St. Dunston in the east

St. Hellen

St. Andrew

Lion Kay

Billingate

THE BRIDGE

Bridge Gate

Mary Ouerts

The Complete Works of Shakespeare

EDITORIAL ADVISORY BOARD

The
Complete Works
of Shakespeare

Fifth Edition

Edited by

David Bevington

The University of Chicago

PEARSON
Longman

New York   San Francisco   Boston
London   Toronto   Sydney   Tokyo   Singapore   Madrid
Mexico City   Munich   Paris   Cape Town   Hong Kong   Montreal

Vice President and Editor-in-Chief: Joseph Terry
Managing Editor: Erika Berg
Development Manager: Janet Lanphier
Development Editor: Michael Greer
Senior Marketing Manager: Melanie Craig
Senior Supplements Editor: Donna Campion
Media Supplements Editor: Nancy Garcia
Senior Production Manager: Valerie Zaborski
Project Coordination and Electronic Page Makeup: Electronic Publishing Services Inc., NYC
Cover Designer/Manager: Wendy Fredericks
Cover Illustration: *The Flower Portrait,* from the RSC Collection with permission of the Governors of the Royal Shakespeare Company.
   (Background photo) Siede Preis/Getty Images.
Front and Back Endpapers: © Copyright The British Museum
Part Opening Photos: Universiteitsbibliotheek Utrecht
Photo Researcher: Photosearch, Inc.
Manufacturing Buyer: Lucy Hebard
Printer and Binder: Hamilton Printing
Cover Printer: Lehigh Press, Inc.

Library of Congress Cataloging-in-Publication Data

Shakespeare, William, 1564–1616.
   [Works. 2003]
   The complete works of Shakespeare / edited by David Bevington.—5th ed.
      p. cm.
   Includes bibliographical references and index.
   ISBN 0-321-09333-X
   I. Bevington, David M. II. Title.
PR2754.B4 2003
822.3'3—dc21   2003045975

Please visit our website at http://www.ablongman.com.

ISBN 0-321-09333-X

1 2 3 4 5 6 7 8 9 10—HT—06 05 04 03

CONTENTS

Preface   vi

Shakespeare's World: **A Visual Portfolio   following page xlviii**

PREFACE

I have had the extraordinary privilege of editing and reediting *The Complete Works of Shakespeare* throughout my career as teacher and scholar, beginning in the early 1970s. What, you may ask, is the need for all this reediting? Is not the text of Shakespeare a fixed entity? As Falstaff asks, in *1 Henry IV*, Is not the truth the truth? Yet these have been times of extraordinary discovery about textual and analytical method. No period in history has seen such an extensive study of Shakespeare, and no period has experienced so many revolutions in critical method: feminist, new historical, deconstructive, post-colonial, and still more. My attempt has been, throughout this period, to reeducate myself, to learn more about the complexities of meaning and the innumerable alternative possibilities that present themselves to the student of Shakespeare. Above all, I have tried to learn how to improve accessibility and clarity for today's reader in the interpretation of this extraordinary body of dramatic literature.

This fifth edition has given me the chance to revisit every aspect of the work, with extensive reworking of much of the volume. The Shakespearean text itself, as one would expect, is not substantially changed overall, though I have thought through again all the emendations of the earlier editions and have chosen to abandon some that seem no longer necessary or advisable. I have rethought the stage directions throughout, with numerous additions or changes, refined modernizations of spelling and punctuation, and taken another look at the complex issue of lineation.

My hope is that the fifth edition offers students and general readers the most accessible and usable Shakespeare anthology on the market.

KEY FEATURES OF THE FIFTH EDITION

- **Thoroughly revised and updated notes and glosses** provide contemporary readers the support they need to understand Elizabethan language and idioms in accessible and clear modern language, line by line.
- **A richly illustrated general introduction** provides readers with the historical and cultural background required to understand Shakespeare's works in context.
- **"Shakespeare's World: A Visual Portfolio"** provides 16 pages of full color illustrations to help readers visualize Renaissance life and culture and to trace the history of significant performances on stage and screen. Nearly half of these color images are new to this edition, including a selection of stills from recent films of Shakespeare's plays.
- **Significantly revised introductory essays on each of the plays and poems** offer new insight into major themes, cultural issues, and critical conflicts.
- **Updated appendices** include the most recent information on sources, textual choices, performance history, dating of the works, and bibliographic resources.

From the start of my editing career I have aimed at explaining difficult passages, not just single words, keeping in mind the questions that readers might ask as to possible meanings. In undertaking this revision I have been astonished to discover how extensively I have wanted to rewrite the commentary notes. The fifth edition incorporates many such changes. Some notes I had written seemed to me just plain wrong; many others seemed to me in need of greater clarity and accessibility. I have been both abashed to see how much improvement was necessary and grateful to be able to profit from my own experience with these texts in the classroom.

Issues of post-colonialism, gender relations, ethnic conflict, attitudes toward war and politics, ambiguities of language, the canon, dating, multiple authorship, and textual revision have been on the march since the early 1980s especially. These are heady times in which to attempt to practice literary criticism. Introductory essays need to be open to recent as well as more traditional critical approaches; they should open up issues for examination rather than offer pronouncements. I have listened carefully to reviewers who have occasionally found my introductions to earlier editions too confident of my own reading of the plays and poems. I have attempted to make an important correction in this matter, especially by adding some examples of production history and recent criticism that offer radically different readings of the dramatic texts. A teaching text should ask questions and offer the reader alternative possibilities. Discussion of recent film and stage history can enhance our appreciation of the plays in performance while at the same time enriching possibilities of interpretation.

This edition differs from other currently available editions of the *Complete Works* in being presented from the viewpoint of a single editor. That is at once its strength and no doubt its weakness. The viewpoint is, I would venture to say, a moderate and inclusive one, deeply interested in new critical approaches while also attuned to the kinds of responses that Shakespeare has evoked in past generations. I like the fact that this edition began in the Middle West, in Chicago, and that it serves a host of colleges and universities many of which are also in the great heartland of America. This edition attempts to be middle American, intended for a broad spectrum of educational uses and for private enjoyment as well.

I hope that the potential hubris of a single editorship is significantly ameliorated by the way in which this edition, like its predecessors, has made extensive use of editorial consultants. Each consultant was asked to respond to a particular play or work, including the notes and commentary. Many of the responses have been extraordinary and have sharpened issues I could never have addressed sufficiently on my own. The consultants, listed in the front of the book, are experts not only in Shakespeare

studies but also in the particular work I asked them to consider. I am deeply grateful for their help. Lois Potter, originally asked to serve as a consultant on performance history, presented so many suggestions that Longman and I asked her to write a new essay on the subject. This essay is her own, though I have helped edit it for this volume. I am honored that such a superb stage historian has been willing to help in this way.

A significant omission from this fifth edition is the poem called "A Funeral Elegy for Master William Peter," which I included in the fourth updated edition albeit with considerable hesitation on the grounds that an interesting case had been made for Shakespeare's authorship and that the issue was still hotly debated at the time (around 1997). By now it has been well established that the poem is by John Ford, and so out it goes. *The Two Noble Kinsmen*, on the other hand, clearly deserves to be included as a collaboration by Shakespeare and John Fletcher, even if it was not included in the First Folio of Shakespeare's plays in 1623. (Neither was *Pericles*.) Other works that might be gathered under the title of a Complete Shakespeare include the anonymous *Edward III*, the miscellany known as *The Passionate Pilgrim* (1599) in which five poems are certainly by Shakespeare but which also appear elsewhere, and the revised fragment from *The Book of Thomas More* dealing with the May Day Riots of 1517. These works all deserve to be known and studied, but are omitted here simply in the interests of keeping the volume within a certain size. The concept of a "Complete" Shakespeare is a flexible one at all events, given the increasing information we have on the collaborative nature of much authorship in the early modern period.

A BRIEF GUIDE TO THE EDITORIAL PRACTICES AND STYLE USED IN THIS EDITION

The running title at the top of each page of text gives the Through Line Numbers (TLN) of each play based on the Norton First Folio of Shakespeare. That facsimile of the original provides line numberings throughout, one number for each line of type. The advantage of this system is that it is universal, applying to all editions whether new or old. Such editions vary in line numbering depending on how the text is divided into scenes and how prose is numbered in columns of varying width. Because the TLN system is truly universal it is often used by textual scholars.

Line numbers in the text indicate that a gloss is to be found at the foot of the column for some word or phrase in the line in question.

Stage directions in square brackets are editorially added. Those without brackets, or in parentheses, are from the original Folio or Quarto text. The same is true of the numberings of acts and scenes.

The notes indicate the place of each scene. These indications should not be read as meaning that the stage needs to "look" like a particular street or house or room. Shakespeare's plays were acted essentially without scenery, as is often the case today. The indications of place are meant solely to give the reader information on the imagined location, since those locations can shift quite rapidly.

When the scansion of verse requires that vowels are to receive a syllable they would not normally receive, the vowel in question is marked with an accent grave. Thus, "lovèd" is to be pronounced in two syllables, "lov-ed." When the word has no such accented vowel it should receive the normal pronunciation. These markings normally correspond with a similar system in the original Folio and Quarto texts, although in those texts "loved" is normally bisyllabic whereas "lov'd" is monosyllabic.

In the commentary notes, capitalization and end punctuation of each note is determined by how the paraphrase in the note fits into the Shakespearean text it represents. If the phrase being glossed begins a sentence, the note will begin with a capital letter, and correspondingly with end punctuation. The idea here is to make the paraphrase as smoothly compatible with the text as possible.

Any reader interested in further discussion on modernizing of spelling is invited to consult the Preface of the fourth updated edition.

ACKNOWLEDGMENTS

I am grateful to the reviewers who made numerous suggestions for improvements in this new edition. For their detailed and thoughtful suggestions, I would like to thank the following: Celia A. Easton, SUNY Geneseo; Peter Greenfield, University of Puget Sound; Glenn Hopp, Howard Payne University; George Justice, Louisiana State University; Joseph Tate, University of Washington; Ann Tippett, Monroe Community College; Lewis Walker, University of North Carolina, Wilmington; Robert F. Wilson Jr., University of Missouri, Kansas City; and David Wilson-Okamura, East Carolina University.

A number of faculty were generous enough to respond to a survey we conducted to learn more about the undergraduate Shakespeare course market today. Thanks to the following for providing guidance and information: Mark Aune, North Dakota State University; Douglas A. Brooks, Texas A&M University; Robert Cirasa, Kean University; Bill Dynes, University of Indianapolis; Lisa Freinkel, University of Oregon; John Hagge, Iowa State University; Ritchie D. Kendall, University of North Carolina, Chapel Hill; Robert Levine, Boston University; Allen Michie, Iowa State University; Neil Nakadate, Iowa State University; Bonnie Nelson, Kansas State University; Robert O'Brien, California State University, Chico; Arlene Okerlund, San Jose State University; George Rowe, University of Oregon; Lisa S. Starks, University of South Florida; and Nathaniel Wallace, South Carolina State University.

I want to acknowledge a special debt of gratitude to the editorial advisory board members, who provided detailed suggestions on the plays, commentaries, notes, and appendixes. The names of our editorial consultants are listed facing the title page.

Lois Potter of the University of Delaware went far beyond the call of duty by completely rewriting Appendix 3 on Shakespeare in Performance. That her work was done under intense deadline pressure makes the achievement of her wonderful and learned essay all the more impressive.

SUPPLEMENTS

The following supplements are available free when ordered with this text. Please consult your local Longman representative if you would like to set up a value pack.

Evaluating a Performance, **by Mike Greenwald,** informs students about stage and theatrical performance and helps them to become more critical viewers of dramatic productions (ISBN 0-321-09541-3).

Screening Shakespeare: Using Film to Understand the Plays, **by Michael Greer,** is a brief, practical guide to select feature films of the most commonly taught plays (ISBN 0-321-19479-9).

I would be most grateful if you would bring to my attention any errors you find. Such errors can be corrected in a subsequent printing. My e-mail address is bevi@uchicago.edu.

David Bevington
2003

GENERAL INTRODUCTION

LIFE IN SHAKESPEARE'S ENGLAND

England during Shakespeare's lifetime (1564–1616) was a proud nation with a strong sense of national identity, but it was also a small nation by modern standards. Probably not more than five million people lived in the whole of England, considerably fewer than now live in London. England's territories in France were no longer extensive, as they had been during the fourteenth century and earlier; in fact, by the end of Queen Elizabeth's reign (1558–1603), England had virtually retired from the territories she had previously controlled on the Continent, especially in France. Wales was a conquered principality. England's overseas empire in America had scarcely begun, with the Virginia settlement established in the 1580s. Scotland was not yet a part of Great Britain; union with Scotland would not take place until 1707, despite the fact that King James VI of Scotland assumed the English throne in 1603 as James I of England. Ireland, although declared a kingdom under English rule in 1541, was more a source of trouble than of economic strength. The last years of Elizabeth's reign, especially from 1597 to 1601, were plagued by the rebellion of the Irish under Hugh O'Neill, Earl of Tyrone. Thus, England of the sixteenth and early seventeenth centuries was both small and isolated.

The Social and Economic Background

By and large, England was a rural land. Much of the kingdom was still wooded, though timber was being used increasingly in manufacturing and shipbuilding. The area of the Midlands, today heavily industrialized, was at that time still a region of great trees, green fields, and clear streams. England's chief means of livelihood was agriculture. This part of the economy was generally in a bad way, however, and people who lived off the land did not share in the prosperity of many Londoners. A problem throughout the sixteenth century was that of "enclosure": the conversion by rich landowners of croplands into pasturage. Farmers and peasants complained bitterly that they were being dispossessed and starved for the benefit of livestock. Rural uprisings and food riots were common, to the dismay of the authorities. Some Oxfordshire peasants arose in 1596, threatening to massacre the gentry and march on London; other riots had occurred in 1586 and 1591. There were thirteen riots in Kent alone during Elizabeth's reign. Unrest continued into the reign of James I, notably the Midlands' rising of 1607. Although the government did what it could to inhibit enclosure, the economic forces at work were too massive and too inadequately understood to be curbed by governmental fiat. The absence of effective bureaucracies or agencies of coercion compounded the difficulty of governmental control. Pasture used large areas with greater efficiency than crop farming, and required far less

"Enclosure" was a problem throughout the sixteenth century in England. Crop lands were converted into pasturage. The livelihood of the plowman was threatened by the pasturing of sheep and the growing production of wool.

labor. The wool produced by the pasturing of sheep was needed in ever increasing amounts for the manufacture of cloth.

The wool industry also experienced occasional economic difficulties, to be sure; overexpansion in the early years of the sixteenth century created a glutted market that collapsed disastrously in 1551, producing widespread unemployment. Despite such fluctuations and reversals, however, the wool industry at least provided handsome profits for some landowners and middlemen. Mining and manufacture in coal, iron, tin, copper, and lead, although insignificant by modern standards, also were expanding at a significant rate. Trading companies exploited the rich new resources of the Americas, as well as of eastern Europe and the Orient. Queen Elizabeth aided economic development by keeping England out of war with her continental enemies as long as possible, despite provocations from those powers and despite the eagerness of some of her advisers to retaliate.

Certainly England's economic condition was better than the economic condition of the rest of the Continent; an Italian called England "the land of comforts." Yet although some prosperity did exist, it was not evenly distributed. Especially during Shakespeare's first years in London, in the late 1580s and the 1590s, the gap between rich and poor grew more and more extreme. Elizabeth's efforts at peacemaking were no longer able to prevent years of war with the Catholic powers of the Continent. Taxation grew heavier, and inflation proceeded at an unusually rapid rate during this period. A succession of bad harvests compounded the miseries of those who dwelled on the land. When the hostilities on the Conti-

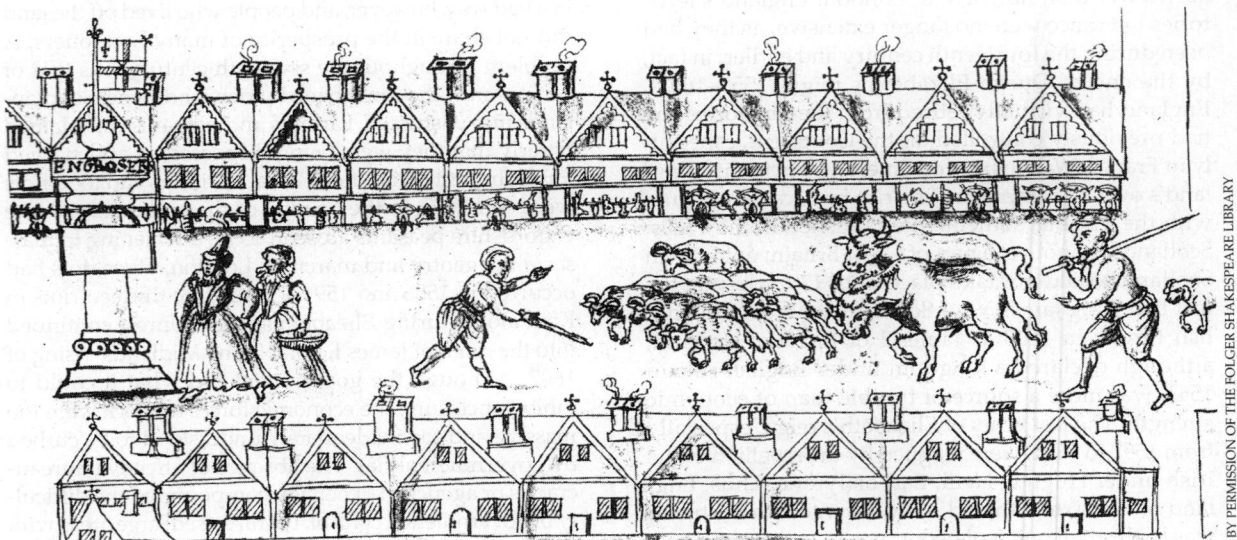

Sixteenth-century London was a city teeming with activity. Pedestrians were often forced to make way for the livestock being driven through the streets.

nent ceased for a time in about 1597, a wave of returning veterans added to unemployment and crime. The rising prosperity experienced by Shakespeare and other fortunate Londoners was undeniably real, but it was not universal. Nowhere was the contrast between rich and poor more visible than in London.

London

Sixteenth-century London was at once more attractive and less attractive than twenty-first-century London. It was full of trees and gardens; meadows and cultivated lands reached in some places to its very walls. Today we can perhaps imagine the way in which it bordered clear streams and green fields when we approach from a distance some noncommercial provincial city such as Lincoln, York, or Hereford. Partly surrounded by its ancient wall, London was by no means a large metropolis. With

190,000 to 200,000 inhabitants in the city proper and its suburbs, it was nonetheless the largest city of Europe, and its dominance among English cities was even more striking; in 1543–1544, London paid thirty times the subsidy of Norwich, then the second-largest city in the kingdom (15,000 inhabitants). Although London's population had expanded into the surrounding area in all directions, the city proper stretched along the north bank of the Thames River from the old Tower of London on the east to St. Paul's Cathedral and the Fleet Ditch on the west—a distance of little more than a mile. Visitors approaching London from the south bank of the Thames (the Bankside) and crossing London Bridge could see virtually all of this exciting city lying before them. London Bridge itself was one of the major attractions of the city, lined with shops and richly decorated on occasion for the triumphal entry of a king or queen.

Yet London had its grim and ugly side as well. On London Bridge could sometimes be seen the heads of executed traitors. The city's houses were generally small and crowded; its streets were often narrow and filthy. In the absence of sewers, open ditches in the streets served to collect and carry off refuse. Frequent epidemics of the bubonic plague were the inevitable result of unsanitary

This detail from a 1572 map of London shows closely packed buildings intersected with throroughfares, with gardens and open spaces on the outskirts.

London Bridge, lined with shops, houses, and severed heads on poles, provided a colorful route for those traveling between the north and south banks of the Thames. A number of Elizabethan theaters, including the Globe, were located on the south bank.

COURTESY, GUILDHALL LIBRARY, CORPORATION OF LONDON

BY PERMISSION OF THE FOLGER SHAKESPEARE LIBRARY

The taverns of Cheapside in London were popular and occasionally rowdy.

conditions and medical ignorance. Lighting of the streets at night was generally nonexistent, and the constabulary was notoriously unreliable. Shakespeare gives us unforgettable satires of night watchmen and bumbling police officials in *Much Ado About Nothing* (Dogberry and the night watch) and *Measure for Measure* (Constable Elbow). Prostitution thrived in the suburbs, conveniently located, although beyond the reach of the London authorities. Again, we are indebted to Shakespeare for a memorable portrayal in *Measure for Measure* of just such a demimonde (Mistress Overdone the bawd, Pompey her pimp, and various customers). Houses of prostitution were often found in the vicinity of the public theaters, since the theaters also took advantage of suburban locations to escape the stringent regulations imposed by London's Lord Mayor and Council of Aldermen. The famous Globe Theatre, for example, was on the south bank of the Thames, a short distance west of London Bridge. Another theatrical building (called simply "The Theatre"), used earlier by Shakespeare and the Lord Chamberlain's players, was located in Finsbury Fields, a short distance across Moorfields from London's northeast corner. The suburbs also housed various con games and illegal operations, some of them brilliantly illustrated (and no doubt exaggerated) in Ben Jonson's *The Alchemist* (1610).

Roughly half of London's total population, perhaps 100,000 people, lived within its walls, and as many more in the suburbs. The royal palace of Whitehall, Westminster Abbey (then known as the Abbey Church of St. Peter), the Parliament House, and Westminster Hall were well outside London, two miles or so to the west on the Thames River. They remain today in the same location, in Westminster, although the metropolis of London has long since surrounded these official buildings.

Travel

Travel was still extremely painful and slow because of the poor condition of the roads. Highway robbers were a constant threat. (The celebrated highway robbery in Shakespeare's *1 Henry IV* takes place at Gads Hill, on the main road between London and Canterbury.) English inns seem to have been good, however, and certainly much better than the inns of the Continent. Travel on horseback was the most common method of transportation, and probably the most comfortable, since coach building was a new and imperfect art. Coaches of state, some of which we see in prints and pictures of the era, were lumbering affairs, no doubt handsome enough in processions, but springless, unwieldly, and hard to pull. Carts and wagons were used for carrying merchandise, but packsaddles were safer and quicker. Under such difficulties, no metropolitan area such as London could possibly have thrived in the interior. London depended for its commercial greatness upon the Thames River and its access to the North Sea.

Commerce

When Elizabeth came to the English throne in 1558, England's chief foreign trade was with Antwerp, Bruges, and other Belgian cities. Antwerp was an especially important market for England's export of wool cloth. This market was seriously threatened, however, since the Low Countries were under the domination of the Catholic King of Spain, Philip II. When Philip undertook to punish his Protestant subjects in the Low Countries for their religious heresy, many of Elizabeth's counselors and subjects urged her to come to the defense of England's Protestant neighbors and trading allies. Elizabeth held back. Philip's armies attacked Antwerp in 1576 and again in 1585, putting an end to the commercial ascendancy of that great northern European metropolis. Perhaps as many as one-third of Antwerp's merchants and artisans settled in London, bringing with them their expert knowledge of commerce and manufacture. The influx of so many skilled workers and merchants into London produced problems of unemployment and overcrowding but contributed nevertheless to London's emergence as a leading port of trade.

English ships assumed a dominant position in Mediterranean trade, formerly carried on mainly by the Venetians. In the Baltic Sea, England competed successfully in trade that had previously been controlled by the Hanseatic League. Bristol thrived on commerce with Ireland and subsequently on trade with the Western Hemisphere. Boston and Hull increased their business with Scandinavian ports. The Russia Company was founded in 1555; the Levant Company became the famous East India Company in 1600; and the Virginia Company opened up trade with the New World in the Western Hemisphere. Fisheries were developed in the North Sea, in the waters north of Ireland, and off the banks of Newfoundland. Elizabeth and her ministers encouraged this commercial expansion.

The Poor Laws and Apprenticeship

Despite the new prosperity experienced by many Elizabethans, especially in London, unemployment remained a serious problem. The suppresssion of the monasteries in 1536–1539, as part of Henry VIII's reformation of the Catholic Church, had dispossessed a large class of persons who were not easily reemployed. Other causes of unemployment, such as the periodic collapse of the wool trade, dispossession of farm workers by enclosure of land, the sudden influx of skilled artisans from Antwerp, and the return of army veterans, have already been mentioned. Elizabethan parliaments attempted to cope with the problem of unemployment but did so in ways that seem unduly harsh today. Several laws were passed between 1531, when the distinction between those poor needing charity and those unwilling to work first became law, and 1597–1598. The harshest of the laws was that of 1547, providing that vagabonds be branded and enslaved for two years; escape was punishable by death or life enslavement. This act was repealed in 1549, but subsequent acts of 1572 and 1576 designated ten classes of vagrants and required municipal authorities to provide work for the healthy unemployed of each town or parish. This localization of responsibility laid the basis for what has been known historically as the "poor rate" (a local tax levied for the support of the poor) and for that sinister institution, the workhouse. The provisions of this act remained in force for centuries. The most comprehensive laws were those of the Parliament of 1597–1598, which repeated many provisions of earlier acts and added harsh, punitive penalties intended to send vagabonds back to the parishes in which they had been born or had last worked. After 1597, no begging was permitted; the poor were supposed to be provided for by the "poor rate" already established.

Regulations for apprentices were no less strict. An act of Parliament of 1563, known as the Statute of Artificers, gave the craft trades of England—still organized as medieval guilds—virtually complete authority over the young persons apprenticed to a trade. The law severely limited access to apprenticeship to sons of families with

Although some Elizabethans rose to great wealth, poverty and unemployment were widespread.

estates worth at least forty shillings of income. Apprenticeship usually began between the ages of fourteen and seventeen, and lasted for a period of not less than seven years. During this time, the young worker lived with the family of the employer. Without such an extensive apprenticeship, entry into the skilled crafts was virtually impossible. Apprenticeships were not open, however, in all guilds, and the law courts subsequently ruled that apprenticeship rules did not apply to crafts developed after 1563, so that exceptions did exist. All able-bodied workers not bound to crafts were supposed to work in agriculture. Acting companies, such as the company Shakespeare joined, were not technically organized as guilds, though the boys who played women's parts were in some cases at least bound by the terms of apprenticeship; a number of the adult actors belonged to one London guild or another and could use that status to apprentice boys. We do not know whether Shakespeare actually served such an indenture before becoming a full member of his acting company.

Social Change

The opportunities for rapid economic advance in Elizabethan England, though limited almost entirely to those who were already prosperous, did produce social change and a quality of restlessness in English society. "New men" at court were an increasing phenomenon under the Tudor monarchs, especially Henry VII and Henry VIII, who tended to rely on loyal counselors of humble origin rather than on the once-too-powerful nobility. Cardinal Wolsey, for example, rose from obscurity to become the most mighty subject of Henry VIII's realm, with a newly built residence (Hampton Court) rivaling the splendor of the King's own palaces. He was detested as an upstart by old aristocrats, such as the Duke of Norfolk, and his sudden fall was as spectacular as had been his rise to power. The Earl of Leicester, Queen Elizabeth's first favorite, was a descendant of the Edmund Dudley who had risen from unpretentious beginnings to great eminence under Henry VII, Queen Elizabeth's grandfather. Although Queen Elizabeth did not contribute substantially to the new aristocracy—she created only three peers from 1573 onward—new and influential families were numerous throughout the century. Conversely, the ancient families discovered that they were no longer entrusted with positions of highest authority. To be sure, the aristocracy remained at the apex of England's social structure. New aspirants to power emulated the aristocracy by purchasing land and building splendid residences, rather than defining themselves as a rich new "middle class." Bourgeois status was something the new men put behind them as quickly as they could. Moreover, social mobility could work in both directions: upward and downward. Many men were quickly ruined by the costly and competitive business of seeking favor at the Tudor court. The poor, in a vast majority, enjoyed virtually no rights at all. Nonetheless, the Elizabethan era was one of greater opportunity for rapid social and economic advancement among persons of wealth than England had heretofore known.

Increased economic contacts with the outside world inevitably led to the importation of new styles of living. Such new fashions, together with the rapid changes now possible in social position, produced a reaction of dismay from those who feared the destruction of traditional English values. Attitudes toward Italy veered erratically between condemnation and admiration: on the one hand, Italy was the home of the Catholic Church and originator of many supposedly decadent fashions, whereas, on the other hand, Italy was the cradle of humanism and the country famed for Venice's experiment in republican government. To many conservative Englishmen, the word *Italianate* connoted a whole range of villainous practices, including diabolical methods of torture and revenge: poisoned books of devotion that would kill the unsuspecting victims who kissed them, ingeniously contrived chairs that would close upon the person who sat in them, and the like. The revenge plays of Shakespeare's contemporaries, such as *Antonio's Revenge* by John Marston, *The Revenger's Tragedy* probably by Thomas Middleton, and *The White Devil* by John Webster, offer spectacular caricatures of the so-called Italianate style in murder. The name of Italy was also associated with licentiousness, immorality, and outlandish fashions in clothes. France, too, was accused of encouraging such extravagances in dress as ornamented headdresses, stiffly pleated ruffs, padded doublets, puffed or double sleeves, and richly decorated hose. Rapid changes in fashion added to the costliness of being up to date and thereby increased the outcry against vanity in dress. Fencing, dicing, the use of cosmetics, the smoking of tobacco, the drinking of imported wines, and almost every vice known to humanity were attributed by angry moralists to the corrupting influence from abroad.

Not all Englishmen deplored continental fashion, of course. Persons of advanced taste saw the importation of European styles as a culturally liberating process. Fashion thus became a subject of debate between moral traditionalists and those who welcomed the new styles. The controversy was a bitter one, with religious overtones, in which the reformers' angry accusations became increasingly extreme. This attack on changing fashion was, in fact, an integral part of the Puritan movement. It therefore stressed the sinfulness, not only of extravagance in clothing, but also of the costliness in building great houses and other such worldly pursuits. Those whose sympathies were Puritan became more and more disaffected with the cultural values represented by the court, and thus English society drifted further and further toward irreconcilable conflict.

This brothel scene, featuring gambling or dicing, illustrates some of the vices that were attributed to the corrupting influence from abroad.

Shakespeare's personal views on this controversy are hard to determine and do not bear importantly on his achievement as an artist. Generally, however, we can observe that his many references to changes in fashion cater neither to the avant-garde nor to reactionary traditionalists. Shakespeare's audience was, after all, a broadly national one. It included many well-informed Londoners who viewed "Italianate" fashion neither with enthusiasm nor with alarm, but with satiric laughter. Such spectators would certainly have seen the point, for example, in Mercutio's witty diatribe at the expense of the new French style in fencing. The object of his scorn is Tybalt, who, according to Mercutio, "fights as you sing prick song" and fancies himself to be "the very butcher of a silk button." "Is not this a lamentable thing," asks Mercutio rhetorically, "that we should be thus afflicted with these strange flies, these fashionmongers, these pardon-me's, who stand so much on the new form that they cannot sit at ease on the old bench?" (*Romeo and Juliet*, 2.4.20–35). In a similar vein, Shakespeare's audience would have appreciated the joking in *The Merchant of Venice* about England's servile imitation of continental styles in clothes. "What say you, then, to Falconbridge, the young baron of England?" asks Nerissa of her mistress Portia concerning one of Portia's many suitors. Portia replies, "How oddly he is suited! I think he bought his doublet in Italy, his round hose in France, his bonnet in Germany, and his behavior everywhere" (1.2.64–74). Court butterflies in Shakespeare's plays who bow and scrape and fondle their plumed headgear, like Le Beau in *As You Like It* and Osric in *Hamlet*, are the objects of ridicule. Hotspur in *1 Henry IV*, proud northern aristocrat that he is, has nothing but contempt for an effeminate courtier, "perfumèd like a milliner," who has come from King Henry to discuss the question of prisoners (1.3.36). Throughout Shakespeare's plays, the use of cosmetics generally has the negative connotation of artificial beauty used to conceal inward corruption, as in Claudius's reference to "the harlot's cheek, beautied with plast'ring art" (*Hamlet*, 3.1.52). Yet Shakespeare's treatment of newness in fashion is never shrill in tone. Nor does he fail in his dramas to give an honorable place to the ceremonial use of wealth and splendid costuming. His plays thus avoid both extremes in the controversy over changing fashions, though they give plentiful evidence as to the liveliness and currency of the topic.

Shakespeare also reflects a contemporary interest in the problem of usury, especially in *The Merchant of Venice*. Although usury was becoming more and more of a necessity, emotional attitudes toward it changed only slowly. The traditional moral view condemned usury as forbidden by Christian teaching; on the other hand, European governments of the sixteenth century found themselves increasingly obliged to borrow large sums of money. The laws against usury were alternatively relaxed and enforced, according to the economic exigencies of the moment. Shakespeare's plays capture the Elizabethan ambivalence of attitude toward this feared but necessary practice (see Introduction to *The Merchant of Venice*). Similarly, most Englishmen had contradictory attitudes toward what we today would call the law of supply and demand in the marketplace. Conservative moralists complained bitterly when merchants exploited the scarcity of some commodity by forcing up prices; the practice was denounced as excessive profit taking and declared to be sinful, like usury. In economic policy, then, as in matters of changing fashion or increased social mobility, many Englishmen were ambivalent about the perennial conflict between the old order and the new.

Elizabethan Houses

Those fortunate Englishmen who grew wealthy in the reign of Elizabeth took special pleasure in building

Tudor mansions were often splendid, with impressive gardens and terraces. Shown here is Little Moreton Hall, in Cheshire, built in 1559.

THE NATIONAL TRUST PHOTOGRAPHIC LIBRARY. PHOTO BY GEOFF MORGAN

themselves fine new houses with furnishings to match. Chimneys were increasingly common, so that smoke no longer had to escape through a hole in the roof. Pewter, or even silver dishes, took the place of the wooden spoon and trencher. Beds, and even pillows, became common. Carpets were replacing rushes as covering for the floors; wainscoting, tapestries or hangings, and pictures appeared on the walls; and glass began to be used extensively for windows.

Despite the warnings of those moralists who preached against the vanity of worldly acquisition, domestic comfort made considerable progress in Elizabethan England. Many splendid Tudor mansions stand today, testifying to the important social changes that had taken place between the strife-torn fifteenth century and the era of relative peace under Elizabeth. The battlement, the moat, the fortified gate, and the narrow window used for archery or firearms generally disappeared in favor of handsome gardens and terraces. At the lower end of the social scale, the agricultural laborers who constituted the great mass of the English population were generally poor, malnourished, and uneducated, but they seem to have enjoyed greater physical security than did their ancestors

in the fifteenth century, and no longer needed to bring their cows, pigs, and poultry into their dwellings at night in order to protect them from thieves. City houses, of which many exist today, were often large and imposing structures, three or four stories in height, and framed usually of strong oak with the walls filled in with brick and plaster. Although the frontage on the streets of London was usually narrow, many houses had trees and handsome gardens at the rear. Of course London also had its plentiful share of tenements for the urban poor.

With the finer houses owned by the fortunate elite came features of privacy that had been virtually unknown to previous generations. Life in the household of a medieval lord had generally focused on the great hall, which could serve variously as the kitchen, dining hall, and sitting room for the entire family and its retainers. The men drank in the hall in the evenings and slept there at night. The new dwellings of prosperous Elizabethans, on the other hand, featured private chambers into which the family and the chief guests could retire.

The Elizabethans built well. Not only do we still admire their houses, but also we can see from their oriel windows and stained glass, their broad staircases, their jewels, and their costumes that they treasured the new beauty of their lives made possible by the culture of the Renaissance. Although the graphic and plastic arts did not thrive in England to the same extent as in Italy, France, and the Low Countries, England made lasting achievements in architecture, as well as in music, drama, and all forms of literature.

The Political and Religious Background

England under the Tudors suffered from almost unceasing religious conflict. The battle over religion affected every aspect of life and none more so than politics. At the very beginning of the Tudor reign, to be sure, England's problem was not religious but dynastic. Henry VII, the first of the Tudor kings, brought an end to the devastating civil wars of the fifteenth century with his overthrow of Richard III at the battle of Bosworth Field in 1485. The civil wars thus ended were the so-called Wars of the Roses, between the Lancastrian House of Henry VI (sym-bolized by the red rose) and the Yorkist House of Edward IV (symbolized by the white rose). Shakespeare chose these eventful struggles as the subject for his first series of English history plays, from *Henry VI* in three parts to *Richard III*. The House of Lancaster drew its title from John of Gaunt, Duke of Lancaster, father of Henry IV and great-grandfather of Henry VI; the House of York drew its title from Edmund Langley, Duke of York, great-grandfather of Edward IV and Richard III. Because John of Gaunt and Edmund Langley had been brothers, virtually all the noble contestants in this War of the Roses were cousins of one another, caught in a remorseless dynastic struggle for control of the English crown. Many of them lost their lives in the fighting. By 1485, England was exhausted from civil conflict. Although Henry VII's own dynastic claim to the throne was weak, he managed to suppress factional opposition and to give England the respite from war so desperately needed. His son, Henry VIII, inherited a throne in 1509 that was more secure than it had been in nearly a century.

On Sundays crowds gathered to listen to the sermon at St. Paul's Cathedral, the subject of this anonymous painting dated 1616.

The Knights of the Garter belonged to the highest order of knighthood; many were influential courtiers and favorites of Queen Elizabeth. A masterful politician, Elizabeth remained unmarried throughout her life. A marriage would have upset the political balance and would have committed her to one foreign nation or to one constituency at home.

Henry VIII's notorious marital difficulties, however, soon brought an end to dynastic security and civil accord. Moreover, religious conflict within the Catholic Church was growing to the extent that a break with Rome appeared inevitable. Henry's marriage troubles precipitated that momentous event. Because he divorced his first wife, Katharine of Aragon, in 1530 without the consent of Rome, he was excommunicated by the pope. His response in 1534 was to have himself proclaimed "Protector and only Supreme Head of the Church and Clergy of England." This decisive act signaled the beginning of the Reformation in England, not many years after Martin Luther's momentous break with the papacy in 1517 and the consequent beginning of Lutheran Protestantism on the Continent. In England, Henry's act of defiance split the Church and the nation. Many persons chose Sir Thomas More's path of martyrdom rather than submit to Henry's new title as supreme head of the English church. Henry's later years did witness a period of retrenchment in religion, after the downfall of Thomas Cromwell in 1540, and indeed Henry's break with Rome had had its origin in political and marital strife as well as in matters of dogma and liturgy. Nevertheless, the establishment of an English church was now an accomplished fact. The accession of Henry's ten-year-old son Edward

VI in 1547 gave reformers an opportunity to bring about rapid changes in English Protestantism. Archbishop Cranmer's forty-two articles of religion (1551) and his prayer book laid the basis for the Anglican Church of the sixteenth century.

The death of the sickly Edward VI in 1553 brought with it an intense crisis in religious politics and a temporary reversal of England's religious orientation. The Duke of Northumberland, Protector and virtual ruler of England in Edward's last years, attempted to secure a Protestant succession and his own power by marrying his son to Lady Jane Grey, a granddaughter of Henry VII, whom Edward had named heir to the throne, but the proclamation of Lady Jane as Queen ended in failure. She was executed, as were her husband and father-in-law. For five years, England returned to Catholicism under the rule of Edward's elder sister Mary, daughter of the Catholic Queen Katharine of Aragon. The crisis accompanying such changes of government during this midcentury period was greatly exacerbated by the fact that all three of Henry VIII's living children were considered illegitimate by one faction or another of the English people. In Protestant eyes, Mary was the daughter of the divorced Queen Katharine, whose marriage to Henry had never been valid because she had previous-

ly been the spouse of Henry VIII's older brother Arthur. This Arthur had died at a young age, in 1502, shortly after his state marriage to the Spanish princess. If, as the Protestants insisted, Arthur had consummated the marriage, then Katharine's subsequent union with her deceased husband's brother was invalid, and Henry was free, instead, to marry Anne Boleyn—the mother-to-be of Elizabeth. In Catholic eyes, however, both Elizabeth and her brother Edward VI (son of Jane Seymour, Henry VIII's third wife) were the bastard issue of Henry's bigamous marriages; Henry's one and only true marriage in the Catholic faith was that to Katharine of Aragon. Edward and Elizabeth were regarded by many Catholics, at home and abroad, not only as illegitimate children, but also as illegitimate rulers, to be disobeyed and even overthrown by force. Thus, dynastic and marital conflicts became matters of grave political consequence.

Because of these struggles, Elizabeth's accession to the throne in 1558 remained an uncertainty until the last moment. Once she actually became ruler, England returned once more to the Protestant faith. Even then, tact and moderation were required to prevent open religious war. Elizabeth's genius at compromise prompted her to seek a middle position for her church, one that combined an episcopal form of church government (owing no allegiance to the pope) with an essentially traditional form of liturgy and dogma. As much as was practicable, she left matters up to individual conscience; she drew the line, however, where matters of conscience tended to "exceed their bounds and grow to be matter of faction." In practice, this meant that she did not tolerate avowed Catholics on the religious right or Protestant sects who denied the doctrine of the Trinity on the religious left. The foundation for this so-called Elizabethan compromise was the thirty-nine articles, adopted in 1563 and based in many respects upon Cranmer's forty-two articles of 1551. The compromise did not please everyone, of course, but it did achieve a remarkable degree of consensus during Elizabeth's long reign.

Queen Elizabeth and Tudor Absolutism

Elizabeth had to cope with a religiously divided nation and with extremists of both the right and the left who wished her downfall. She was a woman, in an age openly skeptical of women's ability or right to rule. Her success in dealing with such formidable odds was in large measure the result of her personal style as a monarch. Her combination of imperious will and femininity and her brilliant handling of her many contending male admirers have become legendary. She remained unmarried throughout her life, in part, at least, because marriage would have upset the delicate balance she maintained among rival groups, both foreign and domestic. Marriage would have committed her irretrievably to either one foreign nation or to one constituency at home. She chose instead to bestow her favor on certain courtiers, notably Robert Dudley (whom she elevated to be the Earl of Leicester) and, after Leicester's death in 1588, Robert Devereux, second Earl of Essex. Her relationship with these men, despite her partiality to them, was marked by her outbursts of tempestuous jealousy. In addition, she relied on the staid counsel of her hard-working ministers: Lord Burghley, Sir Francis Walsingham, Burghley's son Robert Cecil, and a few others.

In her personal style as monarch, Elizabeth availed herself of the theory of absolute supremacy. Under all the Tudors, England was nominally at least an absolute monarchy in an age when many of England's greatest rivals—France, Spain, the Holy Roman Empire—were also under absolutist rule. "Absolutism" meant that the monarch served for life, could not legally be removed from office, and was normally succeeded by his eldest son—all of this bolstered by claims of divine sanction, though the claims were frequently contested. The rise of absolutism throughout Renaissance Europe was the result of an increase of centralized national power and a corresponding decrease in autonomous baronial influence. Henry VII's strong assertion of his royal authority at the expense of the feudal lords corresponded roughly in time with the ascendancy of Francis I of France (1515) and Charles V of the Holy Roman Empire (1519). Yet England had long enjoyed a tradition of rule by consensus. When Elizabeth came to the throne, England was already in some ways a "limited" monarchy. Parliament, and especially the members of the House of Commons, claimed prerogatives of their own and were steadily gaining in both experience and power. In the mid-1560s, for example, the Commons made repeated attempts to use parliamentary tax-levying authority as a means of obliging Elizabeth to name a Protestant successor to the throne. The attempt, despite its failure to achieve its immediate goal, was significant; the Commons had shown that they were a force to be reckoned with. Even though Elizabeth made skillful rhetorical use of the theory of absolutism, portraying herself as God's appointed deputy on earth, her idea of absolutism should not be confused with despotism. To be sure, Elizabeth learned to avoid parliamentary interference in her affairs whenever possible; there were only thirteen sessions of Parliament in her forty-five years of rule. Still, Parliament claimed the right to establish law and to levy taxes on which the monarchy had to depend. Elizabeth needed all her considerable diplomatic skills in dealing with her parliaments and

with the English people, who were self-reliant and proud of their reputation for independence. Elizabeth had more direct authority over her Privy Council, since she could appoint its members herself, yet even here she consulted faithfully with them on virtually everything she did. Nor were her closest advisers reluctant to offer her advice. Many vocal leaders in her government, including Walsingham and Leicester, urged the Queen during the 1570s and 1580s to undertake a more active military role on the Continent against the Catholic powers. So did her later favorite, the Earl of Essex. With remarkable tact, she managed to retain the loyalty of her militant and sometimes exasperated counselors, and yet to keep England out of war with Spain until that country actually launched an invasion attempt in 1588 (the Great Armada).

Catholic Opposition

During her early years, Elizabeth sought through her religious compromise to ease the divisions of her kingdom and attempted to placate her enemies abroad (notably Philip of Spain) rather than involve England in a costly war. For about twelve years, while England's economy gained much-needed strength, this policy of temporizing succeeded. Yet Elizabeth's more extreme Catholic opponents at home and abroad could never be reconciled to the daughter of that Protestant "whore," Anne Boleyn. England's period of relative accommodation came to an end in 1569 and 1570, with Catholic uprisings in the north and with papal excommunication of the English Queen. As a declared heretic, Elizabeth's very life was in danger; her Catholic subjects were encouraged by Rome to disobey her and to seek means for her violent overthrow.

Conspirators did, in fact, make attempts on the Queen's life, notably in the so-called Babington conspiracy of 1586, named for one of the chief participants. This plot, brought to light by Secretary of State Walsingham, sought to place Mary, Queen of Scots on the English throne in Elizabeth's stead. Mary was Elizabeth's kinswoman; Mary's grandmother, sister to Henry VIII, had been married to James IV of Scotland. So long as Elizabeth remained childless, Mary was a prominent heir to the English throne. Catholics pinned their hopes on her succession, by force if necessary; Protestant leaders urged Elizabeth to marry and give birth to a Protestant heir or at least to name a Protestant successor. Mary had abdicated the Scottish throne in 1567 after the sensational murder of her Catholic counselor David Rizzio, the murder of Mary's husband, the Earl of Darnley (in which Mary was widely suspected to have taken part), and her subsequent marriage to Darnley's slayer, the Earl of Bothwell. Taking refuge in England, Mary remained a political prisoner and the inevitable focus of Catholic plotting against Elizabeth for approximately two decades. She, in fact, assented in writing to Babington's plot against Eliz-

UNKNOWN ARTIST, "EXECUTION OF MARY QUEEN OF SCOTS." SCOTTISH NATIONAL PORTRAIT GALLERY

Along with the defeat of the Spanish Armada in 1588, the 1587 beheading of Mary, Queen of Scots, shown holding a crucifix and surrounded by official witnesses in this contemporary illustration, virtually ended any serious Catholic challenge to Elizabeth's throne.

abeth. All that long while Elizabeth resisted demands from her Protestant advisers that she execute her kinswoman and thereby end a constant threat to the throne; Elizabeth was reluctant to kill a fellow monarch and agreed fully with Mary's son James that "anointing by God cannot be defiled by man." Nonetheless, Mary's clear involvement in the Babington conspiracy led to the so-called Bond of Association, in which thousands of Englishmen pledged to prevent the succession of any person plotting Elizabeth's death, and then at last to Mary's execution in 1587. By that time, Spain was mounting an invasion against England, the Great Armada of 1588, and Elizabeth's temporizing tactics were no longer feasible. The long years of peace had done their work, however, and England was considerably stronger and more resolute than thirty years before. With Elizabeth's tacit approval, Sir Francis Drake and other naval commanders carried the fighting to Spain's very shore and to her American colonies. The war with Spain continued from 1588 until about 1597.

Elizabeth's great compromise dealt not only with the political dangers of opposition but also with the more central theological issues. England was sorely divided, as was much of Europe, on such matters as whether Christ's body was transubstantially present in the Mass, as Catholic faith maintained; whether good works were effi-

cacious in salvation or whether people could be saved by God's grace alone, as the Reformers insisted; whether a portion of humankind was predeterminately damned, as the Calvinists believed; and the like. During the turbulent years of the Reformation, many people died for their faith. In general, the Elizabethan compromise insisted on allegiance to the English throne, church, and ecclesiastical hierarchy but allowed some latitude in matters of faith. The degree of elaboration in vestments and ritual was also an explosive issue on which the English church attempted to steer a central and pragmatic course, although conflicts inevitably arose within the church itself.

Protestant Opposition

The threat from the Protestant left was no less worrisome than that from the Catholic right. Protestant reformers had experienced their first taste of power at the time of Henry VIII's break with Rome in 1534. Under Thomas Cromwell, Cardinal Wolsey's successor as the King's chief minister, the monasteries were suppressed and William Tyndale's English Bible was authorized. The execution of Cromwell introduced a period of conservative retrenchment, but the accession of Edward VI in 1547 brought reform once more into prominence. Thereafter, Mary's Catholic reign drove most of the reformers into exile on the Continent. When they returned after 1558, many had been made more radical by their continental experience.

To be sure, reform covered a wide spectrum, from moderation to radicalism. Some preferred to work within the existing hierarchical structure of church and state, whereas others were religious separatists. Only the more radical groups, such as the Brownists and Anabaptists, endorsed ideas of equality and communal living. The abusive epithet "Puritan," applied indiscriminately to all reformers, tended to obscure the wide range of difference in the reform movement. The reformers were, to some extent, united by a dislike for formal ritual and ecclesiastical garments, by a preference for a simple and pious manner of living, and by a belief in the literal word of the Bible rather than the traditional teachings of the church fathers. They stressed personal responsibility in religion and were Calvinist in their emphasis on human depravity and the need for grace through election. Yet at first only the more radical were involved in a movement to separate entirely from the established English church.

The radicals on the religious left, even if they represented at first only a minority of the reformers, posed a serious threat to Elizabeth's government. Their program bore an ironic resemblance to that of the Catholic opposition on the religious right. In their theoretical writings, the extreme reformers justified overthrow of what they considered to be tyrannical rule, just as Catholic spokesmen had absolved Elizabeth's subjects of obedience to her on the grounds that she was illegitimate. Both extremes appealed to disobedience in the name of a higher religious law, as enunciated in Romans 13:1–2: "For there is no power but of God." Among the reforming theoreticians was John Ponet, whose *Short Treatise of Politic Power* (1556) argued that a monarch is subject to a social contract and must rule according to laws that are equally subscribed to by Parliament, the clergy, and the people.

The Doctrine of Passive Obedience

Elizabeth's government countered such assaults on its authority, from both the right and the left, with many arguments, of which perhaps the most central was that of passive obedience. This doctrine condemned rebellion under virtually all circumstances. Its basic assumption was that the king or queen is God's appointed deputy on earth. To depose such a monarch must therefore be an act of disobedience against God's will. Since God is all-wise and all-powerful, his placing of an evil ruler in power must proceed from some divine intention, such as the punishment of a wayward people. Rebellion against God's "scourge" merely displays further disobedience to God's will. A people suffering under a tyrant must wait patiently for God to remove the burden, which he will surely do when the proper time arrives.

This doctrine was included in the official book of homilies of the Church of England and was read from the pulpit at regular intervals. The best-known such homily, entitled *Against Disobedience and Willful Rebellion,* had been preceded by such tracts as William Tyndale's *Obedience of a Christian Man* (1528); a book of homilies, published in 1547, including an "Exhortation Concerning Good Order and Obedience"; Thomas Cranmer's *Notes for a Sermon on the Rebellion of 1549;* and Hugh Latimer's *Sermon on the Lord's Prayer* (1552). Shakespeare heard such homilies often, and he expresses their ideas through several of his characters, such as John of Gaunt and the Bishop of Carlisle in *Richard II* (1.2.37–41, 4.1.115–50). This is not to say that he endorses such ideas, for he sets them in dramatic opposition to other and more heterodox concepts. We can say, nevertheless, that Shakespeare's audience would have recognized in Gaunt's speeches a clear expression of a familiar and officially correct position.

The Political Ideas of Machiavelli

The orthodoxies of the Elizabethan establishment were under attack, not only from the Catholic right and the Protestant left, but also from a new and revolutionary point of view that set aside all criteria of religious morality. Tudor defense of order was based, as we have seen, on the assumption that the monarch rules in accord with a divine plan, a higher Law of Nature to which every just ruler is attuned. Political morality must be at one with religious morality. Catholic and Protestant critiques of the Tudor establishment made similar assumptions, even though they appealed to revolution in the name of that religious morality. To Niccolò Machiavelli, on the other hand, politics was a manipulative science best governed by the dictates of social expediency. His philosophy did not, as many accusingly charged, lead necessarily to the cynical promotion of mere self-interest. Nevertheless, he did argue, in his *Discourses* and *The Prince,* that survival and political stability are the first obligations of any ruler. Machiavelli regarded religion as a tool of the enlightened ruler rather than as a morally absolute guide. He extolled in his ideal leader the quality of *virtù*—a mixture of cunning and forcefulness. He saw history as a subject offering practical lessons in the kind of pragmatic statecraft he proposed.

Machiavelli was a hated name in England, and most of his works were never available in an English printed edition during Shakespeare's lifetime. (The *Florentine History* was translated in 1595; *The Prince* was not translated until 1640.) Nevertheless, his writings were available in Italian, French, and Latin editions, and in manuscript English translations. His ideas certainly had a profound impact on the England of the 1590s. Marlowe caricatures the Italian writer in his *The Jew of Malta,* but he clearly was fascinated by what Machiavelli had to say. Shakespeare, too, reveals a complex awareness. However much he may lampoon the Machiavellian type of conscienceless villain in *Richard III*, he shows us more plausible pragmatists in *Richard II* and *1 Henry IV*. Conservative theories of the divine right of kings are set in debate with the more heterodox ambitions of Henry Bolingbroke (who then adopts the most orthodox of political vocabularies once he is king). Bolingbroke is not a very attractive figure, but he does succeed politically where Richard has failed.

Shakespeare thus reveals himself as less a defender of the established order than as a great dramatist able to give sympathetic expression to the aspirations of all sides in a tense political struggle. His history plays have been variously interpreted either as defenses of monarchy or as subtle pleas for rebellion, but the consensus today is that the plays use political conflict as a way of probing the motivations of social behavior. To be sure, the plays do stress the painful consequences of disorder and present, on the whole, an admiring view of monarchy (especially in *Henry V*), despite the manifest limitations of that institution. Certainly, we can sense that Shakespeare's history plays were written for a generation of Englishmen who had experienced political crisis and who could perceive issues of statecraft in Shakespeare's plays that were relevant to England's struggles in the 1580s and the 1590s. The play of *King John*, for example, deals with a king whose uncertain claim to the throne is challenged by France and the papacy in the name of John's nephew, Arthur; Elizabeth faced a similar situation in her dilemma over her kinswoman, Mary, Queen of Scots. Elizabeth also bitterly acknowledged the cogency of a popular analogy comparing her reign with that of King Richard II, and, when Shakespeare's play about Bolingbroke's overthrow of Richard was apparently revived for political purposes shortly before the Earl of Essex's abortive rebellion against Elizabeth in 1601, Shakespeare's acting company had some explaining to do to the authorities (see Introduction to *Richard II*). Nevertheless, Shakespeare's attitudes toward the issues of his own day are ultimately unknowable and unimportant, since his main concern seems to have been with the dramatization of political conflict rather than with the urging of a polemical position.

Shakespeare on Religion

Our impressions of Shakespeare's personal sympathies in religion are similarly obscured by his refusal to use his art for polemical purposes. To be sure, members of his mother's family in Warwickshire seem to have remained loyal to Catholicism, and his father John Shakespeare may conceivably have undergone financial and other difficulties in Stratford for reasons of faith. (See "Shakespeare's Family" below, in the section on Shakespeare's Life and Work.) Certainly Shakespeare himself displays a familiarity with some Catholic practices and theology,

as when the Ghost of Hamlet's father speaks of being "Unhousled, disappointed, unaneled" (i.e., not having received last rites) at the time of his murder (*Hamlet*, 1.5.78). Nonetheless, we see in his plays a spectrum of religious attitudes portrayed with an extraordinary range of insight. In matters of doctrine, his characters are at various times acquainted with Catholic theology or with the controversy concerning salvation by faith or good works (see *Measure for Measure*, 1.2.24–5), and yet a consistent polemical bias is absent. Some Catholic prelates are schemers, like Pandulph in *King John*. Ordinarily, however, Shakespeare's satirical digs at ecclesiastical pomposity and hypocrisy have little to do with the Catholic question. Cardinal Beaufort in *1 Henry VI* is a political maneuverer, but so are many of his secular rivals. Cardinal Wolsey in *Henry VIII* is motivated by personal ambition, rather than by any sinister conspiracy of the international church. Many of Shakespeare's nominally Catholic clerics, such as Friar Laurence in *Romeo and Juliet* or Friar Francis in *Much Ado About Nothing*, are gentle and well-intentioned people, even if occasionally bumbling. We can certainly say that Shakespeare consistently avoids the chauvinistic anti-Catholic baiting so often found in the plays of his contemporaries.

The same avoidance of extremes can be seen in his portrayal of Protestant reformers, though the instances in this case are few. Malvolio in *Twelfth Night* is fleetingly compared with a "puritan" (2.3.139–46), although Shakespeare insists that no extensive analogy can be made. Angelo in *Measure for Measure* is sometimes thought to be a critical portrait of the Puritan temperament. Even if this were so, Shakespeare's satire is extremely indirect compared with the lampoons written by his contemporaries Ben Jonson and Thomas Dekker.

Stuart Absolutism

Queen Elizabeth's successor, James I of the Scottish house of Stuarts, reigned from 1603 to 1625. Even more than Elizabeth, he was a strong believer in the divinely appointed authority of kings; whereas she had insisted on divine sanction, James and his successor Charles called it a divine right. Although James succeeded easily to the throne in 1603, since he was Protestant with a legitimate claim of descent from Henry VIII, the English people did not take to this foreigner from the north. James was eccentric in his personal habits, and the English were always inclined to be suspicious of the Scots in any case. As a result, James was less successful in dealing with the heterogeneous and antagonistic forces that Elizabeth had kept in precarious balance. At the Hampton Court Conference of 1604, relations quickly broke down between James and the Puritan wing of the church, so that even its more moderate adherents joined forces with the separatists. James had similar difficulties with an increasingly radical group in the House of Commons. In the widening rift between the absolutists and those who defended the supremacy of Parliament, James's court moved toward the right. Catholic sympathies at court became common. Civil war was still a long way off and by no means inevitable; the beheading of King Charles I (James's son) would not occur until 1649. Still, throughout James's reign, the estrangement between the right and the left was becoming more and more uncomfortable. The infamous Gunpowder Plot of 1605, in which Guy Fawkes and other Catholic conspirators were accused of having plotted to blow up the houses of Parliament, raised hysteria to a new intensity. Penal laws against papists were harshly enforced. The Parliament of 1614 included in its membership John Pym, Thomas Wentworth, and John Eliot—men who were to become turbulent spokesmen against taxes imposed without parliamentary grant, imprisonment without the stating of specific criminal charges, and other purported abuses of royal power. The polarization of English society naturally affected the London theaters. Popular London audiences (generally sympathetic with religious reform) eventually grew disaffected with the stage, while even the popular acting companies came under the increasing domination of the court. Shakespeare's late plays reflect the increasing influence of a courtly audience.

THE INTELLECTUAL BACKGROUND

Renaissance Cosmology

In learning, as in politics and religion, Shakespeare's England was a time of conflict and excitement. Medieval ideas of a hierarchical and ordered creation were under attack but were still widely prevalent, and were used to justify a hierarchical order in society itself. According to the so-called Ptolemaic system of the universe, formulated by Ptolemy of Alexandria in the second century A.D., the earth stood at the center of creation. Around it moved, in nine concentric spheres, the heavenly bodies of the visible universe, in order as follows (from the earth outward): the moon, Mercury, Venus, the sun, Mars, Jupiter, Saturn, the fixed stars on a single plane, and lastly the *primum mobile,* imparting motion to the whole system. (See the accompanying illustration.) Some commentators proposed alternate arrangements or speculated as to the existence of one or two additional spheres, in particular a "crystalline sphere" between the fixed stars and the *primum mobile.* These additional spheres were needed to cope with matters not adequately explained in Ptolemaic astronomy, such as the precession of the equinoxes. More troublesomely, the seemingly erratic retrograde motion of the planets—that is, the refusal of Mars and other planets to move around the earth in steady orbit—

called forth increasingly ingenious theories, such as Tycho Brahe's scheme of epicycles. Still, the conservative appeal of the earth-centered cosmos remained very strong. How could one suppose that the earth was not at the center of the universe?

The *primum mobile* was thought to turn the entire universe around the earth once every twenty-four hours. Simultaneously, the individual heavenly bodies moved more slowly around the earth on their individual spheres, constantly changing position with respect to the fixed stars. The moon, being the only heavenly body that seemed subject to change in its monthly waxing and waning, was thought to represent the boundary between the unchanging universe and the incessantly changing world. Beneath the moon, in the "sublunary" sphere, all creation was subject to death as a result of Adam's fall from grace; beyond the moon lay perfection. Hell was imagined to exist deep within the earth, as in Dante's *Inferno,* or else outside the *primum mobile* and far below the created universe in the realm of chaos, as in Milton's *Paradise Lost.*

Heaven or the Empyrean stood, according to most Ptolemaic systems, at the top of the universe. Between heaven and earth dwelled the nine angelic orders, each associated with one of the nine concentric spheres. According to a work attributed to Dionysius the Areopagite, *On the Heavenly Hierarchy* (fifth century A.D.), the nine angelic orders consisted of three hierarchies. Closest to God were the contemplative orders of Seraphim, Cherubim, and Thrones; next, the intermediate orders of Dominions, Powers, and Virtues; and finally the active orders of Principalities, Archangels, and Angels. These last served as God's messengers and intervened from time to time in the affairs of mortals. Ordered life among humans, although manifestly imperfect when compared with the eternal bliss of the angelic orders, still modeled itself on that platonic idea of perfect harmony. Thus the state, the church, and the family all resembled one another because they resembled (however distantly) the kingdom of God. Richard Hooker, in his *Of the Laws of Ecclesiastical Polity* (1594–1597), defends the established Church of England in terms that emanate from a comparable idea of a divine, creative, and ordering law of nature "Whose seat is the bosom of God, whose voice the harmony of the world."

The devils of hell were fallen angels, with Satan as their leader. Such evil spirits might assume any number of shapes, such as demons, goblins, wizards, or witches. Believers in evil spirits generally made no distinction between orthodox Christian explanations of evil and the more primitive folklore of witchcraft. Belief in witchcraft was widespread indeed; King James I took the matter very seriously. So did Reginald Scot's *The Discovery of Witchcraft* (1584), though its author also attempted to confute what he regarded as ignorant superstition and char-

Ptolemy's earth-centered system of the universe (top) was challenged by the sun-centered system of Copernicus (bottom) with the publishing of De revolutionibus orbium coelestium *in 1543. Shakespeare, like other major poets of the English Renaissance, poetically represents the universe in cosmic terms as described by Ptolemy, but also reflects uncertainties generated by the new cosmology.*

latanism. Throughout Shakespeare's lifetime, belief and skepticism about such matters existed side by side.

A similar ambiguity pertained to belief in the Ptolemaic universe itself. All major poets of the Renaissance, including Shakespeare, Spenser, and Milton (who completed *Paradise Lost* after 1660), represented the universe in cosmic terms essentially as described by Ptolemy. Yet Nicolaus Copernicus's revolutionary theory of a sun-centered solar system (*De revolutionibus orbium coelestium*, published on the Continent in 1543) and the discovery of a new star in Cassiopeia in 1572 stimulated much new thought. Galileo Galilei, born in the same year as Shakespeare (1564), published in 1610 the results of his telescopic examinations of the moon, thereby further confirming Copernicus's hypothesis. Although the news of Galileo's astounding discovery came too late to affect any but the latest of Shakespeare's plays, a sense of excitement and dislocation was apparent throughout most of the years of his writing career. Thomas Nashe, in 1595, referred familiarly to Copernicus as the author "who held that the sun remains immobile in the center of the world, and that the earth is moved about the sun" (Nashe, *Works*, ed. R. B. McKerrow, 1904–1910, 3.94). John Donne lamented in 1611–1612 that the "new philosophy" (i.e., the new science) "calls all in doubt." Skeptical uncertainty about the cosmos was on the rise. The poetic affirmations in Renaissance art of traditional ideas of the cosmos can best be understood as a response to uncertainty—a statement of faith in an age of increasing skepticism.

Alchemy and Medicine

In all areas of Renaissance learning, the new and the old science were juxtaposed. Alchemy, for example, made important contributions to learning, despite its superstitious character. Its chief goal was the transformation of base metals into gold, on the assumption that all metals were ranked on a hierarchical scale and could be raised from lower to higher positions on that scale by means of certain alchemical techniques. Other aims of alchemy included the discovery of a universal cure for diseases and of a means for preserving life indefinitely. Such aims encouraged quackery and prompted various exposés, such as Chaucer's "The Canon's Yeoman's Tale" (late fourteenth century) and Jonson's *The Alchemist* (1610). Yet many of the procedures used in alchemy were essentially chemical procedures, and the science of chemistry received a valuable impetus from constant experimentation. Queen Elizabeth was seriously interested in alchemy throughout her life.

In physics, medicine, and psychology, as well, older concepts vied with new. Traditional learning apportioned all physical matter into four elements: earth, air, fire, and water. Each of these was thought to be a different combination of the four "qualities" of the universe: hot, cold,

Gedruckt zu Franckfurt am Mayn/durch Johan Feyerabendt. 1598.

Alchemists employed relatively sophisticated equipment in their futile search for the "philosopher's stone," a reputed substance supposed to possess the property of changing other metals into gold and silver.

moist, and dry. Earth combined cold and dry; air, hot and moist; fire, hot and dry; and water, cold and moist. Earth and water were the baser or lower elements, confined to the physical world; fire and air were aspiring elements, tending upward. Humans, as a microcosm of the larger universe, contained in themselves the four elements. The individual's temperament, or "humor" or "complexion," depended on which "humor" predominated in that person. The four humors in humans corresponded to the four elements of physical matter. The blood was hot and moist, like air; yellow bile or choler was hot and dry, like fire; phlegm was cold and moist, like water; and black bile was cold and dry, like earth. A predominance of blood in an individual created a sanguine or cheerful temperament (or humor), yellow bile produced a choleric or irascible temperament, phlegm produced a phlegmatic or stolid temperament, and black bile produced a melancholic temperament. Diet could affect the balance among these humors, since an excess of a particular food would stimulate overproduction of one humor. The stomach and the liver, which converted food into humors, were regarded as the seat of human passions. The spleen was thought to be the seat of laughter, sudden impulse, or caprice, and also melancholy. (Hotspur, in *1 Henry IV*, is said to be "governed by a spleen," 5.2.19.) Strong emotional reactions could be explained in terms of the physiology of the humors: in anger, the blood rushed to the head and thereby produced a flush of red color and staring eyes; in fear, the blood migrated to the heart and thus left the face and liver pale, and so on. Sighs supposedly cost the heart a drop of blood, while wine could refortify it (as Falstaff insists in *2 Henry IV*, 4.3.90–123). The signs of youth were warmth and moisture, as in Desdemona's "hot and moist"

hand (*Othello*, 3.4.39); those of age were "a moist eye, a dry hand, a yellow cheek, a white beard, a decreasing leg, an increasing belly" (*2 Henry IV*, 1.2.179–81). A common remedy for illness was to let blood and thereby purge the body of unwanted humors.

The name traditionally associated with such theories was that of Galen, the most celebrated of ancient writers on medicine (c. 130 A.D.). A more revolutionary name was that of Paracelsus, a famous German physician (c. 1493–1541) who attacked the traditional medical learning of his time and urged a more unfettered pragmatic research into pharmacy and medicine. Such experimentalism bore fruit in the anatomical research of Vesalius (1514–1564) and in William Harvey's investigations of the circulation of the blood (c. 1616). Nevertheless, the practice of medicine in Renaissance times remained under the influence of the "humors" theory until quite late, and its ideas are found throughout Shakespeare's writings.

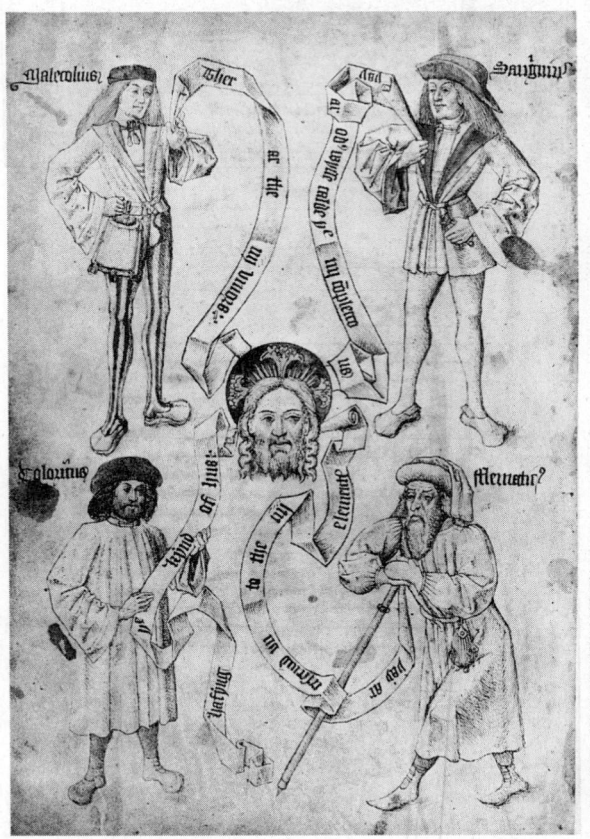

The four humors of black bile, blood, yellow bile or choler, and phlegm, as shown in this illustration from an illuminated manuscript, were believed to govern the human personality by producing a disposition toward melancholic, sanguine, choleric, or phlegmatic temperaments.

Learning

In learning generally, and in theories of education, new ideas conflicted with old. The curriculum of schools and colleges in the Renaissance was inherited largely from the Middle Ages and displayed many traditional characteristics. The curriculum consisted of the seven Liberal Arts: a lower division, called the trivium, comprised of grammar, rhetoric, and logic; and an upper division, called the quadrivium, comprised of arithmetic, geometry, astronomy, and music. In addition, there were the philosophical studies associated chiefly with Aristotle: natural philosophy, ethics, and metaphysics.

Aristotle's name had a towering influence in medieval times and remained important to the Renaissance as well. Even among his Renaissance admirers, however, Aristotle proved more compelling in practical matters than in the abstract scholastic reasoning associated with his name in the Middle Ages. The Italian Aristotelians whose work made its way into England were interested primarily in the science of human behavior. Aristotelian ethics was for them a practical subject, telling people how to live usefully and well and how to govern themselves politically. Rhetoric was the science of persuasion, enabling people to use eloquence for socially useful goals. Poetry was a kind of rhetoric, a language of persuasion which dramatists, too, might use for morally pragmatic ends.

At the same time, new thinkers were daring to attack Aristotle by name as a symbol of traditional medieval thought. The attack was not always fair to Aristotle himself, whose work had been bent to the *a priori* purposes of much medieval scholasticism. Nevertheless, his name had assumed such symbolic importance that he had to be confronted directly. The Huguenot logician Petrus Ramus (1515–1572), defiantly proclaiming that "everything that Aristotle taught is false," argued for rules of logic as derived from observation. He urged, for example, that his students learn about rhetoric from observing in detail Cicero's effect on his listeners, rather than by the rote practice of syllogism. Actually, Ramus's thought was less revolutionary in its concepts of logic than in the tremendous ferment of opinion caused by his iconoclastic teaching.

A basic issue at stake in the anti-Aristotelian movement was that of traditional authority versus independent observation. How do people best acquire true knowledge—through the teachings of their predecessors or through their own discovery? The issue had profound implications for religious truth as well: should individuals heed the collective wisdom of the earthly church or read the Bible with their individual perceptions as their guide? Is "reason" an accretive wisdom handed down by authority or a quality of the individual soul? Obviously, a middle ground exists between the two extremes, and no new thinker of the Renaissance professed to abandon entirely the use of ancient author-

ity. For men like Henricus Agrippa (1486–1535) and Sir Francis Bacon (1561–1626), however, scholastic tradition had exerted its oppressive influence far too long. Authority needed to be examined critically and scientifically. Bacon, in his *The Advancement of Learning* (1605), fought against the blind acceptance of ancient wisdom and argued that "knowledge derived from Aristotle, and exempted from liberty of examination, will not rise again higher than the knowledge of Aristotle." Sir Walter Ralegh and others joined in the excited new search for what human "reason" could discover when set free from scholastic restraint. Such belief in the perfectibility of human reason owed some of its inspiration to Italian Neoplatonic humanists like Giovanni Pico della Mirandola (1463–1494), who, in his *Oration on the Dignity of Man*, celebrated a human race "constrained by no limits" in accordance with the potential of its own free will. The new learning did not seem to trouble these men in their religious faith, although a tension between scientific observation and faith in miracles was to become plentifully evident in the seventeenth century.

The Nature of Humankind

Medieval thought generally assigned to humankind a uniquely superior place in the order of creation on earth. That assumption of superiority rested on biblical and patristic teachings about the hierarchy of creation, in which humanity stood at the apex of physical creation nearest God and the angels. Humankind was thus supreme on earth in the so-called chain of being. Human reason, though subject to error because of sinfulness, enabled humans to aspire toward divinity. Humans were, in the view of medieval philosophers, the great amphibians, as well as the microcosm of the universe, part bestial and part immortal, doomed by Adam's fall to misery and death in this life but promised eternal salvation through Christ's atonement. Right reason, properly employed, could lead to the truths of revealed Christianity and thus give humankind a glimpse of the heavenly perfection one day to be ours. Renaissance Neoplatonism, as expounded, for example, in the writings of Marsilio Ficino, Pico della Mirandola, and Baldassare Castiglione (in *The Courtier*, translated by Sir Thomas Hoby in 1561), offered humanity a vision of a platonic ladder, extending from the perception of physical beauty to contemplation of the platonic idea of beauty and finally to the experiencing of God's transcendent love.

Protestant thought of the Renaissance did not wholly disagree with this formulation, but it did place a major new emphasis on human reprobation. The idea was not new, for Saint Augustine (354–430) had insisted on human depravity and our total dependence on God's inscrutable grace, but, in the years of the Reformation, this theology took on a new urgency. Martin Luther

(1483–1540), by rejecting veneration of the Virgin Mary and the saints, and by taking away the sacraments of confession and penance, by which individual Christians could seek the institutional comforts of the Catholic Church, exposed the individual sinner to agonies of conscience that could result in a sense of alienation and loss. The rewards were great for those who found new faith in God's infinite goodness, but the hazards of predestinate damnation were fearsome to those who were less sure of their spiritual welfare. Luther's God was inscrutable, majestic, and infallible. Luther's God decreed salvation for the elect and damnation for all others, and His will could not be challenged or questioned. The individual was to blame for sin, even though God hardened the hearts of the reprobate. John Calvin (1509–1564) placed even greater stress on predestinate good and evil and insisted that the grace of salvation was founded on God's freely given mercy that humans could not possibly deserve. Salvation was God's to give or withhold as He wished; humans might not repine that in His incomprehensible wisdom God has "barred the door of life to those whom He has given over to damnation." Faced with such

a view of human spiritual destiny, the individual Christian's lot was one of potential tragedy. The human soul was a battleground of good and evil.

Michel de Montaigne (1533–1592), Shakespeare's great French contemporary, provided a very different and heterodox way of thinking about human imperfection. In his "Apology for Raymond Sebond" and other of his essays, Montaigne questioned the assumption of humanity's superiority to the animal kingdom, and in doing so gave Shakespeare a fundamentally different way to consider the nature of humankind—a way that reflects itself, for example, in Hamlet's observations on humans as "quintessence of dust." Montaigne stressed humans' arrogance, vanity, and frailty. He was unconvinced of humanity's purported moral superiority to the animals and argued that animals are no less endowed with a soul. Montaigne undermined, in other words, the hierarchy in which the human race was the unquestioned master of the physical world, just as Copernican science overturned the earth-centered cosmos and Machiavelli's political system dismissed as an improbable fiction the divinely constituted hierarchy of the state. Montaigne's very choice of

This guide, graphically setting forth the ideals to which every English gentlewoman and gentleman should aspire, illustrates the Renaissance concept that outward deportment and accomplishments should correctly and invariably mirror a person's inner nature.

the essay as his favorite literary form bespeaks his commitment to attempts and explorations, rather than to definite solutions; etymologically, the very word "essay" signifies an exploration or inquiry. Montaigne was not alone in his skepticism about human nature; his ideas had much in common with Bernardino Telesio's *De Rerum Natura* and with the writings of the Italian Giordano Bruno. Montaigne was followed in the seventeenth century by that overpowering iconoclast, Thomas Hobbes, who extended the concept of mechanical laws governing human society and human psychology. Hobbes postdates Shakespeare, to be sure, but one has only to consider Iago's philosophy of the assertive individual will (in *Othello*) or Edmund's contempt for his father Gloucester's astrological pieties (in *King Lear*) to see the enormous impact on Shakespeare of the new heterodoxies of his age. Shakespeare makes us aware that skeptical thought can be used by dangerous men like Iago, Edmund, and Richard III to promote their own villainies in a world no longer held together by the certitudes of traditional faith, but he also shows us the gullibility of some traditionalists and the abuses of power that can be perpetrated in the name of ancient and divine privilege by a king like Richard II. Above all, Shakespeare delights in the play of mind among competing ideas, inviting us to wonder, for example, if Caliban in *The Tempest* is not invested with natural qualities that Prospero, his Christian colonizer, does not sufficiently understand, and whether some of the other supposedly civilized Europeans who come to Caliban's island do not have a great deal to learn from its uncivilized beauty.

THE DRAMA BEFORE SHAKESPEARE

When William Shakespeare made his first acquaintance with the professions of acting and playwriting in the late 1580s, the English theater was already a flourishing institution with a long and complex history. In order to understand what opportunities it offered Shakespeare, we need to look briefly at that history.

The Liturgical Drama

The sixth-century Catholic Church had been largely responsible for closing down the late Roman theater, with its bloody gladiatorial contests and its pervasive moral decadence. Thereafter, for about four centuries the theater officially did not exist in western Europe. Paradoxically, it was the Church in the tenth century that sponsored the beginnings of a new dramatic form within the liturgy (the prescribed form of worship) of the Church itself. This dramatic activity perhaps began as an insertion into the regular service of a "trope" or musical composition designed

to be sung antiphonally by members of a monastic community. The earliest of these may have been composed for Easter morning, at the supremely important moment of Christ's Resurrection. The Mass itself had long displayed semidramatic characteristics, and the first Easter expansions must not have seemed particularly revolutionary to anyone involved. The simplest of the early tropes (though perhaps not the first), composed at St. Gall in Switzerland some time early in the tenth century, consists merely of a chanted interrogation, "*Quem quaeritis in sepulchro, Christicolae?*" ("Whom do you seek in the sepulcher, O followers of Christ?"), and a chanted response, "*Jesum Nazarenum crucifixum, o caelicolae*" ("Jesus of Nazareth who was crucified, O heaven-dwellers"), followed by an announcement that Christ is risen as he had predicted. From other early texts of this sort, we can guess that this simple antiphon was accompanied by some stylized semidramatic assignment of roles to members of the religious community as the three Marys visiting Christ's tomb and as the angels guarding the tomb. At any rate, tenth-century tropes of Easter soon included use of simple costumes, physical movement toward the tomb, and appropriate gestures.

Other actions were appropriate to such a dramatic representation of the Resurrection: the visit of the disciples to the sepulchre, the appearance of Christ as a gardener to Mary Magdalene, and his appearance to the disciples on the road to Emmaus. Moreover, other seasons of the year afforded similar opportunities, especially Christmas; the crèche was already a venerable custom, and Christmas tropes may have originated as early as Easter tropes or possibly even earlier.

In any event, Christmas liturgical dramatic activity grew apace, perhaps more rapidly than at Easter because of the sacred inhibitions associated with the Resurrection. By the twelfth century, Christmas liturgical drama had become lengthy and complex, including not only the visit of the shepherds and the Magi but also the slaughter of the innocents and the flight into Egypt. Simultaneously, liturgical plays were developed for other festivals in the liturgical calendar. Some were in the vernacular: by the end of the twelfth century, an Anglo-Norman poet had written a play of Adam featuring the creation of humankind, the expulsion from the garden of Eden, the slaughter of Abel by Cain, and a lengthy procession of prophets announcing the advent of Christ. Such early vernacular plays may well have influenced the development of Latin liturgical drama. The twelfth century also saw a play about Daniel in the lions' den, various Saint Nicholas plays in which that popular saint performed miracles, a play at Tegernsee about the Antichrist, a play about the conversion of Saint Paul, and many others. In other words, by 1200 or thereabouts, the liturgical drama had produced plays of considerable length and complexity for numerous religious festivals throughout the year. Montecassino in Italy had a complex Passion play by this date. The late twelfth or early thirteenth century saw the performance at Benediktbeuren in Germany of the impressive "Carmina Burana" plays for Easter and Christmas.

The Corpus Christi Play

Although one might suppose that these liturgical plays would be gathered together into larger cycles of the divine history of the world, compilations of this sort do not seem generally to have taken place. Liturgical plays continued to be performed individually at appropriate times in the Church calendar. Most religious communities owned and produced one or two such plays year after year, but no communities owned or produced very many such plays. The plays were numerous but scattered throughout western Europe.

What appears to have happened instead of the forming of liturgical plays into a cycle is that the various craft guilds of certain towns, especially in England, banded together with the ecclesiastical authorities to produce a summer festival that would be both civic and religious in nature. One impetus was the institution of the feast of Corpus Christi in the early fourteenth century. The feast was designed to honor the Eucharist (the sacrament of the Lord's Supper) in a joyous mood, uninhibited by the somber reflections on Christ's crucifixion that are appropriate to Passion Week. The date chosen, the Thursday after Trinity Sunday, came during a slack period in the liturgical calendar in very late spring. In May or June the days of the year are longest, and the English weather is generally cooperative. The cycles that thus originated were performed on other festivals of the early summer season besides Corpus Christi day, but that festival has given its name to the genre.

Corpus Christi plays were often performed either in procession on moving pageant wagons or in arena theaters with scaffolds located around the acting area. This illustration shows a procession around a square in Brussels in 1615, using staging methods perhaps not unlike those in use in England during the fifteenth and sixteenth centuries.

The feast of Corpus Christi regularly featured elaborate processions through town, and, indeed, these processions may have preceded the plays themselves. Various guilds were usually assigned events in the divine history of the world for which they undertook to present dramatized renditions. The plays written for such guilds had to be numerous in most towns, since there were many guilds: the York cycle, for example, had forty-eight plays; the so-called Towneley cycle (probably misnamed, perhaps acted at Wakefield), thirty-two; the so-called N-Town or *Ludus Coventriae* cycle (perhaps acted in the vicinity of Lincoln), forty-three. The texts were evidently not translations from the Latin liturgical drama but were English compositions often based on medieval narrative accounts of the divine history of the world. Such versions contained much patristic and legendary material, as well as straightforward biblical narrative; for example, the account of Christ's harrowing of hell, based on the apocryphal Gospel of Saint Thomas rather than on the Bible itself, had become an accepted part of the story. More noncanonical still are accounts of Mary's childhood and of her marriage to Joseph. The cycles varied somewhat as to content, but they tended to choose many of the same traditional stories embodied in Church liturgy. The main figures in these favorite stories—Abel, Noah, Abraham, and Isaac—were often seen as "typological," that is, prefiguring by their piety and suffering the advent of Christ himself.

The common core of most cycles included the following: the creation, the fall of Adam and expulsion from Paradise, Cain's slaying of Abel, Noah's flood, Abraham and Isaac, Moses, the prophets, the Annunciation, the visit of the shepherds and the Magi, the flight into Egypt, the slaughter of the innocents, the baptism, the temptation in the wilderness, the raising of Lazarus, the entry into Jerusalem and the entire Passion sequence, the burial, the harrowing of hell, the Resurrection, Christ's appearances to the disciples, his Ascension, and the day of doom. Other subjects were often added, such as the story of Pentecost, the assumption of the blessed Virgin Mary, and the coming of Antichrist.

Sometimes these medieval "pageants" were acted by individual craft guilds on pageant wagons before a series of audiences gathered at fixed locales throughout the town. Recent investigations have shown, however, the formidable difficulties involved in performing a complete cycle of plays in narrow streets, with each pageant having to wait in line until the preceding pageant had finished. Street processions remained common but may, in some cases, have involved displays in *tableau vivant* rather than a full performance of each play. Certainly, in some towns the plays themselves were acted, not on pageant wagons, but in the round, in arena theaters with several scaffolds on the periphery or even in the center of the acting area. Scaffolds variously represented heaven and hell, Pilate's judgment hall, the house of the Last Supper, and the like.

In the marketplace or in the cathedral close, the pageants may have been ranged in order about the open space so that the spectators themselves could move from scene to scene. Multiple-place staging certainly existed in London and in the south of England, and was the regular form of the mystery-play stage on the Continent. (The Corpus Christi plays are sometimes called "mystery" plays, since they were acted by the "mystery" or trade guilds.)

As many as twenty full-scope plays, mostly of the Corpus Christi type, may have existed at one time in England, though the complete texts of only four have been preserved. The York, Towneley, and N-Town cycles have already been mentioned; a fourth extant cycle was acted at Chester. In addition, two fragments exist of a cycle acted at Coventry, one each from Norwich and Newcastle-on-Tyne, and several other single scenes from places not located. A Cornish cycle, written in Celtic, presents some Old Testament episodes and a Passion sequence more like certain continental religious dramas than the English plays we have been discussing.

Shakespeare probably saw Corpus Christi plays in his youth, before they were suppressed by Protestant authorities, and he appears to recollect them at times in his plays. When Hamlet says disparagingly of bombastic acting that "it out-herods Herod" (*Hamlet*, 3.2.14), he is thinking of the stage bully of the slaughter of the innocents who, in the Coventry version, "ragis in the pagond [pageant] and in the strete also." Herod was indeed legendary for his rant. The Porter in *Macbeth* is surely alluding to Christ's harrowing of hell when he complains, "But this place is too cold for hell. / I'll devil-porter it no further" (2.3.16–17). The medieval heritage adds a remarkable dimension to this scene: Macbeth's castle becomes a kind of hell, as the Porter jokingly observes, and Macduff's arrival takes on an aspect of deliverance through which Macbeth and his "fiend-like Queen" (5.8.70) will be brought to account. Henry V has Herod in mind again in his speech to the beleaguered citizens of Harfleur, when he bids them surrender lest they see their naked infants "spitted upon pikes" and the childrens' mothers howling in grief "as did the wives of Jewry / At Herod's bloody-hunting slaughtermen" (3.3.38–41). More broadly, the cosmic structure of the cycle plays, bound together in their many episodes by an overarching narrative of divine history, offered a model of construction that Shakespeare would apply in modified form to his writing of English history plays.

Saints' Plays and Morality Plays

Saints' plays were also widely current in England, although few examples survive today. These dramas resembled the Corpus Christi cycles in their staging and their panoramic religious spectacle, but they differed from the cycles in that they told about the lives and miracles of individual saints and martyrs rather than, as in the cycles, telling the entire divine history of the human race as incorporated chiefly in the Old and New Testaments. Some particular cases, to be sure, incorporated features of both saints' lives and Corpus Christi drama. The story of Mary Magdalene, for example, was derived in part from the biblical accounts of her meetings with Christ, but the narrative had been enormously expanded to include legendary reports of her travels and miraculous deeds as a saint. St. Paul was another biblical figure whose sudden conversion and subsequent travels gave to his story the characteristics of a typical saint's life. As a group, however, saints' plays offered more emphasis on miraculous conversion from sin to grace and on the wondrous intervention of saints in the lives of ordinary people than did the Corpus Christi cycles.

Shakespeare's debt to saints' plays is indirect and hard to demonstrate. Some of his history plays reveal a pattern of conversion followed by glorious acts, as in the saga of Henry V, but this story was inherent in the myth of Henry V that Shakespeare inherited. Comedies of repentance, such as *Measure for Measure* and *The Winter's Tale,* show us a pattern of redemptive sorrow and renewal in which the protagonist is given an almost miraculous second chance. Shakespeare's late romances are especially illuminated by this tradition of conversion narratives. We cannot be sure, however, that he encountered such stories through saints' plays (which were suppressed by the English Reformation), since nondramatic sources, such as the Legenda Aurea or Golden Legend of the lives of the saints, were more immediately available to him.

Shakespeare's awareness of the morality play is easier to prove. Indeed, this genre had survived well enough into the late sixteenth century to make a significant impact on the plays of Shakespeare, Ben Jonson, and oth-ers. The morality play chose as its distinctive mode the allegorical rendition of humanity's spiritual journey through life to an eventual preparation for death and judgment before God. Allegory was not unknown in the cycles or in the saints' plays, but it became the staple of the morality play. The earliest texts, from the sixteenth century, include *The Castle of Perseverance, Mankind,* and *Everyman.* Although the last of these focuses atypically on the moment of death, more typical early morality plays tell a story of spiritual struggle and eventual triumph over sin. This simple plot had an advantage over the cycles and saints' plays in that it could be adapted to the religious and social controversies of the era. The Corpus Christi cycles and saints' plays were, after all, tied to biblical or legendary events; when Reformation authorities sought to suppress the "idolatrous" representation of God on stage or banned worship of the Virgin Mary and the saints, the cycles and saints' plays were doomed. Even though they were occasionally staged late enough in the sixteenth century for Shakespeare to have seen performances, they belonged chiefly to an earlier, pre-Reformation era. The morality play, on the other hand, thrived on controversy. Its plot of soul struggle between the forces of good and evil for the allegiance of Mankind or Everyman, and his wavering progress toward eventual salvation, could and did frequently serve as a vehicle for portraying many social phenomena of the sixteenth century.

In John Skelton's political morality play called *Magnificence* (1515–1518), for example, the protagonist is a representative king figure who must choose between evil counselors urging fiscal extravagance on the one hand and wise counselors urging fiscal prudence on the other hand. The plot, telling of the King's temptation and his choosing of the wrong path before he is finally awakened to his folly, is essentially that of nonpolitical morality

Four allegorical characters in the morality play Hickescorner *were Contemplation, Perseverance, Imagination, and Free Will.*

plays, such as *Hickescorner* or *Youth* (c. 1513–1520), in which the human protagonist inevitably succumbs to temptation but is eventually rescued through divine guidance. The issues in Skelton's play have embraced secular as well as spiritual concerns, while the simple story line and the dramatic structure have remained virtually unchanged. The study of a "historical" type, in this case a king, enables such a play to comment on contemporary history and yet appeal simultaneously to a universal moral pattern. Skelton's play may allude indirectly to the fiscal recklessness of Henry VIII under Cardinal Wolsey's persuasive tutelage, but it discusses fiscal responsibility in general terms that also apply to any king—or to any human. Shakespeare's English history plays, especially the early plays about Henry VI and Richard III, owe an important debt to the tradition of the political morality, as exemplified by *Magnificence*.

Shakespeare's history play *King John* studies a king who had actually been the protagonist of the first play to represent an English monarch, *King Johan*, by John Bale (1538, later revised). Although Shakespeare may not have consulted Bale's play directly, Bale still had made an impressive contribution to the English history play by demonstrating how the morality structure could be used in the analysis of political crises. His play is an avowedly Protestant tract in the guise of a morality play, depicting its historical protagonist as a victim of Catholic duplicity and hence an example of what sixteenth-century England had to fear from its Catholic enemies. Later popular plays, combining a morality structure with a passionate interest in history and contemporary political theory, include Thomas Preston's *Cambises* (1560–1561) and John Pickering's *Horestes* (1567).

During the Reformation, the morality play was used polemically by both the Protestants and the Catholics. Dramatists were often commissioned by governmental authorities to write plays for public performance by touring actors as weapons of ideological persuasion. In Protestant plays, such as *Lusty Juventus* (c. 1547–1553) or *New Custom* (c. 1570), the villainous Vices were depicted as Catholic tempters; in Catholic plays, such as *Respublica* (1553, during the reign of Queen Mary), the Vices were Protestant. The protean flexibility of the morality formula enabled it to adapt itself to many different situations in this way. Polemical drama put ideology ahead of artistic concern, to be sure, but constant experimentation with new forms provided the popular drama of midcentury England with much-needed practical experience. One permutation of the Reformation morality play, for example, proved of considerable importance to the development of English tragedy. In some Protestant morality plays that Calvinistically stress humankind's innate depravity, such as William Wager's *Enough Is as Good as a Feast* (c. 1559–1570) and Nathaniel Woodes's *The Conflict of Conscience* (1570–1581), spiritual struggle ends in failure rather than in triumph for the human protagonist. Among the great English tragedies of the late sixteenth century, Christopher Marlowe's *Doctor Faustus* (c. 1588) is most obviously indebted to such dramatic renditions of spiritual despair, but Shakespeare's *Macbeth* and other plays may also have learned something from a native homiletic tradition in tragedy.

In staging and acting, as well, the morality play served as an important transition from late medieval religious drama to the drama of the late sixteenth century. In its origins, as seen, for example, in *The Castle of Perseverance* (early fifteenth century), the morality play had been staged like many of the cycles or saints' plays, such as *Mary Magdalene*, that is, in the round, with an open acting area surrounded by acting scaffolds on the periphery. The morality play developed great flexibility in its staging, however, just as it had developed flexibility in its approach to contemporary political or social issues. *Mankind* (c. 1471) required only an acting platform, raised probably on trestles to a height of four or five feet, and a curtain backdrop through which the actors could enter and exit. A stage of this simplicity could be carried anywhere in England and set up at a moment's notice—on a village green, in a town hall, or in the banqueting hall of a lord's manor. The troupe acting *Mankind* was vastly more efficient and transportable than the company of twenty-two or more actors required for *The Castle of Perseverance; Mankind* required only six actors.

Troupes of four or five men and one boy apprentice (for women's roles) were quite standard in early Tudor England. Similar or even smaller troupes enacted folk plays and miracle plays, the texts of which are regrettably not as extensively preserved as those of morality plays. Such troupes traveled the length and breadth of the country, and dominated the field of popular entertainment from the late fifteenth century until Shakespeare's day. They were, in fact, the professional ancestors of the Shakespearean acting company. Under the direction of their leading player, who often acted the part of Vice since it was usually the choice role of the morality play, the actors were organized as repertory companies able to perform a number of plays on short notice and to present a remarkably large number of roles by the doubling of parts. They grew slowly in size as they prospered, but they retained their traditional organization. The best of the troupes gravitated to London, where, in 1576, a troupe of perhaps six or eight men and two boys founded England's first permanent theater. Shakespeare's company, the Lord Chamberlain's men (later the King's men), was only slightly larger than this, with perhaps ten actors who were partners or "sharers" in the company, two or more boys, and a few hired hands. Shakespeare's early plays, moreover, were sometimes structured for presentation by just such a company, much as earlier popular plays had been structured, with considerable doubling of

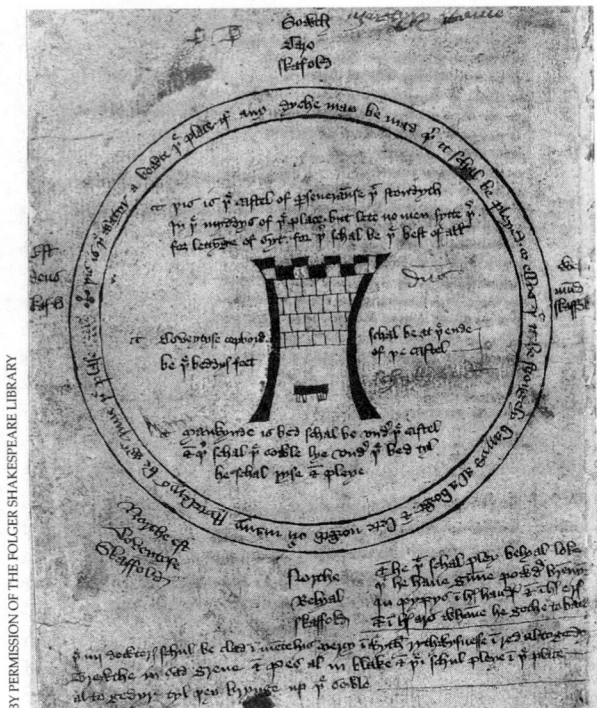

A fifteenth-century diagram for the presentation of The Castle of Perseverance *shows the scaffolds surrounding the open acting area with the castle in the center.*

parts and with a multiplicity of episodes allowing for the sequential presentation of numerous minor roles. The early history plays about Henry VI and Richard III are especially illustrative of this structural tradition.

Shakespeare's references to morality drama suggest a real familiarity. Prince Hal jestingly caricatures Falstaff as "that roasted Manningtree ox with the pudding in his belly, that reverend Vice, that grey iniquity, that father ruffian, that vanity in years . . . that old whitebearded Satan" (*1 Henry IV*, 2.4.447–58). Manningtree in Essex appears to have been renowned for its annual fair at which plays were acted and great-sized oxen were roasted; the Vice, as we have seen, was the chief comic tempter of most morality plays. Falstaff himself refers to the Vice's traditional dagger of lath in his contemptuous remarks about Justice Shallow: "And now is this Vice's dagger become a squire" (*2 Henry IV*, 3.2.317–18). Feste, in *Twelfth Night*, exits at one point with a promise to the audience that he will return soon "Like to the old Vice" with his "dagger of lath" and "his rage and his wrath" (4.2.120–31). Kent, in *King Lear*, speaks of Goneril as having taken "Vanity the puppet's part against the royalty of her father" (2.2.36–7), as though she were a personified representation of Pride in a morality play. The evocation of that

genre strengthens our perception that good and evil are indeed battling over Lear's destiny on a cosmic scale. Richard III explicitly compares himself to "the formal Vice, Iniquity" in his use of sinister double entendres and his boasting to the audience of his cleverness 3.1.82–3).

Shakespeare's specific references to late medieval drama are less important, however, than his larger indebtedness to it. His use of a structural tradition of episodic multiplicity and of alternation between seriousness and comedy is especially evident in the early history plays. Of equal significance is his indebtedness to the Vice, the comic tempter of the morality play whose sinister but fascinating techniques of evil persuasion had become an enduring part of Tudor popular drama. The Vice's boastful and chortling brand of villainy is still clearly recognizable, though transmuted into superb poetry, in the insinuations of Richard III, Aaron the Moor (in *Titus Andronicus*), Iago (in *Othello*), and Edmund (in *King Lear*). As Bernard Spivack has argued, in his *Shakespeare and the Allegory of Evil*, Shakespeare's secular vision of the contest between good and evil for human souls owes much to the morality tradition and to other forms of medieval drama.

Early Tudor Humanist Drama

The development of the morality play and of other medieval drama, briefly sketched in the preceding sections, tells only one part of the story of sixteenth-century drama. The trend we have observed in morality drama, toward the depiction of contemporary English life, manifested itself also in other kinds of plays that were not so plainly derived from the religious drama of the Middle Ages. A relatively new influence was that of classical and neoclassical drama, from the ancient classical world and from Renaissance Europe. Important, too, were the secular kinds of dramatic entertainment that had flourished in the English court even before the advent of neoclassicism. Early Tudor drama for courtly and well-educated audiences was heterogeneous because it reflected so many diverse impulses: the intensified renewal of classical learning that had come about through the activities of the new humanists, the ferment of ideologies introduced by the Reformation, the increase in social mobility in the Tudor court, and the like. In varying proportions, the courtly and intellectual drama of the period borrowed from the English morality play, from courtly pastimes such as the "disguising" (a kind of masque) and the dialogue or *débat*, from secular farce and romance, from classical and neoclassical literature, and even from the Corpus Christi cycles and saints' plays. The mixture, experimental and often uneven, was nonetheless stimulating, because it attempted to fuse English culture with the thought of neoclassical Europe. This drama was usually staged in courtly surroundings, such as the banqueting halls of the aristocracy. (See "The

Tudor Hall" below, in the section on London Theaters and Dramatic Companies.)

Especially important in the development of this early Tudor drama were the humanists who associated themselves with Sir Thomas More and his patron Cardinal Morton. These men were, like their counterparts in Italy and elsewhere on the Continent, intensely devoted to the revival of classical learning in all its aspects—art, architecture, literary texts, historical knowledge, and politics—and thus to the enhancement of the human spirit. Their shared ideals can be seen in the plays that they wrote or sponsored. Henry Medwall, chaplain to Cardinal Morton, wrote a morality play called *Nature* (c. 1490–1501) that reveals an interest in Aristotelian ethics, as well as in traditional Christian ideas of salvation. Medwall also wrote *Fulgens and Lucrece* (c. 1490–1500), the earliest extant play in England to use an ancient Roman setting and a secular romantic love plot. The heroine, Lucrece, chooses the love of a virtuous but untitled "new" man at court in preference to a haughty and degenerate aristocrat. This *débat* was derived from *De Vera Nobilitate* by Buonaccorso of Pistoia, an ardent Italian humanist. Despite its ancient setting and romantic plot, it is also unmistakably relevant to the struggle between "new" men and old aristocrats in the court of Henry VII. Both of Medwall's plays were printed by John Rastell, another humanist in the service of Cardinal Morton. Rastell, who married More's sister, wrote a humanist interlude called *The Nature of the Four Elements* (c. 1517–1518), in which he excitedly discussed the latest scientific theories concerning the roundness of the world and other such new ideas. He is probably the author of *Of Gentleness and Nobility* (c. 1527–1530) as well, a play that iconoclastically asks whether monarchy and the inheritance of property are not social evils that ideally ought to be abolished. The influence of Thomas More's *Utopia* on this play is unmistakable.

John Heywood, son-in-law of John Rastell, was the most important and versatile dramatist of the humanist group. All his plays, except *Witty and Witless*, which has been preserved only in manuscript, were printed by John Rastell or his son, William Rastell. Heywood's plays fall into two groups: the courtly disputations, such as *The Play of Love, The Play of the Weather*, and *Witty and Witless* (c. 1525–1533), and the more popular farces that may have been intended for popular audiences as well, such as *The Pardoner and the Friar, The Four PP*, and *John John the Husband* (c. 1513–1533). In the first group, *Weather* reveals a characteristic attention to humanist and courtly themes. In an obvious analogy to the Tudor concept of an absolutist yet benevolent monarchy, the various petitioners of the play complain to Jupiter about the weather but are finally persuaded to be grateful for the mixed weather that is provided them. Heywood is suggesting, in other words, that the English monarchy must bestow its favors impartially on all classes of persons and that all subjects ought to recognize the essential soundness of the social order as it presently exists. Heywood's second group of plays, on the other hand, eschews such courtly and political themes for a broader slapstick comedy in the vein of Chaucerian *fabliau* and French farce.

In addition to these humanist plays written by members of the Sir Thomas More circle, the learned drama of early Tudor England included many plays written for schoolboys or for the choristers attached to royal and noble households. The plays written under such auspices tended to reveal a much stronger interest in classical and neoclassical drama than did the plays written for popular audiences. Schoolmasters wrote dramatic texts derived from the classics for educational purposes; at court, sophisticated audiences were interested in the latest dramatic fashions from Italy or France. Ancient Greek drama did not receive nearly so much attention, however, as the Latin drama of Terence (c. 186–159 B.C.), Plautus (c. 254–184 B.C.), and Seneca (c. 4 B.C. –65 A.D.). These Latin authors had long been used as schoolboys' texts, though they were frequently expurgated or allegorized into the terms of Christian morality in order to render them suitable for schoolboys' sensibilities. This academic tradition, on the Continent and in England, produced a number of imitative plays that could be acted by boys as part of their training in classical languages. Some plays, such as John Palsgrave's *Acolastus* (1540), were intended to be read rather than acted. Many others were Latin biblical plays in classical guise, such as Thomas Watson's *Absalom* (c. 1535–1544) and George Buchanan's *Jephthes* (1540–1545).

At court and in noble households, choristers were becoming noted for their acting ability. They performed chiefly during seasons of revels, such as in the Christmas season. They did not appear commercially before public audiences during the early Tudor period, as did the players of moralities and popular interludes. The Children of the Royal Chapel are known to have presented plays as early as 1506. The boys of St. Paul's School acted before King Henry VIII in 1528. Later, in the 1570s and 1580s, these children's groups were organized into professional acting companies. Children's plays were generally written by schoolmasters or choirmasters. The plays were heavily influenced by continental traditions and often depicted themes, such as that of the Prodigal Son, that were congenial to boys of school age. *Nice Wanton* (1547–1553) offers an instance of this sort. Biblical themes were common and were sometimes used to urge a political lesson in the presence of a courtly audience. *Godly Queen Hester* (1525–1529), for example, seems to defend the cause of Katharine of Aragon and to denounce the machinations of Cardinal Wolsey. *Jacob and Esau* (1547–1553) draws an unflattering comparison between the unregenerate Esau and those who refuse to abandon the Catholic faith. Classical subjects were, of course, much in

Early Tudor drama employed the talents of boy actors on stage such as this company, the Children of the Royal Chapel.

demand as a way of educating youth, as in *Appius and Virginia* (1559–1567) and in Richard Edwards's *Damon and Pythias* (c. 1565).

Early Comedy

Schoolboys' drama was also vitally important in the development of classical or "regular" comedy on the English stage. Native morality drama was often highly comic, to be sure, especially in its depiction of the resourceful and scheming Vice; but English drama still had much to learn from classical examples about play construction and about the presentation of various types of characters. Perhaps the two best-known early English "regular" comedies were *Ralph Roister Doister* and *Gammer Gurton's Needle*.

Ralph Roister Doister, by Nicholas Udall, at one time headmaster of Eton, was acted probably between 1552 and 1554 by boy actors. Its staging is essentially that of neoclassical comedy, with two houses facing onto a street. The play employs a classical five-act structure and preserves the unities of time and place. (According to classical and neoclassical theory, a play's action should be limited to one location—a city, for example—and to a single day.) Stock comic types include the *miles gloriosus,* or braggart soldier, and the parasite. At the same time, Udall has transformed his heroine, usually a courtesan in Plautus's racy comedies, into a winsomely pious Englishwoman named Christian Custance. Ralph Roister Doister, the braggardly type for whom the play is named, is foiled in his mean-spirited determination to win Christian Custance away from her true love, Gawin Goodluck. Almost all the characters virtuously conspire to expose Ralph for his effrontery and pretended bravery; even Matthew Merrygreek, the fun-loving parasite, proves ultimately to be on the side of decency and fair play. Throughout, Udall has adapted Roman comedy to English customs and mores.

Gammer Gurton's Needle, written by William Stevenson, fellow of Christ's College, Cambridge, at about the

same time as *Roister Doister,* is similarly designed for student acting. Stock Roman characters are transformed into hearty English types. Diccon the Bedlam, who engineers the farcical action of the lost needle, resembles not only the Roman parasite but also the English natural fool or zany. To some extent, he also reminds us of the mischievous and inventive Vice of the morality play. Other characters are even less purely Roman in their origin: Hodge, the clownish servant; Dame Chat, the shrewish neighbor; and Dr. Rat, the impoverished and ill-trained clergyman who spends most of his time drinking and complaining about his wretched lot. The play is an educated college man's indulgent laugh at his country neighbors. Yet the play is, like *Ralph Roister Doister,* classically structured into five acts, with a single stage setting that preserves the unities of time and place.

In 1566, the members of Gray's Inn saw a production of George Gascoigne's *Supposes,* translated from the Italian of Ariosto (1509). Because it was a translation and not an English adaptation, this play preserves essentially in their original form the stock character types of neoclassical comedy: the parasite, the pantaloon or miserly aged rival in love, the overly watchful father, the clever servant, the bawdy nurse, and so on. The heroine, though no longer a Roman courtesan, as in the comedies of the much-imitated Latin dramatist Plautus, is nonetheless a self-possessed and sophisticated young woman who conducts a secret affair for some time without being detected by her father. The mores of this continental play must have seemed challengingly cosmopolitan to its fashionable courtly and intellectual audience. Just as importantly, the play offered graceful prose language as its medium, rather than the homely English verse of *Ralph Roister Doister* and *Gammer Gurton's Needle. Supposes* provided a new model for neoclassical comedy and was to become (with some of its continental morality anglicized) a source for Shakespeare's *The Taming of the Shrew.* Indeed, Shakespeare learned much about play construction, dialogue, and characterization from neoclassical comedies of this sort; perhaps his earliest comedy, *The Comedy of Errors,* owes a great deal to Plautus and to neoclassical imitators of that Latin comic writer. Another early Italian comedy in English, *The Bugbears,* was adapted from Grazzini's *La Spiritata* and acted in about 1563–1565 by boy actors.

Early Tragedy

In early English tragedy, as in early comedy, native and neoclassical traditions coalesced and sometimes clashed. Native conceptions of tragedy had partly originated in two great medieval commonplaces: the "wheel of fortune" and the "fall of princes." Both were incorporated in Chaucer's "The Monk's Tale" and its source, Boccaccio's *De Casibus Virorum Illustrium,* which presented moral examples from the lives of famous men. Chaucer had defined "tragedy" as the story of a great person "that stood in greet prosperitee, / And is yfallen out of heigh degree / Into myserie, and endeth wrecchedly." His examples, taken from Boccaccio, included Lucifer, Adam, Samson, Hercules, Julius Caesar, and others. These were men or evil beings who had either fallen through sinful pride or had been brought low through the inevitable turn of fortune's wheel. Both types of tragedy illustrated to the medieval mind the folly of trusting to worldly expectations. The "fall of princes" tradition was extended into Elizabethan times through John Lydgate's Chaucerian imitation, *The Fall of Princes,* and its Tudor sequel, *The Mirror for Magistrates* (1559, with many subsequent revisions and enlargements). The morality play contributed a pattern similar to that of Satan's tragic fall through pride; and, although the mankind figure of early morality plays invariably was recovered to God's grace by the end of the play, some early Elizabethan Calvinistic moralities (such as *Enough Is as Good as a Feast* or *The Longer Thou Livest the More Fool Thou Art*) featured human protagonists who were eternally damned. As we have already seen, Elizabethan moralities of this sort anticipated the tragic pattern of Marlowe's *Doctor Faustus.*

Native traditions of tragedy evolved quite independent of classical tragic drama and were, in some ways, strikingly different from it. Christian morality often served as a major explanation of the cause of tragic fall in medieval tragedy. Moreover, the focus was broad and cosmic, as in *Doctor Faustus.* Scenes of comic depravity often alternated with scenes of tragic seriousness, especially in the morality plays. Classical tragedy, on the other hand, usually focused on a moment of crisis in the protagonist's life and presented this crisis in its full, tragic intensity without the undercutting of comic effect. In classical tragedy generally, narrative interest was subordinated to dramatic or lyrical interest. Unity of action, as understood by Renaissance theorists of drama, necessarily included unity of time and place. Thus, the gap between native and classical tragedy was potentially vast.

Perhaps the earliest tragedy based on classical models in England was Thomas Norton and Thomas Sackville's *Gorboduc,* presented before Queen Elizabeth at Whitehall on January 18, 1562. The play attempted to offer Queen Elizabeth political advice on the need for naming a Protestant successor, by way of a cautionary example in the fratricidal strife between Gorboduc's two sons. Although Sir Philip Sidney later complained about the play's violation of the unities in the fifth act, he praised it otherwise as "an exact model of all tragedies." To be sure, native concepts of tragedy are observable in *Gorboduc,* especially in its use of an ancient British setting and in its moral and Christian explanations of the causes of tragedy. Nevertheless, the classical element predominates.

This classical element is basically Senecan. Ancient Greek tragedy was relatively unknown to Elizabethan England except through Seneca's Roman adaptations. Seneca's ten plays were all translated into English by 1581 and had long been read in the schools as models of rhetoric (just as Terence and Plautus were also read). Seneca's plays were, in fact, closet dramas, intended to be recited rather than acted. Seneca provided *Gorboduc* with a model for its long declamatory speeches, its occasional passages of stichomythia (rapid one-line exchange of dialogue), its five-act structure punctuated by dumb shows, and its supernatural agents prognosticating doom. Moreover, *Gorboduc*'s blank verse, created to approximate the Latin meters of Seneca, set a style for blank verse tragedy that dominated the English stage throughout Shakespeare's career. (Blank verse had been used shortly before *Gorboduc* by the Earl of Surrey in his translations from Virgil's *Aeneid,* but never before in drama.) *Gorboduc* also made an important contribution to the English history play by its use of chronicle materials in a tragic setting.

Other Senecan plays followed, written at first for gentlemanly audiences of the universities and the Inns of Court, rather than for the popular stage. One such was George Gascoigne's *Jocasta* (1566). In 1588, eight gentlemen of Gray's Inn, including Thomas Hughes and Francis Bacon, presented before the Queen a drama similar in form to *Gorboduc,* called *The Misfortunes of Arthur.* This tragedy borrows from Seneca not only chorus, messengers, and machinery but also ideas, sentiments, and heightened language. Like *Gorboduc, The Misfortunes of Arthur* is somewhat free with the classical unities. Also, it is based upon the chronicle history of Britain, which was to become one of the chief sources of subject matter for English tragedy.

Another principal source for tragic writers was the Italian short story, which, because it was also impassioned and serious, offered many themes to writers of tragedy. *Gismond of Salerne* dramatizes a well-known Italian tale and, like *Gorboduc* and *The Misfortunes of Arthur,* is Senecan in form and nature. It was acted before the Queen in 1566 or 1568. In the same storehouse of narrative,

Shakespeare was later to find his source for *Othello*, as well as for such comedies as *The Merchant of Venice* and *Measure for Measure*. *Romeo and Juliet* was based on a English poem which in turn drew from an Italian source.

Sir Philip Sidney as Dramatic Critic

The kind of tragedy that Shakespeare and other popular dramatists wrote in the late sixteenth and early seventeenth centuries is not rigorously classical. It preserves many of the elements of English tragedy already enumerated: a broad narrative focus, frequent violations or total ignoring of the classical unities of time and place, the inclusion of comedy, and the like. Tragedy of this sort might never have developed in England to so high a point or might never have been accepted as the prevailing form of tragedy but for two things: in the first place, few Elizabethan dramatists learned their craft by studying the classical rules; in the second place, the Elizabethan audience, with a taste for native English drama, demanded new, varied, and sensational plots, accompanied by vaudeville clownery and songs. Such popular drama was often condemned by those critics who were familiar with classical literature, but to have made English tragedy conform with classical rules would have meant changing its nature. In France, where in Shakespeare's time the drama came under the control of the court and the learned classes, tragedy developed according to classical rules into the drama of Corneille and Racine; in England, on the other hand, Shakespeare and his contemporaries created a kind of tragedy particularly their own.

The most famous neoclassical critic of the age, Sir Philip Sidney, took vigorous exception to the kind of tragedy in vogue during the 1580s. His views are set forth in *The Defence of Poesy*, written in 1581 or slightly later:

Our tragedies and comedies not without cause cried out against, observing rules neither of honest civility nor skillful poetry, excepting *Gorboduc*—again I say of those that I have seen. Which notwithstanding as it is full of stately speeches and well-sounding phrases, climbing to the height of Seneca his style, and as full of notable morality, which it doth most delightfully teach, and so obtain the very end of poesy, yet in truth it is very defective in the circumstances, which grieves me, because it might not remain as an exact model of all tragedies. For it is faulty both in place and time, the two necessary companions of all corporal actions. For where the stage should alway represent but one place, and the uttermost time presupposed in it should be, both by Aristotle's precept and common reason, but one day, there is both many days and many places inartificially imagined.

But if it be so in *Gorboduc*, how much more in all the rest? where you shall have Asia of the one side and Afric of the other, and so many other under-kingdoms, that the player, when he comes in, must ever begin with telling where he is, or else the tale will not be conceived. Now you shall have three ladies walk to gather flowers, and then we must believe the stage to be a garden. By and by we hear news of shipwreck in the same place; then we are to blame if we accept it not for a rock. Upon the back of that comes out a hideous monster with fire and smoke, and then the miserable beholders are bound to take it for a cave. While in the meantime two armies fly in, represented with four swords and bucklers, and then what hard heart will not receive it for a pitched field?

Now of time they are much more liberal. For ordinary it is that two young princes fall in love; after many traverses she is got with child, delivered of a fair boy; he is lost, groweth a man, falleth in love, and is ready to get another child,—and all this in two hours space; which how absurd it is in sense even sense may imagine, and art hath taught, and all ancient examples justified, and at this day the ordinary players in Italy will not err in....

Later he tells us that English plays are "neither right tragedies nor right comedies"; instead, they mingle clowns and kings with "neither decency nor discretion."

To be sure, Sidney's criticism is never narrowly classical; in the essay as a whole, he affirms the power of the artist to range freely in the world of wit and imagination and to create artifacts that are more universally "true" than either philosophy or history. At the same time, his strictures against the contemporary English stage do invoke classical ideals of unity that many dramatists and audiences ignored. Popular audiences of the time seem to have had no more difficulty imagining the lapse of twenty years than the lapse of two hours. Nor were they troubled by scenic shifts from one continent to another, or by shifts in tone from the comic to the pathetic, the grotesque, or the tragic. Because native English drama had never paid much attention to classical precept, it worked out its own sense of cohesion according to different criteria of multiplicity, alternating effects, sudden juxtapositions, typological recurrence, and the like.

John Lyly, George Peele, and Robert Greene

In facing the problem of understanding just what Elizabethan drama was and how it became what it was, we must recognize that the classification of drama into comedy and tragedy by the ancients does not tell the whole story. Even when we add the history or chronicle play to these two divisions of drama, we have, at best, a rough classification that leaves out a great deal and implies that these three forms were sharply discriminated. In fact, Elizabethan drama is, generally speaking, a blend of many elements. Nearly all Elizabethan tragedies have in them comic scenes and by-plots; most comedies have in them serious issues that might conceivably result in disaster; and history plays are often capable of being classified as comedies or as tragedies. To appreciate further this protean quality of genre in early Elizabethan drama, we might consider the varied works of a number of dramatists whose practice was successful on the stage and who influenced Shakespeare and his immediate contemporaries. Of these, John Lyly is one of the most important.

John Lyly (1554?–1606), grandson of the grammarian William Lyly or Lilly, educated at Oxford and Cambridge, first acquired fame not as a dramatist, but as a writer of prose. His *Euphues, The Anatomy of Wit,* published in 1578, and its sequel, *Euphues and His England* (1580), stand as the most sensational and brilliant effort in the struggle of English Renaissance prose to acquire a conscious artistic manner. The style is, to a remarkable extent, composed of rhetorical devices: antithesis, personification, rhetorical question, metaphor, simile, and, above all, balance reinforced by alliteration. Recondite tidbits and fanciful legends about natural history are garnered from Plutarch, Pliny, and many other writers. The overall result is a kind of handbook for the courtier, the lover, the traveler, and the statesman. Lyly's deliberately outrageous style was imitated by dozens of other writers, including Robert Greene and Thomas Lodge, and seems to have set a new fashion of smart speech in the court of Queen Elizabeth. "Euphuism" itself had a vast influence on the style of the drama and other literature, both in poetry and in prose. Shakespeare is one of those who imitated and also ridiculed euphuistic speech. (For amusing examples of Shakespeare's parodying of the euphuistic style, see Falstaff's speech in *1 Henry IV,* 2.4.396 ff., beginning "for though the camomile, the more it is trodden on the faster it grows, yet youth, the more it is wasted the sooner it wears," or Don Armado's love letter in *Love's Labor's Lost,* 4.1.61 ff.: "Shall I command thy love? I may. Shall I enforce thy love? I could. Shall I entreat thy love? I will," and so on.)

Lyly was also the author of at least eight comedies, written to suit the taste of the court and possibly all acted before the Queen by the children of the Chapel Royal or of St. Paul's School. The plays are often courtly debates in the tradition of Medwall's *Fulgens and Lucrece,* with much combat of wits and philosophical argument. These comedies are also sufficiently modeled on Plautus or Terence to indicate that the characteristic features of Latin comedy by this time (1580–1590) had become naturalized on the English stage. *Mother Bombie,* for example, is an adaptation of Latin comedy, containing such stock figures as the pedant, the rascally servant, the duped parent, the parasite, and the aged lover, although, as usual, in Lyly the clownery has an English flavor as well.

Indeed, however much Lyly may recall classical Latin comedy, he is most important as the inventor of a fanciful type of love comedy to which Shakespeare was significantly indebted in several of his plays. Lyly's *Sappho and Phao, Endymion,* and *Midas* have romantic plots derived from Ovidian mythology. *Galatea* uses a pastoral setting for its love story and male disguises for the heroines, as in *As You Like It. Love's Metamorphosis* and *The Woman in the Moon* are also pastoral comedies. *Campaspe,* like *The Merchant of Venice,* portrays conflicts of love and friendship. Lyly's flattery of Queen Elizabeth through topical allegory and his appeal to a courtly clientele are, to be sure, modes that Shakespeare does not generally adopt. On the other hand, Shakespeare learned a good deal from Lyly's sensitive portrayal of the psychology of love. The depiction is often wryly comic: Lyly's men abase themselves before women, vacillate between idealization and misogyny, and not infrequently fail as wooers—much as the young lords do in Shakespeare's most Lylyan play, *Love's Labor's Lost.* Shakespeare's lovers generally work toward a more successful and realistic completion of romantic expectations, but Shakespeare's interest in love comedy began, in part, with what Lyly had achieved.

George Peele (1558?–1597) was also active as a dramatist around the time that Shakespeare first came to London. Peele's *The Arraignment of Paris* (1581) offers a quality of blank verse not previously seen in comedy and shows how classical legend could be adapted to a thoroughly English celebration of the nation and its Queen. *The Old Wives' Tale* (c. 1588–1594) is a seemingly naive but actually skillful medley of folk legends in the spirit of popular romance. *David and Bethsabe* (c. 1581–1594) dramatizes a familar biblical narrative in terms of erotic love and kingly power. Peele also contributed importantly to the new and burgeoning genre of the English history play with his *Edward I* (1590–1593); it is, like other history plays of the Armada era, jingoistically anti-Spanish and features a popular folk-hero king who understands and respects the proud local customs of his people. *The Battle of Alcazar* (1588–1589), another play of the Armada era, revels in the exotic world of Africa and the Middle East, in the vaunting heroic vein of Christopher Marlowe's *Tamburlaine.* Peele also devised two London civic pageants.

Robert Greene (1558–1592), more than any other dramatist, opened up for Shakespeare the world of Greek romance—the kind of fiction ultimately derived from Heliodorus, Achilles Tatius, and other protonovelists of the Mediterranean world in the second through fourth centuries. The Greeks of that era were the merchants, traders, sailors, and schoolmasters of the Roman Empire, and the early form of prose romance they created was a reflection of the adventurous life they lived. This romantic fiction reveled in strange and improbable encounters, piracies, the exposure of infant children to the elements and their eventual restoration as grown-ups to their aging parents, the separation and reunion of indistinguishable twins, and many other plot devices rendered familiar to us in the writings of Renaissance authors for whom this kind of sensationalism was every bit as interesting and worthy of imitation as the classics of Virgil and Ovid. Stories of the Greek kind, translated into various languages and ultimately into English, were to serve as models for a number of Shakespeare's late romances, especially *Pericles, The Winter's Tale,* and *Cymbeline.* Indeed, the plot of *The Winter's Tale* came to Shakespeare by way of Greene's prose romance, *Pandosto*.

From Greek romantic fiction, Greene devised a type of plucky romantic heroine for his plays and novels that Shakespeare was to develop further in his comedies. The society depicted by Greek romance gave women great liberty, and, like them, Greene's heroines are independent, witty, and resourceful, though at the same time feminine. Greene's dramas are almost the first modern productions in which women are in any degree represented as assuming a relatively dignified station in a mutually supportive love relationship with a man.

Greene also borrowed from Greek romantic fiction, and from other sources, especially for pastoral fiction. His plays, particularly *James IV* and *Friar Bacon and Friar Bungay* (c. 1589–1592), give us that blend of the pastoral and the romantic which the world has enjoyed in *As You Like It* and *Love's Labor's Lost*. *Friar Bacon* is particularly noteworthy for its multiple plot, its resourceful heroine, and its embracing of serious issues in a comic world. Greene must be regarded as the first great master of plot in English comedy.

Greene may also have written *George a Greene, the Pinner of Wakefield* (1587–1593), a play that exalts the virtues of England's yeoman class in defiance of the aristocracy and all foreign foes. The hero, George, is a patriot, a scorner of hereditary titles, and a representative of the common people against vested interests. As a new breed of English folk hero, he is so invincible that even Robin Hood must yield to his authority. The appeal of this dream of power to the artisans and yeomen in Greene's popular audiences must have been heady indeed.

Shortly before he fell victim to the notorious debaucheries of his bohemian existence (he was reported to have died from a surfeit of pickled herring and Rhenish wine), Greene wrote many pamphlets, some about London roguery, some about his own hard usage at the hands of the world. In one of the latter, *Greene's Groatsworth of Wit Bought with a Million of Repentance* (1592), he gave us our first personal reference to Shakespeare. (See "The Only Shake-scene in a Country" in the biographical account of Shakespeare's life and work, below.) Shakespeare was, of course, not the only dramatist to be influenced by Greene; Anthony Munday, Thomas Dekker, and most of the popular dramatists of the next decade were similarly indebted to Greene's example.

Thomas Kyd and Christopher Marlowe

While romantic comedy was being shaped and developed in the hands of Lyly, Peele, and Greene, Senecan tragedy was also finding its proponents on the English stage. Lucius Annaeus Seneca (c. 4 B.C.–65 A.D.), a Roman statesman and stoic philosopher during the reign of the emperor Nero, wrote tragedies of a severely formal cast

based on the tragedies of Aeschylus, Sophocles, and Euripides. Although never performed in Seneca's lifetime and indeed written as "closet" dramas, they became immensely influential on dramatists of later generations, especially during the Renaissance on the Continent and in England. The greatest genius in adapting Senecan action to the English theater was Thomas Kyd (1558–1594). His influence on his contemporaries and on later dramatists was immense; *The Spanish Tragedy* (c. 1583–1587) was probably acted more times during the sixteenth century than any other English play and became a pattern for subsequent revenge drama. Although Senecan tradition by no means accounts for all of the play's successful qualities, it remains a central part. Kyd catches the unabashed brutality and horror of the Senecan story and reveals it openly. Instead of having the action reported as taking place off the stage, as in Seneca and in most classical tragedy, he presents it directly. For tales of Greek mythology, he substitutes a modern story

Thomas Kyd's The Spanish Tragedy *was perhaps the most popular play of the sixteenth century; it was performed more than any other English drama of the time. The* Spanish Tragedy *served as a pattern and influenced subsequent revenge drama—including Shakespeare's* Hamlet.

of love, conspiracy, murder, and political intrigue. He retains the Senecan ghost, the revenge motive, the spirit of stoicism, and a modified form of the chorus. The play deals both seriously and sensationally with the conflicting codes of revenge and Christian faith in God's providence. The protagonist Hieronimo, confronted with his son's murder and seemingly unable to obtain justice through the state, finds his pleas to the heavens unanswered and turns instead to a revenge that hardens his spirit and requires his own violent death as payment. The action is presided over by the spirit of Revenge, a choruslike figure whose aims share nothing in common with Christian views of justice and mercy. *The Spanish Tragedy* is also noteworthy for a style that is a tour de force of rhetorical figures, such as anaphora and oxymoron—an achievement both imitated and mocked by later dramatists. Probably Kyd is also the author of the first dramatic version of the story of Hamlet.

Kyd's work gave rise to a series of revenge plays, not only in his own time, but also later, in 1600 and the years following, when the revenge tragedy again became fashionable. Moreover, Kyd seems to have had a shaping influence on Greene and on Marlowe. For example, Marlowe's *The Jew of Malta* (c. 1589), in its verbal extravagance and sensational intrigue, seems particularly indebted to *The Spanish Tragedy*.

Nevertheless, however much Kyd may have contributed in matters of style and form, Marlowe remains the leader in the great English type of Elizabethan tragedy. He shaped the genre that subsequently was perfected by Shakespeare. His achievement is all the more remarkable when we consider that he was born in the same year as Shakespeare (1564) and died in 1593, when Shakespeare had written no more than six or seven of his earliest plays. Marlowe's great contribution to English drama was a type of protagonist expressing something of the aspiration of the very Renaissance itself. Tamburlaine thirsts for world conquest; Dr. Faustus would go to the utmost bounds of knowledge and the power which knowledge gives; and Barabas in *The Jew of Malta* sets no limit to his longing for wealth.

Structurally, *Tamburlaine* (1587–1588) is a good deal closer to the English popular morality play than to classical drama. Each of the play's two parts consists of a linear sequence of conquests by the humbly born but seemingly invincible Tamburlaine, until at last death ends his glory. Because many characters appear in one episode only, the cast is large and yet within the capacities of an Elizabethan acting company. Doubling of parts, as in Shakespeare's early history plays, is both common and necessary. Structural unity is achieved through thematic repetition rather than through a narrowing of the narrative focus. At the same time, the language of *Tamburlaine* is rich and new in its vibrant appeal to limitless human aspiration. The Elizabethan playgoer is invited to forget moral considerations

in evaluating the play's ruthless hero and to revel instead in the intoxicating spectacle of a baseborn shepherd "threat'ning the world with high astounding terms."

A profound ambivalence permeates all of Marlowe's plays and gives them a restless, brilliant energy that is characteristic of the times for which they were written. Tamburlaine is both a remorseless butcher of his enemies and a superhuman quester. He is fierce, mysterious, oriental, exotic, unknowable; as the projection of a universal human dream of aspiration, he is to be both admired and feared. Barabas in *The Jew of Malta* is at once colossally rich and colossally evil. Similarly, the protagonist of *Doctor Faustus* (c. 1588–1589) is both a sinner who falls from grace and a noble but doomed Overreacher (as Harry Levin describes him), daring like Icarus to fly toward the sun. In medieval and Christian orthodox terms, Faustus is guilty of pride, the deadliest of the Deadly Sins; but in Renaissance terms he at least fleetingly resembles Prometheus, challenging the hierarchy of an oppressive and outmoded universe. In its free mixture of comedy and tragedy and its wholesale disregard of the classical unities, *Doctor Faustus* brilliantly demonstrates

The title page of the 1616 edition of Christopher Marlowe's Doctor Faustus *shows Faustus's conjuration of the devil. The play illustrates native rather than classical traditions of tragedy in its disregard of the unities and its free use of comedy.*

what the native and homiletic tradition of tragedy had to offer Shakespeare.

Edward II, perhaps Marlowe's last play (1591–1593), is ambivalent toward its paired central figures, Edward and Mortimer Junior. At first, the effeminate King seems chiefly in the wrong, while his baronial opponents lament England's decline. Toward the end of the play, however, the King becomes the sympathetic victim of a power-mad and Machiavellian Mortimer. Queen Isabella also changes radically from a long-suffering, neglected wife into a scheming adulteress. This shift in sympathy from the barons to King Edward is structurally much like that of Shakespeare's *Richard II*, and, unquestionably, Marlowe's history play had a profound effect on Shakespeare. Yet Marlowe's tone, as in his other plays, remains one of naturalistic amorality. He wryly regards England's political struggles as one more manifestation of the restlessness and ambition afflicting all mortal endeavors. His world is one of constant turmoil in which persons of insatiable will assert themselves and rise to the top, at whatever cost to themselves and to society. Shakespeare's world is basically different, even though he learned a great deal from Marlowe's tragic vision.

Marlowe first gave to English tragedy its realization of character and, still more, its dignity and seriousness. He endowed English drama with a spirit of aspiration. His enthusiasm for beauty of language, shared by Spenser, Greene, Peele, and others, provided a rich heritage for the young Shakespeare. Not the least among Marlowe's gifts to English drama was a new and more flexible blank-verse style. In the following prologue to *Tamburlaine the Great*, Part I, Marlowe does not treat each blank-verse line as a separate unit but runs the sense on from line to line in order to produce what might be described as a blank-verse paragraph, a thing most necessary to drama if it is to represent widely varying emotions, thoughts, and characters:

> From jigging veins of rhyming mother-wits,
> And such conceits as clownage keeps in pay,
> We'll lead you to the stately tent of war,
> Where you shall hear the Scythian Tamburlaine
> Threat'ning the world with high astounding terms,
> And scourging kingdoms with his conquering sword.
> View but his picture in this tragic glass,
> And then applaud his fortunes as you please.

This is not only a manifesto of tragic seriousness; it is also, in spite of its elevated style, one of the first examples in English tragedy of vigorous, natural, straightforward expression. Tamburlaine in his utterances is a typical Renaissance poet on the themes of both love and war, as can be seen in the following evocation of the aspiring mind:

> If all the pens that ever poets held
> Had fed the feeling of their masters' thoughts,
> And every sweetness that inspired their hearts,
> Their minds, and muses on admirèd themes;
> If all the heavenly quintessence they still
> From their immortal flowers of poesy,
> Wherein, as in a mirror, we perceive
> The highest reaches of a human wit;
> If these had made one poem's period,
> And all combined in beauty's worthiness,
> Yet should there hover in their restless heads
> One thought, one grace, one wonder, at the least,
> Which into words no virtue can digest.

—*Tamburlaine*, Pt. I, 5.1.161–73

Shakespeare's Dramatic Heritage

Shakespearean tragedy began, roughly speaking, with marked indebtedness to the tragic writing of Marlowe and Kyd: poetry, character, and style from Marlowe; motive, plot, and tragic intensity from Kyd. No evidence suggests that Shakespeare was ever particularly aware of, or influenced by, Aristotelian theories of tragedy. His wish was to hold "the mirror up to nature" and show "virtue her feature, scorn her own image, and the very age and body of the time his form and pressure" (*Hamlet*, 3.2.22–4). Sometimes he approximated Aristotelian ideals in his plays (most nearly, perhaps, in *Othello, Macbeth,* and *Coriolanus*), but not by conscious design. Nor was he a slavish borrower from Marlowe and Kyd, even in his early tragedies, such as *Titus Andronicus*. Greene and many others sought to imitate Marlowe in tragedy, with but indifferent success. Shakespeare, Marlowe's only successful imitator, soon outdistanced Marlowe in those very qualities for which he was indebted to him.

Similarly, the elements of Shakespearean comedy are, in part, derived from Lyly, Peele, and Greene. The contributions of Lyly and Peele were those of style, setting, and movement. Greene, primarily a writer of romance, an adapter of Greek romantic fiction, furnished the element of love and adventure that makes so many Elizabethan plays delightful merely as stories. He also put upon the stage the witty, independent-minded woman, often in boy's clothes, who gives point and naturalness to love intrigue whether in serious drama or in comedy. Not only did Shakespeare, who was a far greater genius than any of them, combine the elements of the comedies of these men and better the instruction, but, as his career went on, he realized on a broad scale the possibilities of the comic point of view in the representation of human life and character.

In the English history play, though he may have learned much from Marlowe, Peele, and others, Shakespeare was clearly an innovator as well. His early history plays on the reigns of Henry VI and Richard III were among the earliest such plays seen in London and were (at least some of them) enormous stage successes. Even here, however, we can see how much Shakespeare learned from such earlier plays as *Gorboduc* and *The Troublesome Reign of King John*.

LONDON THEATERS AND DRAMATIC COMPANIES

Throughout Shakespeare's life, the propriety of acting any plays at all was a matter of bitter controversy. Indeed, when one considers the power and earnestness of the opposition, one is surprised that such a wealth of dramatic excellence could come into being and that Shakespeare's plays should reflect so little the anger and hostility generated by this continuing conflict.

Religious and Moral Opposition to the Theater

From the 1570s onward, and even earlier, the city fathers of London revealed an ever-increasing distrust of the public performance of plays. They fretted about the dangers of plague and of riotous assembly. They objected to the fact that apprentices idly wasted their time instead of working in their shops. And always the municipal authorities suspected immorality. Thus, by an order of the Common Council of London, dated December 6, 1574, the players were put under severe restrictions.

The order cites the reasons. The players, it was charged, had been acting in the innyards of the city, which in consequence were haunted by great multitudes of people, especially youths. These gatherings had been the occasions of frays and quarrels, "evil practices of incontinency in great inns"; the players published "uncomely and unshamefast speeches and doings," withdrew the Queen's subjects from divine service on Sundays and holidays, wasted the money of "poor and fond persons," gave opportunity to pick pockets, uttered "busy and seditious matters," and injured and maimed people by the falling of their scaffolds and by weapons and powder used in plays. The order goes on to state the Common Council's fear that if the plays, which had been forbidden on account of the plague, should be resumed, God's wrath would manifest itself by an increase of the infection. Therefore, no innkeeper, tavernkeeper, or other person might cause or suffer to be openly played "any play, interlude, comedy, tragedy, matter, or show" which had not been first licensed by the mayor and the Court of Aldermen.

The mayor and aldermen did not always state their case plainly, because Queen Elizabeth was a patron of the players, and because the players had friends and patrons in the Privy Council and among the nobility; sometimes,

however, they did so quite boldly. One sees the case against plays stated syllogistically in the following words of Thomas White, a preacher at Paul's Cross in 1577:

Look but upon the common plays of London, and see the multitude that flocketh to them and followeth them! Behold the sumptuous theater houses, a continual monument of London prodigality and folly! But I understand they are now forbidden because of the plague. I like the policy well if it hold still, for a disease is but botched and patched up that is not cured in the cause, and the cause of plagues is sin, if you look to it well, and the cause of sin are plays. Therefore the cause of plagues are plays. (From *A Sermon preached at Paul's Cross . . . in the Time of the Plague*, 1578.)

Moved, no doubt, by the prohibition of the Common Council, James Burbage, with a company of actors under the patronage of the Earl of Leicester, leased a site in Shoreditch, a London suburb in Middlesex, beyond the immediate jurisdiction of the official enemies in the Common Council, whose authority extended only to the city limits. By 1576, he had completed the Theatre. Perhaps he called it "the Theatre" because it had no competitor (other than the Red Lion, established in 1567 and used seemingly as a playing place for feasts and festival days in the performance style of Corpus Christi and saints' plays). Burbage erected what may have been England's first permanent commercial theatrical building. In general, the building combined features of the innyard and the animal-baiting house, having a central and probably paved courtyard open to the sky (like an innyard) and surrounding galleries on all sides (like an animal-baiting house). Burbage erected a stage at one side of the circular arena and put dressing rooms behind it to form the "tiring house" or backstage area for the actors; the facade of this "tiring house" served as a visible backdrop to the stage itself. Burbage's Theatre became the model for other public playhouses, such as the Curtain, the Swan, and the Globe, which were constructed later.

By building his playhouse in Shoreditch, Burbage gained immunity from the London authorities. The city fathers could not suppress plays or control them with perfect success if they were performed in Middlesex, or in the "liberty" of Blackfriars and similar districts exempted by charters from London's civic authority (see "London's Private Theaters," below), or (in the case of later playhouses) on the Bankside across the Thames in Surrey. In order to get at them in these suburban regions, the city authorities had to petition the Queen's Privy Council to give orders to the magistrates and officers of the law in these counties. The Queen's Privy Council, although always on the most polite terms with the Lord Mayor and his brethren of the city and always open to the argument that the assemblage of crowds caused the spread of the plague, was to a much less degree in sympathy with the moral scruples of the city. Current arguments for the plays,

The George Inn of Southwark, England, London's only surviving galleried inn, was destroyed by fire in 1676 but rebuilt the following year with two galleries instead of the original three. Despite these changes, the George Inn gives us the best picture we have of the kind of space in which traveling companies could mount their plays on bare platform stages.

derived from the works of scholars, poets, and playwrights, were numerous and often heard: namely, that classical antiquity gave precedent for dramatic spectacles; that by drawing a true picture of both the bad and the good in life, plays enabled people to choose the good; that people should have wholesome amusement; and that plays provided livelihood for loyal subjects of the Queen.

Of these arguments, to be sure, the Privy Council made little use, resting the case for plays instead on what was, no doubt, an unanswerable argument: that since the players were to appear before Her Majesty, especially during the Christmas/Shrovetide period, the players needed practice in order to prepare themselves to please the royal taste. A good deal of politic fencing ensued, and, so far as orders, complaints, and denunciations were concerned, the reforming opposition had much the better of it. The preachers thundered against plays. Pamphleteers denounced all matters pertaining to the stage: Stephen Gosson in *The School of Abuse, Containing a Pleasant Invective Against Poets, Pipers, Players, Jesters and Suchlike Caterpillars of a Commonwealth* (1579) and other works; Philip

Stubbes in *The Anatomy of Abuses* (1583); and finally and most furiously of all, William Prynne in *Histrio-Mastix: The Players' Scourge or Actor's Tragedy* (1633). Gosson spoke of plays as "the inventions of the devil, the offerings of idolatry, the pomp of worldlings, the blossoms of vanity, the root of apostacy, food of iniquity, riot and adultery." "Detest them," he warned. "Players are masters of vice, teachers of wantonness, spurs to impurity, the sons of idleness."

At first, such diatribes represented an extreme reforming opinion obviously not shared by a majority of London viewers. They kept coming to plays, and the flourishing public theaters attracted the talents of the age's leading dramatists. An ominous note of polarization was sounded, however, early in the reign of James I (1603–1625) when the rift between the Puritans and the court broke into open antagonism. After about 1604, when James alienated the Puritans at the Hampton Court Conference, the split between popular audiences and the best drama of the age became increasingly evident. Shakespeare's company, now the King's men, gravitated, whether through choice or necessity, toward the precinct of the court. Although the public theater, with its capacity for large audiences, continued to serve as a lively center of theatrical activity, Puritan opposition to the stage gathered momentum. Many dramatists, in turn, grew more satirical of London customs and more attuned to courtly tastes. Eventually, Puritan hostility to the theater was at least part of the motive behind Parliament's order to close the theaters in 1642.

The Public Theaters

A year or more after Burbage built the Theatre in 1576, the Curtain was put up near it by Philip Henslowe, or possibly by Henry Laneman, or Lanman. About ten years later, Philip Henslowe built the Rose, the first playhouse on the Bankside (the southern bank of the Thames River). In 1599, James Burbage's sons Richard and Cuthbert dismantled the Theatre because of trouble about the lease of the land and rebuilt it as the Globe on the Bankside. This Globe playhouse burned on June 29, 1613, from the discharge of cannon backstage during a performance of *All Is True*, a play thought to be identical with Shakespeare's *Henry VIII*. The Globe was rebuilt, probably in its original polygonal form, that is, essentially round with a large number of sides. In 1600, Henslowe built the Fortune as a theater for the Lord Admiral's men, who were chief rivals to the Lord Chamberlain's men. The companies were differently organized, in that the Lord Chamberlain's men were joint sharers in their own enterprise and owners of their own theatrical building, whereas Henslowe owned the Fortune (and the Rose before it) and served as landlord to the Admiral's men—no doubt profiting handsomely from their activities.

Various records of these theatrical buildings have survived. One such record is the Fortune contract, preserved at Dulwich College among other invaluable papers of Philip Henslowe, theatrical entrepreneur and father-in-law of the famous Edward Alleyn of the Lord Admiral's men. The contract for building the Fortune was let to the same contractor who had built the new Globe, and, since the specifications required that the Fortune should be like the Globe in all its main features, except that it was to be square instead of polygonal, we may gain from these specifications an idea of the Globe. A second documentary record is a drawing of the Swan, a Bankside theater, accompanying a description of the playhouse by Johannes De Witt, who visited London in 1596. The drawing, which was discovered in the University Library at Utrecht, is the work of one Van Buchell and may be based on drawings by De Witt himself. Besides the Fortune contract and the Swan drawing, we have two or three little pictures of the Elizabethan public stage on the title pages of published plays, the most important being that on the title page of William Alabaster's *Roxana* (1632). Just recently, in 1989, the discovery and excavation of the foundations of the Rose playhouse and partial excavation of the Globe playhouse foundations in Southwark, together with the construction of a modern replica of the Globe playhouse near the site of these two theaters, have added invaluable archeological information about the dimensions of that acting arena.

The London Public Stage

From these documents and pictures and from scattered references to the theaters, as well as from extended studies of stage directions and scenic conditions in plays themselves, we have a fairly clear idea of the public stage in London. Its features are these: a pit about seventy feet in diameter, usually circular and open to the sky; surrounding this, galleries in three tiers, containing the most expensive seats; and a rectangular stage, about forty-three by twenty-seven feet, wider than it was deep, raised about five and one-half feet above the surface of the yard, sometimes built on trestles so that it could be removed if the house was also customarily used for bearbaiting and bullbaiting. The flat, open stage usually contained one trapdoor. Part of the stage was afforded some protection from the weather by a brightly decorated wooden roof supported by posts, constituting the "heavens." Above this roof was a "hut," perhaps containing suspension gear for ascents and descents. (The Rose appears originally to have been generally smaller than what is described here, with a stage that tapered toward the front to a width of only twenty-five feet or so. The building was somewhat expanded in 1592 but was still small compared with other theaters. The original building shows no certain evidence of a roof over the stage supported by pillars, but the later building appears to have had roof pillars at the front of the stage.)

At the back of the stage was a partition wall, the "tiring-house facade," with at least two doors in it connecting the stage with the actors' dressing rooms or "tiring house." In the Rose, the tiring-house facade seems to have curved with the polygonal shape of the theater building, but in the DeWitt drawing the Swan facade looks perfectly straight across. Some theaters appear to have had no more than two doors, left and right, as shown in the Swan drawing; other theaters may have had a third door in the center. The arrangement of the Globe playhouse in this important matter cannot be finally determined, although some particular scenes from Shakespeare's plays seem to demand a third door. In any case, the so-called inner stage, long supposed to have stood at the rear of the Elizabeth stage, almost certainly did not exist. A more modest "discovery space" could be provided at one of the curtained doors when needed, as for example in *The Tempest* when Ferdinand and Miranda are suddenly "discovered" at their game of chess by Prospero. Such scenes never called for extensive action within the

This drawing of an Elizabethan public stage appeared on the title page of the published version of William Alabaster's play Roxana *(1632).*

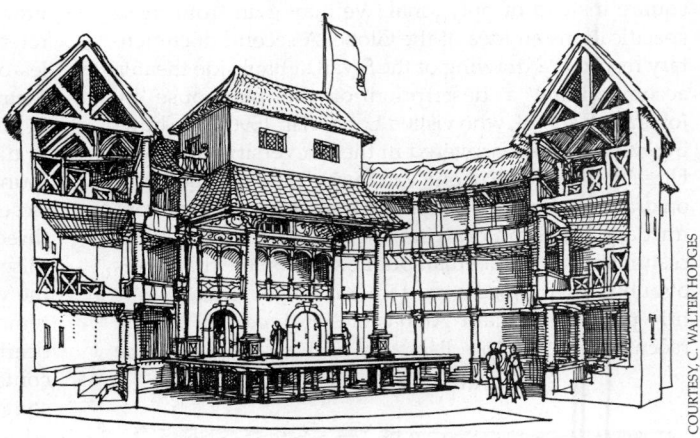

This diagram of the Swan Theatre (left) by Van Buchell (c. 1596), based on the observations of Johannes De Witt, shows features of the public playhouse shared by James Burbage's Theatre and the Globe. A modern sketch of the Swan Theatre (right) shows the open, encircling roof and a full view of the tiring house. Like the Globe and other open theaters, the design of the Swan seems to resemble the Elizabethan innyard with an added stage.

discovery space, however, and, indeed, the number of such discoveries in Elizabethan plays is very few. Well-to-do spectators who may have been seated in the gallery above the rear of the stage could not see into the discovery space. Accordingly, it was used sparingly and only for brief visual effects. Otherwise, the actors performed virtually all their scenes on the open stage. Sometimes curtains were hung over the tiring-house facade between the doors to facilitate scenes of concealment, as when Polonius and Claudius eavesdrop on Hamlet and Ophelia.

An upper station was sometimes used as an acting space, but not nearly so often as was once supposed. The gallery seats above the stage, sometimes known as the "Lord's room," were normally sold to well-to-do spectators. (We can see such spectators in the Swan drawing and in Alabaster's *Roxana*.) Occasionally, these box seats could be used by the actors, as when Juliet appears at her window (it is never called a balcony). In military sequences, as in the *Henry VI* plays, the tiring-house facade could represent the walls of a besieged city, with the city's defenders appearing "on the walls" (i.e., in the gallery above the stage) in order to parley with the besieging enemy standing below on the main stage. Such scenes were relatively infrequent, however, and usually required only a small number of persons to be aloft. A music room,

when needed, could be located in one of the gallery boxes over the stage, but public theaters did not emulate the private stages with music rooms and music between the acts until some time around 1609.

The use of scenery was almost wholly unknown on the Elizabethan public stage, although we do find occasional hints of the use of labels to designate a certain door or area as a fixed location (as, perhaps, in *The Comedy of Errors*). For the most part, the scene was unlimited and the concept of space was fluid. No proscenium arch or curtain stood between the actors and the audience, and so the action could not be easily interrupted. Only belatedly did the public companies adopt the private-theater practice of entr'acte music, as we have seen. Most popular Elizabethan plays were written to be performed nonstop. Five-act structure had little currency, especially at first, and the occasional act divisions in the published versions of Shakespeare's plays may be nonauthorial. Acting tempo was brisk. The Prologue of *Romeo and Juliet* speaks of "the two hours' traffic of our stage." Plays were performed in the afternoons and had to be completed by dark in order to allow the audience to return safely to London. During the winter season, playing time was severely restricted. Outbreaks of plague often occasioned the closing of the theaters, especially in warm weather.

Elizabethan dancers, shown above, perform on a stage below a gallery of musicians. Imported stage designs from Italy made more use of perspective scenery than did the commercial theaters.

A capacity audience for the popular theaters came to about 2,000 to 3,000 persons. (The recently excavated Rose playhouse foundations suggest an audience there of around 2,000.) For the most part, the audience was affluent, consisting chiefly of the gentry and of London's substantial mercantile citizenry who paid two to three pence or more for gallery seats or the "Lord's room," but the ample pit or yard also provided room for small shopkeepers and artisans who stood for a penny. The spectators were lively, demanding, and intelligent. Although Shakespeare does allow Hamlet to refer disparagingly on one occasion to the "groundlings" who "for the most part are capable of nothing but inexplicable dumbshows and noise" (*Hamlet*, 3.2.11–12), Shakespeare appealed to the keenest understanding of his whole audience, thereby achieving a breadth of vision seldom found in continental courtly drama of the same period. The vitality and financial success of the Elizabethan public theater is without parallel in English history. The city of London itself, in 1600 or so, had only about 100,000 inhabitants, yet throughout Shakespeare's career several companies were competing simultaneously for this audience and constantly producing new plays. Most new plays ran for only a few performances, so that the acting companies were always in rehearsal with new shows. The actors needed phenomenal memories and a gift of improvisation as well. Their acting seems to have been of a high caliber, despite the speed with which they worked. Among other things, many of them were expert fencers and singers.

The London public stage inherited many of its practices from native and medieval traditions. The fluid, open stage, with spectators on four sides, recalled the arena staging of many early Corpus Christi cycles, saints' plays, and morality plays. The adult professional companies were, as we have seen, descended from the itinerant troupes that had acted their plays throughout England in guildhalls, private residences, monastic houses and schools, and perhaps occasionally outdoors on booth stages (though the evidence for this last possible venue is scarce). The Elizabethan tiring-house facade and platform stage may have owed much to the kinds of theatrical space that touring actors had known, and perhaps to the arrangement of a booth stage and a trestle platform set up against one wall of an innyard where the guests of the inn could enjoy a performance, along with standing spectators in the yard. When the itinerant actors had set up their plays in noblemen's banqueting halls or at court, at any rate, they encountered another space that had an important influence on their concept of a theater: the Tudor hall. We must next examine the significance of this indoor theatrical setting.

The Tudor Hall

The Tudor banqueting hall played a major part in the staging of much early Tudor drama. Medwall's *Fulgens and Lucrece*, one of the earliest such plays, was written to be performed during the intervals of a state banquet. The patrician guests were seated at tables, while servingmen bustled to and fro or stood crowded together at the doors in the hall "screen." This screen or partition traversed the lower end of the rectangular hall, providing a passageway to the kitchens and to the outside. Its doors—often two, sometimes three—were normally curtained to prevent drafts. This arrangement of the doors bears an interesting resemblance to that of many playhouses in late Elizabethan England, both public and private. Moreover, hall screens and passageways were normally surmounted by a gallery, where musicians could play—an architectural feature markedly resembling the upper galleries of late Elizabethan theaters. Could the Tudor hall screen provide a natural facade for dramatic action? Perhaps it did, although records from Shakespeare's era only rarely document an actual performance in front of the screen, whereas performances were common at the upper end of the hall in front of the dais or in the midst of the hall, where the persons of highest social rank sitting on the dais would have had the best view. The actors of *Fulgens and Lucrece* clearly made use of the doorways in the hall screen, sometimes joking with the servingmen as the actors pushed their way into the hall, but they probably acted in the center, among the spectators' tables. John Heywood's *Play of the Weather* calls for a similar *mise en scène*. Although this ready-made "stage" sufficed for most Tudor plays, the actors sometimes provided additional stage structures; *Weather*, for example, calls for a throne room into which Jupiter can retire without leaving the hall. Similar structures could represent a shop, an orchard, a mountain, or what have you.

Guild and town halls, where players on tour performed before the mayor and council (and sometimes a wider public), provided a similar physical environment except that we cannot be sure that such spaces had galleries in the sixteenth century. Since the gallery is not necessary for many Tudor plays, the players may well have gained experience in halls of this kind that influenced their techniques of staging once they had gravitated to London.

Although both medieval and continental drama offered traditions of multiple staging, in which a series of simultaneously visible and adjacent structures would represent as fixed locations all the playing areas needed for the performance of a play, Tudor indoor staging seems to have made less use of this method than was once supposed. Nor did the various indoor theaters of Tudor England make extensive use of neoclassical staging from

Italy, with its street scene in perspective created by means of lath-and-canvas stage "houses." Italian scenery of this sort came into use sooner in the court masque than in regular drama. Nevertheless, we do find in the Tudor indoor theater a neoclassical tendency toward a fixed locale, in preference to the unlimited open stage. *Gammer Gurton's Needle*, for example, acted probably in a university hall, seems to have used one stage structure, or possibly one door, to represent Gammer's house throughout the action, and another to represent Dame Chat's house. Shakespeare may have been influenced by this kind of fixed-locale staging in *The Comedy of Errors*. (Alan Nelson's *Early Cambridge Theaters*, 1994, is an important resource for school staging.)

The Private Stage

Despite such influences on the public stage, the most significant contribution of the Tudor hall and its hall screen was to the so-called private stage of the late Elizabethan period—"private" in the sense of being intended for a more select and courtly audience than that which frequented the "public" theaters. In the 1570s, choir boys began performing professionally to courtly and intellectual audiences in London. The choir boys had long performed plays for the royal and noble households to which they were attached, but in the 1570s they were, in effect, organized into professional acting companies. Sebastian Westcote and the Children of Paul's may have originated this enterprise. Their theater was apparently

The Tudor banqueting hall provided a place to "stage" much early Tudor drama. The actors performed on the floor among the tables of the guests. The Middle Temple Hall, shown here, later served as the location for a performance of Shakespeare's Twelfth Night *on February 2, 1602. The Middle Temple is one of the Inns of Court, where young men studied law and occasionally relaxed by staging dramatic entertainments.*

Shakespeare's World
A Visual Portfolio

PLATE 1. The Globe Theater. *This eighteenth-century watercolor is based on Claes Janszoon de Visscher's* View of London *(1616). Built in 1599, the Globe was about 80 feet in diameter and accommodated between two and three thousand spectators. Southwark, on the south bank of the Thames river, was also home to the Rose and Swan theaters.*

PLATE 2. London in Shakespeare's Time. *In this anonymous seventeenth-century painting, the theaters of Southwark are clearly visible in the left foreground, flags flying. London Bridge crosses the River Thames into the city, where St Paul's Cathedral dominates the central skyline. The Tower of London is visible on the right. The many boats on the Thames are evidence of the vital role the river played in the city's emerging importance in national and international trade.*

PLATE 3. The Painting of a Lifetime. *This painting of the life of Sir Henry Unton (1557?–1596), probably commissioned by his widow, shows the important events of his life. In the lower right, we see him at birth, in his mother's arms. Above that, we see him as a student at Oxford. The top center depicts his travels to Europe and his expedition to the Netherlands ("Low Countries") under the command of the Earl of Leicester. Below that, we see various scenes in Wadley House, his residence, including a feast with masquers in festive dress, led in procession by Diana and Mercury. His death and burial are pictured in the lower left corner.*

PLATE 4. Queen Elizabeth I. *Few monarchs have ever influenced an age so pervasively and left their stamp on it so permanently as did Elizabeth I during her reign from 1558-1603. Elizabeth is celebrated in this portrait that commemorates the English defeat of the Spanish Armada in 1588. A mythology developed around the Queen, linked to her virginity and devotion to her people. With her right hand on the globe, she is shown here in all her glory as the empress of the world.*

PLATE 5. King James I. *James I, King of England from 1603–1625, was the first of the Stuart dynasty. His name is linked to one of the most creative periods in the history of the theater: that of the Jacobean drama. "Jacobean" is derived from* Jacobus, *the Latin word for James.*

PLATE 6. Social Class in Shakespeare's Time. *Social classes and fashions in Shakespeare's day were clearly defined. People were required by English law to dress according to their social status. Shown here are a workman (top), carrying his tools; "a presumptuous woman" (center), gaudily attired beyond her appointed station; and a "gentleman" (bottom), privileged to wear his apparel.*

PLATE 7. Ben Jonson. *Chief dramatic rival for public acclaim during Shakespeare's later years was Ben Jonson (1572–1637). Jonson, a poet, playwright, and literary critic, was a noted scholar of classical literature and a good friend of Shakespeare. The First Folio of 1623 contains a poetic eulogy of Shakespeare written by Jonson.*

PLATE 8. Edward Alleyn. *Edward Alleyn (1566–1626) won great acclaim in the roles of Tamburlaine and Doctor Faustus, among many others. As leading player of Lord Strange's men and then the Lord Admiral's men, he became a prominent rival of Richard Burbage of the Lord Chamberlain's men. This was the company in which Shakespeare served as actor-sharer and playwright, starting in 1594. Alleyn was also the founder of Dulwich College.*

PLATE 9. Falstaff and Crew. *William Hogarth's painting, "Falstaff Examining His Recruits from Henry IV," dates from 1730. Sir John Falstaff was one of Shakespeare's most popular characters, appearing in parts 1 and 2 of* Henry IV *as well as* The Merry Wives of Windsor. *Falstaff, in the red jacket and feathered hat, here reviews his ragged recruits in a scene from* 2 Henry IV *(3.2).*

PLATE 10. *A Midsummer Night's Dream.* Peter Brook's brilliantly revisionary stage production for the Royal Shakespeare Company in 1970 set A Midsummer Night's Dream *in a brightly lit white box peopled with jugglers and athletic trapeze artists who tumbled and dashed about after one another with abandon. Here, Titania, under the spell of a love potion, embraces the weaver, Bottom, whom Puck has mischievously given an ass's ears and a clown nose. (The clown nose is Brook's invention; Shakespeare's script calls for an ass's head.)*

PLATE 11. *Coriolanus.* Caius Marcius (Ian McKellen), about to be glorified with the surname "Coriolanus" for his triumph over the army of Aufidius at Corioles, is hoisted aloft by his triumphant soldiers in Act 1 of Peter Hall's Coriolanus *at the National Theatre, London, in 1985.*

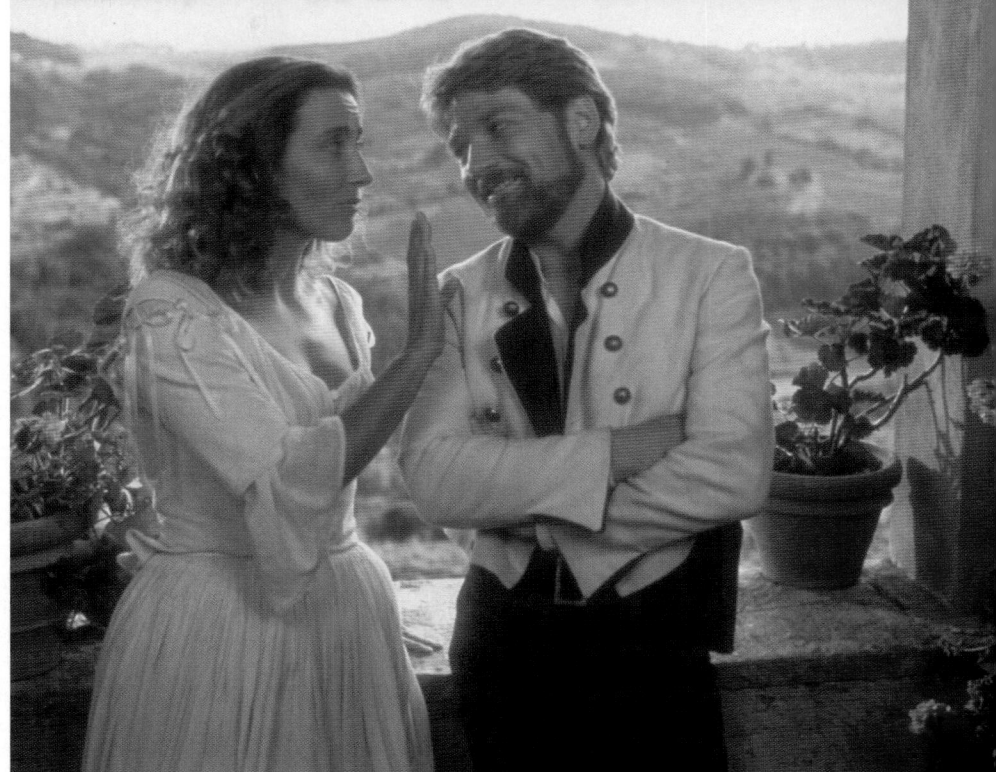

PLATE 12. ***Much Ado About Nothing.*** *Beatrice (Emma Thompson) and Benedick (Kenneth Branagh) in Branagh's 1993 film of* Much Ado About Nothing. *In this scene, (5.2) Beatrice asks Benedick whether or not he has followed through on his promise to challenge Claudio.*

THE KOBAL COLLECTION / SAM GOLDWYN / RENAISSANCE FILMS. PHOTO BY BBC

PLATE 13. ***Twelfth Night.*** *The four lovers in their festive wedding clothes at the very end of Trevor Nunn's film of* Twelfth Night *(1996). Olivia (Helena Bonham Carter) is on the left, with Sebastian (Steven Mackintosh), Viola (Imogen Stubbs), and Orsino (Toby Stephens), left to right.*

PHOTOFEST

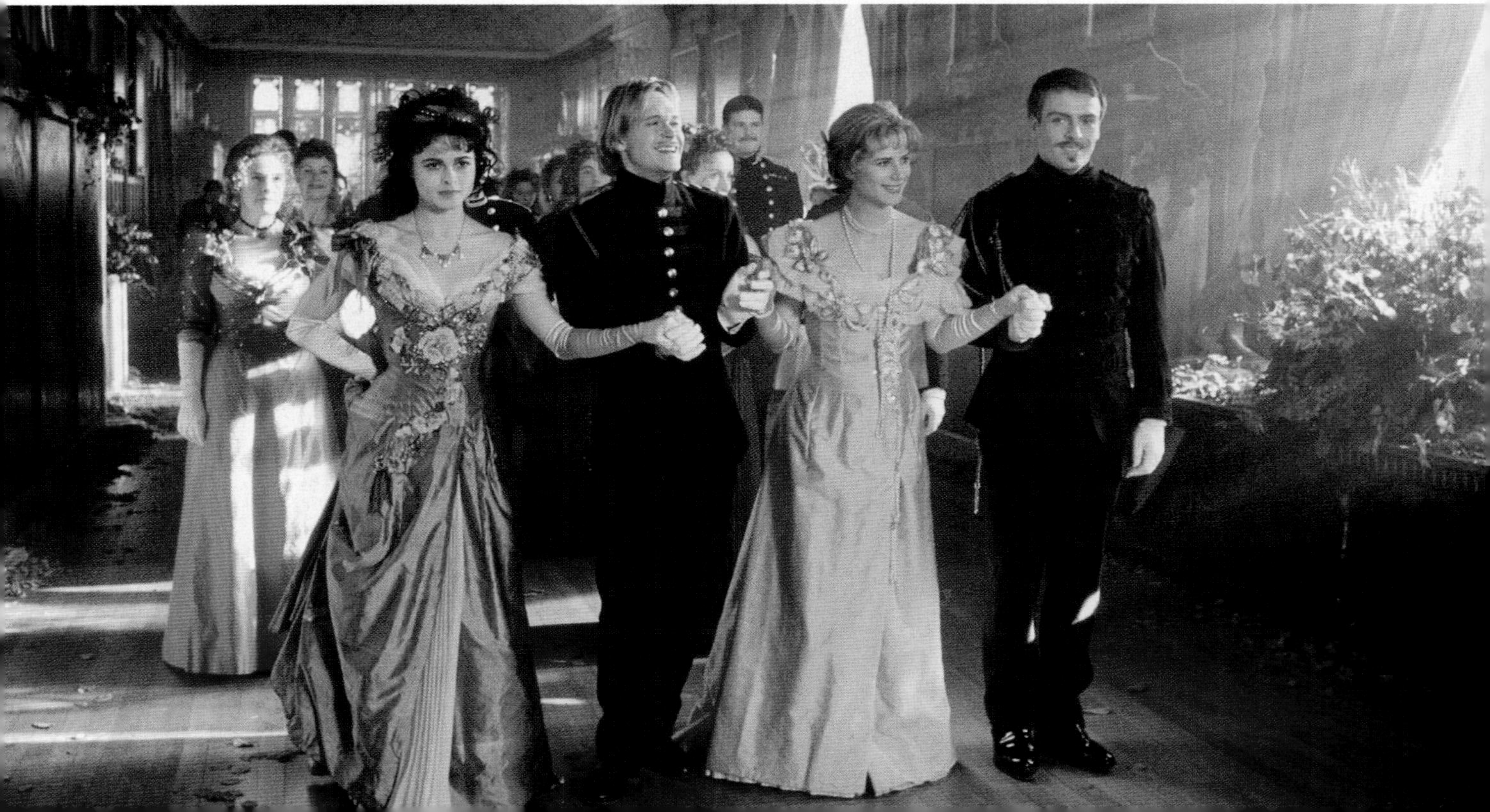

PLATE 14. *Henry V.* Laurence Olivier as King Henry V, about to sail for France at the end of Act 2, Scene 2. "Cheerly to sea! The signs of war advance! / No king of England, if not king of France!" Note how the colorful, patriotic imagery of Olivier's 1944 film contrasts with the gritty realism of Branagh's 1989 film, in Plate 17.

PLATE 15. *Richard III.* Ian McKellen in director Richard Loncraine's 1995 film. In Act 1, Scene 1, Richard appears to be celebrating the Yorkist victory over the Lancastrians, though we as audience perceive the mockery and malice in his words, "Now is the winter of our discontent / Made glorious summer by this son of York." Set in pre-WWII England, Loncraine's film imagines England to be taken over by fascists with Richard Duke of Gloucester as their evil genius.

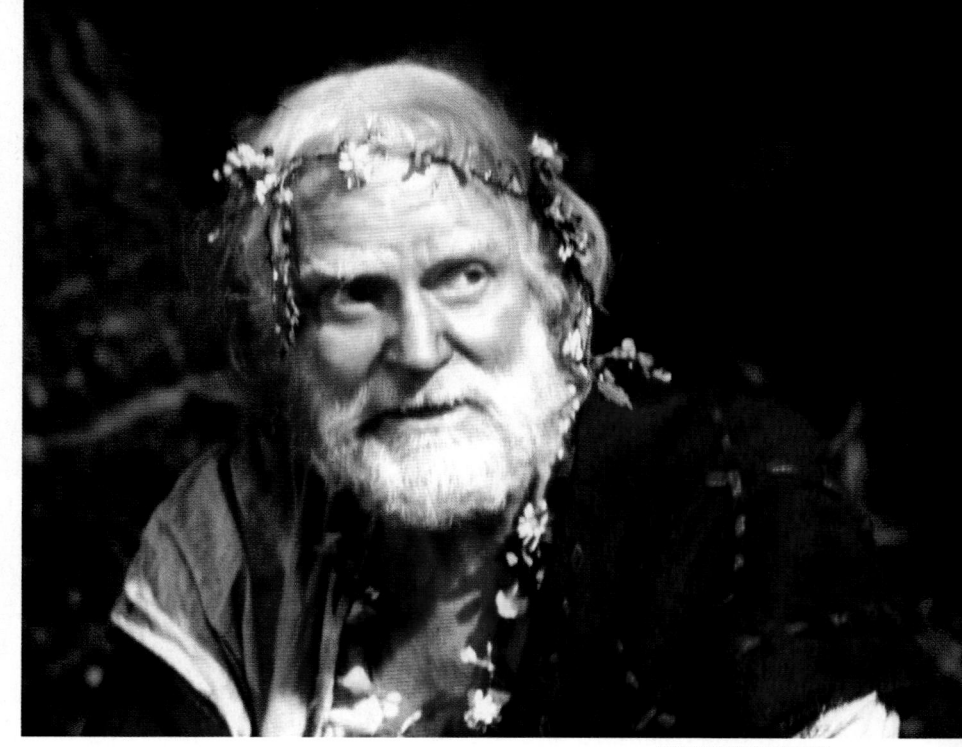

PLATE 16. ***King Lear.*** *Laurence Olivier as King Lear in Granada Television's 1983 production. See Act 4, Scene 6:* Enter Lear [mad, fantastically dressed with wild flowers]. *This was to be Olivier's last performance; he was terminally ill with cancer when this production was televised.*

© YORKSHIRE TELEVISION

TERRY O'NEILL/CORBIS SYGMA

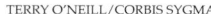

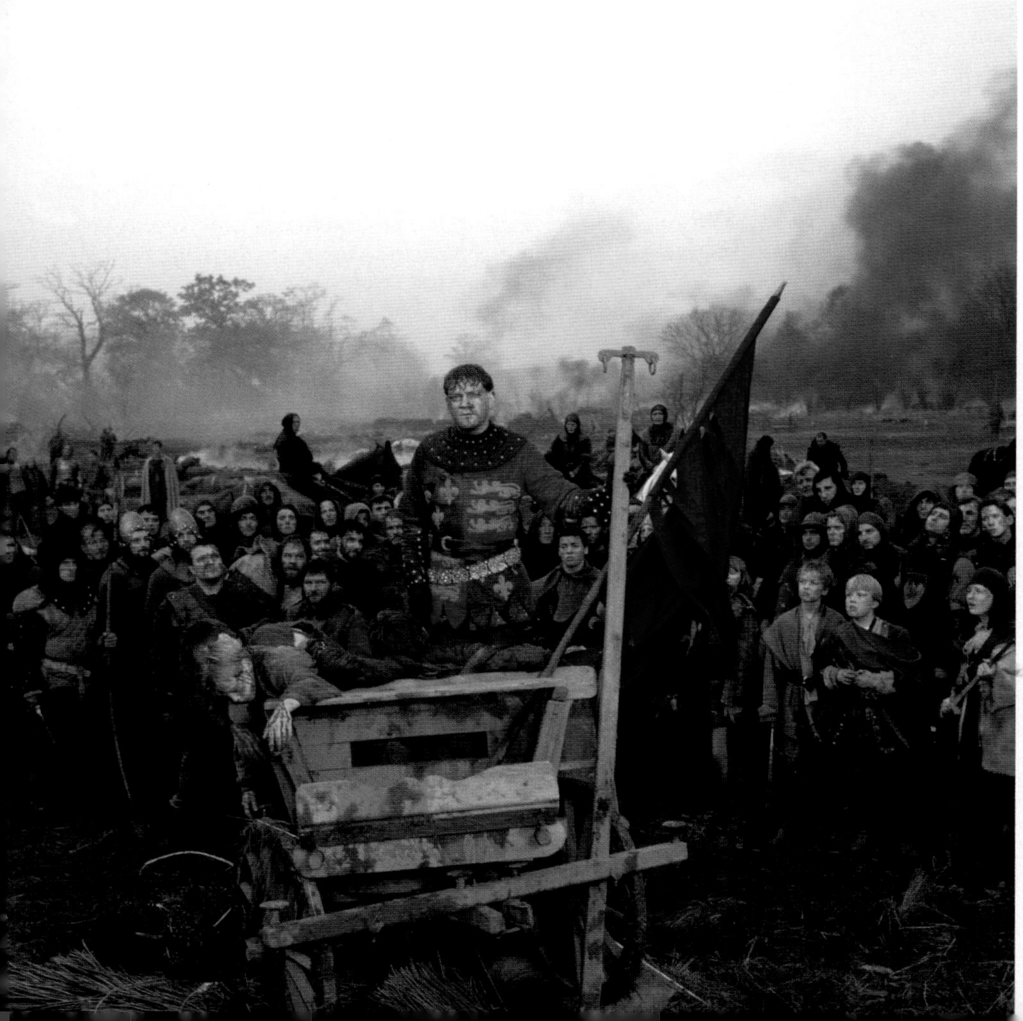

PLATE 17. ***Henry V.*** *King Henry V (Kenneth Branagh), exhausted yet triumphant after his victory over the French at the Battle of Agincourt, surveys the carnage of war amid his devoted followers in Act 4. Compare this image, from Branagh's 1989 film, to Olivier's more nationalistic view in Plate 14.*

PLATE 18. *Hamlet. Hamlet (Mel Gibson) and Ophelia (Helena Bonham Carter) in Franco Zeffirelli's 1990 film of* Hamlet. *In Zeffirelli's direction, this scene from Act 3 takes place without any words being spoken. While Polonius watches, Hamlet grabs Ophelia, looks into her eyes, sighs, and leaves.*

PLATE 19. *Hamlet. Hamlet (Ethan Hawke) and Ophelia (Julia Stiles) in Michael Almereyda's* Hamlet (2000). *Almereyda's* Hamlet *is set in present-day New York City, and in this scene from Act 3, Ophelia is wearing a surveillance microphone (so that Polonius can eavesdrop electronically). Hamlet reaches to embrace her and discovers the wire.*

PLATE 20. *Romeo and Juliet. Juliet (Olivia Hussey) and Romeo (Leonard Whiting), near the end of Franco Zeffirelli's 1968 film. Juliet is about to stab herself with Romeo's dagger: "This is thy sheath. There rust, and let me die" (5.3.170).*

PHOTOFEST

PLATE 21. *Romeo and Juliet. Claire Danes as Juliet in Baz Luhrmann's 1996 film,* William Shakespeare's Romeo + Juliet. *Juliet prepares to take the sleeping potion the Friar has given her, not sure that it may not be poison. "What if this mixture not work at all? / Shall I be married then tomorrow morning?" (4.3.21-2).*

PLATE 22. *Othello.* *Othello (Laurence Fishburne) and Iago (Kenneth Branagh) in Oliver Parker's 1997 film. Iago's insinuations begin their poisonous work, destroying Othello's peace of mind by urging Othello to suspect his wife Desdemona of infidelity. 3.3.178-80: "Oh, beware, my lord, of jealousy. / It is the green-eyed monster which doth mock / The meat it feeds on."*

PLATE 23. *Shakespeare in Love.* *"Will Shakespeare" (Joseph Fiennes) suffers from writer's block in his frustrating attempt to write a play called "Romeo and Ethel the Pirate's Daughter."*

some indoor hall in the vicinity of St. Paul's in London, outfitted much like the typical domestic Tudor hall to which the boys had grown accustomed. Comparable indoor "private" theaters soon followed at Blackfriars and Whitefriars.

At some point, a low stage was constructed in front of the hall screen, and seats were provided for all the spectators. Many of these seats were in the "pit," or what we would call the "orchestra," facing toward the stage at one end of the rectangular room. Other seats were in galleries along both sides of the room; these were quite elaborate in the so-called Second Blackfriars of 1596 and provided two or three tiers of seats. Elegant box seats stood at either side of the stage itself. The Second Blackfriars had a permanently built tiring house to the rear of the stage, with probably three doors. Above it was a gallery used variously as a lord's room, a music room, and an upper station for occasional acting.

The private theater flourished during the 1580s and again after 1598–1599, having been closed down during most of the 1590s because of its satirical activities. Although it was a commercial theater, it was "private" in its clientele, because its high price of admission (sixpence) excluded those who could stand in the yards of the "public" theaters for a penny (roughly the equivalent of an hour's wage for a skilled worker). Plays written for the more select audiences of the "private" theaters tended to be more satirical and oriented to courtly values than those written for the "public" theaters, although the distinction is by no means absolute.

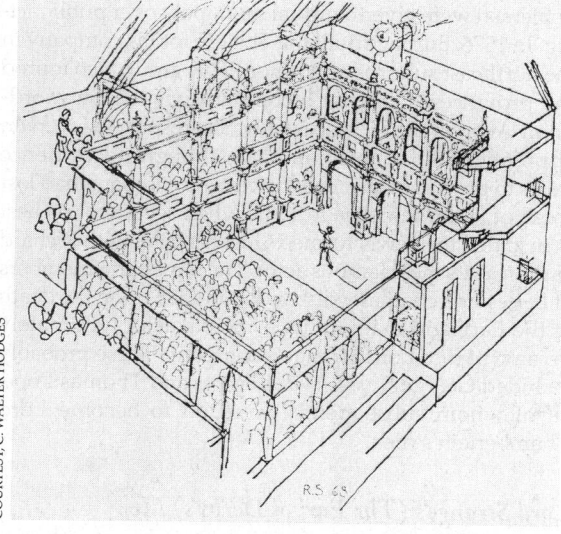

A reconstruction of the Second Blackfriars, featuring a rectangular stage, a tiring house with three doors, and a gallery.

COURTESY, C. WALTER HODGES

London Private Theaters

The important private theaters of Shakespeare's London were two in the precinct, or "liberty," of Blackfriars, an early one in Whitefriars about which little is known, a later one there, and a theater at Paul's, the exact location and nature of which is not known. In the thirteenth century, the mother house of the Dominican friars, or Blackfriars, was established on the sloping ground between St. Paul's Cathedral and the river. It was a sizable institution, ultimately covering about five acres of ground. It stood on the very border of the city and, after the custom of the time, was made a liberty; that is to say, it had its own local government and was removed from the immediate jurisdiction of the city of London. After the suppression of the friary and the confiscation of its lands, the jealousy existing between the Privy Council, representing the crown, and the mayor and aldermen, representing the city and probably also the rights of property holders, prevented the district of the Blackfriars from losing its political independence of the municipality. It was still a liberty and therefore attractive to players and other persons wishing to avoid the London authorities. At the same time, aristocrats residing in the area required protection, and the crown had certain rights still in its control.

From 1576 to 1584, the Children of the Queen's Chapel, one of the two most important companies of boy actors, had used a hall in the precinct of Blackfriars in which to act their plays. Here were acted at least some of John Lyly's plays. In 1596, James Burbage purchased property in this precinct and seems to have spent a good deal of money in its adaptation for use as an indoor theater (the so-called Second Blackfriars). He probably appreciated its advantages over Cripplegate or the Bankside of greater proximity to London and of protection against the elements, particularly for use in winter. But the aristocratic residents of the Blackfriars by petition to the Privy Council prevented him from making use of his theater. Plays within the city proper had only recently been finally and successfully prohibited, and the petitioners no doubt objected to their intrusion into Blackfriars on the grounds that the plays and their crowds were a nuisance.

Burbage's new indoor theater may have lain idle from the time of its preparation until 1600; but, in any case, in that year it became the scene of many plays. It was let by lease for the use of the Children of the Chapel, who in 1604 became the Children of the Queen's Revels. Their theater managers brought into their service a number of new dramatists—Ben Jonson, John Marston, George Chapman, and later John Webster. The vogue of the plays acted by the Children of the Chapel was so great as to damage the patronage of the established companies and to compel them to go on the road. Out of this rivalry between the children and the adult actors arose that open competition alluded to in *Hamlet* (2.2.328–362) and sometimes referred to today as the "War of the Theaters." The skirmishes were relatively brief, arising in part from a clash of personalities among Jonson, Marston, and Thomas Dekker, but the debate between public and private acting companies was significant as an indication of whether London drama would continue to play to large popular audiences or would increasingly turn to a more courtly clientele. In 1608, the Burbage interests secured the evacuation of the lease, so that the theater in Blackfriars became the winter playhouse of Shakespeare's company from that time forward.

System of Patronage

In 1572, common players of interludes, along with minstrels, bearwards, and fencers, were included within the hard terms of the act for the punishment of vagabonds, provided that such common players were not enrolled as the servants of a baron of the realm or of some honorable person of greater degree. The result was a system of patronage of theatrical companies in Elizabethan and Jacobean times, according to which players became the "servants" of some nobleman or of some member of the royal family.

By the time Shakespeare came to London in the late 1580s, many of these companies were already in existence, some of which long antedated the passage of the act of 1572. Provincial records of the visits of players, to be sure, sometimes failed to distinguish actors from acrobats or other public performers who were similarly organized. Nonetheless, we have evidence that various companies of players performed in London and elsewhere in the late 1580s under the patronage of the Queen, the Earl of Worcester, the Earl of Leicester, the Earl of Oxford, the Earl of Sussex, the Lord Admiral, and Charles, Lord Howard of Effingham. These companies were eventually much reduced in number; usually only three adult companies acted at any given time in London during Shakespeare's prime. In addition, the children's companies, privately controlled, acted intermittently but at times very successfully. The most important of these were the Children of the Chapel and Queen's Revels and the Children of Paul's, but there were also boy players of Windsor, Eton College, the Merchant Taylors, Westminster, and other schools.

Shakespeare and the London Theatrical Companies

We know that by 1592 Shakespeare had arrived in London and had achieved sufficient notice as a young playwright to arouse the resentment of a rival dramatist, Robert Greene. In that year, shortly before he died, Greene—or possibly his editor after Greene's death—lashed out at an "upstart crow, beautified with our feathers," who had had the audacity to fancy himself "the only Shake-scene in a country" (*Groats-worth of Wit*). This petulant outburst was plainly directed at Shakespeare, since Greene included in his remarks a parody of some lines from *3 Henry VI*. As a university man and an established dramatist, Greene seems to have resented the intrusion into his profession of a mere player who was not university trained. This "upstart crow" was achieving a very real success on the London stage. Shakespeare had probably already written *The Comedy of Errors, Love's Labor's Lost, The Two Gentlemen of Verona*, the *Henry VI* plays, and *Titus Andronicus*, and perhaps also *Richard III* and *The Taming of the Shrew*.

For which acting company or companies had he written these plays, however? By 1594, we know that Shakespeare was an established member of the Lord Chamberlain's company, important enough, in fact, to have been named, along with Will Kempe and Richard Burbage, as payee for court performances on December 26 and 28 of 1594. But when had he joined the Chamberlain's men, and for whom had he written and acted previously? These are the problems of the so-called dark years, during which Shakespeare came to London (perhaps around 1587) and got started on his career.

One prestigious acting company he could have joined was the Earl of Leicester's company, led by James Burbage, father of Shakespeare's later colleague, Richard Burbage. Leicester was a favorite minister of Queen Elizabeth until his death in 1588, and his company of actors received from the Queen in 1574 an extraordinary patent to perform plays anywhere in England, despite all local prohibitions, provided that the plays were approved beforehand by the master of the Queen's Revels. Since an act of 1572 had outlawed all unlicensed troupes, Leicester's men and similar companies attached to important noblemen were given a virtual monopoly over public acting. In 1576, Burbage built the Theatre for his company in the northeast suburbs of London. This group also toured the provinces: Leicester's company visited Stratford-upon-Avon in 1587. Conceivably, Shakespeare served an apprenticeship in this company, though no evidence exists to prove a connection. Leicester's company had lost some of its prominence in 1583, when several of its best men joined the newly formed Queen's men, with Richard Tarlton as its most famous actor. The remaining members of Leicester's company disbanded in 1588 upon the death of the Earl, and many of its principal actors ultimately became part of Lord Strange's company. These probably included George Bryan, Will Kempe, and Thomas Pope, all of whom subsequently went on to become Lord Chamberlain's men.

Lord Strange's (The Earl of Derby's) Men

The Queen's men gained an extraordinary prominence in the 1580s, as Scott McMillin and Sally-Beth MacLean have shown in the *Queen's Men and Their Plays* (1998). This acting group was assembled under royal sponsorship as an instrument of furthering the Protestant Reformation through its performances of plays, and did so with notable success, although it then declined rapidly in the early 1590s chiefly because as a touring company it was unprepared to compete with the new companies that learned how to succeed in the metropolis by staging a wide variety of plays in a fixed London theater. Prominent among the acting companies to which Shakespeare could have belonged when he came to London, probably in the late 1580s, were Lord Strange's men, the Lord Admiral's men, the Earl of Pembroke's men, and the Earl of Sussex's men. Scholars have long speculated that Shakespeare may have joined the company of Ferdinando Stanley, Lord Strange (who in 1593 became the Earl of Derby). The names of George Bryan, Will Kempe, and Thomas Pope appear on a roster of Strange's company in 1593, along with those of John Heminges and Augustine Phillips. All of these men later became part of the Lord Chamberlain's company, most of them when it was first formed in 1594. Shakespeare's name does not appear on the 1593 Lord Strange's list (which was a license for touring in the provinces), but he may possibly have stayed in London to attend to his writing while the company toured. Certainly, an important number of his later associates belonged to this group.

During the years from 1590 to 1594, some of Lord Strange's men appear to have joined forces on occasion with Edward Alleyn and others of the Admiral's men. This impressive combination of talents enjoyed a successful season in 1591–1592, with six performances at court. Alleyn's father-in-law, Philip Henslowe, recorded in his *Diary* the performances of the combined players in early 1592, probably at the Rose Theatre. Their repertory included a *Harey the vj* and a *Titus & Vespacia*. The latter play is, however, no longer thought to have any connection with Shakespeare's *Titus Andronicus;* and the *Harey the vj* may or may not have been Shakespeare's, since *3 Henry VI* was (according to its 1595 title page) acted by Pembroke's men, rather than Lord Strange's men. If Shakespeare was a member of the Strange-Admiral's combination in 1591–1592, we are at a loss to explain why Henslowe's 1592 list records so many performances of plays by Marlowe, Greene, Kyd, and others, but none that are certainly by Shakespeare. On the other hand, the *Harey the vj* may be his, and the title page of the 1594 Quarto of *Titus Andronicus* does list the Earl of Derby's men as performers of the play, in addition to the Earl of Pembroke's and the Earl of Sussex's men. (Lord Strange's men became officially known as the Earl of Derby's men when Lord Strange was made an earl in September 1593.) At any rate, the company disbanded when the Earl died in April 1594, leaving them without a patron. The connection with the Admiral's men was discontinued, with Alleyn returning to the Admiral's men and the rest of the

Clowns were enormously popular on the Elizabethan stage. Of the many Elizabethan clowns whose names are known to us, Richard Tarlton is one of the most famous. (Will Kempe, in Shakespeare's company, the Lord Chamberlain's men, is another; see pp. lxviii–lxix.) Tarlton is shown here inside an elaborate letter T, dancing a jig with his pipe and tabor. Such jigs were often used at the conclusion of a play.

group forming a new company under the patronage of Henry Carey, first Lord Hunsdon, the Lord Chamberlain.

The Earl of Pembroke's Men

The other company to which Shakespeare is most likely to have belonged prior to 1594 is the Earl of Pembroke's company. This group came to grief in 1593–1594, evidently as a result of virulent outbursts of the plague, which had kept the theaters closed during most of 1592 and 1593. Pembroke's men were forced to tour the provinces and then to sell a number of their best plays to the booksellers. Henslowe wrote to Alleyn in September 1593 of the extreme financial plight of Pembroke's company: "As for my lord of Pembroke's [men], which you desire to know where they be, they are all at home and has been this five or six weeks, for they cannot save their charges [expenses] with travel, as I hear, and were fain to pawn their parell [apparel] for their charge." Soon thereafter this company disbanded.

Pembroke's men were associated with a significant number of Shakespeare's early plays. Among the playbooks they evidently sold in 1593–1594 were *The Taming of a Shrew* and *The True Tragedy of Richard Duke of York.* The first of these was published in 1594 with the assertion that it had been "sundry times acted by the Right Honorable the Earle of Pembroke his Servants." Although the text of this quarto is not Shakespeare's play as we know it but, instead, an anonymous version, most scholars now feel certain that it was an imitation of Shakespeare's play and that the work performed by Pembroke's men was, in fact, Shakespeare's. The same conclusion pertains to a performance in 1594 of *"the Tamynge of a Shrowe"* at Newington Butts, a playhouse south of London Bridge. Henslowe's *Diary* informs us that the actors on this occasion were either the Lord Chamberlain's or the Lord Admiral's men. The probability, then, is that Shakespeare's *The Taming of the Shrew* passed from Pembroke's men to the Chamberlain's men when Pembroke's company collapsed in 1593–1594.

The True Tragedy of Richard Duke of York, published in 1595, was a seemingly unauthorized quarto of Shakespeare's *3 Henry VI.* Its title page declared that it had been "sundry times acted by the Right Honorable the Earl of Pembroke his Servants." Probably they acted *2 Henry VI* as well, to which part three was a sequel. In addition, the 1594 Quarto of *Titus Andronicus* mentions on its title page the Earl of Pembroke's servants, although the Earl of Derby's and the Earl of Sussex's men are named there as well. Thus, Pembroke's men performed as many as four of Shakespeare's early plays—more than we can assign to any other known company. Nevertheless, their claim to Shakespeare remains uncertain. We simply do not know who acted several of Shakespeare's earliest plays, such as *The Comedy of Errors, Love's Labor's Lost,* and *The Two Gentlemen of Verona.* Lord Strange's (Derby's) men, as we have seen, did act something called *Harey the vj* and are named on the 1594 title page of *Titus Andronicus.* Sussex's men may conceivably have owned for a time some early Shakespearean plays that later went to the Lord Chamberlain's men, such as *Titus Andronicus.* The Queen's men, although associated with no known Shakespeare play, other than the old *King Lear* (acted jointly with Sussex's men in 1593), were a leading company during the years in question. All we can say for sure is that the difficulties of 1592–1593 with the plague and the death of the Earl of Derby in 1594 led to a major reshuffling of the London acting companies. From this reshuffling emerged in 1594 the Lord Chamberlain's company, with Shakespeare and Richard Burbage (whose earlier history is also difficult to trace) as two of its earliest and most prominent members.

SHAKESPEARE'S LIFE AND WORK

THE EARLY YEARS, 1564–C. 1594

Stratford-upon-Avon

About Shakespeare's place of birth, Stratford-upon-Avon, there is no doubt. He spent his childhood there and returned periodically throughout his life. During most or all of his long professional career in London, his wife and children lived in Stratford. He acquired property and took some interest in local affairs. He retired to Stratford and chose to be buried there. Its Warwickshire surroundings lived in his poetic imagination.

The Stratford of Shakespeare's day was a "handsome small market town" (as described by William Camden) of perhaps 1,500 inhabitants, with fairly broad streets and half-timbered houses roofed with thatch. It could boast of a long history and an attractive setting on the river Avon. A bridge of fourteen arches, built in 1496 by Sir Hugh Clopton, Lord Mayor of London, spanned the river. Beside the Avon stood Trinity Church, built on the site of a Saxon monastery. The chapel of the Guild of the Holy Trinity, dating from the thirteenth century, and an old King Edward VI grammar school were buildings of note. Strat-

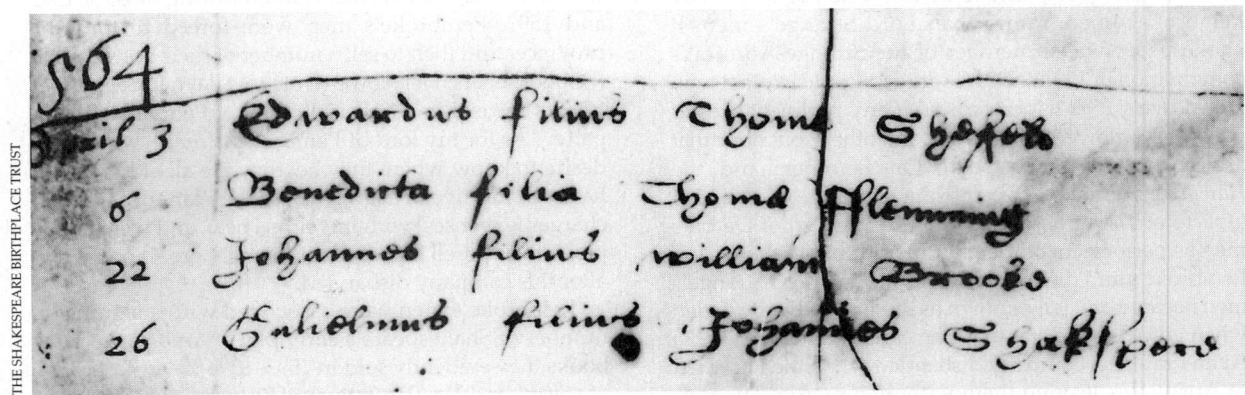

The earliest written reference to William Shakespeare is this record of his christening in the register of Holy Trinity Church at Stratford, April 26, 1564. The entry reads, "Gulielmus filius Johannes Shakspere."

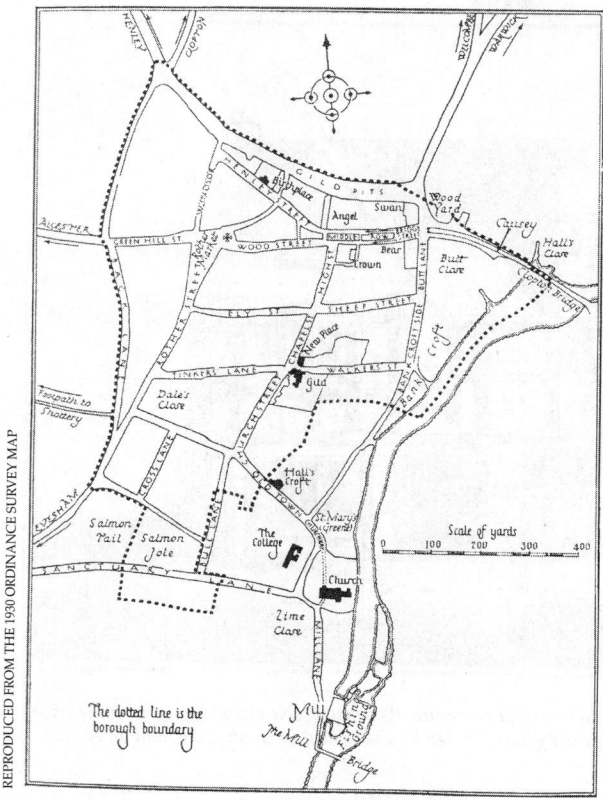

The town of Stratford-upon-Avon as Shakespeare knew it. The house in which he is considered to have been born is on Henley Street; the larger house he purchased in 1597, New Place, is on Chapel Street.

ford had maintained a grammar school at least since 1424 and probably long before that. It was a town without the domination of clergy, aristocracy, or great wealth. It lay in a rich agricultural region, in the county of Warwickshire. To the north of Stratford lay the Forest of Arden.

Shakespeare's Family

The family that bore the name of Shakespeare was well distributed throughout England, but was especially numerous in Warwickshire. A name "Saquespee," in various spellings, is found in Normandy at an early date. It means, according to J. Q. Adams, "to draw out the sword quickly." That name, in the form "Sakspee," with many variants, is found in England; also the name "Saksper," varying gradually to the form "Shakespeare." It may have been wrought into that form by the obvious military meaning of "one who shakes the spear."

Our first substantial records of the family begin with Richard Shakespeare, who was, in all probability, Shakespeare's grandfather, a farmer living in the village of

Snitterfield four miles from Stratford. He was a tenant on the property of Robert Arden of Wilmcote, a wealthy man with the social status of gentleman. Richard Shakespeare died about 1561, possessed of an estate valued at the very respectable sum of thirty-eight pounds and seventeen shillings.

His son John made a great step forward in the world by his marriage with Mary Arden, daughter of his father's landlord. John Shakespeare had some property of his own and through his wife acquired a good deal more. He moved from Snitterfield to Stratford at some date before 1552. He rose to great local importance in Stratford and bought several houses, among which was the one on Henley Street traditionally identified as Shakespeare's birthplace. William Shakespeare was born in 1564 and was baptized on April 26. The exact date of his birth is not known, but traditionally we celebrate it on April 23, the feast day of St. George, England's patron saint. (The date is at least plausible in view of the practice of baptizing infants shortly after birth.) The house in which Shakespeare was probably born, though almost entirely rebuilt and changed in various and unknown ways during the years that have intervened since Shakespeare's birth, still stands. It is of considerable size, having four rooms on the ground floor, and must, therefore, have been an important business house in the Stratford of those days. John Shakespeare's occupation seems to have been that of a tanner and glover; that is, he cured skins, made gloves and some other leather goods, and sold them in his shop. He was also a dealer in wool, grain, malt, and other farm produce.

The long story, beginning in 1552, of John Shakespeare's success and misfortunes in Stratford is attested to by many borough records. He held various city offices. He was ale taster (inspector of bread and malt), burgess (petty constable), affeeror (assessor of fines), city chamberlain (treasurer), alderman, and high bailiff of the town—the highest municipal office in Stratford. At some time around 1576, he applied to the Herald's office for the right to bear arms and style himself a gentleman. This petition was later to be renewed and successfully carried through to completion by his famous son. In 1577 or 1578, however, when William was as yet only thirteen or fourteen years old, John Shakespeare's fortunes began a sudden and mysterious decline. He absented himself from council meetings. He had to mortgage his wife's property and showed other signs of being in financial difficulty. He became involved in serious litigation and was assessed heavy fines. Although he kept his position on the corporation council until 1586 or 1587, he was finally replaced as alderman because of his failure to attend. Conceivably, John Shakespeare's sudden difficulties were the result of persecution for his Catholic faith, since John's wife's family had remained loyal to Catholicism, and the old faith was being attacked with new vigor in the Warwickshire

This house on Henley Street in Stratford is considered to have been the birthplace of Shakespeare. Its considerable size shows what must have been an important house of business. Shakespeare's father dealt chiefly in leather goods, though he also traded in wool, grain, and other farm produce.

region in 1577 and afterwards. This hypothesis is unsubstantial, however, especially in view of the fact that some Catholics and Puritans seemed to have held posts of trust and to have remained prosperous in Stratford during this period. In the last analysis, we have little evidence as to John Shakespeare's religious faith or as to the reasons for his sudden reversal of fortune.

The family of Shakespeare's mother could trace its ancestry back to the time of William the Conqueror, and Shakespeare's father, in spite of his troubles, was a citizen of importance. John Shakespeare made his mark, instead of writing his name, but so did other men of the time who we know could read and write. His offices, particularly that of chamberlain, and the various public functions he discharged indicate that he must have had some education.

Shakespeare in School

Nicholas Rowe, who published in 1709 the first extensive biographical account of Shakespeare, reports the tradition that Shakespeare studied "for some time at a Free-School." Although the list of students who actually attended the King's New School at Stratford-upon-Avon in the late sixteenth century has not survived, we cannot doubt that Rowe is reporting accurately. Shakespeare's father, as a leading citizen of Stratford, would scarcely

have spurned the benefits of one of Stratford's most prized institutions. The town had had a free school since the thirteenth century, at first under the auspices of the Church. During the reign of King Edward VI (1547–1553), the Church lands were expropriated by the crown and the town of Stratford was granted a corporate charter. At this time, the school was reorganized as the King's New School, named in honor of the reigning monarch. It prospered. Its teachers, or "masters," regularly held degrees from Oxford during Shakespeare's childhood and received salaries that were superior to those of most comparable schools.

Much has been learned about the curriculum of such a school. A child would first learn the rudiments of reading and writing English by spending two or three years in a "petty" or elementary school. The child learned to read from a "hornbook," a single sheet of paper mounted on a board and protected by a thin transparent layer of horn, on which was usually printed the alphabet in small and capital letters and the Lord's Prayer. The child would also practice an ABC book with catechism. When the child had demonstrated the ability to read satisfactorily, the child was admitted, at about the age of seven, to the grammar school proper. Here the day was a rigorous one, usually extending from 6 A.M. in the summer or 7 A.M. in the winter until 5 P.M. Intervals for food or brief

The interior of the Stratford grammar school: a late and not very reliable tradition claims that Shakespeare's desk was third from the front on the left-hand side.

recreation came at midmorning, noon, and midafternoon. Holidays occurred at Christmas, Easter, and Whitsuntide (usually late May and June), comprising perhaps forty days in all through the year. Discipline was strict, and physical punishment was common.

Latin formed the basis of the grammar school curriculum. The scholars studied grammar, read ancient writers, recited, and learned to write in Latin. A standard text was the *Grammatica Latina* by William Lilly or Lyly, grandfather of the later Elizabethan dramatist John Lyly. The scholars also became familiar with the *Disticha de Moribus* (moral proverbs) attributed to Cato, *Aesop's Fables,* the *Eclogues* of Baptista Spagnuoli Mantuanus or Mantuan (alluded to in *Love's Labor's Lost*), the *Eclogues* and *Aeneid* of Virgil, the comedies of Plautus or Terence (sometimes performed in Latin by the children), Ovid's *Metamorphoses* and other of his works, and possibly some Horace and Seneca.

Shakespeare plentifully reveals in his dramatic writings an awareness of many of these authors, especially Plautus (in *The Comedy of Errors*), Ovid (in *A Midsummer Night's Dream* and elsewhere), and Seneca (in *Titus Andronicus*). Although he often consulted translations of these authors, he seems to have known the originals as well. He had, in Ben Jonson's learned estimation, "small Latin and less Greek"; the tone is condescending, but the statement does concede that Shakespeare had some of both. He would have acquired some Greek in the last years of his grammar schooling. By twentieth-century standards, Shakespeare had a fairly comprehensive amount of training in the ancient classics, certainly enough to account for the general, if unscholarly, references we find in the plays.

Shakespeare's Marriage

When Shakespeare was eighteen years old, he married Anne Hathaway, a woman eight years his senior. (The inscription on her grave states that she was sixty-seven when she died in August 1623.) The bishop's register of

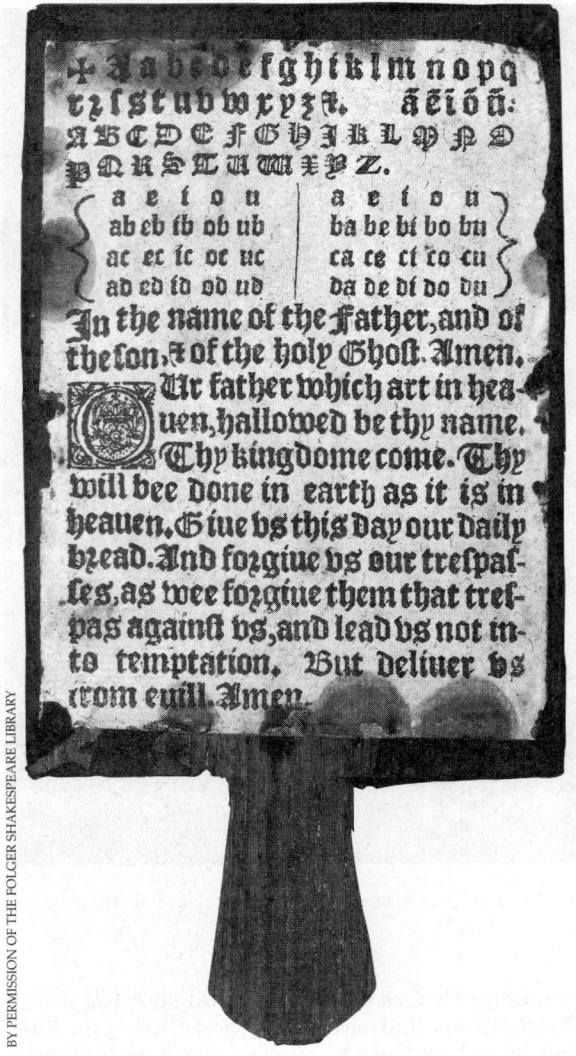

The hornbook pictured here—showing the alphabet and the Lord's Prayer—was part of a child's education in Shakespeare's time.

Worcester, the central city of the diocese, shows for November 27, 1582, the issue of a bishop's license for the marriage of William Shakespeare and Anne "Whately"; the bond of sureties issued next day refers to her as "Hathaway." She has been identified with all reasonable probability as Agnes (or Anne) Hathaway, daughter of the then recently deceased Richard Hathaway of the hamlet of Shottery, a short distance from Stratford.

The obtaining of a license was not normally required for a marriage. William Shakespeare and Anne Hathaway seem to have applied for a license on this occasion because they wished to be married after only one read-ing of the banns rather than the usual three. (The read-ing of the banns, or announcement in church of a forth-coming marriage, usually on three successive Sundays, enabled any party to object to the marriage if he or she knew of any legal impediment.) Since the reading of all banns was suspended for long periods during Advent (before Christmas) and Lent (before Easter), a couple intending to marry shortly before Christmas might have had to wait until April before the banns could be read thrice. Accordingly, the bishop not uncommonly grant-ed a license permitting couples to marry during the win-ter season with only one reading of the banns. To obtain such a license, two friends of the bride's family had to sign a bond obligating themselves to pay the bishop up to forty pounds, should any impediment to the marriage result in a legal action against the bishop for having issued the license.

The actual record of the marriage in a parish register has not survived, but presumably the couple were mar-ried shortly after obtaining the license. They may have been married in Temple Grafton, where Anne had rela-tives. The couple took up residence in Stratford. Anne was already pregnant at the time of the marriage, for she gave birth to a daughter, Susanna, on May 26, 1583. The birth of a child six months after the wedding may explain the need for haste the previous November. These cir-cumstances, and Anne's considerable seniority in age to William, have given rise to much speculation about mat-ters that can never be satisfactorily resolved. We do know that a formal betrothal in the presence of witnesses could legally validate a binding relationship, enabling a couple to consummate their love without social stigma. We know also that Shakespeare dramatized the issue of pre-marital contract and pregnancy in *Measure for Measure*. Whether Shakespeare entered into such a formal rela-tionship with Anne is, however, undiscoverable.

On February 2, 1585, Shakespeare's only other chil-dren, the twins Hamnet and Judith, were baptized in Stratford Church. The twins seem to have been named after Shakespeare's friends and neighbors, Hamnet Sadler, a baker, and his wife, Judith.

The Seven "Dark" Years

From 1585, the year in which his twins were baptized, until 1592, when he was first referred to as an actor and dramatist of growing importance in London, Shake-speare's activities are wholly unknown. Presumably, at some time during this period he made his way to London and entered its theatrical world, but otherwise we can only record traditions and guesses as to what he did between the ages of 21 and 28.

One of the oldest and most intriguing suggestions comes from John Aubrey, who, in collecting information in the late seventeenth century about actors and drama-

J. KOMENSKY, "ORBIS SENSUALUM PICTUS," 1659

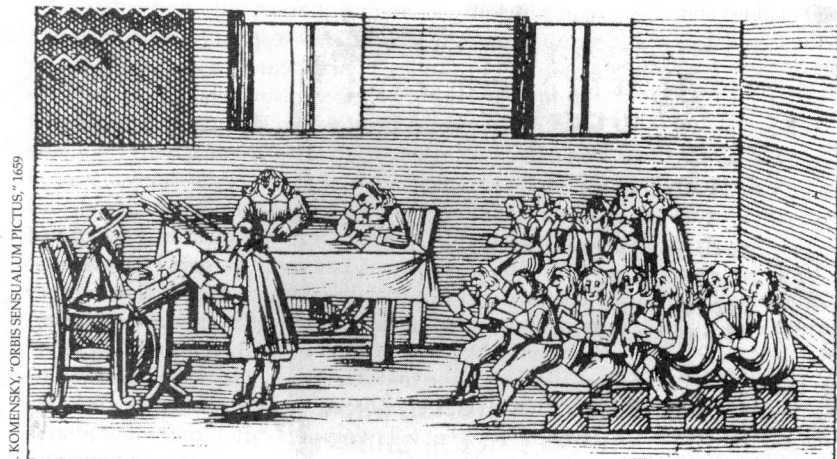

A schoolroom in Tudor England.

tists for his "Minutes of Lives," sought the help of one William Beeston. John Dryden believed Beeston to be "the chronicle of the stage," and Aubrey seems also to have had a high opinion of Beeston's theatrical knowledge. In his manuscript, Aubrey made a note to himself: "W. Shakespeare—quaere [i.e., inquire of] Mr. Beeston, who knows most of him." Aubrey then cites Beeston as his authority for this tradition about Shakespeare:

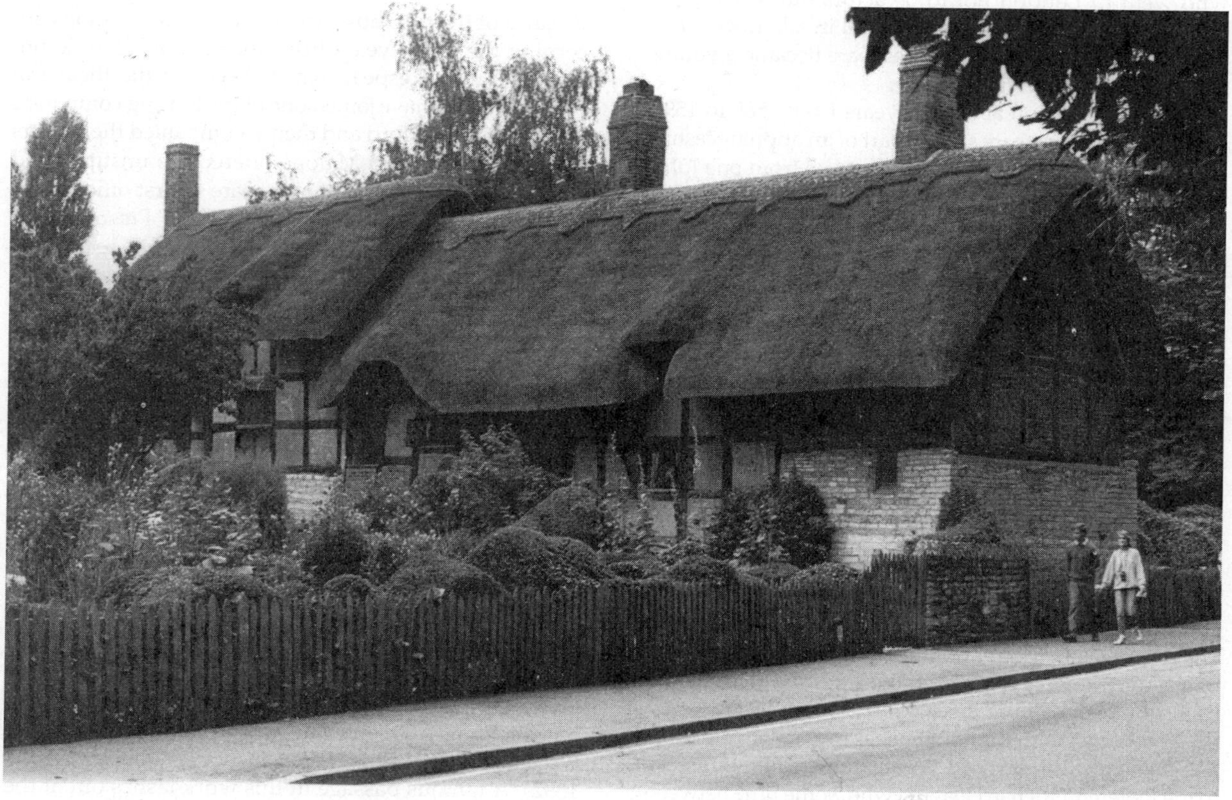

THE SHAKESPEARE BIRTHPLACE TRUST

The substantial farmhouse owned by the Hathaways of Shottery, originally known as "Hewland" but now almost universally famous as Anne Hathaway's Cottage.

Though, as Ben Jonson says of him, that he had but little Latin and less Greek, he understood Latin pretty well, for he had been in his younger years a schoolmaster in the country.

Beeston had been a theatrical manager all his life. He was the son of the actor Christopher Beeston, who had been a member of Shakespeare's company, probably from 1596 until 1602, and who therefore had occasion to know Shakespeare well.

Shakespeare's own grammar school education would not have qualified him to be the master of a school, but he could have served as "usher" or assistant to the master. The idea that Shakespeare may have taught in this way is not unattractive. Although, as we have seen, he had some acquaintance with Plautus, Ovid, and other classical writers through his own grammar school reading, a stint as schoolmaster would have made these authors more familiar and readily accessible to him when he began writing his plays and nondramatic poems. His earliest works—*The Comedy of Errors, Love's Labor's Lost, Titus Andronicus, Venus and Adonis, The Rape of Lucrece*—show most steadily and directly the effect of his classical reading. Schoolteaching experience might have encouraged his ambitions to be a writer, like Marlowe or Greene, who went to London not to be actors but to try their hands at poetry and playwriting. All in all, however, it seems more probable that Shakespeare became a young actor rather than a schoolteacher.

Another tradition about the years from 1585 to 1592 asserts that Shakespeare served part of an apprenticeship in Stratford. This suggestion comes to us from one John Dowdall, who, traveling through Warwickshire in 1693, heard the story from an old parish clerk who was showing him around the town of Stratford. According to this parish clerk, Shakespeare had been bound as apprentice to a butcher but ran away from his master to London where he was received into a playhouse as "servitor." John Aubrey records a similar tradition: "When he [Shakespeare] was a boy he exercised his father's trade." Aubrey believed this trade to have been that of a butcher. Moreover, says Aubrey, "When he killed a calf, he would do it in a high style, and make a speech." No other evidence confirms, however, that Shakespeare was a runaway apprentice. The allusion to "killing a calf" may, instead, refer to an ancient rural amusement in which the slaughter of a calf was staged behind a curtain for the entertainment of visitors at county fairs. Conceivably, Shakespeare's participation in such a game during his youth may have given rise to the tradition that he had been a butcher's apprentice.

Another legend, that of Shakespeare's deer stealing, has enjoyed wide currency. We are indebted for this story to the Reverend Richard Davies, who, some time between 1688 and 1709, jotted down some gossipy interpolations in the manuscripts of the Reverend William Fulman. (Ful-man himself was an antiquarian who had collected a number of notes about Shakespeare and Stratford.) According to Davies, Shakespeare was "much given to all unluckiness in stealing venison and rabbits, particularly from Sir —— Lucy, who had him oft whipped and sometimes imprisoned and at last made him fly his native country, to his great advancement." This tradition has led to speculation by Nicholas Rowe that Justice Shallow of *2 Henry IV* and *The Merry Wives of Windsor* is a satirical portrait of Sir Thomas Lucy of Charlecote Hall and that Shakespeare even composed an irreverent ballad about Lucy that added to the urgency of Shakespeare's departure for London. In fact, however, there is no compelling reason to believe that Shallow is based on Lucy, on Justice William Gardiner of Surrey (as Leslie Hotson insists), or on any live Elizabethan. We don't know that Shakespeare ever drew contemporary portraits in his plays, as is sometimes alleged; is Polonius in *Hamlet* Lord Burghley, for example, or is he Shakespeare's original portrait of a minister of state who is also a busybody? Nor do we know if the deer-slaying incident took place at all. It makes interesting fiction but unreliable biography.

Shakespeare's Arrival in London

Because of the total absence of reliable information concerning the seven years from 1585 to 1592, we do not know how Shakespeare got his start in the theatrical world. He may have joined one of the touring companies that came to Stratford and then accompanied the players to London. Edmund Malone offered the unsupported statement (in 1780) that Shakespeare's "first office in the theater was that of prompter's attendant." Presumably, a young man from the country would have had to begin at the bottom. Shakespeare's later work certainly reveals an intimate and practical acquaintance with technical matters of stagecraft. In any case, his rise to eminence as an actor and a writer seems to have been rapid. He was fortunate also in having at least one prosperous acquaintance in London, Richard Field, formerly of Stratford and the son of an associate of Shakespeare's father. Field was a printer, and in 1593 and 1594 he published two handsome editions of Shakespeare's first serious poems, *Venus and Adonis* and *The Rape of Lucrece*.

"The Only Shake-scene in a Country"

The first allusion to Shakespeare after his Stratford days is a vitriolic attack on him. It occurs in *Greene's Groatsworth of Wit Bought with a Million of Repentance*, written by Robert Greene during the last months of his wretched existence (he died in poverty in September 1592). A famous passage in this work lashes out at the actors of the public theaters for having deserted Greene and for bestowing their favor instead on a certain upstart dramatist. The passage warns three fellow dramatists and University Wits, Christopher Marlowe, Thomas Nashe, and George Peele, to abandon the writing of plays before they fall prey to a similar ingratitude. The diatribe runs as follows:

> . . . Base minded men all three of you, if by my misery you be not warned. For unto none of you (like me) sought those burs to cleave—those puppets, I mean, that spake from our mouths, those antics garnished in our colors. Is it not strange that I, to whom they all have been beholding, is it not like that you, to whom they all have been beholding, shall (were ye in that case as I am now) be both at once of them forsaken? Yes, trust them not. For there is an upstart crow, beautified with our feathers, that with his "Tiger's heart wrapped in a player's hide" supposes he is as well able to bombast out a blank verse as the best of you, and, being an absolute *Johannes Factotum,* is in his own conceit the only Shake-scene in a country.

The "burs" here referred to are the actors who have forsaken Greene in his poverty for the rival playwright "Shake-scene"—an obvious hit at Shakespeare. The sneer at a *"Johannes Factotum"* suggests another dig at Shakespeare for being a jack-of-all-trades—actor, playwright, poet, and theatrical handyman in the directing and producing of plays. The most unmistakable reference to Shakespeare, however, is to be found in the burlesque line, "Tiger's heart wrapped in a player's hide," modeled after "Oh, tiger's heart wrapped in a woman's hide!" from *3 Henry VI* (1.4.137). Shakespeare's success as a dramatist had led to an envious outburst from an older, disappointed rival. (Did Shakespeare possibly have this attack in mind some years later when he has Polonius object, in *Hamlet,* 2.2.111–12, "'beautified' is a vile phrase"?)

Soon after Greene's death, Henry Chettle, who had seen the manuscript through the press (and who today some believe to have written the attack himself), issued an apology in his *Kind-Heart's Dream* that may refer to Shakespeare. The apology begins with a disclaimer of all personal responsibility for the incident and with Chettle's insistence that he has neither known nor wishes to know Marlowe (whom Greene's pamphlet had accused of atheism). Toward another unidentified playwright, on the other hand, Chettle expresses genuine concern and regret that Chettle had not done more to soften the acerbity of Greene's vitriol:

> The other, whom at that time I did not so much spare as since I wish I had, for that, as I have moderated the heat of living writers and might have used my own discretion (especially in such a case, the author being dead), that I did not I am as sorry as if the original fault had been my fault; because myself have seen his demeanor no less civil than he excellent in the quality he professes. Besides, divers of worship have reported his uprightness of dealing, which argues his honesty and his facetious grace in writing that approves his art.

If the unnamed person here is to be understood as Shakespeare, it represents him in a most attractive light. Chettle freely admits to having been impressed by this person's civility. He praises the dramatist as "excellent in the quality he professes," that is, excellent as an actor. Chettle notes with approval that the man he is describing enjoys the favor of certain persons of importance, some of whom have borne witness to his uprightness in dealing. *Greene's Groatsworth of Wit,* then, with its rancorous attack on Shakespeare, has paradoxically led to the plausible inference (though not certain in its identification) that in 1592 Shakespeare was regarded as a man of pleasant demeanor, honest reputation, and acknowledged skill as an actor and writer.

Dramatic Apprenticeship

By the end of the year 1594, when after the long plague the theatrical companies were again permitted to act before London audiences, we find Shakespeare as a member of the Lord Chamberlain's company. Probably he had already written *The Comedy of Errors, Love's Labor's Lost, The Two Gentlemen of Verona,* the *Henry VI* plays, and *Titus Andronicus.* (A *Love's Labor's Won,* mentioned by Francis Meres in 1598, is possibly either a lost play or an alternate title for one of the extant comedies.) He may also have completed *The Taming of the Shrew, A Midsummer Night's Dream, Richard III, King John,* and *Romeo and Juliet.* Although some scholars still question his authorship in part or all of *Titus* and the *Henry VI* plays, no one questions that they are from the period around 1590.

Shakespeare's early development is hard to follow because of difficulties in exact dating of the early plays and because some of the texts (such as *Love's Labor's Lost*) may have been later revised. As a learner making rapid progress in the skill of his art, Shakespeare was also subjected to outside influences that can only partly be determined. Among these influences, we may be sure, were the plays of his contemporary dramatists. If we could define these influences and form an idea of the kinds of plays acceptable on the stage during Shakespeare's early period, we could better understand the milieu in which he began his work.

Fortunately, we know a fair amount concerning the dramatic repertory in London during Shakespeare's early years. Henslowe's *Diary,* for example, records the daily performances of plays by the Lord Strange's men, in conjunction with the Admiral's men, from February 19, 1592 to June 22, 1592. Many of their plays unfortunately are lost, but enough of them are preserved to indicate the sorts of drama then in vogue. The Strange-Admiral's repertory included Christopher Marlowe's *The Jew of Malta,* Robert Greene's *Orlando Furioso* and *Friar Bacon and Friar Bungay,* Robert Greene and Thomas Lodge's *A Looking Glass for London and England,* Thomas Kyd's *The*

Spanish Tragedy, the anonymous *A Knack to Know a Knave,* and possibly George Peele's *The Battle of Alcazar,* and Shakespeare's *1 Henry VI.* We find, in other words, a tragedy with a villain as hero, a romantic comedy masquerading as a heroic play, a love comedy featuring a lot of magic, a biblical moral, England's first great revenge tragedy, a popular satiric comedy aimed at dissolute courtiers and usurers, a history play about Portugal's African empire, and an English history play. The titles of other works now lost suggest a similar amalgam of widely differing genres.

Comparatively few plays may have been written during the period when plays were forbidden because of the long plague of 1592–1594. When the Lord Chamberlain's men and the Lord Admiral's men acted under Henslowe's management at the suburban theater of Newington Butts from June 3–13, 1594, their repertories seem to have consisted largely of old plays. In this brief period, they are thought to have acted *Titus Andronicus, Hamlet* (the pre-Shakespearean version), *The Taming of a Shrew* (quite possibly Shakespeare's version), *The Jew of Malta,* a lost play called *Hester and Ahasuerus,* and others.

The Lord Admiral's men probably moved soon afterwards in 1594 to the Rose on the Bankside, across the river Thames from the city of London, where they continued to play under Henslowe's management until 1603. During the years 1594–1597, Henslowe kept in his *Diary* a careful record of their plays and of the sums of money taken in. This circumstance enables us to know a great deal more about the repertory of Shakespeare's rival company than we can ever know about his own. When the Lord Admiral's men began again in 1594, they had five of Marlowe's plays. They seem also to have had Peele's *Edward I,* Kyd's *The Spanish Tragedy,* and a Henry V play. They may also have had plays by both Greene and Peele (Henslowe's chaotic spelling makes it hard to determine), although some of the principal dramas of these two authors had probably ceased to be acted.

We do not know as much about the repertory of the Lord Chamberlain's company as we do about that of the Lord Admiral's men. We know enough, however, to be sure that in 1594 both companies were acting the same sorts of plays that had been on the boards in 1592. We have, therefore, grounds for assuming that, in spite of the loss of many plays (some of which may have been important), the chief contemporary influences upon Shakespeare during his early period were those of Marlowe, Greene, Peele, and Kyd. As an actor possibly in Lord Strange's company or the Earl of Pembroke's company, he would have been familiar with their plays.

Shakespeare learned also from Lyly, though perhaps more from reading Lyly's plays than from actually seeing or performing in them. The boy actors for whom Lyly wrote were forced by the authorities to suspend acting in about 1591 because of their tendency toward controversial satire, and a number of Lyly's plays were printed at that time. As a theatrical figure, therefore, Lyly belonged really to the previous decade.

The Early Plays

Although Shakespeare's genius manifests itself in his early work, his indebtedness to contemporary dramatists and to classical writers is also more plainly evident than in his later writings. His first tragedy, *Titus Andronicus* (c. 1589–1592), is more laden with quotations and classical references than any other tragedy he wrote. Its genre owes much to the revenge play that had been made so popular by Thomas Kyd. Like Kyd, Shakespeare turns to Seneca but also reveals on stage a considerable amount of sensational violence in a manner that is distinctly not classical. For his first villain, Aaron the Moor, Shakespeare borrows some motifs from the morality play and its gleefully sinister tempter, the Vice. Shakespeare may also have had in mind the boastful antics of Marlowe's Vicelike Barabas, in *The Jew of Malta.* Certainly, Shakespeare reveals an extensive debt in his early works to Ovid and to the vogue of Ovidian narrative poetry in the early 1590s, as, for example, in his repeated allusions to the story of Philomela and Tereus (in *Titus Andronicus*) and in his Ovidian poems, *Venus and Adonis* and *The Rape of Lucrece* (1593, 1594).

Shakespeare was still questing for a suitable mode in tragedy and was discovering that the English drama of the 1590s offered no single, clear model. His only other early tragedy, *Romeo and Juliet* (c. 1594–1596), proved to be as different a tragedy from *Titus Andronicus* as could be imagined. Revenge is still prominent in *Romeo and Juliet* but is ultimately far less compelling a theme than the brevity of love and the sacrifice the lovers make of themselves to one another. Shakespeare's source is not the revenge drama of Seneca or Kyd, but a romantic love narrative derived from the fiction of Renaissance Italy. Elements of comedy so predominate in the play's first half that one senses a closer affinity to *A Midsummer Night's Dream* than to *The Spanish Tragedy.*

Shakespeare discovered his true bent more quickly in comedy than in tragedy. Again, however, he experimented with a wide range of models and genres. *The Comedy of Errors* (c. 1589–1594) brings together elements of two plots from the Latin drama of Plautus. The character types and situations are partly derivative, but Shakespeare still reveals an impressive skill in plot construction. *Love's Labor's Lost* (c. 1588–1597) is Shakespeare's most Lylyan early comedy, with its witty debates and its amicable, if brittle, war between the sexes. The play also features an array of humorous characters, including a clownish bumpkin, a country slut, a fantastic courtier, a pedant, a country curate, and the like, whose mannerisms and wordplay add to the rich feast of language in a play that

A contemporary illustration of Titus Andronicus, *the earliest of Shakespeare's tragedies. Shakespeare's early plays demonstrated that he was more than a slavish imitator of predecessors such as Kyd and Marlowe.*

THE GREAT POND AT ELVETHAM
arranged for the Second Day's Entertainment.

A. Her Majestie's presence seate and traine.   B. Nereus and his followers.   C. The pinnace of Neæra and her musicke.   D. The Ship-ile.
E. A boate with musicke, attending on the pinnace of Neæra.   F. The Fort-mount.   G. The Snaile-mount.   H. The Roome of Estate.
I. Her Majestie's Court.   K. Her Majestie's Wardrop.   L. The place whence Silvanus and his companie issued.

An entertainment presented by the Earl of Hertford to Queen Elizabeth during her visit to Elvetham in 1591 is seemingly referred to by Shakespeare in A Midsummer Night's Dream, *2.1.157–64. The scene shows an elaborate water pageant in honor of the Queen, who appears enthroned at the left of the picture.*

centers its attention on proper and improper styles. *The Two Gentlemen of Verona* (c. 1590–1594) and *The Taming of the Shrew* (c. 1590–1593) are derived from Italianate romantic fiction and comedy. In both, Shakespeare skillfully combines simultaneous plots that offer contrasting views on love and friendship. (*The Taming of the Shrew* makes effective use of a "frame" plot involving a group of characters who serve as audience for the rest of the play.) *A Midsummer Night's Dream* (c. 1595), with its four brilliantly interwoven actions involving court figures, lovers, fairies, and Athenian tradesmen, shows us Shakespeare already at the height of his powers in play construction, even though the comic emphasis on love's irrationality in this play is still in keeping with Shakespeare's early style. The early comedies do not ignore conflict and danger, as we see in the threatened execution of Egeon in

The Comedy of Errors and the failure of courtships in *Love's Labor's Lost*, but these plays do not as yet fully explore the social dilemmas of *The Merchant of Venice*, the narrowly averted catastrophe of *Much Ado About Nothing*, or the melancholy vein of *As You Like It* and *Twelfth Night*. On stage, early comedies such as *The Comedy of Errors* and *The Taming of the Shrew* are as hilariously funny as anything Shakespeare ever wrote.

Shakespeare's early history plays show a marked affinity with those of Marlowe, Peele, and Greene. Yet today Shakespeare is given more credit for pioneering in the genre of the English history play than he once was. If all the *Henry VI* plays (c. 1589–1592) are basically his, as scholars now often allow, he had more imitators in this genre than predecessors. He scored a huge early success with the heroic character of Lord Talbot in *1 Henry VI,* and by the time Richard Duke of Gloucester had emerged from the *Henry VI* plays to become King Richard III, Shakespeare's fame as a dramatist was assured. He had, of course, learned much from Marlowe's "mighty line" in *Tamburlaine* (1587–1588) and perhaps from Peele's *The Battle of Alcazar* (1588–1589). The anonymous *Famous Victories of Henry V* (1583–1588) must have preceded and influenced his work. Even so, Shakespeare had done much more than simply "beautify" himself with the "feathers" of earlier dramatists, as Greene (or Chettle) enviously charged. Even in his earliest work, Shakespeare already displayed an extraordinary ability to transcend the models from which he learned.

SHAKESPEARE IN THE THEATER, C. 1594–1601

By the year 1594, Shakespeare had already achieved a considerable reputation as a poet and dramatist. We should not be surprised that many of his contemporaries thought of his nondramatic writing as his most significant literary achievement. Throughout his lifetime, in fact, his contemporary fame rested, to a remarkable degree, on his nondramatic poems, *Venus and Adonis*, *The Rape of Lucrece*, and the *Sonnets* (which were circulated in manuscript prior to their unauthorized publication in 1609). One of the earliest tributes suggesting the importance of the poems is found in an anonymous commendatory verse prefixed to Henry Willobie's *Willobie His Avisa* (1594). It summarizes the plot and theme of *The Rape of Lucrece*:

> Though *Collatine* have dearly bought,
> To high renown, a lasting life,
> And found—that most in vain have sought—
> To have a fair and constant wife,
>   Yet Tarquin plucked his glittering grape,
>   And Shakespeare paints poor Lucrece' rape.

Richard Barnfield, in his *Poems in Divers Humors* (1598), praised the "honey-flowing vein" of Shakespeare's *Venus and Adonis* and *The Rape of Lucrece*.

Yet Shakespeare's plays were also highly regarded by his contemporaries, even if those plays were accorded a literary status below that given to the narrative and lyrical poems. Francis Meres insisted, in 1598, that Shakespeare deserved to be compared not only with Ovid for his verse but also with Plautus and Seneca for his comedies and tragedies:

As the soul of Euphorbus was thought to live in Pythagoras, so the sweet, witty soul of Ovid lives in mellifluous and honey-tongued Shakespeare: witness his *Venus and Adonis*, his *Lucrece*, his sugared sonnets among his private friends, etc.

As Plautus and Seneca are accounted the best for comedy and tragedy among the Latins, so Shakespeare among the English is the most excellent in both kinds for the stage: for comedy, witness his *Gentlemen of Verona*, his *Errors*, his *Love's*

Labor's Lost, his *Love's Labor's Won*, his *Midsummer Night's Dream*, and his *Merchant of Venice*; for tragedy, his *Richard the II*, *Richard the III*, *Henry the IV*, *King John*, *Titus Andronicus*, and his *Romeo and Juliet*.

Comedy and tragedy were, after all, literary forms sanctioned by classical precept. By calling some of Shakespeare's English history plays "tragedies," Meres endowed them with the respectability of an ancient literary tradition, recognizing, too, that many of Shakespeare's historical plays culminate in the death of an English king.

John Weever, too, in his epigram *Ad Gulielmum Shakespeare* in *Epigrams in the Oldest Cut and Newest Fashion* (1599), mentioned not only the ever-popular narrative poems but also *Romeo and Juliet* and a history play about one of the Richards:

> Honey-tongued Shakespeare! When I saw thine issue,
> I swore Apollo got them and none other:
> Their rosy-tainted features clothed in tissue,
> Some heaven-born goddess said to be their mother;
> Rose-cheeked Adonis, with his amber tresses,
> Fair fire-hot Venus, charming him to love her;
> Chaste Lucretia virgin-like her dresses,
> Proud lust-stung Tarquin seeking still to prove her;
> *Romeo, Richard*—more whose names I know not.
> Their sugared tongues and power-attractive beauty
> Say they are saints, although that saints they show not,
> For thousands vows to them subjective duty;
> They burn in love thy children. Shakespeare het them.
> Go, woo thy muse more nymphish brood beget them.

Even Gabriel Harvey, an esteemed classical scholar and friend of Edmund Spenser, considered Shakespeare's play *Hamlet* to be worthy of no less praise than the best of the Ovidian poems. Harvey's comments are to be found in a marginal note to a copy of Speght's *Chaucer*, written down some time between 1598 and 1601:

The younger sort takes much delight in Shakespeare's *Venus and Adonis*, but his *Lucrece* and his tragedy of *Hamlet, Prince of Denmark* have it in them to please the wiser sort.

Shakespeare's growing fame was even such that his dramatic characters began to enter into the intellectual life of the time. The name of Falstaff became a byword almost as soon as he made his appearance on the stage. The references were not always friendly. A play written to be performed by the rival Admiral's company in answer to *1 Henry IV*, called *Sir John Oldcastle* (1599), took Falstaff to task for being a "pampered glutton" and an "aged counsellor to youthful sin." Evidently, the authors of this attack were offended by the fact that Falstaff had been named "Oldcastle" in an early version of *1 Henry IV*, thereby dishonoring the name of one whom many Puritans regarded as a martyr to their cause (see the Introduction to *1 Henry IV*). Generally, however, the references

Falstaff and Mistress Quickly are shown here in a composite theatrical illustration of about 1662. The engraving, used as the frontispiece to Francis Kirkman's The Wits, or Sport upon Sport, *also shows other theatrical types. Visible are candelabras and footlights for stage lighting and a curtained area used perhaps for "discoveries." Spectators are visible in the gallery above, as they are also in the De Witt drawing of the Swan Theatre on p. xlvi and in Alabaster's* Roxana *on p. xlv.*

during this period to Falstaff and his cronies were fond. In a letter to a friend in London, for example, Sir Charles Percy fretted jocosely that his prolonged stay in the country among his rustic neighbors might cause him to "be taken for Justice Silence or Justice Shallow" (1600). In another letter, from the Countess of Southampton to her husband (written seemingly in 1599), Falstaff's name had become so familiar that it was used apparently as a privately understood substitute for the name of some real person in an item of court gossip:

All the news I can send you, that I think will make you merry, is that I read in a letter from London that Sir John Falstaff is by his Mistress Dame Pintpot made father of a godly miller's thumb, a boy that's all head and very little body; but this is a secret.

Shakespeare's immense popularity as a dramatist was bound to invite some resentment. One irreverent reaction is found in the so-called *Parnassus* trilogy (1598–1603). The three plays in this series consist of *The Pilgrimage to Parnassus* and *The Return from Parnassus,* in two parts, all of which were acted by the students of St. John's College, Cambridge.

These *Parnassus* plays take a mordantly satirical view of English life around 1600, from the point of view of university graduates attempting to find gainful employment. The graduates discover, to their vocal dismay, that they must seek the patronage of fashion-mongering courtiers, complacent justices of the peace, professional acting com-

panies who offer them pitifully small wages, and the like. One especially foolish patron, to whom the witty Ingenioso applies for a position, is a poetaster named Gullio. This courtly fop aspires to be a fashionable poet himself, and agrees to hire Ingenioso if the latter will help him with his verse writing. In fact, however, as Ingenioso scornfully observes in a series of asides, Gullio's verses are "nothing but pure Shakespeare and shreds of poetry that he hath gathered at the theaters." Most of all, Gullio loves to plagiarize from *Venus and Adonis* and *Romeo and Juliet.* With unparalleled presumption, he actually requests Ingenioso to compose poems "in two or three divers veins, in Chaucer's, Gower's and Spenser's and Mr. Shakespeare's," which Gullio will then pass off as his own inspiration. When Ingenioso does so extempore, producing, among other things, a fine parody of *Venus and Adonis,* Gullio is as delighted as a child. Although he admires Spenser, Chaucer, and Gower, Gullio confesses that Shakespeare is his favorite; he longs to hang Shakespeare's portrait "in my study at the court" and vows he will sleep with *Venus and Adonis* under his pillow (*The Return from Parnassus,* Part I, 1009–1217). Later on (lines 1875–1880), some university graduates trying out as actors in Shakespeare's company are requested to recite a few famous lines from the beginning of *Richard III*—lines that, in the satirical context of this play, sound both stereotyped and bombastic. Shakespeare's fame made him an easy target for university "wits" who regarded the theater of London

Henry Fuseli's nineteenth-century interpretation of Falstaff shows him in the tavern in Eastcheap with Doll Tearsheet on his lap while Prince Hal and Poins, disguised as tapsters, enter from behind. Falstaff is perhaps saying, "Peace, good Doll, do not speak like a death's-head" (2 Henry IV, 2.4.232–3).

as lowbrow. Still, the portrait throughout is more satirical of those who plagiarize and idolize Shakespeare than of the dramatist's own work. In their backhanded tribute, the *Parnassus* authors make plain that Shakespeare was a household name even at the universities.

Shakespeare's Career and Private Life

During the years from 1594 to 1601, Shakespeare seems to have prospered as an actor and writer for the Lord Chamberlain's men. Whether he had previously belonged to Lord Strange's company or to the Earl of Pembroke's company, or possibly to some other group, is uncertain, but we know that he took part in 1594 in the general reorganization of the companies, out of which emerged the Lord Chamberlain's company. In 1595, his name appeared, for the first time, in the accounts of the Treasurer of the Royal Chamber as a member of the Chamberlain's company of players, which had presented two comedies before Queen Elizabeth at Greenwich in the Christmas season of 1594. This company usually performed at the Theatre, northeast of London, from 1594

until 1599, when they moved to the Globe playhouse south of the Thames. They seem to have been the victors in the intense economic rivalry between themselves and the Lord Admiral's company at the Rose playhouse under Philip Henslowe's management. Fortunately for all the adult companies, the boys' private theatrical companies were shut down during most of the 1590s. Shakespeare's company enjoyed a phenomenal success, and in short time it became the most successful theatrical organization in England.

The nucleus of the Chamberlain's company in 1594 was the family of Burbage. James Burbage, the father, was owner of the Theatre, Cuthbert Burbage was a manager, and Richard Burbage became the principal actor of the troupe. Together the Burbages owned five "shares" in the company, entitling them to half the profits. Shakespeare and four other principal actors—John Heminges, Thomas Pope, Augustine Phillips, and Will Kempe—owned one share each. Not only was Shakespeare a full sharing actor, but also he was the principal playwright of the company. He was named as a chief actor in the 1616 edition of Ben Jonson's *Every Man in His Humor,* performed by the Chamberlain's company in 1598. Later tradition reports, with questionable reliability, that Shakespeare specialized in "kingly parts" or in the roles of older men, such as Adam in *As You Like It* and the Ghost in *Hamlet.* Shakespeare was more celebrated as a playwright than as an actor, and his acting responsibilities may well have diminished as his writing reputation grew. The last occasion on which he is known to have acted was in Jonson's *Sejanus* in 1603.

His prosperity appears in the first record of his residence in London. The tax returns, or Subsidy Rolls, of a parliamentary subsidy granted to Queen Elizabeth for the year 1596 show that Shakespeare was a resident in the parish of St. Helen's, Bishopsgate, near the Theatre, and was assessed at the respectable sum of five pounds. By the next year, Shakespeare had evidently moved to Southwark, near the Bear Garden, for the returns from

First among the actors in Shakespeare's company was Richard Burbage (1567–1619). He played Hamlet, Othello, King Lear, and presumably other major roles including Macbeth, Antony, Coriolanus, and Prospero.

Bishopsgate show his taxes delinquent. He was later located and the taxes paid.

In 1596, Shakespeare suffered a serious personal loss: the death of his only son Hamnet, at the age of eleven. Hamnet was buried at Stratford in August.

Shakespeare acquired property in Stratford during these years, as well as in London. In 1597 he purchased New Place, a house of importance and one of the two largest in the town. Shakespeare's family entered the house as residents shortly after the purchase and continued to live there until long after Shakespeare's death. The last of his family, his granddaughter, Lady Bernard, died in 1670, and New Place was sold.

Shakespeare was also interested in the purchase of land at Shottery in 1598. He was listed among the chief holders of corn and malt in Stratford that same year and sold a load of stone to the Stratford corporation in 1599.

No less suggestive of Shakespeare's rapid rise in the world is his acquisition of the right to bear arms, or, in other words, his establishment in the rank and title of gentleman. The Herald's College in London preserves two drafts of a grant of arms to Shakespeare's father, devised by one William Dethick and dated October 20, 1596. Although we may certainly believe that the application was put forward by William Shakespeare, John Shakespeare was still living, and the grant was drawn up in the father's name. The device for Shakespeare's coat of arms makes a somewhat easy use of the meaning of his name:

Gold on a bend sables, a spear of the first steeled argent. And for his crest of cognizance a falcon, his wings displayed argent, standing on a wreath of his colors, supporting a spear, gold

steeled as aforesaid, set upon a helmet with mantles and tassels, as hath been accustomed and doth more plainly appear depicted on this margent.

According to one of the documents in the grant, John Shakespeare, at the height of his prosperity as a Stratford burgher, had applied twenty years before to the Herald's College for authority to bear arms. The family may not have been able to meet the expense of seeing the application through, however, until William Shakespeare had made his fortune. The grant of heraldic honors to John Shakespeare was confirmed in 1599.

A lawsuit during this period gives us a rather baffling glimpse into Shakespeare's life in the theater. From a writ discovered by Leslie Hotson (*Shakespeare Versus Shallow*, 1931) in the records of the Court of the Queen's Bench, Michaelmas term 1596, we learn that a person named William Wayte sought "for fear of death" to have William Shakespeare, Francis Langley, and two unknown women bound over to keep the peace. Earlier in the same term, moreover, Francis Langley had sworn out a similar writ against this same William Wayte and his stepfather William Gardiner, a justice of the peace in Surrey. Langley was owner of the Swan playhouse on the bankside, near the later-built Globe. His quarrel with Gardiner and Wayte appears to have jeopardized all the acting companies that performed plays south of the Thames, for William Gardiner's jurisdiction included the Bankside theater district. Gardiner and Wayte vengefully tried to drive the theaters out of the area. Possibly Shakespeare's company acted occasionally at the Swan in 1596. Hotson speculates that Shakespeare retaliated by immortalizing

This recreation of what New Place purportedly looked like during Shakespeare's ownership suggests that it must have indeed been an imposing structure. It was warmed by ten fireplaces and had surrounding grounds that included two gardens and two barns.

Gardiner and Wayte as Shallow and Slender in *The Merry Wives of Windsor*. The date of 1596 is too early for that play, and we do not know that Shakespeare drew contemporary portraits in his drama, but we can wonder if lawsuits of this sort gave him no very high opinion of the law's delay and the insolence of office.

During this period Shakespeare's plays began to appear occasionally in print. His name was becoming such a drawing card that it appeared on the title pages of the Second and Third Quartos of *Richard II* (1598), the Second Quarto of *Richard III* (1598), *Love's Labor's Lost* (1598), and the Second Quarto of *1 Henry IV* (1599).

In 1599, the printer William Jaggard sought to capitalize unscrupulously on Shakespeare's growing reputation by bringing out a slender volume of twenty or twenty-one poems called *The Passionate Pilgrim*, attributed to Shakespeare. In fact, only five of the poems were assuredly his, and none of them was newly composed for the occasion. Three came from *Love's Labor's Lost* (published in 1598) and two from Shakespeare's as yet unpublished sonnet sequence.

Contemporary Drama

Shakespeare was without doubt the leading dramatist of the period from 1594 to 1601, not only in our view, but also in that of his contemporaries. The earlier group of dramatists from whom he had learned so much—Lyly, Greene, Marlowe, Peele, Kyd, Nashe—were either dead or no longer writing plays. The group of dramatists who were to rival him in the 1600s and eventually surpass him in contemporary popularity had not yet become well known.

Ben Jonson's early career is obscure. He may have written an early version of his *A Tale of a Tub* in 1596 and *The Case Is Altered* in 1597, though both were later revised. Unquestionably, his first major play was *Every Man in His Humor* (1598), in which Shakespeare acted. This comedy did much to establish the new vogue of comedy of humors, a realistic and satirical kind of drama featuring "humors" characters whose personalities are dominated by some exaggerated trait. We are invited to laugh at the country simpleton, the jealous husband, the overly careful father, the cowardly braggart soldier, the poetaster, and the like. Shakespeare responded to the vogue of humors comedy in his *Henry IV* plays and *The Merry Wives*. Jonson followed his great success with *Every Man Out of His Humor* (1599), an even more biting vision of human folly. George Chapman also deserves important credit for the establishment of humors comedy, with his *The Blind Beggar of Alexandria* (1596) and *An Humorous Day's Mirth* (1597).

Despite the emergence of humors comedy, however, with its important anticipations of Jacobean and even Restoration comedy of manners, the prevailing comedy to be seen on the London stage between 1595 and 1601 was romantic comedy. William Haughton wrote *Englishmen for My Money* in 1598. Thomas Dekker's *Old Fortunatus*, the dramatization of a German folktale, appeared in 1599. Dekker's *The Shoemaker's Holiday* (1599), despite its seemingly realistic touches of life among the apprentices of London, is a thoroughly romanticized saga of rags to riches. A young aristocrat disguises himself as a shoemaker to woo a mayor's daughter; love conquers social rank, and the King himself sentimentally blesses the union. Thomas Heywood wrote heroical romances and comedies, perhaps including *Godfrey of Boulogne* (1594), although most of his early works have disappeared. The boys' private theaters were closed during most of the 1590s, until 1598–1599, and thus the child actors could not perform the satirical comedies at which they were so adept.

Patriotic history drama also continued to flourish on the public stage during those years when Shakespeare wrote his best history plays. Heywood wrote the two parts of *Edward IV* between 1592 and 1599. The anonymous *Edward III* appeared in 1595 or earlier, enough in the vein of Shakespeare's histories that it is sometimes attributed (albeit on uncertain and impressionistic grounds) to him. *Sir Thomas More*, by Munday, Dekker, Chettle, and perhaps Heywood, was written sometime in the later 1590s and very probably revised by Shakespeare himself. Chettle and Munday wrote a trilogy of plays about *Robert, Earl of Huntingdon*, or Robin Hood (1598–1599), on themes that remind us of Shakespeare's *As You Like It*. These plays were performed by the Admiral's men, who also produced the two parts of *Sir John Oldcastle* (1599–1600) by Drayton, Hathway, Munday, and others, in rivalry with Shakespeare's *Henry IV* plays.

Shakespeare's Work

Shakespeare thus wrote his greatest history plays for an audience that knew the genre well. The history play had first become popular just at the start of Shakespeare's career, during the patriotic aftermath of the defeat of the Spanish Armada (1588). Shakespeare himself did much to establish the genre. He wrote first his four-play series dealing with the Lancastrian wars of the fifteenth century, and then went backwards in historical time to King John's reign and to the famous reigns of Henry IV and Henry V.

His romantic comedies were also written for audiences that knew what to expect from the genre. From the comedies of Greene, Peele, Munday, and the rest, as well as Shakespeare himself, Elizabethan audiences were thoroughly familiar with such conventions as fairy charms, improbable adventures in forests, heroines disguised as young men, shipwrecks, love overcoming differences in social rank, and the like. Yet the conventions also demanded more than mere horseplay or foolish antics. Plays of this sort customarily affirmed "wholesome" moral values and appealed to generosity and decency. They were written, like the history plays, for a socially diversified, though generally intelligent and well-to-do, audience.

Several critical terms have been used to suggest the special quality of Shakespeare's comedies during this period of the later 1590s. "Romantic comedy" implies first of all a story in which the main action is about love, but it can also imply elements of the improbable and the miraculous. (The difference between the "romantic comedies" of the later 1590s and the "romances" of Shakespeare's last years, 1606–1613, is that, in part at least, romantic comedy seeks to "make wonder familiar," whereas the romances seek to make the familiar wonderful.) "Philosophical comedy" emphasizes the moral and sometimes Christian idealism underlying many of these comedies of the 1590s: the quest for deep and honest understanding between men and women in *Much Ado About Nothing*, the awareness of an eternal and spiritual dimension to love in *The Merchant of Venice*, and the theme of love as a mysterious force able to regenerate a corrupted social world from which it has been banished in *As You Like It*. "Love-game comedy" pays particular attention to the witty battle of the sexes that we find in several of these plays. "Festive comedy" urges the celebratory nature of comedy, especially in *Twelfth Night* and the *Henry IV* plays, in which Saturnalian revelry must contend against grim and disapproving forces of sobriety. "Comedy of forgiveness," although applicable to only a limited number of plays of this period (especially *Much Ado*), stresses the unexpected second chance that the world of comedy extends to even the most undeserving of heroes; Claudio is forgiven his ill treatment of Hero, although the play's villain, Don John, is not.

SHAKESPEARE IN THE THEATER, C.1601–1608

When the Globe, the most famous of the London public playhouses, was built in 1599, one-half interest in the property was assigned to the Burbage family, especially to the brothers Cuthbert and Richard Burbage. The other half was divided among five actor-sharers: Shakespeare, Will Kempe, Thomas Pope, Augustine Phillips, and John Heminges. Kempe left the company, however, in 1599 and subsequently became a member of the Earl of Worcester's men. His place as leading comic actor was taken by Robert Armin, an experienced man of the theater and occasional author, whose comic specialty was the role of the wise fool. We can observe in Shakespeare's plays the effects of Kempe's departure and of Armin's arrival. Kempe had apparently specialized in clownish and rustic parts, such as those of Dogberry in *Much Ado,* Lancelot Gobbo in *The Merchant of Venice,* and Bottom in *A Midsummer Night's Dream.* (We know that he played Dogberry because his name appears in the early Quarto, derived from the play manuscript; similar evidence links his name to the role of Peter in *Romeo and Juliet.*) For Armin, on the other hand, Shakespeare evidently created such roles as Touchstone in *As You Like It,* Feste in *Twelfth Night,* Lavatch in *All's Well That Ends Well,* and the Fool in *King Lear.*

Other shifts in personnel can sometimes be traced in Shakespeare's plays, especially changes in the number and ability of the boy actors (whose voices would suddenly start to crack at puberty). Shakespeare makes an amusing point about the relative size of two boy actors, for example, in *A Midsummer Night's Dream* and in *As You Like It*; this option may have been available to him only at certain times. On the other hand, not all changes in the company roster can be related meaningfully to Shake-

Among the members of Shakespeare's acting company were John Lowin, William Sly, and Nathaniel Field.

Will Kempe (above), for whom Shakespeare created several clownish roles, was a member of the Lord Chamberlain's men and a noted Elizabethan comic. Kempe left the company in 1599 and was replaced by Robert Armin (right), an accomplished actor who specialized in fool's roles.

speare's dramatic development. Augustine Phillips, who died in 1605, was a full actor-sharer of long standing in the company, but his "type" of role was probably not sharply differentiated from that of several of his associates. Shakespeare's plays, after all, involve many important supporting roles, and versatility in the undertaking of such parts must have been more common than specialization. (Phillips is remembered also for his last will and testament: he left a bequest of "a thirty shillings piece in gold" to "my fellow, William Shakespeare," and similar bequests to other members of the troupe.)

With the reopening of the boys' acting companies in 1598–1599, a serious economic rivalry sprang up between them and the adult companies. The Children of the Chapel Royal occupied the theater in Blackfriars, and the Children of Paul's probably acted in their own singing school in St. Paul's churchyard. Their plays exploited a new vogue for satire. The satiric laughter was often directed at the city of London and its bourgeois inhabitants: socially ambitious tradesmen's wives, Puritan zealots, and the like. Other favorite targets included parvenu knights at court, would-be poets, and hysterical governmental officials. The price of admission at the private theaters was considerably higher than at the Globe or Rose, so the clientele tended to be more fashionable. Sophisticated authors like Ben Jonson, George Chapman, and John Marston tended to find writing for the boy actors more rewarding literarily than writing for the adult players.

One manifestation of the rivalry between public and private theaters was the so-called War of the Theaters, or Poetomachia. In part, this was a personal quarrel between

Jonson on one side and Marston and Thomas Dekker on the other. Underlying this quarrel, however, was a serious hostility between a public theater and one that catered more to the elite. Dekker, with Marston's encouragement, attacked Jonson as a literary dictator and snob—one who subverted public decency. Jonson replied with a fervent defense of the artist's right to criticize everything that the artist sees wrong. The major plays in the exchange (1600–1601) were Jonson's *Cynthia's Revels,* Dekker and Marston's *Satiromastix,* and Jonson's *The Poetaster.*

Shakespeare allows Hamlet to comment on the theatrical rivalry (2.2.330–62), with seeming regret for the fact that the boys have been overly successful and that many adult troupes have been obliged to tour the provinces. Most of all, though, Hamlet's remarks deplore the needless bitterness on both sides. The tone of kindly remonstrance makes it seem unlikely that Shakespeare took an active part in the fracas. To be sure, in the Cambridge play *2 Return from Parnassus* (1601–1603), the character called Will Kempe does assert that his fellow actor, Shakespeare, had put down the famous Ben Jonson:

Why, here's our fellow Shakespeare puts them all down, ay, and Ben Jonson, too. O, that Ben Jonson is a pestilent fellow! And he brought up Horace giving the poets a pill, but our fellow Shakespeare hath given him a purge that made him bewray his credit (lines 1809–1813).

Nevertheless, no play exists in which Shakespeare did put down Jonson, and the reference may be instead to *Satiromastix,* which was performed by Shakespeare's company. Or perhaps "put down" means simply "surpassed." In fact, Shakespeare and Jonson remained on cordial terms, despite their differences in artistic outlook.

Upon the death of Queen Elizabeth in 1603 and the accession to the throne of King James I, Shakespeare's company added an important new success to their already great prosperity. According to a document of instruction from King James to his Keeper of the Privy Seal, dated May 19, 1603, and endorsed as "The Players' Privilege," the acting company that had formerly been the Lord Chamberlain's men now became the King's company. The document names Shakespeare, Richard Burbage, Augustine Phillips, John Heminges, Henry Condell, Will Sly, Robert Armin, Richard Cowley, and Lawrence Fletcher—the last, an actor who had played before the King and the Scottish court in 1599 and 1601. These players are accorded the usual privileges of exercising their art anywhere within the kingdom and are henceforth to be known as the King's company. The principal members of the troupe also were appointed to the honorary rank of Grooms of the Royal Chamber. We therefore find them duly recorded in the Accounts of the Master of the Wardrobe on March 15, 1604, as recipients of the customary grants of red cloth, so that they, dressed in the royal livery, might take part in the approaching coronation procession of King James. The same men are mentioned in these grants as in the Players' Privilege. Shakespeare's name stands second in the former document and first in the latter. In a somewhat similar manner, the King's players, as Grooms of the Royal Chamber, were called in attendance on the Spanish ambassador at Somerset House in August 1604.

The Revels Accounts of performances at court during the winter season of 1604–1605 contain an unusually full entry, listing several of Shakespeare's plays. The list includes *Othello, The Merry Wives of Windsor, Measure for Measure,* "The play of Errors," *Love's Labor's Lost, Henry V,* and *The Merchant of Venice.* The last play was "again commanded by the King's majesty," and so was performed a second time. This list also sporadically notes the names of "the poets which made the plays," ascribing three of these works to "Shaxberd." (Probably the final *d* is an error for *e,* since the two characters are easily confused in Elizabethan handwriting; the word represents "Shaxbere" or "Shaxpere.") The entire entry was once called into question as a possible forgery but is now generally regarded as authentic.

A number of records during this period show us glimpses of Shakespeare as a man of property. On May 1, 1602, John and William Combe conveyed to Shakespeare one hundred and seven acres of arable land, plus twenty acres of pasture in the parish of Old Stratford, for the sizable payment of three hundred and twenty pounds. The deed was delivered to Shakespeare's brother Gilbert and not to the poet, who was probably at that time occupied in London. On September 28 of the same year, Shake-speare acquired the title to "one cottage and one garden by estimation a quarter of an acre," located opposite his home (New Place) in Stratford.

Shakespeare made still other real-estate investments in his home town. In 1605 he purchased an interest in the tithes of Stratford and adjacent villages from one Ralph Hubaud for the considerable sum of four hundred and forty pounds. The purchasing of tithes was a common financial transaction in Shakespeare's time, though unknown today. Tithes were originally intended for the support of the Church but had, in many cases, become privately owned and hence negotiable. The owners of tithes paid a fixed rental sum for the right to collect as many of these taxes as they could, up to the total amount due under the law. Shakespeare seems, on this occasion in 1605, to have bought from Ralph Hubaud a one-half interest, or "moiety," in certain tithes of Stratford and vicinity. Later, probably in 1609, Shakespeare was one of those who brought a bill of complaint before the Lord Chancellor, requesting that certain other titheholders be required to come into the High Court of Chancery and make answer to the complaints alleged, namely, that they had not paid their proportional part of an annual rental of twenty-seven pounds, thirteen shillings, and four pence on the whole property in the tithes to one Henry Barker. This Barker had the theoretical right to foreclose on the entire property if any one of the forty-two titheholders failed to contribute his share of the annual fee. The suit was, in effect, a friendly one, designed to ensure that all those who were supposed to contribute did so on an equitable and businesslike basis.

We learn from the Stratford Registers of baptism, marriage, and burial of the changes in Shakespeare's family during this period. His father died in 1601, his brother Edmund in 1607, and his mother in 1608. On June 5, 1607, his daughter Susanna was married to Dr. John Hall in Holy Trinity Church, Stratford. Their first child, and Shakespeare's first grandchild, Elizabeth, was christened in the same church on February 21, 1608.

Shakespeare's Reputation, 1601–1608

Allusions to Shakespeare are frequent during this period of his life. One amusing reference is not literary but professes to tell about Shakespeare's prowess as a lover and rival of his good friend and theatrical colleague, Richard Burbage. Perhaps the joke was just a good bawdy story and should not be taken too seriously, but it is nonetheless one of the few anecdotes that date from Shakespeare's lifetime. Our informant is John Manningham, a young law student, who notes in his commonplace book in 1602 the following:

13 March 1601 [1602] . . . Upon a time, when Burbage played Richard III there was a citizen grew so far in liking with him

that, before she went to the play, she appointed him to come that night unto her by the name of Richard the Third. Shakespeare, overhearing their conclusion, went before, and was entertained and at his game ere Burbage came. Then message being brought that Richard the Third was at the door, Shakespeare caused return to be made that William the Conqueror was before Richard the Third. Shakespeare's name William.

Other allusions of the time are more literary. Shakespeare's greatness is, by this time, taken for granted. Anthony Scoloker, for example, in his epistle prefatory to *Diaphantus, or the Passions of Love* (1604), attempts to describe an excellent literary work in this way:

It should be like the never-too-well read Arcadia . . . or to come home to the vulgar's element, like friendly Shakespeare's tragedies, where the comedian rides, when the tragedian stands on tip-toe. Faith, it should please all, like Prince Hamlet.

The antiquarian William Camden includes Shakespeare's name among his list of England's greatest writers in his *Remains of a Greater Work Concerning Britain* (1605):

These may suffice for some poetical descriptions of our ancient poets. If I would come to our time, what a world could I present to you out of Sir Philip Sidney, Edmund Spenser, Samuel Daniel, Hugh Holland, Ben Jonson, Thomas Campion, Michael Drayton, George Chapman, John Marston, William Shakespeare, and other most pregnant wits of these our times, whom succeeding ages may justly admire.

An attempt to use one of Shakespeare's plays for political purposes had some potentially serious repercussions. Two days before the abortive rebellion of the Earl of Essex on February 7, 1601, Shakespeare's company was commissioned to perform a well-known play in its repertory about King Richard II. This play must almost surely have been Shakespeare's. Evidently, the purpose of this extraordinary performance was to awaken public sympathy for Essex by suggesting that Queen Elizabeth was another Richard II, surrounded by corrupt favorites and deaf to the pleas of her subjects. Essex's avowed intention was to remove from positions of influence those men whom he considered his political enemies. Fortunately, Shakespeare's company was later exonerated of any blame in the affair (see the Introduction to *Richard II*).

Perhaps no other allusion to Shakespeare during this period can suggest so well as the following quotation the extent to which Shakespeare's plays had become familiar to English citizens everywhere. The quotation is taken from the notes of a certain Captain Keeling, commander of the East India Company's ship *Dragon*, off Sierra Leone, in the years 1607 and 1608:

1607, Sept. 5. I sent the interpreter, according to his desire, aboard the *Hector*, where he broke fast, and after came aboard me, where we gave the tragedy of *Hamlet*.

30. Captain Hawkins dined with me, where my companions acted *King Richard the Second*.

[March 31.] I invited Captain Hawkins to a fish dinner and had *Hamlet* acted aboard me, which I permit to keep my people from idleness and unlawful games or sleep.

Other Drama of the Period

Even without Shakespeare, the early Jacobean drama in England would rank as one of the most creative periods in the history of all theater. (The word *Jacobean* is derived from *Jacobus,* the Latin form of the name of King James I.) Shakespeare's earlier contemporaries—Lyly, Greene, Marlowe, Peele, Kyd—were dead or silent, but another generation of playwrights was at hand. George Chapman, John Marston, and Ben Jonson all began writing plays shortly before 1600. So did Thomas Dekker and Thomas Heywood, whose dramatic output, often in collaboration, would prove to be considerable. Francis Beaumont, John Fletcher, Cyril Tourneur, and Thomas Middleton emerged into prominence in about 1606 or 1607. John Webster collaborated with Dekker and others in such plays as *Westward Ho* and *Sir Thomas Wyatt* around 1604, although he did not write his great tragedies until 1609–1614. Lesser talents, such as Henry Chettle, Anthony Munday, Henry Porter, John Day, and William Haughton, continued to pour forth an abundant supply of workmanlike plays. As Shakespeare's career developed, therefore, he enjoyed the fellowship and, no doubt, the rivalry of a remarkably gifted and diverse group of practicing dramatists.

Early Jacobean drama is, on the whole, characteristically different from the late Elizabethan drama that had preceded it. Other dramatists besides Shakespeare mirror his shift of focus from romantic comedies and patriotic histories to "problem" plays and tragedies. The boys' companies, reopening in 1598–1599 after virtually a decade of silence, did much to set the new tone. They avoided almost entirely the English history play, with its muscularly heroic style, so unsuited for the acting capabilities of boys. Besides, sophisticated audiences were sated with jingoistic fare, and even in the public theaters the genre had pretty well run its course. The fashion of the moment turned instead to revenge tragedy and satiric comedy.

The Jacobean revenge play owed much of its original inspiration to Thomas Kyd's *The Spanish Tragedy* (c. 1587), with its influential conventions: the intervention of supernatural forces, the feigned madness of the avenger, his difficulty in ascertaining the true facts of the murder, his morbid awareness of the conflict between human injustice and divine justice, his devising of a play within the play, and his invention of ingenious methods of slaughter in the play's gory ending. Kyd may also have written an early version of *Hamlet* featuring similar motifs. Shakespeare confronted cosmic issues of justice and human depravity in his revenge tragedy, *Hamlet* (c. 1599–1601), as indeed Kyd had done, but most followers of Kyd preferred to revel in the sensationalism of the genre. Some private-theater dramatists, such as Marston, subjected the conventions of the genre to caricature. Marston's revenge plays, written chiefly for Paul's boys and (after 1604) for the Children of the Queen's Revels, include *Antonio's Revenge* (1599–1601) and *The Malcontent* (1600–1604). These dramas are marked by flamboyantly overstated cynicism and are, in many ways, as close to satire as they are to tragedy. Marston had, in fact, made his first reputation as a nondramatic satirist, with *The Metamorphosis of Pygmalion's Image* and *The Scourge of Villainy* in 1598. His plays represent a continuation in dramatic form of the techniques of the Roman satirist. The typical Marstonian avenger, such as Malevole in *The Malcontent,* is an exaggeratedly unattractive authorial spokesman, pouring forth venomous hatred upon the loathsome and degenerate court in which he finds himself.

Similar in their exaggerated pursuit of the grotesque and the morbid are Cyril Tourneur's *The Atheist's Tragedy* (1607–1611) and a play formerly attributed to Tourneur but probably by Thomas Middleton, *The Revenger's Tragedy* (1606–1607). These plays are brilliant in the plotting of impossible situations and in the invention of cunning Italianate forms of torture and murder. Any sympathetic identification with the characters of these plays is sacrificed in the interests of technical virtuosity. As a result, the plays are more ironic than cathartic in their effect; we are overwhelmed by life's dark absurdities rather than ennobled by a vision of humanity's tragic grandeur. *The Tragedy of Hoffman, or A Revenge for a Father* by Henry Chettle (Admiral's men, 1602) is similarly grotesque and lacking in sympathy for its revenger hero. To be sure, George Chapman's *Bussy D'Ambois* (1600–1604) and its sequel, *The Revenge of Bussy D'Ambois* (1607–1612), are thoughtful plays about human aspiration, in the vein of Marlowe's *Tamburlaine,* but even these plays employ a good deal of Senecan bloody melodrama.

The revenge play enjoyed a great popularity on the public stage and (in a caricatured form) on the private stage. The public theater did, however, cater also to its Puritan-leaning audiences with more pious and moral tragedy. *Arden of Feversham* (c. 1591) is a good early example of what has come to be called domestic or homiletic tragedy. In the studiously plain style of a broadside ballad, it sets forth the facts of an actual murder that had occurred in 1551 and had been reported in Holinshed's *Chronicles.* The play interprets those events earnestly and providentially. The most famous play in the genre of domestic tragedy is Thomas Heywood's *A Woman Killed with Kindness* (1603). It tells, not of a murder, but of an adultery, for which the goodhearted but offending wife must be perpetually banished by her grieving husband. The play succeeds in elevating the private sorrows of its ordinary characters to tragic stature. The moral stances appear to be unambiguous: adultery is a heinous offense but can be transcended by Christian forgiveness; dueling is evil. Still, a mix of sympathies is perhaps reflective of shifting public attitudes toward the role of women in marriage. Other plays in the vein of domestic tragedy include *A Yorkshire Tragedy* (1605–1608), *The Miseries of Enforced Marriage* (1605–1606), and *Two Lamentable Tragedies* (c. 1594–1598).

In comedy, the greatest writer of the period besides Shakespeare was Ben Jonson. His predilection was toward the private theater, though he continued to write occasionally for the public stage as well. To an ever-increasing extent, he fixed his satirical gaze on those values and institutions which Thomas Heywood cherished: the city of London, its bourgeois citizens, its traditional approach to morality, and its religious zeal. *Every Man Out of His Humor* (1599), written for the Chamberlain's men, features a foolish uxorious citizen, his socially aspiring wife, and her fashionmongering lover—humors types that were to appear again and again in the genre of satirical comedy known as "city comedy." (See Brian Gibbons, *Jacobean City Comedy,* 1968.) *Volpone* (1605–1606), though technically not a London city comedy, since it purportedly takes place in Venice, castigates greed among lawyers, businessmen, and other professional types. *The Alchemist* (1610) ridicules the affectations of petty shopkeepers, lawyers' clerks, Puritan divines, and others. *Bartholomew Fair* (1614) and *The Alchemist* give us Jonson's most memorable indictment of the Puritans.

Numerous other writers contributed to humors comedy and city comedy. George Chapman probably deserves more credit than he usually receives for having helped determine the shape of humors comedy in his *The Blind Beggar of Alexandria* (1596), *An Humorous Day's Mirth* (1597), *All Fools* (1599–1604), *May-Day* (1601–1609), *The Gentleman Usher* (1602–1604), and others. Francis Beaumont, assisted perhaps by John Fletcher, ridicules London grocers and apprentices for their naive tastes in romantic chivalry in *The Knight of the Burning Pestle* (1607–1610). Some satire in this vein, to be sure, is reasonably good-humored. *Eastward Ho* (1605), by Chapman, Jonson, and Marston, is genially sympathetic toward the lifestyle of the small shopkeeper, even though the play contains a good deal of satire directed at social climbing and sharp business practices. Thomas Dekker's collaboration with Thomas Middleton on *The Honest Whore* (Part I, 1604) gives us an amused and yet warm portrayal of a linen draper who succeeds in business by insisting that the customer is always right. Dekker often shows a wry but generous appreciation of bourgeois ethics, as in *The Shoemaker's Holiday* (1599). Yet even he turns against the Puritans in *If This Be Not a Good Play, the Devil Is in It* (1611–1612).

Marston shows his talent for city comedy in *The Dutch Courtesan* (1603–1605). Perhaps the most ingratiating and truly funny of the writers of city comedy, however, is Middleton. His *A Trick to Catch the Old One* (1604–1607) illustrates the tendency of Jacobean comedy to move away both from Shakespeare's romantic vein and Jonson's morally satirical vein toward a more lighthearted comedy of manners, anticipating the style of Restoration comedy. One of Middleton's most hilarious and philosophically unpretentious plays, though plotted with great ingenuity of situation, is *A Mad World, My Masters* (1604–1607). *Michaelmas Term*, written about the same time, exposes the sharp practices of usurers and lawyers. All these Middleton plays were written for Paul's boys.

Romantic comedy, though overshadowed by humors and city comedy during the 1600s, still held forth at the public theaters. A leading exponent was Thomas Heywood, in such plays as *The Fair Maid of the West*, or *A Girl Worth Gold* (1597–1610). Heywood also wrote English history plays designed to prove the sturdiness and historical importance of the London citizenry he so loved, as in *Edward IV* (1597–1599), *The Four Prentices of London* (c. 1600), and *If You Know Not Me You Know Nobody* (1605). Classical tragedy also continued to be written, despite the vogue of revenge tragedy. Ben Jonson rather dogmatically illustrated his classical theories of tragedy in *Sejanus* (1603) and *Catiline* (1611). Samuel Daniel wrote *Philotas* in 1604 and a revision of his *Cleopatra* in 1607. Heywood's *The Rape of Lucrece* appeared in 1606–1608. These are not, however, the immortal tragedies for which the Jacobean period is remembered.

Shakespeare's Work, 1601–1608

Shakespeare's plays of this period are characteristically Jacobean in their fascination with the dark complexities of sexual jealousy, betrayal, revenge, and social conflict.

The comedies are few in number and lack the joyous affirmation we associate with *Twelfth Night* and earlier plays. *Measure for Measure*, for example, is not about young men and women happily in love, but about premarital sex and the insoluble problems that arise when vice-prone men attempt to legislate morality for their fellow mortals. Angelo, self-hating and out of emotional control, is a tragic hero providentially rescued from his own worst self. The Duke and Isabella must use ethically dubious means—the bed trick—to effect their virtuous aims. Comedy in the play deals darkly in terms of prostitution, slander, and police inefficiency.

All's Well That Ends Well, though less grim than *Measure for Measure* in its confrontation of human degeneracy, does apply a similar bed trick as its central plot device. Just as important, the obstacles to love are internal and psychological, rather than external; that is, the happy union of Bertram and Helena is delayed, not by parental objections or by accident (as in *Romeo and Juliet* and *A Midsummer Night's Dream*), but by Bertram's unreadiness for the demands of a mature marital relationship. *Troilus and Cressida* is a play in which love is paralyzed by a combination of external and internal forces. Troilus must hand Cressida over to the Greeks because his code of honor bids him put his country's cause before his own, and yet that code of "honor" is based on Paris's rape of Helen. Cressida simply gives herself up to Diomedes, knowing she is not strong enough to stand alone in a moral wilderness. The combatants in the greatest war in all history turn out to be petty bickerers who play nasty games on one another and sulk when their reputations are impugned. The cause for which both sides fight is squalid and senseless.

Raphael Holinshed's Chronicles of England, Scotland, and Ireland, *which was published (1577, 2nd edition in 1587) before Shakespeare's career began, served as principal historic source for many plays, including* Macbeth, King Lear, *and* Cymbeline, *as well as the history plays. Here, in a woodcut from the* Chronicles, *Macbeth and Banquo are shown encountering the three weird sisters.*

In *Hamlet,* Shakespeare explores similar dilemmas posed by human carnality. Women, in Hamlet's misogynistic angst, are too often frail; men are too often importunate and brutal. How is a thoughtful person to justify his or her own existence? Should one struggle actively against injustice and personal wrong? How can one know what is really true or foresee the complex results of action? How, in *Othello,* can the protagonist resist temptation and inner weakness, prompting him to destroy the very thing on which his happiness depends? Is Macbeth tempted to sin by the weird sisters and his wife, or is the choice to murder Duncan ultimately his? To what extent is humanity responsible for its tragic fate? Most of all, in *King Lear,* are the heavens themselves indifferent to human bestiality? Must Cordelia die? Yet, despite these overwhelmingly pessimistic questions, and the tragic consequences they imply for all human life, Shakespeare's "great" tragedies affirm at least the nobility of humanity's striving to know itself, and the redeeming fact that human goodness does exist (in Desdemona, Duncan, Cordelia), even if those who practice goodness are often slaughtered.

The Roman or classical tragedies are something apart from the "great" tragedies. They are more ironic in tone, more dispiriting, though they, too, affirm an essential nobility in humanity. Brutus misguidedly leads a revolution against Caesar but dies loyal to his great principles. Timon of Athens proves the appalling ingratitude of his fellow creature and resolutely cuts himself off from all human contact. Coriolanus proclaims himself an enemy of the Roman people and seeks to destroy them for their ingratitude, though he is compromised and destroyed at last by his promptings of human feeling. Antony, too, is pulled apart by an irreconcilable conflict. Yet, in this play at least, Shakespeare achieves, partly through the greatness of Cleopatra, a triumph over defeat that seems to offer a new resolution of humanity's tragic dilemma.

THE LATE YEARS: 1608–1616

In the summer of 1608, Shakespeare's acting company signed a twenty-one-year lease for the use of the Blackfriars playhouse, an indoor and rather intimate, artificially lighted theater inside the city of London, close to the site of St. Paul's cathedral. A private theater had existed on this spot since 1576, when the Children of the Chapel and then Paul's boys began acting their courtly plays for paying spectators in a building that had once belonged to the Dominicans, or Black Friars. James Burbage had begun construction in 1596 of the so-called Second Blackfriars theater in the same building. Although James encountered opposition from the residents of the area and died before he could complete the work, James's son Richard did succeed in opening the new theater in 1600. At first, he leased it (for twenty-one

years) to a children's company, but when that company was suppressed in 1608 for offending the French ambassador in a play by George Chapman, Burbage seized the opportunity to take back the unexpired lease and to set up Blackfriars as the winter playhouse for his adult company, the King's men. By this time, the adult troupes could plainly see that they needed to cater more directly to courtly audiences than they once had done. Their popular audiences were becoming increasingly disenchanted with the drama. Puritan fulminations against the stage gained in effect, especially when many playwrights refused to disguise their satirical hostility toward Puritans and the London bourgeoisie.

Several of Shakespeare's late plays may have been acted both at the Globe and at Blackfriars. The plays he wrote after 1608–1609—*Cymbeline, The Winter's Tale,* and *The Tempest*—all show the distinct influence of the dramaturgy of the private theaters. Also, we know that an increasing number of Shakespeare's plays were acted at the court of King James. *Othello, King Lear,* and *The Tempest* are named in court revels accounts, and *Macbeth* dramatizes Scottish history with a seemingly explicit reference to King James as the descendant of Banquo who bears the "twofold balls and treble scepters" (4.1.121); James had received a double coronation as King of England and Scotland, and took seriously his assumed title as King of Great Britain, France, and Ireland. On the other hand, Shakespeare's plays certainly continued to be acted at the Globe to the very end of his career. The 1609 Quarto of *Pericles* advertises that it was acted "by his Majesty's Servants, at the Globe on the Bankside." The 1608 Quarto of *King Lear* mentions a performance at court and assigns the play to "his Majesty's servants playing usually at the Globe on the Bankside." Simon Forman saw *Macbeth, Cymbeline,* and *The Winter's Tale* at the Globe. Finally, a performance of *Henry VIII* on June 29, 1613, resulted in the burning of the Globe to the ground, though afterwards it soon was rebuilt.

Shakespeare's last plays, written with a view to Blackfriars and the court, as well as to the Globe, are now usually called "romances" or "tragicomedies," or sometimes both. Although they were not known by these terms in Shakespeare's day—they were grouped with the comedies in the First Folio of 1623, except for *Cymbeline,* which was placed among the tragedies—the very ambiguity about the genre in this arrangement is suggestive of an uncertainty as to whether they were seen as predominantly comic or tragic. The term "romance" suggests a return to the kind of story Robert Greene had derived from Greek romance: tales of adventure, long separation, and tearful reunion, involving shipwreck, capture by pirates, riddling prophecies, children set adrift in boats or abandoned on foreign shores, the illusion of death and subsequent restoration to life, the revelation of the identity of long-lost children by birthmarks, and the like. The term "tragicomedy" suggests

This section of Wenceslaus Hollar's "Long View" of London dates from 1647, some years after Shakespeare's death, but gives nonetheless a fine view of two theater buildings on the south bank of the Thames River, across from the city. The two labels of "The Globe" and "Beere bayting" should in fact be reversed; the Globe (rebuilt in 1613) appears to the left and below the bearbaiting arena.

a play in which the protagonist commits a seemingly fatal error or crime, or (as in *Pericles*) suffers an extraordinarily adverse fortune to test his patience; in either event, he must experience agonies of contrition and bereavement until he is providentially delivered from his tribulations. The tone is deeply melancholic and resigned, although suffused also with a sense of gratitude for the harmonies that are mysteriously restored.

The appropriateness of such plays to the elegant atmosphere of Blackfriars and the court is subtle but real. Although one might suppose at first that old-fashioned naiveté would seem out of place in a sophisticated milieu, the naiveté is only superficial. Tragicomedy and pastoral romance were, in the period from 1606 to 1610, beginning to enjoy a fashionable courtly revival. The leading practitioners of the new genre were Beaumont and Fletcher, though Shakespeare made a highly significant contribution. Perhaps sophisticated audiences responded to pastoral and romantic drama as the nostalgic evocation of an idealized past, a chivalric "golden world" fleetingly recovered through an artistic journey back to naiveté and

innocence. The evocation of such a world demands the kind of studied but informal artifice we find in many tragicomic plays of the period: the elaborate masques and allegorical shows, the descents of enthroned gods from the heavens (as in *Cymbeline*), the use of quaint Chorus figures like Old Gower or Time (in *Pericles* and *The Winter's Tale*), and the quasi-operatic blend of music and spectacle. At their best, such plays powerfully compel belief in the artistic world thus artificially created. The very improbability of the story becomes, paradoxically, part of the means by which an audience must "awake its faith" in a mysterious truth.

Shakespeare did not merely ape the new fashion in tragicomedy and romance. In fact, he may have done much to establish it. His *Pericles*, written seemingly in about 1606–1608 for the public stage before Shakespeare's company acquired Blackfriars, anticipated many important features, not only of Shakespeare's own later romances, but also of Beaumont and Fletcher's *The Maid's Tragedy* and *Philaster* (c. 1608–1611). Still, Shakespeare was on the verge of retirement, and the future belonged to Beaumont and Fletcher. Gradually, Shakespeare disengaged himself, spending more and more time in Stratford. His last-known stint as an actor was in Jonson's *Sejanus* in 1603. Some time in 1611 or 1612, he probably gave up his lodgings in London, though he still may have returned for such occasions as the opening performance of *Henry VIII* in 1613. He continued to be one of the proprietors of the newly rebuilt Globe, but his involvement in its day-to-day operations dwindled.

Shakespeare's Reputation, 1608–1616

Shakespeare's reputation among his contemporaries was undiminished in his late years, even though Beaumont and Fletcher were the new rage at the Globe and Blackfriars. Among those who apostrophized Shakespeare was John Davies of Hereford in *The Scourge of Folly* (entered in the Stationers' Register in 1610):

> To our English Terence, Mr. Will Shakespeare.
>
> Some say, good Will, which I, in sport, do sing:
> Hadst thou not played some kingly parts in sport,
> Thou hadst been a companion for a king,
> And been a king among the meaner sort.
> Some others rail. But, rail as they think fit,
> Thou hast no railing, but a reigning, wit.
> And honesty thou sow'st, which they do reap,
> So to increase their stock which they do keep.

The following sonnet is from *Run and a Great Cast* (1614) by Thomas Freeman:

> To Master W. Shakespeare.
>
> Shakespeare, that nimble Mercury thy brain

Lulls many hundred Argus-eyes asleep,
So fit, for all thou fashionest thy vein,
At th' horse-foot fountain thou hast drunk full deep.
Virtue's or vice's theme to thee all one is.
Who loves chaste life, there's *Lucrece* for a teacher;
Who list read lust, there's *Venus and Adonis,*
True model of a most lascivious lecher.
Besides, in plays thy wit winds like Meander,
Whence needy new composers borrow more
Than Terence doth from Plautus or Menander.
But to praise thee aright, I want thy store.
  Then let thine own works thine own worth upraise,
  And help t' adorn thee with deservèd bays.

Ben Jonson took a more critical view, though he also admired Shakespeare greatly. In the Induction to his *Bartholomew Fair* (1631 edition), Jonson compared the imaginary world he presented in his play with the more improbable fantasies of romantic drama:

If there be never a servant-monster i' the fair, who can help it? He [the author, Jonson] says; nor a nest of antics? He is loath to make Nature afraid in his plays, like those that beget tales, Tempests, and suchlike drolleries to mix his head with other men's heels.

From this, one judges that Jonson had in mind not only *The Tempest* but also Shakespeare's other late romances. He similarly protested in the Prologue to his 1616 edition of *Every Man in His Humor* that his own playwriting was free of the usual romantic claptrap:

Where neither Chrous wafts you o'er the seas,
Nor creaking throne comes down the boys to please,
Nor nimble squib is seen to make afeard
The gentlewomen, nor rolled bullet heard
To say it thunders, nor tempestuous drum
Rumbles to tell you when the storm doth come.

Still, Shakespeare's reputation was assured. John Webster paid due homage, in his note To the Reader accompanying *The White Devil* (1612), to "the right happy and copious industry of M. *Shakespeare,* M. *Dekker,* & M. *Heywood,*" along with Chapman, Jonson, Beaumont, and Fletcher.

Records of the Late Years

Shakespeare's last recorded investment in real estate was the purchase of a house in Blackfriars, London, in 1613. There is no indication he lived there, for he had retired to Stratford. He did not pay the full purchase price of one hundred and forty pounds, and the mortgage deed executed for the unpaid balance furnishes one of the six unquestioned examples of his signature.

John Combe, a wealthy bachelor of Stratford and Shakespeare's friend, left him a legacy of five pounds in his will at the time of Combe's death in 1613. At about the same time, John's kinsman William Combe began a controversial attempt to enclose Welcombe Common, that is, to convert narrow strips of arable land to pasture. Presumably, Combe was interested in a more efficient means of using the land. Enclosure was, however, an explosive issue, since many people feared they would lose the right to farm the land and would be evicted to make room for cattle and sheep. Combe attempted to guarantee Shakespeare and other titheholders that they would lose no money. He offered similar assurances to the Stratford Council, but the townspeople were adamantly opposed. Shakespeare was consulted by letter as a leading titheholder. The letter is lost, but, presumably, it set forth the Council's reasons for objecting to enclosure. Shakespeare's views on the controversy remain unknown. Eventually, the case went to the Privy Council, where Combe was ordered to restore the land to its original use.

One of the most interesting documents from these years consists of the records of a lawsuit entered into in 1612 by Stephen Belott against his father-in-law, Christopher Mountjoy, a Huguenot maker of women's ornamental headdresses who resided on Silver Street, St. Olave's parish, London. Belott sought to secure the payment of a dower promised him at the time of his marriage to Mountjoy's daughter. In this suit, Shakespeare was summoned as a witness and made deposition on five interrogatories. From this document we learn that Shakespeare was a lodger in Mountjoy's house at the time of the marriage in 1604 and probably for some time before that, since he states in his testimony that he had known Mountjoy for more than ten years. Shakespeare admitted that, at the solicitation of Mountjoy's wife, he had acted as an intermediary in the arrangement of the marriage between Belott and Mountjoy's daughter. Shakespeare declared himself unable, however, to recall the exact amount of the portion or the date on which it was to have been paid. Shakespeare's signature to his deposition is authentic and one of the best samples of his handwriting that we have.

In January of 1615 or 1616, Shakespeare drew up his last will and testament with the assistance of his lawyer Francis Collins, who had aided him earlier in some of his transactions in real estate. On March 25, 1616, Shakespeare revised his will in order to provide for the marriage of his daughter Judith and Thomas Quiney in that same year. Shakespeare's three quavering signatures, one on each page of this document, suggest that he was in failing health. The cause of his death on April 23 is not known. An intriguing bit of Stratford gossip is reported by John Ward, vicar of Holy Trinity in Stratford from 1662 to 1689, in his diary: "Shakespeare, Drayton, and Ben Jonson had a merry meeting, and it seems drank too hard, for Shakespeare died of a fever there contracted." The report comes fifty years after Shakespeare's death, however, and is hardly an expert medical opinion.

The will disposes of all the property of which Shakespeare is known to have died possessing, the greater share of it going to his daughter Susanna. His recently married daughter Judith received a dowry, a provision for any children that might be born of her marriage, and other gifts. Ten pounds went to the poor of Stratford; Shakespeare's sword went to Mr. Thomas Combe; twenty-six shillings and eight pence apiece went to Shakespeare's fellow actors Heminges, Burbage, and Condell to buy them mourning rings; and other small bequests went to various other friends and relatives.

An interlineation contains the bequest of Shakespeare's "second best bed with the furniture," that is, the hangings, to his wife. Anne's name appears nowhere else in the will. Some scholars, beginning with Edmund Malone, have taken this reference as proof of an unhappy marriage, confirming earlier indications, such as the hasty wedding to a woman who was William's senior by eight years and his prolonged residence in London for twenty years or more seemingly without his family. The evidence is inconclusive, however. Shakespeare certainly supported his family handsomely, acquired much property in Stratford, and retired there when he might have remained still in London. Although he showed no great solicitude for Anne's well-being in the will, her rights were protected by law; a third of her husband's estate went to her without having to be mentioned in the will. New Place was to be the home of Shakespeare's favorite daughter Susanna, wife of the distinguished Dr. John Hall. Anne Shakespeare would make her home with her daughter and, with her dower rights secured by law, would be quite as wealthy as she would need to be.

The date of Shakespeare's death (April 23, 1616) and his age (his fifty-third year) are inscribed on his monument. This elaborate structure, still standing in the chancel of Trinity Church, Stratford, was erected some time before 1623 by the London stonecutting firm of Gheerart Janssen and his sons. Janssen's shop was in Southwark, near the Globe, and may have been familiar to the actors. The bust of Shakespeare is a conventional sort of statuary for its time. Still, it is one of the only two contemporary likenesses we have. The other is the Droeshout engraving of Shakespeare in the Folio of 1623.

The epitaph on the monument reads as follows:

Iudicio Phylium, genio Socratem, arte Maronem;
Terra tegit, populus maeret, Olympus habet.
Stay passenger. Why goest thou by so fast?
Read, if thou canst, whom envious Death hath placed
Within this monument: Shakespeare, with whom
Quick Nature died, whose name doth deck this tomb
Far more than cost, sith all that he hath writ
Leaves living art but page to serve his wit.
Obiit anno domini 1616,
Aetatis 53, die 23 April.

These lines, of which the beginning Latin couplet compares Shakespeare with Nestor (King of Pylos) for wise judgment, Socrates for genius, and Virgil (Maro) for poetic art, and avers that the earth covers him, people grieve for him, and Mount Olympus (that is, heaven) has him, indicate the high reputation he enjoyed at the time of his death. More widely known, perhaps, are the four lines inscribed over Shakespeare's grave near the north wall of the chancel. A local tradition assigns them to Shakespeare himself and implies that he wrote them "to suit the capacity of clerks and sextons," whom he wished apparently to frighten out of the idea of opening the grave to make room for a new occupant:

Good friend, for Jesus' sake forbear
To dig the dust enclosèd here.
Blest be the man that spares these stones,
And curst be he that moves my bones.

Whether Shakespeare actually wrote these lines cannot, however, be determined.

Other Dramatists

The most significant new development in the drama of the period from about 1608 to 1616, apart from Shakespeare's

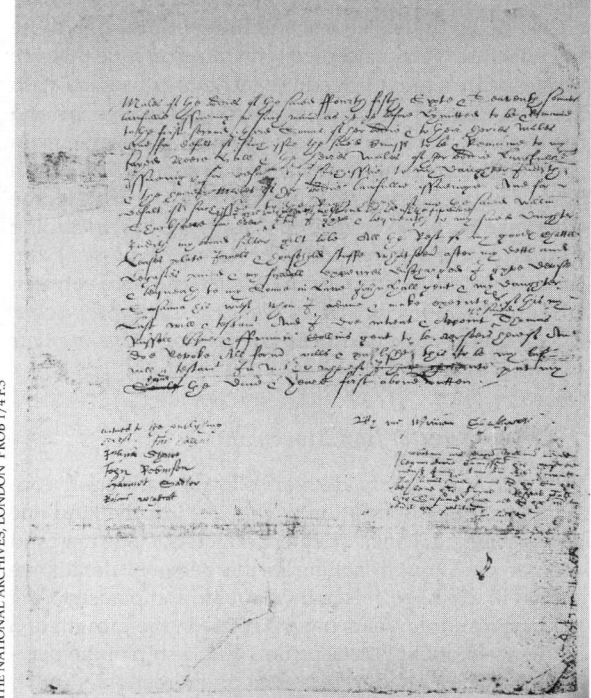

THE NATIONAL ARCHIVES, LONDON PROB 1/4 E3

As with so many other things in his life, the curious terms of Shakespeare's will have led to endless and provocative conjecture.

new interest in romance and tragicomedy, was the emergence of the famous literary partners Francis Beaumont and John Fletcher. Beaumont, the son of a distinguished lawyer, studied for a while at Oxford and then at the Inner Temple before drifting into a literary career. In 1613, he married an heiress and retired almost completely from the theater. John Fletcher was the son of Richard Fletcher, Queen Elizabeth's chaplain and later Bishop of London. The young man probably studied at Cambridge. The father died in 1596 heavily in debt, leaving the young Fletcher to support a family of eight children. Fletcher became a professional writer, earning his living as chief dramatist for the King's men. He was Shakespeare's successor. Fletcher's cousins, Giles and Phineas Fletcher, gained some reputation as poets. Beaumont and Fletcher, who were close friends, regarded themselves also as poets and as members of the "tribe of Ben"—the disciples of the great Ben Jonson who often gathered together at the Mermaid Tavern for an evening of witty literary conversation.

> What things have we seen
> Done at the Mermaid! heard words that have been
> So nimble, and so full of subtle flame,
> As if that every one from whence they came
> Had meant to put his whole wit in a jest,
> And had resolved to live a fool the rest
> Of his dull life!

> *(Master Francis Beaumont's Letter to Ben Jonson)*

Beaumont and Fletcher actually collaborated on only about seven plays: *The Woman Hater,* a comedy (1606); *The Maid's Tragedy,* a tragedy (1608–1611); *Philaster,* a tragicomedy (1608–1610); *Cupid's Revenge,* a tragedy (c. 1607–1612); *The Coxcomb,* a comedy (1608–1610); *A King and No King,* a tragicomedy (1611); *The Scornful Lady,* a tragicomedy (1613–1616); and perhaps one or two others. They may have collaborated on *The Knight of the Burning Pestle* (c. 1607–1610), though it was chiefly Beaumont's. Beaumont also wrote *Mask of the Inner Temple and Gray's Inn* (1613). Fletcher unassisted wrote *The Faithful Shepherdess* (1608–1609), *The Night Walker* (c. 1611), *Bonduca* (1611–1614), *Valentinian* (1610–1614), and others. He also collaborated with several other writers, including Massinger, Middleton, Field, and Rowley. Importantly, he seems to have collaborated with Shakespeare on *The Two Noble Kinsmen* (1613–1616) and, probably, on *Henry VIII.* Eventually, most of these various dramatic enterprises were gathered together in 1647 as the works of Beaumont and Fletcher. They have remained known as such ever since, partly because the original collaboration of these two men did so much to set a new style in coterie drama.

The plays they wrote together, such as *The Maid's Tragedy* and *Philaster,* offer an interesting comparison with Shakespeare's contemporary writing in a similar genre.

Beaumont and Fletcher often employ exotic settings, like Rhodes or Sicily. In such an environment, refined aristocratic characters are caught in dynastic struggles or in a rarified conflict between love and honor. They must cope with stereotyped villains, such as tyrants or shamelessly lustful courtiers. The sentiments are lofty, the rhetoric is mannered; elaborately contrived situations are offered with no pretense of verisimilitude. The characters live according to lofty chivalric codes and despise ill breeding above all else. In the plotting of the tragicomic reversal, the audience is sometimes deliberately deceived into believing something that is not true, so that the sudden happy outcome arrives as a theatrically contrived surprise. Disguising and masking are common motifs. The audience is deliberately made aware throughout of the play's theatrical artifice, statuesque scene building, and titillating sensationalism.

Although Shakespeare wrote no tragedies after *Coriolanus,* great tragedy did continue to appear on the Jacobean stage. John Webster wrote his two most splendid plays, *The White Devil* and *The Duchess of Malfi,* between 1609 and 1614. Both contain elements of the still-popular revenge tradition. They also manage to achieve a vision of triumphant human dignity in defeat that merits comparison with Shakespeare's greatest tragic achievement. Still to come were *The Changeling* (1622) by Thomas Middleton and William Rowley, *Women Beware Women* (c. 1620–1627) by Middleton, *'Tis Pity She's a Whore* (1629?–1633) by John Ford, and others. Although these tragedies are more concerned with the grotesque than are Shakespeare's great tragedies, and more obsessed with abnormal human psychology (incest, werewolfism, and the like), they are nonetheless sublime achievements in art. The genius of the age for tragedy did not die with Shakespeare. During Shakespeare's last years, George Chapman was also writing his best tragedies, including *Charles Duke of Byron* in 1608, *The Revenge of Bussy D'Ambois* in about 1610, and *Chabot, Admiral of France* between 1611 and 1622. Ben Jonson's *Catiline His Conspiracy,* a classical tragedy, appeared in 1611; Marston's *The Insatiate Countess,* in about 1610.

The Anti-Stratfordian Movement

What we know of Shakespeare's life is really quite considerable. The information we have is just the kind one would expect. It hangs together and refers to one man and one career. Though lacking in the personal details we should like to have, it is both adequate and plausible. Yet the past hundred years or so have seen the growth of a tendency to doubt Shakespeare's authorship of the plays and poems ascribed to him. The phenomenon is sometimes called the "anti-Stratfordian" movement, since its attack is leveled at the literary credentials of the man who was born in Stratford and later became an actor in London. Although based on no reliable evidence, the movement has persisted long enough to become a kind of myth. It also has the appeal of a mystery thriller: who really wrote Shakespeare's plays? A brief account must be made here of the origins of the anti-Stratfordian movement.

Beginning in the late eighteenth century, and especially in the mid nineteenth century, a few admirers of Shakespeare began to be troubled by the scantiness of information about England's greatest author. As we have already seen, good reasons exist for the scarcity: the great London fire of 1666 that destroyed many records, the relatively low social esteem accorded to popular dramatists during the Elizabethan period, and the like. Also, we do actually know more about Shakespeare than about most of his contemporaries in the theater, despite the difficulties imposed by the passage of time. Still, some nineteenth-century readers saw only that they knew far less about Shakespeare than about many authors of more recent date.

Moreover, the impressions of the man did not seem to square with his unparalleled literary greatness. William Shakespeare had been brought up in a small country town; were his parents cultured folk or even literate? No record of his schooling has been preserved; was Shakespeare himself able to read and write, much less write immortal plays and poems? The anti-Stratfordians did not deny the existence of a man called Shakespeare from Stratford-upon-Avon, but they found it incredible that such a person should be connected with the works ascribed to him. Mark Twain, himself an anti-Stratfordian, was fond of joking that the plays were not by Shakespeare but by another person of the same name. Beneath the humor in this remark lies a deep-seated mistrust: how could a country boy have written so knowledgeably and eloquently about the lives of kings and queens? Where could such a person have learned so much about the law, about medicine, about the art of war, about heraldry? The puzzle seemed a genuine one, even though no one until the late eighteenth century had thought to question Shakespeare's authorship of the plays—least of all his colleagues and friends, such as Ben Jonson, who admitted that Shakespeare's classical learning was "small" but insisted that Shakespeare was an incomparable genius.

The first candidate put forward in the anti-Stratfordian cause as the "real" author of the plays was Sir Francis Bacon, a reputable Elizabethan writer with connections at court and considerable cultural attainments. Yet the ascription of the plays to Bacon was based on no documentary evidence. It relied, instead, on the essentially snobbish argument that Bacon was better born and purportedly better educated than Shakespeare—an argument that appealed strongly to the nineteenth century in which a university education was becoming more and more a distinctive mark of the cultivated person. The assertion of Bacon's authorship was also based on a conspiratorial theory of history; that is, its believers had to assume the existence of a mammoth conspiracy in Elizabethan times in which Shakespeare would allow his name to be used by Bacon as a *nom de plume* and in which Shakespeare's friends, such as Ben Jonson, would take part. (Jonson knew Shakespeare too well, after all, to have been duped for a period of almost twenty years.) The motive for such an arrangement, presumably, was that Bacon did not deign to lend his dignified name to the writing of popular plays (since they were considered subliterary) and so chose a common actor named Shakespeare to serve as his alter ego. This theory of an elaborate hoax involving England's greatest literary giant has proved powerfully attractive to modern writers like Mark Twain who have sometimes referred to themselves as rebels against the cultural "Establishment" of their own times.

The claim that Bacon wrote Shakespeare's works was soon challenged in the name of other prominent Elizabethans: the Earl of Oxford, the Earl of Southampton, Anthony Bacon, the Earl of Rutland, the Earl of Devonshire, Christopher Marlowe, and others. Since documentary claims as to Bacon's authorship of the Shakespearen canon were nonexistent, other Elizabethans could be proposed to fill his role just as satisfactorily as Bacon himself. The anti-Stratfordian movement gained momentum and came to include several prominent persons, including Delia Bacon and Sigmund Freud, as well as Mark Twain. One of the appeals of the anti-Stratfordian movement in recent years has proved to be a kind of amateur sleuthing or scholarship, carried on by professional lawyers, doctors, and the like, who have explored Shakespeare's interest in law and medicine as a hobby and have convinced themselves that Shakespeare's wisdom in these subjects entitles him to claim a better birth than that of a glover's son from Stratford. Ingenious efforts at "deciphering" hidden meanings in the works have been adduced to prove one authorship claim or another. The academic "Establishments" of modern universities have been accused of perpetuating Shakespeare's name out of mere vested self-interest: Shakespeare scholarship is an industry, and its busy workers need to preserve their source of income.

We must ask in all seriousness, however, whether such assertions are not offering answers to nonexistent questions. Responsible scholarship has admirably dispelled the seeming mystery of Shakespeare's humble beginnings. T. W. Baldwin, for example, in *William Shakespeare's Petty School* (1943) and *William Shakspere's Small Latine and Lesse Greeke* (1944), has shown just what sort of classical training Shakespeare almost surely received in the free grammar school of Stratford. It is precisely the sort of training that would have enabled him to use classical authors as he does, with the familiarity of one who likes to read. His Latin and Greek were passable but not strong; he often consulted modern translations, as well as classical originals. Just as importantly, Shakespeare's social background was, in fact, typical of many of the greatest writers of the English Renaissance. He earned his living by his writing, and thus had one of the strongest of motives for success. So did his contemporaries Marlowe (who came from a shoemaker's family) and Jonson (whose stepfather was a brickmason). Greene, Peele, Nashe, and many others sold plays and other writings for a livelihood. Although a few wellborn persons, such as Bacon and Sir Philip Sidney, also made exceptional contributions to literature, and although a number of courtiers emulated Henry VIII and Elizabeth as gifted amateurs in the arts, the court was not the direct or major source of England's literary greatness. Most courtiers were not, like Shakespeare, professional writers. A man like Bacon lacked Shakespeare's connection with a commercial acting company. Surely the theater was a more relevant "university" for Shakespeare than Oxford or Cambridge, where most of his studies would have been in ancient languages and in divinity.

SHAKESPEARE'S LANGUAGE: HIS DEVELOPMENT AS POET AND DRAMATIST

LANGUAGE AND ARTISTIC DEVELOPMENT

One indication of Shakespeare's greatness is his extraordinary development. As he worked through his writing career of more than twenty years, he constantly explored new themes, perfected genres and moved on to new ones, and saw ever more deeply into the human condition. Many of the works that have made him immortal were not written until he was nearly forty years old or more. The study of his development is, in itself, an interesting and complex subject. It is one that requires an accurate dating of his plays and poems.

The First Folio, published in 1623 as the first "complete edition" of Shakespeare's plays in the large and handsome folio format for which the printed sheet was folded only once, gives no help in determining the order of composition of Shakespeare's plays. They are arranged in three groups—comedies, histories, and tragedies—without regard for dates of composition. The first comedy in the Folio is *The Tempest*, known to be one of Shakespeare's latest plays; the second is *The Two Gentlemen of Verona*, one of the earliest. The histories are arranged in order of the English kings whose reigns they treat, although Shakespeare clearly did not write them in that order. The tragedies show no discernible arrangement by date. Information about dating can partially be recovered from the fact that eighteen of the thirty-six plays in the First Folio had previously been published in single quarto volumes at various times, with dates on their title pages. *Pericles*, which

was not included in the First Folio, appeared in quarto format in 1609. (The quarto format required that the printed sheet be folded twice, resulting in a smaller page than that of a folio volume.) All the quarto editions, except *Romeo and Juliet* and *Love's Labor's Lost*, were entered in the Register of the Stationers' Company of London; two other plays, *As You Like It* (entered in the Stationers' Register in 1600) and *Antony and Cleopatra* (S.R. 1608), although not printed in quarto, were entered in the Stationers' Register possibly in order to forestall publication by printers who had no right to them. The date of entry of a play in the register indicates that, at least by that time, the play was in existence. The quarto editions also have certain information on their title pages regarding date, author, and publisher, and sometimes tell what theatrical company acted the play. Other kinds of external evidence of date include references to Shakespeare's plays in diaries, journals, or accounts of the period, and quotations from his plays in the literary works of Elizabethan and Jacobean writers. Allusions in Shakespeare's plays themselves to contemporary events, although difficult to prove beyond dispute, can sometimes be helpful. See Appendix 1, at the end of this volume, for a detailed discussion on "Canon, Dates, and Early Texts" of each of Shakespeare's plays.

Once Shakespeare's plays have been arranged in approximate chronological order on the basis of the kinds of external evidence already described, we can perceive that his style underwent a continuous development from his earliest work to the end of his career as a dramatist. Matters of style are not easy to talk about precisely, and we can hardly expect to be able to date a particular passage as having been written in 1604, say, as distinguished from 1602. Overall, on the other hand, the early and late Shakespeare are strikingly distinguishable. Take, for example, the following two passages. One is from the Duke of Clarence's description of his dream in *Richard III* (1.4.21–33), written in about 1591–1594, near the start of Shakespeare's career:

> Oh, Lord, methought what pain it was to drown!
> What dreadful noise of waters in my ears!
> What sights of ugly death within my eyes!
> Methoughts I saw a thousand fearful wracks;
> Ten thousand men that fishes gnawed upon;
> Wedges of gold, great anchors, heaps of pearl,
> Inestimable stones, unvalued jewels,
> All scattered in the bottom of the sea.
> Some lay in dead men's skulls, and in the holes
> Where eyes did once inhabit there were crept,
> As 'twere in scorn of eyes, reflecting gems,
> That wooed the slimy bottom of the deep
> And mocked the dead bones that lay scattered by.

The second is Prospero's description of his magic in *The Tempest* (5.1.33–50), from about 1610–1611 when Shakespeare was on the verge of retirement:

Ye elves of hills, brooks, standing lakes, and groves,
And ye that on the sands with printless foot
Do chase the ebbing Neptune, and do fly him
When he comes back; you demi-puppets that
By moonshine do the green sour ringlets make,
Whereof the ewe not bites; and you whose pastime
Is to make midnight mushrooms, that rejoice
To hear the solemn curfew; by whose aid,
Weak masters though ye be, I have bedimmed
The noontide sun, called forth the mutinous winds,
And twixt the green sea and the azured vault
Set roaring war; to the dread rattling thunder
Have I given fire, and rifted Jove's stout oak
With his own bolt; the strong-based promontory
Have I made shake, and by the spurs plucked up
The pine and cedar; graves at my command
Have waked their sleepers, oped, and let 'em forth
By my so potent art.

These two passages have been chosen for comparison, in part because they are both set speeches in blank verse, rich in formal characteristics. Put side by side, they reveal a stylistic shift that we can observe in other less formal poetry and even in prose. The shift is away from rhetorical balance toward a freedom from verse restraint, a deliberate syncopation of blank verse rhythms, and a complication of syntax.

Completely regular blank verse, invariably consisting of ten syllables to each unrhymed line, with an accent falling on every other syllable, soon becomes monotonous. The iambic pattern can, however, be varied by a number of subtle changes. Extra syllables, accented and unaccented, can be added to the line, or a line may occasionally be short by one or more syllables. The regular alternation of accented and unaccented syllables, producing the effect of five iambic "feet" in each line (each foot consisting of an accented and an unaccented syllable), can be interrupted by the occasional inversion of a foot. Pauses, or caesuras, may occur at several points in the line. Most importantly, the line can be "end-stopped"—with a strong pause at the end of the line—or "run on" without interruption into the next line. Variations of this sort can transform blank verse from a formal and rhetorical vehicle into one that is highly conversational and supple.

Shakespeare increasingly abandons formal end-stopped verse for a fluid and more conversational style. In the preceding two passages, the first introduces a grammatical stop at the end of every line, except the ninth, whereas the second passage tends to run on past the end of the line; it does so in all but the fifth and tenth lines. Similarly, the passage from *The Tempest* is more apt to introduce a grammatical pause in the middle of a verse line, whereas the passage from *Richard III* stops between clauses in midline only in line 9. Shakespeare's later style is freer in its use of so-called feminine ends at the ends of lines, that is, endings with an unstressed syllable added on to the final stress of the iambic pattern; "fly him," "pastime," and "thunder" are good examples of this. A corollary of Shakespeare's increased use of feminine line endings and nonstopped blank verse is that the lines of his later verse are more apt to end in conjunctions, prepositions, auxiliary verbs, possessive pronouns, and other lightly stressed words. The *Richard III* passage generally ends in strong verbs and nouns, such as "drown," "ears," "eyes," and so on, whereas the *Tempest* passage makes use of "that," "up," and "forth."

Stylistic traits such as these can be quantified to demonstrate a fairly steady course of progression from the early to later plays. Early plays have low percentages of run-on lines in relation to the total number of lines: *1 Henry VI* has 10.4 percent, *2 Henry VI* 11.4 percent, *3 Henry VI* 9.5 percent, *The Comedy of Errors* 12.9 percent, and *The Two Gentlement of Verona* 12.4 percent, whereas *Cymbeline* has 46.0 percent, *The Winter's Tale* 37.5 percent, *The Tempest* 41.5 percent, and *Henry VIII* 46.3 percent. Feminine or "double" endings run from a total of 9 in *Love's Labor's Lost* and 29 in *A Midsummer Night's Dream* to 708 in *Coriolanus*, 726 in *Cymbeline,* and 1,195 in *Henry VIII.* The actual number of light or weak endings increases from none in *The Comedy of Errors* and *The Two Gentlemen of Verona* to 104 in *Coriolanus*, 130 in *Cymbeline*, and 100 in *The Tempest.*

Other stylistic characteristics, though not discernible in the two examples from *Richard III* and *The Tempest,* spell out a similar development toward flexibility. For example, Shakespeare increasingly divides a verse line between two or more speakers. *The Comedy of Errors* and *1 Henry VI* do so hardly at all, whereas in *Cymbeline* the figures rise to a remarkable 85 percent of all instances in which one speaker stops speaking and another begins; *The Winter's Tale* does so in 87.6 percent of such instances, and *The Tempest*, in 84.5 percent.

Shakespeare's use of prose in his plays depends, to a significant extent, on genre, especially in his early work. At the start of his career, Shakespeare seldom uses prose, except in the speeches of clowns, servants, and rustics, whereas blank verse is his common vehicle of expression in speeches of heightened oratory or dramatic seriousness. *1 Henry VI* and *3 Henry VI, King John,* and *Richard II* are essentially written throughout in verse—usually blank verse. Prose is more common in the early comedies because of the presence of the Dromios, Christopher Sly, and Bottom the Weaver, but the love scenes are generally in verse. Poetry is important to the lyric plays of the mid-1590s, such as *The Merchant of Venice, A Midsummer Night's Dream,* and *Romeo and Juliet.* Prose assumes a major function, on the other hand, in plays of comic wit in the later 1590s, including *1 Henry IV* (45 percent), *2 Henry IV* (54 percent), *Much Ado About Nothing* (74 percent), and *The Merry Wives of Windsor* (81 percent), and here we see that comedy is used not for wisecracking servants so much as for Falstaff, Beatrice, and Benedick. Thereafter, prose is essential to Shakespeare's comic world. It also takes on a major function in *Hamlet* (31 percent), as, for instance, when Hamlet converses with his onetime friends Rosencrantz and Guildenstern, when he plagues Polonius with his satirical wit, or when he philosophizes with Horatio, though verse is, of course, appropriate for the soliloquies and the moments of confrontation with Claudius. In the other great tragedies as well, prose has become for Shakespeare an instrument of limitless flexibility. Although the mixture of prose and blank verse is thus hard to quantify in any steady progression of percentages, the pattern of increased versatility is undeniable. Many of the late plays make less use of prose because of their choice of subject, but all excel in prose comic scenes for Autolycus, Caliban, and many others.

In his use of rhyme, as well, Shakespeare's practice changes from the early to late plays. Early plays and those of the lyric period, such as *A Midsummer Night's Dream* and *Romeo and Juliet*, use a great deal of rhyme, whereas late plays, such as *The Tempest*, use practically none. The commonest form of rhyme is the iambic pentameter measure rhymed in couplet, as when Phoebe, quoting Marlowe's *Hero and Leander*, says in *As You Like It* (3.5.81–2):

> Dead shepherd, now I find thy saw of might,
> "Who ever loved that loved not at first sight?"

Shakespeare does not limit his use of rhyme to the couplet, however. *Romeo and Juliet* and *Love's Labor's Lost* each contains a number of complete sonnets, as well as rhymed sequences made up of a quatrain followed by a couplet, and a good deal of alternate rhyme. Doggerel lines of verse appear in some of the early plays.

One quite formal use of the rhymed couplet does not conform to the statistical pattern that we observe generally in the use of rhyme. Because the Elizabethan theater lacked a front curtain to mark a pause between scenes in a play, Elizabethan dramatists often gave emphasis to a scene ending by means of a rhymed couplet. Possibly the device served also as a cue to those actors backstage who were waiting to begin the next scene. At any rate, the use of scene-ending couplets is common in some plays that otherwise make little use of rhyme. For example, Act 1, scene 5 of *Hamlet* virtually ends with the following concluding statement by the protagonist:

> The time is out of joint. O cursèd spite,
> That ever I was born to set it right!

Apart from this convention, however, use of rhyme in Shakespeare is normally indicative of early style. His lovers in the early plays often speak in rhyme; later, they tend to use prose.

Impossible to quantify, but no less significant in any study of the evolution of Shakespeare's art, is his use of imagery. Images are key to his poetic imagination, and, in part, they can be appreciated out of chronological context, because Shakespeare's mind dwells incessantly on certain image clusters: the family as a metaphor for the state, the garden as an image of social order and disorder, images of medicine and healing applied to the ills of the individual and the commonwealth, images of sexual desire and activity, images of hunting and of other sports, biblical images (Eden, Cain and Abel, Christ's ministry, his Passion, the Last Judgment, etc.), mythological allusions (Danae, Actaeon, Phaethon, Noah, Niobe), and many others. Patterns of imagery have been well studied by Caroline Spurgeon in her *Shakespeare's Imagery and What It Tells Us* (1935), Maurice Charney in *The Function of Imagery in the Drama* (1961), and others. In addition, we can see throughout Shakespeare's career the evolution of an imagistic style, as convincingly demonstrated by Wolfgang Clemen in *The Development of Shakespeare's Imagery* (1951). The early Shakespeare uses figures of speech for decoration and amplification, and learns only gradually to integrate these figures into a presentation of theme, subject, and individual character. In Shakespeare's later work, simile is often transformed into metaphor and assumes an organic function in relation to the entire play. By the end of his career, virtually every aspect of his style has been transformed from one of formal and rhetorical regularity to one of vast flexibility and range.

SHAKESPEARE'S ENGLISH

Pronunciation

How would Shakespeare's plays have sounded to our ears? The distance between Shakespearean and modern English is clearly not as great as in the case of Chaucer, and yet significant differences remain. Spoken English, especially in the pronunciation of vowel sounds, has undergone many striking changes since the early seventeenth century. We can assume that however much Shakespeare's own speech may have been colored by his Warwickshire boyhood, his acting company as a whole was most heavily influenced by London dialect. This form of English had become notably more dominant than in Chaucer's day, though it also included an admixture of northern, eastern, and southern forms because of the cosmopolitan character of the city. Shakespeare often pokes fun at regional dialects in his plays, especially at Welsh, Scottish, and Irish, and at the accents of Frenchmen or other foreigners attempting to speak English (see, for example, *Henry V* and *The Merry Wives of Windsor*).

Reconstructing how early modern English would have sounded is, to be sure, not always easy, since dialect did vary substantially from region to region, and since the ascertaining of pronunciations is often based on rhymes when we cannot be sure how either word in a rhyming pair was pronounced and cannot safely assume that rhymes were exact. Nevertheless, here, in summary form, are some approximate suggestions for pronouncing words in Shakespeare that are not similarly pronounced today. These examples can be applied to similar words: for example, *way* and *say* have the same vowel sound as *day; night,* the same vowel sound as *wide.*

> *folk* (sound the *l*)
> *gnaw* (sound the *g*)
> *knife* (sound the *k; i* as in *wide,* below)
> *brush* (rhymes with *push; r* somewhat trilled)
> *dull* (rhymes with *pull*)
> *seam* (pronounced *same,* with open *a*)
> *old* (pronounced *auld*)
> *now* (pronounced *noo*)
> *house* (pronounced *hoos*)
> *soul* (pronounced *saul*)
> *know* (pronounced *knaw,* with sounded *k*)
> *own* (pronounced *awn*)
> *tune* (pronounced *tiwn*)
> *rule* (pronounced *riwl; r* somewhat trilled)
> *day* (pronounced *die*)
> *time* (pronounced *toime*)
> *wide* (pronounced *woide*)
> *join* (rhymes with *line*)
> *creeping* (pronounced *craypin,* with open *a*)
> *dissention* (in four syllables, without *sh* sound)
> *persuasion* (in four syllables, without *zh* sound)

A matter of more practical importance than phonetic changes is that of differences in Shakespeare's English and ours in the accentuation of syllables. Many cases of variable stress can be found in which he seems to have been at liberty to accent the word in two different ways; in other cases, words were customarily accented on a different syllable from that in current speech. For example, the following accentuations are either usual or frequent: *aspect´, charac´ter, com´mendable, com´plete, con´cealed, con´fessor, consort´* (as a noun), *contract´* (noun), *de´testable, dis´tinct, envy´, for´lorn, hu´mane, instinct´, ob´scure, persev´er, pi´oner, ple´beians, portents´, pur´sue, record´* (noun), *reven´ue, se´cure, sinis´ter, welcome´.*

Not only are *-tion* and *-sion* regularly pronounced as two syllables, but the same situation causes other words in which *e* or *i* stand before vowels to be uttered in Shakespeare's language with one more syllable than in ours; for example, *oce-an, courti-er, marri-age.* We may even have *cre-ature, tre-asure,* and *venge-ance.* Nasals and liquids are frequently pronounced as if an extra vowel were introduced between them and a preceding letter. Accordingly, we have *wrest(e)ler, Eng(e)land, assemb(e)ly,* and *ent(e)rance,* as well as *de-ar, you(e)r,* and *mo-re.* Final *-er*

often has a greater syllabic importance than it has in later poetry. Final *-(e)s* in the genitive singular and the plural of nouns not ending in an *-s* sound may constitute a separate syllable; for example, "To show his teeth as white as whale's bone" (*Love's Labor's Lost,* 5.2.333).

The study of metrics is fraught with peril. Knowledge of syllabification can often be circular in that it has to assume a kind of metrical regularity in the line of a verse. Even so, in scanning of Shakespeare's verse it helps to ascertain as accurately as we can how many syllables he intended a given word to have. As compared to modern-day English, a Shakespearean word may have (1) an additional syllable, or (2) one fewer syllables, or (3) two adjoining syllables in adjoining words that coalesce or elide. Spelling may not always indicate these differences to a modern reader.

1. The following lines give us extra-syllable words in *moon's, juggler, entrance,* and *complexion*:

> I do wander everywhere,
> Swifter than the moon's sphere.
> (*A Midsummer Night's Dream,* 2.1.6–7)

> O me! You juggler! You cankerblossom!
> (*A Midsummer Night's Dream,* 3.2.282)

> After the prompter, for our entrance.
> (*Romeo and Juliet,* 1.4.8)

> Mislike me not for my complexion.
> (*The Merchant of Venice,* 2.1.1)

Similarly, the words *captain, monstrous, esperance, this* (*this is*), *George* (*Richard III,* 5.5.9), *valiant, villain,* and *jealous* sometimes have extra syllables in pronunciation.

2. In the following line, *marry* is elided into one syllable:

> Good mother, do not *marry* me to yond fool.
> (*The Merry Wives of Windsor,* 3.4.83)

Similarly, the words *lineal, journeying, carrion, celestial, herald, royal, malice, absolute, perjury, madame, needle, taken, heaven, spirit, devil, gentleman, unpeople, forward, gather, innocent, violet, Africa, eagle, listen,* and *venomous* have usually one fewer syllables than in current English.

3. The following examples are of elision between the syllables of adjoining words:

> Why should I joy in *an abortive* birth?
> (*Love's Labor's Lost,* 1.1.104)

> The *lover, all* as frantic,
> (*A Midsummer Night's Dream,* 5.1.10)

> Romans, *do me* right.
> (*Titus Andronicus,* 1.1.204)

Differences in accentuation and lengthening or shortening of words thus have great importance in the reading and scanning of Shakespeare's verse. Shortening of words by elision or by slurring is common in Shakespeare, but at least in this matter modern practice forms a good guide. Syllables ending in vowels are not infrequently elided before words beginning with a vowel, as in "How cáme / we ashóre" (*The Tempest*, 1.2.159) and "too hárd / a knót / for mé / t' untíe" (*Twelfth Night*, 2.2.41). Syncopation, or the omission of a syllable, often occurs in words with *r*, as in "I wár-rant / it wíll" (*Hamlet*, 1.2.248); and in final *-er, -el,* and *-le,* as in "Trável you / farre ón" (*The Taming of the Shrew*, 4.2.74). The following words and other similar ones may be treated as monosyllabic in Shakespeare's verse: *whether, ever, hither, other, father, evil, having*. Almost any unaccented syllable of a polysyllabic word (especially if it contains an *i*) may be softened and ignored. This syncopation is frequent in polysyllabic words and proper names: "Thoughts spécu / latíve" (*Macbeth*, 5.4.19) and "Did sláy / this Fórtinbras; / who by / a seáled /compáct" (*Hamlet*, 1.1.90). Other occasions for slurring, as listed by Abbott in his *Shakespearian Grammar*, are light vowels preceded by heavy vowels, as in *power, dying,* and so on; plurals and possessives of nouns ending in an *s* sound, as in *empress'* and *Mars'*; final *-ed* following *d* or *t*, as in "you háve / exceéded / all prómise" (*As You Like It*, 1.2.234); and the *-est* of superlatives (pronounced *-st*) after dentals and liquids, as "the stérn'st / good-níght" (*Macbeth*, 2.2.4) and "thy éldest / son's són" (*King John*, 2.1.177).

Grammar and Rhetoric

Shakespeare's grammar presents but few differences in forms from the grammar of current modern English. The *-eth* ending in the third person singular of the present tense, indicative mood, was very commonly used, especially in serious prose. Shakespeare frequently uses this older form, especially *hath, doth,* and *saith*, but seems to prefer the form in *-s* or *-es*. In a few cases, he also seems to use the old northern plural in *-s* or *-es* in the third person of the present indicative, as " . . . at those springs, / On chaliced flowers that *lies*" (*Cymbeline*, 2.3.22–3). He does not always agree with modern usage in the forms of the past tenses and the perfect participles of the verbs that he employs. He retains some lost forms of the strong verbs, sometimes ignores distinctions we make between the past tense and the perfect participle, and treats some verbs as weak (or regular) which are now strong (or irregular). For example, he uses *arose* for *arisen, swam* for *swum, foughten* for *fought, gave* for *given, took* for *taken, sprung* for *sprang, writ* for *wrote, blowed* for *blew, weaved* for *wove,* and *shaked* for *shaken*. Forms like *degenerate* for *degenerated* and *exhaust* for *exhausted* are especially common. A few instances are to be found of

the archaic *y-* with the past participle, as in *yclad*. For the possessive case of the neuter personal pronoun *it*, Shakespeare normally uses the regular form at that time, *his*; but he also uses the possessive form *it*, and in his plays first published in the First Folio in 1623 we find several occurrences of the new form *its*. Shakespeare uses the old form *moe*, as well as *more,* and *enow* as the plural of *enough*, though these forms have been modernized in this edition because they are used so inconsistently. He uses *near* and *next* along with *nearer* and *nearest*, as the comparative and superlative of *nigh*. These are the most obvious of the formal differences between Shakespeare's grammar and our own.

The functional differences are more considerable. Elizabethan language exercised an extraordinary freedom, even for English, in the use of one part of speech for another. Shakespeare uses verbs, adjectives, adverbs, and pronouns as nouns. He makes verbs out of nouns and adjectives and, of course, uses nouns as adjectives, for this is a distinguishing characteristic of English speech, but he also uses adverbs, verbs, and prepositional phrases as adjectives, as in "Looks he as freshly as he did . . . ?" (*As You Like It*, 3.2.227). Almost any adjective may be freely used as an adverb, as in "And in my house you shall be friendly lodged" (*The Taming of the Shrew*, 4.2.109). He makes active words—both adjectives and verbs—discharge a passive function, as in "the sightless [invisible] couriers of the air" (*Macbeth*, 1.7.23) and "this aspect of mine / Hath feared the valiant," that is, caused the valiant to be afraid (*The Merchant of Venice*, 2.1.8–9). He makes wider use of the infinitive as a verbal noun or as a gerundive participle than do we: "This to be true / I do engage my life" (*As You Like It*, 5.4.164–5), "My operant powers their functions leave to do" (*Hamlet*, 3.2.172), "Nor do I now make moan to be abridged" (*The Merchant of Venice*, 1.1.126), and "You might have saved me my pains, to have taken [by having taken] it away yourself" (*Twelfth Night*, 2.2.5–7). The functions of prepositions in Elizabethan English were so various that one can only refer the student to the notes to the text or to a dictionary.

In certain other features, however, as, for example, in the use of modal auxiliaries, Shakespeare's language is as restricted and conventional as ours is at formal levels, or even more so. *Shall* is regularly used in Shakespeare to express something inevitable in future time and is, therefore, the usual future tense for all persons. *Will*, which originally expressed intention, determination, or willingness, was, to be sure, beginning to encroach on *shall* for the expression of futurity in the second and third persons, but its use usually still retains in Shakespeare a consciousness of its original meaning. *Should* and *would* had their original senses of obligation and volition, respectively, and had other peculiarities, then as now, of considerable difficulty. The subjunctive mood was vital to

Shakespeare as a means of expressing condition, doubt, concession, command, wish, or desire, and, in dependent clauses, indefinitiveness, purpose, or sometimes simple futurity. Note the following examples:

> But if my father *had* not scanted me . . .
> Yourself, renownèd prince, then *stood* as fair.
> (*The Merchant of Venice*, 2.1.17, 20)

> *Live* a thousand years,
> I *shall* not find myself so apt to die.
> (*Julius Caesar*, 3.1.161–2)

> Lest your retirement do *amaze* your friends.
> (*1 Henry IV*, 5.4.6)

> *'Twere* best he speak no harm of Brutus here.
> (*Julius Caesar*, 3.2.70)

> *Melt* Egypt into Nile, and kindly creatures
> *Turn* all to serpents!
> (*Antony and Cleopatra*, 2.5.79–80)

> Yet were it true
> To say this boy *were* like me.
> (*The Winter's Tale*, 1.2.134–5)

> And may direct his course as *please* himself.
> (*Richard III*, 2.2.129)

Some other features of Shakespeare's grammar are as follows: he often omits the relative pronoun; he often uses the nominative case of the pronoun for the accusative case, and vice versa; he uses *him, her, me,* and *them* as true reflexives to mean *himself, herself, myself,* and *themselves;* he employs double negatives and double comparatives and superlatives; he shows a consciousness in the use of *thee* and *thou* of their application to intimates and inferiors and of their insulting quality when addressed to strangers (e.g., "If thou 'thou'-est him some thrice, it shall not be amiss," *Twelfth Night*, 3.2.43–4); he employs *which* to refer to both persons and things; and he does not discriminate closely between *ye*, nominative, and *you*, objective. He makes frequent use of the dative constructions, that is, the objective forms of the pronouns, *me, thee, you, him, her*, and so on, without prepositions where the meaning is "by me," "for me," "with me," "to me," "of me," and the like. For example:

> I am appointed *him* [by him] to murder you.
> (*The Winter's Tale*, 1.2.411)

> She looks *us* [to us] like
> A thing made more of malice than of duty.
> (*Cymbeline*, 3.5.32–3)

One prominent feature of Shakespeare's grammar is his use of the ethical dative, a construction in which the pronoun is generally used to indicate the person interested in the statement. In *King John* (3.4.146), the phrase "John lays you plots," means something like "John lays plots which you may profit by." In the following, *me* means "to my detriment" or "to my disadvantage":

> See how this river comes *me* cranking in
> And cuts *me* from the best of all my land
> A huge half-moon.
> (*1 Henry IV*, 3.1.95–7)

"Whip *me* such honest knaves" (*Othello*, 1.1.51) means "In my judgment such knaves should be whipped." In Quickly's description of Mistress Page, the dative *you* is equivalent to "mark you," "take notice":

> . . . a civil modest wife, and one, I tell you, that will not miss *you* morning nor evening prayer, as any is in Windsor.
> (*The Merry Wives of Windsor*, 2.2.92–4)

At times, however, the ethical dative is idiomatic and virtually without equivalent meaning in modern English; the sense of the passage is best obtained by omitting the pronoun.

Shakespeare, like other Renaissance poets, makes extensive use of the forms and figures of rhetoric. He is fond, for example, of using the abstract for the concrete, as in the words addressed by Surrey to Cardinal Wolsey: "Thou scarlet sin" (*Henry VIII*, 3.2.255). Transpositions are numerous, as are inversions, ellipses, and broken or confused constructions, as in the following examples:

> That thing you speak of,
> I took it for a man. (*Absolute construction.*)
> (*King Lear*, 4.6.77–8)

> Souls and bodies hath he divorced three. (*Transposition of adjective.*)
> (*Twelfth Night*, 3.4.238–9)

> A happy gentleman in blood and lineaments. (*Transposition of adjectival phrase.*)
> (*Richard II*, 3.1.9)

> Your state of fortune and your due of birth. (*Transposition of pronoun.*)
> (*Richard III*, 3.7.120)

> She calls me proud, and [says] that she could not love me. (*Ellipsis.*)
> (*As You Like It*, 4.3.17)

> Returning were as tedious as [to] go o'er. (*Ellipsis.*)
> (*Macbeth*, 3.4.139)

> They call him Doricles, and boasts himself
> To have a worthy feeding. (*Ellipsis of nominative.*)
> (*The Winter's Tale*, 4.4.168–9)

Of all men else I have avoided thee. (*Confusion of two constructions.*)

(*Macbeth,* 5.8.4)

The venom of such looks, we fairly hope,
Have lost their quality. (*Confusion of number arising from proximity.*)

(*Henry V,* 5.2.18–19)

Rather proclaim it, Westmorland, through my host
That he which hath no stomach to this fight,
Let him depart. (*Construction changed by change of thought.*)

(*Henry V,* 4.3.34–6)

For always I am Caesar. (*Inversion of adverb.*)

(*Julius Caesar,* 1.2.212)

Shakespeare often uses rhetorical figures for symmetrical effects, especially in the early, ornamental style of *Richard III* and the nondramatic poems. Following are definitions of some of the most popular figures he uses, with illustrations from *Venus and Adonis:*

1. *Parison.* The symmetrical repetition of words in grammatically parallel phrases: "How love makes young men thrall, and old men dote" (line 837).
2. *Isocolon.* The symmetrical repetition of sounds and words in phrases of equal length, as in the previous example, and in this: "Or as the wolf doth grin before he barketh, /Or as the berry breaks before it staineth" (lines 459–60). Parison and isocolon are frequently combined.
3. *Anaphora.* The symmetrical repetition of a word at the beginning of a sequence of clauses or sentences, often at the beginning of lines. Anaphora is frequently combined with parison and isocolon, as in the second example already given, and in this: " 'Give me my hand,' saith he. 'Why dost thou feel it?' / 'Give me my heart,' saith she, 'and thou shalt have it' " (lines 373–4).
4. *Antimetabole.* The symmetrical repetition of words in inverted order: "She clepes him king of graves and grave for kings" (line 995).
5. *Anadiplosis.* The beginning of a phrase with the final words of the previous phrase: "O, thou didst kill me; kill me once again!" (line 499).
6. *Epanalepsis.* The symmetrical repetition of a word or words at the beginning and ending of a line: "He sees his love, and nothing else he sees" (line 287).
7. *Ploce.* The insistent repetition of a word within the same line or phrase: "Then why not lips on lips, since eyes in eyes?" (line 120).
8. *Epizeuxis.* An intensified form of ploce, repeating the word without another intervening word: " 'Ay me!' she cries, and twenty times, 'Woe, woe!' / And twenty echoes twenty times cry so" (lines 833–4).
9. *Antanaclasis.* The shifting of a repeated word from one meaning to another: "My love to love is love but to disgrace it," or " 'Where did I leave?' 'No matter where,' quoth he, / 'Leave me' " (lines 412, 715–6).

For other figures and illustrations, see Sister Miriam Joseph, *Shakespeare's Use of the Arts of Language* (1947) and Brian Vickers, "Shakespeare's Use of Rhetoric," in *A New Companion to Shakespeare Studies,* edited by Kenneth Muir and S. Schoenbaum (1971).

Vocabulary

Renaissance English was hospitable to foreign importation. Many words taken directly from Latin became a permanent part of the language, serving to enrich its power to express thought and its rhythmical capabilities; others were ultimately discarded. The principal borrowings were in the realm of learning and culture. Such words usually retained a vital sense of their original Latin meaning. Sometimes such words have not replaced native words of the same meaning, so that we have such pairs of synonyms as *acknowledge* and *confess,* just as Shakespeare had *wonder* and *admiration.* Because of this Latin heritage, even a slight knowledge of Latin is a great advantage in the correct understanding of Elizabethan writers, since many Latin borrowings have taken on since the sixteenth century a different shade of meaning from that in which they were borrowed. The Latin sense of *aggravate* ("to add weight to") still struggles for recognition; but *apparent* no longer means primarily "visible to sight," and *intention* does not convey the idea of "intentness." The *Oxford English Dictionary* (*OED*) provides a wealth of information about derivations and changes in meaning.

Latin words were often taken over in their Latin forms, as *objectum* and *subjectum, statua* and *aristocratia,* and later were made to conform to English spelling and stress, though a few, such as *decorum,* still have a Latin form. French continued to be drawn upon and sometimes caused a new Latin borrowing to be adopted in a French form, just as, on the other hand, such words as *adventure* were supplied with a *d* to make them conform to Latin spelling. This principle is illustrated in the pedantry of Holofernes when he objects (*Love's Labor's Lost,* 5.1.20) to "det" as the pronunciation of "debt." Spanish, Italian, and Dutch also supplied many terms. Spanish gave words having to do with commerce, religion, and the New World, such as *mosquito, alligator, ambuscado,* and *grandee.* From Italian came terms of art, learning, and dueling: *bandetto, portico, canto, stoccato.* The Dutch contributed many nautical and oriental words.

These foreign borrowings were a part of what might be called the linguistic ambition of the age, a desire for forcible expression. Language was in a plastic state, so that it had an unparalleled freedom in both vocabulary and form. With this freedom, to be sure, came some confusion, since the Elizabethan era saw few efforts at grammatical precision. Such efforts were later to be made by the age of Dryden and the Royal Society, and by learned men ever since, prompted by an awareness that English was too vague and irregular for use as a means of scientific expression. Still, we readily perceive that English profited from its Renaissance expansion and its subsequent absorption with Shakespeare and the English Bible. It gained, for example, an increased facility in making compounds. Shakespeare, with his *cloud-capped towers* and his *home-keeping wits,* was a genius at this. Also from Shakespeare's time came the English adaptability in the use of prefixes, such as *dis-, re-,* and *en-,* and of suffixes, such as *-ful, -less, -ness,* and *-hood.*

EDITIONS AND EDITORS OF SHAKESPEARE

The earliest complete edition of Shakespeare's plays was the so-called First Folio of 1623, sponsored by Shakespeare's theatrical colleagues, John Heminges and Henry Condell. (A "folio" book was one in which the printing sheets were folded only once, each producing two "leaves," or four rather large printed pages of about 13 ½ × 8 ¼ inches. In a "quarto" book, the sheets were folded twice, producing eight pages on four leaves half the folio size.) The First Folio brought together eighteen plays that had previously been published individually in quarto volumes and eighteen plays that had never before been published. It did not include Shakespeare's nondramatic poetry, of which *Venus and Adonis* and *The Rape of Lucrece* had been published in 1593–1594 and the sonnets in 1609. Nor did it include *Pericles, The Two Noble Kinsmen,* and *Edward III.*

The nature of the early printed texts, and their relationship to what Shakespeare actually wrote, is a complex subject requiring some understanding of the physical process by which Elizabethan plays were written, prepared for staging, licensed, and printed. What sorts of manuscripts lie behind the various printed early editions we have, and how were those manuscripts modified successively by scribes, governmental officials, theatrical producers, actors, editors, compositors, proofreaders, and editors of subsequent editions? The problem is amplified by the fact that none of Shakespeare's manuscripts survives today. Consequently, textual critics can only theorize about the kinds of printer's copy that appear to underlie the printed texts we have. The resulting theories are necessarily conjectural, and they appear increasingly so in an age that general-

ly is wary of attempts to construct an authorial presence in a literary work. What follows here is an attempt to set forth what was once a widely adopted theory of textual origins, as devised by A. W. Pollard, R. B. McKerrow, W. W. Greg, Fredson Bowers, and others. Although, as we shall see, the various hypotheses about manuscript sources and types of quartos do not always account for the evidence, the theory itself still represents a once-prevailing set of assumptions against which the new textual scholarship offers its objections and qualifications, and hence needs to be laid out here. A good place to begin is with the hypothetical reconstruction of manuscripts.

Manuscripts

Most often, it seems, Elizabethan dramatic companies obtained a play by commissioning a known professional dramatist to write a new play, to revise an old one, or to collaborate with another author. Usually, the company paid the dramatist a flat fee. Shakespeare, on the other hand, was a "sharer" in the Chamberlain's (later the King's) company; that is, he was part owner and took a share of the profits. He may then have written plays not for a fee but as his chief contribution to the company's activities. Whatever the financial arrangement between author and company, in any case, the play became the property of the acting company, and the author gave up his individual right to sell it elsewhere. Moreover, he ordinarily wrote the play with a view not to publication, but to performance. Occasionally, a literary-minded author like Ben Jonson would see his plays through the press (and be scoffed at for his pretentiousness). Shakespeare, however, almost certainly did not do this. The quarto texts of his plays that appeared during his lifetime show no trace of having been prepared for the reader. They are playhouse documents.

When Shakespeare had finished writing a play, very likely in consultation with his fellow players, he presumably submitted a readable manuscript to his acting company. A certain amount of deletion, interlineation, inconsistency, and illegibility was inevitable. Authors' manuscripts became the property of the acting company and might be turned over to the printer when the company decided to sell its rights in a play. The company presumably would prefer to hold on to its theatrical copy of the play and to dispose of the authors' manuscript as of little further value if they chose to have a play printed. Such a supposed manuscript naturally would pose some difficulties for the compositor.

Since we lack manuscript copy for any printed play by Shakespeare or indeed generally by other playwrights, the business of determining from the printed plays themselves any clear evidence of their having been printed from mansucript copy is uncertain and provisional. Textual scholars like Greg and Bowers used to be more confident of such deductions than now seems tenable. Nonetheless, some educated guesswork as to whether the play was printed from authors' mansucript, or from a transcript of that manuscript, or from manuscript that had been marked up by the prompter for theatrical use, can be provisionally helpful in thinking about the nature of the printed text and what kinds of printing errors it might be especially prone to. Appendix 1 in this volume records, play by play, a summary of speculation concerning the kinds of manuscript lying behind the printed texts. The characterizations in Appendix 1 should be viewed with skepticism in light of these difficulties.

Among the Shakespearean quarto texts thought by Greg and others to have been based on authorial manuscripts are the first quartos of *Titus Andronicus, Love's Labor's Lost, A Midsummer Night's Dream, Richard II, The Merchant of Venice, Much Ado About Nothing,* and *1* and *2 Henry IV,* and the second quartos of *Romeo and Juliet* and *Hamlet.* Three more first quartos—*Troilus and Cressida, Othello,* and *King Lear*—were also thought to be based on authorial papers, each as an anomolous case. In addition, the First Folio contains several newly printed plays thought to be based on authorial manuscripts or transcripts thereof, including *The Comedy of Errors, The Taming of the Shrew, All's Well That Ends Well, Timon of Athens, Coriolanus,* and *Henry VIII.*

We might expect printed texts based on authorial papers to be close to what Shakespeare wrote but also to contain errors of transcription resulting from difficulties of deletion, illegibility, and the like encountered by the printers as they read their copy. Some printed texts presumably based on authorial manuscripts do indeed seem to preserve Shakespeare's work in an early state of composition: *Timon of Athens,* for example, seems never to have been finished by Shakespeare, since the text we have retains glaring inconsistencies and redundancies that he presumably would have straightened out in a final version. *Love's Labor's Lost* and *Romeo and Juliet* contain uncanceled duplicatory passages. On the other hand, *The Merchant of Venice, Richard II,* and the *Henry IV* plays are very good texts, and *Much Ado* is almost ready for stage production; the names of two actors appear among the speech prefixes, although other irregularities suggest that the manuscript was in the last stages of authorial revision. The hypothesis therefore represents a whole spectrum of states from unrevised manuscript to a text that has been thoroughly worked over.

In addition to the fact that we lack an existing manuscript for any of Shakespeare's plays, we need to recognize that hypothesizing a distinction between texts based on authorial papers and those based on theatrical copy is entirely prone to compromise and unclear distinctions. Authors' papers may well have been used sometimes by the acting company without recopying and without extensive annotation for purposes of production. Authors might well think in terms of production needs and add stage directions intended for the players; Shakespeare was, after all, a member of his acting company. Play texts that scholars have tentatively classified as based on authorial manuscripts not infrequently contain details that sounds like something the prompter would want to add, and conversely texts that are presumed to be based on theatrical copy are not infrequently careless of details that one might have supposed a prompter would have wished to remedy or clarify for the acting company.

Given all these formidable difficulties, we must be cautious. In theory, an author's manuscript is thought to be identifiable behind the printed text through some of the following characteristics: vagueness in specifying the number of supernumeraries needed for a scene, lack of precision in the marking of entrances and especially exits, authorial stage directions that tend to describe stage business or the emotional states of the characters, speech prefixes that inconsistently refer to a character both by personal name and generic title, and so on. Thus, in *Love's Labor's Lost,* Navarre, Armado, and Holofernes are at times referred to as King, Braggart, and Pedant; Navarre is also called Ferdinand.

Licensing for Performance

Before one of Shakespeare's plays could go into production, it had to be licensed by the Master of the Revels, an officer of the royal household responsible for supervising court entertainments. Since the beginning of Elizabeth's reign, and even earlier, dramatic performances throughout England had been made subject to governmental control. Elizabeth had authorized municipal and other local governments to scrutinize plays performed within their jurisdictions. In the vicinity of London, however, where municipal hostility toward the theater was particularly strong, she took the unusual step in 1581 of transferring licensing power to her own Master of the Revels. Since many public plays came to court, as we have seen, Elizabeth was inclined to protect the players against the city authorities in this way and to adopt the useful fiction that public performances were rehearsals of plays intended for her ultimate benefit.

The Master of the Revels did occasionally censor Shakespeare's plays. For example, the scene of Richard II's deposition, omitted from the three earliest quarto editions of the play, may have been disallowed for acting during Elizabeth's lifetime. (She was sensitive to a widespread and libelous analogy comparing her with

A CATALOGVE

of the feuerall Comedies, Hiftories, and Tragedies contained in this Volume.

John Heminges and Henry Condell, Shakespeare's fellow actors, gathered contents for the First Folio, published in 1623. They collected thirty-six plays in the volume, omitting Pericles and The Two Noble Kinsmen. Troilus and Cressida is included in most copies of the First Folio but is not listed here in the contents.

Richard.) More often, one suspects, the mere threat of censorship was sufficient to keep the London dramatic companies in line. The Tudor establishment had no intention of tolerating openly seditious criticism in the drama. Generally, the Master of the Revels was more concerned with questions of religion and politics than with morals. Edmund Tilney served as Master of the Revels from 1579 to 1610, when he was succeeded by his deputy, Sir George Buc. In 1622, the office passed to Sir Henry Herbert.

The Playbook

The document on which the Master of the Revels affixed his seal of approval was the playbook, often referred to in recent scholarship as the "prompt-book" or "prompt-copy," that is, the version prepared by the acting company for use in actual production. Sometimes this version may have been a fair copy of the manuscript, readied for stage performance, that is, with the odd technical inconsistency weeded out and with briefer but sometimes incomplete stage directions added marginally. One possibility is that the author's last draft might be converted into a playbook. Whatever manuscript was thus used, McKerrow once supposed that the playbook would undertake to normalize any inconsistent speech prefixes (such as those already noted in *Love's Labor's Lost*), in order to avoid confusion for actors and stage managers, but this supposition is not well supported by evidence from extant manuscripts. Perhaps the prompter would add some stage directions, concentrating on such technical matters as entrances and occasional specific effects. In *Julius Caesar*, for example, we find such stage directions as *"Enter Brutus in his orchard," "Thunder and lightning. Enter Julius Caesar in his nightgown,"* and *"Brutus goes into the pulpit."* We cannot be sure, however, that these are not authorial stage directions, and, indeed, recent evidence suggests that the acting company often did rather little to an authorial manuscript to ready it for production. Shakespeare was an acting member of his own company and must have known what his colleagues wanted, so that revision of his final draft need not have been extensive. Examination of existing playbooks by dramatists other than Shakespeare suggests that such playbooks were annotated in a variety of ways: sometimes with actors' names, sometimes with warnings for entrances and props, sometimes with calls for sound effects, and sometimes with stage directions repeated in more visible locations in the margins and highlighted with rules. Seldom does annotation follow a now-recoverable pattern within a manuscript or across various manuscripts. The category of "playbook" is not as certain today as it seemed to Greg and others.

Comparatively few of Shakespeare's printed texts are thought to be derived from playbooks, actually, since the playbook, bearing the official license of the Master of the Revels, was an invaluable document if the play was ever to be revived. Of the nineteen Shakespearean plays published in quarto prior to 1623, not one seems to have been printed from a playbook. Nevertheless, the First Folio does contain a few plays seemingly printed from playbooks or transcripts of playbooks, including *As You Like It, Twelfth Night, Julius Caesar*, and *Macbeth* (in a cut version). Two more plays—*The Two Gentlemen of Verona* and *The Merry Wives of Windsor*—were evidently printed from transcriptions by Ralph Crane of playbooks. Three other plays, *1 Henry VI, Antony and Cleopatra*, and *Cymbeline*, have been thought to contain some annotations by the stage adapter.

Playbooks are presumably not as likely to correspond with the author's intentions as his own papers, and indeed, some playbooks probably reflect changes occurring in the theater over a period of years. A playbook might be altered for the revival of an old favorite or might even represent a cut performance intended to be taken on tour—as perhaps in the case of *Macbeth*. Such a text might incorporate non-Shakespearean material; *Macbeth* contains songs and lines attributed to Thomas Middleton.

Playbooks were presumably also used to copy out individual parts for each actor. Although such actors' "rolls," as they were called, could conceivably have been used to assemble a printed text, no Shakespearean play is known to have been printed in this fashion. A few plays, such as *The Two Gentlemen of Verona* and *The Winter's Tale*, were once thought to have been made up out of actors' rolls, since the texts of these plays generally omit stage directions and group characters' names at the head of each scene; however, these traits are now known to be the identifying characteristics of the professional scrivener named Ralph Crane. Apparently, Crane was employed to prepare copies (also including *The Tempest, The Merry Wives of Windsor*, and *Measure for Measure*) for the printers of the First Folio.

The Question of "Unauthorized" Quartos

An acting company presumably had some concern to get its plays into print, chiefly for the purpose of advertising. The acting company's name almost invariably appears prominently on the title page of a play—which, until the seventeenth century, often provided no playwright's name. At the same time, other copies of plays might well exist besides those owned by acting companies, and copies such as these might conceivably find their way into print. According to Humphrey

Moseley's "The Stationer to the Readers" in the Beaumont and Fletcher Folio (1646), actors sometimes sold patrons transcripts of what was acted. Copies might be obtained by other means. If a bookseller chose to risk the capital to print a play that he had somehow obtained, he might then present his copy of it at Stationers' Hall and enter it in the Stationers' Register, or the official record book of the London Company of Stationers (i.e., booksellers). By paying a fee, usually sixpence, he reserved the right to publish the work he had thus entered. Indeed, even if a book was printed without having been entered in the Stationers' Register, it evidently received the protection of copyright by the very act of printing. Copyright had considerable legal force. Although authors and acting companies could not copyright their plays, the stationers or booksellers enjoyed a tight monopoly. Their London Company of Stationers had a patent from the crown to restrict the number of presses operating in London, the number of books that could be printed, and so on.

A. W. Pollard was followed by many twentieth-century textual critics in imagining that the acting companies were concerned to keep their plays out of print as long as the plays could hold the stage and in furthering imagining that the stationers were desperate to get plays into print in whatever form, however corrupt, to feed an presumably bottomless market of play-readers. Consequently Pollard and his followers have argued that acting companies protected themselves by entering into agreements with cooperative booksellers. The acting companies, according to this theory, might allow a friendly bookseller or a printer to register a play for later publication. For example, on July 22, 1598, the printer James Roberts entered in the Stationers' Register "a booke of the Marchaunt of Venyce, or otherwise called the Jewe Of Venyce, Prouided, that yt bee not prynted by the said James Robertes or anye other whatsoeuer without lycence first had from the Right honorable the lord Chamberlen." This is what is generally known as a "staying entry," since Roberts agrees to "stay" or withhold publication pending further authorization from the acting company's patron. Similar entries occur in August 1600 for *Much Ado About Nothing, As You Like It*, and *Henry V*, although a Quarto of *Henry V* appeared in August 1600. The argument that such staying entries were designed to forestall the activities of less scrupulous publishers has been exploded, however, by Peter Blayney ("The Publication of Playbooks," in *A New History of Early English Drama*, ed. John D. Cox and David Scott Kastan, 1997), who shows that a large proportion of books in the Stationers' Register was given only conditional entrance. Moreover, Blayney's research, indicating how small was the proportion of plays in the overall publication schedule of London

publishers, calls into question the idea that stationers were so hungry for plays that they would resort to any means to get them. All in all, Pollard's theory that the printers of the so-called bad quartos were somehow unscrupulous has been thoroughly challenged.

How much credence should we give to complaints that corrupt texts of plays were somehow stolen to be put into print? A prefatory letter "To the great Variety of Readers" of the First Folio signed by Heminges and Condell complains that "before" publication of the Folio, readers "were abused with divers stolen and surreptitious copies, maimed and deformed by the frauds and stealths of injurious imposters." Thomas Heywood similarly protests against unauthorized editions of his plays, which "have (unknown to me, and without any of my direction) accidentally come into the printer's hands, and therefore so corrupt and mangled (copied only by the ear) that I have been unable to know them" (Preface to *The Rape of Lucrece*, 1608).

How were such corrupt and mangled texts obtained? Heywood says they were "copied only by the ear." Elsewhere, in *Pleasant Dialogues and Dramas* (1637), he complains about the pirating of one of his plays "by stenography." Yet the stenographic hypothesis may not account for most cases of reported texts. The apparently corrupted texts we have seem to rely instead on the use of memory.

Most such texts, according to W. W. Greg, were put together by "memorial reconstruction." The agents sometimes may have been one or more actors, especially temporary actors hired to perform minor roles, rather than actor-sharers. Possibly, one or more such minor actors got together and slowly recited what they could remember of a play, while a scribe took down what they recited. The reporter or reporters of a pirated text can sometimes tentatively be identified by the relative accuracy of certain roles. For example, the actor who perhaps played the minor part of Marcellus in *Hamlet* may have helped in the memorial reconstruction of some of the first act of the unauthorized quarto of that play.

A quarto put together in some part by memorial reconstruction reveals itself by certain characteristics, although the matter of identification is in some dispute. Such a text tends to give a fairly accurate rendition of the overall plot but garbles some speeches, transfers or misplaces lines of dialogue or even whole scenes, borrows scraps of phrases from other plays in which the actor-reporters may have acted, mislineates blank verse or crudely versifies passages of prose, ad-libs freely in half-remembered parts of the play, and so on. A memorially reported quarto is always shorter than the regular version. Visual impressions are often vivid, since the actor-reporters are remembering things they have seen on stage. The stage directions tend to be more frequent and more detailed than in either an author's manuscript or a playbook.

The theory of memorial reconstruction was once thought to have application to dozens of plays from Shakespeare's time. Now it is thought to explain, although only in part, the origin of the 1602 Quarto of *The Merry Wives of Windsor* (the text for which Greg originally devised the fullest elaboration of the theory), and, in even smaller part, the origin of the 1603 Quarto of *Hamlet*. The theory has also been attached to the Quarto versions of *2 Henry VI* and *3 Henry VI* known as *The First Part of the Contention betwixt the Two Famous Houses of York and Lancaster* and *The True Tragedy of Richard Duke of York* (1594 and 1595), as well as to the 1597 Quarto of *Romeo and Juliet,* the 1600 Quarto of *Henry V* (1600), and the 1609 Quarto of *Pericles* (the only substantive text we have of this play), but the application of the theory to these texts is very hard to maintain. The title page of the Second Quarto of *Romeo and Juliet* in 1599, advertising itself as "New corrected, augmented, and amended," does suggest a desire to correct the earlier Quarto, but need not necessitate a theory of memorial reconstruction for that earlier edition. A similar phrase, "Newly corrected and augmented," appeared on the title page of the 1598 Quarto of *Love's Labor's Lost,* implying an earlier edition in need of improvement, but if such an edition ever existed, it has disappeared.

A few texts seem to have been put together by unusual circumstances that somewhat resemble memorial reconstruction, so that the number of quartos to be characterized as "bad" remains in dispute. *The Taming of the Shrew* was not printed until the Folio of 1623, but a Quarto did appear in 1594 of a very similar play, called *The Taming of a Shrew.* Its place names and characters' names are different from those of the Folio version, and the language differs throughout. Some scholars still regard the play as a source for Shakespeare. Nevertheless, the generally held view today is that *A Shrew* is a special kind of pirated text, one in which a rival dramatist has changed the language and the names of the characters to make the work seem his own. A different sort of anomaly is seen in *Richard III*. The 1597 Quarto may be one in which the acting company had a hand, putting together an acting version for performance on tour when the original text was not available. Whatever the circumstances, we can see that the category of so-called "bad" quartos is problematic as to how many quartos belong in this group and how their various defects may have come about. Nonetheless, A. W. Pollard's distinction between "good" and "bad" continues to be embraced in some form by some textual critics today.

The So-Called "Good" Quartos

The so-called "good" quartos, according to Pollard's theory, were based generally on Shakespeare's own drafts or on transcripts of them. Good first quartos, as thus defined, include *Titus Andronicus* (1594), *Richard II* (1597), *1 Henry IV* (1598), *Love's Labor's Lost* (1598), *Romeo and Juliet* (1599), *2 Henry IV* (1600), *A Midsummer Night's Dream* (1600), *The Merchant of Venice* (1600), *Much Ado About Nothing* (1600), *Hamlet* (1604–1605), *Troilus and Cressida* (1609, printed seemingly without permission of Shakespeare's company), and the late First Quarto of *Othello* (1622). This is a short list and is sporadic in its time schedule; booksellers, it seems, were wary of plays as investments. Once a play had appeared in print, it sometimes sold well and sometimes not. *Richard II* went through five quartos before the Folio of 1623. At the other extreme, we have *2 Henry IV*, issued in only one quarto prior to 1623; possibly the printers ran off a large number of copies in anticipation of heavy sales, or perhaps, as Peter Blayney argues, the book-buying market may have been glutted with plays. Some quarto texts continued to appear after the Folio of 1623.

Licensing for Printing

Before a play could be printed, it had to be licensed. The licensing agency responsible for printed matter was a panel of London clergymen known as the "correctors of the press," operating under the authority of the Privy Council, the Bishop of London, the Archbishop of Canterbury, and the Lord Chamberlain. In 1606, Parliament passed a law forbidding references to the Deity in the performance of plays. This legislation, though not aimed at publication per se, had a visible effect on printed texts. Plays printed before 1606 and then revised for subsequent publication after that date show the effects of this censorship.

The Pavier Collection of 1619

A few years before the Shakespearean First Folio appeared in 1623, a bookseller named Thomas Pavier and a printer named William Jaggard made an apparent attempt to collect Shakespeare's plays. Pavier already owned the publishing rights to *Henry V*, for in August 1600 he had received assignment of rights to the memorially reconstructed Quarto of the play published in that year. He brought out a Second Quarto of *Henry V* in 1602 and a Third (printed by Jaggard) in 1619 as part of his anthologizing project. In 1602, Pavier had also obtained the rights to *The First Part of the Contention* and *The True Tragedy of Richard Duke of York*, now generally regarded as the unauthorized quartos of *2* and *3 Henry VI*. Pavier issued them in 1619 under the combined title *The Whole Contention between the Two Famous Houses, Lancaster and York*, printed by Jaggard. Pavier also included in his collection two pseudo-Shakespearean plays to which he owned the rights, *A Yorkshire Tragedy* and *Sir John Oldcastle*, and five Shakespearean plays to which he may have obtained rights or which he considered to be unowned: *A Midsummer Night's Dream, The Merchant of Venice, The Merry Wives of Windsor, King Lear*, and *Pericles*.

Pavier's evident intention was to publish these ten plays in a single volume, and, indeed, two such copies exist today—one in the Folger Library and one in the Lewis Collection at Texas Christian University. Pavier's scheme was frustrated, however, seemingly by the Lord Chamberlain at the instigation of Shakespeare's company. Pavier chose the expedient of publishing his plays separately, some with fraudulently early dates and names of publishers on their title pages in an apparent attempt to obscure the fact of new publication. Whether Pavier's texts contain any textual authority is a vexing question. They are, for the most part, copied from earlier quartos, and yet at times (in *Henry V, The Contention*, and *The True Tragedy*), they anticipate Folio readings in departing from their printed copy, and in the latter half of *King Lear*, the Pavier Quarto anticipates Folio line divisions. Possibly, this evidence points to an infusion of new manuscript source material into the Pavier quartos, but it may instead reflect a consultation of the Pavier quartos during the printing of the Folio.

Publishing Rights for the 1623 Folio

Pavier's dubious and abortive undertaking may possibly have given impetus to a more legitimate edition of Shakespeare's collected plays, some seven years after the author's death, although Shakespeare's company may already have been contemplating such an honor to its famous playwright. Ben Jonson's folio collection of plays in 1616 had established a major precedent for such a volume, despite the scorn of those who regarded all plays as subliterary. The large and tomelike folio format, normally reserved for edifying religious tracts, the "works" of classical authorities, and the like, might now be used also for a collection of plays.

The first task facing the supervisors of the Folio collection, Heminges and Condell, was the assembling of publishing rights to those eighteen Shakespearean plays that had already appeared in print. The most efficient means of doing so was to form a syndicate of publishers who already owned the rights to a large number of the plays. The colophon at the very end of the First Folio names those who took part: "Printed at the charges of W. Jaggard, Ed. Blount, I. Smithweeke, and W. Aspley, 1623." William Jaggard had succeeded to the printing business of James Roberts in 1608. Despite Jaggard's part in the printing of the Pavier quartos of 1619, he evident-

Martin Droeshout's engraving on the title page of the First Folio is one of only two authentic likenesses of Shakespeare in existence.

ly remained on good terms with Shakespeare's company and became (together with his son Isaac) the printer of the 1623 Folio. (William Jaggard died in November 1623, but his son continued to carry on the business as he had during his father's blindness.) Edward Blount had registered *Antony and Cleopatra* and *Pericles* in 1608, though he seems to have overlooked the fact, for *Antony* was reregistered in 1623, and *Pericles* never appeared in the Folio. John Smethwick had received from Nicholas Ling the rights to *Love's Labor's Lost, Romeo and Juliet*, and *Hamlet* in 1607. William Aspley owned the rights to *Much Ado About Nothing* and *2 Henry IV*. One other previously published play, *A Midsummer Night's Dream*, was "derelict" or no longer assigned to a publisher.

Some further negotiations must still have been necessary, with Richard Bonian and Henry Walley for *Troilus and Cressida*, with Nathaniel Butter for *King Lear*, with Thomas Pavier for *2* and *3 Henry VI, Titus Andronicus*, and *Henry V*, perhaps also with Edward White for *Titus Andronicus*, with Matthew Law for *Richard III, Richard II*, and *1 Henry IV*, with Thomas Heyes for *The Merchant of*

Venice, with Arthur Johnson for *The Merry Wives of Windsor,* and with Thomas Walkley for *Othello.* The last-minute inclusion of *Troilus and Cressida* between the histories and the tragedies with incomplete pagination may suggest that Bonian and Walley held out for a long time.

Eighteen plays had never before been printed. To secure rights to these plays, Messrs. Blount and Isaac Jaggard caused the following entry to be made in the Stationers' Register on November 8, 1623:

Mr. Blount, Isaac Jaggard: Entered for their copy under the hands of Mr. Dr. Worrall and Mr. Cole, Warden, Mr. William Shakespeare's Comedies, Histories, and Tragedies, so many of the said copies as are not formerly entered to other men, viz.: Comedies: *The Tempest, The Two Gentlemen of Verona, Measure for Measure, The Comedy of Errors, As You Like It, All's Well That Ends Well, Twelfth Night, The Winter's Tale.* Histories: *The Third Part of Henry the Sixth, Henry the Eighth.* Tragedies: *Coriolanus, Timon of Athens, Julius Caesar, Macbeth, Antony and Cleopatra, Cymbeline.*

The Stationers' Register list includes only sixteen names, since *The Taming of the Shrew* and *King John* were considered to have been published previously: *The Taming of a Shrew* and *The Troublesome Reign of King John,* now generally regarded as an adaptation and a source, respectively, had appeared in print in 1594 and 1591. Two plays on the list had actually been registered previously: *As You Like It* and *Antony and Cleopatra.* "The Third Part of Henry the Sixth" refers to *1 Henry VI,* since the other two *Henry VI* plays had already been published as quartos.

The Texts Used for the 1623 Folio

In addition to securing publishing rights, Heminges and Condell and their associates had the further task of selecting copy from which the printers were to set up their work. In the case of the eighteen as yet unpublished plays, the editors selected various manuscripts: the author's draft, or, just as likely, a transcript of it for *All's Well,* perhaps the playbook for *As You Like It,* a scribal transcript for *Twelfth Night,* and so on. Perhaps the editors planned at first to give the printers clean new transcriptions of such plays, for the first four plays in the Folio— *The Tempest, The Two Gentlemen of Verona, The Merry Wives of Windsor,* and *Measure for Measure*—were all printed from copies made by the professional scribe Ralph Crane. If the editors had planned to continue this practice throughout the volume, however, they abandoned it after the fourth play and turned instead to a variety of sorts of copy. An alternative explanation is that the editors had these four clean copies on hand and chose to begin the volume with them simply because they were available and ready for the printer.

The complicated choices involved plays that had already been published. Printers, then as now, preferred to work from printed copy because of its legibility.

Although one might suppose that Heminges and Condell would have set aside unauthorized quartos entirely, they did not always do so, perhaps because the manuscript alternatives were illegible or defective. In other cases, the editors had to make a more subtle choice between a "good" quarto and a still better manuscript. What the editors sometimes did in such cases was to use the inferior printed text but to annotate it by reference to a superior manuscript. This process of annotation might vary widely in its degree of thoroughness.

The use of inferior quartos as copy was, to be sure, unusual. The Folio text of *Henry V* seems to have been sporadically contaminated by the Third Quarto, which was derived from the Quarto of 1600, but probably the Third Quarto did not, in fact, serve as printer's copy. On the other hand, the Folio text of *2 Henry VI* may actually have been set in part from pages of the Third Quarto, derived from the First Quarto, and some editors argue that the same is basically true of *3 Henry VI.* Even in these questionable cases, an attempt seems to have been made to overcome the limitations of the defective quarto copy.

More often, one of the good quartos was corrected by checking it against a manuscript source. The Folio text of *Titus Andronicus,* for example, was evidently derived from a copy of the Third Quarto, but that copy may have been corrected by reference to some other copy, perhaps the playbook. In any case, a portion of Act 3 that is missing from all the early quartos must have been derived from some manuscript source. In some cases, later quartos supplied material missing from earlier ones. In still other instances, as in *Richard III, Troilus and Cressida, Othello, King Lear, Hamlet,* and *2 Henry IV,* the relationship of Quarto text to the Folio text is extraordinarily complicated. See Appendix 1 for statements on the texts of each play.

The Printing of the 1623 Folio

The printing of the 1623 Folio continued from April 1621 to December 1623 in the printing shop of William and Isaac Jaggard. The compositors who actually set the type were, according to Charlton Hinman (*The Printing and Proof-Reading of the First Folio of Shakespeare,* 2 vols., 1963), five in number. For convenient reference, they are designated as compositors A through E. A and B were the principal workmen. E was evidently an inept apprentice, unfortunately brought into the project just in time to work on several of the tragedies. Still other compositors have been proposed since Hinman's time, namely, F, H, I, and J, at least some of which are problematic—F likely being D, and J almost certainly A. (See Peter W. M. Blayney, *The First Folio of Shakespeare,* Folger Shakespeare Library, Washington, D.C., 1991.)

Compositors had to rely on their ability to memorize large segments of their copy—perhaps whole lines of verse—at a time, since they needed to look at the type they were setting manually. Hence, they were apt to make mistakes based on imperfect remembering. Less skillful compositors not infrequently introduced errors by transposing words in a line, substituting a new word for what was in the copy, or maiming the scansion of a line of verse by adding or subtracting syllables.

Compositors were largely responsible for the "pointing" or punctuation of the text. They also usually imposed their own spelling practices on their copy. No copy editor went over the materials first to normalize spelling, and the compositors were free to normalize as they chose. They occasionally used variant spellings to "justify" prose lines. Elizabethan spelling was, in any case, chaotic by our standards. The modern textual business of identifying compositors relies mainly on discovering the characteristic spelling habits of each.

Rather than setting their pages in numbered sequence right through an entire play, as we would assume, the compositors of the Folio used a system known as "casting off": that is, they estimated the amount of copy needed to fill a page of type and divided the whole text up into portions of the estimated correct length. They could then begin by setting pages six and seven, and would immediately start printing these two pages side by side on the same "forme" or side of a sheet. (When three large sheets are folded once and gathered together, the result is a "quire" of twelve pages, with pages one and twelve printed on the outer side or "forme" of the outermost sheet, pages two and eleven on the inner forme of that same sheet, pages three and ten on the outer forme of the middle sheet, and so on.) Since type was expensive and in limited supply in a printing shop, the type had to be redistributed into the type cases as soon as the requisite number of copies of any forme had been run off. Casting off enabled the printers to print and redistribute the type of pages six and seven without having to wait for all the intervening pages to be set up also. (The reappearance of distributed type is, in fact, one clue by which Hinman was able to discover that the Folio had been set up throughout by casting off rather than by printing in sequence.)

Despite the advantages of flexibility, casting off had its disadvantages. If a compositor discovered he had been given too little copy for a page of text, he had to stretch his material by heavy "leading" or spacing. If, on the other hand, he discovered he had been given too much copy for a page, he had to crowd his lines, print verse as prose, or even eliminate words and lines. Knowledge of this sort of printing information is useful to modern editors, since it enables them to determine when the compositors may have interfered with the text that Shakespeare wrote.

When a compositor had completed one entire forme, consisting of two pages of text to be printed on one side of a large printing sheet, the forme went into the press and the requisite number of copies was run off by hand.

One side of the sheet, either the inner or outer forme, was printed at a time. Proofreading, or "press correction," may have been done in part by checking the "foul proof" before the press run began, but further proofreading took place while the printing continued. At first, a number of sides of the sheet would be printed in their uncorrected state, that is, entirely unproofread. When the press corrector found more errors, the presses would be stopped so that the errors might be corrected, after which printing would continue. Such interruptions might occur several times. Uncorrected or partially corrected sheets were not destroyed, however; paper was too costly for that. Later, when the stacks of sheets printed on one side were printed on the other side, errors would again be corrected as printing continued. Ultimately, when the sheets were gathered by threes into a quire of twelve pages and then sewn into a complete volume, no single copy of the Folio was apt to be exactly like another. In fact, the many copies of the First Folio extant today differ from one another in their press variants. Even though we might regard this as evidence of carelessness, Jaggard's work on the First Folio seems to have been scrupulous when judged by the standards of the day.

At a guess, about 750 copies of the First Folio were printed and sold for as much as twenty shillings, though the price could vary depending on markup; the cost of an unbound copy, retail, may have been around fifteen shillings. Approximately 230 copies survive today, of which seventy-nine bound folios, not all complete copies, plus some fragments, are to be found in the collection of the Folger Library, Washington, D.C.

The Later Folios

When, after nine years, the first edition of the Folio had been sold out, a second edition was printed in 1632 by Thomas Cotes. He had succeeded to the Jaggards' business after the death of Isaac in 1627. The Second Folio merely reprinted the text of the First Folio together with a considerable number of editorial emendations. These have no independent textual authority, although some of the more commonsense suggestions have since been adopted by modern editors. A third edition appeared in 1663, based on the second. A second issue of this same third edition in 1664 included seven new plays: *Pericles, The London Prodigal, Thomas Lord Cromwell, Sir John Oldcastle, The Puritan, A Yorkshire Tragedy*, and *Locrine*. Of these, only *Pericles* has gained general acceptance in the Shakespeare canon (see Appendix 1 and the Introduction to the play). A fourth edition of the Folio in 1685, based on the third, also included the seven new plays. Like the second and third editions, this fourth edition offered many emendations or new errors not based on any textual authority.

Later Editions

The first editor of Shakespeare in the modern sense of the term was Nicholas Rowe. His six-volume edition of 1709 (reedited in eight volumes in 1714) was based on the Fourth Folio, to which the publisher Jacob Tonson had acquired the rights. Rowe began many practices we now regard as standard for a reader's edition. He provided a complete list of *dramatis personae* for each play, whereas the earlier folios had done so only sporadically. Similarly, he extended the practice of announcing the locale at the beginning of a scene. He marked entrances and exits with more care than in the folios and provided more extensive division of the plays into acts and scenes. Although he did not consult Shakespeare's early texts, Rowe did offer a number of textual emendations. He also modernized spelling and punctuation.

Alexander Pope was Shakespeare's next editor. Pope's text, completed in 1725 in six volumes (2nd edition, 1728), was printed from a copy of Rowe's edition with Pope's annotations. Pope excluded *Pericles* and the spurious plays that had been added to the Third Folio, although a companion volume containing these plays appeared with the second edition of 1728, lacking Pope's name and perhaps not authorized by him. He completed Rowe's task of indicating locale for each of the scenes, and also completed the division of the text into acts and scenes. In fact, Pope used the "continental" system of marking a new scene whenever a major character comes on stage, so that his text contained many more scenes than did other editions. Most importantly, Pope regarded Shakespeare's text as something to be "improved," because it had been written in a barbaric age for irresponsible actors all too ready to take liberties with the text, and for ignorant spectators. Although he claimed to have consulted the early quartos, Pope excised parts of Shakespeare's text that he considered vulgar, regularized lines that struck him as defective, eliminated anachronisms he regarded as indecorous, and the like. Pope's edition reflected the "refined" eighteenth-century view of Shakespeare as a very rough diamond in need of polishing. Some of the "improvements" are convincing and have been adopted by more recent editors, but most are sophistications that, for a time, moved Shakespearean editing away from the purpose of recovering what Shakespeare had actually written.

A corrective was in order. Lewis Theobald took up the challenge, though he was to be rewarded for his pains by being crowned the King of Dullness in Pope's *The Dunciad* (1728 version). Theobald's edition appeared in 1733 and was later reissued several times. He was the first editor to consult the folios and quartos. He did not, however, wholly recognize the textual value of those quartos. He also failed to base his text directly on the earliest substantive texts; instead, he annotated a copy of Pope's edition, just as Pope had annotated Rowe and Rowe had annotated

the Fourth Folio. Despite his consultation of the early texts and his occasional brilliance as an emender, therefore, Theobald inevitably perpetuated more errors than he eliminated from the Rowe-Pope tradition.

The convention of relying on one's predecessor's edition continued to afflict eighteenth-century editing of Shakespeare. Sir Thomas Hanmer (1743–1744) and William Warburton (1747) contributed some emendations that are used today but tended to follow their predecessors. (This Warburton is not, however, the John Warburton whose cook is said to have burned a number of now-lost early editions of plays by using them to line pie plates.) Even Dr. Johnson (1765), who set a standard of conservatism in admitting emendations to the Shakespearean text, based his edition almost entirely on Theobald's of 1757, with only occasional use of Warburton's. Johnson's account of the text took an unfriendly view toward the interference of scribes, players, and printers; he shared Pope's dismay at the conditions under which Shakespeare wrote but mistrusted Pope's poetic "improvements" as too subjective.

Only with Edward Capell (1768) did an eighteenth-century editor finally base his text on the original Folio and quartos. Capell amassed an admirable collection of quartos and was the first to recognize that they might sometimes be preferred as copy text to the Folio itself. Unlike his eighteenth-century predecessors, who generally dismissed the quartos as based on playbooks and hence contaminated by theatrical revision, Capell thought that they usually represented Shakespeare's own drafts. At the same time, Capell's principle of selection was too eclectic in that he was ready to choose any early reading, whether from the first printing or a derivative one, so long as it offered what he regarded as an improvement. Capell's work heavily influenced George Steevens's 1773 revision of Dr. Johnson's text.

Edmund Malone, at first a collaborator with Steevens and later his rival, issued a ten-volume edition in 1790. Malone reintroduced *Pericles*, which Pope and subsequent editors had eliminated along with the spurious plays of the Third Folio. Malone brought to his editing an extensive knowledge of Elizabethan documents, such as the Stationers' Register, Henslowe's *Diary*, and the records of the Master of the Revels. His most important contribution to theory of editing was to grant authority only to the earliest printing of any version of a play—a principle that he had trouble applying in some cases, however, because the false-dated Pavier quartos had yet to be sorted out. He left uncompleted a variorum edition recording all textual variants; this edition was finished in 1821 by James Boswell, son of Dr. Johnson's biographer, and became known as the Third Variorum because Isaac Reed's earlier editions (1803, 1813) had called themselves the First and Second Variorums. The so-called New Variorum Shakespeare continued this tradition under Henry Howard Furness, beginning in 1871.

Nineteenth-century editions were numerous. One of the most famous and influential was the "bowdlerized" or expurgated *Family Shakespeare* of the Rev. Thomas Bowdler, done with the assistance of his daughter Henrietta; first appearing in 1807 and then in 1818, it soon extended its influence throughout the English-speaking world. Other editions included those of S. W. Singer (1826, 1855–1856), John Payne Collier (1842–1844, 1858, 1875–1878), Charles Knight (1838–1843, 1842–1844, 1867), Alexander Dyce (1857, 1864–1867, 1875–1876), Howard Staunton (1858–1860), Nikolaus Delius (1854–1861, 1864), H. N. Hudson (1851–1856, 1880–1881), Thomas Keightley (1864), and Charles and Mary Cowden Clarke (1864–1868). Editors from this period were generally absorbed with reading different printed versions as if they represented different authorial versions and with an unresolved debate as to whether the "bad" quarto of *Hamlet*, among others, represented authorial versions or else derivative and corrupt versions of fuller texts.

The outstanding scholarly edition of the nineteenth century was the so-called Cambridge Shakespeare of William George Clark and William Aldis Wright (1863–1866), issued in 1864 in a single volume known as the Globe text. Although its choice of copy texts has been challenged in two or three instances by twentieth-century bibliographical research, the Globe text was soundly edited for its day and soon established itself as definitive. Its act and scene divisions and its line numbering became standards of reference for concordances, works of literary criticism, and the like.

Later nineteenth- and early twentieth-century editions included those of W. J. Rolfe (1871–1896), Appleton Morgan (1888), F. A. Marshall and others (The Henry Irving Shakespeare, 1888–1890), Sir Israel Gollancz (The Temple Shakespeare, 1894–1895), W. J. Craig (1891), C. H. Herford (1899), and Helen Porter and Charlotte Clarke (1903–1914). Influential American editions included those of W. A. Neilson (1906) and George Lyman Kittredge (1936).

The twentieth century has seen an enormous increase in the information available on bibliographical matters: printing-house procedures, the mechanics of book production, watermarks, printer's ornaments, Elizabethan handwriting, spelling, punctuation, and the like. Prominent among bibliographical studies are those that laid the basis for the standard "received" theories of editorial scholarship discussed previously. These include A. W. Pollard's *Shakespeare's Folios and Quartos* (1909) and *Shakespeare's Hand in the Play of Sir Thomas More* (1923); R. B. McKerrow's *An Introduction to Bibliography for Literary Students* (1927) and *Prolegomena for the Oxford Shakespeare* (1939) in which, near the end of his life, McKerrow dissents from much of what became the standard "received" theory of Greg; W. W. Greg's *Principles of Emendation in Shakespeare* (1928) and *The Editorial Problem in Shakespeare* (3rd edition, 1954); and E. K. Chambers's *William Shakespeare: A Study of Facts and Problems* (1930). No less important are Alice Walker's *Textual Problems of the First Folio* (1953) and Fredson Bowers's *Bibliography and Textual Criticism* (1964). An updated survey of problems and methods is to be found in Philip Gaskell's *A New Introduction to Bibliography* (1972). Significant studies also have appeared on individual plays, such as that of Peter Alexander on the *Henry VI* plays and *Richard III*, Madeleine Doran also on *Henry VI*, J. Dover Wilson on *Hamlet*, George Williams on *Romeo and Juliet*, G. I. Duthie on *King Lear*, and Peter Blayney on *King Lear*.

During the twentieth century, bibliographical theories have, of course, continued to evolve. Sidney Lee, early in the century, still held by and large to Dr. Johnson's view that Heminges and Condell were right to denigrate the quartos because some of them offered such apparently deficient texts (a totalizing view of the quartos based on only a handful of them) and that the Folio was equally suspect because Heminges and Condell, though having denigrated the quartos, persisted in using some of them as printer's copy. Only in the 1930s and afterward did a consensus begin to develop as to how Shakespeare's play texts got transmitted into print. Pollard's distinction between good and bad quartos, although it relied too much on the notion that the printers of the bad quartos were unscrupulous and led to disagreement as to which quartos might, in fact, be categorized as "bad," established the system of classification that continues, albeit with increasing reservations, to be used today.

Two main challenges face bibliographical scholars currently. The first asks whether the categories proposed by Pollard, Greg, and others, for all their being well established, are, in fact, viable. William B. Long and Paul Werstine have shown with disconcerting precision that many supposed "foul paper" characteristics are to be found in supposed playbooks, and the reverse, so that it is often virtually impossible to determine what was the nature of the copy underlying a printed text. (See, for example, William B. Long, "'A bed for woodstock': A Warning for the Unwary," *Medieval and Renaissance Drama in England*, 2, 1985, pp. 91–118, and Paul Werstine, "Plays in Manuscript," *A New History of Early English Drama*, eds. John D. Cox and David Scott Kastan, New York, 1997, pp. 481–97). Empirical research, based in part on surviving manuscripts by dramatists other than Shakespeare, suggests that manuscripts annotated for use in the theater contain little of the normalization and regularization that Greg and McKerrow argued they would. Perhaps most decisively against Greg and McKerrow is the observation that neither the perfectly regularized and completely annotated playbook nor the first-and-final authorial draft called "foul papers" seems to be represented among extant manuscripts of Shakespeare's period. And, although theories of memorial reconstruction appear still to be useful, not even the theory of memorial reconstruction of a "bad" quarto by an actor or actors quite stands up as a complete explanation of the origin of such a quarto, because there are always discrepancies in the fit between the role(s) of the alleged reporter(s) and the quality of the reproduction of the play text. Steven Urkowitz and others challenge the category of "bad" quartos entirely by attempting to show how theatrical the readings in those quartos sometimes can be represented to be. (See, for example, Steven Urkowitz, "Five Women Eleven Ways: Changing Images of Shakespearean Characters in the Earliest Texts," *Images of Shakespeare*, ed. Werner Habicht et al., 1988, pp. 292–304.)

The other challenge is the hypothesis of authorial revision, especially with regard to *King Lear, Hamlet, Troilus and Cressida, 2 Henry IV, The Contention, The True Tragedy, Richard III, Henry V, Othello*, and, to a lesser extent, *1 Henry IV* and *Richard II*. The case for Shakespeare as a conscious reviser is being made more and more strongly than ever before by Gary Taylor, Stanley Wells, Michael Warren, and others, and it is an argument that, of course, affects the issue of what text to edit. Is the Folio *King Lear* an authorial revision? If so, its claim to precedence over the Quarto version is strong. If, on the other hand, it represents theatrical revision, involving the acting company, then Shakespeare's role is less determinable. Does this uncertainty matter, or should we prefer the theatrically revised versions in any case? Were cuts made for reasons of length? Did actors have trouble with certain lines and wish to see them dropped or altered? Did actors' improvisations sometimes make their way into the text? In what ways did censorship contribute to revision? Were there other practical considerations at work, such as provincial touring, to which Shakespeare may have been asked to accede? Do we want a text that comes closest to what Shakespeare may originally have written, or do we want the product as it emerged from the process of rehearsal and revival? The Folio and Quarto versions of *King Lear* are so unlike each other that we must realize we have been given the play in two states, both arguably authoritative. An edition can choose to print both, as in the new Oxford Shakespeare, but perhaps at the cost of making life unreasonably difficult for many readers and certainly at the cost of added paper. How is an editor to address the question of what is most useful for readers and students? The answer must depend in part on what any given edition is for and what audience it is addressing.

Textual controversies such as these have led to new twentieth-century editions of Shakespeare in which the textual method has been measurably advanced. Among the most significant are the New Cambridge Shakespeare of Sir Arthur Quiller-Couch and J. Dover Wilson, and the still-continuing Arden Shakespeare under a succession of general editors, including W. J. Craig, R. H. Case, Una Ellis-Fermor, Harold Jenkins, Harold Brooks, Richard Proudfoot, Ann Thompson, and David Scott Kastan. Peter Alexander's edition of 1951 is often cited as a standard text.

It was soon followed by C. J. Sisson's edition of 1954 and the London Shakespeare of John Munro, 1958. College editions reedited from original texts include the Pelican Shakespeare, under the general editorship of Alfred Harbage (1956–1969, currently appearing in newly edited individual texts by Stephen Orgel, A. R. Braunmuller, Russ McDonald, and others); the revision of Kittredge's edition by Irving Ribner (1971); the Signet Classic Shakespeare, under the general editorship of Sylvan Barnet (1972); the Riverside Shakespeare (1974, 2nd edition 1997), of which G. Blakemore Evans is the textual editor; this present edition; the still-continuing English New Penguin Shakespeare under the general editorship of T. J. B. Spencer and Stanley Wells; the Bantam Shakespeare, edited by David Bevington (1988); and The New Folger Library Shakespeare, edited by Barbara A. Mowat and Paul Werstine, currently appearing in individual paperbacks. Two major editorial undertakings of the 1980s are the controversial and impressive Oxford Shakespeare in several formats (a one-volume modern-spelling edition and a one-volume old-spelling edition, 1986; a *Textual Companion*, 1987; and individual editions of the plays and poems by various editors, still forthcoming, all under the general editorship of Stanley Wells and Gary Taylor), and the New Cambridge Shakespeare (in individual one-volume editions, still forthcoming, under the general editorship of Philip Brockbank, Brian Gibbons, and A. R. Braunmuller).

Norton has also issued its Norton *Facsimile of The First Folio* of Shakespeare, prepared by Charlton Hinman from the Folios of the Folger Library (1968, updated by Peter Blayney, 1991). Older facsimiles of the First Folio are available in libraries, such as that prepared by Sidney Lee (1902) and J. Dover Wilson (in separate plays), but the Norton facsimile unquestionably sets a new standard of excellence. Facsimiles of the quartos are also available, including those prepared for the Oxford University Press by W. W. Greg and Charlton Hinman, those published as Malone Society Reprints, and, most recently, a one-volume set edited by Kenneth Muir and Michael Allen, chiefly from the holdings of the Huntington Library. They are also available from Early English Books Online. Xerox copies of early printed books, such as Shakespearean quartos, are to be found in many libraries through the S.T.C. (Short Title Catalogue) series of University Microfilms. Photographic copies of early texts are also frequently available on microfilm and online.

SHAKESPEARE CRITICISM

In his own time, Shakespeare achieved a reputation for immortal greatness that is astonishing when we consider the low regard in which playwrights were then generally held. Francis Meres compared him to Ovid, Plautus, and Seneca, and proclaimed Shakespeare to be England's most excellent writer in both comedy and tragedy. John Weever spoke of "honey-tongued Shakespeare." The number of such praising allusions is high. Even Ben Jonson, a learned writer strongly influenced by the classical tradition, lauded Shakespeare as "a monument without a tomb," England's best poet, exceeding Chaucer, Spenser, Beaumont, Kyd, and Marlowe. In tragedy, Jonson compared Shakespeare with Aeschylus, Euripides, and Sophocles; in comedy, he insisted Shakespeare had no rival even in "insolent Greece or haughty Rome." This tribute appeared in Jonson's commendatory poem written for the Shakespeare First Folio of 1623.

To be sure, Jonson had more critical things to say about Shakespeare. Even in the Folio commendatory poem, Jonson could not resist a dig at Shakespeare's "small Latin, and less Greek." To William Drummond of Hawthornden, he objected that Shakespeare "wanted art" because in a play (*The Winter's Tale*) he "brought in a number of men saying they had suffered shipwreck in Bohemia, where there is no sea near by some hundred miles." In *Timber*, or *Discoveries*, Jonson chided Shakespeare for his unrestrained facility in writing. "The players have often mentioned it as an honor to Shakespeare, that in his writing, whatsoever he penned he never blotted out [a] line. My answer hath been, would he had blotted a thousand." In a preface to his own play, *Every Man in His Humor* (1616 edition), Jonson satirized English history plays (such as Shakespeare's) that "with three rusty swords, / And help of some few foot-and-half-foot words, / Fight over York and Lancaster's long jars, / And in the tiring-house bring wounds to scars." He also jeered at plays lacking unity of time in which children grow to the age of sixty or older and at nonsensical romantic plays featuring fireworks, thunder, and a chorus that "wafts you o'er the seas."

These criticisms are all of a piece. As a classicist himself, Jonson held in high regard the classical unities. He deplored much English popular drama, including some of Shakespeare's plays, for their undisciplined mixture of comedy and tragedy. Measured against his cherished ideals of classical decorum and refinement of language, Shakespeare's histories and the late romances—*Pericles, Cymbeline, The Winter's Tale,* and *The Tempest*—seemed irritatingly naive and loose-jointed. Yet Jonson knew that Shakespeare had an incomparable genius, superior even to his own. Jonson's affection and respect for Shakespeare seem to have been quite unforced. In the midst of his critical remarks in *Timber*, he freely conceded that "I loved the man, and do honor his memory (on this side idolatry) as much as any. He was indeed honest, and of an open and free nature, had an excellent fantasy, brave notions, and gentle expressions."

The Age of Dryden and Pope

Jonson's attitude toward Shakespeare lived on into the Restoration period of the late seventeenth century. A commonplace of that age held it proper to "admire" Ben Jonson but to "love" Shakespeare. Jonson was the more correct poet, the better model for imitation. Shakespeare often had to be rewritten according to the sophisticated tastes of the Restoration (see Appendix 3 for an account of Restoration stage adaptations of Shakespeare), but he was also regarded as a natural genius. Dryden reflected this view in his *Essay of Dramatic Poesy* (1668) and his *Essay on the Dramatic Poetry of the Last Age* (1672). Dryden condemned *The Winter's Tale, Pericles,* and several other late romances for "the lameness of their plots" and for their "ridiculous incoherent story" which is usually "grounded on impossibilities." Not only Shakespeare, he charged, but several of his contemporaries "neither understood correct plotting nor that which they call *the decorum of the stage*." Had Shakespeare lived in the Restoration, Dryden believed, he would doubtless have written "more correctly" under the influence of a language that had become more "courtly" and a wit that had grown more "refined." Shakespeare, he thought, had limitless "fancy" but sometimes lacked "judgment." Dryden regretted that Shakespeare had been forced to write in "ignorant" times and for audiences who "knew no better." Like Jonson, nevertheless, Dryden had the magnanimity to perceive that Shakespeare transcended his limitations. Shakespeare, said Dryden, was "the man who of all modern and perhaps ancient poets had the largest and most comprehensive soul." From a classical writer, this was high praise indeed.

Alexander Pope's edition of Shakespeare (1725) was based upon a similar estimate of Shakespeare as an untutored genius. Pope freely "improved" Shakespeare's language, rewriting lines and excising those parts he considered vulgar, in order to rescue Shakespeare from the barbaric circumstances of his Elizabethan milieu. Other critics of the Restoration and early eighteenth century who stressed Shakespeare's "natural" genius and imaginative powers were John Dennis, Joseph Addison, and the editors Nicholas Rowe and Lewis Theobald.

The Age of Johnson

Shakespeare was not without his detractors during the late seventeenth and early eighteenth centuries; after all, classical criticism tended to distrust imagination and fancy. Notable among the harsher critics of the Restoration period was Thomas Rymer, whose *Short View of Tragedy* (1692) included a famous attack on *Othello* for making too much out of Desdemona's handkerchief. In the eighteenth century, Voltaire spoke out sharply against Shakespeare's violation of the classical unities, though Voltaire also had some admiring things to say.

The most considered answer to such criticism in the later eighteenth century was that of Dr. Samuel Johnson, in his edition of Shakespeare's plays and its great preface

(1765). Shakespeare, said Johnson, is the poet of nature who "holds up to his readers a faithful mirror of manners and of life. His characters are not modified by the customs of particular places, unpracticed by the rest of the world. . . . In the writings of other poets a character is too often an individual; in those of Shakespeare it is commonly a species." Johnson's attitudes were essentially classical in that he praised Shakespeare for being universal, for having provided a "just representation of general nature," and for having stood the test of time. Yet Johnson also magnanimously praised Shakespeare for having transcended the classical rules. Johnson triumphantly vindicated the mixture of comedy and tragedy in Shakespeare's plays and the supposed indecorum of his characters.

Of course, Johnson did not praise everything he saw. He objected to Shakespeare's loose construction of plot, careless huddling together of the ends of his plays, licentious humor, and, above all, the punning wordplay. He deplored Shakespeare's failure to satisfy the demands of poetic justice, especially in *King Lear*, and he regretted that Shakespeare seemed more anxious to please than to instruct. Still, Johnson did much to free Shakespeare from the constraint of an overly restrictive classical approach to criticism.

The Age of Coleridge

With the beginning of the Romantic period, in England and on the Continent, Shakespeare criticism increasingly turned away from classical precept in favor of a more spontaneous and enthusiastic approach to Shakespeare's creative genius. The new Shakespeare became indeed a rallying cry for those who now deplored such "regular" dramatic poets as Racine and Corneille. Shakespeare became a seer, a bard with mystic powers of insight into the human condition. Goethe, in *Wilhelm Meister* (1796), conceived of Hamlet as the archetypal "Romantic" poet: melancholic, delicate, and unable to act.

Critical trends in England moved toward similar conclusions. Maurice Morgann, in his *Essay on the Dramatic Character of Sir John Falstaff* (1777), glorified Falstaff into a rare individual of courage, dignity, and—yes—honor. To do so, Morgann had to suppress much evidence as to Falstaff's overall function in the *Henry IV* plays. Dramatic structure, in fact, did not interest him; his passion was "character," and his study of Falstaff reflected a new Romantic preoccupation with character analysis. Like other character critics who followed him, Morgann tended to move away from the play itself and into a world where the dramatic personage being considered might lead an independent existence. What would it have been like to know Falstaff as a real person? How would he have behaved on occasions other than those reported by Shakespeare? Such questions fascinated Morgann and others because they led into grand speculations about human psychology and philosophy. Shakespeare's incomparably penetrating insights into character prompted further investigations of the human psyche.

Other late eighteenth-century works devoted to the study of character included Lord Kames's *Elements of Criticism* (1762), Thomas Whately's *Remarks on Some of the Characters of Shakespeare* (1785), William Richardson's *Philosophical Analysis and Illustration of Some of Shakespeare's Remarkable Characters* (1774), and William Jackson's *Thirty Letters on Various Subjects* (1782). Morgann spoke for this school of critics when he insisted, "It may be fit to consider them [Shakespeare's characters] rather as historic than dramatic beings; and, when occasion requires, to account for their conduct from the whole of character, from general principles, from latent motives, and from policies not avowed."

Samuel Taylor Coleridge, the greatest of the English Romantic critics, was profoundly influenced by character criticism, both English and continental. He himself made important contributions to the study of character. His conception of Hamlet, derived in part from Goethe and Hegel, as one who "vacillates from sensibility, and procrastinates from thought, and loses the power of action in the energy of resolve," was to dominate nineteenth-century interpretations of Hamlet. His insight into Iago's evil nature—"the motive-hunting of a motiveless malignity"— was also influential.

Nevertheless, Coleridge did not succumb to the temptation, as did so many character critics, of ignoring the unity of an entire play. Quite to the contrary, he affirmed in Shakespeare an "organic form" or "innate" sense of shape, developed from within, that gave new meaning to Shakespeare's fusion of comedy and tragedy, his seeming anachronisms, his improbable fictions, and his supposedly rambling plots. Coleridge heaped scorn on the eighteenth-century idea of Shakespeare as a "natural" but untaught genius. He praised Shakespeare not for having mirrored life, as Dr. Johnson had said, but for having created an imaginative world attuned to its own internal harmonies. He saw Shakespeare as an inspired but deliberate artist who fitted together the parts of his imaginative world with consummate skill. "The judgment of Shakespeare is commensurate with his genius."

In all this, Coleridge was remarkably close to his German contemporary and rival, August Wilhelm Schlegel, who insisted that Shakespeare was "a profound artist, and not a blind and wildly luxuriant genius." In Shakespeare's plays, said Schlegel, "The fancy lays claim to be considered as an independent mental power governed according to its own laws." Between them, Coleridge and Schlegel utterly inverted the critical values of the previous age, substituting "sublimity" and "imagination" for universality and trueness to nature.

Other Romantic critics included William Hazlitt (*Characters of Shakespear's Plays*, 1817), Charles Lamb (*On* the *Tragedies of Shakespeare,* 1811), and Thomas De Quincey (*On the Knocking at the Gate in Macbeth,* 1823). Hazlitt reveals a political liberalism characteristic of a number of Romantic writers in his skeptical view of Henry V's absolutism and his imperialist war against the French. John Keats has some penetrating things to say in his letters about Shakespeare's "negative capability," or his ability to see into characters' lives with an extraordinary self-effacing sympathy. As a whole, the Romantics were enthusiasts of Shakespeare, and sometimes even idolaters. Yet they consistently refused to recognize him as a man of the theater. Lamb wrote, "It may seem a paradox, but I cannot help being of opinion that the plays of Shakespeare are less calculated for performance on a stage than those of almost any other dramatist whatever." Hazlitt similarly observed: "We do not like to see our author's plays acted, and least of all, *Hamlet.* There is no play that suffers so much in being transferred to the stage." These hostile attitudes toward the theater reflected, in part, the condition of the stage in nineteenth-century England. In part, however, these attitudes were the inevitable result of character criticism, or what Lamb called the desire "to know the internal workings and movements of a great mind, of an Othello or a Hamlet for instance, the *when* and the *why* and the *how far* they should be moved." This fascination with character swept everything before it during the Romantic period.

A. C. Bradley and the Turn of the Century

The tendency of nineteenth-century criticism, then, was to exalt Shakespeare as a poet and a philosopher rather than as a playwright, and as a creator of immortal characters whose "lives" might be studied as though existing independent of a dramatic text. Not infrequently, this critical approach led to a biographical interpretation of Shakespeare through his plays, on the assumption that what he wrote was his own spiritual autobiography and a key to his own fascinating character. Perhaps the most famous critical study in this line was Edward Dowden's *Shakspere: A Critical Study of His Mind and Art* (1875), in which he traced a progression from Shakespeare's early exuberance and passionate involvement through brooding pessimism to a final philosophical calm.

At the same time, the nineteenth century also saw the rise of a more factual and methodological scholarship, especially in the German universities. Dowden, in fact, reflected this trend as well, for one of the achievements of philological study was to establish with some accuracy the dating of Shakespeare's plays and thus make possible an analysis of his artistic development. Hermann Ulrici's *Über Shakespeares dramatische Kunst* (1839) and Gottfried Gervinus's edition of 1849 were among the earliest studies to interest themselves in Shakespeare's chronological development.

The critic who best summed up the achievement of nineteenth-century Shakespeare criticism was A. C. Bradley, in his *Shakespearean Tragedy* (1904) and other studies. *Shakespearean Tragedy* dealt with the four "great" tragedies: *Hamlet, Othello, King Lear,* and *Macbeth.* Bradley revealed his Romantic tendencies in his focus on psychological analysis of character, but he also brought to his work a scholarly awareness of the text that had been missing in some earlier character critics. His work continues to have considerable influence today, despite modern tendencies to rebel against nineteenth-century idealism. To Bradley, Shakespeare's tragic world was ultimately explicable and profoundly moral. Despite the overwhelming impression of tragic waste in *King Lear,* he argued, we as audience experience a sense of compensation and completion that implies an ultimate pattern in human life. "Good, in the widest sense, seems thus to be the principle of life and health in the world; evil, at least in these worst forms, to be a poison. The world reacts against it violently, and, in the struggle to expel it, is driven to devastate itself." Humanity must suffer because of its fatal tendency to pursue some extreme passion, but humanity learns through suffering about itself and the nature of its world. We as audience are reconciled to our existence through purgative release; we smile through our tears. Cordelia is wantonly destroyed, but the fact of her transcendent goodness is eternal. Although in one sense she fails, said Bradley, she is "in another sense superior to the world in which [she] appears; is, in some way which we do not seek to define, untouched by the doom that overtakes [her]; and is rather set free from life than deprived of it."

Historical Criticism

The first major twentieth-century reaction against character criticism was that of the so-called historical critics. (On the later critical movement known as the New Historicism, see below, following "Jan Kott and the Theater of the Absurd.") These critics insisted on a more hardheaded and skeptical appraisal of Shakespeare through better understanding of his historical milieu: his theater, his audience, and his political and social environment. In good part, this movement was the result of a new professionalism of Shakespearean studies in the twentieth century. Whereas earlier critics—Dryden, Pope, Johnson, and Coleridge—had generally been literary amateurs in the best sense, early twentieth-century criticism became increasingly the province of those who taught in universities. Historical research became a professional activity. Bradley himself was Professor of English Literature at Liverpool and Oxford, and did much to legitimize the incorporation of Shakespeare into the humanities curriculum. German scholarship produced the first regular periodical devoted to Shakespeare studies, *Shakespeare-Jahrbuch,* to be followed in due course in England and

America by *Shakespeare Survey* (beginning in 1948), *Shakespeare Quarterly* (1950), and *Shakespeare Studies* (1965).

From the start, historical criticism took a new look at Shakespeare as a man of the theater. Sir Walter Raleigh (Professor of English Literature at Oxford, not to be confused with his Elizabethan namesake) rejected the Romantic absorption in psychology and turned his attention instead to the artistic methods by which plays affect theater-going spectators. The poet Robert Bridges insisted that Shakespeare had often sacrificed consistency and logic for primitive theatrical effects designed to please his vulgar audience. Bridges's objections were often based on serious lack of information about Shakespeare's stage, but they had a healthy iconoclastic effect nonetheless on the scholarship of his time. In Germany, Levin Schücking pursued a similar line of reasoning in his *Character Problems in Shakespeare's Plays* (1917, translated into English in 1922). Schücking argued that Shakespeare had disregarded coherent structure and had striven instead for vivid dramatic effect ("episodic intensification") in his particular scenes. Schücking's *The Meaning of Hamlet* (1937) explained the strange contradictions of that play as resulting from primitive and brutal Germanic source materials which Shakespeare had not fully assimilated.

A keynote for historical critics of the early twentieth century was the concept of artifice or convention in the construction of a play. Perhaps the leading spokesman for this approach was E. E. Stoll, a student of G. L. Kittredge of Harvard University, himself a leading force in historical scholarship in America. Stoll vigorously insisted, in such works as *Othello: An Historical and Comparative Study* (1915), *Hamlet: An Historical and Comparative Study* (1919), and *Art and Artifice in Shakespeare* (1933), that a critic must never be sidetracked by moral, psychological, or biographical interpretations. A play, he argued, is an artifice arising out of its historical milieu. Its conventions are implicit agreements between playwright and spectator. They alter with time, and a modern reader who is ignorant of Elizabethan conventions is all too apt to be misled by his own post-Romantic preconceptions. For example, a calumniator like Iago in *Othello* is conventionally supposed to be believed by the other characters on stage. We do not need to speculate about the "realities" of Othello's being duped, and, in fact, we are likely to be led astray by such Romantic speculations. Stoll went so far as to affirm, in fact, that Shakespearean drama intentionally distorts reality through its theatrical conventions in order to fulfill its own existence as artifice. *Hamlet* is not a play about delay but a revenge story of a certain length, containing many conventional revenge motifs, such as the ghost and the "mousetrap" scheme used to test the villain, and deriving many of its circumstances from Shakespeare's sources; delay is a conventional device needed to continue the story to its conclusion.

Stoll's zeal led to excessive claims for historical criticism, as one might expect in the early years of a pioneering movement. At its extreme, historical criticism came close to implying that Shakespeare was a mere product of his environment. Indeed, the movement owed many of its evolutionist assumptions to the supposedly scientific "social Darwinism" of Thomas Huxley and other late nineteenth-century social philosophers. In more recent years, however, the crusading spirit has given way to a more moderate historical criticism that continues to be an important part of Shakespearean scholarship.

Alfred Harbage, for example, in *As They Liked It* (1947) and *Shakespeare and the Rival Traditions* (1952), has analyzed the audience for which Shakespeare wrote and the rivalry between popular and elite theaters in the London of his day. Harbage sees Shakespeare as a popular dramatist writing for a highly intelligent, enthusiastic, and socially diversified audience. More recently, in *The Privileged Playgoers of Shakespeare's London, 1576–1642* (1981), Ann Jennalie Cook has qualified Harbage's view, arguing that Shakespeare's audience was, for the most part, affluent and well connected. G. E. Bentley has amassed an invaluable storehouse of information about *The Jacobean and Caroline Stage* (1941–1968), just as E. K. Chambers earlier had collected documents and data on *The Elizabethan Stage* (1923). Other studies by these historical scholars include Chambers's *William Shakespeare: A Study of Facts and Problems* (1930), and Bentley's *Shakespeare and His Theatre* (1964) and *The Profession of Dramatist in Shakespeare's Time* (1971). T. W. Baldwin exemplifies the historical scholar who, like Stoll, claims too much for the method; nevertheless, much information on Shakespeare's schooling, reading, and professional theatrical life is available in such works as *William Shakspere's Small Latine and Lesse Greeke* (1944) and *The Organization and Personnel of the Shakespearean Company* (1927). Hardin Craig uses historical method in *An Interpretation of Shakespeare* (1948).

Historical criticism has contributed greatly to our knowledge of the staging of Shakespeare's plays. George Pierce Baker, in *The Development of Shakespeare as a Dramatist* (1907), continued the line of investigation begun by Walter Raleigh. Harley Granville-Barker brought to his *Prefaces to Shakespeare* (1930, 1946) a wealth of professional theatrical experience of his own. Ever since his time, the new theatrical method of interpreting Shakespeare has been based to an ever increasing extent on a genuine revival of interest in Shakespearean production. John Dover Wilson shows an awareness of the stage in *What Happens in Hamlet* (1935) and *The Fortunes of Falstaff* (1943). At its best, as in John Russell Brown's *Shakespeare's Plays in Performance* (1966), in John Styan's *Shakespeare's Stagecraft* (1967), in Michael Goldman's *Shakespeare and the Energies of Drama* (1972), and in Alan Dessen's *Elizabethan Drama and the Viewer's Eye* (1977) and his *Recovering Shakespeare's Theatrical Vocabulary* (1995), this critical method reveals many insights into the text that are hard to obtain without an awareness of theatrical technique.

Supporting this theatrical criticism, historical research has learned a great deal about the physical nature of Shakespeare's stage. J. C. Adams's well-known model of the Globe Playhouse, as presented in Irwin Smith's *Shakespeare's Globe Playhouse: A Modern Reconstruction* (1956), is now generally discredited in favor of a simpler building, as reconstructed by C. Walter Hodges (*The Globe Restored*, 1953, 2nd edition, 1968), Bernard Beckerman (*Shakespeare at the Globe*, 1962, 2nd edition, 1967), Richard Hosley ("The Playhouses and the Stage" in *A New Companion to Shakespeare Studies*, edited by K. Muir and S. Schoenbaum, 1971, and several other good essays), T. J. King (*Shakespearean Staging, 1599–1642*, 1971), and others. Information on the private theaters, such as the Blackfriars, where Shakespeare's plays were also performed, appears in William Armstrong, *The Elizabethan Private Theatres* (1958); Richard Hosley, "A Reconstruction of the Second Blackfriars" (*The Elizabethan Theatre*, 1969); Glynne Wickham, *Early English Stages* (1959–1972); and others. For further information on innyard theaters and on courtly or private theaters, see the contributions of Herbert Berry, D. F. Rowan, W. Reavley Gair, and others cited in the bibliography at the end of this volume.

A related pursuit of historical criticism has been the better understanding of Shakespeare through his dramatic predecessors and contemporaries. Willard Farnham, in *The Medieval Heritage of Elizabethan Tragedy* (1936), traces the evolution of native English tragedy through the morality plays of the early Tudor period. J. M. R. Margeson's *The Origins of English Tragedy* (1967) broadens the pattern to include still other sources for Elizabethan ideas on dramatic tragedy. Bernard Spivack, in *Shakespeare and the Allegory of Evil* (1958), sees Iago, Edmund, Richard III, and other boasting villains in Shakespeare as descendants of the morality Vice. In *Shakespeare and the Idea of the Play* (1962), Anne Righter (Barton) traces the device of the play-within-the-play and the metaphor of the world as a stage back to medieval and classical ideas of dramatic illusion. Irving Ribner's *The English History Play in the Age of Shakespeare* (1959, revised 1965) examines Shakespeare's plays on English history in the context of the popular Elizabethan genre to which they belonged. Robert Weimann's *Shakespeare and the Popular Tradition in the Theatre* (translated from the German in 1978) is a Marxist study in the social dimension of dramatic form and function. Many other studies of this sort could be cited, including Glynne Wickham's *Shakespeare's Dramatic Heritage* (1969), Oscar J. Campbell's *Shakespeare's Satire* (1943), M. C. Bradbrook's *Themes and Conventions of Elizabethan Tragedy* (1935), and S. L. Bethell's *Shakespeare and the Popular Dramatic Tradition* (1944).

Another important concern of historical criticism has been the relationship between Shakespeare and the ideas of his age—cosmological, philosophical, and political. Among the first scholars to study Elizabethan cosmology were Hardin Craig in *The Enchanted Glass* (1936) and A. O. Lovejoy in *The Great Chain of Being* (1936). As their successor, E. M. W. Tillyard provided in *The Elizabethan World Picture* (1943) a definitive view of the conservative and hierarchical values that Elizabethans were supposed to have espoused. In *Shakespeare's History Plays* (1944), Tillyard extended his essentially conservative view of Shakespeare's philosophical outlook to the histories, arguing that they embody a "Tudor myth" and thereby lend support to the Tudor state. Increasingly, however, critics have disputed the extent to which Shakespeare in fact endorsed the "establishment" values of the Elizabethan world picture. Theodore Spencer, in *Shakespeare and the Nature of Man* (1942), discusses the impact on Shakespeare of radical new thinkers like Machiavelli, Montaigne, and Copernicus. In political matters, Henry A. Kelly's *Divine Providence in the England of Shakespeare's Histories* (1970) has challenged the existence of a single "Tudor myth" and has argued that Shakespeare's history plays reflect contrasting political philosophies set dramatically in conflict with one another. M. M. Reese's *The Cease of Majesty* (1961) also offers a graceful corrective to Tillyard's lucid but occasionally one-sided interpretations. Revisions in this direction continue in the work of the so-called new historicists and cultural materialists, to be discussed below.

Historical criticism has also yielded many profitable specialized studies, in which Shakespeare is illuminated by a better understanding of various sciences of his day. Lily Bess Campbell approaches Shakespearean tragedy through Renaissance psychology in *Shakespeare's Tragic Heroes: Slaves of Passion* (1930). Paul Jorgensen uses Elizabethan documents on the arts of war and generalship in his study *Shakespeare's Military World* (1956). Many similar studies examine Shakespeare in relation to law, medicine, and other professions.

"New" Criticism

As we have seen, historical criticism is still an important part of Shakespeare criticism; for better or worse, it is the stuff of some research-oriented universities and their Ph.D. programs. Since its beginning, however, historical criticism has had to face a critical reaction, generated, in part, by its own utilitarian and fact-gathering tendencies. The suggestions urged by Stoll and others that Shakespeare was the product of his cultural and theatrical environment tended to obscure his achievement as a poet. Amassing of information about Shakespeare's reading or his theatrical company often seemed to inhibit the scholar from responding to the power of words and images.

Such at any rate was the rallying cry of the *Scrutiny* group in England, centered on F. R. Leavis, L. C. Knights, and Derek Traversi, and the "new" critics in America, such as Cleanth Brooks. The new critics demanded close attention to the poetry without the encumbrance of historical research. Especially at first, the new critics were openly hostile to any criticism distracting readers from the text. The satirical force of the movement can perhaps best be savored in L. C. Knights's "How Many Children Had Lady Macbeth?" (1933), prompted by the learned appendices in Bradley's *Shakespearean Tragedy*: "When was the murder of Duncan first plotted? Did Lady Macbeth really faint? Duration of the action in *Macbeth*. Macbeth's age. 'He has no children.'"

In part, the new critical movement was (and still is) a pedagogical movement, a protest against the potential dryness of historical footnoting and an insistence that classroom study of Shakespeare ought to focus on a response to his language. Cleanth Brooks's "The Naked Babe and the Cloak of Manliness" (in *The Well Wrought Urn*, 1947) offers to the teacher a model of close reading that focuses on imagery and yet attempts to see a whole vision of the play through its language. G. Wilson Knight concentrates on imagery and verbal texture, sometimes to the exclusion of the play as a whole, in his *The Wheel of Fire* (1930), *The Imperial Theme* (1931), *The Shakespearian Tempest* (1932), *The Crown of Life* (1947), and others. William Empson is best known for his *Seven Types of Ambiguity* (1930) and *Some Versions of Pastoral* (1935). Derek Traversi's works include *An Approach to Shakespeare* (1938), *Shakespeare: The Last Phase* (1954), *Shakespeare: From Richard II to Henry V* (1957), and *Shakespeare: The Roman Plays* (1963). Perhaps the greatest critic of this school has been L. C. Knights, whose books include *Explorations* (1946), *Some Shakespearean Themes* (1959), *An Approach to Hamlet* (1960), and *Further Explorations* (1965). T. S. Eliot's perceptive and controversial observations have also had an important influence on critics of this school. Other studies making good use of the new critical method include Robert Heilman's *This Great Stage* (1948) and *Magic in the Web* (1956). Many of these critics are concerned not only with language but also with the larger moral and structural implications of Shakespeare's plays as discovered through a sensitive reading of the text.

More specialized studies of Shakespearean imagery and language include Caroline Spurgeon's *Shakespeare's Imagery and What It Tells Us* (1935). Its classifications are now recognized to be overly statistical and restricted in definition, but the work has nonetheless prompted valuable further study. Among later works are Sister Miriam Joseph's *Shakespeare's Use of the Arts of Language* (1947, partly reprinted in *Rhetoric in Shakespeare's Time*, 1962), Wolfgang Clemen's *The Development of Shakespeare's Imagery* (1951), and M. M. Mahood's *Shakespeare's Wordplay* (1957). The study of prose has not received as much attention as that of poetry, although Brian Vickers's *The Artistry of Shakespeare's Prose* (1968) and Milton Crane's

Shakespeare's Prose (1951) make significant contributions. See also Edward Armstrong's *Shakespeare's Imagination* (1963) and Kirby Farrell's *Shakespeare's Creation: The Language of Magic and Play* (1975).

A more recent development in studies of Shakespeare's imagery has led to the examination of visual images in the theater as part of Shakespeare's art. Reginald Foakes ("Suggestions for a New Approach to Shakespeare's Imagery," *Shakespeare Survey*, 5, 1952, 81–92) and Maurice Charney (*Shakespeare's Roman Plays: The Function of Imagery in the Drama*, 1961) were among the first to notice that Caroline Spurgeon and other "new" critics usually excluded stage picture in their focus on verbal image patterns. Yet Shakespeare's extensive involvement with the practicalities of theatrical production might well lead one to suspect that he arranges his stage with care and that the plays are full of hints as to how he communicates through visual means. Costume, properties, the theater building, the blocking of actors in visual patterns onstage, expression, movement—all of these contribute to the play's artistic whole. Francis Fergusson analyzes the way in which the Elizabethan theatrical building provides *Hamlet* with an eloquently expressive idea of order and hierarchy, against which are ironically juxtaposed Claudius's acts of killing a king and marrying his widow (*The Idea of a Theater*, 1949). Other studies of stage imagery include Ann Pasternak Slater's *Shakespeare the Director* (1982) and David Bevington's *Action Is Eloquence: Shakespeare's Language of Gesture* (1984).

Another call for expansion of the occasionally narrow limits of "new" criticism comes from the so-called Chicago school of criticism, centered on R. S. Crane, Richard McKeon, Elder Olson, Bernard Weinberg, and others, who, in the 1950s and 1960s, espoused a formal or structural approach to criticism, using Aristotle as its point of departure. Crane was reacting to the new critics who, in his view, restricted the kinds of answers they could obtain by limiting themselves to one methodology. Critics hostile to the Chicago school have responded, to be sure, that Crane's own approach tends to produce its own dogmatism. Formalist analyses of Shakespeare plays are to be found, for example, in the work of W. R. Keast, Wayne Booth, and Norman Maclean; see *Critics and Criticism*, edited by R. S. Crane (1952) and the bibliography at the back of this book.

Psychological Criticism

In a sense, Freudian and other psychological criticism continues the "character" criticism of the nineteenth century. Freudian critics sometimes follow a character into a world outside the text, analyzing Hamlet (for instance) as though he were a real person whose childhood traumas can be inferred from the symptoms he displays. The most famous work in this vein is *Hamlet and Oedipus* (1910, revised 1949), by Freud's disciple, Ernest Jones. According to Jones, Hamlet's delay is caused by an oedipal trauma. Hamlet's uncle, Claudius, has done exactly what Hamlet himself incestuously and subconsciously wished to do: kill his father and marry his mother. Because he cannot articulate these forbidden impulses to himself, Hamlet is paralyzed into inactivity. Jones's critical analysis thus assumes, as did such Romantic critics as Coleridge, that the central problem of *Hamlet* is one of character and motivation: why does Hamlet delay? (Many modern critics would deny that this is a problem or would insist, at least, that by setting such a problem, Jones has limited the number of possible answers. Avi Erlich proposes an entirely different psychological reading of the play in *Hamlet's Absent Father*, 1977). Psychological criticism sometimes also reveals its affinities with nineteenth-century character criticism in its attempt to analyze Shakespeare's personality through his plays, as though the works constituted a spiritual autobiography. The terminology of psychological criticism is suspect to some readers because it is at least superficially anachronistic when dealing with a Renaissance writer. The terminology is also sometimes overburdened with technical jargon.

Nonetheless, psychological criticism has afforded many insights into Shakespeare not readily available through other modes of perception. Jones's book makes clear the intensity of Hamlet's revulsion toward women as a result of his mother's inconstancy. At a mythic level, Hamlet's story certainly resembles that of Oedipus, and Freudian criticism is often at its best when it shows us this universal aspect of the human psyche. Freudian terminology need not be anachronistic when it deals with timeless truths. Psychological criticism can reveal to us Shakespeare's preoccupation with certain types of women in his plays, such as the domineering and threatening masculine type (Joan of Arc, Margaret of Anjou) or, conversely, the long-suffering and patient heroine (Helena in *All's Well*, Hermione in *The Winter's Tale*). Psychological criticism is perhaps most useful in studying family relationships in Shakespeare. It also has much to say about the psychic or sexual connotations of symbols. Influential books include Norman O. Brown's *Life Against Death: The Psychoanalytical Meaning of History* (1959) and Norman Holland's *Psychoanalysis and Shakespeare* (1966) and *The Shakespearean Imagination* (1964).

Richard Wheeler's *Turn and Counter-Turn: Shakespeare's Development and the Problem Comedies* (1981) applies psychoanalytic method to a study of Shakespeare's development, in which, as Wheeler sees it, the sonnets and the problem plays are pivotal as Shakespeare turns from the safely contained worlds of romantic comedy (with nonthreatening heroines) and the English history play (in which women are generally denied anything more than a marginal role in state affairs) to the tragedies, in which sexual conflict is shown in all its potentially terrifying destructiveness. Wheeler's completion of C. L. Barber's *The Whole Journey: Shakespeare's Power of Development* (1986) continues the study of Shakespeare's development in the late plays. The dichotomies of gender and genre urged in these studies and continued by Linda Bamber (*Comic Women, Tragic Men: A Study of Gender and Genre in Shakespeare*, 1982), among others, have been challenged by Jonathan Goldberg in his essay, "Shakespearean Inscriptions: The Voicing of Power," in *Shakespeare and the Question of Theory* (edited by Patricia Parker and Geoffrey Hartman, 1985). A collection of essays under the editorship of Murray Schwartz and Coppélia Kahn, *Representing Shakespeare* (1980), affords a sample of work by Janet Adelman, David Willbern, Meredith Skura, David Sundelson, Madelon Gohlke Sprengnether, Joel Fineman, and others.

Much psychoanalytic criticism of the 1980s has sought to displace Freud's emphasis upon the relation of son and father in the oedipal triangle in favor of attention to the mother and child preoedipal relation; a model here is the work of Karen Horney (e.g., *Neurosis and Human Growth: The Struggle Toward Self-Realization*, 1950). Jacques Lacan (*Écrits*, translated by Alan Sheridan, 1977) and Erik Erikson (*Childhood and Selfhood*, 1978) are also prominent theorists in the post-Freudian era. Despite such changes, the psychoanalytic critic still attempts to discover in the language of the play the means by which he or she can reconstruct an early stage in the development of one or more of the dramatic characters.

Mythological Criticism

Related to psychological criticism is the search for archetypal myth in literature, as an expression of the "collective unconscious" of the human race. Behind such an approach lie the anthropological and psychological assumptions of Jung and his followers. One of the earliest studies of this sort was Gilbert Murray's *Hamlet and Orestes* (1914), analyzing the archetype of revenge for a murdered father. Clearly this custom goes far back into tribal prehistory and emerges in varying but interrelated forms in many different societies. This anthropological universality enables us to look at Hamlet as the heightened manifestation of an incredibly basic story. *Hamlet* gives shape to urgings that are a part of our innermost social being. The struggle between the civilized and the primitive goes on in us as in the play *Hamlet*.

The vast interdisciplinary character of mythological criticism leaves it vulnerable to charges of speculativeness and glib theorizing. At its best, however, mythological criticism can illuminate the nature of our responses as audience to a work of art. Northrop Frye argues, in *A Natural Perspective* (1965), that we respond to mythic patterns by imagining ourselves participating in them communally. The Greek drama emerged, after all, from

Dionysiac ritual. All drama celebrates in one form or another the primal myths of vegetation, from the death of the year to the renewal or resurrection of life. In his most influential book, *Anatomy of Criticism* (1957), Frye argues that mythic criticism presents a universal scheme for the investigation of all literature, or all art, since art is itself the ordering of our most primal stirrings. Frye sees in drama (as in other literature) a fourfold correspondence to the cyclical pattern of the year: comedy is associated with spring, romance with summer, tragedy with autumn, and satire with winter. Historically, civilization moves through a recurrent cycle from newness to decadence and decay; this cycle expresses itself culturally in a progression from epic and romance to tragedy, to social realism, and, finally, to irony and satire before the cycle renews itself. Thus, according to Frye, the genres of dramatic literature (and of other literary forms as well) have an absolute and timeless relationship to myth and cultural history. That is why we as audience respond so deeply to form and meaning as contained in genre. C. L. Barber, in *Shakespeare's Festive Comedy* (1959), makes a similar argument: our enjoyment of comedy arises from our intuitive appreciation of such "primitive" social customs as Saturnalian revels, May games, and fertility rites. John Holloway offers an anthropological study of Shakespeare's tragedies in *The Story of the Night* (1961).

Frye's critical system has not been without its detractors. For example, Frederick Crews (*Psychoanalysis and Literary Process*, 1970) argues that Frye's system is too self-contained in its ivory tower and too much an abstract artifact of the critical mind to be "relevant" to the social purposes of art. Nevertheless, Frye continues to be one of the most influential critics of the late twentieth century.

Typological Criticism

Another controversy of the later twentieth century has to do with the Christian interpretation of Shakespeare. Do the images and allusions of Shakespeare's plays show him to be deeply immersed in a Christian culture inherited from the Middle Ages? Does he reveal a typological cast of mind, so common in medieval literature, whereby a story can suggest through analogy a universal religious archetype? For example, does the mysterious Duke in *Measure for Measure* suggest to us a God figure, hovering unseen throughout the play to test human will and then to present humanity with an omniscient but merciful judgment? Is the wanton slaughter of the good Cordelia in *King Lear* reminiscent of the Passion of Christ? Can Portia in *The Merchant of Venice* be seen as an angelic figure descending from Belmont into the fallen human world of Venice? Often the operative question we must ask is: "How far should such analogy be pursued?" Richard II unquestionably likens himself to Christ betrayed by the disciples, and at times the play evokes images of Adam

banished from Paradise, but do these allusions coalesce into a sustained analogy?

Among the most enthusiastic searchers after Christian meaning are J. A. Bryant, in *Hippolyta's View* (1961); Roy Battenhouse, in *Shakespearean Tragedy: Its Art and Christian Premises* (1969); and R. Chris Hassel, in *Renaissance Drama and the English Church* (1979) and *Faith and Folly in Shakespeare: Romantic Comedies* (1980). Their efforts have encountered stern opposition, however. One notable dissenter is Roland M. Frye, whose *Shakespeare and Christian Doctrine* (1963) argues that Shakespeare cannot be shown to have known much Renaissance theology and that, in any case, his plays are concerned with human drama rather than with otherworldly questions of damnation or salvation. Frye's argument stresses the incompatibility of Christianity and tragedy, as does also D. G. James's *The Dream of Learning* (1951) and Clifford Leech's *Shakespeare's Tragedies and Other Studies in Seventeenth-Century Drama* (1950). Virgil Whitaker's *The Mirror Up to Nature* (1965) sees religion as an essential element in Shakespeare's plays but argues that Shakespeare uses the religious knowledge of his audience as a shortcut to characterization and meaning, rather than as an ideological weapon. The controversy will doubtless long continue, even though the typological critics have had to assume a defensive posture.

Jan Kott and the Theater of the Absurd

At an opposite extreme from the Christian idealism of most typological critics is the iconoclasm of those who have been disillusioned by recent events in history. One who brilliantly epitomizes political disillusionment in the aftermath of World War II, especially in Eastern Europe, is Jan Kott. The evocative debunking of romantic idealism set forth in his *Shakespeare Our Contemporary* (1964, translated from the Polish) has enjoyed enormous influence since the 1960s, especially in the theater. Kott sees Shakespeare as a dramatist of the absurd and the grotesque. In this view, Shakespearean plays are often close to "black" comedy or comedy of the absurd, as defined by Antonin Artaud (*The Theatre and Its Double*, 1958) and Jerzy Grotowski (*Towards a Poor Theatre*, 1968). Indeed, Kott has inspired productions that expose traditional values to skepticism and ridicule. Portia and Bassanio in *The Merchant of Venice* become scheming adventurers; Henry V becomes a priggish warmonger. History is for Kott a nightmare associated with his country's experience in World War II, and Shakespeare's modernity can be seen in his sardonic portrayal of political opportunism and violence. Even *A Midsummer Night's Dream* is a play of disturbingly erotic brutality, Kott argues. Here is an interpretation of Shakespeare that was bound to have an enormous appeal in a world confronted by the assassinations of the Kennedys and Martin Luther King, Jr.; by incessant war in the Middle East, Southeast Asia, and much of the third world; by the threat of nuclear annihilation and ecological disaster; and by political leadership generally perceived as interested only in the public-relations techniques of self-preservation. An essentially ironic view of politics and, more broadly, of human nature has informed a good deal of criticism since Kott's day and has led to the dethronement of E. M. W. Tillyard and his essentially positive view of English patriotism and heroism in the history plays.

New Historicism and Cultural Materialism

A more recent way of investigating Shakespeare through the demystifying perspective of modern experience—the so-called new historicism— has focused on the themes of political self-fashioning and role playing in terms of power and subversion. This critical school has paid close attention to historians and cultural anthropologists like Lawrence Stone (*The Crisis of the Aristocracy, 1558–1641,* 1965) and Clifford Geertz (*Negara: The Theatre State in Nineteenth-Century Bali,* 1980), who explore new ways of looking at the relationship between historical change and the myths generated to bring it about or to retain power. Geertz analyzes the way in which the ceremonies and myths of political rule can, in effect, become a self-fulfilling reality; kings and other leaders, acting out their roles in ceremonials designed to encapsulate the myth of their greatness and divine origin, essentially become what they have created in their impersonations of power. Such a view of political authority is an inherently skeptical one, seeing government as a process of manipulating illusions. When Shakespeare's English history plays—or indeed any plays dealing with conflicts of authority—are analyzed in these terms, subversion and containment become important issues. Do the plays of Shakespeare and other Renaissance dramatists celebrate the power of the Tudor monarchs, or do they question and undermine assumptions of hierarchy? Did Elizabethan drama serve to increase skepticism and pressure for change, or was it, conversely, a way of easing that pressure so that the power structure could remain in force?

The "new historicism" is a name applied to a kind of literary criticism practiced in America, prominently by Stephen Greenblatt. Especially influential have been his *Renaissance Self-Fashioning* (1980), *Shakespearean Negotiations* (1988), and his editing of the journal *Representations.* Those who pursue similar concerns, including Louis Montrose, Stephen Orgel, Richard Helgerson, Don E. Wayne, Frank Whigham, Richard Strier, Jonathan Goldberg, David Scott Kastan, and Steven Mullaney, share Greenblatt's goals to a greater or lesser extent and think of themselves only with important reservations as "new historicists"; the term is misleadingly categorical, and Greenblatt, among others, is eager to enlarge the parameters of the method rather than to allow it to harden into an orthodoxy. (Greenblatt, in fact, prefers the term "poetics of culture" to "new historicism," even though the latter phrase remains better known.) Still, these critics do generally share a number of common concerns. Among the ways in which new historicists seek to separate themselves from earlier historical critics is by denying that the work of art is a unified and self-contained product of an independent creator in masterful control of the meaning of the work. Instead, the new historicists represent the work as shot through with the multiple and contradictory discourses of its time. New historicists also deny the notion that art merely "reflects" its historical milieu; instead, they argue that art is caught up in, and contributes to, the social practices of its time. Although the boundary between new and old historical criticism is often hard to draw, in general the new historicists are apt to be skeptical of the accepted canon of literary texts and are drawn to a markedly politicized reading of Renaissance plays. One finds everywhere in the new historicism a deep ambivalence toward political authority.

Mikhail Bakhtin's provocative ideas on carnival (*L'Oeuvre de François Rabelais et la Culture Populaire du Moyen Age,* 1970) have had an important influence in new historical circles, as reflected, for example, in the work of Michael Bristol (*Carnival and Theatre: Plebeian Culture and the Structure of Authority in Renaissance England,* 1985), Peter Stallybrass, Gail Paster, and others. Like new historicism, this critical approach looks at so-called high cultural entertainment, including Shakespeare, in relation to the practices of popular culture, thereby breaking down the distinction between "high" and "popular." Literary and nonliterary texts are subjected to the same kind of serious scrutiny. Popular origins of the theater receive new attention, as in Robert Weimann's *Shakespeare and the Popular Tradition in the Theater: Studies in the Social Dimension of Dramatic Form and Function* (published in German in 1967 and in English translation in 1978).

Cultural materialism, in Britain, takes an analogous approach to the dethroning of canonical texts and the emphasis on art as deeply implicated in the social practices of its time but differs from American new historicism on the issue of change. New historicism is sometimes criticized for its lack of a model for change and for its reluctant belief, instead (in Greenblatt's formulation especially), that all attempts at subversion through art are destined to be contained by power structures in society; art permits the expression of heterodox points of view, but only as a way of letting off steam, as it were, and thereby easing the pressures for actual radical change. British cultural materialism, in contrast, is more avowedly committed not only to radical political interpretation but also to rapid political change, partly in response to what are perceived to be more deeply rooted class differences than are found in America. Jonathan Dollimore's *Radical Tragedy* (1984) and *Political Shakespeare* (1985), edited by Dollimore and Alan

Sinfield, enlist the dramatist on the side of class struggle. So do *Alternative Shakespeares,* edited by John Drakakis (1985), and Terry Eagleton's *Shakespeare and Society* (1967) and *William Shakespeare* (1986). Raymond Williams, not himself a Shakespearean critic, is an acknowledged godfather of the movement.

Feminist Criticism

Feminist criticism is such an important and diverse field that it has necessarily and productively reached into a number of related disciplines, such as cultural anthropology and its wealth of information about family structures. In his *The Elementary Structures of Kinship* (1949, translated 1969) and other books, Claude Lévi-Strauss analyzes the way in which men, as fathers and as husbands, control the transfer of women from one family to another in an "exogamous" marital system designed to strengthen commercial and other ties among men. Recent feminist criticism has had a lot to say about patriarchal structures in the plays and poems of Shakespeare, some of it building upon Lévi-Strauss's analysis of patriarchy; see, for example, Karen Newman, "Portia's Ring: Unruly Women and Structures of Exchange in *The Merchant of Venice,*" *Shakespeare Quarterly,* 38 (1987), 10–33, and Lynda Boose, "The Father and the Bride in Shakespeare," *PMLA,* 97 (1982), 325–47. Coppélia Kahn has examined the ideology of rape in *The Rape of Lucrece,* showing how the raped woman is devalued by the shame that attaches to her husband, even though she is innocent (*Shakespeare Studies,* 9, 1976, 45–72).

Another important source of insight for feminist criticism is the anthropological work on rites of passage by Arnold Van Gennep (*The Rites of Passage,* translated by M. B. Vizedom and G. L. Caffee, 1960) and Victor Turner (*The Ritual Process,* 1969), among others. The focus here is on the dangers of transition at times of birth, puberty, marriage, death, and other turning points of human life. Feminist criticism, in dealing with such crises of transition, concerns itself not only with women's roles but also, more broadly, with gender relations, with family structures, and with the problems that males encounter in their quest for mature sexual identity. Coppélia Kahn's *Man's Estate; Masculine Identity in Shakespeare* (1981) looks particularly at the difficulty of the male in confronting the hazards of maturity. Robert Watson's *Shakespeare and the Hazards of Ambition* (1984) also looks at the male in the political context of career and self-fashioning. Marjorie Garber's *Coming of Age in Shakespeare* (1981) takes a broad look at maturation.

As these titles suggest, the models are often psychological, as well as anthropological. One focus of feminist criticism is the role of women in love and marriage. Feminist critics disagree among themselves as to whether the portrait painted by Shakespeare and other Elizabethan

dramatists is a hopeful one, as argued, for example, by Juliet Dusinberre in *Shakespeare and the Nature of Women* (1975, 1996), or repressive, as argued by Lisa Jardine in *Still Harping on Daughters: Women and Drama in the Age of Shakespeare* (1983). Recent historians add an important perspective, especially Lawrence Stone in his *The Family, Sex, and Marriage in England, 1500–1800* (1977). Did the Protestant emphasis on marriage as a morally elevated and reciprocal relationship have the paradoxical effect of arousing in men an increased hostility and wariness toward women and a resulting increase in repression and violence? Or, as David Underdown suggests, should we look to economic explanations of hostility and wariness toward women in the Renaissance? His studies indicate that repression of women is greatest in regions of the country where their place in the economy offers the possibility of their having some control over family finances. (See *Revel, Riot, and Rebellion: Popular Culture in England, 1603–1660,* 1985, pp. 73–105, especially p. 99.)

Certainly, recent criticism has paid a lot of attention to male anxieties about women in Shakespeare's plays, as various male protagonists resolve to teach women a lesson (*The Taming of the Shrew*), succumb to dark fantasies of female unfaithfulness (*Much Ado About Nothing, Othello*), or are overwhelmed by misogynistic revulsion (*Hamlet, King Lear*). It is as though Shakespeare, in his plays and poems, works through the problems that men experience throughout their lives in their relationships with women, from the insecurities of courtship to the desire for possession and control in marriage, and from jealous fears of betrayal to the longing for escape into middle-age sexual adventure (as in *Antony and Cleopatra*). The late plays show us the preoccupation of the aging male with the marriages of his daughters (another form of betrayal) and with the approach of death.

Recently, feminist criticism has begun to increase its historical consciousness. Critics such as Gail Paster, Jean Howard, Phyllis Rackin, Dympna Callaghan, Lorraine Helms, Jyotsna Singh, Alison Findlay, Lisa Jardine, and Karen Newman focus on the construction of gender in early modern England in terms of social and material conditions, abandoning the nonhistorical psychological model of earlier feminist criticism. See the bibliography at the end of this book for feminist studies by these and other feminist critics, including Catherine Belsey, Carol Neely, Peter Erickson, Meredith Skura, Marianne Novy, Margo Hendricks, Kim Hall, Philippa Berry, Frances Dolan, Mary Beth Rose, Valerie Traub, Susan Zimmerman, Lynda Boose, and Ania Loomba. Gender studies concerned with issues of same-sex relationships have made important contributions in recent years, in the work of Bruce Smith, Laurie Shannon, Jonathan Goldberg, Stephen Orgel, Leonard Barkan, Mario DiGangi, and others.

Poststructuralism and Deconstruction

A major influence today in Shakespeare criticism, as in virtually all literary criticism of recent date, is the school of analysis known as poststructuralism or deconstruction; the terms, though not identical, significantly overlap. This school derives its inspiration originally from the work of certain French philosophers and critics, chief among whom are Ferdinand de Saussure, a specialist in linguistics, Michel Foucault, a historian of systems of discourse, and Jacques Derrida, perhaps the most highly visible exponent and practitioner of deconstruction. The ideas of these men were first introduced into American literary criticism by scholars at Yale such as Geoffrey Hartman, J. Hillis Miller, and Paul de Man. The ideas are controversial and difficult.

Poststructuralism and deconstruction begin with an insistence that language is a system of difference—one in which the signifiers (such as words and gestures) are essentially arbitrary to the extent that "meaning" and "authorial intention" are virtually impossible to fix precisely; that is, language enjoys a potentially infinite subjectivity. To an extent, this approach to the subjectivity of meaning in a work of art resembles "new" criticism in its mistrust of "message" in literature, but the new method goes further. It resists all attempts at paraphrase, for example, insisting that the words of a text cannot be translated into other words without altering something vital; indeed, there is no way of knowing if an author's words will strike any two readers or listeners in the same way. The very concept of an author has been challenged by Michel Foucault ("What Is an Author?" in *Language, Counter-Memory, Practice,* edited by Donald F. Bouchard, 1977). Deconstruction proclaims that there is no single identifiable author in the traditional sense; instead of a single text, we have a potentially infinite number of texts.

Both the theory and practice of deconstruction remain highly controversial. Although poststructuralism and deconstruction owe a debt to the general philosophical theory of signs and symbols known as semiotics, in which the function of linguistic signs is perceived to be artificially constructed, the new method also calls into question the very distinctions on which the discipline of semiotics is based. Derrida builds upon the work of Saussure and yet goes well beyond him in an insistence that words (signifiers) be left in play rather than attached to their alleged meaning (signifieds). Frank Lentricchia (*After the New Criticism,* 1980) takes the Yale school critics to task for interpreting Derrida in too formalist and apolitical a sense. Despite disagreements among theorists, nevertheless, the approach has deeply influenced Shakespeare criticism as a whole by urging critics to consider the suppleness with which signifiers (words) in the Shakespearean text are converted by listeners and readers into some approximation of meaning.

The ramifications of poststructuralism and deconstruction are increasingly felt in other forms of criticism, even those at least nominally at odds with poststructuralist assumptions. Some radical textual critics, for example, are fascinated by the unsettling prospects of the deconstructed text. What does one edit and how does one go about editing when words are to be left in play, to the infinite regress of meaning? The problems are acutely examined in a collection of essays called *The Division of the Kingdom,* edited by Gary Taylor and Michael Warren, on the two early and divergent texts of *King Lear* (1983). The method of linguistic analysis known as "speech-act theory," developed by the philosopher Warren Austin as a way of exploring how we perform certain linguistic acts when we swear oaths or make asseverations and the like, is sharply at variance with deconstruction in its premises about a correlation between speech and intended meaning, and yet it, too, can help us understand the instability of spoken or written language in Shakespeare. Joseph Porter's *The Drama of Speech Acts* (1979), for example, looks at ways in which Shakespeare's characters in the plays about Henry IV and Henry V reveal, through their language of oath making and oath breaking, asseveration, and the like, their linguistic adaptability or lack of adaptability to historical change. Richard II resists historical change in the very way he speaks; Prince Hal embraces it. A third related field of analysis that is interested in the instability of meaning in Shakespeare's texts is metadramatic criticism, where the focus is on ways in which dramatic texts essentially talk about the drama itself, about artistic expression, and about the artist's quest for immortality in art. James Calderwood's *Shakespearean Metadrama* (1971) is an influential example.

At its extreme, then, deconstructive criticism comes close to undermining all kinds of "meaningfulness" in artistic utterance and to being thus at war with other methods of interpretation. Still, deconstruction continues to remain influential, because it also usefully challenges complacent formulations of meaning and because it promotes such a subtle view of linguistic complexity.

At its best, late twentieth-century criticism transcends the splintering effect of a heterogeneous critical tradition to achieve a synthesis that is at once unified and multiform in its vision. The pluralistic approach aims at overall balance and a reinforcement of one critical approach through the methodology of another. Many of the works already cited in this introduction refuse to be constricted by methodological boundaries. The best historical criticism makes use of close explication of the text where appropriate; image patterns can certainly reinforce mythological patterns; typological interpretation, when sensibly applied, serves the cause of image study. Some fine books are so eclectic in their method that one hesitates to apply the label of any one critical school. Among such works are Maynard Mack's *King Lear in Our Time* (1965), David Young's *Something of Great Constancy: The Art of A Midsummer Night's Dream* (1966), R. G. Hunter's *Shakespeare and the Comedy of Forgiveness* (1965), Janet Adelman's *The Common Liar: An Essay on "Antony and Cleopatra"* (1973), Stanley Cavell's "The Avoidance of Love: A Reading of King Lear," in *Must We Mean What We Say?* (1969, reprinted in *Disowning Knowledge in Six Plays of Shakespeare*, 1987), and Paul Jorgensen's *Our Naked Frailties: Sensational Art and Meaning in Macbeth* (1971).

INTO THE TWENTY-FIRST CENTURY

The sense of where we are in the twenty-first century in Shakespeare criticism reflects the uncertainties and guardedly hopeful expectations of the academic profession as a whole. The period of the 1970s and 1980s, described previously, was one of extraordinary ferment, brought on by a host of developments: the Vietnam War and its aftermath, the assassinations of the Kennedys and Martin Luther King, the impact of French linguistic and philosophical thought on American intellectual writing, the frustrations of many academics with Reaganomics and their consequent fascination with British Marxism, emerging demands on behalf of minorities and women, a revolution in social and sexual mores accompanied by a backlash in the name of "family values," conflict over American foreign policy in the Middle East (Israel, Iraq), and much more. The result was what must be regarded as a genuine revolution in methods of critical analysis and reading. The literary text became multivalent, ambiguous, deconstructed, dethroned as a unique artifact, and was seen, instead, as a product of and contributing to its social and intellectual environment. The author became a construction of criticism and of a new kind of literary history.

Shakespeare studies have taken a lead in all of this new exploration. Although one of the postmodern demands has been for a recanonizing of literature in favor of newer literature, works by women and minorities, and works from countries other than Britain and the United States instead of the traditional canon of dead white European males, Shakespeare not only has survived this recanonization but also has become more prominent than ever. Other Renaissance writers such as Ben Jonson, John Webster, Thomas Dekker, Thomas Nashe, John Lyly, Edmund Spenser, and even Christopher Marlowe, John Milton, and John Donne have been the victims of declining enrollments in classes generally, but Shakespeare triumphs. Why?

One compelling answer is that Shakespeare is simply indispensable to postmodern critical inquiry. His texts are so extraordinarily responsive that new questions put to them—about the changing role of women, about cynicism in the political process, about the pro-

tean near-indeterminacy of meaning in language—evoke insights that are hard to duplicate in other literary texts. Shakespeare does not seem out of date. The very impulse of so much recent criticism to claim Shakespeare as "our contemporary," attuned to our own skepticisms and disillusionment and even despair (as in the writings of Jan Kott, for example), attests to his unparalleled engagement with the issues about which we care so deeply. Even those who argue that Shakespeare exhibits the male hang-ups of a patriarchal society and that he is a social snob who glorifies aristocracy and warfare do not see Shakespeare as a writer who is out of touch with the values of our contemporary society but, rather, as one who gives eloquent testimonial to structures that were alive in our cultural past and with which we sense a continuum today even if outward circumstances have changed. The best scholarship does not condemn Shakespeare for believing in kingship or for sometimes showing men as victorious in the battle of the sexes; instead, that criticism is interested in the whole process of the literary text's participation in the creation of culture. Even when recent scholarship is concerned with examining class and gender issues to clarify some of the systematic oppressiveness of early modern culture, it does so generally in an attempt to negotiate the relationship of the present to the past, rather than assuming a superiority in our modern world's approaches to issues of class, gender, and ethnicity.

To be sure, a number of Shakespeare's plays are in trouble today because they make us uncomfortable about these issues. *The Merchant of Venice* is, in the eyes of many, almost unproduceable, because the anti-Semitic emotions it explores are so distasteful. It is less often assigned now in classrooms than it once was, even though, when it is taught or produced onstage, it can lead to extraordinarily searching discussions of painful but real issues. The same is true of *The Taming of the Shrew*, which is being taken from the shelves of more than a few libraries because of its apparent flaunting of sexist behavior toward women. *Othello* offends some readers and viewers because of its racist language and, in the view of some, racial stereotypes. Yet, the power of Shakespeare's language continues to exert its spell despite, and in part because of, these troubling conflicts over the role of dramatic art in modern society.

The world of Shakespeare criticism today, after two decades or so of revolution, is seemingly one of consolidation. At a March 1995 meeting of the Shakespeare Association of America in Chicago, many conferees wondered: Where is the profession going? What are the hot new issues? Who are the new critics that no one wants to miss? And, in fact, there seemed to be little dramatic excitement of this sort, little agreement as to any discernible new trend. To some, this is frustrating. Where does one turn for real creativity after a thoroughgoing revolution such as we have experienced?

To others, a time of stocktaking is potentially healthy. There seems to be relatively little interest in turning the clock back; postmodernism and indeterminacy have changed the critical landscape for better and for worse. Now that this new landscape begins to seem familiar, however, new members of the profession seem less anxious to resolve their own identity crises in terms of affiliating with some critical school or other. The critical challenges are there, not so stridently new as they were ten years ago, and adaptable to various uses.

The result is increasing variety in the kinds of critical work being done. Some of it is recognizably traditional, dealing with stage history and conditions of performance during Shakespeare's lifetime, as, for example, in T. J. King, *Casting Shakespeare's Plays: London Actors and Their Roles* (1992); William Ingram, *The Business of Playing: The Beginnings of the Adult Professional Theater in Elizabethan London* (1992); David Bradley, *From Text to Performance in the Elizabethan Theatre: Preparing the Play for the Stage* (1992); David Mann, *The Elizabethan Player: Contemporary Stage Representation* (1991); John H. Astington, ed., *The Development of Shakespeare's Theater* (1992); Andrew Gurr, *Playgoing in Shakespeare's London* (1987, 2nd edition, 1996) and *The Shakespearian Playing Companies* (1996); and Roslyn Lander Knutson, *The Repertory of Shakespeare's Company, 1594–1613* (1991). Background and historical studies of the conditions that helped produce Shakespeare's theater can sometimes be informatively revisionist in the sense of toppling cherished older notions without at the same time being postmodern in approach. Examples here might include Richard Dutton, *Mastering the Revels: The Regulation and Censorship of English Renaissance Drama* (1991); Scott McMillin and Sally-Beth MacLean, *The Queen's Men and Their Plays* (1998); and Leeds Barroll, *Politics, Plague, and Shakespeare's Theater: The Stuart Years* (1991).

Other studies are more openly revisionist in a postmodern vein, sometimes in dealing with hypotheses about bibliography and textual studies, as in Margreta de Grazia, *Shakespeare Verbatim: The Reproduction of Authenticity and the 1790 Apparatus* (1991) and Grace Ioppolo, *Revising Shakespeare* (1991). The New Folger Library Shakespeare, edited by Barbara Mowat and Paul Werstine (1992—), gives a more measured approach. The Arden Shakespeare is currently bringing out new critical editions of all the plays in individual volumes (Arden 3), as are the New Cambridge Shakespeare and the Oxford Shakespeare. Occasionally a conservative counterblast is heard, as in Brian Vickers's entertaining, learned, and feisty polemic, *Appropriating Shakespeare: Contemporary Critical Quarrels* (1993). A forum of essays edited by Ivo Kamps, called *Shakespeare Left and Right*, gives us a chance to weigh arguments from various sides.

What the contemporary critical scene does best is to free critics to be who they are and to write without paying dues to any particular affiliation. The results are refreshingly diverse. Among the books that show this spread of critical approaches are Karen Newman, *Fashioning Femininity and the English Renaissance Drama* (1991); Bruce R. Smith, *Homosexual Desire in Shakespeare's England* (1991); Janet Adelman, *Suffocating Mothers: Fantasies of Maternal Origin in Shakespeare's Plays, "Hamlet" to "The Tempest"* (1992); Alan Sinfield, *Faultlines: Cultural Materialism and the Politics of Dissident Reading* (1992); Valerie Traub, *Desire and Anxiety: Circulations of Sexuality in Shakespearean Drama* (1992); Richard Burt, *Licensed by Authority: Ben Jonson and the Discourses of Censorship* (1993); Linda Charnes, *Notorious Identity: Materializing the Subject in Shakespeare* (1993); Lars Engle, *Shakespearean Pragmatism: Market of His Time* (1993); Gail Kern Paster, *The Body Embarrassed: Drama and the Disciplines of Shame in Early Modern England* (1993); Meredith Anne Skura, *Shakespeare the Actor and the Purposes of Playing* (1993); Frances E. Dolan, *Dangerous Familiars: Representations of Domestic Crime in England, 1550–1700* (1994); Kim F. Hall, *Things of Darkness: Economies of Race and Gender in Early Modern England* (1994); Jean Howard, *The Stage and Social Struggle in Early Modern England* (1994); Robert Watson, *The Rest Is Silence: Death as Annihilation in the English Renaissance* (1994); Katharine Eisaman Maus, *Inwardness and Theatre in the English Renaissance Drama* (1995); Louis Montrose, *The Purpose of Playing: Shakespeare and the Cultural Politics of the Elizabethan Theatre* (1996); Patricia Parker, *Shakespeare from the Margins: Language, Culture, Context* (1996); Jean E. Howard and Phyllis Rackin, *Engendering a Nation: A Feminist Account of Shakespeare's English Histories* (1997); Anthony B. Dawson and Paul Yachnin, *The Culture of Playgoing in Shakespeare's England* (2001); David Scott Kastan, *Shakespeare and the Book* (2001); Mary Beth Rose, *Gender and Heroism in Early Modern English Literature* (2002); and Stephen Orgel, *The Authentic Shakespeare* (2002). For other suggestions, see recent entries in the bibliography at the back of this volume.

The Comedies

The Comedy of Errors

The Comedy of Errors is a superb illustration of Shakespeare's "apprenticeship" in comedy. It is more imitative of classical comedy, especially of Plautus, than is Shakespeare's mature work. Its verbal humor, including the scatological jokes about breaking wind, the bawdy jests about cuckold's horns, and the overly ingenious banter (as in 2.2), is at times adolescent. The play abounds in the farcical humor of physical abuse, so endearing to children of all ages. It is perhaps the most uncomplicatedly funny of all Shakespeare's plays. Yet the softening touches of Shakespeare's maturity are unmistakably present as well. Shakespeare frames his farce of mistaken identity with old Egeon's tragicomic story of separation, threatened death, and eventual reunion. He adds characters to his chief sources, Plautus's *Menaechmi* and *Amphitruo* (see Appendix 2), in order to enhance the love interest and to reconcile Plautus with English moral conventions. He touches upon themes of illusion, madness, and revelry that are to figure prominently in *A Midsummer Night's Dream* and in *Twelfth Night*, a later comedy of mistaken identity. In these respects, *The Comedy of Errors* is both a fascinating prelude to Shakespeare's later development and a rich achievement in its own right. On stage, it has not attracted the greatest Shakespearean actors, since it offers no complex or dominating roles, but it has seldom failed to delight audiences.

We cannot be sure precisely how early the play was written. A performance took place on December 28, 1594, at Gray's Inn, one of the Inns of Court, before an unruly assembly of lawyers, law students, and their guests. This was probably not the first performance, however. Topical allusions offer hints of an earlier date. When Dromio of Syracuse speaks of France as "armed and reverted, making war against her heir" (3.2.123–4), he clearly is referring to the Catholic League's opposition to Henry of Navarre, who was the apparent heir to the French throne until 1593, when he became king. Another allusion, to Spain's sending "whole armadas of carracks" (lines

135–6), would possibly have lost its comic point soon after the Invincible Armada of 1588. The play's style, characterization, and imitative construction are all consistent with a date between 1589 and 1593.

Whatever the exact date, Shakespeare's youthful fascination with Plautus is manifest. Shakespeare's command of Latin, though sneered at by Ben Jonson, was undoubtedly good enough to have let him read Plautus with pleasure. He must have been drilled in Latin for years as a student in the town of Stratford-upon-Avon. Indeed, the influence of not only Plautus but also Ovid and Seneca (together with touches of Horace, Catullus, etc.) is a prominent feature of Shakespeare's early work, dramatic and nondramatic. Shakespeare may have consulted Plautus both in the original and in a contemporary translation, as was frequently his custom with non-English sources. From Renaissance Latin editions of Plautus, he apparently took the odd designation "Antipholis Sereptus" (i.e., "surreptus," snatched away), which appears in the Folio text in a stage direction at 2.1.0 to indicate the twin who was separated from his father. On the other hand, a translation of the *Menaechmi* by "W. W." (? William Warner), published in 1595, was registered in 1594 and might have been available earlier to Shakespeare in manuscript.

Plautus had much to offer Shakespeare and his fellow dramatists, especially in the way of tightly organized and complex plot construction. Native English drama of the sixteenth century tended to be episodic and panoramic in its design. Shakespeare's apprenticeship in neoclassical form can be seen in his precise observation of the unities of time and place—those unities which he openly disregarded in most of his later plays. At the play's beginning, Egeon is informed that he has until sundown to raise his ransom money, and the play then moves toward that point in time with periodic observations that it is now noon, now two o'clock, and so on. (At one point, time even seems to go backwards, but that is part of the illusion of madness.) The action is restricted to the city of Ephesus; events that have happened elsewhere, at an earlier time (such as the separation of the Antipholus family), are told to us by persons in the play, such as old Egeon. Although Shakespeare's company did not employ the sort of painted scenery drawn in perspective used by continental neoclassicists, with fixed locations for houses facing on a street, the original production of this play may nonetheless have used one stage "house" or door to represent the dwelling of Antipholus of Ephesus (the Phoenix) throughout the drama. The entire play can be staged as if all the action occurs in the vicinity of this single "house," with the Courtesan's establishment and abbey near at hand. Never again does Shakespeare utilize such a neoclassical stage.

These unities of time and place are mechanical matters, but they do also harmonize with a more essential unity of action. The story moves, as though in perfect accord with neoclassical five-act theory, from exposition and complication to climax, anagnoresis (discovery), and peripeteia (reversal of fortune). The brilliance of the plotting is decidedly Plautine. Shakespeare pushes to its limit the interweaving of comic misunderstandings only to unravel all these seemingly tightly woven knots with ease. Yet the imitation of Plautus, even in matters of construction, is by no means slavish, for Shakespeare borrows both from Plautus' farce on the mistaken identity of twins (*Menaechmi*) and from Plautus's best-known comedy (*Amphitruo*), in which a husband and his servant are excluded from their own house while a disguised visitor usurps the master's role within. Such ingenious adaptations and rearrangements were common among neoclassical dramatists like Ludovico Ariosto, and, although Shakespeare seems not to have used any of the sixteenth-century analogues to this play, he does reveal an acquaintance with neoclassical comedy and an ability to compete with the best that Europe had to offer in this vein. Such versatility is noteworthy in a young dramatist who was to reveal himself in time as far less of a neoclassicist than a native English writer. Moreover, even if his self-imposed neoclassical training was only an apprenticeship, it was to prove invaluable to Shakespeare. Despite his later tendency toward "romantic" plotting—toward the depiction of multiple actions extending over widely separated spaces and extended periods of time—Shakespeare's greatest comedies continue to point toward the same gratifying resolution of dramatic conflict in a single and well-structured denouement.

For all its Plautine skill of design, *The Comedy of Errors* is quite far removed from *The Menaechmi* in tone and spirit. Gone are the cynicism, the satirical hardness, and the amoral tone of the Roman original. The characters, though still recognizable as types, are humanized. The familiar Plautine parasite is excluded entirely. The usual clever servant happily becomes the Dromio twins.

Plautus's quack Doctor, Medicus, is hilariously transmuted into Dr. Pinch, a pedantic schoolmaster. The Courtesan's role is no longer prominent. Instead, Shakespeare creates Luciana, the virtuous sister of Adriana, who pleads the cause of forbearance in marriage and who eventually becomes the bride of Antipholus of Syracuse. *The Comedy of Errors* does not end, as do most of Shakespeare's later comedies, with a parade of couples to the altar, but the marriage of Antipholus and Luciana is at least one important step in that direction. Besides, we are told of yet another marriage still to come—that of Dromio of Ephesus to Luce, the kitchen wench. This belowstairs parody of wedded affection is thoroughly English in character and recalls a similar mirroring of courtship among the comic servants of Henry Medwall's *Fulgens and Lucrece* (c. 1497). The motif is not sufficiently stressed to threaten the unity of the main plot, but the potentiality for double plotting is unmistakable.

An even more significant contrast to Plautine farce is to be found in the romantic saga of old Egeon and his long-lost wife, the Abbess. Their story is one not of mistaken identity (though that contributes to the denouement) but of painful separation, wandering, and reunion. Indeed, the note struck at the beginning of the play might seem tragic were we not already attuned to the conventional romantic expectation that separated members of a family are likely to be restored to one another again. Egeon, threatened with immediate execution, unfolds to us a narrative of wedded bliss interrupted by the malignancy of Fortune. In contrast to the tightly controlled unity of time of the farcical action, the romantic narrative extends (by recollection) over many years of error and suffering. Egeon's tragicomic story of testing and of patient endurance is very much like that of *Apollonius of Tyre*, a popular tale used by Shakespeare in his late romance *Pericles* (c. 1606–1608). The conventions of this sort of romance, ultimately Greek in origin, stress improbability: identical twins who can be told apart only by birthmarks, a storm at sea splitting a vessel in half and neatly dividing a family, and so on. The sea is emblematic of unpredictable Fortune, taking away with one hand and restoring with the other. The wife who is lost at sea, like her counterpart in *Apollonius* or *Pericles*, takes to a life of cloistered devotion, suggesting a pattern of symbolic death, healing, and ultimate rebirth. The ending of *The Comedy of Errors* has just a hint of death restored mysteriously to life: "After so long grief, such nativity!" (5.1.407).

Egeon's story of endurance counterpoints the farce in yet another way. His arraignment before the Duke of Ephesus introduces into the play a "tragic" world of law, punishment, and death. Egeon's date with the executioner is not illusory. His predicament is the result of the bitter "mortal and intestine jars" (1.1.11) between two cities caught in a frenzy of economic reprisals. The law cannot be merciful, even though the unfairness of Egeon's plight is manifest to everyone, including the Duke. These potentially tragic factors must not be overstressed, for the first scene is brief and we are reassured by the play's hilarious tone (and by our surmising that Egeon is father of the Antipholus twins) that all will be well. Still, Shakespeare's addition of this romance plot suggests his restlessness with pure farce. As in his later comedies, which are virtually all threatened by catastrophes, the denouement of *The Comedy of Errors* is deepened into something approaching miraculous recovery. Moreover, the backdrop of a near-tragic world of genuine suffering heightens our appreciation of comic unreality in the self-contained world of Plautine farce and stresses the illusory nature of the dilemmas arising out of purely mistaken identity. Such delusions are all the more comic because they are the delusions that supposedly sane people suffer: contentiousness and jealousy in marriage, concern for respectable appearances among one's neighbors, and the suspicion that one is always being cheated in money matters. These are the chimeras that, by being made to look so plausible and yet so patently insane, are farcically exploited in Shakespeare's comic device: the inversion of madness and sanity, dreaming and waking, illusion and reality.

What happens when the behavior of one twin is mistaken for that of the other? The situation is, of course, amusing in itself, but it also serves as a test of the other characters, to discover what mad hypotheses they will construct. Adriana, faced with her husband's seeming refusal to come home to dinner, launches into a jealous tirade against husbands who neglect their wives for courtesans. The illusory situation, in other words, brings out her latent fears. We understand better now why she acts shrewishly: she fears rejection and the fading of her beauty, and she imagines that her fading beauty may be the cause of her husband's neglect. Actually, even as she speaks, her husband is busy making arrangements about a chain he means to give Adriana; but, when subsequently he is locked out of his own house and jumps to the conclusion that Adriana is being faithless, he resolves in his fury to bestow the chain on a courtesan in order to "spite my wife." He would actually do so were he not saved from this destructively revengeful impulse by the beneficently comic action of the farcical plot: through mistaken identity, the chain is delivered into the hands of his twin. Once again, illusion has prompted a character to assume the worst, to reveal his suspicions of a plot against him. And so it goes when Antipholus of Ephesus is arrested for nonpayment of the chain (he assumes that all merchants are thieves) or is denied his bail money by the servant he thinks he sent to fetch it (he assumes that all servants are thieves). We laugh at the endless capacity of the human mind for distortions of this self-punishing sort.

The metaphor used most often to convey this sense of bewilderment, even a confusion about one's own identity, is that of metamorphosis. All have drunk of Circe's cup (5.1.271) and have been transformed into animals—most of them into asses. All have hearkened to the mermaid's song and are enchanted. Ephesus, they conclude, must be haunted by sorcerers, witches, goblins, and spirits (4.3.11 ff.). Ephesus is, in fact, associated in the Bible with exorcism (Acts 19:13 ff.), and "Circe" suggests that Antipholus of Syracuse is a becalmed Odysseus. In such a mad world, the characters assume a license to embark on Saturnalian holiday. The experience of transformation thus leads to various forms of "release" from ordinary social behavior, but the experience is also disturbing and continually reminds the characters of exorcism, hell, and devils. The threat of incest hovers over the comic business of two brothers sharing a wife, and indeed there is a dark subtext to the twinning that is unavoidably present throughout the play: the twinned cities of Ephesus and Syracuse, the twinned brothers, the twinned servants, all of whom are trying to discover their identities amid the paradoxes of singleness and doubleness. The play's farcical action is never far from violence. Witches and fat kitchen wenches suggest a fascination with unruly women. The characters can explain their inverted world only by assuming that all men are lunatic, all honest women whores, and all true men thieves. "Do you know me, sir? . . . Am I myself?" "Am I in earth, or heaven, or in hell?/Sleeping or waking, mad or well advised?" (3.2.73–4, 2.2.211–12). Perhaps, as Barbara Freeman suggests, the whole play can be looked at as Egeon's dream. It is both reassuring and hilariously anticlimactic that these questionings can finally be dispelled by the most mundane of explanations: there are two Antipholuses and two Dromios.

Contained within this framework of madness and waking is a playful yet serious examination of the dynamics of courtship and marriage. The two most important women in the play are meaningfully paired and contrasted. Adriana, the shrewish wife, frets at social custom that allows her husband Antipholus to roam abroad while she is domestically confined. Her unmarried sister Luciana endorses the traditional view that husbands enjoy a precedence found everywhere in nature: males "are masters to their females, and their lords" (2.1.24). What Luciana calls obedience (line 29) her married sister calls "servitude" (line 26). Who is right? The debate, left unresolved, nonetheless raises skeptical questions about marital hierarchies. The plot also probes and tests through fantasies of inversion. A wife, believing herself rejected for having aged in her wifely obedience, locks her husband out of the house and dines with a stranger. Luciana meantime finds herself courted by what appears to be her own brother-in-law and thus must face a conflict between desire and loyalty to her sister. Of course, Adriana does not know that she is inverting authority by excluding her husband from his own hearth, but the plot of mistaken identities does allow her to act out her self-assertiveness without being, in fact, guilty of disloyalty. Her husband's role is to play the wandering male and to be eventually forgiven by his wife; presumably his exposure in Act 5 will make him a more tolerant husband, like Count Almaviva in Mozart's *The Marriage of Figaro*. The discovery of identities in Act 5 allows Luciana to marry the man she has learned to love, but without the guilt of her fantasy experience. Patriarchal values are restored by the play's conclusion, yet the partners in love and marriage have been, to some extent, liberated by their role playing in a plot of metamorphosis. These issues of domestic relations will be further explored in *The Taming of the Shrew, Othello,* and other plays.

The playfulness about illusion should not be overemphasized, for the play expends most of its energies in farce. The Dromios, with their incessant drubbings, are often the center of interest in performance, and rightly so. Shakespeare employs no behind-the-scenes manipulator of illusion, such as Puck in *A Midsummer Night's Dream* or the Duke in *Measure for Measure*. His interest in the metaphor of the world as a stage is discernible only as the foreshadowing of greatness to come. Nevertheless, Shakespeare's alterations of Plautus amply reveal the philosophic and idealistic direction that his subsequent comedy is to take.

The Comedy of Errors

[*Dramatis Personae*

SOLINUS, *Duke of Ephesus*
EGEON, *a merchant of Syracuse*
EMILIA, *Lady Abbess at Ephesus, and Egeon's wife*

ANTIPHOLUS OF EPHESUS, } *twin brothers,*
ANTIPHOLUS OF SYRACUSE, } *sons of Egeon and Emilia*

DROMIO OF EPHESUS, } *twin brothers,*
DROMIO OF SYRACUSE, } *bondsmen to the two Antipholuses*

ADRIANA, *wife of Antipholus of Ephesus*
LUCIANA, *her sister*

SCENE: *Ephesus*]

LUCE, *Adriana's kitchen maid (also known as* NELL)

BALTHASAR, *a merchant*
ANGELO, *a goldsmith*
FIRST MERCHANT, *friend to Antipholus of Syracuse*
SECOND MERCHANT, *to whom Angelo is a debtor*
DOCTOR PINCH, *a conjuring schoolmaster*
A COURTESAN
AN OFFICER
A MESSENGER

Jailer, Headsman, Officers, and other Attendants

1.1

Enter the Duke of Ephesus, with [Egeon] the merchant of Syracuse, Jailer, and other attendants.

1.1. Location: Some editors argue that the play was staged according to classical practice with three visible doors backstage representing three "houses"—that of Antipholus of Ephesus (in the center), that of the Courtesan, and that of the Priory—with the stage itself representing a marketplace or open area. More probably, the stage may have been open and unlocalized. The present scene may be at the Duke's court.

EGEON
  Proceed, Solinus, to procure my fall,
  And by the doom of death end woes and all.   2
DUKE
  Merchant of Syracusa, plead no more.   3
  I am not partial to infringe our laws.   4
  The enmity and discord which of late
  Sprung from the rancorous outrage of your Duke   6

2 doom judgment   **3 Syracusa** Syracuse, in Sicily   **4 partial** predisposed, biased   **6 outrage** violence

To merchants, our well-dealing countrymen,
Who, wanting guilders to redeem their lives,   8
Have sealed his rigorous statutes with their bloods, 9
Excludes all pity from our threat'ning looks.
For since the mortal and intestine jars   11
Twixt thy seditious countrymen and us,
It hath in solemn synods been decreed,   13
Both by the Syracusians and ourselves,
To admit no traffic to our adverse towns.   15
Nay, more, if any born at Ephesus   16
Be seen at any Syracusian marts and fairs;   17
Again, if any Syracusian born
Come to the bay of Ephesus, he dies,
His goods confiscate to the Duke's dispose,   20
Unless a thousand marks be levièd   21
To quit the penalty and to ransom him.   22
Thy substance, valued at the highest rate,   23
Cannot amount unto a hundred marks;
Therefore by law thou art condemned to die.

EGEON
Yet this my comfort: when your words are done,
My woes end likewise with the evening sun.

DUKE
Well, Syracusian, say in brief the cause
Why thou departed'st from thy native home
And for what cause thou cam'st to Ephesus.

EGEON
A heavier task could not have been imposed
Than I to speak my griefs unspeakable.   32
Yet, that the world may witness that my end
Was wrought by nature, not by vile offense,   34
I'll utter what my sorrow gives me leave.   35
In Syracusa was I born, and wed
Unto a woman, happy but for me,   37
And by me, had not our hap been bad.   38
With her I lived in joy; our wealth increased
By prosperous voyages I often made
To Epidamnum, till my factor's death   41
And the great care of goods at random left   42
Drew me from kind embracements of my spouse;
From whom my absence was not six months old
Before herself, almost at fainting under
The pleasing punishment that women bear,
Had made provision for her following me,
And soon and safe arrivèd where I was.

There had she not been long but she became
A joyful mother of two goodly sons,
And, which was strange, the one so like the other
As could not be distinguished but by names.   52
That very hour and in the selfsame inn
A mean woman was deliverèd   54
Of such a burden male, twins both alike.
Those, for their parents were exceeding poor,
I bought and brought up to attend my sons.
My wife, not meanly proud of two such boys,   58
Made daily motions for our home return;   59
Unwilling I agreed. Alas, too soon
We came aboard.
A league from Epidamnum had we sailed   62
Before the always-wind-obeying deep
Gave any tragic instance of our harm.   64
But longer did we not retain much hope;
For what obscurèd light the heavens did grant
Did but convey unto our fearful minds
A doubtful warrant of immediate death,   68
Which, though myself would gladly have embraced,
Yet the incessant weepings of my wife—
Weeping before for what she saw must come—
And piteous plainings of the pretty babes,   72
That mourned for fashion, ignorant what to fear,   73
Forced me to seek delays for them and me.   74
And this it was, for other means was none:
The sailors sought for safety by our boat
And left the ship, then sinking-ripe, to us.   77
My wife, more careful for the latter-born,   78
Had fastened him unto a small spare mast
Such as seafaring men provide for storms;
To him one of the other twins was bound,
Whilst I had been like heedful of the other.
The children thus disposed, my wife and I,
Fixing our eyes on whom our care was fixed,   84
Fastened ourselves at either end the mast,
And, floating straight, obedient to the stream,   86
Was carried towards Corinth, as we thought.
At length the sun, gazing upon the earth,
Dispersed those vapors that offended us,   89
And by the benefit of his wishèd light
The seas waxed calm, and we discoverèd
Two ships from far, making amain to us,   92
Of Corinth that, of Epidaurus this.   93
But ere they came—Oh, let me say no more!
Gather the sequel by that went before.   95

DUKE
Nay, forward, old man. Do not break off so,
For we may pity, though not pardon thee.

---

8 **wanting guilders** lacking money; the guilder was a Dutch coin worth about one shilling eight pence. **redeem** ransom 9 **sealed** ratified. **bloods** i.e., lives. (The grim analogy is to red sealing wax.)
11 **mortal** . . . **jars** deadly civil quarrels 13 **synods** assemblies
15 **To** . . . **towns** to allow no trade between our hostile towns.
16 **Ephesus** a port on the Aegean coast of modern Turkey 17 **marts** markets 20 **confiscate** confiscated. **dispose** disposal 21 **marks** money worth thirteen shillings four pence 22 **quit** pay 23 **Thy substance** The sum total of your wealth 32 **unspeakable** indescribable. (But with a punning oxymoron on the literal sense: Egeon will speak that which cannot be spoken.) 34 **by nature** i.e., by natural affection; here, a father's love 35 **gives me leave** allows me.
37–8 **happy** . . . **bad** happy only in having me, and happy indeed through me if we had not suffered misfortune. 41 **Epidamnum** (So spelled in Plautus's *The Menaechmi*); Epidamnus, a port on the coast of modern Albania. **factor's** agent's 42 **care of** anxiety about

52 **As** that they 54 **mean** of low birth 58 **not meanly** to no small degree 59 **motions** proposals, entreaties 62 **league** a measure of distance, about three miles 64 **instance** proof, sign 68 **doubtful** dreadful 72 **plainings** wailings 73 **for fashion** in imitation
74 **delays** i.e., delays from death 77 **sinking-ripe** ready to sink
78 **careful** anxious. **latter-born** (Compare line 124, however, from which we learn that the younger or "latter-born" was saved with the father.) 84 **whom** those on whom, or, him on whom 86 **straight** at once 89 **vapors** clouds 92 **making amain** proceeding at full speed
93 **Epidaurus** a Greek town southwest of Athens and Corinth; or possibly Dubrovnik, on the Adriatic coast 95 **that** that which

EGEON
Oh, had the gods done so, I had not now   98
Worthily termed them merciless to us!   99
For, ere the ships could meet by twice five leagues,
We were encountered by a mighty rock,
Which being violently borne upon,
Our helpful ship was splitted in the midst,   103
So that in this unjust divorce of us
Fortune had left to both of us alike
What to delight in, what to sorrow for.   106
Her part, poor soul, seeming as burdenèd   107
With lesser weight, but not with lesser woe,
Was carried with more speed before the wind,
And in our sight they three were taken up
By fishermen of Corinth, as we thought.
At length, another ship had seized on us,
And, knowing whom it was their hap to save,
Gave healthful welcome to their shipwrecked guests,   114
And would have reft the fishers of their prey   115
Had not their bark been very slow of sail;   116
And therefore homeward did they bend their course.
Thus have you heard me severed from my bliss,
That by misfortunes was my life prolonged,
To tell sad stories of my own mishaps.
DUKE
And, for the sake of them thou sorrowest for,
Do me the favor to dilate at full   122
What have befall'n of them and thee till now.
EGEON
My youngest boy, and yet my eldest care,
At eighteen years became inquisitive
After his brother, and importuned me
That his attendant—so his case was like,   127
Reft of his brother, but retained his name—   128
Might bear him company in the quest of him,
Whom whilst I labored of a love to see,   130
I hazarded the loss of whom I loved.   131
Five summers have I spent in farthest Greece,
Roaming clean through the bounds of Asia,   133
And, coasting homeward, came to Ephesus—   134
Hopeless to find, yet loath to leave unsought   135
Or that or any place that harbors men.   136
But here must end the story of my life,
And happy were I in my timely death   138
Could all my travels warrant me they live.   139
DUKE
Hapless Egeon, whom the fates have marked
To bear the extremity of dire mishap!   141

Now, trust me, were it not against our laws,
Against my crown, my oath, my dignity,   143
Which princes, would they, may not disannul,   144
My soul should sue as advocate for thee.
But though thou art adjudgèd to the death,   146
And passèd sentence may not be recalled   147
But to our honor's great disparagement,   148
Yet will I favor thee in what I can.
Therefore, merchant, I'll limit thee this day   150
To seek thy health by beneficial help.
Try all the friends thou hast in Ephesus;
Beg thou, or borrow, to make up the sum,
And live; if no, then thou art doomed to die.—
Jailer, take him to thy custody.
JAILER
I will, my lord.
EGEON
Hopeless and helpless doth Egeon wend,
But to procrastinate his lifeless end.   *Exeunt.* 158

❖

[1.2]

*Enter Antipholus [of Syracuse], [First] Merchant,
and Dromio [of Syracuse].*

FIRST MERCHANT
Therefore give out you are of Epidamnum,   1
Lest that your goods too soon be confiscate.
This very day a Syracusian merchant
Is apprehended for arrival here
And, not being able to buy out his life,
According to the statute of the town
Dies ere the weary sun set in the west.
There is your money that I had to keep.   8
[*He gives money.*]
S. ANTIPHOLUS [*giving the money to S. Dromio*]
Go bear it to the Centaur, where we host,   9
And stay there, Dromio, till I come to thee.
Within this hour it will be dinnertime.   11
Till that, I'll view the manners of the town,
Peruse the traders, gaze upon the buildings,
And then return and sleep within mine inn,
For with long travel I am stiff and weary.
Get thee away.
S. DROMIO
Many a man would take you at your word
And go indeed, having so good a mean.   18
Exit Dromio [of Syracuse].
S. ANTIPHOLUS
A trusty villain, sir, that very oft,   19
When I am dull with care and melancholy,

98 **had . . . so** i.e., had the gods shown pity   99 **Worthily** justly
103 **helpful ship** i.e., the mast   106 **What** something   107 **as** as if
114 **healthful** saving   115 **reft** bereft   116 **bark** sailing vessel
122 **dilate at full** relate at length   127 **so . . . like** in a similar situation
128 **Reft . . . name** (Evidently Egeon, presuming that the lost son and
servant are dead, has given their names to the surviving twin brothers.) 130–1 **Whom . . . loved** i.e., while I labored lovingly to find the
lost twin, I ran the risk of losing my younger son, whom I loved no
less.   133 **clean** entirely.   **bounds** boundaries, territories   134 **coasting** traveling along the coast   135 **Hopeless** despairing   136 **Or**
either   138 **timely** speedy, opportune   139 **travels** "travails," or
hardships, as well as travels.   **warrant** assure   141 **mishap** (Punning
on *Hapless* in line 140.)

143 **dignity** high office   144 **would they** even if they wished.
disannul annul, cancel   146 **the death** i.e., death by judicial sentence
147 **recalled** revoked   148 **But** except   150 **limit** allow, appoint
158 **procrastinate** postpone
1.2. Location: The street.
1 **give out** say   8 **keep** safeguard.   9 **Centaur** the name of an inn,
identified by its sign over the door. In mythology, a centaur is half
horse, half man.   **host** lodge   11 **dinnertime** i.e., noon   18 **mean**
(1) opportunity (2) money.   19 **villain** servant. (Said good-humoredly.)

Lightens my humor with his merry jests.   21
What, will you walk with me about the town
And then go to my inn and dine with me?

FIRST MERCHANT
I am invited, sir, to certain merchants,
Of whom I hope to make much benefit;
I crave your pardon. Soon at five o'clock,   26
Please you, I'll meet with you upon the mart
And afterward consort you till bedtime.   28
My present business calls me from you now.

S. ANTIPHOLUS
Farewell till then. I will go lose myself   30
And wander up and down to view the city.

FIRST MERCHANT
Sir, I commend you to your own content.   *Exit.*

S. ANTIPHOLUS
He that commends me to mine own content
Commends me to the thing I cannot get.
I to the world am like a drop of water   35
That in the ocean seeks another drop,
Who, falling there to find his fellow forth,   37
Unseen, inquisitive, confounds himself.   38
So I, to find a mother and a brother,
In quest of them, unhappy, lose myself.

Enter Dromio of Ephesus.

Here comes the almanac of my true date.—   41
What now? How chance thou art returned so soon?   42

E. DROMIO
Returned so soon? Rather approached too late:
The capon burns, the pig falls from the spit,
The clock hath strucken twelve upon the bell;
My mistress made it one upon my cheek.   46
She is so hot because the meat is cold;   47
The meat is cold because you come not home;
You come not home because you have no stomach;   49
You have no stomach, having broke your fast.
But we that know what 'tis to fast and pray
Are penitent for your default today.   52

S. ANTIPHOLUS
Stop in your wind, sir. Tell me this, I pray: 53
Where have you left the money that I gave you?

E. DROMIO
Oh—sixpence that I had o'Wednesday last
To pay the saddler for my mistress' crupper?   56
The saddler had it, sir; I kept it not.

S. ANTIPHOLUS
I am not in a sportive humor now.
Tell me, and dally not: where is the money?
We being strangers here, how dar'st thou trust
So great a charge from thine own custody?   61

E. DROMIO
I pray you, jest, sir, as you sit at dinner.
I from my mistress come to you in post;   63
If I return; I shall be post indeed,   64
For she will scour your fault upon my pate.   65
Methinks your maw, like mine, should be your clock   66
And strike you home without a messenger.

S. ANTIPHOLUS
Come, Dromio, come, these jests are out of season;
Reserve them till a merrier hour than this.
Where is the gold I gave in charge to thee?

E. DROMIO
To me, sir? Why, you gave no gold to me.

S. ANTIPHOLUS
Come on, sir knave, have done your foolishness,
And tell me how thou hast disposed thy charge.   73

E. DROMIO
My charge was but to fetch you from the mart
Home to your house, the Phoenix, sir, to dinner;   75
My mistress and her sister stays for you.

S. ANTIPHOLUS
Now, as I am a Christian, answer me
In what safe place you have bestowed my money,
Or I shall break that merry sconce of yours   79
That stands on tricks when I am undisposed.   80
Where is the thousand marks thou hadst of me?

E. DROMIO
I have some marks of yours upon my pate,
Some of my mistress' marks upon my shoulders,
But not a thousand marks between you both.
If I should pay Your Worship those again,
Perchance you will not bear them patiently.

S. ANTIPHOLUS
Thy mistress' marks? What mistress, slave, hast thou?

E. DROMIO
Your Worship's wife, my mistress at the Phoenix,
She that doth fast till you come home to dinner
And prays that you will hie you home to dinner.   90

S. ANTIPHOLUS
What, wilt thou flout me thus unto my face,
Being forbid? There, take you that, sir knave.
                        [He beats Dromio of Ephesus.]

E. DROMIO
What mean you, sir? For God sake, hold your hands!
Nay, an you will not, sir, I'll take my heels.   94
                        Exit Dromio of Ephesus.

S. ANTIPHOLUS
Upon my life, by some device or other
The villain is o'erraught of all my money.   96
They say this town is full of cozenage,   97
As nimble jugglers that deceive the eye,

---

21 humor mood, disposition   **26 Soon at** About   **28 consort** accompany   **30 lose myself** roam freely   **35 to** in relation to   **37 to . . . forth** to find his companion   **38 confounds himself** mingles indistinguishably.   **41 the almanac . . . date** (Being born in the same hour, Dromio serves as an almanac by which Antipholus can see his age.)   **42 How chance** How comes it   **46 My . . . cheek** i.e., your wife slapped my cheek. (Dromio puns on the idea of the clock *striking* the hour.)   **47 hot** angry   **49 stomach** appetite.   **52 penitent** doing penance (i.e., suffering hunger).   **default** fault   **53 wind** i.e., words   **56 crupper** leather strap on a saddle that is passed under the horse's tail in order to keep the saddle from riding forward.   **61 charge** responsibility

63 post haste   **64 post** door-post of a tavern used for keeping reckonings   **65 scour** beat. (With a pun on the idea of keeping score.)   **66 maw** stomach. (Applied usually to animals.)   **73 disposed** disposed of   **75 the Phoenix** the sign of Antipholus of Ephesus's shop. (He lives and carries on his business in the same dwelling.) In mythology, a phoenix is a fabulous bird that periodically is regenerated from its own ashes.   **79 sconce** head   **80 stands on** insists on, engages in   **90 hie** hasten   **94 an** if.   **take my heels** take to my heels.   **96 The . . . money** the rascal has cheated me out of all my money.   **97 cozenage** cheating

Dark-working sorcerers that change the mind,
Soul-killing witches that deform the body,
Disguisèd cheaters, prating mountebanks,   101
And many suchlike liberties of sin.   102
If it prove so, I will be gone the sooner.
I'll to the Centaur to go seek this slave.
I greatly fear my money is not safe.   *Exit.*

❖

2.1

Enter Adriana, wife to Antipholus [of Ephesus],
with Luciana, her sister.

ADRIANA
Neither my husband nor the slave returned
That in such haste I sent to seek his master?
Sure, Luciana, it is two o'clock.

LUCIANA
Perhaps some merchant hath invited him,
And from the mart he's somewhere gone to dinner.
Good sister, let us dine, and never fret.
A man is master of his liberty;
Time is their master, and when they see time   8
They'll go or come. If so, be patient, sister.

ADRIANA
Why should their liberty than ours be more?

LUCIANA
Because their business still lies out o'door.   11

ADRIANA
Look when I serve him so, he takes it ill.   12

LUCIANA
Oh, know he is the bridle of your will.

ADRIANA
There's none but asses will be bridled so.

LUCIANA
Why, headstrong liberty is lashed with woe.   15
There's nothing situate under heaven's eye
But hath his bound, in earth, in sea, in sky.   17
The beasts, the fishes, and the wingèd fowls
Are their males' subjects and at their controls.
Man, more divine, the master of all these,
Lord of the wide world and wild wat'ry seas,
Endued with intellectual sense and souls,   22
Of more preeminence than fish and fowls,
Are masters to their females, and their lords.
Then let your will attend on their accords.   25

ADRIANA
This servitude makes you to keep unwed.

LUCIANA
Not this, but troubles of the marriage bed.

ADRIANA
But, were you wedded, you would bear some sway.

LUCIANA
Ere I learn love, I'll practice to obey.

ADRIANA
How if your husband start some other where?   30

LUCIANA
Till he come home again, I would forbear.

ADRIANA
Patience unmoved! No marvel though she pause;
They can be meek that have no other cause.   33
A wretched soul, bruised with adversity,   34
We bid be quiet when we hear it cry;
But were we burdened with like weight of pain,
As much or more we should ourselves complain.
So thou, that hast no unkind mate to grieve thee,
With urging helpless patience would relieve me;   39
But if thou live to see like right bereft,   40
This fool-begged patience in thee will be left.   41

LUCIANA
Well, I will marry one day, but to try.   42
Here comes your man; now is your husband nigh.   43

Enter Dromio of Ephesus.

ADRIANA
Say, is your tardy master now at hand?

E. DROMIO Nay, he's at two hands with me, and that   45
my two ears can witness.

ADRIANA
Say, didst thou speak with him? Know'st thou his
mind?

E. DROMIO
I? Ay, he told his mind upon mine ear.   48
Beshrew his hand, I scarce could understand it.   49

LUCIANA
Spake he so doubtfully thou couldst not feel his
meaning?   50

E. DROMIO Nay, he struck so plainly I could too well
feel his blows, and withal so doubtfully that I could   52
scarce understand them.

ADRIANA
But say, I prithee, is he coming home?
It seems he hath great care to please his wife.

E. DROMIO
Why, mistress, sure my master is horn-mad.   56

ADRIANA
Horn-mad, thou villain?

E. DROMIO   I mean not cuckold-mad,
But sure he is stark mad.
When I desired him to come home to dinner,

---

101 **mountebanks** charlatans 102 **liberties of sin** persons allowed
improper freedom to sin. (With a suggestion of certain districts, as in
the London area, that were exempt from civic jurisdiction and were,
in a punning sense, places of "license.")
2.1 Location: The house of Antipholus of Ephesus.
8 **Time** Time alone. **see time** see fit 11 **still** constantly 12 **Look
when** Whenever 15 **Why . . . woe** Headstrong liberty (in a wife) is
whipped and punished with unhappiness. (Luciana argues that a
wife is better off obeying her husband.) 17 **his** its 22 **intellectual
sense** reason 25 **accords** consent.

30 **start . . . where** i.e., goes off elsewhere, after other women.
33 **other cause** cause to be otherwise. 34 **A wretched soul** i.e., A
fussy, crying baby 39 **helpless** passive 40–1 **But . . . left** i.e., but if
you live to see your rights similarly taken away, you will abandon
this foolishly urged patience. 42 **but to try** i.e., just to put it to the
test. 43 **man** servant 45 **at two hands** (Alluding to the beating he
received at 1.2.92.) 48 **told** (Punning on "tolled.") 49 **Beshrew** Bad
luck to. **understand** (With pun on "stand up under"; also in line 53.)
50 **doubtfully** ambiguously 52 **doubtfully** dreadfully 56 **horn-
mad** mad as a horned beast. (With a quibble on the sense of rage at
being made a cuckold.)

He asked me for a thousand marks in gold.
" 'Tis dinnertime," quoth I. "My gold!" quoth he.
"Your meat doth burn," quoth I. "My gold!" quoth he.
"Will you come home?" quoth I. "My gold!" quoth he.
"Where is the thousand marks I gave thee, villain?"
"The pig," quoth I, "is burned." "My gold!" quoth he.
"My mistress, sir—" quoth I. "Hang up thy mistress!   66
I know not thy mistress. Out on thy mistress!"

LUCIANA   Quoth who?

E. DROMIO   Quoth my master.
"I know," quoth he, "no house, no wife, no mistress."
So that my errand, due unto my tongue,   71
I thank him, I bare home upon my shoulders;   72
For, in conclusion, he did beat me there.

ADRIANA
Go back again, thou slave, and fetch him home.

E. DROMIO
Go back again and be new beaten home?
For God's sake, send some other messenger.

ADRIANA
Back, slave, or I will break thy pate across.

E. DROMIO
And he will bless that cross with other beating.   78
Between you I shall have a holy head.   79

ADRIANA
Hence, prating peasant! Fetch thy master home.
[She beats Dromio.]

E. DROMIO
Am I so round with you as you with me,   81
That like a football you do spurn me thus?
You spurn me hence, and he will spurn me hither.
If I last in this service, you must case me in leather.
[Exit.]

LUCIANA
Fie, how impatience loureth in your face!   85

ADRIANA
His company must do his minions grace,   86
Whilst I at home starve for a merry look.
Hath homely age th'alluring beauty took   88
From my poor cheek? Then he hath wasted it.   89
Are my discourses dull? Barren my wit?   90
If voluble and sharp discourse be marred,   91
Unkindness blunts it more than marble hard.   92
Do their gay vestments his affections bait?   93
That's not my fault; he's master of my state.   94
What ruins are in me that can be found
By him not ruined? Then is he the ground   96

Of my defeatures. My decayèd fair   97
A sunny look of his would soon repair.
But, too unruly deer, he breaks the pale   99
And feeds from home. Poor I am but his stale.   100

LUCIANA
Self-harming jealousy! Fie, beat it hence!

ADRIANA
Unfeeling fools can with such wrongs dispense.   102
I know his eye doth homage otherwhere,
Or else what lets it but he would be here?   104
Sister, you know he promised me a chain.
Would that alone o' love he would detain,   106
So he would keep fair quarter with his bed!   107
I see the jewel best enamelèd   108
Will lose his beauty; yet the gold bides still   109
That others touch, and often touching will   110
Wear gold; and no man that hath a name   111
By falsehood and corruption doth it shame.   112
Since that my beauty cannot please his eye,
I'll weep what's left away, and weeping die.

LUCIANA
How many fond fools serve mad jealousy!   115

Exeunt.

❖

[2.2]

Enter Antipholus of Syracuse.

S. ANTIPHOLUS
The gold I gave to Dromio is laid up
Safe at the Centaur, and the heedful slave
Is wandered forth in care to seek me out
By computation and mine host's report.   4
I could not speak with Dromio since at first
I sent him from the mart. See, here he comes.

Enter Dromio of Syracuse.

How now, sir, is your merry humor altered?
As you love strokes, so jest with me again.   8
You know no Centaur? You received no gold?
Your mistress sent to have me home to dinner?
My house was at the Phoenix? Wast thou mad,
That thus so madly thou didst answer me?

S. DROMIO
What answer, sir? When spake I such a word?

---

66 Hang up i.e., To hell with   **71 due . . . tongue** which I should have delivered by my tongue   **72 I bare . . . shoulders** I took in the form of a beating   **78 he . . . cross** i.e., he will add further devotion in the form of a beating. (There is a pun on "to bless," to wound, from the French *blesser*. *Cross* is a quibble on *across* in the previous line.)
79 holy (Punning on the sense "full of holes.")   **81 round** plainspoken. (With pun on the sense of "spherical.")   **85 loureth** frowns, scowls   **86 His . . . grace** He bestows favors on his darling paramours   **88 took** taken   **89 wasted** (1) squandered (2) laid waste to, ruined   **90 discourses** conversations   **91–2 If . . . hard** i.e., If my fluent and sometimes too shrewish discourse seems peevish to my husband, unkindness on his part simply blunts it even more than when a sharp instrument is struck against hard marble.   **93 his affections bait** entice his passions   **94 state** outward estate, condition, i.e., clothes.   **96 ground** cause

97 defeatures disfigurements.   **decayèd fair** impaired or perished beauty   **99 pale** enclosure   **100 from** away from.   **stale** rejected lover who has become a laughingstock. (With a pun on *stale*, tiresomely lacking in freshness; she is stale to him, he dear [*deer*] to her.)
102 Unfeeling . . . dispense Only an insensitive fool would condone such wrongs.   **104 lets** hinders   **106 Would . . . detain** Would that he would withhold only that token of his affection (?)   **107 So . . . bed!** provided he would remain faithful to his marriage bed!   **108–12 I see . . . shame** (A difficult passage. Adriana comments that a showy jewel, like a gaudily dressed woman [as in line 93], will lose its beauty in time, whereas a true wife is like gold, which, if properly handled, remains unsullied; no husband of good reputation should be ashamed of virtuous use like this in his wife.)   **109 his** its
115 fond doting
2.2 location: The street before Antipholus of Ephesus' house.
4 computation estimation, reckoning   **8 strokes** blows

S. ANTIPHOLUS
Even now, even here, not half an hour since.

S. DROMIO
I did not see you since you sent me hence
Home to the Centaur with the gold you gave me.

S. ANTIPHOLUS
Villain, thou didst deny the gold's receipt
And told'st me of a mistress and a dinner,
For which I hope thou felt'st I was displeased.

S. DROMIO
I am glad to see you in this merry vein.
What means this jest? I pray you, master, tell me.

S. ANTIPHOLUS
Yea, dost thou jeer and flout me in the teeth? 22
Think'st thou I jest? Hold, take thou that, and that.
Beats Dromio.

S. DROMIO
Hold, sir, for God's sake! Now your jest is earnest. 24
Upon what bargain do you give it me?

S. ANTIPHOLUS
Because that I familiarly sometimes
Do use you for my fool and chat with you,
Your sauciness will jest upon my love 28
And make a common of my serious hours. 29
When the sun shines let foolish gnats make sport,
But creep in crannies when he hides his beams.
If you will jest with me, know my aspect 32
And fashion your demeanor to my looks,
Or I will beat this method in your sconce. 34

S. DROMIO   "Sconce" call you it? So you would leave battering, I had rather have it a head. An you use these 36
blows long, I must get a sconce for my head and in- 37
sconce it too, or else I shall seek my wit in my shoul- 38
ders. But I pray, sir, why am I beaten? 39

S. ANTIPHOLUS   Dost thou not know?

S. DROMIO   Nothing, sir, but that I am beaten.

S. ANTIPHOLUS   Shall I tell you why?

S. DROMIO   Ay, sir, and wherefore; for they say every
why hath a wherefore.

S. ANTIPHOLUS   "Why," first—for flouting me; and then,
"wherefore"—for urging it the second time to me.

S. DROMIO
Was there ever any man thus beaten out of season, 47
When in the why and the wherefore is neither rhyme
nor reason?
Well, sir, I thank you.

S. ANTIPHOLUS   Thank me, sir, for what?

S. DROMIO   Marry, sir, for this something that you gave 51
me for nothing.

S. ANTIPHOLUS   I'll make you amends next, to give you
nothing for something. But say, sir, is it dinnertime?

S. DROMIO   No, sir, I think the meat wants that I have. 55

S. ANTIPHOLUS   In good time, sir, what's that? 56

S. DROMIO   Basting. 57

S. ANTIPHOLUS   Well, sir, then 'twill be dry.

S. DROMIO   If it be, sir, I pray you, eat none of it.

S. ANTIPHOLUS   Your reason?

S. DROMIO   Lest it make you choleric and purchase me 61
another dry basting. 62

S. ANTIPHOLUS   Well, sir, learn to jest in good time.
There's a time for all things.

S. DROMIO   I durst have denied that before you were
so choleric.

S. ANTIPHOLUS   By what rule, sir?

S. DROMIO   Marry, sir, by a rule as plain as the plain bald
pate of Father Time himself.

S. ANTIPHOLUS   Let's hear it.

S. DROMIO   There's no time for a man to recover his hair
that grows bald by nature.

S. ANTIPHOLUS   May he not do it by fine and recovery? 73

S. DROMIO   Yes, to pay a fine for a periwig and recover
the lost hair of another man.

S. ANTIPHOLUS   Why is Time such a niggard of hair,
being, as it is, so plentiful an excrement? 77

S. DROMIO   Because it is a blessing that he bestows on
beasts, and what he hath scanted men in hair he hath
given them in wit.

S. ANTIPHOLUS   Why, but there's many a man hath
more hair than wit.

S. DROMIO   Not a man of those but he hath the wit to 83
lose his hair. 84

S. ANTIPHOLUS   Why, thou didst conclude hairy men
plain dealers without wit.

S. DROMIO   The plainer dealer, the sooner lost. Yet he 87
loseth it in a kind of jollity. 88

S. ANTIPHOLUS   For what reason?

S. DROMIO   For two, and sound ones too.

S. ANTIPHOLUS   Nay, not sound, I pray you. 91

S. DROMIO   Sure ones, then.

S. ANTIPHOLUS   Nay, not sure, in a thing falsing. 93

S. DROMIO   Certain ones, then.

S. ANTIPHOLUS   Name them.

S. DROMIO   The one, to save the money that he spends in
tiring; the other, that at dinner they should not drop in 97
his porridge.

S. ANTIPHOLUS   You would all this time have proved
there is no time for all things.

---

22 in the teeth to my face.   **24 earnest** serious. (With a pun on the financial sense: money paid as an installment to secure a bargain.) **28 jest upon** trifle with   **29 common** public playground   **32 aspect** look, expression; also, astrological favor or disfavor of a planet **34 sconce** head. (With pun on the meaning "fort" in line 35 and "helmet" or "protective covering" in line 37; the *battering*, lines 35–6, is both a beating and assault by a battering ram.)   **36 An** If **37–8 insconce** shelter within a sconce or fortification   **38–9 I shall . . . shoulders** i.e., my head will be beaten into my shoulders. **47 out of season** inappropriately   **51 Marry** i.e., Truly. (A shortened form of the oath "by the Virgin Mary.")

55 wants that lacks that which   **56 In good time** Indeed   **57 Basting** (1) Moistening with butter or drippings during cooking (2) Beating. **61 choleric** (Hot or dry food was thought to produce or aggravate the choleric or irascible humor.)   **62 dry basting** hard beating. **73 fine and recovery** a legal procedure for converting an entailed estate, one in which the property is limited to specified heirs, into a fee simple, one in which the owner has unqualified ownership. **77 excrement** outgrowth (of hair).   **83–4 he . . . hair** (A reference to the venereal diseases in which loss of hair was a symptom.) **87 dealer** i.e., dealer with women   **88 a kind of jollity** i.e., sexual pleasure.   **91 not sound** invalid. (With a pun on "venereally diseased.")   **93 falsing** deceptive. (Continuing the joke on venereal disease.)   **97 tiring** dressing the hair

S. DROMIO Marry, and did, sir; namely, e'en no time to
recover hair lost by nature.
S. ANTIPHOLUS But your reason was not substantial
why there is no time to recover.
S. DROMIO Thus I mend it: Time himself is bald and 105
therefore to the world's end will have bald followers.
S. ANTIPHOLUS I knew 'twould be a bald conclusion. 107
But soft, who wafts us yonder? 108

Enter Adriana [beckoning], and Luciana.

ADRIANA
Ay, ay, Antipholus, look strange and frown. 109
Some other mistress hath thy sweet aspects; 110
I am not Adriana, nor thy wife.
The time was once when thou unurged wouldst vow
That never words were music to thine ear,
That never object pleasing in thine eye,
That never touch well welcome to thy hand,
That never meat sweet-savored in thy taste,
Unless I spake, or looked, or touched, or carved to thee.
How comes it now, my husband, oh, how comes it,
That thou art then estrangèd from thyself? 119
Thyself I call it, being strange to me
That, undividable, incorporate,
Am better than thy dear self's better part.
Ah, do not tear away thyself from me!
For know, my love, as easy mayst thou fall 124
A drop of water in the breaking gulf, 125
And take unmingled thence that drop again
Without addition or diminishing,
As take from me thyself and not me too. 128
How dearly would it touch thee to the quick, 129
Shouldst thou but hear I were licentious
And that this body, consecrate to thee, 131
By ruffian lust should be contaminate! 132
Wouldst thou not spit at me, and spurn at me, 133
And hurl the name of husband in my face,
And tear the stained skin off my harlot brow,
And from my false hand cut the wedding ring,
And break it with a deep-divorcing vow?
I know thou canst, and therefore see thou do it. 138
I am possessed with an adulterate blot; 139
My blood is mingled with the crime of lust. 140
For if we two be one, and thou play false, 141
I do digest the poison of thy flesh, 142
Being strumpeted by thy contagion. 143

Keep then fair league and truce with thy true bed, 144
I live distained, thou undishonorèd. 145
S. ANTIPHOLUS
Plead you to me, fair dame? I know you not.
In Ephesus I am but two hours old,
As strange unto your town as to your talk,
Who, every word by all my wit being scanned, 149
Wants wit in all one word to understand. 150
LUCIANA
Fie, brother, how the world is changed with you!
When were you wont to use my sister thus? 152
She sent for you by Dromio home to dinner.
S. ANTIPHOLUS By Dromio?
S. DROMIO By me?
ADRIANA
By thee; and this thou didst return from him:
That he did buffet thee and in his blows
Denied my house for his, me for his wife.
S. ANTIPHOLUS
Did you converse, sir, with this gentlewoman?
What is the course and drift of your compact? 160
S. DROMIO
I, sir? I never saw her till this time.
S. ANTIPHOLUS
Villain, thou liest, for even her very words
Didst thou deliver to me on the mart.
S. DROMIO
I never spake with her in all my life.
S. ANTIPHOLUS
How can she thus then call us by our names,
Unless it be by inspiration?
ADRIANA
How ill agrees it with your gravity 167
To counterfeit thus grossly with your slave, 168
Abetting him to thwart me in my mood! 169
Be it my wrong you are from me exempt, 170
But wrong not that wrong with a more contempt. 171
Come, I will fasten on this sleeve of thine.
[She clings to him.]
Thou art an elm, my husband, I a vine,
Whose weakness, married to thy stronger state,
Makes me with thy strength to communicate. 175
If aught possess thee from me, it is dross, 176
Usurping ivy, brier, or idle moss, 177
Who, all for want of pruning, with intrusion 178
Infect thy sap and live on thy confusion. 179
S. ANTIPHOLUS *[aside]*
To me she speaks; she moves me for her theme. 180

105 Time . . . bald (Time is conventionally personified as an old bald man, with only a forelock of hair; one must seize opportunity by the forelock, i.e., quickly, or the occasion will be lost.) 107 bald i.e., senseless, stupid. (Continuing the joke about baldness.) 108 soft gently, wait a minute. wafts beckons 109 strange estranged, distant 110 aspects glances 119 then therefore. estrangèd from thyself (1) behaving unlike yourself (2) estranged from me, your other half. 124 fall let fall 125 breaking gulf surf-crested sea 128 and . . . too without taking me from myself (since we are inseparable and indivisible). 129 the quick the most sensitive or vulnerable part 131 consecrate consecrated 132 contaminate contaminated. 133 spurn kick 138–43 I know . . . contagion i.e., Go ahead and divorce me, since you have the right to do it; because we are one flesh as husband and wife, when you commit adultery it taints me also with the guilt of having been a strumpet. (Said with bitter irony.)

144 Keep . . . truce If you remain faithful to your marriage vows 145 distained unstained (by contagion) 149–50 Who . . . understand i.e., and I, though listening intently to every word, cannot understand one word of what you've said. 152 use treat 160 compact plot. 167 gravity social dignity 168 grossly obviously 169 Abetting helping. mood anger. 170–1 Be . . . contempt i.e., Even if it's my fault that your affections wander, don't make it worse with your contempt. 175 with . . . communicate share in your strength. 176 If . . . dross If anything usurps my possession of you, it is an impure substance 177 idle unprofitable 178 Who which. want lack. intrusion forced entry 179 confusion ruin. 180 moves . . . theme appeals to me as her subject of discourse.

What, was I married to her in my dream?
Or sleep I now and think I hear all this?
What error drives our eyes and ears amiss?
Until I know this sure uncertainty,   184
I'll entertain the offered fallacy.   185

LUCIANA
Dromio, go bid the servants spread for dinner.   186

S. DROMIO
Oh, for my beads! I cross me for a sinner.   187
                                    [He crosses himself.]
This is the fairy land. Oh, spite of spites,
We talk with goblins, elves, and sprites!   189
If we obey them not, this will ensue:
They'll suck our breath or pinch us black and blue.   191

LUCIANA
Why prat'st thou to thyself and answer'st not?   192
Dromio, thou drone, thou snail, thou slug, thou sot!   193

S. DROMIO
I am transformèd, master, am not I?

S. ANTIPHOLUS
I think thou art in mind, and so am I.

S. DROMIO
Nay, master, both in mind and in my shape.

S. ANTIPHOLUS
Thou hast thine own form.

S. DROMIO   No, I am an ape.   197

LUCIANA
If thou art changed to aught, 'tis to an ass.

S. DROMIO
'Tis true; she rides me and I long for grass.   199
'Tis so, I am an ass; else it could never be
But I should know her as well as she knows me.

ADRIANA
Come, come, no longer will I be a fool,
To put the finger in the eye and weep
Whilst man and master laughs my woes to scorn.
Come, sir, to dinner.—Dromio, keep the gate.—
Husband, I'll dine above with you today   206
And shrive you of a thousand idle pranks.—   207
Sirrah, if any ask you for your master,   208
Say he dines forth, and let no creature enter.—   209
Come, sister.—Dromio, play the porter well.

S. ANTIPHOLUS [aside]
Am I in earth, in heaven, or in hell?
Sleeping or waking, mad or well-advised?
Known unto these, and to myself disguised?   212
I'll say as they say, and persever so,
And in this mist at all adventures go.   215

S. DROMIO
Master, shall I be porter at the gate?

ADRIANA
Ay, and let none enter, lest I break you pate.

LUCIANA
Come, come, Antipholus, we dine too late.
[Exeunt. Dromio of Syracuse remains as porter,
visible to the audience but not to those approaching
the door.]

❧

3.1

*Enter Antipholus of Ephesus, his man Dromio,
Angelo the goldsmith, and Balthasar the merchant.*

E. ANTIPHOLUS
Good Signor Angelo, you must excuse us all;
My wife is shrewish when I keep not hours.   2
Say that I lingered with you at your shop
To see the making of her carcanet   4
And that tomorrow you will bring it home.—
But here's a villain that would face me down   6
He met me on the mart, and that I beat him
And charged him with a thousand marks in gold,   8
And that I did deny my wife and house.—   9
Thou drunkard, thou, what didst thou mean by this?

E. DROMIO
Say what you will, sir, but I know what I know.
That you beat me at the mart, I have your hand to show.   12
If the skin were parchment and the blows you gave
    were ink,
Your own handwriting would tell you what I think.

E. ANTIPHOLUS
I think thou art an ass.

E. DROMIO   Marry, so it doth appear
By the wrongs I suffer and the blows I bear.
I should kick, being kicked, and, being at that pass,   17
You would keep from my heels and beware of an ass.

E. ANTIPHOLUS
You're sad, Signor Balthasar. Pray God our cheer   19
May answer my good will and your good welcome
    here.   20

BALTHASAR
I hold your dainties cheap, sir, and your welcome
    dear.   21

E. ANTIPHOLUS
Oh, Signor Balthasar, either at flesh or fish,
A table full of welcome makes scarce one dainty
    dish.   23

---

184 **Until . . . uncertainty** Until I can fathom the meaning of what is certainly a mystery. (Stated as an oxymoron.)   185 **entertain** accept. **fallacy** delusive notion, error.   186 **spread** set the table   187 **beads** rosary beads.   189 **sprites** spirits.   191 **suck our breath** (This piece of folklore was perhaps connected with the old idea that the breath of a person was that person's soul. Fairies were famous for sucking and pinching.)   192 **prat'st thou** do you chatter   193 **sot** fool.   197 **ape** i.e., counterfeit.   199 **for grass** for freedom (as a horse put out to pasture).   206 **above** i.e., on the second floor, above Antipholus's shop   207 **shrive** hear confession and give absolution   208 **Sirrah** (Customary form of address to servants.)   209 **forth** away from home   212 **well-advised** in my right mind.   215 **at all adventures** whatever may happen

3.1 Location: Before the house of Antipholus of Ephesus. The scene is continuous with the previous one.
2 **keep not hours** am not punctual.   4 **carcanet** necklace (the *chain* of 2.1.105 and line 115 below)   6 **face me down** maintain to my face that   8 **charged him with** entrusted him with possession of   9 **deny** disown   12 **hand** i.e., handiwork on my body. (With a pun on "handwriting.")   17 **at that pass** in that situation   19 **sad** serious. **cheer** entertainment   20 **answer** agree with, match   21 **dainties** delicacies. **cheap** of minor importance. **dear** of primary importance.
23 **makes scarce** scarcely equals

BALTHASAR
Good meat, sir, is common; that every churl affords. 24

E. ANTIPHOLUS
And welcome more common, for that's nothing
but words.

BALTHASAR
Small cheer and great welcome makes a merry feast.

E. ANTIPHOLUS
Ay, to a niggardly host and more sparing guest. 27
But though my cates be mean, take them in good
part; 28
Better cheer may you have, but not with better heart.
*[They approach the door of Antipholus of Ephesus's
house.]*
But soft! My door is locked. *[To Dromio]* Go bid them
let us in.

E. DROMIO *[calling]*
Maud, Bridget, Marian, Cicely, Gillian, Ginn!

S. DROMIO *[speaking from the other side of the door]*
Mome, malt-horse, capon, coxcomb, idiot, patch! 32
Either get thee from the door or sit down at the
hatch. 33
Dost thou conjure for wenches, that thou call'st for
such store 34
When one is one too many? Go, get thee from the
door.

E. DROMIO
What patch is made our porter? My master stays in
the street. 36

S. DROMIO
Let him walk from whence he came, lest he catch cold
on 's feet. 37

E. ANTIPHOLUS
Who talks within there? Ho, open the door!

S. DROMIO
Right, sir, I'll tell you when, an you'll tell me
wherefore. 39

E. ANTIPHOLUS
Wherefore? For my dinner. I have not dined today.

S. DROMIO
Nor today here you must not. Come again when
you may.

E. ANTIPHOLUS
What art thou that keep'st me out from the house I
owe? 42

S. DROMIO
The porter for this time, sir, and my name is Dromio.

E. DROMIO
O villain! Thou hast stol'n both mine office and my
name.
The one ne'er got me credit, the other mickle blame. 45
If thou hadst been Dromio today in my place,
Thou wouldst have changed thy face for a name or
thy name for an ass. 47

*Enter Luce [above, concealed from Antipholus of
Ephesus and his companions].*

LUCE
What a coil is there, Dromio? Who are those at the
gate? 48

E. DROMIO
Let my master in, Luce.

LUCE   Faith, no, he comes too late,
And so tell your master.

E. DROMIO   Oh, Lord, I must laugh!
Have at you with a proverb: Shall I set in my staff? 51

LUCE
Have at you with another: that's—When, can you
tell? 52

S. DROMIO
If thy name be called Luce, Luce, thou hast answered
him well.

E. ANTIPHOLUS *[to Luce]*
Do you hear, you minion? You'll let us in, I hope? 54

LUCE
I thought to have asked you.

S. DROMIO   And you said no.

E. DROMIO
So, come help. *[They beat the door.]* Well struck!
There was blow for blow.

E. ANTIPHOLUS *[to Luce]*
Thou baggage, let me in.

LUCE   Can you tell for whose sake? 57

E. DROMIO
Master, knock the door hard.

LUCE   Let him knock till it ache.

E. ANTIPHOLUS
You'll cry for this, minion, if I beat the door down.
[He knocks.]

LUCE
What needs all that, and a pair of stocks in the town? 60

*Enter Adriana [above, concealed, like Luce and
Dromio of Syracuse, from those at the door].*

---

24 **every churl** i.e., everyone 27 **sparing** self-denying 28 **cates** provisions, dainties. **mean** plain, simple 32 **s.d.** *speaking . . . door* (Dromio of Syracuse has remained onstage since the end of the previous scene, visible to the audience but not to those at the door. Alternatively, he could exist at the end of 2.2 and speak now *within*, or enter at this point, but neither solution seems satisfactory. Compare the entrances of Luce and Adriana at lines 47 and 60.) 32 **Mome** Dolt, blockhead. **malt-horse** brewer's horse; stupid person. **patch** fool, clown. 33 **hatch** half-door that can be kept closed while the upper half is opened. 34 **conjure for** summon as if by magic. **store** quantity 36 **What . . . porter?** i.e., What clown is this who is acting as gatekeeper? **stays** waits 37 **on 's** in his 39 **an** if. **wherefore** why. 42 **owe** own.

45 **The one . . . blame** i.e., My name has never benefited me, my office of servant has got me much blame. 47 **Thou . . . ass** i.e., you would have been glad to change places with someone else (since I was beaten like a beast of burden). 47.1 *Enter Luce [above]* (Here and at line 60, Luce and then Adriana may enter above in such a way that the audience understands them not to be visible to those who are calling at the door.) 48 **coil** noise, disturbance 51 **Have . . . staff** Let me come at you with a proverb: Shall I take up my abode here? (With a phallic joke.) 52 **When . . . tell?** i.e., Never. (Another proverbial expression, used derisively to turn aside a question.) 54 **minion** hussy. **hope** (A line following with an answering rhyme may be missing; perhaps it would have cleared up the present obscurity of lines 55 and 56.) 57 **baggage** good-for-nothing 60 **What . . . town?** i.e., Why do we need to put up with this disturbance, when the town provides stocks for punishment?

ADRIANA
Who is that at the door that keeps all this noise?   61

S. DROMIO
By my troth, your town is troubled with unruly boys.

E. ANTIPHOLUS
Are you there, wife? You might have come before.

ADRIANA
Your wife, sir knave? Go get you from the door.
                                        [Exit with Luce.]

E. DROMIO
If you went in pain, master, this "knave" would go
    sore.   65

ANGELO
Here is neither cheer, sir, nor welcome. We would
    fain have either.   66

BALTHASAR
In debating which was best, we shall part with
    neither.   67

E. DROMIO
They stand at the door, master. Bid them welcome
    hither.   68

E. ANTIPHOLUS
There is something in the wind, that we cannot
    get in.   69

E. DROMIO
You would say so, master, if your garments were thin.   70
Your cake is warm within; you stand here in the
    cold.
It would make a man mad as a buck to be so bought
    and sold.   72

E. ANTIPHOLUS
Go fetch me something. I'll break ope the gate.

S. DROMIO
Break any breaking here, and I'll break your knave's
    pate.

E. DROMIO
A man may break a word with you, sir, and words
    are but wind,   75
Ay, and break it in your face, so he break it not
    behind.   76

S. DROMIO
It seems thou want'st breaking. Out upon thee, hind!   77

E. DROMIO
Here's too much "Out upon thee!" I pray thee, let
    me in.

S. DROMIO
Ay, when fowls have no feathers and fish have no
    fin.   [Exit.]   79

E. ANTIPHOLUS
Well, I'll break in. Go borrow me a crow.   80

E. DROMIO
A crow without feather? Master, mean you so?
For a fish without a fin, there's a fowl without a
    feather.—
If a crow help us in, sirrah, we'll pluck a crow
    together.   83

E. ANTIPHOLUS
Go, get thee gone. Fetch me an iron crow.

BALTHASAR
Have patience, sir. Oh, let it not be so!
Herein you war against your reputation
And draw within the compass of suspect   87
Th'unviolated honor of your wife.
Once this: your long experience of her wisdom,   89
Her sober virtue, years, and modesty,   90
Plead on her part some cause to you unknown;
And doubt not, sir, but she will well excuse   92
Why at this time the doors are made against you.   93
Be ruled by me. Depart in patience,
And let us to the Tiger all to dinner,   95
And about evening come yourself alone
To know the reason of this strange restraint.
If by strong hand you offer to break in   98
Now in the stirring passage of the day,   99
A vulgar comment will be made of it,   100
And that supposèd by the common rout   101
Against your yet ungallèd estimation,   102
That may with foul intrusion enter in
And dwell upon your grave when you are dead;
For slander lives upon succession,   105
Forever housèd where it gets possession.

E. ANTIPHOLUS
You have prevailed. I will depart in quiet,
And, in despite of mirth, mean to be merry.   108
I know a wench of excellent discourse,
Pretty and witty, wild and yet, too, gentle.
There will we dine. This woman that I mean,
My wife—but, I protest, without desert—   112
Hath oftentimes upbraided me withal.
To her will we to dinner. [To Angelo] Get you home
And fetch the chain; by this I know 'tis made.   115
Bring it, I pray you, to the Porcupine,   116
For there's the house. That chain will I bestow—
Be it for nothing but to spite my wife—
Upon mine hostess there. Good sir, make haste.
Since mine own doors refuse to entertain me,
I'll knock elsewhere, to see if they'll disdain me.

---

61 keeps keeps up   **65 If . . . sore** i.e., Yourself and this "knave" she
mentions are the same person.   **went** i.e., were   **66 fain** gladly
67 part depart   **68 They . . . hither** i.e., Both cheer and welcome have
been barred at the door, master. Invite them in. (Said ironically, as an
impossibility.)   **69 something . . . wind** something strange going on
70 You . . . thin i.e., If you were more thinly dressed (like me), master,
you'd say it's a cold wind indeed that shuts you out this way.
(Dromio takes the proverbial wind of line 69 in a literal sense.)   **72 as
a buck** i.e., as a male deer in rutting season. (Compare *horn-mad*,
2.1.57.)   **bought and sold** i.e., betrayed, ill-treated.   **75 break a word**
exchange words. (Punning on *break* in the previous lines.)   **76 behind**
i.e., in farting.   **77 thou . . . breaking** you need to be broken in by a
beating.   **hind** boor, menial.   **79 s.d. Exit** (If Dromio of Syracuse has
been visible to the audience, he probably leaves at this point.)

80 crow crowbar (Introducing a quibble by Dromio of Ephesus.)
83 pluck . . . together pick a bone together, settle accounts.
87 draw . . . suspect bring under suspicion   **89 Once this** To be brief,
in short   **90 virtue** merit, general excellence   **92 excuse** justify
93 made fastened   **95 the Tiger** (Presumably an inn.)   **98 offer**
attempt   **99 stirring passage** bustle   **100 vulgar** public
101 And . . . rout and it will be presumed true by everyone
102 yet . . . estimation still unsullied reputation   **105 lives upon
succession** passes from generation to generation   **108 in . . . mirth**
despite my not feeling mirthful, or, in spite of the mockery
112 desert my deserving it   **115 this** this time   **116 Porcupine** (The
name of the Courtesan's house.)

ANGELO
I'll meet you at that place some hour hence.

E. ANTIPHOLUS
Do so. This jest shall cost me some expense. *Exeunt.*

❧

[3.2]

Enter Luciana with Antipholus of Syracuse.

LUCIANA
And may it be that you have quite forgot   1
   A husband's office? Shall, Antipholus,   2
Even in the spring of love, thy love springs rot?   3
   Shall love, in building, grow so ruinous?
If you did wed my sister for her wealth,
   Then for her wealth's sake use her with more
      kindness;
Or if you like elsewhere, do it by stealth:
   Muffle your false love with some show of
      blindness.   8
Let not my sister read it in your eye;
   Be not thy tongue thy own shame's orator;
Look sweet, speak fair, become disloyalty;   11
   Apparel vice like virtue's harbinger.   12
Bear a fair presence, though your heart be tainted;
   Teach sin the carriage of a holy saint;   14
Be secret-false. What need she be acquainted?
   What simple thief brags of his own attaint?   16
'Tis double wrong to truant with your bed   17
   And let her read it in thy looks at board.   18
Shame hath a bastard fame, well managèd;   19
   Ill deeds is doubled with an evil word.   20
Alas, poor women! Make us but believe,
   Being compact of credit, that you love us.   22
Though others have the arm, show us the sleeve;
   We in your motion turn and you may move us.   24
Then, gentle brother, get you in again.
   Comfort my sister, cheer her, call her wife.
'Tis holy sport to be a little vain   27
   When the sweet breath of flattery conquers strife.

S. ANTIPHOLUS
Sweet mistress—what your name is else, I know not,   29
   Nor by what wonder you do hit of mine—   30
Less in your knowledge and your grace you show not   31
   Than our earth's wonder, more than earth divine.   32

Teach me, dear creature, how to think and speak;
   Lay open to my earthy-gross conceit,   34
Smothered in errors, feeble, shallow, weak,
   The folded meaning of your words' deceit.   36
Against my soul's pure truth why labor you   37
   To make it wander in an unknown field?   38
Are you a god? Would you create me new?
   Transform me then, and to your power I'll yield.
But if that I am I, then well I know
   Your weeping sister is no wife of mine,
Nor to her bed no homage do I owe.
   Far more, far more to you do I decline.   44
Oh, train me not; sweet mermaid, with thy note,   45
   To drown me in thy sister's flood of tears!
Sing, siren, for thyself, and I will dote.
   Spread o'er the silver waves thy golden hairs,
And as a bed I'll take them and there lie,   49
   And in that glorious supposition think
He gains by death that hath such means to die.   51
   Let Love, being light, be drownèd if she sink!   52

LUCIANA
What, are you mad, that you do reason so?   53

S. ANTIPHOLUS
Not mad, but mated—how, I do not know.   54

LUCIANA
It is a fault that springeth from your eye.

S. ANTIPHOLUS
For gazing on your beams, fair sun, being by.   56

LUCIANA
Gaze where you should, and that will clear your sight.

S. ANTIPHOLUS
As good to wink, sweet love, as look on night.   58

LUCIANA
Why call you me "love"? Call my sister so.

S. ANTIPHOLUS
Thy sister's sister.

LUCIANA   That's my sister.

S. ANTIPHOLUS   No,
It is thyself, mine own self's better part,
Mine eye's clear eye, my dear heart's dearer heart,
My food, my fortune, and my sweet hope's aim,
My sole earth's heaven, and my heaven's claim.   64

LUCIANA
All this my sister is, or else should be.

S. ANTIPHOLUS
Call thyself sister, sweet, for I am thee.   66

3.2 Location: Antipholus of Ephesus's house or in front of it, certainly so by line 163.
1 may can **2 office** duty. **3 love springs** tender shoots of love **8 Muffle** hide. **show of blindness** deceptive appearance. **11 fair** courteously. **become disloyalty** carry off your infidelity gracefully **12 harbinger** messenger, forerunner. **14 carriage** demeanor **16 simple** simple-minded. **attaint** stain, dishonor. **17 truant with** be faithless to **18 board** table. **19–20 Shame . . . word** i.e., Shameful behavior, if cleverly managed, can assume a false reputation for humble conduct, whereas sin is made twice as heinous by callous boasting of it. **22 Being . . . credit** i.e., we who are wholly inclined to believe you **24 We . . . turn** we are governed by your motion, orbit (referring to the motion of the heavenly spheres) **27 holy sport** virtuous jesting. (An oxymoron.) **vain** false **29 else** otherwise **30 wonder** miracle. **hit of** hit upon, guess **31–2 Less . . . divine** i.e., you seem no less wise and graceful than our divine queen, wonder of the earth. (Seemingly a flattering reference to Queen Elizabeth.)

34 Lay . . . conceit explain to my dull understanding **36 folded** concealed **37–8 Against . . . field?** Why do you strive against the pure yearning of my soul, as if desiring it to seek elsewhere? **44 decline** incline. **45 train** entice. **mermaid** siren. (In classical myth, one of a group of nymphs who lured sailors to destruction with their sweet singing.) **note** song **49 take** use **51 die** cease to live. (With a pun on "achieve sexual climax.") **52 Let . . . sink!** i.e., If she whom I love can fail to raise me up, let love itself, which is both braggart and wanton, sink to the bottom! **53 reason** talk, argue **54 mated** amazed, confounded. (With quibble on the sense of "matched with a wife.") **56 by** near. **58 As . . . night** i.e., If I were to close my eyes or avert my gaze from you, I might as well be in darkness, unable to see at all. **64 My sole . . . claim** my sole heaven on earth and my claim on heaven hereafter. **66 Call . . . thee** i.e., You and I are indivisible, as it were, through the bond of spiritual love, and therefore the sister I love is yourself.

Thee will I love and with thee lead my life;
Thou hast no husband yet, nor I no wife.
Give me thy hand.

LUCIANA   Oh, soft, sir! Hold you still.
I'll fetch my sister, to get her good will.   *Exit.*   70

Enter Dromio [of] Syracuse, [running].

S. ANTIPHOLUS   Why, how now, Dromio, where runn'st
thou so fast?

S. DROMIO   Do you know me, sir? Am I Dromio? Am I
your man? Am I myself?

S. ANTIPHOLUS   Thou art Dromio, thou art my man,
thou art thyself.

S. DROMIO   I am an ass, I am a woman's man, and be-   77
sides myself.   78

S. ANTIPHOLUS   What woman's man? And how besides   79
thyself?

S. DROMIO   Marry, sir, besides myself I am due to a
woman: one that claims me, one that haunts me, one
that will have me.

S. ANTIPHOLUS   What claim lays she to thee?

S. DROMIO   Marry, sir, such claim as you would lay to
your horse; and she would have me as a beast—not   86
that, I being a beast, she would have me, but that she
being a very beastly creature, lays claim to me.

S. ANTIPHOLUS   What is she?

S. DROMIO   A very reverend body; ay, such a one as a
man may not speak of without he say "sir-reverence."   91
I have but lean luck in the match, and yet is she a   92
wondrous fat marriage.

S. ANTIPHOLUS   How dost thou mean, a fat marriage?

S. DROMIO   Marry, sir, she's the kitchen wench, and all
grease, and I know not what use to put her to but to   96
make a lamp of her and run from her by her own light.
I warrant her rags and the tallow in them will burn a   98
Poland winter. If she lives till doomsday, she'll burn a   99
week longer than the whole world.

S. ANTIPHOLUS   What complexion is she of?

S. DROMIO   Swart like my shoe, but her face nothing like   102
so clean kept. For why? She sweats a man may go over   103
shoes in the grime of it.   104

S. ANTIPHOLUS   That's a fault that water will mend.

S. DROMIO   No, sir, 'tis in grain. Noah's flood could not   106
do it.

S. ANTIPHOLUS   What's her name?

S. DROMIO   Nell, sir; but her name and three quarters—   109

that's an ell and three quarters—will not measure her   110
from hip to hip.

S. ANTIPHOLUS   Then she bears some breadth?

S. DROMIO   No longer from head to foot than from hip
to hip. She is spherical, like a globe. I could find out
countries in her.

S. ANTIPHOLUS   In what part of her body stands Ireland?

S. DROMIO   Marry, sir, in her buttocks. I found it out by
the bogs.

S. ANTIPHOLUS   Where Scotland?

S. DROMIO   I found it by the barrenness, hard in the   120
palm of the hand.

S. ANTIPHOLUS   Where France?

S. DROMIO   In her forehead, armed and reverted,   123
making war against her heir.   124

S. ANTIPHOLUS   Where England?

S. DROMIO   I looked for the chalky cliffs, but I could find   126
no whiteness in them. But I guess it stood in her chin,   127
by the salt rheum that ran between France and it.   128

S. ANTIPHOLUS   Where Spain?

S. DROMIO   Faith, I saw it not, but I felt it hot in her
breath.

S. ANTIPHOLUS   Where America, the Indies?

S. DROMIO   Oh, sir, upon her nose, all o'er embellished   133
with rubies, carbuncles, sapphires, declining their rich   134
aspect to the hot breath of Spain, who sent whole   135
armadas of carracks to be ballast at her nose.   136

S. ANTIPHOLUS   Where stood Belgia, the Netherlands?

S. DROMIO   Oh, sir, I did not look so low. To conclude,   138
this drudge or diviner laid claim to me, called me   139
Dromio, swore I was assured to her, told me what   140
privy marks I had about me—as the mark of my   141
shoulder, the mole in my neck, the great wart on my
left arm, that I amazed ran from her as a witch.
And, I think, if my breast had not been made of
faith and my heart of steel,
She had transformed me to a curtal dog and made
me turn i'the wheel.   145

S. ANTIPHOLUS
Go, hie thee presently; post to the road.   146

---

70 good will approval. (This is perhaps a mere excuse, but it may be a sign she is attracted.)   **77–8 besides myself** also myself. (With a pun on the sense of "out of my mind.")   **79 besides** (A further quibble: "in addition to.")   **86 a beast** (With a pun on "abased," reflecting Elizabethan pronunciation of beast as "baste.")   **91 without** unless. **"sir-reverence"** i.e.; save your reverence, an expression used in apology for the remark that follows it.   **92 lean** poor, meager   **96 grease** (With a pun on "grace," reflecting Elizabethan pronunciation.) **98–9 a Poland winter** i.e., a long, cold winter.   **102 Swart** Swarthy, dark   **103 She sweats a man** She sweats so much that a man **103–4 over shoes** ankle-deep. (Her sweat makes mud of her face's grime, so deep that a man would be ankle deep in it.)   **106 in grain** indelible, fast dyed.   **109 Nell** (The maidservant appearing in 3.1 is named Luce; usually the two are assumed to be one person.)

110 an ell forty-five inches. (With a pun on "a Nell.")   **120 barrenness** callused hardness and dryness. (Perhaps with a pun on "barren ness," a barren promontory.)   **123 reverted** in rebellion. (See the Introduction for an explanation of the reference to the French war.)   **124 heir** (With a pun on "hair" and a joke about syphilis as causing baldness.) **126 chalky cliffs** i.e., her teeth. (In his geographic metaphor, Dromio of Syracuse identifies white teeth with the cliffs of Dover.)   **127 them** i.e., her teeth.   **128 salt rheum** nasal discharge. (Here Dromio jokingly makes a comparison to the English Channel.)   **133–6 Oh . . . nose** (Dromio imagines whole fleets of Spanish galleons taking on ballast at this woman's nose, embellished as it is with pimples and boils that resemble the treasures pillaged by the Spanish in the Americas. A *carbuncle* is both a precious jewel and a pimple. The eruptions on her nose pay homage (*declining their rich aspect*) to the hot breath of Spain, suggesting both her foul breath and the hot importunity of the Spanish.)   **138 so low** (A joke about the female genitalia. The Netherlands were known as the Low Countries.)   **139 diviner** sorceress **140 assured** affianced   **141 privy** secret, personal   **145 curtal dog** dog with a docked tail. (And hence not used in hunting.)   **turn i'the wheel** run in a wheel to turn the spit.   **146 hie thee presently** hasten at once.   **post** hasten.   **road** harbor, roadstead.

An if the wind blow any way from shore,   147
I will not harbor in this town tonight.
If any bark put forth, come to the mart,   149
Where I will walk till thou return to me.
If everyone knows us and we know none,
'Tis time, I think, to trudge, pack, and be gone.   152

S. DROMIO
As from a bear a man would run for life,
So fly I from her that would be my wife.   *Exit.*

S. ANTIPHOLUS
There's none but witches do inhabit here,
And therefore 'tis high time that I were hence.
She that doth call me husband, even my soul
Doth for a wife abhor. But her fair sister,
Possessed with such a gentle sovereign grace,   159
Of such enchanting presence and discourse,
Hath almost made me traitor to myself.
But, lest myself be guilty to self-wrong,   162
I'll stop mine ears against the mermaid's song.

Enter Angelo with the chain.

ANGELO
    Master Antipholus—
S. ANTIPHOLUS   Ay, that's my name.
ANGELO
    I know it well, sir. Lo, here's the chain.
    I thought to have ta'en you at the Porcupine;   166
    The chain unfinished made me stay thus long.
                            [He presents the chain.]
S. ANTIPHOLUS
    What is your will that I shall do with this?
ANGELO
    What please yourself, sir. I have made it for you.   169
S. ANTIPHOLUS
    Made it for me, sir? I bespoke it not.   170
ANGELO
    Not once, nor twice, but twenty times you have.
    Go home with it and please your wife withal,
    And soon at suppertime I'll visit you
    And then receive my money for the chain.
S. ANTIPHOLUS
    I pray you, sir, receive the money now,
    For fear you ne'er see chain nor money more.
ANGELO
    You are a merry man, sir. Fare you well.   *Exit.*
S. ANTIPHOLUS
    What I should think of this, I cannot tell.
    But this I think: there's no man is so vain   179
    That would refuse so fair an offered chain.
    I see a man here needs not live by shifts,   181
    When in the streets he meets such golden gifts.
    I'll to the mart and there for Dromio stay;
    If any ship put out, then straight away.   *Exit.*   184

❧

147 **An if** If   149 **bark** ship   152 **pack** depart   159 **Possessed with**
Having possession of   162 **to** of   166 **ta'en** overtaken, met up with
169 **What please yourself** Whatever you please   170 **bespoke**
requested   179 **vain** foolish   181 **shifts** stratagems, tricks
184 **straight** at once

4.1

*Enter a [Second] Merchant, [Angelo the]
goldsmith, and an Officer.*

SECOND MERCHANT *[to Angelo]*
    You know since Pentecost the sum is due,   1
    And since I have not much importuned you,   2
    Nor now I had not, but that I am bound
    To Persia and want guilders for my voyage.   4
    Therefore make present satisfaction,   5
    Or I'll attach you by this officer.   6
ANGELO
    Even just the sum that I do owe to you   7
    Is growing to me by Antipholus,   8
    And in the instant that I met with you
    He had of me a chain. At five o'clock
    I shall receive the money for the same.
    Pleaseth you walk with me down to his house,   12
    I will discharge my bond and thank you too.

*Enter Antipholus [and] Dromio of Ephesus from
the Courtesan's.*

OFFICER
    That labor may you save. See where he comes.
E. ANTIPHOLUS *[to Dromio of Ephesus]*
    While I go to the goldsmith's house, go thou
    And buy a rope's end; that will I bestow   16
    Among my wife and her confederates
    For locking me out of my doors by day.
    But soft! I see the goldsmith. Get thee gone.   19
    Buy thou a rope and bring it home to me.
E. DROMIO
    I buy a thousand pound a year! I buy a rope!   21
                            Exit Dromio.
E. ANTIPHOLUS *[to Angelo]*
    A man is well holp up that trusts to you!   22
    I promisèd your presence and the chain,   23
    But neither chain nor goldsmith came to me.
    Belike you thought our love would last too long   25
    If it were chained together, and therefore came not.
ANGELO *[showing a paper]*
    Saving your merry humor, here's the note   27
    How much your chain weighs to the utmost carat,
    The fineness of the gold and chargeful fashion,   29
    Which doth amount to three odd ducats more   30
    Than I stand debted to this gentleman.

4.1. Location: The street.
1 Pentecost the commemoration of the descent of the Holy Ghost
upon the Apostles, celebrated on the seventh Sunday after Easter
2 since since then.   **importuned** harassed with demands, bothered
4 want guilders lack money   **5 present satisfaction** immediate payment   **6 attach** arrest, seize   **7 Even just** Precisely   **8 growing** due,
accruing   **12 Pleaseth** May it please   **16 a rope's end** a fragment of
rope (to be used as a whip).   **bestow** employ   **19 soft** i.e., wait a
minute.   **21 I . . . rope!** (An obscure line. Dromio may mean that in
buying a rope as he is bidden, he is purchasing for himself a thousand poundings or beatings a year.)
23 promisèd was promised   **25 Belike** Perhaps   **27 Saving** With
respect for   **29 chargeful fashion** expensive workmanship
30 ducats gold coins (of several European countries)

I pray you, see him presently discharged,
For he is bound to sea and stays but for it.

E. ANTIPHOLUS
I am not furnished with the present money;
Besides, I have some business in the town.
Good signor, take the stranger to my house,
And with you take the chain, and bid my wife
Disburse the sum on the receipt thereof.
Perchance I will be there as soon as you.

ANGELO
Then you will bring the chain to her yourself?

E. ANTIPHOLUS
No, bear it with you, lest I come not time enough.

ANGELO
Well, sir, I will. Have you the chain about you?

E. ANTIPHOLUS
An if I have not, sir, I hope you have,
Or else you may return without your money.

ANGELO
Nay, come, I pray you, sir, give me the chain.
Both wind and tide stays for this gentleman,
And I, too blame, have held him here too long.

E. ANTIPHOLUS
Good Lord! You use this dalliance to excuse
Your breach of promise to the Porcupine.
I should have chid you for not bringing it,
But, like a shrew, you first begin to brawl.

SECOND MERCHANT [to Angelo]
The hour steals on. I pray you, sir, dispatch.

ANGELO
You hear how he importunes me. The chain!

E. ANTIPHOLUS
Why, give it to my wife and fetch your money.

ANGELO
Come, come, you know I gave it you even now.
Either send the chain or send me by some token.

E. ANTIPHOLUS
Fie, now you run this humor out of breath.
Come, where's the chain? I pray you, let me see it.

SECOND MERCHANT
My business cannot brook this dalliance.
Good sir, say whe'er you'll answer me or no.
If not, I'll leave him to the officer.

E. ANTIPHOLUS
I answer you? What should I answer you?

ANGELO
The money that you owe me for the chain.

E. ANTIPHOLUS
I owe you none till I receive the chain.

ANGELO
You know I gave it you half an hour since.

E. ANTIPHOLUS
You gave me none. You wrong me much to say so.

ANGELO
You wrong me more, sir, in denying it.
Consider how it stands upon my credit.

SECOND MERCHANT
Well, officer, arrest him at my suit.

OFFICER [to Angelo]
I do, and charge you in the Duke's name to obey me.

ANGELO [to Antipholus]
This touches me in reputation.
Either consent to pay this sum for me,
Or I attach you by this officer.

E. ANTIPHOLUS
Consent to pay thee that I never had?
Arrest me, foolish fellow, if thou dar'st.

ANGELO
Here is thy fee. Arrest him, officer. [He gives money.]
I would not spare my brother in this case
If he should scorn me so apparently.

OFFICER [to Antipholus]
I do arrest you, sir. You hear the suit.

E. ANTIPHOLUS
I do obey thee till I give thee bail.—
But, sirrah, you shall buy this sport as dear
As all the metal in your shop will answer.

ANGELO
Sir, sir, I shall have law in Ephesus,
To your notorious shame, I doubt it not.

Enter Dromio [of] Syracuse, from the bay.

S. DROMIO
Master, there's a bark of Epidamnum
That stays but till her owner comes aboard,
And then she bears away. Our freightage, sir,
I have conveyed aboard, and I have bought
The oil, the balsamum, and aqua vitae.
The ship is in her trim; the merry wind
Blows fair from land; they stay for naught at all
But for their owner, master, and yourself.

E. ANTIPHOLUS
How now? A madman? Why, thou peevish sheep,
What ship of Epidamnum stays for me?

S. DROMIO
A ship you sent me to, to hire waftage.

E. ANTIPHOLUS
Thou drunken slave, I sent thee for a rope
And told thee to what purpose and what end.

S. DROMIO
You sent me for a rope's end as soon.
You sent me to the bay, sir, for a bark.

E. ANTIPHOLUS
I will debate this matter at more leisure
And teach your ears to list me with more heed.

---

32 discharged paid **34 present** available **41 time enough** in time.
47 too blame too blameworthy **48 dalliance** idle delay **50 chid**
chided **53 importunes** solicits urgently **56 send me ... token** send
me with some object of yours authorizing me to receive payment.
57 run ... breath i.e., carry the joke too far. **59 brook** endure
60 whe'er whether. **answer** pay, give me satisfaction

68 how ... credit how it affects my reputation for honesty. **69 at my
suit** on my petition. **71 touches** injures, affects **78 apparently**
openly. **84.1 from the bay** i.e., presumably from a side entry which
we understand to represent the direction of the bay. **89 balsamum**
balm, a fragrant and healing resin. **aqua vitae** strong liquor. **90 in
her trim** rigged and ready to sail **93 peevish** silly. **sheep** (With play
on *ship* in next line.) **95 waftage** passage. **98 a rope's end** i.e., a
whipping, or perhaps a hangman's noose; see line 16 and note
101 list listen to

To Adriana, villain, hie thee straight. [*He gives a key.*]
Give her this key, and tell her, in the desk
That's covered o'er with Turkish tapestry
There is a purse of ducats; let her send it.
Tell her I am arrested in the street,
And that shall bail me. Hie thee, slave, begone!
On, officer, to prison till it come.
Exeunt [*all but Dromio of Syracuse*].

S. DROMIO
To Adriana! That is where we dined,
Where Dowsabel did claim me for her husband.   110
She is too big, I hope, for me to compass.   111
Thither I must, although against my will,
For servants must their masters' minds fulfill.   *Exit.*

❖

[4.2]

Enter Adriana and Luciana.

ADRIANA
Ah, Luciana, did he tempt thee so?
    Mightst thou perceive austerely in his eye   2
That he did plead in earnest, yea or no?
    Looked he or red or pale, or sad or merrily?   4
What observation mad'st thou in this case
Of his heart's meteors tilting in his face?   6
LUCIANA
First he denied you had in him no right.   7
ADRIANA
He meant he did me none; the more my spite.   8
LUCIANA
Then swore he that he was a stranger here.
ADRIANA
And true he swore, though yet forsworn he were.   10
LUCIANA
Then pleaded I for you.
ADRIANA   And what said he?
LUCIANA
That love I begged for you he begged of me.
ADRIANA
With what persuasion did he tempt thy love?
LUCIANA
With words that in an honest suit might move.   14
First he did praise my beauty, then my speech.
ADRIANA
Didst speak him fair?
LUCIANA   Have patience, I beseech.   16
ADRIANA
I cannot, nor I will not, hold me still.

My tongue, though not my heart, shall have his will.   18
He is deformèd, crooked, old, and sere,   19
Ill faced, worse bodied, shapeless everywhere;   20
Vicious, ungentle, foolish, blunt, unkind,
Stigmatical in making, worse in mind.   22
LUCIANA
Who would be jealous then of such a one?
No evil lost is wailed when it is gone.
ADRIANA
Ah, but I think him better than I say,
And yet would herein others' eyes were worse.   26
Far from her nest the lapwing cries away;   27
My heart prays for him, though my tongue do curse.

Enter Dromio of Syracuse, [running, with the key].

S. DROMIO
Here, go—the desk, the purse! Sweet, now, make
    haste—   29
LUCIANA
How hast thou lost thy breath?
S. DROMIO   By running fast.
ADRIANA
Where is thy master, Dromio? Is he well?
S. DROMIO
No, he's in Tartar limbo, worse than hell.   32
A devil in an everlasting garment hath him,   33
One whose hard heart is buttoned up with steel;
A fiend, a fairy, pitiless and rough;   35
A wolf, nay, worse, a fellow all in buff;
A back friend, a shoulder clapper, one that
    countermands   37
The passages of alleys, creeks, and narrow lands;   38
A hound that runs counter and yet draws dryfoot
    well;   39
One that before the judgment carries poor souls to
    hell.   40
ADRIANA   Why, man, what is the matter?
S. DROMIO
I do not know the matter. He is 'rested on the case.   42
ADRIANA
What, is he arrested? Tell me at whose suit.
S. DROMIO
I know not at whose suit he is arrested well;

---

18 his its   **19 sere** withered   **20 shapeless** misshapen   **22 Stigmatical in making** deformed in appearance   **26 And . . . worse** i.e., and yet I wish that others would look disapprovingly at his behavior. **27 Far . . . away** i.e., I am like the lapwing (a bird that flies away from its nest to divert the attention of intruders from its young) in that what I say is very different from what I feel   **29 Sweet** (An inoffensive term of endearment. Some editors emend it to Sweat.) **32 Tartar limbo** Tartarus or pagan hell, worse than Christian hell **33 everlasting garment** i.e., buff leather attire of the police officer; everlasting both because of its durability and because of the joke about perpetual durance in limbo or jail. (*Everlasting* is itself the name of a coarse woolen fabric sometimes used for the uniforms of petty officers of justice.)   **35 fairy** i.e., malevolent spirit   **37–9 one . . . well** i.e., one who prohibits the movement of people in alleys and narrow passages; a hound that follows a trail in the direction opposite to that which the game has taken (with a quibble on *counter*, a prison) and skillfully tracks game by the mere scent of the footprint **40 judgment** legal decision. (With a pun on "Judgment Day," continuing the joke about jail as Tartar limbo.)   **42 'rested on the case** arrested in a lawsuit.

---

110 Dowsabel (Used ironically for Nell or Luce; derived from the French *douce et belle*, "gentle and beautiful.")   **111 compass** achieve. (With added meaning of "put my arms around.")
4.2. Location: The house of Antipholus of Ephesus.
2 austerely objectively, strictly   **4 or red** either red-faced.   **or sad** either sad   **6 meteors tilting** i.e., passions warring. (The next line begins a passage of stichomythia, dialogue in which each speech consists of a single line, much used in classical drama.)   **7 no** i.e., any **8 spite** vexation, grief.   **10 true . . . were** i.e., though no foreigner, he spoke true in the sense that he is a stranger to my heart and thus false to his vows.   **14 honest** honorable   **16 Didst . . . fair?** Did you encourage him?

But is in a suit of buff which 'rested him, that can I
  tell.
Will you send him, mistress, redemption, the
  money in his desk?   45

ADRIANA
Go fetch it, sister.   *Exit Luciana.*
               This I wonder at,
That he, unknown to me, should be in debt.
Tell me, was he arrested on a band?   49

S. DROMIO
Not on a band, but on a stronger thing:
A chain, a chain! Do you not hear it ring?

ADRIANA   What, the chain?

S. DROMIO
No, no, the bell. 'Tis time that I were gone.
It was two ere I left him, and now the clock strikes
  one.   54

ADRIANA
The hours come back! That did I never hear.

S. DROMIO
Oh, yes, if any hour meet a sergeant, 'a turns back for
  very fear.   56

ADRIANA
As if Time were in debt. How fondly dost thou
  reason!   57

S. DROMIO
Time is a very bankrupt and owes more than he's
  worth to season.   58
Nay, he's a thief too. Have you not heard men say
That Time comes stealing on by night and day?
If 'a be in debt and theft, and a sergeant in the way,   61
Hath he not reason to turn back an hour in a day?

Enter Luciana [with the purse].

ADRIANA
Go, Dromio, there's the money. Bear it straight,
And bring thy master home immediately.   63
         [Exit Dromio, with the purse.]
Come, sister. I am pressed down with conceit—   65
Conceit, my comfort and my injury.   *Exeunt.*   66

                  ❧

[4.3]

Enter Antipholus of Syracuse, [wearing the chain].

S. ANTIPHOLUS
There's not a man I meet but doth salute me
As if I were their well-acquainted friend,

And everyone doth call me by my name.
Some tender money to me; some invite me;   4
Some other give me thanks for kindnesses;   5
Some offer me commodities to buy.
Even now a tailor called me in his shop
And showed me silks that he had bought for me
And therewithal took measure of my body.
Sure, these are but imaginary wiles,   10
And Lapland sorcerers inhabit here.   11

Enter Dromio of Syracuse, [with the purse].

S. DROMIO   Master, here's the gold you sent me for.
What, have you got the picture of old Adam new-   13
apparelled?   14

S. ANTIPHOLUS   What gold is this? What Adam dost
thou mean?

S. DROMIO   Not that Adam that kept the Paradise, but   16
that Adam that keeps the prison; he that goes in the
calf's skin that was killed for the Prodigal; he that   18
came behind you, sir, like an evil angel, and bid you
forsake your liberty.

S. ANTIPHOLUS   I understand thee not.

S. DROMIO   No? Why, 'tis a plain case: he that went, like
a bass viol, in a case of leather, the man, sir, that,   23
when gentlemen are tired, gives them a sob and 'rests   24
them; he, sir, that takes pity on decayed men and gives 25
them suits of durance; he that sets up his rest to do   26
more exploits with his mace than a morris-pike.   27

S. ANTIPHOLUS   What, thou mean'st an officer?

S. DROMIO   Ay, sir, the sergeant of the band; he that   29
brings any man to answer it that breaks his band; one   30
that thinks a man always going to bed, and says, "God
give you good rest!"   32

S. ANTIPHOLUS   Well, sir, there rest in your foolery. Is
there any ships puts forth tonight? May we be gone?

S. DROMIO   Why, sir, I brought you word an hour since
that the bark *Expedition* put forth tonight, and then
were you hindered by the sergeant to tarry for the hoy   37
Delay. Here are the angels that you sent for to deliver 38
you.   *[He gives the purse.]*

---

45 suit (1) suit of clothes (2) lawsuit   **49 band** bond. (But Dromio puns on the sense "neckband" in the next line.)   **54 one** (*One* and *on* were pronounced very much alike; the word here rhymes with *gone*.) **56 if . . . fear** Time appears to go backwards, like a person in debt (an "over," punning on *hour*), or a whore (pronounced like *hour*) running away from an arresting officer.   **'a it,** she, he   **57 fondly** foolishly **58 Time . . . season** i.e., Having overspent itself, Time is so much in debt that it is of little worth when it comes to fruition. (With a probable pun on *season* and *seisin,* legal possession.)   **to season** to bring to fruition, make acceptable.   **61 theft** i.e., a thief. **in the way** lying in wait to arrest   **63 straight** straight away, immediately   **65 conceit** imaginings   **66 Conceit . . . injury** (Adriana is filled with imaginings, both of the wrongs she has suffered and the comfort she can provide her wayward husband.)
4.3. Location: The street.

4 tender offer   **5 other** others   **10 imaginary wiles** tricks of the imagination   **11 Lapland sorcerers** (Lapland was said to surpass all nations in the practice of witchcraft and sorcery.)   **13–14 What . . . new-apparelled?** (Dromio wonders how his master has managed to evade the arresting officer who apprehended Antipholus (of Ephesus, not Syracuse) in 4.1. *New-apparelled* plays on [1] a new suit of clothes [2] a new lawsuit. Adam, *new-apparelled* in beasts' skins after the fall of man [Genesis 3:21], reminds Dromio of the correcting officer in his buff leather jerkin or jacket.)   **16 kept the Paradise** (This sounds like an allusion to an inn of which the innkeeper was named Adam.) **18 calf's . . . Prodigal** (An allusion to the fatted calf killed for the Prodigal Son's return; see Luke 15:23.)   **23 case** (With a pun on *plain case,* line 22.)   **24 a sob** (1) a sob of pity; see next line (2) a breathing-space given to a horse to allow it to recover from its exertions **24–5 'rests them** (1) arrests them (2) gives them respite   **25 decayed** financially ruined. (With a pun on the usual sense.)   **26 durance** a kind of long-wearing cloth like buff. (With a pun on "imprisonment.") **sets . . . rest** stakes his all. (With a continuing pun on *'rest;* the metaphor of staking all one's venture is from the game of primero.) **27 mace** staff of office carried by a constable.   **morris-pike** a weapon, supposedly of Moorish origin   **29 band** troop   **30 band** bond **32 rest** (Continuing the wordplay on *arrest*.)   **37 hoy** a small coastal vessel   **38 angels** gold coins worth about ten shillings

S. ANTIPHOLUS
The fellow is distract, and so am I,   40
And here we wander in illusions.
Some blessèd power deliver us from hence!

Enter a Courtesan.

COURTESAN
Well met, well met, Master Antipholus.
I see, sir, you have found the goldsmith now.
Is that the chain you promised me today?

S. ANTIPHOLUS
Satan, avoid! I charge thee, tempt me not.   46

S. DROMIO   Master, is this Mistress Satan?

S. ANTIPHOLUS   It is the devil.

S. DROMIO   Nay, she is worse, she is the devil's dam, and   49
here she comes in the habit of a light wench; and   50
thereof comes that the wenches say, "God damn me,"   51
that's as much to say, "God make me a light wench."
It is written they appear to men like angels of light;   53
light is an effect of fire, and fire will burn; ergo, light   54
wenches will burn. Come not near her.   55

COURTESAN
Your man and you are marvelous merry, sir.
Will you go with me? We'll mend our dinner here.   57

S. DROMIO   Master, if you do, expect spoon meat, or   58
bespeak a long spoon.   59

S. ANTIPHOLUS   Why, Dromio?

S. DROMIO   Marry, he must have a long spoon that must   61
eat with the devil.   62

S. ANTIPHOLUS   [*to the Courtesan*]
Avoid then, fiend! What tell'st thou me of supping?   63
Thou art, as you are all, a sorceress.
I conjure thee to leave me and be gone.

COURTESAN
Give me the ring of mine you had at dinner
Or, for my diamond, the chain you promised,
And I'll be gone, sir, and not trouble you.

S. DROMIO
Some devils ask but the parings of one's nail,
A rush, a hair, a drop of blood, a pin,
A nut, a cherrystone;
But she, more covetous, would have a chain.
Master, be wise. An if you give it her,   73
The devil will shake her chain and fright us with it.

COURTESAN
I pray you, sir, my ring, or else the chain!
I hope you do not mean to cheat me so?

S. ANTIPHOLUS
Avaunt, thou witch!—Come, Dromio, let us go.   77

S. DROMIO
"Fly pride," says the peacock. Mistress, that you
know.   *Exeunt* [*Antipholus and Dromio of Syracuse*].   78

COURTESAN
Now, out of doubt Antipholus is mad,
Else would he never so demean himself.   80
A ring he hath of mine worth forty ducats,
And for the same he promised me a chain;
Both one and other he denies me now.
The reason that I gather he is mad,
Besides this present instance of his rage,   85
Is a mad tale he told today at dinner
Of his own doors being shut against his entrance.
Belike his wife, acquainted with his fits,   88
On purpose shut the doors against his way.
My way is now to hie home to his house   90
And tell his wife that, being lunatic,
He rushed into my house and took perforce   92
My ring away. This course I fittest choose,   93
For forty ducats is too much to lose.   [*Exit.*]

[4.4]

Enter Antipholus of Ephesus with a Jailer [*or
Officer*].

E. ANTIPHOLUS
Fear me not, man, I will not break away.
I'll give thee ere I leave thee so much money
To warrant thee as I am 'rested for.   3
My wife is in a wayward mood today   4
And will not lightly trust the messenger.   5
That I should be attached in Ephesus,   6
I tell you, 'twill sound harshly in her ears.

Enter Dromio of Ephesus with a rope's end.

Here comes my man. I think he brings the money.—
How now, sir? Have you that I sent you for?

E. DROMIO   [*giving the rope*]
Here's that, I warrant you, will pay them all.

E. ANTIPHOLUS   But where's the money?

E. DROMIO
Why, sir, I gave the money for the rope.

E. ANTIPHOLUS
Five hundred ducats, villain, for a rope?

E. DROMIO
I'll serve you, sir, five hundred at the rate.   14

---

40 distract deranged, distracted   **46 avoid!** begone! (See Matthew
4:10.)   **49 dam** mother   **50 habit** demeanor, manner; also, dress.
light wanton   **51 damn me** i.e., dam me, make me a mother.
53 angels of light (See 2 Corinthians 11:14, where Satan is referred to
as transformed into an angel of light.)   **54 ergo** therefore   **55 will
burn** i.e., will transmit venereal disease.   **57 mend** supplement, complete   **58 spoon meat** food for infants, hence delicacies   **59 bespeak**
order   **61–2 he . . . devil** (A proverbial idea.)   **63 What** Why   **73 An
If** If   **77 Avaunt** Begone

78 "Fly . . . peacock (The peacock, symbol of vanity, warns hypocritically against pride; similarly, in Dromio's view, this cheating courtesan accuses Antipholus of cheating her. *Pride* can also mean "sexual
desire.")   **80 demean** conduct   **85 rage** madness   **88 Belike** Presumably   **90 My way** My best course   **92 perforce** forcibly
93 fittest as most appropriate
4.4 Location: The street.
3 warrant thee guarantee your security   **4 wayward** perverse, ill
tempered   **5 lightly trust** easily believe   **6 attached** arrested
14 I'll . . . rate I'll supply you with five hundred ropes, sir, for that
amount.

E. ANTIPHOLUS
To what end did I bid thee hie thee home?

E. DROMIO   To a rope's end, sir; and to that end am I
returned.

E. ANTIPHOLUS
And to that end, sir, I will welcome you.
[He starts to beat Dromio of Ephesus.]

OFFICER   Good sir, be patient.

E. DROMIO   Nay, 'tis for me to be patient. I am in adversity.

OFFICER   Good now, hold thy tongue.   22

E. DROMIO   Nay, rather persuade him to hold his hands.

E. ANTIPHOLUS   Thou whoreson, senseless villain!

E. DROMIO   I would I were senseless, sir, that I might not
feel your blows.

E. ANTIPHOLUS   Thou art sensible in nothing but blows,   27
and so is an ass.

E. DROMIO   I am an ass, indeed; you may prove it by my
long ears. I have served him from the hour of my   30
nativity to this instant and have nothing at his hands
for my service but blows. When I am cold, he heats me
with beating; when I am warm, he cools me with
beating. I am waked with it when I sleep, raised with
it when I sit, driven out of doors with it when I go
from home, welcomed home with it when I return.
Nay, I bear it on my shoulders, as a beggar wont her   37
brat, and I think when he hath lamed me I shall beg
with it from door to door.

Enter Adriana, Luciana, Courtesan, and a schoolmaster called Pinch.

E. ANTIPHOLUS
Come, go along. My wife is coming yonder.

E. DROMIO [to Adriana]   Mistress, respice finem, respect   41
your end; or rather, to prophesy like the parrot,
"Beware the rope's end."

E. ANTIPHOLUS   Wilt thou still talk?   Beats Dromio.

COURTESAN [to Adriana]
How say you now? Is not your husband mad?

ADRIANA
His incivility confirms no less.—
Good Doctor Pinch, you are a conjurer;   47
Establish him in his true sense again,   48
And I will please you what you will demand.   49

LUCIANA
Alas, how fiery and how sharp he looks!   50

COURTESAN
Mark how he trembles in his ecstasy!   51

PINCH [to Antipholus]
Give me your hand, and let me feel your pulse.

E. ANTIPHOLUS [striking him]
There is my hand, and let it feel your ear.

PINCH
I charge thee, Satan, housed within this man,
To yield possession to my holy prayers
And to thy state of darkness hie thee straight!
I conjure thee by all the saints in heaven!

E. ANTIPHOLUS
Peace, doting wizard, peace! I am not mad.

ADRIANA
Oh, that thou wert not, poor distressèd soul!

E. ANTIPHOLUS
You minion, you, are these your customers?   60
Did this companion with the saffron face   61
Revel and feast it at my house today,
Whilst upon me the guilty doors were shut
And I denied to enter in my house?

ADRIANA
Oh, husband, God doth know you dined at home,
Where would you had remained until this time,   66
Free from these slanders and this open shame!

E. ANTIPHOLUS
Dined at home? [To E. Dromio] Thou villain, what
sayest thou?

E. DROMIO
Sir, sooth to say, you did not dine at home.

E. ANTIPHOLUS
Were not my doors locked up and I shut out?

E. DROMIO
Pardie, your doors were locked and you shut out.   71

E. ANTIPHOLUS
And did not she herself revile me there?

E. DROMIO
Sans fable, she herself reviled you there.   73

E. ANTIPHOLUS
Did not her kitchen maid rail, taunt, and scorn me?

E. DROMIO
Certes, she did. The kitchen vestal scorned you.   75

E. ANTIPHOLUS
And did not I in rage depart from thence?

E. DROMIO
In verity you did. My bones bears witness,
That since have felt the vigor of his rage.

ADRIANA
Is't good to soothe him in these contraries?   79

PINCH
It is no shame. The fellow finds his vein,   80
And yielding to him humors well his frenzy.   81

---

22 Good now Pray you   **27 sensible in** sensitive to; also, made sensible by   **30 ears** (With a pun on "years"; Dromio says he is an ass for having served his master so long.)   **37 wont** is accustomed to (bear)   **41 respice finem** consider your end. (A pious sentiment on the brevity of life and the approach of death; with a play on *respice funem*, "consider the hangman's rope." A parrot might be taught to say *respice finem*, or perhaps "rope.")   **47 Doctor** (An honorific term for any learned person. Pinch is not a medical doctor.)   **conjurer** (Being able to speak Latin, Pinch could conjure spirits.)   **48 true sense** right mind   **49 please** pay   **50 sharp** angry   **51 ecstasy** fit, frenzy.

60 minion hussy, i.e., Adriana   **61 companion** fellow, i.e., Pinch. **saffron** yellow   **66 would** I wish   **71 Pardie** (An oath, from the French *pardieu*, "by God.")   **73 Sans** Without   **75 Certes** Certainly. **kitchen vestal** (Ironically, her task was like that of the vestal virgins of ancient Rome, to keep the fire burning.)   **79 soothe** encourage, humor.   **contraries** denials, lies.   **80–1 It . . . frenzy** i.e., Such a humoring of Antipholus is not reprehensible. (Dromio grasps the nature of his master's madness, and giving in this way can soothe the patient's frenzy.)

E. ANTIPHOLUS [*to Adriana*]
Thou hast suborned the goldsmith to arrest me.   82
ADRIANA
Alas, I sent you money to redeem you
By Dromio here, who came in haste for it.
E. DROMIO
Money by me? Heart and good will you might,   85
But surely, master, not a rag of money.   86
E. ANTIPHOLUS
Went'st not thou to her for a purse of ducats?
ADRIANA
He came to me, and I delivered it.
LUCIANA
And I am witness with her that she did.
E. DROMIO
God and the rope maker bear me witness
That I was sent for nothing but a rope!
PINCH [*to Adriana*]
Mistress, both man and master is possessed;
I know it by their pale and deadly looks.   93
They must be bound and laid in some dark room.   94
E. ANTIPHOLUS [*to Adriana*]
Say wherefore didst thou lock me forth today?   95
[*To E. Dromio*] And why dost thou deny the bag of gold?
ADRIANA
I did not, gentle husband, lock thee forth.
E. DROMIO
And, gentle master, I received no gold.
But I confess, sir, that we were locked out.
ADRIANA
Dissembling villain, thou speak'st false in both.
E. ANTIPHOLUS
Dissembling harlot, thou art false in all
And art confederate with a damnèd pack   102
To make a loathsome abject scorn of me!   103
But with these nails I'll pluck out those false eyes
That would behold in me this shameful sport.
[*He threatens Adriana.*]
ADRIANA
Oh, bind him, bind him! Let him not come near me.   106

*Enter three or four, and offer to bind him. He
strives.*

PINCH
More company! The fiend is strong within him.
LUCIANA
Ay me, poor man, how pale and wan he looks!
E. ANTIPHOLUS
What, will you murder me?—Thou jailer, thou,
I am thy prisoner. Wilt thou suffer them
To make a rescue?
OFFICER   Masters, let him go.   111
He is my prisoner, and you shall not have him.

PINCH
Go bind his man, for he is frantic too.
[*They bind Dromio of Ephesus.*]
ADRIANA
What wilt thou do, thou peevish officer?   114
Hast thou delight to see a wretched man
Do outrage and displeasure to himself?   116
OFFICER
He is my prisoner. If I let him go,
The debt he owes will be required of me.
ADRIANA
I will discharge thee ere I go from thee.   119
Bear me forthwith unto his creditor,
And, knowing how the debt grows, I will pay it.   121
Good Master Doctor, see him safe conveyed
Home to my house. Oh, most unhappy day!   123
E. ANTIPHOLUS   Oh, most unhappy strumpet!
E. DROMIO
Master, I am here entered in bond for you.   125
E. ANTIPHOLUS
Out on thee, villain! Wherefore dost thou mad me?   126
E. DROMIO   Will you be bound for nothing? Be mad,
good master; cry, "The devil!"
LUCIANA
God help, poor souls, how idly do they talk!   129
ADRIANA
Go bear him hence. Sister, go you with me.   130
*Exeunt [Pinch and his assistants, carrying off
Antipholus and Dromio of Ephesus]. Manent
Officer, Adriana, Luciana, Courtesan.*
Say now, whose suit is he arrested at?
OFFICER
One Angelo, a goldsmith. Do you know him?
ADRIANA
I know the man. What is the sum he owes?
OFFICER
Two hundred ducats.
ADRIANA   Say, how grows it due?
OFFICER
Due for a chain your husband had of him.
ADRIANA
He did bespeak a chain for me, but had it not.   136
COURTESAN
Whenas your husband all in rage today   137
Came to my house and took away my ring—
The ring I saw upon his finger now—
Straight after did I meet him with a chain.
ADRIANA
It may be so, but I did never see it.—
Come, jailer, bring me where the goldsmith is.
I long to know the truth hereof at large.   143

*Enter Antipholus and Dromio [of] Syracuse with
their rapiers drawn.*

---

82 suborned induced **85 Heart . . . might** You might have sent love
and good wishes by me **86 rag** scrap **93 deadly** deathlike
94 bound . . . room (The regular treatment for lunacy in Shakespeare's
day.) **95 forth** out. (Also in line 97.) **102 pack** i.e., of conspirators
103 abject scorn despicable object of contempt **106.1** *offer* attempt
111 make a rescue take a prisoner by force from legal custody.
Masters Good sirs

114 peevish silly, senseless **116 displeasure** injury, wrong **119 discharge** pay, clear the debt for **121 knowing . . . grows** when I know
how the debt accrued **123 unhappy** fatal, miserable **125 entered in
bond** (1) bound up, tied (2) pledged **126 mad** exasperate **129 idly**
senselessly **130.2** *Manent* They remain onstage **136 bespeak** order
137 Whenas When **143 at large** in full, in detail

LUCIANA
God, for thy mercy! They are loose again.

ADRIANA
And come with naked swords. Let's call more help   145
To have them bound again.

OFFICER   Away! They'll kill us.   146

Run all out. Exeunt omnes, as fast as may be,
frighted. [Antipholus and Dromio of Syracuse
remain.]

S. ANTIPHOLUS
I see these witches are afraid of swords.

S. DROMIO
She that would be your wife now ran from you.

S. ANTIPHOLUS
Come to the Centaur. Fetch our stuff from thence.   149
I long that we were safe and sound aboard.

S. DROMIO   Faith, stay here this night. They will surely
do us no harm. You saw they speak us fair, give us   152
gold. Methinks they are such a gentle nation that, but
for the mountain of mad flesh that claims marriage of
me, I could find in my heart to stay here still and turn   155
witch.

S. ANTIPHOLUS
I will not stay tonight for all the town.
Therefore, away, to get our stuff aboard.   *Exeunt.*

❧

5.1

Enter the [Second] Merchant and [Angelo] the
goldsmith.

ANGELO
I am sorry, sir, that I have hindered you;   1
But I protest he had the chain of me,
Though most dishonestly he doth deny it.

SECOND MERCHANT
How is the man esteemed here in the city?

ANGELO
Of very reverend reputation, sir,
Of credit infinite, highly beloved,
Second to none that lives here in the city.
His word might bear my wealth at any time.   8

SECOND MERCHANT
Speak softly. Yonder, as I think, he walks.

Enter Antipholus and Dromio [of Syracuse] again,
[Antipholus wearing the chain].

ANGELO
'Tis so, and that self chain about his neck   10
Which he forswore most monstrously to have.   11
Good sir, draw near to me. I'll speak to him.—
Signor Antipholus, I wonder much
That you would put me to this shame and trouble
And, not without some scandal to yourself,

With circumstance and oaths so to deny   16
This chain which now you wear so openly.
Beside the charge, the shame, imprisonment,   18
You have done wrong to this my honest friend,   19
Who, but for staying on our controversy,   20
Had hoisted sail and put to sea today.
This chain you had of me. Can you deny it?

S. ANTIPHOLUS
I think I had. I never did deny it.

SECOND MERCHANT
Yes, that you did, sir, and forswore it too.

S. ANTIPHOLUS
Who heard me to deny it or forswear it?

SECOND MERCHANT
These ears of mine, thou know'st, did hear thee.
Fie on thee, wretch! 'Tis pity that thou liv'st
To walk where any honest men resort.

S. ANTIPHOLUS
Thou art a villain to impeach me thus.   29
I'll prove mine honor and mine honesty
Against thee presently, if thou dar'st stand.   31

SECOND MERCHANT
I dare, and do defy thee for a villain.   *They draw.* 32

Enter Adriana, Luciana, [the] Courtesan, and
others.

ADRIANA
Hold, hurt him not, for God sake! He is mad.
Some get within him; take his sword away.   34
Bind Dromio too, and bear them to my house.

S. DROMIO
Run, master, run; for God sake, take a house!   36
This is some priory. In, or we are spoiled!   37

Exeunt [Antipholus and Dromio of Syracuse]
to the priory.

Enter [Emilia, the] Lady Abbess.

ABBESS
Be quiet, people. Wherefore throng you hither?

ADRIANA
To fetch my poor distracted husband hence.
Let us come in, that we may bind him fast
And bear him home for his recovery.

ANGELO
I knew he was not in his perfect wits.

SECOND MERCHANT
I am sorry now that I did draw on him.

ABBESS
How long hath this possession held the man?

ADRIANA
This week he hath been heavy, sour, sad,   45
And much different from the man he was;
But till this afternoon his passion

---

145 **naked** drawn   146.1 *omnes* all   149 **stuff** goods, baggage
152 **speak us fair** speak courteously to us   155 **still** always
5.1. Location: Before the priory and Antipholus of Ephesus's house.
1 **hindered you** delayed your journey   8 **might bear** is worth
10 **self** same   11 **forswore** denied under oath

16 **circumstance** details, particulars   18 **charge** cost   19 **honest** honorable   20 **on** as a result of   29 **impeach** accuse   31 **presently** at
once.   **stand** take a fighting stance, put yourself to the test.   32 **defy**
challenge.   **villain** base person.   34 **within him** under his guard
36 **take** take refuge in   37 **spoiled** ruined, done for.   45 **This week**
All this week.   **sad** melancholy

Ne'er brake into extremity of rage.   48

ABBESS
Hath he not lost much wealth by wreck of sea?   49
Buried some dear friend? Hath not else his eye
Strayed his affection in unlawful love—   51
A sin prevailing much in youthful men,
Who give their eyes the liberty of gazing?
Which of these sorrows is he subject to?

ADRIANA
To none of these, except it be the last,
Namely, some love that drew him oft from home.

ABBESS
You should for that have reprehended him.   57

ADRIANA
Why, so I did.

ABBESS   Ay, but not rough enough.

ADRIANA
As roughly as my modesty would let me.

ABBESS
Haply in private.

ADRIANA   And in assemblies too.   60

ABBESS   Ay, but not enough.

ADRIANA
It was the copy of our conference.   62
In bed he slept not for my urging it;   63
At board he fed not for my urging it;
Alone, it was the subject of my theme;
In company I often glancèd it;   66
Still did I tell him it was vile and bad.   67

ABBESS
And thereof came it that the man was mad.
The venom clamors of a jealous woman   69
Poisons more deadly than a mad dog's tooth.
It seems his sleeps were hindered by thy railing,
And thereof comes it that his head is light.
Thou say'st his meat was sauced with thy upbraidings.
Unquiet meals make ill digestions;
Thereof the raging fire of fever bred,
And what's a fever but a fit of madness?
Thou sayest his sports were hindered by thy brawls.
Sweet recreation barred, what doth ensue
But moody and dull melancholy,
Kinsman to grim and comfortless despair,
And at her heels a huge infectious troop
Of pale distemperatures and foes to life?   82
In food, in sport, and life-preserving rest
To be disturbed would mad or man or beast.   84
The consequence is, then, thy jealous fits
Hath scared thy husband from the use of wits.

LUCIANA
She never reprehended him but mildly,
When he demeaned himself rough, rude, and wildly.   88
[To Adriana] Why bear you these rebukes and
    answer not?

ADRIANA
She did betray me to my own reproof.—   90
Good people, enter and lay hold on him.

ABBESS
No, not a creature enters in my house.

ADRIANA
Then let your servants bring my husband forth.

ABBESS
Neither. He took this place for sanctuary,
And it shall privilege him from your hands
Till I have brought him to his wits again
Or lose my labor in assaying it.   97

ADRIANA
I will attend my husband, be his nurse,
Diet his sickness, for it is my office,   99
And will have no attorney but myself;   100
And therefore let me have him home with me.

ABBESS
Be patient, for I will not let him stir
Till I have used the approvèd means I have,   103
With wholesome syrups, drugs, and holy prayers,
To make of him a formal man again.   105
It is a branch and parcel of mine oath,   106
A charitable duty of my order.
Therefore depart and leave him here with me.

ADRIANA
I will not hence and leave my husband here;
And ill it doth beseem your holiness
To separate the husband and the wife.

ABBESS
Be quiet and depart. Thou shalt not have him. [Exit.]

LUCIANA [to Adriana]
Complain unto the Duke of this indignity.

ADRIANA
Come, go. I will fall prostrate at his feet
And never rise until my tears and prayers
Have won His Grace to come in person hither
And take perforce my husband from the Abbess.

SECOND MERCHANT
By this, I think, the dial points at five.   118
Anon, I'm sure, the Duke himself in person
Comes this way to the melancholy vale,
The place of death and sorry execution   121
Behind the ditches of the abbey here.

ANGELO   Upon what cause?

SECOND MERCHANT
To see a reverend Syracusian merchant,
Who put unluckily into this bay
Against the laws and statutes of this town,
Beheaded publicly for his offense.

ANGELO
See where they come. We will behold his death.

LUCIANA
Kneel to the Duke before he pass the abbey.

---

48 brake broke. rage madness 49 wreck of shipwreck at
51 Strayed led astray 57 reprehended rebuked 60 Haply Perhaps
62 copy topic, theme. conference conversation. 63 for because of
66 glancèd alluded to 67 Still continually 69 venom venomous
82 distemperatures physical disorder, illness 84 mad or madden
either 88 demeaned behaved, conducted

90 She . . . reproof i.e., She led me to see my own faults. 97 assaying
attempting 99 office duty 100 attorney agent, deputy
103 approvèd proved, tested 105 formal normal, made in proper
form 106 parcel integral part 118 By this By this time. dial sundial or watch dial 121 sorry sad

Enter the Duke of Ephesus and [Egeon] the
merchant of Syracuse, barehead [and bound], with
the Headsman and other officers.

DUKE
Yet once again proclaim it publicly,
If any friend will pay the sum for him,
He shall not die; so much we tender him.   132

ADRIANA *[kneeling]*
Justice, most sacred Duke, against the Abbess!

DUKE
She is a virtuous and a reverend lady.
It cannot be that she hath done thee wrong.

ADRIANA
May it please Your Grace, Antipholus my husband,
Who I made lord of me and all I had,
At your important letters, this ill day   138
A most outrageous fit of madness took him,
That desperately he hurried through the street—   140
With him his bondman, all as mad as he—   141
Doing displeasure to the citizens   142
By rushing in their houses, bearing thence
Rings, jewels, anything his rage did like.   144
Once did I get him bound and sent him home,
Whilst to take order for the wrongs I went   146
That here and there his fury had committed.
Anon, I wot not by what strong escape,   148
He broke from those that had the guard of him,
And with his mad attendant and himself,
Each one with ireful passion, with drawn swords,
Met us again and, madly bent on us,   152
Chased us away, till raising of more aid
We came again to bind them. Then they fled
Into this abbey, whither we pursued them;
And here the Abbess shuts the gates on us
And will not suffer us to fetch him out,
Nor send him forth that we may bear him hence.
Therefore, most gracious Duke, with thy command
Let him be brought forth and borne hence for help. 160

DUKE *[raising Adriana]*
Long since, thy husband served me in my wars,
And I to thee engaged a prince's word,   162
When thou didst make him master of thy bed,
To do him all the grace and good I could.—
Go, some of you, knock at the abbey gate
And bid the Lady Abbess come to me.
I will determine this before I stir.   167

Enter a [Servant as] messenger.

SERVANT
Oh, mistress, mistress, shift and save yourself!   168
My master and his man are both broke loose,

Beaten the maids a-row, and bound the doctor,   170
Whose beard they have singed off with brands of fire,
And ever as it blazed they threw on him
Great pails of puddled mire to quench the hair.   173
My master preaches patience to him, and the while
His man with scissors nicks him like a fool;   175
And sure, unless you send some present help,
Between them they will kill the conjurer.

ADRIANA
Peace, fool! Thy master and his man are here,
And that is false thou dost report to us.

SERVANT
Mistress, upon my life, I tell you true.
I have not breathed almost since I did see it.
He cries for you, and vows, if he can take you,
To scorch your face and to disfigure you.   183
                                    Cry within.
Hark, hark! I hear him, mistress. Fly, begone!

DUKE
Come, stand by me. Fear nothing.—Guard with
halberds!   185

ADRIANA
Ay me, it is my husband! Witness you
That he is borne about invisible.
Even now we housed him in the abbey here,   188
And now he's there, past thought of human reason.

Enter Antipholus and Dromio of Ephesus.

E. ANTIPHOLUS
Justice, most gracious Duke, oh, grant me justice!
Even for the service that long since I did thee,
When I bestrid thee in the wars and took   192
Deep scars to save thy life; even for the blood
That then I lost for thee, now grant me justice.

EGEON
Unless the fear of death doth make me dote,
I see my son Antipholus and Dromio.

E. ANTIPHOLUS
Justice, sweet prince, against that woman there!
She whom thou gav'st to me to be my wife,
That hath abusèd and dishonored me   199
Even in the strength and height of injury!
Beyond imagination is the wrong
That she this day hath shameless thrown on me.

DUKE
Discover how, and thou shalt find me just.   203

E. ANTIPHOLUS
This day, great Duke, she shut the doors upon me
While she with harlots feasted in my house.   205

DUKE
A grievous fault. Say, woman, didst thou so?

---

132 so . . . him so much consideration we grant him. (With suggestion also of "value" and "have pity on.")   **138 important** importunate, pressing.   **letters** (Adriana would seem to have been ward to the Duke and married at his importunate urging.)   **140 That desperately** so that recklessly   **141 all** totally   **142 displeasure** wrong, injury   **144 rage** madness, insanity   **146 take order** settle, make reparation   **148 wot** know.   **strong** violent   **152 bent** turned   **160 help** cure.   **162 engaged** pledged   **167 determine** settle   **168 shift** escape, depart

170 a-row one after another   **173 puddled** from filthy puddles   **175 nicks . . . fool** gives him a fantastic haircut in the short fashion of the court fool   **183 scorch** (Compare the singeing of Pinch's beard at line 171; also, score, slash.)   **185 halberds** long-handled spears with blades.   **188 housed him in** i.e., drove him into   **192 bestrid** stood over (to defend when fallen in battle)   **199 abusèd** maltreated   **203 Discover** Reveal   **205 harlots** rascals, vile companions

ADRIANA

  No, my good lord. Myself, he, and my sister
  Today did dine together. So befall my soul   208
  As this is false he burdens me withal.   209

LUCIANA

  Ne'er may I look on day nor sleep on night   210
  But she tells to Your Highness simple truth.

ANGELO

  Oh, perjured woman!—They are both forsworn.
  In this the madman justly chargeth them.

E. ANTIPHOLUS

  My liege, I am advisèd what I say,   214
  Neither disturbèd with the effect of wine
  Nor heady-rash provoked with raging ire,
  Albeit my wrongs might make one wiser mad.
  This woman locked me out this day from dinner.
  That goldsmith there, were he not packed with her, 219
  Could witness it, for he was with me then;
  Who parted with me to go fetch a chain,   221
  Promising to bring it to the Porcupine,
  Where Balthasar and I did dine together.
  Our dinner done, and he not coming thither,
  I went to seek him. In the street I met him,
  And in his company that gentleman.
          [*Indicating the Second Merchant.*]
  There did this perjured goldsmith swear me down 227
  That I this day of him received the chain,
  Which, God he knows, I saw not; for the which
  He did arrest me with an officer.
  I did obey, and sent my peasant home
  For certain ducats. He with none returned.
  Then fairly I bespoke the officer   233
  To go in person with me to my house.
  By th' way we met
  My wife, her sister, and a rabble more
  Of vile confederates. Along with them
  They brought one Pinch, a hungry, lean-faced villain,
  A mere anatomy, a mountebank,   239
  A threadbare juggler and a fortune-teller,   240
  A needy, hollow-eyed, sharp-looking wretch,
  A living dead man. This pernicious slave,
  Forsooth, took on him as a conjurer   243
  And, gazing in mine eyes, feeling my pulse,
  And with no face, as 'twere, outfacing me,   245
  Cries out I was possessed. Then all together 246
  They fell upon me, bound me, bore me thence,
  And in a dark and dankish vault at home
  There left me and my man, both bound together,
  Till, gnawing with my teeth my bonds in sunder,
  I gained my freedom and immediately
  Ran hither to Your Grace, whom I beseech
  To give me ample satisfaction

  For these deep shames and great indignities.

ANGELO

  My lord, in truth, thus far I witness with him,
  That he dined not at home but was locked out.

DUKE

  But had he such a chain of thee, or no?

ANGELO

  He had, my lord, and when he ran in here
  These people saw the chain about his neck.

SECOND MERCHANT [*to E. Antipholus*]

  Besides, I will be sworn these ears of mine
  Heard you confess you had the chain of him
  After you first forswore it on the mart,
  And thereupon I drew my sword on you;
  And then you fled into this abbey here,
  From whence, I think, you are come by miracle.

E. ANTIPHOLUS

  I never came within these abbey walls,
  Nor ever didst thou draw thy sword on me.
  I never saw the chain, so help me Heaven!
  And this is false you burden me withal.

DUKE

  Why, what an intricate impeach is this!   270
  I think you all have drunk of Circe's cup.   271
  If here you housed him, here he would have been.
  If he were mad, he would not plead so coldly.   273
  [*To Adriana*] You say he dined at home; the goldsmith
    here
  Denies that saying. [*To E. Dromio*] Sirrah, what say you?

E. DROMIO

  Sir, he dined with her there, at the Porcupine.

COURTESAN

  He did, and from my finger snatched that ring.

E. ANTIPHOLUS

  'Tis true, my liege. This ring I had of her.

DUKE [*to the Courtesan*]

  Saw'st thou him enter at the abbey here?

COURTESAN

  As sure, my liege, as I do see Your Grace.

DUKE

  Why, this is strange. Go call the Abbess hither.
  I think you are all mated or stark mad.   282
              Exit one to the Abbess.

EGEON

  Most mighty Duke, vouchsafe me speak a word.
  Haply I see a friend will save my life
  And pay the sum that may deliver me.

DUKE

  Speak freely, Syracusian, what thou wilt.

EGEON

  Is not your name, sir, called Antipholus?
  And is not that your bondman, Dromio?

E. DROMIO [*to E. Antipholus*]

  Within this hour I was his bondman, sir,
  But he, I thank him, gnawed in two my cords.
  Now am I Dromio and his man, unbound.

---

208 So . . . soul i.e., As I hope to be saved   **209 he . . . withal** he charges
me with.   **210 on at**   **214 am advisèd** know very well   **219 packed in**
conspiracy   **221 parted with** departed from   **227 swear me down**
swear in the face of my denials   **233 fairly** civilly. **bespoke** requested
239 mere anatomy absolute skeleton. **mountebank** quack, charlatan
240 juggler sorcerer   **243 took . . . as** pretended to be   **245 And . . . me**
i.e., and blandly staring me down. (With wordplay on "face" and "outfacing.") **246 possessed** mad.

270 intricate impeach involved accusation   **271 Circe's cup** the
charmed cup, a draft of which turned men into beasts (as told in
Homer's *Odyssey*).   **273 coldly** calmly, rationally.   **282 mated** stupefied

EGEON
I am sure you both of you remember me.

E. DROMIO
Ourselves we do remember, sir, by you;
For lately we were bound, as you are now.
You are not Pinch's patient, are you, sir?

EGEON
Why look you strange on me? You know me well.

E. ANTIPHOLUS
I never saw you in my life till now.

EGEON
Oh, grief hath changed me since you saw me last,
And careful hours with Time's deformèd hand   299
Have written strange defeatures in my face.   300
But tell me yet, dost thou not know my voice?

E. ANTIPHOLUS   Neither.

EGEON   Dromio, nor thou?

E. DROMIO   No, trust me, sir, nor I.

EGEON   I am sure thou dost.

E. DROMIO   Ay, sir, but I am sure I do not; and whatsoever a man denies, you are now bound to believe him.

EGEON
Not know my voice! O time's extremity,
Hast thou so cracked and splitted my poor tongue
In seven short years, that here my only son
Knows not my feeble key of untuned cares?   311
Though now this grainèd face of mine be hid   312
In sap-consuming winter's drizzled snow   313
And all the conduits of my blood froze up,
Yet hath my night of life some memory,
My wasting lamps some fading glimmer left,   316
My dull deaf ears a little use to hear.
All these old witnesses—I cannot err—
Tell me thou art my son Antipholus.

E. ANTIPHOLUS
I never saw my father in my life.

EGEON
But seven years since, in Syracusa, boy,   321
Thou know'st we parted. But perhaps, my son,
Thou sham'st to acknowledge me in misery.

E. ANTIPHOLUS
The Duke and all that know me in the city
Can witness with me that it is not so.
I ne'er saw Syracusa in my life.

DUKE
I tell thee, Syracusian, twenty years
Have I been patron to Antipholus,
During which time he ne'er saw Syracusa.
I see thy age and dangers make thee dote.

*Enter the Abbess, with Antipholus and Dromio of
Syracuse.*

ABBESS
Most mighty Duke, behold a man much wronged.
                              All gather to see them.

ADRIANA
I see two husbands, or mine eyes deceive me.

DUKE
One of these men is genius to the other;   333
And so of these, which is the natural man,
And which the spirit? Who deciphers them?   335

S. DROMIO
I, sir, am Dromio. Command him away.

E. DROMIO
I, sir, am Dromio. Pray, let me stay.

S. ANTIPHOLUS
Egeon art thou not? Or else his ghost?

S. DROMIO
Oh, my old master! Who hath bound him here?

ABBESS
Whoever bound him, I will loose his bonds
And gain a husband by his liberty.
Speak, old Egeon, if thou be'st the man
That hadst a wife once called Emilia
That bore thee at a burden two fair sons.   344
Oh, if thou be'st the same Egeon, speak,
And speak unto the same Emilia!

EGEON
If I dream not, thou art Emilia.
If thou art she, tell me where is that son
That floated with thee on the fatal raft?

ABBESS
By men of Epidamnum he and I
And the twin Dromio all were taken up;
But by and by rude fishermen of Corinth   352
By force took Dromio and my son from them,
And me they left with those of Epidamnum.
What then became of them I cannot tell;
I to this fortune that you see me in.

DUKE
Why, here begins his morning story right: 357
These two Antipholus', these two so like,
And these two Dromios, one in semblance—   359
Besides her urging of her wreck at sea—   360
These are the parents to these children,
Which accidentally are met together.
Antipholus, thou cam'st from Corinth first?

S. ANTIPHOLUS
No, sir, not I. I came from Syracuse.

DUKE
Stay, stand apart. I know not which is which.

E. ANTIPHOLUS
I came from Corinth, my most gracious lord—

E. DROMIO   And I with him.

E. ANTIPHOLUS
Brought to this town by that most famous warrior,
Duke Menaphon, your most renownèd uncle.

ADRIANA
Which of you two did dine with me today?

---

299 careful care-filled   **300 defeatures** disfigurements, blemishes
311 my . . . cares my voice enfeebled by discordant cares.
312 grainèd lined, furrowed   **313 In . . . snow** i.e., by my white hairs,
that have dried up the sap of my youth   **316 wasting lamps** i.e., dimming eyes   **321 But** Only

333 genius attendant spirit   **335 deciphers** distinguishes   **344 burden** birth   **352 rude** rough, simple   **357 his morning story** i.e., the
history Egeon related this morning   **359 semblance** appearance
360 urging urgent account

S. ANTIPHOLUS
I, gentle mistress.

ADRIANA   And are not you my husband?

E. ANTIPHOLUS   No, I say nay to that.

S. ANTIPHOLUS
And so do I. Yet did she call me so,
And this fair gentlewoman, her sister here,
Did call me brother. [*To Luciana*] What I told you then
I hope I shall have leisure to make good,   376
If this be not a dream I see and hear.

ANGELO [*pointing to the chain Antipholus of Syracuse wears*]
That is the chain, sir, which you had of me.

S. ANTIPHOLUS
I think it be, sir. I deny it not.

E. ANTIPHOLUS [*to Angelo*]
And you, sir, for this chain arrested me.

ANGELO
I think I did, sir. I deny it not.

ADRIANA [*to Antipholus of Ephesus*]
I sent you money, sir, to be your bail,
By Dromio, but I think he brought it not.

E. DROMIO   No, none by me.

S. ANTIPHOLUS [*showing his purse to Adriana*]
This purse of ducats I received from you,
And Dromio my man did bring them me.
I see we still did meet each other's man,   387
And I was ta'en for him, and he for me,
And thereupon these errors are arose.

E. ANTIPHOLUS [*offering money*]
These ducats pawn I for my father here.

DUKE
It shall not need. Thy father hath his life.   391

COURTESAN [*to E. Antipholus*]
Sir, I must have that diamond from you.

E. ANTIPHOLUS [*giving the ring*]
There, take it, and much thanks for my good cheer.

ABBESS
Renownèd Duke, vouchsafe to take the pains   394
To go with us into the abbey here
And hear at large discoursèd all our fortunes,   396
And all that are assembled in this place,
That by this sympathizèd one day's error   398
Have suffered wrong. Go, keep us company,

---

376 leisure opportunity   **387 still** continually   **391 life** pardon.
394 vouchsafe deign, agree   **396 at large** at length   **398 sympathizèd**
shared in by all equally

And we shall make full satisfaction.
Thirty-three years have I but gone in travail
Of you, my sons, and till this present hour
My heavy burden ne'er deliverèd.
The Duke, my husband, and my children both,
And you the calendars of their nativity,   405
Go to a gossips' feast, and joy with me;   406
After so long grief, such nativity!

DUKE
With all my heart I'll gossip at this feast.   408
      *Exeunt omnes. Manent the two Dromios and two
                                 brothers [Antipholus].*

S. DROMIO [*to Antipholus of Ephesus*]
Master, shall I fetch your stuff from shipboard?

E. ANTIPHOLUS
Dromio, what stuff of mine hast thou embarked?

S. DROMIO
Your goods that lay at host, sir, in the Centaur.   411

S. ANTIPHOLUS
He speaks to me.—I am your master, Dromio.
Come, go with us. We'll look to that anon.
Embrace thy brother there; rejoice with him.
                  Exeunt [the two brothers Antipholus].

S. DROMIO
There is a fat friend at your master's house
That kitchened me for you today at dinner.   416
She now shall be my sister, not my wife.   417

E. DROMIO
Methinks you are my glass and not my brother.   418
I see by you I am a sweet-faced youth.
Will you walk in to see their gossiping?   420

S. DROMIO   Not I, sir, you are my elder.

E. DROMIO   That's a question. How shall we try it?

S. DROMIO   We'll draw cuts for the senior. Till then, lead   423
thou first.

E. DROMIO   Nay, then, thus:
We came into the world like brother and brother,
And now let's go hand in hand, not one before
      another.   *Exeunt.*

---

405 calendars . . . nativity i.e., the Dromios, since the servants were
born at the same time as their masters   **406 a gossips' feast** a christening feast, here to celebrate, belatedly, the start of life for the two sets of
twins, who were not truly born till now; also, a feast of companionship   **408 gossip** i.e., be a hearty companion, take part   **411 lay at
host** were put up at the inn   **416 kitchened** entertained in the kitchen
417 sister sister-in-law   **418 glass** mirror   **420 gossiping** merrymaking   **423 cuts** lots.

Love's Labor's Lost

In much the same way that *The Comedy of Errors* is Shakespeare's apprenticeship to Plautus and neo-classical comedy, *Love's Labor's Lost* is his apprenticeship to John Lyly's courtly drama of the 1580s, to the court masque, and to conventions of Petrarchan lyric poetry. The play is word conscious and stylistically mannered to an extent that is unusual even for the pun-loving Shakespeare. The humor abounds in the pert repartee for which juvenile actors were especially fitted, and an extraordinarily high percentage of roles are assigned to boys: four women and a diminutive page (Mote) among seventeen named roles. The social setting is patrician and the entertainments aristocratic. In some ways, little seems to happen in *Love's Labor's Lost*. Fast-moving plot is replaced by a structure that includes a series of debates on courtly topics reminiscent of John Lyly: love versus honor, the flesh versus the spirit, pleasure versus instruction, art versus nature. The songs and sonnets composed by the courtiers for the ladies (4.3.23–116) gracefully caricature the excesses of the Petrarchan love convention (named for the influential Italian sonneteer, Francesco Petrarch): the lovers are "sick to death" with unrequited passion, they catalogue the charms of their proud mistresses, they express their exquisitely tortured emotions through elaborate poetical metaphors, and so on. Stage movements are often masquelike; characters group themselves and then pair off two by two, as in a formal dance. Actual masques and pageants, presented by the courtiers or devised for their amusement, are essential ingredients of the spectacle.

Yet beneath the brightly polished surfaces of this sophisticated comedy, we often catch glimpses of a candor and a simplicity that offset the tinsel and glitter. The wits ultimately disclaim (with some qualification) their wittiness, and the ladies confess they have tried too zealously to put down the men; both sides disavow the extreme postures they have striven so hard to maintain. The clowns, though deflated by mocking laughter for their naiveté and pomposity, deflate the courtiers, in turn, for lack of compassion. From this interplay among various forms of courtly wit, Petrarchism, pedantry, and rustic speech emerges a recommended style that is witty but not irresponsibly so, courtly yet sincere, polished and yet free of affectation or empty verbal ornament. This new harmony is aptly expressed by Berowne and Rosaline, whose witty quest for self-understanding in love foreshadows that of Benedick and Beatrice in *Much Ado About Nothing*. The perfect expression of the true style is found in the song at the end of the play; taking the form of a medieval literary debate between Spring and Winter, it beautifully fuses the natural and the artificial into a concordant vision transcending the mundane.

Like *The Comedy of Errors*, *Love's Labor's Lost* is an early comedy that is hard to date with precision. It was published in quarto in 1598 "as it was presented before Her Highness this last Christmas" (1597). The text also purports to be "newly corrected and augmented," though we know of no earlier published version. Perhaps a play that was already several years old may have seemed in need of stylistic revision. Act 4 does, in fact, contain two long duplicatory passages, suggesting that a certain amount of rewriting did take place. The revisions alter the meaning only slightly, however, and give little support to the widely held notion that Shakespeare must have reworked the ending of his play. The unresolved ending, in which no marriages take place and in which the Princess's territorial claims to Aquitaine are left unsettled, should be regarded not as unfinished but as highly imaginative and indeed indispensable. The title, after all, assures us that "love's labors" will be lost, and the Princess affirms the principle of "form confounded."

Some stylistic tests suggest a date between 1592 and 1595, although these characteristics might point to an early play that had been "new corrected and augmented." Topical hypotheses arise from the quest for Shakespeare's sources. Since the plot of *Love's Labor's Lost* is derived from no known literary source, may it have been drawn instead from the Elizabethan contemporary scene, poking fun at the pretentiousness of literary figures and intellectuals, such as John Florio, Thomas Nashe, Gabriel Harvey, Sir Walter Ralegh, and George Chapman? Or should we seek topical meaning in the undoubted currency of such names as Navarre (Henry of Navarre, King Henry IV of France), Berowne (Biron, Henry IV's general), Dumaine (De Mayenne, brother of the Catholic Guise), and others? From the point of view of dating the play, however, such names would have been distastefully controversial in a courtly comedy after 1589. That date saw the beginning in France of a bitter civil conflict between the Catholic Guise and Protestant Navarre, continuing until Henry abjured Protestantism in 1593 and assumed the French throne. In the late 1580s, on the other hand, the tiny kingdom of Navarre would have seemed charmingly appropriate as a setting for Shakespeare's play. Such an early date, although by no means certain, would also help explain the Lylyan tone of the comedy and its early techniques of versification: the high percentage of rhymed lines in couplets and quatrains, the end-stopped blank verse, the use of various sonnet forms and of seven-stress (septenary) couplets, and the like.

The world of *Love's Labor's Lost* seems uneventful at first and remarkably unthreatened by danger or evil; only hintingly do reminders of mortality intrude upon the never-never-land of Navarre. There are, to be sure, occasional references to the Princess's "bedrid" father, to the plague, and to a "death's head," but the courtiers and we as audience are little prepared for the sudden appearance of Marcade in 5.2 and his announcement that the Princess's royal father is dead and that all lighthearted entertainments must now give way to mourning. Prior to this belated moment of reversal, the male characters are menaced by nothing worse than loss of dignity through breaking of their oaths. And although oath breaking was a matter of great seriousness to Elizabethan gentlemen, their doing so here is partly excused by the constancy of their devotion once they have fallen in love. In such an artificial world, the preservation of one's self-esteem assumes undue importance. Using the criteria of wit and self-awareness, Mote and Boyet, as manipulators and controllers of point of view, show us how to laugh at folly in love and pomposity in language. They present to us variations on a theme of courtly behavior, creating, in effect, a scale of manners ranging from the most aristocratic (the King and the Princess, Berowne and Rosaline) to the most absurdly pretentious (Armado, Holofernes, Nathaniel, and Dull). Nearly all the characters are mocked, but those at the lower end of the scale are especially vulnerable because they are grossly un-self-aware and hence unteachable.

The King and his companions deserve to be mocked because of their transparent lack of self-knowledge, their

affectation, and the futility of their vows against love. As Berowne concedes from the start, such defiance of love is at odds with a fundamental natural rhythm that ultimately cannot be thwarted—a rhythm that provides a counterpoint and corrective to the frequently artificial rhythms of courtly life. This natural rhythm asserts itself throughout the play until it becomes starkly insistent in the death of the Princess's royal father and in the resulting twelve-month delay of all marriages.

Hypocritical defiance of love is doomed to comic failure and satirical punishment. The basic devices used to expose this hypocrisy are misdirected love letters and overheard speech, both devices of unmasking. Appropriately, the young ladies administer their most amusing comeuppance to the men by seeing through their Muscovite masks. The code governing this merry conflict is one of "mock for mock" and "sport by sport o'erthrown" (5.2.140, 153). In a prevailing legal metaphor, the young men are guilty of forswearing their written oaths, and must be punished for their perjury. Love is metaphorically a war, a siege, a battle of the sexes in which the women come off virtually unscathed. The language of love is that of parry and thrust (with occasional bawdy overtones). The men naturally are chagrined to be put down by the ladies but are on their way to a cure: they learn to laugh at their own pretentiousness and, even if hyperbolically, vow to cast aside all "affectation" and "maggot ostentation" in favor of "russet yeas and honest kersey noes" (lines 403–16). At the same time, Berowne's renunciation of artful language is cast in the form of a perfect fourteen-line sonnet; Shakespeare is having it both ways.

The clownish types are generally more victimized by their affectations. The fantastical Don Armado, as lover of Jaquenetta the country wench, apes the courtly conventions of the aristocrats to whose company he aspires. Enervated by base passion, penning wretched love letters, and worshiping a dairymaid as though she were an unapproachable goddess, he is a caricature of the Petrarchan lover. Generally, however, the affectations of the comic characters have to do with language rather than love. Armado himself is known as a phrasemaker, "a plume of feathers," a "weathercock": "Did you ever hear better?" (4.1.94–5). His letter to Jaquenetta, read aloud for the Princess's amusement, is an exquisite spoof of John Lyly's exaggeratedly mannered style, called Euphuism: "Shall I command thy love? I may. Shall I enforce thy love? I could. Shall I entreat thy love? I will. What shalt thou exchange for rags? Robes. For tittles? Titles. For thyself? Me" (lines 80–3). Here we see the repeated antitheses, the balanced structure (reflected also in the structure of the play), and the alliterative effects that so intoxicated literary sophisticates of the 1580s. In a similar spirit, other comic types are distinguished by their verbal habits: Constable Dull by his malapropisms (anticipating Dogberry and Elbow); Holofernes by his Latinisms, philological definitions, and varied epithets; Nathaniel by his deference to Holofernes as a fellow bookman; and Costard by his amiable but unlettered confusion over such grandiose terms as "remuneration" and "guerdon" (3.1.167–71). The word-conscious humor of the play gives us parodies of excruciatingly bad verse (as in Holofernes's "extemporal epitaph on the death of the deer," 4.2.49–61), teeth-grating puns (enfranchise, one Frances, 3.1.118–19), and the longest Latin word in existence (*honorificabilitudinitatibus*, 5.1.41).

A little of this sort of thing goes a long way, and occasional scenes of verbal sparring are overdone. Shakespeare tries to have it both ways, reveling in linguistic self-consciousness while laughing at its excesses. Yet the self-possessed characters do at least come to a realization that verbal overkill, like Petrarchan posturing, must be cast aside in favor of decorum and frankness in speech. There will always be "style," but it must be an appropriate style. The comic characters at their best help emphasize this same point. Costard especially is blessed with a pragmatic folk wisdom and simplicity that enable him to stand up unflinchingly to the ladies and gentlemen. He does not hesitate to tell the Princess that she is the "thickest and the tallest" of the ladies, for "truth is truth" (4.1.48). His forbearing description of Nathaniel as "a little o'erparted" (5.2.580–1) in the role of Alexander serves as a gentle rebuke to the wits, whose caustic observations on "The Nine Worthies" have gotten out of hand. Even Holofernes justly chides, before retiring in confusion as Judas Maccabaeus, that "This is not generous, not gentle, not humble" (line 626).

Even if the stylistic self-consciousness makes for labored reading at times, the play can be wonderfully funny in the theater. It provides numerous opportunities for sight gags, and it revels in comic character types who are funny even when their jokes are feeble. For all his indebtedness to Lyly's courtly drama in this play, Shakespeare has shaped it to the demands of a popular audience. Perhaps the greatest source of amusement is in Shakespeare's depiction of the war of the sexes. Nowhere else does he give us male characters who are so consistently baffled and tormented by women. The young women know from the start who they are and what men they are attracted to; we never see the women fall in love, for they have evidently made up their minds already. The men, conversely, flounder about absurdly from one inelegant posture to another, from futile asceticism to curiosity, infatuation, betrayal of their oaths, attempts to conceal their lovesickness from one another, and collapse of all pretenses when they are caught out. They have yet to come to terms with their own inner feelings and must be taught—and tortured—by the self-possessed young ladies. The men are at their most absurd when, having confessed to falling in love, they now rival one another in boasting of their respective mistresses and in striving to see who will succeed first. It never crosses their minds that they might be rejected now that they have deigned to come forward as suitors.

The masquing in Act 5 is thus a device by which the women can test and even humiliate the young men to show them how flighty and uncontrolled are their unfamiliar new emotions. The uncompleted ending of the play expresses an unfinished process: the young men must still apprentice themselves to mature self-reflection before they can be deemed worthy as husbands. Ironically, the young women consign the men to the very sort of celibate exercise in self-understanding that the men thought they were committing themselves to at the play's start. In these terms, too, we can see that some of the play's subplot characters are variations on a theme of male folly in love: Costard is the self-assured peasant, while Armado is the self-abnegating aristocrat. Armado exaggerates everything foolish that the aristocratic men have undergone and in Act 5 is fittingly the center of an absurd pageant, through which he becomes the comic scapegoat. Watching his performance in the pageant of "The Nine Worthies," the young aristocrats can laugh at the absurdities of male posturing and self-abasement that they are now slowly learning to control in themselves.

Above all, then, it is the play's unexpected ending that introduces an invaluable new insight on the courtiers' brittle war of wits. The death of the Princess's father brings everyone back to reality, to sober responsibility, to an awareness that marriage requires thoughtful decision. Devouring Time has entered the never-never-land of Navarre's park. The song at the end, appropriately cast in the form of a dialogue or debate, gives us the two voices of Spring and Winter, love and death, carnival and Lent, to remind us that human happiness and self-understanding are complex and perishable. And the song reminds us as well, in its "living art," of that subtle power of the imagination, which transforms time, love, and death into artistic creation.

Love's Labor's Lost

[*Dramatis Personae*

FERDINAND, *King of Navarre*
BEROWNE,
LONGAVILLE, } *lords attending the King*
DUMAINE,

THE PRINCESS OF FRANCE
ROSALINE,
MARIA, } *ladies attending the Princess*
KATHARINE,
BOYET, *a French lord attending the Princess*
MARCADE, *a French gentleman acting as messenger*
Two French LORDS

SCENE: *Navarre*]

DON ADRIANO DE ARMADO, *a Spanish braggart*
MOTE, *his page*
NATHANIEL, *a curate*
HOLOFERNES, *a schoolmaster, called a pedant*
DULL, *a constable*
COSTARD, *a rustic, also referred to as a clown*
JAQUENETTA, *a dairymaid*
A FORESTER

Lords and Attendants; Attendants disguised as blackamoors

[1.1]

Enter Ferdinand, King of Navarre, Berowne, Longaville, and Dumaine.

KING
Let fame, that all hunt after in their lives,
Live registered upon our brazen tombs, 2
And then grace us in the disgrace of death, 3
When, spite of cormorant devouring Time, 4
Th'endeavor of this present breath may buy 5
That honor which shall bate his scythe's keen edge 6
And make us heirs of all eternity.
Therefore, brave conquerors—for so you are,
That war against your own affections 9
And the huge army of the world's desires—
Our late edict shall strongly stand in force. 11
Navarre shall be the wonder of the world;
Our court shall be a little academe, 13
Still and contemplative in living art. 14
You three, Berowne, Dumaine, and Longaville,
Have sworn for three years' term to live with me
My fellow scholars and to keep those statutes
That are recorded in this schedule here. 18
[He shows a document.]
Your oaths are passed; and now subscribe your
names, 19
That his own hand may strike his honor down 20
That violates the smallest branch herein. 21
If you are armed to do as sworn to do, 22
Subscribe to your deep oaths, and keep it, too.
LONGAVILLE *[signing]*
I am resolved. 'Tis but a three years' fast.
The mind shall banquet, though the body pine. 25
Fat paunches have lean pates, and dainty bits 26
Make rich the ribs but bankrupt quite the wits.

1.1 Location: The King of Navarre's park. (The locale remains the same throughout the play, sometimes immediately outside the gates of Navarre's court.)
2 registered recorded. **brazen** brass **3 grace** honor. **the disgrace of death** (1) the taking away of the grace of life by death (2) the overthrowing of death by proper fame **4 spite of** despite. **cormorant** ravenous, rapacious. (The cormorant is a large, voracious seabird.) **5 breath** breathing time, i.e., life itself; also, speech **6 bate** abate, blunt **9 affections** emotions, passions **11 late** recent

13 academe academy. (From the name of the grove near Athens where Plato and his followers gathered.) **14 Still** constant, calm. **living art** (1) the art of living (an idea probably derived from the *ars vivendi* of the Roman Stoics) (2) infusing learning (*art*) with vitality. **18 schedule** document **19 passed** pledged **20 hand** (1) armed hand of a warrior (2) handwriting **21 branch** i.e., clause **22 armed** i.e., prepared. (With a play on the military sense, as in *hand*, line 20.) **25 pine** languish, waste away. **26 pates** heads. **dainty bits** delicate morsels

DUMAINE [*signing*]
   My loving lord, Dumaine is mortified.   28
   The grosser manner of these world's delights
   He throws upon the gross world's baser slaves.   30
   To love, to wealth, to pomp I pine and die,
   With all these living in philosophy.   32
BEROWNE
   I can but say their protestation over.   33
   So much, dear liege, I have already sworn,   34
   That is, to live and study here three years.
   But there are other strict observances:
   As, not to see a woman in that term,
   Which I hope well is not enrollèd there;
   And one day in a week to touch no food,
   And but one meal on every day beside,
   The which I hope is not enrollèd there;
   And then to sleep but three hours in the night,
   And not be seen to wink of all the day—   43
   When I was wont to think no harm all night,   44
   And make a dark night too of half the day—
   Which I hope well is not enrollèd there.
   Oh, these are barren tasks, too hard to keep:
   Not to see ladies, study, fast, not sleep!
KING
   Your oath is passed to pass away from these.
BEROWNE
   Let me say no, my liege, an if you please.
   I only swore to study with Your Grace   50
   And stay here in your court for three years' space.   52
LONGAVILLE
   You swore to that, Berowne, and to the rest.
BEROWNE
   By yea and nay, sir, then I swore in jest.   54
   What is the end of study, let me know?   55
KING
   Why, that to know which else we should not know.
BEROWNE
   Things hid and barred, you mean, from common
      sense?   57
KING
   Ay, that is study's godlike recompense.   58
BEROWNE
   Come on, then, I will swear to study so   59
   To know the thing I am forbid to know,
   As thus: to study where I well may dine,
      When I to feast expressly am forbid;
   Or study where to meet some mistress fine,
      When mistresses from common sense are hid;

   Or, having sworn too-hard-a-keeping oath,   65
   Study to break it and not break my troth.   66
   If study's gain be thus, and this be so,   67
   Study knows that which yet it doth not know.   68
   Swear me to this, and I will ne'er say no.
KING
   These be the stops that hinder study quite,   70
   And train our intellects to vain delight.   71
BEROWNE
   Why, all delights are vain, but that most vain
   Which, with pain purchased, doth inherit pain: 73
   As, painfully to pore upon a book   74
      To seek the light of truth, while truth the while   75
   Doth falsely blind the eyesight of his look.   76
      Light seeking light doth light of light beguile;   77
   So, ere you find where light in darkness lies,   78
   Your light grows dark by losing of your eyes.   79
   Study me how to please the eye indeed   80
      By fixing it upon a fairer eye,   81
   Who dazzling so, that eye shall be his heed   82
      And give him light that it was blinded by.   83
   Study is like the heaven's glorious sun,
      That will not be deep searched with saucy looks.   85
   Small have continual plodders ever won   86
      Save base authority from others' books.   87
   These earthly godfathers of heaven's lights,   88
      That give a name to every fixèd star,   89
   Have no more profit of their shining nights   90
      Than those that walk and wot not what they are.   91
   Too much to know is to know naught but fame;   92
   And every godfather can give a name.   93
KING
   How well he's read, to reason against reading!
DUMAINE
   Proceeded well, to stop all good proceeding.   95
LONGAVILLE
   He weeds the corn and still lets grow the weeding.   96

---

28 mortified i.e., dead to worldly desire. **30 throws upon** leaves to. **baser slaves** i.e., slaves to passion and pleasure. **32 With . . . philosophy** i.e., thereby choosing instead the philosophical life. (*These* may mean "these acts of renunciation.") **33 say . . . over** repeat their vows. **34 liege** lord **43 wink of all** close the eyes at any time during **44 wont** accustomed. **think no harm** i.e., think it no harm to sleep soundly **50 an if** if **52 space** time. **54 By . . . nay** (A pious equivocation found in Matthew 5:33–7, frequently invoked by those not having a proper answer.) **55 end** goal **57 common sense** ordinary observation or intelligence. **58 recompense** compensation, payment. **59 Come on** (With a quibble on *common*, line 57.)

65 too . . . oath an oath too hard to keep **66 troth** faith. **67–8 If . . . know** If the true purpose of study should be as I've defined it—and indeed it is—then study offers unexpected rewards. **70 stops** obstacles **71 train** lure, entice. **vain** (1) foolish (2) overly proud **73 Which . . . pain** which, acquired by dint of effort and suffering, gains nothing but more pain **74 painfully** laboriously. **upon** over **75–6 while truth . . . look** i.e., while truth meantime eludes the reader's gaze. (Too much study, poorly directed, is counterproductive.) **77–9 Light . . . eyes** i.e., Searching for truth by excessive study paradoxically blinds the reader; and so, before you can bring illumination out of darkness, you lose your ability to see at all. **80 Study me** Let me study **81 fairer** i.e., of a fair lady **82–3 Who dazzling . . . by** i.e., which dazzling eye will occupy all the man's attention and bestow upon him the very light that first blinded him. **85 That . . . looks** i.e., that refuses to be searched or analyzed (literally, penetrated as in "searching" a wound) with insolent gazes. **86 Small** Little **87 Save** except. **base** commonplace, lower **88–9 These . . . star** i.e., Those complacent astronomers who have the audacity to name the stars, as if the astronomers were the stars' godfathers **90 their** i.e., the stars' **91 wot** know **92–3 Too . . . name** i.e., The acquiring of superfluous knowledge leads only to an empty reputation, since anyone who acts as godparent can do what the astronomers do (that is, give a name to something or someone). **95 Proceeded** Advanced. (In the academic sense of taking a degree.) **96 He . . . weeding** He pulls out the wheat and allows the weeds to grow.

BEROWNE
    The spring is near when green geese are a-breeding. 97
DUMAINE
    How follows that?
BEROWNE   Fit in his place and time. 98
DUMAINE
    In reason nothing.
BEROWNE   Something then in rhyme. 99
KING
    Berowne is like an envious sneaping frost 100
        That bites the firstborn infants of the spring. 101
BEROWNE
    Well, say I am. Why should proud summer boast 102
        Before the birds have any cause to sing?
    Why should I joy in an abortive birth? 104
    At Christmas I no more desire a rose
    Than wish a snow in May's newfangled shows, 106
    But like of each thing that in season grows. 107
    So you to study, now it is too late, 108
    Climb o'er the house to unlock the little gate. 109
KING
    Well, sit you out. Go home, Berowne. Adieu. 110
BEROWNE
    No, my good lord, I have sworn to stay with you.
    And though I have for barbarism spoke more 112
        Than for that angel knowledge you can say,
    Yet, confident, I'll keep what I have sworn
    And bide the penance of each three years' day. 115
    Give me the paper. Let me read the same,
    And to the strictest decrees I'll write my name.
                                    [He takes the paper.]
KING
    How well this yielding rescues thee from shame!
BEROWNE [reads] "Item, That no woman shall come
    within a mile of my court—" Hath this been pro-
    claimed?
LONGAVILLE   Four days ago.
BEROWNE   Let's see the penalty—"on pain of losing her
    tongue." Who devised this penalty?
LONGAVILLE
    Marry, that did I.
BEROWNE   Sweet lord, and why? 125
LONGAVILLE
    To fright them hence with that dread penalty.
BEROWNE
    A dangerous law against gentility! 127

[He reads.] "Item, If any man be seen to talk with a
woman within the term of three years, he shall endure
such public shame as the rest of the court can possibly
devise."
This article, my liege, yourself must break,
    For well you know here comes in embassy 133
The French King's daughter with yourself to speak—
    A maid of grace and complete majesty— 135
About surrender up of Aquitaine
    To her decrepit, sick, and bed-rid father. 137
Therefore this article is made in vain,
    Or vainly comes th'admirèd Princess hither.
KING
What say you, lords? Why, this was quite forgot.
BEROWNE
So study evermore is overshot. 141
While it doth study to have what it would, 142
It doth forget to do the thing it should,
And when it hath the thing it hunteth most, 144
'Tis won as towns with fire—so won, so lost. 145
KING
We must of force dispense with this decree. 146
She must lie here, on mere necessity. 147
BEROWNE
Necessity will make us all forsworn 148
    Three thousand times within this three years' space;
For every man with his affects is born, 150
    Not by might mastered, but by special grace. 151
If I break faith, this word shall speak for me: 152
I am forsworn on "mere necessity."
So to the laws at large I write my name. [He signs.] 154
    And he that breaks them in the least degree
Stands in attainder of eternal shame. 156
    Suggestions are to other as to me; 157
But I believe, although I seem so loath, 158
I am the last that will last keep his oath. 159
But is there no quick recreation granted? 160
KING
Ay, that there is. Our court, you know, is haunted 161
    With a refinèd traveler of Spain, 162
A man in all the world's new fashion planted, 163
    That hath a mint of phrases in his brain; 164
One who the music of his own vain tongue 165
    Doth ravish like enchanting harmony;
A man of compliments, whom right and wrong 167

97 The . . . a-breeding (Berowne may be hinting that his fellows are
all foolish, but Dumaine, in lines 98–9, misses the point; to him,
Berowne's quip does not seem to follow logically from what preceded.) 98 Fit in his Appropriate to its 99 In reason nothing i.e.,
It doesn't follow at all logically. rhyme (Berowne, answering
Dumaine, plays upon the proverbial phrase "neither rhyme nor reason": if what I said doesn't seem to follow logically, at least it
rhymes.) 100 envious malignant. sneaping biting, nipping
101 infants buds 102 proud glorious 104 abortive monstrous,
unnatural 106 May's . . . shows i.e., the display of spring flowers
107 like of approve of. in season i.e., in its proper season 108 too
late i.e., too late in our lives to be students 109 Climb . . . gate i.e.,
you begin at the wrong end. 110 sit you out don't take part.
112 for barbarism on the side of ignorance 115 bide endure.
each . . . day every day of the three years. 125 Marry (A mild oath,
derived from "by the Virgin Mary.") 127 gentility civilized custom.

133 in embassy as an ambassador 135 complete perfect 137 bedrid bedridden 141 overshot wide of the mark by shooting over the
target, mistaken. 142 would desires 144–5 And . . . lost i.e., and
when study achieves its desire, it does so by consuming what it
sought, much as towns are conquered by being burned to the ground
or destroyed by artillery. 146 of force necessarily 147 lie lodge.
on mere out of absolute 148 forsworn guilty of breaking an oath,
perjured 150 affects natural passions 151 might i.e., his own
strength. special grace divine intervention. 152 word motto
154 at large as a whole, in general 156 in attainder under penalty
157 Suggestions . . . me i.e., Temptations affect others as much as
they do me. 158 loath reluctant (to sign) 159 I . . . oath I that speak
last will be the last to break my oath. (But with an equivocal meaning
also of being the last person to keep his oath to the last.) 160 quick
lively 161–2 haunted With frequented by 163 planted rooted
164 a mint i.e., a vast sum. (Literally, a place where money is coined.)
165 who whom 167 compliments gentlemanly mannerisms

Have chose as umpire of their mutiny. 168
This child of fancy, that Armado hight, 169
For interim to our studies shall relate 170
In high-borne words the worth of many a knight 171
From tawny Spain, lost in the world's debate. 172
How you delight, my lords, I know not, I, 173
But I protest I love to hear him lie,
And I will use him for my minstrelsy. 175

BEROWNE
Armado is a most illustrious wight, 176
A man of fire-new words, fashion's own knight. 177

LONGAVILLE
Costard the swain and he shall be our sport; 178
And so to study three years is but short.

Enter [Dull,] a constable, with Costard, with a letter.

DULL   Which is the Duke's own person? 180
BEROWNE   This, fellow. What wouldst? 181
DULL   I myself reprehend his own person, for I am His 182
Grace's farborough. But I would see his own person 183
in flesh and blood.
BEROWNE   This is he.
DULL   Señor Arm–Arm–commends you. There's vil- 186
lainy abroad. This letter will tell you more.
[He gives the letter to the King.]
COSTARD   Sir, the contempts thereof are as touching me. 188
KING   A letter from the magnificent Armado. 189
BEROWNE   How low soever the matter, I hope in God 190
for high words. 191
LONGAVILLE   A high hope for a low heaven. God grant 192
us patience!
BEROWNE   To hear, or forbear hearing?
LONGAVILLE   To hear meekly, sir, and to laugh moder-
ately, or to forbear both.
BEROWNE   Well, sir, be it as the style shall give us cause 197
to climb in the merriness.
COSTARD   The matter is to me, sir, as concerning Jaque- 199
netta. The manner of it is, I was taken with the manner. 200
BEROWNE   In what manner?

COSTARD   In manner and form following, sir—all those 202
three. I was seen with her in the manor house, sitting 203
with her upon the form, and taken following her into 204
the park; which, put together, is "in manner and form
following." Now, sir, for the manner—it is the manner
of a man to speak to a woman. For the form—in
some form.
BEROWNE   For the "following," sir?
COSTARD   As it shall follow in my correction; and God 210
defend the right! 211
KING   Will you hear this letter with attention?
BEROWNE   As we would hear an oracle.
COSTARD   Such is the sinplicity of man to hearken after 214
the flesh.
KING [*reads*]   "Great deputy, the welkin's vicegerent, 216
and sole dominator of Navarre, my soul's earth's god, 217
and body's fostering patron—" 218
COSTARD   Not a word of Costard yet.
KING [*reads*]   "So it is—"
COSTARD   It may be so, but if he say it is so, he is, in
telling true, but so. 222
KING   Peace!
COSTARD   Be to me and every man that dares not fight. 224
KING   No words!
COSTARD   Of other men's secrets, I beseech you. 226
KING [*reads*]   "So it is, besieged with sable-colored 227
melancholy, I did commend the black oppressing 228
humor to the most wholesome physic of thy health- 229
giving air, and, as I am a gentleman, betook myself to
walk. The time when? About the sixth hour,
when beasts most graze, birds best peck, and men sit
down to that nourishment which is called supper. So
much for the time when. Now for the ground which—
which, I mean, I walked upon. It is yclept thy park. 235
Then for the place where—where, I mean, I did encounter that obscene and most preposterous event that 237
draweth from my snow-white pen the ebon-colored ink 238
which here thou viewest, beholdest, surveyest, or see'st.
But to the place where. It standeth north-northeast and
by east from the west corner of thy curious-knotted 241

---

168 mutiny discord. (This man of judgment and discretion is able to sort out right from wrong.)   **169 child of fancy** fantastic or grotesque creature.   **hight** is called. (An archaic, affected term.)   **170–2 For . . . debate** i.e., For an interlude in our studies, Armado will tell, in lofty and patrician terms, sagas of many an adventurous knight from sunburned Spain that might otherwise be lost to debate.   **173 How you delight** What delights you   **175 minstrelsy** i.e., entertainment.
176 wight person   **177 fire-new** newly coined   **178 Costard** (The name means a large apple; the term is frequently applied humorously or derisively to the head.)   **swain** rustic young fellow   **180 Duke's** i.e., King's   **181 fellow** (Customary form of address to a servant.)
182 reprehend (Malapropism for "represent.")   **183 farborough** (Malapropism for "tharborough" or "third borough," a petty constable.)   **186 commends you** sends you his greetings   **188 contempts** (Malapropism for "contents.")   **189 magnificent Armado** boastful or grandiose Armado. (With an allusion to the great Armada of Spain.)
190 How low soever However debased   **191 high** lofty, exalted
192 low heaven i.e., small blessing.   **197 be it** so it be.   **style** (With a pun on "stile," giving point to *climb* in the next line.)   **199 is to** applies to   **200 with the manner** with the stolen goods. (An Anglo-French law term *mainoure*, from *manoeuvre*.)

202 In manner and form (A familiar legal formula of the time.)
202–3 those three i.e., manner and form following. (Costard proceeds to illustrate each term as it applies to his case.)   **203 manor** (Playing upon "manner.")   **204 form** bench. (Playing upon *form* in line 202, as also with *following*.)   **210 correction** punishment   **210–11 God defend the right!** (Prayer before mortal combat.)   **214 sinplicity** (This Quarto reading may be a malapropism and has an ironic fitness, although it could also be a simple misprint or variant spelling for "simplicity." Whether the joke is audible in the theater is hard to say.)   **216 welkin's vicegerent** heaven's deputy. (A pompous phrase, as most in the letter are.)   **217 dominator** ruler   **218 fostering** nurturing   **222 but so** i.e., not saying much.   **224 Be to me** (Costard punningly changes the King's "Peace"—i.e., "Be silent!"—to suit his own purposes; *Peace be to me* means "may I go undisturbed with the law's blessing.")   **226 Of . . . secrets** (As in line 224, Costard changes the King's meaning with witty wordplay: "Let's have no talk of other men's secrets, which can get a person into trouble.")   **227 sable-colored** i.e., black   **228–9 black oppressing humor** black bile or melancholy, oppressing with its black essence   **229 physic** medicine   **235 yclept** called. (Archaic usage.)   **237 obscene** disgusting   **238 snow-white pen** i.e., white goose quill.   **ebon-colored** i.e., black. (Like ebony.)   **241 curious-knotted** delicately or intricately designed

garden. There did I see that low-spirited swain, that 242
base minnow of thy mirth—" 243

COSTARD   Me?

KING [*reads*]   "that unlettered, small-knowing soul—" 245

COSTARD   Me?

KING [*reads*]   "that shallow vassal—" 247

COSTARD   Still me?

KING [*reads*]   "which, as I remember, hight Cos- 249
tard—"

COSTARD   Oh! Me.

KING [*reads*]   "sorted and consorted, contrary to thy 252
established proclaimed edict and continent canon, 253
with, with—oh, with—but with this I passion to say 254
wherewith—"

COSTARD   With a wench.

KING [*reads*]   "with a child of our grandmother Eve,
a female; or, for thy more sweet understanding, a
woman. Him I, as my ever-esteemed duty pricks 259
me on, have sent to thee, to receive the meed 260
of punishment, by Thy sweet Grace's officer,
Anthony Dull, a man of good repute, carriage,
bearing, and estimation." 263

DULL   Me, an't shall please you. I am Anthony Dull. 264

KING [*reads*]   "For Jaquenetta—so is the weaker vessel 265
called which I apprehended with the aforesaid
swain—I keep her as a vessel of thy law's fury, and
shall at the least of thy sweet notice bring her to 268
trial. Thine, in all compliments of devoted and heart- 269
burning heat of duty,   Don Adriano de Armado."

BEROWNE   This is not so well as I looked for, but the best
that ever I heard.

KING   Ay, the best for the worst.—But, sirrah, what say 273
you to this?

COSTARD   Sir, I confess the wench.

KING   Did you hear the proclamation?

COSTARD   I do confess much of the hearing it, but little
of the marking of it. 278

KING   It was proclaimed a year's imprisonment to be
taken with a wench.

COSTARD   I was taken with none, sir. I was taken with
a damsel.

KING   Well, it was proclaimed "damsel."

COSTARD   This was no damsel neither, sir. She was a
virgin.

BEROWNE   It is so varied too, for it was proclaimed "virgin." 286

COSTARD   If it were, I deny her virginity. I was taken
with a maid.

KING   This "maid" will not serve your turn, sir. 289

COSTARD   This maid will serve my turn, sir.

KING   Sir, I will pronounce your sentence: you shall fast
a week with bran and water.

COSTARD   I had rather pray a month with mutton and 293
porridge. 294

KING
And Don Armado shall be your keeper.
My Lord Berowne, see him delivered o'er. 296
And go we, lords, to put in practice that
Which each to other hath so strongly sworn.
[*Exeunt the King, Longaville, and Dumaine.*]

BEROWNE
I'll lay my head to any goodman's hat, 299
These oaths and laws will prove an idle scorn. 300
Sirrah, come on.

COSTARD   I suffer for the truth, sir; for true it is, I was
taken with Jaquenetta, and Jaquenetta is a true girl; 303
and therefore, welcome the sour cup of prosperity! 304
Affliction may one day smile again, and till then, sit 305
thee down, sorrow!   *Exeunt.* 306

❦

[1.2]

Enter Armado and Mote, his page.

ARMADO   Boy, what sign is it when a man of great spirit 1
grows melancholy?

MOTE   A great sign, sir, that he will look sad.

ARMADO   Why, sadness is one and the selfsame thing,
dear imp. 5

MOTE   No, no, oh, Lord, sir, no.

ARMADO   How canst thou part sadness and melancholy, 7
my tender juvenal? 8

MOTE   By a familiar demonstration of the working, my 9
tough señor. 10

ARMADO   Why "tough señor"? Why "tough señor"?

MOTE   Why "tender juvenal"? Why "tender juvenal"?

ARMADO   I spoke it, tender juvenal, as a congruent epi- 13
theton appertaining to thy young days, which we may 14
nominate "tender." 15

MOTE   And I, tough señor, as an appertinent title to 16
your old time, which we may name "tough."

ARMADO   Pretty and apt.

MOTE   How mean you, sir? I pretty and my saying apt?
Or I apt and my saying pretty?

---

242 low-spirited ignoble   **243 minnow** contemptible little creature
245 unlettered illiterate   **247 vassal** slavish fellow   **249 hight** is called.
(Archaic usage.)   **252 sorted and consorted** associated   **253 continent
canon** law-enforcing restraint   **254 passion** grieve   **259 pricks** spurs
260 meed reward   **263 estimation** reputation.   **264 an't . . . you** if you
please.   **265 For** As for.   **weaker vessel** i.e., woman. (See 1 Peter 3:7.)
268 at . . . notice i.e., at your first hint   **268–9 bring her to trial** (With
perhaps a bawdy double meaning of testing her mettle as a woman.)
273 best . . . worst i.e., best example of the worst.   **sirrah** (Ordinary
form of address to inferiors.)   **278 the marking of it** paying attention
to it.   **286 so varied** alternatively phrased (in typical legal jargon)
289 serve your turn i.e., get you out of your difficulty. (But Costard, in
the next line, interprets the phrase in a ribald sense.)

293–4 mutton and porridge mutton broth. (With a pun on "mutton,"
whore.)   **296 delivered o'er** handed over.   **299 lay** wager.   **goodman's** i.e., yeoman's   **300 idle scorn** worthless object of mockery.
303 true honest   **304 prosperity** (Malapropism for "adversity"?)
305 Affliction (Costard mixes this up with "prosperity.")
305–6 sit thee down i.e., stay, settle down with me
1.2. Location: The same. Navarre's park.
0.1 Mote (The word in the First Quarto is *Moth*, pronounced identically with *mote* and meaning "dust speck." The sense of "moth" or
tiny winged creature may also be present. There may possibly be a
play also on *mot*, French for "word.")   **1 sign is it** is it a sign of
5 imp young shoot, child.   **7 part** distinguish between   **8 juvenal**
youth; satirist (after Juvenal, the Roman satirist).   **9 familiar** plain,
easily understood.   **working** operation (of these emotions)
10 señor sir. (With pun on "senior.")   **13–14 congruent epitheton**
appropriate epithet   **14 appertaining** belonging, suiting
15 nominate call   **16 appertinent** appropriate

ARMADO   Thou pretty, because little.   21

MOTE   Little pretty, because little. Wherefore apt?

ARMADO   And therefore apt, because quick.   23

MOTE   Speak you this in my praise, master?

ARMADO   In thy condign praise.   25

MOTE   I will praise an eel with the same praise.

ARMADO   What, that an eel is ingenious?

MOTE   That an eel is quick.   28

ARMADO   I do say thou art quick in answers. Thou   29
heat'st my blood.   30

MOTE   I am answered, sir.

ARMADO   I love not to be crossed.   32

MOTE   [aside] He speaks the mere contrary; crosses   33
love not him.

ARMADO   I have promised to study three years with the
Duke.   36

MOTE   You may do it in an hour, sir.

ARMADO   Impossible.

MOTE   How many is one thrice told?   39

ARMADO   I am ill at reckoning; it fitteth the spirit of a   40
tapster.   41

MOTE   You are a gentleman and a gamester, sir.   42

ARMADO   I confess both. They are both the varnish of a   43
complete man.   44

MOTE   Then I am sure you know how much the gross
sum of deuce-ace amounts to.   46

ARMADO   It doth amount to one more than two.

MOTE   Which the base vulgar do call three.   48

ARMADO   True.

MOTE   Why, sir, is this such a piece of study? Now here   50
is three studied ere ye'll thrice wink; and how easy it
is to put "years" to the word "three" and study three
years in two words, the dancing horse will tell you.   53

ARMADO   A most fine figure!   54

MOTE   [aside] To prove you a cipher.   55

ARMADO   I will hereupon confess I am in love; and as it
is base for a soldier to love, so am I in love with a base
wench. If drawing my sword against the humor of   58
affection would deliver me from the reprobate thought   59
of it, I would take Desire prisoner and ransom him to
any French courtier for a new-devised curtsy. I think   61
scorn to sigh; methinks I should outswear Cupid.   62
Comfort me, boy. What great men have been in love?

MOTE   Hercules, master.

ARMADO   Most sweet Hercules! More authority, dear
boy, name more; and, sweet my child, let them be men
of good repute and carriage.   67

MOTE   Samson, master; he was a man of good carriage,
great carriage, for he carried the town gates on his
back like a porter; and he was in love.

ARMADO   O well-knit Samson! Strong-jointed Samson!   71
I do excel thee in my rapier as much as thou didst me   72
in carrying gates. I am in love too. Who was Samson's
love, my dear Mote?

MOTE   A woman, master.

ARMADO   Of what complexion?   76

MOTE   Of all the four, or the three, or the two, or one of
the four.

ARMADO   Tell me precisely of what complexion.

MOTE   Of the sea-water green, sir.

ARMADO   Is that one of the four complexions?

MOTE   As I have read, sir; and the best of them, too.

ARMADO   Green indeed is the color of lovers; but to have   83
a love of that color, methinks Samson had small reason
for it. He surely affected her for her wit.   85

MOTE   It was so, sir, for she had a green wit.   86

ARMADO   My love is most immaculate white and red.

MOTE   Most maculate thoughts, master, are masked   88
under such colors.   89

ARMADO   Define, define, well-educated infant.   90

MOTE   My father's wit and my mother's tongue, assist me!

ARMADO   Sweet invocation of a child, most pretty and
pathetical!   94

MOTE

If she be made of white and red,   95
    Her faults will ne'er be known,   96
For blushing cheeks by faults are bred,   97
    And fears by pale white shown.   98
Then if she fear, or be to blame,
    By this you shall not know,   100
For still her cheeks possess the same   101
    Which native she doth owe.   102

---

21 Thou . . . little. (Armado refers to the commonplace "little things are pretty.") 23 quick quick-witted. 25 condign worthily deserved 28 quick quick at maneuvering. 29–30 Thou . . . blood. You make me angry. 32 crossed thwarted, opposed. 33 mere absolute. crosses coins. (So called because many of them were impressed with crosses.) 36 Duke i.e., King 39 told counted. 40 ill at reckoning no good at arithmetic 41 tapster bartender. 42 gamester gambler 43 varnish finish, ornament 44 complete accomplished 46 deuce-ace are a throw of two and one in dice 48 vulgar common people 50 piece masterpiece 53 dancing horse (Probably a reference to a famous trained horse brought to London in 1591, named Morocco, that could count by tapping with its hoof.) 54 figure figure of speech. 55 cipher zero. (Mote takes Armado's figure in line 54 to mean "numeral.") 58–9 humor of affection inclination to passion 59 deliver me save me. reprobate depraved, degrading 61 new-devised curtsy newfangled manner of bowing; any new fashion. 61–2 think scorn disdain 62 outswear overcome by swearing or, swear to do without

67 carriage bearing. (With pun on "ability to carry" in the following speech; see Judges 16:3 for the account of Samson's deed.) 71 well-knit well-proportioned 72 in my rapier in my swordsmanship. (The rapier replaced the old-fashioned long sword in the 1590s.) 76 complexion skin color; also temperament. (The four complexions were sanguine, choleric, phlegmatic, and melancholic, and were supposedly determined by the relative proportions of the four humors.) 83 Green (A reference to lovers' "greensickness," an anemic condition of puberty.) 85 affected loved. wit intelligence. 86 green immature. (With a punning reference perhaps to the seven green withes with which Samson was bound, Judges 16:7–9.) 88 maculate stained, polluted 89 colors (With a pun on "pretexts.") 90 Define Explain 94 pathetical moving. 95 be made of i.e., has a complexion that is. (With a play on "maid." Mote also hints that the red and white are cosmetic.) 96 Her . . . known i.e., she will never be betrayed by blushes or pallor, since the red and white (perhaps cosmetic) will mask those effects 97 by faults are bred are caused by an awareness of being at fault 98 fears i.e., fears of detection 100 this i.e., her complexion or coloring (which is perhaps produced by cosmetics) 101–2 For . . . owe i.e., for her cheeks are always (and therefore suspiciously) colored with the red and white of her supposedly natural coloration.

A dangerous rhyme, master, against the reason of 103
white and red. 104

ARMADO   Is there not a ballad, boy, of the King and the 105
Beggar? 106

MOTE   The world was very guilty of such a ballad some
three ages since, but I think now 'tis not to be found; 108
or, if it were, it would neither serve for the writing nor 109
the tune. 110

ARMADO   I will have that subject newly writ o'er, that I 111
may example my digression by some mighty prece- 112
dent. Boy, I do love that country girl that I took in the
park with the rational hind Costard. She deserves 114
well.

MOTE [aside]   To be whipped; and yet a better love 116
than my master. 117

ARMADO   Sing, boy. My spirit grows heavy in love.

MOTE [aside]   And that's great marvel, loving a light wench. 119

ARMADO   I say, sing.

MOTE   Forbear till this company be past. 121

*Enter [Costard the] clown, [Dull the] constable,
and [Jaquenetta, a] wench.*

DULL   Sir, the Duke's pleasure is that you keep Costard
safe, and you must suffer him to take no delight nor 123
no penance, but 'a must fast three days a week. For 124
this damsel, I must keep her at the park. She is allowed 125
for the deywoman. Fare you well. 126

ARMADO [aside]   I do betray myself with blushing.—
Maid!

JAQUENETTA   Man?

ARMADO   I will visit thee at the lodge.

JAQUENETTA   That's hereby. 130

ARMADO   I know where it is situate. 131

JAQUENETTA   Lord, how wise you are!

ARMADO   I will tell thee wonders.

JAQUENETTA   With that face? 134

ARMADO   I love thee.

JAQUENETTA   So I heard you say.

ARMADO   And so, farewell.

JAQUENETTA   Fair weather after you!

DULL   Come, Jaquenetta, away!

Exeunt [Dull and Jaquenetta].

ARMADO   Villain, thou shalt fast for thy offenses ere 140
thou be pardoned.

COSTARD   Well, sir, I hope when I do it I shall do it on 142
a full stomach. 143

ARMADO   Thou shalt be heavily punished.

COSTARD   I am more bound to you than your fellows, 145
for they are but lightly rewarded. 146

ARMADO [to Mote]   Take away this villain. Shut him up.

MOTE   Come, you transgressing slave, away!

COSTARD   Let me not be pent up, sir. I will fast, being 149
loose. 150

MOTE   No, sir, that were fast and loose. Thou shalt to 151
prison.

COSTARD   Well, if ever I do see the merry days of deso- 153
lation that I have seen, some shall see. 154

MOTE   What shall some see?

COSTARD   Nay, nothing, Master Mote, but what they
look upon. It is not for prisoners to be too silent in their 157
words, and therefore I will say nothing. I thank God I 158
have as little patience as another man, and therefore I 159
can be quiet. *Exit [with Mote]*.

ARMADO   I do affect the very ground, which is base, 161
where her shoe, which is baser, guided by her foot,
which is basest, doth tread. I shall be forsworn, which 163
is a great argument of falsehood, if I love. And how 164
can that be true love which is falsely attempted? Love
is a familiar; Love is a devil. There is no evil angel but 166
Love. Yet was Samson so tempted, and he had an
excellent strength; yet was Solomon so seduced, and
he had a very good wit. Cupid's butt shaft is too hard 169
for Hercules' club, and therefore too much odds for a 170
Spaniard's rapier. The first and second cause will not 171
serve my turn; the passado he respects not, the duello 172
he regards not. His disgrace is to be called boy, but his
glory is to subdue men. Adieu, valor! Rust, rapier! Be
still, drum! For your manager is in love; yea, he loveth. 175
Assist me, some extemporal god of rhyme, for I am 176
sure I shall turn sonnet. Devise, wit; write, pen; for I 177
am for whole volumes in folio. *Exit*. 178

❖

142–3 on a full stomach (1) when I've had plenty to eat (2) with manly courage.   **145 bound** (1) obliged (2) tied.   **fellows** servants **146 but lightly** only slightly. (Playing on *heavily*, line 144.)   **149–50 I will . . . loose** I promise to fast if you give me my liberty.   **151 fast and loose** a cheating trick.   **Thou shalt** You will go   **153–4 desolation** (Malapropism for "consolation"?)   **154 some shall see** (Costard seems to imply that some who have wronged him will see how he can revenge, although he refuses to say so when Mote queries his meaning.)   **157–8 It is . . . words** (Costard means to say that prisoners should be careful what they utter.)   **159 patience** (Costard means the opposite of what he says.)   **161 affect** love   **163 be forsworn** break my oath   **164 argument** proof   **166 familiar** attendant evil spirit   **169 butt shaft** unbarbed arrow, used in archery practice **170 too much odds** at too great an advantage   **171 first . . . cause** (An allusion to certain situations that necessitated a duel according to the code of honor. Armado complains that Cupid will not follow his code of honor.)   **172 passado** forward thrust with the sword, one foot being advanced at the same time.   **duello** established code of duelists   **175 manager** skilled practitioner   **176 extemporal . . . rhyme** god of impromptu poetry   **177 sonnet** i.e., sonneteer **178 am for** am destined to produce.   **folio** large format.

103–4 A dangerous . . . red i.e., A warning in rhyme against trusting in white and red complexions. (The sentence plays on the contrast of *rhyme* and *reason*.)   **105–6 ballad . . . Beggar** ballad of King Cophetua and the beggar maid. (Compare 4.1.66–7.)   **108 since** ago   **109–10 it would . . . tune** i.e., both the lyrics and the tune would seem out of date.   **serve** suffice   **111 writ o'er** written up   **112 example . . . by** justify my own waywardness by   **114 rational** capable of reason. (Said patronizingly.)   **hind** rustic or clown   **116–17 To be . . . master** i.e., She deserves to be whipped, as prostitutes are whipped, and yet even at that she deserves a better lover than Armado.   **119 light** wanton. (With a play on the opposite of *heavy*, line 118.)   **121 Forbear** Hold off   **123 suffer** allow   **124 penance** (Malapropism for "pleasance," i.e., joy.)   **'a** he.   **For** As for   **125–6 allowed . . . deywoman** approved or assigned to serve as dairymaid.   **130 hereby** close by. **131 situate** located.   **134 With that face?** (A colloquial sarcasm, like "You don't mean it?")   **140 Villain** (1) Servant (2) Rascal

[2.1]

Enter the Princess of France, with three attending Ladies [Rosaline, Maria, and Katharine] and three Lords [one being Boyet].

BOYET
Now, madam, summon up your dearest spirits.   1
Consider who the King your father sends,
To whom he sends, and what's his embassy:
Yourself, held precious in the world's esteem,
To parley with the sole inheritor   5
Of all perfections that a man may owe,   6
Matchless Navarre; the plea of no less weight   7
Than Aquitaine, a dowry for a queen.
Be now as prodigal of all dear grace   9
As Nature was in making graces dear   10
When she did starve the general world beside   11
And prodigally gave them all to you.   12

PRINCESS
Good Lord Boyet, my beauty, though but mean,   13
Needs not the painted flourish of your praise.   14
Beauty is bought by judgment of the eye,
Not uttered by base sale of chapmen's tongues.   16
I am less proud to hear you tell my worth   17
Than you much willing to be counted wise
In spending your wit in the praise of mine.
But now to task the tasker. Good Boyet,   20
You are not ignorant all-telling fame   21
Doth noise abroad Navarre hath made a vow: 22
Till painful study shall outwear three years,
No woman may approach his silent court.
Therefore to 's seemeth it a needful course,   25
Before we enter his forbidden gates,
To know his pleasure; and in that behalf,   27
Bold of your worthiness, we single you   28
As our best-moving fair solicitor.   29
Tell him the daughter of the King of France,
On serious business craving quick dispatch,
Importunes personal conference with His Grace.   32
Haste, signify so much, while we attend,   33
Like humble-visaged suitors, his high will.

BOYET
Proud of employment, willingly I go.

PRINCESS
All pride is willing pride, and yours is so.   36

Exit Boyet.

Who are the votaries, my loving lords,   37
That are vow-fellows with this virtuous duke?   38

A LORD
Lord Longaville is one.

PRINCESS   Know you the man?

MARIA
I know him, madam. At a marriage feast,
Between Lord Perigord and the beauteous heir   41
Of Jaques Falconbridge, solemnizèd
In Normandy, saw I this Longaville.
A man of sovereign parts he is esteemed,   44
Well fitted in arts, glorious in arms.   45
Nothing becomes him ill that he would well.   46
The only soil of his fair virtue's gloss—   47
If virtue's gloss will stain with any soil—   48
Is a sharp wit matched with too blunt a will,   49
Whose edge hath power to cut, whose will still wills   50
It should none spare that come within his power.   51

PRINCESS
Some merry mocking lord, belike. Is't so?   52

MARIA
They say so most that most his humors know.

PRINCESS
Such short-lived wits do wither as they grow.
Who are the rest?

KATHARINE
The young Dumaine, a well-accomplished youth,
Of all that virtue love for virtue loved;   57
Most power to do most harm, least knowing ill,   58
For he hath wit to make an ill shape good   59
And shape to win grace though he had no wit.   60
I saw him at the Duke Alençon's once,
And much too little of that good I saw   62
Is my report to his great worthiness.   63

ROSALINE
Another of these students at that time
Was there with him, if I have heard a truth.
Berowne they call him; but a merrier man,
Within the limit of becoming mirth,   67
I never spent an hour's talk withal.   68
His eye begets occasion for his wit,   69

2.1. Location: The same. Outside the gates of Navarre's court.
1 dearest spirits best thoughts and courage.   **5 parley** negotiate
6 owe own   **7 the plea . . . weight** the point at issue being of no less consequence   **9 Be . . . grace** Be now as lavish of your divine gracefulness   **10 dear** scarce, costly   **11 When . . . beside** when she deprived everyone else of her graces   **12 prodigally** extravagantly, too generously   **13 mean** average, moderate   **14 flourish** adornment
16 uttered (1) spoken (2) offered for sale.   **chapmen's** merchants'
17 tell (1) speak of (2) reckon   **20 task** (1) chastise (2) lay a task upon
21 ignorant unaware that.   **fame** rumor   **22 noise** spread the news
25 to 's to us. (The royal "we.")   **needful** necessary   **27 in that behalf** for that purpose   **28 Bold of** confident of.   **single** choose
29 best-moving most eloquent   **32 Importunes** requests
33 Haste . . . much Quickly deliver this message to him

36 All . . . so (The Princess reminds Boyet that pride is self-glorifying and thus sinful, however much he may have meant that he was honored to be asked to serve.)   **37 votaries** those who have taken vows
38 vow-fellows individuals bound by the same vow   **41 beauteous** beautiful   **44 sovereign parts** excellent qualities   **45 fitted in arts** furnished with learning   **46 Nothing . . . well** Nothing is unbecoming in him that he undertakes to do well.   **47–9 The only . . . will** i.e., The only blot on the appearance of his general excellence, if virtue's fair appearance can sustain any blemish, is a sharp wit matched with too much bluntness   **50 Whose** i.e., the wit's.   **still** continually   **51 his** its   **52 belike** most likely.   **57–60 Of . . . wit** i.e., esteemed for his virtue by those who love virtue; one whose graces give him the power to do much harm, even though he has no such intent, for he has intelligence enough to put a good appearance on things that are not good and an appearance so attractive that he would win favor even if he lacked intelligence.   **62 little** short, inadequate   **63 to** compared with   **67 becoming** suitable   **68 withal** with.   **69 begets occasion** creates opportunities

For every object that the one doth catch
The other turns to a mirth-moving jest,
Which his fair tongue, conceit's expositor,   72
Delivers in such apt and gracious words
That agèd ears play truant at his tales,   74
And younger hearings are quite ravishèd,
So sweet and voluble is his discourse.   76

PRINCESS
God bless my ladies! Are they all in love,
That every one her own hath garnishèd
With such bedecking ornaments of praise?

A LORD
Here comes Boyet.

                    Enter Boyet.

PRINCESS   Now, what admittance, lord?   80
BOYET
Navarre had notice of your fair approach,
And he and his competitors in oath   82
Were all addressed to meet you, gentle lady,   83
Before I came. Marry, thus much I have learned:
He rather means to lodge you in the field,
Like one that comes here to besiege his court,
Than seek a dispensation for his oath
To let you enter his unpeopled house.   88

        Enter [the King of] Navarre, Longaville, Dumaine,
        and Berowne.

Here comes Navarre.
KING   Fair Princess, welcome to the court of Navarre.
PRINCESS   "Fair" I give you back again, and "welcome"
I have not yet. The roof of this court is too high to be   92
yours, and welcome to the wide fields too base to be
mine.
KING
You shall be welcome, madam, to my court.
PRINCESS
I will be welcome, then. Conduct me thither.
KING
Hear me, dear lady: I have sworn an oath.
PRINCESS
Our Lady help my lord! He'll be forsworn.
KING
Not for the world, fair madam, by my will.   99
PRINCESS
Why, will shall break it—will and nothing else.   100
KING
Your Ladyship is ignorant what it is.   101
PRINCESS
Were my lord so, his ignorance were wise,   102
Where now his knowledge must prove ignorance.   103

I hear Your Grace hath sworn out housekeeping.   104
'Tis deadly sin to keep that oath, my lord,
And sin to break it.
But pardon me, I am too sudden-bold;
To teach a teacher ill beseemeth me.   108
Vouchsafe to read the purpose of my coming,   109
And suddenly resolve me in my suit.   110
              [The King is handed a paper.]

KING
Madam, I will, if suddenly I may.
PRINCESS
You will the sooner that I were away,
For you'll prove perjured if you make me stay.   112
              [The King reads silently.]

BEROWNE *[to Rosaline]*
Did not I dance with you in Brabant once?   114
ROSALINE
Did not I dance with you in Brabant once?
BEROWNE
I know you did.
ROSALINE   How needless was it then
To ask the question!
BEROWNE   You must not be so quick.   117
ROSALINE
'Tis long of you, that spur me with such questions.   118
BEROWNE
Your wit's too hot. It speeds too fast; 'twill tire.   119
ROSALINE
Not till it leave the rider in the mire.
BEROWNE
What time o'day?   121
ROSALINE
The hour that fools should ask.
BEROWNE
Now fair befall your mask!   123
ROSALINE
Fair fall the face it covers!   124
BEROWNE
And send you many lovers!
ROSALINE
Amen, so you be none.
BEROWNE
Nay, then will I be gone.   *[He stands aside.]*
KING *[to the Princess]*
Madam, your father here doth intimate   128
The payment of a hundred thousand crowns,   129
Being but the one half of an entire sum
Disbursèd by my father in his wars.   131
But say that he or we—as neither have—   132
Received that sum, yet there remains unpaid
A hundred thousand more, in surety of the which   134

---

72 **conceit's expositor** the part of him that gives expression to his clever ideas   74 **play truant** i.e., neglect important business   76 **voluble** fluent   80 **admittance** reception   82 **competitors** associates   83 **addressed** prepared   88 **unpeopled** inadequately staffed with servants   92 **The roof of this court** i.e., The sky   99 **by my will** willingly. (A common mild oath.)   100 **will** intent   101 **what it is** what it is that we have sworn.   102–3 **Were . . . ignorance** i.e., A better self-knowledge on your part would teach you the wisdom of knowing your own ignorance and thus might save you from the consequences of that imperfect knowledge.

104 **sworn out housekeeping** renounced hospitality.   108 **ill beseemeth me** suits me badly.   109 **Vouchsafe** Deign, agree   110 **suddenly resolve** quickly answer   112 **that . . . away** to procure my departure   114 **Brabant** a province in central Belgium   117 **quick** sharp.   118 **long of** on account of.   **spur** goad   119 **hot** ardent, eager.   121 **What . . . day?** What time of day is it?   123 **fair befall** good luck to   124 **Fair fall** Good luck to   128 **intimate** refer to, discuss, imply   129 **The payment** i.e., that he has already paid   131 **his** i.e., the king of France's   132 **he** i.e., my father   134 **in surety** as a guarantee

One part of Aquitaine is bound to us,
Although not valued to the money's worth.
If then the King your father will restore 136
But that one half which is unsatisfied,
We will give up our right in Aquitaine
And hold fair friendship with His Majesty.
But that, it seems, he little purposeth, 141
For here he doth demand to have repaid 142
A hundred thousand crowns, and not demands, 143
On payment of a hundred thousand crowns,
To have his title live in Aquitaine— 145
Which we much rather had depart withal, 146
And have the money by our father lent,
Than Aquitaine, so gelded as it is. 148
Dear Princess, were not his requests so far
From reason's yielding, your fair self should make
A yielding 'gainst some reason in my breast 151
And go well satisfied to France again.

PRINCESS
You do the King my father too much wrong,
And wrong the reputation of your name,
In so unseeming to confess receipt 155
Of that which hath so faithfully been paid.

KING
I do protest I never heard of it;
And, if you prove it, I'll repay it back
Or yield up Aquitaine.

PRINCESS　　　　　　　　　We arrest your word. 159
Boyet, you can produce acquittances 160
For such a sum from special officers
Of Charles, his father. 162

KING　　　　　　　　　Satisfy me so.

BOYET
So please Your Grace, the packet is not come
Where that and other specialties are bound. 164
Tomorrow you shall have a sight of them.

KING
It shall suffice me, at which interview
All liberal reason I will yield unto. 167
Meantime, receive such welcome at my hand
As honor, without breach of honor, may
Make tender of to thy true worthiness. 170
You may not come, fair Princess, within my gates,
But here without you shall be so received 172
As you shall deem yourself lodged in my heart, 173
Though so denied fair harbor in my house.
Your own good thoughts excuse me, and farewell.
Tomorrow shall we visit you again.

PRINCESS
Sweet health and fair desires consort Your Grace! 177

KING
Thy own wish wish I thee in every place. 178
　　　　　　　　　Exit [with Longaville and Dumaine].

BEROWNE [*to Rosaline*]　Lady, I will commend you to
mine own heart.

ROSALINE　Pray you, do my commendations. I would
be glad to see it.

BEROWNE　I would you heard it groan.

ROSALINE　Is the fool sick? 184

BEROWNE　Sick at the heart.

ROSALINE
Alack, let it blood. 186

BEROWNE
Would that do it good?

ROSALINE
My physic says "ay." 188

BEROWNE
Will you prick't with your eye? 189

ROSALINE
Non point, with my knife. 190

BEROWNE
Now, God save thy life!

ROSALINE
And yours from long living!

BEROWNE
I cannot stay thanksgiving.　　　　　　　*Exit.* 193

　　　　　　　　Enter Dumaine.

DUMAINE [*to Boyet*]
Sir, I pray you, a word. What lady is that same?

BOYET
The heir of Alençon, Katharine her name.

DUMAINE
A gallant lady. Monsieur, fare you well.　　*Exit.*

　　　　　　　[*Enter Longaville.*]

LONGAVILLE [*to Boyet*]
I beseech you a word. What is she in the white? 197

BOYET
A woman sometimes, an you saw her in the light. 198

LONGAVILLE
Perchance light in the light. I desire her name. 199

BOYET
She hath but one for herself; to desire that were a shame. 200

---

136 valued equal in value　**141 little purposeth** scarcely intends
142 demand . . . repaid insists he has already repaid　**143 and not
demands** i.e., instead of proposing or stipulating　**145 To have . . .
Aquitaine** i.e., to regain his title to Aquitaine by paying the 100,000
crowns that are owed to Navarre　**146 depart withal** part with　**148
gelded** emasculated, weakened in value (with one part cut away)
151 A yielding . . . breast i.e., a willingness on my part to compromise, despite the fact that right is on my side　**155 unseeming** being
apparently unwilling　**159 arrest** take as security　**160 acquittances**
receipts for payment of a debt　**162 his father** i.e., the King of
Navarre's father (referred to in lines 131 and 147).　**Satisfy me so**
Prove to me that this is true.　**164 specialties** warrants, special documents　**167 All . . . unto** I will freely yield to all reasonable terms.
170 Make tender of offer　**172 without** outside　**173 As that**

177 consort attend　**178 Thy . . . place** I return your good wishes
wherever you may be.　**184 the fool** (A term of endearment or gentle
raillery.)　**186 let it blood** bleed it. (A reference to the medical practice of drawing blood.)　**188 physic** medical knowledge
189 Will . . . eye? i.e., Will you stab me through the heart with your
glance, smiting me as with Cupid's arrow? (With wordplay on *eye*
and *ay* in line 188.)　**190 Non . . . knife** (By playfully proposing to
stab Berowne's heart with a knife point, rather than a mere glance of
her "killing" eye, Rosaline deflates his flowery metaphors with a dose
of reality.)　**193 I . . . thanksgiving** I can't stay to thank you for that.
(Rosaline has just put Berowne down by saying, in effect, "May you
not live long!")　**197 What** Who　**198 an** if　**199 light in the light**
wanton when her conduct is known or brought to light.　**200 She . . .
shame** (Boyet wittily replies as though Longaville, in desiring her
name, had asked to take Maria's name away from her.)

LONGAVILLE
Pray you, sir, whose daughter?
BOYET
Her mother's, I have heard.
LONGAVILLE
God's blessing on your beard! 203
BOYET
Good sir, be not offended.
She is an heir of Falconbridge.
LONGAVILLE
Nay, my choler is ended. 206
She is a most sweet lady.
BOYET
Not unlike, sir. That may be. *Exit Longaville.* 208

Enter Berowne.

BEROWNE
What's her name in the cap?
BOYET
Rosaline, by good hap. 210
BEROWNE
Is she wedded or no?
BOYET
To her will, sir, or so. 212
BEROWNE
Oh, you are welcome, sir. Adieu.
BOYET
Farewell to me, sir, and welcome to you. 214
Exit Berowne.

MARIA
That last is Berowne, the merry madcap lord.
Not a word with him but a jest.
BOYET And every jest but a word. 216
PRINCESS
It was well done of you to take him at his word. 217
BOYET
I was as willing to grapple as he was to board. 218
KATHARINE
Two hot sheeps, marry.
BOYET And wherefore not ships? 219
No sheep, sweet lamb, unless we feed on your lips.
KATHARINE
You sheep, and I pasture. Shall that finish the jest? 221
BOYET
So you grant pasture for me. *[Offering to kiss her.]*
KATHARINE Not so, gentle beast. 222
My lips are no common, though several they be. 223
BOYET
Belonging to whom?
KATHARINE To my fortunes and me.

PRINCESS
Good wits will be jangling; but, gentles, agree. 225
This civil war of wits were much better used
On Navarre and his bookmen, for here 'tis abused. 227
BOYET
If my observation, which very seldom lies,
By the heart's still rhetoric disclosèd with eyes, 229
Deceive me not now, Navarre is infected.
PRINCESS With what?
BOYET
With that which we lovers entitle "affected." 232
PRINCESS Your reason?
BOYET
Why, all his behaviors did make their retire 234
To the court of his eye, peeping thorough desire. 235
His heart, like an agate, with your print impressed, 236
Proud with his form, in his eye pride expressed. 237
His tongue, all impatient to speak and not see, 238
Did stumble with haste in his eyesight to be; 239
All senses to that sense did make their repair, 240
To feel only looking on fairest of fair. 241
Methought all his senses were locked in his eye,
As jewels in crystal for some prince to buy, 243
Who, tend'ring their own worth from where they
were glassed, 244
Did point you to buy them, along as you passed. 245
His face's own margent did quote such amazes 246
That all eyes saw his eyes enchanted with gazes.
I'll give you Aquitaine and all that is his, 248
An you give him for my sake but one loving kiss. 249
PRINCESS
Come to our pavilion. Boyet is disposed. 250
BOYET
But to speak that in words which his eye hath
disclosed. 251
I only have made a mouth of his eye,
By adding a tongue which I know will not lie.
ROSALINE
Thou art an old lovemonger and speakest skillfully.
MARIA
He is Cupid's grandfather, and learns news of him.

203 **God's . . . beard!** (To insult or pluck a man's beard was a standard Elizabethan way to challenge someone to a duel.) 206 **choler** anger 208 **unlike** unlikely 210 **hap** fortune. 212 **or so** or something of that kind. 214 **Farewell . . . you** You bid me "farewell" and I will say "you're welcome to go." 216 **Not . . . jest** Everything he says is a joke. 217 **take . . . word** (1) vie with him in wordplay (2) take him literally. 218 **grapple, board** (Tactics of sea warfare, here applied to the badinage, with bawdy overtones.) 219 **sheeps, ships** (Pronounced nearly alike by Elizabethans.) 221 **pasture** (With a play on "pastor," shepherd.) 222 **So** Provided 223 **common** common land for pasturing. (With a bawdy suggestion of "available to all men.") 223 **several** (1) private enclosed land (2) more than one (3) parted

225 **jangling** quarreling. **gentles** gentlefolk 227 **bookmen** scholars. **abused** misapplied. 229 **By . . . eyes** seen with the eyes and thus interpreted by the heart's silent rhetoric 232 **affected** being in love. 234 **behaviors** actions. **make their retire** withdraw, retire. (Navarre was dumbstruck, unable to do anything except gaze at the Princess.) 235 **thorough** through 236 **agate** (An allusion to small figures cut in agate stones.) **print impressed** image engraved 237 **Proud . . . expressed** proud of the form (of the Princess) imprinted on it, expressed that pride through the look in his eye. 238 **to speak . . . see** at being able to speak only and not to see 239 **in his . . . be** to take part in his seeing 240 **that sense** i.e., the eyesight. **make their repair** go 241 **To . . . fair** to express themselves solely through looking upon the most beautiful of women. 243 **in crystal** enclosed within crystal glass 244 **Who . . . glassed** which, proclaiming their worth from the crystal glass of the eyes in which they lay encased 245 **point** appoint, direct, invite 246 **His . . . amazes** i.e., His expression of amazement offered such a visible commentary on what his eyes saw. (*Margents* or margins of books often bore commentary on the text proper.) 248 **I'll give you** i.e., I warrant you can have 249 **An** if 250 **disposed** inclined (to be merry). 251 **But** Merely. **his** i.e., the King's

KATHARINE
Then was Venus like her mother, for her father is
but grim.   256
BOYET
Do you hear, my mad wenches?
MARIA   No.
BOYET   What then, do you see?   257
KATHARINE
Ay, our way to be gone.
BOYET   You are too hard for me.   258

Exeunt omnes.

❖

[3.1]

Enter [Armado the] braggart and [Mote,] his boy.

ARMADO   Warble, child. Make passionate my sense of   1
hearing.
MOTE   [*singing*] Concolinel.   3
ARMADO   Sweet air! Go, tenderness of years. [*He gives a*   4
key.] Take this key, give enlargement to the swain,   5
bring him festinately hither. I must employ him in a   6
letter to my love.
MOTE   Master, will you win your love with a French
brawl?   9
ARMADO   How meanest thou? Brawling in French?   10
MOTE   No, my complete master, but to jig off a tune at the   11
tongue's end, canary to it with your feet, humor it with   12
turning up your eyelids, sigh a note and sing a note,
sometime through the throat as if you swallowed love
with singing love, sometime through the nose as if you
snuffed up love by smelling love, with your hat
penthouse-like o'er the shop of your eyes, with your   17
arms crossed on your thin-belly doublet like a rabbit on   18
a spit, or your hands in your pocket like a man after the   19
old painting, and keep not too long in one tune, but   20
a snip and away. These are compliments, these are   21
humors; these betray nice wenches that would be   22

betrayed without these, and make them men of note—   23
do you note?—men that most are affected to these.   24
ARMADO   How hast thou purchased this experience?
MOTE   By my penny of observation.
ARMADO   But oh, but oh—   27
MOTE   "The hobbyhorse is forgot."   28
ARMADO   Call'st thou my love "hobbyhorse"?
MOTE   No, master; the hobbyhorse is but a colt, and   30
your love perhaps a hackney. But have you forgot   31
your love?
ARMADO   Almost I had.
MOTE   Negligent student, learn her by heart.
ARMADO   By heart and in heart, boy.
MOTE   And out of heart, master. All those three I will
prove.   37
ARMADO   What wilt thou prove?
MOTE   A man, if I live; and this, "by," "in," and
"without," upon the instant: "by" heart you love her
because your heart cannot come by her; "in" heart you   41
love her because your heart is in love with her; and
"out" of heart you love her, being out of heart that you   43
cannot enjoy her.
ARMADO   I am all these three.
MOTE   And three times as much more—[*aside*] and yet
nothing at all.
ARMADO   Fetch hither the swain. He must carry me a   48
letter.
MOTE   [*aside*]   A message well sympathized—a horse   50
to be ambassador for an ass.
ARMADO   Ha, ha! What sayest thou?
MOTE   Marry, sir, you must send the ass upon the
horse, for he is very slow-gaited. But I go.
ARMADO   The way is but short. Away!
MOTE   As swift as lead, sir.
ARMADO   The meaning, pretty ingenious?
Is not lead a metal heavy, dull, and slow?
MOTE
Minime, honest master; or rather, master, no.   59
ARMADO
I say lead is slow.
MOTE   You are too swift, sir, to say so.
Is that lead slow which is fired from a gun?
ARMADO   Sweet smoke of rhetoric!
He reputes me a cannon, and the bullet, that's he.
I shoot thee at the swain.
MOTE   Thump, then, and I flee.   64

[*Exit.*]

ARMADO
A most acute juvenal, voluble and free of grace!   65
By thy favor, sweet welkin, I must sigh in thy face.   66

---

256 Then ... grim i.e., Boyet isn't nearly handsome enough to have
given Venus her beauty.   **257 Do you hear** i.e., Won't you listen to
me. (But the ladies parry Boyet's *hear* and *see* to their own witty purposes.)   **mad** high-spirited   **258 our ... gone** the way out of here.
hard sharp, difficult to outwit   **258.1** *omnes* all.
3.1. Location: Navarre's park.
1 passionate impassioned, responsive   **3 Concolinel** (Unidentified;
perhaps the name or refrain of a song.)   **4 air** song   **5 enlargement**
release from confinement   **6 festinately** quickly   **9 brawl** a French
dance figure.   **10 Brawling** Quarreling   **11 complete** accomplished.
jig ... tune sing a jiglike tune   **12 canary** dance. (From the name of a
lively dance; compare *jig*.)   **17 penthouse-like** like the projecting second story of a house built out to shelter the shop on the ground floor
18 arms crossed (Betokening melancholy; compare 4.3.131.)   **thin-
belly doublet** (1) man's jacket over his thin belly, thin because of
lovesickness (2) a jacket thinly padded in the waist   **19 after** in the
style of   **20 old painting** (If Mote refers here to a specific painting, it
remains unidentified, but he may merely mean "some old painting.")
21 a snip and away a snippet or scrap of one song and then on to
another.   **compliments** gentlemanly accomplishments. (Or perhaps
complements, those things that complete or make perfect.)
22 humors moods.   **nice** coy

23 note (1) distinction (2) musical notation   **24 affected** inclined,
drawn   **27–8 But oh ... forgot.** (Probably the refrain of a popular
song; it turns up again in *Hamlet*, 3.2.133. The hobbyhorse was the figure of a horse made of light material and fastened over the torso and
head of a morris dancer.)   **30–1 hobbyhorse, colt, hackney** (Slang
terms for prostitutes or wanton persons.)   **37 prove** demonstrate.
(But Mote then uses the word in line 39 also to mean "turn out to
be.")   **41 come by** possess   **43 out of heart** discouraged, depressed
48 me for me   **50 sympathized** matched   **59** *Minime* Not at all
64 Thump (Representing the sound of cannon.)   **65 voluble** quick-
witted   **66 favor** good will, permission.   **welkin** sky

Most rude melancholy, valor gives thee place.   67
My herald is returned.

Enter [Mote the] page and [Costard the] clown.

MOTE
A wonder, master! Here's a costard broken in a shin.   69
ARMADO
Some enigma, some riddle. Come, thy *l'envoi*; begin.   70
COSTARD   No egma, no riddle, no *l'envoi*, no salve in   71
the mail, sir. Oh, sir, plantain, a plain plantain. No   72
l'envoi, no *l'envoi*, no salve, sir, but a plantain.
ARMADO   By virtue, thou enforcest laughter; thy silly   74
thought, my spleen; the heaving of my lungs provokes   75
me to ridiculous smiling. Oh, pardon me, my stars!   76
Doth the inconsiderate take "salve" for *l'envoi*, and the   77
word *l'envoi* for a salve?
MOTE
Do the wise think them other? Is not *l'envoi* a salve?
ARMADO
No, page, it is an epilogue or discourse to make plain
Some obscure precedence that hath tofore been sain.   81
I will example it: 82
The fox, the ape, and the humble-bee   83
Were still at odds, being but three.   84
There's the moral. Now the *l'envoi*.   85
MOTE
I will add the *l'envoi*. Say the moral again.
ARMADO
The fox, the ape, and the humble-bee
Were still at odds, being but three.
MOTE
Until the goose came out of door,
And stayed the odds by adding four.   90
Now will I begin your moral, and do you follow with
my *l'envoi*.
The fox, the ape, and the humble-bee
Were still at odds, being but three.
ARMADO
Until the goose came out of door,

Staying the odds by adding four.
MOTE   A good *l'envoi*, ending in the goose. Would you   97
desire more?
COSTARD
The boy hath sold him a bargain—a goose, that's flat.   99
Sir, your pennyworth is good, an your goose be fat.   100
To sell a bargain well is as cunning as fast and loose.   101
Let me see: a fat *l'envoi*—ay, that's a fat goose.
ARMADO
Come hither, come hither. How did this argument
begin?
MOTE
By saying that a costard was broken in a shin.   104
Then called you for the *l'envoi*.
COSTARD   True, and I for a plantain. Thus came your
argument in; then the boy's fat *l'envoi*, the goose that
you bought; and he ended the market.   108
ARMADO   But tell me, how was there a costard broken   109
in a shin?
MOTE   I will tell you sensibly.   111
COSTARD   Thou hast no feeling of it, Mote. I will speak
that *l'envoi*:
I Costard, running out, that was safely within,
Fell over the threshold and broke my shin.
ARMADO   We will talk no more of this matter.
COSTARD   Till there be more matter in the shin.   117
ARMADO   Sirrah Costard, I will enfranchise thee.   118
COSTARD   Oh, marry me to one Frances! I smell some
l'envoi, some goose, in this.   120
ARMADO   By my sweet soul, I mean setting thee at lib-
erty, enfreedoming thy person. Thou wert immured,   122
restrained, captivated, bound.
COSTARD   True, true, and now you will be my purga-   124
tion and let me loose.   125
ARMADO   I give thee thy liberty, set thee from durance,   126
and in lieu thereof impose on thee nothing but this:
Bear this significant [*giving a letter*] to the country maid   128
Jaquenetta. There is remuneration. [*He gives money.*]   129
For the best ward of mine honor is rewarding my   130
dependents. —Mote, follow.   [*Exit.*]
MOTE
Like the sequel, I. Seigneur Costard, adieu.   [*Exit.*] 132

---

67 gives thee place gives way to you.   **69 Here's . . . shin** Here's an
apple or a head with a bruised shin. (An *enigma*, as Armado points
out, since apples and heads don't have shins, though Mote means
simply that Costard is limping.)   **70 l'envoi** i.e., postscript or commendatory statement to the reader attached to a composition; here,
an explanation   **71 egma** (Costard's attempt at *enigma*; he evidently
mistakes this strange name, along with *riddle* and *l'envoi*, as a kind of
salve for his hurt shin.)   **salve** (With a play seemingly on *salve*,
meaning "hail!" Armado points out in his next speech that Costard
has mistaken *salve*, a salutation, for *l'envoi*, a farewell.)   **72 mail**
pouch, bag. (Suggesting the bag of a mountebank or seller of cures.)
plantain an old-fashioned herbal remedy (which Costard prefers to
the strange-sounding *egma*, etc.)   **74 By virtue** (A colorful oath.)
75 spleen i.e., laughter. (The *spleen*, supposedly the seat of emotions
and passions, was held to be the organ that controlled excessive mirth
or anger.)   **76 ridiculous** scornful. (But with unintended meaning of
"absurd.")   **my stars** the stars that govern my destiny.   **77 inconsiderate** mindless fellow.   **salve** (Here it is used in the Latin sense of
"hail.")   **81 precedence** preceding discourse.   **tofore** previously.
sain said.   **82 example** give an example of   **83 humble-bee** bumble-
bee   **84 still** continually.   **at odds** (1) at enmity (2) an odd number,
i.e., three   **85 moral** riddle or allegory.   **90 stayed the odds**
(1) stopped the enmity (2) changed odd to even.   **four** a fourth.

97 l'envoi…goose (Mote's joke is based on the fact that *l'envoi* ends
with the same sound as the French word for goose, *oie*. Armado has
made himself the goose by playing Mote's game.)   **99 sold . . .
bargain** i.e., outwitted him.   **flat** certain.   **100 your . . . good** i.e.,
you got your money's worth.   **an if**   **101 fast and loose** a cheating
trick. (See 1.2.151.)   **104 broken in a shin** with a cut or bruised
shin.   **108 and . . . market** (Costard refers to the proverbial expression "Three women and a goose make a market.")   **109 how** in
what sense   **111 sensibly** feelingly. (But Costard protests that Mote
cannot personally know what it *feels* like.)   **117 matter** pus. (Playing on *matter*, business, in line 116.)   **118 enfranchise** release from
confinement. (Costard hears this as *en-Frances*, "provide with a
Frances.")   **120 goose** (Slang for "prostitute.")   **122 immured**
imprisoned   **124–5 be my purgation** purge me of guilt. (With pun
on the sense of giving a purgative so that Costard's bowels will be
let loose.)   **126 set** release.   **durance** imprisonment.   **128 significant** sign, token   **129 remuneration** payment.   **130 ward** guard
132 the sequel that which follows; *l'envoi*

COSTARD

My sweet ounce of man's flesh, my incony Jew! 133
Now will I look to his remuneration. [*He looks at his money.*] Remuneration! Oh, that's the Latin word for three farthings. Three farthings—remuneration. 136
"What's the price of this inkle?"—"One penny."— 137
"No, I'll give you a remuneration." Why, it carries it. 138
Remuneration! Why, it is a fairer name than French 139
crown. I will never buy and sell out of this word. 140

Enter Berowne.

BEROWNE   My good knave Costard, exceedingly well 141
met. 142

COSTARD   Pray you, sir, how much carnation ribbon 143
may a man buy for a remuneration?

BEROWNE   What is a remuneration?

COSTARD   Marry, sir, halfpenny farthing. 146

BEROWNE   Why, then, three farthing worth of silk.

COSTARD   I thank Your Worship. God be wi' you!

[*He starts to leave.*]

BEROWNE   Stay, slave, I must employ thee. 149
As thou wilt win my favor, good my knave, 150
Do one thing for me that I shall entreat.

COSTARD   When would you have it done, sir?

BEROWNE   This afternoon.

COSTARD   Well, I will do it, sir. Fare you well.

BEROWNE   Thou knowest not what it is.

COSTARD   I shall know, sir, when I have done it.

BEROWNE   Why, villain, thou must know first.

COSTARD   I will come to Your Worship tomorrow morning.

BEROWNE   It must be done this afternoon. Hark, slave, it is but this:
The Princess comes to hunt here in the park,
And in her train there is a gentle lady;
When tongues speak sweetly, then they name her name,
And Rosaline they call her. Ask for her,
And to her white hand see thou do commend 166
This sealed-up counsel. There's thy guerdon; go. 167

[*Giving him a letter and a shilling.*]

COSTARD   Gardon, O sweet gardon! Better than remu- 168
neration, a 'levenpence farthing better. Most 169
sweet gardon! I will do it, sir, in print. Gardon! 170
Remuneration! *Exit.*

BEROWNE

And I, forsooth, in love! I that have been Love's whip,
A very beadle to a humorous sigh, 173
A critic, nay, a night-watch constable,
A domineering pedant o'er the boy, 175
Than whom no mortal so magnificent!
This wimpled, whining, purblind, wayward boy, 177
This Senior Junior, giant dwarf, Dan Cupid, 178
Regent of love rhymes, lord of folded arms, 179
Th'anointed sovereign of sighs and groans,
Liege of all loiterers and malcontents,
Dread prince of plackets, king of codpieces, 182
Sole imperator and great general 183
Of trotting paritors—Oh, my little heart! 184
And I to be a corporal of his field 185
And wear his colors like a tumbler's hoop! 186
What? I love, I sue, I seek a wife?
A woman, that is like a German clock,
Still a-repairing, ever out of frame, 189
And never going aright, being a watch,
But being watched that it may still go right? 191
Nay, to be perjured, which is worst of all;
And, among three, to love the worst of all—
A whitely wanton with a velvet brow, 194
With two pitch-balls stuck in her face for eyes; 195
Ay, and, by heaven, one that will do the deed 196
Though Argus were her eunuch and her guard. 197
And I to sigh for her, to watch for her, 198
To pray for her! Go to, it is a plague 199
That Cupid will impose for my neglect
Of his almighty dreadful little might.
Well, I will love, write, sigh, pray, sue, groan. 202
Some men must love milady, and some Joan. [*Exit.*] 203

❖

133 incony fine, rare, delicate. **Jew** (Here it is a term of playful insult, possibly suggested by *juvenile*.) **136 farthings** coins worth a quarter of a penny. **137 inkle** a kind of linen tape. **138 carries it** wins the day. **139–40 French crown** (1) a coin (2) a bald head, the result of syphilis or "the French disease." **140 out of** i.e., without using **141–2 exceedingly well met** i.e., how fortunate to see you just now. **143 carnation** flesh-colored **146 halfpenny farthing** i.e., three farthings (a *halfpenny*, worth two farthings, plus one farthing). **149 slave** i.e., fellow, rascal **150 good my knave** my good fellow **166 commend** entrust **167 counsel** private or secret communication. **guerdon** reward. **167.1 *shilling*** a silver coin worth twelve pence **168 Gardon** (Costard anglicizes the French *guerdon*.) **168–9 Better . . . better** (Costard delights that the shilling he has been given is worth eleven pence and a farthing more than the three farthings he had.) **170 in print** i.e., most exactly.

173 beadle parish officer responsible for whipping minor offenders. **humorous** moody **175 pedant** schoolmaster **177 wimpled** blindfolded. **purblind** quite blind **178 Dan** Don, Sir. (From the Latin *dominus*.) **179 Regent** ruler. **folded arms** (Betokening melancholy; see 3.1.18.) **182 plackets** slits in petticoats. (Referring bawdily to women.) **codpieces** flaps or pouches concealing the opening in the front of men's breeches. (Referring bawdily to men.) **183 imperator** absolute ruler **184 paritors** apparitors, summoners of ecclesiastical courts (who could make a profit by spying out sexual offenders) **185 a corporal . . . field** Cupid's field officer. **186 tumbler's hoop** (Such hoops were usually brightly decorated with silks and ribbons.) **189 Still a-repairing** Always in need of repair. **frame** order **191 But being watched** unless it is watched carefully (like a wandering wife) **194 whitely** pale of complexion. (Considered beautiful; but compare 4.3.250–73, where the lords joke about the darkness of Rosaline's features.) **velvet** i.e., soft-skinned **195 pitch-balls** balls made of pitch, a viscous black substance created by distilling tar **196 do the deed** engage in sex **197 Argus** a fabulous monster with a hundred eyes, some of which were always awake. (Juno gave Argus custody over Io, of whom Jove was enamored.) **eunuch** i.e., guard in a seraglio **198 watch** lose sleep, stay awake **199 Go to** (An expression of impatience.) **202 sue** plead **203 milady, Joan** (Opposite types on the social scale—one a lady or quality and one a peasant woman.)

[4.1]

*Enter the Princess, a Forester, her Ladies, and her
Lords [Boyet and others].*

PRINCESS
Was that the King that spurred his horse so hard
Against the steep uprising of the hill?
BOYET
I know not, but I think it was not he.
PRINCESS
Whoe'er 'a was, 'a showed a mounting mind.   4
Well, lords, today we shall have our dispatch;   5
On Saturday we will return to France.
Then, Forester, my friend, where is the bush
That we must stand and play the murderer in?
FORESTER
Hereby, upon the edge of yonder coppice,   9
A stand where you may make the fairest shoot.   10
PRINCESS
I thank my beauty, I am fair that shoot,
And thereupon thou speak'st "the fairest shoot."
FORESTER
Pardon me, madam, for I meant not so.
PRINCESS
What, what? First praise me and again say no?   14
Oh short-lived pride! Not fair? Alack, for woe!
FORESTER
Yes, madam, fair.
PRINCESS   Nay, never paint me now.   16
Where fair is not, praise cannot mend the brow.   17
Here, good my glass, take this for telling true.   18
                          [*She gives him money.*]
Fair payment for foul words is more than due.
FORESTER
Nothing but fair is that which you inherit.   20
PRINCESS
See, see, my beauty will be saved by merit!   21
Oh, heresy in fair, fit for these days!   22
A giving hand, though foul, shall have fair praise.
But come, the bow. [*She takes the bow.*] Now mercy
    goes to kill,   24
and shooting well is then accounted ill.   25
Thus will I save my credit in the shoot: 26

Not wounding, pity would not let me do't;   27
If wounding, then it was to show my skill,
That more for praise than purpose meant to kill.   29
And, out of question, so it is sometimes,   30
Glory grows guilty of detested crimes,   31
When for fame's sake, for praise, an outward part,   32
We bend to that the working of the heart,   33
As I for praise alone now seek to spill   34
The poor deer's blood that my heart means no ill.   35
BOYET
Do not curst wives hold that self-sovereignty   36
Only for praise' sake when they strive to be   37
Lords o'er their lords?   38
PRINCESS
Only for praise, and praise we may afford
To any lady that subdues a lord.

Enter [Costard the] clown [with a letter].

BOYET
Here comes a member of the commonwealth.   41
COSTARD   God-i-good-e'en all! Pray you, which is the 42
head lady?
PRINCESS   Thou shalt know her, fellow, by the rest that
have no heads.
COSTARD   Which is the greatest lady, the highest?
PRINCESS   The thickest and the tallest.   47
COSTARD
The thickest and the tallest! It is so; truth is truth
An your waist, mistress, were as slender as my wit,   49
One o' these maids' girdles for your waist should be fit.
Are not you the chief woman? You are the thickest
    here.
PRINCESS   What's your will, sir? What's your will?
COSTARD   I have a letter from Monsieur Berowne to one
Lady Rosaline.
PRINCESS [*to Rosaline*]
Oh, thy letter, thy letter! He's a good friend of mine. 55
Stand aside, good bearer. Boyet, you can carve;   56
Break up this capon.   [*The letter is given to Boyet.*]
BOYET   I am bound to serve.   57
This letter is mistook; it importeth none here.   58
It is writ to Jaquenetta.

4.1. Location: Navarre's park. A hunter's station at the edge of a coppice.
4 'a he.   **mounting** (1) rising (2) aspiring   **5 dispatch** settlement
and dismissal   **9 coppice** grove of trees   **10 stand** hunter's station,
toward which the game is driven.   **fairest** most favorable. (The
Princess chooses to play on the word in a compliment to herself.)
14 again i.e., then   **16 paint** flatter   **17 fair** beauty.   **brow** forehead, i.e., face.   **18 good my glass** my true mirror. (I.e., a counselor
who will not flatter. The Princess amuses herself with Renaissance
commonplaces about the value of honest counselors to a true
prince, much to the discomfort of the Forester.)   **20 inherit** possess.
21 my . . . merit i.e., my beauty is complimented again in return for
my giving a gratuity. (To be *saved by merit* was, however, a heresy
according to orthodox Anglican doctrine, which taught salvation by
faith rather than by merit or good works.)   **22 in fair** regarding
beauty.   **these days** i.e., these times of religious controversy.
24 mercy i.e., the Princess, who as a royal woman is an emblem of
mercy   **25 then** i.e., when a merciful person like the Princess goes
hunting   **26 credit** reputation

27 Not . . . do't i.e., I can claim, if I miss, that pity restrained me
29 That . . . kill i.e., I shot to earn praise for my skill rather than for
the sake of killing.   **30–1 And . . . crimes** And undoubtedly it is
occasionally true that an excessive desire for glory prompts us to
commit detestable crimes   **32 an outward part** a superficial thing
33 We . . . heart we deflect the promptings of our heart into an excessive desire for fame   **34 As** just as   **35 The poor . . . ill** the blood of
the poor deer that means me no harm.   **36–8 Do . . . lord?** Don't
shrewish wives show pride when they claim sole sovereignty in
marriage? (But the Princess, in her reply in lines 39–40, defends and
honors such assertive wives.)   **41 commonwealth** ordinary citizenry.   **42 God-i-good-e'en** God give you good afternoon   **47 The
thickest . . . tallest** (The Princess quips that *greatest* could be defined
this way. Costard, in his reply, lines 48–51, undiplomatically observes
that the terms could indeed be applied to her.)   **49 An if**   **55 He's
. . . mine** (Perhaps the Princess says this to explain her excitement
over the letter. *He's* seems to refer to Berowne.)   **56 carve** (1) cut up,
i.e., open (2) make courtly gestures.   **57 Break up** cut up (a technical
term in carving).   **capon** (Like the French *poulet, capon*
designates figuratively a love letter.)   **bound** obliged   **58 mistook**
mis-taken, misdirected.   **importeth** concerns

PRINCESS   We will read it, I swear.
Break the neck of the wax, and everyone give ear. 60
BOYET *(reads)* "By heaven, that thou art fair is most
infallible; true that thou art beauteous; truth itself that 62
thou art lovely. More fairer than fair, beautiful than
beauteous, truer than truth itself, have commiseration 64
on thy heroical vassal! The magnanimous and most 65
illustrate King Cophetua set eye upon the pernicious 66
and indubitate beggar Zenelophon; and he it was that 67
might rightly say, '*Veni, vidi, vici*'; which to annotha- 68
nize in the vulgar—Oh, base and obscure vulgar!— 69
videlicet, 'He came, saw, and overcame.' He came, 70
one; saw, two; overcame, three. Who came? The King.
Why did he come? To see. Why did he see? To overcome. To whom came he? To the beggar. What saw he?
The beggar. Who overcame he? The beggar. The conclusion is victory. On whose side? The King's. The captive is enriched. On whose side? The beggar's. The
catastrophe is a nuptial. On whose side? The King's— 77
no, on both in one, or one in both. I am the King, for 78
so stands the comparison; thou the beggar, for so wit- 79
nesseth thy lowliness. Shall I command thy love? I 80
may. Shall I enforce thy love? I could. Shall I entreat
thy love? I will. What shalt thou exchange for rags?
Robes. For tittles? Titles. For thyself? Me. Thus, expect- 83
ing thy reply, I profane my lips on thy foot, my eyes on 84
thy picture, and my heart on thy every part.
Thine, in the dearest design of industry, 86
                    Don Adriano de Armado.
Thus dost thou hear the Nemean lion roar 88
    'Gainst thee, thou lamb, that standest as his prey.
Submissive fall his princely feet before, 90
    And he from forage will incline to play. 91
But if thou strive, poor soul, what art thou then? 92
Food for his rage, repasture for his den." 93
PRINCESS
What plume of feathers is he that indited this letter? 94
What vane? What weathercock? Did you ever hear
better? 95
BOYET
I am much deceived but I remember the style. 96

PRINCESS
Else your memory is bad, going o'er it erewhile. 97
BOYET
This Armado is a Spaniard that keeps here in court, 98
A phantasime, a Monarcho, and one that makes sport 99
To the Prince and his bookmates.
PRINCESS   [*to Costard*]   Thou fellow, a word. 100
Who gave thee this letter?
COSTARD   I told you—my lord.
PRINCESS
To whom shouldst thou give it?
COSTARD   From my lord to my lady.
PRINCESS
From which lord to which lady?
COSTARD
From my lord Berowne, a good master of mine,
To a lady of France that he called Rosaline.
PRINCESS
Thou hast mistaken his letter. Come, lords, away. 106
[*To Rosaline*] Here, sweet, put up this; 'twill be thine
    another day.   [*Exeunt Princess and attendants.*] 107
BOYET
Who is the shooter? Who is the shooter?
ROSALINE   Shall I teach you to know? 108
BOYET
Ay, my continent of beauty.
ROSALINE   Why, she that bears the bow. 109
Finely put off! 110
BOYET
My lady goes to kill horns, but if thou marry, 111
Hang me by the neck if horns that year miscarry. 112
Finely put on! 113
ROSALINE
Well, then, I am the shooter.
BOYET   And who is your deer? 114
ROSALINE
If we choose by the horns, yourself come not near. 115
Finely put on, indeed!
MARIA
You still wrangle with her, Boyet, and she strikes at
the brow. 117

---

60 **wax** seal   62 **infallible** certain, incontrovertible   64 **commiseration** pity   65 **vassal** humble servant.   66 **illustrate** illustrious.
King Cophetua. (See 1.2.105–6 and note.)   **pernicious** (Armado may
mean "penurious," or the text may be in error.)   67 **indubitate**
undoubted.   **Zenelophon** Penelophon, the beggar maid in the ballad
about King Cophetua   68 ***Veni, vidi, vici*** I came, I saw, I overcame.
(The words are Julius Caesar's terse account of his victory over King
Pharnaces.)   68–9 **annothanize** annotate (pseudo-Latin), or, anatomize, explain, interpret   69 **vulgar** vernacular   70 **videlicet** namely
77 **catastrophe** conclusion   78–9 **for . . . comparison** according to this
analogy   80 **lowliness** low social standing.   83 **tittles** insignificant
specks or dots.   84 **profane** desecrate   86 **dearest . . . industry** most
excellent pattern of zealous gallantry   88 **Nemean lion** lion slain by
Hercules in the first of his twelve labors   90 **Submissive fall** If you
fall submissively   91 **forage** raging, ravening.   **incline** turn, shift
92 **strive** resist   93 **repasture** food   94 **What . . . feathers** What kind
of bird, dandy.   **indited** wrote   95 **vane . . . weathercock** weathervane (because showy and constantly shifting)   96 **I . . . but I** i.e.,
unless my memory fails me, I

97 **Else** Otherwise.   **going o'er it** (1) reading it over (2) climbing over
a *stile*, playing on "style."   **erewhile** just now.   98 **keeps** lives,
dwells   99 **phantasime** one who entertains fantastic notions.
Monarcho (The nickname of an eccentric Italian at the Elizabethan
court who fancied himself the emperor of the world; hence, anyone
who displays absurd pretensions.)   100 **To** for.   **bookmates** fellow
scholars.   106 **mistaken** incorrectly delivered   107 **up** away.   **'twill
be thine** i.e., it will be your turn.   **s.d. attendants** (Perhaps the
Forester exits here.)   108 **shooter** archer. (With a pun on "suitor."
Boyet may be asking who is to shoot, now that the Princess has left.
Perhaps Rosaline has been given the bow.)   109 **continent of** container of all   110 **put off** answered evasively.   111 **horns** i.e., deer
112 **horns** i.e., cuckolds' horns. (Boyet saucily suggests that, if Rosaline marries, cuckolds' horns will not be in short supply.)   **miscarry**
do not appear.   113 **put on** urged, applied.   114 **deer** (With pun on
"dear"; Rosaline is the natural target of all this double entendre about
the huntress who is hunting for a husband, since Berowne is known
to have written her a love letter.)   115 **If . . . near** (Rosaline retorts to
Boyet acerbically by intimating that he couldn't possibly be her
choice.)   117 **she . . . brow** i.e., she takes good aim at you.
(With pun on the idea that she has also put Boyet down with a joke
about cuckoldry.)

BOYET
But she herself is hit lower. Have I hit her now?   118

ROSALINE   Shall I come upon thee with an old saying   119
that was a man when King Pépin of France was a   120
little boy, as touching the hit it?   121

BOYET   So I may answer thee with one as old, that was   122
a woman when Queen Guinevere of Britain was a   123
little wench, as touching the hit it.

ROSALINE
"Thou canst not hit it, hit it, hit it,
Thou canst not hit it, my good man."

BOYET
"An I cannot, cannot, cannot,
An I cannot, another can."   *Exit* [*Rosaline*].

COSTARD
By my troth, most pleasant. How both did fit it!   129

MARIA
A mark marvelous well shot, for they both did hit it.   130

BOYET
A mark! Oh, mark but that mark! "A mark," says my
lady!
Let the mark have a prick in't to mete at, if it may be.   132

MARIA
Wide o'the bow hand! I' faith, your hand is out.   133

COSTARD
Indeed, 'a must shoot nearer, or he'll ne'er hit the
clout.   134

BOYET   [*to Maria*]
An if my hand be out, then belike your hand is in.   135

COSTARD
Then will she get the upshoot by cleaving the pin.   136

MARIA
Come, come, you talk greasily; your lips grow foul.   137

COSTARD
She's too hard for you at pricks, sir. Challenge her to
bowl.   138

BOYET
I fear too much rubbing. Good night, my good owl.   139
[*Exeunt Boyet, Maria, and Katharine.*]

COSTARD
By my soul, a swain, a most simple clown!   140
Lord, Lord, how the ladies and I have put him down!
O' my troth, most sweet jests, most incony vulgar wit!   142
When it comes so smoothly off, so obscenely, as it
were, so fit.   143
Armado o'th'one side—oh, a most dainty man!   144
To see him walk before a lady and to bear her fan!
To see him kiss his hand, and how most sweetly 'a
will swear!
And his page o'th'other side, that handful of wit!
Ah, heavens, it is a most pathetical nit! *Shout within.*   148
Sola, sola!   *Exit* [*Costard, running*].   149

❖

[4.2]

Enter Dull, Holofernes the pedant, and Nathaniel.

NATHANIEL   Very reverend sport, truly, and done in the   1
testimony of a good conscience.   2

HOLOFERNES   The deer was, as you know, *sanguis*, in   3
blood, ripe as the pomewater, who now hangeth like   4
a jewel in the ear of *caelo*, the sky, the welkin, the   5
heaven, and anon falleth like a crab on the face of *terra*,   6
the soil, the land, the earth.

NATHANIEL   Truly, Master Holofernes, the epithets are
sweetly varied, like a scholar at the least. But, sir, I   9
assure ye, it was a buck of the first head.   10

HOLOFERNES   Sir Nathaniel, *haud credo*.   11

DULL   'Twas not a *haud credo*, 'twas a pricket.   12

HOLOFERNES   Most barbarous intimation! Yet a kind of   13
insinuation, as it were, *in via*, in way, of explication;   14
facere, as it were, replication, or rather, *ostentare*, to   15
show, as it were, his inclination, after his undressed,
unpolished, uneducated, unpruned, untrained, or
rather, unlettered, or, ratherest, unconfirmed fashion,   18
to insert again my *haud credo* for a deer.   19

DULL   I said the deer was not a *haud credo*, 'twas a
pricket.

HOLOFERNES   Twice-sod simplicity, *bis coctus!*   22
O thou monster Ignorance, how deformed dost
thou look!

NATHANIEL

Sir, he hath never fed of the dainties that are bred
in a book.

He hath not eat paper, as it were; he hath not drunk 24
ink. His intellect is not replenished. He is only an ani- 25
mal, only sensible in the duller parts;

And such barren plants are set before us that we 27
thankful should be—

Which we of taste and feeling are—for those parts
that do fructify in us more than he. 29

For as it would ill become me to be vain, indiscreet,
or a fool,

So were there a patch set on learning to see him
in a school. 31

But *omne bene*, say I, being of an old Father's mind: 32
"Many can brook the weather that love not the wind." 33

DULL

You two are bookmen. Can you tell me by your wit
What was a month old at Cain's birth that's not
five weeks old as yet?

HOLOFERNES

Dictynna, goodman Dull, Dictynna, goodman Dull. 36

DULL   What is Dictima?

NATHANIEL   A title to Phoebe, to Luna, to the moon. 38

HOLOFERNES

The moon was a month old when Adam was no
more,

And raught not to five weeks when he came to 39
fivescore.

Th'allusion holds in the exchange. 40

DULL   'Tis true indeed. The collusion holds in the ex- 41
change. 42

HOLOFERNES   God comfort thy capacity! I say, th'allu- 44
sion holds in the exchange.

DULL   And I say the pollution holds in the exchange, for 46
the moon is never but a month old; and I say beside
that 'twas a pricket that the Princess killed.

HOLOFERNES   Sir Nathaniel, will you hear an extemporal 49
epitaph on the death of the deer? And, to humor the
ignorant, call I the deer the Princess killed a pricket.

NATHANIEL   *Perge*, good Master Holofernes, *perge*, so it 52
shall please you to abrogate scurrility. 53

HOLOFERNES   I will something affect the letter, for it ar- 54
gues facility. 55

The preyful Princess pierced and pricked a pretty
pleasing pricket; 56

Some say a sore, but not a sore till now made sore
with shooting. 57

The dogs did yell. Put "l" to "sore," then sorel jumps
from thicket, 58

Or pricket sore, or else sorel. The people fall a-hooting. 59

If sore be sore, then "l" to "sore" makes fifty sores
o' sorel. 60

Of one sore I an hundred make by adding but one
more "l."

NATHANIEL   A rare talent!

DULL   [*aside*]   If a talent be a claw, look how he claws 63
him with a talent.

HOLOFERNES   This is a gift that I have, simple, simple—
a foolish extravagant spirit, full of forms, figures,
shapes, objects, ideas, apprehensions, motions, revo- 67
lutions. These are begot in the ventricle of memory, 68
nourished in the womb of *pia mater*, and delivered 69
upon the mellowing of occasion. But the gift is good 70
in those in whom it is acute, and I am thankful for it.

NATHANIEL   Sir, I praise the Lord for you, and so may
my parishioners, for their sons are well tutored by
you, and their daughters profit very greatly under you. 74
You are a good member of the commonwealth.

HOLOFERNES   *Mehercle*, if their sons be ingenious, they 76
shall want no instruction; if their daughters be capa- 77
ble, I will put it to them. But *vir sapit qui pauca loquitur.* 78
A soul feminine saluteth us.

Enter Jaquenetta and [Costard] the clown.

JAQUENETTA   God give you good morrow, Master Person. 80

HOLOFERNES   Master Person, *quasi* pierce-one. And if 81
one should be pierced, which is the one? 82

---

24 of on.   **dainties** delicacies   **25 eat** eaten. (Pronounced "et.")
27 sensible capable of perception   **29 fructify** grow fruitful.   **he** in
him.   **31 were . . . learning** (1) it would be setting a fool or dolt to
learn (2) it would be a disgrace to learning itself   **32 omne bene** all is
well.   **being . . . mind** agreeing as I do with one of the Fathers of the
early Christian Church   **33 Many . . . wind** i.e., One must endure
what one cannot change. (A proverb, and hardly the wisdom of the
Church Fathers.)   **brook** put up with   **36, 38 Dictynna, Phoebe,
Luna** (Classical names for the moon. The first is uncommon and is
appropriate to the pedant. It occurs in Golding's translation of Ovid,
a book that Shakespeare knew.)   **39 no more** no older   **40 raught**
reached, attained   **41 Th'allusion . . . exchange** i.e., The riddle is still
valid even if Cain's name (see line 35) is substituted for Adam's.
42 collusion conspiracy. (Dull's error for "allusion.")   **44 comfort**
have pity on   **46 pollution** (Another error for "allusion," perhaps unintended relevance to the linguistic *pollution* of Holofernes'
Latin.)   **49 extemporal** impromptu   **52 Perge** Proceed   **52–3 so . . .
scurrility** if you will be so good as to refrain from bawdry.

54 something . . . letter somewhat make use of alliteration
54–5 argues demonstrates   **56 preyful** intent upon prey   **57 sore**
buck in its fourth year.   **made sore** wounded   **58 Put "l" to "sore"**
(The "l" is like a yelling noise that alarms the buck.)   **sorel** buck in
its third year   **59 Or** Either   **60 If sore be sore** If it's a sore buck that
is wounded.   **"l"** ("L" is Roman numeral fifty.)   **63 talent** i.e., talon.
claws (1) scratches (2) flatters   **67 motions** impulses   **67–8 revolutions** turns of thought.   **68 ventricle of memory** one of the three sections of the brain, believed to contain the memory   **69 pia mater** the
membrane surrounding the brain; the brain itself   **69–70 delivered . . .
occasion** born when the moment is propitious.   **74 under you** under
your instruction. (With unintended sexual double meaning.)
76 Mehercle By Hercules.   **ingenious** clever   **77 want** lack
77–8 capable (1) apt as pupils (2) able to bear children (an unconscious sexual pun that goes back to *under you* in line 74)   **78 put it to
them** (With unintended sexual meaning.)   **78 vir . . . loquitur** he is a
wise man who says little.   **80 Person** (Normally pronounced "parson" in Elizabethan English, but here pronounced "person," in rustic
speech, thereby eliciting a pedantic witticism from Holofernes.)
81 quasi that is, as if   **82 pierced** (Pronounced "persed"; playing on
pers-one, "pierce one." This is sometimes taken as an allusion to
Nashe's *Pierce Penniless, His Supplication to the Devil*, a fantastic satire
in which the author, in the character of Pierce, comments on the vices
of the times; also to Harvey's answer, *Pierce's Supererogation*, in which
Pierce is referred to as "the hogshead of wit"; compare line 85.)

COSTARD Marry, Master Schoolmaster, he that is likeliest
to a hogshead.   84

HOLOFERNES Of piercing a hogshead! A good luster of 85
conceit in a turf of earth; fire enough for a flint, pearl 86
enough for a swine. 'Tis pretty, it is well.

JAQUENETTA Good Master Person, be so good as read
me this letter. It was given me by Costard and sent me
from Don Armado. I beseech you, read it.
[*She hands the letter to Nathaniel.*]

HOLOFERNES "*Fauste, precor gelida quando pecus omne sub* 91
umbra ruminat," and so forth. Ah, good old Mantuan! 92
I may speak of thee as the traveler doth of Venice:
    Venezia, Venezia,   94
    Chi non ti vede, chi non ti prezia.   95
Old Mantuan, old Mantuan! Who understandeth thee
not, loves thee not. [*He sings.*] Ut, re, sol, la, mi, fa. [*To* 97
Nathaniel, who is examining the letter.] Under pardon, 98
sir, what are the contents? Or rather, as Horace says in
his—What, my soul, verses?

NATHANIEL Ay, sir, and very learned.

HOLOFERNES Let me hear a staff, a stanza, a verse. *Lege*, 102
domine.   103

NATHANIEL [*reads*]
"If love make me forsworn, how shall I swear to
    love?   104
Ah, never faith could hold, if not to beauty vowed!
Though to myself forsworn, to thee I'll faithful prove;
    Those thoughts to me were oaks, to thee like
    osiers bowed.   107
Study his bias leaves and makes his book thine eyes, 108
    Where all those pleasures live that art would
    comprehend.
If knowledge be the mark, to know thee shall suffice; 110
    Well learnd is that tongue that well can thee commend,
All ignorant that soul that sees thee without wonder;
    Which is to me some praise that I thy parts
    admire.   113
Thy eye Jove's lightning bears, thy voice his
    dreadful thunder,
    Which, not to anger bent, is music and sweet fire. 115
Celestial as thou art, oh, pardon love this wrong, 116

That sings heaven's praise with such an earthly
    tongue."   117

HOLOFERNES You find not the apostrophus, and so miss 118
the accent. Let me supervise the canzonet. [*He takes* 119
the letter.] Here are only numbers ratified, but, for the 120
elegancy, facility, and golden cadence of poesy—
caret. Ovidius Naso was the man. And why indeed 122
"Naso" but for smelling out the odoriferous flowers
of fancy, the jerks of invention? *Imitari* is nothing. So 124
doth the hound his master, the ape his keeper, the tired
horse his rider. But, damosella virgin, was this
directed to you?

JAQUENETTA Ay, sir, from one Monsieur Berowne, one
of the strange queen's lords.   129

HOLOFERNES I will overglance the superscript: "To the 130
snow-white hand of the most beauteous Lady Ros-
aline. "I will look again on the intellect of the letter for 132
the nomination of the party writing to the person 133
written unto: "Your Ladyship's in all desired employ- 134
ment, Berowne." Sir Nathaniel, this Berowne is one of 135
the votaries with the King, and here he hath framed a 136
letter to a sequent of the stranger queen's, which 137
accidentally, or by the way of progression, hath mis- 138
carried.—Trip and go, my sweet; deliver this 139
paper into the royal hand of the King. It may con- 140
cern much. [*He gives her the letter.*] Stay not thy com- 141
pliment. I forgive thy duty. Adieu.   142

JAQUENETTA Good Costard, go with me.—Sir, God save
your life!

COSTARD Have with thee, my girl.   145
                    Exit [with Jaquenetta].

NATHANIEL Sir, you have done this in the fear of God,
very religiously; and, as a certain Father saith—   147

HOLOFERNES Sir, tell not me of the Father, I do fear
colorable colors. But to return to the verses: did they 149
please you, Sir Nathaniel?

NATHANIEL Marvelous well for the pen.   151

HOLOFERNES I do dine today at the father's of a certain
pupil of mine, where, if before repast it shall please you 153
to gratify the table with a grace, I will, on my privilege 154
I have with the parents of the foresaid child or pupil,

---

84 likeliest most like. **hogshead** barrel. (With a suggestion also of "fathead.") **85 piercing a hogshead** broaching a barrel, i.e., getting drunk. **85–6 A good . . . earth** A good spark of fancy in one who is close to the soil **91–2 *Fauste . . . ruminat*** (The first line of the first eclogue of the Italian Renaissance poet Mantuan. It was a well-known text in the schools. The passage means "Faustus, I beg, while all the cattle chew their cud in the cool shade.") **94–5 *Venezia . . . prezia*** Venice, Venice, only he who sees you not loves you not. **97 Ut** (Equivalent to the modern *do*. If Holofernes intends to sing the scale, *do, re, mi, fa, sol, la*, he displays his ignorance, but he may be singing a fragment of a melody.) **98 Under pardon** i.e., Excuse me **102 staff** stanza **102–3 *Lege, domine*** Read, master. **104–17 If . . . tongue** (These lines were printed with minor changes in *The Passionate Pilgrim*, 1599, a collection of poems by various authors but attributed to Shakespeare. Two others of the volume are also from this play—that read by Longaville, 4.3.56–69, and that by Dumaine, 4.3.97–116.) **107 osiers** willows **108 Study . . . leaves** i.e., The student leaves his studious inclination **110 mark** target, goal **113 Which . . . admire** which reflects well on me in that I sing your praises. **115 bent** turned, directed **116 pardon . . . wrong** excuse this failure in my loving. (Or else, "Oh, pardon, love, this wrong.")

118 find heed. **apostrophus** apostrophes, marks of elision used to indicate omitted vowels and shortened pronunciation of a word **119 supervise the canzonet** peruse the poem. **120 only numbers ratified** i.e., merely language made metrical **122 caret** it is lacking. **Ovidius Naso** The Roman poet Ovid, born in 43 B.C. (*Naso*, his surname, is derived from *nasus*, nose.) **124 fancy** imagination. **jerks of invention** strokes of imagination. *Imitari* To imitate **129 strange** foreign. (Either Jaquenetta believes mistakenly that Berowne is attached to the Princess's retinue, or she means that the Princess and her ladies regard the young aristocratic men as their "lords," their beaux.) **130 superscript** address **132 intellect** meaning, import, contents **133 nomination** name **134–5 all desired employment** any service you require of me **136 votaries** those who have taken a vow **137 sequent** follower, attendant **138 by . . . progression** in process of delivery **139 Trip and go** Move nimbly and swiftly. (A phrase from a popular song.) **140–1 concern much** be of importance. **141–2 Stay . . . compliment** i.e., Don't stand on ceremony. **142 I forgive thy duty** I set aside the requirement of a curtsy. **145 Have with thee** I'll go with you **147 Father** Church Father **149 colorable colors** i.e., specious authorities. **151 pen** penmanship, or style. **153 repast** the meal **154 gratify** (1) delight (2) grace. **the table** i.e., those at the table

undertake your *ben venuto*; where I will prove those 156
verses to be very unlearned, neither savoring of poetry,
wit, nor invention. I beseech your society.   158

NATHANIEL   And thank you too; for society, saith
the text, is the happiness of life.

HOLOFERNES   And certes the text most infallibly con- 161
cludes it. [*To Dull*] Sir, I do invite you too. You shall not 162
say me nay. *Pauca verba*. Away! The gentles are at their 163
game, and we will to our recreation.   *Exeunt.* 164

❧

[4.3]

Enter Berowne, with a paper in his hand, alone.

BEROWNE   The King, he is hunting the deer; I am
coursing myself. They have pitched a toil; I am toiling 2
in a pitch—pitch that defiles. Defile! A foul word. Well, 3
set thee down, sorrow! For so they say the fool said, 4
and so say I—and I the fool. Well proved, wit! By the 5
Lord, this love is as mad as Ajax. It kills sheep; it kills 6
me, I a sheep. Well proved again o' my side! I will not
love; if I do, hang me. I' faith, I will not. Oh, but her
eye! By this light, but for her eye I would not love her.
Yes, for her two eyes. Well, I do nothing in the world
but lie, and lie in my throat. By heaven, I do love, and 11
it hath taught me to rhyme and to be melancholy; and
here is part of my rhyme, and here my melancholy.
Well, she hath one o' my sonnets already. The clown
bore it, the fool sent it, and the lady hath it—sweet
clown, sweeter fool, sweetest lady! By the world, I
would not care a pin, if the other three were in. Here 17
comes one with a paper. God give him grace to groan! 18
He stands aside.

The King entereth [with a paper].

KING   Ay me!

BEROWNE   [*aside*]   Shot, by heaven! Proceed, sweet
Cupid. Thou hast thumped him with thy bird-bolt 21
under the left pap. In faith, secrets!   22

KING   [*reads*]
"So sweet a kiss the golden sun gives not
    To those fresh morning drops upon the rose
As thy eyebeams, when their fresh rays have smote 25
    The night of dew that on my cheeks down flows. 26
Nor shines the silver moon one-half so bright
    Through the transparent bosom of the deep 28
As doth thy face, through tears of mine, give light;
    Thou shin'st in every tear that I do weep.
No drop but as a coach doth carry thee;
    So ridest thou triumphing in my woe.
Do but behold the tears that swell in me,
    And they thy glory through my grief will show.
But do not love thyself; then thou wilt keep
    My tears for glasses, and still make me weep. 36
O queen of queens! How far dost thou excel,
No thought can think nor tongue of mortal tell."
How shall she know my griefs? I'll drop the paper.
Sweet leaves, shade folly. Who is he comes here? 40

*Enter Longaville [with papers]. The King steps
aside.*

What, Longaville, and reading! Listen, ear.

BEROWNE   [*aside*]
Now, in thy likeness, one more fool appear! 42

LONGAVILLE   Ay me, I am forsworn!

BEROWNE   [*aside*]
Why, he comes in like a perjure, wearing papers. 44

KING   [*aside*]
In love, I hope. Sweet fellowship in shame!

BEROWNE   [*aside*]
One drunkard loves another of the name. 46

LONGAVILLE
Am I the first that have been perjured so?

BEROWNE   [*aside*]
I could put thee in comfort: not by two that I know.
Thou makest the triumviry, the corner-cap of society, 49
The shape of Love's Tyburn, that hangs up
    simplicity.   50

LONGAVILLE
I fear these stubborn lines lack power to move. 51
[*Reading*] "O sweet Maria, empress of my love!"—
These numbers will I tear, and write in prose. 53
[He tears the paper.]

BEROWNE   [*aside*]
Oh, rhymes are guards on wanton Cupid's hose; 54

---

156 undertake your *ben venuto* ensure your welcome   **158 society**
company.   **161–2 certes . . . concludes it** certainly the biblical text
you allude to (perhaps Ecclesiastes 4:8–12) infallibly demonstrates the
point.   **163 *Pauca verba*** Few words.   **gentles** gentlefolk   **164 game**
i.e., hunting.
4.3 Location: Navarre's park.
2 coursing pursuing.   **pitched a toil** set a snare   **2–3 toiling . . . pitch** i.e.,
struggling in the toils of love. (*Pitch* means both "sticky tar" and "a fixed
opinion," with a quibbling reference to Rosaline's eyes, which he has earlier, in 3.1.195, called *two pitch-balls*.)   **3 defiles** corrupts. (See Ecclesiasticus 13:1: "Whoso toucheth pitch shall be defiled withal.")
4 set thee down i.e., stay, settle down with me. (See 1.1.305–6.)   **4 they . . .
said** people attribute that saying to a fool   **5 and I the fool** and the fool
turns out to be myself.   **6 mad as Ajax** (An allusion to the story of Ajax,
who, maddened by his failure in a contest for Achilles's armor, attacked a
flock of sheep, supposing them to be those who had denied him the
prize.)   **11 in my throat** i.e., utterly.   **17 in** involved (i.e., in love).
18 God . . . groan! i.e., May God grant that he be moved to groan for love!
18.1 *He stands aside* (Possibly Berowne hides in some elevated place
understood to be a tree; see 4.3.75, 161.)   **21 bird-bolt** blunt arrow for
shooting birds   **22 left pap** left breast . (Where the heart is located.)
In faith, secrets! i.e., In truth, we will now hear a confession of love!

25 smote struck   **26 night of dew** i.e., tears that flow nightly
28 the deep a body of water reflecting the moonlight   **36 glasses**
mirrors.   **still** continually   **40 shade** conceal   **42 thy** i.e., the King's
44 perjure perjurer.   **wearing papers** (An allusion to the custom of
attaching to a convicted perjurer's breast the papers involved in and
setting forth his offense—in this case, the poem, which is an open
indication of Longaville's having forsworn his vow to eschew love.)
46 One . . . name A drunkard finds comfort in the drunkenness of
another; misery loves company.   **49 Thou . . . society** You make up
the triumvirate, the three-cornered cap of our fellowship   **50 Tyburn**
(A place of public execution in London; with reference here to the triangular structure of the gallows.)   **51 stubborn** rough, harsh
53 numbers verses   **54 guards** trim, decorative embroideries.
hose breeches

Disfigure not his shop.

LONGAVILLE [*taking another paper*] This same shall go.   55
(*He reads the sonnet.*)
"Did not the heavenly rhetoric of thine eye,   56
    'Gainst whom the world cannot hold argument,   57
Persuade my heart to this false perjury?
    Vows for thee broke deserve not punishment.
A woman I forswore, but I will prove,
    Thou being a goddess, I forswore not thee.
My vow was earthly, thou a heavenly love.
    Thy grace being gained cures all disgrace in me.   63
Vows are but breath, and breath a vapor is.
    Then thou, fair sun, which on my earth dost shine,
Exhal'st this vapor vow; in thee it is.   66
    If broken, then, it is no fault of mine.
If by me broke, what fool is not so wise   68
To lose an oath to win a paradise?"   69

BEROWNE [*aside*]   70
This is the liver vein, which makes flesh a deity,
A green goose a goddess. Pure, pure idolatry.   71
God amend us, God amend! We are much out
    o'the way.   72

Enter Dumaine [with a paper].

LONGAVILLE
By whom shall I send this?—Company! Stay.
                               [*He steps aside.*]

BEROWNE [*aside*]
All hid, all hid—an old infant play.   74
Like a demigod here sit I in the sky,   75
And wretched fools' secrets heedfully o'ereye.   76
More sacks to the mill! Oh, heavens, I have my wish!   77
Dumaine transformed! Four woodcocks in a dish!   78

DUMAINE   O most divine Kate!

BEROWNE [*aside*]   O most profane coxcomb!

DUMAINE
By heaven, the wonder in a mortal eye!   81

BEROWNE [*aside*]
By earth, she is not, Corporal. There you lie.   82

DUMAINE
Her amber hairs for foul hath amber quoted.   83

BEROWNE [*aside*]
An amber-colored raven was well noted.   84

DUMAINE
As upright as the cedar.

BEROWNE [*aside*]   Stoop, I say!   85
Her shoulder is with child.

DUMAINE   As fair as day.   86

BEROWNE [*aside*]
Ay, as some days; but then no sun must shine.

DUMAINE
Oh, that I had my wish!

LONGAVILLE [*aside*]   And I had mine!

KING [*aside*]
And I mine too, good Lord!

BEROWNE [*aside*]
Amen, so I had mine. Is not that a good word?   90

DUMAINE
I would forget her, but a fever she   91
Reigns in my blood and will remembered be.   92

BEROWNE [*aside*]
A fever in your blood! Why, then incision   93
Would let her out in saucers. Sweet misprision!   94

DUMAINE
Once more I'll read the ode that I have writ.

BEROWNE [*aside*]
Once more I'll mark how love can vary wit.   96

DUMAINE (*reads his sonnet*)
"On a day—alack the day!—   97
Love, whose month is ever May,
Spied a blossom passing fair   99
Playing in the wanton air.   100
Through the velvet leaves the wind,
All unseen, can passage find,   102
That the lover, sick to death,   103
Wished himself the heaven's breath.
'Air,' quoth he, 'thy cheeks may blow;
Air, would I might triumph so!
But, alack, my hand is sworn
Ne'er to pluck thee from thy thorn—
Vow, alack, for youth unmeet,   109
Youth so apt to pluck a sweet!
Do not call it sin in me
That I am forsworn for thee,
Thou for whom Jove would swear
Juno but an Ethiop were,   114
And deny himself for Jove,   115
Turning mortal for thy love.' "   116
This will I send, and something else more plain,

---

55 **Disfigure . . . shop** Don't deface Cupid's place of workmanship (where love's embroideries are fashioned).   **56–69 Did . . . paradise?** (See the note on 4.2.104–17.)   **57 whom** i.e., which   **63 Thy . . . me** i.e., The fact that you are a goddess exculpates me, since I vowed only to forswear the company of women, not goddesses.   **66 Exhal'st** draws up. (It was thought that the sun drew up vapors from the earth, thereby producing meteors, will-o'-the-wisps, etc.)   **68 If** Even if   **69 To** As to   **70 the liver vein** i.e., the vein or style of a lover. (Since the liver was assumed to be the seat of the passions.)   **71 green goose** gosling, i.e., a young girl, a strumpet   **72 much...way** far gone.   **74 infant play** child's game of hide and seek. (But with a suggestion also of a medieval religious play, in which God appears above.)   **75 in the sky** (Berowne speaks as though he were looking down on the others from some elevated position, possibly the gallery above the stage; see also 4.3.161.)   **76 heedfully o'ereye** attentively observe.   **77 More . . . mill** (A proverbial expression, here suggesting that more food for laughter appears to be on its way.)   **78 woodcocks** (Birds noted for their stupidity.)   **81 mortal** human   **82 Corporal** i.e., field officer for Cupid (see 3.1.185). With a play on "corporeal," fleshly.)   **83 quoted** designated. (Dumaine hyperbolically insists that her amber hair makes real amber seem foul, ugly, by comparison.)

84 An . . . noted i.e. (ironically), Dumaine has aptly described a black fowl (with pun on "foul") as amber-colored.   **85 Stoop** (1) Stooped, Stunted (2) Dumaine should avoid such lofty comparisons   **86 is with child** i.e., is swollen, unshapely.   **90 Is . . . word?** (1) Isn't that kind of me? (2) Isn't *amen* known to be a good word?   **91 a fever** as a fever   **92 and . . . be** and cannot be ignored.   **93 incision** letting blood   **94 in saucers** (1) by the bowlful (2) into bowls to catch the blood.   **misprision** (1) mistake (2) being released from confinement (of the veins).   **96 can vary wit** can inspire variety of expression.   **97–116 On . . . love** (See the note on 4.2.104–17.)   **99 passing** surpassingly   **100 wanton** frolicsome   **102 can** began to   **103 That** so that   **109 unmeet** inappropriate   **114 Ethiop** Ethiopian, black African. (Used here as an example of ugliness.)   **115 for Jove** to be Jove

That shall express my true love's fasting pain.   118
Oh, would the King, Berowne, and Longaville
Were lovers too! Ill, to example ill,   120
Would from my forehead wipe a perjured note,   121
For none offend where all alike do dote.   122

LONGAVILLE [advancing]
Dumaine, thy love is far from charity,   123
That in love's grief desir'st society.   124
You may look pale, but I should blush, I know,
To be o'erheard and taken napping so.

KING [advancing]
Come, sir, you blush! As his, your case is such;
You chide at him, offending twice as much.
You do not love Maria? Longaville
Did never sonnet for her sake compile,
Nor never lay his wreathèd arms athwart   131
His loving bosom to keep down his heart?
I have been closely shrouded in this bush
And marked you both, and for you both did blush.
I heard your guilty rhymes, observed your fashion,
Saw sighs reek from you, noted well your passion.
"Ay me!" says one. "O Jove!" the other cries;
One, her hairs were gold, crystal the other's eyes.
[To Longaville] You would for paradise break faith
    and troth;   139
[To Dumaine] And Jove, for your love, would
    infringe an oath.   140
What will Berowne say when that he shall hear   141
Faith infringèd, which such zeal did swear?
How will he scorn! How will he spend his wit!
How will he triumph, leap, and laugh at it!
For all the wealth that ever I did see
I would not have him know so much by me.   146

BEROWNE [advancing]
Now step I forth to whip hypocrisy.
Ah, good my liege, I pray thee, pardon me.
Good heart, what grace hast thou, thus to reprove   149
These worms for loving, that art most in love?
Your eyes do make no coaches; in your tears   151
There is no certain princess that appears;   152
You'll not be perjured, 'tis a hateful thing—
Tush, none but minstrels like of sonneting!   154
But are you not ashamed? Nay, are you not,
All three of you, to be thus much o'ershot?   156
[To Longaville] You found his mote; the King your
    mote did see;   157
But I a beam do find in each of three.   158
Oh, what a scene of foolery have I seen,
Of sighs, of groans, of sorrow, and of teen!   160

Oh, me, with what strict patience have I sat,
To see a king transformèd to a gnat!   162
To see great Hercules whipping a gig,   163
And profound Solomon to tune a jig,   164
And Nestor play at pushpin with the boys,   165
And critic Timon laugh at idle toys!   166
Where lies thy grief, oh, tell me, good Dumaine?
And, gentle Longaville, where lies thy pain?
And where my liege's? All about the breast.—
A caudle, ho!

KING   Too bitter is thy jest.   170
Are we betrayed thus to thy overview?

BEROWNE
Not you to me, but I betrayed by you.
I, that am honest, I, that hold it sin
To break the vow I am engagèd in,
I am betrayed by keeping company
With men like you, men of inconstancy.
When shall you see me write a thing in rhyme?
Or groan for Joan? Or spend a minute's time
In pruning me? When shall you hear that I   179
Will praise a hand, a foot, a face, an eye,
A gait, a state, a brow, a breast, a waist,   181
A leg, a limb—   [He starts to leave.]

KING   Soft! Whither away so fast?
A true man or a thief, that gallops so?   183

BEROWNE
I post from love. Good lover, let me go.   184

Enter Jaquenetta [with a letter], and [Costard the]
clown.

JAQUENETTA
God bless the King!

KING   What present hast thou there?

COSTARD
Some certain treason.

KING   What makes treason here?   186

COSTARD
Nay, it makes nothing, sir.

KING   If it mar nothing neither,   187
The treason and you go in peace away together.   188

JAQUENETTA
I beseech Your Grace, let this letter be read.
Our parson misdoubts it; 'twas treason, he said.   190
                     [She gives the letter.]

KING   Berowne, read it over.
                     He [Berowne] reads the letter [silently].

[To Jaquenetta] Where hadst thou it?

---

118 **fasting** hungering   120 **Ill . . . ill** i.e., Then perjury, by serving as an example and precedent of sin   121 **note** mark, document. (See 4.3.44.)   122 **dote** love dotingly.   123 **charity** Christian love   124 **That . . . society** you who, in your suffering from love, uncharitably desire others to suffer also. (Proverbial: "Misery loves company.")   131 **lay . . . athwart** i.e., fold his arms in the conventional sign of melancholy; compare 3.1.18   139 **troth** loyalty   140 **infringe** break   141 **when that** when   146 **by** about   149 **grace** graciousness; privilege.   **reprove** rebuke, condemn   151 **Your . . . coaches** (Alluding to the King's sonnet, 4.3.31–2.)   152 **certain** particular   154 **like** approve   156 **o'ershot** wide of the mark, shooting beyond it; i.e., in error.   157, 158 **mote, beam** i.e., small speck, large defect. (See Matthew 7:3–5, Luke 6:41–2.)   160 **teen** affliction, grief.

162 **a gnat** i.e., a tiny creature. (With a play perhaps on *mote*.)   163 **whipping a gig** spinning a top   164 **tune** play or sing   165 **Nestor** wise old Greek chieftain in the Trojan War.   **pushpin** a child's game   166 **critic** critical, censorious.   **Timon** a fifth-century Athenian notorious for his misanthropy.   **laugh . . . toys** take delight in mindless entertainments.   170 **caudle** warm drink given to sick people   179 **pruning me** preening, i.e., trimming, dressing up myself.   181 **state** attitude, bearing   183 **true** honest   184 **post** hasten   186 **What makes treason** What is treason doing   187–8 **If . . . together** (The King acerbically suggests that all will be well if Costard and Jaquenetta just leave. With a play on the common saying, "to make or to mar.")   190 **misdoubts** suspects

JAQUENETTA   Of Costard.
KING   [to Costard]   Where hadst thou it?
COSTARD   Of Dun Adramadio, Dun Adramadio.
                                    [Berowne tears the letter.]

KING
   How now, what is in you? Why dost thou tear it?
BEROWNE
   A toy, my liege, a toy. Your Grace needs not fear it.   197
LONGAVILLE
   It did move him to passion, and therefore let's hear it.
DUMAINE   [gathering up the pieces]
   It is Berowne's writing, and here is his name.
BEROWNE   [to Costard]
   Ah, you whoreson loggerhead! You were born to do
      me shame.—   200
   Guilty, my lord, guilty! I confess, I confess.
KING   What?
BEROWNE
   That you three fools lacked me fool to make up the
      mess.   203
   He, he, and you—and you, my liege!—and I,
   Are pickpurses in love, and we deserve to die.   205
   Oh, dismiss this audience, and I shall tell you more.
DUMAINE
   Now the number is even.
BEROWNE   True, true, we are four.
   Will these turtles be gone?
KING   [to Costard and Jaquenetta]   Hence, sirs. Away!   208
COSTARD
   Walk aside the true folk, and let the traitors stay.   209
                     [Exeunt Costard and Jaquenetta.]
BEROWNE
   Sweet lords, sweet lovers, oh, let us embrace!
   As true we are as flesh and blood can be.
   The sea will ebb and flow, heaven show his face;
      Young blood doth not obey an old decree.
   We cannot cross the cause why we were born;   214
   Therefore of all hands must we be forsworn.   215
KING
   What, did these rent lines show some love of thine?   216
BEROWNE
   Did they, quoth you? Who sees the heavenly Rosaline, 217
   That, like a rude and savage man of Ind   218
      At the first opening of the gorgeous east,   219
   Bows not his vassal head and, strucken blind,
   Kisses the base ground with obedient breast?
   What peremptory eagle-sighted eye   222
   Dares look upon the heaven of her brow
   That is not blinded by her majesty?

KING
   What zeal, what fury hath inspired thee now?
   My love, her mistress, is a gracious moon,
      She an attending star, scarce seen a light.   227
BEROWNE
   My eyes are then no eyes, nor I Berowne.
      Oh, but for my love, day would turn to night!   229
   Of all complexions the culled sovereignty   230
      Do meet as at a fair in her fair cheek,
   Where several worthies make one dignity,   232
      Where nothing wants that want itself doth seek.   233
   Lend me the flourish of all gentle tongues—   234
      Fie, painted rhetoric! Oh, she needs it not.   235
   To things of sale a seller's praise belongs;   236
      She passes praise, then praise too short doth blot. 237
   A withered hermit, fivescore winters worn,   238
      Might shake off fifty, looking in her eye.
   Beauty doth varnish age, as if newborn,   240
      And gives the crutch the cradle's infancy.
   Oh, 'tis the sun that maketh all things shine!
KING
   By heaven, thy love is black as ebony.
BEROWNE
   Is ebony like her? Oh, word divine!
      A wife of such wood were felicity.   245
   Oh, who can give an oath? Where is a book,   246
      That I may swear Beauty doth beauty lack
   If that she learn not of her eye to look?   248
      No face is fair that is not full so black.   249
KING
   Oh, paradox! Black is the badge of hell,
      The hue of dungeons and the school of night;   251
   And beauty's crest becomes the heavens well.   252
BEROWNE
   Devils soonest tempt, resembling spirits of light.   253
   Oh, if in black my lady's brows be decked,   254
      It mourns that painting and usurping hair   255
   Should ravish doters with a false aspect;   256
      And therefore is she born to make black fair.
   Her favor turns the fashion of the days,   258

197 toy trifle   200 whoreson loggerhead i.e., infernal blockhead
203 mess group of four at table.   205 pickpurses pickpockets (i.e.,
cheaters)   208 turtles turtledoves, lovers.   sirs (An acceptable form
of address for both women and men.)   209 Walk . . . folk i.e., Those
who tell the truth are sent away for their efforts. (Costard's wry comment need not be offered as an aside.)   214 We . . . born We cannot
continue to defy natural instinct (i.e., to love)   215 of all hands
inevitably, in every way, on every side   216 rent lines torn verses
217 quoth you forsooth.   218 rude ignorant. Ind India   219 opening i.e., dawning   222 peremptory bold.   eagle-sighted (The eagle
was believed to be the only bird able to look directly at the sun.)

227 She i.e., Rosaline.   scarce . . . light a light scarcely visible.
229 my love the woman I love   230 the culled sovereignty those chosen as supreme   232 worthies excellences.   dignity i.e., supreme
example of beauty   233 wants is lacking.   want desire   234 flourish
adornment, eloquence.   gentle noble   235 painted artificial   236 of
sale for sale   237 She . . . blot she surpasses all praise, and thus any
praise of her falls short and stains her name.   238 fivescore . . . worn a
hundred years old   240 Beauty . . . newborn Beauty is able to transform old age, giving it a new lease on life   245 were would be
246 book i.e., Bible   248 If . . . look? unless Beauty herself learns from
Rosaline's eyes how beauty should truly appear?   249 full fully
251 the school of night The King regards a dark beauty as a contradiction in terms, like a school (either Holofernes's kind of school for
youngsters or the "academy" to which the gentlemen earlier professed
allegiance) devoted to studying dark things.   252 And . . . well
whereas true beauty in all its glory is the adornment of the heavens.
253 spirits of light angels. (This warning against false appearances is
extended in Berowne's following diatribe against cosmetics. Rosaline's
dark beauty need not be covered up in this way.)   254 decked adorned
255–6 It . . . aspect she is in black as though in mourning for the sad fact
that cosmetics and wigs are so often used to seduce doting males with
deceptive appearances   258 Her favor turns Her beauty inverts

For native blood is counted painting now;   259
And therefore red, that would avoid dispraise,   260
Paints itself black to imitate her brow.

DUMAINE
To look like her are chimney sweepers black.

LONGAVILLE
And since her time are colliers counted bright.   263

KING
And Ethiops of their sweet complexion crack.   264

DUMAINE
Dark needs no candles now, for dark is light.

BEROWNE
Your mistresses dare never come in rain,   266
For fear their colors should be washed away.   267

KING
'Twere good yours did; for, sir, to tell you plain,
I'll find a fairer face not washed today.   269

BEROWNE
I'll prove her fair, or talk till doomsday here.

KING
No devil will fright thee then so much as she.   271

DUMAINE
I never knew man hold vile stuff so dear.   272

LONGAVILLE [showing his shoe]
Look, here's thy love; my foot and her face see.

BEROWNE
Oh, if the streets were pavèd with thine eyes,   274
Her feet were much too dainty for such tread!   275

DUMAINE
Oh, vile! Then, as she goes, what upward lies   276
The street should see as she walked overhead.

KING
But what of this? Are we not all in love?

BEROWNE
Nothing so sure, and thereby all forsworn.

KING
Then leave this chat, and, good Berowne, now prove
Our loving lawful and our faith not torn.   281

DUMAINE
Ay, marry, there, some flattery for this evil.   282

LONGAVILLE
Oh, some authority how to proceed,
Some tricks, some quillets, how to cheat the devil.   284

DUMAINE
Some salve for perjury.

BEROWNE   Oh, 'tis more than need.   285
Have at you, then, Affection's men-at-arms!   286

Consider what you first did swear unto:
To fast, to study, and to see no woman—
Flat treason 'gainst the kingly state of youth.   289
Say, can you fast? Your stomachs are too young,
And abstinence engenders maladies.   291
Oh, we have made a vow to study, lords,
And in that vow we have forsworn our books.
For when would you, my liege, or you, or you,
In leaden contemplation have found out   295
Such fiery numbers as the prompting eyes   296
Of beauty's tutors have enriched you with?   297
Other slow arts entirely keep the brain,   298
And therefore, finding barren practicers,
Scarce show a harvest of their heavy toil;
But love, first learnèd in a lady's eyes,
Lives not alone immurèd in the brain,   302
But with the motion of all elements   303
Courses as swift as thought in every power,   304
And gives to every power a double power
Above their functions and their offices.   306
It adds a precious seeing to the eye;
A lover's eyes will gaze an eagle blind.   308
A lover's ear will hear the lowest sound,
When the suspicious head of theft is stopped.   310
Love's feeling is more soft and sensible   311
Than are the tender horns of cockled snails.   312
Love's tongue proves dainty Bacchus gross in taste.   313
For valor, is not Love a Hercules,   314
Still climbing trees in the Hesperides?   315
Subtle as Sphinx, as sweet and musical   316
As bright Apollo's lute strung with his hair.   317
And when Love speaks, the voice of all the gods
Make heaven drowsy with the harmony.
Never durst poet touch a pen to write   320
Until his ink were tempered with Love's sighs.   321
Oh, then his lines would ravish savage ears
And plant in tyrants mild humility.
From women's eyes this doctrine I derive:
They sparkle still the right Promethean fire;   325
They are the books, the arts, the academes
That show, contain, and nourish all the world;

259 For . . . now for nowadays a natural, ruddy complexion is suspected of being cosmetically put on   260 dispraise disparagement, censure   263 colliers coal miners   264 of . . . crack boast to have attractive complexions.   266 come in walk in, be exposed to   267 colors makeup   269 I'll . . . today i.e., many unwashed faces are cleaner and fairer than hers.   271 then i.e., on doomsday   272 hold . . . dear value worthless things so highly.   274–5 Oh, . . . tread! Oh, even if the street were paved with your soft and delicate eyeballs, her feet would be too dainty to walk on such a surface!   276 what upward lies (Dumaine bawdily suggests that a street paved with his eyes would be able to look up constantly under her dress.)   281 torn broken.   282 some . . . evil i.e., give us some plausible way to put a good face on this difficulty.   284 quillets verbal niceties, subtle distinctions   285 'tis . . . need such a comfort is very needful.   286 Have at you I come at you, i.e., here it is.   Affection's Love's

289 state (1) condition (2) majesty   291 maladies (The Quarto here supplies twenty-two lines that appear to be a first start for lines 292–339; seemingly they were meant to be canceled. See Textual Notes.)   295–7 In . . . with? have found in the dull study of books the inspiration to write passionate verses in the way that the prompting eyes of beauty have tutored you to do?   298 arts branches of knowledge.   keep dwell within   302 immurèd walled up, imprisoned   303 elements i.e., earth, air, fire, and water   304 Courses runs.   power faculty, natural capacity   306 Above . . . offices above and beyond their ordinary functions.   308 gaze stare   310 When . . . stopped even when the most sensitive alertness to the danger of being robbed hears nothing.   311 sensible sensitive   312 cockled having a shell   313 Bacchus god of wine and revelry   314 For as for   315 Hesperides where the golden apples grew (the gaining of which was the eleventh of Hercules's twelve labors)   316 Sphinx mythological creature of ancient Thebes who destroyed all passersby who could not solve her riddle.   317 Apollo's lute (Apollo was the Greek god of music, poetry, and prophecy.)   320 durst dares   321 tempered blended, softened   325 They . . . fire they continually emit the true heavenly fire. (From the legend that Prometheus stole fire from heaven and gave it to humankind.)

Else none at all in aught proves excellent.   328
Then fools you were these women to forswear,
Or, keeping what is sworn, you will prove fools.
For wisdom's sake, a word that all men love,
Or for love's sake, a word that loves all men,   332
Or for men's sake, the authors of these women,   333
Or women's sake, by whom we men are men,   334
Let us once lose our oaths to find ourselves,   335
Or else we lose ourselves to keep our oaths.
It is religion to be thus forsworn,
For charity itself fulfills the law,   338
And who can sever love from charity?

KING
Saint Cupid, then! And, soldiers, to the field!

BEROWNE
Advance your standards, and upon them, lords;   341
Pell-mell, down with them! But first advised   342
In conflict that you get the sun of them.   343

LONGAVILLE
Now to plain dealing. Lay these glozes by.   344
Shall we resolve to woo these girls of France?

KING
And win them, too. Therefore let us devise
Some entertainment for them in their tents.

BEROWNE
First, from the park let us conduct them thither;
Then homeward every man attach the hand   349
Of his fair mistress. In the afternoon
We will with some strange pastime solace them,   351
Such as the shortness of the time can shape;
For revels, dances, masques, and merry hours
Forerun fair Love, strewing her way with flowers.   354

KING
Away, away! No time shall be omitted
That will betime and may by us be fitted.   356

BEROWNE
Allons! Allons! Sowed cockle reaped no corn,   357
And justice always whirls in equal measure.   358
Light wenches may prove plagues to men forsworn;   359
If so, our copper buys no better treasure. [*Exeunt.*]   360

❖

[5.1]

*Enter [Holofernes] the pedant, [Nathaniel] the
curate, and Dull [the constable].*

HOLOFERNES   *Satis quod sufficit.*   1
NATHANIEL   I praise God for you, sir. Your reasons at   2
dinner have been sharp and sententious, pleasant
without scurrility, witty without affection, audacious   4
without impudency, learned without opinion, and   5
strange without heresy. I did converse this quondam   6
day with a companion of the King's who is intituled,   7
nominated, or called Don Adriano de Armado.
HOLOFERNES   *Novi hominem tanquam te.* His humor is   9
lofty, his discourse peremptory, his tongue filed, his   10
eye ambitious, his gait majestical, and his general
behavior vain, ridiculous, and thrasonical. He is too   12
picked, too spruce, too affected, too odd, as it were, too   13
peregrinate, as I may call it.   14
NATHANIEL   A most singular and choice epithet.   15
                     [*He*] draw[*s*] *out his table book.*
HOLOFERNES   He draweth out the thread of his ver-   17
bosity finer than the staple of his argument. I abhor   18
such fanatical phantasimes, such insociable and point-   19
devise companions, such rackers of orthography, as to
speak "dout," fine, when he should say "doubt";   20
"det"when he should pronounce "debt"—d, e, b, t, not
d, e, t. He clepeth a calf "cauf," half "hauf"; neighbor   22
vocatur "nebor"; neigh abbreviated "ne." This is   23
abhominable—which he would call "abbominable." It   24
insinuateth me of insanie. *Ne intelligis, domine?* To   25
make frantic, lunatic.
NATHANIEL   *Laus Deo, bone intelligo.*   27
HOLOFERNES   "Bone?" "Bone" for "bene?" Priscian a little   28
scratched; 'twill serve.   29

5.1. Location: Navarre's park.
1 *Satis quod sufficit* Enough is as good as a feast.   **2 reasons** discussions, discourses   **4 affection** affectation   **5 opinion** arrogance, dogmatism   **6 strange** novel, new.   **this quondam** the other
7 intituled entitled, named   **9** *Novi . . . te* I know the man as well as I know you.   **10 peremptory** positive, overbearing.   **filed** polished
12 thrasonical boastful. (From Thraso, a braggart soldier in Terence's play *Eunuchus.*)   **13 picked** fastidious.   **spruce** dapper   **14 peregrinate** touristy.   **15.1 table book** notebook.   **17 staple** fiber, thread.
argument subject matter   **18 phantasimes** persons who entertain fantastic notions.   **insociable** unsociable, unpleasant   **18–19 such . . .
companions** such unsociable and pedantically precise fellows
19 rackers of orthography torturers of spelling. (Holofernes's tirade reflects a conscious attempt of some Renaissance educators to bring the English spelling and pronunciation of certain borrowed words more nearly to their Latin originals.)   **20 fine** mincingly, too thinly. (Or perhaps an error for "*sine* b," "without b.")   **22 clepeth** calls
23 *vocatur* is called   **24 abhominable . . . abominable** (This is pedantic to the point of being simply wrong, since the supposed derivation of *abhominable* from *abhomine*, away from mankind, inhuman, is a false one, but it is a derivation that Shakespeare seems elsewhere to have accepted.)   **24–5 It . . . insanie** (1) To me it savors of insanity (2) It drives me mad.   **25** *Ne intelligis, domine?* Do you understand me, sir?
27 *Laus . . . intelligo* Praise God, I understand well.   **28 "Bone"
for "bene"** i.e., The Latin should be *bene*, "well."   **28–9 Priscian . . .
scratched** i.e., Your Latin is a little faulty. (Priscian was a grammarian of the fifth or sixth century whose textbooks were considered standard.)

328 Else otherwise.   **aught** anything   **332 loves** is lovable to, inspires with love   **333–4 Or . . . men** (Conventionally, men are the active principle in the creation of human life, while women are the vessels in which all infants are nurtured.)   **335 once** for once, one time.   **lose** break   **338 For . . . law** (From Romans 13:8: "for he that loveth another hath fulfilled the law.")   **341 Advance . . . lords**
Advance your standards, raise high your banners. (The military metaphor is not only amorous but bawdy.)   **342 Pell-mell** without keeping ranks, in hand-to-hand combat.   **be first advised** take care first of all   **343 get . . . them** i.e., take field position so that the sun is in their eyes. (With a play on the idea of "begetting a son.")
344 glozes sophistries   **349 attach** seize   **351 strange** novel, fresh.
solace entertain   **354 Forerun** come before, prepare the way for
356 betime happen.   **fitted** used. (The King resolves to take advantage of every minute.)   **357** *Allons!* Come on, let's go!   **cockle** a weed.   **corn** wheat. (Berowne says that without well-planned efforts there will be no results.)   **358 measure** proportion. (Again suggesting that reward comes only from effort.)   **359 Light** Giddy, teasing
360 copper coin of little value. (Berowne's point is that, as beggars and forswearers, the men cannot afford to be choosers.)

Enter [Armado the] braggart, [Mote, his] boy, [and Costard].

NATHANIEL   *Videsne quis venit?*   30

HOLOFERNES   *Video, et gaudeo.*   31

ARMADO   [*to Mote*]   Chirrah!   32

HOLOFERNES   *Quare* "chirrah," not "sirrah"?   33

ARMADO   Men of peace, well encountered.

HOLOFERNES   Most military sir, salutation.

MOTE   [*aside to Costard*]   They have been at a great feast of languages and stolen the scraps.

COSTARD   [*to Mote*]   Oh, they have lived long on the alms basket of words. I marvel thy master hath not eaten thee for a word, for thou art not so long by the head as *honorificabilitudinitatibus*. Thou art easier swallowed than a flapdragon.   39 40 41 42

MOTE   [*to Costard*]   Peace! The peal begins.   43

ARMADO   [*to Holofernes*]   Monsieur, are you not lettered?   45

MOTE   Yes, yes, he teaches boys the hornbook. What is "a, b" spelled backward, with the horn on his head?   46

HOLOFERNES   Ba, *pueritia*, with a horn added.   48

MOTE   Ba, most silly sheep with a horn! You hear his learning.

HOLOFERNES   *Quis, quis,* thou consonant?   51

MOTE   The last of the five vowels, if you repeat them; or the fifth, if I.   52

HOLOFERNES   I will repeat them: a, e, i—

MOTE   The sheep. The other two concludes it—o, u.   55

ARMADO   Now, by the salt wave of the *Mediterraneum*, a sweet touch, a quick venue of wit! Snip, snap, quick and home. It rejoiceth my intellect. True wit!   57

MOTE   Offered by a child to an old man—which is wit-old.   60

HOLOFERNES   What is the figure? What is the figure?   61

MOTE   Horns.

HOLOFERNES   Thou disputes like an infant. Go whip thy gig.   63 64

MOTE   Lend me your horn to make one, and I will whip about your infamy *manu cita*—a gig of a cuckold's horn.   66

COSTARD   An I had but one penny in the world, thou shouldst have it to buy gingerbread. Hold, there is the very remuneration I had of thy master, thou halfpenny purse of wit, thou pigeon egg of discretion. [*He gives money.*] Oh, an the heavens were so pleased that thou wert but my bastard, what a joyful father wouldst thou make me! Go to, thou hast it *ad dunghill*, at the fingers' ends, as they say.   68 70 71

HOLOFERNES   Oh, I smell false Latin! "Dunghill" for "*unguem*."   77

ARMADO   Arts-man, *preambulate*. We will be singuled from the barbarous. Do you not educate youth at the charge-house on the top of the mountain?   78 80

HOLOFERNES   Or *mons*, the hill.

ARMADO   At your sweet pleasure, for the mountain.

HOLOFERNES   I do, sans question.   83

ARMADO   Sir, it is the King's most sweet pleasure and affection to congratulate the Princess at her pavilion in the posteriors of this day, which the rude multitude call the afternoon.   85 86

HOLOFERNES   The posterior of the day, most generous sir, is liable, congruent, and measurable for the afternoon. The word is well culled, choice, sweet, and apt, I do assure you, sir, I do assure.   88 89 90

ARMADO   Sir, the King is a noble gentleman, and my familiar, I do assure ye, very good friend. For what is inward between us, let it pass. I do beseech thee, remember thy courtesy. I beseech thee, apparel thy head. And, among other importunate and most serious designs, and of great import indeed, too—but let that pass; for I must tell thee it will please His Grace, by the world, sometime to lean upon my poor shoulder and with his royal finger thus dally with my excrement, with my mustachio; but, sweetheart, let that pass. By the world, I recount no fable! Some certain special honors it pleaseth his greatness to impart to Armado, a soldier, a man of travel, that hath seen the world, but let that pass. The very all of all is—but, sweetheart, I do implore secrecy—that the King would have me present the Princess, sweet chuck, with some delightful ostentation, or show, or pageant, or antic, or firework. Now, understanding that the curate and your sweet self are good at such eruptions and sudden   93 94 95 99 101 102 105 107 108 109

---

30 *Videsne quis venit?* Do you see who comes? **31 *Video, et gaudeo*** I see and I rejoice. (This trivial Latin dialogue is after the manner of schoolboys' exercises.) **32 Chirrah!** (A dialectal corruption of the Greek *chaere*, "hail," or merely a dialectal pronunciation of *sirrah*, a term of address to a social inferior.) **33 *Quare*** Why **39 alms basket** a basket used to gather scraps for the poor **40 for a word** (Mote's name puns on the French *mot*, "word.") **40–1 so long . . . head** i.e., as tall **41 *honorificabilitudinitatibus*** (Once considered the longest word in existence. It is the dative or ablative plural of a Latin word meaning something like "honorableness.") **42 flapdragon** the raisin or plum in burning brandy to be snapped with the mouth in the game of snapdragon. **43 peal** i.e., clatter of tongues, like a peal of bells **44–5 lettered** i.e., educated. (Mote replies as though *lettered* meant "able to teach boys their letters.") **46 hornbook** printed sheets of paper, covered by a protective thin layer of horn; used for teaching children their alphabet. (The *horn* sets up a joke on the sheep's or cuckold's horn.) **48 *pueritia*** child **51 *Quis . . . consonant?*** i.e., Who, who, you nonentity? (A consonant cannot be sounded without also sounding the vowels.) **52 last** (An error for *third?*) **55 The sheep** i.e., Holofernes, by saying "i," that is, "I," has labeled himself the sheep. **concludes it** (1) completes the list of the five vowels (2) proves my point. **o, u** i.e., oh, you. **57 venue** sally, thrust. (A fencing term, continued in *quick and home*, to the quick.) **wit** intellect **60 wit-old** mentally feeble. (With a pun on "wittol," a contented cuckold.) **61 figure** metaphor, figure of speech. **63 Thou disputes** You reason **63–4 whip thy gig** spin your spinning-top (as a child might do).

66 *manu cita* with a ready hand **68 An** If **70–1 halfpenny purse** a tiny purse **71 pigeon egg** i.e., tiny object **77 *unguem*** i.e., *ad unguem*, "to the fingernail," perfectly **78 Arts-man . . . singuled** Scholar, walk with me. We will set ourselves apart **80 charge-house** some kind of school **83 sans** without **85 affection to congratulate** desire to greet **86 in the posteriors** at the end. **rude** ignorant **88 generous** cultivated, wellborn **89 liable** apt. **measurable** fitted **90 culled** selected **93 familiar** intimate acquaintance **94 inward** private. **let it pass** never mind about that **95 remember thy courtesy** i.e., remember to use your hat courteously. **99 by the world** (A mild oath.) **101 excrement** outgrowth (of hair). **sweetheart** (A term of endearment, here spoken in friendship.) **102 I . . . fable!** I'm telling the truth! **105 very all of all** sum of everything **107 chuck** chick. (A term of endearment.) **108 ostentation** display. **antic** a pageant or entertainment using fantastic costumes **109 firework** pyrotechnic display.

breaking out of mirth, as it were, I have acquainted
you withal, to the end to crave your assistance. 112

HOLOFERNES   Sir, you shall present before her the Nine 114
Worthies.—Sir Nathaniel, as concerning some enter- 115
tainment of time, some show in the posterior of this
day, to be rendered by our assistance, the King's command, and this most gallant, illustrate, and learned
gentleman, before the Princess—I say none so fit as to 119
present the Nine Worthies.

NATHANIEL   Where will you find men worthy enough
to present them?

HOLOFERNES   Joshua, yourself; myself; and this gallant 123
gentleman, Judas Maccabaeus; this swain, because of 124
his great limb or joint, shall pass Pompey the Great; 125
the page, Hercules— 126

ARMADO   Pardon, sir, error. He is not quantity enough
for that Worthy's thumb. He is not so big as the end of
his club.

HOLOFERNES   Shall I have audience? He shall present 130
Hercules in minority. His enter and exit shall be stran- 131
gling a snake; and I will have an apology for that 132
purpose.

MOTE   An excellent device! So, if any of the audience 134
hiss, you may cry, "Well done, Hercules! Now thou 135
crushest the snake!" That is the way to make an 136
offense gracious, though few have the grace to do it.

ARMADO   For the rest of the Worthies?

HOLOFERNES   I will play three myself.

MOTE   Thrice-worthy gentleman!

ARMADO   Shall I tell you a thing?

HOLOFERNES   We attend. 142

ARMADO   We will have, if this fadge not, an antic. I be- 143
seech you, follow.

HOLOFERNES   *Via*, goodman Dull! Thou hast spoken no 145
word all this while.

DULL   Nor understood none neither, sir.

HOLOFERNES   *Allons!* We will employ thee. 148

DULL
I'll make one in a dance or so, or I will play 149
On the tabor to the Worthies, and let them dance
the hay. 150

HOLOFERNES
Most dull, honest Dull! To our sport, away!

Exeunt.

❧

[5.2]

*Enter the ladies [the Princes, Katharine, Rosaline,
and Maria].*

PRINCESS
Sweethearts, we shall be rich ere we depart,
If fairings come thus plentifully in. 2
A lady walled about with diamonds! 3
Look you what I have from the loving King.
[She shows a jewel.]

ROSALINE
Madam, came nothing else along with that?

PRINCESS
Nothing but this? Yes, as much love in rhyme
As would be crammed up in a sheet of paper,
Writ o'both sides the leaf, margent and all, 8
That he was fain to seal on Cupid's name. 9

ROSALINE
That was the way to make his godhead wax, 10
For he hath been five thousand year a boy. 11

KATHARINE
Ay, and a shrewd unhappy gallows, too. 12

ROSALINE
You'll ne'er be friends with him. 'A killed your sister. 13

KATHARINE
He made her melancholy, sad, and heavy, 14
And so she died. Had she been light, like you, 15
Of such a merry, nimble, stirring spirit,
She might ha' been a grandam ere she died. 17
And so may you, for a light heart lives long.

ROSALINE
What's your dark meaning, mouse, of this light word? 19

KATHARINE
A light condition in a beauty dark. 20

ROSALINE
We need more light to find your meaning out.

KATHARINE
You'll mar the light by taking it in snuff; 22
Therefore I'll darkly end the argument. 23

---

112 **withal** with this   114–15 **Nine Worthies** (A conventional subject
familiar to Shakespeare's audience in poems, pageants, and tapestries. The nine were three pagans, Hector of Troy, Alexander the
Great, and Julius Caesar; three Jews, Joshua, David, and Judas Maccabaeus; and three Christians, Arthur, Charlemagne, and Godfrey of
Boulogne. The list varied, but Shakespeare makes an unusual departure when he introduces Pompey and Hercules.)   119 **gentleman** i.e.,
Armado   123–6 **Joshua . . . Hercules** (The assignment of parts here
and in line 139 does not correspond with the actual casting of parts in
5.3.543 ff. Presumably, changes occur in rehearsal.)   130 **have audience** be heard.   131 **in minority** as a child.   **enter** entrance
131–2 **strangling a snake** (According to legend, Hercules as an infant
displayed his great strength by strangling two serpents sent by the
envious Juno to destroy him in his cradle.)   132 **apology** explanatory
prologue   134–6 **if . . . snake** (Any hissing by the audience can thus
be explained away as the hissing of the snake.)   142 **attend** listen.
143 **if this fadge not** i.e., even if this fails.   **an antic** i.e., a show of
some sort, perhaps of "The Owl and the Cuckoo."   145 **Via** Onward!
(A cry of encouragement to troops.)   148 **Allons!** Let's go!
149 **make one** take part   150 **tabor** small drum.   **the hay** a country
dance

5.2. **Location: Navarre's park. Near the ladies' tents.**
2 **fairings** gifts such as might be bought at a fair   3 **A lady . . . diamonds** (The Princess has evidently received a brooch with a dia-
mond-studded frame enclosing a portrait of a lady.)   8 **margent**
margin   9 **That . . . name** i.e., that there was no room for the wax seal
other than on top of Cupid's name.   10 **to make . . . wax** to make
Cupid increase in years. (With pun on the wax of the seal.)   11 **he
hath . . . boy** i.e., Cupid has remained young ever since the world
began.   12 **shrewd unhappy gallows** wicked, mischievous knave,
deserving to be hanged   13 **'A killed your sister** (A mocking hint of
a story, not developed here, of a young woman who died for love.)
'A He   14 **heavy** depressed   15 **light** (1) merry (2) unchaste
17 **grandam** grandmother   19 **dark** hidden.   **mouse** (A term of
endearment.)   **light word** frivolous speech.   20 **light condition**
wanton temperament   22 **taking . . . snuff** (1) trimming the burning
candlewick (2) taking offense   23 **darkly** obscurely, mysteriously

ROSALINE
Look what you do, you do it still i'the dark.   24
KATHARINE
So do not you, for you are a light wench.
ROSALINE
Indeed I weigh not you, and therefore light.   26
KATHARINE
You weigh me not? Oh, that's you care not for me.   27
ROSALINE
Great reason, for past cure is still past care.   28
PRINCESS
Well bandied both! A set of wit well played.   29
But, Rosaline, you have a favor too.   30
Who sent it? And what is it?
ROSALINE   I would you knew.   31
An if my face were but as fair as yours,   32
My favor were as great. Be witness this.   33
                [She shows a love token.]
Nay, I have verses too, I thank Berowne;
The numbers true, and, were the numbering, too,   35
I were the fairest goddess on the ground.   36
I am compared to twenty thousand fairs.   37
Oh, he hath drawn my picture in his letter!
PRINCESS   Anything like?
ROSALINE
Much in the letters, nothing in the praise.   40
PRINCESS
Beauteous as ink—a good conclusion.   41
KATHARINE
Fair as a text B in a copybook.   42
ROSALINE
Ware pencils, ho! Let me not die your debtor,   43
My red dominical, my golden letter.   44
Oh, that your face were not so full of O's!   45
PRINCESS
A pox of that jest! And I beshrew all shrows.   46
But, Katharine, what was sent to you from fair
    Dumaine?

KATHARINE
Madam, this glove.   [She shows a glove.]
PRINCESS   Did he not send you twain?   48
KATHARINE
Yes; madam, and moreover
Some thousand verses of a faithful lover,
A huge translation of hypocrisy,   51
Vilely compiled, profound simplicity.   52
MARIA [showing a letter and a pearl necklace]
This, and these pearls, to me sent Longaville.
The letter is too long by half a mile.
PRINCESS
I think no less. Dost thou not wish in heart
The chain were longer and the letter short?
MARIA
Ay, or I would these hands might never part.   57
PRINCESS
We are wise girls to mock our lovers so.
ROSALINE
They are worse fools to purchase mocking so.   59
That same Berowne I'll torture ere I go.
Oh, that I knew he were but in by th' week!   61
How I would make him fawn, and beg, and seek,
And wait the season, and observe the times,   63
And spend his prodigal wits in bootless rhymes,   64
And shape his service wholly to my hests,   65
And make him proud to make me proud that jests!   66
So pair-taunt-like would I o'ersway his state   67
That he should be my fool and I his fate.   68
PRINCESS
None are so surely caught when they are catched   69
As wit turned fool. Folly in wisdom hatched   70
Hath wisdom's warrant and the help of school   71
And wit's own grace to grace a learnèd fool.   72
ROSALINE
The blood of youth burns not with such excess
As gravity's revolt to wantonness.   74
MARIA
Folly in fools bears not so strong a note   75
As fool'ry in the wise when wit doth dote,   76
Since all the power thereof it doth apply   77
To prove, by wit, worth in simplicity.   78

    Enter Boyet.

PRINCESS
Here comes Boyet, and mirth is in his face.

24 look what Whatever. do it . . . i'the dark (With obvious sexual meaning.) 26 weigh not you don't weigh as much as you 27 weigh regard seriously. that's that means 28 Great reason With good reason. past cure . . . care what can't be helped shouldn't be worried about. (Proverbial.) Rosaline implies that Katharine is incurable, and puns on care, "have fondness," in line 27. 29 Well bandied both! i.e., Both of you have wittily traded insults. (A tennis term, continued in set.) 30 favor love token 31 would wish 32–3 An . . . this If only my face were as attractive as yours, I might have received as great a gift as love token. Here's the evidence. (Favor here also plays on the meaning "personal appearance.") 35 numbers meter. numbering reckoning 36 were would be 37 fairs beautiful women 40 Much . . . praise The lettering (i.e., handwriting) is recognizable, but the praise is unrecognizable (i.e., excessive). 41 ink (Referring to Rosaline's dark complexion.) 42 a text B (Perhaps a heavily ornamented capital B, for Berowne, boldly dark like Rosaline's complexion.) 43 Ware pencils i.e., Be wary of such drawings or paintings. (Pencils here are fine-tipped brushes.) 43–5 Let . . . O's! (Said to Katharine): I'll get even with you, my fine red-cheeked beauty. Oh, if only your face weren't full of smallpox scars! (Red dominical is red lettering used in calendars to mark Sundays and holy days; from Dies dominica, "the Lord's day." Golden suggests both fair hair and the reddish color of gold.) 46 A pox of i.e., A curse on. (Playing also on the O's or smallpox in Katharine's face.) beshrew all shrows I wish a plague on all shrews or scolds. (The Quarto/Folio spelling of "beshrow all Shrowes" makes plain the rhyme with O's.)

48 twain two. 51 translation expression 52 simplicity silliness. 57 would wish. (Perhaps Maria makes an imploring gesture with her joined hands.) 59 purchase earn, invite 61 in . . . week i.e., caught, trapped permanently. 63 And wait . . . times i.e., and wait until it suits me, follow my schedule 64 bootless fruitless 65 hests behests 66 And . . . jests and make him take satisfaction in glorifying me, the one who mocks him. 67 pair-taunt-like like one holding a winning hand (pair-taunt) in the card game of "post-and-pair." (With a pun on taunt.) 68 his fate the controller of his destiny. 69 surely securely 70–1 Folly . . . fool Folly in a seemingly wise person can have the appearance of wisdom, learning, and graceful wit, all serving to grace one who is only a learned fool. 74 As gravity's revolt as when a wise man turns 75–8 Folly . . . simplicity Folly in a genuine fool is not so remarkable as foolishness in doting wise persons, since in the latter case wit uses all its ingenuity.

BOYET
      Oh, I am stabbed with laughter! Where's Her Grace?

PRINCESS
      Thy news, Boyet?

BOYET   Prepare, madam, prepare!
      Arm, wenches, arm! Encounters mounted are   82
      Against your peace. Love doth approach disguised,
      Armèd in arguments. You'll be surprised.   84
      Muster your wits, stand in your own defense,
      Or hide your heads like cowards and fly hence.

PRINCESS
      Saint Denis to Saint Cupid! What are they   87
      That charge their breath against us? Say, scout, say. 88

BOYET
      Under the cool shade of a sycamore
      I thought to close mine eyes some half an hour,
      When, lo, to interrupt my purposed rest,
      Toward that shade I might behold addressed   92
      The King and his companions. Warily
      I stole into a neighbor thicket by
      And overheard what you shall overhear—   95
      That, by and by, disguised they will be here.
      Their herald is a pretty knavish page
      That well by heart hath conned his embassage.   98
      Action and accent did they teach him there: 99
      "Thus must thou speak," and "thus thy body bear."
      And ever and anon they made a doubt   101
      Presence majestical would put him out;   102
      "For," quoth the King, "an angel shalt thou see;
      Yet fear not thou, but speak audaciously."   104
      The boy replied, "An angel is not evil;
      I should have feared her had she been a devil."
      With that, all laughed and clapped him on the shoulder,
      Making the bold wag by their praises bolder.   108
      One rubbed his elbow thus, and fleered, and swore   109
      A better speech was never spoke before.
      Another, with his finger and his thumb,   111
      Cried, "Via! We will do't, come what will come."   112
      The third he capered and cried, "All goes well!"   113
      The fourth turned on the toe, and down he fell.   114
      With that, they all did tumble on the ground
      With such a zealous laughter, so profound,
      That in this spleen ridiculous appears,   117
      To check their folly, passion's solemn tears.

PRINCESS
      But what, but what? Come they to visit us?

BOYET
      They do, they do, and are appareled thus,
      Like Muscovites or Russians, as I guess.   121
      Their purpose is to parle, to court, and dance;   122
      And everyone his love suit will advance
      Unto his several mistress, which they'll know   124
      By favors several which they did bestow.

PRINCESS
      And will they so? The gallants shall be tasked;   126
      For, ladies, we will every one be masked,
      And not a man of them shall have the grace,
      Despite of suit, to see a lady's face.   129
      Hold, Rosaline, this favor thou shalt wear,
      And then the King will court thee for his dear.
      Hold, take thou this, my sweet, and give me thine. 132
      So shall Berowne take me for Rosaline.   133
            [The Princess and Rosaline exchange favors.]
      And change you favors too. So shall your loves   134
      Woo contrary, deceived by these removes.   135
            [Katharine and Maria exchange favors.]

ROSALINE
      Come on, then, wear the favors most in sight.   136

KATHARINE
      But in this changing what is your intent?

PRINCESS
      The effect of my intent is to cross theirs.   138
      They do it but in mockery merriment,   139
      And mock for mock is only my intent.
      Their several counsels they unbosom shall   141
      To loves mistook, and so be mocked withal   142
      Upon the next occasion that we meet,
      With visages displayed, to talk and greet.   144

ROSALINE
      But shall we dance, if they desire us to't?

PRINCESS
      No, to the death we will not move a foot,   146
      Nor to their penned speech render we no grace,   147
      But while 'tis spoke each turn away her face.

BOYET
      Why, that contempt will kill the speaker's heart
      And quite divorce his memory from his part.

PRINCESS
      Therefore I do it; and I make no doubt
      The rest will ne'er come in, if he be out.   152
      There's no such sport as sport by sport o'erthrown,
      To make theirs ours and ours none but our own.   154

---

82 **Encounters mounted are** Skirmishes or assailants are readied, set in position   84 **surprised** assaulted in a surprise attack.   87 **Saint Denis** patron saint of France.   **to** against   88 **charge their breath** aim their words. (To *charge* is to attack at full gallop or to level, as in aiming a weapon.)   92 **I . . . addressed** I could see approaching   95 **overhear** hear over again   98 **conned his embassage** memorized his message.   99 **Action** Gesture   101 **ever and anon** every now and then.   **made a doubt** expressed a fear (that)   102 **put him out** leave him confused and tongue-tied   104 **audaciously** boldly.   108 **wag** young man   109 **rubbed his elbow** (in a gesture of satisfaction, like rubbing the hands).   **fleered** grinned   111 **with . . . thumb** i.e., snapping his fingers   112 *Via!* Onward!   113 **capered** skipped, danced   114 **turned on the toe** pirouetted   117 **spleen ridiculous** ludicrous fit of laughter

121 **Muscovites or Russians** (Costumes not uncommon in court masquerades.)   **guess** (The unrhymed word suggests a missing line.)   122 **parle** parley   124 **several** respective, particular.   **which** whom   126 **tasked** tried, tested   129 **suit** petition, entreaty. (With a play on "suit of clothes.")   132–3 **Hold . . . Rosaline** (Possibly Shakespeare intended this couplet to replace lines 130–1.)   134 **change** exchange   135 **removes** exchanges.   136 **most in sight** conspicuously.   138 **cross** thwart   139 **mockery** mocking   141–2 **Their . . . mistook** They will disclose their various private intentions to the wrong ladies   144 **With visages displayed** we with our masks removed, showing our faces   146 **to the death** (as in "fight to the death")   147 **penned speech** speech composed and written out with care.   **grace** favor   152 **The rest . . . out** The others will give up if the first speaker forgets his lines.   154 **To . . . own** to make their intended sport into one that is ours and ours alone.

So shall we stay, mocking intended game,
And they, well mocked, depart away with shame.
                                    Sound trumpet [within].
BOYET
  The trumpet sounds. Be masked; the maskers come.   157
                                    [The ladies mask.]

  Enter blackamoors with music; [Mote,] the boy,
  with a speech, and [the King, Berowne, and] the
  rest of the lords disguised [as Russians, and
  visored].

MOTE
  All hail, the richest beauties on the earth!
BEROWNE *[aside]*
  Beauties no richer than rich taffeta.   159
MOTE
  A holy parcel of the fairest dames   160
                      The ladies turn their backs to him
  That ever turned their—backs—to mortal views!
BEROWNE *[prompting Mote]* "Their eyes," villain,
  "their eyes."
MOTE
  That ever turned their eyes to mortal views!
  Out—
BOYET   True; out indeed.   166
MOTE
  Out of your favors, heavenly spirits, vouchsafe   167
  Not to behold—
BEROWNE *[to Mote]* "Once to behold," rogue.
MOTE
  Once to behold with your sun-beamèd eyes—
  With your sun-beamèd eyes—
BOYET
  They will not answer to that epithet.
  You were best call it "daughter-beamèd eyes."   173
MOTE
  They do not mark me, and that brings me out.   174
BEROWNE
  Is this your perfectness? Begone, you rogue!   175
                                    [Exit Mote.]
ROSALINE *[speaking as the Princess]*
  What would these strangers? Know their minds,
    Boyet.
                                                       176
  If they do speak our language, 'tis our will
  That some plain man recount their purposes.   178
  Know what they would.
BOYET   What would you with the Princess?
BEROWNE
  Nothing but peace and gentle visitation.   180

ROSALINE   What would they, say they?
BOYET
  Nothing but peace and gentle visitation.
ROSALINE
  Why, that they have, and bid them so be gone.
BOYET
  She says you have it, and you may be gone.
KING
  Say to her we have measured many miles   185
  To tread a measure with her on this grass.   186
BOYET
  They say that they have measured many a mile
  To tread a measure with you on this grass.
ROSALINE
  It is not so. Ask them how many inches
  Is in one mile. If they have measured many,   190
  The measure then of one is eas'ly told.
BOYET
  If to come hither you have measured miles,
  And many miles, the Princess bids you tell
  How many inches doth fill up one mile.
BEROWNE
  Tell her we measure them by weary steps.
BOYET
  She hears herself.
ROSALINE   How many weary steps,
  Of many weary miles you have o'ergone,
  Are numbered in the travel of one mile?
BEROWNE
  We number nothing that we spend for you.
  Our duty is so rich, so infinite,
  That we may do it still without account.   201
  Vouchsafe to show the sunshine of your face,
  That we, like savages, may worship it.
ROSALINE
  My face is but a moon, and clouded too.   204
KING
  Blessed are clouds, to do as such clouds do!   205
  Vouchsafe, bright moon, and these thy stars, to shine,   206
  Those clouds removed, upon our watery eyne.   207
ROSALINE
  Oh, vain petitioner! Beg a greater matter;
  Thou now requests but moonshine in the water.   209
KING
  Then in our measure do but vouchsafe one change.   210
  Thou bid'st me beg; this begging is not strange.
ROSALINE
  Play, music, then! Nay, you must do it soon.
                                    [Music plays.]
  Not yet? No dance! Thus change I like the moon.

157.2 blackamoors i.e., attendants in blackface   **159 Beauties . . .
taffeta** Handsome women no richer in beauty than their masks or
rich taffeta cloth. (Some editors assign the speech to Boyet.)   **160 parcel** company   **166 out** i.e., having forgotten his lines   **167 Out . . .
vouchsafe** Have the goodness, heavenly spirits, to deign
173 daughter-beamèd (Substituting *daughter* for *sun*, i.e., son.)
174 mark pay attention to   **175 Is . . . perfectness?** Is this your idea of
a perfectly memorized speech?   **176 What . . . minds** What do these
strangers want? Learn their intentions. (Rosaline, masquerading as
the Princess, presides.)   **178 plain** plainspoken   **180 visitation** visit.

185 measured traversed   **186 tread a measure** perform a dance
190 measured (1) traversed (2) taken the measurement of
201 account reckoning.   **204 a moon . . . too** i.e., changeable and soon
clouded over with a frown.   **205 to do . . . do** i.e., to be close to such
heavenly beauty (as the masks are close to the ladies' faces).
206 stars i.e., ladies   **207 clouds** i.e., the masks.   **eyne** eyes.
209 moonshine . . . water i.e., nothing at all, mere foolishness.
(Proverbial.)   **210 Then . . . change** Then deign to dance one dance
with us. (With a play on the idea of the moon's changing.)

KING
　　Will you not dance? How come you thus estranged?　214
ROSALINE
　　You took the moon at full, but now she's changed.
KING
　　Yet still she is the moon, and I the man.　216
　　The music plays; vouchsafe some motion to it.　217
ROSALINE
　　Our ears vouchsafe it.
KING　　　　　　　　　　　But your legs should do it.　218
ROSALINE
　　Since you are strangers and come here by chance,　219
　　We'll not be nice. Take hands. We will not dance.　220
　　　　　　　　　　　　　　[She offers her hand.]
KING
　　Why take we hands, then?
ROSALINE　　　　　　　　　Only to part friends.
　　Curtsy, sweethearts, and so the measure ends.
KING
　　More measure of this measure! Be not nice.　223
ROSALINE
　　We can afford no more at such a price.
KING
　　Price you yourselves. What buys your company?　225
ROSALINE
　　Your absence only.
KING　　　　　　　　　That can never be.
ROSALINE
　　Then cannot we be bought. And so, adieu—
　　Twice to your visor, and half once to you.　228
KING
　　If you deny to dance, let's hold more chat.　229
ROSALINE
　　In private, then.
KING　　　　　　　I am best pleased with that.
　　　　　　　　　　　　　　[They converse apart.]
BEROWNE [to the Princess]
　　Whitehanded mistress, one sweet word with thee.
PRINCESS [speaking as Rosaline]
　　Honey, and milk, and sugar—there is three.　232
BEROWNE
　　Nay, then, two treys, an if you grow so nice—　233
　　Metheglin, wort, and malmsey. Well run, dice!　234
　　There's half a dozen sweets.
PRINCESS　　　　　　　　Seventh sweet, adieu.
　　Since you can cog, I'll play no more with you.　236

BEROWNE
　　One word in secret.
PRINCESS　　　　　　　Let it not be sweet.
BEROWNE
　　Thou grievest my gall.
PRINCESS　　　　　　　Gall! Bitter.
BEROWNE　　　　　　　　　　Therefore meet.　238
　　　　　　　　　　　　　　[They converse apart.]
DUMAINE [to Maria]
　　Will you vouchsafe with me to change a word?　239
MARIA [speaking as Katharine]
　　Name it.
DUMAINE　　Fair lady—
MARIA　　　　　　　Say you so? Fair lord!　240
　　Take that for your "fair lady."
DUMAINE　　　　　　　　　Please it you,
　　As much in private, and I'll bid adieu.
　　　　　　　　　　　　　　[They converse apart.]
KATHARINE [speaking as Maria]
　　What, was your vizard made without a tongue?　243
LONGAVILLE
　　I know the reason, lady, why you ask.
KATHARINE
　　Oh, for your reason! Quickly, sir, I long.
LONGAVILLE
　　You have a double tongue within your mask　246
　　And would afford my speechless vizard half.　247
KATHARINE
　　"Veal," quoth the Dutchman. Is not "veal" a calf?　248
LONGAVILLE
　　A calf, fair lady!
KATHARINE　　　　　No, a fair lord calf.
LONGAVILLE
　　Let's part the word.
KATHARINE　　　　　　No, I'll not be your half.　250
　　Take all and wean it; it may prove an ox.　251
LONGAVILLE
　　Look how you butt yourself in these sharp mocks!　252
　　Will you give horns, chaste lady? Do not so.
KATHARINE
　　Then die a calf, before your horns do grow.
LONGAVILLE
　　One word in private with you, ere I die.

214 How . . . estranged? Why are you disaffected?　216 man i.e., man in the moon. (This unrhymed word suggests a missing line.)
217 vouchsafe some motion deign to dance　218 Our . . . it i.e., I deign to hear your *motion* or proposal. (Rosaline pretends not to understand an invitation to dance.)　219 strangers foreigners
220 nice coy.　223 More . . . nice i.e., We wish more quantity of dancing. Don't be coy.　225 Price you yourselves Set your own price on yourselves.　228 Twice . . . you (Rosaline, posing as the Princess, saucily offers more curtsies to the King's visor than to the person behind the mask.)　229 deny refuse　232 Honey . . . sugar (These are words of sweetness, appropriate to women.)　233–4 Nay . . . dice! i.e., Let me counter with three words of my own—words for a spiced drink made from herbs and honey, a sweet unfermented beer, and a strong sweet wine (words that are characteristically masculine). Such is my gambit, my throw of the dice.　236 cog deceive

238 Thou . . . gall i.e., You distress me. (Gall is bile, a bitter secretion of the liver.)　Therefore meet i.e., Then let us converse.　239 vouchsafe . . . word deign to speak with me. (*Change* means "exchange.")
240 Say . . . lord (Maria mischievously takes Dumaine's request for a *word* literally and so cuts off his reply at "Fair lady.")　243 What . . . tongue? i.e., Cat got your tongue?　246–7 You . . . half i.e., You speak with a duplicitous tongue and thus can talk enough for the two of us. (The speech may refer also to a leather "tongue" inside some masks, held in the mouth to keep the mask in place.)　248 Veal i.e., as a Dutchman would pronounce "well." (With a possible pun on *veil*, mask, as well as *veal*, calf; also, in lines 245 and 248, Katharine punningly pronounces Longaville's name—*long veal*—and implies that he is a calf or dunce.)　250 Let's part the word i.e., Let's reach a compromise. (But Katharine wittily insists on the literal meaning; he must take all the word *calf* to himself.)　your half (1) sharer with you of two halves (2) your partner in marriage.　251 wean i.e., raise.　ox (A type of stupidity.)　252 butt injure. (With play on *give horns* in the next line, meaning both to butt with horns and to make a cuckold.)

KATHARINE
    Bleat softly then. The butcher hears you cry.
                         [*They converse apart.*]
BOYET
    The tongues of mocking wenches are as keen
      As is the razor's edge invisible;
    Cutting a smaller hair than may be seen;
    Above the sense of sense, so sensible   260
    Seemeth their conference. Their conceits have wings 261
    Fleeter than arrows, bullets, wind, thought, swifter
      things.
ROSALINE
    Not one word more, my maids. Break off, break off!
          [*The ladies break away from the gentlemen.*]
BEROWNE
    By heaven, all dry-beaten with pure scoff!   264
KING
    Farewell, mad wenches. You have simple wits.
       Exeunt [*King, lords, and blackamoors. The ladies*
                              unmask.]
PRINCESS
    Twenty adieus, my frozen Muscovits.
    Are these the breed of wits so wondered at?
BOYET
        Tapers they are, with your sweet breaths puffed
      out.   268
ROSALINE
    Well-liking wits they have; gross, gross; fat, fat. 269
PRINCESS
    Oh, poverty in wit, kingly-poor flout!   270
    Will they not, think you, hang themselves tonight?
    Or ever but in vizards show their faces?
    This pert Berowne was out of count'nance quite. 273
ROSALINE
    They were all in lamentable cases!   274
    The King was weeping-ripe for a good word.   275
PRINCESS
    Berowne did swear himself out of all suit.   276
MARIA
    Dumaine was at my service, and his sword.
    "*Non point,*" quoth I. My servant straight was
      mute.   278
KATHARINE
    Lord Longaville said I came o'er his heart;
    And trow you what he called me?
PRINCESS
                         Qualm, perhaps. 280

KATHARINE
    Yes, in good faith.
PRINCESS   Go, sickness as thou art!
ROSALINE
    Well, better wits have worn plain statute-caps. 282
    But will you hear? The King is my love sworn.
PRINCESS
    And quick Berowne hath plighted faith to me. 284
KATHARINE
    And Longaville was for my service born.
MARIA
    Dumaine is mine, as sure as bark on tree.   286
BOYET
    Madam, and pretty mistresses, give ear: 287
    Immediately they will again be here
    In their own shapes, for it can never be   289
    They will digest this harsh indignity.   290
PRINCESS
    Will they return?
BOYET   They will, they will, God knows,
    And leap for joy, though they are lame with blows.
    Therefore change favors, and when they repair, 293
    Blow like sweet roses in this summer air.   294
PRINCESS
    How "blow"? How "blow"? Speak to be understood.
BOYET
    Fair ladies masked are roses in their bud;
    Dismasked, their damask sweet commixture shown, 297
    Are angels vailing clouds, or roses blown.   298
PRINCESS
    Avaunt, perplexity!—What shall we do   299
    If they return in their own shapes to woo?
ROSALINE
    Good madam, if by me you'll be advised,
    Let's mock them still, as well known as disguised. 302
    Let us complain to them what fools were here,
    Disguised like Muscovites in shapeless gear,   304
    And wonder what they were, and to what end
    Their shallow shows and prologue vilely penned
    And their rough carriage so ridiculous   307
    Should be presented at our tent to us.
BOYET
    Ladies, withdraw. The gallants are at hand.
PRINCESS
    Whip to our tents, as roes run o'er land.   310
      Exeunt [*Princess, Rosaline, Katharine, and Maria*].

260–1 Above . . . conference The pert talk of women seems so quick-witted as to be beyond the reach of normal sense. **261 conceits** fancies **264 dry-beaten** beaten soundly without blood drawn **268 Tapers . . . out** They are like candles puffed out with your sweet breaths. **269 Well-liking . . . fat** Their wits are amiable but gross. **270 Oh . . . flout** i.e., Their wits and floutings are paradoxically both kinglike and poor. **273 out of count'nance** flustered, embarrassed. (With a play on the literal meaning, "without a face," i.e., masked.) **274 cases** (1) situations (2) masks. **275 weeping-ripe** ready to weep. **good** kind **276 out of all suit** excessively and to no avail. (With a play on the idea of "costume.") **278 Non point** Not at all. (Quibbling also on the *point* of his sword. See the note on 2.1.190.) **servant** servant in love, admirer. **straight** immediately **280 trow you** would you believe. **Qualm** i.e., Heartburn. (With a play perhaps on *came*, line 279, as suggested by Elizabethan pronunciation.)

282 better . . . statute-caps i.e., one could find better wits even among London apprentices (who were required by statute to wear identifiable caps). **284 plighted faith** pledged his love **286 sure** firmly united **287 give ear** listen **289 In their own shapes** i.e., having put off their disguises **290 digest** stomach, put up with **293 change favors** i.e., return the love tokens to their original owners. **repair** return **294 Blow** bloom. (But the Princess wonders if *blow* might mean to give *blows*, as in line 292.) **297–8 Dismasked . . . blown** unmasked, with their sweet mingling of red and white complexion shown to view, they are angels trailing clouds (of glory) or fully blooming roses. **299 Avaunt, perplexity!** i.e., Away, you tease! **302 as . . . disguised.** in their familiar appearances just as previously in their disguises. **304 shapeless gear** unshapely apparel **307 rough carriage** awkward bearing **310 Whip** Move quickly. **roes** female or roe deer. (With a pun on a *rose* sending out runners.)

Enter the King and the rest [Berowne, Longaville, and Dumaine, in their proper dress].

KING
Fair sir, God save you! Where's the Princess?
BOYET
Gone to her tent. Please it Your Majesty
Command me any service to her thither?   313
KING
That she vouchsafe me audience for one word.
BOYET
I will, and so will she, I know, my lord.   *Exit.*
BEROWNE
This fellow pecks up wit as pigeons pease,
And utters it again when God doth please.   317
He is wit's peddler, and retails his wares
At wakes and wassails, meetings, markets, fairs;   319
And we that sell by gross, the Lord doth know,   320
Have not the grace to grace it with such show.   321
This gallant pins the wenches on his sleeve.   322
Had he been Adam, he had tempted Eve.   323
'A can carve too, and lisp. Why, this is he   324
That kissed his hand away in courtesy.   325
This is the ape of form, Monsieur the Nice,   326
That, when he plays at tables, chides the dice   327
In honorable terms. Nay, he can sing   328
A mean most meanly; and in ushering   329
Mend him who can. The ladies call him sweet.   330
The stairs, as he treads on them, kiss his feet.
This is the flower that smiles on everyone,
To show his teeth as white as whale's bone;
And consciences that will not die in debt
Pay him the due of "honey-tongued Boyet."
KING
A blister on his sweet tongue, with my heart,
That put Armado's page out of his part!   337

Enter the ladies [wearing their original favors, with Boyet].

BEROWNE
See where it comes! Behavior, what wert thou   338
Till this madman showed thee? And what art thou
    now?   339
KING
All hail, sweet madam, and fair time of day!

PRINCESS
"Fair" in "all hail" is foul, as I conceive.   341
KING
Construe my speeches better, if you may.   342
PRINCESS
Then wish me better. I will give you leave.   343
KING
We came to visit you, and purpose now   344
    To lead you to our court. Vouchsafe it, then.   345
PRINCESS
This field shall hold me, and so hold your vow.   346
    Nor God nor I delights in perjured men.   347
KING
Rebuke me not for that which you provoke.   348
    The virtue of your eye must break my oath.   349
PRINCESS
You nickname virtue. "Vice," you should have
    spoke,   350
    For virtue's office never breaks men's troth.   351
Now by my maiden honor, yet as pure   352
    As the unsullied lily, I protest,
A world of torments though I should endure,
    I would not yield to be your house's guest,
So much I hate a breaking cause to be   356
Of heavenly oaths, vowed with integrity.
KING
Oh, you have lived in desolation here,
    Unseen, unvisited, much to our shame.
PRINCESS
Not so, my lord. It is not so, I swear.
    We have had pastimes here and pleasant game:
A mess of Russians left us but of late.   362
KING
    How, madam? Russians?
PRINCESS   Ay, in truth, my lord.
Trim gallants, full of courtship and of state.   364
ROSALINE
    Madam, speak true.—It is not so, my lord.
My lady, to the manner of the days,   366
In courtesy gives undeserving praise.
We four indeed confronted were with four
In Russian habit. Here they stayed an hour
And talked apace; and in that hour, my lord,   370
They did not bless us with one happy word.   371
I dare not call them fools; but this I think,

---

313 **Command . . . thither?** Do you wish me to take any message to her there?   317 **utters** (1) speaks (2) peddles.   **when . . . please** i.e., on any occasion.   319 **wakes and wassails** festivals and revels   320–1 **And . . . show** i.e., and even we who deal wholesale in wit are unable to deliver it with such gracefulness as he.   322 **This . . . sleeve** i.e., This dashing fellow is quite a ladies' man, wearing their favors on his garments.   323 **had** would have   324–5 **'A . . . courtesy** i.e., He can woo courteously, too, and speak with courtly affectation. He kisses his hand so often he might wear it away.   326 **ape of form** imitator of courtly manners.   **Nice** Fastidious   327 **tables** backgammon   328–30 **Nay . . . who can** He can sing the tenor part well enough, and, as for fulfilling the role of gentleman-usher, let anyone who would like to do better just try.   337 **That . . . part** that caused Mote to forget his lines.   338 **it** i.e., Boyet.   **Behavior** i.e., Elegant manners   339 **Till . . . now?** i.e., till this madcap (Boyet) showed just how elegant manners can be? And see to what a state of art courtly manners have arrived!

341 **all hail** (The Princess deliberately misconstrues the King to have referred to a hailstorm, foul weather.)   **conceive** understand the matter.   342 **Construe** Interpret   343 **Then . . . leave** i.e., In that case you must greet me better. I will give you permission to try again.   344 **purpose** intend   345 **Vouchsafe it** Consent to it   346 **This . . . vow** i.e., I will stay right here; that way you can still hold true on your vow (not to admit women).   347 **Nor** Neither   348 **Rebuke . . . provoke** Don't blame me for something which you started (by your enchanting eye).   349 **virtue** power. (But the Princess, in the next line, insists on interpreting the word as "moral goodness," the opposite of "vice.")   350 **nickname** misname, mention in error   351 **office** action.   **troth** faith.   352 **yet** still   356 **a breaking . . . to be** to be the cause of your breaking   362 **mess** foursome   364 **Trim** Spruce, neatly got up.   **courtship** courtliness   366 **to . . . days** in the fashion of the time   370 **talked apace** spoke rapidly, i.e., chattered   371 **happy** felicitous

When they are thirsty, fools would fain have drink.   373

BEROWNE

This jest is dry to me. Gentle sweet,   374
Your wits makes wise things foolish. When we greet,   375
With eyes' best seeing, heaven's fiery eye,   376
By light we lose light. Your capacity   377
Is of that nature that to your huge store   378
Wise things seem foolish and rich things but poor.   379

ROSALINE

This proves you wise and rich, for in my eye—   380

BEROWNE

I am a fool, and full of poverty.   381

ROSALINE

But that you take what doth to you belong,   382
It were a fault to snatch words from my tongue.   383

BEROWNE

Oh, I am yours, and all that I possess!

ROSALINE

All the fool mine?

BEROWNE   I cannot give you less.

ROSALINE

Which of the vizards was it that you wore?   386

BEROWNE

Where? When? What vizard? Why demand you this?   387

ROSALINE

There, then, that vizard, that superfluous case   388
That hid the worse and showed the better face.

KING [*aside to his lords*]

We were described. They'll mock us now downright.   390

DUMAINE [*aside to the lords*]

Let us confess and turn it to a jest.

PRINCESS

Amazed, my lord? Why looks Your Highness sad?   392

ROSALINE

Help, hold his brows! He'll swoon! Why look you
   pale?   393
Seasick, I think, coming from Muscovy.

BEROWNE

Thus pour the stars down plagues for perjury.
   Can any face of brass hold longer out?   396
Here stand I, lady. Dart thy skill at me.   397
   Bruise me with scorn, confound me with a flout,   398
Thrust thy sharp wit quite through my ignorance,
Cut me to pieces with thy keen conceit,
And I will wish thee nevermore to dance,   401
   Nor nevermore in Russian habit wait.   402

Oh, never will I trust to speeches penned,
   Nor to the motion of a schoolboy's tongue,
Nor never come in vizard to my friend,   405
   Nor woo in rhyme, like a blind harper's song!   406
Taffeta phrases, silken terms precise,   407
   Three-piled hyperboles, spruce affectation,   408
Figures pedantical—these summer flies   409
   Have blown me full of maggot ostentation.   410
I do forswear them, and I here protest,
   By this white glove—how white the hand, God
     knows!—
Henceforth my wooing mind shall be expressed
   In russet yeas and honest kersey noes.   414
And to begin, wench—so God help me, law!—   415
My love to thee is sound, sans crack or flaw.   416

ROSALINE

Sans "sans," I pray you.

BEROWNE   Yet I have a trick   417
Of the old rage. Bear with me, I am sick;   418
I'll leave it by degrees. Soft, let us see:
Write "Lord have mercy on us" on those three.   420
They are infected; in their hearts it lies;
They have the plague, and caught it of your eyes.   422
These lords are visited; you are not free,   423
For the Lord's tokens on you do I see.   424

PRINCESS

No, they are free that gave these tokens to us.   425

BEROWNE

Our states are forfeit. Seek not to undo us.   426

ROSALINE

It is not so, for how can this be true,   427
That you stand forfeit, being those that sue?   428

BEROWNE

Peace! For I will not have to do with you.   429

ROSALINE

Nor shall not, if I do as I intend.

BEROWNE [*to the other lords*]

Speak for yourselves. My wit is at an end.

KING

Teach us, sweet madam, for our rude transgression
Some fair excuse.

PRINCESS   The fairest is confession.
Were not you here but even now disguised?   434

---

373 When . . . drink i.e., the gentlemen are indistinguishable from fools.   **374 dry** stupid, dull. (Playing on *thirsty* in line 373.) **375–9 Your . . . poor** You wittily invert wisdom into folly. When we human beings look directly at the sun, we blind ourselves by too much light. You, like the sun, are of such godlike capacity that, in comparison to your huge store of wisdom, ordinary sagacity seems foolish and normal supplies of intelligence seem inadequate. **380–1 This . . . poverty** (Paradoxically, the beginning of true wisdom is to know that one is an unknowing fool.)   **382–3 But . . . tongue** If you weren't so right to acknowledge folly in yourself, it would be impolite of you to anticipate what I was about to say.   **386 vizards** masks   **387 demand** ask   **388 case** covering, mask.   **390 descried** discovered.   **392 Amazed** Bewildered   **393 brows** forehead.   **396 face of brass** brazen manner   **397 Dart thy skill** Shoot your verbal dexterity   **398 confound** overthrow.   **flout** jeer, insult   **401 wish** entreat   **402 habit** dress.   **wait** be in attendance

405 friend sweetheart   **406 harper's** minstrel's   **407 precise** fastidious   **408 Three-piled** deep-piled, as in costly velvet.   **spruce** fashionable   **409 Figures** figures of speech   **410 blown me** filled me with maggot eggs, made me foul.   **ostentation** pretension, vanity. **414 russet** simple homespun, russet brown in color.   **kersey** plain woolen cloth   **415 law** lo, indeed   **416 sans** without. (But, as Rosaline points out in the next line, he is still using French expressions.) **417 Yet** Still.   **trick** trace   **418 rage** fever.   **420 Lord . . . us** (Sign posted on houses containing the infectious plague within.)   **those three** i.e., his companions.   **422 of** from   **423 visited** infested by the plague.   **free** free of infection. (But the Princess also quibbles on the meaning "generous with gifts.")   **424 the Lord's tokens** (1) plague sores as visible signs of infection (2) the love tokens given by the lords, *the lords' tokens*   **425 free** i.e., generous, openhanded. (Playing on *free*, plague-free, in line 423.)   **426 Our . . . us** i.e., We are at your mercy. Do not ruin us. (Berowne introduces a legal metaphor that Rosaline pursues in lines 427–8.)   **427–8 It . . . sue?** How can you be legally in danger of forfeiture, being the plaintiffs who bring suit? (With a pun on *sue*, woo.)   **429 have** have anything   **434 but even now** a short while ago

KING
Madam, I was.

PRINCESS   And were you well advised?   435

KING
I was, fair madam.

PRINCESS   When you then were here,
What did you whisper in your lady's ear?

KING
That more than all the world I did respect her.   438

PRINCESS
When she shall challenge this, you will reject her.

KING
Upon mine honor, no.

PRINCESS   Peace, peace! Forbear.
Your oath once broke, you force not to forswear.   441

KING
Despise me when I break this oath of mine.

PRINCESS
I will, and therefore keep it.—Rosaline,
What did the Russian whisper in your ear?

ROSALINE
Madam, he swore that he did hold me dear
As precious eyesight, and did value me
Above this world, adding thereto moreover
That he would wed me or else die my lover.

PRINCESS
God give thee joy of him! The noble lord
Most honorably doth uphold his word.

KING
What mean you, madam? By my life, my troth,
I never swore this lady such an oath.

ROSALINE
By heaven, you did. And to confirm it plain,
You gave me this. But take it, sir, again.
                    [She offers him the Princess's favor.]

KING
My faith and this the Princess I did give.
I knew her by this jewel on her sleeve.

PRINCESS
Pardon me, sir, this jewel did she wear,
And Lord Berowne, I thank him, is my dear.
[To Berowne] What, will you have me, or your pearl
    again?   [She offers Rosaline's favor.]

BEROWNE
Neither of either. I remit both twain.   460
I see the trick on't: here was a consent,   461
Knowing aforehand of our merriment,
To dash it like a Christmas comedy.   463
Some carry-tale, some please-man, some slight zany,   464
Some mumble-news, some trencher-knight, some
    Dick,   465
That smiles his cheek in years and knows the trick   466

To make my lady laugh when she's disposed,   467
Told our intents before; which once disclosed,
The ladies did change favors, and then we,   469
Following the signs, wooed but the sign of she.   470
Now, to our perjury to add more terror,
We are again forsworn, in will and error.
Much upon this 'tis. [To Boyet] And might not you   473
Forestall our sport, to make us thus untrue?
Do not you know my lady's foot by th' squier,   475
    And laugh upon the apple of her eye?   476
And stand between her back, sir, and the fire,   477
    Holding a trencher, jesting merrily?   478
You put our page out. Go, you are allowed;   479
Die when you will, a smock shall be your shroud.   480
You leer upon me, do you? There's an eye   481
Wounds like a leaden sword.

BOYET   Full merrily   482
Hath this brave manage, this career, been run.   483

BEROWNE
Lo, he is tilting straight! Peace, I have done.   484

            Enter [Costard the] clown.

Welcome, pure wit! Thou part'st a fair fray.   485

COSTARD
Oh, Lord, sir, they would know
Whether the three Worthies shall come in or no.

BEROWNE
What, are there but three?

COSTARD   No, sir, but it is vara fine,   488
For every one pursents three.

BEROWNE   And three times thrice is nine.

COSTARD
Not so, sir, under correction, sir, I hope it is not so.   490
You cannot beg us, sir, I can assure you, sir; we
    know what we know.   491
I hope, sir, three times thrice, sir—

BEROWNE   Is not nine?

COSTARD   Under correction, sir, we know whereuntil it   493
doth amount.

BEROWNE   By Jove, I always took three threes for nine.

COSTARD   Oh, Lord, sir, it were pity you should get your   496
living by reckoning, sir.   497

---

435 And . . . advised? And did you know what you were doing?
438 respect value, regard   **441 force not** have no hesitation
460 either the two.   **remit both twain** give up both of them.
461 on't of it.   **consent** agreement, plot   **463 dash** shatter
464–5 Some . . . Dick Some gossipmonger, some flatterer, some
pitiable clown, some prattler, some huge feeder, some very ordinary
person (as in "Tom, Dick, and Harry." A *trencher* is a wooden dish.)
466 That . . . years i.e., who smiles ingratiatingly so hard that he puts
wrinkles of seeming age into his face

467 disposed i.e., disposed to be merry(?)   **469 change** exchange
470 wooed . . . she wooed the mere outward appearance of what we
took to be our own sweethearts.   **473 Much . . . 'tis** i.e., It must have
happened much this way.   **475–6 Do not . . . eye?** i.e., Don't you
know how to suit Rosaline's fancy, and know how to keep her amused
by wittily catching her eye? (*Squier*, rhyming with *fire* in line 477,
means "square," carpenter's rule; Boyet should know the length of her
foot. *Apple* means "pupil of the eye.")   **477–8 And . . . merrily?** And
stand near her at the fire, at her back, ready to offer her refreshment
(in a *trencher*, or wooden dish) and to amuse her?   **479 you are
allowed** i.e., you are an allowed fool, free to make jests   **480 Die . . .
shroud** i.e., You are such a ladies' man, so obsequious in attending on
them, that you'll be buried with a petticoat as your shroud.
481–2 There's . . . sword i.e., Your disapproving glance is about as
threatening to me as a sword of lead.   **482–3 Full . . . run** i.e., What a
fine horseback maneuver and gallop you just executed with your wit!
(Said sardonically.)   **484 Lo . . . straight!** i.e., There he goes, tilting at
me again with a quip!   **485 Thou . . . fray** You interrupt a fine battle.
488 vara very   **490 under** subject to   **491 beg us** i.e., take us for fools,
take us for granted   **493 whereuntil** to what   **496–7 it . . . reckoning**
it would be a shame if you had to earn your living by doing sums

BEROWNE   How much is it?

COSTARD   Oh, Lord, sir, the parties themselves, the actors,
sir, will show whereuntil it doth amount. For mine
own part, I am, as they say, but to parfect one man in   501
one poor man—Pompion the Great, sir.   502

BEROWNE   Art thou one of the Worthies?

COSTARD   It pleased them to think me worthy of
Pompey the Great. For mine own part, I know not the
degree of the Worthy, but I am to stand for him.   506

BEROWNE   Go bid them prepare.

COSTARD
We will turn it finely off, sir. We will take some care.   508
                                                    Exit.

KING
Berowne, they will shame us. Let them not approach.

BEROWNE
We are shame-proof, my lord; and 'tis some policy   510
To have one show worse than the King's and his
company.

KING   I say they shall not come.

PRINCESS
Nay, my good lord, let me o'errule you now.
That sport best pleases that doth least know how,
Where zeal strives to content, and the contents   515
Dies in the zeal of that which it presents.   516
Their form confounded makes most form in mirth,   517
When great things laboring perish in their birth.   518

BEROWNE   [to the King]
A right description of our sport, my lord.   519

        Enter [Armado the] braggart.

ARMADO   [to the King]   Anointed, I implore so much   520
expense of thy royal sweet breath as will utter a
brace of words.   [He delivers the king a paper.]   522

PRINCESS   [to Berowne]   Doth this man serve God?

BEROWNE   Why ask you?

PRINCESS   'A speaks not like a man of God his making.   525

ARMADO   That is all one, my fair, sweet, honey monarch,
for, I protest, the schoolmaster is exceeding fantastical,
too, too vain, too, too vain; but we will put it, as they
say, to fortuna de la guerra. I wish you the peace of   529
mind, most royal couplement!   Exit.   530

KING   [consulting the paper]   Here is like to be a good pres-   531
ence of Worthies. He presents Hector of Troy, the swain
Pompey the Great, the parish curate Alexander, Armado's page Hercules, the pedant Judas Maccabaeus;   534
And if these four Worthies in their first show thrive,
These four will change habits and present the other   536
five.

BEROWNE
There is five in the first show.   537

KING
You are deceived. 'Tis not so.   538

BEROWNE
The pedant, the braggart, the hedge-priest, the fool,
and the boy.   539
Abate throw at novum, and the whole world again   540
Cannot pick out five such, take each one in his vein.   541

KING
The ship is under sail, and here she comes amain.   542

        Enter [Costard, as] Pompey.

COSTARD
"I Pompey am—"

BEROWNE   You lie; you are not he.

COSTARD
"I Pompey am—"

BOYET   With leopard's head on knee.   544

BEROWNE
Well said, old mocker. I must needs be friends with
thee.   545

COSTARD
"I Pompey am, Pompey surnamed the Big—"

DUMAINE   "The Great."

COSTARD
It is "Great," sir.—"Pompey surnamed the Great,
That oft in field, with targe and shield, did make
my foe to sweat.   549
And traveling along this coast, I here am come by
chance,
And lay my arms before the legs of this sweet lass of
France."   [He lays down his weapons.]
If Your Ladyship would say "Thanks, Pompey," I had
done.

PRINCESS   Great thanks, great Pompey.

COSTARD   'Tis not so much worth; but I hope I was per-   555
fect. I made a little fault in "Great."   556

BEROWNE   My hat to a halfpenny Pompey proves the   557
best Worthy.   [Costard stands aside.]   558

        Enter [Nathaniel the] curate, for Alexander.

NATHANIEL
"When in the world I lived, I was the world's
commander;
By east, west, north, and south, I spread my
conquering might.
My scutcheon plain declares that I am Alisander—"   561

---

501 parfect (He means "perform," "present.")   502 Pompion Pumpkin. (Malapropism for Pompey.)   506 degree rank.   stand for represent, play   508 turn . . . off perform it well   510 some policy a
shrewd stratagem   515–16 and the . . . presents and the (feeble) substance of what they perform is obscured by the zeal of the presentation.   517 Their . . . mirth i.e., Their confusion as performers will
provide mirth for us   518 laboring striving to be born   519 right
apt.   our sport i.e., our appearance as Muscovites   520 Anointed
i.e., King   522 brace pair   525 God his God's   529 fortuna . . .
guerra the fortune of war.   530 couplement couple.   531 like likely.
presence assembly   534 pedant schoolmaster   536 habits costumes

537 five (Berowne corrects "These four" in lines 536–7 to five, since
Armado's paper has named five.)   538 You . . . so (The King's point
is that only four will have to change costumes.)   539 hedge-priest
illiterate, rural priest   540 Abate . . . novum Set aside a lucky throw
of the dice in the game of novum or nines—a game that has five and
nine as its principal throws. (With a joke on the business of offering
nine characters with just five actors.)   541 take . . . vein character by
character.   542 amain with full force.   544 leopard's head (A part of
Pompey's ridiculous coat of arms or costume.)   545 I . . . thee Let's
be friends. (Berowne is prepared to forget his quarrel with Boyet; they
join forces, now mocking the pageant.)   549 targe shield   555–6 I . . .
perfect I hope I recited correctly.   557 My hat to I'll wager my hat
against   558.1 for as. (Also at 583.2.)   561 scutcheon coat of arms

BOYET
   Your nose says, no, you are not; for it stands too
      right.   562
BEROWNE   [to Boyet]
   Your nose smells "no" in this, most tender-smelling
      knight.   563
PRINCESS
   The conqueror is dismayed. Proceed, good Alexander.
NATHANIEL
   "When in the world I lived, I was the world's
      commander—"
BOYET
   Most true; 'tis right. You were so, Alisander.
BEROWNE   [to Costard]   Pompey the Great—
COSTARD   Your servant, and Costard.   568
BEROWNE   Take away the conqueror. Take away Alis-
   ander.
   COSTARD   [to Nathaniel]   Oh, sir, you have overthrown
   Alisander the conqueror! You will be scraped out of   572
   the painted cloth for this. Your lion, that holds his   573
   poleax sitting on a closestool, will be given to Ajax; he   574
   will be the ninth Worthy. A conqueror, and afeard to
   speak? Run away for shame, Alisander.
                                          [Exit Nathaniel.]
   There, an't shall please you, a foolish mild man, an   577
   honest man, look you, and soon dashed. He is a mar-   578
   velous good neighbor, faith, and a very good bowler.
   But, for Alisander—alas, you see how 'tis—a, little
   o'erparted. But there are Worthies a-coming will speak   581
   their mind in some other sort.   582
   PRINCESS   Stand aside, good Pompey.
                                    [Costard stands aside.]

   Enter [Holofernes the] pedant, for Judas, and
   [Mote] the boy, for Hercules.

HOLOFERNES   [as presenter]
   "Great Hercules is presented by this imp,   584
      Whose club killed Cerberus, that three-headed
         canus;   585
   And when he was a babe, a child, a shrimp,
      Thus did he strangle serpents in his manus.   587
   Quoniam he seemeth in minority,   588
   Ergo I come with this apology."   589

[To Mote] Keep some state in thy exit, and vanish.   590
                                          Exit Boy.
[As Judas] "Judas I am—"
DUMAINE   A Judas!   592
HOLOFERNES   Not Iscariot, sir.
   "Judas I am, yclept Maccabaeus."   594
DUMAINE   Judas Maccabaeus clipped is plain Judas.   595
BEROWNE   A kissing traitor. How art thou proved Judas?   596
HOLOFERNES   "Judas I am—"
DUMAINE   The more shame for you, Judas.
HOLOFERNES   What mean you, sir?
BOYET   To make Judas hang himself.
HOLOFERNES   Begin, sir. You are my elder.   601
BEROWNE   Well followed. Judas was hanged on an elder.   602
HOLOFERNES   I will not be put out of countenance.   603
BEROWNE   Because thou hast no face.   604
HOLOFERNES   [pointing to his own face]   What is this?
BOYET   A citternhead.   606
DUMAINE   The head of a bodkin.   607
BEROWNE   A death's face in a ring.   608
LONGAVILLE   The face of an old Roman coin, scarce   609
   seen.   610
BOYET   The pommel of Caesar's falchion.   611
DUMAINE   The carved-bone face on a flask.   612
BEROWNE   Saint George's half-cheek in a brooch.   613
DUMAINE   Ay, and in a brooch of lead.   614
BEROWNE   Ay, and worn in the cap of a tooth drawer.   615
   And now forward, for we have put thee in counte-   616
   nance.   617
HOLOFERNES   You have put me out of countenance.   618
BEROWNE   False. We have given thee faces.
HOLOFERNES   But you have outfaced them all.   620
BEROWNE
   An thou wert a lion, we would do so.   621

---

562 **right** straight. (Alexander was supposed to have had a wry neck that twisted his head to one side.)   563 **Your . . . this** (Alexander was reputed to have a body odor of "marvelous good savor," according to Plutarch, as translated by Thomas North.)   **tender-smelling** sensitive to smells   568 **Your . . . Costard** Costard, at your service. 572–3 **You will . . . for this** (The Nine Worthies were frequently depicted in tapestry.)   573–4 **Your lion . . . closestool** (A Renaissance memorial emblem of Alexander described a lion sitting on a throne, holding a battle-ax. Costard here substitutes a *closestool,* or privy, for the throne.)   574 **Ajax** legendary Greek chieftain at the Trojan War who coveted the slain Achilles's armor. (With a pun on *jakes,* privy.) 577 **an't . . . you** if you please   578 **dashed** rattled, daunted. 581 **o'erparted** having a part too difficult.   582 **sort** manner. 584 **presented** played, represented.   **imp** child   585 **Cerberus** three-headed dog at the entrance to Hades, the capturing of which was one of Hercules's twelve labors.   **canus** i.e., *canis,* "dog" in Latin. (*Canus* is needed for the rhyme.)   587 **manus** hands.   588 **Quoniam . . . minor-ity** Since he is a child   589 **Ergo** therefore

590 **state** dignity   592 **A Judas** i.e., A traitor. (The lords deliberately confuse the military hero Judas Maccabaeus with Judas Iscariot, who betrayed Christ.)   594 **yclept** called   595 **clipped** shortened. (With a play on *yclept* in line 594.)   596 **A kissing traitor** i.e., a reference to Judas's embrace and kiss of Jesus by which he betrayed his master. (Playing on *clipped* in line 595, in the sense of "embraced" or "kissed.") 601 **You . . . elder** i.e., You are my senior and so should take precedence.   602 **Well . . . elder** (Berowne answers Holofernes with a pun on *elder,* "elder tree," traditionally the tree on which Judas hanged himself.)   603 **put out of countenance** disconcerted.   604 **Because . . . face** (Berowne counters by taking Holofernes's *countenance* in its literal sense, "face.")   606 **citternhead** head of a cithern or guitar (often grotesquely carved).   607 **bodkin** a long, jeweled pin for a lady's hair, or a small dagger (similarly carved).   608 **A death's . . . ring** i.e., A death's-head ring worn as a *memento mori.*   609–10 **scarce seen** i.e., worn almost smooth.   611 **falchion** curved sword. (The *pommel* or rounded knob on the hilt would be carved.)   612 **flask** i.e., horn powder flask.   613 **half-cheek** profile   614 **of lead** i.e., of inferior quality. 615 **tooth drawer** (Tooth extractors were not highly regarded; a brooch worn by such people in the cap might be of an inferior sort.) 616–17 **we . . . countenance** i.e., (1) we've reversed our putting you *out of countenance,* line 603 (2) we've drawn your portrait.   618 **You . . . countenance** (Holofernes protests: "You've made me forget my lines.")   620 **outfaced them** i.e., mocked them, put them down. (Playing on *faces* in line 619.)   621 **An** If.   **lion** (One of Aesop's fables tells of an ass that wears a lion's skin until he is betrayed by his bray.)

BOYET
　　Therefore, as he is an ass, let him go.
　　And so adieu, sweet Jude! Nay, why dost thou stay?
DUMAINE　　For the latter end of his name.
BEROWNE
　　For the ass to the Jude? Give it him. Jud-as, away!　625
HOLOFERNES
　　This is not generous, not gentle, not humble.　626
BOYET
　　A light for Monsieur Judas! It grows dark; he may
　　stumble.　　　　　　　　　　　　　　　　[Exit Holofernes.]
PRINCESS
　　Alas, poor Maccabaeus, how hath he been baited!　628

　　　　　Enter [Armado the] braggart [as Hector].

BEROWNE　　Hide thy head, Achilles! Here comes Hector　629
in arms.
DUMAINE　　Though my mocks come home by me, I will　631
now be merry.
KING　　Hector was but a Trojan in respect of this.　633
BOYET　　But is this Hector?
KING　　I think Hector was not so clean-timbered.　635
LONGAVILLE　　His leg is too big for Hector's.
DUMAINE　　More calf, certain.　637
BOYET　　No, he is best endued in the small.　638
BEROWNE　　This cannot be Hector.
DUMAINE　　He's a god or a painter, for he makes faces.　640
ARMADO
　　"The armipotent Mars, of lances the almighty,　641
　　Gave Hector a gift—"
DUMAINE　　A gilt nutmeg.　643
BEROWNE　　A lemon.
LONGAVILLE　　Stuck with cloves.
DUMAINE　　No, cloven.　646
ARMADO　　Peace!—
　　"The armipotent Mars, of lances the almighty,
　　Gave Hector a gift, the heir of Ilion;　649
　　A man so breathed that certain he would fight, yea　650
　　From morn till night, out of his pavilion.　651
　　I am that flower—"　652
DUMAINE　　That mint.
LONGAVILLE　　That columbine.
ARMADO　　Sweet Lord Longaville, rein thy tongue.　655
LONGAVILLE　　I must rather give it the rein, for it runs　656
against Hector.

DUMAINE　　Ay, and Hector's a greyhound.　658
ARMADO　　The sweet warman is dead and rotten. Sweet　659
chucks, beat not the bones of the buried. When he
breathed, he was a man. But I will forward with my　661
device. [To the Princess] Sweet royalty, bestow on me　662
the sense of hearing.
　　　Berowne steps forth [to whisper to Costard, and
　　　　　　　　　　　　　　then resumes his place].
PRINCESS
　　Speak, brave Hector. We are much delighted.
ARMADO　　I do adore thy sweet Grace's slipper.
BOYET　　Loves her by the foot.
DUMAINE　　He may not by the yard.　667
ARMADO
　　"This Hector far surmounted Hannibal—"
COSTARD　　The party is gone. Fellow Hector, she is gone!　669
She is two months on her way.　670
ARMADO　　What meanest thou?
COSTARD　　Faith, unless you play the honest Trojan, the　672
poor wench is cast away. She's quick; the child brags　673
in her belly already. 'Tis yours.
ARMADO　　Dost thou infamonize me among potentates?　675
Thou shalt die.
COSTARD　　Then shall Hector be whipped for Jaquenetta
that is quick by him and hanged for Pompey that is　678
dead by him.　679
DUMAINE　　Most rare Pompey!　680
BOYET　　Renowned Pompey!
BEROWNE　　Greater than "Great"! Great, great, great
Pompey! Pompey the Huge!
DUMAINE　　Hector trembles.
BEROWNE　　Pompey is moved. More Ates, more Ates!　685
Stir them on, stir them on!
DUMAINE　　Hector will challenge him.
BEROWNE　　Ay, if 'a have no more man's blood in his　688
belly than will sup a flea.　689
ARMADO　　By the North Pole, I do challenge thee.
COSTARD　　I will not fight with a pole, like a northern　691
man. I'll slash; I'll do it by the sword. I bepray you, let　692
me borrow my arms again.　693
DUMAINE　　Room for the incensed Worthies!　694
COSTARD　　I'll do it in my shirt. [He takes off his doublet.]
DUMAINE　　Most resolute Pompey!

---

625 Jud-as (Jude's *latter end* turns out to be his ass.) **626 gentle** courteous **628 baited** set upon, attacked. **629 Achilles . . . Hector** (These two were great antagonists in the Trojan War.) **631 by me** to mock me **633 a Trojan . . . this** i.e., (1) a resident of Troy (2) a jolly companion, a roisterer in comparison with Armado. **635 clean-timbered** well built. **637 calf** (1) lower part of leg (2) dolt **638 best . . . small** well endowed in the part of the leg below the calf. **640 makes faces** (1) creates images as a god or a painter might do (2) grimaces (being a bad actor). **641 armipotent** powerful in arms **643 gilt** glazed with egg yolk, saffron, etc. **646 No, cloven** i.e., No, "cloven" is more appropriate to a *leman* or lover (varied from *lemon* in line 644) who is *cloven* in the act of love. **649 Ilion** Troy **650 so breathed** in such fit condition **651 pavilion** tent or camp to which the combatant retired when not engaged in fight **652 flower** (Armado is trying to say "flower of chivalry.") **655 rein** restrain, control **656 give it the rein** allow it to run freely

658 a greyhound i.e., famed for his speed as a runner. **659 warman** warrior **661 forward** go forward, continue **662 device** i.e., speech. **667 yard** (Dumaine puns on the slang sense, "penis.") **669 The party is gone** i.e., Jaquenetta has disappeared. (Costard may have received this news from Berowne when Berowne whispered to him.) **670 on her way** i.e., pregnant. **672 play . . . Trojan** i.e., do the honest thing by her **673 quick** pregnant **675 infamonize** slander **678–9 and hanged . . . him** (Costard seems to mean that Armado will have to kill him, the actor of Pompey, if he does not do right by Jaquenetta; Costard will challenge Armado to a duel.) **680 rare** excellent **685 Ates** i.e., incitements to mischief. (Ate was the goddess of discord.) **688 if 'a** even if he **689 sup** feed **691–2 a northern man** a boorish ruffian from the north (for whom the stave or *pole* was a traditional weapon). **692–3 let . . . again** (Costard asks if he can borrow the weapons he lay down before the Princess in line 551.) **694 Room . . . Worthies!** Make room for the incensed Worthies to fight!

MOTE [*to Armado*] Master, let me take you a buttonhole 697
lower. Do you not see Pompey is uncasing for the 698
combat? What mean you? You will lose your reputation. 699

ARMADO   Gentlemen and soldiers, pardon me. I will not
combat in my shirt. 701

DUMAINE   You may not deny it. Pompey hath made the
challenge.

ARMADO   Sweet bloods, I both may and will. 704

BEROWNE   What reason have you for't?

ARMADO   The naked truth of it is, I have no shirt. I go 706
woolward for penance. 707

BOYET   True, and it was enjoined him in Rome for want 708
of linen; since when, I'll be sworn, he wore none but 709
a dishclout of Jaquenetta's, and that 'a wears next his 710
heart for a favor. 711

Enter a messenger, Monsieur Marcade.

MARCADE   God save you, madam!

PRINCESS   Welcome, Marcade,
But that thou interruptest our merriment.

MARCADE
I am sorry, madam, for the news I bring
Is heavy in my tongue. The King your father—

PRINCESS
Dead, for my life!

MARCADE   Even so. My tale is told.

BEROWNE
Worthies, away! The scene begins to cloud.

ARMADO   For mine own part, I breathe free breath. I
have seen the day of wrong through the little hole of 719
discretion, and I will right myself like a soldier. 720
                                Exeunt [*the*] *Worthies.* 721

KING   How fares Your Majesty?

PRINCESS
Boyet, prepare. I will away tonight.

KING
Madam, not so. I do beseech you, stay.

PRINCESS
Prepare, I say. I thank you, gracious lords,
For all your fair endeavors, and entreat,
Out of a new-sad soul, that you vouchsafe
In your rich wisdom to excuse or hide   728
The liberal opposition of our spirits,   729
If overboldly we have borne ourselves
In the converse of breath; your gentleness   731
Was guilty of it. Farewell, worthy lord!   732

A heavy heart bears not a humble tongue.   733
Excuse me so, coming too short of thanks   734
For my great suit so easily obtained.   735

KING
The extreme parts of time extremely forms   736
All causes to the purpose of his speed,   737
And often at his very loose decides   738
That which long process could not arbitrate.
And though the mourning brow of progeny   740
Forbid the smiling courtesy of love   741
The holy suit which fain it would convince,   742
Yet since love's argument was first on foot,
Let not the cloud of sorrow jostle it
From what it purposed, since to wail friends lost 745
Is not by much so wholesome-profitable   746
As to rejoice at friends but newly found.

PRINCESS
I understand you not. My griefs are double.   748

BEROWNE
Honest plain words best pierce the ear of grief,
And by these badges understand the King.   750
For your fair sakes have we neglected time,
Played foul play with our oaths. Your beauty, ladies,
Hath much deformed us, fashioning our humors
Even to the opposèd end of our intents,   754
And what in us hath seemed ridiculous—
As love is full of unbefitting strains,   756
All wanton as a child, skipping and vain,   757
Formed by the eye and therefore, like the eye,
Full of strange shapes, of habits, and of forms,
Varying in subjects as the eye doth roll
To every varied object in his glance;   761
Which parti-coated presence of loose love   762
Put on by us, if in your heavenly eyes
Have misbecomed our oaths and gravities,   764
Those heavenly eyes that look into these faults
Suggested us to make. Therefore, ladies,   766
Our love being yours, the error that love makes   767
Is likewise yours. We to ourselves prove false   768
By being once false forever to be true   769
To those that make us both—fair ladies, you.   770
And even that falsehood, in itself a sin,
Thus purifies itself and turns to grace.

---

697 take . . . lower (1) help remove your doublet (2) "take you down a peg," humiliate you.   **698 uncasing** undressing   **699 You . . . reputation** (A gentleman would lose status fighting with a country bumpkin like Costard.)   **701 combat** duel, fight   **704 bloods** men of mettle and rank   **706–7 go woolward for penance** i.e., with woolen clothing next to the skin and no linen underwear. (Armado's lame excuse is that he does so to punish the flesh.)   **708 enjoined** required of   **708–9 want of linen** lack of a clean shirt, etc. (Boyet sees through the excuse.)   **710 dishclout** dishcloth   **711 favor** love token.   **719–21 For . . . discretion** i.e., For my part, I have things under control. I now perceive how wrongly I have behaved   **721 right myself** i.e., make honorable amends, do the right thing   **728 hide** overlook   **729 liberal opposition** too-free antagonism   **731 in . . . breath** in conversation.   **gentleness** courtesy   **731–2 your . . . of it** i.e., your courteous forbearance encouraged us to tease you so.

733 A heavy . . . tongue My sad heart prevents me from speaking with a proper humility.   **734 so** therefore   **735 suit** i.e., the mission on which the came (which the King evidently has granted)   **736–7 The . . . speed** i.e., A few last moments demand quick decisions   **737, 738 his** i.e., time's   **738 loose** release, discharge. (An archery term.)   **740 the mourning brow of progeny** i.e., mourning worn by the Princess to honor her dead father   **741 Forbid** deny to us   **742 The . . . convince** the virtuous love suit it wishes to pursue   **745 to wail . . . lost** to lament for the dead   **746 by much** nearly   **748 double** i.e., because of my father's death, and because I don't understand you.   **750 badges** signs, i.e., my honest, plain words   **754 opposèd** opposite   **756 strains** impulses   **757 wanton** frivolous. **vain** foolish   **761 his** its   **762 Which . . . love** which jesting appearance of unrestrained love   **764 misbecomed** been unbecoming to   **766 Suggested us to make** tempted us to commit all these follies of love.   **767 Our love being yours** i.e., since our love for you is really your fault   **768–70 We . . . you** i.e., We have been false to our vows this once, abandoning the studies we vowed to pursue in order to be true forever to you, fair ladies, who make us both false and true: false to our former vow but true to you.

PRINCESS
　We have received your letters full of love,
　Your favors, the ambassadors of love,
　And in our maiden council rated them   774
　At courtship, pleasant jest, and courtesy,   775
　As bombast and as lining to the time.   776
　But more devout than this in our respects   777
　Have we not been, and therefore met your loves   778
　In their own fashion, like a merriment.   779

DUMAINE
　Our letters, madam, showed much more than jest.

LONGAVILLE
　So did our looks.

ROSALINE   We did not quote them so.   782

KING
　Now, at the latest minute of the hour,
　Grant us your loves.

PRINCESS   A time, methinks, too short
　To make a world-without-end bargain in.
　No, no, my lord, Your Grace is perjured much,
　Full of dear guiltiness, and therefore this: 787
　If for my love—as there is no such cause—   788
　You will do aught, this shall you do for me: 789
　Your oath I will not trust, but go with speed
　To some forlorn and naked hermitage,   791
　Remote from all the pleasures of the world;
　There stay until the twelve celestial signs   793
　Have brought about the annual reckoning.
　If this austere insociable life
　Change not your offer made in heat of blood;
　If frosts and fasts, hard lodging, and thin weeds   797
　Nip not the gaudy blossoms of your love,
　But that it bear this trial, and last love;   799
　Then, at the expiration of the year,
　Come challenge me, challenge me by these deserts,   801
　And, by this virgin palm now kissing thine,
　　　　　　　　　　[giving him her hand]
　I will be thine; and till that instance shut   803
　My woeful self up in a mourning house,
　Raining the tears of lamentation
　For the remembrance of my father's death.
　If this thou do deny, let our hands part,
　Neither entitled in the other's heart.   808

KING
　If this, or more than this, I would deny,
　　To flatter up these powers of mine with rest,   810
　The sudden hand of death close up mine eye!   811

　Hence, hermit, then. My heart is in thy breast.   812
　　　　　　　　　　[They converse apart.]

DUMAINE [to Katharine]
　But what to me, my love? But what to me?
　A wife?

KATHARINE   A beard, fair health, and honesty.   814
　With threefold love I wish you all these three.

DUMAINE
　Oh, shall I say, "I thank you, gentle wife"?

KATHARINE
　Not so, my lord. A twelvemonth and a day
　I'll mark no words that smooth-faced wooers say.   818
　Come when the King doth to my lady come;
　Then, if I have much love, I'll give you some.

DUMAINE
　I'll serve thee true and faithfully till then.

KATHARINE
　Yet swear not, lest ye be forsworn again.
　　　　　　　　　　[They converse apart.]

LONGAVILLE
　What says Maria?

MARIA   At the twelvemonth's end
　I'll change my black gown for a faithful friend.   824

LONGAVILLE
　I'll stay with patience, but the time is long.   825

MARIA
　The liker you. Few taller are so young.   826
　　　　　　　　　　[They converse apart.]

BEROWNE [to Rosaline]
　Studies my lady? Mistress, look on me.   827
　Behold the window of my heart, mine eye,
　What humble suit attends thy answer there.   829
　Impose some service on me for thy love.

ROSALINE
　Oft have I heard of you, my Lord Berowne,
　Before I saw you; and the world's large tongue   832
　Proclaims you for a man replete with mocks,
　Full of comparisons and wounding flouts,   834
　Which you on all estates will execute   835
　That lie within the mercy of your wit.
　To weed this wormwood from your fruitful brain,   837
　And therewithal to win me, if you please,
　Without the which I am not to be won,
　You shall this twelvemonth term from day to day
　Visit the speechless sick and still converse   841
　With groaning wretches, and your task shall be
　With all the fierce endeavor of your wit
　To enforce the painèd impotent to smile.   844

BEROWNE
　To move wild laughter in the throat of death?
　It cannot be. It is impossible.
　Mirth cannot move a soul in agony.

---

774 **favors** love tokens   775–6 **rated them At** evaluated them as
777 **bombast** (1) a loosely made fabric used for padding or stuffing
garments, for *lining* (2) puffed-up rhetoric, fit only to fill up the time
778–9 **But . . . been** i.e., For our part, we have not taken the matter
any more seriously than we judged you to have done   782 **quote**
interpret   787 **dear** grievous and precious   788 **as . . . cause** i.e.,
though I can't see why it should inspire you in that way   789 **aught**
anything   791 **naked** austere, isolated   793 **twelve celestial signs**
signs of the zodiac (encompassing one year)   797 **hard lodging**
uncomfortable accommodations.   **weeds** garments   799 **last** remain,
continue as   801 **challenge** claim.   **deserts** meritorious actions
803 **instance** instant   808 **entitled in** having a claim to   810 **To . . .
rest** to pamper my five senses with sensual ease   811 **The sudden**
may the sudden

812 **Hence, hermit then** i.e., Then off I go to be a hermit.   814 **A beard**
i.e., May you grow up to be a man   818 **smooth-faced** (1) beardless
(2) smooth-talking   824 **friend** sweetheart.   825 **stay** wait   826 **The
. . . young** i.e., That's just like you. Few tall young men are so callow
and impatient.   827 **Studies my lady?** i.e., Are you in a brown study?
829 **attends** awaits   832 **the world's large tongue** i.e., universal report
834 **comparisons** sardonic similes.   **flouts** jeers, insults   835 **all
estates** all classes of people   837 **weed** i.e., remove.   **wormwood** (A
bitter-tasting herb, hence, "bitterness.")   841 **still converse** constantly
associate   844 **the painèd impotent** helpless sufferers

ROSALINE

Why, that's the way to choke a gibing spirit,   848
Whose influence is begot of that loose grace   849
Which shallow laughing hearers give to fools.
A jest's prosperity lies in the ear
Of him that hears it, never in the tongue
Of him that makes it. Then if sickly ears,
Deafed with the clamors of their own dear groans,   854
Will hear your idle scorns, continue then,
And I will have you and that fault withal;   856
But if they will not, throw away that spirit,
And I shall find you empty of that fault,
Right joyful of your reformation.

BEROWNE

A twelvemonth? Well, befall what will befall,
I'll jest a twelvemonth in an hospital.

PRINCESS [to the King]

Ay, sweet my lord, and so I take my leave.

KING

No, madam, we will bring you on your way.   863

BEROWNE

Our wooing doth not end like an old play;
Jack hath not Jill. These ladies' courtesy
Might well have made our sport a comedy.

KING

Come, sir, it wants a twelvemonth and a day,   867
And then 'twill end.

BEROWNE   That's too long for a play.

Enter [Armado the] braggart.

ARMADO [to the King] Sweet Majesty, vouchsafe me—
PRINCESS   Was not that Hector?
DUMAINE   The worthy knight of Troy.
ARMADO   I will kiss thy royal finger, and take leave. I am
a votary; I have vowed to Jaquenetta to hold the plow   873
for her sweet love three year. But, most esteemed
greatness, will you hear the dialogue that the two   875
learned men have compiled in praise of the owl   876
and the cuckoo? It should have followed in the end of
our show.
KING   Call them forth quickly. We will do so.
ARMADO [calling] Holla! Approach.

Enter all [Holofernes, Nathaniel, Mote, Costard,
Jaquenetta, and others. They stand in two groups.]

This side is Hiems, Winter, this Ver, the Spring; the
one maintained by the owl, th'other by the cuckoo.   882
Ver, begin.

The Song

SPRING [sings]

When daisies pied and violets blue,   884
    And lady-smocks all silver-white,   885
And cuckoo-buds of yellow hue   886
    Do paint the meadows with delight,
The cuckoo then on every tree
Mocks married men, for thus sings he:
        Cuckoo!
Cuckoo, cuckoo! Oh, word of fear,
Unpleasing to a married ear!   892

When shepherds pipe on oaten straws,
    And merry larks are plowmen's clocks,   894
When turtles tread, and rooks and daws,   895
    And maidens bleach their summer smocks,
The cuckoo then on every tree
Mocks married men, for thus sings he:
        Cuckoo!
Cuckoo, cuckoo! Oh, word of fear,
Unpleasing to a married ear!

WINTER [sings]

When icicles hang by the wall,
    And Dick the shepherd blows his nail,   903
And Tom bears logs into the hall,
    And milk comes frozen home in pail,
When blood is nipped, and ways be foul,   906
Then nightly sings the staring owl:
Tu-whit, tu-whoo! A merry note,
While greasy Joan doth keel the pot.   909

When all aloud the wind doth blow,
    And coughing drowns the parson's saw,   911
And birds sit brooding in the snow,
    And Marian's nose looks red and raw,
When roasted crabs hiss in the bowl,   914
Then nightly sings the staring owl:
Tu-whit, tu-whoo! A merry note,
While greasy Joan doth keel the pot.

ARMADO   The words of Mercury are harsh after the   918
songs of Apollo. You that way; we this way.   919
                            Exeunt, [separately].

---

848 **gibing** mocking, scornful   849 **loose grace** carelessly given
approval. (Rosaline is saying that Berowne's mocking manner has
been nurtured by the fact that others have laughed shallowly and too
easily at his foolish raillery.)   854 **dear** heartfelt   856 **withal** in addition   863 **bring** accompany   867 **wants** lacks   873 **hold the plow**
i.e., labor at farming   875 **dialogue** debate   875–6 **the two learned
men** i.e., Holofernes and Nathaniel   882 **maintained** defended,
championed

884 **pied** parti-colored   885 **lady-smocks** cuckooflowers
886 **cuckoo-buds of yellow** buttercups (?)   892 **Unpleasing** i.e.,
because the cuckoo suggests cuckoldry   894 **clocks** i.e., because plow-
men "rise with the lark"   895 **turtles tread** turtledoves mate.   **rooks
and daws** black birds related to the crow   903 **blows his nail** blows
on his fingernails (i.e., to keep warm, and waiting patiently with nothing to do)   906 **nipped** chilled.   **ways** pathways   909 **keel** skim and
stir; cool to prevent boiling   911 **saw** maxim, moral observation
914 **crabs** crab apples   918 **Mercury** messenger of the gods and associated with eloquence or sophistry, in antithesis to Apollo, the god of
music   919 **You . . . this way** (Armado may be directing those
who have presented Winter to exit in one direction and those who
have presented Spring, in another; he may also be referring to
the audience.)

The Two Gentlemen of Verona

If by "romantic comedy" we mean a love story in which the lovers overcome parental obstacles, jealousies, separations, and dangers to be united at last in married bliss, then *The Two Gentlemen of Verona* is perhaps Shakespeare's first. Although *The Comedy of Errors* may be an earlier play, it is a farce of mistaken identity, with only a secondary interest in marriage, whereas *Love's Labor's Lost* is a courtly confection ending in the postponement of all marriages. No mention of *The Two Gentlemen of Verona* occurs until it is mentioned in Francis Meres's *Palladis Tamia: Wit's Treasury* of 1598, but the play is often dated around 1590–1594 on the basis of style: rhymed couplets, end-stopped verse, passages of excessive wit combat, and the like. *The Taming of the Shrew* (c. 1592–1594) is often dated a little later than *The Two Gentlemen of Verona*, if only because its double plotting is more complex and its exploration of the perils and rewards of courtships more challenging. In any event, *The Two Gentlemen of Verona* helps define, at an early stage, the genre of Shakespeare's best-known "festive" comedies, from *A Midsummer Night's Dream* to *Twelfth Night*.

The Two Gentlemen of Verona is also Shakespeare's apprenticeship to the romantic fiction of Italy and other southern European countries, whence he later derived so many plots of threatened love. He locates his story in Italy and gives some of his characters Italian names. He uses the conventional plot devices of romantic fiction: inconstancy in love and in friendship, the disguise of the heroine as a page, the overhearing of false vows, banishment, elopement, capture by outlaws, and so on. Virtually all the characters have a recognizable ancestry, not only in continental fiction but in neoclassical drama as well: Lucetta is the conventional female companion of the heroine, Thurio is the rich but unwelcome rival wooer (the pantaloon), Antonio and the Duke are typically strong-willed fathers opposing the romantic marriages of their children, Speed and Lance are at least supposed to be the clever servants who deliver messages and arrange rendezvous, and the four young lovers are the romantic protagonists.

Even in this early apprenticeship, to be sure, Shakespeare departs from the neoclassical norm of his continental sources. The setting remains nominally Italian, but the tone is often heartily English, and Shakespeare's attitude toward his romantic models borders occasionally on the irreverent. Lucetta is a true friend of Julia and a virtuous counselor in love; the jest about her being a "broker" or a go-between (1.2.41) reminds us how unlike a bawdy duenna of neoclassical comedy she really is. Thurio, Antonio, and the Duke are all portrayed with such amiable forbearance that they often seem inadequately motivated as the opponents of romantic happiness. Most of all, Speed and Lance have departed from their traditional roles as comic manipulators to become vaudeville jokesters.

Moreover, the very conventions of love and friendship are presented in such a way as to cast those conventions in an improbable light. What are we to make of the inconstant Proteus, who rejects his faithful Julia the moment he is away from her, tries instead to win the lady-fair of his dearest friend Valentine, informs the Duke of Valentine's plan to elope with Silvia, and then attempts a violent assault on Silvia's chastity? What sort of romantic hero is this, and why should he be rewarded by being forgiven and restored to his Julia? Most puzzling of all, is it credible that Valentine should respond to all this perfidy by offering to relinquish Silvia to Proteus? By the same token, isn't it absurd that the outlaws in the forest near Mantua should turn out to be gentlemen in exile and that they should offer command of their group to Valentine, whom they have just captured? Isn't the Duke's forgiveness of his eloped daughter Silvia rather sudden and unconvincing? These problems, which have troubled many readers of the play (though they generally seem less formidable to spectators of an actual production), can perhaps best be analyzed in two ways: as a result of Shakespeare's having combined two sources with conflicting conventions, thereby subjecting those conventions to a playfully ironic perspective, and as a result of Shakespeare's conscious interest in the theme of unexpected forgiveness for his erring protagonist.

Using a device of plotting that was to become customary in his romantic comedies, Shakespeare combines two fictional sources and thereby sets up a dramatic tension between the two. His chief source appears to have been *Diana*, a popular pastoral romance in Spanish by the Portuguese Jorge de Montemayor (1520–1561). Its heroine, Felismena (corresponding to Julia), is wooed by Don Felix (Proteus), whose father (Antonio) disapproves of the match and sends Don Felix away to court. Felismena, following after him disguised as a page, stops at an inn and is invited by the Host to listen to some music, whereupon she overhears Don Felix protesting his love to a new lady, Celia (Silvia). At this point, the resemblance between *Diana* and Shakespeare's play breaks off. Even thus far, despite several striking resemblances, the story provides no counterpart for Valentine, Proteus's best friend and the faithful lover of Silvia. Montemayor's romance is primarily concerned with inconstancy in love.

For the motif of true friendship, Shakespeare may have turned to the story of Titus and Gisippus, as told by Sir Thomas Elyot in *The Governor* (1531). Here Gisippus, upon learning that his dear friend Titus has fallen in love with Gisippus's ladylove, not only relinquishes the lady to Titus but also actually smuggles him into bed with her, all unbeknownst to the lady. The point of this story, as of other well-known treatises on friendship, such as John Lyly's *Euphues* (1578) and *Endymion* (1588) or Richard Edwards's *Damon and Pythias* (1565), is that friendship is a higher form of human affection than erotic love, since it is disinterested, platonically pure, and capable of teaching selflessness to others. Such a tale of perfect friendship provides, however, no counterpart for Julia, the lady abandoned by Proteus. Shakespeare has neatly dovetailed the two stories, making a quartet of lovers out of two triangular situations. The false lover of the first story becomes also the false friend of the second—only to be overwhelmed at the end by the generosity of his true friend.

The dramatic problem created by combining these two stories is that they arouse different expectations. The one is dedicated to the virtue of constancy in love; the other, to friendship. Valentine's ultimate function is to demonstrate the triumph of selfless friendship over love, and yet his function in the plot of love rivalry is to demonstrate true loyalty to his Silvia. His relinquishing of her to Proteus seems inconsistent with his vows as a lover. Conversely, Proteus's double perfidy, toward his lover Julia and his friend Valentine, seems to render him unworthy of the generous action Valentine bestows on him. Proteus's very name is synonymous with inconstancy; his namesake in the *Odyssey* was infamous for his ability to change shapes at will. (Valentine's name, on the other hand, betokens constancy in love.) The coupling of

the two plots simultaneously intensifies Proteus's guilt and Valentine's magnanimity.

Yet Shakespeare makes a virtue out of the seeming lack of credibility. First, the very implausibility of Valentine's selflessness in love and of Proteus's sudden conversion to virtue allows Shakespeare to mock gently the literary commonplaces of his sources. At the same time, Shakespeare finds serious value in his conventional topics of love and friendship, through the device of paradox. The more unlikely Valentine's actions seem, the more transcendent and wondrous they are bound to appear. Shakespeare prepares for his climactic scene of forgiveness in several ways. First, he presents Proteus as an essentially noble person who has fallen through a single fault. Proteus is wellborn, accomplished, and handsome. The worthy Julia loves him for his good qualities, and he responds with sincerity and passion. He is equally ardent as a friend to Valentine. Only when he sees Silvia does Proteus become helpless, "dazzlèd" (2.4.207). He cannot completely be blamed for being overwhelmed by passion, for the other lovers are no less obedient to love's command. According to the code of love that infuses this play, love cannot choose its object. Proteus's unhappy fate is to love Silvia. Yet he must also be held responsible for his actions and, indeed, blames himself for the desertion that he has consciously committed. His self-hatred increases as he turns flatterer, liar, betrayer, and finally would-be rapist. Like Angelo in *Measure for Measure*, Proteus is compulsively driven to abhorrent sin, but the choice is ultimately his. The psychological insight of that later dark comedy is lacking—the soliloquies do not create the suffocating atmosphere of a nightmare—but the pattern of a guilty fall is still manifest.

We are probably on the wrong track if we attempt to psychoanalyze Valentine too closely; the choice he must sort out between love and friendship is more a conventional debate on a favorite Renaissance theme than a realistic portrayal of a man caught between conflicting ideals. Shakespeare makes no attempt to conceal what is absurd about Valentine's sudden renunciation of the woman who has been unswervingly loyal to him and who has no wish to be traded from one lover to another as though she were the object of some kind of moralistic barter. Nonetheless, the very implausibility of Valentine's offer to relinquish Silvia accentuates the noble intent behind the gesture. We are surprised, even comically surprised, because we don't expect such selflessness in human nature; but, if friendship is to be seen as a supreme achievement of the human spirit, it must transcend humanity's all-too-common penchant for rivalry and ingratitude. Valentine's generosity is not achieved without inner struggle. In the climactic scene of attempted rape, his first natural reaction is angry denunciation. What changes his mind is the depth and earnestness of Proteus's confession and desire for forgiveness: "If hearty sorrow / Be a sufficient ransom for offense, / I tender't here" (5.4.74–6). Valentine responds in the name of mercy and at the prompting of divine example: "By penitence th'Eternal's wrath's appeased" (line 81). The more undeserved the pardon, the more selfless the act of him who pardons. Only by conquering his desire for Silvia can Valentine teach his friend selflessness and thus reunite all four lovers in perfect joy. *The Two Gentlemen of Verona* is thus in part a comedy of forgiveness, anticipating later plays in which the romantic protagonist is equally culpable and yet equally forgiven: *Much Ado About Nothing, Measure for Measure, All's Well That Ends Well, Cymbeline*, and others (see R. G. Hunter's *Shakespeare and the Comedy of Forgiveness*, 1965.) *The Two Noble Kinsmen*, written very late (c. 1613) in collaboration with John Fletcher, is a sophisticated return to issues of friendship and sexual rivalry that are so prominent in *The Two Gentlemen of Verona*.

Forgiveness of Proteus must proceed no less from Julia than from Valentine. She, too, has much to pardon; as Proteus contritely observes, "O heaven! Were man / But constant, he were perfect" (5.4.110–11). Julia initiates a line of Shakespearean heroines, including Hero, Isabella, Helena, and Imogen in the plays already named, who must similarly cure inconstancy by their constancy. Like many Shakespearean heroines, Julia is plucky, resourceful, modest but witty, patiently obedient in love and yet coyly flirtatious, a true friend, and long-suffering. Disguised as a page, she overhears her lover's infidelity and yet never loses her faith in him. She patiently delivers Proteus' messages to her rival (like Viola in *Twelfth Night*) and gently acts as conscience to her erring master.

Julia's use of male disguise anticipates more complex analyses, in later comedies, of the ambivalent and partly illusory nature of the differences between male and female. When Julia determines to don a male disguise in order to follow Proteus to Milan, she and Lucetta laugh at the necessity of Julia's tying up her hair and dressing herself in breeches festooned with a codpiece (2.7.39–61). Since a boy actor is playing a young woman in disguise as a young male, the theatrical playfulness and artifice positively invite us to see gender as something largely defined by role-playing and social expectations. The scene is an amused reflection on the different ways in which young men and women present themselves to the world.

The repeated device of overhearing, as in later comedies, provides a test for the protagonists' intentions. Thinking themselves unobserved, they reveal their true natures for better or for worse. In the ingeniously devised if improbable climactic scene (5.4), Proteus as would-be ravisher is overheard by both his rejected mistress and his betrayed friend. Conversely, Silvia proves loyal and chaste whenever she is silently observed by Julia (disguised as Sebastian) or by Valentine in the forest scenes. These overhearings suggest not only that humanity's good and evil deeds are witnessed but also that a beneficent providence will protect the virtuous. Valentine's unseen presence assures that Silvia will be saved from rape and that Proteus will be prevented from committing an actual crime of violence. As in later comedies of this sort, forgiveness is possible because the guilt remains one of intent only.

These slightly absurd but happy resolutions of conflict take place in a forest near Mantua, the first of what Northrop Frye calls Shakespeare's "green worlds" (*English Institute Essays 1948*, pp. 58–73). Although sketchily presented, this forest does anticipate the Forest of Arden and other sylvan restorative landscapes. Its inhabitants are banished men protesting the injustice of society at court or fugitives from unkind love. Valentine learns to prefer "unfrequented woods" to "flourishing peopled towns." His "wild faction" of outlaws desist from attacking "silly women or poor passengers" and appropriately swear "By the bare scalp of Robin Hood's fat friar" (5.4.2–3; 4.1.36–7). The outlaws are charmingly suited to their role of threatening and then reuniting the lovers, providentially capturing Silvia just as she is on her way to find Valentine. Their actions are highly improbable and poke fun at the very conventions they illustrate, but then the same can be said of Valentine's forgiveness of Proteus and the Duke's sudden reconciliation with his prospective son-in-law, Valentine. Like Arden, this forest is a strange place in which such changes of heart are expected to occur. The aura of improbability may also partly explain the play's carelessness about social distinctions and the realities of geography: the Duke is sometimes called the Emperor, and at one point Valentine sets sail from Verona to Milan (both located inland).

The buffoonish comedy of Lance and Speed performs a function similar to that of romantic improbability by undercutting the artifice and melodrama of the love story. How can we worry long over Valentine's banishment when Lance bursts out, "Sir, there is a proclamation that you are vanished" (3.1.217)? Or how can we fret about Proteus' courtship of Silvia when the love token he sends her is transformed into Lance's odoriferous dog? This sort of absurd anticlimax occurs at every turn. Lance's first soliloquy, about the dog's refusal to mourn their departure from Verona (2.3), is a brilliant example of what we would call vaudeville or stand-up comic joking, but it also comments on the immediately preceding scene of Proteus' tearful farewell to Julia. Lance's friendship for Speed, and especially his friendship for the dog, delightfully blaspheme the play's serious interest in true friendship. In one of Lance's funniest scenes (4.4.1–38), he describes how he has selflessly taken on himself the punishment meted out to the dog for urinating on Silvia's hooped petticoat. Similarly, the spectacle of Lance in love, cataloguing his mistress's virtues and vices, insures us against too deep an involvement in the hazards of Cupid. The play continually reminds us of the folly of love without denying its exquisite joys or its highest potential for selflessness.

The Two Gentlemen of Verona

The Names of All the Actors

DUKE [OF MILAN], *father to Silvia*
VALENTINE,
PROTEUS, } *the two gentlemen*
ANTONIO, *father to Proteus*
THURIO, *a foolish rival to Valentine*
EGLAMOUR, *agent for Silvia in her escape*
HOST [*of the inn*] *where Julia lodges*
OUTLAWS *with Valentine*

SPEED, *a clownish servant to Valentine*
LANCE, *the like to Proteus*
PANTHINO, *servant to Antonio*

JULIA, *beloved of Proteus*
SILVIA, *beloved of Valentine*
LUCETTA, *waiting-woman to Julia*

[*Servants, Musicians*

SCENE: *Verona; Milan; the frontiers of Mantua*]

1.1

[*Enter*] *Valentine* [*and*] *Proteus.*

VALENTINE
Cease to persuade, my loving Proteus;
Home-keeping youth have ever homely wits.   2
Were't not affection chains thy tender days   3
To the sweet glances of thy honored love,
I rather would entreat thy company
To see the wonders of the world abroad
Than, living dully sluggardized at home,
Wear out thy youth with shapeless idleness.   8
But since thou lov'st, love still, and thrive therein,
Even as I would when I to love begin.

PROTEUS
Wilt thou be gone? Sweet Valentine, adieu!
Think on thy Proteus when thou haply see'st   12
Some rare noteworthy object in thy travel.
Wish me partaker in thy happiness
When thou dost meet good hap; and in thy danger,   15
If ever danger do environ thee,
Commend thy grievance to my holy prayers,   17
For I will be thy beadsman, Valentine.   18

VALENTINE
And on a love book pray for my success?   19

PROTEUS
Upon some book I love I'll pray for thee.

VALENTINE
That's on some shallow story of deep love,   21
How young Leander crossed the Hellespont.   22

PROTEUS
That's a deep story of a deeper love,
For he was more than over shoes in love.

VALENTINE
'Tis true; for you are over boots in love,
And yet you never swam the Hellespont.

PROTEUS
Over the boots? Nay, give me not the boots.   27

VALENTINE
No, I will not, for it boots thee not.   28

PROTEUS   What?

VALENTINE
To be in love, where scorn is bought with groans,
Coy looks with heartsore sighs, one fading moment's
     mirth
With twenty watchful, weary, tedious nights.   32
If haply won, perhaps a hapless gain;   33
If lost, why then a grievous labor won;
However, but a folly bought with wit,   35
Or else a wit by folly vanquishèd.

PROTEUS
So by your circumstance you call me fool.   37

1.1. Location: Verona. A street.
2 homely dull, simple   **3 affection** passion, love.   **tender** youthful
8 shapeless aimless   **12 haply** by chance   **15 hap** fortune   **17 Commend thy grievance** commit your distress   **18 beadsman** one engaged to pray for others, using the beads of the rosary   **19 love book** manual of courtship or a love story (rather than a prayer book)

21 shallow . . . deep (Playing on the oppositions of shallow and deep water, superficial and heartfelt love.)   **22 Leander** famous lover of Greek legend who drowned as he swam the Hellespont to see his love Hero   **27 give . . . boots** i.e., don't make fun of me.   **28 boots** profits, avails. (With play on *boots* in line 27. This passage is full of punning, on *shallow* and *deep, over shoes, over boots,* etc.)   **32 watchful** wakeful   **33 hapless** unlucky   **35 However . . . wit** in either case, being in love is nothing but foolishness acquired through much ingenuity   **37 circumstance** account

VALENTINE
So by your circumstance I fear you'll prove.   38
PROTEUS
'Tis love you cavil at. I am not Love.   39
VALENTINE
Love is your master, for he masters you;
And he that is so yokèd by a fool
Methinks should not be chronicled for wise.   42
PROTEUS
Yet writers say, as in the sweetest bud
The eating canker dwells, so eating love   44
Inhabits in the finest wits of all.   45
VALENTINE
And writers say, as the most forward bud   46
Is eaten by the canker ere it blow,   47
Even so by love the young and tender wit
Is turned to folly, blasting in the bud,   49
Losing his verdure even in the prime,   50
And all the fair effects of future hopes.   51
But wherefore waste I time to counsel thee   52
That art a votary to fond desire?   53
Once more adieu! My father at the road   54
Expects my coming, there to see me shipped.   55
PROTEUS
And thither will I bring thee, Valentine.   56
VALENTINE
Sweet Proteus, no. Now let us take our leave.
To Milan let me hear from thee by letters   58
Of thy success in love, and what news else
Betideth here in absence of thy friend;   60
And I likewise will visit thee with mine.   61
PROTEUS
All happiness bechance to thee in Milan!
VALENTINE
As much to you at home! And so, farewell.   *Exit.*
PROTEUS
He after honor hunts, I after love.
He leaves his friends to dignify them more;   65
I leave myself, my friends, and all, for love.   66
Thou, Julia, thou hast metamorphized me,
Made me neglect my studies, lose my time,   68
War with good counsel, set the world at naught;   69
Made wit with musing weak, heart sick with thought.   70

    [Enter] Speed.

SPEED
Sir Proteus, save you! Saw you my master?   71
PROTEUS
But now he parted hence to embark for Milan.   72
SPEED
Twenty to one, then, he is shipped already,
And I have played the sheep in losing him.   74
PROTEUS
Indeed, a sheep doth very often stray,
An if the shepherd be awhile away.   76
SPEED   You conclude that my master is a shepherd, then,
and I a sheep?
PROTEUS   I do.
SPEED   Why then, my horns are his horns, whether I   80
wake or sleep.
PROTEUS   A silly answer, and fitting well a sheep.
SPEED   This proves me still a sheep.
PROTEUS   True; and thy master a shepherd.
SPEED   Nay, that I can deny by a circumstance.   85
PROTEUS   It shall go hard but I'll prove it by another.   86
SPEED   The shepherd seeks the sheep, and not the sheep
the shepherd; but I seek my master, and my master
seeks not me. Therefore I am no sheep.
PROTEUS   The sheep for fodder follow the shepherd; the
shepherd for food follows not the sheep. Thou for
wages followest thy master; thy master for wages fol-
lows not thee. Therefore thou art a sheep.
SPEED   Such another proof will make me cry "Baa."   94
PROTEUS   But dost thou hear? Gav'st thou my letter to   95
Julia?
SPEED   Ay, sir. I, a lost mutton, gave your letter to her, a   97
laced mutton, and she, a laced mutton, gave me, a lost   98
mutton, nothing for my labor.
PROTEUS   Here's too small a pasture for such store of
muttons.
SPEED   If the ground be overcharged, you were best   102
stick her.   103
PROTEUS   Nay, in that you are astray. 'Twere best   104
pound you.   105
SPEED   Nay, sir, less than a pound shall serve me for   106
carrying your letter.
PROTEUS   You mistake. I mean the pound—a pinfold.   108
SPEED
From a pound to a pin? Fold it over and over,   109

---

38 **circumstance** situation, condition   39 **cavil at** carp at, find fault with.   **Love** i.e., Cupid.   42 **chronicled for wise** set down as being wise.   44 **canker** cankerworm   45 **Inhabits** dwells   46 **forward** early   47 **blow** bloom   49 **blasting** withering   50 **his verdure** its flourishing vigor.   **prime** spring   51 **fair . . . hopes** bright fulfillment of future happiness.   52 **wherefore** why   53 **votary** worshiper.   **fond** foolish   54 **road** roadstead, harbor   55 **shipped** aboard. (Shakespeare evidently assumes that Verona and Milan are connected by water; Proteus also travels by ship, though Julia later makes the journey by land.)   56 **bring** accompany   58 **To Milan** By letters sent to Milan   60 **Betideth** occurs   61 **visit** enrich with a similar benefit   65 **friends** (including family).   **dignify** i.e., honor (by increasing his own fame)   66 **leave** neglect   68 **lose** waste   69 **War . . . counsel** reject good advice   70 **Made . . . thought** You have caused me to weaken my intellect by fanciful imaginings and to make sick my heart through melancholy.

71 **save you** God save you.   72 **But now** Just now.   **parted** departed   74 **played the sheep** behaved sheepishly. (With a pun on *sheep* and *ship*; the words were pronounced similarly.)   76 **An if** if   80 **Why . . . his horns** i.e., Then you hint that I and my master are alike in that we are both horned. (Traditionally, husbands whose wives deceived them were supposed to grow cuckolds' horns.)   85 **circumstance** process of reasoning.   86 **It . . . I'll** I'll be doing pretty badly if I cannot   94 **Baa** (With a pun on *bah*, as in "bah, humbug.")   95 **dost thou hear** i.e., listen here.   97 **to her** (At 1.2.39–40 we learn that Speed gave the letter to Lucetta.)   97–8 **a lost mutton . . . a laced mutton** a lost sheep . . . a whore with tightly laced bodice or laced slashing in her dress. (With a pun on *lost/laced*, similarly pronounced.)   102 **overcharged** overcrowded   103 **stick** (1) stab—with a bawdy suggestion of penetration (2) shut up in a pen   104 **astray** (1) wandering like a lost sheep (2) going too far, missing the point.   105 **pound** (1) impound, shut up in an animal pen (2) beat   106 **pound** (1) twenty shillings (2) a beating   108 **pinfold** pen for stray animals.   109 **a pin** i.e., an object worth very little.   **Fold** (1) as in folding a letter (2) multiply. (*Pin? Fold* plays on *pinfold* in line 108).

'Tis threefold too little for carrying a letter to your
    lover.
PROTEUS   But what said she?
SPEED   [*first nodding*]   Ay.
PROTEUS   Nod—ay—why, that's "noddy."   113
SPEED   You mistook, sir. I say she did nod, and you ask
    me if she did nod, and I say, "Ay."
PROTEUS   And that set together is "noddy."
SPEED   Now you have taken the pains to set it together,
    take it for your pains.   118
PROTEUS   No, no, you shall have it for bearing the letter.
SPEED   Well, I perceive I must be fain to bear with you.   120
PROTEUS   Why, sir, how do you bear with me?
SPEED   Marry, sir, the letter, very orderly, having noth-   122
    ing but the word "noddy" for my pains.
PROTEUS   Beshrew me, but you have a quick wit.   124
SPEED   And yet it cannot overtake your slow purse.
PROTEUS   Come, come, open the matter in brief. What   126
    said she?
SPEED   Open your purse, that the money and the matter
    may be both at once delivered.   129
PROTEUS   [*giving him money*]   Well, sir, here is for your
    pains. What said she?
SPEED   Truly, sir, I think you'll hardly win her.
PROTEUS   Why? Couldst thou perceive so much from her?
SPEED   Sir, I could perceive nothing at all from her, no,   134
    not so much as a ducat for delivering your letter. And   135
    being so hard to me that brought your mind, I fear   136
    she'll prove as hard to you in telling your mind. Give   137
    her no token but stones, for she's as hard as steel.   138
PROTEUS   What said she? Nothing?
SPEED   No, not so much as "Take this for thy pains." To
    testify your bounty, I thank you, you have testerned   141
    me; in requital whereof, henceforth carry your letters   142
    yourself. And so, sir, I'll commend you to my master.   143
PROTEUS
    Go, go, begone, to save your ship from wreck,
    Which cannot perish having thee aboard,   145
    Being destined to a drier death on shore.   146
                                        [*Exit Speed.*]
    I must go send some better messenger.
    I fear my Julia would not deign my lines,   148
    Receiving them from such a worthless post.   *Exit.*   149

                    ♣

113 **noddy** a simpleton.   118 **take . . . pains** take it as your reward.
(With wordplay in *taken the pain / take it for your pains*.)   120 **fain** content.   **bear with** (1) put up with (2) carry for. (Speed sees he is to get no
tip.)   122 **Marry** i.e., Indeed. (Originally an oath, "by the Virgin Mary.")
124 **Beshrew me** (A mild oath.)   126 **open** disclose. (Anticipating a pun
in line 128 on *opening* a purse.)   129 **delivered** (1) handed over (said of
the *money*) (2) reported (said of the *matter* or business being discussed).
134 **perceive** (Punning on *perceive*, "understand," in the previous line.)   135 **a ducat** a silver or gold coin   136 **mind** desires, intentions   137 **in telling** for telling   138 **stones** (1) jewels such as
diamonds, harder than steel and well suited to hard-hearted ladies
(2) testicles   141–2 **testerned me** given me a testern, sixpence (a small
tip)   143 **commend you** deliver your greetings   145–6 **Which . . . shore**
(An allusion to the proverb "He that is born to be hanged shall never be
drowned.")   148 **deign** deign to accept   149 **post** (1) messenger
(2) blockhead.

1.2

Enter Julia and Lucetta.

JULIA
    But say, Lucetta, now we are alone,
    Wouldst thou then counsel me to fall in love?
LUCETTA
    Ay, madam, so you stumble not unheedfully.   3
JULIA
    Of all the fair resort of gentlemen   4
    That every day with parle encounter me,   5
    In thy opinion which is worthiest love?   6
LUCETTA
    Please you repeat their names, I'll show my mind   7
    According to my shallow simple skill.
JULIA
    What think'st thou of the fair Sir Eglamour?   9
LUCETTA
    As of a knight well-spoken, neat, and fine;
    But, were I you, he never should be mine.
JULIA
    What think'st thou of the rich Mercatio?
LUCETTA
    Well of his wealth, but of himself, so-so.
JULIA
    What think'st thou of the gentle Proteus?
LUCETTA
    Lord, Lord, to see what folly reigns in us!
JULIA
    How now? What means this passion at his name?   16
LUCETTA
    Pardon, dear madam, 'tis a passing shame   17
    That I, unworthy body as I am,
    Should censure thus on lovely gentlemen.   19
JULIA
    Why not on Proteus, as of all the rest?
LUCETTA
    Then thus: of many good I think him best.
JULIA   Your reason?
LUCETTA
    I have no other but a woman's reason:
    I think him so because I think him so.
JULIA
    And wouldst thou have me cast my love on him?
LUCETTA
    Ay, if you thought your love not cast away.
JULIA
    Why, he of all the rest hath never moved me.   27
LUCETTA
    Yet he of all the rest I think best loves ye.
JULIA
    His little speaking shows his love but small.
LUCETTA
    Fire that's closest kept burns most of all.

1.2. Location: Verona. Julia's house.
3 so provided that   **4 resort** company, assemblage   **5 parle** talk
6 worthiest love most worthy of love.   **7 Please** If it please
9 Eglamour (Not to be identified with Silvia's friend of the same
name.)   **16 passion** passionate outburst   **17 passing** surpassing
19 censure pass judgment   **27 moved** urged (with a suit of love)

JULIA
    They do not love that do not show their love.
LUCETTA
    Oh, they love least that let men know their love.
JULIA   I would I knew his mind.
LUCETTA   [*giving a letter*]   Peruse this paper, madam.
JULIA   "To Julia." Say, from whom?
LUCETTA   That the contents will show.
JULIA   Say, say, who gave it thee?
LUCETTA
    Sir Valentine's page; and sent, I think, from Proteus.
    He would have given it you, but I, being in the way,   39
    Did in your name receive it. Pardon the fault, I pray.
JULIA
    Now, by my modesty, a goodly broker!   41
    Dare you presume to harbor wanton lines?   42
    To whisper, and conspire against my youth?   43
    Now, trust me, 'tis an office of great worth,
    And you an officer fit for the place.
    There, take the paper. See it be returned,
    Or else return no more into my sight.
                        [*She gives the letter back.*]
LUCETTA
    To plead for love deserves more fee than hate.   48
JULIA
    Will ye be gone?
LUCETTA   That you may ruminate.   *Exit.*   49
JULIA
    And yet I would I had o'erlooked the letter.   50
    It were a shame to call her back again
    And pray her to a fault for which I chid her.   52
    What 'fool is she, that knows I am a maid   53
    And would not force the letter to my view!
    Since maids, in modesty, say no to that
    Which they would have the profferer construe ay.
    Fie, fie, how wayward is this foolish love
    That, like a testy babe, will scratch the nurse   58
    And presently, all humbled, kiss the rod!   59
    How churlishly I chid Lucetta hence,
    When willingly I would have had her here!
    How angerly I taught my brow to frown,   62
    When inward joy enforced my heart to smile!
    My penance is to call Lucetta back
    And ask remission for my folly past.
    What ho! Lucetta!

            [*Enter Lucetta.*]

LUCETTA   What would Your Ladyship?
JULIA
    Is't near dinnertime?
LUCETTA   I would it were,
    That you might kill your stomach on your meat   68

    And not upon your maid.
            [*She drops the letter and stoops to pick it up.*]
JULIA
    What is't that you took up so gingerly?
LUCETTA   Nothing.
JULIA   Why didst thou stoop, then?
LUCETTA
    To take a paper up that I let fall.
JULIA   And is that paper nothing?
LUCETTA   Nothing concerning me.
JULIA
    Then let it lie for those that it concerns.
LUCETTA
    Madam, it will not lie where it concerns,   77
    Unless it have a false interpreter.
JULIA
    Some love of yours hath writ to you in rhyme.
LUCETTA
    That I might sing it, madam, to a tune,   80
    Give me a note. Your ladyship can set.   81
JULIA
    As little by such toys as may be possible.   82
    Best sing it to the tune of "Light o' Love."   83
LUCETTA
    It is too heavy for so light a tune.   84
JULIA
    Heavy! Belike it hath some burden then?   85
LUCETTA
    Ay, and melodious were it, would you sing it.   86
JULIA
    And why not you?
LUCETTA   I cannot reach so high.   87
JULIA
    Let's see your song. How now, minion?   88
                        [*She takes the letter.*]
LUCETTA
    Keep tune there still; so you will sing it out.   89
    And yet methinks I do not like this tune.
JULIA   You do not?
LUCETTA   No, madam, 'tis too sharp.   92
JULIA   You, minion, are too saucy.
LUCETTA   Nay, now you are too flat,   94
    And mar the concord with too harsh a descant.   95

---

39 being . . . way i.e., happening to encounter him   **41 broker** intermediary.   **42–3 Dare . . . youth?** (Said ironically.)   **48 more fee** better recompense   **49 That . . . ruminate.** (I'm leaving) so that you can think carefully about this.   **50 o'erlooked** read   **52 to a fault** to commit a fault   **53 'fool** a fool   **58 testy** fretful   **59 presently** immediately afterward.   **rod** spanking rod.   **62 angerly** angrily   **68 kill your stomach** (1) satisfy your appetite (2) appease your anger.   **meat** (Pronounced "mate," with wordplay on *maid* in the next line.)

77 lie where it concerns tell falsehoods in matters of importance. (Punning on the meaning "be left for those whose business it is" in the preceding line.)   **80 That** In order that   **81 note** (With a punning reference to Proteus's letter.)   **set** (1) set to music (2) write a letter. (But Julia takes the word in the sense of setting store by something, regarding it of value.)   **82 toys** trifles   **83 "Light o' Love"** (A familiar tune of the time.)   **84 heavy** serious   **85 Belike** Perhaps.   **burden** (1) bass accompaniment to a melody (2) heavy load (with an added sexual suggestion of the burden women must bear)   **86 melodious . . . it** it would be melodious if you would sing it.   **87 reach so high** (1) sing so high (2) aspire to a person of Proteus's rank.   **88 minion** hussy. (With a pun on *minim*, half-note.)   **89 tune** (1) pitch (2) temper, mood.   **so . . . out** (1) if you do so, you'll be able to sing the song completely (2) that way you'll get over your bad mood.   **92 sharp** (1) high in pitch (2) saucy, bitter. (Perhaps Julia pinches or slaps Lucetta here and at line 94, or perhaps Lucetta is referring to her mistress' tone of voice.)   **94 flat** (1) low in pitch (2) blunt   **95 descant** (1) soprano counterpoint sung above the melody (2) carping criticism.

There wanteth but a mean to fill your song.   96

JULIA
The mean is drowned with your unruly bass.   97

LUCETTA
Indeed, I bid the base for Proteus.   98

JULIA
This babble shall not henceforth trouble me.   99
Here is a coil with protestation!   100
     [She tears the letter and drops the pieces.]
Go, get you gone, and let the papers lie.
You would be fing'ring them to anger me.

LUCETTA
She makes it strange, but she would be best pleased   103
To be so angered with another letter.   [Exit.]

JULIA
Nay, would I were so angered with the same!   105
     [She picks up some fragments.]
O hateful hands, to tear such loving words!
Injurious wasps, to feed on such sweet honey   107
And kill the bees that yield it with your stings!
I'll kiss each several paper for amends.   109
Look, here is writ "kind Julia." Unkind Julia!   110
As in revenge of thy ingratitude,   111
I throw thy name against the bruising stones,
Trampling contemptuously on thy disdain.
     [She throws down a fragment.]
And here is writ "love-wounded Proteus."
Poor wounded name! My bosom as a bed
Shall lodge thee till thy wound be throughly healed;   116
And thus I search it with a sovereign kiss.   117
But twice or thrice was "Proteus" written down.
Be calm, good wind, blow not a word away
Till I have found each letter in the letter,
Except mine own name; that some whirlwind bear   121
Unto a ragged, fearful, hanging rock
And throw it thence into the raging sea!
Lo, here in one line is his name twice writ,
"Poor forlorn Proteus, passionate Proteus,
To the sweet Julia." That I'll tear away;
And yet I will not, sith so prettily   127
He couples it to his complaining names.
Thus will I fold them, one upon another.
Now kiss, embrace, contend, do what you will.
     [She puts some folded papers in her bosom.]

   [Enter Lucetta.]

LUCETTA Madam,
Dinner is ready, and your father stays.   132

JULIA Well, let us go.

LUCETTA
What, shall these papers lie like telltales here?

JULIA
If you respect them, best to take them up.   135

LUCETTA
Nay, I was taken up for laying them down;   136
Yet here they shall not lie, for catching cold.   137
   [She gathers up the remaining fragments.]

JULIA
I see you have a month's mind to them.   138

LUCETTA
Ay, madam, you may say what sights you see;
I see things too, although you judge I wink.   140

JULIA Come, come, will 't please you go? Exeunt.

❖

1.3

Enter Antonio and Panthino.

ANTONIO
Tell me, Panthino, what sad talk was that   1
Wherewith my brother held you in the cloister?   2

PANTHINO
'Twas of his nephew Proteus, your son.

ANTONIO
Why, what of him?

PANTHINO   He wondered that Your Lordship
Would suffer him to spend his youth at home,   5
While other men, of slender reputation,   6
Put forth their sons to seek preferment out: 7
Some to the wars, to try their fortune there,
Some to discover islands far away,
Some to the studious universities.
For any or for all these exercises
He said that Proteus your son was meet,   12
And did request me to importune you   13
To let him spend his time no more at home,
Which would be great impeachment to his age   15
In having known no travel in his youth.

ANTONIO
Nor need'st thou much importune me to that
Whereon this month I have been hammering.   18
I have considered well his loss of time,
And how he cannot be a perfect man,   20
Not being tried and tutored in the world.   21
Experience is by industry achieved

---

96 wanteth but is lacking only. **mean** (1) middle or tenor voice between the *descant* and the *bass*, i.e., Proteus (2) opportunity **97 unruly bass** (With pun on "base behavior.") **98 bid the base for** i.e., act in behalf of, intercede for. (Referring to the game of "prisoner's base," and with a pun on *base*, "bass, low.") **99 babble** i.e., idle chatter; or else *bauble*, foolish trifle—the letter **100 coil with protestation** commotion or fuss about protestations of love (i.e., about Proteus's letter.) **103 makes it strange** pretends indifference. (Lucetta says this speech for the audience's benefit, but it is a catty third-person reference to Julia rather than an aside, and Julia makes it clear in line 105 that she has heard it.) **105 Nay . . . same!** i.e., Indeed, I wish I had this same letter intact to pretend to be angry about! **107 wasps** i.e., fingers **109 several paper** separate scraps of paper **110 Unkind** Unnatural, cruel **111 As** As if, or, Thus **116 throughly** thoroughly **117 search** probe, cleanse (as one would a wound). **sovereign** healing **121 that . . . bear** may some whirlwind bear *that*, my name **127 sith** since

132 stays waits. **135 respect** prize, esteem. **best to take** it were best you take **136 taken up** scolded. (With a play on *take them up* in the preceding line.) **137 for** for fear of **138 month's mind** inclination, liking **140 wink** close the eyes.
1.3. Location: Verona. Antonio's house.
1 sad serious **2 the cloister** any covered arcade attached to a building. **5 suffer** allow **6 of slender reputation** i.e., of lower station than yourself **7 Put . . . out** send their sons away from home to seek advancement **12 meet** fitted **13 importune** urge **15 impeachment to his age** detriment or cause for reproach to him in his mature years **18 hammering** beating (an idea) into shape. **20 perfect** i.e., educated, mature **21 tried** tested

And perfected by the swift course of time.
Then tell me, whither were I best to send him?   24
PANTHINO
I think Your Lordship is not ignorant
How his companion, youthful Valentine,
Attends the Emperor in his royal court.   27
ANTONIO   I know it well.
PANTHINO
'Twere good, I think, Your Lordship sent him thither.
There shall he practice tilts and tournaments,   30
Hear sweet discourse, converse with noblemen,
And be in eye of every exercise   32
Worthy his youth and nobleness of birth.   33
ANTONIO
I like thy counsel. Well hast thou advised,
And, that thou mayst perceive how well I like it,
The execution of it shall make known.
Even with the speediest expedition   37
I will dispatch him to the Emperor's court.
PANTHINO
Tomorrow, may it please you, Don Alphonso,
With other gentlemen of good esteem,
Are journeying to salute the Emperor
And to commend their service to his will.   42
ANTONIO
Good company. With them shall Proteus go—

    [Enter] Proteus, [reading a letter].

And in good time! Now will we break with him.   44
PROTEUS   [to himself]
Sweet love, sweet lines, sweet life!
Here is her hand, the agent of her heart;
Here is her oath for love, her honor's pawn.   47
Oh, that our fathers would applaud our loves
To seal our happiness with their consents!   49
Oh, heavenly Julia!
ANTONIO
How now? What letter are you reading there?
PROTEUS
May't please Your Lordship, 'tis a word or two
Of commendations sent from Valentine,
Delivered by a friend that came from him.   53
ANTONIO
Lend me the letter. Let me see what news.
PROTEUS
There is no news, my lord, but that he writes
How happily he lives, how well beloved
And daily gracèd by the Emperor,   58
Wishing me with him, partner of his fortune.
ANTONIO
And how stand you affected to his wish?   60

PROTEUS
As one relying on Your Lordship's will,
And not depending on his friendly wish.
ANTONIO
My will is something sorted with his wish.   63
Muse not that I thus suddenly proceed,   64
For what I will, I will, and there an end.
I am resolved that thou shalt spend some time
With Valentinus in the Emperor's court.
What maintenance he from his friends receives,   68
Like exhibition thou shalt have from me.   69
Tomorrow be in readiness to go.
Excuse it not, for I am peremptory.   71
PROTEUS
My lord, I cannot be so soon provided.   72
Please you, deliberate a day or two.
ANTONIO
Look what thou want'st shall be sent after thee.   74
No more of stay. Tomorrow thou must go.—   75
Come on, Panthino. You shall be employed
To hasten on his expedition.

    [Exeunt Antonio and Panthino.]
PROTEUS
Thus have I shunned the fire for fear of burning
And drenched me in the sea, where I am drowned.
I feared to show my father Julia's letter
Lest he should take exceptions to my love,
And with the vantage of mine own excuse
Hath he excepted most against my love.   83
Oh, how this spring of love resembleth
The uncertain glory of an April day,
Which now shows all the beauty of the sun,
And by and by a cloud takes all away!

    [Enter Panthino.]

PANTHINO
Sir Proteus, your father calls for you.
He is in haste; therefore, I pray you, go.
PROTEUS
Why, this it is: my heart accords thereto,
And yet a thousand times it answers no.   Exeunt.

❧

2.1

Enter Valentine [and] Speed.

SPEED
Sir, your glove.   [Offering a glove.]
VALENTINE   Not mine. My gloves are on.
SPEED   Why, then, this may be yours, for this is but one.   2
VALENTINE
Ha! Let me see. Ay, give it me, it's mine.

24 **were I best** would it be best for me   27 **the Emperor** i.e., the Duke
of Milan. (An apparent inconsistency.)   30 **practice** perform, take
part in   32 **in eye of** in a position to see   33 **Worthy** worthy of
37 **expedition** swiftness   42 **commend** commit, dedicate   44 **in good
time** i.e., just at the right time (here he comes).   **break with** reveal,
disclose the plan to   47 **pawn** pledge.   49 **seal** ratify   53 **commendations** greetings   58 **gracèd** favored   60 **stand you affected** are you
disposed, inclined

63 **something sorted** rather in accordance   64 **Muse** Wonder
68 **maintenance** allowance.   **friends** i.e., relatives   69 **exhibition**
allowance of money   71 **Excuse it not** Offer no excuses.   **peremptory** resolved.   72 **provided** equipped.   74 **Look what** Whatever
75 **No more of stay** No more talk of delay.   83 **excepted most against**
most effectively hindered
2.1. **Location:** Milan. Perhaps at the Duke's palace, or in some
unspecified location.
2 **one** (Pronounced like "on," thus providing a pun on the previous line.)

Sweet ornament that decks a thing divine!
Ah, Silvia, Silvia!
SPEED [*calling*] Madam Silvia! Madam Silvia!
VALENTINE How now, sirrah? 7
SPEED She is not within hearing, sir.
VALENTINE Why, sir, who bade you call her?
SPEED Your Worship, sir, or else I mistook.
VALENTINE Well, you'll still be too forward. 11
SPEED And yet I was last chidden for being too slow.
VALENTINE Go to, sir. Tell me, do you know Madam 13
Silvia?
SPEED She that Your Worship loves?
VALENTINE Why, how know you that I am in love?
SPEED Marry, by these special marks: first, you have
learned, like Sir Proteus, to wreathe your arms, like a 18
malcontent; to relish a love song, like a robin redbreast; 19
to walk alone, like one that had the pestilence; to sigh,
like a schoolboy that had lost his A B C; to weep, like 21
a young wench that had buried her grandam; to fast, 22
like one that takes diet; to watch, like one that fears 23
robbing; to speak puling, like a beggar at Hallowmas. 24
You were wont, when you laughed, to crow like a
cock; when you walked, to walk like one of the lions. 26
When you fasted, it was presently after dinner; when
you looked sadly, it was for want of money. And now 28
you are metamorphized with a mistress, that when I 29
look on you I can hardly think you my master.
VALENTINE Are all these things perceived in me?
SPEED They are all perceived without ye. 32
VALENTINE Without me? They cannot. 33
SPEED Without you? Nay, that's certain, for, without 34
you were so simple, none else would. But you are so 35
without these follies that these follies are within you, 36
and shine through you like the water in an urinal, that 37
not an eye that sees you but is a physician to comment
on your malady.
VALENTINE But tell me, dost thou know my lady Silvia?
SPEED She that you gaze on so as she sits at supper?
VALENTINE Hast thou observed that? Even she I mean.
SPEED Why, sir, I know her not.
VALENTINE Dost thou know her by my gazing on her,
and yet know'st her not?
SPEED Is she not hard-favored, sir? 46
VALENTINE Not so fair, boy, as well-favored. 47
SPEED Sir, I know that well enough.
VALENTINE What dost thou know?

SPEED That she is not so fair as, of you, well-favored. 50
VALENTINE I mean that her beauty is exquisite but her
favor infinite. 52
SPEED That's because the one is painted and the other 53
out of all count. 54
VALENTINE How painted? And how out of count?
SPEED Marry, sir, so painted to make her fair that no
man counts of her beauty. 57
VALENTINE How esteem'st thou me? I account of her 58
beauty.
SPEED You never saw her since she was deformed. 60
VALENTINE How long hath she been deformed?
SPEED Ever since you loved her.
VALENTINE I have loved her ever since I saw her, and
still I see her beautiful.
SPEED If you love her, you cannot see her.
VALENTINE Why?
SPEED Because Love is blind. Oh, that you had mine 67
eyes, or your own eyes had the lights they were wont 68
to have when you chid at Sir Proteus for going 69
ungartered! 70
VALENTINE What should I see then?
SPEED Your own present folly and her passing defor- 72
mity; for he, being in love, could not see to garter his
hose, and you, being in love, cannot see to put on your 74
hose. 75
VALENTINE Belike, boy, then you are in love, for last 76
morning you could not see to wipe my shoes.
SPEED True, sir. I was in love with my bed. I thank you,
you swinged me for my love, which makes me the 79
bolder to chide you for yours.
VALENTINE In conclusion, I stand affected to her. 81
SPEED I would you were set; so your affection would 82
cease.
VALENTINE Last night she enjoined me to write some
lines to one she loves.
SPEED And have you?
VALENTINE I have.
SPEED Are they not lamely writ?
VALENTINE No, boy, but as well as I can do them.
Peace, here she comes. 90

[*Enter*] *Silvia.*

SPEED [*aside*] Oh, excellent motion! Oh, exceeding puppet! 91
Now will he interpret to her. 92

---

7 sirrah fellow. (Form of address to inferiors.)   **11 still** always
13 Go to (An expression of remonstrance.)   **18 wreathe** fold. (Folded
arms were a conventional gesture of melancholy, such as love melancholy.)   **19 relish** sing, warble   **21 A B C** primer   **22 grandam**
grandmother   **23 takes diet** diets for reasons of health.   **watch** lie
awake, sit up at night   **24 puling** whiningly.   **Hallowmas** All Saints'
Day, November 1 (a day when beggars asked special alms).
26 like . . . lions i.e., proudly, manfully.   **28 want** lack   **29 with** by.
that so that   **32 without ye** from your outside appearance.   **33 Without me?** In my absence?   **34 without** unless   **35 would** i.e., would
perceive them.   **35–6 you are . . . follies** i.e., you so surround and
encompass these follies   **37 urinal** glass container for medical examination of urine   **46 hard-favored** ugly   **47 fair** beautiful, blond-
haired.   **well-favored** gracious, charming; also, good-looking. (But
Speed takes the word in the sense of "looked upon with approval.")

50 of by.   **well-favored** approved of.   **52 favor** grace, charm
53 painted achieved by cosmetics   **54 out of all count** incalculable.
57 counts of esteems   **58 How . . . me?** i.e., Are you impugning my
judgment?   **account of** esteem   **60 deformed** i.e., transformed by
the distorting perspective of Valentine's love for her.   **67 Love** i.e.,
Cupid, traditionally represented as blind   **68 lights** sight
69–70 going ungartered i.e., neglecting appearance in dress, a traditional sign of love melancholy.   **72 passing** surpassing, very great
74–5 cannot . . . hose i.e., you are in even worse shape than Proteus,
and he was perfectly helpless.   **76 Belike** Probably   **79 you . . . love**
you thrashed me for being too fond of lying abed   **81 I stand
affected to** I am in love with   **82 set** (1) settled, finished (2) seated,
as contrasted with *stand* in line 81 (3) no longer in a condition of
standing, being erect (giving a bawdy sense to Valentine's innocent
use of *stand*)   **90 Peace** Be quiet   **91 motion** puppet show.   **puppet**
i.e., Silvia.   **92 interpret** i.e., supply dialogue or commentary, as for a
puppet show

VALENTINE   Madam and mistress, a thousand good-
morrows.

SPEED   [aside]   Oh, give ye good even! Here's a million   95
of manners.

SILVIA   Sir Valentine and servant, to you two thousand.   97

SPEED   [aside]   He should give her interest, and she gives   98
it him.   99

VALENTINE
As you enjoined me, I have writ your letter
Unto the secret, nameless friend of yours,
Which I was much unwilling to proceed in
But for my duty to Your Ladyship.   [Giving a letter.]   103

SILVIA
I thank you, gentle servant. 'Tis very clerkly done.   104

VALENTINE
Now trust me, madam, it came hardly off,   105
For, being ignorant to whom it goes,
I writ at random, very doubtfully.   107

SILVIA
Perchance you think too much of so much pains?   108

VALENTINE
No, madam. So it stead you, I will write—   109
Please you command—a thousand times as much.
And yet—

SILVIA
A pretty period! Well, I guess the sequel.   112
And yet I will not name it. And yet I care not.
And yet take this again. And yet I thank you,   114
Meaning henceforth to trouble you no more.
[She offers him the letter.]

SPEED   [aside]
And yet you will, and yet another "yet."

VALENTINE
What means Your Ladyship? Do you not like it?

SILVIA   Yes, yes. The lines are very quaintly writ,   118
But since unwillingly, take them again.
Nay, take them.   [She gives back the letter.]

VALENTINE   Madam, they are for you.

SILVIA
Ay, ay. You writ them, sir, at my request,
But I will none of them. They are for you.
I would have had them writ more movingly.

VALENTINE
Please you, I'll write Your Ladyship another.

SILVIA
And when it's writ, for my sake read it over.
And if it please you, so; if not, why, so.   126

VALENTINE
If it please me, madam? What then?

SILVIA
Why, if it please you, take it for your labor.
And so good morrow, servant.   Exit Silvia.

SPEED   [aside]
Oh, jest unseen, inscrutable, invisible
As a nose on a man's face, or a weathercock on a
steeple!
My master sues to her, and she hath taught her suitor,   132
He being her pupil, to become her tutor.
Oh, excellent device! Was there ever heard a better,
That my master, being scribe, to himself should write
the letter?

VALENTINE   How now, sir? What, are you reasoning   136
with yourself?

SPEED   Nay, I was rhyming. 'Tis you that have the   138
reason.

VALENTINE   To do what?

SPEED   To be a spokesman from Madam Silvia.

VALENTINE   To whom?

SPEED   To yourself. Why, she woos you by a figure.   143

VALENTINE   What figure?

SPEED   By a letter, I should say.

VALENTINE   Why, she hath not writ to me.

SPEED   What need she, when she hath made you write
to yourself? Why, do you not perceive the jest?

VALENTINE   No, believe me.

SPEED   No believing you, indeed, sir. But did you per-   150
ceive her earnest?   151

VALENTINE   She gave me none, except an angry word.

SPEED   Why, she hath given you a letter.

VALENTINE   That's the letter I writ to her friend.

SPEED   And that letter hath she delivered, and there an   155
end.   156

VALENTINE   I would it were no worse.

SPEED   I'll warrant you, 'tis as well.
For often have you writ to her, and she, in modesty,
Or else for want of idle time, could not again reply;
Or fearing else some messenger that might her mind
discover,
Herself hath taught her love himself to write unto her
lover.
All this I speak in print, for in print I found it. Why   163
muse you, sir? 'Tis dinnertime.

VALENTINE   I have dined.   165

SPEED   Ay, but hearken, sir: though the chameleon Love   166
can feed on the air, I am one that am nourished by my

---

95 give i.e., God give.   **a million** i.e., an excessive amount   **97 servant** male admirer devoted to serving a lady in love   **98–9 He . . . him** i.e., He is the one who should be showing *interest* in her, as her *servant*, and yet she gives him *interest* by doubling what he has given her. (Playing on the financial meaning of *interest*.)   **103 duty** obedience, submission   **104 clerkly** in a scholarly manner. (And perhaps with good penmanship.)   **105 Now . . . off** Believe me, madam, it was done with difficulty   **107 doubtfully** uncertainly.   **108 Perchance . . . pains?** Perhaps you think I have given you too much trouble?   **109 So** So long as.   **stead** benefit   **112 A pretty period!** A fine conclusion! i.e., To finish your eloquent protestation of devoted service with "And yet" is to spoil all that came before it.   **114 again** back.   **118 quaintly** ingeniously   **126 so** well and good

132 sues to wooes, pleads with   **136, 138 reasoning . . . rhyming** (Playing on the antithesis of *rhyme* and *reason*.)   **143 figure** device.   **150 No believing you** There's no believing anything you say. (Playing on *No, believe me* in the previous line.)   **151 earnest** to be serious. (But Valentine, in line 152, takes the word as a noun meaning "money paid as an installment to secure a bargain.")   **155–6 there an end** (1) there's no more to be said (2) that's where the matter should end, with the letter delivered to you as the intended recipient.   **163 All . . . found it** I say all this with assurance, having seen it in writing. **165 dined** i.e., feasted on the sight of Silvia.   **166 chameleon Love** (The chameleon was popularly thought to be able to live on air. Love is also a chameleon because it is so changeable.)

victuals, and would fain have meat. Oh, be not like 168
your mistress; be moved, be moved!   *Exeunt.* 169

❖

2.2

Enter Proteus [and] Julia.

PROTEUS   Have patience, gentle Julia.
JULIA   I must, where is no remedy.   2
PROTEUS
When possibly I can, I will return.
JULIA
If you turn not, you will return the sooner.   4
Keep this remembrance for thy Julia's sake.
                            [*She gives him a ring.*]
PROTEUS
Why, then, we'll make exchange. Here, take you this.
                            [*He gives her a ring.*]
JULIA
And seal the bargain with a holy kiss.   [*They kiss.*]
PROTEUS
Here is my hand for my true constancy;
And when that hour o'erslips me in the day   9
Wherein I sigh not, Julia, for thy sake,
The next ensuing hour some foul mischance
Torment me for my love's forgetfulness!
My father stays my coming. Answer not.   13
The tide is now—nay, not thy tide of tears;   14
That tide will stay me longer than I should.
Julia, farewell!   [*Exit Julia.*]
              What, gone without a word?
Ay, so true love should do; it cannot speak,
For truth hath better deeds than words to grace it.   18

[Enter] Panthino.

PANTHINO
Sir Proteus, you are stayed for.
PROTEUS   Go. I come, I come.
Alas! This parting strikes poor lovers dumb. *Exeunt.*

❖

2.3

Enter Lance [with his dog, Crab].

LANCE   Nay, 'twill be this hour ere I have done weeping.
All the kind of the Lances have this very fault. I have   2
received my proportion, like the prodigious son, and   3
am going with Sir Proteus to the Imperial's court. I   4
think Crab, my dog, be the sourest-natured dog that
lives. My mother weeping, my father wailing, my sister crying, our maid howling, our cat wringing her

hands, and all our house in a great perplexity, yet did
not this cruel-hearted cur shed one tear. He is a stone,
a very pebblestone, and has no more pity in him than
a dog. A Jew would have wept to have seen our parting. Why, my grandam, having no eyes, look you,
wept herself blind at my parting. Nay, I'll show you
the manner of it. This shoe is my father. No, this left   14
shoe is my father. No, no, this left shoe is my mother.
Nay, that cannot be so neither. Yes, it is so, it is so—it
hath the worser sole. This shoe with the hole in it is my   17
mother, and this my father. A vengeance on't! There   18
'tis. Now, sir, this staff is my sister, for, look you, she is
as white as a lily and as small as a wand. This hat is   20
Nan, our maid. I am the dog. No, the dog is himself,
and I am the dog—Oh, the dog is me, and I am myself.
Ay, so, so. Now come I to my father: "Father, your
blessing." Now should not the shoe speak a word for
weeping. Now should I kiss my father. Well, he weeps
on. Now come I to my mother. Oh, that she could
speak now like a wood woman! Well, I kiss her. Why,   27
there 'tis. Here's my mother's breath up and down.   28
Now come I to my sister; mark the moan she makes.
Now the dog all this while sheds not a tear nor speaks
a word; but see how I lay the dust with my tears.

[Enter] Panthino.

PANTHINO   Lance, away, away, aboard! Thy master is
shipped, and thou art to post after with oars. What's   33
the matter? Why weep'st thou, man? Away, ass! You'll
lose the tide if you tarry any longer.
LANCE   It is no matter if the tied were lost, for it is the   36
unkindest tied that ever any man tied.
PANTHINO   What's the unkindest tide?
LANCE   Why, he that's tied here, Crab, my dog.
PANTHINO   Tut, man, I mean thou'lt lose the flood, and   40
in losing the flood, lose thy voyage, and in losing thy
voyage, lose thy master, and in losing thy master, lose
thy service, and in losing thy service—[*Lance puts his
hand over Panthino's mouth.*] Why dost thou stop my
mouth?
LANCE   For fear thou shouldst lose thy tongue.   46
PANTHINO   Where should I lose my tongue?
LANCE   In thy tale.
PANTHINO   In thy tail!
LANCE   Lose the tide, and the voyage, and the master,
and the service, and the tied? Why, man, if the river
were dry, I am able to fill it with my tears; if the wind
were down, I could drive the boat with my sighs.
PANTHINO   Come, come away, man. I was sent to call   54
thee.

---

168 fain gladly   **169 be moved** (1) be not hard-hearted (2) be persuaded to go to dinner
2.2. Location: Verona. Julia's house.
2 where is where there is   **4 turn not** do not prove to be unfaithful
9 o'erslips me slips by me unnoticed   **13 stays** awaits   **14 The tide**
The high tide for departure by ship   **18 grace** adorn
2.3. Location: Verona. A street.
2 kind kindred, race   **3 proportion** (A malapropism for "portion,
allotment.")   **prodigious** (A malapropism for "prodigal.")   **4 Imperial's** i.e., Emperor's

14 This shoe . . . father (Lance demonstrates.)   **17 sole** (With a pun
on "soul." Lance refers to a common debate as to whether a woman's
soul is inferior to a man's.)   **the hole in it** (Suggesting a bawdy joke
about the feminine sexual anatomy.)   **18 A vengeance on't** (A mild
curse, probably occasioned by the difficulty Lance has in pulling his
shoe off. *There* 'tis in lines 18–19 signals his success in doing so.)
20 small slim   **27 wood** mad, distraught. (With punning allusion to a
wooden shoe.)   **28 up and down** i.e., exactly.   **33 post** hasten.   **with
oars** i.e., in a rowboat, in order to reach the sailing vessel at anchor.
36 the tied i.e., the dog that is tied. (With a pun on *tide*.)   **40 lose the
flood** miss the tide   **46 lose** (1) lose (2) loose   **54 call** summon

LANCE   Sir, call me what thou dar'st.   56
PANTHINO   Wilt thou go?
LANCE   Well, I will go.   *Exeunt.*

❧

2.4

Enter Valentine, Silvia, Thurio, [and] Speed.

SILVIA   Servant!
VALENTINE   Mistress?
SPEED   [*aside to Valentine*]   Master, Sir Thurio frowns on you.
VALENTINE   Ay, boy, it's for love.
SPEED   Not of you.
VALENTINE   Of my mistress, then.
SPEED   'Twere good you knocked him.   [*Exit.*]   7
SILVIA   [*to Valentine*]   Servant, you are sad.
VALENTINE   Indeed, madam, I seem so.
THURIO   Seem you that you are not?   10
VALENTINE   Haply I do.   11
THURIO   So do counterfeits.
VALENTINE   So do you.
THURIO   What seem I that I am not?
VALENTINE   Wise.
THURIO   What instance of the contrary?   16
VALENTINE   Your folly.
THURIO   And how quote you my folly?   18
VALENTINE   I quote it in your jerkin.   19
THURIO   My "jerkin" is a doublet.   20
VALENTINE   Well, then, I'll double your folly.
THURIO   How?   22
SILVIA   What, angry, Sir Thurio? Do you change color?
VALENTINE   Give him leave, madam; he is a kind of
    chameleon.
THURIO   That hath more mind to feed on your blood   26
    than live in your air.   27
VALENTINE   You have said, sir.   28
THURIO   Ay, sir, and done too, for this time.   29
VALENTINE   I know it well, sir; you always end ere you   30
    begin.   31
SILVIA   A fine volley of words, gentlemen, and quickly
    shot off.
VALENTINE   'Tis indeed, madam, we thank the giver.
SILVIA   Who is that, servant?
VALENTINE   Yourself, sweet lady, for you gave the fire. Sir   36
    Thurio borrows his wit from Your Ladyship's looks,

and spends what he borrows kindly in your company.   38
THURIO   Sir, if you spend word for word with me, I shall
    make your wit bankrupt.
VALENTINE   I know it well, sir; you have an exchequer   41
    of words, and, I think, no other treasure to give your
    followers, for it appears, by their bare liveries, that   43
    they live by your bare words.   44
SILVIA   No more, gentlemen, no more. Here comes my
    father.

[Enter the] Duke.

DUKE
    Now, daughter Silvia, you are hard beset.—   47
    Sir Valentine, your father is in good health.
    What say you to a letter from your friends
    Of much good news?
VALENTINE   My lord, I will be thankful
    To any happy messenger from thence.   51
DUKE
    Know ye Don Antonio, your countryman?
VALENTINE
    Ay, my good lord, I know the gentleman
    To be of worth and worthy estimation,
    And not without desert so well reputed.   55
DUKE   Hath he not a son?
VALENTINE
    Ay, my good lord, a son that well deserves
    The honor and regard of such a father.
DUKE   You know him well?
VALENTINE
    I know him as myself, for from our infancy
    We have conversed and spent our hours together.
    And though myself have been an idle truant,
    Omitting the sweet benefit of time   63
    To clothe mine age with angel-like perfection,
    Yet hath Sir Proteus—for that's his name—
    Made use and fair advantage of his days;
    His years but young, but his experience old;
    His head unmellowed, but his judgment ripe.   68
    And in a word—for far behind his worth
    Comes all the praises that I now bestow—
    He is complete in feature and in mind   71
    With all good grace to grace a gentleman.
DUKE
    Beshrew me, sir, but if he make this good,   73
    He is as worthy for an empress' love
    As meet to be an emperor's counselor.   75
    Well, sir, this gentleman is come to me
    With commendation from great potentates,
    And here he means to spend his time awhile.
    I think 'tis no unwelcome news to you.

---

56 **call me what** call me whatever names
2.4. Location: Milan. The Duke's palace.
7 **'Twere . . . him** You'd better hit him.   10 **that** what   11 **Haply** Perhaps   16 **instance** proof   18 **quote** notice, observe. (Pronounced like *coat*, enabling Valentine to pun on that idea.)   19 **jerkin** close-fitting jacket worn over, or in place of, the doublet   20 **My . . . doublet** What you ignorantly call my "jerkin" is in fact a doublet, i.e., another kind of men's jacket. (With a play on *double* in the next line.)   22 **How?** (An expression of annoyance or incredulity.)   26 **That** i.e., One who   27 **in your air** (1) in the air you breathe, i.e., near you (2) listening to your talk. (Chameleons were supposed to be able to live on air alone.)   28 **You have said** i.e., That's a lot of fine talk   29 **done** (1) acted, in contrast to *said* (2) finished. (Thurio hints here that he's prepared to duel with Valentine at some future date.)   30–1 **end . . . begin** i.e., stop before you come to actual blows.   36 **fire** i.e., spark to set off the volley.

38 **kindly** fittingly, naturally, affectionately   41 **exchequer** treasury   43 **bare liveries** threadbare uniforms   44 **bare** mere   47 **hard beset** strongly besieged (with two wooers at once).   51 **happy messenger** bringer of good tidings   55 **without desert** undeservedly   63 **Omitting** neglecting   68 **unmellowed** i.e., unmixed with gray hair   71 **complete in feature** perfect in shape of body and personal appearance   73 **Beshrew me** (A mild oath.)   **make this good** i.e., match your description   75 **meet** suited

VALENTINE
    Should I have wished a thing, it had been he.

DUKE
    Welcome him then according to his worth.
    Silvia, I speak to you, and you, Sir Thurio;
    For Valentine, I need not cite him to it.
    I will send him hither to you presently.   [*Exit.*]   83

VALENTINE
    This is the gentleman I told Your Ladyship
    Had come along with me, but that his mistress   86
    Did hold his eyes locked in her crystal looks.

SILVIA
    Belike that now she hath enfranchised them   88
    Upon some other pawn for fealty.   89

VALENTINE
    Nay, sure, I think she holds them prisoners still.

SILVIA
    Nay, then he should be blind, and being blind
    How could he see his way to seek out you?

VALENTINE
    Why, lady, Love hath twenty pair of eyes.

THURIO
    They say that Love hath not an eye at all.

VALENTINE
    To see such lovers, Thurio, as yourself.
    Upon a homely object Love can wink.   96

SILVIA
    Have done, have done. Here comes the gentleman.   97

        [*Enter*] *Proteus.*

VALENTINE
    Welcome, dear Proteus!—Mistress, I beseech you,
    Confirm his welcome with some special favor.

SILVIA
    His worth is warrant for his welcome hither,
    If this be he you oft have wished to hear from.

VALENTINE
    Mistress, it is. Sweet lady, entertain him   102
    To be my fellow servant to Your Ladyship.

SILVIA
    Too low a mistress for so high a servant.

PROTEUS
    Not so, sweet lady, but too mean a servant   105
    To have a look of such a worthy mistress.   106

VALENTINE
    Leave off discourse of disability.   107
    Sweet lady, entertain him for your servant.

PROTEUS
    My duty will I boast of, nothing else.   109

SILVIA
    And duty never yet did want his meed.   110
    Servant, you are welcome to a worthless mistress.

PROTEUS
    I'll die on him that says so but yourself.   112

SILVIA
    That you are welcome?

PROTEUS   That you are worthless.

        [*Enter a Servant.*]

SERVANT
    Madam, my lord your father would speak with you.

SILVIA
    I wait upon his pleasure.   [*Exit Servant.*]
                    Come, Sir Thurio,
    Go with me.—Once more, new servant, welcome.
    I'll leave you to confer of home affairs.
    When you have done, we look to hear from you.

PROTEUS
    We'll both attend upon Your Ladyship.
        [*Exeunt Sylvia and Thurio.*]

VALENTINE
    Now tell me, how do all from whence you came?

PROTEUS
    Your friends are well and have them much
        commended.   121

VALENTINE
    And how do yours?

PROTEUS   I left them all in health.

VALENTINE
    How does your lady, and how thrives your love?

PROTEUS
    My tales of love were wont to weary you.
    I know you joy not in a love discourse.

VALENTINE
    Ay, Proteus, but that life is altered now.
    I have done penance for contemning Love,   127
    Whose high imperious thoughts have punished me
    With bitter fasts, with penitential groans,
    With nightly tears, and daily heartsore sighs;
    For in revenge of my contempt of love
    Love hath chased sleep from my enthrallèd eyes
    And made them watchers of mine own heart's sorrow.   133
    O gentle Proteus, Love's a mighty lord,
    And hath so humbled me as I confess   135
    There is no woe to his correction,   136
    Nor to his service no such joy on earth.   137
    Now, no discourse except it be of love.
    Now can I break my fast, dine, sup, and sleep
    Upon the very naked name of love.   140

PROTEUS
    Enough. I read your fortune in your eye.
    Was this the idol that you worship so?

VALENTINE
    Even she. And is she not a heavenly saint?

PROTEUS
    No, but she is an earthly paragon.

---

83 **cite** urge   86 **Had** would have   88 **Belike that** Perhaps
88–9 **enfranchised . . . fealty** set free his eyes in return for some other
pledge of fidelity, or, to pledge his fidelity somewhere else, or, now
that some other lover has pledged his service to her.   96 **homely**
plain.   **wink** close the eyes.   97 **Have done** Cease this bickering
102 **entertain** take into service   105 **mean** lowly, unworthy   106 **of**
from   107 **Leave . . . disability**   Stop talking about your unworthiness.   109 **duty** i.e., to Silvia   110 **want his meed** lack its reward.

112 **die on** die fighting with   121 **have . . . commended** have sent
warm greetings.   127 **contemning** scorning   133 **watchers** wakeful
beholders   135 **as** that   136 **to his correction** compared to the woe of
his punishment   137 **to his service** i.e., compared to serving Love
140 **very naked** mere

VALENTINE
    Call her divine.

PROTEUS   I will not flatter her.

VALENTINE
    Oh, flatter me, for love delights in praises.

PROTEUS
    When I was sick, you gave me bitter pills,
    And I must minister the like to you.

VALENTINE
    Then speak the truth by her: if not divine,   148
    Yet let her be a principality,   149
    Sovereign to all the creatures on the earth.

PROTEUS
    Except my mistress.

VALENTINE   Sweet, except not any,   151
    Except thou wilt except against my love.   152

PROTEUS
    Have I not reason to prefer mine own?

VALENTINE
    And I will help thee to prefer her, too.   154
    She shall be dignified with this high honor:
    To bear my lady's train, lest the base earth
    Should from her vesture chance to steal a kiss
    And, of so great a favor growing proud,
    Disdain to root the summer-swelling flower,   159
    And make rough winter everlastingly.

PROTEUS
    Why, Valentine, what braggartism is this?

VALENTINE
    Pardon me, Proteus, all I can is nothing   162
    To her whose worth makes other worthies nothing.   163
    She is alone.

PROTEUS   Then let her alone.   164

VALENTINE
    Not for the world. Why, man, she is mine own,
    And I as rich in having such a jewel
    As twenty seas, if all their sand were pearl,
    The water nectar, and the rocks pure gold.
    Forgive me that I do not dream on thee,   169
    Because thou see'st me dote upon my love.
    My foolish rival, that her father likes
    Only for his possessions are so huge,   172
    Is gone with her along, and I must after;
    For love, thou know'st, is full of jealousy.

PROTEUS   But she loves you?

VALENTINE
    Ay, and we are betrothed. Nay, more, our marriage hour,
    With all the cunning manner of our flight,
    Determined of—how I must climb her window,   178
    The ladder made of cords, and all the means
    Plotted and 'greed on for my happiness.

    Good Proteus, go with me to my chamber,
    In these affairs to aid me with thy counsel.

PROTEUS
    Go on before. I shall inquire you forth.   183
    I must unto the road, to disembark   184
    Some necessaries that I needs must use,
    And then I'll presently attend you.

VALENTINE   Will you make haste?

PROTEUS   I will.   *Exit* [*Valentine*].
    Even as one heat another heat expels,   189
    Or as one nail by strength drives out another,
    So the remembrance of my former love
    Is by a newer object quite forgotten.
    Is it mine eye, or Valentine's praise,
    Her true perfection, or my false transgression
    That makes me, reasonless, to reason thus?   195
    She is fair; and so is Julia that I love—
    That I did love, for now my love is thawed,
    Which like a waxen image 'gainst a fire
    Bears no impression of the thing it was.
    Methinks my zeal to Valentine is cold,
    And that I love him not as I was wont.   201
    Oh, but I love his lady too, too much,
    And that's the reason I love him so little.
    How shall I dote on her with more advice,   204
    That thus without advice begin to love her?   205
    'Tis but her picture I have yet beheld,   206
    And that hath dazzlèd my reason's light;
    But when I look on her perfections,   208
    There is no reason but I shall be blind.   209
    If I can check my erring love, I will;   210
    If not, to compass her I'll use my skill.   *Exit.* 211

❖

2.5

Enter, [*meeting,*] *Speed and Lance* [*with his dog, Crab*].

SPEED   Lance, by mine honesty, welcome to Milan!   1

LANCE   Forswear not thyself, sweet youth, for I am not welcome. I reckon this always, that a man is never un-   3
done till he be hanged, nor never welcome to a place   4
till some certain shot be paid and the hostess say,   5
"Welcome!"

SPEED   Come on, you madcap, I'll to the alehouse with you presently, where, for one shot of five pence, thou   8
shalt have five thousand welcomes. But sirrah, how did thy master part with Madam Julia?

---

148 **by** about 149 **a principality** a member of one of the nine orders of angels 151 **Sweet** (A term of affection used with both men and women.) 152 **Except . . . except** unless you want to cast aspersions 154 **prefer** advance. (With wordplay on *prefer*, like better, in line 153.) 159 **root** provide rooting for 162 **can** i.e., can say of her 163 **To her** compared to her 164 **is alone** is peerless. (But Proteus plays on the sense of "let her be.") 169 **that . . . thee** i.e., that I seem neglectful of you 172 **for** because 178 **Determined of** is decided, arranged

183 **I . . . forth** I will ask after your whereabouts and find you.
184 **road** roadstead, harbor 189 **Even . . . expels** (The application of heat was thought to relieve the pain of a burn.) 195 **reasonless** without justification, wrongly 201 **wont** accustomed. 204–5 **How . . . her?** How will I adore her on further consideration, I who have fallen in love with her so suddenly and rashly? (With wordplay on *advice*.)
206 **picture** i.e., outer appearance 208 **perfections** true qualities, not immediately apparent to view 209 **no reason but** no doubt but that
210 **check** restrain 211 **compass** obtain
2.5. Location: Milan. A street.
1 **by mine honesty** upon my word 3–4 **undone** ruined 5 **shot** tavern reckoning 8 **one . . . pence** a fivepenny drink

LANCE   Marry, after they closed in earnest they parted 11
very fairly in jest. 12

SPEED   But shall she marry him?

LANCE   No.

SPEED   How then? Shall he marry her?

LANCE   No, neither.

SPEED   What, are they broken? 17

LANCE   No, they are both as whole as a fish. 18

SPEED   Why, then, how stands the matter with them?

LANCE   Marry, thus: when it stands well with him, it 20
stands well with her.

SPEED   What an ass art thou! I understand thee not.

LANCE   What a block art thou, that thou canst not! My 23
staff understands me.

SPEED   What thou say'st?

LANCE   Ay, and what I do too. Look thee, I'll but lean,
and my staff under-stands me.

SPEED   It stands under thee, indeed.

LANCE   Why, stand-under and under-stand is all one.

SPEED   But tell me true, will't be a match?

LANCE   Ask my dog. If he say ay, it will; if he say no, it
will; if he shake his tail and say nothing, it will.

SPEED   The conclusion is then that it will.

LANCE   Thou shalt never get such a secret from me but
by a parable. 35

SPEED   'Tis well that I get it so. But Lance, how say'st 36
thou, that my master is become a notable lover? 37

LANCE   I never knew him otherwise.

SPEED   Than how?

LANCE   A notable lubber, as thou reportest him to be. 40

SPEED   Why, thou whoreson ass, thou mistak'st me. 41

LANCE   Why, fool, I meant not thee. I meant thy
master.

SPEED   I tell thee my master is become a hot lover.

LANCE   Why, I tell thee I care not, though he burn 45
himself in love. If thou wilt, go with me to the 46
alehouse; if not, thou art an Hebrew, a Jew, and not
worth the name of a Christian.

SPEED   Why?

LANCE   Because thou hast not so much charity in thee as
to go to the ale with a Christian. Wilt thou go? 51

SPEED   At thy service.   *Exeunt.*

❧

2.6

Enter Proteus solus.

PROTEUS
To leave my Julia shall I be forsworn;
To love fair Silvia shall I be forsworn;
To wrong my friend I shall be much forsworn.
And ev'n that power which gave me first my oath 4
Provokes me to this threefold perjury.
Love bade me swear, and Love bids me forswear.
O sweet-suggesting Love, if thou hast sinned, 7
Teach me, thy tempted subject, to excuse it! 8
At first I did adore a twinkling star,
But now I worship a celestial sun.
Unheedful vows may heedfully be broken, 11
And he wants wit that wants resolvèd will 12
To learn his wit t'exchange the bad for better. 13
Fie, fie, unreverent tongue, to call her bad
Whose sovereignty so oft thou hast preferred 15
With twenty thousand soul-confirming oaths! 16
I cannot leave to love, and yet I do; 17
But there I leave to love where I should love.
Julia I lose, and Valentine I lose.
If I keep them, I needs must lose myself.
If I lose them, thus find I by their loss
For Valentine, myself; for Julia, Silvia.
I to myself am dearer than a friend,
For love is still most precious in itself, 24
And Silvia—witness heaven, that made her fair!—
Shows Julia but a swarthy Ethiop. 26
I will forget that Julia is alive,
Rememb'ring that my love to her is dead;
And Valentine I'll hold an enemy,
Aiming at Silvia as a sweeter friend.
I cannot now prove constant to myself
Without some treachery used to Valentine.
This night he meaneth with a corded ladder
To climb celestial Silvia's chamber window,
Myself in counsel, his competitor. 35
Now presently I'll give her father notice
Of their disguising and pretended flight, 37
Who, all enraged, will banish Valentine;
For Thurio, he intends, shall wed his daughter.
But Valentine being gone, I'll quickly cross 40
By some sly trick blunt Thurio's dull proceeding. 41
Love, lend me wings to make my purpose swift,
As thou hast lent me wit to plot this drift!   *Exit.* 43

❧

2.7

Enter Julia and Lucetta.

JULIA
Counsel, Lucetta. Gentle girl, assist me;
And ev'n in kind love I do conjure thee,
Who art the table wherein all my thoughts   3
Are visibly charactered and engraved,   4
To lesson me and tell me some good mean   5
How, with my honor, I may undertake
A journey to my loving Proteus.

LUCETTA
Alas, the way is wearisome and long!

JULIA
A true-devoted pilgrim is not weary
To measure kingdoms with his feeble steps;   10
Much less shall she that hath Love's wings to fly,
And when the flight is made to one so dear,
Of such divine perfection, as Sir Proteus.

LUCETTA
Better forbear till Proteus make return.

JULIA
Oh, know'st thou not his looks are my soul's food?
Pity the dearth that I have pinèd in   16
By longing for that food so long a time.
Didst thou but know the inly touch of love,   18
Thou wouldst as soon go kindle fire with snow
As seek to quench the fire of love with words.

LUCETTA
I do not seek to quench your love's hot fire,
But qualify the fire's extreme rage,   22
Lest it should burn above the bounds of reason.

JULIA
The more thou dam'st it up, the more it burns.
The current that with gentle murmur glides,
Thou know'st, being stopped, impatiently doth rage;
But when his fair course is not hinderèd,
He makes sweet music with th'enameled stones,   28
Giving a gentle kiss to every sedge   29
He overtaketh in his pilgrimage,
And so by many winding nooks he strays
With willing sport to the wild ocean.
Then let me go, and hinder not my course.
I'll be as patient as a gentle stream
And make a pastime of each weary step,
Till the last step have brought me to my love,
And there I'll rest, as after much turmoil
A blessèd soul doth in Elysium.

LUCETTA
But in what habit will you go along?   39

JULIA
Not like a woman, for I would prevent   40

The loose encounters of lascivious men.
Gentle Lucetta, fit me with such weeds   42
As may beseem some well-reputed page.   43

LUCETTA
Why, then, Your Ladyship must cut your hair.

JULIA
No, girl, I'll knit it up in silken strings
With twenty odd-conceited true-love knots.   46
To be fantastic may become a youth   47
Of greater time than I shall show to be.   48

LUCETTA
What fashion, madam, shall I make your breeches?

JULIA
That fits as well as "Tell me, good my lord,
What compass will you wear your farthingale?"   51
Why, ev'n what fashion thou best likes, Lucetta.

LUCETTA
You must needs have them with a codpiece, madam.   53

JULIA
Out, out, Lucetta! That will be ill-favored.   54

LUCETTA
A round hose, madam, now's not worth a pin,   55
Unless you have a codpiece to stick pins on.   56

JULIA
Lucetta, as thou lov'st me, let me have
What thou think'st meet and is most mannerly.   58
But tell me, wench, how will the world repute me
For undertaking so unstaid a journey?   60
I fear me it will make me scandalized.

LUCETTA
If you think so, then stay at home and go not.

JULIA   Nay, that I will not.

LUCETTA
Then never dream on infamy, but go.
If Proteus like your journey when you come,
No matter who's displeased when you are gone.
I fear me he will scarce be pleased withal.   67

JULIA
That is the least, Lucetta, of my fear.
A thousand oaths, an ocean of his tears,
And instances of infinite of love   70
Warrant me welcome to my Proteus.

LUCETTA
All these are servants to deceitful men.

JULIA
Base men, that use them to so base effect!
But truer stars did govern Proteus' birth;
His words are bonds, his oaths are oracles,   75
His love sincere, his thoughts immaculate,
His tears pure messengers sent from his heart,

---

42 weeds garments **43 beseem** suit **46 odd-conceited** strangely devised **47 fantastic** flamboyantly dressed **48 Of greater time** of more years **51 compass** fullness. **farthingale** hooped petticoat. **53 must needs** will have to. **codpiece** bagged appendage to the front of close-fitting hose or breeches, often conspicuous and ornamented **54 Out** (An expression of reproach or indignation.) **ill-favored** unsightly. **55 round hose** padded breeches **56 stick pins on** (One method used to decorate the codpiece.) **58 meet** suitable **60 unstaid** immodest, unconventional **67 withal** with it. **70 infinite** infinity **75 oracles** infallible indicators

---

2.7. Location: Verona. Julia's house.
3 table tablet **4 charactered** inscribed **5 lesson** teach **10 measure** traverse **16 dearth** famine **18 inly** inward **22 qualify** control, moderate **28 enameled** having shiny, polished surfaces; variegated **29 sedge** grassy, rushlike plant **39 habit** apparel **40 prevent** forestall

His heart as far from fraud as heaven from earth.
LUCETTA
Pray heav'n he prove so when you come to him!
JULIA
Now, as thou lov'st me, do him not that wrong
To bear a hard opinion of his truth.   81
Only deserve my love by loving him,
And presently go with me to my chamber
To take a note of what I stand in need of
To furnish me upon my longing journey.   85
All that is mine I leave at thy dispose,   86
My goods, my lands, my reputation;
Only, in lieu thereof, dispatch me hence.
Come, answer not, but to it presently.
I am impatient of my tarriance.   *Exeunt.*   90

❖

3.1

Enter [the] Duke, Thurio, [and] Proteus.

DUKE
Sir Thurio, give us leave, I pray, awhile.   1
We have some secrets to confer about.   [*Exit Thurio.*]
Now, tell me, Proteus, what's your will with me?
PROTEUS
My gracious lord, that which I would discover   4
The law of friendship bids me to conceal;
But when I call to mind your gracious favors
Done to me, undeserving as I am,
My duty pricks me on to utter that   8
Which else no worldly good should draw from me.
Know, worthy prince, Sir Valentine, my friend,
This night intends to steal away your daughter.
Myself am one made privy to the plot.   12
I know you have determined to bestow her
On Thurio, whom your gentle daughter hates;
And should she thus be stol'n away from you,
It would be much vexation to your age.
Thus, for my duty's sake, I rather chose
To cross my friend in his intended drift   18
Than, by concealing it, heap on your head
A pack of sorrows which would press you down,
Being unprevented, to your timeless grave.   21
DUKE
Proteus, I thank thee for thine honest care,
Which to requite, command me while I live.   23
This love of theirs myself have often seen,
Haply when they have judged me fast asleep,
And oftentimes have purposed to forbid
Sir Valentine her company and my court.
But, fearing lest my jealous aim might err,   28
And so unworthily disgrace the man—

A rashness that I ever yet have shunned—
I gave him gentle looks, thereby to find
That which thyself hast now disclosed to me.
And, that thou mayst perceive my fear of this,
Knowing that tender youth is soon suggested,   34
I nightly lodge her in an upper tower,
The key whereof myself have ever kept;
And thence she cannot be conveyed away.
PROTEUS
Know, noble lord, they have devised a means
How he her chamber window will ascend
And with a corded ladder fetch her down;
For which the youthful lover now is gone,
And this way comes he with it presently,   42
Where, if it please you, you may intercept him.
But, good my lord, do it so cunningly
That my discovery be not aimèd at;   45
For, love of you, not hate unto my friend,
Hath made me publisher of this pretense.   47
DUKE
Upon mine honor, he shall never know
That I had any light from thee of this.
PROTEUS
Adieu, my lord. Sir Valentine is coming.   [*Exit.*]

[Enter] Valentine, [hurrying elsewhere, con-
cealing a rope ladder beneath his cloak].

DUKE
Sir Valentine, whither away so fast?
VALENTINE
Please it Your Grace, there is a messenger
That stays to bear my letters to my friends,
And I am going to deliver them.
DUKE   Be they of much import?
VALENTINE
The tenor of them doth but signify
My health and happy being at your court.
DUKE
Nay then, no matter. Stay with me awhile.
I am to break with thee of some affairs   59
That touch me near, wherein thou must be secret.   60
'Tis not unknown to thee that I have sought
To match my friend Sir Thurio to my daughter.
VALENTINE
I know it well, my lord, and sure the match
Were rich and honorable. Besides, the gentleman   64
Is full of virtue, bounty, worth, and qualities
Beseeming such a wife as your fair daughter.   66
Cannot Your Grace win her to fancy him?
DUKE
No, trust me. She is peevish, sullen, froward,   68
Proud, disobedient, stubborn, lacking duty,
Neither regarding that she is my child
Nor fearing me as if I were her father.

---

81 **truth** faithfulness.   85 **my longing journey** the journey I long to
make.   86 **at thy dispose** in thy charge   90 **tarriance** delaying.
3.1. Location: Milan. The Duke's palace.
1 **give us leave** (A polite form of dismissal.)   4 **discover** reveal
8 **pricks** spurs   12 **Myself . . . plot** I am one who has been given private knowledge of the plot.   18 **cross** thwart.   **drift** scheme
21 **timeless** untimely   23 **command me** ask any favor of me
28 **jealous aim** suspicious conjecture

34 **suggested** tempted   42 **presently** now   45 **discovery** disclosure.
aimèd at guessed   47 **publisher** discloser.   **pretense** intention.
59 **I am . . . thee of** I wish to disclose to you   60 **touch me near** are of
vital concern to me   64 **Were** would be   66 **Beseeming** befitting
68 **trust** believe.   **peevish** willful.   **froward** perverse

And, may I say to thee, this pride of hers,
Upon advice, hath drawn my love from her; 73
And, where I thought the remnant of mine age 74
Should have been cherished by her childlike duty,
I now am full resolved to take a wife,
And turn her out to who will take her in. 77
Then let her beauty be her wedding dower,
For me and my possessions she esteems not.

VALENTINE
What would Your Grace have me to do in this?

DUKE
There is a lady in Verona here 81
Whom I affect, but she is nice and coy 82
And naught esteems my agèd eloquence. 83
Now therefore would I have thee to my tutor— 84
For long agone I have forgot to court; 85
Besides, the fashion of the time is changed—
How and which way I may bestow myself 87
To be regarded in her sun-bright eye.

VALENTINE
Win her with gifts if she respect not words. 89
Dumb jewels often in their silent kind 90
More than quick words do move a woman's mind. 91

DUKE
But she did scorn a present that I sent her.

VALENTINE
A woman sometimes scorns what best contents her.
Send her another. Never give her o'er,
For scorn at first makes after-love the more.
If she do frown, 'tis not in hate of you,
But rather to beget more love in you.
If she do chide, 'tis not to have you gone,
Forwhy the fools are mad if left alone. 99
Take no repulse, whatever she doth say;
For "Get you gone," she doth not mean "Away!" 101
Flatter and praise, commend, extol their graces;
Though ne'er so black, say they have angels' faces. 103
That man that hath a tongue, I say, is no man
If with his tongue he cannot win a woman.

DUKE
But she I mean is promised by her friends 106
Unto a youthful gentleman of worth,
And kept severely from resort of men,
That no man hath access by day to her. 109

VALENTINE
Why then I would resort to her by night.

DUKE
Ay, but the doors be locked and keys kept safe,
That no man hath recourse to her by night.

VALENTINE
What lets but one may enter at her window? 113

DUKE
Her chamber is aloft, far from the ground,
And built so shelving that one cannot climb it 115
Without apparent hazard of his life. 116

VALENTINE
Why then, a ladder quaintly made of cords 117
To cast up, with a pair of anchoring hooks,
Would serve to scale another Hero's tower, 119
So bold Leander would adventure it. 120

DUKE
Now, as thou art a gentleman of blood, 121
Advise me where I may have such a ladder.

VALENTINE
When would you use it? Pray, sir, tell me that.

DUKE
This very night; for Love is like a child
That longs for everything that he can come by.

VALENTINE
By seven o'clock I'll get you such a ladder.

DUKE
But hark thee, I will go to her alone.
How shall I best convey the ladder thither?

VALENTINE
It will be light, my lord, that you may bear it
Under a cloak that is of any length. 130

DUKE
A cloak as long as thine will serve the turn? 131

VALENTINE
Ay, my good lord.

DUKE   Then let me see thy cloak.
I'll get me one of such another length. 133

VALENTINE
Why, any cloak will serve the turn, my lord.

DUKE
How shall I fashion me to wear a cloak?
I pray thee, let me feel thy cloak upon me.
                         [He pulls open Valentine's cloak.]
What letter is this same? What's here? "To Silvia"?
And here an engine fit for my proceeding. 138
I'll be so bold to break the seal for once.   [He reads.]
"My thoughts do harbor with my Silvia nightly, 140
And slaves they are to me, that send them flying. 141
Oh, could their master come and go as lightly, 142
Himself would lodge where, senseless, they are
  lying! 143
My herald thoughts in thy pure bosom rest them, 144
While I, their king, that thither them importune, 145
Do curse the grace that with such grace hath blessed
  them, 146
Because myself do want my servants' fortune. 147

---

73 **Upon advice** after some careful consideration   74 **where** whereas
77 **who** whoever   81 **Verona** (An error for Milan, seemingly, but
Verona fits the line metrically. Some editors emend "in Verona" to "of
Verona.")   82 **affect** am fond of.   **nice** difficult to please   83 **naught**
not at all   84 **to** as, for   85 **agone** ago.   **forgot** forgotten how
87 **bestow** behave, conduct   89 **respect** heed   90 **kind** nature
91 **quick** lively (as contrasted with *Dumb*, silent)   99 **Forwhy the
fools** because women   101 **For** by   103 **black** dark of complexion
106 **friends** i.e., relatives   109 **That** so that. (Also in line 112.)
113 **lets** hinders

115 **shelving** projecting, overhanging   116 **apparent** plain, evident
117 **quaintly** skillfully   119–20 **Hero's . . . Leander** (See the note to
1.1.22.)   120 **So** provided   121 **blood** good family   130 **of any length**
tolerably long.   131 **turn** purpose.   133 **such another** the same
138 **engine** contrivance, i.e., the rope ladder   140 **harbor** reside
141 **that . . . flying** I who send those thoughts as messages.
142 **lightly** easily, quickly   143 **senseless** insensible.   **lying** dwelling.
144 **them** themselves   145 **importune** command   146–7 **Do . . .
fortune** do curse the happiness that is bestowed so gracefully on them,
because I lack the good fortune enjoyed by my servants, i.e., my
thoughts. (They are able to be with you, while I am not.)

I curse myself for they are sent by me,   148
That they should harbor where their lord should be."
What's here?
"Silvia, this night I will enfranchise thee."
'Tis so; and here's the ladder for the purpose.
Why, Phaëthon, for thou art Merops' son,   153
Wilt thou aspire to guide the heavenly car,
And with thy daring folly burn the world?
Wilt thou reach stars because they shine on thee?   156
Go, base intruder, overweening slave!   157
Bestow thy fawning smiles on equal mates,   158
And think my patience, more than thy desert,
Is privilege for thy departure hence.   160
Thank me for this more than for all the favors
Which, all too much, I have bestowed on thee.
But if thou linger in my territories
Longer than swiftest expedition   164
Will give thee time to leave our royal court,
By heaven, my wrath shall far exceed the love
I ever bore my daughter or thyself.
Begone! I will not hear thy vain excuse,
But, as thou lov'st thy life, make speed from hence.
                                                        [*Exit.*]

VALENTINE
And why not death rather than living torment?
To die is to be banished from myself,
And Silvia is myself. Banished from her
Is self from self—a deadly banishment!
What light is light, if Silvia be not seen?
What joy is joy, if Silvia be not by?
Unless it be to think that she is by
And feed upon the shadow of perfection.   177
Except I be by Silvia in the night,   178
There is no music in the nightingale;
Unless I look on Silvia in the day,
There is no day for me to look upon.
She is my essence, and I leave to be   182
If I be not by her fair influence   183
Fostered, illumined, cherished, kept alive.
I fly not death, to fly his deadly doom;   185
Tarry I here, I but attend on death,   186
But, fly I hence, I fly away from life.

                    [*Enter Proteus and*] *Lance.*

PROTEUS   Run, boy, run, run, and seek him out.
LANCE   So-ho, so-ho!   189
PROTEUS   What see'st thou?

LANCE   Him we go to find. There's not a hair on 's head   191
but 'tis a Valentine.   192
PROTEUS   Valentine?
VALENTINE   No.
PROTEUS   Who then? His spirit?
VALENTINE   Neither.
PROTEUS   What then?
VALENTINE   Nothing.
LANCE   Can nothing speak? Master, shall I strike?   199
PROTEUS   Who wouldst thou strike?
LANCE   Nothing.
PROTEUS   Villain, forbear.
LANCE   Why, sir, I'll strike nothing. I pray you—
PROTEUS   Sirrah, I say, forbear.—Friend Valentine, a
word.
VALENTINE
My ears are stopped and cannot hear good news,
So much of bad already hath possessed them.
PROTEUS
Then in dumb silence will I bury mine,   208
For they are harsh, untunable, and bad.   209
VALENTINE   Is Silvia dead?
PROTEUS   No, Valentine.
VALENTINE
No Valentine, indeed, for sacred Silvia.   212
Hath she forsworn me?
PROTEUS   No, Valentine.
VALENTINE
No Valentine, if Silvia have forsworn me.
What is your news?
LANCE   Sir, there is a proclamation that you are van-
ished.
PROTEUS
That thou art banished—Oh, that's the news!—
From hence, from Silvia, and from me thy friend.
VALENTINE
Oh, I have fed upon this woe already,
And now excess of it will make me surfeit.
Doth Silvia know that I am banished?
PROTEUS
Ay, ay; and she hath offered to the doom—   223
Which, unreversed, stands in effectual force—   224
A sea of melting pearl, which some call tears.
Those at her father's churlish feet she tendered;
With them, upon her knees, her humble self,
Wringing her hands, whose whiteness so became
them
As if but now they waxèd pale for woe.
But neither bended knees, pure hands held up,
Sad sighs, deep groans, nor silver-shedding tears
Could penetrate her uncompassionate sire,
But Valentine, if he be ta'en, must die.   233

148 **for** since, in that   153 **Phaëthon, Merops** (Phaëthon was the son of
Helios, the sun god, and of Clymene, lawful wife of Merops. Phaëthon
aspired to guide the sun god's *car* [line 154] or chariot and was slain by
Zeus for his presumption after he had scorched a large portion of the
earth.)   **for** just because   156 **reach** reach for   157 **overweening** presumptuous   158 **equal mates** i.e., women of your own social status
160 **Is privilege for** authorizes   164 **expedition** speed   177 **shadow**
image   178 **Except** Unless   182 **leave** cease   183 **influence** (An astrological term for the emanations supposed to flow from the stars and to
have power over the destinies of men.)   185 **I . . . doom** I shall not
escape death by flying from the Duke's sentence of death, or, from
death's deadly sentence   186 **Tarry I** if I tarry.   **attend on** wait for
189 **So-ho** (Hunting cry used when the game is sighted.)

191 **hair** (With pun on "hare.")   192 **Valentine** (His name means "token
of true love.")   199 **shall I strike** (Lance wonders if he should strike at a
spirit, line 195, to ward off evil effects, as in *Hamlet*, 1.1.144.)   208 **mine**
i.e., my news   209 **they** i.e., the news   212 **No Valentine** (Valentine
jests bitterly on the inappropriateness of his name and on the loss of his
very identity, playing on *No, Valentine* in the previous line.)   223 **to the
doom** to this news of the sentence   224 **Which . . . force** which, if not
reversed, must certainly take effect   233 **But** but that

Besides, her intercession chafed him so,
When she for thy repeal was suppliant,   235
That to close prison he commanded her,   236
With many bitter threats of biding there.   237

VALENTINE
No more, unless the next word that thou speak'st
Have some malignant power upon my life;
If so, I pray thee, breathe it in mine ear,
As ending anthem of my endless dolor.   241

PROTEUS
Cease to lament for that thou canst not help,   242
And study help for that which thou lament'st.   243
Time is the nurse and breeder of all good.
Here if thou stay thou canst not see thy love;
Besides, thy staying will abridge thy life.
Hope is a lover's staff; walk hence with that
And manage it against despairing thoughts.   248
Thy letters may be here, though thou art hence,
Which, being writ to me, shall be delivered
Even in the milk-white bosom of thy love.
The time now serves not to expostulate.   252
Come, I'll convey thee through the city gate,
And ere I part with thee confer at large   254
Of all that may concern thy love affairs.
As thou lov'st Silvia, though not for thyself,   256
Regard thy danger, and along with me!

VALENTINE
I pray thee, Lance, an if thou see'st my boy,
Bid him make haste and meet me at the north gate.

PROTEUS   [to Lance]
Go, sirrah, find him out.—Come, Valentine.

VALENTINE
O my dear Silvia! Hapless Valentine!
              [Exeunt Valentine and Proteus.]

LANCE   I am but a fool, look you, and yet I have the wit
to think my master is a kind of a knave. But that's all   263
one, if he be but one knave. He lives not now that   264
knows me to be in love, yet I am in love. But a team of
horse shall not pluck that from me, nor who 'tis I love.   266
And yet 'tis a woman, but what woman, I will not tell
myself. And yet 'tis a milkmaid. Yet 'tis not a maid, for
she hath had gossips. Yet 'tis a maid, for she is her   269
master's maid, and serves for wages. She hath more
qualities than a water spaniel, which is much in a bare   271
Christian. [Pulling out a paper] Here is the catalog of
her condition. "Imprimis: She can fetch and carry."   273
Why, a horse can do no more. Nay, a horse cannot fetch,   274
but only carry; therefore is she better than a   275

jade. "Item: She can milk." Look you, a sweet virtue in   276
a maid with clean hands.

        [Enter] Speed.

SPEED   How now, Signor Lance, what news with Your
Mastership?

LANCE   With my master's ship? Why, it is at sea.   280

SPEED   Well, your old vice still: mistake the word. What   281
news, then, in your paper?

LANCE   The black'st news that ever thou heard'st.

SPEED   Why, man, how "black"?

LANCE   Why, as black as ink.

SPEED   Let me read them.   286

LANCE   Fie on thee, jolt-head! Thou canst not read.   287

SPEED   Thou liest. I can.

LANCE   I will try thee. Tell me this: who begot thee?

SPEED   Marry, the son of my grandfather.

LANCE   Oh, illiterate loiterer! It was the son of thy grand-   291
mother. This proves that thou canst not read.

SPEED   Come, fool, come. Try me in thy paper.

LANCE   There. [Giving him the paper] And Saint Nicholas   294
be thy speed!   295

SPEED   [reads] "Imprimis: She can milk."

LANCE   Ay, that she can.

SPEED   "Item: She brews good ale."

LANCE   And thereof comes the proverb: "Blessing of
your heart, you brew good ale."

SPEED   "Item: She can sew."

LANCE   That's as much as to say, "Can she so?"

SPEED   "Item: She can knit."

LANCE   What need a man care for a stock with a wench,   304
when she can knit him a stock?   305

SPEED   "Item: She can wash and scour."

LANCE   A special virtue, for then she need not be
washed and scoured.   308

SPEED   "Item: She can spin."

LANCE   Then may I set the world on wheels, when she   310
can spin for her living.   311

SPEED   "Item: She hath many nameless virtues."   312

LANCE   That's as much as to say bastard virtues, that
indeed know not their fathers and therefore have no
names.

SPEED   Here follow her vices.

LANCE   Close at the heels of her virtues.

SPEED   "Item: She is not to be kissed fasting, in respect   318
of her breath."   319

LANCE   Well, that fault may be mended with a breakfast.
Read on.

---

235 **repeal** recall from exile   236 **close** tightly enclosed   237 **biding**
permanently remaining   241 **ending anthem** requiem   242 **that** what
243 **study** devise   248 **manage** wield   252 **expostulate** discuss at
length.   254 **confer at large** discuss at length   256 **though not for thyself** even though not for your own sake   263–4 **that's . . . knave** i.e., it's
all right so long as he's knavish in one thing only (that is, in love).
264 **He lives not now** There is no one alive   266 **horse** horses
269 **gossips** i.e., godparents to a child of hers.   **maid** (Lance quibbles
on [1] maidservant [2] virgin. She is the first, even if no longer the second.)   271 **water spaniel** (A fawning, subservient kind of dog.)   **bare**
(1) mere (2) naked, hairless   273 **condition** qualities.   **Imprimis** In the
first place (to be followed, in a list, with each particular marked *Item*)
274–5 **cannot fetch** cannot be ordered to go and fetch something

276 **jade** (1) ill-conditioned horse (2) hussy.   280 **at sea** (1) on the
high seas (2) adrift, at loose ends.   281 **vice** (With added meaning of
Vice, comic character in morality plays who speaks with double
meaning.)   286 **them** the news.   287 **jolt-head** blockhead.   291 **loiterer** idle person, lazy student.   294 **Saint Nicholas** patron saint of
scholars   295 **speed** protection. (With a play on Speed's name.)
304 **stock** dowry   305 **stock** stocking.   308 **scoured** (1) scrubbed
(2) beaten, drubbed. (*Washed* probably has a similar double meaning.)
310 **set . . . wheels** i.e., take life easy   311 **spin for her living** (Probably with a sexual double meaning, as in *Twelfth Night*, 1.3.100–2: "I
hope to see a huswife take thee between her legs and spin it off.")
312 **nameless** inexpressible   318–9 **in respect of** on account of

SPEED   "Item: She hath a sweet mouth."   322

LANCE   That makes amends for her sour breath.

SPEED   "Item: She doth talk in her sleep."

LANCE   It's no matter for that, so she sleep not in her talk.   325

SPEED   "Item: She is slow in words."

LANCE   Oh, villain, that set this down among her vices! To be slow in words is a woman's only virtue. I pray thee, out with't, and place it for her chief virtue.

SPEED   "Item: She is proud."   331

LANCE   Out with that too. It was Eve's legacy, and cannot be ta'en from her.

SPEED   "Item: She hath no teeth."

LANCE   I care not for that neither, because I love crusts.

SPEED   "Item: She is curst."   336

LANCE   Well, the best is, she hath no teeth to bite.

SPEED   "Item: She will often praise her liquor."

LANCE   If her liquor be good, she shall. If she will not, I will, for good things should be praised.

SPEED   "Item: She is too liberal."   341

LANCE   Of her tongue she cannot, for that's writ down she is slow of; of her purse she shall not, for that I'll keep shut. Now, of another thing she may, and that   344 cannot I help. Well, proceed.

SPEED   "Item: She hath more hair than wit, and more faults than hairs, and more wealth than faults."

LANCE   Stop there; I'll have her. She was mine and not mine twice or thrice in that last article. Rehearse that   349 once more.

SPEED   "Item: She hath more hair than wit—"

LANCE   More hair than wit? It may be: I'll prove it. The cover of the salt hides the salt, and therefore it is more   353 than the salt; the hair that covers the wit is more than the wit, for the greater hides the less. What's next?

SPEED   "And more faults than hairs—"

LANCE   That's monstrous. Oh, that that were out!

SPEED   "And more wealth than faults."

LANCE   Why, that word makes the faults gracious. Well, I'll have her; and if it be a match, as nothing is impossible—

SPEED   What then?

LANCE   Why, then will I tell thee—that thy master stays for thee at the north gate.   364

SPEED   For me?

LANCE   For thee? Ay, who art thou? He hath stayed for a better man than thee.

SPEED   And must I go to him?

LANCE   Thou must run to him, for thou hast stayed so long that going will scarce serve the turn.   370

SPEED   Why didst not tell me sooner? Pox of your love   371 letters!   [Exit.]

LANCE   Now will he be swinged for reading my   373 letter—an unmannerly slave, that will thrust himself into secrets! I'll after, to rejoice in the boy's correction.   375
                                                                      Exit.

❧

322 sweet mouth sweet tooth. (With a wanton sense.)   325 sleep (With a pun on "slip"; pronunciation was similar.)   331 proud (With additional meaning of "lascivious.")   336 curst shrewish.   341 liberal free.   344 another thing (With bawdy suggestion, playing on the idea of her purse, which her husband is to keep shut to strangers.) 349 Rehearse Repeat   353 cover of the salt lid of the salt cellar 364 stays waits   370 going walking   371 Pox i.e., A plague on 373 swinged thrashed   375 correction punishment.

3.2

Enter [the] Duke [and] Thurio.

DUKE
Sir Thurio, fear not but that she will love you,
Now Valentine is banished from her sight.

THURIO
Since his exile she hath despised me most,
Forsworn my company, and railed at me,
That I am desperate of obtaining her.   5

DUKE
This weak impress of love is as a figure   6
Trenchèd in ice, which with an hour's heat   7
Dissolves to water and doth lose his form.   8
A little time will melt her frozen thoughts,
And worthless Valentine shall be forgot.

[Enter] Proteus.

How now, Sir Proteus? Is your countryman,
According to our proclamation, gone?

PROTEUS   Gone, my good lord.

DUKE
My daughter takes his going grievously.

PROTEUS
A little time, my lord, will kill that grief.

DUKE
So I believe, but Thurio thinks not so.
Proteus, the good conceit I hold of thee—   17
For thou hast shown some sign of good desert—
Makes me the better to confer with thee.   19

PROTEUS
Longer than I prove loyal to Your Grace
Let me not live to look upon Your Grace.

DUKE
Thou know'st how willingly I would effect
The match between Sir Thurio and my daughter.

PROTEUS   I do, my lord.

DUKE
And also, I think, thou art not ignorant
How she opposes her against my will.   26

PROTEUS
She did, my lord, when Valentine was here.

DUKE
Ay, and perversely she persevers so.
What might we do to make the girl forget
The love of Valentine, and love Sir Thurio?

PROTEUS
The best way is to slander Valentine
With falsehood, cowardice, and poor descent,
Three things that women highly hold in hate.

DUKE
Ay, but she'll think that it is spoke in hate.

PROTEUS
Ay, if his enemy deliver it;   35
Therefore it must with circumstance be spoken   36
By one whom she esteemeth as his friend.

3.2. Location: Milan. The Duke's palace.
5 That so that   6 impress impression   7 Trenchèd cut   8 his its
17 conceit opinion   19 the better the rather, more willingly   26 her herself   35 deliver speak   36 circumstance confirming detail

DUKE
    Then you must undertake to slander him.
PROTEUS
    And that, my lord, I shall be loath to do.
    'Tis an ill office for a gentleman,
    Especially against his very friend.   41
DUKE
    Where your good word cannot advantage him   42
    Your slander never can endamage him.
    Therefore the office is indifferent,   44
    Being entreated to it by your friend.   45
PROTEUS
    You have prevailed, my lord. If I can do it
    By aught that I can speak in his dispraise,
    She shall not long continue love to him.
    But say this weed her love from Valentine,   49
    It follows not that she will love Sir Thurio.
THURIO
    Therefore, as you unwind her love from him,
    Lest it should ravel and be good to none
    You must provide to bottom it on me;   53
    Which must be done by praising me as much
    As you in worth dispraise Sir Valentine.
DUKE
    And, Proteus, we dare trust you in this kind
    Because we know, on Valentine's report,
    You are already Love's firm votary
    And cannot soon revolt and change your mind.
    Upon this warrant shall you have access
    Where you with Silvia may confer at large;
    For she is lumpish, heavy, melancholy,   62
    And, for your friend's sake, will be glad of you,
    Where you may temper her by your persuasion   64
    To hate young Valentine and love my friend.
PROTEUS
    As much as I can do, I will effect.
    But you, Sir Thurio, are not sharp enough.
    You must lay lime to tangle her desires   68
    By wailful sonnets, whose composèd rhymes
    Should be full-fraught with serviceable vows.   70
DUKE
    Ay, much is the force of heaven-bred poesy.
PROTEUS
    Say that upon the altar of her beauty
    You sacrifice your tears, your sighs, your heart.
    Write till your ink be dry, and with your tears
    Moist it again, and frame some feeling line   75
    That may discover such integrity.   76
    For Orpheus' lute was strung with poets' sinews,   77
    Whose golden touch could soften steel and stones,
    Make tigers tame, and huge leviathans   79

    Forsake unsounded deeps to dance on sands.
    After your dire-lamenting elegies,
    Visit by night your lady's chamber window
    With some sweet consort. To their instruments   83
    Tune a deploring dump. The night's dead silence   84
    Will well become such sweet-complaining grievance. 85
    This, or else nothing, will inherit her.   86
DUKE
    This discipline shows thou hast been in love.   87
THURIO
    And thy advice this night I'll put in practice.
    Therefore, sweet Proteus, my direction-giver,
    Let us into the city presently
    To sort some gentlemen well skilled in music.   91
    I have a sonnet that will serve the turn
    To give the onset to thy good advice.   93
DUKE   About it, gentlemen!
PROTEUS
    We'll wait upon Your Grace till after supper,
    And afterward determine our proceedings.
DUKE
    Even now about it. I will pardon you.   *Exeunt.* 97

❖

4.1

Enter certain Outlaws.

FIRST OUTLAW
    Fellows, stand fast. I see a passenger.   1
SECOND OUTLAW
    If there be ten, shrink not, but down with 'em.   2

    [Enter] Valentine [and] Speed.

THIRD OUTLAW
    Stand, sir! And throw us that you have about ye.   3
    If not, we'll make you sit, and rifle you.   4
SPEED *[to Valentine]*
    Sir, we are undone. These are the villains
    That all the travelers do fear so much.
VALENTINE   My friends—
FIRST OUTLAW
    That's not so, sir. We are your enemies.
SECOND OUTLAW   Peace! We'll hear him.
THIRD OUTLAW
    Ay, by my beard will we, for he is a proper man.   10
VALENTINE
    Then know that I have little wealth to lose.
    A man I am, crossed with adversity;   12
    My riches are these poor habiliments,
    Of which if you should here disfurnish me   14
    You take the sum and substance that I have.
SECOND OUTLAW   Whither travel you?

---

41 very true   **42 advantage** profit   **44 indifferent** neither good nor bad   **45 your friend** i.e., the Duke.   **49 say . . . Valentine** even supposing this should root out the love she feels for Valentine   **53 bottom** wind, as a skein of thread   **62 lumpish** dull, spiritless **64 temper** mold   **68 lime** birdlime, a sticky substance smeared on twigs to ensnare small birds   **70 Should . . . vows** should be fully laden with vows of service.   **75 frame** compose   **76 discover** reveal. **integrity** true devotion.   **77 Orpheus** legendary musician whose music had the power to move inanimate objects as well as animals. **sinews** nerves   **79 leviathans** whales

83 consort company of musicians.   **84 deploring dump** doleful, sad melody.   **85 grievance** grief.   **86 inherit** put you in possession of **87 discipline** teaching   **91 sort** choose   **93 To . . . to** to set in motion **97 pardon you** i.e., excuse you your *waiting upon* or attending upon me. **4.1. Location: The frontiers of Mantua. A forest. 1 passenger** traveler.   **2 If** Even if   **3 Stand** Halt. (But the Third Outlaw puns on *sit*, line 4, as the opposite of "stand up.")   **4 rifle** plunder   **10 proper** good-looking   **12 crossed with** thwarted by **14 disfurnish** deprive

VALENTINE   To Verona.

FIRST OUTLAW   Whence came you?

VALENTINE   From Milan.

THIRD OUTLAW   Have you long sojourned there?

VALENTINE
Some sixteen months, and longer might have stayed
If crooked fortune had not thwarted me.   22

FIRST OUTLAW   What, were you banished thence?

VALENTINE   I was.

SECOND OUTLAW   For what offense?

VALENTINE
For that which now torments me to rehearse: 26
I killed a man, whose death I much repent,   27
But yet I slew him manfully in fight
Without false vantage or base treachery.

FIRST OUTLAW
Why, ne'er repent it, if it were done so.
But were you banished for so small a fault?

VALENTINE
I was, and held me glad of such a doom.   32

SECOND OUTLAW   Have you the tongues?   33

VALENTINE
My youthful travel therein made me happy,   34
Or else I had been often miserable.

THIRD OUTLAW
By the bare scalp of Robin Hood's fat friar,   36
This fellow were a king for our wild faction!   37

FIRST OUTLAW   We'll have him. Sirs, a word.
                              [*The Outlaws confer in whispers.*]

SPEED   Master, be one of them;
It's an honorable kind of thievery.

VALENTINE   Peace, villain!   41

SECOND OUTLAW   [*returning to Valentine*]
Tell us this: have you anything to take to?   42

VALENTINE   Nothing but my fortune.

THIRD OUTLAW
Know, then, that some of us are gentlemen,
Such as the fury of ungoverned youth
Thrust from the company of awful men.   46
Myself was from Verona banishèd
For practicing to steal away a lady,   48
An heir, and near allied unto the Duke.

SECOND OUTLAW
And I from Mantua, for a gentleman
Who, in my mood, I stabbed unto the heart.   51

FIRST OUTLAW
And I for suchlike petty crimes as these.
But to the purpose—for we cite our faults
That they may hold excused our lawless lives;   54
And partly, seeing you are beautified
With goodly shape, and by your own report

A linguist, and a man of such perfection
As we do in our quality much want—   58

SECOND OUTLAW
Indeed, because you are a banished man,
Therefore, above the rest, we parley to you.   60
Are you content to be our general?
To make a virtue of necessity
And live, as we do, in this wilderness?

THIRD OUTLAW
What say'st thou? Wilt thou be of our consort?   64
Say ay, and be the captain of us all.
We'll do thee homage and be ruled by thee,
Love thee as our commander and our king.

FIRST OUTLAW
But if thou scorn our courtesy, thou diest.

SECOND OUTLAW
Thou shalt not live to brag what we have offered.

VALENTINE
I take your offer and will live with you,
Provided that you do no outrages
On silly women or poor passengers.   72

THIRD OUTLAW
No, we detest such vile, base practices.
Come, go with us. We'll bring thee to our crews   74
And show thee all the treasure we have got,
Which, with ourselves, all rest at thy dispose. *Exeunt.*   76

❖

4.2

Enter Proteus.

PROTEUS
Already have I been false to Valentine,
And now I must be as unjust to Thurio.
Under the color of commending him   3
I have access my own love to prefer.   4
But Silvia is too fair, too true, too holy
To be corrupted with my worthless gifts.
When I protest true loyalty to her,
She twits me with my falsehood to my friend.
When to her beauty I commend my vows,   9
She bids me think how I have been forsworn
In breaking faith with Julia, whom I loved.
And notwithstanding all her sudden quips,   12
The least whereof would quell a lover's hope,
Yet, spaniel-like, the more she spurns my love,
The more it grows and fawneth on her still.
But here comes Thurio. Now must we to her window
And give some evening music to her ear.

    [*Enter*] *Thurio* [*and*] *musicians.*

---

22 **crooked** perverse, malignant   26 **rehearse** repeat   27 **I killed a man** (A lie, presumably intended to impress the outlaws.)
32 **held . . . doom** was pleased with such a light sentence.   33 **the tongues** ability in foreign languages.   34 **travel** (The Folio spelling, "trauaile," may also suggest "laborious study.")   **happy** proficient
36 **friar** i.e., Friar Tuck   37 **were** would be suitable as.   **faction** band, set of persons.   41 **villain** i.e., you rogue.   42 **anything to take to** any prospect of a position or occupation.   46 **awful** law-abiding
48 **practicing** plotting   51 **mood** anger, displeasure   54 **hold excused** justify

58 **quality** profession.   **want** lack   60 **above the rest** for this reason chiefly.   **parley to** confer with, negotiate with   64 **consort** company
72 **silly** defenseless.   **passengers** travelers.   74 **crews** bands   76 **dispose** disposal.
4.2. Location: Milan. Outside the Duke's palace, under Silvia's window.
3 **color** pretext   4 **prefer** urge.   9 **commend** offer, direct   12 **quips** sharp, sarcastic remarks

THURIO
How now, Sir Proteus, are you crept before us?

PROTEUS
Ay, gentle Thurio, for you know that love
Will creep in service where it cannot go.   20

THURIO
Ay, but I hope, sir, that you love not here.

PROTEUS
Sir, but I do, or else I would be hence.

THURIO
Who? Silvia?

PROTEUS   Ay, Silvia—for your sake.

THURIO
I thank you for your own.—Now, gentlemen,   24
Let's tune, and to it lustily awhile.   25

    [Enter, at a distance, the] Host [of the inn, and]
    Julia [disguised as a page. They talk apart.]

HOST   Now, my young guest, methinks you're ally-   26
cholly. I pray you, why is it?   27

JULIA   Marry, mine host, because I cannot be merry.

HOST   Come, we'll have you merry. I'll bring you where
you shall hear music and see the gentleman that you
asked for.   31

JULIA   But shall I hear him speak?

HOST   Ay, that you shall.

JULIA   That will be music.   *[Music plays.]*

HOST   Hark, hark!

JULIA   Is he among these?

HOST   Ay, but peace! Let's hear 'em.

    Song

MUSICIAN
Who is Silvia? What is she,
    That all our swains commend her?
Holy, fair, and wise is she;   39
    The heaven such grace did lend her,
That she might admirèd be.   42

Is she kind as she is fair?
    For beauty lives with kindness.
Love doth to her eyes repair
    To help him of his blindness,   45
And, being helped, inhabits there.

Then to Silvia let us sing,
    That Silvia is excelling.
She excels each mortal thing
    Upon the dull earth dwelling.
To her let us garlands bring.

HOST   How now? Are you sadder than you were before?
How do you, man? The music likes you not.   54

JULIA   You mistake. The musician likes me not.   55

HOST   Why, my pretty youth?

JULIA   He plays false, father.   57

HOST   How? Out of tune on the strings?

JULIA   Not so, but yet so false that he grieves my very
heartstrings.

HOST   You have a quick ear.

JULIA   Ay, I would I were deaf. It makes me have a slow 62
heart.

HOST   I perceive you delight not in music.

JULIA   Not a whit, when it jars so.   65

HOST   Hark, what fine change is in the music!   66

JULIA   Ay, that change is the spite.   67

HOST   You would have them always play but one thing? 68

JULIA   I would always have one play but one thing. But
Host, doth this Sir Proteus that we talk on often resort 70
unto this gentlewoman?

HOST   I tell you what Lance, his man, told me: he loved
her out of all nick.   73

JULIA   Where is Lance?

HOST   Gone to seek his dog, which tomorrow, by his master's command, he must carry for a present to his lady.

JULIA
Peace! Stand aside. The company parts.
    [Julia and the Host stand aside.]

PROTEUS
Sir Thurio, fear not you. I will so plead
That you shall say my cunning drift excels.   80

THURIO
Where meet we?

PROTEUS   At Saint Gregory's well.

THURIO   Farewell.
    [Exeunt Thurio and the musicians.]

    [Enter] Silvia [above, at her window].

PROTEUS
Madam, good even to Your Ladyship.

SILVIA
I thank you for your music, gentlemen.
Who is that that spake?

PROTEUS
One, lady, if you knew his pure heart's truth,
You would quickly learn to know him by his voice.

SILVIA   Sir Proteus, as I take it.

PROTEUS
Sir Proteus, gentle lady, and your servant.

SILVIA
What's your will?

PROTEUS   That I may compass yours.   89

SILVIA
You have your wish. My will is even this:
That presently you hie you home to bed.   91

---

20 go walk at an ordinary pace.   **24 I thank . . . own** i.e., It's just as
well, for your own safety, that you added that disclaimer.   **25 lustily**
heartily, with a will   **26–7 allycholly** (A colloquial form of *melancholy*.)
31 asked for inquired about.   **39 swains** youths, wooers   **42 admirèd**
wondered at   **45 repair** hasten, visit   **54 likes** pleases   **55 likes me
not** (1) displeases me with his music (2) does not love me. (The first
meaning is intended for the Host; the second is hidden except from
the audience.)

57 plays false (1) plays out of tune (2) is unfaithful.   **father** (A form
of address to an older man.)   **62 slow** heavy. (Playing also on *slow* as
the opposite of *quick* in line 61.)   **65 jars** is discordant   **66 change**
modulation. (But Julia plays on the sense of "fickleness.")   **67 spite**
injury, annoyance.   **68 play but one thing** play only one musical
piece. (But Julia plays on the sense of "play only one role as lover.")
70 talk on talk of   **73 out of all nick** i.e., beyond all reckoning.
80 drift scheme   **89 compass yours** (1) obtain your good will (2) perform your every wish.   **91 presently** immediately.   **hie** hasten

Thou subtle, perjured, false, disloyal man!   92
Think'st thou I am so shallow, so conceitless,   93
To be seducèd by thy flattery,   94
That hast deceived so many with thy vows?
Return, return, and make thy love amends.
For me, by this pale queen of night I swear,   97
I am so far from granting thy request
That I despise thee for thy wrongful suit,
And by and by intend to chide myself
Even for this time I spend in talking to thee.

PROTEUS
I grant, sweet love, that I did love a lady,
But she is dead.

JULIA [aside]   'Twere false, if I should speak it,   103
For I am sure she is not burièd.

SILVIA
Say that she be, yet Valentine, thy friend,
Survives, to whom—thyself art witness—
I am betrothed. And art thou not ashamed
To wrong him with thy importunacy?   108

PROTEUS
I likewise hear that Valentine is dead.

SILVIA
And so suppose am I, for in his grave,
Assure thyself, my love is buried.

PROTEUS
Sweet lady, let me rake it from the earth.

SILVIA
Go to thy lady's grave and call hers thence.
Or, at the least, in hers sepulchre thine.   114

JULIA [aside]   He heard not that.   115

PROTEUS
Madam, if your heart be so obdurate,
Vouchsafe me yet your picture for my love,
The picture that is hanging in your chamber.
To that I'll speak, to that I'll sigh and weep;
For since the substance of your perfect self
Is else devoted, I am but a shadow,   121
And to your shadow will I make true love.   122

JULIA [aside]
If 'twere a substance, you would, sure, deceive it   123
And make it but a shadow, as I am.   124

SILVIA
I am very loath to be your idol, sir.
But since your falsehood shall become you well   126
To worship shadows and adore false shapes,
Send to me in the morning, and I'll send it.   128

And so, good rest.   92

PROTEUS   As wretches have o'ernight   129
That wait for execution in the morn.
[Exeunt Proteus and Silvia separately.]

JULIA   Host, will you go?
HOST   By my halidom, I was fast asleep.   132
JULIA   Pray you, where lies Sir Proteus?   133
HOST   Marry, at my house. Trust me, I think 'tis almost day.   134
JULIA
Not so; but it hath been the longest night
That e'er I watched, and the most heaviest.   [Exeunt.]   136

❖

4.3

Enter [Sir] Eglamour.

EGLAMOUR
This is the hour that Madam Silvia
Entreated me to call and know her mind.
There's some great matter she'd employ me in.—
Madam, madam!

[Enter] Silvia [above, at her window].

SILVIA   Who calls?
EGLAMOUR   Your servant and your friend;
One that attends Your Ladyship's command.

SILVIA
Sir Eglamour, a thousand times good morrow.

EGLAMOUR
As many, worthy lady, to yourself.
According to Your Ladyship's impose,   10
I am thus early come to know what service
It is your pleasure to command me in.

SILVIA
O Eglamour, thou art a gentleman—
Think not I flatter, for I swear I do not—
Valiant, wise, remorseful, well accomplished.   15
Thou art not ignorant what dear good will   16
I bear unto the banished Valentine,
Nor how my father would enforce me marry
Vain Thurio, whom my very soul abhors.
Thyself hast loved, and I have heard thee say
No grief did ever come so near thy heart
As when thy lady and thy true love died,
Upon whose grave thou vowed'st pure chastity.
Sir Eglamour, I would to Valentine,   24
To Mantua, where I hear he makes abode;
And, for the ways are dangerous to pass,   26
I do desire thy worthy company,
Upon whose faith and honor I repose.
Urge not my father's anger, Eglamour,

92 subtle crafty   93 conceitless witless   94 To be as to be   97 this pale . . . night i.e., the moon, Diana, goddess of chastity   103 if . . . it i.e., even if I should say such a thing in the sense that I am slain in my heart by Proteus's faithlessness and thus transformed into "Sebastian"   108 importunacy importunity.   114 sepulchre bury   115 He heard not that i.e., He will turn a deaf ear to such unwelcome talk. 121 else elsewhere   121–2 I am . . . love (Proteus plays on two meanings of shadow: I am reduced to being nothing, but I will at least worship your picture.)   123–4 If . . . I am (Julia's rueful aside plays on the antithesis of substance and shadow: she fears that Proteus's idea of love is as insubstantial as a mere picture or shadow, and that his love for Silvia is no more realistic or capable of fidelity than his love for Julia has proved to be.)   126 since . . . well i.e., since it befits your false nature   128 Send i.e., send a messenger

129 As wretches i.e., I will enjoy just about as much rest as poor convicts   132 halidom (Originally, a holy relic; here, a mild oath.) 133 lies lodges   134 Marry Indeed. (Originally, an oath, "by the Virgin Mary.")   house inn.   Trust me i.e., On my honor   136 watched stayed awake through
4.3. Location: The same, early in the morning (and perhaps only a short time after 4.2, which ends as it is "almost day," line 134).
10 impose command   15 remorseful compassionate   16 dear affectionate   24 would wish to go   26 for because

But think upon my grief, a lady's grief,
And on the justice of my flying hence
To keep me from a most unholy match,
Which heaven and fortune still rewards with plagues. 33
I do desire thee, even from a heart
As full of sorrows as the sea of sands,
To bear me company and go with me;
If not, to hide what I have said to thee,
That I may venture to depart alone.

EGLAMOUR
Madam, I pity much your grievances,
Which, since I know they virtuously are placed,
I give consent to go along with you,
Recking as little what betideth me   42
As much I wish all good befortune you.   43
When will you go?

SILVIA   This evening coming.

EGLAMOUR
Where shall I meet you?

SILVIA   At Friar Patrick's cell,
Where I intend holy confession.

EGLAMOUR
I will not fail Your Ladyship.
Good morrow, gentle lady.

SILVIA
Good morrow, kind Sir Eglamour.

                              Exeunt [separately].

❖

4.4

                    Enter Lance [with his dog, Crab].

LANCE   When a man's servant shall play the cur with
him, look you, it goes hard—one that I brought up of   2
a puppy, one that I saved from drowning when three
or four of his blind brothers and sisters went to it. I   4
have taught him, even as one would say precisely,
"Thus I would teach a dog." I was sent to deliver him
as a present to Mistress Silvia from my master, and I
came no sooner into the dining chamber but he steps
me to her trencher and steals her capon's leg. Oh, 'tis   9
a foul thing when a cur cannot keep himself in all   10
companies! I would have, as one should say, one that   11
takes upon him to be a dog indeed, to be, as it were, a 12
dog at all things. If I had not had more wit than he, to 13
take a fault upon me that he did, I think verily he had 14
been hanged for't; sure as I live, he had suffered for't.
You shall judge. He thrusts me himself into the company of three or four gentlemanlike dogs, under the

Duke's table. He had not been there—bless the   18
mark!—a pissing while but all the chamber smelt him.   19
"Out with the dog!" says one. "What cur is that?" says
another. "Whip him out," says the third. "Hang him
up," says the Duke. I, having been acquainted with the
smell before, knew it was Crab, and goes me to the   23
fellow that whips the dogs. "Friend," quoth I, "you
mean to whip the dog?" "Ay, marry do I," quoth he.
"You do him the more wrong," quoth I. "'Twas I did
the thing you wot of." He makes me no more ado, but   27
whips me out of the chamber. How many masters
would do this for his servant? Nay, I'll be sworn I have
sat in the stocks for puddings he hath stolen, otherwise 30
he had been executed. I have stood on the pillory for
geese he hath killed, otherwise he had suffered for't.—
Thou think'st not of this now. Nay, I remember the
trick you served me when I took my leave of Madam
Silvia. Did not I bid thee still mark me and do as I do?
When didst thou see me heave up my leg and make
water against a gentlewoman's farthingale? Didst   37
thou ever see me do such a trick?

                    [Enter] Proteus [and] Julia [disguised].

PROTEUS   *[to Julia]*
Sebastian is thy name? I like thee well,
And will employ thee in some service presently.

JULIA
In what you please. I'll do what I can.

PROTEUS
I hope thou wilt. *[To Lance]* How now, you whoreson
      peasant,   42
Where have you been these two days loitering?

LANCE   Marry, sir, I carried Mistress Silvia the dog you
bade me.

PROTEUS   And what says she to my little jewel?   46

LANCE   Marry, she says your dog was a cur, and tells
you currish thanks is good enough for such a present. 48

PROTEUS   But she received my dog?

LANCE   No, indeed, did she not. Here have I brought
him back again.   *[He points to his dog.]*

PROTEUS   What, didst thou offer her this from me?

LANCE   Ay, sir, the other squirrel was stolen from me by 53
the hangman boys in the marketplace, and then I   54
offered her mine own, who is a dog as big as ten of
yours, and therefore the gift the greater.

PROTEUS
Go, get thee hence, and find my dog again,
Or ne'er return again into my sight.
Away, I say! Stayest thou to vex me here?

                              [Exit Lance with Crab.]
A slave, that still an end turns me to shame!—   60

---

33 **still rewards** always reward   42 **Recking** heeding, caring
43 **befortune** befall
4.4. Location: The same, some hours later.
2 **of** from   4 **blind** i.e., with eyes not yet opened.   **to it** i.e., to
drowning.   9 **me** i.e., to my injury, to my detriment. (Compare lines
16, 23, and 27.)   **trencher** wooden dish or plate.   **capon's leg** leg of a
rooster, castrated to make the flesh succulent.   10 **keep** restrain
11–12 **one that . . . him** such a dog as undertakes   12–13 **a dog at**
adept at. (But with literal meaning as well.)   13–14 **to take . . . did** to
take the blame upon myself for the fault he did

18–19 **bless the mark** (A phrase used to apologize for indecorous language.)   19 **a pissing while** a short while. (But with literal meaning
as well.)   23 **goes me** i.e., I went   27 **wot of** know about.   **makes me**
makes   30 **puddings** sausages made by stuffing animal entrails with
spicy minced meat, etc.   37 **farthingale** hooped petticoat.   42 **whoreson peasant** (A term of jocular familiarity.)   46 **jewel** (Proteus is
thinking of the small, elegant dog he intended as a present to Silvia.)
48 **currish** i.e., mean-spirited. (With a play on *cur*.)   53 **squirrel** i.e., little dog   54 **hangman** i.e., fit for the hangman, rascally   60 **A slave . . .
shame** A wretch that continually brings shame upon me.

Sebastian, I have entertainèd thee,   61
Partly that I have need of such a youth
That can with some discretion do my business—
For 'tis no trusting to yond foolish lout—
But chiefly for thy face and thy behavior,
Which, if my augury deceive me not,
Witness good bringing up, fortune, and truth.   67
Therefore know thou, for this I entertain thee.
Go presently and take this ring with thee.
                              [*He gives a ring.*]
Deliver it to Madam Silvia.
She loved me well delivered it to me.   71

JULIA
It seems you loved not her, to leave her token.   72
She is dead, belike?

PROTEUS   Not so. I think she lives.   73

JULIA   Alas!

PROTEUS   Why dost thou cry "Alas"?

JULIA   I cannot choose but pity her.

PROTEUS   Wherefore shouldst thou pity her?

JULIA
Because methinks that she loved you as well
As you do love your lady Silvia.
She dreams on him that has forgot her love;   80
You dote on her that cares not for your love.   81
'Tis pity love should be so contrary;
And thinking on it makes me cry "Alas!"

PROTEUS [*giving a letter*]
Well, give her that ring and therewithal   84
This letter. That's her chamber. Tell my lady
I claim the promise for her heavenly picture.
Your message done, hie home unto my chamber,
Where thou shalt find me sad and solitary.   [*Exit.*]

JULIA
How many women would do such a message?
Alas, poor Proteus! Thou hast entertained
A fox to be the shepherd of thy lambs.
Alas, poor fool, why do I pity him   92
That with his very heart despiseth me?
Because he loves her, he despiseth me;
Because I love him, I must pity him.
This ring I gave him when he parted from me,
To bind him to remember my good will;
And now am I, unhappy messenger,
To plead for that which I would not obtain,
To carry that which I would have refused,
To praise his faith which I would have dispraised.   101
I am my master's true-confirmèd love,
But cannot be true servant to my master
Unless I prove false traitor to myself.
Yet will I woo for him, but yet so coldly

As, heaven it knows, I would not have him speed.   106

              [*Enter*] Silvia [*attended*].

Gentlewoman, good day! I pray you, be my mean
To bring me where to speak with Madam Silvia.   108

SILVIA
What would you with her, if that I be she?

JULIA
If you be she, I do entreat your patience
To hear me speak the message I am sent on.

SILVIA   From whom?

JULIA   From my master, Sir Proteus, madam.

SILVIA   Oh, he sends you for a picture?

JULIA   Ay, madam.

SILVIA   Ursula, bring my picture there.
            [*A servant, Ursula, brings a picture.*]
Go, give your master this. Tell him from me,
One Julia, that his changing thoughts forget,
Would better fit his chamber than this shadow.

JULIA
Madam, please you peruse this letter.—
         [*She offers a letter but then withdraws it.*]
Pardon me, madam, I have unadvised   121
Delivered you a paper that I should not.
                     [*She gives another letter.*]
This is the letter to Your Ladyship.

SILVIA
I pray thee, let me look on that again.   124

JULIA
It may not be. Good madam, pardon me.

SILVIA   There, hold!
I will not look upon your master's lines.
I know they are stuffed with protestations
And full of newfound oaths, which he will break   129
As easily as I do tear his paper.   [*She tears the letter.*]

JULIA [*offering the ring*]
Madam, he sends Your Ladyship this ring.

SILVIA
The more shame for him that he sends it me,
For I have heard him say a thousand times
His Julia gave it him at his departure.
Though his false finger have profaned the ring,
Mine shall not do his Julia so much wrong.

JULIA   She thanks you.

SILVIA   What say'st thou?

JULIA
I thank you, madam, that you tender her.   139
Poor gentlewoman! My master wrongs her much.

SILVIA   Dost thou know her?

---

106 speed succeed.   **106.1 *Enter Silvia*** This entrance is presumably onto the main stage, still imagined as below Silvia's window in her father's palace, where the scene has been located since the beginning of 4.2. Proteus gestures towards her window in line 85 above when he says, "That's her chamber." Silvia is perhaps on her way to confession at Friar Patrick's cell (4.3.45–6) as part of her plan of escape to Mantua with Eglamour's assistance (4.3.24–7).   **108 where to** where I may   **121 unadvised** inadvertently   **124 that** i.e., the first letter   **129 newfound** recently devised   **139 tender** feel sympathetically toward

61 entertainèd taken into service   **67 Witness** bear witness to   **71 delivered** who gave   **72 leave** part with   **73 belike** perhaps.   **80 She . . . that** i.e., Julia dreams on Proteus, who   **81 her** i.e., Silvia   **84 therewithal** with it   **92 poor fool** i.e., Julia herself   **101 would have** desire to have

JULIA
Almost as well as I do know myself.
To think upon her woes I do protest
That I have wept a hundred several times.   144

SILVIA
Belike she thinks that Proteus hath forsook her?

JULIA
I think she doth, and that's her cause of sorrow.

SILVIA   Is she not passing fair?   147

JULIA
She hath been fairer, madam, than she is.
When she did think my master loved her well,
She, in my judgment, was as fair as you;
But since she did neglect her looking glass
And threw her sun-expelling mask away,
The air hath starved the roses in her cheeks   152
And pinched the lily tincture of her face,
That now she is become as black as I.   155

SILVIA   How tall was she?

JULIA
About my stature; for at Pentecost,   157
When all our pageants of delight were played,   158
Our youth got me to play the woman's part,   159
And I was trimmed in Madam Julia's gown,   160
Which servèd me as fit, by all men's judgments,
As if the garment had been made for me.
Therefore I know she is about my height.
And at that time I made her weep agood,   164
For I did play a lamentable part:
Madam, 'twas Ariadne, passioning   166
For Theseus' perjury and unjust flight;
Which I so lively acted with my tears
That my poor mistress, movèd therewithal,
Wept bitterly; and would I might be dead
If I in thought felt not her very sorrow!

SILVIA
She is beholding to thee, gentle youth.   172
Alas, poor lady, desolate and left!
I weep myself to think upon thy words.
Here, youth, there is my purse. [She gives money.] I give
    thee this
For thy sweet mistress' sake, because thou lov'st her.
Farewell.   [Exit Silvia, with attendants.]

JULIA
And she shall thank you for't, if e'er you know her—
A virtuous gentlewoman, mild and beautiful!
I hope my master's suit will be but cold,   180
Since she respects my mistress' love so much.   181

Alas, how love can trifle with itself!
Here is her picture. [She looks at the picture.] Let me
    see, I think
If I had such a tire, this face of mine   184
Were full as lovely as is this of hers;
And yet the painter flattered her a little,
Unless I flatter with myself too much.   187
Her hair is auburn, mine is perfect yellow;
If that be all the difference in his love,
I'll get me such a colored periwig.
Her eyes are gray as glass, and so are mine.
Ay, but her forehead's low, and mine's as high.   192
What should it be that he respects in her
But I can make respective in myself,   194
If this fond Love were not a blinded god?   195
Come, shadow, come, and take this shadow up,   196
For 'tis thy rival. [She picks up the picture.] O thou
    senseless form,   197
Thou shalt be worshiped, kissed, loved, and adored!
And, were there sense in his idolatry,   199
My substance should be statue in thy stead.   200
I'll use thee kindly for thy mistress' sake,
That used me so; or else, by Jove I vow,
I should have scratched out your unseeing eyes,
To make my master out of love with thee!   Exit.

❧

5.1

Enter [Sir] Eglamour.

EGLAMOUR
The sun begins to gild the western sky,
And now it is about the very hour
That Silvia at Friar Patrick's cell should meet me.
She will not fail, for lovers break not hours
Unless it be to come before their time,
So much they spur their expedition.   6

    [Enter] Silvia.

See where she comes.—Lady, a happy evening!

SILVIA
Amen, amen! Go on, good Eglamour,
Out at the postern by the abbey wall.   9
I fear I am attended by some spies.   10

EGLAMOUR
Fear not. The forest is not three leagues off.
If we recover that, we are sure enough.   Exeunt. 12

❧

---

144 **several** different   147 **passing** surpassingly   152 **sun-expelling
mask** mask to keep the complexion fair. (Considered more beautiful
than a tan.)   155 **black** of a dark complexion, tanned   157 **Pentecost**
Whitsuntide (seven weeks after Easter)   158 **pageants of delight**
delightful entertainments   159 **Our youth** the youth of our village
160 **trimmed** dressed up   164 **agood** in earnest   166 **Ariadne** daughter
of Minos, King of Crete. (Ariadne, having fallen in love with one of her
father's captives, Theseus, gave him a clew of thread by which he was
able to find his way out of the labyrinth. He fled with her but abandoned
her on the island of Naxos.)   **passioning** sorrowing   172 **beholding**
indebted, beholden   180 **cold** vain   181 **my mistress'** (Julia ironically
refers thus to herself, as formerly beloved by her master, Proteus.)

184 **tire** headdress   187 **flatter with myself** (1) praise myself with flattery (2) flatter myself with deceiving hopes   192 **mine's as high** i.e., my
forehead's no lower than hers. (High foreheads were much admired, as
was yellow hair.)   194 **But . . . myself** that I cannot make worthy of
regard in myself. (With wordplay on *respects / respective* in lines 193–4.)
195 **fond** foolish   196 **shadow . . . shadow** i.e., the mere shadow of
myself . . . the picture of Silvia. (See also 4.2.120–4.)   **take . . . up** (1) pick
up this picture (2) oppose, accept a challenge   197 **senseless** insensible
199 **sense** reason   200 **My . . . stead** i.e., my real person would be the
object of his veneration, his idol, instead of Silvia's mere picture.
5.1. Location: Milan. An abbey.
6 **expedition** haste.   9 **postern** small back or side door   10 **attended**
followed (for hostile purposes)   12 **recover** reach.   **sure** safe

5.2

Enter Thurio, Proteus, [and] Julia [disguised in page's attire].

THURIO
Sir Proteus, what says Silvia to my suit?

PROTEUS
Oh, sir, I find her milder than she was,
And yet she takes exceptions at your person.   3

THURIO   What, that my leg is too long?

PROTEUS   No, that it is too little.

THURIO
I'll wear a boot, to make it somewhat rounder.

JULIA *[aside]*
But love will not be spurred to what it loathes.   7

THURIO   What says she to my face?

PROTEUS   She says it is a fair one.   9

THURIO
Nay then, the wanton lies. My face is black.   10

PROTEUS
But pearls are fair, and the old saying is,
Black men are pearls in beauteous ladies' eyes.   12

JULIA *[aside]*
'Tis true, such pearls as put out ladies' eyes,   13
For I had rather wink than look on them.   14

THURIO   How likes she my discourse?

PROTEUS   Ill, when you talk of war.   16

THURIO
But well, when I discourse of love and peace.

JULIA *[aside]*
But better, indeed, when you hold your peace.   18

THURIO   What says she to my valor?

PROTEUS   Oh, sir, she makes no doubt of that.   20

JULIA *[aside]*
She needs not, when she knows it cowardice.

THURIO   What says she to my birth?

PROTEUS   That you are well derived.   23

JULIA *[aside]*   True; from a gentleman to a fool.   24

THURIO   Considers she my possessions?

PROTEUS   Oh, ay, and pities them.   26

THURIO   Wherefore?

JULIA *[aside]*   That such an ass should owe them.   28

PROTEUS   That they are out by lease.   29

[Enter the] Duke.

JULIA   Here comes the Duke.

DUKE
How now, Sir Proteus? How now, Thurio?
Which of you saw Eglamour of late?

THURIO   Not I.

PROTEUS   Nor I.

DUKE   Saw you my daughter?

PROTEUS   Neither.

DUKE   Why then,
She's fled unto that peasant Valentine,   38
And Eglamour is in her company.
'Tis true, for Friar Laurence met them both
As he in penance wandered through the forest.
Him he knew well, and guessed that it was she,
But, being masked, he was not sure of it.   43
Besides, she did intend confession
At Patrick's cell this even, and there she was not.   45
These likelihoods confirm her flight from hence.
Therefore, I pray you, stand not to discourse,
But mount you presently and meet with me   48
Upon the rising of the mountain foot
That leads toward Mantua, whither they are fled.
Dispatch, sweet gentlemen, and follow me.   *[Exit.]*   51

THURIO
Why, this it is to be a peevish girl,   52
That flies her fortune when it follows her.   53
I'll after, more to be revenged on Eglamour
Than for the love of reckless Silvia.   *[Exit.]*   55

PROTEUS
And I will follow, more for Silvia's love
Than hate of Eglamour that goes with her.   *[Exit.]*

JULIA
And I will follow, more to cross that love
Than hate for Silvia, that is gone for love.   *Exit.*

❧

5.3

[Enter] Silvia, [led by] Outlaws.

FIRST OUTLAW   Come, come,
Be patient. We must bring you to our captain.

SILVIA
A thousand more mischances than this one
Have learned me how to brook this patiently.   4

SECOND OUTLAW   Come, bring her away.

FIRST OUTLAW
Where is the gentleman that was with her?   6

THIRD OUTLAW
Being nimble-footed, he hath outrun us,
But Moses and Valerius follow him.
Go thou with her to the west end of the wood;
There is our captain. We'll follow him that's fled.
The thicket is beset; he cannot scape.   11
[Exeunt all but the First Outlaw and Silvia.]

5.2. Location: Milan. The Duke's palace.
3 takes exceptions at finds fault with   **7 spurred** incited. (With a quibble on *boot*, i.e., "riding boot," in the preceding line.)   **9 fair** i.e., pale. (Beneath the seeming compliment is a suggestion of effeminacy or fair-faced deception.)   **10 black** dark, tanned (as contrasted with *fair*, "light-skinned").   **12 pearls** i.e., rare and beautiful objects   **13 pearls** i.e., cataracts   **14 wink** close the eyes   **16 Ill . . . war** i.e., (1) You upset her with frightening talk of war (2) Your absurd talk of war shows how ill-suited you are for manly pursuits.   **18 hold your peace** are silent. (With quibble on *peace* in previous line.)   **20 makes . . . of** has no uncertainty about. (Another deliberately ambiguous reply.)   **23 derived** descended.   **24 from . . . fool** (Julia plays on *derived* in another sense—"fallen away from, lowered"—than in line 23.)   **26 pities** (1) shows concern for (2) despises   **28 owe** own   **29 out by lease** (1) rented out (2) beyond Thurio's control.

38 peasant i.e., base scoundrel   **43 being masked** i.e., since Silvia was masked—perhaps with a *sun-expelling mask* (4.4.152) rather than a disguise   **45 even** evening   **48 presently** immediately   **51 Dispatch** Make haste   **52 peevish** perverse   **53 flies her fortune** flees from her good fortune   **55 reckless** uncaring
5.3. Location: The frontiers of Mantua. The forest.
4 learned taught.   **brook** endure   **6 gentleman** i.e., Sir Eglamour
11 beset surrounded

FIRST OUTLAW
     Come, I must bring you to our captain's cave.
     Fear not. He bears an honorable mind
     And will not use a woman lawlessly.

SILVIA
     O Valentine, this I endure for thee!   *Exeunt.*

❦

5.4

Enter Valentine.

VALENTINE
     How use doth breed a habit in a man!   1
     This shadowy desert, unfrequented woods   2
     I better brook than flourishing peopled towns.
     Here can I sit alone, unseen of any,
     And to the nightingale's complaining notes
     Tune my distresses and record my woes.   6
     O thou that dost inhabit in my breast,
     Leave not the mansion so long tenantless,
     Lest, growing ruinous, the building fall
     And leave no memory of what it was!
     Repair me with thy presence, Silvia;
     Thou gentle nymph, cherish thy forlorn swain!
                                 [*Shouting is heard within.*]
     What halloing and what stir is this today?
     These are my mates, that make their wills their law,
     Have some unhappy passenger in chase.   15
     They love me well, yet I have much to do
     To keep them from uncivil outrages.
     Withdraw thee, Valentine. Who's this comes here?
                                     [*He stands aside.*]

     [*Enter*] *Proteus, Silvia,* [*and*] *Julia* [*disguised as
     Sebastian*].

PROTEUS
     Madam, this service I have done for you—
     Though you respect not aught your servant doth—   20
     To hazard life and rescue you from him
     That would have forced your honor and your love:
     Vouchsafe me for my meed but one fair look;   23
     A smaller boon than this I cannot beg,
     And less than this, I am sure, you cannot give.

VALENTINE [*aside*]
     How like a dream is this I see and hear!
     Love, lend me patience to forbear awhile.

SILVIA
     Oh, miserable, unhappy that I am!

PROTEUS
     Unhappy were you, madam, ere I came;
     But by my coming I have made you happy.

SILVIA
     By thy approach thou mak'st me most unhappy.   31

JULIA [*aside*]
     And me, when he approacheth to your presence.

SILVIA
     Had I been seizèd by a hungry lion,
     I would have been a breakfast to the beast
     Rather than have false Proteus rescue me.
     Oh, heaven be judge how I love Valentine,
     Whose life's as tender to me as my soul!   37
     And full as much—for more there cannot be—
     I do detest false, perjured Proteus.
     Therefore begone. Solicit me no more.

PROTEUS
     What dangerous action, stood it next to death,
     Would I not undergo for one calm look?   42
     Oh, 'tis the curse in love, and still approved,   43
     When women cannot love where they're beloved!

SILVIA
     When Proteus cannot love where he's beloved.
     Read over Julia's heart, thy first, best love,
     For whose dear sake thou didst then rend thy faith   47
     Into a thousand oaths, and all those oaths
     Descended into perjury, to love me.
     Thou hast no faith left now, unless thou'dst two,   50
     And that's far worse than none. Better have none
     Than plural faith, which is too much by one.
     Thou counterfeit to thy true friend!

PROTEUS   In love
     Who respects friend?

SILVIA   All men but Proteus.   54

PROTEUS
     Nay, if the gentle spirit of moving words
     Can no way change you to a milder form,
     I'll woo you like a soldier, at arms' end,   57
     And love you 'gainst the nature of love—force ye.

SILVIA
     O heaven!

PROTEUS [*assailing her*]   I'll force thee yield to my desire.

VALENTINE [*coming forward*]
     Ruffian, let go that rude, uncivil touch,
     Thou friend of an ill fashion!

PROTEUS   Valentine!   61

VALENTINE
     Thou common friend, that's without faith or love!   62
     For such is a friend now. Treacherous man,
     Thou hast beguiled my hopes. Naught but mine eye
     Could have persuaded me. Now I dare not say
     I have one friend alive; thou wouldst disprove me.
     Who should be trusted, when one's right hand
     Is perjured to the bosom? Proteus,
     I am sorry I must never trust thee more,
     But count the world a stranger for thy sake.
     The private wound is deepest. Oh, time most accurst,
     'Mongst all foes that a friend should be the worst!

PROTEUS
     My shame and guilt confounds me.
     Forgive me, Valentine. If hearty sorrow
     Be a sufficient ransom for offense,

5.4. Location: The forest.
1 **use** custom   2 **desert** deserted region   6 **record** sing   15 **Have**
Who have.   **unhappy passenger** unlucky traveler   20 **respect** heed
23 **meed** reward.   **fair** kind   31 **approach** amorous advances

37 **tender** dear   42 **undergo** undertake.   **calm** gentle, kind   43 **still
approved** continually reaffirmed by experience   47 **rend** tear
50 **thou'dst** thou hast   54 **respects** takes into consideration
57 **arms' end** sword's point. (With bawdy suggestion.)   61 **fashion**
kind, sort.   62 **common** vulgar, superficial

I tender't here. I do as truly suffer
As e'er I did commit.   76
VALENTINE   Then I am paid,
And once again I do receive thee honest.   77
Who by repentance is not satisfied   78
Is nor of heaven nor earth. For these are pleased;
By penitence th'Eternal's wrath's appeased.   80
And, that my love may appear plain and free,
All that was mine in Silvia I give thee.   82

JULIA   Oh, me unhappy!   [*She swoons.*]

PROTEUS   Look to the boy.

VALENTINE   Why, boy! Why, wag! How now? What's
the matter? Look up. Speak.   86

JULIA [*recovering*]   Oh, good sir, my master charged me
to deliver a ring to Madam Silvia, which, out of my
neglect, was never done.

PROTEUS
Where is that ring, boy?

JULIA [*giving her own ring*]   Here 'tis. This is it.

PROTEUS   How? Let me see.
Why, this is the ring I gave to Julia.

JULIA
Oh, cry you mercy, sir, I have mistook.
This is the ring you sent to Silvia.   94
                          [*She offers another ring.*]

PROTEUS
But how cam'st thou by this ring? At my depart
I gave this unto Julia.

JULIA
And Julia herself did give it me;
And Julia herself hath brought it hither.
                          [*She reveals her identity.*]

PROTEUS   How? Julia?

JULIA
Behold her that gave aim to all thy oaths
And entertained 'em deeply in her heart.   101
How oft hast thou with perjury cleft the root!
Oh, Proteus, let this habit make thee blush!
Be thou ashamed that I have took upon me   104
Such an immodest raiment, if shame live
In a disguise of love.   106
It is the lesser blot, modesty finds,   107
Women to change their shapes than men their minds.

PROTEUS
Than men their minds? 'Tis true. Oh, heaven! Were
man
But constant, he were perfect. That one error
Fills him with faults, makes him run through all
th'sins;

Inconstancy falls off ere it begins.   113
What is in Silvia's face but I may spy
More fresh in Julia's, with a constant eye?   115

VALENTINE
Come, come, a hand from either.
Let me be blest to make this happy close;   117
'Twere pity two such friends should be long foes.
                     [*Proteus and Julia join hands.*]

PROTEUS
Bear witness, heaven, I have my wish forever.

JULIA   And I mine.
          [*Enter the*] Duke [*and*] Thurio, [*led by*] Outlaws.

OUTLAWS   A prize, a prize, a prize!

VALENTINE
Forbear, forbear, I say! It is my lord the Duke.
                   [*The Duke and Thurio are released.*]
Your Grace is welcome to a man disgraced,
Banishèd Valentine.

DUKE   Sir Valentine!

THURIO [*advancing*]
Yonder is Silvia, and Silvia's mine.

VALENTINE [*drawing his sword*]
Thurio, give back, or else embrace thy death.   126
Come not within the measure of my wrath.   127
Do not name Silvia thine; if once again,
Verona shall not hold thee. Here she stands.   129
Take but possession of her with a touch;
I dare thee but to breathe upon my love.

THURIO
Sir Valentine, I care not for her, I.
I hold him but a fool that will endanger
His body for a girl that loves him not.
I claim her not, and therefore she is thine.

DUKE
The more degenerate and base art thou,
To make such means for her as thou hast done   137
And leave her on such slight conditions.—   138
Now, by the honor of my ancestry,
I do applaud thy spirit, Valentine,
And think thee worthy of an empress' love.
Know then I here forget all former griefs,   142
Cancel all grudge, repeal thee home again,   143
Plead a new state in thy unrivaled merit,   144
To which I thus subscribe: Sir Valentine,
Thou art a gentleman and well derived.
Take thou thy Silvia, for thou hast deserved her.

VALENTINE
I thank Your Grace. The gift hath made me happy.
I now beseech you, for your daughter's sake,
To grant one boon that I shall ask of you.

DUKE
I grant it, for thine own, whate'er it be.

---

76 tender't offer it   **77 commit** sin.   **78 receive** believe, acknowledge
80 nor of neither of.   **these** i.e., heaven and earth   **82 love** friendship   **86 wag** (A term of endearment for a youth.)   **94 cry you mercy**
I beg your pardon.   **101 gave aim to** was the object of   **104 habit** i.e.,
page's costume   **106–7 if shame . . . love** if a disguise undertaken for
love can be thought shameful; or, if one who feigns love (such as Proteus) can feel shame.

113 Inconstancy . . . begins i.e., inconstant love falls away from loving almost before it has even begun.   **115 constant** steady, loyal
117 close union, conclusion   **126 give back** stand back   **127 measure**
reach   **129 Verona** (Again, probably an error for *Milan;* see 3.1.81.)
hold thee keep you safe   **137 means** exertions   **138 on . . . conditions** for such a paltry reason.   **142 griefs** grievances   **143 repeal**
recall   **144 Plead . . . state** argue or maintain a new state of affairs

VALENTINE
These banished men, that I have kept withal,   152
Are men endued with worthy qualities.
Forgive them what they have committed here,
And let them be recalled from their exile.
They are reformèd, civil, full of good,
And fit for great employment, worthy lord.

DUKE
Thou hast prevailed. I pardon them and thee.
Dispose of them as thou know'st their deserts.
Come, let us go. We will include all jars   160
With triumphs, mirth, and rare solemnity.   161

VALENTINE
And, as we walk along, I dare be bold

With our discourse to make Your Grace to smile.
What think you of this page, my lord?

DUKE
I think the boy hath grace in him. He blushes.

VALENTINE
I warrant you, my lord, more grace than boy.

DUKE   What mean you by that saying?

VALENTINE
Please you, I'll tell you as we pass along,
That you will wonder what hath fortunèd.   169
Come, Proteus, 'tis your penance but to hear
The story of your loves discoverèd.   171
That done, our day of marriage shall be yours;
One feast, one house, one mutual happiness.

Exeunt.

152 **kept withal** lived with   160 **include all jars** conclude all discords
161 **triumphs** festive celebrations.   **rare solemnity** marvelous festivity.

169 **That . . . fortunèd** in such a way that you will marvel at what has
happened.   171 **discoverèd** declared, disclosed.

The Taming of the Shrew

The Taming of the Shrew (c. 1592–1594) shows Shakespeare's comic genius at its best. At the same time, it shares with his other early plays an anticipation of the directions that his genius is to take in *Much Ado about Nothing* and other comedies of the later 1590s. By skillfully juxtaposing two plots and an induction, or framing plot, it offers contrasting views on the battle of the sexes. This debate on the nature of the love relationship will continue through many later comedies. The play also adroitly manipulates the device of mistaken identity, as in *The Comedy of Errors,* inverting appearance and reality, dreaming and waking, and the master-servant relationship in order to create a transformed Saturnalian world anticipating that of *A Midsummer Night's Dream* and *Twelfth Night.*

The induction sets up the theme of illusion, using an old motif known as "The Sleeper Awakened" (as found, for example, in *The Arabian Nights*). This device frames the main action of the play, giving to it an added perspective. *The Taming of the Shrew* purports, in fact, to be a play within a play, an entertainment devised by a witty nobleman as a practical joke on a drunken tinker, Christopher Sly. The jest is to convince Sly that he is not Sly at all, but an aristocrat suffering delusions. Outlandishly dressed in new finery, Sly is invited to witness a play from the gallery over the stage. In a rendition called *The Taming of a Shrew* (printed in 1594 and now generally thought to be taken from an earlier version of Shakespeare's play, employing a good deal of conscious originality along with some literary borrowing and even plagiarism), the framing plot concludes by actually putting Sly back out on the street in front of the alehouse where he was found. He awakes, recalls the play as a dream, and proposes to put the vision to good use by taming his own wife. Whether this ending reflects an epilogue now lost from the text of Shakespeare's play cannot be said, but it does reinforce the idea of the play as Sly's fantasy. Like Puck at the end of *A Midsummer Night's Dream,* urging us to

dismiss what we have seen as the product of our own slumbering, Sly continually reminds us that the play is only an illusion or shadow.

With repeated daring, Shakespeare calls attention to the contrived nature of his artifact, the play. When, for example, Sly is finally convinced that he is, in fact, a noble lord recovering from madness and lustily proposes to hasten off to bed with his long-neglected wife, we are comically aware that the "wife" is an impostor, a young page in disguise. Yet this counterfeiting of roles is no more unreal than the employment of Elizabethan boy-actors for the parts of Katharina and Bianca in the "real" play. As we watch Sly watching a play, levels of meaning intersect in this evocative fashion. Again, the paintings offered to Sly by his new attendants call attention to art's ability to confound illusion and reality. In one painting, Cytherea is hidden by reeds "Which seem to move and wanton with her breath / Even as the waving sedges play wi'th'wind," and, in another painting, Io appears "As lively painted as the deed was done" (Induction, 2.50–6). Sly's function, then, is that of the naive observer who inverts illusion and reality in his mind, concluding that his whole previous life of tinkers and alehouses and Cicely Hackets has been unreal. As his attendants explain to him, "These fifteen years you have been in a dream, / Or when you waked, so waked as if you slept." We as audience laugh at Sly's naiveté, and yet we, too, are moved and even transformed by an artistic vision that we know to be illusory.

Like Sly, many characters in the main action of the play are persuaded, or contrive, to be what they are not. Lucentio and Tranio exchange roles of master and servant. Bianca's supposed tutors are, in fact, her wooers, using their lessons to disguise messages of love. Katharina is prevailed upon by her husband, Petruchio, to declare that the sun is the moon and that an old gentleman (Vincentio) is a fair young maiden. Vincentio is publicly informed that he is an impostor and that the "real" Vincentio (the Pedant) is at that very moment looking at him out of the window of his son Lucentio's house. This last ruse does not fool the real Vincentio, but it nearly succeeds in fooling everyone else. Baptista Minola is about to commit Vincentio to jail for the infamous slander of asserting that the supposed Lucentio is only a servant in disguise. Vincentio, as the newly arrived stranger, is able to see matters as they really are, but the dwellers of Padua have grown so accustomed to the mad and improbable fictions of their life that they are not easily awakened to reality.

Such illusions have the effect of challenging the norms of social order. If a servant can playact at being the master so successfully that no one can tell the difference, are we to understand that social distinctions are mere arbitrary constructions? If Sly can become a lord by wearing the right clothes and speaking blank verse (as in the Induction, 2.68 and following), might audience members similarly raise their status? The theater promotes such skeptical questions, since it is in the business of dressing actors up as persons of whatever rank the playwright chooses. Surely one of the pleasures of theatrical performance for Elizabethan audiences was that of dreaming of social advancement or social control. At the same time, this theater treats such a liberating experience as holiday or farcical nightmare, and as Saturnalian escape; we realize as audience that we will return to the norms of our daily lives after having visited an imagined space where anything is possible.

Shakespeare multiplies his devices of illusion by combining two entirely distinct plots, each concerned, at least in part, with the comic inversion of appearance and reality: the shrew-taming plot involving Petruchio and Kate, and the more conventional romantic plot involving Lucentio and Bianca. The latter plot is derived from the *Supposes* of George Gascoigne, a play first presented at Gray's Inn (one of the Inns of Court) in 1566, as translated from Ariosto's neoclassical comedy, *I Suppositi*, 1509. (Ariosto's work, in turn, was based upon Terence's *Eunuchus* and Plautus's *Captivi*.) The "Supposes" are mistaken identities or misunderstandings, the kind of hilarious farcical mix-ups with which Shakespeare had already experimented in *The Comedy of Errors*. Shakespeare has, as usual, both romanticized his source and moralized it in a characteristically English way. The heroine, who in the Roman comedy of Plautus and Terence would have been a courtesan, and who in *Supposes* is made pregnant by her clandestine lover, remains thoroughly chaste in Shakespeare's comedy. Consequently, she has no need for a pander, or go-between, such as the bawdy Duenna or Nurse of *Supposes*. The satire directed at the heroine's unwelcome old wooer Gremio is far less savage than in *Supposes*, where the "pantaloon," Dr. Cleander, is a villainously corrupt lawyer epitomizing the depravity of "respectable" society. Despite Shakespeare's modifications, however, the basic plot remains an effort to foil parental authority. The young lovers, choosing each other for romantic reasons, must fend off the materialistic calculations of their parents.

In a stock situation of this sort, the character types are also conventional. Gremio, the aged wealthy wooer, is actually labeled a "pantaloon" in the text (3.1.36–7) to stress his neoclassical ancestry. (Lean and foolish old wooers of this sort were customarily dressed in pantaloons, slippers, and spectacles on the Italian stage.) Gremio is typically "the graybeard," and Baptista Minola is "the narrow-prying father" (3.2.145–6). Even though Shakespeare renders these characters far less unattractive than in *Supposes*, their worldly behavior still invites reprisal from the young. Since Baptista Minola insists on selling his daughter Bianca to the highest bidder, it is fitting that her wealthiest suitor (the supposed Lucentio) should turn out in the end to be a penniless servant (Tranio) disguised as a man of affluence and position. In his traditional role as the clever servant of neoclassical comedy, Tranio skillfully apes the mannerisms of respectable society. He can deal in the mere surfaces— clothes or reputation—out of which a man's social importance is created, and can even furnish himself with a rich father. Gremio and Baptista deserve to be foiled, because they accept the illusion of respectability as real.

Even the romantic lovers of this borrowed plot are largely conventional. To be sure, Shakespeare emphasizes their virtuous qualities and their sincerity. He adds Hortensio (not in *Supposes*) to provide Lucentio with a genuine, if foolish, rival and Bianca with two wooers closer to her age than old Gremio. Lucentio and Bianca deserve their romantic triumph; they are self-possessed, witty, and steadfast to each other. Yet we know very little about them, nor have they seen deeply into each other. Lucentio's love talk is laden with conventional images in praise of Bianca's dark eyes and scarlet lips. At the play's end, he discovers, to his surprise, that she can be willful, even disobedient. Has her appearance of virtue concealed something from him and from us? Because the relationship between these lovers is superficial, they are appropriately destined to a superficial marriage as well. The passive Bianca becomes the proud and defiant wife.

By contrast, Petruchio and Kate are the more interesting lovers, whose courtship involves mutual self-discovery. Admittedly, we must not overstate the case. Especially at first, these lovers are also stock types: the shrew tamer and his proverbially shrewish wife. (The word *shrew*, originally signifying a wicked or malignant man, often applied to the devil or to a malignant planet, had come to mean a scolding or turbulent wife.) Although Shakespeare seems not to have used any single source for this plot, he was well acquainted with crude, misogynistic stories demonstrating the need for putting women in their place. In a ballad called *A Merry Jest of a Shrewd and Curst Wife, Lapped in Morel's Skin* (printed c. 1550), for example, the husband tames his shrewish wife by flaying her bloody with birch rods and then wrapping her in the freshly salted skin of a plow horse named Morel. (This shrewish wife, like Kate, has an obedient and gentle younger sister who is their father's favorite.) Other features of Shakespeare's plot can be found in similar tales: the tailor scolded for devising a gown of outlandish fashion (Gerard Legh's *Accidence of Armory*, 1562), the wife obliged to agree with her husband's assertion of some patent falsehood (Don Juan Manuel's *El Conde Lucanor*, c. 1335), and the three husbands' wager on their wives' obedience (*The Book of the Knight of La Tour-Landry*, printed 1484). In the raw spirit of this sexist tradition, so unlike the refined Italianate sentiment of his other plot, Shakespeare introduces Petruchio as a man of reckless bravado who is ready to marry the ugliest or sharpest-tongued woman alive so long as she is rich. However much he may be later attracted by Kate's fiery spirit, his first attraction to her is crassly financial. Kate is, moreover, a troublesomely defiant young woman at first, described by the men who know her as "intolerable curst / And shrewd and froward," and aggressive in her bullying of Bianca. She and Petruchio meet as grotesque comic counterparts.

At the play's end, the traditional pattern of male dominance and female acquiescence is still prominent. Kate is allowed food, sleep, and sex only when she yields to a socially ordained patriarchal framework in which a husband is the princely ruler of his wife. Kate is not like the young heroines of many other Shakespearean comedies (Portia in *The Merchant of Venice* and Rosalind in *As You Like It*, for example) who wittily guide their immature and overly romantic young men toward a pragmatic view of love and marriage; in this play, Kate is the one who must be mastered by the self-assured male. Her shrewishness is an open threat to male control in the marital bond, and, accordingly, the play's comic finale celebrates containment of this threat in her, along with a sharp reminder of the resistance to be endured by other husbands who have failed to tame their shrews.

Within this male-oriented frame of reference, however, Petruchio and Kate are surprisingly like Benedick and Beatrice of *Much Ado About Nothing*. Petruchio, for all his rant, is increasingly drawn to Kate by her spirit. As wit-combatants, they are worthy of one another's enmity—or love. No one else in the play is a fit match for either of them. Kate, too, is attracted to Petruchio, despite her war of words. Her anger is part defensive protection, part testing of his sincerity. If she is contemptuous of the wooers she has seen till now, she has good reason to be. We share her condescension toward the aged Gremio or the laughably inept Hortensio. She rightly fears that her father wishes to dispose of her so that he may auction off Bianca to the wealthiest competitor. Kate's jaded view of such marriage brokering is entirely defensible. Not surprisingly, she first views Petruchio, whose professed intentions are far from reassuring, as another mere adventurer in love. She is impressed by his "line" in wooing her but needs to test his constancy and sincerity. Marriage for her

would be a serious step, since social convention allows a dominant role for the husband; can she hope that she and Petruchio will arrive at some sort of understanding in which her role as wife and partner will be an honorable one? She puts down most men with a shrewish manner that challenges their very masculinity; Petruchio is the first man to counter her wit and energy with his own. Can she learn to live with this man?

Kate's rejection of men has not left her very happy, however genuine her disdain is for most of those who have come to woo. Petruchio's "schooling" can be seen as addressing that unhappiness, even if his purpose is unremittingly masculine in its assumption that a rebellious wife has to be "tamed" as one would tame a hawk. Having wooed and partly won her, Petruchio tests her with his late arrival at the marriage, his unconventional dress, and his crossing all her desires. Like the hawk-tamer, Petruchio uses harsh physical means, including deprivation of food and drink. He treats Kate as his chattel, and never wavers in his certainty that he is right to do so. Other males applaud his success and wish only to follow his example. The resolution is in these terms manifestly more sexist than in *Much Ado About Nothing*; it is as though Shakespeare works his way through the problems of sexual conflict from this early, very masculine play to a more complex and mutual accommodation in his later comedies.

At the same time, it is possible to see *The Taming of the Shrew* as a play in which a genuine accommodation is reached, even if it is on the man's terms with the woman being given no choice. The play may encourage the view that Petruchio's treatment of Kate, no matter how temporarily harsh, is ultimately benign in its intent. Petruchio, by his outlandish behavior of overturning tables and scolding servants, shows Kate an ugly picture of what her refractoriness is like. He succeeds by insisting on what, arguably, she may desire too: a well-defined relationship tempered by mutual respect and love. In this interpretation, Kate may gain something by the play's end. Her closing speech, with its fine blend of irony and self-conscious hyperbole, together with its seriousness of concern, can be read as expressing the way in which her independence of spirit and her newfound acceptance of a domestic rule are successfully fused, enabling her to gain widespread applause instead of opprobrium.

This is by no means the only way of reading the final scene, as modern productions often make clear: Kate emerges in various stage productions as more or less contented, or as simply resigned, or as cruelly brainwashed, or as only playing the role of obedient wife to get what she wants. The uncertainty of interpretation is one of the great pleasures and challenges today, in a world for which ideas about marriage have manifestly shifted since Shakespeare wrote. Even so, the play offers common ground in its appreciation for the seriousness of the issue and in its wonderful transparency as a text that offers itself up for rival interpretations.

The Taming of the Shrew

❧

[*Dramatis Personae*

CHRISTOPHER SLY, *a tinker and beggar,* }
HOSTESS *of an alehouse,*
A LORD, } *Persons in the Induction*
A PAGE, SERVANTS, HUNTSMEN,
PLAYERS, }

BAPTISTA, *a rich gentleman of Padua*
KATHARINA, *the shrew, also called Katharine and Kate, Baptista's elder daughter*
BIANCA, *Baptista's younger daughter*

PETRUCHIO, *a gentleman of Verona, suitor to Katharina*
GRUMIO, *Petruchio's servant*
CURTIS, NATHANIEL, PHILIP, JOSEPH, NICHOLAS, PETER, *and other servants of Petruchio*

GREMIO, *elderly suitor to Bianca*
HORTENSIO, *suitor to Bianca*
LUCENTIO, *son of Vincentio, in love with Bianca*
TRANIO, *Lucentio's servant*
BIONDELLO, *Lucentio's servant*
VINCENTIO, *a gentleman of Pisa*
A PEDANT (*or Merchant*) *of Mantua*
A WIDOW, *courted by Hortensio*

A TAILOR
A HABERDASHER
AN OFFICER
Other Servants of Baptista and Lucentio

SCENE: *Padua, and Petruchio's country house in Italy; the Induction is located in the countryside and at a Lord's house in England*]

[Induction.1]

Enter Beggar (Christopher Sly) and Hostess.

SLY   I'll feeze you, in faith. 1
HOSTESS   A pair of stocks, you rogue! 2
SLY   You're a baggage. The Slys are no rogues. Look in 3
the chronicles; we came in with Richard Conqueror. 4
Therefore *paucas pallabris,* let the world slide. Sessa! 5
HOSTESS   You will not pay for the glasses you have burst?
SLY   No, not a denier. Go by, Saint Jeronimy, go to thy 8
cold bed and warm thee. 9

HOSTESS   I know my remedy; I must go fetch the third- 10
borough.   [*Exit.*] 11
SLY   Third, or fourth, or fifth borough, I'll answer him 12
by law. I'll not budge an inch, boy. Let him come, and 13
kindly.   *Falls asleep.* 14

Wind horns [within]. Enter a Lord from hunting, with his train.

LORD
Huntsman, I charge thee, tender well my hounds. 15
Breathe Merriman—the poor cur is embossed— 16
And couple Clowder with the deep-mouthed brach. 17
Saw'st thou not, boy, how Silver made it good 18
At the hedge corner, in the coldest fault? 19

Induction.1. Location: **Before an alehouse and, subsequently, before the Lord's house nearby. (See lines 75, 135.)**
1 feeze you i.e., fix you, get even with you   **2 A . . . stocks** i.e., I'll have you put in the stocks   **3 baggage** contemptible woman or prostitute   **4 Richard** (Sly's mistake for "William.")   **5** *paucas pallabris* i.e., *pocas palabras,* "few words." (Spanish.)   **Sessa** (Of doubtful meaning; perhaps "be quiet," "cease," or "let it go.")   **8 denier** French copper coin of little value.   **Go . . . Jeronimy** (Sly's variation of an often quoted line from Kyd's *The Spanish Tragedy,* urging caution.)   **8–9 go . . . thee** (Perhaps a proverb; see *King Lear,* 3.4.46–7.)

10–11 thirdborough constable.   **12 Third** (Sly shows his ignorance; the *third* in "thirdborough" derives from the Old English word *frith,* "peace.")   **13 by law** in the law courts.   **14 kindly** welcome. (Said ironically.)   **14.1** *Wind* Blow   **14.2** *train* retinue.   **15 tender** care for   **16 Breathe Merriman** Give the dog Merriman time to recover its breath.   **embossed** foaming at the mouth from exhaustion   **17 couple** leash together.   **deep-mouthed brach** bitch hound with the deep baying voice.   **18 made it good** i.e., picked up the lost scent   **19 in the coldest fault** when the scent was lost by a *fault* or break in the scent.

I would not lose the dog for twenty pound.

FIRST HUNTSMAN
Why, Bellman is as good as he, my lord.
He cried upon it at the merest loss,   22
And twice today picked out the dullest scent.
Trust me, I take him for the better dog.

LORD
Thou art a fool. If Echo were as fleet,
I would esteem him worth a dozen such.
But sup them well and look unto them all.   27
Tomorrow I intend to hunt again.

FIRST HUNTSMAN   I will, my lord.

LORD [seeing Sly]
What's here? One dead, or drunk? See, doth he
   breathe?

SECOND HUNTSMAN [examining Sly]
He breathes, my lord. Were he not warmed with ale,
This were a bed but cold to sleep so soundly.

LORD
Oh, monstrous beast, how like a swine he lies!
Grim death, how foul and loathsome is thine image!   34
Sirs, I will practice on this drunken man.   35
What think you, if he were conveyed to bed,
Wrapped in sweet clothes, rings put upon his fingers,   37
A most delicious banquet by his bed,   38
And brave attendants near him when he wakes,   39
Would not the beggar then forget himself?

FIRST HUNTSMAN
Believe me, lord, I think he cannot choose.   41

SECOND HUNTSMAN
It would seem strange unto him when he waked.

LORD
Even as a flatt'ring dream or worthless fancy.   43
Then take him up, and manage well the jest.
Carry him gently to my fairest chamber,
And hang it round with all my wanton pictures.
Balm his foul head in warm distillèd waters,   47
And burn sweet wood to make the lodging sweet.
Procure me music ready when he wakes,
To make a dulcet and a heavenly sound.   50
And if he chance to speak, be ready straight,   51
And with a low submissive reverence   52
Say, "What is it Your Honor will command?"
Let one attend him with a silver basin
Full of rosewater and bestrewed with flowers;
Another bear the ewer, the third a diaper,   56
And say, "Will 't please Your Lordship cool your
   hands?"
Someone be ready with a costly suit,
And ask him what apparel he will wear;
Another tell him of his hounds and horse,   60
And that his lady mourns at his disease.   61

Persuade him that he hath been lunatic,
And when he says he is, say that he dreams,   63
For he is nothing but a mighty lord.
This do, and do it kindly, gentle sirs.   65
It will be pastime passing excellent,   66
If it be husbanded with modesty.   67

FIRST HUNTSMAN
My lord, I warrant you we will play our part
As he shall think by our true diligence   69
He is no less than what we say he is.

LORD
Take him up gently, and to bed with him,
And each one to his office when he wakes.   72
         [Some bear out Sly.] Sound trumpets [within].
Sirrah, go see what trumpet 'tis that sounds.   73
                                        [Exit a Servingman.]
Belike some noble gentleman that means,   74
Traveling some journey, to repose him here.

         Enter [a] Servingman.

How now? Who is it?

SERVINGMAN   An't please Your Honor, players   76
That offer service to Your Lordship.

         Enter Players.

LORD
Bid them come near.—Now, fellows, you are welcome.

PLAYERS   We thank Your Honor.

LORD
Do you intend to stay with me tonight?

FIRST PLAYER
So please Your Lordship to accept our duty.   81

LORD
With all my heart. This fellow I remember
Since once he played a farmer's eldest son.—
'Twas where you wooed the gentlewoman so well.
I have forgot your name, but sure that part
Was aptly fitted and naturally performed.

SECOND PLAYER
I think 'twas Soto that Your Honor means.

LORD
'Tis very true. Thou didst it excellent.
Well, you are come to me in happy time,   89
The rather for I have some sport in hand   90
Wherein your cunning can assist me much.   91
There is a lord will hear you play tonight.
But I am doubtful of your modesties,   93
Lest, overeyeing of his odd behavior—   94
For yet His Honor never heard a play—
You break into some merry passion   96

---

22 **cried . . . loss** bayed to signal his recovery of the scent after it had been completely lost   27 **sup them well** feed them a good supper
34 **image** likeness (since sleep was regarded as a likeness of death).
35 **practice on** play a joke on   37 **sweet** perfumed   38 **banquet** light repast   39 **brave** finely arrayed   41 **cannot choose** is bound to.
43 **fancy** flight of imagination.   47 **Balm** Bathe, anoint   50 **dulcet** melodious   51 **straight** at once   52 **reverence** bow   56 **ewer** jug, pitcher.
diaper towel   60 **horse** horses   61 **disease** i.e., mental derangement.

63 **when . . . is** i.e., when he says he must be mad indeed. (The *is* is stressed.)   65 **kindly** naturally (and thus persuasively).   **gentle** kind   66 **passing** surpassingly   67 **husbanded with modesty** managed with decorum.   69 **As** so that.   **by** as a result of   72 **office** duty   73 **Sirrah** (Usual form of address to inferiors.)   74 **Belike** Perhaps   76 **An't** If it   81 **So please** If it please.   **duty** expression of respect and dutiful service.   89 **happy** opportune   90 **The rather for** the more so since   91 **cunning** professional skill   93 **doubtful** apprehensive.   **modesties** discretion, self-control   94 **overeyeing of** witnessing   96 **merry passion** outburst of laughter

And so offend him; for I tell you, sirs,
If you should smile, he grows impatient.

FIRST PLAYER
Fear not, my lord, we can contain ourselves,
Were he the veriest antic in the world.   100

LORD [to a Servingman]
Go, sirrah, take them to the buttery,   101
And give them friendly welcome every one.
Let them want nothing that my house affords.   103

Exit one with the Players.

Sirrah, go you to Barthol'mew my page,
And see him dressed in all suits like a lady.   105
That done, conduct him to the drunkard's chamber,
And call him "madam," do him obeisance.   107
Tell him from me, as he will win my love,   108
He bear himself with honorable action
Such as he hath observed in noble ladies
Unto their lords by them accomplishèd.   111
Such duty to the drunkard let him do
With soft low tongue and lowly courtesy,
And say, "What is't Your Honor will command,
Wherein your lady and your humble wife
May show her duty and make known her love?"
And then with kind embracements, tempting kisses,
And with declining head into his bosom,
Bid him shed tears, as being overjoyed
To see her noble lord restored to health,
Who for this seven years hath esteemèd him   121
No better than a poor and loathsome beggar.
And if the boy have not a woman's gift
To rain a shower of commanded tears,
An onion will do well for such a shift,   125
Which in a napkin being close conveyed   126
Shall in despite enforce a watery eye.   127
See this dispatched with all the haste thou canst.
Anon I'll give thee more instructions.   129

Exit a Servingman.

I know the boy will well usurp the grace,   130
Voice, gait, and action of a gentlewoman.
I long to hear him call the drunkard husband,
And how my men will stay themselves from laughter   133
When they do homage to this simple peasant.
I'll in to counsel them. Haply my presence   135
May well abate the overmerry spleen   136
Which otherwise would grow into extremes.

[Exeunt.]

❧

[Induction.2]

Enter aloft the drunkard [Sly], with attendants;
some with apparel, basin, and ewer and other
appurtenances; and Lord.

SLY For God's sake, a pot of small ale.   1
FIRST SERVINGMAN
Will't please Your Lordship drink a cup of sack?   2
SECOND SERVINGMAN
Will't please Your Honor taste of these conserves?   3
THIRD SERVINGMAN
What raiment will Your Honor wear today?
SLY I am Christophero Sly. Call not me "Honor" nor
"Lordship." I ne'er drank sack in my life; and if you
give me any conserves, give me conserves of beef.   7
Ne'er ask me what raiment I'll wear, for I have no
more doublets than backs, no more stockings than   9
legs, nor no more shoes than feet—nay, sometimes
more feet than shoes, or such shoes as my toes look   11
through the overleather.   12
LORD
Heaven cease this idle humor in Your Honor!   13
Oh, that a mighty man of such descent,
Of such possessions and so high esteem,
Should be infusèd with so foul a spirit!
SLY What, would you make me mad? Am not I Christopher Sly, old Sly's son of Burton-heath, by birth a   18
peddler, by education a cardmaker, by transmutation   19
a bearherd, and now by present profession a tinker?   20
Ask Marian Hacket, the fat alewife of Wincot, if she   21
know me not. If she say I am not fourteen pence on   22
the score for sheer ale, score me up for the lyingest   23
knave in Christendom. What, I am not bestraught: 24
here's—
THIRD SERVINGMAN
Oh, this it is that makes your lady mourn!
SECOND SERVINGMAN
Oh, this is it that makes your servants droop!
LORD
Hence comes it that your kindred shuns your house,
As beaten hence by your strange lunacy.   29
Oh, noble lord, bethink thee of thy birth.
Call home thy ancient thoughts from banishment,   31
And banish hence these abject lowly dreams.
Look how thy servants do attend on thee,
Each in his office ready at thy beck.   34

Induction.2. Location: A bedchamber in the Lord's house.
0.1 aloft i.e., in the gallery over the rear facade of the stage **1 small** weak (and therefore cheap) **2 sack** sweet Spanish wine (suited to a gentleman to drink). **3 conserves** candied fruit. **7 conserves of beef** preserved (salted) beef. **9 doublets** men's jackets **11 as that** **12 overleather** upper leather of the shoe. **13 idle humor** foolish whim **18 Burton-heath** (Perhaps Barton on the Heath, about sixteen miles from Stratford, the home of Shakespeare's aunt.) **19 cardmaker** maker of cards or combs used to prepare wool for spinning **20 bearherd** keeper of a performing bear. **tinker** pot mender. **21 alewife** woman who keeps an alehouse. **Wincot** small village about four miles from Stratford. (The parish register shows that there were Hackets living there in 1591.) **22–3 on the score** in debt (since such reckonings were originally notched or scored on a stick) **23 sheer** nothing but. **score me up for** reckon me to be **24 bestraught** distracted **29 As** as if **31 ancient** former **34 beck** nod.

100 **veriest antic** oddest buffoon or eccentric 101 **buttery** pantry, or a room for storing liquor (in butts) and other provisions 103 **want** lack 105 **in all suits** in every detail. (With a pun on *suits* of clothes.) 107 **do him obeisance** show him dutiful respect. 108 **him** i.e., the page Bartholomew. **as he will** if he wishes to 111 **by them accomplishèd** performed by the ladies. 121 **him** himself 125 **shift** purpose 126 **napkin** handkerchief. **close** secretly 127 **in despite** i.e., notwithstanding a natural inclination to laugh rather than cry 129 **Anon** Soon 130 **usurp** assume 133 **And how** i.e., and to see how 135 **I'll in** I'll go in 136 **spleen** mood. (The spleen was the supposed seat of laughter and anger.)

Wilt thou have music? Hark, Apollo plays,   *Music.*   35
And twenty cagèd nightingales do sing.
Or wilt thou sleep? We'll have thee to a couch,
Softer and sweeter than the lustful bed
On purpose trimmed up for Semiramis.   39
Say thou wilt walk; we will bestrew the ground.   40
Or wilt thou ride? Thy horses shall be trapped,   41
Their harness studded all with gold and pearl.
Dost thou love hawking? Thou hast hawks will soar
Above the morning lark. Or wilt thou hunt?
Thy hounds shall make the welkin answer them   45
And fetch shrill echoes from the hollow earth.

FIRST SERVINGMAN
Say thou wilt course, thy greyhounds are as swift   47
As breathèd stags, ay, fleeter than the roe.   48

SECOND SERVINGMAN
Dost thou love pictures? We will fetch thee straight
Adonis painted by a running brook,   50
And Cytherea all in sedges hid,   51
Which seem to move and wanton with her breath,   52
Even as the waving sedges play wi'th'wind.

LORD
We'll show thee Io as she was a maid,   54
And how she was beguilèd and surprised,
As lively painted as the deed was done.   56

THIRD SERVINGMAN
Or Daphne roaming through a thorny wood,   57
Scratching her legs that one shall swear she bleeds,
And at that sight shall sad Apollo weep,
So workmanly the blood and tears are drawn.   60

LORD
Thou art a lord, and nothing but a lord.
Thou hast a lady far more beautiful
Than any woman in this waning age.   63

FIRST SERVINGMAN
And till the tears that she hath shed for thee
Like envious floods o'errun her lovely face,   65
She was the fairest creature in the world;
And yet she is inferior to none.   67

SLY
Am I a lord? And have I such a lady?
Or do I dream? Or have I dreamed till now?
I do not sleep: I see, I hear, I speak,
I smell sweet savors, and I feel soft things.
Upon my life, I am a lord indeed,
And not a tinker nor Christopher Sly.
Well, bring our lady hither to our sight,

And once again a pot o'th' smallest ale.

SECOND SERVINGMAN
Will 't please Your Mightiness to wash your hands?
Oh, how we joy to see your wit restored!   77
Oh, that once more you knew but what you are!   78
These fifteen years you have been in a dream,
Or when you waked, so waked as if you slept.

SLY
These fifteen years! By my fay, a goodly nap.   81
But did I never speak of all that time?   82

FIRST SERVINGMAN
Oh, yes, my lord, but very idle words;
For though you lay here in this goodly chamber,
Yet would you say ye were beaten out of door,
And rail upon the hostess of the house,   86
And say you would present her at the leet   87
Because she brought stone jugs and no sealed quarts.   88
Sometimes you would call out for Cicely Hacket.

SLY
Ay, the woman's maid of the house.

THIRD SERVINGMAN
Why, sir, you know no house, nor no such maid,
Nor no such men as you have reckoned up,
As Stephen Sly, and old John Naps of Greet,   93
And Peter Turf, and Henry Pimpernel,
And twenty more such names and men as these,
Which never were, nor no man ever saw.

SLY
Now Lord be thankèd for my good amends!   97

ALL
Amen.

Enter [the Page as a] lady, with Attendants.

SLY   I thank thee. Thou shalt not lose by it.   98

PAGE
How fares my noble lord?

SLY
                                    Marry, I fare well,   99
For here is cheer enough. Where is my wife?

PAGE
Here, noble lord. What is thy will with her?

SLY
Are you my wife, and will not call me husband?
My men should call me "lord"; I am your goodman.   103

PAGE
My husband and my lord, my lord and husband;
I am your wife in all obedience.

SLY
I know it well.—What must I call her?

---

35 Apollo i.e., as god of music   **39 Semiramis** legendary queen of Assyria, famous for her voluptuousness.   **40 bestrew** i.e., scatter rushes on   **41 trapped** adorned   **45 welkin** sky, heavens   **47 course** hunt the hare   **48 breathèd** in good physical condition, with good wind.   **roe** small, swift deer.   **50 Adonis** a young huntsman with whom Venus is vainly in love. (See Ovid's *Metamorphoses*, Book 10, and Shakespeare's poem, *Venus and Adonis*.)   **51 Cytherea** one of the names for Venus (because of her association with the island of Cythera).   **sedges** grassy marsh plants   **52 wanton** play seductively   **54 Io** a woman who, according to Ovid, was seduced by Jove concealed in a mist and afterwards transformed into a heifer   **56 as** as if   **57 Daphne** a wood nymph beloved by Apollo, changed by Diana into a laurel tree to preserve her from Apollo's assault (*Metamorphoses*, Book 1)   **60 workmanly** skillfully   **63 waning** degenerate   **65 envious** spiteful   **67 yet** even today

77 wit mental faculties   **78 knew but** only knew   **81 fay** faith   **82 of** during   **86 house** tavern   **87 present** bring accusation against.   **leet** manorial court   **88 sealed quarts** quart containers officially stamped as a guarantee of that capacity. (The irregular stoneware quarts might be used to cheat customers.)   **93 Stephen . . . Greet** (A Stephen Sly lived in Stratford during Shakespeare's day. *Greet* is a Gloucestershire hamlet not far from Stratford. The Folio reading, "Greece," is an easy misreading if Shakespeare wrote "Greete.")   **97 amends** recovery   **98 Thou . . . it** i.e., I will reward your solicitude toward me.   **99 Marry** (A mild oath, derived from "by Mary.")   **fare well** (1) am fine (2) have plenty of good *cheer* (line 100), refreshment   **103 goodman** (A homely term for "husband.")

LORD   Madam.

SLY   Al'ce madam, or Joan madam?

LORD
    Madam, and nothing else. So lords call ladies.

SLY
    Madam wife, they say that I have dreamed
    And slept above some fifteen year or more.

PAGE
    Ay, and the time seems thirty unto me,
    Being all this time abandoned from your bed.   112

SLY
    'Tis much.—Servants, leave me and her alone.—
    Madam, undress you and come now to bed.

PAGE
    Thrice-noble lord, let me entreat of you
    To pardon me yet for a night or two,
    Or, if not so, until the sun be set.
    For your physicians have expressly charged,
    In peril to incur your former malady,
    That I should yet absent me from your bed.
    I hope this reason stands for my excuse.

SLY   Ay, it stands so that I may hardly tarry so long. But   122
    I would be loath to fall into my dreams again. I will
    therefore tarry in despite of the flesh and the blood.

                Enter a [Servingman as] messenger.

SERVINGMAN
    Your Honor's players, hearing your amendment,
    Are come to play a pleasant comedy,
    For so your doctors hold it very meet,   127
    Seeing too much sadness hath congealed your blood,
    And melancholy is the nurse of frenzy,
    Therefore they thought it good you hear a play
    And frame your mind to mirth and merriment,
    Which bars a thousand harms and lengthens life.

SLY   Marry, I will let them play it. Is not a comonty a   133
    Christmas gambold or a tumbling-trick?   134

PAGE
    No, my good lord, it is more pleasing stuff.

SLY   What, household stuff?   136

PAGE   It is a kind of history.   137

SLY   Well, we'll see 't. Come, madam wife, sit by my side
    and let the world slip; we shall ne'er be younger.   139
                        [They sit over the stage.] Flourish.

                            ❧

1.1

                Enter Lucentio and his man, Tranio.

LUCENTIO
    Tranio, since for the great desire I had
    To see fair Padua, nursery of arts,   2
    I am arrived fore fruitful Lombardy,   3
    The pleasant garden of great Italy,
    And by my father's love and leave am armed
    With his good will and thy good company,
    My trusty servant, well approved in all,   7
    Here let us breathe and haply institute   8
    A course of learning and ingenious studies.   9
    Pisa, renownèd for grave citizens,
    Gave me my being, and my father first—   11
    A merchant of great traffic through the world,   12
    Vincentio, come of the Bentivolii.   13
    Vincentio's son, brought up in Florence,   14
    It shall become to serve all hopes conceived   15
    To deck his fortune with his virtuous deeds.   16
    And therefore, Tranio, for the time I study,   17
    Virtue and that part of philosophy
    Will I apply that treats of happiness   19
    By virtue specially to be achieved.
    Tell me thy mind, for I have Pisa left
    And am to Padua come as he that leaves
    A shallow plash to plunge him in the deep,   23
    And with satiety seeks to quench his thirst.

TRANIO
    Mi perdonate, gentle master mine.   25
    I am in all affected as yourself,   26
    Glad that you thus continue your resolve
    To suck the sweets of sweet philosophy.
    Only, good master, while we do admire
    This virtue and this moral discipline,
    Let's be no stoics nor no stocks, I pray,   31
    Or so devote to Aristotle's checks   32
    As Ovid be an outcast quite abjured.   33
    Balk logic with acquaintance that you have,   34
    And practice rhetoric in your common talk.   35
    Music and poesy use to quicken you;   36

1.1 Location: Padua. A street before Baptista's house.
2 Padua . . . arts (Padua's was one of the most renowned of universities during Shakespeare's time.)   **3 am arrived fore** have arrived at, or at the gates of, before. (Padua is not in Lombardy, but imprecise maps may have allowed Shakespeare to think of Lombardy as comprising all of northern Italy.)   **7 approved** tested and proved trustworthy   **8 breathe** pause, settle down.   **haply institute** begin, as circumstances permit   **9 ingenious** i.e., "ingenuous," liberal, befitting a wellborn person   **11 first** i.e., before me   **12 of great traffic** involved in extensive trade   **13 come of** descended from
14–16 Vincentio's . . . deeds It will befit Vincentio's son, brought up in Florence, to fulfill all the hopes of his family by adding virtuous deeds to what fortune has bestowed on him.   **17 for . . . study** for my term of study   **19 apply** study.   **treats of** discusses, concerns
23 plash pool   **25 *Mi perdonate*** Pardon me   **26 affected** disposed
31 stocks persons devoid of feeling, like wooden posts. (With a play on *stoics.*)   **32 devote** devoted.   **checks** restraints   **33 As** so that.
Ovid Latin love poet. (Used here to typify amorous light entertainment, as contrasted with the constraining philosophic study of Aristotle.)   **34 Balk logic** Argue, bandy words.   **acquaintance** acquaintances   **35 common talk** ordinary conversation.
36 Music . . . you Use music and poetry to refresh yourself

---

112 abandoned banished   **122 stands** (1) is the case (2) punningly, "is giving me an erection." The joke picks up on *stands,* meaning "serves," in line 121.   **127 meet** suitable   **133 Marry . . . play it** (Perhaps the Folio punctuation should be emended to "Marry, I will. Let them play it.")   **comonty** (Sly's approximation of "comedy.")   **134 gambold** (Sly's version of "gambol," frolicsome merrymaking and leaping about.)   **136 household stuff** i.e., domestic doings.   **137 history** story.   **139.1 *They sit over the stage*** (Possibly the Lord and some servingmen exeunt here or at line 113. At 1.1.249 ff., a servingman, the Page, and Sly speak, while the Lord is no longer heard from.)

The mathematics and the metaphysics,
Fall to them as you find your stomach serves you. 38
No profit grows where is no pleasure ta'en.
In brief, sir, study what you most affect. 40

LUCENTIO
Gramercies, Tranio, well dost thou advise. 41
If, Biondello, thou wert come ashore, 42
We could at once put us in readiness
And take a lodging fit to entertain
Such friends as time in Padua shall beget.
But stay awhile, what company is this?

TRANIO
Master, some show to welcome us to town. 47

Enter Baptista with his two daughters, Katharina and Bianca; Gremio, a pantaloon; [and] Hortensio, suitor to Bianca. Lucentio [and] Tranio stand by.

BAPTISTA
Gentlemen, importune me no farther,
For how I firmly am resolved you know:
That is, not to bestow my youngest daughter
Before I have a husband for the elder.
If either of you both love Katharina,
Because I know you well and love you well,
Leave shall you have to court her at your pleasure.

GREMIO
To cart her rather. She's too rough for me. 55
There, there, Hortensio, will you any wife?

KATHARINA [to Baptista]
I pray you, sir, is it your will
To make a stale of me amongst these mates? 58

HORTENSIO
"Mates," maid? How mean you that? No mates for you,
Unless you were of gentler, milder mold.

KATHARINA
I'faith, sir, you shall never need to fear;
Iwis it is not halfway to her heart. 62
But if it were, doubt not her care should be
To comb your noddle with a three-legged stool, 64
And paint your face, and use you like a fool. 65

HORTENSIO
From all such devils, good Lord deliver us!

GREMIO   And me too, good Lord!

TRANIO [aside to Lucentio]
Husht, master, here's some good pastime toward. 68

That wench is stark mad or wonderful froward. 69

LUCENTIO [aside to Tranio]
But in other's silence do I see
Maid's mild behavior and sobriety.
Peace, Tranio!

TRANIO [aside to Lucentio]
Well said, master. Mum, and gaze your fill.

BAPTISTA
Gentlemen, that I may soon make good
What I have said—Bianca, get you in.
And let it not displease thee, good Bianca,
For I will love thee ne'er the less, my girl.

KATHARINA   A pretty peat! It is best 78
Put finger in the eye, an she knew why. 79

BIANCA
Sister, content you in my discontent.—
Sir, to your pleasure humbly I subscribe. 81
My books and instruments shall be my company,
On them to look and practice by myself.

LUCENTIO [aside to Tranio]
Hark, Tranio, thou mayst hear Minerva speak. 84

HORTENSIO
Signor Baptista, will you be so strange? 85
Sorry am I that our good will effects 86
Bianca's grief.

GREMIO   Why will you mew her up, 87
Signor Baptista, for this fiend of hell,
And make her bear the penance of her tongue? 89

BAPTISTA
Gentlemen, content ye. I am resolved.
Go in, Bianca.   [Exit Bianca.]
And for I know she taketh most delight 92
In music, instruments, and poetry,
Schoolmasters will I keep within my house
Fit to instruct her youth. If you, Hortensio,
Or, Signor Gremio, you know any such,
Prefer them hither; for to cunning men 97
I will be very kind, and liberal
To mine own children in good bringing up.
And so farewell.—Katharina, you may stay,
For I have more to commune with Bianca.   *Exit.* 101

KATHARINA
Why, and I trust I may go too, may I not?
What, shall I be appointed hours, 103
As though, belike, I knew not what to take, 104
And what to leave? Ha!   *Exit.* 105

GREMIO   You may go to the devil's dam. Your gifts are 106
so good, here's none will hold you.—Their love is not 107

---

38 stomach inclination, appetite   **40 affect** find pleasant.   **41 Gramercies** Many thanks   **42 Biondello** (Lucentio apostrophizes his absent servant.)   **come ashore** (Padua, though inland, is given a harbor by Shakespeare, unless he is thinking of the canals that crossed northern Italy in the sixteenth century.)   **47.2 pantaloon** foolish old man, a stock character in Italian comedy   **55 cart** carry in a cart through the streets by way of punishment or public exposure. (With a play on *court*.)   **58 stale** laughingstock. (With a play on the meaning "harlot," since a harlot might well be carted.)   **mates** rude fellows. (But Hortensio takes the word in the sense of "husband.")   **62 Iwis . . . heart** indeed, marriage is not even halfway suited to my inclination. (Katharina speaks of herself in the third person here and in line 63.)   **64 comb your noddle** rake your head   **65 paint** i.e., make red with scratches   **68 toward** in prospect.

69 wonderful froward incredibly perverse.   **78–9 A . . . why** i.e., A fine spoiled darling she is! She does well to put on a show of weeping, knowing what's good for her. (Said sardonically.)   **81 pleasure** will.   **subscribe** submit.   **84 Minerva** goddess of wisdom   **85 strange** distant, unfeeling.   **86 effects** causes   **87 mew** coop (as one would a falcon)   **89 her . . . her** i.e., Bianca . . . Katharina's   **92 for** because   **97 Prefer** recommend.   **cunning** skillful, learned   **101 commune** discuss   **103 appointed hours** given a timetable   **104–5 As . . . leave?** as though, forsooth, I didn't know how to choose for myself?   **106 dam** mother.   **gifts** endowments. (Said ironically.)   **107 hold** detain.   **Their love** i.e., The love of women

so great, Hortensio, but we may blow our nails to- 108
gether and fast it fairly out. Our cake's dough on both 109
sides. Farewell. Yet, for the love I bear my sweet 110
Bianca, if I can by any means light on a fit man to teach
her that wherein she delights, I will wish him to 112
her father.

HORTENSIO   So will I, Signor Gremio. But a word, I pray.
Though the nature of our quarrel yet never brooked 115
parle, know now, upon advice, it toucheth us both, 116
that we may yet again have access to our fair mistress
and be happy rivals in Bianca's love, to labor and effect
one thing specially.

GREMIO   What's that, I pray?

HORTENSIO   Marry, sir, to get a husband for her sister.

GREMIO   A husband? A devil.

HORTENSIO   I say a husband.

GREMIO   I say a devil. Think'st thou, Hortensio, though
her father be very rich, any man is so very a fool to be 125
married to hell?

HORTENSIO   Tush, Gremio, though it pass your patience 127
and mine to endure her loud alarums, why, man, there 128
be good fellows in the world, an a man could light on 129
them, would take her with all faults, and money 130
enough.

GREMIO   I cannot tell. But I had as lief take her dowry 132
with this condition: to be whipped at the high cross 133
every morning.

HORTENSIO   Faith, as you say, there's small choice in
rotten apples. But come, since this bar in law makes us 136
friends, it shall be so far forth friendly maintained till
by helping Baptista's eldest daughter to a husband we
set his youngest free for a husband, and then have to't 139
afresh. Sweet Bianca! Happy man be his dole! He that 140
runs fastest gets the ring. How say you, Signor 141
Gremio?

gremio   I am agreed, and would I had given him the best
horse in Padua to begin his wooing that would thoroughly woo her, wed her, and bed her and rid the
house of her! Come on.   *Exeunt ambo. Manent* 146
               Tranio and Lucentio.

TRANIO
I pray, sir, tell me, is it possible
That love should of a sudden take such hold?

LUCENTIO
Oh, Tranio, till I found it to be true,
I never thought it possible or likely.
But see, while idly I stood looking on,

I found the effect of love in idleness,   152
And now in plainness do confess to thee,
That art to me as secret and as dear   154
As Anna to the Queen of Carthage was,   155
Tranio, I burn, I pine, I perish, Tranio,
If I achieve not this young modest girl.
Counsel me, Tranio, for I know thou canst;
Assist me, Tranio, for I know thou wilt.

TRANIO
Master, it is no time to chide you now.
Affection is not rated from the heart.   161
If love have touched you, naught remains but so,
"Redime te captum quam queas minimo."   163

LUCENTIO
Gramercies, lad. Go forward. This contents;   164
The rest will comfort, for thy counsel's sound.   165

TRANIO
Master, you looked so longly on the maid,   166
Perhaps you marked not what's the pith of all.   167

LUCENTIO
Oh, yes, I saw sweet beauty in her face,
Such as the daughter of Agenor had,   169
That made great Jove to humble him to her hand,   170
When with his knees he kissed the Cretan strand.   171

TRANIO
Saw you no more? Marked you not how her sister
Began to scold and raise up such a storm
That mortal ears might hardly endure the din?

LUCENTIO
Tranio, I saw her coral lips to move,
And with her breath she did perfume the air.
Sacred and sweet was all I saw in her.

TRANIO *[aside]*
Nay, then, 'tis time to stir him from his trance.—
I pray, awake, sir. If you love the maid,
Bend thoughts and wits to achieve her. Thus it stands:
Her elder sister is so curst and shrewd   181
That till the father rid his hands of her,
Master, your love must live a maid at home,   183
And therefore has he closely mewed her up,
Because she will not be annoyed with suitors.   185

LUCENTIO
Ah, Tranio, what a cruel father's he!
But art thou not advised he took some care   187
To get her cunning schoolmasters to instruct her?   188

TRANIO
Ay, marry, am I, sir; and now 'tis plotted.

108–9 blow . . . together i.e., twiddle our thumbs, wait patiently
109 fast . . . out abstain as best we can   **109–10 Our cake's . . . sides**
i.e., We're both out of luck, getting nowhere.   **112 wish** commend
115-16 brooked parle tolerated conference   **116 advice** reflection.
toucheth concerns   **125 very a** utterly a   **127 pass** exceed
128 alarums i.e., loud, startling noises. (In military terms, a call to
arms.)   **129 an** if   **130 would** who would   **132 I cannot tell** i.e., I
don't know about that, don't know what to say.   **had as lief** would
as willingly   **133 high cross** cross set on a pedestal in a marketplace
or center of a town   **136 bar in law** legal impediment, i.e., Baptista's
refusal to receive suitors for Bianca   **139 have to't** renew combat
140 Happy . . . dole! i.e., May happiness be the reward of him who
wins! (Proverbial.)   **141 the ring** (An allusion to the sport of riding at
the ring, with quibble on "wedding ring" and also sexual sense, "vul-
var ring.")   **146 s.d. *ambo*** both. *Manent* They remain onstage

152 love in idleness i.e., (1) desire bred by idleness (2) a popular name
for the pansy, thought to induce love   **154 secret** trusted, intimate
155 Anna confidante of her sister Dido, Queen of Carthage, beloved of
Aeneas   **161 rated** driven away by chiding   **163 *Redime . . . minimo***
Buy yourself out of bondage for as little as you can. (From Terence's
Eunuchus as quoted in William Lilly's *Latin Grammar*.)   **164 Gramercies** Thanks   **165 The rest** The rest of what you have to say   **166 so
longly** (1) for such a long time (2) so longingly   **167 marked** noted.
pith core, essence   **169 daughter of Agenor** Europa, beloved of Jove;
Jove took the form of a bull in order to abduct her   **170 him** himself
171 kissed i.e., knelt on   **181 curst and shrewd** shrewish and ill-
natured   **183 must . . . home** must remain unattached, unmated
185 Because so that   **187 advised** aware (that)   **188 cunning** expert

LUCENTIO
  I have it, Tranio.
TRANIO   Master, for my hand,   190
  Both our inventions meet and jump in one.   191
LUCENTIO
  Tell me thine first.
TRANIO   You will be schoolmaster
  And undertake the teaching of the maid:
  That's your device.
LUCENTIO   It is. May it be done?
TRANIO
  Not possible; for who shall bear your part
  And be in Padua here Vincentio's son,
  Keep house and ply his book, welcome his friends,   197
  Visit his countrymen, and banquet them?
LUCENTIO
  Basta, content thee, for I have it full.   199
  We have not yet been seen in any house,
  Nor can we be distinguished by our faces
  For man or master. Then it follows thus:
  Thou shalt be master, Tranio, in my stead,
  Keep house, and port, and servants, as I should.   204
  I will some other be, some Florentine,
  Some Neapolitan, or meaner man of Pisa.   206
  'Tis hatched and shall be so. Tranio, at once
  Uncase thee. Take my colored hat and cloak.   208
  When Biondello comes, he waits on thee,
  But I will charm him first to keep his tongue.   210
TRANIO   So had you need.
  In brief, sir, sith it your pleasure is,   212
  And I am tied to be obedient—
  For so your father charged me at our parting,
  "Be serviceable to my son," quoth he,
  Although I think 'twas in another sense—
  I am content to be Lucentio,
  Because so well I love Lucentio.
                              [*They exchange clothes.*]
LUCENTIO
  Tranio, be so, because Lucentio loves.
  And let me be a slave t'achieve that maid
  Whose sudden sight hath thralled my wounded eye.   221

          Enter Biondello.

  Here comes the rogue.—Sirrah, where have you been?
BIONDELLO
  Where have I been? Nay, how now, where are you?
  Master, has my fellow Tranio stol'n your clothes?
  Or you stol'n his? Or both? Pray, what's the news?
LUCENTIO
  Sirrah, come hither. 'Tis no time to jest,
  And therefore frame your manners to the time.   227
  Your fellow Tranio here, to save my life,
  Puts my apparel and my countenance on,   229

And I for my escape have put on his;
For in a quarrel since I came ashore,
I killed a man, and fear I was descried.   232
Wait you on him, I charge you, as becomes,   233
While I make way from hence to save my life.
You understand me?
BIONDELLO   I, sir?—Ne'er a whit.   235
LUCENTIO
And not a jot of Tranio in your mouth.
Tranio is changed into Lucentio.
BIONDELLO
The better for him. Would I were so, too!
TRANIO
So could I, faith, boy, to have the next wish after,
That Lucentio indeed had Baptista's youngest
  daughter.
But, sirrah, not for my sake, but your master's, I
  advise
You use your manners discreetly in all kind of com-
  panies.
When I am alone, why, then I am Tranio,
But in all places else your master Lucentio.
LUCENTIO   Tranio, let's go.
One thing more rests, that thyself execute: 246
To make one among these wooers. If thou ask me
  why,
Sufficeth my reasons are both good and weighty.   248
                                          Exeunt.

          The presenters above speak.

FIRST SERVINGMAN
  My lord, you nod. You do not mind the play.   249
SLY   Yes, by Saint Anne, do I. A good matter, surely.
  Comes there any more of it?
PAGE [*as lady*]   My lord, 'tis but begun.
SLY   'Tis a very excellent piece of work, madam lady.
  Would 'twere done!   *They sit and mark.* 254

                              ❖

[1.2]

          Enter Petruchio and his man, Grumio.

PETRUCHIO
  Verona, for a while I take my leave
  To see my friends in Padua, but of all   2
  My best belovèd and approvèd friend,
  Hortensio; and I trow this is his house.   4
  Here, sirrah Grumio, knock, I say.
GRUMIO   Knock, sir? Whom should I knock? Is there any
  man has rebused Your Worship?   7
PETRUCHIO   Villain, I say, knock me here soundly.   8

---

190 for my hand (A mild oath.)   **191 inventions** plans.   **jump** tally,
agree   **197 keep . . . book** entertain guests and pursue his studies
199 Basta Enough.   **full** i.e., fully thought out.   **204 port** state, style
of living   **206 meaner** of a lower social class   **208 Uncase thee**
Remove your outer garments.   **210 charm** i.e., command, persuade
212 sith since   **221 Whose . . . thralled** the sudden sight of whom has
captured   **227 frame** adapt, suit   **229 countenance** bearing, manner

232 descried observed.   **233 as becomes** as is suitable   **235 I, sir**
(Lucentio may hear this as "Ay, sir.")   **Ne'er a whit** Not in the least.
246 rests remains to be done   **248 Sufficeth** it suffices that
248.2 presenters characters of the Induction, whose role it is to "present" the play proper   **249 mind** attend to   **254 s.d. mark** observe
1.2. Location: Padua. Before Hortensio's house.
2 of all above all   **4 trow** believe   **7 rebused** (A blunder for
"abused.")   **8 Villain** i.e., Wretch. (A term of abuse.)   **me** i.e., for me.
(But Grumio, perhaps intentionally, misunderstands.)

GRUMIO　Knock you here, sir? Why, sir, what am I, sir,
that I should knock you here, sir?

PETRUCHIO
Villain, I say, knock me at this gate,　　　　　　　11
And rap me well, or I'll knock your knave's pate.

GRUMIO
My master is grown quarrelsome. I should knock
　　you first,　　　　　　　　　　　　　　　　　13
And then I know after who comes by the worst.　14

PETRUCHIO　Will it not be?　　　　　　　　　15
Faith, sirrah, an you'll not knock, I'll ring it.　16
I'll try how you can *sol fa* and sing it.　　　17
　　　　　　　　　　　　　He wrings him by the ears.

GRUMIO
Help, masters, help! My master is mad.　　　18

PETRUCHIO
Now knock when I bid you, sirrah villain.

　　　Enter Hortensio.

HORTENSIO　How now, what's the matter? My old
friend Grumio and my good friend Petruchio? How
do you all at Verona?

PETRUCHIO
Signor Hortensio, come you to part the fray?
Con tutto il cuore ben trovato, may I say.　　24

HORTENSIO
Alla nostra casa ben venuto,　　　　　　　25
Molto onorato signor mio Petruchio.—　　　26
Rise, Grumio, rise. We will compound this quarrel.　27

GRUMIO　Nay, 'tis no matter, sir, what he 'leges in Latin.　28
If this be not a lawful cause for me to leave his service!
Look you, sir: he bid me knock him and rap him
soundly, sir. Well, was it fit for a servant to use his
master so, being perhaps, for aught I see, two-and-　32
thirty, a pip out?　　　　　　　　　　　　　33
Whom would to God I had well knocked at first!
Then had not Grumio come by the worst.

PETRUCHIO
A senseless villain! Good Hortensio,
I bade the rascal knock upon your gate,
And could not get him for my heart to do it.　38

GRUMIO　Knock at the gate? Oh, heavens! Spake you
not these words plain, "Sirrah, knock me here, rap me
here, knock me well, and knock me soundly"? And
come you now with "knocking at the gate"?　42

PETRUCHIO
Sirrah, begone, or talk not, I advise you.

HORTENSIO
Petruchio, patience. I am Grumio's pledge.　44
Why, this's a heavy chance twixt him and you,　45
Your ancient, trusty, pleasant servant Grumio.　46
And tell me now, sweet friend, what happy gale
Blows you to Padua here from old Verona?

PETRUCHIO
Such wind as scatters young men through the world
To seek their fortunes farther than at home,
Where small experience grows. But in a few,　51
Signor Hortensio, thus it stands with me:
Antonio, my father, is deceased,
And I have thrust myself into this maze,
Happily to wive and thrive as best I may.　55
Crowns in my purse I have, and goods at home,　56
And so am come abroad to see the world.

HORTENSIO
Petruchio, shall I then come roundly to thee　58
And wish thee to a shrewd, ill-favored wife?　59
Thou'dst thank me but a little for my counsel.
And yet I'll promise thee she shall be rich,
And very rich. But thou'rt too much my friend,
And I'll not wish thee to her.

PETRUCHIO
Signor Hortensio, twixt such friends as we
Few words suffice. And therefore, if thou know
One rich enough to be Petruchio's wife—
As wealth is burden of my wooing dance—　67
Be she as foul as was Florentius' love,　68
As old as Sibyl, and as curst and shrewd　69
As Socrates' Xanthippe, or a worse,　　70
She moves me not, or not removes, at least,　71
Affection's edge in me, were she as rough　72
As are the swelling Adriatic seas.
I come to wive it wealthily in Padua;
If wealthily, then happily in Padua.

GRUMIO　Nay, look you, sir, he tells you flatly what his
mind is. Why, give him gold enough and marry him
to a puppet or an aglet-baby, or an old trot with ne'er　78
a tooth in her head, though she have as many diseases
as two-and-fifty horses. Why, nothing comes amiss, so　80
money comes withal.　　　　　　　　　　　　81

---

11 **gate** door　13–14 **I should . . . worst** i.e., You're asking me to hit
you—and I know who then will get the worst of it.　15 **Will it not
be?** i.e., Aren't you going to do what I said?　16 **an** if.　**ring it** sound
loudly, using a circular knocker or a bell. (With a pun on *wring*.)
17 **I'll . . . sing it** i.e., I'll make you cry out. (To *sol fa* is to sing a scale.)
18 **masters** i.e., sirs. (Addressed to the audience.)　24 *Con . . . trovato*
With all my heart, well met　25–6 *Alla . . . Petruchio* Welcome to our
house, my much-honored Petruchio. (Italian.)　27 **compound** settle
28 **'leges** alleges　32–3 **two . . . out** i.e., drunk, or not quite right in
the head. (Derived from the card game called *one-and-thirty*.)
33 **a pip** a spot on a playing card. (Hence, *a pip out* means "off by
one," or "one in excess of thirty one.")　38 **for my heart** i.e., for my
life　42 **come you now with** do you now change your tune to

44 **pledge** surety.　45 **this's . . . chance** this is a sad occurrence
46 **ancient** long-standing.　**pleasant** merry　51 **in a few** in short
55 **Happily** with good luck. (*Happily* and *haply* were not always distinguished.)　56 **Crowns** Gold coins　58 **come roundly** speak
plainly　59 **shrewd** shrewish.　**ill-favored** ill-natured (? Kate is not
"ugly," the usual meaning of this term; see line 85.)　67 **burden**
undersong, i.e., basis　68 **foul** ugly.　**Florentius' love** (An allusion
to John Gower's version in *Confessio Amantis* of the fairy tale of the
knight who promises to marry an ugly old woman if she solves the
riddle he must answer. After the fulfillment of all promises, she
becomes young and beautiful. Another version of this story is
Chaucer's "Tale of the Wife of Bath," from *The Canterbury Tales.*)
69 **Sibyl** prophetess of Cumae, to whom Apollo gave as many
years of life as she held grains of sand in her hand　70 **Xanthippe**
the philosopher's notoriously shrewish wife　71 **moves** affects,
disturbs. (Setting up wordplay on *removes.*)　72 **Affection's edge**
the keen edge of desire　78 **aglet-baby** small figure carved on the
metal tip of a lace, i.e., a tiny baby.　**trot** hag　80 **so** provided
81 **withal** with it.

HORTENSIO
Petruchio, since we are stepped thus far in,
I will continue that I broached in jest.   83
I can, Petruchio, help thee to a wife
With wealth enough, and young and beauteous,
Brought up as best becomes a gentlewoman.
Her only fault, and that is faults enough,
Is that she is intolerable curst   88
And shrewd, and froward, so beyond all measure   89
That, were my state far worser than it is,   90
I would not wed her for a mine of gold.

PETRUCHIO
Hortensio, peace! Thou know'st not gold's effect.
Tell me her father's name and 'tis enough;
For I will board her, though she chide as loud   94
As thunder when the clouds in autumn crack.   95

HORTENSIO
Her father is Baptista Minola,
An affable and courteous gentleman.
Her name is Katharina Minola,
Renowned in Padua for her scolding tongue.

PETRUCHIO
I know her father, though I know not her,
And he knew my deceasèd father well.
I will not sleep, Hortensio, till I see her;
And therefore let me be thus bold with you
To give you over at this first encounter,   104
Unless you will accompany me thither.

GRUMIO [to Hortensio]   I pray you, sir, let him go while
the humor lasts. O' my word, an she knew him as well   107
as I do, she would think scolding would do little good
upon him. She may perhaps call him half a score
knaves or so. Why, that's nothing; an he begin once,
he'll rail in his rope tricks. I'll tell you what, sir: an she   111
stand him but a little, he will throw a figure in her face   112
and so disfigure her with it that she shall have no more   113
eyes to see withal than a cat. You know him not, sir.   114

HORTENSIO
Tarry, Petruchio, I must go with thee,
For in Baptista's keep my treasure is.   117
He hath the jewel of my life in hold,   118
His youngest daughter, beautiful Bianca,
And her withholds from me and other more,   120
Suitors to her and rivals in my love,
Supposing it a thing impossible,
For those defects I have before rehearsed,   123
That ever Katharina will be wooed.
Therefore this order hath Baptista ta'en,   125
That none shall have access unto Bianca

Till Katharine the curst have got a husband.

GRUMIO   Katharine the curst!
A title for a maid of all titles the worst.

HORTENSIO
Now shall my friend Petruchio do me grace,   130
And offer me disguised in sober robes
To old Baptista as a schoolmaster
Well seen in music, to instruct Bianca,   133
That so I may by this device at least
Have leave and leisure to make love to her,   135
And unsuspected court her by herself.

Enter Gremio [with a paper], and Lucentio disguised [as a schoolmaster].

GRUMIO   Here's no knavery! See, to beguile the old   137
folks, how the young folks lay their heads together!
Master, master, look about you. Who goes there, ha?

HORTENSIO
Peace, Grumio, it is the rival of my love.
Petruchio, stand by awhile.   *[They stand aside.]*

GRUMIO [aside]
A proper stripling and an amorous!   142

GREMIO [to Lucentio]
Oh, very well, I have perused the note.   143
Hark you, sir, I'll have them very fairly bound—
All books of love, see that at any hand—   145
And see you read no other lectures to her.   146
You understand me. Over and beside
Signor Baptista's liberality,
I'll mend it with a largess. Take your paper too,   149
       [giving Lucentio the note]
And let me have them very well perfumed,   150
For she is sweeter than perfume itself
To whom they go to. What will you read to her?

LUCENTIO
Whate'er I read to her, I'll plead for you
As for my patron, stand you so assured,
As firmly as yourself were still in place—   155
Yea, and perhaps with more successful words
Than you, unless you were a scholar, sir.

GREMIO
Oh, this learning, what a thing it is!

GRUMIO [aside]
Oh, this woodcock, what an ass it is!   159

PETRUCHIO   Peace, sirrah!

HORTENSIO [coming forward]
Grumio, mum!—God save you, Signor Gremio.

GREMIO
And you are well met, Signor Hortensio.   162
Trow you whither I am going? To Baptista Minola.   163

---

83 **that I broached** what I began   88–9 **intolerable . . . froward** intolerably ill-natured and willful   90 **state** estate   94 **board** woo aggressively, accost, have intercourse with, rape   95 **crack** make an explosive noise.   104 **give you over** leave you   107 **humor** whim. **O' my word, an** On my word, if   111 **he'll . . . tricks** i.e., he has tricks up his sleeve to answer her scolding.   112–14 **he will . . . cat** i.e., he will utterly dazzle and disable her with his rhetorical tricks. (A *figure* is a figure of speech.)   117 **keep** (1) place to store treasure (2) keeping   118 **in hold** (1) in his custody (2) in his stronghold   120 **And . . . more** and witholds her from me and others besides   123 **rehearsed** related, described   125 **this order** these measures

130 **grace** a favor   133 **seen** skilled   135 **make love to** woo 137 **Here's no knavery!** (Said sarcastically.)   142 **proper stripling** handsome young fellow. (Said ironically, in reference to Gremio.) 143 **note** (Evidently, a list of books for Bianca's tutoring.) 145 **see** see to. **at any hand** in any case   146 **read . . . lectures** teach no other lessons   149 **mend** improve, increase. **largess** gift of money.   150 **them** i.e., the books   155 **as** as if. **still in place** present all the time   159 **woodcock** (A bird easily caught; proverbially stupid.)   162 **you are well met** i.e., how opportune to meet you just now   163 **Trow** Know

I promised to inquire carefully
About a schoolmaster for the fair Bianca,
And by good fortune I have lighted well   166
On this young man, for learning and behavior
Fit for her turn, well read in poetry   168
And other books—good ones, I warrant ye.

HORTENSIO
'Tis well. And I have met a gentleman
Hath promised me to help me to another,   171
A fine musician to instruct our mistress.
So shall I no whit be behind in duty
To fair Bianca, so beloved of me.

GREMIO
Beloved of me, and that my deeds shall prove.

GRUMIO [aside]   And that his bags shall prove. 176

HORTENSIO
Gremio, 'tis now no time to vent our love.   177
Listen to me, and if you speak me fair,   178
I'll tell you news indifferent good for either. 179
Here is a gentleman whom by chance I met,
Upon agreement from us to his liking,
Will undertake to woo curst Katharine,   181
Yea, and to marry her, if her dowry please.

GREMIO   So said, so done, is well.   184
Hortensio, have you told him all her faults?

PETRUCHIO
I know she is an irksome brawling scold.
If that be all, masters, I hear no harm.   187

GREMIO
No? Say'st me so, friend? What countryman?

PETRUCHIO
Born in Verona, old Antonio's son.
My father dead, his fortune lives for me,
And I do hope good days and long to see.   191

GREMIO
Oh, sir, such a life with such a wife were strange. 192
But if you have a stomach, to't, i' God's name. 193
You shall have me assisting you in all.
But will you woo this wildcat?

PETRUCHIO   Will I live?

GRUMIO
Will he woo her? Ay, or I'll hang her.

PETRUCHIO
Why came I hither but to that intent?
Think you a little din can daunt mine ears?
Have I not in my time heard lions roar?
Have I not heard the sea, puffed up with winds,
Rage like an angry boar chafèd with sweat?
Have I not heard great ordnance in the field,   202
And heaven's artillery thunder in the skies?

Have I not in a pitchèd battle heard   204
Loud 'larums, neighing steeds, and trumpets' clang? 205
And do you tell me of a woman's tongue,
That gives not half so great a blow to hear
As will a chestnut in a farmer's fire?   208
Tush, tush! Fear boys with bugs.

GRUMIO   For he fears none. 209

GREMIO   Hortensio, hark.
This gentleman is happily arrived,   211
My mind presumes, for his own good and ours.

HORTENSIO
I promised we would be contributors
And bear his charge of wooing, whatsoe'er.   214

GREMIO
And so we will, provided that he win her.

GRUMIO
I would I were as sure of a good dinner.   216

    Enter Tranio, brave [as Lucentio], and
    Biondello.

TRANIO
Gentlemen, God save you. If I may be bold,
Tell me, I beseech you, which is the readiest way
To the house of Signor Baptista Minola?

BIONDELLO   He that has the two fair daughters, is't he
you mean?

TRANIO   Even he, Biondello.   221

GREMIO
Hark you, sir, you mean not her to—

TRANIO
Perhaps him and her, sir. What have you to do?   224

PETRUCHIO
Not her that chides, sir, at any hand, I pray.   225

TRANIO
I love no chiders, sir.—Biondello, let's away.

LUCENTIO [aside]
Well begun, Tranio.

HORTENSIO   Sir, a word ere you go.
Are you a suitor to the maid you talk of, yea or no?

TRANIO
An if I be, sir, is it any offense?

GREMIO
No, if without more words you will get you hence.

TRANIO
Why, sir, I pray, are not the streets as free
For me as for you?

GREMIO   But so is not she.

TRANIO
For what reason, I beseech you?

GREMIO   For this reason, if you'll know,
That she's the choice love of Signor Gremio.

166 **lighted** alighted   168 **Fit for her turn** suited to her needs. (Something that is true in more ways than Gremio realizes.)   171 **Hath . . . another** who has promised to help me to obtain another   176 **bags** moneybags   177 **vent** express   178 **speak me fair** deal with me courteously   179 **indifferent** equally   181 **Upon . . . liking** who, if we agree to terms satisfactory to him   184 **So . . . is well** i.e., That's all very well, when his deeds match his words (which may not be soon).   187 **masters** good sirs   191 **And . . . see** and I hope to see many happy days.   192 **were** would be   193 **a stomach** an appetite, inclination   202 **ordnance** artillery.   **field** battlefield

204 **a pitchèd battle** a planned battle set in orderly array (unlike a skirmish)   205 **'larums** calls to arms   208 **chestnut** (Chestnuts roasted will pop open or explode with a loud report.)   209 **Fear . . . bugs.** Frighten children with bugbears, bogeymen.   211 **happily** fortunately, just when needed   214 **charge** expense   216.1 *brave* elegantly dressed   221 **Even he** Yes, precisely, he   224 **Perhaps . . . do?** i.e., Perhaps I mean to woo both Baptista Minola and Katharina, sir. What's that to you?   225 **at any hand** on any account

HORTENSIO
  That she's the chosen of Signor Hortensio.

TRANIO
  Softly, my masters! If you be gentlemen,
  Do me this right: hear me with patience.
  Baptista is a noble gentleman,
  To whom my father is not all unknown;   239
  And were his daughter fairer than she is,
  She may more suitors have, and me for one.
  Fair Leda's daughter had a thousand wooers;   242
  Then well one more may fair Bianca have,
  And so she shall. Lucentio shall make one,
  Though Paris came in hope to speed alone.   245

GREMIO
  What, this gentleman will out-talk us all!

LUCENTIO
  Sir, give him head. I know he'll prove a jade.   247

PETRUCHIO
  Hortensio, to what end are all these words?

HORTENSIO [to Tranio]
  Sir, let me be so bold as ask you,   249
  Did you yet ever see Baptista's daughter?

TRANIO
  No, sir, but hear I do that he hath two,
  The one as famous for a scolding tongue
  As is the other for beauteous modesty.

PETRUCHIO
  Sir, sir, the first's for me. Let her go by.   254

GREMIO
  Yea, leave that labor to great Hercules,
  And let it be more than Alcides' twelve.   256

PETRUCHIO
  Sir, understand you this of me, in sooth: 257
  The youngest daughter, whom you hearken for,   258
  Her father keeps from all access of suitors,
  And will not promise her to any man
  Until the elder sister first be wed.
  The younger then is free, and not before.

TRANIO
  If it be so, sir, that you are the man
  Must stead us all, and me amongst the rest;   264
  And if you break the ice and do this feat,
  Achieve the elder, set the younger free
  For our access, whose hap shall be to have her   267
  Will not so graceless be to be ingrate.   268

HORTENSIO
  Sir, you say well, and well you do conceive.   269
  And since you do profess to be a suitor,
  You must, as we do, gratify this gentleman,   271

  To whom we all rest generally beholding.   272

TRANIO
  Sir, I shall not be slack. In sign whereof,
  Please ye we may contrive this afternoon,   274
  And quaff carouses to our mistress' health,   275
  And do as adversaries do in law—   276
  Strive mightily, but eat and drink as friends.

GRUMIO, BIONDELLO
  Oh, excellent motion! Fellows, let's be gone.   278

HORTENSIO
  The motion's good indeed, and be it so.
  Petruchio, I shall be your ben venuto.   Exeunt. 280

❖

[2.1]

  Enter Katharina and Bianca [with her hands tied].

BIANCA
  Good sister, wrong me not, nor wrong yourself,
  To make a bondmaid and a slave of me.
  That I disdain. But for these other goods,   3
  Unbind my hands, I'll pull them off myself,   4
  Yea, all my raiment, to my petticoat,
  Or what you will command me will I do,
  So well I know my duty to my elders.

KATHARINA
  Of all thy suitors here I charge thee tell
  Whom thou lov'st best. See thou dissemble not.

BIANCA
  Believe me, sister, of all the men alive
  I never yet beheld that special face
  Which I could fancy more than any other.

KATHARINA
  Minion, thou liest. Is't not Hortensio?   13

BIANCA
  If you affect him, sister, here I swear   14
  I'll plead for you myself but you shall have him.   15

KATHARINA
  Oh, then belike you fancy riches more.   16
  You will have Gremio to keep you fair.   17

BIANCA
  Is it for him you do envy me so?
  Nay, then, you jest, and now I well perceive
  You have but jested with me all this while.
  I prithee, sister Kate, untie my hands.

KATHARINA (strikes her)
  If that be jest, then all the rest was so.

  Enter Baptista.

---

239 **all** entirely   242 **Leda's daughter** Helen of Troy   245 **Though . . . alone** even if Paris (who abducted Helen from her husband, Menelaus) were to come in hopes of succeeding above all others. 247 **Sir . . . jade** Sir, give him a loose bridle; i.e., let him talk freely. I know he'll prove to be a worthless horse, soon tired.   249 **as ask** as to ask   254 **Let her go by** Pass over her.   256 **And . . . twelve** (Hercules, called *Alcides* because he was the reputed grandson of Alcaeus, had to perform twelve huge labors.)   257 **of me** from me.   **sooth** truth   258 **hearken for** seek to win   264 **Must stead** who must help   267 **whose hap** he whose good fortune   268 **to be ingrate** as to be ungrateful.   269 **conceive** understand.   271 **gratify this gentleman** reward Petruchio

272 **beholding** beholden, indebted.   274 **contrive** manage our affairs, pass the time (?)   275 **quaff carouses** drink toasts   276 **adversaries** opposing lawyers   278 **motion** suggestion.   280 *ben venuto* welcome, i.e., host.
2.1. Location: Padua. Baptista's house.
3 **for** as for.   **goods** i.e., clothes, jewels, love tokens   4 **Unbind** if you will unbind   13 **Minion** Hussy   14 **affect** love   15 **but . . . him** if necessary for you to win him.   16 **belike** perhaps   17 **fair** resplendent with finery.

BAPTISTA
Why, how now, dame, whence grows this
    insolence?—
Bianca, stand aside. Poor girl, she weeps.
Go ply thy needle, meddle not with her.—   25
For shame, thou hilding of a devilish spirit,   26
Why dost thou wrong her that did ne'er wrong thee?
When did she cross thee with a bitter word?   28

KATHARINA
Her silence flouts me, and I'll be revenged.   29
                       [*She*] *flies after Bianca.*

BAPTISTA
What, in my sight? Bianca, get thee in.   *Exit* [*Bianca*].

KATHARINA
What, will you not suffer me? Nay, now I see   31
She is your treasure, she must have a husband;
I must dance barefoot on her wedding day,   33
And for your love to her lead apes in hell.   34
Talk not to me. I will go sit and weep
Till I can find occasion of revenge.   [*Exit.*]

BAPTISTA
Was ever gentleman thus grieved as I?
But who comes here?   38

    Enter Gremio, Lucentio [*as a schoolmaster*] *in the*
    habit of a mean man, Petruchio, with [*Hortensio as*
    a musician, and] *Tranio* [*as Lucentio*] *with his boy*
    [*Biondello*] *bearing a lute and books.*

GREMIO   Good morrow, neighbor Baptista.
BAPTISTA   Good morrow, neighbor Gremio. God save
you, gentlemen.
PETRUCHIO
And you, good sir. Pray, have you not a daughter
Called Katharina, fair and virtuous?

BAPTISTA
I have a daughter, sir, called Katharina.

GREMIO
You are too blunt. Go to it orderly.   45

PETRUCHIO
You wrong me, Signor Gremio; give me leave.—   46
I am a gentleman of Verona, sir,
That, hearing of her beauty and her wit,
Her affability and bashful modesty,
Her wondrous qualities and mild behavior,
Am bold to show myself a forward guest
Within your house, to make mine eye the witness
Of that report which I so oft have heard.
And, for an entrance to my entertainment,   54
I do present you with a man of mine,
                 [*presenting Hortensio*]
Cunning in music and the mathematics,   56

To instruct her fully in those sciences,   57
Whereof I know she is not ignorant.
Accept of him, or else you do me wrong.   59
His name is Litio, born in Mantua.

BAPTISTA
You're welcome, sir, and he, for your good sake.
But for my daughter Katharine, this I know,   62
She is not for your turn, the more my grief.

PETRUCHIO
I see you do not mean to part with her,
Or else you like not of my company.   65

BAPTISTA
Mistake me not, I speak but as I find.
Whence are you, sir? What may I call your name?

PETRUCHIO
Petruchio is my name, Antonio's son,
A man well known throughout all Italy.

BAPTISTA
I know him well. You are welcome for his sake.   70

GREMIO
Saving your tale, Petruchio, I pray,   71
Let us that are poor petitioners speak too.
Bacare! You are marvelous forward.   73

PETRUCHIO
Oh, pardon me, Signor Gremio, I would fain be doing. 74

GREMIO
I doubt it not, sir, but you will curse your wooing.—
Neighbors, this is a gift very grateful, I am sure of   76
it. [*To Baptista*] To express the like kindness, myself, that have been more kindly beholding to you
than any, freely give unto you this young scholar
[*presenting Lucentio*], that hath been long studying at
Rheims, as cunning in Greek, Latin, and other languages, as the other in music and mathematics. His   82
name is Cambio. Pray, accept his service.   83

BAPTISTA   A thousand thanks, Signor Gremio.—Welcome, good Cambio. [*To Tranio*] But, gentle sir,
methinks you walk like a stranger. May I be so bold to
know the cause of your coming?

TRANIO
Pardon me, sir, the boldness is mine own,
That, being a stranger in this city here,
Do make myself a suitor to your daughter,
Unto Bianca, fair and virtuous.
Nor is your firm resolve unknown to me
In the preferment of the eldest sister.   93
This liberty is all that I request,
That, upon knowledge of my parentage,   95
I may have welcome 'mongst the rest that woo,
And free access and favor as the rest.   97

---

25 meddle not with have nothing to do with   **26 hilding** vicious
(hence worthless) beast   **28 cross** contradict, thwart   **29 flouts**
mocks, insults   **31 suffer me** let me have my own way.   **33, 34 dance
. . . day, lead . . . hell** (Popularly supposed to be the fate of old maids.)
38.2 habit dress.   **mean** of low social station. (Said here of a schoolmaster.)   **45 orderly** in a properly orderly manner   **46 give me leave**
excuse me, let me do this my way.   **54 entrance** entrance fee.
entertainment reception.   **56 Cunning** skillful

57 sciences subjects, branches of knowledge   **59 Accept of** Accept
62 for as for   **65 like not of** do not like   **70 know** know of. (See also
lines 104–5.)   **71 Saving** With all due respect for   **73 Bacare!** Stand
back!   **74 fain** gladly.   **doing** getting on with the business. (With
sexual suggestion.)   **76 grateful** pleasing   **82 the other** i.e., Hortensio   **83 Cambio** (In Italian, appropriately, the word means "change"
or "exchange.")   **93 In the preferment of** in the precedence you give
to   **95 upon knowledge of** when you know about   **97 favor** leave,
permission

And toward the education of your daughters
I here bestow a simple instrument,
And this small packet of Greek and Latin books.
If you accept them, then their worth is great.
[*Biondello brings forward the lute and books.*]

BAPTISTA
Lucentio is your name? Of whence, I pray?   102

TRANIO
Of Pisa, sir, son to Vincentio.

BAPTISTA
A mighty man of Pisa. By report
I know him well. You are very welcome, sir.
[*To Hortensio*] Take you the lute, [*to Lucentio*] and
    you the set of books;
You shall go see your pupils presently.—
Holla, within!

Enter a Servant.

        Sirrah, lead these gentlemen
To my daughters, and tell them both
These are their tutors. Bid them use them well.
[*Exit Servant, with Lucentio and Hortensio.*]
We will go walk a little in the orchard,
And then to dinner. You are passing welcome,   112
And so I pray you all to think yourselves.

PETRUCHIO
Signor Baptista, my business asketh haste,
And every day I cannot come to woo.
You knew my father well, and in him me,
Left solely heir to all his lands and goods,
Which I have bettered rather than decreased.
Then tell me, if I get your daughter's love,
What dowry shall I have with her to wife?

BAPTISTA
After my death the one half of my lands,
And in possession twenty thousand crowns.   122

PETRUCHIO
And for that dowry I'll assure her of   123
Her widowhood, be it that she survive me,   124
In all my lands and leases whatsoever.
Let specialties be therefore drawn between us,   126
That covenants may be kept on either hand.

BAPTISTA
Ay, when the special thing is well obtained,
That is, her love; for that is all in all.

PETRUCHIO
Why, that is nothing, for I tell you, father,   130
I am as peremptory as she proud-minded;
And where two raging fires meet together,
They do consume the thing that feeds their fury.
Though little fire grows great with little wind,
Yet extreme gusts will blow out fire and all.
So I to her, and so she yields to me,   136

For I am rough and woo not like a babe.

BAPTISTA
Well mayst thou woo, and happy be thy speed!   138
But be thou armed for some unhappy words.

PETRUCHIO
Ay, to the proof, as mountains are for winds,   140
That shakes not, though they blow perpetually.   141

Enter Hortensio [as Litio], with his head broke.

BAPTISTA
How now, my friend, why dost thou look so pale?

HORTENSIO
For fear, I promise you, if I look pale.   143

BAPTISTA
What, will my daughter prove a good musician?

HORTENSIO
I think she'll sooner prove a soldier.   145
Iron may hold with her, but never lutes.   146

BAPTISTA
Why then, thou canst not break her to the lute?   147

HORTENSIO
Why, no, for she hath broke the lute to me.
I did but tell her she mistook her frets,   149
And bowed her hand to teach her fingering,
When, with a most impatient devilish spirit,
"Frets, call you these?" quoth she, "I'll fume with
    them."
And with that word she struck me on the head,
And through the instrument my pate made way;
And there I stood amazèd for a while,   155
As on a pillory, looking through the lute,   156
While she did call me rascal fiddler
And twangling Jack, with twenty such vile terms,   158
As had she studied to misuse me so.   159

PETRUCHIO
Now, by the world, it is a lusty wench!   160
I love her ten times more than e'er I did.
Oh, how I long to have some chat with her!

BAPTISTA [*to Hortensio*]
Well, go with me, and be not so discomfited.
Proceed in practice with my younger daughter;   164
She's apt to learn and thankful for good turns.—
Signor Petruchio, will you go with us,
Or shall I send my daughter Kate to you?

PETRUCHIO
I pray you, do.   *Exeunt. Manet Petruchio.*
        I'll attend her here,   168
And woo her with some spirit when she comes.

<hr>

102 **Lucentio . . . name?** (Baptista may have learned this information from a note accompanying the books and lute.)   112 **passing** exceedingly   122 **in possession** in immediate possession   123 **for** in exchange for   124 **widowhood** i.e., widow's share of the estate.
be it that she if she should   126 **specialties** terms of contract
130 **father** father-in-law   136 **So I** i.e., So I behave, like an extreme gust of wind

138 **happy . . . speed!** may fortune give you success!   140 **to the proof** i.e., in armor, proof against her shrewishness   141 **shakes** shake.   141.1 *broke* with a bleeding cut. (Hortensio usually appears on stage with his head emerging through a broken lute.)
143 **promise** assure   145 **I think . . . soldier** i.e., She's better suited for the manly career of soldiering.   146 **hold with** hold out against   147 **break** train. (With pun in the next line.)   149 **frets** ridges or bars on the fingerboard of the lute. (But Kate puns on the sense of "fume," "be indignant.")   155 **amazèd** bewildered   156 **As on a pillory** as if with my head in a wooden collar used as punishment   158 **Jack** knave   159 **As . . . so** as if she had planned how to abuse me so.
160 **lusty** lively   164 **practice** instruction   168 **s.d.** *Manet* He remains onstage

Say that she rail, why then I'll tell her plain
She sings as sweetly as a nightingale.
Say that she frown, I'll say she looks as clear   172
As morning roses newly washed with dew.
Say she be mute and will not speak a word,
Then I'll commend her volubility
And say she uttereth piercing eloquence.   176
If she do bid me pack, I'll give her thanks,   177
As though she bid me stay by her a week.
If she deny to wed, I'll crave the day   179
When I shall ask the banns and when be married.   180
But here she comes; and now, Petruchio, speak.

Enter Katharina.

Good morrow, Kate, for that's your name, I hear.

KATHARINA
Well have you heard, but something hard of hearing.   183
They call me Katharine that do talk of me.

PETRUCHIO
You lie, in faith, for you are called plain Kate,
And bonny Kate, and sometimes Kate the curst;
But Kate, the prettiest Kate in Christendom,
Kate of Kate Hall, my superdainty Kate,
For dainties are all Kates, and therefore, Kate,   189
Take this of me, Kate of my consolation: 190
Hearing thy mildness praised in every town,
Thy virtues spoke of, and thy beauty sounded,   192
Yet not so deeply as to thee belongs,
Myself am moved to woo thee for my wife.   194

KATHARINA
Moved? In good time! Let him that moved you hither 195
Remove you hence. I knew you at the first
You were a movable.

PETRUCHIO   Why, what's a movable?   197

KATHARINA
A joint stool.

PETRUCHIO   Thou hast hit it. Come, sit on me.   198

KATHARINA
Asses are made to bear, and so are you.   199

PETRUCHIO
Women are made to bear, and so are you.

KATHARINA
No such jade as you, if me you mean.   201

PETRUCHIO
Alas, good Kate, I will not burden thee,   202

For knowing thee to be but young and light.   203

KATHARINA
Too light for such a swain as you to catch,   204
And yet as heavy as my weight should be.

PETRUCHIO
Should be? Should—buzz!

KATHARINA   Well ta'en, and like a buzzard. 206

PETRUCHIO
Oh, slow-winged turtle, shall a buzzard take thee?

KATHARINA
Ay, for a turtle, as he takes a buzzard.

PETRUCHIO
Come, come, you wasp, i'faith you are too angry.   209

KATHARINA
If I be waspish, best beware my sting.

PETRUCHIO
My remedy is then to pluck it out.

KATHARINA
Ay, if the fool could find it where it lies.

PETRUCHIO
Who knows not where a wasp does wear his sting?
In his tail.

KATHARINA   In his tongue.

PETRUCHIO   Whose tongue?

KATHARINA
Yours, if you talk of tales, and so farewell.   217

PETRUCHIO
What, with my tongue in your tail? Nay, come again.
Good Kate, I am a gentleman—

KATHARINA   That I'll try.
                                        She strikes him.

PETRUCHIO
I swear I'll cuff you if you strike again.

KATHARINA   So may you lose your arms.
If you strike me, you are no gentleman,
And if no gentleman, why then no arms.   223

PETRUCHIO
A herald, Kate? Oh, put me in thy books!   224

KATHARINA   What is your crest, a coxcomb?   225

PETRUCHIO
A combless cock, so Kate will be my hen.   226

KATHARINA
No cock of mine. You crow too like a craven.   227

---

172 clear serene   **176 piercing** moving   **177 pack** begone   **179 deny**
refuse.   **crave the day** ask her to name the day   **180 ask the banns**
have a reading of the required announcement in church of a forthcoming marriage   **183 heard, hard** (Pronounced nearly alike.)
189 all Kates (With a quibble on "cates," confections, delicacies.)
190 of me from me.   **consolation** comfort   **192 sounded** proclaimed.
(With a quibble on "plumbed," as indicated by *deeply* in the next line.)
194 moved impelled. (Followed by wordplay on the more literal
meaning of *move* and *remove*.)   **195 In good time!** Forsooth! Indeed!
197 movable (1) one easily changed or dissuaded (2) an article of furniture.   **198 A joint stool** a well-fitted stool made by an expert crafts-
man.   **199 bear** carry. (With puns in the following lines suggesting
"bear children" and "support a man during sexual intercourse.")
201 jade an ill-conditioned horse   **202 burden** (1) oppress with a
heavy load—a term appropriate to *asses* and *bear* in line 199, since
asses are beasts of *burden* (2) lie on during sexual intercourse, impregnate. (See notes on lines 199 and 203.)

203 For knowing because I know.   **light** (1) of delicate stature (2) lascivious (3) lacking a *burden* (see previous line) in the musical sense of
lacking a bass undersong or accompaniment (4) elusive (in the following line).   **204 swain** young rustic in love   **206 Should . . . buzz!**
(Petruchio puns on *be* and "bee," and uses *buzz* in perhaps three
senses: [1] an interjection of impatience or contempt [2] a bee's sound
[3] a rumor being buzzed about, to which he implies, Kate had better
listen.)   **buzzard** (1) figuratively, a fool (2) in the next line, an inferior
kind of hawk, fit only to overtake a slow-winged *turtle* or turtledove,
as Petruchio might overtake Kate (3) a buzzing insect, caught by a
turtledove.   **209 wasp** i.e., waspish, scolding woman. (But suggested
by *buzzard*, buzzing insect.)   **217 talk of tales** i.e., idly tell stories.
(With pun on "tail.")   **223 no arms** no coat of arms. (With pun on
arms as limbs of the body.)   **224 books** (1) books of heraldry, heraldic
registers (2) grace, favor.   **225 crest** (1) armorial device (2) a rooster's
comb, setting up the joke on *coxcomb*, the cap of the court fool
226 A combless cock i.e., A gentle rooster. (With suggestion of the
male sexual organ.)   **so** provided that   **227 a craven** a cock that is
not "game" or willing to fight.

PETRUCHIO
Nay, come, Kate, come. You must not look so sour.

KATHARINA
It is my fashion when I see a crab. 229

PETRUCHIO
Why, here's no crab, and therefore look not sour.

KATHARINA There is, there is.

PETRUCHIO
Then show it me.

KATHARINA Had I a glass, I would.

PETRUCHIO What, you mean my face?

KATHARINA Well aimed of such a young one. 234

PETRUCHIO
Now, by Saint George, I am too young for you.

KATHARINA
Yet you are withered.

PETRUCHIO 'Tis with cares.

KATHARINA I care not.

PETRUCHIO
Nay, hear you, Kate. In sooth, you scape not so. 237

KATHARINA
I chafe you if I tarry. Let me go. 238

PETRUCHIO
No, not a whit. I find you passing gentle. 239
'Twas told me you were rough, and coy, and sullen, 240
And now I find report a very liar, 241
For thou art pleasant, gamesome, passing courteous, 242
But slow in speech, yet sweet as springtime flowers. 243
Thou canst not frown, thou canst not look askance, 244
Nor bite the lip, as angry wenches will,
Nor hast thou pleasure to be cross in talk; 246
But thou with mildness entertain'st thy wooers, 247
With gentle conference, soft and affable. 248
Why does the world report that Kate doth limp?
Oh, sland'rous world! Kate like the hazel twig
Is straight and slender, and as brown in hue
As hazelnuts, and sweeter than the kernels.
Oh, let me see thee walk. Thou dost not halt. 253

KATHARINA
Go, fool, and whom thou keep'st command. 254

PETRUCHIO
Did ever Dian so become a grove 255
As Kate this chamber with her princely gait?
Oh, be thou Dian, and let her be Kate,
And then let Kate be chaste and Dian sportful! 258

KATHARINA
Where did you study all this goodly speech? 259

PETRUCHIO
It is extempore, from my mother wit. 260

KATHARINA
A witty mother! Witless else her son. 261

PETRUCHIO Am I not wise? 262

KATHARINA Yes, keep you warm. 263

PETRUCHIO
Marry, so I mean, sweet Katharine, in thy bed.
And therefore, setting all this chat aside,
Thus in plain terms: your father hath consented
That you shall be my wife; your dowry 'greed on;
And will you, nill you, I will marry you. 268
Now, Kate, I am a husband for your turn, 269
For by this light, whereby I see thy beauty—
Thy beauty that doth make me like thee well—
Thou must be married to no man but me.

Enter Baptista, Gremio, [and] Tranio [as Lucentio].

For I am he am born to tame you, Kate,
And bring you from a wild Kate to a Kate 274
Conformable as other household Kates. 275
Here comes your father. Never make denial;
I must and will have Katharine to my wife.

BAPTISTA
Now, Signor Petruchio, how speed you with my
daughter? 278

PETRUCHIO
How but well, sir, how but well?
It were impossible I should speed amiss.

BAPTISTA
Why, how now, daughter Katharine, in your dumps? 281

KATHARINA
Call you me daughter? Now, I promise you, 282
You have showed a tender fatherly regard,
To wish me wed to one half-lunatic,
A madcap ruffian and a swearing Jack, 285
That thinks with oaths to face the matter out. 286

PETRUCHIO
Father, 'tis thus: yourself and all the world
That talked of her have talked amiss of her.
If she be curst, it is for policy, 289
For she's not froward, but modest as the dove. 290
She is not hot, but temperate as the morn.
For patience she will prove a second Grissel, 292
And Roman Lucrece for her chastity. 293
And to conclude, we have 'greed so well together
That upon Sunday is the wedding day.

---

229 **crab** crab apple.   234 **aimed of** guessed for.   **young** i.e., inexperienced. (But Petruchio picks up the word in the sense of "strong," "virile.")   237 **scape** escape   238 **chafe** irritate, arouse   239 **passing** very. (Also in line 242.)   240 **coy** disdainful   241 **a very** an utter   242 **pleasant, gamesome** merry, spirited   243 **But slow** never anything but slow   244 **askance** scornfully   246 **cross in talk** always contradicting   247 **entertain'st** receive   248 **conference** conversation   253 **halt** limp.   254 **whom thou keep'st command** i.e., order about those whom you employ, your servants, not me.   255 **Dian** Diana, goddess of the hunt and of chastity.   **become** adorn   258 **sportful** amorous.   259 **study** memorize   260 **mother wit** native intelligence.

261 **Witless . . . son** i.e., Without the intelligence inherited from her, he would have none at all.   262–3 **wise . . . warm** (An allusion to the proverbial phrase "enough wit to keep oneself warm.")   268 **will you, nill you** whether you're willing or not   269 **for your turn** to suit you   274 **wild Kate** (With a quibble on "wildcat.")   275 **Conformable** compliant   278 **speed** fare, get on   281 **in your dumps** in low spirits.   282 **promise** assure   285 **Jack** ill-mannered fellow   286 **face** brazen   289 **policy** cunning, ulterior motive   290 **froward** willful, perverse   292 **Grissel** patient Griselda, the epitome of wifely patience and devotion (whose story was told by Chaucer in "The Clerk's Tale" of *The Canterbury Tales* and earlier by Boccaccio and Petrarch)   293 **Roman Lucrece** Lucretia, a Roman lady who took her own life after her chastity had been violated by the Tarquin prince, Sextus. (Shakespeare tells the story in *The Rape of Lucrece*.)

KATHARINA
I'll see thee hanged on Sunday first.

GREMIO   Hark, Petruchio, she says she'll see thee
hanged first.

TRANIO
Is this your speeding? Nay then, good night our part!   299

PETRUCHIO
Be patient, gentlemen. I choose her for myself.
If she and I be pleased, what's that to you?
'Tis bargained twixt us twain, being alone,
That she shall still be curst in company.
I tell you, 'tis incredible to believe
How much she loves me. Oh, the kindest Kate!
She hung about my neck, and kiss on kiss
She vied so fast, protesting oath on oath,   307
That in a twink she won me to her love.
Oh, you are novices! 'Tis a world to see   309
How tame, when men and women are alone,
A meacock wretch can make the curstest shrew.—   311
Give me thy hand, Kate. I will unto Venice
To buy apparel gainst the wedding day.—   313
Provide the feast, father, and bid the guests.
I will be sure my Katharine shall be fine.   315

BAPTISTA
I know not what to say. But give me your hands.
God send you joy, Petruchio! 'Tis a match.

GREMIO, TRANIO
Amen, say we. We will be witnesses.

PETRUCHIO
Father, and wife, and gentlemen, adieu.
I will to Venice. Sunday comes apace.
We will have rings, and things, and fine array;
And kiss me, Kate. We will be married o'Sunday.   322
        Exeunt Petruchio and Katharine [separately].

GREMIO
Was ever match clapped up so suddenly?   323

BAPTISTA
Faith, gentlemen, now I play a merchant's part,   324
And venture madly on a desperate mart.   325

TRANIO
'Twas a commodity lay fretting by you;   326
'Twill bring you gain, or perish on the seas.

BAPTISTA
The gain I seek is quiet in the match.

GREMIO
No doubt but he hath got a quiet catch.   329
But now, Baptista, to your younger daughter.
Now is the day we long have looked for.
I am your neighbor, and was suitor first.

TRANIO
And I am one that love Bianca more
Than words can witness, or your thoughts can guess.

GREMIO
Youngling, thou canst not love so dear as I.

TRANIO
Graybeard, thy love doth freeze.

GREMIO   But thine doth fry.
Skipper, stand back. 'Tis age that nourisheth.   337

TRANIO
But youth in ladies' eyes that flourisheth.

BAPTISTA
Content you, gentlemen, I will compound this strife.   339
'Tis deeds must win the prize, and he of both   340
That can assure my daughter greatest dower   341
Shall have my Bianca's love.
Say, Signor Gremio, what can you assure her?

GREMIO
First, as you know, my house within the city
Is richly furnishèd with plate and gold,   345
Basins and ewers to lave her dainty hands;   346
My hangings all of Tyrian tapestry;   347
In ivory coffers I have stuffed my crowns;   348
In cypress chests my arras counterpoints,   349
Costly apparel, tents, and canopies,   350
Fine linen, Turkey cushions bossed with pearl,   351
Valance of Venice gold in needlework,   352
Pewter and brass, and all things that belongs
To house or housekeeping. Then at my farm
I have a hundred milch kine to the pail,   355
Sixscore fat oxen standing in my stalls,
And all things answerable to this portion.   357
Myself am struck in years, I must confess,   358
And if I die tomorrow, this is hers,
If whilst I live she will be only mine.

TRANIO
That "only" came well in.—Sir, list to me:
I am my father's heir and only son.
If I may have your daughter to my wife,
I'll leave her houses three or four as good,
Within rich Pisa walls, as any one
Old Signor Gremio has in Padua,
Besides two thousand ducats by the year   367
Of fruitful land, all which shall be her jointure.—   368
What, have I pinched you, Signor Gremio?

GREMIO
Two thousand ducats by the year of land!
[*Aside*] My land amounts not to so much in all.—
That she shall have, besides an argosy   372

---

299 speeding success.   **good night our part** good-bye to what we hoped to get.   **307 vied** went me one better, kiss for kiss   **309 a world** worth a whole world   **311 meacock** cowardly   **313 gainst** in anticipation of   **315 fine** elegantly dressed.   **322 kiss me** (Petruchio probably kisses her.)   **323 clapped up** settled (by a shaking of hands)   **324 Faith** In faith   **325 desperate mart** risky venture.   **326 lay fretting** i.e., which lay in storage being destroyed by moths, weevils, or spoilage. (With a pun on "chafing.")   **329 quiet catch** (Said ironically; Gremio is sure that Kate will be anything but quiet.)

337 Skipper Flighty fellow   **339 compound** settle   **340 deeds** (1) actions (2) legal deeds.   **he of both** the one of you two   **341 dower** portion of a husband's estate settled on his wife in his will. (Also at line 387 and 4.4.45.)   **345 plate** silver utensils   **346 ewers to lave** pitchers to wash   **347 hangings** draperies hung on beds and walls.   **Tyrian** dark red or purple   **348 crowns** five-shilling coins   **349 arras counterpoints** counterpanes of tapestry   **350 tents** bed curtains   **351 Turkey** Turkish.   **bossed** embossed   **352 Valance** fringes of drapery around the canopy or bed frame   **355 milch kine to the pail** dairy cattle   **357 answerable to** on the same scale as   **358 struck** advanced   **367 ducats** gold coins   **368 Of** from.   **jointure** marriage settlement.   **372 argosy** merchant vessel of the largest size

That now is lying in Marseilles road.   373
[*To Tranio*] What, have I choked you with an argosy?

TRANIO
Gremio, 'tis known my father hath no less
Than three great argosies, besides two galliases   376
And twelve tight galleys. These I will assure her,   377
And twice as much, whate'er thou off'rest next.

GREMIO
Nay, I have offered all. I have no more,
And she can have no more than all I have.
[*To Baptista*] If you like me, she shall have me and
    mine.

TRANIO
Why then, the maid is mine from all the world,
By your firm promise. Gremio is outvied.   383

BAPTISTA
I must confess your offer is the best;
And, let your father make her the assurance,   385
She is your own; else, you must pardon me.
If you should die before him, where's her dower?

TRANIO
That's but a cavil. He is old, I young.   388

GREMIO
And may not young men die, as well as old?

BAPTISTA
Well, gentlemen, I am thus resolved:
On Sunday next, you know
My daughter Katharine is to be married.
Now, on the Sunday following shall Bianca
Be bride [*to Tranio*] to you, if you make this assurance;
If not, to Signor Gremio.
And so I take my leave, and thank you both.   *Exit.*

GREMIO
Adieu, good neighbor.—Now I fear thee not.
Sirrah, young gamester, your father were a fool
To give thee all, and in his waning age
Set foot under thy table. Tut, a toy!   400
An old Italian fox is not so kind, my boy.   *Exit.*

TRANIO
A vengeance on your crafty withered hide!
Yet I have faced it with a card of ten.   403
'Tis in my head to do my master good.
I see no reason but supposed Lucentio
Must get a father, called supposed Vincentio—
And that's a wonder. Fathers commonly
Do get their children; but in this case of wooing,   408
A child shall get a sire, if I fail not of my cunning.
    Exit.

❖

3.1

*Enter Lucentio [as Cambio], Hortensio [as
Litio], and Bianca.*

LUCENTIO
Fiddler, forbear. You grow too forward, sir.
Have you so soon forgot the entertainment
Her sister Katharine welcomed you withal?

HORTENSIO
But, wrangling pedant, this is   4
The patroness of heavenly harmony.
Then give me leave to have prerogative,   6
And when in music we have spent an hour,
Your lecture shall have leisure for as much.   8

LUCENTIO
Preposterous ass, that never read so far
To know the cause why music was ordained!   10
Was it not to refresh the mind of man
After his studies or his usual pain?   12
Then give me leave to read philosophy,   13
And, while I pause, serve in your harmony.   14

HORTENSIO
Sirrah, I will not bear these braves of thine.   15

BIANCA
Why, gentlemen, you do me double wrong
To strive for that which resteth in my choice.
I am no breeching scholar in the schools;   18
I'll not be tied to hours nor 'pointed times,
But learn my lessons as I please myself.
And, to cut off all strife, here sit we down.
[*To Hortensio*] Take you your instrument, play you the
    whiles;   22
His lecture will be done ere you have tuned.

HORTENSIO
You'll leave his lecture when I am in tune?

LUCENTIO
That will be never. Tune your instrument.
    [*Hortensio moves aside and tunes.*]

BIANCA   Where left we last?
LUCENTIO   Here, madam. [*He reads.*]
    "Hic ibat Simois; hic est Sigeia tellus;   28
    Hic steterat Priami regia celsa senis."   29
BIANCA   Conster them.   30
LUCENTIO   "Hic ibat," as I told you before, "Simois," I
am Lucentio, "hic est," son unto Vincentio of Pisa, "Sigeia
tellus," disguised thus to get your love; "Hic
steterat," and that Lucentio that comes a-wooing,
"Priami," is my man Tranio, "regia," bearing my port,   35
"celsa senis," that we might beguile the old panta-   36
loon.   37

---

373 **road** roadstead, harbor.   376 **galliases** heavy, low-built vessels
377 **tight** watertight   383 **outvied** outbidden.   385 **let** provided
388 **but a cavil** merely a frivolous objection.   400 **Set . . . toy!** i.e.,
become a dependent in your household. Tut, nonsense!   403 **faced . . .
ten** brazened it out with only a ten-spot of cards.   408 **get** beget.
(With a play on *get*, "obtain," in line 406.)

3.1. Location: The same.
4 this i.e., Bianca   **6 prerogative** precedence   **8 lecture** lesson
10 To know as to know   **12 usual pain** regular labors.   **13 read** teach
14 serve in present, serve up   **15 braves** insults   **18 breeching
scholar** i.e., schoolboy liable to be whipped   **22 the whiles** meantime
28–9 Hic . . . senis Here flowed the river Simois; here is the Sigeian
land; here stood the lofty palace of old Priam. (Ovid, *Heroides*, 1.33–4.)
30 Conster Construe   **35 bearing my port** i.e., pretending to be me
36–7 pantaloon foolish old man, i.e., Gremio

HORTENSIO   Madam, my instrument's in tune.
BIANCA   Let's hear. [*He plays.*] Oh, fie! The treble jars.
LUCENTIO   Spit in the hole, man, and tune again.   40
                          [*Hortensio moves aside.*]
BIANCA   Now let me see if I can conster it: "*Hic ibat
Simois*," I know you not, "*hic est Sigeia tellus*," I trust
you not; "*Hic steterat Priami*," take heed he hear us not,
"*regia*," presume not, "*celsa senis*," despair not.
HORTENSIO
Madam, 'tis now in tune.   [*He plays again.*]
LUCENTIO   All but the bass.
HORTENSIO
The bass is right, 'tis the base knave that jars.
[*Aside*] How fiery and forward our pedant is!
Now, for my life, the knave doth court my love.
Pedascule, I'll watch you better yet.   49
BIANCA   [*to Lucentio*]
In time I may believe, yet I mistrust.
LUCENTIO
Mistrust it not, for, sure, Aeacides   51
Was Ajax, called so from his grandfather.
BIANCA
I must believe my master; else, I promise you,
I should be arguing still upon that doubt.
But let it rest.—Now, Litio, to you:
Good master, take it not unkindly, pray,
That I have been thus pleasant with you both.   57
HORTENSIO   [*to Lucentio*]
You may go walk, and give me leave awhile.
My lessons make no music in three parts.
LUCENTIO
Are you so formal, sir? Well, I must wait.   60
[*Aside*] And watch withal; for, but I be deceived,   61
Our fine musician groweth amorous.
                          [*He moves aside.*]
HORTENSIO
Madam, before you touch the instrument,
To learn the order of my fingering,   64
I must begin with rudiments of art,
To teach you gamut in a briefer sort,   66
More pleasant, pithy, and effectual
Than hath been taught by any of my trade.
And there it is in writing, fairly drawn.   69
                          [*He gives her a paper.*]
BIANCA
Why, I am past my gamut long ago.

HORTENSIO
Yet read the gamut of Hortensio.
BIANCA   [*reads*]
"*Gamut* I am, the ground of all accord,   72
A re, to plead Hortensio's passion;
B mi, Bianca, take him for thy lord,   74
C fa ut, that loves with all affection.   75
D sol re, one clef, two notes have I;   76
E la mi, show pity, or I die."   77
Call you this gamut? Tut, I like it not.
Old fashions please me best; I am not so nice   79
To change true rules for odd inventions.

          Enter a [*Servant as*] *messenger.*

SERVANT
Mistress, your father prays you leave your books
And help to dress your sister's chamber up.
You know tomorrow is the wedding day.
BIANCA
Farewell, sweet masters both. I must be gone.
LUCENTIO
Faith, mistress, then I have no cause to stay.
          [*Exeunt Bianca, Servant, and Lucentio.*]
HORTENSIO
But I have cause to pry into this pedant.
Methinks he looks as though he were in love.
Yet if thy thoughts, Bianca, be so humble
To cast thy wandering eyes on every stale,   89
Seize thee that list. If once I find thee ranging,   90
Hortensio will be quit with thee by changing.   *Exit.*   91

❖

[3.2]

          Enter Baptista, Gremio, Tranio [*as Lucentio*],
          Katharine, Bianca, [*Lucentio as Cambio*], *and
          others, attendants.*

BAPTISTA   [*to Tranio*]
Signor Lucentio, this is the 'pointed day
That Katharine and Petruchio should be married,
And yet we hear not of our son-in-law.
What will be said? What mockery will it be,   4
To want the bridegroom when the priest attends   5
To speak the ceremonial rites of marriage?
What says Lucentio to this shame of ours?

---

40 Spit in the hole i.e., to make the peg stick   **49** *Pedascule* (A word
contemptuously coined by Hortensio, presumably the vocative of an
invented Latinism, *pedasculus*, "little pedant.")   **51 Mistrust** (Lucentio plays upon Bianca's *mistrust* in line 50, in which she expresses
skepticism about his secret wooing; his answer seeks to reassure her,
while at the same time in "Litio's" hearing he seems to emphasize the
truth of his instruction as he goes on with his lesson from the
Heroides. Her reply is ambiguous in the same way.)   **Aeacides**
descendant of Aeacus, King of Aegina, father of Telamon and grandfather of Ajax   **57 pleasant** merry   **60 formal** precise   **61 but** unless
64 order method   **66 gamut** the scale, from the alphabet name
(*gamma*) of the first note plus *ut*, its syllable name, now commonly
called *do.* (The *gamut* of Hortensio begins on G instead of on C.)
69 drawn set out, copied.

72 ground bass note, foundation.   **accord** harmony   **74** *B mi* (With a
suggestion of "be my.")   **75** *fa ut* (The note C is the fourth note, or *fa*,
of a scale based on G but is the first note, *ut*, or *do*, of the more universal major scale based on C. Similarly, D is the fifth note, or *sol*, in the
G scale but is the second, or *re*, in the C scale; similarly, with E as
sixth and third.)   **76 two notes** (Hinting at Hortensio's disguise.)
77 *E la mi* (Suggesting "Ill am I.")   **79 nice** capricious   **89 stale**
ridiculous rival   **90 Seize . . . list** let him who wants you have you.
ranging inconstant. (The metaphor is that of a straying hawk.)
91 be quit get even.   **changing** loving another.
3.2. Location: Padua. Before Baptista's house.
4 What . . . said? What will people say?   **5 want** lack

KATHARINA

No shame but mine. I must, forsooth, be forced
To give my hand opposed against my heart
Unto a mad-brain rudesby full of spleen, 10
Who wooed in haste and means to wed at leisure.
I told you, I, he was a frantic fool,
Hiding his bitter jests in blunt behavior.
And, to be noted for a merry man, 14
He'll woo a thousand, 'point the day of marriage,
Make friends, invite, and proclaim the banns, 16
Yet never means to wed where he hath wooed.
Now must the world point at poor Katharine
And say, "Lo, there is mad Petruchio's wife,
If it would please him come and marry her!"

TRANIO

Patience, good Katharine, and Baptista, too.
Upon my life, Petruchio means but well,
Whatever fortune stays him from his word. 23
Though he be blunt, I know him passing wise; 24
Though he be merry, yet withal he's honest. 25

KATHARINA

Would Katharine had never seen him, though!

Exit weeping.

BAPTISTA

Go, girl, I cannot blame thee now to weep,
For such an injury would vex a very saint,
Much more a shrew of thy impatient humor.

Enter Biondello.

BIONDELLO   Master, master! News, and such old news 30
as you never heard of!

BAPTISTA   Is it new and old too? How may that be?

BIONDELLO   Why, is it not news to hear of Petruchio's
coming?

BAPTISTA   Is he come?

BIONDELLO   Why, no, sir.

BAPTISTA   What, then?

BIONDELLO   He is coming.

BAPTISTA   When will he be here?

BIONDELLO   When he stands where I am and sees you
there.

TRANIO   But say, what to thine old news? 42

BIONDELLO   Why, Petruchio is coming in a new hat and
an old jerkin; a pair of old breeches thrice turned; a 44
pair of boots that have been candle-cases, one buckled, 45
another laced; an old rusty sword ta'en out of the town
armory, with a broken hilt, and chapeless; with two 47
broken points; his horse hipped, with an old mothy 48

saddle and stirrups of no kindred; besides, possessed 49
with the glanders and like to mose in the chine, trou- 50
bled with the lampass, infected with the fashions, full 51
of windgalls, sped with spavins, rayed with the yel- 52
lows, past cure of the fives, stark spoiled with the stag- 53
gers, begnawn with the bots, swayed in the back and 54
shoulder-shotten; near-legged before, and with a half- 55
cheeked bit and a headstall of sheep's leather which, 56
being restrained to keep him from stumbling, hath 57
been often burst and now repaired with knots; one
girth six times pieced, and a woman's crupper of 59
velour, which hath two letters for her name fairly 60
set down in studs, and here and there pieced
with packthread. 62

BAPTISTA   Who comes with him?

BIONDELLO   Oh, sir, his lackey, for all the world capari- 64
soned like the horse; with a linen stock on one leg and 65
a kersey boot-hose on the other, gartered with a red 66
and blue list; an old hat, and the humor of forty fan- 67
cies pricked in 't for a feather—a monster, a very mon- 68
ster in apparel, and not like a Christian footboy or a
gentleman's lackey.

TRANIO

'Tis some odd humor pricks him to this fashion; 71
Yet oftentimes he goes but mean-appareled. 72

BAPTISTA   I am glad he's come, howsoe'er he comes.

BIONDELLO   Why, sir, he comes not.

BAPTISTA   Didst thou not say he comes?

BIONDELLO   Who? That Petruchio came?

BAPTISTA   Ay, that Petruchio came.

BIONDELLO   No, sir, I say his horse comes, with him on
his back.

BAPTISTA   Why, that's all one. 80

BIONDELLO

Nay, by Saint Jamy,

---

10 rudesby unmannerly fellow. **spleen** i.e., changeable temper
14 to be noted for in order to get a reputation as **16 banns** wedding
announcement **23 Whatever . . . word** whatever accident keeps him
from fulfilling his promise. **24 passing** exceedingly **25 merry**
given to joking **30 old** rare; and referring to Petruchio's old clothes
42 to about **44 jerkin** man's jacket. **turned** i.e., with the material
reversed to get more wear **45 candle-cases** i.e., discarded boots,
used only as a receptacle for candle ends **47 chapeless** without the
chape, the metal plate or mounting of a scabbard, especially that
which covers the point **48 points** tagged laces for attaching hose to
doublet. **hipped** lamed in the hip. (Almost all the diseases here
named are described in Gervase Markham's *How to Choose, Ride,
Train, and Diet both Hunting Horses and Running Horses . . . Also a Discourse of Horsemanship*, probably first published in 1593.)

49 of no kindred that don't match **50 glanders** contagious disease in
horses causing swelling beneath the jaw and mucous discharge from
the nostrils **50 mose in the chine** suffer from glanders **51 lampass** a
thick, spongy flesh growing over a horse's upper teeth and hindering
his eating. **fashions** i.e., farcins, or farcy, a disease like glanders.
52 windgalls soft tumors or swellings generally found on the fetlock
joint, so called from having been supposed to contain air. **sped** far
gone. **spavins** a disease of the hock, marked by a small bony enlargement inside the leg. **rayed** bespattered, defiled **52–3 yellows** jaundice **53 fives** avives, a glandular disease causing swelling behind the
ear **53–4 stark . . . staggers** completely destroyed by a disease causing
palsylike staggering **54 bots** parasitic worms **55 shoulder-shotten**
with sprained or dislocated shoulder. **near-legged before** with knock-
kneed forelegs **55–6 half-cheeked bit** one to which the bridle is
attached halfway up the cheek or sidepiece and thus not giving sufficient control over the horse **56 headstall** part of the bridle over the
head. **sheep's leather** (i.e., of inferior quality; pigskin was used for
strongest harness) **57 restrained** drawn back **59 girth** saddle-strap
passing under the horse's belly. **pieced** mended. **crupper** leather
loop passing under the horse's tail and fastened to the saddle
60 velour velvet. **two . . . name** her initials **62 packthread** twine for
securing parcels. **64–5 for . . . caparisoned** in all respects outfitted
65 stock stocking **66 kersey boot-hose** overstocking of coarse material
for wearing under boots **67 list** strip of cloth **67–8 the humor . . .
feather** a trite motto incised in it instead of a feather **68 pricked**
pinned. **for** in place of **71 humor pricks** whim that spurs **72 mean-
appareled** poorly dressed **80 all one** the same thing.

I hold you a penny,
A horse and a man
Is more than one,
And yet not many.

Enter Petruchio and Grumio.

PETRUCHIO
Come, where be these gallants? Who's at home?
BAPTISTA   You are welcome, sir.
PETRUCHIO   And yet I come not well.   88
BAPTISTA   And yet you halt not.   89
TRANIO
Not so well appareled as I wish you were.
PETRUCHIO
Were it better, I should rush in thus.   91
But where is Kate? Where is my lovely bride?
How does my father? Gentles, methinks you frown.
And wherefore gaze this goodly company,
As if they saw some wondrous monument,   95
Some comet, or unusual prodigy?   96
BAPTISTA
Why, sir, you know this is your wedding day.
First were we sad, fearing you would not come,
Now sadder that you come so unprovided.   99
Fie, doff this habit, shame to your estate,   100
An eyesore to our solemn festival!
TRANIO
And tell us, what occasion of import
Hath all so long detained you from your wife
And sent you hither so unlike yourself?
PETRUCHIO
Tedious it were to tell, and harsh to hear.
Sufficeth I am come to keep my word,   106
Though in some part enforcèd to digress,   107
Which at more leisure I will so excuse
As you shall well be satisfied withal.
But where is Kate? I stay too long from her.
The morning wears; 'tis time we were at church.
TRANIO
See not your bride in these unreverent robes.
Go to my chamber. Put on clothes of mine.
PETRUCHIO
Not I, believe me. Thus I'll visit her.
BAPTISTA
But thus, I trust, you will not marry her.
PETRUCHIO
Good sooth, even thus. Therefore ha' done with
    words.   116
To me she's married, not unto my clothes.
Could I repair what she will wear in me   118
As I can change these poor accoutrements,
'Twere well for Kate and better for myself.

But what a fool am I to chat with you,   82
When I should bid good morrow to my bride
And seal the title with a lovely kiss!   *Exit.* 123
TRANIO
He hath some meaning in his mad attire.
We will persuade him, be it possible,
To put on better ere he go to church.
BAPTISTA
I'll after him, and see the event of this.   127
        Exit [with all but Tranio and Lucentio].
TRANIO
But, sir, to love concerneth us to add   128
Her father's liking, which to bring to pass,
As I before imparted to Your Worship,   130
I am to get a man—whate'er he be
It skills not much, we'll fit him to our turn—   132
And he shall be Vincentio of Pisa
And make assurance here in Padua
Of greater sums than I have promisèd.
So shall you quietly enjoy your hope
And marry sweet Bianca with consent.
LUCENTIO
Were it not that my fellow schoolmaster
Doth watch Bianca's steps so narrowly,
'Twere good, methinks, to steal our marriage,   140
Which once performed, let all the world say no,
I'll keep mine own, despite of all the world.
TRANIO
That by degrees we mean to look into,
And watch our vantage in this business.   144
We'll overreach the graybeard, Gremio,
The narrow-prying father, Minola,   146
The quaint musician, amorous Litio,   147
All for my master's sake, Lucentio.

Enter Gremio.

Signor Gremio, came you from the church?
GREMIO
As willingly as e'er I came from school.
TRANIO
And is the bride and bridegroom coming home?
GREMIO
A bridegroom, say you? 'Tis a groom indeed,   152
A grumbling groom, and that the girl shall find.
TRANIO
Curster than she? Why, 'tis impossible.
GREMIO
Why, he 's a devil, a devil, a very fiend.
TRANIO
Why, she's a devil, a devil, the devil's dam.   156

82 **hold** wager   88 **I come not well** i.e., I am not made to feel welcome; or, I come admittedly not well appareled.   89 **halt** limp, move slowly   91 **Were it** Even if it (my apparel) were.   **rush** come quickly. (Referring to *halt not* in line 89.)   95 **monument** portent   96 **prodigy** omen.   99 **unprovided** ill equipped   100 **habit** outfit.   **estate** position, station   106 **Sufficeth** It is enough that   107 **digress** i.e., deviate   116 **Good sooth** i.e., Yes, indeed   118 **Could . . . me** If I could amend in my character what she'll have to put up with

123 **lovely** loving   127 **event** outcome   128 **to love . . . add** besides obtaining the love of the lady, it behooves us to add   130 **to Your Worship** (Tranio privately drops the fiction that he is Lucentio's master.)   132 **skills** matters   140 **steal our marriage** elope   144 **watch our vantage** look out for our best opportunity, advantage   146 **narrow-prying** suspicious, watchful   147 **quaint** skillful   152 **'Tis a groom indeed** A fine bridegroom he is. (Said ironically, with pun on the sense of "servant," "rough fellow.")   156 **dam** mother.

GREMIO
Tut, she's a lamb, a dove, a fool to him. 157
I'll tell you, Sir Lucentio. When the priest
Should ask if Katharine should be his wife, 159
"Ay, by Gog's wouns," quoth he, and swore so loud 160
That all amazed the priest let fall the book,
And as he stooped again to take it up,
This mad-brained bridegroom took him such a cuff 163
That down fell priest and book, and book and priest.
"Now take them up," quoth he, "if any list." 165

TRANIO
What said the wench when he rose again?

GREMIO
Trembled and shook, forwhy he stamped and swore 167
As if the vicar meant to cozen him. 168
But after many ceremonies done
He calls for wine. "A health!" quoth he, as if
He had been aboard, carousing to his mates 171
After a storm; quaffed off the muscatel
And threw the sops all in the sexton's face, 173
Having no other reason
But that his beard grew thin and hungerly 175
And seemed to ask him sops as he was drinking. 176
This done, he took the bride about the neck
And kissed her lips with such a clamorous smack
That at the parting all the church did echo.
And I seeing this came thence for very shame,
And after me, I know, the rout is coming. 181
Such a mad marriage never was before.   *Music plays.*
Hark, hark! I hear the minstrels play.

Enter Petruchio, Kate, Bianca, Hortensio [as Litio],
Baptista, [with Grumio, and train].

PETRUCHIO
Gentlemen and friends, I thank you for your pains.
I know you think to dine with me today,
And have prepared great store of wedding cheer;
But so it is my haste doth call me hence,
And therefore here I mean to take my leave.

BAPTISTA
Is't possible you will away tonight?

PETRUCHIO
I must away today, before night come.
Make it no wonder. If you knew my business, 191
You would entreat me rather go than stay.
And, honest company, I thank you all 193
That have beheld me give away myself
To this most patient, sweet, and virtuous wife.
Dine with my father, drink a health to me,
For I must hence; and farewell to you all.

TRANIO
Let us entreat you stay till after dinner.

PETRUCHIO
It may not be.

GREMIO   Let me entreat you.

PETRUCHIO
It cannot be.

KATHARINA   Let me entreat you.

PETRUCHIO
I am content.

KATHARINA   Are you content to stay?

PETRUCHIO
I am content you shall entreat me stay;
But yet not stay, entreat me how you can.

KATHARINA
Now, if you love me, stay.

PETRUCHIO   Grumio, my horse. 204

GRUMIO Ay, sir, they be ready. The oats have eaten the 205
horses. 206

KATHARINA   Nay, then,
Do what thou canst, I will not go today,
No, nor tomorrow—not till I please myself.
The door is open, sir; there lies your way.
You may be jogging whiles your boots are green. 211
For me, I'll not be gone till I please myself. 212
'Tis like you'll prove a jolly, surly groom, 213
That take it on you at the first so roundly. 214

PETRUCHIO
Oh, Kate, content thee. Prithee, be not angry.

KATHARINA
I will be angry. What hast thou to do?— 216
Father, be quiet. He shall stay my leisure. 217

GREMIO
Ay, marry, sir, now it begins to work. 218

KATHARINA
Gentlemen, forward to the bridal dinner.
I see a woman may be made a fool
If she had not a spirit to resist.

PETRUCHIO
They shall go forward, Kate, at thy command.—
Obey the bride, you that attend on her.
Go to the feast, revel and domineer, 224
Carouse full measure to her maidenhead, 225
Be mad and merry, or go hang yourselves.
But for my bonny Kate, she must with me. 227
Nay, look not big, nor stamp, nor stare, nor fret; 228
I will be master of what is mine own.
She is my goods, my chattels; she is my house,
My household stuff, my field, my barn,
My horse, my ox, my ass, my anything; 232
And here she stands, touch her whoever dare.

---

157 **a fool to** i.e., a pitiable weak creature compared with
159 **Should ask** came to the point (in the service) where he is directed
to ask   160 **Gog's wouns** God's (Christ's) wounds   163 **took** gave,
struck   165 **list** choose   167 **forwhy** for   168 **cozen** cheat
171 **aboard** aboard ship   173 **sops** cakes or bread soaked in the wine
175 **hungerly** hungry looking, having a starved or famished look
176 **And . . . drinking** and seemed to invite the throwing in his face of
what Petruchio was drinking.   181 **rout** crowd, wedding party
191 **Make it no wonder** Don't be surprised.   193 **honest** worthy, kind

204 **horse** horses.   205–6 **oats . . . horses** (A comic inversion.)
211 **be . . . green** (Proverbial for "getting an early start," with a sarcastic allusion to his unseemly attire.)   **green** fresh, new.   212 **For** As
for   213 **like** likely.   **jolly** (Said sarcastically.)   214 **take it on you**
i.e., throw your weight around.   **roundly** unceremoniously.
216 **What . . . do?** What business is it of yours?   217 **stay my leisure**
wait until I am ready.   218 **now . . . work** now it starts.   224 **domineer** feast riotously   225 **to her maidenhead** to her loss of virginity
227 **for** as for   228 **big** threatening   232 **ox . . . anything** (This catalogue of a man's possessions is from the Tenth Commandment.)

I'll bring mine action on the proudest he   234
That stops my way in Padua.—Grumio,
Draw forth thy weapon. We are beset with thieves.   236
Rescue thy mistress, if thou be a man.—
Fear not, sweet wench, they shall not touch thee, Kate!
I'll buckler thee against a million.   239

Exeunt Petruchio, Katharina, [and Grumio].

BAPTISTA
Nay, let them go—a couple of quiet ones!

GREMIO
Went they not quickly, I should die with laughing.

TRANIO
Of all mad matches never was the like.

LUCENTIO
Mistress, what's your opinion of your sister?

BIANCA
That, being mad herself, she's madly mated.

GREMIO
I warrant him, Petruchio is Kated.   245

BAPTISTA
Neighbors and friends, though bride and bridegroom
   wants   246
For to supply the places at the table,   247
You know there wants no junkets at the feast.   248
Lucentio, you shall supply the bridegroom's place,
And let Bianca take her sister's room.

TRANIO
Shall sweet Bianca practice how to bride it?   251

BAPTISTA
She shall, Lucentio.—Come, gentlemen, let's go.

Exeunt.

❖

[4.1]

Enter Grumio.

GRUMIO   Fie, fie on all tired jades, on all mad masters, 1
and all foul ways! Was ever man so beaten? Was ever   2
man so rayed? Was ever man so weary? I am sent be-   3
fore to make a fire, and they are coming after to warm
them. Now, were not I a little pot and soon hot, my   5
very lips might freeze to my teeth, my tongue to the
roof of my mouth, my heart in my belly, ere I should
come by a fire to thaw me. But I with blowing the fire   8
shall warm myself; for, considering the weather, a
taller man than I will take cold.—Holla, ho! Curtis!   10

Enter Curtis.

CURTIS   Who is that calls so coldly?

GRUMIO   A piece of ice. If thou doubt it, thou mayst
slide from my shoulder to my heel with no greater a
run but my head and my neck. A fire, good Curtis!   14

CURTIS   Is my master and his wife coming, Grumio?

GRUMIO   Oh, ay, Curtis, ay, and therefore fire, fire! Cast 16
on no water.   17

CURTIS   Is she so hot a shrew as she's reported?

GRUMIO   She was, good Curtis, before this frost. But,
thou know'st, winter tames man, woman, and beast;
for it hath tamed my old master and my new mistress
and myself, fellow Curtis.

CURTIS   Away, you three-inch fool! I am no beast.   23

GRUMIO   Am I but three inches? Why, thy horn is a foot,   24
and so long am I, at the least. But wilt thou make a fire, 25
or shall I complain on thee to our mistress, whose
hand—she being now at hand—thou shalt soon feel,
to thy cold comfort, for being slow in thy hot office?   28

CURTIS   I prithee, good Grumio, tell me, how goes the
world?

GRUMIO   A cold world, Curtis, in every office but thine,
and therefore fire. Do thy duty, and have thy duty, for   32
my master and mistress are almost frozen to death.

CURTIS   There's fire ready, and therefore, good Grumio,
the news.

GRUMIO   Why, "Jack boy, ho, boy!" and as much news   36
as wilt thou.

CURTIS   Come, you are so full of coney-catching.   38

GRUMIO   Why, therefore fire, for I have caught extreme
cold. Where's the cook? Is supper ready, the house
trimmed, rushes strewed, cobwebs swept, the serv-   41
ingmen in their new fustian, the white stockings, and   42
every officer his wedding garment on? Be the Jacks   43
fair within, the Jills fair without, the carpets laid, and   44
everything in order?

CURTIS   All ready; and therefore, I pray thee, news.

GRUMIO   First, know my horse is tired, my master and
mistress fallen out.   48

CURTIS   How?

GRUMIO   Out of their saddles into the dirt—and thereby   50
hangs a tale.   51

---

234 action (1) lawsuit (2) attack   **236 Draw** (Perhaps Petruchio and
Grumio actually draw their swords.)   **239 buckler** shield, defend
245 Kated (Gremio's invention for "mated and matched with Kate.")
246–7 wants For to supply are not present to fill   **248 there wants no
junkets** there is no lack of sweetmeats   **251 bride it** play the bride.
4.1. Location: Petruchio's country house. A table is set out,
with seats.
1 jades ill-conditioned horses   **2 ways** roads.   **3 rayed** bespattered.
5 a little . . . hot (Proverbial expression for a person of small stature
soon angered.)   **8 come by** find   **10 taller** (With play on the meaning
"better," "finer.")

14 run running start   **16–17 Cast . . . water** (Alludes to the round
"Scotland's burning," in which the phrase "Fire, fire!" is followed by
"Pour on water, pour on water.")   **23 three-inch fool** (Another reference to Grumio's size.)   **I am no beast** (Curtis protests being called
fellow by Grumio, since Grumio in line 20 has paralleled himself with
beast.)   **24–5 Why . . . least** (Grumio hints that Curtis is a beast with a
prominent *horn*, and hence a cuckold; suggesting too that Grumio's
horn, i.e., *penis*, is as long as Curtis's or longer.)   **28 hot office** i.e.,
duty of providing a fire.   **32 have thy duty** have what's coming to
you, your due   **36 Jack . . . boy** (The first line of another round or
catch.)   **38 coney-catching** cheating, trickery. (With wordplay on
catch, or round, like "Jack boy, ho, boy" in line 36.)
41 rushes (Used to cover the floor.)   **42 fustian** coarse cloth of cotton
and flax   **43 officer** household servant.   **Jacks** (1) servingmen (2)
drinking vessels, usually of leather and hence needing to be clean
within   **44 Jills** (1) maidservants (2) "gills," drinking vessels holding
a quarter pint, often of metal and hence in need of polishing *without*.
(Grumio may joke that the maidservants cannot be expected to be
clean *within*.)   **48 fallen out** quarreling. (But with a pun on the literal
sense in line 50.)   **50–1 thereby hangs a tale** there's quite a story to
tell about that. (But with a risible suggestion of hanging by one's *tail*.)

CURTIS   Let's ha 't, good Grumio.   52
GRUMIO   Lend thine ear.
CURTIS   Here.
GRUMIO   There.   [*He cuffs Curtis.*]
CURTIS   This 'tis to feel a tale, not to hear a tale.
GRUMIO   And therefore 'tis called a sensible tale, and   57
this cuff was but to knock at your ear and beseech
listening. Now I begin: Imprimis, we came down a   59
foul hill, my master riding behind my mistress—   60
CURTIS   Both of one horse?   61
GRUMIO   What's that to thee?
CURTIS   Why, a horse.
GRUMIO   Tell thou the tale. But hadst thou not crossed   64
me, thou shouldst have heard how her horse fell and
she under her horse; thou shouldst have heard in how
miry a place, how she was bemoiled, how he left her   67
with the horse upon her, how he beat me because her
horse stumbled, how she waded through the dirt to
pluck him off me, how he swore, how she prayed that
never prayed before, how I cried, how the horses ran
away, how her bridle was burst, how I lost my
crupper, with many things of worthy memory, which   73
now shall die in oblivion and thou return unexperi-
enced to thy grave.
CURTIS   By this reckoning he is more shrew than she.
GRUMIO   Ay, and that thou and the proudest of you all
shall find when he comes home. But what talk I of   78
this? Call forth Nathaniel, Joseph, Nicholas, Philip,
Walter, Sugarsop, and the rest. Let their heads be
sleekly combed, their blue coats brushed, and their   81
garters of an indifferent knit; let them curtsy with their   82
left legs, and not presume to touch a hair of my
master's horsetail till they kiss their hands. Are they
all ready?
CURTIS   They are.
GRUMIO   Call them forth.
CURTIS [*calling*]   Do you hear, ho? You must meet my
master to countenance my mistress.   89
GRUMIO   Why, she hath a face of her own.
CURTIS   Who knows not that?
GRUMIO   Thou, it seems, that calls for company to
countenance her.
CURTIS   I call them forth to credit her.   94

Enter four or five Servingmen.

GRUMIO   Why, she comes to borrow nothing of them.
NATHANIEL   Welcome home, Grumio!
PHILIP   How now, Grumio?
JOSEPH   What, Grumio!
NICHOLAS   Fellow Grumio!
NATHANIEL   How now, old lad?

GRUMIO   Welcome, you; how now, you; what, you; fellow, you—and thus much for greeting. Now, my
spruce companions, is all ready, and all things neat?   103
NATHANIEL   All things is ready. How near is our
master?
GRUMIO   E'en at hand, alighted by this; and therefore
be not—Cock's passion, silence! I hear my master.   107

Enter Petruchio and Kate.

PETRUCHIO
Where be these knaves? What, no man at door
To hold my stirrup nor to take my horse?   109
Where is Nathaniel, Gregory, Philip?
ALL SERVANTS   Here, here, sir, here, sir.
PETRUCHIO
Here, sir! Here, sir! Here, sir! Here, sir!
You loggerheaded and unpolished grooms!
What, no attendance? No regard? No duty?
Where is the foolish knave I sent before?   115
GRUMIO
Here, sir, as foolish as I was before.
PETRUCHIO
You peasant swain, you whoreson, malt-horse
drudge!   117
Did I not bid thee meet me in the park
And bring along these rascal knaves with thee?
GRUMIO
Nathaniel's coat, sir, was not fully made,
And Gabriel's pumps were all unpinked i'the heel.   121
There was no link to color Peter's hat,   122
And Walter's dagger was not come from sheathing.   123
There were none fine but Adam, Ralph, and Gregory;   124
The rest were ragged, old, and beggarly.
Yet, as they are, here are they come to meet you.
PETRUCHIO
Go, rascals, go and fetch my supper in.
                                        Exeunt Servants.
[*He sings.*] "Where is the life that late I led?   128
Where are those—" Sit down, Kate, and welcome.—   129
                                        [*They sit at table.*]
Soud, soud, soud, soud!   130

Enter Servants with supper.

Why, when, I say?—Nay, good sweet Kate, be
merry.—   131
Off with my boots, you rogues! You villains, when?
                        [*A Servant takes off Petruchio's boots.*]
[*He sings.*] "It was the friar of orders gray,   133
As he forth walkèd on his way—"   134

---

52 **ha 't** have it   57 **sensible** (1) capable of being felt (2) showing good sense   59 **Imprimis** In the first place   60 **foul** muddy   61 **of** on   64 **crossed** thwarted, interrupted   67 **bemoiled** befouled with mire   73 **crupper.** (See 3.2.59.)   **of worthy** worthy of   78 **what** why   81 **blue coats** (Usual dress for servingmen.)   82 **indifferent** well-matched, identical   89 **countenance** pay respects to. (With a following pun on the meaning "face.")   94 **credit** pay respects to. (With another pun following, on "extend financial credit.")

103 **spruce** lively, trim in appearance   107 **Cock's passion** By God's (Christ's) suffering   109 **hold my stirrup** i.e., help me dismount   115 **before** ahead. (With pun in next line on "previously.")
117 **swain** rustic.   **whoreson . . . drudge** worthless plodding work animal, such as would be used on a treadmill to grind malt.
121 **pumps** low cut shoes.   **unpinked** lacking in eyelets or in ornamental tracing in the leather   122 **link** blacking made from burnt "links" or torches   123 **sheathing** being fitted with a sheath.
124 **fine** well clothed   128–9 **Where . . . those** (A fragment of a lost ballad, probably lamenting the man's loss of freedom in marriage.)
130 **Soud** (A nonsense song, or expression of impatience, or perhaps "food!")   131 **when** (An exclamation of impatience.)   133–4 **"It . . . way"** (A fragment of a lost ballad, probably bawdy.)

Out, you rogue! You pluck my foot awry.   135
                    [He kicks the Servant.]
Take that, and mend the plucking of the other.—   136
Be merry, Kate.—Some water, here. What, ho!

  Enter one with water.

Where's my spaniel Troilus? Sirrah, get you hence,
And bid my cousin Ferdinand come hither—
           [Exit Servant.]
One, Kate, that you must kiss and be acquainted with.
Where are my slippers? Shall I have some water?
Come, Kate, and wash, and welcome heartily.
   [A Servant offers water, but spills some.]
You whoreson villain, will you let it fall?
        [He strikes the Servant.]

KATHARINA
 Patience, I pray you, 'twas a fault unwilling.   144
PETRUCHIO
 A whoreson, beetleheaded, flap-eared knave!—   145
Come, Kate, sit down. I know you have a stomach.   146
Will you give thanks, sweet Kate, or else shall I?—   147
What's this? Mutton?
FIRST SERVANT Ay.
PETRUCHIO   Who brought it?
PETER   I.
PETRUCHIO
 'Tis burnt, and so is all the meat.
What dogs are these? Where is the rascal cook?
How durst you, villains, bring it from the dresser   151
And serve it thus to me that love it not?
There, take it to you, trenchers, cups, and all.,   153
     [He throws the meat, etc., at them.]
You heedless jolt-heads and unmannered slaves!   154
What, do you grumble? I'll be with you straight.   155
          [They run out.]
KATHARINA
 I pray you, husband, be not so disquiet.
The meat was well, if you were so contented.   157
PETRUCHIO
 I tell thee, Kate, 'twas burnt and dried away,
And I expressly am forbid to touch it;
For it engenders choler, planteth anger,   160
And better 'twere that both of us did fast,
Since, of ourselves, ourselves are choleric,   162
Than feed it with such overroasted flesh.
Be patient. Tomorrow 't shall be mended,
And for this night we'll fast for company.   165
Come, I will bring thee to thy bridal chamber.   166
            Exeunt.

  Enter Servants severally.

NATHANIEL Peter, didst ever see the like?
PETER He kills her in her own humor.   168

  Enter Curtis.

GRUMIO Where is he?
CURTIS In her chamber,
Making a sermon of continency to her,   171
And rails, and swears, and rates, that she, poor soul, 172
Knows not which way to stand, to look, to speak,
And sits as one new risen from a dream.
Away, away! For he is coming hither. *[Exeunt.]*

  Enter Petruchio.

PETRUCHIO
 Thus have I politicly begun my reign,   176
And 'tis my hope to end successfully.
My falcon now is sharp and passing empty,   178
And till she stoop she must not be full-gorged,   179
For then she never looks upon her lure.
Another way I have to man my haggard,   181
To make her come and know her keeper's call:
That is, to watch her, as we watch these kites   183
That bate and beat and will not be obedient.   184
She ate no meat today, nor none shall eat.
Last night she slept not, nor tonight she shall not.
As with the meat, some undeservèd fault
I'll find about the making of the bed,
And here I'll fling the pillow, there the bolster,
This way the coverlet, another way the sheets.
Ay, and amid this hurly I intend   191
That all is done in reverent care of her.
And in conclusion she shall watch all night,   193
And if she chance to nod I'll rail and brawl,
And with the clamor keep her still awake.
This is a way to kill a wife with kindness;
And thus I'll curb her mad and headstrong humor. 197
He that knows better how to tame a shrew,
Now let him speak. 'Tis charity to show. *Exit.* 199

      ❖

[4.2]

  *Enter Tranio [as Lucentio] and Hortensio
  [as Litio].*

TRANIO
 Is't possible, friend Litio, that Mistress Bianca
Doth fancy any other but Lucentio?
I tell you, sir, she bears me fair in hand.   3

---

135 Out (Exclamation of anger or reproach.) **136 mend the plucking of** do a better job of pulling off **144 unwilling** not intentional.
145 beetleheaded i.e., blockheaded (since a *beetle* is a pounding tool)
146 stomach appetite. (With a suggestion also of "temper.")
147 give thanks say grace **151 dresser** one who "dresses" or prepares the food; or, sideboard **153 trenchers** wooden dishes or plates
154 jolt-heads blockheads **155 with you straight** after you at once (to get even for this). **157 if . . . contented** if you had chosen to be pleased with it. **160 choler** the humor or bodily fluid, hot and dry in character, that supposedly produced ill temper and was thought to be aggravated by the eating of roast meat **162 of ourselves** by our natures **165 for company** together. **166.2 *severally*** separately

168 He . . . humor He subdues her shrewishness with his own greater shrewishness. **171 sermon of continency** lecture on self-restraint
172 rates scolds. **that** so that **176 politicly** with skillful calculation
178 sharp hungry. **passing** very **179 stoop** fly down to the lure
181 man tame, assert masculine authority over. **haggard** wild female hawk; hence, an intractable woman **183 watch her** keep her watching, i.e., awake. **kites** a kind of hawk. (With a pun on *Kate*.)
184 bate and beat beat the wings impatiently and flutter away from the hand or perch **191 hurly** commotion. **intend** pretend
193 watch stay awake **197 humor** disposition. **199 'Tis charity to show** This is to perform an act of Christian benevolence. (On the rhyme with *shrew*, see also the play's final lines.)
4.2. Location: Padua. Before Baptista's house.
3 bears . . . hand gives me encouragement, leads me on.

HORTENSIO
    Sir, to satisfy you in what I have said,   4
    Stand by and mark the manner of his teaching.
                                    [They stand aside.]

        Enter Bianca [and Lucentio as Cambio].

LUCENTIO
    Now, mistress, profit you in what you read?   6
BIANCA
    What, master, read you? First resolve me that.   7
LUCENTIO
    I read that I profess, *The Art to Love.*   8
BIANCA
    And may you prove, sir, master of your art!
LUCENTIO
    While you, sweet dear, prove mistress of my heart!
              [They move aside and court each other.]
HORTENSIO *[to Tranio, coming forward]*
    Quick proceeders, marry! Now, tell me, I pray,   11
    You that durst swear that your mistress Bianca
    Loved none in the world so well as Lucentio.
TRANIO
    Oh, despiteful love! Unconstant womankind!   14
    I tell thee, Litio, this is wonderful.   15
HORTENSIO
    Mistake no more. I am not Litio,
    Nor a musician, as I seem to be,
    But one that scorn to live in this disguise   18
    For such a one as leaves a gentleman   19
    And makes a god of such a cullion.   20
    Know, sir, that I am called Hortensio.
TRANIO
    Signor Hortensio, I have often heard
    Of your entire affection to Bianca;   23
    And since mine eyes are witness of her lightness,   24
    I will with you, if you be so contented,
    Forswear Bianca and her love forever.
HORTENSIO
    See how they kiss and court! Signor Lucentio,
    Here is my hand, and here I firmly vow
                           [giving his hand]
    Never to woo her more, but do forswear her,
    As one unworthy all the former favors
    That I have fondly flattered her withal.   31
TRANIO
    And here I take the like unfeignèd oath,
    Never to marry with her though she would entreat.
    Fie on her, see how beastly she doth court him!
HORTENSIO
    Would all the world but he had quite forsworn!   35

    For me, that I may surely keep mine oath,   36
    I will be married to a wealthy widow,
    Ere three days pass, which hath as long loved me
    As I have loved this proud disdainful haggard.   39
    And so farewell, Signor Lucentio.
    Kindness in women, not their beauteous looks,
    Shall win my love. And so I take my leave,
    In resolution as I swore before.   *[Exit.]* 43
TRANIO *[as Lucentio and Bianca come forward again]*
    Mistress Bianca, bless you with such grace
    As 'longeth to a lover's blessèd case!   45
    Nay, I have ta'en you napping, gentle love,   46
    And have forsworn you with Hortensio.
BIANCA
    Tranio, you jest. But have you both forsworn me?
TRANIO
    Mistress, we have.
LUCENTIO   Then we are rid of Litio.
TRANIO
    I' faith, he'll have a lusty widow now,   50
    That shall be wooed and wedded in a day.
BIANCA   God give him joy!
TRANIO   Ay, and he'll tame her.
BIANCA   He says so, Tranio?
TRANIO
    Faith, he is gone unto the taming-school.
BIANCA
    The taming-school! What, is there such a place?
TRANIO
    Ay, mistress, and Petruchio is the master,
    That teacheth tricks eleven-and-twenty long   58
    To tame a shrew and charm her chattering tongue.

        Enter Biondello.

BIONDELLO
    Oh, master, master, I have watched so long
    That I am dog-weary, but at last I spied
    An ancient angel coming down the hill   62
    Will serve the turn.
TRANIO   What is he, Biondello? 63
BIONDELLO
    Master, a marcantant, or a pedant,   64
    I know not what, but formal in apparel,
    In gait and countenance surely like a father.
LUCENTIO   And what of him, Tranio?
TRANIO
    If he be credulous and trust my tale,
    I'll make him glad to seem Vincentio,
    And give assurance to Baptista Minola

---

4 satisfy convince **6 read** (Evidently, both Bianca and "Cambio" carry books.) **7 resolve** answer **8 I read . . . Love** I read what I practice, Ovid's *Ars Amatoria.* **11 proceeders** (1) workers, doers (2) candidates for academic degrees (as suggested by the phrase *master of your art* in line 9) **14 despiteful** cruel **15 wonderful** cause for wonder. **18 scorn** scorns **19 such a one** i.e., Bianca **20 cullion** base fellow. (Referring to "Cambio"; literally, *cullion* means "testicle.") **23 entire** sincere **24 lightness** wantonness **31 fondly** foolishly **35 Would . . . forsworn!** i.e., May everyone in the world forsake her except the penniless "Cambio," and may she thus get what she deserves!

36 For As for **39 haggard** wild hawk. **43 In resolution** determined **45 'longeth** belongs **46 ta'en you napping** taken you by surprise **50 lusty** merry, lively **58 eleven . . . long** i.e., right on the money. (Alluding to the card game called "one-and-thirty" referred to at 1.2.32–3.) **62 ancient angel** i.e., fellow of the good old stamp. (Literally, an "angel" or gold coin bearing the stamp of the archangel Michael and thus distinguishable from more recent debased coinage.) **63 Will . . . turn** who will serve our purposes. **64 marcantant** merchant. **pedant** schoolmaster. (Though at lines 90–1 he speaks more like a merchant.)

As if he were the right Vincentio.
Take in your love, and then let me alone.   72

[*Exeunt Lucentio and Bianca.*]

Enter a Pedant.

PEDANT
God save you, sir!
TRANIO   And you sir! You are welcome.
Travel you farre on, or are you at the farthest?   74
PEDANT
Sir, at the farthest for a week or two,
But then up farther, and as far as Rome,
And so to Tripoli, if God lend me life.
TRANIO
What countryman, I pray?
PEDANT   Of Mantua.
TRANIO
Of Mantua, sir? Marry, God forbid!
And come to Padua, careless of your life?
PEDANT
My life, sir? How, I pray? For that goes hard.   81
TRANIO
'Tis death for anyone in Mantua
To come to Padua. Know you not the cause?
Your ships are stayed at Venice, and the Duke,   84
For private quarrel twixt your Duke and him,
Hath published and proclaimed it openly.
'Tis marvel, but that you are but newly come,
You might have heard it else proclaimed about.
PEDANT
Alas, sir, it is worse for me than so,   89
For I have bills for money by exchange   90
From Florence, and must here deliver them.
TRANIO
Well, sir, to do you courtesy,
This will I do, and this I will advise you—
First, tell me, have you ever been at Pisa?
PEDANT
Ay, sir, in Pisa have I often been,
Pisa renownèd for grave citizens.
TRANIO
Among them know you one Vincentio?
PEDANT
I know him not, but I have heard of him;
A merchant of incomparable wealth.
TRANIO
He is my father, sir, and, sooth to say,
In count'nance somewhat doth resemble you.
BIONDELLO [*aside*]   As much as an apple doth an oy-
ster, and all one.   103
TRANIO
To save your life in this extremity,
This favor will I do you for his sake;
And think it not the worst of all your fortunes
That you are like to Sir Vincentio.

His name and credit shall you undertake,   108
And in my house you shall be friendly lodged.
Look that you take upon you as you should.   110
You understand me, sir. So shall you stay
Till you have done your business in the city.
If this be courtesy, sir, accept of it.
PEDANT
Oh, sir, I do, and will repute you ever   114
The patron of my life and liberty.
TRANIO
Then go with me to make the matter good.   116
This, by the way, I let you understand:
My father is here looked for every day
To pass assurance of a dower in marriage   119
Twixt me and one Baptista's daughter here.
In all these circumstances I'll instruct you.
Go with me to clothe you as becomes you.

                                                Exeunt.

❖

4.[3]

Enter Katharina and Grumio.

GRUMIO
No, no, forsooth, I dare not for my life.
KATHARINA
The more my wrong, the more his spite appears.   2
What, did he marry me to famish me?
Beggars that come unto my father's door
Upon entreaty have a present alms;   5
If not, elsewhere they meet with charity.
But I, who never knew how to entreat,
Nor never needed that I should entreat,
Am starved for meat, giddy for lack of sleep,
With oaths kept waking, and with brawling fed.
And that which spites me more than all these wants,
He does it under name of perfect love,
As who should say, if I should sleep or eat
'Twere deadly sickness or else present death.   13
I prithee, go and get me some repast,
I care not what, so it be wholesome food.   16
GRUMIO   What say you to a neat's foot?   17
KATHARINA
'Tis passing good. I prithee, let me have it.   18
GRUMIO
I fear it is too choleric a meat.
How say you to a fat tripe finely broiled?
KATHARINA
I like it well. Good Grumio, fetch it me.
GRUMIO
I cannot tell. I fear 'tis choleric.   22
What say you to a piece of beef and mustard?

---

72 **let me alone** leave things to me.   74 **farre** farther   81 **goes hard** is serious indeed.   84 **stayed** detained   89 **than** so than that
90 **bills . . . exchange** promissory notes   103 **all one** no matter.

108 **credit** reputation   110 **take upon you** play your part   114 **repute you** regard you as   116 **make . . . good** carry out the plan.   119 **pass assurance** convey a legal guarantee
4.3. Location: Petruchio's house. A table is set out, with seats.
2 **my wrong** the wrong done to me   5 **present** immediate. (As in line 14.)   13 **As who** as if one   16 **so** so long as   17 **neat's** ox's   18 **passing** extremely   22 **I cannot tell** I don't know what to say.

KATHARINA
A dish that I do love to feed upon.

GRUMIO
Ay, but the mustard is too hot a little.

KATHARINA
Why then, the beef, and let the mustard rest.   26

GRUMIO
Nay then, I will not. You shall have the mustard,
Or else you get no beef of Grumio.

KATHARINA
Then both, or one, or anything thou wilt.

GRUMIO
Why then, the mustard without the beef.

KATHARINA
Go, get thee gone, thou false, deluding slave,
                                        [She] beats him.
That feed'st me with the very name of meat!   32
Sorrow on thee and all the pack of you,
That triumph thus upon my misery!
Go, get thee gone, I say.

                Enter Petruchio and Hortensio with meat.

PETRUCHIO
How fares my Kate? What, sweeting, all amort?   36

HORTENSIO
Mistress, what cheer?   Faith, as cold as can be.

KATHARINA

PETRUCHIO
Pluck up thy spirits; look cheerfully upon me.
Here, love, thou see'st how diligent I am
To dress thy meat myself and bring it thee.   40
I am sure, sweet Kate, this kindness merits thanks.
What, not a word? Nay, then thou lov'st it not,
And all my pains is sorted to no proof.—   43
Here, take away this dish.

KATHARINA   I pray you, let it stand.

PETRUCHIO
The poorest service is repaid with thanks,
And so shall mine before you touch the meat.

KATHARINA   I thank you, sir.

HORTENSIO
Signor Petruchio, fie, you are to blame.
Come, Mistress Kate, I'll bear you company.

PETRUCHIO [aside to Hortensio]
Eat it up all, Hortensio, if thou lovest me.—
Much good do it unto thy gentle heart!
Kate, eat apace. And now, my honey love,
Will we return unto thy father's house
And revel it as bravely as the best,   54
With silken coats and caps and golden rings,
With ruffs, and cuffs, and farthingales, and things,   56
With scarves, and fans, and double change of brav'ry,   57
With amber bracelets, beads, and all this knav'ry.

What, hast thou dined? The tailor stays thy leisure,   59
To deck thy body with his ruffling treasure.   60

                Enter Tailor [with a gown].

Come, tailor, let us see these ornaments.
Lay forth the gown.

                Enter Haberdasher [with a cap].

                        What news with you, sir?

HABERDASHER
Here is the cap Your Worship did bespeak.   63

PETRUCHIO
Why, this was molded on a porringer—   64
A velvet dish. Fie, fie, 'tis lewd and filthy.   65
Why, 'tis a cockle or a walnut shell,   66
A knack, a toy, a trick, a baby's cap.   67
Away with it! Come, let me have a bigger.

KATHARINA
I'll have no bigger. This doth fit the time,   69
And gentlewomen wear such caps as these.

PETRUCHIO
When you are gentle, you shall have one too,   71
And not till then.

HORTENSIO [aside]   That will not be in haste.

KATHARINA
Why, sir, I trust I may have leave to speak,
And speak I will. I am no child, no babe.
Your betters have endured me say my mind,   75
And if you cannot, best you stop your ears.
My tongue will tell the anger of my heart,
Or else my heart, concealing it, will break.
And rather than it shall, I will be free
Even to the uttermost, as I please, in words.

PETRUCHIO
Why, thou say'st true. It is a paltry cap,
A custard-coffin, a bauble, a silken pie.   82
I love thee well in that thou lik'st it not.

KATHARINA
Love me or love me not, I like the cap,
And it I will have, or I will have none.

                                        [Exit Haberdasher.]

PETRUCHIO
Thy gown? Why, ay. Come, tailor, let us see't.
Oh, mercy, God, what masquing stuff is here?   87
What's this, a sleeve? 'Tis like a demicannon.   88
What, up and down carved like an apple tart?   89
Here's snip, and nip, and cut, and slish and slash,
Like to a censer in a barber's shop.   91
Why, what i' devil's name, tailor, call'st thou this?

---

26 let . . . rest i.e., forget about the mustard.   32 very mere   36 all
amort dejected, dispirited.   40 dress prepare   43 is . . . proof have
proved to be to no purpose.   54 bravely splendidly   56 farthingales
hooped petticoats   57 bravery finery

59 stays awaits   60 ruffling treasure finery trimmed with ruffles.
63 bespeak order.   64 porringer porridge bowl   65 lewd vile
66 cockle cockleshell   67 trick trifle   69 fit the time suit the current
fashion   71 gentle mild. (Petruchio plays on Kate's gentlewomen,
line 70, i.e., women of high social station.)   75 endured me say
suffered me to say   82 custard-coffin pastry crust for a custard
87 masquing i.e., suited only for a masque   88 demicannon large
cannon.   89 What . . . tart? What, carved from one end to the other
with slits like those in the crust of an apple tart? (Such slits in gowns
were designed to reveal the fabric underneath.)   91 censer perfum-
ing pan having an ornamental lid

HORTENSIO [aside]
    I see she's like to have neither cap nor gown.   93
TAILOR
    You bid me make it orderly and well,
    According to the fashion and the time.
PETRUCHIO
    Marry, and did. But if you be remembered,   96
    I did not bid you mar it to the time.
    Go hop me over every kennel home,   98
    For you shall hop without my custom, sir.
    I'll none of it. Hence, make your best of it.
KATHARINA
    I never saw a better fashioned gown,
    More quaint, more pleasing, nor more
        commendable.   102
    Belike you mean to make a puppet of me.   103
PETRUCHIO
    Why, true, he means to make a puppet of thee.
TAILOR
    She says Your Worship means to make a puppet of her.
PETRUCHIO
    Oh, monstrous arrogance! Thou liest, thou thread,
        thou thimble,   106
    Thou yard, three-quarters, half-yard, quarter, nail!   107
    Thou flea, thou nit, thou winter cricket, thou!   108
    Braved in mine own house with a skein of thread?   109
    Away, thou rag, thou quantity, thou remnant,   110
    Or I shall so be-mete thee with thy yard   111
    As thou shalt think on prating whilst thou liv'st!   112
    I tell thee, I, that thou hast marred her gown.
TAILOR
    Your Worship is deceived. The gown is made
    Just as my master had direction.
    Grumio gave order how it should be done.
GRUMIO   I gave him no order. I gave him the stuff.   117
TAILOR
    But how did you desire it should be made?
GRUMIO   Marry, sir, with needle and thread.
TAILOR
    But did you not request to have it cut?
GRUMIO   Thou hast faced many things.   121
TAILOR   I have.
GRUMIO   Face not me. Thou hast braved many men;   123
    brave not me. I will neither be faced nor braved. I say   124
    unto thee, I bid thy master cut out the gown, but I did
    not bid him cut it to pieces. Ergo, thou liest.   126
TAILOR   Why, here is the note of the fashion to testify.
        [He displays his bill.]
PETRUCHIO   Read it.

GRUMIO   The note lies in 's throat if he say I said so.   129
TAILOR [reads]   "Imprimis, a loose-bodied gown—"   130
GRUMIO   Master, if ever I said loose-bodied gown,   131
    sew me in the skirts of it and beat me to death with a
    bottom of brown thread. I said a gown.   133
PETRUCHIO   Proceed.
TAILOR [reads]   "With a small compassed cape—"   135
GRUMIO   I confess the cape.
TAILOR [reads]   "With a trunk sleeve—"   137
GRUMIO   I confess two sleeves.
TAILOR [reads]   "The sleeves curiously cut."   139
PETRUCHIO   Ay, there's the villainy.
GRUMIO   Error i'the bill, sir, error i'the bill. I commanded
    the sleeves should be cut out and sewed up again, and
    that I'll prove upon thee, though thy little finger be   143
    armed in a thimble.
TAILOR   This is true that I say. An I had thee in place   145
    where, thou shouldst know it.   146
GRUMIO   I am for thee straight. Take thou the bill, give   147
    me thy mete-yard, and spare not me.   148
HORTENSIO   God-a-mercy, Grumio, then he shall have   149
    no odds.   150
PETRUCHIO   Well, sir, in brief, the gown is not for me.
GRUMIO   You are i'the right, sir, 'tis for my mistress.
PETRUCHIO   Go, take it up unto thy master's use.   153
GRUMIO [to the Tailor]   Villain, not for thy life! Take up
    my mistress' gown for thy master's use!
PETRUCHIO   Why sir, what's your conceit in that?   156
GRUMIO
    Oh, sir, the conceit is deeper than you think for: 157
    Take up my mistress' gown to his master's use!
    Oh, fie, fie, fie!
PETRUCHIO [aside to Hortensio]
    Hortensio, say thou wilt see the tailor paid.
    [To Tailor] Go, take it hence. Begone, and say no more.
HORTENSIO [aside to the Tailor]
    Tailor, I'll pay thee for thy gown tomorrow.
    Take no unkindness of his hasty words.
    Away, I say. Commend me to thy master.
                                        Exit Tailor.
PETRUCHIO
    Well, come, my Kate. We will unto your father's
    Even in these honest, mean habiliments.   166
    Our purses shall be proud, our garments poor,
    For 'tis the mind that makes the body rich;
    And as the sun breaks through the darkest clouds,

93 **like** likely   96 **Marry . . remembered** I did indeed. But if you recollect   98 **hop . . . home** hop on home over every street gutter   102 **quaint** elegant   103 **Belike** Perhaps   106–10 **thou thread . . . remnant** Petruchio attacks the tailor's proverbial thinness and effeminacy using metaphors from tailoring.   107 **nail** a measure of length for cloth: 2 ¼ inches.   108 **nit** louse egg   109 **Braved** Defied.   **with** by   110 **quantity** fragment   111 **be-mete** measure, i.e., thrash.   **yard** yardstick   112 **think on prating** i.e., remember this thrashing and think twice before talking so again   117 **stuff** material.
121 **faced** trimmed, decked   123 **Face** Bully.   **braved** dressed finely   124 **brave** defy   126 **Ergo** Therefore

129 **lies in 's throat** i.e., lies utterly   130 **Imprimis** First   131 **loose-bodied gown** (Grumio plays on *loose*, "wanton"; a gown fit for a prostitute.)   133 **bottom** i.e., ball or skein. (A weaver's term for the bobbin.)   135 **compassed** flared, cut on the bias so as to fall in a circle   137 **trunk** full, wide   139 **curiously** elaborately   143 **prove upon thee** prove by fighting you   145–6 **in place where** in a suitable place   147 **bill** (1) the note ordering the gown (2) a weapon, a halberd   148 **mete-yard** measuring stick   149 **God-a-mercy** Thanks   150 **no odds** no advantage. (The contest between Grumio and the Tailor will be evenly matched.)   153 **take it up** take it away.   **use** i.e., whatever use he can make of it. (But Grumio deliberately misinterprets both expressions in a bawdy sense.)   156 **conceit** idea   157 **deeper** more serious. (But continuing the sexual idea of lifting up the dress and entering for sexual "use," as in lines 155 and 158.)   166 **honest, mean habiliments** respectable, plain clothes.

So honor peereth in the meanest habit.   170
What, is the jay more precious than the lark
Because his feathers are more beautiful?
Or is the adder better than the eel
Because his painted skin contents the eye?   174
Oh, no, good Kate; neither art thou the worse
For this poor furniture and mean array.   176
If thou account'st it shame, lay it on me.
And therefore frolic; we will hence forthwith,
To feast and sport us at thy father's house.
[*To Grumio*] Go call my men, and let us straight
    to him;
And bring our horses unto Long Lane end.
There will we mount, and thither walk on foot.
Let's see, I think 'tis now some seven o'clock,
And well we may come there by dinnertime.   184

KATHARINA
I dare assure you, sir, 'tis almost two,
And 'twill be suppertime ere you come there.

PETRUCHIO
It shall be seven ere I go to horse.
Look what I speak, or do, or think to do,   188
You are still crossing it.—Sirs, let 't alone.   189
I will not go today, and ere I do,
It shall be what o'clock I say it is.

HORTENSIO [*aside*]
Why, so this gallant will command the sun.   192

                                            [*Exeunt.*]

                         ❖

[4.4]

Enter Tranio [as Lucentio], and the Pedant
dressed like Vincentio [booted].

TRANIO
Sir, this is the house. Please it you that I call?

PEDANT
Ay, what else? And but I be deceived,   2
Signor Baptista may remember me,   3
Near twenty years ago, in Genoa—   4

TRANIO
Where we were lodgers at the Pegasus.—   5
'Tis well; and hold your own in any case   6
With such austerity as 'longeth to a father.

Enter Biondello.

PEDANT
I warrant you. But, sir, here comes your boy.
'Twere good he were schooled.   9

TRANIO
Fear you not him.—Sirrah Biondello,
Now do your duty throughly, I advise you.   11
Imagine 'twere the right Vincentio.   12

BIONDELLO   Tut, fear not me.   13

TRANIO
But hast thou done thy errand to Baptista?

BIONDELLO
I told him that your father was at Venice
And that you looked for him this day in Padua.

TRANIO [*giving money*]
Thou'rt a tall fellow. Hold thee that to drink.   17
Here comes Baptista. Set your countenance, sir.   18

    Enter Baptista, and Lucentio [as Cambio].
    [The] Pedant [stands] bareheaded.

Signor Baptista, you are happily met.   19
[*To the Pedant*] Sir, this is the gentleman I told you of.
I pray you, stand good father to me now;
Give me Bianca for my patrimony.

PEDANT   Soft, son!—   23
Sir, by your leave, having come to Padua
To gather in some debts, my son Lucentio
Made me acquainted with a weighty cause
Of love between your daughter and himself;
And, for the good report I hear of you   28
And for the love he beareth to your daughter
And she to him, to stay him not too long,   30
I am content, in a good father's care,
To have him matched. And if you please to like   32
No worse than I, upon some agreement
Me shall you find ready and willing
With one consent to have her so bestowed;   35
For curious I cannot be with you,   36
Signor Baptista, of whom I hear so well.

BAPTISTA
Sir, pardon me in what I have to say.
Your plainness and your shortness please me well.
Right true it is your son Lucentio here
Doth love my daughter, and she loveth him,
Or both dissemble deeply their affections.
And therefore, if you say no more than this,
That like a father you will deal with him
And pass my daughter a sufficient dower,   45
The match is made, and all is done.
Your son shall have my daughter with consent.

TRANIO
I thank you, sir. Where then do you know best   48
We be affied and such assurance ta'en   49
As shall with either part's agreement stand?   50

---

170 **peereth . . . habit** peeps through the humblest attire.
174 **painted** colorfully patterned   176 **furniture** furnishings of attire
184 **dinnertime** i.e., about noon.   188 **Look what** Whatever
189 **still crossing** always contradicting or defying   192 **so** at this rate
4.4. **Location: Padua. Before Baptista's house.**
0.2 *booted* (signifying travel)   2 **but** unless   3–4 **Signor . . . Genoa**
(The Pedant rehearses what he is to say.)   5 **Where . . . Pegasus**
(Tranio is coaching the Pedant in further details of his story.)   **the**
Pegasus i.e., an inn, so named after the famous winged horse of classical myth.   6 **hold your own** play your part   9 **schooled** i.e.,
rehearsed in his part.

11 **throughly** thoroughly   12 **right** real   13 **fear not me** don't worry
about my doing my part   17 **tall** fine.   **Hold . . . drink** Take that and
buy a drink.   18 **Set your countenance** i.e., Put on the expression of
an austere father (line 7).   19 **happily** fortunately   23 **Soft** i.e.,
Steady, take it easy   28 **for** because of   30 **to stay him not** not to
keep him waiting   32 **like** i.e., approve of the match   35 **one** i.e.,
firm   36 **curious** overly particular   45 **pass** settle on, give
48–50 **Where . . . stand?** Where in your view is the best place for
us to be betrothed and for legal assurances to be made that will
confirm an agreement satisfactory to both parties?

BAPTISTA
Not in my house, Lucentio, for you know
Pitchers have ears, and I have many servants.
Besides, old Gremio is heark'ning still,   53
And happily we might be interrupted.   54
TRANIO
Then at my lodging, an it like you.   55
There doth my father lie, and there this night   56
We'll pass the business privately and well.   57
Send for your daughter by your servant here.
         [He indicates Lucentio, and winks at him.]
My boy shall fetch the scrivener presently.   59
The worst is this, that at so slender warning
You are like to have a thin and slender pittance.   61
BAPTISTA
It likes me well. Cambio, hie you home,
And bid Bianca make her ready straight.
And if you will, tell what hath happened:
Lucentio's father is arrived in Padua,
And how she's like to be Lucentio's wife.
                                    [Exit Lucentio.]
BIONDELLO
I pray the gods she may with all my heart!
TRANIO
Dally not with the gods, but get thee gone.
                              Exit [Biondello].
Signor Baptista, shall I lead the way?
Welcome! One mess is like to be your cheer.   70
Come, sir, we will better it in Pisa.
BAPTISTA   I follow you.   72
                Exeunt [Tranio, Pedant, and Baptista].

        Enter Lucentio [as Cambio] and Biondello.

BIONDELLO   Cambio!
LUCENTIO   What say'st thou, Biondello?
BIONDELLO   You saw my master wink and laugh upon
you?
LUCENTIO   Biondello, what of that?
BIONDELLO   Faith, nothing; but he's left me here behind
to expound the meaning or moral of his signs and to-   79
kens.
LUCENTIO   I pray thee, moralize them.   81
BIONDELLO   Then thus. Baptista is safe, talking with   82
the deceiving father of a deceitful son.
LUCENTIO   And what of him?
BIONDELLO   His daughter is to be brought by you to
the supper.
LUCENTIO   And then?
BIONDELLO   The old priest at Saint Luke's church is at
your command at all hours.
LUCENTIO   And what of all this?

BIONDELLO   I cannot tell, except they are busied about a   91
counterfeit assurance. Take you assurance of her   92
cum privilegio ad imprimendum solum. To th'   93
church take the priest, clerk, and some sufficient hon-   94
est witnesses.
If this be not that you look for, I have no more to say,   96
But bid Bianca farewell forever and a day.
                          [Biondello starts to leave.]
LUCENTIO   Hear'st thou, Biondello?
BIONDELLO   I cannot tarry. I knew a wench married in
an afternoon as she went to the garden for parsley to
stuff a rabbit, and so may you, sir. And so, adieu, sir.
My master hath appointed me to go to Saint Luke's, to
bid the priest be ready to come against you come with   103
your appendix.   *Exit*.   104
LUCENTIO
I may, and will, if she be so contented.
She will be pleased; then wherefore should I doubt?
Hap what hap may, I'll roundly go about her.   107
It shall go hard if Cambio go without her.   *Exit*. 108

                        ✦

[4.5]

        Enter Petruchio, Kate, [and] Hortensio.

PETRUCHIO
Come on, i'God's name, once more toward our father's.   1
Good Lord, how bright and goodly shines the moon!
KATHARINA
The moon? The sun. It is not moonlight now.
PETRUCHIO
I say it is the moon that shines so bright.
KATHARINA
I know it is the sun that shines so bright.
PETRUCHIO
Now, by my mother's son, and that's myself,
It shall be moon, or star, or what I list   7
Or ere I journey to your father's house.—   8
Go on, and fetch our horses back again—
Evermore crossed and crossed, nothing but crossed!
HORTENSIO [*to Katharina*]
Say as he says, or we shall never go.
KATHARINA
Forward, I pray, since we have come so far,
And be it moon, or sun, or what you please;
An if you please to call it a rush candle,   14

91 except unless   92 counterfeit assurance pretended betrothal
agreement.   Take . . . of her Legalize your claim to her (by marriage)
93 cum . . . solum with exclusive printing rights. (A copyright formula
often appearing on the title pages of books, here jokingly applied to
the marriage and to procreation as an act of imprinting.)   94 sufficient meeting the legal requirement in number and social standing
96 that you look for what you are looking for   103 against you come
in anticipation of your arrival   104 appendix something appended,
i.e., the bride. (Continuing the metaphor of printing.)   107 roundly . . .
her set about marrying her in no uncertain terms.   108 It . . . her i.e.,
I'm determined to have her. (With pun about erection.)
4.5. Location: A road on the way to Padua.
1 our father's our father's house.   7 list please   8 Or ere before
14 a rush candle a rush dipped into tallow; hence a very feeble light

53 hearkening still continually listening   54 happily haply   55 an it
like if it please   56 lie lodge   57 pass transact   59 scrivener notary,
one to draw up contracts.   presently at once.   61 like likely.
slender pittance i.e., scanty banquet.   70 mess dish.   cheer entertainment.   72.1 Exeunt (Technically, the cleared stage may mark a
new scene, but the conversation of Lucentio and Biondello suggests
that they come creeping back on stage as the others leave rather than
doing the errands Baptista and Tranio bid them.)   79 moral hidden
meaning   81 moralize elucidate   82 safe i.e., safely out of the way

Henceforth I vow it shall be so for me.

PETRUCHIO
I say it is the moon.

KATHARINA   I know it is the moon.

PETRUCHIO
Nay, then you lie. It is the blessèd sun.

KATHARINA
Then, God be blessed, it is the blessèd sun.
But, sun it is not, when you say it is not,
And the moon changes even as your mind.
What you will have it named, even that it is,
And so it shall be so for Katharine.

HORTENSIO
Petruchio, go thy ways. The field is won.   23

PETRUCHIO
Well, forward, forward. Thus the bowl should run,
And not unluckily against the bias.   25
But soft! Company is coming here.

           Enter Vincentio.

[*To Vincentio*] Good morrow, gentle mistress. Where
    away?—   27
Tell me, sweet Kate, and tell me truly too,
Hast thou beheld a fresher gentlewoman?
Such war of white and red within her cheeks!
What stars do spangle heaven with such beauty
As those two eyes become that heavenly face?—
Fair lovely maid, once more good day to thee.—
Sweet Kate, embrace her for her beauty's sake.

HORTENSIO [*aside*]
'A will make the man mad, to make a woman of him.   35

KATHARINA [*embracing Vincentio*]
Young budding virgin, fair, and fresh, and sweet,
Whither away, or where is thy abode?
Happy the parents of so fair a child!
Happier the man whom favorable stars
Allots thee for his lovely bedfellow!   40

PETRUCHIO
Why, how now, Kate? I hope thou art not mad.
This is a man, old, wrinkled, faded, withered,
And not a maiden, as thou say'st he is.

KATHARINA
Pardon, old father, my mistaking eyes,
That have been so bedazzled with the sun   46
That everything I look on seemeth green.
Now I perceive thou art a reverend father.
Pardon, I pray thee, for my mad mistaking.

PETRUCHIO
Do, good old grandsire, and withal make known
Which way thou travelest—if along with us,
We shall be joyful of thy company.

VINCENTIO
Fair sir, and you, my merry mistress,
That with your strange encounter much amazed me,

My name is called Vincentio, my dwelling Pisa,
And bound I am to Padua, there to visit
A son of mine, which long I have not seen.

PETRUCHIO
What is his name?

VINCENTIO   Lucentio, gentle sir.

PETRUCHIO
Happily met, the happier for thy son.
And now by law as well as reverend age
I may entitle thee my loving father.
The sister to my wife, this gentlewoman,
Thy son by this hath married. Wonder not,   62
Nor be not grieved. She is of good esteem,   63
Her dowry wealthy, and of worthy birth;
Besides, so qualified as may beseem   65
The spouse of any noble gentleman.
Let me embrace with old Vincentio,
And wander we to see thy honest son,   68
Who will of thy arrival be full joyous.
                              [*He embraces Vincentio.*]

VINCENTIO
But is this true? Or is it else your pleasure,
Like pleasant travelers, to break a jest   71
Upon the company you overtake?

HORTENSIO
I do assure thee, father, so it is.

PETRUCHIO
Come, go along, and see the truth hereof,
For our first merriment hath made thee jealous.   75
                              Exeunt [all but Hortensio].

HORTENSIO
Well, Petruchio, this has put me in heart.   76
Have to my widow! And if she be froward,   77
Then hast thou taught Hortensio to be untoward.   78
                                                    Exit.

                         ❧

[5.1]

*Enter Biondello, Lucentio [no longer disguised],
and Bianca. Gremio is out before [and stands
aside].*

BIONDELLO Softly and swiftly, sir, for the priest is
    ready.

LUCENTIO I fly, Biondello. But they may chance to need
    thee at home; therefore leave us.

BIONDELLO Nay, faith, I'll see the church a' your back,   5
    and then come back to my master's as soon as I can.
                 [*Exeunt Lucentio, Bianca, and Biondello.*]

---

62 by this by this time   **63 esteem** reputation   **65 so qualified** having
such qualities.   **beseem** befit   **68 wander** go (having changed plans)
71 pleasant humorous, jocular.   **break a jest** play a practical joke
75 jealous suspicious.   **76 put me in heart** encouraged me.   **77 Have
to** i.e., Now for.   **froward** perverse   **78 untoward** unmannerly.
5.1. Location: Padua. Before Lucentio's house.
0.2 out before i.e., onstage first. (Gremio does not see Biondello,
Lucentio, and Bianca as they steal to church, or else he does not
recognize Lucentio in his own person.)   **5 a' your back** at your
back, behind you. (Biondello first wants to see them in church
and safely married.)

---

23 go thy ways i.e., well done, carry on.   **25 against the bias** off its
proper course. (The *bias* is an off-center weight in a bowling ball
enabling the bowler to roll the ball in an oblique or curving path.)
27 Where away? Where are you going?   **35 'A** He   **40 Allots** allot
46 green young and fresh.

GREMIO
I marvel Cambio comes not all this while.

Enter Petruchio, Kate, Vincentio, Grumio, with attendants.

PETRUCHIO
Sir, here's the door. This is Lucentio's house.
My father's bears more toward the marketplace;   9
Thither must I, and here I leave you, sir.

VINCENTIO
You shall not choose but drink before you go.   11
I think I shall command your welcome here,
And by all likelihood some cheer is toward.   *Knock.* 13

GREMIO *[advancing]* They're busy within. You were
best knock louder.   15

Pedant looks out of the window.

PEDANT What's he that knocks as he would beat down
the gate?

VINCENTIO Is Signor Lucentio within, sir?

PEDANT He's within, sir, but not to be spoken withal. 19

VINCENTIO What if a man bring him a hundred pound
or two to make merry withal?

PEDANT Keep your hundred pounds to yourself. He
shall need none, so long as I live.

PETRUCHIO *[to Vincentio]* Nay, I told you your son was
well beloved in Padua.—Do you hear, sir? To leave
frivolous circumstances, I pray you, tell Signor Lucen- 26
tio that his father is come from Pisa and is here at the
door to speak with him.

PEDANT Thou liest. His father is come from Padua and 29
here looking out at the window.

VINCENTIO Art thou his father?

PEDANT Ay, sir, so his mother says, if I may believe
her.

PETRUCHIO *[to Vincentio]* Why, how now, gentleman!
Why, this is flat knavery, to take upon you another 35
man's name.

PEDANT Lay hands on the villain. I believe 'a means to
cozen somebody in this city under my countenance.   38

Enter Biondello.

BIONDELLO *[aside]* I have seen them in the church
together, God send 'em good shipping! But who is
here? Mine old master Vincentio! Now we are undone 40
and brought to nothing.

VINCENTIO *[seeing Biondello]* Come hither, crackhemp. 43

BIONDELLO I hope I may choose, sir.   44

VINCENTIO Come hither, you rogue. What, have you
forgot me?

BIONDELLO Forgot you? No, sir. I could not forget you,
for I never saw you before in all my life.

VINCENTIO What, you notorious villain, didst thou
never see thy master's father, Vincentio?

BIONDELLO What, my old worshipful old master? Yes,
marry, sir, see where he looks out of the window.

VINCENTIO Is't so, indeed?   *He beats Biondello.*

BIONDELLO Help, help, help! Here's a madman will
murder me.   *[Exit.]*

PEDANT Help, son! Help, Signor Baptista!
                              [Exit from the window.]

PETRUCHIO Prithee, Kate, let's stand aside and see the
end of this controversy.   *[They stand aside.]*

*Enter [below] Pedant with servants, Baptista,
[and] Tranio [as Lucentio].*

TRANIO Sir, what are you that offer to beat my servant? 59

VINCENTIO What am I, sir? Nay, what are you, sir? O
immortal gods! Oh, fine villain! A silken doublet, a velvet hose, a scarlet cloak, and a copintank hat! Oh, I am 62
undone, I am undone! While I play the good husband 63
at home, my son and my servant spend all at the university.

TRANIO How now, what's the matter?

BAPTISTA What, is the man lunatic?

TRANIO Sir, you seem a sober ancient gentleman by
your habit, but your words show you a madman.   69
Why, sir, what 'cerns it you if I wear pearl and gold? 70
I thank my good father, I am able to maintain it.   71

VINCENTIO Thy father! Oh, villain, he is a sailmaker in
Bergamo.

BAPTISTA You mistake, sir, you mistake, sir. Pray, what
do you think is his name?

VINCENTIO His name! As if I knew not his name! I have
brought him up ever since he was three years old, and
his name is Tranio.

PEDANT Away, away, mad ass! His name is Lucentio,
and he is mine only son, and heir to the lands of me,
Signor Vincentio.

VINCENTIO Lucentio! Oh, he hath murdered his master!
Lay hold on him, I charge you, in the Duke's name.
Oh, my son, my son! Tell me, thou villain, where is my
son Lucentio?

TRANIO Call forth an officer.

[Enter an Officer.]

Carry this mad knave to the jail. Father Baptista, I
charge you see that he be forthcoming.   88

VINCENTIO Carry me to the jail?

GREMIO Stay, officer, he shall not go to prison.

BAPTISTA Talk not, Signor Gremio. I say he shall go to
prison.

---

9 father's i.e., father-in-law's, Baptista's. **bears** lies. (A nautical
term.) **11 You . . . but** i.e., I insist that **13 cheer is toward** entertainment is in prospect. **15.1 window** i.e., probably the gallery to the
rear, over the stage. **19 withal** with. **26 circumstances** matters
29 from Padua i.e., from Padua, where we are right now. (Often
emended to "from Mantua," "from Pisa," "to Padua," etc.)
35 flat downright **38 cozen** cheat. **under my countenance** by pretending to be me. **40 good shipping** bon voyage, good fortune.
43 crackhemp i.e., rogue likely to end up being hanged. **44 choose**
do as I choose

59 offer dare, presume **62 copintank** high-crowned, sugar-loaf
shape **63 good husband** careful provider, manager **69 habit** clothing **70 'cerns** concerns **71 maintain** afford **88 forthcoming** ready
to stand trial when required.

GREMIO   Take heed, Signor Baptista, lest you be coney-   93
catched in this business. I dare swear this is the right   94
Vincentio.

PEDANT   Swear, if thou dar'st.

GREMIO   Nay, I dare not swear it.

TRANIO   Then thou wert best say that I am not Lucentio.   98

GREMIO   Yes, I know thee to be Signor Lucentio.

BAPTISTA   Away with the dotard! To the jail with him!

Enter Biondello, Lucentio, and Bianca.

VINCENTIO   Thus strangers may be haled and abused.   101
—Oh, monstrous villain!

BIONDELLO   Oh! We are spoiled and—yonder he is.   103
Deny him, forswear him, or else we are all undone.
*Exeunt Biondello, Tranio, and Pedant as fast as
may be. [Lucentio and Bianca] kneel.*

LUCENTIO
Pardon, sweet father.

VINCENTIO   Lives my sweet son?

BIANCA
Pardon, dear father.

BAPTISTA   How hast thou offended?
Where is Lucentio?

LUCENTIO   Here's Lucentio,
Right son to the right Vincentio,
That have by marriage made thy daughter mine,
While counterfeit supposes bleared thine eyne.   110

GREMIO
Here's packing, with a witness, to deceive us all!   111

VINCENTIO
Where is that damnèd villain Tranio,
That faced and braved me in this matter so?   113

BAPTISTA
Why, tell me, is not this my Cambio?

BIANCA
Cambio is changed into Lucentio.   115

LUCENTIO
Love wrought these miracles. Bianca's love
Made me exchange my state with Tranio,   117
While he did bear my countenance in the town,   118
And happily I have arrivèd at the last
Unto the wishèd haven of my bliss.
What Tranio did, myself enforced him to;
Then pardon him, sweet father, for my sake.

VINCENTIO   I'll slit the villain's nose, that would have
sent me to the jail.

BAPTISTA   [*to Lucentio*] But do you hear, sir? Have you
married my daughter without asking my good will?

VINCENTIO   Fear not, Baptista, we will content you. Go   127
to. But I will in, to be revenged for this villainy.   128
Exit.

BAPTISTA   And I, to sound the depth of this knavery.
Exit.

LUCENTIO   Look not pale, Bianca. Thy father will not
frown.   *Exeunt [Lucentio and Bianca].*

GREMIO
My cake is dough, but I'll in among the rest,   132
Out of hope of all but my share of the feast.   [*Exit.*] 133

KATHARINA   Husband, let's follow, to see the end of
this ado.

PETRUCHIO   First kiss me, Kate, and we will.

KATHARINA   What, in the midst of the street?

PETRUCHIO   What, art thou ashamed of me?

KATHARINA   No, sir, God forbid, but ashamed to kiss.

PETRUCHIO
Why, then let's home again. [*To Grumio*] Come, sirrah,
let's away.

KATHARINA
Nay, I will give thee a kiss. [*She kisses him.*] Now pray
thee, love, stay.

PETRUCHIO
Is not this well? Come, my sweet Kate.
Better once than never, for never too late.   *Exeunt.* 143

❖

5.[2]

*Enter Baptista, Vincentio, Gremio, the Pedant,
Lucentio, and Bianca; [Petruchio, Kate, Hortensio,] Tranio, Biondello, Grumio, and [the]
Widow; the servingmen with Tranio bringing
in a banquet.*

LUCENTIO
At last, though long, our jarring notes agree,   1
And time it is, when raging war is done,
To smile at scapes and perils overblown.   3
My fair Bianca, bid my father welcome,
While I with selfsame kindness welcome thine.
Brother Petruchio, sister Katharina,
And thou, Hortensio, with thy loving widow,
Feast with the best, and welcome to my house.
My banquet is to close our stomachs up   9
After our great good cheer. Pray you, sit down,   10
For now we sit to chat as well as eat.   [*They sit.*]

PETRUCHIO
Nothing but sit and sit, and eat and eat!

BAPTISTA
Padua affords this kindness, son Petruchio.

PETRUCHIO
Padua affords nothing but what is kind.

93–4 coney-catched tricked   **98 wert best** might as well
101 haled hauled about, maltreated   **103 spoiled** ruined   **110 supposes** suppositions, false appearances. (With an allusion to Gascoigne's *Supposes*, an adaptation of *I Suppositi* by Ariosto, from
which Shakespeare took the Lucentio-Bianca plot of intrigue.)
eyne eyes.   **111 Here's . . . all!** Here's evidence of a conspiracy, no
mistake about it!   **113 faced and braved** stood up to and defied
115 Cambio is changed (A pun. *Cambio* in Italian means "change"
or "exchange.")   **117 state** social station   **118 countenance** appearance, identity

127–8 Go to i.e., Don't worry. (An expression of impatience or annoyance.)   **132 My . . . dough** i.e., I'm out of luck, I failed
133 Out . . . but having hope for nothing other than   **143 once** at
some time. (Compare with "better late than never.")
5.2. Location: Padua. Lucentio's house.
1 long after long time   **3 scapes** close calls   **9 stomachs** (1) appetites
(2) quarrels   **10 cheer** i.e., wedding feast.

HORTENSIO
For both our sakes, I would that word were true.

PETRUCHIO
Now, for my life, Hortensio fears his widow.   16

WIDOW
Then never trust me if I be afeard.   17

PETRUCHIO
You are very sensible, and yet you miss my sense:
I mean Hortensio is afeard of you.

WIDOW
He that is giddy thinks the world turns round.

PETRUCHIO
Roundly replied.

KATHARINA   Mistress, how mean you that?   21

WIDOW   Thus I conceive by him.   22

PETRUCHIO
Conceives by me! How likes Hortensio that?

HORTENSIO
My widow says, thus she conceives her tale.   24

PETRUCHIO
Very well mended. Kiss him for that, good widow.

KATHARINA
"He that is giddy thinks the world turns round":
I pray you, tell me what you meant by that.

WIDOW
Your husband, being troubled with a shrew,
Measures my husband's sorrow by his woe.
And now you know my meaning.   29

KATHARINA
A very mean meaning.

WIDOW   Right, I mean you.   31

KATHARINA
And I am mean indeed, respecting you.   32

PETRUCHIO   To her, Kate!   33

HORTENSIO   To her, widow!

PETRUCHIO
A hundred marks, my Kate does put her down.   35

HORTENSIO   That's my office.

PETRUCHIO
Spoke like an officer. Ha' to thee, lad!   37

                    [He] drinks to Hortensio.

BAPTISTA
How likes Gremio these quick-witted folks?

GREMIO
Believe me, sir, they butt together well.   39

BIANCA
Head, and butt! An hasty-witted body   40
Would say your head and butt were head and horn.   41

VINCENTIO
Ay, mistress bride, hath that awakened you?

BIANCA
Ay, but not frighted me. Therefore I'll sleep again.

PETRUCHIO
Nay, that you shall not. Since you have begun,
Have at you for a bitter jest or two!   45

BIANCA
Am I your bird? I mean to shift my bush;   46
And then pursue me as you draw your bow.
You are welcome all.
        Exit Bianca [with Katharina and the Widow].

PETRUCHIO
She hath prevented me. Here, Signor Tranio,   49
This bird you aimed at, though you hit her not.   50
Therefore a health to all that shot and missed.   51
                        [He offers a toast.]

TRANIO
Oh, sir, Lucentio slipped me like his greyhound,
Which runs himself and catches for his master.   52

PETRUCHIO
A good swift simile, but something currish.   54

TRANIO
'Tis well, sir, that you hunted for yourself.
'Tis thought your deer does hold you at a bay.   56

BAPTISTA
Oho, Petruchio! Tranio hits you now.

LUCENTIO
I thank thee for that gird, good Tranio.   58

HORTENSIO
Confess, confess, hath he not hit you here?

PETRUCHIO
'A has a little galled me, I confess;   60
And as the jest did glance away from me,
'Tis ten to one it maimed you two outright.

BAPTISTA
Now, in good sadness, son Petruchio,   63
I think thou hast the veriest shrew of all.

PETRUCHIO
Well, I say no. And therefore for assurance   65
Let's each one send unto his wife;
And he whose wife is most obedient
To come at first when he doth send for her
Shall win the wager which we will propose.

HORTENSIO
Content. What's the wager?

LUCENTIO   Twenty crowns.

PETRUCHIO   Twenty crowns!
I'll venture so much of my hawk or hound,   72
But twenty times so much upon my wife.

---

16 **for my life** upon my life. **fears** is afraid of   17 **afeard** frightened (by Hortensio)   21 **Roundly** Boldly, bluntly   22 **Thus . . . him** i.e., That's what I think of him, Petruchio. (But Petruchio takes up *conceives* in the sense of "is made pregnant.")   24 **conceives** intends, interprets. (With a possible pun on *tale* and "tail.")   29 **his** his own   31 **very mean** contemptible. (But the Widow takes up *mean* in the sense of "have in mind," and Kate replies in the sense of "moderate in shrewishness.")   32 **respecting** compared to   33 **To her** (A cry used to egg on fighting roosters.)   35 **marks** coins worth thirteen shillings four pence. **put her down** overcome her. (But Hortensio takes up the phrase in a bawdy sense.)   37 **officer** (playing on Hortensio's speaking of his *office* or function.)   **Ha'** Have, i.e., Here's   39 **butt** butt heads   40 **An hasty-witted body** A quick-witted person   41 **head and horn** (Alluding to the familiar joke about cuckolds' horns.)

45 **Have at you for** Here comes   46 **Am . . . bush** i.e., If you mean to shoot your barbs at me, I intend to move out of the way, as a bird would fly to another bush. (With a possible bawdy double meaning; *bush* can suggest pubic hair.)   49 **prevented** forestalled   50 **This bird** i.e., Bianca, whom Tranio courted (*aimed at*) in his disguise as Lucentio   51 **a health** a toast   52 **slipped** unleashed   54 **swift** (1) quick-witted (2) concerning swiftness.   **currish** (1) ignoble (2) concerning dogs.   56 **deer** (Punning on "dear.")   **does . . . bay** turns on you like a cornered animal and holds you at a distance.   58 **gird** sharp, biting jest   60 **galled** scratched, chafed   63 **sadness** seriousness   65 **assurance** proof   72 **of** on

LUCENTIO   A hundred then.
HORTENSIO   Content.
PETRUCHIO   A match. 'Tis done.
HORTENSIO   Who shall begin?
LUCENTIO   That will I.
Go, Biondello, bid your mistress come to me.
BIONDELLO   I go.   *Exit.*
BAPTISTA
Son, I'll be your half Bianca comes.   81
LUCENTIO
I'll have no halves; I'll bear it all myself.

        Enter Biondello.

How now, what news?
BIONDELLO
Sir, my mistress sends you word
That she is busy and she cannot come.
PETRUCHIO
How? She's busy and she cannot come?
Is that an answer?
GREMIO   Ay, and a kind one too.
Pray God, sir, your wife send you not a worse.
PETRUCHIO   I hope better.
HORTENSIO
Sirrah Biondello, go and entreat my wife
To come to me forthwith.   *Exit Biondello.*
PETRUCHIO   Oho, entreat her!
Nay, then she must needs come.
HORTENSIO   I am afraid, sir,
Do what you can, yours will not be entreated.

        Enter Biondello.

Now, where's my wife?
BIONDELLO
She says you have some goodly jest in hand.
She will not come. She bids you come to her.
PETRUCHIO
Worse and worse. She will not come!
Oh, vile, intolerable, not to be endured!—
Sirrah Grumio, go to your mistress.
Say I command her come to me.   *Exit [Grumio].*
HORTENSIO
I know her answer.
PETRUCHIO   What?
HORTENSIO   She will not.
PETRUCHIO
The fouler fortune mine, and there an end.   102

        Enter Katharina.

BAPTISTA
Now, by my halidom, here comes Katharina!   103
KATHARINA
What is your will, sir, that you send for me?
PETRUCHIO
Where is your sister, and Hortensio's wife?

KATHARINA
They sit conferring by the parlor fire.
PETRUCHIO
Go fetch them hither. If they deny to come,
Swinge me them soundly forth unto their husbands.   108
Away, I say, and bring them hither straight.
                        [*Exit Katharina.*]
LUCENTIO
Here is a wonder, if you talk of a wonder.
HORTENSIO
And so it is. I wonder what it bodes.
PETRUCHIO
Marry, peace it bodes, and love, and quiet life,
An awful rule, and right supremacy,   113
And, to be short, what not that's sweet and happy.
BAPTISTA
Now, fair befall thee, good Petruchio!   115
The wager thou hast won, and I will add
Unto their losses twenty thousand crowns,
Another dowry to another daughter,
For she is changed, as she had never been.   119
PETRUCHIO
Nay, I will win my wager better yet,
And show more sign of her obedience,
Her new-built virtue and obedience.

        Enter Kate, Bianca, and [the] Widow.

See where she comes and brings your froward wives
As prisoners to her womanly persuasion.—
Katharine, that cap of yours becomes you not.
Off with that bauble. Throw it underfoot.
                                 [*She obeys.*]
WIDOW
Lord, let me never have a cause to sigh
Till I be brought to such a silly pass!   128
BIANCA
Fie, what a foolish duty call you this?
LUCENTIO
I would your duty were as foolish, too.
The wisdom of your duty, fair Bianca,
Hath cost me a hundred crowns since suppertime.
BIANCA
The more fool you, for laying on my duty.   133
PETRUCHIO
Katharine, I charge thee tell these headstrong women
What duty they do owe their lords and husbands.
WIDOW
Come, come, you're mocking. We will have no telling.
PETRUCHIO
Come on, I say, and first begin with her.
WIDOW   She shall not.
PETRUCHIO
I say she shall—and first begin with her.

---

81 **be your half** take half your bet   102 **there an end** that's that.
103 **by my halidom** (Originally an oath by the holy relics, but confused with an oath to the Virgin Mary.)

108 **Swinge** thrash.   **me** i.e., at my behest. (*Me* is used colloquially.)
113 **awful rule** authority commanding awe or respect   115 **fair befall thee** good luck to you, and congratulations   119 **as . . . been** as if she had never existed, i.e., she is totally changed.   128 **pass** state of affairs.   133 **laying** wagering

KATHARINA

> Fie, fie! Unknit that threatening, unkind brow,
> And dart not scornful glances from those eyes
> To wound thy lord, thy king, thy governor.
> It blots thy beauty as frosts do bite the meads,   143
> Confounds thy fame as whirlwinds shake fair buds,   144
> And in no sense is meet or amiable.
> A woman moved is like a fountain troubled,   146
> Muddy, ill-seeming, thick, bereft of beauty;
> And while it is so, none so dry or thirsty   148
> Will deign to sip or touch one drop of it.
> Thy husband is thy lord, thy life, thy keeper,
> Thy head, thy sovereign; one that cares for thee,
> And for thy maintenance commits his body
> To painful labor both by sea and land,   153
> To watch the night in storms, the day in cold,   154
> Whilst thou liest warm at home, secure and safe;
> And craves no other tribute at thy hands
> But love, fair looks, and true obedience—
> Too little payment for so great a debt.
> Such duty as the subject owes the prince,
> Even such a woman oweth to her husband;
> And when she is froward, peevish, sullen, sour,   161
> And not obedient to his honest will,   162
> What is she but a foul contending rebel
> And graceless traitor to her loving lord?
> I am ashamed that women are so simple   165
> To offer war where they should kneel for peace,
> Or seek for rule, supremacy, and sway,
> When they are bound to serve, love, and obey.
> Why are our bodies soft, and weak, and smooth,
> Unapt to toil and trouble in the world,   170
> But that our soft conditions and our hearts   171
> Should well agree with our external parts?

> Come, come, you froward and unable worms!   173
> My mind hath been as big as one of yours,   174
> My heart as great, my reason haply more,
> To bandy word for word and frown for frown;
> But now I see our lances but straws,
> Our strength as weak, our weakness past compare,   178
> That seeming to be most which we indeed least are.   179
> Then vail your stomachs, for it is no boot,   180
> And place your hands below your husband's foot,
> In token of which duty, if he please,
> My hand is ready; may it do him ease.   183

PETRUCHIO

> Why, there's a wench! Come on, and kiss me, Kate.

[They kiss.]

LUCENTIO

> Well, go thy ways, old lad, for thou shalt ha 't.   185

VINCENTIO

> 'Tis a good hearing when children are toward.   186

LUCENTIO

> But a harsh hearing when women are froward.

PETRUCHIO   Come, Kate, we'll to bed.
> We three are married, but you two are sped.   189
> _[To Lucentio]_ 'Twas I won the wager, though you hit
>   the white,   190
> And, being a winner, God give you good night!   191

Exit Petruchio [with Katharina].

HORTENSIO

> Now go thy ways. Thou hast tamed a curst shrew.   192

LUCENTIO

> 'Tis a wonder, by your leave, she will be tamed so.

[Exeunt.]

143 **meads** meadows   144 **Confounds thy fame** ruins your reputation   146 **moved** angry   148 **none . . . thirsty** there is no one so thirsty that he   153 **painful** onerous   154 **watch** stay awake throughout   161 **peevish** obstinate   162 **to his honest will** (Kate may suggest that she will be obedient when his will is decent and virtuous, not that his will is always so.)   165 **simple** foolish   170 **Unapt to** unfit for   171 **conditions** qualities

173 **unable worms** i.e., poor feeble creatures.   174 **big** haughty   178 **as weak** i.e., as weak as straws   179 **That seeming to be** seeming to be that   180 **Then . . . boot** Then lower your pride, for it is no use striving   183 **do him ease** give him pleasure.   185 **go thy ways** well done.   **ha 't** have it, the prize.   186 **'Tis . . . toward** i.e., One likes to hear when children are obedient.   189 **We . . . sped** i.e., All we three men have taken wives, but you two are done for (*sped*) through disobedient wives.   190 **the white** the center of the target. (With quibble on the name of Bianca, which in Italian means "white.")   191 **being** since I am   192 **shrew** pronounced "shrow" (and thus spelled in the Folio). See also 4.1.198 and 5.2.28.

A Midsummer Night's Dream

One of the many astonishing achievements in *A Midsummer Night's Dream* (c. 1594–1595) is its development of the motif of love as an imaginative journey from a world of social conflict into a fantasy world created by the artist, ending in a return to a reality that has itself been partly transformed by the experience of the journey. As the lovers in this play flee from the Athenian law to lose themselves in the forest, they reveal and discover in themselves the simultaneously hilarious and horrifying effects of sexual desire. Moreover, their journey suggests the extent to which love or desire is itself an act of imagination, not unlike the imagination that underlies the creation of art. The fifth act especially invites us to see theatrical experience as like a dream, at times nightmarish but at its best an emancipating foray into an imagined space wholly beyond the realm of ordinary human happenings. Shakespeare gives us an earlier hint of an imaginary sylvan landscape in *The Two Gentlemen of Verona*, but not until *A Midsummer Night's Dream* is the idea fully realized. The motif of contrasting worlds, one of social convention and the other of visionary fantasy, will remain an enduring preoccupation of Shakespeare to the very last. This visionary world haunts the imagination with some of the most poetic passages of the entire Shakespeare canon, from Titania's evocation of her bond of affection with her votaress "in the spicèd Indian air by night" (2.1.123–37) to Oberon's memory of a mermaid singing on a dolphin's back (2.1.150–4). Containing the highest percentage of rhymed verse in all of Shakespeare's plays, *A Midsummer Night's Dream* calls attention to the seemingly magical capacity of words to weave spells not only on the characters but on the audience as well.

In construction, *A Midsummer Night's Dream* is a skillful interweaving of four plots involving four groups of characters: the court party of Theseus, the four young lovers, the fairies, and the "rude mechanicals" or would-be actors. Felix Mendelssohn's incidental music for the play evokes the contrasting textures of the various groups: Theseus's hunting horns and ceremonial wedding marches, the lovers' soaring and throbbing melodies, the fairies' pianissimo staccato, the tradesmen's clownish bassoon. Moreover, each plot is derived from its own set of source materials. The action involving Theseus and Hippolyta, for example, owes several details to Thomas North's translation (1579) of Plutarch's *Lives of the Noble Grecians and Romans*, to Chaucer's *Knight's Tale* and perhaps to his *Legend of Good Women*, and to Ovid's *Meta-morphoses* (in the Latin text or in Arthur Golding's popular Elizabethan translation). The lovers' story, meanwhile, is Italianate and Ovidian in tone and also, in the broadest sense, follows the conventions of plot in Plautus's and Terence's Roman comedies, although no particular source is known. Shakespeare's rich fairy lore, by contrast, is part folk tradition and part learned. For some of his material he seems to have turned to written sources, such as the French romance *Huon of Bordeaux* (translated into English by 1540), Robert Greene's play *James IV* (c. 1591), and Edmund Spenser's *The Faerie Queene*, II.i.8 (1590). Similarly, he may have taken Titania's name from the *Metamorphoses*, where it is used as an epithet for both Diana and Circe. At the same time, in his creation of Mustardseed, Cobweb, Mote, and Peaseblossom, Shakespeare also pays homage to a rich body of unwritten sources that are, for the most part, no longer accessible. Changeling children, mortals kidnapped by fairy queens, men transformed to beasts by evil spells: these were the stuff of oral tales circulated by firesides on winter nights. Finally, for Bottom the weaver and company, Shakespeare's primary inspiration was doubtless his own theatrical experience, although even here he is indebted to Ovid for the story of Pyramus and Thisbe, and probably to Apuleius's *Golden Ass* (translated by William Adlington, 1566) for Bottom's transformation.

Each of the four main plots in *A Midsummer Night's Dream* contains one or more pairs of lovers whose happiness has been frustrated by misunderstanding or parental opposition. Theseus and Hippolyta, once enemies in battle, become husband and wife; their court marriage, constituting the overplot of the play, provides a framework for other dramatic actions that similarly oscillate between conflict and harmony. In fact, Theseus's actions are instrumental in setting in motion and finally resolving the tribulations of the other characters. In the beginning of the play, for example, the lovers flee from Theseus's Athenian law; at the end, they are awakened by him from their dream. As the king and queen of fairies come to Athens to celebrate Theseus's wedding, they exchange jealous accusations: Oberon accuses his queen of being overly partial to Theseus, while she is critical of Oberon's attentions to Hippolyta. These plots of the Athenian and the fairy monarchs are drawn even more closely together by the common practice in today's theater of doubling the parts of Theseus and Oberon, Hippolyta and Titania (also, frequently, Philostrate and Puck). The broadly comic action of Bottom the Weaver and his companions is drawn into the overall design by means of their deciding to use the forest of Athens as the place where they will rehearse their performance of "Pyramus and Thisbe" in anticipation of the wedding festivities.

The tragic love story of Pyramus and Thisbe, although it seems absurdly ill suited to a wedding, reminds us of the discord and potentially fatal misunderstandings that threaten even the best of relationships between men and women. For all his graceful bearing and princely authority, Theseus is a conquering male who freely admits that he has won the love of Hippolyta with his sword, doing her "injuries" (1.1.17). He never questions that the accord between them should now be stated in terms of male ascendancy over the female. The Amazonian Hippolyta may accept with good grace the marriage she previously resisted with all her might, like Kate in *The Taming of the Shrew*, and yet, in many recent stage productions, the actress playing Hippolyta has found it easy to cast doubt on the presumed tranquility of this forthcoming marriage by a display of feminist impatience at Theseus's urbanely patriarchal ways. The reconciliation of Oberon and Titania, meanwhile, reinforces the hierarchy of male over female in no uncertain terms. Having taught Titania a lesson for trying to keep a changeling boy from him, Oberon relents and eventually frees Titania from her debasing enchantment. She does not reproach him with so much as a word when she is awakened from her "vision." Even so, the very existence of the abundantly female space of Titania's bower where, surrounded by her attendants, she has acted out desires that she thought were her own, poses an alternative to patriarchy. The four young lovers end up happily paired, but only after they have experienced rejection, rivalry, hatred, and the desire to kill; the final resolution of this plot would not be possible if Demetrius were not left under the spell of the fairy love-juice. Thus, Theseus's wedding provides a ceremonial occasion of harmony and reconciliation but in such a way as to highlight the difficulties that have beset the drama's various couples.

Despite Theseus's cheerful preoccupation with marriage, his court embodies at first a stern attitude toward young love. As administrator of the law, Theseus must accede to the remorseless demands of Hermia's father, Egeus. The inflexible Athenian law sides with parentage, age, male dominance, wealth, and position against youth and romantic choice in love. The penalties are harsh: death or perpetual virginity—and virginity is presented in this comedy (despite the nobly chaste examples of Christ, St. Paul, and Queen Elizabeth) as a fate worse than death. Egeus is a familiar type, the interfering parent found in the Roman comedy of Plautus and Terence (and in Shakespeare's *Romeo and Juliet*). Indeed, the lovers' story is distantly derived from Roman comedy, which conventionally celebrated the triumph of young love over the machinations of age and wealth. Lysander reminds us that "the course of true love never did run smooth," and he sees its enemies as being chiefly external: the conflicting interests of parents or friends; mismating with respect to years and blood; war; death; or sickness (1.1.134–42). This description clearly applies to "Pyramus and Thisbe," and it is tested by the action of *A Midsummer Night's Dream* as a whole (as well as by other early Shakespearean plays, such as *Romeo and Juliet*). The archetypal story, whether ending happily or sadly, is an evocation of love's difficulties in the face of social hostility and indifference.

While Shakespeare uses several elements of Roman comedy in setting up the basic conflicts of his drama, he also introduces important modifications from the beginning. For example, he discards one conventional confrontation of classical and neoclassical comedy, in which the heroine must choose between an old, wealthy suitor supported by her family and the young but impecunious darling of her heart. Lysander is equal to his rival in social position, income, and attractiveness. Egeus's demand, therefore—that Hermia marry Demetrius rather than Lysander—seems simply arbitrary and unjust. Shakespeare emphasizes in this way the irrationality of Egeus's harsh insistence on being obeyed and of Theseus's rather complacent acceptance of the law's inequity. Spurned by an unfeeling social order, Lysander and Hermia are compelled to elope. To be sure, in the end Egeus proves to be no formidable threat; even he must admit the logic of permitting the lovers to couple as they ultimately desire. Thus, the obstacles to love are seen from the start as fundamentally superficial and indeed almost whimsical. Egeus is as heavy a villain as we are likely to find in this *jeu d'esprit*. Moreover, the very irrationality of his position prepares the way for an ultimate resolution of the conflict. Nevertheless, by the end of the first act, the supposedly rational world of conformity and duty, by its customary insensitivity to youthful happiness, has set in motion a temporary escape to a fantasy world where the law cannot reach.

In the forest, all the lovers—including Titania and Bottom—undergo a transforming experience engineered by the mischievous Puck. This experience demonstrates the universal power of love, which can overcome the queen of fairies as readily as the lowliest of humans. It also suggests the irrational nature of love and its affinity to enchantment, witchcraft, and even madness. Love is seen as an affliction taken in through the frail senses, particularly the eyes. When it strikes, the victim cannot choose but to embrace the object of his or her infatuation. By his amusing miscalculations, Puck shuffles the four lovers through various permutations with mathematical predictability. First, two gentlemen compete for one lady, leaving the second lady sadly unrequited in love; then everything is at cross-purposes, with each gentleman pursuing the lady who is in love with the other man; then the two gentlemen compete for the lady they both previously ignored. Finally, of course, Jack shall have his Jill—whom else should he have? The couples are properly united, as they evidently were at some time prior to the commencement of the play, when Demetrius had been romantically attached to Helena and Lysander to Hermia.

Their experience in the forest is an unsettling one for the four young lovers. Although some of them seek out the forest as a refuge from the Athenian law, the place rapidly takes on the darker aspect of a nightmare. Hermia awakens from sleep to find Lysander gone and soon discovers that her dream of a serpent eating her heart away while Lysander watches smiling (2.2.155–6) is all too prophetically true. The forest is a place of testing of the lovers, and the test appears at first to show how they are all their own worst enemies. Helena, having been rejected by Demetrius, can only suppose that she is being mocked, with Lysander and Demetrius both paying court to her. Next, it occurs to her that Hermia must be part of their conspiracy, too. Even though Hermia and Helena recall to each other the selfless devotion they have known as young friends, they become hated rivals in their present mood of self-pity and injured self-regard. The threshold of sexual awakening, it would seem, confronts them with a hazardous rite of passage—one that is especially threatening to the nonsexual friendship of their adolescent years. The two young men respond to similar conflicts by turning on one another in characteristically aggressive male ways. Puck allows them to playact their intended mayhem in a way that cannot harm them and then brings all four lovers together where they can awaken from their nightmare of imagined persecution. How much do they remember? Have they been changed by their journey in the forest? The lovers convey a sense of confusion, of an unreconciled dissonance of perspective in which "everything seems double" (4.1.189). As the lovers return to the daylight world of Athens and the court, their experiences assume the unreality of a remembered dream, like "far-off mountains turnèd into clouds" (4.1.187). When they thus awaken and return to the daylight world of Athens and the court, their renewed love and friendship are presumably deepened by their perception of how narrowly they have escaped from their own self-destructive imaginings. Their new happiness, they see, is better than they have deserved.

We sense that Puck is by no means unhappy about his knavish errors and manipulations: "Lord, what fools these mortals be!" Along with the other fairies in this play, Puck takes his being and his complex motivation from many denizens of the invisible world. As the agent of all-powerful love, Puck compares himself to Cupid. The love juice he administers comes from Cupid's flower, "love-in-idleness." Like Cupid, Puck acts at the behest of the gods, and yet he wields a power that the chiefest of the gods themselves cannot resist. Essentially, however, Puck is less a classical love deity than a prankish folk spirit, such as we find in every folklore: gremlin, leprechaun, hobgoblin, and the like. Titania's fairies recognize Puck as the folk figure Robin Goodfellow, able to deprive a beer barrel of its yeast so that it spoils rather than ferments. Puck characterizes himself as a practical joker, pulling stools out from under old ladies.

Folk wisdom imagines the inexplicable and unaccountable events in life to be caused by invisible spirits who laugh at mortals' discomfiture and mock them for mere sport. Puck is related to these mysterious spirits dwelling in nature, who must be placated with gifts and ceremonies. Although Shakespeare restricts Puck to a benign sportive role in dealing with the lovers or with Titania, the actual folk legends about Puck mentioned in this play are frequently disquieting. Puck is known to "mislead night wanderers, laughing at their harm"; indeed, he demonstrates as much with Demetrius and Lysander, leading them on through the forest to the point of exhaustion, even though we perceive the sportful intent. At the play's end, Puck links himself and his fellows with the ghoulish apparitions of death and night: wolves howling at the moon, screech owls, shrouds, gaping graves. Associations of this sort go beyond mere sportiveness to the witchcraft and demonology involving spirits rising from the dead. Even Oberon's assurance that the fairies will bless all the marriages of this play, shielding their progeny against mole, harelip, or other birth defects, carries the implication that such misfortunes can be caused by offended spirits. The magic of this play is thus explicitly related to deep irrational powers and forces capable of doing great harm, although, to be sure, the spirit of comedy keeps such veiled threats safely at a distance in *A Midsummer Night's Dream*.

Oberon and Titania, in their view of the relationship between gods and humans, reflect yet another aspect of the fairies' spiritual ancestry. The king and queen of fairies assert that, because they are immortal, their regal quarrels in love must inevitably have dire consequences on earth, either in the love relationship of Theseus and Hippolyta or in the management of the weather. Floods, storms, diseases, and sterility abound, "And this same progeny of evils comes / From our debate, from our dissension. / We are their parents and original" (2.1.115–17). This motif of the gods' quarreling over human affairs reminds us of Homer and Virgil. At the same time, in this lighthearted play the motif is more nearly mock-epic than truly epic. The consequences of the gods' anger are simply mirth-provoking, most of all in Titania's love affair with Bottom the weaver.

The story of Bottom and Titania is simultaneously classical and folk in nature. In a playfully classical mode, this love affair between a god and an earthy creature underscores humanity's double nature. Bottom himself becomes half man and half beast, even if he is more ludicrously comic than the centaurs, satyrs, griffins, sphinxes, and other amphibious beings of classical mythology. Some ballads of the early modern period tell of humans transformed into beasts, or of mortals kidnapped by a fairy queen; see, for example, "Tam Lin" and "Thomas Rhymer." Bottom is an especially comic example of metamorphosis because he reverses the usual pattern of a human head and an animal body: instead, his head is animal, his body human. His very name suggests the solid nature of his fleshly being (*bottom* is appropriately also a weaving term). He and Titania represent the opposites of flesh and spirit, miraculously yoked for a time in a twofold vision of humankind's absurd and ethereal nature.

A play bringing together fairies and mortals inevitably raises questions of illusion and reality. These questions reach their greatest intensity in the presentation of "Pyramus and Thisbe." This play within a play focuses our attention on the familiarly Shakespearean metaphor of art as illusion and of the world itself as a stage on which men and women are merely players. As Theseus observes, apologizing for the ineptness of the tradesmen's performance, "the best in this kind are but shadows" (5.1.210); that is, Shakespeare's own play is of the same order of reality as Bottom's play. Puck too, in his epilogue, invites any spectator offended by Shakespeare's play to dismiss it as a mere dream—as, indeed, the play's very title suggests. Theseus goes even further, linking dream to the essence of imaginative art, although he does so in a clearly critical and rather patronizing way. The artist, he says, is like the maniac or the lover in his or her frenzy of inspiration, giving "to airy nothing / A local habitation and a name" (5.1.16–17). Artistic achievements are too unsubstantial for Theseus; from his point of view they are the products of mere fantasy and irrationality, mere myths or fairy stories or old wives' tales. Behind this critical persona defending the "real" world of his court, how-

ever, we can hear Shakespeare's characteristically self-effacing defense of "dreaming."

"Pyramus and Thisbe," like the larger play surrounding it, attempts to body forth "the forms of things unknown." The play within the play gives us personified moonshine, a speaking wall, and an apologetic lion. Of course, it is an absurdly bad play, full of lame epithets, bombastic alliteration, and bathos. In part, Shakespeare here is satirizing the abuses of a theater he had helped reform. The players' chosen method of portraying imaginative matters is ridiculous and calls forth deliciously wry comments from the courtly spectators on stage: "Would you desire lime and hair to speak better?" (5.1.164–5). At the same time, those spectators on stage are actors in our play. Their sarcasms render them less sympathetic in our eyes; we see that their kind of sophistication is as restrictive as it is illuminating. Bottom and his friends have conceived moonshine and lion as they did because these simple men are so responsive to the terrifying power of art. A lion might frighten the ladies and get the men hanged. Theirs is a primitive faith, naive but strong, and in this sense it contrasts favorably with the jaded rationality of the court party. Theseus's valuable reminder that all art is only "illusion" is thus juxtaposed with Bottom's insistence that imaginative art has a reality of its own.

Theseus above all embodies the sophistication of the court in his description of art as a frenzy of seething brains. Ironically, Theseus's genial scoffing at "These antique fables" and "these fairy toys" (5.1.3) would seem to efface his own identity as the figure of legend. Limited by his own skepticism, Theseus seems to have forgotten his own forest wanderings, led by Titania through the "glimmering night" (2.1.77). Bottom, contrastingly, has experienced "a most rare vision," such a dream as is "past the wit of man to say what dream it was" (4.1.203–5). He alone can claim to have been the lover of the queen of fairies; and, although his language cannot adequately describe the experience, Bottom will see it made into a ballad called "Bottom's Dream." Shakespeare leaves the status of his fantasy world deliberately complex; Theseus's lofty denial of dreaming is too abrupt. Even if the Athenian forest world can be made only momentarily substantial in the artifact of Shakespeare's play, we as audience respond to its tantalizing vision. We emerge back into our lives wondering if the fairies were "real"; that is, we are puzzled by the relationship of these artistic symbols to the tangible concreteness of our daily existence. Unless our perceptions have been thus enlarged by sharing in the author's dream, we have not surrendered to the imaginative experience.

Recent performances of this enduringly popular play suggest how open it is to varying interpretation and especially to postmodern views of love and politics as thoroughly unsettling in their irrationality. Nineteenth-century staging generally preferred to see the play as a gossamer delight of diminutive gilded-winged fairies and prankish hobgoblins, all underscored by the romantic strains of Mendelssohn's incidental music. More recently, and especially after World War II, theater and film versions have responded to a darker view. Inspired by Jan Kott's *Shakespeare Our Contemporary* (1964), a book written from the perspective of Soviet-dominated eastern Europe of the Cold War, Peter Brook's brilliantly revisionary stage version for the Royal Shakespeare Theater in 1970 set the play in a brightly lit white box peopled with jugglers and athletic trapeze artists who tumbled and dashed about after one another with abandon. Bottom the Weaver, sporting the button nose of a circus clown, thrust his clenched fist from between his legs in a gesture of phallic aggression.

Brook's avowed aim of freeing the play from what he saw as an oppressive tradition has proved to be immensely influential. Ever since, the young lovers have learned to express their sexual energies through vigorous pursuit and physical contact. Feminist insights have enriched the role of Queen Hippolyta: formerly a captive queen resigned to her marriage to Theseus, she has become in many productions a champion of Hermia's right to resist her father's patriarchal insistence on his will. Puck, in many a recent production, is the denizen of a drug culture, with the love potion as the weed he gleefully distributes. The experience of the forest becomes a drug-induced "high," for audiences as for the actors. The fairies, sometimes played by adult and hairy males, can exhibit a steak of cruelty. The doubling of some central roles, notably Theseus/Oberon, Hippolyta/Titania, and Philostrate/Puck, has given ironic emphasis to parallels between human society and fairyland. Throughout, modern productions have tended to exploit disenchantment with traditional social structures and the surging energy of sexual self-discovery. These modern interpretations are arguably neither more nor less "true" to Shakespeare's text than earlier or more "traditional" versions. What they do demonstrate is the play's remarkable permeability and openness to differing views.

A Midsummer Night's Dream

[*Dramatis Personae*

THESEUS, *Duke of Athens*

HIPPOLYTA, *Queen of the Amazons, betrothed to Theseus*
PHILOSTRATE, *Master of the Revels*
EGEUS, *father of Hermia*

HERMIA, *daughter of Egeus, in love with Lysander*
LYSANDER, *in love with Hermia*
DEMETRIUS, *in love with Hermia and favored by Egeus*
HELENA, *in love with Demetrius*

OBERON, *King of the Fairies*
TITANIA, *Queen of the Fairies*
PUCK, *or* ROBIN GOODFELLOW

PEASEBLOSSOM,
COBWEB,
MOTE,   } *fairies attending Titania*
MUSTARDSEED,
Other FAIRIES *attending*

PETER QUINCE, *a carpenter,*	PROLOGUE
NICK BOTTOM, *a weaver,*	PYRAMUS
FRANCIS FLUTE, *a bellows mender,*	*repre-senting* THISBE
TOM SNOUT, *a tinker,*	WALL
SNUG, *a joiner,*	LION
ROBIN STARVELING, *a tailor,*	MOONSHINE

Lords and Attendants on Theseus and Hippolyta

SCENE: *Athens, and a wood near it*]

[1.1]

Enter Theseus, Hippolyta, [and Philostrate,]
with others.

THESEUS
Now, fair Hippolyta, our nuptial hour
Draws on apace. Four happy days bring in
Another moon; but, oh, methinks, how slow
This old moon wanes! She lingers my desires,   4
Like to a stepdame or a dowager   5
Long withering out a young man's revenue.   6

HIPPOLYTA
Four days will quickly steep themselves in night;   7
Four nights will quickly dream away the time;
And then the moon, like to a silver bow
New bent in heaven, shall behold the night
Of our solemnities.

THESEUS   Go, Philostrate,   11
Stir up the Athenian youth to merriments.
Awake the pert and nimble spirit of mirth.
Turn melancholy forth to funerals;
The pale companion is not for our pomp.   15
                          [*Exit Philostrate.*]
Hippolyta, I wooed thee with my sword   16
And won thy love doing thee injuries;
But I will wed thee in another key,
With pomp, with triumph, and with reveling.   19

Enter Egeus and his daughter Hermia, and
Lysander, and Demetrius.

EGEUS
Happy be Theseus, our renownèd duke!

THESEUS
Thanks, good Egeus. What's the news with thee?

EGEUS
Full of vexation come I, with complaint
Against my child, my daughter Hermia.—
Stand forth, Demetrius.—My noble lord,
This man hath my consent to marry her.—
Stand forth, Lysander.—And, my gracious Duke,
This man hath bewitched the bosom of my child.—
Thou, thou Lysander, thou hast given her rhymes
And interchanged love tokens with my child.
Thou hast by moonlight at her window sung
With feigning voice verses of feigning love,   31
And stol'n the impression of her fantasy   32
With bracelets of thy hair, rings, gauds, conceits,   33

Knacks, trifles, nosegays, sweetmeats—messengers   34
Of strong prevailment in unhardened youth.   35
With cunning hast thou filched my daughter's heart,
Turned her obedience, which is due to me,
To stubborn harshness. And, my gracious Duke,
Be it so she will not here before Your Grace   39
Consent to marry with Demetrius,
I beg the ancient privilege of Athens:
As she is mine, I may dispose of her,
Which shall be either to this gentleman
Or to her death, according to our law
Immediately provided in that case.   45

THESEUS
What say you, Hermia? Be advised, fair maid.
To you your father should be as a god—
One that composed your beauties, yea, and one
To whom you are but as a form in wax
By him imprinted, and within his power
To leave the figure or disfigure it.   51
Demetrius is a worthy gentleman.

HERMIA
So is Lysander.

THESEUS   In himself he is;
But in this kind, wanting your father's voice,   54
The other must be held the worthier.

HERMIA
I would my father looked but with my eyes.

THESEUS
Rather your eyes must with his judgment look.

HERMIA
I do entreat Your Grace to pardon me.
I know not by what power I am made bold,
Nor how it may concern my modesty
In such a presence here to plead my thoughts;
But I beseech Your Grace that I may know
The worst that may befall me in this case
If I refuse to wed Demetrius.

THESEUS
Either to die the death or to abjure   65
Forever the society of men.
Therefore, fair Hermia, question your desires,
Know of your youth, examine well your blood,   68
Whether, if you yield not to your father's choice,
You can endure the livery of a nun,   70
For aye to be in shady cloister mewed,   71
To live a barren sister all your life,
Chanting faint hymns to the cold fruitless moon.
Thrice blessèd they that master so their blood
To undergo such maiden pilgrimage;
But earthlier happy is the rose distilled   76
Than that which, withering on the virgin thorn,
Grows, lives, and dies in single blessedness.

1.1. Location: Athens. Theseus's court.
4 lingers frustrates   **5 stepdame** stepmother.   **a dowager** i.e., a
widow (whose right of inheritance from her dead husband is eating
into her son's estate)   **6 withering out** causing to dwindle
7 Four . . . night (The image is of the day sinking into the ocean as
night comes on.)   **11 solemnities** festive ceremonies of marriage.
15 companion fellow. (A pale complexion is linked to melancholy.)
pomp ceremonial magnificence.   **16 with my sword** i.e., in a military
engagement against the Amazons, when Hippolyta was taken captive   **19 triumph** public festivity   **31 feigning** (1) counterfeiting
(2) faining, desirous   **32 And . . . fantasy** and made her fall in love
with you (imprinting your image on her imagination) by stealthy and
dishonest means   **33 gauds, conceits** playthings, fanciful trifles

34 Knacks . . . sweetmeats knickknacks, trinkets, bouquets, candies
35 prevailment in influence on   **39 Be it so** if   **45 Immediately**
directly, with nothing intervening   **51 leave** i.e., leave unaltered
54 kind respect.   **wanting** lacking.   **voice** approval   **65 die the**
death be executed by legal process   **68 blood** passions   **70 livery**
habit, costume   **71 aye** ever.   **mewed** shut in. (Said of a hawk, poultry, etc.)   **76 earthlier happy** happier as respects this world.
distilled i.e., to make perfume

HERMIA

So will I grow, so live, so die, my lord,
Ere I will yield my virgin patent up   80
Unto His Lordship, whose unwishèd yoke
My soul consents not to give sovereignty.

THESEUS

Take time to pause, and by the next new moon—
The sealing day betwixt my love and me
For everlasting bond of fellowship—
Upon that day either prepare to die
For disobedience to your father's will,
Or else to wed Demetrius, as he would,
Or on Diana's altar to protest   89
For aye austerity and single life.

DEMETRIUS

Relent, sweet Hermia, and, Lysander, yield
Thy crazèd title to my certain right.   92

LYSANDER

You have her father's love, Demetrius;
Let me have Hermia's. Do you marry him.

EGEUS

Scornful Lysander! True, he hath my love,
And what is mine my love shall render him.
And she is mine, and all my right of her
I do estate unto Demetrius.   98

LYSANDER

I am, my lord, as well derived as he,   99
As well possessed; my love is more than his; 100
My fortunes every way as fairly ranked,   101
If not with vantage, as Demetrius';   102
And, which is more than all these boasts can be,
I am beloved of beauteous Hermia.
Why should not I then prosecute my right?
Demetrius, I'll avouch it to his head,   106
Made love to Nedar's daughter, Helena,
And won her soul; and she, sweet lady, dotes,
Devoutly dotes, dotes in idolatry
Upon this spotted and inconstant man.   110

THESEUS

I must confess that I have heard so much,
And with Demetrius thought to have spoke thereof;
But, being overfull of self-affairs,   113
My mind did lose it. But, Demetrius, come,
And come, Egeus, you shall go with me;
I have some private schooling for you both. 116
For you, fair Hermia, look you arm yourself 117
To fit your fancies to your father's will,   118
Or else the law of Athens yields you up—
Which by no means we may extenuate—   120
To death or to a vow of single life.
Come, my Hippolyta. What cheer, my love?
Demetrius and Egeus, go along.   123

I must employ you in some business
Against our nuptial, and confer with you   125
Of something nearly that concerns yourselves. 126

EGEUS

With duty and desire we follow you.
          Exeunt [all but Lysander and Hermia].

LYSANDER

How now, my love, why is your cheek so pale?
How chance the roses there do fade so fast?

HERMIA

Belike for want of rain, which I could well   130
Beteem them from the tempest of my eyes.   131

LYSANDER

Ay me! For aught that I could ever read,
Could ever hear by tale or history,
The course of true love never did run smooth;
But either it was different in blood—   135

HERMIA

Oh, cross! Too high to be enthralled to low. 136

LYSANDER

Or else misgrafted in respect of years—   137

HERMIA

Oh, spite! Too old to be engaged to young.

LYSANDER

Or else it stood upon the choice of friends— 139

HERMIA

Oh, hell, to choose love by another's eyes!

LYSANDER

Or if there were a sympathy in choice,   141
War, death, or sickness did lay siege to it,
Making it momentany as a sound,   143
Swift as a shadow, short as any dream,
Brief as the lightning in the collied night   145
That in a spleen unfolds both heaven and earth, 146
And ere a man hath power to say "Behold!"
The jaws of darkness do devour it up.
So quick bright things come to confusion.   149

HERMIA

If then true lovers have been ever crossed,   150
It stands as an edict in destiny.
Then let us teach our trial patience,   152
Because it is a customary cross,
As due to love as thoughts, and dreams, and sighs,
Wishes, and tears, poor fancy's followers.   155

LYSANDER

A good persuasion. Therefore, hear me, Hermia: 156
I have a widow aunt, a dowager
Of great revenue, and she hath no child.
From Athens is her house remote seven leagues; 159
And she respects me as her only son.   160

80 **patent** privilege   89 **protest** vow   92 **crazèd** cracked, unsound
98 **estate unto** settle or bestow upon   99 **as well derived** as well born
and descended   100 **possessed** endowed with wealth   101 **fairly**
handsomely   102 **vantage** superiority   106 **head** i.e., face   110 **spot-**
ted i.e., morally stained   113 **self-affairs** my own concerns
116 **schooling** admonition   117 **look you arm** take care you prepare
118 **fancies** likings, thoughts of love   120 **extenuate** mitigate, relax
123 **go** i.e., come

125 **Against** in preparation for   126 **nearly that** that closely
130 **Belike** Very likely   131 **Beteem** grant, afford   135 **blood** hereditary rank   136 **cross** vexation.   137 **misgrafted** ill grafted, badly
matched   139 **friends** relatives   141 **sympathy** agreement
143 **momentany** lasting but a moment   145 **collied** blackened (as
with coal dust), darkened   146 **in a spleen** in a swift impulse, in a
violent flash.   **unfolds** reveals   149 **confusion** ruin.   150 **ever**
crossed always thwarted   152 **teach . . . patience** i.e., teach ourselves
patience in this trial   155 **fancy's** amorous passion's   156 **persua-**
sion doctrine.   159 **seven leagues** about 21 miles   160 **respects**
regards

There, gentle Hermia, may I marry thee,
And to that place the sharp Athenian law
Cannot pursue us. If thou lovest me, then,
Steal forth thy father's house tomorrow night;
And in the wood, a league without the town,   165
Where I did meet thee once with Helena
To do observance to a morn of May,   167
There will I stay for thee.

HERMIA   My good Lysander!
I swear to thee, by Cupid's strongest bow,
By his best arrow with the golden head,   170
By the simplicity of Venus' doves,   171
By that which knitteth souls and prospers loves,
And by that fire which burned the Carthage queen   173
When the false Trojan under sail was seen,   174
By all the vows that ever men have broke,
In number more than ever women spoke,
In that same place thou hast appointed me
Tomorrow truly will I meet with thee.

LYSANDER
Keep promise, love. Look, here comes Helena.

        Enter Helena.

HERMIA
God speed, fair Helena! Whither away?   180

HELENA
Call you me fair? That "fair" again unsay.
Demetrius loves your fair. Oh, happy fair!   182
Your eyes are lodestars, and your tongue's sweet air   183
More tunable than lark to shepherd's ear   184
When wheat is green, when hawthorn buds appear.
Sickness is catching. Oh, were favor so,   186
Yours would I catch, fair Hermia, ere I go;
My ear should catch your voice, my eye your eye,
My tongue should catch your tongue's sweet melody.
Were the world mine, Demetrius being bated,   190
The rest I'd give to be to you translated.   191
Oh, teach me how you look and with what art
You sway the motion of Demetrius' heart.   193

HERMIA
I frown upon him, yet he loves me still.

HELENA
Oh, that your frowns would teach my smiles such
    skill!

HERMIA
I give him curses, yet he gives me love.

HELENA
Oh, that my prayers could such affection move!   197

HERMIA
The more I hate, the more he follows me.

HELENA
The more I love, the more he hateth me.

HERMIA
His folly, Helena, is no fault of mine.

HELENA
None, but your beauty. Would that fault were mine!

HERMIA
Take comfort. He no more shall see my face.
Lysander and myself will fly this place.
Before the time I did Lysander see   204
Seemed Athens as a paradise to me.   205
Oh, then, what graces in my love do dwell,
That he hath turned a heaven unto a hell?

LYSANDER
Helen, to you our minds we will unfold.
Tomorrow night, when Phoebe doth behold   209
Her silver visage in the watery glass,   210
Decking with liquid pearl the bladed grass,   211
A time that lovers' flights doth still conceal,   212
Through Athens' gates have we devised to steal.

HERMIA
And in the wood, where often you and I
Upon faint primrose beds were wont to lie,   215
Emptying our bosoms of their counsel sweet,   216
There my Lysander and myself shall meet,
And thence from Athens turn away our eyes
To seek new friends and stranger companies.   219
Farewell, sweet playfellow. Pray thou for us,
And good luck grant thee thy Demetrius!
Keep word, Lysander. We must starve our sight
From lovers' food till morrow deep midnight.

LYSANDER
I will, my Hermia.   *Exit Hermia.*
            Helena, adieu!
As you on him, Demetrius dote on you!
                                        Exit Lysander.

HELENA
How happy some o'er other some can be!   226
Through Athens I am thought as fair as she.
But what of that? Demetrius thinks not so;
He will not know what all but he do know.
And as he errs, doting on Hermia's eyes,
So I, admiring of his qualities.
Things base and vile, holding no quantity,   232
Love can transpose to form and dignity.
Love looks not with the eyes, but with the mind,
And therefore is winged Cupid painted blind.

---

165 **without** outside   167 **To do . . . May** to perform the ceremonies
of May Day   170 **best arrow** (Cupid's best gold-pointed arrows were
supposed to induce love; his blunt leaden arrows, aversion.)
171 **simplicity** innocence.   **doves** i.e., those that drew Venus's chariot
173, 174 **Carthage queen, false Trojan** (Dido, Queen of Carthage,
immolated herself on a funeral pyre after having been deserted by
the Trojan hero Aeneas.)   180 **fair** fair-complexioned. (Generally
regarded by the Elizabethans as more beautiful than a dark complexion.)   182 **your fair** your beauty (even though Hermia is dark complexioned).   **happy fair** lucky fair one.   183 **lodestars** guiding stars.
air music   184 **tunable** tuneful, melodious   186 **favor** appearance,
looks   190 **bated** excepted   191 **translated** transformed.   193 **sway
the motion** control the impulses

197 **Oh, that . . . move!** Would that my prayers could arouse such
desire!   204–5 **Before . . . to me** (Love has led to complications and
jealousies, making Athens hell for Hermia.)   209 **Phoebe** Diana, the
moon   210 **glass** reflecting surface (of a lake, etc.)   211 **liquid pearl**
i.e., dew   212 **still** always   215 **faint** pale   216 **counsel** secret
thought   219 **stranger companies** the company of strangers.
226 **o'er . . . can be** can be in comparison to some others.   232 **holding no quantity** i.e., unsubstantial, unshapely

Nor hath Love's mind of any judgment taste;   236
Wings and no eyes figure unheedy haste.   237
And therefore is Love said to be a child,
Because in choice he is so oft beguiled.   239
As waggish boys in game themselves forswear,   240
So the boy Love is perjured everywhere.
For ere Demetrius looked on Hermia's eyne,   242
He hailed down oaths that he was only mine;
And when this hail some heat from Hermia felt,
So he dissolved, and showers of oaths did melt.
I will go tell him of fair Hermia's flight.
Then to the wood will he tomorrow night
Pursue her; and for this intelligence   248
If I have thanks, it is a dear expense.   249
But herein mean I to enrich my pain,
To have his sight thither and back again.   *Exit.*

❖

[1.2]

*Enter Quince the carpenter, and Snug the
joiner, and Bottom the weaver, and Flute the
bellows mender, and Snout the tinker, and
Starveling the tailor.*

QUINCE   Is all our company here?
BOTTOM   You were best to call them generally, man by   2
man, according to the scrip.   3
QUINCE   Here is the scroll of every man's name which
is thought fit, through all Athens, to play in our inter-   5
lude before the Duke and the Duchess on his wedding   6
day at night.
BOTTOM   First, good Peter Quince, say what the play
treats on, then read the names of the actors, and so
grow to a point.   10
QUINCE   Marry, our play is "The most lamentable com-   11
edy and most cruel death of Pyramus and Thisbe."
BOTTOM   A very good piece of work, I assure you, and
a merry. Now, good Peter Quince, call forth your
actors by the scroll. Masters, spread yourselves.
QUINCE   Answer as I call you. Nick Bottom, the weaver.   16
BOTTOM   Ready. Name what part I am for, and proceed.
QUINCE   You, Nick Bottom, are set down for Pyramus.
BOTTOM   What is Pyramus? A lover or a tyrant?
QUINCE   A lover, that kills himself most gallant for love.
BOTTOM   That will ask some tears in the true performing
of it. If I do it, let the audience look to their eyes. I will
move storms; I will condole in some measure. To the   23
rest—yet my chief humor is for a tyrant. I could play   24

Ercles rarely, or a part to tear a cat in, to make all split.   25
    "The raging rocks
    And shivering shocks
    Shall break the locks
       Of prison gates;
    And Phibbus' car   30
    Shall shine from far
    And make and mar
       The foolish Fates."
This was lofty! Now name the rest of the players. This is
Ercles' vein, a tyrant's vein. A lover is more condoling.
QUINCE   Francis Flute, the bellows mender.
FLUTE   Here, Peter Quince.
QUINCE   Flute, you must take Thisbe on you.
FLUTE   What is Thisbe? A wandering knight?
QUINCE   It is the lady that Pyramus must love.
FLUTE   Nay, faith, let not me play a woman. I have a
beard coming.
QUINCE   That's all one. You shall play it in a mask, and   43
you may speak as small as you will.   44
BOTTOM   An I may hide my face, let me play Thisbe too.   45
I'll speak in a monstrous little voice: "Thisne, Thisne!"
"Ah, Pyramus, my lover dear! Thy Thisbe dear, and
lady dear!"
QUINCE   No, no, you must play Pyramus, and Flute, you
Thisbe.
BOTTOM   Well, proceed.
QUINCE   Robin Starveling, the tailor.
STARVELING   Here, Peter Quince.
QUINCE   Robin Starveling, you must play Thisbe's
mother. Tom Snout, the tinker.
SNOUT   Here, Peter Quince.
QUINCE   You, Pyramus' father; myself, Thisbe's father;
Snug, the joiner, you, the lion's part; and I hope here is
a play fitted.
SNUG   Have you the lion's part written? Pray you, if it
be, give it me, for I am slow of study.
QUINCE   You may do it extempore, for it is nothing but
roaring.
BOTTOM   Let me play the lion too. I will roar that I will
do any man's heart good to hear me. I will roar that I
will make the Duke say, "Let him roar again, let him
roar again."
QUINCE   An you should do it too terribly, you would
fright the Duchess and the ladies, that they would
shriek; and that were enough to hang us all.
ALL   That would hang us, every mother's son.
BOTTOM   I grant you, friends, if you should fright the
ladies out of their wits, they would have no more discretion but to hang us; but I will aggravate my voice   74
so that I will roar you as gently as any sucking dove; I   75
will roar you an 'twere any nightingale.   76

---

236 Nor . . . taste i.e., Nor has Love, which dwells in the fancy or
imagination, any least bit of judgment or reason   **237 figure** signify
239 in choice in choosing.   **beguiled** self-deluded, making unaccountable choices.   **240 waggish** playful, mischievous.   **game** sport,
jest   **242 eyne** eyes. (Old form of plural.)   **248 intelligence** information   **249 a dear expense** i.e., a trouble worth taking on my part.
1.2. Location: Athens.
2 generally (Bottom's blunder for "individually.")   **3 scrip** script.
5–6 interlude play   **10 grow to** come to   **11 Marry** (A mild oath;
originally the name of the Virgin Mary.)   **16 Bottom** (As a weaver's
term, a *bottom* was an object around which thread was wound.)
23 condole lament, arouse pity   **24 humor** inclination

---

25 Ercles Hercules. (The tradition of ranting came from Seneca's
Hercules Furens.)   **tear a cat** i.e., rant.   **make all split** i.e., cause a stir,
bring the house down.   **30 Phibbus' car** Phoebus's, the sun god's
chariot   **43 That's all one** It makes no difference.   **44 small** high-
pitched   **45 An** If. (Also at line 68.)   **74 aggravate** (Bottom's blunder
for "moderate.")   **75 roar you** i.e., roar for you.   **sucking dove** (Bottom conflates *sitting dove* and *sucking lamb,* two proverbial images of
innocence.)   **76 an 'twere** as if it were

QUINCE   You can play no part but Pyramus; for Pyramus is a sweet-faced man, a proper man as one shall see in a summer's day, a most lovely gentlemanlike man. Therefore you must needs play Pyramus. 78

BOTTOM   Well, I will undertake it. What beard were I best to play it in?

QUINCE   Why, what you will.

BOTTOM   I will discharge it in either your straw-color beard, your orange-tawny beard, your purple-in-grain beard, or your French-crown-color beard, your perfect yellow. 84 85 86

QUINCE   Some of your French crowns have no hair at all, and then you will play barefaced. But, masters, here are your parts. [He distributes parts.] And I am to entreat you, request you, and desire you to con them by tomorrow night, and meet me in the palace wood, a mile without the town, by moonlight. There will we rehearse; for if we meet in the city, we shall be dogged with company, and our devices known. In the meantime I will draw a bill of properties, such as our play wants. I pray you, fail me not. 88 91 95 96

BOTTOM   We will meet, and there we may rehearse most obscenely and courageously. Take pains, be perfect. Adieu. 99

QUINCE   At the Duke's oak we meet.

BOTTOM   Enough. Hold, or cut bowstrings.   *Exeunt.* 102

❖

[2.1]

Enter a Fairy at one door, and Robin Goodfellow [Puck] at another.

PUCK
How now, spirit, whither wander you?

FAIRY
    Over hill, over dale,
        Thorough bush, thorough brier, 3
    Over park, over pale, 4
        Thorough flood, thorough fire,
    I do wander everywhere,
    Swifter than the moon's sphere; 7
    And I serve the Fairy Queen,
    To dew her orbs upon the green. 9
    The cowslips tall her pensioners be. 10
    In their gold coats spots you see;

    Those be rubies, fairy favors; 12
        In those freckles live their savors. 13
    I must go seek some dewdrops here
    And hang a pearl in every cowslip's ear.
    Farewell, thou lob of spirits; I'll be gone. 16
    Our Queen and all her elves come here anon. 17

PUCK
    The King doth keep his revels here tonight.
    Take heed the Queen come not within his sight.
    For Oberon is passing fell and wrath, 20
    Because that she as her attendant hath
    A lovely boy, stolen from an Indian king;
    She never had so sweet a changeling. 23
    And jealous Oberon would have the child
    Knight of his train, to trace the forests wild. 25
    But she perforce withholds the lovèd boy, 26
    Crowns him with flowers, and makes him all her joy.
    And now they never meet in grove or green,
    By fountain clear, or spangled starlight sheen, 29
    But they do square, that all their elves for fear 30
    Creep into acorn cups and hide them there.

FAIRY
    Either I mistake your shape and making quite,
    Or else you are that shrewd and knavish sprite 33
    Called Robin Goodfellow. Are not you he
    That frights the maidens of the villagery, 35
    Skim milk, and sometimes labor in the quern, 36
    And bootless make the breathless huswife churn, 37
    And sometimes make the drink to bear no barm, 38
    Mislead night wanderers, laughing at their harm? 39
    Those that "Hobgoblin" call you, and "Sweet Puck," 40
    You do their work, and they shall have good luck.
    Are you not he?

PUCK   Thou speakest aright;
    I am that merry wanderer of the night.
    I jest to Oberon and make him smile
    When I a fat and bean-fed horse beguile, 45
    Neighing in likeness of a filly foal; 46
    And sometimes lurk I in a gossip's bowl 47
    In very likeness of a roasted crab, 48
    And when she drinks, against her lips I bob
    And on her withered dewlap pour the ale. 50
    The wisest aunt, telling the saddest tale, 51

78 proper handsome   **84 discharge** perform.   **your** i.e., you know the kind I mean   **85 purple-in-grain** dyed a very deep red. (From *grain,* the name applied to the dried insect used to make the dye.) **86 French-crown-color** i.e., color of a French crown, a gold coin **88 crowns** heads bald from syphilis, the "French disease"   **91 con** memorize   **95 devices** plans   **96 draw a bill** draw up a list **99 obscenely** (An unintentionally funny blunder, whatever Bottom meant to say.)   **perfect** i.e., letter-perfect in memorizing your parts. **102 Hold . . . bowstrings** (An archers' expression, not definitely explained, but probably meaning here "keep your promises, or give up the play.")
2.1. Location: A wood near Athens.
3 Thorough through   **4 pale** enclosure   **7 sphere** orbit   **9 dew** sprinkle with dew.   **orbs** circles, i.e., fairy rings (circular bands of grass, darker than the surrounding area, caused by fungi enriching the soil)   **10 pensioners** retainers, members of the royal bodyguard

12 favors love tokens   **13 savors** sweet smells.   **16 lob** country bumpkin   **17 anon** at once.   **20 passing fell** exceedingly angry. **wrath** wrathful   **23 changeling** child exchanged for another by the fairies.   **25 trace** range through   **26 perforce** forcibly   **29 fountain** spring.   **starlight sheen** shining starlight   **30 square** quarrel **33 shrewd** mischievous.   **sprite** spirit   **35 villagery** village population   **36 Skim milk** i.e., steal the cream.   **quern** hand mill (where Puck presumably hampers the grinding of grain)   **37 bootless** in vain. (Puck prevents the cream from turning to butter.)   **huswife** housewife   **38 barm** head on the ale. (Puck prevents the barm or yeast from producing fermentation.)   **39 Mislead night wanderers** i.e., mislead with false fire those who walk abroad at night (hence earning Puck his other names of Jack o' Lantern and Will o' the Wisp) **40 Those . . . Puck** i.e., Those who call you by the names you favor rather than those denoting the mischief you do   **45 bean-fed** full of beans   **46 a filly foal** a mare (in heat)   **47 gossip's** old woman's **48 crab** crab apple   **50 dewlap** loose skin on neck   **51 aunt** old woman.   **saddest** most serious

Sometime for three-foot stool mistaketh me;
Then slip I from her bum, down topples she,
And "Tailor" cries, and falls into a cough;   54
And then the whole choir hold their hips and laugh,   55
And waxen in their mirth, and neeze, and swear   56
A merrier hour was never wasted there.   57
But, room, fairy! Here comes Oberon.   58

FAIRY
And here my mistress. Would that he were gone!

*Enter [Oberon] the King of Fairies at one door,
with his train, and [Titania] the Queen at
another, with hers.*

OBERON
Ill met by moonlight, proud Titania.

TITANIA
What, jealous Oberon? Fairies, skip hence.
I have forsworn his bed and company.

OBERON
Tarry, rash wanton. Am not I thy lord?   63

TITANIA
Then I must be thy lady; but I know
When thou hast stolen away from Fairyland
And in the shape of Corin sat all day,   66
Playing on pipes of corn and versing love   67
To amorous Phillida. Why art thou here   68
Come from the farthest step of India,   69
But that, forsooth, the bouncing Amazon,
Your buskined mistress and your warrior love,   71
To Theseus must be wedded, and you come
To give their bed joy and prosperity.

OBERON
How canst thou thus for shame, Titania,
Glance at my credit with Hippolyta,   75
Knowing I know thy love to Theseus?
Didst not thou lead him through the glimmering night
From Perigenia, whom he ravishèd?   78
And make him with fair Aegles break his faith,   79
With Ariadne and Antiopa?   80

TITANIA
These are the forgeries of jealousy;
And never, since the middle summer's spring,   82
Met we on hill, in dale, forest, or mead,   83

By pavèd fountain or by rushy brook,   84
Or in the beachèd margent of the sea,   85
To dance our ringlets to the whistling wind,   86
But with thy brawls thou hast disturbed our sport.
Therefore the winds, piping to us in vain,
As in revenge, have sucked up from the sea
Contagious fogs which, falling in the land,   90
Hath every pelting river made so proud   91
That they have overborne their continents.   92
The ox hath therefore stretched his yoke in vain,   93
The plowman lost his sweat, and the green corn   94
Hath rotted ere his youth attained a beard;
The fold stands empty in the drownèd field,   96
And crows are fatted with the murrain flock;   97
The nine-men's morris is filled up with mud,   98
And the quaint mazes in the wanton green   99
For lack of tread are undistinguishable.
The human mortals want their winter here;   101
No night is now with hymn or carol blessed.
Therefore the moon, the governess of floods,   103
Pale in her anger, washes all the air,   104
That rheumatic diseases do abound.   105
And thorough this distemperature we see   106
The seasons alter: hoary-headed frosts
Fall in the fresh lap of the crimson rose,
And on old Hiems' thin and icy crown   109
An odorous chaplet of sweet summer buds
Is, as in mockery, set. The spring, the summer,
The childing autumn, angry winter, change   112
Their wonted liveries, and the mazèd world   113
By their increase now knows not which is which.   114
And this same progeny of evils comes
From our debate, from our dissension.   116
We are their parents and original.   117

OBERON
Do you amend it, then. It lies in you.
Why should Titania cross her Oberon?
I do but beg a little changeling boy
To be my henchman.

TITANIA   Set your heart at rest.   121
The fairy land buys not the child of me.
His mother was a vot'ress of my order,   123

---

54 **"Tailor"** (Seemingly a cry of distress or embarrassment.) 55 **choir** company 56 **waxen** increase. **neeze** sneeze 57 **wasted** spent 58 **room** stand aside, make room 63 **wanton** headstrong creature. 66, 68 **Corin, Phillida** (Conventional names of pastoral lovers.) 67 **corn** (Here, oat stalks.) **versing love** writing love verses 69 **step** farthest limit of travel, or, perhaps, *steep*, "mountain range" 71 **buskined** wearing half-boots called buskins 75 **Glance . . . Hippolyta** make insinuations about my favored relationship with Hippolyta 78 **Perigenia** i.e., Perigouna, one of Theseus's conquests. (This and the following women are named in Thomas North's translation of Plutarch's "Life of Theseus.") 79 **Aegles** i.e., Aegle, for whom Theseus deserted Ariadne according to some accounts 80 **Ariadne** the daughter of Minos, King of Crete, who helped Theseus to escape the labyrinth after killing the Minotaur; later she was abandoned by Theseus. **Antiopa** Queen of the Amazons and wife of Theseus; elsewhere identified with Hippolyta, but here thought of as a separate woman. 82 **middle summer's spring** beginning of midsummer 83 **mead** meadow

84 **pavèd** with pebbled bottom. **rushy** bordered with rushes 85 **in on.** **margent** edge, border 86 **ringlets** dances in a ring. (See *orbs* in line 9.) **to** to the sound of 90 **Contagious** noxious 91 **pelting** paltry 92 **continents** banks that contain them. 93 **stretched his yoke** i.e., pulled at his yoke in plowing 94 **corn** grain of any kind 96 **fold** pen for sheep or cattle 97 **murrain** having died of the plague 98 **nine-men's morris** i.e., portion of the village green marked out in a square for a game played with nine pebbles or pegs 99 **quaint mazes** i.e., intricate paths marked out on the village green to be followed rapidly on foot as a kind of contest. **wanton** luxuriant 101 **want** lack. **winter** i.e., regular winter season; or, proper observances of winter, such as the *hymn* or *carol* in the next line (?) 103 **Therefore** i.e., As a result of our quarrel 104 **washes** saturates with moisture 105 **rheumatic diseases** colds, flu, and other respiratory infections 106 **distemperature** disturbance in nature 109 **Hiems'** the winter god's 112 **childing** fruitful, pregnant 113 **wonted liveries** usual apparel. **mazèd** bewildered 114 **their increase** the increasing pace of change; or, their produce 116 **debate** quarrel 117 **original** origin. 121 **henchman** attendant, page. 123 **was . . . order** had taken a vow to serve me

And in the spicèd Indian air by night
Full often hath she gossiped by my side
And sat with me on Neptune's yellow sands,
Marking th'embarkèd traders on the flood,   127
When we have laughed to see the sails conceive
And grow big-bellied with the wanton wind;   129
Which she, with pretty and with swimming gait,   130
Following—her womb then rich with my young
    squire—
Would imitate, and sail upon the land
To fetch me trifles, and return again
As from a voyage, rich with merchandise.
But she, being mortal, of that boy did die;
And for her sake do I rear up her boy,
And for her sake I will not part with him.

OBERON
How long within this wood intend you stay?

TITANIA
Perchance till after Theseus' wedding day.
If you will patiently dance in our round   140
And see our moonlight revels, go with us;
If not, shun me, and I will spare your haunts.   142

OBERON
Give me that boy, and I will go with thee.

TITANIA
Not for thy fairy kingdom. Fairies, away!
We shall chide downright, if I longer stay.
          Exeunt [*Titania with her train*].

OBERON
Well, go thy way. Thou shalt not from this grove   146
Till I torment thee for this injury.
My gentle Puck, come hither. Thou rememb'rest
Since once I sat upon a promontory,   149
And heard a mermaid on a dolphin's back
Uttering such dulcet and harmonious breath   151
That the rude sea grew civil at her song,   152
And certain stars shot madly from their spheres
To hear the sea-maid's music?

PUCK   I remember.

OBERON
That very time I saw, but thou couldst not,
Flying between the cold moon and the earth
Cupid, all armed. A certain aim he took   157
At a fair vestal thronèd by the west,   158
And loosed his love shaft smartly from his bow   159
As it should pierce a hundred thousand hearts;   160
But I might see young Cupid's fiery shaft   161
Quenched in the chaste beams of the wat'ry moon,
And the imperial vot'ress passèd on,
In maiden meditation, fancy-free.   164
Yet marked I where the bolt of Cupid fell: 165

It fell upon a little western flower,
Before milk-white, now purple with love's wound,
And maidens call it love-in-idleness.   168
Fetch me that flower; the herb I showed thee once.
The juice of it on sleeping eyelids laid
Will make or man or woman madly dote   171
Upon the next live creature that it sees.
Fetch me this herb, and be thou here again
Ere the leviathan can swim a league.   174

PUCK
I'll put a girdle round about the earth
In forty minutes.   [*Exit.*]

OBERON   Having once this juice,
I'll watch Titania when she is asleep
And drop the liquor of it in her eyes.
The next thing then she waking looks upon,
Be it on lion, bear, or wolf, or bull,
On meddling monkey, or on busy ape,
She shall pursue it with the soul of love.
And ere I take this charm from off her sight,
As I can take it with another herb,
I'll make her render up her page to me.
But who comes here? I am invisible,
And I will overhear their conference.

          [*He stands aside.*]

    Enter Demetrius, Helena following him.

DEMETRIUS
I love thee not; therefore pursue me not.
Where is Lysander and fair Hermia?
The one I'll slay; the other slayeth me.
Thou toldst me they were stol'n unto this wood;
And here am I, and wood within this wood   192
Because I cannot meet my Hermia.
Hence, get thee gone, and follow me no more.

HELENA
You draw me, you hardhearted adamant!   195
But yet you draw not iron, for my heart
Is true as steel. Leave you your power to draw,   197
And I shall have no power to follow you.

DEMETRIUS
Do I entice you? Do I speak you fair?   199
Or rather do I not in plainest truth
Tell you I do not nor I cannot love you?

HELENA
And even for that do I love you the more.
I am your spaniel; and, Demetrius,
The more you beat me I will fawn on you.
Use me but as your spaniel, spurn me, strike me,
Neglect me, lose me; only give me leave,
Unworthy as I am, to follow you.
What worser place can I beg in your love—
And yet a place of high respect with me—
Than to be usèd as you use your dog?

---

127 traders trading vessels. **flood** flood tide **129 wanton** (1) playful (2) amorous **130 swimming** smooth, gliding **140 round** circular
dance **142 spare** shun **146 from** go from **149 Since** when
151 dulcet sweet. **breath** voice, song **152 rude** rough **157 all**
fully. **certain** sure **158 vestal** vestal virgin. (Contains a complimentary allusion to Queen Elizabeth as a votaress of Diana and probably
refers to an actual entertainment in her honor at Elvetham in 1591.)
by in the region of **159 loosed** released **160 As** as if **161 might**
could **164 fancy-free** free of love's spell. **165 bolt** arrow

168 love-in-idleness pansy, heartsease. **171 or man** either man
174 leviathan sea monster, whale **192 wood** mad, frantic. (With an
obvious wordplay on *wood*, meaning "woods.") **195 adamant** lodestone, magnet. (With pun on *hardhearted,* since adamant was also
thought to be the hardest of all stones and was confused with the diamond.) **197 Leave you** Give up **199 speak you fair** speak courteously to you.

DEMETRIUS
Tempt not too much the hatred of my spirit,
For I am sick when I do look on thee.

HELENA
And I am sick when I look not on you.

DEMETRIUS
You do impeach your modesty too much   214
To leave the city and commit yourself   215
Into the hands of one that loves you not,
To trust the opportunity of night
And the ill counsel of a desert place   218
With the rich worth of your virginity.

HELENA
Your virtue is my privilege. For that   220
It is not night when I do see your face,
Therefore I think I am not in the night;
Nor doth this wood lack worlds of company,
For you, in my respect, are all the world.   224
Then how can it be said I am alone
When all the world is here to look on me?

DEMETRIUS
I'll run from thee and hide me in the brakes,   227
And leave thee to the mercy of wild beasts.

HELENA
The wildest hath not such a heart as you.
Run when you will. The story shall be changed:
Apollo flies and Daphne holds the chase,   231
The dove pursues the griffin, the mild hind   232
Makes speed to catch the tiger—bootless speed,   233
When cowardice pursues and valor flies!

DEMETRIUS
I will not stay thy questions. Let me go!   235
Or if thou follow me, do not believe
But I shall do thee mischief in the wood.

HELENA
Ay, in the temple, in the town, the field,
You do me mischief. Fie, Demetrius!
Your wrongs do set a scandal on my sex.   240
We cannot fight for love, as men may do;
We should be wooed and were not made to woo.
                                    [Exit Demetrius.]
I'll follow thee and make a heaven of hell,
To die upon the hand I love so well.   [Exit.] 244

OBERON
Fare thee well, nymph. Ere he do leave this grove
Thou shalt fly him, and he shall seek thy love.

                  Enter Puck.

Hast thou the flower there? Welcome, wanderer.

PUCK
Ay, there it is.   [He offers the flower.]
OBERON   I pray thee, give it me.
I know a bank where the wild thyme blows,   249
Where oxlips and the nodding violet grows,   250
Quite overcanopied with luscious woodbine,   251
With sweet muskroses and with eglantine.   252
There sleeps Titania sometime of the night,   253
Lulled in these flowers with dances and delight;
And there the snake throws her enameled skin,   255
Weed wide enough to wrap a fairy in.   256
And with the juice of this I'll streak her eyes   257
And make her full of hateful fantasies.
Take thou some of it, and seek through this grove.
                          [He gives some love juice.]
A sweet Athenian lady is in love
With a disdainful youth. Anoint his eyes,
But do it when the next thing he espies
May be the lady. Thou shalt know the man
By the Athenian garments he hath on.
Effect it with some care, that he may prove
More fond on her than she upon her love;   266
And look thou meet me ere the first cock crow.

PUCK
Fear not, my lord, your servant shall do so.
                                    Exeunt [separately].

                          ❧

[2.2]

          Enter Titania, Queen of Fairies, with her train.

TITANIA
Come, now a roundel and a fairy song;   1
Then, for the third part of a minute, hence—
Some to kill cankers in the muskrose buds,   3
Some war with reremice for their leathern wings   4
To make my small elves coats, and some keep back
The clamorous owl, that nightly hoots and wonders
At our quaint spirits. Sing me now asleep.   7
Then to your offices, and let me rest.

          Fairies sing.

FIRST FAIRY
          You spotted snakes with double tongue,   9
              Thorny hedgehogs, be not seen;
          Newts and blindworms, do no wrong;   11
              Come not near our Fairy Queen.

214 **impeach** call into question   215 **To leave** by leaving   218 **desert** deserted   220 **privilege** safeguard, warrant.   **For that** Because 224 **in my respect** as far as I am concerned, in my esteem 227 **brakes** thickets   231 **Apollo . . . chase** (In the ancient myth, Daphne fled from Apollo and was saved from rape by being transformed into a laurel tree; here it is the female who *holds the chase*, or pursues, instead of the male.)   232 **griffin** a fabulous monster with the head and wings of an eagle and the body of a lion.   **hind** female deer   233 **bootless** fruitless   235 **stay** wait for, put up with. **questions** talk or argument.   240 **Your . . . sex** i.e., The wrongs that you do me cause me to act in a manner that disgraces my sex. 244 **upon** by

249 **blows** blooms   250 **oxlips** flowers resembling cowslip and primrose   251 **woodbine** honeysuckle   252 **muskroses** a kind of large, sweet-scented rose.   **eglantine** sweetbrier, another kind of rose. 253 **sometime of** for part of   255 **throws** sloughs off, sheds 256 **Weed** garment   257 **streak** anoint, touch gently   266 **fond on** doting on
2.2. Location: The wood.
1 **roundel** dance in a ring   3 **cankers** cankerworms (i.e., caterpillars or grubs)   4 **reremice** bats   7 **quaint** dainty   9 **double** forked 11 **Newts** water lizards. (Considered poisonous, as were *blindworms*— small snakes with tiny eyes—and spiders.)

CHORUS [*dancing*]
                Philomel, with melody   13
                Sing in our sweet lullaby;
            Lulla, lulla, lullaby, lulla, lulla, lullaby.
                Never harm
                Nor spell nor charm
            Come our lovely lady nigh.
            So good night, with lullaby.

FIRST FAIRY
            Weaving spiders, come not here;
                Hence, you long-legged spinners, hence!
            Beetles black, approach not near;
                Worm nor snail, do no offense.   23

CHORUS [*dancing*]
                Philomel, with melody
                Sing in our sweet lullaby;
            Lulla, lulla, lullaby, lulla, lulla, lullaby.
                Never harm
                Nor spell nor charm
            Come our lovely lady nigh.
            So good night, with lullaby.   [*Titania sleeps.*]

SECOND FAIRY
            Hence, away! Now all is well.
            One aloof stand sentinel.   32
                    [*Exeunt Fairies, leaving one sentinel.*]

        *Enter Oberon [and squeezes the flower on
        Titania's eyelids].*

OBERON
            What thou see'st when thou dost wake,
            Do it for thy true love take;
            Love and languish for his sake.
            Be it ounce, or cat, or bear,   36
            Pard, or boar with bristled hair,   37
            In thy eye that shall appear
            When thou wak'st, it is thy dear.
            Wake when some vile thing is near.   [*Exit.*]

        Enter Lysander and Hermia.

LYSANDER
            Fair love, you faint with wand'ring in the wood;
                And to speak truth, I have forgot our way.
            We'll rest us, Hermia, if you think it good,
                And tarry for the comfort of the day.

HERMIA
            Be it so, Lysander. Find you out a bed,
            For I upon this bank will rest my head.

LYSANDER
            One turf shall serve as pillow for us both;
            One heart, one bed, two bosoms, and one troth.   48

HERMIA
            Nay, good Lysander, for my sake, my dear,
            Lie further off yet. Do not lie so near.

LYSANDER
            Oh, take the sense, sweet, of my innocence!   51
            Love takes the meaning in love's conference.   52
            I mean that my heart unto yours is knit,
            So that but one heart we can make of it;
            Two bosoms interchainèd with an oath—
            So then two bosoms and a single troth.
            Then by your side no bed-room me deny,
            For lying so, Hermia, I do not lie.   58

HERMIA
            Lysander riddles very prettily.
            Now much beshrew my manners and my pride   60
            If Hermia meant to say Lysander lied.
            But, gentle friend, for love and courtesy
            Lie further off, in human modesty.
            Such separation as may well be said
            Becomes a virtuous bachelor and a maid,
            So far be distant; and, good night, sweet friend.
            Thy love ne'er alter till thy sweet life end!

LYSANDER
            Amen, amen, to that fair prayer, say I,
            And then end life when I end loyalty!
            Here is my bed. Sleep give thee all his rest!

HERMIA
            With half that wish the wisher's eyes be pressed!   71
                    [*They sleep, separated by a short distance.*]

        Enter Puck.

PUCK
            Through the forest have I gone,
            But Athenian found I none
            On whose eyes I might approve   74
            This flower's force in stirring love.
            Night and silence.—Who is here?
            Weeds of Athens he doth wear.
            This is he, my master said,
            Despisèd the Athenian maid;
            And here the maiden, sleeping sound,
            On the dank and dirty ground.
            Pretty soul, she durst not lie
            Near this lack-love, this kill-courtesy.
            Churl, upon thy eyes I throw
            All the power this charm doth owe.   85
                    [*He applies the love juice.*]
            When thou wak'st, let love forbid   86
            Sleep his seat on thy eyelid.   87
            So awake when I am gone,
            For I must now to Oberon.   *Exit.*

        Enter Demetrius and Helena, running.

HELENA
            Stay, though thou kill me, sweet Demetrius!

13 Philomel the nightingale. (Philomela, daughter of King Pandion, was transformed into a nightingale, according to Ovid's *Meta-morphoses* 6, after she had been raped by her sister Procne's husband, Tereus.)   **23 offense** harm.   **32 sentinel** (Presumably Oberon is able to outwit or intimidate this guard.)   **36 ounce** lynx   **37 Pard** leopard   **48 troth** faith, trothplight.

51–2 take . . . conference take my meaning in an innocent sense, with generosity and sympathy! True lovers do so when they converse. **58 lie** tell a falsehood. (With a riddling pun on *lie*, "recline.") **60 beshrew** (A mild oath.)   **71 With . . . pressed!** i.e., I return half that wish, so that you, the wisher, may sleep well too (instead of Sleep giving all his rest to me)!   **74 approve** test   **85 owe** own.   **86–7 let . . . eyelid** may love, heretofore denied, be enthroned in your eyes.

DEMETRIUS

I charge thee, hence, and do not haunt me thus.

HELENA

Oh, wilt thou darkling leave me? Do not so.   92

DEMETRIUS

Stay, on thy peril! I alone will go.   [Exit.] 93

HELENA

Oh, I am out of breath in this fond chase!   94
The more my prayer, the lesser is my grace.   95
Happy is Hermia, wheresoe'er she lies,   96
For she hath blessèd and attractive eyes.
How came her eyes so bright? Not with salt tears;
If so, my eyes are oft'ner washed than hers.
No, no, I am as ugly as a bear,
For beasts that meet me run away for fear.
Therefore no marvel though Demetrius   102
Do, as a monster, fly my presence thus.   103
What wicked and dissembling glass of mine   104
Made me compare with Hermia's sphery eyne?   105
But who is here? Lysander, on the ground?
Dead, or asleep? I see no blood, no wound.
Lysander, if you live, good sir, awake.

LYSANDER [awaking]

And run through fire I will for thy sweet sake.
Transparent Helena! Nature shows art,   110
That through thy bosom makes me see thy heart.
Where is Demetrius? Oh, how fit a word
Is that vile name to perish on my sword!

HELENA

Do not say so, Lysander; say not so.
What though he love your Hermia? Lord, what
   though?
Yet Hermia still loves you. Then be content.

LYSANDER

Content with Hermia? No! I do repent
The tedious minutes I with her have spent.
Not Hermia but Helena I love.
Who will not change a raven for a dove?
The will of man is by his reason swayed,   121
And reason says you are the worthier maid.
Things growing are not ripe until their season;
So I, being young, till now ripe not to reason.   124
And, touching now the point of human skill,   125
Reason becomes the marshal to my will
And leads me to your eyes, where I o'erlook   127
Love's stories written in love's richest book.

HELENA

Wherefore was I to this keen mockery born?   129
When at your hands did I deserve this scorn?
Is't not enough, is't not enough, young man,
That I did never—no, nor never can—
Deserve a sweet look from Demetrius' eye,

But you must flout my insufficiency?
Good troth, you do me wrong, good sooth, you do,   135
In such disdainful manner me to woo.
But fare you well. Perforce I must confess
I thought you lord of more true gentleness.   138
Oh, that a lady, of one man refused,   139
Should of another therefore be abused!   Exit. 140

LYSANDER

She sees not Hermia. Hermia, sleep thou there,
And never mayst thou come Lysander near!
For as a surfeit of the sweetest things
The deepest loathing to the stomach brings,
Or as the heresies that men do leave   145
Are hated most of those they did deceive,   146
So thou, my surfeit and my heresy,
Of all be hated, but the most of me!   148
And, all my powers, address your love and might   149
To honor Helen and to be her knight!   Exit.

HERMIA [awaking]

Help me, Lysander, help me! Do thy best
To pluck this crawling serpent from my breast!
Ay me, for pity! What a dream was here!
Lysander, look how I do quake with fear.
Methought a serpent ate my heart away,
And you sat smiling at his cruel prey.   156
Lysander! What, removed? Lysander! Lord!
What, out of hearing? Gone? No sound, no word?
Alack, where are you? Speak, an if you hear;   159
Speak, of all loves! I swoon almost with fear.   160
No? Then I well perceive you are not nigh.
Either death, or you, I'll find immediately.

          Exit. [The sleeping Titania remains.]

❧

3.1

*Enter the clowns [Quince, Snug, Bottom, Flute,
Snout, and Starveling].*

BOTTOM   Are we all met?

QUINCE   Pat, pat; and here's a marvelous convenient   2
place for our rehearsal. This green plot shall be our
stage, this hawthorn brake our tiring-house, and we   4
will do it in action as we will do it before the Duke.

BOTTOM   Peter Quince?

QUINCE   What sayest thou, bully Bottom?   7

BOTTOM   There are things in this comedy of Pyramus
and Thisbe that will never please. First, Pyramus must
draw a sword to kill himself, which the ladies cannot
abide. How answer you that?

SNOUT   By'r lakin, a parlous fear.   12

92 darkling in the dark   93 on thy peril i.e., on pain of reprisal if you
don't obey me and stay.   94 fond doting   95 my grace the favor I
obtain.   96 lies dwells   102–3 no marvel . . . thus i.e., no wonder
that Demetrius flies from me as from a monster.   104 glass mirror
105 compare compare myself.   sphery eyne eyes as bright as stars in
their spheres.   110 Transparent Radiant, pure.   art skill, magic
power   121 will desire   124 ripe not have not ripened   125 touching . . . skill reaching now the age of mature judgment   127 o'erlook
read over   129 Wherefore Why

135 Good troth, good sooth i.e., Indeed, truly   138 lord of i.e., possessor of.   gentleness courtesy.   139 of by   140 abused ill treated.
145–6 as . . . deceive as renounced heresies are hated most by those
persons who formerly were deceived by them   148 Of . . . of by . . .
by   149 address direct, apply   156 prey act of preying.   159 an if if
160 of all loves for love's sake.
3.1. Location: The action is continuous.
0.1 clowns rustics   2 Pat On the dot, punctually   4 brake thicket.
tiring-house attiring area, hence backstage   7 bully i.e., worthy, jolly,
fine fellow   12 By'r lakin By our ladykin, i.e., the Virgin Mary.
parlous perilous, alarming

STARVELING   I believe we must leave the killing out, when all is done.   14

BOTTOM   Not a whit. I have a device to make all well. Write me a prologue, and let the prologue seem to say,   16 we will do no harm with our swords, and that Pyramus is not killed indeed; and for the more better assurance, tell them that I, Pyramus, am not Pyramus but Bottom the weaver. This will put them out of fear.

QUINCE   Well, we will have such a prologue, and it shall be written in eight and six.   22

BOTTOM   No, make it two more: let it be written in eight and eight.

SNOUT   Will not the ladies be afeard of the lion?

STARVELING   I fear it, I promise you.

BOTTOM   Masters, you ought to consider with yourself, to bring in—God shield us!—a lion among ladies is a   28 most dreadful thing. For there is not a more fearful   29 wildfowl than your lion living, and we ought to look to 't.

SNOUT   Therefore another prologue must tell he is not a lion.

BOTTOM   Nay, you must name his name, and half his face must be seen through the lion's neck, and he himself must speak through, saying thus or to the same defect: "Ladies," or "Fair ladies, I would wish you," or   37 "I would request you," or "I would entreat you, not to fear, not to tremble; my life for yours. If you think I   39 come hither as a lion, it were pity of my life. No, I am   40 no such thing; I am a man as other men are." And there indeed let him name his name, and tell them plainly he is Snug the joiner.

QUINCE   Well, it shall be so. But there is two hard things: that is, to bring the moonlight into a chamber; for, you know, Pyramus and Thisbe meet by moonlight.

SNOUT   Doth the moon shine that night we play our play?

BOTTOM   A calendar, a calendar! Look in the almanac. Find out moonshine, find out moonshine.

[They consult an almanac.]

QUINCE   Yes, it doth shine that night.

BOTTOM   Why then may you leave a casement of the great chamber window where we play open, and the moon may shine in at the casement.

QUINCE   Ay; or else one must come in with a bush of   55 thorns and a lantern and say he comes to disfigure, or   56 to present, the person of Moonshine. Then there is another thing: we must have a wall in the great cham-

ber; for Pyramus and Thisbe, says the story, did talk through the chink of a wall.

SNOUT   You can never bring in a wall. What say you, Bottom?

BOTTOM   Some man or other must present Wall. And let him have some plaster, or some loam, or some rough-   64 cast about him, to signify wall; or let him hold his   65 fingers thus, and through that cranny shall Pyramus and Thisbe whisper.

QUINCE   If that may be, then all is well. Come, sit down, every mother's son, and rehearse your parts. Pyramus, you begin. When you have spoken your speech, enter into that brake, and so everyone according to his cue.

Enter Robin [Puck].

PUCK   *[aside]*
What hempen homespuns have we swagg'ring here   72
So near the cradle of the Fairy Queen?   73
What, a play toward? I'll be an auditor;   74
An actor, too, perhaps, if I see cause.

QUINCE   Speak, Pyramus. Thisbe, stand forth.

BOTTOM   *[as Pyramus]*
"Thisbe, the flowers of odious savors sweet—"

QUINCE   Odors, odors.

BOTTOM   "—Odors savors sweet;
So hath thy breath, my dearest Thisbe dear.
But hark, a voice! Stay thou but here awhile,
And by and by I will to thee appear."   *Exit.*

PUCK   A stranger Pyramus than e'er played here. *[Exit.]*   83

FLUTE   Must I speak now?

QUINCE   Ay, marry, must you; for you must understand he goes but to see a noise that he heard, and is to come again.

FLUTE   *[as Thisbe]*
"Most radiant Pyramus, most lily-white of hue,
Of color like the red rose on triumphant brier,   89
Most brisky juvenal and eke most lovely Jew,   90
As true as truest horse that yet would never tire.
I'll meet thee, Pyramus, at Ninny's tomb."

QUINCE   "Ninus' tomb," man. Why, you must not speak   93 that yet. That you answer to Pyramus. You speak all your part at once, cues and all. Pyramus, enter. Your   95 cue is past; it is "never tire."

FLUTE
Oh—"As true as truest horse that yet would never tire."   97

[Enter Puck, and Bottom as Pyramus with the ass head.]

---

14 when all is done i.e., when all is said and done.   **16 Write me** i.e., Write at my suggestion. (*Me* is used colloquially.)   **22 eight and six** alternate lines of eight and six syllables, a common ballad measure.   **28 lion among ladies** (A contemporary pamphlet tells how, at the christening in 1594 of Prince Henry, eldest son of King James VI of Scotland, later James I of England, a "blackamoor" instead of a lion drew the triumphal chariot, since the lion's presence might have "brought some fear to the nearest.")   **29 fearful** fear-inspiring   **37 defect** (Bottom's blunder for "effect.")   **39 my life for yours** i.e., I pledge my life to make your lives safe.   **40 it were . . . life** i.e., I should be sorry, by my life; or, my life would be endangered.   **55–6 bush of thorns** bundle of thornbush fagots. (Part of the accoutrements of the man in the moon, according to the popular notions of the time, along with his lantern and his dog.)   **56 disfigure** (Quince's blunder for "figure," "represent.")

64–5 roughcast a mixture of lime and gravel used to plaster the outside of buildings   **72 hempen homespuns** i.e., rustics dressed in homespun fabric made from hemp   **73 cradle** i.e., Titania's bower   **74 toward** about to take place.   **83 A stranger . . . here** The strangest Pyramus you ever saw.   **89 triumphant** magnificent   **90 brisky juvenal** lively youth.   **eke** also.   **Jew** (A desperate attempt to rhyme with *hue*, inspired perhaps by the first syllable of *juvenal*.)   **93 Ninus** mythical founder of Nineveh (whose wife, Semiramis, was supposed to have built the walls of Babylon where the story of Pyramus and Thisbe takes place)   **95 part** (An actor's *part* was a script consisting only of his speeches and their cues.)   **97.1–2 with the ass head** (This stage direction, taken from the Folio, presumably refers to a standard stage property.)

BOTTOM
"If I were fair, Thisbe, I were only thine." 98

QUINCE   Oh, monstrous! Oh, strange! We are haunted.
Pray, masters! Fly, masters! Help!

[Exeunt Quince, Snug, Flute,
Snout, and Starveling.]

PUCK
I'll follow you: I'll lead you about a round, 101
    Through bog, through bush, through brake,
        through brier.
Sometimes a horse I'll be, sometimes a hound,
    A hog, a headless bear, sometimes a fire; 104
And neigh, and bark, and grunt, and roar, and burn,
Like horse, hound, hog, bear, fire, at every turn. *Exit.*

BOTTOM   Why do they run away? This is a knavery of
them to make me afeard.

Enter Snout.

SNOUT   Oh, Bottom, thou art changed! What do I see on
thee?

BOTTOM   What do you see? You see an ass head of your
own, do you?   *[Exit Snout.]*

Enter Quince.

QUINCE   Bless thee, Bottom, bless thee! Thou art trans- 113
lated.   *Exit.* 114

BOTTOM   I see their knavery. This is to make an ass of
me, to fright me, if they could. But I will not stir from
this place, do what they can. I will walk up and down
here, and I will sing, that they shall hear I am not
afraid.   *[He sings.]*
    The ouzel cock so black of hue, 120
        With orange-tawny bill,
    The throstle with his note so true, 122
        The wren with little quill— 123

TITANIA *[awaking]*
What angel wakes me from my flow'ry bed?

BOTTOM *[sings]*
    The finch, the sparrow, and the lark,
        The plainsong cuckoo gray, 126
    Whose note full many a man doth mark,
        And dares not answer nay— 128
For indeed, who would set his wit to so foolish a bird? 129
Who would give a bird the lie, though he cry "cuckoo" 130
never so? 131

TITANIA
I pray thee, gentle mortal, sing again.
Mine ear is much enamored of thy note;
So is mine eye enthrallèd to thy shape;
And thy fair virtue's force perforce doth move me 135
On the first view to say, to swear, I love thee.

BOTTOM   Methinks, mistress, you should have little reason for that. And yet, to say the truth, reason and love
keep little company together nowadays—the more the
pity that some honest neighbors will not make them
friends. Nay, I can gleek upon occasion. 141

TITANIA
Thou art as wise as thou art beautiful.

BOTTOM   Not so, neither. But if I had wit enough to get
out of this wood, I have enough to serve mine own 144
turn. 145

TITANIA
Out of this wood do not desire to go.
Thou shalt remain here, whether thou wilt or no.
I am a spirit of no common rate. 148
The summer still doth tend upon my state, 149
And I do love thee. Therefore, go with me.
I'll give thee fairies to attend on thee,
And they shall fetch thee jewels from the deep,
And sing while thou on pressèd flowers dost sleep.
And I will purge thy mortal grossness so
That thou shalt like an airy spirit go.—
Peaseblossom, Cobweb, Mote, and Mustardseed! 156

Enter four Fairies [Peaseblossom, Cobweb,
Mote, and Mustardseed].

PEASEBLOSSOM   Ready.
COBWEB
And I.
MOTE   And I.
MUSTARDSEED   And I.
ALL   Where shall we go?

TITANIA
Be kind and courteous to this gentleman.
Hop in his walks and gambol in his eyes; 160
Feed him with apricots and dewberries, 161
With purple grapes, green figs, and mulberries;
The honey bags steal from the humble-bees,
And for night tapers crop their waxen thighs, 164
And light them at the fiery glowworms' eyes, 165
To have my love to bed and to arise;
And pluck the wings from painted butterflies
To fan the moonbeams from his sleeping eyes.
Nod to him, elves, and do him courtesies.

PEASEBLOSSOM   Hail, mortal!
COBWEB   Hail!
MOTE   Hail!
MUSTARDSEED   Hail!
BOTTOM   I cry Your Worships mercy, heartily. I beseech 174
Your Worship's name.

COBWEB   Cobweb.

---

98 If Even if.   fair handsome.   were would be   101 about a round
roundabout   104 fire will-o'-the-wisp   113–14 translated transformed.   120 ouzel cock male blackbird   122 throstle song thrush
123 with little quill with small pipe, i.e., high-pitched note; or else
with small feathers   126 plainsong singing a melody without variations   128 dares . . . nay i.e., cannot deny that he is a cuckold
129 set his wit to employ his intelligence to answer   130 give . . . lie
call the bird a liar   131 never so ever so much.   135 thy . . . force the
power of your unblemished excellence

141 gleek jest   144–5 serve . . . turn answer my purpose.   148 rate
rank, value.   149 still . . . state always waits upon me as a part of my
royal retinue   156 Mote i.e., speck. (The two words *moth* and *mote*
were pronounced alike, and both meanings may be present.)   160 in
his eyes in his sight (i.e., before him)   161 dewberries blackberries
164 night . . . thighs (The waxen thighs of the bumble-bee are to be
fashioned into wax candles to light Bottom's way in the dark.)   165
eyes (In fact, the light is emitted by the abdomen. *Eyes* may be
metaphorical.)   174 I cry . . . mercy I beg pardon of Your Worships
(for presuming to ask a question)

BOTTOM I shall desire you of more acquaintance, good 177
Master Cobweb. If I cut my finger, I shall make bold 178
with you.—Your name, honest gentleman? 179

PEASEBLOSSOM Peaseblossom.

BOTTOM I pray you, commend me to Mistress Squash, 181
your mother, and to Master Peascod, your father. 182
Good Master Peaseblossom, I shall desire you of more
acquaintance too.—Your name, I beseech you, sir?

MUSTARDSEED Mustardseed.

BOTTOM Good Master Mustardseed, I know your 186
patience well. That same cowardly, giantlike ox-beef 187
hath devoured many a gentleman of your house. I
promise you, your kindred hath made my eyes water 189
ere now. I desire you of more acquaintance, good
Master Mustardseed.

TITANIA
Come wait upon him; lead him to my bower.
The moon methinks looks with a wat'ry eye;
And when she weeps, weeps every little flower, 194
Lamenting some enforcèd chastity. 195
Tie up my lover's tongue; bring him silently. 196

Exeunt.

❧

[3.2]

Enter [Oberon,] King of Fairies.

OBERON
I wonder if Titania be awaked;
Then, what it was that next came in her eye,
Which she must dote on in extremity.

[Enter] Robin Goodfellow [Puck].

Here comes my messenger. How now, mad spirit?
What night-rule now about this haunted grove? 5

PUCK
My mistress with a monster is in love.
Near to her close and consecrated bower, 7
While she was in her dull and sleeping hour, 8
A crew of patches, rude mechanicals, 9
That work for bread upon Athenian stalls, 10
Were met together to rehearse a play
Intended for great Theseus' nuptial day.
The shallowest thickskin of that barren sort, 13
Who Pyramus presented, in their sport 14
Forsook his scene and entered in a brake. 15
When I did him at this advantage take,

An ass's noll I fixèd on his head.
Anon his Thisbe must be answerèd, 17
And forth my mimic comes. When they him spy, 19
As wild geese that the creeping fowler eye, 20
Or russet-pated choughs, many in sort, 21
Rising and cawing at the gun's report,
Sever themselves and madly sweep the sky, 23
So, at his sight, away his fellows fly;
And, at our stamp, here o'er and o'er one falls;
He "Murder!" cries and help from Athens calls.
Their sense thus weak, lost with their fears thus
strong,
Made senseless things begin to do them wrong, 27
For briers and thorns at their apparel snatch; 28
Some, sleeves—some, hats; from yielders all things
catch. 30
I led them on in this distracted fear
And left sweet Pyramus translated there,
When in that moment, so it came to pass,
Titania waked and straightway loved an ass.

OBERON
This falls out better than I could devise.
But hast thou yet latched the Athenian's eyes 36
With the love juice, as I did bid thee do?

PUCK
I took him sleeping—that is finished too—
And the Athenian woman by his side,
That, when he waked, of force she must be eyed. 40

Enter Demetrius and Hermia.

OBERON
Stand close. This is the same Athenian.

PUCK
This is the woman, but not this the man.

[They stand aside.]

DEMETRIUS
Oh, why rebuke you him that loves you so?
Lay breath so bitter on your bitter foe.

HERMIA
Now I but chide; but I should use thee worse,
For thou, I fear, hast given me cause to curse.
If thou hast slain Lysander in his sleep,
Being o'er shoes in blood, plunge in the deep, 48
And kill me too.
The sun was not so true unto the day
As he to me. Would he have stolen away
From sleeping Hermia? I'll believe as soon
This whole earth may be bored, and that the moon 53
May through the center creep, and so displease
Her brother's noontide with th'Antipodes. 55

---

177 **I . . . acquaintance** I crave to be better acquainted with you
178–9 If . . . you (Cobwebs were used to stanch bleeding.)
181 Squash unripe pea pod **182 Peascod** ripe pea pod **186–7 your
patience** what you have endured. (Mustard is eaten with beef.)
189 water (1) weep for sympathy (2) smart, sting **194 And . . .
flower** (Dew was thought to fall from the heavens in greater proportion as the moon shown fully.) **195 enforcèd** violated. (The moon is
associated throughout the play with the goddess Diana and chastity.)
196 Tie . . . tongue (Presumably Bottom is braying like an ass.)
3.2. Location: The wood.
5 night-rule diversion or misrule for the night **7 close** secret **8 dull**
drowsy **9 patches** clowns, fools. **rude mechanicals** ignorant artisans **10 stalls** market booths **13 barren sort** stupid company or
crew **14 presented** acted **15 scene** playing area

17 **noll** noddle, head 19 **mimic** actor 20 **fowler** hunter of game
birds 21 **russet-pated choughs** reddish brown or gray-headed jackdaws. **in sort** in a flock 23 **Sever themselves** i.e., scatter
27–8 Their . . . wrong Their weakened physical senses, disabled by
their strong fears, made it seem to them as though inanimate things
in the forest were attacking them **30 from . . . catch** the forest
snatches away everything from those who yield to it. **36 latched**
snared, taken prisoner **40 of force** perforce **48 Being o'er shoes**
having waded in so far **53 whole** solid **55 Her . . . Antipodes** i.e.,
the sun's noontime on the opposite side of the earth, among the people who live there, the Antipodes.

It cannot be but thou hast murdered him;
So should a murderer look, so dead, so grim.   57

DEMETRIUS

So should the murdered look, and so should I,
Pierced through the heart with your stern cruelty.
Yet you, the murderer, look as bright, as clear
As yonder Venus in her glimmering sphere.

HERMIA

What's this to my Lysander? Where is he?   62
Ah, good Demetrius, wilt thou give him me?

DEMETRIUS

I had rather give his carcass to my hounds.

HERMIA

Out, dog! Out, cur! Thou driv'st me past the bounds
Of maiden's patience. Hast thou slain him, then?
Henceforth be never numbered among men.
Oh, once tell true, tell true, even for my sake: 68
Durst thou have looked upon him being awake?   69
And hast thou killed him sleeping? Oh, brave touch!   70
Could not a worm, an adder, do so much?   71
An adder did it; for with doubler tongue   72
Than thine, thou serpent, never adder stung.

DEMETRIUS

You spend your passion on a misprised mood.   74
I am not guilty of Lysander's blood,
Nor is he dead, for aught that I can tell.

HERMIA

I pray thee, tell me then that he is well.

DEMETRIUS

And if I could, what should I get therefor?   78

HERMIA

A privilege never to see me more.
And from thy hated presence part I so.
See me no more, whether he be dead or no.   *Exit.*

DEMETRIUS

There is no following her in this fierce vein.
Here therefore for a while I will remain.
So sorrow's heaviness doth heavier grow   84
For debt that bankrupt sleep doth sorrow owe,   85
Which now in some slight measure it will pay,   86
If for his tender here I make some stay.   87
                         [*He*] lie[*s*] *down* [*and sleeps*].

OBERON

What hast thou done? Thou hast mistaken quite
And laid the love juice on some true love's sight.
Of thy misprision must perforce ensue   90
Some true love turned, and not a false turned true.

PUCK

Then fate o'errules, that, one man holding troth,   92
A million fail, confounding oath on oath.   93

OBERON

About the wood go swifter than the wind,
And Helena of Athens look thou find.
All fancy-sick she is and pale of cheer   96
With sighs of love, that cost the fresh blood dear.   97
By some illusion see thou bring her here.
I'll charm his eyes against she do appear.   99

PUCK

I go, I go, look how I go,
Swifter than arrow from the Tartar's bow.   [*Exit.*] 101

OBERON [*applying love juice to Demetrius's eyes*]
Flower of this purple dye,
Hit with Cupid's archery,
Sink in apple of his eye.   104
When his love he doth espy,
Let her shine as gloriously
As the Venus of the sky.
When thou wak'st, if she be by,
Beg of her for remedy.

          Enter Puck.

PUCK

Captain of our fairy band,
Helena is here at hand,
And the youth, mistook by me,
Pleading for a lover's fee.   113
Shall we their fond pageant see?   114
Lord, what fools these mortals be!

OBERON

Stand aside. The noise they make
Will cause Demetrius to awake.

PUCK

Then will two at once woo one;
That must needs be sport alone.   119
And those things do best please me
That befall preposterously.   121
                         [*They stand aside.*]

          Enter Lysander and Helena.

LYSANDER

Why should you think that I should woo in scorn?
Scorn and derision never come in tears.
Look when I vow, I weep; and vows so born,   124
In their nativity all truth appears.   125
How can these things in me seem scorn to you,
Bearing the badge of faith to prove them true?

HELENA

You do advance your cunning more and more.   128
When truth kills truth, oh, devilish-holy fray!   129
These vows are Hermia's. Will you give her o'er?
Weigh oath with oath, and you will nothing weigh;

57 **dead** deadly, or deathly pale   62 **to** to do with   68 **once** once and for all   69 **being awake** when he was awake.   70 **brave touch!** fine stroke! (Said ironically.)   71 **worm** serpent   72 **doubler** (1) more forked (2) more deceitful   74 **You . . . mood** Your anger is misdirected.   78 **therefor** in return for that.   84–7 **So . . . stay** The heaviness of sorrow grows still heavier when sleepiness adds to the weariness caused by sorrow, which debt to sleepiness I will now repay in part if I can stop here and accept what sleep has to offer.   90 **misprision** mistake   92–3 **Then . . . oath** If so, then fate prevails; for each male who is able to keep true faith in love, a million will fail, breaking oath on oath.

96 **fancy-sick** lovesick.   **cheer** face   97 **sighs . . . dear** (Each sigh was supposed to cost the heart a drop of blood.)   99 **against . . . appear** in anticipation of her coming.   101 **Tartar's bow** (Tartars were famed for their skill with the bow.)   104 **apple** pupil   113 **fee** privilege, reward.   114 **fond pageant** foolish spectacle   119 **alone** unequaled.   121 **preposterously** out of the natural order.   124 **Look when** Whenever   124–5 **vows . . . appears** i.e., vows made by one who is weeping give evidence thereby of their sincerity.   128 **advance** carry forward, display   129 **When . . . truth** i.e., When one of your vows cancels the other

Your vows to her and me, put in two scales,
Will even weigh, and both as light as tales.

LYSANDER
I had no judgment when to her I swore.   133

HELENA
Nor none, in my mind, now you give her o'er.

LYSANDER
Demetrius loves her, and he loves not you.

DEMETRIUS [awaking]
O Helen, goddess, nymph, perfect, divine!
To what, my love, shall I compare thine eyne?
Crystal is muddy. Oh, how ripe in show
Thy lips, those kissing cherries, tempting grow!   139
That pure congealèd white, high Taurus' snow,   141
Fanned with the eastern wind, turns to a crow   142
When thou hold'st up thy hand. Oh, let me kiss
This princess of pure white, this seal of bliss!

HELENA
Oh, spite! Oh, hell! I see you all are bent   144
To set against me for your merriment.
If you were civil and knew courtesy,   146
You would not do me thus much injury.
Can you not hate me, as I know you do,
But you must join in souls to mock me too?
If you were men, as men you are in show,   150
You would not use a gentle lady so—
To vow, and swear, and superpraise my parts,
When I am sure you hate me with your hearts.   153
You both are rivals, and love Hermia,
And now both rivals to mock Helena.
A trim exploit, a manly enterprise,
To conjure tears up in a poor maid's eyes   157
With your derision! None of noble sort
Would so offend a virgin and extort   159
A poor soul's patience, all to make you sport.   160

LYSANDER
You are unkind, Demetrius. Be not so.
For you love Hermia; this you know I know.
And here, with all good will, with all my heart,
In Hermia's love I yield you up my part;
And yours of Helena to me bequeath,
Whom I do love, and will do till my death.

HELENA
Never did mockers waste more idle breath.

DEMETRIUS
Lysander, keep thy Hermia; I will none.
If e'er I loved her, all that love is gone.   169
My heart to her but as guestwise sojourned,
And now to Helen is it home returned,   171
There to remain.

LYSANDER   Helen, it is not so.

DEMETRIUS
Disparage not the faith thou dost not know,
Lest, to thy peril, thou aby it dear.   175
Look where thy love comes; yonder is thy dear.

Enter Hermia.

HERMIA
Dark night, that from the eye his function takes,   177
The ear more quick of apprehension makes;
Wherein it doth impair the seeing sense,
It pays the hearing double recompense.
Thou art not by mine eye, Lysander, found;
Mine ear, I thank it, brought me to thy sound.
But why unkindly didst thou leave me so?

LYSANDER
Why should he stay, whom love doth press to go?

HERMIA
What love could press Lysander from my side?

LYSANDER
Lysander's love, that would not let him bide—
Fair Helena, who more engilds the night
Than all yon fiery oes and eyes of light.   188
Why seek'st thou me? Could not this make thee
    know
The hate I bear thee made me leave thee so?

HERMIA
You speak not as you think. It cannot be.

HELENA
Lo, she is one of this confederacy!
Now I perceive they have conjoined all three
To fashion this false sport, in spite of me.   194
Injurious Hermia, most ungrateful maid!
Have you conspired, have you with these contrived
To bait me with this foul derision?   197
Is all the counsel that we two have shared—   198
The sisters' vows, the hours that we have spent
When we have chid the hasty-footed time
For parting us—oh, is all forgot?
All schooldays' friendship, childhood innocence?
We, Hermia, like two artificial gods   203
Have with our needles created both one flower,
Both on one sampler, sitting on one cushion,
Both warbling of one song, both in one key,
As if our hands, our sides, voices, and minds
Had been incorporate. So we grew together,   208
Like to a double cherry, seeming parted,
But yet an union in partition,
Two lovely berries molded on one stem;
So, with two seeming bodies but one heart,
Two of the first, like coats in heraldry,   213
Due but to one and crownèd with one crest.   214
And will you rend our ancient love asunder,
To join with men in scorning your poor friend?
It is not friendly, 'tis not maidenly.

Our sex, as well as I, may chide you for it,
Though I alone do feel the injury.

HERMIA
I am amazèd at your passionate words.
I scorn you not. It seems that you scorn me.

HELENA
Have you not set Lysander, as in scorn,
To follow me and praise my eyes and face?
And made your other love, Demetrius,
Who even but now did spurn me with his foot,
To call me goddess, nymph, divine, and rare,
Precious, celestial? Wherefore speaks he this
To her he hates? And wherefore doth Lysander
Deny your love, so rich within his soul,
And tender me, forsooth, affection,   230
But by your setting on, by your consent?
What though I be not so in grace as you,   232
So hung upon with love, so fortunate,
But miserable most, to love unloved?
This you should pity rather than despise.

HERMIA
I understand not what you mean by this.

HELENA
Ay, do! Persever, counterfeit sad looks,   237
Make mouths upon me when I turn my back,   238
Wink each at other, hold the sweet jest up.   239
This sport, well carried, shall be chronicled.   240
If you have any pity, grace, or manners,
You would not make me such an argument.   242
But fare ye well. 'Tis partly my own fault,
Which death, or absence, soon shall remedy.

LYSANDER
Stay, gentle Helena; hear my excuse,
My love, my life, my soul, fair Helena!

HELENA
Oh, excellent!

HERMIA [to Lysander]   Sweet, do not scorn her so.

DEMETRIUS [to Lysander]
If she cannot entreat, I can compel.   248

LYSANDER
Thou canst compel no more than she entreat.
Thy threats have no more strength than her weak
    prayers.—
Helen, I love thee, by my life, I do!
I swear by that which I will lose for thee,
To prove him false that says I love thee not.

DEMETRIUS [to Helena]
I say I love thee more than he can do.

LYSANDER
If thou say so, withdraw, and prove it too.   255

DEMETRIUS
Quick, come!

HERMIA   Lysander, whereto tends all this?

LYSANDER
Away, you Ethiope!

            [He tries to break away from Hermia.]

DEMETRIUS   No, no; he'll   257
Seem to break loose; take on as you would follow,   258
But yet come not. You are a tame man. Go!

LYSANDER [to Hermia]
Hang off, thou cat, thou burr! Vile thing, let loose,   260
Or I will shake thee from me like a serpent!

HERMIA
Why are you grown so rude? What change is this,
Sweet love?

LYSANDER   Thy love? Out, tawny Tartar, out!
Out, loathèd med'cine! O hated potion, hence!   264

HERMIA
Do you not jest?

HELENA   Yes, sooth, and so do you.   265

LYSANDER
Demetrius, I will keep my word with thee.

DEMETRIUS
I would I had your bond, for I perceive
A weak bond holds you. I'll not trust your word.   268

LYSANDER
What, should I hurt her, strike her, kill her dead?
Although I hate her, I'll not harm her so.

HERMIA
What, can you do me greater harm than hate?
Hate me? Wherefore? Oh, me, what news, my love?   272
Am not I Hermia? Are not you Lysander?
I am as fair now as I was erewhile.   274
Since night you loved me; yet since night you left me.
Why, then you left me—oh, the gods forbid!—
In earnest, shall I say?

LYSANDER   Ay, by my life!
And never did desire to see thee more.
Therefore be out of hope, of question, of doubt;
Be certain, nothing truer. 'Tis no jest
That I do hate thee and love Helena.

HERMIA [to Helena]
Oh, me! You juggler! You cankerblossom!   282
You thief of love! What, have you come by night
And stol'n my love's heart from him?

HELENA   Fine, i'faith!
Have you no modesty, no maiden shame,
No touch of bashfulness? What, will you tear
Impatient answers from my gentle tongue?
Fie, fie! You counterfeit, you puppet, you!   288

HERMIA
"Puppet"? Why, so! Ay, that way goes the game.
Now I perceive that she hath made compare
Between our statures; she hath urged her height,
And with her personage, her tall personage,

---

230 **tender** offer   232 **grace** favor   237 **sad** grave, serious
238 **mouths** i.e., mows, faces, grimaces. **upon** at   239 **hold . . . up**
keep up the joke.   240 **carried** carried out, brought off   242 **argument** subject for a jest.   248 **entreat** i.e., succeed by entreaty
255 **withdraw . . . too** i.e., withdraw with me and prove your claim
in a duel. (The two gentlemen are armed.)

257 **Ethiope** (Referring to Hermia's relatively dark hair and complexion; see also *tawny Tartar* six lines later.)   258 **take on as** act as if,
make a fuss as if   260 **Hang off** Let go   264 **med'cine** i.e., poison
265 **sooth** truly   268 **weak bond** i.e., Hermia's arm. (With a pun on
bond, "oath," in the previous line.)   272 **what news** what is the matter   274 **erewhile** just now.   282 **cankerblossom** worm that destroys
the flower bud, or wild rose.   288 **puppet** (1) counterfeit (2) dwarfish
woman (in reference to Hermia's smaller stature)

Her height, forsooth, she hath prevailed with him.
And are you grown so high in his esteem
Because I am so dwarfish and so low?
How low am I, thou painted maypole? Speak!
How low am I? I am not yet so low
But that my nails can reach unto thine eyes.

[*She flails at Helena but is restrained.*]

HELENA
I pray you, though you mock me, gentlemen,
Let her not hurt me. I was never curst;   300
I have no gift at all in shrewishness;
I am a right maid for my cowardice.   302
Let her not strike me. You perhaps may think,
Because she is something lower than myself,   304
That I can match her.

HERMIA   Lower? Hark, again!

HELENA
Good Hermia, do not be so bitter with me.
I evermore did love you, Hermia,
Did ever keep your counsels, never wronged you,
Save that, in love unto Demetrius,
I told him of your stealth unto this wood.   310
He followed you; for love I followed him.
But he hath chid me hence and threatened me   312
To strike me, spurn me, nay, to kill me too.   313
And now, so you will let me quiet go,   314
To Athens will I bear my folly back
And follow you no further. Let me go.
You see how simple and how fond I am.   317

HERMIA
Why, get you gone. Who is't that hinders you?

HELENA
A foolish heart, that I leave here behind.

HERMIA
What, with Lysander?

HELENA   With Demetrius.

LYSANDER
Be not afraid; she shall not harm thee, Helena.

DEMETRIUS
No, sir, she shall not, though you take her part.

HELENA
Oh, when she is angry, she is keen and shrewd.   323
She was a vixen when she went to school;
And though she be but little, she is fierce.

HERMIA
"Little" again? Nothing but "low" and "little"?—
Why will you suffer her to flout me thus?
Let me come to her.

LYSANDER   Get you gone, you dwarf!
You minimus, of hind'ring knotgrass made!   329
You bead, you acorn!

DEMETRIUS   You are too officious
In her behalf that scorns your services.
Let her alone. Speak not of Helena;

Take not her part. For, if thou dost intend   333
Never so little show of love to her,
Thou shalt aby it.

LYSANDER   Now she holds me not.   335
Now follow, if thou dar'st, to try whose right,
Of thine or mine, is most in Helena.   [*Exit.*]

DEMETRIUS
Follow? Nay, I'll go with thee, cheek by jowl.   338

[*Exit, following Lysander.*]

HERMIA
You, mistress, all this coil is 'long of you.   339
Nay, go not back.

HELENA   I will not trust you, I,   340
Nor longer stay in your curst company.
Your hands than mine are quicker for a fray;
My legs are longer, though, to run away.   [*Exit.*]

HERMIA
I am amazed and know not what to say.   *Exit.*

[*Oberon and Puck come forward.*]

OBERON
This is thy negligence. Still thou mistak'st,
Or else commit'st thy knaveries willfully.

PUCK
Believe me, king of shadows, I mistook.
Did not you tell me I should know the man
By the Athenian garments he had on?
And so far blameless proves my enterprise
That I have 'nointed an Athenian's eyes;
And so far am I glad it so did sort,   352
As this their jangling I esteem a sport.   353

OBERON
Thou see'st these lovers seek a place to fight.
Hie therefore, Robin, overcast the night;   355
The starry welkin cover thou anon   356
With drooping fog as black as Acheron,   357
And lead these testy rivals so astray
As one come not within another's way.   359
Like to Lysander sometimes frame thy tongue,   360
Then stir Demetrius up with bitter wrong;   361
And sometimes rail thou like Demetrius.
And from each other look thou lead them thus,
Till o'er their brows death-counterfeiting sleep
With leaden legs and batty wings doth creep.   365
Then crush this herb into Lysander's eye,   366

[*giving herb*]

Whose liquor hath this virtuous property,   367
To take from thence all error with his might   368
And make his eyeballs roll with wonted sight.   369
When they next wake, all this derision   370
Shall seem a dream and fruitless vision,

300 **curst** shrewish   302 **right** true   304 **something** somewhat
310 **stealth** stealing away   312 **chid me hence** driven me away with
his scolding   313 **spurn** kick   314 **so** if only   317 **fond** foolish
323 **keen and shrewd** fierce and shrewish.   329 **minimus** diminutive
creature.   **knotgrass** a weed, an infusion of which was thought to
stunt the growth

333 **intend** give sign of   335 **aby** pay for   338 **cheek by jowl** i.e.,
side by side.   339 **coil** turmoil, dissension.   **'long of** on account of
340 **go not back** i.e., don't retreat. (Hermia is again proposing a fight.)
352 **so far** at least to this extent.   **sort** turn out   353 **As** in that
355 **Hie** Hasten   356 **welkin** sky   357 **Acheron** river of Hades (here
representing Hades itself)   359 **As** that   360 **frame thy tongue** fashion your speech   361 **wrong** insults   365 **batty** batlike   366 **this
herb** i.e., the antidote (mentioned in 2.1.184) to love-in-idleness
367 **virtuous** efficacious   368 **his** its   369 **wonted** accustomed
370 **derision** laughable business

And back to Athens shall the lovers wend
With league whose date till death shall never end.   373
Whiles I in this affair do thee employ,
I'll to my queen and beg her Indian boy;
And then I will her charmèd eye release
From monster's view, and all things shall be peace.

PUCK
My fairy lord, this must be done with haste,
For night's swift dragons cut the clouds full fast,   379
And yonder shines Aurora's harbinger,   380
At whose approach ghosts, wand'ring here and there,
Troop home to churchyards. Damnèd spirits all,
That in crossways and floods have burial,   383
Already to their wormy beds are gone.
For fear lest day should look their shames upon,
They willfully themselves exile from light
And must for aye consort with black-browed night.   387

OBERON
But we are spirits of another sort.
I with the Morning's love have oft made sport,   389
And, like a forester, the groves may tread   390
Even till the eastern gate, all fiery red,
Opening on Neptune with fair blessèd beams,
Turns into yellow gold his salt green streams.
But notwithstanding, haste, make no delay.
We may effect this business yet ere day.   [*Exit.*]

PUCK
          Up and down, up and down,
          I will lead them up and down.
          I am feared in field and town.
          Goblin, lead them up and down.   399
Here comes one.

          Enter Lysander.

LYSANDER
Where art thou, proud Demetrius? Speak thou now.
PUCK [*mimicking Demetrius*]
Here, villain, drawn and ready. Where art thou?   402
LYSANDER
I will be with thee straight.
PUCK   Follow me, then,   403
To plainer ground.
          [*Lysander wanders about, following the voice.*]

          Enter Demetrius.

DEMETRIUS   Lysander! Speak again!   404
Thou runaway, thou coward, art thou fled?
Speak! In some bush? Where dost thou hide thy head?

PUCK [*mimicking Lysander*]
Thou coward, art thou bragging to the stars,
Telling the bushes that thou look'st for wars,
And wilt not come? Come, recreant; come, thou child,   409
I'll whip thee with a rod. He is defiled
That draws a sword on thee.
DEMETRIUS   Yea, art thou there?
PUCK
Follow my voice. We'll try no manhood here.   412
                                        Exeunt.

          [*Lysander returns.*]

LYSANDER
He goes before me and still dares me on.
When I come where he calls, then he is gone.
The villain is much lighter-heeled than I.
I followed fast, but faster he did fly,
That fallen am I in dark uneven way,
And here will rest me. [*He lies down.*] Come, thou
          gentle day!
For if but once thou show me thy gray light,
I'll find Demetrius and revenge this spite. [*He sleeps.*]

          [*Enter*] Robin [*Puck*] *and Demetrius.*

PUCK
Ho, ho, ho! Coward, why com'st thou not?
DEMETRIUS
Abide me, if thou dar'st; for well I wot   422
Thou runn'st before me, shifting every place,
And dar'st not stand nor look me in the face.
Where art thou now?
PUCK   Come hither. I am here.
DEMETRIUS
Nay, then, thou mock'st me. Thou shalt buy this dear,   426
If ever I thy face by daylight see.
Now go thy way. Faintness constraineth me
To measure out my length on this cold bed.
By day's approach look to be visited.
          [*He lies down and sleeps.*]

          Enter Helena.

HELENA
O weary night, O long and tedious night,
     Abate thy hours! Shine comforts from the east,   432
That I may back to Athens by daylight
     From these that my poor company detest;
And sleep, that sometimes shuts up sorrow's eye,
Steal me awhile from mine own company!
          [*She lies down and*] sleep[*s*].

PUCK
          Yet but three? Come one more;
          Two of both kinds makes up four.
          Here she comes, curst and sad.   439
          Cupid is a knavish lad,
          Thus to make poor females mad.

          [*Enter Hermia.*]

---

373 **date** term of existence   379 **dragons** (Supposed here to be yoked to the car of the goddess of night or the moon.)   380 **Aurora's harbinger** the morning star, precursor of dawn   383 **crossways . . . burial** (Those who had committed suicide were buried at crossways, with a stake driven through them; those who intentionally or accidentally drowned [in *floods* or deep water] would be condemned to wander disconsolately for lack of burial rites.)   387 **for aye** forever   389 **the Morning's love** Cephalus, a beautiful youth beloved by Aurora; or perhaps the goddess of the dawn herself   390 **forester** keeper of a royal forest   399 **Goblin** Hobgoblin. (Puck refers to himself.)   402 **drawn** with drawn sword   403 **straight** immediately   404 **plainer** more open.   s.d. *Lysander wanders about* (Lysander may exit here, but perhaps not; neither exit nor reentrance is indicated in the early texts.)

409 **recreant** cowardly wretch   412 **try** test   422 **Abide** Confront, face.   **wot** know   426 **buy this dear** pay for this dearly   432 **Abate** lessen, shorten   439 **curst** ill-tempered

HERMIA

Never so weary, never so in woe,
    Bedabbled with the dew and torn with briers,
I can no further crawl, no further go;
    My legs can keep no pace with my desires.
Here will I rest me till the break of day.
Heavens shield Lysander, if they mean a fray!

[She lies down and sleeps.]

PUCK

        On the ground
        Sleep sound.
        I'll apply
        To your eye,
Gentle lover, remedy.

        [He squeezes the juice on Lysander's eyes.]
        When thou wak'st,
        Thou tak'st
        True delight
        In the sight
Of thy former lady's eye;
And the country proverb known,
That every man should take his own,
In your waking shall be shown: 461
        Jack shall have Jill;
        Naught shall go ill;
The man shall have his mare again, and all shall
    be well. *[Exit. The four sleeping lovers remain.]*

♣

[4.1]

*Enter [Titania,] Queen of Fairies, and [Bottom
the] clown, and Fairies; and [Oberon,] the King,
behind them.*

TITANIA

Come, sit thee down upon this flow'ry bed,
    While I thy amiable cheeks do coy,   2
And stick muskroses in thy sleek smooth head,
    And kiss thy fair large ears, my gentle joy.

[They recline.]

BOTTOM   Where's Peaseblossom?

PEASEBLOSSOM   Ready.

BOTTOM   Scratch my head, Peaseblossom. Where's
Monsieur Cobweb?

COBWEB   Ready.

BOTTOM   Monsieur Cobweb, good monsieur, get you
your weapons in your hand, and kill me a red-hipped
humble-bee on the top of a thistle; and, good monsieur, bring me the honey bag. Do not fret yourself too
much in the action, monsieur; and, good monsieur,
have a care the honey bag break not. I would be loath
to have you overflown with a honey bag, signor.

[Exit Cobweb.]

Where's Monsieur Mustardseed?

MUSTARDSEED   Ready.

BOTTOM   Give me your neaf, Monsieur Mustardseed.   19
Pray you, leave your courtesy, good monsieur.   20

MUSTARDSEED   What's your will?

BOTTOM   Nothing, good monsieur, but to help Cavalery   22
Cobweb to scratch. I must to the barber's, monsieur,   23
for methinks I am marvelous hairy about the face; and
I am such a tender ass, if my hair do but tickle me I
must scratch.

TITANIA

What, wilt thou hear some music, my sweet love?

BOTTOM   I have a reasonable good ear in music. Let's
have the tongs and the bones.   29

[Music: tongs, rural music.]

TITANIA

Or say, sweet love, what thou desirest to eat.

BOTTOM   Truly, a peck of provender. I could munch   31
your good dry oats. Methinks I have a great desire to
a bottle of hay. Good hay, sweet hay, hath no fellow.   33

TITANIA

I have a venturous fairy that shall seek
The squirrel's hoard, and fetch thee new nuts.

BOTTOM   I had rather have a handful or two of dried
peas. But, I pray you, let none of your people stir me.   37
I have an exposition of sleep come upon me.   38

TITANIA

Sleep thou, and I will wind thee in my arms.—
Fairies, begone, and be all ways away.   40

[Exeunt Fairies.]

So doth the woodbine the sweet honeysuckle   41
Gently entwist; the female ivy so
Enrings the barky fingers of the elm.
Oh, how I love thee! How I dote on thee!

[They sleep.]

Enter Robin Goodfellow [Puck].

OBERON *[coming forward]*

Welcome, good Robin. See'st thou this sweet sight?
Her dotage now I do begin to pity.
For, meeting her of late behind the wood
Seeking sweet favors for this hateful fool,   48
I did upbraid her and fall out with her.
For she his hairy temples then had rounded
With coronet of fresh and fragrant flowers;
And that same dew, which sometime on the buds   52
Was wont to swell like round and orient pearls,   53
Stood now within the pretty flowerets' eyes
Like tears that did their own disgrace bewail.
When I had at my pleasure taunted her,

---

461 Jack shall have Jill (Proverbial for "boy gets girl.")
4.1. Location: The action is continuous. The four lovers are still
asleep onstage. (Compare with the Folio stage direction: "They sleep
all the act.")
2 amiable lovely.   **coy** caress

19 neaf fist   **20 leave your courtesy** i.e., stop bowing, or put on your
hat   **22 Cavalery** Cavalier. (Form of address for a gentleman.)
23 Cobweb (Seemingly an error, since Cobweb has been sent to bring
honey, while Peaseblossom has been asked to scratch.)   **29 tongs . . .
bones** instruments for rustic music. (The tongs were played like a triangle, whereas the bones were held between the fingers and used as
clappers.)   **29.1 *Music . . . music*** (This stage direction is added from
the Folio.)   **31 peck of provender** one-quarter bushel of grain.
33 bottle bundle.   **fellow** equal.   **37 stir** disturb   **38 exposition of**
(Bottom's phrase for "disposition to.")   **40 all ways** in all directions
41 woodbine bindweed, a climbing plant   **48 favors** i.e., gifts of
flowers   **52 sometime** formerly   **53 orient** lustrous

And she in mild terms begged my patience,
I then did ask of her her changeling child,
Which straight she gave me, and her fairy sent
To bear him to my bower in Fairyland.
And, now I have the boy, I will undo
This hateful imperfection of her eyes.
And, gentle Puck, take this transformèd scalp
From off the head of this Athenian swain,
That he, awaking when the other do,   65
May all to Athens back again repair,   66
And think no more of this night's accidents
But as the fierce vexation of a dream.
But first I will release the Fairy Queen.
                            [*He squeezes an herb on her eyes.*]
       Be as thou wast wont to be;
       See as thou wast wont to see.
       Dian's bud o'er Cupid's flower   72
       Hath such force and blessèd power.
Now, my Titania, wake you, my sweet queen.

TITANIA [*awaking*]
My Oberon! What visions have I seen!
Methought I was enamored of an ass.

OBERON
There lies your love.

TITANIA   How came these things to pass?
Oh, how mine eyes do loathe his visage now!

OBERON
Silence awhile. Robin, take off this head.
Titania, music call, and strike more dead
Than common sleep of all these five the sense.   81

TITANIA
Music, ho! Music, such as charmeth sleep!   [*Music.*]   82

PUCK [*removing the ass head*]
Now, when thou wak'st, with thine own fool's eyes
   peep.

OBERON
Sound, music! Come, my queen, take hands with me,
And rock the ground whereon these sleepers be.
                                          [*They dance.*]
Now thou and I are new in amity,
And will tomorrow midnight solemnly   87
Dance in Duke Theseus' house triumphantly,
And bless it to all fair prosperity.
There shall the pairs of faithful lovers be
Wedded, with Theseus, all in jollity.

PUCK
Fairy King, attend, and mark:
I do hear the morning lark.

OBERON
Then, my queen, in silence sad,
Trip we after night's shade.   94
We the globe can compass soon,
Swifter than the wand'ring moon.

TITANIA
Come, my lord, and in our flight
Tell me how it came this night
That I sleeping here was found
With these mortals on the ground.
                  Exeunt [*Oberon, Titania, and Puck*].
                              Wind horn [*within*].

Enter Theseus and all his train; [*Hippolyta,
Egeus*].

THESEUS
Go, one of you, find out the forester,
For now our observation is performed;   103
And since we have the vaward of the day,   104
My love shall hear the music of my hounds.
Uncouple in the western valley; let them go.   106
Dispatch, I say, and find the forester.
                              [*Exit an Attendant.*]
We will, fair queen, up to the mountain's top
And mark the musical confusion
Of hounds and echo in conjunction.

HIPPOLYTA
I was with Hercules and Cadmus once   111
When in a wood of Crete they bayed the bear   112
With hounds of Sparta. Never did I hear   113
Such gallant chiding; for, besides the groves,   114
The skies, the fountains, every region near
Seemed all one mutual cry. I never heard
So musical a discord, such sweet thunder.

THESEUS
My hounds are bred out of the Spartan kind,   118
So flewed, so sanded; and their heads are hung   119
With ears that sweep away the morning dew;
Crook-kneed, and dewlapped like Thessalian bulls;   121
Slow in pursuit, but matched in mouth like bells,   122
Each under each. A cry more tunable   123
Was never holloed to nor cheered with horn   124
In Crete, in Sparta, nor in Thessaly.
Judge when you hear. [*He sees the sleepers.*] But soft!
   What nymphs are these?   126

EGEUS
My lord, this is my daughter here asleep,
And this Lysander; this Demetrius is;
This Helena, old Nedar's Helena.
I wonder of their being here together.   130

THESEUS
No doubt they rose up early to observe
The rite of May, and hearing our intent,

---

65 **other** others   66 **repair** return   72 **Dian's bud** (Perhaps the flower of the *agnus castus* or chaste-tree, supposed to preserve chastity; or perhaps referring simply to Oberon's herb by which he can undo the effects of "Cupid's flower," the love-in-idleness of 2.1.166–8.)
81 **these five** i.e., the four lovers and Bottom   82 **charmeth** brings about, as though by a charm   87 **solemnly** ceremoniously
94 **sad** solemn

103 **observation** i.e., observance to a morn of May (1.1.167)
104 **vaward** vanguard, i.e., earliest part   106 **Uncouple** Set free for the hunt   111 **Cadmus** mythical founder of Thebes. (This story about him is unknown.)   112 **bayed** brought to bay   113 **hounds of Sparta** (A breed famous in antiquity for their hunting skill.)   114 **chiding** i.e., yelping   118 **kind** strain, breed   119 **So flewed** similarly having large hanging chaps or fleshy covering of the jaw.   **sanded** of sandy color   121 **dewlapped** having pendulous folds of skin under the neck.   **Thessalian** from Thessaly, in Greece   122–3 **matched . . . each** i.e., harmoniously matched in their various cries like a set of bells, from treble down to bass.   123 **cry** pack of hounds.   **tunable** well tuned, melodious   124 **cheered** encouraged   126 **soft** i.e., gently, wait a minute.   130 **of** at

Came here in grace of our solemnity.   133
But speak, Egeus. Is not this the day
That Hermia should give answer of her choice?

EGEUS   It is, my lord.

THESEUS
Go bid the huntsmen wake them with their horns.

[Exit an Attendant.]

Shout within. Wind horns. They all start up.

Good morrow, friends. Saint Valentine is past.   138
Begin these woodbirds but to couple now?

LYSANDER
Pardon, my lord.   [They kneel.]

THESEUS   I pray you all, stand up.
[They stand.]
I know you two are rival enemies;
How comes this gentle concord in the world,
That hatred is so far from jealousy
To sleep by hate and fear no enmity?

LYSANDER
My lord, I shall reply amazedly,
Half sleep, half waking; but as yet, I swear,
I cannot truly say how I came here.
But, as I think—for truly would I speak,
And now I do bethink me, so it is—
I came with Hermia hither. Our intent
Was to be gone from Athens, where we might,
Without the peril of the Athenian law—

EGEUS
Enough, enough, my lord; you have enough.
I beg the law, the law, upon his head.
They would have stol'n away; they would, Demetrius,
Thereby to have defeated you and me,
You of your wife and me of my consent,
Of my consent that she should be your wife.

DEMETRIUS
My lord, fair Helen told me of their stealth,
Of this their purpose hither to this wood,
And I in fury hither followed them,
Fair Helena in fancy following me.
But, my good lord, I wot not by what power—   162
But by some power it is—my love to Hermia,
Melted as the snow, seems to me now
As the remembrance of an idle gaud   166
Which in my childhood I did dote upon;
And all the faith, the virtue of my heart,
The object and the pleasure of mine eye,
Is only Helena. To her, my lord,
Was I betrothed ere I saw Hermia,
But like a sickness did I loathe this food;
But, as in health, come to my natural taste,
Now I do wish it, love it, long for it,
And will forevermore be true to it.

THESEUS
Fair lovers, you are fortunately met.
Of this discourse we more will hear anon.

Egeus, I will overbear your will;
For in the temple, by and by, with us
These couples shall eternally be knit.
And, for the morning now is something worn,   181
Our purposed hunting shall be set aside.
Away with us to Athens. Three and three,
We'll hold a feast in great solemnity.   184
Come, Hippolyta.

[Exeunt Theseus, Hippolyta, Egeus, and train.]

DEMETRIUS
These things seem small and undistinguishable,
Like far-off mountains turnèd into clouds.

HERMIA
Methinks I see these things with parted eye,   188
When everything seems double.

HELENA   So methinks;
And I have found Demetrius like a jewel,   190
Mine own, and not mine own.

DEMETRIUS   Are you sure   191
That we are awake? It seems to me
That yet we sleep, we dream. Do not you think
The Duke was here, and bid us follow him?

HERMIA
Yea, and my father.

HELENA   And Hippolyta.

LYSANDER
And he did bid us follow to the temple.

DEMETRIUS
Why, then, we are awake. Let's follow him,
And by the way let us recount our dreams.

[Exeunt the lovers.]

BOTTOM [awaking]   When my cue comes, call me, and I
will answer. My next is "Most fair Pyramus." Heigh-
ho! Peter Quince! Flute, the bellows mender! Snout,
the tinker! Starveling! God's my life, stolen hence and   202
left me asleep! I have had a most rare vision. I have
had a dream, past the wit of man to say what dream
it was. Man is but an ass if he go about to expound this   205
dream. Methought I was—there is no man can tell
what. Methought I was—and methought I had—but
man is but a patched fool if he will offer to say what   208
methought I had. The eye of man hath not heard, the   209
ear of man hath not seen, man's hand is not able to   210
taste, his tongue to conceive, nor his heart to report,   211
what my dream was. I will get Peter Quince to write
a ballad of this dream. It shall be called "Bottom's   213
Dream," because it hath no bottom; and I will sing it   214
in the latter end of a play, before the Duke. Peradventure, to make it the more gracious, I shall sing it at her   216
death.
[Exit.]

❖

---

133 in . . . solemnity in honor of our wedding ceremony.   138 Saint
Valentine (Birds were supposed to choose their mates on Saint Valentine's Day.)   162 in fancy driven by love   166 idle gaud worthless
trinket

181 for since.   something somewhat   184 in great solemnity with
great ceremony.   188 parted i.e., improperly focused   190–1 like . . .
own i.e., something precious that seems mine and yet so mysteriously found that I can hardly believe it is mine.   202 God's May God
save   205 go about attempt   208 patched wearing motley, i.e., a
dress of various colors.   offer venture   209–11 The eye . . . report
(Bottom garbles 1 Corinthians 2:9.)   213 ballad (The proper medium
for relating sensational stories and preposterous events.)   214 hath
no bottom is unfathomable   216 her Thisbe's (?)

[4.2]

Enter Quince, Flute, [Snout, and Starveling].

QUINCE   Have you sent to Bottom's house? Is he come
home yet?

STARVELING   He cannot be heard of. Out of doubt he is
transported.   4

FLUTE   If he come not, then the play is marred. It goes
not forward. Doth it?

QUINCE   It is not possible. You have not a man in all
Athens able to discharge Pyramus but he.   8

FLUTE   No, he hath simply the best wit of any handicraft   9
man in Athens.

QUINCE   Yea, and the best person too, and he is a very   11
paramour for a sweet voice.

FLUTE   You must say "paragon." A paramour is, God
bless us, a thing of naught.   14

Enter Snug the joiner.

SNUG   Masters, the Duke is coming from the temple,
and there is two or three lords and ladies more
married. If our sport had gone forward, we had all   17
been made men.   18

FLUTE   Oh, sweet bully Bottom! Thus hath he lost
sixpence a day during his life; he could not have   20
scaped sixpence a day. An the Duke had not given him
sixpence a day for playing Pyramus, I'll be hanged. He
would have deserved it. Sixpence a day in Pyramus,
or nothing.

Enter Bottom.

BOTTOM   Where are these lads? Where are these hearts?   25

QUINCE   Bottom! Oh, most courageous day! Oh, most
happy hour!

BOTTOM   Masters, I am to discourse wonders. But ask   28
me not what; for if I tell you, I am no true Athenian. I
will tell you everything, right as it fell out.

QUINCE   Let us hear, sweet Bottom.

BOTTOM   Not a word of me. All that I will tell you is that   32
the Duke hath dined. Get your apparel together,
good strings to your beards, new ribbons to your   34
pumps; meet presently at the palace; every man look   35
o'er his part; for the short and the long is, our play is
preferred. In any case, let Thisbe have clean linen; and   37
let not him that plays the lion pare his nails, for they
shall hang out for the lion's claws. And, most dear actors, eat no onions nor garlic, for we are to utter sweet
breath; and I do not doubt but to hear them say it is
a sweet comedy. No more words. Away! Go, away!
[Exeunt.]

❧

4.2. Location: Athens.
4 transported carried off by fairies; or, transformed.   **8 discharge**
perform   **9 wit** intellect   **11 person** appearance   **14 a . . . naught** a
shameful thing   **17–18 we . . . men** i.e., we would have had our fortunes made.   **20 sixpence a day** i.e., as a royal pension   **25 hearts**
good fellows.   **28 am . . . wonders** have wonders to relate.   **32 of** out
of   **34 strings** (to attach the beards)   **35 pumps** light shoes or slippers   **37 preferred** selected for consideration.

[5.1]

Enter Theseus, Hippolyta, and Philostrate,
[lords, and attendants].

HIPPOLYTA
'Tis strange, my Theseus, that these lovers speak of.   1

THESEUS
More strange than true. I never may believe   2
These antique fables nor these fairy toys.   3
Lovers and madmen have such seething brains,
Such shaping fantasies, that apprehend   5
More than cool reason ever comprehends.   6
The lunatic, the lover, and the poet
Are of imagination all compact.   8
One sees more devils than vast hell can hold;
That is the madman. The lover, all as frantic,
Sees Helen's beauty in a brow of Egypt.   11
The poet's eye, in a fine frenzy rolling,
Doth glance from heaven to earth, from earth to
heaven;
And as imagination bodies forth
The forms of things unknown, the poet's pen
Turns them to shapes and gives to airy nothing
A local habitation and a name.
Such tricks hath strong imagination
That, if it would but apprehend some joy,
It comprehends some bringer of that joy;   20
Or in the night, imagining some fear,   21
How easy is a bush supposed a bear!

HIPPOLYTA
But all the story of the night told over,
And all their minds transfigured so together,
More witnesseth than fancy's images   25
And grows to something of great constancy;   26
But, howsoever, strange and admirable.   27

Enter lovers: Lysander, Demetrius, Hermia,
and Helena.

THESEUS
Here come the lovers, full of joy and mirth.
Joy, gentle friends! Joy and fresh days of love
Accompany your hearts!

LYSANDER   More than to us
Wait in your royal walks, your board, your bed!

THESEUS
Come now, what masques, what dances shall we
have,   32
To wear away this long age of three hours
Between our after-supper and bedtime?
Where is our usual manager of mirth?

5.1. Location: Athens. The palace of Theseus.
1 that that which   **2 may** can   **3 antique** old-fashioned. (Punning,
too, on *antic*, "strange," "grotesque.")   **fairy toys** trifling stories
about fairies.   **5 fantasies** imaginations.   **apprehend** conceive,
imagine   **6 comprehends** understands.   **8 compact** formed, composed.   **11 Helen's** i.e., of Helen of Troy, pattern of beauty.   **brow
of Egypt** i.e., face of a gypsy.   **20 bringer** i.e., source   **21 fear** object
of fear   **25 More . . . images** testifies to something more substantial
than mere imaginings   **26 constancy** certainty   **27 howsoever** in
any case. **admirable** a source of wonder.   **32 masques** courtly
entertainments

What revels are in hand? Is there no play
To ease the anguish of a torturing hour?
Call Philostrate.

PHILOSTRATE   Here, mighty Theseus.

THESEUS

Say, what abridgment have you for this evening?   39
What masque? What music? How shall we beguile
The lazy time, if not with some delight?

PHILOSTRATE [*giving him a paper*]

There is a brief how many sports are ripe.   42
Make choice of which Your Highness will see first.

THESEUS [*reads*]

"The battle with the Centaurs, to be sung   44
By an Athenian eunuch to the harp"?
We'll none of that. That have I told my love,
In glory of my kinsman Hercules.   47
[*He reads.*] "The riot of the tipsy Bacchanals,   48
Tearing the Thracian singer in their rage"?   49
That is an old device; and it was played   50
When I from Thebes came last a conqueror.
[*He reads.*] "The thrice three Muses mourning for the
    death
Of Learning, late deceased in beggary"?   52
That is some satire, keen and critical,   53
Not sorting with a nuptial ceremony.   55
[*He reads.*] "A tedious brief scene of young Pyramus
And his love Thisbe; very tragical mirth"?
Merry and tragical? Tedious and brief?
That is, hot ice and wondrous strange snow.   59
How shall we find the concord of this discord?

PHILOSTRATE

A play there is, my lord, some ten words long,
Which is as brief as I have known a play;
But by ten words, my lord, it is too long,
Which makes it tedious. For in all the play
There is not one word apt, one player fitted.
And tragical, my noble lord, it is,
For Pyramus therein doth kill himself.
Which, when I saw rehearsed, I must confess,
Made mine eyes water; but more merry tears
The passion of loud laughter never shed.

THESEUS   What are they that do play it?

PHILOSTRATE

Hardhanded men that work in Athens here,
Which never labored in their minds till now,
And now have toiled their unbreathed memories   74

With this same play, against your nuptial.   75

THESEUS

And we will hear it.

PHILOSTRATE   No, my noble lord,
It is not for you. I have heard it over,
And it is nothing, nothing in the world;
Unless you can find sport in their intents,
Extremely stretched and conned with cruel pain   80
To do you service.

THESEUS   I will hear that play;
For never anything can be amiss
When simpleness and duty tender it.
Go, bring them in; and take your places, ladies.
    [*Philostrate goes to summon the players.*]

HIPPOLYTA

I love not to see wretchedness o'ercharged,   85
And duty in his service perishing.   86

THESEUS

Why, gentle sweet, you shall see no such thing.

HIPPOLYTA

He says they can do nothing in this kind.   88

THESEUS

The kinder we, to give them thanks for nothing.
Our sport shall be to take what they mistake;
And what poor duty cannot do, noble respect   91
Takes it in might, not merit.   92
Where I have come, great clerks have purposèd   93
To greet me with premeditated welcomes;
Where I have seen them shiver and look pale,
Make periods in the midst of sentences,
Throttle their practiced accent in their fears,   97
And in conclusion dumbly have broke off,
Not paying me a welcome. Trust me, sweet,
Out of this silence yet I picked a welcome;
And in the modesty of fearful duty
I read as much as from the rattling tongue
Of saucy and audacious eloquence.
Love, therefore, and tongue-tied simplicity
In least speak most, to my capacity.   105

    [*Philostrate returns.*]

PHILOSTRATE

So please Your Grace, the Prologue is addressed.   106

THESEUS   Let him approach.   [*A flourish of trumpets.*]

    Enter the Prologue [*Quince*].

PROLOGUE

If we offend, it is with our good will.
    That you should think, we come not to offend,
But with good will. To show our simple skill,
    That is the true beginning of our end.

---

39 abridgment pastime (to abridge or shorten the evening)
42 brief summary   **44 battle . . . Centaurs** (Probably refers to the battle of the Centaurs and the Lapithae, when the Centaurs attempted to
carry off Hippodamia, bride of Theseus's friend Pirothous. The story
is told in Ovid's *Metamorphoses* 12.)   **47 kinsman** (Plutarch's "Life of
Theseus" states that Hercules and Theseus were near kinsmen. Theseus is referring to a version of the battle of the Centaurs in which
Hercules was said to be present.)   **48–9 The riot . . . rage** (This was
the story of the death of Orpheus, as told in *Metamorphoses* 11.)
50 device show, performance   **52–3 The thrice . . . beggary** (Possibly
an allusion to Spenser's *Teares of the Muses*, 1591, though "satires"
deploring the neglect of learning and the creative arts were commonplace.)   **55 sorting with** befitting   **59 strange** (Sometimes emended
to an adjective that would contrast with *snow*, just as *hot* contrasts
with *ice*.)   **74 toiled** taxed.   **unbreathed** unexercised

75 against in preparation for   **80 conned** memorized   **85 wretchedness o'ercharged** social or intellectual inferiority overburdened
86 his service its attempt to serve   **88 kind** kind of thing.
91–2 noble . . . merit noble consideration values it for the effort made
rather than for the actual worth.   **93 clerks** learned men   **97 practiced accent** i.e., rehearsed speech; or, usual way of speaking
105 least i.e., saying least.   **to my capacity** in my judgment and
understanding.   **106 Prologue** speaker of the prologue.   **addressed**
ready.

Consider, then, we come but in despite.
    We do not come, as minding to content you,   113
Our true intent is. All for your delight
    We are not here. That you should here repent you,
The actors are at hand; and, by their show,
You shall know all that you are like to know.

THESEUS   This fellow doth not stand upon points.   118

LYSANDER   He hath rid his prologue like a rough colt; he   119
knows not the stop. A good moral, my lord: it is not   120
enough to speak, but to speak true.

HIPPOLYTA   Indeed, he hath played on his prologue like
a child on a recorder: a sound, but not in government.   123

THESEUS   His speech was like a tangled chain: nothing   124
impaired, but all disordered. Who is next?

Enter Pyramus [Bottom], and Thisbe [Flute],
and Wall [Snout], and Moonshine [Starveling],
and Lion [Snug].

PROLOGUE
    Gentles, perchance you wonder at this show;
        But wonder on, till truth make all things plain.
    This man is Pyramus, if you would know;
        This beauteous lady Thisbe is, certain.
    This man with lime and roughcast doth present
        Wall, that vile wall which did these lovers sunder;
    And through Wall's chink, poor souls, they are content
        To whisper. At the which let no man wonder.
    This man, with lantern, dog, and bush of thorn,
        Presenteth Moonshine; for, if you will know,
    By moonshine did these lovers think no scorn   136
        To meet at Ninus' tomb, there, there to woo.
    This grisly beast, which Lion hight by name,   138
    The trusty Thisbe coming first by night
    Did scare away, or rather did affright;
    And as she fled, her mantle she did fall,   141
        Which Lion vile with bloody mouth did stain.
    Anon comes Pyramus, sweet youth and tall,   143
        And finds his trusty Thisbe's mantle slain;
    Whereat, with blade, with bloody, blameful blade,
    He bravely broached his boiling bloody breast.   146
    And Thisbe, tarrying in mulberry shade,
        His dagger drew, and died. For all the rest,
    Let Lion, Moonshine, Wall, and lovers twain
    At large discourse, while here they do remain.   150
                    Exeunt Lion, Thisbe, and Moonshine.

THESEUS   I wonder if the lion be to speak.

DEMETRIUS   No wonder, my lord. One lion may, when
many asses do.

WALL
    In this same interlude it doth befall   154
    That I, one Snout by name, present a wall;
    And such a wall as I would have you think

That had in it a crannied hole or chink,
Through which the lovers, Pyramus and Thisbe,
Did whisper often, very secretly.
This loam, this roughcast, and this stone doth show
That I am that same wall; the truth is so.
And this the cranny is, right and sinister,   162
Through which the fearful lovers are to whisper.

THESEUS   Would you desire lime and hair to speak
better?

DEMETRIUS   It is the wittiest partition that ever I heard   166
discourse, my lord.

    [*Pyramus comes forward.*]

THESEUS   Pyramus draws near the wall. Silence!

PYRAMUS
    O grim-looked night! O night with hue so black!   169
        O night, which ever art when day is not!
    O night, O night! Alack, alack, alack,
        I fear my Thisbe's promise is forgot.
    And thou, O wall, O sweet, O lovely wall,
        That stand'st between her father's ground and
            mine,
    Thou wall, O wall, O sweet and lovely wall,
        Show me thy chink, to blink through with mine
            eyne.   [*Wall makes a chink with his fingers.*]
    Thanks, courteous wall. Jove shield thee well for
        this.
    But what see I? No Thisbe do I see.
    O wicked wall, through whom I see no bliss!
    Cursed be thy stones for thus deceiving me!

THESEUS   The wall, methinks, being sensible, should   181
curse again.   182

PYRAMUS   No, in truth, sir, he should not. "Deceiving
me" is Thisbe's cue: she is to enter now, and I am to
spy her through the wall. You shall see, it will fall pat   185
as I told you. Yonder she comes.

    Enter Thisbe.

THISBE
    O wall, full often hast thou heard my moans
        For parting my fair Pyramus and me.
    My cherry lips have often kissed thy stones,
        Thy stones with lime and hair knit up in thee.

PYRAMUS
    I see a voice. Now will I to the chink,
        To spy an I can hear my Thisbe's face.   192
    Thisbe!

THISBE   My love! Thou art my love, I think.

PYRAMUS
    Think what thou wilt, I am thy lover's grace,   194
    And like Limander am I trusty still.   195

THISBE
    And I like Helen, till the Fates me kill.   196

---

113 minding intending   **118 stand upon points** (1) heed niceties or
small points (2) pay attention to punctuation in his reading. (The
humor of Quince's speech is in the blunders of its punctuation.)
119 rid ridden.   **rough** unbroken   **120 stop** (1) stopping of a colt by
reining it in (2) punctuation mark.   **123 recorder** wind instrument
like a flute.   **government** control.   **124 nothing** not at all   **136 think
no scorn** think it no disgraceful matter   **138 hight** is called   **141 fall**
let fall   **143 tall** courageous   **146 broached** stabbed   **150 At large** in
full, at length   **154 interlude** play

162 right and sinister from right to left   **166 partition** (1) wall (2) section of a learned treatise or oration   **169 grim-looked** grim-looking
181 sensible capable of feeling   **182 again** in return.   **185 pat** exactly
192 an if   **194 lover's grace** i.e., gracious lover   **195, 196 Limander,
Helen** (Blunders for "Leander" and "Hero.")

PYRAMUS
    Not Shafalus to Procrus was so true.   197

THISBE
    As Shafalus to Procrus, I to you.

PYRAMUS
    Oh, kiss me through the hole of this vile wall!

THISBE
    I kiss the wall's hole, not your lips at all.

PYRAMUS
    Wilt thou at Ninny's tomb meet me straightway?

THISBE
    'Tide life, 'tide death, I come without delay.   202
                   [Exeunt Pyramus and Thisbe.]

WALL
    Thus have I, Wall, my part dischargèd so;
    And, being done, thus Wall away doth go.   *[Exit.]*

THESEUS   Now is the mural down between the two
    neighbors.

DEMETRIUS   No remedy, my lord, when walls are so
    willful to hear without warning.   208

HIPPOLYTA   This is the silliest stuff that ever I heard.

THESEUS   The best in this kind are but shadows; and the 210
    worst are no worse, if imagination amend them.

HIPPOLYTA   It must be your imagination then, and not
    theirs.

THESEUS   If we imagine no worse of them than they of
    themselves, they may pass for excellent men. Here
    come two noble beasts in, a man and a lion.

Enter Lion and Moonshine.

LION
    You, ladies, you, whose gentle hearts do fear
        The smallest monstrous mouse that creeps on
           floor,
    May now perchance both quake and tremble here,
    When lion rough in wildest rage doth roar.
    Then know that I, as Snug the joiner, am   221
    A lion fell, nor else no lion's dam;   222
    For, if I should as lion come in strife
    Into this place, 'twere pity on my life.

THESEUS   A very gentle beast, and of a good conscience.

DEMETRIUS   The very best at a beast, my lord, that e'er I
    saw.

LYSANDER   This lion is a very fox for his valor.   228

THESEUS   True; and a goose for his discretion.   229

DEMETRIUS   Not so, my lord, for his valor cannot carry
    his discretion, and the fox carries the goose.

THESEUS   His discretion, I am sure, cannot carry his
    valor; for the goose carries not the fox. It is well. Leave
    it to his discretion, and let us listen to the moon.

MOON
    This lanthorn doth the hornèd moon present—   235

DEMETRIUS   He should have worn the horns on his 236
    head.   237

THESEUS   He is no crescent, and his horns are invisible 238
    within the circumference.

MOON
    This lanthorn doth the hornèd moon present;
    Myself the man i'th' moon do seem to be.

THESEUS   This is the greatest error of all the rest. The
    man should be put into the lanthorn. How is it else the
    man i'th' moon?

DEMETRIUS   He dares not come there for the candle, for 245
    you see it is already in snuff.   246

HIPPOLYTA   I am aweary of this moon. Would he would
    change!

THESEUS   It appears, by his small light of discretion, that
    he is in the wane; but yet, in courtesy, in all reason, we
    must stay the time.

LYSANDER   Proceed, Moon.

MOON   All that I have to say is to tell you that the lan-
    thorn is the moon, I, the man i'th' moon, this thorn-
    bush my thornbush, and this dog my dog.

DEMETRIUS   Why, all these should be in the lanthorn,
    for all these are in the moon. But silence! Here comes
    Thisbe.

Enter Thisbe.

THISBE
    This is old Ninny's tomb. Where is my love?

LION *[roaring]* Oh!

DEMETRIUS   Well roared, Lion.
                  [Thisbe runs off, dropping her mantle.]

THESEUS   Well run, Thisbe.

HIPPOLYTA   Well shone, Moon. Truly, the moon shines
    with a good grace.
                  [The Lion worries Thisbe's mantle.]

THESEUS   Well moused, Lion.   265

Enter Pyramus.   *[Exit Lion.]*

DEMETRIUS   And then came Pyramus.

LYSANDER   And so the lion vanished.

PYRAMUS
    Sweet Moon, I thank thee for thy sunny beams;
        I thank thee, Moon, for shining now so bright;
    For, by thy gracious, golden, glittering gleams,
        I trust to take of truest Thisbe sight.
            But stay, oh, spite!
            But mark, poor knight,
        What dreadful dole is here?
                            274
            Eyes, do you see?
            How can it be?

---

197 Shafalus, Procrus (Blunders for "Cephalus" and "Procris," also famous lovers.) **202 'Tide** Betide, come **208 willful** willing. **without warning** i.e., without warning the parents. (Demetrius makes a joke on the proverb "Walls have ears.") **210 in this kind** of this sort. **shadows** likenesses, representations **221–2 am . . . dam** enact the part of a fierce lion, but otherwise am not really a lion. (*Dam* means "mother"; in Shakespeare's source the beast is a lioness.) **228 is . . . valor** i.e., his valor consists of craftiness and discretion. **229 a goose . . . discretion** i.e., as discreet as a goose, that is, more foolish than discreet.

235 lanthorn (This original spelling, "lanthorne," may suggest a play on the *horn* of which lanterns were made and also on a cuckold's horns; however, the spelling "lanthorn" is not used consistently for comic effect in this play or elsewhere. At 5.1.134, for example, the word is "lanterne" in the original.) **236–7 on his head** (As a sign of cuckoldry.) **238 crescent** a waxing moon **245 for** because of, for fear of **246 in snuff** (1) offended (2) in need of snuffing or trimming. **265 moused** shaken, torn, bitten **274 dole** grievous event

Oh, dainty duck! Oh, dear!
　　Thy mantle good,
　　What, stained with blood?
Approach, ye Furies fell!   280
　　O Fates, come, come,   281
　　Cut thread and thrum;   282
Quail, crush, conclude, and quell!   283

THESEUS　This passion, and the death of a dear friend,   284
would go near to make a man look sad.   285

HIPPOLYTA　Beshrew my heart, but I pity the man.   286

PYRAMUS
Oh, wherefore, Nature, didst thou lions frame?   287
Since lion vile hath here deflowered my dear,
Which is—no, no, which was—the fairest dame
That lived, that loved, that liked, that looked with
　　cheer.   290
　　Come, tears, confound,
　　Out, sword, and wound
The pap of Pyramus;   293
　　Ay, that left pap,
　　Where heart doth hop.   [He stabs himself.]
Thus die I, thus, thus, thus.
　　Now am I dead,
　　Now am I fled;
My soul is in the sky.
　　Tongue, lose thy light;
　　Moon, take thy flight.   [Exit Moonshine.]
　　Now die, die, die, die, die. [Pyramus dies.]

DEMETRIUS　No die, but an ace, for him; for he is   303
but one.   304

LYSANDER　Less than an ace, man; for he is dead, he is
nothing.

THESEUS　With the help of a surgeon he might yet
recover, and yet prove an ass.   308

HIPPOLYTA　How chance Moonshine is gone before
Thisbe comes back and finds her lover?

THESEUS　She will find him by starlight.

[Enter Thisbe.]

Here she comes; and her passion ends the play.

HIPPOLYTA　Methinks she should not use a long one for
such a Pyramus. I hope she will be brief.

DEMETRIUS　A mote will turn the balance, which Pyra-   315
mus which Thisbe, is the better: he for a man, God   316
warrant us; she for a woman, God bless us.

LYSANDER　She hath spied him already with those sweet
eyes.

DEMETRIUS　And thus she means, videlicet: 320
THISBE
　　Asleep, my love?
　　What, dead, my dove?
O Pyramus, arise!
　　Speak, speak. Quite dumb?
　　Dead, dead? A tomb
Must cover thy sweet eyes.
　　These lily lips,
　　This cherry nose,
These yellow cowslip cheeks,
　　Are gone, are gone!
Lovers, make moan.
His eyes were green as leeks.
　　O Sisters Three,   333
　　Come, come to me,
With hands as pale as milk;
　　Lay them in gore,
　　Since you have shore   337
With shears his thread of silk.
　　Tongue, not a word.
　　Come, trusty sword,
Come, blade, my breast imbrue!   341
                              [She stabs herself.]
　　And farewell, friends.
　　Thus Thisbe ends.
　　Adieu, adieu, adieu.   [She dies.]

THESEUS　Moonshine and Lion are left to bury the dead.
DEMETRIUS　Ay, and Wall too.
BOTTOM [starting up, as Flute does also]　No, I assure you,
the wall is down that parted their fathers. Will it please
you to see the epilogue, or to hear a Bergomask dance   349
between two of our company?

[The other players enter.]

THESEUS　No epilogue, I pray you; for your play needs
no excuse. Never excuse; for when the players are all
dead, there need none to be blamed. Marry, if he that
writ it had played Pyramus and hanged himself in
Thisbe's garter, it would have been a fine tragedy; and
so it is, truly, and very notably discharged. But, come,
your Bergomask. Let your epilogue alone. [A dance.]
The iron tongue of midnight hath told twelve.   358
Lovers, to bed, 'tis almost fairy time.
I fear we shall outsleep the coming morn
As much as we this night have overwatched.   361
This palpable-gross play hath well beguiled   362
The heavy gait of night. Sweet friends, to bed.   363
A fortnight hold we this solemnity,
In nightly revels and new jollity.
                                         [Exeunt.]

Enter Puck [carrying a broom].

---

280 Furies fell fierce avenging goddesses of Greek myth.　281 Fates
the three goddesses (Clotho, Lachesis, Atropos) of Greek myth who
spun, drew, and cut the thread of human life　282 thread and thrum
i.e., everything—the good and bad alike; literally, the warp in weaving and the loose end of the warp　283 Quail overpower.　quell kill,
destroy.　284–5 This . . . sad i.e., If one had other reason to grieve,
one might be sad, but not from this absurd portrayal of passion.
286 Beshrew Curse. (A mild curse.)　287 frame create.　290 cheer
countenance.　293 pap breast　303 ace the side of the die featuring
the single pip, or spot. (The pun is on die as a singular of dice; Bottom's performance is not worth a whole die but rather one single face
of it, one small portion.)　304 one (1) an individual person
(2) unique.　308 ass (With a pun on ace.)　315 mote small particle
315–16 which . . . which whether . . . or

320 means moans, laments. (With a pun on the meaning, "lodge a formal complaint.")　videlicet to wit　333 Sisters Three the Fates
337 shore shorn　341 imbrue stain with blood.　349 Bergomask
dance a rustic dance named from Bergamo, a province in the state of
Venice　358 iron tongue i.e., of a bell.　told counted, struck
("tolled")　361 overwatched stayed up too late.　362 palpable-gross
palpably gross, obviously crude　363 heavy drowsy, dull

PUCK

Now the hungry lion roars,
    And the wolf behowls the moon,
Whilst the heavy plowman snores,   368
    All with weary task fordone.   369
Now the wasted brands do glow,   370
    Whilst the screech owl, screeching loud,
Puts the wretch that lies in woe
    In remembrance of a shroud.
Now it is the time of night
    That the graves, all gaping wide,
Every one lets forth his sprite,   376
    In the churchway paths to glide.
And we fairies, that do run
    By the triple Hecate's team.   379
From the presence of the sun,
    Following darkness like a dream,
Now are frolic. Not a mouse   382
    Shall disturb this hallowed house.
I am sent with broom before,
    To sweep the dust behind the door.   385

Enter [Oberon and Titania,] King and Queen of
Fairies, with all their train.

OBERON

Through the house give glimmering light,
    By the dead and drowsy fire;
Every elf and fairy sprite
    Hop as light as bird from brier;
And this ditty, after me,
Sing, and dance it trippingly.

TITANIA

First, rehearse your song by rote,   392
To each word a warbling note.
Hand in hand, with fairy grace,
Will we sing, and bless this place.

[Song and dance.]

OBERON

Now, until the break of day,
Through this house each fairy stray.
To the best bride-bed will we,
Which by us shall blessèd be;
And the issue there create   400
Ever shall be fortunate.
So shall all the couples three
Ever true in loving be;
And the blots of Nature's hand
Shall not in their issue stand;
Never mole, harelip, nor scar,
Nor mark prodigious, such as are   407
Despisèd in nativity,
Shall upon their children be.
With this field dew consecrate,   410
Every fairy take his gait,   411
And each several chamber bless,   412
Through this palace, with sweet peace;
And the owner of it blest
Ever shall in safety rest.
Trip away; make no stay;
Meet me all by break of day.

Exeunt [Oberon, Titania, and train].

PUCK [to the audience]

If we shadows have offended,
Think but this, and all is mended,
That you have but slumbered here   420
While these visions did appear.
And this weak and idle theme,
No more yielding but a dream,   423
Gentles, do not reprehend.
If you pardon, we will mend.   425
And, as I am an honest Puck,
If we have unearnèd luck
Now to scape the serpent's tongue,   428
We will make amends ere long;
Else the Puck a liar call.
So, good night unto you all.
Give me your hands, if we be friends,   432
And Robin shall restore amends.   [Exit.] 433

368 heavy tired   369 fordone exhausted.   370 wasted brands
burned-out logs   376 Every . . . sprite every grave lets forth its ghost
379 triple Hecate's (Hecate ruled in three capacities: as Luna or Cynthia in heaven, as Diana on earth, and as Proserpina in hell.)
382 frolic merry.   385 behind from behind, or else like sweeping the
dirt under the carpet. (Robin Goodfellow was a household spirit who
helped good housemaids and punished lazy ones, but he could, of
course, be mischievous.)   392 rehearse recite

400 issue offspring.   create created   407 prodigious monstrous,
unnatural   410 consecrate consecrated   411 take his gait go his way
412 several separate   420 That . . . here i.e., that it is a "midsummer
night's dream"   423 No . . . but yielding no more than   425 mend
improve.   428 serpent's tongue i.e., hissing   432 Give . . . hands
Applaud   433 restore amends give satisfaction in return.

The Merchant of Venice

Although Shylock is the most prominent character in *The Merchant of Venice*, he takes part in neither the beginning nor the ending of the play. And, although the play's title might seem to suggest that he is the "merchant" of Venice, Shylock is, strictly speaking, a moneylender whose usury is portrayed as the very opposite of true commerce. His vengeful struggle to obtain a pound of flesh from Antonio contrasts with the various romantic episodes woven together in this play: Bassanio's choosing of Portia by means of the caskets, Gratiano's wooing of Nerissa, Jessica's elopement with Lorenzo, Lancelot Gobbo's changing of masters, and the episode of the rings. In all these stories, a Christian ethic of generosity, love, and risk-taking friendship is set in pointed contrast with a non-Christian ethic that is seen, from a Christian point of view, as grudging, resentful, and self-calculating. Yet this contrasting vision is made problematic by the deplorable behavior of some Christians. In stage productions today, Belmont and its inhabitants are apt to seem frivolous, pleasure-loving, hedonistic, and above all racist in their insular preference for their own economically and culturally privileged position. The play invites us to question the motives of Shylock's enemies. It makes us (today, at least, after the terrors of the German Holocaust) uncomfortable at the insularity of a Venetian ethic that has no genuine place for non-Christians or cultural outsiders. The most painful question of all, for us, is to wonder whether the play assumes for its own dramatic purposes a Christian point of view, however much it sees a genuine and understandable motive in Shylock's desire for revenge. The problem of divided sympathies is exacerbated because Shylock's structural function in the play is essentially that of the villain in a love comedy. His remorseless pursuit of Antonio darkens the mood of the play, and his overthrow signals the providential triumph of love and friendship, even though that triumph is not without its undercurrent of wry melancholy. Before we examine the painful issue of anti-Semitism more closely,

we need to establish the structural context of this love comedy as a whole.

Like many of Shakespeare's philosophical and festive comedies, *The Merchant of Venice* presents two contrasting worlds—one fantasy-like and the other marked by conflict and anxiety. To an extent, these contrasting worlds can be identified with the locations of Belmont and Venice. Belmont, to which the various happy lovers and their friends eventually retire, is a place of magic and romance. As its name implies, it is on a mountain, and it is reached by a journey across water. As often happens in fairy stories, on this mountain dwells a princess who must be won by means of a riddling contest. We usually see Belmont at night. Music surrounds it, and women preside over it. Even its caskets, houses, and rings are essentially feminine symbols. Venice, on the other hand, is a place of bustle and economic competition, seen most characteristically in the heat of the day. It lies low and flat, at a point where rivers reach the sea. Men preside over its contentious marketplace and its haggling law courts. Actually, the opposition of Venice and Belmont is not quite so clear-cut: Venice contains much compassionate friendship, whereas Belmont is subject to the arbitrary command of Portia's dead father. (Portia somewhat resembles Jessica in being imprisoned by her father's will.) Even though Portia descends to Venice in the angelic role of mercy giver, she also remains very human: sharp-tongued and even venomous in caricaturing her unwelcome wooers, crafty in her legal maneuvering, saucily prankish in her torturing of Bassanio about the rings. For all its warmth and generosity, Belmont is also the embodiment of an insular Christian culture that makes room for outsiders only when they convert to Christian mores. The traits that Shylock carries to an unpleasant extreme are needed in moderation by the Venetians, notably thrift, promise-keeping, and prudent self-interest; only when the Christians temper their penchant for reckless extravagance, legal sophistry or even theft, and risk-taking is a happy resolution possible. Nevertheless, the polarity of two contrasting localities and two groups of characters is vividly real in this play.

The play's opening scene, from which Shylock is excluded, sets forth the interrelated themes of friendship, romantic love, and risk or "hazard." The merchant who seemingly fulfills the title role, Antonio, is the victim of a mysterious melancholy. He is wealthy enough and surrounded by friends, but something is missing from his life. He assures his solicitous companions that he has no financial worries, for he has been too careful to trust all his cargoes to one sea vessel. Antonio, in fact, has no idea why he is so sad. The question is haunting. What is the matter? Perhaps the answer is to be found in a paradox: those who strive to prosper in the world's terms are doomed to frustration, not because prosperity will necessarily elude them, but because it will not satisfy the spirit. "You have too much respect upon the world," argues the carefree Gratiano. "They lose it that do buy it with much care" (1.1.74–5). Portia and Jessica, too, are at first afflicted by a melancholy that stems from the incompleteness of living isolated lives, with insufficient opportunities for love and sacrifice. They must learn, as Antonio learns with the help of his dear friend Bassanio, to seek happiness by daring to risk everything for friendship. Antonio's risk is most extreme: only when he has thrown away concern for his life can he discover what there is to live for.

At first, Bassanio's request for assistance seems just as materialistic as the worldliness from which Antonio suffers. Bassanio proposes to marry a rich young lady, Portia, in order to recoup his fortune lost through prodigality, and he needs money from Antonio so that he may woo Portia in proper fashion. She is "richly left," the heiress of a dead father, a golden fleece for whom this new Jason will make a quest. Bassanio's adventure is partly commercial. Yet his pilgrimage for Portia is magnanimous as well. The occasional modern practice of playing Bassanio and Portia as cynical antiheroes of a "black" comedy points up the problematic character of their materialism and calculation, but it gives only one aspect of the portrayal. Bassanio has lost his previous fortune through the amiable faults of reckless generosity and a lack of concern for financial prudence. The money he must now borrow, and the fortune he hopes to acquire, are to him no more than a means to carefree happiness. Although Portia's rich dowry is a strong consideration, he describes her also as "fair and, fairer than that word,/Of wondrous virtues" (1.1.162–3). Moreover, he enjoys the element of risk in wooing her. It is like shooting a second arrow in order to recover one that has been lost—double or nothing. This gamble, or "hazard," involves risk for Antonio as well as for Bassanio, and it ultimately brings a double reward to them both—spiritual as well as financial. Unless one recognizes these aspects of Bassanio's quest, as well as the clear fairy-tale quality with which Shakespeare deliberately invests this part of the plot, one cannot properly assess Bassanio's role in this romantic comedy.

Bassanio's quest for Portia can, in fact, never succeed until he disavows the very financial considerations that brought him to Belmont in the first place. This is the paradox of the riddle of the three caskets, an ancient parable stressing the need for choosing by true substance rather than by outward show. To choose "what many men desire," as the Prince of Morocco does, is to pin one's hopes on worldly wealth; to believe that one "deserves" good fortune, as the Prince of Aragon does, is to reveal a fatal pride in one's own merit. Bassanio perceives that, in order to win true love, he must "give and hazard all he hath" (2.7.9). He is not "deceived with ornament" (3.2.74). Just as Antonio must risk all for friendship, and just as Bassanio himself must later be willing to risk losing Portia for the sake of true friendship (in the episode of the rings), Bassanio must renounce worldly ambition and beauty before he can be rewarded with success. Paradoxically, only those who learn to subdue such worldly desires may then legitimately enjoy the world's pleasures. Only they have acknowledged the hierarchical subservience of the flesh to the spirit. These are the philosophical truisms of Renaissance Neoplatonism, depicting love as a chain or ladder from the basest carnality to the supreme love of God for humanity. On this ladder, perfect friendship and spiritual union are more sublimely Godlike than sexual fulfillment. This idealism may seem a strange doctrine for Bassanio the fortune hunter, but, actually, its conventional wisdom simply confirms his role as romantic hero. He and Portia are not denied worldly happiness or erotic pleasure; they are merely asked to give first thought to their Christian duty in marriage.

For Portia, marriage represents both a gain and a loss. She can choose only by her dead father's will; the patriarchal system, according to which a woman is given in marriage by her father to a younger man, is seemingly able to extend its control even beyond the grave. The prospect of marrying the Prince of Morocco or the Prince of Aragon dismays her, and yet she persists in her vow of obedience and is eventually rewarded by the man of her choice. It is as though the benign father knew how to set the terms of choice in such a way that the "lottery" of the caskets would turn out right for her. When she accepts Bassanio, too, she must make a difficult choice, for in legal terms she makes Bassanio master over everything she owns. Portia is at once spirited and submissive, able to straighten out Venice's legal tangles when all the men have failed and yet ready to call Bassanio her lord. Her teasing him about the ring is a sign that she will make demands of him in marriage, but it is a testing that cannot produce lasting disharmony so long as Bassanio is truly loyal. Portia is, from Bassanio's male point of view, the perfect woman: humanly attainable and yet never seriously threatening. Guided by her, Bassanio makes the potentially hazardous transition from the male-oriented friendships of Venice (especially with Antonio) to heterosexual union. Portia is more fortunate than Jessica, who must break with her faith and her father in order to find marital happiness. The two women are alike, however, in that they experience the play's central paradox of losing the world in order to gain the world. Through them, we see that this paradox illuminates the casket episode, the struggle for the pound of flesh, the elopement of Jessica, the ring episode, and even the comic foolery of Lancelot Gobbo.

Shylock, in his quest for the pound of flesh, represents, as seen from a Christian point of view, a denial of all the paradoxical truths just described. As a usurer, he refuses to lend money interest-free in the name of friendship. Instead of taking risks, he insists on his bond. He spurns mercy and demands strict justice. By calculating all his chances too craftily, he appears to win at first but must eventually lose all. He has "too much respect upon the world" (1.1.74). His God is the Old Testament God of Moses, the God of wrath, the God of the Ten Commandments, with their forbidding emphasis on "Thou shalt not." (This oversimplified contrast between Judaism and Christianity was commonplace in Shakespeare's time.) Shylock abhors stealing but admires equivocation as a means of out-maneuvering a competitor; he approvingly cites Jacob's ruse to deprive Laban of his sheep (1.3.69–88). Any tactic is permissible so long as it falls within the realm of legality and contract.

Shylock's ethical outlook, then, justifies both usury and the old dispensation of the Jewish law. The two are philosophically combined, just as usury and Judaism had become equated in the popular imagination of Renaissance Europe. Even though lending at interest was becoming increasingly necessary and common, old prejudices against it still persisted. Angry moralists pointed out that the New Testament had condemned usury and that Aristotle had described money as barren. To breed money was therefore regarded as unnatural. Usury was considered sinful because it did not involve the usual risks of commerce; the lender was assured against loss of his principal by the posting of collateral and, at the same time, was sure to earn a handsome interest. The usurer seemed to be getting something for nothing. For these reasons, usury was sometimes declared illegal. Its practitioners were viewed as corrupt and grasping, hated as misers. In some European countries, Jews were permitted to practice this un-Christian living (and permitted to do very little else) and then, hypocritically, were detested for performing un-Christian deeds. Ironically, the moneylenders of England were Christians, and few Jews were to be found in any professions. Nominally excluded since Edward I's reign, the Jews had returned in small numbers to London but did not practice their Judaism openly.

They attended Anglican services as required by law and then worshiped in private, relatively undisturbed by the authorities. Shylock may not be based on observation from London life. He is derived from continental tradition and reflects a widespread conviction that Jews and usurers were alike in being un-Christian and sinister.

Shylock is unquestionably sinister, even if he also invites sympathy. He bears an "ancient grudge" against Antonio simply because Antonio is "a Christian." We recognize in Shylock the archetype of the supposed Jew who wishes to kill a Christian and obtain his flesh. In early medieval anti-Semitic legends of this sort, the flesh thus obtained was imagined to be eaten ritually during Passover. Because some Jews had once persecuted Christ, all were unfairly presumed to be implacable enemies of all Christians. These anti-Semitic superstitions were likely to erupt into hysteria at any time, as in 1594 when Dr. Roderigo Lopez, a Portuguese Jewish physician, was accused of having plotted against the life of Queen Elizabeth and of Don Antonio, pretender to the Portuguese throne. Christopher Marlowe's *The Jew of Malta* was revived for this occasion, enjoying an unusually successful run of fifteen performances, and scholars have often wondered if Shakespeare's play was not written under the same impetus. On this score, the evidence is inconclusive, and the play might have been written any time between 1594 and 1598 (when it is mentioned by Francis Meres), but, in any case, Shakespeare has made no attempt to avoid the anti-Semitic nature of his story.

To offset the portrayal of Jewish villainy, however, the play also dramatizes the possibility of conversion to Christianity, suggesting that Judaism is more a matter of benighted faith than of ethnic origin. Converted Jews were not new on the stage: they had appeared in medieval cycle drama, in the Croxton *Play of the Sacrament* (late fifteenth century), and more recently in *The Jew of Malta*, in which Barabas' daughter Abigail falls in love with a Christian and eventually becomes a nun. Shylock's daughter Jessica similarly embraces Christianity as Lorenzo's wife and is received into the happy comradeship of Belmont. Shylock is forced to accept Christianity, presumably for the benefit of his eternal soul (though today we find this deeply offensive, and it is sometimes cut from stage productions). Earlier in the play, Antonio repeatedly indicates his willingness to befriend Shylock if the latter will only give up usury, and he is even cautiously hopeful when Shylock offers him an interest-free loan: "The Hebrew will turn Christian; he grows kind" (1.3.177). To be sure, Antonio's denunciation of Shylock's usurious Judaism has been vehement and personal; we learn that he has spat on Shylock's gaberdine and kicked him as one would kick a dog. This violent disapproval offers no opportunity for the toleration of cultural and religious differences that we expect today from people of good will, but at least Antonio is prepared to accept Shylock if Shylock will embrace the Christian faith and its ethical responsibilities. Whether the play itself endorses Antonio's Christian point of view as normative or insists on a darker reading by making us uneasy with intolerance is a matter of unceasing critical debate. Quite possibly, the play's power to disturb emanates—at least in part—from the dramatic conflict of irreconcilable sets of values.

To Antonio, then, as well as to other Venetians, true Christianity is both an absolute good from which no deviation is possible without evil and a state of faith to which aliens may turn by abjuring the benighted creeds of their ancestors. By this token, the Prince of Morocco is condemned to failure in his quest for Portia, not so much because he is black as because he is an infidel, one who worships "blind fortune" and therefore chooses a worldly rather than a spiritual reward. Although Portia pertly dismisses him with "Let all of his complexion choose me so" (2.7.79), she professes earlier to find him handsome and agrees that he should not be judged by his complexion (2.1.13–22). Unless she is merely being hypocritical, she means by her later remark that black-skinned people are generally infidels, just as Jews are as a group un-Christian. Such pejorative thinking about persons as types is no doubt distressing and suggests—at least to a modern audience—the cultural limitation of Portia's view, but, in any case, it shows her to be no less well disposed toward black suitors than toward others who are also alien. She is glad not to be won by the Prince of Aragon because he, too, though nominally a Christian, is too self-satisfied and proud. All persons, therefore, may aspire to truly virtuous conduct, and those who choose virtue are equally blessed; however, the terms of defining that ideal in this play are essentially Christian. Jews and Blacks may rise spiritually only by abandoning their pagan creeds for the new dispensation of charity and forgiveness.

The superiority of Christian teaching to the older Jewish dispensation was, of course, a widely accepted notion of Shakespeare's time. After all, these were the years when people fought and died to maintain their religious beliefs. Today, the notion of a single true church is less widely held, and we have difficulty understanding why anyone would wish to force conversion on Shylock. Modern productions find it tempting to portray Shylock as a victim of bigotry and to put great stress on his heartrending assertions of his humanity: "Hath not a Jew eyes? . . . If you prick us, do we not bleed?" (3.1.56–62). Shylock does indeed suffer from his enemies, and his sufferings add a tortured complexity to this play—even, one suspects, for an Elizabethan audience. Those who profess Christianity must surely examine their own motives and conduct. Is it right to steal treasure from Shylock's house along with his eloped daughter? Is it considerate of Jessica and Lorenzo to squander Shylock's turquoise ring, the gift of his wife Leah, on a monkey? Does Shylock's vengeful insistence on law justify the quibbling counter-

measures devised by Portia even as she piously declaims about mercy? Do Shylock's misfortunes deserve the mirthful parodies of Solanio ("My daughter! Oh, my ducats!") or the hostile jeering of Gratiano at the conclusion of the trial? Because he stands outside Christian faith, Shylock can provide a perspective whereby we see the hypocrisies of those who profess a higher ethical code. Nevertheless, Shylock's compulsive desire for vengeance according to an Old Testament code of an eye for an eye cannot be justified by the wrongdoings of any particular Christian. In the play's control of an ethical point of view, such deeds condemn the doer rather than undermine the Christian standards of true virtue as ideally expressed. Shakespeare humanizes Shylock by portraying him as a believable and sensitive man, and he shows much that is to be regretted in Shylock's Christian antagonists, but he also allows Shylock to place himself in the wrong by his refusal to forgive his enemies.

Shylock thus loses everything through his effort to win everything on his own terms. His daughter, Jessica, by her elopement, follows an opposite course. She characterizes her father's home as "hell," and she resents being locked up behind closed windows. Shylock detests music and the sounds of merriment; Jessica's new life in Belmont is immersed in music. He is old, suspicious, miserly; she is young, loving, adventurous. Most important, she seems to be at least part Christian when we first see her. As Lancelot jests half in earnest, "If a Christian did not play the knave and get thee, I am much deceived" (2.3.11–12). Her removal from Shylock's house involves theft, and her running from Venice is, she confesses, an "unthrift love." Paradoxically, however, she sees this recklessness as of more blessed effect than her father's legalistic caution. As she says, "I shall be saved by my husband. He hath made me a Christian" (3.5.17–18).

Lancelot Gobbo's clowning offers a similarly paradoxical comment on the tragedy of Shylock. Lancelot debates whether or not to leave Shylock's service in terms of a soul struggle between his conscience and the devil (2.2.1–29). Conscience bids him stay, for service is a debt, a bond, an obligation, whereas abandonment of one's indenture is a kind of rebellion or stealing away. Yet Shylock's house is "hell" to Lancelot as it is to Jessica. Comparing his new master with his old, Lancelot observes to Bassanio, "You have the grace of God, sir, and he hath enough." Service with Bassanio involves imprudent risks, since Bassanio is a spendthrift. The miserly Shylock rejoices to see the ever hungry Lancelot, this "huge feeder," wasting the substance of a hated Christian. Once again, however, Shylock will lose everything in his grasping quest for security. Another spiritual renewal occurs when Lancelot encounters his old and nearly blind father (2.2). In a scene echoing the biblical stories of the Prodigal Son and of Jacob and Esau, Lancelot teases the old man with false rumors of Lancelot's own death in order to make their reunion seem all the more unexpected and precious. The illusion of loss gives way to joy: Lancelot is, in language adapted from the liturgy, "your boy that was, your son that is, your child that shall be."

In the episode of the rings, we encounter a final playful variation on the paradox of winning through losing. Portia and Nerissa cleverly present their new husbands with a cruel choice: disguised as a doctor of law and his clerk, who have just saved the life of Antonio from Shylock's wrath, the two wives ask nothing more for their services than the rings they see on the fingers of Bassanio and Gratiano. The two husbands, who have vowed never to part with these wedding rings, must therefore choose between love and friendship. Portia knows well enough that Bassanio's obedience to the Neoplatonic ideal of disinterested friendship is an essential part of his virtue. Just as he previously renounced beauty and riches before he could deserve Portia, he must now risk losing her for friendship's sake. The testing of the husbands' constancy does border at times on gratuitous harshness and exercise of power, for it deals with the oldest of masculine nightmares: cuckoldry. Wives are not without weapons in the struggle for control in marriage, and Portia and Nerissa enjoy trapping their new husbands in a no-win situation. Still, the threat is easily resolved by the dispelling of farcically mistaken identities. The young men have been tricked into bestowing their rings on their wives for a second time in the name of perfect friendship, thereby confirming a relationship that is both platonic and fleshly. As Gratiano bawdily points out in the play's last line, the ring is both a spiritual and a sexual symbol of marriage. The resolution of this illusory quarrel also brings to an end the merry battle of the sexes between wives and husbands. Having hinted at the sorts of misunderstandings that afflict even the best of human relationships and having proved themselves wittily able to torture and deceive their husbands, Portia and Nerissa submit at last to the patriarchal norms of their age and to the authority of Bassanio and Gratiano.

Bassanio's marriage to Portia represents a heterosexual fulfillment of their courtship that leaves Antonio without a partner at the play's end. He is, to be sure, included in the camaraderie of Belmont, but a part of the sacrifice he has made for Bassanio is to give that young man the freedom and means to marry as he chooses. Antonio's attachment for Bassanio is a deeply loving one, and is sometimes portrayed as homosexual in modern productions. The force of Antonio's attachment to Bassanio should not be underestimated. At the same time, he does appear to be truly willing for the young man to marry. In this sense, the marriage represents a completion in which friendship and love are fully complementary. Heterosexual union is, in this play and in Shakespearean comedy generally, a dominant and theatrically conventional resolution; but it is so without denying that there are other forms of human happiness. Whether or not Antonio is entirely content with his final role as a kind of benign older friend we cannot be sure, but his pronouncements in the final act are all aimed at encouraging the harmony between husband and wife that he has risked his life to enable.

As defined by the accepted notions of gender relations in Shakespeare's time, then, all appears to be in harmony in Belmont. The disorders of Venice have been left far behind, however imperfectly they may have been resolved. Jessica and Lorenzo contrast their present happiness with the sufferings of less fortunate lovers of long ago: Troilus and Cressida, Pyramus and Thisbe, Aeneas and Dido, Jason and Medea. The tranquil joy found in Belmont is attuned to the music of the spheres, the singing of the "young-eyed cherubins" (5.1.62), although with a proper Christian humility the lovers also realize that the harmony of immortal souls is infinitely beyond their comprehension. Bound in by the grossness of the flesh, "this muddy vesture of decay" (5.1.64), they can only reach toward the bliss of eternity through music and the perfect friendship of true love. Even in their final joy, accordingly, the lovers find an incompleteness that lends a wistful and slightly melancholy reflective tone to the play's ending. That sense of imperfection is accentuated for us by our awareness that the play's serious problems of gender relations, friendship, and anti-Semitism have by no means been fully resolved; the final concord is one that arises out of discord. Even so, this concluding sense of the unavoidable incompleteness of all human life is of a very different order from that earlier melancholy of isolation and lack of commitment experienced by Portia, Jessica, Antonio, and others.

In performance, the play has prompted both hostile and genuinely sympathetic responses for Shylock. The traditional anti-Semitic interpretation in early stage history manifested itself, for instance, in the performance of George Frederick Cooke in 1803–1804, "bent with age and ugly with mental deformity, grinning with deadly malice, with the venom of his heart congealed in the expression of his countenance, sullen, morose, gloomy, inflexible" (these are William Hazlitt's words). Still other renditions made use of the red wig and hooked nose of the stereotypical stage Jew that associated Shylock with Judas Iscariot. Conversely, Edmund Kean, in 1814, evoked such sympathy as to make the Christians in the play seem hypocrites by comparison. Henry Irving in 1879, and Beerbohm Tree in 1908, combined a kind of ancient dignity with pathos. George C. Scott, at the New York Shakespeare Festival in 1962, acted Shylock as a persecuted and desperate man surrounded by powerful enemies. Laurence Olivier's anguished Shylock (1970, subsequently televised) showed up the Christians as complacent members of a bigoted Venetian social world of privilege and exclusivity. A production in Weimar, Germany, in 1995, commemorating the fiftieth anniversary of the liberation of the concentration camp at nearby Buchenwald, captured what is so horrendously problematic in the play by imagining what it would be like if enacted by German officers and guards amusing themselves with amateur theatricals during wartime and assigning three Jewish inmates to the roles of Shylock, Tubal, and Jessica. Perhaps no Shakespeare play raises more painful issues today for us to think hard about than *The Merchant of Venice*.

The Merchant of Venice

[*Dramatis Personae*

THE DUKE OF VENICE
ANTONIO, *a merchant of Venice*
BASSANIO, *his friend, suitor to Portia*
GRATIANO, *a follower of Bassanio, in love with Nerissa*
SOLANIO, ⎫ *friends to Antonio*
SALERIO, ⎭ *and Bassanio*
LORENZO, *in love with Jessica*
LEONARDO, *servant to Bassanio*

PORTIA, *a rich heiress of Belmont*
NERISSA, *her waiting-gentlewoman*
BALTHASAR, *servant to Portia*
STEPHANO, *servant to Portia*

THE PRINCE OF MOROCCO, *suitor to Portia*
THE PRINCE OF ARAGON, *suitor to Portia*
A MESSENGER *to Portia*

SHYLOCK, *a rich Jew*
JESSICA, *his daughter*
TUBAL, *a Jew, Shylock's friend*
LANCELOT GOBBO, *a clown, servant to Shylock and then to Bassanio*
OLD GOBBO, *Lancelot's father*

Magnificoes of Venice, Officers of the Court of Justice, Jailor, Servants to Portia, and other Attendants

SCENE: *Partly at Venice and partly at Belmont, the seat of Portia*]

[1.1]

Enter Antonio, Salerio, and Solanio.

ANTONIO
In sooth, I know not why I am so sad.   1
It wearies me, you say it wearies you;
But how I caught it, found it, or came by it,
What stuff 'tis made of, whereof it is born,
I am to learn;   5
And such a want-wit sadness makes of me
That I have much ado to know myself.   6

SALERIO
Your mind is tossing on the ocean,
There where your argosies with portly sail,
Like signors and rich burghers on the flood,   9
Or as it were the pageants of the sea,   10
Do overpeer the petty traffickers   11
That curtsy to them, do them reverence,   12
As they fly by them with their woven wings.   13
                                                 14
SOLANIO
Believe me, sir, had I such venture forth,   15
The better part of my affections would

1.1. Location: A street in Venice.
1 In sooth Truly.   **sad** morose, dismal-looking.   **5 am to learn** have yet to learn   **6 such . . . of me** such sadness makes me so distracted, lacking in good sense

9 argosies large merchant ships. (So named from *Ragusa*, the modern city of Dubrovnik.)   **portly** majestic   **10 signors** gentlemen.   **flood** sea   **11 pageants** mobile stages used in plays or processions   **12 overpeer** look down upon   **13 curtsy** i.e., bob up and down, or lower topsails in token of respect (*reverence*)   **14 woven wings** canvas sails.   **15 venture forth** investment at risk

Be with my hopes abroad. I should be still   17
Plucking the grass to know where sits the wind,
Peering in maps for ports and piers and roads;   19
And every object that might make me fear
Misfortune to my ventures, out of doubt
Would make me sad.

SALERIO   My wind cooling my broth
Would blow me to an ague when I thought   23
What harm a wind too great might do at sea.
I should not see the sandy hourglass run
But I should think of shallows and of flats,   26
And see my wealthy *Andrew* docked in sand,   27
Vailing her high-top lower than her ribs   28
To kiss her burial. Should I go to church   29
And see the holy edifice of stone
And not bethink me straight of dangerous rocks   31
Which, touching but my gentle vessel's side,
Would scatter all her spices on the stream,
Enrobe the roaring waters with my silks,
And, in a word, but even now worth this,   35
And now worth nothing? Shall I have the thought
To think on this, and shall I lack the thought
That such a thing bechanced would make me sad?   38
But tell not me. I know Antonio
Is sad to think upon his merchandise.

ANTONIO
Believe me, no. I thank my fortune for it,
My ventures are not in one bottom trusted,   42
Nor to one place; nor is my whole estate
Upon the fortune of this present year.   44
Therefore my merchandise makes me not sad.

SOLANIO
Why then, you are in love.

ANTONIO   Fie, fie!

SOLANIO
Not in love neither? Then let us say you are sad
Because you are not merry; and 'twere as easy
For you to laugh and leap, and say you are merry
Because you are not sad. Now, by two-headed
    Janus,   50
Nature hath framed strange fellows in her time: 51
Some that will evermore peep through their eyes   52
And laugh like parrots at a bagpiper,   53
And other of such vinegar aspect   54
That they'll not show their teeth in way of smile
Though Nestor swear the jest be laughable.   56

Enter Bassanio, Lorenzo, and Gratiano.

Here comes Bassanio, your most noble kinsman,
Gratiano, and Lorenzo. Fare ye well.
We leave you now with better company.

SALERIO
I would have stayed till I had made you merry,
If worthier friends had not prevented me.   61

ANTONIO
Your worth is very dear in my regard.
I take it your own business calls on you,
And you embrace th'occasion to depart.   64

SALERIO   Good morrow, my good lords.

BASSANIO
Good signors both, when shall we laugh? Say,
    when?   66
You grow exceeding strange. Must it be so?   67

SALERIO
We'll make our leisures to attend on yours.   68
                           Exeunt Salerio and Solanio.

LORENZO
My lord Bassanio, since you have found Antonio,
We two will leave you, but at dinnertime,
I pray you, have in mind where we must meet.

BASSANIO   I will not fail you.

GRATIANO
You look not well, Signor Antonio.
You have too much respect upon the world.   74
They lose it that do buy it with much care.
Believe me, you are marvelously changed.

ANTONIO
I hold the world but as the world, Gratiano—
A stage where every man must play a part,
And mine a sad one.

GRATIANO   Let me play the fool.
With mirth and laughter let old wrinkles come,
And let my liver rather heat with wine   81
Than my heart cool with mortifying groans.   82
Why should a man whose blood is warm within
Sit like his grandsire cut in alabaster?   84
Sleep when he wakes, and creep into the jaundice   85
By being peevish? I tell thee what, Antonio—
I love thee, and 'tis my love that speaks—
There are a sort of men whose visages
Do cream and mantle like a standing pond,   89
And do a willful stillness entertain   90
With purpose to be dressed in an opinion   91
Of wisdom, gravity, profound conceit,   92
As who should say, "I am Sir Oracle,   93

---

17 still continually   **19 roads** anchorages, open harbors   **23 blow . . .
ague** i.e., start me shivering   **26 flats** shoals   **27** *Andrew* name of a
ship. (Perhaps after the *St. Andrew*, a Spanish galleon captured at
Cadiz in 1596.)   **28 Vailing** lowering. (Usually as a sign of submission.)   **high-top** topmast   **29 burial** burial place.   **31 bethink me
straight** be put in mind immediately   **35 even now** a short while
ago.   **this** i.e., the cargo of spices and silks   **38 bechanced** having
happened   **42 bottom** ship's hold   **44 Upon . . . year** i.e., risked
upon the chance of the present year.   **50 two-headed Janus** a Roman
god of all beginnings, represented by a figure with two faces
51 framed fashioned   **52 peep . . . eyes** i.e., look with eyes narrowed
by laughter   **53 at a bagpiper** i.e., even at a bagpiper, whose music
was regarded as melancholic   **54 other** others.   **vinegar aspect** sour,
sullen looks   **56 Nestor** venerable senior officer in the *Iliad*, noted
for gravity

61 prevented forestalled   **64 th'occasion** the opportunity   **66 laugh**
i.e., be merry together.   **67 strange** distant.   **Must it be so**? Must
you go? or, Must you show reserve?   **68 We'll . . . yours** We'll adjust
our spare time to accommodate your schedule.   **74 respect . . . world**
concern for worldly affairs of business.   **81 heat with wine** (The liver
was regarded as the seat of the passions and wine as an agency for
inflaming them.)   **82 mortifying** penitential and deadly. (Sighs were
thought to cost the heart a drop of blood.)   **84 in alabaster** i.e., in a
stone effigy upon a tomb.   **85 jaundice** (Regarded as arising from the
effects of too much choler or yellow bile, one of the four humors, in
the blood.)   **89 cream and mantle** become covered with scum, i.e.,
acquire a lifeless, stiff expression.   **standing** stagnant   **90–2 And . . .
conceit** and who maintain a willful silence in order to acquire a reputation for gravity and deep thought   **93 As . . . say** as if to say

And when I ope my lips let no dog bark!"   94
Oh, my Antonio, I do know of these
That therefore only are reputed wise
For saying nothing, when, I am very sure,
If they should speak, would almost damn those ears   98
Which, hearing them, would call their brothers
    fools.   99
I'll tell thee more of this another time.
But fish not with this melancholy bait   101
For this fool gudgeon, this opinion.—   102
Come, good Lorenzo.—Fare ye well awhile.
I'll end my exhortation after dinner.

LORENZO [to Antonio and Bassanio]
Well, we will leave you then till dinnertime.
I must be one of these same dumb wise men,   106
For Gratiano never lets me speak.

GRATIANO
Well, keep me company but two years more,   108
Thou shalt not know the sound of thine own
    tongue.

ANTONIO
Fare you well. I'll grow a talker for this gear.   110

GRATIANO
Thanks, i'faith, for silence is only commendable
In a neat's tongue dried and a maid not vendible.   112
                    Exeunt [Gratiano and Lorenzo].

ANTONIO   Is that anything now?   113

BASSANIO   Gratiano speaks an infinite deal of nothing,
more than any man in all Venice. His reasons are as   115
two grains of wheat hid in two bushels of chaff; you
shall seek all day ere you find them, and when you
have them they are not worth the search.

ANTONIO
Well, tell me now what lady is the same   119
To whom you swore a secret pilgrimage,
That you today promised to tell me of.

BASSANIO
'Tis not unknown to you, Antonio,
How much I have disabled mine estate
By something showing a more swelling port   124
Than my faint means would grant continuance.   125
Nor do I now make moan to be abridged   126
From such a noble rate; but my chief care   127
Is to come fairly off from the great debts   128
Wherein my time, something too prodigal,   129
Hath left me gaged. To you, Antonio,   130
I owe the most, in money and in love,

And from your love I have a warranty   132
To unburden all my plots and purposes   133
How to get clear of all the debts I owe.

ANTONIO
I pray you, good Bassanio, let me know it;
And if it stand, as you yourself still do,   136
Within the eye of honor, be assured   137
My purse, my person, my extremest means
Lie all unlocked to your occasions.

BASSANIO
In my schooldays, when I had lost one shaft,   140
I shot his fellow of the selfsame flight   141
The selfsame way with more advisèd watch   142
To find the other forth, and by adventuring both   143
I oft found both. I urge this childhood proof
Because what follows is pure innocence.   145
I owe you much, and, like a willful youth,
That which I owe is lost; but if you please
To shoot another arrow that self way   148
Which you did shoot the first, I do not doubt,
As I will watch the aim, or to find both   150
Or bring your latter hazard back again   151
And thankfully rest debtor for the first.   152

ANTONIO
You know me well, and herein spend but time   153
To wind about my love with circumstance;   154
And out of doubt you do me now more wrong
In making question of my uttermost   156
Than if you had made waste of all I have.
Then do but say to me what I should do
That in your knowledge may by me be done,
And I am prest unto it. Therefore speak.   160

BASSANIO
In Belmont is a lady richly left;   161
And she is fair and, fairer than that word,
Of wondrous virtues. Sometimes from her eyes   163
I did receive fair speechless messages.
Her name is Portia, nothing undervalued   165
To Cato's daughter, Brutus' Portia.   166
Nor is the wide world ignorant of her worth,
For the four winds blow in from every coast
Renownèd suitors, and her sunny locks
Hang on her temples like a golden fleece,
Which makes her seat of Belmont Colchis' strand,   171
And many Jasons come in quest of her.
Oh, my Antonio, had I but the means
To hold a rival place with one of them,

94 let . . . bark i.e., let no creature dare to interrupt me.   98–9 would
. . . fools i.e., would virtually condemn their hearers into calling them
fools. (Compare Matthew 5:22, in which anyone calling another a fool
is threatened with damnation.)   101–2 fish . . . opinion i.e., don't go
fishing for a reputation of being wise, using your melancholy silence as
the bait to fool people. (Gudgeon, a small fish, was thought of as a type
of gullibility.)   106 dumb mute, speechless   108 keep if you keep
110 for this gear in view of what you say.   112 neat's ox's.   not
vendible i.e., not yet salable in the marriage market.   113 Is . . . now?
i.e., Was all that talk about anything?   115 reasons reasonable ideas
119 the same i.e., the one   124 By . . . port by showing a somewhat
more lavish style of living   125 grant continuance allow to continue.
126–7 make . . . rate complain at being cut back from such a high style
of living   128 to . . . off honorably to extricate myself   129 time youthful lifetime   130 gaged pledged, in pawn.

132 warranty authorization   133 unburden disclose   136–7 if . . .
honor if it looks honorable, as your conduct has always done
140 shaft arrow   141 his its.   selfsame flight same kind and range
142 advisèd careful   143 forth out.   adventuring risking   145 innocence ingenuousness, sincerity.   148 self same   150 or either
151 hazard that which was risked   152 rest remain   153 spend but
time only waste time   154 To . . . circumstance i.e., in not asking
plainly what you want. (Circumstance here means "circumlocution.")
156 In . . . uttermost in showing any doubt of my intention to do all I
can   160 prest ready   161 richly left a large fortune (by her
father's will)   163 Sometimes Once   165–6 nothing undervalued To
of no less worth than   166 Portia (The same Portia as in Shakespeare's Julius Caesar.)   171 Colchis' (Jason adventured for the
golden fleece in the land of Colchis, on the Black Sea.)   strand shore

I have a mind presages me such thrift 175
That I should questionless be fortunate.

ANTONIO
Thou know'st that all my fortunes are at sea;
Neither have I money nor commodity 178
To raise a present sum. Therefore go forth. 179
Try what my credit can in Venice do;
That shall be racked even to the uttermost 181
To furnish thee to Belmont, to fair Portia.
Go presently inquire, and so will I, 183
Where money is, and I no question make 184
To have it of my trust or for my sake. *Exeunt.* 185

❧

[1.2]

Enter Portia with her waiting woman, Nerissa.

PORTIA   By my troth, Nerissa, my little body is aweary 1
of this great world.

NERISSA   You would be, sweet madam, if your miseries 3
were in the same abundance as your good fortunes
are; and yet, for aught I see, they are as sick that surfeit 5
with too much as they that starve with nothing. It is
no mean happiness, therefore, to be seated in the 7
mean. Superfluity comes sooner by white hairs, but 8
competency lives longer. 9

PORTIA   Good sentences, and well pronounced. 10

NERISSA   They would be better if well followed.

PORTIA   If to do were as easy as to know what were
good to do, chapels had been churches and poor
men's cottages princes' palaces. It is a good divine that 14
follows his own instructions. I can easier teach twenty
what were good to be done than to be one of the
twenty to follow mine own teaching. The brain may
devise laws for the blood, but a hot temper leaps o'er 18
a cold decree; such a hare is madness, the youth, to
skip o'er the meshes of good counsel, the cripple. But 20
this reasoning is not in the fashion to choose me a 21
husband. Oh, me, the word "choose"! I may neither 22
choose who I would nor refuse who I dislike; so is the
will of a living daughter curbed by the will of a dead 24
father. Is it not hard, Nerissa, that I cannot choose one
nor refuse none?

NERISSA   Your father was ever virtuous, and holy men
at their death have good inspirations; therefore the

lottery that he hath devised in these three chests of
gold, silver, and lead, whereof who chooses his mean- 30
ing chooses you, will no doubt never be chosen by
any rightly but one who you shall rightly love. But 32
what warmth is there in your affection towards any of
these princely suitors that are already come?

PORTIA   I pray thee, overname them, and as thou nam- 35
est them I will describe them; and according to my
description level at my affection. 37

NERISSA   First, there is the Neapolitan prince.

PORTIA   Ay, that's a colt indeed, for he doth nothing but 39
talk of his horse, and he makes it a great appropriation 40
to his own good parts that he can shoe him him- 41
self. I am much afeard my lady his mother played false
with a smith.

NERISSA   Then is there the County Palatine. 44

PORTIA   He doth nothing but frown, as who should say, 45
"An you will not have me, choose." He hears merry 46
tales and smiles not. I fear he will prove the weeping 47
philosopher when he grows old, being so full of un- 48
mannerly sadness in his youth. I had rather be mar- 49
ried to a death's-head with a bone in his mouth than
to either of these. God defend me from these two!

NERISSA   How say you by the French lord, Monsieur 52
Le Bon?

PORTIA   God made him, and therefore let him pass for a
man. In truth, I know it is a sin to be a mocker, but
he! Why, he hath a horse better than the Neapolitan's,
a better bad habit of frowning than the Count Palatine;
he is every man in no man. If a throstle sing, he 58
falls straight a-capering. He will fence with his own 59
shadow. If I should marry him, I should marry twenty
husbands. If he would despise me, I would forgive
him, for if he love me to madness, I shall never re- 62
quite him.

NERISSA   What say you, then, to Falconbridge, the 64
young baron of England?

PORTIA   You know I say nothing to him, for he understands not me, nor I him. He hath neither Latin,
French, nor Italian, and you will come into the court 68
and swear that I have a poor pennyworth in the Eng- 69
lish. He is a proper man's picture, but alas, who can 70
converse with a dumb show? How oddly he is suited! 71
I think he bought his doublet in Italy, his round hose 72

---

175 **presages** i.e., that presages.   **thrift** profit and good fortune
178 **commodity** merchandise   179 **a present sum** ready money.
181 **racked** stretched   183 **presently** immediately   184 **no question make** have no doubt   185 **of my trust** on the basis of my credit as a merchant.   **sake** i.e., personal sake.
1.2. Location: Belmont. Portia's house.
1 **troth** faith   3 **would be** would have reason to be (weary)
5 **surfeit** overindulge   7 **mean** small. (With a pun; see next note.)
7–8 **in the mean** having neither too much nor too little.   8 **comes sooner by** acquires sooner   9 **competency** modest means   10 **sentences** maxims.   **pronounced** delivered.   14 **divine** clergyman
18 **blood** (Thought of as a chief agent of the passions, which in turn were regarded as the enemies of reason.)   20 **meshes** nets. (Used here for hunting hares.)   **good counsel, the cripple** (Wisdom is portrayed as old and no longer agile.)   20–2 **But . . . husband** But this talk is not the way to help me choose a husband.   24 **will . . . will** volition . . . testament

30 **who** whoever.   **his** i.e., the father's   32 **rightly . . . rightly** correctly . . . truly   35 **overname** them name them over   37 **level** aim, guess   39 **colt** i.e., wanton and foolish young man. (With a punning appropriateness to his interest in horses.)   40 **appropriation** addition
41 **good parts** accomplishments   44 **County Palatine** a count entitled to supreme jurisdiction in his province.   45 **as who should say** as one might say   46 **An** If.   **choose** i.e., do as you please.   47–8 **the weeping philosopher** i.e., Heraclitus of Ephesus, a melancholic and retiring philosopher of about 500 B.C., often contrasted with Democritus, the "laughing philosopher"   49 **sadness** melancholy   52 **How . . . by** What do you have to say about   58 **he is . . . no man** i.e., he borrows aspects from everyone but has no character of his own.
throstle thrush   59 **straight** at once   62 **if** even if   64 **say you . . . to** do you say about. (But Portia wittily puns, in her reply, on the literal sense of "speak to.")   68–70 **come . . . English** i.e., bear witness that I can speak very little English.   70 **He . . . picture** i.e., He looks handsome   71 **dumb show** pantomime.   **suited** dressed.   72 **doublet** upper garment corresponding to a jacket.   **round hose** short, puffed-out breeches

in France, his bonnet in Germany, and his behavior 73
everywhere.

NERISSA   What think you of the Scottish lord, his
neighbor?

PORTIA   That he hath a neighborly charity in him, for he
borrowed a box of the ear of the Englishman and swore 78
he would pay him again when he was able. I think the
Frenchman became his surety and sealed under for an- 80
other. 81

NERISSA   How like you the young German, the Duke of
Saxony's nephew?

PORTIA   Very vilely in the morning, when he is sober,
and most vilely in the afternoon, when he is drunk.
When he is best he is a little worse than a man, and
when he is worst he is little better than a beast. An 87
the worst fall that ever fell, I hope I shall make shift to 88
go without him.

NERISSA   If he should offer to choose, and choose the 90
right casket, you should refuse to perform your father's
will if you should refuse to accept him.

PORTIA   Therefore, for fear of the worst, I pray thee, set
a deep glass of Rhenish wine on the contrary casket, 94
for if the devil be within and that temptation without, 95
I know he will choose it. I will do anything, Nerissa, 96
ere I will be married to a sponge.

NERISSA   You need not fear, lady, the having any of
these lords. They have acquainted me with their de-
terminations, which is indeed to return to their home
and to trouble you with no more suit, unless you may
be won by some other sort than your father's imposi- 102
tion depending on the caskets. 103

PORTIA   If I live to be as old as Sibylla, I will die as chaste 104
as Diana, unless I be obtained by the manner of my 105
father's will. I am glad this parcel of wooers are so rea- 106
sonable, for there is not one among them but I dote on
his very absence, and I pray God grant them a fair
departure.

NERISSA   Do you not remember, lady, in your father's
time, a Venetian, a scholar and a soldier, that came
hither in company of the Marquess of Montferrat?

PORTIA   Yes, yes, it was Bassanio—as I think, so was
he called.

NERISSA   True, madam. He, of all the men that ever my
foolish eyes looked upon was the best deserving a fair
lady.

PORTIA   I remember him well, and I remember him
worthy of thy praise.

Enter a Servingman.

How now, what news?

SERVINGMAN   The four strangers seek for you, madam, 121
to take their leave; and there is a forerunner come from 122
a fifth, the Prince of Morocco, who brings word the
Prince his master will be here tonight.

PORTIA   If I could bid the fifth welcome with so good
heart as I can bid the other four farewell, I should be
glad of his approach. If he have the condition of a saint 127
and the complexion of a devil, I had rather he should 128
shrive me than wive me. 129
Come, Nerissa. [*To Servingman*] Sirrah, go before. 130
Whiles we shut the gate upon one wooer, another
    knocks at the door.   *Exeunt.*

❖

[1.3]

Enter Bassanio with Shylock the Jew.

SHYLOCK   Three thousand ducats, well.   1

BASSANIO   Ay, sir, for three months.

SHYLOCK   For three months, well.

BASSANIO   For the which, as I told you, Antonio shall
be bound.

SHYLOCK   Antonio shall become bound, well.

BASSANIO   May you stead me? Will you pleasure me? 7
Shall I know your answer?

SHYLOCK   Three thousand ducats for three months and
Antonio bound.

BASSANIO   Your answer to that.

SHYLOCK   Antonio is a good man.   12

BASSANIO   Have you heard any imputation to the
contrary?

SHYLOCK   Ho, no, no, no, no! My meaning in saying he
is a good man is to have you understand me that he is
sufficient. Yet his means are in supposition. He hath an 17
argosy bound to Tripolis, another to the Indies. I understand, moreover, upon the Rialto, he hath a third 19
at Mexico, a fourth for England, and other ventures he
hath squandered abroad. But ships are but boards, 21
sailors but men. There be land rats and water rats,
water thieves and land thieves—I mean pirates—and
then there is the peril of waters, winds, and rocks. The
man is, notwithstanding, sufficient. Three thousand
ducats. I think I may take his bond.

BASSANIO   Be assured you may.   27

SHYLOCK   I will be assured I may; and that I may be 28
assured, I will bethink me. May I speak with Antonio?

73 bonnet hat   **78 borrowed** received. (But with a play on the idea of something that must be repaid.)   **80–1 became . . . another** offered to back up the Scottish lord and promised (with as solemn a vow as if he were signing and sealing a document) to add a blow of his own. (An allusion to the age-old alliance of the French and the Scots against the English.)   **87 An** If   **88 fall** befall.   **make shift** manage   **90 offer** undertake   **94 Rhenish wine** a German white wine from the Rhine Valley.   **contrary** i.e., wrong   **95 if** even if   **96 it** i.e., the tempting red wine.   **102 sort** means. (With perhaps a suggestion too of "casting or drawing of lots.")   **102–3 imposition** command, charge   **104 Sibylla** the Cumaean Sibyl, to whom Apollo gave as many years as there were grains in her handful of sand   **105 Diana** goddess of chastity and of the hunt   **106 parcel** assembly, group

121 four (Nerissa actually names six suitors; possibly a sign of revision or the author's early draft.)   **122 forerunner** herald   **127 condition** disposition, character   **128 complexion of a devil** (Devils were thought to be black; but *complexion* can also mean "temperament," "disposition.")   **129 shrive me** pardon me, excuse me from having to be wooed. (Literally, act as my confessor and give absolution.)   **130 Sirrah** (Form of address to social inferior.)
1.3. Location: Venice. A public place.
1 ducats gold coins   **7 stead** supply, assist.   **pleasure** oblige   **12 good** (Shylock means "solvent," a good credit risk; Bassanio interprets it in the moral sense.)   **17 sufficient** i.e., a good security.   **in supposition** doubtful, uncertain.   **19 the Rialto** the merchants' exchange in Venice and the center of commercial activity   **21 squandered** scattered   **27, 28 assured** (Bassanio means that Shylock may trust Antonio, whereas Shylock means that he will obtain legal assurances.)

BASSANIO   If it please you to dine with us.

SHYLOCK   Yes, to smell pork, to eat of the habitation
which your prophet the Nazarite conjured the devil   32
into. I will buy with you, sell with you, talk with you,
walk with you, and so following, but I will not eat   34
with you, drink with you, nor pray with you. What
news on the Rialto? Who is he comes here?

       Enter Antonio.

BASSANIO   This is Signor Antonio.

SHYLOCK *[aside]*
How like a fawning publican he looks!   38
I hate him for he is a Christian,   39
But more for that in low simplicity   40
He lends out money gratis and brings down   41
The rate of usance here with us in Venice.   42
If I can catch him once upon the hip,   43
I will feed fat the ancient grudge I bear him.   44
He hates our sacred nation, and he rails,   45
Even there where merchants most do congregate,
On me, my bargains, and my well-won thrift,
Which he calls interest. Cursèd be my tribe
If I forgive him!

BASSANIO   Shylock, do you hear?

SHYLOCK   I am debating of my present store,   50
And, by the near guess of my memory,
I cannot instantly raise up the gross   52
Of full three thousand ducats. What of that?
Tubal, a wealthy Hebrew of my tribe,
Will furnish me. But soft, how many months   55
Do you desire? *[To Antonio]* Rest you fair, good
   signor!
Your Worship was the last man in our mouths.   57

ANTONIO
Shylock, albeit I neither lend nor borrow
By taking nor by giving of excess,   59
Yet, to supply the ripe wants of my friend,   60
I'll break a custom. *[To Bassanio]* Is he yet possessed   61
How much ye would?   62

SHYLOCK   Ay, ay, three thousand ducats.

ANTONIO   And for three months.

SHYLOCK
I had forgot—three months, you told me so.
Well then, your bond. And let me see—but hear
   you,
Methought you said you neither lend nor borrow
Upon advantage.

ANTONIO   I do never use it.   68

SHYLOCK
When Jacob grazed his uncle Laban's sheep—   69
This Jacob from our holy Abram was,   70
As his wise mother wrought in his behalf,
The third possessor; ay, he was the third—   72

ANTONIO
And what of him? Did he take interest?

SHYLOCK
No, not take interest, not as you would say
Directly interest. Mark what Jacob did.
When Laban and himself were compromised   76
That all the eanlings which were streaked and pied   77
Should fall as Jacob's hire, the ewes, being rank,   78
In end of autumn turnèd to the rams,
And when the work of generation was   80
Between these woolly breeders in the act,
The skillful shepherd peeled me certain wands,   82
And in the doing of the deed of kind   83
He stuck them up before the fulsome ewes,   84
Who then conceiving did in eaning time   85
Fall parti-colored lambs, and those were Jacob's.   86
This was a way to thrive, and he was blest;
And thrift is blessing, if men steal it not.   88

ANTONIO
This was a venture, sir, that Jacob served for,   89
A thing not in his power to bring to pass,
But swayed and fashioned by the hand of heaven.
Was this inserted to make interest good?   92
Or is your gold and silver ewes and rams?

SHYLOCK
I cannot tell. I make it breed as fast.   94
But note me, signor—

ANTONIO   Mark you this, Bassanio,
The devil can cite Scripture for his purpose.   96
An evil soul producing holy witness
Is like a villain with a smiling cheek,
A goodly apple rotten at the heart.
Oh, what a goodly outside falsehood hath!

SHYLOCK
Three thousand ducats. 'Tis a good round sum.
Three months from twelve, then let me see, the rate—

ANTONIO
Well, Shylock, shall we be beholding to you?   103

SHYLOCK
Signor Antonio, many a time and oft
In the Rialto you have rated me   105
About my moneys and my usances.
Still have I borne it with a patient shrug,

---

32 Nazarite Nazarene. (For the reference to Christ's casting evil spirits into a herd of swine, see Matthew 8:30–2, Mark 5:1–13, and Luke
8:32–3.) **34 so following** so forth **38 publican** Roman tax gatherer
(a term of opprobrium; see Luke 18:9–14); or, innkeeper **39 for**
because **40 low simplicity** humble foolishness **41 gratis** without
charging interest **42 usance** usury, interest **43 upon the hip** i.e., at
my mercy. (A figure of speech from wrestling; see Genesis 32:24–9.)
44 fat until fatted for the kill **45 our sacred nation** i.e., the Hebrew
people **50 I am . . . store** I am considering my current supply of
money **52 gross** total **55 soft** i.e., wait a minute **57 Your . . .
mouths** i.e., We were just speaking of you. (But with ominous connotation of devouring; compare line 44.) **59 excess** interest **60 ripe
wants** pressing needs **61 possessed** informed **62 ye would** you
want. **68 advantage** interest.

69 Jacob (See Genesis 27, 30:25–43.) **70 Abram** Abraham **72 third**
i.e., after Abraham and Isaac. **possessor** i.e., of the birthright of
which, with the help of Rebecca, he was able to cheat Esau, his elder
brother **76 compromised** agreed **77 eanlings** young lambs or kids.
pied spotted **78 hire** wages, share. **rank** in heat **80 work of generation** mating **82 peeled . . . wands** i.e., partly stripped the bark of
some sticks. (*Me* is used colloquially.) **83 deed of kind** i.e., copulation **84 fulsome** lustful, well-fed **85 eaning** lambing **86 Fall** give
birth to **88 thrift** thriving, profit **89 venture . . . for** uncertain commercial venture on which Jacob risked his wages **92 inserted . . .
good** brought in to justify the practice of usury. **94 I cannot tell** i.e., I
don't know about that. **96 devil . . . Scripture** (See Matthew 4:6.)
103 beholding beholden, indebted **105 rated** berated, rebuked

For sufferance is the badge of all our tribe.   108
You call me misbeliever, cutthroat dog,
And spit upon my Jewish gaberdine,   110
And all for use of that which is mine own.
Well then, it now appears you need my help.
Go to, then. You come to me and you say,   113
"Shylock, we would have moneys"—you say so,
You, that did void your rheum upon my beard   115
And foot me as you spurn a stranger cur   116
Over your threshold. Moneys is your suit.   117
What should I say to you? Should I not say,
"Hath a dog money? Is it possible
A cur can lend three thousand ducats?" Or
Shall I bend low, and in a bondman's key,   121
With bated breath and whispering humbleness,   122
Say this:
"Fair sir, you spit on me on Wednesday last,
You spurned me such a day, another time
You called me dog, and for these courtesies
I'll lend you thus much moneys"?

ANTONIO
I am as like to call thee so again,   128
To spit on thee again, to spurn thee too.
If thou wilt lend this money, lend it not
As to thy friends, for when did friendship take
A breed for barren metal of his friend?   132
But lend it rather to thine enemy,   133
Who, if he break, thou mayst with better face   134
Exact the penalty.
SHYLOCK   Why, look you how you storm!
I would be friends with you and have your love,
Forget the shames that you have stained me with,
Supply your present wants, and take no doit   138
Of usance for my moneys, and you'll not hear me.
This is kind I offer.   140
BASSANIO   This were kindness.   141
SHYLOCK   This kindness will I show.
Go with me to a notary, seal me there
Your single bond; and, in a merry sport,   144
If you repay me not on such a day,
In such a place, such sum or sums as are
Expressed in the condition, let the forfeit
Be nominated for an equal pound   148
Of your fair flesh, to be cut off and taken
In what part of your body pleaseth me.
ANTONIO
Content, in faith. I'll seal to such a bond
And say there is much kindness in the Jew.

BASSANIO
You shall not seal to such a bond for me!
I'll rather dwell in my necessity.   154
ANTONIO
Why, fear not, man, I will not forfeit it.
Within these two months—that's a month before
This bond expires—I do expect return
Of thrice three times the value of this bond.
SHYLOCK
O father Abram, what these Christians are,
Whose own hard dealings teaches them suspect
The thoughts of others! Pray you, tell me this:
If he should break his day, what should I gain
By the exaction of the forfeiture?
A pound of man's flesh taken from a man
Is not so estimable, profitable neither,   165
As flesh of muttons, beefs, or goats. I say
To buy his favor I extend this friendship.
If he will take it, so; if not, adieu.   168
And for my love, I pray you, wrong me not.   169
ANTONIO
Yes, Shylock, I will seal unto this bond.
SHYLOCK
Then meet me forthwith at the notary's.
Give him direction for this merry bond,
And I will go and purse the ducats straight,
See to my house, left in the fearful guard   174
Of an unthrifty knave, and presently
I'll be with you.   Exit.
ANTONIO   Hie thee, gentle Jew.—   176
The Hebrew will turn Christian; he grows kind.
BASSANIO
I like not fair terms and a villain's mind.
ANTONIO
Come on. In this there can be no dismay;
My ships come home a month before the day.
                                              [Exeunt.]

❖

[2.1]

[Flourish of cornets.] Enter [the Prince of]
Morocco, a tawny Moor all in white, and three
or four followers accordingly, with Portia, Nerissa, and their train.

MOROCCO
Mislike me not for my complexion,
The shadowed livery of the burnished sun,   2
To whom I am a neighbor and near bred.   3
Bring me the fairest creature northward born,
Where Phoebus' fire scarce thaws the icicles,   5
And let us make incision for your love

---

108 **sufferance** endurance   110 **gaberdine** loose outer garment like a
cape or mantle   113 **Go to** (An exclamation of impatience or annoyance.)   115 **rheum** spittle   116 **spurn** kick   117 **suit** request.
121 **bondman's key** serf's tone of voice   122 **bated** subdued
128 **like** likely   132 **A breed . . . metal** offspring from money, which
cannot naturally breed. (One of the oldest arguments against usury
was that it was thereby "unnatural.")   **of** from   133 **to** as if to
134 **Who** from whom.   **break** fail to pay on time   138 **doit** a Dutch
coin of very small value   140 **kind** kindly   141 **were** would be (if
seriously offered)   144 **single bond** bond signed alone without other
security; unconditional. (Shylock pretends the *condition*, line 147, is
only a joke.)   148 **nominated for** named, specified as.   **equal** exact

154 **dwell** remain   165 **estimable** valuable   168 **so** well and good
169 **wrong me not** do not think evil of me.   174 **fearful** to be mistrusted   176 **gentle** gracious, courteous. (With a play on "gentile.")
2.1. Location: Belmont. Portia's house.
0.3 *accordingly* similarly (i.e., dressed in white and dark-skinned like
Morocco)   2 **shadowed livery** i.e., dark complexion, worn as though
it were a costume of the sun's servants   3 **near bred** closely related
5 **Phoebus'** i.e., the sun's

To prove whose blood is reddest, his or mine.   7
I tell thee, lady, this aspect of mine   8
Hath feared the valiant. By my love I swear,   9
The best-regarded virgins of our clime
Have loved it too. I would not change this hue,
Except to steal your thoughts, my gentle queen.

PORTIA
In terms of choice I am not solely led
By nice direction of a maiden's eyes;   14
Besides, the lott'ry of my destiny
Bars me the right of voluntary choosing.
But if my father had not scanted me,   17
And hedged me by his wit to yield myself   18
His wife who wins me by that means I told you,   19
Yourself, renownèd prince, then stood as fair   20
As any comer I have looked on yet
For my affection.

MOROCCO   Even for that I thank you.   22
Therefore, I pray you, lead me to the caskets
To try my fortune. By this scimitar
That slew the Sophy and a Persian prince,   25
That won three fields of Sultan Solyman,   26
I would o'erstare the sternest eyes that look,   27
Outbrave the heart most daring on the earth,
Pluck the young sucking cubs from the she-bear,
Yea, mock the lion when 'a roars for prey,   30
To win thee, lady. But alas the while!
If Hercules and Lichas play at dice   32
Which is the better man, the greater throw
May turn by fortune from the weaker hand.
So is Alcides beaten by his page,
And so may I, blind Fortune leading me,
Miss that which one unworthier may attain,
And die with grieving.

PORTIA   You must take your chance,
And either not attempt to choose at all
Or swear before you choose, if you choose wrong
Never to speak to lady afterward
In way of marriage. Therefore be advised.   42

MOROCCO
Nor will not. Come, bring me unto my chance.   43

PORTIA
First, forward to the temple. After dinner   44
Your hazard shall be made.

MOROCCO   Good fortune then!
To make me blest or cursed'st among men.
                    [Cornets, and] exeunt.

7 **reddest** (Red blood was regarded as a sign of courage.)   8 **aspect** visage   9 **feared** frightened   14 **nice direction** careful guidance   17 **scanted** limited   18 **wit** wisdom   18–19 **yield . . . who** give myself to be the wife of him who   20 **then . . . fair** would then have looked as attractive and stood as fair a chance. (With a play on "fair-skinned.")   22 **For my** of gaining my   25 **Sophy** Shah of Persia   26 **fields** battles.   **Solyman** a Turkish sultan ruling from 1520 to 1566   27 **o'erstare** outstare   30 **'a** he   32 **Lichas** a page of Hercules (Alcides). See the note for 3.2.55.   42 **be advised** take warning, consider.   43 **Nor will not** i.e., Nor indeed will I violate the oath.   44 **to the temple** i.e., in order to take the oaths.

[2.2]

Enter [Lancelot] the clown, alone.

LANCELOT   Certainly my conscience will serve me to   1
run from this Jew my master. The fiend is at mine
elbow and tempts me, saying to me, "Gobbo, Lancelot
Gobbo, good Lancelot," or "Good Gobbo," or "Good
Lancelot Gobbo, use your legs, take the start, run
away." My conscience says, "No, take heed, honest
Lancelot, take heed, honest Gobbo," or, as aforesaid,
"Honest Lancelot Gobbo, do not run; scorn running
with thy heels." Well, the most courageous fiend bids   9
me pack. "Fia!" says the fiend. "Away!" says the fiend.   10
"For the heavens, rouse up a brave mind," says the   11
fiend, "and run." Well, my conscience, hanging about   12
the neck of my heart, says very wisely to me, "My hon-   13
est friend Lancelot, being an honest man's son," or
rather an honest woman's son—for indeed my father
did something smack, something grow to, he had a   16
kind of taste—well, my conscience says, "Lancelot,   17
budge not." "Budge," says the fiend "Budge not," says
my conscience. "Conscience," say I, "you counsel
well." "Fiend," say I, "you counsel well." To be ruled by
my conscience, I should stay with the Jew my master,
who, God bless the mark, is a kind of devil; and to run   22
away from the Jew, I should be ruled by the fiend, who,
saving your reverence, is the devil himself. Certainly
the Jew is the very devil incarnation; and, in my con-   25
science, my conscience is but a kind of hard conscience
to offer to counsel me to stay with the Jew. The fiend
gives the more friendly counsel. I will run, fiend. My
heels are at your commandment. I will run.

Enter Old Gobbo, with a basket.

GOBBO   Master young man, you, I pray you, which is   30
the way to master Jew's?

LANCELOT [*aside*] Oh, heavens, this is my true-
begotten father, who, being more than sand-blind,   33
high-gravel-blind, knows me not. I will try confusions   34
with him.

GOBBO   Master young gentleman, I pray you, which is
the way to master Jew's?

LANCELOT   Turn up on your right hand at the next
turning, but at the next turning of all on your left;
marry, at the very next turning, turn of no hand, but   40
turn down indirectly to the Jew's house.

2.2. Location: Venice. A street.
0.1 *clown* (1) country bumpkin (2) comic type in an Elizabethan acting company   **1 serve** permit   **9 with thy heels** i.e., emphatically. (With a pun on the literal sense.)   **10 pack** begone.   **Fia!** i.e., Via, away!   **11 For the heavens** i.e., In heaven's name   **12–13 hanging . . . heart** i.e., timidly   **16–17 something smack . . . taste** i.e., had a tendency to lechery   **22 God . . . mark** (An expression by way of apology for introducing something potentially offensive, as also in *saving your reverence* in line 24.)   **25 incarnation** (Lancelot means "incarnate.")   **30 you** (Gobbo uses the formal *you* but switches to the familiar *thou*, line 88, when he accepts Lancelot as his son.)   **33 sand-blind** dim-sighted   **34 high-gravel-blind** blinder than sand-blind. (A term seemingly invented by Lancelot.)   **try confusions** (Lancelot's blunder for "try conclusions," i.e., experiment, though his error is comically apt.)   **40 marry** i.e., by the Virgin Mary, indeed. (A mild interjection.)   **of no hand** neither right nor left

GOBBO   By God's sonties, 'twill be a hard way to hit. 42
Can you tell me whether one Lancelot, that dwells
with him, dwell with him or no?

LANCELOT   Talk you of young Master Lancelot? [*Aside*]
Mark me now; now will I raise the waters.—Talk you 46
of young Master Lancelot?

GOBBO   No master, sir, but a poor man's son. His father, 48
though I say 't, is an honest exceeding poor man and,
God be thanked, well to live. 50

LANCELOT   Well, let his father be what 'a will, we talk 51
of young Master Lancelot.

GOBBO   Your Worship's friend, and Lancelot, sir. 53

LANCELOT   But I pray you, ergo, old man, ergo, I be- 54
seech you, talk you of young Master Lancelot?

GOBBO   Of Lancelot, an't please Your Mastership?

LANCELOT   Ergo, Master Lancelot. Talk not of Master
Lancelot, father, for the young gentleman, according 58
to Fates and Destinies and such odd sayings, the Sis- 59
ters Three and such branches of learning, is indeed 60
deceased, or, as you would say in plain terms, gone to
heaven.

GOBBO   Marry, God forbid! The boy was the very staff
of my age, my very prop.

LANCELOT   Do I look like a cudgel or a hovel post, a 65
staff, or a prop? Do you know me, father?

GOBBO   Alack the day, I know you not, young gentleman. But I pray you, tell me, is my boy, God rest his
soul, alive or dead?

LANCELOT   Do you not know me, father?

GOBBO   Alack, sir, I am sand-blind. I know you not.

LANCELOT   Nay, indeed, if you had your eyes you
might fail of the knowing me; it is a wise father that 73
knows his own child. Well, old man, I will tell you 74
news of your son. [*He kneels.*] Give me your blessing.
Truth will come to light; murder cannot be hid long; a
man's son may, but in the end truth will out.

GOBBO   Pray you, sir, stand up. I am sure you are not
Lancelot, my boy.

LANCELOT   Pray you, let's have no more fooling about
it, but give me your blessing. I am Lancelot, your 81
boy that was, your son that is, your child that shall be. 82

GOBBO   I cannot think you are my son.

LANCELOT   I know not what I shall think of that; but I
am Lancelot, the Jew's man, and I am sure Margery
your wife is my mother.

GOBBO   Her name is Margery indeed. I'll be sworn, if
thou be Lancelot, thou art mine own flesh and blood.
Lord worshiped might he be, what a beard hast thou 89
got! Thou hast got more hair on thy chin than Dobbin
my fill horse has on his tail. 91

LANCELOT   [*rising*]   It should seem then that Dobbin's
tail grows backward. I am sure he had more hair of 93
his tail than I have of my face when I last saw him. 94

GOBBO   Lord, how art thou changed! How dost thou and
thy master agree? I have brought him a present. How
'gree you now?

LANCELOT   Well, well; but for mine own part, as I have
set up my rest to run away, so I will not rest till 99
I have run some ground. My master's a very Jew. Give 100
him a present? Give him a halter! I am famished in his 101
service; you may tell every finger I have with my ribs. 102
Father, I am glad you are come. Give me your present 103
to one Master Bassanio, who indeed gives rare new 104
liveries. If I serve not him, I will run as far as God has 105
any ground. Oh, rare fortune! Here comes the man. To
him, father, for I am a Jew if I serve the Jew any longer. 107

*Enter Bassanio, with [Leonardo and] a follower
or two.*

BASSANIO   You may do so, but let it be so hasted that 108
supper be ready at the farthest by five of the clock. See 109
these letters delivered, put the liveries to making, and
desire Gratiano to come anon to my lodging.

[*Exit a Servant.*]

LANCELOT   To him, father.

GOBBO [*advancing*]   God bless Your Worship!

BASSANIO   Gramercy. Wouldst thou aught with me? 114

GOBBO   Here's my son, sir, a poor boy— 115

LANCELOT   Not a poor boy, sir, but the rich Jew's man,
that would, sir, as my father shall specify—

GOBBO   He hath a great infection, sir, as one would say, 118
to serve—

LANCELOT   Indeed, the short and the long is, I serve the
Jew, and have a desire, as my father shall specify—

GOBBO   His master and he, saving Your Worship's
reverence, are scarce cater-cousins— 123

LANCELOT   To be brief, the very truth is that the Jew,
having done me wrong, doth cause me, as my father,
being, I hope, an old man, shall frutify unto you— 126

GOBBO   I have here a dish of doves that I would bestow
upon Your Worship, and my suit is—

LANCELOT   In very brief, the suit is impertinent to 129
myself, as Your Worship shall know by this honest old
man, and, though I say it, though old man, yet poor
man, my father.

---

42 sonties little saints   **46 raise the waters** i.e., start tears.   **48 master**
(The title was applied to gentlefolk only.)   **50 well to live** prospering,
in good health.   **51 'a** he   **53 Your . . . Lancelot** (Again, Old Gobbo
denies that Lancelot is entitled to be called "Master.")   **54 ergo** therefore. (But Lancelot may use this Latin word with no particular meaning in mind.)   **58 father** (1) old man (2) father   **59–60 the Sisters
Three** the three Fates   **65 hovel post** post holding up a hovel or open
shed   **73–4 it is . . . child** (Reverses the proverb "It is a wise child
that knows his own father.")   **81–2 your . . . shall be** (Echoes the
Gloria from the Book of Common Prayer: "As it was in the beginning,
is now, and ever shall be.")   **89 beard** (Stage tradition has Old Gobbo
mistaking Lancelot's long hair for a beard.)   **91 fill horse** cart horse

93 grows backward grows at the wrong end.   **94 of** on   **99 set up
my rest** determined, risked all. (A metaphor from the card game
primero, in which a final wager is made, with a pun also on *rest* as
"place of residence.")   **not rest** i.e., not stop running. (More punning
on *rest*.)   **100 very** veritable.   **Jew** (1) Hebrew (2) grasping old
usurer   **101 halter** hangman's noose.   **102 tell** count.   **tell . . . ribs**
(Comically reverses the usual saying of counting one's ribs with one's
fingers.)   **103 Give me** Give. (*Me* suggests "on my behalf.")
104 rare splendid   **105 liveries** uniforms or costumes for servants.
107 a Jew i.e., a villain. (Punning on the literal sense in *the Jew*. Compare with line 100.)   **108 hasted** hastened, hurried   **109 farthest** latest   **114 Gramercy** Many thanks.   **aught** anything   **115 poor**
(1) unfortunate (2) penniless (contrasted with *rich* in the next line)
118 infection (Blunder for "affection" or "inclination.")   **123 cater-
cousins** good friends   **126 frutify** (Lancelot may be trying to say
"fructify," but he means "certify" or "notify.")   **129 impertinent**
(Blunder for "pertinent.")

BASSANIO One speak for both. What would you?

LANCELOT Serve you, sir.

GOBBO That is the very defect of the matter, sir. 135

BASSANIO
I know thee well; thou hast obtained thy suit.
Shylock thy master spoke with me this day,
And hath preferred thee, if it be preferment 138
To leave a rich Jew's service to become
The follower of so poor a gentleman.

LANCELOT The old proverb is very well parted be- 141
tween my master Shylock and you, sir: you have the
grace of God, sir, and he hath enough.

BASSANIO
Thou speak'st it well. Go, father, with thy son.
Take leave of thy old master, and inquire
My lodging out. [To a Servant] Give him a livery
More guarded than his fellows'. See it done. 147

LANCELOT Father, in. I cannot get a service, no! I have
ne'er a tongue in my head, well! [He looks at his palm.]
If any man in Italy have a fairer table which doth offer 150
to swear upon a book, I shall have good fortune. Go 151
to, here's a simple line of life. Here's a small trifle of 152
wives! Alas, fifteen wives is nothing. Eleven widows
and nine maids is a simple coming-in for one man. 154
And then to scape drowning thrice, and to be in peril
of my life with the edge of a feather bed! Here are 156
simple scapes. Well, if Fortune be a woman, she's a 157
good wench for this gear. Father, come. I'll take my 158
leave of the Jew in the twinkling.
Exit clown [Lancelot, with Old Gobbo].

BASSANIO [giving Leonardo a list]
I pray thee, good Leonardo, think on this:
These things being bought and orderly bestowed, 161
Return in haste, for I do feast tonight 162
My best-esteemed acquaintance. Hie thee, go.

LEONARDO
My best endeavors shall be done herein.
[He starts to leave.]

Enter Gratiano.

GRATIANO [to Leonardo]
Where's your master?

LEONARDO
Yonder, sir, he walks.
Exit Leonardo.

GRATIANO Signor Bassanio!

BASSANIO Gratiano!

GRATIANO
I have a suit to you.

BASSANIO You have obtained it.

GRATIANO You must not deny me. I must go with you
to Belmont.

BASSANIO
Why, then you must. But hear thee, Gratiano;
Thou art too wild, too rude and bold of voice—
Parts that become thee happily enough, 173
And in such eyes as ours appear not faults,
But where thou art not known, why, there they show
Something too liberal. Pray thee, take pain 176
To allay with some cold drops of modesty 177
Thy skipping spirit, lest through thy wild behavior
I be misconstered in the place I go to 179
And lose my hopes.

GRATIANO Signor Bassanio, hear me:
If I do not put on a sober habit, 181
Talk with respect and swear but now and then,
Wear prayer books in my pocket, look demurely,
Nay more, while grace is saying, hood mine eyes 184
Thus with my hat, and sigh and say "amen,"
Use all the observance of civility,
Like one well studied in a sad ostent 187
To please his grandam, never trust me more. 188

BASSANIO Well, we shall see your bearing.

GRATIANO
Nay, but I bar tonight. You shall not gauge me
By what we do tonight.

BASSANIO No, that were pity.
I would entreat you rather to put on
Your boldest suit of mirth, for we have friends
That purpose merriment. But fare you well;
I have some business.

GRATIANO
And I must to Lorenzo and the rest,
But we will visit you at suppertime. Exeunt.

❖

[2.3]

Enter Jessica and [Lancelot] the clown.

JESSICA
I am sorry thou wilt leave my father so.
Our house is hell, and thou, a merry devil,
Didst rob it of some taste of tediousness.
But fare thee well. There is a ducat for thee.
[Giving money.]
And, Lancelot, soon at supper shalt thou see
Lorenzo, who is thy new master's guest.
Give him this letter; do it secretly. [Giving a letter.]
And so farewell. I would not have my father
See me in talk with thee.

---

135 defect (Blunder for "effect," i.e., "purport.") 138 preferred recommended 141 proverb i.e., "He who has the grace of God has enough." parted divided 147 guarded trimmed with braided ornament 150 table palm of the hand. (Lancelot now reads the lines of his palm.) 151 book i.e., Bible. (The image is of a hand being laid on the Bible to take an oath.) 151–2 Go to (An expression of impatience.) 152 simple unremarkable. (Said ironically.) line of life curved line at the base of the thumb. 154 simple coming-in modest beginning or income. (With sexual suggestion.) 156 feather bed (Suggesting marriage bed or love bed; Lancelot sees sexual adventure and the dangers of marriage in his palm reading.) 157 scapes 1) adventures (2) transgressions. Fortune . . . woman (Fortune was personified as a goddess.) 158 gear matter. 161 bestowed i.e., stowed on board ship 162 feast give a feast for

173 Parts qualities 176 liberal free of manner. (Often with sexual connotation.) 177 allay temper, moderate. modesty decorum 179 misconstered misconstrued 181 habit demeanor. (With a suggestion of "clothes.") 184 saying being said 187 sad ostent grave appearance 188 grandam grandmother
2.3. Location: Venice. Shylock's house.

LANCELOT   Adieu! Tears exhibit my tongue. Most   10
beautiful pagan, most sweet Jew! If a Christian did not
play the knave and get thee, I am much deceived. But,   12
adieu! These foolish drops do something drown my
manly spirit. Adieu!

JESSICA   Farewell, good Lancelot.   [Exit Lancelot.]
Alack, what heinous sin is it in me
To be ashamed to be my father's child!
But though I am a daughter to his blood,
I am not to his manners. O Lorenzo,
If thou keep promise, I shall end this strife,
Become a Christian and thy loving wife.   Exit.

❧

[2.4]

Enter Gratiano, Lorenzo, Salerio, and Solanio.

LORENZO
Nay, we will slink away in suppertime,   1
Disguise us at my lodging, and return
All in an hour.

GRATIANO
We have not made good preparation.

SALERIO
We have not spoke us yet of torchbearers.   5

SOLANIO
'Tis vile, unless it may be quaintly ordered,   6
And better in my mind not undertook.

LORENZO
'Tis now but four o'clock. We have two hours
To furnish us.

Enter Lancelot [with a letter].

Friend Lancelot, what's the news?

LANCELOT   An it shall please you to break up this, it   10
shall seem to signify.   [Giving the letter.]

LORENZO
I know the hand. In faith, 'tis a fair hand,
And whiter than the paper it writ on
Is the fair hand that writ.

GRATIANO   Love news, in faith.

LANCELOT   By your leave, sir.   [He starts to leave.]

LORENZO   Whither goest thou?

LANCELOT   Marry, sir, to bid my old master the Jew to
sup tonight with my new master the Christian.

LORENZO
Hold here, take this. [He gives money.] Tell gentle
Jessica
I will not fail her. Speak it privately.
         Exit clown [Lancelot].
Go, gentlemen,
Will you prepare you for this masque tonight?
I am provided of a torchbearer.

SALERIO
Ay, marry, I'll be gone about it straight.   24

SOLANIO
And so will I.

LORENZO   Meet me and Gratiano.
At Gratiano's lodging some hour hence.   26

SALERIO   'Tis good we do so.   Exit [with Solanio].

GRATIANO
Was not that letter from fair Jessica?

LORENZO
I must needs tell thee all. She hath directed   29
How I shall take her from her father's house,
What gold and jewels she is furnished with,
What page's suit she hath in readiness.
If e'er the Jew her father come to heaven,
It will be for his gentle daughter's sake;   34
And never dare misfortune cross her foot,   35
Unless she do it under this excuse,   36
That she is issue to a faithless Jew.   37
Come, go with me. Peruse this as thou goest.
         [He gives Gratiano the letter.]
Fair Jessica shall be my torchbearer.   Exeunt.

❧

[2.5]

*Enter [Shylock the] Jew and [Lancelot,] his man
that was, the clown.*

SHYLOCK
Well, thou shalt see, thy eyes shall be thy judge,
The difference of old Shylock and Bassanio.—   2
What, Jessica!—Thou shalt not gormandize,   3
As thou hast done with me—What, Jessica!—
And sleep and snore, and rend apparel out—   5
Why, Jessica, I say!

LANCELOT   Why, Jessica!

SHYLOCK
Who bids thee call? I do not bid thee call.

LANCELOT   Your Worship was wont to tell me I could
do nothing without bidding.

Enter Jessica.

JESSICA   Call you? What is your will?

SHYLOCK
I am bid forth to supper, Jessica.
There are my keys. But wherefore should I go?   13
I am not bid for love—they flatter me—
But yet I'll go in hate, to feed upon
The prodigal Christian. Jessica, my girl,
Look to my house. I am right loath to go.   17
There is some ill a-brewing towards my rest,
For I did dream of moneybags tonight.   19

LANCELOT   I beseech you, sir, go. My young master
doth expect your reproach.   21

---

26 **some hour** about an hour   29 **must needs** must   34 **gentle** (With
pun on "gentile"?)   35 **foot** footpath   36 **she** i.e., Misfortune   37 **she
is issue** i.e., Jessica is daughter.   **faithless** pagan
2.5. Location: Venice. Before Shylock's house.
2 **of** between   3 **gormandize** eat gluttonously   5 **rend apparel out**
i.e., wear out your clothes   13 **wherefore** why   17 **right loath** reluctant   19 **tonight** last night.   21 **reproach** (Lancelot's blunder for
"approach." Shylock takes it in grim humor.)

---

10 **exhibit** (Blunder for "inhibit," "restrain.")   12 **get** beget
2.4. Location: Venice. A street.
1 **in** during   5 **spoke . . . of** yet bespoken, ordered   6 **quaintly
ordered** skillfully and tastefully managed   10 **An** If.   **break up this**
unseal the letter   24 **straight** at once.

SHYLOCK   So do I his.

LANCELOT   And they have conspired together. I will
not say you shall see a masque, but if you do, then it
was not for nothing that my nose fell a-bleeding on
Black Monday last at six o'clock i'th' morning, falling   26
out that year on Ash Wednesday was four year in
th'afternoon.

SHYLOCK
What, are there masques? Hear you me, Jessica:
Lock up my doors, and when you hear the drum
And the vile squealing of the wry-necked fife,   31
Clamber not you up to the casements then,
Nor thrust your head into the public street
To gaze on Christian fools with varnished faces,   34
But stop my house's ears—I mean my casements.
Let not the sound of shallow fopp'ry enter
My sober house. By Jacob's staff I swear   37
I have no mind of feasting forth tonight.
But I will go.—Go you before me, sirrah.
Say I will come.

LANCELOT   I will go before, sir. [Aside to Jessica] Mis-
tress, look out at window, for all this;
There will come a Christian by,
Will be worth a Jewess' eye.   [Exit.]

SHYLOCK
What says that fool of Hagar's offspring, ha?   45

JESSICA
His words were "Farewell, mistress," nothing else.

SHYLOCK
The patch is kind enough, but a huge feeder,   47
Snail-slow in profit, and he sleeps by day   48
More than the wildcat. Drones hive not with me;
Therefore I part with him, and part with him
To one that I would have him help to waste
His borrowed purse. Well, Jessica, go in.
Perhaps I will return immediately.
Do as I bid you. Shut doors after you.
Fast bind, fast find—   55
A proverb never stale in thrifty mind.   Exit.

JESSICA
Farewell, and if my fortune be not crossed,
I have a father, you a daughter, lost.   Exit.

❖

[2.6]

Enter the masquers, Gratiano and Salerio.

GRATIANO
This is the penthouse under which Lorenzo   1

Desired us to make stand.

SALERIO   His hour is almost past.

GRATIANO
And it is marvel he outdwells his hour,   4
For lovers ever run before the clock.

SALERIO
Oh, ten times faster Venus' pigeons fly   6
To seal love's bonds new-made than they are wont
To keep obligèd faith unforfeited.   8

GRATIANO
That ever holds. Who riseth from a feast   9
With that keen appetite that he sits down?
Where is the horse that doth untread again   11
His tedious measures with the unbated fire   12
That he did pace them first? All things that are
Are with more spirit chasèd than enjoyed.
How like a younger or a prodigal   15
The scarfèd bark puts from her native bay,   16
Hugged and embracèd by the strumpet wind!   17
How like the prodigal doth she return,
With overweathered ribs and ragged sails,   19
Lean, rent, and beggared by the strumpet wind!   20

Enter Lorenzo.

SALERIO
Here comes Lorenzo. More of this hereafter.

LORENZO
Sweet friends, your patience for my long abode;   22
Not I, but my affairs, have made you wait.
When you shall please to play the thieves for wives,
I'll watch as long for you then. Approach;   25
Here dwells my father Jew.—Ho! Who's within?   26

[Enter] Jessica, above [in boy's clothes].

JESSICA
Who are you? Tell me for more certainty,
Albeit I'll swear that I do know your tongue.

LORENZO   Lorenzo, and thy love.

JESSICA
Lorenzo, certain, and my love indeed,
For who love I so much? And now who knows
But you, Lorenzo, whether I am yours?   31

LORENZO
Heaven and thy thoughts are witness that thou art.

JESSICA [throwing down a casket]
Here, catch this casket. It is worth the pains.
I am glad 'tis night, you do not look on me,

---

26 **Black Monday** Easter Monday. (Lancelot's talk of omens is perhaps intentional gibberish, a parody of Shylock's fears.)   **31 wry-
necked** i.e., played with the musician's head awry; or possibly
comparing the fife's *vile squealing* to the call of the wryneck, a bird
with a high-pitched call and a writhing movement of head and neck
34 varnished faces i.e., painted masks   **37 Jacob's staff** (See Genesis
32:10 and Hebrews 11:21.)   **45 Hagar's offspring** (Hagar, a gentile
and Abraham's servant, gave birth to Ishmael; both mother and son
were cast out after the birth of Isaac.)   **47 patch** fool   **48 profit** profitable labor   **55 Fast . . . find** i.e., Keep your property secure and you
will always know where it is. (Proverbial.)
2.6. Location: Before Shylock's house, as in 2.5.
1 penthouse projecting roof or upper story of a house

4 **it . . . hour** i.e., it is surprising that he is late   **6–8 Oh, ten . . . unforfeited** i.e., Oh, lovers are ten times more alacritous in their first
pledge of love than in keeping faith in a long-term commitment.
(*Venus' pigeons* are the doves that draw her chariot.)   **9 ever holds**
always holds true.   **11 untread** retrace   **12 measures** paces
15 younger i.e., younger son, as in the parable of the Prodigal Son
(Luke 15). (Often emended to *younker*, youth.)   **16 scarfèd bark** sailing vessel festooned with flags or streamers   **17 strumpet** i.e., inconstant, variable. (Likened metaphorically to the harlots with whom
the Prodigal Son wasted his fortune.)   **19 overweathered ribs** i.e.,
weather-beaten and leaking timbers   **20 rent** torn   **22 your patience**
i.e., I beg your patience.   **abode** delay   **25 watch** keep watch
26 father i.e., father-in-law   **31 But you** better than you

For I am much ashamed of my exchange. 36
But love is blind, and lovers cannot see
The pretty follies that themselves commit, 38
For if they could, Cupid himself would blush
To see me thus transformèd to a boy.

LORENZO
Descend, for you must be my torchbearer.

JESSICA
What, must I hold a candle to my shames? 42
They in themselves, good sooth, are too too light. 43
Why, 'tis an office of discovery, love, 44
And I should be obscured.

LORENZO   So are you, sweet,
Even in the lovely garnish of a boy. 46
But come at once,
For the close night doth play the runaway, 48
And we are stayed for at Bassanio's feast. 49

JESSICA
I will make fast the doors, and gild myself 50
With some more ducats, and be with you straight.
                                    [Exit above.]

GRATIANO
Now, by my hood, a gentle and no Jew. 52

LORENZO
Beshrew me but I love her heartily, 53
For she is wise, if I can judge of her,
And fair she is, if that mine eyes be true,
And true she is, as she hath proved herself;
And therefore, like herself, wise, fair, and true,
Shall she be placèd in my constant soul.

        Enter Jessica [below].

What, art thou come? On, gentlemen, away!
Our masquing mates by this time for us stay. 60
                Exit [with Jessica and Salerio;
                Gratiano is about to follow them].

        Enter Antonio.

ANTONIO   Who's there?
GRATIANO   Signor Antonio?
ANTONIO
Fie, fie, Gratiano! Where are all the rest?
'Tis nine o'clock; our friends all stay for you.
No masque tonight. The wind is come about;
Bassanio presently will go aboard.
I have sent twenty out to seek for you.

GRATIANO
I am glad on 't. I desire no more delight
Than to be under sail and gone tonight.   Exeunt.

♣

[2.7]

[Flourish of cornets.] Enter Portia, with [the
Prince of] Morocco, and both their trains.

PORTIA
Go, draw aside the curtains and discover 1
The several caskets to this noble prince. 2
Now make your choice.   [The curtains are drawn.]

MOROCCO
The first, of gold, who this inscription bears, 4
"Who chooseth me shall gain what many men desire";
The second, silver, which this promise carries,
"Who chooseth me shall get as much as he deserves";
This third, dull lead, with warning all as blunt, 8
"Who chooseth me must give and hazard all he hath."
How shall I know if I do choose the right?

PORTIA
The one of them contains my picture, Prince.
If you choose that, then I am yours withal. 12

MOROCCO
Some god direct my judgment! Let me see,
I will survey th'inscriptions back again.
What says this leaden casket?
"Who chooseth me must give and hazard all he hath."
Must give—for what? For lead? Hazard for lead?
This casket threatens. Men that hazard all
Do it in hope of fair advantages.
A golden mind stoops not to shows of dross. 20
I'll then nor give nor hazard aught for lead. 21
What says the silver with her virgin hue?
"Who chooseth me shall get as much as he deserves."
As much as he deserves! Pause there, Morocco,
And weigh thy value with an even hand. 25
If thou be'st rated by thy estimation, 26
Thou dost deserve enough; and yet enough
May not extend so far as to the lady;
And yet to be afeard of my deserving
Were but a weak disabling of myself. 30
As much as I deserve? Why, that's the lady.
I do in birth deserve her, and in fortunes,
In graces, and in qualities of breeding;
But more than these, in love I do deserve.
What if I strayed no farther, but chose here?
Let's see once more this saying graved in gold: 36
"Who chooseth me shall gain what many men desire."
Why, that's the lady; all the world desires her.
From the four corners of the earth they come
To kiss this shrine, this mortal breathing saint. 40
The Hyrcanian deserts and the vasty wilds 41
Of wide Arabia are as throughfares now
For princes to come view fair Portia.

---

36 **exchange** change of clothes.   38 **pretty** ingenious, artful   **42 hold
a candle** i.e., stand by and witness. (With a play on the idea of acting
as torchbearer.)   **43 light** (1) immodest (2) illuminated.   **44 'tis . . .
discovery** i.e., torchbearing is intended to shed light on matters
46 garnish outfit, trimmings   **48 close** dark, secretive.   **doth . . . runaway** i.e., is quickly passing   **49 stayed** waited   **50 gild** adorn. (Literally, cover with gold.)   **52 by my hood** (An asseveration.)   **gentle**
gracious person. (With pun on "gentile," as at 2.4.34.)   **53 Beshrew**
i.e., A mischief on. (A mild oath.)   **60 stay** wait. (Also in line 64.)

2.7. Location: Belmont. Portia's house.
0.2 trains followers   **1 discover** reveal   **2 several** different, various
4 who which   **8 dull** (1) dull-colored (2) blunt.   **all as blunt** as blunt
as lead   **12 withal** with it.   **20 dross** worthless matter. (Literally, the
impurities cast off in the melting down of metals.)   **21 nor give** neither give   **25 even** impartial   **26 estimation** worth   **30 disabling**
underrating   **36 graved** engraved   **40 mortal breathing** living
41 Hyrcanian (Hyrcania was the country south of the Caspian Sea
celebrated for its wildness.)   **vasty** vast

The watery kingdom, whose ambitious head
Spits in the face of heaven, is no bar   45
To stop the foreign spirits, but they come,   46
As o'er a brook, to see fair Portia.
One of these three contains her heavenly picture.
Is't like that lead contains her? 'Twere damnation   49
To think so base a thought; it were too gross   50
To rib her cerecloth in the obscure grave.   51
Or shall I think in silver she's immured,   52
Being ten times undervalued to tried gold?   53
Oh, sinful thought! Never so rich a gem
Was set in worse than gold. They have in England   55
A coin that bears the figure of an angel   56
Stamped in gold, but that's insculped upon;   57
But here an angel in a golden bed
Lies all within. Deliver me the key.
Here do I choose, and thrive I as I may!

PORTIA
There, take it, Prince; and if my form lie there,   61
Then I am yours.
                        [*He unlocks the golden casket.*]
MOROCCO   Oh, hell! What have we here?
A carrion Death, within whose empty eye   63
There is a written scroll! I'll read the writing.
[*He reads.*]
        "All that glisters is not gold;
        Often have you heard that told.
        Many a man his life hath sold
        But my outside to behold.
        Gilded tombs do worms infold.   68
        Had you been as wise as bold,
        Young in limbs, in judgment old,
        Your answer had not been inscrolled.   72
        Fare you well; your suit is cold."
    Cold, indeed, and labor lost.
    Then, farewell, heat, and welcome, frost!
Portia, adieu. I have too grieved a heart
To take a tedious leave. Thus losers part.   77
                        Exit [*with his train. Flourish of cornets.*]
PORTIA
A gentle riddance. Draw the curtains, go.
Let all of his complexion choose me so.   79
                        [*The curtains are closed, and*] *exeunt.*

❦

45 Spits (The image is of huge waves breaking at sea.)   46 spirits i.e.,
men of courage   49 like likely   50 base (1) ignoble (2) low in the
natural scale, as with lead, a *base* metal   50–1 it were . . . grave i.e., it
would be too gross an insult to inter her, as it were, wrapped in a
waxed cloth, in a lead casket.   52 immured enclosed, confined
53 Being . . . gold which has only one-tenth the value of assayed and
purified gold.   55 set fixed, as a precious stone, in a border of metal
56 coin i.e., the gold coin known as the *angel,* which bore the device
of the archangel Michael treading on the dragon   57 insculped upon
merely engraved upon the surface   61 form image   63 carrion
Death death's-head   68 But only   72 inscrolled i.e., written on this
scroll.   77 part depart.   79 complexion temperament (not merely
skin color)

[2.8]

Enter Salerio and Solanio.

SALERIO
Why, man, I saw Bassanio under sail.
With him is Gratiano gone along,
And in their ship I am sure Lorenzo is not.
SOLANIO
The villain Jew with outcries raised the Duke,   4
Who went with him to search Bassanio's ship.
SALERIO
He came too late. The ship was under sail.
But there the Duke was given to understand
That in a gondola were seen together
Lorenzo and his amorous Jessica.
Besides, Antonio certified the Duke
They were not with Bassanio in his ship.
SOLANIO
I never heard a passion so confused,   12
So strange, outrageous, and so variable
As the dog Jew did utter in the streets:
"My daughter! Oh, my ducats! Oh, my daughter!
Fled with a Christian! Oh, my Christian ducats!
Justice! The law! My ducats, and my daughter!
A sealèd bag, two sealèd bags of ducats,
Of double ducats, stol'n from me by my daughter!
And jewels, two stones, two rich and precious
    stones,
Stol'n by my daughter! Justice! Find the girl!
She hath the stones upon her, and the ducats."
SALERIO
Why, all the boys in Venice follow him,
Crying his stones, his daughter, and his ducats.   24
SOLANIO
Let good Antonio look he keep his day,   25
Or he shall pay for this.
SALERIO   Marry, well remembered.
I reasoned with a Frenchman yesterday,   27
Who told me, in the narrow seas that part   28
The French and English, there miscarrièd
A vessel of our country richly fraught.   30
I thought upon Antonio when he told me,
And wished in silence that it were not his.
SOLANIO
You were best to tell Antonio what you hear.
Yet do not suddenly, for it may grieve him.
SALERIO
A kinder gentleman treads not the earth.
I saw Bassanio and Antonio part.
Bassanio told him he would make some speed
Of his return; he answered, "Do not so.
Slubber not business for my sake, Bassanio,   39
But stay the very riping of the time;   40

2.8. Location: Venice. A street.
4 raised roused   12 passion passionate outburst   24 stones (In the
boys' jeering cry, the *two stones* suggest testicles; see line 20.)   25 look . . .
day see to it that he repays his loan on time   27 reasoned talked
28 narrow seas English Channel   30 fraught freighted.   39 Slubber
not business Don't do the business hastily and badly   40 But . . . time
i.e., Pursue your business at Belmont until it is brought to completion

And for the Jew's bond which he hath of me, 41
Let it not enter in your mind of love. 42
Be merry, and employ your chiefest thoughts
To courtship and such fair ostents of love 44
As shall conveniently become you there."
And even there, his eye being big with tears, 46
Turning his face, he put his hand behind him, 47
And with affection wondrous sensible 48
He wrung Bassanio's hand; and so they parted.

SOLANIO
I think he only loves the world for him. 50
I pray thee, let us go and find him out
And quicken his embracèd heaviness 52
With some delight or other.

SALERIO   Do we so.   *Exeunt.*

❖

[2.9]

Enter Nerissa and a Servitor.

NERISSA
Quick, quick, I pray thee, draw the curtain straight. 1
The Prince of Aragon hath ta'en his oath,
And comes to his election presently. 3
                    [*The curtains are drawn back.*]

[*Flourish of cornets.*] *Enter* [*the Prince of*]
Aragon, his train, and Portia.

PORTIA
Behold, there stand the caskets, noble Prince.
If you choose that wherein I am contained,
Straight shall our nuptial rites be solemnized;
But if you fail, without more speech, my lord,
You must be gone from hence immediately.

ARAGON
I am enjoined by oath to observe three things:
First, never to unfold to anyone 10
Which casket 'twas I chose; next, if I fail
Of the right casket, never in my life
To woo a maid in way of marriage;
Lastly,
If I do fail in fortune of my choice,
Immediately to leave you and be gone.

PORTIA
To these injunctions everyone doth swear
That comes to hazard for my worthless self.

ARAGON
And so have I addressed me. Fortune now 19
To my heart's hope! Gold, silver, and base lead.
"Who chooseth me must give and hazard all he hath."

You shall look fairer ere I give or hazard.
What says the golden chest? Ha, let me see:
"Who chooseth me shall gain what many men desire."
What many men desire! That "many" may be meant
By the fool multitude, that choose by show, 26
Not learning more than the fond eye doth teach, 27
Which pries not to th'interior, but like the martlet 28
Builds in the weather on the outward wall, 29
Even in the force and road of casualty. 30
I will not choose what many men desire,
Because I will not jump with common spirits 32
And rank me with the barbarous multitudes.
Why then, to thee, thou silver treasure-house!
Tell me once more what title thou dost bear:
"Who chooseth me shall get as much as he deserves."
And well said too; for who shall go about
To cozen fortune, and be honorable 38
Without the stamp of merit? Let none presume 39
To wear an undeservèd dignity.
Oh, that estates, degrees, and offices 41
Were not derived corruptly, and that clear honor
Were purchased by the merit of the wearer!
How many then should cover that stand bare? 44
How many be commanded that command? 45
How much low peasantry would then be gleaned 46
From the true seed of honor, and how much honor 47
Picked from the chaff and ruin of the times
To be new-varnished? Well, but to my choice: 49
"Who chooseth me shall get as much as he deserves."
I will assume desert. Give me a key for this,
And instantly unlock my fortunes here.
                    [*He opens the silver casket.*]

PORTIA
Too long a pause for that which you find there.

ARAGON
What's here? The portrait of a blinking idiot,
Presenting me a schedule! I will read it. 55
How much unlike art thou to Portia!
How much unlike my hopes and my deservings!
"Who chooseth me shall have as much as he
   deserves."
Did I deserve no more than a fool's head?
Is that my prize? Are my deserts no better?

PORTIA
To offend and judge are distinct offices 61
And of opposèd natures.

ARAGON   What is here? 62

---

41 **for** as for   42 **of** preoccupied with   44 **ostents** expressions, shows
46 **there** thereupon, then   47 **behind him** (Antonio turns away in
tears while extending his hand back to Bassanio.)   48 **affection wondrous sensible** wondrously sensitive and keen emotion   50 **he . . .
him** i.e., Bassanio is all he lives for   52 **quicken . . . heaviness** lighten
the sorrow he has embraced
2.9. Location: Belmont. Portia's house.
0.1 *Servitor* servant   **1 straight** at once   **3 election presently** choice
immediately   **10 unfold** disclose   **19 addressed me** prepared myself
(by this swearing).

26 **By** for, to signify   27 **fond** foolish   28 **martlet** swift   29 **in**
exposed to   30 **force . . . casualty** power and path of mischance.
32 **jump** agree   38 **cozen** cheat   39 **stamp** seal of approval
41 **estates, degrees** status, social rank   44 **cover . . . bare** i.e., wear
hats (of authority) who now stand bareheaded.   45 **How . . . command?** How many then should be servants that are now masters?
46 **gleaned** culled out and discarded   47 **the true seed of honor** i.e.,
persons of noble descent   49 **new-varnished** i.e., having the luster of
their true nobility restored to them.   55 **schedule** written paper.
61–2 **To offend . . . natures** i.e., You have no right, having submitted
your case to judgment, to attempt to judge your own case; or, it is not
for me to say, since I've been the indirect cause of your discomfiture.

[*He reads.*]"The fire seven times tried this; 63
 Seven times tried that judgment is
 That did never choose amiss.
 Some there be that shadows kiss; 66
 Such have but a shadow's bliss.
 There be fools alive, iwis, 68
 Silvered o'er, and so was this. 69
 Take what wife you will to bed;
 I will ever be your head. 71
 So begone; you are sped." 72

Still more fool I shall appear 73
By the time I linger here. 74
With one fool's head I came to woo,
But I go away with two.
Sweet, adieu. I'll keep my oath,
Patiently to bear my wroth. 78
     [*Exeunt Aragon and train.*]

PORTIA
Thus hath the candle singed the moth.
Oh, these deliberate fools! When they do choose, 80
They have the wisdom by their wit to lose.
NERISSA
The ancient saying is no heresy:
Hanging and wiving goes by destiny.
PORTIA Come, draw the curtain, Nerissa.
     [*The curtains are closed.*]

Enter Messenger.

MESSENGER
 Where is my lady?
PORTIA   Here. What would my lord? 85
MESSENGER
Madam, there is alighted at your gate
A young Venetian, one that comes before
To signify th'approaching of his lord,
From whom he bringeth sensible regreets, 89
To wit, besides commends and courteous breath, 90
Gifts of rich value. Yet I have not seen 91
So likely an ambassador of love.
A day in April never came so sweet,
To show how costly summer was at hand, 94
As this fore-spurrer comes before his lord. 95
PORTIA
No more, I pray thee. I am half afeard
Thou wilt say anon he is some kin to thee,
Thou spend'st such high-day wit in praising him. 98
Come, come, Nerissa, for I long to see
Quick Cupid's post that comes so mannerly. 100

NERISSA
Bassanio, Lord Love, if thy will it be!   *Exeunt.*

❖

[3.1]

[*Enter*] *Solanio and Salerio.*

SOLANIO Now, what news on the Rialto?
SALERIO Why, yet it lives there unchecked that Anto- 2
nio hath a ship of rich lading wrecked on the narrow 3
seas—the Goodwins, I think they call the place, a 4
very dangerous flat, and fatal, where the carcasses of 5
many a tall ship lie buried, as they say, if my gossip 6
Report be an honest woman of her word. 7
SOLANIO I would she were as lying a gossip in that as
ever knapped ginger or made her neighbors believe 9
she wept for the death of a third husband. But it is
true, without any slips of prolixity or crossing the 11
plain highway of talk, that the good Antonio, the 12
honest Antonio—oh, that I had a title good enough to
keep his name company!—
SALERIO Come, the full stop. 15
SOLANIO Ha, what sayest thou? Why, the end is, he
hath lost a ship.
SALERIO I would it might prove the end of his losses.
SOLANIO Let me say "amen" betimes, lest the devil 19
cross my prayer, for here he comes in the likeness of 20
a Jew.

Enter Shylock.

How now, Shylock, what news among the merchants?
SHYLOCK You knew, none so well, none so well as
you, of my daughter's flight.
SALERIO That's certain. I for my part knew the tailor
that made the wings she flew withal. 26
SOLANIO And Shylock for his own part knew the bird
was fledge, and then it is the complexion of them all 28
to leave the dam. 29
SHYLOCK She is damned for it.
SALERIO That's certain, if the devil may be her judge.
SHYLOCK My own flesh and blood to rebel!
SOLANIO Out upon it, old carrion! Rebels it at these 33
years? 34
SHYLOCK I say my daughter is my flesh and my blood.

---

63 **The fire . . . this** This silver has been seven times tested and purified 66 **shadows** illusions 68 **iwis** certainly 69 **Silvered o'er** i.e.,
with silver hair and so apparently wise 71 **I . . . head** i.e., you will
always have a fool's head, be a fool. 72 **sped** done for. 73–4 **Still . . .
here** i.e., I shall seem all the greater fool for wasting any more time
here. 78 **wroth** sorrow, unhappy lot (a variant of *ruth*); or, anger.
80 **deliberate** reasoning, calculating 85 **my lord** (A jesting response
to "my lady.") 89 **sensible regreets** tangible gifts, greetings
90 **commends** greetings. **breath** speech 91 **Yet** Heretofore
94 **costly** lavish, rich 95 **fore-spurrer** herald, harbinger
98 **high-day** holiday (i.e., extravagant) 100 **post** messenger

3.1. Location: Venice. A street.
2 **yet . . . unchecked** i.e., a rumor is spreading undenied **3–4 the narrow seas** the English Channel, as at 2.8.28. **4 Goodwins** Goodwin
Sands, off the Kentish coast near the Thames estuary **5 flat** shoal,
sandbank **6 tall** gallant **6-7 gossip Report** i.e., Dame Rumor
9 knapped nibbled **11 slips of prolixity** lapses into long-winded-
ness; or, long-winded lies. *Slips* may be the cuttings or offshoots of
tediousness. **11–12 crossing . . . talk** deviating from honest, plain
speech **15 Come . . . stop** Finish your sentence; rein in your tongue
as a horse is checked in its manage. **19 betimes** while there is yet
time **20 cross** thwart; make the sign of the cross following
26 the wings . . . withal i.e., the disguise she escaped in. (With a play
on *wings* or ornamented shoulder flaps sewn on garments.)
28 fledge ready to fly. **complexion** natural disposition, as at 2.7.79
29 dam mother. **33–4 Rebels . . . years?** (Solanio pretends to interpret Shylock's cry about the rebellion of his own flesh and blood as
referring to his own carnal desires, his own erection.)

SALERIO   There is more difference between thy flesh and
hers than between jet and ivory, more between your   37
bloods than there is between red wine and Rhenish.   38
But tell us, do you hear whether Antonio have had
any loss at sea or no?

SHYLOCK   There I have another bad match! A bankrupt,   41
a prodigal, who dare scarce show his head on the
Rialto; a beggar, that was used to come so smug upon
the mart! Let him look to his bond. He was wont to   44
call me usurer. Let him look to his bond. He was wont
to lend money for a Christian courtesy. Let him look to
his bond.

SALERIO   Why, I am sure, if he forfeit, thou wilt not take
his flesh. What's that good for?

SHYLOCK   To bait fish withal. If it will feed nothing else,
it will feed my revenge. He hath disgraced me, and
hindered me half a million, laughed at my losses,
mocked at my gains, scorned my nation, thwarted my
bargains, cooled my friends, heated mine enemies;
and what's his reason? I am a Jew. Hath not a Jew
eyes? Hath not a Jew hands, organs, dimensions, senses, affections, passions? Fed with the same food, hurt
with the same weapons, subject to the same diseases,
healed by the same means, warmed and cooled by the
same winter and summer, as a Christian is? If you
prick us, do we not bleed? If you tickle us, do we not
laugh? If you poison us, do we not die? And if you
wrong us, shall we not revenge? If we are like you in
the rest, we will resemble you in that. If a Jew wrong
a Christian, what is his humility? Revenge. If a   65
Christian wrong a Jew, what should his sufferance be   66
by Christian example? Why, revenge. The villainy you
teach me I will execute, and it shall go hard but I will   68
better the instruction.

Enter a Man from Antonio.

MAN   Gentlemen, my master Antonio is at his house
and desires to speak with you both.

SALERIO   We have been up and down to seek him.   72

Enter Tubal.

SOLANIO   Here comes another of the tribe. A third
cannot be matched, unless the devil himself turn Jew.   74
        Exeunt gentlemen [Solanio, Salerio, with Man].

SHYLOCK   How now, Tubal, what news from Genoa?
Hast thou found my daughter?

TUBAL   I often came where I did hear of her, but cannot
find her.

SHYLOCK   Why, there, there, there, there! A diamond
gone, cost me two thousand ducats in Frankfort! The   80
curse never fell upon our nation till now; I never felt it   81

till now. Two thousand ducats in that, and other
precious, precious jewels. I would my daughter were
dead at my foot, and the jewels in her ear! Would she
were hearsed at my foot, and the ducats in her coffin!   85
No news of them? Why, so—and I know not what's
spent in the search. Why, thou loss upon loss! The
thief gone with so much, and so much to find the
thief, and no satisfaction, no revenge! Nor no ill luck
stirring but what lights o' my shoulders, no sighs but
o' my breathing, no tears but o' my shedding.

TUBAL   Yes, other men have ill luck too. Antonio, as I
heard in Genoa—

SHYLOCK   What, what, what? Ill luck, ill luck?

TUBAL   hath an argosy cast away, coming from Tripolis.   95

SHYLCOK   I thank God, I thank God. Is it true, is it true?

TUBAL   I spoke with some of the sailors that escaped the
wreck.

SHYLOCK   I thank thee, good Tubal. Good news, good
news! Ha, ha! Heard in Genoa?

TUBAL   Your daughter spent in Genoa, as I heard, one
night fourscore ducats.

SHYLOCK   Thou stick'st a dagger in me. I shall never see
my gold again. Fourscore ducats at a sitting? Fourscore ducats?

TUBAL   There came divers of Antonio's creditors in my
company to Venice that swear he cannot choose but
break.   108

SHYLOCK   I am very glad of it. I'll plague him, I'll torture
him. I am glad of it.

TUBAL   One of them showed me a ring that he had of
your daughter for a monkey.

SHYLOCK   Out upon her! Thou torturest me, Tubal. It
was my turquoise; I had it of Leah when I was a   114
bachelor. I would not have given it for a wilderness of
monkeys.

TUBAL   But Antonio is certainly undone.

SHYLOCK   Nay, that's true, that's very true. Go, Tubal,
fee me an officer; bespeak him a fortnight before. I will   119
have the heart of him if he forfeit, for were he out of
Venice I can make what merchandise I will. Go, Tubal,   121
and meet me at our synagogue. Go, good Tubal; at our
synagogue, Tubal.   *Exeunt [separately].*

❧

[3.2]

*Enter Bassanio, Portia, Gratiano, [Nerissa,]
and all their trains.*

PORTIA
I pray you, tarry. Pause a day or two
Before you hazard, for in choosing wrong   2
I lose your company. Therefore forbear awhile.
There's something tells me—but it is not love—
I would not lose you; and you know yourself
Hate counsels not in such a quality.   6

37 **jet** a black, hard mineral, here contrasted with the whiteness of
ivory and Jessica's fair complexion   38 **Rhenish** i.e., a German white
wine from the Rhine valley. (Salerio seems to prefer the white wine as
more refined than the red.)   41 **match** bargain.   44 **mart** marketplace, Rialto.   65 **what . . . Revenge** i.e., in what spirit does the Christian receive the injury, that of Christian humility? No, he seeks
revenge.   66 **his sufferance** the Jew's patient endurance   68 **it shall
. . . but** i.e., assuredly; unless difficulties intervene   72 **up and down**
i.e., everywhere   74 **matched** i.e., found to match them   80–1 **The
curse** God's curse (such as the plagues visited upon Egypt in Exodus
7–12)

85 **hearsed** coffined   95 **cast away** shipwrecked   108 **break** go bankrupt.   114 **Leah** Shylock's wife   119 **fee** hire.   **officer** bailiff.
bespeak engage   121 **make . . . I will** drive whatever bargains I
please
3.2. Location: Belmont. Portia's house.
2 **in choosing** if you choose   6 **quality** way, manner.

But lest you should not understand me well—
And yet a maiden hath no tongue but thought—
I would detain you here some month or two
Before you venture for me. I could teach you
How to choose right, but then I am forsworn.
So will I never be. So may you miss me. 12
But if you do, you'll make me wish a sin,
That I had been forsworn. Beshrew your eyes,
They have o'erlooked me and divided me! 15
One half of me is yours, the other half yours—
Mine own, I would say; but if mine, then yours,
And so all yours. Oh, these naughty times 18
Puts bars between the owners and their rights! 19
And so, though yours, not yours. Prove it so, 20
Let Fortune go to hell for it, not I. 21
I speak too long, but 'tis to peise the time, 22
To eke it and to draw it out in length, 23
To stay you from election.

BASSANIO   Let me choose, 24
For as I am, I live upon the rack.

PORTIA
Upon the rack, Bassanio? Then confess 26
What treason there is mingled with your love. 27

BASSANIO
None but that ugly treason of mistrust, 28
Which makes me fear th'enjoying of my love. 29
There may as well be amity and life
'Tween snow and fire, as treason and my love. 31

PORTIA
Ay, but I fear you speak upon the rack,
Where men enforcèd do speak anything.

BASSANIO
Promise me life, and I'll confess the truth.

PORTIA
Well then, confess and live.

BASSANIO   "Confess and love"
Had been the very sum of my confession.
Oh, happy torment, when my torturer
Doth teach me answers for deliverance!
But let me to my fortune and the caskets. 39

PORTIA
Away, then! I am locked in one of them.
If you do love me, you will find me out.
Nerissa and the rest, stand all aloof. 42
Let music sound while he doth make his choice;
Then, if he lose, he makes a swanlike end, 44
Fading in music. That the comparison
May stand more proper, my eye shall be the stream

And wat'ry deathbed for him. He may win;
And what is music then? Then music is
Even as the flourish when true subjects bow 49
To a new-crownèd monarch. Such it is
As are those dulcet sounds in break of day
That creep into the dreaming bridegroom's ear
And summon him to marriage. Now he goes,
With no less presence, but with much more love, 54
Than young Alcides when he did redeem 55
The virgin tribute paid by howling Troy 56
To the sea monster. I stand for sacrifice; 57
The rest aloof are the Dardanian wives, 58
With blearèd visages, come forth to view 59
The issue of th'exploit. Go, Hercules! 60
Live thou, I live. With much, much more dismay 61
I view the fight than thou that mak'st the fray.

*A song, the whilst Bassanio comments on the
caskets to himself.*

Tell me where is fancy bred, 63
Or in the heart or in the head? 64
How begot, how nourishèd?
     Reply, reply.
It is engendered in the eyes, 67
With gazing fed, and fancy dies
In the cradle where it lies. 69
     Let us all ring fancy's knell.
     I'll begin it—Ding, dong, bell.
ALL   Ding, dong, bell.
BASSANIO
So may the outward shows be least themselves; 73
The world is still deceived with ornament. 74
In law, what plea so tainted and corrupt
But, being seasoned with a gracious voice,
Obscures the show of evil? In religion,
What damnèd error but some sober brow 78
Will bless it and approve it with a text, 79
Hiding the grossness with fair ornament?
There is no vice so simple but assumes 81
Some mark of virtue on his outward parts. 82
How many cowards, whose hearts are all as false
As stairs of sand, wear yet upon their chins 84
The beards of Hercules and frowning Mars,
Who, inward searched, have livers white as milk? 86
And these assume but valor's excrement 87

---

12 So i.e., Forsworn.   **So may . . . me** That being the case, you may fail to win me.   **15 o'erlooked** bewitched   **18 naughty** wicked   **19 bars** barriers   **20 though yours, not yours** (I am) yours by right but not by actual possession.   **20–1 Prove . . . not I** i.e., If it turn out thus (that you are cheated of what is justly yours, i.e., of me), let Fortune be blamed for it, not I, for I will not be forsworn.   **22 peise** retard (by hanging on of weights)   **23 eke it** stretch it out, make it last   **24 election** choice.   **26–7 confess What treason** (The rack was used to force traitors to confess.)   **28 mistrust** misapprehension   **29 fear** fearful about   **31 as** as between   **39 fortune . . . caskets** (Presumably the curtains are drawn at about this point, as in the previous "casket" scenes, revealing the three caskets.)   **42 aloof** apart, at a distance.   **44 swan-like** (Swans were believed to sing when they came to die.)

49 flourish sounding of trumpets   **54 presence** noble bearing   **55 Alcides** Hercules (called *Alcides*, as at 2.1.32–5, because he was the grandson of Alcaeus) rescued Hesione, daughter of the Trojan king Laomedon, from a monster to which, by command of Neptune, she was about to be sacrificed. Hercules was rewarded, however, not with the lady's love, but with a famous pair of horses.   **56 howling** lamenting   **57 stand for sacrifice** represent the sacrificial victim   **58 Dardanian** Trojan   **59 blearèd** tear-stained   **60 issue** outcome   **61 Live thou** If you live   **63 fancy** love   **64 Or** either   **67 eyes** (Love entered the heart especially through the eyes.)   **69 In the cradle** i.e., in its infancy, in the eyes   **73 be least themselves** least represent the inner reality   **74 still** ever   **78 sober brow** i.e., solemn-faced clergyman   **79 approve** confirm   **81 simple** unadulterated   **82 his** its   **84 stairs** steps   **86 searched** surgically probed.   **livers** (The liver was thought to be the seat of courage; for it to be deserted by the blood would be the condition of cowardice.)   **87 excrement** outgrowth, here a beard

To render them redoubted. Look on beauty, 88
And you shall see 'tis purchased by the weight, 89
Which therein works a miracle in nature,
Making them lightest that wear most of it. 91
So are those crispèd, snaky, golden locks, 92
Which maketh such wanton gambols with the wind
Upon supposèd fairness, often known 94
To be the dowry of a second head, 95
The skull that bred them in the sepulcher. 96
Thus ornament is but the guilèd shore 97
To a most dangerous sea, the beauteous scarf
Veiling an Indian beauty; in a word, 99
The seeming truth which cunning times put on
To entrap the wisest. Therefore, thou gaudy gold,
Hard food for Midas, I will none of thee; 102
Nor none of thee, thou pale and common drudge 103
'Tween man and man. But thou, thou meager lead, 104
Which rather threaten'st than dost promise aught,
Thy paleness moves me more than eloquence;
And here choose I. Joy be the consequence!

PORTIA [*aside*]
How all the other passions fleet to air,
As doubtful thoughts, and rash-embraced despair, 109
And shuddering fear, and green-eyed jealousy!
O love, be moderate, allay thy ecstasy,
In measure rain thy joy, scant this excess! 112
I feel too much thy blessing. Make it less,
For fear I surfeit.

BASSANIO [*opening the leaden casket*]
                    What find I here?
Fair Portia's counterfeit! What demigod
Hath come so near creation? Move these eyes? 115
Or whether, riding on the balls of mine,
Seem they in motion? Here are severed lips,
Parted with sugar breath; so sweet a bar 119
Should sunder such sweet friends. Here in her hairs 120
The painter plays the spider, and hath woven
A golden mesh t'entrap the hearts of men
Faster than gnats in cobwebs. But her eyes— 123
How could he see to do them? Having made one,
Methinks it should have power to steal both his
And leave itself unfurnished. Yet look how far 126
The substance of my praise doth wrong this shadow 127
In underprizing it, so far this shadow 128
Doth limp behind the substance. Here's the scroll, 129

The continent and summary of my fortune. 130
[*He reads.*] "You that choose not by the view
            Chance as fair, and choose as true. 132
        Since this fortune falls to you,
        Be content and seek no new.
        If you be well pleased with this,
        And hold your fortune for your bliss,
        Turn you where your lady is
        And claim her with a loving kiss."
A gentle scroll. Fair lady, by your leave,
I come by note, to give and to receive. 140
Like one of two contending in a prize, 141
That thinks he hath done well in people's eyes,
Hearing applause and universal shout,
Giddy in spirit, still gazing in a doubt
Whether those peals of praise be his or no, 145
So, thrice-fair lady, stand I, even so,
As doubtful whether what I see be true,
Until confirmed, signed, ratified by you.

PORTIA
You see me, Lord Bassanio, where I stand,
Such as I am. Though for myself alone
I would not be ambitious in my wish
To wish myself much better, yet for you
I would be trebled twenty times myself,
A thousand times more fair, ten thousand times
    more rich,
That only to stand high in your account 155
I might in virtues, beauties, livings, friends, 156
Exceed account. But the full sum of me 157
Is sum of something, which, to term in gross, 158
Is an unlessoned girl, unschooled, unpracticèd;
Happy in this, she is not yet so old
But she may learn; happier than this,
She is not bred so dull but she can learn;
Happiest of all is that her gentle spirit
Commits itself to yours to be directed
As from her lord, her governor, her king.
Myself and what is mine to you and yours
Is now converted. But now I was the lord 167
Of this fair mansion, master of my servants,
Queen o'er myself; and even now, but now,
This house, these servants, and this same myself
Are yours, my lord's. I give them with this ring,
Which when you part from, lose, or give away,
Let it presage the ruin of your love
And be my vantage to exclaim on you. 174
                [*She puts a ring on his finger.*]

BASSANIO
Madam, you have bereft me of all words.
Only my blood speaks to you in my veins,

---

88 redoubted feared.   **89 purchased by the weight** bought (as cosmetics) at so much per ounce   **91 lightest** most frivolous or lascivious. (With pun on the sense of "least heavy.")   **92 crispèd** curly   **94 Upon supposèd fairness** i.e., on a woman supposed beautiful and fair-haired   **95–6 To . . . sepulcher** i.e., to be a wig of hair taken from a woman now dead.   **97 guilèd** treacherous   **99 Indian** i.e., swarthy, not fair   **102 Midas** the Phrygian king whose touch turned everything to gold, including his food   **103–4 pale . . . man** i.e., silver, used in commerce.   **104 meager** wanting in richness   **109 As** such as   **112 rain** rain down, or perhaps "rein."   **scant** lessen   **115 counterfeit** portrait.   **demigod** i.e., the painter as creator   **119–20 so . . . friends** i.e., only so sweet a barrier as her mouth and breath should be allowed to part such sweet friends as her two lips.   **123 Faster** (1) more tightly (2) quicker   **126 unfurnished** i.e., without a companion.   **look how far** however far   **127 shadow** painting, semblance   **128 underprizing it** failing to do it justice.   **so far** to a similar extent   **129 the substance** the subject, i.e., Portia.

130 continent container   **132 Chance as fair** take your chances fortunately   **140 by note** by a bill of dues (i.e., the scroll). The commercial metaphor continues in *confirmed, signed, ratified* (line 148), *account* (155), *sum* (157), *term in gross* (158), etc.   **141 prize** competition   **145 his** for him   **155 account** estimation   **156 livings** possessions   **157 account** calculation. (Playing on *account*, estimation, in line 155.)   **157–8 But . . . something** i.e., But the full sum of my worth can only be the sum of whatever I am   **158 term in gross** denote in full   **167 But now** A moment ago   **174 vantage to exclaim on** opportunity to reproach

And there is such confusion in my powers   177
As, after some oration fairly spoke
By a belovèd prince, there doth appear
Among the buzzing pleasèd multitude,
Where every something being blent together   181
Turns to a wild of nothing save of joy   182
Expressed and not expressed. But when this ring   183
Parts from this finger, then parts life from hence.
Oh, then be bold to say Bassanio's dead!

NERISSA
My lord and lady, it is now our time,
That have stood by and seen our wishes prosper,   187
To cry, "good joy." Good joy, my lord and lady!

GRATIANO
My lord Bassanio and my gentle lady,
I wish you all the joy that you can wish—
For I am sure you can wish none from me.   191
And when Your Honors mean to solemnize
The bargain of your faith, I do beseech you
Even at that time I may be married too.

BASSANIO
With all my heart, so thou canst get a wife.   195

GRATIANO
I thank Your Lordship, you have got me one.
My eyes, my lord, can look as swift as yours.
You saw the mistress, I beheld the maid;   198
You loved, I loved; for intermission   199
No more pertains to me, my lord, than you.
Your fortune stood upon the caskets there,
And so did mine too, as the matter falls;   202
For wooing here until I sweat again,   203
And swearing till my very roof was dry   204
With oaths of love, at last, if promise last,   205
I got a promise of this fair one here
To have her love, provided that your fortune
Achieved her mistress.

PORTIA   Is this true, Nerissa?

NERISSA
Madam, it is, so you stand pleased withal.   209

BASSANIO
And do you, Gratiano, mean good faith?

GRATIANO   Yes, faith, my lord.

BASSANIO
Our feast shall be much honored in your marriage.

GRATIANO   We'll play with them the first boy for a thou-   213
sand ducats.

NERISSA   What, and stake down?   215

GRATIANO   No, we shall ne'er win at that sport, and
stake down.

Enter Lorenzo, Jessica, and Salerio, a messenger
from Venice.

But who comes here? Lorenzo and his infidel?
What, and my old Venetian friend Salerio?

BASSANIO
Lorenzo and Salerio, welcome hither,
If that the youth of my new interest here   221
Have power to bid you welcome.—By your leave,
I bid my very friends and countrymen,   223
Sweet Portia, welcome.

PORTIA   So do I, my lord.
They are entirely welcome.

LORENZO
I thank Your Honor. For my part, my lord,
My purpose was not to have seen you here,
But, meeting with Salerio by the way,
He did entreat me, past all saying nay,
To come with him along.

SALERIO   I did, my lord,
And I have reason for it. Signor Antonio
Commends him to you.   [*He gives Bassanio a letter.*]

BASSANIO   Ere I ope his letter,   232
I pray you tell me how my good friend doth.

SALERIO
Not sick, my lord, unless it be in mind,
Nor well, unless in mind. His letter there
Will show you his estate.   [*Bassanio*] *open*[*s*] *the letter.* 236

GRATIANO [*indicating Jessica*]
Nerissa, cheer yond stranger, bid her welcome.   237
Your hand, Salerio. What's the news from Venice?
How doth that royal merchant, good Antonio?   239
I know he will be glad of our success.
We are the Jasons; we have won the fleece.   241

SALERIO
I would you had won the fleece that he hath lost.

PORTIA
There are some shrewd contents in yond same paper   243
That steals the color from Bassanio's cheek—
Some dear friend dead, else nothing in the world
Could turn so much the constitution
Of any constant man. What, worse and worse?   247
With leave, Bassanio; I am half yourself,   248
And I must freely have the half of anything
That this same paper brings you.

BASSANIO   O sweet Portia,
Here are a few of the unpleasant'st words
That ever blotted paper! Gentle lady,
When I did first impart my love to you,
I freely told you all the wealth I had
Ran in my veins, I was a gentleman;
And then I told you true. And yet, dear lady,

---

177 powers faculties   **181–3 Where . . . expressed** i.e., in which every individual utterance, being blended and confused, turns into a hubbub of joy.   **187 That** we who   **191 For . . . me** i.e., I'm sure I can't wish you any more joy than you could wish for yourselves, or, I'm sure your wishes for happiness cannot take away from my happiness. **195 so** provided   **198 maid** (Nerissa is a lady-in-waiting, not a house servant.)   **199 intermission** delay (in loving)   **202 falls** falls out, happens   **203 sweat again** sweated repeatedly   **204 roof** roof of my mouth   **205 if promise last** i.e., if Nerissa's promise should last, hold out. (With a play on *last* and *at last,* "finally.")   **209 so** provided **213 We'll . . . boy** We'll wager with them to see who has the first male heir   **215 stake down** cash placed in advance. (But Gratiano, in his reply, turns the phrase into a bawdy joke; *stake down* to him suggests a non-erect phallus.)

221 youth . . . interest i.e., newness of my household authority **223 very** true   **232 Commends him** desires to be remembered **236 estate** situation.   **237 stranger** alien   **239 royal merchant** i.e., chief among merchants   **241 Jasons . . . fleece** (Compare with 1.1.170–2.)   **243 shrewd** cursed, grievous   **247 constant** settled, not swayed by passion   **248 With leave** With your permission

Rating myself at nothing, you shall see
How much I was a braggart. When I told you
My state was nothing, I should then have told you   259
That I was worse than nothing; for indeed
I have engaged myself to a dear friend,
Engaged my friend to his mere enemy,   262
To feed my means. Here is a letter, lady,
The paper as the body of my friend,
And every word in it a gaping wound
Issuing lifeblood. But is it true, Salerio?
Hath all his ventures failed? What, not one hit?   267
From Tripolis, from Mexico, and England,
From Lisbon, Barbary, and India,
And not one vessel scape the dreadful touch
Of merchant-marring rocks?

SALERIO   Not one, my lord.   271
Besides, it should appear that if he had
The present money to discharge the Jew   273
He would not take it. Never did I know   274
A creature that did bear the shape of man
So keen and greedy to confound a man.   276
He plies the Duke at morning and at night,
And doth impeach the freedom of the state   278
If they deny him justice. Twenty merchants,
The Duke himself, and the magnificoes   280
Of greatest port have all persuaded with him,   281
But none can drive him from the envious plea   282
Of forfeiture, of justice, and his bond.

JESSICA
When I was with him I have heard him swear
To Tubal and to Chus, his countrymen,   285
That he would rather have Antonio's flesh
Than twenty times the value of the sum
That he did owe him; and I know, my lord,
If law, authority, and power deny not,
It will go hard with poor Antonio.

PORTIA [to Bassanio]
Is it your dear friend that is thus in trouble?

BASSANIO
The dearest friend to me, the kindest man,
The best-conditioned and unwearied spirit   293
In doing courtesies, and one in whom
The ancient Roman honor more appears
Than any that draws breath in Italy.

PORTIA   What sum owes he the Jew?

BASSANIO
For me, three thousand ducats.

PORTIA   What, no more?
Pay him six thousand, and deface the bond;   299
Double six thousand, and then treble that,
Before a friend of this description

Shall lose a hair through Bassanio's fault.
First go with me to church and call me wife,
And then away to Venice to your friend;
For never shall you lie by Portia's side
With an unquiet soul. You shall have gold
To pay the petty debt twenty times over.
When it is paid, bring your true friend along.
My maid Nerissa and myself meantime
Will live as maids and widows. Come, away!
For you shall hence upon your wedding day.
Bid your friends welcome, show a merry cheer;   312
Since you are dear bought, I will love you dear.   313
But let me hear the letter of your friend.

BASSANIO [reads]   "Sweet Bassanio, my ships have all
miscarried, my creditors grow cruel, my estate is
very low, my bond to the Jew is forfeit; and since in
paying it, it is impossible I should live, all debts are
cleared between you and I if I might but see you at
my death. Notwithstanding, use your pleasure. If
your love do not persuade you to come, let not my
letter."

PORTIA
O love, dispatch all business, and begone!

BASSANIO
Since I have your good leave to go away,
I will make haste; but till I come again
No bed shall e'er be guilty of my stay,
Nor rest be interposer twixt us twain.   Exeunt.

❧

[3.3]

Enter [Shylock] the Jew and Solanio and Antonio
and the Jailer.

SHYLOCK
Jailer, look to him. Tell not me of mercy.
This is the fool that lent out money gratis.   2
Jailer, look to him.

ANTONIO   Hear me yet, good Shylock.

SHYLOCK
I'll have my bond. Speak not against my bond.
I have sworn an oath that I will have my bond.
Thou called'st me dog before thou hadst a cause,
But since I am a dog, beware my fangs.
The Duke shall grant me justice. I do wonder,
Thou naughty jailer, that thou art so fond   9
To come abroad with him at his request.   10

ANTONIO   I pray thee, hear me speak.

SHYLOCK
I'll have my bond. I will not hear thee speak.
I'll have my bond, and therefore speak no more.
I'll not be made a soft and dull-eyed fool,   14
To shake the head, relent, and sigh, and yield
To Christian intercessors. Follow not.
I'll have no speaking. I will have my bond.   *Exit Jew.*

---

259 **state** estate   262 **mere** absolute   267 **hit** success.   271 **merchant-marring** capable of damaging a merchant ship   273 **present** available. **discharge** pay off   274 **He** i.e., Shylock   276 **confound** destroy   278 **doth . . . state** i.e., calls in question the ability of Venice to defend legally the freedom of commerce of its citizens   280 **magnificoes** chief men of Venice   281 **port** dignity.   **persuaded** argued   282 **envious** malicious   285 **Chus** the Bishops' Bible spelling of *Cush*, son of Ham and grandson of Noah. *Tubal* was son of Japheth and grandson of Noah (Genesis 10:2, 6).   293 **best-conditioned** best-natured   299 **deface** erase

312 **cheer** countenance   313 **dear . . . dear** at great cost . . . dearly.
3.3. Location: Venice. A street.
2 **gratis** free (of interest).   9 **naughty** worthless, wicked.   **fond** foolish   10 **abroad** outside   14 **dull-eyed** easily duped

SOLANIO
    It is the most impenetrable cur
    That ever kept with men.

ANTONIO   Let him alone.   19
    I'll follow him no more with bootless prayers.   20
    He seeks my life. His reason well I know:
    I oft delivered from his forfeitures
    Many that have at times made moan to me;
    Therefore he hates me.

SOLANIO   I am sure the Duke
    Will never grant this forfeiture to hold.

ANTONIO
    The Duke cannot deny the course of law;
    For the commodity that strangers have   27
    With us in Venice, if it be denied,
    Will much impeach the justice of the state,
    Since that the trade and profit of the city   30
    Consisteth of all nations. Therefore go.
    These griefs and losses have so bated me   32
    That I shall hardly spare a pound of flesh
    Tomorrow to my bloody creditor.—
    Well, jailer, on. Pray God Bassanio come
    To see me pay his debt, and then I care not.   *Exeunt.*

❖

[3.4]

*Enter Portia, Nerissa, Lorenzo, Jessica, and
[Balthasar,] a man of Portia's.*

LORENZO
    Madam, although I speak it in your presence,
    You have a noble and a true conceit   2
    Of godlike amity, which appears most strongly   3
    In bearing thus the absence of your lord.
    But if you knew to whom you show this honor,   5
    How true a gentleman you send relief,
    How dear a lover of my lord your husband,   7
    I know you would be prouder of the work
    Than customary bounty can enforce you.   9

PORTIA
    I never did repent for doing good,
    Nor shall not now; for in companions
    That do converse and waste the time together,   12
    Whose souls do bear an equal yoke of love,
    There must be needs a like proportion   14
    Of lineaments, of manners, and of spirit;   15
    Which makes me think that this Antonio,
    Being the bosom lover of my lord,   17
    Must needs be like my lord. If it be so,
    How little is the cost I have bestowed
    In purchasing the semblance of my soul   20

    From out the state of hellish cruelty!   21
    This comes too near the praising of myself;
    Therefore no more of it. Hear other things:
    Lorenzo, I commit into your hands
    The husbandry and manage of my house   25
    Until my lord's return. For mine own part,
    I have toward heaven breathed a secret vow
    To live in prayer and contemplation,
    Only attended by Nerissa here,
    Until her husband and my lord's return.
    There is a monastery two miles off,
    And there we will abide. I do desire you
    Not to deny this imposition,   33
    The which my love and some necessity
    Now lays upon you.

LORENZO   Madam, with all my heart,
    I shall obey you in all fair commands.

PORTIA
    My people do already know my mind,   37
    And will acknowledge you and Jessica
    In place of Lord Bassanio and myself.
    So fare you well till we shall meet again.

LORENZO
    Fair thoughts and happy hours attend on you!

JESSICA
    I wish Your Ladyship all heart's content.

PORTIA
    I thank you for your wish and am well pleased
    To wish it back on you. Fare you well, Jessica.
                    Exeunt [Jessica and Lorenzo].
    Now, Balthasar,
    As I have ever found thee honest-true,
    So let me find thee still. Take this same letter,
                    [giving a letter]
    And use thou all th'endeavor of a man
    In speed to Padua. See thou render this
    Into my cousin's hands, Doctor Bellario;
    And look what notes and garments he doth give thee,   51
    Bring them, I pray thee, with imagined speed   52
    Unto the traject, to the common ferry   53
    Which trades to Venice. Waste no time in words,   54
    But get thee gone. I shall be there before thee.

BALTHASAR
    Madam, I go with all convenient speed.   *[Exit.]*

PORTIA
    Come on, Nerissa, I have work in hand
    That you yet know not of. We'll see our husbands
    Before they think of us.

NERISSA   Shall they see us?

PORTIA
    They shall, Nerissa, but in such a habit   60
    That they shall think we are accomplishèd   61
    With that we lack. I'll hold thee any wager,   62

---

19 kept associated, dwelt **20 bootless** unavailing **27 commodity** facilities or privileges for trading. **strangers** noncitizens, including Jews **30 Since that** since **32 bated** reduced **3.4. Location:** Belmont. Portia's house.
2 conceit understanding **3 amity** friendship and love **5 to whom ... honor** i.e., Antonio, who you honor by sending money to relieve him **7 lover** friend **9 Than ... you** than ordinary benevolence can make you. **12 waste** spend **14 must be needs** must be **15 lineaments** physical features **17 bosom lover** dear friend **20 the semblance of my soul** i.e., Antonio, so like my Bassanio.

21 From . . . cruelty from the cruel state in which he presently stands.
25 husbandry and manage care and management **33 deny this imposition** refuse this charge imposed **37 people** servants **51 look what** whatever **52 imagined** all imaginable **53 traject** ferry. (Italian *traghetto*.) **common** public **54 trades** plies back and forth **60 habit** apparel, garb **61 accomplishèd** supplied **62 that** that which. (With a bawdy suggestion.)

When we are both accoutered like young men
I'll prove the prettier fellow of the two,
And wear my dagger with the braver grace,
And speak between the change of man and boy
With a reed voice, and turn two mincing steps
Into a manly stride, and speak of frays
Like a fine bragging youth, and tell quaint lies, 69
How honorable ladies sought my love,
Which I denying, they fell sick and died—
I could not do withal! Then I'll repent, 72
And wish, for all that, that I had not killed them;
And twenty of these puny lies I'll tell, 74
That men shall swear I have discontinued school 75
Above a twelvemonth. I have within my mind 76
A thousand raw tricks of these bragging Jacks, 77
Which I will practice.
NERISSA Why, shall we turn to men? 78
PORTIA Fie, what a question's that,
If thou wert near a lewd interpreter!
But come, I'll tell thee all my whole device 81
When I am in my coach, which stays for us
At the park gate; and therefore haste away,
For we must measure twenty miles today. *Exeunt.* 84

♣

[3.5]

Enter [Lancelot the] clown and Jessica.

LANCELOT Yes, truly, for look you, the sins of the father are to be laid upon the children; therefore, I prom- 2
ise you, I fear you. I was always plain with you, and 3
so now I speak my agitation of the matter. Therefore 4
be o' good cheer, for truly I think you are damned.
There is but one hope in it that can do you any good,
and that is but a kind of bastard hope, neither. 7
JESSICA And what hope is that, I pray thee?
LANCELOT Marry, you may partly hope that your father got you not, that you are not the Jew's daughter. 10
JESSICA That were a kind of bastard hope, indeed! So
the sins of my mother should be visited upon me.
LANCELOT Truly, then, I fear you are damned both by
father and mother. Thus when I shun Scylla, your 14
father, I fall into Charybdis, your mother. Well, you 15
are gone both ways. 16
JESSICA I shall be saved by my husband. He hath made 17
me a Christian.

LANCELOT Truly, the more to blame he! We were 19
Christians enough before, e'en as many as could well 20
live one by another. This making of Christians will 21
raise the price of hogs. If we grow all to be pork eaters,
we shall not shortly have a rasher on the coals for 23
money. 24

Enter Lorenzo.

JESSICA I'll tell my husband, Lancelot, what you say.
Here he comes.
LORENZO I shall grow jealous of you shortly, Lancelot,
if you thus get my wife into corners.
JESSICA Nay, you need not fear us, Lorenzo. Lancelot
and I are out. He tells me flatly there's no mercy for me 30
in heaven because I am a Jew's daughter; and he says
you are no good member of the commonwealth, for in
converting Jews to Christians you raise the price of
pork.
LORENZO [*to Lancelot*] I shall answer that better to the
commonwealth than you can the getting up of the
Negro's belly. The Moor is with child by you, Lancelot. 37
LANCELOT It is much that the Moor should be more 38
than reason; but if she be less than an honest woman, 39
she is indeed more than I took her for. 40
LORENZO How every fool can play upon the word! I
think the best grace of wit will shortly turn into 42
silence, and discourse grow commendable in none
only but parrots. Go in, sirrah, bid them prepare for
dinner.
LANCELOT That is done, sir. They have all stomachs. 46
LORENZO Goodly Lord, what a wit-snapper are you!
Then bid them prepare dinner.
LANCELOT That is done too, sir, only "cover" is the 49
word.
LORENZO Will you cover then, sir? 51
LANCELOT Not so, sir, neither. I know my duty. 52
LORENZO Yet more quarreling with occasion! Wilt thou 53
show the whole wealth of thy wit in an instant? I pray
thee, understand a plain man in his plain meaning: go
to thy fellows, bid them cover the table, serve in the
meat, and we will come in to dinner. 57
LANCELOT For the table, sir, it shall be served in; for the 58
meat, sir, it shall be covered; for your coming in to 59

69 quaint elaborate, clever **72 do withal** help it. **74 puny** childish **75–6 I . . . twelvemonth** i.e., that I am no mere schoolboy. **76 Above** more than **77 Jacks** fellows **78 turn to** turn into. (But Portia sees the occasion for a bawdy quibble on the idea of "turning toward, lying next to.") **81 device** plan **84 measure** traverse **3.5. Location: Belmont. Outside Portia's house.** **2–3 promise** assure **3 fear you** fear for you. **4 my agitation of** my sense of agitation about **7 bastard** i.e., unfounded. (But also anticipating the usual meaning in lines 9–10.) **neither** i.e., to be sure. **10 got begot 14, 15 Scylla, Charybdis** twin dangers of the *Odyssey*, 12.255, a monster and a whirlpool guarding the straits presumably between Italy and Sicily. (*Fall into* plays on the idea of entering the female sexual anatomy.) **16 gone** done for **17 I . . . husband** (Compare 1 Corinthians 7:14: "the unbelieving wife is sanctified by the husband.")

19–20 We . . . enough There were enough of us Christians **21 one by another** (1) as neighbors (2) off one another. **23 rasher** i.e., of bacon **23–4 for money** even for ready money, at any price. **30 are out** have fallen out. **37 The Moor** (Lancelot has evidently impregnated some woman of the household, who, being of African heritage, is referred to as both "Negro" and "Moor.") **38–40 It is . . . for** i.e., It is a matter of concern that the Moor is larger (being pregnant) than usual, larger than she should be; but if it turns out that she is less than perfectly chaste, she is something more than I originally supposed. (Lancelot professes to be surprised by what has happened. With wordplay on *less/more* and *more/Moor*.) **42 the best . . . wit** true wittiness **46 They . . . stomachs** The guests all have appetites, and are prepared in that sense. (Lancelot quibbles with Lorenzo's meaning that the cooks and servants should be told to get dinner ready.) **49, 51 cover** spread the table for the meal. (But in line 52 Lancelot uses the word to mean "put on one's hat.") **52 my duty** i.e., my duty to remain bareheaded. **53 Yet . . . occasion!** i.e., Still quibbling at every opportunity! **57 meat** food **58 For** As for. **table** (Here Lancelot quibblingly uses the word to mean the food itself.) **59 covered** (Here used in the sense of providing a cover for each separate dish.)

dinner, sir, why, let it be as humors and conceits shall 60
govern.   *Exit [Lancelot the] clown.*

LORENZO
Oh, dear discretion, how his words are suited!   62
The fool hath planted in his memory
An army of good words; and I do know
A many fools, that stand in better place,   65
Garnished like him, that for a tricksy word   66
Defy the matter. How cheer'st thou, Jessica?   67
And now, good sweet, say thy opinion:
How dost thou like the Lord Bassanio's wife?

JESSICA
Past all expressing. It is very meet   70
The Lord Bassanio live an upright life,
For, having such a blessing in his lady,
He finds the joys of heaven here on earth;
And if on earth he do not merit it,
In reason he should never come to heaven.   75
Why, if two gods should play some heavenly match
And on the wager lay two earthly women,   77
And Portia one, there must be something else   78
Pawned with the other, for the poor rude world   79
Hath not her fellow.

LORENZO   Even such a husband   80
Hast thou of me as she is for a wife.

JESSICA
Nay, but ask my opinion too of that!

LORENZO
I will anon. First let us go to dinner.

JESSICA
Nay, let me praise you while I have a stomach.   84

LORENZO
No, pray thee, let it serve for table talk;
Then, howsome'er thou speak'st, 'mong other things
I shall digest it.

JESSICA   Well, I'll set you forth.   *Exeunt.* 87

❧

[4.1]

Enter the Duke, the Magnificoes, Antonio, Bas-
sanio, [Salerio,] and Gratiano [with others. The
judges take their places.]

DUKE   What, is Antonio here?
ANTONIO   Ready, so please Your Grace.

DUKE
I am sorry for thee. Thou art come to answer   3
A stony adversary, an inhuman wretch
Uncapable of pity, void and empty
From any dram of mercy.

ANTONIO   I have heard   6
Your Grace hath ta'en great pains to qualify   7
His rigorous course; but since he stands obdurate
And that no lawful means can carry me
Out of his envy's reach, I do oppose   10
My patience to his fury and am armed
To suffer with a quietness of spirit
The very tyranny and rage of his.   13

DUKE
Go one, and call the Jew into the court.

SALERIO
He is ready at the door. He comes, my lord.

Enter Shylock.

DUKE
Make room, and let him stand before our face.—   16
Shylock, the world thinks, and I think so too,
That thou but leadest this fashion of thy malice 18
To the last hour of act, and then 'tis thought   19
Thou'lt show thy mercy and remorse more strange   20
Than is thy strange apparent cruelty;   21
And where thou now exacts the penalty,
Which is a pound of this poor merchant's flesh,
Thou wilt not only loose the forfeiture,   24
But, touched with human gentleness and love,
Forgive a moiety of the principal,   26
Glancing an eye of pity on his losses
That have of late so huddled on his back—
Enough to press a royal merchant down
And pluck commiseration of his state   30
From brassy bosoms and rough hearts of flint,   31
From stubborn Turks and Tartars never trained
To offices of tender courtesy.
We all expect a gentle answer, Jew.

SHYLOCK
I have possessed Your Grace of what I purpose,   35
And by our holy Sabbath have I sworn
To have the due and forfeit of my bond.
If you deny it, let the danger light   38
Upon your charter and your city's freedom!   39
You'll ask me why I rather choose to have
A weight of carrion flesh than to receive
Three thousand ducats. I'll not answer that,
But say it is my humor. Is it answered?   43
What if my house be troubled with a rat
And I be pleased to give ten thousand ducats

---

60 humors and conceits whims and fancies   **62 Oh, dear discretion**
Oh, what precious discrimination.   **suited** suited to the occasion
65 A many many.   **better place** higher social station   **66 Garnished**
i.e., furnished with words, or with garments   **66–7 that . . . matter**
who for the sake of ingenious wordplay torture the plain meaning.
67 How cheer'st thou i.e., What cheer, how are you doing   **70 meet**
fitting   **75 In reason** it stands to reason. (Jessica jokes that for Bassanio to receive unmerited bliss on earth—unmerited because no person can earn bliss through his or her own deserving—is to run the
risk of eternal damnation.)   **77 lay** stake   **78 else** more   **79 Pawned**
staked, wagered   **80 fellow** equal.   **84 stomach** (1) appetite (2) inclination.   **87 digest** (1) ponder, analyze (2) "swallow," put up with.
(With a play also on the gastronomic sense.)   **set you forth** (1) serve
you up, as at a feast (2) set forth your praises.
4.1. Location: Venice. A court of justice. Benches, etc., are provided
for the justices.

3 answer defend yourself against. (A legal term.)   **6 dram** sixty
grains apothecaries' weight, a tiny quantity   **7 qualify** moderate
10 envy's malice's   **13 tyranny** cruelty   **16 our** (The royal plural.)
18 That . . . fashion that you only maintain this pretense or form
19 the last . . . act the brink of action   **20 remorse** pity.   **strange**
remarkable   **21 strange** unnatural, foreign.   **apparent** (1) manifest,
overt (2) seeming   **24 loose** release, waive   **26 moiety** part, portion
30 of for   **31 brassy** unfeeling, hard like brass   **35 possessed**
informed   **38 danger** injury   **39 Upon . . . freedom** (See 3.2.278.)
43 humor whim.

To have it baned? What, are you answered yet?   46
Some men there are love not a gaping pig,   47
Some that are mad if they behold a cat,
And others, when the bagpipe sings i'th' nose,
Cannot contain their urine; for affection,   50
Mistress of passion, sways it to the mood
Of what it likes or loathes. Now, for your answer:
As there is no firm reason to be rendered
Why he cannot abide a gaping pig,   54
Why he a harmless necessary cat,   55
Why he a woolen bagpipe, but of force   56
Must yield to such inevitable shame
As to offend, himself being offended,
So can I give no reason, nor I will not,
More than a lodged hate and a certain loathing   60
I bear Antonio, that I follow thus
A losing suit against him. Are you answered?   62

BASSANIO
This is no answer, thou unfeeling man,
To excuse the current of thy cruelty.   64

SHYLOCK
I am not bound to please thee with my answers.

BASSANIO
Do all men kill the things they do not love?

SHYLOCK
Hates any man the thing he would not kill?

BASSANIO
Every offense is not a hate at first.

SHYLOCK
What, wouldst thou have a serpent sting thee twice?

ANTONIO
I pray you, think you question with the Jew.   70
You may as well go stand upon the beach
And bid the main flood bate his usual height;   72
You may as well use question with the wolf   73
Why he hath made the ewe bleat for the lamb;
You may as well forbid the mountain pines
To wag their high tops and to make no noise
When they are fretten with the gusts of heaven;   77
You may as well do anything most hard
As seek to soften that—than which what's harder?—
His Jewish heart. Therefore, I do beseech you,
Make no more offers, use no farther means,
But with all brief and plain conveniency
Let me have judgment, and the Jew his will.

BASSANIO [to Shylock]
For thy three thousand ducats here is six.

SHYLOCK
If every ducat in six thousand ducats
Were in six parts, and every part a ducat,
I would not draw them. I would have my bond.   87

DUKE
How shalt thou hope for mercy, rendering none?

SHYLOCK
What judgment shall I dread, doing no wrong?   89
You have among you many a purchased slave,
Which, like your asses and your dogs and mules,
You use in abject and in slavish parts,   92
Because you bought them. Shall I say to you,
"Let them be free, marry them to your heirs!
Why sweat they under burdens? Let their beds
Be made as soft as yours, and let their palates
Be seasoned with such viands"? You will answer   97
"The slaves are ours." So do I answer you:
The pound of flesh which I demand of him
Is dearly bought, is mine, and I will have it.
If you deny me, fie upon your law!
There is no force in the decrees of Venice.
I stand for judgment. Answer: shall I have it?

DUKE
Upon my power I may dismiss this court,   104
Unless Bellario, a learnèd doctor,   105
Whom I have sent for to determine this,   106
Come here today.

SALERIO   My lord, here stays without   107
A messenger with letters from the doctor,
New come from Padua.

DUKE
Bring us the letters. Call the messenger.   [Exit one.]

BASSANIO
Good cheer, Antonio. What, man, courage yet!
The Jew shall have my flesh, blood, bones, and all,
Ere thou shalt lose for me one drop of blood.

ANTONIO
I am a tainted wether of the flock,   114
Meetest for death. The weakest kind of fruit   115
Drops earliest to the ground, and so let me.
You cannot better be employed, Bassanio,
Than to live still and write mine epitaph.

Enter Nerissa [dressed like a lawyer's clerk].

DUKE
Came you from Padua, from Bellario?

NERISSA
From both, my lord. Bellario greets Your Grace.
[She presents a letter. Shylock whets his knife on his shoe.]

BASSANIO
Why dost thou whet thy knife so earnestly?

SHYLOCK
To cut the forfeiture from that bankrupt there.

GRATIANO
Not on thy sole, but on thy soul, harsh Jew,
Thou mak'st thy knife keen; but no metal can,
No, not the hangman's ax, bear half the keenness   125
Of thy sharp envy. Can no prayers pierce thee?   126

---

46 **baned** poisoned   47 **love** who love.   **gaping pig** pig roasted
whole with its mouth open   50 **affection** feeling, desire   **54, 55, 56
he, he, he** one person, another, yet another   55 **necessary** i.e., useful
for catching rats and mice   56 **woolen** i.e., with flannel-covered bag
60 **lodged** settled, steadfast.   **certain** unwavering, fixed   62 **losing**
unprofitable   64 **current** flow, tendency   70 **think** bear in mind.
question argue   72 **And . . . height** and bid the ocean put an end to
its usual high tide   73 **use question with** interrogate   77 **fretten** fretted, i.e., disturbed, ruffled   87 **draw** receive

89 **wrong** legal wrong.   92 **parts** duties, capacities   97 **such viands**
food such as you eat.   104 **Upon** In accordance with   105 **doctor**
person of learning. (Here, of law.)   106 **determine this** resolve this
legal dispute   107 **stays without** waits outside   114 **wether** ram,
especially a castrated ram   115 **Meetest** fittest   125 **hangman's** executioner's.   **keenness** (1) sharpness (2) savagery   126 **envy** malice.

SHYLOCK
No, none that thou hast wit enough to make.

GRATIANO
Oh, be thou damned, inexecrable dog,   128
And for thy life let Justice be accused!   129
Thou almost mak'st me waver in my faith
To hold opinion with Pythagoras   131
That souls of animals infuse themselves
Into the trunks of men. Thy currish spirit
Governed a wolf who, hanged for human slaughter,   134
Even from the gallows did his fell soul fleet,   135
And, whilst thou layest in thy unhallowed dam,   136
Infused itself in thee; for thy desires
Are wolvish, bloody, starved, and ravenous.

SHYLOCK
Till thou canst rail the seal from off my bond,   139
Thou but offend'st thy lungs to speak so loud.   140
Repair thy wit, good youth, or it will fall
To cureless ruin. I stand here for law.   142

DUKE
This letter from Bellario doth commend
A young and learnèd doctor to our court.
Where is he?

NERISSA   He attendeth here hard by
To know your answer, whether you'll admit him.

DUKE
With all my heart. Some three or four of you
Go give him courteous conduct to this place.
                                    [Exeunt some.]
Meantime the court shall hear Bellario's letter.
[He reads.] "Your Grace shall understand that at the   150
receipt of your letter I am very sick; but in the instant
that your messenger came, in loving visitation was
with me a young doctor of Rome. His name is Balthasar. I acquainted him with the cause in controversy
between the Jew and Antonio the merchant. We
turned o'er many books together. He is furnished with
my opinion, which, bettered with his own learning,
the greatness whereof I cannot enough commend,
comes with him, at my importunity, to fill up Your   159
Grace's request in my stead. I beseech you, let his lack
of years be no impediment to let him lack a reverend 161
estimation, for I never knew so young a body with so
old a head. I leave him to your gracious acceptance,
whose trial shall better publish his commendation."   164

    Enter Portia for Balthasar [dressed like a doctor
    of laws, escorted].

You hear the learn'd Bellario, what he writes;
And here, I take it, is the doctor come.—
Give me your hand. Come you from old Bellario?

PORTIA
I did, my lord.

DUKE   You are welcome. Take your place.
                                    [Portia takes her place.]
Are you acquainted with the difference   169
That holds this present question in the court?

PORTIA
I am informèd throughly of the cause.   171
Which is the merchant here, and which the Jew?

DUKE
Antonio and old Shylock, both stand forth.
                    [Antonio and Shylock stand forth.]

PORTIA
Is your name Shylock?

SHYLOCK   Shylock is my name.

PORTIA
Of a strange nature is the suit you follow,
Yet in such rule that the Venetian law   176
Cannot impugn you as you do proceed.—   177
You stand within his danger, do you not?

ANTONIO
Ay, so he says.

PORTIA   Do you confess the bond?

ANTONIO
I do.

PORTIA   Then must the Jew be merciful.

SHYLOCK
On what compulsion must I? Tell me that.

PORTIA
The quality of mercy is not strained.   182
It droppeth as the gentle rain from heaven
Upon the place beneath. It is twice blest: 184
It blesseth him that gives and him that takes.
'Tis mightiest in the mightiest; it becomes
The thronèd monarch better than his crown.
His scepter shows the force of temporal power,   188
The attribute to awe and majesty,   189
Wherein doth sit the dread and fear of kings.
But mercy is above this sceptered sway;
It is enthronèd in the hearts of kings;
It is an attribute to God himself;
And earthly power doth then show likest God's
When mercy seasons justice. Therefore, Jew,
Though justice be thy plea, consider this,
That in the course of justice none of us   197
Should see salvation. We do pray for mercy,
And that same prayer doth teach us all to render
The deeds of mercy. I have spoke thus much
To mitigate the justice of thy plea,   201
Which if thou follow, this strict court of Venice
Must needs give sentence 'gainst the merchant there.

128 **inexecrable** thoroughly execrable   **129 And . . . accused!** and may
Justice herself be accused for allowing you to live!   **131 Pythagoras**
ancient Greek philosopher who argued for the transmigration of souls
134 hanged for human slaughter (A possible allusion to the Elizabethan practice of trying and punishing animals for various crimes.)
135 fell fierce, cruel.   **fleet** flit, i.e., pass from the body   **136 dam**
mother. (Usually used of animals.)   **139 rail** remove by your abusive
language   **140 Thou but offend'st** you merely injure   **142 cureless**
incurable   **150 [He reads.]** (In many modern editions, the reading of
the letter is assigned to a clerk, but the original text gives no such indication.)   **159 comes with him** accompanies him in the form of my
learned opinion.   **importunity** insistence   **161 to let him lack** such as
would deprive him of   **164 whose . . . commendation** the demonstration of whose excellence will proclaim what is commendable in him
better than my letter can.   **164.1 for** i.e., disguised as

169 **difference** argument   **171 throughly** thoroughly.   **cause** case.
176 rule order   **177 impugn** find fault with   **182 strained** forced,
constrained.   **184 is twice blest** grants a double blessing   **188 His**
i.e., The monarch's   **189 attribute to** symbol of   **197 justice** divine
justice   **201 To . . . plea** i.e., to show the way in which your call for
justice needs to be mitigated or reduced in severity

SHYLOCK
My deeds upon my head! I crave the law,　　204
The penalty and forfeit of my bond.

PORTIA
Is he not able to discharge the money?

BASSANIO
Yes, here I tender it for him in the court,
Yea, twice the sum. If that will not suffice,
I will be bound to pay it ten times o'er,
On forfeit of my hands, my head, my heart.
If this will not suffice, it must appear
That malice bears down truth. And I beseech you,　　212
Wrest once the law to your authority.　　213
To do a great right, do a little wrong,
And curb this cruel devil of his will.

PORTIA
It must not be. There is no power in Venice
Can alter a decree establishèd.
'Twill be recorded for a precedent,
And many an error by the same example
Will rush into the state. It cannot be.

SHYLOCK
A Daniel come to judgment! Yea, a Daniel!　　221
O wise young judge, how I do honor thee!

PORTIA
I pray you, let me look upon the bond.

SHYLOCK [giving the bond]
Here 'tis, most reverend doctor, here it is.

PORTIA
Shylock, there's thrice thy money offered thee.

SHYLOCK
An oath, an oath! I have an oath in heaven.
Shall I lay perjury upon my soul?
No, not for Venice.

PORTIA　　　　　　　　Why, this bond is forfeit,
And lawfully by this the Jew may claim
A pound of flesh, to be by him cut off
Nearest the merchant's heart.—Be merciful.
Take thrice thy money; bid me tear the bond.

SHYLOCK
When it is paid according to the tenor.　　233
It doth appear you are a worthy judge.
You know the law. Your exposition
Hath been most sound. I charge you by the law,
Whereof you are a well-deserving pillar,
Proceed to judgment. By my soul I swear
There is no power in the tongue of man
To alter me. I stay here on my bond.　　240

ANTONIO
Most heartily I do beseech the court
To give the judgment.

PORTIA　　　　　　　　Why then, thus it is:
You must prepare your bosom for his knife.

SHYLOCK
O noble judge! O excellent young man!

PORTIA
For the intent and purpose of the law
Hath full relation to the penalty　　246
Which here appeareth due upon the bond.

SHYLOCK
'Tis very true. O wise and upright judge!
How much more elder art thou than thy looks!

PORTIA
Therefore lay bare your bosom.

SHYLOCK　　　　　　　　　Ay, his breast.
So says the bond, doth it not, noble judge?
"Nearest his heart," those are the very words.

PORTIA
It is so. Are there balance here　　253
To weigh the flesh?

SHYLOCK　　　　　　I have them ready.

PORTIA
Have by some surgeon, Shylock, on your charge,　　255
To stop his wounds, lest he do bleed to death.

SHYLOCK
Is it so nominated in the bond?

PORTIA
It is not so expressed, but what of that?
'Twere good you do so much for charity.

SHYLOCK
I cannot find it. 'Tis not in the bond.

PORTIA
You, merchant, have you anything to say?

ANTONIO
But little. I am armed and well prepared.—　　262
Give me your hand, Bassanio; fare you well!
Grieve not that I am fall'n to this for you,
For herein Fortune shows herself more kind
Than is her custom. It is still her use　　266
To let the wretched man outlive his wealth
To view with hollow eye and wrinkled brow
An age of poverty; from which ling'ring penance
Of such misery doth she cut me off.
Commend me to your honorable wife.
Tell her the process of Antonio's end,　　272
Say how I loved you, speak me fair in death;　　273
And, when the tale is told, bid her be judge
Whether Bassanio had not once a love.　　275
Repent but you that you shall lose your friend,　　276
And he repents not that he pays your debt.
For if the Jew do cut but deep enough,
I'll pay it instantly with all my heart.　　279

BASSANIO
Antonio, I am married to a wife,
Which is as dear to me as life itself;
But life itself, my wife, and all the world

204 My . . . head! (Compare the cry of the crowd at Jesus' crucifixion: "His blood be on us, and on our children," Matthew 27:25.) 212 bears down truth overwhelms righteousness. 213 Wrest once for once, forcibly subject 221 Daniel (In the Apocrypha's story of Susannah and the Elders, Daniel is the young man who rescues Susannah from her false accusers.) 233 tenor conditions. 240 stay stand, insist

246 Hath . . . to is fully in accord with 253 balance scales 255 Have by Have ready at hand. on your charge at your personal expense 262 armed i.e., fortified in spirit 266 still her use i.e., commonly Fortune's practice 272 process story, manner 273 speak me fair speak well of me 275 a love a friend's love. 276 Repent but you Grieve only 279 with . . . heart (1) wholeheartedly (2) literally, with my heart's blood.

Are not with me esteemed above thy life.
I would lose all, ay, sacrifice them all
Here to this devil, to deliver you.

PORTIA
Your wife would give you little thanks for that,
If she were by to hear you make the offer.   287

GRATIANO
I have a wife who, I protest, I love;
I would she were in heaven, so she could
Entreat some power to change this currish Jew.

NERISSA
'Tis well you offer it behind her back;
The wish would make else an unquiet house.

SHYLOCK
These be the Christian husbands. I have a daughter;
Would any of the stock of Barabbas   294
Had been her husband rather than a Christian!—
We trifle time. I pray thee, pursue sentence.   296

PORTIA
A pound of that same merchant's flesh is thine.
The court awards it, and the law doth give it.

SHYLOCK   Most rightful judge!

PORTIA
And you must cut this flesh from off his breast.
The law allows it, and the court awards it.

SHYLOCK
Most learnèd judge! A sentence!—Come, prepare.

PORTIA
Tarry a little; there is something else.
This bond doth give thee here no jot of blood;
The words expressly are "a pound of flesh."
Take then thy bond, take thou thy pound of flesh,
But in the cutting it if thou dost shed
One drop of Christian blood, thy lands and goods
Are by the laws of Venice confiscate
Unto the state of Venice.

GRATIANO
O upright judge! Mark, Jew. O learnèd judge!

SHYLOCK
Is that the law?

PORTIA   Thyself shalt see the act;
For, as thou urgest justice, be assured
Thou shalt have justice, more than thou desir'st.

GRATIANO
O learnèd judge! Mark, Jew, a learnèd judge!

SHYLOCK
I take this offer, then. Pay the bond thrice
And let the Christian go.

BASSANIO   Here is the money.

PORTIA   Soft!   318
The Jew shall have all justice. Soft, no haste.   319
He shall have nothing but the penalty.

GRATIANO
O Jew! An upright judge, a learnèd judge!

PORTIA
Therefore prepare thee to cut off the flesh.
Shed thou no blood, nor cut thou less nor more
But just a pound of flesh. If thou tak'st more
Or less than a just pound, be it but so much
As makes it light or heavy in the substance   326
Or the division of the twentieth part   327
Of one poor scruple, nay, if the scale do turn   328
But in the estimation of a hair,
Thou diest, and all thy goods are confiscate.

GRATIANO
A second Daniel, a Daniel, Jew!   331
Now, infidel, I have you on the hip.   332

PORTIA
Why doth the Jew pause? Take thy forfeiture.

SHYLOCK
Give me my principal, and let me go.

BASSANIO
I have it ready for thee. Here it is.

PORTIA
He hath refused it in the open court.
He shall have merely justice and his bond.

GRATIANO
A Daniel, still say I, a second Daniel!
I thank thee, Jew, for teaching me that word.

SHYLOCK
Shall I not have barely my principal?

PORTIA
Thou shalt have nothing but the forfeiture,
To be so taken at thy peril, Jew.

SHYLOCK
Why, then the devil give him good of it!
I'll stay no longer question.   [*He starts to go.*]

PORTIA   Tarry, Jew!   344
The law hath yet another hold on you.
It is enacted in the laws of Venice,
If it be proved against an alien
That by direct or indirect attempts
He seek the life of any citizen,
The party 'gainst the which he doth contrive
Shall seize one half his goods; the other half
Comes to the privy coffer of the state,   352
And the offender's life lies in the mercy   353
Of the Duke only, 'gainst all other voice.   354
In which predicament, I say, thou stand'st;
For it appears, by manifest proceeding,
That indirectly and directly too
Thou hast contrived against the very life
Of the defendant; and thou hast incurred
The danger formerly by me rehearsed.   360
Down therefore, and beg mercy of the Duke.   361

---

287 **by** nearby   294 **Barabbas** a thief whom Pontius Pilate set free
instead of Christ in response to the people's demand (see Mark 15);
also, the villainous protagonist of Marlowe's *The Jew of Malta*
296 **trifle** waste.   **pursue** proceed with   318 **Soft!** i.e., Not so fast!
319 **all justice** precisely what the law provides.

326 **substance** mass or gross weight   327 **division** fraction
328 **scruple** twenty grains apothecaries' weight, a small quantity
331 **Daniel** (See line 221 above and note.)   332 **on the hip** i.e., at a
disadvantage. (A phrase from wrestling.)   344 **I'll . . . question** I'll
stay no further pursuing of the case.   352 **privy coffer** private treasury   353 **lies in** lies at   354 **'gainst . . . voice** without appeal
360 **The danger . . . rehearsed** the penalty already cited by me.
361 **Down** Down on your knees

GRATIANO

Beg that thou mayst have leave to hang thyself!
And yet, thy wealth being forfeit to the state,
Thou hast not left the value of a cord;
Therefore thou must be hanged at the state's charge.   365

DUKE

That thou shalt see the difference of our spirit,
I pardon thee thy life before thou ask it.
For half thy wealth, it is Antonio's;   368
The other half comes to the general state,
Which humbleness may drive unto a fine.   370

PORTIA

Ay, for the state, not for Antonio.   371

SHYLOCK

Nay, take my life and all! Pardon not that!
You take my house when you do take the prop
That doth sustain my house. You take my life
When you do take the means whereby I live.

PORTIA

What mercy can you render him, Antonio?

GRATIANO

A halter gratis! Nothing else, for God's sake.   377

ANTONIO

So please my lord the Duke and all the court
To quit the fine for one half of his goods,   379
I am content, so he will let me have   380
The other half in use, to render it,   381
Upon his death, unto the gentleman
That lately stole his daughter.
Two things provided more: that for this favor
He presently become a Christian;
The other, that he do record a gift   385
Here in the court of all he dies possessed
Unto his son Lorenzo and his daughter.   387

DUKE

He shall do this, or else I do recant
The pardon that I late pronouncèd here.   389

PORTIA

Art thou contented, Jew? What dost thou say?

SHYLOCK

I am content.

PORTIA   Clerk, draw a deed of gift.

SHYLOCK

I pray you, give me leave to go from hence;
I am not well. Send the deed after me,
And I will sign it.

DUKE   Get thee gone, but do it.

GRATIANO

In christening shalt thou have two godfathers.
Had I been judge, thou shouldst have had ten more,   397

To bring thee to the gallows, not the font.

                    Exit [Shylock].

DUKE [to Portia]

Sir, I entreat you home with me to dinner.

PORTIA

I humbly do desire Your Grace of pardon.
I must away this night toward Padua,
And it is meet I presently set forth.   402

DUKE

I am sorry that your leisure serves you not.
Antonio, gratify this gentleman,   404
For in my mind you are much bound to him.

                    Exeunt Duke and his train.

BASSANIO [to Portia]

Most worthy gentleman, I and my friend
Have by your wisdom been this day acquitted
Of grievous penalties, in lieu whereof,   408
Three thousand ducats due unto the Jew
We freely cope your courteous pains withal.   410

                    [He offers money.]

ANTONIO

And stand indebted over and above
In love and service to you evermore.

PORTIA

He is well paid that is well satisfied,
And I, delivering you, am satisfied,
And therein do account myself well paid.
My mind was never yet more mercenary.
I pray you, know me when we meet again.   417
I wish you well, and so I take my leave.

                    [She starts to leave.]

BASSANIO

Dear sir, of force I must attempt you further.   419
Take some remembrance of us as a tribute,
Not as fee. Grant me two things, I pray you:
Not to deny me, and to pardon me.   422

PORTIA

You press me far, and therefore I will yield.
Give me your gloves, I'll wear them for your sake.   424
And, for your love, I'll take this ring from you.   425
Do not draw back your hand; I'll take no more,
And you in love shall not deny me this.

BASSANIO

This ring, good sir? Alas, it is a trifle!
I will not shame myself to give you this.

PORTIA

I will have nothing else but only this;
And now, methinks, I have a mind to it.

BASSANIO

There's more depends on this than on the value.

The dearest ring in Venice will I give you,   433
And find it out by proclamation.
Only for this, I pray you, pardon me.

PORTIA
I see, sir, you are liberal in offers.   436
You taught me first to beg, and now, methinks,
You teach me how a beggar should be answered.

BASSANIO
Good sir, this ring was given me by my wife,
And when she put it on she made me vow
That I should neither sell nor give nor lose it.

PORTIA
That 'scuse serves many men to save their gifts.
An if your wife be not a madwoman,   443
And know how well I have deserved this ring,
She would not hold out enemy forever
For giving it to me. Well, peace be with you!
                                        Exeunt [Portia and Nerissa].

ANTONIO
My lord Bassanio, let him have the ring.
Let his deservings and my love withal
Be valued 'gainst your wife's commandement.   449

BASSANIO
Go, Gratiano, run and overtake him;
Give him the ring, and bring him, if thou canst,
Unto Antonio's house. Away, make haste!
                                        Exit Gratiano [with the ring].
Come, you and I will thither presently,
And in the morning early will we both
Fly toward Belmont. Come, Antonio.   Exeunt.

❖

[4.2]

Enter [Portia and] Nerissa [still disguised].

PORTIA [giving a deed to Nerissa]
Inquire the Jew's house out; give him this deed   1
And let him sign it. We'll away tonight
And be a day before our husbands home.
This deed will be well welcome to Lorenzo.

Enter Gratiano.

GRATIANO   Fair sir, you are well o'erta'en.   5
My lord Bassanio upon more advice   6
Hath sent you here this ring and doth entreat
Your company at dinner.   [He gives a ring.]

PORTIA   That cannot be.
His ring I do accept most thankfully,
And so, I pray you, tell him. Furthermore,
I pray you, show my youth old Shylock's house.

GRATIANO
That will I do.

NERISSA   Sir, I would speak with you.
[Aside to Portia] I'll see if I can get my husband's
   ring,
Which I did make him swear to keep forever.

PORTIA [aside to Nerissa]
Thou mayst, I warrant. We shall have old swearing   15
That they did give the rings away to men;
But we'll outface them, and outswear them too.—   17
Away, make haste! Thou know'st where I will tarry.

NERISSA [to Gratiano]
Come, good sir, will you show me to this house?
                        [Exeunt, Portia separately from the others.]

❖

[5.1]

Enter Lorenzo and Jessica.

LORENZO
The moon shines bright. In such a night as this,
When the sweet wind did gently kiss the trees
And they did make no noise, in such a night
Troilus methinks mounted the Trojan walls   4
And sighed his soul toward the Grecian tents
Where Cressid lay that night.

JESSICA   In such a night
Did Thisbe fearfully o'ertrip the dew,   7
And saw the lion's shadow ere himself,
And ran dismayed away.

LORENZO   In such a night
Stood Dido with a willow in her hand   10
Upon the wild sea banks, and waft her love   11
To come again to Carthage.

JESSICA   In such a night
Medea gathered the enchanted herbs   13
That did renew old Aeson.

LORENZO   In such a night
Did Jessica steal from the wealthy Jew   15
And with an unthrift love did run from Venice   16
As far as Belmont.

JESSICA   In such a night
Did young Lorenzo swear he loved her well,
Stealing her soul with many vows of faith,
And ne'er a true one.

LORENZO   In such a night
Did pretty Jessica, like a little shrew,
Slander her love, and he forgave it her.

JESSICA
I would out-night you, did nobody come.   23
But hark, I hear the footing of a man.   24

Enter [Stephano,] a messenger.

LORENZO
Who comes so fast in silence of the night?

---

433 **dearest** most expensive   436 **liberal** generous   443 **An if** If
449 **commandement** (Pronounced in four syllables.)
4.2. Location: Venice. A street.
1 **this deed** i.e., the deed of gift   5 **you . . . o'erta'en** I'm happy to
have caught up with you.   6 **advice** consideration

15 **old** plenty of   17 **outface** boldly contradict
5.1. Location: Belmont. Outside Portia's house.
4 **Troilus** Trojan prince deserted by his beloved, Cressida, after she had
been transferred to the Greek camp   7 **Thisbe** beloved of Pyramus
who, arranging to meet him by night, was frightened by a lion and fled;
the tragic misunderstanding of her absence led to the suicides of both
lovers. (See *A Midsummer Night's Dream*, Act 5.)   10 **Dido** Queen of
Carthage, deserted by Aeneas.   **willow** (A symbol of forsaken love.)
11 **waft** wafted, beckoned   13 **Medea** famous sorceress of Colchis who,
after falling in love with Jason and helping him to gain the Golden
Fleece, used her magic to restore youth to Aeson, Jason's father
15 **steal** (1) escape (2) rob   16 **unthrift** prodigal   23 **out-night** i.e.,
outdo in the verbal games we've been playing   24 **footing** footsteps

STEPHANO   A friend.

LORENZO

  A friend? What friend? Your name, I pray you,
  friend?

STEPHANO

  Stephano is my name, and I bring word
  My mistress will before the break of day
  Be here at Belmont. She doth stray about
  By holy crosses, where she kneels and prays   31
  For happy wedlock hours.

LORENZO   Who comes with her?

STEPHANO

  None but a holy hermit and her maid.
  I pray you, is my master yet returned?

LORENZO

  He is not, nor we have not heard from him.
  But go we in, I pray thee, Jessica,
  And ceremoniously let us prepare
  Some welcome for the mistress of the house.

       Enter [Lancelot, the] clown.

LANCELOT   Sola, sola! Wo ha, ho! Sola, sola!   39
LORENZO   Who calls?
LANCELOT   Sola! Did you see Master Lorenzo? Master
  Lorenzo, sola, sola!
LORENZO   Leave holloing, man! Here.
LANCELOT   Sola! Where, where?
LORENZO   Here.
LANCELOT   Tell him there's a post come from my mas-   46
  ter, with his horn full of good news: my master will be   47
  here ere morning.   *[Exit.]*

LORENZO

  Sweet soul, let's in, and there expect their coming.   49
  And yet no matter. Why should we go in?
  My friend Stephano, signify, I pray you,   51
  Within the house, your mistress is at hand,
  And bring your music forth into the air.

                [Exit Stephano.]

  How sweet the moonlight sleeps upon this bank!
  Here will we sit and let the sounds of music
  Creep in our ears. Soft stillness and the night
  Become the touches of sweet harmony.   57
  Sit, Jessica. *[They sit.]* Look how the floor of heaven
  Is thick inlaid with patens of bright gold.   59
  There's not the smallest orb which thou behold'st
  But in his motion like an angel sings,
  Still choiring to the young-eyed cherubins.   62
  Such harmony is in immortal souls,
  But whilst this muddy vesture of decay   64
  Doth grossly close it in, we cannot hear it.   65

      [Enter musicians.]

  Come, ho, and wake Diana with a hymn!   66
  With sweetest touches pierce your mistress' ear
  And draw her home with music.   *Play music.*

JESSICA

  I am never merry when I hear sweet music.

LORENZO

  The reason is, your spirits are attentive.   70
  For do but note a wild and wanton herd,
  Or race of youthful and unhandled colts,   72
  Fetching mad bounds, bellowing and neighing loud,
  Which is the hot condition of their blood;
  If they but hear perchance a trumpet sound,
  Or any air of music touch their ears,
  You shall perceive them make a mutual stand,   77
  Their savage eyes turned to a modest gaze
  By the sweet power of music. Therefore the poet   79
  Did feign that Orpheus drew trees, stones, and
    floods,
                                80
  Since naught so stockish, hard, and full of rage   81
  But music for the time doth change his nature.   82
  The man that hath no music in himself,
  Nor is not moved with concord of sweet sounds,
  Is fit for treasons, stratagems, and spoils;   85
  The motions of his spirit are dull as night
  And his affections dark as Erebus.   87
  Let no such man be trusted. Mark the music.

      Enter Portia and Nerissa.

PORTIA

  That light we see is burning in my hall.
  How far that little candle throws his beams!
  So shines a good deed in a naughty world.   91

NERISSA

  When the moon shone, we did not see the candle.

PORTIA

  So doth the greater glory dim the less.
  A substitute shines brightly as a king
  Until a king be by, and then his state   95
  Empties itself, as doth an inland brook
  Into the main of waters. Music! Hark!   97

NERISSA

  It is your music, madam, of the house.

PORTIA

  Nothing is good, I see, without respect.   99
  Methinks it sounds much sweeter than by day.

NERISSA

  Silence bestows that virtue on it, madam.

PORTIA

  The crow doth sing as sweetly as the lark
  When neither is attended; and I think   103
  The nightingale, if she should sing by day,

---

31 holy crosses wayside shrines   **39 Sola** (Imitation of a post horn.)
46 post courier   **47 horn** (Lancelot jestingly compares the courier's
post horn to a cornucopia; perhaps too with a glance at the frayed jest
about cuckolds' horns.)   **49 expect** await   **51 signify** make known
57 Become suit.   **touches** strains, notes (produced by the fingering of
an instrument)   **59 patens** thin, circular plates of metal   **62 Still
choiring** continually singing.   **young-eyed** eternally clear-sighted.
(In Ezekiel 10:12, the bodies and wings of cherubim are "full of eyes
round about.")   **64 muddy . . . decay** i.e., mortal flesh   **65 close it in**
i.e., enclose the soul.   **hear it** i.e., hear the music of the spheres.

66 Diana (Here, goddess of the moon; compare with 1.2.105.)
70 spirits are attentive (The spirits would be in motion within the
body in merriment, whereas in sadness they would be drawn to the
heart and, as it were, busy listening.)   **72 race** herd   **77 mutual** common or simultaneous   **79 poet** perhaps Ovid, with whom the story of
Orpheus was a favorite theme   **80 Orpheus** legendary musician.
drew attracted, charmed.   **floods** rivers   **81 stockish** unfeeling
82 his its (a tree, a stone, etc.)   **87 Erebus** a
place of primeval darkness on the way to Hades.   **91 naughty**
wicked   **95 his** i.e., the substitute's   **97 main of waters** sea.
99 respect comparison, context.   **103 attended** listened to

When every goose is cackling, would be thought
No better a musician than the wren.
How many things by season seasoned are   107
To their right praise and true perfection!
Peace, ho! The moon sleeps with Endymion   109
And would not be awaked.   [*The music ceases.*]

LORENZO   That is the voice,
Or I am much deceived, of Portia.

PORTIA
He knows me as the blind man knows the cuckoo,
By the bad voice.

LORENZO   Dear lady, welcome home.

PORTIA
We have been praying for our husbands' welfare,
Which speed, we hope, the better for our words.   115
Are they returned?

LORENZO   Madam, they are not yet;
But there is come a messenger before,
To signify their coming.

PORTIA   Go in, Nerissa.
Give order to my servants that they take
No note at all of our being absent hence;
Nor you, Lorenzo; Jessica, nor you. [*A tucket sounds.*] 121

LORENZO
Your husband is at hand. I hear his trumpet.
We are no telltales, madam, fear you not.

PORTIA
This night, methinks, is but the daylight sick;   124
It looks a little paler. 'Tis a day
Such as the day is when the sun is hid.

> *Enter Bassanio, Antonio, Gratiano, and their*
> *followers.*

BASSANIO
We should hold day with the Antipodes,   127
If you would walk in absence of the sun.   128

PORTIA
Let me give light, but let me not be light;   129
For a light wife doth make a heavy husband,   130
And never be Bassanio so for me.
But God sort all! You are welcome home, my lord.   132

BASSANIO
I thank you, madam. Give welcome to my friend.
This is the man, this is Antonio,
To whom I am so infinitely bound.

PORTIA
You should in all sense be much bound to him,   136
For, as I hear, he was much bound for you.   137

ANTONIO
No more than I am well acquitted of.   138

PORTIA
Sir, you are very welcome to our house.
It must appear in other ways than words;
Therefore I scant this breathing courtesy.   141

GRATIANO [*to Nerissa*]
By yonder moon I swear you do me wrong!
In faith, I gave it to the judge's clerk.
Would he were gelt that had it, for my part,   144
Since you do take it, love, so much at heart.

PORTIA
A quarrel, ho, already? What's the matter?

GRATIANO
About a hoop of gold, a paltry ring
That she did give me, whose posy was   148
For all the world like cutler's poetry
Upon a knife, "Love me, and leave me not."

NERISSA
What talk you of the posy or the value?
You swore to me, when I did give it you,
That you would wear it till your hour of death
And that it should lie with you in your grave.
Though not for me, yet for your vehement oaths
You should have been respective and have kept it.   156
Gave it a judge's clerk! No, God's my judge,
The clerk will ne'er wear hair on 's face that had it.

GRATIANO
He will, an if he live to be a man.   159

NERISSA
Ay, if a woman live to be a man.

GRATIANO
Now, by this hand, I gave it to a youth,
A kind of boy, a little scrubbèd boy   162
No higher than thyself, the judge's clerk,
A prating boy, that begged it as a fee.   164
I could not for my heart deny it him.

PORTIA
You were to blame—I must be plain with you—
To part so slightly with your wife's first gift,
A thing stuck on with oaths upon your finger,
And so riveted with faith unto your flesh.
I gave my love a ring and made him swear
Never to part with it; and here he stands.
I dare be sworn for him he would not leave it,
Nor pluck it from his finger, for the wealth
That the world masters. Now, in faith, Gratiano,   174
You give your wife too unkind a cause of grief.
An 'twere to me, I should be mad at it.   176

BASSANIO [*aside*]
Why, I were best to cut my left hand off
And swear I lost the ring defending it.

GRATIANO
My lord Bassanio gave his ring away

---

107 season fit occasion. (But playing on the idea of seasoning, spices.) **109 Endymion** a shepherd loved by the moon goddess, who caused him to sleep a perennial sleep in a cave on Mount Latmos where she could visit him   **115 Which . . . words** who prosper and return speedily, we hope, because we prayed for them.   **121 s.d. *tucket*** flourish on a trumpet   **124 sick** i.e., made pale by the approach of dawn   **127–8 We . . . sun** i.e., If you, Portia, like a second sun, would always walk about during the sun's absence, we should never have night but would enjoy daylight even when the Antipodes, those who dwell on the opposite side of the globe, enjoy daylight.   **129 be light** be wanton, unchaste   **130 heavy** sad. (With wordplay on the antithesis of *light* and *heavy*.)   **132 sort** decide, dispose   **136 in all sense** in every way, with every reason   **136–7 bound . . . bound** Portia plays on (1) obligated (2) indebted and imprisoned.

138 acquitted of freed from and amply repaid (by thanks and love). **141 scant . . . courtesy** make brief these empty (i.e., merely verbal) compliments.   **144 gelt** gelded, castrated.   **for my part** as far as I'm concerned   **148 posy** a motto on a ring   **156 respective** mindful, careful   **159 an if** if   **162 scrubbèd** diminutive   **164 prating** chattering   **174 masters** owns.   **176 An** If.   **mad** beside myself

Unto the judge that begged it and indeed
Deserved it too; and then the boy, his clerk,
That took some pains in writing, he begged mine;
And neither man nor master would take aught   183
But the two rings.

PORTIA [to Bassanio] What ring gave you, my lord?
Not that, I hope, which you received of me.

BASSANIO
If I could add a lie unto a fault,
I would deny it; but you see my finger
Hath not the ring upon it. It is gone.

PORTIA
Even so void is your false heart of truth.
By heaven, I will ne'er come in your bed
Until I see the ring!

NERISSA [to Gratiano] Nor I in yours
Till I again see mine.

BASSANIO   Sweet Portia,
If you did know to whom I gave the ring,
If you did know for whom I gave the ring,
And would conceive for what I gave the ring,
And how unwillingly I left the ring,
When naught would be accepted but the ring,
You would abate the strength of your displeasure.

PORTIA
If you had known the virtue of the ring,   199
Or half her worthiness that gave the ring,
Or your own honor to contain the ring,   201
You would not then have parted with the ring.
What man is there so much unreasonable,
If you had pleased to have defended it
With any terms of zeal, wanted the modesty   205
To urge the thing held as a ceremony?   206
Nerissa teaches me what to believe:
I'll die for't but some woman had the ring.

BASSANIO
No, by my honor, madam! By my soul,
No woman had it, but a civil doctor,   210
Which did refuse three thousand ducats of me
And begged the ring, the which I did deny him
And suffered him to go displeased away—   213
Even he that had held up the very life
Of my dear friend. What should I say, sweet lady?
I was enforced to send it after him.
I was beset with shame and courtesy.
My honor would not let ingratitude
So much besmear it. Pardon me, good lady!   219
For by these blessèd candles of the night,   220
Had you been there, I think you would have begged
The ring of me to give the worthy doctor.

PORTIA
Let not that doctor e'er come near my house.
Since he hath got the jewel that I loved,
And that which you did swear to keep for me,
I will become as liberal as you:

I'll not deny him anything I have,   226
No, not my body nor my husband's bed.
Know him I shall, I am well sure of it.
Lie not a night from home. Watch me like Argus;   229
If you do not, if I be left alone,   230
Now, by mine honor, which is yet mine own,
I'll have that doctor for my bedfellow.   232

NERISSA
And I his clerk; therefore be well advised
How you do leave me to mine own protection.   234

GRATIANO
Well, do you so. Let not me take him, then!
For if I do, I'll mar the young clerk's pen.   236

ANTONIO   237
I am th'unhappy subject of these quarrels.

PORTIA
Sir, grieve not you; you are welcome notwithstanding.

BASSANIO
Portia, forgive me this enforcèd wrong,
And in the hearing of these many friends
I swear to thee, even by thine own fair eyes
Wherein I see myself—

PORTIA   Mark you but that!
In both my eyes he doubly sees himself;
In each eye, one. Swear by your double self,
And there's an oath of credit.   245

BASSANIO   Nay, but hear me.
Pardon this fault, and by my soul I swear   246
I never more will break an oath with thee.

ANTONIO
I once did lend my body for his wealth,
Which, but for him that had your husband's ring,   249
Had quite miscarried. I dare be bound again,
My soul upon the forfeit, that your lord
Will nevermore break faith advisedly.   252

PORTIA   253
Then you shall be his surety. Give him this,
And bid him keep it better than the other.   254
[She gives the ring to Antonio, who gives it to Bassanio.]

ANTONIO
Here, Lord Bassanio. Swear to keep this ring.

BASSANIO
By heaven, it is the same I gave the doctor!

PORTIA
I had it of him. Pardon me, Bassanio,
For by this ring the doctor lay with me.

NERISSA
And pardon me, my gentle Gratiano,
For that same scrubbèd boy, the doctor's clerk,
In lieu of this last night did lie with me.
[Presenting her ring.] 262

---

183 **aught** anything   199 **virtue** moral efficacy   201 **contain** keep
safe   205 **wanted the modesty** who would have been so lacking in
consideration as   206 **urge** insist upon receiving.   **ceremony** something sacred.   210 **civil doctor** i.e., doctor of civil law   213 **suffered**
allowed   219 **it** i.e., my honor.   220 **blessèd . . . night** i.e., stars

226 **liberal** generous (sexually as well as otherwise)   229 **Know**
(With the suggestion of carnal knowledge.)   230 **from** away from.
Argus mythological monster with a hundred eyes   232 **honor**
(1) honorable name (2) chastity   234 **be well advised** take care
236 **take** apprehend   237 **pen** (With sexual double meaning.)
245 **double** i.e., deceitful   246 **of credit** worthy to be believed. (Said
ironically.)   249 **wealth** welfare   252 **My . . . forfeit** at the risk of
eternal damnation   253 **advisedly** intentionally   254 **surety** guarantor.   262 **In lieu of** in return for

GRATIANO
Why, this is like the mending of highways
In summer, where the ways are fair enough.   264
What, are we cuckolds ere we have deserved it?   265

PORTIA
Speak not so grossly. You are all amazed.
Here is a letter; read it at your leisure.
                                        [*She gives a letter.*]
It comes from Padua, from Bellario.
There you shall find that Portia was the doctor,
Nerissa there her clerk. Lorenzo here
Shall witness I set forth as soon as you,
And even but now returned; I have not yet
Entered my house. Antonio, you are welcome,
And I have better news in store for you
Than you expect. Unseal this letter soon.
                                        [*She gives him a letter.*]
There you shall find three of your argosies
Are richly come to harbor suddenly.
You shall not know by what strange accident
I chancèd on this letter.

ANTONIO   I am dumb.   279

BASSANIO [*to Portia*]
Were you the doctor and I knew you not?

GRATIANO [*to Nerissa*]
Were you the clerk that is to make me cuckold?

NERISSA
Ay, but the clerk that never means to do it,
Unless he live until he be a man.

BASSANIO
Sweet doctor, you shall be my bedfellow.

When I am absent, then lie with my wife.

ANTONIO
Sweet lady, you have given me life and living;
For here I read for certain that my ships
Are safely come to road.

PORTIA   How now, Lorenzo?   288
My clerk hath some good comforts too for you.

NERISSA
Ay, and I'll give them him without a fee.
                                        [*She gives a deed.*]
There do I give to you and Jessica,
From the rich Jew, a special deed of gift,
After his death, of all he dies possessed of.

LORENZO
Fair ladies, you drop manna in the way   294
Of starved people.

PORTIA   It is almost morning,
And yet I am sure you are not satisfied
Of these events at full. Let us go in;
And charge us there upon inter'gatories,   298
And we will answer all things faithfully.

GRATIANO
Let it be so. The first inter'gatory
That my Nerissa shall be sworn on is
Whether till the next night she had rather stay   302
Or go to bed now, being two hours to day.
But were the day come, I should wish it dark
Till I were couching with the doctor's clerk.   305
Well, while I live I'll fear no other thing
So sore as keeping safe Nerissa's ring.   *Exeunt.*   307

---

264 are fair enough i.e., are not in need of repair. **265 cuckolds** husbands whose wives are unfaithful **279 dumb** at a loss for words.

288 road anchorage. **294 manna** the food from heaven that was miraculously supplied to the Israelites in the wilderness (Exodus 16) **298 And . . . inter'gatories** and put questions to us (as in a court of law) **302 stay** wait **305 couching** going to bed **307 ring** (With sexual suggestion.)

Much Ado About Nothing

*M*uch Ado About Nothing belongs to a group of Shakespeare's most mature romantic comedies, linked by similar titles, that also includes *As You Like It* and *Twelfth Night* (subtitled *what You will*). All date from the period 1598 to 1600. These plays are the culmination of Shakespeare's exuberant, philosophical, and festive vein in comedy, with only an occasional anticipation of the darker problem comedies of the early 1600s. They also parallel the culmination of Shakespeare's writing of history plays, in *Henry IV* and *V*.

Much Ado excels in combative wit and in swift, colloquial prose. It differs, too, from several other comedies (including *A Midsummer Night's Dream* and *The Merchant of Venice*) in that it features no journey of the lovers, no heroine disguised as a man, no envious court or city contrasted with an idealized landscape of the artist's imagination. Instead, the prevailing motif is that of the mask. Prominent scenes include a masked ball (2.1), a charade offstage in which the villainous Borachio misrepresents himself as the lover of Hero (actually Margaret in disguise), and a marriage ceremony with the supposedly dead bride masking as her own cousin (5.3). The word *Nothing* in the play's title, pronounced rather like *noting* in the English of Elizabethan London and vicinity, suggests a pun on the idea of overhearing as well as of musical notation; it also has a bawdy connotation, as when Hamlet wryly suggests to Ophelia that "Nothing" is "a fair thought to lie between maids' legs" (*Hamlet*, 3.2.116–18; see also *Othello*, 3.3.317, where Iago responds to his wife's "I have a thing for you" with a degrading sexual insult). Overhearings are constant and are essential to the process of both misunderstanding (as in the false rumor of Don Pedro's wooing Hero for himself) and clarification (as in the discovery by the night watch of the slander done to Hero's reputation, or in the revelation to Beatrice and Benedick of each other's true state of mind). The masks, or roles, that the characters incessantly assume are, for the most part, defensive and inimical to mutual understanding. How can they be dispelled? It is the search for candor and self-awareness in relationships with others, the quest for honesty and respect beneath conventional outward appearances, that provides the journey in this play.

Structurally, the play contrasts two pairs of lovers. The ladies, Beatrice and Hero, are cousins and close friends. The gentlemen, Benedick and Claudio, Italian gentlemen and fellow officers under the command of Don Pedro, have returned from the war, in which they have fought bravely. These similarities chiefly serve, however, to accentuate the differences between the two couples. Hero is modest, retiring, usually silent, and obedient to her father's will. Claudio appears ideally suited to her, since he is also respectful and decorous. They are conventional lovers in the roles of romantic hero and naive heroine. Beatrice and Benedick, on the other hand, are renowned for "a kind of merry war" between them. Although obviously destined to come together, they are seemingly too independent and skeptical of convention to be tolerant and accepting in love. They scoff so at romantic sentimentality that they cannot permit themselves to drop their satirical masks. Yet, paradoxically, their relationship is ultimately more surefooted because of their refusal to settle for the illusory cliches of many young wooers.

As in some of his other comic double plots (*The Taming of the Shrew*, for example), Shakespeare has linked together two stories of diverse origins and contrasting tones in order to set off one against the other. The Hero-Claudio plot is Italianate in flavor and origin, sensational, melodramatic, and potentially tragic. In fact, the often told story of the maiden falsely slandered did frequently end in disaster—as, for example, in Edmund Spenser's *Faerie Queene*, 2.4 (1590). Spenser was apparently indebted to Ariosto's *Orlando Furioso* (translated into English by Sir John Harington, 1591), as were Peter Beverly in *The Historie of Ariodanto and Ieneura* (1566) and Richard Mulcaster in his play *Ariodante and Genevora* (1583).

Shakespeare seems to have relied more on the Italian version by Matteo Bandello (Lucca, 1554) and its French translation by Belleforest, *Histoires Tragiques* (1569). Still other versions have been discovered, both nondramatic and dramatic, although it cannot be established that Shakespeare was reworking an old play. Various factual inconsistencies in Shakespeare's text (such as Leonato's wife Imogen and a "kinsman" who are named briefly in both Quarto and Folio but have no roles in the play) can perhaps be explained by Shakespeare's having worked quickly from more than one source.

Shakespeare's other plot, of Benedick and Beatrice, is much more English and his own. The battle of the sexes is a staple of English medieval humor (Chaucer's Wife of Bath, the Wakefield play of *Noah*) and of Shakespeare's own early comedy: Berowne and Rosaline in *Love's Labor's Lost*, Petruchio and Katharina in *The Taming of the Shrew*. The merry war of Benedick and Beatrice is Shakespeare's finest achievement in this vein and was to become a rich legacy in the later English comedy of William Congreve, Oscar Wilde, and George Bernard Shaw. The tone is lighthearted, bantering, and reassuring, in contrast with the Italianate mood of vengeance and duplicity in the Claudio-Hero plot. No less English are the clownish antics of Dogberry and his crew, representing still another group of characters although not a separate plot. Like Constable Dull in *Love's Labor's Lost* or the tradesmen of *A Midsummer Night's Dream*, the buffoons of *Much Ado* function in a nominally Mediterranean setting but are nonetheless recognizable London types. Their preposterous antics not only puncture the ominous mood threatening our enjoyment of the main plot but also, absurdly enough, even help to abort a potential crime. When Dogberry comes, laughter cannot be far behind.

The two plots provide contrasting perspectives on the nature of love. Because it is sensational and melodramatic, the Claudio-Hero plot stresses situation at the expense of character. The conspiracy that nearly overwhelms the lovers is an engrossing story, but they themselves remain one-dimensional. They interest us more as conventional types, and hence as foils to Benedick and Beatrice, than as lovers in their own right. Benedick and Beatrice, on the other hand, are psychologically complex. Clearly, they are fascinated with each other. Beatrice's questions in the first scene, although abusive in tone, betray her concern for Benedick's welfare. Has he safely returned from the wars? How did he bear himself in battle? Who are his companions? She tests his moral character by high standards, suspecting that he will fail because she demands so much. We are not surprised when she lectures her docile cousin, Hero, on the folly of submitting to parental choice in marriage: "It is my cousin's duty to make curtsy and say, 'Father, as it please you.' But yet for all that, cousin, let him be a handsome fellow, or else

make another curtsy and say, 'Father, as it please me' " (2.1.49–52). Beatrice remains single not from love of spinsterhood but from insistence on a nearly perfect mate. Paradoxically, she who is the inveterate scoffer is the true idealist. And we know from her unceasing fascination with Benedick that he, of all the men in her acquaintance, comes closest to her mark. The only fear preventing the revelation of her love—a not unnatural fear, in view of the insults she and Benedick exchange—is that he will prove faithless and jest at her weakness.

Benedick is similarly hemmed in by his posturing as "a professed tyrant to their sex." Despite his reputation as a perennial bachelor and his wry amusement at Claudio's newfound passion, Benedick confesses in soliloquy (2.3.8–34) that he could be won to affection by the ideal woman. Again, his criteria are chiefly those of temperament and moral character, although he by no means spurns wealth, beauty, and social position; the happiest couples are those well matched in fortune's gifts. "Rich she shall be, that's certain; wise, or I'll none; virtuous, or I'll never cheapen her; fair, or I'll never look on her; mild, or come not near me; noble, or not I for an angel; of good discourse, an excellent musician, and her hair shall be of what color it please God." This last self-mocking concession indicates that Benedick is aware of how impossibly much he is asking. Still, there is one woman, Beatrice, who may well possess all of these qualities except mildness. Even her sharp wit is part of her admirable intelligence. She is a match for Benedick, and he is a man who would never tolerate the submissive conventionality of someone like Hero. All that appears to be lacking, in fact, is any sign of fondness on Beatrice's part. For him to make overtures would be to invite her withering scorn—not to mention the I-told-you-so mockery of his friends.

Benedick and Beatrice have been playing the game of verbal abuse for so long that they scarcely remember how it started—perhaps as a squaring-off between the only two intelligences worthy of contending with each other, perhaps as a more profoundly defensive reaction of two sensitive persons not willing to part lightly with their independence. They seem to have had a prior relationsip with each other that ended unhappily. They know that intimate involvement with another person is a complex matter—one that can cause heartache. Yet the masks they wear with each other are scarcely satisfactory. At the masked ball (2.1), we see how hurtful the "merry war" has become. Benedick, attempting to pass himself off as a stranger in a mask, abuses Beatrice by telling her of her reputation for disdain; but she, perceiving who he is, retaliates by telling him as a purported stranger what she "really" thinks of Benedick. These devices cut deeply and confirm the worst fears of each. Ironically, these fears can be dispelled only by the virtuous deceptions practiced on them by their friends. Once Benedick is assured that Beatrice secretly loves him, masking her affection with scorn, he acquires the confidence he needs to make a commitment, and vice versa in her case. The beauty of the virtuous deceptions, moreover, is that they are so plausible—because, indeed, they are essentially true. Benedick overhears himself described as a person so satirical that Beatrice dare not reveal her affection, for fear of being repulsed (2.3). Beatrice learns that she is indeed called disdainful by her friends (3.1). Both lovers respond generously to these revelations, accepting the accusations as richly deserved and placing no blame on the other. As Beatrice proclaims to herself, "Contempt, farewell, and maiden pride, adieu!" The relief afforded by this honesty is genuine and lasting.

Because Claudio knows so little about Hero and is content with superficial expectations, he is vulnerable to a far uglier sort of deception. Claudio's first questions about Hero betray his romantically stereotyped attitudes and his willingness to let Don Pedro and Hero's father, Leonato, arrange a financially advantageous match. Claudio treasures Hero's outward reputation for modesty, an appearance easily besmirched. When a false rumor suggests that Don Pedro is wooing the lady for himself, Claudio's response is predictably cliché-ridden: all's fair in love and war, you can't trust friends in an affair of the heart, and so farewell Hero. The rumor has a superficial plausibility about it, especially when the villainous Don John steps into the situation. Motivated in part by pure malice and the sport of ruining others' happiness, Don John speaks to the masked Claudio at the ball (2.1) as though he were speaking to Benedick and, in this guise, pretends to reveal the secret "fact" of Don Pedro's duplicity in love. (The device is precisely that used by Beatrice to put down Benedick in the same scene.) With this specious confirmation, Claudio leaps to a wrong conclusion, thereby judging both his friend and mistress to be false. He gives them no chance to speak in their own defense. To be sure, Hero's father and uncle have also believed in the false report and have welcomed the prospect of Don Pedro as Hero's husband. She herself raises no objection to the prospect of marriage with the older man. Don Pedro is, after all, a prince of presumably enormous wealth, power, and social status, well above that of Leonato and his well-to-do but bourgeois family; when he asks (perhaps as a pleasantry) if Beatrice will have him as her husband, her polite refusal seems tinged with a note of regret (2.1.303–21). These attractive features in Don Pedro tend to excuse the general willingness to accept the idea of him as a splendidly suitable husband for Hero. Even so, Claudio has revealed a lack of faith resulting from his slender knowledge of Hero and of himself.

The nearly tragic "demonstration" of Hero's infidelity follows the same course, because Claudio has not learned from his first experience. Once again, the villainous Don John first implants the insidious suggestion in Claudio's mind, then creates an illusion entirely plausible to the senses, and finally confirms it with Borachio's testimony. What Claudio and Don Pedro have actually seen is Margaret wooed at Hero's window, shrouded in the dark of night and seen from "afar off in the orchard." The power of suggestion is enough to do the rest. Don John's method, and his pleasure in evil, are much like those of his later counterparts, Iago in *Othello* and Edmund in *King Lear*. Indeed, John is compared with the devil, who has power over mortals' frail senses but must rely on their complicity and acquiescence in evil. Claudio is once again led to denounce faithlessly the virtuous woman whose loyalty he no longer deserves. Yet his fault is typically human and is shared by Don Pedro. Providence gives him a second chance, through the ludicrous and bumbling intervention of Dogberry's night watch. These men overhear the plot of Don John as soon as it is announced to us, so that we know justice will eventually prevail, even though it will also be farcically delayed. Once again, misunderstanding has become "much ado about nothing," an escalating of recriminations based on a purely chimerical assumption that must eventually be deflated. The painful experience is not without value, for it tests the characters' spiritual worth in a crisis. Beatrice, like Friar Francis, shows herself to be a person of unshakable faith in goodness. Benedick, though puzzled and torn in his loyalties, also passes the test and proves himself worthy of Beatrice. Claudio is found wanting, and indeed is judged by many modern readers and audiences to be wholly inadequate, but Hero forgives and accepts him anyway. In her role as the granter of a merciful second chance, she foreshadows the beatifically symbolic nature of many of Shakespeare's later heroines.

Much Ado comes perhaps closer to potentially tragic action than Shakespeare's other festive comedies, though *The Merchant of Venice* is another, and so are late romances like *Cymbeline* and *The Winter's Tale* that *Much Ado* can be said to anticipate in the serious matter of slander against a virtuous heroine. Most strikingly, Claudio's failure is unnervingly like that of Othello. The fact that both men are too easily persuaded to reject and humiliate the innocent women they love suggests a deep inadequacy in each. The tempters (Don John, Iago) cannot alone be blamed; the male lovers themselves are too prone to believe the worst of women. In Claudio we can see a vulnerability in the very way he looks at courtship and marriage. As Benedick jests, Claudio talks almost as though he wants to buy Hero (1.1.172). Certainly his attitude is acquisitive and superficial; as the conquering hero returned from the wars, he is ready to settle down into married respectability, and he needs a socially eligible wife. He desires Hero for her beauty, for her wealth and family connections, and above all for her modesty and her reputation for virginal purity. These are attributes easily impugned by false apearances, and in his too-quick rejection of Hero we see in Claudio a deep cynicism about women. He fears the betrayal and loss of masculine self-esteem that a woman can inflict on him by sexual infidelity. To Claudio, Hero is a saint one moment and a whore the next.

Nor is he the only man to demean her (and women) thus. Don Pedro, his patron and older friend, is no less ready to believe Don John's lies, even though Don Pedro has been deceived by his brother before and should know better. Hero's father collapses in shame when he hears his daughter publicly accused of promiscuity, for Leonato's own reputation is on the line: as a father in a patriarchal society, his responsibility is to guarantee the chastity of his daughter to the younger man who proposes to receive her. Leonato's first assumption is that she must be guilty if other men say so; even he is altogether ready to believe the worst of women. Virtually the whole male world of Messina is victimized by its own fear of womanly perfidy—a fear that seems to arise from male lack of self-assurance and a deep inner conviction of being unloved. Benedick is much to be commended for his skepticism about the slanderous attacks on Hero; in no way does he better prove his worthiness of being Beatrice's husband than in his defense of a traduced and innocent woman. Yet Benedick, too, suffers to such a degree from his own male insecurity that he nearly gives up Beatrice at the very end of the play, even as she is nearly ready to give up him. Despite their self-awareness, these lovers must be rescued from their autonomous self-defensiveness by one more intervention on the part of their friends. Benedick and Beatrice are not wholly unlike Claudio and Hero after all. Both pairs of lovers are saved from their own worst selves by a harmonizing force that works its will through strange and improbable means—even through Constable Dogberry and his watch.

Performance history has abundantly illustrated the durable quality of this remarkable play. Perhaps no other comedy by Shakespeare has been as influential as *Much Ado*, providing as it does a model for wit combat and comedy of manners in William Congreve's *The Way of the World*, Oscar Wilde's *The Importance of Being Earnest*, George Bernard Shaw's *Man and Superman*, Noel Coward's *Private Lives*, Tom Stoppard's *The Real Thing*, and many others. Onstage the play has always been a favorite in the repertory, featuring such couples as Hannah Pritchard and David Garrick, Ellen Terry and Henry Irving, Peggy Ashcroft and John Gielgud, Diana Wynyard and Anthony Quayle, Janet Suzman and Alan Howard, Maggie Smith and Robert Stephens, Judi Dench and Donald Sinden, Sinead Cusack and Derek Jacobi, and many more. A commercial television production by A. J. Antoon, originating in New York's Delacorte Theater in 1972, was witnessed by more viewers on that occasion than had seen the play in its entire stage history. Kenneth Branagh's 1993 film, with Emma Thompson and Branagh in the leading roles, along with Denzel Washington as Don Pedro and Michael Keaton as Dogberry, capitalized on a gorgeous Italian villa and its star-laden cast to produce one of the most popular of Shakespeare cinemas. Emma Thompson shows us a Beatrice who is strong, independent, not easily fooled, undaunted by men, and willing to marry Benedick (Branagh) only after she has tested him and made clear the mutuality of respect that she demands. In recent years the play has been located in a wide variety of updated settings: frontier Texas, small-town America right after the Spanish-American War, Victorian India of the British Raj, Regency England, the Edwardian era, mafiosa Sicily, and still more. The incessant updating testifies paradoxically to the play's engaging timelessness; it works anywhere and any time. The play continues to succeed because it is so genuinely open to such interpretations.

Much Ado About Nothing

※

[*Dramatis Personae*

DON PEDRO, *Prince of Aragon*
LEONATO, *Governor of Messina*
ANTONIO, *his brother*

BENEDICK, *a young lord of Padua*
BEATRICE, *Leonato's niece*
CLAUDIO, *a young lord of Florence*
HERO, *Leonato's daughter*
MARGARET, } *gentlewomen attending Hero*
URSULA,

DON JOHN, *Don Pedro's bastard brother*
BORACHIO, } *followers of Don John*
CONRADE,

DOGBERRY, *Constable in charge of the Watch*
VERGES, *the Headborough, or parish constable, Dogberry's partner*
A SEXTON (FRANCIS SEACOAL)
FIRST WATCHMAN
SECOND WATCHMAN (GEORGE SEACOAL)

BALTHASAR, *a singer attending Don Pedro*
FRIAR FRANCIS
A BOY
MESSENGER *to Leonato*
Another MESSENGER

Attendants, Musicians, Members of the Watch, Antonio's Son and other Kinsmen

SCENE: *Messina*]

[1.1]

Enter Leonato, Governor of Messina, Hero his daughter, and Beatrice his niece, with a Messenger.

LEONATO [*holding a letter*]   I learn in this letter that Don Pedro of Aragon comes this night to Messina.

MESSENGER   He is very near by this. He was not three leagues off when I left him.   4

LEONATO   How many gentlemen have you lost in this action?   6

MESSENGER   But few of any sort and none of name.   7

LEONATO   A victory is twice itself when the achiever brings home full numbers. I find here that Don Pedro hath bestowed much honor on a young Florentine called Claudio.

MESSENGER   Much deserved on his part and equally remembered by Don Pedro. He hath borne himself   13 beyond the promise of his age, doing in the figure of a lamb the feats of a lion. He hath indeed better bettered expectation than you must expect of me to tell   16 you how.

LEONATO   He hath an uncle here in Messina will be   18 very much glad of it.

MESSENGER   I have already delivered him letters, and there appears much joy in him, even so much that joy   21 could not show itself modest enough without a badge   22 of bitterness.   23

LEONATO   Did he break out into tears?

MESSENGER   In great measure.

LEONATO   A kind overflow of kindness. There are no   26 faces truer than those that are so washed. How much better is it to weep at joy than to joy at weeping!

BEATRICE   I pray you, is Signor Mountanto returned   29 from the wars or no?

MESSENGER   I know none of that name, lady. There was none such in the army of any sort.

LEONATO   What is he that you ask for, niece?

1.1. Location: Messina. Before Leonato's house.
4 leagues units of about three miles   **6 action** battle.   **7 sort** rank **name** reputation, or noble name   **13 remembered** rewarded

16 bettered surpassed   **18 will** who will   **21–3 joy . . . bitterness** joy could not show a decorous moderation only by weeping at the same time.   **26 kind** natural   **29 Mountanto** montanto, an upward blow or thrust in fencing

HERO   My cousin means Signor Benedick of Padua.

MESSENGER   Oh, he's returned, and as pleasant as ever 35
he was.

BEATRICE   He set up his bills here in Messina and chal- 37
lenged Cupid at the flight; and my uncle's fool, reading 38
the challenge, subscribed for Cupid and challenged 39
him at the bird-bolt. I pray you, how many hath he 40
killed and eaten in these wars? But how many hath he
killed? For indeed I promised to eat all of his killing.

LEONATO   Faith, niece, you tax Signor Benedick too 43
much, but he'll be meet with you, I doubt it not. 44

MESSENGER   He hath done good service, lady, in these
wars.

BEATRICE   You had musty victual, and he hath holp to 47
eat it. He is a very valiant trencherman; he hath an 48
excellent stomach. 49

MESSENGER   And a good soldier too, lady.

BEATRICE   And a good soldier to a lady, but what is he 51
to a lord? 52

MESSENGER   A lord to a lord, a man to a man, stuffed 53
with all honorable virtues.

BEATRICE   It is so, indeed, he is no less than a stuffed 55
man. But for the stuffing—well, we are all mortal. 56

LEONATO   You must not, sir, mistake my niece. There is
a kind of merry war betwixt Signor Benedick and her.
They never meet but there's a skirmish of wit between
them.

BEATRICE   Alas! He gets nothing by that. In our last
conflict, four of his five wits went halting off, and now 62
is the whole man governed with one; so that if he have
wit enough to keep himself warm, let him bear it for a
difference between himself and his horse, for it is all 65
the wealth that he hath left to be known a reasonable 66
creature. Who is his companion now? He hath every 67
month a new sworn brother. 68

MESSENGER   Is't possible?

BEATRICE   Very easily possible. He wears his faith but as 70
the fashion of his hat; it ever changes with the next
block. 72

MESSENGER   I see, lady, the gentleman is not in your 73
books. 74

BEATRICE   No. An he were, I would burn my study. But 75
I pray you, who is his companion? Is there no young
squarer now that will make a voyage with him to the 77
devil?

MESSENGER   He is most in the company of the right
noble Claudio.

BEATRICE   Oh, Lord, he will hang upon him like a 81
disease! He is sooner caught than the pestilence, and
the taker runs presently mad. God help the noble 83
Claudio! If he have caught the Benedick, it will cost 84
him a thousand pound ere 'a be cured. 85

MESSENGER   I will hold friends with you, lady. 86

BEATRICE   Do, good friend.

LEONATO   You will never run mad, niece. 88

BEATRICE   No, not till a hot January. 89

MESSENGER   Don Pedro is approached.

*Enter Don Pedro, Claudio, Benedick, Balthasar,
and [Don] John the Bastard.*

DON PEDRO   Good Signor Leonato, are you come to
meet your trouble? The fashion of the world is to 92
avoid cost, and you encounter it. 93

LEONATO   Never came trouble to my house in the
likeness of Your Grace. For trouble being gone,
comfort should remain; but when you depart from
me, sorrow abides and happiness takes his leave.

DON PEDRO   You embrace your charge too willingly.—I 98
think this is your daughter.

[*Presenting himself to Hero.*]

LEONATO   Her mother hath many times told me so.

BENEDICK   Were you in doubt, sir, that you asked her?

LEONATO   Signor Benedick, no; for then were you a
child.

DON PEDRO   You have it full, Benedick. We may guess 104
by this what you are, being a man. Truly, the lady
fathers herself. Be happy, lady, for you are like an 106
honorable father.

BENEDICK   If Signor Leonato be her father, she would
not have his head on her shoulders for all Messina, as 109
like him as she is.   [*Don Pedro and Leonato talk aside.*]

BEATRICE   I wonder that you will still be talking, Signor
Benedick. Nobody marks you.

BENEDICK   What, my dear Lady Disdain! Are you yet
living?

BEATRICE   Is it possible disdain should die while she
hath such meet food to feed it as Signor Benedick? 116

35 pleasant jocular   **37 bills** placards, advertisements   **38 at the flight** to a long-distance archery contest. (Beatrice mocks Benedick's pretentions as a lady killer.)   **my uncle's fool** (Perhaps a professional fool in her uncle's service.)   **39 subscribed for** accepted on behalf of   **40 bird-bolt** a blunt-headed arrow used for fowling. (Sometimes used by children because of its relative harmlessness and thus conventionally appropriate to Cupid.)   **43 tax** disparage   **44 meet** even, quits   **47 musty victual** stale food.   **holp** helped   **48 valiant trencherman** great eater   **49 stomach** appetite. (With a mocking suggestion also of "courage.")   **51 soldier to a lady** lady killer. (With a play on *to/too*.)   **52 to** compared to   **53 stuffed** amply supplied   **55–6 a stuffed man** i.e., a figure stuffed to resemble a man   **56 the stuffing** i.e., what he's truly made of.   **well . . . mortal** i.e., well, we all have our faults.   **62 five wits** i.e., not the five senses, but the five faculties: memory, imagination, judgment, fantasy, common sense.   **halting** limping   **65 difference** heraldic feature distinguishing a junior member or branch of a family. (With a play on the usual sense.)   **65–7 it is . . . creature** i.e., his feeble wit is all he has left to identify him as rationally human.   **68 sworn brother** brother in arms (*frater juratus*, an allusion to the ancient practice of swearing brotherhood).   **70 faith** allegiance, or fidelity   **72 block** mold for shaping hats.

73–4 in your books in favor with you, in your good books. (But Beatrice, in her reply, takes *books* in the literal sense of something to be found in a library.)   **75 An** If. (Also in line 131.)   **77 squarer** quarreler   **81 he** i.e., Benedick   **83 presently** immediately   **84 the Benedick** i.e., as if this were a disease   **85 'a** he   **86 hold friends** keep on friendly terms (so as not to earn your enmity)   **88 run mad** i.e., "catch the Benedick"   **89 not . . . January** i.e., not any time soon.   **92 your trouble** i.e., the expense of entertaining me and my retinue.   **93 encounter** go to meet   **98 charge** social responsibility and expense.   **104 have it full** are well answered   **106 fathers herself** shows by appearance who her father is.   **109 his head** i.e., with Leonato's white beard and signs of age   **116 meet** suitable. (With a pun on "meat.")

Courtesy itself must convert to disdain, if you come in 117
her presence.

BENEDICK   Then is courtesy a turncoat. But it is certain
I am loved of all ladies, only you excepted; and I
would I could find in my heart that I had not a hard
heart, for truly I love none.

BEATRICE   A dear happiness to women! They would 123
else have been troubled with a pernicious suitor. I
thank God and my cold blood I am of your humor for 125
that. I had rather hear my dog bark at a crow than a 126
man swear he loves me.

BENEDICK   God keep Your Ladyship still in that mind!
So some gentleman or other shall scape a predestinate 129
scratched face.

BEATRICE   Scratching could not make it worse, an 'twere
such a face as yours were.   132

BENEDICK   Well, you are a rare parrot-teacher.   133

BEATRICE   A bird of my tongue is better than a beast of 134
yours.   135

BENEDICK   I would my horse had the speed of your
tongue and so good a continuer. But keep your way, 137
i'God's name; I have done.

BEATRICE   You always end with a jade's trick. I know 139
you of old.

DON PEDRO   That is the sum of all, Leonato. Signor 141
Claudio and Signor Benedick, my dear friend Leonato
hath invited you all. I tell him we shall stay here at the
least a month, and he heartily prays some occasion
may detain us longer. I dare swear he is no hypocrite,
but prays from his heart.

LEONATO   If you swear, my lord, you shall not be forsworn. [To Don John] Let me bid you welcome, my
lord, being reconciled to the Prince your brother. I owe 149
you all duty.

DON JOHN   I thank you. I am not of many words, but I
thank you.

LEONATO   Please it Your Grace lead on?   153

DON PEDRO   Your hand, Leonato. We will go together. 154
            Exeunt. Manent Benedick and Claudio.

CLAUDIO   Benedick, didst thou note the daughter of
Signor Leonato?

BENEDICK   I noted her not, but I looked on her.   157

CLAUDIO   Is she not a modest young lady?

BENEDICK   Do you question me as an honest man
should do, for my simple true judgment? Or would

you have me speak after my custom, as being a
professed tyrant to their sex?   162

CLAUDIO   No, I pray thee, speak in sober judgment.

BENEDICK   Why, i'faith, methinks she's too low for a 164
high praise, too brown for a fair praise, and too little
for a great praise. Only this commendation I can afford
her, that were she other than she is, she were unhandsome, and being no other but as she is, I do not like
her.

CLAUDIO   Thou thinkest I am in sport. I pray thee, tell
me truly how thou lik'st her.

BENEDICK   Would you buy her, that you inquire after
her?

CLAUDIO   Can the world buy such a jewel?

BENEDICK   Yea, and a case to put it into. But speak you 175
this with a sad brow? Or do you play the flouting Jack, 176
to tell us Cupid is a good hare-finder and Vulcan a rare 177
carpenter? Come, in what key shall a man take you, to 178
go in the song?   179

CLAUDIO   In mine eye she is the sweetest lady that ever
I looked on.

BENEDICK   I can see yet without spectacles, and I see no
such matter. There's her cousin, an she were not possessed with a fury, exceeds her as much in beauty as the 184
first of May doth the last of December. But I hope you
have no intent to turn husband, have you?

CLAUDIO   I would scarce trust myself, though I had
sworn the contrary, if Hero would be my wife.

BENEDICK   Is't come to this? In faith, hath not the world 189
one man but he will wear his cap with suspicion? Shall 190
I never see a bachelor of threescore again? Go to, 191
i'faith; an thou wilt needs thrust thy neck into a yoke,
wear the print of it and sigh away Sundays. Look, Don 193
Pedro is returned to seek you.

            Enter Don Pedro.

DON PEDRO   What secret hath held you here, that you
followed not to Leonato's?

BENEDICK   I would Your Grace would constrain me to 197
tell.

DON PEDRO   I charge thee on thy allegiance.

BENEDICK   You hear, Count Claudio. I can be secret as a
dumb man—I would have you think so—but on my
allegiance, mark you this, on my allegiance! He is in
love. With who? Now that is Your Grace's part. Mark 203
how short his answer is: with Hero, Leonato's short
daughter.

117 convert change   **123 dear happiness** precious piece of luck
125–6 I am . . . that I am of the same disposition in that matter, i.e., of
loving no one.   **129 scape** escape.   **predestinate** inevitable (for any
man who should woo Beatrice)   **132 were** i.e., is.   **133 rare** outstanding.   **parrot-teacher** i.e., one who would teach a parrot well, because
you merely "parrot" my lines.   **134 of my tongue** taught to speak
like me, i.e., incessantly   **134–5 of yours** taught to speak like you.
137 and . . . continuer i.e., and as much staying power in running as
you have in talking.   **139 a jade's trick** i.e., an ill-tempered horse's
habit of slipping its head out of the collar or stopping suddenly (just
as Benedick proposes to abandon this exchange of witticisms when
he thinks he has had the last word).   **141 sum of all** (Don Pedro and
Leonato have been conversing apart on other matters.)   **149 being**
since you are   **153 Please it** May it please   **154 go together** i.e., go
arm in arm (thus avoiding the question of precedence in order of
leaving).   **154.1 Manent** They remain onstage   **157 noted her not**
gave her no special attention

162 tyrant one cruel or pitiless in attitude   **164 low** short   **175 case**
(1) jewel case (2) clothing, outer garments. (There is also a bawdy
play on the meaning "female pudenda.")   **176 sad** serious.   **flouting
Jack** i.e., mocking rascal   **177–8 to tell . . . carpenter?** i.e., are you
mocking us with nonsense? (Cupid was blind, not sharp-eyed like a
hunter, and Vulcan was a blacksmith, not a carpenter.)   **178–9 to . . .
song** as the song expresses it. (Alluding perhaps to some popular
song.)   **184 with a fury** by an avenging, infernal spirit   **189–90 hath
. . . suspicion?** i.e., isn't there a man left alive who will regard marriage with a jaundiced eye? (A cap might be used, unsuccessfully perhaps, in an attempt to hide a cuckold's horns.)   **191 Go to** (An
expression of impatience.)   **193 wear . . . Sundays** i.e., display the
marks of your domestic enslavement resignedly.   **197 constrain**
order   **203 part** speaking part. (I.e., to say, "With who?")

CLAUDIO   If this were so, so were it uttered.   206

BENEDICK   Like the old tale, my lord: "It is not so, nor   207
'twas not so, but indeed, God forbid it should be so."

CLAUDIO   If my passion change not shortly, God forbid
it should be otherwise.

DON PEDRO   Amen, if you love her, for the lady is very
well worthy.

CLAUDIO   You speak this to fetch me in, my lord.   213

DON PEDRO   By my troth, I speak my thought.   214

CLAUDIO   And in faith, my lord, I spoke mine.

BENEDICK   And by my two faiths and troths, my lord, I   216
spoke mine.

CLAUDIO   That I love her, I feel.

DON PEDRO   That she is worthy, I know.

BENEDICK   That I neither feel how she should be loved
nor know how she should be worthy is the opinion
that fire cannot melt out of me. I will die in it at the
stake.

DON PEDRO   Thou wast ever an obstinate heretic in the
despite of beauty.   225

CLAUDIO   And never could maintain his part but in the   226
force of his will.   227

BENEDICK   That a woman conceived me, I thank her;
that she brought me up, I likewise give her most humble thanks. But that I will have a recheat winded in my   230
forehead or hang my bugle in an invisible baldrick, all   231
women shall pardon me. Because I will not do them   232
the wrong to mistrust any, I will do myself the right to
trust none; and the fine is, for the which I may go the   234
finer, I will live a bachelor.   235

DON PEDRO   I shall see thee, ere I die, look pale with
love.

BENEDICK   With anger, with sickness, or with hunger,
my lord, not with love. Prove that ever I lose more   239
blood with love than I will get again with drinking,   240
pick out mine eyes with a ballad-maker's pen and   241
hang me up at the door of a brothel house for the sign   242
of blind Cupid.

DON PEDRO   Well, if ever thou dost fall from this faith,
thou wilt prove a notable argument.   245

BENEDICK   If I do, hang me in a bottle like a cat and   246
shoot at me, and he that hits me, let him be clapped on
the shoulder and called Adam.   248

DON PEDRO   Well, as time shall try:
"In time the savage bull doth bear the yoke."   250

BENEDICK   The savage bull may; but if ever the sensible
Benedick bear it, pluck off the bull's horns and set
them in my forehead, and let me be vilely painted, and
in such great letters as they write, "Here is good horse
to hire," let them signify under my sign, "Here you
may see Benedick the married man."

CLAUDIO   If this should ever happen, thou wouldst be
horn-mad.   258

DON PEDRO   Nay, if Cupid have not spent all his quiver
in Venice, thou wilt quake for this shortly.   260

BENEDICK   I look for an earthquake too, then.   261

DON PEDRO   Well, you will temporize with the hours. In   262
the meantime, good Signor Benedick, repair to
Leonato's. Commend me to him, and tell him I will
not fail him at supper, for indeed he hath made great
preparation.

BENEDICK   I have almost matter enough in me for such   267
an embassage; and so I commit you—   268

CLAUDIO   To the tuition of God. From my house, if I had   269
it—

DON PEDRO   The sixth of July. Your loving friend,
Benedick.

BENEDICK   Nay, mock not, mock not. The body of your
discourse is sometime guarded with fragments, and   274
the guards are but slightly basted on neither. Ere you   275
flout old ends any further, examine your conscience.   276
And so I leave you.   *Exit.*

CLAUDIO
My liege, Your Highness now may do me good.   278

DON PEDRO
My love is thine to teach. Teach it but how,
And thou shalt see how apt it is to learn
Any hard lesson that may do thee good.

CLAUDIO
Hath Leonato any son, my lord?

DON PEDRO
No child but Hero; she's his only heir.
Dost thou affect her, Claudio?

CLAUDIO   O my lord,   284

206 If . . . uttered If this were true, it might be told in words to this effect.   **207 old tale** (In the English fairy tale known as "Mr. Fox," a murderous wooer, discovered in his crimes by the lady he seeks to marry and victimize, repeatedly disclaims her recital of what she has seen by the refrain here set in quotations. The story is a variant of the theme known as "the Robber Bridegroom." Benedick uses it mock-ingly here to characterize Claudio's reluctance to admit his "crime" of falling in love.)   **213 fetch me in** get me to confess   **214 By my troth** By my faith, upon my word. (A mild oath.)   **216 by . . . troths** as it were, by my loyalty to you both   **225 despite** contempt   **226–7 in . . . will** by mere obstinacy (which, as defined by the Schoolmen, was the state of the heretic).   **230–2 But that . . . me** i.e., Women must pardon me for refusing to have a horn placed on my head as if I were a cuck-old. (A *recheat* is a hunting call sounded [*winded*] on a horn to assem-ble the hounds; a *baldrick* is a strap that supports the horn, here *invisible* because the horn is the metaphorical one of cuckoldry.)   **234 fine** conclusion   **234–5 go the finer** be more finely dressed (since without a wife I will have more money to spend on clothing)   **239 Prove** If you can prove   **239–40 lose . . . drinking** (According to Elizabethan theory, each sigh cost the heart a drop of blood, whereas blood was replenished by wine.)   **241 ballad-maker's pen** i.e., such as would be used to write love ballads or satires   **242 sign** painted sign, such as hung over inns and shops   **245 notable argument** noto-rious subject for conversation, example.

246 bottle wicker or leather basket (to hold the cat sometimes used as an archery target)   **248 Adam** (Probably refers to Adam Bell, archer outlaw of the ballads.)   **250 In . . . yoke** (Proverbial.)   **258 horn-mad** stark mad. (From the fury of horned beasts; with allusion to cuck-oldry.)   **260 Venice** (A city noted for licentiousness.)   **261 I . . . then** i.e., My falling in love will be at least as rare as an earthquake.   **262 temporize . . . hours** come to terms, or become milder, in time. (With perhaps a bawdy pun on *hours*, "whores," pronounced something like "hoors.")   **267 matter** wit, intelligence   **268 embassage** mission.   **and so . . . you** (A conventional close, which Claudio and Don Pedro mockingly play with as though it were the complimentary close of a letter.)   **269 tuition** protection   **274 guarded** ornamented, trimmed   **275 guards . . . neither** trimmings are tenuously stitched on at best, have only the flimsiest connection.   **276 flout old ends** quote or recite mockingly proverbial tags of wisdom (as well as fragments of cloth, or the *ends* of letters that Claudio and Don Pedro have been parodying). **examine your conscience** look to your own behavior or speech.   **278 do me good** do me some good, help me.   **284 affect** love

When you went onward on this ended action,   285
I looked upon her with a soldier's eye,
That liked, but had a rougher task in hand
Than to drive liking to the name of love.
But now I am returned and that war thoughts   289
Have left their places vacant, in their rooms
Come thronging soft and delicate desires,
All prompting me how fair young Hero is,
Saying, I liked her ere I went to wars.

DON PEDRO
Thou wilt be like a lover presently
And tire the hearer with a book of words.
If thou dost love fair Hero, cherish it,
And I will break with her and with her father,   297
And thou shalt have her. Was't not to this end
That thou began'st to twist so fine a story?   299

CLAUDIO
How sweetly you do minister to love,
That know love's grief by his complexion!   301
But lest my liking might too sudden seem,
I would have salved it with a longer treatise.   303

DON PEDRO
What need the bridge much broader than the flood?   304
The fairest grant is the necessity.   305
Look what will serve is fit. 'Tis once: thou lovest,   306
And I will fit thee with the remedy.
I know we shall have reveling tonight;
I will assume thy part in some disguise
And tell fair Hero I am Claudio,
And in her bosom I'll unclasp my heart
And take her hearing prisoner with the force
And strong encounter of my amorous tale.
Then after to her father will I break,
And the conclusion is, she shall be thine.
In practice let us put it presently.   *Exeunt.*

❖

[1.2]

*Enter Leonato and an old man [Antonio],
brother to Leonato, [meeting].*

LEONATO   How now, brother, where is my cousin,   1
your son? Hath he provided this music?

ANTONIO   He is very busy about it. But brother, I can
tell you strange news that you yet dreamt not of.

LEONATO   Are they good?   5

ANTONIO   As the event stamps them, but they have a   6
good cover; they show well outward. The Prince and   7

Count Claudio, walking in a thick-pleached alley in   8
mine orchard, were thus much overheard by a man of   9
mine: the Prince discovered to Claudio that he loved   10
my niece your daughter and meant to acknowledge it
this night in a dance, and if he found her accordant, he   12
meant to take the present time by the top and instantly   13
break with you of it.

LEONATO   Hath the fellow any wit that told you this?   15

ANTONIO   A good sharp fellow. I will send for him, and
question him yourself.

LEONATO   No, no; we will hold it as a dream till it
appear itself. But I will acquaint my daughter withal,
that she may be the better prepared for an answer, if
peradventure this be true. Go you and tell her of it.

*[Enter Antonio's Son, with a musician and
others.]*

Cousins, you know what you have to do.—Oh, I cry   22
you mercy, friend; go you with me, and I will use your   23
skill.—Good cousin, have a care this busy time.

                                        Exeunt.

❖

[1.3]

*Enter Sir [Don] John the Bastard and Conrade,
his companion.*

CONRADE   What the goodyear, my lord! Why are you   1
thus out of measure sad?   2

DON JOHN   There is no measure in the occasion that
breeds; therefore the sadness is without limit.

CONRADE   You should hear reason.   5

DON JOHN   And when I have heard it, what blessing
brings it?

CONRADE   If not a present remedy, at least a patient
sufferance.   9

DON JOHN   I wonder that thou, being, as thou say'st
thou art, born under Saturn, goest about to apply a   11
moral medicine to a mortifying mischief. I cannot hide   12
what I am: I must be sad when I have cause and smile
at no man's jests, eat when I have stomach and wait   14
for no man's leisure, sleep when I am drowsy and
tend on no man's business, laugh when I am merry   16
and claw no man in his humor.   17

CONRADE   Yea, but you must not make the full show of
this till you may do it without controlment. You have   19
of late stood out against your brother, and he hath   20
ta'en you newly into his grace, where it is impossible   21
you should take true root but by the fair weather that

---

285 ended action military action now ended   **289 now** now that
297 break open the subject. (As also in line 314.)   **299 twist** draw out
the thread of   **301 his complexion** its outward appearance.
303 salved soothed, eased the way for   **304 What need** Why need be.
flood river.   **305 The fairest . . . necessity** The best thing to do is simply what is necessary.   **306 Look what** Whatever.   **'Tis once** In
short, once and for all. (This speech of Don Pedro's is overheard by a
servant of Antonio's, as we learn in the next scene.)
1.2 Location: Leonato's house.
1 cousin kinsman   **5 they** i.e., the news. (Often treated as a plural
noun, as at 2.1.167.)   **6 event** outcome   **6–7 they . . . cover** (The
image is of a printed book, promising well by its cover.)

8 thick-pleached alley walk lined with dense hedges of intertwined
shrubs   **9 orchard** garden.   **9 man** servant   **10 discovered** disclosed
12 accordant agreeing, consenting   **13 take . . . top** i.e., seize the
opportunity. (Proverbially, Occasion was imagined bald in the back of
the head but with a forelock hair in the front that opportunistically
could be grabbed.)   **15 wit** sense, intelligence   **22–3 cry you mercy**
beg your pardon   **23 friend** (Addressed perhaps to the musician.)
1.3. Location: Leonato's house.
1 What the goodyear i.e., What the deuce   **2 out of measure** immoder-
ately   **5 hear** listen to   **9 sufferance** endurance.   **11 under Saturn**
(Hence, of a morose disposition.)   **11–12 goest . . . mischief** endeavor
to cure with moral commonplaces a deadly disease.   **14 stomach**
appetite   **16 tend on** attend to   **17 claw** flatter.   **humor** whim.
19 controlment restraint.   **20 stood out** rebelled   **21 grace** favor

you make yourself. It is needful that you frame the   23
season for your own harvest.

DON JOHN   I had rather be a canker in a hedge than a   25
rose in his grace, and it better fits my blood to be dis-   26
dained of all than to fashion a carriage to rob love from   27
any. In this, though I cannot be said to be a flattering
honest man, it must not be denied but I am a plain-
dealing villain. I am trusted with a muzzle and   30
enfranchised with a clog; therefore I have decreed not   31
to sing in my cage. If I had my mouth, I would bite; if
I had my liberty, I would do my liking. In the
meantime let me be that I am, and seek not to alter me.

CONRADE   Can you make no use of your discontent?

DON JOHN   I make all use of it, for I use it only. Who   36
comes here?

Enter Borachio.

What news, Borachio?

BORACHIO   I came yonder from a great supper. The
Prince your brother is royally entertained by Leonato,
and I can give you intelligence of an intended mar-   41
riage.

DON JOHN   Will it serve for any model to build mischief
on? What is he for a fool that betroths himself to   44
unquietness?

BORACHIO   Marry, it is your brother's right hand.   46

DON JOHN   Who, the most exquisite Claudio?

BORACHIO   Even he.

DON JOHN   A proper squire! And who, and who? Which   49
way looks he?

BORACHIO   Marry, one Hero, the daughter and heir of
Leonato.

DON JOHN   A very forward March chick! How came   53
you to this?

BORACHIO   Being entertained for a perfumer, as I was   55
smoking a musty room, comes me the Prince and   56
Claudio, hand in hand, in sad conference. I whipped   57
me behind the arras, and there heard it agreed upon   58
that the Prince should woo Hero for himself and,
having obtained her, give her to Count Claudio.

DON JOHN   Come, come, let us thither. This may prove
food to my displeasure. That young start-up hath all   62
the glory of my overthrow. If I can cross him any way,   63
I bless myself every way. You are both sure, and will   64
assist me?

CONRADE   To the death, my lord.

DON JOHN   Let us to the great supper. Their cheer is the
greater that I am subdued. Would the cook were o' my   68
mind! Shall we go prove what's to be done?   69

BORACHIO   We'll wait upon Your Lordship.   *Exeunt.*

[2.1]

*Enter Leonato, his brother [Antonio], Hero his
daughter, and Beatrice his niece [with Margaret
and Ursula].*

LEONATO   Was not Count John here at supper?

ANTONIO   I saw him not.

BEATRICE   How tartly that gentleman looks! I never can   3
see him but I am heartburned an hour after.   4

HERO   He is of a very melancholy disposition.

BEATRICE   He were an excellent man that were made   6
just in the midway between him and Benedick. The
one is too like an image and says nothing, and the   8
other too like my lady's eldest son, evermore tattling.   9

LEONATO   Then half Signor Benedick's tongue in Count
John's mouth, and half Count John's melancholy in
Signor Benedick's face—

BEATRICE   With a good leg and a good foot, uncle, and
money enough in his purse, such a man would win
any woman in the world, if 'a could get her good will.   15

LEONATO   By my troth, niece, thou wilt never get thee a
husband if thou be so shrewd of thy tongue.   17

ANTONIO   In faith, she's too curst.   18

BEATRICE   Too curst is more than curst. I shall lessen
God's sending that way; for it is said, "God sends a   20
curst cow short horns," but to a cow too curst he sends   21
none.

LEONATO   So, by being too curst, God will send you no
horns.

BEATRICE   Just, if he send me no husband, for the which   25
blessing I am at him upon my knees every morning
and evening. Lord, I could not endure a husband with
a beard on his face! I had rather lie in the woolen.   28

LEONATO   You may light on a husband that hath no
beard.

BEATRICE   What should I do with him? Dress him in my
apparel and make him my waiting-gentlewoman? He
that hath a beard is more than a youth, and he that
hath no beard is less than a man; and he that is more
than a youth is not for me, and he that is less than a
man, I am not for him. Therefore I will even take

23 frame fashion   **25 canker** dog rose, one that grows wild rather
than being cultivated in formal gardens   **26 blood** mood, disposition
27 fashion . . . love counterfeit a behavior to gain undeserved attention   **30–1 I . . . clog** I am trusted only with my muzzle on and am
allowed freedom only to the extent of being hampered by a heavy
wooden block   **31 decreed** determined   **36 I . . . only** Discontent is
my only resource, and I cultivate it alone.   **41 intelligence** news
44 What . . . fool What kind of fool is he   **46 Marry** By the Virgin
Mary, i.e., indeed   **49 proper squire** fine young man. (Said contemptuously.)   **53 forward March chick** precocious young thing (like a
chick hatched early)   **55 entertained for** hired as   **56 smoking**
sweetening the air of (with aromatic smoke).   **comes me** comes. (*Me*
is used colloquially, as also in line 58.)   **57 sad** serious   **58 arras**
tapestry, wall hanging   **62 start-up** upstart   **63 cross** thwart
64 sure trustworthy

68–9 o' my mind i.e., of a mind to poison the food.   **69 prove** try out
2.1. Location: Leonato's house.
3 tartly sour of disposition   **4 heartburned** afflicted with heartburn or
indigestion   **6 He were** A man would be   **8 image** statue   **9 my . . .
son** i.e., a spoiled child.   **tattling** chattering.   **15 'a** he   **17 shrewd**
sharp   **18 curst** shrewish   **20 that way** in that respect   **21 curst** i.e.,
savage, vicious. (God proverbially takes care that vicious are limited
in their ability to do harm.)   **25 Just** Right, exactly so.   **no husband**
If Beatrice has no husband, there can be no prospect of cuckold's
horns. (She may also be jesting about a short penis here and in lines
20–2.)   **28 in the woolen** between blankets, without sheets.

sixpence in earnest of the bearward, and lead his apes   37
into hell.   38

LEONATO   Well, then, go you into hell?

BEATRICE   No, but to the gate; and there will the devil
meet me, like an old cuckold, with horns on his head,
and say, "Get you to heaven, Beatrice, get you to
heaven, here's no place for you maids." So deliver I up
my apes, and away to Saint Peter, for the heavens; he   44
shows me where the bachelors sit, and there live we   45
as merry as the day is long.

ANTONIO   [to Hero]   Well, niece, I trust you will be ruled
by your father.

BEATRICE   Yes, faith, it is my cousin's duty to make
curtsy and say, "Father, as it please you." But yet for
all that, cousin, let him be a handsome fellow, or else
make another curtsy and say, "Father, as it please me."

LEONATO   Well, niece, I hope to see you one day fitted
with a husband.

BEATRICE   Not till God make men of some other metal   55
than earth. Would it not grieve a woman to be overmastered with a piece of valiant dust? To make an
account of her life to a clod of wayward marl? No,   58
uncle, I'll none. Adam's sons are my brethren, and   59
truly I hold it a sin to match in my kindred.   60

LEONATO   [to Hero]   Daughter, remember what I told
you. If the Prince do solicit you in that kind, you know 62
your answer.

BEATRICE   The fault will be in the music, cousin, if you
be not wooed in good time. If the Prince be too   65
important, tell him there is measure in everything,   66
and so dance out the answer. For, hear me, Hero:
wooing, wedding, and repenting is as a Scotch jig, a   68
measure, and a cinquepace. The first suit is hot and   69
hasty, like a Scotch jig, and full as fantastical; the
wedding, mannerly-modest, as a measure, full of state   71
and ancientry; and then comes Repentance, and with   72
his bad legs falls into the cinquepace faster and faster
till he sink into his grave.

LEONATO   Cousin, you apprehend passing shrewdly.   75

BEATRICE   I have a good eye, uncle; I can see a church by 76
daylight.   77

LEONATO   The revelers are entering, brother. Make good
room.   [The men put on their masks.]

Enter [as maskers] Prince [Don] Pedro, Claudio, and Benedick, and Balthasar, [Borachio,]
and Don John.

DON PEDRO   Lady, will you walk a bout with your   80
friend?   [The couples pair off for the dance.] 81

HERO   So you walk softly and look sweetly and say
nothing, I am yours for the walk, and especially when
I walk away.

DON PEDRO   With me in your company?

HERO   I may say so, when I please.

DON PEDRO   And when please you to say so?

HERO   When I like your favor, for God defend the lute 88
should be like the case!   89

DON PEDRO   My visor is Philemon's roof; within the   90
house is Jove.

HERO   Why, then, your visor should be thatched.   92

DON PEDRO   Speak low, if you speak love.   93
                              [They dance to one side.]

BALTHASAR   Well, I would you did like me.   94

MARGARET   So would not I for your own sake, for I have
many ill qualities.

BALTHASAR   Which is one?

MARGARET   I say my prayers aloud.

BALTHASAR   I love you the better. The hearers may cry
Amen.

MARGARET   God match me with a good dancer!

BALTHASAR   Amen.

MARGARET   And God keep him out of my sight when
the dance is done! Answer, clerk.   104

BALTHASAR   No more words. The clerk is answered.   105
                              [They dance to one side.]

URSULA   I know you well enough. You are Signor
Antonio.

ANTONIO   At a word, I am not.   108

URSULA   I know you by the waggling of your head.

ANTONIO   To tell you true, I counterfeit him.

URSULA   You could never do him so ill-well unless you 111
were the very man. Here's his dry hand up and down.   112
You are he, you are he.

ANTONIO   At a word, I am not.

URSULA   Come, come, do you think I do not know you
by your excellent wit? Can virtue hide itself? Go to,
mum, you are he. Graces will appear, and there's an   117
end.   [They dance to one side.] 118

---

37 in earnest in token advance payment for.   **bearward** one who
keeps and exhibits a bear (and sometimes apes)   **37–8 lead . . . hell**
(An ancient proverb says, "Such as die maids do all lead apes in
hell.")   **44 for the heavens** (A common interjection, like "Good heavens!" but here also carrying its literal meaning, i.e., bound for
heaven.)   **45 bachelors** unmarried persons of either sex   **55 metal**
substance. (With play on "mettle.")   **58 marl** clay, earth (such as was
used by God to make Adam in Genesis 2).   **59–60 Adam's . . . kindred** (Beatrice jests that since men and women are all descended from
Adam, it would be incestuous for her to marry a man.)   **62 in that
kind** to that effect (i.e., to marriage)   **65 in good time** (1) soon (2) in
time to the music, rhythmically.   **66 important** importunate, urgent.
measure (1) moderation (2) rhythm, dance   **68–9 a measure** a formal
dance   **69 cinquepace** five-step lively dance, galliard. (The pun on
"sink apace," as it was pronounced, is evident in lines 72–4: repentance will *sink faster and faster,* with a suggestion of detumescence.)
71–2 state and ancientry dignity and traditional stateliness
75 apprehend passing shrewdly understand with unusual perspicac-
ity.   **76–7 see . . . daylight** i.e., see something as plain as the nose on
your face.

---

80 walk a bout take a turn, join in a section of a dance. (Here probably a slow, stately pavane.)   **81 friend** wooer.   **88 favor** face
88–9 God . . . case! i.e., God forbid the face within should be as
unhandsome as its cover, your visor!   **90 Philemon's roof** i.e., the
humble cottage in which the peasants Philemon and Baucis entertained Jove, or Jupiter, unawares. (See Ovid, *Metamorphoses,* 8.)
90–3 My . . . love (A fourteen-syllable rhymed couplet, the verse form
of Arthur Golding's translation of the *Metamorphoses,* 1567.)   **92 visor**
mask.   **thatched** i.e., whiskered, to resemble the thatch of a humble
cottage.   **94–105 BALTHASAR** (The speech prefixes in the Quarto text
for Balthasar's lines read *Bene.* and *Balth.* Some editors speculate that
Borachio is intended.)   **104 clerk** (So addressed because of Balthasar's
repeatedly answering "Amen" like the parish clerk saying the
responses.)   **108 At a word** In short   **111 do . . . ill-well** imitate his
imperfections so perfectly   **112 dry hand** (A sign of age.)   **up and
down** up exactly.   **117 mum** be silent   **117–18 an end** no more to
be said.

BEATRICE   Will you not tell me who told you so?

BENEDICK   No, you shall pardon me.

BEATRICE   Nor will you not tell me who you are?

BENEDICK   Not now.

BEATRICE   That I was disdainful and that I had my good
wit out of the *Hundred Merry Tales*—well, this was 124
Signor Benedick that said so.

BENEDICK   What's he?

BEATRICE   I am sure you know him well enough.

BENEDICK   Not I, believe me.

BEATRICE   Did he never make you laugh?

BENEDICK   I pray you, what is he?

BEATRICE   Why, he is the Prince's jester, a very dull fool.
Only his gift is in devising impossible slanders. None 132
but libertines delight in him, and the commendation 133
is not in his wit but in his villainy, for he both pleases 134
men and angers them, and then they laugh at him and 135
beat him. I am sure he is in the fleet. I would he had 136
boarded me. 137

BENEDICK   When I know the gentleman, I'll tell him 138
what you say.

BEATRICE   Do, do. He'll but break a comparison or two 140
on me, which peradventure not marked or not laughed 141
at strikes him into melancholy; and then there's a partridge wing saved, for the fool will eat no supper that
night. [*Music.*] We must follow the leaders. 144

BENEDICK   In every good thing.

BEATRICE   Nay, if they lead to any ill, I will leave them
at the next turning. 147

*Dance. Exeunt [all except Don John, Borachio, and
Claudio. Don John and Borachio are unmasked.]*

DON JOHN *[to Borachio]*   Sure my brother is amorous on
Hero and hath withdrawn her father to break with
him about it. The ladies follow her, and but one visor
remains.

BORACHIO   And that is Claudio. I know him by his
bearing.

DON JOHN *[advancing to Claudio]*   Are not you Signor
Benedick?

CLAUDIO   You know me well. I am he.

DON JOHN   Signor, you are very near my brother in his 157
love. He is enamored on Hero. I pray you, dissuade 158
him from her; she is no equal for his birth. You may do 159
the part of an honest man in it.

CLAUDIO   How know you he loves her?

DON JOHN   I heard him swear his affection.

BORACHIO   So did I, too, and he swore he would marry
her tonight.

DON JOHN   Come, let us to the banquet. 165

Exeunt. Manet Claudio.

CLAUDIO

Thus answer I in name of Benedick,
But hear these ill news with the ears of Claudio.
'Tis certain so. The Prince woos for himself.
Friendship is constant in all other things
Save in the office and affairs of love;
Therefore all hearts in love use their own tongues.
Let every eye negotiate for itself
And trust no agent; for beauty is a witch
Against whose charms faith melteth into blood. 174
This is an accident of hourly proof, 175
Which I mistrusted not. Farewell therefore Hero! 176

Enter Benedick [unmasked].

BENEDICK   Count Claudio?

CLAUDIO   Yea, the same.

BENEDICK   Come, will you go with me?

CLAUDIO   Whither?

BENEDICK   Even to the next willow, about your own 181
business, County. What fashion will you wear the gar- 182
land of? About your neck, like an usurer's chain? Or 183
under your arm, like a lieutenant's scarf? You must 184
wear it one way, for the Prince hath got your Hero. 185

CLAUDIO   I wish him joy of her.

BENEDICK   Why, that's spoken like an honest drover; so 187
they sell bullocks. But did you think the Prince would 188
have served you thus?

CLAUDIO   I pray you, leave me.

BENEDICK   Ho, now you strike like the blind man. 'Twas 191
the boy that stole your meat, and you'll beat the post. 192

CLAUDIO   If it will not be, I'll leave you.   *Exit.* 193

BENEDICK   Alas, poor hurt fowl! Now will he creep into 194
sedges. But that my Lady Beatrice should know me, 195
and not know me! The Prince's fool! Ha? It may be I 196
go under that title because I am merry. Yea, but so I am
apt to do myself wrong. I am not so reputed. It is the 198
base, though bitter, disposition of Beatrice that puts the 199
world into her person and so gives me out. Well, I'll be 200
revenged as I may.

*Enter the Prince [Don Pedro], Hero, [and]
Leonato. [All are unmasked.]*

---

124 Hundred Merry Tales (A popular collection of anecdotes first published by John Rastell in 1526.) **132 Only his gift** His only talent.
impossible incredible **133 libertines** i.e., those who disregard conventional moral laws **134 villainy** i.e., mocking, raillery; also,
clownishness **134–5 pleases . . . angers them** i.e., amuses some
with his rudeness and angers others with his slanders **136 fleet** i.e.,
crowd, company sailing past in the dance. **137 boarded** i.e.,
accosted. (Continuing the nautical metaphor begun in *fleet*.)
138 know become acquainted with **140 break a comparison** i.e.,
make a scornful simile (as in a tilting or breaking of lances) **141 peradventure** if it is **144 leaders** i.e., of the dance. **147 turning** turning
figure in the dance. **157–8 near . . . love** close to my brother.
159 birth aristocratic rank.

165 banquet light repast of fruit, wine, and dessert. **165.1 Manet**
He remains onstage **174 faith . . . blood** loyalty gives way to passion. **175 accident** occurrence **176 mistrusted** suspected **181 willow** (An emblem of disappointed love.) **182 County** count.
182–3 garland i.e., of willow **183 usurer's chain** heavy gold chain,
worn by rich men as if it were a badge of office. **184 scarf** sling.
185 one way one way or the other **187 drover** cattle dealer
188 bullocks oxen. **191 strike . . . man** lash out blindly in every
direction. **191–2 'Twas . . . post** i.e., You're ready to blame anything
but the true cause of your distress. (Benedick seemingly alludes to
some fable about a boy and an innocent postman that demonstrates
this object lesson.) **193 If . . . be** i.e., If you won't leave me as I asked
194–5 creep into sedges i.e., hide himself away, as wounded fowl
creep into rushes along the river. **195–6 know me, and not know
me** i.e., be of my long acquaintance, and yet misjudge me so cruelly.
198–200 It is . . . out It is Beatrice's low and harsh disposition to assume
that she speaks for everyone when she characterizes me this way.

DON PEDRO   Now, signor, where's the Count? Did you see him?

BENEDICK   Troth, my lord, I have played the part of Lady 204 Fame. I found him here as melancholy as a lodge in a 205 warren. I told him, and I think I told him true, that 206 Your Grace had got the good will of this young lady, and I offered him my company to a willow tree, either 208 to make him a garland, as being forsaken, or to bind 209 him up a rod, as being worthy to be whipped.   210

DON PEDRO   To be whipped! What's his fault?

BENEDICK   The flat transgression of a schoolboy, who, 212 being overjoyed with finding a bird's nest, shows it his companion, and he steals it.

DON PEDRO   Wilt thou make a trust a transgression? The 215 transgression is in the stealer.

BENEDICK   Yet it had not been amiss the rod had been made, and the garland too; for the garland he might have worn himself, and the rod he might have bestowed on you, who, as I take it, have stolen his bird's nest.

DON PEDRO   I will but teach them to sing and restore 222 them to the owner.

BENEDICK   If their singing answer your saying, by my 224 faith, you say honestly.

DON PEDRO   The Lady Beatrice hath a quarrel to you. 226 The gentleman that danced with her told her she is much wronged by you.

BENEDICK   Oh, she misused me past the endurance of a block! An oak but with one green leaf on it would have 230 answered her. My very visor began to assume life and scold with her. She told me, not thinking I had been myself, that I was the Prince's jester, that I was duller than a great thaw; huddling jest upon jest with such 234 impossible conveyance upon me that I stood like a 235 man at a mark, with a whole army shooting at me. She 236 speaks poniards, and every word stabs. If her breath 237 were as terrible as her terminations, there were no liv- 238 ing near her; she would infect to the North Star. I 239 would not marry her, though she were endowed with all that Adam had left him before he transgressed. She 241 would have made Hercules have turned spit, yea, and 242 have cleft his club to make the fire, too. Come, talk not 243 of her. You shall find her the infernal Ate in good 244 apparel. I would to God some scholar would conjure 245 her, for certainly, while she is here, a man may live as 246 quiet in hell as in a sanctuary, and people sin upon purpose because they would go thither; so indeed all disquiet, horror, and perturbation follows her.

Enter Claudio and Beatrice.

DON PEDRO   Look, here she comes.

BENEDICK   Will Your Grace command me any service to the world's end? I will go on the slightest errand now to the Antipodes that you can devise to send me on; I 253 will fetch you a toothpicker now from the furthest inch 254 of Asia, bring you the length of Prester John's foot, 255 fetch you a hair off the great Cham's beard, do you any 256 embassage to the Pygmies, rather than hold three 257 words' conference with this harpy. You have no 258 employment for me?

DON PEDRO   None but to desire your good company.

BENEDICK   Oh, God, sir, here's a dish I love not! I cannot endure my Lady Tongue.   *Exit.*

DON PEDRO   Come, lady, come, you have lost the heart of Signor Benedick.

BEATRICE   Indeed, my lord, he lent it me awhile, and I 265 gave him use for it, a double heart for his single one. 266 Marry, once before he won it of me with false dice; 267 therefore Your Grace may well say I have lost it.

DON PEDRO   You have put him down, lady, you have 269 put him down.

BEATRICE   So I would not he should do me, my lord, lest I should prove the mother of fools. I have brought Count Claudio, whom you sent me to seek.

DON PEDRO   Why, how now, Count? Wherefore are you sad?

CLAUDIO   Not sad, my lord.

DON PEDRO   How then? Sick?

CLAUDIO   Neither, my lord.

BEATRICE   The Count is neither sad, nor sick, nor merry, nor well; but civil count, civil as an orange, and some- 280 thing of that jealous complexion.   281

DON PEDRO   I'faith, lady, I think your blazon to be true, 282 though I'll be sworn, if he be so, his conceit is false. 283 Here, Claudio, I have wooed in thy name, and fair

---

204 Troth By my faith   204–5 Lady Fame Dame Rumor
205–6 lodge in a warren isolated gamekeeper's hut in a large game preserve.   208 offered . . . to offered to accompany him to
209–10 bind . . . rod tie several willow switches into a scourge for him   212 flat plain   215 a trust a trusted assignment (here, the Prince's having taken in trust the wooing of Hero for Claudio, not himself)   222 them i.e., the young birds in the nest   224 answer your saying correspond to what you say   226 to with   230 block (of wood).   234 great thaw i.e., time when roads are muddy and impassable, obliging one to stay dully at home.   huddling piling, heaping up   235 impossible conveyance incredible dexterity
236 at a mark at the target, marking where the arrows hit
237 poniards daggers   238 terminations terms, expressions
239 North Star (Popularly supposed to be the most remote of stars.)
241 all . . . him i.e., Paradise before the fall of man   242 Hercules . . . spit (The Amazon Omphale forced the captive Hercules to wear women's clothing and spin; turning the spit would be an even more menial kitchen duty.)   243 cleft split   244 Ate goddess of discord

245 scholar . . . conjure (Scholars were supposed to be able to conjure evil spirits back into hell by addressing them in Latin.)   246 here i.e., on earth. (As long as Beatrice is on earth, hell will seem like a place of refuge.)   253 Antipodes people and region on the opposite side of the earth   254 toothpicker toothpick   255 Prester John a legendary Christian king of the Far East   256 great Cham the Khan of Tartary, ruler of the Mongols   257 Pygmies legendary small race thought to live in India   258 harpy legendary creature with a woman's face and body and a bird's wings and claws.   265–7 he . . . dice (Beatrice refers seemingly to a previous courtship in which she feels that Benedick prevailed over her unfairly, in return for which she now has paid him back with use or interest, two to one.)   269 put him down got the better of him. (But Beatrice plays with the phrase in its literal and sexual sense.)   280 civil serious, grave. (Punning on Seville for the city in Spain whence came bitter-tasting oranges.)   280–1 something somewhat   281 jealous complexion, i.e., yellow, associated with melancholy and symbolic of jealousy.   282 blazon description. (A heraldic term.)   283 conceit (1) notion, idea (2) heraldic device. (Continuing the metaphor of blazon.)

Hero is won. I have broke with her father and his good 285
will obtained. Name the day of marriage, and God
give thee joy!

LEONATO   Count, take of me my daughter and with her
my fortunes. His Grace hath made the match, and all 289
grace say Amen to it. 290

BEATRICE   Speak, Count, 'tis your cue.

CLAUDIO   Silence is the perfectest herald of joy. I were
but little happy if I could say how much!—Lady, as
you are mine, I am yours. I give away myself for you
and dote upon the exchange.

BEATRICE   Speak, cousin, or if you cannot, stop his
mouth with a kiss, and let not him speak neither.
                                    [*Claudio and Hero kiss.*]

DON PEDRO   In faith, lady, you have a merry heart.

BEATRICE   Yea, my lord; I thank it, poor fool, it keeps on
the windy side of care. My cousin tells him in his ear 300
that he is in her heart.

CLAUDIO   And so she doth, cousin.

BEATRICE   Good Lord, for alliance! Thus goes everyone 303
to the world but I, and I am sunburnt. I may sit in a 304
corner and cry, "Heigh-ho for a husband!" 305

DON PEDRO   Lady Beatrice, I will get you one.

BEATRICE   I would rather have one of your father's
getting. Hath Your Grace ne'er a brother like you? 308
Your father got excellent husbands, if a maid could come
by them.

DON PEDRO   Will you have me, lady?

BEATRICE   No, my lord, unless I might have another for
working days. Your Grace is too costly to wear every
day. But I beseech Your Grace, pardon me. I was born
to speak all mirth and no matter. 315

DON PEDRO   Your silence most offends me, and to be
merry best becomes you, for out o' question you were
born in a merry hour.

BEATRICE   No, sure, my lord, my mother cried; but then
there was a star danced, and under that was I born.
Cousins, God give you joy!

LEONATO   Niece, will you look to those things I told you
of?

BEATRICE   I cry you mercy, uncle. [*To Don Pedro*] By Your 324
Grace's pardon.   *Exit Beatrice.* 325

DON PEDRO   By my troth, a pleasant-spirited lady.

LEONATO   There's little of the melancholy element in 327
her, my lord. She is never sad but when she sleeps, and
not ever sad then; for I have heard my daughter say 329
she hath often dreamt of unhappiness and waked 330
herself with laughing.

DON PEDRO   She cannot endure to hear tell of a husband.

LEONATO   Oh, by no means. She mocks all her wooers 333
out of suit. 334

DON PEDRO   She were an excellent wife for Benedick.

LEONATO   Oh, Lord, my lord, if they were but a week
married they would talk themselves mad.

DON PEDRO   County Claudio, when mean you to go to
church?

CLAUDIO   Tomorrow, my lord. Time goes on crutches till
Love have all his rites.

LEONATO   Not till Monday, my dear son, which is hence
a just sevennight and a time too brief, too, to have all 343
things answer my mind. 344

DON PEDRO   Come, you shake the head at so long a
breathing, but I warrant thee, Claudio, the time shall 346
not go dully by us. I will in the interim undertake one
of Hercules' labors, which is to bring Signor Benedick
and the Lady Beatrice into a mountain of affection
th'one with th'other. I would fain have it a match, and 350
I doubt not but to fashion it, if you three will but
minister such assistance as I shall give you direction. 352

LEONATO   My lord, I am for you, though it cost me ten
nights' watchings. 354

CLAUDIO   And I, my lord.

DON PEDRO   And you too, gentle Hero?

HERO   I will do any modest office, my lord, to help my 357
cousin to a good husband.

DON PEDRO   And Benedick is not the unhopefullest hus- 359
band that I know. Thus far can I praise him: he is of a
noble strain, of approved valor and confirmed honesty. 361
I will teach you how to humor your cousin, that she
shall fall in love with Benedick; and I, with your two
helps, will so practice on Benedick that, in despite of
his quick wit and his queasy stomach, he shall fall in 365
love with Beatrice. If we can do this, Cupid is no longer
an archer; his glory shall be ours, for we are the
only love gods. Go in with me, and I will tell you my
drift.   *Exeunt.* 369

❧

[2.2]

Enter [Don] John and Borachio.

DON JOHN   It is so. The Count Claudio shall marry the 1
daughter of Leonato.

BORACHIO   Yea, my lord, but I can cross it. 3

DON JOHN   Any bar, any cross, any impediment will be 4
medicinable to me. I am sick in displeasure to him, 5

---

285 **broke** spoken   289–90 **all . . . to it** i.e., we thank God for this
union.   300 **windy** windward, safe. (In sailing, the ship to windward
has the advantage.)   303 **alliance** relationship by marriage. (Claudio
has just called her "cousin.")   303–4 **goes . . . world** i.e., everyone
gets married   304 **sunburnt** (The Renaissance considered dark complexions unattractive.)   305 **Heigh-ho . . . husband!** (The title of a
ballad.)   308 **getting** begetting. (Playing on *get*, "procure," in the previous speech.)   315 **matter** substance.   324 **cry you mercy** beg your
pardon (for not having obeyed earlier)   324–5 **By . . . pardon** i.e., I
beg you to excuse my departure.   327 **melancholy element** i.e.,
earth, associated with the humor of melancholy in the old physiology
329 **ever** always   330 **unhappiness** misfortune

333–4 **She . . . suit** She discomfits and discourages all her wooers.
343 **a just sevennight** exactly a week   344 **answer my mind** suit my
wishes.   346 **breathing** pause, interval   350 **fain** gladly   352 **minister** furnish, supply   354 **watchings** staying awake.   357 **do . . . office**
play any seemly role   359 **unhopefullest** most unpromising
361 **strain** ancestry. **approved** tested. **honesty** honor.   365 **queasy**
squeamish, delicate (about marriage)   369 **drift** purpose.
2.2. Location: Leonato's house.
1 **shall** is going to   3 **cross** thwart. (Also in line 7.)   4 **bar** obstacle
5 **medicinable** medicinal.   **in displeasure to** with dislike of

and whatsoever comes athwart his affection ranges 6
evenly with mine. How canst thou cross this mar- 7
riage?

BORACHIO   Not honestly, my lord, but so covertly that
no dishonesty shall appear in me.

DON JOHN   Show me briefly how.

BORACHIO   I think I told Your Lordship, a year since, 12
how much I am in the favor of Margaret, the waiting
gentlewoman to Hero.

DON JOHN   I remember.

BORACHIO   I can, at any unseasonable instant of the 16
night, appoint her to look out at her lady's chamber
window.

DON JOHN   What life is in that, to be the death of this
marriage?

BORACHIO   The poison of that lies in you to temper. Go 21
you to the Prince your brother; spare not to tell him
that he hath wronged his honor in marrying the renowned Claudio—whose estimation do you mightily 24
hold up—to a contaminated stale, such a one as Hero. 25

DON JOHN   What proof shall I make of that?

BORACHIO   Proof enough to misuse the Prince, to vex 27
Claudio, to undo Hero, and kill Leonato. Look you for
any other issue? 29

DON JOHN   Only to despite them I will endeavor any- 30
thing.

BORACHIO   Go, then, find me a meet hour to draw Don 32
Pedro and the Count Claudio alone. Tell them that you
know that Hero loves me. Intend a kind of zeal both to 34
the Prince and Claudio, as—in love of your brother's 35
honor, who hath made this match, and his friend's
reputation, who is thus like to be cozened with the 37
semblance of a maid—that you have discovered thus. 38
They will scarcely believe this without trial. Offer
them instances, which shall bear no less likelihood 40
than to see me at her chamber window, hear me call
Margaret Hero, hear Margaret term me Claudio; and 42
bring them to see this the very night before the
intended wedding—for in the meantime I will so
fashion the matter that Hero shall be absent—and
there shall appear such seeming truth of Hero's
disloyalty that jealousy shall be called assurance and 47
all the preparation overthrown. 48

DON JOHN   Grow this to what adverse issue it can, I will 49
put it in practice. Be cunning in the working this, and
thy fee is a thousand ducats. 51

BORACHIO   Be you constant in the accusation, and my
cunning shall not shame me.

DON JOHN   I will presently go learn their day of mar- 54
riage.   *Exit* [*with Borachio*].

❖

[2.3]

Enter Benedick alone.

BENEDICK   Boy!

[*Enter Boy.*]

BOY   Signor?

BENEDICK   In my chamber window lies a book. Bring it
hither to me in the orchard. 4

BOY   I am here already, sir. 5

BENEDICK   I know that, but I would have thee hence and
here again.   *Exit* [*Boy*].
I do much wonder that one man, seeing how much
another man is a fool when he dedicates his behaviors
to love, will, after he hath laughed at such shallow follies in others, become the argument of his own scorn 11
by falling in love; and such a man is Claudio. I have
known when there was no music with him but the 13
drum and the fife, and now had he rather hear the 14
tabor and the pipe. I have known when he would have 15
walked ten mile afoot to see a good armor, and now 16
will he lie ten nights awake carving the fashion of a 17
new doublet. He was wont to speak plain and to the 18
purpose, like an honest man and a soldier, and now is
he turned orthography—his words are a very fantas- 20
tical banquet, just so many strange dishes. May I be so
converted and see with these eyes? I cannot tell; I think
not. I will not be sworn but Love may transform me to
an oyster, but I'll take my oath on it, till he have made
an oyster of me, he shall never make me such a fool.
One woman is fair, yet I am well; another is wise, yet
I am well; another virtuous, yet I am well; but till all
graces be in one woman, one woman shall not come
in my grace. Rich she shall be, that's certain; wise, or
I'll none; virtuous, or I'll never cheapen her; fair, or I'll 30
never look on her; mild, or come not near me; noble, 31
or not I for an angel; of good discourse, an excellent 32
musician, and her hair shall be of what color it please
God. Ha! The Prince and Monsieur Love. I will hide
me in the arbor.   [*He hides.*]

Enter Prince [*Don Pedro*], *Leonato, Claudio.*

DON PEDRO   Come, shall we hear this music?

6–7 whatsoever . . . mine whatever crosses his inclination runs parallel
with mine.   **12 since** ago   **16 unseasonable** unsuitable, unseemly
21 lies in rests with.   **temper** mix, compound.   **24–5 whose . . . up** and
emphasize how much you admire his reputation   **25 stale** prostitute
27 misuse abuse, deceive   **29 issue** outcome. (With a pun on children
as the product of marriage; cf. 4.1.132.)   **30 despite** torture, injure
32 meet suitable   **34 Intend** Pretend   **35 as** i.e., saying as follows. (The
words between the dashes are to be understood as instructions to Don
John as to what he is to say.)   **37 like** likely.   **cozened** deceived,
cheated   **38 semblance** semblance only, outward appearance.
discovered revealed   **40 instances** proofs   **42 hear . . . Claudio** (Many
editors read *Borachio* for *Claudio*. The present reading may be defended
if one imagines that, by arrangement with Margaret, Borachio is playing
the part of Claudio, but the reading may also be an inconsistency.)
47 jealousy suspicion.   **assurance** certainty   **48 preparation** i.e., for
marriage   **49 Grow this** Let this ripen   **51 ducats** gold coins.

54 presently immediately
2.3. Location: Leonato's garden.
4 orchard garden   **5 I . . . already** i.e., I will be so quick as to use no
time at all. (But Benedick quibbles on the literal sense.)   **11 argument**
subject   **13-14 there was . . . fife** i.e., his only commitment was to soldiering   **15 tabor . . . pipe** (Symbols of peaceful merriment and wooing.)   **16 armor** suit of armor   **17 carving** planning   **18 doublet** jacket.
20 turned orthography become fastidious and fashionable in his choice
of language   **30 I'll none** I'll have none of her.   **30 cheapen** make a bid
for. (The idea of lessening her value by using her may also be suggested,
though historically it is a later meaning.)   **31, 32 noble, angel** (Each of
these words involves a pun on the meaning "a coin," a noble being
worth six shillings eightpence and an angel, ten shillings.)

CLAUDIO
  Yea, my good lord. How still the evening is,
  As hushed on purpose to grace harmony!   38
DON PEDRO *[apart to them]*
  See you where Benedick hath hid himself?
CLAUDIO *[apart in reply]*
  Oh, very well, my lord. The music ended,   40
  We'll fit the kid-fox with a pennyworth.   41

      Enter Balthasar with music.

DON PEDRO
  Come, Balthasar, we'll hear that song again.
BALTHASAR
  Oh, good my lord, tax not so bad a voice   43
  To slander music any more than once.
DON PEDRO
  It is the witness still of excellency   45
  To put a strange face on his own perfection.   46
  I pray thee, sing, and let me woo no more.   47
BALTHASAR
  Because you talk of wooing, I will sing,   48
  Since many a wooer doth commence his suit   49
  To her he thinks not worthy, yet he woos,   50
  Yet will he swear he loves.
DON PEDRO   Nay, pray thee, come,   51
  Or if thou wilt hold longer argument,
  Do it in notes.
BALTHASAR   Note this before my notes: 53
  There's not a note of mine that's worth the noting.
DON PEDRO
  Why, these are very crotchets that he speaks!   55
  Note, notes, forsooth, and nothing.   *[Music.]*   56
BENEDICK *[aside]* Now, divine air! Now is his soul rav- 57
ished! Is it not strange that sheeps' guts should hale 58
souls out of men's bodies? Well, a horn for my money, 59
when all's done.

      The Song.

BALTHASAR
    Sigh no more, ladies, sigh no more.
      Men were deceivers ever,
    One foot in sea and one on shore,
      To one thing constant never.

    Then sigh not so, but let them go,
      And be you blithe and bonny,   66
    Converting all your sounds of woe
      Into Hey nonny, nonny.   68

    Sing no more ditties, sing no moe,   69
      Of dumps so dull and heavy;   70
    The fraud of men was ever so,
      Since summer first was leavy.   72
    Then sigh not so, but let them go,
      And be you blithe and bonny,
    Converting all your sounds of woe
      Into Hey nonny, nonny.

DON PEDRO   By my troth, a good song.
BALTHASAR   And an ill singer, my lord.
DON PEDRO   Ha, no, no, faith, thou sing'st well enough
for a shift.   80
BENEDICK *[aside]* An he had been a dog that should 81
have howled thus, they would have hanged him, and
I pray God his bad voice bode no mischief. I has as
lief have heard the night raven, come what plague 84
could have come after it.
DON PEDRO   Yea, marry, dost thou hear, Balthasar? I 86
pray thee, get us some excellent music, for tomorrow
night we would have it at the Lady Hero's chamber
window.
BALTHASAR   The best I can, my lord.
DON PEDRO   Do so. Farewell.   *Exit Balthasar.*
Come hither, Leonato. What was it you told me of
today, that your niece Beatrice was in love with Signor
Benedick?
CLAUDIO   Oh, ay! *[Aside to Pedro]* Stalk on, stalk on; the 95
fowl sits.—I did never think that lady would have 96
loved any man.
LEONATO   No, nor I neither, but most wonderful that she
should so dote on Signor Benedick, whom she hath in
all outward behaviors seemed ever to abhor.
BENEDICK *[aside]* Is't possible? Sits the wind in that 101
corner?   102
LEONATO   By my troth, my lord, I cannot tell what to
think of it but that she loves him with an enraged 104
affection; it is past the infinite of thought.   105
DON PEDRO   Maybe she doth but counterfeit.
CLAUDIO   Faith, like enough.   107
LEONATO   Oh, God, counterfeit? There was never counterfeit of passion came so near the life of passion as she
discovers it.   110
DON PEDRO   Why, what effects of passion shows she?
CLAUDIO *[aside to them]* Bait the hook well; this fish will
bite.

---

38 As as if. **grace harmony** do honor to music. **40 The music ended** When the music is over **41 We'll . . . pennyworth** i.e., we'll give our sly victim more than he bargained for. (A *kid-fox* is presumably a young fox, as in beast fable; *kid*, i.e., young goat, also suggests one whom they are stalking as their quarry. Claudio may be referring to some children's game.) **43 tax** task **45–6 It . . . perfection** It is always characteristic of excellence to pretend not to know its own skill. **47 woo** entreat **48–51 Because . . . he loves** (Balthasar modestly claims to be unworthy of being *wooed,* i.e., entreated, but will comply, since he knows Don Pedro speaks with the hyperbole all wooers use in addressing women they actually consider unworthy.) **53 notes** music. **55 crotchets** (1) whims, fancies (2) musical notes of brief duration **56 nothing** (With a pun on *noting;* the two words were pronounced alike. Compare the same pun in the title of the play, where *Nothing* suggests "noting," or eavesdropping.) **57 air** melody. **58 sheeps' guts** strings on musical instruments. **hale** draw **59 a horn** a hunting horn, a more masculine instrument than a lute. (But with a perhaps unconscious allusion to a cuckold's horns.)

66 blithe and bonny cheerful and carefree **68 Hey nonny, nonny** (A nonsense refrain.) **69 moe** more **70 dumps** mournful songs; also, dances **72 leavy** leafy. **80 for a shift** in a pinch. **81 An** If. (Also in line 161.) **84 lief** willingly. **night raven** a bird of night, portending disaster **86 Yea, marry** (A continuation of Don Pedro's speech preceding Benedick's aside.) **95–6 Stalk . . . sits** i.e., Proceed stealthily; the hunted bird is hiding in the bush. **101–2 Sits . . . corner?** Is that the way the wind is blowing? **104 enraged** maddened with passion **105 infinite** farthest reach. (It's unbelievable but true.) **107 like** likely **110 discovers** betrays

LEONATO   What effects, my lord? She will sit you—you 114
heard my daughter tell you how.

CLAUDIO   She did indeed.

DON PEDRO   How, how, I pray you? You amaze me. I
would have thought her spirit had been invincible
against all assaults of affection.

LEONATO   I would have sworn it had, my lord—especially against Benedick.

BENEDICK [*aside*]   I should think this a gull but that the 122
white-bearded fellow speaks it. Knavery cannot, sure,
hide himself in such reverence.

CLAUDIO [*apart to them*]   He hath ta'en th'infection.
Hold it up.   126

DON PEDRO   Hath she made her affection known to
Benedick?

LEONATO   No, and swears she never will. That's her
torment.

CLAUDIO   'Tis true, indeed. So your daughter says.
"Shall I," says she, "that have so oft encountered him 132
with scorn, write to him that I love him?"

LEONATO   This says she now when she is beginning to
write to him, for she'll be up twenty times a night, and
there will she sit in her smock till she have writ a sheet 136
of paper. My daughter tells us all.

CLAUDIO   Now you talk of a sheet of paper, I remember
a pretty jest your daughter told us of.

LEONATO   Oh, when she had writ it and was reading it
over, she found "Benedick" and "Beatrice" between
the sheet?

CLAUDIO   That.   143

LEONATO   Oh, she tore the letter into a thousand half- 144
pence; railed at herself, that she should be so immod- 145
est to write to one that she knew would flout her. "I 146
measure him," says she, "by my own spirit, for I
should flout him if he writ to me. Yea, though I love
him, I should."

CLAUDIO   Then down upon her knees she falls, weeps,
sobs, beats her heart, tears her hair, prays, curses: "O
sweet Benedick! God give me patience!"

LEONATO   She doth indeed; my daughter says so. And
the ecstasy hath so much overborne her that my 154
daughter is sometime afeard she will do a desperate
outrage to herself. It is very true.

DON PEDRO   It were good that Benedick knew of it by
some other, if she will not discover it.   158

CLAUDIO   To what end? He would make but a sport of
it and torment the poor lady worse.

DON PEDRO   An he should, it were an alms to hang him. 161
She's an excellent sweet lady, and, out of all suspicion, 162
she is virtuous.

CLAUDIO   And she is exceeding wise.

DON PEDRO   In everything but in loving Benedick.

LEONATO   O my lord, wisdom and blood combating in 166

so tender a body, we have ten proofs to one that blood
hath the victory. I am sorry for her, as I have just
cause, being her uncle and her guardian.

DON PEDRO   I would she had bestowed this dotage on 170
me. I would have doffed all other respects and made 171
her half myself. I pray you, tell Benedick of it, and hear 172
what 'a will say.

LEONATO   Were it good, think you?

CLAUDIO   Hero thinks surely she will die; for she says
she will die if he love her not, and she will die ere she
make her love known, and she will die if he woo her,
rather than she will bate one breath of her accustomed 178
crossness.   179

DON PEDRO   She doth well. If she should make tender 180
of her love, 'tis very possible he'll scorn it; for the man,
as you know all, hath a contemptible spirit.   182

CLAUDIO   He is a very proper man.   183

DON PEDRO   He hath indeed a good outward happiness. 184

CLAUDIO   Before God, and in my mind, very wise.   185

DON PEDRO   He doth indeed show some sparks that are
like wit.

CLAUDIO   And I take him to be valiant.

DON PEDRO   As Hector, I assure you; and in the manag- 189
ing of quarrels you may say he is wise, for either he
avoids them with great discretion or undertakes them
with a most Christian-like fear.

LEONATO   If he do fear God, 'a must necessarily keep
peace. If he break the peace, he ought to enter into a
quarrel with fear and trembling.

DON PEDRO   And so will he do, for the man doth fear
God, howsoever it seems not in him by some large 197
jests he will make. Well, I am sorry for your niece. Shall
we go seek Benedick and tell him of her love?

CLAUDIO   Never tell him, my lord. Let her wear it out 200
with good counsel.   201

LEONATO   Nay, that's impossible. She may wear her
heart out first.

DON PEDRO   Well, we will hear further of it by your
daughter. Let it cool the while. I love Benedick well,
and I could wish he would modestly examine himself,
to see how much he is unworthy so good a lady.

LEONATO   My lord, will you walk? Dinner is ready.

[*They walk aside.*]

CLAUDIO   If he do not dote on her upon this, I will never 209
trust my expectation.

DON PEDRO   Let there be the same net spread for her;
and that must your daughter and her gentlewomen
carry. The sport will be when they hold one an opinion 213
of another's dotage, and no such matter; that's the 214

114 **sit you** i.e., sit. (*You* is used idiomatically.)   122 **gull** trick, deception.   **but** except for the fact   126 **Hold it up** Keep up the jest.
132 **she** i.e., Beatrice   136 **smock** chemise   143 **That** i.e., That's it.
144–5 **halfpence** i.e., small pieces   146 **flout** mock   154 **overborne**
overwhelmed   158 **discover** reveal   161 **alms** good deed. (Hanging
would be too good for him.)   162 **out of** beyond   166 **blood** natural
feeling

170 **dotage** doting affection   171 **doffed** put or turned aside.
respects considerations   172 **half myself** i.e., my wife.   178 **bate**
abate   179 **crossness** perversity, contrariety.   180 **tender** offer
182 **contemptible** contemptuous   183 **proper** handsome   184 **outward happiness** fortune in his good looks.   185 **Before God** i.e., By
God, you're absolutely right   189 **Hector** the mightiest of the Trojans   197 **by** to judge by.   **large** broad, indelicate   200 **wear it out**
eradicate it   201 **counsel** reflection, deliberation.   209 **upon** as a
result of, after   213 **carry** carry out.   213–14 **they . . . dotage** each
believes the other to be in love   214 **no such matter** the reality is
quite otherwise

scene that I would see, which will be merely a dumb 215
show. Let us send her to call him in to dinner. 216

[*Exeunt Don Pedro, Claudio, and Leonato.*]

BENEDICK [*coming forward*]   This can be no trick. The
conference was sadly borne. They have the truth of 218
this from Hero. They seem to pity the lady. It seems
her affections have their full bent. Love me? Why, it 220
must be requited. I hear how I am censured. They say
I will bear myself proudly if I perceive the love come
from her; they say too that she will rather die than give
any sign of affection. I did never think to marry. I must
not seem proud; happy are they that hear their detrac- 225
tions and can put them to mending. They say the lady 226
is fair; 'tis a truth, I can bear them witness; and virtuous; 'tis so, I cannot reprove it; and wise but for loving 228
me; by my troth, it is no addition to her wit, nor no
great argument of her folly, for I will be horribly in
love with her. I may chance have some odd quirks and 231
remnants of wit broken on me, because I have railed
so long against marriage. But doth not the appetite
alter? A man loves the meat in his youth that he cannot endure in his age. Shall quips and sentences and 235
these paper bullets of the brain awe a man from the 236
career of his humor? No, the world must be peopled. 237
When I said I would die a bachelor, I did not think I
should live till I were married. Here comes Beatrice.
By this day, she's a fair lady! I do spy some marks of
love in her.

Enter Beatrice.

BEATRICE   Against my will I am sent to bid you come in
to dinner.
BENEDICK   Fair Beatrice, I thank you for your pains.
BEATRICE   I took no more pains for those thanks than
you take pains to thank me. If it had been painful I
would not have come.
BENEDICK   You take pleasure then in the message?
BEATRICE   Yea, just so much as you may take upon a 249
knife's point and choke a daw withal. You have no 250
stomach, signor. Fare you well.   *Exit.* 251
BENEDICK   Ha! "Against my will I am sent to bid you
come in to dinner." There's a double meaning in that.
"I took no more pains for those thanks than you took
pains to thank me." That's as much as to say, "Any
pains that I take for you is as easy as thanks." If I do
not take pity of her, I am a villain; if I do not love her,
I am a Jew. I will go get her picture.   *Exit.*

215–16 dumb show pantomime (lacking their usual banter)
218 sadly borne soberly conducted.   **220 have . . . bent** i.e., are fully
engaged. (The image is of a bow pulled taut.)   **225–6 that . . . mending** that can hear themselves criticized and undertake to remedy the
defect.   **228 reprove** refute   **231 quirks** witty conceits or jokes
235 sentences saws, maxims   **236 paper bullets** i.e., words
237 career of his humor pursuit of his inclination. (In horsemanship,
a *career* is a short gallop.)   **249–50 just . . . withal** i.e., very little. (A
daw or jackdaw is a common blackbird, smaller than a crow.)
251 stomach appetite

[3.1]

*Enter Hero and two gentlewomen, Margaret
and Ursula.*

HERO
Good Margaret, run thee to the parlor.
There shalt thou find my cousin Beatrice
Proposing with the Prince and Claudio.   3
Whisper her ear and tell her I and Ursley   4
Walk in the orchard, and our whole discourse
Is all of her. Say that thou overheard'st us,
And bid her steal into the pleachèd bower,   7
Where honeysuckles, ripened by the sun,
Forbid the sun to enter, like favorites,
Made proud by princes, that advance their pride   10
Against that power that bred it. There will she hide
  her,   11
To listen our propose. This is thy office.   12
Bear thee well in it and leave us alone.   13
MARGARET
I'll make her come, I warrant you, presently.   [*Exit.*] 14
HERO
Now, Ursula, when Beatrice doth come,
As we do trace this alley up and down,   16
Our talk must only be of Benedick.
When I do name him, let it be thy part
To praise him more than ever man did merit.
My talk to thee must be how Benedick
Is sick in love with Beatrice. Of this matter
Is little Cupid's crafty arrow made,
That only wounds by hearsay.

Enter Beatrice [behind].

                              Now begin,   23
For look where Beatrice, like a lapwing, runs   24
Close by the ground, to hear our conference.
URSULA [*to Hero*]
The pleasant'st angling is to see the fish
Cut with her golden oars the silver stream   27
And greedily devour the treacherous bait.
So angle we for Beatrice, who even now
Is couchèd in the woodbine coverture.   30
Fear you not my part of the dialogue.   31
HERO [*to Ursula*]
Then go we near her, that her ear lose nothing
Of the false sweet bait that we lay for it.
                        [*They approach the bower.*]
No, truly, Ursula, she is too disdainful;
I know her spirits are as coy and wild   35
As haggards of the rock.
URSULA   But are you sure   36

3.1 Location: Leonato's garden.
3 Proposing conversing   **4 Ursley** (A nickname for *Ursula*)
7 pleachèd formed by densely interwoven branches   **10–11 that . . . it**
i.e., who dare set themselves up against the very princes who advanced
them.   **12 listen our propose** listen to our conversation.   **office** responsibility.   **13 leave us alone** leave the rest to us.   **14 presently** immediately.   **16 trace** walk   **23 only . . . hearsay** wounds by mere report.
24 lapwing bird of the plover family   **27 oars** i.e., fins   **30 Is . . . coverture** is hid in the honeysuckle bower.   **31 Fear . . . dialogue** Don't worry
about my not holding up my part in the conversation.   **35 coy** disdainful   **36 As . . . rock** as untamed female hawks in mountainous terrain.

That Benedick loves Beatrice so entirely?

HERO
So says the Prince and my new-trothèd lord.

URSULA
And did they bid you tell her of it, madam?

HERO
They did entreat me to acquaint her of it;
But I persuaded them, if they loved Benedick,
To wish him wrestle with affection
And never to let Beatrice know of it.

URSULA
Why did you so? Doth not the gentleman
Deserve as full as fortunate a bed   45
As ever Beatrice shall couch upon?   46

HERO
O god of love! I know he doth deserve
As much as may be yielded to a man;
But Nature never framed a woman's heart
Of prouder stuff than that of Beatrice.
Disdain and scorn ride sparkling in her eyes,
Misprizing what they look on, and her wit   52
Values itself so highly that to her
All matter else seems weak. She cannot love,   54
Nor take no shape nor project of affection,   55
She is so self-endearèd.

URSULA   Sure I think so,   56
And therefore certainly it were not good
She knew his love, lest she'll make sport at it.

HERO
Why, you speak truth. I never yet saw man,
How wise, how noble, young, how rarely featured,   60
But she would spell him backward. If fair-faced,   61
She would swear the gentleman should be her
   sister;
If black, why, Nature, drawing of an antic,   63
Made a foul blot; if tall, a lance ill-headed;
If low, an agate very vilely cut;   65
If speaking, why, a vane blown with all winds;
If silent, why, a block movèd with none.
So turns she every man the wrong side out
And never gives to truth and virtue that
Which simpleness and merit purchaseth.   70

URSULA
Sure, sure, such carping is not commendable.

HERO
No, not to be so odd and from all fashions   72
As Beatrice is cannot be commendable.
But who dare tell her so? If I should speak,
She would mock me into air; oh, she would laugh me   75
Out of myself, press me to death with wit.   76

Therefore let Benedick, like covered fire,
Consume away in sighs, waste inwardly.   78
It were a better death than die with mocks,
Which is as bad as die with tickling.

URSULA
Yet tell her of it. Hear what she will say.

HERO
No, rather I will go to Benedick
And counsel him to fight against his passion.
And truly, I'll devise some honest slanders   84
To stain my cousin with. One doth not know
How much an ill word may empoison liking.

URSULA
Oh, do not do your cousin such a wrong!
She cannot be so much without true judgment—
Having so swift and excellent a wit
As she is prized to have—as to refuse   90
So rare a gentleman as Signor Benedick.

HERO
He is the only man of Italy,
Always excepted my dear Claudio.

URSULA
I pray you, be not angry with me, madam,
Speaking my fancy: Signor Benedick,
For shape, for bearing, argument, and valor,   96
Goes foremost in report through Italy.

HERO
Indeed, he hath an excellent good name.

URSULA
His excellence did earn it ere he had it.
When are you married, madam?

HERO
Why, every day, tomorrow. Come, go in.   101
I'll show thee some attires and have thy counsel
Which is the best to furnish me tomorrow.
                              [They walk away.]

URSULA [to Hero]
She's limed, I warrant you. We have caught her,
   madam.   104

HERO [to Ursula]
If it prove so, then loving goes by haps;   105
Some Cupid kills with arrows, some with traps.   106
                    [Exeunt Hero and Ursula.]

BEATRICE [coming forward]
What fire is in mine ears? Can this be true?   107
   Stand I condemned for pride and scorn so much?
Contempt, farewell, and maiden pride, adieu!
   No glory lives behind the back of such.   110
And Benedick, love on; I will requite thee,
   Taming my wild heart to thy loving hand.   112

45–6 as full . . . upon i.e., as good a wife as Beatrice. 52 Misprizing
undervaluing, despising 54 weak unimportant. 55 project conception,
idea 56 self-endearèd full of self-love. 60 How however.
rarely excellently 61 spell him backward i.e., speak contrarily of
him by characterizing his virtues as vices. 63 black dark. antic
buffoon, grotesque figure 65 agate i.e., diminutive person. (Alluding to the small figures cut in agate for rings.) 70 simpleness
integrity, plainness. purchaseth earn, deserve. 72 from contrary to
75–6 she . . . myself she would mockingly put me down 76 press
me to death (Pressing to death with weights was the usual punishment for those accused of crimes who refused to plead either guilty
or not guilty.)

78 Consume . . . sighs (An allusion to the belief that each sigh cost the
heart a drop of blood.) 84 honest slanders i.e., slanders that do not
involve her virtue 90 prized esteemed 96 argument skill in discourse 101 every day, tomorrow tomorrow and every day thereafter. 104 limed caught, like a bird in birdlime, a sticky substance
spread on branches to trap the birds that perch on them 105 by haps
by chance 106 Some Cupid kills Cupid kills some 107 What . . .
ears? (An allusion to the old saying that a person's ears burn when
one is being discussed in one's absence.) 110 No . . . such Nothing is
gained by hiding behind such defenses. 112 Taming . . . hand
(A figure derived from the taming of the hawk by the hand of
the falconer.)

If thou dost love, my kindness shall incite thee
  To bind our loves up in a holy band;   114
For others say thou dost deserve, and I
  Believe it better than reportingly.   *Exit.*   116

❖

[3.2]

*Enter Prince [Don Pedro], Claudio, Benedick,
and Leonato.*

DON PEDRO   I do but stay till your marriage be con-   1
  summate, and then go I toward Aragon.   2
CLAUDIO   I'll bring you thither, my lord, if you'll   3
  vouchsafe me.   4
DON PEDRO   Nay, that would be as great a soil in the   5
  new gloss of your marriage as to show a child his new
  coat and forbid him to wear it. I will only be bold with   7
  Benedick for his company, for from the crown of his
  head to the sole of his foot he is all mirth. He hath
  twice or thrice cut Cupid's bowstring, and the little
  hangman dare not shoot at him. He hath a heart as   11
  sound as a bell, and his tongue is the clapper, for what
  his heart thinks his tongue speaks.
BENEDICK   Gallants, I am not as I have been.
LEONATO   So say I. Methinks you are sadder.   15
CLAUDIO   I hope he be in love.
DON PEDRO   Hang him, truant! There's no true drop of   17
  blood in him, to be truly touched with love. If he be
  sad, he wants money.   19
BENEDICK   I have the toothache.   20
DON PEDRO   Draw it.   21
BENEDICK   Hang it!   22
CLAUDIO   You must hang it first and draw it after-
  wards.
DON PEDRO   What, sigh for the toothache?
LEONATO   Where is but a humor or a worm.   26
BENEDICK   Well, everyone can master a grief but he that   27
  has it.
CLAUDIO   Yet say I, he is in love.
DON PEDRO   There is no appearance of fancy in him,   30
  unless it be a fancy that he hath to strange disguises;   31
  as, to be a Dutchman today, a Frenchman tomorrow,
  or in the shape of two countries at once, as, a German
  from the waist downward, all slops, and a Spaniard   34
  from the hip upward, no doublet. Unless he have a   35

fancy to this foolery, as it appears he hath, he is no fool   36
  for fancy, as you would have it appear he is.   37
CLAUDIO   If he be not in love with some woman, there
  is no believing old signs. 'A brushes his hat o'
  mornings. What should that bode?
DON PEDRO   Hath any man seen him at the barber's?
CLAUDIO   No, but the barber's man hath been seen with
  him, and the old ornament of his cheek hath already   43
  stuffed tennis balls.   44
LEONATO   Indeed he looks younger than he did by the
  loss of a beard.
DON PEDRO   Nay, 'a rubs himself with civet. Can you   47
  smell him out by that?   48
CLAUDIO   That's as much as to say the sweet youth's in
  love.
DON PEDRO   The greatest note of it is his melancholy. 51
CLAUDIO   And when was he wont to wash his face?   52
DON PEDRO   Yea, or to paint himself? For the which I   53
  hear what they say of him.   54
CLAUDIO   Nay, but his jesting spirit, which is now crept
  into a lute string and now governed by stops.   56
DON PEDRO   Indeed, that tells a heavy tale for him.
  Conclude, conclude he is in love.
CLAUDIO   Nay, but I know who loves him.
DON PEDRO   That would I know too. I warrant, one that
  knows him not.
CLAUDIO   Yes, and his ill conditions; and, in despite of   62
  all, dies for him.
DON PEDRO   She shall be buried with her face upwards. 64
BENEDICK   Yet is this no charm for the toothache. Old
  signor, walk aside with me. I have studied eight or
  nine wise words to speak to you, which these hobby-   67
  horses must not hear.   [*Exeunt Benedick and Leonato.*]   68
DON PEDRO   For my life, to break with him about   69
  Beatrice.
CLAUDIO   'Tis even so. Hero and Margaret have by this 71
  played their parts with Beatrice, and then the two
  bears will not bite one another when they meet.

Enter [Don] John the Bastard.

DON JOHN   My lord and brother, God save you!
DON PEDRO   Good e'en, brother.   75
DON JOHN   If your leisure served, I would speak with
  you.
DON PEDRO   In private?

---

114 band bond   **116 better than reportingly** on better evidence than
mere report
3.2. Location: Leonato's house.
1–2 consummate consummated   **3 bring** escort   **4 vouchsafe** allow
5 soil stain   **7 be bold with** ask   **11 hangman** executioner; rogue.
(Playfully applied to Cupid.)   **15 sadder** more serious.   **17 truant**
i.e., from love.   **19 wants** lacks   **20 toothache** (Thought to be a common ailment of lovers.)   **21 Draw** Extract. (But Claudio jokes on the
method of executing traitors, who were hanged first and then cut
down alive and drawn, i.e., disemboweled, and finally quartered.)
22 Hang it! Confound it!   **26 Where** Where there.   **humor or a
worm** (A toothache was ascribed to "humors," or unhealthy secre-
tions, and to actual worms in the teeth.)   **27 grief** pain.   **but** except
30 fancy love   **31 fancy** whim, liking   **34 slops** loose breeches
35 no doublet i.e., with a hip-length cloak in place of, or covering, the
close-fitting doublet.

36–7 fool for fancy i.e., lover   **43–4 the old . . . tennis balls** i.e.,
Benedick's beard has gone to stuff tennis balls. (He appears onstage
beardless in this scene for the first time.)   **47 civet** perfume derived
from the civet cat.   **48 smell him out** (1) discern his secret (2) smell
him coming   **51 note** mark   **52 wont** accustomed.   **wash** i.e., with
cosmetics; similarly with *paint* in the next line   **53–4 For . . . him**
That's what I hear people saying about him.   **56 stops** (1) frets on the
fingerboard (2) restraints.   **62 ill conditions** bad qualities   **64 buried
. . . upwards** i.e., as the faithful, not as a suicide, who were sometimes
buried face downwards (?). (There is also a sexual suggestion of her
being smothered under Benedick, continuing the joke on *dies for him*,
meaning to have an orgasm.)   **67–8 hobbyhorses** i.e., buffoons.
(Originally, figures in a morris dance made to resemble a horse and
rider.)   **69 For** Upon.   **break** speak   **71 Margaret** (Ursula joined
Hero in playing the trick on Beatrice, but Margaret has been in on it.)
75 e'en evening, i.e., afternoon

DON JOHN   If it please you. Yet Count Claudio may hear, for what I would speak of concerns him.

DON PEDRO   What's the matter?

DON JOHN   [to Claudio]   Means Your Lordship to be married tomorrow?

DON PEDRO   You know he does.

DON JOHN   I know not that, when he knows what I know.

CLAUDIO   If there be any impediment, I pray you discover it.   88

DON JOHN   You may think I love you not. Let that appear hereafter, and aim better at me by that I now   90 will manifest. For my brother, I think he holds you   91 well and in dearness of heart hath holp to effect your   92 ensuing marriage—surely suit ill spent and labor ill bestowed.

DON PEDRO   Why, what's the matter?

DON JOHN   I came hither to tell you, and, circumstances   96 shortened—for she has been too long a-talking of—   97 the lady is disloyal.   98

CLAUDIO   Who, Hero?

DON JOHN   Even she—Leonato's Hero, your Hero, every man's Hero.

CLAUDIO   Disloyal?

DON JOHN   The word is too good to paint out her   103 wickedness. I could say she were worse; think you of a worse title, and I will fit her to it. Wonder not till fur-   105 ther warrant. Go but with me tonight, you shall see her   106 chamber window entered, even the night before her wedding day. If you love her then, tomorrow wed her; but it would better fit your honor to change your mind.

CLAUDIO   May this be so?

DON PEDRO   I will not think it.

DON JOHN   If you dare not trust that you see, confess not   113 that you know. If you will follow me, I will show you   114 enough; and when you have seen more and heard more, proceed accordingly.

CLAUDIO   If I see anything tonight why I should not marry her, tomorrow in the congregation, where I should wed, there will I shame her.

DON PEDRO   And, as I wooed for thee to obtain her, I will join with thee to disgrace her.

DON JOHN   I will disparage her no farther till you are my witnesses. Bear it coldly but till midnight, and let the   123 issue show itself.   124

DON PEDRO   O day untowardly turned!   125

CLAUDIO   O mischief strangely thwarting!

DON JOHN   O plague right well prevented! So will you say when you have seen the sequel.   [Exeunt.]

❧

[3.3]

Enter Dogberry and his compartner [Verges] with the Watch.

DOGBERRY   Are you good men and true?

VERGES   Yea, or else it were pity but they should suffer salvation, body and soul.   3

DOGBERRY   Nay, that were a punishment too good for them, if they should have any allegiance in them,   5 being chosen for the Prince's watch.

VERGES   Well, give them their charge, neighbor Dog-   7 berry.

DOGBERRY   First, who think you the most desartless   9 man to be constable?

FIRST WATCH   Hugh Oatcake, sir, or George Seacoal, for they can write and read.

DOGBERRY   Come hither, neighbor Seacoal. [*Seacoal, or Second Watch, steps forward.*] God hath blessed you with a good name. To be a well-favored man is the gift   15 of fortune, but to write and read comes by nature.

SEACOAL   Both which, Master Constable—

DOGBERRY   You have. I knew it would be your answer. Well, for your favor, sir, why, give God thanks, and make no boast of it; and for your writing and reading, let that appear when there is no need of such vanity. You are thought here to be the most senseless and fit   22 man for the constable of the watch; therefore bear you the lantern. This is your charge: you shall comprehend   24 all vagrom men; you are to bid any man stand, in the   25 Prince's name.

SEACOAL   How if 'a will not stand?

DOGBERRY   Why, then, take no note of him, but let him go, and presently call the rest of the watch together and thank God you are rid of a knave.

VERGES   If he will not stand when he is bidden, he is none of the Prince's subjects.

DOGBERRY   True, and they are to meddle with none but the Prince's subjects. You shall also make no noise in the streets; for, for the watch to babble and to talk is most tolerable and not to be endured.   36

WATCH   We will rather sleep than talk. We know what belongs to a watch.   38

DOGBERRY   Why, you speak like an ancient and most   39 quiet watchman, for I cannot see how sleeping should offend. Only have a care that your bills be not stolen.   41 Well, you are to call at all the alehouses and bid those that are drunk get them to bed.

WATCH   How if they will not?

---

88 **discover** reveal   90 **aim better at** judge better of.   **that** that which 91–2 **holds you well** thinks well of you   92 **holp** helped   96–7 **circumstances shortened** without unnecessary details   97 **a-talking of** under discussion (by us)   98 **disloyal** unfaithful.   103 **paint out** portray in full   105–6 **till further warrant** till further proof appears. 113–14 **If . . . know** i.e., If you are unwilling to believe what you see, then don't claim to know the truth.   123 **coldly** calmly   124 **issue** outcome   125 **untowardly turned** wretchedly altered

3.3. Location: A street.
3 salvation (A blunder for "damnation.")   **5 allegiance** (For "treachery.")   **7 charge** instructions   **9 desartless** (For "deserving.") **15 a good name** (Sea coal was high-grade coal shipped from Newcastle, not the charcoal usually sold by London colliers.)   **well-favored** good-looking   **22 senseless** (For "sensible.")   **24 comprehend** (For "apprehend.")   **25 vagrom** vagrant.   **stand** stand still, stop   **36 tolerable** (For "intolerable.")   **37 WATCH** (Here and at lines 44, 48, 53, and 66 Shakespeare's text does not specify which watchman speaks. These lines are sometimes assigned to the Second Watch, Seacoal, but could be spoken by others of the watch.)   **38 belongs to** are the duties of   **39 ancient** venerable, experienced   **41 bills** pikes, with axes fixed to long poles

DOGBERRY   Why, then, let them alone till they are sober. If they make you not then the better answer, you may say they are not the men you took them for.

WATCH   Well, sir.

DOGBERRY   If you meet a thief, you may suspect him, by virtue of your office, to be no true man; and for such 50 kind of men, the less you meddle or make with them, 51 why, the more is for your honesty. 52

WATCH   If we know him to be a thief, shall we not lay hands on him?

DOGBERRY   Truly, by your office you may, but I think they that touch pitch will be defiled. The most 56 peaceable way for you, if you do take a thief, is to let him show himself what he is and steal out of your company.

VERGES   You have been always called a merciful man, partner.

DOGBERRY   Truly, I would not hang a dog by my will, much more a man who hath any honesty in him.

VERGES   If you hear a child cry in the night, you must call to the nurse and bid her still it.

WATCH   How if the nurse be asleep and will not hear us?

DOGBERRY   Why, then, depart in peace and let the child wake her with crying, for the ewe that will not hear her lamb when it baas will never answer a calf when he bleats.

VERGES   'Tis very true.

DOGBERRY   This is the end of the charge: you, Constable, are to present the Prince's own person. If you meet 74 the Prince in the night, you may stay him. 76

VERGES   Nay, by'r Lady, that I think 'a cannot.

DOGBERRY   Five shillings to one on't, with any man that knows the statutes, he may stay him; marry, not without the Prince be willing, for indeed the watch ought to offend no man, and it is an offense to stay a man against his will.

VERGES   By'r Lady, I think it be so.

DOGBERRY   Ha, ah ha! Well, masters, good night. An there be any matter of weight chances, call up me. Keep your fellows' counsels and your own, and good night. Come, neighbor. [*He starts to leave with Verges.*]

SEACOAL   Well, masters, we hear our charge. Let us go sit here upon the church bench till two, and then all to bed.

DOGBERRY   One word more, honest neighbors. I pray you, watch about Signor Leonato's door, for the wedding being there tomorrow, there is a great coil 92 tonight. Adieu. Be vigitant, I beseech you. 93

Exeunt [*Dogberry and Verges*].

Enter Borachio and Conrade.

BORACHIO   What, Conrade!

SEACOAL [*aside*]   Peace! Stir not.

BORACHIO   Conrade, I say!

CONRADE   Here, man. I am at thy elbow.

BORACHIO   Mass, and my elbow itched; I thought there 98 would a scab follow. 99

CONRADE   I will owe thee an answer for that. And now, 100 forward with thy tale.

BORACHIO   Stand thee close, then, under this penthouse, 102 for it drizzles rain, and I will, like a true drunkard, 103 utter all to thee.

SEACOAL [*aside*]   Some treason, masters. Yet stand 105 close. 106

BORACHIO   Therefore know I have earned of Don John a thousand ducats.

CONRADE   Is it possible that any villainy should be so dear? 110

BORACHIO   Thou shouldst rather ask if it were possible any villainy should be so rich; for when rich villains 112 have need of poor ones, poor ones may make what price they will.

CONRADE   I wonder at it.

BORACHIO   That shows thou art unconfirmed. Thou 116 knowest that the fashion of a doublet, or a hat, or a cloak, is nothing to a man. 118

CONRADE   Yes, it is apparel.

BORACHIO   I mean, the fashion. 120

CONRADE   Yes, the fashion is the fashion.

BORACHIO   Tush, I may as well say the fool's fool. But see'st thou not what a deformed thief this fashion 123 is?

SEACOAL [*aside*]   I know that Deformed. 'A has been a vile thief this seven year; 'a goes up and down like a 126 gentleman. I remember his name.

BORACHIO   Didst thou not hear somebody?

CONRADE   No, 'twas the vane on the house.

BORACHIO   See'st thou not, I say, what a deformed thief this fashion is, how giddily 'a turns about all the hot bloods between fourteen and five-and-thirty, sometimes fashioning them like Pharaoh's soldiers in the reechy painting, sometime like god Bel's priests in the 134 old church-window, sometime like the shaven 135 Hercules in the smirched worm-eaten tapestry, where 136 his codpiece seems as massy as his club? 137

---

98 Mass i.e., By the Mass.   **my elbow itched** (Proverbially, a warning against questionable companions.)   **99 scab** i.e., scoundrel. (With play on literal meaning.)   **100 owe thee an answer** answer later   **102 penthouse** overhanging structure   **103 true drunkard** (Alludes to the commonplace that the drunkard tells all; Borachio's name in Spanish means "drunkard.")   **105–6 stand close** stay hidden.   **110 dear** expensive.   **112 rich** well-paid   **116 unconfirmed** inexperienced.   **118 is . . . man** does not make the man. (But Conrade plays on the phrase in the sense of "means nothing to a man.")   **120 I . . . fashion** i.e., My emphasis was on the mere fashion, not on the apparel itself. (But Conrade wittily refuses to allow the difference.)   **123 deformed thief** i.e., so called because fashion takes such varied and extreme shapes and because it impoverishes those who follow fashion   **126 up and down** about, here and there   **134 reechy** dirty, grimy. (Perhaps this painting is of the Israelites passing through the Red Sea.)   **god Bel's priests** (Probably alludes to the story of Bel and the Dragon, from the apocryphal Book of Daniel, depicted in a stained-glass window.)   **135–6 shaven Hercules** (A reference either to young Hercules at the crossroads, choosing between virtue and vice, or in the service of Omphale—see 2.1.242, note—or, confusedly, to the story of Samson.)   **137 codpiece** decorative pouch at the front of a man's breeches (indelicately conspicuous in this tapestry)

---

50 true honest   **51 meddle or make** have to do   **52 is** it is   **56 they . . . defiled** (A commonplace, derived from Ecclesiasticus 13:1.)   **74 present** represent   **76 by'r Lady** i.e., by Our Lady. (A mild oath.)   **92 coil** to-do   **93 vigitant** (For "vigilant.")

CONRADE   All this I see, and I see that the fashion wears 138
out more apparel than the man. But art not thou 139
thyself giddy with the fashion, too, that thou hast
shifted out of thy tale into telling me of the fashion?

BORACHIO   Not so, neither. But know that I have tonight
wooed Margaret, the Lady Hero's gentlewoman, by
the name of Hero. She leans me out at her mistress' 144
chamber window, bids me a thousand times good
night—I tell this tale vilely; I should first tell thee how
the Prince, Claudio, and my master, planted and
placed and possessed by my master Don John, saw 148
afar off in the orchard this amiable encounter. 149

CONRADE   And thought they Margaret was Hero?

BORACHIO   Two of them did, the Prince and Claudio,
but the devil my master knew she was Margaret; and
partly by his oaths, which first possessed them, partly
by the dark night, which did deceive them, but chiefly
by my villainy, which did confirm any slander that
Don John had made, away went Claudio enraged;
swore he would meet her, as he was appointed, next
morning at the temple, and there, before the whole
congregation, shame her with what he saw o'ernight
and send her home again without a husband.

SEACOAL   We charge you, in the Prince's name, stand!

FIRST WATCH   Call up the Right Master Constable. We 162
have here recovered the most dangerous piece of 163
lechery that ever was known in the commonwealth. 164

SEACOAL   And one Deformed is one of them. I know
him; 'a wears a lock. 166

CONRADE   Masters, masters—

FIRST WATCH   You'll be made bring Deformed forth, I
warrant you.

CONRADE   Masters—

SEACOAL   Never speak, we charge you. Let us obey you 171
to go with us.

BORACHIO   We are like to prove a goodly commodity, 173
being taken up of these men's bills. 174

CONRADE   A commodity in question, I warrant you. 175
Come, we'll obey you.   *Exeunt.*

❖

[3.4]

Enter Hero, and Margaret and Ursula.

HERO   Good Ursula, wake my cousin Beatrice, and
desire her to rise.

URSULA   I will, lady.

HERO   And bid her come hither.

URSULA   Well.   [*Exit.*] 5

MARGARET   Troth, I think your other rabato were better. 6

HERO   No, pray thee, good Meg, I'll wear this.

MARGARET   By my troth, 's not so good, and I warrant 8
your cousin will say so.

HERO   My cousin's a fool, and thou art another. I'll wear
none but this.

MARGARET   I like the new tire within excellently, if the 12
hair were a thought browner; and your gown's a most 13
rare fashion, i'faith. I saw the Duchess of Milan's gown
that they praise so.

HERO   Oh, that exceeds, they say. 16

MARGARET   By my troth, 's but a nightgown in respect 17
of yours: cloth o' gold, and cuts, and laced with silver, 18
set with pearls, down sleeves, side sleeves, and skirts, 19
round underborne with a bluish tinsel. But for a fine, 20
quaint, graceful, and excellent fashion, yours is worth 21
ten on't. 22

HERO   God give me joy to wear it! For my heart is
exceeding heavy.

MARGARET   'Twill be heavier soon by the weight of a
man.

HERO   Fie upon thee! Art not ashamed?

MARGARET   Of what, lady? Of speaking honorably? Is
not marriage honorable in a beggar? Is not your lord 29
honorable without marriage? I think you would have
me say, "saving your reverence, a husband." An bad 31
thinking do not wrest true speaking, I'll offend 32
nobody. Is there any harm in "the heavier for a husband"? None, I think, an it be the right husband and
the right wife; otherwise 'tis light, and not heavy. Ask 35
my Lady Beatrice else. Here she comes.

Enter Beatrice.

HERO   Good morrow, coz.

BEATRICE   Good morrow, sweet Hero.

HERO   Why, how now? Do you speak in the sick tune? 39

BEATRICE   I am out of all other tune, methinks.

MARGARET   Clap 's into "Light o 'love." That goes 41
without a burden; do you sing it, and I'll dance it. 42

BEATRICE   Ye light o' love with your heels! Then, if your 43
husband have stables enough, you'll see he shall lack
no barns. 45

MARGARET   Oh, illegitimate construction! I scorn that 46
with my heels. 47

6 **rabato** tall collar supporting a ruff, stiffened with wire or starch
8 **troth, 's** faith, it is   12 **tire within** headdress in the inner room
13 **hair** hairpiece attached to the *tire* (line 12)   16 **exceeds** i.e., exceeds
comparison   17 **nightgown** dressing gown   17–18 **in respect of** compared to   18 **cuts . . . silver** slashes in a garment revealing the underlying fabic, and laced with silver thread   19 **down sleeves** tight-fitting
sleeves to the wrist.   **side sleeves** secondary ornamental sleeves hanging from the shoulder   20 **round underborne** with a lining around the
edge of the skirt.   **tinsel** cloth, usually silk, interwoven with threads of
silver or gold.   21 **quaint** elegant   22 **on't** of it.   29 **in** even in
31 **saving . . . husband** (By this apologetic formula, Margaret suggests
that Hero is too prudish even to hear the word *husband* mentioned.)
An bad If bawdy   32 **wrest** misinterpret   35 **light** harmless. (With a
play on the meaning "wanton.")   39 **tune** i.e., mood.   41 **Clap 's** Let's
shift.   **Light o' love** (A popular song.)   42 **burden** bass accompaniment. (With play on the idea of "the weight of a man.")   43 **Ye . . .
heels** i.e., You're light-heeled, wanton!   45 **barns** (With pun on
"bairns," children.)   46 **illegitimate construction** false inference. (But
with a play on the idea of bastard "bairns.")   47 **with my heels** (A
proverbial expression of scorn.)

138–9 **fashion . . . man** i.e., fashion prompts the discarding of clothes
faster than honest use.   144 **leans me** leans. (*Me* is an emphatic
marker.)   148 **possessed** (misleadingly) informed; also, perhaps, possessed, as by the devil   149 **amiable** amorous   162 **Right Master
Constable** (A comic title on the pattern of "Right Worshipful," etc.)
163 **recovered** (For "discovered.")   164 **lechery** (For "treachery.")
166 **lock** lock of hair hanging down on the left shoulder; the lovelock.
171 **obey** (For "oblige," "command.")   173 **commodity** goods
acquired   174 **taken up** (1) arrested (2) obtained on credit.   **bills**
(1) pikes (2) bonds given as security.   175 **in question** (1) subject to
judicial examination (2) of doubtful value
3.4. Location: Leonato's house.
5 **Well** Very well, as you wish.

BEATRICE   'Tis almost five o'clock, cousin; 'tis time you
were ready. By my troth, I am exceeding ill. Heigh-ho!
MARGARET   For a hawk, a horse, or a husband?   50
BEATRICE   For the letter that begins them all, H.   51
MARGARET   Well, an you be not turned Turk, there's no   52
more sailing by the star.   53
BEATRICE   What means the fool, trow?   54
MARGARET   Nothing, I; but God send everyone their
heart's desire!
HERO   These gloves the Count sent me, they are an
excellent perfume.   58
BEATRICE   I am stuffed, cousin. I cannot smell.   59
MARGARET   A maid, and stuffed! There's goodly catch-
ing of cold.
BEATRICE   Oh, God help me, God help me! How long
have you professed apprehension?   63
MARGARET   Ever since you left it. Doth not my wit   64
become me rarely?
BEATRICE   It is not seen enough; you should wear it in   66
your cap. By my troth, I am sick.   67
MARGARET   Get you some of this distilled *carduus bene-*   68
dictus, and lay it to your heart. It is the only thing for a   69
qualm.   70
HERO   There thou prick'st her with a thistle.
BEATRICE   *Benedictus!* Why *benedictus?* You have some
moral in this *benedictus.*   73
MARGARET   Moral? No, by my troth, I have no moral
meaning, I meant plain holy thistle. You may think   75
perchance that I think you are in love. Nay, by'r Lady,
I am not such a fool to think what I list, nor I list not to   77
think what I can, nor indeed I cannot think, if I would
think my heart out of thinking, that you are in love or   79
that you will be in love or that you can be in love. Yet
Benedick was such another, and now is he become a   81
man. He swore he would ever marry, and yet now, in   82
despite of his heart, he eats his meat without grudg-   83
ing; and how you may be converted I know not, but   84
methinks you look with your eyes as other women do.
BEATRICE   What pace is this that thy tongue keeps?
MARGARET   Not a false gallop.   87

Enter Ursula.

URSULA   Madam, withdraw. The Prince, the Count,
Signor Benedick, Don John, and all the gallants of the
town are come to fetch you to church.
HERO   Help to dress me, good coz, good Meg, good
Ursula.   [*Exeunt.*]

✿

[3.5]

*Enter Leonato and the Constable [Dogberry]
and the Headborough [Verges].*

LEONATO   What would you with me, honest neighbor?
DOGBERRY   Marry, sir, I would have some confidence   2
with you that decerns you nearly.   3
LEONATO   Brief, I pray you, for you see it is a busy time
with me.
DOGBERRY   Marry, this it is, sir.
VERGES   Yes, in truth it is, sir.
LEONATO   What is it, my good friends?
DOGBERRY   Goodman Verges, sir, speaks a little off the   9
matter—an old man, sir, and his wits are not so blunt   10
as, God help, I would desire they were, but, in faith,
honest as the skin between his brows.   12
VERGES   Yes, I thank God I am as honest as any man
living that is an old man and no honester than I.
DOGBERRY   Comparisons are odorous. *Palabras,* neigh-   15
bor Verges.
LEONATO   Neighbors, you are tedious.
DOGBERRY   It pleases Your Worship to say so, but we are
the poor Duke's officers. But truly, for mine own part,   19
if I were as tedious as a king, I could find in my heart   20
to bestow it all of Your Worship.   21
LEONATO   All thy tediousness on me, ah?
DOGBERRY   Yea, an 'twere a thousand pound more than
'tis; for I hear as good exclamation on Your Worship as   24
of any man in the city, and though I be but a poor man,
I am glad to hear it.
VERGES   And so am I.
LEONATO   I would fain know what you have to say.
VERGES   Marry, sir, our watch tonight, excepting Your   29
Worship's presence, ha' ta'en a couple of as arrant   30
knaves as any in Messina.
DOGBERRY   A good old man, sir; he will be talking. As
they say, when the age is in, the wit is out. God help   33
us, it is a world to see! Well said, i'faith, neighbor   34

---

50 For . . . husband? (*Heigh-ho* might be a cry of encouragement in the hunt or else "Heigh-ho for a husband!" as at 2.1.305.)   **51 H** (With a pun on "ache," pronounced "aitch." Beatrice complains of aching with a cold.)   **52 turned Turk** i.e., turned apostate to the true faith (by violating your oath not to become a lover)   **52–3 no . . . star** no more navigating by the North Star, i.e., no certain truth in which to trust.   **54 trow** I wonder.   **58 perfume** (Gloves were often perfumed.)   **59 stuffed** i.e., stuffed up with a cold. (But Margaret takes it in a bawdy sense.)   **63 professed apprehension** made claim to be witty.   **64 left it** gave it up. (Margaret gibes at Beatrice's pretending not to know what the joking is all about.)   **66–7 wear . . . cap** i.e., wear it prominently visible, as a fool wears his coxcomb. (Beatrice jokes that Margaret's supposed wit is imperceptible.)   **68–9 carduus benedictus** the blessed thistle, noted for medicinal properties. (With a pun on "Benedick.")   **70 a qualm** an attack of nausea (or misgiving).   **73 moral** hidden meaning   **75 holy thistle** the blessed thistle or *carduus benedictus* of 68–9.   **77 list** please   **79 think . . . thinking** i.e., rack my brains   **81 such another** i.e., seemingly proof against love   **81–2 a man** i.e., like other men.   **83–4 eats . . . grudging** i.e., is content to be like other men, to be in love   **87 Not . . . gallop.** i.e., I'm not speaking at a false pace, at a canter; I speak the truth.

3.5. Location: Leonato's house.
0.2 *Headborough* local constable   **2 confidence** (A blunder for "conference.")   **3 decerns** (For "concerns.")   **9 Goodman** (Title of a person under the social rank of gentleman.)   **10 blunt** (He means "sharp.")   **12 honest . . . brows** (Proverbial expression of honesty.)   **15 odorous** (For "odious.")   ***Palabras*** (For *pocas palabras,* "few words" in Spanish.)   **19 poor Duke's officers** (For "Duke's poor officers.")   **20 tedious** (Dogberry evidently thinks *tedious* means "rich.")   **21 of** on   **24 exclamation** (Possibly for "acclamation.")   **29 tonight** last night.   **29–30 excepting . . . presence** (The normal meaning, "with the exception of your honored self," comically implies that Leonato is an even more arrant knave than the men arrested. Verges probably means, "begging Your Worship's pardon.")   **30 ha' ta'en** have taken   **33 when . . . out** (An adaptation of the proverb, "When ale is in, wit is out.")   **34 a world** i.e., wonderful. (Proverbial.)

Verges. Well, God's a good man. An two men ride   35
of a horse, one must ride behind. An honest soul,   36
i'faith, sir, by my troth he is, as ever broke bread. But, God
is to be worshiped, all men are not alike, alas, good
neighbor!

LEONATO   Indeed, neighbor, he comes too short of you.

DOGBERRY   Gifts that God gives.

LEONATO   I must leave you.

DOGBERRY   One word, sir. Our watch, sir, have indeed
comprehended two aspicious persons, and we would   44
have them this morning examined before Your Worship.

LEONATO   Take their examination yourself and bring
it me. I am now in great haste, as it may appear
unto you.

DOGBERRY   It shall be suffigance.   50

LEONATO   Drink some wine ere you go. Fare you well.

[Enter a Messenger.]

MESSENGER   My lord, they stay for you to give your
daughter to her husband.

LEONATO   I'll wait upon them. I am ready.   54
[Exeunt Leonato and Messenger.]

DOGBERRY   Go, good partner, go, get you to Francis Sea-   55
coal. Bid him bring his pen and inkhorn to the jail. We   56
are now to examination these men.   57

VERGES   And we must do it wisely.

DOGBERRY   We will spare for no wit, I warrant you.
Here's that shall drive some of them to a noncome.   60
Only get the learned writer to set down our excom-   61
munication, and meet me at the jail.   [Exeunt.]   62

❧

[4.1]

*Enter Prince [Don Pedro], [Don John the]
Bastard, Leonato, Friar [Francis], Claudio,
Benedick, Hero, and Beatrice [with attendants].*

LEONATO   Come, Friar Francis, be brief—only to the
plain form of marriage, and you shall recount their
particular duties afterwards.

FRIAR   You come hither, my lord, to marry this lady?

CLAUDIO   No.

LEONATO   To be married to her. Friar, you come to
marry her.

FRIAR   Lady, you come hither to be married to this
Count?

HERO   I do.

FRIAR   If either of you know any inward impediment   11

why you should not be conjoined, I charge you on
your souls to utter it.

CLAUDIO   Know you any, Hero?

HERO   None, my lord.

FRIAR   Know you any, Count?

LEONATO   I dare make his answer: none.

CLAUDIO   Oh, what men dare do! What men may do!
What men daily do, not knowing what they do!

BENEDICK   How now? Interjections? Why, then, some be   20
of laughing, as, ah, ha, he!   21

CLAUDIO
Stand thee by, Friar.—Father, by your leave,   22
Will you with free and unconstrainèd soul
Give me this maid, your daughter?

LEONATO
As freely, son, as God did give her me.

CLAUDIO
And what have I to give you back, whose worth
May counterpoise this rich and precious gift?   27

DON PEDRO
Nothing, unless you render her again.

CLAUDIO
Sweet Prince, you learn me noble thankfulness.   29
[He hands Hero to Leonato.]
There, Leonato, take her back again.
Give not this rotten orange to your friend;
She's but the sign and semblance of her honor.   32
Behold how like a maid she blushes here!
Oh, what authority and show of truth
Can cunning sin cover itself withal!
Comes not that blood as modest evidence   36
To witness simple virtue? Would you not swear,   37
All you that see her, that she were a maid,
By these exterior shows? But she is none:
She knows the heat of a luxurious bed.   40
Her blush is guiltiness, not modesty.

LEONATO
What do you mean, my lord?

CLAUDIO   Not to be married,   42
Not to knit my soul to an approvèd wanton.   43

LEONATO
Dear my lord, if you, in your own proof,   44
Have vanquished the resistance of her youth,
And made defeat of her virginity—

CLAUDIO
I know what you would say: if I have known her,   47
You will say, she did embrace me as a husband,
And so extenuate the forehand sin.   49
No, Leonato,
I never tempted her with word too large,   51

35 God's . . . man i.e., God is good. (A proverbial saying.)   **36 of** on
44 comprehended (For "apprehended.")   **aspicious** (For "suspicious.")   **50 suffigance** (For "sufficient.")   **54 wait upon** attend
55–6 Francis Seacoal i.e., the Sexton of 4.2, not George, the member of
the watch in 3.3.   **57 examination** (For "examine.")   **60 noncome**
(Probably an unintended contraction for *non compos mentis*, "not of
sound mind," but Dogberry may have intended "nonplus.")
61–2 excommunication (For "examination" or "communication.")
4.1. Location: A church.
11 inward secret

20–1 some . . . he (Benedick quotes from Lilly's Latin grammar on the
subject of interjections; according to Lilly, these are to be classified as
laughing interjections.)   **22 Stand thee by** Stand aside   **27 counterpoise** balance, be equivalent to   **29 learn** teach   **32 sign and semblance** pretense and outward show   **36 blood** i.e., blush.   **modest
evidence** evidence of modesty   **37 witness** bear witness to   **40 luxurious** lascivious, lustful   **42 mean** imply, suggest. (But Claudio bitterly replies in the sense of "intend.")   **43 approvèd** proved   **44 in . . .
proof** in making trial of her yourself   **47 known her** i.e., known her
sexually   **49 extenuate** excuse, lessen.   **forehand sin** sin of anticipating (marriage).)   **51 large** broad, immodest

But, as a brother to his sister, showed
Bashful sincerity and comely love.

HERO
And seemed I ever otherwise to you?

CLAUDIO
Out on thee, seeming! I will write against it.   55
You seem to me as Dian in her orb,   56
As chaste as is the bud ere it be blown;   57
But you are more intemperate in your blood
Than Venus, or those pampered animals
That rage in savage sensuality.

HERO
Is my lord well, that he doth speak so wide?   61

LEONATO
Sweet Prince, why speak not you?

DON PEDRO   What should I speak?
I stand dishonored, that have gone about   63
To link my dear friend to a common stale.   64

LEONATO
Are these things spoken, or do I but dream?

DON JOHN
Sir, they are spoken, and these things are true.

BENEDICK   This looks not like a nuptial.

HERO   "True"! Oh, God!   68

CLAUDIO   Leonato, stand I here?
Is this the Prince? Is this the Prince's brother?
Is this face Hero's? Are our eyes our own?

LEONATO
All this is so. But what of this, my lord?

CLAUDIO
Let me but move one question to your daughter,   73
And by that fatherly and kindly power   74
That you have in her, bid her answer truly.

LEONATO [to Hero]
I charge thee do so, as thou art my child.

HERO
Oh, God defend me, how am I beset!
What kind of catechizing call you this?   78

CLAUDIO
To make you answer truly to your name.

HERO
Is it not Hero? Who can blot that name
With any just reproach?

CLAUDIO   Marry, that can Hero!   82
Hero itself can blot out Hero's virtue.
What man was he talked with you yesternight
Out at your window betwixt twelve and one?
Now, if you are a maid, answer to this.

HERO
I talked with no man at that hour, my lord.

DON PEDRO
Why, then are you no maiden. Leonato,
I am sorry you must hear. Upon mine honor,
Myself, my brother, and this grievèd Count   89
Did see her, hear her, at that hour last night
Talk with a ruffian at her chamber window,
Who hath indeed, most like a liberal villain,   92
Confessed the vile encounters they have had
A thousand times in secret.

DON JOHN
Fie, fie, they are not to be named, my lord,
Not to be spoke of!
There is not chastity enough in language
Without offense to utter them. Thus, pretty lady,
I am sorry for thy much misgovernment.   99

CLAUDIO
O Hero, what a Hero hadst thou been
If half thy outward graces had been placed
About thy thoughts and counsels of thy heart!
But fare thee well, most foul, most fair! Farewell,
Thou pure impiety and impious purity!
For thee I'll lock up all the gates of love,   105
And on my eyelids shall conjecture hang,   106
To turn all beauty into thoughts of harm,
And never shall it more be gracious.   108

LEONATO
Hath no man's dagger here a point for me?
                              [Hero swoons.]

BEATRICE
Why, how now, cousin, wherefore sink you down?

DON JOHN
Come, let us go. These things, come thus to light,
Smother her spirits up.
         [Exeunt Don Pedro, Don John, and Claudio.]

BENEDICK
How doth the lady?

BEATRICE   Dead, I think. Help, uncle!
Hero, why, Hero! Uncle! Signor Benedick! Friar!

LEONATO
O Fate, take not away thy heavy hand!
Death is the fairest cover for her shame
That may be wished for.

BEATRICE   How now, cousin Hero?

FRIAR   Have comfort, lady.

LEONATO
Dost thou look up?

FRIAR   Yea, wherefore should she not?   119

LEONATO
Wherefore? Why, doth not every earthly thing
Cry shame upon her? Could she here deny
The story that is printed in her blood?   122
Do not live, Hero, do not ope thine eyes;
For, did I think thou wouldst not quickly die,
Thought I thy spirits were stronger than thy shames,   125

---

55 Out . . . seeming! i.e., Shame on you, a mere semblance of good!
56 Dian . . . orb i.e., Diana, goddess of chastity, enthroned in the
moon   **57 be blown** open, flower   **61 wide** wide of the mark.
63 gone about undertaken   **64 stale** whore.   **68 True** (A response
to Don John's use of the term.)   **73 move** put   **74 kindly** natural
78 catechizing formal questioning used by the Church to teach the
principles of faith. The first question in the Church of England's
catechism is, "What is your name?"   **82 Hero itself** The very name
of Hero (who, in the story of Hero and Leander, is the faithful
tragic heroine)

89 grievèd (1) aggrieved, wronged (2) struck with grief   **92 liberal**
licentious   **99 much misgovernment** gross misconduct.   **105 For
thee** Because of you   **106 conjecture** evil suspicion   **108 be gracious**
seem attractive, graceful.   **119 wherefore** why   **122 blood** i.e.,
blushes.   **125 spirits** life-giving energies, vital powers

Myself would, on the rearward of reproaches,   126
Strike at thy life. Grieved I I had but one?
Chid I for that at frugal nature's frame?   128
Oh, one too much by thee! Why had I one?
Why ever wast thou lovely in my eyes?
Why had I not with charitable hand
Took up a beggar's issue at my gates,   132
Who, smirchèd thus and mired with infamy,
I might have said, "No part of it is mine;
This shame derives itself from unknown loins"?
But mine, and mine I loved, and mine I praised,   136
And mine that I was proud on, mine so much
That I myself was to myself not mine,   138
Valuing of her—why, she, oh, she, is fallen   139
Into a pit of ink, that the wide sea   140
Hath drops too few to wash her clean again
And salt too little which may season give   142
To her foul-tainted flesh!

BENEDICK   Sir, sir, be patient.
For my part, I am so attired in wonder,
I know not what to say.

BEATRICE
Oh, on my soul, my cousin is belied!

BENEDICK
Lady, were you her bedfellow last night?

BEATRICE
No, truly, not; although, until last night,
I have this twelvemonth been her bedfellow.

LEONATO
Confirmed, confirmed! Oh, that is stronger made
Which was before barred up with ribs of iron!
Would the two princes lie and Claudio lie,   151
Who loved her so that, speaking of her foulness,
Washed it with tears? Hence from her! Let her die.

FRIAR   Hear me a little;
For I have only been silent so long
And given way unto this course of fortune   157
By noting of the lady. I have marked
A thousand blushing apparitions
To start into her face, a thousand innocent shames
In angel whiteness beat away those blushes,
And in her eye there hath appeared a fire
To burn the errors that these princes hold
Against her maiden truth. Call me a fool;
Trust not my reading nor my observations,
Which with experimental seal doth warrant   166
The tenor of my book; trust not my age,   167
My reverence, calling, nor divinity,
If this sweet lady lie not guiltless here
Under some biting error.

LEONATO   Friar, it cannot be.
Thou see'st that all the grace that she hath left
Is that she will not add to her damnation

A sin of perjury; she not denies it.
Why seek'st thou then to cover with excuse
That which appears in proper nakedness?   175

FRIAR
Lady, what man is he you are accused of?

HERO
They know that do accuse me; I know none.
If I know more of any man alive
Than that which maiden modesty doth warrant,   179
Let all my sins lack mercy! O my father,
Prove you that any man with me conversed   181
At hours unmeet or that I yesternight   182
Maintained the change of words with any creature,   183
Refuse me, hate me, torture me to death!   184

FRIAR
There is some strange misprision in the princes.   185

BENEDICK
Two of them have the very bent of honor;   186
And if their wisdoms be misled in this,
The practice of it lives in John the Bastard,   188
Whose spirits toil in frame of villainies.   189

LEONATO
I know not. If they speak but truth of her,
These hands shall tear her; if they wrong her honor,
The proudest of them shall well hear of it.
Time hath not yet so dried this blood of mine,
Nor age so eat up my invention,   194
Nor fortune made such havoc of my means,
Nor my bad life reft me so much of friends,   196
But they shall find, awaked in such a kind,   197
Both strength of limb and policy of mind,   198
Ability in means, and choice of friends,
To quit me of them throughly.

FRIAR   Pause awhile,   200
And let my counsel sway you in this case.
Your daughter here the princes left for dead,   202
Let her awhile be secretly kept in,   203
And publish it that she is dead indeed.
Maintain a mourning ostentation,   205
And on your family's old monument   206
Hang mournful epitaphs, and do all rites
That appertain unto a burial.

LEONATO
What shall become of this? What will this do?   209

FRIAR
Marry, this, well carried, shall on her behalf   210
Change slander to remorse. That is some good.
But not for that dream I on this strange course,   212

126 on . . . reproaches following this public disgrace   128 Chid
Chided.   frame plan, order.   132 Took . . . issue taken up a beggar's
child   136 mine i.e., my own daughter   138–9 That . . . her i.e., that I
set no value on myself in caring so much for her   140 that such that
142 season preservative   151 before already   157 given . . . fortune
yielded to this turn of events   166–7 Which . . . book i.e., by means
of which observations and experience I have confirmed what I
learned from books

175 proper true   179 warrant sanction, permit   181 Prove you if you
prove   182 unmeet improper   183 Maintained the change held
exchange   184 Refuse disown   185 misprision mistake, misunderstanding   186 Two . . . honor i.e., Don Pedro and Claudio are wholly
honorable   188 practice scheming   189 frame contriving   194 eat
eaten. (Pronounced "et.")   invention power to plan (vengeance)
196 reft robbed   197 kind manner   198 policy shrewdness
200 quit . . . throughly settle accounts with them thoroughly.
202 the princes i.e., (whom) Don Pedro and Claudio   203 in in hiding, at home   205 Maintain . . . ostentation Perform all the outward
signs of mourning   206 monument burial vault   209 become of
result from   210 carried managed   212 not for that not for that
reason alone

But on this travail look for greater birth.   213
She—dying, as it must be so maintained,
Upon the instant that she was accused—
Shall be lamented, pitied, and excused
Of every hearer; for it so falls out
That what we have we prize not to the worth   218
Whiles we enjoy it, but, being lacked and lost,
Why then we rack the value, then we find   220
The virtue that possession would not show us
Whiles it was ours. So will it fare with Claudio.
When he shall hear she died upon his words,   223
Th'idea of her life shall sweetly creep
Into his study of imagination,   225
And every lovely organ of her life   226
Shall come appareled in more precious habit,   227
More moving-delicate, and full of life,
Into the eye and prospect of his soul,   229
Than when she lived indeed. Then shall he mourn,
If ever love had interest in his liver,   231
And wish he had not so accusèd her,
No, though he thought his accusation true.
Let this be so, and doubt not but success   234
Will fashion the event in better shape   235
Than I can lay it down in likelihood.   236
But if all aim but this be leveled false,   237
The supposition of the lady's death
Will quench the wonder of her infamy.
And if it sort not well, you may conceal her,   240
As best befits her wounded reputation,
In some reclusive and religious life,   242
Out of all eyes, tongues, minds, and injuries.   243

BENEDICK
Signor Leonato, let the Friar advise you.
And though you know my inwardness and love   245
Is very much unto the Prince and Claudio,
Yet, by mine honor, I will deal in this
As secretly and justly as your soul
Should with your body.

LEONATO   Being that I flow in grief,   249
The smallest twine may lead me.

FRIAR
'Tis well consented. Presently away;   251
    For to strange sores strangely they strain the cure.   252
Come, lady, die to live. This wedding day
    Perhaps is but prolonged. Have patience, and
    endure.   254
                    Exit [with all but Benedick and Beatrice].
BENEDICK   Lady Beatrice, have you wept all this while?

BEATRICE   Yea, and I will weep a while longer.
BENEDICK   I will not desire that.
BEATRICE   You have no reason. I do it freely.   258
BENEDICK   Surely I do believe your fair cousin is
    wronged.
BEATRICE   Ah, how much might the man deserve of me
    that would right her!
BENEDICK   Is there any way to show such friendship?
BEATRICE   A very even way, but no such friend.   264
BENEDICK   May a man do it?
BEATRICE   It is a man's office, but not yours.   266
BENEDICK   I do love nothing in the world so well as you.
    Is not that strange?
BEATRICE   As strange as the thing I know not. It were as
    possible for me to say I loved nothing so well as you.
    But believe me not; and yet I lie not. I confess nothing,
    nor I deny nothing. I am sorry for my cousin.
BENEDICK   By my sword, Beatrice, thou lovest me.
BEATRICE   Do not swear and eat it.   274
BENEDICK   I will swear by it that you love me, and I will
    make him eat it that says I love not you.   276
BEATRICE   Will you not eat your word?
BENEDICK   With no sauce that can be devised to it. I
    protest I love thee.   279
BEATRICE   Why, then, God forgive me!
BENEDICK   What offense, sweet Beatrice?
BEATRICE   You have stayed me in a happy hour. I was   282
    about to protest I loved you.
BENEDICK   And do it with all thy heart.
BEATRICE   I love you with so much of my heart that
    none is left to protest.   286
BENEDICK   Come, bid me do anything for thee.
BEATRICE   Kill Claudio.
BENEDICK   Ha! Not for the wide world.
BEATRICE   You kill me to deny it. Farewell.   [Going.]
BENEDICK   Tarry, sweet Beatrice.
BEATRICE   I am gone, though I am here. There is no love   292
    in you. Nay, I pray you, let me go.
BENEDICK   Beatrice—
BEATRICE   In faith, I will go.
BENEDICK   We'll be friends first.
BEATRICE   You dare easier be friends with me than fight
    with mine enemy.
BENEDICK   Is Claudio thine enemy?
BEATRICE   Is 'a not approved in the height a villain, that   300
    hath slandered, scorned, dishonored my kinswoman?
    Oh, that I were a man! What, bear her in hand until   302
    they come to take hands, and then, with public accus-
    ation, uncovered slander, unmitigated rancor—Oh,   304
    God, that I were a man! I would eat his heart in the
    marketplace.

---

213 **on this travail** from this effort (which is metaphorically like the *travail*, or labor, of childbirth) 218 **to the worth** as fully as it deserves 220 **rack** stretch, extend 223 **upon** in consequence of 225 **Into . . . imagination** into his thoughts 226 **organ . . . life** aspect of her when she was alive 227 **habit** apparel 229 **prospect** range of vision 231 **interest in** claim upon. **liver** (The supposed seat of the passion of love.) 234 **success** i.e., what succeeds or happens in time as my plan unfolds 235 **event** outcome 236 **lay . . . likelihood** anticipate its probable course. 237 **if . . . false** i.e., if every other aim miscarry 240 **sort** turn out 242 **reclusive** cloistered 243 **injuries** insults. 245 **inwardness and love** close friendship 249 **Being . . . grief** Since I overflow in grief 251 **Presently** Immediately 252 **For . . . cure** for strange diseases require strange and desperate cures. 254 **prolonged** deferred.

258 **You . . . reason** (Beatrice twists Benedick's "I wish you weren't so unhappy," line 257, into "There's no need for you to bid me stop weeping.") 264 **even** direct, straightforward 266 **office** duty 274 **eat it** i.e., eat your words. 276 **eat it** i.e., eat my sword, be stabbed by it 279 **protest** affirm. (Also in line 283.) 282 **stayed** stopped. **in . . . hour** at an appropriate moment. 286 **protest** object. (With a play on the sense of "affirm" in 279 and 283.) 292 **gone** i.e., in spirit 300 **approved in the height** proved in the highest degree 302 **bear her in hand** delude Hero with false hopes 304 **uncovered** open, unconcealed

BENEDICK   Hear me, Beatrice—

BEATRICE   Talk with a man out at a window! A proper 308
saying! 309

BENEDICK   Nay, but Beatrice—

BEATRICE   Sweet Hero! She is wronged, she is slandered,
she is undone.

BENEDICK   Beat—

BEATRICE   Princes and counties! Surely, a princely testi- 314
mony, a goodly count, Count Comfect; a sweet gallant, 315
surely! Oh, that I were a man for his sake! Or that I had
any friend would be a man for my sake! But manhood
is melted into curtsies, valor into compliment, and
men are only turned into tongue, and trim ones too. 319
He is now as valiant as Hercules that only tells a lie 320
and swears it. I cannot be a man with wishing, there- 321
fore I will die a woman with grieving.

BENEDICK   Tarry, good Beatrice. By this hand, I love
thee.

BEATRICE   Use it for my love some other way than
swearing by it.

BENEDICK   Think you in your soul the Count Claudio
hath wronged Hero?

BEATRICE   Yea, as sure as I have a thought or a soul.

BENEDICK   Enough, I am engaged. I will challenge him. 330
I will kiss your hand, and so I leave you. By this hand,
Claudio shall render me a dear account. As you hear 332
of me, so think of me. Go comfort your cousin. I must
say she is dead. And so, farewell. [*Exeunt separately.*]

❖

[4.2]

*Enter the Constables [Dogberry and Verges]
and the Town Clerk [Sexton] in gowns, Borachio, [Conrade, and Watch].*

DOGBERRY   Is our whole dissembly appeared? 1

VERGES   Oh, a stool and a cushion for the sexton.
[*Stool and cushion are brought. The Sexton sits.*]

SEXTON   Which be the malefactors?

DOGBERRY   Marry, that am I and my partner. 4

VERGES   Nay, that's certain; we have the exhibition to 5
examine.

SEXTON   But which are the offenders that are to be
examined? Let them come before Master Constable.

DOGBERRY   Yea, marry, let them come before me. [*The
prisoners are brought forward.*] What is your name,
friend?

BORACHIO   Borachio.

DOGBERRY   Pray, write down Borachio.—Yours, sirrah? 13

CONRADE   I am a gentleman, sir, and my name is
Conrade.

DOGBERRY   Write down Master Gentleman Conrade.
Masters, do you serve God?

CONRADE, BORACHIO   Yea, sir, we hope.

DOGBERRY   Write down that they hope they serve God;
and write God first, for God defend but God should 20
go before such villains! Masters, it is proved already
that you are little better than false knaves, and it will
go near to be thought so shortly. How answer you for
yourselves?

CONRADE   Marry, sir, we say we are none.

DOGBERRY   A marvelous witty fellow, I assure you, but 26
I will go about with him. [*To Borachio*] Come you 27
hither, sirrah. A word in your ear. Sir, I say to you, it is
thought you are false knaves.

BORACHIO   Sir, I say to you we are none.

DOGBERRY   Well, stand aside. 'Fore God, they are both
in a tale. Have you writ down that they are none? 32

SEXTON   Master Constable, you go not the way to
examine. You must call forth the watch that are their
accusers.

DOGBERRY   Yea, marry, that's the eftest way. Let the 36
watch come forth.—Masters, I charge you in the
Prince's name accuse these men.

SEACOAL   This man said, sir, that Don John, the Prince's
brother, was a villain.

DOGBERRY   Write down Prince John a villain. Why, this
is flat perjury, to call a prince's brother villain. 42

BORACHIO   Master Constable—

DOGBERRY   Pray thee, fellow, peace. I do not like thy
look, I promise thee.

SEXTON   What heard you him say else?

FIRST WATCH   Marry, that he had received a thousand
ducats of Don John for accusing the Lady Hero
wrongfully.

DOGBERRY   Flat burglary as ever was committed.

VERGES   Yea, by Mass, that it is. 51

SEXTON   What else, fellow?

SEACOAL   And that Count Claudio did mean, upon his 53
words, to disgrace Hero before the whole assembly, 54
and not marry her.

DOGBERRY   Oh, villain! Thou wilt be condemned into
everlasting redemption for this. 57

SEXTON   What else?

WATCH   This is all. 59

SEXTON   And this is more, masters, than you can deny:
Prince John is this morning secretly stolen away. Hero
was in this manner accused, in this very manner
refused, and upon the grief of this suddenly died.—
Master Constable, let these men be bound and
brought to Leonato's. I will go before and show him
their examination. [*Exit.*]

308–9 proper saying likely story.   **314 counties** counts.   **315 count**
(1) the title (2) declaration of complaint in an indictment (3) account.
Comfect candy or sweetmeat   **319 are . . . tongue** have become mere
(flattering) voices.   **trim** nice, elegant, fine. (Used ironically.)
320–1 He . . . swears it A man need only tell lies and swear they are
true to gain a reputation for bravery nowadays.   **330 I am engaged** I
pledge myself.   **332 dear** costly
4.2. Location: The jail.
1 dissembly (A blunder for "assembly.")   **4 that am I** (Dogberry evidently understands *malefactors* to mean "factors," agents.)   **5 exhibition** (Possibly for "commission.")   **13 sirrah** (Used to address
inferiors; Conrade objects.)

20 defend forbid   **26 witty** clever, cunning   **27 go about with** get
the better of, deal with   **32 in a tale** in agreement.   **36 eftest** (Some
sort of invention for "easiest" or "deftest.")   **42 perjury** (Dogberry
means "slander.")   **51 by Mass** by the Mass   **53–4 upon his words**
on the basis of Borachio's testimony   **57 redemption** (Dogberry
means "damnation.")   **59 WATCH** (Perhaps both Seacoal and his partner speak.)

DOGBERRY   Come, let them be opinioned.   67
VERGES   Let them be in the hands—
CONRADE   Off, coxcomb!
DOGBERRY   God's my life, where's the sexton? Let him   70
write down the Prince's officer coxcomb. Come, bind
them. Thou naughty varlet!   72
CONRADE   Away! You are an ass, you are an ass.
DOGBERRY   Dost thou not suspect my place? Dost thou   74
not suspect my years? Oh, that he were here to write   75
me down an ass! But masters, remember that I am an
ass; though it be not written down, yet forget not that
I am an ass. No, thou villain, thou art full of piety, as   78
shall be proved upon thee by good witness. I am a
wise fellow, and, which is more, an officer, and, which
is more, a householder, and, which is more, as pretty
a piece of flesh as any is in Messina, and one that
knows the law, go to, and a rich fellow enough, go to,
and a fellow that hath had losses, and one that hath
two gowns and everything handsome about him.—
Bring him away. Oh, that I had been writ down an ass!
Exeunt.

❖

5.1

Enter Leonato and his brother [Antonio].

ANTONIO
If you go on thus, you will kill yourself;
And 'tis not wisdom thus to second grief   2
Against yourself.
LEONATO   I pray thee, cease thy counsel,
Which falls into mine ears as profitless
As water in a sieve. Give not me counsel,
Nor let no comforter delight mine ear
But such a one whose wrongs do suit with mine.   7
Bring me a father that so loved his child,
Whose joy of her is overwhelmed like mine,
And bid him speak of patience;
Measure his woe the length and breadth of mine,   11
And let it answer every strain for strain,   12
As thus for thus, and such a grief for such,
In every lineament, branch, shape, and form;
If such a one will smile and stroke his beard,
Bid sorrow wag, cry "hem!" when he should groan,   16
Patch grief with proverbs, make misfortune drunk   17
With candle wasters, bring him yet to me,   18
And I of him will gather patience.
But there is no such man. For, brother, men
Can counsel and speak comfort to that grief
Which they themselves not feel; but tasting it,

Their counsel turns to passion, which before
Would give preceptial medicine to rage,   24
Fetter strong madness in a silken thread,
Charm ache with air and agony with words.   26
No, no, 'tis all men's office to speak patience   27
To those that wring under the load of sorrow,   28
But no man's virtue nor sufficiency   29
To be so moral when he shall endure   30
The like himself. Therefore give me no counsel.
My griefs cry louder than advertisement.   32
ANTONIO
Therein do men from children nothing differ.   33
LEONATO
I pray thee, peace. I will be flesh and blood;
For there was never yet philosopher
That could endure the toothache patiently,
However they have writ the style of gods   37
And made a push at chance and sufferance.   38
ANTONIO
Yet bend not all the harm upon yourself.
Make those that do offend you suffer, too.
LEONATO
There thou speak'st reason. Nay, I will do so.
My soul doth tell me Hero is belied,
And that shall Claudio know; so shall the Prince
And all of them that thus dishonor her.

Enter Prince [Don Pedro] and Claudio.

ANTONIO
Here comes the Prince and Claudio hastily.
DON PEDRO
Good e'en, good e'en.
CLAUDIO   Good day to both of you.
LEONATO
Hear you, my lords—
DON PEDRO   We have some haste, Leonato.
LEONATO
Some haste, my lord! Well, fare you well, my lord.
Are you so hasty now? Well, all is one.   49
DON PEDRO
Nay, do not quarrel with us, good old man.
ANTONIO
If he could right himself with quarreling,   51
Some of us would lie low.
CLAUDIO   Who wrongs him?   52
LEONATO
Marry, thou dost wrong me, thou dissembler, thou!   53
Nay, never lay thy hand upon thy sword;
I fear thee not.
CLAUDIO   Marry, beshrew my hand   55
If it should give your age such cause of fear.
In faith, my hand meant nothing to my sword.   57

---

67 **opinioned** (For "pinioned.")   70 **God's** May God save
72 **naughty** wicked   74 **suspect** (For "respect.")   75 **my years** (With
an unconscious suggestion of "my ears," i.e., ass's ears.)   78 **piety**
(For "impiety.")
5.1. Location: Near Leonato's house.
2 **second** assist, encourage   7 **suit with** match   11 **Measure his woe**
let his woe equal in scope   12 **answer . . . for strain** correspond, pang
for pang. (With a musical sense also of echoing a refrain.)   16 **wag** be
off.   **cry "hem"** i.e., clear the throat as before some wordy speech
17 **drunk** i.e., insensible to pain   18 **candle wasters** those who waste
candles by late study, bookworms, moral philosophers

24 **preceptial** consisting of precepts   26 **air** mere breath, words
27 **office** duty   28 **wring** writhe   29 **sufficiency** ability, power
30 **moral** prone to moralizing   32 **advertisement** advice, counsel.
33 **Therein . . . differ** i.e., It is childish to be so inconsolable.   37 **writ . . .**
gods uttered godlike wisdom   38 **made . . . sufferance** scoffed at misfortune and suffering.   49 **all is one** it makes no difference.   51 **he** i.e.,
Leonato   52 **Some of us** i.e., Don Pedro and Claudio   53 **thou** (Used
contemptuously instead of the more polite *you.*)   55 **beshrew** curse
57 **my . . . sword** I had no intention of using my sword.

LEONATO
    Tush, tush, man, never fleer and jest at me.   58
    I speak not like a dotard nor a fool,
    As under privilege of age to brag
    What I have done being young or what would do
    Were I not old. Know, Claudio, to thy head,   62
    Thou hast so wronged mine innocent child and me
    That I am forced to lay my reverence by,   64
    And with gray hairs and bruise of many days
    Do challenge thee to trial of a man.   66
    I say thou hast belied mine innocent child.
    Thy slander hath gone through and through her
        heart,
    And she lies buried with her ancestors—
    Oh, in a tomb where never scandal slept,
    Save this of hers, framed by thy villainy!   71
CLAUDIO
    My villainy?
LEONATO   Thine, Claudio, thine, I say.
DON PEDRO
    You say not right, old man.
LEONATO   My lord, my lord,
    I'll prove it on his body if he dare,
    Despite his nice fence and his active practice,   75
    His May of youth and bloom of lustihood.   76
CLAUDIO
    Away! I will not have to do with you.
LEONATO
    Canst thou so daff me? Thou hast killed my child.
    If thou kill'st me, boy, thou shalt kill a man.   78
ANTONIO
    He shall kill two of us, and men indeed.
    But that's no matter; let him kill one first.
    Win me and wear me! Let him answer me.
    Come follow me, boy. Come, sir boy, come follow me,   82
    Sir boy, I'll whip you from your foining fence!
    Nay, as I am a gentleman, I will.   84
LEONATO   Brother—
ANTONIO
    Content yourself. God knows I loved my niece,   87
    And she is dead, slandered to death by villains
    That dare as well answer a man indeed
    As I dare take a serpent by the tongue.
    Boys, apes, braggarts, jacks, milksops!
LEONATO   Brother Antony—
ANTONIO
    Hold you content. What, man! I know them, yea,
    And what they weigh, even to the utmost scruple—   94
    Scambling, outfacing, fashionmonging boys,   95
    That lie and cog and flout, deprave and slander,   96

Go anticly, show outward hideousness,   97
And speak off half a dozen dangerous words   98
How they might hurt their enemies, if they durst,
And this is all.
LEONATO
    But brother Antony—
ANTONIO   Come, 'tis no matter.
    Do not you meddle; let me deal in this.
DON PEDRO
    Gentlemen both, we will not wake your patience.   103
    My heart is sorry for your daughter's death;
    But, on my honor, she was charged with nothing
    But what was true and very full of proof.
LEONATO   My lord, my lord—
DON PEDRO   I will not hear you.
LEONATO
    No? Come, brother, away! I will be heard.
ANTONIO
    And shall, or some of us will smart for it.   110
                    Exeunt ambo [Leonato and Antonio].

            Enter Benedick.

DON PEDRO
    See, see, here comes the man we went to seek.
CLAUDIO   Now, signor, what news?
BENEDICK   Good day, my lord.
DON PEDRO   Welcome, signor. You are almost come to
    part almost a fray.
CLAUDIO   We had like to have had our two noses   116
    snapped off with two old men without teeth.   117
DON PEDRO   Leonato and his brother. What think'st
    thou? Had we fought, I doubt we should have been   119
    too young for them.
BENEDICK   In a false quarrel there is no true valor. I came
    to seek you both.
CLAUDIO   We have been up and down to seek thee, for
    we are high-proof melancholy and would fain have it   124
    beaten away. Wilt thou use thy wit?
BENEDICK   It is in my scabbard. Shall I draw it?
DON PEDRO   Dost thou wear thy wit by thy side?
CLAUDIO   Never any did so, though very many have
    been beside their wit. I will bid thee draw as we do the   129
    minstrels, draw to pleasure us.   130
DON PEDRO   As I am an honest man, he looks pale. Art
    thou sick, or angry?
CLAUDIO   What, courage, man! What though care killed
    a cat, thou hast mettle enough in thee to kill care.
BENEDICK   Sir, I shall meet your wit in the career, an you 135
    charge it against me. I pray you, choose another sub-   136
    ject.

---

58 **fleer** sneer, jeer   62 **head** i.e., face   64 **my reverence** i.e., the reverence due old age   66 **trial of a man** manly contest, i.e., duel.
71 **framed** devised   75 **nice fence** dexterous swordsmanship. (Said
contemptuously.)   76 **lustihood** bodily vigor   78 **daff** doff, brush
aside   82 **Win . . . me!** (A proverbial expression, used as a challenge,
meaning he'll have to overcome me before he can claim me as a
prize.)   **answer me** i.e., in a duel.   84 **foining** thrusting   87 **Content
yourself** i.e., Don't try to stop me.   94 **scruple** small measure of
weight   95 **Scambling . . . boys** contentious, swaggering, dandified
boys   96 **cog** cheat.   **deprave** defame, traduce

97 **anticly** fantastically dressed.   **hideousness** frightening appearance   98 **dangerous** threatening, haughty   103 **wake your patience**
put your patience to any further test.   110.1 *ambo* both   116 **We had
. . . had** We almost had   117 **with** by   119 **doubt** fear, suspect. (Said
ironically.)   124 **high-proof** to the highest degree.   **fain** gladly
129 **beside their wit** out of their wits. (Playing on *by thy side* in line
127.)   130 **draw** (1) draw your weapon (2) draw a bow across a musical instrument   135 **career** short gallop at full speed (as in a tourney).
an if   136 **charge** level (as a weapon)

CLAUDIO   Nay, then, give him another staff. This last 138
was broke cross. 139

DON PEDRO   By this light, he changes more and more. I
think he be angry indeed.

CLAUDIO   If he be, he knows how to turn his girdle. 142

BENEDICK   Shall I speak a word in your ear?

CLAUDIO   God bless me from a challenge!

BENEDICK [aside to Claudio]   You are a villain. I jest not. I
will make it good how you dare, with what you dare,
and when you dare. Do me right, or I will protest your 147
cowardice. You have killed a sweet lady, and her death
shall fall heavy on you. Let me hear from you.

CLAUDIO   Well, I will meet you, so I may have good
cheer. 151

DON PEDRO   What, a feast, a feast?

CLAUDIO   I'faith, I thank him, he hath bid me to a calf's 153
head and a capon, the which if I do not carve most 154
curiously, say my knife's naught. Shall I not find a 155
woodcock too? 156

BENEDICK   Sir, your wit ambles well; it goes easily. 157

DON PEDRO   I'll tell thee how Beatrice praised thy wit
the other day. I said thou hadst a fine wit. "True," said
she, "a fine little one." "No," said I, "a great wit."
"Right," says she, "a great gross one." "Nay," said I, "a
good wit." "Just," said she, "it hurts nobody." "Nay," 162
said I, "the gentleman is wise." "Certain," said she,
"a wise gentleman." "Nay," said I, "he hath the 164
tongues." "That I believe," said she, "for he swore a 165
thing to me on Monday night which he forswore on
Tuesday morning. There's a double tongue; there's
two tongues." Thus did she, an hour together, trans- 168
shape thy particular virtues. Yet at last she concluded 169
with a sigh, thou wast the proper'st man in Italy. 170

CLAUDIO   For the which she wept heartily and said she
cared not.

DON PEDRO   Yea, that she did. But yet for all that, an if
she did not hate him deadly, she would love him
dearly. The old man's daughter told us all. 175

CLAUDIO   All, all. And, moreover, God saw him when 176
he was hid in the garden. 177

DON PEDRO   But when shall we set the savage bull's
horns on the sensible Benedick's head?

CLAUDIO   Yea, and text underneath, "Here dwells 180
Benedick, the married man"?

BENEDICK   Fare you well, boy. You know my mind. I
will leave you now to your gossiplike humor. You
break jests as braggarts do their blades, which, God be 184
thanked, hurt not.—My lord, for your many courtesies I thank you. I must discontinue your company.
Your brother the bastard is fled from Messina. You
have among you killed a sweet and innocent lady. For
my Lord Lackbeard there, he and I shall meet, and till
then peace be with him. [Exit.]

DON PEDRO   He is in earnest.

CLAUDIO   In most profound earnest, and, I'll warrant
you, for the love of Beatrice.

DON PEDRO   And hath challenged thee?

CLAUDIO   Most sincerely.

DON PEDRO   What a pretty thing man is when he goes 196
in his doublet and hose and leaves off his wit! 197

CLAUDIO   He is then a giant to an ape; but then is an ape 198
a doctor to such a man. 199

DON PEDRO   But, soft you, let me be. Pluck up, my heart, 200
and be sad. Did he not say my brother was fled? 201

*Enter Constables, [Dogberry and Verges, and
the Watch, with] Conrade and Borachio.*

DOGBERRY   Come you, sir. If Justice cannot tame you,
she shall ne'er weigh more reasons in her balance. 203
Nay, an you be a cursing hypocrite once, you must be 204
looked to.

DON PEDRO   How now, two of my brother's men
bound? Borachio one!

CLAUDIO   Hearken after their offense, my lord. 208

DON PEDRO   Officers, what offense have these men
done?

DOGBERRY   Marry, sir, they have committed false report;
moreover, they have spoken untruths; secondarily,
they are slanders; sixth and lastly, they have belied a 213
lady; thirdly, they have verified unjust things; and to
conclude, they are lying knaves.

DON PEDRO   First, I ask thee what they have done;
thirdly, I ask thee what's their offense; sixth and lastly,
why they are committed; and to conclude, what you
lay to their charge.

CLAUDIO   Rightly reasoned, and in his own division; 220
and, by my troth, there's one meaning well suited. 221

DON PEDRO   Who have you offended, masters, that you
are thus bound to your answer? This learned consta- 223
ble is too cunning to be understood. What's your
offense?

---

138 staff spear shaft.   **139 broke cross** i.e., broken by clumsily allowing the spear to break crosswise against the opponent's shield. (In
other words, Claudio accuses Benedick of having failed in his sally of
wit.)   **142 turn his girdle** i.e., turn his sword belt around so that he's
ready to fight. (A proverbial expression of uncertain meaning.)
147 Do me right Give me satisfaction.   **protest** proclaim before witnesses   **151 cheer** entertainment. (Claudio is ready to fight, he says,
for the pleasant diversion it should offer.)   **153–6 calf's head, capon,
woodcock** (In the proposed feast of dueling, Claudio plans to carve
various dishes connoting foolishness, effeminate cowardice, and stupidity.)   **155 curiously** daintily.   **naught** good for nothing.
157 ambles i.e., minces along   **162 good** (1) keen (2) harmless.   **Just**
Exactly   **164 a wise gentleman** i.e., an old fool.   **164–5 hath the
tongues** masters several languages   **168–9 trans-shape** distort, turn
the wrong side out   **170 proper'st** handsomest   **175 old man's
daughter** i.e., Hero   **176–7 God . . . garden** (Alluding to the trick
played on Benedick to love Beatrice, and also to Genesis 3:8.)
180 text (In 1.1.251–6, Benedick vowed that, if he were ever to fall in
love, his friends might set a bull's horns on his head and label him
"Benedick the married man.")

184 as . . . blades i.e., as braggarts furtively damage their blades to
make it appear they have been fighting fiercely   **196–7 goes . . . wit**
goes about fully dressed like a rational creature but forgets to equip
himself with good sense.   **198–9 He . . . man** i.e., Such a man looks
like a hero in a fool's eyes, but actually the fool is a wise man compared to him.   **200–1 soft . . . be sad** wait a minute, not so fast; let me
think. Rouse yourself, my heart, and be serious.   **201.1–2** (The Quarto
placement of this stage direction after line 197 suggests that Dogberry
is visible, strutting and fussing with his prisoners, before he speaks.)
203 ne'er . . . balance never again weigh arguments of reason in her
scales. (But the pronunciation of *reason* as "raisin" invokes the comic
image of a shopkeeper weighing produce.)   **204 cursing** accursed.
once in a word   **208 Hearken after** Inquire into   **213 slanders** (For
"slanderers.")   **220 his own division** its own partition in a logical
arrangement. (Said ironically.)   **221 well suited** nicely dressed up in
the trappings of language.   **223 bound** (Playing on the meanings
"pinioned" and "headed for a destination.")   **answer** trial, account.

BORACHIO   Sweet Prince, let me go no farther to mine
answer. Do you hear me, and let this count kill me. I
have deceived even your very eyes. What your
wisdoms could not discover, these shallow fools have
brought to light, who in the night overheard me confessing to this man how Don John your brother
incensed me to slander the Lady Hero, how you were 231
brought into the orchard and saw me court Margaret
in Hero's garments, how you disgraced her when you
should marry her. My villainy they have upon record,
which I had rather seal with my death than repeat
over to my shame. The lady is dead upon mine and 236
my master's false accusation; and, briefly, I desire
nothing but the reward of a villain.

DON PEDRO [*to Claudio*]
Runs not this speech like iron through your blood?

CLAUDIO
I have drunk poison whiles he uttered it.

DON PEDRO [*to Borachio*]
But did my brother set thee on to this?

BORACHIO   Yea, and paid me richly for the practice of it. 242

DON PEDRO
He is composed and framed of treachery,
And fled he is upon this villainy.   244

CLAUDIO
Sweet Hero! Now thy image doth appear
In the rare semblance that I loved it first.   246

DOGBERRY   Come, bring away the plaintiffs. By this time 247
our sexton hath reformed Signor Leonato of the 248
matter. And masters, do not forget to specify, when 249
time and place shall serve, that I am an ass.

VERGES   Here, here comes Master Signor Leonato, and
the sexton, too.

      *Enter Leonato, his brother [Antonio], and the
      Sexton.*

LEONATO
Which is the villain? Let me see his eyes,
That when I note another man like him,
I may avoid him. Which of these is he?

BORACHIO
If you would know your wronger, look on me.

LEONATO
Art thou the slave that with thy breath hast killed
Mine innocent child?

BORACHIO   Yea, even I alone.

LEONATO
No, not so, villain, thou beliest thyself.
Here stand a pair of honorable men—   260
A third is fled—that had a hand in it.
I thank you, princes, for my daughter's death.
Record it with your high and worthy deeds.
'Twas bravely done, if you bethink you of it.

CLAUDIO
I know not how to pray your patience,
Yet I must speak. Choose your revenge yourself;

Impose me to what penance your invention   267
Can lay upon my sin. Yet sinned I not
But in mistaking.

DON PEDRO   By my soul, nor I.
And yet, to satisfy this good old man,
I would bend under any heavy weight
That he'll enjoin me to.

LEONATO
I cannot bid you bid my daughter live—
That were impossible—but, I pray you both,
Possess the people in Messina here   275
How innocent she died; and if your love
Can labor aught in sad invention,   277
Hang her an epitaph upon her tomb,
And sing it to her bones; sing it tonight.
Tomorrow morning come you to my house,
And since you could not be my son-in-law,
Be yet my nephew. My brother hath a daughter,
Almost the copy of my child that's dead,
And she alone is heir to both of us.   284
Give her the right you should have giv'n her cousin, 285
And so dies my revenge.

CLAUDIO   O noble sir,
Your overkindness doth wring tears from me!
I do embrace your offer; and dispose   288
For henceforth of poor Claudio.   289

LEONATO
Tomorrow then I will expect your coming;
Tonight I take my leave. This naughty man   291
Shall face to face be brought to Margaret,
Who I believe was packed in all this wrong,   293
Hired to it by your brother.

BORACHIO   No, by my soul, she was not,
Nor knew not what she did when she spoke to me,
But always hath been just and virtuous
In anything that I do know by her.   298

DOGBERRY   Moreover, sir, which indeed is not under 299
white and black, this plaintiff here, the offender, did 300
call me ass. I beseech you, let it be remembered in his
punishment. And also the watch heard them talk of
one Deformed. They say he wears a key in his ear and 303
a lock hanging by it and borrows money in God's 304
name, the which he hath used so long and never paid 305
that now men grow hardhearted and will lend nothing for God's sake. Pray you, examine him upon that
point.

LEONATO   I thank thee for thy care and honest pains.

DOGBERRY   Your Worship speaks like a most thankful
and reverend youth, and I praise God for you.

LEONATO   There's for thy pains.   [*He gives money.*]

DOGBERRY   God save the foundation!   313

---

267 Impose me to Impose on me   **275 Possess** inform   **277 aught** to
any extent   **284 heir to both** (Leonato overlooks Antonio's son mentioned in 1.2.2.)   **285 right** equitable treatment. (Quibbling on "rite,"
"ceremony.")   **288 dispose** you may dispose   **289 For henceforth** for
the future   **291 naughty** wicked   **293 packed** involved as an accomplice   **298 by** concerning   **299–300 under . . . black** written down in
black and white   **303–4 key . . . by it** (This is what Dogberry has
made out of the lovelock mentioned in 3.3.166.)   **304–5 in God's
name** (A phrase of the professional beggar.)   **313 God . . . foundation!** (A formula of those who received alms at religious houses or
charitable foundations.)

---

231 incensed incited   **236 upon** in consequence of   **242 practice** cunning execution   **244 upon** i.e., having committed   **246 rare semblance** splendid likeness   **247 plaintiffs** (For "defendants.")
248 reformed (For "informed.")   **249 specify** (For "testify"?)
260 honorable men i.e., Don Pedro and Claudio, men of rank

LEONATO   Go, I discharge thee of thy prisoner, and I
thank thee.
DOGBERRY   I leave an arrant knave with Your Worship,
which I beseech Your Worship to correct yourself, for
the example of others. God keep Your Worship! I wish
Your Worship well. God restore you to health! I
humbly give you leave to depart; and if a merry meet- 320
ing may be wished, God prohibit it! Come, neighbor. 321
                        [*Exeunt Dogberry and Verges.*]
LEONATO
Until tomorrow morning, lords, farewell.
ANTONIO
Farewell, my lords. We look for you tomorrow.
DON PEDRO
We will not fail.
CLAUDIO   Tonight I'll mourn with Hero.
LEONATO [*to the Watch*]
Bring you these fellows on.—We'll talk with Margaret,
How her acquaintance grew with this lewd fellow. 326
                        Exeunt [*separately*].

[5.2]

Enter Benedick and Margaret, [*meeting*].

BENEDICK   Pray thee, sweet Mistress Margaret, deserve
well at my hands by helping me to the speech of   2
Beatrice.
MARGARET   Will you then write me a sonnet in praise of
my beauty?
BENEDICK   In so high a style, Margaret, that no man   6
living shall come over it, for in most comely truth thou 7
deservest it.
MARGARET   To have no man come over me! Why, shall
I always keep below stairs?   10
BENEDICK   Thy wit is as quick as the greyhound's
mouth; it catches.
MARGARET   And yours as blunt as the fencer's foils,
which hit but hurt not.
BENEDICK   A most manly wit, Margaret; it will not hurt
a woman. And so, I pray thee, call Beatrice. I give thee 16
the bucklers.   17
MARGARET   Give us the swords. We have bucklers of
our own.
BENEDICK   If you use them, Margaret, you must put in
the pikes with a vice, and they are dangerous weapons 21
for maids.

MARGARET   Well, I will call Beatrice to you, who I think
hath legs.   *Exit Margaret.*
BENEDICK   And therefore will come.
[*He sings.*] "The god of love,   26
          That sits above,
          And knows me, and knows me,
          How pitiful I deserve—"   29
I mean in singing; but in loving, Leander the good   30
swimmer, Troilus the first employer of panders, and a 31
whole bookful of these quondam carpetmongers,   32
whose names yet run smoothly in the even road of a
blank verse, why, they were never so truly turned over 34
and over as my poor self in love. Marry, I cannot show 35
it in rhyme. I have tried. I can find out no rhyme to
"lady" but "baby," an innocent rhyme; for "scorn,"   37
"horn," a hard rhyme; for "school," "fool," a babbling 38
rhyme; very ominous endings. No, I was not born
under a rhyming planet, nor I cannot woo in festival
terms.

Enter Beatrice.

Sweet Beatrice, wouldst thou come when I called thee?
BEATRICE   Yea, signor, and depart when you bid me.
BENEDICK   Oh, stay but till then! [*She starts to leave.*]
BEATRICE   "Then" is spoken; fare you well now. And
yet, ere I go, let me go with that I came, which is, with 46
knowing what hath passed between you and Claudio.
BENEDICK   Only foul words; and thereupon I will kiss
thee.
BEATRICE   Foul words is but foul wind, and foul wind
is but foul breath, and foul breath is noisome; there- 51
fore I will depart unkissed.
BENEDICK   Thou hast frighted the word out of his right 53
sense, so forcible is thy wit. But I must tell thee plainly,
Claudio undergoes my challenge; and either I must
shortly hear from him, or I will subscribe him a   56
coward. And I pray thee now tell me, for which of my
bad parts didst thou first fall in love with me?
BEATRICE   For them all together, which maintained so
politic a state of evil that they will not admit any good 60
part to intermingle with them. But for which of my
good parts did you first suffer love for me?   62
BENEDICK   Suffer love! A good epithet. I do suffer love 63
indeed, for I love thee against my will.
BEATRICE   In spite of your heart, I think. Alas, poor
heart, if you spite it for my sake I will spite it for yours,
for I will never love that which my friend hates.
BENEDICK   Thou and I are too wise to woo peaceably.

---

320 **give you leave** (For "ask your leave.")   321 **prohibit** (For "permit.")   326 **lewd** wicked, worthless
**5.2. Location: Leonato's garden (? At the scene's end, Leonato's
house is some distance away.)**
2 to the speech of to speak with   **6 style** (1) poetic style (2) stile,
stairs over a fence   **7 come over** (1) excel beyond (2) traverse, as one
would cross a stile (3) in Margaret's next speech, the phrase is taken
to mean "mount sexually."   **comely** good. (With an allusion to Margaret's beauty.)   **10 keep below stairs** dwell in the servants' quarters.
16–17 I . . . bucklers i.e., I acknowledge myself beaten (in repartee).
(Bucklers are shields with spikes [pikes] in their centers. Margaret
uses the word in a bawdy sense in her reply.)   **21 pikes** spikes in the
center of a shield.   **vice** screw. (Benedick's bawdy sense continues
Margaret's jest.)

26–9 **The god . . . deserve** (The beginning of an old song by William
Elderton.)   29 **How . . . deserve** how I deserve pity. (But Benedick
uses the phrase to mean "how little I deserve.")   30 **Leander** lover of
Hero of Sestos; he swam the Hellespont nightly to see her until he
drowned   31 **Troilus** lover of Cressida, whose affair was assisted by
her uncle Pandarus   32 **quondam carpetmongers** ladies' men of old,
such as one might find in the carpeted boudoirs of the women they
woo   34-5 **over and over** i.e., head over heels   37 **innocent** childish
38 **hard** (1) exact (2) unpleasant, because of the association with cuckold's horns   46 **that I came** what I came for   51 **noisome** noxious
53 **his** its   56 **subscribe** formally proclaim in writing   60 **politic** prudently governed   62 **suffer** (1) experience (2) feel the pain of
63 **epithet** expression.

BEATRICE   It appears not in this confession. There's not 69
one wise man among twenty that will praise himself.

BENEDICK   An old, an old instance, Beatrice, that lived 71
in the time of good neighbors. If a man do not erect in 72
this age his own tomb ere he dies, he shall live no 73
longer in monument than the bell rings and the 74
widow weeps. 75

BEATRICE   And how long is that, think you?

BENEDICK   Question: why, an hour in clamor and a 77
quarter in rheum. Therefore is it most expedient for 78
the wise, if Don Worm, his conscience, find no imped- 79
iment to the contrary, to be the trumpet of his own
virtues, as I am to myself. So much for praising myself,
who, I myself will bear witness, is praiseworthy. And
now tell me, how doth your cousin?

BEATRICE   Very ill.

BENEDICK   And how do you?

BEATRICE   Very ill too.

BENEDICK   Serve God, love me, and mend. There will I
leave you too, for here comes one in haste.

Enter Ursula.

URSULA   Madam, you must come to your uncle. Yonder's old coil at home. It is proved my lady Hero hath 90
been falsely accused, and the Prince and Claudio mightily
abused, and Don John is the author of all, who is fled 92
and gone. Will you come presently? 93

BEATRICE   Will you go hear this news, signor?

BENEDICK   I will live in thy heart, die in thy lap, and be 95
buried in thy eyes; and moreover I will go with thee to
thy uncle's.   *Exeunt.*

❧

[5.3]

*Enter Claudio, Prince [Don Pedro, Balthasar],
and three or four with tapers.*

CLAUDIO   Is this the monument of Leonato?

A LORD   It is, my lord.

CLAUDIO   [*reading from a scroll*]

Epitaph.

"Done to death by slanderous tongues
    Was the Hero that here lies.
Death, in guerdon of her wrongs,
    Gives her fame which never dies. 5
So the life that died with shame
Lives in death with glorious fame."

Hang thou there upon the tomb,
Praising her when I am dumb.
                [*He hangs up the scroll.*]
Now, music, sound, and sing your solemn hymn.

Song.

BALTHASAR
Pardon, goddess of the night, 12
Those that slew thy virgin knight; 13
For the which, with songs of woe,
Round about her tomb they go.
    Midnight, assist our moan;
    Help us to sigh and groan,
        Heavily, heavily.
    Graves, yawn and yield your dead,
    Till death be utterèd, 20
        Heavily, heavily.

CLAUDIO
Now, unto thy bones good night!
Yearly will I do this rite.

DON PEDRO
Good morrow, masters. Put your torches out.
    The wolves have preyed; and look, the gentle day, 25
Before the wheels of Phoebus, round about 26
    Dapples the drowsy east with spots of gray.
Thanks to you all, and leave us. Fare you well.

CLAUDIO
Good morrow, masters. Each his several way. 29

DON PEDRO
Come, let us hence, and put on other weeds, 30
    And then to Leonato's we will go.

CLAUDIO
And Hymen now with luckier issue speed's 32
    Than this for whom we rendered up this woe.
                                  Exeunt.

❧

[5.4]

*Enter Leonato, Benedick, [Beatrice], Margaret,
Ursula, old man [Antonio], Friar [Francis, and]
Hero.*

FRIAR
Did I not tell you she was innocent?

LEONATO
So are the Prince and Claudio, who accused her
Upon the error that you heard debated. 3
But Margaret was in some fault for this,
Although against her will, as it appears 5
In the true course of all the question. 6

---

69 **It . . . confession** i.e., You don't show your wisdom in praising
yourself for being wise.   71 **instance** proverb (i.e., "He has ill neighbors that is fain to praise himself").   72 **time . . . neighbors** good old
times (when one's neighbors spoke well of one).   73–5 **he shall . . .
weeps** i.e., he will be memorialized only during the (brief) time of the
funeral service and the official mourning.   77 **Question** i.e., An easy
question, which I will answer as follows.   **clamor** noise (of the bell)
78 **rheum** tears (of the widow).   79 **Don . . . conscience** (The action
of the conscience was traditionally described as the gnawing of a
worm; compare with Mark 9:44–8.)   90 **old coil** great confusion
92 **abused** deceived   93 **presently** immediately.   95 **die** (With the
common connotation of "experience sexual climax.")
5.3. Location: A churchyard.
5 **guerdon** recompense

12 **goddess of the night** i.e., Diana, moon goddess, patroness of
chastity   13 **knight** i.e., follower   20 **utterèd** fully expressed
25 **have preyed** i.e., have done their preying   26 **wheels of Phoebus**
i.e., chariot of the sun god   29 **several** separate   30 **weeds** garments
32 **And . . . speed's** And may the god of marriage favor us with better
fortune
5.4. Location: Leonato's house.
3 **Upon** on the basis of   5 **against her will** unintentionally   6 **question** investigation.

ANTONIO
   Well, I am glad that all things sorts so well.   7

BENEDICK
   And so am I, being else by faith enforced   8
   To call young Claudio to a reckoning for it.

LEONATO
   Well, daughter, and you gentlewomen all,
   Withdraw into a chamber by yourselves,
   And when I send for you, come hither masked.
   The Prince and Claudio promised by this hour
   To visit me. You know your office, brother:
   You must be father to your brother's daughter,
   And give her to young Claudio.   *Exeunt ladies.*

ANTONIO
   Which I will do with confirmed countenance.   17

BENEDICK
   Friar, I must entreat your pains, I think.   18

FRIAR   To do what, signor?

BENEDICK
   To bind me or undo me—one of them.   20
   Signor Leonato, truth it is, good signor,
   Your niece regards me with an eye of favor.

LEONATO
   That eye my daughter lent her. 'Tis most true.   23

BENEDICK
   And I do with an eye of love requite her.

LEONATO
   The sight whereof I think you had from me,   25
   From Claudio, and the Prince. But what's your will?   26

BENEDICK
   Your answer, sir, is enigmatical.
   But, for my will, my will is your good will   28
   May stand with ours, this day to be conjoined
   In the state of honorable marriage,
   In which, good Friar, I shall desire your help.

LEONATO
   My heart is with your liking.

FRIAR   And my help.
   Here comes the Prince and Claudio.

     Enter Prince [Don Pedro] and Claudio, and
     two or three other.

DON PEDRO
   Good morrow to this fair assembly.

LEONATO
   Good morrow, Prince. Good morrow, Claudio.
   We here attend you. Are you yet determined   35
   Today to marry with my brother's daughter?

CLAUDIO
   I'll hold my mind, were she an Ethiope.

LEONATO
   Call her forth, brother. Here's the Friar ready.
                   [*Exit Antonio.*]

DON PEDRO
   Good morrow, Benedick. Why, what's the matter,
   That you have such a February face,
   So full of frost, of storm, and cloudiness?

CLAUDIO
   I think he thinks upon the savage bull.   42
   Tush, fear not, man! We'll tip thy horns with gold,
   And all Europa shall rejoice at thee,   44
   As once Europa did at lusty Jove   45
   When he would play the noble beast in love.

BENEDICK
   Bull Jove, sir, had an amiable low,
   And some such strange bull leapt your father's cow
   And got a calf in that same noble feat
   Much like to you, for you have just his bleat.

     Enter [Leonato's] brother [Antonio], Hero,
     Beatrice, Margaret, [and] Ursula, [the ladies
     masked].

CLAUDIO
   For this I owe you. Here comes other reckonings.   51
   Which is the lady I must seize upon?

ANTONIO
   This same is she, and I do give you her.

CLAUDIO
   Why then, she's mine. Sweet, let me see your face.

LEONATO
   No, that you shall not, till you take her hand
   Before this friar and swear to marry her.

CLAUDIO
   Give me your hand before this holy friar.
   I am your husband, if you like of me.   58

HERO [*unmasking*]
   And when I lived, I was your other wife;
   And when you loved, you were my other husband.

CLAUDIO
   Another Hero!

HERO   Nothing certainer.
   One Hero died defiled, but I do live,
   And surely as I live, I am a maid.

DON PEDRO
   The former Hero! Hero that is dead!

LEONATO
   She died, my lord, but whiles her slander lived.   65

FRIAR
   All this amazement can I qualify,   66
   When, after that the holy rites are ended,
   I'll tell you largely of fair Hero's death.   68
   Meantime let wonder seem familiar,   69
   And to the chapel let us presently.   70

BENEDICK
   Soft and fair, Friar. Which is Beatrice?   71

---

7 sorts turn out   **8 being . . . enforced** since otherwise I would be enforced by my promise to Beatrice   **17 confirmed countenance** straight face.   **18 entreat your pains** beg your help   **20 undo** (1) ruin (2) untie, unbind   **23 That . . . her** (Alludes to Hero's role in tricking Beatrice into confessing her love for Benedick.)   **25–6 The sight . . . Prince** (Alludes to their role in tricking Benedick into confessing his love for Beatrice.)   **28 for** as for.   **is** that   **35 yet** still

42 I . . . bull (A jocular reminiscence of the conversation in 1.1.250 ff.)   **44 Europa** Europe   **45 Europa** a princess whom Jove approached in the form of a white bull and bore on his back through the sea to Crete   **51 I owe you** i.e., I'll pay you back later (for calling me a calf and a bastard).   **other reckonings** i.e., other matters to be settled first.   **58 like of** care for   **65 but whiles** only while   **66 qualify** moderate   **68 largely** at large, in full   **69 let . . . familiar** treat these marvels as ordinary matters   **70 let us presently** let us go at once.   **71 Soft and fair** i.e., Wait a minute

BEATRICE [*unmasking*]
    I answer to that name. What is your will?
BENEDICK
    Do not you love me?
BEATRICE   Why, no, no more than reason.
BENEDICK
    Why, then your uncle and the Prince and Claudio
    Have been deceived. They swore you did.
BEATRICE
    Do not you love me?
BENEDICK   Troth, no, no more than reason.
BEATRICE
    Why, then my cousin, Margaret, and Ursula   77
    Are much deceived, for they did swear you did.
BENEDICK
    They swore that you were almost sick for me.
BEATRICE
    They swore that you were well-nigh dead for me.
BENEDICK
    'Tis no such matter. Then you do not love me?
BEATRICE
    No, truly, but in friendly recompense.
LEONATO
    Come, cousin, I am sure you love the gentleman.   83
CLAUDIO
    And I'll be sworn upon't that he loves her;
    For here's a paper written in his hand,
    A halting sonnet of his own pure brain,   86
    Fashioned to Beatrice.   [*He shows a paper.*]
HERO   And here's another
    Writ in my cousin's hand, stol'n from her pocket,
    Containing her affection unto Benedick.
                  [*She shows another paper.*]
BENEDICK   A miracle! Here's our own hands against our   90
    hearts. Come, I will have thee, but by this light I take   91
    thee for pity.
BEATRICE   I would not deny you, but by this good day,
    I yield upon great persuasion, and partly to save your
    life, for I was told you were in a consumption.   95

BENEDICK   Peace! I will stop your mouth. [*Kissing her.*]
DON PEDRO   How dost thou, Benedick, the married
    man?
BENEDICK   I'll tell thee what, Prince: a college of wit-   99
    crackers cannot flout me out of my humor. Dost thou
    think I care for a satire or an epigram? No. If a man   101
    will be beaten with brains, 'a shall wear nothing hand-   102
    some about him. In brief, since I do purpose to marry,   103
    I will think nothing to any purpose that the world can
    say against it; and therefore never flout at me for what   105
    I have said against it; for man is a giddy thing, and this
    is my conclusion. For thy part, Claudio, I did think to
    have beaten thee, but in that thou art like to be my   108
    kinsman, live unbruised, and love my cousin.
CLAUDIO   I had well hoped thou wouldst have denied
    Beatrice, that I might have cudgeled thee out of thy
    single life, to make thee a double-dealer, which out of   112
    question thou wilt be, if my cousin do not look   113
    exceeding narrowly to thee.   114
BENEDICK   Come, come, we are friends. Let's have a
    dance ere we are married, that we may lighten our
    own hearts and our wives' heels.
LEONATO   We'll have dancing afterward.
BENEDICK   First, of my word! Therefore play, music.   119
    Prince, thou art sad. Get thee a wife, get thee a wife.
    There is no staff more reverend than one tipped with   121
    horn.   122

       Enter Messenger.

MESSENGER
    My lord, your brother John is ta'en in flight
    And brought with armèd men back to Messina.
BENEDICK   Think not on him till tomorrow. I'll devise
    thee brave punishments for him. Strike up, pipers!   126
              Dance. [*Exeunt.*]

---

77 my cousin i.e., Hero   **83 cousin** i.e., niece   **86 halting** limping. **his own pure** purely his own   **90–1 against our hearts** i.e., to prove our hearts guilty as charged.   **95 in a consumption** i.e., wasting away in sighs.

99 college assembly   **101–3 If ... him** i.e., If a man allows himself to be cowed by ridicule, he'll never dare dress handsomely or do anything conspicuous that will draw attention.   **105 flout** mock   **108 in that** in view of the fact that.   **like** likely   **112 a double-dealer** (1) a married man (2) a deceiver, adulterer   **113–14 look ... narrowly** to keep close watch over   **119 of** on   **121–2 tipped with horn** (Alludes to the usual joke about cuckolds, as at line 43).   **126 brave** fine

The Merry Wives of Windsor

According to an early eighteenth-century tradition, Shakespeare composed *The Merry Wives of Windsor* at the behest of Queen Elizabeth. John Dennis, a critic and dramatist, asserted in 1702 that the Queen "was so eager to see it acted, that she commanded it to be finished in fourteen days." The editor Nicholas Rowe added in 1709 that the Queen, having been so pleased with Falstaff in the *Henry IV* plays, wished to see him in love. Such legends, emerging more than a century after the event, must be regarded with caution. Whether true or not, however, they do point to a passage of courtly flattery in the play that strongly suggests the presence of the court at some performance. The fairy blessing bestowed on Windsor Castle in Act 5 in unquestionably intended to celebrate the famous Order of the Garter. Mistress Quickly, disguised as leader of the fairies, orders her charges to sing nightly "Like to the Garter's compass, in a ring," to write "*Honi soit qui mal y pense*," the motto of the Garter, and to tend carefully the "several chairs of order"—those decorated stalls in the Chapel of St. George belonging to the illustrious lords who made up the Order of the Garter. Every such "installment" receives her blessing, along with each knight's "coat," "crest," and "blazon" (5.5.36–75). The topical nature of this passage is stressed by its apparent lack of relevance to the plot.

Other extraneous bits of action may allude to courtly matters or to Windsor gossip. The business about the purported three German horse thieves and their Duke (4.3, 5), which makes little sense in the play as it stands, can perhaps be explained as an in-group joke on Frederick of Würtemburg, Count Mömpelgard, a German nobleman obsessively intent on joining the Garter. He was the object of much anti-German scorn. His name, Mömpelgard or Mömpelgart, is possibly scrambled into "garmombles" in the corrupt 1602 Quarto text, where the Folio text reads "cozen-germans" (4.5.74). Also, the geography of Windsor is rendered with loving and accurate attention to detail, as though for an audience familiar with its environs.

Such topical flourishes do not rob the drama of its general appeal; it has had great success, both as a stage play and in Verdi's and Nicolai's operatic versions, and was presumably popular with Shakespeare's London audience. Shakespeare never composed exclusively for special audiences, so far as we know, and indeed the blessing of Windsor Castle could have been added to a commercial play in order to render it particularly suitable for royal performance. The allusion to "the fat woman of Brentford," a notorious tavern keeper of Brentford (halfway between London and Windsor), would have been as meaningful to Shakespeare's London audience as to the court. The same may be true of the "luces" in the coat of arms of Justice Shallow (1.1.14), sometimes thought to ridicule Shakespeare's Stratford neighbor Sir Thomas Lucy, but believed by scholar-critic Leslie Hotson to be a dig at William Gardiner, a Justice of the Peace in Surrey near London. The dig at the Brooke family, the lords of Cobham, in the disguise name (Brook) of the jealous Ford (as recorded in the unauthorized quarto of 1602), must have amused knowledgeable Londoners; indeed, the satirical hit was evidently so offensive that the name had to be changed to "Broome" (as in the Folio text). Nevertheless, *The Merry Wives* could have been originally planned as entertainment to please Queen Elizabeth. A Feast of St. George in honor of the Garter was held at Westminster on April 23, 1597, in the Queen's presence. Among those elected to the Order was George Carey, Lord Hunsdon, the patron of Shakespeare's company and the new Lord Chamberlain. He was actually installed in the Order at Windsor in May. This date is early for a play that appears to borrow several comic figures from the *Henry IV* plays and perhaps from *Henry V* (usually dated 1599) as well. Recently, however, it has been argued persuasively that *The Merry Wives* may have been written while *2 Henry IV* was in the process of composition, making use of its comic types, but before they had actually appeared on the London stage. According to this theory, Nym was created first for *The Merry Wives* and was then reintroduced into *Henry V*. The dating and order of composition of these plays are still controversial, so that the dating of *The Merry Wives* must remain uncertain from 1597 to 1601.

Despite this uncertainty, Shakespeare's comic strategy in *The Merry Wives* seems reasonably clear: to translate highly popular comic figures, such as Falstaff, Bardolph, Pistol, and Slender, from the history plays into a ludicrously different kind of situation. Falstaff, the once resourceful and self-aware companion of Prince Hal, becomes the buffoonish wooer of two virtuously married women who thoroughly best him and subject him to a series of amusingly humiliating punishments. Prince Hal, too, of course, treats Falstaff as a scapegoat in the *Henry IV* plays and ultimately rejects him, but the farcical nature of the action in *The Merry Wives* exposes Falstaff to more openly satirical laughter and discomfiture than in the history plays. Some admirers of Falstaff have been dismayed by the falling off and dismiss the play as an insult to his greatness, but surely to view the play thus is to create false expectations and thereby miss the point of Shakespeare's comic intent. Falstaff and his companions should not be judged against their counterparts in the history plays, even though an awareness of their existence in that different context is an essential part of the jest. To see Falstaff in love as a wooer of women much younger than himself—this tour de force required that Shakespeare devise a multiple plot as unlike that of the history plays as possible, in order to stress the comic discrepancy.

The result is a structurally complex comic plot that appropriately bears more resemblance to Shakespeare's other comedies than to the history plays. At the center of *The Merry Wives* is a familiar plot of romantic intrigue, featuring a young heroine (Anne Page) whose parents object to her attachment to young Fenton. They pester her with unwelcome rival wooers (Slender and Dr. Caius), obliging her finally to dupe her parents by a cleverly engineered elopement. This plot to outwit parents and rivals in the name of young love has its ancestry in the classical comedy of Plautus and in neoclassical comedy, though Shakespeare uses no particular recognizable source. To this plot he adds a second and parallel story of a lover (Falstaff) caught in the act of wooing two women. Italian *novelle* provide many situations of this sort, including that in which the husband is deceived by concealment of the lover in a clothes basket; see especially "Of Two Brethren and Their Wives" from *Riche His Farewell to Military Profession*, 1581, "Two Lovers of Pisa" from *Tarlton's News Out of Purgatory*, 1590, and the second story of the first day from Ser Giovanni Fiorentino's *Il Pecorone*, 1558. The effect of the combined plots is often farcelike, especially in the emphasis on swift, hilarious action and comic physical abuse at the expense of consistency in character. For example, we must accept as a given the preference of wise Master Page for Slender as his son-in-law and the inexplicable preference of Mistress Page for the suit of Dr. Caius. Reasons are stated, but symmetry of the design is paramount.

In addition, Shakespeare enriches these two plot situations with minor characters, such as the rival wooers, go-betweens, and informers, who inevitably come in conflict with one another and thereby reveal their "humors" or idiosyncrasies. Only tangentially connected with the plot, these characters are prized for their eccentricity. The Welsh Parson Evans and the French Dr. Caius nearly come to blows over Caius's courtship of Anne Page. They are safely kept apart by the genial Host of the Garter Inn and are reconciled to the extent of plotting against the Host for having deceived them both. (Perhaps they carry out their threat in the guise of the mysterious Germans who purportedly steal the Host's horses, though the text is murky on this point.) Justice Shallow, a humorous character in *2 Henry IV*, is given nominal justification in this play as cousin of Anne's second unwanted suitor, Slender, but Shallow's essential function is to quarrel with Falstaff about the latter's poaching and riotous behavior. This plot goes nowhere and indeed is little more than a means for the revelation of humorous characters. Shallow's is a cameo role, like many others, enabling him to assume the fatuous postures we also encounter in *2 Henry IV*. Pistol and Nym, similarly requiring some pretext for being on hand, avenge their dismissal from Falstaff's service by informing the two husbands of Falstaff's designs on the two merry wives. Bardolph finds suitable employment as a bartender. Mistress Quickly's transformation is perhaps the most gloriously improbable of all: she becomes confidante of all three wooers of Anne Page (offering equal encouragement to each and receiving payment from each), as well as go-between for Falstaff and the two wives. She is no longer a married and then widowed hostess of a London tavern, but an unmarried housekeeper of Windsor. She triumphs over Falstaff in a way not possible in the history plays, joining the entire cast as they jeer at the discomfited horn-browed knight.

By providing occasion for the exhibition of idiosyncratic character for its own sake, side by side with his fast-moving farcical action, Shakespeare seems to have been responding to the newest dramatic genre of the late 1590s: the humors comedy. George Chapman's *The Blind Beggar of Alexandria* (1596) had done much to establish the new fashion. Ben Jonson's *Every Man in His Humor* (1598) either influenced Shakespeare or was influenced by him, depending upon the dates. Jonson's plot, like Shakespeare's, is chiefly a vehicle for displaying various humors or comically obsessed types: the overly watchful father, the jealous husband, the braggart soldier, the country simpleton intent on learning to quarrel like a gentleman, the waspishly impatient man. Similar types appear in *The Merry Wives*, although Shakespeare characteristically does not satirize affectation so much as cherish it.

Shakespeare's comic types endear themselves chiefly through their verbal traits: Nym with his use of the word "humor"; Pistol with his anachronistic terms, recondite allusions, stilted poetic inversions, and hyperboles ("O base Hungarian wight! Wilt thou the spigot wield?", 1.3.19–20); Mistress Quickly with her pungent homely metaphors (comparing a beard to "a glover's paring knife," 1.4.19–20) and her pat phrases ("But let that pass," line 14); Shallow with his legal jargon; and the French Caius and the Welsh Evans with their ability to "keep their limbs whole and hack our English" (3.1.73). Shakespeare also caricatures these humorous types by distinctive physical traits, such as Bardolph's "tinderbox" nose (1.3.23) or Slender's unappealing face and little yellow beard that so aptly suit his passion for bearbaiting and his idiotic deference to his superiors. We laugh at these deformities and yet see that no one is incorrigible. The characters amiably poke fun at one another, and every discomfiture leads ultimately to a reconciliation. Few escape laughter, even those we might regard as normative characters if this were a satire; the Host, for example, loses his horses, and Mistress Page is tricked at last by her daughter's elopement.

Nevertheless, the merry wives of the play's title come as close as any to representing the normative vision of the play, functioning as witty manipulators in a plot to expose hypocrisy and lechery. The devices they invent for Falstaff are rather like Maria's schemes for Malvolio in *Twelfth Night*, since all depend upon the complicity of the self-blinded victim. Falstaff is the dominant humors character of the play, obsessed both with lust and greed, amusing to us because the greed is predominant. His hypocritical reasons for wooing deserve comic reprisal, or "vengeance." His greed and his fatuous belief in his own charm overwhelm his natural sagacity and leave him vulnerable. He credulously accepts the bribes of the jealous Ford, disguised as Brook, and is deceived by the wives on no less than three occasions. For their part, the wives are delighted with their "sport," for they must devise increasingly clever schemes to offset Falstaff's growing suspicions. The more unlikely he is to return for more punishment, the greater must be their ingenuity in order to fool him once again. Mistress Ford enjoys the added pleasure of teaching her husband a lesson about jealousy. The wives' humorous plotting derives its sharpness from their potential to be faithless, if they choose, and hence from the power they enjoy over men like Ford and Falstaff, who are obsessed with groundless fantasies

of betrayal or are compulsively in need of validating their masculinity through conquest of the female. The cleverness of the wives' sport is justified by its moral intent, and, conversely, the moral point is deprived of any tedious didacticism by the good humor of the jest. In his final humiliation, plagued by virtually all the play's characters, reduced to an absurd belief in fairies, Falstaff becomes a scapegoat in the truest sense of that term: a horned figure who embodies the faults of an entire society and whose chastisement brings about purification. Yet, as Mistress Quickly observes, "nobody but has his fault" (1.4.13–14), and this comic rejection of Falstaff leads not to banishment but to a reconciling feast at the Pages' house. Without intending it, Falstaff has cured Ford's jealousy and has helped show that "Wives may be merry, and yet honest too." (4.2.97).

The Merry Wives is a remarkable play in terms of its relationship to comedy and history, the two genres most evident in Shakespeare's dramatic writing of the 1590s. The romantic plot of love's triumph, though nominally at the center of the plot, is decidedly secondary in importance. The more dominant motif of scapegoating and renewal gives the central roles to married women rather than the young lovers of romantic comedy. Falstaff's claim to wit and vitality in *1 Henry IV* and *2 Henry IV* gives place here to the ascendancy of domestic women; the comic principle shifts to them. Mistress Quickly, translated like Falstaff and his crew from the history plays into comedy, shares in this vindication of women's wit and virtue; no longer a tavern keeper or widow enduring Falstaff's broken promises or patiently supplying him with women, Quickly becomes a go-between in a comic plot of exposure of male philandering. Women are no longer on the periphery of a male-dominated world, as in the history plays, but in their element. At the same time, the women of this play embody married virtues for the most part, rather than the youthful companionship (Portia, Beatrice, Rosalind, Viola) of the romantic comedies. The location of the play in a part of England not far from where Shakespeare grew up, the inclusion of place names familiar from his youth, the fond portrait of a schoolboy's terror in coping with Latin paradigms, all suggest a kind of tribute to the world in which Shakespeare's own family affairs remained while he sought professional advancement in London. The mildly satiric celebration of bourgeois life, found nowhere else to such an extent in Shakespeare, gives a meaningful insight into an author who profited from the limited but increasing social mobility of his age.

The Merry Wives of Windsor

[*Dramatis Personae*

MISTRESS MARGARET PAGE, *a wife of Windsor*
MASTER GEORGE PAGE, *her husband*
ANNE PAGE, *their daughter*
WILLIAM PAGE, *a schoolboy, their son*

MISTRESS ALICE FORD, *a wife of Windsor*
MASTER FRANK FORD, *her husband*
JOHN,
ROBERT, } *their servants*

SIR JOHN FALSTAFF
ROBIN, *his page*
BARDOLPH,
PISTOL, } *his followers*
NYM,

SIR HUGH EVANS, *a Welsh parson*

DOCTOR CAIUS, *a French physician*
MISTRESS QUICKLY, *his housekeeper*
JOHN RUGBY, *his servant*

ROBERT SHALLOW, *a country justice of the peace*
ABRAHAM SLENDER, *his nephew*
PETER SIMPLE, *Slender's servant*

HOST *of the Garter Inn*
FENTON, *a gentleman in love with Anne Page*

Children of Windsor, disguised as fairies

SCENE: *Windsor, and the neighborhood*]

1.1

Enter Justice Shallow, Slender, [and] Sir Hugh Evans.

SHALLOW Sir Hugh, persuade me not. I will make a Star 1
Chamber matter of it. If he were twenty Sir John 2
Falstaffs, he shall not abuse Robert Shallow, Esquire.
SLENDER In the county of Gloucester, Justice of Peace
and Coram. 5
SHALLOW Ay, cousin Slender, and Custalorum. 6
SLENDER Ay, and Ratolorum too. And a gentleman 7
born, Master Parson, who writes himself "Armigero" in 8
any bill, warrant, quittance, or obligation: "Armigero." 9

SHALLOW Ay, that I do, and have done any time these
three hundred years.
SLENDER All his successors gone before him hath 12
done't, and all his ancestors that come after him may. 13
They may give the dozen white luces in their coat. 14
SHALLOW It is an old coat.
EVANS The dozen white louses do become an old coat
well. It agrees well, passant. It is a familiar beast to 17
man, and signifies love.
SHALLOW The luce is the fresh fish. The salt fish is an 19
old coat. 20
SLENDER I may quarter, coz 21
SHALLOW You may, by marrying.
EVANS It is marring indeed, if he quarter it.
SHALLOW Not a whit.

1.1. Location: Windsor. Before Master Page's house.
0.1 *Sir* courtesy title for a priest. **1 persuade** argue with **1–2 Star Chamber matter** (The court of Star Chamber, composed chiefly of the King's Privy Council, was the highest and most powerful court in the realm.) **5 Coram** i.e., quorum, a title of certain justices whose presence was necessary to constitute a bench. **6 cousin** kinsman. **Custalorum** A corruption of Latin *custos rotulorum*, "keeper of the rolls." **7 Ratolorum** (For *rotulorum*.) **8 Armigero** Esquire, one entitled to bear arms. (A heraldic term.) **9 bill** bill of financial exchange. **quittance** discharge from legal agreement. **obligation** contract

12–13 successors . . . ancestors (Slender comically gets these words backwards.) **14 give** display heraldically. **luces** pikes, fresh-water fish. **coat** coat of arms. **17 passant** (1) walking (in heraldic language) (2) passing, exceeding. **familiar** (1) well-known and part of the family (2) overfamiliar (taking *louse* in the sense of a tiny biting insect) **19–20 The luce . . . coat** (The meaning is unclear, though Shallow is seemingly joking about Evans's pronunciation of *coat* as "cod.") **21 quarter** combine the arms of two families by adding to one's own coat the arms of another family in one quarter of the escutcheon. **coz** cousin, kinsman.

EVANS   Yes, py'r Lady. If he has a quarter of your coat, 25
there is but three skirts for yourself, in my simple 26
conjectures. But that is all one. If Sir John Falstaff have
committed disparagements unto you, I am of the
Church, and will be glad to do my benevolence to
make atonements and compromises between you. 30

SHALLOW   The Council shall hear it. It is a riot. 31

EVANS   It is not meet the Council hear a riot. There is no 32
fear of Got in a riot. The Council, look you, shall desire
to hear the fear of Got, and not to hear a riot. Take 34
your visaments in that. 35

SHALLOW   Ha! O' my life, if I were young again, the
sword should end it.

EVANS   It is petter that friends is the sword, and end it. 38
And there is also another device in my prain, which
peradventure prings goot discretions with it: there is
Anne Page, which is daughter to Master George Page,
which is pretty virginity.

SLENDER   Mistress Anne Page? She has brown hair and 43
speaks small like a woman? 44

EVANS   It is that fery person for all the 'orld, as just as 45
you will desire. And seven hundred pounds of
moneys, and gold, and silver, is her grandsire upon 47
his death's-bed—Got deliver to a joyful resurrec- 48
tions!—give, when she is able to overtake seventeen 49
years old. It were a goot motion if we leave our pribbles 50
and prabbles, and desire a marriage between 51
Master Abraham and Mistress Anne Page.

SLENDER   Did her grandsire leave her seven hundred
pound?

EVANS   Ay, and her father is make her a petter penny. 55

SHALLOW   I know the young gentlewoman. She has
good gifts. 57

EVANS   Seven hundred pounds and possibilities is goot 58
gifts.

SHALLOW   Well, let us see honest Master Page. Is Fal- 60
staff there?

EVANS   Shall I tell you a lie? I do despise a liar as I do
despise one that is false, or as I despise one that is not
true. The knight Sir John is there, and I beseech you
be ruled by your well-willers. I will peat the door for 65
Master Page. [He knocks.] What ho! Got pless your
house here!

PAGE [within]   Who's there?

EVANS   Here is Got's plessing, and your friend, and
Justice Shallow, and here young Master Slender, that
peradventures shall tell you another tale, if matters 71
grow to your likings.

[Enter] Master Page.

PAGE   I am glad to see Your Worships well. I thank you
for my venison, Master Shallow.

SHALLOW   Master Page, I am glad to see you. Much
good do it your good heart! I wished your venison
better; it was ill killed. How doth good Mistress 77
Page?—And I thank you always with my heart, la,
with my heart.

PAGE   Sir, I thank you.

SHALLOW   Sir, I thank you. By yea and no I do.

PAGE   I am glad to see you, good Master Slender.

SLENDER   How does your fallow greyhound, sir? I heard 83
say he was outrun on Cotswold. 84

PAGE   It could not be judged, sir. 85

SLENDER   You'll not confess, you'll not confess. 86

SHALLOW   That he will not. 'Tis your fault, 'tis your 87
fault. 'Tis a good dog.

PAGE   A cur, sir.

SHALLOW   Sir, he's a good dog, and a fair dog. Can
there be more said? He is good and fair. Is Sir John
Falstaff here?

PAGE   Sir, he is within; and I would I could do a good 93
office between you.

EVANS   It is spoke as a Christians ought to speak.

SHALLOW   He hath wronged me, Master Page.

PAGE   Sir, he doth in some sort confess it. 97

SHALLOW   If it be confessed, it is not redressed. Is not
that so, Master Page? He hath wronged me, indeed he
hath; at a word, he hath. Believe me, Robert Shallow, 100
Esquire, saith he is wronged.

[Enter Sir John] Falstaff, Bardolph, Nym, [and]
Pistol.

PAGE   Here comes Sir John.

FALSTAFF   Now, Master Shallow, you'll complain of me
to the King?

SHALLOW   Knight, you have beaten my men, killed my
deer, and broke open my lodge. 106

FALSTAFF   But not kissed your keeper's daughter?

SHALLOW   Tut, a pin! This shall be answered. 108

FALSTAFF   I will answer it straight: I have done all this. 109
That is now answered.

SHALLOW   The Council shall know this.

---

25 py'r Lady by Our Lady. (Evans' Welsh dialect often substitutes "p"
for "b" at the start of words, as in *petter*, *prain*, and *prings*, lines 38–40;
substitutes "f" for "v" and "t" for "d," as in *Fery goot*, line 133; leaves
out initial "w," as in *'orld* and *'oman*, lines 45, 210; etc.)   **26 skirts** the
tails of a long doublet or coat. (Evans is still thinking of a literal coat
that would be marred by quartering, i.e., cutting into quarters.)
30 atonements reconciliations.   **compromises** i.e., settlement by arbitration   **31 The Council . . . riot.** (The King's Privy Council, sitting in
Star Chamber, frequently concerned itself with riots. Evans, however,
understands *Council* to refer to an ecclesiastical council.)   **32 meet** fitting   **34–5 Take . . . that** Take that into consideration. (*Visaments*
means "advisements.")   **38 that friends is the sword** i.e., that the
quarrel be ended by friendly motions   **43 Mistress** (Used of married
or unmarried women.)   **44 small** with a gentle, high voice   **45 as
just** exactly   **47–9 is . . . give** has . . . given (her)   **50 motion** plan
50–1 pribbles and prabbles i.e., petty disputes   **55 is make . . .
penny** will provide her a pretty penny more.   **57 gifts** natural
endowments.   **58 possibilities** pecuniary prospects   **60 honest** worthy   **65 well-willers** well-wishers.   **peat** beat, knock

71 tell . . . tale i.e., have something more to say to you   **77 ill** i.e., illegally, by Falstaff. (See below, lines 105–6.)   **83 fallow** fawn-colored
84 on Cotswold i.e., in games held in the Cotswold hills in Gloucestershire.   **85 judged** fairly decided   **86 confess** admit (that your dog
lost)   **87 That . . . fault** i.e., He (Page) certainly won't admit that. You
(Slender) are in the wrong. (*Fault* also suggests "loss of scent.")
93 within i.e., at dinner in Page's house; see lines 179–80 below
97 in some sort to some extent   **100 at a word** in a word   **106 lodge**
forest keeper's dwelling.   **108 pin** trifle.   **answered** accounted for.
(But Falstaff plays on the meaning "replied to.")   **109 straight** (1) at
once (2) straightforwardly

FALSTAFF 'Twere better for you if it were known in 112
counsel. You'll be laughed at. 113

EVANS *Pauca verba*, Sir John, good worts. 114

FALSTAFF Good worts? Good cabbage!—Slender, I 115
broke your head. What matter have you against me? 116

SLENDER Marry, sir, I have matter in my head against 117
you, and against your coney-catching rascals, 118
Bardolph, Nym, and Pistol.

BARDOLPH You Banbury cheese! 120

SLENDER Ay, it is no matter.

PISTOL How now, Mephistopheles? 122

SLENDER Ay, it is no matter.

NYM Slice, I say! *Pauca, pauca*. Slice, that's my humor. 124

SLENDER Where's Simple, my man? Can you tell,
cousin?

EVANS Peace, I pray you. Now let us understand. There
is three umpires in this matter, as I understand; that
is, Master Page, fidelicet Master Page; and there is myself, 129
fidelicet myself; and the three party is, lastly and 130
finally, mine Host of the Garter. 131

PAGE We three to hear it, and end it between them.

EVANS Fery goot. I will make a prief of it in my notebook, 133
and we will afterwards 'ork upon the cause with
as great discreetly as we can. 135

FALSTAFF Pistol!

PISTOL He hears with ears.

EVANS The tevil and his tam! What phrase is this, "He 138
hears with ear"? Why, it is affectations.

FALSTAFF Pistol, did you pick Master Slender's purse?

SLENDER Ay, by these gloves, did he—or I would I
might never come in mine own great chamber again 142
else—of seven groats in mill-sixpences, and two 143
Edward shovelboards, that cost me two shilling and 144
twopence apiece of Yed Miller, by these gloves. 145

FALSTAFF Is this true, Pistol?

EVANS No, it is false, if it is a pickpurse. 147

PISTOL
Ha, thou mountain-foreigner!—Sir John and master
mine, 148
I combat challenge of this latten bilbo. 149

Word of denial in thy *labras* here! 150
Word of denial! Froth and scum, thou liest!

SLENDER [*indicating Nym*] By these gloves, then 'twas
he.

NYM Be advised, sir, and pass good humors. I will say 153
"marry, trap with you" if you run the nuthook's 154
humor on me. That is the very note of it. 155

SLENDER By this hat, then, he in the red face had it. 156
For though I cannot remember what I did when you
made me drunk, yet I am not altogether an ass.

FALSTAFF [*to Bardolph*] What say you, Scarlet and John? 159

BARDOLPH Why, sir, for my part, I say the gentleman
had drunk himself out of his five sentences.

EVANS It is his five "senses." Fie, what the ignorance is!

BARDOLPH And being fap, sir, was, as they say, 163
cashiered. And so conclusions passed the careers. 164

SLENDER Ay, you spake in Latin then, too. But 'tis no
matter. I'll ne'er be drunk whilst I live again, but in
honest, civil, godly company, for this trick. If I be
drunk, I'll be drunk with those that have the fear of
God, and not with drunken knaves.

EVANS So Got 'udge me, that is a virtuous mind. 170

FALSTAFF You hear all these matters denied, gentlemen.
You hear it.

[*Enter*] Anne Page [*with wine*]; *Mistress Ford*
[*and*] *Mistress Page* [*following*].

PAGE Nay, daughter, carry the wine in; we'll drink
within. [*Exit Anne Page.*]

SLENDER Oh, heaven! This is Mistress Anne Page.

PAGE How now, Mistress Ford?

FALSTAFF Mistress Ford, by my troth, you are very well
met. By your leave, good mistress. [*He kisses her.*]

PAGE Wife, bid these gentlemen welcome.—Come,
we have a hot venison pasty to dinner. Come, gentle- 180
men, I hope we shall drink down all unkindness.
[*Exeunt all except Shallow, Slender, and Evans.*]

SLENDER I had rather than forty shillings I had my
book of songs and sonnets here. 183

[*Enter*] Simple.

How now, Simple, where have you been? I must wait
on myself, must I? You have not the book of riddles 185
about you, have you?

112–13 in counsel secretly. (Playing on *Council*.) **114 *Pauca verba***
(Let's have) few words **115 worts** vegetables, cabbages. (A quibble
on Sir Hugh's pronunciation of *words*.) **116 broke your head** made a
slight bleeding wound on your head. **116, 117 matter** (1) cause of
complaint (2) matter of consequence; pus **118 coney-catching** cheating. (A *coney* is literally a rabbit, a proverbially gullible animal.)
120 Banbury cheese (Banbury cheeses were noted for their thinness;
a reference to Slender's name and physique.) **122 Mephistopheles**
name of the devil in Marlowe's *Doctor Faustus*. **124 Slice** (1) Speak
briefly (2) I will slice with my sword (3) a reference to Bardolph's calling Slender a cheese (?) *Pauca* Speak briefly. **humor** mood.
129 fidelicet i.e., *videlicet*, namely **130 three** third **131 Garter** the
name of an inn in Windsor. **133 prief** brief, summary **135 discreetly** discretion **138 tam** dam, mother. **142 great chamber** hall
143 groats coins equal to four pence. **mill-sixpences** coins stamped
by means of the mill and press **144 Edward shovelboards** shillings
coined in the reign of Edward VI. (So called from their use in the gambling game of shovelboard.) **145 Yed** Ed, Edward **147 it is false** i.e.,
Pistol is false, not *true* ("honest"). **if it** if he **148 mountain-foreigner** i.e., Welshman. **149 combat challenge** (A flowery way of issuing a challenge to a duel.) **latten bilbo** *Latten* (literally, a yellow
brasslike alloy) refers to the inferior color and *bilbo* (from Bilbao in
Spain) to the thinness of a Spanish sword. Both make fun of Slender.

150 labras lips, i.e., face **153 Be . . . humors** i.e., Be careful what you
say and don't say anything to rile me up. **154 marry, trap with you**
(An insulting phrase meaning something like "run off," "beat it.")
154–5 run . . . me threaten me with a constable, or behave like one. (A
nuthook literally is a hooked stick used to pull nuts from trees; applied
to a constable.) **155 very note of it** truth of the matter. **156 he . . .
face** (as in *1* and *2 Henry IV* and *Henry V*, Bardolph's face is flushed
and inflamed from habitual drinking.) **it** Slender's purse.
159 Scarlet and John (Names of Robin Hood's companions, Will
Scarlet and Little John. *Scarlet* is humorously applied to Bardolph's
red face.) **163 fap** drunk **164 cashiered** deprived (of his senses; but
perhaps suggesting, too, that he was fleeced). **164 conclusions . . .
careers** i.e., they got out of control. (*Careers* means "short gallops at
full speed.") **170 'udge** judge. (For "judge.") **mind** intent. **180 pasty** to
meat pie for **183 book of songs and sonnets** (Probably refers to Tottel's *Miscellany*, published in 1557 and quite old-fashioned by the late
1590s.) **185 book of riddles** (Such a book is mentioned as in the
library of Captain Cox in *Laneham's Letter*, 1575. No copy is extant earlier than 1629.)

SIMPLE   Book of riddles? Why, did you not lend it to
Alice Shortcake upon Allhallowmas last, a fortnight 188
afore Michaelmas? 189

SHALLOW   Come, coz, come, coz, we stay for you. A 190
word with you, coz—marry, this, coz: there is as 191
'twere a tender, a kind of tender, made afar off by Sir 192
Hugh here. Do you understand me?

SLENDER   Ay, sir, you shall find me reasonable. If it be
so, I shall do that that is reason.

SHALLOW   Nay, but understand me.

SLENDER   So I do, sir.

EVANS   Give ear to his motions. Master Slender, I will 198
description the matter to you, if you be capacity of it. 199

SLENDER   Nay, I will do as my cousin Shallow says. I
pray you, pardon me. He's a Justice of Peace in his
country, simple though I stand here. 202

EVANS   But that is not the question. The question is
concerning your marriage.

SHALLOW   Ay, there's the point, sir.

EVANS   Marry, is it, the very point of it—to Mistress
Anne Page.

SLENDER   Why, if it be so, I will marry her upon any
reasonable demands. 209

EVANS   But can you affection the 'oman? Let us command to know that of your mouth or of your lips; for
divers philosophers hold that the lips is parcel of the 212
mouth. Therefore, precisely, can you carry your good
will to the maid?

SHALLOW   Cousin Abraham Slender, can you love her?

SLENDER   I hope, sir, I will do as it shall become one
that would do reason.

EVANS   Nay, Got's lords and his ladies! You must speak
positable, if you can carry her your desires towards 219
her.

SHALLOW   That you must. Will you, upon good dowry, 221
marry her?

SLENDER   I will do a greater thing than that upon your
request, cousin, in any reason.

SHALLOW   Nay, conceive me, conceive me, sweet coz. 225
What I do is to pleasure you, coz. Can you love the 226
maid?

SLENDER   I will marry her, sir, at your request. But if
there be no great love in the beginning, yet heaven
may decrease it upon better acquaintance, when we 230
are married and have more occasion to know one another. I hope upon familiarity will grow more content. 232

But if you say, "Marry her," I will marry her. That I am
freely dissolved, and dissolutely. 234

EVANS   It is a fery discretion answer; save the faul is in 235
the 'ort "dissolutely." The 'ort is, according to our 236
meaning, "resolutely." His meaning is good.

SHALLOW   Ay, I think my cousin meant well.

SLENDER   Ay, or else I would I might be hanged, la!

[Enter Anne Page.]

SHALLOW   Here comes fair Mistress Anne.—Would I
were young for your sake, Mistress Anne!

ANNE   The dinner is on the table. My father desires Your
Worships' company.

SHALLOW   I will wait on him, fair Mistress Anne. 244

EVANS   'Od's plessed will! I will not be absence at the 245
grace.   *[Exeunt Shallow and Evans.]*

ANNE   Will 't please Your Worship to come in, sir?

SLENDER   No, I thank you, forsooth, heartily. I am very
well.

ANNE   The dinner attends you, sir. 250

SLENDER   I am not ahungry, I thank you, forsooth. *[To
Simple]* Go, sirrah, for all you are my man, go wait 252
upon my cousin Shallow.   *[Exit Simple.]*
A Justice of Peace sometime may be beholding to his 254
friend for a man. I keep but three men and a boy yet,
till my mother be dead. But what though? Yet I live 256
like a poor gentleman born. 257

ANNE   I may not go in without Your Worship. They will
not sit till you come.

SLENDER   I'faith, I'll eat nothing. I thank you as much
as though I did.

ANNE   I pray you, sir, walk in.

SLENDER   I had rather walk here, I thank you. I bruised
my shin th'other day with playing at sword and 264
dagger with a master of fence—three veneys for a 265
dish of stewed prunes—and, by my troth, I cannot 266
abide the smell of hot meat since. Why do your dogs
bark so? Be there bears i'th' town?

ANNE   I think there are, sir. I heard them talked of.

SLENDER   I love the sport well, but I shall as soon quarrel 270
at it as any man in England. You are afraid if you see 271
the bear loose, are you not?

ANNE   Ay, indeed, sir.

SLENDER   That's meat and drink to me, now. I have
seen Sackerson loose twenty times, and have taken 275
him by the chain. But, I warrant you, the women have
so cried and shrieked at it that it passed. But women, 277

188–9 Allhallowmas . . . Michaelmas (Simple's blunder. Michaelmas
occurs on September 29; Allhallowmas or All Saints' Day is November 1.) **190 stay** wait **191 marry** (A mild oath, originally "by the
Virgin Mary.") **192 tender** offer (of marriage). **afar off** indirectly
198 motions proposal. **199 description** describe. **be . . . of it** have
the capacity to understand. **202 country** district. **simple though** as
sure as. (But also suggesting "however humble I, his kinsman, may
appear to be.") **209 demands** requests, terms. **212 parcel** part
219 positable (For "positively.") **221 upon good dowry** if a suitable
dowry is arranged **225 conceive** understand **226 pleasure** please
230 decrease (For "increase." But with unintended comic meaning;
the proverb "Marry first and love will after" contends with "Familiarity breeds contempt" in line 232.) **232 hope** hope that. **content**
(Unwittingly suggesting "contempt," as in the proverb cited in note
230 above.)

234 dissolved (For "resolved.") **dissolutely** (For "resolutely.")
235 faul i.e., fault **236 'ort** word **244 wait on him** join him
245 'Od's God's **250 attends** waits for **252 sirrah** (Usual form of
address to a social inferior.) **for all** even though **252–3 wait upon**
attend **254 beholding** beholden **256 till . . . dead** (Slender's widowed mother evidently controls a sizable portion of the family estate
until she dies.) **what though?** what of it? **256–7 Yet . . . born** (Slender lives like a gentleman, but one without much income at present.)
264 playing at practicing with **265 fence** fencing. **veneys** bouts in
fencing **266 stewed prunes** (A comically homespun sort of prize for
fencing, and one also associated with the "stews" or brothel houses,
where they might be served.) **270–1 quarrel at it** i.e., become
involved in altercations or competition with other men at the bearbaiting arena **275 Sackerson** a famous bear at the Paris Garden near the
theaters on the Bankside **277 passed** i.e., surpassed description.

indeed, cannot abide 'em—they are very ill-favored, 278 rough things.

[*Enter Page.*]

PAGE   Come, gentle Master Slender, come. We stay for you.

SLENDER   I'll eat nothing, I thank you, sir.

PAGE   By cock and pie, you shall not choose, sir. 283 Come, come.

SLENDER   Nay, pray you, lead the way.

PAGE   Come on, sir.

SLENDER   Mistress Anne, yourself shall go first.

ANNE   Not I, sir. Pray you, keep on.   288

SLENDER   Truly, I will not go first, truly, la! I will not do you that wrong.

ANNE   I pray you, sir.

SLENDER   I'll rather be unmannerly than troublesome. You do yourself wrong, indeed, la!   *Exeunt.*

❖

1.2

Enter Evans [from dinner] and Simple.

EVANS   Go your ways, and ask of Doctor Caius' house 1 which is the way. And there dwells one Mistress Quickly, which is in the manner of his nurse, or his dry nurse, or his cook, or his laundry, his washer, and 4 his wringer.

SIMPLE   Well, sir.

EVANS   Nay, it is petter yet. Give her this letter. [*He gives a letter.*] For it is a 'oman that altogether's 8 acquaintance with Mistress Anne Page. And the letter 9 is to desire and require her to solicit your master's 10 desires to Mistress Anne Page. I pray you, begone. I will make an end of my dinner; there's pippins and 12 cheese to come.   *Exeunt [separately].*

❖

1.3

Enter Falstaff, Host, Bardolph, Nym, Pistol, [and Robin, Falstaff's] Page.

FALSTAFF   Mine Host of the Garter!

HOST   What says my bully rook? Speak scholarly and 2 wisely.

FALSTAFF   Truly, mine Host, I must turn away some of my followers.

HOST   Discard, bully Hercules, cashier. Let them wag; 6 trot, trot.

FALSTAFF   I sit at ten pounds a week.   8

HOST   Thou'rt an emperor—Caesar, Kaiser, and Phee- 9 zer. I will entertain Bardolph; he shall draw, he 10 shall tap. Said I well, bully Hector?   11

FALSTAFF   Do so, good mine Host.

HOST   I have spoke; let him follow. [*To Bardolph*] Let me see thee froth and lime. I am at a word. Follow.   14

[*Exit.*]

FALSTAFF   Bardolph, follow him. A tapster is a good trade. An old cloak makes a new jerkin; a withered 16 servingman a fresh tapster. Go; adieu.

BARDOLPH   It is a life that I have desired. I will thrive.

[*Exit Bardolph.*]

PISTOL   O base Hungarian wight! Wilt thou the spigot 19 wield?

NYM   He was gotten in drink. Is not the humor con- 21 ceited?   22

FALSTAFF   I am glad I am so acquit of this tinderbox. 23 His thefts were too open. His filching was like an un- skillful singer: he kept not time.   25

NYM   The good humor is to steal at a minute's rest.   26

PISTOL   "Convey," the wise it call. "Steal"? Foh! A fico 27 for the phrase!

FALSTAFF   Well, sirs, I am almost out at heels.   29

PISTOL   Why then, let kibes ensue.   30

FALSTAFF   There is no remedy; I must coney-catch, I 31 must shift.   32

PISTOL   Young ravens must have food.   33

FALSTAFF   Which of you know Ford of this town?

PISTOL   I ken the wight. He is of substance good.   35

FALSTAFF   My honest lads, I will tell you what I am 36 about.   37

PISTOL   Two yards, and more.

FALSTAFF   No quips now, Pistol. Indeed, I am in the waist two yards about. But I am now about no waste; 40 I am about thrift. Briefly, I do mean to make love to

---

278 **ill-favored** ugly   283 **By cock and pie** (A popular oath, combining *cock,* a euphemism for "God," with *pie,* a dig at the service book for the pre-Reformation church.)   **shall not choose** must   288 **keep on** go ahead.
1.2. Location: The same scene, a short time later, essentially continuous.
1 **ask of** inquire concerning   4 **dry nurse** i.e., attendant to an adult, not a child; a housekeeper.   **laundry** laundress   8–9 **altogether's acquaintance** is well acquainted   10 **solicit your master's** plead the case for Master Slender's   12 **pippins** a kind of apple
1.3. Location: The Garter Inn.
2 **bully rook** i.e., fine fellow. (An abusive epithet, used jocularly here as an endearment; a *rook* is often a slang term for a swindler or a gull.)

6 **cashier** dismiss.   **wag** move on   8 **I sit at** My expenses are
9 **Kaiser** emperor   9–10 **Pheezer** i.e., Vizier. (Another extravagant epithet, like *Kaiser.*)   10 **entertain** employ.   **draw** draw liquor
11 **tap** serve as tapster.   **bully Hector** the hero of Troy, and a type of manliness, like *Hercules* in line 6. (*Bully* means "worthy," "gallant.")
14 **froth** draw liquor in such a way as to make it frothy, filling the glass with less beer.   **lime** adulterate wine by putting lime into it to mask the sour taste.   **I am at a word** I say no more.   16 **jerkin** jacket
19 **Hungarian wight** i.e., beggarly person.   21 **gotten** begotten
21–2 **conceited** ingenious.   23 **acquit** rid.   **tinderbox** (Alluding to Bardolph's fiery complexion.)   25 **he . . . time** i.e., he moved too slowly and didn't know when to stop.   26 **The good . . . rest** i.e., The smart thing is to steal quickly, within a minute's time.   27 **"Convey . . . call** i.e., *Convey* is the cant phrase for stealing used by those in the know.   **fico** Italian for *fig,* an insulting phrase and obscene gesture of putting the thumb between the second and third fingers   29 **out at heels** i.e., out of money. (Literally, with stockings or shoes worn through at the heel.)   30 **kibes** chilblains. (Pistol interprets *out at heels* literally.)   31 **coney-catch** catch rabbits, i.e., cheat victims in a con game   32 **shift** devise a stratagem.   33 **Young . . . food** (Young ravens are always hungry.)   35 **I ken . . . good** I know the chap. He is a person of means.   36–7 **what I am about** what I am up to. (But Pistol plays with the meaning "what I measure round about the waist.")   40 **waste** (With wordplay on *waist* and on the antithesis of *waste* and *thrift.*)

Ford's wife. I spy entertainment in her. She discourses, 42
she carves, she gives the leer of invitation. I 43
can construe the action of her familiar style; and the 44
hardest voice of her behavior, to be Englished rightly, 45
is, "I am Sir John Falstaff's."

PISTOL [to Nym]   He hath studied her well and translated her will—out of honesty into English. 48

NYM   The anchor is deep. Will that humor pass? 49

FALSTAFF   Now, the report goes she has all the rule of
her husband's purse. He hath a legion of angels. 51

PISTOL   As many devils entertain; and "To her, boy!" 52
say I.

NYM   The humor rises; it is good. Humor me the an- 54
gels. 55

FALSTAFF [showing letters]   I have writ me here a letter 56
to her; and here another to Page's wife, who even now 57
gave me good eyes too, examined my parts with most
judicious oeillades. Sometimes the beam of her view 59
gilded my foot, sometimes my portly belly.

PISTOL [to Nym]   Then did the sun on dunghill shine.

NYM [to Pistol]   I thank thee for that humor.

FALSTAFF   Oh, she did so course o'er my exteriors, with 63
such a greedy intention that the appetite of her eye did 64
seem to scorch me up like a burning glass! Here's 65
another letter to her. She bears the purse too; she is a
region in Guiana, all gold and bounty. I will be cheat- 67
ers to them both, and they shall be exchequers to me. 68
They shall be my East and West Indies, and I will trade
to them both. [To Pistol] Go bear thou this letter to
Mistress Page. [To Nym] And thou this to Mistress
Ford. We will thrive, lads, we will thrive.

PISTOL [giving the letter back]
Shall I Sir Pandarus of Troy become, 73
And by my side wear steel? Then Lucifer take all! 74

NYM   I will run no base humor. Here, take the humor-

letter. [He gives the letter back.] I will keep the havior of 76
reputation. 77

FALSTAFF [to Robin]
Hold, sirrah, bear you these letters tightly. 78
[He gives the letters.]
Sail like my pinnace to these golden shores.— 79
Rogues, hence, avaunt! Vanish like hailstones, go!
Trudge, plod away o'th' hoof! Seek shelter, pack! 81
Falstaff will learn the humor of the age: 82
French thrift, you rogues—myself and skirted page. 83
[Exeunt Falstaff and Robin.]

PISTOL
Let vultures gripe thy guts! For gourd and fullam holds, 84
And high and low beguiles the rich and poor. 85
Tester I'll have in pouch when thou shalt lack, 86
Base Phrygian Turk! 87

NYM   I have operations which be humors of revenge. 88

PISTOL   Wilt thou revenge?

NYM   By welkin and her star! 90

PISTOL   With wit or steel? 91

NYM
With both the humors, I. 92
I will discuss the humor of this love to Page. 93

PISTOL   And I to Ford shall eke unfold 94
How Falstaff, varlet vile,
His dove will prove, his gold will hold, 96
And his soft couch defile.

NYM   My humor shall not cool. I will incense Page to
deal with poison; I will possess him with yellowness, 99
for the revolt of mine is dangerous. That is my true 100
humor.

PISTOL   Thou art the Mars of malcontents. I second 102
thee. Troop on.   Exeunt.

❖

1.4

Enter Mistress Quickly [and] Simple.

QUICKLY [calling]   What, John Rugby!

[Enter Rugby.]

---

42 **entertainment** (1) readiness to receive me (2) a source of supply
43 **carves** i.e., is welcoming and affable.   **leer** come-hither glance
44 **construe** interpret. (Introducing an extended grammatical pun,
continued in *style*, *voice*, and *Englished*.)   **44–5 the hardest . . . rightly**
the most severe construction that could be placed on her behavior
toward me, if translated into English speech   48 **will** (1) intent (2) sexual desire.   **honesty** chastity   49 **The anchor . . . pass?** The plan is
well anchored and secure. Will it work? Or, Will my newly coined
expression pass muster?   51 **angels** coins stamped with the figure of
the archangel Michael, worth about ten shillings.   52 **As . . . entertain**
(Pistol, taking *legion of angels* in the sense of "heavenly host," plays on
the idea of a battle between them and a legion of devils. Falstaff, with
his devilish devices, is to take on the angels and *entertain* them to his
own use.)   **To her, boy!** (A cry of encouragement to a hunting
hound.)   **54–5 Humor me the angels** i.e., Yes, take the money by this
device. (Nym is seconding Pistol's advice; the *humor* of the enterprise
takes shape.)   56 **writ me** written. (*Me* is used colloquially.)   57 **even
now** just now   59 **oeillades** amorous glances.   **the beam . . . view** her
eyebeam. (Eyes were thought to emit rays toward the object being
looked at.)   63 **course o'er** run her eyes over   64 **intention** intentness
of gaze   65 **burning glass** magnifying glass to focus rays of the sun.
67 **region in Guiana** (A possible reference to Sir Walter Ralegh's
Discovery of the Large, Rich, and Beautiful Empire of Guiana, published
1596.)   **67–8 cheaters** escheaters, officers appointed to look after the
King's escheats, i.e., land reverted to the crown. (With a quibble on the
ordinary sense of "those who cheat.")   68 **exchequers** treasuries
73 **Sir Pandarus** uncle of Cressida, and go-between in the story of
Troilus and Cressida. (From his name originated the word *pander*.)
74 **And . . . steel**? i.e., even though I am a soldier?

76–7 I . . . reputation I will guard my reputation (as one who refuses
to pimp).   78 **tightly** deftly, securely.   79 **pinnace** a small, swift sailing vessel   81 **pack!** be off!   82 **humor** fashion   83 **French thrift**
(Alludes to the current practice of economizing with one French page
instead of a more numerous retinue.)   **skirted** wearing a doublet
with long skirts or tails   84 **gourd and fullam** two kinds of false dice.
holds hold good, can still be used as a means of livelihood   85 **high
and low** i.e., false dice weighted so as to produce high and low numbers   86 **Tester** Sixpence.   **pouch** purse   87 **Phrygian Turk** (A term
of opprobrium.)   88 **operations** plans   90 **welkin** sky   91 **wit or
steel** i.e., cunning or violence.   92 **both the humors** i.e., wit and
sword   93 **discuss** declare   94 **eke** also   96 **His . . . prove** will test
the virtue of Ford's wife.   **hold** seize   99 **possess** fill.   **yellowness**
i.e., jealousy. (In the Folio text, Nym plans to incense *Ford* with jealousy, which seems more appropriate to Ford's jealous temperament,
while in line 94 Pistol plans to speak to Page; however, in 2.1.104 ff.,
Nym speaks to Page, trying to make him jealous, and Pistol to Ford,
and so it seems best to follow the Quarto assignments here in lines
93–4 and 98. See Textual Notes.)   100 **the revolt . . . dangerous** i.e.,
my turning against Falstaff will harm him.   102 **the Mars** i.e., the
most warlike and mighty
1.4. Location: Doctor Caius' house.

I pray thee, go to the casement and see if you can see 1
my master, Master Doctor Caius, coming. If he do,
i'faith, and find anybody in the house, here will be an
old abusing of God's patience and the King's English. 5

RUGBY   I'll go watch.

QUICKLY   Go; and we'll have a posset for't soon at 7
night, in faith, at the latter end of a sea-coal fire. 8
[*Rugby goes to look out the window.*] An honest, willing, 9
kind fellow as ever servant shall come in house 10
withal, and, I warrant you, no telltale nor no breed- 11
bate. His worst fault is that he is given to prayer. He is 12
something peevish that way, but nobody but has his 13
fault. But let that pass. Peter Simple you say your
name is?

SIMPLE   Ay, for fault of a better. 16

QUICKLY   And Master Slender's your master?

SIMPLE   Ay, forsooth.

QUICKLY   Does he not wear a great round beard, like a
glover's paring knife?

SIMPLE   No, forsooth. He hath but a little whey face, 21
with a little yellow beard, a Cain-colored beard. 22

QUICKLY   A softly spirited man, is he not? 23

SIMPLE   Ay, forsooth. But he is as tall a man of his hands 24
as any is between this and his head. He hath fought 25
with a warrener. 26

QUICKLY   How say you? Oh, I should remember him. Does
he not hold up his head, as it were, and strut in his gait?

SIMPLE   Yes indeed does he.

QUICKLY   Well, heaven send Anne Page no worse
fortune! Tell Master Parson Evans I will do what I can
for your master. Anne is a good girl, and I wish—

[*Rugby returns.*]

RUGBY   Out, alas! Here comes my master. 33

QUICKLY   We shall all be shent. Run in here, good 34
young man; go into this closet. He will not stay long. 35
[*She shuts Simple in.*] What, John Rugby! John!
What, John, I say! Go, John, go inquire for my master.
I doubt he be not well, that he comes not home. 38

[*Exit Rugby.*]

[*Singing*] "And down, down, adown-a," etc. 39

[*Enter*] Doctor Caius.

CAIUS   Vat is you sing? I do not like dese toys. Pray 40
you, go and vetch me in my closet *un boîtier vert*, a box, 41
a green-a box. Do intend vat I speak? A green-a box. 42

QUICKLY   Ay, forsooth, I'll fetch it you. [*Aside*] I am
glad he went not in himself. If he had found the
young man, he would have been horn-mad. 45

[*She goes to the door.*]

CAIUS   *Fe, fe, fe, fe! Ma foi, il fait fort chaud. Je m'en vais à* 46
la cour—la grande affaire. 47

QUICKLY   Is it this, sir? [*She offers him a box.*]

CAIUS   *Oui; mets-le à ma* pocket. *Dépêche,* quickly! Vere is 49
dat knave Rugby?

QUICKLY   What, John Rugby! John!

[*Enter Rugby.*]

RUGBY   Here, sir.

CAIUS   You are John Rugby, and you are Jack Rugby.
Come, take-a your rapier, and come after my heel to 54
the court.

RUGBY   'Tis ready, sir, here in the porch.

CAIUS   By my trot, I tarry too long. 'Od's me, *qu'ai-j'oublié?* 57
Dere is some simples in my closet dat I vill not 58
for the varld I shall leave behind.

QUICKLY   [*aside*] Ay me, he'll find the young man
there, and be mad!

CAIUS   [*going to the room*] O *diable, diable!* Vat is in my 62
closet? Villainy! *Larron!* [*Pulling Simple out.*] Rugby, 63
my rapier!

QUICKLY   Good master, be content. 65

CAIUS   Wherefore shall I be content-a?

QUICKLY   The young man is an honest man.

CAIUS   What shall de honest man do in my closet? Dere
is no honest man dat shall come in my closet.

QUICKLY   I beseech you, be not so phlegmatic. Hear the 70
truth of it: he came of an errand to me from Parson 71
Hugh.

CAIUS   Vell?

SIMPLE   Ay, forsooth, to desire her to—

QUICKLY   Peace, I pray you.

CAIUS   Peace-a your tongue.—Speak-a your tale.

SIMPLE   To desire this honest gentlewoman, your maid,
to speak a good word to Mistress Anne Page for my
master in the way of marriage.

QUICKLY   This is all, indeed, la! But I'll ne'er put my 80
finger in the fire, and need not. 81

CAIUS   Sir Hugh send-a you? Rugby, *baille* me some 82
paper. [*To Simple*] Tarry you a little-a while. [*Rugby
fetches paper, and Dr. Caius writes.*]

QUICKLY   [*aside to Simple*] I am glad he is so quiet. If he
had been throughly moved, you should have heard 85
him so loud and so melancholy. But notwithstanding, 86

---

1 **casement** window   5 **old** plentiful, great   7 **a posset** a drink of hot
milk curdled with ale or wine   7–8 **soon at night** as soon as night
comes   8 **sea-coal** mineral coal brought by sea (as distinguished from
charcoal)   9 **s.d.** *window* (Rugby perhaps looks offstage.)   10–11 **as
ever . . . withal** i.e., as good a servant as ever served in a household
11–12 **breed-bate** mischief maker.   13 **something peevish** somewhat
whimsical, fussy   16 **for fault of** for lack of   21 **whey** i.e., pallid
22 **Cain-colored** (Cain is often pictured in old tapestries with a yellow
or reddish beard.)   23 **softly spirited** gentle   24 **as tall . . . hands** as
valiant a man, as stout of arms   25 **between . . . head** i.e., in these
parts, anywhere. (Proverbial.)   26 **warrener** gamekeeper   33 **Out** (A
cry of dismay.)   34 **shent** blamed, disgraced.   35 **closet** closet or private room.   38 **doubt** fear   39 **And . . . adown-a** (A balled refrain.)
40 **toys** trifles, i.e., songs.   41 *un boîtier vert* a green box   42 **Do
intend** Do you understand. (French *entendre*.)

45 **horn-mad** (1) enraged, like a horned beast (2) enraged like a jealous cuckold.   46–7 *Ma foi . . . affaire* By my faith, it is very hot; I am
going to court—the great affair.   49 *Oui . . . Dépêche* Yes, put it in my
pocket; be quick   54 **your rapier** i.e., your master's rapier   57 **trot**
truth, faith.   '**Od's me** God save me.   *qu'ai-j'oublié?* what have I
forgotten?   58 **simples** medicinal herbs   62 *diable* devil   63 *Larron!*
Robber!   65 **content** calm.   70 **phlegmatic** (Probably a blunder for
"choleric," hot-tempered; *phlegmatic* is the very opposite in the physiology of humors.)   71 **of an** on an   80–1 **I'll . . . not** i.e., I'll never
meddle and risk hurting myself if I don't need to.   82 *baille* fetch
85 **throughly moved** thoroughly angered   86 **melancholy** (Perhaps a
blunder again, like *phlegmatic,* above.)

man, I'll do you your master what good I can. And the 87
very yea and the no is, the French doctor, my master— 88
I may call him my master, look you, for I keep his
house, and I wash, wring, brew, bake, scour, dress 90
meat and drink, make the beds, and do all myself— 91

SIMPLE [*aside to Quickly*] 'Tis a great charge to come 92
under one body's hand.

QUICKLY [*aside to Simple*] Are you advised o' that? 94
You shall find it a great charge. And to be up early
and down late. But notwithstanding—to tell you in
your ear; I would have no words of it—my master 97
himself is in love with Mistress Anne Page. But
notwithstanding that, I know Anne's mind: that's
neither here nor there.

CAIUS [*giving Simple a letter*] You jack'nape, give-a this 101
letter to Sir Hugh. By gar, it is a shallenge. I will cut 102
his troat in de park, and I will teach a scurvy jackanape
priest to meddle or make. You may be gone; it is not 104
good you tarry here.   [*Exit Simple.*]
By gar, I will cut all his two stones. By gar, he shall not 106
have a stone to throw at his dog.

QUICKLY Alas, he speaks but for his friend.

CAIUS It is no matter-a ver dat. Do not you tell-a me dat 109
I shall have Anne Page for myself? By gar, I vill kill de
jack priest; and I have appointed mine Host of de 111
Jarteer to measure our weapon. By gar, I will myself 112
have Anne Page.

QUICKLY Sir, the maid loves you, and all shall be well.
We must give folks leave to prate. What the goodyear! 115

CAIUS Rugby, come to the court with me. [*To Mistress
Quickly*] By gar, if I have not Anne Page, I shall turn
your head out of my door.—Follow my heels, Rugby.
                              [*Exeunt Caius and Rugby.*]

QUICKLY You shall have An fool's head of your own. 119
No, I know Anne's mind for that. Never a woman in
Windsor knows more of Anne's mind than I do, nor
can do more than I do with her, I thank heaven.

FENTON [*within*] Who's within there, ho?

QUICKLY Who's there, I trow? Come near the house, I 124
pray you.

                    [*Enter*] Fenton.

FENTON How now, good woman, how dost thou?

QUICKLY The better that it pleases Your good Worship
to ask.

FENTON What news? How does pretty Mistress Anne?

QUICKLY In truth, sir, and she is pretty, and honest, and 130
gentle, and one that is your friend, I can tell you that 131
by the way, I praise heaven for it.

FENTON Shall I do any good, think'st thou? Shall I not
lose my suit?

QUICKLY Troth, sir, all is in His hands above. But
notwithstanding, Master Fenton, I'll be sworn on a 136
book she loves you. Have not Your Worship a wart 137
above your eye?

FENTON Yes, marry, have I. What of that?

QUICKLY Well, thereby hangs a tale. Good faith, it is 140
such another Nan! But, I detest, an honest maid as 141
ever broke bread. We had an hour's talk of that wart.
I shall never laugh but in that maid's company! But 143
indeed she is given too much to allicholy and musing. 144
But for you—well, go to. 145

FENTON Well, I shall see her today. Hold, there's money
for thee. [*He gives money.*] Let me have thy voice in my 147
behalf. If thou see'st her before me, commend me.

QUICKLY Will I? I'faith, that I will. And I will tell Your
Worship more of the wart the next time we have
confidence, and of other wooers. 151

FENTON Well, farewell. I am in great haste now.

QUICKLY Farewell to Your Worship.   [*Exit Fenton.*]
Truly, an honest gentleman. But Anne loves him not,
for I know Anne's mind as well as another does.—
Out upon't! What have I forgot?   *Exit.* 156

❖

2.1

Enter Mistress Page [with a letter].

MRS. PAGE What, have I scaped love letters in the
holiday time of my beauty, and am I now a subject for
them? Let me see.   [*She reads.*]
"Ask me no reason why I love you, for though Love
use Reason for his precisian, he admits him not for his 5
counselor. You are not young; no more am I. Go to, 6
then, there's sympathy. You are merry; so am I. Ha, 7
ha! Then there's more sympathy. You love sack, and 8
so do I. Would you desire better sympathy? Let it
suffice thee, Mistress Page—at the least, if the love of
soldier can suffice—that I love thee. I will not say, "pity
me"—'tis not a soldierlike phrase—but I say, "love
me." By me,
      Thine own true knight,
      By day or night
      Or any kind of light,
      With all his might
      For thee to fight,
                                  John Falstaff."

---

87 **you** for you, since you ask me   87–8 **the very yea and the no** the
long and short of it   90–1 **scour . . . meat** scrub, prepare food
92 **charge** responsibility   94 **Are . . . that?** i.e., Do you understand
that? You can say that again.   97 **I would . . . of it** I wouldn't want
the word to get out   101 **jack'nape** i.e., coxcomb, conceited fop. (A
contemptuous epithet; literally, Jack of Naples, an ape or tame monkey.)   102 **gar** i.e., God   104 **meddle or make** meddle.   106 **cut . . .
stones** castrate him.   109 **ver** for   111 **jack** (A contemptuous epithet.)   112 **Jarteer** Garter.   **measure our weapon** i.e., act as second or
referee. (Literally, to make sure that the swords are of equal length.)
115 **What the goodyear!** i.e., What the deuce!   119 **An** (The Folio uses
the same spelling, *An*, for *Anne*, in lines 120 and 121, suggesting a
pun on *Anne Page*; Caius is to have a fool's head for wooing Anne.)
124 **trow** wonder.   **Come near** Enter

130 **honest** chaste   131 **gentle** well-bred.   **your friend** friendly disposed toward you.   136–7 **a book** i.e., a Bible   140–1 **it is . . . Nan** i.e.,
you wouldn't believe it if I told you about Ann; she's a wonder.
141 **detest** (For "protest.")   143 **but** except   144 **allicholy** (For
"melancholy.")   145 **go to** i.e., enough; come, come.   147 **voice** word
of support   151 **confidence** (For "conference," blurred here with the
notion of confiding.)   156 **Out upon't!** i.e., Deuce take it!
2.1. Location: Before Page's house.
5 **precisian** strict adviser   6 **counselor** personal guide.   7 **sympathy**
congeniality.   8 **sack** a Spanish wine

What a Herod of Jewry is this! Oh, wicked, wicked world! 20
One that is well-nigh worn to pieces with age, to show
himself a young gallant! What an unweighed behavior 22
hath this Flemish drunkard picked, i'th' devil's 23
name, out of my conversation, that he dares in this 24
manner assay me? Why, he hath not been thrice in my 25
company. What should I say to him? I was then frugal 26
of my mirth. Heaven forgive me! Why, I'll exhibit a 27
bill in the Parliament for the putting down of men. 28
How shall I be revenged on him? For revenged I will
be, as sure as his guts are made of puddings. 30

[*Enter*] Mistress Ford.

MRS. FORD   Mistress Page! Trust me, I was going to 31
your house.

MRS. PAGE   And, trust me, I was coming to you. You
look very ill. 34

MRS. FORD   Nay, I'll ne'er believe that. I have to show 35
to the contrary.

MRS. PAGE   Faith, but you do, in my mind.

MRS. FORD   Well, I do, then. Yet I say I could show you
to the contrary. Oh, Mistress Page, give me some
counsel!

MRS. PAGE   What's the matter, woman?

MRS. FORD   Oh, woman, if it were not for one trifling
respect, I could come to such honor! 43

MRS. PAGE   Hang the trifle, woman, take the honor.
What is it? Dispense with trifles. What is it?

MRS. FORD   If I would but go to hell for an eternal
moment or so, I could be knighted.

MRS. PAGE   What? Thou liest! Sir Alice Ford? These 48
knights will hack, and so thou shouldst not alter the 49
article of thy gentry. 50

MRS. FORD   We burn daylight. Here, read, read. Perceive 51
how I might be knighted. [*She gives a letter.*] I shall
think the worse of fat men as long as I have an eye to 53
make difference of men's liking. And yet he would not 54
swear, praised women's modesty, and gave such 55
orderly and well-behaved reproof to all uncomeliness 56
that I would have sworn his disposition would have
gone to the truth of his words. But they do no more 58
adhere and keep place together than the Hundredth
Psalm to the tune of "Greensleeves." What tempest, I 60
trow, threw this whale, with so many tuns of oil in his 61

belly, ashore at Windsor? How shall I be revenged on
him? I think the best way were to entertain him with 63
hope, till the wicked fire of lust have melted him in his 64
own grease. Did you ever hear the like?

MRS. PAGE   Letter for letter, but that the name of Page
and Ford differs! To thy great comfort in this mystery 67
of ill opinions, here's the twin brother of thy letter. 68
[*She shows her letter.*] But let thine inherit first, for I 69
protest mine never shall. I warrant he hath a thousand
of these letters, writ with blank space for different
names—sure, more—and these are of the second
edition. He will print them, out of doubt; for he cares 73
not what he puts into the press, when he would put 74
us two. I had rather be a giantess and lie under Mount
Pelion. Well, I will find you twenty lascivious turtles 76
ere one chaste man.

MRS. FORD   [*comparing the letters*]   Why, this is the very
same: the very hand, the very words. What doth he 79
think of us?

MRS. PAGE   Nay, I know not. It makes me almost ready
to wrangle with mine own honesty. I'll entertain my- 82
self like one that I am not acquainted withal; for, sure, 83
unless he know some strain in me that I know not 84
myself, he would never have boarded me in this fury. 85

MRS. FORD   "Boarding," call you it? I'll be sure to keep
him above deck.

MRS. PAGE   So will I. If he come under my hatches, I'll
never to sea again. Let's be revenged on him. Let's
appoint him a meeting, give him a show of comfort in
his suit, and lead him on with a fine-baited delay till 91
he hath pawned his horses to mine Host of the Garter. 92

MRS. FORD   Nay, I will consent to act any villainy 93
against him that may not sully the chariness of our 94
honesty. Oh, that my husband saw this letter! It would 95
give eternal food to his jealousy.

MRS. PAGE   Why, look where he comes, and my good- 97
man too. He's as far from jealousy as I am from giving 98
him cause, and that, I hope, is an unmeasurable 99
distance.

MRS. FORD   You are the happier woman. 101

MRS. PAGE   Let's consult together against this greasy
knight. Come hither.   [*They retire.*]

[*Enter*] Master Page [*with*] Nym, Master Ford
[*with*] Pistol.

---

20 Herod of Jewry bombastic ranter, like the comic villain of the Corpus Christi plays   **22 unweighed** unconsidered, inadvertent
23 Flemish drunkard (The Flemish were proverbially heavy drinkers.)
24 conversation conduct   **25 assay** accost, address (with proposals of love)   **26 should I say** was I to say   **27 exhibit** introduce   **28 putting down** suppression. (But with bawdy suggestion.)   **30 puddings** mixture of meat, herbs, etc., stuffed into intestines of animals, as sausage.
31 Trust me Believe me   **34 ill** unhappy, out of sorts. (But Mistress Ford, in replying, plays on the sense of "ugly.")   **35 have** have something, i.e., the letter   **43 respect** matter, consideration   **48–50 These . . . gentry** i.e., These knights are a quarrelsome and promiscuous lot, and so you should not risk your social respectability for the dubious honor of being a knight's lover.   **51 burn daylight** i.e., waste time.   **53–4 to make . . . liking** to discriminate among men.   **54–5 he . . . swear** he would not use profanity in my presence   **56 uncomeliness** unseemly behavior   **58 gone . . . words** matched his language.   **60 Greensleeves** (A popular tune, to which many sets of words have been sung, some of them erotic and thus wholly unlike the Hundredth Psalm; compare 5.5.19.)   **61 trow** wonder.   **tuns** (1) large casks (2) tons

63–4 entertain . . . hope lead him on   **67–8 mystery . . . opinions** i.e., revelation of the low opinion Falstaff has of us, and thus of our low opinion of Falstaff   **69 inherit** come into possession, as of a legacy
73 out of without   **74 into the press** (1) into the printing press (2) under his weight   **76 Pelion** mountain in Thessaly. (The giants, according to Greek mythology, heaped it on a neighboring mountain, Ossa, and Ossa on Olympus, in their attempts to overthrow the gods.)   **turtles** turtledoves, proverbially faithful to their mates and therefore not likely to be promiscuous   **79 hand** handwriting
82 wrangle with quarrel with, doubt.   **honesty** chastity.   **entertain** treat   **83 withal** with   **84 strain** quality   **85 boarded** accosted, made advances to. (A term of naval warfare.)   **91 fine-baited** with the hook well baited   **91–2 till . . . Garter** i.e., until Falstaff is even more in debt than he is now.   **93 Nay** i.e., Indeed   **94–5 the chariness . . . honesty** the integrity of our chaste virtue.   **95 that** if only
97–8 goodman husband   **99 unmeasurable** infinite   **101 happier** more fortunate (than I)

FORD   Well, I hope it be not so.

PISTOL
Hope is a curtal dog in some affairs.   105
Sir John affects thy wife.   106

FORD   Why, sir, my wife is not young.

PISTOL
He woos both high and low, both rich and poor
Both young and old, one with another, Ford.
He loves the gallimaufry. Ford, perpend.   110

FORD   Love my wife?

PISTOL
With liver burning hot. Prevent, or go thou,   112
Like Sir Actaeon, he, with Ringwood at thy heels.—   113
Oh, odious is the name!   114

FORD   What name, sir?

PISTOL   The horn, I say. Farewell.
Take heed, have open eye, for thieves do foot by night.   117
Take heed, ere summer comes or cuckoo birds do sing.   118
Away, Sir Corporal Nym!   119
Believe it, Page, he speaks sense.   [Exit.]

FORD   [aside]   I will be patient. I will find out this.

NYM   [to Page]   And this is true. I like not the humor of
lying. He hath wronged me in some humors. I   123
should have borne the humored letter to her; but I   124
have a sword, and it shall bite upon my necessity.   125
He loves your wife; there's the short and the long.
My name is Corporal Nym. I speak and I avouch 'tis
true. My name is Nym, and Falstaff loves your wife.
Adieu. I love not the humor of bread and cheese,   129
and there's the humor of it. Adieu.

PAGE   [aside]   "The humor of it," quoth 'a! Here's a
fellow frights English out of his wits.   132

FORD   [aside]   I will seek out Falstaff.

PAGE   [aside]   I never heard such a drawling, affecting   134
rogue.

FORD   [aside]   If I do find it—well.   136

PAGE   [aside]   I will not believe such a Cathayan, though   137
the priest o'th' town commended him for a true man.

FORD   [aside]   'Twas a good sensible fellow. Well.

[Mistress Page and Mistress Ford come forward.]

PAGE   How now, Meg?

MRS. PAGE   Whither go you, George? Hark you.
[They converse apart.]

MRS. FORD   How now, sweet Frank, why art thou
melancholy?

FORD   I melancholy? I am not melancholy. Get you
home, go.

MRS. FORD   Faith, thou hast some crotchets in thy head   146
now.—Will you go, Mistress Page?

MRS. PAGE   Have with you. You'll come to dinner, George?   148

[Enter Mistress] Quickly.

[Aside to Mistress Ford] Look who comes yonder. She
shall be our messenger to this paltry knight.

MRS. FORD   [aside to Mistress Page]   Trust me, I thought
on her. She'll fit it.   152

MRS. PAGE   [to Mistress Quickly]   You are come to see
my daughter Anne?

QUICKLY   Ay, forsooth; and, I pray, how does good Mistress Anne?

MRS. PAGE   Go in with us and see. We have an hour's
talk with you.
[Exeunt Mistress Page, Mistress Ford, and
Mistress Quickly.]

PAGE   How now, Master Ford?

FORD   You heard what this knave told me, did you not?

PAGE   Yes, and you heard what the other told me?

FORD   Do you think there is truth in them?

PAGE   Hang 'em, slaves! I do not think the knight would
offer it. But these that accuse him in his intent towards   164
our wives are a yoke of his discarded men—very   165
rogues, now they be out of service.

FORD   Were they his men?

PAGE   Marry, were they.

FORD   I like it never the better for that. Does he lie at the   169
Garter?

PAGE   Ay, marry, does he. If he should intend this   171
voyage toward my wife, I would turn her loose to him;
and what he gets more of her than sharp words, let it
lie on my head.   174

FORD   I do not misdoubt my wife, but I would be loath   175
to turn them together. A man may be too confident. I   176
would have nothing lie on my head. I cannot be thus
satisfied.

[Enter] Host.

PAGE   Look where my ranting Host of the Garter comes.   179
There is either liquor in his pate or money in his purse
when he looks so merrily.—How now, mine Host?

HOST   How now, bully rook? Thou'rt a gentleman. [He   182
turns and calls.] Cavaleiro Justice, I say!   183

[Enter] Shallow.

---

105 Hope . . . affairs i.e., Hope is not to be trusted. (A *curtal dog* is one
with docked tail, often used to run a treadwheel, perhaps likened here
to a creature turning Fortune's wheel.)   106 affects loves, aims at
110 gallimaufry a dish of miscellaneous ingredients; hence, the whole
lot.   perpend consider.   112 liver burning hot (The liver was considered the seat of the passions.)   113 Actaeon huntsman who was
changed into a stag by Diana as punishment for watching her and her
nymphs at their bath and was torn to pieces by his own hounds. (Pistol urges Ford to avoid the fate of the horned beast: that of wearing a
cuckold's horns.)   Ringwood one of Actaeon's hounds. (Mentioned
in Golding's translation of Ovid.)   114 the name i.e., the name of
Actaeon or cuckold.   117 foot walk   118 cuckoo birds (Associated
with cuckoldry because of their call, "cuckoo," and because they lay
eggs in other birds' nests.)   119 Away Come away   123–4 I . . . borne
i.e., He wanted me to carry   125 upon my necessity when I have
need.   129 humor . . . cheese (Alludes to the scant rations Nym
received as Falstaff's retainer.)   132 his its   134 affecting affected
136 If . . . well If I find it's true, well, I'll take steps.   137 Cathayan
person from Cathay, i.e., China, and therefore assumed by Page to be
a scoundrel.   though even if

146 crotchets whims, fancies   148 Have with you I'll go along with
you.   152 She'll fit it She is just the person for the part.   164 offer
venture   165 yoke pair   169 lie lodge   171 intend propose making   174 lie on my head be my responsibility. (But Ford, in his
reply, sees a reference to cuckold's horns.)   175 misdoubt mistrust
176 turn them together i.e., let them loose together in the same pasture, as in line 172 above.   179 ranting speaking in a high-flown,
bombastic style   182 bully rook i.e., fine fellow. (See 1.3.2 and note.
Similarly in lines 187 and 191 below.)   183 Cavaleiro Justice Gallant Justice Shallow. (Put here in the form of an honorific title. The
Spanish *caballero* is a gentleman trained in arms; the Italian *cavaliere*
is a knight.)

SHALLOW   I follow, mine Host, I follow.—Good even 184
and twenty, good Master Page! Master Page, will you 185
go with us? We have sport in hand.

HOST   Tell him, Cavaleiro Justice. Tell him, bully rook.

SHALLOW   Sir, there is a fray to be fought between Sir
Hugh the Welsh priest and Caius the French doctor.

FORD   Good mine Host o'th' Garter, a word with you.

HOST   What say'st thou, my bully rook?

[They converse apart.]

SHALLOW   [*to Page*]   Will you go with us to behold it?
My merry Host hath had the measuring of their weap- 193
ons, and, I think, hath appointed them contrary 194
places; for, believe me, I hear the parson is no jester. 195
Hark, I will tell you what our sport shall be.

[They converse apart.]

HOST   [*to Ford*]   Hast thou no suit against my knight, 197
my guest cavalier? 198

FORD   None, I protest. But I'll give you a pottle of burnt 199
sack to give me recourse to him and tell him my name 200
is Brook—only for a jest. 201

HOST   My hand, bully. Thou shalt have egress and 202
regress—said I well?—and thy name shall be Brook. 203
It is a merry knight.—Will you go, mynheers? 204

SHALLOW   Have with you, mine Host. 205

PAGE   I have heard the Frenchman hath good skill in his
rapier.

SHALLOW   Tut, sir, I could have told you more. In these
times you stand on distance—your passes, stoccados, 209
and I know not what. 'Tis the heart, Master Page; 'tis 210
here, 'tis here. I have seen the time, with my long 211
sword I would have made you four tall fellows skip 212
like rats.

HOST   Here, boys, here, here! Shall we wag? 214

PAGE   Have with you. I had rather hear them scold than
fight.   *Exeunt [Host, Shallow, and Page].*

FORD   Though Page be a secure fool, and stands so 217
firmly on his wife's frailty, yet I cannot put off my
opinion so easily. She was in his company at Page's 219
house, and what they made there I know not. Well, I 220
will look further into't, and I have a disguise to sound 221

Falstaff. If I find her honest, I lose not my labor; if she
be otherwise, 'tis labor well bestowed.   *[Exit.]*

❖

2.2

Enter Falstaff [and] Pistol.

FALSTAFF   I will not lend thee a penny.

PISTOL

Why, then the world's mine oyster,
Which I with sword will open.
I will retort the sum in equipage. 4

FALSTAFF   Not a penny. I have been content, sir, you
should lay my countenance to pawn. I have grated 6
upon my good friends for three reprieves for you and 7
your coach-fellow Nym, or else you had looked 8
through the grate like a gemini of baboons. I am 9
damned in hell for swearing to gentlemen my friends 10
you were good soldiers and tall fellows. And when 11
Mistress Bridget lost the handle of her fan, I took't 12
upon mine honor thou hadst it not. 13

PISTOL

Didst not thou share? Hadst thou not fifteen pence?

FALSTAFF   Reason, you rogue, reason. Think'st thou I'll 15
endanger my soul gratis? At a word, hang no more 16
about me. I am no gibbet for you. Go. A short knife 17
and a throng! To your manor of Pickt-hatch, go. You'll 18
not bear a letter for me, you rogue? You stand upon
your honor? Why, thou unconfinable baseness, it is as 20
much as I can do to keep the terms of my honor 21
precise. Ay, ay, I myself sometimes, leaving the fear of 22
God on the left hand and hiding mine honor in my 23
necessity, am fain to shuffle, to hedge, and to lurch; 24
and yet you, you rogue, will ensconce your rags, your
cat-a-mountain looks, your red-lattice phrases, and 26
your bold-beating oaths, under the shelter of your 27
honor! You will not do it? You?

PISTOL   I do relent. What would thou more of man?

[Enter] Robin.

ROBIN   Sir, here's a woman would speak with you.

FALSTAFF   Let her approach.

[Enter Mistress] Quickly.

184–5 **Good . . . twenty** i.e., Good afternoon, many times over
193–4 **hath had . . . weapons** i.e., has been appointed referee
194–5 **contrary places** different meeting places   195 **the parson . . .
jester** i.e., Parson Evans is serious about this challenge to a duel, and
is a swordsman to be reckoned with. (Earlier, Evans played peacemaker with Falstaff and Shallow, but the present quarrel is, for him, a
matter of honor in defending his candidate for Anne Page's hand,
Slender, against Doctor Caius.)   197–8 **my . . . cavalier** Falstaff,
residing in the Host's inn.   199 **protest** insist.   **pottle** two-quart
measure.   **burnt** heated   200 **recourse** access   201 **Brook** (Ford's
alias, usually spelled *Brooke* in the 1602 Quarto, was changed to
Broome in the Folio because Brooke was the family name of Lord Cobham. See Introduction.)   202–3 **egress and regresss** i.e., free access to
come and go   204 **mynheers** gentlemen. (Dutch.)   205 **Have with
you** I'll come with you. (Also in line 215.)   209 **you stand on distance** one attaches great importance to prescribed space between
fencers.   **passes** lunges.   **stoccados** thrusts   210–11 **'Tis . . . 'tis here**
i.e., Real fencing, Master Page, is a matter of the heart, not of this
affected modern etiquette. (Shallow perhaps taps his chest as he says,
"'Tis here.")   211–12 **long sword** an old-fashioned, heavy weapon
212 **tall** valiant   214 **wag** go. (See 1.3.6.)   217 **secure** overconfident
219 **She** i.e., Mistress Ford.   **his** i.e., Falstaff's   220 **made** did
221 **sound** test, plumb the depths of

2.2. Location: The Garter Inn.
4 **retort . . . equipage** i.e., pay back the whole amount in military
equipment.   6 **lay . . . pawn** i.e., borrow money on the strength of my
patronage.   6–7 **grated upon** i.e., persistently and irritatingly begged
8 **coach-fellow** partner (like a fellow horse in harness)   9 **grate** i.e., of
a debtors' prison window.   **gemini** pair   10 **gentlemen my friends**
my gentlemen friends   11 **tall** brave   12–13 **took't upon** swore by
15 **Reason** With good reason   16 **gratis** for free.   **At a word** In short.
hang loiter. (With pun on hanging from a *gibbet* in line 17.)
17–18 **A short . . . throng!** i.e., With a short knife you might cut purses
in a crowd!   18 **Pickt-hatch** (A quarter in London, notorious in Elizabethan times for criminal types and prostitutes, the houses having
hatches, or half-doors, the lower half-door surmounted with spikes.)
20 **unconfinable** infinite   21–2 **to keep . . . precise** i.e., to keep my
reputation unsullied by associating with you. (*Precise* is a term often
associated with puritanism.)   22–3 **leaving . . . hand** i.e., disregarding a proper fear of God   24 **fain . . . lurch** obliged to practice trickery, to dodge, and to steal   26 **cat-a-mountain** catamount, leopard or
panther, wildcat.   **red-lattice phrases** alehouse talk. (Lattices painted
red identified an alehouse.)   27 **bold-beating oaths** the oaths of a
rowdy braggart, oaths as violent as blows

QUICKLY   Give Your Worship good morrow.

FALSTAFF   Good morrow, goodwife.

QUICKLY   Not so, an't please Your Worship.   34

FALSTAFF   Good maid, then.

QUICKLY   I'll be sworn: as my mother was, the first   36
hour I was born.   37

FALSTAFF   I do believe the swearer. What with me?

QUICKLY   Shall I vouchsafe Your Worship a word or two?   39

FALSTAFF   Two thousand, fair woman, and I'll vouchsafe
thee the hearing.

QUICKLY   There is one Mistress Ford, sir—I pray, come
a little nearer this ways. I myself dwell with Master
Doctor Caius—

FALSTAFF   Well, on. Mistress Ford, you say—

QUICKLY   Your Worship says very true. I pray Your
Worship, come a little nearer this ways.

FALSTAFF   I warrant thee, nobody hears. Mine own
people, mine own people.

QUICKLY   Are they so? God bless them and make them
His servants!

FALSTAFF   Well; Mistress Ford: what of her?

QUICKLY   Why, sir, she's a good creature. Lord, Lord,
Your Worship's a wanton! Well, heaven forgive you
and all of us, I pray!

FALSTAFF   Mistress Ford; come, Mistress Ford—

QUICKLY   Marry, this is the short and the long of it: you
have brought her into such a canaries as 'tis wonder-   58
ful. The best courtier of them all, when the court lay at   59
Windsor, could never have brought her to such a
canary. Yet there has been knights, and lords, and
gentlemen, with their coaches, I warrant you, coach
after coach, letter after letter, gift after gift, smelling so
sweetly, all musk, and so rushling, I warrant you, in   64
silk and gold, and in such alligant terms, and in such   65
wine and sugar of the best and the fairest, that would
have won any woman's heart; and, I warrant you,
they could never get an eye-wink of her. I had myself
twenty angels given me this morning; but I defy all   69
angels, in any such sort, as they say, but in the way of   70
honesty; and, I warrant you, they could never get her   71
so much as sip on a cup with the proudest of them all.
And yet there has been earls, nay, which is more,
pensioners, but I warrant you all is one with her.   74

FALSTAFF   But what says she to me? Be brief, my good
she-Mercury.   76

QUICKLY   Marry, she hath received your letter, for the
which she thanks you a thousand times, and she gives   78
you to notify that her husband will be absence from   79
his house between ten and eleven.

FALSTAFF   Ten and eleven?

QUICKLY   Ay, forsooth; and then you may come and see
the picture, she says, that you wot of. Master Ford, her   83
husband, will be from home. Alas, the sweet woman
leads an ill life with him. He's a very jealousy man.
She leads a very frampold life with him, good heart.   86

FALSTAFF   Ten and eleven. Woman, commend me to
her. I will not fail her.

QUICKLY   Why, you say well. But I have another mes-   89
senger to Your Worship. Mistress Page hath her hearty   90
commendations to you, too; and let me tell you in your
ear, she's as fartuous a civil modest wife, and one, I   92
tell you, that will not miss you morning nor evening   93
prayer, as any is in Windsor, whoe'er be the other.
And she bade me tell Your Worship that her husband
is seldom from home, but she hopes there will come
a time. I never knew a woman so dote upon a man.
Surely I think you have charms, la! Yes, in truth.   98

FALSTAFF   Not I, I assure thee. Setting the attraction of
my good parts aside, I have no other charms.   100

QUICKLY   Blessing on your heart for't!

FALSTAFF   But, I pray thee, tell me this: has Ford's wife
and Page's wife acquainted each other how they love
me?

QUICKLY   That were a jest indeed! They have not so little
grace, I hope. That were a trick indeed! But Mistress
Page would desire you to send her your little page, of   107
all loves. Her husband has a marvelous infection to the   108
little page; and truly Master Page is an honest man.   109
Never a wife in Windsor leads a better life than she
does. Do what she will, say what she will, take all, pay
all, go to bed when she list, rise when she list—all is   112
as she will. And truly she deserves it, for if there be a
kind woman in Windsor, she is one. You must send
her your page, no remedy.   115

FALSTAFF   Why, I will.

QUICKLY   Nay, but do so, then. And, look you, he may
come and go between you both. And in any case have
a nayword, that you may know one another's mind,   119
and the boy never need to understand anything; for
'tis not good that children should know any wickedness.
Old folks, you know, have discretion, as they
say, and know the world.

FALSTAFF   Fare thee well. Commend me to them both.
There's my purse; I am yet thy debtor. [*He gives
money.*] Boy, go along with this woman.

[*Exeunt Mistress Quickly and Robin.*]

This news distracts me!   127

---

34 Not so i.e., I am not a wife. **an't** if it **36 I'll be sworn** I'll swear
to that **36–7 as . . . born** (Mistress Quickly probably means "as much
a maid as when I was born, just like my mother before me," but manages instead to allege the impossible, that her mother was a virgin
when Mistress Quickly was born.) **39 vouchsafe** deign to grant.
(The comic pompousness of *vouchsafe* prompts Falstaff to use it in his
reply.) **58 canaries** state of excitement. (Confusing "quandary" with
the dance called the canary?) **59 lay** resided **64 rushling** i.e.,
rustling **65 alligant** i.e., elegant, or eloquent (?) **69 twenty angels**
i.e., as a bribe to act as go-between. *Angels* are gold coins. **defy**
reject, spurn **70 sort** manner **71 they** the supposed admirers of
Mistress Ford **74 pensioners** crown pensioners, who were required
to pray twice a day for the monarch in return for their pension. (In
elevating them above earls in the social order, Mistress Quickly is
either confused or exaggerating in order to flatter Falstaff.) **all is
one** it's a matter of indifference **76 she-Mercury** woman messenger.

78–9 gives you to notify bids you take notice **79 absence** (For
"absent.") **83 wot** know **86 frampold** disagreeable **89–90 messenger** (For "message.") **92 fartuous** (For "virtuous.") **modest**
decent, proper **93 miss you** miss. (*You* is used colloquially.)
98 have charms use magic. **100 parts** qualities **107–8 of all loves**
for love's sake. **108 infection to** (For "affection for.") **109 an honest** a worthy **112 list** wishes **115 no remedy** no two ways about it.
119 nayword watchword **127 distracts** bewilders (with ecstasy)

PISTOL [aside]
    This punk is one of Cupid's carriers.   128
    Clap on more sails! Pursue! Up with your fights!   129
    Give fire! She is my prize, or ocean whelm them all!   130
                   [Exit.]

FALSTAFF   Say'st thou so, old Jack? Go thy ways. I'll 131
make more of thy old body than I have done. Will they
yet look after thee? Wilt thou, after the expense of so 133
much money, be now a gainer? Good body, I thank
thee. Let them say 'tis grossly done; so it be fairly 135
done, no matter. 136

        [Enter] Bardolph [with wine].

BARDOLPH   Sir John, there's one Master Brook below
would fain speak with you and be acquainted with
you, and hath sent Your Worship a morning's draft of
sack.
FALSTAFF   Brook is his name?
BARDOLPH   Ay, sir.
FALSTAFF   Call him in. Such Brooks are welcome to me,
that o'erflows such liquor.   [Exit Bardolph.]
Aha! Mistress Ford and Mistress Page, have I encom- 145
passed you? Go to. Via! 146

        [Enter Bardolph, with] Ford [disguised].

FORD   Bless you, sir.
FALSTAFF   And you, sir. Would you speak with me?
FORD   I make bold to press with so little preparation 149
upon you.
FALSTAFF   You're welcome. What's your will? [To Bar-
dolph] Give us leave, drawer.   [Exit Bardolph.] 152
FORD   Sir, I am a gentleman that have spent much. My
name is Brook.
FALSTAFF   Good Master Brook, I desire more acquaintance of you.
FORD   Good Sir John, I sue for yours—not to charge 157
you, for I must let you understand I think myself in 158
better plight for a lender than you are, the which hath
something emboldened me to this unseasoned intru- 160
sion; for they say if money go before, all ways do lie
open.
FALSTAFF   Money is a good soldier, sir, and will on.
FORD   Troth, and I have a bag of money here troubles
me. If you will help to bear it, Sir John, take all, or half,
for easing me of the carriage. 166
FALSTAFF   Sir, I know not how I may deserve to be your
porter.

FORD   I will tell you, sir, if you will give me the hearing.
FALSTAFF   Speak, good Master Brook. I shall be glad to
be your servant.
FORD   Sir, I hear you are a scholar—I will be brief with
you—and you have been a man long known to me,
though I had never so good means as desire to make
myself acquainted with you. I shall discover a thing to 175
you wherein I must very much lay open mine own
imperfection. But, good Sir John, as you have one eye
upon my follies, as you hear them unfolded, turn
another into the register of your own, that I may pass 179
with a reproof the easier, sith you yourself know how 180
easy it is to be such an offender.
FALSTAFF   Very well, sir. Proceed.
FORD   There is a gentlewoman in this town; her husband's name is Ford.
FALSTAFF   Well, sir.
FORD   I have long loved her, and, I protest to you, bestowed much on her, followed her with a doting ob- 187
servance, engrossed opportunities to meet her, fee'd 188
every slight occasion that could but niggardly give me
sight of her, not only bought many presents to give
her but have given largely to many to know what she 191
would have given. Briefly, I have pursued her as love 192
hath pursued me, which hath been on the wing of all
occasions. But whatsoever I have merited—either in
my mind or in my means—meed I am sure I have 195
received none, unless experience be a jewel. That I
have purchased at an infinite rate, and that hath
taught me to say this:
"Love like a shadow flies when substance love
    pursues, 199
Pursuing that that flies, and flying what pursues." 200
FALSTAFF   Have you received no promise of satisfaction
at her hands?
FORD   Never.
FALSTAFF   Have you importuned her to such a purpose?
FORD   Never.
FALSTAFF   Of what quality was your love, then?
FORD   Like a fair house built on another man's ground,
so that I have lost my edifice by mistaking the place
where I erected it.
FALSTAFF   To what purpose have you unfolded this to
me?
FORD   When I have told you that, I have told you all.
Some say that though she appear honest to me, yet in 213
other places she enlargeth her mirth so far that there is 214
shrewd construction made of her. Now, Sir John, here 215
is the heart of my purpose. You are a gentleman of
excellent breeding, admirable discourse, of great ad- 217
mittance, authentic in your place and person, gener- 218

---

128 punk whore. carriers messengers. 129 Clap Put. fights fighting sails, i.e., screens raised during naval engagements to conceal and
protect the crew. 130 prize booty. ocean whelm let the ocean overwhelm. (Pistol, having refused to carry Falstaff's love notes, sees Mistress Quickly as an adversary.) 131 Say'st . . . ways i.e., What do you
think of that, Jack, my boy? Not bad. 133 look after i.e., lust after
135–6 Let . . . matter i.e., My enemies can criticize me all they want
for indelicacy (and fatness), but so long as my plan succeeds, that is
all that matters. 145–6 encompassed you achieved you. 146 Go to
i.e., Well, then. Via! Go on! (A shout of encouragement.)
149 preparation advance notice 152 Give . . . drawer Leave us
alone, tapster. 157–8 charge you put you to expense 160 something somewhat. unseasoned unseasonable 166 the carriage the
carrying of it.

175 discover reveal 179 register record 180 sith since
187–8 observance attentiveness 188 engrossed seized. fee'd purchased 191 largely generously 191–2 what . . . given what she would
like to have given to her. 195 meed reward 199–200 Love . . . pursues
i.e., Love runs away when pursued but pursues when run away from,
just as a shadow seems to run away from a body (a substance) running
in its direction but follows a body running the other way. (Proverbial.)
213 honest chaste 214 enlargeth gives free scope to 215 shrewd construction malicious interpretation 217–18 of great admittance i.e.,
widely received in society 218 authentic entitled to respect

ally allowed for your many warlike, courtlike, and ²¹⁹
learned preparations.   ²²⁰

FALSTAFF Oh, sir!

FORD Believe it, for you know it. There is money. Spend
it, spend it; spend more; spend all I have. [*He offers
money.*] Only give me so much of your time in exchange of it as to lay an amiable siege to the honesty of ²²⁵
this Ford's wife. Use your art of wooing; win her to
consent to you. If any man may, you may as soon as
any.

FALSTAFF Would it apply well to the vehemency of your
affection that I should win what you would enjoy?
Methinks you prescribe to yourself very preposterously.

FORD Oh, understand my drift. She dwells so securely
on the excellency of her honor that the folly of my soul
dares not present itself; she is too bright to be looked
against. Now, could I come to her with any detection ²³⁶
in my hand, my desires had instance and argument to ²³⁷
commend themselves. I could drive her then from the
ward of her purity, her reputation, her marriage vow, ²³⁹
and a thousand other her defenses, which now are too ²⁴⁰
too strongly embattled against me. What say you to't,
Sir John?

FALSTAFF Master Brook, I will first make bold with your
money; next, give me your hand; and last, as I am a
gentleman, you shall, if you will, enjoy Ford's wife.
[*He accepts the money and takes Ford's hand.*]

FORD Oh, good sir!

FALSTAFF I say you shall.

FORD Want no money, Sir John, you shall want none.   ²⁴⁸

FALSTAFF Want no Mistress Ford, Master Brook, you
shall want none. I shall be with her, I may tell you, by
her own appointment. Even as you came in to me, her
assistant or go-between parted from me. I say I shall
be with her between ten and eleven, for at that time
the jealous rascally knave her husband will be forth. ²⁵⁴
Come you to me at night; you shall know how I
speed.   ²⁵⁶

FORD I am blest in your acquaintance. Do you know
Ford, sir?

FALSTAFF Hang him, poor cuckoldly knave! I know him
not. Yet I wrong him to call him poor. They say the
jealous wittolly knave hath masses of money, for the ²⁶¹
which his wife seems to me well-favored. I will use her ²⁶²
as the key of the cuckoldly rogue's coffer, and there's
my harvest home.   ²⁶⁴

FORD I would you knew Ford, sir, that you might avoid
him if you saw him.

FALSTAFF Hang him, mechanical salt-butter rogue! I ²⁶⁷
will stare him out of his wits. I will awe him with my

cudgel; it shall hang like a meteor o'er the cuckold's ²⁶⁹
horns. Master Brook, thou shalt know I will predomi- ²⁷⁰
nate over the peasant, and thou shalt lie with his wife. ²⁷¹
Come to me soon at night. Ford's a knave, and I will
aggravate his style: thou, Master Brook, shalt know ²⁷³
him for knave and cuckold. Come to me soon at night.
[*Exit.*]

FORD What a damned Epicurean rascal is this! My heart ²⁷⁵
is ready to crack with impatience. Who says this is
improvident jealousy? My wife hath sent to him, the
hour is fixed, the match is made. Would any man
have thought this? See the hell of having a false
woman! My bed shall be abused, my coffers ransacked, my reputation gnawn at; and I shall not only
receive this villainous wrong but stand under the ²⁸²
adoption of abominable terms, and by him that does ²⁸³
me this wrong. Terms! Names! "Amaimon" sounds ²⁸⁴
well, "Lucifer" well, "Barbason" well, yet they are ²⁸⁵
devils' additions, the names of fiends. But "Cuckold!" ²⁸⁶
"Wittol!"—"Cuckold!" The devil himself hath not
such a name. Page is an ass, a secure ass. He will trust ²⁸⁸
his wife; he will not be jealous. I will rather trust a
Fleming with my butter, Parson Hugh the Welshman
with my cheese, an Irishman with my aqua vitae ²⁹¹
bottle, or a thief to walk my ambling gelding, than my ²⁹²
wife with herself. Then she plots, then she ruminates,
then she devises; and what they think in their hearts ²⁹⁴
they may effect, they will break their hearts but they
will effect. Heaven be praised for my jealousy! Eleven
o'clock the hour. I will prevent this, detect my wife, be ²⁹⁷
revenged on Falstaff, and laugh at Page. I will about it;
better three hours too soon than a minute too late. Fie,
fie, fie! Cuckold, cuckold, cuckold!   *Exit.*

❖

2.3

Enter Caius [and] Rugby.

CAIUS Jack Rugby!

RUGBY Sir?

CAIUS Vat is de clock, Jack?

RUGBY 'Tis past the hour, sir, that Sir Hugh promised
to meet.

CAIUS By gar, he has save his soul dat he is no come; he
has pray his Pible well dat he is no come. By gar, Jack
Rugby, he is dead already if he be come.

RUGBY He is wise, sir. He knew Your Worship would
kill him if he came.

---

219 allowed acknowledged and approved   **220 preparations** accomplishments.   **225 of it** for it.   **amiable** amorous   **236 against** directly
toward (like looking at the sun).   **237 had instance** would have proof
and precedent   **239 ward** defensive posture in fencing   **240 other
her defenses** other defenses of hers   **254 forth** away
from home.   **256 speed** succeed.   **261 wittolly** willingly cuckolded
261–2 for the which for which reason   **262 well-favored** attractive.
264 harvest home occasion for reaping a profit.   **267 mechanical** i.e.,
base. (Literally, one engaged in manual occupation).   **salt-butter** butter preserved with salt, often old and of inferior quality

269 meteor (An ominous sign.)   **270–1 predominate** be in the ascendancy. (An astrological term.)   **273 aggravate his style** increase or
add to his title (by adding *cuckold*)   **275 Epicurean** pleasure-loving
282–3 stand . . . terms have to put up with being called names
284, 285 Amaimon, Lucifer, Barbason (Names of devils; they occur in
Scot's *Discovery of Witchcraft*, 1584.)   **286 additions** titles   **288 a
secure ass** an overconfident fool.   **291 aqua vitae** any strong spirit
like brandy. (Irish were known for their drinking, just as Welshmen
for eating of cheese and Flemish for love of butter.)   **292 to walk . . .
gelding** i.e., to exercise my good riding horse. (*Geldings*, or castrated
male horses, are gentle and well suited to going at a comfortable
pace.)   **294 they** i.e., scheming wives   **297 prevent** come there before
2.3. Location: A field near Windsor.

CAIUS   By gar, de herring is no dead so as I vill kill him. 11
Take your rapier, Jack. I vill tell you how I vill kill him.

RUGBY   Alas, sir, I cannot fence.

CAIUS   Villainy, take your rapier. 14

RUGBY   Forbear. Here's company.

[Enter] Page, Shallow, Slender, [and] Host.

HOST   Bless thee, bully Doctor!

SHALLOW   Save you, Master Doctor Caius!

PAGE   Now, good Master Doctor! 17

SLENDER   Give you good morrow, sir.

CAIUS   Vat be all you, one, two, tree, four, come for?

HOST   To see thee fight, to see thee foin, to see thee 21
traverse; to see thee here, to see thee there; to see thee 22
pass thy punto, thy stock, thy reverse, thy distance, 23
thy montant. Is he dead, my Ethiopian? Is he dead, 24
my Francisco? Ha, bully? What says my Aesculapius, 25
my Galen, my heart of elder, ha? Is he dead, bully 26
stale? Is he dead? 27

CAIUS   By gar, he is de coward jack priest of de vorld.
He is not show his face.

HOST   Thou art a Castilian King-Urinal. Hector of 30
Greece, my boy!

CAIUS   I pray you, bear witness that me have stay six or 32
seven, two, tree hours for him, and he is no come.

SHALLOW   He is the wiser man, Master Doctor. He is a
curer of souls, and you a curer of bodies. If you should
fight, you go against the hair of your professions. Is it 36
not true, Master Page?

PAGE   Master Shallow, you have yourself been a great
fighter, though now a man of peace.

SHALLOW   Bodykins, Master Page, though I now be old 40
and of the peace, if I see a sword out, my finger itches
to make one. Though we are justices and doctors and 42
churchmen, Master Page, we have some salt of our 43
youth in us. We are the sons of women, Master Page. 44

PAGE   'Tis true, Master Shallow.

SHALLOW   It will be found so, Master Page.—Master Doctor Caius, I am come to fetch you home. I am sworn of
the peace. You have showed yourself a wise physician,

and Sir Hugh hath shown himself a wise and patient
churchman. You must go with me, Master Doctor.

HOST   Pardon, guest Justice. A word, Monsieur Mock- 51
water. 52

CAIUS   Mockvater? Vat is dat?

HOST   "Mockwater," in our English tongue, is "valor,"
bully.

CAIUS   By gar, den, I have as mush mockvater as de
Englishman. Scurvy jack-dog priest! By gar, me vill cut 57
his ears.

HOST   He will clapper-claw thee tightly, bully. 59

CAIUS   Clapper-de-claw? Vat is dat?

HOST   That is, he will make thee amends.

CAIUS   By gar, me do look he shall clapper-de-claw me,
for, by gar, me vill have it.

HOST   And I will provoke him to't, or let him wag. 64

CAIUS   Me tank you for dat.

HOST   And, moreover, bully—*[aside to the others]* but
first, master guest and Master Page, and eke Cavaleiro
Slender, go you through the town to Frogmore. 68

PAGE   Sir Hugh is there, is he?

HOST   He is there. See what humor he is in, and I will
bring the Doctor about by the fields. Will it do well?

SHALLOW   We will do it.

PAGE, SHALLOW, AND SLENDER   Adieu, good Master
Doctor.   *[Exeunt Page, Shallow, and Slender.]*

CAIUS *[drawing his rapier]*   By gar, me vill kill de priest,
for he speak for a jackanape to Anne Page. 76

HOST   Let him die. But first, sheathe thy impatience;
throw cold water on thy choler. Go about the fields
with me through Frogmore. I will bring thee where
Mistress Anne Page is, at a farmhouse a-feasting; and
thou shalt woo her. Cried game? Said I well? 81

CAIUS *[sheathing his rapier]*   By gar, me dank you vor dat.
By gar, I love you; and I shall procure-a you de good
guest: de earl, de knight, de lords, de gentlemen, my
patients.

HOST   For the which I will be thy adversary toward 86
Anne Page. Said I well?

CAIUS   By gar, 'tis good. Vell said.

HOST   Let us wag, then.

CAIUS   Come at my heels, Jack Rugby.   *Exeunt.*

✤

3.1

Enter Evans [and] Simple.

EVANS   I pray you now, good Master Slender's servingman, and friend Simple by your name, which way
have you looked for Master Caius, that calls himself
doctor of physic?

---

11 **no dead so** not so dead. (Compare with "dead as a herring.")
14 **Villainy** i.e., Villain   17 **Save** God save   21 **foin** thrust. (A fencing term, like those that follow here.)   22 **traverse** move from side to
side.   23–4 **pass . . . montant** employ your stroke or thrust with the
point of the sword, your stoccado or thrust, your backhand stroke,
your keeping of the prescribed distance between contestants, your
upright thrust.   24 **Ethiopian** (An extravagant epithet applied to
Doctor Caius, perhaps in acknowledgment of a dark complexion.)
25 **Francisco** i.e., Frenchman.   **Aesculapius** i.e., doctor. (Literally,
Greek god of medicine.)   26 **Galen** famous Greek physician.   **heart
of elder** i.e., opposite of "heart of oak." (The elder has no heart,
though Caius, with his halting English, presumably is unaware of the
insult.)   27 **stale** i.e., doctor. (Literally, "urine," which is used to
make medical diagnosis; see also *urinal* in Host's next speech, and
Mockwater, lines 51–2. A *stale* is also a dupe.)
30 **Castilian** i.e., Spanish. (An insulting term in a time of war with
Spain, though Caius, with his imperfect English, is presumably oblivious of this. The term also suggests *Castalian* [Folio: Castalion], relating to the sacred spring on Mount Parnassus.)   **Urinal** (Comically
appropriate to a doctor, who uses urine for diagnosis.)   **Hector** chief
warrior of ancient Troy (not Greece)   32 **me have stay** I have stayed
36 **go . . . of** i.e., act contrary to. (Literally, rub hair the wrong way.)
40 **Bodykins** i.e., By God's little body   42 **make one** join in.   43 **salt**
savor   44 **We . . . women** i.e., We are men. (Proverbial.)

51 **guest Justice** i.e., a justice of the peace who is a paying guest in my
inn. (Said to Shallow.)   51–2 **Mockwater** (See the note to line 27,
above; said to Caius.)   57 **jack-dog** mongrel   59 **clapper-claw**
thrash.   **tightly** soundly   64 **wag** go on his way, run for his life.
68 **Frogmore** small village near Windsor.   76 **for a jackanape** on
behalf of an ape, i.e., Slender   81 **Cried game?** Have I announced
good sport? (A hunting cry.)   86 **adversary** (The Host again takes
advantage of Caius' poor English; the expected word is "emissary" or
"advocate.")
3.1. Location: A field near Frogmore.

SIMPLE   Marry, sir, the Petty-ward, the Park-ward, 5
every way; Old Windsor way, and every way but the
town way.

EVANS   I most fehemently desire you you will also look
that way.

SIMPLE   I will, sir.   [*Going aside.*]

EVANS   Pless my soul, how full of cholers I am, and
trempling of mind! I shall be glad if he have deceived
me. How melancholies I am! I will knog his urinals 13
about his knave's costard when I have good opportu- 14
nities for the 'ork. Pless my soul!   [*He sings.*]

"To shallow rivers, to whose falls 16
Melodious birds sings madrigals;
There will we make our peds of roses,
And a thousand fragrant posies.
To shallow—"

Mercy on me! I have a great dispositions to cry.
                                                   [*He sings.*]

"Melodious birds sing madrigals—
Whenas I sat in Pabylon— 23
And a thousand vagram posies. 24
To shallow," etc. 25

[*Simple returns.*]

SIMPLE   Yonder he is, coming this way, Sir Hugh.

EVANS   He's welcome.   [*He sings.*]
"To shallow rivers, to whose falls—"
God prosper the right! What weapons is he? 29

SIMPLE   No weapons, sir. There comes my master, Master Shallow, and another gentleman, from Frogmore,
over the stile, this way.

EVANS   Pray you, give me my gown; or else keep it in
your arms.   [*He reads in a book.*]

[*Enter*] Page, Shallow, [*and*] Slender.

SHALLOW   How now, Master Parson? Good morrow,
good Sir Hugh. Keep a gamester from the dice and a 36
good student from his book, and it is wonderful. 37

SLENDER [*aside*]   Ah, sweet Anne Page!

PAGE   God save you, good Sir Hugh!

EVANS   God pless you from His mercy sake, all of you! 40

SHALLOW   What, the sword and the Word? Do you 41
study them both, Master Parson?

PAGE   And youthful still—in your doublet and hose 43
this raw rheumatic day?

EVANS   There is reasons and causes for it.

PAGE   We are come to you to do a good office, Master
Parson.

EVANS   Fery well. What is it?

PAGE   Yonder is a most reverend gentleman, who,
belike having received wrong by some person, is at 50
most odds with his own gravity and patience that ever
you saw.

SHALLOW   I have lived fourscore years and upward; I
never heard a man of his place, gravity, and learning
so wide of his own respect. 55

EVANS   What is he?

PAGE   I think you know him: Master Doctor Caius, the
renowned French physician.

EVANS   Got's will and His passion of my heart! I had as 59
lief you would tell me of a mess of porridge. 60

PAGE   Why?

EVANS   He has no more knowledge in Hibbocrates and 62
Galen—and he is a knave besides, a cowardly knave
as you would desires to be acquainted withal.

PAGE [*to Shallow*]   I warrant you, he's the man should 65
fight with him.

SLENDER [*aside*]   Oh, sweet Anne Page!

SHALLOW [*to Page*]   It appears so by his weapons. Keep
them asunder; here comes Doctor Caius. 69

[*Enter*] Host, Caius, [*and*] Rugby. [*Evans and
Caius offer to fight.*]

PAGE   Nay, good Master Parson, keep in your weapon.

SHALLOW   So do you, good Master Doctor.

HOST   Disarm them and let them question. Let them 72
keep their limbs whole and hack our English.
                            [*Caius and Evans are disarmed.*]

CAIUS [*to Evans*]   I pray you, let-a me speak a word
with your ear. Vherefore vill you not meet-a me?

EVANS [*aside to Caius*]   Pray you, use your patience.
[*Aloud*] In good time. 77

CAIUS   By gar, you are de coward, de jack dog, john
ape.

EVANS [*aside to Caius*]   Pray you, let us not be
laughingstocks to other men's humors; I desire you
in friendship, and I will one way or other make you
amends. [*Aloud*] I will knog your urinal about your
knave's cogscomb for missing your meetings and
appointments.

CAIUS   *Diable!* Jack Rugby—mine Host de Jarteer—have
I not stay for him to kill him? Have I not, at de 87
place I did appoint?

EVANS   As I am a Christians soul now, look you, this is
the place appointed. I'll be judgment by mine Host of 90
the Garter.

HOST   Peace, I say, Gallia and Gaul, French and Welsh, 92
soul curer and body curer!

CAIUS   Ay, dat is very good, *excellent.*

HOST   Peace, I say! Hear mine Host of the Garter. Am I

5 the Petty-ward toward Windsor Petty (or Little) Park.   **the Park-
ward** toward Windsor Great Park   **13 knog** knock   **14 costard** i.e.,
head. (Literally, apple.)   **16–25 To shallow rivers,** etc. (Lines from
Marlowe's "Come live with me and be my love.")   **23 Whenas . . .
Pabylon** (An insertion of a line from the metrical Psalms, number
137.)   **24 vagram** i.e., vagrant. (But Evans means "fragrant.")   **29 is
he** he is carrying.   **36–7 Keep . . . wonderful** i.e., It's as hard to keep
a true student from his book as to keep a gamester from dice.   **40
from His mercy sake** (The correct phrase is "for His mercy's sake.")
41 the Word i.e., the Bible.   **43 in . . . hose** i.e., without a cloak, in
close-fitting jacket and breeches

50 belike it would seem   **55 so . . . respect** i.e., so out of keeping with
the gravity and patience that he is respected for (see lines 50–2), having lost control.   **59–60 had as lief** would just as soon   **62 Hibbocrates** Hippocrates, ancient Greek physician   **65 he's** i.e., Evans is.
should who is supposed to   **69.2 offer** make as if, prepare. (The stage
direction is substantially from the Quarto.)   **72 question** talk, discuss.   **77 In good time** All in good time.   **87 stay** waited   **90 judgment** judged   **92 Gallia and Gaul** Wales and France

politic? Am I subtle? Am I a Machiavel? Shall I lose my 96
doctor? No, he gives me the potions and the motions. 97
Shall I lose my parson, my priest, my Sir Hugh? No,
he gives me the proverbs and the no-verbs. Give me 99
thy hand, terrestrial; so. Give me thy hand, celestial; 100
so. [*He joins their hands.*] Boys of art, I have deceived 101
you both; I have directed you to wrong places. Your
hearts are mighty, your skins are whole, and let burnt 103
sack be the issue. Come, lay their swords to pawn. 104
Follow me, lads of peace, follow, follow, follow.

SHALLOW   Trust me, a mad host. Follow, gentlemen, 106
follow.

SLENDER [*aside*]   Oh, sweet Anne Page!

[*Exeunt Shallow, Slender, Page, and Host.*]

CAIUS   Ha, do I perceive dat? Have you make-a de sot 109
of us, ha, ha?

EVANS   This is well! He has made us his vloutingstog. I 111
desire you that we may be friends; and let us knog our
prains together to be revenge on this same scall, 113
scurvy, cogging companion, the Host of the Garter. 114

CAIUS   By gar, with all my heart. He promise to bring
me where is Anne Page. By gar, he deceive me too.

EVANS   Well, I will smite his noddles. Pray you, follow. 117

[*Exeunt.*]

❖

3.2

[*Enter*] Mistress Page [*and*] Robin.

MRS. PAGE   Nay, keep your way, little gallant. You were 1
wont to be a follower, but now you are a leader.
Whether had you rather, lead mine eyes or eye your 3
master's heels?

ROBIN   I had rather, forsooth, go before you like a man
than follow him like a dwarf.

MRS. PAGE   Oh, you are a flattering boy. Now I see you'll
be a courtier.

[*Enter*] Ford.

FORD   Well met, Mistress Page. Whither go you?

MRS. PAGE   Truly, sir, to see your wife. Is she at home?

FORD   Ay, and as idle as she may hang together, for 11
want of company. I think if your husbands were dead 12
you two would marry.

MRS. PAGE   Be sure of that—two other husbands.

FORD   Where had you this pretty weathercock? 15

MRS. PAGE   I cannot tell what the dickens his name is
my husband had him of.—What do you call your 17
knight's name, sirrah?

ROBIN   Sir John Falstaff.

FORD   Sir John Falstaff!

MRS. PAGE   He, he. I can never hit on 's name. There is
such a league between my goodman and he! Is your 22
wife at home indeed?

FORD   Indeed she is.

MRS. PAGE   By your leave, sir. I am sick till I see her.

[*Exeunt Mistress Page and Robin.*]

FORD   Has Page any brains? Hath he any eyes? Hath he
any thinking? Sure they sleep; he hath no use of them.
Why, this boy will carry a letter twenty mile as easy as
a cannon will shoot point-blank twelve score. He 29
pieces out his wife's inclination; he gives her folly 30
motion and advantage. And now she's going to my 31
wife, and Falstaff's boy with her. A man may hear this 32
shower sing in the wind. And Falstaff's boy with her! 33
Good plots! They are laid; and our revolted wives share
damnation together. Well, I will take him, then torture 35
my wife, pluck the borrowed veil of modesty from the
so-seeming Mistress Page, divulge Page himself for a
secure and willful Actaeon; and to these violent pro- 38
ceedings all my neighbors shall cry aim. [*A clock* 39
strikes.] The clock gives me my cue, and my assurance 40
bids me search. There I shall find Falstaff. I shall be
rather praised for this than mocked, for it is as positive
as the earth is firm that Falstaff is there. I will go.

[*Enter*] Page, Shallow, Slender, Host, Evans,
Caius, [*and Rugby*].

SHALLOW, PAGE, ETC   Well met, Master Ford.

FORD [*aside*]   Trust me, a good knot. [*To them*] I have 45
good cheer at home, and I pray you all go with me. 46

SHALLOW   I must excuse myself, Master Ford.

SLENDER   And so must I, sir. We have appointed to dine
with Mistress Anne, and I would not break with her 49
for more money than I'll speak of.

SHALLOW   We have lingered about a match between
Anne Page and my cousin Slender, and this day we 52
shall have our answer.

SLENDER   I hope I have your good will, father Page.

PAGE   You have, Master Slender; I stand wholly for you.
But my wife, Master Doctor, is for you altogether.

CAIUS   Ay, by gar, and de maid is love-a me. My
nursh-a Quickly tell me so mush.

---

96 Machiavel i.e., an intriguer, modeled on Niccolò Machiavelli, the Italian political philosopher who symbolized crafty and ruthless ambition to Elizabethans.   **97 motions** purges.   **99 proverbs . . . no-verbs** i.e., proverbial wisdom and Thou-shalt-not's.   **100 terrestrial** i.e., the Doctor, who treats the body   **101 art** learning   **103–4 burnt sack** heated and mulled wine, as at 2.1.199–200   **104 issue** outcome. **to pawn** as a pledge or surety.   **106 Trust me** Believe me.   **109 you** i.e., the Host.   **sot** fool   **111 vloutingstog** flouting-stock, i.e., laughingstock.   **113–14 scall . . . companion** scurvy cheating rascal   **117 noddles** head.
3.2. Location: A street in Windsor.
1 keep your way keep on your way (in front of me)   **3 Whether** Which of the two   **11–12 as idle . . . company** i.e., women as idle as my wife (and you, Mistress Page) may band together for lack of better company.

15 Where . . . weathercock? i.e., Where did you find this sprucely dressed little fellow? (A *weathercock*, literally a weathervane in the shape of rooster, shifts direction quickly, as a young lad might in fashion of dress.)   **17 had him of** got him from.   **22 league** friendship. **goodman** husband   **29 point-blank** in a straight trajectory.   **twelve score** i.e., 240 paces.   **29–30 He pieces out** Page positively encourages   **30 folly** wantonness   **31 motion and advantage** encouragement and opportunity.   **32–3 hear . . . wind** tell from the rising wind that a storm is coming up, i.e., that trouble is brewing.   **35 take him** take him by surprise   **38 secure** overconfident.   **Actaeon** i.e., horned man, cuckold. (See the note for 2.1.113.)   **39 cry aim** applaud. (A term from archery.)   **40 assurance** foreknowledge   **45 knot** group, company.   **46 cheer** fare   **49 break with** break my promise to   **52 cousin** kinsman, i.e., nephew

HOST What say you to young Master Fenton? He capers, he dances, he has eyes of youth, he writes verses, he speaks holiday, he smells April and May. 61 He will carry't, he will carry't. 'Tis in his buttons he 62 will carry't. 63

PAGE Not by my consent, I promise you. The gentleman is of no having. He kept company with the wild 65 Prince and Poins. He is of too high a region; he knows 66 too much. No, he shall not knit a knot in his fortunes 67 with the finger of my substance. If he take her, let him take her simply. The wealth I have waits on my 69 consent, and my consent goes not that way.

FORD I beseech you heartily, some of you go home with me to dinner. Besides your cheer, you shall have sport: I will show you a monster. Master Doctor, you shall go. So shall you, Master Page, and you, Sir Hugh.

SHALLOW Well, fare you well. We shall have the freer 75 wooing at Master Page's. 76

[*Exeunt Shallow and Slender.*]

CAIUS Go home, John Rugby. I come anon.

[*Exit Rugby.*]

HOST Farewell, my hearts. I will to my honest knight 78 Falstaff, and drink canary with him. [*Exit.*] 79

FORD [*aside*] I think I shall drink in pipe-wine first 80 with him; I'll make him dance.—Will you go, gentles? 81

ALL Have with you to see this monster. *Exeunt.* 82

❧

3.3

Enter Mistress Ford [and] Mistress Page.

MRS. FORD What, John! What, Robert! 1
MRS. PAGE Quickly, quickly! Is the buck basket— 2
MRS. FORD I warrant. What, Robert, I say!

[*Enter*] *Servants [with a great basket].*

MRS. PAGE Come, come, come.
MRS. FORD Here, set it down.
MRS. PAGE Give your men the charge. We must be brief. 6
MRS. FORD Marry, as I told you before, John and Robert, be ready here hard by in the brewhouse; and when I 8 suddenly call you, come forth, and without any pause or staggering take this basket on your shoulders. That done, trudge with it in all haste, and carry it among

the whitsters in Datchet Mead, and there empty it in 12 the muddy ditch close by the Thames' side.

MRS. PAGE You will do it?
MRS. FORD I ha' told them over and over; they lack no direction.—Begone, and come when you are called.

[*Exeunt Servants.*]

MRS. PAGE Here comes little Robin.

[*Enter*] *Robin.*

MRS. FORD How now, my eyas musket, what news 18 with you?

ROBIN My master, Sir John, is come in at your back door, Mistress Ford, and requests your company.

MRS. PAGE You little Jack-a-Lent, have you been true 22 to us?

ROBIN Ay, I'll be sworn. My master knows not of your being here and hath threatened to put me into everlasting liberty if I tell you of it; for he swears he'll 26 turn me away. 27

MRS. PAGE Thou'rt a good boy. This secrecy of thine shall be a tailor to thee and shall make thee a new doublet and hose.—I'll go hide me.

MRS. FORD Do so.—Go tell thy master I am alone.

[*Exit Robin.*]

Mistress Page, remember you your cue.

MRS. PAGE I warrant thee. If I do not act it, hiss me.

[*Exit.*]

MRS. FORD Go to, then. We'll use this unwholesome 34 humidity, this gross watery pumpkin. We'll teach him to know turtles from jays. 36

[*Enter*] *Falstaff.*

FALSTAFF "Have I caught thee, my heavenly jewel?" 37 Why, now let me die, for I have lived long enough. This is the period of my ambition. Oh, this blessed hour! 39

MRS. FORD O sweet Sir John!

FALSTAFF Mistress Ford, I cannot cog, I cannot prate, 41 Mistress Ford. Now shall I sin in my wish: I would thy husband were dead. I'll speak it before the best lord: 43 I would make thee my lady.

MRS. FORD I your lady, Sir John? Alas, I should be a pitiful lady!

FALSTAFF Let the court of France show me such another. I see how thine eye would emulate the diamond. Thou hast the right arched beauty of the brow that be- 49 comes the ship-tire, the tire-valiant, or any tire of 50 Venetian admittance. 51

MRS. FORD A plain kerchief, Sir John. My brows be- 52 come nothing else, nor that well neither. 53

---

61 holiday in a fashion appropriate to a holiday, elegantly **62 carry't** carry it off **62–3 'Tis . . . carry't** i.e., He's sure to succeed. **65 having** estate. **65–6 wild . . . Poins** i.e., Prince Hal and Poins of *1 Henry IV* and *2 Henry IV.* **66 region** social status **67 knit a knot in** mend **69 simply** i.e., by herself, without a dowry. **waits on** is subject to **75–6 We shall . . . Page's** i.e., Slender's wooing of Anne will be less constrained if Caius, Evans, and Anne's father are not there. **78 my hearts** my hearties. **79 canary** a sweet wine from the Canary Islands. (*Canary* is also a dance, and this sense of the word may inspire Ford's metaphor of dancing in the next line.) **80 pipe-wine** wine from the cask, or wood. (With a pun on *pipe* as a musical instrument played for the *dance,* line 81. See next note.) **81 I'll . . . dance** i.e., I'll make Falstaff jump, make it hot for him. **gentles** gentlemen. **82 Have with you** We'll go with you
3.3. Location: Ford's house.
1 What i.e., Move quickly **2 buck basket** basket for soiled clothes. (*Bucking* means "washing.") **6 charge** instructions. **8 hard by** close at hand

12 whitsters bleachers of linen. **Datchet Mead** a meadow along the Thames, near Windsor Park **18 eyas musket** young male sparrow hawk **22 Jack-a-Lent** figure of a man set up during Lent to be pelted by boys, a puppet **26 liberty** i.e., unemployment **27 turn me away** dismiss me. **34 use** trick **36 turtles** turtledoves, models of constancy in love. **jays** i.e., loose women. **37 Have . . . jewel?** (From Sir Philip Sidney's *Astrophel and Stella.*) **39 period** goal **41 cog** deceive, flatter. (Also in line 63.) **43 I'll speak . . . lord** I will proclaim this publicly in the presence of the most distinguished lord in England **49–50 that . . . ship-tire** that suits the elaborate woman's headdress shaped to resemble a ship **50 tire-valiant** (An invented word seemingly describing a headdress of daunting proportions.) **51 admittance** fashion. **52–3 become** suit

FALSTAFF   By the Lord, thou art a tyrant to say so. Thou
wouldst make an absolute courtier, and the firm   55
fixture of thy foot would give an excellent motion to   56
thy gait in a semicircled farthingale. I see what thou   57
wert, if Fortune thy foe were not, Nature thy friend.   58
Come, thou canst not hide it.

MRS. FORD   Believe me, there's no such thing in me.

FALSTAFF   What made me love thee? Let that persuade
thee there's something extraordinary in thee. Come, I
cannot cog and say thou art this and that, like a many
of these lisping hawthorn buds, that come like women   64
in men's apparel and smell like Bucklersbury in sim-   65
ple time. I cannot. But I love thee, none but thee; and   66
thou deserv'st it.

MRS. FORD   Do not betray me, sir. I fear you love Mis-   68
tress Page.

FALSTAFF   Thou mightst as well say I love to walk by
the Counter gate, which is as hateful to me as the reek   71
of a limekiln.

MRS. FORD   Well, heaven knows how I love you, and
you shall one day find it.

FALSTAFF   Keep in that mind. I'll deserve it.

MRS. FORD   Nay, I must tell you, so you do, or else I
could not be in that mind.

[Enter Robin.]

ROBIN   Mistress Ford, Mistress Ford! Here's Mistress
Page at the door, sweating and blowing and looking   79
wildly, and would needs speak with you presently.   80

FALSTAFF   She shall not see me. I will ensconce me   81
behind the arras.   82

MRS. FORD   Pray you, do so. She's a very tattling
woman.   *[Falstaff hides himself behind the arras.]*

[Enter Mistress Page.]

What's the matter? How now!

MRS. PAGE   Oh, Mistress Ford, what have you done?
You're shamed, you're overthrown, you're undone
forever!

MRS. FORD   What's the matter, good Mistress Page?

MRS. PAGE   Oh, welladay, Mistress Ford, having an hon-   90
est man to your husband, to give him such cause of   91
suspicion!

MRS. FORD   What cause of suspicion?

MRS. PAGE   What cause of suspicion? Out upon you!   94
How am I mistook in you!

MRS. FORD   Why, alas, what's the matter?

MRS. PAGE   Your husband's coming hither, woman,
with all the officers in Windsor, to search for a

gentleman that he says is here now in the house, by
your consent, to take an ill advantage of his absence.
You are undone.

MRS. FORD   'Tis not so, I hope.

MRS. PAGE   Pray heaven it be not so, that you have
such a man here! But 'tis most certain your husband's
coming, with half Windsor at his heels, to search for
such a one. I come before to tell you. If you know
yourself clear, why, I am glad of it. But if you have a   107
friend here, convey, convey him out. Be not amazed!   108
Call all your senses to you; defend your reputation, or
bid farewell to your good life forever.   110

MRS. FORD   What shall I do? There is a gentleman, my
dear friend; and I fear not mine own shame so much
as his peril. I had rather than a thousand pound he
were out of the house.

MRS. PAGE   For shame! Never stand "you had rather"   115
and "you had rather." Your husband's here at hand!
Bethink you of some conveyance. In the house you   117
cannot hide him. Oh, how have you deceived me! Look,
here is a basket. If he be of any reasonable stature, he
may creep in here; and throw foul linen upon him, as
if it were going to bucking. Or—it is whiting time—   121
send him by your two men to Datchet Mead.

MRS. FORD   He's too big to go in there. What shall I do?

FALSTAFF   *[coming forward]*   Let me see't, let me see't,
oh, let me see't! I'll in, I'll in. Follow your friend's
counsel. I'll in.

MRS. PAGE   What, Sir John Falstaff? *[Aside to him]* Are
these your letters, knight?

FALSTAFF   *[aside to her]*   I love thee. Help me away. Let
me creep in here. I'll never—
        [He gets into the basket; they cover him with foul
linen.]

MRS. PAGE   Help to cover your master, boy.—Call your
men, Mistress Ford.—You dissembling knight!

MRS. FORD   What, John! Robert! John!

[Enter Servants.]

Go take up these clothes here quickly. Where's the
cowlstaff? Look how you drumble! Carry them to the   135
laundress in Datchet Mead. Quickly! Come.
        [The Servants lift the basket and start to leave.]

[Enter] Ford, Page, Caius, [and] Evans.

FORD   Pray you, come near. If I suspect without cause,
why then make sport at me. Then let me be your jest;
I deserve it.—How now? Whither bear you this?

SERVANT   To the laundress, forsooth.

MRS. FORD   Why, what have you to do whither they
bear it? You were best meddle with buck washing.   142

---

55 **absolute** perfect   55–6 **the firm . . . foot** your firm and assured
way of putting your feet on the ground   57 **semicircled farthingale**
petticoat with hoops at the sides and back but not extending in front.
57–8 **I see . . . friend** i.e., I can imagine how impressive you would be
at court if Fortune had not cast you in a lowly lot with only your natural beauty to assist you. ("Fortune My Foe" is the name of a popular
ballad tune.)   64 **hawthorn buds** i.e., young fops   65 **Bucklersbury**
a London street inhabited by herbalists   65–6 **simple time** midsummer, the time when apothecaries were supplied with simples or
herbs.   68 **betray** deceive   71 **Counter gate** gate of the Counter or
debtors' prison in London   79 **blowing** puffing   80 **presently** at
once.   81 **ensconce me** hide myself   82 **arras** tapestry wall hanging.
90 **welladay** alas   91 **to** as   94 **Out upon you!** i.e., For shame!

107 **clear** clear of blame   108 **friend** lover.   **amazed** stunned, bewildered.   110 **your good life** your respectability   115 **stand** lose time
over   117 **conveyance** means of conveying him.   121 **bucking** washing.   **whiting time** bleaching time   135 **cowlstaff** pole on which a
"cowl" or basket is carried between two persons.   **drumble** are sluggish.   142 **buck washing** washing clothes. (But Ford puns on *buck* in
the sense of "horned male deer," resembling the cuckold, and also of
"copulating.")

FORD   Buck? I would I could wash myself of the buck! Buck, buck, buck! Ay, buck! I warrant you, buck— and of the season too, it shall appear.   145

[*Exeunt Servants with the basket.*]

Gentlemen, I have dreamed tonight; I'll tell you my 146 dream. Here, here, here be my keys. Ascend my chambers. Search, seek, find out. I'll warrant we'll unkennel the fox. Let me stop this way first. [*He locks* 149 *the door.*] So, now uncape.   150

PAGE   Good Master Ford, be contented. You wrong 151 yourself too much.   152

FORD   True, Master Page. Up, gentlemen, you shall see 153 sport anon. Follow me, gentlemen.   [*Exit.*]

EVANS   This is fery fantastical humors and jealousies.

CAIUS   By gar, 'tis no the fashion of France. It is not jealous in France.

PAGE   Nay, follow him, gentlemen. See the issue of his 158 search.   [*Exeunt Page, Caius, and Evans.*]

MRS. PAGE   Is there not a double excellency in this?

MRS. FORD   I know not which pleases me better, that my husband is deceived, or Sir John.

MRS. PAGE   What a taking was he in when your hus- 163 band asked who was in the basket!

MRS. FORD   I am half afraid he will have need of 165 washing, so throwing him into the water will do him 166 a benefit.

MRS. PAGE   Hang him, dishonest rascal! I would all of the same strain were in the same distress.   169

MRS. FORD   I think my husband hath some special suspicion of Falstaff's being here, for I never saw him so gross in his jealousy till now.

MRS. PAGE   I will lay a plot to try that, and we will yet 173 have more tricks with Falstaff. His dissolute disease will scarce obey this medicine.   175

MRS. FORD   Shall we send that foolish carrion Mistress 176 Quickly to him, and excuse his throwing into the 177 water, and give him another hope, to betray him to another punishment?

MRS. PAGE   We will do it. Let him be sent for tomorrow eight o'clock, to have amends.

[*Enter Ford, Page, Caius, and Evans.*]

FORD   I cannot find him. Maybe the knave bragged of that he could not compass.   183

MRS. PAGE   [*aside to Mistress Ford*]   Heard you that?

MRS. FORD   You use me well, Master Ford, do you?

FORD   Ay, I do so.

MRS. FORD   Heaven make you better than your thoughts!

FORD   Amen!

MRS. PAGE   You do yourself mighty wrong, Master Ford.

FORD   Ay, ay, I must bear it.

EVANS   If there be anybody in the house, and in the chambers, and in the coffers, and in the presses, 192 heaven forgive my sins at the day of judgment!

CAIUS   By gar, nor I too. There is nobodies.

PAGE   Fie, fie, Master Ford, are you not ashamed? What spirit, what devil suggests this imagination? I would 196 not ha' your distemper in this kind for the wealth of 197 Windsor Castle.

FORD   'Tis my fault, Master Page. I suffer for it.

EVANS   You suffer for a pad conscience. Your wife is as honest a 'omans as I will desires among five thousand, and five hundred too.

CAIUS   By gar, I see 'tis an honest woman.

FORD   Well, I promised you a dinner. Come, come, walk in the park. I pray you, pardon me. I will 205 hereafter make known to you why I have done this.—Come, wife, come, Mistress Page, I pray you, pardon me. Pray, heartily, pardon me.

PAGE   Let's go in, gentlemen; but, trust me, we'll mock 209 him. I do invite you tomorrow morning to my house to breakfast. After, we'll a-birding together. I have a 211 fine hawk for the bush. Shall it be so?   212

FORD   Anything.

EVANS   If there is one, I shall make two in the company.

CAIUS   If there be one or two, I shall make-a the turd.

FORD   Pray you, go, Master Page.

[*Exeunt Ford and Page.*]

EVANS   [*to Caius*]   I pray you now, remembrance 217 tomorrow on the lousy knave, mine Host.   218

CAIUS   Dat is good, by gar; with all my heart!

EVANS   A lousy knave, to have his gibes and his mockeries!   *Exeunt.*

❖

3.4

Enter Fenton [and] Anne Page.

FENTON
I see I cannot get thy father's love;   1
Therefore no more turn me to him, sweet Nan.   2

ANNE
Alas, how then?

FENTON   Why, thou must be thyself.   3
He doth object I am too great of birth,
And that, my state being galled with my expense,   5
I seek to heal it only by his wealth.
Besides these, other bars he lays before me—
My riots past, my wild societies;   8

145 **of the season** in the rutting season   146 **tonight** last night
149 **unkennel** dislodge, unearth   150 **uncape** unkennel (as in line
149), dislodge, uncase (?).   151–2 **wrong yourself** put yourself in the
wrong   153 **True** (Ford may mean that he is indeed too much
wronged, or else placates Page by seeming to agree with him.)
158 **issue** outcome   163 **taking** fright   165–6 **will . . . washing** i.e.,
will have befouled himself in fright   169 **strain** character, kind
173 **try** test   175 **obey this medicine** i.e., yield to this first dose.
176 **carrion** rotten old flesh, bawd (?)   177 **excuse** make excuses for
183 **that** that which.   **compass** accomplish.

192 **presses** cupboards, clothes presses   196 **suggests** incites,
prompts you to.   **imagination** wild suspicion.   197 **distemper . . .
kind** mental disorder of this sort   205 **walk . . . park** i.e., stroll till
dinnertime.   209 **go in** i.e., go in to dinner at the proper time   211 **a-
birding** go hunting small birds of the bush with a hawk and guns
212 **for the bush** for driving the small birds into the bush (where they
can be shot).   217–18 **remembrance . . . Host** (A seeming allusion to
the conversation at the end of 3.1 and to the plot carried out in 4.5.)
3.4. Location: Before Page's house.
1 **love** good will   2 **turn** direct   3 **be thyself** be your own mistress.
5 **my state . . . expense** my estate being wasted away by my extravagance   8 **societies** companionships

And tells me 'tis a thing impossible
I should love thee but as a property.

ANNE   Maybe he tells you true.

FENTON

No, heaven so speed me in my time to come!   12
Albeit I will confess thy father's wealth   13
Was the first motive that I wooed thee, Anne,
Yet, wooing thee, I found thee of more value
Than stamps in gold or sums in sealèd bags;   16
And 'tis the very riches of thyself
That now I aim at.

ANNE   Gentle Master Fenton,
Yet seek my father's love; still seek it, sir.
If opportunity and humblest suit
Cannot attain it, why, then—hark you hither.

[They converse apart.]

[Enter] Shallow, Slender, [and Mistress] Quickly.

SHALLOW   Break their talk, Mistress Quickly. My kins-   22
man shall speak for himself.

SLENDER   I'll make a shaft or a bolt on't. 'Slid, 'tis but   24
venturing.

SHALLOW   Be not dismayed.

SLENDER   No, she shall not dismay me. I care not
for that, but that I am afeard.   28

QUICKLY *[to Anne]* Hark ye, Master Slender would
speak a word with you.

ANNE

I come to him. *[Aside]* This is my father's choice.
Oh, what a world of vile ill-favored faults
Looks handsome in three hundred pounds a year!   32

QUICKLY   And how does good Master Fenton? Pray you,
a word with you.   *[She draws him aside.]*

SHALLOW   She's coming. To her, coz! O boy, thou hadst   36
a father!   37

SLENDER   I had a father, Mistress Anne; my uncle can
tell you good jests of him.—Pray you, uncle, tell
Mistress Anne the jest how my father stole two geese
out of a pen, good uncle.

SHALLOW   Mistress Anne, my cousin loves you.   42

SLENDER   Ay, that I do, as well as I love any woman in
Gloucestershire.

SHALLOW   He will maintain you like a gentlewoman.

SLENDER   Ay, that I will, come cut and longtail, under   46
the degree of a squire.   47

SHALLOW   He will make you a hundred and fifty   48
pounds jointure.   49

ANNE   Good Master Shallow, let him woo for himself.

SHALLOW   Marry, I thank you for it; I thank you for that
good comfort.—She calls you, coz. I'll leave you.

[He moves aside.]

ANNE   Now, Master Slender—

SLENDER   Now, good Mistress Anne—

ANNE   What is your will?

SLENDER   My will? 'Od's heartlings, that's a pretty jest   56
indeed! I ne'er made my will yet, I thank heaven; I am
not such a sickly creature, I give heaven praise.

ANNE   I mean, Master Slender, what would you with
me?

SLENDER   Truly, for mine own part, I would little or
nothing with you. Your father and my uncle hath
made motions. If it be my luck, so; if not, happy man   63
be his dole! They can tell you how things go better   64
than I can. You may ask your father. Here he comes.

[Enter] Page [and] Mistress Page.

PAGE

Now, Master Slender. Love him, daughter Anne.—
Why, how now? What does Master Fenton here?
You wrong me, sir, thus still to haunt my house.
I told you, sir, my daughter is disposed of.

FENTON

Nay, Master Page, be not impatient.

MRS. PAGE

Good Master Fenton, come not to my child.

PAGE   She is no match for you.

FENTON   Sir, will you hear me?

PAGE   No, good Master Fenton.
Come, Master Shallow; come, son Slender, in.—
Knowing my mind, you wrong me, Master Fenton.

[Exeunt Page, Shallow, and Slender.]

QUICKLY *[to Fenton]* Speak to Mistress Page.

FENTON

Good Mistress Page, for that I love your daughter   78
In such a righteous fashion as I do,
Perforce, against all checks, rebukes, and manners   80
I must advance the colors of my love   81
And not retire. Let me have your good will.

ANNE   Good mother, do not marry me to yond fool.

MRS. PAGE   I mean it not; I seek you a better husband.   84

QUICKLY *[aside to Anne]* That's my master, Master Doctor.

ANNE

Alas, I had rather be set quick i'th' earth   86
And bowled to death with turnips!   87

MRS. PAGE

Come, trouble not yourself. Good Master Fenton,
I will not be your friend nor enemy.
My daughter will I question how she loves you,
And, as I find her, so am I affected.   91

---

12 heaven . . . come i.e., as I hope to be saved. **speed** prosper
13 Albeit Although   **16 stamps in gold** gold coins   **22 Break** Interrupt   **24 I'll . . . on't** i.e., I'll try it one way or another. (A *shaft* is a
slender arrow; a *bolt*, a thick and blunt one.)   **'Slid** By his (God's)
eyelid   **28 but . . . afeard** except that I am afraid. (Slender evidently
doesn't understand what *dismayed* means.)   **32 ill-favored** unattractive   **36–7 thou hadst a father** i.e., remember that your father wooed
a woman; be like him. (But Slender misses the point.)   **42 cousin** i.e.,
kinsman   **46 come . . . longtail** i.e., come what may. (Literally, horses
or dogs with docked and long tails, i.e., all sorts.)   **46–7 under . . .
squire** (Slender promises to provide Anne with the lifestyle to which
squires are entitled. A squire is here a landed gentleman, often a Justice of the Peace.)   **48 make** give, assure   **49 jointure** settlement in
the marriage contract providing for the wife's widowhood.

56 'Od's heartlings By God's little heart   **63 motions** proposals.   **so**
well and good.   **63–4 happy . . . dole** i.e., may whoever succeeds
with you be happy. (Literally, may his lot in life be that of a happy
man.)   **78 for that** because   **80 checks** reproofs.   **manners** usage,
(hostile) behavior   **81 advance the colors** raise high the standard (as
in anticipation of battle)   **84 mean** intend   **86 quick** alive
87 bowled i.e., pelted with turnips as bowling balls   **91 affected**
inclined.

Till then farewell, sir. She must needs go in;
Her father will be angry.

FENTON
Farewell, gentle mistress. Farewell, Nan.
                        [*Exeunt Mistress Page and Anne.*]

QUICKLY   This is my doing, now. "Nay," said I, "will
you cast away your child on a fool, and a physician?
Look on Master Fenton." This is my doing.

FENTON
I thank thee; and I pray thee, once tonight   98
Give my sweet Nan this ring. There's for thy pains.
                        [*He gives a ring and money.*]

QUICKLY   Now heaven send thee good fortune!
                                    [*Exit Fenton.*]

A kind heart he hath. A woman would run
through fire and water for such a kind heart. But yet I
would my master had Mistress Anne; or I would
Master Slender had her; or, in sooth, I would Master
Fenton had her. I will do what I can for them all three;
for so I have promised, and I'll be as good as my
word—but speciously for Master Fenton. Well, I must   107
of another errand to Sir John Falstaff from my two   108
mistresses. What a beast am I to slack it!   *Exit.*

❧

3.5

Enter Falstaff.

FALSTAFF   Bardolph, I say!

[*Enter*] *Bardolph.*

BARDOLPH   Here, sir.

FALSTAFF   Go fetch me a quart of sack; put a toast in't.   3
                                    [*Exit Bardolph.*]

Have I lived to be carried in a basket,
like a barrow of butcher's offal, and to be thrown in   5
the Thames? Well, if I be served such another trick, I'll
have my brains ta'en out and buttered, and give them
to a dog for a New Year's gift. The rogues slighted me   8
into the river with as little remorse as they would have   9
drowned a blind bitch's puppies, fifteen i'th' litter!   10
And you may know by my size that I have a kind of
alacrity in sinking; if the bottom were as deep as hell,
I should down. I had been drowned, but that the   13
shore was shelvy and shallow—a death that I abhor;   14
for the water swells a man, and what a thing should I
have been when I had been swelled! I should have
been a mountain of mummy.   17

[*Enter Bardolph with sack.*]

BARDOLPH   Here's Mistress Quickly, sir, to speak with
you.

FALSTAFF   Come, let me pour in some sack to the
Thames water, for my belly's as cold as if I had

swallowed snowballs for pills to cool the reins. [*He*   22
drinks.] Call her in.

BARDOLPH   Come in, woman!

[*Enter Mistress*] *Quickly.*

QUICKLY   By your leave; I cry you mercy. Give Your   25
Worship good morrow.

FALSTAFF [*to Bardolph*]   Take away these chalices. Go   27
brew me a pottle of sack finely.   28

BARDOLPH   With eggs, sir?

FALSTAFF   Simple of itself. I'll no pullet sperm in my   30
brewage.   [*Exit Bardolph.*]   31
How now?   32

QUICKLY   Marry, sir, I come to Your Worship from
Mistress Ford.

FALSTAFF   Mistress Ford? I have had ford enough. I was   35
thrown into the ford. I have my belly full of ford.

QUICKLY   Alas the day, good heart, that was not her
fault. She does so take on with her men; they mistook   38
their erection.   39

FALSTAFF   So did I mine, to build upon a foolish
woman's promise.

QUICKLY   Well, she laments, sir, for it, that it would   42
yearn your heart to see it. Her husband goes this   43
morning a-birding. She desires you once more to come
to her, between eight and nine. I must carry her word
quickly. She'll make you amends, I warrant you.

FALSTAFF   Well, I will visit her; tell her so. And bid her
think what a man is. Let her consider his frailty, and   48
then judge of my merit.

QUICKLY   I will tell her.

FALSTAFF   Do so. Between nine and ten, say'st thou?

QUICKLY   Eight and nine, sir.

FALSTAFF   Well, begone. I will not miss her.   53

QUICKLY   Peace be with you, sir.   [*Exit.*]

FALSTAFF   I marvel I hear not of Master Brook; he sent
me word to stay within. I like his money well. Oh, here
he comes.

[*Enter*] *Ford* [*disguised*].

FORD   Bless you, sir!

FALSTAFF   Now, Master Brook, you come to know
what hath passed between me and Ford's wife?

FORD   That, indeed, Sir John, is my business.

FALSTAFF   Master Brook, I will not lie to you. I was at
her house the hour she appointed me.

FORD   And sped you, sir?   64

FALSTAFF   Very ill-favoredly, Master Brook.   65

---

98 once sometime   **107 speciously** (For "specially.")   **107–8 must of** must undertake
3.5. Location: The Garter Inn.
3 toast piece of toast   **5 barrow** wheelbarrowful   **8 slighted me** dumped me heedlessly   **9 remorse** compunction   **10 a blind bitch's puppies** a bitch's puppies, blind at birth   **13 down** sink.   **14 shore** bottom near the edge.   **17 mummy** dead flesh.

22 reins kidneys.   **25 cry you mercy** beg your pardon.   **27 chalices** (A lofty name for drinking cups.)   **27–8 Go . . . finely** Go fix me a two-quart measure of sack (a sweet white wine) tastefully brewed. (*Brew* and *brewage*, lines 28 and 31, signify that such a drink might well have been heated and spiced, perhaps with ginger and with other possible ingredients as well, though on this occasion Falstaff declines the offer of eggs.)   **30 Simple of itself** Unadulterated. **I'll** I'll have   **35 ford** i.e., river, stream. (Literally, a shallow place in the river where one may cross.)   **38 take on with** berate, scold   **39 erection** (Blunder for "direction"; Falstaff plays bawdily on her malapropism.)   **42 that** so that   **43 yearn** grieve   **48 his** i.e., man's   **53 miss** fail   **64 sped you** did you succeed   **65 ill-favoredly** badly

FORD   How so, sir? Did she change her determination? 66
FALSTAFF   No, Master Brook, but the peaking cornuto 67
her husband, Master Brook, dwelling in a continual
larum of jealousy, comes me in the instant of our en- 69
counter, after we had embraced, kissed, protested, 70
and, as it were, spoke the prologue of our comedy;
and at his heels a rabble of his companions, thither
provoked and instigated by his distemper, and, forsooth, to search his house for his wife's love.
FORD   What, while you were there?
FALSTAFF   While I was there.
FORD   And did he search for you, and could not find you?
FALSTAFF   You shall hear. As good luck would have it,
comes in one Mistress Page, gives intelligence of Ford's
approach, and, in her invention and Ford's wife's distraction, they conveyed me into a buck basket.
FORD   A buck basket?
FALSTAFF   By the Lord, a buck basket! Rammed me in
with foul shirts and smocks, socks, foul stockings,
greasy napkins, that, Master Brook, there was the 85
rankest compound of villainous smell that ever offended nostril.
FORD   And how long lay you there?
FALSTAFF   Nay, you shall hear, Master Brook, what I
have suffered to bring this woman to evil for your
good. Being thus crammed in the basket, a couple of
Ford's knaves, his hinds, were called forth by their 92
mistress to carry me in the name of foul clothes to
Datchet Lane. They took me on their shoulders, met 94
the jealous knave their master in the door, who asked
them once or twice what they had in their basket. I
quaked for fear lest the lunatic knave would have
searched it; but fate, ordaining he should be a cuckold,
held his hand. Well, on went he for a search, and away
went I for foul clothes. But mark the sequel, Master
Brook. I suffered the pangs of three several deaths: first, 101
an intolerable fright to be detected with a jealous rot- 102
ten bellwether; next, to be compassed, like a good 103
bilbo, in the circumference of a peck, hilt to point, heel 104
to head; and then, to be stopped in, like a strong dis- 105
tillation, with stinking clothes that fretted in their own 106
grease. Think of that—a man of my kidney. Think of 107
that—that am as subject to heat as butter; a man of
continual dissolution and thaw. It was a miracle to 109
scape suffocation. And in the height of this bath,
when I was more than half stewed in grease, like a

Dutch dish, to be thrown into the Thames and cooled,
glowing hot, in that surge, like a horseshoe! Think of
that—hissing hot—think of that, Master Brook!
FORD   In good sadness, sir, I am sorry that for my sake 115
you have suffered all this. My suit then is desperate;
you'll undertake her no more?
FALSTAFF   Master Brook, I will be thrown into Etna, as 118
I have been into Thames, ere I will leave her thus. Her
husband is this morning gone a-birding. I have
received from her another embassy of meeting. Twixt 121
eight and nine is the hour, Master Brook.
FORD   'Tis past eight already, sir.
FALSTAFF   Is it? I will then address me to my appoint- 124
ment. Come to me at your convenient leisure, and
you shall know how I speed; and the conclusion shall
be crowned with your enjoying her. Adieu. You shall
have her, Master Brook; Master Brook, you shall
cuckold Ford.   [*Exit.*]
FORD   Hum! Ha! Is this a vision? Is this a dream? Do I
sleep? Master Ford, awake! Awake, Master Ford!
There's a hole made in your best coat, Master Ford. 132
This 'tis to be married! This 'tis to have linen and
buck baskets! Well, I will proclaim myself what I am. 134
I will now take the lecher. He is at my house. He can- 135
not scape me. 'Tis impossible he should. He cannot
creep into a halfpenny purse, nor into a pepperbox. 137
But, lest the devil that guides him should aid him, I
will search impossible places. Though what I am I can- 139
not avoid, yet to be what I would not shall not make 140
me tame. If I have horns to make one mad, let the 141
proverb go with me: I'll be horn-mad.   *Exit.* 142

❧

4.1

*Enter Mistress Page, [Mistress] Quickly, [and]
William.*

MRS. PAGE   Is he at Master Ford's already, think'st thou?
QUICKLY   Sure he is by this, or will be presently. But
truly he is very courageous mad about his throwing 3
into the water. Mistress Ford desires you to come
suddenly.   5
MRS. PAGE   I'll be with her by and by. I'll but bring my
young man here to school.

[Enter Sir Hugh] Evans.

Look where his master comes. 'Tis a playing day, I 8
see.—How now, Sir Hugh, no school today?

---

66 change her determination change her mind.   **67 peaking cornuto**
sneaking horned person, i.e., cuckold   **69 larum** i.e., state of surprise
and fear.   **comes me** comes. (*Me* is used colloquially.)   **70 protested**
i.e., solemnly swore our vows of love   **85 that** so that   **92 hinds** servants   **94 took . . . shoulders** i.e., shouldered the heavy basket by
means of a cowlstaff. (See 3.3.135.)   **101 several** distinct   **102 with**
by   **103 bellwether** castrated or old ram, leader of a flock (provided
with a noisy bell and horned like a cuckold).   **compassed** (1) encompassed, surrounded (2) bent into a circle   **104 bilbo** finely tempered
and flexible sword of Bilbao in Spain.   **peck** container holding a
quarter of a bushel; i.e., a very small space.   **hilt to point** (Falstaff is
bent over, head to toes, like a fine Spanish sword that could be bent
thus without breaking.)   **105 stopped** shut, stoppered   **106 fretted**
fermented, stewed   **107 kidney** temperament, constitution.
109 dissolution liquefaction

115 good sadness all seriousness.   **118 Etna** volcano in Sicily
121 embassy message   **124 address me to** prepare myself for, betake
myself to   **132 There's . . . coat** (A proverb warning of unseen dangers and of hidden faults that may come to light.)   **134 what I am**
i.e., a cuckold.   **135 take** apprehend   **137 halfpenny purse** small
purse for small coins   **139–41 Though . . . tame** i.e., Though I cannot
avoid being a cuckold, I will not be so complacently; I won't take it
lying down.   **142 horn-mad** frenzied like a horned animal in rutting
season. (As at 1.4.45.)
4.1. Location: A street in Windsor.
3 courageous (For "outrageously" or "ragingly"?)   **5 suddenly** at
once.   **8 playing day** holiday

EVANS   No. Master Slender is let the boys leave to play.   10

QUICKLY   Blessing of his heart!   11

MRS. PAGE   Sir Hugh, my husband says my son profits   12
nothing in the world at his book. I pray you, ask him   13
some questions in his accidence.   14

EVANS   Come hither, William. Hold up your head.
Come.

MRS. PAGE   Come on, sirrah, hold up your head.
Answer your master. Be not afraid.

EVANS   William, how many numbers is in nouns?   19

WILLIAM   Two.

QUICKLY   Truly, I thought there had been one number
more, because they say "'Od's nouns."   22

EVANS   Peace your tattlings!—What is "fair," William?   23

WILLIAM   *Pulcher.*

QUICKLY   Polecats? There are fairer things than pole-   25
cats, sure.

EVANS   You are a very simplicity 'oman. I pray you,
peace.—What is *lapis*, William?

WILLIAM   A stone.

EVANS   And what is "a stone," William?

WILLIAM   A pebble.

EVANS   No, it is *lapis*. I pray you, remember in your
prain.

WILLIAM   *Lapis.*

EVANS   That is a good William. What is he, William,
that does lend articles?

WILLIAM   Articles are borrowed of the pronoun, and be   37
thus declined, *singulariter, nominativo, hic, haec, hoc.*   38

EVANS   *Nominativo, hig, hag, hog.* Pray you, mark: *genitivo, huius.* Well, what is your accusative case?

WILLIAM   *Accusativo, hinc.*

EVANS   I pray you, have your remembrance, child.
Accusativo, hung, hang, hog.

QUICKLY   "Hang-hog" is Latin for bacon, I warrant   44
you.

EVANS   Leave you prabbles, 'oman.—What is the
focative case, William?

WILLIAM   *O—vocativo,* O.

EVANS   Remember, William, focative is *caret.*   49

QUICKLY   And that's a good root.

EVANS   'Oman, forbear.

MRS. PAGE   [*to Mistress Quickly*]   Peace!

EVANS   What is your genitive case plural, William?

WILLIAM   Genitive case?

EVANS   Ay.

WILLIAM   *Genitivo—horum, harum, horum.*

QUICKLY   Vengeance of Jenny's case! Fie on her! Never   57
name her, child, if she be a whore.

EVANS   For shame, 'oman!

QUICKLY   You do ill to teach the child such words. He
teaches him to hick and to hack, which they'll do fast   61
enough of themselves, and to call "whorum." Fie
upon you!

EVANS   'Oman, art thou lunatics? Hast thou no understandings for thy cases and the numbers of the
genders? Thou art as foolish Christian creatures as I
would desires.

MRS. PAGE   [*to Mistress Quickly*]   Prithee, hold thy peace.

EVANS   Show me now, William, some declensions of
your pronouns.

WILLIAM   Forsooth, I have forgot.

EVANS   It is *qui, quae, quod.* If you forget your *qui's,*
your *quae's,* and your *quod's,* you must be
preeches. Go your ways and play, go.   74

MRS. PAGE   He is a better scholar than I thought he
was.

EVANS   He is a good sprag memory. Farewell, Mistress   77
Page.

MRS. PAGE   Adieu, good Sir Hugh.   [*Exit Sir Hugh.*]
Get you home, boy.   [*Exit William.*]
Come, we stay too long.   *Exeunt.*

❋

4.2

Enter Falstaff [and] Mistress Ford.

FALSTAFF   Mistress Ford, your sorrow hath eaten up   1
my sufferance. I see you are obsequious in your love,   2
and I profess requital to a hair's breadth, not only,   3
Mistress Ford, in the simple office of love, but in all   4
the accoutrement, complement, and ceremony of it.   5
But are you sure of your husband now?

MRS. FORD   He's a-birding, sweet Sir John.

MRS. PAGE   [*within*]   What ho, gossip Ford! What ho!   8

MRS. FORD   Step into the chamber, Sir John.

[*Exit Falstaff.*]

[*Enter*] *Mistress Page.*

MRS. PAGE   How now, sweetheart, who's at home
besides yourself?

MRS. FORD   Why, none but mine own people.   12

MRS. PAGE   Indeed?

10 Master . . . play (As nephew of Robert Shallow, Justice of the
Peace, Slender has the authority to interrupt the school calendar; the
schoolmaster serves at the pleasure of the county's first family. Presumably Slender wants Evans free of his teaching duties so that he
can work to further the marriage of Slender to Anne.)   **11 of** on
12–13 profits . . . book isn't making any progress in his studies.
14 accidence rudiments of Latin grammar.   **19 numbers** i.e., singular
and plural   **22 'Od's nouns** by God's wounds. (Confused with *odd*
numbers, e.g., three.)   **23 Peace your tattlings!** Cease your prattle!
25 Polecats (Many of Quickly's misconstruings are bawdy: *polecats,*
"prostitutes"; *horum,* "whores"; *harum,* "hare," "prostitute"; *Jenny's
case,* "a whore's pudendum," or, "her pregnancy"; etc.)   **37 Articles
. . . pronoun** (William is reciting uncomprehendingly from William
Lilly's widely used Latin grammar, which followed the ancient stoic
grammarians in regarding demonstrative pronouns—*hic, haec, hoc*—
as a sort of article, like *the.*)   **38 *singulariter*** in the singular.
nominativo. (Similarly with *genitivo, accusativo,* and
vocativo.)   **44 Hang-hog** (Bacon is made by hanging up a hog.)
49 *caret* is lacking. (But Quickly interprets it as "carrot.")

57 Vengeance of i.e., A plague on   **61 to hick and to hack** i.e., to
drink and engage in sex; see 2.1.49   **74 preeches** breeched, i.e.,
whipped on the bare buttocks.   **77 sprag** sprack, lively, alert
4.2. Location: Ford's house.
1–2 your . . . sufferance i.e., your sorrow for what I have suffered has
taken away my distress.   **2 obsequious** zealously devoted   **3 I profess . . . breadth** I declare that I return your love in full measure
3–5 not only . . . of it i.e., not only in the simple fact of my loving you,
but in the outward ceremonies and flourishes that embellish that
love.   **8 gossip** i.e., friend, neighbor. (Literally, fellow godparent.)
12 people household servants.

MRS. FORD   No, certainly. [*Aside to her*] Speak louder.

MRS. PAGE   Truly, I am so glad you have nobody here.

MRS. FORD   Why?

MRS. PAGE   Why, woman, your husband is in his old lines again. He so takes on yonder with my husband, so rails against all married mankind, so curses all Eve's daughters, of what complexion soever, and so buffets himself on the forehead, crying, "Peer out, peer out!", that any madness I ever yet beheld seemed but tameness, civility, and patience to this his distemper he is in now. I am glad the fat knight is not here. 18

MRS. FORD   Why, does he talk of him?

MRS. PAGE   Of none but him, and swears he was carried out, the last time he searched for him, in a basket; protests to my husband he is now here, and hath drawn him and the rest of their company from their sport, to make another experiment of his suspicion. But I am glad the knight is not here. Now he shall see his own foolery. 30, 32

MRS. FORD   How near is he, Mistress Page?

MRS. PAGE   Hard by, at street end. He will be here anon.

MRS. FORD   I am undone! The knight is here.

MRS. PAGE   Why, then, you are utterly shamed, and he's but a dead man. What a woman are you! Away with him, away with him! Better shame than murder.

MRS. FORD   Which way should he go? How should I bestow him? Shall I put him into the basket again?

[*Enter Falstaff.*]

FALSTAFF   No, I'll come no more i'th' basket. May I not go out ere he come?

MRS. PAGE   Alas, three of Master Ford's brothers watch the door with pistols, that none shall issue out; otherwise you might slip away ere he came. But what make you here? 45, 46

FALSTAFF   What shall I do? I'll creep up into the chimney.

MRS. FORD   There they always use to discharge their birding pieces. 49, 50

MRS. PAGE   Creep into the kilnhole. 51

FALSTAFF   Where is it?

MRS. FORD   He will seek there, on my word. Neither press, coffer, chest, trunk, well, vault, but he hath an abstract for the remembrance of such places, and goes to them by his note. There is no hiding you in the house. 54, 55

FALSTAFF   I'll go out, then.

MRS. PAGE   If you go out in your own semblance, you die, Sir John—unless you go out disguised.

MRS. FORD   How might we disguise him?

MRS. PAGE   Alas the day, I know not! There is no woman's gown big enough for him; otherwise he might put on a hat, a muffler, and a kerchief, and so escape.

FALSTAFF   Good hearts, devise something. Any extremity rather than a mischief. 67

MRS. FORD   My maid's aunt, the fat woman of Brentford, has a gown above. 68, 69

MRS. PAGE   On my word, it will serve him; she's as big as he is. And there's her thrummed hat and her muffler too. Run up, Sir John. 71

MRS. FORD   Go, go, sweet Sir John. Mistress Page and I will look some linen for your head. 74

MRS. PAGE   Quick, quick! We'll come dress you straight. Put on the gown the while.   [*Exit Falstaff.*] 75

MRS. FORD   I would my husband would meet him in this shape. He cannot abide the old woman of Brentford. He swears she's a witch, forbade her my house, and hath threatened to beat her.

MRS. PAGE   Heaven guide him to thy husband's cudgel, and the devil guide his cudgel afterwards!

MRS. FORD   But is my husband coming?

MRS. PAGE   Ay, in good sadness, is he, and talks of the basket too, howsoever he hath had intelligence. 84

MRS. FORD   We'll try that; for I'll appoint my men to carry the basket again, to meet him at the door with it, as they did last time. 86

MRS. PAGE   Nay, but he'll be here presently. Let's go dress him like the witch of Brentford. 89, 90

MRS. FORD   I'll first direct my men what they shall do with the basket. Go up. I'll bring linen for him straight.   [*Exit.*]

MRS. PAGE   Hang him, dishonest varlet! We cannot misuse him enough. 94
We'll leave a proof, by that which we will do,
Wives may be merry, and yet honest too. 97
We do not act that often jest and laugh; 98
'Tis old, but true, "Still swine eats all the draff." 99
    [*Exit.*]

[*Enter Mistress Ford with two*] *Servants.*

MRS. FORD   Go, sirs, take the basket again on your shoulders. Your master is hard at door. If he bid you set it down, obey him. Quickly, dispatch!   [*Exit.*] 101, 102

FIRST SERVANT   Come, come, take it up.

SECOND SERVANT   Pray heaven it be not full of knight again.

FIRST SERVANT   I hope not. I had as lief bear so much lead.   [*They take up the basket.*] 106

[*Enter*] *Ford, Page, Caius, Evans,* [*and*] *Shallow.*

---

18 **lines** fits of temper or madness.   **He . . . with** He argues with, harangues   21 **Peer out** i.e., Let my cuckold's horns come forth and be visible   23 **to** compared to   30 **experiment** trial   32 **his** Ford's   45–6 **what . . . here?** what are you doing here?   49–50 **There . . . pieces** (After the hunt, the hunters fire off any gun that is still loaded, using the chimney as a convenient place to do so and also as a way of scouring the chimney; removing the bullet, powder, etc., is too cumbersome.)   51 **kilnhole** oven.   54 **press** clothes cupboard   55 **abstract** inventory

67 **mischief** calamity.   68–9 **Brentford** a nearby village   69 **above** upstairs.   71 **thrummed** made of or fringed with the unwoven ends of the warp threads   74 **look** look for   75 **straight** at once.   84 **in good sadness** in all seriousness   86 **try** test   89 **presently** right away.   90 **him** Falstaff   94 **dishonest** lecherous   97 **honest** chaste   98–9 **We . . . draff** i.e., We wives are often merry, but that does not mean we act unchastely; as the proverb says, "It is the quiet ones whom you have to watch for licentious conduct."   101 **hard at door** right at the door.   102 **dispatch** get it done, hurry.   106 **I had as lief** I would just as soon

FORD   Ay, but if it prove true, Master Page, have you
any way then to unfool me again?—Set down the bas- 109
ket, villain! Somebody call my wife. Youth in a basket!
Oh, you panderly rascals! There's a knot, a ging, a pack, 111
a conspiracy against me. Now shall the devil be 112
shamed.—What, wife, I say! Come, come forth! Be- 113
hold what honest clothes you send forth to bleaching!

PAGE   Why, this passes, Master Ford. You are not to go 115
loose any longer; you must be pinioned. 116

EVANS   Why, this is lunatics. This is mad as a mad dog.

SHALLOW   Indeed, Master Ford, this is not well, indeed.

FORD   So say I, too, sir. 119

   [Enter Mistress Ford.]

Come hither, Mistress Ford—Mistress Ford, the honest woman, the modest wife, the virtuous creature,
that hath the jealous fool to her husband! I suspect
without cause, mistress, do I?

MRS. FORD   Heaven be my witness you do, if you
suspect me in any dishonesty.

FORD   Well said, brazenface! Hold it out.—Come forth, 126
sirrah!   [He pulls clothes out of the basket.]

PAGE   This passes!

MRS. FORD   Are you not ashamed? Let the clothes alone.

FORD   I shall find you anon.

EVANS   'Tis unreasonable. Will you take up your wife's 131
clothes? Come, away.

FORD   Empty the basket, I say!

MRS. FORD   Why, man, why?

FORD   Master Page, as I am a man, there was one
conveyed out of my house yesterday in this basket.
Why may not he be there again? In my house I am
sure he is. My intelligence is true; my jealousy is 138
reasonable.—Pluck me out all the linen. 139

MRS. FORD   If you find a man there, he shall die a flea's 140
death. 141

PAGE   Here's no man.

SHALLOW   By my fidelity, this is not well, Master Ford. 143
This wrongs you. 144

EVANS   Master Ford, you must pray, and not follow the
imaginations of your own heart. This is jealousies.

FORD   Well, he's not here I seek for.

PAGE   No, nor nowhere else but in your brain.

FORD   Help to search my house this one time. If I find
not what I seek, show no color for my extremity; let 150
me forever be your table sport. Let them say of me, 151

"As jealous as Ford, that searched a hollow walnut for
his wife's leman." Satisfy me once more; once more 153
search with me.   [Exeunt Servants with basket.]

MRS. FORD   [calling upstairs]   What ho, Mistress Page!
Come you and the old woman down. My husband
will come into the chamber.

FORD   Old woman? What old woman's that?

MRS. FORD   Why, it is my maid's aunt of Brentford.

FORD   A witch, a quean, an old, cozening quean! Have 160
I not forbid her my house? She comes of errands, does 161
she? We are simple men; we do not know what's
brought to pass under the profession of fortunetelling.
She works by charms, by spells, by th' figure, 164
and such daubery as this is, beyond our element; we 165
know nothing.—Come down, you witch, you hag,
you! Come down, I say!

MRS. FORD   Nay, good sweet husband!—Good gentlemen, let him not strike the old woman.

   [Enter Falstaff in woman's clothes, and Mistress
   Page.]

MRS. PAGE   Come, Mother Prat, come, give me your
hand.

FORD   I'll prat her. [Beating him.] Out of my door, you 172
witch, you rag, you baggage, you polecat, you 173
ronyon! Out, out! I'll conjure you, I'll fortune-tell you. 174
   [Exit Falstaff.]

MRS. PAGE   Are you not ashamed? I think you have
killed the poor woman.

MRS. FORD   Nay, he will do it.—'Tis a goodly credit for 177
you. 178

FORD   Hang her, witch!

EVANS   By Jeshu, I think the 'oman is a witch indeed. I
like not when a 'oman has a great peard. I spy a great
peard under his muffler.

FORD   Will you follow, gentlemen? I beseech you,
follow. See but the issue of my jealousy. If I cry out 184
thus upon no trail, never trust me when I open again. 185

PAGE   Let's obey his humor a little further. Come, 186
gentlemen.
   [Exeunt Ford, Page, Shallow, Caius, and Evans.]

MRS. PAGE   Trust me, he beat him most pitifully.

MRS. FORD   Nay, by th' Mass, that he did not; he beat
him most unpitifully, methought.

MRS. PAGE   I'll have the cudgel hallowed and hung o'er
the altar. It hath done meritorious service.

MRS. FORD   What think you? May we, with the warrant
of womanhood and the witness of a good conscience,
pursue him with any further revenge?

---

109 unfool me disburden me of a reputation for folly   111 a knot . . .
pack a company, a gang, a confederacy   112–13 Now . . . shamed i.e.,
Now truth will out. (From the proverb "Tell the truth and shame the
devil.")   115 passes surpasses, goes beyond all bounds   116 be pinioned (Such restraint was standard procedure in treating insanity.)
119 So say I, too (Ford means that something is amiss; not, as Shallow
intended to say, that Ford's behavior is deplorable.)   126 Hold it out
i.e., Continue to maintain your falsehood.   131 take up pick up. (But
with unintended bawdy suggestion of lifting his wife's dress.)
138 intelligence information   139 Pluck me out Pluck out for me
140–1 he . . . death i.e., he will die an ignominious death, squashed
like a flea.   143 By my fidelity Upon my word   144 wrongs you
does you dishonor.   150 show . . . extremity make no attempt to
excuse my extreme behavior   151 your table sport butt or laughingstock of the company.

153 leman lover.   160 quean slut, hussy.   cozening deceiving
161 of on   164 by the figure i.e., by making wax figures and sticking
pins in them, or, by astrological charts   165 daubery false show.
beyond our element beyond our comprehension, belonging to
another world   172 prat beat, teach a lesson, practice tricks on (?)
173–4 you rag . . . ronyon! i.e., you worthless wretch, you slut, you
whore, you bitch!   177–8 'Tis . . . you It does you great credit. (Said
ironically.)   184 issue conclusion   184–5 cry . . . trail bay like a hunting dog despite the absence of a scent   185 open give voice (like a
hunting dog)   186 obey his humor humor him

MRS. PAGE   The spirit of wantonness is, sure, scared 196
out of him. If the devil have him not in fee simple, 197
with fine and recovery, he will never, I think, in the 198
way of waste, attempt us again. 199

MRS. FORD   Shall we tell our husbands how we have
served him?

MRS. PAGE   Yes, by all means, if it be but to scrape the
figures out of your husband's brains. If they can find 203
in their hearts the poor, unvirtuous, fat knight shall be
any further afflicted, we two will still be the ministers. 205

MRS. FORD   I'll warrant they'll have him publicly
shamed, and methinks there would be no period 207
to the jest, should he not be publicly shamed.

MRS. PAGE   Come, to the forge with it, then shape it. I 209
would not have things cool.   *Exeunt.*

4.3

Enter Host and Bardolph.

BARDOLPH   Sir, the Germans desire to have three of
your horses. The Duke himself will be tomorrow at
court, and they are going to meet him.

HOST   What duke should that be comes so secretly? I
hear not of him in the court. Let me speak with the
gentlemen. They speak English?

BARDOLPH   Ay, sir. I'll call them to you.

HOST   They shall have my horses, but I'll make them
pay; I'll sauce them. They have had my house a week 9
at command. I have turned away my other guests. 10
They must come off. I'll sauce them. Come.   *Exeunt.* 11

❧

4.4

*Enter Page, Ford, Mistress Page, Mistress
Ford, and Evans.*

EVANS   'Tis one of the best discretions of a 'oman as 1
ever I did look upon. 2

PAGE   And did he send you both these letters at an 3
instant? 4

MRS. PAGE   Within a quarter of an hour.

FORD
Pardon me, wife. Henceforth do what thou wilt;
I rather will suspect the sun with cold 7
Than thee with wantonness. Now doth thy honor
    stand,

---

196 **wantonness** lust   197 **fee simple** estate belonging to an owner
and his heirs forever; hence, absolute possession   198 **fine and
recovery** procedures by which an entailed estate was converted into
fee simple. (Unless Falstaff already belongs to the devil outright, says
Mistress Page, he won't try us again.)   199 **waste** spoliation, despoiling. (Another legal term.)   203 **figures** fantasies, conceits   205 **ministers** agents   207 **period** suitable conclusion   209 **Come . . . shape
it** i.e., Strike while the iron is hot.
4.3. Location: The Garter Inn.
9 **sauce them** i.e., make them pay dearly.   10 **at command** retained
for their use upon their expected arrival.   11 **come off** pay up.
4.4. Location: Page's house.
1–2 **'Tis . . . upon** i.e., This joke played on Falstaff by the merry wives is
one of the best instances of feminine wit and adroit management I have
ever seen.   3–4 **at an instant** at the same time.   7 **with** with being

---

In him that was of late an heretic,
As firm as faith.

PAGE   Tis well, 'tis well. No more.
Be not as extreme in submission as in offense.
But let our plot go forward. Let our wives
Yet once again, to make us public sport,
Appoint a meeting with this old fat fellow,
Where we may take him and disgrace him for it.

FORD
There is no better way than that they spoke of.

PAGE   How? To send him word they'll meet him in
the park at midnight? Fie, fie, he'll never come.

EVANS   You say he has been thrown in the rivers and
has been grievously peaten as an old 'oman. Methinks 20
there should be terrors in him that he should not 21
come. Methinks his flesh is punished; he shall have no 22
desires.

PAGE   So think I too.

MRS. FORD
Devise but how you'll use him when he comes, 25
And let us two devise to bring him thither.

MRS. PAGE
There is an old tale goes that Herne the hunter,
Sometime a keeper here in Windsor Forest, 28
Doth all the wintertime, at still midnight,
Walk round about an oak, with great ragg'd horns; 30
And there he blasts the tree, and takes the cattle, 31
And makes milch kine yield blood, and shakes a
    chain 32
In a most hideous and dreadful manner.
You have heard of such a spirit, and well you know
The superstitious idle-headed eld 35
Received and did deliver to our age
This tale of Herne the hunter for a truth.

PAGE
Why, yet there want not many that do fear 38
In deep of night to walk by this Herne's oak.
But what of this?

MRS. FORD   Marry, this is our device: 40
That Falstaff at that oak shall meet with us,
Disguised like Herne, with huge horns on his head.

PAGE
Well, let it not be doubted but he'll come.
And in this shape when you have brought him thither,
What shall be done with him? What is your plot?

MRS. PAGE
That likewise have we thought upon, and thus:
Nan Page my daughter, and my little son,
And three or four more of their growth, we'll dress 48
Like urchins, aufs, and fairies, green and white, 49
With rounds of waxen tapers on their heads, 50
And rattles in their hands. Upon a sudden,

20–2 **Methinks . . . come** I should think he'd be too afraid to come.
25 **use** treat   28 **Sometime** formerly   30 **ragg'd** shaggy, pronged
31 **blasts** blights, or blasts with lightning.   **takes** bewitches
32 **milch kine** dairy cattle   35 **idle-headed eld** ignorant folk of olden
time   38 **yet . . . many** even today there are many   40 **device** plan
48 **growth** size, age   49 **urchins, aufs** (Terms for goblins or elves.)
50 **rounds** circlets, coronets

As Falstaff, she, and I are newly met,
Let them from forth a sawpit rush at once   53
With some diffusèd song. Upon their sight,   54
We two in great amazedness will fly.
Then let them all encircle him about,
And, fairylike, to pinch the unclean knight,
And ask him why, that hour of fairy revel,
In their so sacred paths he dares to tread
In shape profane.
MRS. FORD   And till he tell the truth,
Let the supposèd fairies pinch him sound   61
And burn him with their tapers.
MRS. PAGE   The truth being known,
We'll all present ourselves, dis-horn the spirit,
And mock him home to Windsor.
FORD   The children must
Be practiced well to this, or they'll ne'er do't.
EVANS   I will teach the children their behaviors, and I
will be like a jackanapes also, to burn the knight with   67
my taber.   68
FORD
That will be excellent. I'll go buy them vizards.   69
MRS. PAGE
My Nan shall be the queen of all the fairies,
Finely attirèd in a robe of white.
PAGE
That silk will I go buy. [Aside] And in that tire   72
Shall Master Slender steal my Nan away
And marry her at Eton. [To Mistress Page] Go,
    send to Falstaff straight.   74
FORD
Nay, I'll to him again in name of Brook.
He'll tell me all his purpose. Sure he'll come.
MRS. PAGE
Fear not you that. Go get us properties   77
And tricking for our fairies.   78
EVANS   Let us about it. It is admirable pleasures and
fery honest knaveries. [Exeunt Page, Ford, and Evans.]
MRS. PAGE   Go, Mistress Ford,
Send quickly to Sir John, to know his mind.
                              [Exit Mistress Ford.]
I'll to the Doctor. He hath my good will,
And none but he, to marry with Nan Page.
That Slender, though well landed, is an idiot;   85
And he my husband best of all affects.   86
The Doctor is well moneyed, and his friends
Potent at court. He, none but he, shall have her,
Though twenty thousand worthier come to crave her.
                                             [Exit.]

❖

4.5

Enter Host [and] Simple.

HOST   What wouldst thou have, boor? What, thickskin?   1
Speak, breathe, discuss; brief, short, quick, snap.   2
SIMPLE   Marry, sir, I come to speak with Sir John
Falstaff from Master Slender.
HOST   There's his chamber, his house, his castle, his
standing bed and truckle bed. 'Tis painted about with   6
the story of the Prodigal, fresh and new. Go knock and   7
call. He'll speak like an Anthropophaginian unto thee.   8
Knock, I say.
SIMPLE   There's an old woman, a fat woman, gone up
into his chamber. I'll be so bold as stay, sir, till she
come down. I come to speak with her, indeed.
HOST   Ha, a fat woman? The knight may be robbed. I'll   13
call.—Bully knight! Bully Sir John! Speak from thy
lungs military. Art thou there? It is thine Host, thine
Ephesian, calls.   16
FALSTAFF [within]   How now, mine Host?
HOST   Here's a Bohemian Tartar tarries the coming   18
down of thy fat woman. Let her descend, bully, let
her descend. My chambers are honorable. Fie, pri-   20
vacy? Fie!

        [Enter] Falstaff.

FALSTAFF   There was, mine Host, an old fat woman even
now with me, but she's gone.
SIMPLE   Pray you, sir, was't not the wise woman of   24
Brentford?
FALSTAFF   Ay, marry, was it, mussel shell. What would   26
you with her?
SIMPLE   My master, sir, my Master Slender, sent to her,
seeing her go through the streets, to know, sir,
whether one Nym, sir, that beguiled him of a chain,
had the chain or no.
FALSTAFF   I spake with the old woman about it.
SIMPLE   And what says she, I pray, sir?
FALSTAFF   Marry, she says that the very same man that be- 34
guiled Master Slender of his chain cozened him of it.   35
SIMPLE   I would I could have spoken with the woman
herself. I had other things to have spoken with her too
from him.
FALSTAFF   What are they? Let us know.
HOST   Ay, come. Quick.

4.5. Location: The Garter Inn.
1 thickskin one slow or dull of feeling.   **2 discuss** declare   **6 truckle bed** trundle bed, low bed stored under the *standing bed* or regular bed.   **7 the Prodigal** (Compare *1 Henry IV,* 4.2.34 and *2 Henry IV,* 2.1.143, where this story from Luke 15:11–32 is again associated with Falstaff.)   **8 Anthropophaginian** (One of the Host's extravagant epithets, perhaps intended to frighten Simple. Literally, a cannibal.)
13 The knight . . . robbed (The Host is worried that an unaccompanied woman going up to man's chambers is likely to be a prostitute and a thief.)   **16 Ephesian** i.e., boon companion   **18 Bohemian Tartar** i.e., barbarian, wild man.   **tarries** (who) awaits   **20 My . . . honorable** i.e., I won't have any whores in my inn.   **24 wise woman** i.e., fortune-teller   **26 mussel shell** i.e., one who gapes.   **34–5 Marry . . . of it** (Falstaff wittily answers Simple as a soothsayer might, with a seeming profundity that merely restates the obvious: the beguiler was the cozener or cheater.)

---

53 sawpit a pit over which wood was sawed   **54 diffusèd** confused, disorderly   **61 sound** soundly   **67 like a jackanapes** disguised as an ape or monkey. (Evans actually disguises himself as a satyr.)   **68 taber** taper, candle.   **69 vizards** visors, masks.   **72 tire** attire   **74 Eton** town across the Thames from Windsor.   **77 properties** theatrical props   **78 tricking** adornment, costumes   **85 well landed** rich in land   **86 he** i.e., him. **affects** prefers.

SIMPLE   I may not conceal them, sir.   41

HOST   Conceal them or thou diest.

SIMPLE   Why, sir, they were nothing but about Mistress
Anne Page, to know if it were my master's fortune to
have her or no.

FALSTAFF   'Tis, 'tis his fortune.

SIMPLE   What, sir?

FALSTAFF   To have her, or no. Go, say the woman told   48
me so.

SIMPLE   May I be bold to say so, sir?

FALSTAFF   Ay, sir; like who more bold.   51

SIMPLE   I thank Your Worship. I shall make my master
glad with these tidings.   [*Exit.*]

HOST   Thou art clerkly, thou art clerkly, Sir John. Was   54
there a wise woman with thee?

FALSTAFF   Ay, that there was, mine Host, one that hath
taught me more wit than ever I learned before in my
life. And I paid nothing for it, neither, but was paid for   58
my learning.

[*Enter*] *Bardolph.*

BARDOLPH   Out, alas, sir! Cozenage, mere cozenage!   60

HOST   Where be my horses? Speak well of them,   61
varletto.   62

BARDOLPH   Run away with the cozeners. For so soon as
I came beyond Eton, they threw me off from behind
one of them, in a slough of mire, and set spurs and   65
away, like three German devils, three Doctor Faus-   66
tuses.   67

HOST   They are gone but to meet the Duke, villain. Do
not say they be fled. Germans are honest men.

[*Enter*] *Evans.*

EVANS   Where is mine Host?

HOST   What is the matter, sir?

EVANS   Have a care of your entertainments. There is a   72
friend of mine come to town tells me there is three
cozen-germans that has cozened all the hosts of   74
Reading, of Maidenhead, of Colnbrook, of horses and   75
money. I tell you for good will, look you. You are
wise, and full of gibes and vloutingstocks, and 'tis not   77
convenient you should be cozened. Fare you well.   78
[*Exit.*]

[*Enter*] *Caius.*

CAIUS   Vere is mine Host de Jarteer?

HOST   Here, Master Doctor, in perplexity and doubtful   80
dilemma.

CAIUS   I cannot tell vat is dat. But it is tell-a me dat you
make grand preparation for a duke de Jamany. By my   83
trot, dere is no duke that the court is know to come. I   84
tell you for good will. Adieu.   [*Exit.*]

HOST   Hue and cry, villain, go!—Assist me, knight. I am   86
undone!—Fly, run, hue and cry, villain! I am undone!
[*Exeunt Host and Bardolph.*]

FALSTAFF   I would all the world might be cozened, for I
have been cozened and beaten too. If it should come
to the ear of the court how I have been transformed,
and how my transformation hath been washed and
cudgeled, they would melt me out of my fat drop by
drop and liquor fishermen's boots with me. I warrant   93
they would whip me with their fine wits till I were as
crestfallen as a dried pear. I never prospered since I   95
forswore myself at primero. Well, if my wind were but   96
long enough to say my prayers, I would repent.

[*Enter Mistress*] *Quickly.*

Now, whence come you?

QUICKLY   From the two parties, forsooth.

FALSTAFF   The devil take one party and his dam the   100
other! And so they shall be both bestowed. I have   101
suffered more for their sakes, more than the villainous
inconstancy of man's disposition is able to bear.

QUICKLY   And have not they suffered? Yes, I warrant,
speciously one of them. Mistress Ford, good heart, is   105
beaten black and blue, that you cannot see a white
spot about her.

FALSTAFF   What tell'st thou me of black and blue? I was
beaten myself into all the colors of the rainbow, and I
was like to be apprehended for the witch of Brentford.   110
But that my admirable dexterity of wit, my counter-   111
feiting the action of an old woman, delivered me, the
knave constable had set me i'the stocks, i'th'
common stocks, for a witch.

QUICKLY   Sir, let me speak with you in your chamber,   115
you shall hear how things go, and, I warrant, to your
content. Here is a letter will say somewhat. [*She gives
a letter.*] Good hearts, what ado is here to bring you
together! Sure, one of you does not serve heaven well,
that you are so crossed.   120

FALSTAFF   Come up into my chamber.   *Exeunt.*

❧

---

41 **conceal** (For "reveal." The Host answers ironically with the same misused word.)   48 **To have . . . no** (As in lines 34-5, Falstaff again speaks in oracular ambiguities that say nothing: either Slender will succeed or he won't.)   51 **like . . . bold** i.e., who could possibly have a right to be bolder than you? (Said with mock politeness.)   54 **clerkly** scholarly, wise, clever. (The Host admires Falstaff's wit at Simple's expense.)   58 **was paid** i.e., with a beating   60 **Cozenage** Double-dealing.   **mere** absolute   61–2 **Speak . . . varletto** i.e., Tell me good news of them, you rascal.   65 **one of them** one of the horses   66–7 **Doctor Faustuses** (Named for the German scholar-magician who practices devilish arts in Marlowe's play.)   72 **your entertainments** i.e., your guests.   74 **cozen-germans** (1) first cousins (2) cozening or cheating Germans; see note 83 below for a topical reference   75 **Reading** a town not far from Windsor. (Also true of *Maidenhead* and *Colnbrook*.)   77 **vloutingstocks** i.e., taunts   78 **convenient** fitting

80 **doubtful** full of doubts   83 **duke de Jamany** duke of Germany. (Seemingly a satirical reference to Count Mömpelgard, later Duke of Württemberg, who offended many observers by his self-serving maneuvering to be elected Knight of the Garter in 1592 and afterwards. The Quarto's "cosen garmombles" in place of the Folio's "three Cozen-Iermans" in lines 73–4 hints topically at Mömpelgard.)   84 **trot** troth.   **that . . . to come** whose arrival is expected at court.   86 **Hue and cry, villain** (The Host bids Bardolph go raise the cry for pursuit of a felon.)   93 **liquor** saturate with oil to make waterproof   95 **crestfallen** i.e., shriveled   96 **forswore . . . primero** i.e., swore a false oath that I had never cheated at primero, a gambling card game, and was detected in the lie.   100 **dam** mother   101 **bestowed** i.e., lodged where they deserve.   105 **speciously** (For "specially.")   110 **like** likely, about   111 **But that** Were it not that   115 **let** if you will let   120 **crossed** thwarted.

4.6

Enter Fenton [and] Host.

HOST Master Fenton, talk not to me. My mind is
heavy. I will give over all.   2

FENTON
Yet hear me speak. Assist me in my purpose,
And, as I am a gentleman, I'll give thee
A hundred pound in gold more than your loss.

HOST I will hear you, Master Fenton, and I will at the
least keep your counsel.   7

FENTON
From time to time I have acquainted you
With the dear love I bear to fair Anne Page,
Who mutually hath answered my affection,
So far forth as herself might be her chooser,   11
Even to my wish. I have a letter from her   12
Of such contents as you will wonder at,
The mirth whereof so larded with my matter   14
That neither singly can be manifested
Without the show of both. Fat Falstaff
Hath a great scene; the image of the jest   17
I'll show you here at large. [*He shows a letter.*] Hark,
good mine Host.   18
Tonight at Herne's oak, just twixt twelve and one,
Must my sweet Nan present the Fairy Queen—   20
The purpose why is here—in which disguise,
While other jests are something rank on foot,   22
Her father hath commanded her to slip
Away with Slender, and with him at Eton
Immediately to marry. She hath consented.
Now, sir,
Her mother, even strong against that match   27
And firm for Doctor Caius, hath appointed
That he shall likewise shuffle her away,   29
While other sports are tasking of their minds,   30
And at the deanery, where a priest attends,
Straight marry her. To this her mother's plot
She, seemingly obedient, likewise hath
Made promise to the Doctor. Now, thus it rests: 34
Her father means she shall be all in white,
And in that habit, when Slender sees his time   36
To take her by the hand and bid her go,
She shall go with him. Her mother hath intended,   38
The better to denote her to the Doctor—
For they must all be masked and vizarded—
That quaint in green she shall be loose enrobed,   41
With ribbons pendent, flaring 'bout her head;
And when the Doctor spies his vantage ripe,
To pinch her by the hand, and on that token
The maid hath given consent to go with him.

HOST
Which means she to deceive, father or mother?

FENTON
Both, my good Host, to go along with me.
And here it rests: that you'll procure the vicar
To stay for me at church twixt twelve and one,
And, in the lawful name of marrying,
To give our hearts united ceremony.

HOST
Well, husband your device. I'll to the vicar.   52
Bring you the maid, you shall not lack a priest.   53

FENTON
So shall I evermore be bound to thee.
Besides, I'll make a present recompense.   *Exeunt.* 55

❖

5.1

Enter Falstaff [and Mistress] Quickly.

FALSTAFF Prithee, no more prattling; go. I'll hold. This   1
is the third time; I hope good luck lies in odd numbers. Away, go. They say there is divinity in odd   3
numbers, either in nativity, chance, or death. Away!

QUICKLY I'll provide you a chain, and I'll do what I can
to get you a pair of horns.

FALSTAFF Away, I say! Time wears. Hold up your   7
head, and mince.   [*Exit Mistress Quickly.*] 8

[Enter] Ford [disguised].

How now, Master Brook? Master Brook, the matter
will be known tonight or never. Be you in the park
about midnight, at Herne's oak, and you shall see
wonders.

FORD Went you not to her yesterday, sir, as you told   13
me you had appointed?

FALSTAFF I went to her, Master Brook, as you see, like
a poor old man, but I came from her, Master Brook,
like a poor old woman. That same knave Ford, her
husband, hath the finest mad devil of jealousy in him,
Master Brook, that ever governed frenzy. I will tell you:
he beat me grievously, in the shape of a woman; for
in the shape of man, Master Brook, I fear not Goliath 21
with a weaver's beam, because I know also life is a   22
shuttle. I am in haste. Go along with me; I'll tell you 23
all, Master Brook. Since I plucked geese, played   24
truant, and whipped top, I knew not what 'twas to be   25
beaten till lately. Follow me. I'll tell you strange things
of this knave Ford, on whom tonight I will be

4.6. Location: The Garter Inn, as before.
2 give over abandon **7 keep your counsel** keep your secret. **11 So
far forth** insofar **12 to** according to **14 larded . . . matter** intermin-
gled with what concerns me **17 image** form, idea **18 at large** at
length. **20 present** represent **22 something . . . foot** abundantly
being devised **27 even** equally **29 shuffle** smuggle, steal **30 tasking of** busily occupying **34 it rests** matters stand **36 habit** dress
38 intended arranged **41 quaint** decorously

52 husband manage prudently **53 Bring you** If you bring **55 present** immediate
5.1. Location: The Garter Inn, as before.
1 hold persevere, keep the appointment. **3 divinity** mysterious
power **7–8 Hold . . . mince** Hold your head proudly erect as you
trip away. **13 yesterday** (Actually, the meeting appears to have been
earlier this same day.) **21–2 Goliath . . . beam** (See 1 Samuel 17:7:
"The staff of his [Goliath's] spear was like a weaver's beam." See also
2 Samuel 21:19. A weaver's beam is a wooden cylinder in a loom.)
22–3 life is a shuttle (See Job 7:6: "My days are swifter than a
weaver's shuttle.") **24–5 plucked . . . top** i.e., committed various
boyhood pranks. To whip a top is to set it spinning.

revenged, and I will deliver his wife into your hand. Follow. Strange things in hand, Master Brook! Follow.   *Exeunt.*

❦

5.2

Enter Page, Shallow, [and] Slender.

PAGE   Come, come. We'll couch i'th' castle ditch till we 1
see the light of our fairies. Remember, son Slender, my daughter.

SLENDER   Ay, forsooth. I have spoke with her, and we have a nayword how to know one another. I come to 5
her in white and cry "mum," she cries "budget," and 6
by that we know one another.

SHALLOW   That's good too. But what needs either your 8
"mum" or her "budget"? The white will decipher her 9
well enough.—It hath struck ten o'clock.

PAGE   The night is dark; light and spirits will become it 11
well. Heaven prosper our sport! No man means evil but the devil, and we shall know him by his horns. Let's away. Follow me.   *Exeunt.*

❦

5.3

Enter Mistress Page, Mistress Ford, [and] Caius.

MRS. PAGE   Master Doctor, my daughter is in green. When you see your time, take her by the hand, away with her to the deanery, and dispatch it quickly. Go 3
before into the park. We two must go together.

CAIUS   I know vat I have to do. Adieu.

MRS. PAGE   Fare you well, sir.   *[Exit Caius.]*
My husband will not rejoice so much at the abuse of Falstaff as he will chafe at the Doctor's marrying my daughter. But 'tis no matter. Better a little chiding than a great deal of heartbreak.

MRS. FORD   Where is Nan now, and her troop of fairies, and the Welsh devil Hugh?

MRS. PAGE   They are all couched in a pit hard by Herne's Oak, with obscured lights, which, at the very instant of Falstaff's and our meeting, they will at once display to the night.

MRS. FORD   That cannot choose but amaze him.   17

MRS. PAGE   If he be not amazed, he will be mocked. If 18
he be amazed, he will every way be mocked.   19

MRS. FORD   We'll betray him finely.

MRS. PAGE
Against such lewdsters and their lechery,
Those that betray them do no treachery.

MRS. FORD   The hour draws on. To the oak, to the oak!
Exeunt.

❦

5.4

Enter Evans [as a satyr] and [children disguised as] fairies.

EVANS   Trib, trib, fairies. Come, and remember your 1
parts. Be pold, I pray you. Follow me into the pit, and when I give the watch'ords, do as I pid you. Come, come; trib, trib.   *Exeunt.*

❦

5.5

Enter Falstaff [disguised as Herne, wearing a buck's head].

FALSTAFF   The Windsor bell hath struck twelve; the minute draws on. Now, the hot-blooded gods assist me! Remember, Jove, thou wast a bull for thy Europa; 3
love set on thy horns. O powerful Love, that in some respects makes a beast a man, in some other a man a beast! You were also, Jupiter, a swan for the love of 6
Leda. O omnipotent Love, how near the god drew to 7
the complexion of a goose! A fault done first in the form of a beast—O Jove, a beastly fault!—and then another fault in the semblance of a fowl; think on 't, Jove, a foul fault! When gods have hot backs, what shall poor men do? For me, I am here a Windsor stag, and the fattest, I think, i'th' forest. Send me a cool rut-time, Jove, or who can blame me to piss my 14
tallow? Who comes here? My doe?   15

[Enter] Mistress Page [and] Mistress Ford.

MRS. FORD   Sir John? Art thou there, my deer, my male 16
deer?

FALSTAFF   My doe with the black scut! Let the sky rain 18
potatoes; let it thunder to the tune of "Greensleeves," 19
hail kissing-comfits, and snow eringoes; let there 20
come a tempest of provocation, I will shelter me here. 21
[He embraces her.]

MRS. FORD   Mistress Page is come with me, sweetheart.

FALSTAFF   Divide me like a bribed buck, each a haunch. 23
I will keep my sides to myself, my shoulders for the fellow of this walk, and my horns I bequeath your 25
husbands. Am I a woodman, ha? Speak I like Herne 26

5.2. Location: On the way to Windsor Park.
1 couch hide   5 nayword password, watchword   6 mum, budget
(*Mumbudget* connotes silence, as in a children's game by that name.)
8 what needs what need is there for   9 decipher identify
11 become suit
5.3. Location: Somewhere in Windsor.
3 dispatch conclude   17 cannot choose but amaze is certain to
astound and terrify   18–19 mocked . . . mocked deceived . . .
ridiculed.

5.4. Location: Windsor Park, as before.
1 Trib Trip, move nimbly
5.5. Location: Windsor Park, as before.
3, 6–7 bull . . . Europa, swan . . . Leda (References to legends of
Jupiter's animal disguises when engaged in various amours.)
14 rut-time mating season   14–15 piss my tallow i.e., sweat off and
excrete excess fat during mating season, like a stag.   16 deer (With a
pun on "dear.")   18 scut tail, pudendum.   19 potatoes i.e., sweet
potatoes. (Regarded by Elizabethans as aphrodisiac.)   Greensleeves
(A popular tune; see the note for 2.1.60.)   20 kissing-comfits perfumed sweetmeats for sweetening the breath.   eringoes candied root
of a plant called sea holly. (Regarded as aphrodisiac.)   21 provocation i.e., sexual stimulation   23 bribed stolen (and then quickly cut
up and divided by the poachers)   25 fellow . . . walk i.e., keeper of
the forest. (Traditionally, the forester received the shoulders of
slaughtered beasts as his fee.)   25-6 my horns . . . husbands (Falstaff
will make the husbands wear cuckold's horns.)   26 woodman
(1) hunter (2) woman chaser

the hunter? Why, now is Cupid a child of conscience;   27
he makes restitution. As I am a true spirit, welcome!
[A noise within.]

MRS. PAGE   Alas, what noise?

MRS. FORD   Heaven forgive our sins!

FALSTAFF   What should this be?

MRS. FORD, MRS. PAGE   Away, away!   [They run off.]

FALSTAFF   I think the devil will not have me damned,
lest the oil that's in me should set hell on fire. He
would never else cross me thus.   35

[Enter] Evans, [disguised as a satyr, Mistress]
Quickly [as the Fairy Queen], Anne Page [and
children as] fairies, [with tapers, and] Pistol [as
Hobgoblin].

QUICKLY [as Fairy Queen]
Fairies, black, gray, green, and white,
You moonshine revelers, and shades of night,   37
You orphan heirs of fixèd destiny,   38
Attend your office and your quality.   39
Crier Hobgoblin, make the fairy oyes.   40

PISTOL [as Hobgoblin]
Elves, list your names. Silence, you airy toys!   41
Cricket, to Windsor chimneys shalt thou leap.
Where fires thou find'st unraked and hearths
   unswept,   43
There pinch the maids as blue as bilberry.   44
Our radiant Queen hates sluts and sluttery.   45

FALSTAFF
They are fairies. He that speaks to them shall die.   46
I'll wink and couch; no man their works must eye.   47
[He lies face downward.]

EVANS [as a satyr]
Where's Bead? Go you, and where you find a maid
That, ere she sleep, has thrice her prayers said,
Raise up the organs of her fantasy;   50
Sleep she as sound as careless infancy.   51
But those as sleep and think not on their sins,   52
Pinch them, arms, legs, backs, shoulders, sides, and
   shins.

QUICKLY   About, about!   54
Search Windsor Castle, elves, within and out.
Strew good luck, aufs, on every sacred room,   56
That it may stand till the perpetual doom   57
In state as wholesome as in state 'tis fit,   58
Worthy the owner, and the owner it.

The several chairs of order look you scour   60
With juice of balm and every precious flower.
Each fair installment, coat, and several crest   62
With loyal blazon evermore be blest!   63
And nightly, meadow fairies, look you sing,
Like to the Garter's compass, in a ring.   65
Th'expressure that it bears, green let it be,   66
More fertile-fresh than all the field to see;
And "Honi soit qui mal y pense" write   68
In em'rald tufts, flow'rs purple, blue, and white,
Like sapphire, pearl, and rich embroidery,
Buckled below fair knighthood's bending knee;
Fairies use flowers for their charactery.   72
Away, disperse! But till 'tis one o'clock,
Our dance of custom, round about the oak   74
Of Herne the hunter, let us not forget.

EVANS   Pray you,
Lock hand in hand. Yourselves in order set;
And twenty glowworms shall our lanterns be
To guide our measure round about the tree.   79
But stay! I smell a man of middle-earth.   80

FALSTAFF   Heavens defend me from that Welsh fairy,
lest he transform me to a piece of cheese!   82
[They discover Falstaff hiding.]

PISTOL
Vile worm, thou wast o'erlooked even in thy birth.   83

QUICKLY [to Fairies]
With trial-fire touch me his finger end.
If he be chaste, the flame will back descend
And turn him to no pain; but if he start,   86
It is the flesh of a corrupted heart.

PISTOL
A trial, come.

EVANS
Come, will this wood take fire?   88
[They put the tapers to his fingers, and he starts.]

FALSTAFF   Oh, Oh, Oh!

QUICKLY
Corrupt, corrupt, and tainted in desire!
About him, fairies. Sing a scornful rhyme,
And, as you trip, still pinch him to your time.   92

The Song.

FAIRIES
Fie on sinful fantasy!
Fie on lust and luxury!   94

27 is Cupid . . . conscience i.e., Cupid is keeping faith with me
35 cross thwart   37 shades spirits   38 orphan i.e., parentless.
(Fairies were thought to be not of human parentage.)   heirs . . . destiny i.e., inheritors of commissions to specific fairy assignments
39 Attend . . . quality attend to your duties and particular functions.
40 oyes oyez, hear ye. (The call of the public crier.)   41 list listen for.
toys substanceless beings.   43 unraked not raked together to last
through the night   44 bilberry a kind of blueberry.   45 sluttery sluttishness.   46 He . . . die (A widespread tradition about fairies.)
47 wink and couch close my eyes and lie hidden   50 Raise . . . fantasy i.e., give her pleasant dreams   51 Sleep she let her sleep.
careless free of care   52 as who   54 About i.e., Get to work   56 aufs
elves   57 perpetual doom Day of Judgment   58 In . . . fit i.e., in a
healthy condition, as befits its dignity

60 The several . . . order i.e., The individual stalls of the Garter
knights (in Saint George's chapel at Windsor)   62 Each . . . crest Each
place in which a knight is installed, coat of arms, and separate
heraldic device   63 loyal blazon coat of arms, armorial bearings of a
loyal knight.   65 compass circle. (The garter was worn below the left
knee by knights of the order.)   66 Th'expressure the image, picture
68 Honi . . . pense Evil to him who evil thinks. (The motto of the
Order of the Garter.)   72 charactery writing.   74 dance of custom
customary dance   79 measure stately dance   80 middle-earth i.e.,
the earth, the center of the universe, conceived of as between the
heavens and the underworld.   82 cheese (The Welshman's favorite
food; compare 2.2.290–1.)   83 o'erlooked bewitched, looked on with
an evil eye   86 turn put   88.1 fingers fingertips. (The stage direction
is from the Quarto.)   92 still continually   94 luxury lechery.

Lust is but a bloody fire,
Kindled with unchaste desire,
Fed in heart, whose flames aspire,
As thoughts do blow them, higher and higher.
Pinch him, fairies, mutually! 99
Pinch him for his villainy.
Pinch him, and burn him, and turn him about,
Till candles and starlight and moonshine be out.

*[During this song they pinch Falstaff. Doctor] Caius
[enters one way, and steals away a fairy in
green]; Slender, [another way, and takes off a
fairy in white; and] Fenton [enters, and steals
away Mistress Anne page. A noise of hunting is
heard within. Mistress Quickly, Evans, pistol, and
all the Fairies run away. Falstaff pulls off his
buck's head, and rises.]*

*[Enter] Page, Ford, [Mistress Page, and Mistress
Ford].*

PAGE
Nay, do not fly. I think we have watched you now. 103
Will none but Herne the hunter serve your turn? 104

MRS. PAGE
I pray you, come, hold up the jest no higher. 105
Now, good Sir John, how like you Windsor wives?
[She points to Falstaff's horns.]
See you these, husband? Do not these fair yokes 107
Become the forest better than the town?

FORD   Now, sir, who's a cuckold now? Master Brook,
Falstaff's a knave, a cuckoldly knave; here are his
horns, Master Brook. And, Master Brook, he hath
enjoyed nothing of Ford's but his buck basket, his
cudgel, and twenty pounds of money, which must be
paid to Master Brook. His horses are arrested for it, 114
Master Brook.

MRS. FORD   Sir John, we have had ill luck; we could
never meet. I will never take you for my love again, 117
but I will always count you my deer. 118

FALSTAFF   I do begin to perceive that I am made an ass.

FORD   Ay, and an ox too. Both the proofs are extant. 120

FALSTAFF   And these are not fairies? I was three or four
times in the thought they were not fairies; and yet the
guiltiness of my mind, the sudden surprise of my
powers, drove the grossness of the foppery into a 124
received belief, in despite of the teeth of all rhyme and 125
reason, that they were fairies. See now how wit may
be made a Jack-a-Lent when 'tis upon ill employment! 127

EVANS   Sir John Falstaff, serve Got, and leave your
desires, and fairies will not pinse you.

FORD   Well said, fairy Hugh.

95 EVANS   And leave you your jealousies too, I pray you.

FORD   I will never mistrust my wife again till thou art
able to woo her in good English.

FALSTAFF   Have I laid my brain in the sun and dried it,
that it wants matter to prevent so gross o'erreaching as 135
this? Am I ridden with a Welsh goat too? Shall I have 136
a coxcomb of frieze? 'Tis time I were choked with a 137
piece of toasted cheese.

EVANS   Seese is not good to give putter. Your belly is all
putter.

FALSTAFF   "Seese" and "putter"! Have I lived to stand
at the taunt of one that makes fritters of English? This
is enough to be the decay of lust and late walking 143
through the realm.

MRS. PAGE   Why, Sir John, do you think, though we
would have thrust virtue out of our hearts by the head
and shoulders, and have given ourselves without scruple to hell, that ever the devil could have made you
our delight?

FORD   What, a hodge pudding? A bag of flax? 150

MRS. PAGE   A puffed man? 151

PAGE   Old, cold, withered and of intolerable entrails? 152

FORD   And one that is as slanderous as Satan?

PAGE   And as poor as Job? 154

FORD   And as wicked as his wife? 155

EVANS   And given to fornications, and to taverns, and
sack, and wine, and metheglins, and to drinkings, 157
and swearings, and starings, pribbles and prabbles? 158

FALSTAFF   Well, I am your theme. You have the start of 159
me. I am dejected. I am not able to answer the Welsh 160
flannel. Ignorance itself is a plummet o'er me. Use me 161
as you will.

FORD   Marry, sir, we'll bring you to Windsor, to one
Master Brook, that you have cozened of money, to
whom you should have been a pander. Over and 165
above that you have suffered, I think to repay that 166
money will be a biting affliction.

PAGE   Yet be cheerful, knight. Thou shalt eat a posset 168
tonight at my house, where I will desire thee to laugh
at my wife that now laughs at thee. Tell her Master
Slender hath married her daughter.

MRS. PAGE *[aside]*   Doctors doubt that. If Anne Page 172
be my daughter, she is, by this, Doctor Caius' wife. 173

[Enter Slender.]

95 **bloody fire** fire in the blood   99 **mutually** jointly, in unison.
103 **watched you** caught you in the act   104 **serve your turn** do for
you. (Addressed to Falstaff in the disguise of Herne or in mock
reproof to Mistress Page—part of "the jest" of line 105.)   105 **hold . . .
higher** maintain the jest no longer.   107 **these fair yokes** i.e., the
horns   114 **arrested** seized by warrant as a security for paying
117 **meet** (With a pun on "mate.")   118 **deer** (With a pun on "dear.")
120 **ox** i.e., fool. (With reference to the ox's horns, the *proofs* that are
extant, i.e., still in existence and also protuberant.)   124 **powers** faculties.   **foppery** deceit   125 **received** accepted.   **in despite of the
teeth of** in the teeth of, in defiance of   127 **Jack-a-Lent** butt. (See the
note for 3.3.22.)

135 **wants matter** lacks means   136 **ridden with** mastered by
137 **coxcomb of frieze** fool's cap of coarse woolen cloth, common in
Wales.   143 **decay** ruin.   **late walking** keeping late hours (in pursuit of women)   150 **hodge pudding** large "pudding," or sausage,
made with a medley of ingredients.   **bag of flax** i.e., a large, shapeless bag of flax.   151 **puffed** dropsied, corpulent   152 **intolerable**
excessive   154 **Job** (See Job 1 for Job's sudden descent into poverty.)
155 **his wife** i.e., Job's wife, who advised him to curse God (Job 2:9).
157 **metheglins** spiced drink made from wort and honey, Welsh in
origin   158 **starings** glaring, madly raving   159 **theme** i.e., subject
of mirth.   **start advantage   160 **dejected** (1) overthrown (2) disheartened.   161 **flannel** a Welsh cloth.   **plummet** (A quibble on
plumbet, a woolen fabric, suggested by *flannel*, and *plummet*, "a line
for fathoming." Falstaff laments that he has been fathomed even by
an ignorant Welshman.)   165 **should have been** were to have been
166 **above that** above that which   168 **eat a posset** imbibe a nightcap
of curdled ale or wine   172 **Doctors doubt that** i.e., The wise are
skeptical; things may turn out differently from what you expected.
(Proverbial.)   173 **this** this time

SLENDER Whoa, ho, ho, father Page!

PAGE Son, how now? How now, son? Have you
dispatched? 176

SLENDER Dispatched? I'll make the best in Gloucestershire know on't. Would I were hanged, la, else! 178

PAGE Of what, son?

SLENDER I came yonder at Eton to marry Mistress Anne
Page, and she's a great lubberly boy. If it had not been
i' th' church, I would have swinged him, or he should 182
have swinged me. If I did not think it had been Anne
Page, would I might never stir! And 'tis a postmaster's 184
boy. 185

PAGE Upon my life, then, you took the wrong.

SLENDER What need you tell me that? I think so, when
I took a boy for a girl. If I had been married to him,
for all he was in woman's apparel, I would not have
had him.

PAGE Why, this is your own folly. Did not I tell you
how you should know my daughter by her garments?

SLENDER I went to her in white and cried "mum," and
she cried "budget," as Anne and I had appointed.
And yet it was not Anne, but a postmaster's boy.

MRS. PAGE Good George, be not angry. I knew of your
purpose, turned my daughter into green, and indeed
she is now with the Doctor at the deanery, and there
married.

[*Enter Caius.*]

CAIUS Vere is Mistress Page? By gar, I am cozened! I
ha' married *un garçon*, a boy; *un paysan*, by gar, a boy. 201
It is not Anne Page. By gar, I am cozened.

MRS. PAGE Why, did you take her in green?

CAIUS Ay, by gar, and 'tis a boy. By gar, I'll raise all
Windsor.

FORD This is strange. Who hath got the right Anne?

PAGE My heart misgives me. Here comes Master
Fenton.

[*Enter Fenton and Anne Page.*]

How now, Master Fenton?

ANNE Pardon, good father! Good my mother, pardon!

PAGE Now, mistress, how chance you went not with
Master Slender?

MRS. PAGE Why went you not with Master Doctor, maid?

FENTON

You do amaze her. Hear the truth of it. 214
You would have married her most shamefully,
Where there was no proportion held in love. 216
The truth is, she and I, long since contracted, 217
Are now so sure that nothing can dissolve us. 218
Th'offense is holy that she hath committed,
And this deceit loses the name of craft,
Of disobedience, or unduteous title, 221
Since therein she doth evitate and shun 222
A thousand irreligious cursèd hours
Which forcèd marriage would have brought upon
her.

FORD

Stand not amazed. Here is no remedy.
In love the heavens themselves do guide the state;
Money buys lands, and wives are sold by fate. 227

FALSTAFF I am glad, though you have ta'en a special
stand to strike at me, that your arrow hath glanced. 229

PAGE

Well, what remedy? Fenton, heaven give thee joy!
What cannot be eschewed must be embraced.

FALSTAFF

When night dogs run, all sorts of deer are chased.

MRS. PAGE

Well, I will muse no further. Master Fenton, 233
Heaven give you many, many merry days!
Good husband, let us every one go home
And laugh this sport o'er by a country fire—
Sir John and all.

FORD   Let it be so.—Sir John,
To Master Brook you yet shall hold your word,
For he tonight shall lie with Mistress Ford. *Exeunt.*

---

176 dispatched finished the business. **178 on't** of it. **else** if I don't
182 swinged thrashed **184–5 postmaster's boy** boy of the master of
the post-horses. **201 *paysan*** peasant, i.e., yokel

214 amaze bewilder **216 proportion** equality **217 contracted**
betrothed **218 sure** fast knit **221 unduteous title** title of undutiful-
ness **222 evitate** avoid **227 Money . . . fate** (A variant of the proverb
"Marriage and hanging go by destiny.") **229 stand** concealed place
for shooting. **glanced** (Falstaff takes comfort in the fact that, though
he was the main target of the plot of exposure, others have suffered
mild humiliation as well.) **233 muse** grumble, complain

As You Like It

❧

As You Like It represents, together with *Much Ado About Nothing* and *Twelfth Night*, the summation of Shakespeare's achievement in festive, happy comedy during the years 1598–1601. *As You Like It* contains several motifs found in other Shakespearean comedies: the journey from a jaded court into a transforming sylvan environment and back to a revitalized court (as in *A Midsummer Night's Dream*); hence, a contrasting of two worlds in the play—one presided over by a virtuous but exiled older brother and the other, by a usurping younger brother (as in *The Tempest*); the heroine disguised as a man (as in *The Merchant of Venice, The Two Gentlemen of Verona, Cymbeline,* and *Twelfth Night*); and a structure of multiple plotting in which numerous groups of characters are thematically played off against one another (as in several of Shakespeare's comedies). What chiefly distinguishes this play from the others, however, is the nature and function of its pastoral setting—the Forest of Arden.

The Forest of Arden is seen in many perspectives. As a natural wilderness, it is probably most like the real forest Shakespeare knew near Stratford-upon-Avon in Warwickshire—a place capable of producing the vulgarity of an Audrey or the bumptuous clowning of a William. The forest bears the name of Shakespeare's mother, Mary Arden, the daughter of a prosperous Warwickshire farmer. Its name also owes something to the forest in Shakespeare's source, *Rosalynde,* based in turn on the forest of Ardennes in France. No less vividly, the place recalls for us Nottinghamshire and the Sherwood Forest of Robin Hood, where persons in retreat from a society seemingly beyond repair find refuge in a mythic folk world purged of social injustice. As the "golden world" (1.1.114), the forest evokes an even deeper longing for a mythological past age of innocence and plenty, when humans shared some attributes of the giants and the gods. This myth has its parallel in the biblical Garden of Eden, before the human race experienced "the penalty of Adam" (2.1.5). Finally, in another of its aspects, the forest is Arcadia, a pastoral landscape embodied in an ancient and sophisticated literary tradition and peopled by the likes of Corin, Silvius, and Phoebe.

All but the first of these Ardens, compared and contrasted with one another, involve some idealization, not only of nature and the natural landscape, but also of the human condition. These various Ardens place our real life in a complex perspective and force us to a fresh appraisal of our own ordinary existence. Duke Senior, for example, describes the forest environment as a corrective for the evils of society. He addresses his followers in the forest as "my co-mates and brothers in exile" (2.1.1), suggesting a kind of social equality that he could never know in the cramped formality of his previous official existence. The banished Duke Senior and his followers have had to leave behind their lands and revenues in the grip of the usurping Duke Frederick. No longer rich, though adequately provided with life's necessities, the Duke and his "merry men" live "like the old Robin Hood of England" and "fleet the time carelessly as they did in the golden world" (1.1.111–14). In this friendly society, a strong communal sense replaces the necessity for individual proprietorship. All comers are welcome, with food for all.

There are no luxuries in the forest, to be sure, but even this spare existence affords relief from the decadence of courtly life. "Sweet are the uses of adversity" (2.1.12), insists Duke Senior. He welcomes the cold of winter because it teaches him the true condition of humanity and of himself. The forest is serenely impartial: neither malicious nor compassionate. Death, and even killing for food, are an inevitable part of forest existence. The Duke concedes that his presence in the forest means the slaughter of deer, who were the original inhabitants; Orlando and Adam find that death through starvation in the forest is all too real a possibility. The forest is never guilty of the degrading perversity of humans at their worst, but it is also incapable of charity and forgiveness.

Shakespeare's sources reflect the complexity of his vision of Arden. The original of the Orlando story, which Shakespeare may not have used directly, is *The Cook's Tale of Gamelyn*, found in a number of manuscripts of *The Canterbury Tales* and wrongly attributed to Chaucer. This hearty English romance glorifies the rebellious and even violent spirit of its Robin Hood hero, the neglected youngest son Gamelyn, who, aided by faithful old Adam the Spencer, evades his wicked eldest brother in a cunning and bloody escape. As king of the outlaws in Sherwood Forest, Gamelyn eventually triumphs over his eldest brother (now the sheriff) and sees him hanged. Here, then, originates the motif of refuge from social injustice in Arden, even though most of the actual violence has been omitted from Shakespeare's version. (A trio of Robin Hood plays on a similar theme, beginning in 1598 with Anthony Munday's *The Downfall of Robert Earl of Huntingdon After Called Robin Hood,* was being performed with great success by the Admiral's company, chief rivals of the Lord Chamberlain's company to which Shakespeare belonged.)

As You Like It is clearly indebted to Thomas Lodge's *Rosalynde: Euphues' Golden Legacy* (published in 1590), a prose narrative version of the Gamelyn story in the ornate Euphuistic style of the 1580s. (Lodge's Epistle to the Gentleman Readers, casually inviting them to be pleased with this story if they are so inclined—"*If you like it, so*"—probably gave Shakespeare a hint for the name of his play.) Lodge accentuated the love story with its courtship in masquerade, provided some charming songs, and introduced the pastoral love motif involving Corin, Silvius, Phoebe, and Ganymede. Shakespeare's ordering of episode is generally close to that of Lodge. Pastoral literature, which had become a literary rage in the 1580s and early 1590s, owing particularly to Edmund Spenser's *Shepheardes Calendar* (1579) and Philip Sidney's *Arcadia* (1590), traced its ancestry through such Renaissance continental writers as Jorge de Montemayor, Jacopo Sannazaro, and Giovanni Battista Guarini to the so-called Greek romances, and finally back to the eclogues of Virgil, Theocritus, and Bion. A literary mode that had begun originally as a realistic evocation of difficult country life had become, in the Renaissance, an elegant vehicle for the loftiest and most patrician sentiments in love, for philosophic debate, and even for extensive political analysis and satire of the clergy.

Shakespeare's alterations and additions give us insight into his method of construction and his thematic focus. Whereas Lodge cheerfully accepts the pastoral conventions of his day, Shakespeare exposes those conventions to some criticism and considerable irony. Alongside the mannered and literary Silvius and Phoebe, he places William and Audrey, as peasantlike a couple as ever drew milk from a cow's teat. The juxtaposition holds up to critical perspective the rival claims of the literary and natural worlds by examining the defects of each in relation to the strengths of the other. William and Audrey are Shakespeare's own creation, based presumably on observation and also on the dramatic convention of the rustic clown and wench, as exemplified earlier in his Costard and Jaquenetta (*Love's Labor's Lost*).

Equally original, and essential to the many-sided debate concerning the virtues of the court versus those of the country, are Touchstone and Jaques. Touchstone is a professional court fool, dressed in motley, a new comic type in Shakespeare, created apparently in response to the recent addition to the Lord Chamberlain's company of the brilliant actor Robert Armin. Jaques is also a new type, the malcontent satirist, reflecting the very latest literary vogue in the nondramatic poetry and in drama of George Chapman, John Marston, and Ben Jonson. (The so-called private theaters, featuring boy actors, reopened in 1598–1599 after nearly a decade of enforced silence and proceeded at once to specialize in satirical drama; the public theaters like the Globe, the Rose, and the Swan sometimes joined in.) Touchstone and Jaques complement one another as critics and observers—one laughing at human folly with quizzical comic detachment and the other satirizing it with self-righteous scorn. Once we have been exposed to this assortment of newly created characters, we can no longer view either pastoral life or pastoral love as simply as Lodge and some other writers of the period portray them.

When *As You Like It* is compared with its chief source, Shakespeare can also be seen to have altered and considerably softened the characters of the wicked brothers Oliver and Frederick. Whereas Lodge's Saladyne is motivated by a greedy desire to seize his younger brother Rosader's property, Shakespeare's Oliver is envious of Orlando's natural goodness and popularity. As he confesses in soliloquy, Orlando is "so much in the heart of the world and especially of my own people . . . that I am altogether misprized" (1.1.159–61). In his warped way, Oliver desires to be more like Orlando, and in the enchanted forest of Arden he eventually becomes so. Duke Frederick, too, is plainly envious of goodness. Trying to persuade his daughter Celia of the need for banishing Rosalind, he argues, "thou wilt show more bright and seem more virtuous / When she is gone" (1.3.79–80). In spite of his obsession with the mere "seeming" of virtue, Duke Frederick acknowledges the power of a goodness that will eventually convert him along with the rest. Penitence and conciliation replace the vengeful conclusion of Lodge's novel, in which the nobles of France finally overthrow and execute the usurping king. Although Shakespeare's resolutions are sudden, like all miracles they attest to the inexplicable power of goodness.

The court of Duke Frederick is "the envious court," identified by this fixed epithet. In it, brothers turn unnaturally against brothers: the younger Frederick usurps his older brother's throne, whereas the older Oliver denies the younger Orlando his birthright of education. In still another parallel, both Rosalind and Orlando find themselves mistrusted as the children of Frederick's political enemies, Duke Senior and Sir Rowland de Boys. A daughter and a son are held to be guilty by association. "Thou art thy father's daughter. There's enough" (1.3.56), Frederick curtly retorts in explaining Rosalind's exile. And to Orlando, triumphant in wrestling with Charles, Frederick asserts, "I would thou hadst been son to some man else" (1.2.214). Here again, Frederick plaintively reveals his envy of goodness, even if at present any potential for goodness in him is thwarted by tyrannous whim. Many of Frederick's entourage might also be better persons if they only knew how to escape the insincerities of their courtly life. Charles the wrestler, for example, places himself at Oliver's service, and yet he would happily avoid breaking Orlando's neck if to do so were consistent with self-interest. Even Le Beau, the giddy fop so delighted at first with the cruel sport of wrestling, takes Orlando aside at some personal risk to warn him of Duke Frederick's foul humor. Ideally, Le Beau would prefer to be a companion of Orlando's "in a better world than this" (1.2.275). The vision of a regenerative Utopia secretly abides in the heart of this courtly creature.

It is easier to anatomize the defects of a social order than to propound solutions. As have other creators of visionary landscapes (including Thomas More in his *Utopia*), Shakespeare uses playful debate to elicit complicated responses on the part of his audience. Which is preferable, the court or the country? Jaques and Touchstone are adept gadflies, incessantly pointing out contradictions and ironies. Jaques, the malcontent railer derived from literary satire, takes delight in being out of step with everyone. Seemingly, his chief reason for having joined the others in the forest is to jibe at their motives for being there. To their song about the rejection of courtly ambition he mockingly supplies another verse, charging them with having left their wealth and ease out of mere willfulness (2.5.46–54). With ironic appropriateness, Jaques eventually decides to remain in the forest in the company of Frederick; Jaques cannot thrive on resolution and harmony. His humor is "melancholy," from which, as he observes, he draws consolation as a weasel sucks eggs (2.5.11–12). The others treat him as a sort of profane jester whose soured conceits add relish to their enjoyment of the forest life.

Despite his affectation, however, Jaques is serious and even excited in his defense of satire as a curative form of laughter (2.7.47–87). The appearance of Touchstone in the forest has reaffirmed in Jaques his profound commitment to a view of life as an absurd process of decay governed by inexorable time. His function in such a life is to be mordant, unsparing. As literary satirist, he must be free to awaken people's minds to their own folly. To Duke Senior's protestation that the satirist is merely self-indulgent and licentious, Jaques counters with a thoughtful and classically Horatian defense of satire as an art form devoted not to libelous attacks on individuals but to exposing types of folly. Any observer who feels individually portrayed merely condemns himself or herself by confessing his or her resemblance to the type. This particular debate between Duke Senior and Jaques ends, appropriately, in a draw. The Duke's point is well taken, for Jaques's famous "Seven Ages of Man" speech, so often read out of context, occurs in a scene that also witnesses the sacrifices and brave deeds that Orlando and Adam are prepared to undertake for each other. The feeling bond between the generations that they share refutes Jaques's wry narrative of isolated self-interest. As though in answer to Jaques's acid depiction of covetous old age, we see old Adam's self-sacrifice and trust in Providence. Instead of "mere oblivion," we see charitable compassion prompting Duke Senior to aid Orlando and Orlando to aid Adam. Perhaps this vision seems of a higher spiritual order than that of Jaques. Nonetheless, without him the forest would lack a satirical perspective that continually requires us to reexamine our romantic assumptions about human happiness.

Touchstone's name suggests that he similarly offers a multiplicity of viewpoints. (A touchstone is a kind of stone used to test for gold and silver.) He shares with Jaques a skeptical view of life, but for Touchstone the inconsistency and absurdity of life are occasions for wit and humor rather than melancholy and cynicism. As a professional fool, he observes that many supposedly sane men are more foolish than he—as, for example, in their elaborate dueling code of the Retort Courteous and the Reply Churlish, leading finally to the Lie Circumstantial and the Lie Direct. He is fascinated by the games people make of their lives and is amused by their inability to be content with what they already have. Of the shepherd's life, he comments, "In respect that it is solitary, I like it very well; but in respect that it is private, it is a very vile life" (3.2.15–16). This paradox, though nonsensical, captures the restlessness of human striving for a life that can somehow combine the peaceful solitude of nature with the convenience and excitement of city life. Although Touchstone marries, even his marriage is a spoof of the institution rather than a serious attempt at commitment. Like all fools, who in Renaissance times were regarded as a breed apart, Touchstone exists outside the realm of ordinary human responses. There he can comment disinterestedly on human folly. He is prevented, however, from sharing fully in the human love and conciliation with which the play ends. He and Jaques are not touched by the play's regenerative magic; Jaques will remain in the forest, and Touchstone will remain forever a childlike entertainer.

The regenerative power of Arden, as we have seen, is not the forest's alone. What saves Orlando is the human charity practiced by him and by Duke Senior, who, for all his love of the forest, longs to rejoin that human society where he has "with holy bell been knolled to church" (2.7.120). Civilization at its best is no less necessary to the human spirit than is the natural order of the forest. In love, also, perception and wisdom must be combined with nature's gifts. Orlando, when we first see him, is a young man of the finest natural qualities but admittedly lacking experience in the nuances of complex human relationships. Nowhere does his lack of sophistication betray him more unhappily than in his first encounter with Rosalind, following the wrestling match. In response to her unmistakable hints of favor, he stands ox-like, tongue-tied. Later, in the forest, his first attempts at self-education in love lead him into an opposite danger: an excess of platitudinous manners parading in the guise of Petrarchism. (The Italian sonneteer Francis Petrarch has given to the language a name for the stereotypical literary mannerisms we associate with courtly love: the sighing and self-abasement of the young man, the chaste denial of love by the woman whom he worships, and the like.) Orlando's newfound self-abasement and idealization of his absent mistress are as unsatisfactory as his former naiveté. The sonnets he hangs on trees are too deserving of the delicious parody they get from Touchstone. Orlando must learn from Rosalind that a quest for true understanding in love avoids the extreme of pretentious mannerism as well as that of mere artlessness. Orlando as Petrarchan lover too much resembles Silvius, the lovesick young man, cowering before the imperious will of his coy mistress Phoebe. This stereotyped relationship, taken from the pages of fashionable pastoral romance, represents a posturing that Rosalind hopes to cure in Silvius and Phoebe even as she will also cure Orlando.

Rosalind is, above all, the realistic one, the plucky Shakespearean heroine showing her mettle in the world of men, emotionally more mature than her lover. Her concern is with a working and clear-sighted relationship in love, and to that end she daringly insists that Orlando learn something of woman's changeable mood. Above all, she must disabuse him of the dangerously misleading clichés of the Petrarchan love myth. When he protests he would die for love of Rosalind, she lectures him mockingly in her guise of Ganymede: "No, faith, die by attorney. The poor world is almost six thousand years old, and in all this time there was not any man died in his own person, videlicet, in a love cause." She debunks the legends of Troilus and Leander, youths supposed to have died for love who, if they had ever really existed, would no doubt have met with more prosaic ends. "But these are all lies. Men have died from time to time, and worms have eaten them, but not for love" (4.1.89–102). Rosalind wants Orlando to know that women are not goddesses but frail human beings who can be giddy, jealous, infatuated with novelty, irritatingly talkative, peremptory, and hysterical (4.1.142–9), though she is circumspect as to whether women can also be unfaithful. Orlando must be taught that love is a madness (3.2.390), and he must be cured, not of loving Rosalind, but of worshiping her with unrealistic expectations that can lead only to disillusionment. Rosalind teases him, as Portia does Bassanio in *The Merchant of Venice*, but she does not seriously threaten him with wantonness. Her disguise as Ganymede provides for her the perfect role in Orlando's approach to sexual manhood: he can learn to love "Ganymede" as a friend and then make the transition to heterosexual union in his blessed discovery that the friend is also the lover. Rosalind's own rite of passage is easier; for all her reliance on her loving friendship with Celia, or "Aliena," she is ready to exclaim, "But what talk we of fathers, when there is such a man as Orlando?" (3.4.36–7). She is spiritedly independent, even more so than Portia; whereas Portia's choice of husband is controlled by her father from his grave, Rosalind picks for herself. To be sure, Duke Senior is certainly happy that she marries Orlando, and she is glad to be reunited with her father, but her choice in marriage is very much her own. The forest is indeed a place where she can encounter her father "man to man," as it were, and be liberated from him while coming to terms with a patriarchal world. She is ready to give herself to Orlando, but she must educate him first. When Orlando has been sufficiently tested as to patience, loyalty, and understanding, she unmasks herself to him and simultaneously unravels the plot of ridiculous love we have come to associate with Silvius and Phoebe.

Rosalind's disguise name, Ganymede, has connotations that suggest ways in which human sexuality can be partly understood as socially constructed. If Rosalind in disguise as Ganymede wins the affection and eventually the love of Orlando, while her father and the other forest dwellers are equally taken in by the disguise, are maleness and femaleness chiefly matters of sartorial convention and superficial appearance? When Phoebe falls in love with Ganymede, is not her infatuation a way of showing that the roles of the sexes can be put on and off? Theatrically, the device of having a young male actor play Rosalind who then disguises him/herself as a young man adds to the witty confusion of sexual identities by introducing homoerotic possibilities. Not only can the roles of the sexes be put on and off, sexual desire itself is unstable, attaching itself to effeminate or sexually indeterminate young men like Ganymede, who is described as being "Of female favor" and "Like a ripe sister" (4.3.87–8; compare *Twelfth Night*, 1.4.31–4, where Orsino says of "Cesario" that "all is semblative a woman's part"). Both Phoebe and Orlando are in some ways attracted to Ganymede; when Rosalind says of Orlando that "his kissing is as full of sanctity as the touch of holy bread" (3.4.13–14), she seems to suggest that Orlando has kissed her in her male disguise. Mythologically Ganymede is Zeus's or Jupiter's young male lover as well as cupbearer. The very role of boy actors in an all-male acting company must have struck some viewers as homoerotically suggestive.

At the same time, the motif of disguise enables the play to pursue a serious point about love and friendship. Orlando can speak frankly and personally to "Ganymede" as a perfect friend, one who can enable him as a young man still faced with the uncertainties and hazards of courtship to traverse the potentially difficult transition from male-to-male friendship into adult heterosexuality. The relationship closely anticipates that of "Cesario" and Orsino in *Twelfth Night*, where once again a powerful and loving attraction to a sexually ambiguous young man/woman ripens into mature love when the older man has been educated by the experience of loving friendship. Both plays depict heterosexual courtship as full of dangers for the male. In *As You Like It*, Rosalind is at pains to coach Orlando in what to expect from unruly women; and indeed, Rosalind's very readiness to wear male apparel bespeaks her daring intrusion into a man's world, even if Shakespeare carefully hedges this threat by insisting on Rosalind's hesitancy in being so bold. Rosalind is thus, like Portia in *The Merchant of Venice*, both spirited and eventually ready to comply with the mores of a male-dominated world.

By becoming Orlando's teacher, Rosalind is able to claim a strong position in their friendship and in our estimate of her remarkable worthiness. Posing as Ganymede, Rosalind can observe and test Orlando and thereby learn the truth about his capability for lifelong fidelity as only another man would have the opportunity to do. Once a loving friendship has grown strong between them, the unmasking of Rosalind's sexual identity makes possible a physical union between them to confirm and express the spiritual. In these terms, the play's happy ending affirms marriage as an institution, not simply as the expected denouement. The procession to the altar is synchronous with the return to civilization's other institutions, made whole again not solely by the forest but by the power of goodness embodied in Rosalind, Orlando, Duke Senior, and the others who persevere.

As You Like It

[*Dramatis Personae*

DUKE SENIOR, *a banished duke*
DUKE FREDERICK, *his usurping brother*
ROSALIND, *daughter of Duke Senior, later disguised as*
GANYMEDE
CELIA, *daughter of Duke Frederick, later disguised as* ALIENA

OLIVER,
JAQUES, } *sons of Sir Rowland de Boys*
ORLANDO,

AMIENS, } *lords attending Duke Senior*
JAQUES,

LE BEAU, *a courtier attending Duke Frederick*
CHARLES, *a wrestler in the court of Duke Frederick*

ADAM, *an aged servant of Oliver and then Orlando*
DENNIS, *a servant of Oliver*

TOUCHSTONE, *the* CLOWN *or* FOOL

CORIN, *an old shepherd*
SILVIUS, *a young shepherd, in love with Phoebe*
PHOEBE, *a shepherdess*
WILLIAM, *a country youth, in love with Audrey*
AUDREY, *a country wench*
SIR OLIVER MAR-TEXT, *a country vicar*

HYMEN, *god of marriage*

Lords and Attendants waiting on Duke Frederick and Duke Senior

SCENE: *Oliver's house; Duke Frederick's court; and the Forest of Arden*]

1.1

Enter Orlando and Adam.

ORLANDO   As I remember, Adam, it was upon this fash- 1
ion bequeathed me by will but poor a thousand 2
crowns and, as thou say'st, charged my brother on his 3
blessing to breed me well; and there begins my 4
sadness. My brother Jaques he keeps at school, and 5
report speaks goldenly of his profit. For my part, he 6
keeps me rustically at home—or, to speak more
properly, stays me here at home unkept; for call you 8
that "keeping" for a gentleman of my birth, that
differs not from the stalling of an ox? His horses are
bred better, for besides that they are fair with their 11
feeding, they are taught their manage, and to that end 12

riders dearly hired. But I, his brother, gain nothing 13
under him but growth, for the which his animals on
his dunghills are as much bound to him as I. Besides
this nothing that he so plentifully gives me, the
something that nature gave me his countenance 17
seems to take from me. He lets me feed with his
hinds, bars me the place of a brother, and as much as 19
in him lies, mines my gentility with my education. 20
This is it, Adam, that grieves me; and the spirit of my
father, which I think is within me, begins to mutiny
against this servitude. I will no longer endure it,
though yet I know no wise remedy how to avoid it.

Enter Oliver.

ADAM   Yonder comes my master, your brother.
ORLANDO   Go apart, Adam, and thou shalt hear how 26
he will shake me up.   [*Adam stands aside.*] 27
OLIVER   Now, sir, what make you here? 28

1.1 Location: The garden of Oliver's house.
1–3 it was . . . crowns it was in this way that I was left, by the terms of my father's will, a mere thousand crowns or £250   **3 crowns** coins worth five shillings.   **3–4 charged . . . well** my brother was instructed as a condition of my father's blessing to educate me well   **5 My . . . school** My oldest brother Oliver maintains my other brother, Jaques, at university   **6 profit** progress.   **8 stays** detains.   **unkept** poorly supported   **11–12 fair . . . feeding** kept well groomed with good diet   **12 manage** manège, paces and maneuvers in the art of horsemanship

13 riders trainers.   **dearly** expensively   **17 countenance** behavior; (neglectful) patronage   **19 hinds** farm hands.   **bars me** excludes me from   **19–20 as much . . . education** with all the power at his disposal, undermines my right to be educated as a gentleman.   **26 Go apart** Stand aside   **27 shake me up** abuse me.   **28 make** do. (But Orlando takes it in the more usual sense.)

ORLANDO Nothing. I am not taught to make anything.

OLIVER What mar you then, sir? 30

ORLANDO Marry, sir, I am helping you to mar that 31 which God made, a poor unworthy brother of yours, with idleness.

OLIVER Marry, sir, be better employed, and be naught 34 awhile. 35

ORLANDO Shall I keep your hogs and eat husks with 36 them? What prodigal portion have I spent, that I 37 should come to such penury? 38

OLIVER Know you where you are, sir? 39

ORLANDO Oh, sir, very well: here in your orchard. 40

OLIVER Know you before whom, sir?

ORLANDO Ay, better than him I am before knows me. I know you are my eldest brother, and in the gentle 43 condition of blood you should so know me. The cour- 44 tesy of nations allows you my better, in that you are 45 the firstborn, but the same tradition takes not away my blood, were there twenty brothers betwixt us. I 47 have as much of my father in me as you, albeit I con- fess your coming before me is nearer to his reverence. 49

OLIVER What, boy!   [He strikes Orlando.]

ORLANDO Come, come, elder brother, you are too young in this.   [He seizes Oliver by the throat.] 52

OLIVER Wilt thou lay hands on me, villain? 53

ORLANDO I am no villain. I am the youngest son of Sir Rowland de Boys. He was my father, and he is thrice 55 a villain that says such a father begot villains. Wert thou not my brother, I would not take this hand from thy throat till this other had pulled out thy tongue for saying so. Thou hast railed on thyself. 59

ADAM Sweet masters, be patient! For your father's 60 remembrance, be at accord. 61

OLIVER Let me go, I say.

ORLANDO I will not till I please. You shall hear me. My father charged you in his will to give me good educa- tion. You have trained me like a peasant, obscuring and hiding from me all gentlemanlike qualities. The 66 spirit of my father grows strong in me, and I will no longer endure it; therefore allow me such exercises as 68 may become a gentleman, or give me the poor allotery 69 my father left me by testament. With that I will go buy my fortunes.   [He releases Oliver.]

OLIVER And what wilt thou do? Beg when that is spent? Well, sir, get you in. I will not long be troubled with you; you shall have some part of your will. I pray 74 you, leave me.

ORLANDO I will no further offend you than becomes me for my good.

OLIVER [to Adam] Get you with him, you old dog.

ADAM Is "old dog" my reward? Most true, I have lost my teeth in your service. God be with my old master! He would not have spoke such a word.

Exeunt Orlando [and] Adam.

OLIVER Is it even so? Begin you to grow upon me? I will 82 physic your rankness and yet give no thousand 83 crowns neither.—Holla, Dennis! 84

Enter Dennis.

DENNIS Calls Your Worship?

OLIVER Was not Charles, the Duke's wrestler, here to speak with me?

DENNIS So please you, he is here at the door and 88 importunes access to you.

OLIVER Call him in.   [Exit Dennis.] 'Twill be a good way; and tomorrow the wrestling is.

Enter Charles.

CHARLES Good morrow to Your Worship. 92

OLIVER Good Monsieur Charles, what's the new news at the new court?

CHARLES There's no news at the court, sir, but the old news: that is, the old Duke is banished by his younger brother the new Duke, and three or four loving lords have put themselves into voluntary exile with him, whose lands and revenues enrich the new Duke; 99 therefore he gives them good leave to wander. 100

OLIVER Can you tell if Rosalind, the Duke's daughter, be banished with her father?

CHARLES Oh, no; for the Duke's daughter, her cousin, so loves her, being ever from their cradles bred together, 104 that she would have followed her exile or have died to 105 stay behind her. She is at the court and no less beloved 106 of her uncle than his own daughter, and never two ladies loved as they do.

OLIVER Where will the old Duke live?

CHARLES They say he is already in the Forest of Arden, and a many merry men with him; and there they live like the old Robin Hood of England. They say many young gentlemen flock to him every day and fleet the 113 time carelessly as they did in the golden world. 114

OLIVER What, you wrestle tomorrow before the new Duke?

---

30 mar ("To make or mar" is a commonplace antithesis.) **31 Marry** i.e., Indeed. (Originally an oath by the Virgin Mary.) **34–5 be naught awhile** i.e., stay in your place, don't grumble. **36–8 Shall . . . penury?** (Alluding to the story of the Prodigal Son, in Matthew 25:14–30 and Luke 15:11–32, who, having wasted his "portion" or inheritance, had to tend swine and eat with them.) **39 where** in whose presence. (But Orlando sarcastically takes the more literal meaning.) **40 orchard** garden. **43–4 in . . . blood** acknowledging the bond of our being of gentle birth **44–5 courtesy of nations** recognized custom (of primogeniture, whereby the eldest son inherits all the land) **47 blood** (1) gentlemanly lineage (2) spirit **49 is nearer . . . reverence** is closer to his position of authority (as head of family). **52 young** inexperienced (at fighting) **53 villain** i.e., wicked fellow. (But Orlando plays on the literal meaning of "bondman" or "serf," as well as Oliver's meaning.) **55 he** anyone **59 railed on thyself** insulted your own blood. **60–1 your father's remembrance** the sake of your father's memory **66 qualities** (1) characteristics (2) accomplishments. **68 exercises** employments **69 allotery** portion

74 will (1) desire (2) portion from your father's will (3) willfulness (i.e., you'll get what is coming to you). **82 grow upon me** take liberties with me; grow too big for your breeches. **83 physic your rankness** apply medicine to your overweening **84 neither** either.
88 So please you If you please **92 Good morrow** Good morning **99 whose** all of whose **100 good leave** full permission **104 being** they being **105–6 died to stay** died from being forced to stay **113 fleet** pass **114 carelessly** free from care. **golden world** the primal age of innocence and ease from which humankind was thought to have degenerated. (See Ovid, *Metamorphoses* 1.)

CHARLES   Marry, do I, sir; and I came to acquaint you with a matter. I am given, sir, secretly to understand that your younger brother Orlando hath a disposition to come in disguised against me to try a fall. Tomor- 120 row, sir, I wrestle for my credit, and he that escapes 121 me without some broken limb shall acquit him well. 122 Your brother is but young and tender, and for your love I would be loath to foil him, as I must for my 124 own honor if he come in. Therefore, out of my love to you, I came hither to acquaint you withal, that either 126 you might stay him from his intendment or brook 127 such disgrace well as he shall run into, in that it is a thing of his own search and altogether against my will. 129

OLIVER   Charles, I thank thee for thy love to me, which thou shalt find I will most kindly requite. I had myself notice of my brother's purpose herein and have by underhand means labored to dissuade him from it, but 133 he is resolute. I'll tell thee, Charles, it is the stubbornest young fellow of France, full of ambition, an envious emulator of every man's good parts, a secret and 136 villainous contriver against me his natural brother. 137 Therefore use thy discretion. I had as lief thou didst 138 break his neck as his finger. And thou wert best look 139 to't; for if thou dost him any slight disgrace, or if he 140 do not mightily grace himself on thee, he will practice 141 against thee by poison, entrap thee by some treacherous device, and never leave thee till he hath ta'en thy life by some indirect means or other; for I assure thee, and almost with tears I speak it, there is not one so young and so villainous this day living. I speak but brotherly of him, but should I anatomize him to thee as 147 he is, I must blush and weep, and thou must look pale and wonder.

CHARLES   I am heartily glad I came hither to you. If he come tomorrow, I'll give him his payment. If ever he go alone again, I'll never wrestle for prize more. And 152 so God keep Your Worship!

OLIVER   Farewell, good Charles.   *Exit [Charles].* Now will I stir this gamester. I hope I shall see an end of 155 him; for my soul, yet I know not why, hates nothing more than he. Yet he's gentle, never schooled and yet 157 learned, full of noble device, of all sorts enchantingly 158 beloved, and indeed so much in the heart of the world and especially of my own people, who best know him, 160 that I am altogether misprized. But it shall not be so 161 long; this wrestler shall clear all. Nothing remains but 162 that I kindle the boy thither, which now I'll go about. 163 *Exit.*

1.2

Enter Rosalind and Celia.

CELIA   I pray thee, Rosalind, sweet my coz, be merry.   1

ROSALIND   Dear Celia, I show more mirth than I am mistress of, and would you yet I were merrier? Unless you could teach me to forget a banished father, you must not learn me how to remember any extraordi- 5 nary pleasure.

CELIA   Herein I see thou lov'st me not with the full weight that I love thee. If my uncle, thy banished 8 father, had banished thy uncle, the Duke my father, so thou hadst been still with me, I could have taught 10 my love to take thy father for mine. So wouldst thou, if the truth of thy love to me were so righteously 12 tempered as mine is to thee.   13

ROSALIND   Well, I will forget the condition of my estate 14 to rejoice in yours.

CELIA   You know my father hath no child but I, nor none is like to have. And truly, when he dies thou 17 shalt be his heir, for what he hath taken away from thy father perforce I will render thee again in affection. By 19 mine honor, I will, and when I break that oath, let me turn monster. Therefore, my sweet Rose, my dear Rose, be merry.

ROSALIND   From henceforth I will, coz, and devise sports. Let me see, what think you of falling in love?

CELIA   Marry, I prithee, do, to make sport withal. But 25 love no man in good earnest, nor no further in sport neither than with safety of a pure blush thou mayst in 27 honor come off again.   28

ROSALIND   What shall be our sport, then?

CELIA   Let us sit and mock the good huswife Fortune 30 from her wheel, that her gifts may henceforth be bestowed equally.

ROSALIND   I would we could do so, for her benefits are mightily misplaced, and the bountiful blind woman 34 doth most mistake in her gifts to women.

CELIA   'Tis true, for those that she makes fair she scarce 36 makes honest, and those that she makes honest she 37 makes very ill-favoredly.   38

---

120 a fall a bout of wrestling.   **121 credit** reputation   **122 shall . . . well** (1) must exert himself very skillfully (2) will be lucky indeed. **124 foil** defeat   **126 withal** with this   **127 stay . . . intendment** restrain him from his intent.   **brook** endure   **129 search** seeking **133 underhand** unobtrusive   **136 envious emulator** malicious disparager.   **parts** qualities   **137 contriver** plotter.   **natural** blood **138 lief** willingly   **139–40 thou . . . to't** you'd better beware   **140–1 if he . . . on thee** if he fails to distinguish himself at your expense **141 practice** plot   **147 brotherly** as a brother should.   **anatomize** analyze   **152 go alone** walk unassisted   **155 gamester** sportsman. (Said sardonically.)   **157 gentle** gentlemanly   **158 noble device** lofty aspiration.   **sorts** classes of people.   **enchantingly** as if they were under his spell   **160 people** servants   **161 misprized** undervalued, scorned

162 clear all solve everything.   **163 kindle . . . thither** inflame Orlando with desire to go to the wrestling match **1.2 Location: Duke Frederick's court. A place suitable for wrestling. 1 sweet my coz** my sweet cousin   **5 learn** teach   **8 that** with which **10 so** provided that   **12–13 righteously tempered** harmoniously composed   **14 condition of my estate** state of my fortunes   **17 like** likely   **19 perforce** by force   **25 sport** pastimes   **27 pure** (1) mere (2) innocent   **28 come off** retire, leave   **30 huswife** one who manages household affairs and operates the spinning wheel. (Shakespeare conflates this wheel with the commonplace wheel of Fortune.) *Huswife* is used derogatorily here, with a suggestion of "hussy." **34 bountiful blind woman** i.e., Fortune   **36 scarce** rarely   **37 honest** chaste   **38 ill-favoredly** ugly.

ROSALIND   Nay, now thou goest from Fortune's office to Nature's. Fortune reigns in gifts of the world, not in the lineaments of Nature. 40 41

Enter [Touchstone the] Clown.

CELIA   No; when Nature hath made a fair creature, may she not by Fortune fall into the fire? Though Nature hath given us wit to flout at Fortune, hath not Fortune sent in this fool to cut off the argument? 43 44

ROSALIND   Indeed, there is Fortune too hard for Nature, when Fortune makes Nature's natural the cutter-off of Nature's wit. 46 47 48

CELIA   Peradventure this is not Fortune's work neither but Nature's, who perceiveth our natural wits too dull to reason of such goddesses and hath sent this natural for our whetstone; for always the dullness of the fool is the whetstone of the wits.—How now, wit, whither wander you? 49 51 52 53 54

TOUCHSTONE   Mistress, you must come away to your father.

CELIA   Were you made the messenger?

TOUCHSTONE   No, by mine honor, but I was bid to come for you.

ROSALIND   Where learned you that oath, Fool?

TOUCHSTONE   Of a certain knight that swore by his honor they were good pancakes and swore by his honor the mustard was naught. Now I'll stand to it the pancakes were naught and the mustard was good, and yet was not the knight forsworn. 62 63 65

CELIA   How prove you that in the great heap of your knowledge?

ROSALIND   Ay, marry, now unmuzzle your wisdom.

TOUCHSTONE   Stand you both forth now. Stroke your chins, and swear by your beards that I am a knave.

CELIA   By our beards, if we had them, thou art.

TOUCHSTONE   By my knavery, if I had it, then I were; but if you swear by that that is not, you are not forsworn. No more was this knight, swearing by his honor, for he never had any; or if he had, he had sworn it away before ever he saw those pancakes or that mustard.

CELIA   Prithee, who is't that thou mean'st?

TOUCHSTONE   One that old Frederick, your father, loves.

CELIA   My father's love is enough to honor him enough. Speak no more of him; you'll be whipped for taxation one of these days. 81

TOUCHSTONE   The more pity that fools may not speak wisely what wise men do foolishly.

CELIA   By my troth, thou sayest true; for since the little wit that fools have was silenced, the little foolery that wise men have makes a great show. Here comes Monsieur Le Beau. 85 86

Enter Le Beau.

ROSALIND   With his mouth full of news.

CELIA   Which he will put on us as pigeons feed their young. 90

ROSALIND   Then shall we be news-crammed.

CELIA   All the better; we shall be the more marketable.—*Bonjour*, Monsieur Le Beau. What's the news? 93 94

LE BEAU   Fair princess, you have lost much good sport.

CELIA   Sport? Of what color? 97

LE BEAU   What color, madam? How shall I answer you?

ROSALIND   As wit and fortune will.

TOUCHSTONE   Or as the Destinies decrees.

CELIA   Well said. That was laid on with a trowel. 101

TOUCHSTONE   Nay, if I keep not my rank— 102

ROSALIND   Thou loosest thy old smell.

LE BEAU   You amaze me, ladies. I would have told you of good wrestling, which you have lost the sight of. 104

ROSALIND   Yet tell us the manner of the wrestling.

LE BEAU   I will tell you the beginning, and if it please Your Ladyships you may see the end, for the best is yet to do, and here, where you are, they are coming to perform it. 108 109

CELIA   Well, the beginning, that is dead and buried. 111

LE BEAU   There comes an old man and his three sons—

CELIA   I could match this beginning with an old tale.

LE BEAU   Three proper young men, of excellent growth and presence— 114

ROSALIND   With bills on their necks, "Be it known unto all men by these presents." 116 117

LE BEAU   The eldest of the three wrestled with Charles, the Duke's wrestler, which Charles in a moment threw him and broke three of his ribs, that there is little hope of life in him. So he served the second, and so the third. Yonder they lie, the poor old man their father making such pitiful dole over them that all the beholders take his part with weeping. 121 123

ROSALIND   Alas!

TOUCHSTONE   But what is the sport, monsieur, that the ladies have lost?

LE BEAU   Why, this that I speak of.

---

40 gifts of the world e.g., riches and power   **41 the lineaments of Nature** the features that Nature provides (like beauty or ugliness). **41.1** *Touchstone* a stone used to test for gold and silver   **43 she** the woman whom Nature has made beautiful   **44 flout** scoff   **46 there** in that instance   **47–8 when . . . wit** i.e., when Fortune makes this natural half-wit (Touchstone) the cutter-off of witty dialogue that our natural gifts enable us to engage in. (A *natural* here means a born idiot; also in line 51.)   **49 Peradventure** Perhaps   **51 to reason . . . goddesses** to engage in debate about Reason and Nature   **52 whetstone** grinding stone against which to sharpen things (in this case, wit)   **52–3 the dullness . . . wits** i.e., the mindless things said by an idiot serve as material on which to sharpen our wits.   **53–4 whither wander you** (An allusion to the expression "wandering wits.") **62 pancakes** fritters (which might be made of meat and so require mustard)   **63 naught** worthless.   **stand to it** maintain, argue **65 forsworn** perjured.   **81 taxation** censure, slander

85–6 since . . . silenced (Perhaps refers specifically to the Bishops' order of June 1599 banning satirical books.)   **90 put on** force upon **93–4 marketable** i.e., like animals that have been crammed with food before being sent to market.   **97 color** kind.   **101 with a trowel** i.e., thick.   **102 rank** i.e., status as a wit. (But Rosalind plays on the sense of "stench.")   **104 amaze** bewilder   **108–9 yet to do** still to come **111 the beginning** tell us what has already occurred   **114 proper** handsome   **116 bills** proclamations   **117 these presents** the present document. (Rosalind uses this legal phrase to pun on *presence* in line 115.)   **121 So** Similarly   **123 dole** lamentation

TOUCHSTONE   Thus men may grow wiser every day. It is the first time that ever I heard breaking of ribs was sport for ladies.

CELIA   Or I, I promise thee.   132

ROSALIND   But is there any else longs to see this broken 133 music in his sides? Is there yet another dotes upon rib 134 breaking?—Shall we see this wrestling, cousin?

LE BEAU   You must if you stay here, for here is the place appointed for the wrestling, and they are ready to perform it.

CELIA   Yonder, sure, they are coming. Let us now stay and see it.

Flourish. Enter Duke [Frederick], Lords,
Orlando, Charles, and attendants.

DUKE FREDERICK   Come on. Since the youth will not be entreated, his own peril on his forwardness.   142

ROSALIND [*to Le Beau*]   Is yonder the man?

LE BEAU   Even he, madam.

CELIA   Alas, he is too young! Yet he looks successfully.   145

DUKE FREDERICK   How now, daughter and cousin? Are 146 you crept hither to see the wrestling?

ROSALIND   Ay, my liege, so please you give us leave.   148

DUKE FREDERICK   You will take little delight in it, I can tell you, there is such odds in the man. In pity of the 150 challenger's youth I would fain dissuade him, but he 151 will not be entreated. Speak to him, ladies; see if you can move him.

CELIA   Call him hither, good Monsieur Le Beau.

DUKE FREDERICK   Do so. I'll not be by.   [*He steps aside.*]

LE BEAU [*to Orlando*]   Monsieur the challenger, the princess calls for you.

ORLANDO [*approaching the ladies*]   I attend them with all respect and duty.

ROSALIND   Young man, have you challenged Charles the wrestler?

ORLANDO   No, fair princess. He is the general chal- 162 lenger. I come but in, as others do, to try with him the 163 strength of my youth.

CELIA   Young gentleman, your spirits are too bold for your years. You have seen cruel proof of this man's strength. If you saw yourself with your eyes or knew 167 yourself with your judgment, the fear of your adven- 168 ture would counsel you to a more equal enterprise. We 169 pray you, for your own sake, to embrace your own safety and give over this attempt.

ROSALIND   Do, young sir. Your reputation shall not therefore be misprized. We will make it our suit to the 173 Duke that the wrestling might not go forward.

ORLANDO   I beseech you, punish me not with your hard thoughts, wherein I confess me much guilty to deny 176 so fair and excellent ladies anything. But let your fair eyes and gentle wishes go with me to my trial, wherein if I be foiled, there is but one shamed that was never gracious, if killed, but one dead that is willing to 180 be so. I shall do my friends no wrong, for I have none to lament me; the world no injury, for in it I have nothing. Only in the world I fill up a place which may 183 be better supplied when I have made it empty.

ROSALIND   The little strength that I have, I would it were with you.

CELIA   And mine, to eke out hers.

ROSALIND   Fare you well. Pray heaven I be deceived 188 in you!   189

CELIA   Your heart's desires be with you!

CHARLES   Come, where is this young gallant that is so desirous to lie with his mother earth?

ORLANDO   Ready, sir, but his will hath in it a more modest working.   194

DUKE FREDERICK   You shall try but one fall.

CHARLES   No, I warrant Your Grace, you shall not entreat him to a second, that have so mightily persuaded him from a first.

ORLANDO   You mean to mock me after; you should not have mocked me before. But come your ways.   200

ROSALIND   Now Hercules be thy speed, young man!   201

CELIA   I would I were invisible, to catch the strong fellow by the leg.   [*Orlando and Charles*] *wrestle.*

ROSALIND   Oh, excellent young man!

CELIA   If I had a thunderbolt in mine eye, I can tell who 205 should down.   *Shout. [Charles is thrown.]*   206

DUKE FREDERICK   No more, no more.

ORLANDO   Yes, I beseech Your Grace. I am not yet well 208 breathed.   209

DUKE FREDERICK
How dost thou, Charles?

LE BEAU   He cannot speak, my lord.

DUKE FREDERICK
Bear him away.—What is thy name, young man?
    [*Charles is borne out.*]

ORLANDO   Orlando, my liege, the youngest son of Sir Rowland de Boys.

DUKE FREDERICK
I would thou hadst been son to some man else.
The world esteemed thy father honorable,
But I did find him still mine enemy.
Thou shouldst have better pleased me with this deed
Hadst thou descended from another house.
But fare thee well; thou art a gallant youth.
I would thou hadst told me of another father.
    Exit Duke [with train, and others. Rosalind and
    Celia remain; Orlando stands apart from them.]

---

132 promise assure   **133 any else** anyone else who   **133–4 broken music** literally, music arranged in parts for different instruments; here applied to the breaking of ribs   **134 another** another who
142 entreated . . . forwardness i.e., entreated to desist, let the risk be blamed upon his own rashness.   **145 successfully** i.e., as if he would be successful.   **146 cousin** i.e., niece   **148 so . . . leave** if you will permit us.   **150 there . . . man** Charles is such an odds-on favorite to win.   **151 fain** willingly   **162–3 the general challenger** the one who is ready to take on all comers. (Orlando is the challenger in a more limited sense.)   **167–8 If . . . judgment** If you saw yourself objectively   **169 equal** i.e., where the odds are more equal   **173 misprized** despised, undervalued.

176 wherein though.   **to deny** in denying   **180 gracious** looked upon with favor   **183 Only . . . I** In the world I merely
188–9 deceived in you i.e., mistaken in fearing you will lose.
194 modest working decorous endeavor (than to lie with one's mother earth. For a man to lie with his mother is to commit incest.)
200 come your ways come on.   **201 Hercules be thy speed** may Hercules help you   **205 If . . . eye** i.e., If I were Zeus or Jupiter
206 down fall.   **208–9 well breathed** warmed up.

CELIA [*to Rosalind*]

Were I my father, coz, would I do this?

ORLANDO [*to no one in particular*]

I am more proud to be Sir Rowland's son,
His youngest son, and would not change that calling   223
To be adopted heir to Frederick.

ROSALIND [*to Celia*]

My father loved Sir Rowland as his soul,
And all the world was of my father's mind.
Had I before known this young man his son,
I should have given him tears unto entreaties   228
Ere he should thus have ventured.

CELIA [*to Rosalind*]   Gentle cousin,

Let us go thank him and encourage him.
My father's rough and envious disposition
Sticks me at heart.—Sir, you have well deserved.   232
If you do keep your promises in love
But justly as you have exceeded all promise,   234
Your mistress shall be happy.

ROSALIND [*giving him a chain from her neck*]   Gentleman,   235

Wear this for me, one out of suits with fortune,   236
That could give more, but that her hand lacks means.   237
[*To Celia*] Shall we go, coz?

CELIA   Ay.—Fare you well, fair gentleman.

[*Rosalind and Celia start to leave.*]

ORLANDO [*aside*]

Can I not say, "I thank you"? My better parts
Are all thrown down, and that which here stands up
Is but a quintain, a mere lifeless block.   241

ROSALIND [*to Celia*]

He calls us back. My pride fell with my fortunes;
I'll ask him what he would.—Did you call, sir?   243
Sir, you have wrestled well and overthrown
More than your enemies.

CELIA   Will you go, coz?

ROSALIND   Have with you.—Fare you well.   247

Exit [*with Celia*].

ORLANDO

What passion hangs these weights upon my tongue?
I cannot speak to her, yet she urged conference.   249
O poor Orlando, thou art overthrown!
Or Charles or something weaker masters thee.   251

Enter Le Beau.

LE BEAU

Good sir, I do in friendship counsel you
To leave this place. Albeit you have deserved
High commendation, true applause, and love,
Yet such is now the Duke's condition   255
That he misconsters all that you have done.   256
The Duke is humorous. What he is indeed   257
More suits you to conceive than I to speak of.   258

ORLANDO

I thank you, sir. And, pray you, tell me this:
Which of the two was daughter of the Duke
That here was at the wrestling?

LE BEAU

Neither his daughter, if we judge by manners,
But yet indeed the taller is his daughter.   263
The other is daughter to the banished Duke,
And here detained by her usurping uncle
To keep his daughter company, whose loves
Are dearer than the natural bond of sisters.
But I can tell you that of late this Duke
Hath ta'en displeasure gainst his gentle niece,
Grounded upon no other argument   270
But that the people praise her for her virtues
And pity her for her good father's sake;
And, on my life, his malice gainst the lady
Will suddenly break forth. Sir, fare you well.   274
Hereafter, in a better world than this,   275
I shall desire more love and knowledge of you.

ORLANDO

I rest much bounden to you. Fare you well.   277

[*Exit Le Beau.*]

Thus must I from the smoke into the smother,   278
From tyrant Duke unto a tyrant brother.
But heavenly Rosalind!   *Exit.*

❧

1.3

Enter Celia and Rosalind.

CELIA   Why, cousin, why, Rosalind! Cupid have mercy!
Not a word?

ROSALIND   Not one to throw at a dog.

CELIA   No, thy words are too precious to be cast away
upon curs. Throw some of them at me. Come, lame   5
me with reasons.   6

ROSALIND   Then there were two cousins laid up, when
the one should be lamed with reasons and the other
mad without any.

CELIA   But is all this for your father?

ROSALIND   No, some of it is for my child's father. Oh,   11
how full of briers is this working-day world!

CELIA   They are but burs, cousin, thrown upon thee in   13
holiday foolery. If we walk not in the trodden paths,   14
our very petticoats will catch them.   15

ROSALIND   I could shake them off my coat. These burs
are in my heart.

263 taller (Perhaps a textual error for *smaller* or *lesser*, or else an inconsistency on Shakespeare's part; at 1.3.113, Rosalind is shown to be the taller.)   **270 argument** reason   **274 suddenly** very soon   **275 in . . . world** in better times   **277 bounden** indebted   **278 from . . . smother** i.e., out of the frying pan into the fire. (*Smother* means "a dense suffocating smoke.")

1.3 Location: Duke Frederick's court.

5–6 lame . . . reasons throw some explanations (for your silence) at me.   **11 my child's father** one who might father my children, i.e., Orlando.   **13–15 They . . . them** i.e., You are making too much of minor difficulties; one catches such burs on one's clothes constantly if one strays from the path of propriety (by falling into the folly of love). (*Holiday* and *working-day*, lines 12 and 14, form a crucial comic binary in this play.)

223 change that calling exchange that name and vocation   **228 unto** in addition to   **232 Sticks** stabs   **234 But justly** exactly   **235 s.d. chain** (See 3.2.178, where Celia speaks of a chain given to Orlando by Rosalind.)   **236 out . . . fortune** (1) whose petitions to Fortune are rejected (2) not wearing the livery of Fortune, not in her service   **237 could** would   **241 quintain** wooden figure used as a target in tilting   **243 would** wants.   **247 Have with you** I'll go with you.   **249 urged conference** invited conversation.   **251 Or** Either   **255 condition** disposition   **256 misconsters** misconstrues   **257 humorous** capricious.   **258 conceive** imagine, understand

CELIA　Hem them away.　18

ROSALIND　I would try, if I could cry "hem" and have　19
him.

CELIA　Come, come, wrestle with thy affections.

ROSALIND　Oh, they take the part of a better wrestler than
myself.

CELIA　Oh, a good wish upon you! You will try in time,　24
in despite of a fall. But, turning these jests out of　25
service, let us talk in good earnest. Is it possible, on　26
such a sudden, you should fall into so strong a liking
with old Sir Rowland's youngest son?

ROSALIND　The Duke my father loved his father dearly.

CELIA　Doth it therefore ensue that you should love his
son dearly? By this kind of chase, I should hate him,　31
for my father hated his father dearly; yet I hate not　32
Orlando.

ROSALIND　No, faith, hate him not, for my sake.　34

CELIA　Why should I not? Doth he not deserve well?　35

Enter Duke [Frederick], with Lords.

ROSALIND　Let me love him for that, and do you love
him because I do.—Look, here comes the Duke.

CELIA　With his eyes full of anger.

DUKE FREDERICK　[to Rosalind]
Mistress, dispatch you with your safest haste
And get you from our court.

ROSALIND　　　　　　　　　Me, uncle?

DUKE FREDERICK　　　　　　　　You, cousin.　40
Within these ten days if that thou be'st found
So near our public court as twenty miles,
Thou diest for it.

ROSALIND　　　　　　I do beseech Your Grace
Let me the knowledge of my fault bear with me.
If with myself I hold intelligence　45
Or have acquaintance with mine own desires,
If that I do not dream or be not frantic—　47
As I do trust I am not—then, dear uncle,
Never so much as in a thought unborn
Did I offend Your Highness.

DUKE FREDERICK　　　　　　Thus do all traitors.
If their purgation did consist in words,　51
They are as innocent as grace itself.
Let it suffice thee that I trust thee not.

ROSALIND
Yet your mistrust cannot make me a traitor.
Tell me whereon the likelihood depends.

DUKE FREDERICK
Thou art thy father's daughter. There's enough.　56

ROSALIND
So was I when Your Highness took his dukedom;
So was I when Your Highness banished him.
Treason is not inherited, my lord;
Or, if we did derive it from our friends,　60
What's that to me? My father was no traitor.
Then, good my liege, mistake me not so much
To think my poverty is treacherous.　63

CELIA　Dear sovereign, hear me speak.

DUKE FREDERICK
Ay, Celia, we stayed her for your sake,　65
Else had she with her father ranged along.　66

CELIA
I did not then entreat to have her stay;
It was your pleasure and your own remorse.　68
I was too young that time to value her,　69
But now I know her. If she be a traitor,
Why, so am I. We still have slept together,　71
Rose at an instant, learned, played, eat together,　72
And wheresoe'er we went, like Juno's swans　73
Still we went coupled and inseparable.

DUKE FREDERICK
She is too subtle for thee; and her smoothness,
Her very silence, and her patience
Speak to the people, and they pity her.
Thou art a fool. She robs thee of thy name,　78
And thou wilt show more bright and seem more
virtuous
When she is gone. Then open not thy lips.
Firm and irrevocable is my doom　81
Which I have passed upon her; she is banished.

CELIA
Pronounce that sentence then on me, my liege!
I cannot live out of her company.

DUKE FREDERICK
You are a fool.—You, niece, provide yourself.　85
If you outstay the time, upon mine honor,
And in the greatness of my word, you die.　87
　　　　　　　　　　　Exit Duke [with Lords].

CELIA
O my poor Rosalind, whither wilt thou go?
Wilt thou change fathers? I will give thee mine.　89
I charge thee, be not thou more grieved than I am.

ROSALIND
I have more cause.

CELIA　　　　　　Thou hast not, cousin.
Prithee, be cheerful. Know'st thou not the Duke
Hath banished me, his daughter?

ROSALIND　　　　　　　　　That he hath not.

---

18 Hem (1) Tuck (2) Cough (since you say they are in the chest.) A *bur* can be something that sticks in the throat.　**19 cry "hem"** attract Orlando's attention by coughing. (But with the suggestion too of a bawd's warning cry to the lovers whose secrecy is being guarded. With a pun on *"hem"* and *him*.)　**24–5 Oh . . . fall** i.e., Good luck to you; you'll undertake to wrestle with Orlando sooner or later, despite the danger of your being thrown down. (With sexual suggestion.)　**25–6 turning . . . service** i.e., dismissing this banter　**31 By . . . chase** To pursue this line of reasoning　**32 dearly** intensely　**34 faith** in truth　**35 Why . . . not?** Why shouldn't I hate him, i.e., love him? (Celia has just argued by chop-logic, in lines 30-2, that to love is to hate and vice versa.)　**40 cousin** i.e., niece.　**45 If . . . intelligence** If I understand my own feelings　**47 If that** If.　**frantic** insane　**51 purgation** clearing of guilt. (A medical, legal, and theological metaphor.)

56 There's enough That's reason enough.　**60 friends** relatives **63 To think** as to think　**65 stayed** kept　**66 ranged** roamed **68 remorse** compassion.　**69 that time** at that time　**71 still** continually　**72 at an instant** at the same time.　**eat** ate　**73 Juno's swans** i.e., yoked together. (Though according to Ovid it was Venus, not Juno, who used swans to draw her chariot.)　**78 name** reputation **81 doom** sentence　**85 provide yourself** get ready　**87 in . . . word** upon my authority as Duke　**89 change** exchange

CELIA
No, hath not? Rosalind lacks then the love
Which teacheth thee that thou and I am one.
Shall we be sundered? Shall we part, sweet girl?
No, let my father seek another heir.
Therefore devise with me how we may fly,
Whither to go, and what to bear with us.
And do not seek to take your change upon you,   100
To bear your griefs yourself and leave me out;
For, by this heaven, now at our sorrows pale,   102
Say what thou canst, I'll go along with thee.

ROSALIND   Why, whither shall we go?

CELIA
To seek my uncle in the Forest of Arden.

ROSALIND
Alas, what danger will it be to us,
Maids as we are, to travel forth so far!
Beauty provoketh thieves sooner than gold.

CELIA
I'll put myself in poor and mean attire   109
And with a kind of umber smirch my face;   110
The like do you. So shall we pass along
And never stir assailants.

ROSALIND   Were it not better,
Because that I am more than common tall,
That I did suit me all points like a man?   114
A gallant curtal ax upon my thigh,   115
A boar spear in my hand, and—in my heart
Lie there what hidden woman's fear there will—
We'll have a swashing and a martial outside,   118
As many other mannish cowards have
That do outface it with their semblances.   120

CELIA
What shall I call thee when thou art a man?

ROSALIND
I'll have no worse a name than Jove's own page,
And therefore look you call me Ganymede.   123
But what will you be called?

CELIA
Something that hath a reference to my state:
No longer Celia, but Aliena.   126

ROSALIND
But, cousin, what if we assayed to steal
The clownish fool out of your father's court?   127
Would he not be a comfort to our travel?   129

CELIA
He'll go along o'er the wide world with me.
Leave me alone to woo him. Let's away,   131
And get our jewels and our wealth together,
Devise the fittest time and safest way
To hide us from pursuit that will be made

After my flight. Now go we in content   135
To liberty, and not to banishment.   *Exeunt.*

❖

2.1

*Enter Duke Senior, Amiens, and two or three
Lords, [dressed] like foresters.*

DUKE SENIOR
Now, my co-mates and brothers in exile,
Hath not old custom made this life more sweet   2
Than that of painted pomp? Are not these woods
More free from peril than the envious court?
Here feel we not the penalty of Adam,   5
The seasons' difference, as the icy fang   6
And churlish chiding of the winter's wind,
Which when it bites and blows upon my body
Even till I shrink with cold, I smile and say
"This is no flattery; these are counselors
That feelingly persuade me what I am."
Sweet are the uses of adversity,
Which, like the toad, ugly and venomous,   13
Wears yet a precious jewel in his head;   14
And this our life, exempt from public haunt,   15
Finds tongues in trees, books in the running brooks,
Sermons in stones, and good in everything.

AMIENS
I would not change it. Happy is Your Grace
That can translate the stubbornness of fortune
Into so quiet and so sweet a style.

DUKE SENIOR
Come, shall we go and kill us venison?
And yet it irks me the poor dappled fools,   22
Being native burghers of this desert city,   23
Should in their own confines with forkèd heads   24
Have their round haunches gored.

FIRST LORD   Indeed, my lord,
The melancholy Jaques grieves at that,
And in that kind swears you do more usurp   27
Than doth your brother that hath banished you.
Today my lord of Amiens and myself
Did steal behind him as he lay along   30
Under an oak whose antique root peeps out   31
Upon the brook that brawls along this wood,   32
To the which place a poor sequestered stag   33
That from the hunter's aim had ta'en a hurt
Did come to languish. And indeed, my lord,
The wretched animal heaved forth such groans

---

100 **change** change of fortune   102 **pale** (Heaven is pale in sympathy with their plight.)   109 **mean** lowly   110 **umber** yellow-brown pigment (to give a tanned appearance appropriate to countrywomen)   114 **suit me all points** outfit myself in all ways   115 **curtal ax** broad cutting sword   118 **swashing** swaggering   120 **outface . . . semblances** bluff their way through with mere appearances.   123 **Ganymede** Jupiter's cupbearer. (The name used for disguise also in Lodge's *Rosalynde*.)   126 **Aliena** the estranged one.   127 **assayed** tried   129 **travel** (1) movement from place to place (2) labor, hardship (*travail*)   131 **Leave . . . him** Leave it to me to persuade him.

135 **content** contentment
2.1 Location: The Forest of Arden.
2 **old custom** long experience   5–6 **feel . . . difference** we don't mind the consequences of Adam's original sin—the hardship of the seasons. (*Not* is often emended to *but*.)   6 **as** such as   13–14 **like . . . head** (Alludes to the widespread belief that the toad was a poisonous creature but with a jewel embedded in its head that worked as an antidote.)   15 **exempt** cut off.   **haunt** society   22 **fools** innocents   23 **burghers** citizens.   **desert city** uninhabited place   24 **forkèd heads** barbed hunting arrows, but also suggesting antlers   27 **kind** regard   30 **along** stretched out   31 **antique** (1) ancient or (2) *antic*, "gnarled"   32 **brawls** noisily flows   33 **sequestered** separated (from the herd)

That their discharge did stretch his leathern coat
Almost to bursting, and the big round tears
Coursed one another down his innocent nose   39
In piteous chase. And thus the hairy fool,
Much markèd of the melancholy Jaques,   41
Stood on th'extremest verge of the swift brook,   42
Augmenting it with tears.

DUKE SENIOR   But what said Jaques?
Did he not moralize this spectacle?   44

FIRST LORD
Oh, yes, into a thousand similes.
First, for his weeping into the needless stream: 46
"Poor deer," quoth he, "thou mak'st a testament   47
As worldings do, giving thy sum of more   48
To that which had too much." Then, being there alone,   49
Left and abandoned of his velvet friends: 50
"'Tis right," quoth he, "thus misery doth part   51
The flux of company." Anon a careless herd,   52
Full of the pasture, jumps along by him   53
And never stays to greet him. "Ay," quoth Jaques,
"Sweep on, you fat and greasy citizens;   55
'Tis just the fashion. Wherefore do you look   56
Upon that poor and broken bankrupt there?"   57
Thus most invectively he pierceth through   58
The body of the country, city, court,
Yea, and of this our life, swearing that we
Are mere usurpers, tyrants, and what's worse,   61
To fright the animals and to kill them up   62
In their assigned and native dwelling place.

DUKE SENIOR
And did you leave him in this contemplation?

SECOND LORD
We did, my lord, weeping and commenting
Upon the sobbing deer.

DUKE SENIOR   Show me the place.
I love to cope him in these sullen fits,   67
For then he's full of matter.   68

FIRST LORD   I'll bring you to him straight.   *Exeunt.*   69

❧

2.2

Enter Duke [Frederick], with Lords.

DUKE FREDERICK
Can it be possible that no man saw them?
It cannot be. Some villains of my court
Are of consent and sufferance in this.   3

FIRST LORD
I cannot hear of any that did see her.   4
The ladies, her attendants of her chamber,
Saw her abed, and in the morning early
They found the bed untreasured of their mistress.

SECOND LORD
My lord, the roynish clown, at whom so oft   8
Your Grace was wont to laugh, is also missing.
Hisperia, the princess' gentlewoman,
Confesses that she secretly o'erheard
Your daughter and her cousin much commend
The parts and graces of the wrestler   13
That did but lately foil the sinewy Charles,
And she believes wherever they are gone
That youth is surely in their company.

DUKE FREDERICK
Send to his brother. Fetch that gallant hither.   17
If he be absent, bring his brother to me;   18
I'll make him find him. Do this suddenly,   19
And let not search and inquisition quail   20
To bring again these foolish runaways.   *Exeunt.*   21

❧

2.3

Enter Orlando and Adam, [meeting].

ORLANDO   Who's there?

ADAM
What, my young master? Oh, my gentle master,
Oh, my sweet master, oh, you memory   3
Of old Sir Rowland! Why, what make you here?   4
Why are you virtuous? Why do people love you?
And wherefore are you gentle, strong, and valiant?
Why would you be so fond to overcome   7
The bonny prizer of the humorous Duke?   8
Your praise is come too swiftly home before you.
Know you not, master, to some kind of men
Their graces serve them but as enemies?
No more do yours. Your virtues, gentle master,   12
Are sanctified and holy traitors to you.

---

39 Coursed chased   **41 markèd of** observed by   **42 th'extremest
verge** the very edge   **44 moralize** draw out the hidden meaning of
46 needless having no need of more water. (Weeping deer are common in literature.)   **47 testament** will   **48 worldings** worldly men
48–9 giving . . . much bequeathing your superabundance of wealth
to heirs who are already too wealthy.   **49 being** the deer being
50 of by.   **velvet** i.e., prosperous. (Velvet was an appropriately rich
dress for a courtier; the term also alludes here to the deers' velvety
coat or to the covering of their antlers during rapid growth.)
51 'Tis right i.e., That's how it goes   **51–2 thus . . . company** thus
the miserable are separated from and forgotten by the herd.
52 careless (1) carefree (2) uncaring   **53 the pasture** i.e., good food
55 greasy fat and unctuously prosperous, like rich burghers or *citizens*   **56–7 Wherefore . . . there?** Why do you even bother to glance
at that poor physically shattered deer there? (*Broken* also hints at a
financial ruin appropriate to *citizens* in line 55.)   **58 invectively** in
the most bitter terms   **61 what's worse** whatever is worse than
these   **62 up** off, utterly   **67 cope** encounter   **68 matter** substance.
69 straight at once.

2.2 Location: Duke Frederick's court.
3 Are . . . this have conspired in and permitted this.   **4 her** Celia.
8 roynish scurvy, rascally. (Literally, covered with scale or scurf.)
13 parts good qualities   **17 Send . . . hither** i.e., Send word to Oliver
to bring Orlando here.   **18 he** i.e., Orlando.   **his brother** i.e., Oliver.
(Or possibly referring to Jaques de Boys, the other brother.)   **19 suddenly** speedily   **20 inquisition quail** investigation fail   **21 again**
back
2.3 Location: Before Oliver's house.
3 memory likeness, reminder   **4 what make you** what are you doing
7 fond to foolish as to   **8 bonny prizer** sturdy prizefighter.
humorous temperamental   **12 No . . . yours** Your fine qualities serve
you no better than that.

Oh, what a world is this, when what is comely
Envenoms him that bears it!

ORLANDO
Why, what's the matter?

ADAM   O unhappy youth,
Come not within these doors! Within this roof
The enemy of all your graces lives.
Your brother—no, no brother; yet the son—
Yet not the son, I will not call him son
Of him I was about to call his father—
Hath heard your praises, and this night he means   22
To burn the lodging where you use to lie   23
And you within it. If he fail of that,
He will have other means to cut you off.
I overheard him and his practices.   26
This is no place, this house is but a butchery.   27
Abhor it, fear it, do not enter it.

ORLANDO
Why, whither, Adam, wouldst thou have me go?

ADAM
No matter whither, so you come not here.   30

ORLANDO
What, wouldst thou have me go and beg my food?
Or with a base and boist'rous sword enforce   32
A thievish living on the common road?
This I must do or know not what to do;
Yet this I will not do, do how I can.
I rather will subject me to the malice
Of a diverted blood and bloody brother.   37

ADAM
But do not so. I have five hundred crowns,
The thrifty hire I saved under your father,   39
Which I did store to be my foster nurse
When service should in my old limbs lie lame   41
And unregarded age in corners thrown.   42
Take that, and He that doth the ravens feed,   43
Yea, providently caters for the sparrow,   44
Be comfort to my age! Here is the gold; [offering gold]
All this I give you. Let me be your servant.
Though I look old, yet I am strong and lusty,   47
For in my youth I never did apply
Hot and rebellious liquors in my blood,
Nor did not with unbashful forehead woo   50
The means of weakness and debility;   51
Therefore my age is as a lusty winter,
Frosty but kindly. Let me go with you.   53
I'll do the service of a younger man
In all your business and necessities.

ORLANDO
Oh, good old man, how well in thee appears
The constant service of the antique world,   57
When service sweat for duty, not for meed!   58
Thou art not for the fashion of these times,
Where none will sweat but for promotion,
And having that do choke their service up   61
Even with the having. It is not so with thee.   62
But, poor old man, thou prun'st a rotten tree,
That cannot so much as a blossom yield
In lieu of all thy pains and husbandry.   65
But come thy ways. We'll go along together,
And ere we have thy youthful wages spent,
We'll light upon some settled low content.   68

ADAM
Master, go on, and I will follow thee
To the last gasp, with truth and loyalty.
From seventeen years till now almost fourscore
Here lived I, but now live here no more.
At seventeen years many their fortunes seek,
But at fourscore it is too late a week;   74
Yet fortune cannot recompense me better
Than to die well and not my master's debtor.

                                        Exeunt.

❖

2.4

*Enter Rosalind for Ganymede, Celia for Aliena,
and Clown, alias Touchstone.*

ROSALIND   Oh, Jupiter, how weary are my spirits!

TOUCHSTONE   I care not for my spirits, if my legs were
not weary.

ROSALIND   I could find in my heart to disgrace my man's
apparel and to cry like a woman; but I must comfort   5
the weaker vessel, as doublet and hose ought to show   6
itself courageous to petticoat. Therefore courage, good
Aliena!

CELIA   I pray you, bear with me. I cannot go no further.

TOUCHSTONE   For my part, I had rather bear with you
than bear you; yet I should bear no cross if I did bear   11
you, for I think you have no money in your purse.

ROSALIND   Well, this is the Forest of Arden.

TOUCHSTONE   Ay, now am I in Arden; the more fool I.
When I was at home I was in a better place, but
travelers must be content.

Enter Corin and Silvius.

ROSALIND   Ay, be so, good Touchstone.—Look you
who comes here, a young man and an old in solemn
talk.   [*They stand aside and listen.*]

CORIN
That is the way to make her scorn you still.

SILVIUS
Oh, Corin, that thou knew'st how I do love her!

CORIN
I partly guess, for I have loved ere now.

SILVIUS
No, Corin, being old, thou canst not guess,
Though in thy youth thou wast as true a lover
As ever sighed upon a midnight pillow.
But if thy love were ever like to mine—
As sure I think did never man love so—
How many actions most ridiculous
Hast thou been drawn to by thy fantasy?   29

CORIN
Into a thousand that I have forgotten.

SILVIUS
Oh, thou didst then never love so heartily!
If thou remember'st not the slightest folly
That ever love did make thee run into,
Thou hast not loved.
Or if thou hast not sat as I do now,
Wearing thy hearer in thy mistress' praise,   36
Thou hast not loved.
Or if thou hast not broke from company
Abruptly, as my passion now makes me,
Thou has not loved.
O Phoebe, Phoebe, Phoebe!   *Exit.*

ROSALIND
Alas, poor shepherd! Searching of thy wound,   42
I have by hard adventure found mine own.   43

TOUCHSTONE   And I mine. I remember, when I was in
love I broke my sword upon a stone and bid him take   45
that for coming a-night to Jane Smile; and I remember   46
the kissing of her batler and the cow's dugs that her   47
pretty chapped hands had milked; and I remember   48
the wooing of a peascod instead of her, from whom I   49
took two cods and, giving her them again, said with   50
weeping tears, "Wear these for my sake." We that are   51
true lovers run into strange capers; but as all is mortal   52
in nature, so is all nature in love mortal in folly.   53

ROSALIND   Thou speak'st wiser than thou art ware of.   54

TOUCHSTONE   Nay, I shall ne'er be ware of mine own   55
wit till I break my shins against it.   56

ROSALIND
Jove, Jove! This shepherd's passion
Is much upon my fashion.   58

TOUCHSTONE
And mine, but it grows something stale with me.   59

CELIA
I pray you, one of you question yond man
If he for gold will give us any food.
I faint almost to death.

TOUCHSTONE [*to Corin*]   Holla: you, clown!   62

ROSALIND
Peace, Fool! He's not thy kinsman.

CORIN   Who calls?

TOUCHSTONE
Your betters, sir.

CORIN   Else are they very wretched.

ROSALIND
Peace, I say.—Good even to you, friend.   65

CORIN
And to you, gentle sir, and to you all.

ROSALIND
I prithee, shepherd, if that love or gold   67
Can in this desert place buy entertainment,   68
Bring us where we may rest ourselves and feed.
Here's a young maid with travel much oppressed,
And faints for succor.

CORIN   Fair sir, I pity her   71
And wish, for her sake more than for mine own,
My fortunes were more able to relieve her;
But I am shepherd to another man
And do not shear the fleeces that I graze.   75
My master is of churlish disposition,   76
And little recks to find the way to heaven   77
By doing deeds of hospitality.
Besides, his cote, his flocks, and bounds of feed   79
Are now on sale, and at our sheepcote now,
By reason of his absence, there is nothing
That you will feed on. But what is, come see,   82
And in my voice most welcome shall you be.   83

ROSALIND
What is he that shall buy his flock and pasture?   84

CORIN
That young swain that you saw here but erewhile,   85
That little cares for buying anything.

ROSALIND
I pray thee, if it stand with honesty,   87
Buy thou the cottage, pasture, and the flock,
And thou shalt have to pay for it of us.   89

---

29 **fantasy** love imaginings.   36 **Wearing** wearing out   42 **Searching of** Probing   43 **hard adventure** painful experience   45–6 **I broke . . . Smile** (In his parody of a distraught lover, Touchstone imagines himself attacking a stone as if it were his rival for a country maiden named Jane Smile. *A-night* means "by night.")   47 **batler** club for beating clothes in process of washing.   **dugs** udder   48–51 **and I . . . sake** (Touchstone absurdly imagines himself courting a pea plant as though it were Jane Smile and exchanging pea pods with her by way of love tokens.)   52 **mortal** subject to death   53 **mortal** typically human, frail   54 **ware** aware   55–6 **Nay . . . against it** (Touchstone, as a professional fool, laughs at the idea of stumbling on or discovering his own capacity for saying something wise. His use of *ware* plays on [1] aware [2] wary.)

58 **upon** after, according to   59 **something** somewhat   62 **clown** yokel. (But Rosalind then alludes to the word as it applies to Touchstone as a court fool or clown.)   65 **even** evening, i.e., afternoon   67 **if that** if   68 **desert** uninhabited.   **entertainment** hospitality, provision   71 **for succor** for lack of food.   75 **do . . . fleeces** i.e., do not obtain the profits from the flock   76 **churlish** miserly   77 **recks** reckons   79 **cote** cottage.   **bounds of feed** range of pasture   82 **That . . . feed on** suitable for your refined tastes.   83 **in my voice** insofar as I have authority to speak   84 **What** Who   85 **but erewhile** just now   87 **stand** be consistent   89 **have to pay** have the money

CELIA
  And we will mend thy wages. I like this place   90
  And willingly could waste my time in it.   91

CORIN
  Assuredly the thing is to be sold.
  Go with me. If you like upon report
  The soil, the profit, and this kind of life,
  I will your very faithful feeder be   95
  And buy it with your gold right suddenly.   *Exeunt.* 96

❖

2.5

*Enter Amiens, Jaques, and others. [A table is
set out.]*

Song.

AMIENS [*sings*]
          Under the greenwood tree
          Who loves to lie with me,
          And turn his merry note   2
          Unto the sweet bird's throat,   3
      Come hither, come hither, come hither.   4
          Here shall he see
          No enemy
      But winter and rough weather.

JAQUES   More, more, I prithee, more.
AMIENS   It will make you melancholy, Monsieur Jaques.
JAQUES   I thank it. More, I prithee, more. I can suck mel-
  ancholy out of a song as a weasel sucks eggs. More, I
  prithee, more.
AMIENS   My voice is ragged. I know I cannot please you.   14
JAQUES   I do not desire you to please me, I do desire
  you to sing. Come, more, another stanzo. Call you   16
  'em "stanzos"?
AMIENS   What you will, Monsieur Jaques.
JAQUES   Nay, I care not for their names; they owe me   19
  nothing. Will you sing?   20
AMIENS   More at your request than to please myself.
JAQUES   Well then, if ever I thank any man, I'll thank
  you; but that they call "compliment" is like th'en-   23
  counter of two dog-apes, and when a man thanks   24
  me heartily, methinks I have given him a penny and
  he renders me the beggarly thanks. Come, sing; and   26
  you that will not, hold your tongues.
AMIENS   Well, I'll end the song.—Sirs, cover the while;   28
  the Duke will drink under this tree.—He hath been all
  this day to look you.   [*Food and drink are set out.*] 30

JAQUES   And I have been all this day to avoid him. He
  is too disputable for my company. I think of as many 32
  matters as he, but I give heaven thanks and make no
  boast of them. Come, warble, come.

Song.

AMIENS [*sings*]
          Who doth ambition shun
          And loves to live i'th' sun,   36
          Seeking the food he eats   37
          And pleased with what he gets,
                              All together here.
      Come hither, come hither, come hither.
          Here shall he see
          No enemy
      But winter and rough weather.

JAQUES   I'll give you a verse to this note that I made   43
  yesterday in despite of my invention.   44
AMIENS   And I'll sing it.
JAQUES   Thus it goes:

          If it do come to pass
          That any man turn ass,
          Leaving his wealth and ease,
          A stubborn will to please,
      Ducdame, ducdame, ducdame.   51
          Here shall he see
          Gross fools as he,
      An if he will come to me.

AMIENS   What's that "ducdame"?
JAQUES   'Tis a Greek invocation, to call fools into a circle.
  I'll go sleep, if I can; if I cannot, I'll rail against all the
  firstborn of Egypt.   58
AMIENS   And I'll go seek the Duke. His banquet is pre-   59
  pared.   *Exeunt [separately].*

❖

2.6

Enter Orlando and Adam.

ADAM   Dear master, I can go no further. Oh, I die for
  food! Here lie I down and measure out my grave.
  Farewell, kind master.   [*He lies down.*]

---

90 **mend** improve   91 **waste** spend   95 **feeder** dependent, servant
96 **right suddenly** without delay.
2.5 Location: The forest.
2 **Who** anyone who.   **lie** dwell   3–4 **And . . . throat** and tune his
song to the bird's voice   14 **ragged** hoarse.   16 **stanzo** (The word
stanza, variously spelled, was newfangled and therefore of ironic
interest to Jaques.)   19–20 **they owe me nothing** (Jaques speaks of
names as of something valuable only when written as signatures to a
bond of indebtedness.)   23 **that** what.   **"compliment"** courtesy
24 **dog-apes** dog-faced baboons   26 **beggarly** effusive, like the
thanks of a beggar   28 **cover the while** set the table for a meal
meanwhile   30 **to look** looking for

32 **disputable** inclined to dispute   36 **live i'th' sun** dwell in the open
air, without the cares of the court   37 **Seeking** hunting for   43 **note**
tune   44 **in . . . invention** i.e., without needing to make use of my
powerful rhetorical skills. (The nonsense that follows will make a
mockery of true invention.)   51 **Ducdame** (Probably a nonsense term
devised to puzzle Jaques's hearers, although with intriguing resemblances to phrases in Romany, *dukrà me*, "I foretell," or Welsh *Dewch
da mi*, "Come with (or to) me," or dog-Latin *Duc ad me*, "Lead him to
me," or simply "Duke damn me.")   58 **firstborn of Egypt** (In Exodus
12:28–33, the firstborn of Egypt are slain by the Lord as the enemies
of Moses and the Israelites, who, like the Duke and his followers, are
in exile.)   59 **banquet** wine and dessert after dinner. (This repast,
now prepared on stage, seemingly is to remain there during the short
following scene.)
2.6. Location: The forest. The scene is continuous. By convention
we understand that Adam and Orlando are in a different part of the
forest and do not "see" the table remaining onstage.

ORLANDO   Why, how now, Adam? No greater heart in
thee? Live a little, comfort a little, cheer thyself a little.   5
If this uncouth forest yield anything savage, I will   6
either be food for it or bring it for food to thee. Thy   7
conceit is nearer death than thy powers. For my sake   8
be comfortable; hold death awhile at the arm's end. I   9
will here be with thee presently, and if I bring thee not
something to eat, I will give thee leave to die; but if
thou diest before I come, thou art a mocker of my
labor. Well said! Thou look'st cheerly, and I'll be with   13
thee quickly. Yet thou liest in the bleak air. Come, I   14
will bear thee to some shelter; and thou shalt not die
for lack of a dinner, if there live anything in this desert.
[*He picks up Adam.*] Cheerly, good Adam!   *Exeunt.*

❖

2.7

Enter Duke Senior and Lords, like outlaws.

DUKE SENIOR
I think he be transformed into a beast,
For I can nowhere find him like a man.

FIRST LORD
My lord, he is but even now gone hence.
Here was he merry, hearing of a song.

DUKE SENIOR
If he, compact of jars, grow musical,   5
We shall have shortly discord in the spheres.   6
Go seek him. Tell him I would speak with him.

Enter Jaques.

FIRST LORD
He saves my labor by his own approach.

DUKE SENIOR
Why, how now, monsieur, what a life is this,
That your poor friends must woo your company!
What, you look merrily.

JAQUES
A fool, a fool! I met a fool i'th' forest,
A motley fool. A miserable world!   13
As I do live by food, I met a fool,
Who laid him down and basked him in the sun,
And railed on Lady Fortune in good terms,
In good set terms, and yet a motley fool.   17
"Good morrow, Fool," quoth I. "No, sir," quoth he,
"Call me not fool till heaven hath sent me fortune."   19
And then he drew a dial from his poke   20
And, looking on it with lackluster eye,
Says very wisely, "It is ten o'clock.

Thus we may see," quoth he, "how the world wags.   23
'Tis but an hour ago since it was nine,
And after one hour more 'twill be eleven;
And so from hour to hour we ripe and ripe,
And then from hour to hour we rot and rot,
And thereby hangs a tale." When I did hear
The motley fool thus moral on the time,   29
My lungs began to crow like Chanticleer,   30
That fools should be so deep-contemplative,
And I did laugh sans intermission   32
An hour by his dial. Oh, noble fool!
A worthy fool! Motley's the only wear.   34

DUKE SENIOR   What fool is this?

JAQUES
Oh, worthy fool! One that hath been a courtier,
And says, if ladies be but young and fair,
They have the gift to know it. And in his brain,   38
Which is as dry as the remainder biscuit   39
After a voyage, he hath strange places crammed   40
With observation, the which he vents   41
In mangled forms. Oh, that I were a fool!
I am ambitious for a motley coat.

DUKE SENIOR
Thou shalt have one.

JAQUES   It is my only suit,   44
Provided that you weed your better judgments
Of all opinion that grows rank in them   46
That I am wise. I must have liberty
Withal, as large a charter as the wind,   48
To blow on whom I please, for so fools have.
And they that are most gallèd with my folly,   50
They most must laugh. And why, sir, must they so?
The "why" is plain as way to parish church:
He that a fool doth very wisely hit   53
Doth very foolishly, although he smart,   54
Not to seem senseless of the bob. If not,   55
The wise man's folly is anatomized   56
Even by the squand'ring glances of the fool.   57
Invest me in my motley; give me leave   58
To speak my mind, and I will through and through
Cleanse the foul body of th'infected world,   60
If they will patiently receive my medicine.

DUKE SENIOR
Fie on thee! I can tell what thou wouldst do.

JAQUES
What, for a counter, would I do but good?   63

---

5 **comfort** comfort yourself   6 **uncouth** strange, wild   7–8 **Thy conceit . . . powers** You imagine you are nearer death than you really are.
9 **comfortable** comforted   13 **Well said!** Well done!   14 **Yet** Still
2.7. Location: The forest; the scene is continuous. (A repast, set out
for the Duke in 2.5, has remained onstage during 2.6.)
5 **compact of jars** composed of discords   6 **the spheres** the concentric spheres of the old Ptolemaic solar system (which, by their movement, were thought to produce harmonious music)   13 **motley**
wearing motley, the parti-colored dress of the professional jester
17 **set** carefully composed   19 **Call . . . fortune** (An allusion to the
proverb "Fortune favors fools.")   20 **dial** pocket sundial or watch.
poke pouch or pocket

23 **wags** goes.   29 **moral** moralize   30 **crow** i.e., laugh merrily.
Chanticleer a rooster   32 **sans** without   34 **only wear** only thing
worth wearing.   38 **know it** i.e., put their beauty to advantage.
39 **dry** (According to Elizabethan physiology, a dry brain was marked
by a strong memory but a slowness of apprehension.)   **remainder**
left over   40 **places** (1) nooks and corners (2) rhetorical topics
41 **vents** utters   44 **suit** (1) request (2) suit of clothes   46 **rank** wildly,
coarsely   48 **Withal** in addition.   **charter** license, privilege   50 **gallèd** rubbed sore   53–5 **He . . . bob** He whom a fool wittily attacks
behaves very foolishly, no matter how much he feels the sting, unless
he pretends to be unaware of the taunt.   55–7 **If not . . . fool** Otherwise, the folly of even a wise person is dissected and laid open even
by the variously directed shots of wit made by the fool.   58 **Invest**
Array   60 **Cleanse** purge. (A medical metaphor.)   63 **counter**
(1) thing of no intrinsic value, a metal disk used in counting (2) parry

DUKE SENIOR

Most mischievous foul sin, in chiding sin.
For thou thyself hast been a libertine,
As sensual as the brutish sting itself;
And all th'embossèd sores and headed evils   66
That thou with license of free foot hast caught   67
Wouldst thou disgorge into the general world.   68

JAQUES   Why, who cries out on pride   69
That can therein tax any private party?   70
Doth it not flow as hugely as the sea,   71
Till that the weary very means do ebb?   72
What woman in the city do I name,
When that I say the city woman bears
The cost of princes on unworthy shoulders?   75
Who can come in and say that I mean her,   76
When such a one as she, such is her neighbor?   77
Or what is he of basest function
That says his bravery is not on my cost,   79
Thinking that I mean him, but therein suits   80
His folly to the mettle of my speech?   81
There then, how then? What then? Let me see   82
        wherein
My tongue hath wronged him. If it do him right,   84
Then he hath wronged himself. If he be free,   85
Why then my taxing like a wild goose flies,   86
Unclaimed of any man.—But who comes here?   87

Enter Orlando [with his sword drawn].

ORLANDO

Forbear, and eat no more!

JAQUES   Why, I have eat none yet. 88

ORLANDO

Nor shalt not, till necessity be served.

JAQUES

Of what kind should this cock come of?   90

DUKE SENIOR

Art thou thus boldened, man, by thy distress,
Or else a rude despiser of good manners,
That in civility thou seem'st so empty?

ORLANDO

You touched my vein at first. The thorny point   94
Of bare distress hath ta'en from me the show
Of smooth civility; yet am I inland bred   96

---

66 **brutish sting** carnal impulse   67 **th'embossèd** the swollen.
headed evils sores that have come to a head   68 **license . . . foot** the
licentious freedom of a libertine   69 **disgorge** vomit   70–1 **who . . .
party?** what true satirist inveighs against extravagance in dress with
only some private individual in mind?   72–3 **Doth . . . ebb?** Is not
pride as universal as the sea, overflowing everywhere until it finally
ebbs like the tide, having exhausted what it fed upon?   75–6 **when . . .
shoulders?** when I characterize the typical citizen's wife as dressing
herself in finery that is costly enough to adorn a prince?   77 **come in**
i.e., come into court as a complainant   79–82 **Or . . . speech?** Or who
is he of even the lowest social standing that does not object to my
saying that sartorial finery is a fit subject for my satirical spleen,
thinking I am satirizing him when his own folly shows how well he
fits the contents of my speech?   84–7 **If . . . man** If my satirical sketch
fits him, then he condemns himself by resembling my portrait of
folly. If he does not resemble my sketch, my criticism does him no
harm.   88 **have eat** have eaten. (Pronounced "et.")   90 **Of . . . of?**
What sort of fighting cock is this?   94 **You . . . first** Your first supposition is correct.   96 **inland bred** i.e., raised in the center of civilization rather than on the outskirts

---

And know some nurture. But forbear, I say.   97
He dies that touches any of this fruit
Till I and my affairs are answerèd.   99

JAQUES

An you will not be answered with reason, I must die. 100

DUKE SENIOR

What would you have? Your gentleness shall force
More than your force move us to gentleness.

ORLANDO

I almost die for food, and let me have it!

DUKE SENIOR

Sit down and feed, and welcome to our table.

ORLANDO

Speak you so gently? Pardon me, I pray you.
I thought that all things had been savage here,
And therefore put I on the countenance
Of stern commandment. But whate'er you are
That in this desert inaccessible,
Under the shade of melancholy boughs,   110
Lose and neglect the creeping hours of time;
If ever you have looked on better days,
If ever been where bells have knolled to church,   113
If ever sat at any good man's feast,
If ever from your eyelids wiped a tear
And know what 'tis to pity and be pitied,
Let gentleness my strong enforcement be,
In the which hope I blush and hide my sword.

            [He sheathes his sword.]

DUKE SENIOR

True is it that we have seen better days,
And have with holy bell been knolled to church,
And sat at good men's feasts, and wiped our eyes
Of drops that sacred pity hath engendered.
And therefore sit you down in gentleness,
And take upon command what help we have   124
That to your wanting may be ministered.   125

ORLANDO

Then but forbear your food a little while,
Whiles, like a doe, I go to find my fawn
And give it food. There is an old poor man
Who after me hath many a weary step
Limped in pure love. Till he be first sufficed,
Oppressed with two weak evils, age and hunger,   131
I will not touch a bit.

DUKE SENIOR   Go find him out,
And we will nothing waste till you return.   133

ORLANDO

I thank ye; and be blest for your good comfort!

            [Exit.]

DUKE SENIOR

Thou see'st we are not all alone unhappy.
This wide and universal theater
Presents more woeful pageants than the scene
Wherein we play in.

JAQUES   All the world's a stage,

---

97 **nurture** education, training.   99 **answerèd** satisfied.   100 **An** If.
reason (A pun on "raisin" plays upon *fruit* in line 98.)   110 **melancholy** dark, shadowy   113 **knolled** knelled, rung   124 **upon command** for the asking   125 **wanting** need   131 **weak evils** disabilities
causing weakness   133 **waste** consume

And all the men and women merely players.
They have their exits and their entrances,
And one man in his time plays many parts,
His acts being seven ages. At first the infant,
Mewling and puking in the nurse's arms. 143
Then the whining schoolboy, with his satchel
And shining morning face, creeping like snail
Unwillingly to school. And then the lover,
Sighing like furnace, with a woeful ballad
Made to his mistress' eyebrow. Then a soldier,
Full of strange oaths and bearded like the pard, 149
Jealous in honor, sudden, and quick in quarrel, 150
Seeking the bubble reputation
Even in the cannon's mouth. And then the justice,
In fair round belly with good capon lined, 153
With eyes severe and beard of formal cut,
Full of wise saws and modern instances; 155
And so he plays his part. The sixth age shifts
Into the lean and slippered pantaloon, 157
With spectacles on nose and pouch on side,
His youthful hose, well saved, a world too wide
For his shrunk shank; and his big manly voice, 160
Turning again toward childish treble, pipes
And whistles in his sound. Last scene of all, 162
That ends this strange, eventful history,
Is second childishness and mere oblivion, 164
Sans teeth, sans eyes, sans taste, sans everything. 165

Enter Orlando, with Adam.

DUKE SENIOR
Welcome. Set down your venerable burden
And let him feed.
ORLANDO   I thank you most for him.
                  [He sets down Adam.]
ADAM   So had you need.
I scarce can speak to thank you for myself.
DUKE SENIOR
Welcome. Fall to. I will not trouble you
As yet to question you about your fortunes.—
Give us some music, and, good cousin, sing. 173
        [They eat, while Orlando and Duke Senior
                          converse apart.]

Song.

AMIENS *[sings]*
    Blow, blow, thou winter wind.
    Thou art not so unkind
      As man's ingratitude.
    Thy tooth is not so keen,
    Because thou art not seen,
      Although thy breath be rude. 180

Heigh-ho, sing heigh-ho, unto the green holly. 181
Most friendship is feigning, most loving mere
    folly.
      Then heigh-ho, the holly!
        This life is most jolly.
Freeze, freeze, thou bitter sky,
That dost not bite so nigh 186
    As benefits forgot.
Though thou the waters warp, 188
Thy sting is not so sharp
    As friend remembered not.
Heigh-ho, sing heigh-ho, unto the green holly.
Most friendship is feigning, most loving mere
    folly.
      Then heigh-ho, the holly!
        This life is most jolly.

DUKE SENIOR *[to Orlando]*
If that you were the good Sir Rowland's son, 195
As you have whispered faithfully you were 196
And as mine eye doth his effigies witness 197
Most truly limned and living in your face, 198
Be truly welcome hither. I am the Duke
That loved your father. The residue of your fortune, 200
Go to my cave and tell me.—Good old man,
Thou art right welcome as thy master is.—
Support him by the arm. Give me your hand,
And let me all your fortunes understand.   *Exeunt.* 204

❧

3.1

Enter Duke [Frederick], Lords, and Oliver.

DUKE FREDERICK
Not see him since? Sir, sir, that cannot be. 1
But were I not the better part made mercy, 2
I should not seek an absent argument 3
Of my revenge, thou present. But look to it: 4
Find out thy brother, wheresoe'er he is.
Seek him with candle. Bring him dead or living 6
Within this twelvemonth, or turn thou no more 7
To seek a living in our territory.
Thy lands and all things that thou dost call thine
Worth seizure do we seize into our hands, 10
Till thou canst quit thee by thy brother's mouth 11
Of what we think against thee.

---

181 **holly** (An emblem of Christmastime and holiday cheer, as in "the holly and the ivy.") 186 **nigh** deeply, near (to the heart) 188 **warp** freeze so that the surface of the ice cracks and forces up ridges 195 **If that** If 196 **faithfully** persuasively and honestly 197 **doth . . . witness** witnesses the likeness of the dead Sir Rowland 198 **limned** painted 200 **The . . . fortune** The rest of your adventure 204 **s.d. *Exeunt*** (The table must be removed at this point.)
3.1. Location: Duke Frederick's court.
1 **Not . . . since?** i.e., You mean to tell me you claim not to have seen Orlando since the disappearance of Celia and Rosalind? 2 **were . . . mercy** i.e., if I were not a merciful man. (Literally, if I were not composed mostly of mercy.) 3–4 **I . . . present** i.e., I would seek revenge not on the absent Orlando, but on you, who are right here. 6 **Seek . . . candle** i.e., Look for him everywhere, even in the darkest corners. (See Luke 15:8.) 7 **turn** return 10 **we . . . our** (The royal plural.) 11 **quit . . . mouth** acquit yourself by the direct testimony of Orlando. (The Duke suspects that Oliver has murdered Orlando.)

---

143 **Mewling** crying with a catlike noise 149 **bearded . . . pard** having bristling mustaches like the leopard's 150 **Jealous in honor** quick to anger in matters of honor 153 **capon** rooster castrated to make the flesh more tender for eating (and often presented to judges as a bribe) 155 **saws** sayings. **modern instances** commonplace illustrations 157 **pantaloon** ridiculous, enfeebled old man. (A stock type in Italian *commedia dell'arte*.) 160 **shank** calf 162 **his** its 164 **mere oblivion** total forgetfulness 165 **Sans** without 173 **cousin** (A term used by sovereigns to address their nobility.) 180 **rude** rough

OLIVER
Oh, that Your Highness knew my heart in this!
I never loved my brother in my life.

DUKE FREDERICK
More villain thou.—Well, push him out of doors,
And let my officers of such a nature   16
Make an extent upon his house and lands.   17
Do this expediently, and turn him going.   *Exeunt.*   18

❧

3.2

Enter Orlando [with a paper].

ORLANDO
Hang there, my verse, in witness of my love;
    And thou, thrice-crownèd queen of night, survey   2
With thy chaste eye, from thy pale sphere above,
    Thy huntress' name that my full life doth sway.   4
O Rosalind! These trees shall be my books,
    And in their barks my thoughts I'll character,   6
That every eye which in this forest looks
    Shall see thy virtue witnessed everywhere.
Run, run, Orlando, carve on every tree
The fair, the chaste, and unexpressive she.   *Exit.*   10

Enter Corin and [Touchstone the] Clown.

CORIN   And how like you this shepherd's life, Master
Touchstone?

TOUCHSTONE   Truly, shepherd, in respect of itself, it is a   13
good life; but in respect that it is a shepherd's life, it is
naught. In respect that it is solitary, I like it very well;   15
but in respect that it is private, it is a very vile life.
Now in respect it is in the fields, it pleaseth me well;
but in respect it is not in the court, it is tedious. As it
is a spare life, look you, it fits my humor well; but as   19
there is no more plenty in it, it goes much against my
stomach. Hast any philosophy in thee, shepherd?

CORIN   No more but that I know the more one sickens
the worse at ease he is; and that he that wants money,   23
means, and content is without three good friends; that
the property of rain is to wet and fire to burn; that
good pasture makes fat sheep and that a great cause
of the night is lack of the sun; that he that hath learned
no wit by nature nor art may complain of good   28
breeding or comes of a very dull kindred.

TOUCHSTONE   Such a one is a natural philosopher.
Wast ever in court, shepherd?

CORIN   No, truly.

TOUCHSTONE   Then thou art damned.

CORIN   Nay, I hope.   34

TOUCHSTONE   Truly, thou art damned, like an ill-
roasted egg, all on one side.

CORIN   For not being at court? Your reason.

TOUCHSTONE   Why, if thou never wast at court, thou
never saw'st good manners; if thou never saw'st good   39
manners, then thy manners must be wicked; and   40
wickedness is sin, and sin is damnation. Thou art in
a parlous state, shepherd.   42

CORIN   Not a whit, Touchstone. Those that are good
manners at the court are as ridiculous in the country as
the behavior of the country is most mockable at the
court. You told me you salute not at the court but you   46
kiss your hands; that courtesy would be uncleanly, if   47
courtiers were shepherds.

TOUCHSTONE   Instance, briefly; come, instance.   49

CORIN   Why, we are still handling our ewes, and their   50
fells you know are greasy.   51

TOUCHSTONE   Why, do not your courtier's hands sweat?   52
And is not the grease of a mutton as wholesome as the   53
sweat of a man? Shallow, shallow. A better instance, I   54
say. Come.

CORIN   Besides, our hands are hard.

TOUCHSTONE   Your lips will feel them the sooner.
Shallow again. A more sounder instance. Come.

CORIN   And they are often tarred over with the surgery   59
of our sheep; and would you have us kiss tar? The
courtier's hands are perfumed with civet.   61

TOUCHSTONE   Most shallow man! Thou worms'meat, in   62
respect of a good piece of flesh indeed! Learn of the   63
wise, and perpend: civet is of a baser birth than tar,   64
the very uncleanly flux of a cat. Mend the instance,   65
shepherd.

CORIN   You have too courtly a wit for me. I'll rest.

TOUCHSTONE   Wilt thou rest damned? God help thee,
shallow man! God make incision in thee! Thou art   69
raw.   70

CORIN   Sir, I am a true laborer: I earn that I eat, get that   71
I wear, owe no man hate, envy no man's happiness,
glad of other men's good, content with my harm, and   73
the greatest of my pride is to see my ewes graze and
my lambs suck.

TOUCHSTONE   That is another simple sin in you, to bring   76
the ewes and the rams together and to offer to get your   77

---

16 of such a nature who attend to such duties   **17 extent** writ of
seizure   **18 expediently** expeditiously.   **turn him going** send him
packing.
3.2. Location: The forest.
2 thrice-crownèd . . . night i.e., Diana in the three aspects of her
divinity: as Luna or Cynthia, goddess of the moon; as Diana, goddess
on earth; and as Hecate or Proserpina, goddess in the lower world
4 Thy huntress' i.e., Rosalind's, who is here thought of as accompanying Diana, patroness of the hunt and of chastity.   **sway** control.
6 character inscribe   **10 unexpressive** inexpressible   **13 in respect of
itself** considered in and for itself   **15 naught** vile, of no social consequence.   **19 spare** frugal.   **humor** temperament   **23 wants** lacks
28 wit wisdom.   **art** study.   **complain of** lament the lack of

34 hope i.e., hope not.   **39 manners** etiquette   **40 manners** morals
42 parlous perilous   **46 salute** greet   **46–7 but . . . hands** without
kissing the other person's hands   **49 Instance** Proof   **50 still** constantly   **51 fells** skins with the wool, or fleeces   **52 your courtier's**
your typical courtier's   **53–4 And . . . man?** (Human sweat was
thought to be fat oozing from the pores.)   **59 tarred over** anointed
with tar on their cuts and sores   **61 civet** a musky perfume derived
from glands in the anal pouch of the civet cat. (As Touchstone points
out.)   **62–3 Thou . . . indeed!** You miserable creature (literally, you
food for worms, subject to the decay of death), if we compare you
with any worthy sample of humankind!   **64 perpend** consider
65 flux secretion.   **Mend** Improve   **69 incision** a cut, perhaps for the
purpose of letting blood (here, to let out folly); or for seasoning as
raw meat is scored and salted before cooking   **70 raw** (1) wet behind
the ears (2) uncooked (3) afflicted with a raw wound.   **71 earn . . . eat**
earn my living   **73 content . . . harm** patient with my ill fortune
76 simple sin sin arising from simplicity   **77 offer** undertake

living by the copulation of cattle; to be bawd to a bell- 78
wether, and to betray a she-lamb of a twelvemonth to 79
a crooked-pated old cuckoldly ram, out of all reasonable 80
match. If thou be'st not damned for this, the devil him- 81
self will have no shepherds; I cannot see else how thou 82
shouldst scape. 83

CORIN   Here comes young Master Ganymede, my new
mistress's brother.

Enter Rosalind [with a paper, reading].

ROSALIND
"From the east to western Ind,   86
No jewel is like Rosalind.
Her worth, being mounted on the wind,
Through all the world bears Rosalind.
All the pictures fairest lined   90
Are but black to Rosalind.   91
Let no face be kept in mind
But the fair of Rosalind."   93

TOUCHSTONE   I'll rhyme you so eight years together, 94
dinners and suppers and sleeping hours excepted. It 95
is the right butter-women's rank to market. 96

ROSALIND   Out, fool! 97

TOUCHSTONE   For a taste:
If a hart do lack a hind,   99
Let him seek out Rosalind.
If the cat will after kind,   101
So, be sure, will Rosalind.
Wintered garments must be lined,   103
So must slender Rosalind.
They that reap must sheaf and bind;   105
Then to cart with Rosalind.   106
Sweetest nut hath sourest rind;
Such a nut is Rosalind.
He that sweetest rose will find
Must find love's prick and Rosalind.   110

This is the very false gallop of verses. Why do you 111
infect yourself with them?

ROSALIND   Peace, you dull fool! I found them on a tree.

TOUCHSTONE   Truly, the tree yields bad fruit.

ROSALIND   I'll graft it with you, and then I shall graft it 115
with a medlar. Then it will be the earliest fruit i'th' 116
country; for you'll be rotten ere you be half ripe, and
that's the right virtue of the medlar. 118

TOUCHSTONE   You have said; but whether wisely or no,
let the forest judge.

Enter Celia, with a writing.

ROSALIND   Peace! Here comes my sister, reading. Stand
aside.

CELIA [*reads*]
"Why should this a desert be?
For it is unpeopled? No.   124
Tongues I'll hang on every tree,
That shall civil sayings show: 126
Some, how brief the life of man
Runs his erring pilgrimage,   128
That the stretching of a span   129
Buckles in his sum of age;   130
Some, of violated vows
Twixt the souls of friend and friend;
But upon the fairest boughs,
Or at every sentence end,
Will I 'Rosalinda' write,
Teaching all that read to know
The quintessence of every sprite   137
Heaven would in little show.   138
Therefore heaven Nature charged   139
That one body should be filled
With all graces wide-enlarged.   141
Nature presently distilled
Helen's cheek, but not her heart,   143
Cleopatra's majesty,
Atalanta's better part,   145
Sad Lucretia's modesty.   146
Thus Rosalind of many parts
By heavenly synod was devised   148
Of many faces, eyes, and hearts
To have the touches dearest prized.   150
Heaven would that she these gifts should have,   151
And I to live and die her slave."   152

78 cattle livestock   **78–9 bellwether** the leading male sheep of a
flock, wearing a bell   **80 crooked-pated** with crooked horns.
cuckoldly i.e., horned like a cuckold (husband of an unfaithful wife).
out of contrary to   **81–2 If . . . shepherds** i.e., Your only possible
escape from damnation would be if the devil should find shepherds
too objectionable to have in hell under any circumstances   **83 scape**
escape.   **86 Ind** Indies   **90 lined** drawn   **91 black to** dark-complec-
tioned and hence ugly compared to   **93 fair** beauty   **94 together**
without stop   **95–6 It is . . . market** i.e., The rhymes, all alike, follow
each other precisely like a line of butter women or dairy women jogging along to market.   **97 Out** (An exclamation here denoting comic
indignation.)   **99 If . . . hind** If a male deer longs for a female deer.
(Touchstone wryly suggests in his verses that Rosalind is the responsive object of male desire.)   **101 after kind** follow its natural instinct
103 Wintered Old, worn; used in winter.   **lined** (1) given a winter
lining (2) stuffed. (The term was sometimes used for the copulating of
dogs.)   **105 sheaf and bind** tie in a bundle   **106 to cart** (1) onto the
harvest cart (2) onto the cart used to carry prostitutes through the
streets, exposing them to public ridicule   **110 prick** thorn. (With
bawdy suggestion.)   **111 false gallop** canter

115 you (With a pun on "yew.")   **116 medlar** a fruit like a small
brown-skinned apple that is eaten when it starts to decay. (With a
pun on "meddler.")   **118 right virtue** true quality   **124 For** Because
126 civil sayings maxims of civilized life   **128 his erring** its wandering   **129–30 That . . . age** i.e., so that a very brief span encompasses
his whole life. (A *span* is a handbreadth. See Psalm 39:5.)   **137 quintessence** highest perfection. (Literally, the fifth essence or element of
the medieval alchemists, purer even than fire.)   **sprite** spirit
138 Heaven . . . show that heaven wishes to show in one small person, Rosalind (who, in microcosm, embodies the supreme essence of
the heavens, or macrocosm).   **139 heaven . . . charged** heaven commanded Nature   **141 wide-enlarged** all-encompassing   **143 Helen's
. . . heart** i.e., the beauty of Helen of Troy but not her false heart
145 Atalanta's better part i.e., her beauty or her fleetness of foot, not
her scornfulness and greed. (She refused to marry any man who was
unable to defeat her in a foot race and, when challenged by Hippomenes, lost to him because Hippomenes dropped in her way three
golden apples of the Hesperides.)   **146 Lucretia** an honorable Roman
lady raped by Tarquin (whose story Shakespeare tells in *The Rape of
Lucrece*).   **148 synod** assembly   **150 touches** traits   **151 would**
decree   **152 And I to** and that I should

ROSALIND   Oh, most gentle Jupiter, what tedious homily 153
of love have you wearied your parishioners withal,
and never cried, "Have patience, good people!"

CELIA   How now? Back, friends. Shepherd, go off a 156
little. [To Touchstone] Go with him, sirrah.   157

TOUCHSTONE   Come, shepherd, let us make an honorable retreat, though not with bag and baggage, yet 159
with scrip and scrippage.   Exit [with Corin]. 160

CELIA   Didst thou hear these verses?

ROSALIND   Oh, yes, I heard them all, and more, too, for
some of them had in them more feet than the verses
would bear.

CELIA   That's no matter. The feet might bear the verses.

ROSALIND   Ay, but the feet were lame and could not
bear themselves without the verse and therefore stood 167
lamely in the verse.

CELIA   But didst thou hear without wondering how thy
name should be hanged and carved upon these trees?

ROSALIND   I was seven of the nine days out of the 171
wonder before you came; for look here what I found 172
on a palm tree. I was never so berhymed since
Pythagoras' time, that I was an Irish rat, which I can 174
hardly remember.

CELIA   Trow you who hath done this?   176

ROSALIND   Is it a man?

CELIA   And a chain that you once wore about his neck. 178
Change you color?

ROSALIND   I prithee, who?

CELIA   Oh, Lord, Lord, it is a hard matter for friends to 181
meet; but mountains may be removed with earth- 182
quakes and so encounter.   183

ROSALIND   Nay, but who is it?

CELIA   Is it possible?   185

ROSALIND   Nay, I prithee now with most petitionary
vehemence, tell me who it is.

CELIA   Oh, wonderful, wonderful, and most wonderful,
wonderful! And yet again wonderful, and after that,
out of all whooping!   190

ROSALIND   Good my complexion! Dost thou think, 191
though I am caparisoned like a man, I have a doublet 192
and hose in my disposition? One inch of delay more 193
is a South Sea of discovery. I prithee, tell me who is it 194
quickly, and speak apace. I would thou couldst stam-

mer, that thou mightst pour this concealed man out of
thy mouth as wine comes out of a narrow-mouthed
bottle, either too much at once or none at all. I prithee,
take the cork out of thy mouth that I may drink thy
tidings.

CELIA   So you may put a man in your belly.   201

ROSALIND   Is he of God's making? What manner of 202
man? Is his head worth a hat, or his chin worth a
beard?

CELIA   Nay, he hath but a little beard.

ROSALIND   Why, God will send more, if the man will be
thankful. Let me stay the growth of his beard, if thou 207
delay me not the knowledge of his chin.

CELIA   It is young Orlando, that tripped up the wrestler's heels and your heart both in an instant.

ROSALIND   Nay, but the devil take mocking. Speak sad 211
brow and true maid.   212

CELIA   I'faith, coz, 'tis he.

ROSALIND   Orlando?

CELIA   Orlando.

ROSALIND   Alas the day, what shall I do with my
doublet and hose? What did he when thou saw'st him?
What said he? How looked he? Wherein went he? 218
What makes he here? Did he ask for me? Where 219
remains he? How parted he with thee? And when 220
shalt thou see him again? Answer me in one word.

CELIA   You must borrow me Gargantua's mouth first; 222
'tis a word too great for any mouth of this age's size.
To say ay and no to these particulars is more than to 224
answer in a catechism.   225

ROSALIND   But doth he know that I am in this forest
and in man's apparel? Looks he as freshly as he did
the day he wrestled?

CELIA   It is as easy to count atomies as to resolve the 229
propositions of a lover. But take a taste of my finding 230
him, and relish it with good observance. I found him 231
under a tree, like a dropped acorn.

ROSALIND   It may well be called Jove's tree, when it 233
drops forth such fruit.

CELIA   Give me audience, good madam.   235

ROSALIND   Proceed.

CELIA   There lay he, stretched along, like a wounded
knight.

ROSALIND   Though it be pity to see such a sight, it well
becomes the ground.   240

CELIA   Cry "holla" to thy tongue, I prithee; it curvets 241
unseasonably. He was furnished like a hunter.   242

153 Jupiter (Often emended to "pulpiter.")   **156 Back** i.e., Move back,
away. (Addressed to Corin and Touchstone.)   **157 sirrah** a form of
address to inferiors (here, Touchstone).   **159 bag and baggage** i.e.,
equipment appropriate to a retreating army   **160 scrip and scrippage**
shepherd's pouch and its contents.   **167 without** (1) without the help
of (2) outside   **171–2 seven . . . wonder** (A reference to the common
phrase "a nine days' wonder.")   **174 Pythagoras** Greek philosopher
credited with the doctrine of the transmigration of souls.   **that** when.
Irish rat (Refers to a current belief that Irish enchanters could rhyme
rats and other animals to death.)   **which** a thing which   **176 Trow
you** Have you any idea   **178 And a chain** And with a chain   **181–3 it
is . . . encounter** (A playful inversion of the proverb, "Friends may
meet, but mountains never greet." Celia appears to be teasing Rosalind's eagerness to meet Orlando.)   **removed with** moved by
185 possible i.e., possible you don't know   **190 out . . . whooping**
beyond all power to utter.   **191 Good my complexion!** Oh, my (feminine) temperament, my woman's curiosity!   **192 caparisoned**
bedecked. (Usually said of a horse.)   **192–3 I have . . . disposition?**
i.e., that I have a man's patience?   **194 a South Sea of discovery** i.e.,
as tedious as a long exploratory voyage to the South Pacific Ocean.

201 belly (1) stomach (2) womb.   **202 of God's making** i.e., a real
man, not of a tailor's making.   **207 stay** wait for   **211–12 sad . . .
maid** i.e., seriously and truthfully.   **218 Wherein went he?** In what
clothes was he dressed?   **219 makes** does   **220 remains** dwells
222 Gargantua's mouth (Gargantua is the giant of popular literature
who, in Rabelais' novel, swallowed five pilgrims in a salad.)
224–5 To . . . catechism To give even yes and no answers to these
questions would take longer than to go through the catechism (i.e.,
the formal questioning used in the Church to teach the principles of
faith).   **229 atomies** motes, specks of dirt   **230 propositions** questions   **231 relish it** heighten its pleasant taste.   **observance** attention.   **233 Jove's tree** the oak   **235 Give me audience** Listen to me
240 becomes adorns   **241 holla** stop.   **curvets** prances   **242 furnished** equipped, dressed

ROSALIND Oh, ominous! He comes to kill my heart. 243

CELIA I would sing my song without a burden. Thou 244
bring'st me out of tune. 245

ROSALIND Do you not know I am a woman? When I
think, I must speak. Sweet, say on.

Enter Orlando and Jaques.

CELIA You bring me out.—Soft, comes he not here? 248

ROSALIND 'Tis he. Slink by, and note him.
[They stand aside and listen.]

JAQUES *[to Orlando]* I thank you for your company,
but, good faith, I had as lief have been myself alone.

ORLANDO And so had I; but yet, for fashion sake, I 252
thank you too for your society.

JAQUES God b'wi'you. Let's meet as little as we can. 254

ORLANDO I do desire we may be better strangers.

JAQUES I pray you, mar no more trees with writing
love songs in their barks.

ORLANDO I pray you, mar no more of my verses with
reading them ill-favoredly. 259

JAQUES Rosalind is your love's name?

ORLANDO Yes, just. 261

JAQUES I do not like her name.

ORLANDO There was no thought of pleasing you when
she was christened.

JAQUES What stature is she of?

ORLANDO Just as high as my heart.

JAQUES You are full of pretty answers. Have you not
been acquainted with goldsmiths' wives, and conned 268
them out of rings? 269

ORLANDO Not so; but I answer you right painted cloth, 270
from whence you have studied your questions.

JAQUES You have a nimble wit; I think 'twas made of
Atalanta's heels. Will you sit down with me? And we 273
two will rail against our mistress the world and all our
misery.

ORLANDO I will chide no breather in the world but 276
myself, against whom I know most faults.

JAQUES The worst fault you have is to be in love.

ORLANDO 'Tis a fault I will not change for your best
virtue. I am weary of you.

JAQUES By my troth, I was seeking for a fool when I
found you.

ORLANDO He is drowned in the brook. Look but in,
and you shall see him.

JAQUES There I shall see mine own figure. 285

ORLANDO Which I take to be either a fool or a cipher. 286

JAQUES I'll tarry no longer with you. Farewell, good
Seigneur Love.

ORLANDO I am glad of your departure. Adieu, good
Monsieur Melancholy. *[Exit Jaques.]*

ROSALIND *[aside to Celia]* I will speak to him like a
saucy lackey and under that habit play the knave 292
with him.—Do you hear, forester?

ORLANDO Very well. What would you?

ROSALIND I pray you, what is't o'clock?

ORLANDO You should ask me what time o' day.
There's no clock in the forest.

ROSALIND Then there is no true lover in the forest, else
sighing every minute and groaning every hour would
detect the lazy foot of Time as well as a clock. 300

ORLANDO And why not the swift foot of Time? Had
not that been as proper?

ROSALIND By no means, sir. Time travels in divers
paces with divers persons. I'll tell you who Time
ambles withal, who Time trots withal, who Time 305
gallops withal, and who he stands still withal.

ORLANDO I prithee, who doth he trot withal?

ROSALIND Marry, he trots hard with a young maid
between the contract of her marriage and the day it is
solemnized. If the interim be but a se'nnight, Time's 310
pace is so hard that it seems the length of seven year.

ORLANDO Who ambles Time withal?

ROSALIND With a priest that lacks Latin and a rich man
that hath not the gout, for the one sleeps easily
because he cannot study and the other lives merrily
because he feels no pain, the one lacking the burden of
lean and wasteful learning, the other knowing no 317
burden of heavy tedious penury. These Time ambles
withal.

ORLANDO Who doth he gallop withal?

ROSALIND With a thief to the gallows, for though he go
as softly as foot can fall, he thinks himself too soon
there.

ORLANDO Who stays it still withal?

ROSALIND With lawyers in the vacation; for they sleep
between term and term, and then they perceive not 326
how Time moves.

ORLANDO Where dwell you, pretty youth?

ROSALIND With this shepherdess, my sister, here in the
skirts of the forest, like fringe upon a petticoat.

ORLANDO Are you native of this place?

ROSALIND As the coney that you see dwell where she is 332
kindled. 333

ORLANDO Your accent is something finer than you 334
could purchase in so removed a dwelling. 334

ROSALIND I have been told so of many. But indeed an
old religious uncle of mine taught me to speak, who 337
was in his youth an inland man, one that knew 338
courtship too well, for there he fell in love. I have 339

243 **heart** (With pun on "hart.") 244 **burden** refrain, or bass part.
244–5 **Thou bring'st** You put 248 **Soft** i.e., Wait a minute, or, stop
talking 252 **fashion** fashion's 254 **God b'wi'you** God be with you,
good-bye 259 **ill-favoredly** unsympathetically. 261 **just** just so.
268 **conned** memorized 269 **rings** (Verses or "posies" were often
inscribed in rings.) 270 **right painted cloth** in the true spirit of a
painted cloth decorated with commonplace pictures and cliché mottoes (frequently mythological or scriptural) 273 **Atalanta's heels**
(See above, the note for line 145.) 276 **breather** living being
285 **figure** reflection. (Narcissus fell in love with his own reflection in
a pool.) 286 **cipher** nonentity, zero.

292 **and under . . . knave** and in that disguise (1) pose as a boy
(2) deal mischievously 300 **detect** reveal 305 **withal** with
310 **se'nnight** week 317 **lean** unremunerative. **wasteful** making
one waste away 326 **term** court session 332 **coney** rabbit 333 **kindled** littered, born. 334 **something** somewhat 335 **purchase**
acquire. **removed** remote 337 **religious** i.e., belonging to a religious order 338 **inland** from a center of civilization 339 **courtship**
(1) wooing (2) knowledge of courtly manners

heard him read many lectures against it, and I thank 340 God I am not a woman, to be touched with so many 341 giddy offences as he hath generally taxed their whole sex withal.

ORLANDO   Can you remember any of the principal evils that he laid to the charge of women?

ROSALIND   There were none principal; they were all like one another as halfpence are, every one fault seeming monstrous till his fellow fault came to match it. 348

ORLANDO   I prithee, recount some of them.

ROSALIND   No, I will not cast away my physic but on 350 those that are sick. There is a man haunts the forest that abuses our young plants with carving "Rosalind" on their barks, hangs odes upon hawthorns and elegies on brambles, all, forsooth, deifying the name of Rosalind. If I could meet that fancy-monger, I would 355 give him some good counsel, for he seems to have the quotidian of love upon him. 357

ORLANDO   I am he that is so love-shaked. I pray you, tell me your remedy.

ROSALIND   There is none of my uncle's marks upon you. He taught me how to know a man in love, in which cage of rushes I am sure you are not prisoner. 362

ORLANDO   What were his marks?

ROSALIND   A lean cheek, which you have not; a blue eye 364 and sunken, which you have not; an unquestionable 365 spirit, which you have not; a beard neglected, which you have not—but I pardon you for that, for simply 367 your having in beard is a younger brother's revenue. 368 Then your hose should be ungartered, your bonnet un- 369 banded, your sleeve unbuttoned, your shoe untied, 370 and everything about you demonstrating a careless desolation. But you are no such man. You are rather point-device in your accoutrements, as loving your- 373 self, than seeming the lover of any other.

ORLANDO   Fair youth, I would I could make thee believe I love.

ROSALIND   Me believe it? You may as soon make her that you love believe it, which I warrant she is apter to do than to confess she does. That is one of the points in the which women still give the lie to their con- 380 sciences. But in good sooth, are you he that hangs the 381 verses on the trees, wherein Rosalind is so admired?

ORLANDO   I swear to thee, youth, by the white hand of Rosalind, I am that he, that unfortunate he.

ROSALIND   But are you so much in love as your rhymes speak?

ORLANDO   Neither rhyme nor reason can express how much.

ROSALIND   Love is merely a madness and, I tell you, 390 deserves as well a dark house and a whip as madmen 391 do; and the reason why they are not so punished and cured is that the lunacy is so ordinary that the whippers are in love too. Yet I profess curing it by 394 counsel.

ORLANDO   Did you ever cure any so?

ROSALIND   Yes, one, and in this manner. He was to imagine me his love, his mistress; and I set him every day to woo me. At which time would I, being but a moonish youth, grieve, be effeminate, changeable, 399 longing and liking, proud, fantastical, apish, shallow, inconstant, full of tears, full of smiles; for every passion something and for no passion truly anything, as boys and women are for the most part cattle of this color; would now like him, now loathe him; then entertain 404 him, then forswear him; now weep for him, then spit at him; that I drave my suitor from his mad humor of 406 love to a living humor of madness, which was to for- 407 swear the full stream of the world and to live in a nook merely monastic. And thus I cured him; and this way 409 will I take upon me to wash your liver as clean as a 410 sound sheep's heart, that there shall not be one spot of love in't.

ORLANDO   I would not be cured, youth.

ROSALIND   I would cure you, if you would but call me Rosalind and come every day to my cote and woo me. 415

ORLANDO   Now by the faith of my love, I will. Tell me where it is.

ROSALIND   Go with me to it, and I'll show it you; and by the way you shall tell me where in the forest you 419 live. Will you go?

ORLANDO   With all my heart, good youth.

ROSALIND   Nay, you must call me Rosalind.—Come, sister, will you go?   *Exeunt.*

✦

3.3

Enter [Touchstone the] Clown, Audrey; and Jaques [apart].

TOUCHSTONE   Come apace, good Audrey. I will fetch up 1 your goats, Audrey. And how, Audrey, am I the man 2 yet? Doth my simple feature content you? 3

AUDREY   Your features, Lord warrant us! What features? 4

TOUCHSTONE   I am here with thee and thy goats, as the most capricious poet, honest Ovid, was among the 6 Goths. 7

---

340 read many lectures deliver many admonitory speeches **341 touched** tainted   **348 his** its   **350 physic** medicine   **355 fancy-monger** love peddler   **357 quotidian** fever recurring daily. (See *love-shaked*, line 358).   **362 cage of rushes** i.e., flimsy prison   **364 blue eye** i.e., having dark circles   **365 unquestionable** unwilling to be conversed with   **367–8 simply . . . revenue** what beard you have is like a younger brother's inheritance (i.e., small)   **369–70 bonnet unbanded** hat lacking a band around the crown   **373 point-device** faultless **380 still** continually   **381 good sooth** honest truth

390 merely utterly   **391 dark . . . whip** (The common treatment of lunatics.)   **394 profess** am expert in   **399 moonish** changeable **404 entertain** receive cordially   **406 that** with the result that.   **drave** drove   **406–7 mad . . . madness** mad fancy of love to a real madness **409 merely** utterly   **410 liver** (Supposed seat of the emotions, especially love.)   **415 cote** cottage   **419 by** on **3.3 Location: The forest.** **1 apace** quickly   **2 And how** i.e., What do you say   **3 simple feature** plain appearance. (But Audrey, in her answer, may have her mind on *features* as "parts of the body.")   **4 warrant** protect   **6 capricious** witty, fanciful. (Derived from the Latin *caper,* "male goat"; hence, "goatish, lascivious.")   **7 Goths** (With pun on "goats"; the two words were pronounced alike.)

JAQUES [*aside*]   Oh, knowledge ill-inhabited, worse than   8
Jove in a thatched house!   9

TOUCHSTONE   When a man's verses cannot be under-   10
stood, nor a man's good wit seconded with the   11
forward child, understanding, it strikes a man more   12
dead than a great reckoning in a little room. Truly, I   13
would the gods had made thee poetical.

AUDREY   I do not know what "poetical" is. Is it honest
in deed and word? Is it a true thing?

TOUCHSTONE   No, truly; for the truest poetry is the most
feigning, and lovers are given to poetry, and what   18
they swear in poetry may be said as lovers they do   19
feign.   20

AUDREY   Do you wish then that the gods had made me
poetical?

TOUCHSTONE   I do, truly; for thou swear'st to me thou
art honest. Now, if thou wert a poet, I might have   24
some hope thou didst feign.   25

AUDREY   Would you not have me honest?

TOUCHSTONE   No, truly, unless thou wert hard-   27
favored; for honesty coupled to beauty is to have   28
honey a sauce to sugar.

JAQUES [*aside*]   A material fool!   30

AUDREY   Well, I am not fair, and therefore I pray the
gods make me honest.

TOUCHSTONE   Truly, and to cast away honesty upon a
foul slut were to put good meat into an unclean dish.   34

AUDREY   I am not a slut, though I thank the gods I am   35
foul.   36

TOUCHSTONE   Well, praised be the gods for thy foulness!
Sluttishness may come hereafter. But be it as it
may be, I will marry thee, and to that end I have been
with Sir Oliver Mar-text, the vicar of the next village,   40
who hath promised to meet me in this place of the
forest and to couple us.

JAQUES [*aside*]   I would fain see this meeting.   43

AUDREY   Well, the gods give us joy!

TOUCHSTONE   Amen. A man may, if he were of a
fearful heart, stagger in this attempt; for here we have   46
no temple but the wood, no assembly but horn-beasts.   47

But what though? Courage! As horns are odious, they   48
are necessary. It is said, "Many a man knows no end   49
of his goods." Right! Many a man has good horns and   50
knows no end of them. Well, that is the dowry of his   51
wife; 'tis none of his own getting. Horns? Even so.   52
Poor men alone? No, no, the noblest deer hath them   53
as huge as the rascal. Is the single man therefore   54
blessed? No. As a walled town is more worthier than
a village, so is the forehead of a married man more
honorable than the bare brow of a bachelor; and by
how much defense is better than no skill, by so much   58
is a horn more precious than to want.   59

Enter Sir Oliver Mar-text.

Here comes Sir Oliver.—Sir Oliver Mar-text, you are
well met. Will you dispatch us here under this tree, or   61
shall we go with you to your chapel?

SIR OLIVER   Is there none here to give the woman?   63

TOUCHSTONE   I will not take her on gift of any man.

SIR OLIVER   Truly, she must be given, or the marriage is
not lawful.

JAQUES [*advancing*]   Proceed, proceed. I'll give her.

TOUCHSTONE   Good even, good Master What-ye-call-'t.   68
How do you, sir? You are very well met. God 'ild you   69
for your last company. I am very glad to see you. Even   70
a toy in hand here, sir.—Nay, pray be covered.   71

JAQUES   Will you be married, motley?

TOUCHSTONE   As the ox hath his bow, sir, the horse his   73
curb, and the falcon her bells, so man hath his desires;   74
and as pigeons bill, so wedlock would be nibbling.   75

JAQUES   And will you, being a man of your breeding,
be married under a bush like a beggar? Get you to   77
church, and have a good priest that can tell you what   78
marriage is. This fellow will but join you together as   79
they join wainscot; then one of you will prove a
shrunk panel and, like green timber, warp, warp.   81

---

8 ill-inhabited ill-lodged   **9 Jove . . . house!** (An allusion to Ovid's
Metamorphoses 8, containing the story of Jupiter and Mercury lodging
disguised in the humble cottage of Baucis and Philemon.)
10–11 verses . . . understood (Ovid's verses were misunderstood by
the barbaric Goths, among whom he lived in exile, just as Touchstone's wit is misunderstood by Audrey.)   **11–12 nor . . . understanding** (Wisdom, understanding, and memory were thought to occupy
three main ventricles in the brain, and to be interconnected in the
process of thought. *Forward* means "precocious.")   **13 great . . . room**
exorbitant charge for refreshment or lodging in a cramped tavern
room. (Some scholars see in this passage an allusion to the death of
Christopher Marlowe, who was stabbed by Ingram Frysar at an inn
in Deptford in a quarrel over a tavern reckoning, May 30, 1593.)
18 feigning inventive, imaginative. (But Touchstone plays on the
sense of "false, lying.")   **19 may be said** i.e., it may be said   **20 feign**
(With a further play on "desire.")   **24 honest** chaste.   **25 feign**
(1) pretend (2) desire.   **27–8 hard-favored** ugly   **28 honesty** chastity
30 material full of pithy matter   **34 foul** ugly   **35–6 I thank . . . foul**
i.e., my unattractive looks are what destiny has allotted to me.
40 Sir (Courtesy title for a clergyman.)   **43 fain** gladly   **46 stagger**
hesitate   **47 horn-beasts** antlered animals like deer and cattle, and
therefore resembling cuckolded men with their cuckolds' horns.

48 what though what though it be so.   **As** Though   **49 necessary**
(1) useful to horned animals (2) unavoidable to cuckolds.
49–50 knows . . . goods is endlessly well provided.   **51 knows . . .
them** i.e., is endlessly supplied with cuckold's horns. (A sardonic
interpretation of the proverb in lines 49–50.)   **dowry** marriage gift
52 getting (1) obtaining (2) begetting (in the sense that his wife's children will not be his).   **Even so** That's just how it is.   **53 deer**
(1) horned animal (2) dear husband   **54 rascal** (1) young deer that are
lean and out of season (2) poor ordinary husband.   **single** unmarried
58 defense (1) fortifications (including a type known as "hornwork")
(2) the art of self-defense   **59 than to want** i.e., than to be without a
horn. (Recalling the "horn of plenty," which is indeed precious.)
61 dispatch us finish off our business   **63 give the woman** give away
the bride; conventionally, the bride's father answered the question,
"Who giveth this woman to be married to this man?"   **68 What-ye-
call-'t** (Probably joking on *Jakes* as "outhouse.")   **69 'ild you** yield
you, reward you   **70 last** most recent   **71 a toy in hand** a trifle to be
attended to, or literally by the hand.   **be covered** put on your hat,
i.e., no need to show respect; or, cover up your bosom. (Said to
Audrey, or perhaps to Jaques, who may have removed his hat in sardonic deference to the ceremony.)   **73 bow** yoke   **74 curb** chain or
strap attached to the horse's bit and used to control it.   **bells**
(Attached to a falcon's leg during training.)   **75 bill** stroke bill with
bill   **77 under a bush** i.e., by a "hedge-priest," an uneducated clergyman   **78–9 tell . . . is** expound the obligations of marriage   **81 warp**
(1) shrivel and fit badly together (2) stray from the true path.

TOUCHSTONE   I am not in the mind but I were better 82
to be married of him than of another, for he is not 83
like to marry me well; and not being well married, 84
it will be a good excuse for me hereafter to leave my
wife.

JAQUES   Go thou with me, and let me counsel thee.

TOUCHSTONE
Come, sweet Audrey.
We must be married, or we must live in bawdry. 89
Farewell, good Master Oliver; not
      "O sweet Oliver, 91
      O brave Oliver, 92
   Leave me not behind thee";
but
      "Wind away, 95
      Begone, I say,
   I will not to wedding with thee." 97
            [*Exeunt Jaques, Touchstone, and Audrey.*]

SIR OLIVER   'Tis no matter. Ne'er a fantastical knave of 98
them all shall flout me out of my calling.   *Exit.*

❖

3.4

Enter Rosalind and Celia.

ROSALIND   Never talk to me. I will weep.

CELIA   Do, I prithee, but yet have the grace to consider
that tears do not become a man.

ROSALIND   But have I not cause to weep?

CELIA   As good cause as one would desire; therefore
weep.

ROSALIND   His very hair is of the dissembling color. 7

CELIA   Something browner than Judas's. Marry, his 8
kisses are Judas's own children. 9

ROSALIND   I'faith, his hair is of a good color.

CELIA   An excellent color. Your chestnut was ever the 11
only color. 12

ROSALIND   And his kissing is as full of sanctity as the
touch of holy bread. 14

CELIA   He hath bought a pair of cast lips of Diana. A 15
nun of winter's sisterhood kisses not more religiously; 16
the very ice of chastity is in them.

ROSALIND   But why did he swear he would come this
morning, and comes not?

CELIA   Nay, certainly, there is no truth in him.

ROSALIND   Do you think so?

CELIA   Yes. I think he is not a pickpurse nor a horse-
stealer, but for his verity in love, I do think him as
concave as a covered goblet or a worm-eaten nut. 24

ROSALIND   Not true in love?

CELIA   Yes, when he is in, but I think he is not in.

ROSALIND   You have heard him swear downright he
was.

CELIA   "Was" is not "is." Besides, the oath of a lover is
no stronger than the word of a tapster; they are both
the confirmer of false reckonings. He attends here in 31
the forest on the Duke your father.

ROSALIND   I met the Duke yesterday and had much
question with him. He asked me of what parentage I 34
was. I told him, of as good as he; so he laughed and let
me go. But what talk we of fathers, when there is such 36
a man as Orlando?

CELIA   Oh, that's a brave man! He writes brave verses, 38
speaks brave words, swears brave oaths, and breaks
them bravely, quite traverse, athwart the heart of his 40
lover, as a puny tilter, that spurs his horse but on 41
one side, breaks his staff like a noble goose. But all's 42
brave that youth mounts and folly guides. Who comes 43
here?

Enter Corin.

CORIN
Mistress and master, you have oft inquired
After the shepherd that complained of love, 46
Who you saw sitting by me on the turf,
Praising the proud disdainful shepherdess
That was his mistress.

CELIA   Well, and what of him?

CORIN
If you will see a pageant truly played
Between the pale complexion of true love 51
And the red glow of scorn and proud disdain,
Go hence a little, and I shall conduct you,
If you will mark it.

ROSALIND   Oh, come, let us remove! 54
The sight of lovers feedeth those in love.
Bring us to this sight, and you shall say
I'll prove a busy actor in their play.   *Exeunt.*

---

82 **I am ... better** I do not know but that it would be better for me.
(Touchstone may be speaking aside here.)   83 **of** by   84 **like** likely.
well (1) suitably (2) legally   89 **married** i.e., properly married, as
Jaques suggests, not by a hedge-priest. (Having been found out,
Touchstone wryly defers matters for the present.)   91–7 **"O ... thee."**
(Phrases from a current ballad.)   92 **brave** worthy   95 **Wind** Wend,
go   98 **fantastical** affected
3.4 Location: The forest.
7 **the dissembling color** i.e., reddish, traditionally the color of Judas's
hair.   8 **Something** Somewhat   9 **Judas's own children** i.e., as false
and betraying as the kiss given by Judas to Jesus when he betrayed
him to the high priests.   11 **Your chestnut** i.e., This chestnut color
that people talk about   12 **only** only fashionable   14 **holy bread**
either the unleavened bread of the Eucharist or ordinary leavened
bread that was blessed after the Eucharist and distributed to those
who had not received communion.   15 **cast** (1) chaste, cold
(2) molded, or (3) cast off.   **Diana** goddess of chastity.   16 **of winter's sisterhood** i.e., devoted to barrenness and cold

24 **concave** hollow, i.e., insincere   31 **false reckonings** (Tapsters, or
barkeeps, were notorious for inflating bills.)   34 **question** conversation   36 **what** why   38 **brave** fine, excellent   40 **traverse** across,
awry. (A term from medieval jousting or tilting; hence *tilters*, line 41.)
41 **puny** inexperienced. (Literally, junior.)   **but** only   42 **a noble
goose** i.e., a goose-headed young gallent.   42–3 **But ... guides** But
everything is admirable that youth undertakes under the influence
of folly. (Said sardonically.)   46 **complained of** uttered a lament
against   51 **pale complexion** (Sighing was believed to draw the
blood from the heart.)   54 **will mark** wish to observe.   **remove**
leave here and go.

3.5

Enter Silvius and Phoebe.

SILVIUS
Sweet Phoebe, do not scorn me, do not, Phoebe!
Say that you love me not, but say not so
In bitterness. The common executioner,
Whose heart th'accustomed sight of death makes
    hard,
Falls not the ax upon the humbled neck   5
But first begs pardon. Will you sterner be   6
Than he that dies and lives by bloody drops?   7

Enter Rosalind, Celia, and Corin [behind].

PHOEBE
I would not be thy executioner;
I fly thee, for I would not injure thee.
Thou tell'st me there is murder in mine eye.
'Tis pretty, sure, and very probable,   11
That eyes, that are the frail'st and softest things,
Who shut their coward gates on atomies,   13
Should be called tyrants, butchers, murderers!
Now I do frown on thee with all my heart,
And if mine eyes can wound, now let them kill thee.
Now counterfeit to swoon; why, now fall down,
Or if thou canst not, oh, for shame, for shame,
Lie not, to say mine eyes are murderers!   19
Now show the wound mine eye hath made in thee.
Scratch thee but with a pin, and there remains
Some scar of it; lean upon a rush,   22
The cicatrice and capable impressure   23
Thy palm some moment keeps; but now mine eyes,   24
Which I have darted at thee, hurt thee not,
Nor, I am sure, there is no force in eyes
That can do hurt.
SILVIUS   O dear Phoebe,
If ever—as that "ever" may be near—
You meet in some fresh cheek the power of fancy,   29
Then shall you know the wounds invisible
That love's keen arrows make.
PHOEBE   But till that time
Come not thou near me; and when that time comes,
Afflict me with thy mocks; pity me not,
As till that time I shall not pity thee.   34
ROSALIND *[advancing]*
And why, I pray you? Who might be your mother,   35
That you insult, exult, and all at once,   36

Over the wretched? What though you have no
    beauty—   37
As, by my faith, I see no more in you   38
Than without candle may go dark to bed—   39
Must you be therefore proud and pitiless?
Why, what means this? Why do you look on me?
I see no more in you than in the ordinary   42
Of nature's sale-work. 'Od's my little life,   43
I think she means to tangle my eyes too!   44
No, faith, proud mistress, hope not after it.
'Tis not your inky brows, your black silk hair,
Your bugle eyeballs, nor your cheek of cream   47
That can entame my spirits to your worship.   48
[To Silvius] You foolish shepherd, wherefore do you
    follow her,
Like foggy south, puffing with wind and rain?   50
You are a thousand times a properer man   51
Than she a woman. 'Tis such fools as you
That makes the world full of ill-favored children.   53
'Tis not her glass, but you, that flatters her,   54
And out of you she sees herself more proper   55
Than any of her lineaments can show her.—   56
But, mistress, know yourself. Down on your knees,
And thank heaven, fasting, for a good man's love!
For I must tell you friendly in your ear,
Sell when you can. You are not for all markets.
Cry the man mercy, love him, take his offer;   61
Foul is most foul, being foul to be a scoffer.—   62
So take her to thee, shepherd. Fare you well.
PHOEBE
Sweet youth, I pray you, chide a year together.   64
I had rather hear you chide than this man woo.
ROSALIND *[to Phoebe]*   He's fallen in love with your foulness, *[to Silvius]* and she'll fall in love with my anger. If it be so, as fast as she answers thee with frowning looks, I'll sauce her with bitter words. *[To*   69 *Phoebe]* Why look you so upon me?
PHOEBE   For no ill will I bear you.
ROSALIND
I pray you, do not fall in love with me,
For I am falser than vows made in wine.   73
Besides, I like you not. *[To Silvius]* If you will know
    my house,
'Tis at the tuft of olives here hard by.—
Will you go, sister?—Shepherd, ply her hard.—

3.5 Location: The forest.
5 Falls lets fall   **6 But first begs pardon** without first begging pardon (as executioners did in Elizabethan times).   **7 dies . . . drops** makes his living by the deaths of others. (Stated as an oxymoron.)   **11 sure** to be sure   **13 coward gates on atomies** i.e., sensitive eyelids to protect against specks of dirt   **19 to say** by saying   **22 a rush** a reed **23–4 The cicatrice . . . keeps** the scarlike and perceptible impression is retained by one's palm for a moment   **29 You . . . fancy** you yourself feel the powerful spell of love for some new face   **34 As** since **35 Who . . . mother** (1) What human mother could have produced so inhuman a daughter (2) From what sort of a mother did you learn such scorn   **36 insult** exult scornfully.   **all at once** all at the same time

37 have no beauty are not particularly beautiful   **38–9 I see . . . bed** i.e., I see nothing in your beauty that might not go entirely unnoticed, nothing to distinguish you from other young women   **42 ordinary** common run   **43 sale-work** ready-made products, not of the best quality, not distinctive.   **'Od's** May God save   **44 tangle** ensnare **47 bugle** beadlike, black and glassy   **48 to your worship** (1) to the worship of you (2) to adore Your Worship (as such beauty deserved an honorific title).   **50 south** south wind (from which came fog and rain; hence, Silvius's sighs and tears)   **51 properer** better-looking (since handsome is as handsome does)   **53 ill-favored** ugly **54 glass** mirror   **55 out of you** i.e., with you as her mirror   **56 lineaments** features   **61 Cry . . . mercy** Beg the man's pardon   **62 Foul . . . scoffer** i.e., unattractive behavior like yours is at its most foul when it consists of scoffing. (Plays on two meanings of *foul*.)   **64 together** without intermission.   **69 sauce** rebuke   **73 in wine** while drunk.

Come, sister.—Shepherdess, look on him better, 76
And be not proud. Though all the world could see,
None could be so abused in sight as he.— 78
Come, to our flock.   *Exit [with Celia and Corin].* 79

PHOEBE
Dead shepherd, now I find thy saw of might,
"Who ever loved that loved not at first sight?" 81

SILVIUS   82
Sweet Phoebe—

PHOEBE   Ha, what say'st thou, Silvius?

SILVIUS   Sweet Phoebe, pity me.

PHOEBE
Why, I am sorry for thee, gentle Silvius.

SILVIUS
Wherever sorrow is, relief would be.
If you do sorrow at my grief in love,
By giving love, your sorrow and my grief 86
Were both extermined.

PHOEBE   89
Thou hast my love. Is not that neighborly?

SILVIUS   90
I would have you.

PHOEBE   Why, that were covetousness.
Silvius, the time was that I hated thee, 91
And yet it is not that I bear thee love;
But since that thou canst talk of love so well, 93
Thy company, which erst was irksome to me, 94
I will endure, and I'll employ thee too. 95
But do not look for further recompense
Than thine own gladness that thou art employed.

SILVIUS
So holy and so perfect is my love,
And I in such a poverty of grace,
That I shall think it a most plenteous crop 100
To glean the broken ears after the man
That the main harvest reaps. Loose now and then
A scattered smile, and that I'll live upon.

PHOEBE
Know'st thou the youth that spoke to me erewhile? 104

SILVIUS
Not very well, but I have met him oft, 105
And he hath bought the cottage and the bounds
That the old carlot once was master of. 107

PHOEBE   108
Think not I love him, though I ask for him.
'Tis but a peevish boy—yet he talks well—
But what care I for words? Yet words do well

When he that speaks them pleases those that hear.
It is a pretty youth—not very pretty—
But sure he's proud—and yet his pride becomes him.
He'll make a proper man. The best thing in him
Is his complexion; and faster than his tongue 115
Did make offense, his eye did heal it up.
He is not very tall—yet for his years he's tall.
His leg is but so-so—and yet 'tis well.
There was a pretty redness in his lip,
A little riper and more lusty red
Than that mixed in his cheek; 'twas just the difference
Betwixt the constant red and mingled damask.
There be some women, Silvius, had they marked him 123
In parcels as I did, would have gone near
To fall in love with him; but for my part, 125
I love him not nor hate him not; and yet 126
I have more cause to hate him than to love him.
For what had he to do to chide at me?
He said mine eyes were black and my hair black, 129
And, now I am remembered, scorned at me.
I marvel why I answered not again. 131
But that's all one; omittance is no quittance. 132
I'll write to him a very taunting letter, 133
And thou shalt bear it. Wilt thou, Silvius?

SILVIUS
Phoebe, with all my heart.

PHOEBE   I'll write it straight;
The matter's in my head and in my heart. 136
I will be bitter with him and passing short.
Go with me, Silvius.   *Exeunt.* 138

❖

4.1

Enter Rosalind and Celia, and Jaques.

JAQUES   I prithee, pretty youth, let me be better acquainted with thee.

ROSALIND   They say you are a melancholy fellow.

JAQUES   I am so. I do love it better than laughing.

ROSALIND   Those that are in extremity of either are
abominable fellows and betray themselves to every 5
modern censure worse than drunkards.

JAQUES   Why, 'tis good to be sad and say nothing. 7

ROSALIND   Why then, 'tis good to be a post.

JAQUES   I have neither the scholar's melancholy, which
is emulation, nor the musician's, which is fantastical,
nor the courtier's, which is proud, nor the soldier's, 11
which is ambitious, nor the lawyer's, which is politic,
nor the lady's, which is nice, nor the lover's, which is 13

---

76 **ply her hard** woo her energetically.   78 **could see** could look at
you   79 **abused in sight** deceived through the eyes   81 **Dead shepherd** i.e., Christopher Marlowe, who died in 1593.   **saw** saying.   **of
might** forceful, convincing   82 **Who . . . sight?** (From Marlowe's *Hero
and Leander,* Sestiad 1, 176, first published in 1598.)   86 **Wherever . . .
be** Sorrow cries out for relief.   89 **Were both extermined** would both
be exterminated, ended.   90 **Is . . . neighborly?** i.e., May not I love
you in the sense of loving one's neighbor as oneself?   91 **covetousness** (The tenth commandment forbids coveting anything that is
one's neighbor's.)   93 **yet it is not** the time has not yet come
94 **since that** since   95 **erst** formerly   100 **poverty of grace** lack of
reciprocated affection   104 **scattered** thrown negligently, as in the
gleanings of the harvest   105 **erewhile** just now.   107 **bounds** pastures   108 **carlot** churl, countryman. (Perhaps a proper name.)

115 **proper** handsome   123 **mingled damask** mingled red and white,
the color of the damask rose.   125 **In parcels** bit by bit   125–6 **gone . . .
fall** been on the point of falling   129 **what . . . do** what business had
he   131 **am remembered** remember   132 **again** back.   133 **But . . .
quittance** i.e., But just the same, my failure to answer him doesn't
mean I won't do so later.   136 **straight** immediately   138 **passing
short** exceedingly curt.
4.1. Location: The forest.
5 **are . . . of** go to extremes in   7 **modern censure** common judgment
11 **emulation** envy (of the fellow scholar).   **fantastical** extravagantly
fanciful   13 **politic** grave and diplomatic, calculated

all these; but it is a melancholy of mine own, com- 14
pounded of many simples, extracted from many 15
objects, and indeed the sundry contemplation of my 16
travels, in which my often rumination wraps me in a 17
most humorous sadness. 18

ROSALIND   A traveler! By my faith, you have great 19
reason to be sad. I fear you have sold your own lands
to see other men's. Then to have seen much and to
have nothing is to have rich eyes and poor hands.

JAQUES   Yes, I have gained my experience.

Enter Orlando.

ROSALIND   And your experience makes you sad. I had
rather have a fool to make me merry than experience
to make me sad—and to travel for it too!

ORLANDO   Good day and happiness, dear Rosalind! 27

JAQUES   Nay, then, God b'wi'you, an you talk in blank 29
verse.

ROSALIND   Farewell, Monsieur Traveler. Look you lisp
and wear strange suits, disable all the benefits of your 31
own country, be out of love with your nativity, and 32
almost chide God for making you that countenance 33
you are, or I will scarce think you have swam in a
gondola.   [*Exit Jaques.*] 35
Why, how now, Orlando, where have you been all this 36
while? You a lover? An you serve me such another
trick, never come in my sight more.

ORLANDO   My fair Rosalind, I come within an hour of
my promise.

ROSALIND   Break an hour's promise in love? He that will
divide a minute into a thousand parts and break but
a part of the thousandth part of a minute in the affairs
of love, it may be said of him that Cupid hath clapped
him o'th' shoulder, but I'll warrant him heart-whole. 45

ORLANDO   Pardon me, dear Rosalind. 46

ROSALIND   Nay, an you be so tardy, come no more in
my sight. I had as lief be wooed of a snail.

ORLANDO   Of a snail? 49

ROSALIND   Ay, of a snail; for though he comes slowly,
he carries his house on his head—a better jointure, I
think, than you make a woman. Besides, he brings his 52
destiny with him. 53

ORLANDO   What's that?

ROSALIND   Why, horns, which such as you are fain to
be beholding to your wives for. But he comes armed in 56

his fortune and prevents the slander of his wife. 57

ORLANDO   Virtue is no horn-maker, and my Rosalind is 58
virtuous.

ROSALIND   And I am your Rosalind.

CELIA   It pleases him to call you so; but he hath a Rosalind of a better leer than you.

ROSALIND   Come, woo me, woo me, for now I am in a 63
holiday humor and like enough to consent. What
would you say to me now, an I were your very, very
Rosalind?

ORLANDO   I would kiss before I spoke.

ROSALIND   Nay, you were better speak first, and when
you were graveled for lack of matter, you might take
occasion to kiss. Very good orators, when they are out, 70
they will spit; and for lovers lacking—God warrant 71
us!—matter, the cleanliest shift is to kiss. 72

ORLANDO   How if the kiss be denied? 73

ROSALIND   Then she puts you to entreaty, and there
begins new matter.

ORLANDO   Who could be out, being before his beloved
mistress?

ROSALIND   Marry, that should you, if I were your
mistress, or I should think my honesty ranker than
my wit. 80

ORLANDO   What, of my suit?

ROSALIND   Not out of your apparel, and yet out of your 82
suit. Am not I your Rosalind?

ORLANDO   I take some joy to say you are, because I
would be talking of her.

ROSALIND   Well, in her person I say I will not have you.

ORLANDO   Then in mine own person, I die.

ROSALIND   No, faith, die by attorney. The poor world is
almost six thousand years old, and in all this time 89
there was not any man died in his own person, 90
videlicet, in a love cause. Troilus had his brains 91
dashed out with a Grecian club, yet he did what he 92
could to die before, and he is one of the patterns of 93
love. Leander, he would have lived many a fair year
though Hero had turned nun, if it had not been for a 95
hot midsummer night; for, good youth, he went but
forth to wash him in the Hellespont and being taken
with the cramp was drowned; and the foolish chron-

---

14 **nice** fastidious   15–19 **compounded . . . sadness** made up of
many ingredients, extracted from the many objects of my observation
and, indeed, from the diversified considerations of my travels, my
frequent rumination upon which wraps me in a most whimsical and
moody sadness.   27 **travel** (Meaning also "travail," labor.)   29 **an** if
31 **Look** Be sure. (Said ironically.)   **lisp** i.e., affect a foreign accent
32 **disable** disparage   33 **nativity** country of birth   35 **are** i.e., have
35–6 **swam . . . gondola** floated in a gondola, i.e., been in Venice,
where almost all travelers go.   45–6 **Cupid . . . heart-whole** Cupid
may have tried to arrest him, but I'm sure his heart remains unen-
gaged. (Arresting officers customarily grasped the culprit by the
shoulder.)   49 **lief** willingly.   **of** by   52 **jointure** marriage settlement   53 **than . . . woman** than you, Orlando, are able to settle on
your prospective wife.   56 **horns** (1) snails' horns (2) cuckold's
horns, signs of an unfaithful wife.   **fain** obliged

57 **beholding** beholden, indebted   57–8 **But . . . fortune** The snail
comes already provided with the horns that are his nature and his
destiny, thereby forestalling the scandal that would otherwise attach
to his wife. (Since a snail is naturally horned, no scandal can be
adduced from them.)   63 **leer** appearance, color   70 **graveled** stuck.
(Literally, run aground on a shoal.)   71 **out** at a loss through forgetfulness or confusion   72 **warrant** defend   73 **shift** tactic   80 **honesty ranker** chastity more corrupt. (Rosalind would rely on her wit to
keep her lover off balance and thus defend her chastity. She may use
Orlando's *out*, line 77, in a sexual sense of not being admitted.)   82 **of
my suit** (Orlando means "out of my suit," at a loss for words in my
wooing; but Rosalind puns on the meaning "suit of clothes"; to be out
of apparel would be to be undressed.)   89 **attorney** proxy.   90 **six . . .
old** (A common figure in biblical calculation.)   91 **died** who died
92 **videlicet** namely.   **Troilus** hero of the story of Troilus and Cressida, in which he remains faithful to her, but she is faithless to him
92–3 **had . . . club** (Troilus was slain by Achilles with sword or spear
in more traditional accounts. Rosalind's version is calculatedly unro-
mantic.)   95 **Leander** the hero of the story of Hero and Leander, who
lost his life swimming the Hellespont to visit his sweetheart. (Rosalind's account of the cramp again undercuts romantic idealism.)

iclers of that age found it was—Hero of Sestos. But these are all lies. Men have died from time to time, 100 and worms have eaten them, but not for love.

ORLANDO   I would not have my right Rosalind of this mind, for I protest her frown might kill me.   103

ROSALIND   By this hand, it will not kill a fly. But come, 104 now I will be your Rosalind in a more coming-on disposition; and ask me what you will, I will grant it. 106

ORLANDO   Then love me, Rosalind.

ROSALIND   Yes, faith, will I, Fridays and Saturdays and all.

ORLANDO   And wilt thou have me?

ROSALIND   Ay, and twenty such.

ORLANDO   What sayest thou?

ROSALIND   Are you not good?

ORLANDO   I hope so.

ROSALIND   Why then, can one desire too much of a good thing?—Come, sister, you shall be the priest and marry us.—Give me your hand, Orlando.— What do you say, sister?

ORLANDO   Pray thee, marry us.

CELIA   I cannot say the words.

ROSALIND   You must begin, "Will you, Orlando—"

CELIA   Go to. Will you, Orlando, have to wife this Rosalind?   123

ORLANDO   I will.

ROSALIND   Ay, but when?

ORLANDO   Why now, as fast as she can marry us.

ROSALIND   Then you must say, "I take thee, Rosalind, for wife."

ORLANDO   I take thee, Rosalind, for wife.

ROSALIND   I might ask you for your commission; but I do take thee, Orlando, for my husband. There's a girl 131 goes before the priest, and certainly a woman's thought runs before her actions.   133

ORLANDO   So do all thoughts; they are winged.   134

ROSALIND   Now tell me how long you would have her after you have possessed her.

ORLANDO   For ever and a day.

ROSALIND   Say "a day," without the "ever." No, no, Or-lando, men are April when they woo, December when they wed. Maids are May when they are maids, but the sky changes when they are wives. I will be more jealous of thee than a Barbary cock-pigeon over his hen, more clamorous than a parrot against rain, more 143 newfangled than an ape, more giddy in my desires 144 than a monkey. I will weep for nothing, like Diana in 145 the fountain, and I will do that when you are disposed 146 to be merry; I will laugh like a hyena, and that when 147 thou art inclined to sleep.

ORLANDO   But will my Rosalind do so?

ROSALIND   By my life, she will do as I do.

ORLANDO   Oh, but she is wise.

ROSALIND   Or else she could not have the wit to do this. The wiser, the waywarder. Make the doors upon a woman's wit, and it will out at the casement; shut 154 that, and 'twill out at the keyhole; stop that, 'twill fly 155 with the smoke out at the chimney.

ORLANDO   A man that had a wife with such a wit, he might say, "Wit, whither wilt?"

ROSALIND   Nay, you might keep that check for it till 159 you met your wife's wit going to your neighbor's bed. 160

ORLANDO   And what wit could wit have to excuse that?

ROSALIND   Marry, to say she came to seek you there. You shall never take her without her answer unless you take her without her tongue. Oh, that woman that cannot make her fault her husband's occasion, let her never nurse her child herself, for she will breed it like 166 a fool!   167

ORLANDO   For these two hours, Rosalind, I will leave thee.

ROSALIND   Alas, dear love, I cannot lack thee two hours!

ORLANDO   I must attend the Duke at dinner. By two o'clock I will be with thee again.

ROSALIND   Ay, go your ways, go your ways. I knew what you would prove. My friends told me as much, and I thought no less. That flattering tongue of yours won me. 'Tis but one cast away, and so, come, death! Two o'clock is your hour?   177

ORLANDO   Ay, sweet Rosalind.

ROSALIND   By my troth, and in good earnest, and so God mend me, and by all pretty oaths that are not dangerous, if you break one jot of your promise or come one minute behind your hour, I will think you 182 the most pathetical break-promise, and the most hollow lover, and the most unworthy of her you call 184 Rosalind, that may be chosen out of the gross band of the unfaithful. Therefore beware my censure, and 186 keep your promise.

ORLANDO   With no less religion than if thou wert indeed my Rosalind. So adieu.   189

---

100 **found it was** arrived at the verdict that the cause (of his death) was   103 **right** real   104 **protest** insist, proclaim   106 **coming-on** compliant   123 **Go to** (An exclamation of mild impatience.)   131 **ask . . . commission** ask you what authority you have for taking her (since no one is here to give the bride away and since she herself has not yet consented)   133 **goes . . . priest** who anticipates before the "priest" has even asked the question   134 **runs . . . actions** i.e., goes flightily on, outstripping sane conduct.   143 **Barbary cock-pigeon** an ornamental pigeon actually from the orient, not the Barbary (north) coast of Africa. (Following Pliny, the cock-pigeon's jealousy was often contrasted with the mildness of the hen.)   144 **against** in expectation of   145 **newfangled** infatuated with novelty

146 **for nothing** for no apparent reason   146–7 **Diana in the fountain** (Diana frequently appeared as the centerpiece of fountains. Stow's *Survey of London* describes the setting up of a fountain with a Diana in green marble in the year 1596.)   154 **The wiser, the waywarder** i.e., The more experienced in the war of the sexes, the more insisting on her own way.   **Make** Make fast, shut   155 **casement** hinged window   159 **Wit, whither wilt?** Wit, where are you going? (A common Eliza-bethan expression implying that one is talking fantastically, with a wildly wandering wit.)   160 **check** retort   166 **make . . . occasion** i.e., turn a defense of her own conduct into an accusation against her husband   167 **breed it** bring it up   177 **but one cast away** only one woman jilted   182 **dangerous** i.e., blasphemous. (Rosalind's oaths are decorous.)   184 **pathetical** awful, miserable   186 **gross band** whole troop   189 **religion** strict fidelity

ROSALIND   Well, Time is the old justice that examines all such offenders, and let Time try. Adieu. 192

Exit [Orlando].

CELIA   You have simply misused our sex in your love 193 prate. We must have your doublet and hose plucked 194 over your head and show the world what the bird 195 hath done to her own nest. 196

ROSALIND   Oh, coz, coz, coz, my pretty little coz, that thou didst know how many fathom deep I am in love! But it cannot be sounded; my affection hath an unknown 199 bottom, like the Bay of Portugal.

CELIA   Or rather, bottomless, that as fast as you pour 201 affection in, it runs out.

ROSALIND   No, that same wicked bastard of Venus, that 203 was begot of thought, conceived of spleen, and born of 204 madness, that blind rascally boy that abuses every- 205 one's eyes because his own are out, let him be judge 206 how deep I am in love. I'll tell thee, Aliena, I cannot be out of the sight of Orlando. I'll go find a shadow and 208 sigh till he come.

CELIA   And I'll sleep. *Exeunt.*

❖

4.2

Enter Jaques and Lords [dressed as] foresters.

JAQUES   Which is he that killed the deer?

FIRST LORD   Sir, it was I.

JAQUES   Let's present him to the Duke, like a Roman conqueror, and it would do well to set the deer's horns upon his head for a branch of victory. Have you no 5 song, Forester, for this purpose?

SECOND LORD   Yes, sir.

JAQUES   Sing it. 'Tis no matter how it be in tune, so it 8 make noise enough. *Music.*

Song.

SECOND LORD *[sings]*
What shall he have that killed the deer?
His leather skin and horns to wear.
Then sing him home; the rest shall bear 12
This burden. 13
Take thou no scorn to wear the horn; 14
It was a crest ere thou wast born.
Thy father's father wore it,
And thy father bore it.
The horn, the horn, the lusty horn
Is not a thing to laugh to scorn. *Exeunt.*

❖

4.3

Enter Rosalind and Celia.

ROSALIND   How say you now? Is it not past two o'clock? And here much Orlando! 2

CELIA   I warrant you, with pure love and troubled brain 3 he hath ta'en his bow and arrows and is gone forth—to sleep.

Enter Silvius [with a letter].

Look who comes here.

SILVIUS *[to Rosalind]*
My errand is to you, fair youth.
My gentle Phoebe bid me give you this.

[He gives the letter.]

I know not the contents, but as I guess,
By the stern brow and waspish action
Which she did use as she was writing of it,
It bears an angry tenor. Pardon me;
I am but as a guiltless messenger.

ROSALIND *[examining the letter]*
Patience herself would startle at this letter 14
And play the swaggerer. Bear this, bear all! 15
She says I am not fair, that I lack manners;
She calls me proud, and that she could not love me
Were man as rare as phoenix. 'Od's my will! 18
Her love is not the hare that I do hunt.
Why writes she so to me? Well, shepherd, well,
This is a letter of your own device.

SILVIUS
No, I protest, I know not the contents.
Phoebe did write it.

ROSALIND   Come, come, you are a fool,
And turned into the extremity of love. 24
I saw her hand; she has a leathern hand, 25
A freestone-colored hand. I verily did think 26
That her old gloves were on, but 'twas her hands;
She has a huswife's hand—but that's no matter. 28
I say she never did invent this letter;
This is a man's invention and his hand.

SILVIUS   Sure it is hers.

ROSALIND
Why, 'tis a boisterous and a cruel style,
A style for challengers. Why, she defies me,
Like Turk to Christian. Women's gentle brain
Could not drop forth such giant-rude invention,

---

192 **try** determine, judge.   **193 simply misused** absolutely slandered
194–6 We . . . nest i.e., We must expose you for what you are, a woman, and show everyone how a woman has defamed her own kind just as a foul bird proverbially fouls its own nest.   **199 sounded** measured for depth   **201 that** so that   **203 bastard of Venus** i.e., Cupid, son of Venus and Mercury (or Zeus) rather than Vulcan, Venus's husband   **204 thought** fancy.   **spleen** i.e., impulse
205 abuses deceives   **206 out** blinded   **208 shadow** shady spot
4.2 Location: The forest.
5 branch wreath   **8 so** provided that   **12–13 bear This burden** (1) sing this refrain (2) wear the horns that all cuckolds must wear.   **14 Take . . . scorn** Be not ashamed. (Alludes to joke about cuckold's horns.)

4.3 Location: The forest.
2 much (Said ironically: A fat lot we see of Orlando!)   **3 warrant** assure   **14–15 Patience . . . all!** Patience herself would be startled into a violent display by this letter. If one were to put up with such a missive, one would have to accept any insult!   **15 play the swaggerer** (Patience herself would bluster and rant at such a letter.)
18 phoenix a fabulous bird of Arabia, the only one of its kind, which lived five hundred years, died in flames, and was reborn of its own ashes.   **'Od's my will!** (An oath: "May God's will be done!")
24 turned transformed   **25 leathern** leathery   **26 freestone-colored** sandstone-colored, brownish-yellow   **28 hand** handwriting. (With play on "dishpan hands.")

Such Ethiop words, blacker in their effect   36
Than in their countenance. Will you hear the letter?   37

SILVIUS
So please you, for I never heard it yet;
Yet, heard too much of Phoebe's cruelty.

ROSALIND
She Phoebes me. Mark how the tyrant writes.   40
    (*Read*) "Art thou god to shepherd turned,
    That a maiden's heart hath burned?"
Can a woman rail thus?

SILVIUS   Call you this railing?

ROSALIND
    (*Read*) "Why, thy godhead laid apart,   45
    War'st thou with a woman's heart?"
Did you ever hear such railing?
    "Whiles the eye of man did woo me,
    That could do no vengeance to me."—   49
Meaning me a beast.   50
    "If the scorn of your bright eyne   51
    Have power to raise such love in mine,
    Alack, in me what strange effect
    Would they work in mild aspect!   54
    Whiles you chid me, I did love;   55
    How then might your prayers move!
    He that brings this love to thee
    Little knows this love in me;
    And by him seal up thy mind,   59
    Whether that thy youth and kind   60
    Will the faithful offer take
    Of me and all that I can make,   62
    Or else by him my love deny,
    And then I'll study how to die."

SILVIUS   Call you this chiding?

CELIA   Alas, poor shepherd!

ROSALIND   Do you pity him? No, he deserves no pity.—
Wilt thou love such a woman? What, to make thee an   68
instrument and play false strains upon thee? Not to be   69
endured! Well, go your way to her, for I see love hath
made thee a tame snake, and say this to her: that if she   71
love me, I charge her to love thee; if she will not, I will
never have her unless thou entreat for her. If you be a
true lover, hence, and not a word; for here comes
more company.   *Exit Silvius.*

    Enter Oliver.

OLIVER
Good morrow, fair ones. Pray you, if you know,

Where in the purlieus of this forest stands   77
A sheepcote fenced about with olive trees?

CELIA
West of this place, down in the neighbor bottom;   79
The rank of osiers by the murmuring stream   80
Left on your right hand brings you to the place.   81
But at this hour the house doth keep itself;
There's none within.

OLIVER
If that an eye may profit by a tongue,
Then should I know you by description,
Such garments and such years: "The boy is fair,
Of female favor, and bestows himself   87
Like a ripe sister; the woman, low   88
And browner than her brother." Are not you
The owner of the house I did inquire for?

CELIA
It is no boast, being asked, to say we are.

OLIVER
Orlando doth commend him to you both,   92
And to that youth he calls his Rosalind
He sends this bloody napkin. Are you he?   94
    [*He produces a bloody handkerchief.*]

ROSALIND
I am. What must we understand by this?

OLIVER
Some of my shame, if you will know of me
What man I am, and how, and why, and where
This handkerchief was stained.

CELIA   I pray you, tell it.

OLIVER
When last the young Orlando parted from you
He left a promise to return again
Within an hour, and, pacing through the forest,
Chewing the food of sweet and bitter fancy,   102
Lo, what befell! He threw his eye aside,
And mark what object did present itself:
Under an old oak, whose boughs were mossed with
    age
And high top bald with dry antiquity,
A wretched, ragged man, o'ergrown with hair,
Lay sleeping on his back. About his neck
A green and gilded snake had wreathed itself,
Who with her head, nimble in threats, approached
The opening of his mouth; but suddenly,
Seeing Orlando, it unlinked itself   112
And with indented glides did slip away   113
Into a bush, under which bush's shade
A lioness, with udders all drawn dry,   115
Lay couching, head on ground, with catlike watch,
When that the sleeping man should stir; for 'tis   117

---

36 Ethiop i.e., black   **36–7 blacker . . . countenance** even blacker in what they say than in their black appearance on the page.
40 Phoebes me i.e., addresses me in her cruel style.   **45 thy . . . apart** having laid aside your godhead (for human shape)   **49 vengeance** mischief, harm   **50 Meaning me** i.e., Implying that I am   **51 eyne** eyes   **54 in mild aspect** i.e., if they looked on me mildly. (Suggests also astrological influence.)   **55 chid** chided   **59 by . . . mind** i.e., send your thoughts in a letter via Silvius   **60 Whether . . . kind** if your youthful nature   **62 make** make offer of   **68–9 to make . . . instrument** to make an instrument (i.e., messenger) of you. (With a suggestion of making a person into a musical instrument; cf. *Hamlet*, 3.2.363, "You would play upon me," etc.)   **69 strains** parts of a piece of music   **71 tame snake** i.e., pathetic wretch

77 purlieus borders, boundaries   **79 neighbor bottom** neighboring dell   **80 rank of osiers** row of willows   **81 Left** left behind, passed   **87 favor** features.   **bestows** comports   **88 ripe** mature or elder   **92 doth commend him** sends his greetings   **94 napkin** handkerchief.   **102 Chewing . . . fancy** ruminating on the bittersweet nature of love   **112 unlinked** uncoiled   **113 indented** zigzag   **115 with . . . dry** (It would therefore be fierce with hunger.)   **117 When** for the moment

The royal disposition of that beast
To prey on nothing that doth seem as dead.
This seen, Orlando did approach the man
And found it was his brother, his elder brother.

CELIA
Oh, I have heard him speak of that same brother,
And he did render him the most unnatural   123
That lived amongst men.

OLIVER   And well he might so do,
For well I know he was unnatural.

ROSALIND
But to Orlando: did he leave him there,
Food to the sucked and hungry lioness?

OLIVER
Twice did he turn his back and purposed so;
But kindness, nobler ever than revenge,
And nature, stronger than his just occasion,   130
Made him give battle to the lioness,
Who quickly fell before him; in which hurtling   132
From miserable slumber I awaked.

CELIA
Are you his brother?

ROSALIND   Was't you he rescued?

CELIA
Was't you that did so oft contrive to kill him?

OLIVER
'Twas I, but 'tis not I. I do not shame   136
To tell you what I was, since my conversion
So sweetly tastes, being the thing I am.

ROSALIND
But for the bloody napkin?

OLIVER   By and by.   139
When from the first to last betwixt us two
Tears our recounts had most kindly bathed,   141
As how I came into that desert place,
In brief, he led me to the gentle Duke,
Who gave me fresh array and entertainment,   144
Committing me unto my brother's love;
Who led me instantly unto his cave,
There stripped himself, and here upon his arm
The lioness had torn some flesh away,
Which all this while had bled; and now he fainted
And cried, in fainting, upon Rosalind.
Brief, I recovered him, bound up his wound,   151
And after some small space, being strong at heart,
He sent me hither, stranger as I am,
To tell this story, that you might excuse
His broken promise, and to give this napkin
Dyed in his blood unto the shepherd youth
That he in sport doth call his Rosalind.
                                    [Rosalind swoons.]

CELIA
Why, how now, Ganymede, sweet Ganymede!

OLIVER
Many will swoon when they do look on blood.

CELIA
There is more in it.—Cousin Ganymede!

OLIVER   Look, he recovers.

ROSALIND   I would I were at home.

CELIA   We'll lead you thither.—
I pray you, will you take him by the arm?
                        [They help Rosalind up.]

OLIVER   Be of good cheer, youth. You a man? You lack
a man's heart.

ROSALIND   I do so, I confess it. Ah, sirrah, a body would 167
think this was well counterfeited. I pray you, tell your
brother how well I counterfeited. Heigh-ho!

OLIVER   This was not counterfeit. There is too great testimony in your complexion that it was a passion of   171
earnest.   172

ROSALIND   Counterfeit, I assure you.

OLIVER   Well then, take a good heart and counterfeit to
be a man.

ROSALIND   So I do; but, i'faith, I should have been a
woman by right.

CELIA   Come, you look paler and paler. Pray you, draw
homewards.—Good sir, go with us.

OLIVER
That will I, for I must bear answer back
How you excuse my brother, Rosalind.

ROSALIND   I shall devise something. But, I pray you,
commend my counterfeiting to him. Will you go?
                                            Exeunt.

❧

5.1

Enter [Touchstone the] Clown and Audrey.

TOUCHSTONE   We shall find a time, Audrey. Patience,
gentle Audrey.

AUDREY   Faith, the priest was good enough, for all the   3
old gentleman's saying.   4

TOUCHSTONE   A most wicked Sir Oliver, Audrey, a most
vile Mar-text. But Audrey, there is a youth here in the
forest lays claim to you.

AUDREY   Ay, I know who 'tis. He hath no interest in me   8
in the world. Here comes the man you mean.

Enter William.

TOUCHSTONE   It is meat and drink to me to see a clown.   10
By my troth, we that have good wits have much to   11
answer for. We shall be flouting; we cannot hold.   12

WILLIAM   Good even, Audrey.

AUDREY   God gi' good even, William.   14

WILLIAM   And good even to you, sir.
                                    [He removes his hat.]

---

123 **render him** describe him as   130 **just occasion** just opportunity
and motive (for revenge)   132 **hurtling** conflict, tumult   136 **do not
shame** am not ashamed   139 **for** as regards   141 **recounts**
relating of events (to one another)   144 **array** attire.   **entertainment**
hospitality, provision   151 **Brief** In brief.   **recovered** revived

167 **a body** anybody   171–2 **a passion of earnest** a genuine swoon.
5.1 Location: The forest.
3–4 **the old gentleman's** i.e., Jaques's   8 **interest in** claim to
10 **clown** i.e., country yokel.   11–12 **we . . . hold** i.e., we professional
fools have much to answer for in providing a model of folly that
yokels like William are too apt to imitate. We fools are always scoffing; we can't restrain ourselves.   14 **God gi' good even** God give you
good evening. (Here, afternoon.)

TOUCHSTONE   Good even, gentle friend. Cover thy head, cover thy head. Nay, prithee be covered. How old are you, friend?

WILLIAM   Five-and-twenty, sir.

TOUCHSTONE   A ripe age. Is thy name William?

WILLIAM   William, sir.

TOUCHSTONE   A fair name. Wast born i'th' forest here?

WILLIAM   Ay, sir, I thank God.

TOUCHSTONE   "Thank God"—a good answer. Art rich?

WILLIAM   Faith, sir, so-so.

TOUCHSTONE   "So-so" is good, very good, very excellent good; and yet it is not, it is but so-so. Art thou wise?

WILLIAM   Ay, sir, I have a pretty wit.

TOUCHSTONE   Why, thou say'st well. I do now remember a saying, "The fool doth think he is wise, but the wise man knows himself to be a fool." The heathen 31 philosopher, when he had a desire to eat a grape, 32 would open his lips when he put it into his mouth, 33 meaning thereby that grapes were made to eat and 34 lips to open. You do love this maid? 35

WILLIAM   I do, sir.

TOUCHSTONE   Give me your hand. Art thou learned?

WILLIAM   No, sir.

TOUCHSTONE   Then learn this of me: to have is to have. For it is a figure in rhetoric that drink, being poured 40 out of a cup into a glass, by filling the one doth empty 41 the other. For all your writers do consent that *ipse* is 42 he. Now, you are not *ipse*, for I am he. 43

WILLIAM   Which he, sir?

TOUCHSTONE   He, sir, that must marry this woman. Therefore, you clown, abandon—which is in the vulgar "leave"—the society—which in the boorish is "company"—of this female—which in the common is "woman"; which together is, abandon the society of this female, or, clown, thou perishest; or, to thy better understanding, diest; or, to wit, I kill thee, make thee away, translate thy life into death, thy liberty into bondage. I will deal in poison with thee, or in basti- 53 nado, or in steel; I will bandy with thee in faction, I 54 will o'errun thee with policy; I will kill thee a hundred 55 and fifty ways. Therefore tremble, and depart.

AUDREY   Do, good William.

WILLIAM   God rest you merry, sir.   *Exit.* 58

Enter Corin.

CORIN   Our master and mistress seeks you. Come, away, away!

TOUCHSTONE   Trip, Audrey, trip, Audrey!—I attend, I 61 attend.   *Exeunt.*

❧

5.2

Enter Orlando [with his wounded arm in a sling] and Oliver.

ORLANDO   Is't possible that on so little acquaintance you should like her? That but seeing, you should love her? And loving, woo? And, wooing, she should grant? And will you persevere to enjoy her?

OLIVER   Neither call the giddiness of it in question, the 5 poverty of her, the small acquaintance, my sudden wooing, nor her sudden consenting; but say with me, "I love Aliena"; say with her that she loves me; consent with both that we may enjoy each other. It shall be to your good; for my father's house and all the revenue that was old Sir Rowland's will I estate upon 11 you, and here live and die a shepherd.

Enter Rosalind.

ORLANDO   You have my consent. Let your wedding be tomorrow. Thither will I invite the Duke and all 's 14 contented followers. Go you and prepare Aliena; for look you, here comes my Rosalind.

ROSALIND   God save you, brother. 17

OLIVER   And you, fair sister.   [*Exit.*] 18

ROSALIND   O my dear Orlando, how it grieves me to see thee wear thy heart in a scarf! 20

ORLANDO   It is my arm.

ROSALIND   I thought thy heart had been wounded with the claws of a lion.

ORLANDO   Wounded it is, but with the eyes of a lady.

ROSALIND   Did your brother tell you how I counterfeited to swoon when he showed me your handkerchief?

ORLANDO   Ay, and greater wonders than that.

ROSALIND   Oh, I know where you are. Nay, 'tis true. 28 There was never anything so sudden but the fight of two rams and Caesar's thrasonical brag of "I came, 30 saw, and overcame." For your brother and my sister 31 no sooner met but they looked, no sooner looked but they loved, no sooner loved but they sighed, no sooner sighed but they asked one another the reason, no sooner knew the reason but they sought the remedy; and in these degrees have they made a pair of 36

31–5 The heathen . . . open (This bit of fatuously self-evident wisdom parodies the logical proofs of the ancient philosophers. William, whose mouth is no doubt gaping like a rustic's, is invited to consider the consequences of his desire.)   **40 figure** figure of speech, trope **40–2 drink . . . other** i.e., both Touchstone and William cannot possess Audrey.   **42–3 For . . . am he** For all the ancient authorities concur that the word *ipse* in Latin means "he." But you are not *ipse*, i.e., the man of the hour, the one destined to win Audrey, for I am that man. **53–4 bastinado** beating with a cudgel   **54 bandy** contend.   **in fac-tion** factiously   **55 o'errun . . . policy** overwhelm you with craft, cun-ning   **58 God . . . merry** (A common salutation at parting.)

61 Trip Go nimbly
5.2 Location: The forest.
5 giddiness sudden speed   **11 estate** settle as an estate, bestow **14 all 's** all his   **17 brother** i.e., brother-in-law to be.   **18 sister** (Ros-alind is still dressed as a man, but Oliver evidently adopts the fiction that "Ganymede" is Orlando's Rosalind. See 4.3.92 ff.)   **20 scarf** sling.   **28 where you are** i.e., what you mean.   **30 thrasonical** boast-ful. (From Thraso, the boaster in Terence's *Eunuchus*.)   **30–1 "I came . . . overcame"** (Julius Caesar's famous pronouncement, *Veni, vidi, vici*, on the occasion of his victory over Pharnaces at Zela in 47 B.C.) **36 degrees** (Plays on the original meaning, "steps," and also on the rhetorical figure of climax illustrated by Rosalind's sentence as it moves from one step to the next by linked words, *looked, loved, sighed,* etc.)   **pair** flight

stairs to marriage which they will climb incontinent, or 37
else be incontinent before marriage. They are in the
very wrath of love, and they will together. Clubs 39
cannot part them.

ORLANDO   They shall be married tomorrow, and I will
bid the Duke to the nuptial. But oh, how bitter a thing
it is to look into happiness through another man's
eyes! By so much the more shall I tomorrow be at the
height of heart-heaviness, by how much I shall think
my brother happy in having what he wishes for.

ROSALIND   Why, then, tomorrow I cannot serve your
turn for Rosalind?

ORLANDO   I can live no longer by thinking.

ROSALIND   I will weary you then no longer with idle
talking. Know of me then—for now I speak to some
purpose—that I know you are a gentleman of good con- 52
ceit. I speak not this that you should bear a good opin- 53
ion of my knowledge, insomuch I say I know you are; 54
neither do I labor for a greater esteem than may in 55
some little measure draw a belief from you to do 56
yourself good, and not to grace me. Believe then, if you 57
please, that I can do strange things. I have, since I was
three year old, conversed with a magician, most 59
profound in his art and yet not damnable. If you do 60
love Rosalind so near the heart as your gesture cries it 61
out, when your brother marries Aliena shall you 62
marry her. I know into what straits of fortune she is 63
driven; and it is not impossible to me, if it appear not
inconvenient to you, to set her before your eyes 65
tomorrow, human as she is, and without any danger. 66

ORLANDO   Speak'st thou in sober meanings? 67

ROSALIND   By my life, I do, which I tender dearly, 68
though I say I am a magician. Therefore, put you in 69
your best array; bid your friends; for if you will be 70
married tomorrow, you shall, and to Rosalind, if you
will.

Enter Silvius and Phoebe.

Look, here comes a lover of mine and a lover of hers.

PHOEBE *[to Rosalind]*
Youth, you have done me much ungentleness, 74
To show the letter that I writ to you.

ROSALIND
I care not if I have. It is my study 76
To seem despiteful and ungentle to you.
You are there followed by a faithful shepherd.
Look upon him; love him. He worships you.

PHOEBE *[to Silvius]*
Good shepherd, tell this youth what 'tis to love.

SILVIUS
It is to be all made of sighs and tears;
And so am I for Phoebe.

PHOEBE   And I for Ganymede.

ORLANDO   And I for Rosalind.

ROSALIND   And I for no woman.

SILVIUS
It is to be all made of faith and service;
And so am I for Phoebe.

PHOEBE   And I for Ganymede.

ORLANDO   And I for Rosalind.

ROSALIND   And I for no woman.

SILVIUS
It is to be all made of fantasy, 91
All made of passion and all made of wishes,
All adoration, duty, and observance, 93
All humbleness, all patience and impatience,
All purity, all trial, all observance; 95
And so am I for Phoebe.

PHOEBE   And so am I for Ganymede.

ORLANDO   And so am I for Rosalind.

ROSALIND   And so am I for no woman.

PHOEBE *[to Rosalind]*
If this be so, why blame you me to love you? 100

SILVIUS *[to Phoebe]*
If this be so, why blame you me to love you?

ORLANDO
If this be so, why blame you me to love you?

ROSALIND   Why do you speak too, "Why blame you me
to love you?"

ORLANDO   To her that is not here, nor doth not hear.

ROSALIND   Pray you, no more of this; 'tis like the
howling of Irish wolves against the moon. *[To Silvius]*
I will help you, if I can. *[To Phoebe]* I would love you, if
I could.—Tomorrow meet me all together. *[To Phoebe]* I
will marry you, if ever I marry woman, and I'll be
married tomorrow. *[To Orlando]* I will satisfy you, if
ever I satisfied man, and you shall be married
tomorrow. *[To Silvius]* I will content you, if what
pleases you contents you, and you shall be married
tomorrow. *[To Orlando]* As you love Rosalind, meet.
[To Silvius] As you love Phoebe, meet. And as I love
no woman, I'll meet. So fare you well. I have left you
commands.

SILVIUS   I'll not fail, if I live.

PHOEBE   Nor I.

ORLANDO   Nor I.   *Exeunt [separately].*

37 **incontinent** immediately. (Followed by a pun on the meaning
"unchaste or sexually unrestrained.")   39 **wrath** impetuosity, ardor.
Clubs i.e., Physical force, such as that employed by nightwatchmen
armed with clubs   52–3 **conceit** intelligence, understanding.   53 **that**
in order that   54 **insomuch . . . are** from my saying I know you to be
intelligent   55–7 **neither . . . grace me** nor am I interested in winning
approval except insofar as it may, by inspiring your confidence in my
ability, prompt you to do something for your own benefit; it is not
intended to bring favor on myself.   59 **conversed** associated   60 **not
damnable** not a practicer of forbidden or black magic, worthy of execution and damnation.   61 **gesture** bearing   61–2 **cries it out** proclaims   63 **she** Rosalind   65 **inconvenient** inappropriate   66 **human**
i.e., the real Rosalind, not a phantom.   **danger** i.e., the danger to the
soul from one's involvement in magic or witchcraft.   67 **in sober
meanings** seriously.   68 **tender dearly** value highly   69 **though . . .
magician** (According to Elizabethan antiwitchcraft statutes, some
forms of witchcraft were punishable by death; Rosalind thus endan-
gers her life by what she has said.)   70 **bid** invite.   **friends** family
and friends   74 **ungentleness** discourtesy

76 **study** conscious endeavor   91 **fantasy** fancy, imagination
93 **observance** devotion, respect   95 **observance** (Perhaps a compositor's error, repeated from two lines previous; many editors emend it
to *obedience*.)   100 **to love you** for loving you.

5.3

Enter [Touchstone the] Clown and Audrey.

TOUCHSTONE   Tomorrow is the joyful day, Audrey;
tomorrow will we be married.

AUDREY   I do desire it with all my heart; and I hope it is
no dishonest desire to desire to be a woman of the   4
world. Here come two of the banished Duke's pages.   5

Enter two Pages.

FIRST PAGE   Well met, honest gentleman.   6

TOUCHSTONE   By my troth, well met. Come, sit, sit,
and a song.   *[They sit.]*

SECOND PAGE   We are for you. Sit i'th' middle.   9

FIRST PAGE   Shall we clap into't roundly, without hawk-   10
ing or spitting or saying we are hoarse, which are the   11
only prologues to a bad voice?   12

SECOND PAGE   I'faith, i'faith, and both in a tune, like   13
two gypsies on a horse.   14

Song.

BOTH PAGES

It was a lover and his lass,
　　With a hey, and a ho, and a hey-nonny-no,
That o'er the green cornfield did pass   17
　　In springtime, the only pretty ring time,   18
When birds do sing, hey ding a ding, ding,
Sweet lovers love the spring.

Between the acres of the rye,   21
　　With a hey, and a ho, and a hey-nonny-no,
These pretty country folks would lie
　　In springtime, the only pretty ring time,
When birds do sing, hey ding a ding, ding,
Sweet lovers love the spring.

This carol they began that hour,
　　With a hey, and a ho, and hey-nonny-no,
How that a life was but a flower
　　In springtime, the only pretty ring time,
When birds do sing, hey ding a ding, ding,
Sweet lovers love the spring.

And therefore take the present time,
　　With a hey, and a ho, and a hey-nonny-no,
For love is crownèd with the prime   35
　　In springtime, the only pretty ring time,
When birds do sing, hey ding a ding, ding,
Sweet lovers love the spring.

TOUCHSTONE   Truly, young gentlemen, though there
was no great matter in the ditty, yet the note was very   40
untunable.   41

FIRST PAGE   You are deceived, sir. We kept time, we lost   42
not our time.

TOUCHSTONE   By my troth, yes; I count it but time lost
to hear such a foolish song. God b'wi'you, and God
mend your voices! Come, Audrey. *Exeunt [separately].*

❖

5.4

*Enter Duke Senior, Amiens, Jaques, Orlando,
Oliver, [and] Celia.*

DUKE SENIOR

Dost thou believe, Orlando, that the boy
Can do all this that he hath promisèd?

ORLANDO

I sometimes do believe, and sometimes do not,
As those that fear they hope and know they fear.   4

Enter Rosalind, Silvius, and Phoebe.

ROSALIND

Patience once more, whiles our compact is urged.   5
[To the Duke] You say, if I bring in your Rosalind
You will bestow her on Orlando here?

DUKE SENIOR

That would I, had I kingdoms to give with her.

ROSALIND *[to Orlando]*

And you say you will have her when I bring her?

ORLANDO

That would I, were I of all kingdoms king.

ROSALIND *[to Phoebe]*

You say you'll marry me if I be willing?

PHOEBE

That will I, should I die the hour after.

ROSALIND

But if you do refuse to marry me
You'll give yourself to this most faithful shepherd?

PHOEBE   So is the bargain.

ROSALIND *[to Silvius]*

You say that you'll have Phoebe if she will?

SILVIUS

Though to have her and death were both one thing.

ROSALIND

I have promised to make all this matter even.   18
Keep you your word, O Duke, to give your daughter;
You yours, Orlando, to receive his daughter;
Keep you your word, Phoebe, that you'll marry me,
Or else, refusing me, to wed this shepherd;
Keep your word, Silvius, that you'll marry her
If she refuse me; and from hence I go,
To make these doubts all even.

Exeunt Rosalind and Celia.

DUKE SENIOR

I do remember in this shepherd boy
Some lively touches of my daughter's favor.   27

5.3 **Location: The forest.**
4 dishonest immodest   **4–5 woman of the world** married woman;
also, one who advances herself socially.   **6 honest** worthy   **9 We are
for you** i.e., Fine, we're ready.   **10 clap . . . roundly** begin briskly and
with spirit   **10–11 hawking** clearing the throat   **12 only** customary
13 in a tune (1) in unison (2) keeping time   **14 on a** on one   **17 cornfield** field of grain   **18 ring time** time most apt for marriage
21 Between the acres On unplowed strips between the fields
35 prime (1) height of perfection (2) spring   **40 matter** sense, meaning.   **note** music   **41 untunable** discordant.

---

42 deceived mistaken
5.4 Location: The forest.
4 they hope i.e., that they merely hope   **5 urged** put forward.
18 make . . . even set all this to rights, square accounts.   **27 lively**
lifelike.   **favor** appearance.

ORLANDO
My lord, the first time that I ever saw him
Methought he was a brother to your daughter.
But, my good lord, this boy is forest-born
And hath been tutored in the rudiments
Of many desperate studies by his uncle,   32
Whom he reports to be a great magician,
Obscurèd in the circle of this forest.   34

Enter [Touchstone the] Clown and Audrey.

JAQUES   There is, sure, another flood toward, and these 35
couples are coming to the ark. Here comes a pair of   36
very strange beasts, which in all tongues are called
fools.
TOUCHSTONE   Salutation and greeting to you all!
JAQUES   [*to the Duke*]   Good my lord, bid him welcome.
This is the motley-minded gentleman that I have so often
met in the forest. He hath been a courtier, he swears.
TOUCHSTONE   If any man doubt that, let him put me to
my purgation. I have trod a measure; I have flattered a   44
lady; I have been politic with my friend, smooth with   45
mine enemy; I have undone three tailors; I have had   46
four quarrels and like to have fought one.   47
JAQUES   And how was that ta'en up?   48
TOUCHSTONE   Faith, we met and found the quarrel was
upon the seventh cause.
JAQUES   How seventh cause?—Good my lord, like this
fellow.
DUKE SENIOR   I like him very well.
TOUCHSTONE   God 'ild you, sir, I desire you of the like. 54
I press in here, sir, amongst the rest of the country   55
copulatives, to swear and to forswear, according as   56
marriage binds and blood breaks. A poor virgin, sir,   57
an ill-favored thing, sir, but mine own; a poor humor   58
of mine, sir, to take that that no man else will. Rich
honesty dwells like a miser, sir, in a poor house, as   60
your pearl in your foul oyster.   61
DUKE SENIOR   By my faith, he is very swift and senten-   62
tious.   63
TOUCHSTONE   According to the fool's bolt, sir, and such 64
dulcet diseases.   65
JAQUES   But for the seventh cause. How did you find
the quarrel on the seventh cause?

TOUCHSTONE   Upon a lie seven times removed—bear
your body more seeming, Audrey—as thus, sir. I did   69
dislike the cut of a certain courtier's beard. He sent me 70
word if I said his beard was not cut well, he was in
the mind it was: this is called the Retort Courteous. If I
sent him word again it was not well cut, he would
send me word he cut it to please himself: this is called
the Quip Modest. If again it was not well cut, he dis-   75
abled my judgment: this is called the Reply Churlish. If   76
again it was not well cut, he would answer I spake
not true: this is called the Reproof Valiant. If again it
was not well cut, he would say I lie: this is called the
Countercheck Quarrelsome. And so to the Lie Cir-   80
cumstantial and the Lie Direct.
JAQUES   And how oft did you say his beard was not well
cut?
TOUCHSTONE   I durst go no further than the Lie Circumstantial, nor he durst not give me the Lie Direct;
and so we measured swords and parted.   86
JAQUES   Can you nominate in order now the degrees of
the lie?
TOUCHSTONE   Oh, sir, we quarrel in print, by the book, as 89
you have books for good manners. I will name you the
degrees. The first, the Retort Courteous; the second,
the Quip Modest; the third, the Reply Churlish; the
fourth, the Reproof Valiant; the fifth, the Countercheck
Quarrelsome; the sixth, the Lie with Circumstance;
the seventh, the Lie Direct. All these you may
avoid but the Lie Direct; and you may avoid that, too,
with an If. I knew when seven justices could not take   97
up a quarrel, but when the parties were met them-   98
selves, one of them thought but of an If, as, "If you
said so, then I said so"; and they shook hands and
swore brothers. Your If is the only peacemaker; much   101
virtue in If.
JAQUES   Is not this a rare fellow, my lord? He's as good
at anything and yet a fool.
DUKE SENIOR   He uses his folly like a stalking-horse,   105
and under the presentation of that he shoots his wit.   106

Enter Hymen, Rosalind, and Celia. Still music.
[Rosalind and Celia are no longer disguised.]

HYMEN
Then is there mirth in heaven,   107
When earthly things made even   108
    Atone together.   109
Good Duke, receive thy daughter;
Hymen from heaven brought her,
    Yea, brought her hither,

32 desperate dangerous   **34 Obscurèd** hidden.   **circle** compass,
boundaries. (With a possible allusion to the magic circle that protected the magician from the devil during incantation.)   **35 toward**
coming on   **36 a pair** (In Genesis 7:2, God commands Noah to take
on board every "clean" beast by sevens, but those that are not clean,
by twos.)   **44 purgation** proof, trial.   **measure** slow, stately dance
45 politic cunning, Machiavellian.   **smooth** insinuating   **46 undone**
bankrupted (by refusing to pay debts owed them)   **47 like** came
close   **48 ta'en up** settled, made up.   **54 'ild** yield, reward.   **I . . .
like** I wish the same to you. (A polite phrase used to reply to a compliment.)   **55–6 country copulatives** country couples about to marry
and with sex on their minds   **57 blood breaks** as desire bursts forth.
58 humor whim   **60 honesty** chastity   **61 your pearl** i.e., the pearl
that one hears about   **62–3 swift and sententious** quick-witted and
good at aphorisms.   **64 fool's bolt** (Alluding to the proverb "A fool's
bolt [arrow] is soon shot.")   **65 dulcet diseases** pleasant afflictions,
entertaining yet sharp. (Touchstone wryly agrees with the Duke's
assessment of the Fool as swift and sententious.)

69 seeming seemly   **70 dislike** express dislike of   **75–6 disabled** dis-
paraged   **80 Countercheck** Rebuff   **86 measured swords** i.e., as in
the mere preliminary to a duel   **89 in . . . book** in a precise way.
(Touchstone is travestying books on the general subject of honor and
arms, which dealt with occasions and circumstances of the duel.)
97–8 take up settle   **101 swore brothers** became sworn brothers.
105 stalking-horse a real or artificial horse under cover of which the
hunter approached his game   **106 presentation** semblance
106.1 *Hymen* Roman god of faithful marriage.   ***Still*** Soft   **107 mirth**
joy   **108 made even** set straight   **109 Atone** are at one

That thou mightst join her hand with his
Whose heart within his bosom is.   114

ROSALIND [*to the Duke*]
    To you I give myself, for I am yours.
    [*To Orlando*] To you I give myself, for I am yours.

DUKE SENIOR
    If there be truth in sight, you are my daughter.

ORLANDO
    If there be truth in sight, you are my Rosalind.

PHOEBE
    If sight and shape be true,
    Why then, my love adieu!

ROSALIND [*to the Duke*]
    I'll have no father, if you be not he.
    [*To Orlando*] I'll have no husband, if you be not he.
    [*To Phoebe*] Nor ne'er wed woman, if you be not she.

HYMEN
        Peace, ho! I bar confusion.
        'Tis I must make conclusion
            Of these most strange events.
        Here's eight that must take hands
        To join in Hymen's bands,
            If truth holds true contents.   129
    [*To Orlando and Rosalind*]
        You and you no cross shall part.   130
    [*To Oliver and Celia*]
        You and you are heart in heart.
    [*To Phoebe*]
        You to his love must accord   132
        Or have a woman to your lord.   133
    [*To Touchstone and Audrey*]
        You and you are sure together,   134
        As the winter to foul weather.
    [*To all*]
        Whiles a wedlock hymn we sing,
        Feed yourselves with questioning,   137
        That reason wonder may diminish   138
        How thus we met, and these things finish.

                        Song.

        Wedding is great Juno's crown,   140
            O blessèd bond of board and bed!   141
        'Tis Hymen peoples every town;
            High wedlock then be honorèd.   143
        Honor, high honor and renown
            To Hymen, god of every town!

DUKE SENIOR [*to Celia*]
    O my dear niece, welcome thou art to me!
    Even daughter, welcome, in no less degree.   147

PHOEBE [*to Silvius*]
    I will not eat my word, now thou art mine;
    Thy faith my fancy to thee doth combine.   149

            Enter Second Brother [*Jaques de Boys*].

JAQUES DE BOYS
    Let me have audience for a word or two.
    I am the second son of old Sir Rowland,
    That bring these tidings to this fair assembly.
    Duke Frederick, hearing how that every day
    Men of great worth resorted to this forest,
    Addressed a mighty power, which were on foot   155
    In his own conduct, purposely to take   156
    His brother here and put him to the sword;
    And to the skirts of this wild wood he came,
    Where, meeting with an old religious man,
    After some question with him, was converted   160
    Both from his enterprise and from the world,
    His crown bequeathing to his banished brother,
    And all their lands restored to them again
    That were with him exiled. This to be true
    I do engage my life.

DUKE SENIOR   Welcome, young man.   165
    Thou offer'st fairly to thy brothers' wedding: 166
    To one his lands withheld and to the other   167
    A land itself at large, a potent dukedom.   168
    First, in this forest let us do those ends   169
    That here were well begun and well begot;   170
    And after, every of this happy number   171
    That have endured shrewd days and nights with us   172
    Shall share the good of our returnèd fortune
    According to the measure of their states.   174
    Meantime, forget this new-fall'n dignity,   175
    And fall into our rustic revelry.
    Play, music! And you, brides and bridegrooms all,
    With measure heaped in joy, to th' measures fall.   178

JAQUES
    Sir, by your patience.—If I heard you rightly,   179
    The Duke hath put on a religious life
    And thrown into neglect the pompous court.   181

JAQUES DE BOYS   He hath.

JAQUES
    To him will I. Out of these convertites   183
    There is much matter to be heard and learned.   184
    [*To the Duke*] You to your former honor I bequeath;
    Your patience and your virtue well deserves it.
    [*To Orlando*] You to a love that your true faith doth
        merit;

---

114 **Whose** (Refers to Rosalind.)   129 **If . . . contents** if the newly revealed truths are indeed true and bring true contentment.
130 **cross** vexation, mischance   132 **his** i.e., Silvius's   **accord** agree
133 **to your lord** for your husband.   134 **sure** closely united
137 **Feed** satisfy   138 **That . . . diminish** that understanding may lessen your wonder   140 **Juno's** (Juno was the Roman queen of the gods, presiding, in the Renaissance view, over faithful wedlock.)
141 **board and bed** sustenance and lodging; the household.
143 **High** solemn   147 **Even . . . degree** You are as welcome as a daughter.

149 **Thy faith . . . combine** your faithful love for me ties my love to you.   155 **Addressed** prepared.   **power** army   156 **In . . . conduct** under his own command   160 **question** conversation   165 **engage** pledge   166 **Thou offer'st fairly** You contribute handsomely   167 **To one** to Duke Senior   167–8 **to the other . . . large** to Orlando an entire dukedom (since, as husband of Rosalind, Orlando will eventually inherit as duke).   169 **do those ends** accomplish those purposes   170 **begot** conceived   171 **every** every one   172 **shrewd** hard, trying   174 **According . . . states** according to their degrees.   175 **new-fall'n** newly acquired   178 **With . . . fall** with an overflowing measure of joy, fall to dancing. (With wordplay on *measure* and *measures*, "dances.")   179 **by your patience** by your leave, i.e., let the music wait a moment.   181 **pompous** ceremonious   183 **convertites** converts   184 **matter** sound sense

[*To Oliver*] You to your land and love and great allies; 188
[*To Silvius*] You to a long and well-deservèd bed;
[*To Touchstone*] And you to wrangling, for thy loving
    voyage
Is but for two months victualed. So, to your pleasures. 191
I am for other than for dancing measures.

DUKE SENIOR   Stay, Jaques, stay.

JAQUES
To see no pastime I. What you would have
I'll stay to know at your abandoned cave.   *Exit.*

DUKE SENIOR
Proceed, proceed. We'll begin these rites,
As we do trust they'll end, in true delights.
            [*They dance.*] *Exeunt* [*all but Rosalind*].

❖

[Epilogue]

ROSALIND
It is not the fashion to see the lady the epilogue;
but it is no more unhandsome than to see the   2

---

188 **allies** kinfolk   191 **victualed** provisioned.
Epilogue
2 **unhandsome** in bad taste

---

lord the prologue. If it be true that good wine needs   3
no bush, 'tis true that a good play needs no epilogue.   4
Yet to good wine they do use good bushes, and good
plays prove the better by the help of good epilogues.
What a case am I in then, that am neither a good epilogue nor cannot insinuate with you in the behalf of a   8
good play! I am not furnished like a beggar; therefore   9
to beg will not become me. My way is to conjure you,   10
and I'll begin with the women. I charge you, O
women, for the love you bear to men, to like as much
of this play as please you; and I charge you, O men,
for the love you bear to women—as I perceive by your
simpering, none of you hates them—that between
you and the women the play may please. If I were a   16
woman I would kiss as many of you as had beards   17
that pleased me, complexions that liked me, and   18
breaths that I defied not; and I am sure as many as   19
have good beards or good faces or sweet breaths will,
for my kind offer, when I make curtsy, bid me fare-   21
well.   *Exit.*   22

3–4 good . . . bush (A proverb derived from the custom of displaying
a piece of ivy or holly at the tavern door to denote that wine was for
sale there.)   **8 insinuate** ingratiate myself   **9 furnished** equipped,
decked out   **10 conjure** adjure, earnestly charge   **16–17 If . . .
woman** (Womens's parts on the Elizabethan stage were played by
boys in feminine costume.)   **18 liked** pleased   **19 defied** rejected,
disdained   **21–2 bid me farewell** i.e., applaud me.

Twelfth Night; or, What You Will

*T*welfth Night is possibly the latest of the three festive comedies, including *Much Ado About Nothing* and *As You Like It*, with which Shakespeare climaxed his distinctively philosophical and joyous vein of comic writing. Performed on February 2, 1602, at the Middle Temple and written possibly as early as 1599, *Twelfth Night* is usually dated 1600 or 1601. This play is indeed the most festive of the lot. Its keynote is Saturnalian release and the carnival pursuit of love and mirth. Along with such familiar motifs as the plucky heroine disguised as a man (found earlier in *The Two Gentlemen of Verona, As You Like It*, and *The Merchant of Venice*), *Twelfth Night* also returns to the more farcical routines of mistaken identity found in Shakespeare's early comedy. As a witness of the 1602 performance, John Manningham, observes, the play is "much like the *Comedy of Errors*, or *Menaechmi* in Plautus, but most like and near to that in Italian called *Inganni*."

The carnival atmosphere is appropriate to the season designated in the play's title: the twelfth night of Christmas, January 6, the Feast of Epiphany. (The prologue to *Gl'Ingannati*, perhaps the Italian play referred to by Manningham, speaks of "La Notte di Beffania," Epiphany night.) Along with its primary Christian significance as the Feast of the Magi, Epiphany was also in Renaissance times the last day of the Christmas revels. Over a twelve-day period, from Christmas until January 6, noble households sponsored numerous performances of plays, masks, banquets, and every kind of festivity. (Leslie Hotson argues, in fact, that *Twelfth Night* was first performed on twelfth night in early 1601, in the presence of Queen Elizabeth.) Students left schools for vacations, celebrating release from study with plays and revels of their own. The stern rigors of a rule-bound society gave way temporarily to playful inversions of authority. The reign of the Boy Bishop and the Feast of Fools, for example, gave choristers and minor church functionaries the cherished opportunity to boss the hierarchy around, mock the liturgy with outrageous lampooning, and generally let off steam. Although such customs occasionally got out of hand, the idea was to channel potentially destructive insubordination into playacting and thereby promote harmony. Behind these Elizabethan midwinter customs lies the Roman Saturnalia, with its pagan spirit of gift giving, sensual indulgence, and satirical hostility to those who would curb merriment. Shakespeare's play captures the medieval and Renaissance spirit of Epiphany by its often playful allusions to religious practice: Feste's disguise as "Sir Topas," the priest, Feste's joke about living by the church (3.1.3–7), Sir Toby's defense of "cakes and ale," Feste's swearing by Saint Anne, mother of the Virgin Mary (2.3.115–16), Feste's joking about "clerestories" (4.2.38), and the like. Shakespeare lovingly evokes a tradition of festivals and ceremonies that incorporates self-mockery into its celebration of renewal at Christmas time.

Shakespeare's choice of sources for *Twelfth Night* underscores his commitment to mirth. Renaissance literature offered numerous instances of mistaken identity among twins and of the disguised heroine serving as page to her beloved. Among those in English were the anonymous play *Sir Clyomon and Sir Clamydes* (c. 1570–1583), Sir Philip Sidney's *Arcadia* (1590), and the prose romance *Parismus* by Emmanuel Forde (1598), featuring both a shipwreck and two characters with the names of Olivia and Violetta. Of particular significance, though partly for negative reasons, is Barnabe Riche's tale of "Apollonius and Silla" in *Riche His Farewell to Military Profession* (1581), which was based on François de Belleforest's 1571 French version of Matteo Bandello's *Novelle* (1554). Here we find most of the requisite plot elements: the shipwreck; Silla's disguise as a page in Duke Apollonius' court; her office as ambassador of love from Apollonius to the lady Julina, who thereupon falls in love with Silla; and the arrival of Silla's twin brother Silvio and his consequent success in winning Julina's affection. To Riche, however, this tale is merely a long warning against the enervating power of infatuation. Silvio gets Julina with child and disappears forthwith, making his belated reappearance almost too late to save the wrongly accused Silla. Riche's moralizing puts the blame on the gross and drunken appetite of carnal love. The total mismatching of affection with which the story begins, and the sudden realignments of desire based on mere outward resemblances, are seen as proofs of love's unreasonableness. Shakespeare, of course, retains and capitalizes on the irrational quality of love, as in *A Midsummer Night's Dream*, but in doing so he minimizes the harm done (Olivia is not made pregnant) and repudiates any negative moral judgments. The added subplot, with its rebuking of Malvolio's censoriousness, may have been conceived as a further answer to Riche, Fenton, and their sober school.

Shakespeare's festive spirit owes much, as Manningham observed, to Plautus and the neoclassical Italian comic writers. At least three Italian comedies called *Gl'Inganni* ("The Frauds") employ the motif of mistaken identity, and one of them, by Curzio Gonzaga (1592), supplies Viola's assumed name of "Cesare," or Cesario. Another play with the same title appeared in 1562. More useful is *Gl'Ingannati* ("The Deceived"), performed in 1531 and translated into French in 1543. Besides a plot line generally similar to *Twelfth Night* and the reference to La Notte di Beffania (Epiphany), this play offers the suggestive name *Malevolti*, "evil-faced," and *Fabio* (which resembles "Fabian"). It also contains possible hints for Malvolio, Sir Toby, and company, although the plot of the counterfeit letter is original with Shakespeare. Essentially, Shakespeare combines his own plot with an Italianate novella plot, as he did in *The Taming of the Shrew* and *Much Ado About Nothing*. And it is in the Malvolio story that Shakespeare most pointedly defends merriment. Feste the professional fool, an original stage type for Shakespeare in *Twelfth Night* and in *As You Like It*, also reinforces the theme of seizing the moment of mirth.

This great lesson, of savoring life's pleasures while one is still young, is something that Orsino and Olivia have not yet learned when the play commences. Although suited to one another in rank, wealth, and attractiveness, they are unable to overcome their own willful posturing in the elaborate charade of courtship. Like Silvius in *As You Like It*, Orsino is the conventional wooer trapped in the courtly artifice of love's rules. He opens the play on a cloying note of self-pity. He is fascinated with his own degradation as a rejected suitor and bores his listeners with his changeable moods and fondness for poetical "conceits." He sees himself as a hart pursued by his desires "like fell and cruel hounds," reminding us that enervating lovesickness has, in fact, robbed him of his manly occupation, hunting. He sends ornately contrived messages to Olivia but has not seen her in so long that his passion has become unreal and fantastical, feeding on itself.

Olivia plays the opposite role of chaste, denying womanhood. She explains her retirement from the world as mourning for a dead brother (whose name we never learn), but this withdrawal from life is another unreal vision. Olivia's practice of mourning, whereby she will "water once a day her chamber round / With eye-offending brine" (1.1.28–9), is a lifeless ritual. As others view the matter, she is senselessly wasting her beauty and affection on the dead. "What a plague means my niece to take the death of her brother thus?" Sir Toby expostulates (1.3.1–2). Viola, though she, too, has seemingly lost a brother, is an important foil in this regard, for she continues to hope for her brother's safety, trusts his soul is in heaven if he is dead, and refuses to give up her commitment to life in any case. We suspect that Olivia takes a willful pleasure in self-denial not unlike Orsino's self-congratulatory suffering. She appears to derive satisfaction from the power she holds over Orsino, a power of refusal. And she must know that she looks stunning in black.

Olivia's household reflects, in part, her mood of self-denial. She keeps Malvolio as steward because he, too, dresses somberly, insists on quiet as befits a house in mourning, and maintains order. Yet Olivia also retains a fool, Feste, who is Malvolio's opposite in every way. Hard-pressed to defend his mirthful function in a household so given over to melancholy, Feste must find some way of persuading his mistress that her very gravity is itself the essence of folly. This is a paradox, because sobriety and order appeal to the conventional wisdom of the world. Malvolio, sensing that his devotion to propriety is being challenged by the fool's prating, chides Olivia for taking "delight in such a barren rascal" (1.5.80–1).

Feste must argue for an inversion of appearance and reality whereby many of the world's ordinary pursuits can be seen to be ridiculous. As he observes, in his habitually elliptical manner of speech, *"Cucullus non facit monachum* [the cowl doesn't make the monk]; that's as much to say as I wear not motley in my brain" (1.5.52–4). Feste wins his case by making Olivia laugh at her own illogic in grieving for a brother whose soul she assumes to be in heaven. By extension, Olivia has indeed been a fool for allowing herself to be deprived of happiness in love by her brother's death ("there is no true cuckold but calamity") and for failing to consider the brevity of youth ("beauty's a flower"). Yet, paradoxically, only one who professes to be a fool can point this out, enabled by his detachment and innocence to perceive simple but profound truths denied to supposedly rational persons. This vision of the fool as naturally wise, and of society as self-indulgently insane, fascinated Renaissance writers, from Erasmus's *In Praise of Folly* and Cervantes's *Don Quixote* to Shakespeare's *King Lear*.

Viola, although not dressed in motley, aligns herself with Feste's rejection of self-denial. Refreshingly, even comically, she challenges the staid artifice of Orsino's and Olivia's lives. She is an ocean traveler, like many of Shakespeare's later heroines (Marina in *Pericles*, Perdita in *The Winter's Tale),* arriving on Illyria's shore plucky and determined. On her first embassy to Olivia from Orsino, she exposes with disarming candor the willfully ritualistic quality of Olivia's existence. Viola discards the flowery set speech she had prepared and memorized at Orsino's behest; despite her charmingly conceited assertion that the speech has been "excellently well penned," she senses that its elegant but empty rhetoric is all too familiar to the disdainful Olivia. Instead, Viola departs from her text to urge seizing the moment of happiness. "You do usurp yourself," she lectures Olivia, "for what is yours to bestow is not yours to reserve" (1.5.183–4). Beauty is a gift of nature, and failure to use it is a sin against nature. Or, again, "Lady, you are the cruel'st she alive / If you will lead these graces [Olivia's beauty] to the grave / And leave the world no copy" (lines 236–8). An essential argument in favor of love, as in Shakespeare's sonnets, is the necessity of marriage and childbearing in order to perpetuate beauty. This approach is new to Olivia and catches her wholly by surprise. In part, she reacts, like Phoebe in *As You Like It,* with perverse logic, rejecting a too-willing wooer for one who is hard to get. Yet Olivia is also attracted by a new note of sincerity, prompting her to reenter life and accept maturely both the risks and rewards of romantic involvement. Her longing for "Cesario" is, of course, sexually misdirected, but the appearance of Viola's identical twin, Sebastian, soon puts all to rights.

The motifs of Olivia's attraction for another woman (both actors would have been boys) and of Orsino's deep fondness for a seeming young man ("Cesario"), which matures into sexual love, raise delicate suggestions of love between members of the same sex, as in *As You Like It.* Once again, the ambiguities of disguise point toward the socially constructed nature of sexual difference. Viola as "Cesario" strikes those who meet her as almost sexually indeterminate. Orsino puts the matter well, in conversing with "Cesario," when he observes, "they shall yet belie thy happy years / That say thou art a man. Diana's lip / Is not more smooth and rubious; thy small pipe / Is as the maiden's organ, shrill and sound, / And all is semblative a woman's part" (1.4.30–4). Male adolescence and femininity are seen as virtually indistinguishable—a point that is wittily reinforced in the theater by the fact that a boy actor is playing Viola disguised as "Cesario."

At the same time, this playful confusion of sexual difference becomes the vehicle for a serious exploration of love and friendship. Like Rosalind in *As You Like It,* Viola uses her male attire to win Orsino's pure affection in a friendship nominally devoid of sexual interest, since both seemingly are men. Friendship must come first; the Renaissance generally accorded a higher value to friend-

ship than to erotic passion. Yet Shakespeare also insists, as did many of his contemporaries (including Montaigne), that friendship is not only possible between men and women but also that such a relationship, formalized in marriage, offers the best of all worlds; hence, the importance of Viola's male disguise. As "Cesario," she can teach Orsino about the conventions of love in relaxed and frank conversations that would not be possible if she were known to be a woman. She teaches him to avoid the beguiling but misleading myths of Petrarchan love (named after the Italian sonneteer Francis Petrarch, whose poems embody the idealization of courtly love) and so prepares him for the realities of marriage. Comparing men and women in love, she confides, "We men may say more, swear more, but indeed / Our shows are more than will; for still we prove / Much in our vows, but little in our love" (2.4.116–18). Once she and Orsino have achieved an instinctive rapport—all the more remarkable for their talking so often at cross-purposes—Viola's unmasking can make possible a physical communion as well. Orsino, no longer trapped in the futile worship of a seemingly unapproachable goddess, can come to terms with his sexuality as part of a unified and loving human relationship.

The friendship of Sebastian and Antonio, meanwhile, sorely tested by the mix-ups of the mistaken identity plot, similarly places Sebastian in a love-and-friendship triangle like that involving Bassanio, Portia, and Antonio in *The Merchant of Venice.* Sebastian and Antonio are loving friends, so much so that Antonio willingly risks his life to be with Sebastian in a country where Antonio has many enemies. Antonio's expressions of fondness for Sebastian are extraordinarily warm. "If you will not murder me for my love, let me be your servant," he pleads. "I do adore thee so / That danger shall seem sport, and I will go" (2.1.33–4, 45–6). A desire "More sharp than filèd steel" spurs Antonio to seek out his friend, despite the manifest danger (3.3.4–5). "A witchcraft" draws him to Sebastian (5.1.72). Whether the attachment is homosexual, as it is often played on the modern stage, is debatable; expressions of warmth between men seem to have been more common in Elizabethan times than today, and centuries of intervening time have no doubt altered our understanding of same-sex relationships; the term *homosexual* is of much later date. What remains true for the play is that this portrayal of emotional and loving closeness between two men gives way to the marriage of one of them to a woman (as in *The Merchant of Venice*). The depiction of love and friendship between two men is a repeated motif in the play, embodied most of all in the loving relationship of Orsino and "Cesario." Shakespeare chooses to resolve his plot by defining heterosexual marriage as the completion of relationships begun in friendship and incorporating that friendship in a union that finally offers heterosexual fulfillment as well.

The below-stairs characters of the subplot, Sir Toby and the rest, share with Feste and Viola a commitment to joy. As Sir Toby proclaims in his first speech, "care's an enemy to life" (1.3.2–3). Even the simpleton Sir Andrew, although gulled by Sir Toby into spending his money on a hopeless pursuit of Olivia, seems none the worse for his treatment; he loves to drink in Sir Toby's company and can afford to pay for his entertainment. Sir Toby gives us some of the richly inventive humor of Falstaff, another lovable fat roguish knight. In this subplot, however, the confrontations between merriment and sobriety are more harshly drawn than in the main plot. Whereas the gracious Olivia is won away from her folly, the obdurate Malvolio can only be exposed to ridicule. He is chiefly to blame for the polarization of attitudes, for he insists on rebuking the mirth of others. His name (*Mal-volio,* the "ill-wisher") implies a self-satisfied determination to impose his rigid moral code on others. As Sir Toby taunts him, "Dost thou think, because thou art virtuous, there shall be no more cakes and ale?" (2.3.114–15). Malvolio's inflexible hostility provokes a desire for comic vengeance. The method is satiric: the clever manipulators, Maria and Sir Toby, invent a scheme to entrap Malvolio in his own self-deceit. The punishment fits the crime, for he has long dreamed of himself as "Count Malvolio," rich, powerful, and in a position to demolish Sir Toby and the rest. Without Malvolio's infatuated predisposition to believe that Olivia could actually love him and write such a letter as he finds, Maria's scheme would have no hope of success. He tortures the text to make it yield a suitable meaning, much in the style of Puritan theologizing. His conviction that Jove is

with him (2.5.169) reminds us of the Puritan belief that prosperity of the "elect" is a sign of God's grace.

Indeed, Malvolio in some ways does resemble a Puritan, as Maria observes (2.3.139–47), even though she qualifies the assertion by saying that he is not a religious fanatic but a "time-pleaser." She directs her observation not at a religious group but at all who would be killjoys; if the Puritans are like that, she intimates, so much the worse for them. This uncharacteristic lack of charity gives a sharp tone to the vengeance practiced on Malvolio, evoking from Olivia a protest that "he hath been most notoriously abused" (5.1.379). The belated attempt to make a reconciliation with him seems, however, doomed to failure, in light of his grim resolve to "be revenged on the whole pack of you." At the height of his discomfiture, he has been tricked into doing the two things he hates most: smiling affably and wearing sportive attire. The appearance of merriment is so grossly unsuited to him that he is declared mad and put into safekeeping. The apostle of sobriety in this play thus comes before us as a declared madman, while the fool Feste offers him sage comment in the guise of a priest. Wisdom and folly have changed places. The upside-down character of the play is epitomized in Malvolio's plaintive remark to Feste (no longer posing as the priest): "I am as well in my wits, Fool, as thou art" (4.2.88). Malvolio's comeuppance is richly deserved, but the severity of vengeance and countervengeance suggests that the triumph of festival will not last long. This brevity is, of course, inherent in the nature of such holiday release from responsibility. As Feste sings, "What's to come is still unsure. / In delay there lies no plenty."

Twelfth Night; or, What You Will

[*Dramatis Personae*

ORSINO, *Duke (sometimes called Count) of Illyria*
VALENTINE, *gentleman attending on Orsino*
CURIO, *gentleman attending on Orsino*

VIOLA, *a shipwrecked lady, later disguised as Cesario*
SEBASTIAN, *twin brother of Viola*
ANTONIO, *a sea captain, friend to Sebastian*
CAPTAIN *of the shipwrecked vessel*

OLIVIA, *a rich countess of Illyria*
MARIA, *gentlewoman in Olivia's household*

  SCENE: *Illyria*]

SIR TOBY BELCH, *Olivia's uncle*
SIR ANDREW AGUECHEEK, *a companion of Sir Toby*
MALVOLIO, *steward of Olivia's household*
FABIAN, *a member of Olivia's household*
FESTE, *a clown, also called* FOOL, *Olivia's jester*

A PRIEST
FIRST OFFICER
SECOND OFFICER

Lords, Sailors, Musicians, and other Attendants

1.1

Enter Orsino Duke of Illyria, Curio, and other lords [with musicians].

ORSINO
If music be the food of love, play on;
Give me excess of it, that surfeiting,
The appetite may sicken and so die.
That strain again! It had a dying fall;   4
Oh, it came o'er my ear like the sweet sound
That breathes upon a bank of violets,
Stealing and giving odor. Enough, no more.
'Tis not so sweet now as it was before.
O spirit of love, how quick and fresh art thou,   9
That, notwithstanding thy capacity
Receiveth as the sea, naught enters there,
Of what validity and pitch soe'er,   12
But falls into abatement and low price   13
Even in a minute! So full of shapes is fancy   14
That it alone is high fantastical.   15

CURIO
Will you go hunt, my lord?
ORSINO   What, Curio?
CURIO   The hart.
ORSINO
Why, so I do, the noblest that I have.   17
Oh, when mine eyes did see Olivia first,
Methought she purged the air of pestilence.
That instant was I turned into a hart,
And my desires, like fell and cruel hounds,   21
E'er since pursue me.

Enter Valentine.

       How now, what news from her?   22
VALENTINE
So please my lord, I might not be admitted,
But from her handmaid do return this answer:
The element itself, till seven years' heat,   25
Shall not behold her face at ample view;
But like a cloistress she will veilèd walk,   27
And water once a day her chamber round
With eye-offending brine—all this to season   29

1.1 Location: Orsino's court.
0.1 *Illyria* Nominally on the east coast of the Adriatic Sea, but with a suggestion also of "illusion" and "delirium." **4 fall** cadence **9 quick and fresh** keen and hungry **12 validity** value. **pitch** superiority. (Literally, the highest point of a falcon's flight.) **13 abatement** depreciation. (The lover's brain entertains innumerable fantasies but soon tires of them all.) **14 shapes** imagined forms. **fancy** love **15 it … fantastical** it surpasses everything else in imaginative power.

17 the noblest . . . have i.e., my noblest part, my heart. (Punning on *hart.*) **21 fell** fierce **22 pursue me** (Alludes to the story in Ovid of Actaeon, who, having seen Diana bathing, was transformed into a stag and killed by his own hounds.) **25 element** sky. **seven years' heat** seven summers **27 cloistress** nun secluded in a religious community **29 season** keep fresh. (Playing on the idea of the salt in her tears.)

A brother's dead love, which she would keep fresh 30
And lasting in her sad remembrance.
ORSINO
Oh, she that hath a heart of that fine frame 32
To pay this debt of love but to a brother,
How will she love, when the rich golden shaft 34
Hath killed the flock of all affections else 35
That live in her; when liver, brain, and heart, 36
These sovereign thrones, are all supplied, and filled 37
Her sweet perfections, with one self king! 38
Away before me to sweet beds of flowers.
Love-thoughts lie rich when canopied with bowers.
                                                    Exeunt.

❖

1.2

Enter Viola, a Captain, and sailors.

VIOLA   What country, friends, is this?
CAPTAIN   This is Illyria, lady.
VIOLA
And what should I do in Illyria?
My brother he is in Elysium. 4
Perchance he is not drowned. What think you, sailors? 5
CAPTAIN
It is perchance that you yourself were saved. 6
VIOLA
Oh, my poor brother! And so perchance may he be.
CAPTAIN
True, madam, and to comfort you with chance, 8
Assure yourself, after our ship did split,
When you and those poor number saved with you
Hung on our driving boat, I saw your brother, 11
Most provident in peril, bind himself,
Courage and hope both teaching him the practice,
To a strong mast that lived upon the sea; 14
Where, like Arion on the dolphin's back, 15
I saw him hold acquaintance with the waves
So long as I could see.
VIOLA   For saying so, there's gold.   [*She gives money.*]
Mine own escape unfoldeth to my hope, 19
Whereto thy speech serves for authority, 20
The like of him. Know'st thou this country? 21

CAPTAIN
Ay, madam, well, for I was bred and born
Not three hours' travel from this very place.
VIOLA   Who governs here?
CAPTAIN   A noble duke, in nature as in name.
VIOLA   What is his name?
CAPTAIN   Orsino.
VIOLA
Orsino! I have heard my father name him.
He was a bachelor then.
CAPTAIN
And so is now, or was so very late; 30
For but a month ago I went from hence,
And then 'twas fresh in murmur—as, you know, 32
What great ones do the less will prattle of— 33
That he did seek the love of fair Olivia.
VIOLA   What's she?
CAPTAIN
A virtuous maid, the daughter of a count
That died some twelvemonth since, then leaving her
In the protection of his son, her brother,
Who shortly also died; for whose dear love,
They say, she hath abjured the sight
And company of men.
VIOLA   Oh, that I served that lady,
And might not be delivered to the world 42
Till I had made mine own occasion mellow, 43
What my estate is!
CAPTAIN   That were hard to compass, 44
Because she will admit no kind of suit,
No, not the Duke's. 46
VIOLA
There is a fair behavior in thee, Captain,
And though that nature with a beauteous wall 48
Doth oft close in pollution, yet of thee
I will believe thou hast a mind that suits
With this thy fair and outward character. 51
I prithee, and I'll pay thee bounteously,
Conceal me what I am, and be my aid
For such disguise as haply shall become 54
The form of my intent. I'll serve this duke. 55
Thou shalt present me as an eunuch to him. 56
It may be worth thy pains, for I can sing
And speak to him in many sorts of music
That will allow me very worth his service. 59
What else may hap, to time I will commit;
Only shape thou thy silence to my wit. 61
CAPTAIN
Be you his eunuch, and your mute I'll be; 62
When my tongue blabs, then let mine eyes not see.
VIOLA   I thank thee. Lead me on.   *Exeunt.*

❖

30 A brother's dead love her love for her dead brother and the memory of his love for her   **32 frame** construction   **34 golden shaft** Cupid's golden-tipped arrow, causing love. (His lead-tipped arrow causes aversion.)   **35 affections else** other feelings   **36–8 when . . . king** i.e., when passion, thought, and feeling all sit in majesty in their proper thrones (liver, brain, and heart), and her sweet perfections are brought to completion by her union with a single lord and husband.
1.2 Location: The seacoast.
4 Elysium classical abode of the blessed dead   **5-6 Perchance . . . perchance** Perhaps . . . by mere chance   **8 chance** i.e., what one may hope that chance will bring about   **11 driving** drifting, driven by the seas   **14 lived** i.e., kept afloat   **15 Arion** a Greek poet who so charmed the dolphins with his lyre that they saved him when he leaped into the sea to escape murderous sailors   **19-21 unfoldeth . . . him** offers a hopeful example that he may have escaped similarly, to which hope your speech provides support.

30 late lately   **32 murmur** rumor   **33 less** social inferiors   **42 delivered** revealed, made known. (With suggestion of "born.")   **43 Till . . . mellow** until the time is ripe for my purpose   **44 estate** social rank. **compass** encompass, bring about   **46 not** not even   **48 though that** though   **51 character** face or features as indicating moral qualities. **54–5 as haply . . . intent** as may suit the nature of my purpose. **56 eunuch** castrato, high-voiced singer   **59 allow** prove   **61 wit** plan, invention.   **62 mute** silent attendant. (Sometimes used of nonspeaking actors.)

1.3

Enter Sir Toby [Belch] and Maria.

SIR TOBY   What a plague means my niece to take the death of her brother thus? I am sure care's an enemy to life.

MARIA   By my troth, Sir Toby, you must come in earlier o'nights. Your cousin, my lady, takes great exceptions   5 to your ill hours.

SIR TOBY   Why, let her except before excepted.   7

MARIA   Ay, but you must confine yourself within the modest limits of order.   9

SIR TOBY   Confine? I'll confine myself no finer than I am.   10 These clothes are good enough to drink in, and so be these boots too. An they be not, let them hang them-   12 selves in their own straps.

MARIA   That quaffing and drinking will undo you. I heard my lady talk of it yesterday, and of a foolish knight that you brought in one night here to be her wooer.

SIR TOBY   Who, Sir Andrew Aguecheek?

MARIA   Ay, he.

SIR TOBY   He's as tall a man as any's in Illyria.   20

MARIA   What's that to the purpose?

SIR TOBY   Why, he has three thousand ducats a year.   22

MARIA   Ay, but he'll have but a year in all these ducats.   23 He's a very fool and a prodigal.

SIR TOBY   Fie, that you'll say so! He plays o'th' viol-de-   25 gamboys, and speaks three or four languages word   26 for word without book, and hath all the good gifts of   27 nature.

MARIA   He hath indeed, almost natural, for, besides that   29 he's a fool, he's a great quarreler, and but that he hath the gift of a coward to allay the gust he hath in quar-   31 reling, 'tis thought among the prudent he would quickly have the gift of a grave.

SIR TOBY   By this hand, they are scoundrels and sub-   34 stractors that say so of him. Who are they?   35

MARIA   They that add, moreover, he's drunk nightly in your company.

SIR TOBY   With drinking healths to my niece. I'll drink to her as long as there is a passage in my throat and drink in Illyria. He's a coward and a coistrel that will   40 not drink to my niece till his brains turn o'th' toe like

a parish top. What, wench? *Castiliano vulgo!* For here   42 comes Sir Andrew Agueface.   43

Enter Sir Andrew [Aguecheek].

SIR ANDREW   Sir Toby Belch! How now, Sir Toby Belch?

SIR TOBY   Sweet Sir Andrew!

SIR ANDREW   [*to Maria*]   Bless you, fair shrew.   46

MARIA   And you too, sir.

SIR TOBY   Accost, Sir Andrew, accost.   48

SIR ANDREW   What's that?

SIR TOBY   My niece's chambermaid.   50

SIR ANDREW   Good Mistress Accost, I desire better acquaintance.

MARIA   My name is Mary, sir.

SIR ANDREW   Good Mistress Mary Accost—

SIR TOBY   You mistake, knight. "Accost" is front her,   55 board her, woo her, assail her.   56

SIR ANDREW   By my troth, I would not undertake her in   57 this company. Is that the meaning of "accost"?

MARIA   Fare you well, gentlemen.   [*Going.*]

SIR TOBY   An thou let part so, Sir Andrew, would thou   60 mightst never draw sword again.

SIR ANDREW   An you let part so, mistress, I would I might never draw sword again. Fair lady, do you think you have fools in hand?   64

MARIA   Sir, I have not you by the hand.

SIR ANDREW   Marry, but you shall have, and here's my   66 hand.   [*He gives her his hand.*]

MARIA   Now, sir, thought is free. I pray you, bring your   68 hand to th' buttery-bar, and let it drink.   69

SIR ANDREW   Wherefore, sweetheart? What's your metaphor?

MARIA   It's dry, sir.   72

SIR ANDREW   Why, I think so. I am not such an ass but I can keep my hand dry. But what's your jest?

MARIA   A dry jest, sir.   75

SIR ANDREW   Are you full of them?

MARIA   Ay, sir, I have them at my fingers' ends. Marry,   77 now I let go your hand, I am barren.   78

[*She lets go his hand.*] *Exit Maria.*

---

42 parish top a large top provided by the parish to be spun by whip-ping, apparently for exercise.   ***Castiliano vulgo!*** (Of uncertain mean-ing. Possibly Sir Toby is saying "Speak of the devil!" Castiliano is the name adopted by a devil in Haughton's *Grim the Collier of Croydon*.)   **43 Agueface** (Like *Aguecheek*, this name betokens the thin, pale coun-tenance of one suffering from an ague or fever.)   **46 shrew** i.e., diminutive creature. (But with probably unintended suggestion of shrewishness.)   **48 Accost** Go alongside (a nautical term), i.e., greet her, address her   **50 chambermaid** lady-in-waiting (a gentlewoman, not one who would do menial tasks).   **55 front** confront, come along-side   **56 board** greet, approach (as though preparing to board in a naval encounter)   **57 undertake** have to do with. (Here with unin-tended sexual suggestion, to which Maria mirthfully replies with her jokes about *dry jests, barren,* and *buttery-bar.*)   **60 An . . . part** If you let her leave   **64 have . . . hand** i.e., have to deal with fools. (But Maria puns on the literal sense.)   **66 Marry** i.e., Indeed. (Originally, "By the Virgin Mary.")   **68 thought is free** i.e., I may think what I like. (Proverbial; replying to *do you think . . . in hand,* above.)   **69 buttery-bar** ledge on top of the half-door to the buttery or the wine cellar. (Maria's language is sexually suggestive, though Sir Andrew seems oblivious to that.)   **72 dry** thirsty; also dried up, a sign of age and sexual debility   **75 dry** (1) ironic (2) dull, barren. (Referring to Sir Andrew.)   **77 at my fingers' ends** (1) at the ready (2) by the hand. **78 barren** i.e., empty of jests and of Sir Andrew's hand.

1.3 Location: Olivia's house.
5 cousin kinswoman   **7 let . . . excepted** i.e., let her take exception to my conduct all she wants; I don't care. (Plays on the legal phrase *exceptis excipiendis,* "with the exceptions before named.")   **9 modest** moderate   **10 I'll . . . finer** (1) I'll constrain myself no more rigor-ously (2) I'll dress myself no more finely   **12 An** If   **20 tall** brave. (But Maria pretends to take the word in the common sense.) **22 ducats** coins worth about four or five shillings   **23 he'll . . . ducats** he'll spend all his money within a year.   **25–6 viol-de-gamboys** viola da gamba, leg-viol, bass viol   **27 without book** by heart **29 natural** (With a play on the sense "born idiot.")   **31 gift** natural ability. (But shifted to mean "present" in line 33.)   **allay the gust** moderate the taste   **34–5 substractors** detractors   **40 coistrel** horse-groom, base fellow

SIR TOBY   Oh, knight, thou lack'st a cup of canary! When 79
did I see thee so put down?

SIR ANDREW   Never in your life, I think, unless you see
canary put me down. Methinks sometimes I have no 82
more wit than a Christian or an ordinary man has. But
I am a great eater of beef, and I believe that does harm
to my wit.

SIR TOBY   No question.

SIR ANDREW   An I thought that, I'd forswear it. I'll ride
home tomorrow, Sir Toby.

SIR TOBY   *Pourquoi,* my dear knight? 89

SIR ANDREW   What is *"pourquoi"*? Do or not do? I would
I had bestowed that time in the tongues that I 91
have in fencing, dancing, and bearbaiting. Oh, had I 92
but followed the arts! 93

SIR TOBY   Then hadst thou had an excellent head of hair.

SIR ANDREW   Why, would that have mended my hair? 95

SIR TOBY   Past question, for thou see'st it will not curl by
nature.

SIR ANDREW   But it becomes me well enough, does't
not?

SIR TOBY   Excellent. It hangs like flax on a distaff; and I 100
hope to see a huswife take thee between her legs and
spin it off. 102

SIR TOBY   Faith, I'll home tomorrow, Sir Toby. Your
niece will not be seen, or if she be, it's four to one
she'll none of me. The Count himself here hard by 105
woos her.

SIR TOBY   She'll none o'th' Count. She'll not match
above her degree, neither in estate, years, nor wit; I 108
have heard her swear't. Tut, there's life in't, man. 109

SIR ANDREW   I'll stay a month longer. I am a fellow o'th'
strangest mind i'th' world; I delight in masques and
revels sometimes altogether.

SIR TOBY   Art thou good at these kickshawses, knight? 113

SIR ANDREW   As any man in Illyria, whatsoever he be,
under the degree of my betters, and yet I will not 115
compare with an old man. 116

SIR TOBY   What is thy excellence in a galliard, knight? 117

SIR ANDREW   Faith, I can cut a caper. 118

SIR TOBY   And I can cut the mutton to't.

SIR ANDREW   And I think I have the back-trick simply 120
as strong as any man in Illyria.

SIR TOBY   Wherefore are these things hid? Wherefore
have these gifts a curtain before 'em? Are they like to 123
take dust, like Mistress Mall's picture? Why dost thou 124
not go to church in a galliard and come home in a
coranto? My very walk should be a jig; I would not so 126
much as make water but in a sink-a-pace. What dost 127
thou mean? Is it a world to hide virtues in? I did think, 128
by the excellent constitution of thy leg, it was formed
under the star of a galliard. 130

SIR ANDREW   Ay, 'tis strong, and it does indifferent well 131
in a dun-colored stock. Shall we set about some 132
revels?

SIR TOBY   What shall we do else? Were we not born
under Taurus? 135

SIR ANDREW   Taurus? That's sides and heart.

SIR TOBY   No, sir, it is legs and thighs. Let me see thee
caper. [*Sir Andrew capers.*] Ha, higher! Ha, ha, excellent!   *Exeunt.*

❧

1.4

Enter Valentine, and Viola in man's attire.

VALENTINE   If the Duke continue these favors towards
you, Cesario, you are like to be much advanced. He 2
hath known you but three days, and already you are
no stranger.

VIOLA   You either fear his humor or my negligence, 5
that you call in question the continuance of his love. Is
he inconstant, sir, in his favors?

VALENTINE   No, believe me.

Enter Duke [Orsino], Curio, and attendants.

VIOLA   I thank you. Here comes the Count.

ORSINO   Who saw Cesario, ho?

VIOLA   On your attendance, my lord, here. 11

ORSINO
Stand you awhile aloof. [*The others stand aside.*]
Cesario, 12
Thou know'st no less but all. I have unclasped
To thee the book even of my secret soul.
Therefore, good youth, address thy gait unto her; 15
Be not denied access, stand at her doors,

79 thou . . . canary i.e., you look as if you need a drink. (*Canary* is a sweet wine from the Canary Islands.)   **82 put me down** (1) baffle my wits (2) lay me out flat.   **89 *Pourquoi*** Why   **91 tongues** languages. (Sir Toby then puns on "tongs," curling irons.)   **92 bearbaiting** the sport of setting dogs on a chained bear.   **93 the arts** the liberal arts, learning. (But Sir Toby plays on the phrase as meaning "artifice," the antithesis of *nature*.)   **95 mended** improved   **100 distaff** a staff for holding the flax, tow, or wool in spinning   **102 spin it off** i.e., (1) treat your flaxen hair as though it were flax on a distaff to be spun (2) cause you to lose hair as a result of venereal disease (3) make you ejaculate. (*Huswife* suggests "hussy," "whore.")   **105 Count** i.e., Duke Orsino, sometimes referred to as Count.   **hard** near   **108 degree** social position.   **estate** fortune, social position   **109 there's life in't** i.e., while there's life there's hope   **113 kickshawses** delicacies, fancy trifles. (From the French, *quelque chose.*)   **115 under . . . betters** excepting those who are above me   **116 old man** i.e., one experienced through age.   **117 galliard** lively dance in triple time   **118 cut a caper** make a lively leap. (But Sir Toby puns on the *caper* used to make a sauce served with mutton. *Mutton,* in turn, suggests "whore.")

120 back-trick backward step in the galliard. (With sexual innuendo; the back was associated with sexual vigor.)   **123–4 like to take** likely to collect   **124 Mistress Mall's picture** i.e., perhaps the portrait of some woman protected from light and dust, as many pictures were, by curtains. (*Mall* is a diminutive of *Mary.*)   **126 coranto** lively running dance.   **127 sink-a-pace** dance like the galliard. (French *cinquepace. Sink* also suggests a cesspool into which one might urinate.)   **128 virtues** talents   **130 under . . . galliard** i.e., under a star favorable to dancing.   **131 indifferent well** well enough. (Said complacently.)   **132 dun-colored stock** mouse-colored stocking.
135 Taurus zodiacal sign. (Sir Andrew is mistaken, since Leo governed sides and hearts in medical astrology. Taurus governed legs and thighs, or, more commonly, neck and throat.)
1.4 Location: Orsino's court.
2 like likely   **5 humor** changeableness   **11 On your attendance** Ready to do you service   **12 aloof** aside.   **15 address thy gait** go

And tell them, there thy fixèd foot shall grow
Till thou have audience.

VIOLA   Sure, my noble lord,
If she be so abandoned to her sorrow
As it is spoke, she never will admit me.

ORSINO
Be clamorous and leap all civil bounds   21
Rather than make unprofited return.

VIOLA
Say I do speak with her, my lord, what then?

ORSINO
Oh, then unfold the passion of my love;
Surprise her with discourse of my dear faith.   25
It shall become thee well to act my woes;   26
She will attend it better in thy youth
Than in a nuncio's of more grave aspect.   28

VIOLA
I think not so, my lord.

ORSINO   Dear lad, believe it;
For they shall yet belie thy happy years
That say thou art a man. Diana's lip
Is not more smooth and rubious; thy small pipe   32
Is as the maiden's organ, shrill and sound,   33
And all is semblative a woman's part.   34
I know thy constellation is right apt   35
For this affair.—Some four or five attend him.
All, if you will, for I myself am best
When least in company.—Prosper well in this,
And thou shalt live as freely as thy lord,
To call his fortunes thine.

VIOLA   I'll do my best
To woo your lady. [Aside] Yet a barful strife!   41
Whoe'er I woo, myself would be his wife.   Exeunt.

❧

1.5

Enter Maria and Clown [Feste].

MARIA   Nay, either tell me where thou hast been, or I
will not open my lips so wide as a bristle may enter in
way of thy excuse. My lady will hang thee for thy
absence.

FESTE   Let her hang me. He that is well hanged in this
world needs to fear no colors.   6

MARIA   Make that good.   7

FESTE   He shall see none to fear.   8

MARIA   A good Lenten answer. I can tell thee where   9
that saying was born, of "I fear no colors."

FESTE   Where, good Mistress Mary?

MARIA   In the wars, and that may you be bold to say in   12
your foolery.

FESTE   Well, God give them wisdom that have it; and   13
those that are fools, let them use their talents.   15

MARIA   Yet you will be hanged for being so long absent;
or to be turned away, is not that as good as a hanging   17
to you?

FESTE   Many a good hanging prevents a bad marriage;   19
and for turning away, let summer bear it out.   20

MARIA   You are resolute, then?

FESTE   Not so, neither, but I am resolved on two
points.   23

MARIA   That if one break, the other will hold; or if both
break, your gaskins fall.   25

FESTE   Apt, in good faith, very apt. Well, go thy way. If
Sir Toby would leave drinking, thou wert as witty a   27
piece of Eve's flesh as any in Illyria.   28

MARIA   Peace, you rogue, no more o' that. Here comes
my lady. Make your excuse wisely, you were best.   30

[*Exit.*]

*Enter Lady Olivia with Malvolio, [and
attendants].*

FESTE   [*aside*]   Wit, an't be thy will, put me into good 31
fooling! Those wits that think they have thee do very
oft prove fools, and I that am sure I lack thee may pass
for a wise man. For what says Quinapalus? "Better a   34
witty fool than a foolish wit."—God bless thee, lady!

OLIVIA   [*to attendants*]   Take the fool away.

FESTE   Do you not hear, fellows? Take away the lady.

OLIVIA   Go to, you're a dry fool. I'll no more of you.   38
Besides, you grow dishonest.

FESTE   Two faults, madonna, that drink and good   40
counsel will amend. For give the dry fool drink, then
is the fool not dry. Bid the dishonest man mend
himself; if he mend, he is no longer dishonest; if he
cannot, let the botcher mend him. Anything that's   44
mended is but patched; virtue that transgresses is but   45
patched with sin, and sin that amends is but patched
with virtue. If that this simple syllogism will serve, so; 47
if it will not, what remedy? As there is no true cuckold   48
but calamity, so beauty's a flower. The lady bade take   49

17 them i.e., Olivia's servants   21 civil bounds bounds of civility
25 Surprise Take by storm. (A military term.)   dear heartfelt
26 become suit   28 nuncio's messenger's   32 rubious ruby red.
pipe voice, throat   33 shrill and sound high and clear, uncracked
34 semblative resembling, like   35 constellation i.e., nature as determined by your horoscope   41 barful strife endeavor full of impediments.
1.5 Location: Olivia's house.
6 fear no colors i.e., fear no foe, fear nothing. (With pun on *colors*,
worldly deceptions, and "collars," halters or nooses.)   7 Make that
good Explain that.   8 He . . . fear i.e., The hanged man will be dead
and unable to see anything.   9 Lenten meager, scanty (like Lenten
fare), and morbid

12 In the wars (Where *colors* would mean "military standards, enemy
flags"—the literal meaning of the proverb.)   12–13 that . . . foolery
that's an answer you may be bold to use in your fool's conundrums.
(*Colors* here refer to military banners and insignia used to align rows
of fighting men in battle.)   15 talents abilities. (Also alluding to the
parable of the talents, Matthew 25:14–29, and to "talons," claws.)
17 turned away dismissed. (Possibly also meaning "turned off,"
"hanged.")   19 good hanging (With possible bawdy pun on "being
well hung.")   20 for as for.   let . . . out i.e., let mild weather make
dismissal endurable.   23 points (Maria plays on the meaning "laces
used to hold up hose or breeches.")   25 gaskins wide breeches
27–8 thou . . . Illyria (Feste may be hinting ironically that Maria
would be a suitable mate for Sir Toby.)   30 you were best it would be
best for you.   31 an't if it   34 Quinapalus (Feste's invented authority.)   38 Go to (An expression of annoyance or expostulation.)   dry
dull   40 madonna my lady   44 botcher mender of old clothes and
shoes. (Playing on two senses of *mend*: "reform" and "repair.")
44–5 Anything . . . patched i.e., Life is patched or parti-colored like
the Fool's garment, a mix of good and bad   47 so well and good
48–9 As . . . flower (Nonsense, yet with a suggestion that Olivia has
wedded calamity but should not be faithful to it, for the natural
course is to seize the moment of youth and beauty before we lose it.)

away the fool; therefore I say again, take her away.

OLIVIA   Sir, I bade them take away you.

FESTE   Misprision in the highest degree! Lady, *cucullus* 52
non facit monachum; that's as much to say as I wear not 53
motley in my brain. Good madonna, give me leave to 54
prove you a fool.

OLIVIA   Can you do it?

FESTE   Dexteriously, good madonna.

OLIVIA   Make your proof.

FESTE   I must catechize you for it, madonna. Good my 59
mouse of virtue, answer me. 60

OLIVIA   Well, sir, for want of other idleness, I'll bide 61
your proof.

FESTE   Good madonna, why mourn'st thou?

OLIVIA   Good fool, for my brother's death.

FESTE   I think his soul is in hell, madonna.

OLIVIA   I know his soul is in heaven, fool.

FESTE   The more fool, madonna, to mourn for your
brother's soul, being in heaven.—Take away the fool,
gentlemen.

OLIVIA   What think you of this fool, Malvolio? Doth he
not mend? 71

MALVOLIO   Yes, and shall do till the pangs of death
shake him. Infirmity, that decays the wise, doth ever
make the better fool.

FESTE   God send you, sir, a speedy infirmity for the
better increasing your folly! Sir Toby will be sworn
that I am no fox, but he will not pass his word for 77
twopence that you are no fool.

OLIVIA   How say you to that, Malvolio?

MALVOLIO   I marvel Your Ladyship takes delight in such
a barren rascal. I saw him put down the other day
with an ordinary fool that has no more brain than a 82
stone. Look you now, he's out of his guard already. 83
Unless you laugh and minister occasion to him, he is 84
gagged. I protest I take these wise men that crow so at 85
these set kind of fools no better than the fools' zanies. 86

OLIVIA   Oh, you are sick of self-love, Malvolio, and taste
with a distempered appetite. To be generous, guiltless, 88
and of free disposition is to take those things for bird- 89
bolts that you deem cannon bullets. There is no slan- 90
der in an allowed fool, though he do nothing but rail; 91
nor no railing in a known discreet man, though he do 92
nothing but reprove. 93

FESTE   Now Mercury endue thee with leasing, for thou 94
speak'st well of fools!

Enter Maria.

MARIA   Madam, there is at the gate a young gentleman
much desires to speak with you.

OLIVIA   From the Count Orsino, is it?

MARIA   I know not, madam. 'Tis a fair young man, and
well attended.

OLIVIA   Who of my people hold him in delay?

MARIA   Sir Toby, madam, your kinsman.

OLIVIA   Fetch him off, I pray you. He speaks nothing
but madman. Fie on him!   [*Exit Maria.*] 104
Go you, Malvolio. If it be a suit from the Count, I am
sick or not at home; what you will, to dismiss it.
Exit Malvolio.
Now you see, sir, how your fooling grows old, and 107
people dislike it.

FESTE   Thou hast spoke for us, madonna, as if thy eldest
son should be a fool; whose skull Jove cram with
brains, for—here he comes—

Enter Sir Toby.

one of thy kin has a most weak *pia mater.* 112

OLIVIA   By mine honor, half drunk.—What is he at the
gate, cousin?

SIR TOBY   A gentleman.

OLIVIA   A gentleman? What gentleman?

SIR TOBY   'Tis a gentleman here—[*He belches.*] A plague
o' these pickle-herring! [*To Feste*] How now, sot? 118

FESTE   Good Sir Toby.

OLIVIA   Cousin, cousin, how have you come so early by 120
this lethargy?

SIR TOBY   Lechery? I defy lechery. There's one at the
gate.

OLIVIA   Ay, marry, what is he?

SIR TOBY   Let him be the devil an he will, I care not.
Give me faith, say I. Well, it's all one.   *Exit.* 126

OLIVIA   What's a drunken man like, Fool?

FESTE   Like a drowned man, a fool, and a madman.
One draft above heat makes him a fool, the second 129
mads him, and a third drowns him.

OLIVIA   Go thou and seek the crowner, and let him sit 131
o' my coz; for he's in the third degree of drink, he's 132
drowned. Go, look after him.

FESTE   He is but mad yet, madonna; and the fool shall
look to the madman.   [*Exit.*]

Enter Malvolio.

MALVOLIO   Madam, yond young fellow swears he will
speak with you. I told him you were sick; he takes on
him to understand so much, and therefore comes to
speak with you. I told him you were asleep; he seems

---

52 Misprision Mistake, misunderstanding. (A legal term meaning a
wrongful action or misdemeanor.)   **52–3 cucullus . . . monachum** the
cowl does not make the monk   **54 motley** the many-colored garment
of jesters   **59–60 Good . . . virtue** My good, virtuous mouse. (A term
of endearment.)   **bide** endure   **71 mend** i.e.,
improve, grow more amusing. (But Malvolio uses the word to mean
"grow more like a fool.")   **77 pass** give   **82 with** by   **83 out of his
guard** defenseless, unprovided with a witty answer   **84 minister
occasion** provide opportunity (for his fooling)   **85 protest** avow,
declare.   **crow** laugh stridently   **86 set** artificial, stereotyped.
zanies assistants, aping attendants.   **88 distempered** diseased.
generous noble-minded   **89 free** magnanimous   **89–90 bird-bolts**
blunt arrows for shooting small birds   **91 allowed** licensed (to speak
freely)   **90–3 There . . . reprove** Both a licensed fool and a man
known for discretion can criticize freely without being accused of
slander in the first instance or railing in the second. (In rebuking
Malvolio here, Olivia implies that he is not behaving like a "known
discreet man.")

94 Now . . . leasing i.e., May Mercury, the god of deception, make
you a skillful liar   **104 madman** i.e., the words of madness.   **107 old**
stale   **112 pia mater** i.e., brain. (Actually the soft membrane enclosing the brain.)   **118 sot** (1) fool (2) drunkard.   **120 Cousin** Kinsman.
(Here, uncle.)   **126 Give me faith** i.e., to resist the devil.   **it's all one**
it doesn't matter.   **129 draft above heat** helping of drink raising his
temperature above normal bodily warmth   **131 crowner** coroner
131–2 sit o' my coz hold an inquest on my kinsman (Sir Toby)

to have a foreknowledge of that too, and therefore comes to speak with you. What is to be said to him, lady? He's fortified against any denial.

OLIVIA   Tell him he shall not speak with me.

MALVOLIO   He's been told so; and he says he'll stand at your door like a sheriff's post, and be the supporter to 145 a bench, but he'll speak with you.

OLIVIA   What kind o' man is he?

MALVOLIO   Why, of mankind.

OLIVIA   What manner of man?

MALVOLIO   Of very ill manner. He'll speak with you, will you or no.

OLIVIA   Of what personage and years is he?

MALVOLIO   Not yet old enough for a man, nor young enough for a boy; as a squash is before 'tis a peascod, 154 or a codling when 'tis almost an apple. 'Tis with him in 155 standing water between boy and man. He is very 156 well-favored, and he speaks very shrewishly. One 157 would think his mother's milk were scarce out of him.

OLIVIA   Let him approach. Call in my gentlewoman.

MALVOLIO   Gentlewoman, my lady calls.   *Exit.*

Enter Maria.

OLIVIA

Give me my veil. Come, throw it o'er my face.
We'll once more hear Orsino's embassy. [*Olivia veils.*]

Enter Viola.

VIOLA   The honorable lady of the house, which is she?

OLIVIA   Speak to me; I shall answer for her. Your will?

VIOLA   Most radiant, exquisite, and unmatchable beauty—I pray you, tell me if this be the lady of the house, for I never saw her. I would be loath to cast away my speech; for besides that it is excellently well penned, I have taken great pains to con it. Good 170 beauties, let me sustain no scorn; I am very comptible, 171 even to the least sinister usage. 172

OLIVIA   Whence came you, sir?

VIOLA   I can say little more than I have studied, and that question's out of my part. Good gentle one, give me modest assurance if you be the lady of the house, 176 that I may proceed in my speech.

OLIVIA   Are you a comedian? 178

VIOLA   No, my profound heart; and yet, by the very 179 fangs of malice, I swear I am not that I play. Are you 180 the lady of the house?

OLIVIA   If I do not usurp myself, I am. 182

VIOLA   Most certain, if you are she, you do usurp your- 183 self; for what is yours to bestow is not yours to reserve. 184

But this is from my commission. I will on with my 185 speech in your praise, and then show you the heart of my message.

OLIVIA   Come to what is important in't. I forgive you 188 the praise.

VIOLA   Alas, I took great pains to study it, and 'tis poetical.

OLIVIA   It is the more like to be feigned. I pray you, keep it in. I heard you were saucy at my gates, and allowed your approach rather to wonder at you than to hear you. If you be not mad, begone; if you have 195 reason, be brief. 'Tis not that time of moon with me to 196 make one in so skipping a dialogue. 197

MARIA   Will you hoist sail, sir? Here lies your way.

VIOLA   No, good swabber, I am to hull here a little 199 longer.—Some mollification for your giant, sweet 200 lady. Tell me your mind; I am a messenger.

OLIVIA   Sure you have some hideous matter to deliver, when the courtesy of it is so fearful. Speak your office. 203

VIOLA   It alone concerns your ear. I bring no overture of 204 war, no taxation of homage. I hold the olive in my 205 hand; my words are as full of peace as matter.

OLIVIA   Yet you began rudely. What are you? What 207 would you?

VIOLA   The rudeness that hath appeared in me have I learned from my entertainment. What I am and what 210 I would are as secret as maidenhead—to your ears, 211 divinity; to any other's, profanation. 212

OLIVIA   [*to the others*]   Give us the place here alone. We will hear this divinity.   [*Exeunt Maria and attendants.*] Now, sir, what is your text?

VIOLA   Most sweet lady—

OLIVIA   A comfortable doctrine, and much may be said 217 of it. Where lies your text?

VIOLA   In Orsino's bosom.

OLIVIA   In his bosom? In what chapter of his bosom?

VIOLA   To answer by the method, in the first of his 221 heart.

OLIVIA   Oh, I have read it. It is heresy. Have you no more to say?

VIOLA   Good madam, let me see your face.

OLIVIA   Have you any commission from your lord to negotiate with my face? You are now out of your text. 227 But we will draw the curtain and show you the

---

145 **sheriff's post** post before the sheriff's door to mark a residence of authority, often elaborately carved and decorated.   **supporter** prop   154 **squash** unripe pea pod.   **peascod** ripe pea pod. (The image suggests that the boy's testicles have not yet dropped.)   155 **codling** unripe apple   155–6 **in standing water** at the turn of the tide   157 **well-favored** good-looking.   **shrewishly** sharply.   170 **con** memorize   171 **comptible** susceptible, sensitive   172 **least sinister** slightest discourteous   176 **modest** reasonable   178 **comedian** actor.   179 **my profound heart** my most wise lady; or, in all sincerity   179–80 **by . . . I play** (Viola hints at her true identity, with a touch of malice against her rival.)   182 **do . . . myself** am not an impostor   183–4 **usurp yourself** i.e., misappropriate yourself, by withholding yourself from love and marriage

185 **from** outside of   188 **forgive you** excuse you from repeating   195 **not mad** i.e., not altogether mad   196 **reason** sanity.   **moon** (The moon was thought to affect lunatics according to its changing phases.)   197 **make one** take part   199 **swabber** one in charge of washing the decks. (A nautical retort to *hoist sail.*)   **hull** lie with sails furled   200 **Some . . . for** i.e., Please mollify, pacify.   **giant** i.e., the diminutive Maria who, like many giants in medieval romances, is guarding the lady   203 **courtesy** i.e., complimentary, "poetical" introduction. (Or Olivia may refer to Cesario's importunate manner at her gate, as reported by Malvolio.)   **office** commission, business.   204 **overture** declaration. (Literally, opening.)   205 **taxation of homage** demand for tribute.   **olive** olive-branch (signifying peace)   207 **Yet . . . rudely** i.e., Yet you were saucy at my gates.   210 **entertainment** reception.   211 **maidenhead** virginity   212 **divinity** sacred discourse   217 **comfortable** comforting   221 **To . . . method** i.e., To continue the metaphor of delivering a sermon, begun with *divinity* and *what is your text* and continued in *doctrine, heresy,* etc.   227 **out of** straying from

picture. [*Unveiling.*] Look you, sir, such a one I was 229
this present. Is't not well done? 230

VIOLA   Excellently done, if God did all.

OLIVIA   'Tis in grain, sir; 'twill endure wind and 232
weather.

VIOLA
'Tis beauty truly blent, whose red and white 234
Nature's own sweet and cunning hand laid on. 235
Lady, you are the cruel'st she alive
If you will lead these graces to the grave
And leave the world no copy. 238

OLIVIA   Oh, sir, I will not be so hardhearted. I will give
out divers schedules of my beauty. It shall be invento- 240
ried, and every particle and utensil labeled to my 241
will: as, item, two lips, indifferent red; item, two gray 242
eyes, with lids to them; item, one neck, one chin, and
so forth. Were you sent hither to praise me? 244

VIOLA
I see you what you are: you are too proud.
But, if you were the devil, you are fair. 246
My lord and master loves you. Oh, such love 247
Could be but recompensed, though you were
crowned 248
The nonpareil of beauty!

OLIVIA   How does he love me? 249

VIOLA
With adorations, fertile tears, 250
With groans that thunder love, with sighs of fire.

OLIVIA
Your lord does know my mind; I cannot love him.
Yet I suppose him virtuous, know him noble,
Of great estate, of fresh and stainless youth,
In voices well divulged, free, learned, and valiant, 255
And in dimension and the shape of nature 256
A gracious person. But yet I cannot love him. 257
He might have took his answer long ago.

VIOLA
If I did love you in my master's flame, 259
With such a suff'ring, such a deadly life, 260
In your denial I would find no sense;
I would not understand it.

OLIVIA   Why, what would you?

VIOLA
Make me a willow cabin at your gate 263
And call upon my soul within the house; 264
Write loyal cantons of contemnèd love 265

And sing them loud even in the dead of night;
Hallow your name to the reverberate hills, 267
And make the babbling gossip of the air 268
Cry out "Olivia!" Oh, you should not rest
Between the elements of air and earth 270
But you should pity me!

OLIVIA   You might do much.
What is your parentage?

VIOLA
Above my fortunes, yet my state is well: 273
I am a gentleman.

OLIVIA   Get you to your lord.
I cannot love him. Let him send no more—
Unless, perchance, you come to me again
To tell him how he takes it. Fare you well.
I thank you for your pains. Spend this for me.
[*She offers a purse.*]

VIOLA
I am no fee'd post, lady. Keep your purse. 279
My master, not myself, lacks recompense.
Love make his heart of flint that you shall love, 281
And let your fervor, like my master's, be
Placed in contempt! Farewell, fair cruelty. *Exit.*

OLIVIA   "What is your parentage?"
"Above my fortunes, yet my state is well:
I am a gentleman." I'll be sworn thou art!
Thy tongue, thy face, thy limbs, actions, and spirit
Do give thee fivefold blazon. Not too fast! Soft, soft! 288
Unless the master were the man. How now? 289
Even so quickly may one catch the plague?
Methinks I feel this youth's perfections
With an invisible and subtle stealth
To creep in at mine eyes. Well, let it be.—
What ho, Malvolio!

Enter Malvolio.

MALVOLIO   Here, madam, at your service.

OLIVIA
Run after that same peevish messenger,
The County's man. He left this ring behind him, 296
[*giving a ring*]
Would I or not. Tell him I'll none of it. 297
Desire him not to flatter with his lord, 298
Nor hold him up with hopes; I am not for him.
If that the youth will come this way tomorrow,
I'll give him reasons for't. Hie thee, Malvolio. 301

MALVOLIO   Madam, I will. *Exit.*

OLIVIA
I do I know not what, and fear to find
Mine eye too great a flatterer for my mind. 304

229–30 such . . . present this is a recent portrait of me. (Since it was customary to hang curtains in front of pictures, Olivia in unveiling speaks as if she were displaying a picture of herself.) **232 in grain** fast dyed   **234 blent** blended   **235 cunning** skillful   **238 copy** i.e., a child. (But Olivia uses the word to mean "transcript.")   **240 schedules** inventories   **241 utensil** article, item.   **labeled** added as a codicil   **242 indifferent** somewhat   **244 praise** (With pun on "appraise.")   **246 if** even if   **247–9 Oh . . . beauty!** i.e., Even if you were the most beautiful woman alive, that beauty could do no more than repay my master's love for you!   **250 fertile** copious   **255 In . . . divulged** well spoken of.   **free** generous   **256 in . . . nature** in his physical form   **257 gracious** graceful, attractive   **259 flame** passion **260 deadly** deathlike   **263 willow cabin** shelter, hut. (Willow was a symbol of unrequited love.)   **264 my soul** i.e., Olivia   **265 cantons** songs.   **contemnèd** rejected

267 Hallow (1) halloo (2) bless   **268 babbling . . . air** echo **270 Between . . . air** i.e., anywhere   **273 state** social standing **279 fee'd post** messenger to be tipped   **281 Love . . . love** May Cupid make the heart of the man you love as hard as flint   **288 blazon** heraldic description.   **Soft** Wait a minute   **289 Unless . . . man** i.e., Unless Cesario and Orsino changed places.   **296 County's** Count's, i.e., Duke's   **297 Would I or not** whether I wanted it or not. **298 flatter with** encourage   **301 Hie thee** Hasten   **304 Mine . . . mind** i.e., that my eyes (through which love enters the soul) have deceived my reason.

Fate, show thy force. Ourselves we do not owe.   305
What is decreed must be; and be this so.   [*Exit.*]

❧

2.1

Enter Antonio and Sebastian.

ANTONIO   Will you stay no longer? Nor will you not   1
that I go with you?

SEBASTIAN   By your patience, no. My stars shine darkly   3
over me. The malignancy of my fate might perhaps   4
distemper yours; therefore I shall crave of you your   5
leave that I may bear my evils alone. It were a bad
recompense for your love to lay any of them on you.

ANTONIO   Let me yet know of you whither you are
bound.

SEBASTIAN   No, sooth, sir; my determinate voyage is   10
mere extravagancy. But I perceive in you so excellent   11
a touch of modesty that you will not extort from me
what I am willing to keep in; therefore it charges me in   13
manners the rather to express myself. You must know   14
of me then, Antonio, my name is Sebastian, which I
called Roderigo. My father was that Sebastian of
Messaline whom I know you have heard of. He left   17
behind him myself and a sister, both born in an hour.   18
If the heavens had been pleased, would we had so
ended! But you, sir, altered that, for some hour before   20
you took me from the breach of the sea was my sister   21
drowned.

ANTONIO   Alas the day!

SEBASTIAN   A lady, sir, though it was said she much resembled me, was yet of many accounted beautiful. But
though I could not with such estimable wonder over-   26
far believe that, yet thus far I will boldly publish her: 27
she bore a mind that envy could not but call fair. She   28
is drowned already, sir, with salt water, though I seem
to drown her remembrance again with more.

ANTONIO   Pardon me, sir, your bad entertainment.   31

SEBASTIAN   O good Antonio, forgive me your trouble.   32

ANTONIO   If you will not murder me for my love, let me   33
be your servant.

SEBASTIAN   If you will not undo what you have done,
that is, kill him whom you have recovered, desire it   36
not. Fare ye well at once. My bosom is full of

kindness, and I am yet so near the manners of my   38
mother that upon the least occasion more mine eyes   39
will tell tales of me. I am bound to the Count Orsino's
court. Farewell.   *Exit.*

ANTONIO
The gentleness of all the gods go with thee!
I have many enemies in Orsino's court,
Else would I very shortly see thee there.
But come what may, I do adore thee so
That danger shall seem sport, and I will go.   *Exit.*

❧

2.2

Enter Viola and Malvolio, at several doors.

MALVOLIO   Were not you even now with the Countess
Olivia?

VIOLA   Even now, sir. On a moderate pace I have since
arrived but hither.

MALVOLIO   She returns this ring to you, sir. You might
have saved me my pains, to have taken it away   6
yourself. She adds, moreover, that you should put
your lord into a desperate assurance she will none of   8
him. And one thing more: that you be never so hardy   9
to come again in his affairs, unless it be to report your   10
lord's taking of this. Receive it so.

VIOLA   She took the ring of me. I'll none of it.   12

MALVOLIO   Come, sir, you peevishly threw it to her,
and her will is it should be so returned. [*He throws
down the ring.*] If it be worth stooping for, there it lies,
in your eye; if not, be it his that finds it.   *Exit.*   16

VIOLA   [*picking up the ring*]
I left no ring with her. What means this lady?
Fortune forbid my outside have not charmed her!   18
She made good view of me, indeed so much
That sure methought her eyes had lost her tongue,   20
For she did speak in starts, distractedly.
She loves me, sure! The cunning of her passion
Invites me in this churlish messenger.   23
None of my lord's ring? Why, he sent her none.
I am the man. If it be so—as 'tis—   25
Poor lady, she were better love a dream.
Disguise, I see, thou art a wickedness
Wherein the pregnant enemy does much.   28
How easy is it for the proper false   29
In women's waxen hearts to set their forms!   30
Alas, our frailty is the cause, not we,   31
For such as we are made of, such we be.   32

---

305 owe own, control
2.1 Location: Somewhere in Illyria.
1 Nor will you not Do you not wish   **3 patience** leave   **4 malignancy** malevolence (of the stars; also in a medical sense)   **5 distemper** infect   **10 sooth** truly.   **determinate** intended, determined upon
11 extravagancy aimless wandering   **13 am willing . . . in** wish to
keep secret   **13–14 it . . . manners** it is incumbent upon me in all
courtesy   **14 express** reveal   **17 Messaline** possibly Messina, or,
more likely, Massila (the modern Marseilles). In Plautus's *Menaechmi*,
Massilians and Illyrians are mentioned together.   **18 in an hour** in
the same hour   **20 some hour** about an hour   **21 breach of the sea**
surf   **26 estimable wonder** admiring judgment   **27 publish** proclaim   **28 envy** even malice   **31 Pardon . . . entertainment** i.e., I'm
sorry I cannot offer you better hospitality and comfort.   **32 your
trouble** the trouble I put you to   **33 murder . . . love** i.e., cause me to
die from lacking your love   **36 recovered** rescued, restored

38 kindness emotion, affection   **38–9 manners of my mother** i.e.,
womanly inclination to weep
2.2 Location: Near Olivia's house.
0.1 *several* different   **6 to have taken** by taking   **8 desperate** without hope   **9–10 so hardy to come** so bold as to come   **12 She . . . it**
(Viola tells a quick and friendly lie to shield Olivia.)   **16 in your eye**
in plain sight   **18 charmed** enchanted   **20 her eyes . . . tongue** i.e.,
the sight of me had deprived her of speech   **23 in** in the person of
25 the man the man of her choice.   **28 the pregnant enemy** the
resourceful enemy (either Satan or Cupid)   **29 the proper false**
deceptively handsome men   **30 waxen** i.e., malleable, impressionable.   **set their forms** stamp their images (as of a seal).   **31–2 our . . .
be** i.e., the fault lies not in us as individuals, but in the frailty of
female nature.

How will this fadge? My master loves her dearly,   33
And I, poor monster, fond as much on him;   34
And she, mistaken, seems to dote on me.
What will become of this? As I am man,
My state is desperate for my master's love;
As I am woman—now, alas the day!—
What thriftless sighs shall poor Olivia breathe!   39
O Time, thou must untangle this, not I;
It is too hard a knot for me t'untie.   [*Exit.*]

❖

2.3

Enter Sir Toby and Sir Andrew.

SIR TOBY   Approach, Sir Andrew. Not to be abed after
midnight is to be up betimes; and *diluculo surgere*, thou   2
know'st—
SIR ANDREW   Nay, by my troth, I know not, but I know
to be up late is to be up late.
SIR TOBY   A false conclusion. I hate it as an unfilled can.   6
To be up after midnight and to go to bed then, is early;
so that to go to bed after midnight is to go to bed
betimes. Does not our lives consist of the four   9
elements?   10
SIR ANDREW   Faith, so they say, but I think it rather
consists of eating and drinking.
SIR TOBY   Thou'rt a scholar; let us therefore eat and
drink.—Marian, I say, a stoup of wine!   14

Enter Clown [Feste].

SIR ANDREW   Here comes the Fool, i'faith.
FESTE   How now, my hearts! Did you never see the
picture of "we three"?   17
SIR TOBY   Welcome, ass. Now let's have a catch.   18
SIR ANDREW   By my troth, the Fool has an excellent
breast. I had rather than forty shillings I had such a   20
leg, and so sweet a breath to sing, as the Fool has. In   21
sooth, thou wast in very gracious fooling last night,
when thou spok'st of Pigrogromitus, of the Vapians   23
passing the equinoctial of Queubus. 'Twas very good,   24
i'faith. I sent thee sixpence for thy leman. Hadst it?   25
FESTE   I did impeticos thy gratillity; for Malvolio's nose   26
is no whipstock. My lady has a white hand, and the   27
Myrmidons are no bottle-ale houses.   28

SIR ANDREW   Excellent! Why, this is the best fooling,
when all is done. Now, a song.
SIR TOBY   Come on, there is sixpence for you. [*He gives
money.*] Let's have a song.
SIR ANDREW   There's a testril of me too. [*He gives money.*]   33
If one knight give a—
FESTE   Would you have a love song, or a song of good   35
life?   36
SIR TOBY   A love song, a love song.
SIR ANDREW   Ay, ay, I care not for good life.
FESTE (*sings*)
          O mistress mine, where are you roaming?
          Oh, stay and hear, your true love 's coming,
                    That can sing both high and low.
          Trip no further, pretty sweeting;
          Journeys end in lovers' meeting,
                    Every wise man's son doth know.

SIR ANDREW   Excellent good, i'faith.
SIR TOBY   Good, good.
FESTE [*sings*]
          What is love? 'tis not hereafter;
          Present mirth hath present laughter;
                    What's to come is still unsure.   49
          In delay there lies no plenty.
          Then come kiss me, sweet and twenty;   51
                    Youth's a stuff will not endure.

SIR ANDREW   A mellifluous voice, as I am true knight.
SIR TOBY   A contagious breath.   54
SIR ANDREW   Very sweet and contagious, i'faith.
SIR TOBY   To hear by the nose, it is dulcet in contagion.   56
But shall we make the welkin dance indeed? Shall we   57
rouse the night owl in a catch that will draw three   58
souls out of one weaver? Shall we do that?   59
SIR ANDREW   An you love me, let's do't. I am dog at a   60
catch.   61
FESTE   By'r Lady, sir, and some dogs will catch well.   62
SIR ANDREW   Most certain. Let our catch be "Thou   63
knave."   64
FESTE   "Hold thy peace, thou knave," knight? I shall be   65
constrained in't to call thee knave, knight.   66
SIR ANDREW   'Tis not the first time I have constrained
one to call me knave. Begin, Fool. It begins, "Hold thy
peace."

---

33 **fadge** turn out   34 **monster** i.e., being both man and woman.
fond dote   39 **thriftless** unprofitable
2.3. Location: Olivia's house.
2 **betimes** early. *diluculo surgere* (*saluberrimum est*) to rise early is
most healthful. (A sentence from Lilly's *Latin Grammar*.)   6 **can**
tankard.   9-10 **four elements** i.e., fire, air, water, and earth, the elements that were thought to make up all matter.   14 **stoup** drinking
vessel   17 **picture of "we three"** picture of two fools or asses
inscribed "we three," the spectator being the third.   18 **catch** round.
20 **breast** voice.   21 **leg** (for dancing)   23-4 **Pigrogromitus . . .
Queubus** (Feste's mock erudition.)   25 **leman** sweetheart.
26 **impeticos thy gratillity** (Suggests "impetticoat, or pocket up, thy
gratuity.")   27 **is no whipstock** is no whip-handle. (More nonsense,
but perhaps suggesting that Malvolio's nose for smelling out faults
does not give him the right to punish, so that he need not be feared.)
has a white hand i.e., is lady-like. (But Feste's speech may be mere
nonsense.)   28 **Myrmidons** followers of Achilles.   **bottle-ale houses**
(Used contemptuously of taverns because they sold low-class drink.)

33 **testril** tester, a coin worth sixpence   35-6 **good life** virtuous living. (Or perhaps Feste means simply "life's pleasures," but is misunderstood by Sir Andrew to mean "virtuous living.")   49 **still** always
51 **sweet and twenty** i.e., sweet and twenty times sweet, or twenty
years old   54 **contagious** infectiously delightful   56 **To . . . contagion** i.e., If we were to describe hearing in olfactory terms, we could
say it is sweet in stench.   57 **make . . . dance** i.e., drink till the sky
seems to turn around   58-9 **draw three souls** (Refers to the threefold
nature of the soul—vegetal, sensible, and intellectual—or to the three
singers of the three-part catch; or, just a comic exaggeration.)
59 **weaver** (Weavers were often associated with psalm singing.)
60 **dog at** very clever at. (But Feste uses the word literally.)   61 **catch**
round. (But Feste uses it to mean "seize.")   62 **By 'r Lady** (An oath,
originally, "by the Virgin Mary.")   63-4 **"Thou knave"** (This popular
round is arranged so that the three singers repeatedly accost one
another with "Thou knave.")   65-6 **"Hold . . . knight** ("Knight and
knave" is a common antithesis, like "rich and poor.")

FESTE   I shall never begin if I hold my peace.

SIR ANDREW   Good, i'faith. Come, begin.   *Catch sung.*

Enter Maria.

MARIA   What a caterwauling do you keep here! If my 72
lady have not called up her steward Malvolio and bid
him turn you out of doors, never trust me.

SIR TOBY   My lady's a Cataian, we are politicians, 75
Malvolio's a Peg-o'-Ramsey, and [*he sings*] "Three 76
merry men be we." Am not I consanguineous? Am I 77
not of her blood? Tillyvally! Lady! [*He sings.*] "There 78
dwelt a man in Babylon, lady, lady." 79

FESTE   Beshrew me, the knight's in admirable fooling. 80

SIR ANDREW   Ay, he does well enough if he be disposed,
and so do I too. He does it with a better grace,
but I do it more natural. 83

SIR TOBY   [*sings*]
"O' the twelfth day of December"— 84

MARIA   For the love o' God, peace!

Enter Malvolio.

MALVOLIO   My masters, are you mad? Or what are you?
Have you no wit, manners, nor honesty but to gabble 87
like tinkers at this time of night? Do ye make an alehouse of my lady's house, that ye squeak out your coz- 89
iers' catches without any mitigation or remorse of 90
voice? Is there no respect of place, persons, nor time in
you?

SIR TOBY   We did keep time, sir, in our catches. Sneck 93
up! 94

MALVOLIO   Sir Toby, I must be round with you. My 95
lady bade me tell you that though she harbors you as
her kinsman, she's nothing allied to your disorders. If
you can separate yourself and your misdemeanors,
you are welcome to the house; if not, an it would
please you to take leave of her, she is very willing to
bid you farewell.

SIR TOBY   [*sings*]
"Farewell, dear heart, since I must needs be gone." 102

MARIA   Nay, good Sir Toby.

FESTE   [*sings*]
"His eyes do show his days are almost done."

MALVOLIO   Is't even so?

SIR TOBY   [*sings*]
"But I will never die."

FESTE
"Sir Toby, there you lie."

MALVOLIO   This is much credit to you.

SIR TOBY   [*sings*]
"Shall I bid him go?"

FESTE   [*sings*]
"What an if you do?"

SIR TOBY   [*sings*]
"Shall I bid him go, and spare not?"

FESTE   [*sings*]
"Oh, no, no, no, no, you dare not."

SIR TOBY   Out o' tune, sir? Ye lie. Art any more than a 113
steward? Dost thou think, because thou art virtuous,
there shall be no more cakes and ale?

FESTE   Yes, by Saint Anne, and ginger shall be hot i'th' 116
mouth, too.

SIR TOBY   Thou'rt i'the right.—Go, sir, rub your chain 118
with crumbs.—A stoup of wine, Maria! 119

MALVOLIO   Mistress Mary, if you prized my lady's
favor at anything more than contempt, you would not
give means for this uncivil rule. She shall know of it, 122
by this hand.   *Exit.*

MARIA   Go shake your ears. 124

SIR ANDREW   'Twere as good a deed as to drink when a
man's a-hungry to challenge him the field and then to 126
break promise with him and make a fool of him.

SIR TOBY   Do't, knight. I'll write thee a challenge, or I'll
deliver thy indignation to him by word of mouth.

MARIA   Sweet Sir Toby, be patient for tonight. Since the
youth of the Count's was today with my lady, she is
much out of quiet. For Monsieur Malvolio, let me 132
alone with him. If I do not gull him into a nayword 133
and make him a common recreation, do not think I 134
have wit enough to lie straight in my bed. I know I can
do it.

SIR TOBY   Possess us, possess us. Tell us something of 137
him.

MARIA   Marry, sir, sometimes he is a kind of puritan. 139

SIR ANDREW   Oh, if I thought that, I'd beat him like a
dog.

SIR TOBY   What, for being a puritan? Thy exquisite
reason, dear knight?

SIR ANDREW   I have no exquisite reason for't, but I
have reason good enough.

---

72 keep keep up   **75 Cataian** Cathayan, i.e., Chinese, a trickster or inscrutable; or, just nonsense.   **politicians** schemers, intriguers   **76 Peg-o'-Ramsey** character in a popular song. (Used here contemptuously.)   **76–7 "Three . . . we"** (A snatch of an old song.)   **77 consanguineous** i.e., a blood relative of Olivia.   **78 Tillyvally!** Nonsense, fiddle-faddle!   **78–9 "There . . . lady"** (The first line of a ballad, "The Constancy of Susanna," together with the refrain, "Lady, lady.")   **80 Beshrew** i.e., The devil take. (A mild curse.)   **83 natural** naturally. (But unconsciously suggesting idiocy.)   **84 "O' . . . December"** (Possibly part of a ballad about the Battle of Musselburgh Field, or Toby's error for the "twelfth day of Christmas," i.e., Twelfth Night.)   **87 wit** common sense.   **honesty** decency   **89–90 coziers'** cobblers'   **90 mitigation or remorse** i.e., considerate lowering   **93–4 Sneck up!** Go hang!   **95 round** blunt   **102 "Farewell . . . gone"** (From the ballad "Corydon's Farewell to Phyllis.")

113 Out o' tune (Perhaps a quibbling reply—"We did too keep time in our tune"—to Malvolio's accusation of having no respect for place or time, line 91. Often emended to *Out o' time*, easily misread in secretary hand.)   **116 Saint Anne** mother of the Virgin Mary. (Her cult was derided in the Reformation, much as Puritan reformers also derided the tradition of *cakes and ale* at church feasts.)   **ginger** (Commonly used to spice ale.)   **118–19 rub . . . crumbs** i.e., scour or polish your steward's chain; attend to your own business and remember your station   **122 give means** i.e., supply drink.   **rule** conduct.   **124 your ears** i.e., your ass's ears.   **126 the field** i.e., to a duel   **132 For** As for   **132–3 let . . . him** leave him to me.   **133 gull** trick.   **nayword** byword. (His name will be synonymous with "dupe.")   **134 recreation** sport   **137 Possess** Inform   **139 puritan** (Maria's point is that Malvolio is sometimes a *kind* of puritan, insofar as he is precise about moral conduct and censorious of others for immoral conduct, but that he is nothing consistently except a time-server. He is not, then, simply a satirical type of the Puritan sect. The extent of the resemblance is left unstated.)

MARIA   The devil a puritan that he is, or anything con- 146
stantly, but a time-pleaser; an affectioned ass, that cons 147
state without book and utters it by great swaths; the 148
best persuaded of himself, so crammed, as he thinks, 149
with excellencies, that it is his grounds of faith that all 150
that look on him love him; and on that vice in him
will my revenge find notable cause to work.

SIR TOBY   What wilt thou do?

MARIA   I will drop in his way some obscure epistles of 154
love, wherein by the color of his beard, the shape of
his leg, the manner of his gait, the expressure of his 156
eye, forehead, and complexion, he shall find himself
most feelingly personated. I can write very like my 158
lady your niece; on a forgotten matter we can hardly 159
make distinction of our hands.   160

SIR TOBY   Excellent! I smell a device.

SIR ANDREW   I have't in my nose too.

SIR TOBY   He shall think, by the letters that thou wilt
drop, that they come from my niece, and that she's in
love with him.

MARIA   My purpose is indeed a horse of that color.

SIR ANDREW   And your horse now would make him an
ass.

MARIA   Ass, I doubt not.   169

SIR ANDREW   Oh, 'twill be admirable!

MARIA   Sport royal, I warrant you. I know my physic 171
will work with him. I will plant you two, and let the
Fool make a third, where he shall find the letter. Ob-
serve his construction of it. For this night, to bed, 174
and dream on the event. Farewell.   *Exit.* 175

SIR TOBY   Good night, Penthesilea.   176

SIR ANDREW   Before me, she's a good wench.   177

SIR TOBY   She's a beagle true-bred and one that adores 178
me. What o'that?

SIR ANDREW   I was adored once, too.

SIR TOBY   Let's to bed, knight. Thou hadst need send
for more money.

SIR ANDREW   If I cannot recover your niece, I am a foul 183
way out.   184

SIR TOBY   Send for money, knight. If thou hast her not
i'th' end, call me cut.   186

SIR ANDREW   If I do not, never trust me, take it how
you will.

SIR TOBY   Come, come, I'll go burn some sack. 'Tis too 189
late to go to bed now. Come, knight; come, knight. 190
                                                Exeunt.

❖

2.4

Enter Duke [Orsino], Viola, Curio, and others.

ORSINO
Give me some music. Now, good morrow, friends.   1
Now, good Cesario, but that piece of song,   2
That old and antique song we heard last night.   3
Methought it did relieve my passion much,
More than light airs and recollected terms   5
Of these most brisk and giddy-pacèd times.
Come, but one verse.

CURIO   He is not here, so please Your Lordship, that
should sing it.

ORSINO   Who was it?

CURIO   Feste the jester, my lord, a fool that the Lady
Olivia's father took much delight in. He is about the
house.

ORSINO
Seek him out, and play the tune the while.
                    [*Exit Curio.*] *Music plays.*
[*To Viola*] Come hither, boy. If ever thou shalt love,
In the sweet pangs of it remember me;
For such as I am, all true lovers are,
Unstaid and skittish in all motions else   18
Save in the constant image of the creature
That is beloved. How dost thou like this tune?

VIOLA
It gives a very echo to the seat   21
Where Love is throned.

ORSINO   Thou dost speak masterly.
My life upon't, young though thou art, thine eye
Hath stayed upon some favor that it loves.   24
Hath it not, boy?

VIOLA   A little, by your favor.   25

ORSINO
What kind of woman is't?

VIOLA   Of your complexion.

ORSINO
She is not worth thee, then. What years, i'faith?

VIOLA   About your years, my lord.

ORSINO
Too old, by heaven. Let still the woman take   29
An elder than herself. So wears she to him;   30
So sways she level in her husband's heart.   31
For, boy, however we do praise ourselves,

Our fancies are more giddy and unfirm,
More longing, wavering, sooner lost and worn,
Than women's are.   34

VIOLA   I think it well, my lord.

ORSINO
Then let thy love be younger than thyself,
Or thy affection cannot hold the bent;   37
For women are as roses, whose fair flower
Being once displayed, doth fall that very hour.   39

VIOLA
And so they are. Alas that they are so,
To die even when they to perfection grow!   41

Enter Curio and Clown [Feste].

ORSINO
Oh, fellow, come, the song we had last night.
Mark it, Cesario, it is old and plain;
The spinsters and the knitters in the sun,   44
And the free maids that weave their thread with
    bones,   45
Do use to chant it. It is silly sooth,   46
And dallies with the innocence of love,   47
Like the old age.   48

FESTE   Are you ready, sir?

ORSINO   Ay, prithee, sing.   *Music.*

The Song.

FESTE *[sings]*
    Come away, come away, death,   51
        And in sad cypress let me be laid.   52
    Fly away, fly away, breath;
        I am slain by a fair cruel maid.
    My shroud of white, stuck all with yew,   55
        Oh, prepare it!
    My part of death, no one so true   57
        Did share it.   58

    Not a flower, not a flower sweet
        On my black coffin let there be strown;   60
    Not a friend, not a friend greet
        My poor corpse, where my bones shall be
            thrown.
    A thousand thousand sighs to save,
        Lay me, oh, where
    Sad true lover never find my grave,
        To weep there!

ORSINO *[offering money]*   There's for thy pains.
FESTE   No pains, sir. I take pleasure in singing, sir.
ORSINO   I'll pay thy pleasure then.

FESTE   Truly, sir, and pleasure will be paid, one time   70
    or another.   71

ORSINO   Give me now leave to leave thee.   72

FESTE   Now, the melancholy god protect thee, and the   73
    tailor make thy doublet of changeable taffeta, for thy   74
    mind is a very opal. I would have men of such con-   75
    stancy put to sea, that their business might be every-   76
    thing and their intent everywhere, for that's it that   77
    always makes a good voyage of nothing. Farewell.   78

                                                    Exit.

ORSINO
Let all the rest give place.

                    [Curio and attendants withdraw.]
                    Once more, Cesario,   79
Get thee to yond same sovereign cruelty.
Tell her, my love, more noble than the world,
Prizes not quantity of dirty lands;
The parts that fortune hath bestowed upon her,   83
Tell her, I hold as giddily as fortune;   84
But 'tis that miracle and queen of gems   85
That nature pranks her in attracts my soul.   86

VIOLA   But if she cannot love you, sir?

ORSINO
I cannot be so answered.

VIOLA   Sooth, but you must.   88
Say that some lady—as perhaps there is—
Hath for your love as great a pang of heart
As you have for Olivia. You cannot love her;
You tell her so. Must she not then be answered?   92

ORSINO   There is no woman's sides
Can bide the beating of so strong a passion   94
As love doth give my heart; no woman's heart
So big, to hold so much. They lack retention.   96
Alas, their love may be called appetite,
No motion of the liver, but the palate,   98
That suffer surfeit, cloyment, and revolt;   99
But mine is all as hungry as the sea,
And can digest as much. Make no compare   101
Between that love a woman can bear me
And that I owe Olivia.

VIOLA   Ay, but I know—   103
ORSINO   What dost thou know?

---

34 worn exhausted. (Sometimes emended to *won*.)   **37 hold the bent**
hold steady, keep the intensity (like the tension of a bow)   **39 displayed** full blown   **41 even when** just as   **44 spinsters** spinners
45 free carefree, innocent.   **bones** bobbins on which bone-lace was
made   **46 Do use** are accustomed.   **silly sooth** simple truth   **47 dallies with** dwells lovingly on, sports with   **48 Like . . . age** as in the
good old times.   **51 Come away** Come hither   **52 cypress** i.e., a coffin of cypress wood, or bier strewn with sprigs of cypress   **55 yew**
yew sprigs. (Emblematic of mourning, like cypress.)   **57–8 My . . . it**
No one died for love so true to love as I.   **60 strown** strewn

70–1 pleasure . . . another sooner or later one must pay for indulgence.   **72 leave to leave** permission to take leave of, dismiss   **73 the
melancholy god** i.e., Saturn, whose planet was thought to control the
melancholy temperament   **74 doublet** close-fitting jacket.
changeable taffeta a silk so woven of various-colored threads that its
color shifts with changing perspective   **75 opal** an iridescent precious stone that changes color when seen from various angles or in
different lights.   **76–7 that . . . everywhere** i.e., so that in the changeableness of the sea their inconstancy could always be exercised
77–8 for . . . nothing because that's the quality that is satisfied with
an aimless voyage.   **79 give place** withdraw.   **83 parts** attributes
such as wealth or rank   **84 I . . . fortune** I esteem as carelessly as I do
fortune, that fickle goddess   **85 that miracle . . . gems** i.e., her beauty
86 pranks adorns.   **attracts** that attracts   **88 Sooth** In truth   **92 be
answered** be satisfied with your answer.   **94 bide** withstand   **96 to
hold** as to contain.   **retention** constancy, the power of retaining
98 motion impulse.   **liver . . . palate** (Real love is a passion of the
liver, whereas fancy, light love, is born in the eye and nourished in
the palate.)   **99 cloyment** satiety.   **revolt** revulsion   **101 compare**
comparison   **103 owe** have for

VIOLA
Too well what love women to men may owe.
In faith, they are as true of heart as we.
My father had a daughter loved a man
As it might be, perhaps, were I a woman,
I should Your Lordship.

ORSINO   And what's her history?

VIOLA
A blank, my lord. She never told her love,
But let concealment, like a worm i'th' bud,
Feed on her damask cheek. She pined in thought,   112
And with a green and yellow melancholy;   113
She sat like Patience on a monument,   114
Smiling at grief. Was not this love indeed?
We men may say more, swear more, but indeed
Our shows are more than will; for still we prove   117
Much in our vows, but little in our love.

ORSINO
But died thy sister of her love, my boy?

VIOLA
I am all the daughters of my father's house,
And all the brothers too—and yet I know not.
Sir, shall I to this lady?

ORSINO   Ay, that's the theme.
To her in haste; give her this jewel. [*He gives a jewel.*]
Say
My love can give no place, bide no denay.   124
                              Exeunt [*separately*].

❖

2.5

Enter Sir Toby, Sir Andrew, and Fabian.

SIR TOBY   Come thy ways, Signor Fabian.   1

FABIAN   Nay, I'll come. If I lose a scruple of this sport,   2
let me be boiled to death with melancholy.   3

SIR TOBY   Wouldst thou not be glad to have the niggardly rascally sheep-biter come by some notable   5
shame?

FABIAN   I would exult, man. You know he brought me
out o'favor with my lady about a bearbaiting here.   8

SIR TOBY   To anger him we'll have the bear again, and
we will fool him black and blue. Shall we not, Sir An- 10
drew?

SIR ANDREW   An we do not, it is pity of our lives.   12

Enter Maria [*with a letter*].

SIR TOBY   Here comes the little villain.—How now, my   13
metal of India!   14

MARIA   Get ye all three into the boxtree. Malvolio's   15
coming down this walk. He has been yonder i'the sun
practicing behavior to his own shadow this half hour.
Observe him, for the love of mockery, for I know this
letter will make a contemplative idiot of him. Close, in   19
the name of jesting! [*The others hide.*] Lie thou there
[*throwing down a letter*]; for here comes the trout that
must be caught with tickling.   *Exit.*   22

Enter Malvolio.

MALVOLIO   'Tis but fortune; all is fortune. Maria once
told me she did affect me; and I have heard herself   24
come thus near, that should she fancy, it should be   25
one of my complexion. Besides, she uses me with a
more exalted respect than anyone else that follows   27
her. What should I think on't?

SIR TOBY   Here's an overweening rogue!

FABIAN   Oh, peace! Contemplation makes a rare turkey-   30
cock of him. How he jets under his advanced plumes!   31

SIR ANDREW   'Slight, I could so beat the rogue!   32

SIR TOBY   Peace, I say.

MALVOLIO   To be Count Malvolio.

SIR TOBY   Ah, rogue!

SIR ANDREW   Pistol him, pistol him.

SIR TOBY   Peace, peace!

MALVOLIO   There is example for't. The lady of the Stra-   38
chy married the yeoman of the wardrobe.   39

SIR ANDREW   Fie on him, Jezebel!   40

FABIAN   Oh, peace! Now he's deeply in. Look how imagination blows him.   42

MALVOLIO   Having been three months married to her,
sitting in my state—   44

SIR TOBY   Oh, for a stone-bow, to hit him in the eye!   45

MALVOLIO   Calling my officers about me, in my
branched velvet gown; having come from a daybed,   47
where I have left Olivia sleeping—

SIR TOBY   Fire and brimstone!

FABIAN   Oh, peace, peace!

MALVOLIO   And then to have the humor of state; and   51
after a demure travel of regard, telling them I know   52
my place as I would they should do theirs, to ask for
my kinsman Toby.   54

SIR TOBY   Bolts and shackles!

FABIAN   Oh, peace, peace, peace! Now, now.

---

112 **damask** pink and white like the damask rose   113 **green and yellow** pale and sallow   114 **on a monument** carved in statuary on a
tomb   117 **shows** displays of passion.   **more than will** greater than
our determination.   **still** always   124 **can . . . denay** cannot yield or
endure denial.
2.5 Location: Olivia's garden.
1 **Come thy ways** Come along   2 **a scruple** the least bit   3 **boiled**
(With a pun on "biled"; black bile was the "humor" of melancholy
and was thought to be a cold humor.)   5 **sheep-biter** a dog that bites
sheep, i.e., a scoundrel   8 **bearbaiting** (A special target of Puritan
disapproval.)   10 **fool . . . blue** mock him until he is figuratively
black and blue.   12 **An** If.   **pity of our lives** a pity we should live.

13 **villain** (Here, a term of endearment.)   14 **metal** gold, i.e., priceless
one   15 **boxtree** an evergreen shrub.   19 **contemplative** i.e., from
his musings.   **Close** i.e., Keep close, stay hidden   22 **tickling**
(1) stroking gently about the gills—an actual method of fishing
(2) deception.   24 **she** Olivia.   **affect** have fondness for   25 **fancy**
fall in love   27 **follows** serves   30 **rare** extraordinary   31 **jets** struts.
advanced prominent   32 **'Slight** By His (God's) light   38 **example**
precedent   38–9 **lady of the Strachy** (Apparently a lady who had
married below her station; no certain identification.)   40 **Jezebel** the
proud queen of Ahab, King of Israel.   42 **blows** puffs up   44 **state**
chair of state   45 **stone-bow** crossbow that shoots stones
47 **branched** adorned with a figured pattern suggesting branched
leaves or flowers.   **daybed** sofa, couch   51 **have . . . state** adopt the
imperious manner of authority   52 **demure . . . regard** grave survey
of the company.   54 **Toby** (Malvolio omits the title *Sir*.)

MALVOLIO   Seven of my people, with an obedient start, make out for him. I frown the while, and perchance wind up my watch, or play with my—some rich jewel. Toby approaches; curtsies there to me— 59 60

SIR TOBY   Shall this fellow live?

FABIAN   Though our silence be drawn from us with cars, yet peace. 62 63

MALVOLIO   I extend my hand to him thus, quenching my familiar smile with an austere regard of control— 65

SIR TOBY   And does not Toby take you a blow o'the lips then? 66

MALVOLIO   Saying, "Cousin Toby, my fortunes having cast me on your niece give me this prerogative of speech—"

SIR TOBY   What, what?

MALVOLIO   "You must amend your drunkenness."

SIR TOBY   Out, scab! 73

FABIAN   Nay, patience, or we break the sinews of our plot. 74

MALVOLIO   "Besides, you waste the treasure of your time with a foolish knight—"

SIR ANDREW   That's me, I warrant you.

MALVOLIO   "One Sir Andrew."

SIR ANDREW   I knew 'twas I, for many do call me fool.

MALVOLIO   What employment have we here? 81
[Taking up the letter.]

FABIAN   Now is the woodcock near the gin. 82

SIR TOBY   Oh, peace, and the spirit of humors intimate reading aloud to him! 83

MALVOLIO   By my life, this is my lady's hand. These be her very c's, her u's, and her t's; and thus makes she her great P's. It is in contempt of question her hand. 86 87

SIR ANDREW   Her c's, her u's, and her t's. Why that?

MALVOLIO   [reads] "To the unknown beloved, this, and my good wishes."—Her very phrases! By your leave, wax. Soft! And the impressure her Lucrece, with which she uses to seal. 'Tis my lady. To whom should this be? 90 91 92
[He opens the letter.]

FABIAN   This wins him, liver and all. 94

MALVOLIO   [reads]
"Jove knows I love,
      But who?
Lips, do not move;
      No man must know."
"No man must know." What follows? The numbers altered! "No man must know." If this should be thee, Malvolio? 99 100

SIR TOBY   Marry, hang thee, brock! 102

MALVOLIO   [reads]
"I may command where I adore,
      But silence, like a Lucrece knife,
With bloodless stroke my heart doth gore;
      M.O.A.I. doth sway my life."

FABIAN   A fustian riddle! 107

SIR TOBY   Excellent wench, say I.

MALVOLIO   "M.O.A.I. doth sway my life." Nay, but first, let me see, let me see, let me see.

FABIAN   What dish o'poison has she dressed him! 111

SIR TOBY   And with what wing the staniel checks at it! 112 113

MALVOLIO   "I may command where I adore." Why, she may command me; I serve her, she is my lady. Why, this is evident to any formal capacity. There is no obstruction in this. And the end—what should that alphabetical position portend? If I could make that resemble something in me! Softly! "M.O.A.I."— 116 118

SIR TOBY   Oh, ay, make up that. He is now at a cold scent. 120

FABIAN   Sowter will cry upon't for all this, though it be as rank as a fox. 121 122

MALVOLIO   "M"—Malvolio. "M"! Why, that begins my name!

FABIAN   Did not I say he would work it out? The cur is excellent at faults. 126

MALVOLIO   "M"—But then there is no consonancy in the sequel that suffers under probation: "A" should follow, but "O" does. 127 128

FABIAN   And "O" shall end, I hope. 130

SIR TOBY   Ay, or I'll cudgel him, and make him cry "Oh!"

MALVOLIO   And then "I" comes behind.

FABIAN   Ay, an you had any eye behind you, you might see more detraction at your heels than fortunes before you. 133 134

MALVOLIO   "M.O.A.I." This simulation is not as the former. And yet, to crush this a little, it would bow to me, for every one of these letters are in my name. Soft! Here follows prose. 136

---

59 play with my (Malvolio perhaps means his steward's chain but checks himself in time; as "Count Malvolio," he would not be wearing it. A bawdy meaning of playing with himself is also suggested.) **60 curtsies** bows **62–3 with cars** with chariots, i.e., pulling apart by force **65 familiar** (1) customary (2) friendly. **regard of control** look of authority **66 take** deliver **73 scab** scurvy fellow. **74 break . . . of** hamstring, disable **81 employment** business **82 woodcock** (A bird proverbial for its stupidity.) **gin** snare. **83 humors** whim, caprice **86 c's . . . t's** i.e., *cut*, slang for the female pudenda **87 great** (1) uppercase (2) copious. (P suggests "pee.") **in contempt of** beyond **90–1 By . . . wax** (Addressed to the seal on the letter.) **91 Soft** Softly, not so fast. **impressure** device imprinted on the seal. **Lucrece** Lucretia, chaste matron who, ravished by Tarquin, committed suicide **92 uses** is accustomed **94 liver** i.e., the seat of passion **99–100 The numbers altered!** More verses, in a different meter!

102 brock badger. (Used contemptuously.) **107 fustian** bombastic, ridiculously pompous **111 What** What a. **dressed** prepared for **112 wing** speed. **staniel** kestrel, a sparrow hawk. (The word is used contemptuously because of the uselessness of the staniel for falconry.) **112–13 checks at it** turns to fly at it. **116 formal capacity** normal understanding. **118 position** arrangement **120 Oh, ay** (Playing on *O.I.* of *M.O.A.I.*) **make up** work out **121–2 Sowter . . . fox** The hound Sowter (literally, "Cobbler") will bay triumphantly at picking up this false scent, even though the smell is as rank as a fox. ("M.O.A.I." is a false lead that reeks.) **126 at faults** i.e., at maneuvering his way past breaks in the line of scent—in this case, on a false trail. **127–8 no consonancy . . . probation** no pattern in the following letters that stands up under examination. (In fact, the letters "M.O.A.I." represent the first, last, second, and next to last letters of Malvolio's name.) **130 "O" shall end** (1) "O" ends Malvolio's name (2) *omega* ends the Greek alphabet and is thus a symbol for the ending of the world, *alpha* to *omega* (3) Malvolio's cry of pain will end the matter, as Sir Toby suggests in the next line. **133 eye** (punning on the "I" of "Oh, ay" and "M.O.A.I.") **134 detraction . . . heels** defamation pursuing you **136 simulation** disguise, puzzle

[*He reads.*] "If this fall into thy hand, revolve. In my 140
stars I am above thee, but be not afraid of greatness. 141
Some are born great, some achieve greatness, and
some have greatness thrust upon 'em. Thy Fates open 143
their hands; let thy blood and spirit embrace them; 144
and, to inure thyself to what thou art like to be, cast 145
thy humble slough and appear fresh. Be opposite with 146
a kinsman, surly with servants. Let thy tongue tang 147
arguments of state; put thyself into the trick of 148
singularity. She thus advises thee that sighs for thee. 149
Remember who commended thy yellow stockings,
and wished to see thee ever cross-gartered. I say, 151
remember. Go to, thou art made, if thou desir'st to be 152
so. If not, let me see thee a steward still, the fellow of
servants, and not worthy to touch Fortune's fingers.
Farewell. She that would alter services with thee, 155
                                    The Fortunate-Unhappy."
Daylight and champaign discovers not more! This is 157
open. I will be proud, I will read politic authors, I will 158
baffle Sir Toby, I will wash off gross acquaintance, I 159
will be point-devise the very man. I do not now fool 160
myself, to let imagination jade me; for every reason 161
excites to this, that my lady loves me. She did com- 162
mend my yellow stockings of late, she did praise my
leg being cross-gartered; and in this she manifests her- 164
self to my love, and with a kind of injunction drives
me to these habits of her liking. I thank my stars, I am 166
happy. I will be strange, stout, in yellow stockings 167
and cross-gartered, even with the swiftness of putting
on. Jove and my stars be praised! Here is yet a postscript. [*He reads.*] "Thou canst not choose but know who
I am. If thou entertain'st my love, let it appear in thy 171
smiling; thy smiles become thee well. Therefore in my
presence still smile, dear my sweet, I prithee." 173
Jove, I thank thee. I will smile; I will do everything that
thou wilt have me.   *Exit.*

[*Sir Toby, Sir Andrew, and Fabian come from hiding.*]

FABIAN   I will not give my part of this sport for a
pension of thousands to be paid from the Sophy. 177
SIR TOBY   I could marry this wench for this device.
SIR ANDREW   So could I too.
SIR TOBY   And ask no other dowry with her but such
another jest.

                    Enter Maria.

SIR ANDREW   Nor I neither.
FABIAN   Here comes my noble gull-catcher. 183
SIR TOBY   Wilt thou set thy foot o' my neck?
SIR ANDREW   Or o' mine either?
SIR TOBY   Shall I play my freedom at tray-trip, and 186
become thy bondslave?
SIR ANDREW   I'faith, or I either?
SIR TOBY   Why, thou hast put him in such a dream that
when the image of it leaves him he must run mad.
MARIA   Nay, but say true, does it work upon him?
SIR TOBY   Like aqua vitae with a midwife. 192
MARIA   If you will then see the fruits of the sport, mark
his first approach before my lady. He will come to her
in yellow stockings, and 'tis a color she abhors, and
cross-gartered, a fashion she detests; and he will smile
upon her, which will now be so unsuitable to her
disposition, being addicted to a melancholy as she is,
that it cannot but turn him into a notable contempt. If 199
you will see it, follow me.
SIR TOBY   To the gates of Tartar, thou most excellent 201
devil of wit!
SIR ANDREW   I'll make one too.   *Exeunt.* 203

❖

3.1

*Enter Viola, and Clown [Feste, playing his pipe
and tabor].*

VIOLA   Save thee, friend, and thy music. Dost thou live 1
by thy tabor? 2
FESTE   No, sir, I live by the church.
VIOLA   Art thou a churchman?
FESTE   No such matter, sir. I do live by the church, for
I do live at my house, and my house doth stand by the
church.
VIOLA   So thou mayst say the king lies by a beggar if 8
a beggar dwell near him, or the church stands by thy 9
tabor if thy tabor stand by the church. 10
FESTE   You have said, sir. To see this age! A sentence is 11
but a cheveril glove to a good wit. How quickly the 12
wrong side may be turned outward!
VIOLA   Nay, that's certain. They that dally nicely with 14
words may quickly make them wanton. 15
FESTE   I would therefore my sister had had no name,
sir.
VIOLA   Why, man?

---

140 revolve consider.   **141 stars** fortune   **143–4 open their hands**
offer their bounty   **145 inure** accustom.   **like** likely.   **cast** cast off
146 slough skin of a snake; hence, former demeanor of humbleness.
opposite contradictory   **147 tang** sound loud with   **148 state** politics, statecraft   **148–9 trick of singularity** eccentricity of manner.
151 cross-gartered wearing garters above and below the knee so as to
cross behind it.   **152 Go to** (An expression of remonstrance.)
155 alter services i.e., exchange place of mistress and servant
157 champaign open country.   **discovers** discloses   **158 politic** dealing with state affairs   **159 baffle** deride, degrade. (A technical chivalric term used to describe the disgrace of a perjured knight.)   **gross**
base   **160 point-devise** correct to the letter   **161 to let** by letting.
jade me trick me, make me look ridiculous (as an unruly horse might
do)   **162 excites to this** prompts this conclusion   **164 this** this letter
166 these habits this attire   **167 happy** fortunate.   **strange, stout**
aloof, haughty   **171 thou entertain'st** you accept   **173 still** continually   **177 Sophy** Shah of Persia.

183 gull-catcher tricker of *gulls* or dupes.   **186 play** gamble.   **tray-
trip** a game of dice, success in which depended on throwing a three
(*tray*)   **192 aqua vitae** brandy or other distilled liquor   **199 notable
contempt** notorious object of contempt   **201 Tartar** Tartarus, the
infernal regions   **203 make one** i.e., tag along
3.1 Location: Olivia's garden.
1 Save God save   **1–2 live by** earn your living with. (But Feste uses
the phrase to mean "dwell near.")   **2 tabor** small drum.   **8 lies by**
(1) lies sexually with (2) dwells near   **9–10 stands by . . . stand by**
(1) is maintained by (2) is placed near   **11 You have said** You've
expressed your opinion.   **sentence** maxim, judgment, opinion
12 cheveril kidskin   **14 dally nicely** (1) play subtly (2) toy amorously
15 wanton (1) equivocal (2) licentious, unchaste. (Feste then "dallies"
with the word in its sexual sense; see line 20.)

FESTE   Why, sir, her name's a word, and to dally with
that word might make my sister wanton. But indeed,
words are very rascals since bonds disgraced them.   21

VIOLA   Thy reason, man?

FESTE   Troth, sir, I can yield you none without words,
and words are grown so false I am loath to prove
reason with them.

VIOLA   I warrant thou art a merry fellow and car'st for   26
nothing.   27

FESTE   Not so, sir, I do care for something; but in my
conscience, sir, I do not care for you. If that be to care
for nothing, sir, I would it would make you invisible.   30

VIOLA   Art not thou the Lady Olivia's fool?

FESTE   No indeed, sir. The Lady Olivia has no folly. She
will keep no fool, sir, till she be married, and fools are
as like husbands as pilchers are to herrings—the   34
husband's the bigger. I am indeed not her fool but   35
her corrupter of words.

VIOLA   I saw thee late at the Count Orsino's.   37

FESTE   Foolery, sir, does walk about the orb like the   38
sun; it shines everywhere. I would be sorry, sir, but   39
the fool should be as oft with your master as with my   40
mistress. I think I saw Your Wisdom there.   41

VIOLA   Nay, an thou pass upon me, I'll no more with   42
thee. Hold, there's expenses for thee.

[She gives a coin.]

FESTE   Now Jove, in his next commodity of hair, send   44
thee a beard!

VIOLA   By my troth, I'll tell thee, I am almost sick for   46
one—*[aside]* though I would not have it grow on my   47
chin.—Is thy lady within?

FESTE   Would not a pair of these have bred, sir?

VIOLA   Yes, being kept together and put to use.   50

FESTE   I would play Lord Pandarus of Phrygia, sir, to   51
bring a Cressida to this Troilus.

VIOLA   I understand you, sir. 'Tis well begged.

[She gives another coin.]

FESTE   The matter, I hope, is not great, sir, begging   54
but a beggar; Cressida was a beggar. My lady is   55
within, sir. I will conster to them whence you come.   56
Who you are and what you would are out of my
welkin—I might say "element," but the word is   58
overworn.   *Exit.*

VIOLA
This fellow is wise enough to play the fool,
And to do that well craves a kind of wit.
He must observe their mood on whom he jests,
The quality of persons, and the time,   63
Not, like the haggard, check at every feather   64
That comes before his eye. This is a practice   65
As full of labor as a wise man's art;
For folly that he wisely shows is fit,   67
But wise men, folly-fall'n, quite taint their wit.   68

Enter Sir Toby and [Sir] Andrew.

SIR TOBY   Save you, gentleman.

VIOLA   And you, sir.

SIR ANDREW   *Dieu vous garde, monsieur.*   71

VIOLA   *Et vous aussi; votre serviteur.*   72

SIR ANDREW   I hope, sir, you are, and I am yours.

SIR TOBY   Will you encounter the house? My niece is   74
desirous you should enter, if your trade be to her.   75

VIOLA   I am bound to your niece, sir; I mean, she is the   76
list of my voyage.   77

SIR TOBY   Taste your legs, sir. Put them to motion.   78

VIOLA   My legs do better understand me, sir, than I un-   79
derstand what you mean by bidding me taste my legs.

SIR TOBY   I mean, to go, sir, to enter.

VIOLA   I will answer you with gait and entrance.—But   82
we are prevented.   83

Enter Olivia and gentlewoman [Maria].

Most excellent accomplished lady, the heavens rain
odors on you!

SIR ANDREW   *[to Sir Toby]*   That youth's a rare courtier.
"Rain odors"—well.

VIOLA   *[to Sir Toby]*   My matter hath no voice, lady, but   88
to your own most pregnant and vouchsafed ear.   89

SIR ANDREW   *[to Sir Toby]*   "Odors," "pregnant," and
"vouchsafed." I'll get 'em all three all ready.   91

OLIVIA   Let the garden door be shut, and leave me to
my hearing. *[Exeunt Sir Toby, Sir Andrew, and Maria.]*
Give me your hand, sir.

VIOLA
My duty, madam, and most humble service.

OLIVIA   What is your name?

VIOLA
Cesario is your servant's name, fair princess.

21 since . . . them i.e., since bonds have been needed to make sworn statements good. (Words cannot be relied on since not even contractual promises are reliable.)   **26–7 car'st for nothing** are without any worries. (But Feste puns on *care for* in lines 29–30 in the sense of "like.")   **30 invisible** i.e., nothing; absent.   **34 pilchers** pilchards, fish resembling herring but smaller   **35 the bigger** (1) the larger (2) the bigger fool.   **37 late** recently   **38 orb** earth   **39–41 I would . . . mistress** (1) I should be sorry not to visit Orsino's house often (2) It would be a shame if folly were no less common there than in Olivia's household.   **41 Your Wisdom** i.e., you. (A title of mock courtesy.)   **42 an . . . me** if you fence (verbally) with me, pass judgment on me   **44 commodity** supply   **46–7 sick for one** (1) eager to have a beard (2) in love with a bearded man   **50 put to use** put out at interest.   **51 Pandarus** the go-between in the love story of Troilus and Cressida; uncle to Cressida   **54–5 begging . . . was a beggar** (A reference to Henryson's *Testament of Cresseid* in which Cressida became a leper and a beggar. Feste desires another coin to be the mate of the one he has, just as Cressida, the beggar, was mate to Troilus.)   **56 conster** construe, explain   **58 welkin** sky. **element** (The word can be synonymous with *welkin*, but the common phrase *out of my element* means "beyond my scope.")

63 quality character, rank   **64 haggard** untrained adult hawk, hence unmanageable   **64–5 check . . . eye** strike at every bird it sees, i.e., dart from subject to subject.   **65 practice** exercise of skill   **67–8 For . . . wit** for the folly he judiciously displays is appropriate and clever, whereas when wise men fall into folly they utterly infect their own intelligence.   **71 Dieu . . . monsieur** God keep you, sir.   **72 Et . . . serviteur** And you, too; (I am) your servant. (Sir Andrew is not quite up to a reply in French.)   **74 encounter** (High-sounding word to express "approach.")   **75 trade** business. (Suggesting also a commercial venture.)   **76 I am bound** (1) I am on a journey. (Continuing Sir Toby's metaphor in *trade.*) (2) I am confined, obligated   **77 list** limit, destination   **78 Taste** Try   **79 understand** stand under, support   **82 gait and entrance** going and entering. (With a pun on *gate*: [1] stride [2] entryway.)   **83 prevented** anticipated.   **88 hath no voice** cannot be uttered   **89 pregnant and vouchsafed** receptive and attentive   **91 all ready** committed to memory for future use.

OLIVIA
My servant, sir? 'Twas never merry world   98
Since lowly feigning was called compliment.   99
You're servant to the Count Orsino, youth.

VIOLA
And he is yours, and his must needs be yours;   101
Your servant's servant is your servant, madam.

OLIVIA
For him, I think not on him. For his thoughts,   103
Would they were blanks, rather than filled with me!   104

VIOLA
Madam, I come to whet your gentle thoughts
On his behalf.

OLIVIA   Oh, by your leave, I pray you.   106
I bade you never speak again of him.
But, would you undertake another suit,
I had rather hear you to solicit that
Than music from the spheres.

VIOLA   Dear lady—   110

OLIVIA
Give me leave, beseech you. I did send,
After the last enchantment you did here,
A ring in chase of you; so did I abuse   113
Myself, my servant, and, I fear me, you.
Under your hard construction must I sit,   115
To force that on you in a shameful cunning   116
Which you knew none of yours. What might you
think?
Have you not set mine honor at the stake   118
And baited it with all th'unmuzzled thoughts   119
That tyrannous heart can think? To one of your
receiving   120
Enough is shown; a cypress, not a bosom,   121
Hides my heart. So, let me hear you speak.   122

VIOLA
I pity you.

OLIVIA   That's a degree to love.

VIOLA
No, not a grece; for 'tis a vulgar proof   124
That very oft we pity enemies.

OLIVIA
Why then, methinks 'tis time to smile again.   126
Oh, world, how apt the poor are to be proud!   127
If one should be a prey, how much the better

To fall before the lion than the wolf!   *Clock strikes.*   129
The clock upbraids me with the waste of time.
Be not afraid, good youth, I will not have you;
And yet, when wit and youth is come to harvest
Your wife is like to reap a proper man.   133
There lies your way, due west.

VIOLA   Then westward ho!   134
Grace and good disposition attend Your Ladyship.   135
You'll nothing, madam, to my lord by me?

OLIVIA   Stay.
I prithee, tell me what thou think'st of me.

VIOLA
That you do think you are not what you are.   139

OLIVIA
If I think so, I think the same of you.   140

VIOLA
Then think you right. I am not what I am.

OLIVIA
I would you were as I would have you be!

VIOLA
Would it be better, madam, than I am?
I wish it might, for now I am your fool.   144

OLIVIA *[aside]*
Oh, what a deal of scorn looks beautiful
In the contempt and anger of his lip!
A murderous guilt shows not itself more soon
Than love that would seem hid; love's night is noon.—   148
Cesario, by the roses of the spring,
By maidhood, honor, truth, and everything,
I love thee so that, maugre all thy pride,   151
Nor wit nor reason can my passion hide.   152
Do not extort thy reasons from this clause,   153
For that I woo, thou therefore hast no cause.   154
But rather reason thus with reason fetter: 155
Love sought is good, but given unsought is better.

VIOLA
By innocence I swear, and by my youth,
I have one heart, one bosom, and one truth,
And that no woman has, nor never none
Shall mistress be of it save I alone.
And so adieu, good madam. Nevermore
Will I my master's tears to you deplore.   162

OLIVIA
Yet come again, for thou perhaps mayst move
That heart, which now abhors, to like his love.
                              Exeunt [separately].

❧

98–9 'Twas . . . compliment Things have never been the same since affected humility (like calling oneself another's servant) began to be mistaken for courtesy.   **101 yours** your servant.   **his** those belonging to him   **103 For** As for   **104 blanks** blank coins ready to be stamped or empty sheets of paper   **106 by your leave** i.e., allow me to interrupt   **110 music from the spheres** (The heavenly bodies were thought to be fixed in hollow concentric spheres that revolved one about the other, producing a harmony too exquisite to be heard by human ears.)   **113 abuse** wrong, mislead   **115 hard construction** harsh interpretation   **116 To force** for forcing the ring   **118 at the stake** (The figure is from bearbaiting.)   **119 baited** harassed. (Literally, set the unmuzzled dogs on to bite the bear.)   **120 receiving** capacity, intelligence   **121–2 a cypress . . . heart** i.e., I have shown my heart to you, veiled only with thin, gauzelike cypress cloth rather than the opaque flesh of my bosom.   **124 grece** step. (Synonymous with *degree* in the preceding line.)   **vulgar proof** common experience   **126 smile** i.e., cast off love's melancholy   **127 how . . . proud!** how ready the unfortunate and rejected (like myself) are to find something to be proud of in their distress! Or, how apt are persons of comparatively low social station like yourself to show pride in rejecting love!

129 To fall . . . wolf! i.e., to fall before a noble adversary rather than to a person like you who attacks me thus!   **133 like** likely.   **proper** handsome, worthy   **134 westward ho** (The cry of Thames watermen to attract westward-bound passengers.)   **135 Grace . . . Ladyship** May you enjoy God's blessing and a happy frame of mind.   **139 That . . . are** i.e., That you think you are in love with a man, and you are mistaken.   **140 If . . . you** (Olivia may interpret Viola's cryptic statement as suggesting that Olivia "does not know herself," i.e., is distracted with passion; she may also hint at her suspicion that "Cesario" is higher born than he admits.)   **144 fool** butt.   **148 love's . . . noon** i.e., love, despite its attempt to be secret, reveals itself as plain as day.   **152 maugre** in spite of   **152 Nor** neither   **153–4 Do . . . cause** Do not rationalize your indifference along these lines, that because I am the wooer you have no cause to reciprocate.   **155 But . . . fetter** But instead control your reasoning with the following reason   **162 deplore** beweep.

3.2

Enter Sir Toby, Sir Andrew, and Fabian.

SIR ANDREW   No, faith, I'll not stay a jot longer.

SIR TOBY   Thy reason, dear venom, give thy reason.   2

FABIAN   You must needs yield your reason, Sir Andrew.

SIR ANDREW   Marry, I saw your niece do more favors to the Count's servingman than ever she bestowed upon me. I saw't i'th' orchard.   6

SIR TOBY   Did she see thee the while, old boy? Tell me that.

SIR ANDREW   As plain as I see you now.

FABIAN   This was a great argument of love in her toward you.   10

SIR ANDREW   'Slight, will you make an ass o'me?   12

FABIAN   I will prove it legitimate, sir, upon the oaths of judgment and reason.   13

SIR TOBY   And they have been grand-jurymen since before Noah was a sailor.

FABIAN   She did show favor to the youth in your sight only to exasperate you, to awake your dormouse valor,   18
to put fire in your heart and brimstone in your liver. You should then have accosted her, and with some excellent jests, fire-new from the mint, you should   21
have banged the youth into dumbness. This was   22
looked for at your hand, and this was balked. The dou-   23
ble gilt of this opportunity you let time wash off, and   24
you are now sailed into the north of my lady's opinion,   25
where you will hang like an icicle on a Dutchman's   26
beard unless you do redeem it by some laudable at-   27
tempt either of valor or policy.   28

SIR ANDREW   An't be any way, it must be with valor, for policy I hate. I had as lief be a Brownist as a poli-   30
tician.   31

SIR TOBY   Why, then, build me thy fortunes upon the   32
basis of valor. Challenge me the Count's youth to fight   33
with him; hurt him in eleven places. My niece shall take note of it; and assure thyself, there is no love-broker in the world can more prevail in man's   36
commendation with woman than report of valor.

FABIAN   There is no way but this, Sir Andrew.

SIR ANDREW   Will either of you bear me a challenge to him?

SIR TOBY   Go, write it in a martial hand. Be curst and   41
brief; it is no matter how witty, so it be eloquent and full of invention. Taunt him with the license of ink. If   43

thou "thou"-est him some thrice, it shall not be amiss;   44
and as many lies as will lie in thy sheet of paper,   45
although the sheet were big enough for the bed of   46
Ware in England, set 'em down. Go, about it. Let   47
there be gall enough in thy ink, though thou write   48
with a goose pen, no matter. About it.   49

SIR ANDREW   Where shall I find you?

SIR TOBY   We'll call thee at the cubiculo. Go.   51

Exit Sir Andrew.

FABIAN   This is a dear manikin to you, Sir Toby.   52

SIR TOBY   I have been dear to him, lad, some two   53
thousand strong or so.

FABIAN   We shall have a rare letter from him; but you'll   55
not deliver't?

SIR TOBY   Never trust me, then; and by all means stir on the youth to an answer. I think oxen and wainropes   58
cannot hale them together. For Andrew, if he were   59
opened and you find so much blood in his liver as will   60
clog the foot of a flea, I'll eat the rest of th'anatomy.   61

FABIAN   And his opposite, the youth, bears in his   62
visage no great presage of cruelty.

Enter Maria.

SIR TOBY   Look where the youngest wren of nine   64
comes.

MARIA   If you desire the spleen, and will laugh your-   66
selves into stitches, follow me. Yond gull Malvolio is turned heathen, a very renegado; for there is no   68
Christian that means to be saved by believing rightly can ever believe such impossible passages of gross-   70
ness. He's in yellow stockings.   71

SIR TOBY   And cross-gartered?

MARIA   Most villainously, like a pedant that keeps a   73
school i'th' church. I have dogged him like his murderer. He does obey every point of the letter that I dropped to betray him. He does smile his face into more lines than is in the new map with the augmen-   77
tation of the Indies. You have not seen such a thing as   78
'tis. I can hardly forbear hurling things at him. I know my lady will strike him. If she do, he'll smile and take't for a great favor.

SIR TOBY   Come, bring us, bring us where he is.

Exeunt omnes.

44 **"thou"-est** ("Thou" was used only between friends or to inferiors.) 45 **lies** charges of lying   46–7 **bed of Ware** a famous bedstead capable of holding twelve persons, about eleven feet square, said to have been at the Stag Inn in Ware, Hertfordshire   48 **gall** (1) bitterness, rancor (2) a growth found on certain oaks, used as an ingredient of ink 49 **goose pen** (1) goose quill (2) foolish style   51 **call thee** call for you. **cubiculo** little chamber, bedchamber.   52 **manikin** puppet   53 **dear** expensive. (Playing on *dear,* "fond," in the previous speech.)   55 **rare** extraordinary   58 **wainropes** wagon ropes   59 **hale** haul.   **For** As for   60 **liver** (A pale and bloodless liver was a sign of cowardice.) 61 **th'anatomy** the cadaver   62 **opposite** adversary   64 **youngest . . . nine** the last hatched and smallest of a nest of wrens   66 **the spleen** a laughing fit. (The spleen was thought to be the seat of immoderate laughter.)   68 **renegado** renegade, deserter of his religion 70–1 **impossible . . . grossness** gross impossibilities (i.e., in the letter). 73 **villainously** i.e., abominably.   **pedant** schoolmaster   77–8 **the new . . . Indies** (Probably a reference to a map made by Emmeric Mollineux in 1599–1600 to be printed in Hakluyt's *Voyages,* showing more of the East indies, including Japan, than had ever been mapped before.)

3.2. Location: Olivia's house.
2 **venom** i.e., person filled with venomous anger   6 **orchard** garden. 10 **argument** proof   12 **'Slight** By his (God's) light   13 **it** my contention.   **oaths** i.e., testimony under oath   18 **dormouse** i.e., sleepy and timid   21 **fire-new . . . mint** newly coined   22 **banged** struck 23 **balked** missed, neglected.   23–4 **double gilt** thick layer of gold, i.e., rare worth   25 **into . . . opinion** i.e., out of the warmth and sunshine of Olivia's favor   26–7 **icicle . . . beard** (Alludes to the arctic voyage of William Barents in 1596–1597.)   28 **policy** stratagem. 28 **policy** stratagem.   30 **Brownist** (An early name of the Congregationalists, from the name of the founder, Robert Browne.) 30–1 **politician** intriguer. (Sir Andrew misinterprets Sir Toby's more neutral use of *policy,* "clever stratagem.")   32–3 **build me . . . Challenge me** build . . . Challenge. ("Me" is idiomatic.)   36 **love-broker** agent between lovers   41 **curst** fierce   43 **with . . . ink** i.e., with the freedom that may be risked in writing but not in conversation.

3.3

Enter Sebastian and Antonio.

SEBASTIAN
I would not by my will have troubled you,
But since you make your pleasure of your pains,
I will no further chide you.

ANTONIO
I could not stay behind you. My desire,
More sharp than filèd steel, did spur me forth,
And not all love to see you—though so much   6
As might have drawn one to a longer voyage—
But jealousy what might befall your travel,   8
Being skilless in these parts, which to a stranger, 9
Unguided and unfriended, often prove
Rough and unhospitable. My willing love,
The rather by these arguments of fear,   12
Set forth in your pursuit.

SEBASTIAN   My kind Antonio,
I can no other answer make but thanks,
And thanks; and ever oft good turns   15
Are shuffled off with such uncurrent pay.   16
But were my worth, as is my conscience, firm,   17
You should find better dealing. What's to do?   18
Shall we go see the relics of this town?   19

ANTONIO
Tomorrow, sir. Best first go see your lodging.

SEBASTIAN
I am not weary, and 'tis long to night.
I pray you, let us satisfy our eyes
With the memorials and the things of fame
That do renown this city.

ANTONIO   Would you'd pardon me.   24
I do not without danger walk these streets.
Once in a sea fight 'gainst the Count his galleys   26
I did some service, of such note indeed
That were I ta'en here it would scarce be answered. 28

SEBASTIAN
Belike you slew great number of his people?   29

ANTONIO
Th'offense is not of such a bloody nature,
Albeit the quality of the time and quarrel
Might well have given us bloody argument.   32
It might have since been answered in repaying   33
What we took from them, which for traffic's sake   34
Most of our city did. Only myself stood out,
For which, if I be lapsèd in this place,   36
I shall pay dear.

SEBASTIAN   Do not then walk too open.

ANTONIO
It doth not fit me. Hold, sir, here's my purse.
                              [*He gives his purse.*]
In the south suburbs, at the Elephant,   39
Is best to lodge. I will bespeak our diet,   40
Whiles you beguile the time and feed your knowl-
   edge
With viewing of the town. There shall you have me. 42

SEBASTIAN   Why I your purse?

ANTONIO
Haply your eye shall light upon some toy   44
You have desire to purchase; and your store   45
I think is not for idle markets, sir.   46

SEBASTIAN
I'll be your purse-bearer and leave you
For an hour.

ANTONIO   To th'Elephant.

SEBASTIAN   I do remember.
                              Exeunt [separately].

❧

3.4

Enter Olivia and Maria.

OLIVIA [*aside*]
I have sent after him; he says he'll come.   1
How shall I feast him? What bestow of him?   2
For youth is bought more oft than begged or
   borrowed.
I speak too loud.—
Where's Malvolio? He is sad and civil,   5
And suits well for a servant with my fortunes.
Where is Malvolio?

MARIA   He's coming, madam, but in very strange
   manner. He is, sure, possessed, madam.   9

OLIVIA   Why, what's the matter? Does he rave?

MARIA   No, madam, he does nothing but smile. Your
   Ladyship were best to have some guard about you if he
   come, for sure the man is tainted in's wits.   13

OLIVIA
Go call him hither. [*Maria summons Malvolio.*] I am as
   mad as he,
If sad and merry madness equal be.   15

   *Enter Malvolio, [cross-gartered and in yellow
   stockings].*

How now, Malvolio?

MALVOLIO   Sweet lady, ho, ho!

OLIVIA   Smil'st thou? I sent for thee upon a sad   18
   occasion.

3.3. Location: A Street.
6 all only, merely.   **so much** i.e., that was great enough   **8 jealousy** anxiety   **9 skilless in** unacquainted with   **12 The rather** made all the more willing   **15 And . . . turns** (this probably corrupt line is usually made to read, "And thanks and ever thanks; and oft good turns.")   **16 shuffled off** turned aside.   **uncurrent** worthless (such as mere thanks)   **17 worth** wealth.   **conscience** i.e., moral inclination to assist   **18 dealing** treatment, payment.   **19 relics** antiquities   **24 renown** make famous   **26 Count his** Count's, i.e., Duke's   **28 it . . . answered** I'd be hard put to offer a defense.   **29 Belike** Perhaps   **32 bloody argument** cause for bloodshed.   **33 answered** compensated   **34 traffic's** trade's   **36 lapsèd** caught off guard, surprised

39 Elephant the name of an inn   **40 bespeak our diet** order our food   **42 have** find   **44 Haply** Perhaps.   **toy** trifle   **45 store** store of money   **46 is not . . . markets** cannot afford luxuries
3.4. Location: Olivia's garden.
1 he . . . come i.e., suppose he says he'll come.   **2 of** on   **5 sad and civil** sober and decorous   **9 possessed** (1) possessed with an evil spirit (2) mad   **13 in's** in his   **15 If . . . equal be** i.e., if love melancholy and smiling madness are essentially alike. (Love melancholy was regarded as a kind of madness.)   **18 sad** serious

MALVOLIO   Sad, lady? I could be sad. This does make 20
some obstruction in the blood, this cross-gartering,
but what of that? If it please the eye of one, it is with
me as the very true sonnet is, "Please one and please 23
all." 24

OLIVIA   Why, how dost thou, man? What is the matter
with thee?

MALVOLIO   Not black in my mind, though yellow in my 27
legs. It did come to his hands, and commands shall be 28
executed. I think we do know the sweet roman hand. 29

OLIVIA   Wilt thou go to bed, Malvolio? 30

MALVOLIO   To bed! "Ay, sweetheart, and I'll come to 31
thee." 32

OLIVIA   God comfort thee! Why dost thou smile so and
kiss thy hand so oft?

MARIA   How do you, Malvolio?

MALVOLIO   At your request? Yes, nightingales answer 36
daws. 37

MARIA   Why appear you with this ridiculous boldness
before my lady?

MALVOLIO   "Be not afraid of greatness." 'Twas well writ.

OLIVIA   What mean'st thou by that, Malvolio?

MALVOLIO   "Some are born great—"

OLIVIA   Ha?

MALVOLIO   "Some achieve greatness—"

OLIVIA   What say'st thou?

MALVOLIO   "And some have greatness thrust upon them."

OLIVIA   Heaven restore thee!

MALVOLIO   "Remember who commended thy yellow
stockings—"

OLIVIA   Thy yellow stockings?

MALVOLIO   "And wished to see thee cross-gartered."

OLIVIA   Cross-gartered?

MALVOLIO   "Go to, thou art made, if thou desir'st to
be so—"

OLIVIA   Am I made?

MALVOLIO   "If not, let me see thee a servant still."

OLIVIA   Why, this is very midsummer madness. 57

Enter Servant.

SERVANT   Madam, the young gentleman of the Count
Orsino's is returned. I could hardly entreat him back.
He attends Your Ladyship's pleasure.

OLIVIA   I'll come to him.   [*Exit Servant.*]
Good Maria, let this fellow be looked to. Where's my
cousin Toby? Let some of my people have a special
care of him. I would not have him miscarry for the half 64
of my dowry.

Exeunt [Olivia and Maria, different ways].

MALVOLIO   Oho, do you come near me now? No worse 66
man than Sir Toby to look to me! This concurs directly
with the letter. She sends him on purpose that I may
appear stubborn to him, for she incites me to that in
the letter. "Cast thy humble slough," says she; "be opposite with a kinsman, surly with servants; let thy
tongue tang with arguments of state; put thyself into
the trick of singularity." And consequently sets down 73
the manner how: as, a sad face, a reverend carriage, a 74
slow tongue, in the habit of some sir of note, and so 75
forth. I have limed her, but it is Jove's doing, and Jove 76
make me thankful! And when she went away now,
"Let this fellow be looked to." "Fellow!" Not "Malvo- 78
lio," nor after my degree, but "fellow." Why, every- 79
thing adheres together, that no dram of a scruple, no 80
scruple of a scruple, no obstacle, no incredulous or un- 81
safe circumstance—what can be said?—nothing that 82
can be can come between me and the full prospect of
my hopes. Well, Jove, not I, is the doer of this, and he
is to be thanked.

Enter [Sir] Toby, Fabian, and Maria.

SIR TOBY   Which way is he, in the name of sanctity? If
all the devils of hell be drawn in little, and Legion him- 87
self possessed him, yet I'll speak to him.

FABIAN   Here he is, here he is.—How is't with you,
sir? How is't with you, man?

MALVOLIO   Go off. I discard you. Let me enjoy my
private. Go off. 92

MARIA   Lo, how hollow the fiend speaks within him!
Did not I tell you? Sir Toby, my lady prays you to have
a care of him.

MALVOLIO   Aha, does she so?

SIR TOBY   Go to, go to! Peace, peace, we must deal
gently with him. Let me alone.—How do you, 98
Malvolio? How is't with you? What, man, defy the 99
devil! Consider, he's an enemy to mankind.

MALVOLIO   Do you know what you say?

MARIA   La you, an you speak ill of the devil, how he 102
takes it at heart! Pray God he be not bewitched!

FABIAN   Carry his water to th' wisewoman. 104

MARIA   Marry, and it shall be done tomorrow morning,
if I live. My lady would not lose him for more than
I'll say.

MALVOLIO   How now, mistress?

---

20 sad (1) serious (2) melancholy.   **23 sonnet** song, ballad
23–4 "Please . . . all" "To please one special person is as good as to
please everybody." (The refain of a ballad.)   **27 black** i.e., melancholic
28 It i.e., The letter.   **his** Malvolio's   **29 roman hand** fashionable italic
or Italian style of handwriting rather than English "secretary" handwriting.   **30 go to bed** i.e., try to sleep off your mental distress. (But
Malvolio misinterprets as a sexual invitation.)   **31–2 "Ay . . . thee"**
(Malvolio quotes from a popular song of the day.)   **36–7 nightingales
answer daws** i.e. (to Maria), do you suppose a fine fellow like me
would answer a lowly creature (a *daw*, a "jackdaw") like you?
57 midsummer madness (A proverbial phrase; the midsummer
moon was supposed to cause madness.)

64 miscarry come to harm   **66 come near** understand, appreciate
73 consequently thereafter   **74 sad** serious   **75 habit . . . note** attire
suited to a man of distinction   **76 limed** caught like a bird with
birdlime (a sticky substance spread on branches)   **78 Fellow** (Malvolio takes the basic meaning, "companion.")   **79 after my degree**
according to my position   **80 dram** (Literally, one-eighth of a fluid
ounce.)   **scruple** (Literally, one-third of a dram.)   **81 incredulous**
incredible   **81–2 unsafe** uncertain, unreliable   **87 drawn in little**
(1) portrayed in miniature (2) gathered into a small space.   **Legion**
an unclean spirit. ("My name is Legion, for we are many," Mark 5:9.)
92 private privacy.   **98 Let me alone** Leave him to me.   **99 defy**
renounce   **102 La you** Look you   **104 water** urine (for medical
analysis)

MARIA Oh, Lord!

SIR TOBY Prithee, hold thy peace; this is not the way. Do you not see you move him? Let me alone with 111 him.

FABIAN No way but gentleness, gently, gently. The fiend is rough, and will not be roughly used.

SIR TOBY Why, how now, my bawcock! How dost 115 thou, chuck? 116

MALVOLIO Sir!

SIR TOBY Ay, biddy, come with me. What, man, 'tis 118 not for gravity to play at cherry-pit with Satan. Hang 119 him, foul collier! 120

MARIA Get him to say his prayers, good Sir Toby, get him to pray.

MALVOLIO My prayers, minx?

MARIA No, I warrant you, he will not hear of godliness.

MALVOLIO Go hang yourselves all! You are idle, shal- 125 low things; I am not of your element. You shall know 126 more hereafter. *Exit.* 127

SIR TOBY Is't possible?

FABIAN If this were played upon a stage, now, I could condemn it as an improbable fiction.

SIR TOBY His very genius hath taken the infection of 131 the device, man.

MARIA Nay, pursue him now, lest the device take air 133 and taint. 134

FABIAN Why, we shall make him mad indeed.

MARIA The house will be the quieter.

SIR TOBY Come, we'll have him in a dark room and 137 bound. My niece is already in the belief that he's mad. 138 We may carry it thus for our pleasure and his penance 139 till our very pastime, tired out of breath, prompt us to have mercy on him, at which time we will bring the device to the bar and crown thee for a finder of 142 madmen. But see, but see! 143

Enter Sir Andrew [with a letter].

FABIAN More matter for a May morning. 144

SIR ANDREW Here's the challenge. Read it. I warrant there's vinegar and pepper in't.

FABIAN Is't so saucy? 147

SIR ANDREW Ay, is't, I warrant him. Do but read. 148

SIR TOBY Give me. [*He reads.*] "Youth, whatsoever thou art, thou art but a scurvy fellow."

FABIAN Good, and valiant.

SIR TOBY [*reads*] "Wonder not, nor admire not in thy 152 mind, why I do call thee so, for I will show thee no reason for't."

FABIAN A good note, that keeps you from the blow of 155 the law.

SIR TOBY [*reads*] "Thou com'st to the Lady Olivia, and in my sight she uses thee kindly. But thou liest in thy throat; that is not the matter I challenge thee for."

FABIAN Very brief, and to exceeding good sense—less.

SIR TOBY [*reads*] "I will waylay thee going home, where if it be thy chance to kill me—"

FABIAN Good.

SIR TOBY [*reads*] "Thou kill'st me like a rogue and a villain."

FABIAN Still you keep o' th' windy side of the law. 166 Good.

SIR TOBY [*reads*] "Fare thee well, and God have mercy upon one of our souls! He may have mercy upon mine, but my hope is better, and so look to thyself. 170 Thy friend, as thou usest him, and thy sworn enemy, Andrew Aguecheek."

If this letter move him not, his legs cannot. I'll give't 173 him.

MARIA You may have very fit occasion for't. He is now in some commerce with my lady, and will by and by 176 depart.

SIR TOBY Go, Sir Andrew. Scout me for him at the 178 corner of the orchard like a bum-baily. So soon as ever 179 thou see'st him, draw, and as thou draw'st, swear hor- 180 rible; for it comes to pass oft that a terrible oath, with 181 a swaggering accent sharply twanged off, gives man- hood more approbation than ever proof itself would 183 have earned him. Away!

SIR ANDREW Nay, let me alone for swearing. *Exit.* 185

SIR TOBY Now will not I deliver his letter, for the behav- ior of the young gentleman gives him out to be of good capacity and breeding; his employment between his lord and my niece confirms no less. Therefore this letter, being so excellently ignorant, will breed no ter- ror in the youth. He will find it comes from a clodpoll. 191 But, sir, I will deliver his challenge by word of mouth, set upon Aguecheek a notable report of valor, and drive the gentleman—as I know his youth will aptly 194 receive it—into a most hideous opinion of his rage, 195 skill, fury, and impetuosity. This will so fright them both that they will kill one another by the look, like cockatrices. 198

Enter Olivia and Viola.

FABIAN Here he comes with your niece. Give them way 199 till he take leave, and presently after him. 200

---

111 **move** upset, excite 115 **bawcock** fine fellow. (From the French *beau-coq*.) 116 **chuck** (A form of "chick," term of endearment.) 118 **biddy** chicken 119 **for gravity** suitable for a man of your dig- nity. **cherry-pit** a children's game consisting of throwing cherry stones into a little hole 120 **collier** i.e., Satan. (Literally, a coal ven- dor.) 125 **idle** foolish 126 **element** sphere. 126–7 **know more** i.e. hear about this 131 **genius** i.e., soul, spirit 133–4 **take . . . taint** become exposed to air (i.e., become known) and thus spoil. 137–8 **have . . . bound** (The standard treatment for insanity at this time.) 139 **carry** manage 142 **bar** i.e., bar of judgment 142–3 **finder of madmen** member of a jury changed with "finding" if the accused is insane. 144 **matter . . . morning** sport for Mayday plays or games. 147 **saucy** (1) spicy (2) insolent. 148 **him** it. 152 **admire** marvel

155 **note** observation, remark 166 **windy** windward, i.e., safe, where one is less likely to be driven onto legal rocks and shoals 170 **my hope is better** (Sir Andrew's comically inept way of saying he hopes to be the survivor; instead, he seems to say, "May I be damned.") 173 **move** (1) stir up (2) set in motion 176 **commerce** transaction 178 **Scout me** Keep watch 179 **bum-baily** minor sheriff's officer employed in making arrests. 180–1 **horrible** horribly 183 **approba- tion** reputation (for courage). **proof** performance 185 **let . . . swearing** don't worry about my ability in swearing. 191 **clodpoll** blockhead. 194–5 **his . . . it** his inexperience will make him all the more ready to believe it 198 **cockatrices** basilisks, fabulous serpents reputed to be able to kill by a mere look. 199 **Give them way** Stay out of their way 200 **presently** immediately

SIR TOBY   I will meditate the while upon some horrid 201
message for a challenge.

[*Exeunt Sir Toby, Fabian, and Maria.*]

OLIVIA
I have said too much unto a heart of stone
And laid mine honor too unchary on't. 204
There's something in me that reproves my fault,
But such a headstrong potent fault it is
That it but mocks reproof.

VIOLA
With the same havior that your passion bears 208
Goes on my master's griefs. 209

OLIVIA [*giving a locket*]
Here, wear this jewel for me. 'Tis my picture.
Refuse it not; it hath no tongue to vex you.
And I beseech you come again tomorrow.
What shall you ask of me that I'll deny,
That honor, saved, may upon asking give? 214

VIOLA
Nothing but this: your true love for my master.

OLIVIA
How with mine honor may I give him that
Which I have given to you?

VIOLA   I will acquit you. 217

OLIVIA
Well, come again tomorrow. Fare thee well.
A fiend like thee might bear my soul to hell. [*Exit.*] 219

Enter [Sir] Toby and Fabian.

SIR TOBY   Gentleman, God save thee.

VIOLA   And you, sir.

SIR TOBY   That defense thou hast, betake thee to't. Of 222
what nature the wrongs are thou hast done him, I
know not, but thy intercepter, full of despite, bloody 224
as the hunter, attends thee at the orchard end. 225
Dismount thy tuck, be yare in thy preparation, for thy 226
assailant is quick, skillful, and deadly.

VIOLA   You mistake sir. I am sure no man hath any
quarrel to me. My remembrance is very free and clear 229
from any image of offense done to any man.

SIR TOBY   You'll find it otherwise, I assure you. Therefore, if you hold your life at any price, betake you to
your guard, for your opposite hath in him what youth, 233
strength, skill, and wrath can furnish man withal. 234

VIOLA   I pray you, sir, what is he?

SIR TOBY   He is knight, dubbed with unhatched rapier 236
and on carpet consideration, but he is a devil in 237
private brawl. Souls and bodies hath he divorced
three, and his incensement at this moment is so implacable that satisfaction can be none but by pangs of
death and sepulchre. Hob, nob is his word; give't or 241
take't.

VIOLA   I will return again into the house and desire
some conduct of the lady. I am no fighter. I have 244
heard of some kind of men that put quarrels purposely
on others, to taste their valor. Belike this is a 246
man of that quirk. 247

SIR TOBY   Sir, no. His indignation derives itself out of a
very competent injury; therefore, get you on and give 249
him his desire. Back you shall not to the house unless
you undertake that with me which with as much
safety you might answer him. Therefore, on, or strip 252
your sword stark naked; for meddle you must, that's 253
certain, or forswear to wear iron about you. 254

VIOLA   This is as uncivil as strange. I beseech you, do
me this courteous office as to know of the knight what 256
my offense to him is. It is something of my negligence, 257
nothing of my purpose. 258

SIR TOBY   I will do so.—Signor Fabian, stay you by this
gentleman till my return.   *Exit [Sir] Toby.*

VIOLA   Pray you, sir, do you know of this matter?

FABIAN   I know the knight is incensed against you,
even to a mortal arbitrament, but nothing of the 263
circumstance more.

VIOLA   I beseech you, what manner of man is he?

FABIAN   Nothing of that wonderful promise, to read 266
him by his form, as you are like to find him in the 267
proof of his valor. He is, indeed, sir, the most skillful,
bloody, and fatal opposite that you could possibly
have found in any part of Illyria. Will you walk 270
towards him, I will make your peace with him if I can.

VIOLA   I shall be much bound to you for't. I am one
that had rather go with Sir Priest than Sir Knight. I 273
care not who knows so much of my mettle.   *Exeunt.*

Enter [Sir] Toby and [Sir] Andrew.

SIR TOBY   Why, man, he's a very devil; I have not seen
such a firago. I had a pass with him, rapier, scabbard, 276
and all, and he gives me the stuck-in with such a 277
mortal motion that it is inevitable; and on the answer, 278
he pays you as surely as your feet hits the ground they
step on. They say he has been fencer to the Sophy. 280

SIR ANDREW   Pox on't, I'll not meddle with him.

---

201 horrid terrifying. (Literally, "bristling.")   **204 laid** hazarded.
unchary on't recklessly on it.   **208–9 With . . . griefs** i.e., Orsino's sufferings in love are as reckless and uncontrollable as your feelings.
214 That . . . give? that can be granted without compromising my
honor?   **217 acquit you** release you of your promise.   **219 A fiend . . .
hell** i.e., You are my torment. (*Like thee* means "in your likeness.")
222 That . . . to't Get ready to deploy whatever skill you have in fencing.   **224 intercepter** he who lies in wait.   **despite** defiance, ill will
224–5 bloody as the hunter bloodthirsty as a hunting dog   **226 Dismount thy tuck** Draw your rapier.   **yare** ready, nimble   **229 to** with
233 opposite opponent.   **what** whatsoever   **234 withal** with.
236 unhatched unhacked, unused in battle

237 carpet consideration (A carpet knight was one whose title was
obtained, not in battle, but through connections at court.)   **241 Hob,
nob** Have or have not, i.e., give it or take it, kill or be killed.   **word**
motto   **244 conduct** safe-conduct, escort   **246 taste** test, prove
Belike Probably   **247 quirk** peculiar humor.   **249 competent** sufficient   **252–3 strip . . . naked** draw your sword from its sheath
253 meddle engage (in conflict)   **254 forswear . . . iron** give up your
right to wear a sword   **256 know of** inquire from   **257–8 It is . . .
purpose** It is the result of some oversight, not anything I intended.
263 mortal arbitrament trial to the death   **266–7 read . . . form** judge
him by his appearance   **267 like** likely   **270 Will you** If you will
273 go with associate with.   **Sir Priest** (*Sir* was a courtesy title for
priests.)   **276 firago** virago.   **pass** bout   **277 stuck-in** stoccado, a
thrust in fencing   **278 answer** return hit   **280 to** in the service of

SIR TOBY   Ay, but he will not now be pacified. Fabian can scarce hold him yonder.

SIR ANDREW   Plague on't, an I thought he had been valiant and so cunning in fence, I'd have seen him damned ere I'd have challenged him. Let him let the matter slip and I'll give him my horse, gray Capilet. 287

SIR TOBY   I'll make the motion. Stand here, make a 288 good show on't. This shall end without the perdition 289 of souls. [Aside, as he crosses to meet Fabian] Marry, I'll 290 ride your horse as well as I ride you.

Enter Fabian and Viola.

[Aside to Fabian] I have his horse to take up the 292 quarrel. I have persuaded him the youth's a devil.

FABIAN   He is as horribly conceited of him, and pants 294 and looks pale as if a bear were at his heels.

SIR TOBY   [to Viola] There's no remedy, sir, he will fight with you for's oath's sake. Marry, he hath better bethought him of his quarrel, and he finds that now scarce to be worth talking of. Therefore draw, for the supportance of his vow; he protests he 300 will not hurt you.

VIOLA   [aside] Pray God defend me! A little thing 302 would make me tell them how much I lack of a man. 303

FABIAN   Give ground, if you see him furious.

SIR TOBY   [crossing to Sir Andrew] Come, Sir Andrew, there's no remedy. The gentleman will, for his honor's sake, have one bout with you. He cannot by the *duello* avoid it. But he has promised me, as he is 308 a gentleman and a soldier, he will not hurt you. Come on, to't.

SIR ANDREW   Pray God he keep his oath!

Enter Antonio.

VIOLA   [to Fabian]   I do assure you, 'tis against my will.
                                              [They draw.]

ANTONIO   [drawing, to Sir Andrew]
Put up your sword. If this young gentleman
Have done offense, I take the fault on me;
If you offend him, I for him defy you.

SIR TOBY   You, sir? Why, what are you?

ANTONIO
One, sir, that for his love dares yet do more
Than you have heard him brag to you he will.

SIR TOBY   [drawing]
Nay, if you be an undertaker, I am for you. 319

Enter Officers.

FABIAN   Oh, good Sir Toby, hold! Here come the officers.

SIR TOBY   [to Antonio]   I'll be with you anon.

VIOLA   [to Sir Andrew]   Pray, sir, put your sword up, if you please.

SIR ANDREW   Marry, will I, sir; and for that I promised 324 you, I'll be as good as my word. He will bear you 325 easily, and reins well.

FIRST OFFICER   This is the man. Do thy office.

SECOND OFFICER
Antonio, I arrest thee at the suit
Of Count Orsino.

ANTONIO   You do mistake me, sir.

FIRST OFFICER
No, sir, no jot. I know your favor well,   330
Though now you have no sea-cap on your head.—
Take him away. He knows I know him well.

ANTONIO
I must obey. [To Viola] This comes with seeking you.
But there's no remedy; I shall answer it.   334
What will you do, now my necessity
Makes me to ask you for my purse? It grieves me
Much more for what I cannot do for you
Than what befalls myself. You stand amazed,
But be of comfort.

SECOND OFFICER   Come, sir, away.

ANTONIO   [to Viola]
I must entreat of you some of that money.

VIOLA   What money, sir?
For the fair kindness you have showed me here,
And part being prompted by your present trouble,   343
Out of my lean and low ability
I'll lend you something. My having is not much;   345
I'll make division of my present with you.   346
Hold, there's half my coffer.   [She offers money.] 347

ANTONIO   Will you deny me now?
Is't possible that my deserts to you   349
Can lack persuasion? Do not tempt my misery,   350
Lest that it make me so unsound a man   351
As to upbraid you with those kindnesses
That I have done for you.

VIOLA   I know of none,
Nor know I you by voice or any feature.
I hate ingratitude more in a man
Than lying, vainness, babbling drunkenness,   356
Or any taint of vice whose strong corruption
Inhabits our frail blood.

ANTONIO   Oh, heavens themselves!

SECOND OFFICER   Come, sir, I pray you, go.

ANTONIO
Let me speak a little. This youth that you see here
I snatched one half out of the jaws of death,
Relieved him with such sanctity of love,   363
And to his image, which methought did promise   364
Most venerable worth, did I devotion.   365

287 Capilet i.e., "little horse." (From "capel," a nag.)   288 motion offer.   289–90 perdition of souls i.e., loss of lives.   292 take up settle, make up   294 He . . . him i.e., Cesario has as horrible a conception of Sir Andrew   300 supportance upholding   302–3 A little . . . man (With bawdy suggestion of the penis.)   308 duello dueling code   319 undertaker one who takes upon himself a task or business; here, a challenger.   for you ready for you.

324 for that as for what   325 He i.e., The horse   330 favor face   334 answer it stand trial and make reparation for it.   343 part partly   345 having wealth   346 present present store   347 coffer purse. (Literally, strongbox.)   349–50 deserts . . . persuasion claims on you can fail to persuade you to help me.   350 tempt try too severely   351 unsound morally weak, lacking in self-control   356 vainness vaingloriousness   363 such . . . love i.e., such veneration as is due to a sacred relic   364 image what he appeared to be. (Playing on the idea of a religious icon to be venerated.)   365 venerable worth worthiness of being venerated

FIRST OFFICER

What's that to us? The time goes by. Away!

ANTONIO

But, Oh, how vile an idol proves this god!
Thou hast, Sebastian, done good feature shame.   368
In nature there's no blemish but the mind;
None can be called deformed but the unkind.   370
Virtue is beauty, but the beauteous evil   371
Are empty trunks o'erflourished by the devil.   372

FIRST OFFICER

The man grows mad. Away with him! Come, come,
sir.

ANTONIO   Lead me on.   Exit [with Officers].

VIOLA [aside]

Methinks his words do from such passion fly
That he believes himself. So do not I.   376
Prove true, imagination, oh, prove true,
That I, dear brother, be now ta'en for you!

SIR TOBY   Come hither, knight. Come hither, Fabian.
We'll whisper o'er a couplet or two of most sage saws.   380
[They gather apart from Viola.]

VIOLA

He named Sebastian. I my brother know   381
Yet living in my glass; even such and so   382
In favor was my brother, and he went   383
Still in this fashion, color, ornament,   384
For him I imitate. Oh, if it prove,   385
Tempests are kind, and salt waves fresh in love!
[Exit.]

SIR TOBY   A very dishonest paltry boy, and more a   387
coward than a hare. His dishonesty appears in leaving   388
his friend here in necessity and denying him; and for   389
his cowardice, ask Fabian.

FABIAN   A coward, a most devout coward, religious in it.   391

SIR ANDREW   'Slid, I'll after him again and beat him.   392

SIR TOBY   Do, cuff him soundly, but never draw thy
sword.

SIR ANDREW   An I do not—   [Exit.]

FABIAN   Come, let's see the event.   396

SIR TOBY   I dare lay any money 'twill be nothing yet.   397
Exeunt.

❧

4.1

Enter Sebastian and Clown [Feste].

FESTE   Will you make me believe that I am not sent for
you?

SEBASTIAN   Go to, go to, thou art a foolish fellow. Let
me be clear of thee.

FESTE   Well held out, i'faith! No, I do not know you,   5
nor I am not sent to you by my lady to bid you come
speak with her, nor your name is not Master Cesario,
nor this is not my nose, neither. Nothing that is so is so.

SEBASTIAN   I prithee, vent thy folly somewhere else.   9
Thou know'st not me.

FESTE   Vent my folly! He has heard that word of some   11
great man, and now applies it to a fool. Vent my folly!
I am afraid this great lubber, the world, will prove a   13
cockney. I prithee now, ungird thy strangeness and   14
tell me what I shall vent to my lady. Shall I vent to her
that thou art coming?

SEBASTIAN   I prithee, foolish Greek, depart from me.   17
There's money for thee. [He gives money.] If you tarry
longer, I shall give worse payment.

FESTE   By my troth, thou hast an open hand. These   20
wise men that give fools money get themselves a good
report—after fourteen years' purchase.   22

Enter [Sir] Andrew, [Sir] Toby, and Fabian.

SIR ANDREW   Now, sir, have I met you again? There's
for you!   [He strikes Sebastian.]

SEBASTIAN   Why, there's for thee, and there, and there!
[He beats Sir Andrew with the hilt of his dagger.]
Are all the people mad?

SIR TOBY   Hold, sir, or I'll throw your dagger o'er the
house.

FESTE   This will I tell my lady straight. I would not be in   29
some of your coats for twopence.   [Exit.]   30

SIR TOBY   Come on, sir, hold!   [He grips Sebastian.]

SIR ANDREW   Nay, let him alone. I'll go another way to
work with him. I'll have an action of battery against   33
him, if there be any law in Illyria. Though I struck him
first, yet it's no matter for that.

SEBASTIAN   Let go thy hand!

SIR TOBY   Come, sir, I will not let you go. Come, my
young soldier, put up your iron. You are well fleshed.   38
Come on.

SEBASTIAN

I will be free from thee. [He breaks free and draws his
sword.] What wouldst thou now?
If thou dar'st tempt me further, draw thy sword.   41

SIR TOBY   What, what? Nay, then I must have an ounce
or two of this malapert blood from you.   [He draws.]   43

Enter Olivia.

---

368 **Thou . . . shame** i.e., You have shamed physical beauty by showing that it does not always reflect inner beauty.   370 **unkind** ungrateful, unnatural.   371 **beauteous evil** those who are outwardly beautiful but evil within   372 **trunks** (1) chests (2) bodies. **o'erflourished** (1) covered with ornamental carvings (2) made outwardly beautiful   376 **So . . . I** i.e., I do not believe myself (in the hope that has arisen in me).   380 **We'll . . . saws** i.e., Let's converse privately. (*Saws* are sayings.)   381–2 **I . . . glass** i.e., I know that my brother's likeness lives in me   383 **favor** appearance   384 **Still** always   385 **prove** prove true   387 **dishonest** dishonorable   388 **dishonesty** dishonor   389 **denying** refusing to acknowledge   391 **religious in it** making a religion of cowardice.   392 **'Slid** By his (God's) eyelid   396 **event** outcome.   397 **lay** wager.   **yet** nevertheless, after all.
4.1. Location: Before Olivia's house.

5 **held out** kept up   9 **vent** (1) utter (2) void, excrete, get rid of   11 **of** from, suited to the diction of; or, with reference to   13 **lubber** lout   14 **cockney** effeminate or foppish fellow. (Feste comically despairs of finding common sense anywhere if people start using affected phrases like those Sebastian uses.)   **ungird thy strangeness** put off your affectation of being a stranger. (Feste apes the kind of highflown speech he has just deplored.)   17 **Greek** (1) one who speaks gibberish (as in "It's all Greek to me") (2) buffoon (as in "merry Greek")   20 **open** generous. (With money or with blows.)   22 **report** reputation.   **after . . . purchase** i.e., at great cost and after long delays. (Land was ordinarily valued at the price of twelve years' rental; the Fool adds two years to this figure.)   29 **straight** at once.   29–30 **in . . . coats** i.e., in your shoes   33 **action of battery** lawsuit for physical assault   38 **fleshed** initiated into battle   41 **tempt** make trial of   43 **malapert** saucy, impudent

OLIVIA
Hold, Toby! On thy life I charge thee, hold!

SIR TOBY   Madam—

OLIVIA
Will it be ever thus? Ungracious wretch,
Fit for the mountains and the barbarous caves,
Where manners ne'er were preached! Out of my
    sight!—
Be not offended, dear Cesario.—
Rudesby, begone!
    [Exeunt Sir Toby, Sir Andrew, and Fabian.]
                    I prithee, gentle friend,   50
Let thy fair wisdom, not thy passion, sway
In this uncivil and unjust extent   52
Against thy peace. Go with me to my house,
And hear thou there how many fruitless pranks
This ruffian hath botched up, that thou thereby   55
Mayst smile at this. Thou shalt not choose but go.   56
Do not deny. Beshrew his soul for me!   57
He started one poor heart of mine, in thee.   58

SEBASTIAN   [aside]
What relish is in this? How runs the stream?   59
Or I am mad, or else this is a dream.   60
Let fancy still my sense in Lethe steep;   61
If it be thus to dream, still let me sleep!

OLIVIA
Nay, come, I prithee. Would thou'dst be ruled by me!

SEBASTIAN
Madam, I will.

OLIVIA   Oh, say so, and so be!   Exeunt.

❖

4.2

*Enter Maria [carrying a gown and a false
beard], and Clown [Feste].*

MARIA   Nay, I prithee, put on this gown and this beard;
make him believe thou art Sir Topas the curate. Do it   2
quickly. I'll call Sir Toby the whilst.   [Exit.]   3

FESTE   Well, I'll put it on, and I will dissemble myself   4
in't, and I would I were the first that ever dissembled
in such a gown. [He disguises himself in gown and
beard.] I am not tall enough to become the function   7
well, nor lean enough to be thought a good student;   8

but to be said an honest man and a good housekeeper   9
goes as fairly as to say a careful man and a great   10
scholar. The competitors enter.   11

Enter [Sir] Toby [and Maria].

SIR TOBY   Jove bless thee, Master Parson.

FESTE   *Bonos dies*, Sir Toby. For, as the old hermit of   13
Prague, that never saw pen and ink, very wittily said   14
to a niece of King Gorboduc, "That that is, is"; so I,   15
being Master Parson, am Master Parson; for what is
"that" but "that," and "is" but "is"?

SIR TOBY   To him, Sir Topas.

FESTE   What, ho, I say! Peace in this prison!
                [He approaches the door
                behind which Malvolio is confined.]

SIR TOBY   The knave counterfeits well; a good knave.

MALVOLIO   (within)   Who calls there?

FESTE   Sir Topas the curate, who comes to visit Malvolio
the lunatic.

MALVOLIO   Sir Topas, Sir Topas, good Sir Topas, go to
my lady—

FESTE   Out, hyperbolical fiend! How vexest thou this   26
man! Talkest thou nothing but of ladies?

SIR TOBY   Well said, Master Parson.

MALVOLIO   Sir Topas, never was man thus wronged.
Good Sir Topas, do not think I am mad. They have
laid me here in hideous darkness.

FESTE   Fie, thou dishonest Satan! I call thee by the most
modest terms, for I am one of those gentle ones that   33
will use the devil himself with courtesy. Say'st thou
that house is dark?   35

MALVOLIO   As hell, Sir Topas.

FESTE   Why, it hath bay windows transparent as barri-   37
cadoes, and the clerestories toward the south north   38
are as lustrous as ebony; and yet complainest thou of
obstruction?

MALVOLIO   I am not mad, Sir Topas. I say to you this
house is dark.

FESTE   Madman, thou errest. I say there is no darkness
but ignorance, in which thou art more puzzled than
the Egyptians in their fog.   45

MALVOLIO   I say this house is as dark as ignorance,
though ignorance were as dark as hell; and I say there
was never man thus abused. I am no more mad than
you are. Make the trial of it in any constant question.   49

---

50 **Rudesby** Ruffian   52 **extent** attack   55 **botched up** clumsily contrived   56 **Thou . . . go** I insist on your going with me.   57 **deny**
refuse.   **Beshrew** Curse. (A mild oath.)   **for me** for my part.
58 **He . . . thee** i.e., He alarmed that part of my heart which lies in
your bosom. (To *start* is also to drive an animal such as a *hart* [*heart*]
from its cover.)   59 **What . . . this?** i.e., What am I to make of this?
(*Relish* means "taste.")   60 **Or** Either   61 **Let . . . steep** i.e., Let this
fantasy continue to steep my senses in forgetfulness. (*Lethe* is the river
of forgetfulness in the underworld.)
4.2. Location: Olivia's house.
2 **Sir** (An honorific title for priests.)   **Topas** (A name perhaps derived
from Chaucer's comic knight in the "Rime of Sir Thopas" or from a
similar character in Lyly's *Endymion*. Topaz, a semiprecious stone,
was believed to be a cure for lunacy.)   3 **the whilst** in the meantime.
4 **dissemble** disguise. (With a play on "feign.")   7 **become the function** adorn the priestly office   8 **lean** (Scholars were proverbially
sparing of diet.)   **student** scholar (in divinity)

9–11 **to be . . . scholar** to be accounted honest and hospitable is as
good as being known as a painstaking scholar. (Feste suggests that
honesty and charity are found as often in ordinary men as in clerics.)
11 **competitors** associates, partners (in this plot)   13 *Bonos dies* Good
day   13–14 **hermit of Prague** (Probably another invented authority.)
15 **King Gorboduc** a legendary king of ancient Britain, protagonist in
the English tragedy *Gorboduc* (1562)   26 **hyperbolical** vehement,
boisterous.   **fiend** i.e., the devil supposedly possessing Malvolio.
33 **modest** moderate   35 **house** i.e., room   37–8 **barricadoes** barricades. (Which are opaque. Feste speaks comically in impossible paradoxes, but Malvolio seems not to notice.)   38 **clerestories** windows
in an upper wall   45 **Egyptians . . . fog** (Alluding to the darkness
brought upon Egypt by Moses; see Exodus 10:21–3.)   49 **constant
question** problem that requires consecutive reasoning.

FESTE   What is the opinion of Pythagoras concerning 50
wildfowl? 51

MALVOLIO   That the soul of our grandam might haply 52
inhabit a bird.

FESTE   What think'st thou of his opinion?

MALVOLIO   I think nobly of the soul, and no way
approve his opinion.

FESTE   Fare thee well. Remain thou still in darkness.
Thou shalt hold th'opinion of Pythagoras ere I will
allow of thy wits, and fear to kill a woodcock lest thou 59
dispossess the soul of thy grandam. Fare thee well.
   [*He moves away from Malvolio's prison.*]

MALVOLIO   Sir Topas, Sir Topas!

SIR TOBY   My most exquisite Sir Topas!

FESTE   Nay, I am for all waters. 63

MARIA   Thou mightst have done this without thy beard
and gown. He sees thee not.

SIR TOBY   To him in thine own voice, and bring me
word how thou find'st him.—I would we were well rid
of this knavery. If he may be conveniently delivered, I 68
would he were, for I am now so far in offense with
my niece that I cannot pursue with any safety this
sport to the upshot. Come by and by to my chamber. 71
   Exit [*with Maria*].

FESTE [*singing as he approaches Malvolio's prison*]
   "Hey, Robin, jolly Robin, 72
   Tell me how thy lady does." 73

MALVOLIO   Fool!

FESTE   "My lady is unkind, pardie." 75

MALVOLIO   Fool!

FESTE   "Alas, why is she so?"

MALVOLIO   Fool, I say!

FESTE   "She loves another—" Who calls, ha?

MALVOLIO   Good Fool, as ever thou wilt deserve well at
my hand, help me to a candle, and pen, ink, and
paper. As I am a gentleman, I will live to be thankful
to thee for't.

FESTE   Master Malvolio?

MALVOLIO   Ay, good Fool.

FESTE   Alas, sir, how fell you besides your five wits? 86

MALVOLIO   Fool, there was never man so notoriously 87
abused. I am as well in my wits, Fool, as thou art. 88

FESTE   But as well? Then you are mad indeed, if you be 89
no better in your wits than a fool.

MALVOLIO   They have here propertied me, keep me in 91
darkness, send ministers to me—asses—and do all
they can to face me out of my wits. 93

FESTE   Advise you what you say. The minister is here. 94
[*He speaks as Sir Topas.*] Malvolio, Malvolio, thy wits
the heavens restore! Endeavor thyself to sleep, and
leave thy vain bibble-babble.

MALVOLIO   Sir Topas!

FESTE [*in Sir Topas's voice*]   Maintain no words with
him, good fellow. [*In his own voice*] Who, I, sir? Not
I, sir. God b'wi'you, good Sir Topas. [*In Sir Topas's
voice*] Marry, amen. [*In his own voice*] I will, sir, I will.

MALVOLIO   Fool! Fool! Fool, I say!

FESTE   Alas, sir, be patient. What say you, sir? I am
shent for speaking to you. 105

MALVOLIO   Good Fool, help me to some light and some
paper. I tell thee I am as well in my wits as any man in
Illyria.

FESTE   Welladay that you were, sir! 109

MALVOLIO   By this hand, I am. Good Fool, some ink,
paper, and light; and convey what I will set down to
my lady. It shall advantage thee more than ever the
bearing of letter did.

FESTE   I will help you to't. But tell me true, are you
not mad indeed, or do you but counterfeit?

MALVOLIO   Believe me, I am not. I tell thee true.

FESTE   Nay, I'll ne'er believe a madman till I see his
brains. I will fetch you light and paper and ink.

MALVOLIO   Fool, I'll requite it in the highest degree. I
prithee, begone.

FESTE [*sings*]
   I am gone, sir,
   And anon, sir,
I'll be with you again,
   In a trice,
   Like to the old Vice, 125
Your need to sustain;

   Who, with dagger of lath, 127
   In his rage and his wrath,
Cries, "Aha!" to the devil;
   Like a mad lad,
   "Pare thy nails, dad? 131
Adieu, goodman devil!" *Exit.* 132

❖

4.3

Enter Sebastian [*with a pearl*].

SEBASTIAN
   This is the air; that is the glorious sun;

50–1 Pythagoras . . . wildfowl (An opening for the discussion of transmigration of souls, a doctrine held by Pythagoras.) 52 haply perhaps 59 allow of thy wits certify your sanity. woodcock (A proverbially stupid bird, easily caught.) 63 Nay . . . waters i.e., Indeed, I can turn my hand to anything. 68 delivered i.e., delivered from prison 71 upshot conclusion. 72–3 "Hey, Robin . . . does" (Another fragment of an old song, a version of which is attributed to Sir Thomas Wyatt.) 75 pardie i.e., by God, certainly. 86 besides out of. five wits The intellectual faculties, usually listed as common wit, imagination, fantasy, judgment, and memory. 87–8 notoriously abused egregiously ill treated. 89 But Only 91 propertied me i.e., treated me as property and thrown me into the lumber-room 93 face . . . wits brazenly represent me as having lost my wits.

94 Advise you Take care 105 shent scolded, rebuked 109 Welladay Alas, would that 125 Vice comic tempter of the "old" morality plays 127 dagger of lath comic weapon of the Vice in at least some morality plays 131 Pare thy nails (This may allude to the belief that evil spirits could use nail parings to get control of their victims; cf. Dromio of Syracuse in *The Comedy of Errors*, 4.3.69, "Some devils ask but the parings of one's nail," and the Boy's characterization of Pistol in *Henry V*, 4.4.72–3, as "this roaring devil i'th' old play, that everyone may pare his nails with a wooden dagger.") 132 goodman title for a person of substance but not of gentle birth. (This line could be Feste's farewell to Malvolio and his "devil.")
4.3. Location: Olivia's garden.

This pearl she gave me, I do feel't and see't;
And though 'tis wonder that enwraps me thus,
Yet 'tis not madness. Where's Antonio, then?
I could not find him at the Elephant;
Yet there he was, and there I found this credit,   6
That he did range the town to seek me out.
His counsel now might do me golden service;
For though my soul disputes well with my sense   9
That this may be some error, but no madness,
Yet doth this accident and flood of fortune   11
So far exceed all instance, all discourse,   12
That I am ready to distrust mine eyes
And wrangle with my reason that persuades me
To any other trust but that I am mad,   15
Or else the lady's mad. Yet if 'twere so,
She could not sway her house, command her
    followers,   17
Take and give back affairs and their dispatch   18
With such a smooth, discreet, and stable bearing
As I perceive she does. There's something in't
That is deceivable. But here the lady comes.   21

Enter Olivia and Priest.

OLIVIA
Blame not this haste of mine. If you mean well,
Now go with me and with this holy man
Into the chantry by. There, before him,   24
And underneath that consecrated roof,
Plight me the full assurance of your faith,
That my most jealous and too doubtful soul   27
May live at peace. He shall conceal it
Whiles you are willing it shall come to note,   29
What time we will our celebration keep   30
According to my birth. What do you say?   31

SEBASTIAN
I'll follow this good man, and go with you,
And having sworn truth, ever will be true.

OLIVIA
Then lead the way, good father, and heavens so shine
That they may fairly note this act of mine!   *Exeunt.* 35

❖

5.1

Enter Clown [Feste] and Fabian.

FABIAN   Now, as thou lov'st me, let me see his letter.
FESTE   Good Master Fabian, grant me another request.
FABIAN   Anything.

6 was was previously.   **credit** report   **9 my soul . . . sense** i.e., both my rational faculties and my physical senses come to the conclusion   **11 accident** unexpected event   **12 instance** precedent.   **discourse** reason   **15 trust** belief   **17 sway** rule   **18 Take . . . dispatch** receive reports on matters of household business and see to their execution   **21 deceivable** deceptive.   **24 chantry by** private endowed chapel nearby (where mass would be said for the souls of the dead, including Olivia's brother).   **27 jealous** anxious, mistrustful.   **doubtful** full of doubts   **29 Whiles** until.   **come to note** become known   **30 What time** at which time.   **our celebration** i.e., the actual marriage. (What they are about to perform is a binding betrothal.)   **31 birth** social position.   **35 fairly note** look upon with favor   **5.1. Location: Before Olivia's house.**

FESTE   Do not desire to see this letter.
FABIAN   This is to give a dog and in recompense desire   5
my dog again.   6

Enter Duke [Orsino], Viola, Curio, and lords.

ORSINO   Belong you to the Lady Olivia, friends?
FESTE   Ay, sir, we are some of her trappings.   8
ORSINO   I know thee well. How dost thou, my good fellow?
FESTE   Truly, sir, the better for my foes and the worse   10
for my friends.
ORSINO   Just the contrary—the better for thy friends.
FESTE   No, sir, the worse.
ORSINO   How can that be?
FESTE   Marry, sir, they praise me, and make an ass of   15
me. Now my foes tell me plainly I am an ass, so that   16
by my foes, sir, I profit in the knowledge of myself,
and by my friends I am abused; so that, conclusions to 18
be as kisses, if your four negatives make your two   19
affirmatives, why then the worse for my friends and   20
the better for my foes.
ORSINO   Why, this is excellent.
FESTE   By my troth, sir, no, though it please you to be   23
one of my friends.   24
ORSINO   Thou shalt not be the worse for me. There's gold.
                                        [*He gives a coin.*]
FESTE   But that it would be double-dealing, sir, I would 26
you could make it another.
ORSINO   Oh, you give me ill counsel.
FESTE   Put your grace in your pocket, sir, for this once, 29
and let your flesh and blood obey it.   30
ORSINO   Well, I will be so much a sinner to be a   31
double-dealer. There's another. [*He gives another coin.*]
FESTE   *Primo, secundo, tertio,* is a good play, and the old 33
saying is, the third pays for all. The triplex, sir, is a   34
good tripping measure; or the bells of Saint Bennet,   35
sir, may put you in mind—one, two, three.
ORSINO   You can fool no more money out of me at this
throw. If you will let your lady know I am here to   38
speak with her, and bring her along with you, it may
awake my bounty further.
FESTE   Marry, sir, lullaby to your bounty till I come
again. I go, sir, but I would not have you to think that

5–6 This . . . again (Apparently a reference to a well-known reply of Dr. Bulleyn when Queen Elizabeth asked for his dog and promised a gift of his choosing in return; he asked to have his dog back.)   **8 trappings** ornaments, decorations.   **10 for** because of   **15–16 make an ass of me** i.e., flatter me into foolishly thinking well of myself.   **18 abused** flatteringly deceived   **18–20 conclusions . . . affirmatives** i.e., as when a young lady, asked for a kiss, says "no, no" really meaning "yes"; or, as in grammar, two negatives make an affirmative   **23 though** even though   **24 friends** i.e., those who, according to Feste's syllogism, flatter him.   **26 But** Except for the fact.   **double-dealing** (1) giving twice (2) deceit, duplicity   **29 Put . . . pocket** (1) Pay no attention to your honor, put it away (2) Reach in your pocket or purse and show your customary grace or munificence. (*Your Grace* is also the formal way of addressing a duke.)   **30 it** i.e., my "ill counsel."   **31 to be** as to be   **33 Primo . . . tertio** Latin ordinals: first, second, third.   **play** (Perhaps a mathematical game or game of dice.)   **34 the third . . . all** the third time is lucky. (Proverbial.)   **triplex** triple time in music   **35 Saint Bennet** church of St. Benedict   **38 throw** (1) time (2) throw of the dice.

my desire of having is the sin of covetousness. But as
you say, sir, let your bounty take a nap. I will awake
it anon.   *Exit.*

Enter Antonio and Officers.

VIOLA
Here comes the man, sir, that did rescue me.

ORSINO
That face of his I do remember well,
Yet when I saw it last it was besmeared
As black as Vulcan in the smoke of war.   49
A baubling vessel was he captain of,   50
For shallow draft and bulk unprizable,   51
With which such scatheful grapple did he make   52
With the most noble bottom of our fleet   53
That very envy and the tongue of loss   54
Cried fame and honor on him. What's the matter?

FIRST OFFICER
Orsino, this is that Antonio
That took the *Phoenix* and her freight from Candy,   57
And this is he that did the *Tiger* board
When your young nephew Titus lost his leg.
Here in the streets, desperate of shame and state,   60
In private brabble did we apprehend him.   61

VIOLA
He did me kindness, sir, drew on my side,
But in conclusion put strange speech upon me.   63
I know not what 'twas but distraction.   64

ORSINO
Notable pirate, thou saltwater thief,   65
What foolish boldness brought thee to their mercies
Whom thou in terms so bloody and so dear   67
Hast made thine enemies?

ANTONIO   Orsino, noble sir,
Be pleased that I shake off these names you give me.   69
Antonio never yet was thief or pirate,
Though, I confess, on base and ground enough   71
Orsino's enemy. A witchcraft drew me hither.
That most ingrateful boy there by your side
From the rude sea's enraged and foamy mouth
Did I redeem; a wreck past hope he was.   75
His life I gave him, and did thereto add
My love, without retention or restraint,   77
All his in dedication. For his sake   78
Did I expose myself—pure for his love—   79
Into the danger of this adverse town,   80
Drew to defend him when he was beset;

Where being apprehended, his false cunning,
Not meaning to partake with me in danger,
Taught him to face me out of his acquaintance   84
And grew a twenty years' removèd thing   85
While one would wink; denied me mine own purse,   86
Which I had recommended to his use   87
Not half an hour before.

VIOLA   How can this be?

ORSINO   When came he to this town?

ANTONIO
Today, my lord; and for three months before,
No interim, not a minute's vacancy,
Both day and night did we keep company.

Enter Olivia and attendants.

ORSINO
Here comes the Countess. Now heaven walks on
   earth.
But for thee, fellow—fellow, thy words are madness.   95
Three months this youth hath tended upon me;
But more of that anon.—Take him aside.

OLIVIA [*to Orsino*]
What would my lord—but that he may not have—   98
Wherein Olivia may seem serviceable?—
Cesario, you do not keep promise with me.

VIOLA   Madam?

ORSINO   Gracious Olivia—

OLIVIA
What do you say, Cesario?—Good my lord—   103

VIOLA
My lord would speak. My duty hushes me.

OLIVIA
If it be aught to the old tune, my lord,
It is as fat and fulsome to mine ear   106
As howling after music.

ORSINO   Still so cruel?

OLIVIA   Still so constant, lord.

ORSINO
What, to perverseness? You uncivil lady,
To whose ingrate and unauspicious altars   111
My soul the faithfull'st off'rings have breathed out
That e'er devotion tendered! What shall I do?

OLIVIA
Even what it please my lord that shall become him.   114

ORSINO
Why should I not, had I the heart to do it,
Like to th'Egyptian thief at point of death   116
Kill what I love?—a savage jealousy
That sometime savors nobly. But hear me this: 118

Since you to nonregardance cast my faith,   119
And that I partly know the instrument   120
That screws me from my true place in your favor,   121
Live you the marble-breasted tyrant still.
But this your minion, whom I know you love,   123
And whom, by heaven I swear, I tender dearly,   124
Him will I tear out of that cruel eye   125
Where he sits crownèd in his master's spite.—   126
Come, boy, with me. My thoughts are ripe in
    mischief.
I'll sacrifice the lamb that I do love,   128
To spite a raven's heart within a dove.   [Going.] 129

VIOLA
And I, most jocund, apt, and willingly,   130
To do you rest, a thousand deaths would die.   131
                                            [Going.]

OLIVIA
Where goes Cesario?

VIOLA   After him I love
More than I love these eyes, more than my life,
More by all mores than e'er I shall love wife.   134
If I do feign, you witnesses above
Punish my life for tainting of my love!   136

OLIVIA
Ay me, detested! How am I beguiled!   137

VIOLA
Who does beguile you? Who does do you wrong?

OLIVIA
Hast thou forgot thyself? Is it so long?
Call forth the holy father.   [Exit an attendant.]

ORSINO [to Viola]   Come, away!

OLIVIA
Whither, my lord?—Cesario, husband, stay.

ORSINO
Husband?

OLIVIA   Ay, husband. Can he that deny?

ORSINO [to Viola]
Her husband, sirrah?

VIOLA   No, my lord, not I.   143

OLIVIA
Alas, it is the baseness of thy fear
That makes thee strangle thy propriety.   145
Fear not, Cesario, take thy fortunes up;
Be that thou know'st thou art, and then thou art   147
As great as that thou fear'st.

            Enter Priest.

                        Oh, welcome, father!   148
Father, I charge thee by thy reverence

Here to unfold—though lately we intended
To keep in darkness what occasion now   151
Reveals before 'tis ripe—what thou dost know
Hath newly passed between this youth and me.

PRIEST
A contract of eternal bond of love,
Confirmed by mutual joinder of your hands,   155
Attested by the holy close of lips,   156
Strengthened by interchangement of your rings,
And all the ceremony of this compact
Sealed in my function, by my testimony;   159
Since when, my watch hath told me, toward my
    grave
I have traveled but two hours.

ORSINO [to Viola]
Oh, thou dissembling cub! What wilt thou be
When time hath sowed a grizzle on thy case?   163
Or will not else thy craft so quickly grow
That thine own trip shall be thine overthrow?   165
Farewell, and take her, but direct thy feet
Where thou and I henceforth may never meet.

VIOLA
My Lord, I do protest—

OLIVIA   Oh, do not swear!
Hold little faith, though thou hast too much fear.   169

            Enter Sir Andrew.

SIR ANDREW   For the love of God, a surgeon! Send one
presently to Sir Toby.   171

OLIVIA   What's the matter?

SIR ANDREW   He's broke my head across, and has given   173
Sir Toby a bloody coxcomb too. For the love of God,   174
your help! I had rather than forty pound I were at
home.

OLIVIA   Who has done this, Sir Andrew?

SIR ANDREW   The Count's gentleman, one Cesario. We
took him for a coward, but he's the very devil
incarnate.   180

ORSINO   My gentleman, Cesario?

SIR ANDREW   'Od's lifelings, here he is!—You broke my 182
head for nothing, and that that I did I was set on to
do't by Sir Toby.

VIOLA
Why do you speak to me? I never hurt you.
You drew your sword upon me without cause,
But I bespake you fair, and hurt you not.   187

SIR ANDREW   If a bloody coxcomb be a hurt, you have
hurt me. I think you set nothing by a bloody cox-   189
comb.

            Enter [Sir] Toby and Clown [Feste].

---

119 **nonregardance** neglect   120 **that** since   121 **screws** pries, forces
123 **minion** darling, favorite   124 **tender** regard   125–6 **Him . . . spite**
I will tear Cesario away from Olivia, in whose cruel eye he sits like a
king to spite me, his true master.   128–9 **I'll . . . dove** i.e., I'll kill
Cesario, whom I love, to revenge myself on this seemingly gracious
but black-hearted lady.   130 **apt** readily   131 **do you rest** give you
ease   134 **by all mores** by all such comparisons   136 **Punish . . . love!**
Punish me with death for being disloyal to the love I feel!
137 **detested** hated and denounced by another.   143 **sirrah** (The normal way of addressing an inferior.)   145 **strangle thy propriety** i.e.,
deny what is properly yours, disavow your marriage to me.   147 **that**
that which   148 **as that thou fear'st** as him you fear, i.e., Orsino.

151 **occasion** necessity   155 **joinder** joining   156 **close** meeting
159 **Sealed . . . function** ratified through my carrying out of my
priestly office   163 **a grizzle** scattering of gray hair.   **case** skin.
165 **trip** wrestling trick used to throw an opponent. (You'll get over-
clever and trip yourself up.)   169 **Hold . . . fear** Keep to your oath as
well as you can, even if you are frightened by Orsino's threats.
171 **presently** immediately   173 **broke** broken the skin, cut   174 **coxcomb** fool's cap resembling the crest of a cock; here, head   180 **incar-
dinate** (For "incarnate.")   182 **'Od's lifelings** By God's little lives
187 **bespake you fair** addressed you courteously   189 **set nothing by**
regard as insignificant

Here comes Sir Toby, halting. You shall hear more. 191
But if he had not been in drink, he would have tickled
you othergates than he did. 193

ORSINO   How now, gentleman? How is't with you?

SIR TOBY   That's all one. He's hurt me, and there's 195
th'end on't.—Sot, didst see Dick surgeon, sot? 196

FESTE   Oh, he's drunk, Sir Toby, an hour agone; his eyes 197
were set at eight i'th' morning. 198

SIR TOBY   Then he's a rogue, and a passy measures 199
pavane. I hate a drunken rogue. 200

OLIVIA   Away with him! Who hath made this havoc
with them?

SIR ANDREW   I'll help you, Sir Toby, because we'll be 203
dressed together. 204

SIR TOBY   Will you help? An ass-head and a coxcomb
and a knave, a thin-faced knave, a gull!

OLIVIA

Get him to bed, and let his hurt be looked to.
    [Exeunt Feste, Fabian, Sir Toby, and Sir Andrew.]

    Enter Sebastian.

SEBASTIAN

I am sorry, madam, I have hurt your kinsman;
But, had it been the brother of my blood, 209
I must have done no less with wit and safety.— 210
You throw a strange regard upon me, and by that 211
I do perceive it hath offended you.
Pardon me, sweet one, even for the vows
We made each other but so late ago.

ORSINO

One face, one voice, one habit, and two persons, 215
A natural perspective, that is and is not! 216

SEBASTIAN

Antonio, O my dear Antonio!
How have the hours racked and tortured me 218
Since I have lost thee!

ANTONIO   Sebastian are you?

SEBASTIAN   Fear'st thou that, Antonio? 221

ANTONIO

How have you made division of yourself?
An apple cleft in two is not more twin
Than these two creatures. Which is Sebastian?

OLIVIA   Most wonderful!

SEBASTIAN   [seeing Viola]

Do I stand there? I never had a brother;
Nor can there be that deity in my nature
Of here and everywhere. I had a sister, 228
Whom the blind waves and surges have devoured. 229
Of charity, what kin are you to me?

What countryman? What name? What parentage? 230

VIOLA

Of Messaline. Sebastian was my father.
Such a Sebastian was my brother, too.
So went he suited to his watery tomb. 234
If spirits can assume both form and suit, 235
You come to fright us.

SEBASTIAN   A spirit I am indeed,
But am in that dimension grossly clad 237
Which from the womb I did participate. 238
Were you a woman, as the rest goes even, 239
I should my tears let fall upon your cheek
And say, "Thrice welcome, drownèd Viola!"

VIOLA

My father had a mole upon his brow.

SEBASTIAN   And so had mine.

VIOLA

And died that day when Viola from her birth
Had numbered thirteen years.

SEBASTIAN

Oh, that record is lively in my soul! 246
He finishèd indeed his mortal act
That day that made my sister thirteen years.

VIOLA

If nothing lets to make us happy both 249
But this my masculine usurped attire,
Do not embrace me till each circumstance
Of place, time, fortune, do cohere and jump 252
That I am Viola—which to confirm
I'll bring you to a captain in this town
Where lie my maiden weeds, by whose gentle help 255
I was preserved to serve this noble count.
All the occurrence of my fortune since
Hath been between this lady and this lord.

SEBASTIAN   [to Olivia]

So comes it, lady, you have been mistook.
But nature to her bias drew in that. 260
You would have been contracted to a maid,
Nor are you therein, by my life, deceived.
You are betrothed both to a maid and man. 263

ORSINO   [to Olivia]

Be not amazed; right noble is his blood.
If this be so, as yet the glass seems true, 265
I shall have share in this most happy wreck. 266
[To Viola] Boy, thou hast said to me a thousand times
Thou never shouldst love woman like to me. 268

VIOLA

And all those sayings will I over swear, 269
And all those swearings keep as true in soul

---

191 halting limping.   **193 othergates** otherwise   **195 That's all one** It doesn't matter; never mind.   **195–6 there's . . . on't** that's all there is to it.   **196 Sot** (1) Fool (2) Drunkard   **197 agone** ago   **198 set** fixed or closed   **199–200 passy measures pavane** passe-measure pavane, a slow-moving, stately dance. (Suggesting Sir Toby's impatience to have his wounds dressed.)   **203–4 be dressed** have our wounds surgically dressed   **209 the brother . . . blood** my own brother   **210 with wit and safety** with intelligent concern for my own safety.   **211 You . . . me** You look strangely at me   **215 habit** dress   **216 A natural perspective** an optical device or illusion created in this instance by nature   **218 racked** tortured   **221 Fear'st thou that** Do you doubt that   **228 here and everywhere** omnipresence.   **229 blind** heedless, indiscriminate

230 Of charity (Tell me) in kindness   **234 suited** dressed; clad in human form   **235 form and suit** physical appearance and dress   **237 in . . . clad** clothed in that fleshly shape   **238 participate** possess in common with all humanity.   **239 as . . . even** since everything else agrees   **246 record** recollection   **249 lets** hinders   **252 jump** coincide, fit exactly   **255 weeds** clothes   **260 nature . . . that** nature followed her bent in that. (The metaphor is from the game of bowls.)   **263 a maid** i.e., a virgin man   **265 the glass** i.e., the *natural perspective* of line 216   **266 wreck** shipwreck, accident.   **268 like to me** as well as you love me.   **269 over swear** swear again

As doth that orbèd continent the fire 271
That severs day from night.

ORSINO   Give me thy hand,
And let me see thee in thy woman's weeds.

VIOLA
The captain that did bring me first on shore
Hath my maid's garments. He upon some action 275
Is now in durance, at Malvolio's suit, 276
A gentleman and follower of my lady's.

OLIVIA
He shall enlarge him. Fetch Malvolio hither. 278
And yet, alas, now I remember me,
They say, poor gentleman, he's much distract.

Enter Clown [Feste] with a letter, and Fabian.

A most extracting frenzy of mine own 281
From my remembrance clearly banished his. 282
How does he, sirrah?

FESTE   Truly, madam, he holds Beelzebub at the stave's 284
end as well as a man in his case may do. He's here 285
writ a letter to you; I should have given't you today
morning. But as a madman's epistles are no gospels, 287
so it skills not much when they are delivered. 288

OLIVIA   Open't and read it.

FESTE   Look then to be well edified when the fool
delivers the madman. [*He reads loudly.*] "By the Lord, 291
madam—"

OLIVIA   How now, art thou mad?

FESTE   No, madam, I do but read madness. An Your
Ladyship will have it as it ought to be, you must allow
vox. 296

OLIVIA   Prithee, read i'thy right wits.

FESTE   So I do, madonna; but to read his right wits is to 298
read thus. Therefore perpend, my princess, and give 299
ear.

OLIVIA [*to Fabian*]   Read it you, sirrah.

FABIAN (*reads*)   "By the Lord, madam, you wrong me,
and the world shall know it. Though you have put me
into darkness and given your drunken cousin rule
over me, yet have I the benefit of my senses as well
as Your Ladyship. I have your own letter that induced
me to the semblance I put on, with the which I 307
doubt not but to do myself much right or you much
shame. Think of me as you please. I leave my duty 309
a little unthought of, and speak out of my injury. 310
The madly used Malvolio."

OLIVIA   Did he write this?

FESTE   Ay, madam.

ORSINO   This savors not much of distraction.

OLIVIA
See him delivered, Fabian. Bring him hither. 315
[*Exit Fabian.*]
My lord, so please you, these things further thought
on, 316
To think me as well a sister as a wife, 317
One day shall crown th'alliance on't, so please you, 318
Here at my house and at my proper cost. 319

ORSINO
Madam, I am most apt t'embrace your offer. 320
[*To Viola*] Your master quits you; and for your
service done him, 321
So much against the mettle of your sex, 322
So far beneath your soft and tender breeding,
And since you called me master for so long,
Here is my hand. You shall from this time be
Your master's mistress.

OLIVIA   A sister! You are she.

Enter [Fabian, with] Malvolio.

ORSINO
Is this the madman?

OLIVIA   Ay, my lord, this same.
How now, Malvolio?

MALVOLIO   Madam, you have done me wrong,
Notorious wrong.

OLIVIA   Have I, Malvolio? No.

MALVOLIO [*showing a letter*]
Lady, you have. Pray you, peruse that letter.
You must not now deny it is your hand.
Write from it, if you can, in hand or phrase, 332
Or say 'tis not your seal, not your invention. 333
You can say none of this. Well, grant it then,
And tell me, in the modesty of honor, 335
Why you have given me such clear lights of favor, 336
Bade me come smiling and cross-gartered to you,
To put on yellow stockings, and to frown
Upon Sir Toby and the lighter people? 339
And, acting this in an obedient hope, 340
Why have you suffered me to be imprisoned,
Kept in a dark house, visited by the priest, 342
And made the most notorious geck and gull 343
That e'er invention played on? Tell me why? 344

OLIVIA
Alas, Malvolio, this is not my writing,
Though, I confess, much like the character; 346

---

271 As . . . fire i.e., as the sphere of the sun keeps the fire **275 action** legal charge **276 in durance** imprisoned **278 enlarge** release **281 extracting** i.e., that obsessed me and drew all thoughts except of Cesario from my mind **282 his** i.e., his madness. **284–5 holds . . . end** i.e., keeps the devil at a safe distance. (The metaphor is of fighting with quarterstaffs or long poles.) **287 a madman's . . . gospels** i.e., there is no truth in a madman's letters. (An allusion to readings in the church service of selected passages from the epistles and the gospels.) **288 skills** matters. **delivered** (1) delivered to their recipient (2) read aloud. **291 delivers** speaks the words of **296 vox** voice, i.e., an appropriately loud voice. **298 to read . . . wits** to express his true state of mind **299 perpend** consider, attend. (A deliberately lofty word.) **307 the which** i.e., the letter **309–10 I leave . . . injury** I leave unsaid the expressions of duty with which I would normally conclude, and convey instead my sense of having been wronged.

315 delivered released. **316 so . . . on** if you are pleased on further consideration of all that has happened **317 To . . . wife** to regard me as favorably as a sister-in-law as you had hoped to regard me as a wife **318 crown . . . on't** i.e., serve as occasion for two marriages confirming our new relationships **319 proper** own **320 apt** ready **321 quits** releases **322 mettle** natural disposition **332 from it** differently **333 invention** composition. **335 in . . . honor** in the name of all that is decent and honorable **336 clear lights** evident signs **339 lighter** lesser **340 acting . . . hope** when I acted thus out of obedience to you and in hope of your favor **342 priest** i.e., Feste **343 geck** dupe **344 invention played on** contrivance sported with. **346 the character** my handwriting

But out of question 'tis Maria's hand.
And now I do bethink me, it was she
First told me thou wast mad; then cam'st in smiling,   349
And in such forms which here were presupposed   350
Upon thee in the letter. Prithee, be content.
This practice hath most shrewdly passed upon thee;   352
But when we know the grounds and authors of it,
Thou shalt be both the plaintiff and the judge
Of thine own cause.

FABIAN   Good madam, hear me speak,
And let no quarrel nor no brawl to come   356
Taint the condition of this present hour,   357
Which I have wondered at. In hope it shall not,
Most freely I confess, myself and Toby
Set this device against Malvolio here,
Upon some stubborn and uncourteous parts   361
We had conceived against him. Maria writ   362
The letter at Sir Toby's great importance,   363
In recompense whereof he hath married her.
How with a sportful malice it was followed   365
May rather pluck on laughter than revenge,   366
If that the injuries be justly weighed   367
That have on both sides passed.

OLIVIA [to Malvolio]
Alas, poor fool, how have they baffled thee!   369

FESTE Why, "Some are born great, some achieve greatness, and some have greatness thrown upon them." I was one, sir, in this interlude, one Sir Topas,   372
sir, but that's all one. "By the Lord, fool, I am not   373
mad." But do you remember? "Madam, why laugh you at such a barren rascal? An you smile not, he's gagged." And thus the whirligig of time brings in his   376
revenges.

MALVOLIO I'll be revenged on the whole pack of you!
[Exit.]

347 out of beyond 349 cam'st you came 350 presupposed specified beforehand 352 practice plot. shrewdly passed mischievously been perpetrated 356 to come in the future 357 condition (happy) nature 361 Upon on account of. parts qualities, deeds 362 conceived against him seen and resented in him. 363 importance importunity 365 followed carried out 366 pluck on induce 367 If that if 369 baffled disgraced, quelled 372 interlude little play 373 that's all one no matter for that. 376 whirligig spinning top

OLIVIA
He hath been most notoriously abused.

ORSINO
Pursue him, and entreat him to a peace.
He hath not told us of the captain yet.
When that is known, and golden time convents,   382
A solemn combination shall be made
Of our dear souls. Meantime, sweet sister,
We will not part from hence. Cesario, come—
For so you shall be, while you are a man;
But when in other habits you are seen,   387
Orsino's mistress and his fancy's queen.   388

Exeunt [all, except Feste].

FESTE (sings)
When that I was and a little tiny boy,   389
    With hey, ho, the wind and the rain,
A foolish thing was but a toy,   391
    For the rain it raineth every day.

But when I came to man's estate,
    With hey, ho, the wind and the rain,
'Gainst knaves and thieves men shut their gate,
    For the rain it raineth every day.

But when I came, alas, to wive,
    With hey, ho, the wind and the rain,
By swaggering could I never thrive,
    For the rain it raineth every day.

But when I came unto my beds,   401
    With hey, ho, the wind and the rain,
With tosspots still had drunken heads,   403
    For the rain it raineth every day.

A great while ago the world begun,
    With hey, ho, the wind and the rain,
But that's all one, our play is done,
    And we'll strive to please you every day.
[Exit.]

382 convents (1) summons, calls together (2) suits 387 habits attire 388 fancy's love's 389 and a little a little 391 toy trifle 401 unto my beds i.e., (1) drunk to bed, or, perhaps, (2) in the evening of life 403 tosspots drunkards

All's Well That Ends Well

All's Well That Ends Well belongs to that period of Shakespeare's creative life when he concentrated on his great tragedies and wrote little comedy. The few apparent exceptions do not fit readily into conventional dramatic genres. *Measure for Measure* (1603–1604), usually called a problem play, is darkly preoccupied with human carnality and injustice. *Troilus and Cressida* (c. 1601–1602), printed between the histories and the tragedies in the Folio of 1623, is a disillusioning satire of love and war somewhat akin to the black comedy of our modern theater. *All's Well* shares, to an extent, the satiric and brooding spirit of these two plays. Its "bed trick," in which one woman is substituted for another in an assignation with the protagonist, Bertram, poses ethical problems for the audience (as does a similar trick in *Measure for Measure*). Helena, in arranging the substitution, may seem too much of a schemer. The relations between the sexes are problematic in this play, written, as it seemingly was, at a time when Shakespeare was preoccupied with tragedies that are haunted by images of destructive femaleness and of debasing sexuality. The action of *All's Well* is, to a large extent, controlled by an admirable and attractive woman, and yet the play dwells more than do earlier comedies on the potential hazards of sexuality. For these and other reasons, *All's Well* is often grouped with the problem plays.

At the same time, the play also looks forward to Shakespeare's late romances, *Pericles, Cymbeline, The Winter's Tale*, and *The Tempest*. Here the mode of comedy turns toward the miraculous and tragicomic, with journeys of separation ending in tearful reunion, and sinful error ending in spiritual rebirth. This mode was not unknown in Shakespeare's comedies of the late 1590s: *As You Like it* ends with the sudden and implausible conversion of its villains, and *Much Ado About Nothing* offers forgiveness to the undeserving Claudio while restoring his traduced fiancée, Hero, to a new life. *Measure for Measure* follows a similar pattern of redemptive pardon for the corrupted

Angelo and providential deliverance for Isabella. Both *All's Well* and *Measure for Measure* contain features of this comedy of forgiveness, even if admittedly the ironies surrounding the gesture of forgiving are far less controlled than in the late romances.

Certainly, in any case, *All's Well* occupies a central position in the line of development from the early comedies to the late romances. Helena points back to earlier comic women in her role as engineer of the love plot and points forward to women of the late romances in her role as daughter, victim, and savior (though early comedy and late romance are, to be sure, not as neatly distinguishable as this antithesis suggests). Bertram, who is virtually without precedent in earlier comedies, anticipates, to a degree, Posthumus in *Cymbeline*, Florizel in *The Winter's Tale*, and Ferdinand in *The Tempest* in that he takes part in a marriage sanctioned and defined largely by paternal intervention. *All's Well*, like the romances and unlike the earlier comedies, affords a remarkably prominent role to the older generation.

The probable date of *All's Well* is consistent with such a transitional function. Its dates are hard to fix by external evidence, for it was neither registered nor printed until 1623, and allusions to it are scarce. Some scholars think that it is the *Love's Labor's Won* intriguingly mentioned by Francis Meres in *Palladis Tamia* in 1598, which Shakespeare might then have revised some time around 1601–1604. Portions of the play do feature the rhymed couplets, letters in sonnet form, and witty conceits that we normally associate with Shakespeare's early style. These old-fashioned effects may have been deliberate on Shakespeare's part, however, not unlike the anachronisms he later introduces in *Pericles* and *Cymbeline*. Certainly, a major portion of the play dates stylistically from 1601–1604 or even later. Here the language is elliptical and compact, the images complexly interwoven, the verse rhythms free.

In any event, with its two contrasting styles poised between romance and satire, *All's Well* juxtaposes the reassurances of comedy with the pessimistic ironies of Shakespeare's tragic period. It lacks many of the felicities we associate with the festive comedies of the 1590s: the love songs, the innocently hedonistic joy, and the well-mated young lovers escaping from stern parents or an envious court. *All's Well* has too often been judged negatively for its failure to achieve a festive mood that Shakespeare probably did not intend it to have. Both of its central figures are flawed, to the extent that they seem oddly cast in the roles normally demanded by romantic comedy of young men and women who fall in love and eventually marry. Bertram as nominal hero quickly loses our sympathy when he runs away from his marriage vows to pursue warmongering, male camaraderie, and the attempted seduction of a virgin; Helena as nominal heroine complicates our response by the ethically dubious ways in which she tricks Bertram into marrying her and then becoming her partner in bed when he has sworn he will never do so. As the undeserving hero, forgiven in spite of his waywardness, however, Bertram plays an essential role in the play's problematic resolution—or failure to achieve complete resolution. He is, in the common Renaissance view of all humanity, unworthy of the forgiveness he receives, whereas Helena's generosity in forgiving him suggests at least a capability in humanity for decency and compassion. We are left, as in *Measure for Measure*, with a sense of the perennially unbridgeable gap between human ideals and their achievement, and yet we view this dilemma in a comic context where second chances and hope are bestowed even on those who appear to deserve them least.

The satiric mode in *All's Well* is conveyed chiefly through Lavatch the clown and through Parolles, the boastful, cowardly knave who accompanies Bertram to the wars. Lavatch, with the bitter and riddling wit of the professional fool, gives expression to many of the satirical themes that are also illustrated by the exposure of Parolles. Lavatch jests about cuckoldry and the other marital difficulties that cause men to flee from women; he pokes fun at court manners and apes the prodigal disobedience of his master Bertram. He is, like Parolles, called a "foulmouthed and calumnious knave" (1.3.56–7), although the inversion of appearance and reality is evident here, as with all Shakespearean fools: Parolles is truly more fool and knave than his mocking counterpart. Parolles is all pretense. Full of sound, but hollow like the drum to which he is compared, he is a swaggerer and a fashionmonger whose clothes conceal his lack of inner substance. He is a recognizable satiric type that goes back to the Latin dramatists Plautus and Terence: the braggart soldier. He is, to be sure, endearing in his outrageousness; Shakespeare endows him with that vitality we find also in those earlier braggart soldiers, Falstaff and Pistol. He enlists sympathy and fellow-feeling from an audience when, having been exposed and humiliated by his mili-

tary comrades for his cowardice, he rejoins, "Who cannot be crushed with a plot?", and goes on to insist in soliloquy that "Simply the thing I am / Shall make me live" (4.3.326–36). Ultimately, his ebullient vitality leads to his being forgiven even by old Lafew, who has long been on to Parolles's tricks but finds him irresistible nonetheless. Because Parolles lacks the self-awareness of Falstaff, we merely laugh at him rather than with him. To the impressionable young Bertram, hungry for fame, Parolles represents smartness and military style. Bertram rejects the true worth of Helena because she lacks family position and, ironically, embraces the false worth of a parvenu. Parolles and Helena are foils from their first encounter, when the braggart sardonically derides virginity as unnatural and out of fashion. Parolles stands opposite also to Lafew, the Countess, and the King—those dignified embodiments of a traditional chivalrous order, whose generous teachings Bertram rejects for the company of Parolles and of women he hopes to seduce. By disguising his slick insolence in the guise of fashionable manliness, Parolles is able to win Bertram's friendship for a time. Parolles is not really a tempter, for we never see him bending Bertram from his true inclination; rather, Bertram is himself too much in love with sham reputation, too rebellious against the civilized decencies of his elders. He is the Prodigal Son, or Youth in the old morality play, perversely eager to prove his own worst enemy.

Yet Bertram is not without a redeeming nobleness—he bears himself bravely in the Florentine wars—and cannot be fooled indefinitely by his roguish companion. The exposure of Parolles is one of satiric humiliation, even if he is eventually forgiven and reconciled in a way that Mavolio in *Twelfth Night* or many of Ben Jonson's humorous gulls are not. The engineers of Parolles's exposure use the language of Jonsonian satire in their devices to outwit him: their game is a "sport" done "for the love of laughter," employing a snare whereby the "fox" or the "woodcock" will entrap himself (3.6.34–102 and 4.1.92). The device of public humiliation is particularly appropriate, because Parolles is himself a railing slanderer, like Lucio in *Measure for Measure*, caustically brilliant in his invective but nonetheless a slayer of men's reputations. The punishment of ridicule fits his particular crime. His callous disregard for the good name of various French military commanders is parallel to Bertram's indifference to the public shame he has heaped upon his virtuous wife. Once Parolles's bluff has been called, Bertram is, in part, disabused of his folly; but other means are needed to convince him of the wrong he has done to Helena. Indeed, Bertram's very coldness in turning away from Parolles shows a lack of humility. Bertram must learn to know himself better by being tricked, exposed, and humiliated.

The fabulous romancelike aspect of *All's Well* is conveyed chiefly through its folktale plot and through the character of Helena. The story is derived from the third "day" of Giovanni Boccaccio's *Decameron*, a day devoted to tales of lovers obliged to overcome seemingly impossible obstacles in order to achieve love's happiness. The story was translated into English by William Painter in *The Palace of Pleasure* (1566). To win the nobly born Beltramo, Giletta of Narbona must cure the French king with her physician-father's secret remedy and then must perform the riddling tasks assigned her by Beltramo as his means of being rid of her. Both these motifs have ancient antecedents in folklore, and, as in his late romances, Shakespeare puts great stress on the wondrous and improbable nature of these events.

All common sense warns against the likelihood of Helena's success. She is vastly below Bertram in social station or in "blood," even though she excels in "virtue." (This low station is unique among Shakespeare's comic heroines, and it contributes to what is so unusual about this play.) Her only hope is a desperate gamble: to cure the ailing King and so win Bertram as her reward. No one supposes at first she will even be admitted to the King, who has given up all hope of living; his "congregated college" of learned doctors "have concluded / That laboring art can never ransom nature / From her inaidible estate" (2.1.119–21). Helena transcends these rational doubts through resourcefulness and, above all, through a faith in help from above. She is willing to "hazard" all for love. She senses that her father's legacy will "be sanctified / By th' luckiest stars in heaven" (1.3.243–4), and she manages to convince not only the Countess and Lafew (persons who do not appear in Boccaccio) but also the King himself. Believing, like George Bernard Shaw's Saint Joan, that God will perform his greatest works through the humblest of his creatures, Helena inspires her listeners with faith in the impossible. Lafew is so moved by her simple eloquence that he proclaims to the King, "I have seen a medicine / That's able to breathe life into a stone" (2.1.73–4). Soon the King, too, is persuaded that in Helena "some blessèd spirit doth speak / His powerful sound within an organ weak" (lines 177–8). Once the King's cure has been effected, even Parolles and Bertram must agree with Lafew that the age of miracles, long thought to have passed, is with them again. The King's cure by the "Very hand of heaven," through the agency of a "weak—/ And debile minister," is matter for a pious ballad or an old tale (2.3.31–4). At the same time, Helena is very determined and is willing to use whatever means are necessary to get what she wants.

Helena's assuming the role of wooer is a problem for Bertram—as indeed it was for many a male reader in Victorian times, who found her worrisomely guilty of transgressing the boundaries between acceptable and unacceptable female behavior. Bertram nominally objects to her lower social station, but that is a matter the King can remedy. Evidently, Bertram is daunted by something else: by the very prospect of marriage with a virtuous and attractive young woman who unmistakably wants him. He reacts with subterfuge and flight, subscribing to Parolles's notion that it is better to be a soldier than to be one who "hugs his kicky-wicky here at home, / Spending his manly marrow in her arms" (2.3:281–2). War gives Bertram his excuse to evade the responsibilities of marriage. In Italy, to be sure, he finds the prospect of sexual encounter with Diana irresistible, since he thinks he can obtain and then discard her when the affair is done. He is prepared to cheapen "available" women this way but not to commit himself to the complex and mutual commitment that marriage requires. In these terms, Helena's task is to bring Bertram to the point of understanding that sexuality and deep friendship can and should exist in a single relationship, and that women must not be bifurcated by his imagination into those who are respectable but untouchable (like his mother) or cheap and violable. Bertram's unself-knowing friendship with Parolles is symptomatic of his immaturity, and hence the exposure of Parolles is a necessary part of Bertram's education, but Helena must also find a way to help Bertram get over his mistrust of her sexuality.

In so doing, she resembles other Shakespeare heroines, such as Desdemona in *Othello*, Rosalind in *As You Like It*, and Silvia in *The Two Gentlemen of Verona*, who take the initiative in wooing. Helena is fully aware that her intrepidity offends Bertram. Yet she is abundantly admired by the King, Lafew, the Countess, and other rightminded persons in the play, all of whom find Bertram's reluctance immature and virtually incomprehensible. Moreover, her enterprising spirit (see 1.1.216–29) finds its reward in marital success at the end. Throughout his romantic comedies, Shakespeare invites us to admire women who take the lead in wooing, even if he problematizes the issue in *All's Well* by emphasizing Bertram's hostility and Helena's consequent need for deceptive stratagems, and even if he also sees how such a story can end tragically in *Romeo and Juliet* and *Othello*.

The impossible tasks Helena must perform are stated as riddles, as is usual in a folktale, and must be solved by riddling or paradoxical means. Bertram writes that she must "get the ring upon my finger, which never shall come off, and show me a child begotten of thy body that I am father to" (3.2.57–9). Such a challenge invites ingenuity, as in Boccaccio, but in Shakespeare the solution also requires providential aid. Helena's first sad response is to set Bertram free and renounce her audacious pretensions. Her pilgrimage of grief takes her to Florence, where Bertram happens to be serving in the wars. This cannot be mere coincidence, and yet we do not accuse her of scheming in any opprobrious sense. Throughout, her motives are at once virtuous and deceitful, lawful and sinful, just as her very sexuality is wholesome and yet is seen by us in a context of debased human nature (as is generally not the case with Shakespeare's earlier heroines). Her acts are prompted at once by providence and by shrewd calculation. Even if providence must be credited with introducing her to Diana, the very lady whom Bertram is importuning in love, Helena makes the most of such opportunities afforded her, never doubting that "heaven" has "fated" her both to help Diana and simultaneously to serve her own turn (4.4.18–20). The bed trick is a "plot," but a virtuous one, a "deceit" that is "lawful," a deed that is "not sin, and yet a sinful fact" (3.7.38–47). Diana repeatedly plays upon these same riddles in accusing Bertram before the King: he is "guilty, and he is not guilty" (5.3.290).

These conundrums, although playful and entertaining in Shakespeare's highly complicated denouement (not found in Boccaccio), also hint at paradoxes in the nature of humanity. Bertram's typically human waywardness justifies a cunning response. "I think't no sin," argues Diana, "To cozen him that would unjustly win" (4.2.75–6). Justice on earth, as in *Measure for Measure*, must take forms only roughly approximating those of heavenly justice, for human depravity sometimes requires a harsh remedy in kind. Yet, by a providential paradox, humanity's thwarted and evil nature, seemingly so fatal, leads instead to regeneration: by being humbled, humanity is enabled to rise: "The web of our life is of a mingled yarn, good and ill together," says a sympathetic observer of Bertram. "Our virtues would be proud if our faults whipped them not, and our crimes would despair if they were not cherished by our virtues" (4.3.70–3). Human perversity accentuates the need for divine grace.

Helena is a romantic heroine, only metaphorically the "angel" who must "Bless this unworthy husband," reprieving him by her "prayers" from "the wrath / Of greatest justice" (3.4.25–9). Indeed, she is capable of being quite threatening to Bertram. If Bertram typifies the "Natural rebellion" of all youth and Helena, the "herb of grace" whom he has willfully rejected (5.3.6 and 4.5.17), Helena is also an aggressive woman whose clever plans to win Bertram against his will produce an understandable reluctance in the young man. Still, the spiritual overtones are not extraneous to this bittersweet comedy. However much we may sympathize with his desire to choose in love for himself, Bertram's revolt is incomprehensible to every witness except Parolles. Bertram himself concedes, too late it seems, that he has recognized Helena's precious worth. This note of "love that comes too late," wherein the penitent sinner confesses "That's good that's gone," hovers over the play with its tragicomic mood (5.3.58–61). Helena is a "jewel" thrown away and seemingly forever lost (5.3.1). The semblance of her death is, in fact, only another one of her inventive

schemes, along with the bewildering contretemps of the final scene. Yet, when she reappears, setting all to rights, she comes as "one that's dead" but is now "quick," alive again, merely a "shadow" of her former self (5.3.304–8). Bertram has not actually committed the evil he intended; by a providential sophistry, he is innocent, like Claudio in *Much Ado* or Angelo in *Measure for Measure,* and so is reconciled to the goodness he has failed to merit. Even Parolles is given a second chance by the magnanimous Lafew. As the play's title implies, all might have miscarried through humanity's "rash faults" that "Make trivial price of serious things we have" (5.3.61–2), were it not for a forgiving power that can make people's worst failings an instrument of their penitence and recovery. This resolution fleetingly comforts us in the final scene, even though it must do battle with such manifest imbalances as the prolonged shaming of Bertram and the scant attention paid to his reunion with Helena. The web of human life remains a mingled yarn.

The balance in this remarkable play between comedy and tragedy is very much subject to decisions made in performance. For many years after it was written and presumably performed in London, the theatrical decision was to avoid the play entirely or to transform it into something else. An operatic version in 1832 attempted to compensate for the play's purported ethical dubieties with a medley of songs from other plays. Not until the twentieth century did the play begin to come into its own. Even then, Helena remained troublesome for some directors and audiences. In a 1955 production at Stratford-upon-Avon by Noel Willman, Helena was persistent and even aggressive in her pursuit of a Bertram whose responses were plainly triggered by male anxieties about female dominance. In Michael Benthall's Old Vic production of 1953, on the other hand, Helena (Claire Bloom) was a Cinderella fairy princess eventually reunited with her truculent Prince Charming (John Neville). In Trevor Nunn's production for the Royal Shakespeare Company in 1981, Bertram's caddish behavior was made distinctly unsympathetic, to the extent that he was allowed no opportunity to redeem himself at the end. The military action of the play has lent itself to disenchantment engendered by the Vietnam War, as in John Barton's 1967 production for the Royal Shakespeare Company. War becomes a gentleman's game, or (as in Nunn's version) a reminiscence of the Crimea or the trenches of World War I. David Jones's highly successful production at Stratford, Canada, in 1977 was autumnal in mood. Yet the play can succeed also as hilarious comedy throughout. Performance history demonstrates how fluid interpretation can be: there are many Helenas, many Bertrams, many Parolles.

All's Well That Ends Well

⚬⚬⚬

[Dramatis Personae

COUNTESS OF ROSSILLION, *Bertram's mother and Helena's guardian*
BERTRAM, *Count of Rossillion*
HELENA (*or* HELEN), *orphaned daughter of the Countess's physician*
PAROLLES, *a follower of Bertram*
RINALDO, *a steward*,
LAVATCH, *a clown or fool*, } *servants of the Countess of Rossillion*
PAGE,

KING OF FRANCE
LAFEW, *an old lord*

Two FRENCH LORDS, *the brothers Dumain, later captains in the Florentine army*
Other LORDS
Two FRENCH SOLDIERS
A GENTLEMAN
A MESSENGER

DUKE OF FLORENCE
WIDOW CAPILET *of Florence*
DIANA, *her daughter*
MARIANA, *neighbor and friend of the Widow*

Lords, Attendants, Soldiers, Citizens

SCENE: *Rossillion; Paris; Florence; Marseilles*]

1.1

Enter young Bertram, Count of Rossillion, his mother [the Countess], and Helena, [with] Lord Lafew, all in black.

COUNTESS In delivering my son from me, I bury a 1
second husband.
BERTRAM And I in going, madam, weep o'er my
father's death anew. But I must attend His Majesty's 4
command, to whom I am now in ward, evermore in 5
subjection.
LAFEW You shall find of the King a husband, madam; 7
you, sir, a father. He that so generally is at all times 8
good must of necessity hold his virtue to you, whose 9
worthiness would stir it up where it wanted rather 10
than lack it where there is such abundance. 11
COUNTESS What hope is there of His Majesty's amend- 12
ment? 13
LAFEW He hath abandoned his physicians, madam,
under whose practices he hath persecuted time with 15
hope, and finds no other advantage in the process but 16
only the losing of hope by time.
COUNTESS This young gentlewoman had a father—oh,
that "had," how sad a passage 'tis!—whose skill was 19
almost as great as his honesty; had it stretched so far, 20
would have made nature immortal, and death should
have play for lack of work. Would for the King's sake 22
he were living! I think it would be the death of the
King's disease.
LAFEW How called you the man you speak of, madam?

1.1. Location: Rossillion, i.e., Roussillon, in southern France, on the Spanish border near the Mediterranean. The Count's residence.
1 delivering sending. (With play on "giving birth to" and "freeing.")
4 attend obey   **5 in ward** (According to a feudal custom, the King became the guardian of orphaned heirs to estates, who remained "in ward" so long as they were minors. The King's jurisdiction extended even so far as the bestowal of his ward in marriage, but only to someone of equal rank.)   **7 of** in the person of.   **husband** i.e., protector
8 generally to all people

9 hold continue to devote   **9–11 whose . . . abundance** you whose virtue is such that it would inspire generosity even in those who normally lack it, and who therefore cannot fail to find it in a king who is so abundantly generous.   **10 wanted** is lacking   **12–13 amendment** recovery.   **15–16 hath . . . hope** has tormented his time with painful treatments in vain hope of cure   **19 passage** (1) phrase, expression (2) passing away   **20 honesty** integrity of character   **22 Would** Would that

COUNTESS   He was famous, sir, in his profession, and it was his great right to be so: Gerard de Narbonne.

LAFEW   He was excellent indeed, madam. The King very lately spoke of him admiringly and mourningly. He was skillful enough to have lived still, if knowledge could be set up against mortality. 30

BERTRAM   What is it, my good lord, the King languishes of?

LAFEW   A fistula, my lord.

BERTRAM   I heard not of it before. 34

LAFEW   I would it were not notorious.—Was this gentlewoman the daughter of Gerard de Narbonne?

COUNTESS   His sole child, my lord, and bequeathed to my overlooking. I have those hopes of her good that 39 her education promises her dispositions she inherits, 40 which makes fair gifts fairer; for where an unclean 41 mind carries virtuous qualities, there commendations 42 go with pity—they are virtues and traitors too. In her 43 they are the better for their simpleness. She derives 44 her honesty and achieves her goodness. 45

LAFEW   Your commendations, madam, get from her tears.

COUNTESS   'Tis the best brine a maiden can season her 48 praise in. The remembrance of her father never approaches her heart but the tyranny of her sorrows takes all livelihood from her cheek.—No more of this, 51 Helena. Go to, no more, lest it be rather thought you 52 affect a sorrow than to have— 53

HELENA   I do affect a sorrow indeed, but I have it too. 54

LAFEW   Moderate lamentation is the right of the dead, 55 excessive grief the enemy to the living.

COUNTESS   If the living be enemy to the grief, the excess 57 makes it soon mortal. 58

BERTRAM   Madam, I desire your holy wishes.

LAFEW   How understand we that? 60

COUNTESS
Be thou blest, Bertram, and succeed thy father
In manners as in shape! Thy blood and virtue 62
Contend for empire in thee, and thy goodness 63
Share with thy birthright! Love all, trust a few, 64

Do wrong to none. Be able for thine enemy 65
Rather in power than use, and keep thy friend 66
Under thy own life's key. Be checked for silence 67
But never taxed for speech. What heaven more will, 68
That thee may furnish and my prayers pluck down, 69
Fall on thy head! Farewell. [To Lafew] My lord, 70
'Tis an unseasoned courtier; good my lord, 71
Advise him.

LAFEW   He cannot want the best 72
That shall attend his love. 73

COUNTESS   Heaven bless him!—Farewell, Bertram.

BERTRAM   The best wishes that can be forged in your 75
thoughts be servants to you!   [Exit Countess.] 76
[To Helena] Be comfortable to my mother, your 77
mistress, and make much of her. 78

LAFEW   Farewell, pretty lady. You must hold the credit 79
of your father.   [Exeunt Bertram and Lafew.]

HELENA   Oh, were that all! I think not on my father,
And these great tears grace his remembrance more 82
Than those I shed for him. What was he like? 83
I have forgot him. My imagination
Carries no favor in't but Bertram's. 85
I am undone. There is no living, none,
If Bertram be away. 'Twere all one 87
That I should love a bright particular star 88
And think to wed it, he is so above me.
In his bright radiance and collateral light 90
Must I be comforted, not in his sphere.
Th'ambition in my love thus plagues itself;
The hind that would be mated by the lion 93
Must die for love. 'Twas pretty, though a plague, 94
To see him every hour, to sit and draw
His archèd brows, his hawking eye, his curls, 96
In our heart's table—heart too capable 97
Of every line and trick of his sweet favor. 98
But now he's gone, and my idolatrous fancy 99
Must sanctify his relics. Who comes here?

Enter Parolles.

[Aside] One that goes with him. I love him for his sake; 101
And yet I know him a notorious liar,

---

30 still (1) now as before (2) forever   **34 fistula** ulcerous sore
39 overlooking supervision.   **39–45 I have . . . goodness** I have those high hopes for her future well-being which her education will further, nurturing the goodness which she was born with, and enhancing her innate gifts; for where a corrupted mind carries a veneer of learned goodness, praise is mingled with regret for good qualities betrayed by their opposite. In her there is no such division: she inherits a pure heart and nourishes it with good deeds.   **48 season** (1) add flavor to (2) preserve (as with salt)   **51 livelihood** animation   **52 Go to** i.e., Come, come   **53 affect** are enamored of, make an exaggerated show of.   **than** rather than   **54 I do . . . too** I do put on an outward show of sorrow, but I feel it as well.   **55 right** rightful due   **57–8 If . . . mortal** i.e., If grief is by its nature injurious to human happiness, excess of it soon proves fatal.   **60 How . . . that?** What do you mean? (Spoken perhaps in response to the Countess in lines 57–8, simultaneously with Bertram's speech in line 59.)   **62 manners** conduct.   **Thy blood** May your noble birth   **63–4 thy goodness . . . birthright** may the good qualities you achieve share with your inherited qualities in ruling your life.

65–7 Be able . . . key Be powerful enough to resist your enemy without having to use that power, and hold your friend's life as dearly as your own.   **67 checked** reproved   **68–70 What . . . head!** May such blessings heaven intends for you, such as will assist you and that my prayers can draw down from heaven, bestow their goodness upon you!   **71 unseasoned** inexperienced   **72–3 He . . . love** He will not be without the best advice that my love can provide him with.
75–6 The best . . . you! May the best wishes you can imagine always assist you!   **77 comfortable** comforting, serviceable   **78 make much of** be devoted to   **79 hold the credit** uphold the reputation   **82 his** Bertram's   **83 for him** i.e., for my father when he died.   **85 favor** (1) image, face (2) preference   **87–8 'Twere . . . That** It would be all the same if   **90 collateral** distant and parallel, shed from a different sphere. (The different Ptolemaic spheres were said to move collaterally, the implication here being that the distance cannot be closed.)
93 hind female deer. (With pun on "servant.")   **94 pretty** pleasing
96 hawking keen   **97 table** drawing board or tablet   **97–8 capable Of** susceptible to   **98 trick** characteristic expression.   **favor** face.
99 fancy (1) imagination, fantasy (2) love   **101 his** Bertram's

Think him a great way fool, solely a coward. 103
Yet these fixed evils sit so fit in him 104
That they take place when virtue's steely bones 105
Looks bleak i'th' cold wind. Withal, full oft we see 106
Cold wisdom waiting on superfluous folly. 107

PAROLLES Save you, fair queen! 108

HELENA And you, monarch!

PAROLLES No.

HELENA And no.

PAROLLES Are you meditating on virginity?

HELENA Ay. You have some stain of soldier in you; let 113
me ask you a question. Man is enemy to virginity;
how may we barricado it against him? 115

PAROLLES Keep him out.

HELENA But he assails, and our virginity, though
valiant, in the defense yet is weak. Unfold to us some 118
warlike resistance.

PAROLLES There is none. Man setting down before you 120
will undermine you and blow you up. 121

HELENA Bless our poor virginity from underminers and
blowers-up! Is there no military policy how virgins 123
might blow up men?

PAROLLES Virginity being blown down, man will 125
quicklier be blown up. Marry, in blowing him down 126
again, with the breach yourselves made you lose your 127
city. It is not politic in the commonwealth of nature to 128
preserve virginity. Loss of virginity is rational increase, 129
and there was never virgin got till virginity was 130
first lost. That you were made of is metal to make vir- 131
gins. Virginity by being once lost may be ten times 132
found; by being ever kept, it is ever lost. 'Tis too cold 133
a companion. Away with't!

HELENA I will stand for't a little, though therefore I die 135
a virgin.

PAROLLES There's little can be said in't; 'tis against the 137
rule of nature. To speak on the part of virginity is to 138

accuse your mothers, which is most infallible disobedience. He that hangs himself is a virgin; virginity 140
murders itself, and should be buried in highways out 141
of all sanctified limit, as a desperate offendress against 142
nature. Virginity breeds mites, much like a cheese,
consumes itself to the very paring, and so dies with 144
feeding his own stomach. Besides, virginity is peevish, 145
proud, idle, made of self-love, which is the most
inhibited sin in the canon. Keep it not; you cannot 147
choose but lose by't. Out with't! Within th'one year 148
it will make itself two, which is a goodly increase, and
the principal itself not much the worse. Away with't! 150

HELENA How might one do, sir, to lose it to her own 151
liking?

PAROLLES Let me see. Marry, ill, to like him that ne'er 153
it likes. 'Tis a commodity will lose the gloss with lying; 154
the longer kept, the less worth. Off with't while 'tis
vendible; answer the time of request. Virginity, like 156
an old courtier, wears her cap out of fashion, richly
suited, but unsuitable, just like the brooch and the 158
toothpick, which wear not now. Your date is better in 159
your pie and your porridge than in your cheek; and 160
your virginity, your old virginity, is like one of our
French withered pears—it looks ill, it eats drily. Marry, 162
'tis a withered pear; it was formerly better; marry,
yet 'tis a withered pear. Will you anything with it?

HELENA
Not my virginity, yet . . . 165
There shall your master have a thousand loves, 166
A mother, and a mistress, and a friend, 167
A phoenix, captain, and an enemy, 168
A guide, a goddess, and a sovereign, 169
A counselor, a traitress, and a dear; 170
His humble ambition, proud humility, 171
His jarring concord, and his discord dulcet, 172
His faith, his sweet disaster, with a world 173

---

103 a great way in large measure a. **solely** completely **104 fixed** ineradicable, firmly established. **sit so fit** are so natural and plausible (in him) **105–6 take . . . wind** find acceptance and take precedence, while virtue, in its uncompromising severity, is left out in the cold. **106 Withal** Consequently **107 Cold . . . folly** wisdom lacking warmth obliged to dance attendance on a useless display of comfortable foolishness. **108 Save** i.e., God save. **queen** (A hyperbolical compliment, which Helena answers in kind, whereupon they both deny their titles.) **113 stain** tinge **115 barricado** barricade **118 Unfold** Reveal **120–1 setting . . . you** laying siege (as though to a town, but with bawdy quibbling that is elaborated in the following lines. To *undermine* is to tunnel under and into [in both a military and sexual sense]; to *blow up* is to explode with mines and impregnate.) **123 policy** stratagem **125–8 Virginity . . . city** Continuing the metaphor of siege warfare, Parolles argues that virginity's attempts to defend itself against male assault are doomed to self-defeat, just as a defending city, by digging countermines, opens up more breaches through which the defenses can be undermined. Virginal resistance will only sharpen a man's appetite and blow him up—i.e., make him erect. (*Marry* is a mild oath derived from "by the Virgin Mary.") **128 politic** expedient **129 rational increase** (1) an increase by the law of nature (2) an increase of rational beings **130 got** begotten **131 That** That which. **metal** substance, as in minting of coins or compounding of interest. (With idea also of *mettle*, "spirit," "temperament.") **132–3 may . . . found** i.e., may reproduce itself tenfold **135 stand for't** fight, stand up. (With a sexual quibble.) **die** (With probable quibble on "experience orgasm.") **137 in't** in its behalf **138 on the part of** in behalf of

140 is a virgin i.e., is like a virgin, since virginity is a kind of suicide **141–2 buried . . . limit** (Suicides were customarily buried at crossroads of highways, not in consecrated ground.) **144 paring** covering rind **145 his** its. **stomach** (1) maw (2) pride. **147 inhibited** prohibited. **canon** catalogue of sins. (Pride is the first of the Deadly Sins.) **147–8 Keep . . . by't** (With a play on the idea of losing one's virginity.) **148 Out with't!** (1) Away with it! (2) Put it out at interest! **150 the principal** the original investment **151 How** What **153–4 ill . . . likes** i.e., one must do ill, by liking a man that dislikes virginity. **154 will . . . lying** that will lose the gloss of newness with being unused. (With a quibble on "lying down.") **156 vendible** marketable. **the time of request** when there is still demand. **158 unsuitable** unfashionable **159 wear not** are not in fashion. (Brooches in hats and the affectation of using toothpicks, once fashionable, are no longer so.) **159–60 Your . . . cheek** i.e., The date does better as an ingredient in cooking than as an emblem of withering in your cheek. (*Date* also suggests age.) **162 withered pears** poppering pears, a variety that are not edible until partly decayed (and that physically resemble the aging female genitalia, as does the *date*, line 159) **eats drily** is dry to eat. **165 Not . . . yet** The moment for surrendering my virginity has not yet arrived (?) (There may be a textual omission here.) **166 There** i.e., At court **167–73 A mother . . . disaster** (Helena here provides a catalogue of the various emotional relationships and paradoxical emotional attitudes found in Elizabethan courtly love poetry.) **168 phoenix** i.e., nonpareil. (Literally, a fabulous bird of which only one exists at any given time.) **173 disaster** unlucky star

Of pretty, fond, adoptious christendoms 174
That blinking Cupid gossips. Now shall he— 175
I know not what he shall. God send him well!
The court's a learning place, and he is one—
PAROLLES   What one, i'faith?
HELENA   That I wish well. 'Tis pity—
PAROLLES   What's pity?
HELENA

That wishing well had not a body in't 181
Which might be felt, that we, the poorer born, 182
Whose baser stars do shut us up in wishes, 183
Might with effects of them follow our friends 184
And show what we alone must think, which never 185
Returns us thanks. 186

Enter Page.

PAGE   Monsieur Parolles, my lord calls for you.   [*Exit.*]
PAROLLES   Little Helen, farewell. If I can remember
thee, I will think of thee at court:
HELENA   Monsieur Parolles, you were born under a
charitable star.
PAROLLES   Under Mars, I.
HELENA   I especially think under Mars.
PAROLLES   Why under Mars?
HELENA   The wars hath so kept you under that you 195
must needs be born under Mars.
PAROLLES   When he was predominant. 197
HELENA   When he was retrograde, I think rather. 198
PAROLLES   Why think you so?
HELENA   You go so much backward when you fight.
PAROLLES   That's for advantage. 201
HELENA   So is running away, when fear proposes the
safety. But the composition that your valor and fear 203
makes in you is a virtue of a good wing, and I like the 204
wear well. 205
PAROLLES   I am so full of businesses I cannot answer
thee acutely, I will return perfect courtier, in the which 207
my instruction shall serve to naturalize thee, so thou 208
wilt be capable of a courtier's counsel and understand 209
what advice shall thrust upon thee; else thou diest in
thine unthankfulness, and thine ignorance makes thee 211
away. Farewell. When thou hast leisure, say thy pray- 212

ers; when thou hast none, remember thy friends. Get 213
thee a good husband, and use him as he uses thee. So,
farewell.   [*Exit.*]
HELENA

Our remedies oft in ourselves do lie
Which we ascribe to heaven. The fated sky 217
Gives us free scope, only doth backward pull
Our slow designs when we ourselves are dull. 219
What power is it which mounts my love so high, 220
That makes me see and cannot feed mine eye? 221
The mightiest space in fortune nature brings 222
To join like likes and kiss like native things. 223
Impossible be strange attempts to those 224
That weigh their pains in sense and do suppose 225
What hath been cannot be. Who ever strove 226
To show her merit that did miss her love? 227
The King's disease—my project may deceive me,
But my intents are fixed and will not leave me.   *Exit.*

❖

[1.2]

*Flourish cornets. Enter the King of France, with
letters, and [two Lords and] divers attendants.*

KING

The Florentines and Senoys are by th' ears, 1
Have fought with equal fortune and continue
A braving war.
FIRST LORD   So 'tis reported, sir. 3
KING

Nay, 'tis most credible. We here receive it
A certainty, vouched from our cousin Austria, 5
With caution that the Florentine will move us 6
For speedy aid, wherein our dearest friend 7
Prejudicates the business, and would seem 8
To have us make denial.
FIRST LORD   His love and wisdom, 9
Approved so to Your Majesty, may plead 10
For amplest credence.
KING   He hath armed our answer, 11
And Florence is denied before he comes.
Yet for our gentlemen that mean to see 13

174–5 Of . . . gossips of pretty, foolish lovers who give pet names to their mistresses and at whose love-christenings Cupid acts as godfather.   **181–6 That . . . thanks** It is a pity that wishing good fortune to someone does not command a tangible reality enabling us of humble station, whose lesser fortune confines us to mere wishing, to be able instead to bestow positive effects of that wishing on those whom we love, thereby yielding a benefit which, as things now stand, we can only ponder in our private thoughts without receiving any thanks.
195 under down, in an inferior position. (Playing on Parolles's *Under*, line 192, in the sense of "governed by.")   **197 predominant** in the ascendant, ruling.   **198 retrograde** moving backward (i.e., in a direction from east to west relative to the fixed positions of the signs of the zodiac)   **201 for advantage** to gain tactical advantage. (But Helena caustically interprets it as "craven self-protection.")   **203 composition** mixture   **204 of a good wing** strong in flight (and hence useful in rapid retreat; with a quibble on a sartorial sense of *wing*, meaning "an ornamental shoulder flap")   **205 wear** fashion   **207 perfect** complete.   **in the which** i.e., in which courtly behavior   **208 naturalize** familiarize; also, deflower.   **so** provided that   **209 capable** receptive. (With bawdy double meaning, continued in *understand, thrust,* and *diest.*)   **211–12 makes thee away** destroys, puts an end to you.

213 when . . . friends i.e., (patronizingly) don't forget to say your prayers, but remember you have friends who can help you out.   **217 fated** invested with the power of destiny   **219 dull** slow, sluggish.   **220 so high** to so exalted an object, i.e., to Bertram   **221 That . . . eye?** that puts Bertram before me as an object of desire but gives my gazing no fulfillment?   **222–3 The . . . things** i.e., Natural affection can cause even those separated by the widest diversity in social status to come together as if they belonged together.   **224–6 Impossible . . . be** Extraordinary attempts (at surmounting social barriers) seem impossible to those who calculate too carefully the extent and cost of their difficulties and suppose something to be impossible even though it has been done before.   **227 miss** fail to achieve
1.2. Location: Paris. The royal court.
1 Senoys natives of Siena.   **by th' ears** at variance, quarreling. (The King plans to deny Florence help [see 3.1], though allowing his lords free choice in what they do.)   **3 braving war** war of mutual defiance.
5 our cousin my fellow sovereign of   **6 move** petition   **7 friend** i.e., the Duke of Austria   **8 Prejudicates** prejudges   **8–9 would . . . denial** appears to wish that we deny aid (to the Florentines).
10 Approved demonstrated, proved   **11 credence** belief.   **armed** fortified (against denial)   **13 for** as for.   **see** i.e., participate in

The Tuscan service, freely have they leave
To stand on either part.

SECOND LORD   It well may serve   15
A nursery to our gentry, who are sick   16
For breathing and exploit.

KING   What's he comes here?   17

Enter Bertram, Lafew, and Parolles.

FIRST LORD
It is the Count Rossillion, my good lord,   18
Young Bertram.

KING [*to Bertram*]   Youth, thou bear'st thy father's face.
Frank nature, rather curious than in haste,   20
Hath well composed thee. Thy father's moral parts   21
Mayst thou inherit too! Welcome to Paris.

BERTRAM
My thanks and duty are Your Majesty's.

KING
I would I had that corporal soundness now   24
As when thy father and myself in friendship
First tried our soldiership! He did look far   26
Into the service of the time, and was   27
Discipled of the bravest. He lasted long,   28
But on us both did haggish age steal on,   29
And wore us out of act. It much repairs me   30
To talk of your good father. In his youth
He had the wit which I can well observe
Today in our young lords; but they may jest   33
Till their own scorn return to them unnoted   34
Ere they can hide their levity in honor.   35
So like a courtier, contempt nor bitterness   36
Were in his pride or sharpness; if they were,   37
His equal had awaked them, and his honor,   38
Clock to itself, knew the true minute when   39
Exception bid him speak, and at this time   40
His tongue obeyed his hand. Who were below him   41
He used as creatures of another place   42
And bowed his eminent top to their low ranks,   43
Making them proud of his humility   44
In their poor praise he humbled. Such a man   45

Might be a copy to these younger times,   46
Which, followed well, would demonstrate them now   47
But goers backward.

BERTRAM   His good remembrance, sir,   48
Lies richer in your thoughts than on his tomb.
So in approof lives not his epitaph   50
As in your royal speech.

KING
Would I were with him! He would always say—
Methinks I hear him now; his plausive words   53
He scattered not in ears, but grafted them   54
To grow there and to bear—"Let me not live—"   55
This his good melancholy oft began
On the catastrophe and heel of pastime,   57
When it was out—"Let me not live," quoth he,   58
"After my flame lacks oil, to be the snuff   59
Of younger spirits, whose apprehensive senses   60
All but new things disdain, whose judgments are   61
Mere fathers of their garments, whose constancies   62
Expire before their fashions." This he wished.   63
I, after him, do after him wish too,   64
Since I nor wax nor honey can bring home,   65
I quickly were dissolvèd from my hive
To give some laborers room.

SECOND LORD   You're lovèd, sir.
They that least lend it you shall lack you first.   68

KING
I fill a place, I know't.—How long is't, Count,
Since the physician at your father's died?
He was much famed.

BERTRAM   Some six months since, my lord.

KING
If he were living, I would try him yet.—
Lend me an arm.—The rest have worn me out   73
With several applications. Nature and sickness   74
Debate it at their leisure. Welcome, Count;   75
My son's no dearer.

BERTRAM   Thank Your Majesty.

Exeunt. Flourish.

❖

[1.3]

Enter Countess, Steward [Rinaldo], and Clown [Lavatch].

---

15 **stand** serve, fight.   **part** side.   **serve** serve as   16 **nursery** training school   16–17 **sick . . . exploit** longing for, or sick for lack of, action. 18 **Rossillion** (The Folio "*Rosignoll*" suggests a nightingale: French *rossignol*.)   20 **Frank** Generous, bountiful. **curious** careful, skillful 21 **parts** qualities   24 **corporal soundness** physical health   26 **tried** tested   26–7 **He did . . . time** He had a deep understanding of the affairs of war   27–8 **was Discipled of** had as his pupils (or, perhaps, "was taught by")   29 **haggish** like a hag, malevolent   30 **wore . . . act** wore us down into inactivity. **repairs** restores   33–5 **but . . . honor** but the young men of today may jest until their witty scorn goes scornfully unheeded sooner than they can hide the effects of their frivolous jesting with truly honorable action.   36–45 **So . . . humbled** True courtier that he was, he allowed neither contempt nor asperity to darken his proper self-esteem and sharpness of wit; if he ever showed contempt or asperity, it was to a social equal who had done something to deserve such a response; and his honor, self-governing, knew the exact minute when unacceptable behavior (such as an insult) bade him speak, at which time he did exactly what he said he would do and no more. Those who were below him in social station he treated as though they were not in fact his inferiors, bowing his head graciously to their humbleness, making them proud that he should humble his own eminence in acknowledgment of them.

46 **copy** model   47–8 **demonstrate . . . backward** show today's young men to be inferior to him.   50 **So . . . epitaph** The epitaph on his tomb is nowhere so amply confirmed   53 **plausive** praiseworthy 54 **scattered not** did not strew haphazardly   55 **bear** bear fruit 57–8 **On . . . out** at the drawing to a close of some sport (such as hunting), when the sport was over   59 **snuff** burned wick that interferes with proper burning of the candle, hence, hindrance   60 **apprehensive** quick to perceive, keen but impatient   61–2 **whose . . . garments** i.e., whose wisdom produces nothing but new fashions   62 **constancies** loyalties   63 **before** even before   64 **I . . . too** I, surviving him, wish as he did. (With a suggestion also of wishing to follow him in death.)   65 **nor wax** neither wax   68 **lend it you** give love to you. **lack** miss   73 **The rest** i.e., My physicians   74 **several applications** various medical treatments.   75 **Debate . . . leisure** i.e., contend over my condition at length.
1.3. Location: Rossillion.

COUNTESS   I will now hear. What say you of this 1
gentlewoman? 2

RINALDO   Madam, the care I have had to even your con- 3
tent I wish might be found in the calendar of my past 4
endeavors; for then we wound our modesty, and 5
make foul the clearness of our deservings, when of 6
ourselves we publish them. 7

COUNTESS   What does this knave here?—Get you
gone, sirrah. The complaints I have heard of you I do 9
not all believe. 'Tis my slowness that I do not, for I
know you lack not folly to commit them and have
ability enough to make such knaveries yours.

LAVATCH   'Tis not unknown to you, madam, I am a
poor fellow.

COUNTESS   Well, sir.

LAVATCH   No, madam, 'tis not so well that I am poor, 16
though many of the rich are damned; but if I may have
Your Ladyship's good will to go to the world, Isbel 18
the woman and I will do as we may. 19

COUNTESS   Wilt thou needs be a beggar?

LAVATCH   I do beg your good will in this case.

COUNTESS   In what case?

LAVATCH   In Isbel's case and mine own. Service is no 23
heritage, and I think I shall never have the blessing of 24
God till I have issue o' my body; for they say bairns are 25
blessings.

COUNTESS   Tell me thy reason why thou wilt marry.

LAVATCH   My poor body, madam, requires it. I am
driven on by the flesh, and he must needs go that the 29
devil drives.

COUNTESS   Is this all Your Worship's reason? 31

LAVATCH   Faith, madam, I have other holy reasons, 32
such as they are.

COUNTESS   May the world know them?

LAVATCH   I have been, madam, a wicked creature, as
you and all flesh and blood are, and indeed I do marry
that I may repent. 37

COUNTESS   Thy marriage, sooner than thy wickedness. 38

LAVATCH   I am out o' friends, madam, and I hope to
have friends for my wife's sake. 40

COUNTESS   Such friends are thine enemies, knave.

LAVATCH   You're shallow, madam, in great friends, for 42
the knaves come to do that for me which I am aweary
of. He that ears my land spares my team and gives me 44
leave to in the crop. If I be his cuckold, he's my 45
drudge. He that comforts my wife is the cherisher of 46
my flesh and blood; he that cherishes my flesh and
blood loves my flesh and blood; he that loves my flesh
and blood is my friend. Ergo, he that kisses my wife
is my friend. If men could be contented to be what 50
they are, there were no fear in marriage; for young 51
Charbon the puritan and old Poysam the papist, how- 52
some'er their hearts are severed in religion, their heads
are both one—they may jowl horns together like any 54
deer i'th' herd.

COUNTESS   Wilt thou ever be a foulmouthed and calum- 56
nious knave? 57

LAVATCH   A prophet I, madam, and I speak the truth
the next way: 59
    For I the ballad will repeat
        Which men full true shall find:
    Your marriage comes by destiny,
        Your cuckoo sings by kind. 63

COUNTESS   Get you gone, sir. I'll talk with you more
anon.

RINALDO   May it please you, madam, that he bid Helen
come to you. Of her I am to speak.

COUNTESS   [to Lavatch]   Sirrah, tell my gentlewoman I
would speak with her—Helen, I mean.

LAVATCH   [sings]
    "Was this fair face the cause," quoth she, 70
        "Why the Grecians sackèd Troy?
    Fond done, done fond, 72
        Was this King Priam's joy?" 73
    With that she sighèd as she stood,
    With that she sighèd as she stood,
        And gave this sentence then: 76
    "Among nine bad if one be good, 77
    Among nine bad if one be good,
        There's yet one good in ten."

COUNTESS   What, one good in ten? You corrupt the 80
song, sirrah. 81

1–2 this gentlewoman Helena.   3–4 to . . . content to meet your
expectations   4 calendar record. (Rinaldo hopes that his blameless
record will clear him of blame in what he is about to say to the
Countess about Helena.)   5–7 and make . . . them (Rinaldo expresses
an unwillingness to insist on his own deservings or reliability as a
witness, for fear of protesting too much.)   7 publish make known
9 sirrah (Form of address to a social inferior.)   16 well (The Clown
plays on the Countess's "Well" in line 15, i.e., "Well, go ahead"; he
means "satisfactory." He also plays on poor in lines 14 and 16:
[1] wretched [2] impoverished.)   18 go . . . world i.e., marry
18–19 Isbel the woman Lavatch appears to be interested amorously
in Isbel or Isabel, a woman presumably serving in the Countess's
household. She does not appear onstage in the play.   19 do (1) get
along (2) copulate   23 case (With a bawdy pun on "female
pudenda.")   23–4 Service is no heritage i.e., Being a servant gives
me little to bequeath to my posterity   25 bairns children   29 needs
necessarily   31 Your Worship's (The Countess uses a mock title.)
32 holy reasons i.e., reasons sanctioned by the marriage service.
(With obscene puns on "holey" and "raisings.")   37 repent i.e.,
(1) atone for my carnal ways by making them legitimate (2) regret
marrying.   38 Thy marriage i.e., You'll repent your marriage (since
proverbially hasty marriage leads to regret)   40 for . . . sake to keep
my wife company. (With a suggestion of sexual activity as a result.)

42 shallow . . . in a superficial judge of   44–5 He . . . crop i.e., He that
plows (ears) my wife sexually takes the load off my team, my sexual
organs, and provides me with a crop of children.   45 in bring in, harvest.   cuckold a man whose wife is unfaithful   46 drudge menial
laborer.   50–1 what they are i.e., cuckolds   52 Charbon . . . papist
the meat-eating Puritan and the fish-eating Catholic. (Corruptions of
chairbonne, good meat, and poisson, fish, the fast-day diets of Puritans
and Catholics, respectively.)   54 both one alike (in having cuckolds'
horns.)   jowl dash, knock   56 ever always   56–7 calumnious slandering   59 next nearest, most direct   63 kind nature (since cuckoldry is natural).   70 fair face i.e., Helen of Troy's face.   she i.e.,
Hecuba, wife of Priam, or Helen, or the singer of the ballad   72 Fond
Foolishly   73 Was . . . joy? i.e., Was the taking of Helen, that led to
the Trojan War and the eventual sacking of Priam's palace, his joy?
76 sentence maxim   77 Among along with   80–1 You . . . song (The
song must have had "nine good in ten," or "one bad in ten."

LAVATCH   One good woman in ten, madam, which is a   82
purifying o'th' song. Would God would serve the   83
world so all the year! We'd find no fault with the tithe-   84
woman if I were the parson. One in ten, quoth 'a? An   85
we might have a good woman born but or every blaz-   86
ing star, or at an earthquake, 'twould mend the lottery   87
well. A man may draw his heart out ere 'a pluck one.   88

COUNTESS   You'll be gone, sir knave, and do as I
command you?

LAVATCH   That man should be at woman's command,   91
and yet no hurt done! Though honesty be no Puritan,   92
yet it will do no hurt; it will wear the surplice of humil-   93
ity over the black gown of a big heart. I am going,   94
forsooth. The business is for Helen to come hither.

Exit.

COUNTESS   Well, now.

RINALDO   I know, madam, you love your gentlewoman
entirely.

COUNTESS   Faith, I do. Her father bequeathed her to
me, and she herself, without other advantage, may   100
lawfully make title to as much love as she finds. There   101
is more owing her than is paid, and more shall be paid
her than she'll demand.

RINALDO   Madam, I was very late more near her than I   104
think she wished me. Alone she was, and did
communicate to herself her own words to her own
ears; she thought, I dare vow for her, they touched not
any stranger sense. Her matter was, she loved your   108
son. Fortune, she said, was no goddess, that had put   109
such difference betwixt their two estates; Love no god,   110
that would not extend his might only where qualities   111
were level; Dian no queen of virgins, that would suffer   112
her poor knight surprised without rescue in the first   113
assault or ransom afterward. This she delivered in the   114
most bitter touch of sorrow that e'er I heard virgin   115

exclaim in, which I held my duty speedily to acquaint
you withal, sithence, in the loss that may happen, it   117
concerns you something to know it.   118

COUNTESS   You have discharged this honestly. Keep it   119
to yourself. Many likelihoods informed me of this   120
before, which hung so tottering in the balance that I
could neither believe nor misdoubt. Pray you, leave   122
me. Stall this in your bosom, and I thank you for your   123
honest care. I will speak with you further anon.

Exit Steward [Rinaldo].

Enter Helena.

Even so it was with me when I was young.   125
    If ever we are nature's, these are ours. This thorn   126
Doth to our rose of youth rightly belong;
    Our blood to us, this to our blood is born.   128
It is the show and seal of nature's truth,   129
Where love's strong passion is impressed in youth.   130
By our remembrances of days forgone,
Such were our faults, or then we thought them
    none.   132
Her eye is sick on't. I observe her now.   133

HELENA   What is your pleasure, madam?

COUNTESS
You know, Helen, I am a mother to you.

HELENA
Mine honorable mistress.

COUNTESS   Nay, a mother.
Why not a mother? When I said "a mother,"
Methought you saw a serpent. What's in "mother"
That you start at it? I say I am your mother,
And put you in the catalogue of those
That were enwombèd mine. 'Tis often seen
Adoption strives with nature, and choice breeds   142
A native slip to us from foreign seeds.   143
You ne'er oppressed me with a mother's groan,   144
Yet I express to you a mother's care.
God's mercy, maiden, does it curd thy blood
To say I am thy mother? What's the matter,
That this distempered messenger of wet,   148
The many-colored Iris, rounds thine eye?   149
Why? That you are my daughter?

HELENA   That I am not.   150

COUNTESS
I say I am your mother.

HELENA   Pardon, madam;

82–3 which . . . song which corrects the song's incorrect statistics.
83–8 Would . . . one If only God would give us one good woman in
ten as a regular thing! I'd settle for that. (Literally, if I were the parson, I'd settle for that tithing, or payment to the church of one-tenth
of one's income.) If only we could find one good woman born on the
occasion of rare events like comets or earthquakes, it would improve
the odds. A man might just as easily pull his own heart out of his
chest as draw one good woman by lottery.   **91–2 That . . . done!**
Lavatch sardonically professes to be horrified at the idea of a man
being at a woman's command, in disregard of the Saint Paul's insistence that the man should be the head of the woman. (*That* means "To
think that.")   **92–4 Though . . . heart** i.e., Though my outspokenness
has no desire to be hypocritical, it will, like the Puritan, hide its proud
spirit (*big heart*) beneath the guise of humble obedience. (Many Puritans who demurred at the rubrics and canons of the Established
Church, in order to *do no hurt*, conformed outwardly by wearing the
prescribed surplice while still wearing underneath that surplice the
black gown customarily worn by Calvinists.)   **100–1 may . . . finds**
i.e., may claim love of me, which she will find in abundance. (The
Countess's metaphor is of the inheritance of a valuable property that
is entitled to high regard in its own right.)   **104 late** recently
108 any stranger sense any other person's sense of hearing.   **matter**
theme   **109 was no goddess** i.e., was a thing of accident only, not
divine   **110–14 Love . . . afterward** Cupid, she said, was capricious
and unworthy of being worshiped as a god, in that Cupid would give
his blessing and assistance only to couples who were socially equal;
and Diana unworthy of being called the patron goddess of virgins, in
that she would allow her hapless devotee, her *poor knight*, to be captured and left unransomed in the war of the sexes.   **114 delivered**
spoke   **115 touch** note, pang

117 withal with.   **sithence . . . happen** since in view of the harm that
may come of this   **118 something** somewhat   **119 discharged** performed   **120 likelihoods** indications   **122 misdoubt** doubt.   **123 Stall**
Lodge   **125 Even so** (The Countess speaks without being heard by
Helena, who has entered.)   **126 these** i.e., these pangs of love (signs of
which the Countess sees manifested in Helena)   **128–9 Our . . . truth**
Sexual passion is an inborn part of us, and these pangs of love are born
of that passion. It is the sign and guarantee of nature's authority
130 impressed imprinted (as by a seal in wax, or a thorn)   **132 or . . .
none** or rather things we didn't consider faults at the time.   **133 on't**
with it.   **142 strives** vies (in strength of attachment)   **142–3 choice . . .
seeds** grafting from an unrelated stock makes wholly ours what was
originally foreign.   **144 with a mother's groan** i.e., in childbirth
148–9 That . . . eye? that the many-colored rainbow, representing Juno's
messenger Iris as the bringer of sad news and rain, is refracted in your
tearful eyes?   **150 not** i.e., not daughter-in-law.

The Count Rossillion cannot be my brother.
I am from humble, he from honored name;
No note upon my parents, his all noble.   154
My master, my dear lord he is, and I
His servant live and will his vassal die.
He must not be my brother.

COUNTESS   Nor I your mother?

HELENA
You are my mother, madam. Would you were—
So that my lord your son were not my brother—   159
Indeed my mother! Or were you both our mothers,   160
I care no more for than I do for heaven,   161
So I were not his sister. Can't no other   162
But, I your daughter, he must be my brother?   163

COUNTESS
Yes, Helen, you might be my daughter-in-law.
God shield you mean it not! "Daughter" and
    "mother"
So strive upon your pulse. What, pale again?   165
My fear hath catched your fondness. Now I see   167
The mystery of your loneliness and find
Your salt tears' head. Now to all sense 'tis gross: 169
You love my son. Invention is ashamed,   170
Against the proclamation of thy passion,   171
To say thou dost not. Therefore tell me true,
But tell me then 'tis so, for look, thy cheeks
Confess it th'one to th'other, and thine eyes
See it so grossly shown in thy behaviors
That in their kind they speak it. Only sin   176
And hellish obstinacy tie thy tongue,
That truth should be suspected. Speak, is't so?   178
If it be so, you have wound a goodly clew;   179
If it be not, forswear't. Howe'er, I charge thee,   180
As heaven shall work in me for thine avail,   181
To tell me truly.

HELENA   Good madam, pardon me!

COUNTESS
Do you love my son?

HELENA   Your pardon, noble mistress!

COUNTESS
Love you my son?

HELENA   Do not you love him, madam?

COUNTESS
Go not about. My love hath in't a bond   185
Whereof the world takes note. Come, come, disclose   186

The state of your affection, for your passions
Have to the full appeached.

HELENA *[kneeling]*   Then I confess   188
Here on my knee, before high heaven and you,
That before you, and next unto high heaven,   190
I love your son.
My friends were poor but honest, so's my love.   192
Be not offended, for it hurts not him
That he is loved of me. I follow him not
By any token of presumptuous suit,   195
Nor would I have him till I do deserve him,
Yet never know how that desert should be.
I know I love in vain, strive against hope;
Yet in this captious and intenible sieve   199
I still pour in the waters of my love
And lack not to lose still. Thus, Indian-like,   201
Religious in mine error, I adore
The sun, that looks upon his worshiper
But knows of him no more. My dearest madam,   204
Let not your hate encounter with my love   205
For loving where you do; but if yourself,
Whose agèd honor cites a virtuous youth,   207
Did ever in so true a flame of liking   208
Wish chastely and love dearly, that your Dian   209
Was both herself and Love, oh, then, give pity   210
To her whose state is such that cannot choose
But lend and give where she is sure to lose;
That seeks not to find that her search implies,   213
But riddle-like lives sweetly where she dies.   214

COUNTESS
Had you not lately an intent—speak truly—
To go to Paris?

HELENA   Madam, I had.

COUNTESS   Wherefore?   216
Tell true.

HELENA
I will tell truth, by grace itself I swear.
You know my father left me some prescriptions
Of rare and proved effects, such as his reading
And manifest experience had collected   221
For general sovereignty; and that he willed me   222
In heedfull'st reservation to bestow them,   223
As notes whose faculties inclusive were   224
More than they were in note. Amongst the rest   225
There is a remedy, approved, set down,   226

---

154 note mark of distinction.   **parents** ancestors   **159 So** provided that   **160 both our mothers** mother of us both   **161 I . . . heaven** (Helena ambiguously, suggests [1] she wouldn't care much for this [2] she would care for it as much as she longs for heaven.)   **162 So** so long as   **162–3 Can't . . . daughter** Must it be that if I'm your daughter   **165 shield** forbid. (But the construction with *not* is ambiguous.)   **167 catched** caught.   **fondness** love (of Bertram); or foolishness. (The Countess speaks ambiguously while she tests Helena.)   **169 head** source.   **sense** perception.   **gross** palpable, apparent   **170 Invention** i.e., Your ability to invent excuses   **171 Against** in the face of   **176 in their kind** according to their nature, i.e., by weeping   **178 suspected** surmised (by me) rather than openly declared; or, rendered suspect, brought into disrepute.   **179 wound . . . clew** wound up a fine ball of twine, i.e., snarled things up beautifully   **180 forswear't** deny it under oath.   **Howe'er** In any case   **181 avail** benefit   **185 Go not about** Don't evade me.   **bond** i.e., maternal bond   **186 Whereof . . . note** which society acknowledges

188 appeached informed against (you).   **190 before you** even more than (I love) you: or, even more than you love him   **192 friends** kinfolk   **195 By . . . suit** with any indication of my presumptuous love   **199 captious** deceptive; also, capacious.   **intenible** incapable of holding   **201 lack . . . still** still have enough to keep pouring without diminishing my supply; also, continually lose.   **Indian-like** idolatrously, like the savage (who worships the sun)   **204 no more** nothing else.   **205 encounter with** oppose   **207 agèd honor cites** honorable old age bespeaks, gives evidence of   **208 liking** love   **209 that so** so that   **210 both . . . Love** i.e., both Diana and Venus, chaste and passionate   **213 that . . . implies** what her search is for   **214 riddle-like** paradoxically, with an unguessed mystery   **216 Wherefore?** Why?   **221 manifest experience** i.e., the practice, in antithesis to the theory (*reading*)   **222 general sovereignty** universal efficacy and use   **222–5 he . . . note** he exhorted me to take great care in making use of them, as prescriptions whose comprehensive powers were greater than recognized.   **226 approved** tested

To cure the desperate languishings whereof
The King is rendered lost.   228

COUNTESS
This was your motive for Paris, was it? Speak.

HELENA
My lord your son made me to think of this,
Else Paris and the medicine and the King
Had from the conversation of my thoughts   232
Haply been absent then.

COUNTESS   But think you, Helen,   133
If you should tender your supposèd aid,   234
He would receive it? He and his physicians
Are of a mind: he, that they cannot help him,
They, that they cannot help. How shall they credit 237
A poor unlearnèd virgin, when the schools,
Emboweled of their doctrine, have left off   239
The danger to itself?

HELENA   There's something in't
More than my father's skill—which was the great'st
Of his profession—that his good receipt   242
Shall for my legacy be sanctified
By th' luckiest stars in heaven; and would your honor 244
But give me leave to try success, I'd venture   245
The well-lost life of mine on His Grace's cure   246
By such a day and hour.   247

COUNTESS   Dost thou believe't?

HELENA   Ay, madam, knowingly.   249

COUNTESS
Why, Helen, thou shalt have my leave and love,
Means and attendants, and my loving greetings
To those of mine in court. I'll stay at home
And pray God's blessing into thy attempt.   253
Begone tomorrow, and be sure of this:
What I can help thee to thou shalt not miss.   *Exeunt.* 255

❖

2.1

*Enter the King [in his chair] with divers young
Lords taking leave for the Florentine war,
[Bertram] Count Rossillion, and Parolles.
Flourish cornets.*

KING
Farewell, young lords. These warlike principles   1
Do not throw from you. And you, my lords, farewell. 2
Share the advice betwixt you; if both gain all,   3
The gift doth stretch itself as 'tis received,   4
And is enough for both.

FIRST LORD   'Tis our hope, sir,

After well-entered soldiers, to return   6
And find Your Grace in health.

KING
No, no, it cannot be; and yet my heart
Will not confess he owes the malady   9
That doth my life besiege. Farewell, young lords.
Whether I live or die, be you the sons
Of worthy Frenchmen. Let higher Italy—   12
Those bated that inherit but the fall   13
Of the last monarchy—see that you come   14
Not to woo honor, but to wed it. When   15
The bravest questant shrinks, find what you seek, 16
That fame may cry you loud. I say, farewell.   17

SECOND LORD
Health at your bidding serve Your Majesty!

KING
Those girls of Italy, take heed of them.
They say our French lack language to deny   20
If they demand. Beware of being captives   21
Before you serve.

BOTH   Our hearts receive your warnings. 22

KING
Farewell.—Come hither to me.   [*The King converses
                                privately with various lords; Bertram, Parolles,
                                        and their companions move apart.*]

FIRST LORD [*to Bertram*]
Oh my sweet lord, that you will stay behind us!

PAROLLES
'Tis not his fault, the spark.

SECOND LORD   Oh, 'tis brave wars!   25

PAROLLES   Most admirable. I have seen those wars.

BERTRAM   I am commanded here and kept a coil with 27
"Too young" and "The next year" and "'Tis too early."

PAROLLES   An thy mind stand to't, boy, steal away   29
bravely.   30

BERTRAM
I shall stay here the forehorse to a smock,   31
Creaking my shoes on the plain masonry,   32
Till honor be bought up, and no sword worn   33
But one to dance with. By heaven, I'll steal away! 34

FIRST LORD
There's honor in the theft.

PAROLLES   Commit it, Count.

---

228 **rendered lost** reckoned to be incurable.   232 **conversation** movement, train   233 **Haply** perhaps   234 **tender** offer   237 **credit** trust   239 **Emboweled** emptied.   **left off** abandoned   242 **that** whereby.   **receipt** prescription   244 **th' luckiest** i.e., the most able to confer luck   245 **venture** risk, wager   246 **well-lost** i.e., well lost in such a cause, worthless otherwise   247 **such a** i.e., a specific   249 **knowingly** with confidence.   253 **into** upon   255 **miss** be lacking.
2.1. Location: Paris. The royal court.
1–2 **These . . . you** i.e., Remember this military advice.   3–4 **if . . . received** if both groups wish to profit fully from my advice, it will stretch to the extent that it is accepted

6 **After . . . soldiers** after having become seasoned soldiers; or, in the manner of experienced soldiers   9 **he owes** it owns   12 **higher Italy** (1) the knightly class of Italy, corresponding to *worthy Frenchmen,* or (2) Tuscany, of which Florence and Siena are cities   13–14 **Those . . . monarchy** i.e., except those who inherit unworthily the poor remains of the Holy Roman Empire. (Such undeserving knights are not to be taken into account.)   15 **woo** flirt with.   **wed** possess as your own   16 **questant** seeker (after honor)   17 **cry you loud** proclaim you loudly.   20–2 **They . . . serve** People say we French have low resistance to the sexual blandishments of women. Beware of being captive to their charms even before you enter into military action.   25 **spark** elegant young man.   **brave** splendid   27 **here** i.e., to remain here.   **kept a coil** pestered, fussed over   29 **An** If   30 **bravely** (1) worthily (2) valiantly.   31 **the forehorse . . . smock** the lead horse of a team driven by a woman   32 **plain masonry** smooth masonry floor (instead of a battlefield)   33 **Till . . . up** till opportunity for winning honor in the wars is past, all consumed   34 **one . . . with** i.e., a light ornamental weapon.

SECOND LORD
I am your accessory. And so, farewell.

BERTRAM   I grow to you, and our parting is a tortured   37
body.   38

FIRST LORD   Farewell, Captain.

SECOND LORD   Sweet Monsieur Parolles!

PAROLLES   Noble heroes, my sword and yours are kin.
Good sparks and lustrous, a word, good metals: you   42
shall find in the regiment of the Spinii one Captain
Spurio, with his cicatrice, an emblem of war, here on   44
his sinister cheek; it was this very sword entrenched it.   45
Say to him I live, and observe his reports for me.   46

FIRST LORD   We shall, noble Captain.

PAROLLES   Mars dote on you for his novices!   48

[To Bertram] What will ye do?   [Exeunt Lords.]

BERTRAM   Stay the King.   50

PAROLLES   Use a more spacious ceremony to   51
the noble lords; you have restrained yourself within
the list of too cold an adieu. Be more expressive to   53
them, for they wear themselves in the cap of the time;   54
there do muster true gait, eat, speak, and move under   55
the influence of the most received star; and, though the   56
devil lead the measure, such are to be followed. After   57
them, and take a more dilated farewell.   58

BERTRAM   And I will do so.

PAROLLES   Worthy fellows, and like to prove most sin-   60
ewy swordmen.   Exeunt [Bertram and Parolles].   61

Enter Lafew [and approaches the King].

LAFEW [kneeling]
Pardon, my lord, for me and for my tidings.   62

KING   I'll fee thee to stand up.   63

LAFEW [rising]
Then here's a man stands that has brought his pardon.   64
I would you had kneeled, my lord, to ask me mercy,   65
And that at my bidding you could so stand up.   66

KING
I would I had, so I had broke thy pate   67
And asked thee mercy for't.

LAFEW   Good faith, across!   68

But, my good lord, 'tis thus: will you be cured
Of your infirmity?

KING   No.   37

LAFEW   Oh, will you eat   70
No grapes, my royal fox? Yes, but you will   71
My noble grapes, an if my royal fox   72
Could reach them. I have seen a medicine   73
That's able to breathe life into a stone,
Quicken a rock, and make you dance canary   75
With sprightly fire and motion, whose simple touch   76
Is powerful to araise King Pepin, nay,   77
To give great Charlemain a pen in's hand
And write to her a love line.

KING   What "her" is this?   79

LAFEW
Why, Doctor She! My lord, there's one arrived,
If you will see her. Now by my faith and honor,
If seriously I may convey my thoughts
In this my light deliverance, I have spoke   83
With one that in her sex, her years, profession,   84
Wisdom, and constancy hath amazed me more   85
Than I dare blame my weakness. Will you see her,   86
For that is her demand, and know her business?
That done, laugh well at me.

KING   Now, good Lafew,
Bring in the admiration, that we with thee   89
May spend our wonder too, or take off thine   90
By wondering how thou took'st it.

LAFEW   Nay, I'll fit you,   91
And not be all day neither.   [He goes to the door.]

KING
Thus he his special nothing ever prologues.   93

LAFEW [to Helena]   Nay, come your ways.   94

Enter Helena.

KING   This haste hath wings indeed.

LAFEW   Nay, come your ways.
This is His Majesty. Say your mind to him.
A traitor you do look like, but such traitors   98
His Majesty seldom fears. I am Cressid's uncle,   99
That dare leave two together. Fare you well.   Exit.

KING
Now, fair one, does your business follow us?   101

37 grow to grow deeply attached to, become as one with   37–8 a tortured body i.e., as painful as a body being torn apart by torture.
42 metals i.e., "blades"; spirits of mettle   44 Spurio (This name suggests "spurious," "counterfeit.")   cicatrice scar   45 sinister left.   it
was . . . entrenched it mine was the sword that dug that trench-like
scar.   46 reports reply   48 Mars May Mars.   novices devotees.
50 Stay the King Support or wait on the King. (But also interpreted,
with different punctuation, as "Stay; the King wills it" or "Stay; the
King approaches.")   51 spacious ceremony effusive courtesy
53 list boundary. (Literally, the selvage or finished edge of cloth.)
54 wear . . . time stand out as ornaments of the fashionable world
55 muster true gait set the right pace, move gracefully   56 received
fashionable   57 measure dance   58 dilated protracted; expansive
60 like likely   60–1 sinewy energetic, forceful   62 tidings news,
information.   63 I'll . . . up i.e., I bid you rise; or, I will rather reward
you for rising.   64 pardon i.e., something to win the King's indulgence.   65–8 I would . . . for't (Lafew hyperbolically suggests that he
and the King really ought to change places, turning the King into the
petitioner, since Lafew has brought something worth begging for. The
King, not knowing what is in store, jests that he might be willing to
beg forgiveness of Lafew if he could first give Lafew a sharp blow to
the head for his seeming insolence, thus providing the King an occasion for begging pardon.)   68 across i.e., well parried.

70–1 will . . . fox? i.e., will you be like the fox in Aesop's fable and call
the grapes sour because they are beyond your reach?   72 an if if
73 medicine i.e., physician   75 Quicken bring to life.   canary a
lively Spanish dance   76 simple (1) mere (2) medicinal, making use
of "simples" or herbs   77 to araise . . . Pepin to raise from the dead
King Pepin, a French king of the eighth century and father of Charlemagne. (The name has a folklorish ring.)   79 love line (Some of
Lafew's terms, such as stone, quicken, fire and motion, touch, araise, and
pen, in 's hand, have possible erotic undertones that link recovery to
restored potency.)   83 deliverance manner of speaking   84 profession what she professes to be able to do.   85–6 more . . . weakness
more than I can attribute to my feebleness or susceptibility as an old
man.   89 admiration wonder   90 spend expend.   take off dispel,
end   91 took'st conceived. (With a play on take in the previous line.)
fit satisfy   93 special nothing particular trifles.   prologues introduces.   94 come your ways come along.   98 traitor (Lafew's joke
depends on the idea that it is dangerous to leave an unknown person
alone with a king, for fear of a plot.)   99 Cressid's uncle Pandarus,
go-between for the lovers Troilus and Cressida   101 follow concern

HELENA   Ay, my good lord.
        Gerard de Narbonne was my father;
        In what he did profess, well found.
KING   I knew him.   104
HELENA
        The rather will I spare my praises towards him;
        Knowing him is enough. On 's bed of death
        Many receipts he gave me, chiefly one   107
        Which, as the dearest issue of his practice,   108
        And of his old experience th'only darling,   109
        He bade me store up as a triple eye   110
        Safer than mine own two, more dear. I have so;   111
        And hearing Your High Majesty is touched
        With that malignant cause wherein the honor   113
        Of my dear father's gift stands chief in power,   114
        I come to tender it and my appliance   115
        With all bound humbleness.
KING   We thank you, maiden,   116
        But may not be so credulous of cure   117
        When our most learnèd doctors leave us and
        The congregated college have concluded   119
        That laboring art can never ransom nature   120
        From her inaidible estate. I say we must not
        So stain our judgment, or corrupt our hope,   122
        To prostitute our past-cure malady   123
        To empirics, or to dissever so   124
        Our great self and our credit, to esteem   125
        A senseless help when help past sense we deem.   126
HELENA
        My duty then shall pay me for my pains.   127
        I will no more enforce mine office on you,   128
        Humbly entreating from your royal thoughts
        A modest one to bear me back again.   130
KING
        I cannot give thee less, to be called grateful.
        Thou thought'st to help me, and such thanks I give
        As one near death to those that wish him live.
        But what at full I know, thou know'st no part,   134
        I knowing all my peril, thou no art.   135
HELENA
        What I can do can do no hurt to try,
        Since you set up your rest 'gainst remedy.   137
        He that of greatest works is finisher   138

        Oft does them by the weakest minister.
        So holy writ in babes hath judgment shown,   140
        When judges have been babes; great floods have
        flown   141
        From simple sources; and great seas have dried   142
        When miracles have by the great'st been denied.
        Oft expectation fails, and most oft there
        Where most it promises, and oft it hits   145
        Where hope is coldest and despair most fits.
KING
        I must not hear thee. Fare thee well, kind maid.
        Thy pains, not used, must by thyself be paid;   148
        Proffers not took reap thanks for their reward.   149
HELENA
        Inspirèd merit so by breath is barred.   150
        It is not so with Him that all things knows
        As 'tis with us that square our guess by shows;   152
        But most it is presumption in us when
        The help of heaven we count the act of men.   154
        Dear sir, to my endeavors give consent;
        Of heaven, not me, make an experiment.   156
        I am not an impostor that proclaim   157
        Myself against the level of mine aim;   158
        But know I think, and think I know most sure,   159
        My art is not past power, nor you past cure.   160
KING
        Art thou so confident? Within what space   161
        Hop'st thou my cure?
HELENA   The great'st grace lending grace,   162
        Ere twice the horses of the sun shall bring
        Their fiery torcher his diurnal ring,   164
        Ere twice in murk and occidental damp   165
        Moist Hesperus hath quenched her sleepy lamp,   166
        Or four-and-twenty times the pilot's glass   167
        Hath told the thievish minutes how they pass,
        What is infirm from your sound parts shall fly,
        Health shall live free, and sickness freely die.
KING
        Upon thy certainty and confidence
        What dar'st thou venture?
HELENA   Tax of impudence,   172
        A strumpet's boldness, a divulgèd shame

---

104 In . . . found in his medical practice he was reputed to be skilled. **107 receipts** remedies **108–9 the dearest . . . darling** the favorite child or product of his many years of practice **110 triple** third **111 Safer** more safely **113–14 With . . . power** with that malignant disease which my father had become renowned for treating successfully with his special discovery and skill **115 tender** offer **appliance** treatment **116 bound** dutiful **117 credulous of** ready to believe in **119 congregated college** college of physicians **120 art** skill, i.e., medicine **122 stain** sully **123–6 To . . . deem** by basely submitting my past-cure illness to quack doctors, or by divorcing my kingly greatness from my reputation to such an extent as to put credulous faith in a cure too improbable to be believed when the disease exceeds all reasonable hope. **127 My . . . pains** My thanks then must be that I have dutifully offered my aid. **128 office** dutiful service **130 A modest . . . again** i.e., a favorable regard commensurate with my humble station and with my maidenly modesty to take back with me. **134 no part** not at all **135 thou no art** i.e., you having no medical skill capable of saving my life. **137 set . . . rest** stake your all. (A figure from the gambling game of primero.) **138 He** God

140–1 So . . . babes (See, for example, Matthew 11:25 and 1 Corinthians 1:27.) **141 babes** i.e., babyish, foolish. (The inversion of babes and wise men appears often in the Bible.) **142 simple** small, insignificant. **great seas** (Probably the Red Sea; *the great'st* in line 143 is presumably Pharaoh.) **145 hits** succeeds, is confirmed **148 by . . . paid** i.e., be their own reward **149 Proffers . . . thanks** offers not accepted reap thanks (and only thanks) **150 Inspirèd . . . barred** Divinely inspired virtue is thus denied by mere spoken words. **152 square . . . shows** support our conjectures on the basis of appearances **154 count** account **156 experiment** trial. **157–8 that . . . aim** who claims to be more of a marksman than my ability to aim would warrant **159–60 But . . . power** but I have every confidence, given the uncertainty of all human knowing, that what I claim to be able to do is not beyond my power to perform **161 space** period of time **162 Hop'st thou** do you hope for. **The great'st . . . grace** i.e., With God's help **164 Their . . . ring** i.e., the fiery sun-god on his daily round **165 occidental** western, sunset **166 Hesperus** evening star (actually Venus) **167 glass** hour-glass **172 venture** risk, wager. **Tax** Accusation

Traduced by odious ballads; my maiden's name 174
Seared otherwise; nay, worse of worst, extended 175
With vilest torture let my life be ended.

KING
Methinks in thee some blessèd spirit doth speak
His powerful sound within an organ weak;
And what impossibility would slay 179
In common sense, sense saves another way. 180
Thy life is dear, for all that life can rate 181
Worth name of life in thee hath estimate: 182
Youth, beauty, wisdom, courage, all
That happiness and prime can happy call. 184
Thou this to hazard needs must intimate 185
Skill infinite, or monstrous desperate. 186
Sweet practicer, thy physic I will try, 187
That ministers thine own death if I die. 188

HELENA
If I break time or flinch in property 189
Of what I spoke, unpitied let me die,
And well deserved. Not helping, death's my fee; 191
But, if I help, what do you promise me?

KING
Make thy demand.

HELENA   But will you make it even? 193

KING
Ay, by my scepter and my hopes of heaven.

HELENA
Then shalt thou give me with thy kingly hand
What husband in thy power I will command.
Exempted be from me the arrogance
To choose from forth the royal blood of France,
My low and humble name to propagate
With any branch or image of thy state;
But such a one, thy vassal, whom I know
Is free for me to ask, thee to bestow.

KING
Here is my hand. The premises observed, 203
Thy will by my performance shall be served.
So make the choice of thy own time, for I,
Thy resolved patient, on thee still rely. 206
More should I question thee, and more I must—
Though more to know could not be more to trust—
From whence thou cam'st, how tended on; but rest 209
Unquestioned welcome and undoubted blest.— 210

Give me some help here, ho!—If thou proceed
As high as word, my deed shall match thy meed. 212
Flourish. Exeunt, [the King carried in].

❖

[2.2]

Enter Countess and Clown [Lavatch].

COUNTESS   Come on, sir. I shall now put you to the 1
height of your breeding. 2
LAVATCH   I will show myself highly fed and lowly 3
taught. I know my business is but to the court. 4
COUNTESS   "To the court"? Why, what place make you 5
special, when you put off that with such contempt? 6
"But to the court"!
LAVATCH   Truly, madam, if God have lent a man any
manners, he may easily put it off at court. He that 9
cannot make a leg, put off's cap, kiss his hand, and 10
say nothing has neither leg, hands, lip, nor cap; and
indeed such a fellow, to say precisely, were not for the
court. But for me, I have an answer will serve all men.
COUNTESS   Marry, that's a bountiful answer that fits all
questions.
LAVATCH   It is like a barber's chair that fits all buttocks:
the pin-buttock, the quatch-buttock, the brawn-but- 17
tock, or any buttock.
COUNTESS   Will your answer serve fit to all questions?
LAVATCH   As fit as ten groats is for the hand of an 20
attorney, as your French crown for your taffety punk, 21
as Tib's rush for Tom's forefinger, as a pancake for 22
Shrove Tuesday, a morris for May Day, as the nail to 23
his hole, the cuckold to his horn, as a scolding quean 24
to a wrangling knave, as the nun's lip to the friar's
mouth, nay, as the pudding to his skin. 26
COUNTESS   Have you, I say, an answer of such fitness
for all questions?
LAVATCH   From below your duke to beneath your
constable, it will fit any question.
COUNTESS   It must be an answer of most monstrous
size that must fit all demands.
LAVATCH   But a trifle neither, in good faith, if the 33
learned should speak truth of it. Here it is, and all that
belongs to't. Ask me if I am a courtier. It shall do you
no harm to learn.

---

174 Traduced slandered   **175 Seared otherwise** branded in other ways as well.   **extended** stretched out on the rack; or, drawn out in time   **179–80 what . . . way** what common sense would regard as impossible, a higher sense (faith) can regard as possible.   **181–2 for . . . estimate** for everything that life can consider worthy the name of life is to be found and esteemed in you.   **rate** value   **184 That . . . call** that good fortune and the "springtime" of youth can call happy.   **185–6 Thou . . . desperate** The fact that you are prepared to hazard all this argues infinite skill or desperation.   **187 physic** medicine   **188 ministers** administers   **189 If . . . property** If I fail to meet my deadline or fall short in any respect   **191 Not helping** If I do not help   **193 make it even** carry it out.   **203 The premises observed** The conditions of the agreement having been fulfilled   **206 still** continually   **209 tended on** attended   **210 Unquestioned** (1) without being questioned (2) unquestionably

212 As high as word as fully as you have promised.   **meed** merit, worth.
2.2. Location: Rossillion.
1–2 put . . . breeding test your good manners.   **3–4 highly . . . taught** overfed and underdisciplined. ("Better fed than taught" was prover-bial for a spoiled child.)   **5–6 make you special** do you consider spe-cial   **6 put off** dismiss   **9 put it off** carry it off. (With a play on *put off* in line 6 and anticipating the meaning "doff" in line 10.)   **10 leg** respectful bow or curtsy   **17 pin** narrow, pointed.   **quatch** fat, wide.   **brawn** hefty, fleshy   **20 ten groats** forty pence   **21 French crown** (1) coin (2) *corona veneris,* a scab on the head symptomatic of syphilis, the "French disease."   **taffety punk** finely dressed prostitute
22 Tib's rush (Refers to a folk custom of exchanging rings made of reed in a marriage without benefit of clergy.)   **pancake** (Traditionally eaten as a last feast on the final day before Lent, Shrove Tuesday.)
23 morris morris dance, country dance common at May Day celebra-tions   **24 his** its.   **quean** wench   **26 pudding** sausage.   **his** its
33 But . . . neither On the contrary, it's only a trifle

COUNTESS   To be young again, if we could! I will be a
fool in question, hoping to be the wiser by your
answer. I pray you, sir, are you a courtier?

LAVATCH   Oh, Lord, sir!—There's a simple putting off. 40
More, more, a hundred of them.

COUNTESS   Sir, I am a poor friend of yours, that loves
you.

LAVATCH   Oh, Lord, sir!—Thick, thick, spare not me. 44

COUNTESS   I think, sir, you can eat none of this homely 45
meat. 46

LAVATCH   Oh, Lord, sir!—Nay, put me to't, I warrant you.

COUNTESS   You were lately whipped, sir, as I think.

LAVATCH   Oh, Lord, sir!—Spare not me.

COUNTESS   Do you cry, "Oh, Lord, sir!" at your whipping, and "spare not me"? Indeed your "Oh, Lord, sir!"
is very sequent to your whipping. You would answer 52
very well to a whipping, if you were but bound to't. 53

LAVATCH   I ne'er had worse luck in my life in my "Oh,
Lord, sir!" I see things may serve long, but not serve
ever.

COUNTESS
I play the noble huswife with the time,
To entertain it so merrily with a fool.

LAVATCH   Oh, Lord, sir!—Why, there't serves well again.

COUNTESS
An end, sir! To your business. Give Helen this,
                              [giving a letter]
And urge her to a present answer back. 61
Commend me to my kinsmen and my son. 62
This is not much.

LAVATCH   Not much commendation to them?

COUNTESS   Not much employment for you. You understand me?

LAVATCH   Most fruitfully. I am there before my legs. 67

COUNTESS   Haste you again.   Exeunt [separately]. 68

❧

[2.3]

Enter Count [Bertram], Lafew, and Parolles.

LAFEW   They say miracles are past, and we have our 1
philosophical persons to make modern and familiar 2
things supernatural and causeless. Hence is it that we 3
make trifles of terrors, ensconcing ourselves into seem- 4

ing knowledge when we should submit ourselves to
an unknown fear. 6

PAROLLES   Why, 'tis the rarest argument of wonder 7
that hath shot out in our latter times. 8

BERTRAM   And so 'tis.

LAFEW   To be relinquished of the artists— 10

PAROLLES   So I say, both of Galen and Paracelsus. 11

LAFEW   Of all the learned and authentic fellows— 12

PAROLLES   Right, so I say.

LAFEW   That gave him out incurable— 14

PAROLLES   Why, there 'tis; so say I too.

LAFEW   Not to be helped.

PAROLLES   Right! As 'twere a man assured of a—

LAFEW   Uncertain life and sure death.

PAROLLES   Just, you say well; so would I have said. 19

LAFEW   I may truly say it is a novelty to the world.

PAROLLES   It is, indeed. If you will have it in showing, 21
you shall read it in—what-do-ye-call there?
                    [*He points to a ballad in Lafew's hand.*]

LAFEW [*reading*]   "A showing of a heavenly effect in
an earthly actor."

PAROLLES   That's it, I would have said the very same.

LAFEW   Why, your dolphin is not lustier. 'Fore me, I 26
speak in respect— 27

PAROLLES   Nay, 'tis strange, 'tis very strange, that is the 28
brief and the tedious of it; and he's of a most faci- 29
norous spirit that will not acknowledge it to be the— 30

LAFEW   Very hand of heaven.

PAROLLES   Ay, so I say.

LAFEW   In a most weak—

PAROLLES   And debile minister, great power, great 34
transcendence, which should indeed give us a further
use to be made than alone the recovery of the King, as
to be—

LAFEW   Generally thankful. 38

*Enter King, Helena, and attendants. [The King
sits.]*

PAROLLES   I would have said it; you say well. Here
comes the King.

LAFEW   Lustig, as the Dutchman says. I'll like a maid 41
the better whilst I have a tooth in my head. Why, he's 42
able to lead her a coranto. 43

PAROLLES   *Mort du vinaigre!* Is not this Helen? 44

---

40 Oh, Lord, sir (A foppish phrase currently in vogue at court. Here it suggests, "I do indeed presume to be a courtier; isn't that plain enough from my appearance?") **putting off** evasion. **44 Thick** Quickly **45–6 homely meat** plain fare. **52 is very sequent to** is a pertinent response to (because it would be a plea for mercy) **52–3 answer . . . to** (1) reply cleverly to (2) serve as a suitable subject for **53 bound to't** (1) obliged to reply (2) tied up for it. **61 present** immediate **62 Commend me** Give my greetings **67 before my legs** (A comically absurd hyperbole suggesting incredible speed.) **68 again** back again.
2.3 Location: Paris. The royal court.
1 They . . . past (It was commonplace wisdom that the miracles described in the Bible and other early religious writings were some-how unique to an era long past.) **2–3 philsophical . . . causeless** scientists who can cause happenings that strike us as supernatural and inexplicable seem commonplace and familiar. (*Modern* means ordi-nary or commonplace.) **4 ensconcing** taking refuge, fortifying

6 unknown fear awe of the unknown. **7–8 'tis . . . times** it is the most remarkable demonstration of the extraordinary that has suddenly appeared in recent times. **10 relinquished . . . artists** abandoned by the physicians **11 Galen** Greek physician of the second century; the traditional authority. **Paracelsus** Swiss physician of the sixteenth century; the new and more radical authority. **12 authentic fellows** those properly licensed to practice **14 gave him out** proclaimed him **19 Just** Exactly **21 in showing** i.e., in print **26 dolphin** (A sportive and vigorous sea animal; with a pun perhaps on *dauphin*, "French crown prince.") **'Fore me** i.e., Upon my soul **27 in respect** intending no disrespect **28–9 the brief . . . it** i.e., the short and the long of it **29–30 facinorous** infamous, wicked **34 debile minister** weak agent **38 Generally** universally **41 Lustig** Lusty, sportive. **Dutchman** i.e., from any Germanic country **42 have a tooth** (With a play on the meaning "have a sweet tooth, a taste for the pleasures of the senses.") **43 coranto** lively dance. **44 *Mort du vinaigre!*** (An oath, perhaps referring to the vinegar offered by a a bystander to Christ to drink as he hung dying on the cross; see Matthew 27.48, Mark 15.36, and John, 19.29; literally, "death of vinegar.")

LAFEW   'Fore God, I think so.   45

KING
Go, call before me all the lords in court.
[*Exit one or more attendants.*]
Sit, my preserver, by thy patient's side,   [*She sits.*]
And with this healthful hand, whose banished sense   48
Thou hast repealed, a second time receive   49
The confirmation of my promised gift,
Which but attends thy naming.   51

Enter four Lords.

Fair maid, send forth thine eye. This youthful parcel   52
Of noble bachelors stand at my bestowing,   53
O'er whom both sovereign power and father's voice
I have to use. Thy frank election make;   55
Thou hast power to choose, and they none to forsake.   56

HELENA
To each of you one fair and virtuous mistress
Fall, when Love please! Marry, to each but one!   58

LAFEW [*aside*]
I'd give bay Curtal and his furniture   59
My mouth no more were broken than these boys',   60
And writ as little beard.

KING   Peruse them well.   61
Not one of those but had a noble father.

HELENA   Gentlemen,
Heaven hath through me restored the King to health.

ALL THE LORDS
We understand it, and thank heaven for you.

HELENA
I am a simple maid, and therein wealthiest
That I protest I simply am a maid.—   67
Please it Your Majesty, I have done already.
The blushes in my cheeks thus whisper me,
"We blush that thou shouldst choose; but, be refused,   70
Let the white death sit on thy cheek forever,   71
We'll ne'er come there again."

KING   Make choice and see.
Who shuns thy love shuns all his love in me.   73

HELENA
Now, Dian, from thy altar do I fly,   74
And to imperial Love, that god most high,   75
Do my sighs stream. (*She addresses her to a Lord.*) Sir,
will you hear my suit?

FIRST LORD
And grant it.

HELENA   Thanks, sir. All the rest is mute.   77

LAFEW [*aside*] I had rather be in this choice than
throw ambs-ace for my life.   79

HELENA [*to Second Lord*]
The honor, sir, that flames in your fair eyes
Before I speak too threateningly replies.
Love make your fortunes twenty times above   82
Her that so wishes, and her humble love!   83

SECOND LORD
No better, if you please.

HELENA   My wish receive,   84
Which great Love grant! And so I take my leave.

LAFEW [*aside*] Do all they deny her? An they were   86
sons of mine, I'd have them whipped, or I would
send them to the Turk to make eunuchs of.

HELENA [*to Third Lord*]
Be not afraid that I your hand should take;
I'll never do you wrong for your own sake.
Blessing upon your vows, and in your bed
Find fairer fortune, if you ever wed!

LAFEW [*aside*] These boys are boys of ice; they'll none
have her. Sure they are bastards to the English; the   94
French ne'er got 'em.   95

HELENA [*to Fourth Lord*]
You are too young, too happy, and too good   96
To make yourself a son out of my blood.

FOURTH LORD   Fair one, I think not so.

LAFEW [*aside*] There's one grape yet; I am sure thy father   99
drunk wine. But if thou be'st not an ass, I am a   100
youth of fourteen; I have known thee already.   101

HELENA [*to Bertram*]
I dare not say I take you, but I give
Me and my service, ever whilst I live,
Into your guiding power.—This is the man.

KING
Why, then, young Bertram, take her; she's thy wife.

BERTRAM
My wife, my liege? I shall beseech Your Highness,
In such a business give me leave to use
The help of mine own eyes.

KING   Know'st thou not, Bertram,
What she has done for me?

BERTRAM   Yes, my good lord,
But never hope to know why I should marry her.

KING
Thou know'st she has raised me from my sickly bed.

BERTRAM
But follows it, my lord, to bring me down   112

---

45 **I think so** i.e., I should say it is. (Lafew knows it is Helena.)
48 **banished sense** loss of feeling   49 **repealed** recalled (from death)
51 **attends** waits upon   52 **parcel** group   53 **stand . . . bestowing** i.e.,
are my wards, whom I may give in marriage   55 **frank election** free
choice   56 **forsake** refuse.   58 **Love** Cupid   59 **bay Curtal** my bay
horse, Curtal. (From the French *court*, short- or docked-tail.)   **furniture** trappings   60 **My . . . broken** i.e., (1) that I had lost no more
teeth (2) that I, like a young horse, were no more "broken to the bit"
61 **writ** i.e., and that I laid claim to. (Lafew wishes he were young
enough to be a suitor of Helena.)   67 **protest** avow   70 **be refused**
i.e., if you are refused   71 **the white death** i.e., death in its pallor
73 **Who** He who   74 **Dian** Diana, the goddess of chastity   75 **imperial Love** i.e., the god of love, Cupid   77 **All . . . mute** I have nothing
more to say to you.

79 **ambs-ace** two aces, the lowest possible throw in dice. (To throw
ambs-ace with one's life at stake is to risk all on a throw.)   82 **Love
make** May Love make   83 **Her . . . love** her that speaks this wish—
i.e., myself—and the humble love I deserve or can give.   84 **No better** i.e., I want nothing better than your humble love.   **My wish
receive** i.e., Take my *wish* for your fortunate marriage, rather than me
86 **Do . . . her?** (Lafew, unable to hear, misinterprets her passing from
one to another.)   **An** if   94 **Sure** Certainly.   **bastards to** illegitimate
children of   95 **got** begot   96 **happy** fortunate   99 **grape** i.e., scion
of a good family.   **thy** i.e., Bertram's.   100 **drunk wine** i.e., was red-
blooded.   101 **known** i.e., seen through   112 **bring me down** i.e.,
lower me to a socially inferior wife, to the (marriage) bed. (With sexual wordplay in *bring me down*, and *raising* in line 113.)

Must answer for your raising? I know her well;
She had her breeding at my father's charge. 114
A poor physician's daughter my wife? Disdain 115
Rather corrupt me ever! 116

KING

'Tis only title thou disdain'st in her, the which 117
I can build up. Strange is it that our bloods,
Of color, weight, and heat, poured all together,
Would quite confound distinction, yet stands off 120
In differences so mighty. If she be 121
All that is virtuous save what thou dislik'st—
A poor physician's daughter—thou dislik'st
Of virtue for the name. But do not so. 124
From lowest place when virtuous things proceed, 125
The place is dignified by th' doer's deed.
Where great additions swell's, and virtue none, 127
It is a dropsied honor. Good alone 128
Is good without a name; vileness is so; 129
The property by what it is should go, 130
Not by the title. She is young, wise, fair;
In these to nature she's immediate heir, 132
And these breed honor. That is honor's scorn 133
Which challenges itself as honor's born 134
And is not like the sire. Honors thrive 135
When rather from our acts we them derive
Than our foregoers. The mere word's a slave
Debauched on every tomb, on every grave 138
A lying trophy, and as oft is dumb 139
Where dust and damned oblivion is the tomb
Of honored bones indeed. What should be said? 141
If thou canst like this creature as a maid,
I can create the rest. Virtue and she 143
Is her own dower; honor and wealth from me. 144

BERTRAM

I cannot love her, nor will strive to do't.

KING

Thou wrong'st thyself, if thou shouldst strive to
choose. 146

HELENA

That you are well restored, my lord, I'm glad.
Let the rest go.

KING

My honor's at the stake, which to defeat, 149
I must produce my power. Here, take her hand,

Proud, scornful boy, unworthy this good gift,
That dost in vile misprision shackle up 152
My love and her desert; that canst not dream, 153
We, poising us in her defective scale, 154
Shall weigh thee to the beam; that wilt not know 155
It is in us to plant thine honor where 156
We please to have it grow. Check thy contempt; 157
Obey our will, which travails in thy good; 158
Believe not thy disdain, but presently 159
Do thine own fortunes that obedient right 160
Which both thy duty owes and our power claims,
Or I will throw thee from my care forever
Into the staggers and the careless lapse 163
Of youth and ignorance, both my revenge and hate
Loosing upon thee in the name of justice 165
Without all terms of pity. Speak; thine answer. 166

BERTRAM

Pardon, my gracious lord, for I submit
My fancy to your eyes. When I consider 168
What great creation and what dole of honor 169
Flies where you bid it, I find that she, which late 170
Was in my nobler thoughts most base, is now
The praisèd of the King, who, so ennobled,
Is as 'twere born so.

KING   Take her by the hand,
And tell her she is thine, to whom I promise
A counterpoise, if not to thy estate, 175
A balance more replete.

BERTRAM   I take her hand. 176

KING

Good fortune and the favor of the King
Smile upon this contract, whose ceremony 178
Shall seem expedient on the now-born brief 179
And be performed tonight. The solemn feast 180
Shall more attend upon the coming space, 181
Expecting absent friends. As thou lov'st her, 182
Thy love's to me religious; else, does err. 183

Exeunt. Parolles and Lafew stay behind,
commenting of this wedding.

114 charge cost.   115–16 Disdain . . . ever! i.e., Rather let my disdain for thy ruin me forever in your favor! (With unintentional irony; disdain does indeed corrupt Bertram.)   117 title i.e., her lack of title   120–1 Would . . . mighty (blood) is indistinguishable from one person to the next, yet is made the basis of such mighty differences in rank.   124 name i.e., lack of a name (title).   125 proceed emanate   127 great . . . swell's pompous titles puff us up   128 dropsied unhealthily swollen   128–9 Good . . . so What is in itself good is so without a title; the same is true of vileness   130 property quality.   go i.e., be judged, be valued.   132 In . . . heir in these qualities she inherits directly from nature   133–5 That . . . sire True honor is scornful of any claim to honor based only on birth that is not validated by behavior worthy of one's heritage.   138 Debauched corrupted   139 trophy memorial. dumb silent   141 honored bones indeed i.e., the remains of those who were genuinely honorable.   143–4 Virtue . . . dower i.e., Her marriage gift to you will be her virtue and herself   146 strive to choose try to assert your own choice.   149 which i.e., which threat to my honor

152–5 That . . . beam you who with base mistaking fetter both my love and her worth; you who cannot imagine how I, adding my royal weight to her deficiency in order to counterbalance your wealth and position, will equalize the cross-beam of the balance scales. (We is the royal plural, continued in lines 157–8.)   156 in us within my royal power   157 Check Curb, restrain   158 travails in labors for   159 Believe not do not place faith in or obey.   presently at once   160 obedient right right of obedience   163 staggers giddy decline. (Literally, a horse disease.)   careless lapse irresponsible fall   165 Loosing turning loose   166 all . . . pity pity in any form.   168 fancy desires   169 great creation creating of greatness.   dole share, doing out   170 which late who lately   175–6 A counterpoise . . . replete i.e., an equal weight of wealth as dowry, if not an amount even exceeding your estate.   178–9 whose . . . brief whose performing ceremoniously will seem appropriate to the present statement of contract. (Brief suggests both "short" and "expeditious." The King specifies a marriage contract rather than a full wedding ceremony.)   180–2 The solemn . . . friends The full festival of celebration must be delayed for a time until absent friends and relatives can arrive. (Following the formal betrothal just completed onstage, there is to be a wedding tonight and a celebratory feast later on when all can gather.)   182–3 As . . . err So long as you love her truly, I will regard your love for me as holy and true; otherwise, regarding your obligations to me you are a heretic and a traitor.   183.2 of on

LAFEW   Do you hear, monsieur? A word with you.

PAROLLES   Your pleasure, sir?

LAFEW   Your lord and master did well to make his recantation.

PAROLLES   Recantation? My lord? My master?

LAFEW   Ay. Is it not a language I speak?

PAROLLES   A most harsh one, and not to be understood without bloody succeeding. My master?   191

LAFEW   Are you companion to the Count Rossillion?   192

PAROLLES   To any count, to all counts, to what is man.   193

LAFEW   To what is count's man. Count's master is of another style.   194 / 195

PAROLLES   You are too old, sir; let it satisfy you, you are too old.   196

LAFEW   I must tell thee, sirrah, I write man, to which title age cannot bring thee.   198

PAROLLES   What I dare too well do, I dare not do.   200

LAFEW   I did think thee, for two ordinaries, to be a pretty wise fellow; thou didst make tolerable vent of thy travel; it might pass. Yet the scarves and the bannerets about thee did manifoldly dissuade me from believing thee a vessel of too great a burden. I have now found thee. When I lose thee again, I care not; yet art thou good for nothing but taking up, and that thou'rt scarce worth.   201–207

PAROLLES   Hadst thou not the privilege of antiquity upon thee—

LAFEW   Do not plunge thyself too far in anger, lest thou hasten thy trial; which if—Lord have mercy on thee for a hen! So, my good window of lattice, fare thee well. Thy casement I need not open, for I look through thee. Give me thy hand.   212 / 213 / 214

PAROLLES   My lord, you give me most egregious indignity.   216

LAFEW   Ay, with all my heart, and thou art worthy of it.

PAROLLES   I have not, my lord, deserved it.

LAFEW   Yes, good faith, every dram of it, and I will not bate thee a scruple.   220 / 221

PAROLLES   Well, I shall be wiser.   222

LAFEW   Even as soon as thou canst, for thou hast to pull at a smack o'th' contrary. If ever thou be'st bound in thy scarf and beaten, thou shall find what it is to be proud of thy bondage. I have a desire to hold my acquaintance with thee, or rather my knowledge, that I may say in the default, "He is a man I know."   223 / 224 / 225 / 226 / 228

PAROLLES   My lord, you do me most insupportable vexation.

LAFEW   I would it were hell-pains for thy sake, and my poor doing eternal; for doing I am past, as I will by thee, in what motion age will give me leave.   *Exit.*   231 / 232 / 233

PAROLLES   Well, thou hast a son shall take this disgrace off me—scurvy, old, filthy, scurvy lord! Well, I must be patient; there is no fettering of authority. I'll beat him, by my life, if I can meet him with any convenience, an he were double and double a lord. I'll have no more pity of his age than I would have of—I'll beat him, an if I could but meet him again.   234 / 235 / 236 / 237 / 238 / 240

Enter Lafew.

LAFEW   Sirrah, your lord and master's married; there's news for you. You have a new mistress.

PAROLLES   I most unfeignedly beseech Your Lordship to make some reservation of your wrongs. He is my good lord; whom I serve above is my master.   244 / 245

LAFEW   Who? God?

PAROLLES   Ay, sir.

LAFEW   The devil it is that's thy master. Why dost thou garter up thy arms o' this fashion? Dost make hose of thy sleeves? Do other servants so? Thou wert best set thy lower part where thy nose stands. By mine honor, if I were but two hours younger, I'd beat thee. Methink'st thou art a general offense, and every man   248 / 249 / 250 / 251

191 **bloody succeeding** outcome with bloodshed, attendant on change of faith. (Sustaining the language of religion and treachery from lines 182–3.)   192 **companion** (1) comrade (2) rascally knave   193 **what is man** i.e., any true man; or, what is manly.   194–5 **Count's . . . style** i.e., "Man" and "master" are worlds apart, and you belong to the first.   196 **too old** i.e., for me to duel with.   **let . . . you** i.e., take that as a satisfaction instead of a duel   198 **write man** i.e., account myself a man, lay claim to that title   200 **What . . . not do** i.e., What I could too easily accomplish—thrash you—I must not do because of your age.   201 **for two ordinaries** during the space of two meals   202 **didst . . . of** discoursed tolerably upon   203–4 **scarves, bannerets** i.e., soldiers' scarves, reminding Lafew of a ship's pennants   205 **burden** cargo, capacity.   206 **found** found out. (With a play on the antithesis of "find" and "lose.")   207 **yet . . . taking up** you are like a commodity one *takes up* in the sense of taking a loan at exorbitant rates of interest and being paid in shoddy goods not worth the amount borrowed   212 **thy trial** i.e., the testing of your supposed valor   213 **hen** i.e., cackling, cowardly female.   **window of lattice** wooden frame with cross-hatched slats (instead of glass), often painted red and used as the sign of an alehouse; something easily seen through and common, disreputable   214 **casement** window sash   216 **give** offer. (But Lafew mockingly replies as though he were indeed making a valuable gift. He plays with *deserved* the same way in lines 220–1: "Oh, you *deserved* it, all right.")   **egregious** outrageous, flagrant   220 **dram** bit. (Literally, one-eighth of an ounce.)   221 **bate** abate, remit.   **scruple** smallest bit. (Literally, one-third of a dram.)

222 **wiser** i.e., wiser than to deal with such dotards in the future. (But Lafew jestingly answers that Parolles indeed has to learn to be wise, i.e., less foolish.)   223–4 **for . . . contrary** i.e., because it's necessary for you to have a taste of your own folly before you can be called self-knowing and wise.   224–5 **If . . . beaten** i.e., If even you are subjected to one of the greatest indignities an officer can suffer, to be tied up in the scarves you festoon yourself with and thrashed as a poltroon. (See note 248–50 below.)   226 **bondage** i.e., the scarf, in which you would be bound and of which you are now vainly proud.   **hold** continue   228 **in the default** when you default, i.e., show your emptiness on being brought to trial   231–2 **my poor doing** i.e., my inadequate power to teach you a lesson   232 **for doing** for energetic activity. (With a sexual suggestion.)   232–3 **will by thee** i.e., will pass by you. (Punning on *past*, "passed.")   233 **in . . . leave** with whatever speed age will allow me.   234–5 **shall . . . me** i.e., on whom I will vindicate myself for these insults. (Parolles, pretending to be unwilling to fight Lafew because of the latter's older years, asserts that only a son of Lafew would be a fit opponent for Parolles in a duel.)   236 **there . . . authority** there's no use trying to bring a figure of authority like Lafew to account.   237–8 **with any convenience** on a suitable occasion   238 **an** even if   240 **an if** if   244 **make . . . wrongs** put some restraint upon your insults, qualify the insults you've given me.   245 **good lord** i.e., patron (not master, as Lafew has insultingly said.)   **whom** i.e., he whom (God)   248–50 **Why . . . sleeves?** (Parolles apparently has decorative scarves tied around the sleeves of his outfit. Lafew acidly points out that the *hose* or breeches would be a fitter place for such decorations in Parolles's case.)   249 **o'** of, in   250–1 **Thou . . . stands** i.e., Mixing up sleeves and breeches is turning things upside down, as if your ass were where your nose is. (With a scatological suggestion of smelling one's own excrement.)

should beat thee. I think thou wast created for men to
breathe themselves upon thee.   255

PAROLLES   This is hard and undeserved measure, my
lord.

LAFEW   Go to, sir. You were beaten in Italy for picking   258
a kernel out of a pomegranate. You are a vagabond   259
and no true traveler. You are more saucy with lords   260
and honorable personages than the commission of   261
your birth and virtue gives you heraldry. You are not   262
worth another word, else I'd call you knave. I leave
you.   *Exit.*

PAROLLES   Good, very good! It is so, then. Good, very
good. Let it be concealed awhile.

Enter [Bertram] Count Rossillion.

BERTRAM   Undone, and forfeited to cares forever!

PAROLLES   What's the matter, sweetheart?

BERTRAM   Although before the solemn priest I have
sworn, I will not bed her.

PAROLLES   What, what, sweetheart?

BERTRAM
Oh, my Parolles, they have married me!
I'll to the Tuscan wars, and never bed her.

PAROLLES   France is a dog-hole, and it no more merits
the tread of a man's foot. To th' wars!

BERTRAM   There's letters from my mother. What th'im-   276
port is I know not yet.

PAROLLES   Ay, that would be known. To th' wars, my
boy, to th' wars!
He wears his honor in a box unseen
That hugs his kicky-wicky here at home,   281
Spending his manly marrow in her arms,   282
Which should sustain the bound and high curvet   283
Of Mars's fiery steed. To other regions!
France is a stable, we that dwell in't jades.   285
Therefore, to th' war!

BERTRAM
It shall be so. I'll send her to my house,
Acquaint my mother with my hate to her
And wherefore I am fled, write to the King
That which I durst not speak. His present gift
Shall furnish me to those Italian fields   291
Where noble fellows strike. Wars is no strife
To the dark house and the detested wife.   293

PAROLLES
Will this capriccio hold in thee? Art sure?   294

BERTRAM
Go with me to my chamber and advise me.

I'll send her straight away. Tomorrow   296
I'll to the wars, she to her single sorrow.

PAROLLES
Why, these balls bound; there's noise in it. 'Tis hard! 298
A young man married is a man that's marred.
Therefore away, and leave her bravely. Go.
The King has done you wrong, but hush, 'tis so.
                                                   Exeunt.

[2.4]

Enter Helena [with a letter], and Clown [Lavatch].

HELENA
My mother greets me kindly. Is she well?

LAVATCH   She is not well, but yet she has her health.   2
She's very merry, but yet she is not well. But thanks
be given, she's very well and wants nothing i'th'
world; but yet she is not well.

HELENA   If she be very well, what does she ail that she's
not very well?

LAVATCH   Truly, she's very well indeed, but for two
things.

HELENA   What two things?

LAVATCH   One, that she's not in heaven, whither God
send her quickly. The other, that she's in earth, from
whence God send her quickly.

Enter Parolles.

PAROLLES   Bless you, my fortunate lady!

HELENA   I hope, sir, I have your good will to have mine   15
own good fortunes.   16

PAROLLES   You had my prayers to lead them on, and to   17
keep them on have them still.—Oh, my knave, how   18
does my old lady?

LAVATCH   So that you had her wrinkles and I her   20
money, I would she did as you say.   21

PAROLLES   Why, I say nothing.

LAVATCH   Marry, you are the wiser man, for many a
man's tongue shakes out his master's undoing. To say   24
nothing, to do nothing, to know nothing, and to have
nothing is to be a great part of your title, which is   26
within a very little of nothing.

PAROLLES   Away! Thou'rt a knave.

255 **breathe** exercise   258–9 **for . . . pomegranate** i.e., for some petty
offense, or, on a slight pretext.   259 **vagabond** (A word used by the
authorities to describe actors—thus inviting sympathy for Parolles, a
play-actor to the core, whose business, like theirs, is words.)
260 **saucy** unbecomingly familiar   261 **commission** warrant
262 **gives you heraldry** entitles you to be.   276 **letters** i.e., a letter
281 **kicky-wicky** woman. (With sexual suggestion as also in *box* in the
previous line and *Spending* and *marrow* in the following line.)
282 **manly marrow** masculine essence, semen   283 **curvet** leap
285 **jades** worn-out horses.   291 **furnish me** (Knights customarily
provided themselves with trappings and armed retainers when
enlisting in warlike enterprises.)   293 **To . . . house** i.e., compared to
the madhouse (of marriage)   294 **capriccio** caprice, whim

296 **straight** at once   298 **Why . . . hard!** i.e., Now you're talking;
that's the way! (*Balls* here are tennis balls.)
2.4. Location: Paris. The royal court.
2 **not well** (Referring to the Elizabethan euphemism by which the
dead were spoken of as "well," i.e., well rid of this life and well off in
heaven.)   15–16 **I hope . . . fortunes** I hope my good fortunes need
not depend on your good wishes, if you don't mind my saying so.
17 **them** i.e., your good fortunes. (A plural concept.)   17–18 **to . . .
still** to maintain your good fortune, you have my prayers continually.
20–1 **So . . . say** Provided you were old (and wise), like her, and I had
her wealth, I'd be happy to have her follow your advice.   24 **man's**
servant's.   **shakes out** i.e., brings about by talking too freely
26 **your title** i.e., your reputation for being all bluster and no substance. (With wordplay on *title/tittle,* any tiny amount.)

LAVATCH   You should have said, sir, "Before a knave 29
thou'rt a knave"; that's, "Before me thou'rt a knave." 30
This had been truth, sir.

PAROLLES   Go to, thou art a witty fool. I have found 32
thee. 33

LAVATCH   Did you find me in yourself, sir? Or were 34
you taught to find me? The search, sir, was profitable;
and much fool may you find in you, even to the
world's pleasure and the increase of laughter.

PAROLLES
A good knave, i'faith, and well fed.— 38
Madam, my lord will go away tonight;
A very serious business calls on him.
The great prerogative and rite of love,
Which, as your due time claims, he does
    acknowledge, 42
But puts if off to a compelled restraint, 43
Whose want and whose delays is strewed with
    sweets, 44
Which they distill now in the curbèd time, 45
To make the coming hour o'erflow with joy
And pleasure drown the brim.

HELENA   What's his will else? 47

PAROLLES
That you will take your instant leave o'th' King
And make this haste as your own good proceeding, 49
Strengthened with what apology you think
May make it probable need.

HELENA   What more commands he? 51

PAROLLES
That, having this obtained, you presently
Attend his further pleasure. 53

HELENA
In every thing I wait upon his will.

PAROLLES   I shall report it so.

HELENA   I pray you.   Exit Parolles.
[To Lavatch]   Come, sirrah.   Exeunt.

❧

[2.5]

Enter Lafew and Bertram.

LAFEW   But I hope Your Lordship thinks not him a
soldier.

BERTRAM   Yes, my lord, and of very valiant approof. 3

LAFEW   You have it from his own deliverance. 4

BERTRAM   And by other warranted testimony.

LAFEW   Then my dial goes not true. I took this lark for 6
a bunting. 7

BERTRAM   I do assure you, my lord, he is very great in
knowledge, and accordingly valiant. 9

LAFEW   I have then sinned against his experience and
transgressed against his valor; and my state that way 11
is dangerous, since I cannot yet find in my heart to 12
repent. Here he comes. I pray you, make us friends; I
will pursue the amity.

Enter Parolles.

PAROLLES   [*to Bertram*]   These things shall be done, sir.

LAFEW   [*to Bertram*]   Pray you, sir, who's his tailor? 16

PAROLLES   Sir?

LAFEW   Oh, I know him well. Ay, sir, he, sir, 's a good 18
workman, a very good tailor. 19

BERTRAM   [*aside to Parolles*]   Is she gone to the King?

PAROLLES   She is.

BERTRAM   Will she away tonight?

PAROLLES   As you'll have her.

BERTRAM
I have writ my letters, casketed my treasure,
Given order for our horses; and tonight,
When I should take possession of the bride,
End ere I do begin.

LAFEW   A good traveler is something at the latter end of 28
a dinner; but one that lies three thirds, and uses a 29
known truth to pass a thousand nothings with, should
be once heard and thrice beaten. God save you, Captain.

BERTRAM   [*to Parolles*]   Is there any unkindness between 33
my lord and you, monsieur?

PAROLLES   I know not how I have deserved to run into
my lord's displeasure.

LAFEW   You have made shift to run into't, boots and 37
spurs and all, like him that leapt into the custard; and 38
out of it you'll run again, rather than suffer question 39
for your residence. 40

BERTRAM   It may be you have mistaken him, my lord. 41

LAFEW   And shall do so ever, though I took him at 's
prayers. Fare you well, my lord, and believe this of

---

29 **Before** In presence of   30 **Before me** i.e., Upon my soul. (But, by substituting *me* for *knave*, Lavatch suggests that Parolles call himself a knave.)   32–3 **found thee** found you out, found you to be a fool.   34 **Did . . . sir?** i.e., Did you find folly in yourself, sir? (Since I, Lavatch, am a fool.)   38 **well fed** (Referring to the proverb "better fed than taught," as at 2.2.3.)   42 **Which . . . acknowledge** he does acknowledge as your due, in the fullness of time, the rite and privi-lege of sexual consummation   43 **to** owing to   44 **Whose . . . sweets** the desire for which, being delayed, is made all the sweeter by wait-ing, like perfume made sweeter by distillation. (*Sweets* are sweet-smelling flowers.)   45 **Which . . . time** which sweet-smelling flowers of desire and delay distill their essence into this period of restraint   47 **drown** overflow.   **else** besides.   49 **make** represent.   **proceeding** course of action   51 **probable need** a plausible necessity.   53 **Attend** await.   **pleasure** command.
2.5. Location: Paris. The royal court.
3 **valiant approof** proven valor.

4 **deliverance** testimony, word.   6 **dial** clock, compass, i.e., judgment   6–7 **I . . . bunting** i.e., I underestimated him. (The bunting resembles the lark but lacks the lark's beautiful song. Lafew suggests that Parolles is all show and no substance. Compare 1.2.18, where, in the Folio, Bertram is called Count *Rosignoll*, nightingale.)   9 **accordingly** correspondingly   11 **my state** i.e., the state of my soul. (Lafew uses an elaborate metaphor of religious penitence ironically.)   12 **find in** find it in   16 **who's his tailor?** i.e., what tailor made this stuffed (bombast) figure? (Lafew says this to Bertram but is taunting Parolles, who replies indignantly.)   18–19 **Oh . . . tailor** (Lafew mockingly takes Parolles's *Sir* in line 17 as the name of his tailor.)   28–9 **A good . . . dinner** i.e., A person with many traveling experiences is an asset as a storyteller after dinner   29 **three thirds** i.e., all the time   33 **unkindness** ill will   37 **made shift** contrived (at our previous meeting)   38 **like . . . custard** i.e., like a clown at a city entertainment jumping into a large, deep custard   39 **you'll run** you will want to run   39–40 **suffer . . . residence** undergo questioning about your being there, i.e., explain how your cowardice displeased me.   41 **mistaken him** misjudged him. (But Lafew deliberately takes the phrase in the sense of "taken exception to his behavior.")

me: there can be no kernel in this light nut. The soul
of this man is his clothes. Trust him not in matter of
heavy consequence. I have kept of them tame, and   46
know their natures.—Farewell, monsieur. I have
spoken better of you than you have or will to deserve 48
at my hand; but we must do good against evil.

              [Exit.]

PAROLLES An idle lord, I swear.   50
BERTRAM I think so.   51
PAROLLES Why, do you not know him?
BERTRAM
Yes, I do know him well, and common speech
Gives him a worthy pass. Here comes my clog. 54

     Enter Helena.

HELENA
I have, sir, as I was commanded from you,
Spoke with the King, and have procured his leave
For present parting; only he desires
Some private speech with you.
BERTRAM   I shall obey his will.
You must not marvel, Helen, at my course,
Which holds not color with the time, nor does 60
The ministration and requirèd office   61
On my particular. Prepared I was not   62
For such a business; therefore am I found
So much unsettled. This drives me to entreat you
That presently you take your way for home;
And rather muse than ask why I entreat you, 66
For my respects are better than they seem,   67
And my appointments have in them a need   68
Greater than shows itself at the first view
To you that know them not. This to my mother.

         [He gives a letter.]

'Twill be two days ere I shall see you, so
I leave you to your wisdom.
HELENA   Sir, I can nothing say 72
But that I am your most obedient servant.
BERTRAM
Come, come, no more of that.
HELENA   And ever shall
With true observance seek to eke out that   75
Wherein toward me my homely stars have failed 76
To equal my great fortune.
BERTRAM   Let that go.
My haste is very great. Farewell. Hie home. 78

         [He starts to go.]

HELENA
 Pray, sir, your pardon.
BERTRAM   Well, what would you say?
HELENA
I am not worthy of the wealth I owe,   80
Nor dare I say 'tis mine, and yet it is;
But, like a timorous thief, most fain would steal 82
What law does vouch mine own.
BERTRAM   What would you have? 83
HELENA
Something, and scarce so much; nothing, indeed.
I would not tell you what I would, my lord. Faith,
  yes—
Strangers and foes do sunder, and not kiss. 86
BERTRAM
I pray you, stay not, but in haste to horse.   87
HELENA
I shall not break your bidding, good my lord.
BERTRAM *[to Parolles]*
Where are my other men, monsieur?—Farewell.

          Exit [Helena.]

Go thou toward home, where I will never come
Whilst I can shake my sword or hear the drum.
Away, and for our flight.
PAROLLES   Bravely, *coraggio!* *[Exeunt.]* 92

       ❖

3.1

 Flourish. Enter the Duke of Florence [attended];
 the two Frenchmen, with a troop of soldiers.

DUKE
So that from point to point now have you heard
The fundamental reasons of this war,
Whose great decision hath much blood let forth, 3
And more thirsts after.
FIRST LORD   Holy seems the quarrel. 4
Upon Your Grace's part, black and fearful
On the opposer.   6
DUKE
Therefore we marvel much our cousin France 7
Would in so just a business shut his bosom
Against our borrowing prayers.
SECOND LORD   Good my lord, 9
The reasons of our state I cannot yield   10
But like a common and an outward man   11
That the great figure of a council frames   12
By self-unable motion, therefore dare not 13

---

46 heavy serious. **I . . . tame** I have kept tame creatures of this kind
(for the amusement they provide) **48 have . . . deserve** have
deserved or are likely to deserve **50 idle** foolish **51 I think so** i.e., I
suppose you're right. (Parolles emphasizes *know* in the next line to
contrast with *think*.) **54 pass** reputation. **clog** a heavy weight
attached to the leg or neck of a man or animal to prevent freedom of
movement. **60–2 Which . . . particular** which does not appear to suit
with the occasion (of our marriage), nor does it fulfill what is incumbent upon me as a husband. **66 muse** wonder **67 my respects** the
circumstances prompting me **68 appointments** purposes **72 to
your wisdom** to do what you think best. **75 observance** dutiful and
reverential service. **eke out** add to **76 homely stars** i.e., lowly origin **78 Hie** Hasten

80 owe own **82 fain** gladly **83 vouch** affirm to be **86 Strangers . . .
kiss** i.e, Only strangers and enemies depart from one another without
a farewell kiss. **87 stay** delay **92** *coraggio!* courage, bravo!
3.1. Location: Florence.
3–4 Whose . . . after the violent deciding of which has led to much
shedding of blood and a thirsting after still more. **6 the opposer** the
opposer's part. **7 cousin** i.e., fellow sovereign **9 borrowing
prayers** prayers for assistance. **10–13 The reasons . . . motion** I cannot explain to you the rationale of our statecraft other than as an ordinary citizen, not being privy to the workings of the state; I am one
who constructs in his own imagination an imperfect idea of whatever
grand schemes the King and his counsel may be devising

Say what I think of it, since I have found
Myself in my incertain grounds to fail
As often as I guessed.

DUKE   Be it his pleasure.   16

FIRST LORD
But I am sure the younger of our nature,   17
That surfeit on their ease, will day by day   18
Come here for physic.

DUKE   Welcome shall they be,   19
And all the honors that can fly from us   20
Shall on them settle. You know your places well;
When better fall, for your avails they fell.   22
Tomorrow to the field.   *Flourish. [Exeunt.]*

❖

[3.2]

Enter Countess and Clown [Lavatch].

COUNTESS   It hath happened all as I would have had it,
save that he comes not along with her.

LAVATCH   By my troth, I take my young lord to be a   3
very melancholy man.

COUNTESS   By what observance, I pray you?   5

LAVATCH   Why, he will look upon his boot and sing,
mend the ruff and sing, ask questions and sing, pick   7
his teeth and sing. I know a man that had this trick of   8
melancholy sold a goodly manor for a song.   9

COUNTESS   Let me see what he writes and when he
means to come.   *[Opening a letter.]*

LAVATCH   I have no mind to Isbel since I was at court.
Our old lings and our Isbels o'th' country are nothing   13
like your old ling and your Isbels o'th' court. The
brains of my Cupid's knocked out, and I begin to love
as an old man loves money, with no stomach.   16

COUNTESS   What have we here?

LAVATCH   E'en that you have there.   *Exit.*   18

COUNTESS *[reads] a letter.*   "I have sent you a daughter-
in-law. She hath recovered the King and undone me.   20
I have wedded her, not bedded her, and sworn to
make the 'not' eternal. You shall hear I am run away;   22
know it before the report come. If there be breadth
enough in the world, I will hold a long distance. My   24
duty to you.

Your unfortunate son,
Bertram."

This is not well, rash and unbridled boy,
To fly the favors of so good a king,

To pluck his indignation on thy head   30
By the misprizing of a maid too virtuous   31
For the contempt of empire.   32

Enter Clown [Lavatch].

LAVATCH   O madam, yonder is heavy news within   33
between two soldiers and my young lady!

COUNTESS   What is the matter?

LAVATCH   Nay, there is some comfort in the news,
some comfort. Your son will not be killed so soon as I
thought he would.

COUNTESS   Why should he be killed?

LAVATCH   So say I, madam, if he run away, as I hear he
does. The danger is in standing to't; that's the loss of   41
men, though it be the getting of children. Here they   42
come will tell you more. For my part, I only hear your
son was run away.   *[Exit.]*   44

*Enter Helena and [the] two [French] Gentlemen
[or Lords].*

SECOND LORD   Save you, good madam.

HELENA
Madam, my lord is gone, forever gone!

FIRST LORD   Do not say so.

COUNTESS
Think upon patience.—Pray you, gentlemen,
I have felt so many quirks of joy and grief
That the first face of neither, on the start,   50
Can woman me unto't. Where is my son, I pray you?   51

FIRST LORD
Madam, he's gone to serve the Duke of Florence.
We met him thitherward; for thence we came,   53
And, after some dispatch in hand at court,   54
Thither we bend again.   55

HELENA
Look on his letter, madam; here's my passport.   56
[She reads.] "When thou canst get the ring upon my
finger, which never shall come off, and show me a
child begotten of thy body that I am father to, then call
me husband; but in such a 'then' I write a 'never.' "
This is a dreadful sentence.   61

COUNTESS
Brought you this letter, gentlemen?

FIRST LORD   Ay, madam,
And for the contents' sake are sorry for our pains.

COUNTESS
I prithee, lady, have a better cheer.

---

16 Be . . . pleasure i.e., Be it as the King of France wishes.   **17 nature**
outlook, disposition   **18 surfeit** grow sick   **19 physic** i.e., cure of
their surfeit (through bloodletting).   **20 can fly from us** i.e., we can
grant   **22 When . . . fell** whenever better places fall vacant, they will
have done so for you to fill.
3.2. Location: Rossillion.
3 troth faith   **5 observance** observation   **7 mend the ruff** adjust the
loose turned-over flap at the top of his boot or his frilled collar
7–8 pick his teeth (An affected mannerism, as at 1.1.159.)   **9 sold**
who sold   **13 lings** cunts. Lavatch is saying that all women, both old
("old lings") and young ("Isbels"), are much better at the court than
in the country.   **16 stomach** appetite.   **18 E'en . . . there** (The Clown
is playfully literal: to the Countess's "What's this?" he replies, "It
looks like a letter.")   **20 recovered** cured   **22 not** (With a pun on
"knot.")   **24 hold a long distance** stay far away.

30 pluck bring down   **31 misprizing** scorning, failing to appreciate
32 of empire of even an emperor.   **33 heavy** sad   **41 standing to't**
standing one's ground. (With sexual pun. The Clown jests on running
from a battle and running from a woman; in both cases, a soldier can
avoid the *danger* of dying; with its suggestion of sexual climax.)
42 getting begetting   **44 was** has   **50–1 That . . . unto't** i.e., that neither
joy nor grief, no matter how suddenly either appears, can make me
weep as women are supposed to do.   **53 thitherward** on his way there
54 dispatch in hand business to be taken care of   **55 Thither . . .**
again to Florence we will direct our steps.   **56 passport** license to
wander as a beggar.   **61 sentence** (1) sentence of punishment
(2) statement, utterance.

If thou engrossest all the griefs are thine,   65
Thou robb'st me of a moi'ty. He was my son,   66
But I do wash his name out of my blood,
And thou art all my child.—Towards Florence is he?   68

FIRST LORD
    Ay, madam.

COUNTESS   And to be a soldier?

FIRST LORD
    Such is his noble purpose; and, believe't,
The Duke will lay upon him all the honor
That good convenience claims.

COUNTESS   Return you thither?   72

SECOND LORD
    Ay, madam, with the swiftest wing of speed.

HELENA [reading]
    "Till I have no wife, I have nothing in France."
'Tis bitter.

COUNTESS   Find you that there?

HELENA   Ay, madam.

SECOND LORD
    'Tis but the boldness of his hand, haply,   76
Which his heart was not consenting to.

COUNTESS
    Nothing in France, until he have no wife!
There's nothing here that is too good for him
But only she, and she deserves a lord
That twenty such rude boys might tend upon
And call her, hourly, mistress. Who was with him?

SECOND LORD
    A servant only, and a gentleman
Which I have sometime known.

COUNTESS   Parolles, was it not?

SECOND LORD   Ay, my good lady, he.

COUNTESS
    A very tainted fellow, and full of wickedness.
My son corrupts a well-derivèd nature   88
With his inducement.

SECOND LORD   Indeed, good lady,   89
The fellow has a deal of that too much   90
Which holds him much to have.   91

COUNTESS   You're welcome, gentlemen.
I will entreat you, when you see my son,
To tell him that his sword can never win
The honor that he loses. More I'll entreat you
Written to bear along.

FIRST LORD   We serve you, madam,   96
In that and all your worthiest affairs.

COUNTESS
    Not so, but as we change our courtesies.   98
Will you draw near?   Exit [with Gentlemen].   99

HELENA
    "Till I have no wife, I have nothing in France."
Nothing in France, until he has no wife!
Thou shalt have none, Rossillion, none in France;   102
Then hast thou all again. Poor lord, is't I
That chase thee from thy country and expose
Those tender limbs of thine to the event   105
Of the none-sparing war? And is it I
That drive thee from the sportive court, where thou   107
Wast shot at with fair eyes, to be the mark   108
Of smoky muskets? O you leaden messengers,   109
That ride upon the violent speed of fire,
Fly with false aim; move the still-piecing air,   111
That sings with piercing; do not touch my lord!   112
Whoever shoots at him, I set him there;
Whoever charges on his forward breast,   114
I am the caitiff that do hold him to't;   115
And, though I kill him not, I am the cause
His death was so effected. Better 'twere
I met the ravin lion when he roared   118
With sharp constraint of hunger; better 'twere
That all the miseries which nature owes   120
Were mine at once. No, come thou home, Rossillion,
Whence honor but of danger wins a scar,   122
As oft it loses all. I will be gone.   123
My being here it is that holds thee hence.
Shall I stay here to do't? No, no, although   125
The air of paradise did fan the house
And angels officed all. I will be gone,   127
That pitiful rumor may report my flight   128
To consolate thine ear. Come, night; end, day!   129
For with the dark, poor thief, I'll steal away.   Exit.   130

❧

[3.3]

*Flourish. Enter the Duke of Florence, [Bertram,
Count] Rossillion, drum and trumpets, soldiers,
Parolles.*

DUKE
    The General of our Horse thou art, and we,
Great in our hope, lay our best love and credence   2
Upon thy promising fortune.

BERTRAM   Sir, it is
A charge too heavy for my strength, but yet

65–6 If thou . . . moi'ty If you refuse to share your griefs, you rob me
of my right to half of them (in that Bertram is my son).   **68 all my** my
only   **72 That . . . claims** that he can in propriety claim.   **76 haply**
perhaps   **88–9 My . . . inducement** My son corrupts the fine qualities
he inherited from his ancestors, owing to Parolles's corrupt influence.
90–1 The fellow . . . have The fellow has a great supply of that
"excess" which it would be beholding to him much to restrain or
withhold.   **96 Written . . . along** to take with you in the form of a letter.   **98 but . . . courtesies** i.e., only if I can repay or exchange your
courtesy with my own.   **99 draw near** come with me.

102 Rossillion i.e., Bertram (whom Helena refers to by his title)
105 event hazard, outcome   **107 sportive** amorous   **108 mark** target
109 leaden messengers i.e., bullets   **111–12 move . . . piercing** part
the always-observing air, which appears to be still but which whistles
musically when a bullet passes through it. (The Folio reading, "still-
peering," is here emended to "still-piecing," always closing or repairing itself again.)   **114 forward** facing forward in battle, in the van
115 caitiff base wretch   **118 ravin** ravenous   **120 nature owes**
human nature possesses, suffers   **122–3 Whence . . . all** i.e., from war,
in which honor is at best rewarded for danger with a scar, and often
loses life itself.   **125 do't** i.e., keep you hence.   **although** even if
127 officed all performed all domestic duties.   **128 pitiful** compassionate   **129 consolate** console   **130 poor thief** (The night is thief of
the light of day; Helen is an unwilling thief in having "stolen" the
title of wife and in having to steal away.)
3.3. Location: Florence.
2 Great pregnant, expectant.   **lay** wager.   **credence** trust

We'll strive to bear it for your worthy sake
To th'extreme edge of hazard.
DUKE   Then go thou forth,   6
And Fortune play upon thy prosperous helm,   7
As thy auspicious mistress!
BERTRAM   This very day,
Great Mars, I put myself into thy file.   9
Make me but like my thoughts, and I shall prove   10
A lover of thy drum, hater of love.   *Exeunt omnes.*

❧

[3.4]

Enter Countess and Steward [Rinaldo].

COUNTESS
Alas! And would you take the letter of her?
Might you not know she would do as she has done,
By sending me a letter? Read it again.
RINALDO [*reads the*] letter
"I am Saint Jaques' pilgrim, thither gone.   4
Ambitious love hath so in me offended
That barefoot plod I the cold ground upon,
With sainted vow my faults to have amended.   7
Write, write, that from the bloody course of war
My dearest master, your dear son, may hie.   9
Bless him at home in peace, whilst I from far
His name with zealous fervor sanctify.
His taken labors bid him me forgive;   12
I, his despiteful Juno, sent him forth   13
From courtly friends, with camping foes to live   14
Where death and danger dogs the heels of worth.
He is too good and fair for death and me;
Whom I myself embrace, to set him free."   17
COUNTESS
Ah, what sharp stings are in her mildest words!
Rinaldo, you did never lack advice so much   19
As letting her pass so. Had I spoke with her,
I could have well diverted her intents,
Which thus she hath prevented.
RINALDO   Pardon me, madam.   22
If I had given you this at overnight,   23
She might have been o'erta'en; and yet she writes
Pursuit would be but vain.
COUNTESS   What angel shall
Bless this unworthy husband? He cannot thrive,

Unless her prayers, whom heaven delights to hear   27
And loves to grant, reprieve him from the wrath
Of greatest justice. Write, write, Rinaldo,
To this unworthy husband of his wife.   30
Let every word weigh heavy of her worth   31
That he does weigh too light. My greatest grief,
Though little he do feel it, set down sharply.
Dispatch the most convenient messenger.
When haply he shall hear that she is gone,
He will return; and hope I may that she,
Hearing so much, will speed her foot again,
Led hither by pure love. Which of them both
Is dearest to me, I have no skill in sense   39
To make distinction. Provide this messenger.   40
My heart is heavy and mine age is weak;
Grief would have tears, and sorrow bids me speak.
                                        Exeunt.

❧

[3.5]

*A tucket afar off. Enter old Widow of Florence,
her daughter [Diana], and Mariana, with other
citizens.*

WIDOW   Nay, come, for if they do approach the city we
shall lose all the sight.   2
DIANA   They say the French count has done most
honorable service.
WIDOW   It is reported that he has taken their great'st   5
commander, and that with his own hand he slew the
Duke's brother. [*Tucket.*] We have lost our labor; they
are gone a contrary way. Hark! You may know by
their trumpets.
MARIANA   Come, let's return again and suffice ourselves   10
with the report of it.—Well, Diana, take heed of
this French earl. The honor of a maid is her name, and   12
no legacy is so rich as honesty.   13
WIDOW [*to Diana*]   I have told my neighbor how you   14
have been solicited by a gentleman, his companion.
MARIANA   I know that knave, hang him! One Parolles,
a filthy officer he is in those suggestions for the young   17
earl. Beware of them, Diana; their promises, enticements, oaths, tokens, and all these engines of lust are   19
not the things they go under. Many a maid hath been   20
seduced by them; and the misery is, example, that so   21
terrible shows in the wreck of maidenhood, cannot for   22
all that dissuade succession, but that they are limed   23
with the twigs that threatens them. I hope I need not   24

6 **edge of hazard** limit of peril.   7 **helm** helmet   9 **file** battle line; ranks, catalogue.   10 **like my thoughts** i.e., as valiant as I aspire to be   **3.4. Location:** Rossillion.
4–17 (The letter is in the form of a sonnet.)   4 **Saint Jaques' pilgrim** i.e., a pilgrim to the shrine of Saint James, presumably the famous shrine of Santiago de Compostela in Spain   4 **Jaques'** (Pronounced in two syllables.)   7 **sainted** (1) holy (2) offered to a saint   9 **hie** hasten.   12 **His taken labors** The labors he has undertaken   13 **despiteful Juno** spitefully jealous queen of Olympus, who imposed on Hercules his twelve labors because he was the product of one of Jupiter's many amours. She was also partisan in the Trojan War on the Greek side because of the abduction of Helen.   14 **camping** encamped, contending. (Playing on the antithesis of court and military camp.)   17 **Whom** i.e., death   19 **advice** judgment   22 **prevented** forestalled.   23 **at overnight** last night

27 **her** i.e., Helena's. (Helena is likened to saints who can intercede with heaven on behalf of a sinner.)   30 **unworthy . . . wife** husband unworthy of his wife.   31 **weigh heavy of** emphasize   39 **in sense** in perception   40 **this messenger** a messenger to carry this letter.
3.5. Location: Florence. Outside the walls.
0.1 tucket a trumpet fanfare   2 **lose . . . sight** miss seeing them.   5 **their** i.e., the Sienese's   10 **suffice** content   12 **earl** i.e., Count Bertram.   **her name** her reputation (for chastity)   13 **honesty** chastity.   14 **my neighbor** i.e., Mariana   17 **officer** agent.   **suggestions for** solicitings on behalf of, or, temptations to be.   19 **engines** artifices, devices   20 **go under** pretend to be.   21–3 **example . . . succession** the dreadful example of what happens with the loss of virginity nonetheless cannot dissuade another from a similar course   23–4 **they . . . twigs** i.e., other maidens are caught in the same trap. (Birdlime was smeared on twigs to ensnare birds.)

to advise you further, but I hope your own grace will 25
keep you where you are, though there were no further 26
danger known but the modesty which is so lost. 27

DIANA   You shall not need to fear me. 28

Enter Helena [disguised like a pilgrim].

WIDOW   I hope so.—Look, here comes a pilgrim. I
know she will lie at my house; thither they send one 30
another. I'll question her.—God save you, pilgrim!
Whither are bound? 32

HELENA   To Saint Jaques le Grand.
Where do the palmers lodge, I do beseech you? 34

WIDOW
At the Saint Francis here beside the port. 35

HELENA   Is this the way?   *(A march afar.)*

WIDOW
Ay, marry, is't. Hark you, they come this way.
If you will tarry, holy pilgrim,
But till the troops come by,
I will conduct you where you shall be lodged,
The rather for I think I know your hostess
As ample as myself. 42

HELENA   Is it yourself?

WIDOW   If you shall please so, pilgrim.

HELENA
I thank you, and will stay upon your leisure. 45

WIDOW
You came, I think, from France?

HELENA   I did so.

WIDOW
Here you shall see a countryman of yours
That has done worthy service.

HELENA   His name, I pray you?

DIANA
The Count Rossillion. Know you such a one?

HELENA
But by the ear, that hears most nobly of him.
His face I know not.

DIANA   Whatsome'er he is,
He's bravely taken here. He stole from France, 52
As 'tis reported, for the King had married him 53
Against his liking. Think you it is so?

HELENA
Ay, surely, mere the truth. I know his lady. 55

DIANA
There is a gentleman that serves the Count
Reports but coarsely of her.

HELENA   What's his name?

DIANA
Monsieur Parolles.

HELENA   Oh, I believe with him. 58
In argument of praise, or to the worth 59

Of the great Count himself, she is too mean 60
To have her name repeated. All her deserving 61
Is a reservèd honesty, and that 62
I have not heard examined.

DIANA   Alas, poor lady! 63
'Tis a hard bondage to become the wife
Of a detesting lord.

WIDOW
I warrant, good creature, wheresoe'er she is,
Her heart weighs sadly. This young maid might do
    her
A shrewd turn, if she pleased.

HELENA   How do you mean? 68
Maybe the amorous Count solicits her
In the unlawful purpose?

WIDOW   He does indeed,
And brokes with all that can in such a suit 71
Corrupt the tender honor of a maid.
But she is armed for him and keeps her guard
In honestest defense. 74

*Drum and colors. Enter [Bertram] Count
Rossillion, Parolles, and the whole army.*

MARIANA   The gods forbid else! 75

WIDOW   So, now they come.
That is Antonio, the Duke's eldest son;
That, Escalus.

HELENA   Which is the Frenchman?

DIANA   He,
That with the plume. 'Tis a most gallant fellow.
I would he loved his wife. If he were honester 80
He were much goodlier. Is't not a handsome
    gentleman?

HELENA   I like him well.

*[The warriors pass in file and exit in succession.
Parolles comes last.]*

DIANA   'Tis pity he is not honest. Yond's that same knave
That leads him to these places. Were I his lady
I would poison that vile rascal.

HELENA   Which is he?

DIANA
That jackanapes with scarves. Why is he melancholy? 86

HELENA   Perchance he's hurt i'th' battle.

PAROLLES   Lose our drum? Well.

MARIANA   He's shrewdly vexed at something. Look, he 89
has spied us.

WIDOW *[to Parolles]*   Marry, hang you!

MARIANA *[to Parolles]*   And your courtesy, for a ring- 92
carrier! 93

*Exeunt [Bertram and the last of the army,
Parolles among them].*

---

25 **grace** virtuous strength of grace given by God to resist temptation
26 **though** even though   26–7 **further danger** i.e., pregnancy
27 **modesty** chastity and chaste reputation   28 **fear** worry about
30 **lie** lodge   32 **are** are you   34 **palmers** pilgrims   35 **the Saint
Francis** the inn with the sign of Saint Francis.   **port** city gate
42 **ample** fully, completely   45 **stay . . . leisure** await your convenience.   52 **bravely taken** highly regarded   53 **for** because   55 **mere**
absolutely   58 **believe** agree   59 **In argument of** As a subject for.
to compared to

60 **mean** lowly   61–2 **All . . . honesty** Her only merit is a well-
guarded chastity   63 **examined** doubted, questioned.   68 **shrewd**
malicious, hurtful   71 **brokes** bargains   74 **honestest** most chaste
75 **else** that it should be otherwise.   80 **honester** more honorable
(and more chaste)   86 **jackanapes** monkey   89 **shrewdly** sorely
92 **courtesy** ceremonious bow   92–3 **ring-carrier** go-between.

WIDOW
The troop is past. Come, pilgrim, I will bring you
Where you shall host. Of enjoined penitents   95
There's four or five, to great Saint Jaques bound,
Already at my house.

HELENA   I humbly thank you.
Please it this matron and this gentle maid   98
To eat with us tonight, the charge and thanking   99
Shall be for me; and, to requite you further,   100
I will bestow some precepts of this virgin   101
Worthy the note.

BOTH   We'll take your offer kindly.   102

Exeunt.

❖

[3.6]

*Enter [Bertram] Count Rossillion and the [two]
Frenchmen, as at first.*

FIRST LORD   Nay, good my lord, put him to't. Let him   1
have his way.

SECOND LORD   If Your Lordship find him not a hilding,   3
hold me no more in your respect.

FIRST LORD   On my life, my lord, a bubble.

BERTRAM   Do you think I am so far deceived in him?

FIRST LORD   Believe it, my lord, in mine own direct
knowledge, without any malice, but to speak of him   8
as my kinsman, he's a most notable coward, an infi- 9
nite and endless liar, an hourly promise-breaker, the
owner of no one good quality worthy Your Lordship's
entertainment.   12

SECOND LORD   It were fit you knew him, lest, reposing 13
too far in his virtue, which he hath not, he might at
some great and trusty business in a main danger fail 15
you.

BERTRAM   I would I knew in what particular action to
try him.   18

SECOND LORD   None better than to let him fetch off his 19
drum, which you hear him so confidently undertake
to do.

FIRST LORD   I, with a troop of Florentines, will suddenly
surprise him; such I will have whom I am sure   23
he knows not from the enemy. We will bind and
hoodwink him so that he shall suppose no other but   25
that he is carried into the leaguer of the adversary's, 26
when we bring him to our own tents. Be but Your
Lordship present at his examination. If he do not, for
the promise of his life and in the highest compulsion
of base fear, offer to betray you and deliver all the intel- 30
ligence in his power against you, and that with the 31

divine forfeit of his soul upon oath, never trust my
judgment in anything.

SECOND LORD   Oh, for the love of laughter, let him fetch
his drum. He says he has a stratagem for't. When Your
Lordship sees the bottom of his success in't, and to   36
what metal this counterfeit lump of ore will be melted,
if you give him not John Drum's entertainment, your 38
inclining cannot be removed. Here he comes.   39

Enter Parolles.

FIRST LORD   [*aside to Bertram*]   Oh, for the love of
laughter, hinder not the honor of his design. Let him
fetch off his drum in any hand.   42

BERTRAM   How now, monsieur? This drum sticks sorely 43
in your disposition.   44

SECOND LORD   A pox on't, let it go. 'Tis but a drum.   45

PAROLLES   But a drum! Is't but a drum? A drum so lost!
There was excellent command—to charge in with our
horse upon our own wings and to rend our own   48
soldiers!

SECOND LORD   That was not to be blamed in the com-   50
mand of the service. It was a disaster of war that   51
Caesar himself could not have prevented, if he had
been there to command.

BERTRAM   Well, we cannot greatly condemn our success. 54
Some dishonor we had in the loss of that drum,
but it is not to be recovered.

PAROLLES   It might have been recovered.

BERTRAM   It might, but it is not now.

PAROLLES   It is to be recovered. But that the merit of 59
service is seldom attributed to the true and exact
performer, I would have that drum or another, or *hic* 61
jacet.   62

BERTRAM   Why, if you have a stomach, to't, monsieur! 63
If you think your mystery in stratagem can bring this 64
instrument of honor again into his native quarter, be 65
magnanimous in the enterprise and go on. I will grace 66
the attempt for a worthy exploit. If you speed well in 67
it, the Duke shall both speak of it and extend to you
what further becomes his greatness, even to the   69
utmost syllable of your worthiness.

PAROLLES   By the hand of a soldier, I will undertake it.

BERTRAM   But you must not now slumber in it.

PAROLLES   I'll about it this evening, and I will presently 73
pen down my dilemmas, encourage myself in my   74
certainty, put myself into my mortal preparation; and 75
by midnight look to hear further from me.

95 host lodge.   enjoined penitents those bound by oath to undertake a pilgrimage as penance for sin   98 Please it If it please.
99–100 the charge . . . me i.e., I will bear the expense and be grateful
at the same time   101 of on   102 kindly gratefully.
3.6. Location: The Florentine camp.
0.2 *as at first* (See 3.1.0.2.)   1 to't i.e., to the test.   3 hilding good-
for-nothing   8–9 to speak . . . kinsman to speak as candidly and
fairly as I would even if he were my own kinsman   12 entertainment patronage.   13 reposing trusting   15 trusty demanding trustworthiness   18 try test   19 fetch off recapture   23 surprise capture
25 hoodwink blindfold   26 leaguer camp   30–1 intelligence in his
power information at his command

36 bottom extent   38 John Drum's entertainment (Slang phrase for a
thorough beating and unceremonious dismissal.)   39 inclining partiality (for Parolles)   42 in any hand in any case.   43–4 sticks . . .
disposition i.e., greatly troubles you.   45 A pox on't Plague take it
48 wings flanks.   rend cut up, attack   50–1 in . . . service upon the
orders given for the action.   54 we . . . success i.e., we were successful enough.   59 But that Were it not that   61–2 *hic jacet* Latin for
here lies, the beginning phrase of tomb inscriptions. Hence, Parolles
means "I would die in the attempt."   63 stomach appetite   64 mystery skill   65 again . . . quarter back home again   66 grace honor
67 speed succeed   69 becomes does credit to   73 presently immediately   74 pen . . . dilemmas make note of my difficult choices
75 my mortal preparation spiritual preparedness for my death; or,
death-dealing readiness

BERTRAM   May I be bold to acquaint His Grace you are
gone about it?

PAROLLES   I know not what the success will be, my
lord, but the attempt I vow.

BERTRAM   I know thou'rt valiant, and to the possibility   81
of thy soldiership will subscribe for thee. Farewell.   82

PAROLLES   I love not many words.   *Exit.*

FIRST LORD   No more than a fish loves water. Is not this
a strange fellow, my lord, that so confidently seems to
undertake this business, which he knows is not to be
done, damns himself to do, and dares better be   87
damned than to do't?   88

SECOND LORD   You do not know him, my lord, as we
do. Certain it is that he will steal himself into a man's
favor and for a week escape a great deal of discover-   91
ies; but when you find him out, you have him ever   92
after.

BERTRAM   Why, do you think he will make no deed at   94
all of this that so seriously he does address himself
unto?

FIRST LORD   None in the world, but return with an
invention, and clap upon you two or three probable   98
lies. But we have almost embossed him. You shall see   99
his fall tonight; for indeed he is not for Your Lordship's   100
respect.   101

SECOND LORD   We'll make you some sport with the fox
ere we case him. He was first smoked by the old lord   103
Lafew. When his disguise and he is parted, tell me   104
what a sprat you shall find him, which you shall see   105
this very night.

FIRST LORD
I must go look my twigs. He shall be caught.   107

BERTRAM
Your brother he shall go along with me.   108

FIRST LORD
As't please Your Lordship. I'll leave you.   [*Exit.*]

BERTRAM
Now will I lead you to the house and show you
The lass I spoke of.

SECOND LORD   But you say she's honest.   111

BERTRAM
That's all the fault. I spoke with her but once
And found her wondrous cold; but I sent to her,
By this same coxcomb that we have i'th' wind,   114
Tokens and letters, which she did re-send,   115
And this is all I have done. She's a fair creature.

Will you go see her?

SECOND LORD   With all my heart, my lord.
Exeunt.

❧

[3.7]

Enter Helena and Widow.

HELENA
If you misdoubt me that I am not she,   1
I know not how I shall assure you further
But I shall lose the grounds I work upon.   3

WIDOW
Though my estate be fall'n, I was well born,   4
Nothing acquainted with these businesses,
And would not put my reputation now
In any staining act.

HELENA   Nor would I wish you.
First give me trust the Count he is my husband,   8
And what to your sworn counsel I have spoken   9
Is so from word to word; and then you cannot,   10
By the good aid that I of you shall borrow,   11
Err in bestowing it.

WIDOW   I should believe you,
For you have showed me that which well approves   13
You're great in fortune.

HELENA [*giving money*]   Take this purse of gold,
And let me buy your friendly help thus far,
Which I will overpay and pay again
When I have found it. The Count he woos your
daughter,   17
Lays down his wanton siege before her beauty,
Resolved to carry her. Let her in fine consent,   19
As we'll direct her how 'tis best to bear it.   20
Now his important blood will naught deny   21
That she'll demand. A ring the County wears,   22
That downward hath succeeded in his house
From son to son some four or five descents
Since the first father wore it. This ring he holds
In most rich choice, yet, in his idle fire,   26
To buy his will it would not seem too dear,   27
Howe'er repented after.

WIDOW
Now I see the bottom of your purpose.

HELENA
You see it lawful, then. It is no more
But that your daughter, ere she seems as won,
Desires this ring; appoints him an encounter;   32
In fine, delivers me to fill the time,

---

81 possibility capacity   **82 subscribe** vouch   **87–8 damns . . . do't**
i.e., swears perjured oaths to carry out the mission, but ends up
damned if he does and damned if he doesn't.   **91–2 escape . . . discoveries** i.e., almost get away with it   **92 have him** have a true
knowledge of him   **94 deed** attempt   **98 invention** fabrication.
probable plausible   **99 embossed** driven to exhaustion, cornered. (A
hunting term.)   **100 not for** not worthy of   **101 respect** regard.
103 case skin, strip, unmask.   **smoked** smelled out; smoked out into
the open   **104 is parted** are separated   **105 sprat** a small fish; a contemptible creature   **107 look my twigs** i.e., see to my trap (as in
catching birds with birdlime on twigs).   **108 Your brother** i.e., The
Second Lord   **111 honest** chaste.   **114 coxcomb** fool.   **have i'th'
wind** have to our downwind side, whom we are tracking   **115 re-
send** send back

3.7. Location: Florence. The Widow's house.
1 misdoubt doubt   **3 But . . . upon** i.e., without abandoning my disguise and thus forfeiting the ground upon which my plans are built.
4 estate worldly condition   **8 give me trust** believe me (that)
9 to . . . counsel to your private understanding, guarded by your oath
of secrecy   **10 Is so . . . word** is true in every word   **11 By** with
regard to   **13 approves** proves   **17 found it** i.e., received your help
with success.   **19 carry** win.   **in fine** finally, or, to sum up. (As also
in line 33.)   **20 bear** manage   **21 important blood** importunate passion   **22 That** what.   **County** Count   **26 choice** estimation, regard.
idle fire foolish passion   **27 will** sexual desire   **32 appoints him an
encounter** arranges a rendezvous

Herself most chastely absent. After,
To marry her, I'll add three thousand crowns   35
To what is passed already.

WIDOW   I have yielded.
Instruct my daughter how she shall persever,
That time and place with this deceit so lawful
May prove coherent. Every night he comes   39
With musics of all sorts, and songs composed   40
To her unworthiness. It nothing steads us   41
To chide him from our eaves, for he persists   42
As if his life lay on't.

HELENA   Why then tonight   43
Let us essay our plot, which, if it speed,   44
Is wicked meaning in a lawful deed,   45
And lawful meaning in a wicked act,   46
Where both not sin, and yet a sinful fact.   47
But let's about it.   [Exeunt.]

❖

4.1

Enter one of the Frenchmen [the First Lord]
with five or six other Soldiers, in ambush.

FIRST LORD   He can come no other way but by this
hedge corner. When you sally upon him, speak what   2
terrible language you will. Though you understand it 3
not yourselves, no matter; for we must not seem to
understand him, unless someone among us whom   5
we must produce for an interpreter.

FIRST SOLDIER   Good Captain, let me be th'interpreter.

FIRST LORD   Art not acquainted with him? Knows he
not thy voice?

FIRST SOLDIER   No, sir, I warrant you.

FIRST LORD   But what linsey-woolsey hast thou to   11
speak to us again?   12

FIRST SOLDIER   E'en such as you speak to me.

FIRST LORD   He must think us some band of strangers 14
i'th'adversary's entertainment. Now he hath a smack   15
of all neighboring languages. Therefore we must every 16
one be a man of his own fancy, not to know what we   17
speak one to another; so we seem to know is to know   18
straight our purpose: choughs' language, gabble   19
enough and good enough. As for you, interpreter,

you must seem very politic. But couch, ho! Here he   21
comes, to beguile two hours in a sleep, and then to   22
return and swear the lies he forges.   [They hide.]

Enter Parolles.

PAROLLES   Ten o'clock. Within these three hours 'twill
be time enough to go home. What shall I say I have
done? It must be a very plausive invention that carries 26
it. They begin to smoke me, and disgraces have of late 27
knocked too often at my door. I find my tongue is too
foolhardy; but my heart hath the fear of Mars before it, 29
and of his creatures, not daring the reports of my   30
tongue.   31

FIRST LORD [aside]   This is the first truth that e'er thine
own tongue was guilty of.

PAROLLES   What the devil should move me to undertake the recovery of this drum, being not ignorant of
the impossibility, and knowing I had no such purpose?
I must give myself some hurts, and say I got
them in exploit. Yet slight ones will not carry it—they
will say, "Came you off with so little?"—and great
ones I dare not give. Wherefore? What's the instance? 40
Tongue, I must put you into a butter-woman's mouth   41
and buy myself another of Bajazeth's mule, if you   42
prattle me into these perils.

FIRST LORD [aside]   Is it possible he should know what
he is, and be that he is?

PAROLLES   I would the cutting of my garments would
serve the turn, or the breaking of my Spanish sword. 47

FIRST LORD [aside]   We cannot afford you so.   48

PAROLLES   Or the baring of my beard, and to say it was 49
in stratagem.   50

FIRST LORD [aside]   'Twould not do.

PAROLLES   Or to drown my clothes, and say I was
stripped.

FIRST LORD [aside]   Hardly serve.

PAROLLES   Though I swore I leapt from the window of
the citadel—

FIRST LORD [aside]   How deep?

PAROLLES   Thirty fathom.   58

FIRST LORD [aside]   Three great oaths would scarce
make that be believed.

PAROLLES   I would I had any drum of the enemy's. I
would swear I recovered it.

FIRST LORD [aside]   You shall hear one anon.   63

PAROLLES   A drum now of the enemy's—   64

Alarum within.

---

35 To marry her as her dowry   **39 coherent** suitable.   **40 musics**
musicians   **41 To her unworthiness** to her, my humble daughter; or,
to the end of persuading her to do an unworthy deed.   **nothing
steads us** profits us not at all   **42 chide . . . eaves** i.e., drive him away
43 lay depended   **44 essay** try.   **speed** succeed   **45–6 Is . . . act** i.e.,
is wicked intention (on Bertram's part) converted into a lawful act of
sex between married partners, and lawful intent (on Helena's part)
carried out in an ethically dubious way   **47 fact** deed (which would
have been sinful as Bertram intended it).
4.1. Location: Outside the Florentine camp.
2 sally rush out   **3 terrible** terrifying   **5 unless** except for   **11 linsey-woolsey** a fabric woven from wool and flax; figuratively, a
hodge-podge   **12 again** in reply.   **14 strangers** foreigners   **15 entertainment** service.   **smack** smattering   **16–19 we . . . purpose** each of
us must make up his own imaginative language, unintelligible to the
others; so long as we seem to know what is said, we'll accomplish our
purpose   **19 choughs' language** the chattering of a small species of
the crow family, the jackdaw

21 politic shrewd, cunning.   **couch** take concealment   **22 beguile**
while away.   **sleep** nap   **26 plausive** plausible   **26–7 carries it** carries
it off.   **27 smoke** suspect   **29–31 hath . . . tongue** is frightened by the
prospect of the god of war and his followers, and dare not carry out
my boast.   **40 Wherefore . . . instance?** (Parolles may be saying "Why
did I ever open my mouth?" or "Where's the evidence to be produced
from?")   **41 butter-woman** dairywoman, i.e., a proverbial scold and
garrulous talker   **42 of Bajazeth's mule** i.e., from a Turkish mule, since
mules are notoriously mute (?) (Many emendations have been proposed, including *mute* for *mule.*)   **47 serve the turn** suffice   **48 afford
you so** i.e., let you off so lightly.   **50 in stratagem** shaving an act of cunning.   **58 fathom** (A fathom is a unit of measure equal to
six feet.)   **63 anon** immediately.   **64–1 Alarum** Call to arms

FIRST LORD [*coming forward*]   *Throca movousus, cargo,*
cargo, cargo.

ALL   *Cargo, cargo, cargo, villianda par corbo, cargo.*
[*They seize and blindfold him.*]

PAROLLES
Oh, ransom, ransom! Do not hide mine eyes.

FIRST SOLDIER   *Boskos thromuldo boskos.*

PAROLLES
I know you are the Muskos' regiment,   70
And I shall lose my life for want of language.   71
If there be here German, or Dane, Low Dutch,
Italian, or French, let him speak to me,
I'll discover that which shall undo the Florentine.   74

FIRST SOLDIER   *Boskos vauvado.* I understand thee and
can speak thy tongue. *Kerelybonto.* Sir, betake thee to   76
thy faith, for seventeen poniards are at thy bosom.   77

PAROLLES   Oh!

FIRST SOLDIER   Oh, pray, pray, pray! *Manka revania*
dulche.

FIRST LORD   *Oscorbidulchos volivorco.*

FIRST SOLDIER
The General is content to spare thee yet,
And, hoodwinked as thou art, will lead thee on   83
To gather from thee. Haply thou mayst inform   84
Something to save thy life.

PAROLLES   Oh, let me live,
And all the secrets of our camp I'll show,
Their force, their purposes; nay, I'll speak that
Which you will wonder at.

FIRST SOLDIER   But wilt thou faithfully?

PAROLLES
If I do not, damn me.

FIRST SOLDIER   *Acordo linta.*
Come on; thou art granted space.   *Exit* [*with Parolles* 90
guarded]. *A short alarum within.*

FIRST LORD
Go tell the Count Rossillion and my brother
We have caught the woodcock and will keep him
muffled   92
Till we do hear from them.

SECOND SOLDIER   Captain, I will.

FIRST LORD
'A will betray us all unto ourselves.   94
Inform on that.   95

SECOND SOLDIER   So I will, sir.

FIRST LORD
Till then I'll keep him dark and safely locked. *Exeunt.*

❖

[4.2]

Enter Bertram and the maid called Diana.

BERTRAM
They told me that your name was Fontibell.

DIANA
No, my good lord, Diana.

BERTRAM   Titled goddess,   2
And worth it, with addition! But, fair soul,   3
In your fine frame hath love no quality?   4
If the quick fire of youth light not your mind,   5
You are no maiden, but a monument.   6
When you are dead, you should be such a one
As you are now; for you are cold and stern,
And now you should be as your mother was
When your sweet self was got.   10

DIANA
She then was honest.

BERTRAM   So should you be.

DIANA   No.   11
My mother did but duty—such, my lord,
As you owe to your wife.

BERTRAM   No more o' that.
I prithee, do not strive against my vows.   14
I was compelled to her, but I love thee
By love's own sweet constraint and will forever
Do thee all rights of service.

DIANA   Ay, so you serve us
Till we serve you; but when you have our roses,   18
You barely leave our thorns to prick ourselves   19
And mock us with our bareness.

BERTRAM   How have I sworn!   20

DIANA
'Tis not the many oaths that makes the truth,
But the plain single vow that is vowed true.
What is not holy, that we swear not by,   23
But take the High'st to witness. Then pray you, tell me,   24
If I should swear by Jove's great attributes
I loved you dearly, would you believe my oaths
When I did love you ill? This has no holding,   27
To swear by Him whom I protest to love   28
That I will work against Him. Therefore your oaths   29
Are words and poor conditions but unsealed,   30
At least in my opinion.

BERTRAM   Change it, change it!   31
Be not so holy-cruel. Love is holy,   32
And my integrity ne'er knew the crafts   33
That you do charge men with. Stand no more off,

2–3 **Titled . . . addition!** You who have the name of a goddess, and
who deserve that and more!   **4 frame** makeup, being.   **quality** position, part   **5 quick** lively   **6 monument** statue, lifeless effigy   **10 got**
begotten.   **11 honest** chaste, true to marriage vows. (But Bertram
uses it to mean "frank.")   **14 vows** i.e., vows to live apart from
Helena.   **18 serve you** i.e., serve you sexually. (The sexual suggestion
is continued in *roses* and in *prick*, line 19.)   **19 You . . . thorns** you
leave us with only the bare thorns (of shame and guilt)   **20 our bare-**
ness i.e., the loss of our rose of virginity.   **23–4 What . . . witness**
When we swear an oath, we do so not in the name of unholy things,
but with God as our witness.   **27 ill** perfidiously and hence contrary
to the purport of an oath sworn to God.   **holding** power to bind;
consistency   **28 protest** profess   **29 work against Him** oppose His
will by my sinful action.   **30 Are words . . . unsealed** are mere words
and invalid provisos, unratified and hence lacking in legally binding
force   **31 it** i.e., your opinion   **32 holy-cruel** i.e., cruel to me in your
holiness   **33 crafts** deceits

---

70 **Muskos'** Muscovites'   **71 want** lack   **74 discover** reveal
76–7 betake . . . faith i.e., say your prayers   **77 poniards** daggers
83 hoodwinked blindfolded.   **on** onward, elsewhere   **84 gather** get
information.   **Haply** Perhaps   **90 space** time.   **92 woodcock** (A
proverbially stupid bird.)   **muffled** blindfolded   **94 'A** He
95 Inform on Report
4.2. Location: Florence. The Widow's house.

But give thyself unto my sick desires,   35
Who then recovers. Say thou art mine, and ever   36
My love as it begins shall so persever.

DIANA
I see that men may rope 's in such a snare
That we'll forsake ourselves. Give me that ring.   38

BERTRAM
I'll lend it thee, my dear, but have no power
To give it from me.

DIANA   Will you not, my lord?

BERTRAM
It is an honor 'longing to our house,
Bequeathèd down from many ancestors,
Which were the greatest obloquy i'th' world   44
In me to lose.

DIANA   Mine honor's such a ring.
My chastity's the jewel of our house,
Bequeathèd down from many ancestors,
Which were the greatest obloquy i'th' world
In me to lose. Thus your own proper wisdom   49
Brings in the champion Honor on my part   50
Against your vain assault.

BERTRAM   Here, take my ring!
My house, mine honor, yea, my life, be thine,
And I'll be bid by thee.   [He gives the ring.]   53

DIANA
When midnight comes, knock at my chamber
window.
I'll order take my mother shall not hear.   55
Now will I charge you in the bond of truth,
When you have conquered my yet maiden bed,
Remain there but an hour, nor speak to me.
My reasons are most strong, and you shall know
them   59
When back again this ring shall be delivered.   60
And on your finger in the night I'll put
Another ring, that what in time proceeds   62
May token to the future our past deeds.   63
Adieu till then; then, fail not. You have won
A wife of me, though there my hope be done.   65

BERTRAM
A heaven on earth I have won by wooing thee.
                                              [Exit.]

DIANA
For which live long to thank both heaven and me!
You may so in the end.
My mother told me just how he would woo,
As if she sat in 's heart. She says all men

Have the like oaths. He had sworn to marry me   71
When his wife's dead; therefore I'll lie with him   72
When I am buried. Since Frenchmen are so braid,   73
Marry that will, I live and die a maid.   74
Only in this disguise I think 't no sin
To cozen him that would unjustly win.   Exit. 76

❧

[4.3]

*Enter the two French Captains and some two or
three Soldiers.*

FIRST LORD   You have not given him his mother's letter?

SECOND LORD   I have delivered it an hour since. There   2
is something in 't that stings his nature, for on the
reading it he changed almost into another man.

FIRST LORD   He has much worthy blame laid upon him   5
for shaking off so good a wife and so sweet a lady.

SECOND LORD   Especially he hath incurred the everlasting displeasure of the King, who had even tuned his   8
bounty to sing happiness to him. I will tell you a   9
thing, but you shall let it dwell darkly with you.   10

FIRST LORD   When you have spoken it, 'tis dead, and I
am the grave of it.

SECOND LORD   He hath perverted a young gentlewoman   13
here in Florence, of a most chaste renown, and this
night he fleshes his will in the spoil of her honor. He   15
hath given her his monumental ring and thinks him-   16
self made in the unchaste composition.   17

FIRST LORD   Now, God delay our rebellion! As we are   18
ourselves, what things are we!   19

SECOND LORD   Merely our own traitors. And as in the   20
common course of all treasons we still see them reveal   21
themselves till they attain to their abhorred ends, so   22
he that in this action contrives against his own   23
nobility, in his proper stream o'erflows himself.   24

FIRST LORD   Is it not meant damnable in us to be 25
trumpeters of our unlawful intents? We shall not then 26
have his company tonight?

SECOND LORD   Not till after midnight, for he is dieted 28
to his hour. 29

FIRST LORD   That approaches apace. I would gladly have
him see his company anatomized, that he might take 31
a measure of his own judgments wherein so curiously 32
he had set this counterfeit. 33

SECOND LORD   We will not meddle with him till he 34
come, for his presence must be the whip of the other. 35

FIRST LORD   In the meantime, what hear you of these
wars?

SECOND LORD   I hear there is an overture of peace.

FIRST LORD   Nay, I assure you, a peace concluded.

SECOND LORD   What will Count Rossillion do then?
Will he travel higher or return again into France? 41

FIRST LORD   I perceive, by this demand, you are not 42
altogether of his council. 43

SECOND LORD   Let it be forbid, sir! So should I be a great
deal of his act. 45

FIRST LORD   Sir, his wife some two months since fled
from his house. Her pretense is a pilgrimage to Saint 47
Jaques le Grand, which holy undertaking with most
austere sanctimony she accomplished. And, there 49
residing, the tenderness of her nature became as a
prey to her grief; in fine, made a groan of her last 51
breath, and now she sings in heaven.

SECOND LORD   How is this justified? 53

FIRST LORD   The stronger part of it by her own letters,
which makes her story true even to the point of her 55
death. Her death itself, which could not be her office
to say is come, was faithfully confirmed by the rector
of the place.

SECOND LORD   Hath the Count all this intelligence?

FIRST LORD   Ay, and the particular confirmations, point
from point, to the full arming of the verity. 61

SECOND LORD   I am heartily sorry that he'll be glad of
this.

FIRST LORD   How mightily sometimes we make us 64
comforts of our losses! 65

SECOND LORD   And how mightily some other times we 66
drown our gain in tears! The great dignity that his 67
valor hath here acquired for him shall at home be
encountered with a shame as ample.

FIRST LORD   The web of our life is of a mingled yarn,

good and ill together. Our virtues would be proud if 71
our faults whipped them not, and our crimes would 72
despair if they were not cherished by our virtues. 73

Enter a [Servant as] messenger.

How now? Where's your master?

SERVANT   He met the Duke in the street, sir, of whom
he hath taken a solemn leave. His Lordship will next 76
morning for France. The Duke hath offered him letters
of commendations to the King.

SECOND LORD   They shall be no more than needful 79
there, if they were more than they can commend. 80

Enter [Bertram] Count Rossillion.

FIRST LORD   They cannot be too sweet for the King's
tartness. Here's His Lordship now.—How now, my
lord, is't not after midnight?

BERTRAM   I have tonight dispatched sixteen businesses,
a month's length apiece, by an abstract of success: I 85
have congeed with the Duke, done my adieu with his 86
nearest, buried a wife, mourned for her, writ to my 87
lady mother I am returning, entertained my convoy, 88
and between these main parcels of dispatch effected 89
many nicer needs. The last was the greatest, but that 90
I have not ended yet.

SECOND LORD   If the business be of any difficulty, and
this morning your departure hence, it requires haste
of Your Lordship.

BERTRAM   I mean, the business is not ended, as fearing 95
to hear of it hereafter. But shall we have this dialogue 96
between the fool and the soldier? Come, bring forth
this counterfeit module; he's deceived me like a 98
double-meaning prophesier. 99

SECOND LORD   [*to the Soldiers*]   Bring him forth.
[*Exit one or more.*]
He's sat i'the stocks all night, poor gallant knave.

BERTRAM   No matter; his heels have deserved it, in
usurping his spurs so long. How does he carry
himself?

SECOND LORD   I have told Your Lordship already, the
stocks carry him. But to answer you as you would be
understood, he weeps like a wench that had shed her 107
milk. He hath confessed himself to Morgan, whom he
supposes to be a friar, from the time of his remem- 109
brance to this very instant disaster of his setting i'th' 110
stocks. And what think you he hath confessed?

BERTRAM   Nothing of me, has 'a?

25–6 Is it . . . intents? Is it not a sign of our fallen natures to be proud proclaimers of our sinful intents?   **28–9 dieted to his hour** tied to his schedule.   **31 his company** the company he keeps, his companion. **anatomized** dissected, exposed   **32 curiously** carefully, elaborately **33 counterfeit** false jewel, i.e., Parolles.   **34 him** Parolles.   **he** Bertram   **35 his . . . the other** i.e., Bertram's . . . Parolles.   **41 higher** farther   **42 demand** question   **43 of his council** in his confidence.   **45 of his act** an accessory to his misdeeds.   **47 pretense** intent **49 sanctimony** holiness   **51 in fine** at last   **53 justified** made certain.   **55 point** time, moment   **61 arming** corroboration, strengthening.   **verity** truth.   **64–7 make . . . tears** perversely take comfort in misfortune and at other times weep when we are fortunate. (Bertram is glad to lose Helena, having previously grieved at gaining her.)

71–3 Our virtues . . . virtues Our virtues would become arrogant if they were not chastized by our faults, and our wickednesses would despair if the presence of our virtues did not comfort them.   **76 will** i.e., intends to depart   **79–80 They . . . commend** Even if they were stronger than any recommendation could be, they would still be no more than what is needed (to calm the King's anger at Bertram).   **85 by . . . success** by a series of successful moves, as follows, or, by a series of moves that may be summarized as follows   **86 congeed with** taken leave of **86–7 his nearest** those persons nearest him   **88 entertained my convoy** hired my transportation   **89 main . . . dispatch** major items to be settled **90 nicer** more delicate.   **The last** i.e., The affair with Diana   **95–6 the business . . . hereafter** Bertram fears that Diana may be pregnant, with inevitable consequences.   **98 module** mere image   **99 double-meaning** ambiguous, equivocating   **107 shed** spilled. (With the implication of crying over spilt milk.)   **109–10 the time . . . remembrance** as far back as he can recall   **110 instant** present

SECOND LORD   His confession is taken, and it shall be read to his face. If Your Lordship be in't, as I believe you are, you must have the patience to hear it.

Enter Parolles [guarded and blindfolded] with [First Soldier as] his interpreter.

BERTRAM   A plague upon him! Muffled! He can say 116
nothing of me.

FIRST LORD   Hush, hush! Hoodman comes!—*Portotar-* 118
tarosa.

FIRST SOLDIER   *[to Parolles]*   He calls for the tortures. What will you say without 'em?

PAROLLES   I will confess what I know without con- straint. If ye pinch me like a pasty, I can say no more. 123

FIRST SOLDIER   *Bosko chimurcho.*

FIRST LORD   *Boblibindo chicurmurco.*

FIRST SOLDIER   You are a merciful general.—Our gener- al bids you answer to what I shall ask you out of a note. 127

PAROLLES   And truly, as I hope to live.

FIRST SOLDIER   *[as if reading]*   "First demand of him how 129 many horse the Duke is strong." What say you to that? 130

PAROLLES   Five or six thousand, but very weak and unserviceable. The troops are all scattered and the commanders very poor rogues, upon my reputation and credit and as I hope to live.

FIRST SOLDIER   Shall I set down your answer so?
                          [He makes as though to write.]

PAROLLES   Do. I'll take the sacrament on't, how and which way you will.

BERTRAM   *[aside to the Lords]*   All's one to him. What a 139 past-saving slave is this!

FIRST LORD   *[aside to Bertram]*   You're deceived, my lord. This is Monsieur Parolles, the gallant militarist—that was his own phrase—that had the whole theoric of 142 war in the knot of his scarf, and the practice in the chape of his dagger. 144

SECOND LORD   *[aside]*   I will never trust a man again for keeping his sword clean, nor believe he can have 146 everything in him by wearing his apparel neatly.

FIRST SOLDIER   *[to Parolles]*   Well, that's set down.

PAROLLES   "Five or six thousand horse," I said—I will say true—"or thereabouts," set down, for I'll speak truth.

FIRST LORD   *[aside]*   He's very near the truth in this.

BERTRAM   *[aside]*   But I con him no thanks for't, in the 153 nature he delivers it. 154

PAROLLES   "Poor rogues," I pray you, say.

FIRST SOLDIER   Well, that's set down.

PAROLLES   I humbly thank you, sir. A truth's a truth. The rogues are marvelous poor.

FIRST SOLDIER   *[as if reading]*   "Demand of him of what strength they are afoot." What say you to that? 160

PAROLLES   By my troth, sir, if I were to live this present 161 hour, I will tell true. Let me see: Spurio, a hundred and fifty; Sebastian, so many; Corambus, so many; Jaques, 163 so many; Guiltian, Cosmo, Lodowick, and Gratii, two hundred fifty each; mine own company, Chitopher, Vaumond, Bentii, two hundred fifty each; so that the muster-file, rotten and sound, upon my life, amounts 167 not to fifteen thousand poll, half of the which dare not 168 shake the snow from off their cassocks, lest they shake 169 themselves to pieces.

BERTRAM   *[aside to the Lords]*   What shall be done to him?

FIRST LORD   *[aside]*   Nothing, but let him have thanks.— Demand of him my condition and what credit I have with the Duke.

FIRST SOLDIER   Well, that's set down. *[As if reading]* "You shall demand of him whether one Captain Dumain be i'th' camp, a Frenchman; what his reputation is with the Duke; what his valor, honesty, and expertness in wars; or whether he thinks it were not possible, with well-weighing sums of gold, to 181 corrupt him to a revolt." What say you to this? What 182 do you know of it?

PAROLLES   I beseech you, let me answer to the particu- lar of the inter'gatories. Demand them singly. 185

FIRST SOLDIER   Do you know this Captain Dumain?

PAROLLES   I know him. 'A was a botcher's prentice in 187 Paris, from whence he was whipped for getting the sheriff's fool with child—a dumb innocent that could 189 not say him nay.

BERTRAM   *[aside to First Lord, who makes as if to strike Parolles]*   Nay, by your leave, hold your hands— though I know his brains are forfeit to the next tile 193 that falls. 194

FIRST SOLDIER   Well, is this captain in the Duke of Flor- ence's camp?

PAROLLES   Upon my knowledge, he is, and lousy. 197

FIRST LORD   *[aside to Bertram]*   Nay, look not so upon me. We shall hear of Your Lordship anon.

FIRST SOLDIER   What is his reputation with the Duke?

PAROLLES   The Duke knows him for no other but a poor officer of mine, and writ to me this other day to turn him out o'th' band. I think I have his letter in my 203 pocket.

FIRST SOLDIER   Marry, we'll search.
                          [They search his pockets.]

PAROLLES   In good sadness, I do not know; either it is 206 there, or it is upon a file with the Duke's other letters in my tent.

FIRST SOLDIER   Here 'tis, here's a paper. Shall I read it to you?

PAROLLES   I do not know if it be it or no.

---

116 **Muffled!** Blindfolded!   118 **Hoodman comes** (Customary call in the game of blindman's buff.)   123 **pasty** meat pie   127 **note** memo- randum or list.   129 **demand** ask   130 **horse** horsemen, cavalry troops   139 **past-saving** beyond redemption. (Referring back to "sacrament" in line 136.)   142 **theoric** theory   144 **chape** scabbard tip   146 **clean** i.e., polished   153 **con** offer. (Literally, "know.") 153–4 **in . . . it** considering what sort of truth it is that he tells. 160 **afoot** in numbers of foot soldiers.

161 **live** i.e., live only   163 **so many** the same number   167 **file** roll 168 **poll** heads   169 **cassocks** cloaks   181 **well-weighing** heavy and persuasive   182 **revolt** desertion.   185 **inter'gatories** questions. 187 **botcher's** mender's, especially a tailor or cobbler who makes "botch-job" repairs   189 **sheriff's fool** feeble-minded girl in the sher- iff's custody   193–4 **his . . . falls** i.e., such a liar is headed straight for sudden and violent death.   197 **lousy** (1) contemptible (2) infested with lice.   203 **band** company, army.   206 **sadness** seriousness

BERTRAM [aside]   Our interpreter does it well.

FIRST LORD [aside]   Excellently.

FIRST SOLDIER [reads]

"Dian, the Count's a fool, and full of gold—"

PAROLLES   That is not the Duke's letter, sir. That is an
advertisement to a proper maid in Florence, one 216
Diana, to take heed of the allurement of one Count
Rossillion, a foolish idle boy, but for all that very
ruttish. I pray you, sir, put it up again. 219

FIRST SOLDIER   Nay, I'll read it first, by your favor.

PAROLLES   My meaning in 't, I protest, was very honest
in the behalf of the maid, for I knew the young Count
to be a dangerous and lascivious boy, who is a whale
to virginity, and devours up all the fry it finds. 224

BERTRAM [aside]   Damnable both-sides rogue!

FIRST SOLDIER [reads the] letter

"When he swears oaths, bid him drop gold, and
take it; 226
After he scores, he never pays the score. 227
Half won is match well made; match, and well make
it. 228
He ne'er pays after-debts; take it before. 229
And say a soldier, Dian, told thee this:
Men are to mell with, boys are not to kiss. 231
For count of this, the Count's a fool, I know it, 232
Who pays before, but not when he does owe it. 233
Thine, as he vowed to thee in thine ear,
Parolles."

BERTRAM [aside]   He shall be whipped through the
army with this rhyme in's forehead.

SECOND LORD [aside]   This is your devoted friend, sir,
the manifold linguist and the armipotent soldier. 239

BERTRAM [aside]   I could endure anything before but a
cat, and now he's a cat to me. 241

FIRST SOLDIER   I perceive, sir, by our general's looks,
we shall be fain to hang you. 243

PAROLLES   My life, sir, in any case! Not that I am afraid
to die, but that, my offenses being many, I would
repent out the remainder of nature. Let me live, sir, in 246
a dungeon, i'th' stocks, or anywhere, so I may live.

FIRST SOLDIER   We'll see what may be done, so you
confess freely. Therefore, once more to this Captain
Dumain. You have answered to his reputation with
the Duke, and to his valor. What is his honesty?

PAROLLES   He will steal, sir, an egg out of a cloister. For
rapes and ravishments he parallels Nessus. He pro- 253
fesses not keeping of oaths; in breaking 'em he is 254
stronger than Hercules. He will lie, sir, with such
volubility that you would think truth were a fool. 256
Drunkenness is his best virtue, for he will be swine-
drunk, and in his sleep he does little harm, save to his
bedclothes about him; but they know his conditions, 259
and lay him in straw. I have but little more to say, sir,
of his honesty. He has everything that an honest man
should not have; what an honest man should have, he
has nothing.

FIRST LORD [aside]   I begin to love him for this.

BERTRAM [aside]   For this description of thine honesty?
A pox upon him for me, he's more and more a cat.

FIRST SOLDIER   What say you to his expertness in war?

PAROLLES   Faith, sir, he's led the drum before the 268
English tragedians. To belie him I will not, and more 269
of his soldiership I know not, except in that country he
had the honor to be the officer at a place there called
Mile End, to instruct for the doubling of files. I would 272
do the man what honor I can, but of this I am not
certain.

FIRST LORD [aside]   He hath out-villained villainy so far 275
that the rarity redeems him. 276

BERTRAM [aside]   A pox on him, he's a cat still.

FIRST SOLDIER   His qualities being at this poor price, I
need not to ask you if gold will corrupt him to revolt.

PAROLLES   Sir, for a cardecu he will sell the fee simple of 280
his salvation, the inheritance of it, and cut th'entail 281
from all remainders, and a perpetual succession for it 282
perpetually. 283

FIRST SOLDIER   What's his brother, the other Captain
Dumain?

SECOND LORD [aside]   Why does he ask him of me?

FIRST SOLDIER   What's he?

PAROLLES   E'en a crow o'th' same nest; not altogether
so great as the first in goodness, but greater a great
deal in evil. He excels his brother for a coward, yet his
brother is reputed one of the best that is. In a retreat he
outruns any lackey; marry, in coming on he has the 292
cramp.

FIRST SOLDIER   If your life be saved, will you undertake
to betray the Florentine?

PAROLLES   Ay, and the Captain of his Horse, Count 296
Rossillion.

---

216 advertisement warning.   **proper** respectable   **219 ruttish** lecherous.   **224 fry** small fish   **226 drop** i.e., offer, pay.   **take it** i.e., you should take it.   **227 scores** (1) buys on credit (2) hits the mark, scores sexually.   **score** bill.   **228 Half . . . make it** i.e., One is halfway to success if the *match* or bargain is well stated with clearly defined agreements, so be sure to do this.   **229 after-debts** debts payable after the goods are received.   **it** i.e., payment   **231 Men . . . kiss** i.e., Don't fool around with mere boys (like Bertram), but with real men (like me). (*Mell with* means "mingle with in intercourse.")   **232 For count of** On account of, or, therefore take note of   **233 before** in advance (when he is required to do so).   **does owe it** (1) owes payment for something already received (2) possess it, i.e., her maidenhead.   **239 manifold linguist** speaker of many languages.   **armipotent** powerful in arms   **241 cat** (A term of contempt.)   **243 fain** obliged   **246 the remainder of nature** what is left of my natural life.

253 Nessus a centaur who attempted to rape the wife of Hercules.   **253–4 professes** makes a practice of   **256 volubility** fluency, facility.   **truth were a fool** i.e., truth here seems so easily put down and made to look foolish.   **259 they** i.e., his servants.   **conditions** habits   **268–9 led . . . tragedians** (It was a custom of actors entering a village or town to parade in the street before the performance of a play.)   **272 Mile End** place near London where citizen militiamen were regularly exercised. (A slur of amateurism.)   **doubling of files** simple drill maneuver in which the soldiers stand in a row two deep   **275–6 He . . . him** His villainy has so surpassed ordinary villainy that its extraordinariness redeems him.   **280 cardecu** quart d'écu, one-quarter of a French crown.   **fee simple** total and perpetual ownership   **281–3 cut . . . perpetually** prevent it from being passed on successively to subsequent heirs.   **292 lackey** running footman.   **coming on** moving forward   **296 Captain of his Horse** cavalry commander

FIRST SOLDIER   I'll whisper with the General and know his pleasure.

PAROLLES [*to himself*]   I'll no more drumming. A plague of all drums! Only to seem to deserve well, and to beguile the supposition of that lascivious young boy, 302 the Count, have I run into this danger. Yet who would have suspected an ambush where I was taken?

FIRST SOLDIER   There is no remedy, sir, but you must die. The General says, you that have so traitorously discovered the secrets of your army and made such 307 pestiferous reports of men very nobly held can serve 308 the world for no honest use; therefore you must die.—Come, headsman, off with his head.

PAROLLES   Oh, Lord, sir, let me live, or let me see my 311 death!

FIRST SOLDIER   That shall you, and take your leave of all your friends. [*Unblindfolding him.*] So, look about you. Know you any here?

BERTRAM   Good morrow, noble Captain.

SECOND LORD   God bless you, Captain Parolles.

FIRST LORD   God save you, noble Captain.

SECOND LORD   Captain, what greeting will you to my 319 Lord Lafew? I am for France. 320

FIRST LORD   Good Captain, will you give me a copy of the sonnet you writ to Diana in behalf of the Count Rossillion? An I were not a very coward, I'd compel it 323 of you; but fare you well. *Exeunt [Bertram and Lords].*

FIRST SOLDIER   You are undone, Captain, all but your scarf; that has a knot on't yet.

PAROLLES   Who cannot be crushed with a plot?

FIRST SOLDIER   If you could find out a country where but women were that had received so much shame, you might begin an impudent nation. Fare ye well, sir. 330 I am for France too. We shall speak of you there.
                                        Exit [with Soldiers].

PAROLLES
Yet am I thankful. If my heart were great,   332
'Twould burst at this. Captain I'll be no more,
But I will eat and drink, and sleep as soft
As captain shall. Simply the thing I am
Shall make me live. Who knows himself a braggart,   336
Let him fear this, for it will come to pass
That every braggart shall be found an ass.
Rust, sword! Cool, blushes! And, Parolles, live
Safest in shame! Being fooled, by fool'ry thrive!   340
There's place and means for every man alive.
I'll after them.   *Exit.*

❖

[4.4]

Enter Helena, Widow, and Diana.

HELENA
That you may well perceive I have not wronged you,
One of the greatest in the Christian world   2
Shall be my surety; 'fore whose throne 'tis needful,   3
Ere I can perfect mine intents, to kneel.
Time was, I did him a desirèd office,
Dear almost as his life, which gratitude   6
Through flinty Tartar's bosom would peep forth   7
And answer thanks. I duly am informed
His Grace is at Marseilles, to which place
We have convenient convoy. You must know   10
I am supposèd dead. The army breaking,   11
My husband hies him home, where, heaven aiding,   12
And by the leave of my good lord the King,
We'll be before our welcome.

WIDOW   Gentle madam,   14
You never had a servant to whose trust
Your business was more welcome.

HELENA   Nor you, mistress,
Ever a friend whose thoughts more truly labor
To recompense your love. Doubt not but heaven
Hath brought me up to be your daughter's dower,   19
As it hath fated her to be my motive   20
And helper to a husband. But oh, strange men!,
That can such sweet use make of what they hate,
When saucy trusting of the cozened thoughts   23
Defiles the pitchy night! So lust doth play   24
With what it loathes for that which is away.   25
But more of this hereafter. You, Diana,
Under my poor instructions yet must suffer   27
Something in my behalf.

DIANA   Let death and honesty   28
Go with your impositions, I am yours   29
Upon your will to suffer.

HELENA   Yet, I pray you;   30
But with the word the time will bring on summer,   31
When briers shall have leaves as well as thorns,   32
And be as sweet as sharp. We must away;
Our wagon is prepared, and time revives us.   34

4.4. Location: Florence. The Widow's house.
2 One . . . world i.e., the French King   **3 surety** guarantee   **6 which gratitude** gratitude for which   **7 Through** even through   **10 convenient convoy** suitable transport.   **11 breaking** disbanding   **12 hies him** hastens   **14 we'll be . . . welcome** we will arrive before we are expected.   **19 Hath . . . dower** i.e., has groomed me for the role of providing a dowry for your daughter   **20 motive** means
23–4 When . . . night when lustful confidence in deceived fancies sullies the darkness of night. (Recalling the proverbial idea that "pitch doth defile"; here man's lust defiles pitch, i.e., night.)   **24–5 So . . . away** i.e., Thus Bertram's lust enjoys itself with Helena, the loathed wife, supposing her to be Diana.   **27 yet** for a time yet   **28–30 Let . . . suffer** Even if a chaste death were a result of what you ask of me, I am yours, ready to accede to your will.   **30 Yet** A little longer
31–2 But . . . thorns i.e., but soon enough, time will bring on a happier state of affairs, with rewards to compensate for our suffering.
34 revives will revive

302 **supposition** judgment   307 **discovered** revealed   308 **pestifer-ous** malicious, pernicious.   **held** regarded   311 **Oh, Lord, sir** (Unconsciously echoing Lavatch's parody of the courtier at 2.2.49–59.)   319 **will you** do you wish to send   320 **for** bound for, off to   323 **An** If   330 **impudent** shameless   332 **heart** (Thought to be the seat of courage.)   336 **Who** He who   340 **Being . . . thrive!** i.e., Since they have made a fool of me, I will now thrive by being what I am, a fool!

All's well that ends well. Still the fine's the crown;   35
Whate'er the course, the end is the renown.   *Exeunt.*   36

❧

[4.5]

Enter Clown [Lavatch], Old Lady [Countess],
and Lafew.

LAFEW   No, no, no, your son was misled with a   1
snipped-taffeta fellow there, whose villainous saffron   2
would have made all the unbaked and doughy youth   3
of a nation in his color. Your daughter-in-law had
been alive at this hour, and your son here at home,
more advanced by the King than by that red-tailed
humble-bee I speak of.   7

COUNTESS   I would I had not known him! It was the
death of the most virtuous gentlewoman that ever
nature had praise for creating. If she had partaken of
my flesh, and cost me the dearest groans of a mother,   11
I could not have owed her a more rooted love.   12

LAFEW   'Twas a good lady, 'twas a good lady. We may
pick a thousand salads ere we light on such another
herb.

LAVATCH   Indeed, sir, she was the sweet marjoram of
the salad, or rather the herb of grace.   17

LAFEW   They are not herbs, you knave, they are nose-   18
herbs.   19

LAVATCH   I am no great Nebuchadnezzar, sir. I have   20
not much skill in grass.   21

LAFEW   Whether dost thou profess thyself, a knave or a   22
fool?

LAVATCH   A fool, sir, at a woman's service, and a knave
at a man's.

LAFEW   Your distinction?

LAVATCH   I would cozen the man of his wife and do his   27
service.   28

LAFEW   So you were a knave at his service, indeed.

LAVATCH   And I would give his wife my bauble, sir, to   30
do her service.

LAFEW   I will subscribe for thee, thou art both knave   32
and fool.

LAVATCH   At your service.

LAFEW   No, no, no!   35

LAVATCH   Why, sir, if I cannot serve you, I can serve as
great a prince as you are.

LAFEW   Who's that, a Frenchman?

LAVATCH   Faith, sir, 'a has an English name, but his   39
physnomy is more hotter in France than there.   40

LAFEW   What prince is that?

LAVATCH   The black prince, sir, alias the prince of
darkness, alias the devil.

LAFEW   Hold thee, there's my purse. [*He gives money.*] I
give thee not this to suggest thee from thy master thou   45
talk'st of; serve him still.

LAVATCH   I am a woodland fellow, sir, that always   47
loved a great fire, and the master I speak of ever keeps
a good fire. But sure he is the prince of the world; let   49
his nobility remain in 's court. I am for the house with
the narrow gate, which I take to be too little for pomp   51
to enter. Some that humble themselves may, but the
many will be too chill and tender, and they'll be for the   53
flowery way that leads to the broad gate and the great   54
fire.   55

LAFEW   Go thy ways. I begin to be aweary of thee; and   56
I tell thee so before, because I would not fall out with   57
thee. Go thy ways. Let my horses be well looked to,
without any tricks.

LAVATCH   If I put any tricks upon 'em, sir, they shall be
jades' tricks, which are their own right by the law of   61
nature.   *Exit.*

LAFEW   A shrewd knave and an unhappy.   63

COUNTESS   So 'a is. My lord that's gone made himself   64
much sport out of him. By his authority he remains
here, which he thinks is a patent for his sauciness; and
indeed he has no pace, but runs where he will.   67

LAFEW   I like him well; 'tis not amiss. And I was about
to tell you, since I heard of the good lady's death, and   69
that my lord your son was upon his return home, I
moved the King my master to speak in the behalf of
my daughter, which, in the minority of them both, His   72
Majesty, out of a self-gracious remembrance, did first   73
propose. His Highness hath promised me to do it, and
to stop up the displeasure he hath conceived against

---

35 the fine's the crown the end is the crown of all   **36 Whate'er . . .
renown** by whatever means we proceed, the conclusion is what
makes for worth. (I.e., the end justifies the means.)
4.5. Location: Rossillion.
1 with by   **2 snipped-taffeta** wearing taffeta silk garments with
slashes to allow the under material to be visible (suggestive of
Parolles' hollow flashiness).   **saffron** bright yellow spice used in
making pastry and also in dyeing starched ruffs and collars
3 unbaked and doughy raw and unformed   **7 humble-bee** bumble-
bee (noisy and useless)   **11 dearest** (1) direst (2) most loving.
groans of a mother pains of childbirth   **12 rooted** firm   **17 herb of
grace** rue for remembrance. (Also picking up on the theological
theme of "grace.")   **18 not herbs** i.e., not edible salad herbs or greens
18–19 nose-herbs fragrant herbs used for bouquets, not salads.
20–1 Nebuchadnezzar . . . grass In Daniel 4:28–37, King Nebuchadnezzar is reported to have gone mad and eaten grass like a grazing ox.
(With a pun on *grass/grace* and also *graze*; the word in the Folio is
"grace.")   **22 Whether** Which of the two   **27 cozen** cheat   **27–8 do
his service** i.e., usurp his sexual role.   **30 bauble** stick carried by a
court fool. (With bawdy suggestion.)   **32 subscribe** vouch

35 No, no, no! i.e., Not under the terms of service you have
described!   **39 English name** i.e., the Black Prince, a widely known
name for the eldest son of Edward III who defeated the French.
40 physnomy physiognomy.   **more hotter** (1) more choleric in the
fury of fighting (2) more susceptible to the "French disease," syphilis
45 suggest tempt   **47 woodland** rustic   **49 a good fire** i.e., hellfire.
51 narrow gate (Compare with Matthew 7:14: "Strait is the gate, and
narrow is the way, which leadeth unto life.")   **53 many** multitude.
chill and tender sensitive to cold and pampered. (Most people are so
fond of a good fire that they are not keeping in mind the great fire
(lines 54–5) of hell.   **53–5 the flowery . . . fire** (Compare with
Matthew 7:13: "Wide is the gate, and broad is the way, that leadeth to
destruction.")   **56 Go thy ways** Get along with you.   **57 before** i.e.,
before I grow thoroughly weary   **61 jades' tricks** (1) the vicious
behavior of *jades* or ill-tempered horses (2) malicious tricks that
hostlers might play on horses, such as greasing their teeth or their
hay   **63 shrewd** sharp-tongued and witty.   **unhappy** discontented
64 gone dead   **67 has no pace** observes no restraint. (A term from
horse training.)   **69 the good lady's** Helena's   **72 in . . . both** i.e.,
since both my daughter and Bertram are legally minors or wards
73 self-gracious remembrance thoughtful recollection that came to
him without prompting

your son there is no fitter matter. How does Your
Ladyship like it?

COUNTESS   With very much content, my lord, and I
wish it happily effected.

LAFEW   His Highness comes post from Marseilles, of as   80
able body as when he numbered thirty. 'A will be here   81
tomorrow, or I am deceived by him that in such   82
intelligence hath seldom failed.   83

COUNTESS   It rejoices me that I hope I shall see him ere
I die. I have letters that my son will be here tonight. I
shall beseech Your Lordship to remain with me till they
meet together.

LAFEW   Madam, I was thinking with what manners I
might safely be admitted.   89

COUNTESS   You need but plead your honorable privi-   90
lege.   91

LAFEW   Lady, of that I have made a bold charter, but I   92
thank my God it holds yet.

Enter Clown [Lavatch].

LAVATCH   Oh, madam, yonder's my lord your son with a
patch of velvet on 's face. Whether there be a scar
under't or no, the velvet knows, but 'tis a goodly
patch of velvet. His left cheek is a cheek of two pile   97
and a half, but his right cheek is worn bare.   98

LAFEW   A scar nobly got, or a noble scar, is a good livery   99
of honor; so belike is that.   100

LAVATCH   But it is your carbonadoed face.   101

LAFEW   Let us go see your son, I pray you. I long to talk
with the young noble soldier.

LAVATCH   Faith, there's a dozen of 'em, with delicate
fine hats, and most courteous feathers, which bow the
head and nod at every man.   *Exeunt.*

❖

5.1

*Enter Helena, Widow, and Diana, with two
attendants.*

HELENA
But this exceeding posting day and night   1
Must wear your spirits low. We cannot help it.
But since you have made the days and nights as one
To wear your gentle limbs in my affairs,   4
Be bold you do so grow in my requital   5
As nothing can unroot you.

Enter a Gentleman.

In happy time!   6

This man may help me to His Majesty's ear,
If he would spend his power.—God save you, sir.   8

GENTLEMAN   And you.

HELENA
Sir, I have seen you in the court of France.

GENTLEMAN   I have been sometimes there.

HELENA
I do presume, sir, that you are not fall'n
From the report that goes upon your goodness;
And therefore, goaded with most sharp occasions   14
Which lay nice manners by, I put you to   15
The use of your own virtues, for the which
I shall continue thankful.

GENTLEMAN   What's your will?

HELENA   That it will please you
To give this poor petition to the King
    [showing a petition]
And aid me with that store of power you have
To come into his presence.

GENTLEMAN
The King's not here.

HELENA   Not here, sir?

GENTLEMAN   Not indeed.
He hence removed last night, and with more haste   23
Than is his use.

WIDOW   Lord, how we lose our pains!   24

HELENA   All's well that ends well yet,
Though time seem so adverse and means unfit.
I do beseech you, whither is he gone?

GENTLEMAN
Marry, as I take it, to Rossillion,
Whither I am going.

HELENA   I do beseech you, sir,
Since you are like to see the King before me,
Commend the paper to his gracious hand,   31
    [giving the petition]
Which I presume shall render you no blame
But rather make you thank your pains for it.
I will come after you with what good speed
Our means will make us means.

GENTLEMAN   This I'll do for you.   35

HELENA   And you shall find yourself to be well
thanked,
Whate'er falls more. We must to horse again.—   37
Go, go, provide.   *[Exeunt separately.]*

❖

[5.2]

Enter Clown [Lavatch], and Parolles.

PAROLLES   Good Monsieur Lavatch, give my Lord
Lafew this letter [*He offers a letter.*] I have ere now, sir,
been better known to you, when I have held familiarity with fresher clothes; but I am now, sir, muddied in

80 **post** posthaste   81 **numbered thirty** was thirty years old.   82 **him**
i.e., a messenger   83 **intelligence** news   89 **admitted** i.e., allowed to
be present at that meeting.   90–1 **honorable privilege** privilege due
your honor.   92 **made . . . charter** asserted my claim as far as I dare
97–8 **two . . . half** i.e., a thick velvet   98 **worn bare** i.e., without a velvet patch.   99 **livery** uniform   100 **belike** probably   101 **But** Unless.
carbonadoed slashed or scored across with gashes, as to broil meat
(here suggesting a cut made to drain a venereal ulcer and covered
with a velvet patch)
5.1. **Location:** Marseilles. A street.
1 **posting** riding in haste   4 **wear** wear out   5 **bold** confident.
requital i.e., debt, thankfulness   6 **happy** opportune

8 **spend** expend   14 **sharp occasions** urgent circumstances   15 **nice**
scrupulous.   **put** urge   23 **removed** departed   24 **use** usual practice.   31 **Commend** present as worthy of favorable consideration
35 **Our . . . means** our resources will allow us.   37 **falls more** else
may happen.
5.2. **Location:** Rossillion.

Fortune's mood, and smell somewhat strong of her strong displeasure.

LAVATCH   Truly, Fortune's displeasure is but sluttish if it smell so strongly as thou speak'st of. I will henceforth eat no fish of Fortune's buttering. Prithee, allow 9 the wind. 10

PAROLLES   Nay, you need not to stop your nose, sir. I spake but by a metaphor.

LAVATCH   Indeed, sir, if your metaphor stink, I will stop my nose, or against any man's metaphor. Prithee, get thee further.

PAROLLES   Pray you, sir, deliver me this paper. 16

LAVATCH   Foh! Prithee, stand away. A paper from Fortune's close-stool to give to a nobleman! Look, here 18 he comes himself.

Enter Lafew.

Here is a purr of Fortune's sir, or of Fortune's cat—but 20 not a musk cat—that has fallen into the unclean fish- 21 pond of her displeasure, and, as he says, is muddied withal. Pray you, sir, use the carp as you may, for he 23 looks like a poor, decayed, ingenious, foolish, rascally 24 knave. I do pity his distress in my similes of comfort, 25 and leave him to Your Lordship.   [*Exit.*]

PAROLLES   My lord, I am a man whom Fortune hath cruelly scratched.

LAFEW   And what would you have me to do? 'Tis too late to pare her nails now. Wherein have you played the knave with Fortune that she should scratch you, who of herself is a good lady and would not have knaves thrive long under her? There's a cardecu for 33 you. [*He gives money.*] Let the justices make you and 34 Fortune friends; I am for other business.

[*He starts to leave.*]

PAROLLES   I beseech Your Honor to hear me one single word.

LAFEW   You beg a single penny more. Come, you shall ha't. Save your word.

PAROLLES   My name, my good lord, is Parolles.

LAFEW   You beg more than "word," then. Cox my 41 passion! Give me your hand. How does your drum? 42

PAROLLES   O my good lord, you were the first that found me. 44

LAFEW   Was I, in sooth? And I was the first that lost 45 thee.

PAROLLES   It lies in you, my lord, to bring me in some grace, for you did bring me out. 48

LAFEW   Out upon thee, knave! Dost thou put upon me at once both the office of God and the devil? One brings thee in grace and the other brings thee out. [*Trumpets sound.*] The King's coming; I know by his trumpets. Sirrah, inquire further after me. I had talk of you last night. Though you are a fool and a knave, you shall eat. Go to, follow.

PAROLLES   I praise God for you.   [*Exeunt.*]

❧

[5.3]

Flourish. Enter King, Old Lady [Countess], Lafew, the two French Lords, with attendants.

KING
We lost a jewel of her, and our esteem   1
Was made much poorer by it; but your son,
As mad in folly, lacked the sense to know   3
Her estimation home.

COUNTESS   'Tis past, my liege,   4
And I beseech Your Majesty to make it   5
Natural rebellion, done i'th' blade of youth,   6
When oil and fire, too strong for reason's force,
O'erbears it and burns on.

KING   My honored lady,
I have forgiven and forgotten all,
Though my revenges were high bent upon him   10
And watched the time to shoot.

LAFEW   This I must say—   11
But first I beg my pardon—the young lord   12
Did to His Majesty, his mother, and his lady
Offense of mighty note, but to himself
The greatest wrong of all. He lost a wife
Whose beauty did astonish the survey   16
Of richest eyes, whose words all ears took captive, 17
Whose dear perfection hearts that scorned to serve   18
Humbly called mistress.

KING   Praising what is lost   19
Makes the remembrance dear. Well, call him hither.
We are reconciled, and the first view shall kill

---

9 **of Fortune's buttering** i.e., prepared and served by Fortune
9–10 **allow the wind** stand downwind of me. (The hunter stands downwind of the deer so that that the prey won't smell him. Lavatch responds with jesting literalness to Parolles's lament has been befouled by evil-smelling Fortune.)   16 **me** for me   18 **close-stool** privy   20 **purr** (The multiple pun here may include "male child," "piece of dung," "the purr of a cat," and the name given to the jack or knave in the card game post and pair.)   Or perhaps the word should be *paw*; Parolles is a cat's paw; he has been fishing as a cat does in Fortune's pond and has fallen in himself. Fortune's paw has scratched.) 21 **musk cat** (Both the civet cat and musk deer were prized for their musk scent, used in perfumes.)   23 **carp** (1) a fish often bred in sewage-rich fish ponds or moats (2) a chatterer   24 **ingenious** stupid, lacking in genius or intellect (?)   25 **similes of comfort** comforting or instructive similes   33 **cardecu** quart d'écu, one-quarter of a French crown   34 **justices** i.e., Justices of the Peace, responsible in Elizabethan England for beggars under the Elizabethan poor law   41 **more than "word"** i.e., many words; *Parolles* suggests a plural of the French *parole*, "word"   41–2 **Cox my passion!** i.e., By God's (Christ's) passion on the cross!   44 **found me** found me out.

45 **lost** abandoned. (Playing on *lost* and *found*, and recalling the parable of the lost sheep.)   48 **grace** favor. (With perhaps a suggesting of "graze.")   **out** (1) out of favor, out of safe pasture (2) "out" in the theatrical sense of having forgotten one's lines.
5.3. Location: Rossillion.
0.2 *Lafew* (Lafew may remain onstage from the end of the previous scene.)   1 **of** in.   **our esteem** my own value   3–4 **know . . . home** appreciate her value fully.   5 **make account,** consider   6 **Natural rebellion** rebellion by the passions.   **blade** greenness, freshness
10 **high bent** i.e., as with a fully drawn bow   11 **watched** waited for   12 **But . . . pardon** (Lafew ceremoniously begs pardon for expressing an opinion that may seem critical.)   16 **astonish the survey** dazzle the sight   17 **richest** (1) richest in experience (2) nobly born
18–19 **Whose . . . mistress** whose dear perfection was such that gallants who scorned to owe service to anyone humbly did so to her.

All repetition. Let him not ask our pardon.   22
The nature of his great offense is dead,   23
And deeper than oblivion we do bury
Th'incensing relics of it. Let him approach   25
A stranger, no offender; and inform him   26
So 'tis our will he should.

GENTLEMAN   I shall, my liege.   [*Exit.*]   27
KING [*to Lafew*]
What says he to your daughter? Have you spoke?

LAFEW
All that he is hath reference to Your Highness.   29

KING
Then shall we have a match. I have letters sent me
That sets him high in fame.

                Enter Count Bertram.

LAFEW   He looks well on't.
KING   I am not a day of season,   33
For thou mayst see a sunshine and a hail
In me at once. But to the brightest beams
Distracted clouds give way; so stand thou forth.   36
The time is fair again.

BERTRAM   My high-repented blames,   37
Dear sovereign, pardon to me.

KING   All is whole;   38
Not one word more of the consumèd time.   39
Let's take the instant by the forward top;   40
For we are old, and on our quick'st decrees   41
Th'inaudible and noiseless foot of Time
Steals ere we can effect them. You remember
The daughter of this lord?

BERTRAM   Admiringly, my liege. At first
I stuck my choice upon her, ere my heart   46
Durst make too bold a herald of my tongue;
Where the impression of mine eye infixing,   48
Contempt his scornful perspective did lend me,   49
Which warped the line of every other favor,   50
Scorned a fair color, or expressed it stolen,   51
Extended or contracted all proportions   52
To a most hideous object. Thence it came   53
That she whom all men praised and whom myself,   54

Since I have lost, have loved, was in mine eye
The dust that did offend it.

KING   Well excused.   56
That thou didst love her strikes some scores away
From the great compt. But love that comes too late,   58
Like a remorseful pardon slowly carried,   59
To the great sender turns a sour offense,   60
Crying, "That's good that's gone." Our rash faults
Make trivial price of serious things we have,   62
Not knowing them until we know their grave.   63
Oft our displeasures, to ourselves unjust,   64
Destroy our friends, and after weep their dust;   65
Our own love waking cries to see what's done,
While shameful hate sleeps out the afternoon.   67
Be this sweet Helen's knell, and now forget her.
Send forth your amorous token for fair Maudlin.   69
The main consents are had; and here we'll stay
To see our widower's second marriage day.

COUNTESS
Which better than the first, O dear heaven, bless!
Or, ere they meet, in me, O nature, cesse!   73

LAFEW
Come on, my son, in whom my house's name
Must be digested: give a favor from you   75
To sparkle in the spirits of my daughter,   76
That she may quickly come. [*Bertram gives a ring.*]
    By my old beard,
And every hair that's on't, Helen that's dead
Was a sweet creature; such a ring as this,
The last that e'er I took her leave at court,   80
I saw upon her finger.

BERTRAM   Hers it was not.
KING
Now, pray you, let me see it, for mine eye,
While I was speaking, oft was fastened to't.
            [*The ring is given to the King.*]
This ring was mine, and when I gave it Helen
I bade her, if her fortunes ever stood   85
Necessitied to help, that by this token   86
I would relieve her. Had you that craft to reave her   87
Of what should stead her most?

BERTRAM   My gracious sovereign,   88
Howe'er it pleases you to take it so,
The ring was never hers.

COUNTESS   Son, on my life,
I have seen her wear it, and she reckoned it
At her life's rate.

LAFEW   I am sure I saw her wear it.   92

---

22 **repetition** reviewing of past wrongs, with recurrence of my anger.
23 **dead** i.e., forgotten   25 **Th'incensing relics** reminders that kindle
anger   26 **A stranger** i.e., as one whose story is unknown
27 GENTLEMAN (This could be one of the two French lords or some
other person in attendance.)   29 **hath reference to** defers to   33 **of
season** i.e., of one consistent kind of weather   36 **Distracted . . . way**
clouds disperse and give way   37 **high-repented blames** sorely
repented failings   38 **whole** mended, well   39 **consumèd** past
40 **take . . . top** take time by the forelock   41 **quick'st** most urgent
46 **stuck** fixed   48 **Where . . . infixing** i.e., the image of her entering
first at my eye and then fixing itself in my heart. (Bertram seems to
say, in lines 45-56, that he loved Lafew's daughter some time ago but
dared not speak of his love, and that, on her account, he came to
scorn all women, especially Helena, who was like an offending speck
in his eye, though since then he has learned to love the memory of
the wife he lost.)   49 **perspective** an optical glass for producing distorted images   50 **favor** face   51 **expressed it stolen** declared it to be
painted cosmetically   52–3 **Extended . . . object** elongated or compressed all other forms until they made a hideous sight.   54 **she** i.e.,
Helena

56 **offend it** (1) give it offense (2) blur its vision.   58 **compt** account,
reckoning. (With a suggestion of the Day of Judgment.)   59 **remorseful** compassionate.   **slowly carried** i.e., arriving too late   60 **turns . . .
offense** i.e., turns sour on him   62 **Make trivial price of** greatly under-
value   63 **knowing** i.e., appreciating.   **know their grave** i.e., are
aware of their irrevocable loss.   64 **displeasures** offenses   65 **weep
their dust** mourn over their remains   67 **sleeps . . . afternoon** i.e.,
sleeps at ease, having done its work.   69 **Maudlin** i.e., Magdalen, the
daughter of Lafew.   73 **ere they meet** i.e., before the two marriages
come to resemble one another in unhappiness.   **cesse** cease.
75 **digested** incorporated.   **favor** token   76 **To sparkle in** i.e., to cheer
with its luster   80 **The last** the last time.   **took her leave** took leave of
her   85 **bade her** i.e., bade her remember   86 **Necessitied to** in need
of   87 **reave** deprive, rob   88 **stead** help   92 **rate** value.

BERTRAM   You are deceived, my lord; she never saw it.
In Florence was it from a casement thrown me,
Wrapped in a paper, which contained the name
Of her that threw it. Noble she was, and thought
I stood engaged but when I had subscribed   97
To mine own fortune, and informed her fully   98
I could not answer in that course of honor   99
As she had made the overture, she ceased   100
In heavy satisfaction, and would never   101
Receive the ring again.
KING   Plutus himself,   102
That knows the tinct and multiplying med'cine,   103
Hath not in nature's mystery more science   104
Than I have in this ring. 'Twas mine, 'twas Helen's,
Whoever gave it you. Then, if you know   106
That you are well acquainted with yourself,   107
Confess 'twas hers, and by what rough enforcement
You got it from her. She called the saints to surety   109
That she would never put it from her finger
Unless she gave it to yourself in bed,
Where you have never come, or sent it us
Upon her great disaster.
BERTRAM   She never saw it.   113
KING
Thou speak'st it falsely, as I love mine honor,
And mak'st conjectural fears to come into me   115
Which I would fain shut out. If it should prove   116
That thou art so inhuman—'twill not prove so,
And yet I know not. Thou didst hate her deadly,
And she is dead, which nothing but to close
Her eyes myself could win me to believe,
More than to see this ring.—Take him away.
My forepast proofs, howe'er the matter fall,   122
Shall tax my fears of little vanity,   123
Having vainly feared too little. Away with him!   124
We'll sift this matter further.
BERTRAM   If you shall prove
This ring was ever hers, you shall as easy
Prove that I husbanded her bed in Florence,
Where yet she never was.   [Exit, guarded.]

        Enter a Gentleman.

KING
I am wrapped in dismal thinkings.
GENTLEMAN   Gracious sovereign,
Whether I have been to blame or no, I know not.

Here's a petition from a Florentine,   [giving petition]
Who hath for four or five removes come short   132
To tender it herself. I undertook it,   133
Vanquished thereto by the fair grace and speech   134
Of the poor suppliant, who by this I know   135
Is here attending. Her business looks in her   136
With an importing visage, and she told me,   137
In a sweet verbal brief, it did concern   138
Your Highness with herself.
KING [reads] a letter   "Upon his many protestations to
marry me when his wife was dead, I blush to say it,
he won me. Now is the Count Rossillion a widower,
his vows are forfeited to me, and my honor's paid to
him. He stole from Florence, taking no leave, and I   144
follow him to his country for justice. Grant it me, O
King! In you it best lies; otherwise a seducer flour-
ishes and a poor maid is undone.   Diana Capilet"
LAFEW   I will buy me a son-in-low in a fair, and toll for   148
this, I'll none of him.   149
KING
The heavens have thought well on thee, Lafew,
To bring forth this discovery.—Seek these suitors.   151
Go speedily and bring again the Count.
            [Exeunt one or more attendants.]
I am afeard the life of Helen, lady,
Was foully snatched.
COUNTESS   Now, justice on the doers!

        Enter Bertram [guarded].

KING
I wonder, sir, since wives are monsters to you,
And that you fly them as you swear them lordship,   156
Yet you desire to marry.

        Enter Widow [and] Diana.

                              What woman's that?   157
DIANA
I am, my lord, a wretched Florentine,
Derivèd from the ancient Capilet.   159
My suit, as I do understand, you know,
And therefore know how far I may be pitied.
WIDOW
I am her mother, sir, whose age and honor
Both suffer under this complaint we bring,
And both shall cease, without your remedy.   164
KING
Come hither, Count. Do you know these women?

---

97 **engaged** i.e., pledged to her; or, possibly, not pledged to another. (The Folio spelling, "ingag'd," may suggest a negative prefix.) 97–8 **subscribed . . . fortune** i.e., explained my true situation (of my marriage)   99–100 **in that . . . overture** in the same honorable way that she had followed when she proposed   101 **heavy satisfaction** doleful resignation   102 **Plutus** the god of wealth   103 **the tinct . . . med'cine** the alchemical elixir for transmuting base metals into gold   104 **science** knowledge   106–7 **if . . . yourself** i.e., if you are willing to examine yourself and your motives (something that Bertram has been notoriously unable to do)   109 **to surety** to witness   113 **Upon . . . disaster** when a catastrophe befell her.   115 **conjectural fears** fearful conjectures   116 **fain** willingly   122 **My fore-past proofs** The evidence I already have.   **fall** turn out   123–4 **Shall . . . too little** will hardly censure my fears (concerning Helena) as inconsequential; indeed, I have foolishly been too little apprehensive.

132 **for . . . short** on account of four or five shifts of residence of the court (as it moved from Marseilles to Rossillion) come too late   133 **tender** offer   134 **Vanquished** won   135 **by this** by this time   136 **looks** manifests itself   137 **importing** urgent and full of import   138 **brief** summary   144 **taking no leave** not even saying goodbye   148 **in a fair** i.e., where stolen and disreputable merchandise are common. (Lafew says he can do better at such a place than with Bertram.)   148–9 **toll for this** i.e., put Bertram up for sale. (Merchants wishing to sell at market paid a toll or fee in order to enter their goods in a register.)   151 **suitors** petitioners.   156 **as . . . lordship** as soon as you swear to be their lord and husband   157 **Yet** still   159 **Derivèd** descended   164 **both** i.e., both age and honor. (I will die dishonored.)

BERTRAM
  My lord, I neither can nor will deny
  But that I know them. Do they charge me further?
DIANA
  Why do you look so strange upon your wife?
BERTRAM
  She's none of mine, my lord.
DIANA   If you shall marry,
  You give away this hand, and that is mine;   170
  You give away heaven's vows, and those are mine;
  You give away myself, which is known mine;
  For I by vow am so embodied yours
  That she which marries you must marry me,
  Either both or none.
LAFEW [to Bertram]   Your reputation comes too short
  for my daughter; you are no husband for her.
BERTRAM
  My lord, this is a fond and desp'rate creature,   178
  Whom sometime I have laughed with. Let Your
    Highness
  Lay a more noble thought upon mine honor
  Than for to think that I would sink it here.
KING
  Sir for my thoughts, you have them ill to friend   182
  Till your deeds gain them. Fairer prove you honor
  Than in my thought it lies!
DIANA   Good my lord,
  Ask him upon his oath if he does think
  He had not my virginity.
KING   What say'st thou to her?
BERTRAM   She's impudent, my lord,   188
  And was a common gamester to the camp.   189
DIANA   He does me wrong, my lord. If I were so,
  He might have bought me at a common price.
  Do not believe him. Oh, behold this ring,
                   [showing a ring]
  Whose high respect and rich validity   193
  Did lack a parallel; yet for all that
  He gave it to a commoner o'th' camp,
  If I be one.
COUNTESS   He blushes, and 'tis hit.   196
  Of six preceding ancestors, that gem,
  Conferred by testament to th' sequent issue,   198
  Hath it been owed and worn. This is his wife;   199
  That ring's a thousand proofs.
KING [to Diana]   Methought you said
  You saw one here in court could witness it.
DIANA
  I did, my lord, but loath am to produce
  So bad an instrument. His name's Parolles.
LAFEW
  I saw the man today, if man he be.
KING
  Find him, and bring him hither.   [Exit an Attendant.]
BERTRAM   What of him?

  He's quoted for a most perfidious slave,   206
  With all the spots o'th' world taxed and debauched,   207
  Whose nature sickens but to speak a truth.
  Am I or that or this for what he'll utter,   209
  That will speak anything?
KING   She hath that ring of yours.
BERTRAM
  I think she has. Certain it is I liked her,
  And boarded her i'th' wanton way of youth.   212
  She knew her distance and did angle for me,   213
  Madding my eagerness with her restraint,   214
  As all impediments in fancy's course   215
  Are motives of more fancy; and, in fine,   216
  Her infinite cunning, with her modern grace,   217
  Subdued me to her rate. She got the ring,   218
  And I had that which any inferior might
  At market price have bought.
DIANA   I must be patient.
  You that have turned off a first so noble wife
  May justly diet me. I pray you yet—   222
  Since you lack virtue, I will lose a husband—
  Send for your ring, I will return it home,
  And give me mine again.
BERTRAM   I have it not.
KING [to Diana]   What ring was yours, I pray you?
DIANA
  Sir, much like the same upon your finger.
KING
  Know you this ring? This ring was his of late.
DIANA
  And this was it I gave him, being abed.
KING
  The story then goes false you threw it him   231
  Out of a casement?
DIANA   I have spoke the truth.

          Enter Parolles [attended].

BERTRAM
  My lord, I do confess the ring was hers.
KING
  You boggle shrewdly; every feather starts you.—   234
  Is this the man you speak of?
DIANA   Ay, my lord.
KING [to Parolles]
  Tell me, sirrah—but tell me true, I charge you,
  Not fearing the displeasure of your master,
  Which on your just proceeding I'll keep off—   238
  By him and by this woman here what know you?   239

---

206 quoted for set down as   **207 With . . . debauched** accused of, and corrupted by, all the stains of the world   **209 Am I . . . utter** Am I to be considered either one thing or another on the evidence of what he will say   **212 boarded her** accosted her sexually   **213 knew her distance** i.e., knew how to keep her distance, knew her value   **214 Madding** making mad, exciting   **215 fancy's** love's   **216 motives** causes.   **in fine** in conclusion   **217 modern** commonplace   **218 her rate** her terms.   **222 diet me** refuse me as part of your fare, as you did her. (Bertram has turned away Helena as he would a dish, and thus does the same to Diana.)   **231 The story . . . false** The story then is not true that   **234 boggle shrewdly** shy away violently.   **starts** startles **238 on . . . proceeding** if you speak honestly   **239 By** concerning

170 this hand i.e., Bertram's hand   **178 fond** foolish   **182 for** as for. **you . . . friend** they are not well disposed toward you   **188 impudent** shameless   **189 gamester** prostitute   **193 validity** value   **196 'tis hit** i.e., that point scored.   **198 sequent issue** next heir   **199 owed** owned

PAROLLES So please Your Majesty, my master hath been an honorable gentleman. Tricks he hath had in him, which gentlemen have.

KING Come, come, to th' purpose. Did he love this woman?

PAROLLES Faith, sir, he did love her; but how?

KING How, I pray you?

PAROLLES He did love her, sir, as a gentleman loves a woman.

KING How is that?

PAROLLES He loved her, sir, and loved her not.   250

KING As thou art a knave and no knave. What an equivocal companion is this!   252

PAROLLES I am a poor man, and at Your Majesty's command.

LAFEW He's a good drum, my lord, but a naughty orator.   255

DIANA Do you know he promised me marriage?

PAROLLES Faith, I know more than I'll speak.

KING But wilt thou not speak all thou know'st?

PAROLLES Yes, so please Your Majesty. I did go between them, as I said; but more than that, he loved her, for indeed he was mad for her, and talked of Satan and of Limbo and of Furies and I know not what. Yet I was in that credit with them at that time that I knew of   264
their going to bed, and of other motions, as promising   265
her marriage, and things which would derive me ill   266
will to speak of. Therefore I will not speak what I know.

KING Thou hast spoken all already, unless thou canst say they are married. But thou art too fine in thy   269
evidence; therefore stand aside.—
This ring, you say, was yours?

DIANA   Ay, my good lord.

KING
Where did you buy it? Or who gave it you?

DIANA
It was not given me, nor I did not buy it.

KING
Who lent it you?

DIANA   It was not lent me neither.

KING
Where did you find it, then?

DIANA   I found it not.

KING
If it were yours by none of all these ways,
How could you give it him?

DIANA   I never gave it him.

LAFEW This woman's an easy glove, my lord; she goes off and on at pleasure.

KING
This ring was mine. I gave it his first wife.

DIANA
It might be yours or hers, for aught I know.

KING
Take her away; I do not like her now.
To prison with her. And away with him.—

250 **loved her not** i.e., desired her only sexually. 252 **equivocal companion** equivocating knave 255 **drum** drummer (capable of mere noise). **naughty** worthless 264 **in . . . with them** so much in their confidence 265 **motions** proposals 266 **derive** gain 269 **fine** subtle

Unless thou tell'st me where thou hadst this ring,
Thou diest within this hour.

DIANA   I'll never tell you.

KING
Take her away.

DIANA   I'll put in bail, my liege.   286

KING
I think thee now some common customer.   287

DIANA
By Jove, if ever I knew man, 'twas you.   288

KING
Wherefore hast thou accused him all this while?   289

DIANA
Because he's guilty, and he is not guilty.
He knows I am no maid, and he'll swear to't;
I'll swear I am a maid, and he knows not.
Great King, I am no strumpet, by my life;
I am either maid or else this old man's wife.
                    [Pointing to Lafew.]

KING
She does abuse our ears. To prison with her!

DIANA Good mother, fetch my bail.   [Exit Widow.]
                    Stay, royal sir.
The jeweler that owes the ring is sent for,   297
And he shall surety me. But for this lord,   298
Who hath abused me, as he knows himself,
Though yet he never harmed me, here I quit him.   300
He knows himself my bed he hath defiled,
And at that time he got his wife with child.
Dead though she be, she feels her young one kick.
So there's my riddle: one that's dead is quick—   304
And now behold the meaning.

Enter Helena and Widow.

KING   Is there no exorcist   305
Beguiles the truer office of mine eyes?
Is't real that I see?

HELENA   No, my good lord,
'Tis but the shadow of a wife you see,
The name and not the thing.

BERTRAM   Both, both. Oh, pardon!

HELENA
Oh, my good lord, when I was like this maid,   310
I found you wondrous kind. There is your ring,   311
And, look you, here's your letter. [*She produces a letter.*] This it says:
"When from my finger you can get this ring
And are by me with child," et cetera. This is done.
Will you be mine, now you are doubly won?

BERTRAM
If she, my liege, can make me know this clearly,
I'll love her dearly, ever, ever dearly.

286 **put in bail** make bail, i.e., produce evidence to assure my liberty 287 **customer** i.e., prostitute. 288 **if . . . you** i.e., I have known no man sexually any more than I have slept with Your Majesty. 289 **Wherefore** Why 297 **owes** owns 298 **surety me** be my security. 300 **quit** (1) acquit (2) repay 304 **quick** alive (and pregnant) 305 **exorcist** one who conjures up spirits 310 **like this maid** i.e., disguised as Diana 311 **There** i.e., On Diana's finger (unless Diana has returned the ring to Helena.)

HELENA

If it appear not plain and prove untrue,
Deadly divorce step between me and you!—
O my dear mother, do I see you living?   319

LAFEW

Mine eyes smell onions; I shall weep anon.
[*To Parolles*] Good Tom Drum, lend me a handkerchief.
So, I thank thee. Wait on me home, I'll make sport
with thee. Let thy curtsies alone; they are scurvy ones.   324

KING

Let us from point to point this story know,
To make the even truth in pleasure flow.   326
[*To Diana*] If thou be'st yet a fresh uncropped flower,
Choose thou thy husband, and I'll pay thy dower;   328
For I can guess that by thy honest aid
Thou kept'st a wife herself, thyself a maid.
Of that and all the progress, more and less,
Resolvedly more leisure shall express.   332

All yet seems well, and if it end so meet,   333
The bitter past, more welcome is the sweet.   *Flourish.*   334

✤

[Epilogue]

KING [*advancing*]

The king's a beggar, now the play is done.
All is well ended, if this suit be won,
That you express content; which we will pay,   3
With strife to please you, day exceeding day.   4
Ours be your patience then, and yours our parts;   5
Your gentle hands lend us, and take our hearts.   6
                                        Exeunt omnes.

---

319 Deadly divorce may divorcing death   **324 curtsies** courteous
bows. (A word applied to men as well as women.)   **326 even** precise,
plain   **328 Choose . . . dower** (The king offers Diana what he offered
earlier to Helena.)   **332 Resolvedly** in such a way that all doubts are
removed

333 meet fittingly   **334 past** being past
Epilogue
3 express content i.e., applaud   **3–4 which . . . day** which we will
repay by striving to please you, day after day.   **5 Ours . . . parts** i.e.,
We will patiently attend, like an audience, while you undertake the
active role by applauding   **6 Your . . . us** i.e., please applaud.   **hearts**
i.e., gratitude.

Measure for Measure

"A play Caled Mesur for Mesur" by "Shaxberd" was performed at court, for the new King James I, by "his Maiesties plaiers" on December 26, 1604. Probably it had been composed that same year or in late 1603. The play dates from the very height of Shakespeare's tragic period, three years or so after *Hamlet*, contemporary with *Othello*, shortly before *King Lear* and *Macbeth*. This period includes very little comedy of any sort, and what there is differs markedly from the festive comedy of the 1590s. *Troilus and Cressida* (c. 1601–1602), hovering between satire and tragedy, bleakly portrays a hopeless love affair caught in the toils of a pointless and stalemated war. *All's Well That Ends Well* (c. 1601–1604) resembles *Measure for Measure* in its portrayal of an undeserving protagonist who must be deceived into marriage by the ethically ambiguous trick of substituting one woman for another in the protagonist's bed. *Measure for Measure*, perhaps the last such comedy from the tragic period, illustrates most clearly of all what critics usually mean by "problem comedy" or "problem play."

Its chief concern is not with the triumphs of love, as in the happy comedies, but with moral and social problems: "filthy vices" arising from sexual desire and the abuses of judicial authority. Images of disease abound in this play. We see corruption in Vienna "boil and bubble / Till it o'errun the stew" (5.1.326–7). The protagonist, Angelo, is for most of the play a deeply torn character, abhorring his own perverse sinfulness, compulsively driven to an attempted murder in order to cover up his lust for the heroine, Isabella. His soliloquies are introspective, tortured, focused on the psychological horror of an intelligent mind succumbing to criminal desire. The disguised Duke Vincentio, witnessing this fall into depravity and despair, can offer Angelo's intended victims no better philosophical counsel than Christian renunciation of the world and all its vain hopes. Tragedy is averted only by providential intervention and by the harsh trickery of "Craft against vice" (3.2.270), in which the Duke becomes

involved as chief manipulator and stage manager. Of the concluding marriages, two are foisted on the bridegrooms (Angelo and Lucio) against their wills, whereas that of the Duke and Isabella jars oddly with his stoical teachings and with her previous determination to be a nun. The ending thus seems arbitrary; both justice and romantic happiness are so perilously achieved in this play that they seem inconsistent with the injustice and lechery that have prevailed until the last.

Yet the very improbability of the ending and the sense of tragedy narrowly averted are perhaps intentional. These features are appropriate, not only for problem comedy, but also for tragicomedy or comedy of forgiveness, overlapping genres toward which Shakespeare gravitated in his late romances. Angelo is, like Leontes in *The Winter's Tale* (or like Bertram in *All's Well That Ends Well* and Claudio in *Much Ado About Nothing*), an erring protagonist forgiven in excess of his deserving, spared by a benign, overseeing providence from destroying that which is most precious to him.

That providence is partly ascribed to divine intervention, as when the disguised Duke, at a loss for a means of saving Claudio from imminent death, and learning that a prisoner named Ragozine has just died and is enough like Claudio physically that his head can be substituted for that of Claudio as proof that an execution has taken place, exclaims, "Oh, 'tis an accident that heaven provides!" (4.3.77). Yet most of the "providential" oversight in this play is essentially theatrical and humanly devised. It is engineered by "the old fantastical duke of dark corners" (4.3.156–7), the resourceful Vincentio. Indeed, this mysterious Duke becomes a kind of embodiment of the manipulations and sleights of hand through which this dark comedy achieves its improbable ends.

The play's title, *Measure for Measure*, introduces a paradox of human justice which this "problem" play cannot wholly resolve. How are fallible humans to judge the sins of their fellow mortals and still obey Christ's injunction of the Sermon on the Mount: "Judge not that ye be not judged"? Three positions emerge from the debate: absolute justice at one extreme, mercy at the other, and equity as a middle ground. Isabella speaks for mercy, and her words ring with biblical authority. Since all humanity would be condemned to eternal darkness were God not merciful as well as just, should not humans also be merciful? The difficulty, however, is that Vienna shows all too clearly the effects of leniency under the indulgent Duke. Vice is rampant; stern measures are needed. Though he has not wished to crack the whip himself, the Duke firmly endorses "strict statutes and most biting laws, / The needful bits and curbs to headstrong steeds" (1.3.19–20). To carry out necessary reform, the Duke has chosen Angelo, spokesman for absolute justice, to represent him. Angelo's position is cold but consistent. Only by a literal and impartial administering of the statutes, he maintains, can the law deter potential offenders. If the judge is found guilty, he must pay the penalty as well. One difficulty here, however, is that literal enforcement of the statute on fornication seems ironically to catch the wrong culprits. Claudio and Juliet, who are about to be married and are already joined by a "true contract" of betrothal, are sentenced to the severest limit of the law, whereas the pimps and whores of Vienna's suburbs manage at first to evade punishment entirely. Angelo's deputy, Escalus, can only shake his head in dismay at this unjust result of strict justice. Angelo has not remembered fully the terms of his commission from the Duke: to practice both "Mortality and mercy" in Vienna, to "enforce or qualify the laws / As to your soul seems good." The attributes of a ruler, like those of God, must include "terror" but also "love" (1.1.20–67).

Escalus's compassionate and pragmatic approach to law illustrates equity or the flexible application of the law to particular cases. Because Claudio is only technically guilty (though still guilty), Escalus would pronounce for him a light sentence. Pompey and Mistress Overdone, on the other hand, require vigorous prosecution. The problem of policing vice is compounded by the law's inefficiency, as well as by erring human nature, which will never be wholly tamed. Constable Elbow, like Dogberry in *Much Ado*, is a pompous user of malapropisms, less clever by far than the criminals he would arrest. His evidence against Pompey is so absurdly circumstantial that Escalus is first obliged to let off this engaging pimp with a stern warning. Yet Escalus patiently and tenaciously attends to such proceedings, unlike Angelo, whose interest in the law is too theoretical. Escalus deals with day-to-day problems effectively. He orders reforms of the system by which constables are selected, instructs Elbow in the rudiments of his office, and so proceeds, ultimately, to an effective arrest. Vice is not eliminated; as Pompey defiantly points out, unless someone plans to "geld and splay all the youth of the city," they "will to't then" (2.1.229–33). Still, vice is held in check. Law can shape the outer person and hope for some inner reform. Even Pompey is taught a trade, albeit a grisly one, as an apprentice hangman. The law must use both "correction" and "instruction."

The solutions arrived at in the comic subplot do not fit the case of Angelo, for he is powerful enough to be above the Viennese law. Indeed, he tries finally to brazen it out, pitting his authority against that of the seemingly friendless Isabella, much like the biblical Elders when justly accused of immorality by the innocent Susannah. Society is on Angelo's side—even the well-meaning Escalus; only a seeming providence can rescue the defenseless. The Duke of Vienna, hovering in the background and seeing all that happens, intervenes just at those points when tragedy threatens to become irreversible. Moreover, the Duke is testing those he observes. As he says to Friar Thomas, explaining why he has delegated his power to Angelo: "Hence shall we see, / If power change purpose, what our seemers be" (1.3.53–4). The Duke obviously expects Angelo to fall. Indeed, he has known all along that Angelo had dishonorably repudiated his solemn contract to Mariana when her marriage dowry disappeared at sea (3.1.215–25). Like an all-seeing deity who keeps a reckoning of humanity's good and evil deeds, the Duke has found out Angelo's great weakness. As Angelo confesses, "I perceive Your Grace, like power divine, / Hath looked upon my passes" (5.1.377–8). Paradoxically, this seemingly tragic story of temptation and fall yields precious benefits of remorse and humility. Angelo is rescued from his self-made nightmare of seduction, murder, and tyranny. Knowing now that he is prone like other mortals to fleshly weakness, he knows also that he needs spiritual assistance and that, as judge, he ought to use mercy. Seen in retrospect, his panic, despair, and humiliation are curative.

The Duke is no less a problematic character than Angelo, Isabella, and the rest. Vienna's deep corruption is, in part, the result of his unwillingness to bear down on vice, and yet, rather than undertake to remedy the failure himself, this strange monarch elects to leave the business to one he suspects will make matters worse. The Duke has a great deal to learn about his own dislike of crowds, his complacent tolerance of human weakness, and his naive supposition that all his subjects speak well of him. He is a highly manipulative character, the one most responsible in the play for the ethically dubious solutions through which craft must be employed against vice. The comforting words of spiritual counsel he offers Claudio, Juliet, and the rest are spoken by a secular ruler fraudulently disguised as a friar. Certainly, the Duke is no allegorized god-figure, for all his omniscience and final role as both punisher and forgiver. As *deux ex machina* of this problem comedy, the Duke is human, frail, and vulnerable—as indeed he ought to be in a play that explores with such rich complexity the ironic distance between divine and human justice.

Yet, for all his manifest and even comic weaknesses, the Duke is finally the authority figure who must attempt to bring order to the imperfect world of Vienna. The devices he employs, including the bed trick, seem morally questionable and yet are palpable comic fictions that unmistakably notify us what genre we are watching. If the Duke's role is more that of artist than ruler or diety, his being so is appropriate to the artistically contrived and theatrical world that Shakespeare presents to us. Within the world of this play, the disguised Duke's chief function is to test the other characters and to mislead them intentionally into expecting the worst, in order to try their resolve. On a comic level, he exposes the amiable but loose-tongued Lucio as a slanderer against the Duke himself and devises for Lucio a suitably satirical exposure and witty punishment. More seriously, as confessor to Juliet, he assures her that her beloved Claudio must die on the morrow. As she ought, she penitentially accepts "shame with joy" and so is cleansed (2.3.37). Because the Duke is not really a friar, he does not have the spiritual authority to do this, and the ruse strikes us as theatrical, employing devices of illusion that actors and dramatists use. Even so, it provides real comfort for Juliet. The very theatricality of the illusion, by reminding us that we are in the theater, enables us to see the Duke as a kind of morally persuasive playwright who can change the lives of his characters for the better.

Similarly, the counsel of Christian renunciation offered to Claudio by the bogus friar (3.1) is at once illusory and comforting. The Duke's poignant reflection on the vanity of human striving is made ironic but not invalid by our awareness that we are viewing a deception with a seemingly benign purpose—that of persuading Claudio to see matters in their true perspective. The Duke characterizes life as a breath, a dreamlike "after-dinner's sleep," a fever of inconstancy in which timorous humans long fretfully for what they do not have and spurn those things they have. Claudio responds as he ought, resolving to "find life" by "seeking death" (3.1.5–43). He achieves this calm, however, in the face of certain execution; ironically, what he must then learn to overmaster is the desperate hope of living by means of his sister's dishonor. Claudio is broken by this test and perversely begs for a few years of guilty life at the cost of eternal shame for himself and Isabella. From this harrowing experience, he emerges at length with a better understanding of his own weakness and a greater compassion toward the weakness of others.

The searing encounter between Claudio and Isabella puts her to the test as well, and her response seems hysterical and no doubt prudish to modern audiences. She has much to learn about the complexities of human behavior. Although she is sincere in protesting that she would lay down her life for her brother and is correct, in the play's terms, to prefer virtue to mere existence, her tone is too strident. Like other major characters, she must be humbled before she can rise. She and Claudio must heed the Duke's essential admonition: "Do not satisfy your resolution with hopes that are fallible" (3.1.170–1). Only then, paradoxically, can Isabella and Claudio go on to achieve earthly happiness.

Isabella and Angelo are paradoxically alike. Both have retreated from the world of carnal pleasure into havens they regard as safe but that turn out not to work in the way they had hoped. Isabella longs for the restraints of the sisterhood into which she is about to enter. Her suspicions about human frailty can be seen in her testing of her brother; she fears he will fail her by begging life at the cost of her eternal shame, and when he does just that, she reacts with shrill condemnation and even hatred. This is a dark moment for Isabella, and she needs the spiritual counsel of the disguised Duke to enable her to forgive not only her brother but also herself. Angelo, meanwhile, has attempted to put down the rebellion of the flesh by suppressing and denying all such feeling in himself. We see him at first as the workaholic official who is not hesitant to condemn in others what he believes he is free of personally. He cherishes restraint as much as Isabella does, and that is why he is so terrified when the apparent absence of his only superior, the Duke, opens up to him the abyss of his own licentiousness. Once his word is law, Angelo perceives that he can play the tyrant and seducer without check. He is horrified to discover not only that he has ungovernable sexual longings within him but also that they perversely direct themselves toward a woman who is virginal and saintly. Why does he yearn to "raze the sanctuary" thus (2.2.178)? The revelation to him of his own innate evil is virtually tragic in the intensity of his self-loathing, and yet, in this strange comedy, this revelation is a first step toward coming to terms with his reprobate self. Until Angelo acknowledges the carnal within, he cannot begin looking for a way to understand and accept this frailty. The Duke's test provides the means of self-discovery that Angelo cannot fashion on his own.

In her final testing, Isabella shows greatness of spirit. Here, Shakespeare significantly alters his chief sources, George Whetstone's *Promos and Cassandra* (1578), Giovanni Baptista Giraldi Cinthio's *Hecatommithi*, and Whetstone's *Heptameron of Civil Discourses*. In all these versions, the character corresponding to Angelo does actually ravish the heroine, and in the *Hecatommithi* he also murders her brother. Shakespeare, by withholding these irreversible acts, not only gives to Angelo a technical innocence, but also allows the Duke, as *deus ex machina*, to practice virtuous deception on Isabella one more time. Can she forgive the supposed murderer of her brother? Her affirmative answer confutes the Old Testament ethic of "An Angelo for Claudio, death for death" whereby "Like doth quit like, and measure still for measure" (5.1.417–19). Although Angelo concedes that he deserves to die for what he intended, the forfeit need not be paid so long as humanity can reveal itself capable of Isabella's godlike mercy.

With its apparently unsuitable marriages and its improbable plotting, *Measure for Measure* does end by dealing directly with the problems of human nature confronted in the earlier scenes. The bed trick (switching Mariana for Isabella) may seem a legalistic and contrived way to bring Angelo to terms with his own carnality, but it is instructive not only to him but also to Isabella; she, like Angelo, must learn to accept the realities of the human condition. By helping Mariana to achieve her legitimate desire to couple and marry, Isabella sees into her own need. Her begging for Angelo's life is not merely an act of forgiveness to an enemy; it is a gift of continued marriage to Mariana. This realization helps to prepare Isabella herself for a marriage that, although dramatically surprising on stage (and even rejected by her in some modern productions), may be intended to demonstrate her having given up the cloistered life for all that marriage signifies. *Measure for Measure* is thus essentially comic (unlike *Troilus and Cressida*), despite its harrowing scenes of conflict and its awareness of vice everywhere in human nature. The play celebrates the *felix culpa* of human nature, the fall from grace that is an integral part of humanity's rise to happiness and self-knowledge. Throughout, in the play's finest scenes, poignancy is tempered by a wit and humor that are ultimately gracious. The formal and substantive emphasis on marriage stresses not just the benefits of remorse and humility but also the real possibility of psychic and spiritual growth: Isabella can acknowledge that she is a woman, Angelo can be genuinely freed from repression, and Claudio can value life more intensely because he has confronted death. All these recognitions affirm the acceptance and proper use of the physical and sexual side of human nature, and yet they are achieved only through charity and forgiveness. Humanity can learn, however slowly and painfully, that the talents entrusted to it by providence are to be used wisely.

The guardedly hopeful reading of the play offered here is, to be sure, not the only way in which it can be understood. The stage history of *Measure for Measure* highlights much that is problematic and troubling about

it. For virtually all of the seventeenth, eighteenth, and nineteenth centuries, after its initial production, the play disappeared from the theater, other than in a heavily rewritten adaptation of the Restoration period and an even more radically recast nineteenth-century operatic version by Richard Wagner called *Das Liebesverbot* ("Forbidden Love"). The play was, it seems, too disagreeable for audiences in those centuries, too given over to vice and moral ambiguity. Readers were sometimes warned away from it. The twentieth and twenty-first centuries, conversely, have found in *Measure for Measure* a persuasive and even devastating dramatization of human imperfection. In an age that has learned to distrust authority figures, Duke Vincentio can come across as officious and sadistic in his manipulation of human lives, rather than ultimately benign. The director Keith Hack, at Stratford-upon-Avon in 1974, saw the Duke as devious, hypocritical, deeply implicated in the corruption of his city, and bitterly resented by the characters whose lives are intrusively managed by him. Some productions have asked if Lucio is justified in his suspicions that the Duke is really a fleshmonger after all. Isabella's longing for the cloistered life of the convent is sometimes seen today as psychologically driven by a fear of sexuality more than by religious faith. Some stage productions revel in the tawdriness of the bordello world of a corrupted Vienna, as for example in Michael Bogdanov's production at Stratford, Canada, in 1985. To Keith Hack, in 1974, the play was as fable of social impression in the vein of Bertolt Brecht. The marriages with which the play ends are often held up to skeptical scrutiny. Is Angelo chastised by his searing experience into resolving to be a good husband to Mariana, or does he snarl at her when he is led off with her to be married? Most significantly, perhaps, does Isabella accept the surprising offer of marriage from the Duke who has protected her but also deceived her into believing that her brother was dead? Today, beginning with Estelle Kohler in John Barton's production at Stratford-upon-Avon in 1970, actresses and directors get to choose; since Isabella is given no lines indicating her acceptance, the actress may simply be bewildered or may decide, with a gesture of defiance or indifference, to have nothing to do with men. The range of options is extraordinary, and helps demonstrate the way in which Shakespeare provides such an unsettling challenge to actors, directors, and audiences alike.

Measure for Measure

The Names of All the Actors

VINCENTIO, *the Duke*
ANGELO, *the deputy*
ESCALUS, *an ancient lord*
CLAUDIO, *a young gentleman*
LUCIO, *a fantastic*
Two other like GENTLEMEN
PROVOST
THOMAS, ⎫
PETER, ⎬ *two friars*
[A JUSTICE]
[VARRIUS, *a friend of the Duke*]

ELBOW, *a simple constable*
FROTH, *a foolish gentleman*
CLOWN [*POMPEY, a servant to Mistress Overdone*]

ABHORSON, *an executioner*
BARNARDINE, *a dissolute prisoner*

ISABELLA, *sister to Claudio*
MARIANA, *betrothed to Angelo*
JULIET, *beloved of Claudio*
FRANCISCA, *a nun*
MISTRESS OVERDONE, *a bawd*

[A SERVANT *of Angelo*
BOY *singer*
A MESSENGER *from Angelo*

Lords, Officers, Citizens, Servants, and other Attendants]

THE SCENE: *Vienna*

1.1

Enter Duke, Escalus, lords, [and attendants].

DUKE Escalus.
ESCALUS My lord.
DUKE
Of government the properties to unfold   3
Would seem in me t'affect speech and discourse,   4
Since I am put to know that your own science   5
Exceeds, in that, the lists of all advice   6
My strength can give you. Then no more remains   7
But that to your sufficiency   8
. . . . as your worth is able,   9
And let them work. The nature of our people,

Our city's institutions, and the terms   11
For common justice, you're as pregnant in   12
As art and practice hath enrichèd any   13
That we remember. There is our commission,
[giving a paper]
From which we would not have you warp.—Call
   hither,   15
I say, bid come before us Angelo.   *[Exit one.]*
What figure of us think you he will bear?   17
For you must know, we have with special soul   18
Elected him our absence to supply,   19
Lent him our terror, dressed him with our love,   20
And given his deputation all the organs   21
Of our own power. What think you of it?
ESCALUS
If any in Vienna be of worth
To undergo such ample grace and honor,   24

1.1 Location: Vienna. The court of Duke Vincentio.
3–4 Of . . . discourse For me to deliver an oration on the qualities needed in governing well would make me seem enamored of my own pomposity   **5 put to know** obliged to admit.   **science** knowledge   **6 that** i.e., properties of government (line 3).   **lists** limits   **7 strength** power of mind   **8–9 But . . . able** (The passage appears in the Folio as a single line. Several attempts at emendation have been made, but the most plausible explanation is that something has been deleted or inadvertently omitted.)

11 terms terms of court; or, modes of procedure   **12 pregnant** well-informed   **13 art** learning, theory   **15 warp** deviate.   **17 What . . . bear?** i.e., How do you think he will do as my substitute?   **18 special soul** all the powers of the mind; whole heart   **19 Elected** chosen.   **supply** fill, make up for   **20 terror** power to inspire awe and fear   **21 his deputation** him as deputy.   **organs** instruments   **24 undergo** bear the weight of

It is Lord Angelo.

Enter Angelo.

DUKE   Look where he comes.
ANGELO
  Always obedient to Your Grace's will,
  I come to know your pleasure.
DUKE   Angelo,
  There is a kind of character in thy life
  That to th'observer doth thy history
  Fully unfold. Thyself and thy belongings   30
  Are not thine own so proper as to waste   31
  Thyself upon thy virtues, they on thee.   32
  Heaven doth with us as we with torches do,   33
  Not light them for themselves; for if our virtues
  Did not go forth of us, 'twere all alike   35
  As if we had them not. Spirits are not finely touched   36
  But to fine issues, nor Nature never lends   37
  The smallest scruple of her excellence   38
  But, like a thrifty goddess, she determines   39
  Herself the glory of a creditor,   40
  Both thanks and use. But I do bend my speech   41
  To one that can my part in him advertise.   42
  Hold, therefore, Angelo:
  In our remove be thou at full ourself.   44
  Mortality and mercy in Vienna   45
  Live in thy tongue and heart. Old Escalus,
  Though first in question, is thy secondary.   47
  Take thy commission.   [*He gives a paper.*]
ANGELO   Now, good my lord,
  Let there be some more test made of my mettle   49
  Before so noble and so great a figure
  Be stamped upon it.
DUKE   No more evasion.
  We have with a leavened and preparèd choice   52
  Proceeded to you; therefore take your honors.
  Our haste from hence is of so quick condition   54
  That it prefers itself and leaves unquestioned   55
  Matters of needful value. We shall write to you,
  As time and our concernings shall importune,   57
  How it goes with us, and do look to know   58

What doth befall you here. So, fare you well.
  To th' hopeful execution do I leave you   60
  Of your commissions.
ANGELO   Yet give leave, my lord,   61
  That we may bring you something on the way.   62
DUKE   My haste may not admit it;   63
  Nor need you, on mine honor, have to do   64
  With any scruple. Your scope is as mine own,   65
  So to enforce or qualify the laws
  As to your soul seems good. Give me your hand.
  I'll privily away. I love the people   68
  But do not like to stage me to their eyes;   69
  Though it do well, I do not relish well   70
  Their loud applause and "aves" vehement,   71
  Nor do I think the man of safe discretion   72
  That does affect it. Once more, fare you well.   73
ANGELO
  The heavens give safety to your purposes!
ESCALUS
  Lead forth and bring you back in happiness!   75
DUKE   I thank you. Fare you well.   *Exit.*
ESCALUS
  I shall desire you, sir, to give me leave
  To have free speech with you; and it concerns me 78
  To look into the bottom of my place.   79
  A power I have, but of what strength and nature
  I am not yet instructed.
ANGELO
  'Tis so with me. Let us withdraw together,
  And we may soon our satisfaction have
  Touching that point.
ESCALUS   I'll wait upon Your Honor.
                                          Exeunt.

❖

1.2

Enter Lucio and two other Gentlemen.

LUCIO   If the Duke with the other dukes come not to
  composition with the King of Hungary, why then all   2
  the dukes fall upon the King.   3
FIRST GENTLEMAN   Heaven grant us its peace, but not
  the King of Hungary's!
SECOND GENTLEMAN   Amen.
LUCIO   Thou conclud'st like the sanctimonious pirate
  that went to sea with the Ten Commandments but
  scraped one out of the table.   9
SECOND GENTLEMAN   "Thou shalt not steal"?
LUCIO   Ay, that he razed.   11

30 **belongings** attributes, endowments   31 **proper** exclusively
31–2 as to . . . thee that you can expend all your efforts developing
your own talents or use them solely for your own advantage.
33 torches (Compare Jesus' command that we not hide our light
under a bushel, Matthew 5:14–16.)   35 **forth of us** out of us and into
the world.   **'twere all alike** it would be exactly the same   36–7 **Spirits . . . issues** Souls are not deeply moved unless for noble purposes
38 scruple bit. (Literally, a small weight.)   **39–41 But . . . use** unless,
like a thrifty goddess, she gathers to herself the glory due to a creditor, gaining both thanks from her debtor and interest on the loan.
41 bend direct   **42 that . . . advertise** who can instruct my role as
duke now vested in him, i.e., who knows already more about governing in my absence than I can tell him.   **44 In . . . ourself** During my
absence be in every respect my deputy. (The royal plural.)   **45 Mortality** The full rigor of the law, the death sentence   **47 first in question** senior and first appointed   **49 mettle** substance, quality. (With
play on "metal," a common variant spelling, continued in the coining
imagery of lines 50–1.)   **52 leavened** i.e., carefully considered (just as
yeast is given time to leaven dough)   **54–5 Our . . . itself** The cause
for my hasty departure is so urgent that it takes precedence over all
other matters   **55 unquestioned** not yet considered   **57 concernings**
affairs.   **importune** urge   **58 look to know** expect to be informed

60 **th' hopeful** exciting hopes of success.   **execution** carrying out
61 leave permission   **62 bring you something** accompany you for a
short distance   **63 admit** permit   **64–5 have . . . scruple** have the
least doubt or hesitation about what is to be done.   **68 I'll privily
away** I'll go away secretly.   **69 stage me** make a show of myself
70 do well i.e., serves a political purpose   **71 aves** hails of acclamation   **72 safe** sound   **73 affect** desire, court   **75 Lead** May the heavens conduct you   **78 free** frank   **79 the bottom of my place** the
extent of my commission.
1.2. Location: A public place.
2 composition agreement   **3 fall upon** attack   **9 table** tablet.
11 razed scraped out. (The word may also suggest *rased*, "erased.")

FIRST GENTLEMAN   Why, 'twas a commandment to command the captain and all the rest from their function; they put forth to steal. There's not a soldier of us all that, in the thanksgiving before meat, do relish the petition well that prays for peace. 14 15

SECOND GENTLEMAN   I never heard any soldier dislike it.

LUCIO   I believe thee, for I think thou never wast where grace was said.

SECOND GENTLEMAN   No? A dozen times at least.

FIRST GENTLEMAN   What, in meter?

LUCIO   In any proportion or in any language. 22

FIRST GENTLEMAN   I think, or in any religion.

LUCIO   Ay, why not? Grace is grace, despite of all controversy; as, for example, thou thyself art a wicked villain, despite of all grace. 24 25

FIRST GENTLEMAN   Well, there went but a pair of shears between us. 27 28

LUCIO   I grant; as there may between the lists and the velvet. Thou art the list. 29 30

FIRST GENTLEMAN   And thou the velvet. Thou art good velvet; thou'rt a three-piled piece, I warrant thee. I had as lief be a list of an English kersey as be piled, as thou art piled, for a French velvet. Do I speak feelingly now? 32 33 34

LUCIO   I think thou dost, and indeed with most painful feeling of thy speech. I will, out of thine own confession, learn to begin thy health, but, whilst I live, forget to drink after thee. 37 38

FIRST GENTLEMAN   I think I have done myself wrong, have I not? 39

SECOND GENTLEMAN   Yes, that thou hast, whether thou art tainted or free. 42

Enter bawd [Mistress Overdone].

LUCIO   Behold, behold, where Madam Mitigation comes! I have purchased as many diseases under her roof as come to— 43

SECOND GENTLEMAN   To what, I pray?

LUCIO   Judge. 47

SECOND GENTLEMAN   To three thousand dolors a year. 48

FIRST GENTLEMAN   Ay, and more.

LUCIO   A French crown more. 50

FIRST GENTLEMAN   Thou art always figuring diseases in me, but thou art full of error. I am sound. 51

LUCIO   Nay, not, as one would say, healthy, but so sound as things that are hollow. Thy bones are hollow; impiety has made a feast of thee. 54 55

FIRST GENTLEMAN   [*to Mistress Overdone*]   How now, which of your hips has the most profound sciatica? 57

MISTRESS OVERDONE   Well, well; there's one yonder arrested and carried to prison was worth five thousand of you all.

SECOND GENTLEMAN   Who's that, I pray thee?

MISTRESS OVERDONE   Marry, sir, that's Claudio, Signor Claudio. 62

FIRST GENTLEMAN   Claudio to prison? 'Tis not so.

MISTRESS OVERDONE   Nay, but I know 'tis so. I saw him arrested, saw him carried away; and, which is more, within these three days his head to be chopped off. 66

LUCIO   But, after all this fooling, I would not have it so. Art thou sure of this? 68

MISTRESS OVERDONE   I am too sure of it; and it is for getting Madam Julietta with child.

LUCIO   Believe me, this may be. He promised to meet me two hours since, and he was ever precise in promise-keeping. 73

SECOND GENTLEMAN   Besides, you know, it draws something near to the speech we had to such a purpose. 75 76 77

FIRST GENTLEMAN   But most of all agreeing with the proclamation.

LUCIO   Away! Let's go learn the truth of it.

Exit [Lucio with the Gentlemen].

MISTRESS OVERDONE   Thus, what with the war, what with the sweat, what with the gallows, and what with poverty, I am custom-shrunk. 82 83

Enter Clown [Pompey].

How now, what's the news with you?

POMPEY   Yonder man is carried to prison.

MISTRESS OVERDONE   Well, what has he done? 86

POMPEY   A woman.

MISTRESS OVERDONE   But what's his offense?

POMPEY   Groping for trouts in a peculiar river. 89

---

14 put forth set out to sea   **15 thanksgiving before meat** saying of grace before a meal. (As in line 19.)   **22 proportion** form **24–5 Grace . . . controversy** (Refers to the Catholic-Protestant *controversy*, line 25, as to whether humanity can be saved by works or by grace alone; with punning on *grace* as "thanks for a meal," line 19, and "gracefulness" or "becomingness," line 26.)   **27–8 there . . . between us** i.e., we're cut from the same cloth.   **29–30 as . . . list** (Lucio jokes that the shears might also cut between, i.e., distinguish between, the mere *lists* or selvages, edges of a woven fabric, and the *velvet* betokening a true gentlemen. Lucio wittily asserts himself to be a true gentleman; the other speaker, not.)   **32 three-piled** having a threefold pile or nap, the best grade. (Velvet patches might be used to conceal syphilitic sores or scars.)   **33 as lief** as soon, rather.   **kersey** a coarse woolen fabric. (The First Gentleman turns the joke on Lucio by saying he would rather be a plain, homespun Englishman than a Frenchified velvet gentleman in decay and threadbare. *Velvet* suggests prostitutes and venereal disease, as in the following notes.)   **be piled** (1) have a cloth nap (2) suffer from hemorrhoids (3) be pilled or peeled, i.e., hairless, bald, as a result of mercury treatment for syphilis (known as the "French disease"; see *French velvet* in the next line and *French crown*, line 50)   **34 feelingly** to the purpose, so as to hit home. (But Lucio's reply quibbles on "painfully," meaning the Gentleman's mouth is affected by the French disease; hence, Lucio will not drink from the same cup after him.)   **37 begin thy health** drink to your health   **37–8 forget . . . thee** take care not to drink from your cup.   **39 done myself wrong** i.e., asked for that   **42 tainted** infected   **43 Mitigation** (So called because her function is to relieve desire.)

47 Judge Guess.   **48 dolors** (Quibbling on *dollars;* spelled "Dollours" in the Folio.)   **50 French crown** (1) gold coin (2) bald head incurred through syphilis, the "French disease"   **51 figuring** (1) imagining (2) reckoning. (Recalling the monetary puns of lines 48 and 50.) **54 sound** (1) healthy (2) resounding (because of hollow bones caused by syphilis)   **55 impiety** wickedness   **57 sciatica** a disease affecting the sciatic nerve in the hip and thigh, thought to be a symptom of syphilis.   **62 Marry** i.e., By the Virgin Mary   **66 which** what **68 after** notwithstanding   **73 ever** always   **75–6 draws . . . near to** approaches, sounds somewhat like   **76–7 to . . . purpose** on that topic.   **82 sweat** sweating sickness (often fatal), or the plague; also, the sweating tub, a treatment for syphilis   **83 custom-shrunk** having fewer customers.   **86 done** (Pompey quibbles in line 87 on a sexual sense of the word, present also in Mistress Overdone's name.) **89 peculiar** privately owned. (With bawdy suggestion.)

MISTRESS OVERDONE   What? Is there a maid with child by him?

POMPEY   No, but there's a woman with maid by him. 92
You have not heard of the proclamation, have you?

MISTRESS OVERDONE   What proclamation, man?

POMPEY   All houses in the suburbs of Vienna must be 95
plucked down.

MISTRESS OVERDONE   And what shall become of those
in the city?

POMPEY   They shall stand for seed. They had gone 99
down too, but that a wise burgher put in for them. 100

MISTRESS OVERDONE   But shall all our houses of resort
in the suburbs be pulled down?

POMPEY   To the ground, mistress.

MISTRESS OVERDONE   Why, here's a change indeed in
the commonwealth! What shall become of me?

POMPEY   Come, fear not you. Good counselors lack no 106
clients. Though you change your place, you need not 107
change your trade; I'll be your tapster still. Courage! 108
There will be pity taken on you. You that have worn 109
your eyes almost out in the service, you will be con- 110
sidered.

MISTRESS OVERDONE   What's to do here, Thomas Tapster? Let's withdraw.

POMPEY   Here comes Signor Claudio, led by the Pro- 114
vost to prison; and there's Madam Juliet.   *Exeunt.* 115

*Enter Provost, Claudio, Juliet, Officers; Lucio
and two Gentlemen [follow].*

CLAUDIO *[to the Provost]*
Fellow, why dost thou show me thus to the world?
Bear me to prison, where I am committed.

PROVOST
I do it not in evil disposition
But from Lord Angelo by special charge.

CLAUDIO
Thus can the demigod Authority
Make us pay down for our offense, by weight,   121
The words of heaven. On whom it will, it will;   122
On whom it will not, so; yet still 'tis just.   123

LUCIO
Why, how now, Claudio? Whence comes this
restraint?

CLAUDIO
From too much liberty, my Lucio, liberty.

As surfeit is the father of much fast,   126
So every scope, by the immoderate use,   127
Turns to restraint. Our natures do pursue,
Like rats that ravin down their proper bane,   129
A thirsty evil, and when we drink we die.

LUCIO   If I could speak so wisely under an arrest, I 131
would send for certain of my creditors. And yet, to say 132
the truth, I had as lief have the foppery of freedom as 133
the morality of imprisonment. What's thy offense,
Claudio?

CLAUDIO
What but to speak of would offend again.

LUCIO
What, is't murder?

CLAUDIO   No.

LUCIO   Lechery?

CLAUDIO
Call it so.

PROVOST   Away, sir, you must go.

CLAUDIO
One word, good friend.—Lucio, a word with you.

LUCIO
A hundred, if they'll do you any good.
Is lechery so looked after?   141

CLAUDIO
Thus stands it with me: upon a true contract   142
I got possession of Julietta's bed.
You know the lady; she is fast my wife,   144
Save that we do the denunciation lack   145
Of outward order. This we came not to,   146
Only for propagation of a dower   147
Remaining in the coffer of her friends,   148
From whom we thought it meet to hide our love   149
Till time had made them for us. But it chances   150
The stealth of our most mutual entertainment
With character too gross is writ on Juliet.   152

LUCIO
With child, perhaps?

CLAUDIO   Unhappily, even so.
And the new deputy now for the Duke—
Whether it be the fault and glimpse of newness,   155
Or whether that the body public be
A horse whereon the governor doth ride,
Who, newly in the seat, that it may know
He can command, lets it straight feel the spur;   159

---

92 woman with maid (Pompey playfully corrects Mistress Overdone's use of the word "maid," joking that a pregnant woman cannot
be a virgin [*maid*] though the child she carries is one.)   **95 houses** i.e.,
brothels.   **suburbs** (Location of the brothels in Shakespeare's London, as in other walled cities.)   **99 for seed** to preserve the species.
(With ribald pun.)   **100 burgher** citizen.   **put . . . them** interceded on
their behalf, offered to acquire them.   **106–7 Good . . . clients** Good
lawyers (and, by implication, pimps and bawds) are never at a loss
for clients.   **108 tapster** one who draws beer in an alehouse
109–10 worn . . . out i.e., worked so hard. (Perhaps with an ironic reference to the traditional image of the blind Cupid, often depicted on
signs hung at the doors of brothels.)   **114–15 Provost** officer charged
with apprehension, custody, and punishment of offenders
121–2 Make . . . heaven make us pay the full penalty for our offenses
called for in the Bible.   **122–3 On whom . . . 'tis just** (Compare
Romans 9:18: "Therefore hath he [God] mercy on whom he will have
mercy, and whom he will he hardeneth.")

126 As . . . fast Just as excessive indulgence inevitably leads to revulsion and abstinence   **127 scope** liberty, license   **129 ravin . . . bane**
greedily devour what is poisonous to them   **131–2 If . . . creditors** If
imprisonment would gain me such wisdom, I would send for those
to whom I owe money and thus be arrested for debt.   **133 lief** willingly.   **foppery** folly   **141 looked after** kept under observation.
142 a true contract i.e., one made in the presence of witnesses, though
without a religious ceremony. (Such a precontract was binding but, in
the eyes of the Church, did not confer the right of sexual consummation before the nuptials.)   **144 fast my wife** i.e., firmly bound by precontract   **145 denunciation** formal declaration   **146 outward order**
public ceremony.   **147 propagation** increase, begetting   **148 friends**
relatives   **149 meet** fitting, necessary   **150 made . . . us** disposed
them in our favor.   **152 character too gross** writing too evident
155 the fault . . . newness the faulty flashiness of novelty
159 straight at once

Whether the tyranny be in his place,   160
Or in his eminence that fills it up,   161
I stagger in—but this new governor   162
Awakes me all the enrollèd penalties   163
Which have, like unscoured armor, hung by the wall
So long that nineteen zodiacs have gone round   165
And none of them been worn; and for a name   166
Now puts the drowsy and neglected act
Freshly on me. 'Tis surely for a name.

LUCIO   I warrant it is, and thy head stands so tickle on   169
  thy shoulders that a milkmaid, if she be in love, may
  sigh it off. Send after the Duke and appeal to him.

CLAUDIO
I have done so, but he's not to be found.
I prithee, Lucio, do me this kind service:
This day my sister should the cloister enter   174
And there receive her approbation.   175
Acquaint her with the danger of my state;
Implore her, in my voice, that she make friends
To the strict deputy; bid herself assay him.   178
I have great hope in that, for in her youth
There is a prone and speechless dialect   180
Such as move men; beside, she hath prosperous art   181
When she will play with reason and discourse,
And well she can persuade.

LUCIO   I pray she may, as well for the encouragement of   184
  the like, which else would stand under grievous impo-   185
  sition, as for the enjoying of thy life, who I would   186
  be sorry should be thus foolishly lost at a game of tick- 187
  tack. I'll to her.   188

CLAUDIO   I thank you, good friend Lucio.

LUCIO   Within two hours.

CLAUDIO   Come, officer, away!   *Exeunt.*

❖

1.[3]

Enter Duke and Friar Thomas.

DUKE
No, holy Father, throw away that thought;
Believe not that the dribbling dart of love   2
Can pierce a complete bosom. Why I desire thee   3
To give me secret harbor hath a purpose   4
More grave and wrinkled than the aims and ends   5
Of burning youth.

FRIAR THOMAS   May Your Grace speak of it?

DUKE
My holy sir, none better knows than you
How I have ever loved the life removed   8
And held in idle price to haunt assemblies   9
Where youth and cost witless bravery keeps.   10
I have delivered to Lord Angelo,
A man of stricture and firm abstinence,   12
My absolute power and place here in Vienna,
And he supposes me traveled to Poland;
For so I have strewed it in the common ear,
And so it is received. Now, pious sir,
You will demand of me why I do this.

FRIAR THOMAS   Gladly, my lord.

DUKE
We have strict statutes and most biting laws,
The needful bits and curbs to headstrong steeds,   20
Which for this fourteen years we have let slip,   21
Even like an o'ergrown lion in a cave   22
That goes not out to prey. Now, as fond fathers,   23
Having bound up the threat'ning twigs of birch
Only to stick it in their children's sight
For terror, not to use, in time the rod
Becomes more mocked than feared, so our decrees,
Dead to infliction, to themselves are dead;   28
And liberty plucks justice by the nose,   29
The baby beats the nurse, and quite athwart   30
Goes all decorum.

FRIAR THOMAS   It rested in Your Grace   31
To unloose this tied-up justice when you pleased;
And it in you more dreadful would have seemed
Than in Lord Angelo.

DUKE   I do fear, too dreadful.
Sith 'twas my fault to give the people scope,   35
'Twould be my tyranny to strike and gall them   36
For what I bid them do; for we bid this be done   37
When evil deeds have their permissive pass   38
And not the punishment. Therefore indeed, my father,
I have on Angelo imposed the office,   40
Who may in th'ambush of my name strike home,   41
And yet my nature never in the fight   42
To do in slander. And to behold his sway   43
I will, as 'twere a brother of your order,
Visit both prince and people. Therefore, I prithee,
Supply me with the habit, and instruct me   46
How I may formally in person bear   47

---

160 **in his place** inherent in the office   161 **his eminence** the eminence of him   162 **I stagger in** I am uncertain   163 **Awakes me** i.e.,
awakes, activates. (*Me* is used colloquially.)   **enrollèd** written on a
roll or deed   165 **zodiacs** i.e., years   166 **for a name** for reputation's
sake   169 **tickle** uncertain, unstable   174 **cloister** i.e., convent
175 **approbation** novitiate, period of probation.   178 **To** with.   **assay**
try, test   180 **prone** eager, apt, supplicating.   **dialect** language
181 **prosperous art** skill or ability to gain favorable results   184–6 **as
well . . . life** both for the encouragement of similar sexual activity,
which otherwise would be subject to grave charges or accusations,
and for you to continue to live   187–8 **tick-tack** a form of backgammon in which pegs were fitted into holes. (Here applied bawdily.)
1.3. Location: A friary.
2 **dribbling** falling short or wide of the mark   3 **complete** perfect,
whole, strong   4 **harbor** shelter   5 **wrinkled** i.e., mature

8 **removed** retired   9 **in idle price** as little worth. *Idle* means
"unprofitable."   10 **Where . . . keeps** where youth and costly expenditure put themselves foolishly on display.   12 **stricture** strictness
20 **steeds** (The Folio reading, "weedes," is possible in the sense of
"lawless and uncontrolled impulses.")   21 **fourteen** (Claudio mentions nineteen years at 1.2.165; possibly the compositor confused *xiv*
and *xix*.)   22 **o'ergrown** too old and large   23 **fond** doting   28 **Dead
to infliction** dead in that they are not executed   29 **liberty** license
30 **athwart** wrongly, awry   31 **decorum** social order.   **It rested . . .
Grace** It lay in your ducal authority, was incumbent on you   35 **Sith**
Since   36 **gall** chafe, injure   37 **we . . . done** i.e., we virtually order a
crime to be committed   38 **pass** sanction   40 **office** duty   41 **Who . . .
home** who may, under cover of my ducal authority, strike to the heart
of the matter   42 **nature** i.e., personal identity (as distinguished from
official capacity)   43 **do in slander** act so as to invite slander (for
being too repressive).   **sway** rule   46 **habit** garment (of a friar)
47 **formally** in outward appearance.   **bear** bear myself

Like a true friar. More reasons for this action
At our more leisure shall I render you.
Only this one: Lord Angelo is precise,   50
Stands at a guard with envy, scarce confesses   51
That his blood flows or that his appetite   52
Is more to bread than stone. Hence shall we see, 53
If power change purpose, what our seemers be.

                                    Exeunt.

❖

1.[4]

Enter Isabella and Francisca, a nun.

ISABELLA
And have you nuns no farther privileges?
FRANCISCA   Are not these large enough?
ISABELLA
Yes, truly. I speak not as desiring more,
But rather wishing a more strict restraint
Upon the sisterhood, the votarists of Saint Clare.   5
LUCIO   (*within*)
Ho! Peace be in this place!
ISABELLA   Who's that which calls?
FRANCISCA
It is a man's voice. Gentle Isabella,
Turn you the key, and know his business of him.
You may, I may not; you are yet unsworn.   9
When you have vowed, you must not speak with men
But in the presence of the prioress;
Then if you speak you must not show your face,
Or if you show your face you must not speak.
He calls again. I pray you, answer him.   [*Exit.*]
ISABELLA
Peace and prosperity! Who is 't that calls?

[She opens the door. Enter Lucio.]

LUCIO
Hail, virgin, if you be, as those cheek roses   16
Proclaim you are no less. Can you so stead me   17
As bring me to the sight of Isabella,   18
A novice of this place, and the fair sister
To her unhappy brother Claudio?   20
ISABELLA
Why "her unhappy brother"? Let me ask,
The rather for I now must make you know   22
I am that Isabella, and his sister.
LUCIO
Gentle and fair, your brother kindly greets you.
Not to be weary with you, he's in prison.   25

ISABELLA   Woe me! For what?
LUCIO
For that which, if myself might be his judge,
He should receive his punishment in thanks:
He hath got his friend with child.
ISABELLA
Sir, make me not your story.
LUCIO   'Tis true.   30
I would not—though 'tis my familiar sin   31
With maids to seem the lapwing, and to jest,   32
Tongue far from heart—play with all virgins so.
I hold you as a thing enskied and sainted   34
By your renouncement, an immortal spirit
And to be talked with in sincerity
As with a saint.
ISABELLA
You do blaspheme the good in mocking me.   38
LUCIO
Do not believe it. Fewness and truth, 'tis thus: 39
Your brother and his lover have embraced.
As those that feed grow full, as blossoming time   41
That from the seedness the bare fallow brings   42
To teeming foison, even so her plenteous womb   43
Expresseth his full tilth and husbandry.   44
ISABELLA
Someone with child by him? My cousin Juliet?
LUCIO   Is she your cousin?
ISABELLA
Adoptedly, as schoolmaids change their names   47
By vain though apt affection.
LUCIO   She it is.   48
ISABELLA
Oh, let him marry her.
LUCIO   This is the point.
The Duke is very strangely gone from hence;
Bore many gentlemen, myself being one,   51
In hand and hope of action; but we do learn,   52
By those that know the very nerves of state,
His givings-out were of an infinite distance   54
From his true-meant design. Upon his place,   55
And with full line of his authority,   56
Governs Lord Angelo, a man whose blood
Is very snow broth; one who never feels   58
The wanton stings and motions of the sense,   59
But doth rebate and blunt his natural edge   60

49 **more** greater 50 **precise** strict, puritanical 51 **Stands . . . envy**
guards himself severely against calumny 52–3 **or . . . stone** or that
he has an appetite for bread (i.e., food or physical pleasure) any more
than if it were stone. (See Matthew 4.3, where the devil tempts Jesus
to turn stone into bread.)
1.4. Location: A convent.
5 **votarists of Saint Clare** An order founded in 1212 by Saint Francis
of Assisi and Saint Clare; its members were enjoined to a life of
poverty, service, and contemplation. 9 **you . . . unsworn** i.e., you
have not yet taken your formal vows to enter the convent. 16 **cheek
roses** i.e., blushes 17 **stead** help 18 **As** as to 20 **unhappy** unfortunate 22 **The rather for** the more so because 25 **weary** wearisome

30 **story** subject for mirth. 31 **familiar** customary 32 **lapwing** pee-
wit or plover. (The lapwing runs away from its nest in order to draw
away enemies from its young, much as Lucio throws up smoke-
screens in his seductive talk with young women.) 34 **enskied** placed
in heaven 38 **You . . . me** You blaspheme goodness itself when you
mockingly praise me, unworthy as I am, for saintliness. 39 **it** i.e.,
that I am mocking. **Fewness and truth** In few words and truly
41–3 **As . . . foison** Just as the season of blossoming brings the sowing
of the bare untilled land to teeming fruitfulness 44 **Expresseth . . .
husbandry** makes plainly visible Claudio's tilling of the crop, i.e., his
plowing and fertilizing Juliet's body. 47 **change** exchange 48 **vain
though apt** girlish though natural and suitable 51–2 **Bore . . . action**
i.e., he misleadingly kept us in expectation of some military action
54 **givings-out** public statements 55 **Upon** In 56 **line** extent
58 **snow broth** melted snow (i.e., ice water) 59 **motions . . . sense**
promptings of sexual desire 60 **But . . . edge** but dulls and blunts
the sharp desire of sexuality

With profits of the mind, study, and fast.
He—to give fear to use and liberty,   62
Which have for long run by the hideous law
As mice by lions—hath picked out an act,
Under whose heavy sense your brother's life   65
Falls into forfeit. He arrests him on it
And follows close the rigor of the statute
To make him an example. All hope is gone,
Unless you have the grace by your fair prayer
To soften Angelo. And that's my pith of business   70
Twixt you and your poor brother.

ISABELLA   Doth he so
Seek his life?

LUCIO   He's censured him already,   72
And, as I hear, the Provost hath a warrant
For 's execution.

ISABELLA   Alas, what poor
Ability's in me to do him good?

LUCIO   Assay the power you have.   76

ISABELLA
My power? Alas, I doubt.

LUCIO   Our doubts are traitors,
And makes us lose the good we oft might win,   78
By fearing to attempt. Go to Lord Angelo,
And let him learn to know, when maidens sue
Men give like gods, but when they weep and kneel,
All their petitions are as freely theirs   82
As they themselves would owe them.   83

ISABELLA   I'll see what I can do.

LUCIO   But speedily.

ISABELLA   I will about it straight,
No longer staying but to give the Mother   87
Notice of my affair. I humbly thank you.
Commend me to my brother. Soon at night   89
I'll send him certain word of my success.   90

LUCIO
I take my leave of you.

ISABELLA   Good sir, adieu.

Exeunt [separately].

❧

2.1

Enter Angelo, Escalus, and servants, [a] Justice.

ANGELO
We must not make a scarecrow of the law,
Setting it up to fear the birds of prey,   2
And let it keep one shape till custom make it
Their perch and not their terror.

ESCALUS   Ay, but yet
Let us be keen and rather cut a little   5

Than fall and bruise to death. Alas, this gentleman   6
Whom I would save had a most noble father!
Let but Your Honor know,   8
Whom I believe to be most strait in virtue,   9
That, in the working of your own affections,   10
Had time cohered with place, or place with wishing,
Or that the resolute acting of your blood   12
Could have attained th'effect of your own purpose,   13
Whether you had not sometime in your life   14
Erred in this point which now you censure him,   15
And pulled the law upon you.

ANGELO
'Tis one thing to be tempted, Escalus,
Another thing to fall. I not deny
The jury, passing on the prisoner's life,
May in the sworn twelve have a thief or two
Guiltier than him they try. What's open made to
    justice,
That justice seizes. What knows the laws   22
That thieves do pass on thieves? 'Tis very pregnant,   23
The jewel that we find, we stoop and take't
Because we see it; but what we do not see
We tread upon and never think of it.
You may not so extenuate his offense
For I have had such faults; but rather tell me,   28
When I that censure him do so offend,
Let mine own judgment pattern out my death   30
And nothing come in partial. Sir, he must die.   31

Enter Provost.

ESCALUS
Be it as your wisdom will.

ANGELO   Where is the Provost?

PROVOST
Here, if it like Your Honor.

ANGELO   See that Claudio   33
Be executed by nine tomorrow morning.
Bring him his confessor; let him be prepared.
For that's the utmost of his pilgrimage.   36

[Exit Provost.]

ESCALUS
Well, heaven forgive him, and forgive us all!
Some rise by sin, and some by virtue fall;
Some run from breaks of ice and answer none,   39
And some condemnèd for a fault alone.   40

Enter Elbow, Froth, Clown [Pompey], officers.

---

62 **use and liberty** habitual licentiousness   65 **heavy sense** severe
interpretation   70 **my pith of business** the essence of my business
72 **censured** sentenced   76 **Assay** Try   78 **makes** make   82 **their
petitions** i.e., the things the maidens ask for   83 **As . . . them** as they
themselves would wish to have them.   87 **but** than.   **Mother**
Mother Superior, prioress   89 **Soon at night** Early tonight   90 **my
success** how I have succeeded.
2.1 Location: A court of justice.
2 fear frighten   **5 keen** sharp

6 **fall** let fall heavily.   **bruise** i.e., crush   8 **know** consider   9 **strait**
strict   10 **affections** desires   12 **blood** passion   13 **effect** realization
14 **had** would have.   **sometime** on some occasion   15 **censure him**
sentence him for   22–3 **What . . . on thieves?** Who knows what laws
thieves apply to their fellow thieves?   23 **pregnant** clear   28 **For**
because   30–1 **Let . . . partial** let the sentence I have imposed serve as
a model in sentencing me if I commit a crime, no partiality or extenu-
ating circumstances being admitted.   33 **like** please   36 **that's . . .
pilgrimage** that's the furthest point of his life's journey.   39 **Some . . .
none** some break the ice repeatedly (i.e., commit serious infractions of
the law) and yet escape punishment. (A famous crux; the Folio reads
"brakes of Ice.")   40 **a fault alone** one single infraction.

ELBOW   Come, bring them away. If these be good 41
people in a commonweal that do nothing but use their 42
abuses in common houses, I know no law. Bring them 43
away.

ANGELO   How now, sir, what's your name? And what's
the matter?

ELBOW   If it please Your Honor, I am the poor Duke's 47
constable, and my name is Elbow. I do lean upon 48
justice, sir, and do bring in here before Your good Honor
two notorious benefactors.

ANGELO   Benefactors? Well, what benefactors are they?
Are they not malefactors?

ELBOW   If it please Your Honor, I know not well what
they are; but precise villains they are, that I am sure of, 54
and void of all profanation in the world that good 55
Christians ought to have.

ESCALUS   [to Angelo]   This comes off well. Here's a
wise officer.

ANGELO   Go to. What quality are they of?—Elbow is 59
your name? Why dost thou not speak, Elbow?

POMPEY   He cannot, sir; he's out at elbow. 61

ANGELO   What are you, sir?

ELBOW   He, sir? A tapster, sir, parcel-bawd, one that 63
serves a bad woman, whose house, sir, was, as they
say, plucked down in the suburbs; and now she
professes a hothouse, which I think is a very ill house 66
too.

ESCALUS   How know you that?

ELBOW   My wife, sir, whom I detest before heaven and 69
Your Honor—

ESCALUS   How? Thy wife?

ELBOW   Ay, sir; whom I thank heaven is an honest
woman—

ESCALUS   Dost thou detest her therefore?

ELBOW   I say, sir, I will detest myself also, as well as
she, that this house, if it be not a bawd's house, it is
pity of her life, for it is a naughty house. 77

ESCALUS   How dost thou know that, Constable?

ELBOW   Marry, sir, by my wife, who, if she had been a
woman cardinally given, might have been accused in 80
fornication, adultery, and all uncleanliness there.

ESCALUS   By the woman's means?

ELBOW   Ay, sir, by Mistress Overdone's means; but as
she spit in his face, so she defied him. 84

POMPEY   Sir, if it please Your Honor, this is not so.

ELBOW   Prove it before these varlets here, thou honor- 86
able man, prove it. 87

ESCALUS   [to Angelo]   Do you hear how he misplaces?

POMPEY   Sir, she came in great with child, and longing,
saving Your Honor's reverence, for stewed prunes. Sir, 90
we had but two in the house, which at that very
distant time stood, as it were, in a fruit dish, a 92
dish of some threepence. Your Honors have seen such
dishes; they are not China dishes, but very good
dishes—

ESCALUS   Go to, go to. No matter for the dish, sir.

POMPEY   No, indeed, sir, not of a pin; you are therein 97
in the right. But to the point. As I say, this Mistress
Elbow, being, as I say, with child, and being great-
bellied, and longing, as I said, for prunes; and having
but two in the dish, as I said, Master Froth here, this
very man, having eaten the rest, as I said, and, as I
say, paying for them very honestly—for, as you
know, Master Froth, I could not give you threepence
again. 105

FROTH   No, indeed.

POMPEY   Very well. You being then, if you be
remembered, cracking the stones of the foresaid 108
prunes—

FROTH   Ay, so I did indeed.

POMPEY   Why, very well; I telling you then, if you be
remembered, that such a one and such a one were
past cure of the thing you wot of, unless they kept 113
very good diet, as I told you— 114

FROTH   All this is true.

POMPEY   Why, very well, then—

ESCALUS   Come, you are a tedious fool. To the purpose.
What was done to Elbow's wife, that he hath cause to
complain of? Come me to what was done to her. 119

POMPEY   Sir, Your Honor cannot come to that yet.

ESCALUS   No, sir, nor I mean it not.

POMPEY   Sir, but you shall come to it, by Your Honor's
leave. And, I beseech you, look into Master Froth here,
sir, a man of fourscore pound a year, whose father 124
died at Hallowmas.—Was 't not at Hallowmas, Mas- 125
ter Froth?

FROTH   All-hallond eve. 127

POMPEY   Why, very well. I hope here be truths. He, sir,
sitting, as I say, in a lower chair, sir—'twas in the 129
Bunch of Grapes, where indeed you have a delight to 130
sit, have you not?

41 away onward.   42–3 use . . . houses practice their vices in bawdy
houses   47 poor Duke's i.e., Duke's poor   48 lean upon rely on,
appeal to. (With an unintended comic reference to the idea of leaning
on one's elbow.)   54 precise complete. (Or perhaps a blunder for "precious." *Precise* unintentionally recalls the description of Angelo as
precise, i.e., strict or puritanical, at 1.3.50.)   55 profanation (A blunder
for "profession," or a word meaning "irreverence" where Elbow
intends "reverence." Elbow already has used several malapropisms,
including *lean upon*, *benefactors*, and *precise*.)   59 Go to An expression
of impatience or reproof.   quality social standing, occupation   61 out
at elbow (1) impoverished, threadbare, hence without any ideas (2)
missing his cue, i.e., at a loss for words after being called by his name.
63 parcel-bawd part-time bawd (and part-time tapster)   66 professes
a hothouse professes to run a bathhouse   69 detest (For "protest.")
77 pity of her life a great pity.   naughty wicked   80 cardinally (For
"carnally.")   given inclined   84 she spit . . . face Elbow's wife spit in
the face of Pompey (who, as pimp, was acting as Mistress Overdone's
means, line 83).

86–7 varlets . . . honorable (Elbow reverses or *misplaces* these epithets.)   90 saving . . . reverence i.e., begging your pardon for what
I'm about to say.   stewed prunes (Commonly served in houses of
prostitution, or *stews*, and therefore suggesting prostitutes. The dialogue throughout is sexually suggestive.)   92 distant (Blunder for
"instant"?)   97 a pin i.e., an insignificant trifle   105 again back.
108 stones pits. (With suggestion also of "testicles.")   113 the thing . . .
of you know what I mean (i.e., venereal disease)   114 diet strict regimen prescribed for medical treatment   119 Come me i.e., Come. (*Me*
is used colloquially. Pompey makes a vulgar joke on the words *come*
and *done*; see note at line 140.)   124 of . . . year i.e., well off   125 Hallowmas All Saints' Day, November 1   127 All-hallond eve Hal-
loween, October 31.   129 a lower chair i.e., an easy chair (?)
130 Bunch of Grapes (It was not uncommon to designate particular
rooms in inns by such names.)

FROTH   I have so, because it is an open room and good 132
for winter.

POMPEY   Why, very well, then. I hope here be truths.

ANGELO
This will last out a night in Russia,
When nights are longest there. I'll take my leave
And leave you to the hearing of the cause,   137
Hoping you'll find good cause to whip them all.

ESCALUS
I think no less. Good morrow to Your Lordship.   139
                                        Exit [Angelo].
Now, sir, come on. What was done to Elbow's wife,   140
once more?

POMPEY   Once, sir? There was nothing done to her
once.   143

ELBOW   I beseech you, sir, ask him what this man did
to my wife.

POMPEY   I beseech Your Honor, ask me.

ESCALUS   Well, sir, what did this gentleman to her?

POMPEY   I beseech you, sir, look in this gentleman's
face. Good Master Froth, look upon His Honor; 'tis for
a good purpose. Doth Your Honor mark his face?   150

ESCALUS   Ay, sir, very well.

POMPEY   Nay, I beseech you, mark it well.

ESCALUS   Well, I do so.

POMPEY   Doth Your Honor see any harm in his face?

ESCALUS   Why, no.

POMPEY   I'll be supposed upon a book, his face is the 156
worst thing about him. Good, then; if his face be the
worst thing about him, how could Master Froth do the
Constable's wife any harm? I would know that of Your
Honor.

ESCALUS   He's in the right, Constable. What say you
to it?

ELBOW   First, an it like you, the house is a respected 163
house; next, this is a respected fellow; and his mistress
is a respected woman.

POMPEY   By this hand, sir, his wife is a more respected
person than any of us all.

ELBOW   Varlet, thou liest! Thou liest, wicked varlet! The
time is yet to come that she was ever respected with
man, woman, or child.

POMPEY   Sir, she was respected with him before he
married with her.

ESCALUS   Which is the wiser here, Justice or Iniquity?— 173
Is this true?

ELBOW   O thou caitiff! O thou varlet! O thou wicked 175
Hannibal! I respected with her before I was married to 176
her?—If ever I was respected with her, or she with
me, let not Your Worship think me the poor Duke's

officer.—Prove this, thou wicked Hannibal, or I'll
have mine action of battery on thee.   180

ESCALUS   If he took you a box o'th'ear, you might have 181
your action of slander too.

ELBOW   Marry, I thank Your good Worship for it. What
is't Your Worship's pleasure I shall do with this
wicked caitiff?

ESCALUS   Truly, officer, because he hath some offenses
in him that thou wouldst discover if thou couldst, let 187
him continue in his courses till thou know'st what 188
they are.

ELBOW   Marry, I thank Your Worship for it.—Thou see'st,
thou wicked varlet, now, what's come upon thee: thou
art to continue now, thou varlet, thou art to continue. 192

ESCALUS   [to Froth]   Where were you born, friend?

FROTH   Here in Vienna, sir.

ESCALUS   Are you of fourscore pounds a year?   195

FROTH   Yes, an't please you, sir.

ESCALUS   So. [To Pompey] What trade are you of, sir?

POMPEY   A tapster, a poor widow's tapster.

ESCALUS   Your mistress' name?

POMPEY   Mistress Overdone.

ESCALUS   Hath she had any more than one husband?

POMPEY   Nine, sir. Overdone by the last.   202

ESCALUS   Nine?—Come hither to me, Master Froth.
Master Froth, I would not have you acquainted with
tapsters. They will draw you, Master Froth, and you 205
will hang them. Get you gone, and let me hear no 206
more of you.

FROTH   I thank Your Worship. For mine own part, I
never come into any room in a taphouse but I am 209
drawn in.   210

ESCALUS   Well, no more of it, Master Froth. Farewell.
                                        [Exit Froth.]
Come you hither to me, Master Tapster. What's your
name, Master Tapster?

POMPEY   Pompey.

ESCALUS   What else?

POMPEY   Bum, sir.

ESCALUS   Troth, and your bum is the greatest thing
about you, so that in the beastliest sense you are Pompey the Great. Pompey, you are partly a bawd, Pompey, howsoever you color it in being a tapster, are you 220
not? Come, tell me true. It shall be the better for you.

POMPEY   Truly, sir, I am a poor fellow that would live.

ESCALUS   How would you live, Pompey? By being a 223
bawd? What do you think of the trade, Pompey? Is it
a lawful trade?

POMPEY   If the law would allow it, sir.

132 open public   **137 cause** case. (With word play on *cause,* "reason,"
in the next line. See also the play on *leave* in 136–7.)   **139 I . . . less** I
think so, too.   **140 done** (Pompey, in his answer, uses *done* in a sexual
sense.)   **143 once** only once. (Pompey replies wittily to Escalus's *once
more* in 141, meaning "once again.")   **150 mark** observe   **156 supposed** (A malapropism for "deposed," i.e., sworn.)   **book** i.e., Bible
163 an it like if it please.   **respected** (For "suspected.")   **173 Justice
or Iniquity** (Personified characters in a morality play.)   **175 caitiff**
knave, villain.   **176 Hannibal** (A blunder for "cannibal," perhaps
also suggested by the fact that Hannibal and Pompey were both
famous generals in the classical world.)

180 battery (An error for "slander," as Escalus amusedly points
out.)   **181 took** gave.   **o'** on   **187 discover** (1) detect (2) reveal
188 courses courses of action   **192 continue** (Elbow may confuse the
word with its opposite.)   **195 of** possessed of   **202 Overdone . . . last**
(1) Her name, Overdone, was given her by her last husband (2) She
has been worn out *(overdone)* by the last one.   **205 draw** (1) cheat,
take in (2) empty, deplete. (With a pun on the tapster's trade of drawing liquor from a barrel, and on Froth's name.) (3) disembowel, or
drag to execution   **206 will hang them** will be the cause of their
hanging   **209 taphouse** alehouse   **210 drawn in** enticed. (Still
another meaning of *draw,* line 205.)   **220 color** disguise   **223 live**
make a living

ESCALUS   But the law will not allow it, Pompey; nor it
shall not be allowed in Vienna.

POMPEY   Does Your Worship mean to geld and splay all 229
the youth of the city?

ESCALUS   No, Pompey.

POMPEY   Truly, sir, in my poor opinion they will to't
then. If Your Worship will take order for the drabs and 233
the knaves, you need not to fear the bawds.

ESCALUS   There is pretty orders beginning, I can tell
you. It is but heading and hanging. 236

POMPEY   If you head and hang all that offend that way
but for ten year together, you'll be glad to give out a 238
commission for more heads. If this law hold in Vienna 239
ten year, I'll rent the fairest house in it after threepence 240
a bay. If you live to see this come to pass, say Pompey 241
told you so.

ESCALUS   Thank you, good Pompey. And, in requital of 243
your prophecy, hark you: I advise you let me not find
you before me again upon any complaint whatsoever;
no, not for dwelling where you do. If I do, Pompey, I
shall beat you to your tent and prove a shrewd Caesar 247
to you; in plain dealing, Pompey, I shall have you
whipped. So for this time, Pompey, fare you well.

POMPEY   I thank Your Worship for your good counsel.
[Aside] But I shall follow it as the flesh and fortune
shall better determine.
Whip me? No, no, let carman whip his jade. 253
The valiant heart's not whipped out of his trade.

                                                    Exit.

ESCALUS   Come hither to me, Master Elbow; come
hither, Master Constable. How long have you been in
this place of constable?

ELBOW   Seven year and a half, sir.

ESCALUS   I thought, by the readiness in the office, you 259
had continued in it some time. You say, seven years
together?

ELBOW   And a half, sir.

ESCALUS   Alas, it hath been great pains to you. They do
you wrong to put you so oft upon't. Are there not
men in your ward sufficient to serve it? 265

ELBOW   Faith, sir, few of any wit in such matters. As
they are chosen, they are glad to choose me for them. 267
I do it for some piece of money and go through with 268
all. 269

ESCALUS   Look you bring me in the names of some six 270
or seven, the most sufficient of your parish.

ELBOW   To Your Worship's house, sir?

ESCALUS   To my house. Fare you well.   [Exit Elbow.]
What's o'clock, think you?

JUSTICE   Eleven, sir.

ESCALUS
I pray you home to dinner with me. 276

JUSTICE   I humbly thank you.

ESCALUS
It grieves me for the death of Claudio;
But there's no remedy.

JUSTICE   Lord Angelo is severe.

ESCALUS   It is but needful.
Mercy is not itself, that oft looks so; 281
Pardon is still the nurse of second woe. 282
But yet—poor Claudio! There is no remedy.
Come, sir.   Exeunt.

❖

2.2

Enter Provost [and a] Servant.

SERVANT
He's hearing of a cause; he will come straight. 1
I'll tell him of you.

PROVOST   Pray you, do.   [Exit Servant.]
                                  I'll know
His pleasure; maybe he will relent. Alas,
He hath but as offended in a dream! 4
All sects, all ages smack of this vice—and he 5
To die for't!

        Enter Angelo.

ANGELO   Now, what's the matter, Provost?

PROVOST
Is it your will Claudio shall die tomorrow?

ANGELO
Did not I tell thee yea? Hadst thou not order?
Why dost thou ask again?

PROVOST   Lest I might be too rash.
Under your good correction, I have seen 11
When, after execution, judgment hath
Repented o'er his doom. 13

ANGELO   Go to; let that be mine. 14
Do you your office, or give up your place,
And you shall well be spared. 16

PROVOST   I crave Your Honor's pardon.
What shall be done, sir, with the groaning Juliet? 18
She's very near her hour. 19

ANGELO   Dispose of her
To some more fitter place, and that with speed.

        [Enter a Servant.]

---

276 **dinner** (Dinner was customarily eaten just before midday.)
281 **Mercy . . . so** i.e., What seems merciful may not really be so (since
it may encourage crime and hence lead to more punishment)
282 **Pardon . . . woe** i.e., pardon continually nurtures and encourages
a repetition of offenses and hence of punishment.
2.2 Location: Adjacent to the court of justice, perhaps at Angelo's
official residence.
1 **hearing . . . cause** listening to a case.   **straight** immediately.   4 **He . . .
dream** i.e., Claudio offended without conscious intent.   5 **All sects . . .
smack** All classes of people of all ages (and in all past history) partake   11 **Under . . . correction** i.e., Allow me to say   13 **doom** sentence.   14 **mine** my business.   16 **well be spared** easily be done
without.   18 **groaning** (with labor pains)   19 **hour** time of delivery.

---

229 **splay** spay   233 **take order** take measures.   **drabs** prostitutes
236 **It . . . hanging** Beheading and hanging are the order of the day.
238 **year together** years at a stretch   239 **commission** order.   **hold**
remain in force   240 **after** at the rate of   241 **bay** division of a house
included under one gable.   243 **requital of** return for   247 **shrewd**
harsh, severe.   **Caesar** (Julius Caesar defeated Pompey at Pharsalia
in 48 B.C.)   253 **carman** cart driver.   **jade** broken-down horse.
259 **readiness** proficiency, alacrity   265 **sufficient** able   267 **for them**
i.e., to take their place.   268–9 **go . . . all** i.e., perform my duties thoroughly.   270 **Look** See to it that

SERVANT
  Here is the sister of the man condemned
  Desires access to you.
ANGELO   Hath he a sister?   22
PROVOST
  Ay, my good lord, a very virtuous maid,
  And to be shortly of a sisterhood,
  If not already.
ANGELO   Well, let her be admitted.
                              [Exit Servant.]
  See you the fornicatress be removed.
  Let her have needful but not lavish means.
  There shall be order for't.

        Enter Lucio and Isabella.

PROVOST   Save Your Honor!   28
ANGELO [to Provost]
  Stay a little while. [To Isabella] You're welcome.
      What's your will?
ISABELLA
  I am a woeful suitor to Your Honor,
  Please but Your Honor hear me.
ANGELO   Well, what's your suit? 31
ISABELLA
  There is a vice that most I do abhor,
  And most desire should meet the blow of justice,
  For which I would not plead, but that I must;
  For which I must not plead, but that I am
  At war twixt will and will not.
ANGELO   Well, the matter?
ISABELLA
  I have a brother is condemned to die.
  I do beseech you, let it be his fault,   38
  And not my brother.
PROVOST [aside]   Heaven give thee moving graces!
ANGELO
  Condemn the fault, and not the actor of it?
  Why, every fault's condemned ere it be done.
  Mine were the very cipher of a function,
  To fine the faults, whose fine stands in record, 43
  And let go by the actor.
ISABELLA   Oh, just but severe law!
  I had a brother, then. Heaven keep your honor!
LUCIO [aside to Isabella]
  Give't not o'er so. To him again, entreat him!   47
  Kneel down before him; hang upon his gown.
  You are too cold. If you should need a pin,   49
  You could not with more tame a tongue desire it.
  To him, I say!
ISABELLA [to Angelo]
  Must he needs die?
ANGELO   Maiden, no remedy.
ISABELLA
  Yes, I do think that you might pardon him,
  And neither heaven nor man grieve at the mercy.

ANGELO
  I will not do't.
ISABELLA   But can you, if you would?
ANGELO
  Look what I will not, that I cannot do.   56
ISABELLA
  But might you do't, and do the world no wrong,
  If so your heart were touched with that remorse   58
  As mine is to him?
ANGELO   He's sentenced. 'Tis too late.
LUCIO [aside to Isabella]   You are too cold.
ISABELLA
  Too late? Why, no; I that do speak a word
  May call it back again. Well, believe this:
  No ceremony that to great ones 'longs,   64
  Not the king's crown, nor the deputed sword,   65
  The marshal's truncheon, nor the judge's robe,   66
  Become them with one half so good a grace
  As mercy does.
  If he had been as you, and you as he,
  You would have slipped like him; but he, like you, 70
  Would not have been so stern.
ANGELO   Pray you, begone.
ISABELLA
  I would to heaven I had your potency,
  And you were Isabel. Should it then be thus?
  No, I would tell what 'twere to be a judge   74
  And what a prisoner.
LUCIO [aside to Isabella]   Ay, touch him; there's the vein. 75
ANGELO
  Your brother is a forfeit of the law,   76
  And you but waste your words.
ISABELLA   Alas, alas!
  Why, all the souls that were were forfeit once,   78
  And He that might the vantage best have took   79
  Found out the remedy. How would you be,   80
  If He, which is the top of judgment, should   81
  But judge you as you are? Oh, think on that,
  And mercy then will breathe within your lips,
  Like man new-made.
ANGELO   Be you content, fair maid.   84
  It is the law, not I, condemn your brother.
  Were he my kinsman, brother, or my son,
  It should be thus with him. He must die tomorrow.
ISABELLA
  Tomorrow! Oh, that's sudden! Spare him, spare him!
  He's not prepared for death. Even for our kitchens
  We kill the fowl of season. Shall we serve heaven 90
  With less respect than we do minister

22 Desires who desires   28 Save May God save   31 Please . . . me if
Your Honor will please hear me.   38 let . . . fault i.e., let the fault die,
be condemned   43 To fine . . . record to punish only the faults, for
which the penalty stands in the statute books   47 Give't . . . so Don't
give up so soon.   49 need a pin i.e., ask for the smallest trifle

56 Look what Whatever   58 remorse pity   64 'longs is fitting,
belongs   65 deputed sword sword of justice entrusted to the ruler
66 truncheon staff borne by military officers   70 like you in your situation   74 tell make known   75 there's the vein i.e., that's the right
approach. (Vein means "lode to be profitably mined," or perhaps
"vein for bloodletting.")   76 a forfeit one who must incur the
penalty   78–80 Why . . . remedy (A reference to God's redemption of
sinful humanity when He would have been justified in destroying
humankind.)   81 top of judgment supreme judge   84 new-made
i.e., created new by salvation, born again.   90 of season that is in season and properly mature.

To our gross selves? Good, good my lord, bethink
    you:
Who is it that hath died for this offense?
There's many have committed it.
LUCIO [*aside to Isabella*]   Ay, well said.
ANGELO
The law hath not been dead, though it hath slept.
Those many had not dared to do that evil
If the first that did th'edict infringe
Had answered for his deed. Now 'tis awake,
Takes note of what is done, and like a prophet
Looks in a glass that shows what future evils,   100
Either now, or by remissness new-conceived   101
And so in progress to be hatched and born,   102
Are now to have no successive degrees,   103
But ere they live, to end.
ISABELLA   Yet show some pity.   104
ANGELO
I show it most of all when I show justice;
For then I pity those I do not know,
Which a dismissed offense would after gall,   107
And do him right that, answering one foul wrong,   108
Lives not to act another. Be satisfied;
Your brother dies tomorrow. Be content.
ISABELLA
So you must be the first that gives this sentence,
And he that suffers. Oh, it is excellent
To have a giant's strength, but it is tyrannous
To use it like a giant.
LUCIO [*aside to Isabella*]   That's well said.
ISABELLA   Could great men thunder
As Jove himself does, Jove would never be quiet,   116
For every pelting, petty officer   117
Would use his heaven for thunder,
Nothing but thunder. Merciful heaven,
Thou rather with thy sharp and sulfurous bolt   120
Splits the unwedgeable and gnarlèd oak   121
Than the soft myrtle; but man, proud man,
Dressed in a little brief authority,
Most ignorant of what he's most assured,   124
His glassy essence, like an angry ape   125
Plays such fantastic tricks before high heaven
As makes the angels weep; who, with our spleens,   127
Would all themselves laugh mortal.   128

LUCIO [*aside to Isabella*]
Oh, to him, to him, wench! He will relent.
He's coming, I perceive't.
PROVOST [*aside*]   Pray heaven she win him!   130
ISABELLA
We cannot weigh our brother with ourself.   131
Great men may jest with saints; 'tis wit in them,   132
But in the less, foul profanation.   133
LUCIO [*aside to Isabella*]
Thou'rt i'th' right, girl. More o' that.
ISABELLA
That in the captain's but a choleric word   135
Which in the soldier is flat blasphemy.
LUCIO [*aside to Isabella*]   Art advised o' that? More on't.   137
ANGELO
Why do you put these sayings upon me?   138
ISABELLA
Because authority, though it err like others,   139
Hath yet a kind of medicine in itself   140
That skins the vice o'th' top. Go to your bosom;   141
Knock there, and ask your heart what it doth know
That's like my brother's fault. If it confess
A natural guiltiness such as is his,
Let it not sound a thought upon your tongue
Against my brother's life.
ANGELO [*aside*]   She speaks, and 'tis such sense   147
That my sense breeds with it.—Fare you well.   148
            [*He starts to go.*]
ISABELLA   Gentle my lord, turn back.   149
ANGELO
I will bethink me. Come again tomorrow.   150
ISABELLA
Hark how I'll bribe you. Good my lord, turn back.
ANGELO   How? Bribe me?
ISABELLA
Ay, with such gifts that heaven shall share with you.   153
LUCIO [*aside to Isabella*]   You had marred all else.   154
ISABELLA
Not with fond sicles of the tested gold,   155
Or stones whose rate are either rich or poor   156
As fancy values them, but with true prayers   157
That shall be up at heaven and enter there
Ere sunrise—prayers from preservèd souls,   159

---

100 glass magic crystal   **101 Either . . . new-conceived** i.e., both evils already hatched and those that would be encouraged by continued laxity of enforcement   **102 in progress** in the course of time   **103 successive degrees** successors or future stages. (Future evils are to be aborted before they are born and propagate.)   **104 ere they live** i.e., before they can be committed   **107 Which . . . gall** whom a forgiven offense would give trouble to later on   **108 do . . . answering** do justice to that person who, by paying the penalty for   **116 be quiet** have any quiet   **117 pelting** paltry   **120 bolt** thunderbolt   **121 unwedgeable** unsplittable   **124–5 Most . . . essence** i.e., most ignorant of what should give him best comfort and assurance, his immortal soul. (*Glassy* suggests the reflective qualities of the soul as a mirror of God.)   **125 angry ape** i.e., ludicrous buffoon   **127–8 who . . . mortal** who, if they had the organs of laughter that we have, would laugh themselves mortal, becoming like us. (The *spleen* was thought to be the seat of laughter.)

130 coming coming around   **131–3 We . . . profanation** We cannot judge our fellow mortals by the same standards we use in judging ourselves. Persons of great authority are allowed liberties that in lesser persons would be condemned as blasphemies. (Lines 135–6 make much the same point.)   **135 That . . . word** i.e., We treat the abusive language a commanding officer uses in anger merely as an outburst; we are indulgent toward the failings of *great men*. (As in lines 131–3, Isabella's point seems to be that our judgments are biased by our inordinate regard for authority.)   **137 advised** informed, aware. **on't** of it.   **138 put . . . me** apply these sayings to me.   **139–41 Because . . . top** Because authority, though prone to sinfulness like all of humankind, has a way of seeming to heal itself by covering over the boil with a film of skin, leaving the sore unhealed.   **147–8 sense . . . sense** import . . . sensuality   **149 Gentle my lord** My noble lord   **150 bethink me** think it over.   **153 that** as   **154 else** otherwise.   **155 Not . . . gold** Not with foolishly valued shekels of pure gold. (*Shekels* are Hebrew coins.)   **156–7 Or . . . them** or jewels the value of which is merely subjective and transitory   **159 preservèd souls** devout religious who have withdrawn from the world

From fasting maids whose minds are dedicate   160
To nothing temporal.
ANGELO   Well, come to me tomorrow.
LUCIO [*aside to Isabella*]   Go to, 'tis well. Away!
ISABELLA
Heaven keep Your Honor safe!
ANGELO [*aside*]   Amen!
For I am that way going to temptation,
Where prayers cross.
ISABELLA   At what hour tomorrow   165
Shall I attend Your Lordship?
ANGELO   At any time 'fore noon.
ISABELLA   Save Your Honor!   168
            [*Exeunt Isabella, Lucio, and Provost.*]
ANGELO   From thee, even from thy virtue!
What's this, what's this? Is this her fault or mine?
The tempter or the tempted, who sins most, ha?
Not she, nor doth she tempt; but it is I
That, lying by the violet in the sun,
Do, as the carrion does, not as the flower,   174
Corrupt with virtuous season. Can it be   175
That modesty may more betray our sense   176
Than woman's lightness? Having waste ground
   enough,   177
Shall we desire to raze the sanctuary
And pitch our evils there? Oh, fie, fie, fie!   179
What dost thou, or what art thou, Angelo?
Dost thou desire her foully for those things
That make her good? Oh, let her brother live!
Thieves for their robbery have authority
When judges steal themselves. What, do I love her,
That I desire to hear her speak again
And feast upon her eyes? What is't I dream on?
Oh, cunning enemy that, to catch a saint,   187
With saints dost bait thy hook! Most dangerous
Is that temptation that doth goad us on
To sin in loving virtue. Never could the strumpet,
With all her double vigor—art and nature—   191
Once stir my temper; but this virtuous maid   192
Subdues me quite. Ever till now,
When men were fond, I smiled and wondered how.   194
                                           Exit.

❖

2.3

*Enter, [meeting,] Duke [disguised as a friar]
and Provost.*

DUKE
Hail to you, Provost—so I think you are.

160 fasting maids i.e., nuns.   **dedicate** dedicated   **165 cross** are at
cross purposes.   **168 Save** May God save   **174 carrion** decaying
flesh   **175 Corrupt . . . season** i.e., putrefy while all else flourishes.
(The warmth of flowering time causes the violet, Isabella, to blossom
but causes the carrion lying beside it, Angelo, to rot.)   **176 modesty**
virtue, chastity.   **sense** sensual nature   **177 lightness** immodesty,
lust.   **179 pitch our evils there** i.e., erect a privy, not on *waste ground*
(line 177), but on sanctified ground. (*Evils* also has the more common
meaning of "wickedness.")   **187 enemy** i.e., Satan   **191 double . . .**
nature twofold power (of alluring men) through artifice and a sensuous nature   **192 temper** temperament   **194 fond** foolishly in love
2.3 Location: A prison.

PROVOST
I am the Provost. What's your will, good Friar?
DUKE
Bound by my charity and my blest order,
I come to visit the afflicted spirits
Here in the prison. Do me the common right   5
To let me see them and to make me know
The nature of their crimes, that I may minister
To them accordingly.
PROVOST
I would do more than that, if more were needful.

        Enter Juliet.

Look, here comes one: a gentlewoman of mine,
Who, falling in the flaws of her own youth,   11
Hath blistered her report. She is with child,   12
And he that got it, sentenced—a young man   13
More fit to do another such offense
Than die for this.
DUKE
When must he die?
PROVOST   As I do think, tomorrow.
[*To Juliet*] I have provided for you. Stay awhile,   17
And you shall be conducted.   18
DUKE
Repent you, fair one, of the sin you carry?
JULIET
I do, and bear the shame most patiently.
DUKE
I'll teach you how you shall arraign your conscience,   21
And try your penitence, if it be sound   22
Or hollowly put on.   23
JULIET   I'll gladly learn.
DUKE   Love you the man that wronged you?
JULIET
Yes, as I love the woman that wronged him.
DUKE
So then it seems your most offenseful act
Was mutually committed?
JULIET   Mutually.
DUKE
Then was your sin of heavier kind than his.
JULIET
I do confess it and repent it, Father.
DUKE
'Tis meet so, daughter. But lest you do repent   31
As that the sin hath brought you to this shame, 32
Which sorrow is always toward ourselves, not heaven,   33
Showing we would not spare heaven as we love it, 34
But as we stand in fear—
JULIET
I do repent me as it is an evil,

5 common right i.e., right of all clerics   **11 flaws** (1) weaknesses, fis-
sures (2) sudden gusts (of passion)   **12 blistered her report** marred
her reputation.   **13 got** begot   **17 provided** provided a place to stay
18 conducted taken there.   **21 arraign** accuse   **22 try** test   **23 hol-**
lowly falsely   **31 'Tis meet so** It is fitting that you do so   **32 As that**
merely because   **33 toward ourselves** i.e., narrowly self-concerned
rather than loving virtue for its own sake   **34 Showing . . . it** showing that we wish to avoid offending heaven not out of sheer love of
goodness

And take the shame with joy.

DUKE   There rest.   37
　Your partner, as I hear, must die tomorrow,
　And I am going with instruction to him.
　Grace go with you. *Benedicite!*   *Exit.*   40

JULIET

　Must die tomorrow? O injurious love,   41
　That respites me a life whose very comfort   42
　Is still a dying horror!

PROVOST   'Tis pity of him.   *Exeunt.*   43

❧

2.4

Enter Angelo.

ANGELO

　When I would pray and think, I think and pray
　To several subjects. Heaven hath my empty words,   2
　Whilst my invention, hearing not my tongue,   3
　Anchors on Isabel; Heaven in my mouth,
　As if I did but only chew His name,   5
　And in my heart the strong and swelling evil
　Of my conception. The state, whereon I studied,   7
　Is like a good thing, being often read,
　Grown sere and tedious. Yea, my gravity,   9
　Wherein—let no man hear me—I take pride,
　Could I with boot change for an idle plume,   11
　Which the air beats for vain. O place, O form,   12
　How often dost thou with thy case, thy habit,   13
　Wrench awe from fools and tie the wiser souls   14
　To thy false seeming! Blood, thou art blood.   15
　Let's write "good angel" on the devil's horn,   16
　'Tis not the devil's crest.

Enter Servant.

                          How now? Who's there?   17

SERVANT

　One Isabel, a sister, desires access to you.
ANGELO   Teach her the way.   *[Exit Servant.]*
                     Oh, heavens!   19
　Why does my blood thus muster to my heart,   20

Making both it unable for itself   21
And dispossessing all my other parts
Of necessary fitness?
So play the foolish throngs with one that swoons,   24
Come all to help him, and so stop the air
By which he should revive; and even so
The general subject to a well-wished king   27
Quit their own part and in obsequious fondness   28
Crowd to his presence, where their untaught love   29
Must needs appear offense.

Enter Isabella.

                          How now, fair maid?   30
ISABELLA   I am come to know your pleasure.
ANGELO
　That you might know it would much better please me 32
　Than to demand what 'tis. Your brother cannot live. 33
ISABELLA
　Even so. Heaven keep Your Honor!   34
                          [She turns to leave.]
ANGELO
　Yet may he live awhile; and, it may be,
　As long as you or I. Yet he must die.
ISABELLA   Under your sentence?
ANGELO   Yea.
ISABELLA
　When, I beseech you? That in his reprieve,
　Longer or shorter, he may be so fitted   40
　That his soul sicken not.
ANGELO
　Ha? Fie, these filthy vices! It were as good   42
　To pardon him that hath from nature stolen   43
　A man already made, as to remit   44
　Their saucy sweetness that do coin heaven's image 45
　In stamps that are forbid. 'Tis all as easy   46
　Falsely to take away a life true made
　As to put metal in restrainèd means   48
　To make a false one.
ISABELLA
　'Tis set down so in heaven, but not in earth.   50
ANGELO
　Say you so? Then I shall pose you quickly: 51
　Which had you rather, that the most just law
　Now took your brother's life, or, to redeem him,
　Give up your body to such sweet uncleanness

---

37 There rest. Hold fast to that truth.　**40 *Benedicite!*** Blessings on
you!　**41–3 O . . . horror!** i.e., O sinful pregnancy, that prolongs a life
whose greatest comfort will always be a deadly horror! (Pregnancy
could save a woman from being executed. However, *love* is sometimes emended to *law*.)　**43 pity of** a pity about
2.4 Location: Angelo's official residence.
2 several separate　**3 invention** imagination　**5 His** i.e., heaven's,
God's　**7 conception** thought.　**The state** Statecraft　**9 sere** withered,
old　**11–12 Could . . . vain** I would willingly exchange (my gravity)
for the frivolity of a pleasure-loving gallant, sporting a feather that
seems to beat the air in its vanity (or, perhaps, is beaten by the air in
reproof of its vanity).　**12 O place, O form** O authority of high position, O ceremonial dignity of office　**13 thy case . . . habit** your mere
outward appearance and garb　**14–15 Wrench . . . seeming** intimidate
ordinary foolish men and subjugate even the wise to the seeming
virtue of authority.　**15 Blood . . . blood** i.e., No position of authority
or birth, no matter how lofty, can protect a person from the instinctual
power of desire.　**16–17 Let's . . . crest** i.e., No matter how hard we try
to disguise evil under the semblance of good, it remains recognizably
evil still. (In heraldic terms, the devil is known by his baleful horns;
the heraldic crest on his coat of arms does not alter his true identity.)
19 Teach Show　**20 muster to** assemble like soldiers in

21 unable ineffectual　**24 play** behave　**27 general subject** i.e., commoners, subjects.　**well-wished** attended by good wishes　**28 Quit . . .
part** abandon their proper function and (politely distant) place
29 untaught ignorant, unmannerly　**30 Must needs** will necessarily
32–3 That . . . 'tis i.e., I wish you could know the nature of my desire
without your asking and my having to be explicit. (*Know* suggests
carnal knowledge.)　**34 Even so** So be it.　**40 fitted** prepared
42–6 It were . . . forbid One might as well pardon the murderer of a
man already alive as pardon the wanton pleasures of those persons
who produce illegitimate offspring, like counterfeit coiners.
(*Heaven's image* is humankind, made in God's likeness; Genesis 1:27.)
48 metal i.e., the metal used in coining (lines 45–6), with a play on
mettle, natural vigor or spirit.　**restrainèd** prohibited, illicit (both in
counterfeiting coinage and in begetting illegitimate children)
50 'Tis . . . earth i.e., Equating murder and bastardizing accords with
divine law but not with human law, according to which murder is
more heinous.　**51 pose you** put a perplexing question to you

As she that he hath stained?
ISABELLA   Sir, believe this,
I had rather give my body than my soul.   56
ANGELO
I talk not of your soul. Our compelled sins   57
Stand more for number than for account.
ISABELLA   How say you?   58
ANGELO
Nay, I'll not warrant that, for I can speak   59
Against the thing I say. Answer to this:
I, now the voice of the recorded law,
Pronounce a sentence on your brother's life;
Might there not be a charity in sin
To save this brother's life?
ISABELLA   Please you to do't,   64
I'll take it as a peril to my soul;   65
It is no sin at all, but charity.
ANGELO
Pleased you to do't at peril of your soul   67
Were equal poise of sin and charity.   68
ISABELLA
That I do beg his life, if it be sin,
Heaven let me bear it! You granting of my suit,
If that be sin, I'll make it my morn prayer
To have it added to the faults of mine,
And nothing of your answer.
ANGELO   Nay, but hear me.   73
Your sense pursues not mine. Either you are ignorant
Or seem so craftily; and that's not good.
ISABELLA
Let me be ignorant, and in nothing good,
But graciously to know I am no better.   77
ANGELO
Thus wisdom wishes to appear most bright
When it doth tax itself, as these black masks   79
Proclaim an enshield beauty ten times louder   80
Than beauty could, displayed. But mark me.
To be received plain, I'll speak more gross: 82
Your brother is to die.
ISABELLA So.
ANGELO
And his offense is so, as it appears,
Accountant to the law upon that pain.   86
ISABELLA True.
ANGELO
Admit no other way to save his life—   88
As I subscribe not that, nor any other,   89
But in the loss of question—that you, his sister,   90

Finding yourself desired of such a person   91
Whose credit with the judge, or own great place,
Could fetch your brother from the manacles
Of the all-binding law; and that there were
No earthly means to save him, but that either
You must lay down the treasures of your body
To this supposed, or else to let him suffer.   97
What would you do?
ISABELLA
As much for my poor brother as myself:
That is, were I under the terms of death,
Th'impression of keen whips I'd wear as rubies,   100
And strip myself to death as to a bed
That longing have been sick for, ere I'd yield   103
My body up to shame.
ANGELO   Then must your brother die.
ISABELLA   And 'twere the cheaper way.
Better it were a brother died at once   107
Than that a sister, by redeeming him,
Should die forever.
ANGELO
Were not you then as cruel as the sentence
That you have slandered so?
ISABELLA
Ignomy in ransom and free pardon   112
Are of two houses. Lawful mercy   113
Is nothing kin to foul redemption.   114
ANGELO
You seemed of late to make the law a tyrant,
And rather proved the sliding of your brother   116
A merriment than a vice.
ISABELLA
Oh, pardon me, my lord. It oft falls out,
To have what we would have, we speak not what
   we mean.
I something do excuse the thing I hate   120
For his advantage that I dearly love.
ANGELO
We are all frail.
ISABELLA   Else let my brother die,
If not a fedary but only he   123
Owe and succeed thy weakness.   124
ANGELO   Nay, women are frail too.
ISABELLA
Ay, as the glasses where they view themselves,   126
Which are as easy broke as they make forms.   127

---

56 **give** i.e., give to death or punishment. (Isabella avoids or does not understand the drift of the question.) **57–8 Our . . . account** Our sins committed under compulsion are recorded but not charged to our spiritual account. **59 I'll . . . that** i.e., I'm not necessarily endorsing the view I just expressed **64 Please you** If you please **65 take** accept **67 Pleased** If it pleased **68 Were equal poise** there would be equal balance **73 of your answer** to which you will have to answer. **77 graciously** through divine grace **79 tax itself** accuse itself (of ignorance). **these** (Generically referring to any.) **80 enshield** shielded, protected from view behind the black masks **82 received plain** plainly understood. **gross** (1) openly (2) offensively **86 Accountant** accountable. **pain** penalty. **88 Admit** Suppose **89–90 As . . . question** since I will admit no alternative possibility in our discussion. (*Loss of question* means "forfeiting the terms of our debate.")

91 of by **97 supposed** hypothetical person. **him** i.e., Claudio **100 terms** sentence **103 That . . . for** i.e., that I have been sick with longing for. (Isabella's images are of love, death, and flagellation.) **107 died at once** should die once for all, rather than *die forever* (line 109) in the death of the soul through sin **112–14 Ignomy . . . redemption** Being ransomed under ignominious circumstances and being released without conditions are two entirely different things. Mercy under law bears no relation to being spared under foul stipulations. **116 proved** argued **120 something** to some extent **123 fedary** confederate, companion who is equally guilty **124 Owe . . . weakness** possess and inherit the weakness you speak of, or the weakness to which all men as a class are prone. (Isabella argues that Claudio should die only if he is the only man who is frail.) **126 glasses** mirrors **127 forms** (1) images (2) copies of themselves, i.e., children

Women? Help, heaven! Men their creation mar   128
In profiting by them. Nay, call us ten times frail,   129
For we are soft as our complexions are,   130
And credulous to false prints.

ANGELO   I think it well.   131
And from this testimony of your own sex—   132
Since I suppose we are made to be no stronger   133
Than faults may shake our frames—let me be bold.   134
I do arrest your words. Be that you are,   135
That is, a woman; if you be more, you're none.   136
If you be one, as you are well expressed   137
By all external warrants, show it now   138
By putting on the destined livery.   139

ISABELLA
I have no tongue but one. Gentle my lord,   140
Let me entreat you speak the former language.   141

ANGELO   Plainly conceive, I love you.

ISABELLA   My brother did love Juliet,
And you tell me that he shall die for't.

ANGELO
He shall not, Isabel, if you give me love.

ISABELLA
I know your virtue hath a license in't,   146
Which seems a little fouler than it is   147
To pluck on others.

ANGELO   Believe me, on mine honor,   148
My words express my purpose.

ISABELLA
Ha! Little honor to be much believed,
And most pernicious purpose! Seeming, seeming!
I will proclaim thee, Angelo, look for't!
Sign me a present pardon for my brother,   153
Or with an outstretched throat I'll tell the world
    aloud
What man thou art.

ANGELO   Who will believe thee, Isabel?
My unsoiled name, th'austereness of my life,
My vouch against you, and my place i'th' state   157
Will so your accusation overweigh
That you shall stifle in your own report
And smell of calumny. I have begun,   160
And now I give my sensual race the rein.   161
Fit thy consent to my sharp appetite;
Lay by all nicety and prolixious blushes   163
That banish what they sue for. Redeem thy brother   164

By yielding up thy body to my will,
Or else he must not only die the death,   166
But thy unkindness shall his death draw out
To ling'ring sufferance. Answer me tomorrow,   168
Or, by the affection that now guides me most,   169
I'll prove a tyrant to him. As for you,
Say what you can, my false o'erweighs your true.
                                                        Exit.

ISABELLA
To whom should I complain? Did I tell this,   172
Who would believe me? O perilous mouths,   173
That bear in them one and the selfsame tongue,   174
Either of condemnation or approof,   175
Bidding the law make curtsy to their will,   176
Hooking both right and wrong to th'appetite,   177
To follow as it draws! I'll to my brother.   178
Though he hath fall'n by prompture of the blood,   179
Yet hath he in him such a mind of honor
That, had he twenty heads to tender down   181
On twenty bloody blocks, he'd yield them up
Before his sister should her body stoop
To such abhorred pollution.
Then, Isabel, live chaste, and, brother, die;
More than our brother is our chastity.
I'll tell him yet of Angelo's request,
And fit his mind to death, for his soul's rest.   Exit.

❧

3.1

*Enter Duke [disguised as before], Claudio, and
Provost.*

DUKE
So then you hope of pardon from Lord Angelo?

CLAUDIO
The miserable have no other medicine
    But only hope.
I have hope to live and am prepared to die.

DUKE
Be absolute for death. Either death or life
Shall thereby be the sweeter. Reason thus with life:
If I do lose thee, I do lose a thing
That none but fools would keep. A breath thou art,
Servile to all the skyey influences   9
That dost this habitation where thou keep'st   10
Hourly afflict. Merely, thou art death's fool,   11
For him thou labor'st by thy flight to shun,
And yet run'st toward him still. Thou art not noble,   13

128–9 Men . . . them Men mar their creation in God's likeness by taking advantage of women.   130 complexions constitutions, appearance   131 credulous . . . prints susceptible to false impressions. (The metaphor is from the stamping of coins and other metal.)   132 of about   133 we i.e., men and women   134 than than that   135 arrest your words take what you have said and hold you to it.   that what   136 if . . . none i.e., if you insist on remaining a virgin and free of fleshly desire, you are no woman as we have defined the term—that is, frail and susceptible.   137–8 expressed . . . warrants shown to be by your physical beauty   139 putting . . . livery i.e., assuming the characteristic frailty that all women possess.   140 tongue language   141 speak . . . language speak to be understood, in the language I understand.   146–8 I know . . . others i.e., I am sure that you, out of virtuous motives, are speaking licentiously (and with the license of authority) in order to put me to the test.   153 present immediate   157 vouch testimony   160 calumny slander.   161 I give . . . rein I give free rein to my sensual desires to gallop as they please.   163–4 Lay . . . sue for Set aside all the coyness and time-wasting blushes that make a pretense of repulsing the embrace they actually beg for.

166 die the death be put to death   168 sufferance torture.   169 affection passion   172 Did I tell If I told   173–8 O perilous . . . draws! O dangerous voices of authority, able with one tongue either to condemn or approve, forcing both right and wrong to obey the willful appetite!   179 prompture prompting, suggestion   181 tender down lay down in payment
3.1 Location: The prison.
9 skyey influences influence of the stars   10 this habitation i.e., the earth (and the body as well).   keep'st dwell   11 Merely Utterly, only   13 still always.

For all th'accommodations that thou bear'st 14
Are nursed by baseness. Thou'rt by no means valiant, 15
For thou dost fear the soft and tender fork 16
Of a poor worm. Thy best of rest is sleep, 17
And that thou oft provok'st, yet grossly fear'st 18
Thy death, which is no more. Thou art not thyself,
For thou exists on many a thousand grains
That issue out of dust. Happy thou art not,
For what thou hast not, still thou striv'st to get,
And what thou hast, forget'st. Thou art not certain, 23
For thy complexion shifts to strange effects, 24
After the moon. If thou art rich, thou'rt poor, 25
For, like an ass whose back with ingots bows,
Thou bear'st thy heavy riches but a journey,
And death unloads thee. Friend hast thou none,
For thine own bowels which do call thee sire, 29
The mere effusion of thy proper loins, 30
Do curse the gout, serpigo, and the rheum 31
For ending thee no sooner. Thou hast nor youth
    nor age, 32
But as it were an after-dinner's sleep 33
Dreaming on both, for all thy blessèd youth 34
Becomes as agèd and doth beg the alms 35
Of palsied eld; and, when thou art old and rich, 36
Thou hast neither heat, affection, limb, nor beauty 37
To make thy riches pleasant. What's yet in this
That bears the name of life? Yet in this life
Lie hid more thousand deaths; yet death we fear,
That makes these odds all even.

CLAUDIO   I humbly thank you. 41
To sue to live, I find I seek to die, 42
And, seeking death, find life. Let it come on.

Enter Isabella.

ISABELLA
What, ho! Peace here; grace and good company! 44
PROVOST
Who's there? Come in. The wish deserves a welcome.
                          [*He goes to greet her.*]
DUKE [*to Claudio*]
Dear sir, ere long I'll visit you again.
CLAUDIO   Most holy sir, I thank you.
ISABELLA
My business is a word or two with Claudio.
PROVOST
And very welcome.—Look, signor, here's your sister.
DUKE [*aside to the Provost*]   Provost, a word with you.

PROVOST   As many as you please.
DUKE
Bring me to hear them speak, where I may be
Concealed.   [*The Duke and the Provost withdraw.*]
CLAUDIO   Now, sister, what's the comfort?
ISABELLA   Why,
As all comforts are: most good, most good indeed.
Lord Angelo, having affairs to heaven,
Intends you for his swift ambassador,
Where you shall be an everlasting leiger. 57
Therefore your best appointment make with speed; 58
Tomorrow you set on.
CLAUDIO   Is there no remedy? 59
ISABELLA
None but such remedy as, to save a head,
To cleave a heart in twain.
CLAUDIO   But is there any?
ISABELLA   Yes, brother, you may live.
There is a devilish mercy in the judge,
If you'll implore it, that will free your life
But fetter you till death.
CLAUDIO   Perpetual durance? 66
ISABELLA
Ay, just; perpetual durance, a restraint, 67
Though all the world's vastidity you had, 68
To a determined scope.
CLAUDIO   But in what nature? 69
ISABELLA
In such a one as, you consenting to't,
Would bark your honor from that trunk you bear 71
And leave you naked.
CLAUDIO   Let me know the point.
ISABELLA
Oh, I do fear thee, Claudio, and I quake 73
Lest thou a feverous life shouldst entertain, 74
And six or seven winters more respect 75
Than a perpetual honor. Dar'st thou die?
The sense of death is most in apprehension, 77
And the poor beetle that we tread upon
In corporal sufferance finds a pang as great
As when a giant dies.
CLAUDIO   Why give you me this shame?
Think you I can a resolution fetch 82
From flow'ry tenderness? If I must die, 83
I will encounter darkness as a bride
And hug it in mine arms.
ISABELLA
There spake my brother! There my father's grave
Did utter forth a voice. Yes, thou must die.
Thou art too noble to conserve a life

---

14 **accommodations** conveniences, civilized comforts   **15 nursed by baseness** nurtured by ignoble means.   **16 fork** forked tongue   **17 worm** (1) snake (2) grave worm.   **18 thou oft provok'st** you often invoke, summon   **23 certain** steadfast   **24 complexion** constitution. **strange effects** new appearances, manifestations   **25 After** in obedience to, under the influence of   **29 bowels** i.e., offspring   **30 mere** very.   **proper** own   **31 serpigo** a skin eruption.   **rheum** catarrh   **32 nor youth** neither youth   **33 after-dinner's** i.e., afternoon's   **34–6 all . . . eld** your happy youth must decline all too soon into old age and become like a beggar, pleading for the little comfort that palsied infirmity can provide. (Youth is penniless and dependent on the aged, whereas the old lack the physical capacity of youth.)   **37 heat, affection** vigor, passion   **41 makes . . . even** makes all equal.   **42 To sue** Suing, petitioning   **44 grace** God's grace

57 leiger resident ambassador.   **58 appointment** preparation   **59 set on** set forward.   **66 durance** imprisonment.   **67 just** just so   **67–9 a restraint . . . scope** a confinement to fixed limits or bounds (i.e., to inescapable guilt and perpetual remorse for the sinful bargain you had struck), even if you had the entire vastness of the world to wander in.   **71 bark** strip off (as one strips bark from a tree *trunk*)   **73 fear** fear for   **74 feverous** feverish.   **entertain** maintain, desire   **75 respect** value   **77 apprehension** anticipation   **82–3 Think . . . tenderness?** Do you think I can find the courage to face death in flowery figures of speech?

In base appliances. This outward-sainted deputy,   89
Whose settled visage and deliberate word   90
Nips youth i'th' head, and follies doth enew   91
As falcon doth the fowl, is yet a devil;   92
His filth within being cast, he would appear   93
A pond as deep as hell.

CLAUDIO   The prenzie Angelo?   94

ISABELLA
Oh, 'tis the cunning livery of hell,   95
The damned'st body to invest and cover   96
In prenzie guards! Dost thou think, Claudio: 97
If I would yield him my virginity,
Thou mightst be freed!

CLAUDIO   Oh, heavens, it cannot be.

ISABELLA
Yes, he would give't thee, from this rank offense,   100
So to offend him still. This night's the time   101
That I should do what I abhor to name,
Or else thou diest tomorrow.

CLAUDIO   Thou shalt not do't.

ISABELLA   Oh, were it but my life,
I'd throw it down for your deliverance
As frankly as a pin.

CLAUDIO   Thanks, dear Isabel.   107

ISABELLA
Be ready, Claudio, for your death tomorrow.

CLAUDIO
Yes. Has he affections in him,   109
That thus can make him bite the law by th' nose   110
When he would force it? Sure it is no sin,   111
Or of the deadly seven it is the least.

ISABELLA   Which is the least?

CLAUDIO
If it were damnable, he being so wise,
Why would he for the momentary trick   115
Be perdurably fined? Oh, Isabel!   116

ISABELLA
What says my brother?

CLAUDIO   Death is a fearful thing.

ISABELLA   And shamèd life a hateful.

CLAUDIO
Ay, but to die, and go we know not where,
To lie in cold obstruction and to rot,   120
This sensible warm motion to become   121

A kneaded clod, and the delighted spirit   122
To bathe in fiery floods, or to reside
In thrilling region of thick-ribbèd ice;   124
To be imprisoned in the viewless winds   125
And blown with restless violence round about
The pendent world; or to be worse than worst   127
Of those that lawless and incertain thought   128
Imagine howling—'tis too horrible!
The weariest and most loathèd worldly life
That age, ache, penury, and imprisonment
Can lay on nature is a paradise
To what we fear of death.   133

ISABELLA   Alas, alas!

CLAUDIO   Sweet sister, let me live.
What sin you do to save a brother's life,
Nature dispenses with the deed so far   137
That it becomes a virtue.

ISABELLA   Oh, you beast!
Oh, faithless coward! Oh, dishonest wretch!   139
Wilt thou be made a man out of my vice?
Is't not a kind of incest, to take life
From thine own sister's shame? What should I think?
Heaven shield my mother played my father fair!   143
For such a warpèd slip of wilderness   144
Ne'er issued from his blood. Take my defiance,
Die, perish! Might but my bending down   146
Reprieve thee from thy fate, it should proceed.
I'll pray a thousand prayers for thy death,
No word to save thee.

CLAUDIO
Nay, hear me, Isabel.

ISABELLA   Oh, fie, fie, fie!
Thy sin's not accidental, but a trade.   151
Mercy to thee would prove itself a bawd;   152
'Tis best that thou diest quickly.

CLAUDIO   Oh, hear me, Isabella!

[*The Duke comes forward.*]

DUKE
Vouchsafe a word, young sister, but one word.   155

ISABELLA   What is your will?

DUKE   Might you dispense with your leisure, I would
by and by have some speech with you. The satisfaction I would require is likewise your own benefit.   159

ISABELLA   I have no superfluous leisure—my stay
must be stolen out of other affairs—but I will attend   161
you awhile.   [*She walks apart.*]

DUKE   Son, I have overheard what hath passed between
you and your sister. Angelo had never the purpose to

89 In base appliances by means of ignoble devices, remedies.
89–92 This . . . fowl This outwardly holy deputy, who with composed
features and judiciously chosen words swoops down on youth like a
falcon and drives his prey into covert. (To *enew* is to drive prey down
into the water or into hiding.)   **93 cast** dug out; diagnosed, sounded;
vomited (?)   **94, 97 prenzie** (A word unknown elsewhere, perhaps
meaning "princely" or "precise.")   **95–7 'tis . . . guards** it is the cunning ruse of the devil to clothe and conceal the wickedest man imaginable in decorously proper trimmings   **97 Dost thou think** i.e.,
Would you believe   **100–1 he would . . . still** he would grant you
license, in return for your committing this foul crime, to continue
with your fornication.   **107 frankly** freely   **109 affections** passions
110 bite . . . nose i.e., flout the law   **111 force** enforce. (Claudio wonders that lust can drive Angelo to make a mockery of the law even
while seeking to enforce it.)   **115 trick** trifle   **116 perdurably fined**
everlastingly punished.   **120 obstruction** cessation of vital functions
121 sensible endowed with feeling.   **motion** organism

122 kneaded clod shapeless lump of earth.   **delighted spirit** spirit
that is now attended with delight, or capable of being so
124 thrilling piercingly cold   **125 viewless** invisible   **127 pendent**
hanging in space. (A Ptolemaic concept.)   **128 lawless . . . thought**
i.e., wild conjecture   **133 To** compared to   **137 dispenses with**
grants a dispensation for, excuses   **139 dishonest** dishonorable
143 shield forfend, forbid   **144 warpèd . . . wilderness** perverse,
licentious scion, one that reverts to the original wild stock   **146 but**
merely   **151 accidental** casual.   **trade** established habit.   **152 prove . . .
bawd** i.e., provide opportunity for sexual license   **155 Vouchsafe**
Allow   **159 require** ask   **161 attend** await; listen to

corrupt her; only he hath made an assay of her virtue 165
to practice his judgment with the disposition of na- 166
tures. She, having the truth of honor in her, hath made 167
him that gracious denial which he is most glad to re- 168
ceive. I am confessor to Angelo, and I know this to be
true; therefore prepare yourself to death. Do not satisfy
your resolution with hopes that are fallible. Tomorrow
you must die. Go to your knees and make ready.

CLAUDIO   Let me ask my sister pardon. I am so out of
love with life that I will sue to be rid of it.

DUKE   Hold you there. Farewell.   [Claudio retires.] 175
Provost, a word with you.

[The Provost comes forward.]

PROVOST   What's your will, Father?

DUKE   That now you are come, you will be gone. Leave
me awhile with the maid. My mind promises with my 179
habit no loss shall touch her by my company. 180

PROVOST   In good time.   Exit [Provost with Claudio]. 181

[Isabella comes forward.]

DUKE   The hand that hath made you fair hath made you
good. The goodness that is cheap in beauty makes 183
beauty brief in goodness; but grace, being the soul of 184
your complexion, shall keep the body of it ever fair. 185
The assault that Angelo hath made to you, fortune
hath conveyed to my understanding; and, but that 187
frailty hath examples for his falling, I should wonder 188
at Angelo. How will you do to content this substitute 189
and to save your brother?

ISABELLA   I am now going to resolve him. I had rather 191
my brother die by the law than my son should be
unlawfully born. But, oh, how much is the good Duke
deceived in Angelo! If ever he return and I can speak
to him, I will open my lips in vain, or discover his 195
government. 196

DUKE   That shall not be much amiss. Yet, as the matter
now stands, he will avoid your accusation; he made 198
trial of you only. Therefore fasten your ear on my
advisings. To the love I have in doing good a remedy
presents itself. I do make myself believe that you may
most uprighteously do a poor wronged lady a merited
benefit, redeem your brother from the angry law, do
no stain to your own gracious person, and much
please the absent Duke, if peradventure he shall ever
return to have hearing of this business.

ISABELLA   Let me hear you speak farther. I have spirit 207
to do anything that appears not foul in the truth of my 208
spirit. 209

DUKE   Virtue is bold, and goodness never fearful. Have
you not heard speak of Mariana, the sister of Frederick, the great soldier who miscarried at sea?

ISABELLA   I have heard of the lady, and good words
went with her name.

DUKE   She should this Angelo have married, was 215
affianced to her by oath, and the nuptial appointed;
between which time of the contract and limit of the 217
solemnity, her brother Frederick was wrecked at sea, 218
having in that perished vessel the dowry of his sister.
But mark how heavily this befell to the poor gentlewoman. There she lost a noble and renowned brother,
in his love toward her ever most kind and natural;
with him, the portion and sinew of her fortune, her 223
marriage dowry; with both, her combinate husband, 224
this well-seeming Angelo.

ISABELLA   Can this be so? Did Angelo so leave her?

DUKE   Left her in her tears, and dried not one of them
with his comfort; swallowed his vows whole, pretend- 228
ing in her discoveries of dishonor; in few, bestowed 229
her on her own lamentation, which she yet wears for 230
his sake; and he, a marble to her tears, is washed with 231
them but relents not.

ISABELLA   What a merit were it in death to take this
poor maid from the world! What corruption in this
life, that it will let this man live! But how out of this can
she avail? 236

DUKE   It is a rupture that you may easily heal, and the
cure of it not only saves your brother but keeps you
from dishonor in doing it.

ISABELLA   Show me how, good Father.

DUKE   This forenamed maid hath yet in her the continuance of her first affection; his unjust unkindness, that
in all reason should have quenched her love, hath, like
an impediment in the current, made it more violent
and unruly. Go you to Angelo; answer his requiring
with a plausible obedience; agree with his demands to 246
the point. Only refer yourself to this advantage: first, 247
that your stay with him may not be long, that the time
may have all shadow and silence in it, and the place 249
answer to convenience. This being granted in
course—and now follows all—we shall advise this
wronged maid to stead up your appointment, go in 252
your place. If the encounter acknowledge itself here- 253
after, it may compel him to her recompense. And here, 254
by this, is your brother saved, your honor untainted,
the poor Mariana advantaged, and the corrupt deputy
scaled. The maid will I frame and make fit for his at- 257

165 **only he hath** he has only.   **assay** test   166–7 **his judgment . . .
natures** his ability to judge people's characters.   168 **gracious** virtuous   175 **Hold you there** Hold fast to that resolution.
179–80 **with my habit** as well as my priestly garb (that)   181 **In good
time** i.e., Very well.   183–84 **The goodness . . . in goodness** i.e., The
physical attractions that come easily with beauty make beauty soon
cease to be morally good   185 **complexion** character and appearance
187 **but that** were it not that   188 **examples** precedents   189 **this
substitute**, the deputy, Angelo   191 **resolve him** set his mind at
rest.   195–6 **discover his government** expose Angelo's misconduct.
198 **avoid** evade, refute.   **he made** i.e., he will say that he made
207 **spirit** courage   208 **truth** righteousness   209 **spirit** soul.

215 **She . . . married** Angelo was supposed to have married her.
was i.e., he was   217–18 **limit . . . solemnity** date set for the ceremony   223 **the portion and sinew** i.e., the mainstay   224 **combinate
husband** i.e., betrothed   228–9 **pretending . . . dishonor** falsely alleging to have found evidence of unchastity in her   229–30 **in few . . .
lamentation** in short, left her to her grief. (With quibble on *bestowed*,
meaning "gave in marriage.")   230 **wears** i.e., carries in her heart
231 **a marble to** i.e., unmoved by   236 **avail** benefit.   246–7 **to the
point** precisely.   247 **refer . . . advantage** obtain these conditions
249 **shadow** darkness, secrecy   252 **stead . . . appointment** go in your
stead   253–4 **If the . . . hereafter** i.e., If she should become pregnant
257 **scaled** weighed in the scales of justice (and found wanting).
frame prepare

tempt. If you think well to carry this as you may, the doubleness of the benefit defends the deceit from reproof. What think you of it?

ISABELLA   The image of it gives me content already, and I trust it will grow to a most prosperous perfection.

DUKE   It lies much in your holding up. Haste you speed- 264 ily to Angelo. If for this night he entreat you to his bed, give him promise of satisfaction. I will presently to Saint Luke's; there, at the moated grange, resides 267 this dejected Mariana. At that place call upon me; and dispatch with Angelo, that it may be quickly. 269

ISABELLA   I thank you for this comfort. Fare you well, good Father.   *Exit. [The Duke remains.]*

❧

[3.2]

Enter [to the Duke] Elbow, Clown [Pompey, and] officers.

ELBOW   Nay, if there be no remedy for it but that you will needs buy and sell men and women like beasts, we shall have all the world drink brown and white bastard. 4

DUKE [*aside*]   Oh, heavens, what stuff is here?

POMPEY   'Twas never merry world since, of two usur- 6 ies, the merriest was put down, and the worser al- 7 lowed by order of law a furred gown to keep him 8 warm, and furred with fox on lambskins too, to signify that craft, being richer than innocency, stands 10 for the facing. 11

ELBOW   Come your way, sir.—Bless you, good Father Friar.

DUKE   And you, good Brother Father. What offense hath 14 this man made you, sir?

ELBOW   Marry, sir, he hath offended the law; and, sir, we take him to be a thief too, sir, for we have found upon him, sir, a strange picklock, which we have sent 18 to the deputy.

DUKE [*to Pompey*]
Fie, sirrah, a bawd, a wicked bawd!
The evil that thou causest to be done,
That is thy means to live. Do thou but think
What 'tis to cram a maw or clothe a back 23
From such a filthy vice; say to thyself,
From their abominable and beastly touches 25
I drink, I eat, array myself, and live.

Canst thou believe thy living is a life,
So stinkingly depending? Go mend, go mend. 28

POMPEY   Indeed, it does stink in some sort, sir. But yet, sir, I would prove— 30

DUKE
Nay, if the devil have given thee proofs for sin, 31
Thou wilt prove his.—Take him to prison, officer. 32
Correction and instruction must both work
Ere this rude beast will profit.

ELBOW   He must before the deputy, sir; he has given 35 him warning. The deputy cannot abide a whoremaster. If he be a whoremonger and comes before him, he 37 were as good go a mile on his errand. 38

DUKE
That we were all, as some would seem to be, 39
From our faults, as faults from seeming, free! 40

Enter Lucio.

ELBOW   His neck will come to your waist—a cord, sir. 41

POMPEY   I spy comfort, I cry bail. Here's a gentleman and a friend of mine.

LUCIO   How now, noble Pompey? What, at the wheels of Caesar? Art thou led in triumph? What, is there 45 none of Pygmalion's images, newly made woman, to 46 be had now, for putting the hand in the pocket and extracting it clutched? What reply, ha? What say'st thou 48 to this tune, matter, and method? Is 't not drowned i'th' 49 last rain, ha? What say'st thou, trot? Is the world 50 as it was, man? Which is the way? Is it sad, and few 51 words? Or how? The trick of it? 52

DUKE   Still thus, and thus; still worse!

LUCIO   How doth my dear morsel, thy mistress? Procures she still, ha?

POMPEY   Troth, sir, she hath eaten up all her beef, and 56 she is herself in the tub. 57

LUCIO   Why, 'tis good. It is the right of it, it must be so. Ever your fresh whore and your powdered bawd; an 59 unshunned consequence, it must be so. Art going to 60 prison, Pompey?

---

264 **holding up** ability to carry it off.   267 **moated grange** country house surrounded by a ditch   269 **dispatch** settle, conclude business
3.2 Location: Scene continues. The Duke remains onstage.
4 **bastard** sweet Spanish wine. (Used quibblingly.)   6–7 **two usuries** i.e., moneylending (the *worser*) and procuring for fornication (the *merriest*), both of which yield increase   8 **furred gown** (Characteristic attire of usurers.)   10–11 **stands . . . facing** represents the outer covering. (Fox symbolizes *craft* or craftiness, lambskin, *innocency*.)
14 **Brother Father** (The Duke's retort to Elbow's *Father Friar*, i.e., Father Brother.)   18 **picklock** skeleton key, or perhaps a chastity belt in Pompey's possession as pimp; it might seem *strange* to the innocent Elbow   23 **cram . . . back** fill a stomach or provide clothing
25 **touches** sexual encounters

28 **depending** supported.   30 **prove** i.e., argue, demonstrate
31 **proofs for** arguments in defense of   32 **prove** turn out to be
35 **must** must go.   **deputy** i.e., Angelo. (Though Escalus gave Pompey the warning.)   37–8 **he . . . errand** i.e., he will have a hard road to travel.   39 **That** Would that   40 **From . . . free** i.e., free from faults, and our faults free from dissembling.   41 **His . . . cord** i.e., He is likely to hang by a cord like that around your waist. (The Duke is habited as a friar.)   45 **Caesar** (Who defeated Pompey at Pharsalia and led his sons in triumph after defeating them at Munda.)   46 **Pygmalion's images** i.e., prostitutes, so called because they "painted" with cosmetics like a painted statue. (Pygmalion was a sculptor, according to legend, whose female statue came to life "newly made.")   48 **clutched** i.e., with money in it. (But also with sexual suggestion.)   48–50 **What say'st . . . rain** i.e., What do you say now to this latest turn of events? Are our prospects a little dampened?   50 **trot** old bawd.   51–2 **Which . . . words?** i.e., What is the latest fashion? Is melancholy now in vogue? (A wry comment on Pompey's silence.)   52 **trick** fashion   56 **eaten . . . beef** (1) consumed all her salt beef, which had been prepared in a powder-tub like that also used to treat venereal disease (2) run through all her prostitutes   57 **in the tub** being treated for venereal disease by the sweating-tub treatment (much as beef was salted down in a tub to preserve it).   59 **Ever . . . bawd** i.e., It is always thus with young whores and old bawds, *powdered* like beef in a tub and caked with cosmetics   60 **unshunned** unshunnable, unavoidable

POMPEY   Yes, faith, sir.

LUCIO   Why, 'tis not amiss, Pompey. Farewell. Go, say I sent thee thither. For debt, Pompey? Or how?

ELBOW   For being a bawd, for being a bawd.

LUCIO   Well, then, imprison him. If imprisonment be the due of a bawd, why, 'tis his right. Bawd is he doubtless, and of antiquity too; bawd-born. Farewell, 68 good Pompey. Commend me to the prison, Pompey. You will turn good husband now, Pompey; you will 70 keep the house. 71

POMPEY   I hope, sir, Your good Worship will be my bail.

LUCIO   No, indeed, will I not, Pompey; it is not the wear. I will pray, Pompey, to increase your bondage. 74 If you take it not patiently, why, your mettle is the 75 more. Adieu, trusty Pompey.—Bless you, Friar. 76

DUKE   And you.

LUCIO   Does Bridget paint still, Pompey, ha? 78

ELBOW   [to Pompey]   Come your ways, sir, come. 79

POMPEY   [to Lucio]   You will not bail me, then, sir?

LUCIO   Then, Pompey, nor now.—What news abroad, 81 Friar? What news?

ELBOW   Come your ways, sir, come.

LUCIO   Go to kennel, Pompey, go.

[Exeunt Elbow, Pompey, and Officers.]

What news, Friar, of the Duke?

DUKE   I know none. Can you tell me of any?

LUCIO   Some say he is with the Emperor of Russia; other 87 some, he is in Rome. But where is he, think you? 88

DUKE   I know not where; but wheresoever, I wish him well.

LUCIO   It was a mad fantastical trick of him to steal from 91 the state and usurp the beggary he was never born to. 92 Lord Angelo dukes it well in his absence; he puts 93 transgression to't. 94

DUKE   He does well in't.

LUCIO   A little more lenity to lechery would do no harm in him. Something too crabbed that way, Friar. 97

DUKE   It is too general a vice, and severity must cure it.

LUCIO   Yes, in good sooth, the vice is of a great kindred; 99 it is well allied. But it is impossible to extirp it quite, 100 Friar, till eating and drinking be put down. They say this Angelo was not made by man and woman after 102 this downright way of creation. Is it true, think you? 103

DUKE   How should he be made, then?

LUCIO   Some report a sea maid spawned him; some, 105 that he was begot between two stockfishes. But it is 106

certain that when he makes water his urine is congealed ice; that I know to be true. And he is a motion 108 ungenerative; that's infallible. 109

DUKE   You are pleasant, sir, and speak apace. 110

LUCIO   Why, what a ruthless thing is this in him, for the rebellion of a codpiece to take away the life of a man! 112 Would the Duke that is absent have done this? Ere he would have hanged a man for the getting a hundred bastards, he would have paid for the nursing a thousand. He had some feeling of the sport; he knew the service, and that instructed him to mercy. 117

DUKE   I never heard the absent Duke much detected for 118 women. He was not inclined that way.

LUCIO   Oh, sir, you are deceived.

DUKE   'Tis not possible.

LUCIO   Who, not the Duke? Yes, your beggar of fifty; and his use was to put a ducat in her clack-dish. The 123 Duke had crotchets in him. He would be drunk too, that let me inform you.

DUKE   You do him wrong, surely.

LUCIO   Sir, I was an inward of his. A shy fellow was the 127 Duke, and I believe I know the cause of his withdrawing.

DUKE   What, I prithee, might be the cause?

LUCIO   No, pardon. 'Tis a secret must be locked within the teeth and the lips. But this I can let you understand: the greater file of the subject held the Duke to 133 be wise.

DUKE   Wise? Why, no question but he was.

LUCIO   A very superficial, ignorant, unweighing fellow. 136

DUKE   Either this is envy in you, folly, or mistaking. The 137 very stream of his life and the business he hath helmed 138 must, upon a warranted need, give him a better proc- 139 lamation. Let him be but testimonied in his own 140 bringings-forth, and he shall appear to the envious a 141 scholar, a statesman, and a soldier. Therefore you speak unskillfully; or, if your knowledge be more, it is 143 much darkened in your malice.

LUCIO   Sir, I know him, and I love him.

DUKE   Love talks with better knowledge, and knowledge with dearer love.

LUCIO   Come, sir, I know what I know.

DUKE   I can hardly believe that, since you know not what you speak. But if ever the Duke return, as our prayers are he may, let me desire you to make your answer before him. If it be honest you have spoke, you have courage to maintain it. I am bound to call upon you; and, I pray you, your name?

---

68 **antiquity** long continuance.   **bawd-born** a born bawd and born of a bawd.   70 **good husband** thrifty manager   71 **keep the house** stay indoors. (With pun on the pimp's function as doorkeeper.)   74 **wear** fashion.   75–6 **your . . . more** (1) your spirit is revealed all the more (2) your shackles will be made heavier. (Playing on *mettle/metal*.) 78 **paint** use cosmetics   79 **Come your ways** Come along   81 **Then** Neither then.   **abroad** about town   87–8 **other some** some others 91 **steal** steal away   92 **beggary** i.e., status of a wanderer or traveler. (With unconscious ironic appropriateness; Lucio clearly does not see through the Duke's disguise as a mendicant friar.)   93–4 **puts . . . to't** puts lawbreaking under severe restraint.   97 **Something too crabbed** Somewhat too harsh   99 **kindred** i.e., family, numerous and well connected   100 **extirp** eradicate   102 **after** in accordance with 103 **downright** straightforward, usual   105 **sea maid** mermaid 106 **stockfishes** dried codfish.

108–9 **motion ungenerative** masculine puppet, without sexual potency   110 **pleasant** jocose.   **apace** fast and idly.   112 **codpiece** an appendage to the front of close-fitting hose or breeches worn by men, often indelicately and indelicately conspicuous; hence, slang for "penis"   117 **the service** i.e., prostitution   118 **detected** accused 123 **his . . . clack-dish** his custom was to put a coin in her wooden beggar's bowl, with its lid that was "clacked" to attract attention. (Lucio hints that the Duke had sex with her.)   127 **inward** intimate 133 **the greater . . . subject** most of his subjects   136 **unweighing** injudicious   137 **envy** malice   138 **helmed** steered   139 **upon . . . need** if a warrant were needed   139–40 **give . . . proclamation** proclaim him better (than you assert).   140–1 **in . . . bringings-forth** by his own public actions   141 **to the envious** even to the malicious 143 **unskillfully** in ignorance

LUCIO   Sir, my name is Lucio, well known to the Duke.

DUKE   He shall know you better, sir, if I may live to report you.

LUCIO   I fear you not.

DUKE   Oh, you hope the Duke will return no more, or you imagine me too unhurtful an opposite. But indeed 160 I can do you little harm; you'll forswear this again. 161

LUCIO   I'll be hanged first. Thou art deceived in me, Friar. But no more of this. Canst thou tell if Claudio die tomorrow or no?

DUKE   Why should he die, sir?

LUCIO   Why? For filling a bottle with a tundish. I would 166 the Duke we talk of were returned again. This ungen- 167 itured agent will unpeople the province with conti- 168 nency. Sparrows must not build in his house eaves, 169 because they are lecherous. The Duke yet would have dark deeds darkly answered; he would never bring 171 them to light. Would he were returned! Marry, this Claudio is condemned for untrussing. Farewell, good 173 Friar. I prithee, pray for me. The Duke, I say to thee again, would eat mutton on Fridays. He's now past it, 175 yet, and I say to thee, he would mouth with a beggar, 176 though she smelt brown bread and garlic. Say that I 177 said so. Farewell.   *Exit.*

DUKE
No might nor greatness in mortality   179
Can censure scape; back-wounding calumny   180
The whitest virtue strikes. What king so strong   181
Can tie the gall up in the slanderous tongue?
But who comes here?

Enter Escalus, Provost, and [officers with] bawd [Mistress Overdone].

ESCALUS   Go, away with her to prison.

MISTRESS OVERDONE   Good my lord, be good to me. Your Honor is accounted a merciful man. Good my lord.

ESCALUS   Double and treble admonition, and still forfeit 188 in the same kind! This would make mercy swear and 189 play the tyrant.

PROVOST   A bawd of eleven years' continuance, may it please Your Honor.

MISTRESS OVERDONE   My lord, this is one Lucio's infor- 193 mation against me. Mistress Kate Keepdown was with 194 child by him in the Duke's time; he promised her mar-

riage. His child is a year and a quarter old, come Philip 196 and Jacob. I have kept it myself; and see how he goes 197 about to abuse me!   198

ESCALUS   That fellow is a fellow of much license. Let him be called before us. Away with her to prison! Go to, no more words.   *[Exeunt Officers with Mistress Overdone.]*
Provost, my brother Angelo will not be al- 202 tered; Claudio must die tomorrow. Let him be fur- nished with divines and have all charitable 204 preparation. If my brother wrought by my pity, it 205 should not be so with him.

PROVOST   So please you, this friar hath been with him, and advised him for th'entertainment of death.   208

ESCALUS   Good even, good Father.

DUKE   Bliss and goodness on you!

ESCALUS   Of whence are you?

DUKE
Not of this country, though my chance is now
To use it for my time. I am a brother   213
Of gracious order, late come from the See   214
In special business from His Holiness.

ESCALUS   What news abroad i'th' world?

DUKE   None but that there is so great a fever on good- ness that the dissolution of it must cure it. Novelty is 218 only in request, and, as it is, as dangerous to be aged 219 in any kind of course as it is virtuous to be constant 220 in any undertaking. There is scarce truth enough alive 221 to make societies secure, but security enough to make 222 fellowships accursed. Much upon this riddle runs the 223 wisdom of the world. This news is old enough, yet it is every day's news. I pray you, sir, of what disposi- tion was the Duke?

ESCALUS   One that, above all other strifes, contended 227 especially to know himself.

DUKE   What pleasure was he given to?

ESCALUS   Rather rejoicing to see another merry than merry at anything which professed to make him re- 231 joice—a gentleman of all temperance. But leave we him to his events, with a prayer they may prove pros- 233 perous, and let me desire to know how you find Clau- dio prepared. I am made to understand that you have lent him visitation.   236

196–7 **Philip and Jacob** the Feast of Saint Philip and Saint James (*Jacobus* in Latin), May 1.   197–8 **goes about** busies himself
202 **brother** i.e., fellow officer of state   204 **divines** clergymen
205 **wrought . . . pity** acted in accord with my impulses of pity
208 **th'entertainment** the reception, acceptance   213 **To . . . time** to dwell here for my present purposes.   214 **the See** Rome   218 **the dissolution . . . cure it** i.e., only by dying can goodness be rid of the disease.   218–19 **is only in request** is the only thing people seek
219–21 **as it . . . undertaking** as things currently stand, (it is) as dangerous to be constant in any undertaking as it is virtuous to be thus constant.   221–3 **There . . . accursed** i.e., There is hardly enough integrity extant to establish secure and trusting associations among men, but binding contractual obligations enough to be the curse of friendship. (The Duke thus puns on *security* [1] a sense of trust [2] financial pledge required to borrow money, and on *fellowship* [1] friendship [2] corporations formed for trading ventures.)
223 **upon this riddle** in this riddling fashion   227 **strifes** endeavors
231 **professed** attempted   233 **his events** the outcome of his affairs
236 **lent him visitation** paid him a visit.

160 **too . . . opposite** too harmless an adversary.   161 **forswear this again** deny another time what you have said under oath.
166 **tundish** funnel. (Here representing the penis.)   167–8 **ungeni- tured agent** sexless deputy   169 **Sparrows** (Proverbially lecherous birds.)   171 **darkly** secretly   173 **untrussing** undressing. (Specifi- cally, untying the points used to fasten hose to doublet.)   175 **eat . . . Fridays** i.e., frequent loose women in flagrant disregard of the law. (Literally, violate religious observance by eating meat on fast days.)
past it beyond the age for sex   176 **mouth** kiss   177 **smelt brown bread** smelled of coarse bran bread   179 **mortality** humankind; human life   180–1 **Can . . . strikes** can escape censure; backbiting slander strikes even the purest of virtues.   181 **so** be he never so
188–9 **forfeit . . . kind** guilty of the same offense.   189 **mercy** i.e., even mercy   193–4 **information** accusation

DUKE   He professes to have received no sinister measure 237
from his judge, but most willingly humbles himself to
the determination of justice; yet had he framed to him- 239
self, by the instruction of his frailty, many deceiving 240
promises of life, which I, by my good leisure, have
discredited to him, and now is he resolved to die.

ESCALUS   You have paid the heavens your function, and
the prisoner the very debt of your calling. I have la- 244
bored for the poor gentleman to the extremest shore of 245
my modesty, but my brother justice have I found so 246
severe that he hath forced me to tell him he is indeed
Justice.

DUKE   If his own life answer the straitness of his 249
proceeding, it shall become him well; wherein if he
chance to fail, he hath sentenced himself.

ESCALUS   I am going to visit the prisoner. Fare you well.

DUKE   Peace be with you!

                           [Exeunt Escalus and Provost.]

He who the sword of heaven will bear
Should be as holy as severe;
Pattern in himself to know,   256
Grace to stand, and virtue go;   257
More nor less to others paying   258
Than by self-offenses weighing.   259
Shame to him whose cruel striking
Kills for faults of his own liking!
Twice treble shame on Angelo,
To weed my vice and let his grow!   263
Oh, what may man within him hide,
Though angel on the outward side!
How may likeness made in crimes,   266
Making practice on the times,   267
To draw with idle spiders' strings   268
Most ponderous and substantial things!   269
Craft against vice I must apply.
With Angelo tonight shall lie
His old betrothèd but despisèd;
So disguise shall, by the disguisèd,   273
Pay with falsehood false exacting   274
And perform an old contracting.   *Exit.* 275

                        ❖

4.1

Enter Mariana, and Boy singing.

        Song.

BOY

Take, oh, take those lips away,
   That so sweetly were forsworn,
And those eyes, the break of day,
   Lights that do mislead the morn;   4
But my kisses bring again, bring again,   5
Seals of love, but sealed in vain, sealed in vain.   6

Enter Duke [disguised as before].

MARIANA

Break off thy song, and haste thee quick away.
Here comes a man of comfort, whose advice
Hath often stilled my brawling discontent. [*Exit Boy.*]   9
I cry you mercy, sir, and well could wish   10
You had not found me here so musical.
Let me excuse me, and believe me so,
My mirth it much displeased, but pleased my woe.   13

DUKE

'Tis good; though music oft hath such a charm
To make bad good, and good provoke to harm.   15
I pray you, tell me, hath anybody inquired for me here
today? Much upon this time have I promised here   17
to meet.

MARIANA   You have not been inquired after. I have sat
here all day.

Enter Isabella.

DUKE   I do constantly believe you. The time is come   21
even now. I shall crave your forbearance a little. May-   22
be I will call upon you anon, for some advantage to   23
yourself.

MARIANA   I am always bound to you.   *Exit.*

DUKE   Very well met, and welcome.
What is the news from this good deputy?

ISABELLA

He hath a garden circummured with brick,   28
Whose western side is with a vineyard backed;
And to that vineyard is a planchèd gate,   30
That makes his opening with this bigger key.   31

                    [She shows keys.]

---

237 **sinister measure** unfair treatment meted out to him
239–40 **framed to himself** formulated in his mind   240 **by . . . frailty**
at the prompting of his natural human weakness   244 **the**
prisoner . . . calling what your calling as a friar obliges you to give
the prisoner, i.e., the comforts of spiritual counsel.   245–6 **shore . . .**
modesty limit of propriety   249 **straitness** strictness   256–9 **Pat-**
tern . . . weighing he must know himself and be a pattern for others
to emulate, with the grace to stand firm and the virtue to guide himself in the straight path, judging and punishing others with neither
more nor less severity than he applies to his own offenses.   263 **my**
vice i.e., vice in everyone except Angelo. (The Duke speaks chorically
on behalf of everyone generally.)   266–9 **How . . . things!** How may
false seeming of a criminal sort, practicing deception on the world,
make weighty and substantial matters seem as illusory and unsubstantial as spider webs!   273–5 **So . . . contracting** so shall disguise,
employed by those in disguise (i.e., Mariana and the Duke himself),
use a kind of (virtuous) falsehood to pay back what was exacted
through deception (by Angelo), and thereby fulfill an old contract.

4.1 Location: The moated grange at Saint Luke's.
4 **Lights . . . morn** eyes that mislead the morning (the goddess of
dawn, Eos or Aurora) into taking them for the rising sun   5 **again**
back   6 **Seals** confirmations, pledges   9 **brawling** clamorous
10 **cry you mercy** beg your pardon   13 **My . . . woe** i.e., it suited not a
merry but a melancholy mood.   15 **bad good** i.e., bad seem good,
attractive. (The Duke, echoing Renaissance conceptions of the psychological effects of music, warns that music may soothe melancholy
at times but may also produce unvirtuous effects on the mind.)
17 **Much upon** Pretty nearly about   21 **constantly** confidently
22 **crave . . . little** i.e., ask you to withdraw briefly.   23 **anon**
presently   28 **circummured** walled about   30 **planchèd** made of
boards, planks   31 **his** its

This other doth command a little door
Which from the vineyard to the garden leads;
There have I made my promise, upon the   34
Heavy middle of the night, to call upon him.
DUKE
But shall you on your knowledge find this way?
ISABELLA
I have ta'en a due and wary note upon't.
With whispering and most guilty diligence,
In action all of precept, he did show me   39
The way twice o'er.
DUKE   Are there no other tokens
Between you 'greed concerning her observance?   41
ISABELLA
No, none, but only a repair i'th' dark,   42
And that I have possessed him my most stay   43
Can be but brief; for I have made him know
I have a servant comes with me along,
That stays upon me, whose persuasion is   46
I come about my brother.
DUKE   'Tis well borne up.   47
I have not yet made known to Mariana
A word of this.—What, ho, within! Come forth!

Enter Mariana.

I pray you, be acquainted with this maid;
She comes to do you good.
ISABELLA   I do desire the like.
DUKE
Do you persuade yourself that I respect you?   52
MARIANA
Good Friar, I know you do, and have found it.   53
DUKE
Take then this your companion by the hand,
Who hath a story ready for your ear.
I shall attend your leisure. But make haste;
The vaporous night approaches.
MARIANA   Will't please you walk aside?
                                    Exit [with Isabella].
DUKE
O place and greatness! Millions of false eyes
Are stuck upon thee. Volumes of report   60
Run with these false and most contrarious quests   61
Upon thy doings; thousand escapes of wit   62
Make thee the father of their idle dream   63
And rack thee in their fancies.

Enter Mariana and Isabella.

                        Welcome. How agreed? 64

ISABELLA
She'll take the enterprise upon her, Father,
If you advise it.
DUKE   It is not my consent,   66
But my entreaty too.
ISABELLA   Little have you to say 67
When you depart from him but, soft and low,
"Remember now my brother."
MARIANA   Fear me not.   69
DUKE
Nor, gentle daughter, fear you not at all.
He is your husband on a precontract;   71
To bring you thus together, 'tis no sin,
Sith that the justice of your title to him   73
Doth flourish the deceit. Come, let us go.   74
Our corn's to reap, for yet our tithe's to sow. *Exeunt.* 75

❖

4.2

Enter Provost and Clown [Pompey].

PROVOST   Come hither, sirrah. Can you cut off a man's
head?
POMPEY   If the man be a bachelor, sir, I can; but if he be
a married man, he's his wife's head, and I can never   4
cut off a woman's head.   5
PROVOST   Come, sir, leave me your snatches, and yield 6
me a direct answer. Tomorrow morning are to die
Claudio and Barnardine. Here is in our prison a com-   8
mon executioner, who in his office lacks a helper. If 9
you will take it on you to assist him, it shall redeem
you from your gyves; if not, you shall have your full 11
time of imprisonment and your deliverance with an
unpitied whipping, for you have been a notorious
bawd.
POMPEY   Sir, I have been an unlawful bawd time out of
mind, but yet I will be content to be a lawful hangman.
I would be glad to receive some instruction from
my fellow partner.
PROVOST   What, ho, Abhorson! Where's Abhorson,
there?

Enter Abhorson.

ABHORSON   Do you call, sir?
PROVOST   Sirrah, here's a fellow will help you tomorrow
in your execution. If you think it meet, compound   23
with him by the year, and let him abide here with
you; if not, use him for the present and dismiss him.

---

34 **upon** during, at   39 **In action . . . precept** i.e., teaching by demonstration   41 **her observance** what she is supposed to do.   42 **repair** act of going or coming to a place   43 **possessed** informed.   **my most stay** my stay at the longest   46 **stays upon** waits for.   **persuasion** belief   47 **borne up** sustained, carried out.   52 **respect you** are concerned for your welfare.   53 **found it** found it to be true.   60 **stuck** fastened   60–2 **Volumes . . . doings** Innumerable rumors follow a false scent and hunt counter in pursuing your activities   62 **escapes** sallies   63 **Make . . . dream** credit you with being the source of their fantasies   64 **rack** stretch as on the rack, distort

66 **not** not only   67 **Little . . . say** Say little   69 **Fear me not** i.e., Don't worry about my carrying out my part.   71 **precontract** legally binding agreement entered into before any church ceremony. (Compare Claudio's and Juliet's *true contract* at 1.2.142.)   73 **Sith that** since   74 **flourish** adorn, make fair   75 **Our corn's . . . sow** We must first sow grain before we can expect to reap a harvest; i.e., we must get started.   **tithe** grain sown for tithe dues; or, an error for "tilth"   **4.2 Location:** The prison.   4 **he's . . . head** (Compare Ephesians 5:23: "The husband is the head of the wife.")   5 **head** (With wordplay on "maidenhead.")   6 **leave . . . snatches** leave off your quibbles   8–9 **common** public   11 **gyves** fetters, shackles   23 **compound** make an agreement

He cannot plead his estimation with you; he hath   26
been a bawd.

ABHORSON   A bawd, sir? Fie upon him! He will dis-   29
credit our mystery.

PROVOST   Go to, sir, you weigh equally; a feather will
turn the scale.   *Exit.*

POMPEY   Pray, sir, by your good favor—for surely, sir,   32
a good favor you have, but that you have a hanging   33
look—do you call, sir, your occupation a mystery?   34

ABHORSON   Ay, sir, a mystery.

POMPEY   Painting, sir, I have heard say, is a mystery,   36
and your whores, sir, being members of my occupation, using painting, do prove my occupation a
mystery. But what mystery there should be in hanging, if I should be hanged, I cannot imagine.

ABHORSON   Sir, it is a mystery.

POMPEY   Proof?

ABHORSON   Every true man's apparel fits your thief. If it   43
be too little for your thief, your true man thinks it big   44
enough; if it be too big for your thief, your thief thinks   45
it little enough. So every true man's apparel fits your   46
thief.   47

Enter Provost.

PROVOST   Are you agreed?

POMPEY   Sir, I will serve him, for I do find your hangman is a more penitent trade than your bawd: he doth   50
oftener ask forgiveness.   51

PROVOST   You, sirrah, provide your block and your ax
tomorrow four o'clock.

ABHORSON   Come on, bawd. I will instruct thee in my
trade. Follow!

POMPEY   I do desire to learn, sir; and I hope, if you have
occasion to use me for your own turn, you shall find   57
me yare. For truly, sir, for your kindness I owe you a   58
good turn.

PROVOST
Call hither Barnardine and Claudio.
               Exit [*Pompey, with Abhorson*].
Th'one has my pity; not a jot the other,
Being a murderer, though he were my brother.

Enter Claudio.

Look, here's the warrant, Claudio, for thy death.
'Tis now dead midnight, and by eight tomorrow
Thou must be made immortal. Where's Barnardine?   65

CLAUDIO
As fast locked up in sleep as guiltless labor   66
When it lies starkly in the traveler's bones.   67
He will not wake.

PROVOST   Who can do good on him?
Well, go, prepare yourself. [*Knocking within.*] But hark,
   what noise?
Heaven give your spirits comfort!   [*Exit Claudio.*]
                        [*calling*] By and by.—
I hope it is some pardon or reprieve
For the most gentle Claudio.

      Enter Duke [*disguised as before*].

                        Welcome, Father.

DUKE
The best and wholesom'st spirits of the night
Envelop you, good Provost! Who called here of late?

PROVOST   None since the curfew rung.

DUKE
Not Isabel?

PROVOST   No.

DUKE   They will, then, ere't be long.

PROVOST   What comfort is for Claudio?

DUKE
There's some in hope.

PROVOST   It is a bitter deputy.

DUKE
Not so, not so. His life is paralleled   79
Even with the stroke and line of his great justice.   80
He doth with holy abstinence subdue
That in himself which he spurs on his power   82
To qualify in others. Were he mealed with that   83
Which he corrects, then were he tyrannous;
But this being so, he's just. [*Knocking within.*] Now
   are they come.   [*The Provost goes to the door.*]
This is a gentle provost; seldom when   86
The steelèd jailer is the friend of men.   87
                        [*Knocking within.*]
How now? What noise? That spirit's possessed with
   haste
That wounds th'unsisting postern with these strokes.   89

PROVOST [*speaking at the door*]
There he must stay until the officer
Arise to let him in. He is called up.
                        [*He returns to the Duke.*]

DUKE
Have you no countermand for Claudio yet,
But he must die tomorrow?

PROVOST   None, sir, none.

DUKE
As near the dawning, Provost, as it is,

---

26 plead his estimation claim any respect on account of his reputation   **29 mystery** craft, occupation.   **32 favor** leave, permission
33 favor face   **33–4 hanging look** (1) downcast look (2) look of a
hangman   **36 Painting** (1) Painting of pictures (2) Applying cosmetics   **43–7 Every . . . thief** (Abhorson alludes to the custom of giving
to the hangman the garments of the executed criminal. Whether the
clothes are too little or too big, the hangman has to make do with
what he gets, just as the thief must make do with what he steals.)
44–5 big enough i.e., enough of a loss   **46 little enough** little enough
for his efforts.   **50–1 he doth . . . forgiveness** (The executioner per-
functorily asked forgiveness of those whose lives he was about to
take.)   **57 for . . . turn** (1) as a pimp to provide for your sexual needs
(2) as your hangman when it is your turn to be hanged or "turned
off" the ladder   **58 yare** ready, alacritous.   **65 made immortal** i.e.,
executed.

66 fast firmly, soundly.   **guiltless labor** (A personification of the
well-earned weariness that tires the innocent laborer.)   **67 starkly**
stiffly.   **traveler's bones** bones of one who travails or labors or journeys.   **79–80 His . . . justice** His life runs parallel and in exact conformity with the stroke of his pen as he carries out justice.   **82 spurs on**
encourages, urges   **83 qualify** mitigate.   **mealed** spotted, stained
86 seldom when i.e., it is seldom that   **87 steelèd** hardened
89 unsisting unassisting, unresting, or unresisting (?).   **postern**
small door

You shall hear more ere morning.

PROVOST   Happily 95
You something know, yet I believe there comes
No countermand. No such example have we; 97
Besides, upon the very siege of justice 98
Lord Angelo hath to the public ear
Professed the contrary.

Enter a Messenger.

                    This is His Lordship's man.

DUKE
And here comes Claudio's pardon.

MESSENGER [*giving a paper*] My lord hath sent you
this note, and by me this further charge, that you
swerve not from the smallest article of it, neither in
time, matter, or other circumstance. Good morrow;
for, as I take it, it is almost day.

PROVOST   I shall obey him.   [*Exit Messenger.*]

DUKE [*aside*]
This is his pardon, purchased by such sin
For which the pardoner himself is in. 109
Hence hath offense his quick celerity, 110
When it is borne in high authority. 111
When vice makes mercy, mercy's so extended 112
That for the fault's love is th'offender friended.— 113
Now, sir, what news?

PROVOST   I told you. Lord Angelo, belike thinking me 115
remiss in mine office, awakens me with this un- 116
wonted putting-on—methinks strangely, for he hath 117
not used it before.

DUKE   Pray you, let's hear.

PROVOST [*reads*] *the letter* "Whatsoever you may hear
to the contrary, let Claudio be executed by four of
the clock, and in the afternoon Barnardine. For my
better satisfaction, let me have Claudio's head sent 123
me by five. Let this be duly performed, with a
thought that more depends on it than we must yet
deliver. Thus fail not to do your office, as you will 126
answer it at your peril." What say you to this, sir?

DUKE   What is that Barnardine who is to be executed in
th'afternoon?

PROVOST   A Bohemian born, but here nursed up and 131
bred; one that is a prisoner nine years old. 132

DUKE   How came it that the absent Duke had not either
delivered him to his liberty or executed him? I have
heard it was ever his manner to do so.

PROVOST   His friends still wrought reprieves for him;
and indeed his fact, till now in the government of Lord 137
Angelo, came not to an undoubtful proof.

DUKE   It is now apparent?

PROVOST   Most manifest, and not denied by himself.

DUKE   Hath he borne himself penitently in prison? How
seems he to be touched? 142

PROVOST   A man that apprehends death no more dread- 143
fully but as a drunken sleep—careless, reckless, and 144
fearless of what's past, present, or to come; insensible 145
of mortality, and desperately mortal. 146

DUKE   He wants advice. 147

PROVOST   He will hear none. He hath evermore had the 148
liberty of the prison; give him leave to escape hence, 149
he would not. Drunk many times a day, if not many
days entirely drunk. We have very oft awaked him, as
if to carry him to execution, and showed him a
seeming warrant for it; it hath not moved him at all.

DUKE   More of him anon. There is written in your brow,
Provost, honesty and constancy; if I read it not truly,
my ancient skill beguiles me, but, in the boldness of 156
my cunning, I will lay myself in hazard. Claudio, 157
whom here you have warrant to execute, is no greater
forfeit to the law than Angelo who hath sentenced him.
To make you understand this in a manifested effect, I 160
crave but four days' respite, for the which you are to
do me both a present and a dangerous courtesy. 162

PROVOST   Pray, sir, in what?

DUKE   In the delaying death.

PROVOST   Alack, how may I do it, having the hour
limited, and an express command, under penalty, to 166
deliver his head in the view of Angelo? I may make
my case as Claudio's, to cross this in the smallest.

DUKE   By the vow of mine order I warrant you, if my
instructions may be your guide. Let this Barnardine
be this morning executed, and his head borne to
Angelo.

PROVOST   Angelo hath seen them both and will discover 173
the favor. 174

DUKE   Oh, death's a great disguiser, and you may add to
it. Shave the head, and tie the beard, and say it was 176
the desire of the penitent to be so bared before his
death. You know the course is common. If anything 178
fall to you upon this more than thanks and good 179
fortune, by the saint whom I profess, I will plead 180
against it with my life.

PROVOST   Pardon me, good Father, it is against my oath.

DUKE   Were you sworn to the Duke or to the deputy?

PROVOST   To him, and to his substitutes.

DUKE   You will think you have made no offense if the
Duke avouch the justice of your dealing? 186

PROVOST   But what likelihood is in that?

DUKE   Not a resemblance, but a certainty. Yet since I see
you fearful, that neither my coat, integrity, nor

---

95 **Happily** Haply, perhaps   97 **example** precedent   98 **siege** seat
109 **in** engaged.   110–11 **Hence . . . authority** Hence it is that criminal
behavior in high places has its (*his*) own quick way of covering its
tracks.   112–13 **When . . . friended** When criminality acts to save a
life, as in this case, mercy is so strangely broadened in definition that
the offender (here, Claudio) is spared for the fault committed by the
person in authority.   115 **belike** perchance   116–17 **unwonted
putting-on** unaccustomed urging   123 **better satisfaction** greater
assurance   126 **deliver** make known.   131 **here** i.e., in Vienna
132 **a prisoner . . . old** nine years a prisoner.   137 **fact** crime

142 **touched** affected, touched by remorse.   143–4 **no more dreadfully but** with no more dread than   145–6 **insensible . . . mortal**
incapable of comprehending the meaning of death, and incorrigible.
147 **wants advice** needs spiritual counsel.   148 **evermore** constantly
148–9 **the liberty . . . prison** freedom to go anywhere within the
prison   156–7 **in the . . . hazard** confident in my knowledge (of
human character), I will put myself at risk.   160 **in . . . effect** by
means of concrete proof   162 **present** immediate   166 **limited** fixed,
set   173–4 **discover the favor** recognize the face.   176 **tie** tie up, tidy
up   178 **course** practice   179 **fall to** befall   180 **the saint . . . profess**
i.e., St. Benedict, whose example I follow   186 **avouch** confirm

persuasion can with ease attempt you, I will go further 190
than I meant, to pluck all fears out of you. Look you,
sir, here is the hand and seal of the Duke. [*He shows a*
letter.] You know the character, I doubt not, and the 193
signet is not strange to you. 194

PROVOST   I know them both.

DUKE   The contents of this is the return of the Duke.
You shall anon overread it at your pleasure, where
you shall find within these two days he will be here.
This is a thing that Angelo knows not, for he this very
day receives letters of strange tenor, perchance of the
Duke's death, perchance entering into some monas- 201
tery, but by chance nothing of what is writ. Look, th'un- 202
folding star calls up the shepherd. Put not yourself 203
into amazement how these things should be; all difficulties are but easy when they are known. Call your
executioner, and off with Barnardine's head. I will
give him a present shrift and advise him for a better 207
place. Yet you are amazed, but this shall absolutely 208
resolve you. Come away; it is almost clear dawn. 209

Exit [*with Provost*].

❧

4.3

Enter Clown [*Pompey*].

POMPEY   I am as well acquainted here as I was in our 1
house of profession. One would think it were Mistress
Overdone's own house, for here be many of her old
customers. First, here's young Master Rash; he's in for 4
a commodity of brown paper and old ginger, nine- 5
score and seventeen pounds, of which he made five 6
marks, ready money. Marry, then ginger was not 7
much in request, for the old women were all dead. 8
Then is there here one Master Caper, at the suit of 9
Master Three-pile the mercer, for some four suits of 10
peach-colored satin, which now peaches him a beggar. 11
Then have we here young Dizzy, and young 12
Master Deep-vow, and Master Copper-spur, and 13

Master Starve-lackey the rapier and dagger man, and 14
young Drop-heir that killed lusty Pudding, and Mas- 15
ter Forthlight the tilter, and brave Master Shoe-tie the 16
great traveler, and wild Half-can that stabbed Pots, 17
and I think forty more, all great doers in our trade, and
are now "for the Lord's sake." 19

Enter Abhorson.

ABHORSON   Sirrah, bring Barnardine hither.

POMPEY [*calling*]   Master Barnardine! You must rise and 21
be hanged, Master Barnardine! 22

ABHORSON   What, ho, Barnardine!

BARNARDINE (*within*)   A pox o' your throats! Who
makes that noise there? What are you?

POMPEY   Your friends, sir, the hangman. You must be
so good, sir, to rise and be put to death.

BARNARDINE [*within*]   Away, you rogue, away! I am
sleepy.

ABHORSON   Tell him he must awake, and that quickly,
too.

POMPEY   Pray, Master Barnardine, awake till you are executed, and sleep afterwards.

ABHORSON   Go in to him, and fetch him out.

POMPEY   He is coming, sir, he is coming. I hear his
straw rustle.

Enter Barnardine.

ABHORSON   Is the ax upon the block, sirrah?

POMPEY   Very ready, sir.

BARNARDINE   How now, Abhorson? What's the news
with you?

ABHORSON   Truly, sir, I would desire you to clap into 41
your prayers; for, look you, the warrant's come.

BARNARDINE   You rogue, I have been drinking all night.
I am not fitted for 't.

POMPEY   Oh, the better, sir, for he that drinks all night
and is hanged betimes in the morning may sleep the 46
sounder all the next day.

Enter Duke [*disguised as before*].

ABHORSON   Look you, sir, here comes your ghostly 48
father. Do we jest now, think you?

DUKE   Sir, induced by my charity, and hearing how
hastily you are to depart, I am come to advise you,
comfort you, and pray with you.

BARNARDINE   Friar, not I. I have been drinking hard all
night, and I will have more time to prepare me, or

---

190 attempt win, tempt   **193 character** handwriting   **194 strange**
unknown   **201 entering** of his entering   **202 writ** i.e., written here.
202-3 unfolding star i.e., morning star, Venus, which bids the shepherd lead his sheep from the fold   **207 present shrift** immediate
absolution for sins (after confession)   **207–8 advise . . . place** counsel
him on the comforts of heaven.   **208 Yet** Still   **209 resolve you** dispel
your uncertainties.
4.3 Location: The prison.
1 well widely   **4 Rash** (All the names mentioned by Pompey apparently glance at contemporary social affectations and defects. *Rash*
means "reckless.")   **5–8 a commodity . . . dead** (To circumvent the
laws against excessive rates of interest, moneylenders often advanced
cheap commodities to gullible borrowers in lieu of cash. Master Rash,
having agreed to a valuation of 197 pounds for such merchandise,
has been able to resell it for only five marks, each mark worth about
two-thirds of a pound, and has been thrown into prison for debt. The
ginger has not fetched a good price, owing to lack of customers, since
the old women who are proverbially fond of ginger are no longer
alive.)   **9 Caper** (To *caper* was to dance or leap gracefully.)
10 Three-pile the thickest nap and most expensive grade of velvet.
mercer cloth merchant.   **suits** (With a play on *suit*, line 9.)
11 peaches him denounces him as. (With a play on *peach*.)   **12 Dizzy**
i.e., giddy, foolish   **13 Deep-vow** one who swears earnestly and
often.   **Copper-spur** (Copper was often used fraudulently to simu-
late gold.)

14 Starve-lackey (Spendthrift gallants often virtually starved their
pages.)   **15 Drop-heir** (Perhaps referring to those who disinherited
or preyed on unsuspecting heirs; or else *Drop-hair*, losing hair from
syphilis.)   **lusty** vigorous.   **Pudding** i.e., sausage   **16 Forthlight**
(Unexplained; perhaps an error for *Forthright*, referring to a style of
tilting.)   **tilter** jouster.   **brave** showy, splendidly dressed.   **Shoe-tie**
(Evidently a nickname for travelers and others who affected the foreign fashion of elaborate rosettes on the tie of the shoe.)   **17 Half-can**
i.e., a small drinking tankard.   **Pots** i.e., ale pots   **19 "for . . . sake"**
(The cry of prisoners from jail grates to passers-by to give them food
or alms.)   **22 be hanged** (With a play on the imprecation; compare
"go to the devil.")   **41 clap into** quickly begin   **46 betimes** early
48 ghostly spiritual

they shall beat out my brains with billets. I will not 55
consent to die this day, that's certain.

DUKE
Oh, sir, you must, and therefore I beseech you
Look forward on the journey you shall go.

BARNARDINE   I swear I will not die today for any man's
persuasion.

DUKE   But hear you—

BARNARDINE   Not a word. If you have anything to say
to me, come to my ward, for thence will not I today. 63
Exit.

Enter Provost.

DUKE
Unfit to live or die. Oh, gravel heart!   64
After him, fellows. Bring him to the block.
[*Exeunt Abhorson and Pompey.*]

PROVOST
Now, sir, how do you find the prisoner?

DUKE
A creature unprepared, unmeet for death;   67
And to transport him in the mind he is   68
Were damnable.

PROVOST   Here in the prison, Father,
There died this morning of a cruel fever
One Ragozine, a most notorious pirate,
A man of Claudio's years, his beard and head
Just of his color. What if we do omit   73
This reprobate till he were well inclined,
And satisfy the deputy with the visage
Of Ragozine, more like to Claudio?

DUKE
Oh, 'tis an accident that heaven provides!
Dispatch it presently; the hour draws on   78
Prefixed by Angelo. See this be done,   79
And sent according to command, whiles I
Persuade this rude wretch willingly to die.   81

PROVOST
This shall be done, good Father, presently.
But Barnardine must die this afternoon.
And how shall we continue Claudio,   84
To save me from the danger that might come
If he were known alive?

DUKE   Let this be done:
Put them in secret holds, both Barnardine and
Claudio.
Ere twice the sun hath made his journal greeting   87
To yond generation, you shall find   88
Your safety manifested.   89

PROVOST   I am your free dependent.   91

DUKE
Quick, dispatch, and send the head to Angelo.
Exit [*Provost*].
Now will I write letters to Varrius—   93
The Provost, he shall bear them—whose contents
Shall witness to him I am near at home,
And that, by great injunctions, I am bound   96
To enter publicly. Him I'll desire
To meet me at the consecrated fount   98
A league below the city; and from thence,   99
By cold gradation and well-balanced form,   100
We shall proceed with Angelo.

Enter Provost [*with Ragozine's head*].

PROVOST
Here is the head. I'll carry it myself.

DUKE
Convenient is it. Make a swift return,   103
For I would commune with you of such things   104
That want no ear but yours.

PROVOST   I'll make all speed.   *Exit.* 105

ISABELLA (*within*)   Peace, ho, be here!

DUKE
The tongue of Isabel. She's come to know
If yet her brother's pardon be come hither.
But I will keep her ignorant of her good,
To make her heavenly comforts of despair   110
When it is least expected.

Enter Isabella.

ISABELLA   Ho, by your leave!

DUKE
Good morning to you, fair and gracious daughter.

ISABELLA
The better, given me by so holy a man.
Hath yet the deputy sent my brother's pardon?

DUKE
He hath released him, Isabel, from the world.
His head is off and sent to Angelo.

ISABELLA
Nay, but it is not so!

DUKE   It is no other.
Show your wisdom, daughter, in your close patience. 118

ISABELLA
Oh, I will to him and pluck out his eyes!

DUKE
You shall not be admitted to his sight.

ISABELLA
Unhappy Claudio! Wretched Isabel!
Injurious world! Most damnèd Angelo!

---

55 billets cudgels, blocks of wood.   **63 ward** cell   **64 gravel** stony
67 unmeet unready, unfit   **68 transport him** i.e., send him to his
doom.   **he is** he is in   **73 omit** ignore, overlook   **78 presently**
immediately. (As also in line 82.)   **79 Prefixed** appointed beforehand,
stipulated   **81 rude** uncivilized   **84 continue** preserve
87 holds cells, dungeons   **88 journal** daily   **89 yond** i.e., beyond
these walls, outside the perpetually dark prison (?). Sometimes it is
emended to *th' under*, the people of the Antipodes, on the opposite
side of the earth, or, people under the sun, the human race.   **91 free
dependent** willing servant.

93 to Varrius (The Folio reads "to Angelo," but see line 99 below and
4.5.12–14; evidently, the Duke's plan is to meet Varrius "a league
below the city" and then proceed to the rendezvous with Angelo.)
96 by great injunctions by powerful precedent or for compelling reasons   **98 fount** spring   **99 league** (A measure of varying length but
usually about three miles.)   **100 cold . . . form** i.e., moving deliberately and with proper observance of all formalities   **103 Convenient**
Timely, fitting   **104 commune** converse   **105 want** require   **110 of**
from, transformed out of   **118 close patience** silent enduring.

DUKE
>This nor hurts him nor profits you a jot.   123
>Forbear it therefore; give your cause to heaven.
>Mark what I say, which you shall find
>By every syllable a faithful verity.   126
>The Duke comes home tomorrow. Nay, dry your eyes;
>One of our convent, and his confessor,
>Gives me this instance. Already he hath carried   129
>Notice to Escalus and Angelo,
>Who do prepare to meet him at the gates,
>There to give up their pow'r. If you can, pace your
>   wisdom   132
>In that good path that I would wish it go,
>And you shall have your bosom on this wretch,   134
>Grace of the Duke, revenges to your heart,   135
>And general honor.

ISABELLA   I am directed by you.

DUKE
>This letter, then, to Friar Peter give.
>   [*He gives her a letter.*]
>'Tis that he sent me of the Duke's return.   138
>Say, by this token, I desire his company
>At Mariana's house tonight. Her cause and yours
>I'll perfect him withal, and he shall bring you   141
>Before the Duke, and to the head of Angelo   142
>Accuse him home and home. For my poor self,   143
>I am combinèd by a sacred vow,   144
>And shall be absent. Wend you with this letter.
>Command these fretting waters from your eyes   146
>With a light heart. Trust not my holy order
>If I pervert your course. Who's here?

Enter Lucio.

LUCIO   Good even. Friar, where's the Provost?
DUKE   Not within, sir.
LUCIO   Oh, pretty Isabella, I am pale at mine heart to see   151
thine eyes so red. Thou must be patient. I am fain to   152
dine and sup with water and bran; I dare not for my   153
head fill my belly; one fruitful meal would set me   154
to't. But they say the Duke will be here tomorrow.   155
By my troth, Isabel, I loved thy brother. If the old fantastical Duke of dark corners had been at home, he
had lived.   [*Exit Isabella.*]
DUKE   Sir, the Duke is marvelous little beholding to   159
your reports; but the best is, he lives not in them.   160
LUCIO   Friar, thou knowest not the Duke so well as I
do. He's a better woodman than thou tak'st him for.   162

DUKE   Well, you'll answer this one day. Fare ye well.
>   [*He starts to go.*]
LUCIO   Nay, tarry, I'll go along with thee. I can tell thee
pretty tales of the Duke.
DUKE   You have told me too many of him already, sir, if
they be true; if not true, none were enough.
LUCIO   I was once before him for getting a wench with
child.
DUKE   Did you such a thing?
LUCIO   Yes, marry, did I, but I was fain to forswear it.
They would else have married me to the rotten medlar.   172
DUKE   Sir, your company is fairer than honest. Rest you
well.
LUCIO   By my troth, I'll go with thee to the lane's end.
If bawdy talk offend you, we'll have very little of it.
Nay, Friar, I am a kind of burr; I shall stick.   *Exeunt.*

❖

4.4

Enter Angelo and Escalus, [reading letters].

ESCALUS   Every letter he hath writ hath disvouched   1
other.
ANGELO   In most uneven and distracted manner. His
actions show much like to madness. Pray heaven his
wisdom be not tainted! And why meet him at the   5
gates and redeliver our authorities there?
ESCALUS   I guess not.   7
ANGELO   And why should we proclaim it in an hour be- 8
fore his entering, that if any crave redress of injustice,
they should exhibit their petitions in the street?   10
ESCALUS   He shows his reason for that: to have a
dispatch of complaints, and to deliver us from devices 12
hereafter, which shall then have no power to stand
against us.
ANGELO   Well, I beseech you, let it be proclaimed.
Betimes i'th' morn I'll call you at your house. Give   16
notice to such men of sort and suit as are to meet him. 17
ESCALUS   I shall, sir. Fare you well.
ANGELO   Good night.   *Exit [Escalus].*
>This deed unshapes me quite, makes me unpregnant 20
>And dull to all proceedings. A deflowered maid,
>And by an eminent body that enforced   22
>The law against it! But that her tender shame   23
>Will not proclaim against her maiden loss,
>How might she tongue me! Yet reason dares her no, 25
>For my authority bears of a credent bulk   26
>That no particular scandal once can touch
>But it confounds the breather. He should have lived, 28

---

123 **nor hurts** neither hurts   126 **By** with respect to   129 **instance** proof.   132 **pace** teach to move in response to your will, as with a horse   134 **bosom** heart's desire   135 **Grace of** manifestation of favor from.   **to your heart** to your heart's content   138 **that** that which.   **of** concerning   141 **perfect** acquaint completely.   **withal** with   142 **head** i.e., face   143 **home and home** thoroughly.   144 **combinèd** bound   146 **fretting** corroding   151 **pale . . . heart** i.e., pale from sighing (since sighs cost the heart loss of blood)   152 **fain** compelled. (As also in line 171.)   153–4 **for my head** i.e., on my life   154 **fruitful** abundant   154–5 **set me to't** i.e., awaken my lust and thus place me in danger of Angelo's edict.   159 **marvelous** marvelously.   **beholding** beholden   160 **he . . . them** i.e., he is not accurately described by them.   162 **woodman** i.e., hunter (of women)

172 **medlar** a fruit that was eaten after it had begun to rot; here, signifying a prostitute.
4.4. Location: In Vienna.
1 **disvouched** contradicted   5 **tainted** diseased.   7 **guess not** cannot guess.   8 **in an hour** i.e., a full hour   10 **exhibit** present   12 **dispatch** prompt settlement.   **devices** contrived complaints   16 **Betimes** Early   17 **men . . . suit** men of rank with a retinue   20 **unpregnant** unapt   22 **body** person   23 **But that** Were it not that   25 **tongue** i.e., reproach, accuse.   **dares her no** i.e., frightens her to say nothing   26 **bears . . . bulk** bears such a huge credibility   28 **But . . . breather** without its confuting the person who speaks.

Save that his riotous youth, with dangerous sense,   29
Might in the times to come have ta'en revenge
By so receiving a dishonored life   31
With ransom of such shame. Would yet he had lived!
Alack, when once our grace we have forgot,
Nothing goes right; we would, and we would not.

                                        Exit.

❖

4.5

Enter Duke [in his own habit] and Friar Peter.

DUKE
These letters at fit time deliver me.   [*Giving letters.*]   1
The Provost knows our purpose and our plot.
The matter being afoot, keep your instruction,   3
And hold you ever to our special drift,   4
Though sometimes you do blench from this to that   5
As cause doth minister. Go call at Flavius' house,   6
And tell him where I stay. Give the like notice
To Valencius, Rowland, and to Crassus,
And bid them bring the trumpets to the gate;   9
But send me Flavius first.
FRIAR PETER   It shall be speeded well.   [*Exit.*]   11

        Enter Varrius.

DUKE
I thank thee, Varrius. Thou hast made good haste.
Come, we will walk. There's other of our friends
Will greet us here anon. My gentle Varrius!   *Exeunt.*

❖

4.6

Enter Isabella and Mariana.

ISABELLA
To speak so indirectly I am loath.
I would say the truth, but to accuse him so,
That is your part. Yet I am advised to do it,
He says, to veil full purpose.
MARIANA   Be ruled by him.
ISABELLA
Besides, he tells me that if peradventure   5
He speak against me on the adverse side,
I should not think it strange, for 'tis a physic   7
That's bitter to sweet end.

        Enter [Friar] Peter.

MARIANA
I would Friar Peter—
ISABELLA   Oh, peace, the Friar is come.

FRIAR PETER
Come, I have found you out a stand most fit,   10
Where you may have such vantage on the Duke
He shall not pass you. Twice have the trumpets
    sounded.
The generous and gravest citizens   13
Have hent the gates, and very near upon   14
The Duke is entering. Therefore hence, away!

                                    Exeunt.

❖

5.1

*Enter Duke, Varrius, lords, Angelo, Escalus,
Lucio, [Provost, officers, and] citizens at several
doors.*

DUKE
My very worthy cousin, fairly met!   1
Our old and faithful friend, we are glad to see you.   2
ANGELO, ESCALUS
Happy return be to Your Royal Grace!
DUKE
Many and hearty thankings to you both.
We have made inquiry of you, and we hear
Such goodness of your justice that our soul
Cannot but yield you forth to public thanks,   7
Forerunning more requital.   8
ANGELO   You make my bonds still greater.   9
DUKE
Oh, your desert speaks loud, and I should wrong it
To lock it in the wards of covert bosom,   11
When it deserves with characters of brass   12
A forted residence 'gainst the tooth of time   13
And razure of oblivion. Give me your hand,   14
And let the subject see, to make them know   15
That outward courtesies would fain proclaim   16
Favors that keep within. Come, Escalus,   17
You must walk by us on our other hand,
And good supporters are you.

    Enter [Friar] Peter and Isabella.

FRIAR PETER [*to Isabella*]
Now is your time. Speak loud, and kneel before him.
ISABELLA [*kneeling*]
Justice, O royal Duke! Vail your regard   21
Upon a wronged—I would fain have said a maid.
O worthy prince, dishonor not your eye
By throwing it on any other object
Till you have heard me in my true complaint
And given me justice, justice, justice, justice!

29 **sense** passion, intention   31 **By** for, because of
4.5. Location: Outside the city.
1 **me** for me   3 **keep** keep to   4 **drift** plot   5 **blench . . . that** swerve
from one expedient to another   6 **minister** prompt, provide occasion.
9 **trumpets** trumpeters   11 **speeded** accomplished, expedited
4.6. Location: Near the city gate.
5 **peradventure** perhaps   7 **physic** remedy

10 **stand** place to stand   13 **generous** highborn   14 **hent** reached,
occupied.   **very near upon** almost immediately now
5.1 Location: The city gate.
0.2 *several* separate   1 **cousin** fellow nobleman. (Addressed to
Angelo.)   2 **friend** i.e., Escalus   7 **yield . . . to** to call you forth to give
you   8 **more requital** further reward.   9 **bonds** obligations   11 **To
lock . . . bosom** i.e., to keep it locked up in my heart   12 **characters**
writing, letters   13 **forted** fortified   14 **razure** effacement   15 **the
subject** those who are subjects   16–17 **That . . . within** that public
ceremonies serve as outward manifestations of the approval my heart
feels for you.   21 **Vail your regard** Look down

DUKE
Relate your wrongs. In what? By whom? Be brief.
Here is Lord Angelo shall give you justice.   28
Reveal yourself to him.

ISABELLA   O worthy Duke,
You bid me seek redemption of the devil.
Hear me yourself; for that which I must speak
Must either punish me, not being believed,   32
Or wring redress from you.
Hear me, oh, hear me, hear!

ANGELO
My lord, her wits, I fear me, are not firm.
She hath been a suitor to me for her brother
Cut off by course of justice.

ISABELLA [standing]   By course of justice!

ANGELO
And she will speak most bitterly and strange.   38

ISABELLA
Most strange, but yet most truly, will I speak.
That Angelo's forsworn, is it not strange?
That Angelo's a murderer, is 't not strange?
That Angelo is an adulterous thief,
An hypocrite, a virgin-violator,
Is it not strange, and strange?

DUKE   Nay, it is ten times strange.

ISABELLA
It is not truer he is Angelo
Than this is all as true as it is strange.   47
Nay, it is ten times true, for truth is truth
To th'end of reck'ning.

DUKE   Away with her! Poor soul,   49
She speaks this in th'infirmity of sense.   50

ISABELLA
O prince, I conjure thee, as thou believ'st
There is another comfort than this world,
That thou neglect me not with that opinion   53
That I am touched with madness. Make not
     impossible   54
That which but seems unlike. 'Tis not impossible   55
But one, the wicked'st caitiff on the ground,   56
May seem as shy, as grave, as just, as absolute   57
As Angelo; even so may Angelo,
In all his dressings, characts, titles, forms,   59
Be an archvillain. Believe it, royal prince,
If he be less, he's nothing; but he's more,   61
Had I more name for badness.

DUKE   By mine honesty,
If she be mad—as I believe no other—
Her madness hath the oddest frame of sense,   64
Such a dependency of thing on thing,   65

As e'er I heard in madness.

ISABELLA   O gracious Duke,
Harp not on that, nor do not banish reason   67
For inequality, but let your reason serve   68
To make the truth appear where it seems hid,
And hide the false seems true.   70

DUKE   Many that are not mad
Have, sure, more lack of reason. What would
     you say?

ISABELLA
I am the sister of one Claudio,
Condemned upon the act of fornication
To lose his head, condemned by Angelo.
I, in probation of a sisterhood,   76
Was sent to by my brother; one Lucio
As then the messenger—

LUCIO   That's I, an't like Your Grace.   78
I came to her from Claudio and desired her
To try her gracious fortune with Lord Angelo
For her poor brother's pardon.

ISABELLA   That's he indeed.

DUKE [to Lucio]
You were not bid to speak.

LUCIO   No, my good lord,
Nor wished to hold my peace.

DUKE   I wish you now, then.
Pray you, take note of it. And when you have
A business for yourself, pray heaven you then
Be perfect.   86   87

LUCIO   I warrant Your Honor.

DUKE
The warrant's for yourself. Take heed to 't.

ISABELLA
This gentleman told somewhat of my tale—

LUCIO   Right.

DUKE
It may be right, but you are i'the wrong
To speak before your time.—Proceed.

ISABELLA   I went
To this pernicious caitiff deputy—

DUKE
That's somewhat madly spoken.

ISABELLA   Pardon it;
The phrase is to the matter.   95

DUKE   Mended again. The matter; proceed.   96

ISABELLA
In brief, to set the needless process by,   97
How I persuaded, how I prayed and kneeled,
How he refelled me, and how I replied—   99
For this was of much length—the vile conclusion

28 shall who shall   32 not being if I am not   38 strange strangely.
47 Than than that   49 To . . . reck'ning to the end of time and Day of
Judgment, always.   50 in . . . sense out of a sick mind, out of the
weakness of passion.   53 with that opinion out of a supposition
54 Make not Do not consider as   55 unlike unlikely.   56 But but
that.   ground earth   57 shy quietly dignified.   absolute flawless
59 dressings, characts ceremonial robes, insignia of office   61 If . . .
nothing i.e., even if he were less than an archvillain, he would be
worthless   64 frame of sense form of reason   65 dependency . . .
on thing coherence

67–8 do . . . inequality i.e., do not assume lack of reason on my part
because of the inconsistency between my story and Angelo's refutation, or because of the inequality in our reputations   70 hide put out
of sight, remove from consideration.   seems that seems   76 in probation i.e., a novice   78 As then being at that time.   an't like if it
please   86 perfect prepared.   87 warrant assure. (The Duke, however, quibbles in line 88 on the meaning "judicial writ.")   95 to the
matter to the purpose.   96 Mended . . . proceed That sets things
right. Proceed to the main point.   97 to set . . . by not to dwell on
unnecessary details in the story   99 refelled refuted, repelled

I now begin with grief and shame to utter.
He would not, but by gift of my chaste body
To his concupiscible intemperate lust,   103
Release my brother; and after much debatement   104
My sisterly remorse confutes mine honor,   105
And I did yield to him. But the next morn betimes, 106
His purpose surfeiting, he sends a warrant   107
For my poor brother's head.
DUKE   This is most likely!
ISABELLA
Oh, that it were as like as it is true!   109
DUKE
By heaven, fond wretch, thou know'st not what thou
    speak'st,   110
Or else thou art suborned against his honor   111
In hateful practice. First, his integrity   112
Stands without blemish. Next, it imports no reason 113
That with such vehemency he should pursue
Faults proper to himself. If he had so offended, 115
He would have weighed thy brother by himself   116
And not have cut him off. Someone hath set you on.
Confess the truth, and say by whose advice
Thou cam'st here to complain.
ISABELLA   And is this all?
Then, O you blessèd ministers above,
Keep me in patience, and with ripened time
Unfold the evil which is here wrapped up   122
In countenance! Heaven shield Your Grace from woe, 123
As I thus wronged hence unbelievèd go!
                            [She starts to leave.]
DUKE
I know you'd fain be gone.—An officer!
To prison with her. Shall we thus permit
A blasting and a scandalous breath to fall   127
On him so near us? This needs must be a practice.
Who knew of your intent and coming hither?
ISABELLA
One that I would were here, Friar Lodowick.
DUKE
A ghostly father, belike. Who knows that Lodowick? 131
LUCIO
My lord, I know him; 'tis a meddling friar.
I do not like the man. Had he been lay, my lord, 133
For certain words he spake against Your Grace
In your retirement, I had swinged him soundly. 135
DUKE
Words against me? This' a good friar, belike!   136
And to set on this wretched woman here

Against our substitute! Let this friar be found.
                    [Exit one or more attendants.]
LUCIO
But yesternight, my lord, she and that friar,
I saw them at the prison. A saucy friar,
A very scurvy fellow.
FRIAR PETER   Blessed be Your Royal Grace!
I have stood by, my lord, and I have heard
Your royal ear abused. First, hath this woman
Most wrongfully accused your substitute,
Who is as free from touch or soil with her
As she from one ungot.   147
DUKE   We did believe no less.
Know you that Friar Lodowick that she speaks of?
FRIAR PETER
I know him for a man divine and holy,
Not scurvy, nor a temporary meddler,   151
As he's reported by this gentleman;
And, on my trust, a man that never yet
Did, as he vouches, misreport Your Grace.
LUCIO
My lord, most villainously, believe it.
FRIAR PETER
Well, he in time may come to clear himself;
But at this instant he is sick, my lord,
Of a strange fever. Upon his mere request,   158
Being come to knowledge that there was complaint 159
Intended 'gainst Lord Angelo, came I hither,
To speak, as from his mouth, what he doth know
Is true and false, and what he with his oath
And all probation will make up full clear,   163
Whensoever he's convented. First, for this woman, 164
To justify this worthy nobleman,
So vulgarly and personally accused,   166
Her shall you hear disprovèd to her eyes,   167
Till she herself confess it.   [Exit Isabella, guarded.]
DUKE   Good Friar, let's hear it.
                [Friar Peter goes to bring in Mariana.]
Do you not smile at this, Lord Angelo?
Oh, heaven, the vanity of wretched fools!   170
Give us some seats.   [Seats are provided.]
                    Come, cousin Angelo,
In this I'll be impartial. Be you judge
Of your own cause.   [The Duke and Angelo sit.]

    Enter Mariana, [veiled, with Friar Peter].

                    Is this the witness, Friar?
First, let her show her face, and after speak.
MARIANA
Pardon, my lord, I will not show my face
Until my husband bid me.

---

103 concupiscible lustful   **104 debatement** argument, debate
105 remorse pity.   **confutes** confounds, silences   **106 betimes** early
107 surfeiting being satiated   **109 like** likely   **110 fond** foolish
111 suborned induced to give false testimony   **112 practice** machination, conspiracy.   **113 imports no reason** i.e., makes no sense
115 proper to himself of which he himself is guilty.   **116 weighed**
judged   **122 Unfold** disclose   **122–3 wrapped . . . countenance** concealed by the privilege of authority.   **127 blasting** blighting   **131 A
ghostly . . . belike** A cleric, apparently.   **133 lay** not a cleric   **135 In
your retirement** during your absence.   **had swinged** would have
beaten   **136 This'** This is

147 ungot unbegotten.   **151 temporary meddler** meddler in temporal
affairs.   **158 Upon . . . request** Solely at his request   **159 Being . . .
knowledge** he having learned   **163 probation** proof   **164 convented**
summoned.   **166 vulgarly** publicly   **167 to her eyes** i.e., to her face
168 s.d. Exit Isbella, guarded (Isabella seemingly must leave the stage
here or soon afterwards. She is described as "gone" at line 250, and is
summoned at line 278. The phrase "to her eyes" in line 167 may mean
"incontrovertibly.")   **170 vanity** folly

DUKE   What, are you married?

MARIANA   No, my lord.

DUKE   Are you a maid?

MARIANA   No, my lord.

DUKE   A widow, then?

MARIANA   Neither, my lord.

DUKE   Why, you are nothing then, neither maid,
widow, nor wife?

LUCIO   My lord, she may be a punk, for many of them   185
are neither maid, widow, nor wife.

DUKE
Silence that fellow. I would he had some cause
To prattle for himself.   188

LUCIO   Well, my lord.

MARIANA
My lord, I do confess I ne'er was married,
And I confess besides I am no maid.
I have known my husband, yet my husband   192
Knows not that ever he knew me.

LUCIO   He was drunk then, my lord; it can be no better.

DUKE   For the benefit of silence, would thou wert so too!

LUCIO   Well, my lord.

DUKE
This is no witness for Lord Angelo.

MARIANA   Now I come to 't, my lord.
She that accuses him of fornication
In selfsame manner doth accuse my husband,
And charges him, my lord, with such a time   201
When, I'll depose, I had him in mine arms   202
With all th'effect of love.   203

ANGELO   Charges she more than me?   204

MARIANA   Not that I know.

DUKE   No? You say your husband?

MARIANA
Why, just, my lord, and that is Angelo,   207
Who thinks he knows that he ne'er knew my body,
But knows he thinks that he knows Isabel's.

ANGELO
This is a strange abuse. Let's see thy face.   210

MARIANA
My husband bids me. Now I will unmask.
                              [She unveils.]
This is that face, thou cruel Angelo,
Which once thou swor'st was worth the looking on;
This is the hand which, with a vowed contract,
Was fast belocked in thine; this is the body   215
That took away the match from Isabel,   216
And did supply thee at thy garden house
In her imagined person.

DUKE [to Angelo]   Know you this woman?

LUCIO   Carnally, she says.

DUKE   Sirrah, no more!

LUCIO   Enough, my lord.

ANGELO
My lord, I must confess I know this woman,
And five years since there was some speech of
marriage
Betwixt myself and her, which was broke off,
Partly for that her promisèd proportions   226
Came short of composition, but in chief   227
For that her reputation was disvalued   228
In levity. Since which time of five years   229
I never spake with her, saw her, nor heard from her,
Upon my faith and honor.

MARIANA [kneeling]   Noble prince,
As there comes light from heaven and words from
breath,
As there is sense in truth and truth in virtue,
I am affianced this man's wife as strongly
As words could make up vows; and, my good lord,
But Tuesday night last gone in's garden house
He knew me as a wife. As this is true,
Let me in safety raise me from my knees,
Or else forever be confixèd here,   239
A marble monument!

ANGELO   I did but smile till now.
Now, good my lord, give me the scope of justice.   242
My patience here is touched. I do perceive   243
These poor informal women are no more   244
But instruments of some more mightier member   245
That sets them on. Let me have way, my lord,
To find this practice out.

DUKE   Ay, with my heart,
And punish them to your height of pleasure.—
Thou foolish friar, and thou pernicious woman,
Compact with her that's gone, think'st thou thy oaths,   250
Though they would swear down each particular saint,   251
Were testimonies against his worth and credit
That's sealed in approbation?—You, Lord Escalus,   253
Sit with my cousin; lend him your kind pains
To find out this abuse, whence 'tis derived.
There is another friar that set them on;
Let him be sent for.
                [The Duke rises; Escalus takes his chair.]

FRIAR PETER
Would he were here, my lord! For he indeed
Hath set the women on to this complaint.
Your Provost knows the place where he abides,
And he may fetch him.

DUKE   Go do it instantly.
                              [Exit Provost.]
And you, my noble and well-warranted cousin,
Whom it concerns to hear this matter forth,   263
Do with your injuries as seems you best,   264

---

185 punk harlot   **188 To . . . himself** to speak in his own defense. (The Duke hints that there might well be charges pending against Lucio.)   **192 known** had sexual intercourse with   **201 with . . . time** with doing the deed at just the same time   **202 depose** testify under oath   **203 With . . . love** i.e., with sexual fulfillment.   **204 Charges . . . me?** Does she (Isabella) bring charges against persons besides myself?   **207 just** just so   **210 abuse** deception.   **215 fast belocked** firmly locked   **216 match** assignation

226 for that because.   **proportions** dowry   **227 composition** agreement   **228–9 disvalued In levity** discredited for lightness.   **239 confixèd** firmly fixed   **242 scope** full authority   **243 touched** injured, affected.   **244 informal** rash, distracted   **245 But** than   **250 Compact . . . gone** i.e., in collusion with Isabella   **251 swear . . . saint** call down to witness every single saint   **253 sealed in approbation** ratified by proof, like weights and measures being given a stamp or seal to attest to their genuineness.   **263 forth** through   **264 Do . . . best** respond to the wrongs done you as seems best to you

In any chastisement. I for a while
Will leave you; but stir not you till you have
Well determined upon these slanderers.   267

ESCALUS   My lord, we'll do it throughly.   *Exit [Duke].* 268
Signor Lucio, did not you say you knew that Friar
Lodowick to be a dishonest person?

LUCIO   *Cucullus non facit monachum*; honest in nothing 271
but in his clothes, and one that hath spoke most
villainous speeches of the Duke.

ESCALUS   We shall entreat you to abide here till he come,
and enforce them against him. We shall find this friar 275
a notable fellow.   276

LUCIO   As any in Vienna, on my word.

ESCALUS   Call that same Isabel here once again. I would
speak with her.   *[Exit an Attendant.]*
Pray you, my lord, give me leave to question. You shall
see how I'll handle her.

LUCIO   Not better than he, by her own report.   282

ESCALUS   Say you?

LUCIO   Marry, sir, I think, if you handled her privately, 284
she would sooner confess; perchance publicly she'll
be ashamed.

ESCALUS   I will go darkly to work with her.   287

LUCIO   That's the way, for women are light at midnight. 288

*Enter Duke [disguised as a friar], Provost, Isabella,
[and officers].*

ESCALUS   Come on, mistress. Here's a gentlewoman
denies all that you have said.

LUCIO   My lord, here comes the rascal I spoke of, here
with the Provost.

ESCALUS   In very good time. Speak not you to him till
we call upon you.

LUCIO   Mum.

ESCALUS   Come, sir, did you set these women on to
slander Lord Angelo? They have confessed you did.

DUKE   'Tis false.

ESCALUS   How? Know you where you are?

DUKE
Respect to your great place! And let the devil   300
Be sometime honored for his burning throne!   301
Where is the Duke? 'Tis he should hear me speak.

ESCALUS
The Duke's in us, and we will hear you speak.
Look you speak justly.

DUKE
Boldly, at least. But oh, poor souls,
Come you to seek the lamb here of the fox?
Good night to your redress! Is the Duke gone?
Then is your cause gone too. The Duke's unjust,
Thus to retort your manifest appeal,   309

And put your trial in the villain's mouth
Which here you come to accuse.

LUCIO
This is the rascal. This is he I spoke of.

ESCALUS
Why, thou unreverend and unhallowed friar,
Is't not enough thou hast suborned these women
To accuse this worthy man, but, in foul mouth
And in the witness of his proper ear,   316
To call him villain? And then to glance from him
To th'Duke himself, to tax him with injustice?—   318
Take him hence. To th' rack with him!—We'll touse
you   319
Joint by joint, but we will know his purpose.   320
What, "unjust"?

DUKE   Be not so hot. The Duke
Dare no more stretch this finger of mine than he
Dare rack his own. His subject am I not,
Nor here provincial. My business in this state   324
Made me a looker-on here in Vienna,
Where I have seen corruption boil and bubble
Till it o'errun the stew; laws for all faults,   327
But faults so countenanced that the strong statutes   328
Stand like the forfeits in a barber's shop,   329
As much in mock as mark.

ESCALUS   Slander to th' state!   330
Away with him to prison.

ANGELO
What can you vouch against him, Signor Lucio?
Is this the man that you did tell us of?

LUCIO   'Tis he, my lord.—Come hither, Goodman 334
Baldpate. Do you know me?   335

DUKE   I remember you, sir, by the sound of your voice.
I met you at the prison, in the absence of the Duke.

LUCIO   Oh, did you so? And do you remember what you
said of the Duke?

DUKE   Most notedly, sir.   340

LUCIO   Do you so, sir? And was the Duke a fleshmonger, a fool, and a coward, as you then reported him to be?

DUKE   You must, sir, change persons with me ere you 344
make that my report. You indeed spoke so of him, and
much more, much worse.

LUCIO   Oh, thou damnable fellow! Did not I pluck thee by
the nose for thy speeches?

DUKE   I protest I love the Duke as I love myself.

ANGELO   Hark how the villain would close now, after 350
his treasonable abuses!

---

267 **determined** reached judgment   268 **throughly** thoroughly.
271 *Cucullus . . . monachum* A cowl doesn't make a monk
275 **enforce them** forcefully urge your charges   276 **notable** notorious   282 **Not . . . report** (Lucio salaciously turns Escalus's *handle her*
into a sexual slur: You, Escalus, will do no better at "handling"
Isabella than did Angelo, according to Isabella's testimony.)   284 **if
. . . privately** (Lucio continues his sexual joke about "handling.")
287 **darkly** subtly, slyly   288 **light** wanton, unchaste   300–1 **let . . .
throne** i.e., may all authority be respected, even the devil's. (Said
sardonically.)   309 **retort** turn back.   **manifest** obviously just

316 **in . . . ear** within his own hearing   318 **tax him with** accuse him
of   319 **touse** tear   320 **but we will** i.e., if necessary to; until we
324 **provincial** subject to the religious authority of this province or
state.   327 **stew** (1) stewpot (2) brothel   328 **countenanced** tolerated
and protected by corrupt authority   329 **forfeits** cautionary displays,
or lists of rules and fines for handling razors, etc., which barbers
(who also acted as dentists and surgeons) hung in their shops
330 **As . . . mark** as often flouted as observed.   334–5 **Goodman
Baldpate** (Lucio refers to the tonsure that he assumes the Duke must
have under his hood, though the Duke is clearly hooded at this
point.)   340 **notedly** particularly   344 **change** exchange   350 **close**
come to terms, compromise

ESCALUS   Such a fellow is not to be talked withal. Away
with him to prison! Where is the Provost? Away with
him to prison! Lay bolts enough upon him. Let him   354
speak no more. Away with those giglots too, and with   355
the other confederate companion!   356

[*The Provost lays hands on the Duke.*]

DUKE [*to Provost*]   Stay, sir, stay awhile.

ANGELO   What, resists he? Help him, Lucio.

LUCIO   Come, sir, come, sir, come, sir; foh, sir! Why,
you bald-pated, lying rascal, you must be hooded,
must you? Show your knave's visage, with a pox to
you! Show your sheep-biting face, and be hanged an   362
hour! Will't not off?   363

[*He pulls off the friar's hood, and discovers
the Duke. Angelo and Escalus rise.*]

DUKE
Thou art the first knave that e'er mad'st a duke.
First, Provost, let me bail these gentle three.   365
[*To Lucio*] Sneak not away, sir, for the Friar and you
Must have a word anon.—Lay hold on him.

LUCIO   This may prove worse than hanging.

DUKE [*to Escalus*]
What you have spoke I pardon. Sit you down.
We'll borrow place of him. [*To Angelo*] Sir, by your
leave.   [*He takes Angelo's seat. Escalus also sits.*]
Hast thou or word, or wit, or impudence,   371
That yet can do thee office? If thou hast,   372
Rely upon it till my tale be heard,
And hold no longer out.

ANGELO [*kneeling*]   O my dread lord,   374
I should be guiltier than my guiltiness
To think I can be undiscernible,
When I perceive Your Grace, like power divine,
Hath looked upon my passes. Then, good prince,   378
No longer session hold upon my shame,
But let my trial be mine own confession.
Immediate sentence then and sequent death   381
Is all the grace I beg.

DUKE   Come hither, Mariana.—
Say, wast thou e'er contracted to this woman?

ANGELO   I was, my lord.

DUKE
Go take her hence and marry her instantly.
Do you the office, Friar, which consummate,   386
Return him here again. Go with him, Provost.

Exit [*Angelo, with Mariana, Friar Peter, and
Provost*].

ESCALUS
My lord, I am more amazed at his dishonor
Than at the strangeness of it.

DUKE   Come hither, Isabel.
Your friar is now your prince. As I was then

Advertising and holy to your business,   391
Not changing heart with habit, I am still
Attorneyed at your service.

ISABELLA   Oh, give me pardon,   393
That I, your vassal, have employed and pained   394
Your unknown sovereignty!

DUKE   You are pardoned, Isabel.
And now, dear maid, be you as free to us.   396
Your brother's death, I know, sits at your heart;
And you may marvel why I obscured myself,
Laboring to save his life, and would not rather
Make rash remonstrance of my hidden power   400
Than let him so be lost. O most kind maid,
It was the swift celerity of his death,
Which I did think with slower foot came on,
That brained my purpose. But peace be with him!   404
That life is better life past fearing death
Than that which lives to fear. Make it your comfort,
So happy is your brother.

*Enter Angelo, Mariana, [Friar] Peter, [and]
Provost.*

ISABELLA   I do, my lord.   407

DUKE
For this new-married man approaching here,
Whose salt imagination yet hath wronged   409
Your well-defended honor, you must pardon
For Mariana's sake. But as he adjudged your
brother—
Being criminal, in double violation
Of sacred chastity and of promise-breach   413
Thereon dependent, for your brother's life—   414
The very mercy of the law cries out   415
Most audible, even from his proper tongue,   416
"An Angelo for Claudio, death for death!"
Haste still pays haste, and leisure answers leisure;   418
Like doth quit like, and measure still for measure.   419
Then, Angelo, thy fault's thus manifested,
Which, though thou wouldst deny, denies thee
vantage.   421
We do condemn thee to the very block
Where Claudio stooped to death, and with like haste.
Away with him!

MARIANA   O my most gracious lord,
I hope you will not mock me with a husband!

DUKE
It is your husband mocked you with a husband.
Consenting to the safeguard of your honor,
I thought your marriage fit; else imputation,   428
For that he knew you, might reproach your life   429

---

354 **bolts** iron fetters   355 **giglots** wanton women   356 **confederate companion** i.e., Friar Peter.   362 **sheep-biting** knavish. (From the action of wolves or dogs that prey on sheep.)   362–3 **hanged an hour** (A sardonic way of saying "hanged.")   365 **gentle three** i.e., Mariana, Isabella, and Friar Peter.   371 **or word** either word   372 **office** service.   374 **hold . . . out** then persist no longer.   378 **passes** actions, trespasses.   381 **sequent** subsequent   386 **Do . . . office** Please perform the service.   **consummate** being completed

391 **Advertising and holy** attentive and wholly dedicated (in my priestly role)   393 **Attorneyed at** serving as agent in   394 **pained** put to trouble   396 **as free to us** i.e., as generous in pardoning me   400 **rash remonstrance** sudden manifestation   404 **brained** dashed, defeated   407 **So** thus   409 **salt** lecherous   413–14 **promise-breach . . . dependent** i.e., breaking his promise made in return for the yielding up of chastity   415 **The very . . . law** i.e., even mercy itself   416 **his proper** its own   418 **still** always   419 **quit** requite   421 **though** even if. **vantage** i.e., any advantage. (Angelo must suffer the same penalty as Claudio.)   428 **fit** appropriate.   **imputation** accusation, slander   429 **For that he knew you** since he knew you sexually

And choke your good to come. For his possessions,   430
Although by confiscation they are ours,
We do instate and widow you withal,   432
To buy you a better husband.

MARIANA   O my dear lord,
I crave no other, nor no better man.

DUKE
Never crave him; we are definitive.   435

MARIANA [kneeling]
Gentle my liege—

DUKE   You do but lose your labor.—
Away with him to death! [To Lucio] Now, sir, to you.

MARIANA
O my good lord!—Sweet Isabel, take my part!
Lend me your knees, and all my life to come
I'll lend you all my life to do you service.

DUKE
Against all sense you do importune her.
Should she kneel down in mercy of this fact,   442
Her brother's ghost his pavèd bed would break,   443
And take her hence in horror.

MARIANA   Isabel,
Sweet Isabel, do yet but kneel by me!
Hold up your hands, say nothing; I'll speak all.
They say best men are molded out of faults,   447
And, for the most, become much more the better   448
For being a little bad. So may my husband.
O Isabel, will you not lend a knee?

DUKE
He dies for Claudio's death.

ISABELLA [kneeling]   Most bounteous sir,
Look, if it please you, on this man condemned
As if my brother lived. I partly think
A due sincerity governed his deeds,
Till he did look on me. Since it is so,
Let him not die. My brother had but justice,
In that he did the thing for which he died.
For Angelo,
His act did not o'ertake his bad intent,
And must be buried but as an intent   460
That perished by the way. Thoughts are no subjects,   461
Intents but merely thoughts.

MARIANA   Merely, my lord.

DUKE
Your suit's unprofitable. Stand up, I say.

[They stand.]

I have bethought me of another fault.
Provost, how came it Claudio was beheaded
At an unusual hour?

PROVOST   It was commanded so.

DUKE
Had you a special warrant for the deed?

PROVOST
No, my good lord, it was by private message.

DUKE
For which I do discharge you of your office.
Give up your keys.

PROVOST   Pardon me, noble lord.
I thought it was a fault, but knew it not,   472
Yet did repent me after more advice;   473
For testimony whereof, one in the prison,
That should by private order else have died,
I have reserved alive.

DUKE   What's he?

PROVOST   His name is Barnardine.

DUKE
I would thou hadst done so by Claudio.
Go fetch him hither. Let me look upon him.

[Exit Provost.]

ESCALUS
I am sorry one so learnèd and so wise
As you, Lord Angelo, have still appeared,   482
Should slip so grossly, both in the heat of blood
And lack of tempered judgment afterward.

ANGELO
I am sorry that such sorrow I procure,   485
And so deep sticks it in my penitent heart
That I crave death more willingly than mercy.
'Tis my deserving, and I do entreat it.   488

Enter Barnardine and Provost, Claudio [muffled],
[and] Juliet.

DUKE
Which is that Barnardine?

PROVOST   This, my lord.

DUKE
There was a friar told me of this man.—
Sirrah, thou art said to have a stubborn soul
That apprehends no further than this world,
And squar'st thy life according. Thou'rt condemned;   493
But, for those earthly faults, I quit them all,   494
And pray thee take this mercy to provide
For better times to come.—Friar, advise him;
I leave him to your hand.—What muffled fellow's
    that?

PROVOST
This is another prisoner that I saved,
Who should have died when Claudio lost his head,
As like almost to Claudio as himself.

[He unmuffles Claudio.]

DUKE [to Isabella]
If he be like your brother, for his sake
Is he pardoned, and for your lovely sake,
Give me your hand and say you will be mine;
He is my brother too. But fitter time for that.
By this Lord Angelo perceives he's safe;
Methinks I see a quick'ning in his eye.
Well, Angelo, your evil quits you well.   507
Look that you love your wife, her worth worth yours.   508

---

430 For As for   **432 widow** endow with a widow's rights
435 definitive firmly resolved.   **442 in . . . fact** pleading mercy for
this crime   **443 pavèd bed** grave covered with a stone slab   **447 best
men** even the best of men   **448 most** most part   **460 buried** i.e., forgotten   **461 no subjects** i.e., not subject to the state's authority

472 knew it not was not sure   **473 advice** consideration   **482 still** always   **485 procure** cause, prompt   **488.1 muffled** wrapped up so as to
conceal identity. (As also in line 497.)   **493 squar'st** regulates   **494 for**
as for.   **quit** pardon   **507 quits** rewards, requites   **508 her . . . yours**
her worthiness richly deserving your love and worthy of your estate.

I find an apt remission in myself; 509
And yet here's one in place I cannot pardon. 510
[*To Lucio*] You, sirrah, that knew me for a fool, a
coward,
One all of luxury, an ass, a madman— 512
Wherein have I so deserved of you
That you extol me thus?

LUCIO   Faith, my lord, I spoke it but according to the
trick. If you will hang me for it, you may; but I had 516
rather it would please you I might be whipped.

DUKE
Whipped first, sir, and hanged after.—
Proclaim it, Provost, round about the city,
If any woman wronged by this lewd fellow—
As I have heard him swear himself there's one
Whom he begot with child—let her appear,
And he shall marry her. The nuptial finished,
Let him be whipped and hanged.

LUCIO   I beseech Your Highness, do not marry me to a
whore. Your Highness said even now I made you a 526
duke; good my lord, do not recompense me in making me a cuckold.

DUKE
Upon mine honor, thou shalt marry her.
Thy slanders I forgive and therewithal 530
Remit thy other forfeits.—Take him to prison, 531

And see our pleasure herein executed. 532

LUCIO   Marrying a punk, my lord, is pressing to death, 533
whipping, and hanging.

DUKE
Slandering a prince deserves it.
                    [*Exeunt officers with Lucio.*]
She, Claudio, that you wronged, look you restore. 536
Joy to you, Mariana! Love her, Angelo.
I have confessed her, and I know her virtue.
Thanks, good friend Escalus, for thy much goodness;
There's more behind that is more gratulate. 540
Thanks, Provost, for thy care and secrecy;
We shall employ thee in a worthier place.
Forgive him, Angelo, that brought you home
The head of Ragozine for Claudio's;
Th'offense pardons itself. Dear Isabel,
I have a motion much imports your good, 546
Whereto if you'll a willing ear incline,
What's mine is yours, and what is yours is mine.—
So, bring us to our palace, where we'll show 549
What's yet behind, that's meet you all should know. 550
                              [*Exeunt.*]

---

509 **apt remission** readiness to show mercy   510 **in place** present
512 **luxury** lechery   516 **trick** fashion.   526 **even** just   530–1 **and
therewithal . . . forfeits** i.e., and therefore will not have you whipped
and hanged.

---

532 **see . . . executed** i.e., see that my order be carried out that Lucio
marry Kate Keepdown (see 3.2.194–6).   533 **pressing to death** i.e., by
having heavy weights placed on the chest. (A standard form of executing those who refused to plead to a felony charge.) Lucio wryly
complains that marrying a whore is as bad as death by torture.
536 **She . . . restore** i.e., See to it that you marry Juliet.   540 **behind** in
store, to come.   **gratulate** gratifying.   546 **motion** proposal (which)
549 **bring** escort   550 **What's yet behind** what is still to be told

Troilus and Cressida

Shakespeare must have had some relative failures in the theater, as well as enormous successes. *Troilus and Cressida* seems to have been a relative failure, at least onstage in its original run. As we shall see, questions arise as to whether it was produced at all. It is a bitter play about an inconclusive war and a failed love affair, quite unlike anything Shakespeare had written before in his romantic comedies and English history plays. Its bleak satire of political stalemate seems directed, in part, at the unhappy story of the abortive rebellion of the Earl of Essex in 1601; like many of the warriors in *Troilus and Cressida*, Essex was a tarnished hero whose charisma fell victim to his own egomaniacal ambitions and to the mood of anxious helplessness that hovered over Queen Elizabeth's last years. The play is unusually elliptical in its language, as though Shakespeare deliberately adopted a new, contorted style to express the unresolvable paradoxes of the political and psychological no-man's-land he wanted to describe. A major topic of the play is fame, or rather notoriety, for most of Shakespeare's major characters came to him in the story with full-blown legendary identities as antiheroes: Cressida, the faithless woman; Troilus, the rejected male; Pandarus, the go-between; and Achilles, the butcherer of Hector. Shakespeare's language has to deal with shattered identities, with the unstable subjectivity of human willfulness, and with spiritual exhaustion and neurosis. Perhaps some members of Shakespeare's audience were not quite prepared for all of this.

Today, on the other hand, the play enjoys high critical esteem and has shown itself to be theatrically powerful. What we perceive is that its mordant wit, its satirical depiction of war, and its dispiriting portrayal of sexual infidelity call for a response very different from the one required for an appreciation of *A Midsummer Night's Dream* and *As You Like It* or *1 Henry IV. Troilus and Cressida*, written probably in 1601–1602, shortly before the Stationers' Register entry of 1603, is attuned to a new and darker mood emerging during this period in Shakespeare's work and in the work of his contemporaries.

In the early 1600s, dramatic satire enjoyed a sudden and highly visible notoriety. Catering, in large part, to select and courtly audiences, and given new impetus by the reopening of the boys' acting companies at the indoor theaters in 1599, satirical drama quickly employed the talents of Ben Jonson, John Marston, and George Chapman, as well as other sophisticated dramatists. Jonson launched a series of plays he called comical satires, in which he rebuked the London citizenry and presumed to teach manners to the court as well. The so-called War of the Theaters among Jonson, Marston, and Thomas Dekker, although partly a personality clash of no consequence, was also a serious debate between public and more courtly or select stages on the proper uses of satire. Public dramatists complained about the libelous boldness of the new satire and were galled by the preference of some audiences for this new theatrical phenomenon; even Shakespeare fretted in *Hamlet* (2.2.353–79) about the rivalry. Yet, as an artist in search of new forms, he also responded with positive interest. He experimented with a Jonsonian type of satirical plot in the exposure of Malvolio in *Twelfth Night* (1600–1602). *Troilus and Cressida* seems to have been another and more ambitious experiment, embracing a different kind of satire, not of witty exposure, but of disillusionment.

This satiric genre is hard to classify according to the conventional definitions of tragedy, comedy, or history even though it does have its own clearly defined rationale that makes special sense in terms of our modern theater. The play is partly tragic in that it presents the fall of great Hector and adumbrates the fall of Troy, yet its love story merely dwindles into frustrated estrangement without the death of either lover. The play is comic only insofar as it is black comedy or comedy of the absurd. Its leering sexual titillation and its mood of spiritual paralysis link *Troilus and Cressida* to the problem comedies *All's Well*

That Ends Well (c. 1601–1604) and *Measure for Measure* (1603–1604). The play is called a "history" on both its early title pages and assuredly deals with the great events of history's most famous war, but history has become essentially ironic. In this, *Troilus and Cressida* represents a culmination of Shakespeare's ironic exploration of history as begun in the impasses of *Richard II* or *Henry IV* and as portrayed more fully in the sustained ambiguities of *Julius Caesar* (1599). However much Shakespeare may have been influenced by the contemporary vogue of satire in the boys' theater, his own satire of disillusion is integral to his development as an artist. *Troilus and Cressida* is a fitting companion and contemporary for *Hamlet* (c. 1599–1601). Like that play, it evokes a universal disorder that may well reflect the loss of an assured sense of philosophical reliance on the medieval hierarchies of the old Ptolemaic earth-centered cosmos.

Troilus and Cressida achieves its disillusioning effect through repeated ironic juxtaposition of heroic ideals and tarnished realities. Although it deals with the greatest war in history and a renowned love affair, we as audience know that Troy and the lovers will be overthrown by cunning and infidelity. Shakespeare partly inherited from his sources this duality of epic grandeur and dispiriting conclusion. To learn of the war itself, he must have known George Chapman's translation of Homer's *Iliad* (of which seven books were published in 1598) and, of course, Virgil's account of the destruction of Troy, but he relied more particularly on medieval romances: Raoul Lefevre's *Recueil des Histoires de Troyes*, as translated and published by William Caxton, and perhaps John Lydgate's *Troy Book*, derived in part from Guido delle Colonne's *Historia Trojana*. These romances were Trojan in point of view and hence concerned with the fall of that city. For the bitter love story, Shakespeare went to Geoffrey Chaucer's *Troilus and Criseyde* (c. 1385–1386), which had been derived from the twelfth-century medieval romance of Benoit de Sainte-Maure, *Le Roman de Troie*, as amplified and retold in Boccaccio's *Il Filostrato*. Chaucer's Criseyde is an admirably self-possessed young woman, and her love for Troilus captures the spirit of the courtly love tradition upon which the story was based. After the late fourteenth century, however, Chaucer's heroine suffered a drastic decline in esteem. In Robert Henryson's *Testament of Cresseid*, for example, Cressida becomes a leper and beggar, the "lazar kite of Cressid's kind" to whom Pistol alludes in *Henry V*. Her name has become synonymous with womanly infidelity, as Shakespeare wryly points out in *Troilus and Cressida*: "Let all constant men be Troiluses, all false women Cressids, and all brokers-between Pandars" (3.2.201–3). Shakespeare is fascinated by this phenomenon of declining reputations. Just as the illustrious warrior Achilles must learn that envious time detracts from our best achievements and stigmatizes us for our worst failings, Troilus, Cressida, and Pandarus all anticipate the lasting consequences to their reputations of a failed love relationship. The passion to which they commit themselves eternally becomes not only an emblem of lost hopes and promises but also a caricature to later generations of enervating and frustrated desire, promiscuity, and pandering. Thus, Shakespeare finds in his materials both chivalric splendor and a deflation of it.

Stylistically, Shakespeare exploits this juxtaposition. He employs epic conventions more than is his custom. The narrative commences, as the chorus informs us, *in medias res*, "Beginning in the middle." Epic similes adorn the formal speeches of Ulysses, Agamemnon, and Nestor. The rhetoric of persuasion plays an important role, as in *Julius Caesar* and other Roman plays. The great names of antiquity are paraded past us in a roll call of heroes. Hector, above all, is an epic hero, although in the fashion of medieval romance he is also the prince of chivalry. He longs to resolve the war by a challenge to single combat, in tournament, with the breaking of lances and with each warrior defending the honor of his lady-fair (1.3.264–83). The Greeks respond for a time to this stirring call to arms. Yet, in the broader context of the war itself, with its unworthy causes, its frustrating irresolution, and its debilitating effect on the morale of both sides, Hector's idealism cannot prevail. On the Greek side, Ulysses's ennobling vision of "degree, priority, and place" (1.3.86), by which the heavens show to humanity the value of harmonious order, serves more to criticize and mock the present disorder of the Greek army than to offer guidance toward a restoration of that order. Epic convention becomes hollow travesty, as chivalric aspirations repeatedly dissolve into the sordid insinuations of Thersites or Pandarus. Despite the play's epic machinery, the gods are nowhere to be found.

A prevailing metaphor is that of disease (as also in *Hamlet*). Insubordinate conduct "infects" (1.3.187) the body politic. The Greek commanders hope to "physic" (1.3.378) Achilles lest his virtues, "like fair fruit in an unwholesome dish," rot untasted (2.3.119). Hector deplores the way his fellow Trojans "infectiously" enslave themselves to willful appetite (2.2.59). Elsewhere, love is described as an open ulcer and as an itch that must be scratched; Helen is "contaminated carrion" (4.1.73). Thersites, most of all, invites us to regard both love and war as disease-ridden, afflicted by boils, plagues, scabs, the "Neapolitan bone-ache" (syphilis), "lethargies, cold palsies, raw eyes, dirt-rotten livers, wheezing lungs, bladders full of imposthume [abscesses], sciaticas," and still more (2.3.18 and 5.1.19–21). Pandarus ends the play on a similarly tawdry note by jesting about prostitutes (Winchester geese, he calls them) and the "sweating" or venereal diseases.

The war is both glorious and absurd. It calls forth brave deeds and heroic sacrifices. Yet it is correctly labeled by the choric Prologue as a "quarrel," begun over an "old aunt," whom the Greeks have held captive, and Helen, whom the Trojans abducted in reprisal. No one believes the original cause to justify the bloodletting that has ensued. Menelaus's cuckoldry is the subject of obscene mirth in the Greek camp. Among the Trojans, Troilus can argue only that one does not return soiled goods; since all Troy consented to Helen's abduction, Troy must continue the war to maintain its honor. The war thus assumes a grim momentum of its own. The combatants repeatedly discover that they are trapped in the ironies of a situation they helped make but can no longer unmake. Hector's challenge to single combat falls upon Ajax, his "father's sister's son." Achilles, too, has allegiances in the enemy's camp, since he is enamored of Priam's daughter Polyxena. In the parleys between the two sides, the warriors greet one another as long-lost brothers, though they vow to slaughter one another on the morrow. With fitting oxymoron, Paris comments on the paradox of this "most despiteful gentle greeting," this "noblest hateful love" (4.1.34–5). Only a barbarian could be free of regret for a peace that seems so near and is yet so far. The war offers insidious temptations to potentially worthy men, perverting Achilles's once-honorable quest for fame into maniacal ambition and an irresistible impulse to murder Hector. History and tradition, we know, will mock Achilles for this craven deed. It will put him down as a bully rather than as a brave soldier, just as Troilus, Cressida, and Pandarus will come to be regarded in time as stereotypes of the cheated man, the whore, and the procurer. Even before the murder of Hector, Achilles sees his reputation for bravery tarnished by his inaction, while Ajax is hoisted into prominence by the machinations of Ulysses and the other generals.

Hector's tragedy is, in its own way, no less ironic. Even though he emerges as the most thoughtful and courageous man on either side and advises his fellow Trojans to let Helen go in response to the "moral laws / Of nature and of nations" (2.2.184–5), he nonetheless ends the Trojan council of war by resolving to fight on with them. This conclusion may represent, in part, a realization that the others will fight on, in any case, and that he must therefore be loyal to them, but the choice also reflects hubris. Hector is not unlike Julius Caesar in his proud repudiation of his wife Andromache's ominous dreams, his sister Cassandra's mad but oracular prophecies, and his own conviction that Troy's pursuit of honor stems from a sickened appetite. He goes to his death because "The gods have heard me swear" (5.3.15). His character is his fate. Even his humane compunctions, like Brutus's, are held against him; he spares the life of Achilles and is murdered in reward. War is no place for men of scruple, as Troilus reminds his older brother. Yet, Hector, at least, is the better man for refusing to be corrupted by the savagery of war; we honor his memory, even if we also view him as senselessly victimized by a meaningless conflict.

The lovers, as well, are caught in war's trap—not only Troilus and Cressida, but also Paris and Helen, Achilles and Polyxena. Achilles vows to Polyxena not to fight and thereby misses his cherished opportunity for fame; ironically, he is aroused to vengeful action only by the death of a male friend, Patroclus, who is whispered to be his "male varlet" or "masculine whore" (5.1.15–17). Paris is obliged to ask his brother Troilus to return Cressida to the Greeks, so that Paris may continue to enjoy Helen. What else can Paris do? "There is no help," he complains. "The bitter disposition of the time / Will have it so" (4.1.49–51). Troilus prepares his own undoing when he argues in the Trojan council of war that Helen must be kept at all cost; the cost, it turns out, is his own Cressida. He sees this irony at once: "How my achievements mock me!" (4.2.71); that is, he has no sooner achieved her sexually than he must give her up so that the war may go on with Trojan honor intact and Helen still in Paris's bed. The love of Troilus and Cressida is dwarfed by the war, which has no regard for their private concerns. Troilus wins Cressida after many months of wooing, only to lose her the next day. Yet how could Cressida's father Calchas know of her personal situation? He wishes only to have his daughter back. And, although the Trojan leaders do know of Troilus's affair, they must pay heed first to such matters of state as the exchange of prisoners.

So, too, must Troilus. Perhaps the greatest irony is that he must himself choose to send Cressida to the Greeks, placing duty above personal longing. He appears to have no real choice, but the result is surrounded by absurdities, and it is something that Cressida cannot comprehend. She has determined to stay no matter what the world may think; passionate love is more important to her. Although Cressida was first introduced to us as a sardonic and worldly young woman, urbane, mocking, self-possessed, witty, unsentimental, even scheming and opportunistic, and, above all, wary of emotional commitment, her brief involvement with Troilus does touch deep emotion. For a moment, she catches a glimpse of something precious to which she would cling, something genuine in her unstable world. Yet Troilus, caught between love and duty, consents to her departure to the Greek camp. There she reverts to her former disillusioned self, behaving as is expected of her. Who has deserted whom? Cressida gives up, hating herself for doing so. She knows she cannot be true because, like too many women in her experience, she is led by "The error of our eye" and is thus a prey to male importunity (5.2.113). Alone and friendless in the Greek camp except for her neglectful father, she turns to a self-assured and opportunistic man (Diomedes) who is perfectly cynical about women generally but who will at least protect her against the other sex-starved Greek officers. Sometimes she seems, to Ulysses at least, one of those "sluttish spoils of opportunity / And daughters of the game" (4.5.63–4). Still, this surrender to will and appetite in her is not unsympathetic, and does not happen without inner struggle. Her weakness is emblematic of a universal disorder and is partly caused by it. In the grim interplay of war and love, both men and women are powerless to assert their true selves. As the malcontent Thersites concludes, "Lechery, lechery, still wars and lechery; nothing else holds fashion."

The printing history of *Troilus and Cressida* is full of obscurities that may give some insight into the play's apparent lack of stage success. On February 7, 1603, the printer James Roberts entered his name on the Register of the Company of Stationers (i.e., publishers and booksellers) to print, "when he hath gotten sufficient authority for it, the book of Troilus and Cressida as it is acted by my Lord Chamberlain's Men." Evidently, the authority was not forthcoming, for in 1609 the play was reregistered to R. Bonian and H. Walley and published by them that year in quarto as *The History of Troilus and Cressida. As it was acted by the King's Majesty's servants at the Globe. Written by William Shakespeare*. Immediately afterward, and well before this first printing had sold out, a new title page was substituted as follows: *The Famous History of Troilus and Cresseid. Excellently expressing the beginning of their loves, with the conceited wooing of Pandarus Prince of Lycia. Written by William Shakespeare*. This second version had, moreover, a preface to the reader (something found in no other Shakespearean quarto) declaring *Troilus and Cressida* to be "a new play, never staled with the stage, never clapper-clawed with the palms of the vulgar," nor "sullied with the smoky breath of the multitude." The preface goes on to imply that the play's "grand possessors" (i.e., Shakespeare's acting company) had not wished to see the play released at all. What this substituted title page and added preface may suggest is that Bonian and Walley felt constrained to present their text as a new one—a literary rather than a theatrical text—and hence different from the version entered in the Stationers' Register "as it is acted by my Lord Chamberlain's Men." Because that version had been legally registered in the name of James Roberts, the new publishers made their case for legal possession by offering a "new" play.

Later, the editors of the First Folio edition of 1623 seemed to have had difficulty in obtaining permission to print *Troilus and Cressida*. Three pages of the play were actually printed to follow *Romeo and Juliet*, among the tragedies, but were then withdrawn to be replaced by *Timon of Athens*. Ultimately, the play appeared in the Folio almost without pagination, unlisted in the table of contents, and placed with fitting ambiguity between the histories and the tragedies.

This unusual printing history offers conflicting information about original stage performance. Against the evidence of the second version of the 1609 Quarto, with its preface proclaiming a play "never staled with the stage," we have the evidence of the first title page mentioning the King's Majesty's servants at the Globe and of the Stationers' Register entry in 1603 referring to the play "as it is acted." Since the 1609 preface may be part of a legal maneuver designed to represent the play as new, the case in favor of actual performance has some weight. We cannot be sure, however, that the performance was successful or that it reached a very large audience. Some scholars have hypothesized that Shakespeare's company mounted a special production of the play for a private audience at the Inns of Court (where young men studied law) or a similar place, even though an arrangement of this sort would have been most unusual, if not unique; Shakespeare's company often took its regular plays to court or other special audiences, but no instance is positively known in which Shakespeare wrote on commission for a private showing. More likely, *Troilus and Cressida* was performed publicly without great success. A sequel, promised in the closing lines of the play by Pandarus to be presented "some two months hence," evidently did not materialize, perhaps because public demand was insufficient. The 1609 Quarto, with its revised title page and added preface, may have attempted to capitalize on the play's public failure by touting it as sophisticated fare, to be appreciated only by discerning readers. Possibly, Shakespeare and his company took another look at *Troilus and Cressida* in 1608, after they had acquired the right to perform in their indoor theater at Blackfriars, where audiences tended to be more select, only to discover anew that the play was not a great success on the stage. Its subsequent stage history, in any case, is largely a blank until the twentieth century, except for a much changed Restoration adaptation by John Dryden (1679) in which Cressida remains true to Troilus and slays herself when accused of infidelity.

Since 1907, on the other hand, when the play was finally revived on the London stage, it has enjoyed a genuine and growing success. Its disillusionment about war seems admirably suited to an era of world conflict, superpower confrontations, and deepening cynicism about politics. Thersites and Pandarus sound positively choric today in their chortling and obscene reflections on the perversions of human sexuality. Helen as insipid sex goddess and Paris as her languid admirer strike us as boldly modern, as in Michael Macowan's antiwar production for the London Mask Theatre Company on the eve of World War II, in 1938. Most of all, perhaps, Cressida as failed heroine has come into her own. Centuries of disparaging sexist dismissal of her as a typically faithless woman have given way to nuanced interpretations in which male importunity is at least as much to blame for her desertion of Troilus as her own admitted weakness. Once Troilus has possessed her sexually, he seems less obsessively interested in her and consents, even if unwillingly, to her return to the Greeks. Her awareness that something of this sort was bound to happen provides modern actresses with a potent indictment of the male species, as in Juliet Stevenson's sympathetic portrayal of Cressida as a victim of war and male violence in Howard Davies's 1985 production for the Royal Shakespeare Company. Paradoxically, this searing play about the decay of "notorious identities" (Linda Charnes's phrase) has led to a resuscitation of reputation for the woman who was once the most notorious of them all.

The following is a complete text of the preface to the reader from the second "state" of the 1609 Quarto.

A Never Writer, to an Ever Reader. News.

Eternal reader, you have here a new play, never staled with the stage, never clapper-clawed with the palms of the vulgar, and yet passing full of the palm comical; for it is a birth of your brain that never undertook anything comical vainly. And were but the vain names of comedies changed for the titles of commodities, or of plays for pleas, you should see all those grand censors, that now style them such vanities, flock to them for the main grace of their gravities, especially this author's comedies, that are so framed to the life that they serve for the most common commentaries of all the actions of our lives, showing such a dexterity and power of wit that the most displeased with plays are pleased with his comedies. And all such dull and heavy-witted worldlings as were never capable of the wit of a comedy, coming by report of them to his representations, have found that wit there that they never found in themselves and have parted better witted than they came, feeling an edge of wit set upon them more than ever they dreamed they had brain to grind it on. So much and such savored salt of wit is in his comedies that they seem, for their height of pleasure, to be born in that sea that brought forth Venus. Amongst all there is none more witty than this; and had I time I would comment upon it, though I know it needs not, for so much as will make you think your testern well bestowed, but for so much worth as even poor I know to be stuffed in it. It deserves such a labor as well as the best comedy in Terence or Plautus. And believe this, that when he is gone and his comedies out of sale, you will scramble for them and set up a new English Inquisition. Take this for a warning, and at the peril of your pleasure's loss, and judgment's, refuse not, nor like this the less for not being sullied with the smoky breath of the multitude; but thank fortune for the scape it hath made amongst you, since by the grand possessors' wills I believe you should have prayed for them rather than been prayed. And so I leave all such to be prayed for, for the states of their wits' healths, that will not praise it. *Vale.*

Troilus and Cressida

[**Dramatis Personae**

PROLOGUE

PRIAM, *King of Troy*
HECTOR,
TROILUS,
PARIS
DEIPHOBUS, } *his sons*
HELENUS, *a priest,*
MARGARETON, *a bastard,*
AENEAS } *Trojan commanders*
ANTENOR
CALCHAS, *a Trojan priest, Cressida's father, and defector to
   the Greeks*
PANDARUS, *Cressida's uncle*
SERVANT *to Troilus*
SERVANT *to Paris*

CASSANDRA, *Priam's daughter, a prophetess*
ANDROMACHE, *Hector's wife*
HELEN, *former wife of Menelaus, now Paris's mistress*
CRESSIDA, *Calchas's daughter, loved by Troilus*
ALEXANDER, *Cressida's servant*

AGAMEMNON, *the Greek General*
MENELAUS, *brother of Agamemnon*
ACHILLES,
AJAX,
ULYSSES, } *Greek commanders*
NESTOR,
DIOMEDES,
PATROCLUS, *Achilles's friend*
THERSITES, *a scurrilous fool*
SERVANT *to Diomedes*

Trojan and Greek Soldiers, and Attendants

SCENE: *Troy, and the Greek camp before it*]

Prologue

[*Enter the Prologue, in armor.*]

PROLOGUE
In Troy, there lies the scene. From isles of Greece
The princes orgulous, their high blood chafed,   2
Have to the port of Athens sent their ships,
Fraught with the ministers and instruments   4
Of cruel war. Sixty and nine, that wore
Their crownets regal, from th'Athenian bay   6
Put forth toward Phrygia, and their vow is made   7
To ransack Troy, within whose strong immures   8
The ravished Helen, Menelaus' queen,   9
With wanton Paris sleeps; and that's the quarrel.
To Tenedos they come,   11
And the deep-drawing barks do there disgorge   12
Their warlike freightage. Now on Dardan plains   13
The fresh and yet unbruisèd Greeks do pitch
Their brave pavilions. Priam's six-gated city—   15
Dardan, and Timbria, Helias, Chetas, Troien,   16
And Antenorides—with massy staples   17
And corresponsive and fulfilling bolts,   18
Spar up the sons of Troy.   19
Now expectation, tickling skittish spirits   20
On one and other side, Trojan and Greek,

Prologue
2 orgulous proud.   **chafed** heated, angered   **4 Fraught** laden.
ministers agents, i.e., soldiers   **6 crownets** coronets, crowns worn by
nobles   **7 Phrygia** district in western Asia Minor, identified as Troy
by the Roman poets, and hence in Renaissance poetry   **8 immures**
walls   **9 ravished** abducted

11 Tenedos small island in the Aegean Sea off the coast of Asia Minor
12 deep-drawing barks ships lying low in the water (with their
heavy cargo)   **13 Dardan** Trojan. (From *Dardanus*, son of Zeus and
Electra, daughter of Atlas. According to legend, Dardanus was the
ancestor of the Trojan race.)   **15 brave pavilions** splendid tents.
16–17 Dardan . . . Antenorides (The names of Troy's six gates.)
17–18 massy . . . bolts i.e., massive posts fitted with sockets to receive
matching and well-fitted bolts   **19 Spar** close   **20 skittish** lively

Sets all on hazard. And hither am I come,   22
A prologue armed, but not in confidence   23
Of author's pen or actor's voice, but suited   24
In like conditions as our argument,   25
To tell you, fair beholders, that our play
Leaps o'er the vaunt and firstlings of those broils,   27
Beginning in the middle, starting thence away   28
To what may be digested in a play.
Like or find fault; do as your pleasures are;
Now, good or bad, 'tis but the chance of war.

                                                          [*Exit.*]

♣

[1.1]

Enter Pandarus and Troilus.

TROILUS
Call here my varlet; I'll unarm again.   1
Why should I war without the walls of Troy,
That find such cruel battle here within?
Each Trojan that is master of his heart,
Let him to field; Troilus, alas, hath none.   5
PANDARUS   Will this gear ne'er be mended?   6
TROILUS
The Greeks are strong, and skillful to their strength,   7
Fierce to their skill, and to their fierceness valiant;   8
But I am weaker than a woman's tear,
Tamer than sleep, fonder than ignorance,   10
Less valiant than the virgin in the night,
And skilless as unpracticed infancy.
PANDARUS   Well, I have told you enough of this. For
my part, I'll not meddle nor make no farther. He that   14
will have a cake out of the wheat must tarry the   15
grinding.
TROILUS   Have I not tarried?
PANDARUS   Ay, the grinding, but you must tarry the
bolting.   19
TROILUS   Have I not tarried?
PANDARUS   Ay, the bolting, but you must tarry the leav-
ening.
TROILUS   Still have I tarried.
PANDARUS   Ay, to the leavening, but here's yet in the
word "hereafter" the kneading, the making of the
cake, the heating the oven, and the baking; nay, you
must stay the cooling too, or ye may chance burn   27
your lips.
TROILUS
Patience herself, what goddess e'er she be,   29

Doth lesser blench at suff'rance than I do.   30
At Priam's royal table do I sit,
And when fair Cressid comes into my thoughts—
So, traitor! When she comes? When is she thence?   33
PANDARUS   Well, she looked yesternight fairer than ever
I saw her look, or any woman else.
TROILUS
I was about to tell thee—when my heart,
As wedgèd with a sigh, would rive in twain,   37
Lest Hector or my father should perceive me,
I have, as when the sun doth light a-scorn,   39
Buried this sigh in wrinkle of a smile;
But sorrow that is couched in seeming gladness   41
Is like that mirth fate turns to sudden sadness.
PANDARUS   An her hair were not somewhat darker than   43
Helen's—well, go to—there were no more comparison   44
between the women. But, for my part, she is my
kinswoman; I would not, as they term it, praise her.
But I would somebody had heard her talk yesterday,
as I did. I will not dispraise your sister Cassandra's
wit, but—
TROILUS
Oh, Pandarus! I tell thee, Pandarus—
When I do tell thee there my hopes lie drowned,
Reply not in how many fathoms deep
They lie indrenched. I tell thee I am mad   53
In Cressid's love. Thou answer'st she is fair;
Pour'st in the open ulcer of my heart
Her eyes, her hair, her cheek, her gait, her voice,
Handlest in thy discourse—oh!—that her hand,   57
In whose comparison all whites are ink   58
Writing their own reproach, to whose soft seizure   59
The cygnet's down is harsh, and spirit of sense   60
Hard as the palm of plowman. This thou tell'st me,
As true thou tell'st me, when I say I love her;
But saying thus, instead of oil and balm   63
Thou lay'st in every gash that love hath given me
The knife that made it.
PANDARUS   I speak no more than truth.
TROILUS   Thou dost not speak so much.   67
PANDARUS   Faith, I'll not meddle in it. Let her be as she
is. If she be fair, 'tis the better for her; an she be not,
she has the mends in her own hands.   70

---

22 **Sets . . . hazard** puts all at risk.   23 **armed** in armor   23–4 **not . . .
voice** i.e., not overconfident in the value of the play or the acting
24–5 **suited . . . argument** i.e., dressed in armor to match the character
of the military plot. (*Argument* means both "plot of the story" and
"quarrel.")   27 **vaunt and firstlings** beginnings   28 **Beginning in
the middle** (Alluding to the tradition of beginning epic poetry *in
medias res.*)
1.1. Location: Troy.
1 **varlet** page or servant of a knight   5 **none** i.e., no heart to fight.
6 **gear** business   7, 8 **to** in addition to, in proportion to   10 **fonder**
more foolish   14 **meddle nor make** have anything more to do with it
15 **tarry** wait for   19 **bolting** sifting.   27 **stay** wait for   29 **what . . .
be** however much a goddess; or, if she is a goddess

30 **Doth . . . suff'rance** flinches under suffering with less fortitude
33 **So, traitor . . . thence?** (Troilus rebukes himself as a traitor to Love
for implying that Cressida is ever out of his thoughts, as she would
have to be before she could come into them.)   37 **As wedgèd** as if
cleft by a wedge.   **rive** split   39 **a-scorn** scornfully, mockingly.
(Troilus compares his face to that of the sun, putting on a false look of
joviality.)   41 **couched** hidden   43 **An** If.   **darker** (A dark complexion was considered less handsome; Helen is blonde.)   44 **go to** (An
exclamation of impatience or irritation.)   **were** would be
53 **indrenched** drowned.   57 **Handlest . . . hand** you discourse on
that wondrous hand of hers   58 **In whose comparison** in comparison with which   59 **to . . . seizure** in comparison with whose soft
clasp   60 **cygnet's** young swan's.   **spirit of sense** the most delicate of
all material substances. (According to Renaissance physiology, spirits
were the invisible vapors that transmitted sense impressions to the
soul.)   63 **oil and balm** ointments, salves   67 **Thou . . . much** i.e., You
cannot possibly speak the whole truth about Cressida (since she is indescribable).   70 **has . . . hands** i.e., can apply remedy, such as cosmetics.

TROILUS   Good Pandarus, how now, Pandarus?

PANDARUS   I have had my labor for my travail; ill 72
thought on of her and ill thought on of you; gone be- 73
tween and between, but small thanks for my labor

TROILUS   What, art thou angry, Pandarus? What, with
me?

PANDARUS   Because she's kin to me, therefore she's not
so fair as Helen. An she were not kin to me, she would 78
be as fair o' Friday as Helen is on Sunday. But what 79
care I? I care not an she were a blackamoor. 'Tis all one 80
to me.

TROILUS   Say I she is not fair?

PANDARUS   I do not care whether you do or no. She's a
fool to stay behind her father. Let her to the Greeks, 84
and so I'll tell her the next time I see her. For my part,
I'll meddle nor make no more i'th' matter.

TROILUS   Pandarus—

PANDARUS   Not I.

TROILUS   Sweet Pandarus—

PANDARUS   Pray you, speak no more to me. I will leave
all as I found it, and there an end.   *Exit.* 91
                                         Sound alarum.

TROILUS
Peace, you ungracious clamors! Peace, rude sounds!
Fools on both sides! Helen must needs be fair,
When with your blood you daily paint her thus.   94
I cannot fight upon this argument;   95
It is too starved a subject for my sword.   96
But Pandarus—O gods, how do you plague me!
I cannot come to Cressid but by Pandar,
And he's as tetchy to be wooed to woo   99
As she is stubborn-chaste against all suit.
Tell me, Apollo, for thy Daphne's love,   101
What Cressid is, what Pandar, and what we?   102
Her bed is India, there she lies, a pearl;
Between our Ilium and where she resides,   104
Let it be called the wild and wand'ring flood,   105
Ourself the merchant, and this sailing Pandar
Our doubtful hope, our convoy, and our bark.

Alarum. Enter Aeneas.

AENEAS
How now, Prince Troilus, wherefore not afield?

TROILUS
Because not there. This woman's answer sorts,   109
For womanish it is to be from thence.
What news, Aeneas, from the field today?

AENEAS
That Paris is returnèd home and hurt.

TROILUS
By whom, Aeneas?

AENEAS   Troilus, by Menelaus.

TROILUS
Let Paris bleed. 'Tis but a scar to scorn;   114
Paris is gored with Menelaus' horn.   *Alarum.* 115

AENEAS
Hark, what good sport is out of town today!   116

TROILUS
Better at home, if "would I might" were "may."   117
But to the sport abroad. Are you bound thither?

AENEAS
In all swift haste.

TROILUS   Come, go we then together. *Exeunt.*

[1.2]

Enter Cressida and her man [Alexander].

CRESSIDA
Who were those went by?

ALEXANDER   Queen Hecuba and Helen.

CRESSIDA
And whither go they?

ALEXANDER   Up to the eastern tower,
Whose height commands as subject all the vale,
To see the battle. Hector, whose patience
Is as a virtue fixed, today was moved.   5
He chid Andromache and struck his armorer,
And, like as there were husbandry in war,   7
Before the sun rose he was harnessed light,   8
And to the field goes he, where every flower
Did as a prophet weep what it foresaw   10
In Hector's wrath.

CRESSIDA   What was his cause of anger?

ALEXANDER
The noise goes, this: there is among the Greeks   12
A lord of Trojan blood, nephew to Hector;   13
They call him Ajax.

CRESSIDA   Good; and what of him?

ALEXANDER
They say he is a very man per se   15
And stands alone.   16

72 had had only   **73 of** by   **78–9 An . . . Sunday** i.e., If I were free to
praise her unreservedly, without appearing to be biased as her kinsman, I would pronounce her to be as attractive in her plainest attire
as Helen in her Sunday best.   **80 blackamoor** dark-skinned African.
84 her father i.e., Calchas, a Trojan priest, who, advised by the oracle
of Apollo that Troy would fall, fled to the Greeks.   **91.1 alarum** trumpet signal to arms.   **94 paint** (As though the blood were cosmetic,
reddening her complexion.)   **95 upon this argument** for this cause,
theme   **96 starved** empty, trivial. (Troilus would have to fight on an
empty stomach, as it were.)   **99 tetchy to be** irritable at being
101 Apollo (The ardent pursuer of the nymph Daphne who, coy like
Cressida, was changed into a bay tree to elude Apollo's pursuit.)
102 we i.e., I.   **104 Ilium** i.e., Troy generally, but here Priam's palace
105 flood open sea   **109 sorts** is appropriate

114 a scar to scorn (1) a wound not sufficiently serious to be regarded
(2) a scar in return for Paris' scorn of Menelaus   **115 horn** i.e., cuckold's horn, since Paris had stolen Helen from Menelaus.   **116 out of
town** outside the walls   **117 Better . . . "may"** If I had my wish, I'd
have better entertainment at home in amorous pursuit.
1.2. Location: Troy.
5 fixed steadfast.   **moved** angry. (With wordplay on the antithesis
between *fixed* and *moved*.)   **7 like as** as if.   **husbandry** good management (by rising early and getting to work. Hector is a stern "husband" in marriage and in war.)   **8 harnessed light** dressed in light
armor   **10 weep** (The early morning dew on the flowers suggests
tears and extends the metaphor of a husbandman or farmer going
into the field.)   **12 noise** rumor   **13 nephew** i.e., kinsmen, first
cousin   **15 per se** all to himself, without peer   **16 alone** without
peer. (But Cressida sardonically takes it to mean literally "all by himself, without support.")

CRESSIDA   So do all men, unless they are drunk, sick, or have no legs.

ALEXANDER   This man, lady, hath robbed many beasts of their particular additions. He is as valiant as the 20 lion, churlish as the bear, slow as the elephant; a man into whom nature hath so crowded humors that his 22 valor is crushed into folly, his folly sauced with discretion. There is no man hath a virtue that he hath not a glimpse of, nor any man an attaint but he carries some 25 stain of it. He is melancholy without cause and merry against the hair. He hath the joints of everything, but 27 everything so out of joint that he is a gouty Briareus, 28 many hands and no use, or purblind Argus, all eyes 29 and no sight.

CRESSIDA   But how should this man, that makes me smile, make Hector angry?

ALEXANDER   They say he yesterday coped Hector in the 33 battle and struck him down, the disdain and shame whereof hath ever since kept Hector fasting and waking.

[Enter Pandarus.]

CRESSIDA   Who comes here?

ALEXANDER   Madam, your uncle Pandarus.

CRESSIDA   Hector's a gallant man.

ALEXANDER   As may be in the world, lady.

PANDARUS   What's that? What's that?

CRESSIDA   Good morrow, uncle Pandarus.

PANDARUS   Good morrow, cousin Cressid. What do you 43 talk of?—Good morrow, Alexander.—How do you, cousin? When were you at Ilium? 45

CRESSIDA   This morning, uncle.

PANDARUS   What were you talking of when I came? Was Hector armed and gone ere ye came to Ilium? Helen was not up, was she?

CRESSIDA   Hector was gone, but Helen was not up?

PANDARUS   E'en so. Hector was stirring early.

CRESSIDA   That were we talking of, and of his anger.

PANDARUS   Was he angry?

CRESSIDA   So he says here.

PANDARUS   True, he was so. I know the cause too. He'll lay about him today, I can tell them that; and there's 56 Troilus will not come far behind him. Let them take heed of Troilus, I can tell them that too.

CRESSIDA   What, is he angry too?

PANDARUS   Who, Troilus? Troilus is the better man of the two.

CRESSIDA   O Jupiter! There's no comparison.

PANDARUS   What, not between Troilus and Hector? Do you know a man if you see him? 64

CRESSIDA   Ay, if I ever saw him before and knew him.

PANDARUS   Well, I say Troilus is Troilus. 66

CRESSIDA   Then you say as I say, for I am sure he is not Hector.

PANDARUS   No, nor Hector is not Troilus in some de- 69 grees.

CRESSIDA   'Tis just to each of them; he is himself. 71

PANDARUS   Himself? Alas, poor Troilus! I would he 72 were.

CRESSIDA   So he is.

PANDARUS   Condition, I had gone barefoot to India. 75

CRESSIDA   He is not Hector.

PANDARUS   Himself? No, he's not himself. Would 'a 77 were himself! Well, the gods are above; time must friend or end. Well, Troilus, well, I would my heart 79 were in her body. No, Hector is not a better man than Troilus.

CRESSIDA   Excuse me. 82

PANDARUS   He is elder.

CRESSIDA   Pardon me, pardon me.

PANDARUS   Th'other's not come to't. You shall tell me 85 another tale, when th'other's come to't. Hector shall not have his wit this year. 87

CRESSIDA   He shall not need it, if he have his own.

PANDARUS   Nor his qualities.

CRESSIDA   No matter.

PANDARUS   Nor his beauty.

CRESSIDA   'Twould not become him; his own's better.

PANDARUS   You have no judgment, niece. Helen herself swore th'other day that Troilus, for a brown favor— 94 for so 'tis, I must confess—not brown neither—

CRESSIDA   No, but brown. 96

PANDARUS   Faith, to say truth, brown and not brown.

CRESSIDA   To say the truth, true and not true.

PANDARUS   She praised his complexion above Paris'.

CRESSIDA   Why, Paris hath color enough.

PANDARUS   So he has.

CRESSIDA   Then Troilus should have too much. If she 102 praised him above, his complexion is higher than his. 103 He having color enough, and the other higher, is too flaming a praise for a good complexion. I had as lief 105 Helen's golden tongue had commended Troilus for a copper nose. 107

PANDARUS   I swear to you, I think Helen loves him better than Paris.

CRESSIDA   Then she's a merry Greek indeed. 110

20 **additions** qualities bestowing special distinction.   **22 humors** temperamental characteristics   **25 glimpse** trace.   **attaint** defect, stain.   **but** but that   **27 against the hair** contrary to natural tendency.   **28 Briareus** Greek mythological monster with fifty heads and one hundred hands; here, all those hands are gouty   **29 Argus** a monster with one hundred eyes; here, all are blind (*purblind*)   **33 coped** encountered, came to blows with   **43 cousin** kinswoman, i.e., niece   **45 Ilium** the palace.   **56 lay about him** fight fiercely   **64 know a man** recognize a complete man. (But Cressida, pretending to misunderstand, takes it to mean simply "recognize.")

66 is Troilus is that extraordinary individual known far and wide as Troilus. (But, again, Cressida reduces it to the literal.)   **69 in some** by several   **71 he** each   **72 Himself** (Pandarus plays with the expression "not to be oneself," to be out of sorts.)   **75 Condition . . . India** i.e., Troilus is about as likely to be himself again as I am to have walked barefoot on pilgrimage to India, which of course I haven't.   **77 'a** he   **79 friend** befriend   **82 Excuse me** i.e., I beg to differ. (Line 84 means the same.)   **85 to't** i.e., to Hector's age, to maturity.   **87 his wit** i.e., Troilus's intelligence   **94 for a brown favor** considering he has a dark complexion   **96 No, but brown** (Cressida mocks her uncle's hairsplitting: "It isn't brown, but it's brown.")   **102 should** would of necessity   **103 higher than his** i.e., ruddier than Paris's.   **105 flaming** (1) flamboyant (2) inflamed with pimples. **lief** willingly   **107 copper** red (with drinking)   **110 merry Greek** (Slang for a frivolous person, loose in morals.)

PANDARUS   Nay, I am sure she does. She came to him th'other day into the compassed window—and, you 112 know, he has not past three or four hairs on his chin—

CRESSIDA   Indeed, a tapster's arithmetic may soon bring 114 his particulars therein to a total.

PANDARUS   Why, he is very young; and yet will he, within three pound, lift as much as his brother Hector.

CRESSIDA   Is he so young a man and so old a lifter? 118

PANDARUS   But to prove to you that Helen loves him: she came and puts me her white hand to his cloven chin— 120

CRESSIDA   Juno have mercy! How came it cloven?

PANDARUS   Why, you know, 'tis dimpled. I think his smiling becomes him better than any man in all Phrygia.

CRESSIDA   Oh, he smiles valiantly.

PANDARUS   Does he not?

CRESSIDA   Oh, yes, an 'twere a cloud in autumn. 127

PANDARUS   Why, go to, then. But to prove to you that Helen loves Troilus—

CRESSIDA   Troilus will stand to the proof, if you'll prove 130 it so.

PANDARUS   Troilus? Why, he esteems her no more than I esteem an addle egg. 133

CRESSIDA   If you love an addle egg as well as you love an idle head, you would eat chickens i'th' shell. 135

PANDARUS   I cannot choose but laugh to think how she tickled his chin. Indeed, she has a marvelous white 137 hand, I must needs confess—

CRESSIDA   Without the rack. 139

PANDARUS   And she takes upon her to spy a white hair on his chin.

CRESSIDA   Alas, poor chin! Many a wart is richer.

PANDARUS   But there was such laughing! Queen Hecuba laughed that her eyes ran o'er.

CRESSIDA   With millstones. 145

PANDARUS   And Cassandra laughed.

CRESSIDA   But there was a more temperate fire under the 147 pot of her eyes. Did her eyes run o'er too?

PANDARUS   And Hector laughed.

CRESSIDA   At what was all this laughing?

PANDARUS   Marry, at the white hair that Helen spied on Troilus' chin.

CRESSIDA   An't had been a green hair, I should have 153 laughed too.

PANDARUS   They laughed not so much at the hair as at his pretty answer.

CRESSIDA   What was his answer?

PANDARUS   Quoth she, "Here's but two-and-fifty hairs 158 on your chin, and one of them is white."

CRESSIDA   This is her question.

PANDARUS   That's true, make no question of that. "Two-and-fifty hairs," quoth he, "and one white. That white hair is my father, and all the rest are his sons." "Jupiter!" quoth she, "which of these hairs is Paris my husband?" "The forked one," quoth he, "pluck't out, 165 and give it him." But there was such laughing! And Helen so blushed, and Paris so chafed, and all the rest 167 so laughed, that it passed. 168

CRESSIDA   So let it now, for it has been a great while 169 going by.

PANDARUS   Well, cousin, I told you a thing yesterday. Think on't.

CRESSIDA   So I do.

PANDARUS   I'll be sworn 'tis true. He will weep you an 174 'twere a man born in April. 175

CRESSIDA   And I'll spring up in his tears an 'twere a 176 nettle against May.   *Sound a retreat.* 177

PANDARUS   Hark, they are coming from the field. Shall we stand up here and see them as they pass toward Ilium? Good niece, do, sweet niece Cressida.

CRESSIDA   At your pleasure.

PANDARUS   Here, here, here's an excellent place; here we may see most bravely. I'll tell you them all by their 183 names as they pass by, but mark Troilus above the rest.

Enter Aeneas [and passes across the stage].

CRESSIDA   Speak not so loud.

PANDARUS   That's Aeneas. Is not that a brave man? He's 187 one of the flowers of Troy, I can tell you. But mark Troilus; you shall see anon.

Enter Antenor [and passes across the stage].

CRESSIDA   Who's that?

PANDARUS   That's Antenor. He has a shrewd wit, I can tell you, and he's a man good enough. He's one o'th' soundest judgments in Troy whosoever, and a proper 193 man of person. When comes Troilus? I'll show you Troilus anon. If he see me, you shall see him nod at me.

CRESSIDA   Will he give you the nod? 197

PANDARUS   You shall see.

CRESSIDA   If he do, the rich shall have more. 199

Enter Hector [and passes across the stage].

112 **compassed** bay   114 **tapster** barkeep. (Proverbially slow at simple addition.)   118 **old** experienced.   **lifter** (With a pun on the meaning "thief.")   120 **puts me** i.e., puts. (*Me* is merely an emphatic marker implying "listen to this.")   127 **an** as if.   **an . . . autumn** i.e., his smile is like a dark and threatening rain cloud in autumn. (Cressida is teasing her uncle by dispraising Troilus.)   130 **stand . . . proof** i.e., not shrink from the test. (With bawdy pun on *stand,* be erect.)   133 **addle** spoiled   135 **idle** foolish. (With wordplay on *addle.*)   **you . . . shell** i.e., you would positively devour addled eggs (which are often spoiled in the sense of being several days old, so that the chick is starting to develop).   137 **marvelous** marvelously   139 **rack** torture device (used to elicit confessions).   145 **With millstones** i.e., Mirthlessly, since nothing has been said funny enough to make the eyes weep tears of laughter. (To *weep millstones* is to be cruel and heartless.)   147 **temperate** (since Cassandra was an unheeded prophetess who seldom laughed)   153 **An't** If it

158 **two-and-fifty** (Priam had fifty sons. Perhaps the forked hair is to count for two.)   **hairs** (With a pun on "heirs"; the Quarto spelling is "heires.")   165 **forked** (1) bifurcated (2) bearing a cuckold's horns. (The suggestion is that Helen will cheat Paris in love as she has done Menelaus.)   167 **so chafed** was so angry   168 **it passed** it exceeded all description. (But Cressida puns on the sense of "passed by.")   169 **it** i.e., Pandarus' story   174–5 **an 'twere** as if he were   175 **April** i.e., the season of showers.   176–7 **an 'twere . . . May** as if I were a nettle in anticipation of May. (Cressida will "nettle" Troilus.)   177 **s.d.** *retreat* trumpet signal for withdrawal.   183 **bravely** excellently.   187 **brave** excellent   193 **proper** handsome   197 **nod** nod of recognition. (With a pun on *noddy,* fool, simpleton.)   199 **the rich . . . more** i.e., the fool will become more foolish as you are, will receive the *nod,* or noddy (line 197).

PANDARUS   That's Hector, that, that, look you, that. There's a fellow! Go thy way, Hector! There's a brave man, niece. O brave Hector! Look how he looks! There's a countenance! Is't not a brave man?

CRESSIDA   Oh, a brave man!

PANDARUS   Is 'a not? It does a man's heart good. Look you what hacks are on his helmet! Look you yonder, do you see? Look you there. There's no jesting; there's laying on, take't off who will, as they say. There be hacks.   206 ... 208

CRESSIDA   Be those with swords?

Enter Paris [and passes across the stage].

PANDARUS   Swords, anything, he cares not; an the devil come to him, it's all one. By God's lid, it does one's heart good. Yonder comes Paris, yonder comes Paris. Look ye yonder, niece. Is't not a gallant man, too, is't not? Why, this is brave now. Who said he came hurt home today? He's not hurt. Why, this will do Helen's heart good now, ha! Would I could see Troilus now! You shall see Troilus anon.   212

CRESSIDA   Who's that?

Enter Helenus [and passes across the stage].

PANDARUS   That's Helenus. I marvel where Troilus is. That's Helenus. I think he went not forth today. That's Helenus.   221

CRESSIDA   Can Helenus fight, uncle?

PANDARUS   Helenus? No. Yes, he'll fight indifferent well. I marvel where Troilus is. Hark, do you not hear the people cry "Troilus"? Helenus is a priest.   224 ... 225

CRESSIDA   What sneaking fellow comes yonder?

Enter Troilus [and passes across the stage].

PANDARUS   Where? Yonder? That's Deiphobus. 'Tis Troilus! There's a man, niece! Hem! Brave Troilus! The prince of chivalry!

CRESSIDA   Peace, for shame, peace!

PANDARUS   Mark him, note him. O brave Troilus! Look well upon him, niece. Look you how his sword is bloodied and his helm more hacked than Hector's, and how he looks, and how he goes! O admirable youth! He ne'er saw three-and-twenty. Go thy way, Troilus, go thy way! Had I a sister were a grace, or a daughter a goddess, he should take his choice. O admirable man! Paris? Paris is dirt to him; and I warrant Helen, to change, would give an eye to boot.   234 ... 235 ... 237 ... 240 ... 241

[Enter common soldiers and pass across the stage.]

CRESSIDA   Here comes more.

PANDARUS   Asses, fools, dolts! Chaff and bran, chaff and bran! Porridge after meat! I could live and die i'th'eyes of Troilus. Ne'er look, ne'er look. The eagles are gone; crows and daws, crows and daws! I had rather be such a man as Troilus than Agamemnon and all Greece.   244 ... 246

CRESSIDA   There is among the Greeks Achilles, a better man than Troilus.

PANDARUS   Achilles? A drayman, a porter, a very camel.   251

CRESSIDA   Well, well.

PANDARUS   "Well, well"! Why, have you any discretion? Have you any eyes? Do you know what a man is? Is not birth, beauty, good shape, discourse, manhood, learning, gentleness, virtue, youth, liberality, and so forth, the spice and salt that season a man?

CRESSIDA   Ay, a minced man; and then to be baked with no date in the pie, for then the man's date is out.   258 ... 259

PANDARUS   You are such another woman! One knows not at what ward you lie.   261

CRESSIDA   Upon my back to defend my belly, upon my wit to defend my wiles, upon my secrecy to defend mine honesty, my mask to defend my beauty, and you to defend all these, and at all these wards I lie, at a thousand watches.   263 ... 264 ... 265 ... 266

PANDARUS   Say one of your watches.

CRESSIDA   Nay, I'll watch you for that; and that's one of the chiefest of them too. If I cannot ward what I would not have hit, I can watch you for telling how I took the blow—unless it swell past hiding, and then it's past watching.   269 ... 271 ... 272

PANDARUS   You are such another!   273

Enter [Troilus'] Boy.

BOY   Sir, my lord would instantly speak with you.

PANDARUS   Where?

BOY   At your own house. There he unarms him.

PANDARUS   Good boy, tell him I come.   *[Exit Boy.]*
I doubt he be hurt. Fare ye well, good niece.   278

CRESSIDA   Adieu, uncle.

PANDARUS   I'll be with you, niece, by and by.

CRESSIDA   To bring, uncle?   281

PANDARUS   Ay, a token from Troilus.

---

244 Porridge Soup (usually eaten before the meat course; after, it would be an anticlimax)   **246 daws** jackdaws (glossy, black crowlike birds)   **251 drayman** one who draws a cart   **258 minced** (1) chopped up fine (2) affected, effeminate   **259 the man's date is out** (1) the man is like a pie without any dates, a common ingredient used for flavoring (2) the man is past his prime. (With a suggestion, too, of his being a sexual failure.)   **261 at what . . . lie** what defensive postures you adopt. (*Ward* and *lie* are technical terms from fencing. Cressida picks up *lie* in a sexual sense.)   **263 my secrecy** (1) my ability to keep a secret (2) my sexual anatomy   **264 honesty** (1) chastity (2) reputation for chastity.   **mask** (Used to protect fair skin from tanning, considered unhandsome, and also to ward against public gaze.)   **265–6 at a thousand watches** i.e., guarding myself in a thousand ways. (Subsequently, in the wordplay, *watch* means "devotional exercises" or "night watches," line 267, "keep under observation," line 268, and "watch out lest you tell," line 270.)   **269 ward** shield   **271 swell** i.e., in pregnancy   **271–2 past watching** too late to do anything about.   **273 You . . . another!** i.e., What a woman you are!   **278 doubt** fear   **281 To bring** i.e., Are you bringing someone or something? (But Cressida's phrase also completes a colloquial expression, "be with you to bring," meaning roughly, "I'll get even with you.")

---

206 hacks dents, gashes   **208 laying on** i.e., evidence of blows exchanged.   **take't off who will** whatever anyone may say to the contrary. (With a pun on *taking off* as contrasted with *laying on*.)   **212 all one** all the same to him.   **By God's lid** By God's eyelid. (An oath.)   **221 he** Troilus   **224 indifferent** moderately   **225 marvel** wonder   **234 helm** helmet   **235 goes** walks.   **237 a grace** one of the three Graces, the personification of loveliness   **240–1 to change . . . boot** would give Paris plus one of her eyes besides to have Troilus in exchange.

CRESSIDA   By the same token, you are a bawd.

[Exit Pandarus.]

Words, vows, gifts, tears, and love's full sacrifice
He offers in another's enterprise;
But more in Troilus thousandfold I see
Than in the glass of Pandar's praise may be.   287
Yet hold I off. Women are angels, wooing;   288
Things won are done; joy's soul lies in the doing.
That she beloved knows naught that knows not this: 290
Men prize the thing ungained more than it is.   291
That she was never yet that ever knew   292
Love got so sweet as when desire did sue.   293
Therefore this maxim out of love I teach: 294
Achievement is command; ungained, beseech.   295
Then though my heart's contents firm love doth
    bear,   296
Nothing of that shall from mine eyes appear.

Exit [with Alexander].

❖

[1.3]

*[Sennet.] Enter Agamemnon, Nestor, Ulysses,
Diomedes, Menelaus, with others.*

AGAMEMNON   Princes,
What grief hath set the jaundice on your cheeks?   2
The ample proposition that hope makes   3
In all designs begun on earth below   4
Fails in the promised largeness. Checks and disasters 5
Grow in the veins of actions highest reared,   6
As knots, by the conflux of meeting sap,   7
Infects the sound pine and diverts his grain   8
Tortive and errant from his course of growth.   9
Nor, princes, is it matter new to us
That we come short of our suppose so far   11
That after seven years' siege yet Troy walls stand,   12
Sith every action that hath gone before,   13
Whereof we have record, trial did draw   14
Bias and thwart, not answering the aim   15
And that unbodied figure of the thought   16
That gave't surmisèd shape. Why then, you princes,   17

Do you with cheeks abashed behold our works
And think them shames, which are indeed naught
    else
But the protractive trials of great Jove   20
To find persistive constancy in men?   21
The fineness of which metal is not found
In Fortune's love; for then the bold and coward,   23
The wise and fool, the artist and unread,   24
The hard and soft, seem all affined and kin.   25
But in the wind and tempest of her frown,   26
Distinction, with a broad and powerful fan,   27
Puffing at all, winnows the light away,   28
And what hath mass or matter by itself
Lies rich in virtue and unminglèd.   30

NESTOR
With due observance of thy godly seat,   31
Great Agamemnon, Nestor shall apply   32
Thy latest words. In the reproof of chance   33
Lies the true proof of men. The sea being smooth,
How many shallow bauble boats dare sail   35
Upon her patient breast, making their way
With those of nobler bulk!
But let the ruffian Boreas once enrage   38
The gentle Thetis, and anon behold   39
The strong-ribbed bark through liquid mountains
    cut,
Bounding between the two moist elements   41
Like Perseus' horse. Where's then the saucy boat   42
Whose weak untimbered sides but even now   43
Corrivaled greatness? Either to harbor fled
Or made a toast for Neptune. Even so   45
Doth valor's show and valor's worth divide   46
In storms of Fortune. For in her ray and brightness   47
The herd hath more annoyance by the breese   48
Than by the tiger; but when the splitting wind
Makes flexible the knees of knotted oaks,
And flies fled under shade, why, then the thing of
    courage,   51
As roused with rage, with rage doth sympathize,   52
And with an accent tuned in selfsame key
Retorts to chiding Fortune.

ULYSSES   Agamemnon,

---

287 **glass** mirror   288 **wooing** being wooed   290 **That she** Any
woman. (Also in line 292.)   291 **than it is** than its intrinsic worth.
292–3 **That she . . . sue** No woman has ever lived who experienced
love so sweet as when the man still desires what he has not yet
obtained; the love once *got* or obtained by him is never the same.
294 **out of love** as from love's book   295 **Achievement . . . beseech**
To achieve and win a woman is to command her; not yet won, she
must be entreated.   296 **though . . . bear** though I carry firm love in
my heart
1.3. Location: The Greek camp. Before Agamemnon's tent.
0.1 *Sennet* trumpet call signaling a processional entrance or exit
2 jaundice sallowness of complexion   3–5 **The ample . . . largeness**
The ample hopes and desires that we humans propose for ourselves
fail to materialize fully as promised.   5–9 **Checks . . . growth** i.e.,
Hindrances and disasters attend great enterprises, just as knots, at the
points where a pine tree's sap should fully flow, adversely affect the
health of the tree by twisting and diverting the proper course of its
growth. (*Veins* are sap vessels in plants.)   7 **conflux** flowing together
8,9 **his** its   9 **Tortive and errant** twisted and deviating   11 **suppose**
expectation, purpose   12 **yet** still   13–17 **Sith . . . shape** since every
military action on record has gone awry in the doing of it, not corresponding to our aims and imaginings as to how it should go.

20 **protractive** drawn out   21 **persistive** enduring   23 **In Fortune's
love** i.e., when Fortune smiles   24 **artist** scholar   25 **affined** related
26 **her** Fortune's   27–8 **Distinction . . . away** (Fortune is a winnowing
tool, blowing away like chaff those who do not persevere and leaving
behind like grain those who do.)   30 **virtue** excellence.   **unminglèd**
unalloyed, uncontaminated.   31 **observance of** respect for.   **seat**
throne, i.e., dignity of office   32 **apply** explore the implications of
33 **In . . . chance** In the harsh test of misfortune   35 **bauble** toylike
38 **Boreas** north wind   39 **Thetis** a sea deity, mother of Achilles; here,
used for the sea itself. (Probably confused with Tethys, the wife of
Oceanus.)   41 **moist elements** air and water   42 **Perseus' horse** Pegasus, a winged horse that sprang from the blood of Medusa when
Perseus cut off her head. (The horse was given to Bellerophon by the
gods. It is associated, however, with Perseus, probably because Ovid
relates that the latter hero was mounted on Pegasus when he rescued
Andromeda from the sea monster.)   43 **but even now** only a moment
ago   45 **toast** rich morsel to be swallowed, like toasted bread floating in
liquor   46 **show** mere appearance   47 **storms of Fortune** trials and
tests visited by misfortune.   **her** Fortune's   48 **breese** gadfly   51 **fled**
are fled.   **the thing of courage** any brave heart   52 **As** being.
sympathize correspond

Thou great commander, nerves and bone of Greece,   55
Heart of our numbers, soul and only sprite,   56
In whom the tempers and the minds of all   57
Should be shut up, hear what Ulysses speaks.   58
Besides th'applause and approbation   59
The which, [*to Agamemnon*] most mighty for thy
        place and sway,
[*To Nestor*] And thou most reverend for thy
        stretched-out life,
I give to both your speeches, which were such
As Agamemnon and the hand of Greece
Should hold up high in brass, and such again   64
As venerable Nestor, hatched in silver,   65
Should with a bond of air, strong as the axletree   66
On which the heavens ride, knit all Greeks' ears   67
To his experienced tongue, yet let it please both,
Thou great, and wise, to hear Ulysses speak.

AGAMEMNON
Speak, Prince of Ithaca, and be't of less expect   70
That matter needless, of importless burden,   71
Divide thy lips, than we are confident,   72
When rank Thersites opes his mastic jaws,   73
We shall hear music, wit, and oracle.

ULYSSES
Troy, yet upon his basis, had been down,   75
And the great Hector's sword had lacked a master,
But for these instances.
The specialty of rule hath been neglected;   78
And look how many Grecian tents do stand   79
Hollow upon this plain, so many hollow factions.   80
When that the general is not like the hive   81
To whom the foragers shall all repair,   82
What honey is expected? Degree being vizarded,   83
Th'unworthiest shows as fairly in the mask.   84
The heavens themselves, the planets, and this center   85
Observe degree, priority, and place,
Insisture, course, proportion, season, form,   87
Office, and custom, in all line of order.
And therefore is the glorious planet Sol   89
In noble eminence enthroned and sphered   90

Amidst the other, whose med'cinable eye   91
Corrects the ill aspects of planets evil   92
And posts, like the commandment of a king,   93
Sans check, to good and bad. But when the planets   94
In evil mixture to disorder wander,   95
What plagues and what portents, what mutiny,
What raging of the sea, shaking of earth,
Commotion in the winds, frights, changes, horrors,
Divert and crack, rend and deracinate   99
The unity and married calm of states
Quite from their fixure! Oh, when degree is shaked,   101
Which is the ladder to all high designs,
The enterprise is sick. How could communities,
Degrees in schools, and brotherhoods in cities,   104
Peaceful commerce from dividable shores,   105
The primogeneity and due of birth,   106
Prerogative of age, crowns, scepters, laurels,
But by degree stand in authentic place?
Take but degree away, untune that string,
And hark what discord follows. Each thing meets
In mere oppugnancy. The bounded waters   111
Should lift their bosoms higher than the shores
And make a sop of all this solid globe;   113
Strength should be lord of imbecility,   114
And the rude son should strike his father dead;   115
Force should be right; or rather, right and wrong,
Between whose endless jar justice resides,   117
Should lose their names, and so should justice too.
Then everything includes itself in power,   119
Power into will, will into appetite;
And appetite, an universal wolf,
So doubly seconded with will and power,
Must make perforce an universal prey   123
And last eat up himself. Great Agamemnon,
This chaos, when degree is suffocate,   125
Follows the choking.   126
And this neglection of degree it is   127
That by a pace goes backward in a purpose   128
It hath to climb. The general's disdained   129
By him one step below, he by the next,
That next by him beneath; so every step,
Exampled by the first pace that is sick   132
Of his superior, grows to an envious fever   133
Of pale and bloodless emulation.

55 nerves sinews   **56 numbers** armies.   **sprite** spirit, animating principle   **57 tempers** dispositions   **58 shut up** gathered in, embodied   **59 approbation** approval   **64 Should . . . brass** should hold up for emulation, immortalized in brass inscription   **65 hatched in silver** (1) adorned with silver hair, a sign of age and wisdom (2) born wise   **66 bond of air** i.e., his breath or words as speech, powerful oration   **66–7 axletree . . . ride** axis on which the heavens, in the Ptolemaic cosmology, revolve around the earth   **70–2 be't . . . than** be it even less to be expected that matters of importance pass through your lips than that   **73 rank** disgusting, foul-smelling.   **mastic** gummy, abusive, scouring   **75 yet . . . basis** still standing on its foundations   **78 specialty of rule** particular rights and responsibilities of supreme authority   **79 look how many** however many, just as many   **80 Hollow** (1) empty, because of the present assembly (2) symbolizing faction   **81 When . . . hive** i.e., When General Agamemnon, and the general state he embodies, fail to serve as the focus of activity, the command center   **82 repair** return   **83 Degree being vizarded** When the hierarchical function of authority is masked   **84 shows as fairly** appears as attractive (as the most noble)   **85 this center** the earth, center of the Ptolemaic universe   **87 Insisture** steady continuance in their path   **89 Sol** sun. (Regarded as a planet because of its apparent movement around the earth.)   **90 sphered** placed in its sphere

91 other others.   **med'cinable** healing   **92 aspects** relative positions of the heavenly bodies as they appear to an observer on the earth's surface at a given time, and the influence attributed thereto   **93 posts** speeds   **94 Sans . . . bad** without pause, to foster the good and chastise the bad.   **95 mixture** conjunction   **99 deracinate** uproot   **101 fixure** stability.   **104 Degrees in schools** academic rank. **brotherhoods** corporations, guilds   **105 from . . . shores** between countries separated by the sea   **106 primogeneity** right of the eldest son to succeed to his father's estate   **111 mere oppugnancy** total strife.   **113 sop** piece of bread or cake floating in liquor; pulp   **114 imbecility** weakness   **115 rude** brutal   **117 Between . . . resides** i.e., justice is arrived at only through an unceasing adjudication between right and wrong. (*Jar* means "collision.")   **119 includes** subsumes   **123 Must . . . prey** must inevitably prey on everything   **125 suffocate** suffocated   **126 choking** act of suffocation.   **127 neglection** neglect   **128 by a pace** step by step   **128–9 in . . . climb** when it intends to climb.   **132–3 Exampled . . . superior** shown a precedent by the first envious step that his superior takes

And 'tis this fever that keeps Troy on foot,
Not her own sinews. To end a tale of length,
Troy in our weakness lives, not in her strength.

NESTOR
Most wisely hath Ulysses here discovered   138
The fever whereof all our power is sick.   139

AGAMEMNON
The nature of the sickness found, Ulysses,
What is the remedy?

ULYSSES
The great Achilles, whom opinion crowns
The sinew and the forehand of our host,   143
Having his ear full of his airy fame,   144
Grows dainty of his worth and in his tent   145
Lies mocking our designs. With him Patroclus
Upon a lazy bed the livelong day
Breaks scurril jests,
And with ridiculous and awkward action,
Which, slanderer, he imitation calls,
He pageants us. Sometime, great Agamemnon,   151
Thy topless deputation he puts on,   152
And like a strutting player, whose conceit   153
Lies in his hamstring, and doth think it rich   154
To hear the wooden dialogue and sound   155
Twixt his stretched footing and the scaffoldage,   156
Such to-be-pitied and o'erwrested seeming   157
He acts thy greatness in; and when he speaks,
'Tis like a chime a-mending, with terms unsquared,   159
Which, from the tongue of roaring Typhon dropped,   160
Would seem hyperboles. At this fusty stuff   161
The large Achilles, on his pressed bed lolling,   162
From his deep chest laughs out a loud applause,
Cries, "Excellent! 'Tis Agamemnon just.   164
Now play me Nestor; hem, and stroke thy beard,   165
As he being dressed to some oration."   166
That's done, as near as the extremest ends   167
Of parallels, as like as Vulcan and his wife,   168
Yet god Achilles still cries, "Excellent!
'Tis Nestor right. Now play him me, Patroclus,
Arming to answer in a night alarm."   171
And then, forsooth, the faint defects of age   172
Must be the scene of mirth; to cough and spit,
And with a palsy, fumbling on his gorget,   174

Shake in and out the rivet. And at this sport
Sir Valor dies; cries, "Oh, enough, Patroclus,
Or give me ribs of steel! I shall split all
In pleasure of my spleen." And in this fashion,   178
All our abilities, gifts, natures, shapes,
Severals and generals of grace exact,   180
Achievements, plots, orders, preventions,   181
Excitements to the field, or speech for truce,   182
Success or loss, what is or is not, serves
As stuff for these two to make paradoxes.   184

NESTOR
And in the imitation of these twain—
Who, as Ulysses says, opinion crowns   186
With an imperial voice—many are infect.   187
Ajax is grown self-willed and bears his head
In such a rein, in full as proud a place   189
As broad Achilles; keeps his tent like him;   190
Makes factious feasts; rails on our state of war,   191
Bold as an oracle; and sets Thersites,
A slave whose gall coins slanders like a mint,   193
To match us in comparisons with dirt,
To weaken and discredit our exposure,   195
How rank soever rounded in with danger.   196

ULYSSES
They tax our policy and call it cowardice,   197
Count wisdom as no member of the war,   198
Forestall prescience, and esteem no act   199
But that of hand. The still and mental parts   200
That do contrive how many hands shall strike
When fitness calls them on and know by measure   202
Of their observant toil the enemy's weight—   203
Why, this hath not a finger's dignity.   204
They call this bed-work, mapp'ry, closet war;   205
So that the ram that batters down the wall,   206
For the great swinge and rudeness of his poise,   207
They place before his hand that made the engine,   208
Or those that with the fineness of their souls   209
By reason guide his execution.   210

NESTOR
Let this be granted, and Achilles' horse   211
Makes many Thetis' sons.   [Tucket.]   212

---

138 discovered revealed   **139 power** army   **143 forehand** first in might.   **host** army   **144 airy fame** unsubstantial reputation **145 dainty** fastidious   **151 pageants** mimics   **152 topless deputation** supreme power   **153–4 whose . . . hamstring** i.e., whose wits are in his thighs   **154 rich** admirable   **155–6 To hear . . . scaffoldage** i.e., to hear the echoing sound of his marching to and fro on the stage or scaffolding   **157 to-be-pitied . . . seeming** pitiful and exaggerated acting   **159 a-mending** being repaired or retuned.   **terms unsquared** expressions unadapted to their subject, ill-fitted (like unsquared timbers or stones in architecture)   **160 from** even if from. **Typhon** Greek mythological monster with a hundred heads that breathed fire; he made war against the gods and was destroyed by one of Zeus's thunderbolts   **161 fusty** stale. (And suggesting *fustian,* bombastic.)   **162 pressed** weighed down (by its occupant)   **164 just** exactly.   **165 me** for my benefit. (Also in line 170.)   **166 dressed** addressed   **167–8 as near . . . parallels** (Parallel lines never meet, no matter how far they are extended.)   **168 Vulcan . . . wife** i.e., the ugliest god, and Venus, the most beautiful goddess   **171 answer . . . alarm** respond to a nighttime military alert.   **172 faint** weak **174 palsy** tremor.   **gorget** piece of armor for the throat

178 spleen (Regarded as the seat of laughter.)   **180 Severals . . . exact** well-ordered gifts, individual and general   **181 preventions** defensive precautions   **182 Excitements** exhortations   **184 paradoxes** absurdities.   **186–7 crowns . . . voice** i.e., regards most highly, adulates **189 In . . . rein** i.e., so haughtily   **190 broad** hefty.   **keeps** keeps to **191 factious** for his faction; seditious   **our state of war** our state of preparedness for war; our soldiers in their readiness   **193 slave** contemptible person.   **gall** the seat of bile and rancor   **195 exposure** vulnerable situation   **196 rank** thickly.   **rounded in with** surrounded by   **197 tax our policy** censure our prudent management   **198 no member** no fit guide or companion   **199 Forestall prescience** condemn beforehand any attempts at foresight   **200 that of hand** any immediate physical response.   **202 fitness** suitability of occasion **202–3 know . . . weight** figure out by laborious calculation the enemy's strength   **204 hath . . . dignity** is not worth a snap of the fingers. **205 bed-work . . . war** i.e., armchair strategy, mere map-making, war planned in the study   **206–10 So . . . execution** so that they put more value on the great battering ram, because of it huge impetus and roughness of impact, than they give to military planners and generals who, with their superior insight, guide its operation.   **211–12 Let . . . sons** If this is granted, then Achilles's horse in its brute strength outvalues many an Achilles (the son of Thetis).   **212 s.d. Tucket** signal given on a trumpet

AGAMEMNON   What trumpet? Look, Menelaus.
MENELAUS   From Troy.

[*Enter Aeneas with a trumpeter.*]

AGAMEMNON   What would you 'fore our tent?
AENEAS
    Is this great Agamemnon's tent, I pray you?
AGAMEMNON   Even this.
AENEAS
    May one that is a herald and a prince
    Do a fair message to his kingly ears?
AGAMEMNON
    With surety stronger than Achilles' arm   220
    'Fore all the Greekish host, which with one voice   221
    Call Agamemnon head and general.
AENEAS
    Fair leave and large security. How may   223
    A stranger to those most imperial looks
    Know them from eyes of other mortals?
AGAMEMNON   How?
AENEAS
    Ay. I ask, that I might waken reverence,
    And bid the cheek be ready with a blush
    Modest as morning when she coldly eyes   229
    The youthful Phoebus.   230
    Which is that god in office, guiding men?
    Which is the high and mighty Agamemnon?
AGAMEMNON
    This Trojan scorns us, or the men of Troy
    Are ceremonious courtiers.
AENEAS
    Courtiers as free, as debonair, unarmed,   235
    As bending angels—that's their fame in peace.   236
    But when they would seem soldiers, they have galls,   237
    Good arms, strong joints, true swords, and—Jove's
        accord—   238
    Nothing so full of heart. But peace, Aeneas,   239
    Peace, Trojan; lay thy finger on thy lips!
    The worthiness of praise distains his worth,   241
    If that the praised himself bring the praise forth.   242
    But what the repining enemy commends,   243
    That breath fame blows; that praise, sole pure,
        transcends.   244
AGAMEMNON
    Sir, you of Troy, call you yourself Aeneas?
AENEAS   Ay, Greek, that is my name.
AGAMEMNON   What's your affair, I pray you?

AENEAS
    Sir, pardon. 'Tis for Agamemnon's ears.
AGAMEMNON
    He hears naught privately that comes from Troy.
AENEAS
    Nor I from Troy come not to whisper him.   250
    I bring a trumpet to awake his ear,   251
    To set his sense on the attentive bent,   252
    And then to speak.
AGAMEMNON   Speak frankly as the wind;
    It is not Agamemnon's sleeping hour.
    That thou shalt know, Trojan, he is awake,
    He tells thee so himself.
AENEAS   Trumpet, blow loud;
    Send thy brass voice through all these lazy tents,
    And every Greek of mettle, let him know
    What Troy means fairly shall be spoke aloud.
                                        Sound trumpet.
    We have, great Agamemnon, here in Troy
    A prince called Hector—Priam is his father—
    Who in this dull and long-continued truce
    Is resty grown. He bade me take a trumpet   263
    And to this purpose speak: Kings, princes, lords!
    If there be one among the fair'st of Greece
    That holds his honor higher than his ease,
    That seeks his praise more than he fears his peril,
    That knows his valor and knows not his fear,
    That loves his mistress more than in confession   269
    With truant vows to her own lips he loves,   270
    And dare avow her beauty and her worth
    In other arms than hers—to him this challenge.   272
    Hector, in view of Trojans and of Greeks,
    Shall make it good, or do his best to do it,
    He hath a lady, wiser, fairer, truer,
    Than ever Greek did compass in his arms,   276
    And will tomorrow with his trumpet call
    Midway between your tents and walls of Troy
    To rouse a Grecian that is true in love.
    If any come, Hector shall honor him;
    If none, he'll say in Troy when he retires,
    The Grecian dames are sunburnt and not worth   282
    The splinter of a lance. Even so much.   283
AGAMEMNON
    This shall be told our lovers, Lord Aeneas.
    If none of them have soul in such a kind,   285
    We left them all at home. But we are soldiers;
    And may that soldier a mere recreant prove   287
    That means not, hath not, or is not in love!   288
    If then one is, or hath, or means to be,
    That one meets Hector; if none else, I am he.

---

220 surety security   **221 'Fore . . . voice** leading into battle the entire
Greek army, who with one voice   **223 Fair leave** Courteous permission   **229 she** i.e., Aurora, the blushing dawn goddess.   **coldly**
demurely   **230 Phoebus** Apollo, here referred to as the sun-god.
235 free generous.   **debonair** gracious in manner   **236 bending**
bowing.   **fame** reputation   **237 galls** i.e., spirit to resent injury. (See
line 193.)   **238 Jove's accord** Jove being in full accord, God willing
239 Nothing . . . heart nothing is so full of unequaled courage as they.
241 distains his sullies its own   **242 If . . . forth** if the person being
praised is the one who speaks this praise.   **243–4 But . . . transcends**
But whenever an enemy offers praise, being naturally reluctant to do
so, that praise is trumpeted by Fame herself; such praise is transcendent because it is unmixed with unworthy motives.

250 whisper whisper to   **251 trumpet** trumpeter   **252 set . . . bent**
i.e., bend his sense of hearing attentively toward me   **263 resty** sluggish, inactive, restive   **269–70 That . . . loves** i.e., who shows his love
for his beloved more in deeds of arms than in sweet nothings
promised lip to lip   **272 In . . . hers** i.e., in the arms of warfare rather
than those of his mistress   **276 compass** encompass, embrace
282 sunburnt i.e., unattractive, according to Elizabethan tastes in
beauty   **283 Even so much** (A formulaic conclusion to a delivered
message, meaning, "that is the totality of what I am bid to say.")
285 have . . . kind i.e., have the spirit to undertake this challenge
287 mere recreant utter coward   **288 means not** intends not to be

NESTOR
Tell him of Nestor, one that was a man
When Hector's grandsire sucked. He is old now,
But if there be not in our Grecian host
One noble man that hath one spark of fire
To answer for his love, tell him from me
I'll hide my silver beard in a gold beaver,   296
And in my vambrace put this withered brawn,   297
And meeting him will tell him that my lady
Was fairer than his grandam and as chaste   299
As may be in the world. His youth in flood,   300
I'll prove this truth with my three drops of blood.

AENEAS
Now heavens forbid such scarcity of youth!

ULYSSES   Amen.

AGAMEMNON
Fair Lord Aeneas, let me touch your hand;
To our pavilion shall I lead you first.
Achilles shall have word of this intent;
So shall each lord of Greece, from tent to tent.
Yourself shall feast with us before you go,
And find the welcome of a noble foe.   309

[*Exeunt. Manent Ulysses and Nestor.*]

ULYSSES   Nestor!

NESTOR   What says Ulysses?

ULYSSES
I have a young conception in my brain;
Be you my time to bring it to some shape.   313

NESTOR   What is't?

ULYSSES   This 'tis:
Blunt wedges rive hard knots; the seeded pride   316
That hath to this maturity blown up   317
In rank Achilles must or now be cropped   318
Or, shedding, breed a nursery of like evil   319
To overbulk us all.

NESTOR   Well, and how?   320

ULYSSES
This challenge that the gallant Hector sends,
However it is spread in general name,
Relates in purpose only to Achilles.

NESTOR
The purpose is perspicuous even as substance,   324
Whose grossness little characters sum up;   325
And, in the publication, make no strain   326
But that Achilles, were his brain as barren
As banks of Libya—though, Apollo knows,   328
'Tis dry enough—will, with great speed of judgment,   329
Ay, with celerity, find Hector's purpose

Pointing on him.

ULYSSES   And wake him to the answer, think you?

NESTOR
Yes, 'tis most meet. Who may you else oppose   333
That can from Hector bring his honor off   334
If not Achilles? Though 't be a sportful combat,
Yet in this trial much opinion dwells,   336
For here the Trojans taste our dear'st repute   337
With their fin'st palate. And trust to me, Ulysses,   338
Our imputation shall be oddly poised   339
In this wild action. For the success,   340
Although particular, shall give a scantling   341
Of good or bad unto the general;   342
And in such indices, although small pricks   343
To their subsequent volumes, there is seen   344
The baby figure of the giant mass
Of things to come at large. It is supposed
He that meets Hector issues from our choice;
And choice, being mutual act of all our souls,
Makes merit her election and doth boil,   349
As 'twere from forth us all, a man distilled
Out of our virtues; who miscarrying,   351
What heart from hence receives the conquering part,   352
To steel a strong opinion to themselves?   353
Which entertained, limbs are his instruments,   354
In no less working than are swords and bows   355
Directive by the limbs.   356

ULYSSES   Give pardon to my speech:
Therefore 'tis meet Achilles meet not Hector.   358
Let us, like merchants, show our foulest wares,
And think perchance they'll sell; if not,
The lustre of the better yet to show
Shall show the better. Do not consent
That ever Hector and Achilles meet;
For both our honor and our shame in this
Are dogged with two strange followers.

NESTOR
I see them not with my old eyes. What are they?

ULYSSES
What glory our Achilles shares from Hector,   367
Were he not proud, we all should wear with him.
But he already is too insolent,
And we were better parch in Afric sun

---

296 beaver face guard of a helmet   **297 vambrace** armor for the front
part of the arm.   **brawn** i.e., arm   **299 grandam** grandmother
300 His . . . flood i.e., Though Hector's manhood and vigor be at their
height   **309.1 *Manent*** They remain   **313 Be . . . time** i.e., Act as midwife to my newly conceived plan   **316 rive** split, break apart. **seeded
pride** pride that has gone to seed, overblown   **317 blown up**
sprouted, puffed up   **318 rank** overripe, swollen.   **or** either
319 shedding if it scatters its seeds.   **nursery** (1) breeding ground
(2) crop   **320 overbulk** overwhelm, outgrow   **324–5 perspicuous . . .
up** as perceivable as great wealth or matter, the size of which can be
rendered in little figures   **326 in . . . strain** when it is publicly announced, have no doubt   **328 banks** sandbanks; shores
329 dry dull

333 meet fitting.   **else oppose** otherwise put forward as opponent
334 That . . . off who can acquit himself honorably in doing battle
with Hector   **336 opinion** reputation   **337 taste our dear'st repute**
i.e., put to the test Achilles, our warrior of greatest reputation
338 their fin'st palate i.e., Hector.   **339 Our imputation** what is
imputed to us, our reputation.   **oddly poised** unequally balanced
340 wild rash.   **success** outcome   **341 particular** relating to (two)
particular men.   **scantling** specimen, sample   **342 general** army at
large   **343 indices** indications, table of contents   **343–4 small . . .
volumes** small indicators in comparison with the volumes that follow
349 election basis of choice   **351 miscarrying** i.e., if he should fail
352 What . . . part what cheer will the conquering party, i.e., the Trojans, receive from this   **353 steel** strengthen   **354–6 Which . . . limbs**
And in that strengthening of opinion, the limbs that direct the use of
weapons are held no less effective than the weapons themselves. (The
implication is that those who choose a challenger to Hector will be
held as fully to account as the challenger himself.)   **358 meet** fitting
367 shares from gains at the expense of

Than in the pride and salt scorn of his eyes,
Should he scape Hector fair. If he were foiled, 372
Why then we did our main opinion crush 373
In taint of our best man. No, make a lottery, 374
And, by device, let blockish Ajax draw
The sort to fight with Hector. Among ourselves 376
Give him allowance as the worthier man; 377
For that will physic the great Myrmidon 378
Who broils in loud applause, and make him fall 379
His crest that prouder than blue Iris bends. 380
If the dull brainless Ajax come safe off,
We'll dress him up in voices; if he fail, 382
Yet go we under our opinion still
That we have better men. But, hit or miss,
Our project's life this shape of sense assumes: 385
Ajax employed plucks down Achilles' plumes.

NESTOR
Now, Ulysses, I begin to relish thy advice;
And I will give a taste of it forthwith
To Agamemnon. Go we to him straight.
Two curs shall tame each other; pride alone
Must tar the mastiffs on, as 'twere their bone. 391

Exeunt.

❖

[2.1]

Enter Ajax and Thersites.

AJAX   Thersites!

THERSITES   Agamemnon—how if he had boils, full, all
over, generally?

AJAX   Thersites!

THERSITES   And those boils did run? Say so. Did not the
General run, then? Were not that a botchy core? 6

AJAX   Dog!

THERSITES   Then there would come some matter from 8
him. I see none now.

AJAX   Thou bitch-wolf's son, canst thou not hear?
[*Strikes him.*] Feel, then.

THERSITES   The plague of Greece upon thee, thou mon- 12
grel beef-witted lord! 13

AJAX   Speak then, thou vinewed'st leaven, speak. I will 14
beat thee into handsomeness.

THERSITES   I shall sooner rail thee into wit and holiness;
but I think thy horse will sooner con an oration than 17
thou learn a prayer without book. Thou canst strike, 18
canst thou? A red murrain o' thy jade's tricks! 19

AJAX   Toadstool, learn me the proclamation. 20

THERSITES   Dost thou think I have no sense, thou strik- 21
est me thus?

AJAX   The proclamation!

THERSITES   Thou art proclaimed a fool, I think.

AJAX   Do not, porcupine, do not. My fingers itch. 25

THERSITES   I would thou didst itch from head to foot.
An I had the scratching of thee, I would make thee the
loathsomest scab in Greece. When thou art forth in the
incursions, thou strikest as slow as another. 29

AJAX   I say, the proclamation!

THERSITES   Thou grumblest and railest every hour on
Achilles, and thou art as full of envy at his greatness as
Cerberus is at Proserpina's beauty, ay, that thou 33
bark'st at him.

AJAX   Mistress Thersites!

THERSITES   Thou shouldst strike him— 36

AJAX   Cobloaf! 37

THERSITES   He would pun thee into shivers with his 38
fist, as a sailor breaks a biscuit.

AJAX   [*beating him*]   You whoreson cur!

THERSITES   Do, do. 41

AJAX   Thou stool for a witch! 42

THERSITES   Ay, do, do, thou sodden-witted lord! Thou 43
hast no more brain than I have in mine elbows; an
asinego may tutor thee. Thou scurvy-valiant ass! Thou 45
art here but to thrash Trojans, and thou art bought 46
and sold among those of any wit, like a barbarian 47
slave. If thou use to beat me, I will begin at thy heel 48
and tell what thou art by inches, thou thing of no 49
bowels, thou! 50

AJAX   You dog!

THERSITES   You scurvy lord!

AJAX   [*beating him*]   You cur!

THERSITES   Mars his idiot! Do, rudeness, do, camel, 54
do, do.

[*Enter Achilles and Patroclus.*]

ACHILLES   Why, how now, Ajax, wherefore do ye thus? 56
How now, Thersites, what's the matter, man?

THERSITES   You see him there, do you?

ACHILLES   Ay; what's the matter?

THERSITES   Nay, look upon him.

ACHILLES   So I do. What's the matter?

THERSITES   Nay, but regard him well.

---

372 scape Hector fair come off undefeated in fighting Hector. (Ulysses's argument is that Achilles, already too proud, will be insufferable if he wins, and that, if he loses, the Greeks will undergo the humiliation of losing with their best-reputed warrior.)   **373–4 we . . . taint** we would destroy the mainstay of our reputation in the dishonor   **376 sort** lot   **377 allowance as** acknowledgment as   **378 physic** purge medically.   **Myrmidon** i.e., Achilles. (So called here because accompanied by a band of Myrmidon warriors, from a tribe living in Thessaly.)   **379 broils in** basks in.   **379–80 and make . . . bends** and cause him to lower the plumes of his helmet that now arch and wave more proudly than the rainbow. (Literally, Iris, the many-colored messenger of Juno.)   **382 voices** applause   **385 life** success   **391 tar** provoke
2.1. Location: The Greek camp; Achilles's tent.
6 botchy core central hard mass of a boil or tumor.   **8 matter** (1) sense (2) pus   **12–13 mongrel** (Ajax's mother was a Trojan, the sister of Priam; compare 2.2.77 [note], 4.5.84, and 4.5.121.)   **13 beef-witted** i.e., slow-witted. (Perhaps this refers to the belief that eating beef made one dull, or Thersites may merely be calling Ajax a "stupid ox.")   **14 vinewed'st leaven** moldiest dough

17 con memorize   **18 without book** by heart   **19 murrain** plague. **jade's tricks** i.e., ill-tempered kicking and rearing, as of a worthless horse   **20 learn me** find out for me   **21 sense** feeling   **25 porcupine** (A term of abuse for one who is prickly and small.)   **29 incursions** i.e., attacks upon the Trojan forces   **33 Cerberus** three-headed dog that guarded the entrance to Hades.   **Proserpina** Queen of Hades **36 Thou** If thou   **37 Cobloaf** Small round loaf; a bun   **38 pun** pound.   **shivers** fragments   **41 Do** i.e., Go ahead, I dare you **42 stool** privy   **43 sodden-witted** boiled-brained   **45 asinego** little ass   **46–7 bought and sold** i.e., treated like merchandise   **48 use** continue   **49 by inches** methodically, inch by inch   **50 bowels** sensitivity, human feeling   **54 Mars his** Mars's   **56 wherefore** why

ACHILLES   Well, why, I do so.

THERSITES   But yet you look not well upon him; for, whomsomever you take him to be, he is Ajax.   65

ACHILLES   I know that, fool.

THERSITES   Ay, but that fool knows not himself.   67

AJAX   Therefore I beat thee.   68

THERSITES   Lo, lo, lo, lo, what modicums of wit he utters! His evasions have ears thus long. I have bobbed his brain more than he has beat my bones. I will buy nine sparrows for a penny, and his pia mater is not worth the ninth part of a sparrow. This lord, Achilles —Ajax, who wears his wit in his belly and his guts in his head—I'll tell you what I say of him.   69 70 71 72

ACHILLES   What?

THERSITES   I say, this Ajax—   [Ajax threatens him.]

ACHILLES   Nay, good Ajax.

THERSITES   Has not so much wit—

ACHILLES   Nay, I must hold you.

THERSITES   As will stop the eye of Helen's needle, for whom he comes to fight.   81

ACHILLES   Peace, fool!

THERSITES   I would have peace and quietness, but the fool will not—he there, that he. Look you there.

AJAX   Oh, thou damned cur! I shall—

ACHILLES   Will you set your wit to a fool's?   87

THERSITES   No, I warrant you, for a fool's will shame it.   88

PATROCLUS   Good words, Thersites.   89

ACHILLES   What's the quarrel?

AJAX   I bade the vile owl go learn me the tenor of the proclamation, and he rails upon me.

THERSITES   I serve thee not.

AJAX   Well, go to, go to.

THERSITES   I serve here voluntary.   95

ACHILLES   Your last service was suff'rance, 'twas not voluntary; no man is beaten voluntary. Ajax was here the voluntary, and you as under an impress.   96 98

THERSITES   E'en so. A great deal of your wit, too, lies in your sinews, or else there be liars. Hector shall have a great catch an 'a knock out either of your brains; 'a were as good crack a fusty nut with no kernel.   99 100 101 102

ACHILLES   What, with me too, Thersites?

THERSITES   There's Ulysses and old Nestor, whose wit was moldy ere your grandsires had nails on their toes, yoke you like draft-oxen and make you plow up the war.

ACHILLES   What? What?

THERSITES   Yes, good sooth. To, Achilles! To, Ajax! To!   109

AJAX   I shall cut out your tongue.

THERSITES   'Tis no matter. I shall speak as much wit as thou afterwards.   112

PATROCLUS   No more words, Thersites. Peace!

THERSITES   I will hold my peace when Achilles' brach bids me, shall I?   114

ACHILLES   There's for you, Patroclus.

THERSITES   I will see you hanged like clodpolls ere I come any more to your tents. I will keep where there is wit stirring and leave the faction of fools.   Exit.   117

PATROCLUS   A good riddance.

ACHILLES
Marry, this, sir, is proclaimed through all our host:
That Hector, by the fifth hour of the sun,   122
Will with a trumpet twixt our tents and Troy
Tomorrow morning call some knight to arms
That hath a stomach, and such a one that dare   125
Maintain—I know not what, 'tis trash. Farewell.

AJAX   Farewell. Who shall answer him?

ACHILLES   I know not. 'Tis put to lottery. Otherwise
He knew his man.   [Exit with Patroclus.]   129

AJAX   Oh, meaning you? I will go learn more of it.
                                                                        Exit.

❖

[2.2]

Enter Priam, Hector, Troilus, Paris, and Helenus.

PRIAM
After so many hours, lives, speeches spent,
Thus once again says Nestor from the Greeks:
"Deliver Helen, and all damage else—   3
As honor, loss of time, travail, expense,   4
Wounds, friends, and what else dear that is consumed
In hot digestion of this cormorant war—   6
Shall be struck off." Hector, what say you to't?   7

HECTOR
Though no man lesser fears the Greeks than I
As far as toucheth my particular,   9
Yet, dread Priam,
There is no lady of more softer bowels,   11
More spongy to suck in the sense of fear,
More ready to cry out, "Who knows what follows?"
Than Hector is. The wound of peace is surety,   14
Surety secure; but modest doubt is called   15
The beacon of the wise, the tent that searches   16

---

65 **Ajax** (With probable pun on *a jakes,* a latrine.)   67 **that fool . . . himself** (Thersites answers as though Achilles had said, "I know that fool.")   68 **Therefore . . . thee** i.e., I beat you because you are the real fool, not me. (This attempt at wit draws Thersites's sarcasm in the next speech.)   69 **modicums** small amounts   70 **have . . . long** i.e., are those of an ass, are asinine.   **bobbed** thumped   71 **will** can   **pia mater** (Literally, membrane cover of the brain; used here for the brain.)   81 **stop** stop up, fill. (Perhaps with a bawdy sense.)   **Helen's needle** (Aristocratic women customarily did needlework as an avocation.)   87 **set your wit to** match wits with   88 **a fool's . . . shame it** i.e., Ajax's intelligence is even less than a fool's.   89 **Good words** i.e., Speak gently   95 **voluntary** voluntarily.   96 **suff'rance** something imposed   98 **impress** (1) impressment, military draft (2) imprint (of blows).   99 **E'en so** Exactly.   100 **or . . . liars** unless Report is a liar.   101 **an 'a** if he   101–2 **'a . . . good** he might as well   102 **fusty** moldy

109 **To . . . To!** (Thersites impersonates Nestor and Ulysses as drivers of a team, urging Achilles and Ajax to plow.)   112 **afterwards** i.e., even after my tongue is cut out.   114 **brach** bitch hound. (The Quarto reading, "brooch," could mean "bauble, plaything," referring to Patroclus.)   117 **clodpolls** blockheads   122 **fifth hour** eleven o'clock   125 **stomach** appetite (for fighting)   129 **knew** would know
2.2. Location: Troy. The palace.
3 **Deliver** Hand over   4 **travail** strenuous effort   6 **cormorant** voracious (like the seabird)   7 **struck off** canceled.   9 **my particular** me personally   11 **bowels** i.e., mercy, pity   14 **The . . . surety** The danger of peace is in the sense of overconfidence and security it breeds   15 **secure** overconfident.   **modest doubt** a reasonable estimate of danger   16 **beacon** warning signal.   **tent** surgical probe

To th'bottom of the worst. Let Helen go.
Since the first sword was drawn about this question,
Every tithe soul, 'mongst many thousand dismes,   19
Hath been as dear as Helen; I mean, of ours.
If we have lost so many tenths of ours   21
To guard a thing not ours—nor worth to us,
Had it our name, the value of one ten—   23
What merit's in that reason which denies   24
The yielding of her up?

TROILUS   Fie, fie, my brother!
Weigh you the worth and honor of a king
So great as our dread father in a scale
Of common ounces? Will you with counters sum   28
The past-proportion of his infinite,   29
And buckle in a waist most fathomless   30
With spans and inches so diminutive   31
As fears and reasons? Fie, for godly shame!   32

HELENUS [to Troilus]
No marvel, though you bite so sharp at reasons,   33
You are so empty of them. Should not our father   34
Bear the great sway of his affairs with reason,
Because your speech hath none that tell him so?   36

TROILUS
You are for dreams and slumbers, brother priest;
You fur your gloves with reason. Here are your
    reasons: 38
You know an enemy intends you harm;
You know a sword employed is perilous,
And reason flies the object of all harm.   41
Who marvels then, when Helenus beholds
A Grecian and his sword, if he do set
The very wings of reason to his heels
And fly like chidden Mercury from Jove   45
Or like a star disorbed? Nay, if we talk of reason,   46
Let's shut our gates and sleep. Manhood and honor
Should have hare hearts, would they but fat their
    thoughts   48
With this crammed reason. Reason and respect   49
Make livers pale and lustihood deject.   50

HECTOR [to Troilus]
Brother, she is not worth what she doth cost

The holding.

TROILUS   What's aught but as 'tis valued?
HECTOR
But value dwells not in particular will;   53
It holds his estimate and dignity   54
As well wherein 'tis precious of itself   55
As in the prizer. 'Tis mad idolatry   56
To make the service greater than the god;
And the will dotes that is inclinable   58
To what infectiously itself affects   59
Without some image of th'affected merit.   60

TROILUS
I take today a wife, and my election   61
Is led on in the conduct of my will—
My will enkindled by mine eyes and ears,
Two traded pilots twixt the dangerous shores   64
Of will and judgment. How may I avoid,   65
Although my will distaste what it elected,   66
The wife I chose? There can be no evasion
To blench from this and to stand firm by honor.   68
We turn not back the silks upon the merchant
When we have soiled them, nor the remainder viands   70
We do not throw in unrespective sieve   71
Because we now are full. It was thought meet
Paris should do some vengeance on the Greeks.   73
Your breath of full consent bellied his sails;   74
The seas and winds, old wranglers, took a truce   75
And did him service. He touched the ports desired,
And for an old aunt whom the Greeks held captive   77
He brought a Grecian queen, whose youth and
    freshness
Wrinkles Apollo's and makes stale the morning.   79
Why keep we her? The Grecians keep our aunt.
Is she worth keeping? Why, she is a pearl
Whose price hath launched above a thousand ships   82
And turned crowned kings to merchants.   83
If you'll avouch 'twas wisdom Paris went—
As you must needs, for you all cried, "Go, go"—
If you'll confess he brought home noble prize—
As you must needs, for you all clapped your hands
And cried, "Inestimable!"—why do you now

19 Every . . . dismes every human life exacted by the war as a tithe or tenth, amongst many thousand such exactions   **21 tenths** i.e., lives exacted by the war   **23 Had . . . name** i.e., even if Helen were a Trojan.   **one ten** one tithe exacted by the war, one Trojan life   **24 reason** reasoning   **28–32 Will . . . reasons?** Will you employ the valueless disks used by shopkeepers in their commercial bargaining to sum up Priam's infinite worth exceeding all calculation, and attempt to confine his unfathomable greatness with fears and pretexts that are as puny as the nine-inch span from hand to thumb?   **33 reasons** (Pronounced like "raisins," with pun.)   **34 not our father** our father not   **36 Because . . . so?** i.e., simply because you unreasonably urge him to govern unreasonably?   **38 fur** line with soft fur. (Troilus accuses Helenus of using reason as a justification for personal comfort, explaining cowardly flight as prudence.)   **41 And . . . harm** and such cowardly "reason" flees at the sight of anything threatening.   **45 chidden Mercury** (Mercury as Jove's errand boy was subject to his chiding or impatient bidding.)   **46 disorbed** removed from its sphere (like a shooting star).   **48–9 Should . . . reason** would have the craven hearts of hares if they would cram their thoughts with this "reason."   **49 respect** caution   **50 livers pale** (A bloodless liver was thought to be a sign of cowardice.)   **and . . . deject** and bodily vigor overthrown.

53 particular will i.e., one person's preference merely   **54 his** its.   **dignity** worth   **55–6 As well . . . prizer** as much in its intrinsic worth as in the opinion of the person who prizes or appraises it.   **58–60 the will . . . merit** any will is mere willfulness that is derived from the will's own diseased affection without some visible appearance of merit in the thing desired.   **61 I take today a wife** (Troilus, in setting up a hypothetical case that applies to Paris, is also stating his own credo about love.)   **election** choice   **64 traded** skillful in their trade; trafficking back and forth   **65 avoid** rid myself of   **66 distaste** dislike (in time)   **68 blench** shrink.   **and** and simultaneously   **70 remainder viands** leftover food   **71 unrespective sieve** undiscriminating receptacle, i.e., garbage can   **73 vengeance** i.e., in return for Hesione's abduction; see line 77 and note   **74 bellied** swelled   **75 old wranglers** traditional enemies   **77 an old aunt** i.e., Hesione, Priam's sister, rescued from the wrath of Poseidon by Hercules and bestowed by him on the Greek, Telamon, father of Ajax; we learn in 4.5.84 and 4.5.121 that she was Ajax' mother   **79 Wrinkles Apollo's** makes Apollo's youthful countenance look old and ugly by comparison   **82 Whose . . . ships** (Perhaps echoes the famous line from Marlowe's *Doctor Faustus:* "Was this the face that launched a thousand ships?")   **83 turned . . . merchants** i.e., has made kings behave like merchants seeking a rare pearl. (Compare Matthew 13:45.)

The issue of your proper wisdoms rate   89
And do a deed that never Fortune did,   90
Beggar the estimation which you prized   91
Richer than sea and land? Oh, theft most base,
That we have stol'n what we do fear to keep!
But thieves unworthy of a thing so stol'n,   94
That in their country did them that disgrace   95
We fear to warrant in our native place!   96

> Enter Cassandra, [*raving,*] *with her hair about
> her ears.*

CASSANDRA
    Cry, Trojans, cry!
PRIAM   What noise? What shriek is this?
TROILUS
    'Tis our mad sister. I do know her voice.
CASSANDRA   Cry, Trojans!
HECTOR   It is Cassandra.
CASSANDRA
    Cry, Trojans, cry! Lend me ten thousand eyes,
    And I will fill them with prophetic tears.
HECTOR   Peace, sister, peace!
CASSANDRA
    Virgins and boys, mid-age and wrinkled old,   104
    Soft infancy, that nothing canst but cry,   105
    Add to my clamor! Let us pay betimes   106
    A moiety of that mass of moan to come.   107
    Cry, Trojans, cry! Practice your eyes with tears!   108
    Troy must not be, nor goodly Ilium stand;
    Our firebrand brother, Paris, burns us all.   110
    Cry, Trojans, cry! A Helen and a woe!
    Cry, cry! Troy burns, or else let Helen go.   *Exit.*
HECTOR
    Now, youthful Troilus, do not these high strains
    Of divination in our sister work
    Some touches of remorse? Or is your blood
    So madly hot that no discourse of reason,
    Nor fear of bad success in a bad cause,
    Can qualify the same?
TROILUS   Why, brother Hector,   118
    We may not think the justness of each act   119
    Such and no other than th'event doth form it,   120
    Nor once deject the courage of our minds   121
    Because Cassandra's mad. Her brainsick raptures   122
    Cannot distaste the goodness of a quarrel   123

Which hath our several honors all engaged   124
To make it gracious. For my private part,   125
I am no more touched than all Priam's sons,   126
And Jove forbid there should be done amongst us   127
Such things as might offend the weakest spleen   128
To fight for and maintain!   129
PARIS
    Else might the world convince of levity   130
    As well my undertakings as your counsels.   131
    But I attest the gods, your full consent   132
    Gave wings to my propension and cut off   133
    All fears attending on so dire a project.
    For what, alas, can these my single arms?   135
    What propugnation is in one man's valor   136
    To stand the push and enmity of those
    This quarrel would excite? Yet, I protest,
    Were I alone to pass the difficulties,   139
    And had as ample power as I have will,
    Paris should ne'er retract what he hath done
    Nor faint in the pursuit.
PRIAM   Paris, you speak   142
    Like one besotted on your sweet delights.   143
    You have the honey still, but these the gall.
    So to be valiant is no praise at all.   145
PARIS
    Sir, I propose not merely to myself
    The pleasures such a beauty brings with it,
    But I would have the soil of her fair rape   148
    Wiped off in honorable keeping her.
    What treason were it to the ransacked queen,   150
    Disgrace to your great worths, and shame to me,
    Now to deliver her possession up   152
    On terms of base compulsion! Can it be
    That so degenerate a strain as this   154
    Should once set footing in your generous bosoms?   155
    There's not the meanest spirit on our party   156
    Without a heart to dare or sword to draw   157
    When Helen is defended, nor none so noble
    Whose life were ill bestowed or death unfamed   159
    Where Helen is the subject. Then I say,
    Well may we fight for her whom we know well
    The world's large spaces cannot parallel.   162
HECTOR
    Paris and Troilus, you have both said well,
    And on the cause and question now in hand

---

89 The issue . . . rate condemn the results of your own wise deliberation   90 do . . . did act more capriciously than Fortune ever did
91 Beggar . . . which consider valueless the once esteemed object that
94 But i.e., We are but   95–6 That . . . place who disgraced the Greeks
in their own country through an act (the abducting of Helen) that we
are now too cowardly to justify right here in our own native land.
96.1–2 about her ears (Betokening unmarried status and also distraction. Perhaps Cassandra's wild appearance helps explain why the
Trojans do not recognize her at first.)   104 old old persons
105 nothing canst can do nothing   106 betimes before it is too late
107 moiety part   108 Practice Make use of   110 firebrand (Paris's
mother, Hecuba, dreamed when pregnant with Paris that she would
be delivered of a firebrand destined to burn down Troy.)   118 qualify
moderate   119–22 We . . . mad we must not judge the justice of our
proceedings on the outcome, nor abate our courage solely because of
Cassandra's mad warnings.   123 distaste render distasteful

124 our several honors the honor of each of us   125 gracious righteous, dignified. (Because our honorable selves "grace" the enterprise.)   126 touched affected   127–9 Jove . . . maintain! Jove forbid
that any act done by any of Priam's sons (such as abducting Helen)
should be such that even the least courageous among us would not
willingly fight to maintain!   130 convince convict   131 As well . . .
as both . . . and   132 attest call to witness   133 propension propensity, inclination   135 can . . . arms? can my arms alone accomplish?
136 propugnation defense, might   139 pass experience, undergo
142 faint lose heart   143 besotted drunk   145 So Thus, under these
circumstances.   praise merit   148 soil stain.   rape abduction
150 ransacked carried off   152 her possession possession of her
154 strain muddied thought   155 generous noble   156–7 There's . . .
heart Not even the most low-born Trojan would lack the courage
159 Whose . . . unfamed whose life would be unworthily given or
whose death would be neglected by fame   162 The world's . . .
spaces all the world

Have glozed—but superficially, not much   165
Unlike young men, whom Aristotle thought
Unfit to hear moral philosophy.   167
The reasons you allege do more conduce   168
To the hot passion of distempered blood
Than to make up a free determination   170
Twixt right and wrong, for pleasure and revenge
Have ears more deaf than adders to the voice   172
Of any true decision. Nature craves   173
All dues be rendered to their owners. Now,
What nearer debt in all humanity
Than wife is to the husband? If this law
Of nature be corrupted through affection,   177
And that great minds, of partial indulgence   178
To their benumbèd wills, resist the same,
There is a law in each well-ordered nation
To curb those raging appetites that are
Most disobedient and refractory.   182
If Helen then be wife to Sparta's king,
As it is known she is, these moral laws
Of nature and of nations speak aloud
To have her back returned. Thus to persist
In doing wrong extenuates not wrong
But makes it much more heavy. Hector's opinion
Is this in way of truth; yet ne'ertheless,   189
My sprightly brethren, I propend to you   190
In resolution to keep Helen still,
For 'tis a cause that hath no mean dependence   192
Upon our joint and several dignities.   193

TROILUS
Why, there you touched the life of our design!
Were it not glory that we more affected   195
Than the performance of our heaving spleens,   196
I would not wish a drop of Trojan blood
Spent more in her defense. But, worthy Hector,
She is a theme of honor and renown,
A spur to valiant and magnanimous deeds,
Whose present courage may beat down our foes,   201
And fame in time to come canonize us;   202
For I presume brave Hector would not lose
So rich advantage of a promised glory
As smiles upon the forehead of this action   205
For the wide world's revenue.

HECTOR   I am yours,
You valiant offspring of great Priamus.
I have a roisting challenge sent amongst   208
The dull and factious nobles of the Greeks
Will strike amazement to their drowsy spirits.   210

I was advertised their great general slept,   211
Whilst emulation in the army crept.   212
This, I presume, will wake him.   *Exeunt.*

❖

[2.3]

Enter Thersites, solus.

THERSITES   How now, Thersites? What, lost in the labyrinth of thy fury? Shall the elephant Ajax carry it   2
thus? He beats me, and I rail at him. Oh, worthy
satisfaction! Would it were otherwise, that I could beat
him whilst he railed at me. 'Sfoot, I'll learn to conjure   5
and raise devils but I'll see some issue of my spiteful   6
execrations. Then there's Achilles, a rare engineer! If   7
Troy be not taken till these two undermine it, the walls
will stand till they fall of themselves. O thou great
thunder-darter of Olympus, forget that thou art Jove,
the king of gods, and, Mercury, lose all the serpentine   11
craft of thy caduceus, if ye take not that little little less   12
than little wit from them that they have, which short-   13
armed ignorance itself knows is so abundant scarce it   14
will not in circumvention deliver a fly from a spider   15
without drawing their massy irons and cutting the   16
web! After this, the vengeance on the whole camp! Or
rather, the Neapolitan bone-ache! For that, methinks,   18
is the curse dependent on those that war for a placket.   19
I have said my prayers, and devil Envy say
"Amen."—What ho! My lord Achilles!

[Enter Patroclus at the door of the tent.]

PATROCLUS   Who's there? Thersites? Good Thersites,
come in and rail.   *[Exit.]*

THERSITES   If I could ha' remembered a gilt counterfeit,   24
thou wouldst not have slipped out of my contemplation. But it is no matter; thyself upon thyself! The   26
common curse of mankind, folly and ignorance, be
thine in great revenue! Heaven bless thee from a tutor,   28
and discipline come not near thee! Let thy blood be   29

---

165 glozed commented on   **167 moral philosophy** (Aristotle says
this of political philosophy in the *Nichomachean Ethics*.)   **168 conduce**
lead, tend   **170 free** unbiased   **172 adders** (Psalms 58:4–5 speaks of
adders as deaf.)   **173 craves** demands   **177 affection** erotic passion
178 that if that, if.   **of partial** out of self-interested   **182 refractory**
obstinate.   **189 truth** abstract principle   **190 sprightly** full of spirit.
propend incline   **192–3 'tis . . . dignities** i.e., it is a cause upon which
depends our collective and individual honors, and they on it.
195 more affected desired more   **196 heaving spleens** i.e., aroused
anger   **201 Whose . . . foes** the ready and courageous spirit of which
will enable us to beat down our foes   **202 canonize** enroll among
famous persons   **205 forehead** i.e., prospect, beginning   **208 roisting** roistering, clamorous   **210 Will** that will

211 advertised informed.   **their great general** i.e., Achilles; or possibly Agamemnon   **212 emulation** ambitious or jealous rivalry
2.3. Location: The Greek camp. Before Achilles's tent.
2 carry it carry off the honors   **5 'Sfoot** By His (God's) foot   **6 but . . .
issue** i.e., if it takes that to see some result   **7 execrations** curses.
engineer one who digs countermines or tunnels underneath the
enemy's battlements, or devises plans for such undertakings
11–12 serpentine . . . caduceus (Alludes to Mercury's wand, having
two serpents twined round it.)   **13–14 short-armed** inadequate in its
reach, finding everything beyond its grasp   **15 circumvention** craft,
stratagem   **16 massy irons** massive swords. (Used with overkill on a
mere spider's web.)   **18 Neapolitan bone-ache** i.e., venereal disease.
19 dependent on hanging over.   **placket** slit in a petticoat; hence
(indecently) a woman.   **24 ha'** have.   **gilt counterfeit** counterfeit
coin. (Often called a "slip"; hence the quibble in line 25.)   **26 thyself
upon thyself** (Thersites, after alleging that he would have cursed
Patroclus along with Ajax and Achilles if he were not counterfeit and
hence so easily overlooked, now undertakes to curse Patroclus with
the most dire curse imaginable: may Patroclus simply be himself, be
plagued by himself.)   **28 great revenue** generous amounts.   **bless
thee from** bless you by protecting you from (so as to preserve your
native ignorance)   **29 discipline** instruction.   **blood** violent passion

thy direction till thy death; then if she that lays thee   30
out says thou art a fair corpse, I'll be sworn and sworn   31
upon't she never shrouded any but lazars.   32

[*Enter Patroclus.*]

Amen.—Where's Achilles?

PATROCLUS   What, art thou devout? Wast thou in
prayer?

THERSITES   Ay. The heavens hear me!

PATROCLUS   Amen.

Enter Achilles.

ACHILLES   Who's there?

PATROCLUS   Thersites, my lord.

ACHILLES   Where, where? Oh, where?—Art thou come?
Why, my cheese, my digestion, why hast thou not   41
served thyself in to my table so many meals? Come,
what's Agamemnon?

THERSITES   Thy commander, Achilles.—Then tell me,
Patroclus, what's Achilles?

PATROCLUS   Thy lord, Thersites. Then tell me, I pray
thee, what's thyself?

THERSITES   Thy knower, Patroclus. Then tell me, Patroclus, what art thou?

PATROCLUS   Thou mayst tell that knowest.

ACHILLES   Oh, tell, tell.

THERSITES   I'll decline the whole question. Agamemnon   52
commands Achilles, Achilles is my lord, I am Patroclus' knower, and Patroclus is a fool.

PATROCLUS   You rascal!

THERSITES   Peace, fool! I have not done.

ACHILLES   He is a privileged man.—Proceed, Thersites.   57

THERSITES   Agamemnon is a fool, Achilles is a fool,
Thersites is a fool, and, as aforesaid, Patroclus is a fool.   60

ACHILLES   Derive this. Come.

THERSITES   Agamemnon is a fool to offer to command   61
Achilles, Achilles is a fool to be commanded of
Agamemnon, Thersites is a fool to serve such a fool,
and Patroclus is a fool positive.   64

PATROCLUS   Why am I a fool?

THERSITES   Make that demand to the Creator. It suffices   66
me thou art. Look you, who comes here?

Enter [at a distance] *Agamemnon, Ulysses,
Nestor, Diomedes, Ajax, and Calchas.*

ACHILLES   Patroclus, I'll speak with nobody.—Come in
with me, Thersites.   [*Exit.*]

THERSITES   Here is such patchery, such juggling, and   70

such knavery! All the argument is a whore and a   71
cuckold, a good quarrel to draw emulous factions and   72
bleed to death upon. Now, the dry serpigo on the   73
subject, and war and lechery confound all!   [*Exit.*]   74

AGAMEMNON   Where is Achilles?

PATROCLUS   Within his tent, but ill disposed, my lord.

AGAMEMNON   Let it be known to him that we are here.
He shent our messengers, and we lay by   78
Our appertainments, visiting of him.   79
Let him be told so, lest perchance he think
We dare not move the question of our place,   81
Or know not what we are.

PATROCLUS   I shall so say to him. [*Exit.*]

ULYSSES   We saw him at the opening of his tent. He is
not sick.

AJAX   Yes, lion-sick, sick of proud heart. You may call it   85
melancholy if you will favor the man, but, by my
head, 'tis pride. But why, why? Let him show us the
cause.—A word, my lord. [*He takes Agamemnon aside.*]

NESTOR   What moves Ajax thus to bay at him?

ULYSSES   Achilles hath inveigled his fool from him.

NESTOR   Who, Thersites?

ULYSSES   He.

NESTOR   Then will Ajax lack matter, if he have lost his   93
argument.   94

ULYSSES   No, you see, he is his argument that has his   95
argument—Achilles.   96

NESTOR   All the better; their fraction is more our wish   97
than their faction. But it was a strong council that a   98
fool could disunite.   99

ULYSSES   The amity that wisdom knits not, folly may
easily untie.

Enter Patroclus.

Here comes Patroclus.

NESTOR   No Achilles with him.

ULYSSES   The elephant hath joints, but none for courtesy.   104
His legs are legs for necessity, not for flexure.

PATROCLUS
Achilles bids me say he is much sorry
If anything more than your sport and pleasure
Did move your greatness and this noble state   108
To call upon him. He hopes it is no other
But for your health and your digestion sake,   110

30–1 she . . . out the woman who prepares your body for burial
32 lazars lepers.   **41 cheese** (Supposed, proverbially, to aid digestion.)   **52 decline** go through in order from beginning to end (as
when declining a noun)   **57 privileged man** (Fools were permitted to
speak without restraint.)   **60 Derive** Explain, give the origin of. (The
grammatical metaphor is continued here and also in line 64.)
61 offer undertake   **64 positive** absolute.   **66 Make that demand**
Ask that question   **70 patchery** knavery

71–3 All . . . upon i.e., This war is nothing but a quarrel about a
whore and a cuckold (Helen and Menelaus), a fine quarrelsome basis
upon which to draw rival factions into bloody and fatal conflict.
73 serpigo skin eruption   **74 confound** destroy; throw into turmoil
78 shent sent back insultingly   **79 appertainments** rights, prerogatives   **81 move the question** insist upon the prerogatives   **85 lion-
sick** i.e., sick with pride   **93 matter** subject matter (to rail upon)
93–4 his argument i.e., the subject of his railing, Thersites.
95–6 No . . . Achilles i.e., No, Ajax has not lost something to rail on,
since Achilles, who now has Thersites, has become Ajax's latest object
of quarreling.   **97–9 their fraction . . . disunite** i.e., this discord
between Achilles and Ajax better suits our wishes than their uniting
in faction against us. But the alliance between them cannot have been
strong in any case if a fool like Thersites was able to undo it.
104 The elephant hath joints (Refers to a common belief that elephants'
joints did not enable them to lie down.)   **108 state** council of state
110 digestion digestion's

An after-dinner's breath.

AGAMEMNON   Hear you, Patroclus:
We are too well acquainted with these answers;
But his evasion, winged thus swift with scorn,   114
Cannot outfly our apprehensions.
Much attribute he hath, and much the reason   115
Why we ascribe it to him. Yet all his virtues,
Not virtuously on his own part beheld,   117
Do in our eyes begin to lose their gloss,
Yea, like fair fruit in an unwholesome dish,
Are like to rot untasted. Go and tell him   120
We come to speak with him. And you shall not sin   121
If you do say we think him overproud
And underhonest, in self-assumption greater   123
Than in the note of judgment; and worthier than
himself   124
Here tend the savage strangeness he puts on,   125
Disguise the holy strength of their command,
And underwrite in an observing kind   127
His humorous predominance—yea, watch   128
His pettish lunes, his ebbs, his flows, as if   129
The passage and whole carriage of this action   130
Rode on his tide. Go tell him this, and add
That if he overhold his price so much,   132
We'll none of him, but let him, like an engine   133
Not portable, lie under this report: 134
"Bring action hither; this cannot go to war."   135
A stirring dwarf we do allowance give   136
Before a sleeping giant. Tell him so.

PATROCLUS
I shall, and bring his answer presently.   138

AGAMEMNON
In second voice we'll not be satisfied.   139
We come to speak with him.—Ulysses, enter you.
      [*Exit Ulysses with Patroclus.*]

AJAX   What is he more than another?

AGAMEMNON   No more than what he thinks he is.

AJAX   Is he so much? Do you not think he thinks
himself a better man than I am?

AGAMEMNON   No question.

AJAX   Will you subscribe his thought and say he is?   146

AGAMEMNON   No, noble Ajax, you are as strong, as
valiant, as wise, no less noble, much more gentle, and
altogether more tractable.

AJAX   Why should a man be proud? How doth pride   111
grow? I know not what it is.

AGAMEMNON   Your mind is the clearer, Ajax, and your
virtues the fairer. He that is proud eats up himself.
Pride is his own glass, his own trumpet, his own   154
chronicle; and whatever praises itself but in the deed   155
devours the deed in the praise.

            Enter Ulysses.

AJAX   I do hate a proud man as I hate the engend'ring
of toads.

NESTOR [*aside*]   Yet he loves himself. Is't not
strange?

ULYSSES
Achilles will not to the field tomorrow.

AGAMEMNON
What's his excuse?

ULYSSES   He doth rely on none,
But carries on the stream of his dispose   163
Without observance or respect of any,
In will peculiar and in self-admission.   165

AGAMEMNON
Why, will he not upon our fair request
Untent his person and share th' air with us?

ULYSSES
Things small as nothing, for request's sake only,   168
He makes important. Possessed he is with greatness,
And speaks not to himself but with a pride
That quarrels at self-breath. Imagined worth   171
Holds in his blood such swoll'n and hot discourse
That twixt his mental and his active parts
Kingdomed Achilles in commotion rages   174
And batters down himself. What should I say?
He is so plaguey proud that the death tokens of it   176
Cry "No recovery."

AGAMEMNON   Let Ajax go to him.—
Dear lord, go you and greet him in his tent.
'Tis said he holds you well and will be led,   179
At your request, a little from himself.   180

ULYSSES
O Agamemnon, let it not be so!
We'll consecrate the steps that Ajax makes   182
When they go from Achilles. Shall the proud lord   183
That bastes his arrogance with his own seam   184
And never suffers matter of the world   185
Enter his thoughts, save such as do revolve   186
And ruminate himself, shall he be worshiped   187
Of that we hold an idol more than he?   188

---

111 breath i.e., stroll for a breath of fresh air.   **114 apprehensions**
(1) power of arrest (2) understanding.   **115 attribute** credit, reputation   **117 Not . . . beheld** not being modestly observed or kept by
him   **120 like** likely   **121 sin** err   **123 self-assumption** self-impor-
tance   **124 Than . . . judgment** than men of true judgment know him
to be; or, than in qualities of wise judgment   **124–5 worthier . . . on**
worthier persons than himself stand here in attendance while he
assumes an uncivil aloofness   **127–8 underwrite . . . predominance**
deferentially subscribe to the humor now dominant in him—i.e., arrogant pride   **129 pettish lunes** ill-humored tantrums   **130 this action**
the Trojan war   **132 overhold** overvalue   **133 engine** military
machine   **134 lie under** suffer under   **135 "Bring . . . war"** i.e., "Let
the war come to me; I am too proud to accommodate myself to it."
136 stirring active.   **allowance** approbation, praise
138 presently right away.   **139 In second voice** i.e., With a mere
messenger's report   **146 subscribe** concur in

154–5 Pride . . . chronicle Pride is its own mirror and proclaimer of its
greatness   **155 but in the deed** in any way other than in doing
(praiseworthy) deeds   **163 dispose** bent of mind   **165 will peculiar**
his own independent will.   **self-admission** self-approbation.
168 for . . . only only because they are requested   **171 quarrels at
self-breath** i.e., is almost too proud to speak to himself.   **174 Kingdomed** i.e., like a microcosm of a state   **176 death tokens** fatal symptoms   **179 holds** regards   **180 from himself** i.e., from his usual
arrogant behavior.   **182–3 We'll . . . Achilles** i.e., Let us instead venerate Ajax when he puts as much distance between himself and
Achilles as possible.   **184 seam** fat, grease (by means of which
Achilles feeds his own pride)   **185 suffers** allows   **186–7 save . . .
himself** other than thoughts that serve for endless self-contemplation
188 Of . . . idol by one whom we venerate

No, this thrice worthy and right valiant lord
Must not so stale his palm, nobly acquired,   190
Nor, by my will, assubjugate his merit,   191
As amply titled as Achilles' is,   192
By going to Achilles.
That were to enlard his fat-already pride
And add more coals to Cancer when he burns   195
With entertaining great Hyperion.   196
This lord go to him? Jupiter forbid,
And say in thunder, "Achilles, go to him."

NESTOR [aside to Diomedes]
Oh, this is well. He rubs the vein of him.   199

DIOMEDES [aside to Nestor]
And how his silence drinks up this applause!

AJAX
If I go to him, with my armèd fist
I'll pash him o'er the face.   202

AGAMEMNON   Oh, no, you shall not go.

AJAX
An 'a be proud with me, I'll feeze his pride.   204
Let me go to him.

ULYSSES
Not for the worth that hangs upon our quarrel.   206

AJAX   A paltry, insolent fellow!

NESTOR [aside]   How he describes himself!

AJAX   Can he not be sociable?

ULYSSES [aside]   The raven chides blackness.

AJAX   I'll let his humor's blood.   211

AGAMEMNON [aside]   He will be the physician that
should be the patient.

AJAX   An all men were o' my mind—

ULYSSES [aside]   Wit would be out of fashion.

AJAX   'A should not bear it so. 'A should eat swords first.   216
Shall pride carry it?

NESTOR [aside]   An 'twould, you'd carry half.   218

ULYSSES [aside]   'A would have ten shares.   219

AJAX   I will knead him; I'll make him supple.

NESTOR [aside]   He's not yet through warm. Farce him   221
with praises. Pour in, pour in; his ambition is dry.

ULYSSES [to Agamemnon]
My lord, you feed too much on this dislike.   223

NESTOR
Our noble general, do not do so.

DIOMEDES
You must prepare to fight without Achilles.

ULYSSES
Why, 'tis this naming of him does him harm.   226

Here is a man—but 'tis before his face;
I will be silent.

NESTOR   Wherefore should you so?
He is not emulous, as Achilles is.   229

ULYSSES
Know the whole world, he is as valiant—   230

AJAX   A whoreson dog, that shall palter thus with us!   231
Would he were a Trojan!

NESTOR   What a vice were it in Ajax now—

ULYSSES   If he were proud—

DIOMEDES   Or covetous of praise—

ULYSSES   Ay, or surly borne—   236

DIOMEDES   Or strange, or self-affected!   237

ULYSSES [to Ajax]
Thank the heavens, lord, thou art of sweet
     composure.   238
Praise him that got thee, she that gave thee suck;   239
Famed be thy tutor, and thy parts of nature   240
Thrice famed, beyond, beyond all erudition;   241
But he that disciplined thine arms to fight,   242
Let Mars divide eternity in twain
And give him half; and, for thy vigor,
Bull-bearing Milo his addition yield   245
To sinewy Ajax. I will not praise thy wisdom,   246
Which, like a bourn, a pale, a shore, confines   247
Thy spacious and dilated parts. Here's Nestor,   248
Instructed by the antiquary times;   249
He must, he is, he cannot but be wise.
But pardon, father Nestor, were your days
As green as Ajax' and your brain so tempered,   252
You should not have the eminence of him,   253
But be as Ajax.

AJAX   Shall I call you father?

ULYSSES
Ay, my good son.

DIOMEDES   Be ruled by him, Lord Ajax.

ULYSSES
There is no tarrying here; the hart Achilles
Keeps thicket. Please it our great general   257
To call together all his state of war.   258
Fresh kings are come to Troy; tomorrow
We must with all our main of power stand fast.   260
And here's a lord—come knights from east to west,
And cull their flower, Ajax shall cope the best.   262

---

190 stale . . . acquired sully his nobly won honor. (Palm means "palm
leaf.") 191 assubjugate debase, reduce to subjection 192 As . . . is
having as great a name as Achilles's. (Or, if Achilles is not a possessive, this could mean, "granted that Achilles is also rich in titles.")
195–6 add . . . Hyperion i.e., add a fire to the heat of summer. (Cancer
is the sign of the zodiac into which the sun [Hyperion] enters at the
beginning of summer.) 199 vein humor, disposition 202 pash
smash 204 An . . . pride i.e., If he puts on airs with me, I'll settle his
hash. 206 our quarrel i.e., with the Trojans. 211 let . . . blood bleed
him (as a physician would) to cure his excessive humors. 216 'A He.
eat swords swallow my sword, i.e., be beaten in fight 218 An If
219 ten shares i.e., the whole without sharing. 221 through thoroughly. Farce Stuff 223 this dislike i.e., Achilles's truculence.
226 this . . . harm this continual citing of Achilles as our chief hero
that creates the difficulty.

229 emulous envious, eager for glory 230 Know . . . world Let the
whole world know 231 that shall palter who thinks he can trifle,
dodge 236 surly borne bearing himself in a surly fashion
237 strange distant. self-affected in love with himself. 238 composure temperament, constitution. 239 got begot 240–1 thy parts . . .
erudition i.e., your natural gifts thrice exceeding what erudition can
add thereto. (With an ironic double meaning, suggesting that erudition can add little.) 242 But he but as for him 245 Bull-bearing . . .
yield let bull-bearing Milo yield up his title. (Milo, a celebrated ath-
lete of phenomenal strength, was able to carry a bull on his shoulders.) 246 I will not (1) I will forbear to (2) I won't 247 bourn
boundary. pale fence 248 dilated parts extensive and well-known
qualities. (But also hinting at Ajax's beefy build.) 249 antiquary
ancient 252 green immature. tempered composed 253 have . . .
of be reckoned superior to 257 Keeps thicket i.e., stays hidden. (A
thicket is a dense growth of shrubs or trees.) 258 state council
260 main full force 262 cull their flower choose their flower of
chivalry. cope prove a match for

AGAMEMNON
Go we to council. Let Achilles sleep.
Light boats sail swift, though greater hulks draw
  deep.   *Exeunt.* 264

✤

[3.1]

[*Music sounds within.*] *Enter Pandarus* [*and a
Servant*].

PANDARUS   Friend, you, pray you, a word. Do not you
follow the young Lord Paris?   2

SERVANT   Ay, sir, when he goes before me.   3

PANDARUS   You depend upon him, I mean?   4

SERVANT   Sir, I do depend upon the lord.   5

PANDARUS   You depend upon a notable gentleman; I
must needs praise him.   7

SERVANT   The Lord be praised!

PANDARUS   You know me, do you not?

SERVANT   Faith, sir, superficially.

PANDARUS   Friend, know me better. I am the Lord   10
Pandarus.

SERVANT   I hope I shall know Your Honor better.   13

PANDARUS   I do desire it.

SERVANT   You are in the state of grace.   15

PANDARUS   Grace? Not so, friend. "Honor" and "lordship" are my titles. What music is this?

SERVANT   I do but partly know, sir. It is music in parts. 18

PANDARUS   Know you the musicians?

SERVANT   Wholly, sir.

PANDARUS   Who play they to?

SERVANT   To the hearers, sir.

PANDARUS   At whose pleasure, friend?

SERVANT   At mine, sir, and theirs that love music.

PANDARUS   Command, I mean, friend.

SERVANT   Who shall I command, sir?

PANDARUS   Friend, we understand not one another; I
am too courtly and thou too cunning. At whose
request do these men play?

SERVANT   That's to't indeed, sir. Marry, sir, at the   30
request of Paris my lord, who's there in person; with
him, the mortal Venus, the heart-blood of beauty,
love's visible soul—

PANDARUS   Who, my cousin Cressida?

SERVANT   No, sir, Helen. Could not you find out that
by her attributes?

PANDARUS   It should seem, fellow, that thou hast not
seen the Lady Cressida. I come to speak with Paris

from the Prince Troilus. I will make a complimental   39
assault upon him, for my business seethes.   40

SERVANT   Sodden business! There's a stewed phrase, 41
indeed!

Enter Paris and Helen [*attended*].

PANDARUS   Fair be to you, my lord, and to all this fair 43
company! Fair desires, in all fair measure, fairly guide 44
them! Especially to you, fair queen, fair thoughts be
your fair pillow!

HELEN   Dear lord, you are full of fair words.

PANDARUS   You speak your fair pleasure, sweet
queen.—Fair prince, here is good broken music.   49

PARIS   You have broke it, cousin, and, by my life, you 50
shall make it whole again; you shall piece it out with 51
a piece of your performance.—Nell, he is full of harmony.

PANDARUS   Truly, lady, no.

HELEN   Oh, sir—

PANDARUS   Rude, in sooth; in good sooth, very rude. 56

PARIS   Well said, my lord. Well, you say so in fits.   57

PANDARUS   I have business to my lord, dear
queen.—My lord, will you vouchsafe me a word?   59

HELEN   Nay, this shall not hedge us out. We'll hear you 60
sing, certainly.

PANDARUS   Well, sweet queen, you are pleasant with 62
me.—But, marry, thus, my lord: my dear lord and
most esteemed friend, your brother Troilus—

HELEN   My lord Pandarus, honey-sweet lord—

PANDARUS   Go to, sweet queen, go to—commends 66
himself most affectionately to you—

HELEN   You shall not bob us out of our melody. If you 68
do, our melancholy upon your head!

PANDARUS   Sweet queen, sweet queen, that's a sweet
queen, i' faith.

HELEN   And to make a sweet lady sad is a sour offense.

PANDARUS   Nay, that shall not serve your turn, that shall
it not, in truth, la. Nay, I care not for such words, no, 74
no.—And, my lord, he desires you, that if the King
call for him at supper you will make his excuse.

HELEN   My lord Pandarus—

PANDARUS   What says my sweet queen, my very very
sweet queen?

PARIS   What exploit's in hand? Where sups he tonight?

HELEN   Nay, but, my lord—

PANDARUS   What says my sweet queen? My cousin will 82
fall out with you.   83

---

264 hulks big, unwieldy ships
3.1. Location: Troy. The palace.
2 follow serve. (But the servant takes it in the sense of "follow after.")
3 goes walks   **4 depend upon** serve as dependent to. (The servant
mockingly uses a more spiritual sense.)   **5 lord** (Quibbling on *lord*,
referring to Paris, and "Lord" as "God.")   **7 needs** necessarily
10 superficially (1) slightly (2) as a superficial person.   **13 know . . .
better** (1) become better acquainted with you (2) see you become a
more humble man. (*Your Honor* is a polite form of address to one of
social consequence.)   **15 in . . . grace** i.e., in the way of salvation
because of desiring to be better. (Pandarus answers as though *grace*
referred to the courtly title applicable to a duke or prince.)   **18 partly**
(1) partially (2) in parts   **30 to't** to the point

39 complimental courteous   **40 seethes** boils, requires haste.
41 Sodden, stewed (A play on *seethes* and with quibbling reference to
stews or brothels and to the sweating treatment for venereal disease.)
43 Fair Fair wishes, good fortune. (With wordplay in subsequent uses
of *fair*: attractive, pleasing, just, clean.)   **44 fairly** favorably   **49 broken music** music arranged for different families of instruments.
50 broke interrupted.   **cousin** (Often used at court in addressing a
social equal.)   **51 piece it out** mend it   **56 Rude** (I am) unpolished
57 in fits (1) by fits and starts (2) in divisions of a song, in stanzas.
59 vouchsafe permit   **60 hedge** shut   **62 pleasant** jocular   **66 Go to**
(An expression of mild protest.)   **68 bob** cheat   **74 la** (An exclamation accompanying a conventional phrase.)   **82–3 My . . . you** i.e.,
Paris will be angry with you for interrupting so.

HELEN [to Paris] You must not know where he sups. 84
PARIS I'll lay my life, with my disposer Cressida. 85
PANDARUS No, no, no such matter; you are wide. 86
   Come, your disposer is sick.
PARIS Well, I'll make 's excuse. 88
PANDARUS Ay, good my lord. Why should you say
   Cressida? No, your poor disposer's sick.
PARIS I spy. 91
PANDARUS You spy! What do you spy?—Come, give
   me an instrument. [He is handed a musical instrument.]
   Now, sweet queen.
HELEN Why, this is kindly done.
PANDARUS My niece is horribly in love with a thing
   you have, sweet queen.
HELEN She shall have it, my lord, if it be not my lord
   Paris.
PANDARUS He? No, she'll none of him. They two are
   twain. 101
HELEN Falling in, after falling out, may make them 102
   three. 103
PANDARUS Come, come, I'll hear no more of this. I'll
   sing you a song now.
HELEN Ay, ay, prithee. Now, by my troth, sweet lord,
   thou hast a fine forehead.
PANDARUS Ay, you may, you may. 108
HELEN Let thy song be love. This love will undo us all.
   Oh, Cupid, Cupid, Cupid!
PANDARUS Love? Ay, that it shall, i'faith.
PARIS Ay, good now, "Love, love, nothing but love." 112
PANDARUS In good truth, it begins so: [He sings.]
   Love, love, nothing but love, still love, still more!
     For, oh, love's bow
     Shoots buck and doe. 116
     The shaft confounds 117
     Not that it wounds, 118
   But tickles still the sore. 119
   These lovers cry, "Oh! Oh!", they die! 120
     Yet that which seems the wound to kill 121
   Doth turn "Oh! Oh!" to "ha, ha, he!"
     So dying love lives still. 123
   "Oh! Oh!" awhile, but "ha, ha, ha!"
   "Oh! Oh!" groans out for "ha! ha! ha!"—
   Heigh-ho!
HELEN In love, i'faith, to the very tip of the nose.
PARIS He eats nothing but doves, love, and that breeds
   hot blood, and hot blood begets hot thoughts, and hot
   thoughts beget hot deeds, and hot deeds is love.

PANDARUS Is this the generation of love? Hot blood, hot 131
   thoughts, and hot deeds? Why, they are vipers. Is love
   a generation of vipers? Sweet lord, who's afield 133
   today?
PARIS Hector, Deiphobus, Helenus, Antenor, and all
   the gallantry of Troy. I would fain have armed today,
   but my Nell would not have it so. How chance my
   brother Troilus went not?
HELEN He hangs the lip at something.—You know all, 139
   Lord Pandarus.
PANDARUS Not I, honey-sweet queen. I long to hear
   how they sped today.—You'll remember your broth- 142
   er's excuse?
PARIS To a hair. 144
PANDARUS Farewell, sweet queen.
HELEN Commend me to your niece.
PANDARUS I will, sweet queen.   [Exit.]
                      Sound a retreat.
PARIS
   They're come from field. Let us to Priam's hall
   To greet the warriors. Sweet Helen, I must woo you
   To help unarm our Hector. His stubborn buckles,
   With these your white enchanting fingers touched,
   Shall more obey than to the edge of steel
   Or force of Greekish sinews. You shall do more
   Than all the island kings: disarm great Hector. 154
HELEN
   'Twill make us proud to be his servant, Paris.
   Yea, what he shall receive of us in duty
   Gives us more palm in beauty than we have, 157
   Yea, overshines ourself.
PARIS Sweet, above thought I love thee.   Exeunt.

                      ❧

[3.2]

Enter Pandarus and Troilus' Man, [meeting].

PANDARUS How now, where's thy master? At my cousin Cressida's?
MAN No, sir, he stays for you to conduct him thither.

        [Enter Troilus.]

PANDARUS Oh, here he comes.—How now, how now?
TROILUS Sirrah, walk off.   [Exit Man.]
PANDARUS Have you seen my cousin?
TROILUS
   No, Pandarus. I stalk about her door,
   Like a strange soul upon the Stygian banks 8
   Staying for waftage. Oh, be thou my Charon, 9

---

84 **You must not** i.e., Pandarus does not want you to. **he** i.e., Troilus
85 **lay** wager. **my disposer** i.e., one who may do what she likes
(with me or Troilus)   86 **wide** wide of the mark.   **88 make 's excuse**
make his (Troilus's) excuse (to Priam).   **91 I spy** I get it.   **101 twain**
not in accord.   **102–3 Falling . . . three** (Helen bawdily jokes that
Cressida's game will result in the birth of a child, a third person.)
108 you may go on, have your joke.   **112 good now** please
116 buck and doe i.e., male and female.   **117 confounds** overwhelms
118 Not that (1) not that which, or (2) not so much that. (The erotic
suggestion is that love does its harm by penetrating and tickling.)
119 sore (1) wound (2) buck in its fourth year.   **120, 123 die, dying**
(Quibbling on the idea of experiencing orgasm.)   **121 wound to kill**
fatal wound

131 generation genealogy   **133 generation of vipers** (See Matthew
3:7, 12:34, and 23:33.)   **139 He hangs the lip** Pandarus pouts, sulks
142 sped succeeded   **144 To a hair** To the last detail.   **154 island
kings** i.e., Greek chieftains   **157 Gives . . . have** bestows more honor
on me than my own beauty does. (Helen uses the royal plural.)
**3.2. Location: The garden of Cressida's house (formerly her father's
house until he abandoned Troy).**
0.1 Man servant. (Probably the *varlet* referred to in 1.1.1.)
8–9 a strange . . . Charon (Refers to the Greek mythological conception of the fate of departed souls who had to wait on the banks of the
Styx or Acheron until the boatman Charon ferried them across to the
infernal region.)

And give me swift transportation to those fields   10
Where I may wallow in the lily beds
Proposed for the deserver! O gentle Pandar,   12
From Cupid's shoulder pluck his painted wings,
And fly with me to Cressid!

PANDARUS   Walk here i'th'orchard. I'll bring her   15
straight.   [*Exit Pandarus.*]

TROILUS
I am giddy; expectation whirls me round.
Th'imaginary relish is so sweet
That it enchants my sense. What will it be
When that the wat'ry palates taste indeed   20
Love's thrice repurèd nectar? Death, I fear me,   21
Swooning destruction, or some joy too fine,
Too subtle-potent, tuned too sharp in sweetness
For the capacity of my ruder powers.
I fear it much; and I do fear besides
That I shall lose distinction in my joys,   26
As doth a battle, when they charge on heaps   27
The enemy flying.

[*Enter Pandarus.*]

PANDARUS   She's making her ready; she'll come
straight. You must be witty now. She does so blush,   30
and fetches her wind so short, as if she were frayed   31
with a spirit. I'll fetch her. It is the prettiest villain! She   32
fetches her breath as short as a new-ta'en sparrow.
    Exit Pandarus.

TROILUS
Even such a passion doth embrace my bosom.
My heart beats thicker than a feverous pulse,   35
And all my powers do their bestowing lose,   36
Like vassalage at unawares encount'ring   37
The eye of majesty.

Enter Pandarus, and Cressida, [veiled].

PANDARUS   Come, come, what need you blush?
Shame's a baby.—Here she is now. Swear the oaths
now to her that you have sworn to me. [*Cressida draws
back.*] What, are you gone again? You must be watched   42
ere you be made tame, must you? Come your ways,
come your ways; an you draw backward, we'll put
you i'th' thills.—Why do you not speak to her?—   45
Come, draw this curtain, and let's see your picture.   46
[*She is unveiled.*] Alas the day, how loath you are
to offend daylight! An 'twere dark, you'd close sooner.   48

So, so, rub on, and kiss the mistress. [*They kiss.*] How   49
now, a kiss in fee-farm? Build there, carpenter, the air   50
is sweet. Nay, you shall fight your hearts out ere I part   51
you—the falcon as the tercel, for all the ducks i'th'   52
river. Go to, go to.   53

TROILUS   You have bereft me of all words, lady.

PANDARUS   Words pay no debts; give her deeds. But
she'll bereave you o'th' deeds too, if she call your ac-   56
tivity in question. What, billing again? Here's "In wit-   57
ness whereof the parties interchangeably"—Come in,   58
come in. I'll go get a fire.   [*Exit.*]   59

CRESSIDA   Will you walk in, my lord?

TROILUS   Oh, Cressida, how often have I wished me thus!

CRESSIDA   Wished, my lord? The gods grant—Oh, my
lord!

TROILUS   What should they grant? What makes this
pretty abruption? What too curious dreg espies my   65
sweet lady in the fountain of our love?

CRESSIDA   More dregs than water, if my fears have eyes.

TROILUS   Fears make devils of cherubins; they never see   68
truly.

CRESSIDA   Blind fear, that seeing reason leads, finds   70
safer footing than blind reason stumbling without
fear. To fear the worst oft cures the worse.   72

TROILUS   Oh, let my lady apprehend no fear. In all
Cupid's pageant there is presented no monster.

CRESSIDA   Nor nothing monstrous neither?

TROILUS   Nothing but our undertakings, when we vow   76
to weep seas, live in fire, eat rocks, tame tigers, thinking it harder for our mistress to devise imposition   78
enough than for us to undergo any difficulty imposed.
This is the monstrosity in love, lady, that the will is
infinite and the execution confined, that the desire is
boundless and the act a slave to limit.

CRESSIDA   They say all lovers swear more performance
than they are able, and yet reserve an ability that they
never perform, vowing more than the perfection of ten   85
and discharging less than the tenth part of one. They
that have the voice of lions and the act of hares, are
they not monsters?

TROILUS   Are there such? Such are not we. Praise us as
we are tasted, allow us as we prove; our head shall go   90

---

10 **fields** the Elysian fields   12 **Proposed for** promised to
15 **orchard** garden.   20 **wat'ry palates** i.e., sense of taste watering
with anticipation   21 **repurèd** refined, repurified   26 **lose . . . joys** be
unable to distinguish one delight from another   27 **battle** army
30 **witty** alert, resourceful in easy conversation   31 **fetches . . . short**
is short of breath   31–2 **frayed . . . spirit** frightened by a ghost.
32 **villain** (Used endearingly.)   35 **thicker** faster   36 **bestowing**
proper use   37 **vassalage at unawares** vassals unexpectedly
42 **watched** kept awake (like a hawk that is being tamed through
sleeplessness)   45 **thills** shafts of a cart or wagon. (An image of
domesticating the woman, as in hawking.)   46 **curtain** veil. (Curtains
were hung in front of pictures.)   48 **close** (1) encounter (2) come
to terms

49 **kiss the mistress** (In bowls, to touch the central target; to *rub* is to
maneuver obstacles as the ball rolls; *mistress* is analogous to "master,"
short for "master bowl," a small bowl placed as a mark for players to
aim at.)   50 **in fee-farm** i.e., unending, as with land that is held in perpetuity.   50–1 **Build . . . sweet** (1) Erect your house in this fresh and
unspoiled location (2) Place your love here where her breath is sweet.
52–3 **the falcon . . . river** i.e., I'll bet all the ducks in the river that the
female hawk will be as eager as the male.   56–7 **activity** virility. (Pandarus jests that Cressida will wear Troilus down in lovemaking.)
57 **billing** kissing   57–8 "**In . . . interchangeably**" (A legal formula
used for contracts, ending "have set their hand and seals.")   59 **get a
fire** order a fire (for the bedroom).   65 **abruption** breaking off.   **curious dreg** finicky and anxiety-causing impurity   68 **make . . . cherubins** i.e., make things seem worst rather than best   70 **that . . . leads**
that is led by clear-sighted reason   72 **oft . . . worse** enables us to avoid
lesser dangers.   76 **undertakings** vows   78 **to devise imposition** to
think up tasks to impose   85 **perfection of ten** accomplishment of ten
perfect lovers   90 **tasted** tried, proved.   **allow** acknowledge, approve

bare till merit crown it. No perfection in reversion shall 91
have a praise in present; we will not name desert before his birth, and, being born, his addition shall be 93
humble. Few words to fair faith. Troilus shall be such 94
to Cressid as what envy can say worst shall be a mock 95
for his truth, and what truth can speak truest not truer 96
than Troilus.

CRESSIDA   Will you walk in, my lord?

[*Enter Pandarus.*]

PANDARUS   What, blushing still? Have you not done
talking yet?

CRESSIDA   Well, uncle, what folly I commit, I dedicate 101
to you.

PANDARUS   I thank you for that. If my lord get a boy of
you, you'll give him me. Be true to my lord. If he
flinch, chide me for it.

TROILUS   You know now your hostages: your uncle's
word and my firm faith.

PANDARUS   Nay, I'll give my word for her too. Our
kindred, though they be long ere they are wooed,
they are constant being won. They are burrs, I can tell
you; they'll stick where they are thrown.   111

CRESSIDA
Boldness comes to me now and brings me heart.
Prince Troilus, I have loved you night and day
For many weary months.

TROILUS
Why was my Cressid then so hard to win?

CRESSIDA
Hard to seem won; but I was won, my lord,
With the first glance that ever—pardon me;
If I confess much, you will play the tyrant.
I love you now, but till now not so much
But I might master it. In faith, I lie;
My thoughts were like unbridled children, grown   121
Too headstrong for their mother. See, we fools!
Why have I blabbed? Who shall be true to us,
When we are so unsecret to ourselves?
But, though I loved you well, I wooed you not;
And yet, good faith, I wished myself a man,
Or that we women had men's privilege
Of speaking first. Sweet, bid me hold my tongue,
For in this rapture I shall surely speak
The thing I shall repent. See, see, your silence,
Cunning in dumbness, in my weakness draws
My soul of counsel from me! Stop my mouth.   132

TROILUS
And shall, albeit sweet music issues thence.

[*He kisses her.*]

PANDARUS   Pretty, i'faith.

CRESSIDA
My lord, I do beseech you, pardon me;
'Twas not my purpose thus to beg a kiss.
I am ashamed. Oh, heavens, what have I done?
For this time will I take my leave, my lord.

TROILUS   Your leave, sweet Cressid?

PANDARUS   Leave? An you take leave till tomorrow 140
morning—

CRESSIDA   Pray you, content you.   142

TROILUS   What offends you, lady?

CRESSIDA   Sir, mine own company.

TROILUS   You cannot shun yourself.

CRESSIDA   Let me go and try.
I have a kind of self resides with you,
But an unkind self that itself will leave   148
To be another's fool. Where is my wit?   149
I would be gone. I speak I know not what.

TROILUS
Well know they what they speak that speak so wisely. 151

CRESSIDA
Perchance, my lord, I show more craft than love,   152
And fell so roundly to a large confession   153
To angle for your thoughts. But you are wise,   154
Or else you love not, for to be wise and love   155
Exceeds man's might; that dwells with gods above.   156

TROILUS
Oh, that I thought it could be in a woman—
As, if it can, I will presume in you—   158
To feed for aye her lamp and flames of love,
To keep her constancy in plight and youth,   160
Outliving beauty's outward, with a mind   161
That doth renew swifter than blood decays!   162
Or that persuasion could but thus convince me
That my integrity and truth to you
Might be affronted with the match and weight   165
Of such a winnowed purity in love;   166
How were I then uplifted! But, alas,
I am as true as truth's simplicity,   168
And simpler than the infancy of truth.   169

CRESSIDA
In that I'll war with you.

TROILUS   Oh, virtuous fight,
When right with right wars who shall be most right!
True swains in love shall in the world to come
Approve their truth by Troilus. When their rhymes,   173

91 No . . . reversion No promise of perfection to come   93 addition
title   94 Few . . . faith (Compare the proverb: "Where many words
are, the truth goes by.")   95–6 as what . . . truth that the worst that
malice can do is to mock Troilus's loyalty   101 folly foolishness.
(Pandarus understands it to mean "lechery.")   111 thrown (1) tossed
(2) thrown down in the act of seduction.   121 unbridled unrestrained   132 My . . . counsel my inmost thoughts

140 An If   142 content you don't be upset.   148 unkind unnatural
148–9 that . . . fool that will desert its true nature to be your dupe or
plaything.   149 Where . . . wit? What am I saying?   151 Well . . .
wisely Anyone who speaks as wisely as you do knows what he or
she is saying.   152 Perchance Perchance you think that.   craft cunning   153 roundly outspokenly.   large free   154 To . . . thoughts to
draw forth a confession from you.   155–6 Or . . . might or, to put it
another way, you are too wise to be really in love, since to be wise
and love at the same time is beyond human capacity   158 presume
presume that it is   160 To . . . youth to keep her pledged constancy
fresh   161 outward appearance   162 blood decays passions wane.
165–6 affronted . . . love matched with an equal quantity of purified
love (in you).   winnowed separated from the chaff   168 truth's simplicity the simple truth   169 the infancy of truth i.e., pure, innocent
truth.   173 Approve attest.   by Troilus i.e., using Troilus as an ideal
comparison.

Full of protest, of oath and big compare,   174
Wants similes, truth tired with iteration—   175
"As true as steel, as plantage to the moon,   176
As sun to day, as turtle to her mate,   177
As iron to adamant, as earth to th' center"—   178
Yet, after all comparisons of truth,   179
As truth's authentic author to be cited,   180
"As true as Troilus" shall crown up the verse   181
And sanctify the numbers.
CRESSIDA   Prophet may you be!   182
If I be false or swerve a hair from truth,
When time is old and hath forgot itself,
When waterdrops have worn the stones of Troy,
And blind oblivion swallowed cities up,
And mighty states characterless are grated   187
To dusty nothing, yet let memory,
From false to false, among false maids in love,   189
Upbraid my falsehood! When they've said "as false
As air, as water, wind, or sandy earth,
As fox to lamb, or wolf to heifer's calf,
Pard to the hind, or stepdame to her son,"   193
Yea, let them say, to stick the heart of falsehood,   194
"As false as Cressid."
PANDARUS   Go to, a bargain made. Seal it, seal it; I'll be
the witness. Here I hold your hand, here my cousin's.
If ever you prove false one to another, since I have
taken such pains to bring you together, let all pitiful 199
goers-between be called to the world's end after my
name: call them all Pandars. Let all constant men be
Troiluses, all false women Cressids, and all brokers-
between Pandars! Say "Amen."
TROILUS   Amen.
CRESSIDA   Amen.
PANDARUS   Amen. Whereupon I will show you a chamber with a bed, which bed, because it shall not speak
of your pretty encounters, press it to death. Away!   208
                    Exeunt [Troilus and Cressida].
And Cupid grant all tongue-tied maidens here   209
Bed, chamber, pander to provide this gear!   *Exit.* 210

❖

[3.3]

*Flourish. Enter Ulysses, Diomedes, Nestor,
Agamemnon, [Ajax, Menelaus,] and Calchas.*

CALCHAS   174
Now, princes, for the service I have done you,
Th'advantage of the time prompts me aloud   2
To call for recompense. Appear it to your mind   3
That, through the sight I bear in things to come,   4
I have abandoned Troy, left my possessions,
Incurred a traitor's name, exposed myself,
From certain and possessed conveniences,   7
To doubtful fortunes, sequest'ring from me all   8
That time, acquaintance, custom, and condition
Made tame and most familiar to my nature;   10
And here, to do you service, am become   11
As new into the world, strange, unacquainted.
I do beseech you, as in way of taste,   13
To give me now a little benefit
Out of those many registered in promise
Which, you say, live to come in my behalf.   16
AGAMEMNON
What wouldst thou of us, Trojan, make demand?
CALCHAS
You have a Trojan prisoner called Antenor
Yesterday took. Troy holds him very dear.
Oft have you—often have you thanks therefor—
Desired my Cressid in right great exchange,   21
Whom Troy hath still denied; but this Antenor,   22
I know, is such a wrest in their affairs   23
That their negotiations all must slack,
Wanting his manage, and they will almost   25
Give us a prince of blood, a son of Priam,
In change of him. Let him be sent, great princes,   27
And he shall buy my daughter; and her presence
Shall quite strike off all service I have done
In most accepted pain.
AGAMEMNON   Let Diomedes bear him,   30
And bring us Cressid hither. Calchas shall have
What he requests of us. Good Diomed,
Furnish you fairly for this interchange.
Withal bring word if Hector will tomorrow   34
Be answered in his challenge. Ajax is ready.   35
DIOMEDES
This shall I undertake, and 'tis a burden
Which I am proud to bear.   *Exit [with Calchas].* 37

Achilles and Patroclus stand in their tent.

ULYSSES
Achilles stands i'th'entrance of his tent.
Please it our general pass strangely by him,
As if he were forgot; and, princes all,   39
Lay negligent and loose regard upon him.

174 protest protestation (of love). **big compare** extravagant comparisons **175 Wants . . . iteration** are in need of new similes, having
worn out their usual expressions of love through too much repetition
176 plantage vegetation (waxing in growth by the moon's influence)
177 turtle turtledove **178 adamant** lodestone (magnetic). **center**
center of the earth, axis **179 comparisons** illustrative similes
180 As . . . cited when we want to cite as our authority the very foun-
tainhead of truth **181 crown up** give the finishing touches to
182 numbers verses. **187 characterless** unrecorded, without a mark
left. **grated** pulverized **189 From . . . love** passing from one false
one to another among false-hearted young women **193 Pard** leopard or panther. **hind** doe. **stepdame** stepmother **194 stick the
heart** pierce the center of the target **199 pitiful** compassionate
208 press . . . death (Alludes to the usual punishment by weights for
accused persons refusing to plead or "speak.") **209 here** i.e., in the
audience **210 gear** equipment.
3.3. Location: The Greek camp. Before Achilles's tent.

2 advantage of favorable opportunity offered by **3 Appear it** Let it
appear **4 bear** am endowed with **7 From** turning from
8 sequest'ring separating, removing **10 tame** familiar, domestic
11 am have **13 taste** foretaste **16 live to come** await fulfillment
21 right great exchange exchange for distinguished captives **22 still**
continually **23 wrest** tuning key, i.e., one producing harmony and
order **25 Wanting his manage** lacking his management **27 change
of** exchange for **30 In . . . pain** in pains (troubles, hardships) which I
have endured most willingly. **bear** escort **34 Withal** In addition
35 Be answered in meet the answerer of **37.1 stand in** i.e., enter on
stage and stand in the entrance of **39 strangely** i.e., as one who pretends to be a stranger

I will come last. 'Tis like he'll question me
Why such unplausive eyes are bent, why turned, on
   him.   43
If so, I have derision medicinable   44
To use between your strangeness and his pride,   45
Which his own will shall have desire to drink.   46
It may do good. Pride hath no other glass   47
To show itself but pride, for supple knees   48
Feed arrogance and are the proud man's fees.   49

AGAMEMNON
We'll execute your purpose and put on   50
A form of strangeness as we pass along.
So do each lord, and either greet him not
Or else disdainfully, which shall shake him more
Than if not looked on. I will lead the way.
        [They move in procession past Achilles' tent.]

ACHILLES
What, comes the general to speak with me?
You know my mind. I'll fight no more 'gainst Troy.

AGAMEMNON
What says Achilles? Would he aught with us?   57

NESTOR
Would you, my lord, aught with the general?

ACHILLES   No.
NESTOR   Nothing, my lord.
AGAMEMNON   The better.   61
        [Exeunt Agamemnon and Nestor.]
ACHILLES *[to Menelaus]*   Good day, good day.
MENELAUS   How do you? How do you?   *[Exit.]*
ACHILLES   What, does the cuckold scorn me?
AJAX   How now, Patroclus!
ACHILLES   Good morrow, Ajax.
AJAX   Ha?
ACHILLES   Good morrow.
AJAX   Ay, and good next day too.
        Exit. [*Ulysses remains behind, reading.*]

ACHILLES
What mean these fellows? Know they not Achilles?

PATROCLUS
They pass by strangely. They were used to bend,   71
To send their smiles before them to Achilles,
To come as humbly as they use to creep   73
To holy altars.
ACHILLES   What, am I poor of late?
'Tis certain, greatness, once fall'n out with fortune,
Must fall out with men too. What the declined is   76
He shall as soon read in the eyes of others
As feel in his own fall; for men, like butterflies,
Show not their mealy wings but to the summer,   79

And not a man, for being simply man,   80
Hath any honor but honor for those honors   81
That are without him—as place, riches, and favor,   82
Prizes of accident as oft as merit;
Which, when they fall, as being slippery standers,   84
The love that leaned on them, as slippery too,
Doth one pluck down another and together
Die in the fall. But 'tis not so with me;
Fortune and I are friends. I do enjoy
At ample point all that I did possess,   89
Save these men's looks, who do, methinks, find out
Something not worth in me such rich beholding   91
As they have often given. Here is Ulysses;
I'll interrupt his reading.—How now, Ulysses?
ULYSSES   Now, great Thetis' son!
ACHILLES   What are you reading?
ULYSSES   A strange fellow here
Writes me that man, how dearly ever parted,   97
How much in having, or without or in,   98
Cannot make boast to have that which he hath,
Nor feels not what he owes, but by reflection;   100
As when his virtues, shining upon others,
Heat them, and they retort that heat again   102
To the first givers.
ACHILLES   This is not strange, Ulysses.
The beauty that is borne here in the face
The bearer knows not, but commends itself   105
To others' eyes; nor doth the eye itself,
That most pure spirit of sense, behold itself,   107
Not going from itself, but eye to eye opposed   108
Salutes each other with each other's form.   109
For speculation turns not to itself   110
Till it hath traveled and is mirrored there
Where it may see itself. This is not strange at all.
ULYSSES
I do not strain at the position—   113
It is familiar—but at the author's drift,   114
Who, in his circumstance, expressly proves   115
That no man is the lord of anything,
Though in and of him there be much consisting,   117
Till he communicate his parts to others;
Nor doth he of himself know them for aught   119
Till he behold them formed in the applause

80–2 not . . . him no one is honored for himself but, rather, for those marks of distinction that are external to him   **82 as** such as **84 being . . . standers** standing on uncertain foundation   **89 At ample point** to the full   **91 Something . . . beholding** something in me not worthy of such high respect   **97–8 Writes . . . or in** writes that any individual, however richly endowed with natural good qualities both external and internal   **100 owes** owns.   **but by reflection** i.e., except as reflected in others' opinions   **102 retort** reflect   **105 but** (1) unless it (2) but instead   **107 most . . . sense** most exquisite of the five senses. (Compare 1.1.60.)   **108–9 Not . . . form** since it cannot go out from itself; instead, two persons' eyes gazing into each other must convey to both persons a sense of what they look like from another's point of view.   **110 speculation** power of sight   **113 strain . . . position** find difficulty in the writer's general stance   **114 drift** i.e., particular application   **115 circumstance** detailed argument **117 Though . . . consisting** though he enjoys many fine qualities that cohere and harmonize   **119 aught** anything of value

---

43 unplausive disapproving   **44 derision medicinable** curative scorn   **45 use** i.e., make connection.   **strangeness** aloofness **46 Which . . . drink** which medicine his own pride will thirst for. **47 glass** mirror   **48 To show . . . pride** in which to see its image except the pride of others   **48–9 for supple . . . fees** i.e., since obsequiousness merely encourages arrogance by rewarding pride with the adulation it expects.   **50 We'll** I will. (The royal "we.") **57 Would he aught** Does he want anything   **61 The better** So much the better.   **71 used** accustomed   **73 use** are accustomed   **76 the declined** the man brought low   **79 mealy** powdery

Where they're extended; who, like an arch, reverb'rate

The voice again, or, like a gate of steel   121

Fronting the sun, receives and renders back   123

His figure and his heat. I was much rapt in this   124

And apprehended here immediately

Th'unknown Ajax. Heavens, what a man is there!   126

A very horse, that has he knows not what.   127

Nature, what things there are

Most abject in regard and dear in use!   129

What things again most dear in the esteem   130

And poor in worth! Now shall we see tomorrow—

An act that very chance doth throw upon him—

Ajax renowned. Oh, heavens, what some men do,

While some men leave to do!   134

How some men creep in skittish Fortune's hall,   135

Whiles others play the idiots in her eyes!   136

How one man eats into another's pride,   137

While pride is fasting in his wantonness!   138

To see these Grecian lords—why, even already

They clap the lubber Ajax on the shoulder,   140

As if his foot were on brave Hector's breast

And great Troy shrinking.

ACHILLES   I do believe it,

For they passed by me as misers do by beggars,

Neither gave to me good word nor look.

What, are my deeds forgot?

ULYSSES

Time hath, my lord, a wallet at his back,   146

Wherein he puts alms for oblivion,   147

A great-sized monster of ingratitudes.

Those scraps are good deeds past, which are devoured

As fast as they are made, forgot as soon

As done. Perseverance, dear my lord,

Keeps honor bright; to have done is to hang

Quite out of fashion, like a rusty mail   153

In monumental mock'ry. Take the instant way,   154

For honor travels in a strait so narrow

Where one but goes abreast. Keep then the path,   156

For emulation hath a thousand sons   157

That one by one pursue. If you give way,   158

Or hedge aside from the direct forthright,   159

Like to an entered tide they all rush by

And leave you hindmost;

Or, like a gallant horse fall'n in first rank,

Lie there for pavement to the abject rear,   163

O'errun and trampled on. Then what they do in present,   164

Though less than yours in past, must o'ertop yours;

For Time is like a fashionable host

That slightly shakes his parting guest by th' hand,   167

And with his arms outstretched, as he would fly,   168

Grasps in the comer. The welcome ever smiles,   169

And farewell goes out sighing. Let not virtue seek   170

Remuneration for the thing it was;   171

For beauty, wit,

High birth, vigor of bone, desert in service,

Love, friendship, charity, are subjects all

To envious and calumniating Time.   175

One touch of nature makes the whole world kin,   176

That all with one consent praise newborn gauds,

Though they are made and molded of things past,   178

And give to dust that is a little gilt   179

More laud than gilt o'erdusted.   180

The present eye praises the present object.

Then marvel not, thou great and complete man,   182

That all the Greeks begin to worship Ajax,

Since things in motion sooner catch the eye

Than what not stirs. The cry went once on thee,   185

And still it might, and yet it may again,

If thou wouldst not entomb thyself alive

And case thy reputation in thy tent,   188

Whose glorious deeds but in these fields of late   189

Made emulous missions 'mongst the gods themselves   190

And drave great Mars to faction.

ACHILLES   Of this my privacy   191

I have strong reasons.

ULYSSES   But 'gainst your privacy

The reasons are more potent and heroical.   193

'Tis known, Achilles, that you are in love

With one of Priam's daughters.

ACHILLES   Ha! Known?   195

ULYSSES   Is that a wonder?

The providence that's in a watchful state   197

Knows almost every grain of Pluto's gold,   198

Finds bottom in th'uncomprehensive deeps,   199

---

121 Where they're extended of those persons to whom they are displayed.   **who** i.e., the applauders   **123 Fronting** facing   **124 His** its, the sun's   **126 unknown** as yet obscure in reputation   **127 has . . . what** does not know his own strength.   **129 abject . . . use** lowly esteemed and yet valuable, of practical value.   **130 again** on the other hand   **134 to do** undone.   **135 creep** i.e., are unobtrusive, draw no attention to themselves.   **skittish** fickle   **136 Whiles . . . eyes** while others attract the attention of the goddess Fortune by making fools of themselves.   **137–8 How . . . wantonness!** i.e., How one man, like Ajax, encroaches on another's glory, while that other man, like Achilles, starves his own glory through self-indulgence or caprice!   **140 lubber** clumsy lout   **146 wallet** knapsack   **147 alms for oblivion** i.e., noble deeds destined to be forgotten   **153 mail** suit of armor   **154 In . . . mock'ry** serving as a mocking trophy of forgotten noble deeds.   **instant way** way that lies immediately before you now   **156 one but** only one   **157 emulation** envious rivalry   **158 one by one pursue** crowd after one another in single file, vying for supremacy.   **159 Or . . . forthright** or veer from the straight path

163–4 for pavement . . . on as a pavement to be trampled on by the cowardly and inferior troops who bring up the rear.   **167 slightly** negligently   **168 as . . . fly** as if he were about to depart   **169 Grasps in** welcomes, embraces   **170–1 Let . . . was** Don't be so naive as to expect reward for past achievements   **175 calumniating** slandering   **176 nature** i.e., natural human weakness; here, the propensity of men to praise frivolous novelty (*newborn gauds*)   **178 Though . . . past** i.e., even though their apparent novelty is all derivative   **179–80 And . . . o'erdusted** i.e., and give more praise to trivial things that have been made to look glittering than to objects of true worth that have been covered by the dust of oblivion.   **182 complete** accomplished   **185 cry** acclaim   **188 case** box up, enclose   **189 but . . . late** only recently on the battlefield   **190–1 Made . . . faction** i.e., caused the gods themselves to join in the fighting on opposing sides, emulously, and even drove the god of war to be partisan.   **193 heroical** suitable to a hero.   **195 one . . . daughters** i.e., Polyxena.   **197 providence** foresight   **198 Pluto's** (Pluto, god of the underworld, was often confused with Plutus, god of riches.)   **199 th'uncomprehensive** the unfathomable

Keeps place with thought and almost, like the gods,   200
Do thoughts unveil in their dumb cradles.   201
There is a mystery—with whom relation   202
Durst never meddle—in the soul of state,   203
Which hath an operation more divine
Than breath or pen can give expressure to.   205
All the commerce that you have had with Troy   206
As perfectly is ours as yours, my lord;   207
And better would it fit Achilles much
To throw down Hector than Polyxena.
But it must grieve young Pyrrhus now at home,   210
When Fame shall in our islands sound her trump,   211
And all the Greekish girls shall tripping sing,
"Great Hector's sister did Achilles win,
But our great Ajax bravely beat down him."   214
Farewell, my lord. I as your lover speak.   215
The fool slides o'er the ice that you should break.   216

                                                        [*Exit.*]

PATROCLUS
To this effect, Achilles, have I moved you.
A woman impudent and mannish grown   218
Is not more loathed than an effeminate man
In time of action. I stand condemned for this;
They think my little stomach to the war   221
And your great love to me restrains you thus.
Sweet, rouse yourself, and the weak wanton Cupid
Shall from your neck unloose his amorous fold   224
And, like a dewdrop from the lion's mane,
Be shook to air.

ACHILLES   Shall Ajax fight with Hector?
PATROCLUS
Ay, and perhaps receive much honor by him.

ACHILLES
I see my reputation is at stake;
My fame is shrewdly gored.

PATROCLUS   Oh, then, beware!   229
Those wounds heal ill that men do give themselves.
Omission to do what is necessary
Seals a commission to a blank of danger;   232
And danger, like an ague, subtly taints   233
Even then when we sit idly in the sun.

ACHILLES
Go call Thersites hither, sweet Patroclus.
I'll send the fool to Ajax and desire him
T'invite the Trojan lords after the combat
To see us here unarmed. I have a woman's longing,

An appetite that I am sick withal,   239
To see great Hector in his weeds of peace,   240
To talk with him and to behold his visage,
Even to my full of view.

                    Enter Thersites.

                    A labor saved.   242

THERSITES   A wonder!
ACHILLES   What?
THERSITES   Ajax goes up and down the field, asking for
himself.   246
ACHILLES   How so?
THERSITES   He must fight singly tomorrow with Hector
and is so prophetically proud of an heroical cudgeling
that he raves in saying nothing.
ACHILLES   How can that be?
THERSITES   Why, 'a stalks up and down like a peacock—
a stride and a stand; ruminates like an hostess that   253
hath no arithmetic but her brain to set down her reck-   254
oning; bites his lip with a politic regard, as who   255
should say, "There were wit in this head, an 'twould   256
out"—and so there is, but it lies as coldly in him as
fire in a flint, which will not show without knocking.
The man's undone forever, for if Hector break not his
neck i'th' combat, he'll break't himself in vainglory.
He knows not me. I said, "Good morrow, Ajax," and
he replies, "Thanks, Agamemnon." What think you of
this man, that takes me for the general? He's grown a
very land-fish, languageless, a monster. A plague of   264
opinion! A man may wear it on both sides, like a   265
leather jerkin.   266
ACHILLES   Thou must be my ambassador to him, Thersites.
THERSITES   Who, I? Why, he'll answer nobody; he
professes not answering. Speaking is for beggars; he   270
wears his tongue in 's arms. I will put on his presence.   271
Let Patroclus make demands to me; you shall see
the pageant of Ajax.
ACHILLES   To him, Patroclus. Tell him I humbly desire
the valiant Ajax to invite the most valorous Hector to
come unarmed to my tent, and to procure safe-conduct
for his person of the magnanimous and most illus-
trious six-or-seven-times-honored Captain-General of
the Grecian army, Agamemnon, et cetera. Do this.
PATROCLUS   Jove bless great Ajax!
THERSITES   Hum!
PATROCLUS   I come from the worthy Achilles—
THERSITES   Ha?
PATROCLUS   Who most humbly desires you to invite
Hector to his tent—
THERSITES   Hum!

---

200 **Keeps . . . thought** keeps up with what is being thought
201 **Do . . . cradles** uncover thoughts as they are conceived in the
mind and before they are spoken.   202–3 **with . . . meddle** that can
never be talked about   205 **expressure** expression   206 **commerce**
dealings (i.e., with Polyxena)   207 **As perfectly . . . as yours** is
known to us of the Greek council as completely as to you
210 **Pyrrhus** Achilles's son, also called Neoptolemus   211 **trump**
trumpet   214 **him** i.e., Hector.   215 **lover** friend   216 **The fool . . .
break** i.e., The fool easily escapes dangers that to a man of your dignity would be fatal.   218 **impudent** shameless   221 **little stomach to**
lack of enthusiasm for   224 **fold** embrace   229 **shrewdly gored**
severely wounded.   232 **Seals . . . danger** i.e., gives danger unlimited
license, a blank check. (Literally, a warrant with blank spaces.)
233 **ague** fever.   **taints** infects. (Meat spoils when left lying in the sun.)

239 **withal** with   240 **weeds** garments   242 **to . . . view** to the fullest
satisfaction of my eyes.   246 **himself** i.e., "Ajax." (With a quibble on
"a jakes" or latrine.)   253–4 **hostess . . . arithmetic** (Tavern keepers
were proverbially poor at addition; compare 1.2.114.)   255–6 **with
a . . . say** with an assumption of a knowing manner, as if one should
say   264 **land-fish** i.e., monstrous creature   264–6 **A plague . . .
jerkin** A curse on the way men flirt with reputation! It can be turned
inside out, like a man's close-fitting jacket.   270 **professes** i.e., makes
a point of   271 **arms** weapons.   **put . . . presence** assume his
demeanor.

PATROCLUS   And to procure safe-conduct from Agamemnon.

THERSITES   Agamemnon?

PATROCLUS   Ay, my lord.

THERSITES   Ha!

PATROCLUS   What say you to't?

THERSITES   God b'wi'you, with all my heart.

PATROCLUS   Your answer, sir.

THERSITES   If tomorrow be a fair day, by eleven o'clock
it will go one way or other. Howsoever, he shall 296
pay for me ere he has me.

PATROCLUS   Your answer, sir.

THERSITES   Fare ye well, with all my heart.

ACHILLES   Why, but he is not in this tune, is he?   300

THERSITES   No, but he's out o' tune thus. What music
will be in him when Hector has knocked out his
brains, I know not; but, I am sure, none, unless the 303
fiddler Apollo get his sinews to make catlings on.   304

ACHILLES
Come, thou shalt bear a letter to him straight.

THERSITES   Let me carry another to his horse, for that's
the more capable creature.   307

ACHILLES
My mind is troubled, like a fountain stirred,
And I myself see not the bottom of it.
                                    [*Exeunt Achilles and Patroclus.*]

THERSITES   Would the fountain of your mind were clear
again, that I might water an ass at it! I had rather be a
tick in a sheep than such a valiant ignorance.   [*Exit.*] 312

❖

[4.1]

*Enter, at one door, Aeneas, [with a torch;] at
another, Paris, Deiphobus, Antenor, Diomedes
the Grecian [and others[, with torches.*

PARIS   See, ho! Who is that there?

DEIPHOBUS   It is the Lord Aeneas.

AENEAS   Is the prince there in person?
Had I so good occasion to lie long
As you, Prince Paris, nothing but heavenly business
Should rob my bedmate of my company.

DIOMEDES
That's my mind too. Good morrow, Lord Aeneas.   7

PARIS
A valiant Greek, Aeneas; take his hand.
Witness the process of your speech, wherein   9
You told how Diomed, a whole week by days,   10
Did haunt you in the field.

AENEAS   Health to you, valiant sir,
During all question of the gentle truce;   13

But when I meet you armed, as black defiance   14
As heart can think or courage execute.

DIOMEDES
The one and other Diomed embraces.   16
Our bloods are now in calm; and so long, health!   17
But when contention and occasion meet,   18
By Jove, I'll play the hunter for thy life
With all my force, pursuit, and policy.   20

AENEAS   And thou shalt hunt a lion that will fly
With his face backward. In humane gentleness,   22
Welcome to Troy! Now, by Anchises' life,   23
Welcome, indeed! By Venus' hand I swear,   24
No man alive can love in such a sort   25
The thing he means to kill more excellently.

DIOMEDES
We sympathize. Jove, let Aeneas live,   27
If to my sword his fate be not the glory,
A thousand complete courses of the sun!
But, in mine emulous honor, let him die   30
With every joint a wound, and that tomorrow!

AENEAS   We know each other well.

DIOMEDES
We do, and long to know each other worse.

PARIS
This is the most despiteful gentle greeting,   34
The noblest hateful love, that e'er I heard of.
What business, lord, so early?

AENEAS
I was sent for to the King, but why, I know not.

PARIS
His purpose meets you. 'Twas to bring this Greek   38
To Calchas' house, and there to render him,   39
For the enfreed Antenor, the fair Cressid.
Let's have your company, or, if you please,
Haste there before us. [*Aside to Aeneas*] I constantly
do think—   42
Or rather, call my thought a certain knowledge—
My brother Troilus lodges there tonight.
Rouse him and give him note of our approach,   45
With the whole quality whereof. I fear   46
We shall be much unwelcome.

AENEAS   That I assure you.
Troilus had rather Troy were borne to Greece
Than Cressid borne from Troy.

PARIS   There is no help.
The bitter disposition of the time   50
Will have it so. On, lord; we'll follow you.

AENEAS   Good morrow, all.   [*Exit Aeneas.*]

PARIS
And tell me, noble Diomed, faith, tell me true,

---

14 as black defiance defiance as black   **16 The one and other** i.e.,
Aeneas's promises of *health* and *defiance*   **17 so long** for as long as
this truce lasts   **18 when . . . meet** i.e., when the battle gives us
opportunity   **20 policy** cunning.   **22 face backward** i.e., bravely facing the enemy.   **23, 24 Anchises, Venus** (Aeneas's parents)   **25 in . . .
sort** to such a degree   **27 sympathize** share your feeling.   **30 emulous** ambitious   **34 despiteful** contemptuous   **38 His . . . you** i.e., I
can tell you, since the matter is at hand.   **39 render** give   **42 constantly** confirmedly   **45 note** news, notice   **46 the . . . whereof** all
the causes thereof, reasons why.   **50 disposition** (1) temperament
(2) arrangement, ordering

---

296 Howsoever In either case   **300 tune** i.e., mood, disposition
303–4 the fiddler Apollo i.e., Apollo, as god of music   **304 catlings**
catgut, of which strings for instruments were made   **307 capable**
able to understand   **312 ignorance** ignoramus, fool.
4.1. Location: Troy. A street, in an unspecified place.
0.1, 3 torch, torches (These directions may indicate torchbearers.)
7 mind opinion   **9 process** drift   **10 a whole . . . days** every day for a
week   **13 question** discussion, parley (allowed by the truce)

Even in the soul of sound good-fellowship,   54
Who, in your thoughts, merits fair Helen most,
Myself or Menelaus?
DIOMEDES   Both alike.
He merits well to have her that doth seek her,   57
Not making any scruple of her soilure,   58
With such a hell of pain and world of charge;   59
And you as well to keep her that defend her,
Not palating the taste of her dishonor,   61
With such a costly loss of wealth and friends.
He, like a puling cuckold, would drink up   63
The lees and dregs of a flat 'tamèd piece;   64
You, like a lecher, out of whorish loins   65
Are pleased to breed out your inheritors.   66
Both merits poised, each weighs nor less nor more;   67
But he as he, the heavier for a whore.   68
PARIS
You are too bitter to your countrywoman.
DIOMEDES
She's bitter to her country. Hear me, Paris:
For every false drop in her bawdy veins
A Grecian's life hath sunk; for every scruple   72
Of her contaminated carrion weight   73
A Trojan hath been slain. Since she could speak,
She hath not given so many good words breath
As for her Greeks and Trojans suffered death.
PARIS
Fair Diomed, you do as chapmen do,   77
Dispraise the thing that you desire to buy.
But we in silence hold this virtue well:
We'll not commend what we intend to sell.   80
Here lies our way.   *Exeunt.*

❖

[4.2]

Enter Troilus and Cressida.

TROILUS
Dear, trouble not yourself. The morn is cold.
CRESSIDA
Then, sweet my lord, I'll call mine uncle down.
He shall unbolt the gates.
TROILUS   Trouble him not.
To bed, to bed! Sleep kill those pretty eyes,   4
And give as soft attachment to thy senses   5
As infants' empty of all thought!   6

CRESSIDA
Good morrow, then.
TROILUS   I prithee now, to bed.
CRESSIDA   Are you aweary of me?
TROILUS
Oh, Cressida! But that the busy day,
Waked by the lark, hath roused the ribald crows,   10
And dreaming night will hide our joys no longer,
I would not from thee.
CRESSIDA   Night hath been too brief.
TROILUS
Beshrew the witch! With venomous wights she stays   13
As tediously as hell, but flies the grasps of love   14
With wings more momentary-swift than thought.
You will catch cold, and curse me.
CRESSIDA
Prithee, tarry. You men will never tarry.
O foolish Cressid! I might have still held off,
And then you would have tarried. Hark, there's one
up.
PANDARUS [*within*]   What's all the doors open here?   20
TROILUS   It is your uncle.

[Enter Pandarus.]

CRESSIDA
A pestilence on him! Now will he be mocking.
I shall have such a life!
PANDARUS   How now, how now, how go maiden-   24
heads? Here, you maid! Where's my cousin Cressid?   25
CRESSIDA
Go hang yourself, you naughty mocking uncle!
You bring me to do—and then you flout me too.
PANDARUS   To do what, to do what?—Let her say
what.—What have I brought you to do?
CRESSIDA
Come, come, beshrew your heart! You'll ne'er be
good,   30
Nor suffer others.   31
PANDARUS   Ha, ha! Alas, poor wretch! Ah, poor *capoc-*   32
chia! Has 't not slept tonight? Would he not—a   33
naughty man—let it sleep? A bugbear take him!   34
CRESSIDA
Did not I tell you? Would he were knocked i'th' head!
                                                    One knocks.
Who's that at door? Good uncle, go and see.—
My lord, come you again into my chamber.
You smile and mock me, as if I meant naughtily.
TROILUS   Ha, ha!
CRESSIDA
Come, you are deceived. I think of no such thing.
                                                    Knock.

---

54 **soul** spirit   57 **He** Menelaus, or any cuckolded husband
58 **Not . . . scruple** not worrying about.   **soilure** dishonor, stain
59 **charge** cost   61 **Not palating** not tasting, being insensible of
63 **puling** complaining   64 **flat 'tamèd piece** wine so long opened
that it is flat; hence, a used woman   65–6 **out of . . . inheritors** are
content to breed your heirs out of a whore's belly.   67 **poised**
weighed, balanced.   **nor less** neither less   68 **he as he** the one like
the other   72 **scruple** little bit. (Literally, one twenty-fourth of an
ounce.)   73 **carrion** putrefied and rotten, like a carcass   77 **chapmen**
traders, merchants   80 **We'll . . . sell** i.e., We won't praise Helen,
even though we intend to trade her to you at a high price.
4.2. Location: Troy. The courtyard of Calchas' house.
4 **Sleep kill** Let sleep overpower, put to rest   5 **attachment** arrest,
confinement   6 **infants'** i.e., infants' eyes

10 **ribald** offensively noisy, irreverent   13–14 **Beshrew . . . hell** i.e.,
Curse the night! She lingers endlessly with malignant beings (since
night and villainy accord)   20 **What's** Why are   24 **how go** what
price   25 **Where's . . . Cressid?** (Pandarus pretends not to recognize
Cressida now that she is no longer a virgin.)   30–1 **You'll . . . others**
i.e., You think such dirty thoughts that you can't imagine others to be
otherwise.   32–3 *capocchia* dolt, simpleton. (Italian.)   33 **Has 't** Has
it. (Pandarus condescendingly uses the neuter pronoun, as one might
in referring to a baby. [Also in line 34.])   34 **bugbear** hobgoblin

How earnestly they knock! Pray you, come in.
I would not for half Troy have you seen here.
        Exeunt [Troilus and Cressida].
PANDARUS   Who's there? What's the matter? Will you
beat down the door? [*He opens the door.*] How now,
what's the matter?

[*Enter Aeneas.*]

AENEAS   Good morrow, lord, good morrow.
PANDARUS   Who's there? My lord Aeneas? By my troth
I knew you not. What news with you so early?
AENEAS   Is not Prince Troilus here?
PANDARUS   Here? What should he do here?   50
AENEAS
Come, he is here, my lord. Do not deny him.
It doth import him much to speak with me.   52
PANDARUS   Is he here, say you? It's more than I know,
I'll be sworn. For my own part, I came in late. What   54
should he do here?
AENEAS   Hoo!—Nay, then. Come, come, you'll do him
wrong ere you are ware. You'll be so true to him, to be   57
false to him. Do not you know of him, but yet go fetch   58
him hither. Go.

[*Enter Troilus.*]

TROILUS   How now, what's the matter?
AENEAS
My lord, I scarce have leisure to salute you,   61
My matter is so rash. There is at hand   62
Paris your brother and Deiphobus,
The Grecian Diomed, and our Antenor
Delivered to us; and for him forthwith,
Ere the first sacrifice, within this hour,   66
We must give up to Diomedes' hand
The Lady Cressida.
TROILUS   Is it so concluded?
AENEAS
By Priam and the general state of Troy.   69
They are at hand and ready to effect it.
TROILUS
How my achievements mock me!
I will go meet them. And, my lord Aeneas,
We met by chance; you did not find me here.   73
AENEAS
Good, good, my lord, the secrets of nature
Have not more gift in taciturnity.
        Exeunt [Troilus and Aeneas].
PANDARUS   Is't possible? No sooner got but lost? The
devil take Antenor! The young prince will go mad. A
plague upon Antenor! I would they had broke's neck!

Enter Cressida.

CRESSIDA
How now? What's the matter? Who was here?
PANDARUS   Ah, ah!
CRESSIDA
Why sigh you so profoundly? Where's my lord?
Gone? Tell me, sweet uncle, what's the matter?
PANDARUS   Would I were as deep under the earth as I
am above!
CRESSIDA   O the gods! What's the matter?
PANDARUS   Pray thee, get thee in. Would thou hadst
ne'er been born! I knew thou wouldst be his death. Oh,
poor gentleman! A plague upon Antenor!
CRESSIDA   Good uncle, I beseech you, on my knees I
beseech you, what's the matter?
PANDARUS   Thou must be gone, wench, thou must be
gone. Thou art changed for Antenor. Thou must to thy   92
father and be gone from Troilus. 'Twill be his death,
'twill be his bane; he cannot bear it.   94
CRESSIDA
O you immortal gods! I will not go.
PANDARUS   Thou must.
CRESSIDA
I will not, uncle. I have forgot my father.
I know no touch of consanguinity;   98
No kin, no love, no blood, no soul so near me
As the sweet Troilus. O you gods divine!
Make Cressid's name the very crown of falsehood
If ever she leave Troilus! Time, force, and death,
Do to this body what extremes you can;
But the strong base and building of my love
Is as the very center of the earth,
Drawing all things to it. I'll go in and weep—
PANDARUS   Do, do.
CRESSIDA
Tear my bright hair and scratch my praisèd cheeks,
Crack my clear voice with sobs and break my heart
With sounding "Troilus." I will not go from Troy.   110
        [Exeunt.]

❖

[4.3]

*Enter Paris, Troilus, Aeneas, Deiphobus,
Antenor, [and] Diomedes.*

PARIS
It is great morning, and the hour prefixed   1
For her delivery to this valiant Greek
Comes fast upon. Good my brother Troilus,
Tell you the lady what she is to do,
And haste her to the purpose.
TROILUS   Walk into her house.
I'll bring her to the Grecian presently;   6
And to his hand when I deliver her,
Think it an altar, and thy brother Troilus
A priest there off'ring to it his own heart.   *[Exit.]*

50 should he do would he be doing **52 import** concern **57–8 You'll
. . . know of him** i.e., In seeking to guard Troilus' secret, you'll protect
him from knowing of a matter that concerns him. Go ahead and pretend you don't know he is here **61 salute** greet **62 rash** urgent,
pressing. **66 Ere . . . sacrifice** before the first religious ceremony of
the day **69 state** council **73 We met** i.e., Remember to say that we
met. (This is the fiction to which Aeneas agrees.)

92 changed exchanged **94 bane** death **98 touch of consanguinity**
sense or tiniest bit of kinship **110 sounding** uttering
4.3. Location: Troy. Before Cressida's house.
1 great morning broad day. **prefixed** earlier agreed upon **6 to . . .
presently** to Diomedes immediately

PARIS   I know what 'tis to love;
And would, as I shall pity, I could help!   11
Please you walk in, my lords?   *Exeunt.*

❖

[4.4]

Enter Pandarus and Cressida.

PANDARUS   Be moderate, be moderate.

CRESSIDA
Why tell you me of moderation?
The grief is fine, full, perfect, that I taste,   3
And violenteth in a sense as strong   4
As that which causeth it. How can I moderate it?
If I could temporize with my affection,   6
Or brew it to a weak and colder palate,   7
The like allayment could I give my grief.   8
My love admits no qualifying dross;   9
No more my grief, in such a precious loss.

Enter Troilus.

PANDARUS   Here, here, here he comes. Ah, sweet
ducks!
CRESSIDA   Oh, Troilus! Troilus!   [*Embracing him.*]
PANDARUS   What a pair of spectacles is here! Let me   14
embrace, too. "O heart," as the goodly saying is,
      "O heart, heavy heart,
      Why sigh'st thou without breaking?"
where he answers again,   18
      "Because thou canst not ease thy smart
      By friendship nor by speaking."   20
There was never a truer rhyme. Let us cast away noth-
ing, for we may live to have need of such a verse. We   22
see it, we see it. How now, lambs?   23
TROILUS
Cressid, I love thee in so strained a purity   24
That the blest gods, as angry with my fancy,   25
More bright in zeal than the devotion which   26
Cold lips blow to their deities, take thee from me.   27
CRESSIDA   Have the gods envy?
PANDARUS   Ay, ay, ay, ay; 'tis too plain a case.
CRESSIDA
And is it true that I must go from Troy?
TROILUS
A hateful truth.
CRESSIDA   What, and from Troilus too?
TROILUS
From Troy and Troilus.
CRESSIDA   Is't possible?

TROILUS
And suddenly, where injury of chance   33
Puts back leave-taking, jostles roughly by   34
All time of pause, rudely beguiles our lips
Of all rejoindure, forcibly prevents   36
Our locked embrasures, strangles our dear vows   37
Even in the birth of our own laboring breath.
We two, that with so many thousand sighs
Did buy each other, must poorly sell ourselves
With the rude brevity and discharge of one.   41
Injurious Time now with a robber's haste
Crams his rich thiev'ry up, he knows not how.   43
As many farewells as be stars in heaven,
With distinct breath and consigned kisses to them,   45
He fumbles up into a loose adieu,   46
And scants us with a single famished kiss,   47
Distasted with the salt of broken tears.   48
AENEAS   (*within*)   My lord, is the lady ready?
TROILUS
Hark! You are called. Some say the genius so   50
Cries "Come!" to him that instantly must die.—
Bid them have patience. She shall come anon.
PANDARUS   Where are my tears? Rain, to lay this wind,   53
or my heart will be blown up by the root.   [*Exit.*]   54
CRESSIDA
I must then to the Grecians?
TROILUS   No remedy.
CRESSIDA
A woeful Cressid 'mongst the merry Greeks!
When shall we see again?   57
TROILUS
Hear me, my love. Be thou but true of heart—
CRESSIDA
I true? How now? What wicked deem is this?   59
TROILUS
Nay, we must use expostulation kindly,   60
For it is parting from us.   61
I speak not "Be thou true" as fearing thee,   62
For I will throw my glove to Death himself   63
That there's no maculation in thy heart;   64
But "Be thou true," say I, to fashion in   65
My sequent protestation: Be thou true,   66
And I will see thee.

33–4 injury . . . leave-taking injurious Fortune prevents leisurely
farewells   **36 rejoindure** reunion (in a farewell kiss)   **37 embrasures**
embraces   **41 discharge of one** (1) exhalation of a single sigh
(2) making of a single payment.   **43 thiev'ry** stolen property.   **he . . .
how** every which way, distractedly.   **45 With . . . them** with the
words of farewell and the kisses with which those words are confirmed, sealed   **46 He fumbles up** Time clumsily huddles together
47 scants inadequately supplies   **48 Distasted** rendered distasteful.
broken interrupted with sobs   **50 genius** attendant spirit supposed
to be assigned to a person at birth   **53 Rain . . . wind** i.e., Tears, to
allay my sighs   **54 by the root** i.e., as though the heart were a tree in
a storm of sighs. (Sighs were thought to deprive the heart of its
blood.)   **57 see** see each other   **59 deem** thought, surmise   **60–1 we
must . . . from us** i.e., we must expostulate gently, for soon even this
opportunity for speech will be lost to us.   **62 as fearing thee** i.e., as if
not trusting your constancy   **63 throw . . . to** i.e., challenge   **64 maculation** stain of impurity   **65 fashion in** serve as introduction for
66 sequent ensuing

---

11 as as much as
4.4. Location: Troy. Cressida's house.
3 fine refined, pure   **4 violenteth** is violent   **6 temporize** compromise, come to terms   **7 brew** dilute.   **palate** taste   **8 allayment** dilu-
tion, mitigation   **9 qualifying dross** foreign matter making it less
pure   **14 spectacles** sights. (With suggestion of "eyeglasses.")   **18 he**
the heart   **20 By . . . speaking** by mere friendship or words alone.
22–3 We see it i.e., We see how verses can console   **24 strained** purified as by filtering   **25 as** as if.   **fancy** love   **26–7 More . . . deities** a
love that is more zealous than the devotion which the chaste lips of
vestal virgins breathe to the gods

CRESSIDA

Oh, you shall be exposed, my lord, to dangers
As infinite as imminent! But I'll be true.

TROILUS

And I'll grow friend with danger. Wear this sleeve.   70
[They exchange favors.]

CRESSIDA

And you this glove. When shall I see you?

TROILUS

I will corrupt the Grecian sentinels,
To give thee nightly visitation.   72
But yet, be true.

CRESSIDA   Oh, heavens, "Be true" again?

TROILUS   Hear why I speak it, love.
The Grecian youths are full of quality;   76
Their loving well composed with gifts of nature,   77
And flowing o'er with arts and exercise.   78
How novelty may move, and parts with person,   79
Alas, a kind of godly jealousy—
Which, I beseech you, call a virtuous sin—   80
Makes me afeard.

CRESSIDA   Oh, heavens! You love me not.

TROILUS   Die I a villain, then!
In this I do not call your faith in question
So mainly as my merit. I cannot sing,   85
Nor heel the high lavolt, nor sweeten talk,   86
Nor play at subtle games—fair virtues all,   87
To which the Grecians are most prompt and pregnant.   88
But I can tell that in each grace of these
There lurks a still and dumb-discursive devil
That tempts most cunningly. But be not tempted.   90

CRESSIDA   Do you think I will?

TROILUS

No. But something may be done that we will not;   94
And sometimes we are devils to ourselves,
When we will tempt the frailty of our powers,   96
Presuming on their changeful potency.   97

AENEAS (within)

Nay, good my lord—

TROILUS   Come, kiss, and let us part.

PARIS (within)

Brother Troilus!

TROILUS   Good brother, come you hither,
And bring Aeneas and the Grecian with you.

CRESSIDA   My lord, will you be true?

TROILUS

Who, I? Alas, it is my vice, my fault.

Whiles others fish with craft for great opinion,   103
I with great truth catch mere simplicity;   104
Whilst some with cunning gild their copper crowns,   105
With truth and plainness I do wear mine bare.

[Enter Aeneas, Paris, Antenor, Deiphobus, and Diomedes.]

Fear not my truth. The moral of my wit   107
Is "plain and true"; there's all the reach of it.—   108
Welcome, Sir Diomed. Here is the lady
Which for Antenor we deliver you.
At the port, lord, I'll give her to thy hand,   111
And by the way possess thee what she is.   112
Entreat her fair, and by my soul, fair Greek,   113
If e'er thou stand at mercy of my sword,
Name Cressid, and thy life shall be as safe
As Priam is in Ilium.

DIOMEDES   Fair Lady Cressid,
So please you, save the thanks this prince expects.   117
The luster in your eye, heaven in your cheek,
Pleads your fair usage; and to Diomed
You shall be mistress, and command him wholly.

TROILUS

Grecian, thou dost not use me courteously,
To shame the zeal of my petition to thee
In praising her. I tell thee, lord of Greece,
She is as far high-soaring o'er thy praises
As thou unworthy to be called her servant.   125
I charge thee use her well, even for my charge;   126
For, by the dreadful Pluto, if thou dost not,
Though the great bulk Achilles be thy guard,   128
I'll cut thy throat.

DIOMEDES   Oh, be not moved, Prince Troilus.   129
Let me be privileged by my place and message
To be a speaker free. When I am hence,
I'll answer to my lust. And know you, lord,   132
I'll nothing do on charge. To her own worth   133
She shall be prized; but that you say "Be 't so,"   134
I'll speak it in my spirit and honor, "No."   135

TROILUS

Come, to the port.—I'll tell thee, Diomed,
This brave shall oft make thee to hide thy head.—   137
Lady, give me your hand, and, as we walk,
To our own selves bend we our needful talk.
[Exeunt Troilus, Cressida, and Diomedes.] Sound
trumpet [within].

PARIS
Hark! Hector's trumpet.

AENEAS   How have we spent this morning! 140
The Prince must think me tardy and remiss,
That swore to ride before him to the field.

PARIS
'Tis Troilus' fault. Come, come, to field with him.

DEIPHOBUS   Let us make ready straight.

AENEAS
Yea, with a bridegroom's fresh alacrity,
Let us address to tend on Hector's heels.   146
The glory of our Troy doth this day lie
On his fair worth and single chivalry.   *Exeunt.* 148

❖

[4.5]

Enter Ajax, armed, Achilles, Patroclus,
Agamemnon, Menelaus, Ulysses, Nestor, etc.

AGAMEMNON
Here art thou in appointment fresh and fair,   1
Anticipating time with starting courage.   2
Give with thy trumpet a loud note to Troy,
Thou dreadful Ajax, that the appallèd air   4
May pierce the head of the great combatant
And hale him hither.

AJAX   Thou, trumpet, there's my purse. 6
                    [*He throws money to his trumpeter.*]
Now crack thy lungs and split thy brazen pipe.
Blow, villain, till thy spherèd bias cheek   8
Outswell the colic of puffed Aquilon.   9
Come, stretch thy chest, and let thy eyes spout blood;
Thou blowest for Hector.   [*Trumpet sounds.*] 11

ULYSSES   No trumpet answers.

ACHILLES   'Tis but early days.   13

[*Enter Diomedes, with Cressida.*]

AGAMEMNON
Is not yond Diomed, with Calchas' daughter?

ULYSSES
'Tis he. I ken the manner of his gait;   15
He rises on the toe. That spirit of his
In aspiration lifts him from the earth.

AGAMEMNON
Is this the Lady Cressid?

DIOMEDES   Even she.

AGAMEMNON
Most dearly welcome to the Greeks, sweet lady.
                         [*He kisses her.*]

NESTOR
Our general doth salute you with a kiss.

ULYSSES
Yet is the kindness but particular;   21
'Twere better she were kissed in general.   22

NESTOR
And very courtly counsel. I'll begin. [*He kisses her.*]
So much for Nestor.

ACHILLES
I'll take that winter from your lips, fair lady.   25
Achilles bids you welcome.   [*He kisses her.*]

MENELAUS
I had good argument for kissing once.   27

PATROCLUS
But that's no argument for kissing now;
For thus popped Paris in his hardiment,   29
And parted thus you and your argument.
                         [*He kisses her.*]

ULYSSES
Oh, deadly gall and theme of all our scorns,   31
For which we lose our heads to gild his horns! 32

PATROCLUS
The first was Menelaus' kiss; this, mine.
Patroclus kisses you.   [*He kisses her again.*]

MENELAUS   Oh, this is trim!   34

PATROCLUS
Paris and I kiss evermore for him.   35

MENELAUS
I'll have my kiss, sir.—Lady, by your leave.

CRESSIDA
In kissing, do you render or receive?

MENELAUS
Both take and give.

CRESSIDA   I'll make my match to live, 38
The kiss you take is better than you give;
Therefore no kiss.

MENELAUS
I'll give you boot; I'll give you three for one.   41

CRESSIDA
You are an odd man; give even, or give none.   42

MENELAUS
An odd man, lady? Every man is odd.

CRESSIDA
No, Paris is not, for you know 'tis true
That you are odd, and he is even with you.

MENELAUS
You fillip me o'th' head.

CRESSIDA   No, I'll be sworn.   46

---

140 spent consumed wastefully   **146 address** get ready.   **tend** attend
148 single chivalry individual prowess.
4.5. Location: Near the Greek camp. Lists set out as an arena for combat.
1 appointment equipment, accoutrement   **2 starting** bold, eager to begin   **4 dreadful** inspiring dread   **6 trumpet** trumpeter   **8 bias** puffed out (and shaped like a weighted bowling ball used in bowls)   **9 colic** i.e., swelling (like that caused by colic).   **Aquilon** the north wind (here personified as distended by colic)   **11 for Hector** to summon Hector.   **13 days** in the day.   **15 ken** recognize

21 particular single, limited to one   **22 in general** by everyone. (With a play on "by the general.")   **25 that winter** (Alludes to Nestor's old age.)   **27 argument** theme, i.e., Helen. (But Patroclus answers in the sense of "supporting reason.")   **29 popped** came in suddenly. (With sexual suggestion.)   **hardiment** bold exploits, boldness. (With bawdy double meaning of "hardness.")   **31–2 Oh . . . horns!** Oh, fatal bitterness and the theme that brings scorn on us all, in which we lose our lives to gild over the fact of Menelaus's having been made a cuckold!   **34 trim** fine. (Said ironically.)   **35 Paris . . . him** i.e., I take the kiss Menelaus hoped for, just as Paris does in kissing Helen.   **38 I'll . . . to live** I'll wager my life   **41 boot** odds, advantage   **42 odd** (The wordplay here and in lines 43–5 includes [1] strange [2] single, no longer having a wife [3] unique, standing alone [4] odd man out [5] the opposite of *even*.)   **46 fillip . . . head** i.e., touch a sensitive spot, by alluding to my cuckold's horns.

ULYSSES
It were no match, your nail against his horn.   47
May I, sweet lady, beg a kiss of you?

CRESSIDA
You may.

ULYSSES   I do desire it.

CRESSIDA   Why, beg too.   49

ULYSSES
Why then for Venus' sake, give me a kiss
When Helen is a maid again, and his.   51

CRESSIDA
I am your debtor; claim it when 'tis due.

ULYSSES
Never's my day, and then a kiss of you.   53

DIOMEDES
Lady, a word. I'll bring you to your father.
                                    [*They talk apart.*]

NESTOR
A woman of quick sense.

ULYSSES   Fie, fie upon her!   55
There's language in her eye, her cheek, her lip,
Nay, her foot speaks; her wanton spirits look out
At every joint and motive of her body.   58
Oh, these encounterers, so glib of tongue,   59
That give accosting welcome ere it comes,   60
And wide unclasp the tables of their thoughts   61
To every ticklish reader! Set them down   62
For sluttish spoils of opportunity   63
And daughters of the game.   64
                    Exeunt [Diomedes and Cressida].

        Flourish. Enter all of Troy: [Hector, Paris,
        Aeneas, Helenus, Troilus, and attendants].

ALL
The Trojan's trumpet.

AGAMEMNON   Yonder comes the troop.   65

AENEAS
Hail, all you state of Greece! What shall be done   66
To him that victory commands? Or do you purpose   67
A victor shall be known? Will you the knights   68
Shall to the edge of all extremity   69
Pursue each other, or shall they be divided   70
By any voice or order of the field?   71

Hector bade ask.

AGAMEMNON   Which way would Hector have it?

AENEAS
He cares not; he'll obey conditions.   73

AGAMEMNON
'Tis done like Hector.

ACHILLES   But securely done,   74
A little proudly, and great deal disprising   75
The knight opposed.

AENEAS   If not Achilles, sir,
What is your name?

ACHILLES   If not Achilles, nothing.

AENEAS
Therefore Achilles. But, whate'er, know this:
In the extremity of great and little,   79
Valor and pride excel themselves in Hector,   80
The one almost as infinite as all,
The other blank as nothing. Weigh him well,
And that which looks like pride is courtesy.
This Ajax is half made of Hector's blood,   84
In love whereof half Hector stays at home;
Half heart, half hand, half Hector comes to seek
This blended knight, half Trojan and half Greek.

ACHILLES
A maiden battle, then? Oh, I perceive you.   88

            [*Enter Diomedes.*]

AGAMEMNON
Here is Sir Diomed. Go, gentle knight,
Stand by our Ajax. As you and Lord Aeneas
Consent upon the order of their fight,   91
So be it, either to the uttermost,
Or else a breath. The combatants being kin   93
Half stints their strife before their strokes begin.
                    [*Ajax and Hector enter the lists.*]

ULYSSES   They are opposed already.

AGAMEMNON [*to Ulysses*]
What Trojan is that same that looks so heavy?   96

ULYSSES
The youngest son of Priam, a true knight,
Not yet mature, yet matchless firm of word,
Speaking in deeds and deedless in his tongue;   99
Not soon provoked, nor being provoked soon
    calmed;
His heart and hand both open and both free.   101
For what he has he gives; what thinks, he shows;
Yet gives he not till judgment guide his bounty,
Nor dignifies an impair thought with breath;   104
Manly as Hector, but more dangerous,
For Hector in his blaze of wrath subscribes   106
To tender objects, but he in heat of action   107

---

47 It . . . horn i.e., Your fingernail is not nearly tough enough to make any impression on his cuckold's horn.   49 Why, beg too i.e., You must do more than merely *desire* a kiss; you must humble yourself as a petitionary male.   51 When . . . his when Helen is once again the chaste wife of Menelaus. (A virtually impossible condition.)
53 Never's . . . you i.e., I'll never claim that kiss.   55 of quick sense of lively wit and vibrant sensuality.   58 motive moving limb or organ   59 encounterers seductive women   60–2 That . . . reader! who sidle up to men without waiting to be invited, and allow their thoughts to be read avidly by every susceptible male! (With sexual suggestiveness in the image of unclasping, though *tables* are literally writing tablets, as in *Hamlet*, 1.5.108.)   63 sluttish . . . opportunity "corrupt wenches, of whose chastity every opportunity may make a prey" (Johnson)   64 daughters of the game i.e., prostitutes.   65 The Trojan's Hector's   66 state noble lords.   What . . . done i.e., What honors shall be afforded   67 that . . . commands that wins the victory.   68 known adjudged and declared.   68–71 Will . . . field? Do you desire that the combatants fight to the death, or that they be required to separate on order of the marshals, according to set regulations of the field of honor?

73 conditions whatever conditions are agreed upon.   74 securely overconfidently   75 disprising disdaining, underrating   79–80 In . . . Hector i.e., Hector's valor is extremely great; his pride, extremely little   84 Ajax . . . blood (Compare 2.2.77, note, and 4.5.121.)
88 maiden battle combat without bloodshed.   perceive understand
91 Consent agree.   order procedure, rules   93 a breath a friendly bout for exercise.   96 heavy sad.   99 Speaking . . . tongue letting his deeds speak for him and never boasting   101 free open, generous.
104 impair unconsidered, unsuitable   106–7 subscribes . . . objects yields mercy to the defenseless

Is more vindicative than jealous love.   108
They call him Troilus, and on him erect
A second hope, as fairly built as Hector.
Thus says Aeneas, one that knows the youth
Even to his inches, and with private soul   112
Did in great Ilium thus translate him to me.   113
         Alarum. [*Hector and Ajax fight.*]

AGAMEMNON   They are in action.
NESTOR   Now, Ajax, hold thine own!
TROILUS   Hector, thou sleep'st. Awake thee!
AGAMEMNON
His blows are well disposed. There, Ajax!   117
         Trumpets cease.

DIOMEDES
You must no more.
AENEAS   Princes, enough, so please you.
AJAX
I am not warm yet. Let us fight again.
DIOMEDES
As Hector pleases.
HECTOR   Why, then will I no more.
Thou art, great lord, my father's sister's son,
A cousin-german to great Priam's seed.   122
The obligation of our blood forbids
A gory emulation twixt us twain.   124
Were thy commixtion Greek and Trojan so   125
That thou couldst say, "This hand is Grecian all,
And this is Trojan; the sinews of this leg
All Greek, and this all Troy; my mother's blood
Runs on the dexter cheek, and this sinister   129
Bounds in my father's," by Jove multipotent,
Thou shouldst not bear from me a Greekish member
Wherein my sword had not impressure made   132
Of our rank feud. But the just gods gainsay   133
That any drop thou borrow'dst from thy mother,
My sacred aunt, should by my mortal sword
Be drainèd! Let me embrace thee, Ajax.
By him that thunders, thou hast lusty arms!   137
Hector would have them fall upon him thus.
Cousin, all honor to thee!   [*They embrace.*]
  AJAX   I thank thee, Hector.
Thou art too gentle and too free a man.
I came to kill thee, cousin, and bear hence
A great addition earnèd in thy death.   142
HECTOR
Not Neoptolemus so mirable,   143
On whose bright crest Fame with her loud'st "Oyez"   144
Cries, "This is he," could promise to himself   145
A thought of added honor torn from Hector.   146

AENEAS
There is expectance here from both the sides   147
What further you will do.
HECTOR   We'll answer it;
The issue is embracement. Ajax, farewell.   149
         [*They embrace.*]
AJAX
If I might in entreaties find success—
As seld I have the chance—I would desire   151
My famous cousin to our Grecian tents.
DIOMEDES
'Tis Agamemnon's wish, and great Achilles
Doth long to see unarmed the valiant Hector.
HECTOR
Aeneas, call my brother Troilus to me,
And signify this loving interview   156
To the expecters of our Trojan part;   157
Desire them home. Give me thy hand, my cousin.   158
I will go eat with thee and see your knights.
        [*Agamemnon and the rest approach them.*]
AJAX
Great Agamemnon comes to meet us here.
HECTOR [*to Aeneas*]
The worthiest of them tell me name by name;
But for Achilles, mine own searching eyes
Shall find him by his large and portly size.   163
AGAMEMNON
Worthy of arms! As welcome as to one   164
That would be rid of such an enemy—
But that's no welcome. Understand more clear:
What's past and what's to come is strewed with
   husks
And formless ruin of oblivion;
But in this extant moment, faith and troth,   169
Strained purely from all hollow bias-drawing,   170
Bids thee, with most divine integrity,
From heart of very heart, great Hector, welcome.
HECTOR
I thank thee, most imperious Agamemnon.   173
AGAMEMNON [*to Troilus*]
My well-famed lord of Troy, no less to you.
MENELAUS
Let me confirm my princely brother's greeting.
You brace of warlike brothers, welcome hither.
HECTOR
Who must we answer?
AENEAS   The noble Menelaus.
HECTOR
Oh, you, my lord? By Mars his gauntlet, thanks!   178

---

108 **vindicative** vindictive   112 **Even . . . inches** i.e., every inch of
him.   **with private soul** in private confidence   113 **translate** interpret   117 **disposed** placed.   122 **cousin-german** first cousin
124 **gory emulation** bloody rivalry   125 **commixtion** mixture
129 **dexter** right.   **sinister** left   132 **impressure** impression
133 **rank** hot, intemperate.   **gainsay** forbid   137 **By . . . thunders** i.e.,
By Jove   142 **addition** honorable title   143–6 **Not . . . Hector** i.e., Not
even the much-wondered-at Achilles, on whose heraldic badge Fame
herself in the role of the public crier announces "This is the man,"
could assure himself of added honor by defeating Hector.
(*Neoptolemus* is actually the name of Achilles's son.)

147 **expectance** eager desire to know   149 **issue** outcome   151 **seld**
seldom.   **desire** invite   156 **signify** announce   157 **the expecters . . .
part** those awaiting the outcome on our Trojan side   158 **home** to go
home.   163 **portly** stately, dignified   164 **of arms** (1) to bear
weapons (2) to receive embracements.   **as to one** as it is possible to
one   169 **extant** present   169–70 **faith . . . bias-drawing** faithfulness
and honesty, purified of all insincerities or obliquities (such as the
bias weight inserted in bowling balls in the game of bowls)
173 **imperious** imperial   178 **By . . . gauntlet** By Mars's armored
leather glove

Mock not that I affect th'untraded oath;   179
Your quondam wife swears still by Venus' glove.   180
She's well, but bade me not commend her to you.

MENELAUS
Name her not now, sir. She's a deadly theme.   182

HECTOR   Oh, pardon! I offend.

NESTOR
I have, thou gallant Trojan, seen thee oft,
Laboring for destiny, make cruel way   185
Through ranks of Greekish youth, and I have seen
  thee,
As hot as Perseus, spur thy Phrygian steed,   187
And seen thee scorning forfeits and subduements,   188
When thou hast hung thy advancèd sword i'th'air,   189
Not letting it decline on the declined,   190
That I have said to some my standers-by,   191
"Lo, Jupiter is yonder, dealing life!"   192
And I have seen thee pause and take thy breath,
When that a ring of Greeks have hemmed thee in,   194
Like an Olympian, wrestling. This have I seen;   195
But this thy countenance, still locked in steel,   196
I never saw till now. I knew thy grandsire   197
And once fought with him. He was a soldier good,
But, by great Mars, the captain of us all,
Never like thee. Let an old man embrace thee;
And, worthy warrior, welcome to our tents.
                                          [They embrace.]

AENEAS   'Tis the old Nestor.

HECTOR
Let me embrace thee, good old chronicle,
That hast so long walked hand in hand with Time.   203
Most reverend Nestor, I am glad to clasp thee.

NESTOR
I would my arms could match thee in contention
As they contend with thee in courtesy.

HECTOR   I would they could.

NESTOR   Ha!
By this white beard, I'd fight with thee tomorrow.
Well, welcome, welcome! I have seen the time!   211

ULYSSES
I wonder now how yonder city stands
When we have here her base and pillar by us.

HECTOR
I know your favor, Lord Ulysses, well.   214
Ah, sir, there's many a Greek and Trojan dead

Since first I saw yourself and Diomed   216
In Ilium, on your Greekish embassy.   217

ULYSSES
Sir, I foretold you then what would ensue.
My prophecy is but half his journey yet,
For yonder walls, that pertly front your town,   220
Yon towers, whose wanton tops do buss the clouds,   221
Must kiss their own feet.

HECTOR   I must not believe you.
There they stand yet, and modestly I think   223
The fall of every Phrygian stone will cost
A drop of Grecian blood. The end crowns all,
And that old common arbitrator, Time,
Will one day end it.

ULYSSES   So to him we leave it.
Most gentle and most valiant Hector, welcome!
After the general, I beseech you next
To feast with me and see me at my tent.

ACHILLES
I shall forestall thee, Lord Ulysses, thou!—   231
Now, Hector, I have fed mine eyes on thee;
I have with exact view perused thee, Hector,
And quoted joint by joint.

HECTOR   Is this Achilles?   234

ACHILLES   I am Achilles.

HECTOR
Stand fair, I pray thee. Let me look on thee.   236

ACHILLES
Behold thy fill.

HECTOR   Nay, I have done already.

ACHILLES
Thou art too brief. I will the second time,
As I would buy thee, view thee limb by limb.

HECTOR
Oh, like a book of sport thou'lt read me o'er;
But there's more in me than thou understand'st.
Why dost thou so oppress me with thine eye?

ACHILLES
Tell me, you heavens, in which part of his body
Shall I destroy him? Whether there, or there, or there?
That I may give the local wound a name
And make distinct the very breach whereout
Hector's great spirit flew. Answer me, heavens!

HECTOR
It would discredit the blest gods, proud man,
To answer such a question. Stand again.
Think'st thou to catch my life so pleasantly   250
As to prenominate in nice conjecture   251
Where thou wilt hit me dead?

ACHILLES   I tell thee, yea.

HECTOR
Wert thou the oracle to tell me so,

---

179 th'untraded the unhackneyed. (Hector insists that his newly minted oath, "by Mars his gauntlet," is suited to a war fought over a woman. In line 180 he contrasts this warlike oath with Helen's favorite, "by Venus' glove.")   **180 quondam** former   **182 deadly theme** (1) subject for mortal strife (2) gloomy topic of discourse.
185 Laboring for destiny employed in the service of fate, putting people to death   **187 Perseus** (See the note for 1.3.42.)   **188 scorning . . . subduements** i.e., ignoring those already vanquished, whose lives were forfeit; refusing easy prey   **189 advancèd** raised aloft   **190 the declined** those already vanquished   **191 to . . . my standers-by** to some of my followers   **192 dealing life** i.e., mercifully sparing the weak.   **194 When that** when   **195 Olympian** Olympian god, or a wrestler in the Olympic games   **196 still** always   **197 grandsire** i.e., Laomedon, builder of the walls of Troy and defender of the city against an earlier Greek army under Hercules   **203 chronicle** i.e., storehouse of memories   **211 I have . . . time!** i.e., There was a time when I could have taken you on!   **214 favor** face

216–17 Since . . . embassy (Hector refers to a non-Homeric episode, early in the war, when Ulysses and Diomedes visited Troy to offer peace in return for Helen.)   **220 pertly front** boldly stand before   **221 wanton** insolent, reckless. (With suggestion of amorousness in the metaphor of kissing.)   **buss** kiss   **223 modestly** without exaggeration   **231 forestall** prevent   **234 quoted joint by joint** scrutinized limb by limb.   **236 fair** in full view   **250 pleasantly** jocosely, easily   **251 prenominate** name beforehand.   **nice** precise

I'd not believe thee. Henceforth guard thee well;
For I'll not kill thee there, nor there, nor there,
But, by the forge that stithied Mars his helm,   256
I'll kill thee everywhere, yea, o'er and o'er.—
You wisest Grecians, pardon me this brag;
His insolence draws folly from my lips.
But I'll endeavor deeds to match these words,
Or may I never—

AJAX   Do not chafe thee, cousin.   261
And you, Achilles, let these threats alone,   262
Till accident or purpose bring you to't.   263
You may have every day enough of Hector,
If you have stomach. The general state, I fear,   265
Can scarce entreat you to be odd with him.   266

HECTOR *[to Achilles]*
I pray you, let us see you in the field.
We have had pelting wars since you refused   268
The Grecians' cause.

ACHILLES   Dost thou entreat me, Hector?
Tomorrow do I meet thee, fell as death;   270
Tonight all friends.

HECTOR   Thy hand upon that match.
                       [They grasp hands.]

AGAMEMNON
First, all you peers of Greece, go to my tent;
There in the full convive we. Afterwards,   273
As Hector's leisure and your bounties shall
Concur together, severally entreat him.   275
Beat loud the taborins, let the trumpets blow,   276
That this great soldier may his welcome know.
       [Flourish.] Exeunt [all except Troilus and Ulysses].

TROILUS
My lord Ulysses, tell me, I beseech you,
In what place of the field doth Calchas keep?   279

ULYSSES
At Menelaus' tent, most princely Troilus.
There Diomed doth feast with him tonight,
Who neither looks on heaven nor on earth
But gives all gaze and bent of amorous view
On the fair Cressid.

TROILUS
Shall I, sweet lord, be bound to you so much,
After we part from Agamemnon's tent,
To bring me thither?

ULYSSES   You shall command me, sir.
As gentle tell me, of what honor was   288
This Cressida in Troy? Had she no lover there
That wails her absence?

TROILUS
Oh, sir, to such as boasting show their scars   291
A mock is due. Will you walk on, my lord?

She was beloved, she loved; she is, and doth.
But still sweet love is food for fortune's tooth.   294
                           Exeunt.

❖

[5.1]

Enter Achilles and Patroclus.

ACHILLES
I'll heat his blood with Greekish wine tonight,
Which with my scimitar I'll cool tomorrow.   2
Patroclus, let us feast him to the height.

PATROCLUS
Here comes Thersites.

Enter Thersites.

ACHILLES   How now, thou core of envy!   4
Thou crusty batch of nature, what's the news?   5

THERSITES   Why, thou picture of what thou seemest   6
and idol of idiot-worshipers, here's a letter for thee.

ACHILLES   From whence, fragment?   8

THERSITES   Why, thou full dish of fool, from Troy.
           [He gives a letter. Achilles reads it.]

PATROCLUS   Who keeps the tent now?   10

THERSITES   The surgeon's box, or the patient's wound.   11

PATROCLUS   Well said, adversity! And what need these   12
tricks?

THERSITES   Prithee, be silent, boy. I profit not by thy
talk. Thou art thought to be Achilles' male varlet.

PATROCLUS   Male varlet, you rogue? What's that?

THERSITES   Why, his masculine whore. Now, the rotten
diseases of the south, the guts-griping, ruptures,   18
catarrhs, loads o'gravel i'th' back, lethargies, cold   19
palsies, raw eyes, dirt-rotten livers, wheezing lungs,   20
bladders full of imposthume, sciaticas, limekilns   21
i'th' palm, incurable bone-ache, and the riveled fee sim-   22
ple of the tetter, take and take again such preposterous   23
discoveries!   24

PATROCLUS   Why, thou damnable box of envy, thou,
what mean'st thou to curse thus?

THERSITES   Do I curse thee?

PATROCLUS   Why, no, you ruinous butt, you whoreson   28
indistinguishable cur, no.   29

---

256 stithied Mars his helm forged Mars's helmet   **261 chafe thee** anger yourself   **262–3 let . . . to't** stop making such boastful threats until, by accident or on purpose, you come face to face with Hector. **265 stomach** appetite (for fighting).   **general state** i.e., Greek commanders in council   **266 be odd** be at odds, undertake to fight **268 pelting** paltry   **270 fell** fierce   **273 convive we** let us feast together.   **275 severally entreat** individually invite   **276 taborins** drums   **279 keep** dwell.   **288 As gentle** Be so courteous as to. **honor** reputation   **291 such as** those who

294 But . . . tooth i.e., Love will always prove to be the plaything (literally, the sweet tooth) of fickle Fortune.
5.1. Location: The Greek camp. Before Achilles's tent.
2 scimitar sword. (Literally, a short, curved, single-bladed sword.)
4 core central hard mass of a boil or tumor   **5 batch of nature** sample of humankind in its unimproved natural state   **6 picture** mere image **8 fragment** leftover, crust.   **10 Who . . . now?** i.e., Who is looking after or occupying Achilles's tent these days? (Patroclus implies that Achilles can no longer be taunted with languishing here.)
11 surgeon's box (Thersites puns on *tent* in the previous line, i.e., a probe for cleaning a wound.)   **12 adversity** perversity, contrariety.
18–24 guts-griping . . . discoveries! may abdominal spasms, hernias, respiratory infections, severe cases of kidney stones, lethargy, paralysis, eye inflammations, liver diseases, asthma, abscesses of the bladder, lower back pain, gout or psoriasis, syphilitic bone-ache, and incurable wrinkling caused by skin eruptions strike repeatedly with disease such unnatural perversions as are discovered here!
28 ruinous butt dilapidated cask   **29 indistinguishable** misshapen

THERSITES   No? Why art thou then exasperate, thou idle 30
immaterial skein of sleave silk, thou green sarcenet 31
flap for a sore eye, thou tassel of a prodigal's purse, 32
thou? Ah, how the poor world is pestered with such
waterflies, diminutives of nature!

PATROCLUS   Out, gall!   35

THERSITES   Finch egg!   36

ACHILLES
My sweet Patroclus, I am thwarted quite
From my great purpose in tomorrow's battle.
Here is a letter from Queen Hecuba,
A token from her daughter, my fair love,
Both taxing me and gaging me to keep   41
An oath that I have sworn. I will not break it.
Fall, Greeks; fail, fame; honor, or go or stay.   43
My major vow lies here; this I'll obey.
Come, come, Thersites, help to trim my tent.   45
This night in banqueting must all be spent.
Away, Patroclus!   Exit [with Patroclus].

THERSITES   With too much blood and too little brain,   48
these two may run mad; but if with too much brain   49
and too little blood they do, I'll be a curer of madmen.   50
Here's Agamemnon, an honest fellow enough and   51
one that loves quails, but he has not so much brain as   52
earwax. And the goodly transformation of Jupiter   53
there, his brother, the bull—the primitive statue and   54
oblique memorial of cuckolds, a thrifty shoeing-horn   55
in a chain, hanging at his brother's leg—to what form   56
but that he is should wit larded with malice and mal-   57
ice farced with wit turn him to? To an ass were noth-   58
ing, he is both ass and ox; to an ox were nothing, he's   59
both ox and ass. To be a dog, a mule, a cat, a fitchew,   60
a toad, a lizard, an owl, a puttock, or a herring   61
without a roe, I would not care; but to be Menelaus! I   62
would conspire against destiny. Ask me not what I
would be if I were not Thersites, for I care not to be   64

the louse of a lazar, so I were not Menelaus. Heyday!   65
Sprites and fires!   66

Enter [Hector, Troilus, Ajax,] Agamemnon,
Ulysses, Nestor, [Menelaus,] and Diomed[es],
with lights.

AGAMEMNON
We go wrong, we go wrong.

AJAX   No, yonder 'tis,
There, where we see the light.

HECTOR   I trouble you.

AJAX
No, not a whit.

[Enter Achilles.]

ULYSSES   Here comes himself to guide you.

ACHILLES
Welcome, brave Hector; welcome, princes all.

AGAMEMNON
So now, fair Prince of Troy, I bid good night.
Ajax commands the guard to tend on you.

HECTOR
Thanks and good night to the Greeks' general.

MENELAUS   Good night, my lord.

HECTOR   Good night, sweet Lord Menelaus.

THERSITES [aside]   Sweet draft. "Sweet," quoth 'a?   76
Sweet sink, sweet sewer.   77

ACHILLES
Good night and welcome, both at once, to those
That go or tarry.

AGAMEMNON   Good night.
                    Exeunt Agamemnon [and] Menelaus.

ACHILLES
Old Nestor tarries; and you too, Diomed,
Keep Hector company an hour or two.

DIOMEDES
I cannot, lord. I have important business,
The tide whereof is now. Good night, great Hector.   84

HECTOR   Give me your hand.

ULYSSES [aside to Troilus]
Follow his torch; he goes to Calchas' tent.   86
I'll keep you company.

TROILUS [aside to Ulysses]   Sweet sir, you honor me.

HECTOR
And so, good night.
            [Exit Diomedes; Ulysses and Troilus following.]

ACHILLES   Come, come, enter my tent.
                Exeunt [Achilles, Hector, Ajax, and Nestor].

THERSITES   That same Diomed's a false-hearted rogue, a
most unjust knave. I will no more trust him when he   90
leers than I will a serpent when he hisses. He will   91
spend his mouth and promise, like Brabbler the   92

---

30 exasperate exasperated, angry   **30–2 thou idle ... purse** you useless, flimsy coil of floss silk, you eye-patch of soft green silk, you
fringed ornamental pendant on a spendthrift's purse   **31 skein** coil.
sleave silk floss silk, i.e., unwoven and hence worthless *(immaterial)*.
sarcenet fine, soft silk   **35 gall** (1) bitter railer (2) blister.   **36 Finch
egg** (The finch is a small bird.)   **41 taxing** urging.   **gaging** binding,
pledging   **43 or go** either go   **45 trim** prepare   **48 blood** passion,
willfulness   **49–50 but ... madmen** (Thersites considers it extremely
unlikely that Patroclus and Achilles should ever suffer from too much
intelligence or a lack of willful behavior; it's about as likely as if he,
Thersites, could cure mad folk.)   **51 honest ... enough** good enough
chap   **52 quails** i.e., prostitutes. (Cant term.)   **53–4 transformation ...
bull** (Alludes ironically to the myth of Jupiter's rape of Europa,
whom he encountered in a meadow after changing himself into a
bull. Thersites has in mind the bull's horns, which are like Menelaus's
cuckold's horns.)   **54–5 the primitive ... cuckolds** i.e., the prototype
and indirect reminder of cuckolds in having horns   **55–6 a thrifty ...
leg** i.e., a convenient tool, always available to do Agamemnon's will
(the *shoeing-horn* having been suggested in Thersites's mind by the
cuckold's horns)   **56–8 to what ... him to?** to what new shape other
than his own should my malicious wit and witty malice transform
him? (*Farced* means covered, adorned, stuffed, seasoned; or *faced*,
trimmed.)   **58–9 To ... nothing** To transform him into an ass
would be to accomplish nothing at all   **60 fitchew** polecat
61 puttock bird of prey of the kite kind   **61–2 a herring ... roe** i.e.,
a sexually emaciated or "spent" herring   **64 I care not to be** I
wouldn't mind being

65 lazar leper.   **so** provided   **66 Sprites and fires** (Thersites sees
those who are entering with lights, reminding him of will-o'-the-
wisps and other spirits.)   **76 Sweet draft** Sweet cesspool. (An ironic
echo of Hector's "Sweet Lord Menelaus," line 75.)   **'a** he   **77 sink**
privy   **84 tide** time   **86 his** Diomedes's   **90 unjust** dishonest,
perfidious   **91–2 He ... mouth** He will bay loudly as though promising that he has caught the scent   **92 Brabbler** (An apt name for such a
noisy hound.)

hound, but when he performs, astronomers foretell it; 93
it is prodigious, there will come some change. The sun 94
borrows of the moon when Diomed keeps his word. 95
I will rather leave to see Hector than not to dog him. 96
They say he keeps a Trojan drab and uses the traitor 97
Calchas his tent. I'll after. Nothing but lechery! All incon- 98
tinent varlets!   [*Exit.*] 99

✣

[5.2]

Enter Diomedes.

DIOMEDES   What, are you up here, ho? Speak.
CALCHAS [*within*]   Who calls?
DIOMEDES
   Diomed. Calchas, I think. Where's your daughter?
CALCHAS [*within*]   She comes to you.

       [*Enter Troilus and Ulysses at a distance; after
        them, Thersites.*]

ULYSSES [*to Troilus*]
   Stand where the torch may not discover us.   5
       [*He and Troilus conceal themselves in one place,
        Thersites in another. In the ensuing dialogue,
        Ulysses and Troilus continue to speak in asides
        to each other; Thersites utters his asides in
        commentary on the entire scene.*]

   Enter Cressida.

TROILUS
   Cressid comes forth to him.
DIOMEDES [*to Cressida*]   How now, my charge?   6
CRESSIDA
   Now, my sweet guardian! Hark, a word with you.
                                      [*She whispers.*]
TROILUS   Yea, so familiar?
ULYSSES   She will sing any man at first sight.   9
THERSITES [*aside*]   And any man may sing her, if he can
   take her clef. She's noted.   11
DIOMEDES   Will you remember?
CRESSIDA   Remember? Yes.
DIOMEDES   Nay, but do, then,
   And let your mind be coupled with your words.
TROILUS   What should she remember?
ULYSSES   List.   17
CRESSIDA
   Sweet honey Greek, tempt me no more to folly.

THERSITES [*aside*]   Roguery!
DIOMEDES   Nay, then—
CRESSIDA   I'll tell you what—
DIOMEDES
   Foh, foh! Come, tell a pin. You are forsworn.   22
CRESSIDA
   In faith, I cannot. What would you have me do?   23
THERSITES [*aside*]   A juggling trick—to be secretly   24
   open.   25
DIOMEDES
   What did you swear you would bestow on me?
CRESSIDA
   I prithee, do not hold me to mine oath.
   Bid me do anything but that, sweet Greek.
DIOMEDES   Good night.   [*He starts to go.*]
TROILUS   Hold, patience!
ULYSSES   How now, Trojan?
CRESSIDA   Diomed—
DIOMEDES
   No, no, good night. I'll be your fool no more.   33
TROILUS   Thy better must.   34
CRESSIDA   Hark, one word in your ear.
TROILUS   Oh, plague and madness!
ULYSSES
   You are moved, Prince. Let us depart, I pray you,
   Lest your displeasure should enlarge itself
   To wrathful terms. This place is dangerous,   39
   The time right deadly. I beseech you, go.
                          [*He tries to lead Troilus away.*]
TROILUS
   Behold, I pray you!
ULYSSES   Nay, good my lord, go off.
   You flow to great distraction. Come, my lord.   42
TROILUS
   I prithee, stay.
ULYSSES   You have not patience. Come.
TROILUS
   I pray you, stay. By hell and all hell's torments,
   I will not speak a word!
DIOMEDES
   And so, good night.   [*He starts to go.*]
CRESSIDA   Nay, but you part in anger.
TROILUS
   Doth that grieve thee? Oh, witherèd truth!
ULYSSES
   Why, how now, lord?
TROILUS   By Jove, I will be patient.
CRESSIDA
   Guardian!—Why, Greek!
DIOMEDES   Foh, foh! Adieu. You palter.   49

93–4 astronomers . . . change i.e., it is a rare and portentous event.
95 borrows of borrows reflected light from (reversing the natural superiority of the sun—something that will never happen)   **96 leave to see** cease looking upon.   **him** Diomedes.   **97 drab** whore.   **uses** frequents   **98–9 incontinent** (1) unchaste (2) incorrigible
5.2. Location: The Greek camp. Before the tent where Calchas stays with Menelaus. See 4.5.279–87.
5 discover reveal   **6 charge** person entrusted to my care.   **9 sing** i.e., sing the Sirens' song to; play upon   **11 clef** key. (With obscene pun on "cleft," i.e., vulva.)   **noted** set to music. (With pun on the meaning "known," i.e., notorious, or "used sexually.")   **17 List** Listen.

22 tell a pin i.e., don't trifle with me.   **23 I cannot** i.e., I cannot do what I promised.   **24 juggling trick** magic trick (since to be *secretly open* is an apparent contradiction in terms)   **25 open** (1) frank (2) sexually available.   **33 fool** dupe   **34 Thy better must** i.e., Better men than you (including myself) must play the fool to women like Cressida.   **39 wrathful terms** i.e., a fight.   **42 You . . . distraction** Your overfull heart will vent itself in emotional turmoil.   **49 palter** use trickery.

CRESSIDA

In faith, I do not. Come hither once again.

ULYSSES

You shake, my lord, at something. Will you go?
You will break out.

TROILUS   She strokes his cheek!

ULYSSES   Come, Come.

TROILUS

Nay, stay. By Jove, I will not speak a word.
There is between my will and all offenses   54
A guard of patience. Stay a little while.   55

THERSITES [aside]   How the devil Luxury, with his fat   56
rump and potato finger, tickles these together! Fry,   57
lechery, fry!

DIOMEDES [to Cressida]   But will you, then?

CRESSIDA

In faith, I will, la. Never trust me else.

DIOMEDES

Give me some token for the surety of it.

CRESSIDA   I'll fetch you one.   Exit.

ULYSSES

You have sworn patience.

TROILUS   Fear me not, sweet lord.
I will not be myself, nor have cognition
Of what I feel. I am all patience.

        Enter Cressida, [with Troilus' sleeve].

THERSITES [aside]   Now the pledge; now, now, now!

CRESSIDA   Here, Diomed, keep this sleeve.
                        [She gives it to him.]

TROILUS

O beauty, where is thy faith?

ULYSSES   My lord—

TROILUS

I will be patient; outwardly I will.

CRESSIDA

You look upon that sleeve. Behold it well.
He loved me—O false wench!—Give't me again.
                        [She takes it back again.]

DIOMEDES   Whose was 't?

CRESSIDA

It is no matter, now I ha 't again.
I will not meet with you tomorrow night.
I prithee, Diomed, visit me no more.

THERSITES [aside]   Now she sharpens. Well said, whet-   76
stone!

DIOMEDES

I shall have it.

CRESSIDA   What, this?

DIOMEDES   Ay, that.

CRESSIDA

O all you gods! O pretty, pretty pledge!
Thy master now lies thinking on his bed
Of thee and me, and sighs, and takes my glove,
And gives memorial dainty kisses to it,   82

As I kiss thee. Nay, do not snatch it from me;
He that takes that doth take my heart withal.   84

DIOMEDES

I had your heart before; this follows it.

TROILUS   I did swear patience.

CRESSIDA

You shall not have it, Diomed, faith, you shall not.   87
I'll give you something else.

DIOMEDES   I will have this. Whose was it?
                        [He gets the sleeve from her.]

CRESSIDA   It is no matter.

DIOMEDES   Come, tell me whose it was.

CRESSIDA

'Twas one's that loved me better than you will.
But, now you have it, take it.

DIOMEDES   Whose was it?

CRESSIDA

By all Diana's waiting-women yond,   94
And by herself, I will not tell you whose.

DIOMEDES

Tomorrow will I wear it on my helm
And grieve his spirit that dares not challenge it.   97

TROILUS

Wert thou the devil, and wor'st it on thy horn,   98
It should be challenged.

CRESSIDA

Well, well, 'tis done, 'tis past. And yet it is not;
I will not keep my word.

DIOMEDES   Why, then, farewell.
Thou never shalt mock Diomed again.
                        [He starts to go.]

CRESSIDA

You shall not go. One cannot speak a word
But it straight starts you.

DIOMEDES   I do not like this fooling.   104

THERSITES [aside]   Nor I, by Pluto; but that that likes not   105
you pleases me best.

DIOMEDES   What, shall I come? The hour?

CRESSIDA

Ay, come—O Jove!—do come—I shall be plagued.

DIOMEDES

Farewell till then.   [Exit Diomedes.]

CRESSIDA   Good night. I prithee, come.—
Troilus, farewell! One eye yet looks on thee,
But with my heart the other eye doth see.   111
Ah, poor our sex! This fault in us I find:
The error of our eye directs our mind.
What error leads must err. Oh, then conclude:
Minds swayed by eyes are full of turpitude.   Exit. 115

THERSITES [aside]

A proof of strength she could not publish more,   116
Unless she said, "My mind is now turned whore."

ULYSSES
All's done, my lord.

TROILUS   It is.

ULYSSES   Why stay we, then?

TROILUS
To make a recordation to my soul   119
Of every syllable that here was spoke.
But if I tell how these two did coact,
Shall I not lie in publishing a truth?
Sith yet there is a credence in my heart,   123
An esperance so obstinately strong,   124
That doth invert th'attest of eyes and ears,   125
As if those organs had deceptious functions   126
Created only to calumniate.   127
Was Cressid here?

ULYSSES   I cannot conjure, Trojan.

TROILUS
She was not, sure.

ULYSSES   Most sure she was.

TROILUS
Why, my negation hath no taste of madness.   130

ULYSSES
Nor mine, my lord. Cressid was here but now.

TROILUS
Let it not be believed, for womanhood!   132
Think, we had mothers. Do not give advantage
To stubborn critics, apt, without a theme   134
For depravation, to square the general sex   135
By Cressid's rule. Rather think this not Cressid.   136

ULYSSES
What hath she done, Prince, that can soil our
    mothers?

TROILUS
Nothing at all, unless that this were she.

THERSITES [aside] Will 'a swagger himself out on 's own   139
eyes?   140

TROILUS
This she? No, this is Diomed's Cressida.
If beauty have a soul, this is not she;
If souls guide vows, if vows be sanctimonies,   143
If sanctimony be the gods' delight,
If there be rule in unity itself,   145
This is not she. Oh, madness of discourse,   146
That cause sets up with and against itself!   147
Bifold authority, where reason can revolt   148
Without perdition, and loss assume all reason   149
Without revolt! This is and is not Cressid.   150

Within my soul there doth conduce a fight   151
Of this strange nature, that a thing inseparate   152
Divides more wider than the sky and earth,
And yet the spacious breadth of this division
Admits no orifex for a point as subtle   155
As Ariachne's broken woof to enter.   156
Instance, oh, instance, strong as Pluto's gates,   157
Cressid is mine, tied with the bonds of heaven;
Instance, oh, instance, strong as heaven itself,
The bonds of heaven are slipped, dissolved, and
    loosed,
And with another knot, five-finger-tied,   161
The fractions of her faith, orts of her love,   162
The fragments, scraps, the bits and greasy relics
Of her o'ereaten faith, are bound to Diomed.   164

ULYSSES
May worthy Troilus be half attached   165
With that which here his passion doth express?

TROILUS
Ay, Greek; and that shall be divulgèd well
In characters as red as Mars his heart   168
Inflamed with Venus. Never did young man fancy   169
With so eternal and so fixed a soul.
Hark, Greek: as much as I do Cressid love,
So much by weight hate I her Diomed.   172
That sleeve is mine that he'll bear on his helm.
Were it a casque composed by Vulcan's skill,   174
My sword should bite it. Not the dreadful spout   175
Which shipmen do the hurricano call,
Constringed in mass by the almighty sun,   177
Shall dizzy with more clamor Neptune's ear   178
In his descent than shall my prompted sword
Falling on Diomed.

THERSITES [aside] He'll tickle it for his concupy.   181

TROILUS
O Cressid! O false Cressid! False, false, false!
Let all untruths stand by thy stainèd name,
And they'll seem glorious.

ULYSSES   Oh, contain yourself.
Your passion draws ears hither.

        Enter Aeneas.

AENEAS
I have been seeking you this hour, my lord.
Hector, by this, is arming him in Troy;   187

119 recordation record   123 Sith Since.   credence belief   124 esperance hope   125 th'attest the witness   126 deceptious deceiving
127 calumniate slander, defame.   130 negation denial   132 for for
the sake of   134 stubborn hostile   134–6 apt . . . rule apt enough,
even when they lack grounds for negative comment, to make Cressida
the standard by which all womankind is measured. (To square is to use
a carpenter's square or measuring tool.)   139–40 Will . . . eyes? Will
he succeed, with his blustering talk, in denying the evidence of his
own eyes?   143 sanctimonies sacred things   145 If . . . itself i.e., if an
entity (like Cressida) can only be itself and not two entities   146–7 Oh
. . . itself! Oh, mad and paradoxical reasoning, that sets up an argument for and against the very proposition being debated!
148–50 Bifold . . . revolt! Inherent contradiction, when reason can
revolt against itself (by denying the testimony of the senses that this
is indeed Cressida) without actually seeming to contradict itself!

151 conduce take place   152 a thing inseparate i.e., Cressida, an
indivisible entity   155–6 Admits . . . enter provides not even an ori-
fice large enough for a fine-spun spider's web to enter. (Arachne [the
normal spelling] challenged Minerva to a weaving contest; the goddess became angered, tore up Arachne's work, and turned her into a
spider.)   157 Instance Proof, evidence.   Pluto's gates the gates of
hell   161 five-finger-tied i.e., tied indissolubly by giving her hand to
Diomedes   162 fractions fragments.   orts leftovers, fragments
164 o'ereaten i.e., surfeiting through overfeeding, or begnawed, eaten
away   165 half attached half as much affected (as it appears)
168 red bloody. (Troilus will manifest his passion now in warlike
deeds.)   Mars his Mars's   169 fancy love   172 So . . . weight to the
same extent   174 casque headpiece, helmet   175 spout waterspout
177 Constringed compressed   178 dizzy make dizzy   181 He'll . . .
concupy He'll rain ineffectual blows on Diomed's helmet, fighting it
out with Diomed for the sake of his concubine (Cressida) and his concupiscence (his lust).   187 him himself

Ajax, your guard, stays to conduct you home.

TROILUS
Have with you, Prince.—My courteous lord, adieu.   189
Farewell, revolted fair! And, Diomed,
Stand fast, and wear a castle on thy head!   191

ULYSSES   I'll bring you to the gates.

TROILUS   Accept distracted thanks.

Exeunt Troilus, Aeneas, and Ulysses.

THERSITES   Would I could meet that rogue Diomed! I
would croak like a raven; I would bode, I would bode.   195
Patroclus will give me anything for the intelligence of   196
this whore. The parrot will not do more for an almond
than he for a commodious drab. Lechery, lechery, still   198
wars and lechery; nothing else holds fashion. A burn-   199
ing devil take them!   *Exit.*   200

❖

[5.3]

Enter Hector, [armed,] and Andromache.

ANDROMACHE
When was my lord so much ungently tempered
To stop his ears against admonishment?
Unarm, unarm, and do not fight today.

HECTOR
You train me to offend you. Get you in.   4
By all the everlasting gods, I'll go!

ANDROMACHE
My dreams will, sure, prove ominous to the day.   6

HECTOR
No more, I say.

Enter Cassandra.

CASSANDRA   Where is my brother Hector?

ANDROMACHE
Here, sister, armed, and bloody in intent.
Consort with me in loud and dear petition;   9
Pursue we him on knees. For I have dreamt
Of bloody turbulence, and this whole night
Hath nothing been but shapes and forms of slaughter.

CASSANDRA
Oh, 'tis true.

HECTOR *[calling]*   Ho! Bid my trumpet sound.

CASSANDRA
No notes of sally, for the heavens, sweet brother.   14

HECTOR
Begone, I say. The gods have heard me swear.

CASSANDRA
The gods are deaf to hot and peevish vows.
They are polluted off'rings, more abhorred   16
Than spotted livers in the sacrifice.   18

ANDROMACHE
Oh, be persuaded! Do not count it holy
To hurt by being just. It is as lawful,
For we would give much, to use violent thefts,   21
And rob in the behalf of charity.

CASSANDRA
It is the purpose that makes strong the vow,
But vows to every purpose must not hold.   24
Unarm, sweet Hector.

HECTOR   Hold you still, I say.
Mine honor keeps the weather of my fate.   26
Life every man holds dear, but the dear man   27
Holds honor far more precious-dear than life.

Enter Troilus.

How now, young man, mean'st thou to fight today?

ANDROMACHE
Cassandra, call my father to persuade.   30

Exit Cassandra.

HECTOR
No, faith, young Troilus, doff thy harness, youth;   31
I am today i'th' vein of chivalry.
Let grow thy sinews till their knots be strong,
And tempt not yet the brushes of the war.   34
Unarm thee, go, and doubt thou not, brave boy,
I'll stand today for thee and me and Troy.

TROILUS
Brother, you have a vice of mercy in you,
Which better fits a lion than a man.   38

HECTOR
What vice is that? Good Troilus, chide me for it.

TROILUS
When many times the captive Grecian falls,   40
Even in the fan and wind of your fair sword,
You bid them rise and live.

HECTOR
Oh, 'tis fair play.

TROILUS   Fool's play, by heaven, Hector.

HECTOR
How now, how now?

TROILUS   For th' love of all the gods,
Let's leave the hermit Pity with our mothers,
And when we have our armors buckled on,
The venomed vengeance ride upon our swords,   47
Spur them to ruthful work, rein them from ruth.   48

HECTOR
Fie, savage, fie!

TROILUS   Hector, then 'tis wars.   49

HECTOR
Troilus, I would not have you fight today.

---

189 Have . . . Prince I am ready to go with you, Aeneas.   **lord** Ulysses
191 castle fortress, i.e., strong helmet   **195 bode** warn, prognosticate
196 intelligence of information about   **198 commodious drab** accommodating harlot.   **199–200 A burning . . . them!** (1) May a devil take them all to hell! (2) May venereal disease infect them!
5.3. Location: Troy. The palace.
4 train tempt, induce   **6 ominous to** prophetic regarding   **9 Consort** Join.   **dear** ardent   **14 sally** sallying, going forth to battle.   **for the heavens** for heaven's sake   **16 peevish** headstrong   **18 spotted** tainted and hence ill-omened

21 For . . . give because we want to give   **24 vows . . . hold** not every vow must be held sacred (since not all purposes are valid).   **26 keeps the weather of** keeps to the windward side of (for tactical advantage), takes precedence over   **27 dear man** worthy man, man of nobility
30 father father-in-law, i.e., Priam   **31 doff thy harness** take off your armor   **34 tempt** attempt, assay.   **brushes** hostile encounters
38 better fits a lion (Lions were thought to be merciful to submissive prey.)   **40 captive** overpowered in battle, wretched   **47 The venomed vengeance** may the envenomed spirit of vengeance   **48 ruthful** lamentable, i.e., causing lamentation.   **ruth** pity, mercy.   **49 then 'tis wars** i.e., war is like that.

TROILUS   Who should withhold me?
Not fate, obedience, nor the hand of Mars
Beck'ning with fiery truncheon my retire,   53
Not Priamus and Hecuba on knees,
Their eyes o'ergallèd with recourse of tears,   55
Nor you, my brother, with your true sword drawn
Opposed to hinder me, should stop my way,
But by my ruin.

Enter Priam and Cassandra.

CASSANDRA
Lay hold upon him, Priam, hold him fast;
He is thy crutch. Now if thou loose thy stay,   60
Thou on him leaning, and all Troy on thee,
Fall all together.
PRIAM   Come, Hector, come. Go back.
Thy wife hath dreamt, thy mother hath had visions,
Cassandra doth foresee, and I myself
Am like a prophet suddenly enrapt   65
To tell thee that this day is ominous.
Therefore, come back.
HECTOR   Aeneas is afield,
And I do stand engaged to many Greeks,
Even in the faith of valor, to appear   69
This morning to them.
PRIAM   Ay, but thou shalt not go.
HECTOR   I must not break my faith.
You know me dutiful; therefore, dear sir,
Let me not shame respect, but give me leave   73
To take that course by your consent and voice
Which you do here forbid me, royal Priam.
CASSANDRA
O Priam, yield not to him!
ANDROMACHE   Do not, dear father.
HECTOR
Andromache, I am offended with you.
Upon the love you bear me, get you in.
                                        Exit Andromache.
TROILUS
This foolish, dreaming, superstitious girl
Makes all these bodements.
CASSANDRA   Oh, farewell, dear Hector!   80
Look how thou diest! Look how thy eye turns pale!
Look how thy wounds do bleed at many vents!
Hark, how Troy roars, how Hecuba cries out,
How poor Andromache shrills her dolors forth!   84
Behold, distraction, frenzy, and amazement,
Like witless antics, one another meet,   86
And all cry, "Hector! Hector's dead! Oh Hector!"
TROILUS   Away! away!
CASSANDRA
Farewell. Yet soft! Hector, I take my leave.   89
Thou dost thyself and all our Troy deceive.   *[Exit.]*

HECTOR
You are amazed, my liege, at her exclaim.   91
Go in and cheer the town. We'll forth and fight,
Do deeds of praise, and tell you them at night.
PRIAM
Farewell. The gods with safety stand about thee!
        [Exeunt Priam and Hector separately.] Alarum.
TROILUS
They are at it, hark!—Proud Diomed, believe,
I come to lose my arm, or win my sleeve.

Enter Pandarus.

PANDARUS   Do you hear, my lord? Do you hear?
TROILUS   What now?
PANDARUS   Here's a letter come from yond poor girl.
                                        [He gives a letter.]
TROILUS   Let me read.
PANDARUS   A whoreson phthisic, a whoreson rascally   101
phthisic so troubles me, and the foolish fortune of this
girl, and what one thing, what another, that I shall
leave you one o' these days. And I have a rheum in   104
mine eyes, too, and such an ache in my bones that,
unless a man were cursed, I cannot tell what to think
on't.—What says she there?
TROILUS
Words, words, mere words, no matter from the heart;
Th'effect doth operate another way.   109
                    [He tears the letter and tosses it away.]
Go, wind, to wind! There turn and change together.   110
My love with words and errors still she feeds,   111
But edifies another with her deeds.   *Exeunt.*   112

❧

[5.4]

[Alarum.] Enter Thersites. Excursions.

THERSITES   Now they are clapper-clawing one another.   1
I'll go look on. That dissembling abominable varlet,
Diomed, has got that same scurvy doting foolish
young knave's sleeve of Troy there in his helm. I
would fain see them meet, that that same young
Trojan ass that loves the whore there might send that
Greekish whoremasterly villain with the sleeve back to
the dissembling luxurious drab, of a sleeveless errand.   8
O'th'other side, the policy of those crafty swearing   9
rascals—that stale old mouse-eaten dry cheese,
Nestor, and that same dog-fox, Ulysses—is proved   11
not worth a blackberry. They set me up, in policy,   12

---

53 Beck'ning . . . retire beckoning me with a flaming baton to withdraw my staff of office.   **55 o'ergallèd . . . tears** inflamed with the flow of tears   **60 loose thy stay** let go your prop   **65 enrapt** carried away, inspired   **69 the faith of valor** a warrior's honor   **73 shame respect** i.e., violate my filial duty   **80 Makes** causes.   **bodements** omens of ill fortune.   **84 shrills her dolors** wails her grief   **86 antics** fools   **89 soft** i.e., gently; wait.

91 amazed dumbstruck.   **exclaim** outcry.   **101 phthisic** consumptive cough   **104 rheum** watery discharge   **109 Th'effect . . . way** i.e., her actions belie her words.   **110 Go, wind, to wind!** Go, empty words, to the air!   **111 errors** deceits   **112 edifies** i.e., elevates to the role of being her lover   **112 s.d. Exeunt** (In the Folio version, Pandarus is angrily dismissed at this point using the lines printed by the Quarto at 5.10.32–4.)
5.4. Location: Between Troy and the Greek camp. The battlefield is the setting for the rest of the play.
0.1 Excursions sorties or issuings forth of soldiers   **1 clapper-clawing** mauling, thrashing   **8 luxurious drab** lecherous slut.   **sleeveless** futile   **9 policy** craftiness   **11 dog-fox** male fox   **12 set me** set me. (*Me* is used colloquially.)

that mongrel cur, Ajax, against that dog of as bad a
kind, Achilles. And now is the cur Ajax prouder than
the cur Achilles, and will not arm today, whereupon
the Grecians began to proclaim barbarism, and policy   16
grows into an ill opinion.

[*Enter Diomedes, and Troilus following.*]

Soft! Here comes Sleeve, and t'other.

TROILUS
Fly not, for shouldst thou take the River Styx,   19
I would swim after.

DIOMEDES   Thou dost miscall retire.   20
I do not fly, but advantageous care   21
Withdrew me from the odds of multitude.   22
Have at thee!   [*They fight.*]

THERSITES   Hold thy whore, Grecian!—Now for thy   24
whore, Trojan!—Now the sleeve, now the sleeve!

[*Exeunt Troilus and Diomedes, fighting.*]

Enter Hector.

HECTOR
What art thou, Greek? Art thou for Hector's match?
Art thou of blood and honor?   27

THERSITES   No, no, I am a rascal, a scurvy railing knave,
a very filthy rogue.

HECTOR   I do believe thee. Live.   [*Exit.*]

THERSITES   God-a-mercy, that thou wilt believe me; but   31
a plague break thy neck for frighting me! What's become of the wenching rogues? I think they have swallowed one another. I would laugh at that miracle—
yet, in a sort, lechery eats itself. I'll seek them.   *Exit.*   35

[5.5]

Enter Diomedes and Servant.

DIOMEDES
Go, go, my servant, take thou Troilus' horse;
Present the fair steed to my lady Cressid.
Fellow, commend my service to her beauty;
Tell her I have chastised the amorous Trojan
And am her knight by proof.

SERVANT   I go, my lord.   [*Exit.*]   5

Enter Agamemnon.

AGAMEMNON
Renew, renew! The fierce Polydamas   6
Hath beat down Menon; bastard Margareton
Hath Doreus prisoner,

And stands colossus-wise, waving his beam   9
Upon the pashèd corpses of the kings   10
Epistrophus and Cedius; Polyxenes is slain,
Amphimachus and Thoas deadly hurt,
Patroclus ta'en or slain, and Palamedes
Sore hurt and bruised. The dreadful Sagittary   14
Appals our numbers. Haste we, Diomed,   15
To reinforcement, or we perish all.

Enter Nestor [and soldiers].

NESTOR
Go, bear Patroclus' body to Achilles,
And bid the snail-paced Ajax arm for shame.

[*Exeunt some.*]

There is a thousand Hectors in the field.
Now here he fights on Galathe his horse,
And there lacks work; anon he's there afoot,
And there they fly or die, like scalèd schools   22
Before the belching whale; then is he yonder,
And there the strawy Greeks, ripe for his edge,   24
Fall down before him, like the mower's swath.   25
Here, there, and everywhere he leaves and takes,   26
Dexterity so obeying appetite
That what he will he does, and does so much
That proof is called impossibility.   29

Enter Ulysses.

ULYSSES
Oh, courage, courage, princes! Great Achilles
Is arming, weeping, cursing, vowing vengeance.
Patroclus' wounds have roused his drowsy blood,
Together with his mangled Myrmidons,   33
That noseless, handless, hacked and chipped, come
    to him,
Crying on Hector. Ajax hath lost a friend   35
And foams at mouth, and he is armed and at it,
Roaring for Troilus, who hath done today
Mad and fantastic execution,   38
Engaging and redeeming of himself   39
With such a careless force and forceless care   40
As if that luck, in very spite of cunning,   41
Bade him win all.   42

Enter Ajax.

---

16 **proclaim barbarism** set up ignorance in place of authority; they
will be governed by *policy* or statecraft no longer   19 **take** enter (by
way of escape).   **Styx** river of the underworld   20 **miscall retire** call
my tactical withdrawal by the wrong name of flight.   21–2 **advantageous . . . multitude** desire for better military advantage prompted
me to withdraw from the general melee, where I faced heavy odds.
24 **Hold** Defend your right to.   **for** fight for   27 **blood** noble blood
31 **God-a-mercy** Thank God, thanks   35 **in a sort** in a way
5.5. **Location: As before; the battle continues.**
5 **by proof** by proof of arms.   6 **Renew** To it again

9 **colossus-wise** like the Colossus (the great bronze statue of Apollo
at Rhodes, one of the seven wonders of the ancient world).   **beam**
lance   10 **pashèd** battered   14 **Sagittary** (Literally, the archer; a centaur, i.e., a monster half man, half horse, who according to medieval
legends fought in the Trojan War against the Greeks.)   15 **Appals our
numbers** dismays our troops.   22 **scalèd schools** scattering schools
of scaly fish   24 **strawy** like straw ready for mowing.   **his edge** the
edge of his sword   25 **swath** felled row of grain.   26 **he leaves and
takes** like a mower, he drops or *leaves* one cut of the grain and rhythmically engages the next cut with his scythelike sword   29 **proof**
fact, accomplished deed   33 **Myrmidons** soldiers of Thessaly (whom
Achilles led to Troy)   35 **Crying on** exclaiming against   38 **execution** deeds   39–42 **Engaging . . . all** committing himself to battle and
emerging unhurt with such nonchalant use of strength and effortless
self-defense as if Fortune herself cheered him on to victory, in defiance of his enemies' skill in arms.

AJAX
Troilus! Thou coward Troilus!   *Exit.*
DIOMEDES   Ay, there, there.   *Exit.*
NESTOR
So, so, we draw together.

Enter Achilles.

ACHILLES   Where is this Hector?   44
Come, come, thou boy-queller, show thy face!   45
Know what it is to meet Achilles angry.
Hector! Where's Hector? I will none but Hector.
                        Exit [with others].

❖

[5.6]

Enter Ajax.

AJAX
Troilus, thou coward Troilus, show thy head!

Enter Diomedes.

DIOMEDES
Troilus, I say! Where's Troilus?
AJAX   What wouldst thou?
DIOMEDES   I would correct him.
AJAX
Were I the general, thou shouldst have my office
Ere that correction.—Troilus, I say! What, Troilus!   5

Enter Troilus.

TROILUS
O traitor Diomed! Turn thy false face, thou traitor,
And pay the life thou owest me for my horse!
DIOMEDES   Ha, art thou there?
AJAX
I'll fight with him alone. Stand, Diomed.   9
DIOMEDES
He is my prize. I will not look upon.   10
TROILUS
Come, both you cogging Greeks, have at you both!   11
        [Exit Troilus with Ajax and Diomedes, fighting.]

[Enter Hector.]

HECTOR
Yea, Troilus? Oh, well fought, my youngest brother!

Enter Achilles.

ACHILLES
Now do I see thee. Ha! Have at thee, Hector!
                   [They fight; Achilles tires.]
HECTOR   Pause, if thou wilt.

ACHILLES
I do disdain thy courtesy, proud Trojan.
Be happy that my arms are out of use.   16
My rest and negligence befriends thee now,
But thou anon shalt hear of me again;
Till when, go seek thy fortune.   *Exit.*
HECTOR   Fare thee well.
I would have been much more a fresher man,
Had I expected thee.

Enter Troilus.

                   How now, my brother!
TROILUS
Ajax hath ta'en Aeneas. Shall it be?
No, by the flame of yonder glorious heaven,
He shall not carry him. I'll be ta'en too,   24
Or bring him off. Fate, hear me what I say!   25
I reck not though thou end my life today.   *Exit.* 26

Enter one in armor.

HECTOR
Stand, stand, thou Greek! Thou art a goodly mark.   27
No? Wilt thou not? I like thy armor well;
I'll frush it and unlock the rivets all,   29
But I'll be master of it.   *[Exit one in armor.]*
                   Wilt thou not, beast, abide?   30
Why then, fly on. I'll hunt thee for thy hide.   31
                        Exit [in pursuit].

❖

[5.7]

Enter Achilles, with Myrmidons.

ACHILLES
Come here about me, you my Myrmidons;
Mark what I say. Attend me where I wheel.   2
Strike not a stroke, but keep yourselves in breath,
And when I have the bloody Hector found,
Empale him with your weapons round about;   5
In fellest manner execute your arms.   6
Follow me, sirs, and my proceedings eye.   7
It is decreed Hector the great must die.   *Exeunt.*

Enter Thersites; Menelaus [and] Paris [fighting].

THERSITES   The cuckold and the cuckold maker are at it.
Now, bull! Now, dog! 'Loo, Paris, 'loo! Now my dou-   10
ble-horned Spartan! 'Loo, Paris, 'loo! The bull has the   11
game. Ware horns, ho!   *Exeunt Paris and Menelaus.*   12

Enter Bastard [Margareton].

---

16 use practice.   **24 carry** prevail over   **25 bring him off** rescue him.
26 reck care   **27 mark** target.   **29–30 I'll ... of it** I'll win it, if I have
to smash it and pry open the rivets to do so.   **31 hide** i.e., armor.
5.7. Location: As before; the battle continues.
2 wheel execute a circling turning maneuver.   **5 Empale** fence
6 fellest fiercest.   **execute your arms** bring your weapons into operation.   **7 my proceedings eye** watch what I do.   **10 bull** i.e., Menelaus, a cuckold, a horned creature.   **'Loo** (A cry to incite a dog
against the bull in the sport of bullbaiting in Shakespeare's England.)
11 Spartan i.e., Menelaus, King of Sparta.   **11–12 has the game** wins.
12 Ware Beware

44 we draw together i.e., at last we Greeks are pulling together, with
Ajax and Achilles engaged to fight.   **45 boy-queller** boy killer, i.e.,
slayer of Patroclus
5.6. Location: As before; the battle continues.
5 Ere that correction i.e., sooner than take from me the privilege of
chastising Troilus.   **9 Stand** i.e., Stand aside   **10 look upon** remain
an onlooker.   **11 cogging** deceitful

MARGARETON   Turn, slave, and fight.

THERSITES   What art thou?

MARGARETON   A bastard son of Priam's.

THERSITES   I am a bastard too; I love bastards. I am bastard begot, bastard instructed, bastard in mind, bastard in valor, in everything illegitimate. One bear will not bite another, and wherefore should one bastard? Take heed, the quarrel's most ominous to us. If the son of a whore fight for a whore, he tempts judgment. Farewell, bastard.   [Exit.]

MARGARETON   The devil take thee, coward!   Exit.

❧

[5.8]

Enter Hector, [dragging the one in armor he has slain].

HECTOR
Most putrefièd core, so fair without,   1
Thy goodly armor thus hath cost thy life.
Now is my day's work done. I'll take good breath.
Rest, sword; thou hast thy fill of blood and death.
    [He disarms.]

Enter Achilles and [his] Myrmidons.

ACHILLES
Look, Hector, how the sun begins to set,
How ugly night comes breathing at his heels.
Even with the vail and dark'ning of the sun,   7
To close the day up, Hector's life is done.

HECTOR
I am unarmed. Forgo this vantage, Greek.

ACHILLES
Strike, fellows, strike! This is the man I seek.
    [They fall upon Hector and kill him.]
So, Ilium, fall thou! Now, Troy, sink down!
Here lies thy heart, thy sinews, and thy bone.
On, Myrmidons, and cry you all amain,   13
"Achilles hath the mighty Hector slain."
    Retreat [sounded].
Hark! A retire upon our Grecian part.   15

MYRMIDON
The Trojans trumpets sound the like, my lord.

ACHILLES
The dragon wing of night o'erspreads the earth,
And, stickler-like, the armies separates.   18
My half-supped sword, that frankly would have fed,   19
Pleased with this dainty bait, thus goes to bed.   20
    [He sheathes his sword.]
Come, tie his body to my horse's tail.   21
Along the field I will the Trojan trail.
    Exeunt [with Hector's body].

❧

[5.9]

[Sound retreat.] Enter Agamemnon, Ajax, Menelaus, Nestor, Diomedes, and the rest, marching. [Shout within.]

AGAMEMNON   Hark! Hark! What shout is that?

NESTOR   Peace, drums!

SOLDIERS   (within)
Achilles! Achilles! Hector's slain! Achilles!

DIOMEDES
The bruit is, Hector's slain, and by Achilles.   4

AJAX
If it be so, yet bragless let it be;   5
Great Hector was a man as good as he.

AGAMEMNON
March patiently along. Let one be sent
To pray Achilles see us at our tent.
If in his death the gods have us befriended,
Great Troy is ours, and our sharp wars are ended.
    Exeunt.

❧

[5.10]

Enter Aeneas, Paris, Antenor, [and] Deiphobus.

AENEAS
Stand, ho! Yet are we masters of the field.   1
Never go home; here starve we out the night.   2

Enter Troilus.

TROILUS
Hector is slain.

ALL   Hector! The gods forbid!

TROILUS
He's dead, and at the murderer's horse's tail,
In beastly sort, dragged through the shameful field.
Frown on, you heavens, effect your rage with speed!
Sit, gods, upon your thrones and smite at Troy!
I say, at once: let your brief plagues be mercy,   8
And linger not our sure destructions on!   9

AENEAS
My lord, you do discomfort all the host.   10

TROILUS
You understand me not that tell me so.
I do not speak of flight, of fear, of death,
But dare all imminence that gods and men   12
Address their dangers in. Hector is gone.   13
Who shall tell Priam so, or Hecuba?   14
Let him that will a screech owl aye be called
Go into Troy, and say their Hector's dead.

5.8. Location: As before; the battle continues.
1 **core** i.e., the body of the Greek whom Hector has killed for his armor   7 **vail** going down   13 **amain** with all your might   15 **retire** call to retreat   18 **And . . . separates** and, like a referee, separates the armies.   19 **frankly** abundantly; greedily   20 **dainty bait** tasty snack   21 **his** Hector's

5.9. Location: The battlefield; the battle has concluded.
4 **bruit** rumor, noise   5 **bragless** without boasting
5.10. Location: The battlefield after the battle.
1 **Yet** Still   2 **starve we out** let us endure, outlast   8 **let . . . mercy** let your afflictions end us quickly, be mercifully brief   9 **linger** draw out, protract   10 **discomfort** discourage.   **host** army   12 **of flight** merely of disordered retreat   13 **imminence** impending evils, threats of imminent disaster   14 **Address . . . in** prepare to endanger us with.

There is a word will Priam turn to stone,   18
Make wells and Niobes of the maids and wives,   19
Cold statues of the youth, and, in a word,
Scare Troy out of itself. But march away.
Hector is dead. There is no more to say.
Stay yet.—You vile abominable tents,
Thus proudly pitched upon our Phrygian plains,
Let Titan rise as early as he dare,   25
I'll through and through you! And, thou great-sized
    coward,   26
No space of earth shall sunder our two hates.   27
I'll haunt thee like a wicked conscience still,
That moldeth goblins swift as frenzy's thoughts.   29
Strike a free march! To Troy with comfort go.   30
Hope of revenge shall hide our inward woe.
                                [*They proceed to march away.*]

                Enter Pandarus.

PANDARUS [*to Troilus*]   But hear you, hear you!
TROILUS
    Hence, broker-lackey! Ignomy and shame   33
    Pursue thy life, and live aye with thy name!
                                Exeunt all but Pandarus.
PANDARUS   A goodly medicine for my aching bones! Oh,
    world, world, world! Thus is the poor agent despised.

---

18 **will Priam turn** that will turn Priam   19 **Niobes** (Niobe boasted that her six sons and six daughters made her superior to Latona, mother of Apollo and Diana, for which she was punished by seeing them put to death by the arrows of these two deities. While weeping, she was changed into a stone, but her tears continued to flow from the rock. *Wells* are springs.)   25 **Titan** i.e., Helios, the sun-god, one of the Titans   26 **coward** i.e., Achilles, cowardly slayer of Hector   27 **sunder** keep apart   29 **moldeth** conjures up, creates in the imagination   30 **free** unregimented, quick   33 **broker-lackey** pander. **Ignomy** Ignominy

---

O traitors and bawds, how earnestly are you set
a-work, and how ill requited! Why should our endeavor be so desired and the performance so loathed?
What verse for it? What instance for it? Let me see: 40

    Full merrily the humble-bee doth sing,   41
    Till he hath lost his honey and his sting;
    And being once subdued in armèd tail,   43
    Sweet honey and sweet notes together fail.

Good traders in the flesh, set this in your painted   45
cloths: 46
As many as be here of Panders' hall,   47
Your eyes, half out, weep out at Pandar's fall;   48
Or if you cannot weep, yet give some groans,
Though not for me, yet for your aching bones.   50
Brethren and sisters of the hold-door trade,   51
Some two months hence my will shall here be made.
It should be now, but that my fear is this:
Some gallèd goose of Winchester would hiss.   54
Till then I'll sweat and seek about for eases,   55
And at that time bequeath you my diseases.   [*Exit.*]

---

40 **instance** illustrative example   41 **humble-bee** bumblebee   43 **being . . . tail** having lost its sting. (Much as a lover is emptied and perhaps infected in the sexual act.)   45–6 **painted cloths** cheap wall hangings worked or painted with scenes and mottoes   47 **of Panders' hall** of the liveried company of panders   48 **half out** i.e., already half destroyed by weeping and venereal disease   50 **aching bones** (A symptom of venereal disease, as in line 35.)   51 **hold-door trade** i.e., brothel keeping   54 **gallèd . . . Winchester** i.e., a prostitute having venereal disease; so called because the brothels of Southwark were under the jurisdiction of the Bishop of Winchester.   55 **sweat** (A common treatment for venereal disease.)

The Histories

The First Part
of King Henry the Sixth

Throughout much of the fifteenth century, England had suffered the ravages of civil war. From the long struggles between the Lancastrians and the Yorkists, the so-called Wars of the Roses, the country had emerged in 1485 shaken but united at last under the strong rule of the Tudors. To Elizabethans, this period of civil war was still a recent event that had tested and almost destroyed England's nationhood. They were, moreover, still troubled by political and dynastic uncertainties of their own. Queen Elizabeth, granddaughter of the first Tudor king, Henry VII, was unmarried and aging, and her successor unchosen. Her Catholic enemies at home and abroad plotted a return to the ancient faith renounced by Henry VIII in his reformation of the church. Spain had attempted an invasion of England with the great Armada in 1588, perhaps two years before Shakespeare began writing his *Henry VI* plays. It was in such an era of crisis and patriotic excitement that the *Henry VI* plays first appeared. Indeed, they helped to establish the vogue of the English history play, which was to flourish throughout the 1590s. England's civil wars could be studied and analyzed now, from a perspective of over one hundred years later, and perhaps could provide a key to the present time. At hand was a new edition of Raphael Holinshed's *Chronicles*, 1587, along with the earlier chronicle writings of Robert Fabyan, John Stow, and Richard Grafton, as well as Edward Hall's *Union of the Two Noble and Illustre Families of Lancaster and York*, John Foxe's *Acts and Monuments of Martyrs*, and *A Mirror for Magistrates*.

How had these wars begun? Elizabethans searched for an answer, not in economic or social terms, but in religious and moral ones. According to a traditional and government-sponsored explanation, reflected to a large extent (though with many contradictions) in the chronicles of Edward Hall, and familiar to Shakespeare whether he agreed with it or not, the Wars of the Roses were a manifestation of God's wrath, a divine punishment inflicted on the English people for their wayward behav-

ior. The people and their rulers had brought civil war on themselves by self-serving ambition, arrogance, and disloyalty. King Henry VI's grandfather, Henry IV, had come to the throne in 1399 by deposing and then executing his own cousin, Richard II (a momentous event, to be portrayed by Shakespeare in a later history play). Henry VI was himself an infant when he succeeded to the throne in 1422, owing to the untimely death of his father, Henry V. Too young at first to rule and never blessed with his father's ability to act decisively, Henry VI was utterly unable to halt the struggle for power that developed among members of his large and discordant family. Ultimately, his very title to the throne was challenged by his kinsman Richard Plantagenet, Duke of York, who claimed to be rightful king by virtue of his descent from Henry IV's uncle Lionel, Duke of Clarence. The Yorkist faction marched to battle against Henry VI's Lancastrian faction (so named because for generations the family had been possessors of the dukedom of Lancaster), and the war was on.

The providential view of these events was never wholly endorsed by the chroniclers and certainly not by Shakespeare. Edward Hall's overall scheme is undeniably providential, and yet, as a historian, he presents a multiplicity of detail that cumulatively raises difficult issues of interpretation. At the same time, the providential view made good propaganda for the Tudor regime, and as such it gave widespread currency to the theory of God's anger toward a rebellious people. The outcome of the war seemed to confirm this pattern: universal devastation and the deaths of those most responsible for the conflict led eventually, according to the theory, to appeasement of God's anger and a restoration of order. Richard Plantagenet died in the struggle, as did Henry VI, Henry's son Edward, and much of the English nobility. Richard's son Edward survived to become Edward IV, but his manner of obtaining the throne was so manifestly offensive to Providence that (according to the theory) he suffered a retributive death at the hands of an angry God and was succeeded by his younger brother, Richard III. This last Yorkist ruler governed only two years, 1483–1485, and it was through Richard's insane vengeance that God finally settled all his scores against the wayward English people. Having completed this purgation, God chose as his instrument of a new order Henry Tudor, Earl of Richmond, Henry VII. Although Henry's return to England and defeat of Richard at the battle of Bosworth Field might outwardly resemble Henry IV's seizure of power from Richard II, the difference was crucial to Tudor apologists. Richard III had to be seen, from the Tudor point of view, not as a flawed legitimate monarch, but as a mad usurper and tyrant; his defeat was not the disobedient act of one man but a rising up of the entire English nation at the prompting of divine command. Henry VII's accession to power was officially viewed not as a precedent for further rebellion but as a manifestation of divine will without parallel in human history.

The essence of this providential view of events was that divine retribution and eventual reconciliation revealed themselves in the history of the war. The theory, of course, served the interests of the Tudor state and was in part a propaganda weapon calculatedly employed by the ruling class. Shakespeare's commitment to it should not be taken for granted, and indeed a number of recent studies have expressed a profound skepticism toward the theory as the basis of Shakespeare's dramaturgy. Especially in his later tetralogy, or four-play series, from *Richard II* to *Henry V*, Shakespeare reveals considerably more interest in the clash of personalities than in patterns of divine retribution. Shakespeare does not endorse the orthodox view that Bolingbroke's seizure of the throne is a violation of divine purpose for which he and England must be humbled; instead, Shakespeare portrays the issues as many-sided and subject to varying interpretations.

Throughout his history plays, indeed, Shakespeare avoids expressing the Tudor view of recent history through didactic narrators or chorus figures who might seem to represent the point of view of the entire plays; instead, he puts this interpretation into the mouths of avowedly biased and self-interested characters whose motives and testimony the audience can then evaluate as it sees fit. In *1 Henry VI*, for example, the most detailed exposition of the official historical view is given to Mortimer (2.5), whose interpretation, though given special authority by the fact that a dying man is speaking, is self-interestedly consistent with his own frustrated claim to the English throne. His nephew, Richard Plantagenet, who of course endorses the anti-Lancastrian logic of Mortimer's speech, is portrayed as consumed with ambition for the crown. In Shakespeare's depiction of the Lancastrian-Yorkist conflict, neither side maintains a consistent ideological position but, instead, shifts argument

as required by the expediency of the moment. Although in his earlier tetralogy from *1 Henry VI* to *Richard III* Shakespeare does sometimes allow his contending characters to hearken back to the deposition of Richard II in order to explain the misfortunes of England's civil wars, those characters often speak from self-interest and interpret history to their own advantage.

The individual plays of this earlier tetralogy, if seen or read separately, do not consistently comfort the spectator or reader with an assurance that all is working out according to God's plan. The events themselves, seen from the immediate perspective of the moment, provide little comfort. At the end of *1 Henry VI*, King Henry has surrendered to a disastrous marriage and has lost most of France; at the end of *2 Henry VI*, the good Duke Humphrey of Gloucester is dead and his opportunistic political enemies are about to take King Henry off of his throne. The hostilities of Lancaster and York end at the conclusion of *3 Henry VI*, to be sure, but prospects for a stable peace are doubtful in view of Richard of Gloucester's baleful presence. The reciprocity of slaughter visited on both sides appears to stem as much from humanity's insane desire for vengeance as from God's evening of the score. Only in *Richard III* do we retroactively see a pattern of divine anger, retribution, and eventual appeasement that can then be applied to the tetralogy as a continuous narrative. E. M. W. Tillyard's argument for a providential reading of these plays (in his *Shakespeare's History Plays*, 1944) is based not coincidentally on a view of the tetralogy as a cohesive whole. What about the playgoers who saw the plays one at a time? The plays, so far as we know, were written and produced singly and were never staged in a continuous series. Even though the tetralogy as a whole may harmonize in part with the chronicles of Edward Hall and others, written to glorify the Tudor state and to give thanks for its having ended the prolonged anarchy of the fifteenth century, we can see that Shakespeare is no apologist for the Tudor state. He gives expression to a widely felt anxiety about political chaos. In each individual play and throughout the tetralogy, the overriding cosmic irony stressing the gulf between foolish humanity and the inscrutable intentions of Providence offers a potentially stirring conflict of which Shakespeare makes rich use.

Shakespeare wrote his first tetralogy some time between 1589 and 1592. Thomas Nashe's *Pierce Penniless*, 1592, refers to *1 Henry VI* as a huge crowd-pleaser; Robert Greene's *A Groatsworth of Wit* rephrases a line from *3 Henry VI* in that same year; Philip Henslowe's diary records performances of "harey VI" in the spring of 1592; and in that same year, the Earl of Pembroke's Men, who staged a version of *3 Henry VI* under the title *The True Tragedy of Richard, Duke of York*, went out of business. Just how much of this first tetralogy may have been planned out when Shakespeare began work is hard to say. In fact, the very order of composition has long been in dispute. Despite the commonsense pleading of Dr. Johnson that Part Two follows from Part One as a logical consequence, some scholars argue that Part One was composed last. One piece of evidence is that a corrupt version of Part Two was published in quarto version in 1594 as *The First Part of the Contention Betwixt the Two Famous Houses of York and Lancaster* and that a corrupt version of Part Three was published in octavo in 1595 as *The True Tragedy of Richard Duke of York*. Part One had to await publication in the First Folio of 1623 and was registered for publication at that time as "The third part of Henry the sixth." It seems odd, moreover, that Parts Two and Three make no mention of Lord Talbot, so prominent in Part One. If, however, as seems likely, the early printed versions of Parts Two and Three were memorial reconstructions without the authority of the official playbook, the claim of Part Two to have been written first may be unsubstantial. The very fact of prior publication of Parts Two and Three could explain why Part One was called "The third part" in 1623. Although Talbot is not mentioned in Parts Two and Three, these texts do recall important aspects of Part One. It is certainly possible that Shakespeare wrote all three parts in normal order.

Equally vexing is the question of authorship. Many Elizabethan plays were written by teams of authors, and Shakespeare might have collaborated with others, especially at the beginning of his career. Perhaps he rewrote older works by such writers as Thomas Nashe, Robert Greene, and Christopher Marlowe. Theories of multiple authorship, once a commonplace of nineteenth-century scholarship and then discounted by much twentieth-century criticism, have recently been argued anew by the editors of the *Oxford Shakespeare* (1986). Yet there is much reason to believe that Shakespeare is essentially the author of the entire *Henry VI* series. Greene's famous resentment toward Shakespeare as the "upstart crow beautified with our feathers" seems more the envy of a lesser talent than the righteous indignation of one who has been plagiarized. The chief criteria used to "disintegrate" the plays into the hands of various supposed contributors are those of taste and style; for example, the low comic scenes of Joan of Arc were long held to be too coarse for Shakespeare's genius. Today most critics see a consistency of view throughout the *Henry VI* plays, despite minor inconsistencies of fact that might be the result of simple error or of using multiple sources, and they find nothing in these plays inimical to Shakespeare's budding genius. This belief confirms the judgment of Heminges and Condell, Shakespeare's fellow actors and editors of the 1623 Folio, who placed all the *Henry VI* plays among Shakespeare's collected works in their historical order.

If Shakespeare was at least chiefly responsible for the *Henry VI* series, he may also have been an important innovator in the new genre of the history play. Only the anonymous *Famous Victories of Henry V* is certainly earlier in dealing with recent English history. There were, to be sure, plays about legendary British history, such as *Gorboduc* or *The Misfortunes of Arthur*, or about far-off lands, such as *Cambises* or Marlowe's *Tamburlaine*. All these plays had explored by analogy political questions fascinating to Elizabethan England, and *Tamburlaine's* immense success had certainly established a vogue for grand scenes of military conquest. Still, the English history play as a recognizable form came into being with *Henry VI*. The success was evidently tremendous and established Shakespeare as a major playwright.

1 Henry VI, like all the plays in Shakespeare's first tetralogy, comprises a large number of episodes, a sizable cast of characters, and a wide geographical range. The subject is England's loss of French territories because of political division at home. The structure of the play is one of sequential action displayed in great variety and in alternating scenes that are thematically juxtaposed and contrasted with one another. In the rapid shifting back and forth between the English and French court, for example, Shakespeare establishes a paradoxical theme: France triumphs in England's weakness, not in her own strength. The French court is merely one of debased sexual frivolity. The English are naturally superior but are torn apart by internal dissension, by a "jarring discord of nobility," and by a "shouldering of each other in the court" (4.1.188–9) among those attempting to take advantage of Henry VI's weak minority rule and his vulnerable genealogical claim. Two of young Henry's kinsmen jockeying for position are Humphrey, Duke of Gloucester, and the Bishop of Winchester. Humphrey's intentions are virtuous, but he is unable to prevent the opportunistic scheming of his rival. Winchester, despite his ecclesiastical calling, is a man of evil ambition and corrupt life, wholly intent on destroying the right-minded Gloucester. Shakespeare employs derisive anticlerical humor against Winchester and enlists the Protestant sympathies of his Elizabethan audience against the meddling Catholic Church's attempts to exploit England's weak kingship for its own ulterior purposes.

Even so, the menace threatening England is not seen as a Catholic conspiracy throughout; Winchester is only one opportunist seeking to exploit the political vacillation and factionalism at court. Of greater danger in the long term is Richard Plantagenet, scion of the Yorkist claim. From the start, Shakespeare portrays him as cunning, able to ingratiate himself and bide his time, and ultimately ruthless. In these qualities, he ominously foreshadows his youngest son and namesake, Richard III. In this play, Plantagenet's strategy is to allow England to wear herself down by the various conflicts at court and military losses abroad; once the situation is reduced to anarchy, Plantagenet will be able to move in. The strategy works only too well.

Chief defender of England's military might in France, and eventual victim of the bickering among the English nobility, is Lord Talbot. He is the heroic figure of this play with whom Elizabethan audiences identified. As Thomas Nashe wrote in his *Pierce Penniless*, 1592: "How would it have joyed brave Talbot (the terror of the French) to think that after he had lain two hundred years in his tomb, he should triumph again on the stage, and have his bones new embalmed with the tears of ten thousand spectators at least (at several times) who, in the tragedian that represents his person, imagine they behold him fresh bleeding?" As the undiminished hero of *1 Henry VI*, Lord Talbot pleads for political and military unity against the French and demonstrates that with such unity England would be invincible. Talbot is "the terror of the French" (1.4.42), able to hold off a troop of French soldiers with his bare fists, and reputed to twist bars of steel. As the embodiment of chivalry, he delivers a richly deserved rebuke to Sir John Falstaff (historically "Fastolfe," but called "Falstaff" in the Folio text of this play), the cowardly soldier who foreshadows the fat knight of *1 Henry IV*. In *1 Henry VI*, cowardice and honor are rendered in black and white extremes. Talbot is a model general, illustrating all the qualities of great leadership advocated by the textbooks of the age: he is a stirring orator, fearless, witty, and concerned with a proper lasting fame. In the touching scenes with his son, Talbot rises triumphantly above death to become the immortal embodiment of brave soldiership. Yet, even if *1 Henry VI* offers this one important model of rhetoric and arts of leadership put to right use, Talbot's presence nonetheless lends itself more to a profound anxiety about historical events than to a reassuring confidence in divine assistance. Talbot's unnecessary death offers a devastating critique of the weak leadership that has allowed authority in France to be divided among political rivals.

The relations between men and women in this play are also used to create thematic contrasts. Talbot's chief military rival in France is Joan of Arc; and, although many earlier scholars have wanted to deny Shakespeare's authorship of the Joan of Arc scenes, their thematic function is central. As a woman in armor, Joan is the embodiment of the domineering Amazonian woman to whom the effete and self-indulgent dauphin, Charles, weakly capitulates. The sexual roles have been reversed; Venus triumphs over Mars. Joan's role as virgin-warrior, her trafficking in demonology, and her obscenely parodic resemblance to the Virgin Mary all suggest a profound male-oriented ambivalence toward women in positions of authority—including, by implication, Queen Elizabeth. Joan's sexuality is not only demonic but also obsessive in its promiscuity and seeming insatiability. Her English captors at the end of the play (5.4) mock Joan for claiming to be a virgin even while she attempts to save her life by asserting that she is pregnant. York scoffs, "Now heaven forfend! The hold maid with child?" When she appears not to know who the father might be, since she has had so many sexual partners, his glee is unrestrained: "And yet, forsooth, she is a virgin pure!" (5.4.65, 83). Irreverence toward her claim to be *la Pucelle* is thus combined with a Protestant swipe at Catholic Mariolatry. She even attempts to practice her witchcraft (with sexual overtones) on Talbot and his son, but in vain. Talbot's sense of duty never succumbs to Circean voluptuousness. In his encounter with the Countess of Auvergne, Talbot resourcefully outwits another woman who, like Joan, seeks to entrap him. The Countess finally submits to Talbot's courteous but firm authority, thereby reestablishing the traditional relationship of male and female. Talbot stands for every kind of decency and order that ought to prevail but is senselessly destroyed through England's political division.

The last woman introduced in the play, Margaret of Anjou, is another domineering female. Her adulterous relationship with the fleshly Suffolk, and her ascendancy over the weak Henry VI, are to be of fateful consequence in the ensuing plays. Her scenes, although once dismissed as an afterthought, linking *1 Henry VI* with the following plays, in fact recapitulate the motifs of female dominance with great dramatic effect. Young Henry VI is no Talbot; inexperienced in love and highly impressionable, he surrenders to the mere description of a woman he has not even seen and refuses a politically advantageous match arranged by Duke Humphrey in order that he may marry a conniving Frenchwoman without dowry. The marriage also anticipates that of Edward IV (in *3 Henry VI*) to a penniless widow who has caught his roving eye, when Edward could have obtained a handsome dowry and a favorable alliance by marrying the French King's sister-in-law. Such dismal triumphs of passion over reason are emblematic of the general decay among the English aristocracy. Despite Henry's weakness, he is the central character of this play after all, and his enervating surrender in love is a fitting anticlimax with which to end the first installment of England's decline. In the theater we are left at the end of *1 Henry VI* with an appalling sense of dislocation and loss for which no remedies appear to be at hand.

The First Part
of King Henry the Sixth

[*Dramatis Personae*

KING HENRY THE SIXTH
DUKE OF GLOUCESTER, *uncle of the King, and Lord Protector*
DUKE OF BEDFORD, *uncle of the King, and Regent of France*
DUKE OF EXETER, *Thomas Beaufort, great-uncle of the King*
BISHOP OF WINCHESTER, *Henry Beaufort, great-uncle of the King, later* CARDINAL
DUKE OF SOMERSET, *John Beaufort, formerly Earl of Somerset*
RICHARD PLANTAGENET, *son of Richard, late Earl of Cambridge, later* DUKE OF YORK *and Regent of France*
EARL OF WARWICK
EARL OF SALISBURY
EARL OF SUFFOLK, *William de la Pole*
LORD TALBOT, *later Earl of Shrewsbury*
JOHN TALBOT, *his son*
EDMUND MORTIMER
SIR JOHN FALSTAFF
SIR WILLIAM LUCY
SIR WILLIAM GLASDALE
SIR THOMAS GARGRAVE
MAYOR *of London*
WOODVILLE, *Lieutenant of the Tower of London*
VERNON, *of the White Rose or York faction*
BASSET, *of the Red Rose or Lancaster faction*
A LAWYER, *of the York faction*
A PAPAL LEGATE
MESSENGERS
WARDERS *of the Tower of London*
SERVINGMEN

AN OFFICER *serving the Lord Mayor*
A SOLDIER *in Talbot's army*
CAPTAINS
A KEEPER *or Jailer of Mortimer*
WATCH *at the gates of Rouen*

CHARLES, *Dauphin, and afterward King, of France*
REIGNIER, *Duke of Anjou, and titular King of Naples*
MARGARET, *his daughter*
DUKE OF ALENÇON
BASTARD OF ORLEANS
DUKE OF BURGUNDY

GENERAL *of the French forces at Bordeaux*
COUNTESS *of Auvergne*
PORTER *to the Countess*
MASTER GUNNER *of Orleans*
A BOY, *his son*
JOAN LA PUCELLE, *Joan of Arc*
SHEPHERD, *her father*
SERGEANT *of a French detachment*
SENTINEL *of a French detachment*
SOLDIER *with Pucelle at Rouen*
A SCOUT *in the Dauphin's army at Angiers*

English and French Heralds, Soldiers, Officers, Sentinels, Servingmen, Keepers or Jailers, Attendants, the Governor of Paris, Ambassadors, Fiends attending on La Pucelle

SCENE: *Partly in England, and partly in France*]

1.1

Dead march. Enter the funeral of King Henry the Fifth, attended on by the Duke of Bedford, Regent of France; the Duke of Gloucester, Protector; the Duke of Exeter, [the Earl of] Warwick, the Bishop of Winchester, and the Duke of Somerset, [heralds, etc.].

1.1. Location: Westminster Abbey.

BEDFORD
Hung be the heavens with black! Yield, day, to night! 1
Comets, importing change of times and states, 2
Brandish your crystal tresses in the sky, 3

1 Hung . . . black (A metaphor from the theatrical practice of draping the "heavens" or roof projecting over the stage in black when a tragedy was to be performed.) **2 importing** foretelling, portending **3 crystal tresses** shining hair, i.e., the trail of the comet

And with them scourge the bad revolting stars   4
That have consented unto Henry's death—
King Henry the Fifth, too famous to live long!
England ne'er lost a king of so much worth.

GLOUCESTER
England ne'er had a king until his time.   8
Virtue he had, deserving to command.   9
His brandished sword did blind men with his beams;   10
His arms spread wider than a dragon's wings;
His sparkling eyes, replete with wrathful fire,
More dazzled and drove back his enemies
Than midday sun fierce bent against their faces.
What should I say? His deeds exceed all speech.
He ne'er lift up his hand but conquerèd.   16

EXETER
We mourn in black. Why mourn we not in blood?
Henry is dead and never shall revive.
Upon a wooden coffin we attend,
And death's dishonorable victory
We with our stately presence glorify,
Like captives bound to a triumphant car.   22
What? Shall we curse the planets of mishap   23
That plotted thus our glory's overthrow?
Or shall we think the subtle-witted French
Conjurers and sorcerers, that, afraid of him,
By magic verses have contrived his end?   27

WINCHESTER
He was a king blest of the King of kings.
Unto the French the dreadful Judgment Day
So dreadful will not be as was his sight.   30
The battles of the Lord of hosts he fought;
The Church's prayers made him so prosperous.   32

GLOUCESTER
The Church? Where is it? Had not churchmen prayed,   33
His thread of life had not so soon decayed.   34
None do you like but an effeminate prince,   35
Whom like a schoolboy you may overawe.

WINCHESTER
Gloucester, whate'er we like, thou art Protector,   37
And lookest to command the Prince and realm.
Thy wife is proud. She holdeth thee in awe   39
More than God or religious churchmen may.

GLOUCESTER
Name not religion, for thou lov'st the flesh,
And ne'er throughout the year to church thou go'st
Except it be to pray against thy foes.

BEDFORD
Cease, cease these jars and rest your minds in peace!   44

Let's to the altar. Heralds, wait on us.   45
   [*Exeunt Warwick, Somerset, and heralds
                                with the coffin.*]
Instead of gold we'll offer up our arms,   46
Since arms avail not now that Henry's dead.
Posterity, await for wretched years,   48
When at their mothers' moistened eyes babes shall
   suck,   49
Our isle be made a nourish of salt tears,   50
And none but women left to wail the dead.
Henry the Fifth, thy ghost I invoke: 52
Prosper this realm; keep it from civil broils;   53
Combat with adverse planets in the heavens!
A far more glorious star thy soul will make
Than Julius Caesar or bright—

   Enter a Messenger.

FIRST MESSENGER
My honorable lords, health to you all.
Sad tidings bring I to you out of France,
Of loss, of slaughter, and discomfiture.
Guyenne, Champagne, Rouen, Rheims, Orleans,   60
Paris, Gisors, Poitiers, are all quite lost.

BEDFORD
What say'st thou, man, before dead Henry's corpse?
Speak softly, or the loss of those great towns
Will make him burst his lead and rise from death.   64

GLOUCESTER
Is Paris lost? Is Rouen yielded up?
If Henry were recalled to life again,
These news would cause him once more yield the
   ghost.

EXETER
How were they lost? What treachery was used?

FIRST MESSENGER
No treachery, but want of men and money.   69
Amongst the soldiers this is mutterèd,
That here you maintain several factions,   71
And whilst a field should be dispatched and fought,   72
You are disputing of your generals.   73
One would have ling'ring wars with little cost;
Another would fly swift, but wanteth wings;   75
A third thinks, without expense at all,
By guileful fair words peace may be obtained.
Awake, awake, English nobility!
Let not sloth dim your honors new-begot.

---

4 **scourge** (As if the tresses were whips.) **revolting** rebelling
8 **a king** a king in the fullest sense 9 **Virtue** Excellence, authority
10 **his** its 16 **lift** lifted. **but conquerèd** without conquering.
22 **car** chariot. 23 **planets of mishap** misfortune-causing planets
27 **verses** spells 30 **his sight** the sight of him. 32 **prosperous** successful. 33 **prayed** (With pun on "preyed"; also in line 43.)
34 **decayed** been destroyed. 35 **effeminate prince** ineffectual, unmanly ruler 37 **Protector** head of state during the king's minority
39 **Thy wife is proud** (A reference to Gloucester's ambitious wife, Eleanor, whose inordinate desire for greatness is depicted in *2 Henry VI*.) **holdeth . . . awe** overawes you 44 **jars** discords

45 **wait on us** i.e., lead the procession. **45.1–2 *Exeunt . . . coffin*** (Here or later in the scene, the various members of the funeral procession not specifically mentioned in the exits at lines 166–77, including Warwick, Somerset, and the heralds, must leave the stage.) 46 **arms** weapons 48 **await for** expect 49 **When . . . suck** i.e., when mothers will feed their children with tears only 50 **a nourish . . . tears** i.e., a nurse feeding with tears only 52 **invocate** invoke, as one would call on a saint 53 **Prosper** make prosperous 60 **Champagne** Compiègne 64 **lead** leaden inner coffin or wrapping, inside the wooden coffin (line 19) 69 **want** lack 71 **several** separate (and divisive) 72 **field** (1) battle (2) combat force 73 **disputing . . . generals** disputing what strategy the military commanders in the field should employ. 75 **wanteth** lacks

Cropped are the flower-de-luces in your arms;   80
Of England's coat one half is cut away.   [*Exit.*]

EXETER
Were our tears wanting to this funeral,   82
These tidings would call forth her flowing tides.   83

BEDFORD
Me they concern; Regent I am of France.   84
Give me my steelèd coat. I'll fight for France.
Away with these disgraceful wailing robes!
Wounds will I lend the French instead of eyes,   87
To weep their intermissive miseries.   88

Enter to them another Messenger, [with letters].

SECOND MESSENGER
Lords, view these letters, full of bad mischance.
France is revolted from the English quite,   90
Except some petty towns of no import.
The Dauphin Charles is crownèd king in Rheims;
The Bastard of Orleans with him is joined;
Reignier, Duke of Anjou, doth take his part;   94
The Duke of Alençon flieth to his side.   *Exit.*

EXETER
The Dauphin crownèd king? All fly to him?   96
Oh, whither shall we fly from this reproach?   97

GLOUCESTER
We will not fly but to our enemies' throats!
Bedford, if thou be slack, I'll fight it out.   98

BEDFORD
Gloucester, why doubt'st thou of my forwardness?
An army have I mustered in my thoughts,
Wherewith already France is overrun.

Enter another Messenger.

THIRD MESSENGER
My gracious lords, to add to your laments,
Wherewith you now bedew King Henry's hearse,
I must inform you of a dismal fight   105
Betwixt the stout Lord Talbot and the French.   106

WINCHESTER
What? Wherein Talbot overcame, is't so?

THIRD MESSENGER
Oh, no! Wherein Lord Talbot was o'erthrown.
The circumstance I'll tell you more at large.   109
The tenth of August last, this dreadful lord,   110

Retiring from the siege of Orleans,
Having full scarce six thousand in his troop,   112
By three-and-twenty thousand of the French
Was round encompassèd and set upon.   114
No leisure had he to enrank his men.   115
He wanted pikes to set before his archers,   116
Instead whereof sharp stakes plucked out of hedges
They pitchèd in the ground confusedly,
To keep the horsemen off from breaking in.
More than three hours the fight continuèd,
Where valiant Talbot above human thought   121
Enacted wonders with his sword and lance.
Hundreds he sent to hell, and none durst stand him;   123
Here, there, and everywhere, enragèd he slew.
The French exclaimed the devil was in arms;
All the whole army stood agazed on him.   126
His soldiers, spying his undaunted spirit,
"A Talbot! a Talbot!" crièd out amain   128
And rushed into the bowels of the battle.
Here had the conquest fully been sealed up   130
If Sir John Falstaff had not played the coward.   131
He, being in the vaward, placed behind   132
With purpose to relieve and follow them,
Cowardly fled, not having struck one stroke.
Hence grew the general wrack and massacre.   135
Enclosèd were they with their enemies.   136
A base Walloon, to win the Dauphin's grace,   137
Thrust Talbot with a spear into the back,
Whom all France with their chief assembled strength
Durst not presume to look once in the face.

BEDFORD
Is Talbot slain, then? I will slay myself
For living idly here in pomp and ease
Whilst such a worthy leader, wanting aid,
Unto his dastard foemen is betrayed.

THIRD MESSENGER
Oh, no, he lives, but is took prisoner,
And Lord Scales with him, and Lord Hungerford;
Most of the rest slaughtered or took likewise.

BEDFORD
His ransom there is none but I shall pay.   148
I'll hale the Dauphin headlong from his throne;
His crown shall be the ransom of my friend.
Four of their lords I'll change for one of ours.   151
Farewell, my masters; to my task will I.   152
Bonfires in France forthwith I am to make,   153

---

80 Cropped Plucked. **flower-de-luces** the *fleur-de-lis,* or iris, national emblem of France. (According to the Treaty of Troyes, 1420, the crown of France was ceded to England but was nominally to belong to the French king, Charles VI, as long as he lived. Henry V's title was designated "King of England and Heir of France." At his death, this title passed to Henry VI, but, within two months after this took place, Charles VI died and his son Charles VII was proclaimed king. The loss of the French crown would deprive the English king of the right to display the *fleur-de-lis* in his coat of arms.) **82 wanting** lacking **83 her . . . tides** England's abundant tears. **84 Regent** ruler in the king's absence **87–8 Wounds . . . miseries** I will give the French wounds so that they can shed real blood instead of tears at the misfortunes they are now to suffer at regular intervals. **90 quite** entirely **94 Reignier** René **96 fly** flock **97 fly** flee **98 fly** (Gloucester turns the word to mean "fly at their throats.") **105 dismal** savage, terrible **106 stout** brave **109 circumstance** particulars. **at large** in full detail. **110 dreadful** to be dreaded

112 full scarce scarce full, barely **114 round encompassèd** surrounded **115 enrank** draw up in battle array **116 wanted pikes** lacked iron-bound stakes, sharpened at the ends and set in the ground in front of archers as protection against cavalry **121 above human thought** beyond imagining **123 stand him** stand up against him **126 agazed on** astounded at **128 "A Talbot!"** Rally to Talbot! **amain** with full force **130 sealed up** completed **131 Falstaff** ("Fastolfe" in the chronicles, but the Shakespearean spelling used here shows us the origin of the name used in the *Henry IV* plays.) **132 vaward** vanguard **135 wrack** wreckage, destruction **136 with** by **137 Walloon** an inhabitant of that province, now a part of southern Belgium and the adjoining part of France **148 His . . . pay** i.e., I'll pay all the ransom there's going to be, by retaliating. **151 change** i.e., kill in exchange **152 my masters** my good sirs **153 am** intend

To keep our great Saint George's feast withal.   154
Ten thousand soldiers with me I will take,
Whose bloody deeds shall make all Europe quake.

THIRD MESSENGER
So you had need, for Orleans is besieged;   157
The English army is grown weak and faint;
The Earl of Salisbury craveth supply   159
And hardly keeps his men from mutiny,
Since they, so few, watch such a multitude.   [Exit.] 161

EXETER
Remember, lords, your oaths to Henry sworn,
Either to quell the Dauphin utterly
Or bring him in obedience to your yoke.

BEDFORD
I do remember it, and here take my leave
To go about my preparation.   Exit Bedford.

GLOUCESTER
I'll to the Tower with all the haste I can   167
To view th'artillery and munition,
And then I will proclaim young Henry king.
                                      Exit Gloucester.

EXETER
To Eltham will I, where the young King is,   170
Being ordained his special governor,   171
And for his safety there I'll best devise.   Exit.

WINCHESTER
Each hath his place and function to attend.
I am left out; for me nothing remains.
But long I will not be jack-out-of-office.   175
The King from Eltham I intend to steal
And sit at chiefest stern of public weal.   Exit. 177

❧

[1.2]

*Sound a flourish. Enter Charles, Alençon, and
Reignier, marching with drum and soldiers.*

CHARLES
Mars his true moving, even as in the heavens   1
So in the earth, to this day is not known.
Late did he shine upon the English side;   3
Now we are victors, upon us he smiles.

What towns of any moment but we have?   5
At pleasure here we lie near Orleans;   6
Otherwhiles the famished English, like pale ghosts,   7
Faintly besiege us one hour in a month.

ALENÇON
They want their porridge and their fat bull-beeves.
Either they must be dieted like mules   10
And have their provender tied to their mouths,
Or piteous they will look, like drownèd mice.

REIGNIER
Let's raise the siege. Why live we idly here?   13
Talbot is taken, whom we wont to fear.   14
Remaineth none but mad-brained Salisbury,
And he may well in fretting spend his gall;   16
Nor men nor money hath he to make war.   17

CHARLES
Sound, sound alarum! We will rush on them.   18
Now for the honor of the forlorn French!   19
Him I forgive my death that killeth me
When he sees me go back one foot or fly.   Exeunt.

*Here alarum. They are beaten back by the English
with great loss. Enter Charles, Alençon,
and Reignier.*

CHARLES
Who ever saw the like? What men have I!
Dogs, cowards, dastards! I would ne'er have fled
But that they left me 'midst my enemies.

REIGNIER
Salisbury is a desperate homicide;
He fighteth as one weary of his life.   26
The other lords, like lions wanting food,
Do rush upon us as their hungry prey.   28

ALENÇON
Froissart, a countryman of ours, records   29
England all Olivers and Rolands bred   30
During the time Edward the Third did reign.
More truly now may this be verified,
For none but Samsons and Goliases   33
It sendeth forth to skirmish. One to ten!
Lean raw-boned rascals! Who would e'er suppose   35
They had such courage and audacity?

CHARLES
Let's leave this town; for they are harebrained slaves,   37
And hunger will enforce them to be more eager.   38

---

154 **Saint George's feast** the twenty-third of April. (Saint George was
the patron saint of England. To celebrate his day in France would be
to assert England's claim to that territory.)   157 **Orleans is besieged**
(At line 60, a messenger says that Orleans has fallen; at 1.2.8 ff., an
English siege to recover Orleans is under way. The messenger here
must mean that the besieging English army needs help.)   159 **supply**
reinforcements   161 **watch** find themselves face to face with
167 **Tower** Tower of London, ancient palace-fortress, later a prison for
persons of eminence   170 **Eltham** a royal residence southeast of London   171 **Being** I being   175 **jack-out-of-office** i.e., a dismissed fellow with nothing to do.   177 **at chiefest stern** in the steersman's seat,
in a position of supreme control
1.2. Location: France. Before Orleans.
0.1 *flourish* trumpet fanfare.   0.2 *drum* drummer   1 **Mars . . . moving** Mars's precise orbit. (The planet's seemingly eccentric orbit was a
source of perplexity in Shakespeare's day; here, its influence on earth
in human affairs is likewise mysterious. Mars is also the god of war.)
3 **Late** Lately, recently

5 **What . . . have?** What towns of any consequence do we not possess?
6 **At . . . lie** We are encamped and free to move about. (Charles and
his forces are not in the city of Orleans itself, but are encamped outside in an attempt to repulse the English siege of the city.)   7 **Otherwhiles** at times   10 **dieted** fed. (The eating of beef, line 9, was
believed to confer courage.)   13 **raise the siege** drive off the besieging English.   14 **wont** were accustomed   16 **spend his gall** expend
his bitterness of spirit   17 **Nor** neither   18 **alarum** call to arms.
19 **forlorn** in desperate straits   26 **as one** like one who is   28 **hungry
prey** prey for which they hunger.   29 **Froissart** a fourteenth-century
French chronicler who wrote of contemporary events in Flanders,
France, Spain, and England   30 **Olivers and Rolands** paladins in the
Charlemagne legends, the most famous of the twelve for their daring
exploits   33 **Samsons, Goliases** (i.e., Goliaths), biblical characters
typifying great physical strength   35 **rascals** (Literally, young, lean
deer.)   37 **slaves** wretches   38 **eager** (1) fierce (2) hungry.

Of old I know them. Rather with their teeth
The walls they'll tear down than forsake the siege.

REIGNIER
I think by some odd gimmers or device   41
Their arms are set, like clocks, still to strike on;   42
Else ne'er could they hold out so as they do.
By my consent, we'll even let them alone.   44

ALENÇON Be it so.

Enter the Bastard of Orleans.

BASTARD
Where's the Prince Dauphin? I have news for him.

CHARLES
Bastard of Orleans, thrice welcome to us.

BASTARD
Methinks your looks are sad, your cheer appalled.   48
Hath the late overthrow wrought this offense?   49
Be not dismayed, for succor is at hand.
A holy maid hither with me I bring,
Which, by a vision sent to her from heaven,
Ordainèd is to raise this tedious siege
And drive the English forth the bounds of France.   54
The spirit of deep prophecy she hath,
Exceeding the nine sibyls of old Rome.   56
What's past and what's to come she can descry.
Speak, shall I call her in? Believe my words,
For they are certain and unfallible.

CHARLES
Go, call her in.   [*The Bastard goes to the door.*]
           But first, to try her skill,
Reignier, stand thou as Dauphin in my place.
Question her proudly; let thy looks be stern.
By this means shall we sound what skill she hath.   63
                        [*They exchange places.*]

Enter Joan [la] Pucelle, [the Bastard escorting her].

REIGNIER
Fair maid, is't thou wilt do these wondrous feats?

PUCELLE
Reignier, is't thou that thinkest to beguile me?
Where is the Dauphin?—Come, come from behind;
I know thee well, though never seen before.
Be not amazed. There's nothing hid from me.
In private will I talk with thee apart.
Stand back, you lords, and give us leave awhile.
                        [*The lords stand aside.*]

REIGNIER
She takes upon her bravely at first dash.   71

PUCELLE
Dauphin, I am by birth a shepherd's daughter,
My wit untrained in any kind of art.   73
Heaven and Our Lady gracious hath it pleased
To shine on my contemptible estate.

Lo, whilst I waited on my tender lambs
And to sun's parching heat displayed my cheeks,
God's mother deignèd to appear to me,
And in a vision full of majesty
Willed me to leave my base vocation
And free my country from calamity.
Her aid she promised, and assured success.
In complete glory she revealed herself;
And, whereas I was black and swart before,   84
With those clear rays which she infused on me   85
That beauty am I blest with which you may see.
Ask me what question thou canst possible,
And I will answer unpremeditated.
My courage try by combat, if thou dar'st,
And thou shalt find that I exceed my sex.
Resolve on this: thou shalt be fortunate   91
If thou receive me for thy warlike mate.   92

CHARLES
Thou hast astonished me with thy high terms.   93
Only this proof I'll of thy valor make: 94
In single combat thou shalt buckle with me,   95
And if thou vanquishest, thy words are true.
Otherwise I renounce all confidence.   97

PUCELLE
I am prepared. Here is my keen-edged sword,
Decked with five flower-de-luces on each side,   99
The which at Touraine, in Saint Katharine's church-
    yard,   100
Out of a great deal of old iron I chose forth.   101

CHARLES
Then come, i'God's name! I fear no woman.

PUCELLE
And while I live, I'll ne'er fly from a man.   103
        Here they fight, and Joan la Pucelle overcomes.

CHARLES
Stay, stay thy hands! Thou art an Amazon,   104
And fightest with the sword of Deborah.   105

PUCELLE
Christ's mother helps me, else I were too weak.

CHARLES
Whoe'er helps thee, 'tis thou that must help me!
Impatiently I burn with thy desire.   108
My heart and hands thou hast at once subdued.
Excellent Pucelle, if thy name be so,
Let me thy servant and not sovereign be.   111
'Tis the French Dauphin sueth to thee thus.

PUCELLE
I must not yield to any rites of love,

---

41 **gimmers** gimmals, joints or connecting parts for transmitting motion
42 **still** continually   44 **consent** advice.   **even** i.e., do nothing but
48 **cheer appalled** countenances made pale.   49 **late . . . offense** recent
defeat brought about this harm.   54 **forth** out of   56 **nine . . . Rome**
inspired women of the ancient world. (Not only of Rome, however; the
phrase here is probably owing to a confusion with the Cumaean sibyl
who came to Tarquin with nine prophetic books.)   63 **sound** test, determine   63.2 *Pucelle* virgin   71 **She . . . dash** She shows a dauntless
spirit right at first.   73 **wit** mind, intelligence.   **art** learning

84 **black and swart** i.e., heavily tanned   85 **infused** poured
91 **Resolve on** Be sure of   92 **warlike mate** (With sexual suggestion,
as in the military terms throughout this interview.)   93 **high** lofty
94 **proof** trial, test   95 **buckle** join in close combat. (With bawdy suggestion.)   97 **confidence** (1) trust in your speech (2) intimacy.
99–101 **Decked . . . forth** Holinshed skeptically reports the tradition
that Joan's sword, adorned on each side with the five *fleur-de-lis* of the
French royal coat of arms (cf. 1.1.80), was found in a secret place
among old iron in Saint Katherine's church in Touraine.   103 **ne'er . . .
man** (With bawdy suggestion.)   104 **Amazon** race of warrior women
105 **Deborah** Hebrew prophetess who "judged" Israel in the fourteenth century B.C. (She led an army against the Canaanite oppressors,
whom she overcame: Judges 4, 5.)   108 **thy desire** desire for you.
111 **thy servant** i.e., your adorer, ready to fulfill your commands

For my profession's sacred from above.
When I have chasèd all thy foes from hence,
Then will I think upon a recompense.

CHARLES
Meantime, look gracious on thy prostrate thrall. 117

REIGNIER [to the other lords apart] My lord, methinks, is
very long in talk.

ALENÇON
Doubtless he shrives this woman to her smock, 119
Else ne'er could he so long protract his speech.

REIGNIER
Shall we disturb him, since he keeps no mean? 121

ALENÇON
He may mean more than we poor men do know. 122
These women are shrewd tempters with their
tongues. 123

REIGNIER [to Charles]
My lord, where are you? What devise you on? 124
Shall we give o'er Orleans, or no?

PUCELLE
Why, no, I say. Distrustful recreants, 126
Fight till the last gasp. I'll be your guard.

CHARLES
What she says I'll confirm. We'll fight it out.

PUCELLE
Assigned am I to be the English scourge. 129
This night the siege assuredly I'll raise.
Expect Saint Martin's summer, halcyon days, 131
Since I have enterèd into these wars.
Glory is like a circle in the water,
Which never ceaseth to enlarge itself
Till by broad spreading it disperse to naught.
With Henry's death the English circle ends;
Dispersèd are the glories it included.
Now am I like that proud insulting ship 138
Which Caesar and his fortune bare at once. 139

CHARLES
Was Mahomet inspirèd with a dove? 140
Thou with an eagle art inspirèd then.
Helen, the mother of great Constantine, 142
Nor yet Saint Philip's daughters, were like thee. 143
Bright star of Venus, fall'n down on the earth, 144

How may I reverently worship thee enough?

ALENÇON
Leave off delays, and let us raise the siege.

REIGNIER
Woman, do what thou canst to save our honors.
Drive them from Orleans and be immortalized.

CHARLES
Presently we'll try. Come, let's away about it. 149
No prophet will I trust, if she prove false. *Exeunt.*

❦

[1.3]

*Enter [the Duke of] Gloucester, with his Serv-
ingmen [in blue coats].*

GLOUCESTER
I am come to survey the Tower this day. 1
Since Henry's death, I fear, there is conveyance. 2
Where be these warders, that they wait not here? 3
Open the gates! 'Tis Gloucester that calls.
[They knock.]

FIRST WARDER [within]
Who's there that knocks so imperiously?

FIRST SERVINGMAN
It is the noble Duke of Gloucester.

SECOND WARDER [within]
Whoe'er he be, you may not be let in.

FIRST SERVINGMAN
Villains, answer you so the Lord Protector?

FIRST WARDER [within]
The Lord protect him! So we answer him.
We do no otherwise than we are willed. 10

GLOUCESTER
Who willèd you? Or whose will stands but mine? 11
There's none Protector of the realm but I.—
Break up the gates. I'll be your warrantize. 13
Shall I be flouted thus by dunghill grooms? 14
*Gloucester's men rush at the Tower gates, and
Woodville the Lieutenant speaks within.*

WOODVILLE [within]
What noise is this? What traitors have we here?

GLOUCESTER
Lieutenant, is it you whose voice I hear?
Open the gates. Here's Gloucester that would enter.

WOODVILLE [within]
Have patience, noble Duke. I may not open;
The Cardinal of Winchester forbids. 19
From him I have express commandement
That thou nor none of thine shall be let in.

GLOUCESTER
Fainthearted Woodville, prizest him 'fore me?

---

117 look . . . thrall look with favor on your abject servant in love.
119 shrives hears confession, i.e., examines.   **to her smock** to her undergarment, i.e., completely. (With bawdy suggestion.)   **121 keeps no mean**
observes no moderation.   **122 mean** intend. (With a play on *mean*, moderation, in line 121.)   **123 shrewd** cunning, mischievous   **124 where are
you?** i.e., what are you up to?   **devise** decide   **126 Distrustful recreants**
Faithless cowards   **129 the English scourge** scourge of the English
131 Saint Martin's summer i.e., Indian summer; Saint Martin's Day is
November 11.   **halcyon days** i.e., unseasonably fair weather. (The halcyon is the kingfisher, which, according to fable, nested at midwinter on
the seas, which became calm for that purpose.)   **138–9 Now . . . once**
(North's translation of Plutarch relates how Caesar, encountering a storm,
said to the mariners, "Fear not, for thou hast Caesar and his fortune with
thee.")   **140 Was . . . dove** (Mohammed supposedly claimed that he
received divine inspiration from a dove whispering in his ear.)
142 Helen mother of the emperor Constantine and supposed discoverer of
the holy cross and sepulcher of the Lord   **143 Saint Philip's daughters**
the four daughters of Philip the Evangelist, said in Acts 21:9 to have the
power of prophecy   **144 Bright . . . earth** Charles conflates the legend of
Venus come down to earth to look for Cupid with Christian interpretation
of Isaiah 14:12, "How art thou fallen from heaven, O Lucifer, son of the
morning," as referring to the fall of Satan from heaven (though more plausibly it describes Venus as the evening star). Charles's offer to worship
Joan is thus laden with unintended diabolical resonances.

149 Presently Immediately
1.3. Location: Before the Tower of London.
1 survey inspect   **2 conveyance** trickery.   **3 warders** guards
10 willed commanded.   **11 stands** has authority   **13 warrantize**
authorization.   **14 dunghill grooms** i.e., base fellows.   **14.1 rush . . .
gates** (Gloucester's men assault the facade of the tiring-house wall
backstage, which represents the Tower gates; Woodville and the
warders are "within," or behind that wall, invisible to the audience.)
19 Cardinal (An inconsistency with 5.1.28 ff., where Winchester has
just been installed as cardinal.)

Arrogant Winchester, that haughty prelate,
Whom Henry, our late sovereign, ne'er could brook?   24
Thou art no friend to God or to the King.
Open the gates, or I'll shut thee out shortly.   26

SERVINGMEN
Open the gates unto the Lord Protector,
Or we'll burst them open, if that you come not
    quickly.   28

Enter to the Protector at the Tower gates
Winchester and his men in tawny coats.

WINCHESTER
How now, ambitious Humphrey, what means this?

GLOUCESTER
Peeled priest, dost thou command me to be shut out?   30

WINCHESTER
I do, thou most usurping proditor,   31
And not Protector, of the King or realm.

GLOUCESTER
Stand back, thou manifest conspirator,
Thou that contrived'st to murder our dead lord,   34
Thou that giv'st whores indulgences to sin.   35
I'll canvass thee in thy broad cardinal's hat   36
If thou proceed in this thy insolence.

WINCHESTER
Nay, stand thou back. I will not budge a foot.
This be Damascus, be thou cursèd Cain,   39
To slay thy brother Abel, if thou wilt.   40

GLOUCESTER
I will not slay thee, but I'll drive thee back.
Thy scarlet robes as a child's bearing cloth   42
I'll use to carry thee out of this place.

WINCHESTER
Do what thou dar'st! I beard thee to thy face.   44

GLOUCESTER
What, am I dared and bearded to my face?
Draw, men, for all this privilegèd place—   46
Blue coats to tawny coats. Priest, beware your beard.
I mean to tug it and to cuff you soundly.
Under my feet I stamp thy cardinal's hat.
In spite of Pope or dignities of Church,
Here by the cheeks I'll drag thee up and down.

WINCHESTER
Gloucester, thou wilt answer this before the Pope.   52

GLOUCESTER
Winchester goose! I cry, a rope, a rope!   53
[*To his Servingmen*] Now beat them hence. Why do you
    let them stay?—
Thee I'll chase hence, thou wolf in sheep's array.
Out, tawny coats! Out, scarlet hypocrite!

Here Gloucester's men beat out the Cardinal's
men, and enter in the hurly-burly the Mayor of
London and his Officers.

MAYOR
Fie, lords, that you, being supreme magistrates,   57
Thus contumeliously should break the peace!   58

GLOUCESTER
Peace, Mayor! Thou know'st little of my wrongs.
Here's Beaufort, that regards nor God nor king,   60
Hath here distrained the Tower to his use.   61

WINCHESTER
Here's Gloucester, a foe to citizens,   62
One that still motions war and never peace,   63
O'ercharging your free purses with large fines,   64
That seeks to overthrow religion
Because he is Protector of the realm,
And would have armor here out of the Tower
To crown himself king and suppress the Prince.   68

GLOUCESTER
I will not answer thee with words, but blows.
                            Here they skirmish again.

MAYOR
Naught rests for me in this tumultuous strife   70
But to make open proclamation.
Come, officer, as loud as e'er thou canst,
Cry.

OFFICER   All manner of men assembled here in arms
this day against God's peace and the King's, we charge
and command you, in His Highness' name, to repair
to your several dwelling places, and not to wear, han-   77
dle, or use any sword, weapon, or dagger hence-for-
ward, upon pain of death.   79

GLOUCESTER
Cardinal, I'll be no breaker of the law.
But we shall meet and break our minds at large.   81

WINCHESTER
Gloucester, we'll meet to thy cost, be sure.
Thy heart-blood I will have for this day's work.

MAYOR
I'll call for clubs, if you will not away.   84
This cardinal's more haughty than the devil.

---

24 brook endure.   **26 I'll . . . shortly** i.e., I'll take possession and shut
you out.   **28 if that** if   **30 Peeled** Shaven, tonsured   **31 proditor**
traitor   **34–5 Thou . . . sin** (Gloucester, in his bill of particulars
against Winchester, charged that the cleric had suborned someone to
attempt the murder of the prince who later became Henry V. Here he
refers also to the fact that Winchester collected revenues from houses
of prostitution on the south bank of the Thames.)   **35 indulgences**
forgiveness of sins. (One could buy indulgences from the Church.)
36 canvass i.e., deal with severely. (The metaphor is that of tossing
someone in a canvas or blanket as sport or punishment.)   **39 This be
Damascus** Let this be Damascus (a city reputed to have been built on
the site of Cain's slaying of his brother Abel)   **40 thy brother** (Winchester is Gloucester's half-uncle.)   **42 child's bearing cloth** a sling
in which the child could be carried on the mother's back   **44 beard**
openly defy   **46 for . . . place** despite this being a place under royal
jurisdiction. (The drawing of weapons as forbidden by the law of
arms in such a royal residence; cf. 2.4.86 and n.)   **52 answer** render
an account of, pay for

53 Winchester goose (A colloquialism for a venereal infection, and
for a prostitute. Gloucester derides Winchester for licensing of brothels in Southwark.)   **a rope** i.e., a halter for hanging or whipping
57 magistrates rulers   **58 contumeliously** arrogantly, contemptuously   **60 regards nor** has a proper respect for neither   **61 distrained**
confiscated   **62 citizens** inhabitants of a city, especially one possessing civic rights and privileges   **63 still motions** incessantly advo-
cates   **64 O'ercharging . . . fines** overburdening you with excessive
taxation   **68 Prince** i.e., Henry VI.   **70 rests for me** remains for me to
do   **77 several** various   **79 pain** punishment   **81 break our minds**
(1) say what's on our minds (2) crack heads.   **at large** at length.
84 call for clubs i.e., sound the rallying cry for London apprentices
armed with clubs

GLOUCESTER
Mayor, farewell. Thou dost but what thou mayst.

WINCHESTER
Abominable Gloucester, guard thy head,
For I intend to have it ere long.

*Exeunt, [separately, Gloucester and Winchester
with their Servingmen].*

MAYOR
See the coast cleared, and then we will depart.
Good God, these nobles should such stomachs bear!　90
I myself fight not once in forty year.　*Exeunt.*

❧

[1.4]

*Enter the Master Gunner of Orleans and his
Boy.*

MASTER GUNNER
Sirrah, thou know'st how Orleans is besieged　1
And how the English have the suburbs won.

BOY
Father, I know, and oft have shot at them,
Howe'er unfortunate I missed my aim.　4

MASTER GUNNER
But now thou shalt not. Be thou ruled by me.
Chief master gunner am I of this town;
Something I must do to procure me grace.　7
The Prince's espials have informèd me　8
How the English, in the suburbs close entrenched,
Wont through a secret grate of iron bars　10
In yonder tower to overpeer the city
And thence discover how with most advantage
They may vex us with shot or with assault.
To intercept this inconvenience,　14
A piece of ordnance 'gainst it I have placed,　15
And even these three days have I watched,
If I could see them. Now do thou watch,
For I can stay no longer.
If thou spy'st any, run and bring me word,
And thou shalt find me at the governor's.　*Exit.*

BOY
Father, I warrant you; take you no care.　21
I'll never trouble you, if I may spy them.　*Exit.*　22

*Enter Salisbury and Talbot on the turrets, with
[Sir William Glasdale, Sir Thomas Gargrave,
and] others.*

SALISBURY
Talbot, my life, my joy, again returned?
How wert thou handled being prisoner?
Or by what means got'st thou to be released?
Discourse, I prithee, on this turret's top.

TALBOT
The Duke of Bedford had a prisoner
Called the brave Lord Ponton de Santrailles;
For him was I exchanged and ransomèd.
But with a baser man-of-arms by far　30
Once in contempt they would have bartered me;
Which I disdaining scorned, and cravèd death
Rather than I would be so pilled esteemed.　33
In fine, redeemed I was as I desired.　34
But oh, the treacherous Falstaff wounds my heart,
Whom with my bare fists I would execute
If I now had him brought into my power.

SALISBURY
Yet tell'st thou not how thou wert entertained.　38

TALBOT
With scoffs and scorns and contumelious taunts.　39
In open marketplace produced they me
To be a public spectacle to all.
"Here," said they, "is the terror of the French,
The scarecrow that affrights our children so."
Then broke I from the officers that led me
And with my nails digged stones out of the ground
To hurl at the beholders of my shame.
My grisly countenance made others fly;
None durst come near for fear of sudden death.
In iron walls they deemed me not secure;
So great fear of my name 'mongst them were spread
That they supposed I could rend bars of steel
And spurn in pieces posts of adamant.　52
Wherefore a guard of chosen shot I had　53
That walked about me every minute while;　54
And if I did but stir out of my bed,
Ready they were to shoot me to the heart.　56

Enter the Boy with a linstock.

SALISBURY
I grieve to hear what torments you endured.
But we will be revenged sufficiently.
Now it is suppertime in Orleans.
Here, through this grate, I count each one
And view the Frenchmen how they fortify.
Let us look in; the sight will much delight thee.—
Sir Thomas Gargrave and Sir William Glasdale,
Let me have your express opinions　64
Where is best place to make our batt'ry next.　65

GARGRAVE
I think at the north gate, for there stands lords.

GLASDALE
And I here, at the bulwark of the bridge.　67

TALBOT
For aught I see, this city must be famished　68

---

90 these that these.　**stomachs** i.e., angry tempers
1.4. Location: France. Orleans.
1 Sirrah (Customary form of address to an inferior.)　**4 Howe'er
unfortunate** although unfortunately　**7 grace** honor, credit.
8 espials spies　**10 Wont** are accustomed　**14 inconvenience** mischief　**15 'gainst** directed toward　**21 take you no care** don't you
worry.　**22.1 turrets** i.e., some high point of vantage in the theater,
above the main stage

30 baser of lower rank　**33 pilled** peeled, i.e., despoiled of honor
34 In fine Finally.　**redeemed** ransomed　**38 entertained** treated.
39 contumelious insolent　**52 spurn** kick.　**adamant** a legendary
substance supposedly of incredible hardness, like diamond, or like a
magnet.　**53 chosen shot** carefully selected marksmen　**54 every
minute while** i.e., constantly, at minute intervals　**56.1 linstock**
forked stick used to hold a lighted match for firing cannon.
64 express precise　**65 batt'ry** attack　**67 bulwark** fortification
(protecting the bridge)　**68 must be famished** will have to be
reduced to famine

Or with light skirmishes enfeeblèd.   69
    Here they shoot, and Salisbury falls down [together
                    with Gargrave].

SALISBURY
  O Lord, have mercy on us, wretched sinners!

GARGRAVE
  O Lord, have mercy on me, woeful man!

TALBOT
  What chance is this that suddenly hath crossed us?   72
  Speak, Salisbury—at least, if thou canst, speak.
  How far'st thou, mirror of all martial men?   74
  One of thy eyes and thy cheek's side struck off?
  Accursèd tower! Accursèd fatal hand
  That hath contrived this woeful tragedy!
  In thirteen battles Salisbury o'ercame;
  Henry the Fifth he first trained to the wars.
  Whilst any trump did sound or drum struck up,
  His sword did ne'er leave striking in the field.   81
  Yet liv'st thou, Salisbury? Though thy speech doth
    fail,
  One eye thou hast to look to heaven for grace.
  The sun with one eye vieweth all the world.   84
  Heaven, be thou gracious to none alive
  If Salisbury wants mercy at thy hands!   86
  Sir Thomas Gargrave, hast thou any life?
  Speak unto Talbot. Nay, look up to him.—
  Bear hence his body; I will help to bury it.
              [Gargrave's body is borne off.]
  Salisbury, cheer thy spirit with this comfort:
  Thou shalt not die whiles—
  He beckons with his hand and smiles on me,
  As who should say, "When I am dead and gone,   93
  Remember to avenge me on the French."
  Plantagenet, I will; and Nero-like   95
  Play on the lute, beholding the towns burn.
  Wretched shall France be only in my name.   97
      Here an alarum, and it thunders and lightens.
  What stir is this? What tumult's in the heavens?
  Whence cometh this alarum and the noise?

      Enter a Messenger.

MESSENGER
  My lord, my lord, the French have gathered head!   100
  The Dauphin, with one Joan la Pucelle joined,
  A holy prophetess new risen up,
  Is come with a great power to raise the siege.   103
      Here Salisbury lifteth himself up and groans.

TALBOT
  Hear, hear how dying Salisbury doth groan!
  It irks his heart he cannot be revenged.
  Frenchmen, I'll be a Salisbury to you.

Pucelle or pussel, Dauphin or dogfish,   107
Your hearts I'll stamp out with my horse's heels
And make a quagmire of your mingled brains.—
Convey me Salisbury into his tent,   110
And then we'll try what these dastard Frenchmen
    dare.   *Alarum. Exeunt, [bearing out Salisbury].*

                ❖

[1.5]

    Here an alarum again, and Talbot pursueth the
    Dauphin and driveth him. Then enter Joan la
    Pucelle, driving Englishmen before her [and exit
    after them]. Then enter [again] Talbot.

TALBOT
  Where is my strength, my valor, and my force?
  Our English troops retire; I cannot stay them.   2
  A woman clad in armor chaseth them.

    Enter [Joan la] Pucelle.

  Here, here she comes.—I'll have a bout with thee;   4
  Devil or devil's dam, I'll conjure thee.   5
  Blood will I draw on thee—thou art a witch—   6
  And straightway give thy soul to him thou serv'st.   7

PUCELLE
  Come, come, 'tis only I that must disgrace thee.
                  Here they fight.

TALBOT
  Heavens, can you suffer hell so to prevail?
  My breast I'll burst with straining of my courage
  And from my shoulders crack my arms asunder
  But I will chastise this high-minded strumpet.   12
                They fight again.

PUCELLE
  Talbot, farewell. Thy hour is not yet come.
  I must go victual Orleans forthwith.   14
      A short alarum. Then enter the town with soldiers.
  O'ertake me if thou canst! I scorn thy strength.
  Go, go, cheer up thy hungry starvèd men;
  Help Salisbury to make his testament.
  This day is ours, as many more shall be.   *Exit.*

TALBOT
  My thoughts are whirlèd like a potter's wheel.
  I know not where I am nor what I do.
  A witch by fear, not force, like Hannibal   21
  Drives back our troops and conquers as she lists.   22
  So bees with smoke and doves with noisome stench   23

---

107 pussel drab, slut. (A punning spelling variant of *pucelle,* "maid.")
Dauphin (The usual Folio spelling of *Dauphin* is *Dolphin.* The sea
mammal by that name is included in the meaning and is contrasted
with *dogfish,* a very low form of sea life.) **110 Convey me** Convey.
(*Me* is used colloquially.)
1.5. Location: Scene continues at Orleans.
2 stay halt **4 bout** encounter in the fighting. (But with sexual overtones.) **5 dam** dame, mother **6 Blood . . . witch** (Anyone who succeeded in drawing blood from a witch was thought to be
invulnerable to her magic.) **7 him** i.e., the devil **12 But I will** if I
do not. **high-minded** arrogant **14 victual** supply with provisions.
14.1 enter i.e., they, the French, enter Orleans; Joan follows four lines
later **21 Hannibal** Carthaginian general who once repulsed a
Roman army by tying firebrands to the horns of a herd of oxen and
driving the animals toward the Romans **22 lists** pleases. **23 noisome** noxious

69.1 *Here they shoot* i.e., the French (probably offstage, though the
Boy's appearance with the linstock at line 56 visually symbolizes the
action of preparing to fire). **72 chance** misfortune. **crossed** afflicted
74 mirror of example to **81 leave** leave off **84 The sun . . . world**
i.e., With one eye one can still see, and look to heaven for grace. (The
sun was often described as a burning eye.) **86 wants** lacks **93 As
who** as one who **95 Plantagenet** (The Earl of Salisbury was Thomas
Montacute; he was descended from the Plantagenet Edward I.)
Nero-like (Talbot compares himself to Nero, who played music while
Rome burned.) **97 only in** at the mere sound of **100 gathered head**
drawn their forces together. **103 power** army

Are from their hives and houses driven away.
They called us, for our fierceness, English dogs;
Now, like to whelps, we crying run away.
                                        A short alarum.
Hark, countrymen! Either renew the fight
Or tear the lions out of England's coat!   28
Renounce your soil; give sheep in lions' stead.   29
Sheep run not half so treacherous from the wolf,   30
Or horse or oxen from the leopard,
As you fly from your oft-subduèd slaves.   32
                        Alarum. Here another skirmish.
It will not be. Retire into your trenches.   33
You all consented unto Salisbury's death,
For none would strike a stroke in his revenge.   35
Pucelle is entered into Orleans
In spite of us or aught that we could do.
Oh, would I were to die with Salisbury!
The shame hereof will make me hide my head.   39
                        Exit Talbot. Alarum. Retreat.

❧

[1.6]

*Flourish. Enter, on the walls, Pucelle, Dauphin
[Charles], Reignier, Alençon, and soldiers.*

PUCELLE
    Advance our waving colors on the walls;   1
    Rescued is Orleans from the English!
    Thus Joan la Pucelle hath performed her word.

CHARLES
    Divinest creature, Astraea's daughter,   4
    How shall I honor thee for this success?
    Thy promises are like Adonis' garden,   6
    That one day bloomed and fruitful were the next.
    France, triumph in thy glorious prophetess!
    Recovered is the town of Orleans.
    More blessèd hap did ne'er befall our state.   10

REIGNIER
    Why ring not out the bells aloud throughout the
        town?
    Dauphin, command the citizens make bonfires
    And feast and banquet in the open streets
    To celebrate the joy that God hath given us.

ALENÇON
    All France will be replete with mirth and joy
    When they shall hear how we have played the men.   16

CHARLES
    'Tis Joan, not we, by whom the day is won;
    For which I will divide my crown with her,
    And all the priests and friars in my realm
    Shall in procession sing her endless praise.
    A statelier pyramid to her I'll rear
    Than Rhodope's of Memphis ever was.   22
    In memory of her when she is dead,
    Her ashes, in an urn more precious
    Than the rich-jeweled coffer of Darius,   25
    Transported shall be at high festivals
    Before the kings and queens of France.
    No longer on Saint Denis will we cry,   28
    But Joan la Pucelle shall be France's saint.
    Come in, and let us banquet royally
    After this golden day of victory.   *Flourish. Exeunt.*

❧

2.1

*Enter [on the walls] a [French] Sergeant of a
band, with two Sentinels.*

SERGEANT
    Sirs, take your places and be vigilant.
    If any noise or soldier you perceive
    Near to the walls, by some apparent sign   3
    Let us have knowledge at the court of guard.   4

A SENTINEL   Sergeant, you shall.   *[Exit Sergeant.]*
                        Thus are poor servitors,   5
    When others sleep upon their quiet beds,   6
    Constrained to watch in darkness, rain, and cold.   7

*Enter Talbot, Bedford, and Burgundy, [and
forces,] with scaling ladders.*

TALBOT
    Lord Regent, and redoubted Burgundy,
    By whose approach the regions of Artois,   9
    Walloon, and Picardy are friends to us,
    This happy night the Frenchmen are secure,   11
    Having all day caroused and banqueted.
    Embrace we then this opportunity
    As fitting best to quittance their deceit,   14
    Contrived by art and baleful sorcery.   15

BEDFORD
    Coward of France, how much he wrongs his fame,   16
    Despairing of his own arm's fortitude,

---

28 lions . . . coat i.e., the three lions passant displayed in the English coat of arms.   **29 Renounce . . . stead** Renounce your native soil; give up the emblem of the lion that you should display heraldically and display a sheep instead.   **30 treacherous** i.e., cowardly   **32 from . . . slaves** from the wretches you have often overcome.   **33 It will not be** i.e., It's hopeless.   **35 his revenge** revenge of him.   **39.1 Retreat** trumpet call to signal a withdrawal from the attack.
1.6. Location: Scene continues at Orleans.
0.1 on the walls i.e., in the gallery backstage, above the main doors of the tiring-house facade. (When Joan enters Orleans at 1.5.14, she enters the tiring-house through one of its doors, and that tiring-house facade remains the visual equivalent of the walls of Orleans through 2.1.)   **1 Advance** Lift up   **4 Astraea** goddess of Justice   **6 Adonis' garden** mythical garden of eternal fecundity   **10 hap** event   **16 played the men** showed manly courage.

22 Rhodope a Greek courtesan who became the wife of the king of Egypt. (A legend was current that she built the third pyramid.)   **Memphis** an ancient city of Egypt near which stand the pyramids of Ramses II   **25 Darius** King of Persia conquered by Alexander the Great. Alexander, according to legend, used Darius' *rich-jeweled coffer* to carry about the poems of Homer.   **28 Saint Denis** patron saint of France
2.2. Location: Before Orleans, as in the previous scenes; the time is later that night.
0.1 band detachment of soldiers   **3 apparent** plain   **4 court of guard** guardhouse.   **5 servitors** servants, common soldiers   **6 upon their quiet beds** quietly in their beds   **7.1 Burgundy** the Duke of Burgundy, allied to the English by the Treaty of Troyes, 1420. (His support brought with it the cooperation of territories near to Burgundy, in the Low Countries, such as Walloon and Picardy.)   **9 By whose approach** by means of whose joining our alliance   **11 secure** overconfident   **14 quittance** requite   **15 art** i.e., black magic   **16 Coward of France** i.e., the Dauphin.   **fame** reputation

To join with witches and the help of hell!

BURGUNDY
Traitors have never other company.
But what's that Pucelle whom they term so pure?

TALBOT
A maid, they say.

BEDFORD   A maid, and be so martial?

BURGUNDY
Pray God she prove not masculine ere long,   22
If underneath the standard of the French
She carry armor as she hath begun.

TALBOT
Well, let them practice and converse with spirits.
God is our fortress, in whose conquering name
Let us resolve to scale their flinty bulwarks.

BEDFORD
Ascend, brave Talbot. We will follow thee.

TALBOT
Not all together. Better far, I guess,
That we do make our entrance several ways,   30
That, if it chance the one of us do fail,   31
The other yet may rise against their force.

BEDFORD
Agreed. I'll to yond corner.

BURGUNDY   And I to this.

TALBOT
And here will Talbot mount, or make his grave.
Now, Salisbury, for thee, and for the right
Of English Henry, shall this night appear   36
How much in duty I am bound to both.

SENTINELS
Arm, arm! The enemy doth make assault!   38
    [The English scale the walls, Talbot in the center,
               and exeunt above into the city.]
                      Cry: "Saint George! A Talbot!"
    The French leap o'er the walls in their shirts. Enter,
    several ways, [the] Bastard [of Orleans], Alençon,
    [and] Reignier, half ready, and half unready.

ALENÇON
How now, my lords? What, all unready so?

BASTARD
Unready? Ay, and glad we scaped so well.

REIGNIER
'Twas time, I trow, to wake and leave our beds,   41
Hearing alarums at our chamber doors.

ALENÇON
Of all exploits since first I followed arms,   43

Ne'er heard I of a warlike enterprise
More venturous or desperate than this.

BASTARD
I think this Talbot be a fiend of hell.

REIGNIER
If not of hell, the heavens sure favor him.

ALENÇON
Here cometh Charles. I marvel how he sped.   48

    Enter Charles and Joan [la Pucelle].

BASTARD
Tut, holy Joan was his defensive guard.

CHARLES
Is this thy cunning, thou deceitful dame?   50
Didst thou at first, to flatter us withal,   51
Make us partakers of a little gain
That now our loss might be ten times so much?

PUCELLE
Wherefore is Charles impatient with his friend?
At all times will you have my power alike?
Sleeping or waking must I still prevail,   56
Or will you blame and lay the fault on me?—
Improvident soldiers! Had your watch been good,
This sudden mischief never could have fall'n.

CHARLES
Duke of Alençon, this was your default,   60
That, being captain of the watch tonight,   61
Did look no better to that weighty charge.   62

ALENÇON
Had all your quarters been as safely kept
As that whereof I had the government,
We had not been thus shamefully surprised.

BASTARD
Mine was secure.   And so was mine, my lord.

REIGNIER

CHARLES
And, for myself, most part of all this night
Within her quarter and mine own precinct   68
I was employed in passing to and fro
About relieving of the sentinels.
Then how or which way should they first break in?

PUCELLE
Question, my lords, no further of the case,
How or which way. 'Tis sure they found some place
But weakly guarded, where the breach was made.
And now there rests no other shift but this: 75
To gather our soldiers, scattered and dispersed,
And lay new platforms to endamage them.   77

    Alarum. Enter a[n English] Soldier, crying "A
    Talbot! A Talbot!" They fly, leaving their clothes
    behind.

---

22 prove not masculine (1) turn out to be a man after all (2) prove herself feminine by becoming pregnant. (The bawdy punning continues in
standard, "that which stands up," carry armor, "bear the weight of a
man," practice and converse, "engage in sexual contact," etc.) 30 several
ways i.e., on ladders at different points. (The three leaders place their
ladders against the tiring-house facade, one in the middle for Talbot and
one on each wing, and actually ascend to the gallery or top of the
"walls," where they surprise the French. Some of the French, thus surprised, leap from the gallery down onto the main stage, where the Bastard, Alençon, and others consult in a state of disorder about their
situation.) 31 That so that 36 shall it shall 38.6 unready not fully
clothed. (This scene is based on an incident occurring at Le Mans, a year
prior to the siege of Orleans.) 41 trow believe 43 followed arms
practiced soldiership

48 marvel wonder. sped fared. 50 cunning skill 51 flatter lead on
with false hopes. withal with it 56 still prevail always succeed
60 default failure 61 tonight this previous night 62 charge responsibility. 68 her i.e., Joan's. (With a suggestion of sexual intercourse, continued in passing to and fro, line 69.) 75 rests remains. shift strategy
77 platforms plans

SOLDIER
    I'll be so bold to take what they have left.
    The cry of "Talbot" serves me for a sword,
    For I have loaden me with many spoils,   80
    Using no other weapon but his name.
                                    Exit, [bearing spoils].

❖

[2.2]

*Enter Talbot, Bedford, Burgundy, [a Captain,
and soldiers].*

BEDFORD
    The day begins to break, and night is fled,
    Whose pitchy mantle overveiled the earth.   2
    Here sound retreat and cease our hot pursuit.   3
                                    Retreat [is sounded].

TALBOT
    Bring forth the body of old Salisbury
    And here advance it in the marketplace,   5
    The middle center of this cursèd town.

        *[Enter a funeral procession with Salisbury's
        body,] their drums beating a dead march.*

    Now have I paid my vow unto his soul:
    For every drop of blood was drawn from him   8
    There hath at least five Frenchmen died tonight.
    And that hereafter ages may behold
    What ruin happened in revenge of him,
    Within their chiefest temple I'll erect
    A tomb, wherein his corpse shall be interred;
    Upon the which, that everyone may read,
    Shall be engraved the sack of Orleans,
    The treacherous manner of his mournful death,
    And what a terror he had been to France.
                            [Exit funeral procession.]
    But, lords, in all our bloody massacre,
    I muse we met not with the Dauphin's grace,   19
    His new-come champion, virtuous Joan of Arc,   20
    Nor any of his false confederates.
BEDFORD
    'Tis thought, Lord Talbot, when the fight began,
    Roused on the sudden from their drowsy beds,
    They did amongst the troops of armèd men
    Leap o'er the walls for refuge in the field.
BURGUNDY
    Myself, as far as I could well discern
    For smoke and dusky vapors of the night,
    Am sure I scared the Dauphin and his trull,   28
    When arm in arm they both came swiftly running,
    Like to a pair of loving turtledoves
    That could not live asunder day or night.
    After that things are set in order here,

    We'll follow them with all the power we have.

        Enter a Messenger.

MESSENGER
    All hail, my lords! Which of this princely train
    Call ye the warlike Talbot, for his acts
    So much applauded through the realm of France?
TALBOT
    Here is the Talbot. Who would speak with him?
MESSENGER
    The virtuous lady, Countess of Auvergne,
    With modesty admiring thy renown,
    By me entreats, great lord, thou wouldst vouchsafe
    To visit her poor castle where she lies,   41
    That she may boast she hath beheld the man
    Whose glory fills the world with loud report.   43
BURGUNDY
    Is it even so? Nay, then, I see our wars
    Will turn unto a peaceful comic sport,
    When ladies crave to be encountered with.   46
    You may not, my lord, despise her gentle suit.   47
TALBOT
    Ne'er trust me then; for when a world of men   48
    Could not prevail with all their oratory,
    Yet hath a woman's kindness overruled.   50
    And therefore tell her I return great thanks,
    And in submission will attend on her.   52
    Will not Your Honors bear me company?
BEDFORD
    No, truly, 'tis more than manners will;   54
    And I have heard it said unbidden guests
    Are often welcomest when they are gone.
TALBOT
    Well then, alone, since there's no remedy,
    I mean to prove this lady's courtesy.
    Come hither, Captain. (*Whispers.*) You perceive my   58
        mind?
CAPTAIN
    I do, my lord, and mean accordingly.   *Exeunt.*   60

❖

[2.3]

Enter [the] Countess [and her Porter].

COUNTESS
    Porter, remember what I gave in charge,   1
    And when you have done so, bring the keys to me.
PORTER   Madam, I will.   *Exit.*
COUNTESS
    The plot is laid. If all things fall out right,
    I shall as famous be by this exploit

80 **loaden me** laden myself
2.2. Location: Orleans. Within the town.
2 pitchy pitch black   **3 retreat** pull back from the attack   **5 advance**
raise aloft (on a bier)   **8 was** that was   **19 muse** wonder.   **the
Dauphin's grace** His Grace the Dauphin   **20 virtuous** (Said ironically.)   **28 trull** strumpet (i.e., Joan)

41 lies dwells   **43 report** (1) acclaim (2) noise of battle.   **46 encountered with** i.e., encountered socially, as an adversary in the battle of
the sexes, and as the object of wooing.   **47 gentle** gracious, courteous
48 a world of many   **50 overruled** prevailed.   **52 in . . . on her** will
visit her in compliance with her wishes.   **54 will** require   **58 prove**
test   **60 mean** intend to act
2.3. Location: Auvergne. The Countess' castle.
1 gave in charge commanded

As Scythian Tomyris by Cyrus' death.   6
Great is the rumor of this dreadful knight,   7
And his achievements of no less account.
Fain would mine eyes be witness with mine ears,
To give their censure of these rare reports.   10

Enter Messenger and Talbot.

MESSENGER   Madam,
According as Your Ladyship desired,
By message craved, so is Lord Talbot come.

COUNTESS
And he is welcome. What? Is this the man?

MESSENGER
Madam, it is.

COUNTESS   Is this the scourge of France?
Is this the Talbot, so much feared abroad   16
That with his name the mothers still their babes?   17
I see report is fabulous and false.
I thought I should have seen some Hercules,   19
A second Hector, for his grim aspect   20
And large proportion of his strong-knit limbs.   21
Alas, this is a child, a silly dwarf!   22
It cannot be this weak and writhled shrimp   23
Should strike such terror to his enemies.

TALBOT
Madam, I have been bold to trouble you;
But since Your Ladyship is not at leisure,
I'll sort some other time to visit you.   [*Going.*] 27

COUNTESS   [*to the Messenger*]
What means he now? Go ask him whither he goes.

MESSENGER
Stay, my Lord Talbot, for my lady craves
To know the cause of your abrupt departure.

TALBOT
Marry, for that she's in a wrong belief,   31
I go to certify her Talbot's here.   32

Enter Porter with keys.

COUNTESS
If thou be he, then art thou prisoner.

TALBOT
Prisoner? To whom?

COUNTESS   To me, bloodthirsty lord;
And for that cause I trained thee to my house.   35
Long time thy shadow hath been thrall to me,   36
For in my gallery thy picture hangs;
But now the substance shall endure the like,
And I will chain these legs and arms of thine

That hast by tyranny these many years   40
Wasted our country, slain our citizens,
And sent our sons and husbands captivate.   42

TALBOT   Ha, ha, ha!

COUNTESS
Laughest thou, wretch? Thy mirth shall turn to moan.

TALBOT
I laugh to see Your Ladyship so fond   45
To think that you have aught but Talbot's shadow
Whereon to practice your severity.

COUNTESS   Why, art not thou the man?

TALBOT   I am indeed.

COUNTESS   Then have I substance too.

TALBOT
No, no, I am but shadow of myself.
You are deceived. My substance is not here;
For what you see is but the smallest part
And least proportion of humanity.   54
I tell you, madam, were the whole frame here,   55
It is of such a spacious lofty pitch   56
Your roof were not sufficient to contain't.

COUNTESS
This is a riddling merchant for the nonce!   58
He will be here, and yet he is not here.
How can these contrarieties agree?

TALBOT
That will I show you presently.   61

*Winds his horn. Drums strike up. A peal of ord-
nance. Enter soldiers.*

How say you, madam? Are you now persuaded
That Talbot is but shadow of himself?
These are his substance, sinews, arms, and strength,
With which he yoketh your rebellious necks,
Razeth your cities, and subverts your towns,   66
And in a moment makes them desolate.

COUNTESS
Victorious Talbot, pardon my abuse.   68
I find thou art no less than fame hath bruited,   69
And more than may be gathered by thy shape.
Let my presumption not provoke thy wrath,
For I am sorry that with reverence
I did not entertain thee as thou art.   73

TALBOT
Be not dismayed, fair lady, nor misconster   74
The mind of Talbot, as you did mistake
The outward composition of his body.
What you have done hath not offended me;
Nor other satisfaction do I crave
But only, with your patience, that we may   79

---

6 Scythian Tomyris tribal queen of the Massagetae, who slew Cyrus the Great when he invaded her territory and, in revenge for her son's death, had the head of Cyrus placed in a wineskin filled with blood **7 rumor** reputation. **dreadful** inspiring dread **10 censure** judgment. **rare** remarkable **16 abroad** everywhere **17 still** quiet **19–20 Hercules, Hector** (Types of great physical strength.) **20 for** because of. **aspect** facial appearance **21 proportion** size **22 silly** i.e., frail, mere **23 writhled** wrinkled **27 sort** choose **31 Marry** (A mild interjection; originally an oath, "by the Virgin Mary.") **for that** because **32 I . . . here** i.e., I am about to prove to her that the real Talbot, not the legendary figure of popular report, is here. (*I go* might suggest that he is on the point of going to summon his soldiers, though at lines 61 ff. he need only sound his horn.) **35 trained** lured, enticed **36 shadow** image, likeness. **thrall** slave

40 tyranny cruelty **42 captivate** into captivity. **45 fond** foolish **54 proportion of humanity** (1) part of the whole man (2) portion of my army. **55 frame** structure, construct, i.e., of man and of the army **56 pitch** height **58 riddling merchant** dealer in riddles. **for the nonce** (A colloquialism, conveying a note of scornful incredulity: "This is a fine riddling rascal, if you please!") **61 presently** immediately. **61.1 Winds** Sounds **66 subverts** overthrows **68 abuse** (1) error (2) deception. **69 than . . . bruited** than your reputation has declared you to be **73 entertain** receive **74 misconster** misconstrue **79 patience** permission

Taste of your wine and see what cates you have;   80
For soldiers' stomachs always serve them well.   81

COUNTESS
With all my heart, and think me honorèd
To feast so great a warrior in my house.   *Exeunt.*

❖

[2.4]

Enter Richard Plantagenet, Warwick, Somerset,
[William de la] Pole, [Earl of Suffolk, Vernon],
and others [including a Lawyer. A rose-bush is
provided onstage.]

PLANTAGENET
Great lords and gentlemen, what means this silence?
Dare no man answer in a case of truth?

SUFFOLK
Within the Temple hall we were too loud.
The garden here is more convenient.   3

PLANTAGENET
Then say at once if I maintained the truth;
Or else was wrangling Somerset in th'error?   6

SUFFOLK
Faith, I have been a truant in the law   7
And never yet could frame my will to it,   8
And therefore frame the law unto my will.

SOMERSET
Judge you, my lord of Warwick, then, between us.

WARWICK
Between two hawks, which flies the higher pitch,   11
Between two dogs, which hath the deeper mouth,   12
Between two blades, which bears the better temper,
Between two horses, which doth bear him best,   14
Between two girls, which hath the merriest eye,
I have perhaps some shallow spirit of judgment;
But in these nice sharp quillets of the law,   17
Good faith, I am no wiser than a daw.   18

PLANTAGENET
Tut, tut, here is a mannerly forbearance.   19
The truth appears so naked on my side
That any purblind eye may find it out.   21

SOMERSET
And on my side it is so well appareled,
So clear, so shining, and so evident,
That it will glimmer through a blind man's eye.

PLANTAGENET
Since you are tongue-tied and so loath to speak,
In dumb significants proclaim your thoughts.   26
Let him that is a trueborn gentleman
And stands upon the honor of his birth,
If he suppose that I have pleaded truth,   29
From off this brier pluck a white rose with me.   30
    [He plucks a white rose.]

SOMERSET
Let him that is no coward nor no flatterer,
But dare maintain the party of the truth,   32
Pluck a red rose from off this thorn with me.   33
    [He plucks a red rose. The others similarly pluck
    roses as they speak.]

WARWICK
I love no colors, and without all color   34
Of base insinuating flattery
I pluck this white rose with Plantagenet.   36

SUFFOLK
I pluck this red rose with young Somerset
And say withal I think he held the right.   38

VERNON
Stay, lords and gentlemen, and pluck no more
Till you conclude that he upon whose side
The fewest roses are cropped from the tree
Shall yield the other in the right opinion.   42

SOMERSET
Good Master Vernon, it is well objected.   43
If I have fewest, I subscribe in silence.   44

PLANTAGENET   And I.

VERNON
Then, for the truth and plainness of the case,
I pluck this pale and maiden blossom here,
Giving my verdict on the white rose side.

SOMERSET
Prick not your finger as you pluck it off,
Lest, bleeding, you do paint the white rose red,
And fall on my side so against your will.

VERNON
If I, my lord, for my opinion bleed,
Opinion shall be surgeon to my hurt   53
And keep me on the side where still I am.

---

80 **cates** delicacies, dainty confections   81 **stomachs** (1) appetites 2) bravery
2.4. Location: London. The Temple Garden, with rosebushes. (The Temple was a district of London taking its name from the Knights Templar, who owned it during the twelfth and thirteenth centuries. Its buildings were converted into Inns of Court, housing the legal societies of London, including the Inner Temple and the Middle Temple, in the fourteenth century.)
3 **were** (1) were (2) would have been   6 **Or else** i.e., in other words (?) (Or Plantagenet may be saying, lines 5–6, with intended humor, "Am I right, or is Somerset wrong?")   7 **a truant** a neglectful student
8 **frame** adapt   11 **pitch** elevation in flight   12 **mouth** voice
14 **bear him** carry himself   17 **nice sharp quillets** subtle distinctions
18 **daw** jackdaw. (A type of foolishness.)   19 **here . . . forbearance** (Plantagenet sardonically deplores this offering of polite excuses.)
21 **purblind** dim-sighted

26 **dumb significants** silent tokens, signs   29 **pleaded** argued. (One of many legal terms occurring throughout this scene.)   30 **white rose** badge of the Mortimers and subsequently of the house of York
32 **party** side (in law)   33 **red rose** badge of the house of Lancaster
34 **colors** pretexts. (Playing on the literal meaning.)   36 **Plantagenet** (The nickname of Geoffrey of Anjou, founder of the Angevin dynasty, which ruled England from the reign of Geoffrey's son, Henry II, to that of Richard III. None of Geoffrey's descendants assumed the name until Richard, Duke of York, adopted it in order to proclaim his superior right to the crown. He also adopted the white rose as a badge to be an emblem of his line of descent. The red rose had been the symbol of the House of Lancaster since the thirteenth century. The evidence of use of these badges during the civil wars as emblems of the two contending houses is, however, scant; the iconographic concept is basically Tudor propaganda established by Henry VII.)
38 **withal** besides   42 **yield** concede. (Another legal term, like *objected* and *subscribe* in the following two lines and *verdict* at line 48.)
43 **objected** urged.   44 **subscribe** submit, concur (literally, by signature)   53 **Opinion** public opinion, i.e., my reputation. (Punning on *opinion* in the sense of "conviction" in the previous line.)

SOMERSET Well, well, come on, who else?

LAWYER [*to Somerset*]
Unless my study and my books be false,
The argument you held was wrong in law;
In sign whereof I pluck a white rose too.

PLANTAGENET
Now, Somerset, where is your argument?

SOMERSET
Here in my scabbard, meditating that   60
Shall dye your white rose in a bloody red.

PLANTAGENET
Meantime your cheeks do counterfeit our roses;   62
For pale they look with fear, as witnessing
The truth on our side.

SOMERSET   No, Plantagenet,
'Tis not for fear, but anger, that thy cheeks
Blush for pure shame to counterfeit our roses,
And yet thy tongue will not confess thy error.

PLANTAGENET
Hath not thy rose a canker, Somerset?   68

SOMERSET
Hath not thy rose a thorn, Plantagenet?

PLANTAGENET
Ay, sharp and piercing, to maintain his truth,   70
Whiles thy consuming canker eats his falsehood.

SOMERSET
Well, I'll find friends to wear my bleeding roses
That shall maintain what I have said is true,
Where false Plantagenet dare not be seen.

PLANTAGENET
Now, by this maiden blossom in my hand,
I scorn thee and thy fashion, peevish boy.   76

SUFFOLK
Turn not thy scorns this way, Plantagenet.

PLANTAGENET
Proud Pole, I will, and scorn both him and thee.   78

SUFFOLK
I'll turn my part thereof into thy throat.   79

SOMERSET
Away, away, good William de la Pole!
We grace the yeoman by conversing with him.   81

WARWICK
Now, by God's will, thou wrong'st him, Somerset.
His grandfather was Lionel, Duke of Clarence,   83
Third son to the third Edward, King of England.
Spring crestless yeomen from so deep a root?   85

PLANTAGENET
He bears him on the place's privilege,   86
Or durst not, for his craven heart, say thus.

SOMERSET
By him that made me, I'll maintain my words
On any plot of ground in Christendom.
Was not thy father, Richard, Earl of Cambridge,
For treason executed in our late king's days?   91
And by his treason stand'st not thou attainted, 92
Corrupted, and exempt from ancient gentry?   93
His trespass yet lives guilty in thy blood,
And till thou be restored, thou art a yeoman.

PLANTAGENET
My father was attachèd, not attainted,   96
Condemned to die for treason, but no traitor;
And that I'll prove on better men than Somerset,
Were growing time once ripened to my will.   99
For your partaker Pole, and you yourself,   100
I'll note you in my book of memory
To scourge you for this apprehension.   102
Look to it well, and say you are well warned.

SOMERSET
Ah, thou shalt find us ready for thee still,   104
And know us by these colors for thy foes,   105
For these my friends in spite of thee shall wear. 106

PLANTAGENET
And, by my soul, this pale and angry rose,
As cognizance of my blood-drinking hate,   108
Will I forever, and my faction, wear
Until it wither with me to my grave
Or flourish to the height of my degree.   111

SUFFOLK
Go forward, and be choked with thy ambition!
And so farewell until I meet thee next.   *Exit.*

SOMERSET
Have with thee, Pole.—Farewell, ambitious Richard. 114
                                           Exit.

PLANTAGENET
How I am braved and must perforce endure it!   115

WARWICK
This blot that they object against your house   116
Shall be wiped out in the next parliament,

---

60 that that which   **62 counterfeit** imitate   **68 canker** cankerworm
(that feeds on buds)   **70 his** its. (Also in line 71.)   **76 fashion** sort, or,
the fashion of wearing red roses.   **peevish** silly   **78 Pole** family
name of the Duke of Suffolk. (See also line 80.)   **79 I'll … throat** I'll
throw the lies or slanders back into the throat from which they proceeded.   **81 grace** do honor to.   **yeoman** a small freeholder, below
the rank of landed gentleman. (A gibe at Plantagenet for having lost
his lands and titles when his father, Richard, Earl of Cambridge, was
executed in 1415 by Henry V for treason.)   **83 His … Clarence**
(Lionel was actually Richard's maternal great-great-grandfather, but
Edmund, Duke of York, fifth son of Edward III, was his paternal
grandfather. Richard thus could trace his descent from Edward III
through both Lionel and Edmund.)   **85 crestless** lacking heraldic
titles. (With a suggestion also of cowardice.)

86 He … privilege i.e., Somerset presumes upon the safety of a privileged place (since engaging in quarrels with drawn weapons was
prohibited in certain precincts, including the Inns of Court, which lay
outside the jurisdiction of the city of London; see note at 1.3.46).
91 late king's i.e., Henry V's   **92 attainted** convicted and condemned. (According to law, the heirs of a person so attainted were
deprived of all the rights and titles of their forebears; their blood was
pronounced *corrupted*.)   **93 exempt … gentry** cut off from the privileges of hereditary rank.   **96 attachèd, not attainted** (Historically, as
Plantagenet insists, his father was *attached*, i.e., arrested, and summar-
ily executed for treason without a bill of attainder that would deny
rights of inheritance to his heirs.)   **99 Were … will** i.e., if the unfolding of time provides me opportunity.   **100 For your partaker** As for
your supporter   **102 apprehension** conception. (But suggesting also
"attempted arrest.")   **104 still** always   **105 know … foes** i.e., recognize us by these red badges as your enemies   **106 these … wear** my
supporters will wear these (red roses) in spite of you.   **108 cognizance** badge   **111 degree** noble rank.   **114 Have with thee** I'll go
along with you   **115 braved** defied.   **perforce** necessarily
116 object urge, allege

Called for the truce of Winchester and Gloucester;   118
And if thou be not then created York,
I will not live to be accounted Warwick.
Meantime, in signal of my love to thee,
Against proud Somerset and William Pole,
Will I upon thy party wear this rose.
And here I prophesy: this brawl today,
Grown to this faction in the Temple Garden,
Shall send, between the red rose and the white,
A thousand souls to death and deadly night.

PLANTAGENET
Good Master Vernon, I am bound to you
That you on my behalf would pluck a flower.

VERNON
In your behalf still will I wear the same.

LAWYER   And so will I.

PLANTAGENET   Thanks, gentlemen.
Come, let us four to dinner. I dare say
This quarrel will drink blood another day.   *Exeunt.*

❖

[2.5]

Enter Mortimer, brought in a chair, and Jailers.

MORTIMER
Kind keepers of my weak decaying age,
Let dying Mortimer here rest himself.
Even like a man new-halèd from the rack,
So fare my limbs with long imprisonment;
And these gray locks, the pursuivants of death,   5
Nestor-like agèd in an age of care,   6
Argue the end of Edmund Mortimer.   7
These eyes, like lamps whose wasting oil is spent,
Wax dim, as drawing to their exigent;   9
Weak shoulders, overborne with burdening grief,
And pithless arms, like to a withered vine   11
That droops his sapless branches to the ground.
Yet are these feet, whose strengthless stay is numb,   13
Unable to support this lump of clay,
Swift-wingèd with desire to get a grave,
As witting I no other comfort have.   16
But tell me, keeper, will my nephew come?   17

FIRST KEEPER
Richard Plantagenet, my lord, will come.
We sent unto the Temple, unto his chamber,
And answer was returned that he will come.

MORTIMER
Enough. My soul shall then be satisfied.
Poor gentleman, his wrong doth equal mine.   22
Since Henry Monmouth first began to reign,   23

Before whose glory I was great in arms,
This loathsome sequestration have I had;   25
And even since then hath Richard been obscured,
Deprived of honor and inheritance.
But now the arbitrator of despairs,
Just Death, kind umpire of men's miseries,
With sweet enlargement doth dismiss me hence.   30
I would his troubles likewise were expired,   31
That so he might recover what was lost.

Enter Richard [Plantagenet].

FIRST KEEPER
My lord, your loving nephew now is come.

MORTIMER
Richard Plantagenet, my friend, is he come?

PLANTAGENET
Ay, noble uncle, thus ignobly used,
Your nephew, late despisèd Richard, comes.   36

MORTIMER
Direct mine arms I may embrace his neck,   37
And in his bosom spend my latter gasp.   38
Oh, tell me when my lips do touch his cheeks,
That I may kindly give one fainting kiss.
    [He embraces Richard.]
And now declare, sweet stem from York's great stock,
Why didst thou say of late thou wert despised?

PLANTAGENET
First, lean thine agèd back against mine arm,
And, in that ease, I'll tell thee my disease.   44
This day, in argument upon a case,
Some words there grew twixt Somerset and me;
Among which terms he used his lavish tongue
And did upbraid me with my father's death;
Which obloquy set bars before my tongue,
Else with the like I had requited him.
Therefore, good uncle, for my father's sake,
In honor of a true Plantagenet,
And for alliance' sake, declare the cause   53
My father, Earl of Cambridge, lost his head.

MORTIMER
That cause, fair nephew, that imprisoned me
And hath detained me all my flow'ring youth
Within a loathsome dungeon, there to pine,
Was cursèd instrument of his decease.

PLANTAGENET
Discover more at large what cause that was,   59
For I am ignorant and cannot guess.

MORTIMER
I will, if that my fading breath permit   61

---

118 **Called . . . of** assembled to make peace between
2.5. Location: The Tower of London.
5 **pursuivants** heralds   6 **Nestor-like** i.e., extremely old. (Nestor, the oldest of the Greek chieftains at the siege of Troy, came to represent a type of old age.)   7 **Argue** portend   9 **exigent** end   11 **pithless** marrowless, weak   13 **stay** support   16 **As witting** as if knowing
17 **nephew** (Richard Plantagenet was son of the fifth Earl of March's sister, Anne Mortimer, who married Richard, Earl of Cambridge.)
22 **his wrong** the wrong done him   23 **Henry Monmouth** i.e., Henry V

25 **sequestration** imprisonment. (Shakespeare, following the chroniclers, confuses Edmund Mortimer, fifth Earl of March and great-grandson of Lionel, Duke of Clarence, hence potential heir to the throne, with his uncle Sir Edmund Mortimer, who was imprisoned by Glendower, and also with the Earl of March's cousin, Sir John Mortimer, who was imprisoned and finally executed for agitating in behalf of Edmund's royal claim. The Earl of March remained loyal to Henry V.)   30 **enlargement** release from confinement   31 **his** i.e., Richard's   36 **late** lately   37 **I may** so that I may   38 **latter** last
44 **disease** unease, trouble, grievance.   53 **alliance'** kinship's
59 **Discover** Make known.   **at large** at length   61 **if that** if

And death approach not ere my tale be done.
Henry the Fourth, grandfather to this king,
Deposed his nephew Richard, Edward's son,   64
The first-begotten and the lawful heir
Of Edward king, the third of that descent;
During whose reign the Percys of the north,   67
Finding his usurpation most unjust,
Endeavored my advancement to the throne.
The reason moved these warlike lords to this   70
Was for that—young King Richard thus removed,   71
Leaving no heir begotten of his body—
I was the next by birth and parentage;
For by my mother I derivèd am   74
From Lionel, Duke of Clarence, third son
To King Edward the Third; whereas he   76
From John of Gaunt doth bring his pedigree,
Being but fourth of that heroic line.
But mark. As in this haughty great attempt   79
They laborèd to plant the rightful heir,   80
I lost my liberty and they their lives.
Long after this, when Henry the Fifth,
Succeeding his father Bolingbroke, did reign,   83
Thy father, Earl of Cambridge then, derived
From famous Edmund Langley, Duke of York,
Marrying my sister that thy mother was,
Again, in pity of my hard distress,
Levied an army, weening to redeem   88
And have installed me in the diadem.   89
But, as the rest, so fell that noble earl
And was beheaded. Thus the Mortimers,
In whom the title rested, were suppressed.

PLANTAGENET
Of which, my lord, Your Honor is the last.

MORTIMER
True, and thou see'st that I no issue have,   94
And that my fainting words do warrant death.   95
Thou art my heir. The rest I wish thee gather;   96
But yet be wary in thy studious care.   97

PLANTAGENET
Thy grave admonishments prevail with me.
But yet methinks my father's execution
Was nothing less than bloody tyranny.

MORTIMER
With silence, nephew, be thou politic.   101
Strong-fixèd is the house of Lancaster
And like a mountain, not to be removed.
But now thy uncle is removing hence,   104
As princes do their courts, when they are cloyed
With long continuance in a settled place.

PLANTAGENET
O uncle, would some part of my young years
Might but redeem the passage of your age!   108

MORTIMER
Thou dost then wrong me, as that slaughterer doth
Which giveth many wounds when one will kill.
Mourn not, except thou sorrow for my good;   111
Only give order for my funeral.   112
And so farewell, and fair be all thy hopes,
And prosperous be thy life in peace and war!   *Dies.*

PLANTAGENET
And peace, no war, befall thy parting soul!
In prison hast thou spent a pilgrimage
And like a hermit overpassed thy days.   117
Well, I will lock his counsel in my breast,
And what I do imagine, let that rest.—   119
Keepers, convey him hence, and I myself
Will see his burial better than his life.
          Exeunt [Keepers, bearing out the body of
                    Mortimer].

Here dies the dusky torch of Mortimer,
Choked with ambition of the meaner sort.   123
And for those wrongs, those bitter injuries,   124
Which Somerset hath offered to my house,
I doubt not but with honor to redress;
And therefore haste I to the parliament,
Either to be restorèd to my blood   128
Or make mine ill th'advantage of my good.   *Exit.*   129

❖

3.1

*Flourish. Enter King, Exeter, Gloucester,
Winchester, Warwick, Somerset, Suffolk,
Richard Plantagenet, [and others]. Gloucester
offers to put up a bill; Winchester snatches it,
[and] tears it.*

WINCHESTER
Com'st thou with deep premeditated lines,
With written pamphlets studiously devised?
Humphrey of Gloucester, if thou canst accuse,
Or aught intend'st to lay unto my charge,   4
Do it without invention, suddenly,   5
As I with sudden and extemporal speech
Purpose to answer what thou canst object.   7

GLOUCESTER
Presumptuous priest, this place commands my
          patience,   8

---

64 his nephew . . . son his cousin, Richard II, son of Edward the Black Prince   67 whose i.e., Henry IV's   70 moved that moved   71 for that that   74 mother (Shakespeare appears to confuse this Edmund with his uncle, Edmund Mortimer, second son of Lionel's daughter Philippa.)   76 he i.e., Henry IV, and, by extension of the family line, Henry VI. (See line 63.)   79 haughty proud, exalted   80 They the Percys and Mortimers   83 Bolingbroke Henry Bolingbroke, King Henry IV   88 weening to redeem thinking to free from imprisonment   89 installed . . . diadem crowned me king.   94 issue children, heirs   95 warrant promise, assure   96 gather (1) infer (2) take as your own   97 studious diligent   101 politic prudent.   104 thy . . . hence I thy uncle am departing from here, i.e., dying

108 redeem the passage buy back the passing   111 except . . . good other than to mourn ceremonially for my being transported to a better world   112 give order make arrangements   117 overpassed passed   119 let that rest leave it alone, i.e., let that be my business.   123 Choked . . . sort choked by the ambition of less noble men (i.e., the supporters of the Lancastrian claim).   124 for as for   128 blood hereditary rights   129 Or . . . good or use my being wronged to the advancement of my cause.
3.1. Location: London. The Parliament House.
0.4 offers tries, starts.   bill (Here, a written accusation.)   4 lay unto my charge charge me with   5 invention, suddenly premeditated design, unpremeditatedly   7 object urge, present.   8 this place i.e., Parliament, with the King presiding

Or thou shouldst find thou hast dishonored me.
Think not, although in writing I preferred   10
The manner of thy vile outrageous crimes,
That therefore I have forged, or am not able
Verbatim to rehearse the method of my pen.   13
No, prelate, such is thy audacious wickedness,
Thy lewd, pestiferous, and dissentious pranks,   15
As very infants prattle of thy pride.   16
Thou art a most pernicious usurer,
Froward by nature, enemy to peace,
Lascivious, wanton, more than well beseems   18
A man of thy profession and degree.
And for thy treachery, what's more manifest?   21
In that thou laid'st a trap to take my life,
As well at London Bridge as at the Tower.   23
Besides, I fear me, if thy thoughts were sifted,
The King, thy sovereign, is not quite exempt
From envious malice of thy swelling heart.

WINCHESTER
Gloucester, I do defy thee.—Lords, vouchsafe
To give me hearing what I shall reply.   28
If I were covetous, ambitious, or perverse,
As he will have me, how am I so poor?
Or how haps it I seek not to advance   31
Or raise myself, but keep my wonted calling?   32
And for dissension, who preferreth peace
More than I do, except I be provoked?   34
No, my good lords, it is not that offends;   35
It is not that that hath incensed the Duke.
It is because no one should sway but he,   37
No one but he should be about the King;   38
And that engenders thunder in his breast
And makes him roar these accusations forth.
But he shall know I am as good—

GLOUCESTER   As good?
Thou bastard of my grandfather!   42

WINCHESTER
Ay, lordly sir! For what are you, I pray,
But one imperious in another's throne?   44

GLOUCESTER
Am I not Protector, saucy priest?

WINCHESTER
And am not I a prelate of the Church?

GLOUCESTER
Yes, as an outlaw in a castle keeps   47
And useth it to patronage his theft.   48

WINCHESTER
Unreverent Gloucester!

GLOUCESTER   Thou art reverend   49
Touching thy spiritual function, not thy life.   50

WINCHESTER
Rome shall remedy this.

WARWICK   Roam thither, then.

SOMERSET [to Warwick]
My lord, it were your duty to forbear.   52

WARWICK
Ay, see the Bishop be not overborne.   53

SOMERSET
Methinks my lord should be religious   54
And know the office that belongs to such.   55

WARWICK
Methinks His Lordship should be humbler.   56
It fitteth not a prelate so to plead.

SOMERSET
Yes, when his holy state is touched so near.   58

WARWICK
State holy or unhallowed, what of that?
Is not His Grace Protector to the King?   60

PLANTAGENET [aside]
Plantagenet, I see, must hold his tongue,
Lest it be said, "Speak, sirrah, when you should;
Must your bold verdict enter talk with lords?"   63
Else would I have a fling at Winchester.

KING
Uncles of Gloucester and of Winchester,
The special watchmen of our English weal,   66
I would prevail, if prayers might prevail,
To join your hearts in love and amity.
Oh, what a scandal is it to our crown
That two such noble peers as ye should jar!   70
Believe me, lords, my tender years can tell   71
Civil dissension is a viperous worm
That gnaws the bowels of the commonwealth.
    A noise within, "Down with the tawny coats!"
What tumult's this?

WARWICK   An uproar, I dare warrant,
Begun through malice of the Bishop's men.
    A noise again, "Stones! Stones!"

Enter Mayor.

MAYOR
O my good lords, and virtuous Henry,
Pity the city of London, pity us!
The Bishop and the Duke of Gloucester's men,   80

---

10 **preferred** put forward. (See 1.3.34–5 and note.)   **13 Verbatim . . .
pen** orally to recount what I have written.   **15 lewd, pestiferous**
wicked, deadly   **16 As** that   **18 Froward** perverse   **21 for** as for.
(Also in line 33.)   **23 at London Bridge** (Gloucester's articles of accusation against Winchester presented to the Parliament stated that the
latter had "set men-of-arms and archers at the end of London Bridge
next Southwark," to prevent Gloucester's going to Eltham to interfere
with the Bishop's plans regarding the young King.)   **28 To . . . reply**
to hear what I shall say in reply.   **31 haps** happens   **32 wonted calling** customary profession.   **34 except** unless   **35 that** that that
37 sway govern   **38 about** near to   **42 Thou bastard** (Winchester,
son of John of Gaunt and Katharine Swynford before their marriage,
was, with his two brothers and one sister, legitimatized by act of Parliament in Richard II's reign.)   **44 imperious** (1) exercising rule
(2) domineering   **47 keeps** dwells   **48 patronage** maintain

49 **Unreverent . . . reverend** Irreverent, hostile to spiritual authority
. . . respected, revered. (The Folio spellings, "Vnreuerent" and
"reuerent," accentuate the wordplay.)   **50 Touching . . . function** i.e.,
in ecclesiastical title only   **52 were** should be   **53 overborne** prevailed over.   **54 my lord** i.e., Winchester.   **should be** i.e., should be
regarded as. (But Warwick, two lines below, uses the phrase in the
sense "ought to be." Alternatively, Somerset here criticizes Warwick
or Gloucester for showing disrespect toward a bishop.)   **55 office**
duty   **56 His Lordship** i.e., Winchester   **58 state** degree, rank.
touched so near so closely concerned.   **60 His Grace** i.e., Gloucester
63 Must . . . lords? must you venture your audacious opinions in
such distinguished company?   **66 weal** common good   **70 jar** quarrel.   **71 my tender years** (The King was actually five years old at the
time of this episode.)   **80 Bishop** Bishop's

Forbidden late to carry any weapon,   81
Have filled their pockets full of pebblestones
And, banding themselves in contrary parts,   83
Do pelt so fast at one another's pate
That many have their giddy brains knocked out.
Our windows are broke down in every street,
And we for fear compelled to shut our shops.

Enter [Servingmen of both parties] , in skirmish
with bloody pates.

KING
We charge you, on allegiance to ourself,
To hold your slaughtering hands and keep the peace!
Pray, uncle Gloucester, mitigate this strife.
FIRST SERVINGMAN   Nay, if we be forbidden stones,
we'll fall to it with our teeth.
SECOND SERVINGMAN
Do what ye dare, we are as resolute.   *Skirmish again.*
GLOUCESTER
You of my household, leave this peevish broil   94
And set this unaccustomed fight aside.   95
THIRD SERVINGMAN
My lord, we know Your Grace to be a man
Just and upright, and for your royal birth
Inferior to none but to His Majesty;
And ere that we will suffer such a prince,   99
So kind a father of the commonweal,
To be disgracèd by an inkhorn mate,   101
We and our wives and children all will fight
And have our bodies slaughtered by thy foes.
FIRST SERVINGMAN
Ay, and the very parings of our nails
Shall pitch a field when we are dead.   *Begin again.*
GLOUCESTER   Stay, stay, I say! 105
An if you love me, as you say you do,   106
Let me persuade you to forbear awhile.
KING
Oh, how this discord doth afflict my soul!
Can you, my lord of Winchester, behold
My sighs and tears and will not once relent?
Who should be pitiful, if you be not?
Or who should study to prefer a peace,   112
If holy churchmen take delight in broils?
WARWICK
Yield, my Lord Protector; yield, Winchester,
Except you mean with obstinate repulse   115
To slay your sovereign and destroy the realm.
You see what mischief, and what murder too,
Hath been enacted through your enmity.
Then be at peace, except ye thirst for blood.
WINCHESTER
He shall submit, or I will never yield.
GLOUCESTER
Compassion on the King commands me stoop,

Or I would see his heart out ere the priest
Should ever get that privilege of me.   123
WARWICK
Behold, my lord of Winchester, the Duke
Hath banished moody discontented fury,   125
As by his smoothèd brows it doth appear.
Why look you still so stern and tragical?
GLOUCESTER
Here, Winchester, I offer thee my hand.
   [*He offers his hand, which Winchester refuses.*]
KING
Fie, uncle Beaufort! I have heard you preach
That malice was a great and grievous sin;
And will not you maintain the thing you teach,
But prove a chief offender in the same?
WARWICK
Sweet King! The Bishop hath a kindly gird.   133
For shame, my lord of Winchester, relent!
What, shall a child instruct you what to do?
WINCHESTER
Well, Duke of Gloucester, I will yield to thee.
Love for thy love and hand for hand I give.
                              [*They clasp hands.*]
GLOUCESTER [*aside*]
Ay, but, I fear me, with a hollow heart.—
See here, my friends and loving countrymen,
This token serveth for a flag of truce   140
Betwixt ourselves and all our followers.
So help me God, as I dissemble not!
WINCHESTER [*aside*]
So help me God, as I intend it not!
KING
O loving uncle, kind Duke of Gloucester,
How joyful am I made by this contract!
[*To Servingmen*] Away, my masters. Trouble us no
   more,   146
But join in friendship, as your lords have done.
FIRST SERVINGMAN
Content. I'll to the surgeon's.
SECOND SERVINGMAN   And so will I.
THIRD SERVINGMAN
And I will see what physic the tavern affords.   149
                    Exeunt [Servingmen and Mayor].
WARWICK [*proffering scroll*]
Accept this scroll, most gracious sovereign,
Which in the right of Richard Plantagenet
We do exhibit to Your Majesty.   152
GLOUCESTER
Well urged, my lord of Warwick. For, sweet prince,
An if Your Grace mark every circumstance,
You have great reason to do Richard right,
Especially for those occasions   156
At Eltham Place I told Your Majesty.

---

81 **late** lately   83 **contrary parts** contending factions   94 **peevish**
petty, senseless   95 **unaccustomed** contrary to custom and normality
99 **ere that** before   101 **inkhorn mate** scribbler. (Alludes scornfully to
Winchester as a cleric or clerk.)   105 **pitch a field** fight a battle, set in
array for fighting (with defensive stakes)   106 **An if** If   112 **prefer**
propose, assist in arranging   115 **Except** unless.   **repulse** refusal

123 **privilege of** advantage over   125 **moody** haughty   133 **kindly**
gird appropriate rebuke.   140 **This token** i.e., the handshake
146 **masters** good sirs.   149 **physic** medicine, remedy   152 **exhibit**
present for official consideration   156 **occasions** reasons which

KING
  And those occasions, uncle, were of force.   158
  Therefore, my loving lords, our pleasure is
  That Richard be restorèd to his blood.   160
WARWICK
  Let Richard be restorèd to his blood.
  So shall his father's wrongs be recompensed.
WINCHESTER
  As will the rest, so willeth Winchester.
KING
  If Richard will be true, not that alone
  But all the whole inheritance I give
  That doth belong unto the house of York,
  From whence you spring by lineal descent.
PLANTAGENET
  Thy humble servant vows obedience
  And humble service till the point of death.
KING
  Stoop then and set your knee against my foot.
                              [Richard kneels.]
  And in reguerdon of that duty done,   171
  I gird thee with the valiant sword of York.
  Rise, Richard, like a true Plantagenet,
  And rise created princely Duke of York.
PLANTAGENET [rising]
  And so thrive Richard as thy foes may fall!
  And as my duty springs, so perish they
  That grudge one thought against Your Majesty!   177
ALL
  Welcome, high prince, the mighty Duke of York!
SOMERSET [aside]
  Perish, base prince, ignoble Duke of York!
GLOUCESTER
  Now will it best avail Your Majesty
  To cross the seas and to be crowned in France.
  The presence of a king engenders love
  Amongst his subjects and his loyal friends,
  As it disanimates his enemies.   184
KING
  When Gloucester says the word, King Henry goes,
  For friendly counsel cuts off many foes.
GLOUCESTER
  Your ships already are in readiness.   187
              Sennet. Flourish. Exeunt. Manet Exeter.
EXETER
  Ay, we may march in England or in France,
  Not seeing what is likely to ensue.
  This late dissension grown betwixt the peers   190
  Burns under feignèd ashes of forged love   191
  And will at last break out into a flame.
  As festered members rot but by degree
  Till bones and flesh and sinews fall away,
  So will this base and envious discord breed.
  And now I fear that fatal prophecy

Which in the time of Henry named the Fifth
Was in the mouth of every sucking babe:
That Henry born at Monmouth should win all   199
And Henry born at Windsor lose all;   200
Which is so plain that Exeter doth wish
His days may finish ere that hapless time.   Exit.

❖

3.2

Enter [Joan la] Pucelle disguised, with four Soldiers with sacks upon their backs.

PUCELLE
  These are the city gates, the gates of Rouen,   1
  Through which our policy must make a breach.   2
  Take heed, be wary how you place your words;
  Talk like the vulgar sort of marketmen   4
  That come to gather money for their corn.   5
  If we have entrance, as I hope we shall,
  And that we find the slothful watch but weak,   7
  I'll by a sign give notice to our friends
  That Charles the Dauphin may encounter them.   9
FIRST SOLDIER
  Our sacks shall be a mean to sack the city,   10
  And we be lords and rulers over Rouen.
  Therefore we'll knock.   Knock.
WATCH [within]   Qui là?   13
PUCELLE
  Paysans, la pauvre gens de France,
  Poor market folks that come to sell their corn.
WATCH [opening the gates]
  Enter, go in. The market bell is rung.
PUCELLE [aside]
  Now, Rouen, I'll shake thy bulwarks to the ground.
                          Exeunt [to the town].

  Enter Charles, [the] Bastard [of Orleans],
  Alençon, [Reignier, and forces].

CHARLES
  Saint Denis bless this happy stratagem!
  And once again we'll sleep secure in Rouen.
BASTARD
  Here entered Pucelle and her practisants.   20
  Now she is there, how will she specify
  Here is the best and safest passage in?   22
REIGNIER
  By thrusting out a torch from yonder tower,
  Which, once discerned, shows that her meaning is,

---

158 **of force** compelling.   160 **blood** hereditary right, inherited from his father.   171 **reguerdon** reward   177 **grudge one thought** harbor one grudging thought   184 **disanimates** discourages   187.1 **Sennet** set of notes played on a trumpet as a signal for the approach or departure of processions.   *Manet* He remains onstage   190 **late** recent   191 **forged** feigned

199 **Henry born at Monmouth** i.e., Henry V   200 **Henry born at Windsor** i.e., Henry VI
3.2. Location: France. Before Rouen.
1 **Rouen** (As at Orleans in 1.5 through 2.1, the city gates here are represented by doors in the tiring-house facade, the "walls" of Rouen. Appearances "on the walls," as at line 40.4 take place on the gallery backstage.)   2 **policy** stratagem   4 **vulgar** common   5 **corn** grain.   7 **that** if   9 **them** i.e., the English soldiers guarding Rouen   10 **mean** means   13 *Qui là? Qui est là,* Who is there? (Rustic French.)   20 **practisants** fellow conspirators.   22 **Here . . . in** i.e., that here (the same spot she entered) is the best and safest place for us to enter as well.

No way to that, for weakness, which she entered. 25

Enter Pucelle on the top, thrusting out a torch
burning.

PUCELLE
Behold, this is the happy wedding torch
That joineth Rouen unto her countrymen,
But burning fatal to the Talbonites! 28

BASTARD
See, noble Charles, the beacon of our friend!
The burning torch in yonder turret stands.

CHARLES
Now shine it like a comet of revenge, 31
A prophet to the fall of all our foes!

REIGNIER
Defer no time! Delays have dangerous ends.
Enter, and cry "The Dauphin!" presently, 34
And then do execution on the watch. 35
    Alarum. [They storm the gates.]

An alarum. [Enter] Talbot in an excursion
[from within].

TALBOT
France, thou shalt rue this treason with thy tears,
If Talbot but survive thy treachery.
Pucelle, that witch, that damnèd sorceress,
Hath wrought this hellish mischief unawares, 39
That hardly we escaped the pride of France. *Exit.* 40

An alarum. Excursions. Bedford brought in sick
in a chair. Enter Talbot and Burgundy without;
within, Pucelle, Charles, Bastard, [Alençon,]
and Reignier, on the walls.

PUCELLE
Good morrow, gallants. Want ye corn for bread?
I think the Duke of Burgundy will fast 42
Before he'll buy again at such a rate. 43
'Twas full of darnel. Do you like the taste? 44

BURGUNDY
Scoff on, vile fiend and shameless courtesan!
I trust ere long to choke thee with thine own 46
And make thee curse the harvest of that corn.

CHARLES
Your Grace may starve, perhaps, before that time.

BEDFORD
Oh, let no words, but deeds, revenge this treason!

PUCELLE
What will you do, good graybeard, break a lance
And run atilt at Death within a chair? 51

TALBOT
Foul fiend of France and hag of all despite, 52
Encompassed with thy lustful paramours! 53
Becomes it thee to taunt his valiant age
And twit with cowardice a man half dead?
Damsel, I'll have a bout with you again, 56
Or else let Talbot perish with this shame.

PUCELLE
Are ye so hot, sir?—Yet, Pucelle, hold thy peace. 58
If Talbot do but thunder, rain will follow. 59
    They [the English] whisper together in council.
God speed the parliament! Who shall be the speaker? 60

TALBOT
Dare ye come forth and meet us in the field?

PUCELLE
Belike Your Lordship takes us then for fools, 62
To try if that our own be ours or no.

TALBOT
I speak not to that railing Hecate, 64
But unto thee, Alençon, and the rest.
Will ye, like soldiers, come and fight it out?

ALENÇON   Seigneur, no.

TALBOT
Seigneur, hang! Base muleteers of France! 68
Like peasant footboys do they keep the walls 69
And dare not take up arms like gentlemen.

PUCELLE
Away, captains. Let's get us from the walls,
For Talbot means no goodness by his looks.—
Good-bye, my lord. We came but to tell you
That we are here.   *Exeunt from the walls.*

TALBOT
And there will we be too, ere it be long,
Or else reproach be Talbot's greatest fame! 76
Vow, Burgundy, by honor of thy house,
Pricked on by public wrongs sustained in France, 78
Either to get the town again or die.
And I, as sure as English Henry lives
And as his father here was conqueror, 81
As sure as in this late-betrayèd town 82
Great Coeur de Lion's heart was buried, 83
So sure I swear to get the town or die.

---

25 **No . . . entered** no other place can be compared to the one where
she entered for weakness; it is the most weakly defended.
25.1 **on the top** i.e., at some upper vantage point in the theater
28 **Talbonites** followers of Talbot.   31 **shine it** may it shine
34 **presently** immediately   35 **do . . . watch** kill all the guards.
35.2 **excursion** skirmish, sortie   39 **unawares** unexpectedly   40 **pride**
princely power   40.1 *Bedford . . . sick* (Actually, Bedford outlived
Joan of Arc by four years. The entire episode of the capture of Rouen,
as presented here, is unhistorical; the English did not relinquish the
city until 1449, some eighteen years after Joan's death.)   40.2 *without*
i.e., on the main stage.   40.3 *within* i.e., in the gallery backstage
42–3 **will fast . . . rate** i.e., will be hesitant to do business with us
again, having been sold a bill of goods.   44 **darnel** injurious weed.
46 **thine own** i.e., your own bread

51 **And . . . chair?** and, sitting in your chair, joust with Death?
52 **hag of all despite** malicious witch   53 **Encompassed with** surrounded by   56 **bout** encounter with weapons. (With sexual overtones, as earlier at 1.5.4.)   58 **hot** (1) hot-tempered (2) lustful
59 **If . . . follow** (A proverb, suggesting that angry talk is to be followed
by fighting.)   60 **speaker** spokesman. (Playing on the sense of "parliamentary leader.")   62 **Belike** Perhaps   64 **Hecate** goddess of night
and of black magic   68 **muleteers** mule drivers   69 **keep** keep safely
within   76 **fame** reputation.   78 **Pricked on** goaded   81 **father . . .
conqueror** (Henry V captured Rouen in 1419.)   82 **late-betrayèd**
recently lost to the enemy through treachery   83 **Great . . . heart**
(According to Holinshed, Richard Coeur de Lion, "the lion-hearted"
King of England 1189–1199, had willed that "his heart be conveyed
unto Rouen and there buried, in testimony of the love which he had
ever borne unto that city.")

BURGUNDY

My vows are equal partners with thy vows.

TALBOT

But ere we go, regard this dying prince,   86
The valiant Duke of Bedford.—Come, my lord,
We will bestow you in some better place,
Fitter for sickness and for crazy age.   89

BEDFORD

Lord Talbot, do not so dishonor me.
Here will I sit before the walls of Rouen
And will be partner of your weal or woe.   92

BURGUNDY

Courageous Bedford, let us now persuade you.

BEDFORD

Not to be gone from hence; for once I read
That stout Pendragon in his litter sick   95
Came to the field and vanquishèd his foes.
Methinks I should revive the soldiers' hearts,
Because I ever found them as myself.

TALBOT

Undaunted spirit in a dying breast!
Then be it so. Heavens keep old Bedford safe!
And now no more ado, brave Burgundy,
But gather we our forces out of hand   102
And set upon our boasting enemy.
            Exeunt [all but Bedford and attendants].

*An alarum. Excursions. Enter Sir John Falstaff
and a Captain.*

CAPTAIN

Whither away, Sir John Falstaff, in such haste?

FALSTAFF

Whither away? To save myself by flight.
We are like to have the overthrow again.   106

CAPTAIN

What? Will you fly, and leave Lord Talbot?

FALSTAFF   Ay,
All the Talbots in the world, to save my life.   *Exit.*

CAPTAIN

Cowardly knight, ill fortune follow thee!   *Exit.*

*Retreat. Excursions. Pucelle, Alençon, and
Charles fly.*

BEDFORD

Now, quiet soul, depart when heaven please,   110
For I have seen our enemies' overthrow.   111
What is the trust or strength of foolish man?
They that of late were daring with their scoffs

Are glad and fain by flight to save themselves.   114
            Bedford dies, and is carried in by two in his chair.

*An alarum. Enter Talbot, Burgundy, and the
rest [of the English soldiers].*

TALBOT

Lost and recovered in a day again!
This is a double honor, Burgundy.
Yet heavens have glory for this victory!

BURGUNDY

Warlike and martial Talbot, Burgundy
Enshrines thee in his heart and there erects
Thy noble deeds as valor's monuments.

TALBOT

Thanks, gentle Duke. But where is Pucelle now?   121
I think her old familiar is asleep.   122
Now where's the Bastard's braves, and Charles his
    gleeks?   123
What, all amort? Rouen hangs her head for grief   124
That such a valiant company are fled.
Now will we take some order in the town,   126
Placing therein some expert officers,
And then depart to Paris to the King,
For there young Henry with his nobles lie.

BURGUNDY

What wills Lord Talbot pleaseth Burgundy.

TALBOT

But yet, before we go, let's not forget
The noble Duke of Bedford late deceased,
But see his exequies fulfilled in Rouen.   133
A braver soldier never couchèd lance;   134
A gentler heart did never sway in court.   135
But kings and mightiest potentates must die,
For that's the end of human misery.   *Exeunt.*

❖

3.3

*Enter Charles, [the] Bastard [of Orleans], Alençon,
Pucelle, [and French soldiers].*

PUCELLE

Dismay not, princes, at this accident,   1
Nor grieve that Rouen is so recoverèd.
Care is no cure, but rather corrosive,   3
For things that are not to be remedied.
Let frantic Talbot triumph for a while
And like a peacock sweep along his tail;
We'll pull his plumes and take away his train,   7
If Dauphin and the rest will be but ruled.   8

---

86 **regard** attend to   89 **crazy** decrepit   92 **weal** welfare   95 **Pendragon** (According to Holinshed, it was the brother of Uther Pendragon who, "even sick as he was, caused himself to be carried forth in a litter; with whose presence his people were so encouraged that, encountering with the Saxons, they won the victory." Geoffrey of Monmouth, on the other hand, credits this feat to Uther himself. Uther was father of King Arthur.)   102 **out of hand** at once   106 **like to . . . overthrow** likely to be overthrown   110–11 **Now . . . overthrow** (A secular version of Luke 2:29–30, "Lord, now lettest thou thy servant depart in peace," etc., sung as the *Nunc dimittis* in evensong in the Book of Common Prayer.)

114 **fain** eager   114.1 *carried in* carried offstage   121 **gentle** noble   122 **old familiar** customary attendant demon   123 **braves** boasts. **Charles his gleeks** Charles's gibes, jests.   124 **amort** sick to death, dispirited.   126 **take some order** establish order and government   133 **exequies** funeral rites   134 **couchèd lance** carried his lance lowered, in the position of attack   135 **gentler** more noble.   **sway** exercise influence
3.3. Location: Near Rouen.
1 **Dismay not** Be not dismayed, disheartened.   **accident** bad luck, untoward event   3 **Care** Sorrow   7 **train** (1) peacock's tail (2) army   8 **will . . . ruled** will follow my advice.

CHARLES
  We have been guided by thee hitherto,
  And of thy cunning had no diffidence.   10
  One sudden foil shall never breed distrust.   11

BASTARD
  Search out thy wit for secret policies,   12
  And we will make thee famous through the world.

ALENÇON
  We'll set thy statue in some holy place
  And have thee reverenced like a blessèd saint.
  Employ thee then, sweet virgin, for our good.

PUCELLE
  Then thus it must be; this doth Joan devise:
  By fair persuasions, mixed with sugared words,
  We will entice the Duke of Burgundy
  To leave the Talbot and to follow us.

CHARLES
  Ay, marry, sweeting, if we could do that,
  France were no place for Henry's warriors,
  Nor should that nation boast it so with us,
  But be extirpèd from our provinces.   24

ALENÇON
  Forever should they be expulsed from France
  And not have title of an earldom here.

PUCELLE
  Your Honors shall perceive how I will work
  To bring this matter to the wishèd end.
                    Drum sounds afar off.
  Hark, by the sound of drum you may perceive
  Their powers are marching unto Paris-ward.   30
                Here sounds an English march.
  There goes the Talbot, with his colors spread,
  And all the troops of English after him.
                          French march.
  Now in the rearward comes the Duke and his.
  Fortune in favor makes him lag behind.   34
  Summon a parley. We will talk with him.   35
                Trumpets sound a parley.

[*Enter the Duke of Burgundy.*]

CHARLES
  A parley with the Duke of Burgundy!

BURGUNDY
  Who craves a parley with the Burgundy?

PUCELLE
  The princely Charles of France, thy countryman.

BURGUNDY
  What sayst thou, Charles? For I am marching hence.

CHARLES
  Speak, Pucelle, and enchant him with thy words.   40

PUCELLE
  Brave Burgundy, undoubted hope of France,   41
  Stay. Let thy humble handmaid speak to thee.

BURGUNDY
  Speak on, but be not overtedious.

PUCELLE
  Look on thy country, look on fertile France,
  And see the cities and the towns defaced
  By wasting ruin of the cruel foe.
  As looks the mother on her lowly babe   47
  When death doth close his tender-dying eyes,   48
  See, see the pining malady of France!   49
  Behold the wounds, the most unnatural wounds,   50
  Which thou thyself hast given her woeful breast.
  Oh, turn thy edgèd sword another way!
  Strike those that hurt, and hurt not those that help!
  One drop of blood drawn from thy country's bosom
  Should grieve thee more than streams of foreign gore.
  Return thee therefore with a flood of tears
  And wash away thy country's stainèd spots.   57

BURGUNDY [*aside*]
  Either she hath bewitched me with her words,
  Or nature makes me suddenly relent.

PUCELLE
  Besides, all French and France exclaims on thee,   60
  Doubting thy birth and lawful progeny.   61
  Who join'st thou with but with a lordly nation
  That will not trust thee but for profit's sake?
  When Talbot hath set footing once in France
  And fashioned thee that instrument of ill,   65
  Who then but English Henry will be lord,
  And thou be thrust out like a fugitive?   67
  Call we to mind, and mark but this for proof: 68
  Was not the Duke of Orleans thy foe?
  And was he not in England prisoner?
  But when they heard he was thine enemy,
  They set him free without his ransom paid,
  In spite of Burgundy and all his friends.
  See, then, thou fight'st against thy countrymen
  And join'st with them will be thy slaughtermen.   75
  Come, come, return. Return, thou wandering lord!
  Charles and the rest will take thee in their arms.

BURGUNDY [*aside*]
  I am vanquished. These haughty words of hers   78
  Have battered me like roaring cannon-shot
  And made me almost yield upon my knees.—
  Forgive me, country, and sweet countrymen!
  And, lords, accept this hearty kind embrace.
  My forces and my power of men are yours.
  So farewell, Talbot. I'll no longer trust thee.

PUCELLE
  Done like a Frenchman—[*aside*] turn and turn again!

---

10 **diffidence** distrust.   11 **foil** repulse, defeat   12 **policies** stratagems   24 **extirpèd** rooted out   30.1 *Here . . . march* (Probably the
English are heard from offstage, and the French at line 32, but conceivably soldiers could pass over the stage.)   34 **in favor** benevolently, i.e., in our favor   35 **Summon a parley** Sound a trumpet
signal requesting negotiations.   40 **enchant** put spells on
41 **undoubted** i.e., whose bravery and strength are sure bulwarks

47 **lowly** little, or humbled by misfortune   48 **tender-dying** dying at
a tender age   49 **malady of France** (With comic double meaning; the
phrase normally refers to venereal disease.)   50 **unnatural** i.e.,
turned against the doer's own country   57 **thy . . . spots** blemishes to
your country's reputation.   60 **exclaims on** denounces, accuses
61 **progeny** ancestry.   65 **fashioned thee** turned you into   67 **fugitive** renegade, deserter of your own nation.   68 **Call we to mind** Let
us remember   75 **them** those who   78 **I am vanquished** (Historically, Burgundy did not desert the English alliance until four years
after Joan's death, and five years before the Duke of Orleans was
released by the English; see lines 69–73.)   **haughty** lofty

CHARLES
Welcome, brave Duke! Thy friendship makes us fresh.

BASTARD
And doth beget new courage in our breasts.

ALENÇON
Pucelle hath bravely played her part in this   88
And doth deserve a coronet of gold.

CHARLES
Now let us on, my lords, and join our powers,   90
And seek how we may prejudice the foe.   *Exeunt.*   91

❖

3.4

*Enter the King, Gloucester, Winchester, [Richard,
Duke of] York, Suffolk, Somerset, Warwick,
Exeter, [Vernon, wearing a white rose, Basset,
wearing a red rose, and others]. To them, with
his soldiers, Talbot.*

TALBOT
My gracious prince, and honorable peers,
Hearing of your arrival in this realm,
I have awhile given truce unto my wars
To do my duty to my sovereign;   4
In sign whereof, this arm, that hath reclaimed
To your obedience fifty fortresses,
Twelve cities, and seven walled towns of strength,
Beside five hundred prisoners of esteem,
Lets fall his sword before Your Highness' feet,
And with submissive loyalty of heart
Ascribes the glory of his conquest got
First to my God and next unto Your Grace.
                                               [He kneels.]

KING
Is this the Lord Talbot, uncle Gloucester,
That hath so long been resident in France?

GLOUCESTER
Yes, if it please Your Majesty, my liege.

KING
Welcome, brave captain and victorious lord!
When I was young—as yet I am not old—
I do remember how my father said   18
A stouter champion never handled sword.   19
Long since we were resolvèd of your truth,   20
Your faithful service, and your toil in war;
Yet never have you tasted our reward
Or been reguerdoned with so much as thanks,   23
Because till now we never saw your face.
Therefore, stand up. *[Talbot rises.]* And for these good
   deserts
We here create you Earl of Shrewsbury;   25

And in our coronation take your place.   27
       *Sennet. Flourish. Exeunt. Manent Vernon and
                                             Basset.*

VERNON
Now, sir, to you, that were so hot at sea,   28
Disgracing of these colors that I wear   29
In honor of my noble lord of York:
Dar'st thou maintain the former words thou spak'st?

BASSET
Yes, sir, as well as you dare patronage   32
The envious barking of your saucy tongue
Against my lord the Duke of Somerset.

VERNON
Sirrah, thy lord I honor as he is.   35

BASSET
Why, what is he? As good a man as York.

VERNON
Hark ye, not so. In witness, take ye that.
                                            Strikes him.

BASSET
Villain, thou knowest the law of arms is such   38
That whoso draws a sword, 'tis present death,   39
Or else this blow should broach thy dearest blood.   40
But I'll unto His Majesty and crave
I may have liberty to venge this wrong,   42
When thou shalt see I'll meet thee to thy cost.

VERNON
Well, miscreant, I'll be there as soon as you,
And after meet you, sooner than you would. *Exeunt.* 45

❖

4.1

*Enter King, Gloucester, Winchester, [Richard,
Duke of] York, Suffolk, Somerset, Warwick, Talbot, Exeter, Governor [of Paris, and others].*

GLOUCESTER
Lord Bishop, set the crown upon his head.

WINCHESTER
God save King Henry, of that name the sixth!
                                      [The King is crowned.]

GLOUCESTER
Now, Governor of Paris, take your oath,
                                    [The governor kneels.]
That you elect no other king but him,   4
Esteem none friends but such as are his friends,

27.1 *Manent* They remain onstage   28 **so hot at sea** (The details of
this quarrel are given below, at 4.1.87–97.)   29 **Disgracing . . . colors**
i.e., insulting the white rose of York   32 **patronage** defend   35 **as he
is** i.e., for what he is—a person of no worth.   38 **law of arms** (This
law forbade the drawing of weapons near a royal residence; see 1.3.46
and note, and 2.4.86 and note.)   39 **present** instant   40 **broach . . .
blood** tap and draw out your lifeblood (as from a keg).   42 **wrong**
insult   45 **after** i.e., once the royal permission to fight a duel has been
obtained
**4.1. Location: Paris. Scene continues. (The action appears to go on
immediately after the events of 3.4.)**
0.2 *York* i.e., Richard Plantagenet, created Duke of York in 3.1 and
hereafter identified by the speech prefix YORK   4 **elect** acknowledge

---

88 **bravely** courageously and excellently   90 **powers** armed forces
91 **prejudice** harm
3.4. Location: Paris. The royal court.
4 **duty** homage   18 **I . . . said** (Historically, Henry VI was an infant of
nine months at his father's death.)   19 **stouter** more intrepid   20 **we**
i.e., I. (The royal "we.")   **resolvèd** convinced.   **truth** loyalty
23 **reguerdoned** rewarded   25 **deserts** deservings

And none your foes but such as shall pretend   6
Malicious practices against his state.   7
This shall ye do, so help you righteous God!
                              [*The Governor retires.*]

        Enter [*Sir John*] *Falstaff.*

FALSTAFF
My gracious sovereign, as I rode from Calais
To haste unto your coronation,
A letter was delivered to my hands,
Writ to Your Grace from th' Duke of Burgundy.
                              [*He presents a letter.*]

TALBOT
Shame to the Duke of Burgundy and thee!
I vowed, base knight, when I did meet thee next,
To tear the Garter from thy craven's leg,   15
                              [*plucking it off*]
Which I have done, because unworthily
Thou wast installèd in that high degree.—
Pardon me, princely Henry, and the rest.
This dastard, at the battle of Poitiers,   19
When but in all I was six thousand strong   20
And that the French were almost ten to one,
Before we met or that a stroke was given,
Like to a trusty squire did run away;   23
In which assault we lost twelve hundred men.
Myself and divers gentlemen beside
Were there surprised and taken prisoners.   26
Then judge, great lords, if I have done amiss,
Or whether that such cowards ought to wear
This ornament of knighthood, yea or no?

GLOUCESTER
To say the truth, this fact was infamous   30
And ill beseeming any common man,
Much more a knight, a captain, and a leader.

TALBOT
When first this order was ordained, my lords,
Knights of the Garter were of noble birth,
Valiant and virtuous, full of haughty courage,   35
Such as were grown to credit by the wars—   36
Not fearing death, nor shrinking for distress,
But always resolute in most extremes.   38
He then that is not furnished in this sort   39
Doth but usurp the sacred name of knight,
Profaning this most honorable order,
And should, if I were worthy to be judge,
Be quite degraded, like a hedge-born swain   43
That doth presume to boast of gentle blood.   44

KING [*to Falstaff*]
Stain to thy countrymen, thou hear'st thy doom.   45
Be packing, therefore, thou that wast a knight.   46
Henceforth we banish thee, on pain of death.
                              [*Exit Falstaff.*]
And now, my Lord Protector, view the letter
Sent from our uncle Duke of Burgundy.   49

GLOUCESTER [*taking the letter*]
What means His Grace, that he hath changed his
    style?   50
No more but, plain and bluntly, "To the King"?
Hath he forgot he is his sovereign?
Or doth this churlish superscription   53
Pretend some alteration in good will?   54
What's here? [*He reads.*] "I have, upon especial cause,
Moved with compassion of my country's wrack,   56
Together with the pitiful complaints
Of such as your oppression feeds upon,
Forsaken your pernicious faction
And joined with Charles, the rightful King of France."
Oh, monstrous treachery! Can this be so,
That in alliance, amity, and oaths
There should be found such false dissembling guile?

KING
What? Doth my uncle Burgundy revolt?   64

GLOUCESTER
He doth, my lord, and is become your foe.

KING
Is that the worst this letter doth contain?

GLOUCESTER
It is the worst, and all, my lord, he writes.

KING
Why, then, Lord Talbot there shall talk with him
And give him chastisement for this abuse.   69
[*To Talbot*] How say you, my lord? Are you not
    content?

TALBOT
Content, my liege? Yes. But that I am prevented,   71
I should have begged I might have been employed.

KING
Then gather strength and march unto him straight.   73
Let him perceive how ill we brook his treason,   74
And what offense it is to flout his friends.

TALBOT
I go, my lord, in heart desiring still   76
You may behold confusion of your foes.   [*Exit.*]   77

        Enter Vernon and Basset, [*wearing a white and
        a red rose respectively, as before*].

VERNON
Grant me the combat, gracious sovereign.   78

6 **pretend** purpose, intend   7 **practices** stratagems   15 **Garter** badge of the Knights of the Garter, a ribbon of blue velvet edged and buckled with gold, worn below the left knee. (Historically, the Garter was apparently taken from Fastolfe by the Duke of Bedford; Talbot, who was a captive of the French at the time of Henry VI's coronation in Paris, was opposed to the restoration of the Garter to Fastolfe.) 19 **Poitiers** (Seemingly confused with Patay.)   20 **but in all** all told 23 **trusty squire** (Said contemptuously.)   26 **surprised** ambushed 30 **fact** deed   35 **haughty** exalted   36 **were grown to credit** had achieved renown   38 **most** greatest   39 **furnished . . . sort** endowed thus   43 **degraded** lowered in rank.   **hedge-born swain** lowly born rustic   44 **gentle** noble

45 **doom** sentence.   46 **Be packing** Be off   49 **uncle** (The Lancastrian and Burgundian houses were allied by the marriage of the Duke of Bedford, the King's uncle, to Anne, sister of the Duke of Burgundy.) 50 **style** form of address.   53 **churlish superscription** insolent form of address on the outside of the letter   54 **Pretend** portend, import 56 **wrack** ruin   64 **revolt** fall away to the other side.   69 **abuse** deception.   71 **prevented** anticipated   73 **straight** immediately. 74 **brook** endure   76 **still** always   77 **confusion** destruction   78 **the combat** permission to fight a trial by duel

BASSET
And me, my lord. Grant me the combat too.

YORK
This is my servant. Hear him, noble prince.

SOMERSET   80
And this is mine. Sweet Henry, favor him.

KING
Be patient, lords, and give them leave to speak.—
Say, gentlemen, what makes you thus exclaim?
And wherefore crave you combat, or with whom?

VERNON
With him, my lord, for he hath done me wrong.

BASSET
And I with him, for he hath done me wrong.

KING
What is that wrong whereof you both complain?
First let me know, and then I'll answer you.

BASSET
Crossing the sea from England into France,
This fellow here, with envious carping tongue,   90
Upbraided me about the rose I wear,
Saying the sanguine color of the leaves   92
Did represent my master's blushing cheeks,
When stubbornly he did repugn the truth   94
About a certain question in the law
Argued betwixt the Duke of York and him;
With other vile and ignominious terms.
In confutation of which rude reproach,
And in defense of my lord's worthiness,
I crave the benefit of law of arms.   100

VERNON
And that is my petition, noble lord.
For though he seem with forgèd quaint conceit   102
To set a gloss upon his bold intent,   103
Yet know, my lord, I was provoked by him,
And he first took exceptions at this badge,
Pronouncing that the paleness of this flower
Bewrayed the faintness of my master's heart.   107

YORK
Will not this malice, Somerset, be left?   108

SOMERSET
Your private grudge, my lord of York, will out,   109
Though ne'er so cunningly you smother it.

KING
Good Lord, what madness rules in brainsick men,
When for so slight and frivolous a cause
Such factious emulations shall arise!   113
Good cousins both, of York and Somerset,   114
Quiet yourselves, I pray, and be at peace.

YORK
Let this dissension first be tried by fight,
And then Your Highness shall command a peace.

SOMERSET
The quarrel toucheth none but us alone;   118
Betwixt ourselves let us decide it then.

YORK
There is my pledge. Accept it, Somerset.   120
                              [He throws down a gage.]

VERNON
Nay, let it rest where it began at first.   121

BASSET
Confirm it so, mine honorable lord.   122

GLOUCESTER
Confirm it so? Confounded be your strife!
And perish ye, with your audacious prate!
Presumptuous vassals, are you not ashamed
With this immodest clamorous outrage   126
To trouble and disturb the King and us?
And you, my lords, methinks you do not well   128
To bear with their perverse objections,   129
Much less to take occasion from their mouths
To raise a mutiny betwixt yourselves.   131
Let me persuade you take a better course.

EXETER
It grieves His Highness. Good my lords, be friends.

KING
Come hither, you that would be combatants:
Henceforth I charge you, as you love our favor,
Quite to forget this quarrel and the cause.
And you, my lords: remember where we are—
In France, amongst a fickle wavering nation.
If they perceive dissension in our looks
And that within ourselves we disagree,   140
How will their grudging stomachs be provoked   141
To willful disobedience, and rebel!
Besides, what infamy will there arise
When foreign princes shall be certified   144
That for a toy, a thing of no regard,   145
King Henry's peers and chief nobility
Destroyed themselves and lost the realm of France!
Oh, think upon the conquest of my father,
My tender years, and let us not forgo   149
That for a trifle that was bought with blood!   150
Let me be umpire in this doubtful strife.   151
I see no reason, if I wear this rose,
                              [putting on a red rose]
That anyone should therefore be suspicious
I more incline to Somerset than York.

80 **servant** follower.   90 **envious** malicious   92 **sanguine** bloodred.
leaves petals   94 **repugn** oppose   100 **benefit . . . arms** right to protect my honor in a duel.   102 **forgèd quaint conceit** false ingenious
rhetoric   103 **gloss** speciously fair appearance   107 **Bewrayed**
revealed   108 **left** given up, forgotten.   109 **out** appear, be revealed
113 **factious emulations** contentions between rivals   114 **cousins**
kinsmen

118 **toucheth** concerns   120 **pledge** i.e., a glove or gauntlet flung
down as a gage in a duel.   121 **let . . . first** i.e., let the quarrel remain
with me and Basset, who began it. (Said perhaps to York or to the King.
Let it rest can also mean, "do not pick up the gage.")   122 **Confirm . . .
lord** i.e., Confirm the suggestion that Vernon and I be allowed to fight
it out between ourselves. (Said perhaps to Somerset or to the King.)
126 **immodest** arrogant, impudent   128 **my lords** i.e., York and Somerset. (Also in line 137.)   129 **objections** charges, accusations
131 **mutiny** quarrel, strife   140 **within** among   141 **grudging stomachs** resentful tempers   144 **certified** informed   145 **toy** trifle
149–50 **let . . . blood!** i.e., let us not allow these trivial quarrels to cause
us to lose France, bought with many English lives!   151 **doubtful**
causing apprehension

Both are my kinsmen, and I love them both.
As well they may upbraid me with my crown
Because, forsooth, the King of Scots is crowned.
But your discretions better can persuade
Than I am able to instruct or teach;
And therefore, as we hither came in peace,
So let us still continue peace and love.   161
Cousin of York, we institute Your Grace
To be our regent in these parts of France.
And, good my lord of Somerset, unite
Your troops of horsemen with his bands of foot;   165
And like true subjects, sons of your progenitors,
Go cheerfully together and digest   167
Your angry choler on your enemies.
Ourself, my Lord Protector, and the rest
After some respite will return to Calais;
From thence to England, where I hope ere long
To be presented, by your victories,
With Charles, Alençon, and that traitorous rout.   173
　　　　Flourish. Exeunt. Manent York, Warwick, Exeter,
　　　　　　　　　　　　　　　　　　　　　　[and] Vernon.

WARWICK
My lord of York, I promise you, the King   174
Prettily, methought, did play the orator.

YORK
And so he did; but yet I like it not
In that he wears the badge of Somerset.

WARWICK
Tush, that was but his fancy. Blame him not.
I dare presume, sweet prince, he thought no harm.

YORK
An if I wist he did—But let it rest.   180
Other affairs must now be managèd.
　　　　　　　　　　　　　　　　　　Exeunt. Manet Exeter.

EXETER
Well didst thou, Richard, to suppress thy voice;
For, had the passions of thy heart burst out,
I fear we should have seen deciphered there   184
More rancorous spite, more furious raging broils,
Than yet can be imagined or supposed.
But howsoe'er, no simple man that sees   187
This jarring discord of nobility,
This shouldering of each other in the court,
This factious bandying of their favorites,   190
But that it doth presage some ill event.   191
'Tis much when scepters are in children's hands,
But more when envy breeds unkind division.   193
There comes the ruin, there begins confusion.   *Exit.*   194

❧

4.2

Enter Talbot, with trump and drum [and forces],
before Bordeaux.

TALBOT
Go to the gates of Bordeaux, trumpeter.   1
Summon their general unto the wall.

　　　　[Trumpet] sounds. Enter General, aloft.

English John Talbot, captains, calls you forth,
Servant in arms to Harry King of England,
And thus he would: Open your city gates,   5
Be humble to us, call my sovereign yours,
And do him homage as obedient subjects,
And I'll withdraw me and my bloody power.   8
But if you frown upon this proffered peace,
You tempt the fury of my three attendants,
Lean famine, quartering steel, and climbing fire,   11
Who in a moment even with the earth   12
Shall lay your stately and air-braving towers,   13
If you forsake the offer of their love.   14

GENERAL
Thou ominous and fearful owl of death,   15
Our nation's terror and their bloody scourge,   16
The period of thy tyranny approacheth.   17
On us thou canst not enter but by death,
For I protest we are well fortified
And strong enough to issue out and fight.
If thou retire, the Dauphin, well appointed,   21
Stands with the snares of war to tangle thee.
On either hand thee there are squadrons pitched,   23
To wall thee from the liberty of flight;
And no way canst thou turn thee for redress
But death doth front thee with apparent spoil   26
And pale destruction meets thee in the face.   27
Ten thousand French have ta'en the Sacrament   28
To rive their dangerous artillery   29
Upon no Christian soul but English Talbot.
Lo, there thou stand'st, a breathing valiant man
Of an invincible unconquered spirit.
This is the latest glory of thy praise   33
That I, thy enemy, due thee withal;   34
For ere the glass that now begins to run   35
Finish the process of his sandy hour,   36

4.2. Location: France. Before Bordeaux.
0.1 *trump and drum* trumpeter and drummer   **1 gates** (As before at
Orleans and Rouen, these city gates are represented by a door in the
tiring-house facade, which is imagined to be the walls of Bordeaux.
Occupants of Bordeaux appearing *aloft* or on the walls are seen in the
gallery backstage.)   **5 would** wishes   **8 bloody power** bloodthirsty
army.   **11 quartering** dismembering   **12 even** level   **13 air-braving**
defying the heavens (by their height)   **14 forsake** refuse.   **their** i.e.,
famine, steel, and *fire*   **15 owl** i.e., portent   **16 their** our people's
17 period termination.   **tyranny** cruelty   **21 appointed** equipped
23 thee of you.   **pitched** set in battle array   **26 front** face.   **apparent
spoil** certain destruction   **27 pale** (Because Death is portrayed as
pale.)   **28 ta'en the Sacrament** i.e., confirmed their solemn oaths by
taking the Sacrament   **29 rive** burst, fire   **33 latest** final   **34 due**
endue, invest   **35 glass** hourglass   **36 sandy hour** hour as measured
by the running of the sand

161 still ever   **165 bands of foot** troops of infantry   **167 digest**
expend, dissipate   **173 rout** rabble.   **173.1 *Manent*** They remain
onstage   **174 promise** assure   **180 An . . . wist** If I knew for certain
184 deciphered detected, expressed   **187 simple** common
190 bandying contending.   **favorites** followers   **191 But that** i.e.,
but sees that.   **event** outcome.   **193 envy** malice.   **unkind** unnatural   **194 confusion** destruction.

These eyes, that see thee now well colorèd,   37
Shall see thee withered, bloody, pale, and dead.
                                    Drum afar off.
Hark, hark! The Dauphin's drum, a warning bell,
Sings heavy music to thy timorous soul,
And mine shall ring thy dire departure out.   *Exit.* 41

TALBOT
He fables not. I hear the enemy.
Out, some light horsemen, and peruse their wings.   43
                            [*Exeunt some.*]
Oh, negligent and heedless discipline!   44
How are we parked and bounded in a pale—   45
A little herd of England's timorous deer,
Mazed with a yelping kennel of French curs!   47
If we be English deer, be then in blood: 48
Not rascal-like to fall down with a pinch,   49
But rather, moody-mad and desperate stags,   50
Turn on the bloody hounds with heads of steel   51
And make the cowards stand aloof at bay.
Sell every man his life as dear as mine
And they shall find dear deer of us, my friends.   54
God and Saint George, Talbot and England's right,
Prosper our colors in this dangerous fight!   [*Exeunt.*] 56

❧

[4.3]

*Enter a Messenger that meets York. Enter York
with trumpet and many soldiers.*

YORK
Are not the speedy scouts returned again
That dogged the mighty army of the Dauphin?

MESSENGER
They are returned, my lord, and give it out   3
That he is marched to Bordeaux with his power   4
To fight with Talbot. As he marched along,
By your espials were discoverèd   6
Two mightier troops than that the Dauphin led,
Which joined with him and made their march for
Bordeaux.

YORK
A plague upon that villain Somerset,
That thus delays my promisèd supply   10
Of horsemen that were levied for this siege!
Renownèd Talbot doth expect my aid,
And I am louted by a traitor villain   13
And cannot help the noble chevalier.

God comfort him in this necessity!
If he miscarry, farewell wars in France.   16

Enter another Messenger, [Sir William Lucy].

LUCY
Thou princely leader of our English strength,
Never so needful on the earth of France,
Spur to the rescue of the noble Talbot,
Who now is girdled with a waist of iron
And hemmed about with grim destruction.
To Bordeaux, warlike Duke! To Bordeaux, York!
Else, farewell Talbot, France, and England's honor.

YORK
Oh, God, that Somerset, who in proud heart
Doth stop my cornets, were in Talbot's place!   25
So should we save a valiant gentleman
By forfeiting a traitor and a coward.
Mad ire and wrathful fury makes me weep
That thus we die while remiss traitors sleep.

LUCY
Oh, send some succor to the distressed lord!   30

YORK
He dies, we lose; I break my warlike word;
We mourn, France smiles; we lose, they daily get;
All 'long of this vile traitor Somerset.   33

LUCY
Then God take mercy on brave Talbot's soul,
And on his son young John, who two hours since
I met in travel toward his warlike father.
This seven years did not Talbot see his son,
And now they meet where both their lives are done.

YORK
Alas, what joy shall noble Talbot have
To bid his young son welcome to his grave?
Away! Vexation almost stops my breath,   41
That sundered friends greet in the hour of death.
Lucy, farewell. No more my fortune can   43
But curse the cause I cannot aid the man.
Maine, Blois, Poitiers, and Tours are won away,
'Long all of Somerset and his delay.
                        Exit [with his soldiers].

LUCY
Thus, while the vulture of sedition
Feeds in the bosom of such great commanders,
Sleeping neglection doth betray to loss
The conquest of our scarce-cold conqueror,   50
That ever-living man of memory,   51
Henry the Fifth. Whiles they each other cross,
Lives, honors, lands, and all hurry to loss.

❧

---

37 well colorèd in the pink of health   **41 departure** i.e., death
43 peruse their wings reconnoiter their flanks.   **44 discipline** military management.   **45 parked** enclosed.   **pale** fenced-in space
47 Mazed with (1) bewildered, amazed by (2) enclosed by, as in a labyrinth   **48 in blood** in prime condition   **49 rascal-like** (1) like young or inferior deer (2) like rascals.   **pinch** nip   **50 moody-mad** high-spirited and mad with rage   **51 heads of steel** (1) swordlike antlers (2) helmeted heads   **54 dear** (1) costly (in terms of casualties) (2) precious   **56 our colors** i.e., our cause. (Literally, our insignia, banners.)
4.3. Location: France. Plains in Gascony.
3 give it out report   **4 power** army   **6 espials** spies   **10 supply** reinforcements   **13 louted** made a fool of, mocked

16 miscarry come to grief   **25 Doth . . . cornets** detains my cavalry units   **30 distressed** in difficulties   **33 'long of** on account of
41 Vexation Anguish   **43 can** is able to do   **50 scarce-cold** only recently dead. (Shakespeare is compressing time; historically, thirty years intervened between the deaths of Henry V and Talbot.)
51 ever-living . . . memory man of ever-living memory

[4.4]

Enter Somerset, with his army; [a Captain of Talbot's with him].

SOMERSET
It is too late. I cannot send them now.
This expedition was by York and Talbot
Too rashly plotted. All our general force   3
Might with a sally of the very town   4
Be buckled with. The overdaring Talbot   5
Hath sullied all his gloss of former honor
By this unheedful, desperate, wild adventure.
York set him on to fight and die in shame,
That, Talbot dead, great York might bear the name.   9

CAPTAIN
Here is Sir William Lucy, who with me
Set from our o'ermatched forces forth for aid.

[Sir William Lucy comes forward.]

SOMERSET
How now, Sir William, whither were you sent?

LUCY
Whither, my lord? From bought and sold Lord Talbot,
Who, ringed about with bold adversity,
Cries out for noble York and Somerset
To beat assailing death from his weak legions;
And whiles the honorable captain there
Drops bloody sweat from his war-wearied limbs
And, in advantage lingering, looks for rescue,   19
You, his false hopes, the trust of England's honor,   20
Keep off aloof with worthless emulation.   21
Let not your private discord keep away
The levied succors that should lend him aid,   23
While he, renownèd noble gentleman,
Yield up his life unto a world of odds.   25
Orleans the Bastard, Charles, Burgundy,
Alençon, Reignier, compass him about,
And Talbot perisheth by your default.

SOMERSET
York set him on. York should have sent him aid.

LUCY
And York as fast upon Your Grace exclaims,   30
Swearing that you withhold his levied horse
Collected for this expedition.

SOMERSET
York lies. He might have sent and had the horse.   33
I owe him little duty and less love,
And take foul scorn to fawn on him by sending.   35

LUCY
The fraud of England, not the force of France,
Hath now entrapped the noble-minded Talbot.
Never to England shall he bear his life,
But dies betrayed to fortune by your strife.

SOMERSET
Come, go. I will dispatch the horsemen straight.
Within six hours they will be at his aid.

LUCY
Too late comes rescue. He is ta'en or slain;
For fly he could not, if he would have fled;
And fly would Talbot never, though he might.

SOMERSET
If he be dead, brave Talbot, then adieu!

LUCY
His fame lives in the world, his shame in you.
Exeunt [separately].

❖

[4.5]

Enter Talbot and his son [John].

TALBOT
O young John Talbot, I did send for thee
To tutor thee in stratagems of war,
That Talbot's name might be in thee revived
When sapless age and weak unable limbs
Should bring thy father to his drooping chair.   5
But, O malignant and ill-boding stars!
Now thou art come unto a feast of death,
A terrible and unavoided danger.   8
Therefore, dear boy, mount on my swiftest horse,
And I'll direct thee how thou shalt escape
By sudden flight. Come, dally not, begone.

JOHN
Is my name Talbot, and am I your son,
And shall I fly? Oh, if you love my mother,
Dishonor not her honorable name
To make a bastard and a slave of me!   15
The world will say he is not Talbot's blood
That basely fled when noble Talbot stood.

TALBOT
Fly to revenge my death if I be slain.

JOHN
He that flies so will ne'er return again.

TALBOT
If we both stay, we both are sure to die.

JOHN
Then let me stay, and, father, do you fly.
Your loss is great; so your regard should be.   22
My worth unknown, no loss is known in me.   23
Upon my death the French can little boast;
In yours they will, in you all hopes are lost.

4.4. Location: France. Scene continues. Lucy does not leave the stage.
3–5 All . . . with i.e., Our entire army might be successfully encountered by a sortie of the mere French garrison in Bordeaux, unsupported by the other French armies coming to the relief of Bordeaux. **9 That** so that.   **bear the name** i.e., receive all honor as supreme commander in France.   **19 in advantage lingering** making the best he can out of delaying tactics, or finding every way he can to delay matters   **20 trust** guardian   **21 worthless emulation** ignoble rivalry.   **23 levied succors** raised reinforcements   **25 a world of** huge **30 upon . . . exclaims** accuses Your Grace   **33 might . . . had** i.e., had and could have sent   **35 take foul scorn** consider it humiliating

4.5. Location: France. A field of battle near Bordeaux.
5 drooping invalid   **8 unavoided** unavoidable   **15 To . . . me** by prompting me to act the part of a bastard and contemptible low person.   **22 Your loss is great** The loss of you would be a severe setback. **regard** heed for yourself   **23 no loss . . . me** the loss of me would scarcely be noticed.

Flight cannot stain the honor you have won;
But mine it will, that no exploit have done.
You fled for vantage, everyone will swear,   27
But if I bow they'll say it was for fear.   28
There is no hope that ever I will stay,
If the first hour I shrink and run away.
Here on my knee I beg mortality,   32
Rather than life preserved with infamy.

TALBOT
Shall all thy mother's hopes lie in one tomb?

JOHN
Ay, rather than I'll shame my mother's womb.

TALBOT
Upon my blessing I command thee go.

JOHN
To fight I will, but not to fly the foe.

TALBOT
Part of thy father may be saved in thee.

JOHN
No part of him but will be shame in me.

TALBOT
Thou never hadst renown, nor canst not lose it.

JOHN
Yes, your renownèd name. Shall flight abuse it?   41

TALBOT
Thy father's charge shall clear thee from that stain.   42

JOHN
You cannot witness for me, being slain.   43
If death be so apparent, then both fly.

TALBOT
And leave my followers here to fight and die?
My age was never tainted with such shame.   46

JOHN
And shall my youth be guilty of such blame?
No more can I be severed from your side
Than can yourself yourself in twain divide.
Stay, go, do what you will—the like do I;
For live I will not, if my father die.

TALBOT
Then here I take my leave of thee, fair son,
Born to eclipse thy life this afternoon.
Come, side by side together live and die,   53
And soul with soul from France to heaven fly.

                                        Exeunt.

❧

[4.6]

*Alarum. Excursions, wherein Talbot's son is
hemmed about, and Talbot rescues him.*

TALBOT
Saint George and victory! Fight, soldiers, fight!
The Regent hath with Talbot broke his word   2

And left us to the rage of France his sword.   3
Where is John Talbot?—Pause, and take thy breath.
I gave thee life and rescued thee from death.

JOHN
Oh, twice my father, twice am I thy son!
The life thou gav'st me first was lost and done
Till with thy warlike sword, despite of fate,   8
To my determined time thou gav'st new date.   9

TALBOT
When from the Dauphin's crest thy sword struck fire, 10
It warmed thy father's heart with proud desire
Of boldfaced victory. Then leaden age,   12
Quickened with youthful spleen and warlike rage,   13
Beat down Alençon, Orleans, Burgundy,
And from the pride of Gallia rescued thee.   15
The ireful bastard Orleans, that drew blood
From thee, my boy, and had the maidenhood   17
Of thy first fight, I soon encounterèd,   18
And interchanging blows, I quickly shed
Some of his bastard blood; and in disgrace   20
Bespoke him thus: "Contaminated, base,
And misbegotten blood I spill of thine,
Mean and right poor, for that pure blood of mine   23
Which thou didst force from Talbot, my brave boy."
Here, purposing the Bastard to destroy,   25
Came in strong rescue. Speak, thy father's care.
Art thou not weary, John? How dost thou fare?
Wilt thou yet leave the battle, boy, and fly,
Now thou art sealed the son of chivalry?   29
Fly, to revenge my death when I am dead.
The help of one stands me in little stead.
Oh, too much folly is it, well I wot,   32
To hazard all our lives in one small boat!
If I today die not with Frenchmen's rage,
Tomorrow I shall die with mickle age.   35
By me they nothing gain an if I stay;
'Tis but the shortening of my life one day.
In thee thy mother dies, our household's name,
My death's revenge, thy youth, and England's fame.
All these and more we hazard by thy stay;
All these are saved if thou wilt fly away.

JOHN
The sword of Orleans hath not made me smart;   42
These words of yours draw lifeblood from my heart.
On that advantage, bought with such a shame,   44
To save a paltry life and slay bright fame,
Before young Talbot from old Talbot fly,
The coward horse that bears me fall and die!   47
And like me to the peasant boys of France,   48

---

27 that I who   **28 vantage** military advantage   **32 mortality** death
41 abuse dishonor   **42 charge** giving you an order   **43 being slain**
you having been slain.   **46 age** lifetime   **53 eclipse** (Suggesting a
pun on *son, sun* in the previous line.)
4.6. Location: The battlefield still, moments later; the scene is continuous.
2 The Regent i.e., The Duke of York. (Compare this with 4.1.162–3.)

3 France his France's   **8 despite of fate** defying what fate had seemingly decreed   **9 determined** having been determined to end.   **date**
limit, termination.   **10 crest** i.e., helmet   **12 Then leaden age** i.e., Then
I, though slowed down by my many years   **13 Quickened** revived.
spleen i.e., courage, ardor   **15 Gallia** France   **17–18 had . . . fight**
(Talbot speaks of initiation into battle as a ritual of coming into manhood analogous to the loss of virginity.)   **20 in disgrace** by way of
insult   **23 Mean** base, inferior   **25 purposing** as I purposed   **29 sealed**
certified   **32 wot** know   **35 mickle** great   **42 smart** feel pain   **44 On
that advantage** i.e., To gain that advantage of safety   **47 fall** i.e., may it
fall   **48 like** liken

To be shame's scorn and subject of mischance!
Surely, by all the glory you have won,
An if I fly, I am not Talbot's son.
Then talk no more of flight. It is no boot.   52
If son to Talbot, die at Talbot's foot.

TALBOT
Then follow thou thy desperate sire of Crete,
Thou Icarus. Thy life to me is sweet.   55
If thou wilt fight, fight by thy father's side;
And, commendable proved, let's die in pride.
                                                    Exeunt.

❖

[4.7]

*Alarum. Excursions. Enter old Talbot led [by a
Servant].*

TALBOT
Where is my other life? Mine own is gone.
Oh, where's young Talbot? Where is valiant John?
Triumphant Death, smeared with captivity,   3
Young Talbot's valor makes me smile at thee.
When he perceived me shrink and on my knee,   5
His bloody sword he brandished over me,
And like a hungry lion did commence
Rough deeds of rage and stern impatience.
But when my angry guardant stood alone,   9
Tend'ring my ruin and assailed of none,   10
Dizzy-eyed fury and great rage of heart   11
Suddenly made him from my side to start
Into the clust'ring battle of the French,   13
And in that sea of blood my boy did drench   14
His overmounting spirit; and there died
My Icarus, my blossom, in his pride.   16

Enter [soldiers], with John Talbot, borne.

SERVANT
O my dear lord, lo, where your son is borne!

TALBOT
Thou antic Death, which laugh'st us here to scorn,   18
Anon, from thy insulting tyranny,
Coupled in bonds of perpetuity,
Two Talbots, wingèd through the lither sky,   21

In thy despite shall scape mortality.—   22
O thou, whose wounds become hard-favored Death,   23
Speak to thy father ere thou yield thy breath!
Brave Death by speaking, whether he will or no;   25
Imagine him a Frenchman and thy foe.—
Poor boy! He smiles, methinks, as who should say,   27
"Had Death been French, then Death had died today."
Come, come, and lay him in his father's arms.
                    [John is laid in his father's arms.]
My spirit can no longer bear these harms.
Soldiers, adieu! I have what I would have,
Now my old arms are young John Talbot's grave.   32
                            Dies. [Exeunt soldiers.]

*Enter Charles, Alençon, Burgundy, Bastard, and
Pucelle.*

CHARLES
Had York and Somerset brought rescue in,
We should have found a bloody day of this.

BASTARD
How the young whelp of Talbot's, raging wood,   35
Did flesh his puny sword in Frenchmen's blood!   36

PUCELLE
Once I encountered him, and thus I said:
"Thou maiden youth, be vanquished by a maid."   38
But with a proud, majestical high scorn
He answered thus: "Young Talbot was not born
To be the pillage of a giglot wench."   41
So, rushing in the bowels of the French,
He left me proudly, as unworthy fight.   43

BURGUNDY
Doubtless he would have made a noble knight.
See where he lies inhearsèd in the arms   45
Of the most bloody nurser of his harms!   46

BASTARD
Hew them to pieces, hack their bones asunder,
Whose life was England's glory, Gallia's wonder.   48

CHARLES
Oh, no, forbear! For that which we have fled
During the life, let us not wrong it dead.

*Enter [Sir William] Lucy [attended; Herald of the
French preceding].*

LUCY
Herald, conduct me to the Dauphin's tent,
To know who hath obtained the glory of the day.

CHARLES
On what submissive message art thou sent?

---

52 **boot** use. 55 **Thou Icarus** (Daedalus of Crete and his son
Icarus escaped from the labyrinth by means of wings that the
father's ingenuity had devised. As they flew across the sea, Icarus
mounted too high, the sun's heat melted the wax by which his
wings were attached, and he fell into the sea, hence called the Icar-
ian Sea, and was lost.)
4.7. Location: The battlefield still; the scene is continuous.
3 **smeared with captivity** i.e., stained with the blood of captives.
(The image is of a triumphal procession.) 5 **shrink** fall back in
battle 9 **guardant** guardian 10 **Tend'ring** being concerned for.
of by 11 **Dizzy-eyed** (Staring, dazzled eyes were thought of as a
conventional feature of wrath.) 13 **clust'ring battle** swarming
army 14 **drench** drown 16 **pride** glory. 18 **antic** i.e., grinning,
mocking like a jester. (A personification probably suggested by
grotesque pictorial representations in the Middle Ages and early
Renaissance, such as the Dance of Death.) **here** here on earth
21 **lither** yielding

22 **In . . . mortality** in spite of you will escape the bonds of death
(through immortality). 23 **thou** i.e., John. **become . . . Death** make
Death, otherwise hideous, seem beautiful 25 **Brave** Defy 27 **as
who** as if one 32.1 **Dies** (Historically, Talbot did not die until some
twenty-two years after Henry VI's coronation in Paris. Talbot's campaign in the Bordeaux region was successful and included the taking
of the city.) 35 **whelp of Talbot's** (Talbot is the name of a species of
hound.) **wood** mad 36 **flesh** use for the first time in battle. **puny**
inexperienced in bloodshed. (See note at 4.6.17–18.) 38 **maiden** i.e.,
not yet initiated in warfare 41 **giglot** wanton 43 **unworthy** unworthy of 45 **inhearsèd** as in a coffin 46 **Of . . . harms** of the father
who gave him his capacity for doing harm to the enemy. 48 **Gallia's
wonder** a source of amazement and consternation for the French.

LUCY

    Submission, Dauphin? 'Tis a mere French word.
    We English warriors wot not what it means.
    I come to know what prisoners thou hast ta'en
    And to survey the bodies of the dead.

CHARLES

    For prisoners ask'st thou? Hell our prison is.
    But tell me whom thou seek'st.   58

LUCY

    But where's the great Alcides of the field,   60
    Valiant Lord Talbot, Earl of Shrewsbury,
    Created for his rare success in arms
    Great Earl of Wexford, Waterford, and Valence,
    Lord Talbot of Goodrich and Urchinfield,
    Lord Strange of Blackmere, Lord Verdun of Alton,
    Lord Cromwell of Wingfield, Lord Furnival of
      Sheffield,
    The thrice-victorious Lord of Falconbridge,
    Knight of the noble order of Saint George,
    Worthy Saint Michael, and the Golden Fleece,
    Great Marshal to Henry the Sixth
    Of all his wars within the realm of France?

PUCELLE

    Here is a silly, stately style indeed!   72
    The Turk, that two-and-fifty kingdoms hath,   73
    Writes not so tedious a style as this.
    Him that thou magnifi'st with all these titles
    Stinking and flyblown lies here at our feet.

LUCY

    Is Talbot slain, the Frenchmen's only scourge,   77
    Your kingdom's terror and black nemesis?   78
    Oh, were mine eyeballs into bullets turned,
    That I in rage might shoot them at your faces!
    Oh, that I could but call these dead to life!
    It were enough to fright the realm of France.
    Were but his picture left amongst you here,
    It would amaze the proudest of you all.   84
    Give me their bodies, that I may bear them hence
    And give them burial as beseems their worth.   86

PUCELLE

    I think this upstart is old Talbot's ghost,
    He speaks with such a proud commanding spirit.
    For God's sake, let him have them! To keep them here,
    They would but stink and putrefy the air.

CHARLES   Go, take their bodies hence.

LUCY

    I'll bear them hence; but from their ashes shall be
      reared
    A phoenix that shall make all France afeard.   93

CHARLES

    So we be rid of them, do with them what thou wilt.   94
      [*Exeunt Lucy, Herald, and attendants with the*
             bodies.]
    And now to Paris in this conquering vein.
    All will be ours, now bloody Talbot's slain.   *Exeunt.*

❖

[5.1]

Sennet. Enter King, Gloucester, and Exeter,
[and others].

KING

    Have you perused the letters from the Pope,   1
    The Emperor, and the Earl of Armagnac?   2

GLOUCESTER

    I have, my lord, and their intent is this:
    They humbly sue unto Your Excellence   4
    To have a godly peace concluded of
    Between the realms of England and of France.

KING

    How doth Your Grace affect their motion?   7

GLOUCESTER

    Well, my good lord, and as the only means
    To stop effusion of our Christian blood
    And stablish quietness on every side.

KING

    Ay, marry, uncle; for I always thought
    It was both impious and unnatural
    That such immanity and bloody strife   13
    Should reign among professors of one faith.   14

GLOUCESTER

    Beside, my lord, the sooner to effect
    And surer bind this knot of amity,
    The Earl of Armagnac, near knit to Charles,   17
    A man of great authority in France,
    Proffers his only daughter to Your Grace
    In marriage, with a large and sumptuous dowry.

KING

    Marriage, uncle! Alas, my years are young,
    And fitter is my study and my books
    Than wanton dalliance with a paramour.
    Yet call th'ambassadors.   [*Exit one or more.*]
              And, as you please,
    So let them have their answers every one.
    I shall be well content with any choice
    Tends to God's glory and my country's weal.   27

Enter Winchester [in cardinal's habit], and
three Ambassadors, [one a Papal Legate].

---

58 Hell . . . is i.e., We have slain and thus sent our enemies to hell rather than take any prisoners.   60 Alcides Hercules. (Literally, descendant of Alcaeus, who was the father of Hercules's stepfather.)   72 style list of titles, manner of address   73 The Turk i.e., The Sultan of Turkey   77 only supreme   78 nemesis agent for retribution or punishment.   84 amaze stun, throw into confusion   86 beseems their worth befits their rank.   93 phoenix fabulous bird, the only one of its kind, which every five hundred years built itself a funeral pile and died upon it; from the ashes a new phoenix arose

94 So As long as
5.1. Location: London. The royal court.
1–2 Pope . . . Armagnac (During the years 1434–1435, efforts were made by the Emperor Sigismund and other potentates to effect a peace. The marriage proposal of the King to the Earl of Armagnac's daughter, however, was made eight or nine years later.)   4 sue petition   7 affect their motion incline toward their proposal.   13 immanity atrocious savagery   14 among . . . faith i.e., among fellow-Christians.   17 knit i.e., by ties of kinship   27 Tends that tends

EXETER [aside]
 What? Is my lord of Winchester installed
 And called unto a cardinal's degree?   29
 Then I perceive that will be verified
 Henry the Fifth did sometime prophesy: 31
 "If once he come to be a cardinal,
 He'll make his cap coequal with the crown."   33

KING
 My Lords Ambassadors, your several suits   34
 Have been considered and debated on.
 Your purpose is both good and reasonable,
 And therefore are we certainly resolved
 To draw conditions of a friendly peace,   38
 Which by my lord of Winchester we mean
 Shall be transported presently to France.   40

GLOUCESTER [to the Ambassadors from Armagnac]
 And for the proffer of my lord your master,   41
 I have informed His Highness so at large   42
 As, liking of the lady's virtuous gifts,
 Her beauty, and the value of her dower,
 He doth intend she shall be England's queen.

KING
 In argument and proof of which contract,
 Bear her this jewel, pledge of my affection.
         [A jewel is presented to the Ambassadors.]
 And so, my Lord Protector, see them guarded
 And safely brought to Dover, wherein shipped,   49
 Commit them to the fortune of the sea.
         Exeunt [all but Winchester and Legate].

WINCHESTER
 Stay, my Lord Legate. You shall first receive
 The sum of money which I promisèd
 Should be delivered to His Holiness
 For clothing me in these grave ornaments.   54

LEGATE
 I will attend upon Your Lordship's leisure.
         [He steps aside.]

WINCHESTER [aside]
 Now Winchester will not submit, I trow,
 Or be inferior to the proudest peer.
 Humphrey of Gloucester, thou shalt well perceive
 That neither in birth or for authority
 The bishop will be overborne by thee.
 I'll either make thee stoop and bend thy knee,
 Or sack this country with a mutiny.   Exeunt. 62

❧

[5.2]

Enter Charles, Burgundy, Alençon, Bastard,
Reignier, and Joan [la Pucelle].

CHARLES
 These news, my lords, may cheer our drooping spirits:

'Tis said the stout Parisians do revolt   2
And turn again unto the warlike French.

ALENÇON
 Then march to Paris, royal Charles of France,
 And keep not back your powers in dalliance.   5

PUCELLE
 Peace be amongst them, if they turn to us;
 Else, ruin combat with their palaces!   7

         Enter Scout.

SCOUT
 Success unto our valiant general,
 And happiness to his accomplices!   9

CHARLES
 What tidings send our scouts? I prithee, speak.

SCOUT
 The English army, that divided was
 Into two parties, is now conjoined in one
 And means to give you battle presently.

CHARLES
 Somewhat too sudden, sirs, the warning is,
 But we will presently provide for them.

BURGUNDY
 I trust the ghost of Talbot is not there.
 Now he is gone, my lord, you need not fear.

PUCELLE
 Of all base passions, fear is most accurst.
 Command the conquest, Charles, it shall be thine,
 Let Henry fret and all the world repine.

CHARLES
 Then on, my lords, and France be fortunate!
         Exeunt.

❧

[5.3]

Alarum. Excursions. Enter Joan la Pucelle.

PUCELLE
 The Regent conquers, and the Frenchmen fly.   1
 Now help, ye charming spells and periapts,   2
 And ye choice spirits that admonish me   3
 And give me signs of future accidents.   Thunder.   4
 You speedy helpers, that are substitutes   5
 Under the lordly monarch of the north,   6
 Appear and aid me in this enterprise!

         Enter Fiends.

 This speedy and quick appearance argues proof   8
 Of your accustomed diligence to me.
 Now, ye familiar spirits, that are culled
 Out of the powerful regions under earth,

29 called . . . degree (Winchester's being newly made a cardinal is inconsistent with 1.3.19 and 36.)   31 sometime at one time   33 cap i.e., cardinal's skullcap   34 several various   38 draw draw up   40 presently immediately   41 for as for, regarding   42 at large in full   49 shipped embarked   54 grave ornaments solemn robes of ecclesiastical office.   62 mutiny rebellion.
5.2. Location: France. Fields before Angiers.

2 stout courageous   5 powers forces   7 Else . . . palaces! otherwise, let ruin destroy their palaces!   9 accomplices allies.
5.3. Location: Before Angiers still. The scene is continuous.
1 The Regent i.e., The Duke of York   2 charming working by charms. periapts amulets   3 admonish forewarn   4 accidents occurrences.   5 substitutes deputies, agents   6 north (Evil spirits were frequently associated with the North.)   8 argues proof gives evidence

Help me this once, that France may get the field.   12
> *They walk, and speak not.*

Oh, hold me not with silence overlong!
Where I was wont to feed you with my blood,   14
I'll lop a member off and give it you
In earnest of a further benefit,   16
So you do condescend to help me now.   17
> *They hang their heads.*

No hope to have redress? My body shall
Pay recompense, if you will grant my suit.
> *They shake their heads.*

Cannot my body nor blood sacrifice
Entreat you to your wonted furtherance?   21
Then take my soul—my body, soul, and all—
Before that England give the French the foil.   23
> *They depart.*

See, they forsake me! Now the time is come
That France must vail her lofty-plumèd crest   25
And let her head fall into England's lap.
My ancient incantations are too weak,   27
And hell too strong for me to buckle with.   28
Now, France, thy glory droopeth to the dust.   *Exit.*

> *Excursions. Burgundy and York fight hand to hand. French fly. [Joan la Pucelle is taken.]*

YORK
Damsel of France, I think I have you fast.
Unchain your spirits now with spelling charms,   31
And try if they can gain your liberty.
A goodly prize, fit for the devil's grace!   33
See how the ugly witch doth bend her brows
As if, with Circe, she would change my shape!   35

PUCELLE
Changed to a worser shape thou canst not be.

YORK
Oh, Charles the Dauphin is a proper man!   37
No shape but his can please your dainty eye.   38

PUCELLE
A plaguing mischief light on Charles and thee!   39
And may ye both be suddenly surprised   40
By bloody hands in sleeping on your beds!

YORK
Fell banning hag! Enchantress, hold thy tongue!   42

PUCELLE
I prithee, give me leave to curse awhile.

YORK
Curse, miscreant, when thou com'st to the stake.   44
> *Exeunt.*

> *Alarum. Enter Suffolk, with Margaret in his hand.*

SUFFOLK
Be what thou wilt, thou art my prisoner.
> *Gazes on her.*

O fairest beauty, do not fear nor fly!
For I will touch thee but with reverent hands.
I kiss these fingers for eternal peace   48
And lay them gently on thy tender side.   49
Who art thou? Say, that I may honor thee.

MARGARET
Margaret my name, and daughter to a king,
The King of Naples, whosoe'er thou art.

SUFFOLK
An earl I am, and Suffolk am I called.
Be not offended, nature's miracle,
Thou art allotted to be ta'en by me.   55
So doth the swan her downy cygnets save,
Keeping them prisoner underneath her wings.
Yet if this servile usage once offend,   58
Go and be free again as Suffolk's friend.   *She is going.*   59
Oh, stay! [*Aside*] I have no power to let her pass;
My hand would free her, but my heart says no.
As plays the sun upon the glassy streams,   62
Twinkling another counterfeited beam,   63
So seems this gorgeous beauty to mine eyes.
Fain would I woo her, yet I dare not speak.
I'll call for pen and ink and write my mind.
Fie, de la Pole, disable not thyself!   67
Hast not a tongue? Is she not here?   68
Wilt thou be daunted at a woman's sight?   69
Ay, beauty's princely majesty is such
Confounds the tongue and makes the senses rough.   71

MARGARET
Say, Earl of Suffolk—if thy name be so—
What ransom must I pay before I pass?
For I perceive I am thy prisoner.

SUFFOLK [*aside*]
How canst thou tell she will deny thy suit
Before thou make a trial of her love?

MARGARET
Why speak'st thou not? What ransom must I pay?

SUFFOLK [*aside*]
She's beautiful, and therefore to be wooed;
She is a woman, therefore to be won.

---

12 get the field win the battle.   **14 Where** (1) Whereas (2) Where **16 earnest** advance payment.   **further benefit** (With sexual suggestion, as in *member*, line 15, and *Pay recompense*, line 19.)   **17 So** provided.   **condescend** agree   **21 wonted furtherance** customary aid. **23 Before that** before.   **foil** defeat.   **25 vail** lower.   **lofty-plumèd crest** plume proudly waving at the top of the helmet (in token of arrogant pride)   **27 ancient** former   **28 buckle with** do combat with. (Continuing the sexual suggestion of lines 15–19.)   **31 spirits** i.e., the demons—"familiars"—attending on Joan. (Compare with line 10.)   **spelling charms** charms that cast a spell   **33 the devil's grace** His Grace the devil. (Said sardonically.)   **35 with** like.   **Circe** sorceress celebrated for her power to change men into swine **37 proper** handsome. (Said sardonically.)   **38 dainty** fastidious **39 mischief** misfortune   **40 surprised** assailed, taken   **42 Fell banning** Malignant cursing

44.2–3 in his hand by the hand.   **48–9 I kiss . . . side** i.e., I kiss your hand (which I am holding) in token of eternal peace between us, and then I release your hand to hang by your side in token of giving you your freedom. (See line 61, where Suffolk speaks of wishing to free her hand, even though his heart tells him to keep her.)   **55 allotted** destined   **58 servile usage** being treated as a captive   **59 friend** (With suggestion of "lover.")   **62 As . . . streams** Just as the sun plays upon the glassy surface of a stream   **63 Twinkling** causing to twinkle.   **counterfeited** i.e., reflected   **67 disable** disparage   **68 here** i.e., here with me, ready to be wooed.   **69 a woman's sight** the sight of a woman.   **71 Confounds** that it confounds.   **rough** dull.

MARGARET
  Wilt thou accept of ransom, yea or no?
SUFFOLK [*aside*]
  Fond man, remember that thou hast a wife.   81
  Then how can Margaret be thy paramour?
MARGARET
  I were best to leave him, for he will not hear.
SUFFOLK [*aside*]
  There all is marred; there lies a cooling card.   84
MARGARET
  He talks at random. Sure the man is mad.
SUFFOLK [*aside*]
  And yet a dispensation may be had.   86
MARGARET
  And yet I would that you would answer me.
SUFFOLK [*aside*]
  I'll win this Lady Margaret. For whom?
  Why, for my king. Tush, that's a wooden thing!   89
MARGARET
  He talks of wood. It is some carpenter.
SUFFOLK [*aside*]
  Yet so my fancy may be satisfied,   91
  And peace establishèd between these realms.
  But there remains a scruple in that too;
  For though her father be the King of Naples,
  Duke of Anjou and Maine, yet is he poor,
  And our nobility will scorn the match.
MARGARET
  Hear ye, captain, are you not at leisure?
SUFFOLK [*aside*]
  It shall be so, disdain they ne'er so much.
  Henry is youthful and will quickly yield.—
  Madam, I have a secret to reveal.
MARGARET [*aside*]
  What though I be enthralled? He seems a knight,   101
  And will not any way dishonor me.
SUFFOLK
  Lady, vouchsafe to listen what I say.
MARGARET [*aside*]
  Perhaps I shall be rescued by the French,
  And then I need not crave his courtesy.
SUFFOLK
  Sweet madam, give me hearing in a cause—
MARGARET [*aside*]
  Tush, women have been captivate ere now.   107
SUFFOLK
  Lady, wherefore talk you so?
MARGARET
  I cry you mercy, 'tis but quid for quo.   109
SUFFOLK
  Say, gentle princess, would you not suppose
  Your bondage happy, to be made a queen?   111

MARGARET
  To be a queen in bondage is more vile
  Than is a slave in base servility,
  For princes should be free.
SUFFOLK   And so shall you,   114
  If happy England's royal king be free.   115
MARGARET
  Why, what concerns his freedom unto me?
SUFFOLK
  I'll undertake to make thee Henry's queen,
  To put a golden scepter in thy hand,
  And set a precious crown upon thy head,
  If thou wilt condescend to be my—
MARGARET   What?   120
SUFFOLK   His love.
MARGARET
  I am unworthy to be Henry's wife.
SUFFOLK
  No, gentle madam. I unworthy am
  To woo so fair a dame to be his wife
  And have no portion in the choice myself.   125
  How say you, madam, are ye so content?
MARGARET
  An if my father please, I am content.   127
SUFFOLK
  Then call our captains and our colors forth.   128
  And, madam, at your father's castle walls
  We'll crave a parley, to confer with him.   130

          Sound [a parley]. Enter Reignier on the walls.

  See, Reignier, see thy daughter prisoner!
REIGNIER
  To whom?
SUFFOLK   To me.
REIGNIER   Suffolk, what remedy?
  I am a soldier, and unapt to weep
  Or to exclaim on fortune's fickleness.   134
SUFFOLK
  Yes, there is remedy enough, my lord.
  Consent, and for thy honor give consent,   136
  Thy daughter shall be wedded to my king,
  Whom I with pain have wooed and won thereto;   138
  And this her easy-held imprisonment   139
  Hath gained thy daughter princely liberty.
REIGNIER
  Speaks Suffolk as he thinks?
SUFFOLK   Fair Margaret knows
  That Suffolk doth not flatter, face, or feign.   142

81 Fond Foolish   **84 cooling card** something that cools one's ardor or dashes one's hopes. (A metaphor from card playing.)   **86 dispensation** papal permission (to divorce a wife)   **89 wooden** stupid (i.e., either King Henry, or Suffolk's plan)   **91 fancy** desire in love   **101 enthralled** captured.   **107 captivate** taken captive   **109 I . . . quo** i.e., I beg your pardon, my speaking in asides was only tit for tat in response to your having done so (in lines 78–99).   **111 to be** if you were to be

114 princes i.e., men or women of royal birth   **115 happy** fortunate   **120 condescend** consent   **125 And have . . . myself** (Suffolk seems to say to Margaret that he is only the unworthy agent, not deserving to have any other role, but his double meaning points to his having a "piece" out of this for himself.)   **choice** (1) choosing (2) person chosen   **127 An if** If   **128 Then . . . forth** (Suffolk probably calls offstage to attendants.)   **130.1 on the walls** (As in previous sieges, the "walls" of Angiers are here represented by the tiring-house facade, with Reignier appearing above, in the gallery backstage.)   **134 exclaim on** complain against   **136 Consent . . . consent** Consent, and do so for the sake of your honor   **138 Whom** i.e., Margaret   **139 easy-held** easily endured   **142 face** show a false face, deceive

REIGNIER
Upon thy princely warrant, I descend
To give thee answer of thy just demand. 143

[Exit from the walls.]

SUFFOLK
And here I will expect thy coming. 145

Trumpets sound. Enter Reignier [below].

REIGNIER
Welcome, brave earl, into our territories.
Command in Anjou what Your Honor pleases.

SUFFOLK
Thanks, Reignier, happy for so sweet a child, 148
Fit to be made companion with a king.
What answer makes Your Grace unto my suit?

REIGNIER
Since thou dost deign to woo her little worth 151
To be the princely bride of such a lord,
Upon condition I may quietly
Enjoy mine own, the country Maine and Anjou, 154
Free from oppression or the stroke of war,
My daughter shall be Henry's, if he please.

SUFFOLK
That is her ransom. I deliver her, 157
And those two counties I will undertake
Your Grace shall well and quietly enjoy.

REIGNIER
And I again, in Henry's royal name, 160
As deputy unto that gracious king, 161
Give thee her hand for sign of plighted faith.

SUFFOLK
Reignier of France, I give thee kingly thanks,
Because this is in traffic of a king. 164
[Aside] And yet methinks I could be well content
To be mine own attorney in this case.—
I'll over then to England with this news
And make this marriage to be solemnized.
So farewell, Reignier. Set this diamond safe
In golden palaces, as it becomes. 170

REIGNIER
I do embrace thee, as I would embrace
The Christian prince, King Henry, were he here.

[He embraces Suffolk.]

MARGARET
Farewell, my lord. Good wishes, praise, and prayers
Shall Suffolk ever have of Margaret. She is going.

SUFFOLK
Farewell, sweet madam. But hark you, Margaret—
No princely commendations to my king?

MARGARET
Such commendations as becomes a maid,
A virgin, and his servant, say to him.

SUFFOLK
Words sweetly placed and modestly directed. 179
But, madam, I must trouble you again—
No loving token to His Majesty?

MARGARET
Yes, my good lord: a pure unspotted heart,
Never yet taint with love, I send the King. 183

SUFFOLK   And this withal. Kiss her. 184

MARGARET
That for thyself. I will not so presume
To send such peevish tokens to a king. 186

[Exeunt Reignier and Margaret.]

SUFFOLK
Oh, wert thou for myself! But, Suffolk, stay.
Thou mayest not wander in that labyrinth; 188
There Minotaurs and ugly treasons lurk.
Solicit Henry with her wondrous praise; 190
Bethink thee on her virtues that surmount,
And natural graces that extinguish art; 192
Repeat their semblance often on the seas, 193
That, when thou com'st to kneel at Henry's feet,
Thou mayest bereave him of his wits with wonder.

Exit.

❖

[5.4]

Enter York, Warwick, Shepherd, [and] Pucelle
[guarded].

YORK
Bring forth that sorceress condemned to burn.

SHEPHERD
Ah, Joan, this kills thy father's heart outright!
Have I sought every country far and near, 3
And, now it is my chance to find thee out, 4
Must I behold thy timeless cruel death? 5
Ah, Joan, sweet daughter Joan, I'll die with thee!

PUCELLE
Decrepit miser, base ignoble wretch! 7
I am descended of a gentler blood. 8
Thou art no father nor no friend of mine. 9

SHEPHERD
Out, out! My lords, an please you, 'tis not so. 10
I did beget her, all the parish knows.
Her mother liveth yet, can testify
She was the first fruit of my bach'lorship. 13

WARWICK [to Joan]
Graceless, wilt thou deny thy parentage?

143 warrant assurance   145 expect await   148 happy for fortunate in having   151 her little worth her, little worthy as she is   154 country i.e., district or region including   157 deliver free. (Her *ransom* having been agreed upon, Suffolk releases her.)   160 again in return. (In return for promises made in the name of King Henry, Reignier gives back his daughter into the hands of Suffolk, who released her to her father three lines earlier.)   161 As deputy i.e., to you, Suffolk, as deputy   164 traffic business   170 as it becomes as befits such a jewel.

179 placed arranged   183 taint tainted   184 withal in addition.
186 peevish trivial   188 labyrinth a structure built by Daedalus consisting of intricate passageways where the Minotaur—a monster born from the union of the Cretan king's wife with a bull—was confined   190 her wondrous praise praise of her wondrous beauty   192 extinguish eclipse   193 Repeat their semblance rehearse mentally the image of her virtues
5.4. Location: France. Camp of the Duke of York in Anjou.
3 country district   4 And . . . out and, now that fortune has enabled me to find you   5 timeless premature, untimely   7 miser wretch   8 gentler more noble   9 friend kinsman   10 an please you if you please   13 was . . . bach'lorship i.e., was my firstborn. (With a risible suggestion that Joan was born out of wedlock.)

YORK
This argues what her kind of life hath been,
Wicked and vile; and so her death concludes.   16

SHEPHERD
Fie, Joan, that thou wilt be so obstacle!   17
God knows thou art a collop of my flesh,   18
And for thy sake have I shed many a tear.
Deny me not, I prithee, gentle Joan.

PUCELLE
Peasant, avaunt!—You have suborned this man   21
Of purpose to obscure my noble birth.   22

SHEPHERD
'Tis true, I gave a noble to the priest   23
The morn that I was wedded to her mother.
Kneel down and take my blessing, good my girl.
Wilt thou not stoop? Now cursèd be the time
Of thy nativity! I would the milk
Thy mother gave thee when thou suckèd'st her breast
Had been a little ratsbane for thy sake!   29
Or else, when thou didst keep my lambs afield,   30
I wish some ravenous wolf had eaten thee!
Dost thou deny thy father, cursèd drab?—   32
Oh, burn her, burn her! Hanging is too good.   *Exit.*

YORK [*to guards*]
Take her away, for she hath lived too long,
To fill the world with vicious qualities.

PUCELLE
First, let me tell you whom you have condemned:
Not me begotten of a shepherd swain,   37
But issued from the progeny of kings,
Virtuous and holy, chosen from above
By inspiration of celestial grace
To work exceeding miracles on earth.   41
I never had to do with wicked spirits.
But you, that are polluted with your lusts,
Stained with the guiltless blood of innocents,
Corrupt and tainted with a thousand vices—
Because you want the grace that others have,   46
You judge it straight a thing impossible   47
To compass wonders but by help of devils.   48
No, misconceivèd! Joan of Arc hath been   49
A virgin from her tender infancy,
Chaste and immaculate in very thought,
Whose maiden blood, thus rigorously effused,   52
Will cry for vengeance at the gates of heaven.

YORK
Ay, ay.—Away with her to execution.

WARWICK
And hark ye, sirs: because she is a maid,
Spare for no faggots. Let there be enough.

Place barrels of pitch upon the fatal stake,   57
That so her torture may be shortenèd.

PUCELLE
Will nothing turn your unrelenting hearts?
Then, Joan, discover thine infirmity,   60
That warranteth by law to be thy privilege: 61
I am with child, ye bloody homicides.
Murder not then the fruit within my womb,
Although ye hale me to a violent death.

YORK
Now heaven forfend! The holy maid with child?   65

WARWICK
The greatest miracle that e'er ye wrought.
Is all your strict preciseness come to this?   67

YORK
She and the Dauphin have been juggling.   68
I did imagine what would be her refuge.

WARWICK
Well, go to. We'll have no bastards live,   70
Especially since Charles must father it.   71

PUCELLE
You are deceived. My child is none of his.
It was Alençon that enjoyed my love.

YORK
Alençon, that notorious Machiavel?   74
It dies an if it had a thousand lives.

PUCELLE
Oh, give me leave, I have deluded you.
'Twas neither Charles nor yet the Duke I named,
But Reignier, King of Naples, that prevailed.

WARWICK
A married man! That's most intolerable.

YORK
Why, here's a girl! I think she knows not well,
There were so many, whom she may accuse.

WARWICK
It's sign she hath been liberal and free.   82

YORK
And yet, forsooth, she is a virgin pure!—
Strumpet, thy words condemn thy brat and thee.
Use no entreaty, for it is in vain.

PUCELLE
Then lead me hence; with whom I leave my curse.
May never glorious sun reflex his beams   87
Upon the country where you make abode,
But darkness and the gloomy shade of death
Environ you, till mischief and despair   90

---

16 concludes (1) confirms (2) ends.   **17 obstacle** (For "obstinate.")
18 collop slice   **21 avaunt!** begone!   **suborned this man** induced this
man to give perjured testimony   **22 Of** on   **23 noble** coin worth six
shillings eight pence   **29 ratsbane** rat poison   **30 keep** tend   **32 drab**
whore.   **37 me** (An error for "one"? In the early modern handwriting
known as secretary hand, used in legal documents, the words would
look much alike.)   **41 exceeding** exceptional   **46 want** lack
47 straight straightaway, at once   **48 compass** encompass, bring about
49 misconceivèd you who have a wrong idea. (The word has an ironic
application to Joan.)   **52 rigorously effused** mercilessly shed

57 pitch (Pitch would produce hot flames and also heavy smoke,
asphyxiating the person being burned and thereby shortening the suffering. Warwick may be speaking sardonically, however: "We're going
to give her a nice quick death.")   **60 discover** reveal   **61 warranteth**
guarantees.   **privilege** i.e., to be spared until the birth of her supposed
child   **65 forfend** forbid. (Said sardonically.)   **67 preciseness** propriety, modesty   **68 juggling** playing conjuring tricks. (With sexual suggestion.)   **70 go to** (An expression of impatience.)   **71 must father it** is
evidently the father.   **74 Machiavel** (In the popular Elizabethan conception, Niccolò Machiavelli, Italian political philosopher, symbolized
political immorality and ruthless ambition.)   **82 liberal** unrestrained,
licentious. (With a mocking glance at a more innocent meaning, "generous.")   **87 reflex** reflect, shed   **90 mischief** misfortune

Drive you to break your necks or hang yourselves!
                                        Exit [guarded].

*Enter [Winchester, now] Cardinal [Beaufort,
with letters, attended].*

YORK *[to Joan as she exits]*
Break thou in pieces and consume to ashes,   92
Thou foul accursèd minister of hell!   93
CARDINAL
Lord Regent, I do greet Your Excellence
With letters of commission from the King.
For know, my lords, the states of Christendom,
Moved with remorse of these outrageous broils,   97
Have earnestly implored a general peace
Betwixt our nation and the aspiring French;
And here at hand the Dauphin and his train   100
Approacheth, to confer about some matter.
YORK
Is all our travail turned to this effect?   102
After the slaughter of so many peers,
So many captains, gentlemen, and soldiers,
That in this quarrel have been overthrown
And sold their bodies for their country's benefit,
Shall we at last conclude effeminate peace?
Have we not lost most part of all the towns,
By treason, falsehood, and by treachery,
Our great progenitors had conquerèd?
Oh, Warwick, Warwick! I foresee with grief
The utter loss of all the realm of France.
WARWICK
Be patient, York. If we concluded a peace,
It shall be with such strict and severe covenants   114
As little shall the Frenchmen gain thereby.   115

Enter Charles, Alençon, Bastard, Reignier.

CHARLES
Since, lords of England, it is thus agreed
That peaceful truce shall be proclaimed in France,
We come to be informèd by yourselves
What the conditions of that league must be.
YORK
Speak, Winchester, for boiling choler chokes   120
The hollow passage of my poisoned voice
By sight of these our baleful enemies.   122
CARDINAL
Charles, and the rest, it is enacted thus:
That, in regard King Henry gives consent,   124
Of mere compassion and of lenity,   125
To ease your country of distressful war
And suffer you to breathe in fruitful peace,
You shall become true liegemen to his crown.   128
And, Charles, upon condition thou wilt swear
To pay him tribute and submit thyself,

Thou shalt be placed as viceroy under him,
And still enjoy thy regal dignity.
ALENÇON
Must he be then as shadow of himself?
Adorn his temples with a coronet,
And yet in substance and authority   135
Retain but privilege of a private man?
This proffer is absurd and reasonless.
CHARLES
'Tis known already that I am possessed
With more than half the Gallian territories   139
And therein reverenced for their lawful king.
Shall I, for lucre of the rest unvanquished,   141
Detract so much from that prerogative   142
As to be called but viceroy of the whole?   143
No, Lord Ambassador, I'll rather keep
That which I have than, coveting for more,
Be cast from possibility of all.   146
YORK
Insulting Charles, hast thou by secret means
Used intercession to obtain a league,
And, now the matter grows to compromise,   149
Stand'st thou aloof upon comparison?   150
Either accept the title thou usurp'st,
Of benefit proceeding from our king   152
And not of any challenge of desert,   153
Or we will plague thee with incessant wars.
REIGNIER *[aside to Charles]*
My lord, you do not well in obstinacy
To cavil in the course of this contract.   156
If once it be neglected, ten to one
We shall not find like opportunity.
ALENÇON *[aside to Charles]*
To say the truth, it is your policy   159
To save your subjects from such massacre
And ruthless slaughters as are daily seen
By our proceeding in hostility;
And therefore take this compact of a truce,
Although you break it when your pleasure serves.
WARWICK
How say'st thou, Charles? Shall our condition stand? 165
CHARLES   It shall;
Only reserved, you claim no interest   167
In any of our towns of garrison.   168
YORK
Then swear allegiance to His Majesty,
As thou art knight, never to disobey
Nor be rebellious to the crown of England,
Thou nor thy nobles, to the crown of England.
        [Charles and his nobles pledge their allegiance.]

92–3 **Break . . . hell!** (Winchester's entrance in time to hear these lines
seemingly directed at Joan provides added irony, since Winchester is
also a villain.)   97 **remorse** of pity for   100 **train** entourage
102 **travail** labor   114 **convenants** articles of agreement   115 **As** that
120 **choler** i.e., anger   122 **By** at the   124 **in regard** inasmuch as
125 **Of mere** out of pure   128 **true liegemen** loyal subjects

135 **in . . . authority** in actual power   139 **Gallian** French   141 **for
lucre of** in order to gain   142 **Detract . . . prerogative** i.e., yield up
my right to be called king in the territories I already possess   143 **As**
so as, in order to   146 **cast** excluded   149 **grows to compromise**
moves toward a peaceful settlement   150 **upon comparison** i.e.,
quibbling about the proposed articles.   152 **Of benefit** as a feudal
bestowal   153 **challenge of desert** claim of inherent right   156 **cavil
. . . contract** raise frivolous or fault-finding objections during this
period of negotiation.   159 **policy** politic course   165 **condition**
treaty, contract   167 **Only reserved** with this single proviso, that
168 **towns of garrison** fortified towns.

So, now dismiss your army when ye please.
Hang up your ensigns, let your drums be still,
For here we entertain a solemn peace.   *Exeunt.* 175

❧

5.[5]

Enter Suffolk in conference with the King,
Gloucester, and Exeter.

KING
Your wondrous rare description, noble earl,
Of beauteous Margaret hath astonished me.
Her virtues gracèd with external gifts
Do breed love's settled passions in my heart; 4
And like as rigor of tempestuous gusts 5
Provokes the mightiest hulk against the tide, 6
So am I driven by breath of her renown 7
Either to suffer shipwreck or arrive
Where I may have fruition of her love.

SUFFOLK
Tush, my good lord, this superficial tale
Is but a preface of her worthy praise. 11
The chief perfections of that lovely dame,
Had I sufficient skill to utter them,
Would make a volume of enticing lines
Able to ravish any dull conceit; 15
And, which is more, she is not so divine,
So full replete with choice of all delights, 17
But with as humble lowliness of mind
She is content to be at your command—
Command, I mean, of virtuous chaste intents,
To love and honor Henry as her lord.

KING
And otherwise will Henry ne'er presume.
Therefore, my Lord Protector, give consent
That Margaret may be England's royal queen.

GLOUCESTER
So should I give consent to flatter sin. 25
You know, my lord, Your Highness is betrothed
Unto another lady of esteem. 27
How shall we then dispense with that contract
And not deface your honor with reproach?

SUFFOLK
As doth a ruler with unlawful oaths,
Or one that, at a triumph having vowed 31
To try his strength, forsaketh yet the lists 32
By reason of his adversary's odds.
A poor earl's daughter is unequal odds,
And therefore may be broke without offense. 35

GLOUCESTER
Why, what, I pray, is Margaret more than that?
Her father is no better than an earl,
Although in glorious titles he excel.

SUFFOLK
Yes, my lord, her father is a king,
The King of Naples and Jerusalem,
And of such great authority in France
As his alliance will confirm our peace 42
And keep the Frenchmen in allegiance.

GLOUCESTER
And so the Earl of Armagnac may do,
Because he is near kinsman unto Charles.

EXETER
Besides, his wealth doth warrant a liberal dower, 46
Where Reignier sooner will receive than give. 47

SUFFOLK
A dower, my lords? Disgrace not so your king
That he should be so abject, base, and poor
To choose for wealth and not for perfect love.
Henry is able to enrich his queen,
And not to seek a queen to make him rich.
So worthless peasants bargain for their wives, 53
As marketmen for oxen, sheep, or horse.
Marriage is a matter of more worth
Than to be dealt in by attorneyship. 56
Not whom we will, but whom His Grace affects, 57
Must be companion of his nuptial bed.
And therefore, lords, since he affects her most,
That most of all these reasons bindeth us
In our opinions she should be preferred.
For what is wedlock forcèd but a hell,
An age of discord and continual strife?
Whereas the contrary bringeth bliss,
And is a pattern of celestial peace.
Whom should we match with Henry, being a king,
But Margaret, that is daughter to a king?
Her peerless feature, joinèd with her birth, 68
Approves her fit for none but for a king.
Her valiant courage and undaunted spirit,
More than in women commonly is seen,
Will answer our hope in issue of a king; 72
For Henry, son unto a conqueror,
Is likely to beget more conquerors,
If with a lady of so high resolve
As is fair Margaret he be linked in love.
Then yield, my lords, and here conclude with me
That Margaret shall be queen, and none but she.

KING
Whether it be through force of your report,
My noble lord of Suffolk, or for that 80
My tender youth was never yet attaint 81
With any passion of inflaming love,
I cannot tell; but this I am assured,

---

175 **entertain** accept, embrace
5.5. Location: London. The royal court.
4 **settled** fixed, rooted   5 **like as rigor** just as the severity
6 **Provokes . . . tide** drives the mightiest vessel through the seas
7 **breath** (1) report (2) wind in the sails   11 **her worthy praise** the
praise she is truly worth.   15 **conceit** imagination   17 **full** fully
25 **flatter** countenance, excuse   27 **another lady** i.e., the Earl of
Armagnac's daughter. (See 5.1.17 ff.)   31 **triumph** tournament
32 **lists** place of combat in a tournament   35 **may be broke** i.e., the
contract with her may be broken

42 **As** that.   **confirm** strengthen   46 **warrant** guarantee   47 **Where**
whereas   53 **So** Thus do   56 **attorneyship** haggling proxies.
57 **affects** desires   63 **age** lifetime   68 **feature** beauty, figure
72 **Will . . . king** i.e., will fulfill our hopes of royal progeny   80 **for**
that because   81 **attaint** infected

I feel such sharp dissension in my breast,
Such fierce alarums both of hope and fear,
As I am sick with working of my thoughts.
Take therefore shipping; post, my lord, to France.   87
Agree to any covenants, and procure   88
That Lady Margaret do vouchsafe to come
To cross the seas to England and be crowned
King Henry's faithful and anointed queen.
For your expenses and sufficient charge,   92
Among the people gather up a tenth.   93
Begone, I say, for till you do return
I rest perplexèd with a thousand cares.   95
And you, good uncle, banish all offense.   96
If you do censure me by what you were,   97
Not what you are, I know it will excuse   98

---

87 post hasten   **88 procure** bring it about   **92 charge** money
93 gather up a tenth levy a tax of ten percent of the produce of
lands and industry.   **95 rest** remain   **96 offense** feeling of resentment and disapproval   **97–8 censure . . . are** i.e., judge me (in my
lovesickness) in comparison to your own youthful ways, not to your
present wisdom

This sudden execution of my will.
And so, conduct me where, from company,   100
I may revolve and ruminate my grief.   101
                    Exit [with Exeter].
GLOUCESTER
Ay, grief, I fear me, both at first and last.   102
                    Exit Gloucester.
SUFFOLK
Thus Suffolk hath prevailed; and thus he goes,
As did the youthful Paris once to Greece,   104
With hope to find the like event in love,   105
But prosper better than the Trojan did.
Margaret shall now be Queen and rule the King;
But I will rule both her, the King, and realm.   *Exit.*

---

100 from company alone   **101 grief** love melancholy.   **102 grief**
remorse   **104 Paris** Trojan prince whose abduction of Helen of Sparta
instigated the Trojan war   **105 the like event** a similar outcome

The Second Part
of King Henry the Sixth

*H*enry VI, *Part Two* is at once a continuation of the historical narrative begun in *1 Henry VI* (based indeed on the same chronicle sources) and an independent play that must have been staged on a separate occasion in Shakespeare's theater. As the second play of a four-play series, it is openended, commencing in a state of political flux and concluding with a civil war in its early phase. Providential consolation seems far away, even if there are signs of divine wrath at work in human affairs. At the same time, this play has its own integrity of theme and dramatic form.

2 Henry VI picks up where *1 Henry VI* ends (in the year 1445) and continues down to the very eve of actual civil war at the Battle of St. Albans (1455). The major events portrayed are the downfall of Humphrey, Duke of Gloucester, and the angry stirrings of the commoners, leading finally to Jack Cade's rebellion. Popular agitation brings about the death of the Duke of Suffolk, thereby claiming the life of one of those most cynically responsible for England's troubles. The villainous Cardinal of Winchester also dies a horrible and edifying death, suggesting that divine retribution is beginning to reveal its inexorable force. Yet throughout this declining action we witness in countermovement the ominous rise of Richard Plantagenet, Duke of York.

Richard's strategy, like that of his son and namesake in *Richard III*, is to exploit antagonisms at the English court, turning feuding nobles against one another until his potential rivals for power have destroyed themselves. In particular, he takes advantage of the animosity between the new Queen Margaret and Duke Humphrey. Margaret, daughter of a foreign prince, is a consort in the autocratic European style. She haughtily insists on the privileges of her exalted rank and spurns those who govern in the name of justice. "Is this the guise, / Is this the fashion in the court of England?" she incredulously inquires of Suffolk, her lover and political ally (1.3.42–3). Suffolk is an apt mate for Margaret, since he, too,

oppresses the commoners. A petition "against the Duke of Suffolk, for enclosing the commons of Melford" (lines 23–4) is one of many heartfelt grievances brought to the attention of the throne by the common people. Margaret naturally resents the moderate and fair-minded counsel of Duke Humphrey, who urges King Henry to remedy the distress of the commoners.

Richard of York has no inherent admiration for Suffolk and Margaret but cynically backs them as a way of destroying the good Duke of Gloucester. He advises his partners Salisbury and Warwick, "Wink at the Duke of Suffolk's insolence, / At Beaufort's pride, at Somerset's ambition, / At Buckingham, and all the crew of them, / Till they have snared the shepherd of the flock, / That virtuous prince, the good Duke Humphrey" (2.2.70–4). And Humphrey has, in fact, a fatal weakness through which he can be pulled down: the ambition of his wife, Eleanor. Intent on being first lady of the land, Eleanor comes into inevitable conflict with the remorseless Queen Margaret. Winchester and Suffolk, knowing Eleanor's self-blinding pride, find it pathetically easy to plant spies in her household who will encourage her penchant for witchcraft. Humphrey is never contaminated personally by his wife's pride but is doomed nonetheless. King Henry knows of Humphrey's goodness but cannot save him. This fall of a courageous moderate, highlighted in the title of the 1594 Quarto text ("with the death of the good Duke Humphrey"), singles Humphrey out as the most prominent victim of the second play, like Talbot in Part One. He is cut down by an insincere and temporary alliance of extremists from both sides: those such as Margaret and Suffolk who cling to despotic privilege and those such as York who wish to stir up the commoners for their own ulterior purposes. In times of confrontation, the middle position is inherently vulnerable, and its destruction leads to escalating polarization.

As York both foresees and desires, the commoners are indeed unruly when deprived of Humphrey's moderating leadership. Shakespeare has already shown that they tend to ape the quarrels of their elders (as in the ludicrous duel between Horner the Armorer and his man Peter Thump) and are superstitiously gullible (as in the episode of Simpcox the fraudulent blind man). Now, no longer able to petition through channels, their voice becomes importunate. "The commons, like an angry hive of bees / That want their leader, scatter up and down / And care not who they sting in his revenge" (3.2.125–7). At first, their grievances are plausible and their wrath directed at guilty objects. They suspect rightly that their hero, Humphrey, has been destroyed by Suffolk and the Cardinal, and they demand Suffolk's banishment. The request is laudably motivated by a desire to act in behalf of king and country, and does prompt the weak King Henry to remove Suffolk from office as he should have done long ago, but their insistence appears to establish a precedent for activism by the commons that has unsettling implications throughout Shakespeare's plays. Unless Suffolk is banished, they warn, they will take him by force from the palace. Poor King Henry, lamenting the lost conciliatory authority of Humphrey, aptly points up the central issue of royal prerogative: "And had I not been cited so by them, / Yet did I purpose as they do entreat" (3.2.281–2). In the perspective of this play, Henry's yielding to popular force is both a comment on his own incapacity as ruler and a worrisome indication of what is to come. The next step, indeed, is that Suffolk is captured and executed by mariners taking justice into their own hands. Even though they are privateers and kidnappers, their Lieutenant speaks of them as the avengers of Duke Humphrey's death (4.1.70–102). However much Suffolk deserves to be condemned, his summary execution bypasses the norms of a trial before a lawfully constituted authority. Servant has turned against master; the commoners have begun to feel their own power.

The popular rebellion itself, Cade's uprising, is a travesty of popular longings for social justice and suggests that any movement of this sort is bound to end in absurdity. Shakespeare, for all his appreciative depiction of individual commoners, is wary of the consequences of mob rule. Although Cade's rebellion did, in the view of most historians, arise from deplorable economic conditions of poverty and oppression, Shakespeare ignores any circumstances that might give sympathy to the plight of those who strike back at their masters. To the contrary, he accentuates the dangers of popular agitation by unhistorically bringing together the worst excesses of the Cade rebellion itself (1450) and the famous Peasants' Revolt of 1381. The Cade scenes abound in degrading comedy in the shape of lower-class self-assertion. We laugh at the contrast between Cade's professed Utopian notions of abundance for all and his petty ambition to be king. He kills those who refer to him as Jack Cade rather than by his pretended title of Lord Mortimer. His movement is fiercely anti-intellectual. Yet the sour joke does not indict the commoners alone. Cade's insolent pretensions and his claptrap genealogical claims are an exaggerated but recognizable parody of aristocratic behavior. More important, we remember that Cade was whetted on to his rebellion by the demagogic York. That schemer has "seduced" Cade to make commotion while York himself raises a huge personal army and advances his fortunes in Ireland. "This devil here shall be my substitute" (3.1.371). The commoners can indeed prove irresponsible when goaded, but, throughout *2 Henry VI*, feuding aristocrats must bear the chief blame for causing popular discontent.

In view of the need for some kind of coherence amid this universal decline into anarchy and strife, prophecy assumes a structural importance in *2 Henry VI* that is to be accentuated in later plays of the tetralogy. As in ancient Greek drama, prophecies are always eventually fulfilled. They reveal divine necessity but in such ambiguous and riddling language that the persons affected by the prophecy do not comprehend the true nature of the utterance until the event itself is upon them. In this play, for example, the spirit conjured to appear before the Duchess of Gloucester (1.4) predicts that Suffolk will die "by water" and that Somerset should "shun castles." What sorts of warnings are these? When his time comes, Suffolk dies at the hands of a man named Walter (pronounced "water," though Suffolk tries desperately to insist on the French "Gualtier"), whereas Somerset dies at the Castle Inn near St. Albans, at the play's end. Through such paltry quibbles, as in *Macbeth*, great men are misled into a false security. No less riddling is the prophecy about King Henry and his political antagonist: "The duke yet lives that Henry shall depose, / But him outlive, and die a violent death" (1.4.31–2). The first phrase of this oracle is perfectly ambiguous: it can mean that a still living duke will depose Henry or that Henry will depose this duke. Both interpretations turn out to be valid; during the wars of Lancaster and York shown in *3 Henry VI*, King Henry and his Yorkist opponent will, by turns, take the throne from each other. In such prophecy, there is already the concept of an eye for an eye, a Lancastrian for a Yorkist, through which Providence will finally impose its penalty on a rebellious people. Prophecy then serves not to allow human beings to escape their destiny, which is unavoidable, but to give them the opportunity to perceive at last the pattern of divine justice. The audience realizes that prophecy is a divine warning too often unheeded by foolish human beings, and acknowledges the necessity of a fulfillment that is tragic and dispiriting but also comforting to the extent that it shows the heavens to be just.

The role of prophecy is thus central in *2 Henry VI* in that it gives to the play a dominant pattern of prediction and eventual fulfillment. Yet the experience of *2 Henry VI* is one of turbulence. Events increasingly take on their own unstoppable momentum. Ceremonies and institutions employed to control the flux are not successful. Abstract ideas conflict with stern realities; the idea of kingship is appealed to as a rallying cry for authority and stability, but the fact of King Henry's inept leadership and the self-serving ambitions of his antagonists invite continual disarray. As a work of art, 2 *Henry VI* thus grapples with the problem of making something artistically coherent out of chaos. It does so, as does 3 *Henry VI*, by containing the instability within the recurring pattern of an eye for an eye.

Any sense of comfort is slow to arrive in this play. England's political and moral decline remains unchecked. The commoners' rebellion, cynically fomented by Richard, Duke of York, has established the precedent for further rebellion. Knowing his enemies to be weak and divided, Richard no longer conceals the ambition that has led him to accept an assignment in Ireland and thereby raise an army. His excuse for returning to England in arms, to rid King Henry of the hated adviser Somerset, is similarly shown to be no more than a pretext for declaring open civil war. His final justification for challenging King Henry, despite all the fine talk about genealogies, is

that Richard has the ambition and the raw power to carry out his plan. Henry's assertions of right are no less governed by expediency, for he privately confesses the weakness of his claim. The admirable example, shown late in this play, of a Kentish gentleman named Iden who is content to live peaceably on his estate, serves as a contrast to the dismaying ambitions that have infected not only Richard of York and his allies but also the remorseless Queen Margaret and those loyal to her. If, as A. P. Rossiter has cogently argued, 2 *Henry VI* is a "morality of state" in which forces of good and evil struggle for the soul of that beleaguered heroine, Respublica or the commonwealth, then the play must ultimately be viewed as one in which the forces of good do not fare well. To be sure, the haughty Suffolk meets his dire fate, though by a means that encourages further private revenge; Somerset falls as predicted at St. Albans; and Winchester suffers a death of edifying horror. Still, Richard of York and Queen Margaret, having profited from the victimization of the virtuous Duke Humphrey, are more powerful than ever, and Richard's son and namesake is only beginning to make his presence felt. Many scores remain to be settled at the close of 2 *Henry VI*.

The Second Part
of King Henry the Sixth

[Dramatis Personae

KING HENRY THE SIXTH
QUEEN MARGARET
Humphrey, DUKE OF GLOUCESTER, *King Henry's uncle, and Lord Protector*
DUCHESS OF GLOUCESTER, *Dame Eleanor Cobham*
CARDINAL BEAUFORT, *Bishop of Winchester, the King's great-uncle*
DUKE OF SOMERSET, *Edmund Beaufort, second Duke, younger brother of the first Duke of Somerset, John Beaufort*
DUKE OF SUFFOLK, *William de la Pole, earlier Marquess of Suffolk*
DUKE OF BUCKINGHAM
LORD CLIFFORD
YOUNG CLIFFORD, *his son*

RICHARD PLANTAGENET, DUKE OF YORK, *leader of the York faction*
EDWARD, *Earl of March, his eldest son*
RICHARD, *his son*
EARL OF SALISBURY,
EARL OF WARWICK, *his son,* } *supporters of the Yorkist claim*

LORD SCALES,
LORD SAYE,
SIR HUMPHREY STAFFORD,
WILLIAM STAFFORD, *his* BROTHER, } *supporters of King Henry against Cade's rebellion*

SIR JOHN STANLEY, *custodian of the Duchess of Gloucester*
SHERIFF *of London, custodian of the Duchess of Gloucester*

SIR JOHN HUME, *a priest*
JOHN SOUTHWELL, *a priest*
MARGERY JORDAN, *a witch*
ROGER BOLINGBROKE, *a conjurer*
A SPIRIT *named* ASNATH

SCENE: *England*]

Two or Three PETITIONERS
THOMAS HORNER, *the Armorer*
PETER THUMP, *the Armorer's man*
Three NEIGHBORS *of Horner*
Three Fellow PRENTICES *of Peter*

A TOWNSMAN *of St. Albans*
SIMPCOX *or Simon, supposedly restored to sight*
His WIFE
MAYOR *of St. Albans*
A BEADLE *of St. Albans*

LIEUTENANT *or Captain of a ship*
MASTER *of the ship*
WALTER WHITMORE
Two GENTLEMEN *prisoners*

JACK CADE, *rebel leader from Kent*
GEORGE BEVIS,
JOHN HOLLAND,
DICK, *the butcher,* } *followers of Cade*
SMITH, *the weaver,*
MICHAEL,

MESSENGERS
Two SERVINGMEN, *of Gloucester and York*
A HERALD
POST *or Messenger to Parliament*
Two MURDERERS *of Gloucester*
VAUX, *a messenger*
A CLERK *of Chartham*
ALEXANDER IDEN, *a gentleman of Kent*

Falconers, Townsmen and Aldermen, Commoners, Rebels, a Sawyer, Soldiers, Servingmen, Attendants, Guards, Officers, Matthew Gough

1.1

Flourish of trumpets, then hautboys. Enter [the]
King, Duke Humphrey [of Gloucester], Salisbury,
Warwick, and [Cardinal] Beaufort on the one side;
the Queen, Suffolk, York, Somerset, and Bucking-
ham on the other.

SUFFOLK
　As by Your High Imperial Majesty
　I had in charge at my depart for France,　　　　　　2
　As procurator to Your Excellence,　　　　　　　　3
　To marry Princess Margaret for Your Grace,
　So, in the famous ancient city Tours,
　In presence of the Kings of France and Sicil,　　　6
　The Dukes of Orleans, Calaber, Brittaine, and Alençon,　7
　Seven earls, twelve barons, and twenty reverend
　　bishops,
　I have performed my task and was espoused;　　　9
　And humbly now upon my bended knee, [*kneeling*]
　In sight of England and her lordly peers,
　Deliver up my title in the Queen
　To your most gracious hands, that are the substance
　Of that great shadow I did represent:　　　　　　14
　The happiest gift that ever marquess gave,　　　　15
　The fairest queen that ever king received.

KING
　Suffolk, arise. Welcome, Queen Margaret.
　　　　　　　　　　　　　　[*Suffolk rises.*]
　I can express no kinder sign of love　　　　　　　18
　Than this kind kiss. [*He kisses her.*] O Lord, that lends
　　me life,　　　　　　　　　　　　　　　　　19
　Lend me a heart replete with thankfulness!
　For thou hast given me in this beauteous face
　A world of earthly blessings to my soul,
　If sympathy of love unite our thoughts.

QUEEN
　Great King of England and my gracious lord,
　The mutual conference that my mind hath had　　25
　By day, by night, waking and in my dreams,
　In courtly company or at my beads,　　　　　　　27
　With you, mine alderliefest sovereign,　　　　　　28
　Makes me the bolder to salute my king
　With ruder terms, such as my wit affords　　　　　30
　And overjoy of heart doth minister.　　　　　　　31

KING
　Her sight did ravish, but her grace in speech,　　32
　Her words yclad with wisdom's majesty,　　　　　33

Makes me from wond'ring fall to weeping joys,　　　34
Such is the fullness of my heart's content.
Lords, with one cheerful voice welcome my love.

ALL (*kneeling*)
　Long live Queen Margaret, England's happiness!

QUEEN We thank you all.　　　*Flourish.* [*They all rise.*]

SUFFOLK
　My Lord Protector, so it please Your Grace,
　Here are the articles of contracted peace
　Between our sovereign and the French king Charles,
　For eighteen months concluded by consent.

GLOUCESTER (*reads*) "Inprimis, it is agreed between　43
　the French king Charles and William de la Pole, Mar-　44
　quess of Suffolk, ambassador for Henry, King of Eng-　45
　land, that the said Henry shall espouse the Lady Mar-
　garet, daughter unto Reignier, King of Naples, Sicilia,
　and Jerusalem, and crown her Queen of England ere
　the thirtieth of May next ensuing. Item, that the duchy　49
　of Anjou and the county of Maine shall be released and
　delivered to the King her father"—
　　　　　　　　　　　　　　[*He lets the paper fall.*]

KING
　Uncle, how now?

GLOUCESTER Pardon me, gracious lord.
　Some sudden qualm hath struck me at the heart
　And dimmed mine eyes, that I can read no further.　54

KING
　Uncle of Winchester, I pray, read on.　　　　　　55

CARDINAL [*reads*] "Item, it is further agreed between
　them that the duchies of Anjou and Maine shall be　57
　released and delivered over to the King her father, and
　she sent over of the King of England's own proper cost　59
　and charges, without having any dowry."

KING
　They please us well. Lord Marquess, kneel down.
　　　　　　　　　　　　　　[*Suffolk kneels.*]
　We here create thee the first Duke of Suffolk,
　And gird thee with the sword. [*Suffolk rises.*] Cousin of
　　York,　　　　　　　　　　　　　　　　　63
　We here discharge Your Grace from being regent
　I'th' parts of France, till term of eighteen months　65
　Be full expired. Thanks, uncle Winchester,
　Gloucester, York, Buckingham, Somerset,
　Salisbury, and Warwick;
　We thank you all for this great favor done
　In entertainment to my princely queen.　　　　　70
　Come, let us in, and with all speed provide
　To see her coronation be performed.　　　　　　　72
　　　　　　　　　　Exeunt King, Queen, and Suffolk.
　　　　　　　　　　　　　　Manent the rest.

1.1 Location: London. The Royal Court.
0.1 *Flourish* fanfare.　**hautboys** oboelike instruments.　**2 had in
charge** was commissioned.　**depart** departure　**3 procurator to**
agent, proxy for　**6 Sicil** Sicily. (Titularly ruled by Margaret's father,
the Duke of Anjou.)　**7 Calaber** Calabria, in southern Italy.
Brittaine Brittany　**9 I have . . . espoused** (The Duke of Suffolk has
acted as the proxy for King Henry VI in a ceremony of betrothal, at
Tours in 1444. Historically, he then acted as proxy in a marriage ceremony in 1445 at Nancy. Shakespeare conflates the two events.)
14 shadow image, i.e., of royalty　**15 happiest** most fortunate
18 kinder more natural　**19 kind** loving　**25 mutual conference** intimate communication (of the mind with itself)　**27 In . . . beads** in
courtly society or at my prayers (with the rosary)　**28 alderliefest**
most loved　**30 ruder** less polished.　**wit** intelligence　**31 minister**
supply.　**32 Her sight** The sight of her　**33 yclad** clad, clothed

34 wond'ring admiring　**43 Inprimis** Imprimis, in the first place
44–5 Marquess (William de la Pole was fourth Earl and then first
Duke of Suffolk. Edward Hall writes that he was elevated from earl
to marquess "when the marriage contract was agreed.")　**49 Item**
Also　**54 that** so that　**55 Uncle** (Actually, great-uncle.)　**57 duchies
. . . Maine** i.e., the duchy of Anjou and the county of Maine, as in
lines 49–50 above. (Perhaps the text is in error.)　**59 of** at. **proper** personal　**63 Cousin** (An appropriate title for the King to use toward
any peer, but York is also his distant cousin.)　**65 parts** territories.
term . . . months i.e., the period of the truce between England and
France　**70 entertainment to** gracious reception of　**72.2 Manent**
They remain onstage

GLOUCESTER

Brave peers of England, pillars of the state,
To you Duke Humphrey must unload his grief,
Your grief, the common grief of all the land.
What? Did my brother Henry spend his youth,   76
His valor, coin, and people in the wars?
Did he so often lodge in open field,
In winter's cold and summer's parching heat,
To conquer France, his true inheritance?
And did my brother Bedford toil his wits   81
To keep by policy what Henry got?   82
Have you yourselves, Somerset, Buckingham,
Brave York, Salisbury, and victorious Warwick,
Received deep scars in France and Normandy?
Or hath mine uncle Beaufort and myself,
With all the learnèd Council of the realm,
Studied so long, sat in the Council House
Early and late, debating to and fro
How France and Frenchmen might be kept in awe,   90
And had His Highness in his infancy
Crowned in Paris in despite of foes?
And shall these labors and these honors die?
Shall Henry's conquest, Bedford's vigilance,
Your deeds of war, and all our counsel die?
O peers of England, shameful is this league!
Fatal this marriage, canceling your fame,
Blotting your names from books of memory,   98
Razing the characters of your renown,   99
Defacing monuments of conquered France,
Undoing all, as all had never been!   101

CARDINAL

Nephew, what means this passionate discourse,
This peroration with such circumstance?   103
For France, 'tis ours; and we will keep it still.   104

GLOUCESTER

Ay, uncle, we will keep it if we can,
But now it is impossible we should.
Suffolk, the new-made duke that rules the roast,   107
Hath given the duchy of Anjou, and Maine,
Unto the poor King Reignier, whose large style   109
Agrees not with the leanness of his purse.

SALISBURY

Now, by the death of Him that died for all,
These counties were the keys of Normandy.
But wherefore weeps Warwick, my valiant son?

WARWICK

For grief that they are past recovery;
For, were there hope to conquer them again,
My sword should shed hot blood, mine eyes no tears.
Anjou and Maine? Myself did win them both!
Those provinces these arms of mine did conquer.
And are the cities that I got with wounds

Delivered up again with peaceful words?
Mort Dieu!   121

YORK

For Suffolk's duke, may he be suffocate,   122
That dims the honor of this warlike isle!
France should have torn and rent my very heart
Before I would have yielded to this league.   125
I never read but England's kings have had   126
Large sums of gold and dowries with their wives;
And our King Henry gives away his own
To match with her that brings no vantages.   129

GLOUCESTER

A proper jest, and never heard before,   130
That Suffolk should demand a whole fifteenth   131
For costs and charges in transporting her!
She should have stayed in France and starved in
    France
Before—

CARDINAL

My lord of Gloucester, now ye grow too hot.
It was the pleasure of my lord the King.

GLOUCESTER

My lord of Winchester, I know your mind.
'Tis not my speeches that you do mislike,
But 'tis my presence that doth trouble ye.
Rancor will out. Proud prelate, in thy face
I see thy fury. If I longer stay,
We shall begin our ancient bickerings.
Lordings, farewell; and say, when I am gone,   143
I prophesied France will be lost ere long.
                                    Exit Humphrey.

CARDINAL

So, there goes our Protector in a rage.
'Tis known to you he is mine enemy,
Nay, more, an enemy unto you all,
And no great friend, I fear me, to the King.
Consider, lords, he is the next of blood   149
And heir apparent to the English crown.
Had Henry got an empire by his marriage,
And all the wealthy kingdoms of the west,   152
There's reason he should be displeased at it.   153
Look to it, lords; let not his smoothing words   154
Bewitch your hearts. Be wise and circumspect.
What though the common people favor him,
Calling him "Humphrey, the good Duke of Gloucester,"
Clapping their hands and crying with loud voice,
"Jesu maintain Your Royal Excellence!"
With "God preserve the good Duke Humphrey!"

---

76 Henry i.e., Henry V **81 Bedford** (As portrayed in *1 Henry VI.*)
82 policy prudent management **90 awe** subjection **98 books of
memory** i.e., chronicles **99 Razing the characters** scraping away the
records, or *rasing*, "erasing" **101 as** as if **103 peroration** formal discourse. **circumstance** detailed examples. (The terms are from the art
of rhetoric.) **104 For** As for. **still** always. **107 rules the roast** i.e.,
domineers, like a master at table. (The Folio spelling, "rost," may also
suggest "roost," but the etymology is uncertain.) **109 large style**
lavish title

121 Mort Dieu! By God's (Christ's) death! **122 For** As for. **suffocate** (Punning on *Suffolk.*) **125 yielded** consented **126 I . . . but** I
have already read that **129 vantages** benefits, profits. **130 proper**
real, true **131 whole fifteenth** i.e., tax levy consisting of one-fif-
teenth of the produce of lands and industry. (Compare this with *1
Henry VI*, 5.5.92–3, where the figure is put at one-tenth.) **143 Lordings** My lords, gentlemen **149 next of blood** i.e., in line to succeed
to the throne, as Henry's eldest uncle. (Henry was as yet childless.)
152 the wealthy . . . west (Seemingly an anachronistic reference to
New World possessions.) **153 he** Humphrey of Gloucester (who, in
the Cardinal's biased view, would be distressed at seeing his hopes as
heir apparent to the throne interfered with by the birth of an heir to
King Henry) **154 Look to it** Beware. **smoothing** flattering

I fear me, lords, for all this flattering gloss,   161
He will be found a dangerous Protector.

BUCKINGHAM
Why should he, then, protect our sovereign,
He being of age to govern of himself?   164
Cousin of Somerset, join you with me,   165
And all together, with the Duke of Suffolk,
We'll quickly hoist Duke Humphrey from his seat.

CARDINAL
This weighty business will not brook delay;   168
I'll to the Duke of Suffolk presently.   *Exit Cardinal.* 169

SOMERSET
Cousin of Buckingham, though Humphrey's pride   170
And greatness of his place be grief to us,   171
Yet let us watch the haughty Cardinal.
His insolence is more intolerable
Than all the princes in the land beside.   174
If Gloucester be displaced, he'll be Protector.

BUCKINGHAM
Or thou or I, Somerset, will be Protector,   176
Despite Duke Humphrey or the Cardinal.
          Exeunt Buckingham and Somerset.

SALISBURY
Pride went before, Ambition follows him.   178
While these do labor for their own preferment,   179
Behooves it us to labor for the realm.
I never saw but Humphrey, Duke of Gloucester,   181
Did bear him like a noble gentleman.   182
Oft have I seen the haughty Cardinal,
More like a soldier than a man o'th' Church,
As stout and proud as he were lord of all,   185
Swear like a ruffian and demean himself   186
Unlike the ruler of a commonweal.
Warwick, my son, the comfort of my age,
Thy deeds, thy plainness, and thy housekeeping   189
Hath won thee greatest favor of the commons,
Excepting none but good Duke Humphrey.   191
And, brother York, thy acts in Ireland,   192
In bringing them to civil discipline,
Thy late exploits done in the heart of France,
When thou wert regent for our sovereign,
Have made thee feared and honored of the people.
Join we together for the public good,
In what we can, to bridle and suppress
The pride of Suffolk and the Cardinal,
With Somerset's and Buckingham's ambition;
And, as we may, cherish Duke Humphrey's deeds,   201
While they do tend the profit of the land.   202

WARWICK
So God help Warwick, as he loves the land
And common profit of his country!

YORK
And so says York—[*aside*] for he hath greatest cause. 205

SALISBURY
Then let's away and look unto the main.   206

WARWICK
Unto the main? O father, Maine is lost!
That Maine which by main force Warwick did win,
And would have kept so long as breath did last!
Main chance, father, you meant; but I meant Maine,
Which I will win from France, or else be slain.   211
          Exeunt Warwick and Salisbury. Manet York.

YORK
Anjou and Maine are given to the French;
Paris is lost; the state of Normandy
Stands on a tickle point now they are gone.   214
Suffolk concluded on the articles,   215
The peers agreed, and Henry was well pleased
To change two dukedoms for a duke's fair daughter.
I cannot blame them all. What is't to them?
'Tis thine they give away, and not their own.   219
Pirates may make cheap pennyworths of their
     pillage,   220
And purchase friends, and give to courtesans,   221
Still reveling like lords till all be gone;   222
Whileas the silly owner of the goods   223
Weeps over them, and wrings his hapless hands,   224
And shakes his head, and trembling stands aloof, 225
While all is shared and all is borne away,
Ready to starve and dare not touch his own.   227
So York must sit and fret and bite his tongue,
While his own lands are bargained for and sold.
Methinks the realms of England, France, and Ireland
Bear that proportion to my flesh and blood   231
As did the fatal brand Althaea burnt   232
Unto the Prince's heart of Calydon.   233
Anjou and Maine both given unto the French!
Cold news for me, for I had hope of France,   235
Even as I have of fertile England's soil.
A day will come when York shall claim his own;
And therefore I will take the Nevilles' parts   238
And make a show of love to proud Duke Humphrey,

---

205 **greatest cause** i.e., as hopeful claimant to the throne.   **206 unto the main** to the most important business. (With several puns in the following lines: [1] *Maine,* a French province lost in the treaty [2] *main force,* brute force [3] *Main chance,* a gambling term from the dice game called hazard.)   **211.1 *Manet*** He remains onstage   **214 Stands . . . point** is at risk   **215 concluded on the articles** negotiated the exact terms (of the marriage agreement)   **219 thine** (York speaks to himself.)   **220 make cheap pennyworths of** i.e., practically give away   **221 purchase friends** i.e., win friends through reckless generosity   **222 Still** continually   **223 Whileas** while.   **silly** wretched, helpless   **224 hapless** unfortunate   **225 stands aloof** stands to one side (unable to intervene)   **227 Ready . . . and** he being on the point of starvation and yet   **231 proportion** relationship   **232 Althaea** mother of Meleager, prince of Calydon. (At his birth, she was told that her son would live only as long as a brand of wood remained unconsumed. She snatched the brand from the fire, but years later, when Meleager quarreled with Althaea's brothers and slew them, she resentfully threw the fatal brand into the fire, thus causing his death.)   **233 Unto . . . Calydon** to the heart of the Prince of Calydon.   **235 Cold** Unfortunate   **238 take . . . parts** ally myself with the Nevilles, i.e., with Salisbury and his son Warwick. (Richard married Cecill or Cicely Neville, sister of Salisbury.)

161 fear me fear.   **flattering gloss** (1) flattering comment (2) deceivingly fair semblance   **164 He** i.e., King Henry   **165 join you** if you join   **168 brook** endure, permit   **169 presently** immediately.   **170 Cousin** Kinsman, fellow peer   **171 grief** grievance   **174 Than** i.e., than that of.   **princes** peers   **176 Or** Either   **178 Pride** i.e., Winchester.   **Ambition** i.e., Buckingham and Somerset   **179 preferment** advancement   **181 I . . . but** I always saw that   **182 him** himself   **185 stout** haughty.   **as** as if   **186 demean** conduct   **189 plainness** plain dealing.   **housekeeping** hospitality   **191 Excepting none but** second only to   **192 brother** i.e., brother-in-law; see note to line 238 below   **201 cherish** support   **202 tend** tend to, serve

And, when I spy advantage, claim the crown,   240
For that's the golden mark I seek to hit.   241
Nor shall proud Lancaster usurp my right,   242
Nor hold the scepter in his childish fist,
Nor wear the diadem upon his head,
Whose churchlike humors fits not for a crown.   245
Then, York, be still awhile, till time do serve.
Watch thou and wake when others be asleep,
To pry into the secrets of the state,
Till Henry, surfeiting in joys of love
With his new bride and England's dear-bought
   queen,
And Humphrey with the peers be fall'n at jars.   251
Then will I raise aloft the milk-white rose,   252
With whose sweet smell the air shall be perfumed,
And in my standard bear the arms of York,   254
To grapple with the house of Lancaster;
And force perforce I'll make him yield the crown,   256
Whose bookish rule hath pulled fair England down.   257

Exit York.

❖

[1.2]

Enter Duke Humphrey and his wife Eleanor.

DUCHESS
Why droops my lord, like overripened corn,   1
Hanging the head at Ceres' plenteous load?   2
Why doth the great Duke Humphrey knit his brows,
As frowning at the favors of the world?   4
Why are thine eyes fixed to the sullen earth,
Gazing on that which seems to dim thy sight?
What see'st thou there? King Henry's diadem,
Enchased with all the honors of the world?   8
If so, gaze on, and grovel on thy face,
Until thy head be circled with the same.
Put forth thy hand; reach at the glorious gold.
What, is't too short? I'll lengthen it with mine;   12
And having both together heaved it up,   13
We'll both together lift our heads to heaven
And nevermore abase our sight so low
As to vouchsafe one glance unto the ground.

GLOUCESTER
O Nell, sweet Nell, if thou dost love thy lord,
Banish the canker of ambitious thoughts!   18
And may that hour when I imagine ill
Against my king and nephew, virtuous Henry,
Be my last breathing in this mortal world!
My troublous dream this night doth make me sad.   22

DUCHESS
What dreamed my lord? Tell me, and I'll requite it

With sweet rehearsal of my morning's dream.   24

GLOUCESTER
Methought this staff, mine office badge in court,   25
Was broke in twain—by whom, I have forgot,
But, as I think, it was by th' Cardinal—
And on the pieces of the broken wand
Were placed the heads of Edmund, Duke of Somerset,
And William de la Pole, first Duke of Suffolk.
This was my dream. What it doth bode, God knows.

DUCHESS
Tut, this was nothing but an argument   32
That he that breaks a stick of Gloucester's grove   33
Shall lose his head for his presumption.
But list to me, my Humphrey, my sweet duke: 35
Methought I sat in seat of majesty
In the cathedral church of Westminster,
And in that chair where kings and queens are
   crowned,
Where Henry and Dame Margaret kneeled to me
And on my head did set the diadem.

GLOUCESTER
Nay, Eleanor, then must I chide outright.
Presumptuous dame, ill-nurtured Eleanor,   42
Art thou not second woman in the realm,
And the Protector's wife, beloved of him?
Hast thou not worldly pleasure at command
Above the reach or compass of thy thought?   46
And wilt thou still be hammering treachery,   47
To tumble down thy husband and thyself
From top of honor to disgrace's feet?
Away from me, and let me hear no more!

DUCHESS
What, what, my lord? Are you so choleric   51
With Eleanor for telling but her dream?   52
Next time I'll keep my dreams unto myself,
And not be checked.   54

GLOUCESTER
Nay, be not angry. I am pleased again.

Enter Messenger.

MESSENGER
My Lord Protector, 'tis His Highness' pleasure
You do prepare to ride unto Saint Albans,
Whereas the King and Queen do mean to hawk.   58

GLOUCESTER
I go.—Come, Nell, thou wilt ride with us?

DUCHESS
Yes, my good lord, I'll follow presently.   60
Exit Humphrey [with Messenger].
Follow I must; I cannot go before   61

---

240 advantage opportunity   **241 mark** archery target   **242 Lancaster** i.e., Henry VI, here demoted to his title of duke   **245 humors** temperament   **251 at jars** in discords, quarreling.   **252 milk-white rose** (Emblem of the Yorkist dynasty.)   **254 standard** battle standard, ensign.   **arms** coat of arms   **256 force perforce** by violent compulsion   **257 bookish** scholarly and ineffectual
1.2. Location: The Duke of Gloucester's house.
1 corn grain   **2 Ceres** goddess of the harvest and agriculture
4 As as if   **8 Enchased** adorned as with gems   **12 is't** i.e., is your arm   **13 heaved it** i.e., lifted the crown   **18 canker** ulcer   **22 this night** this past night

24 rehearsal recounting.   **morning's dream** (Morning dreams were, in folklore, regarded as foretelling true things.)   **25 mine office badge** the symbol of my office of Protector   **32 argument** proof, evidence   **33 breaks . . . grove** i.e., harms Gloucester in the slightest. (The image of the stick is suggested by the broken staff.)   **35 list** listen   **42 ill-nurtured** ill-bred   **46 compass** encompassing   **47 hammering** i.e., devising   **51 choleric** angry. (A term derived from the four humors in which a preponderance of any one of the fluids led to an imbalance in temperament. See 1.3.152.)   **52 for telling** only for telling   **54 checked** rebuked   **58 Whereas** where.   **hawk** hunt with hawks.   **60 presently** at once.   **61 go before** i.e., advance my own ambitions to be second to none

While Gloucester bears this base and humble mind.
Were I a man, a duke, and next of blood,
I would remove these tedious stumbling blocks
And smooth my way upon their headless necks;
And, being a woman, I will not be slack
To play my part in Fortune's pageant.—   67
Where are you there? Sir John! Nay, fear not, man,   68
We are alone; here's none but thee and I.

    Enter Hume.

HUME
Jesus preserve Your Royal Majesty!
DUCHESS
What say'st thou? "Majesty"? I am but "Grace."   71
HUME
But by the grace of God and Hume's advice
Your Grace's title shall be multiplied.   73
DUCHESS
What say'st thou, man? Hast thou as yet conferred
With Margery Jordan, the cunning witch,   75
With Roger Bolingbroke, the conjurer?
And will they undertake to do me good?
HUME
This they have promisèd: to show Your Highness
A spirit raised from depth of underground
That shall make answer to such questions
As by Your Grace shall be propounded him.
DUCHESS
It is enough. I'll think upon the questions.
When from Saint Albans we do make return,
We'll see these things effected to the full.
Here, Hume, take this reward. [*She gives money.*] Make
    merry, man,
With thy confederates in this weighty cause.
                      Exit Eleanor.

HUME
Hume must make merry with the Duchess' gold.
Marry, and shall! But, how now, Sir John Hume?   88
Seal up your lips, and give no words but mum;
The business asketh silent secrecy.   90
Dame Eleanor gives gold to bring the witch;
Gold cannot come amiss, were she a devil.
Yet have I gold flies from another coast—   93
I dare not say, from the rich Cardinal
And from the great and new-made Duke of Suffolk,
Yet I do find it so; for, to be plain,
They, knowing Dame Eleanor's aspiring humor,   97
Have hirèd me to undermine the Duchess
And buzz these conjurations in her brain.   99
They say "A crafty knave does need no broker,"   100
Yet am I Suffolk and the Cardinal's broker.

Hume, if you take not heed, you shall go near   102
To call them both a pair of crafty knaves.   103
Well, so it stands; and thus, I fear, at last
Hume's knavery will be the Duchess' wrack,   105
And her attainture will be Humphrey's fall.   106
Sort how it will, I shall have gold for all.   *Exit.* 107

                 ❖

[1.3]

    *Enter three or four Petitioners, [Peter,] the
    Armorer's man, being one.*

FIRST PETITIONER   My masters, let's stand close. My   1
  Lord Protector will come this way by and by, and then
  we may deliver our supplications in the quill.   3
SECOND PETITIONER   Marry, the Lord protect him, for
  he's a good man! Jesu bless him!

    Enter Suffolk and Queen.

FIRST PETITIONER   Here 'a comes, methinks, and the   6
  Queen with him. I'll be the first, sure.
              [*He starts forward.*]
SECOND PETITIONER   Come back, fool. This is the Duke
  of Suffolk, and not my Lord Protector.
SUFFOLK   How now, fellow? Wouldst anything with
  me?
FIRST PETITIONER   I pray, my lord, pardon me. I took
  ye for my Lord Protector.
QUEEN   "For my Lord Protector"? Are your supplications to His Lordship? Let me see them. What is
  thine?   [*She takes the petition.*]
FIRST PETITIONER   Mine is, an't please Your Grace,   17
  against John Goodman, my Lord Cardinal's man, for   18
  keeping my house, and lands, and wife and all, from
  me.
SUFFOLK   Thy wife too? That's some wrong, indeed.—
  What's yours? What's here? [*He takes a petition.*]
  "Against the Duke of Suffolk, for enclosing the   23
  commons of Melford." How now, sir knave?   24
SECOND PETITIONER   Alas, sir, I am but a poor petitioner
  of our whole township.   26
PETER [*giving his petition*] Against my master, Thomas
  Horner, for saying that the Duke of York was rightful
  heir to the crown.
QUEEN   What say'st thou? Did the Duke of York say he
  was rightful heir to the crown?
PETER   That my master was? No, forsooth; my master
  said that he was, and that the King was an usurper.
SUFFOLK [*calling*]   Who is there?

    [*Enter a Servant.*]

---

67 pageant spectacular entertainment.   **68 Sir John** (Conventional
form of addressing a priest.)   **71 Grace** (Appropriate address to a
duchess.)   **73 multiplied** augmented. (The line plays on 1 Peter 1.2:
"Grace and peace be multiplied unto you.")   **75 cunning** learned in
magic or fortune telling. (See 4.1.34.)   **88 Marry, and shall** i.e.,
Indeed he will. (*Marry* was originally an oath, "by the Virgin Mary.")
90 asketh requires   **93 flies** i.e., that flies, approaches.   **coast** quarter, source   **97 humor** temperament, fancy   **99 buzz** whisper
100 They say People say.   **broker** agent

102–3 go near To call come close to calling   **105 wrack** ruin
106 attainture conviction and disgrace   **107 Sort . . . all** Whichever
way it turns out, I shall prosper.
1.3. Location: London. The royal court.
1 close near together.   **3 in the quill** i.e., simultaneously, in a body.
6 'a he   **17 an't** if it   **18 man** servant   **23–4 enclosing the commons**
the action of a lord of a manor in enclosing or converting into private
property lands formerly undivided and used by the community as a
whole   **24 sir knave** (A socially oxymoronic insult.)   **26 of** on behalf of

Take this fellow in and send for his master with a pursuivant   35
presently. We'll hear more of your matter before the King.   36

Exit [Servant with Peter].

QUEEN *[to the Petitioners]*
And as for you, that love to be protected
Under the wings of our Protector's grace,   38
Begin your suits anew and sue to him.

Tear the supplication.

Away, base cullions! Suffolk, let them go.   40
ALL   Come, let's be gone.   *Exeunt [Petitioners].*
QUEEN
My lord of Suffolk, say, is this the guise,   42
Is this the fashions in the court of England?
Is this the government of Britain's isle,
And this the royalty of Albion's king?   45
What, shall King Henry be a pupil still
Under the surly Gloucester's governance?
Am I a queen in title and in style,   48
And must be made a subject to a duke?
I tell thee, Pole, when in the city Tours   50
Thou ran'st atilt in honor of my love   51
And stol'st away the ladies' hearts of France,
I thought King Henry had resembled thee
In courage, courtship, and proportion.   54
But all his mind is bent to holiness,
To number Ave Marys on his beads.
His champions are the prophets and apostles,
His weapons holy saws of sacred writ,   58
His study is his tiltyard, and his loves   59
Are brazen images of canonized saints.   60
I would the College of the Cardinals   61
Would choose him Pope and carry him to Rome
And set the triple crown upon his head;   63
That were a state fit for his holiness.   64
SUFFOLK
Madam, be patient. As I was cause
Your Highness came to England, so will I
In England work Your Grace's full content.
QUEEN
Beside the haughty Protector, have we Beaufort   68
The imperious churchman, Somerset, Buckingham,
And grumbling York; and not the least of these
But can do more in England than the King.
SUFFOLK
And he of these that can do most of all
Cannot do more in England than the Nevilles.
Salisbury and Warwick are no simple peers.

QUEEN
Not all these lords do vex me half so much
As that proud dame, the Lord Protector's wife.
She sweeps it through the court with troops of ladies,   77
More like an empress than Duke Humphrey's wife.
Strangers in court do take her for the Queen.   79
She bears a duke's revenues on her back,   80
And in her heart she scorns our poverty.
Shall I not live to be avenged on her?
Contemptuous baseborn callet as she is,   83
She vaunted 'mongst her minions t'other day   84
The very train of her worst wearing gown   85
Was better worth than all my father's lands,   86
Till Suffolk gave two dukedoms for his daughter.   87
SUFFOLK
Madam, myself have limed a bush for her,   88
And placed a choir of such enticing birds   89
That she will light to listen to the lays   90
And never mount to trouble you again.   91
So let her rest. And, madam, list to me,   92
For I am bold to counsel you in this:
Although we fancy not the Cardinal,   94
Yet must we join with him and with the lords
Till we have brought Duke Humphrey in disgrace.
As for the Duke of York, this late complaint   97
Will make but little for his benefit.
So one by one we'll weed them all at last,
And you yourself shall steer the happy helm.   100

*Sound a sennet. Enter the King, Duke Humphrey
[of Gloucester], Cardinal [Beaufort], Buckingham,
York, [Somerset,] Salisbury, Warwick, and the
Duchess [of Gloucester].*

KING
For my part, noble lords, I care not which;   101
Or Somerset or York, all's one to me.   102
YORK
If York have ill demeaned himself in France,
Then let him be denied the regentship.   103
SOMERSET
If Somerset be unworthy of the place,

---

35 pursuivant minor messenger or officer with authority to execute warrants   **36 presently** at once   **38 our Protector's grace** i.e., Duke Humphrey, His Grace the Protector   **40 cullions** base fellows. (Originally, *cullion* meant "testicle.")   **42 guise** custom, manner   **45 Albion's** England's   **48 style** official designation, with a related sense of "manner of life"   **50 Pole** i.e., Suffolk   **51 ran'st atilt** jousted in a tournament   **54 courtship, and proportion** courtliness, and figure.   **58 saws** sayings   **59 tiltyard** enclosed space for tilts or tournaments   **60 brazen images** bronze statues   **61 the College . . . Cardinals** the church body that elected the Pope   **63 the triple crown** i.e., the diadem of the papacy—a large hat enriched by three gold crowns symbolizing perhaps the Church militant, suffering, and triumphant   **64 state** status.   **his holiness** Henry's piety (but playing on the Pope's title, "His Holiness").   **68 Beaufort** Cardinal Beaufort, Bishop of Winchester

77 sweeps it moves majestically, with trailing garments   **79 Strangers** Visiting foreigners   **80 on her back** i.e., in her garments   **83 Contemptuous** (1) Contemptible (2) Full of contempt.   **callet** lewd woman   **84 vaunted** boasted.   **minions** followers, attendants (with overtones of "saucy women")   **85–7 The very . . . daughter** i.e., (Eleanor boasted that) the mere trailing part of her least expensive gown was worth more than all the lands possessed by Reignier until Suffolk arranged a dowry whereby the Duke received two rich dukedoms (Anjou and Maine) in return for the marriage of me, his daughter, to King Henry.   **88 limed a bush** set a trap. (A metaphor from the practice of catching birds by putting sticky birdlime on twigs of trees.)   **89 enticing birds** i.e., decoys   **90 light** alight.   **lays** songs   **91 mount** (1) fly off, fly aloft (2) aspire   **92 let her rest** i.e., forget about her.   **list** listen   **94 fancy not** do not like   **97 late complaint** i.e., recent allegation made by Peter that his master, the armorer, had spoken of York as the proper King of England   **100.1 sennet** trumpet signal for the approach or departure of processions.   **101 For my part** (The Quarto stage direction makes it clear that York and Somerset enter "on both sides of the King, whispering with him." The King is answering their requests.)   **102 Or** either   **103 have . . . himself** has conducted himself badly

Let York be regent. I will yield to him.

WARWICK
Whether Your Grace be worthy, yea or no,
Dispute not that. York is the worthier.

CARDINAL
Ambitious Warwick, let thy betters speak.

WARWICK
The Cardinal's not my better in the field.   110

BUCKINGHAM
All in this presence are thy betters, Warwick.

WARWICK
Warwick may live to be the best of all.

SALISBURY
Peace, son!—And show some reason, Buckingham,
Why Somerset should be preferred in this.

QUEEN
Because the King, forsooth, will have it so.   115

GLOUCESTER
Madam, the King is old enough himself
To give his censure. These are no women's matters.   117

QUEEN
If he be old enough, what needs Your Grace
To be Protector of His Excellence?

GLOUCESTER
Madam, I am Protector of the realm,
And at his pleasure will resign my place.

SUFFOLK
Resign it then, and leave thine insolence.
Since thou wert king—as who is king but thou?—
The commonwealth hath daily run to wrack,
The Dauphin hath prevailed beyond the seas,   125
And all the peers and nobles of the realm
Have been as bondmen to thy sovereignty.   127

CARDINAL
The commons hast thou racked; the clergy's bags   128
Are lank and lean with thy extortions.

SOMERSET
Thy sumptuous buildings and thy wife's attire
Have cost a mass of public treasury.

BUCKINGHAM
Thy cruelty in execution
Upon offenders hath exceeded law,
And left thee to the mercy of the law.

QUEEN
Thy sale of offices and towns in France—
If they were known, as the suspect is great—   136
Would make thee quickly hop without thy head.
          Exit Humphrey. [The Queen drops her fan.]
Give me my fan. What, minion, can ye not?   138
          She gives the Duchess a box on the ear.

I cry you mercy, madam. Was it you?   139

DUCHESS
Was 't I? Yea, I it was, proud Frenchwoman.
Could I come near your beauty with my nails,
I'd set my ten commandments in your face.   142

KING
Sweet aunt, be quiet. 'Twas against her will.   143

DUCHESS
Against her will, good King? Look to't in time.
She'll hamper thee and dandle thee like a baby.   145
Though in this place most master wear no breeches,   146
She shall not strike Dame Eleanor unrevenged.
                              Exit Eleanor.

BUCKINGHAM [*aside to the Cardinal*]
Lord Cardinal, I will follow Eleanor,
And listen after Humphrey, how he proceeds.   149
She's tickled now; her fume needs no spurs.   150
She'll gallop far enough to her destruction.
                              Exit Buckingham.

          Enter Humphrey.

GLOUCESTER
Now, lords, my choler being overblown   152
With walking once about the quadrangle,
I come to talk of commonwealth affairs.
As for your spiteful false objections,
Prove them, and I lie open to the law;
But God in mercy so deal with my soul
As I in duty love my king and country!
But, to the matter that we have in hand:
I say, my sovereign, York is meetest man   160
To be your regent in the realm of France.

SUFFOLK
Before we make election, give me leave   162
To show some reason, of no little force,
That York is most unmeet of any man.

YORK
I'll tell thee, Suffolk, why I am unmeet:
First, for I cannot flatter thee in pride;   166
Next, if I be appointed for the place,
My lord of Somerset will keep me here
Without discharge, money, or furniture   169
Till France be won into the Dauphin's hands.
Last time I danced attendance on his will   171
Till Paris was besieged, famished, and lost.

WARWICK
That can I witness, and a fouler fact   173
Did never traitor in the land commit.

---

110 field field of combat.   **115 forsooth** in truth. (With a hint of derision at Henry's expense.)   **117 censure** opinion, judgment.
125 Dauphin (Suffolk here uses the title of the heir apparent of France to refer to King Charles VII because Suffolk, like most Englishmen, considers Henry VI the rightful King of France. The old spelling, "Dolphin," reinforces the nautical flavor of the line.)
127 bondmen slaves   **128 racked** (Literally, tortured; here, strained beyond endurance in matters of taxation.)   **bags** money bags
136 suspect suspicion   **138 minion** hussy

139 cry you mercy beg your pardon. (The Queen pretends that she thought she was merely slapping one of her ladies in attendance for being slow to obey.)   **142 ten commandments** i.e., ten fingernails (like the fingernails Moses, or God, is proverbially thought to have used in inscribing the ten commandments)   **143 against her will** unintentional.
145 hamper (1) fetter (2) cradle   **146 most master** the one most in command (i.e., the Queen)   **149 listen** inquire   **150 tickled** (1) vexed, irritated (2) like a fish about to be caught by tickling.   **fume** smoke, i.e., rage   **152 choler . . . overblown** anger being dissipated   **160 meetest** fittest   **162 election** choice   **166 for** because   **169 discharge** payment of what is owed.   **furniture** military equipment   **171 Last time** (See *1 Henry VI*, 4.3.)   **173 fact** crime, deed

SUFFOLK   Peace, headstrong Warwick!

WARWICK

Image of pride, why should I hold my peace?   176

Enter [Horner, the] Armorer, and his man
[Peter, guarded].

SUFFOLK

Because here is a man accused of treason.
Pray God the Duke of York excuse himself!

YORK

Doth anyone accuse York for a traitor?   179

KING

What mean'st thou, Suffolk? Tell me, what are these?   180

SUFFOLK

Please it Your Majesty, this is the man
That doth accuse his master of high treason.
His words were these: that Richard, Duke of York,
Was rightful heir unto the English crown,
And that Your Majesty was an usurper.

KING   Say, man, were these thy words?

HORNER   An't shall please Your Majesty, I never said   187
nor thought any such matter. God is my witness, I am
falsely accused by the villain.

PETER   By these ten bones; my lords, he did speak them   190
to me in the garret one night as we were scouring my
lord of York's armor.

YORK

Base dunghill villain and mechanical,   193
I'll have thy head for this thy traitor's speech!
[*To the King*] I do beseech Your Royal Majesty,
Let him have all the rigor of the law.

HORNER   Alas, my lord, hang me if ever I spake the
words. My accuser is my prentice; and when I did
correct him for his fault the other day, he did vow   199
upon his knees he would be even with me. I have
good witness of this. Therefore I beseech Your Majesty,
do not cast away an honest man for a villain's   202
accusation.

KING   [*to Gloucester*]

Uncle, what shall we say to this in law?

GLOUCESTER

This doom, my lord, if I may judge: 205
Let Somerset be regent o'er the French,
Because in York this breeds suspicion;   207
And let these have a day appointed them   208
For single combat in convenient place,   209
For he hath witness of his servant's malice.
This is the law, and this Duke Humphrey's doom.

KING

Then be it so. My lord of Somerset,
We make Your Grace regent over the French.

SOMERSET

I humbly thank Your Royal Majesty.

HORNER   And I accept the combat willingly.

PETER   Alas, my lord, I cannot fight; for God's sake, pity
my case. The spite of man prevaileth against me. O
Lord, have mercy upon me! I shall never be able to
fight a blow. Oh, Lord, my heart!

GLOUCESTER

Sirrah, or you must fight or else be hanged.   220

KING   Away with them to prison; and the day of combat
shall be the last of the next month. Come, Somerset,
we'll see thee sent away.   *Flourish. Exeunt.*

❖

[1.4]

Enter [Margery Jordan] the Witch, the two priests
[Hume and Southwell], and Bolingbroke.

HUME   Come, my masters. The Duchess, I tell you, ex-   1
pects performance of your promises.

BOLINGBROKE   Master Hume, we are therefore pro-   3
vided. Will Her Ladyship behold and hear our exor-   4
cisms?   5

HUME   Ay, what else? Fear you not her courage.   6

BOLINGBROKE   I have heard her reported to be a woman
of an invincible spirit. But it shall be convenient, Master Hume, that you be by her aloft, while we be busy
below; and so, I pray you, go in God's name and
leave us.   *Exit Hume.*
Mother Jordan, be you prostrate and grovel on the earth.
John Southwell, read you; and let us to our work.   13

[*Margery Jordan lies face downward.*]

Enter [Duchess] Eleanor aloft, [Hume following].

DUCHESS   Well said, my masters, and welcome all. To   14
this gear, the sooner the better.   15

BOLINGBROKE

Patience, good lady; wizards know their times.
Deep night, dark night, the silent of the night,
The time of night when Troy was set on fire,
The time when screech owls cry and bandogs howl,   18
And spirits walk, and ghosts break up their graves—   19
That time best fits the work we have in hand.
Madam, sit you and fear not. Whom we raise

---

220 Sirrah (Customary form of address to servants.)   **or you** either you
1.4. Location: Gloucester's house.
1 my masters good sirs.   **3 therefore** for that very purpose
4–5 exorcisms conjurations.   **6 Fear** Doubt   **13 read you** (In the
stage direction at line 23.2, Southwell or Bolingbroke *reads* or recites a
black magic spell.)   **13.2 aloft** (The Quarto specifies that the Duchess
"goes up to the tower," i.e., some elevated place in the theater, perhaps the gallary over the stage.)   **14 Well said** Well done   **14–15 To
this gear** Get on with this business   **18 set on fire** (i.e., by the Greeks
concealed in the Trojan horse; described in Virgil, *Aeneid*, Book 2)
19 bandogs leashed watchdogs

---

176 Image i.e., Symbol   **179 for** of being   **180 what** who   **187 An't** If
it   **190 bones** i.e., fingers   **193 mechanical** common workman
199 correct punish.   **fault** mistake   **202 for** because of   **205 doom**
judgment   **207 in York . . . suspicion** i.e., this arouses suspicions
about York's loyalty   **208 these** i.e., Peter and Horner   **209 single
combat** combat one-on-one

We will make fast within a hallowed verge.   23

> *Here [they] do the ceremonies belonging, and*
> *make the circle. Bolingbroke or Southwell reads*
> *Conjuro te, etc. It thunders and lightens terri-*
> *bly; then the Spirit riseth.*

SPIRIT *Adsum.*   24
MARGERY JORDAN   Asnath,   25
  By the eternal God, whose name and power
  Thou tremblest at, answer that I shall ask,   27
  For till thou speak thou shalt not pass from hence.

SPIRIT
  Ask what thou wilt. That I had said and done!   29

BOLINGBROKE [*reading out of a paper*]
  "First, of the King: what shall of him become?"

SPIRIT
  The duke yet lives that Henry shall depose,   31
  But him outlive, and die a violent death.   32
          [*As the Spirit speaks, Southwell writes the answer.*]

BOLINGBROKE
  "What fates await the Duke of Suffolk?"

SPIRIT
  By water shall he die and take his end.   34

BOLINGBROKE
  "What shall befall the Duke of Somerset?"

SPIRIT   Let him shun castles;   36
  Safer shall he be upon the sandy plains
  Than where castles mounted stand.   38
  Have done, for more I hardly can endure.   39

BOLINGBROKE
  Descend to darkness and the burning lake!
  False fiend, avoid!   41

> *Thunder and lightning. Exit Spirit, [sinking down*
> *again].*

> *Enter the Duke of York and the Duke of Buck-*
> *ingham with their guard and break in. [They*
> *seize Jordan and her cohorts, with their papers.]*

YORK
  Lay hands upon these traitors and their trash.
  [*To Jordan*] Beldam, I think we watched you at an inch.   43
  [*To the Duchess*] What, madam, are you there? The
      King and commonweal
  Are deeply indebted for this piece of pains.   45
  My Lord Protector will, I doubt it not,

See you well guerdoned for these good deserts.   47
DUCHESS
  Not half so bad as thine to England's king,
  Injurious Duke, that threatest where's no cause.   49
BUCKINGHAM
  True, madam, none at all. What call you this?
            [*He shows her the papers he has seized.*]
  Away with them! Let them be clapped up close   51
  And kept asunder. You, madam, shall with us.
  Stafford, take her to thee.   53
            [*Exeunt above Duchess and Hume, guarded.*]
  We'll see your trinkets here all forthcoming.   54
  All away!   *Exit [guard with Jordan, Southwell, and*
                                       Bolingbroke].

YORK
  Lord Buckingham, methinks you watched her well.   56
  A pretty plot, well chosen to build upon!   57
  Now, pray, my lord, let's see the devil's writ.
  What have we here?   *Reads.*
  "The duke yet lives that Henry shall depose;
  But him outlive, and die a violent death."
  Why, this is just "*Aio te, Aeacida,*   62
  Romanos vincere posse." Well, to the rest: 63
  "Tell me what fate awaits the Duke of Suffolk?"
  "By water shall he die and take his end."
  "What shall betide the Duke of Somerset?"
  "Let him shun castles;
  Safer shall he be upon the sandy plains
  Than where castles mounted stand."
  Come, come, my lords, these oracles
  Are hardly attained and hardly understood.   71
  The King is now in progress towards Saint Albans;   72
  With him the husband of this lovely lady.
  Thither goes these news, as fast as horse can carry
      them—
  A sorry breakfast for my Lord Protector.
BUCKINGHAM
  Your Grace shall give me leave, my lord of York,
  To be the post, in hope of his reward.   77
YORK
  At your pleasure, my good lord.   [*Exit Buckingham.*]
  Who's within there, ho!

      Enter a Servingman.

  Invite my lords of Salisbury and Warwick
  To sup with me tomorrow night. Away!   *Exeunt.*

❖

---

23 **hallowed verge** magic circle.   **23.1** *the ceremonies belonging* i.e., the "hocus-pocus" necessary to conjure spirits, such as drawing a magic circle and reciting a formula.   **23.3** *Conjuro te* I conjure you.
23.4 riseth (Presumably a trapdoor is used on the main stage.)
24 *Adsum* I am here.   **25 Asnath** (An anagram for *Sathan.*)   **27 that** that which   **29 That** Would that. (The Spirit is reluctant to answer questions.)   **31–2 The duke . . . death** (The first line of the prophecy, as is characteristic of such utterances, is capable of a double construction: "whom Henry will depose" or "who will depose Henry." The second line is fulfilled in *3 Henry VI* and *Richard III*. "The duke" may refer ambiguously both to Edward IV and to his father, who preceded him as Duke of York.)   **34 By water** (See 4.1.31–5 for an explanation of this riddle.)   **36 Let him shun castles** (The warning is riddlingly fulfilled in 5.2.65 ff.)   **38 mounted** on mounts   **39 Have done** Finish up
41 False Treacherous.   **avoid** begone.   **43 Beldam** Witch, hag.   **at an inch** i.e., closely.   **45 piece of pains** trouble undergone. (Said ironically.)

47 guerdoned rewarded.   **deserts** deserving acts. (Said ironically.)
49 Injurious insulting   **51 clapped up close** imprisoned securely
53 Stafford (Presumably one of Buckingham's kinsmen, perhaps Sir Humphrey Stafford, acting as an officer of the arresting guard.)
54 trinkets trifles, rubbish (used in performing magical acts, and now confiscated to be *forthcoming*, used as legal evidence)   **56 watched** kept surveillance over   **57 plot** clever plan. (With pun on the sense of "plot of ground.")   **build upon** erect a scheme on (continuing the architectural pun).   **62 just** precisely   **62–3** *Aio . . . posse* I say to you, Aeacides, the Romans can conquer. (This prophecy, given by the Delphic oracle to Pyrrhus, descendant of Aeacus, is grammatically ambiguous in just the same fashion as the English oracle about Henry and the Yorkists, lines 31–2.)   **71 hardly attained** with difficulty obtained, or comprehended   **72 in progress** on a state journey   **77 post** messenger

[2.1]

Enter the King, Queen [with her hawk on her fist], Protector [Gloucester], Cardinal, and Suffolk, with falconers halloing.

QUEEN
Believe me, lords, for flying at the brook   1
I saw not better sport these seven years' day.   2
Yet, by your leave, the wind was very high,
And ten to one old Joan had not gone out.   4

KING [*to Gloucester*]
But what a point, my lord, your falcon made,   5
And what a pitch she flew above the rest!   6
To see how God in all his creatures works!
Yea, man and birds are fain of climbing high.   8

SUFFOLK
No marvel, an it like Your Majesty,   9
My Lord Protector's hawks do tower so well;   10
They know their master loves to be aloft
And bears his thoughts above his falcon's pitch.

GLOUCESTER
My lord, 'tis but a base ignoble mind
That mounts no higher than a bird can soar.

CARDINAL
I thought as much. He would be above the clouds.

GLOUCESTER
Ay, my Lord Cardinal, how think you by that?
Were it not good Your Grace could fly to heaven?

KING
The treasury of everlasting joy.

CARDINAL [*to Gloucester*]
Thy heaven is on earth; thine eyes and thoughts
Beat on a crown, the treasure of thy heart.   20
Pernicious Protector, dangerous peer,
That smooth'st it so with King and commonweal!   22

GLOUCESTER
What, Cardinal, is your priesthood grown
    peremptory?
Tantaene animis caelestibus irae?   24
Churchmen so hot? Good uncle, hide such malice.
With such holiness, can you do it?

SUFFOLK
No malice, sir, no more than well becomes
So good a quarrel and so bad a peer.

GLOUCESTER
As who, my lord?

SUFFOLK   Why, as you, my lord,
An't like Your lordly Lord-Protectorship.

GLOUCESTER
Why, Suffolk, England knows thine insolence.   31

QUEEN
And thy ambition, Gloucester.

KING   I prithee, peace,
Good Queen, and whet not on these furious peers;   33
For blessèd are the peacemakers on earth.   34

CARDINAL
Let me be blessèd for the peace I make
Against this proud Protector with my sword!

GLOUCESTER [*aside to Cardinal*]
Faith, holy uncle, would 'twere come to that!

CARDINAL [*aside to Gloucester*]   Marry, when thou dar'st.

GLOUCESTER [*aside to Cardinal*]
Make up no factious numbers for the matter;   39
In thine own person answer thy abuse.   40

CARDINAL [*aside to Gloucester*]
Ay, where thou dar'st not peep. An if thou dar'st,   41
This evening, on the east side of the grove.

KING
How now, my lords?

CARDINAL [*aloud*]   Believe me, cousin Gloucester,
Had not your man put up the fowl so suddenly,   44
We had had more sport. [*Aside to Gloucester*] Come
with thy two-hand sword.

GLOUCESTER [*aloud*] True, uncle.
[*Aside to Cardinal*] Are ye advised? The east side of the
grove.   47

CARDINAL [*aside to Gloucester*]
I am with you.

KING   Why, how now, uncle Gloucester?

GLOUCESTER
Talking of hawking; nothing else, my lord.
[*Aside to Cardinal*] Now by God's mother, priest, I'll
shave your crown for this,   50
Or all my fence shall fail.

CARDINAL [*aside to Gloucester*]   *Medice, teipsum*—   51
Protector, see to't well. Protect yourself.   52

KING
The winds grow high; so do your stomachs, lords.   53
How irksome is this music to my heart!
When such strings jar, what hope of harmony?
I pray, my lords, let me compound this strife.   56

*Enter one [a Townsman of Saint Albans] crying
"A miracle!"*

2.1. Location: St. Albans.
1 flying . . . brook i.e., hawking for waterfowl   **2 these . . . day** for the last seven years up to today.   **4 old . . . out** i.e., the hawk named old Joan would not have flown in such a high wind.   **5 point** advantageous position from which the hawk attacks the bird   **6 pitch** height to which a hawk soars before descending on its prey   **8 fain** fond   **9 an it like** if it please. (Also lines 30 and 78.)   **10 hawks** (Refers not only to the hawks flown by Gloucester in this hunt but also to the falcon with a maiden's head portrayed on Gloucester's heraldic badge.)   **tower** rise wheeling up to the *point* from which the hawk swoops down   **20 Beat on** dwell on, think about constantly   **22 smooth'st it** flatters   **24 Tantaene . . . irae?** Can there be such resentment in heavenly minds? (Virgil, *Aeneid*, 1.11.)

31 England all England   **33 whet not on** do not encourage   **34 blessèd . . . earth** (King Henry cites the Sermon on the Mount, Matthew 5:9.)   **39 Make . . . matter** Do not bring a party of your quarrelsome supporters into the quarrel   **40 abuse** offense, insult.   **41 peep** i.e., show your face.   **An if** If   **44 man** i.e., falconer.   **put . . . fowl** startled the game into flight   **47 Are ye advised?** Do you understand?   **50 I'll shave your crown** (Since a priest is already tonsured, this would be to give him a close shave indeed.)   **51 fence** skill in fighting with a sword.   *Medice, teipsum* Physician, (heal) thyself. (Luke 4:23.)   **52 Protect** (With a pun on *Protector*.)   **53 stomachs** tempers   **56 compound** settle.   **56.1 *Saint Albans*** a shrine and a town named for Saint Alban, supposedly the first Christian martyr in Britain, executed under the edicts of Diocletian in A.D. 304 for sheltering a Christian priest

GLOUCESTER What means this noise?
Fellow, what miracle dost thou proclaim?

TOWNSMAN A miracle! A miracle!

SUFFOLK
Come to the King and tell him what miracle.

TOWNSMAN
Forsooth, a blind man at Saint Albans' shrine
Within this half hour hath received his sight—
A man that ne'er saw in his life before.

KING
Now, God be praised, that to believing souls
Gives light in darkness, comfort in despair!   65

Enter the Mayor of Saint Albans and his brethren,
bearing the man [Simpcox] between two in a chair,
[Simpcox's Wife and others following].

CARDINAL
Here comes the townsmen on procession,   66
To present Your Highness with the man.

KING
Great is his comfort in this earthly vale,   68
Although by his sight his sin be multiplied.   69

GLOUCESTER
Stand by, my masters. Bring him near the King;   70
His Highness' pleasure is to talk with him.

KING
Good fellow, tell us here the circumstance,
That we for thee may glorify the Lord.
What, hast thou been long blind and now restored?

SIMPCOX Born blind, an't please Your Grace.

WIFE Ay, indeed, was he.

SUFFOLK What woman is this?

WIFE His wife, an't like Your Worship.

GLOUCESTER Hadst thou been his mother, thou couldst
have better told.

KING Where wert thou born?

SIMPCOX
At Berwick in the north, an't like Your Grace.

KING
Poor soul, God's goodness hath been great to thee.
Let never day nor night unhallowed pass,   84
But still remember what the Lord hath done.   85

QUEEN
Tell me, good fellow, cam'st thou here by chance,
Or of devotion, to this holy shrine?

SIMPCOX
God knows, of pure devotion, being called
A hundred times and oft'ner in my sleep
By good Saint Alban, who said, "Simon, come,   90
Come, offer at my shrine and I will help thee."   91

WIFE
Most true, forsooth; and many time and oft
Myself have heard a voice to call him so.

CARDINAL   What, art thou lame?

SIMPCOX Ay, God Almighty help me!

SUFFOLK How cam'st thou so?

SIMPCOX A fall off of a tree.

WIFE A plum tree, master.   98

GLOUCESTER How long hast thou been blind?

SIMPCOX Oh, born so, master.

GLOUCESTER What, and wouldst climb a tree?

SIMPCOX But that in all my life, when I was a youth.   102

WIFE
Too true, and bought his climbing very dear.

GLOUCESTER Mass, thou lov'dst plums well, that   104
wouldst venture so.

SIMPCOX Alas, good master, my wife desired some
damsons and made me climb, with danger of my life. 107

GLOUCESTER
A subtle knave! But yet it shall not serve.   108
Let me see thine eyes. Wink now. Now open them.   109
In my opinion yet thou see'st not well.

SIMPCOX Yes, master, clear as day, I thank God and
Saint Alban.

GLOUCESTER
Say'st thou me so? What color is this cloak of?

SIMPCOX Red, master, red as blood.

GLOUCESTER
Why, that's well said. What color is my gown of?

SIMPCOX Black, forsooth, coal black as jet.

KING
Why, then, thou know'st what color jet is of?

SUFFOLK
And yet, I think, jet did he never see.

GLOUCESTER
But cloaks and gowns, before this day, a many.   119

WIFE
Never, before this day, in all his life.

GLOUCESTER Tell me, sirrah, what's my name?

SIMPCOX Alas, master, I know not.

GLOUCESTER [pointing] What's his name?

SIMPCOX I know not.

GLOUCESTER [pointing to another] Nor his?

SIMPCOX No, indeed, master.

GLOUCESTER What's thine own name?

SIMPCOX Sander Simpcox, an if it please you, master.

GLOUCESTER Then, Sander, sit there, the lying'st 129
knave in Christendom. If thou hadst been born
blind, thou mightst as well have known all our names
as thus to name the several colors we do wear. Sight
may distinguish of colors, but suddenly to nominate 133
them all, it is impossible.—My lords, Saint Alban here
hath done a miracle; and would ye not think his

65.1 brethren aldermen, fellow members of the corporation or guild
66 on in   **68 this . . . vale** i.e., this vale of tears, this transitory world
69 by his sight . . . multiplied i.e., he may now be subject to more
temptations, being able to see.   **70 my masters** my good sirs.
84 unhallowed unblessed by your prayers   **85 still** continually
90 Simon (His proper name; *Simpcox* is a variant.)   **91 offer** make
an offering

98 A plum tree (1) A fruit tree (2) A slang phrase for the female
pudenda that sets up an elaborate ribald joke here about a husband
risking his life to try to satisfy his wife's craving   **102 But that** Only
that once   **104 Mass** By the Mass. (An oath.)   **107 damsons** a variety of
plum. (Commonly used as a slang phrase for testicles.)   **108 shall not
serve** won't serve to fool me.   **109 Wink** Close your eyes   **119 many**
multitude.   **129 sit there** there you sit   **133 nominate** call by name

cunning to be great that could restore this cripple to
his legs again?

SIMPCOX   Oh, master, that you could!

GLOUCESTER   My masters of Saint Albans, have you not
beadles in your town, and things called whips?   140

MAYOR   Yes, my lord, if it please Your Grace.

GLOUCESTER   Then send for one presently.   142

MAYOR [to an Attendant]
Sirrah, go fetch the beadle hither straight.   143

Exit [an Attendant.]

GLOUCESTER   Now fetch me a stool hither by and by. [*A*   144
stool is brought.] Now, sirrah, if you mean to save
yourself from whipping, leap me over this stool and   146
run away.

SIMPCOX   Alas, master, I am not able to stand alone. You
go about to torture me in vain.

Enter a Beadle with whips.

GLOUCESTER   Well, sir, we must have you find your
legs.—Sirrah beadle, whip him till he leap over that
same stool.

BEADLE   I will, my lord.—Come on, sirrah, off with
your doublet quickly.   154

SIMPCOX   Alas, master, what shall I do? I am not able to
stand.

*After the Beadle hath hit him once, he leaps over
the stool and runs away; and they follow and
cry, "A miracle!"*

KING
O God, see'st Thou this, and bearest so long?   157

QUEEN
It made me laugh to see the villain run.

GLOUCESTER [to the Beadle]
Follow the knave, and take this drab away.   159

WIFE   Alas, sir, we did it for pure need.

GLOUCESTER   Let them be whipped through every market town till they come to Berwick, from whence they
came.   *Exit [Wife, with Beadle, Mayor, etc.].*

CARDINAL
Duke Humphrey has done a miracle today.

SUFFOLK
True; made the lame to leap and fly away.

GLOUCESTER
But you have done more miracles than I;
You made in a day, my lord, whole towns to fly.   167

Enter Buckingham.

KING
What tidings with our cousin Buckingham?

BUCKINGHAM
Such as my heart doth tremble to unfold: 170

A sort of naughty persons, lewdly bent,   171
Under the countenance and confederacy
Of Lady Eleanor, the Protector's wife,   173
The ringleader and head of all this rout,   174
Have practiced dangerously against your state,
Dealing with witches and with conjurers,   176
Whom we have apprehended in the fact,
Raising up wicked spirits from under ground,   178
Demanding of King Henry's life and death
And other of Your Highness' Privy Council,   180
As more at large Your Grace shall understand.

CARDINAL
And so, my Lord Protector, by this means   182
Your lady is forthcoming yet at London.
[*Aside to Gloucester*] This news, I think, hath turned
    your weapon's edge;   184
'Tis like, my lord, you will not keep your hour.

GLOUCESTER   185
Ambitious churchman, leave to afflict my heart.
Sorrow and grief have vanquished all my powers;
And, vanquished as I am, I yield to thee   188
Or to the meanest groom.

KING
O God, what mischiefs work the wicked ones,   190
Heaping confusion on their own heads thereby!

QUEEN   191
Gloucester, see here the tainture of thy nest,   192
And look thyself be faultless, thou wert best.

GLOUCESTER   193
Madam, for myself, to heaven I do appeal
How I have loved my king and commonweal;   195
And, for my wife, I know not how it stands.
Sorry I am to hear what I have heard.
Noble she is; but if she have forgot   198
Honor and virtue, and conversed with such
As, like to pitch, defile nobility,
I banish her my bed and company
And give her as a prey to law and shame
That hath dishonored Gloucester's honest name.

KING
Well, for this night we will repose us here;
Tomorrow toward London back again,
To look into this business thoroughly,
And call these foul offenders to their answers,   207
And poise the cause in Justice' equal scales,
Whose beam stands sure, whose rightful cause   208
    prevails.   *Flourish. Exeunt.*

❖

140 beadles parish officers charged with punishing minor offenses,
often by whipping   142 presently immediately.   143 straight
immediately.   144 by and by at once.   146 leap me leap. (*Me* is used
colloquially.)   154 doublet close-fitting jacket   157 bearest do you
endure (such sinfulness)   159 drab slut   167 You . . . fly i.e., you
gave away French towns in a day, as part of Queen Margaret's dowry.
170 sort lot, gang.   naughty wicked.   lewdly evilly

171 Under . . . confederacy with the authorization and even complicity   73 rout crew   174 practiced conspired   176 fact crime, deed
178 Demanding of inquiring about   180 at large in detail
182 forthcoming ready to appear (in court)   184 like likely.   hour
appointment (for the duel between Gloucester and the Cardinal).
185 leave to afflict cease afflicting   188 meanest of lowest degree
190 confusion destruction   191 tainture defilement   192 look take
care, see to it.   thou wert best you'd be well advised.   193, 195 for
as for   198 conversed had to do with   207 poise weigh   208 beam
stands sure cross-beam is perfectly steadfast and level

[2.2]

Enter York, Salisbury, and Warwick.

YORK
Now, my good lords of Salisbury and Warwick,
Our simple supper ended, give me leave,
In this close walk, to satisfy myself   3
In craving your opinion of my title,
Which is infallible, to England's crown.

SALISBURY
My lord, I long to hear it at full.

WARWICK
Sweet York, begin; and if thy claim be good,
The Nevilles are thy subjects to command.

YORK Then thus:
Edward the Third, my lords, had seven sons;
The first, Edward the Black Prince, Prince of Wales;
The second, William of Hatfield, and the third,
Lionel, Duke of Clarence; next to whom
Was John of Gaunt, the Duke of Lancaster;
The fifth was Edmund Langley, Duke of York;
The sixth was Thomas of Woodstock, Duke of
   Gloucester;
William of Windsor was the seventh and last.
Edward the Black Prince died before his father
And left behind him Richard, his only son,   19
Who after Edward the Third's death reigned as king
Till Henry Bolingbroke, Duke of Lancaster,
The eldest son and heir of John of Gaunt,
Crowned by the name of Henry the Fourth,
Seized on the realm, deposed the rightful king,
Sent his poor queen to France, from whence she came,
And him to Pomfret; where, as all you know,
Harmless Richard was murdered traitorously.

WARWICK
Father, the Duke hath told the truth.
Thus got the house of Lancaster the crown.

YORK
Which now they hold by force and not by right;
For Richard, the first son's heir, being dead,
The issue of the next son should have reigned.   32

SALISBURY
But William of Hatfield died without an heir.

YORK
The third son, Duke of Clarence, from whose line
I claim the crown, had issue, Philippe, a daughter,
Who married Edmund Mortimer, Earl of March.
Edmund had issue, Roger Earl of March;
Roger had issue, Edmund, Anne, and Eleanor.

SALISBURY
This Edmund, in the reign of Bolingbroke,   39

As I have read, laid claim unto the crown,
And, but for Owen Glendower, had been king,
Who kept him in captivity till he died.   42
But to the rest.

YORK   His eldest sister, Anne,
My mother, being heir unto the crown,
Married Richard, Earl of Cambridge, who was son
To Edmund Langley, Edward the Third's fifth son.
By her I claim the kingdom. She was heir
To Roger, Earl of March, who was the son
Of Edmund Mortimer, who married Philippe,
Sole daughter unto Lionel, Duke of Clarence.
So, if the issue of the elder son
Succeed before the younger, I am king.

WARWICK
What plain proceeding is more plain than this?
Henry doth claim the crown from John of Gaunt,
The fourth son; York claims it from the third.
Till Lionel's issue fails, his should not reign.   56
It fails not yet, but flourishes in thee   57
And in thy sons, fair slips of such a stock.   58
Then, father Salisbury, kneel we together,
And in this private plot be we the first   60
That shall salute our rightful sovereign
With honor of his birthright to the crown.

BOTH [*kneeling*]
Long live our sovereign Richard, England's king!

YORK
We thank you, lords. [*They rise.*] But I am not your king 64
Till I be crowned, and that my sword be stained   65
With heart-blood of the house of Lancaster;
And that's not suddenly to be performed,
But with advice and silent secrecy.   68
Do you as I do in these dangerous days:
Wink at the Duke of Suffolk's insolence,   70
At Beaufort's pride, at Somerset's ambition,
At Buckingham, and all the crew of them,
Till they have snared the shepherd of the flock,
That virtuous prince, the good Duke Humphrey.
'Tis that they seek, and they in seeking that
Shall find their deaths, if York can prophesy.

SALISBURY
My lord, break we off. We know your mind at full.

WARWICK
My heart assures me that the Earl of Warwick
Shall one day make the Duke of York a king.

YORK
And, Neville, this I do assure myself: 80
Richard shall live to make the Earl of Warwick
The greatest man in England but the King.   *Exeunt.*

❧

2.2. **Location: London. The Duke of York's garden.**
3 close private   **19 Richard** i.e., Richard II   **32 issue** offspring
39 This Edmund (A historical error, found also in the chronicles, of
confusing Edmund Mortimer, fifth Earl of March, who was named
heir to the throne by Richard II, with his uncle Edmund, brother of
Roger, who married Glendower's daughter. See *1 Henry VI*, 2.5, and *1
Henry IV*, 1.3.)

42 Who i.e., Glendower   **56 his** i.e., John of Gaunt's   **57 It fails
not** i.e., Lionel's line of descent has not died out   **58 slips** cuttings
60 plot plot of ground   **64 We** (The royal "we"!)   **65 and that** and
until the time that   **68 advice** careful reflection   **70 Wink at**
Shut your eyes to   **80 Neville** (York addresses Warwick by his
family name.)

[2.3]

Sound trumpets. Enter the King and state, [the Queen, Gloucester, York, Suffolk, Salisbury, and others,] with guard, to banish the Duchess [of Gloucester, who is brought on under guard with Margery Jordan, Southwell, Hume, and Bolingbroke].

KING
Stand forth, Dame Eleanor Cobham, Gloucester's
wife.
In sight of God and us, your guilt is great.
Receive the sentence of the law for sins
Such as by God's book are adjudged to death.   4
[*To Margery and the others*] You four, from hence to
prison back again;
From thence unto the place of execution.
The witch in Smithfield shall be burnt to ashes,
And you three shall be strangled on the gallows.
[*To the Duchess*] You, madam, for you are more nobly
born,   9
Despoilèd of your honor in your life,   10
Shall, after three days' open penance done,
Live in your country here in banishment
With Sir John Stanley in the Isle of Man.   13

DUCHESS
Welcome is banishment. Welcome were my death.   14

GLOUCESTER
Eleanor, the law, thou see'st, hath judged thee.
I cannot justify whom the law condemns.
            [*Exeunt Duchess and other prisoners, guarded.*]
Mine eyes are full of tears, my heart of grief.
Ah, Humphrey, this dishonor in thine age
Will bring thy head with sorrow to the grave!
I beseech Your Majesty, give me leave to go;
Sorrow would solace, and mine age would ease.   21

KING
Stay, Humphrey, Duke of Gloucester. Ere thou go,
Give up thy staff. Henry will to himself   23
Protector be; and God shall be my hope,
My stay, my guide, and lantern to my feet.
And go in peace, Humphrey, no less beloved
Than when thou wert Protector to thy king.

QUEEN
I see no reason why a king of years   28
Should be to be protected like a child.   29
God and King Henry govern England's realm!
Give up your staff, sir, and the King his realm.   31

GLOUCESTER
My staff? Here, noble Henry, is my staff.
            [*He lays down his staff.*]
As willingly do I the same resign
As ere thy father Henry made it mine;   34
And even as willingly at thy feet I leave it
As others would ambitiously receive it.
Farewell, good King. When I am dead and gone,
May honorable peace attend thy throne!
                                            Exit Gloucester.

QUEEN
Why, now is Henry king and Margaret queen,
And Humphrey, Duke of Gloucester scarce himself,
That bears so shrewd a maim. Two pulls at once: 41
His lady banished, and a limb lopped off.   42
This staff of honor raught, there let it stand   43
Where it best fits to be, in Henry's hand.

SUFFOLK
Thus droops this lofty pine and hangs his sprays;   45
Thus Eleanor's pride dies in her youngest days.   46

YORK
Lords, let him go. Please it Your Majesty,   47
This is the day appointed for the combat,
And ready are the appellant and defendant—   49
The armorer and his man—to enter the lists,   50
So please Your Highness to behold the fight.

QUEEN
Ay, good my lord, for purposely therefor
Left I the court, to see this quarrel tried.

KING
I' God's name, see the lists and all things fit.
Here let them end it, and God defend the right!

YORK
I never saw a fellow worse bestead,   56
Or more afraid to fight, than is the appellant,
The servant of this armorer, my lords.   58

Enter at one door, the Armorer [Horner] and his Neighbors, drinking to him so much that he is drunk; and he enters with a drum before him and his staff with a sandbag fastened to it; and at the other door his man [Peter], with a drum and sandbag, and Prentices drinking to him.

FIRST NEIGHBOR   Here, neighbor Horner, I drink to
you in a cup of sack; and fear not, neighbor, you shall   60
do well enough.

SECOND NEIGHBOR   And here, neighbor, here's a cup
of charneco.   63

THIRD NEIGHBOR   And here's a pot of good double   64
beer, neighbor. Drink, and fear not your man.

2.3. Location: London. A place of justice.
0.2–3 *and others* (In the Quarto, the Cardinal, Buckingham, and Warwick are also named. Warwick, York, and Salisbury enter "to them," i.e., meeting the royal party.)   **4 by God's book** i.e., according to the commandments in the Bible against witches, Exodus 22:18, and enchantments, Leviticus 19:26, among other passages   **9 for** because **10 Despoilèd** deprived.   **in your life** during the remainder of your life   **13 With . . . Stanley** (An error for Sir Thomas Stanley, the Duchess's custodian and the Lord Stanley of *Richard III*.)   **14 were** would be   **21 would** wishes to have   **23 staff** staff of office.   **28 of years** who is of age   **29 be to be** need to be   **31 Give . . . realm** Give up your staff of office and the control over the King's realm that it symbolizes; give the King his realm back.

34 **ere** at an earlier time. (The Quarto reading, "erst," conveys the same meaning.)   **41 bears . . . maim** endures so grievous a mutilation.   **pulls** pluckings   **42 a limb lopped off** i.e., his staff of office taken away, so much a part of him that the severing was like an amputation.   **43 raught** attained, seized   **45 lofty pine** (An emblem adopted by Henry IV, Gloucester's father.)   **sprays** branches   **46 in her youngest days** i.e., when her ambition and pride were at their height.   **47 Please it** If it please   **49 appellant** challenger   **50 lists** enclosing barricades that surround the combatants   **56 worse bestead** in worse condition   **58.2 drinking to him** offering toasts to him (to which he is obliged to drink in return, drink for drink)   **58.3 drum** drummer   **60 sack** a dry Spanish or Canary wine   **63 charneco** a sweet Portuguese wine.   **64 double** strong

HORNER Let it come, i'faith, and I'll pledge you all; and 66
a fig for Peter! 67

FIRST PRENTICE Here, Peter, I drink to thee, and be not
afraid.

SECOND PRENTICE Be merry, Peter, and fear not thy
master. Fight for credit of the prentices. 71

PETER I thank you all. Drink, and pray for me, I pray
you, for I think I have taken my last draft in this world.
Here, Robin, an if I die, I give thee my apron; and Will,
thou shalt have my hammer; and here, Tom, take all
the money that I have. [*He gives away his things.*] O
Lord bless me, I pray God, for I am never able to deal
with my master, he hath learned so much fence 78
already.

SALISBURY Come, leave your drinking and fall to
blows. Sirrah, what's thy name?

PETER Peter, forsooth.

SALISBURY Peter? What more?

PETER Thump.

SALISBURY Thump! Then see thou thump thy master
well.

HORNER Masters, I am come hither, as it were, upon
my man's instigation, to prove him a knave and
myself an honest man; and touching the Duke of
York, I will take my death, I never meant him any ill, 90
nor the King, nor the Queen. And therefore, Peter,
have at thee with a downright blow! 92

YORK
Dispatch. This knave's tongue begins to double. 93
Sound, trumpets, alarum to the combatants! 94
[*Alarum.*] *They fight, and Peter strikes him down.*

HORNER Hold, Peter, hold! I confess, I confess treason.
[*He dies.*]

YORK Take away his weapon. Fellow, thank God and
the good wine in thy master's way. 97

PETER O God, have I overcome mine enemies in this
presence? O Peter, thou hast prevailed in right!

KING
Go, take hence that traitor from our sight; 100
For by his death we do perceive his guilt,
And God in justice hath revealed to us
The truth and innocence of this poor fellow,
Which he had thought to have murdered wrongfully. 104
[*To Peter*] Come, fellow, follow us for thy reward.
Sound a flourish. Exeunt [*with Horner's body*].

❖

[2.4]

Enter Duke Humphrey [*of Gloucester*] *and his
Men in mourning cloaks.*

GLOUCESTER
Thus sometimes hath the brightest day a cloud,
And after summer evermore succeeds
Barren winter, with his wrathful nipping cold;
So cares and joys abound, as seasons fleet. 4
Sirs, what's o'clock?

SERVANT Ten, my lord.

GLOUCESTER
Ten is the hour that was appointed me
To watch the coming of my punished duchess.
Uneath may she endure the flinty streets, 9
To tread them with her tender-feeling feet.
Sweet Nell, ill can thy noble mind abrook 11
The abject people gazing on thy face, 12
With envious looks laughing at thy shame, 13
That erst did follow thy proud chariot wheels 14
When thou didst ride in triumph through the streets.
But, soft! I think she comes, and I'll prepare 16
My tearstained eyes to see her miseries. 17

Enter the Duchess [*of Gloucester, barefoot*], *in a
white sheet,* [*with verses pinned upon her back,*]
and a taper burning in her hand; with [*Sir John
Stanley,*] *the Sheriff, and officers* [*with bills and
halberds*].

SERVANT
So please Your Grace, we'll take her from the sheriff. 18

GLOUCESTER
No, stir not for your lives. Let her pass by.

DUCHESS
Come you, my lord, to see my open shame?
Now thou dost penance too. Look how they gaze! 21
See how the giddy multitude do point
And nod their heads and throw their eyes on thee!
Ah, Gloucester, hide thee from their hateful looks, 24
And, in thy closet pent up, rue my shame, 25
And ban thine enemies, both mine and thine! 26

GLOUCESTER
Be patient, gentle Nell. Forget this grief.

DUCHESS
Ah, Gloucester, teach me to forget myself!
For whilst I think I am thy married wife
And thou a prince, Protector of this land,
Methinks I should not thus be led along,

---

66 **Let it come** i.e., Let the drink be passed around. **pledge you**
drink your health   67 **a fig** (An obscene insult, accompanied by the
gesture of putting the thumb between the first and second fingers.)
71 **credit** reputation, good name   78 **fence** skill in fighting   90 **take
my death** i.e., take an oath on pain of death   92 **have at thee** here I
come at you   93 **double** thicken and slur (with intoxication).
94 **alarum** call to arms   97 **in thy master's way** i.e., that marred
your master's fighting ability.   100 **that traitor** i.e., Horner
104 **Which he** i.e., whom Horner

2.4. Location: London. A street.
4 **fleet** pass by quickly.   9 **Uneath** With difficulty, scarcely
11 **abrook** endure   12 **abject** lowly born   13 **envious** full of malice
14 **erst** formerly   16 **soft!** wait a minute!   17.4–5 *with bills and
halberds* with long-handled axlike weapons. (The bracketed stage
directions are derived from the Quarto.)   18 **take her** rescue her by
force   21 **Look how they gaze!** (The crowd of commoners may be
represented onstage, or the Duchess may gesture offstage.)
24 **hateful** full of hate   25 **closet** private room   26 **ban** curse

Mailed up in shame, with papers on my back,   32
And followed with a rabble that rejoice   33
To see my tears and hear my deep-fet groans.   34
The ruthless flint doth cut my tender feet,
And when I start, the envious people laugh   36
And bid me be advisèd how I tread.   37
Ah, Humphrey, can I bear this shameful yoke?
Trowest thou that e'er I'll look upon the world,   39
Or count them happy that enjoys the sun?   40
No, dark shall be my light and night my day;
To think upon my pomp shall be my hell.
Sometime I'll say I am Duke Humphrey's wife,
And he a prince and ruler of the land;
Yet so he ruled, and such a prince he was,
As he stood by whilst I, his forlorn duchess,   46
Was made a wonder and a pointing-stock   47
To every idle rascal follower.
But be thou mild and blush not at my shame,
Nor stir at nothing till the ax of death
Hang over thee, as, sure, it shortly will.
For Suffolk, he that can do all in all
With her that hateth thee and hates us all,
And York and impious Beaufort, that false priest,
Have all limed bushes to betray thy wings,
And fly thou how thou canst, they'll tangle thee.
But fear not thou until thy foot be snared,
Nor never seek prevention of thy foes.

GLOUCESTER
Ah, Nell, forbear! Thou aimest all awry.
I must offend before I be attainted;
And had I twenty times so many foes,   60
And each of them had twenty times their power,
All these could not procure me any scathe
So long as I am loyal, true, and crimeless.   63
Wouldst have me rescue thee from this reproach?
Why, yet thy scandal were not wiped away,
But I in danger for the breach of law.   66
Thy greatest help is quiet, gentle Nell.   68
I pray thee, sort thy heart to patience;   69
These few days' wonder will be quickly worn.   70

Enter a Herald.

HERALD
I summon Your Grace to His Majesty's Parliament,

Holden at Bury the first of this next month.   72
GLOUCESTER
And my consent ne'er asked herein before?
This is close dealing. Well, I will be there.   74
        [*Exit Herald.*]
My Nell, I take my leave. And, Master Sheriff,
Let not her penance exceed the King's commission.
SHERIFF
An't please Your Grace, here my commission stays,   77
And Sir John Stanley is appointed now
To take her with him to the Isle of Man.
GLOUCESTER
Must you, Sir John, protect my lady here?
STANLEY
So am I given in charge, may't please Your Grace.   81
GLOUCESTER
Entreat her not the worse in that I pray   82
You use her well. The world may laugh again,   83
And I may live to do you kindness if
You do it her. And so, Sir John, farewell.
        [*He starts to leave.*]
DUCHESS
What, gone, my lord, and bid me not farewell?
GLOUCESTER
Witness my tears, I cannot stay to speak.
        Exit Gloucester [with his men].
DUCHESS
Art thou gone too? All comfort go with thee!
For none abides with me. My joy is death—
Death, at whose name I oft have been afeard,
Because I wished this world's eternity.   91
Stanley, I prithee, go, and take me hence.
I care not whither, for I beg no favor;
Only convey me where thou art commanded.
STANLEY
Why, madam, that is to the Isle of Man,
There to be used according to your state.   96
DUCHESS
That's bad enough, for I am but reproach;   97
And shall I then be used reproachfully?
STANLEY
Like to a duchess and Duke Humphrey's lady,
According to that state you shall be used.
DUCHESS
Sheriff, farewell, and better than I fare,   101
Although thou hast been conduct of my shame.   102
SHERIFF
It is my office; and, madam, pardon me.
DUCHESS
Ay, ay, farewell. Thy office is discharged.
        [*Exit Sheriff and his men.*]
Come, Stanley, shall we go?

32 **Mailed up** enveloped. (Used in hawking to prevent the hawk from struggling, just as Eleanor is wrapped in a white sheet.)   **papers on my back** (The verses pinned upon her back describe the sin for which she is doing penance.)   33 **with** by   34 **deep-fet** fetched from the depths   36 **start** flinch, wince.   **envious** malicious   37 **advisèd** careful   39 **Trowest thou** Do you believe   40 **Or . . . happy** or be numbered among those who account themselves happy   46 **As** that   47 **pointing-stock** one pointed at in scorn   53 **her** i.e., Queen Margaret   55 **limed** put out sticky birdlime as a trap on   56 **fly . . . thee** no matter how you try to fly away, they will ensnare you.   57–8 **But . . . foes** (The Duchess ironically urges her husband to wait until it is too late. *Seek prevention of* means "seek means of forestalling.")   60 **attained** condemned for treason or other serious wrongdoing   63 **scathe** injury   66 **were not** would not be   68 **quiet** i.e., patient endurance   69 **sort** adapt   70 **These . . . wonder** i.e., This passing notoriety (as in the phrase "a nine-days' wonder").   **worn** worn out, i.e., forgotten.

72 **Holden at Bury** to be held at Bury St. Edmunds (in Suffolk)   74 **close** secret, underhand   77 **stays** stops, ends   81 **given in charge** commanded   82 **Entreat** Treat.   **in that** merely because   83 **The world . . . again** i.e., We may see happier times. (Proverbial.)   91 **this world's eternity** endless worldly happiness.   96 **state** noble rank. (But Eleanor plays on *state* in the sense of "condition.")   97 **I . . . reproach** I am the embodiment of reproach or disgrace, deserve only my shame   101 **better . . . fare** may you fare better than I   102 **conduct** conductor

STANLEY
Madam, your penance done, throw off this sheet,
And go we to attire you for our journey.

DUCHESS
My shame will not be shifted with my sheet.   108
No, it will hang upon my richest robes
And show itself, attire me how I can.
Go, lead the way. I long to see my prison.   *Exeunt.*

❧

[3.1]

*Sound a sennet. Enter King, Queen, Cardinal
[Beaufort], Suffolk, York, Buckingham, Salisbury, and Warwick to the Parliament.*

KING
I muse my lord of Gloucester is not come.   1
'Tis not his wont to be the hindmost man,   2
Whate'er occasion keeps him from us now.

QUEEN
Can you not see, or will ye not observe,
The strangeness of his altered countenance?   5
With what a majesty he bears himself?
How insolent of late he is become?
How proud, how peremptory, and unlike himself?
We know the time since he was mild and affable,   9
And if we did but glance a far-off look,
Immediately he was upon his knee,
That all the court admired him for submission;   12
But meet him now, and, be it in the morn,
When everyone will give the time of day,   14
He knits his brow and shows an angry eye
And passeth by with stiff unbowèd knee,
Disdaining duty that to us belongs.   17
Small curs are not regarded when they grin,   18
But great men tremble when the lion roars—
And Humphrey is no little man in England.
First note that he is near you in descent,
And should you fall, he is the next will mount.   22
Me seemeth then it is no policy,   23
Respecting what a rancorous mind he bears   24
And his advantage following your decease,
That he should come about your royal person
Or be admitted to Your Highness' Council;
By flattery hath he won the commons' hearts;
And when he please to make commotion,   29
'Tis to be feared they all will follow him.
Now 'tis the spring, and weeds are shallow-rooted;
Suffer them now, and they'll o'ergrow the garden   32

And choke the herbs for want of husbandry.   33
The reverent care I bear unto my lord
Made me collect these dangers in the Duke.   35
If it be fond, call it a woman's fear—   36
Which fear, if better reasons can supplant,
I will subscribe and say I wronged the Duke.   38
My lord of Suffolk, Buckingham, and York,
Reprove my allegation if you can,   40
Or else conclude my words effectual.   41

SUFFOLK
Well hath Your Highness seen into this duke,
And, had I first been put to speak my mind,
I think I should have told Your Grace's tale.
The Duchess by his subornation,   45
Upon my life, began her devilish practices;   46
Or if he were not privy to those faults,   47
Yet, by reputing of his high descent—   48
As next the King he was successive heir,
And such high vaunts of his nobility—   50
Did instigate the bedlam brainsick Duchess   51
By wicked means to frame our sovereign's fall.   52
Smooth runs the water where the brook is deep,
And in his simple show he harbors treason.   54
The fox barks not when he would steal the lamb.
No, no, my sovereign, Gloucester is a man
Unsounded yet and full of deep deceit.   57

CARDINAL
Did he not, contrary to form of law,
Devise strange deaths for small offenses done?

YORK
And did he not, in his protectorship,
Levy great sums of money through the realm
For soldiers' pay in France, and never sent it,
By means where of the towns each day revolted?   63

BUCKINGHAM
Tut, these are petty faults to faults unknown,   64
Which time will bring to light in smooth Duke
    Humphrey.

KING
My lords, at once: the care you have of us   66
To mow down thorns that would annoy our foot   67
Is worthy praise; but, shall I speak my conscience,   68
Our kinsman Gloucester is as innocent
From meaning treason to our royal person
As is the sucking lamb or harmless dove.
The Duke is virtuous, mild, and too well given   72
To dream on evil or to work my downfall.

QUEEN
Ah, what's more dangerous than this fond affiance?   74

---

108 shifted changed. (With a pun on *shift*, a chemise.)
3.1. Location: A hall for a session of Parliament at Bury St.
Edmunds (historically, the Abbey).
0.1 *Sound a sennet* (The Quarto stage direction specifies that two heralds enter first, leading a formal procession.)   **1 muse** wonder why
2 wont custom   **5 strangeness** aloofness   **9 know** remember.
since when   **12 admired** wondered at   **14 give . . . day** say good
morning   **17 Disdaining . . . belongs** disdaining to show the ceremonial respect that is our (or my) due.   **18 grin** bare their teeth
22 will mount who will mount the throne.   **23 Me seemeth** It seems
to me.   **policy** prudent course   **24 Respecting** considering
29 make commotion foment unrest   **32 Suffer** Allow

33 want of husbandry lack of proper cultivation.   **35 collect** gather,
infer   **36 fond** foolish   **38 subscribe** agree. (Literally, "undersign.")
40 Reprove disprove   **41 effectual** conclusive, legally valid.
45 subornation instigation   **46 Upon my life** i.e., I swear this on
pain of death.   **practices** intrigues   **47 privy to those faults**
informed as to those crimes   **48 reputing** boasting, overvaluing
50 vaunts boasts   **51 bedlam** crazy   **52 frame** devise   **54 simple**
show innocent outward appearance   **57 Unsounded** with depths
still undiscovered   **63 By means whereof** on which account
64 to compared with   **66 at once** answering all of you; or, without
more ado; or, once and for all   **67 annoy** injure   **68 shall I speak** if
I may speak in accordance with   **72 well given** kindly disposed
74 fond affiance foolish confidence.

Seems he a dove? His feathers are but borrowed,
For he's disposèd as the hateful raven.
Is he a lamb? His skin is surely lent him,   76
For he's inclined as is the ravenous wolves.
Who cannot steal a shape that means deceit?   79
Take heed, my lord. The welfare of us all
Hangs on the cutting short that fraudful man.   81

Enter Somerset.

SOMERSET
All health unto my gracious sovereign!

KING
Welcome, Lord Somerset. What news from France?

SOMERSET
That all your interest in those territories
Is utterly bereft you. All is lost.

KING
Cold news, Lord Somerset; but God's will be done!

YORK *[aside]*
Cold news for me, for I had hope of France
As firmly as I hope for fertile England.
Thus are my blossoms blasted in the bud,   89
And caterpillars eat my leaves away;
But I will remedy this gear ere long,   91
Or sell my title for a glorious grave.   92

Enter Gloucester.

GLOUCESTER
All happiness unto my lord the King!
Pardon, my liege, that I have stayed so long.   94

SUFFOLK
Nay, Gloucester, know that thou art come too soon,
Unless thou wert more loyal than thou art.
I do arrest thee of high treason here.

GLOUCESTER
Well, Suffolk, thou shalt not see me blush
Nor change my countenance for this arrest.
A heart unspotted is not easily daunted.
The purest spring is not so free from mud
As I am clear from treason to my sovereign.
Who can accuse me? Wherein am I guilty?

YORK
'Tis thought, my lord, that you took bribes of France
And, being Protector, stayed the soldiers' pay,   105
By means whereof His Highness hath lost France.

GLOUCESTER
Is it but thought so? What are they that think it?   107
I never robbed the soldiers of their pay,
Nor ever had one penny bribe from France.
So help me God as I have watched the night,   110
Ay, night by night, in studying good for England!
That doit that e'er I wrested from the King,   112
Or any groat I hoarded to my use,   113

Be brought against me at my trial day!   114
No, many a pound of mine own proper store,   115
Because I would not tax the needy commons,
Have I dispursèd to the garrisons   117
And never asked for restitution.

CARDINAL
It serves you well, my lord, to say so much.

GLOUCESTER
I say no more than truth, so help me God!

YORK
In your protectorship you did devise
Strange tortures for offenders, never heard of,
That England was defamed by tyranny.   123

GLOUCESTER
Why, 'tis well known that, whiles I was Protector,
Pity was all the fault that was in me;
For I should melt at an offender's tears,   126
And lowly words were ransom for their fault.   127
Unless it were a bloody murderer,
Or foul felonious thief that fleeced poor passengers,   129
I never gave them condign punishment.   130
Murder indeed, that bloody sin, I tortured
Above the felon or what trespass else.   132

SUFFOLK
My lord, these faults are easy, quickly answered;   133
But mightier crimes are laid unto your charge
Whereof you cannot easily purge yourself.
I do arrest you in His Highness' name,
And here commit you to my Lord Cardinal
To keep until your further time to trial.   138

KING
My lord of Gloucester, 'tis my special hope
That you will clear yourself from all suspense.   140
My conscience tells me you are innocent.

GLOUCESTER
Ah, gracious lord, these days are dangerous!
Virtue is choked with foul ambition,
And charity chased hence by rancor's hand;
Foul subornation is predominant,   145
And equity exiled Your Highness' land.   146
I know their complot is to have my life,   147
And if my death might make this island happy
And prove the period of their tyranny,   149
I would expend it with all willingness.
But mine is made the prologue to their play;   151
For thousands more, that yet suspect no peril,
Will not conclude their plotted tragedy.   153

---

76 he's disposèd as he has the disposition of   **79 Who . . . deceit?** Who is there, intending to deceive, that cannot assume an appropriate disguise?   **81 cutting short** stopping. (With a grisly suggestion of beheading.)   **89 blasted . . . bud** i.e., withered before they develop   **91 gear** business   **92 sell** exchange   **94 stayed** delayed   **105 stayed** held back   **107 What** Who   **110 watched the night** remained awake all night   **112, 113 doit, groat** coins of small value

114 Be may it be.   **trial day** (1) date of trial for treason (2) Day of Judgment before God.   **115 proper** personal   **117 dispursèd** disbursed   **123 That** so that.   **was defamed by** became notorious for   **126 should would**   **127 And . . . fault** and humble contrite words were sufficient to atone for the offenders' offenses.   **129 fleeced poor passengers** robbed unfortunate travelers   **130 condign** worthily deserved   **132 Above . . . else** beyond any other kind of felony or misdemeanor.   **133 easy** slight   **138 further** future   **140 suspense** i.e., doubt as to your innocence.   **145 subornation** instigating others to commit crimes, including perjury   **146 equity exiled** justice is exiled from   **147 complot** plot, conspiracy   **149 prove the period** turn out to be the end   **151 mine** i.e., my death   **153 Will . . . tragedy** will not suffice to bring to an end this tragedy they have devised. (With a suggestion of plotting a play.)

Beaufort's red sparkling eyes blab his heart's malice,
And Suffolk's cloudy brow his stormy hate;   155
Sharp Buckingham unburdens with his tongue   156
The envious load that lies upon his heart;
And dogged York, that reaches at the moon,   158
Whose overweening arm I have plucked back,   159
By false accuse doth level at my life.   160
[To the Queen] And you, my sovereign lady, with the
            rest,
Causeless have laid disgraces on my head,
And with your best endeavor have stirred up
My liefest liege to be mine enemy.   164
Ay, all of you have laid your heads together—
Myself had notice of your conventicles—   166
And all to make away my guiltless life.
I shall not want false witness to condemn me   168
Nor store of treasons to augment my guilt.
The ancient proverb will be well effected: 170
"A staff is quickly found to beat a dog."

CARDINAL [to the King]
My liege, his railing is intolerable.
If those that care to keep your royal person   173
From treason's secret knife and traitors' rage
Be thus upbraided, chid, and rated at,   175
And the offender granted scope of speech,   176
'Twill make them cool in zeal unto Your Grace.

SUFFOLK
Hath he not twit our sovereign lady here   178
With ignominious words, though clerkly couched,   179
As if she had subornèd some to swear
False allegations to o'erthrow his state?

QUEEN
But I can give the loser leave to chide.   182

GLOUCESTER
Far truer spoke than meant. I lose, indeed;
Beshrew the winners, for they played me false!   184
And well such losers may have leave to speak.

BUCKINGHAM
He'll wrest the sense and hold us here all day.   186
Lord Cardinal, he is your prisoner.

CARDINAL [to his attendants]
Sirs, take away the Duke and guard him sure.

GLOUCESTER
Ah, thus King Henry throws away his crutch
Before his legs be firm to bear his body.
Thus is the shepherd beaten from thy side,
And wolves are gnarling who shall gnaw thee first.   192
Ah, that my fear were false; ah, that it were!
For, good King Henry, thy decay I fear.   194
            Exit Gloucester [guarded by the Cardinal's men].

KING [rising]
My lords, what to your wisdoms seemeth best
Do or undo, as if ourself were here.

QUEEN
What, will Your Highness leave the Parliament?

KING
Ay, Margaret. My heart is drowned with grief,
Whose flood begins to flow within mine eyes,
My body round engirt with misery;   200
For what's more miserable than discontent?
Ah, uncle Humphrey, in thy face I see
The map of honor, truth, and loyalty;
And yet, good Humphrey, is the hour to come
That e'er I proved thee false or feared thy faith.   205
What louring star now envies thy estate,   206
That these great lords and Margaret our queen
Do seek subversion of thy harmless life?   208
Thou never didst them wrong nor no man wrong.
And as the butcher takes away the calf
And binds the wretch and beats it when it strains,   211
Bearing it to the bloody slaughterhouse,
Even so remorseless have they borne him hence;
And as the dam runs lowing up and down,   214
Looking the way her harmless young one went,   215
And can do naught but wail her darling's loss,
Even so myself bewails good Gloucester's case
With sad unhelpful tears, and with dimmed eyes
Look after him and cannot do him good,
So mighty are his vowèd enemies.
His fortunes I will weep, and twixt each groan
Say "Who's a traitor? Gloucester he is none."   222
            Exeunt [King, Buckingham, Salisbury, and
            Warwick with attendants; Somerset remains
                                            apart].

QUEEN
Free lords, cold snow melts with the sun's hot beams.   223
Henry my lord is cold in great affairs,   224
Too full of foolish pity; and Gloucester's show   225
Beguiles him, as the mournful crocodile   226
With sorrow snares relenting passengers,   227
Or as the snake, rolled in a flow'ring bank,   228
With shining checkered slough, doth sting a child   229
That for the beauty thinks it excellent.
Believe me, lords, were none more wise than I—   231
And yet herein I judge mine own wit good—   232
This Gloucester should be quickly rid the world,   233

200 engirt encircled   205 feared thy faith doubted your loyalty.
206 What . . . estate What threatening planet determines your loss of
great position   208 subversion overthrow   211 strains strives. (The
Folio reading, "strayes," is perhaps possible if binds means "pens in.")
214 dam mother   215 Looking seeking   222.1 Exeunt (The Quarto
version has Salisbury and Warwick exit here with the King. Buckingham, with no further role in the scene, possibly leaves, too. But the Folio
reads Exit, and it is possible the King departs alone, leaving the others
in little groups, trying to conduct a parliament without a king.)
223 Free Noble   224 cold i.e., faint, neglectful, and ready to melt or
give way   225 show false appearance   226 mournful crocodile
(Crocodiles were popularly supposed to weep "crocodile tears" in order
to lure their prey, and then while devouring the victim.)   227 relenting passengers gullible passersby   228 rolled coiled   229 slough
skin   231 were . . . than I i.e., I would venture my opinion, were there
not wiser heads than I   232 wit intelligence   233 rid removed from

155 cloudy threatening   156 Sharp cutting, harsh   158 dogged
(1) relentless (2) currish   159 overweening overreaching, presumptuous   160 accuse accusation.   level aim   164 liefest liege dearest sovereign   166 conventicles private or secret meetings
168 want lack   170 effected fulfilled, realized   173 care take care
175 rated scolded   176 scope freedom   178 twit twitted
179 clerkly couched learnedly and cleverly phrased   182 leave permission   184 Beshrew curse   186 wrest the sense twist the
meaning   192 gnarling snarling over   194 decay downfall

To rid us from the fear we have of him.

CARDINAL

That he should die is worthy policy,   235
But yet we want a color for his death.   236
'Tis meet he be condemned by course of law.   237

SUFFOLK

But, in my mind, that were no policy.   238
The King will labor still to save his life,   239
The commons haply rise to save his life;   240
And yet we have but trivial argument,   241
More than mistrust, that shows him worthy death.   242

YORK

So that, by this, you would not have him die.   243

SUFFOLK

Ah, York, no man alive so fain as I!   244

YORK

'Tis York that hath more reason for his death.
But, my Lord Cardinal, and you, my lord of Suffolk,
Say as you think, and speak it from your souls:
Were't not all one an empty eagle were set   248
To guard the chicken from a hungry kite   249
As place Duke Humphrey for the King's Protector?

QUEEN

So the poor chicken should be sure of death.

SUFFOLK

Madam, 'tis true; and were't not madness then
To make the fox surveyor of the fold?   253
Who, being accused a crafty murderer,
His guilt should be but idly posted over   255
Because his purpose is not executed.
No, let him die in that he is a fox,
By nature proved an enemy to the flock,
Before his chaps be stained with crimson blood,   259
As Humphrey proved, by reasons, to my liege.   260
And do not stand on quillets how to slay him—   261
Be it by gins, by snares, by subtlety,   262
Sleeping or waking, 'tis no matter how,
So he be dead. For that is good deceit   264
Which mates him first that first intends deceit.   265

QUEEN

Thrice-noble Suffolk, 'tis resolutely spoke.

SUFFOLK

Not resolute, except so much were done,   267
For things are often spoke and seldom meant;
But that my heart accordeth with my tongue,   269
Seeing the deed is meritorious,

And to preserve my sovereign from his foe,
Say but the word and I will be his priest.   272

CARDINAL

But I would have him dead, my lord of Suffolk,
Ere you can take due orders for a priest.   274
Say you consent and censure well the deed,   275
And I'll provide his executioner,
I tender so the safety of my liege.   277

SUFFOLK

Here is my hand. The deed is worthy doing.

QUEEN And so say I.

YORK And I. And now we three have spoke it,
It skills not greatly who impugns our doom.   281

Enter a Post.

POST

Great lords, from Ireland am I come amain   282
To signify that rebels there are up   283
And put the Englishmen unto the sword.
Send succors, lords, and stop the rage betimes,   285
Before the wound do grow uncurable;
For, being green, there is great hope of help.   [*Exit.*]   287

CARDINAL

A breach that craves a quick expedient stop!   288
What counsel give you in this weighty cause?

YORK

That Somerset be sent as regent thither.
'Tis meet that lucky ruler be employed—   291
Witness the fortune he hath had in France.

SOMERSET

If York, with all his far-fet policy,   293
Had been the regent there instead of me,
He never would have stayed in France so long.

YORK

No, not to lose it all, as thou hast done.
I rather would have lost my life betimes   297
Than bring a burden of dishonor home
By staying there so long till all were lost.   299
Show me one scar charactered on thy skin.   300
Men's flesh preserved so whole do seldom win.   301

QUEEN

Nay, then, this spark will prove a raging fire
If wind and fuel be brought to feed it with.
No more, good York; sweet Somerset, be still.
Thy fortune, York, hadst thou been regent there,
Might happily have proved far worse than his.   306

YORK

What, worse than naught? Nay, then a shame take all!

---

235 **is worthy policy** is a sound scheme   236 **want a color** lack a pretext   237 **meet** fitting   238 **were no policy** would be a poor stratagem.   239 **still** continually   240 **haply rise** perhaps rise in rebellion   241 **argument** evidence   242 **More than mistrust** other than suspicion   243 **by this** i.e., by this reasoning   244 **fain** glad, eager   248 **all one** just the same, as if.   **empty** hungry   249 **kite** scavenger bird, a kind of hawk   253 **surveyor** guardian.   **fold** sheepfold.   255 **idly posted over** foolishly ignored or hastened over. (Suffolk argues that it would be foolish to place a fox in charge of a sheepfold and then exonerate it of being a killer simply because it hasn't yet killed the sheep.)   259 **chaps** jaws   260 **As . . . liege** since Humphrey has amply demonstrated, and we have shown, is a threat to the King.   261 **quillets** subtle distinctions or disputes   262 **gins** engines, traps   264 **So** so long as   265 **mates** checkmates, foils (i.e., strikes quickly before the enemy can move first)   267 **except . . . done** unless what I've spoken is converted into action   269 **that** i.e., to prove that

272 **be his priest** perform the last rites for him, i.e., preside over his death.   274 **take . . . priest** (1) make arrangements to have a priest there (2) prepare yourself for the priesthood.   275 **censure well** approve   277 **tender** am concerned for, care for   281 **It . . . doom** It doesn't really matter who questions our decision.   281.1 *Post* messenger.   282 **amain** with full speed   283 **signify** report.   **up** up in arms   285 **betimes** early, swiftly   287 **green** fresh   288 **craves** demands   291 **meet** fitting. (Said ironically; York is hostile toward Somerset.)   293 **far-fet** farfetched, artful, deep. (Said ironically.)   297 **betimes** forthwith, sooner   299 **staying . . . long** temporizing   300 **charactered** inscribed   301 **Men's . . . win** Men who can show no wounds are seldom victors.   306 **happily** haply, perhaps

SOMERSET
And, in the number, thee that wishest shame! 308

CARDINAL
My lord of York, try what your fortune is.
Th'uncivil kerns of Ireland are in arms 310
And temper clay with blood of Englishmen. 311
To Ireland will you lead a band of men,
Collected choicely, from each county some,
And try your hap against the Irishmen? 314

YORK
I will, my lord, so please His Majesty.

SUFFOLK
Why, our authority is his consent,
And what we do establish he confirms.
Then, noble York, take thou this task in hand.

YORK
I am content. Provide me soldiers, lords,
Whiles I take order for mine own affairs. 320

SUFFOLK
A charge, Lord York, that I will see performed.
But now return we to the false Duke Humphrey. 322

CARDINAL
No more of him; for I will deal with him
That henceforth he shall trouble us no more.
And so, break off. The day is almost spent. 325
Lord Suffolk, you and I must talk of that event. 326

YORK
My lord of Suffolk, within fourteen days
At Bristol I expect my soldiers,
For there I'll ship them all for Ireland.

SUFFOLK
I'll see it truly done, my lord of York. 330

Exeunt. Manet York.

YORK
Now, York, or never, steel thy fearful thoughts 331
And change misdoubt to resolution. 332
Be that thou hop'st to be, or what thou art 333
Resign to death; it is not worth th'enjoying.
Let pale-faced fear keep with the mean-born man 335
And find no harbor in a royal heart.
Faster than springtime show'rs comes thought on
thought,
And not a thought but thinks on dignity. 338
My brain, more busy than the laboring spider,
Weaves tedious snares to trap mine enemies. 340
Well, nobles, well, 'tis politicly done 341
To send me packing with an host of men. 342
I fear me you but warm the starvèd snake, 343
Who, cherished in your breasts, will sting your hearts.
'Twas men I lacked, and you will give them me;
I take it kindly. Yet be well assured

You put sharp weapons in a madman's hands. 347
Whiles I in Ireland nourish a mighty band,
I will stir up in England some black storm
Shall blow ten thousand souls to heaven or hell; 350
And this fell tempest shall not cease to rage 351
Until the golden circuit on my head, 352
Like to the glorious sun's transparent beams,
Do calm the fury of this mad-bred flaw. 354
And, for a minister of my intent, 355
I have seduced a headstrong Kentishman,
John Cade of Ashford,
To make commotion, as full well he can,
Under the title of John Mortimer. 359
In Ireland have I seen this stubborn Cade
Oppose himself against a troop of kerns,
And fought so long till that his thighs with darts 362
Were almost like a sharp-quilled porcupine;
And in the end being rescued, I have seen
Him caper upright like a wild Morisco, 365
Shaking the bloody darts as he his bells. 366
Full often, like a shag-haired crafty kern,
Hath he conversèd with the enemy,
And undiscovered come to me again
And given me notice of their villainies.
This devil here shall be my substitute;
For that John Mortimer, which now is dead, 372
In face, in gait, in speech, he doth resemble.
By this I shall perceive the commons' mind,
How they affect the house and claim of York. 375
Say he be taken, racked, and torturèd, 376
I know no pain they can inflict upon him
Will make him say I moved him to those arms. 378
Say that he thrive, as 'tis great like he will, 379
Why then from Ireland come I with my strength
And reap the harvest which that rascal sowed.
For, Humphrey being dead, as he shall be,
And Henry put apart, the next for me. *Exit.* 383

❧

[3.2]

*Enter two or three running over the stage, from
the murder of Duke Humphrey.*

FIRST MURDERER
Run to my lord of Suffolk. Let him know

308 in . . . shame! i.e., among the "all" to whom you wish shame, may you be included! 310 uncivil kerns disorderly and irregular light-armed Irish soldiers 311 temper clay moisten the soil 314 hap fortune 320 take order for arrange 322 return we let's get back to talking about 325 break off cease conversation. 326 event affair, business. 330.1 *Manet* He remains onstage 331 fearful apprehensive 332 misdoubt suspicion, fear 333 that that which 335 keep dwell. mean-born lowly born 338 dignity i.e., the dignity of high office—kingship. 340 tedious intricate 341 politicly shrewdly. (Said ironically.) 342 packing away, a-journeying 343 starvèd i.e., deathlike with cold. (One of Aesop's fables is about a man who puts a snake next to his chest to warm it and is stung by it.)

347 put . . . hands (A proverbial expression for foolishly putting oneself at risk.) 350 Shall that shall 351 fell fierce 352 circuit circlet, crown 354 mad-bred flaw i.e., sudden squall or violent flare-up of lower-class rebellion bred by irrational ambition. 355 minister agent 359 Mortimer (The name of a powerful family claiming descent from Lionel, Duke of Clarence, and hence entitled to the crown. See *1 Henry VI*, 2.5.) 362 till that until. darts light spears or arrows 365 Morisco morris dancer, always fancily or grotesquely dressed; or the dance itself 366 he i.e., the morris dancer, with bells on his shins 372 For that because 375 affect incline toward 376 Say he be taken If he were to be captured 378 Will that will. moved incited, prompted 379 great like very likely 383 put apart ousted, deposed 3.2. Location: Bury St. Edmunds, in a room of state adjoining the place of imprisonment where Gloucester has been murdered. Seats are prepared, as for his trial. 0.1–2 *from the murder* (In the Quarto version, "the curtains being drawn, Duke Humphrey is discovered in his bed, and two men lying on his breast and smothering him in his bed." Suffolk enters to them. The curtains are closed as the Murderers exit at line 14.)

We have dispatched the Duke, as he commanded.

SECOND MURDERER

Oh, that it were to do! What have we done?
Didst ever hear a man so penitent?   3

Enter Suffolk.

FIRST MURDERER   Here comes my lord.

SUFFOLK

Now, sirs, have you dispatched this thing?

FIRST MURDERER   Ay, my good lord, he's dead.

SUFFOLK

Why, that's well said. Go get you to my house.   8
I will reward you for this venturous deed.
The King and all the peers are here at hand.
Have you laid fair the bed? Is all things well,   11
According as I gave directions?

FIRST MURDERER   'Tis, my good lord.

SUFFOLK   Away! Begone.   *Exeunt [Murderers].*

*Sound trumpets. Enter the King, the Queen,
Cardinal [Beaufort], Somerset, with attendants.*

KING

Go call our uncle to our presence straight.   15
Say we intend to try His Grace today
If he be guilty, as 'tis publishèd.   17

SUFFOLK

I'll call him presently, my noble lord.   *Exit.* 18

KING

Lords, take your places; and, I pray you all,
Proceed no straiter 'gainst our uncle Gloucester   20
Than from true evidence of good esteem   21
He be approved in practice culpable.   22
                              [They take their places.]

QUEEN

God forbid any malice should prevail
That faultless may condemn a nobleman!   24
Pray God he may acquit him of suspicion!   25

KING

I thank thee, Meg. These words content me much.

Enter Suffolk.

How now? Why look'st thou pale? Why tremblest
  thou?
Where is our uncle? What's the matter, Suffolk?

SUFFOLK

Dead in his bed, my lord. Gloucester is dead.

QUEEN   Marry, God forfend!   30

CARDINAL

God's secret judgment. I did dream tonight   31
The Duke was dumb and could not speak a word.
                                   King swoons.

QUEEN

How fares my lord? Help, lords, the King is dead!

SOMERSET

Rear up his body. Wring him by the nose.   34

QUEEN

Run, go, help, help! O Henry, ope thine eyes!
                        [They revive the King.]

SUFFOLK

He doth revive again. Madam, be patient.

KING

O heavenly God!

QUEEN   How fares my gracious lord?

SUFFOLK

Comfort, my sovereign! Gracious Henry, comfort!

KING

What, doth my lord of Suffolk comfort me?
Came he right now to sing a raven's note,   40
Whose dismal tune bereft my vital powers,
And thinks he that the chirping of a wren,
By crying comfort from a hollow breast,   43
Can chase away the first-conceivèd sound?   44
Hide not thy poison with such sugared words.
Lay not thy hands on me. Forbear, I say!
Their touch affrights me as a serpent's sting.
Thou baleful messenger, out of my sight!
Upon thy eyeballs murderous Tyranny   49
Sits in grim majesty to fright the world.
Look not upon me, for thine eyes are wounding.
Yet do not go away. Come, basilisk,   52
And kill the innocent gazer with thy sight;
For in the shade of death I shall find joy,   54
In life but double death, now Gloucester's dead.

QUEEN

Why do you rate my lord of Suffolk thus?   56
Although the Duke was enemy to him,
Yet he most Christian-like laments his death.
And for myself, foe as he was to me,   59
Might liquid tears or heart-offending groans   60
Or blood-consuming sighs recall his life,
I would be blind with weeping, sick with groans,
Look pale as primrose with blood-drinking sighs,
And all to have the noble Duke alive.
What know I how the world may deem of me?   65
For it is known we were but hollow friends.
It may be judged I made the Duke away;
So shall my name with slander's tongue be wounded
And princes' courts be filled with my reproach.   69
This get I by his death. Ay me, unhappy,
To be a queen, and crowned with infamy!

KING

Ah, woe is me for Gloucester, wretched man!

---

3 **that . . . do!** i.e., would that it were not yet done and thus could be avoided!   8 **well said** well done.   11 **laid fair the bed** i.e., straightened the bed linen to conceal the signs of struggle.   15 **straight** straightway.   17 **If** whether.   **publishèd** publicly proclaimed.   18 **presently** at once   20 **straiter** more severely   21 **of good esteem** worthy of belief   22 **approved . . . culpable** proved guilty of culpable acts.   24 **faultless** (Modifies *nobleman*.)   25 **acquit him** exonerate himself   30 **forfend** forbid.   31 **tonight** this past night

34 **Wring . . . nose** (Evidently a common first-aid remedy for restoring consciousness; compare with *Venus and Adonis*, line 475.)   40 **right now** just now.   **raven's note** a supposed omen of death   43 **hollow** (1) not ringing true (2) reverberating loudly despite the bird's small size   44 **the . . . sound** the sound that was perceived first, i.e., the raven's ominous croaking.   49 **Tyranny** cruelty   52 **basilisk** fabulous reptile, said to kill with its glance   54 **shade** shadow   56 **rate** berate   59 **for** as for   60 **heart-offending** (It was commonly believed that groans and sighs cost the heart a drop of blood. The idea is continued in lines 61 and 63.)   65 **deem** judge   69 **my reproach** blame of me.

QUEEN

Be woe for me, more wretched than he is.   73
What, dost thou turn away and hide thy face?
I am no loathsome leper. Look on me.
What? Art thou, like the adder, waxen deaf?   76
Be poisonous too, and kill thy forlorn queen.
Is all thy comfort shut in Gloucester's tomb?
Why, then, Dame Margaret was ne'er thy joy.
Erect his statue and worship it,
And make my image but an alehouse sign.
Was I for this nigh wrecked upon the sea
And twice by awkward wind from England's bank   83
Drove back again unto my native clime?   84
What boded this, but well forewarning wind   85
Did seem to say, "Seek not a scorpion's nest,
Nor set no footing on this unkind shore"?
What did I then but cursed the gentle gusts
And he that loosed them forth their brazen caves,   89
And bid them blow towards England's blessèd shore
Or turn our stern upon a dreadful rock?   91
Yet Aeolus would not be a murderer,
But left that hateful office unto thee.
The pretty-vaulting sea refused to drown me,   94
Knowing that thou wouldst have me drowned on
   shore
With tears as salt as sea, through thy unkindness.
The splitting rocks cow'red in the sinking sands   97
And would not dash me with their ragged sides,
Because thy flinty heart, more hard than they,   99
Might in thy palace perish Margaret.   100
As far as I could ken thy chalky cliffs,   101
When from thy shore the tempest beat us back,
I stood upon the hatches in the storm,
And when the dusky sky began to rob
My earnest-gaping sight of thy land's view,   105
I took a costly jewel from my neck—
A heart it was, bound in with diamonds—
And threw it towards thy land. The sea received it,
And so I wished thy body might my heart.
And even with this I lost fair England's view,
And bid mine eyes be packing with my heart,   111
And called them blind and dusky spectacles   112
For losing ken of Albion's wishèd coast.   113

How often have I tempted Suffolk's tongue,   114
The agent of thy foul inconstancy,   115
To sit and witch me, as Ascanius did   116
When he to madding Dido would unfold   117
His father's acts commenced in burning Troy!   118
Am I not witched like her, or thou not false like him?   119
Ay me, I can no more. Die, Margaret!
For Henry weeps that thou dost live so long.

*Noise within. Enter Warwick, [Salisbury,] and
many Commons.*

WARWICK

It is reported, mighty sovereign,
That good Duke Humphrey traitorously is murdered
By Suffolk and the Cardinal Beaufort's means.
The commons, like an angry hive of bees
That want their leader, scatter up and down   126
And care not who they sting in his revenge.   127
Myself have calmed their spleenful mutiny,   128
Until they hear the order of his death.   129

KING

That he is dead, good Warwick, 'tis too true;
But how he died God knows, not Henry.
Enter his chamber, view his breathless corpse,
And comment then upon his sudden death.

WARWICK

That shall I do, my liege.—Stay, Salisbury,
With the rude multitude till I return.   [*Exit.*] 135
                     [*Exit Salisbury with the Commons.*]

KING

O Thou that judgest all things, stay my thoughts,   136
My thoughts that labor to persuade my soul
Some violent hands were laid on Humphrey's life!
If my suspect be false, forgive me, God,   139
For judgment only doth belong to Thee.
Fain would I go to chafe his paly lips   141
With twenty thousand kisses, and to drain
Upon his face an ocean of salt tears,
To tell my love unto his dumb deaf trunk
And with my fingers feel his hand unfeeling.
But all in vain are these mean obsequies.   146

*Bed put forth [bearing Gloucester's body. Enter
Warwick.]*

---

73 woe sorry   **76 waxen deaf** grown deaf. (Snakes were popularly supposed to be deaf.)   **83 awkward** adverse.   **bank** shore   **84 Drove** driven.   **clime** country.   **85 but** but that   **89 he** i.e., Aeolus, god of the winds.   **forth** forth from.   **brazen** (In Homer's *Odyssey*, 10.3–4, the floating island of Aeolus is enclosed by a rampart of bronze.)   **91 Or . . . rock?** i.e., or else cast our ship on some dreadful rock? (Margaret hyperbolically claims that she would have wished to die if she were unable to reach England's blessed shore and her forthoming marriage to Henry.)   **94 pretty-vaulting** handsomely rising and falling   **97 The splitting . . . sands** i.e., The rocks that could have split open our ship cowered in the treacherous sandbars where ships so often founder and sink   **99 Because** so that   **100 perish** cause to perish   **101 ken** discern   **105 My earnest-gaping . . . view** my ardent peering toward your land   **111 be packing** begone.   **my heart** (1) my affection, left behind in England (2) my heart-shaped jewel   **112 spectacles** instruments of sight   **113 ken** sight.   **Albion's wishèd** England's longed-for

114–18 How . . . Troy! (Margaret portrays herself as having been mad with infatuation for King Henry, like Dido, Queen of Carthage, so much so that she pleaded with Suffolk, the negotiator of the marriage treaty between herself and Henry, to play the role of Cupid in augmenting her love for Henry. (In Virgil's *Aeneid*, Book I, during Aeneas's narration to Queen Dido of his escape from burning Troy, Aeneas's mother, Venus, sends Cupid disguised as Aeneas's son Ascanius to afflict the Queen with love for Aeneas. *Witch* in line 116 means "bewitch"; *madding* and *unfold* in line 117 mean "become frantic with love" and "narrate.")   **119 witched** bewitched.   **him** i.e., Aeneas.   **126 want** lack   **127 his revenge** revenge of him.   **128 spleenful mutiny** wrathful uprising   **129 order** manner   **135 rude** turbulent, ignorant   **136 stay** restrain   **139 suspect** suspicion   **141 Fain** Gladly.   **chafe** rub, warm.   **paly** pale   **146 mean obsequies** deficient funeral rites.   **146.1 Bed put forth** (In the Quarto version, Warwick need not leave the stage [see line 135] to view Gloucester's dead body; he simply "draws the curtain and shows Duke Humphrey in his bed." In the present Folio version, the bed must be thrust forth onto the stage with Humphrey in it.)

And to survey his dead and earthy image,
What were it but to make my sorrow greater?

WARWICK
Come hither, gracious sovereign. View this body.

KING
That is to see how deep my grave is made.
For with his soul fled all my worldly solace;
For seeing him I see my life in death.   152

WARWICK
As surely as my soul intends to live
With that dread King that took our state upon Him   154
To free us from His Father's wrathful curse,
I do believe that violent hands were laid
Upon the life of this thrice-famèd duke.   157

SUFFOLK
A dreadful oath, sworn with a solemn tongue!
What instance gives Lord Warwick for his vow?   159

WARWICK
See how the blood is settled in his face.
Oft have I seen a timely-parted ghost,   161
Of ashy semblance, meager, pale, and bloodless,
Being all descended to the laboring heart,   163
Who, in the conflict that it holds with death,   164
Attracts the same for aidance 'gainst the enemy,   165
Which with the heart there cools and ne'er returneth 166
To blush and beautify the cheek again.   167
But see, his face is black and full of blood;
His eyeballs further out than when he lived,
Staring full ghastly, like a strangled man;
His hair upreared, his nostrils stretched with
    struggling;   171
His hands abroad displayed, as one that grasped   172
And tugged for life and was by strength subdued.
Look, on the sheets his hair, you see, is sticking;
His well-proportioned beard made rough and rugged,
Like to the summer's corn by tempest lodged.   176
It cannot be but he was murdered here.
The least of all these signs were probable.   178

SUFFOLK
Why, Warwick, who should do the Duke to death?
Myself and Beaufort had him in protection,
And we, I hope, sir, are no murderers.

WARWICK
But both of you were vowed Duke Humphrey's foes,
[*To Cardinal*] And you, forsooth, had the good Duke to
    keep.   183
'Tis like you would not feast him like a friend,   184
And 'tis well seen he found an enemy.   185

QUEEN
Then you, belike, suspect these noblemen   186

As guilty of Duke Humphrey's timeless death.   187

WARWICK
Who finds the heifer dead and bleeding fresh
And sees fast by a butcher with an ax,   189
But will suspect 'twas he that made the slaughter?
Who finds the partridge in the puttock's nest   191
But may imagine how the bird was dead,
Although the kite soar with unbloodied beak?
Even so suspicious is this tragedy.

QUEEN
Are you the butcher, Suffolk? Where's your knife?
Is Beaufort termed a kite? Where are his talons?   196
[*The bed is withdrawn. Exeunt Cardinal, Somerset,*
and others.]

SUFFOLK   I wear no knife to slaughter sleeping men;
But here's a vengeful sword, rusted with ease,   198
That shall be scourèd in his rancorous heart
That slanders me with murder's crimson badge.
Say, if thou dar'st, proud lord of Warwickshire,
That I am faulty in Duke Humphrey's death.

WARWICK
What dares not Warwick, if false Suffolk dare him?

QUEEN
He dares not calm his contumelious spirit,   204
Nor cease to be an arrogant controller,   205
Though Suffolk dare him twenty thousand times.

WARWICK
Madam, be still—with reverence may I say—
For every word you speak in his behalf
Is slander to your royal dignity.

SUFFOLK
Blunt-witted lord, ignoble in demeanor!
If ever lady wronged her lord so much,
Thy mother took into her blameful bed
Some stern untutored churl, and noble stock   213
Was graft with crab-tree slip—whose fruit thou art   214
And never of the Nevilles' noble race.

WARWICK
But that the guilt of murder bucklers thee   216
And I should rob the deathsman of his fee,   217
Quitting thee thereby of ten thousand shames,   218
And that my sovereign's presence makes me mild,   219
I would, false murderous coward, on thy knee
Make thee beg pardon for thy passèd speech   221
And say it was thy mother that thou meant'st,   222
That thou thyself wast born in bastardy;
And after all this fearful homage done,   224

---

152 **For ... death** i.e., for in his death I see an image of how transitory
is our life (including my own) in its passage toward death.   154 **King**
i.e., Christ.   **state** i.e., human nature   157 **thrice-famèd** very famous
159 **instance** proof   161 **a timely-parted ghost** the remains of one
having died in the natural course of events   163 **Being all descended**
i.e., the blood having all descended   164 **Who** which, i.e., the heart
165 **the same** i.e., the blood.   **aidance** aid.   **the enemy** i.e., death
166 **Which** i.e., the blood   167 **blush** cause to take on sanguine color
171 **upreared** standing on end   172 **abroad displayed** spread apart
176 **corn** grain.   **lodged** beaten down.   178 **were probable** would be
sufficient confirmation.   183 **to keep** in your custody.   184 **like**
likely   185 **well seen** obvious   186 **belike** perchance

187 **timeless** untimely   189 **fast by** close by   191 **puttock's** kite's
196.1–2 *Exeunt ... others* (The Cardinal's exit is marked in the Quarto
at 202.1, not in the Folio. Somerset's exit here is even more uncertain,
but he is not needed for the ensuing quarrel and may help the ailing
and guilt-ridden Cardinal off-stage. Also, at some point, the bed and
its dead occupant must be withdrawn or concealed by curtains.)
198 **ease** i.e., disuse   204 **contumelious** contemptuous, contentious
205 **controller** critic, detractor   213–14 **Some ... slip** some bold,
ignorant peasant, and thus the noble lineage of the Neville family tree
was grafted with a cutting of a wild variety, resulting in bastardy.
(*Slip* may also suggest "moral lapse.")   216 **But that** Were it not that.
bucklers shields   217 **deathsman** executioner   218 **Quitting** ridding
219 **that** were it not that   221 **passèd** just spoken   222 **And ... thy**
mother i.e., and force you to admit it was your own mother. (The
emphasis is on *thy*.)   224 **fearful homage** craven submission

Give thee thy hire and send thy soul to hell,   225
Pernicious bloodsucker of sleeping men!   226

SUFFOLK
Thou shalt be waking while I shed thy blood,   227
If from this presence thou dar'st go with me.   228

WARWICK
Away, even now, or I will drag thee hence!
Unworthy though thou art, I'll cope with thee   230
And do some service to Duke Humphrey's ghost.
                              Exeunt [*Suffolk and Warwick*].

KING
What stronger breastplate than a heart untainted?
Thrice is he armed that hath his quarrel just,
And he but naked, though locked up in steel,   234
Whose conscience with injustice is corrupted.
                              A noise within.

QUEEN   What noise is this?

         *Enter Suffolk and Warwick with their weapons
         drawn.*

KING
Why, how now, lords? Your wrathful weapons
    drawn
Here in our presence? Dare you be so bold?
Why, what tumultuous clamor have we here?

SUFFOLK
The trait'rous Warwick, with the men of Bury,
Set all upon me, mighty sovereign.

         Enter Salisbury.

SALISBURY [*to the Commons, within*]
Sirs, stand apart. The King shall know your mind.—
Dread lord, the commons send you word by me,
Unless Lord Suffolk straight be done to death   244
Or banishèd fair England's territories,
They will by violence tear him from your palace
And torture him with grievous ling'ring death.
They say, by him the good Duke Humphrey died;
They say, in him they fear Your Highness' death;
And mere instinct of love and loyalty,   250
Free from a stubborn opposite intent,   251
As being thought to contradict your liking,   252
Makes them thus forward in his banishment.   253
They say, in care of your most royal person,
That if Your Highness should intend to sleep,
And charge that no man should disturb your rest
In pain of your dislike or pain of death,   257
Yet, notwithstanding such a strait edict,   258

Were there a serpent seen with forkèd tongue
That slyly glided towards Your Majesty,
It were but necessary you were waked,
Lest, being suffered in that harmful slumber,   262
The mortal worm might make the sleep eternal.   263
And therefore do they cry, though you forbid,
That they will guard you, whe'er you will or no,   265
From such fell serpents as false Suffolk is—   266
With whose envenomèd and fatal sting   267
Your loving uncle, twenty times his worth,   268
They say, is shamefully bereft of life.   269

COMMONS (*within*)
An answer from the King, my lord of Salisbury!

SUFFOLK
'Tis like the commons, rude unpolished hinds,   271
Could send such message to their sovereign!
[*To Salisbury*] But you, my lord, were glad to be
    employed,
To show how quaint an orator you are.   274
But all the honor Salisbury hath won
Is that he was the lord ambassador
Sent from a sort of tinkers to the King.   277

COMMONS (*within*)
An answer from the King, or we will all break in!

KING
Go, Salisbury, and tell them all from me,
I thank them for their tender loving care;
And had I not been cited so by them,   281
Yet did I purpose as they do entreat.
For, sure, my thoughts do hourly prophesy
Mischance unto my state by Suffolk's means.   284
And therefore, by His majesty I swear,   285
Whose far unworthy deputy I am,
He shall not breathe infection in this air   287
But three days longer, on the pain of death.
                              [*Exit Salisbury.*]

QUEEN
Oh, Henry, let me plead for gentle Suffolk!   289

KING
Ungentle queen, to call him gentle Suffolk!
No more, I say! If thou dost plead for him,
Thou wilt but add increase unto my wrath.
Had I but said, I would have kept my word,   293
But when I swear, it is irrevocable.
[*To Suffolk*] If, after three days' space, thou here be'st
    found
On any ground that I am ruler of,
The world shall not be ransom for thy life.—

---

225 **Give** i.e., I would give.   **hire** reward (i.e., death)   226 **bloodsucker . . . men** (Warwick accuses Suffolk of killing Gloucester in his
sleep, suggesting further that he is a sort of vampire.)   227 **waking**
(Suffolk responds sarcastically to the accusation of killing sleeping
men.)   228 **If . . . me** if you will withdraw with me from this royal
presence to a place where we can fight a duel. (Drawing swords is not
allowed in the King's presence, as also at lines 237–8.)   230 **cope
with** encounter   234 **naked** i.e., unprotected, spiritually vulnerable.
locked . . . steel encased in armor   244 **straight** at once   250 **mere
instinct** pure impulse   251–2 **Free . . . liking** innocent of any stubborn willfulness that might be interpreted as crossing your wishes
253 **forward in** bold, insistent upon   257 **In pain** under penalty
258 **strait** strict

262 **being suffered** you being permitted to remain   263 **mortal
worm** deadly serpent   265 **whe'er** whether   266 **fell** cruel
267–9 **With . . . life** with whose venomous and fatal sting, they say,
your uncle (who is twenty times more worthy than Suffolk) is
deprived of life.   271 **'Tis like** i.e., What a strange coincidence that.
(Suffolk sarcastically implies that Salisbury has put the commons up
to this importuning.)   **hinds** boors, rustics   274 **quaint** skilled,
clever   277 **sort** gang   281 **cited** incited, urged   284 **Mischance**
disaster   285 **His** i.e., God's   287 **breathe** breathe out, spread
289 **gentle** noble   293 **but said** merely spoken, without an oath

Come, Warwick, come, good Warwick, go with me.
I have great matters to impart to thee.   299
           Exit [with all but Queen and Suffolk].
QUEEN [*to the King and Warwick, as they depart*]
Mischance and sorrow go along with you!
Heart's discontent and sour affliction
Be playfellows to keep you company!
There's two of you; the devil make a third,   303
And threefold vengeance tend upon your steps!   304
SUFFOLK
Cease, gentle Queen, these execrations,
And let thy Suffolk take his heavy leave.   306
QUEEN
Fie, coward woman and softhearted wretch!
Hast thou not spirit to curse thine enemies?
SUFFOLK
A plague upon them, wherefore should I curse them?
Could curses kill, as doth the mandrake's groan,   310
I would invent as bitter searching terms,   311
As curst, as harsh, and horrible to hear,   312
Delivered strongly through my fixèd teeth,
With full as many signs of deadly hate,
As lean-faced Envy in her loathsome cave.
My tongue should stumble in mine earnest words,
Mine eyes should sparkle like the beaten flint,
My hair be fixed on end, as one distract;   318
Ay, every joint should seem to curse and ban;   319
And even now my burdened heart would break,
Should I not curse them. Poison be their drink!
Gall, worse than gall, the daintiest that they taste!
Their sweetest shade a grove of cypress trees!   323
Their chiefest prospect murdering basilisks!   324
Their softest touch as smart as lizards' stings!   325
Their music frightful as the serpent's hiss,
And boding screech owls make the consort full!   327
All the foul terrors in dark-seated hell—
QUEEN
Enough, sweet Suffolk. Thou torment'st thyself,
And these dread curses, like the sun 'gainst glass,   330
Or like an overchargèd gun, recoil   331
And turn the force of them upon thyself.
SUFFOLK
You bade me ban, and will you bid me leave?   333
Now, by the ground that I am banished from,
Well could I curse away a winter's night,   335
Though standing naked on a mountain top,

Where biting cold would never let grass grow,
And think it but a minute spent in sport.
QUEEN
Oh, let me entreat thee cease! Give me thy hand,
That I may dew it with my mournful tears;
Nor let the rain of heaven wet this place
To wash away my woeful monuments.   342
                    [*She kisses his hand.*]
Oh, could this kiss be printed in thy hand,
That thou mightst think upon these by the seal,   344
Through whom a thousand sighs are breathed for
   thee!   345
So, get thee gone, that I may know my grief;   346
'Tis but surmised whiles thou art standing by,
As one that surfeits thinking on a want.   348
I will repeal thee, or, be well assured,   349
Adventure to be banishèd myself;   350
And banishèd I am, if but from thee.
Go, speak not to me. Even now, begone!
Oh, go not yet! Even thus two friends condemned
Embrace and kiss and take ten thousand leaves,
Loather a hundred times to part than die.
                    [*They embrace.*]
Yet now farewell, and farewell life with thee!
SUFFOLK
Thus is poor Suffolk ten times banishèd,
Once by the King, and three times thrice by thee.
'Tis not the land I care for, wert thou thence.
A wilderness is populous enough,
So Suffolk had thy heavenly company;   361
For where thou art, there is the world itself,
With every several pleasure in the world,   363
And where thou art not, desolation.
I can no more. Live thou to joy thy life;   365
Myself no joy in naught but that thou liv'st.

           Enter Vaux.

QUEEN
Whither goes Vaux so fast? What news, I prithee?
VAUX
To signify unto His Majesty   368
That Cardinal Beaufort is at point of death;
For suddenly a grievous sickness took him
That makes him gasp and stare and catch the air,
Blaspheming God and cursing men on earth.
Sometime he talks as if Duke Humphrey's ghost
Were by his side; sometimes he calls the King,
And whispers to his pillow as to him
The secrets of his overchargèd soul;   376

299.1 *Exit* (Possibly the bed and Gloucester's body are concealed or withdrawn at this point; see line 196.1.)   303 two i.e., the King and Warwick   304 tend upon follow   306 heavy sorrowful   310 mandrake's groan (Folk belief held that when the forked and man-shaped mandrake root was pulled from the ground, it uttered a shriek that was fatal to the hearer or would drive him or her mad; compare with *Romeo and Juliet*, 4.3.47–8.)   311 searching probing, cutting   312 curst malignant   318 distract mad   319 ban curse   323 cypress trees (Associated with death because they were often planted in graveyards.)   324 prospect view.   basilisks (See line 52 above.)   325 smart stinging   327 boding portending evil.   consort ensemble of musicians   330 'gainst glass being reflected in a mirror   331 overchargèd overloaded   333 leave leave off.   335 Well . . . night I would gladly curse the duration of a winter's night when nights are longest

342 monuments i.e., tears as memorials of sorrow.   344 these i.e., my lips.   seal imprint   345 Through whom i.e., through which lips   346 know fully comprehend   348 As . . . want like a person (such as myself) who, enjoying plenty, anticipates a time of deprivation.   349 repeal thee bring about your recall   350 Adventure risk   361 So so long as   363 several distinct   365 I . . . more I cannot go on.   joy enjoy   368 signify report   376 overchargèd overburdened with guilt

And I am sent to tell His Majesty
That even now he cries aloud for him.

QUEEN
Go tell this heavy message to the King.   *Exit [Vaux].*
Ay me, what is this world? What news are these!
But wherefore grieve I at an hour's poor loss,   381
Omitting Suffolk's exile, my soul's treasure?   382
Why only, Suffolk, mourn I not for thee,
And with the southern clouds contend in tears—   384
Theirs for the earth's increase, mine for my sorrows?   385
Now get thee hence. The King, thou know'st, is coming.
If thou be found by me, thou art but dead.   387

SUFFOLK
If I depart from thee, I cannot live,
And in thy sight to die, what were it else
But like a pleasant slumber in thy lap?
Here could I breathe my soul into the air,
As mild and gentle as the cradle babe
Dying with mother's dug between its lips—   393
Where, from thy sight, I should be raging mad   394
And cry out for thee to close up mine eyes,
To have thee with thy lips to stop my mouth.
So shouldst thou either turn my flying soul,   397
Or I should breathe it so into thy body,
And then it lived in sweet Elysium.   399
To die by thee were but to die in jest;   400
From thee to die were torture more than death.   401
Oh, let me stay, befall what may befall!

QUEEN
Away! Though parting be a fretful corrosive,   403
It is applièd to a deathful wound.   404
To France, sweet Suffolk. Let me hear from thee,
For wheresoe'er thou art in this world's globe,
I'll have an Iris that shall find thee out.   407

SUFFOLK   I go.
QUEEN   And take my heart with thee.
SUFFOLK
A jewel, locked into the woefull'st cask   410
That ever did contain a thing of worth.
Even as a splitted bark, so sunder we.   412
This way fall I to death.
QUEEN   This way for me.   413
                        Exeunt [separately].

❖

381 an hour's (i.e., the Cardinal has figuratively but an hour left to
live in any case)   382 Omitting neglecting   384 southern i.e., especially moist   385 Theirs . . . increase the clouds' moisture being
intended to make crops grow   387 by me near me. but dead as good as
dead.   393 dug nipple, breast   394 Where whereas. from out of
397 turn . . . soul turn back and prevent the soul's escape, preserve my
life. (The soul was thought to leave the body through the mouth.)
399 lived would live. Elysium classical abode after death of those
favored by the gods.   400 die in jest i.e., not truly to die at all. (To die carries the suggestion of experiencing orgasm.)   401 From away from
403 fretful corrosive painful and caustic course of treatment   404 deathful fatal (since Suffolk's remaining would prove fatal)   407 Iris Juno's
messenger   410 cask casket   412 splitted bark sailing vessel split in two
413.1 Exeunt (Gloucester's body in its bed is probably concealed or
removed earlier, perhaps at line 196.1 or line 299.1; since the bed is
needed immediately in the next scene, it almost certainly does not remain
onstage until the end of this scene.)

[3.3]

*Enter the King, Salisbury, and Warwick, to the
Cardinal in bed, [raving and staring as if he
were mad].*

KING
How fares my lord? Speak, Beaufort, to thy sovereign.
CARDINAL
If thou be'st Death, I'll give thee England's treasure,
Enough to purchase such another island,
So thou wilt let me live and feel no pain.   4
KING
Ah, what a sign it is of evil life,
Where death's approach is seen so terrible!
WARWICK
Beaufort, it is thy sovereign speaks to thee.
CARDINAL
Bring me unto my trial when you will.
Died he not in his bed? Where should he die?   9
Can I make men live, whe'er they will or no?   10
Oh, torture me no more! I will confess.
Alive again? Then show me where he is.
I'll give a thousand pound to look upon him.
He hath no eyes! The dust hath blinded them.
Comb down his hair. Look, look! It stands upright,
Like lime-twigs set to catch my wingèd soul.   16
Give me some drink, and bid the apothecary
Bring the strong poison that I bought of him.   18
KING
O thou eternal mover of the heavens,
Look with a gentle eye upon this wretch!
Oh, beat away the busy meddling fiend
That lays strong siege unto this wretch's soul,
And from his bosom purge this black despair!
WARWICK
See, how the pangs of death do make him grin!   24
SALISBURY
Disturb him not. Let him pass peaceably.
KING
Peace to his soul, if God's good pleasure be!
Lord Card'nal, if thou think'st on heaven's bliss,
Hold up thy hand. Make signal of thy hope.
                        [The Cardinal dies.]
He dies and makes no sign. O God, forgive him!
WARWICK
So bad a death argues a monstrous life.
KING
Forbear to judge, for we are sinners all.
Close up his eyes and draw the curtain close,   32
And let us all to meditation. *[The curtains are closed.]*
                        Exeunt.

❖

3.3. Location: The Cardinal's bedchamber.
0.2 in bed (In the Quarto version, the curtains are drawn and the
Cardinal "is discovered in his bed," raving and staring; compare with
3.2.0.1–2.)   4 So provided   9 he i.e., Gloucester   10 whe'er whether
16 lime-twigs twigs smeared with sticky birdlime to trap birds
18 of from   24 grin bare his teeth.   32 curtain (The bed itself, presumably "thrust out" onstage for this brief scene, would have to be removed
at this point; the curtains here are presumably bed curtains, although in
the Quarto version they are drawn open at line 1 in such a way that the
Cardinal is brought into view without having to be brought in on a bed,
i.e., using a curtained area backstage.)

[4.1]

*Alarum [within]. Fight at sea. Ordnance goes
off. Enter Lieutenant, [a Master, a Master's
Mate, Walter Whitmore, and others; with them]
Suffolk [disguised], and others, [prisoners].*

LIEUTENANT
The gaudy, blabbing, and remorseful day   1
Is crept into the bosom of the sea,
And now loud-howling wolves arouse the jades   3
That drag the tragic melancholy night,
Who, with their drowsy, slow, and flagging wings   5
Clip dead men's graves, and from their misty jaws   6
Breathe foul contagious darkness in the air.
Therefore bring forth the soldiers of our prize;   8
For, whilst our pinnace anchors in the Downs,   9
Here shall they make their ransom on the sand,   10
Or with their blood stain this discolored shore.   11
Master, this prisoner freely give I thee;   12
And thou that art his mate, make boot of this;   13
The other, Walter Whitmore, is thy share.   14
*[Three gentlemen prisoners, one of them Suffolk,
are apportioned and handed over.]*

FIRST GENTLEMAN
What is my ransom, Master? Let me know.

MASTER
A thousand crowns, or else lay down your head.

MATE *[to the Second Gentleman]*
And so much shall you give, or off goes yours.   17

WHITMORE
What, think you much to pay two thousand crowns,
And bear the name and port of gentlemen?   19
Cut both the villains' throats! For die you shall.
The lives of those which we have lost in fight   21
Be counterpoised with such a petty sum?   22

FIRST GENTLEMAN
I'll give it, sir, and therefore spare my life.

SECOND GENTLEMAN
And so will I, and write home for it straight.   24

WHITMORE *[to Suffolk]*
I lost mine eye in laying the prize aboard,   25
And therefore to revenge it shalt thou die;
And so should these, if I might have my will.

LIEUTENANT
Be not so rash. Take ransom; let him live.   28

SUFFOLK
Look on my George; I am a gentleman.   29
Rate me at what thou wilt, thou shalt be paid.   30

WHITMORE
And so am I. My name is Walter Whitmore.   31
[Suffolk starts.]
How now, why starts thou? What, doth death affright?

SUFFOLK
Thy name affrights me, in whose sound is death.   33
A cunning man did calculate my birth   34
And told me that by water I should die.
Yet let not this make thee be bloody-minded;
Thy name is Gualtier, being rightly sounded.

WHITMORE
Gualtier or Walter, which it is, I care not.
Never yet did base dishonor blur our name   39
But with our sword we wiped away the blot.
Therefore, when merchantlike I sell revenge,   41
Broke be my sword, my arms torn and defaced,   42
And I proclaimed a coward through the world!

SUFFOLK *[revealing his face]*
Stay, Whitmore, for thy prisoner is a prince,
The Duke of Suffolk, William de la Pole.

WHITMORE
The Duke of Suffolk muffled up in rags?

SUFFOLK
Ay, but these rags are no part of the Duke.
Jove sometime went disguised, and why not I?   48

LIEUTENANT
But Jove was never slain, as thou shalt be.

SUFFOLK
Obscure and lousy swain, King Henry's blood,   50
The honorable blood of Lancaster,
Must not be shed by such a jaded groom.   52
Hast thou not kissed thy hand and held my stirrup?
Bareheaded plodded by my footcloth mule   54
And thought thee happy when I shook my head?   55

4.1. Location: The coast of Kent.
0.2 Lieutenant i.e., captain in charge of the fighting; see lines 65 and 107. (He is called "Captain of the ship" in the Quarto stage direction, but the Master is the mariner in charge of sailing the vessel.) **1 blabbing** telltale, revealing. **remorseful** compassionate (as contrasted with the menacing night) **3 the jades** i.e., the winged dragons of Hecate that draw the chariot of the night **5 flagging** drooping **6 Clip** embrace, open. **their** the graves' **8 soldiers . . . prize** i.e., those taken from the vessel we have captured **9 pinnace** one-masted vessel. **Downs** anchorage off the Kentish coast **10 make their ransom** pay ransom money to obtain their release. **sand** shore **11 discolored** i.e., to be discolored by blood **12 this prisoner** i.e., the First Gentleman **13 his** i.e., the shipmaster's. **make . . . this** i.e., make a profit by ransoming this Second Gentleman **14 The other** i.e., Suffolk **17 so much** an equal sum **19 port** manners and demeanor appropriate to a rank or social station **21–2 The lives . . . sum** (An indignant question, and one that should seemingly be spoken by Whitmore rather than the Lieutenant, to whom the Folio assigns lines 18–22; see lines 25–8.) **22 counterpoised with** compensated, weighed (in a balance) against **24 straight** immediately. **25 laying . . . aboard** capturing the booty

28 Be . . . live (The Lieutenant's caution about killing the prisoners seems to contradict the threatening speech assigned to him in F at lines 18–22. Accordingly, those lines are here assigned to Whitmore, even though it is possible that the Lieutenant is simply being pragmatic in line 28, advising against killing the goose with the golden egg.) **29 George** the gold or jeweled figure of Saint George, worn as the insignium of the Order of the Knights of the Garter **30 Rate** Value, assess **31 am I** i.e., am I a gentleman. (Whitmore denies Suffolk's assertion of distinction in rank.) **33 Thy name** (i.e., Walter, pronounced like "water." In line 37 below, Suffolk tries to avert the prophecy referred to in lines 34–5 [compare with 1.4.33–4] by urging the French form of the name, Gualtier or Gaultier.) **34 A . . . birth** A fortune-teller cast my horoscope **39 blur** blot, stain **41 sell revenge** i.e., give up revenge (for my lost eye) in return for ransom money **42 arms** coat of arms **48 Jove . . . disguised** (Jupiter or Zeus sometimes adopted humble disguises, as when he was entertained by Philemon and Baucis in their lowly cottage, or appeared as a shepherd to the Titaness Mnemosyne.) **50 lousy** louse-infested, scurvy. **King Henry's blood** (Suffolk's claim to be connected to the house of Lancaster is a dubious one.) **52 jaded** ignoble. (With a play in the next line on one who deals with jades, or "horses.") **54 Bareheaded** (Servants went bareheaded in the presence of their masters, who kept their headgear on.) **footcloth** with a large, richly ornamented cloth laid over the back of a horse or mule, hanging down to the ground on each side **55 happy** fortunate. **shook** i.e., nodded

How often hast thou waited at my cup,
Fed from my trencher, kneeled down at the board,   57
When I have feasted with Queen Margaret?   59
Remember it, and let it make thee crestfall'n,   60
Ay, and allay this thy abortive pride,
How in our voiding lobby hast thou stood   61
And duly waited for my coming forth?   62
This hand of mine hath writ in thy behalf,   63
And therefore shall it charm thy riotous tongue.   64

WHITMORE
Speak, Captain, shall I stab the forlorn swain?   65

LIEUTENANT
First let my words stab him, as he hath me.

SUFFOLK
Base slave, thy words are blunt, and so art thou.   67

LIEUTENANT
Convey him hence, and on our longboat's side
Strike off his head.

SUFFOLK   Thou dar'st not, for thy own.   69

LIEUTENANT
Yes, Pole.

SUFFOLK   Pole?

LIEUTENANT   Pool! Sir Pool! Lord!   70
Ay, kennel, puddle, sink, whose filth and dirt   71
Troubles the silver spring where England drinks.
Now will I dam up this thy yawning mouth   73
For swallowing the treasure of the realm.   74
Thy lips that kissed the Queen shall sweep the
    ground,
And thou that smiledst at good Duke Humphrey's
    death
Against the senseless winds shalt grin in vain,   77
Who in contempt shall hiss at thee again.   78
And wedded be thou to the hags of hell   79
For daring to affy a mighty lord   80
Unto the daughter of a worthless king,
Having neither subject, wealth, nor diadem.   82
By devilish policy art thou grown great,   83
And, like ambitious Sylla, overgorged   84
With gobbets of thy mother's bleeding heart.   85

By thee Anjou and Maine were sold to France.
The false revolting Normans thorough thee   87
Disdain to call us lord, and Picardy
Hath slain their governors, surprised our forts,
And sent the ragged soldiers wounded home.
The princely Warwick, and the Nevilles all,
Whose dreadful swords were never drawn in vain,
As hating thee, are rising up in arms;   93
And now the house of York, thrust from the crown
By shameful murder of a guiltless king   95
And lofty, proud, encroaching tyranny,   96
Burns with revenging fire, whose hopeful colors
Advance our half-faced sun, striving to shine,   98
Under the which is writ, "Invitis nubibus."   99
The commons here in Kent are up in arms,
And, to conclude, reproach and beggary
Is crept into the palace of our King,
And all by thee.—Away! Convey him hence.

SUFFOLK
Oh, that I were a god, to shoot forth thunder
Upon these paltry, servile, abject drudges!
Small things make base men proud. This villain here,
Being captain of a pinnace, threatens more
Than Bargulus, the strong Illyrian pirate.   108
Drones suck not eagles' blood, but rob beehives.   109
It is impossible that I should die
By such a lowly vassal as thyself.
Thy words move rage and not remorse in me.
I go of message from the Queen to France;   113
I charge thee waft me safely cross the Channel.   114

LIEUTENANT   Walter—

WHITMORE
Come, Suffolk, I must waft thee to thy death.

SUFFOLK
Paene gelidus timor occupat artus.   117
It is thee I fear.

WHITMORE
Thou shalt have cause to fear before I leave thee.
What, are ye daunted now? Now will ye stoop.

FIRST GENTLEMAN [*to Suffolk*]
My gracious lord, entreat him, speak him fair.   121

SUFFOLK
Suffolk's imperial tongue is stern and rough,
Used to command, untaught to plead for favor.
Far be it we should honor such as these
With humble suit. No, rather let my head
Stoop to the block than these knees bow to any

---

57 trencher wooden dish or plate.   **kneeled . . . board** kneeled down as a sign of deferential service at my dining table.   **59 it** all this.   **crestfall'n** (1) downcast, abashed (2) deprived of the coat of arms boasted of in line 42   **60 allay** quell, put down.   **abortive** monstrous, unlikely to develop successfully to a promised or intended end   **61 our voiding lobby** my anteroom   **62 duly** dutifully   **63 writ . . . behalf** i.e., written to recommend you   **64 charm** put a spell on, silence   **65 Captain** (Appropriate courtesy title for the Lieutenant, since he is the military commander.)   **forlorn swain** desolate, wretched fellow. (Perhaps also mocking Suffolk as a lover of Margaret by invoking terms appropriate to the stereotyped unfortunate lover in Petrarchan love poetry.)   **67 blunt** blunted like an arrow with no point, harmless   **69 for thy own** i.e., for fear of losing your own head.   **70 Pole, Pool** (With verbal play on *poll*, head, *Pole*, Suffolk's family name, and *pool*, a pool of water, all similar in pronunciation.)   **71 kennel** gutter.   **sink** cesspool   **73 yawning** greedily gaping   **74 For swallowing** (1) lest it swallow (2) for having swallowed   **77 senseless** insensible. (Suffolk's head is to be put up on display.)   **78 Who** which, i.e., the winds.   **again** in return.   **79 the hags of hell** i.e., the Furies   **80 affy** betroth.   **lord** i.e., King Henry   **82 Having** i.e., he, Reignier, and Margaret, having   **83 policy** political cunning   **84 ambitious Sylla** i.e., Sulla (138–78 B.C.), Roman dictator, notorious for his cruel proceedings against his adversaries   **85 gobbets** pieces of raw flesh.   **mother's** i.e., England's

87 thorough through, because of   **93 As hating** because they hate   **95 shameful . . . king** i.e., the murder of Richard II by Bolingbroke, who thereupon sidestepped the Yorkist claim and became King Henry IV   **96 encroaching** seizing what is not its own   **98 Advance** raise, display.   **half-faced sun** (Edward III's and Richard II's banner displayed the rays of the sun dispersing themselves out of a cloud.)   **99 "Invitis nubibus"** "in spite of the clouds."   **108 Bargulus** (A pirate, Bardulis; mentioned in Cicero's *De Officiis*, 2.11.)   **109 Drones** Beetles, worthless parasites. (The legends referred to here, that beetles suck the blood of eagles and that drone bees rob beehives of honey, are typical of much imaginary natural history during the Renaissance.)   **113 of message** as messenger   **114 waft** transport, convey   **117 Paene . . . artus** Cold fear takes hold of my limbs almost entirely.   **121 speak him fair** speak courteously to him.

Save to the God of heaven and to my king;
And sooner dance upon a bloody pole   128
Than stand uncovered to the vulgar groom.   129
True nobility is exempt from fear.
More can I bear than you dare execute.

LIEUTENANT
Hale him away, and let him talk no more.   132

SUFFOLK
Come, soldiers, show what cruelty ye can,
That this my death may never be forgot!
Great men oft die by vile bezonians: 135
A Roman sworder and banditto slave   136
Murdered sweet Tully; Brutus' bastard hand   137
Stabbed Julius Caesar; savage islanders   138
Pompey the Great; and Suffolk dies by pirates.
     Exit Walter [Whitmore and others] with Suffolk.

LIEUTENANT
And as for these whose ransom we have set,
It is our pleasure one of them depart;
Therefore [*to the Second Gentleman*] come you with us
and let him go.   *Exeunt Lieutenant and the rest.* 142
     Manet the First Gentleman.

     *Enter Walter [Whitmore] with the body [and
     severed head of Suffolk].*

WHITMORE
There let his head and lifeless body lie,
Until the Queen his mistress bury it.   *Exit Walter.*

FIRST GENTLEMAN
Oh, barbarous and bloody spectacle!
His body will I bear unto the King.
If he revenge it not, yet will his friends;   147
So will the Queen, that living held him dear.   148
     [*Exit with the body and head.*]

     ♣

[4.2]

     *Enter [George] Bevis and John Holland, [with
     long staves].*

BEVIS Come, and get thee a sword, though made of a
lath. They have been up these two days.   2
HOLLAND They have the more need to sleep now, then.   3

BEVIS I tell thee, Jack Cade the clothier means to dress   4
the commonwealth, and turn it, and set a new nap   5
upon it.
HOLLAND So he had need, for 'tis threadbare. Well, I say   7
it was never merry world in England since gentlemen
came up.   9
BEVIS Oh, miserable age! Virtue is not regarded in hand-   10
icraftsmen.
HOLLAND The nobility think scorn to go in leather   12
aprons.
BEVIS Nay, more, the King's Council are no good
workmen.   15
HOLLAND True. And yet it is said, "Labor in thy vocation,"   16
which is as much to say as, "Let the magistrates be la-
boring men." And therefore should we be magistrates.
BEVIS Thou hast hit it, for there's no better sign of a brave   19
mind than a hard hand.   20
HOLLAND I see them, I see them! There's Best's son,
the tanner of Wingham—   22
BEVIS He shall have the skins of our enemies to make
dog's leather of.   24
HOLLAND And Dick the butcher—
BEVIS Then is sin struck down like an ox, and iniquity's
throat cut like a calf.
HOLLAND And Smith the weaver—
BEVIS Argo, their thread of life is spun.   29
HOLLAND Come, come, let's fall in with them.   30

     *Drum. Enter Cade, Dick [the] butcher, Smith
     the weaver, and a Sawyer, with infinite num-
     bers, [bearing long staves].*

CADE We, John Cade, so termed of our supposed   31
father—
DICK [*aside*] Or rather, of stealing a cade of herrings.   33
CADE For our enemies shall fall before us, inspired   34
with the spirit of putting down kings and princes—
command silence.
DICK Silence!
CADE My father was a Mortimer—   38
DICK [*aside*] He was an honest man, and a good
bricklayer.   40
CADE My mother a Plantagenet—
DICK [*aside*] I knew her well. She was a midwife.
CADE My wife descended of the Lacys—   43

---

128 And . . . pole i.e., and rather have my head stuck on a blood-stained pole on London Bridge for treason 129 uncovered bareheaded. groom menial. 132 Hale Drag 135 bezonians needy beggars, rascals 136 sworder gladiator. banditto bandit 137 Tully Cicero. bastard (According to an unreliable tradition, Brutus was thought to be Caesar's bastard son.) 138 savage islanders i.e., inhabitants of Lesbos. (But Plutarch reports, quite to the contrary, that Pompey the Great was stabbed by his former officers at the instigation of Ptolemy, in Egypt after his defeat by Caesar at Pharsalus.) 142 him i.e., the First Gentleman. 142.2 Manet He remains onstage 147 his i.e., Suffolk's 148 living while he was living 4.2. Location: Blackheath, a heath in Kent near London. 0.1 John Holland (The name of the actor assigned to a bit part in this scene; probably George Bevis is similarly a hired man in the company.) 2 lath wood strip. (A dagger of lath was often used by the comic Vice character in the morality plays.) They The Kentish peasants of the Cade rebellion. up up in rebellion 3 They . . . then (Holland's joke is that if they've been up, awake, for two days, they must be sleepy.)

4 dress (1) clothe, array (2) remedy 5 turn (1) turn inside out (as a way of refurbishing old cloth) (2) turn upside down socially. nap (1) fuzz or down on the surface of cloth (2) surface of the social structure 7 threadbare (1) shabby (2) down-at-heels. 9 came up came into fashion, rose to prominence. 10 regarded esteemed 12 think scorn disdain 15 workmen (1) laborers (2) masters of their calling. 16 "Labor . . . vocation" (A common exhortation, found in sermons, proclamations, and the official Homilies, and derived from 1 Cor. 7:20: "Let every man abide in the same vocation wherein he was called.") 19 hit it hit the nail on the head. brave noble 20 hard callused 22 Wingham a village near Canterbury 24 dog's leather (Used in the manufacture of gloves.) 29 Argo i.e., Ergo, therefore 30.2–3 infinite numbers i.e., as many supers as the theater can provide 31 We (The royal "we," fatuously misappropriated.) so termed of named after 33 of on account of. cade barrel, cask 34 For Because. fall (With a pun on the Latin cado, I fall.) 38 Mortimer (See 3.1.359 and note.) 40 bricklayer (With a play on Mortimer and "mortarer.") 43 Lacys the family name of the Earls of Lincoln. (But Dick makes an obvious pun in lines 44–5 on laces.)

DICK [*aside*] She was, indeed, a peddler's daughter, and sold many laces.

SMITH [*aside*] But now of late, not able to travel with her furred pack, she washes bucks here at home. 46

CADE Therefore am I of an honorable house.

DICK [*aside*] Ay, by my faith, the field is honorable; and there was he born, under a hedge, for his father had never a house but the cage. 49 51

CADE Valiant I am.

SMITH [*aside*] 'A must needs, for beggary is valiant. 53

CADE I am able to endure much.

DICK [*aside*] No question of that; for I have seen him whipped three market days together. 56

CADE I fear neither sword nor fire.

SMITH [*aside*] He need not fear the sword, for his coat is of proof. 59

DICK [*aside*] But methinks he should stand in fear of fire, being burnt i'th' hand for stealing of sheep. 61

CADE Be brave, then, for your captain is brave, and vows reformation. There shall be in England seven halfpenny loaves sold for a penny, the three-hooped pot shall have ten hoops, and I will make it felony to drink small beer. All the realm shall be in common, and in Cheapside shall my palfry go to grass. And when I am king, as king I will be— 64 65 66 67

ALL God save Your Majesty!

CADE I thank you, good people—there shall be no money. All shall eat and drink on my score; and I will apparel them all in one livery, that they may agree like brothers and worship me their lord. 71 72

DICK The first thing we do, let's kill all the lawyers.

CADE Nay, that I mean to do. Is not this a lamentable thing, that of the skin of an innocent lamb should be made parchment? That parchment, being scribbled o'er, should undo a man? Some say the bee stings, but I say 'tis the bee's wax; for I did but seal once to a thing, and I was never mine own man since. How now? Who's there? 79

Enter [some, bringing forward] a Clerk [of Chartham]. 82

SMITH The clerk of Chartham. He can write and read and cast account. 83

CADE Oh, monstrous!

SMITH We took him setting of boys' copies. 85

CADE Here's a villain!

SMITH H'as a book in his pocket with red letters in't. 87

CADE Nay, then, he is a conjurer.

DICK Nay, he can make obligations and write court hand. 89 90

CADE I am sorry for't. The man is a proper man, of mine honor; unless I find him guilty, he shall not die.— Come hither, sirrah, I must examine thee. What is thy name? 91

CLERK Emmanuel. 95

DICK They use to write it on the top of letters. 'Twill go hard with you. 96

CADE Let me alone.—Dost thou use to write thy name? Or hast thou a mark to thyself, like an honest, plain-dealing man? 98

CLERK Sir, I thank God, I have been so well brought up that I can write my name.

ALL He hath confessed. Away with him! He's a villain and a traitor.

CADE Away with him, I say! Hang him with his pen and inkhorn about his neck.   *Exit one with the Clerk.*

Enter Michael.

MICHAEL Where's our general?

CADE Here I am, thou particular fellow. 108

MICHAEL Fly, fly, fly! Sir Humphrey Stafford and his brother are hard by, with the King's forces.

CADE Stand, villain, stand, or I'll fell thee down. He shall be encountered with a man as good as himself. He is but a knight, is 'a? 112

MICHAEL No. 114

CADE To equal him, I will make myself a knight presently. [*He kneels.*] Rise up Sir John Mortimer. [*He rises.*] Now have at him! 116 117

Enter Sir Humphrey Stafford and his Brother, with drum and soldiers.

STAFFORD
Rebellious hinds, the filth and scum of Kent, 118
Marked for the gallows, lay your weapons down!
Home to your cottages, forsake this groom. 120
The King is merciful, if you revolt. 121

BROTHER
But angry, wrathful, and inclined to blood
If you go forward. Therefore yield, or die.

CADE
As for these silken-coated slaves, I pass not. 124
It is to you, good people, that I speak,
Over whom, in time to come, I hope to reign;

---

46 travel (Suggesting also *travail*, "work.") **47 furred pack** peddler's pack made of hides turned hair outward. (With a pun on "herd of deer.") **bucks** soiled clothes treated with *buck* or lye. (There is a bawdy suggestion of a loose woman, a vagabond's daughter, who has given up streetwalking with her *furred pack*, her genital organs, to service men [*bucks*] at home.) **49 field** (1) field in a coat of arms (2) out in the fields **51 cage** prison for petty malefactors. **53 'A must needs** He must be. **valiant** sturdy, able to work. (Ordinances forbade those who were sturdy to beg.) **56 whipped** i.e., for vagabondage **59 of proof** (1) impenetrable, tried by experience and hence reliable (2) well-worn. **61 burnt i'th' hand** branded **64–5 three-hooped pot** wooden quart-pot made with three metal bands or staves. (A ten-hooped pot would presumably hold a lot more.) **66 small** weak. (Cade intends that everyone shall drink strong beer.) **be in common** belong to everyone, be free from enclosure. (See 1.3.23–4 and note.) **67 Cheapside** chief location for markets in London (which Cade wishes to abolish) **71 on my score** at my expense **72 livery** uniform mode of dress as officially allowed to the retainers of certain great households **79 seal** i.e., sign and seal (with sealing wax) a legal agreement **82 Chartham** a town near Canterbury; or perhaps Chatham, near Rochester. **83 cast account** i.e., do arithmetic.

85 setting . . . copies setting out passages to be reproduced by school-boys. **87 H'as** He has. **book . . . in't** a schoolbook, probably a primer, with "rubricated" or red-lettered capitals. **89 make obligations** draw up bonds **89–90 court hand** professional hand used in preparing legal documents. **91 proper** handsome-looking **of** upon **95 Emmanuel** i.e., God with us. (Used frequently as heading for letters and documents.) **96 use** make it a practice **98 Let me alone** Let me handle this. **108 particular** private (as opposed to *general* in the previous line) **112 encountered with** opposed by **114 No** i.e., He is only a knight. **116 presently** immediately. **117 have at him** let me at him. **117.2 *drum*** drummer **118 hinds** peasants **120 groom** i.e., low wretch. **121 revolt** turn back. **124 pass** care

For I am rightful heir unto the crown.

STAFFORD
Villain, thy father was a plasterer,
And thou thyself a shearman, art thou not?   129

CADE
And Adam was a gardener.

BROTHER   And what of that?   130

CADE
Marry, this: Edmund Mortimer, Earl of March,
Married the Duke of Clarence' daughter, did he not?

STAFFORD   Ay, sir.

CADE
By her he had two children at one birth.

BROTHER   That's false.

CADE
Ay, there's the question. But I say 'tis true.
The elder of them, being put to nurse,
Was by a beggar-woman stol'n away,
And, ignorant of his birth and parentage,
Became a bricklayer when he came to age.
His son am I. Deny it if you can.

DICK
Nay, 'tis too true. Therefore he shall be king   142

SMITH   Sir, he made a chimney in my father's house,   143
and the bricks are alive at this day to testify it.
Therefore deny it not.

STAFFORD
And will you credit this base drudge's words,
That speaks he knows not what?

ALL
Ay, marry, will we. Therefore get ye gone.

BROTHER
Jack Cade, the Duke of York hath taught you this.

CADE [aside]   He lies, for I invented it myself.—Go to,   150
sirrah, tell the King from me that for his father's
sake, Henry the Fifth, in whose time boys went to
span-counter for French crowns, I am content he   153
shall reign; but I'll be Protector over him.

DICK   And furthermore, we'll have the Lord Saye's   155
head for selling the dukedom of Maine.

CADE   And good reason; for thereby is England
mained, and fain to go with a staff, but that my   158
puissance holds it up. Fellow kings, I tell you that that   159
Lord Saye hath gelded the commonwealth and made
it an eunuch; and more than that, he can speak
French, and therefore he is a traitor.

STAFFORD
Oh, gross and miserable ignorance!

CADE   Nay, answer, if you can. The Frenchmen are our
enemies. Go to, then, I ask but this: can he that speaks
with the tongue of an enemy be a good counselor,
or no?

ALL   No, no! And therefore we'll have his head.

BROTHER [to Stafford]
Well, seeing gentle words will not prevail,
Assail them with the army of the King.

STAFFORD
Herald, away, and throughout every town
Proclaim them traitors that are up with Cade,
That those which fly before the battle ends   173
May, even in their wives' and children's sight,
Be hanged up for example at their doors.
And you that be the King's friends, follow me.
                Exeunt [the two Staffords, and soldiers].

CADE
And you that love the commons, follow me.
Now show yourselves men; 'tis for liberty!
We will not leave one lord, one gentleman;
Spare none but such as go in clouted shoon,   180
For they are thrifty honest men and such
As would, but that they dare not, take our parts.

DICK   They are all in order and march toward us.   183

CADE   But then are we in order when we are most out
of order. Come, march forward.   [Exeunt.]

❦

[4.3]

*Alarums to the fight, wherein both the Staffords
are slain. Enter Cade and the rest.*

CADE   Where's Dick, the butcher of Ashford?

DICK   Here, sir.

CADE   They fell before thee like sheep and oxen, and
thou behaved'st thyself as if thou hadst been in thine
own slaughterhouse. Therefore thus will I reward
thee: the Lent shall be as long again as it is, and thou   6
shalt have a license to kill for a hundred lacking one.   7

DICK   I desire no more.

CADE   And, to speak truth, thou deserv'st no less. This
monument of the victory will I bear [putting on Sir   10
Humphrey's armor]; and the bodies shall be dragged at
my horse heels till I do come to London, where we
will have the Mayor's sword borne before us.

DICK   If we mean to thrive and do good, break open the   14
jails and let out the prisoners.

CADE   Fear not that, I warrant thee. Come, let's march   16
towards London.   Exeunt [with the Staffords' bodies].

❦

---

129 **shearman** one who shears the excess nap (see line 5) from woolen cloth during its manufacture   **130 Adam . . . gardener** (Adam's having been a gardener in the Garden of Eden, as described in the Book of Genesis, was often cited as biblical authority for radical ideas of abolishing all social rank.)   **142 too** very   **143 he** i.e., Cade's father   **150 Go to** (An expression of impatient scorn; also in line 165.)   **153 span-counter** a boys' game, in which one throws a counter or a piece of money that the other wins if he can throw another that hits it or falls within a span (nine inches) of it.   **crowns** (1) coins (2) kingdoms   **155 Lord Saye** (A peer implicated with Suffolk in the loss of Anjou and Maine.)   **158 mained** maimed. (With a pun on *Maine*.)   **fain to go** obliged to walk   **158–9 but . . . puissance** were it not that my power

173 **That . . . fly** i.e., so that those cowardly traitors who will surely flee   **180 clouted shoon** hobnailed or patched shoes   **183 in order** in battle array. (But Cade, in reply, plays on the contrast between public order and rebellion.)
4.3. Location: Scene continues at Blackheath.
0.1–2 (The bodies of the slain Staffords must be removed at some point.)   **6–7 Lent . . . one** (For Dick the butcher's benefit, Cade proposes to double the length of Lent, during which animals could be butchered only by special license in order to supply the sick and others with particular needs; during this period, Dick is to have license to kill ninety-nine animals a week, or to supply ninety-nine persons, or for ninety-nine years.)   **10 monument** memorial   **14 do good** succeed   **16 Fear** Doubt.   **warrant** promise

[4.4]

*Enter the King with a supplication, and the
Queen with Suffolk's head, the Duke of Buckingham, and the Lord Saye.*

QUEEN [*to herself*]
Oft have I heard that grief softens the mind
And makes it fearful and degenerate.
Think therefore on revenge and cease to weep.
But who can cease to weep and look on this?
Here may his head lie on my throbbing breast,
But where's the body that I should embrace?

BUCKINGHAM [*to the King*]   What answer makes Your
Grace to the rebels' supplication?

KING
I'll send some holy bishop to entreat,
For God forbid so many simple souls
Should perish by the sword! And I myself,
Rather than bloody war shall cut them short,
Will parley with Jack Cade their general.
But stay, I'll read it over once again.   [*He reads.*]

QUEEN [*to herself*]
Ah, barbarous villains! Hath this lovely face
Ruled, like a wandering planet, over me,   16
And could it not enforce them to relent
That were unworthy to behold the same?

KING
Lord Saye, Jack Cade hath sworn to have thy head.

SAYE
Ay, but I hope Your Highness shall have his.

KING [*to the Queen*]   How now, madam?
Still lamenting and mourning for Suffolk's death?
I fear me, love, if that I had been dead,
Thou wouldst not have mourned so much for me.

QUEEN
No, my love, I should not mourn, but die for thee.

Enter a Messenger.

KING
How now, what news? Why com'st thou in such
haste?

FIRST MESSENGER
The rebels are in Southwark. Fly, my lord!   27
Jack Cade proclaims himself Lord Mortimer,
Descended from the Duke of Clarence' house,
And calls Your Grace usurper, openly,
And vows to crown himself in Westminster.
His army is a ragged multitude
Of hinds and peasants, rude and merciless.
Sir Humphrey Stafford and his brother's death
Hath given them heart and courage to proceed.
All scholars, lawyers, courtiers, gentlemen,
They call false caterpillars and intend their death.   37

KING
Oh, graceless men! They know not what they do.   38

BUCKINGHAM
My gracious lord, retire to Killingworth   39
Until a power be raised to put them down.   40

QUEEN
Ah, were the Duke of Suffolk now alive,
These Kentish rebels would be soon appeased!   42

KING
Lord Saye, the traitors hateth thee;
Therefore away with us to Killingworth.

SAYE
So might Your Grace's person be in danger.
The sight of me is odious in their eyes;
And therefore in this city will I stay
And live alone as secret as I may.

Enter another Messenger.

SECOND MESSENGER
Jack Cade hath gotten London Bridge!
The citizens fly and forsake their houses.
The rascal people, thirsting after prey,
Join with the traitor, and they jointly swear
To spoil the city and your royal court.   53

BUCKINGHAM
Then linger not, my lord. Away, take horse!

KING
Come, Margaret. God, our hope, will succor us.

QUEEN
My hope is gone, now Suffolk is deceased.

KING [*to Saye*]
Farewell, my lord. Trust not the Kentish rebels.

BUCKINGHAM
Trust nobody, for fear you be betrayed.

SAYE
The trust I have is in mine innocence,
And therefore am I bold and resolute.   *Exeunt.*

❧

[4.5]

*Enter Lord Scales upon the Tower, walking.
Then enter two or three Citizens below.*

SCALES How now, is Jack Cade slain?

FIRST CITIZEN No, my lord, nor likely to be slain; for they
have won the bridge, killing all those that withstand
them. The Lord Mayor craves aid of Your Honor from
the Tower to defend the city from the rebels.

SCALES
Such aid as I can spare you shall command.
But I am troubled here with them myself;
The rebels have essayed to win the Tower.
But get you to Smithfield and gather head,   9
And thither I will send you Matthew Gough.
Fight for your king, your country, and your lives.
And so, farewell, for I must hence again.   *Exeunt.*

❧

4.4. Location: London. The royal court.
16 wandering i.e., not like the fixed stars   **27 Southwark** suburb on
the south bank of the Thames, just across the river from London.
37 caterpillars i.e., thieves, despoilers   **38 They . . . do** (An echo of
Christ's "Father, forgive them, for they know not what they do,"
Luke 23:34.)

39 Killingworth Kenilworth (in Warwickshire)   **40 power** army
42 appeased pacified.   **53 spoil** despoil, sack
4.5. Location: The Tower of London.
0.1 upon the Tower i.e., probably in the rear gallery above the main
stage   **9 Smithfield** area of open fields to the northwest, just outside London's walls.   **head** an armed force

[4.6]

Enter Jack Cade and the rest, and strikes his staff on London Stone.

CADE   Now is Mortimer lord of this city. And here, sitting upon London Stone, I charge and command that, of the city's cost, the Pissing Conduit run nothing but claret wine this first year of our reign. And now henceforward it shall be treason for any that calls me other than Lord Mortimer.   3

Enter a Soldier, running.

SOLDIER   Jack Cade! Jack Cade!

CADE   Knock him down there.   *They kill him.*

SMITH   If this fellow be wise, he'll never call ye Jack Cade more. I think he hath a very fair warning.

DICK   My lord, there's an army gathered together in Smithfield.

CADE   Zounds, then, let's go fight with them. But first go and set London Bridge on fire, and, if you can, burn down the Tower too. Come, let's away.   13

Exeunt omnes.

✣

[4.7]

Alarums. Matthew Gough is slain, and all the rest. Then enter Jack Cade, with his company.

CADE   So, sirs. Now go some and pull down the Savoy; others to th' Inns of Court. Down with them all.   1, 2

DICK   I have a suit unto Your Lordship.

CADE   Be it a lordship, thou shalt have it for that word.   4

DICK   Only that the laws of England may come out of your mouth.   5, 6

HOLLAND   *[aside]*   Mass, 'twill be sore law then, for he was thrust in the mouth with a spear, and 'tis not whole yet.   7, 9

SMITH   *[aside]*   Nay, John, it will be stinking law, for his breath stinks with eating toasted cheese

CADE   I have thought upon it. It shall be so. Away! Burn all the records of the realm. My mouth shall be the Parliament of England.

HOLLAND   *[aside]*   Then we are like to have biting statutes, unless his teeth be pulled out.

CADE   And henceforward all things shall be in common.

Enter a Messenger.

MESSENGER   My lord, a prize, a prize! Here's the Lord Saye, which sold the towns in France; he that made us pay one-and-twenty fifteens, and one shilling to the pound, the last subsidy.   19, 20, 21

Enter George [Bevis], with the Lord Saye.

CADE   Well, he shall be beheaded for it ten times.—Ah, thou say, thou serge, nay, thou buckram lord! Now art thou within point-blank of our jurisdiction regal. What canst thou answer to My Majesty for giving up of Normandy unto Monsieur Basimecu, the Dauphin of France? Be it known unto thee by these presence, even the presence of Lord Mortimer, that I am the besom that must sweep the court clean of such filth as thou art. Thou hast most traitorously corrupted the youth of the realm in erecting a grammar school; and whereas, before, our forefathers had no other books but the score and the tally, thou hast caused printing to be used, and contrary to the King his crown and dignity thou hast built a paper mill. It will be proved to thy face that thou hast men about thee that usually talk of a noun and a verb and such abominable words as no Christian ear can endure to hear. Thou hast appointed justices of peace to call poor men before them about matters they were not able to answer. Moreover, thou hast put them in prison, and because they could not read thou hast hanged them, when indeed only for that cause they have been most worthy to live. Thou dost ride on a footcloth, dost thou not?   23, 24, 26, 27, 28, 29, 33, 34, 37, 42, 43, 44

SAYE   What of that?

CADE   Marry, thou oughtst not to let thy horse wear a cloak, when honester men than thou go in their hose and doublets.   47, 48

DICK   And work in their shirt too—as myself, for example, that am a butcher.

SAYE   You men of Kent—

DICK   What say you of Kent?

SAYE   Nothing but this: 'tis *bona terra, mala gens.*   53

CADE   Away with him, away with him! He speaks Latin.

4.6. Location: London.
0.2 *London Stone* ancient landmark, located in Cannon Street **3 of** at.   **Pissing Conduit** popular name of a conduit, or common fountain, near the Royal Exchange   **13 Zounds** By God's wounds. (An oath.)

4.7. Location: London. The rebellion continues. (The historical location moves from Cannon Street to Smithfield, but onstage the action is continuous.)
0.1–2 *all the rest* i.e., the King's forces. (The bodies of Gough and other slain must be removed at some point.)   **1 the Savoy** (This palace, residence of the Duke of Lancaster, was actually destroyed during Wat Tyler's rebellion in 1381 and was not rebuilt until the sixteenth century.)   **2 th' Inns of Court** sets of buildings in London belonging to legal societies training persons in the law   **4 lordship** title and estates of a noble lord. (Playing on the honorific *Your Lordship* in line 3, by which Cade is flattered.)   **5–6 Only . . . mouth** i.e., That your word would be the only law in England; cf. lines 13–14. **7 Mass** By the Mass. (An oath.)   **9 whole** healed

19–21 he . . . subsidy (The Messenger greatly inflates the amount of the subsidy. This taxation was of course deeply resented.)   **23 say, serge, buckram** kinds of cloth, of silk, wool, and coarse linen, respectively. (With a pun on "say/Saye.")   **24 point-blank** so close that a missile will travel straight to the target   **26 Basimecu** *baise mon cul* (French), "kiss my ass"   **27–8 these presence** i.e., Cade's error, or joke, for "these presents, this present document." (A legal phrase.) **29 besom** broom   **33 score . . . tally** means of reckoning accounts or keeping score, in which a stick was notched and then split lengthwise, thereby giving both debtor and creditor a record of what was owed   **34 printing** (An anachronism; the first printing press was set up in England twenty-seven years after Cade's rebellion, and the first paper mill was set up in 1495.)   **King his** King's   **37 usually** habitually   **42 could not read** i.e., could not demonstrate their literacy in Latin and thereby claim exemption from criminal prosecution through "benefit of clergy"   **43 only . . . cause** for that reason alone **44 footcloth** richly ornamented horse covering; see the note for 4.1.54 **47–8 hose and doublets** breeches and jacket (without a cloak). **53 bona . . . gens** good land, bad people.

SAYE
  Hear me but speak, and bear me where you will.
  Kent, in the *Commentaries* Caesar writ,
  Is termed the civil'st place of all this isle.
  Sweet is the country, because full of riches,
  The people liberal, valiant, active, wealthy,   60
  Which makes me hope you are not void of pity.
  I sold not Maine, I lost not Normandy,
  Yet to recover them would lose my life.
  Justice with favor have I always done;   64
  Prayers and tears have moved me, gifts could never.
  When have I aught exacted at your hands   66
  But to maintain the King, the realm, and you?
  Large gifts have I bestowed on learnèd clerks,   68
  Because my book preferred me to the King;   69
  And, seeing ignorance is the curse of God,
  Knowledge the wing wherewith we fly to heaven,
  Unless you be possessed with devilish spirits
  You cannot but forbear to murder me.
  This tongue hath parleyed unto foreign kings   74
  For your behoof—   75
CADE   Tut, when struck'st thou one blow in the field?
SAYE
  Great men have reaching hands. Oft have I struck   77
  Those that I never saw, and struck them dead.
BEVIS   Oh, monstrous coward! What, to come behind
  folks?
SAYE
  These cheeks are pale for watching for your good.   81
CADE   Give him a box o'th'ear, and that will make 'em
  red again.
SAYE
  Long sitting to determine poor men's causes   84
  Hath made me full of sickness and diseases.
CADE   Ye shall have a hempen caudle, then, and the   86
  help of hatchet.   87
DICK   Why dost thou quiver, man?
SAYE
  The palsy, and not fear, provokes me.
CADE   Nay, he nods at us, as who should say, "I'll be   90
  even with you." I'll see if his head will stand steadier
  on a pole or no. Take him away and behead him.
SAYE
  Tell me wherein have I offended most?
  Have I affected wealth or honor? Speak.   94
  Are my chests filled up with extorted gold?

  Is my apparel sumptuous to behold?
  Whom have I injured, that ye seek my death?
  These hands are free from guiltless blood-shedding,   98
  This breast from harboring foul deceitful thoughts.
  Oh, let me live!
CADE   [*aside*]   I feel remorse in myself with his words,
  but I'll bridle it. He shall die, an it be but for   102
  pleading so well for his life.—Away with him! He
  has a familiar under his tongue; he speaks not i'   104
  God's name. Go, take him away, I say, and strike
  off his head presently; and then break into his   106
  son-in-law's house, Sir James Cromer, and strike off
  his head, and bring then both upon two poles hither.
ALL   It shall be done.
SAYE
  Ah, countrymen! If when you make your prayers,
  God should be so obdurate as yourselves,
  How would it fare with your departed souls?   112
  And therefore yet relent, and save my life.
CADE
  Away with him! And do as I command ye.
                          [*Exeunt some with Lord Saye.*]
  The proudest peer in the realm shall not wear a head
  on his shoulders unless he pay me tribute. There shall
  not a maid be married but she shall pay to me her
  maidenhead ere they have it. Men shall hold of me *in*   118
  capite; and we charge and command that their wives   119
  be as free as heart can wish or tongue can tell.   120
DICK   My lord, when shall we go to Cheapside and   121
  take up commodities upon our bills?   122
CADE   Marry, presently.
ALL   Oh, brave!   124

  Enter one with the heads [*of Lord Saye and Sir
  John Cromer upon two poles*].

CADE   But is not this braver? Let them kiss one another,
  for they loved well when they were alive. [*The heads
  are made to touch one another.*] Now part them again,
  lest they consult about the giving up of some more
  towns in France. Soldiers, defer the spoil of the city   129
  until night, for with these borne before us instead of
  maces will we ride through the streets, and at every   131
  corner have them kiss. Away!   *Exeunt.*

                          ❖

60 liberal generous, free, refined   64 favor compassion   66 aught . . .
hands taken any taxes from you (in my capacity as Lord Treasurer)
68 clerks scholars   69 my . . . King my book learning gained me preferment at court   74 parleyed unto entered into negotiations with
75 behoof benefit   77 reaching far-reaching   81 for watching from
remaining awake, on watch   84 Long . . . determine Lengthy sitting
on the judge's bench to hear and adjudicate   86 caudle warm gruel,
given to sick people. (*Hempen caudle* means that his restorative is to be
a hanging.)   86–7 the help of hatchet i.e., the assistance of the executioner's ax. (Possibly a variant of, or error for, "pap with a hatchet,"
the administering of punishment under the ironical guise of kindly
correction.)   90 as who should as one might   94 affected preferred, striven for

98 guiltless blood-shedding shedding of guiltless blood   102 an it be
but if only   104 familiar familiar spirit, attendant demon   106 presently
immediately   112 your departed souls your souls when you die.
118 maidenhead (Cade claims the *droit de seigneur*, presumed customary right of a feudal lord to be the first to enjoy a bride sexually on her
marriage night.)   hold hold property   118–19 in capite as tenant in
chief, i.e., directly from the crown. (The Latin *caput*, "head," also puns
on *maidenhead*.)   120 free (1) legally independent (2) licentious
121–2 take . . . bills obtain goods on credit. (With a pun on *bills*, military weapons having wooden handles and a blade or ax-shaped
head.)   124 brave fine, splendid.   129 spoil plundering   131 maces
staffs of office carried by sergeants

[4.8]

Alarum and retreat. Enter again Cade and all
his rabblement.

CADE Up Fish Street! Down Saint Magnus' Corner! Kill   1
and knock down! Throw them into Thames! (*Sound a*
parley.) What noise is this I hear? Dare any be so bold   3
to sound retreat or parley when I command them kill?

Enter Buckingham and old Clifford [attended].

BUCKINGHAM
  Ay, here they be that dare and will disturb thee.
  Know, Cade, we come ambassadors from the King
  Unto the commons, whom thou hast misled,
  And here pronounce free pardon to them all   8
  That will forsake thee and go home in peace.

CLIFFORD
  What say ye, countrymen? Will ye relent,
  And yield to mercy whilst 'tis offered you,
  Or let a rebel lead you to your deaths?
  Who loves the King and will embrace his pardon,   13
  Fling up his cap and say "God save His Majesty!"
  Who hateth him and honors not his father,
  Henry the Fifth, that made all France to quake,
  Shake he his weapon at us and pass by.   17

ALL God save the King! God save the King!
                    [They fling up their caps.]

CADE What, Buckingham and Clifford, are ye so brave?   19
  And you, base peasants, do ye believe him? Will you   20
  needs be hanged with your pardons about your necks?   21
  Hath my sword therefore broke through London
  gates, that you should leave me at the White Hart in   23
  Southwark? I thought ye would never have given out   24
  these arms till you had recovered your ancient freedom. But you are all recreants and dastards, and de-   26
  light to live in slavery to the nobility. Let them break
  your backs with burdens, take your houses over your
  heads, ravish your wives and daughters before your
  faces. For me, I will make shift for one, and so God's   30
  curse light upon you all!

ALL We'll follow Cade, we'll follow Cade!

CLIFFORD
  Is Cade the son of Henry the Fifth,
  That thus you do exclaim you'll go with him?
  Will he conduct you through the heart of France
  And make the meanest of you earls and dukes?   36

Alas, he hath no home, no place to fly to,
  Nor knows he how to live but by the spoil,   38
  Unless by robbing of your friends and us.
  Were't not a shame that, whilst you live at jar,   40
  The fearful French, whom you late vanquishèd,   41
  Should make a start o'er seas and vanquish you?   42
  Methinks already in this civil broil
  I see them lording it in London streets,
  Crying "*Villiago!*" unto all they meet.   45
  Better ten thousand baseborn Cades miscarry   46
  Than you should stoop unto a Frenchman's mercy.
  To France, to France, and get what you have lost!   48
  Spare England, for it is your native coast.   49
  Henry hath money; you are strong and manly;
  God on our side, doubt not of victory.

ALL A Clifford! A Clifford! We'll follow the King and   52
  Clifford!

CADE [*aside*] Was ever feather so lightly blown to and
  fro as this multitude? The name of Henry the Fifth
  hales them to an hundred mischiefs and makes them   56
  leave me desolate. I see them lay their heads together   57
  to surprise me. My sword make way for me, for here   58
  is no staying.—In despite of the devils and hell, have   59
  through the very middest of you! And heavens and   60
  honor be witness that no want of resolution in me, but
  only my followers' base and ignominious treasons,
  makes me betake me to my heels.   63
              Exit [Cade, running through the crowd,
                          weapon in hand].

BUCKINGHAM
  What, is he fled? Go some, and follow him,
  And he that brings his head unto the King
  Shall have a thousand crowns for his reward.
                          Exeunt some of them.
  Follow me, soldiers. We'll devise a mean
  To reconcile you all unto the King.   *Exeunt omnes.*

❦

[4.9]

Sound trumpets. Enter King, Queen, and Som-
erset, on the terrace [aloft].

KING
  Was ever king that joyed an earthly throne   1
  And could command no more content than I?
  No sooner was I crept out of my cradle
  But I was made a king, at nine months old.

4.8. **Location: Southwark. The rebellion continues. (The historical location moves from Smithfield to Southwark, but the onstage action is uninterrupted.)**
0.1 *retreat* signal to cease attack. **1 Fish Street, Saint Magnus' Corner** locations in London near London Bridge, directly across from Southwark. **3 s.d.** *parley* trumpet signal requesting a conference between the contending forces. (Also in line 4.) **8 pronounce** proclaim **13 Who** Anyone who. (Also in line 15.) **17 Shake he** let him shake (in a gesture of brave resolution) **19 brave** haughty. **20–1 Will . . . necks?** i.e., Will you credulously trust in offered pardons that will only hang you once you have surrendered? **23 that** to the end that. **White Hart** a famous inn in Southwark **24 out** up **26 recreants** those who break faith, cowards **30 For** As for. **make shift for one** manage for myself **36 meanest** lowest born

38 the spoil pillaging **40 at jar** in discord **41 fearful** timid. **late** lately **42 make a start** suddenly arouse themselves **45 "Villiago!"** "Coward, scoundrel!" (Italian.) **46 miscarry** encounter misfortune **48 get** recapture **49 coast** land. **52 A Clifford!** Rally to Clifford! **56 hales** draws **57 lay . . . together** conspire **58 surprise** capture. **My sword** Let my sword **58–9 here . . . staying** there's no staying here. **59 despite** spite **59–60 have through** i.e., here I come through **63.1 Exit** (In the Quarto version, Cade "runs through them with his staff and flies away.")
4.9. **Location: A castle, historically identified as Kenilworth Castle in Warwickshire, though in the theater we only know that the King receives the submission of the rebels shortly after the fighting in London.**
0.2 *on the terrace* i.e., probably in the gallery to the rear above the main stage **1 joyed** enjoyed

Was never subject longed to be a king
As I do long and wish to be a subject.

Enter Buckingham and [old] Clifford.

BUCKINGHAM
Health and glad tidings to Your Majesty!

KING
Why, Buckingham, is the traitor Cade surprised?   8
Or is he but retired to make him strong?   9

*Enter [below] multitudes, with halters about
their necks.*

CLIFFORD
He is fled, my lord, and all his powers do yield,   10
And humbly thus, with halters on their necks,
Expect Your Highness' doom, of life or death.   12

KING
Then, heaven, set ope thy everlasting gates
To entertain my vows of thanks and praise!   14
Soldiers, this day have you redeemed your lives
And showed how well you love your prince and
    country.
Continue still in this so good a mind,
And Henry, though he be infortunate,
Assure yourselves, will never be unkind.
And so, with thanks and pardon to you all,
I do dismiss you to your several countries.   21

ALL God save the King! God save the King!
[Exeunt the multitudes.]

Enter a Messenger.

MESSENGER
Please it. Your Grace to be advertisèd   23
The Duke of York is newly come from Ireland,
And with a puissant and a mighty power
Of gallowglasses and stout kerns   26
Is marching hitherward in proud array,
And still proclaimeth, as he comes along,   28
His arms are only to remove from thee
The Duke of Somerset, whom he terms a traitor.

KING
Thus stands my state, twixt Cade and York distressed, 31
Like to a ship that, having scaped a tempest,
Is straightway calmed and boarded with a pirate.   33
But now is Cade driven back, his men dispersed,   34
And now is York in arms to second him.
I pray thee, Buckingham, go and meet him,
And ask him what's the reason of these arms.   37
Tell him I'll send Duke Edmund to the Tower;   38
And, Somerset, we will commit thee thither,
Until his army be dismissed from him.

SOMERSET My lord,
I'll yield myself to prison willingly,
Or unto death, to do my country good.

KING *[to Buckingham]*
In any case, be not too rough in terms,
For he is fierce and cannot brook hard language.   45

BUCKINGHAM
I will, my lord, and doubt not so to deal
As all things shall redound unto your good.   47

KING
Come, wife, let's in, and learn to govern better,
For yet may England curse my wretched reign.
Flourish. Exeunt.

❖

[4.10]

Enter Cade.

CADE Fie on ambitions! Fie on myself, that have a
sword and yet am ready to famish! These five days
have I hid me in these woods and durst not peep out,
for all the country is laid for me. But now am I so   4
hungry that, if I might have a lease of my life for a
thousand years, I could stay no longer. Wherefore, o'er   6
a brick wall have I climbed into this garden to see if I
can eat grass or pick a sallet another while, which is   8
not amiss to cool a man's stomach this hot weather.
And I think this word "sallet" was born to do me
good; for many a time, but for a sallet, my brainpan
had been cleft with a brown bill; and many a time,   12
when I have been dry and bravely marching, it hath
served me instead of a quart pot to drink in; and now
the word "sallet" must serve me to feed on.   15

Enter Iden [and his men].

IDEN
Lord, who would live turmoilèd in the court,
And may enjoy such quiet walks as these?
This small inheritance my father left me
Contenteth me, and worth a monarchy.   17
I seek not to wax great by others' waning,
Or gather wealth, I care not with what envy.
Sufficeth that I have maintains my state
And sends the poor well pleasèd from my gate.   21

CADE *[aside]* Zounds, here's the lord of the soil come to   22
seize me for a stray, for entering his fee simple with-   23
out leave.—Ah, villain, thou wilt betray me and get a
thousand crowns of the King by carrying my head to   25

---

45 **brook** endure   47 **redound unto** turn out for
4.10. Location: Kent. Iden's garden.
4 **is laid** is lying in wait   6 **stay** wait   8 **sallet** salad greens. (With a
pun in the following lines on *sallet*, "light helmet.")   **another while**
yet again   12 **brown bill** brown-handled weapon with a blade or ax-
shaped head   15.1 **and his men** (The Quarto reads, "Enter *Iacke Cade*
at one doore, and at the other maister *Alexander Eyden* and his men,"
and at lines 38–9 Cade refers to Iden's "five men.")   17 **And may**
when he might   21 **I care . . . envy** no matter with what cost of being
envied.   22–3 **Sufficeth . . . gate** It suffices that what I have maintains my position (as country gentleman) and also provides enough
to feed the poor who come to my gate.   25 **stray** stray animal, which
might be seized.   **fee simple** estate belonging to an owner and his
heirs forever

---

8 **surprised** captured.   9.1 *halters* nooses   10 **powers** troops. (Also
at line 25.)   12 **Expect** await.   **doom** judgment   14 **entertain**
receive   21 **several countries** various localities.   23 **advertisèd**
informed   26 **gallowglasses, kerns** Irish horsemen and foot soldiers,
armed with heavy and light weapons, respectively   28 **still** continually   31 **state** condition, situation   33 **calmed** becalmed.   **with** by
34 **But now** Even now, just now   37 **of** for   38 **Duke Edmund** i.e.,
Edmund Beaufort, the Duke of Somerset

him; but I'll make thee eat iron like an ostrich and   28
swallow my sword like a great pin, ere thou and I part.

IDEN
Why, rude companion, whatsoe'er thou be,   30
I know thee not. Why then should I betray thee?
Is't not enough to break into my garden,
And like a thief to come to rob my grounds,
Climbing my walls in spite of me the owner,
But thou wilt brave me with these saucy terms?   35

CADE   Brave thee? Ay, by the best blood that ever was   36
broached, and beard thee too. Look on me well. I have   37
eat no meat these five days, yet come thou and thy   38
five men, an if I do not leave you all as dead as a   39
doornail, I pray God I may never eat grass more.

IDEN
Nay, it shall ne'er be said, while England stands,
That Alexander Iden, an esquire of Kent,
Took odds to combat a poor famished man.   43
Oppose thy steadfast-gazing eyes to mine;
See if thou canst outface me with thy looks.   45
Set limb to limb, and thou art far the lesser;   46
Thy hand is but a finger to my fist,
Thy leg a stick comparèd with this truncheon;   48
My foot shall fight with all the strength thou hast;
And if mine arm be heavèd in the air,   50
Thy grave is digged already in the earth.   51
As for words, whose greatness answers words,   52
Let this my sword report what speech forbears.   53

CADE   By my valor, the most complete champion that   54
ever I heard! Steel, if thou turn the edge, or cut not out   55
the burly-boned clown in chines of beef ere thou sleep   56
in the sheath, I beseech God on my knees thou mayst
be turned to hobnails.   Here they fight. [Cade falls.]   58
Oh, I am slain! Famine and no other hath slain me. Let
ten thousand devils come against me, and give me but
the ten meals I have lost, and I'd defy them all. Wither,
garden! And be henceforth a burying place to all that
do dwell in this house, because the unconquered soul
of Cade is fled.

IDEN
Is't Cade that I have slain, that monstrous traitor?
Sword, I will hallow thee for this thy deed
And hang thee o'er my tomb when I am dead.
Ne'er shall this blood be wiped from thy point,
But thou shalt wear it as a herald's coat
To emblaze the honor that thy master got.   70

CADE   Iden, farewell, and be proud of thy victory. Tell
Kent from me she hath lost her best man, and exhort   72
all the world to be cowards; for I, that never feared   73
any, am vanquished by famine, not by valor.   Dies.

IDEN
How much thou wrong'st me, heaven be my judge.   75
Die, damnèd wretch, the curse of her that bare thee!   76
And as I thrust thy body in with my sword,
So wish I, I might thrust thy soul to hell.
Hence will I drag thee headlong by the heels   79
Unto a dunghill, which shall be thy grave,
And there cut off thy most ungracious head,
Which I will bear in triumph to the King,
Leaving thy trunk for crows to feed upon.
Exit, [dragging out the body].

✢

[5.1]

*Enter York and his army of Irish, with drum
and colors.*

YORK
From Ireland thus comes York to claim his right
And pluck the crown from feeble Henry's head.
Ring, bells, aloud! Burn, bonfires, clear and bright
To entertain great England's lawful king!   4
Ah, *sancta maiestas*, who would not buy thee dear?   5
Let them obey that knows not how to rule;
This hand was made to handle naught but gold.
I cannot give due action to my words   8
Except a sword or scepter balance it.   9
A scepter shall it have, have I a soul,   10
On which I'll toss the flower-de-luce of France.   11

Enter Buckingham.

Whom have we here? Buckingham, to disturb me?
The King hath sent him, sure. I must dissemble.
BUCKINGHAM
York, if thou meanest well, I great thee well.
YORK
Humphrey of Buckingham, I accept thy greeting.
Art thou a messenger, or come of pleasure?
BUCKINGHAM
A messenger from Henry, our dread liege,   17
To know the reason of these arms in peace;
Or why thou, being a subject as I am,
Against thy oath and true allegiance sworn

28 eat . . . ostrich Ostriches were thought to consume iron objects,
such as horseshoes.   30 rude companion base fellow   35 brave
defy, taunt.   saucy insolent   36–7 by . . . broached i.e., by Christ's
blood. (An oath. *Broached* means "stabbed, shed, tapped from a
cask.")   37 beard defy   38 eat eaten. (Pronounced "et.")   39 an if
if   43 odds advantage (i.e., the "five men" Cade refers to in line 39)
45 outface defy   46 Set Compare   48 truncheon heavy staff (i.e.,
Iden's leg)   50–1 And . . . earth i.e., if I but lift my arm, you're as
good as dead already.   52 whose . . . words i.e., I whose might is
more than a match for your words   53 report . . . forbears i.e., speak
through actions in place of words.   54 complete accomplished
55 turn the edge fail to cut   56 clown peasant.   chines roasts
58 turned to hobnails i.e., melted down and recast as boot nails.
70 emblaze proclaim as by a heraldic device

72–3 exhort . . . cowards i.e., explain to everyone, using me as an example, that bravery may prove unavailing; cowardice is the safest policy
75 How . . . judge i.e., Heaven can bear witness how unjust it is of you to
say that you were not overcome by my valor.   76 her i.e., you mother.
bare bore, gave birth to   79 headlong head downmost
5.1. Location: In the theater, Act 5 appears to take place in one continuous sweep, though historically the action begins between Dart-
ford and Blackheath just southeast of London in 1452–1453 (see line
46) and then shifts to a battlefield between London and St. Albans,
near the Castle Inn, in 1455.
0.1–2 *drum and colors* drummer and flag bearer.   4 entertain welcome
5 *sancta maiestas* sacred majesty   8–11 I cannot . . . France I can achieve
my avowed aims only through military might or kingly rule. Just as sure
as I have a soul, my hand will hold a scepter, by means of which I shall
hold aloft on my sword's point the heraldic emblem of France's royal coat
of arms.   17 dread leige awe-commanding lord

Should raise so great a power without his leave,   21
Or dare to bring thy force so near the court.

YORK [*aside*]
Scarce can I speak, my choler is so great.   23
Oh, I could hew up rocks and fight with flint,
I am so angry at these abject terms!   25
And now, like Ajax Telamonius,   26
On sheep or oxen could I spend my fury.
I am far better born than is the King,
More like a king, more kingly in my thoughts.
But I must make fair weather yet awhile,   30
Till Henry be more weak and I more strong.—
Buckingham, I prithee, pardon me,
That I have given no answer all this while;
My mind was troubled with deep melancholy.
The cause why I have brought this army hither
Is to remove proud Somerset from the King,
Seditious to His Grace and to the state.

BUCKINGHAM
That is too much presumption on thy part.
But if thy arms be to no other end,
The King hath yielded unto thy demand:
The Duke of Somerset is in the Tower.

YORK
Upon thine honor, is he prisoner?

BUCKINGHAM
Upon mine honor, he is prisoner.

YORK
Then, Buckingham, I do dismiss my powers.—
Soldiers, I thank you all. Disperse yourselves;
Meet me tomorrow in Saint George's field;   46
You shall have pay and everything you wish.
                            [*Exeunt soldiers*].
And let my sovereign, virtuous Henry,
Command my eldest son, nay, all my sons,   49
As pledges of my fealty and love;   50
I'll send them all as willing as I live.
Lands, goods, horse, armor, anything I have
Is his to use, so Somerset may die.   53

BUCKINGHAM
York, I commend this kind submission.
We twain will go into His Highness' tent.
                            [*They walk arm in arm.*]

Enter King and attendants.

KING
Buckingham, doth York intend no harm to us,
That thus he marcheth with thee arm in arm?

YORK
In all submission and humility
York doth present himself unto Your Highness.

KING
Then what intends these forces thou dost bring?

YORK
To heave the traitor Somerset from hence
And fight against that monstrous rebel Cade,
Who since I heard to be discomfited.   63

Enter Iden, with Cade's head.

IDEN
If one so rude and of so mean condition   64
May pass into the presence of a king,
Lo, I present Your Grace a traitor's head,
The head of Cade, whom I in combat slew.

KING
The head of Cade? Great God, how just art Thou!
Oh, let me view his visage, being dead,
That living wrought me such exceeding trouble.
Tell me, my friend, art thou the man that slew him?

IDEN I was, an't like Your Majesty.   72

KING
How art thou called, and what is thy degree?   73

IDEN
Alexander Iden, that's my name,
A poor esquire of Kent that loves his king.

BUCKINGHAM [*to the King*]
So please it you, my lord, 'twere not amiss
He were created knight for his good service.

KING
Iden, kneel down. [*Iden kneels.*] Rise up a knight.
                                    [*Iden rises.*]
We give thee for reward a thousand marks,   79
And will that thou henceforth attend on us.   80

IDEN
May Iden live to merit such a bounty,
And never live but true unto his liege!

Enter Queen and Somerset.

KING
See, Buckingham, Somerset comes with th' Queen.
Go bid her hide him quickly from the Duke.   84

QUEEN
For thousand Yorks he shall not hide his head,
But boldly stand and front him to his face.   86

YORK
How now? Is Somerset at liberty?
Then, York, unloose thy long-imprisoned thoughts
And let thy tongue be equal with thy heart.
Shall I endure the sight of Somerset?
False king, why hast thou broken faith with me,
Knowing how hardly I can brook abuse?   92
"King" did I call thee? No, thou art not king,
Not fit to govern and rule multitudes,
Which dar'st not—no, nor canst not—rule a traitor.   95
That head of thine doth not become a crown;
Thy hand is made to grasp a palmer's staff,   97

---

21 **power** armed force   23 **choler** anger. (See 1.2.51.)   25 **abject terms** degrading, insulting words.   26 **Ajax Telamonius** Ajax, the son of Telamon, one of the Greek heroes of the Trojan War, who, when the weapons of Achilles were allotted to Odysseus, slaughtered in his fury a flock of sheep, mistaking them for the enemy   30 **make fair weather** i.e., dissemble   46 **Saint George's field** an open area south of the Thames River near Southwark   49 **Command** demand   50 **pledges** hostages   53 **so** as long as

63 **discomfited** routed.   64 **rude** unpolished.   **mean condition** low rank   72 **an't like** if it please   73 **degree** social rank.   79 **marks** (Valued at two-thirds of a pound.)   80 **will** command   84 **the Duke** i.e., of York.   86 **front** confront   92 **brook abuse** tolerate deception. 95 **Which** you who   97 **palmer's** pilgrim's

And not to grace an awful princely scepter.   98
That gold must round engirt these brows of mine,
Whose smile and frown, like to Achilles' spear,   100
Is able with the change to kill and cure.
Here is a hand to hold a scepter up
And with the same to act controlling laws.   103
Give place. By heaven, thou shalt rule no more
O'er him whom heaven created for thy ruler.

SOMERSET
Oh, monstrous traitor! I arrest thee, York,
Of capital treason 'gainst the King and crown.   107
Obey, audacious traitor. Kneel for grace.

YORK
Wouldst have me kneel? First let me ask of these,   109
If they can brook I bow a knee to man.   110
[*To an attendant*] Sirrah, call in my sons to be my bail.
                                   [*Exit attendant.*]
I know, ere they will have me go to ward,   112
They'll pawn their swords for my enfranchisement.   113

QUEEN [*to Buckingham*]
Call hither Clifford. Bid him come amain,   114
To say if that the bastard boys of York   115
Shall be the surety for their traitor father.   116
                                   [*Exit Buckingham.*]

YORK [*to the Queen*]
O blood-bespotted Neapolitan,   117
Outcast of Naples, England's bloody scourge!
The sons of York, thy betters in their birth,
Shall be their father's bail, and bane to those   120
That for my surety will refuse the boys!   121

Enter Edward and Richard [Plantagenet, with
drum and soldiers, at one door].

See where they come. I'll warrant they'll make it good.

Enter [old] Clifford [and his Son, with drum
and soldiers, at the other door].

QUEEN
And here comes Clifford to deny their bail.

CLIFFORD [*kneeling before King Henry*]
Health and all happiness to my lord the King!
                                   [*He rises.*]

YORK
I thank thee, Clifford. Say, what news with thee?
Nay, do not fright us with an angry look.
We are thy sovereign, Clifford, kneel again.
For thy mistaking so, we pardon thee.

CLIFFORD
This is my king, York. I do not mistake,
But thou mistakes me much to think I do.—
To Bedlam with him! Is the man grown mad?   131

KING
Ay, Clifford, a bedlam and ambitious humor
Makes him oppose himself against his king.   132

CLIFFORD
He is a traitor. Let him to the Tower,   134
And chop away that factious pate of his.   135

QUEEN
He is arrested, but will not obey.
His sons, he says, shall give their words for him.

YORK Will you not, sons?

EDWARD
Ay, noble father, if our words will serve.

RICHARD
And if words will not, then our weapons shall.

CLIFFORD
Why, what a brood of traitors have we here!

YORK
Look in a glass, and call thy image so.   142
I am thy king, and thou a false-heart traitor.
Call hither to the stake my two brave bears,   144
That with the very shaking of their chains
They may astonish these fell-lurking curs.—   146
Bid Salisbury and Warwick come to me.
                    [*An attendant goes to summon them.*]

Enter the Earls of Warwick and Salisbury, [with
drum and soldiers].

CLIFFORD
Are these thy bears? We'll bait thy bears to death
And manacle the bearherd in their chains,   149
If thou dar'st bring them to the baiting place.   150

RICHARD
Oft have I seen a hot o'erweening cur   151
Run back and bite, because he was withheld,   152
Who, being suffered, with the bear's fell paw   153
Hath clapped his tail between his legs and cried;
And such a piece of service will you do,
If you oppose yourselves to match Lord Warwick.   156

---

98 awful awe-inspiring   **100 Achilles' spear** (Telephus, wounded by Achilles's spear, learned from an oracle that he could be cured only by the instrument that had wounded him. He was eventually cured by an application of rust from the point of the spear.)   **103 act** enact   **107 capital** punishable by death   **109 these** i.e., my sons, who are waiting outside, or followers   **110 brook . . . man** tolerate that I should bow my knee in submission to anyone.   **112 to ward** into custody   **113 pawn** pledge.   **enfranchisement** freedom.   **114–16 Bid . . . father** i.e., Bid Clifford come swiftly to express his views as to whether the illegitimate sons of York will be allowed to deliver their father from arrest as a traitor. (Implying that Clifford will forcefully oppose this attempt.)   **116.1 Exit Buckingham** (Buckingham must exit somewhere before an attendant is sent to find him at line 192, and here seems a likely place.)   **117 Neapolitan** (Margaret's father Reignier, or René, was titular King of Naples.)   **120–1 Shall . . . boys** will rescue York by force from this arrest, and visit destruction on those who oppose the attempt.   **121.2 drum** drummer.   *at one door* (The Quarto version is explicit that Plantagenet's sons enter "at one door" and Clifford with his son and forces "at the other.")

131 Bedlam hospital of St. Mary of Bethlehem in London, used as an asylum for the mentally deranged   **132 bedlam** mad.   **humor** disposition   **134 Let him** Let him be sent   **135 factious pate** rebellious head   **142 glass** mirror   **144 brave bears** i.e., Salisbury and his son Warwick. (Compare with lines 202–3 below, where Warwick describes the badge of his house as a *rampant bear chained to the ragged staff*. The image is from bearbaiting, in which bears were chained to a stake and attacked by *fell-lurking curs*, "cruelly waiting dogs," line 146.)   **146 astonish** frighten   **149 bearherd** bear handler, keeper (i.e., York)   **150 baiting place** bearbaiting pit.   **151 hot o'erweening** hot-tempered and overconfident   **152 bite** i.e., at its trainer, who is restraining it   **153 Who . . . paw** which cur, being released to attach the bear, at one blow of the bear's savage paw   **156 oppose yourselves** set yourselves up as opponents

CLIFFORD
Hence, heap of wrath, foul indigested lump,   157
As crooked in thy manners as thy shape!

YORK
Nay, we shall heat you thoroughly anon.   159

CLIFFORD
Take heed, lest by your heat you burn yourselves.

KING
Why, Warwick, hath thy knee forgot to bow?
Old Salisbury, shame to thy silver hair,
Thou mad misleader of thy brainsick son!
What, wilt thou on thy deathbed play the ruffian,
And seek for sorrow with thy spectacles?   165
Oh, where is faith? Oh, where is loyalty?
If it be banished from the frosty head,
Where shall it find a harbor in the earth?
Wilt thou go dig a grave to find out war,
And shame thine honorable age with blood?
Why art thou old and want'st experience?   171
Or wherefore dost abuse it if thou hast it?   172
For shame! In duty bend thy knee to me
That bows unto the grave with mickle age.   174

SALISBURY
My lord, I have considered with myself
The title of this most renownèd duke,
And in my conscience do repute His Grace
The rightful heir to England's royal seat.

KING
Hast thou not sworn allegiance unto me?

SALISBURY I have.

KING
Canst thou dispense with heaven for such an oath?   181

SALISBURY
It is great sin to swear unto a sin,
But greater sin to keep a sinful oath.
Who can be bound by any solemn vow
To do a murd'rous deed, to rob a man,
To force a spotless virgin's chastity,
To reave the orphan of his patrimony,   187
To wring the widow from her customed right,   188
And have no other reason for this wrong
But that he was bound by a solemn oath?

QUEEN
A subtle traitor needs no sophister.   191

KING [to an attendant]
Call Buckingham, and bid him arm himself.
                                    [Exit attendant.]

YORK [to King Henry]
Call Buckingham and all the friends thou hast,   193
I am resolved for death or dignity.   194

CLIFFORD
The first I warrant thee, if dreams prove true.

WARWICK
You were best to go to bed and dream again,   196
To keep thee from the tempest of the field.

CLIFFORD
I am resolved to bear a greater storm
Than any thou canst conjure up today;
And that I'll write upon thy burgonet,   200
Might I but know thee by thy household badge.   201

WARWICK
Now, by my father's badge, old Neville's crest,   202
The rampant bear chained to the ragged staff,
This day I'll wear aloft my burgonet,   204
As on a mountaintop the cedar shows   205
That keeps his leaves in spite of any storm,   206
Even to affright thee with the view thereof.

CLIFFORD
And from thy burgonet I'll rend thy bear
And tread it underfoot with all contempt,
Despite the bearherd that protects the bear.

YOUNG CLIFFORD
And so to arms, victorious father,
To quell the rebels and their complices.   212

RICHARD
Fie! Charity, for shame! Speak not in spite,
For you shall sup with Jesu Christ tonight.

YOUNG CLIFFORD
Foul stigmatic, that's more than thou canst tell.   215

RICHARD
If not in heaven, you'll surely sup in hell.
                                    Exeunt [separately].

                              ✤

[5.2]

[Alarums to the battle.] Enter Warwick.

WARWICK
Clifford of Cumberland, 'tis Warwick calls!
And if thou dost not hide thee from the bear,
Now, when the angry trumpet sounds alarum   3
And dead men's cries do fill the empty air,   4
Clifford, I say, come forth and fight with me!
Proud northern lord, Clifford of Cumberland,
Warwick is hoarse with calling thee to arms.

Enter York.

---

157 indigested lump (Bear cubs were supposedly born unformed [indigested] and had to be licked into shape by their mother. See *3 Henry VI,* 3.2.161, where Richard's hunched back and other deformities are compared with those of *an unlicked bear whelp.*) **159 heat you** i.e., warm you in the fighting. **anon** soon. **165 spectacles** (A sign of advanced age, like *silver hair,* line 162, and *frosty,* "white-haired," line 167.) **171–2 Why . . . hast it?** Why are you old before you are wise? Or why do you misuse your wisdom and experience if you have them? (*Want'st* means "lack.") **174 That bows** you that bow or your knee that bows. **mickle** great **181 dispense with heaven for** expect or obtain dispensation from heaven for breaking **187 reave** bereave **188 customed right** i.e., right to inherit a portion of her husband's estate **191 sophister** equivocator, expert in casuistry.

193 Call Even if you call **194 resolved for** determined to have. **dignity** exalted rank. **196 You were best** You had better **200 burgonet** light helmet or steel cap (upon which the wearer's heraldic device was often mounted) **201 Might . . . badge** if I can identify you in the battle by your family crest. **202 old Neville's crest** (The Nevilles' crest was, in fact, a bull; Warwick inherited his badge of a chained bear from his wife's family, the Beauchamps.) **204 aloft** on high **205 shows** shows itself **206 his leaves** its needles **212 complices** accomplices. **215 stigmatic** one branded with the mark of his crime (just as Richard is marked by his deformities) **5.2. Location:** Scene continues at the battlefield near the Castle Inn. **3 alarum** call to arms **4 dead** dying

How now, my noble lord? What, all afoot?

YORK
The deadly-handed Clifford slew my steed,
But match to match I have encountered him   10
And made a prey for carrion kites and crows
Even of the bonny beast he loved so well.

Enter [old] Clifford.

WARWICK [*to Clifford*]
Of one or both of us the time is come.

YORK
Hold, Warwick, seek thee out some other chase,   14
For I myself must hunt this deer to death.

WARWICK
Then, nobly, York! 'Tis for a crown thou fight'st.—
As I intend, Clifford, to thrive today,
It grieves my soul to leave thee unassailed.

          Exit Warwick.

CLIFFORD
What see'st thou in me, York? Why dost thou pause?

YORK
With thy brave bearing should I be in love,   20
But that thou art so fast mine enemy.   21

CLIFFORD
Nor should thy prowess want praise and esteem,   22
But that 'tis shown ignobly and in treason.

YORK
So let it help me now against thy sword
As I in justice and true right express it.

CLIFFORD
My soul and body on the action both!   26

YORK
A dreadful lay! Address thee instantly.   27
          [*They fight, and Clifford falls.*]

CLIFFORD
La fin couronne les oeuvres.   [*He dies.*] 28

YORK
Thus war hath given thee peace, for thou art still.
Peace with his soul, heaven, if it be thy will!   [*Exit.*]

Enter young Clifford.

YOUNG CLIFFORD
Shame and confusion! All is on the rout.   31
Fear frames disorder, and disorder wounds   32
Where it should guard. O war, thou son of hell,   33
Whom angry heavens do make their minister,   34
Throw in the frozen bosoms of our part   35
Hot coals of vengeance! Let no soldier fly.
He that is truly dedicate to war   37
Hath no self-love, nor he that loves himself   38

Hath not essentially but by circumstance   39
The name of valor. [*Seeing his dead father.*] Oh, let the
vile world end   40
And the premisèd flames of the last day   41
Knit earth and heaven together!
Now let the general trumpet blow his blast,   43
Particularities and petty sounds   44
To cease! Wast thou ordained, dear father,
To lose thy youth in peace, and to achieve   46
The silver livery of advisèd age,   47
And in thy reverence and thy chair days, thus   48
To die in ruffian battle? Even at this sight
My heart is turned to stone, and while 'tis mine   50
It shall be stony. York not our old men spares;   51
No more will I their babes. Tears virginal   52
Shall be to me even as the dew to fire,   53
And beauty, that the tyrant oft reclaims,   54
Shall to my flaming wrath be oil and flax.   55
Henceforth I will not have to do with pity.
Meet I an infant of the house of York,   57
Into as many gobbets will I cut it   58
As wild Medea young Absyrtus did.   59
In cruelty will I seek out my fame.   60
Come, thou new ruin of old Clifford's house:
As did Aeneas old Anchises bear,   62
So bear I thee upon my manly shoulders;
But then Aeneas bare a living load,   64
Nothing so heavy as these woes of mine.   65
       [*Exit, bearing off his father.*]

*Enter Richard and Somerset to fight. [Somerset
is killed under the sign of the Castle Inn.]*

RICHARD   So, lie thou there;
For underneath an alehouse' paltry sign,
The Castle in Saint Albans, Somerset
Hath made the wizard famous in his death.   69
Sword, hold thy temper; heart, be wrathful still.   70
Priests pray for enemies, but princes kill.   [*Exit.*] 71

Fight. Excursions. Enter King, Queen, and others.

39–40 Hath . . . valor is valiant only by happenstance, not in essence. (Such a person is not truly courageous.) **41 premisèd** foreordained. **last day** Day of judgment **43 general** i.e., summoning all humanity **44 Particularities** individual affairs **46 lose** expend **47 The silver . . . age** the silvery white hair that is emblematic of wise and cautious old age **48 And . . . days** and, in your days of being revered and confined to an invalid's chair **50 while 'tis mine** i.e., as long as my heart continues to beat **51 York . . . spares** York does not spare even our old men **52 virginal** of young maidens **53 as . . . fire** as tiny drops of water to a conflagration, i.e., ineffectual **54 that . . . reclaims** which often softens the temper of the tyrant **55 oil and flax** Proverbial means to make a fire burn hotter. **57 Meet I** If I should meet **58 gobbets** pieces or lumps of flesh **59 As . . . did** i.e., as Medea, daughter of King Aeetes of Colchis, did with her brother Absyrtus in order to help Jason recover the Golden Fleece. (Medea killed her brother and left pieces of his dismembered body in the father's path in order to facilitate her escape with Jason.) **60 fame** reputation. **62 As . . . bear** (In Virgil's *Aeneid*, Aeneas, fleeing from Troy, carried his aged father Anchises on his shoulders.) **64 bare** bore **65 Nothing** not at all. **heavy** (1) weighty (2) sorrowful **69 Hath . . . death** i.e., has confirmed by his death the prophecy that he would die *where castles mounted stand*. (See 1.4.36–8.) **70 still** always. **71 s.d. Exit** (The body of the slain Somerset must be removed at some point.) **71.1 Excursions** Sorties.

10 match to match equal to equal (or horse for horse) **14 chase** game, prey **20 bearing** demeanor **21 fast** unalterably, completely **22 want** lack **26 action** outcome of action **27 lay** wager, oath. **Address thee** Prepare yourself **28 La . . . oeuvres** The end crowns the work. **31 confusion** destruction. **on the rout** i.e., in disorderly retreat. **32 frames** causes **32–3 and disorder . . . guard** i.e., and disorderly retreat makes for casualties instead of effective defense. **34 minister** agent **35 frozen** i.e., unwarmed by wrathful courage. **part** party, faction **37 dedicate** dedicated **38 Hath no self-love** i.e., gives no thought to his own safety. **nor** conversely

QUEEN
 Away, my lord! You are slow. For shame, away!
KING
 Can we outrun the heavens? Good Margaret, stay.
QUEEN
 What are you made of? You'll nor fight nor fly.   74
 Now is it manhood, wisdom, and defense
 To give the enemy way, and to secure us   76
 By what we can, which can no more but fly.   77

Alarum afar off.

 If you be ta'en, we then should see the bottom
 Of all our fortunes; but if we haply scape,   79
 As well we may, if not through your neglect,   80
 We shall to London get, where you are loved
 And where this breach now in our fortunes made
 May readily be stopped.

Enter [young] Clifford.

YOUNG CLIFFORD
 But that my heart's on future mischief set,
 I would speak blasphemy ere bid you fly;
 But fly you must. Uncurable discomfit   86
 Reigns in the hearts of all our present parts.   87
 Away, for your relief! And we will live
 To see their day and them our fortune give.   89
 Away, my lord, away!   *Exeunt.*

❧

[5.3]

*Alarum. Retreat. Enter York, Richard, War-
wick, and soldiers, with drum and colors.*

YORK
 Of Salisbury, who can report of him,
 That winter lion, who in rage forgets   2
 Agèd contusions and all brush of time,   3

And like a gallant in the brow of youth   4
Repairs him with occasion? This happy day   5
Is not itself, nor have we won one foot,   6
If Salisbury be lost.

RICHARD   My noble father,
 Three times today I holp him to his horse,   8
 Three times bestrid him; thrice I led him off,   9
 Persuaded him from any further act.
 But still, where danger was, still there I met him,   11
 And like rich hangings in a homely house,   12
 So was his will in his old feeble body.
 But, noble as he is, look where he comes.

Enter Salisbury.

SALISBURY
 Now, by my sword, well hast thou fought today!
 By th' Mass, so did we all. I thank you, Richard.
 God knows how long it is I have to live,
 And it hath pleased Him that three times today
 You have defended me from imminent death.
 Well, lords, we have not got that which we have;   20
 'Tis not enough our foes are this time fled,
 Being opposites of such repairing nature.   22
YORK
 I know our safety is to follow them;
 For, as I hear, the King is fled to London
 To call a present court of Parliament.   25
 Let us pursue him ere the writs go forth.   26
 What says Lord Warwick? Shall we after them?
WARWICK
 After them? Nay, before them, if we can.
 Now, by my faith, lords, 'twas a glorious day.
 Saint Albans battle won by famous York
 Shall be eternized in all age to come.   31
 Sound drum and trumpets, and to London all,
 And more such days as these to us befall!

[Flourish.] Exeunt.

---

74 **nor fight** neither fight   76–7 **To . . . fly** to give way before the
enemy, and to protect our military situation by whatever means we
can, we who have no options other than to retreat.   79 **haply scape**
by chance escape   80 **if not** unless   86 **Uncurable discomfit** Hopeless discouragement   87 **our present parts** those forces still remaining to us.   89 **To . . . give** to see a day of success like theirs and let
them experience our misfortune.
5.3. Location: Scene continues at the battlefield.
2 **winter** i.e., aged   3 **brush** assault, collision

4–5 **And . . . occasion?** and as though he were a gallant young man
again renews his youth through brave action?   6 **foot** foot of ground
8 **holp** helped   9 **bestrid him** i.e., stood over him to defend him
when he was down   11 **still** continually   12 **hangings** tapestries.
homely modest   20 **got** secured   22 **Being . . . nature** they being
adversaries with such ability to recover quickly.   25 **present** immediate   26 **writs** official summonses issued by the King to members of
Parliament   31 **eternized** immortalized

The Third Part of King Henry the Sixth

enry VI, Part III, must be regarded not only as a part of Shakespeare's first historical four-play series, but also as a play in its own right, presumably seen on its first showing by an Elizabethan audience who, though aware of a larger context, witnessed this dramatic action as a self-contained event. Because *3 Henry VI* represents nearly the entire military phase of the civil war, it is the most crowded and bustling play of the series. Historically, it covers the period from the battles of Wakefield and second St. Albans (1460–1461) to the decisive Yorkist victories at Barnet and Tewkesbury (1471). These and other battles are actually represented onstage in a kind of theatrical shorthand making efficient use of a limited number of actors. The conventional method of representing armed conflict is by means of alarums and excursions (i.e., sudden assaults and forays by armed soldiers in response to a signal to attack), employing as many soldiers as the acting company could muster, with martial music and numerous entrances and exits in rapid succession. Battles are usually preceded by florid boastful rhetorical exchanges, or *flytings*, between the combatants. The military contests focus on heroic confrontations between individual leaders. Staging of battles often uses the Elizabethan playhouse to its physical capacity, with appearances "on the walls" of some town (i.e., from the upper gallery), scaling operations, sieges, and the like. *3 Henry VI* abounds in spectacular deaths, often performed as gruesome rituals. Young Rutland is dragged from his tutor by the implacable Clifford, and Richard of York is mocked with a paper crown by Queen Margaret; Clifford dies with an arrow in his neck, and Warwick the kingmaker dies lamenting the vanity of all earthly achievement; King Henry dies in the Tower, a defenseless prisoner in the hands of Richard of Gloucester. The play is perhaps confusing to the reader, but it breathes with violent energy onstage.

Symbolic of the chaos is the lack of a single central character. The title of the 1595 Octavo edition pairs the deaths of Richard of York and King Henry as the play's most memorable episodes; and in this dual focus we see the dominant motif of reciprocity, a Yorkist death for a Lancastrian death. This pattern will continue into *Richard III*, for *3 Henry VI* ends with an ominous amount of unfinished business; Clarence, for example, later sees that he must die in atonement for his part in the slaughter of Edward, the Lancastrian Prince of Wales. Just as the deaths are balanced and contrasted with one another, the military action also seesaws back and forth. Both Henry VI and Edward IV are at times imprisoned. The wheel of fortune elevates one side and then the other. Political alliances shift the balance of power one way and then the other. The action is painfully indecisive, the carnage leading pointlessly only to further violence. The spectacle is made infinitely more agonizing by the realization that all this is a family quarrel. The commoners suffer accordingly: we witness the grief of a father who has mistakenly killed his son in battle and of a son who has killed his father (2.5) at the battle of Towton, where historically 24,000 were killed in one day. The people, seldom seen, are no longer political troublemakers (as they were briefly in *2 Henry VI*) but mere victims, waiting patiently for an end. A recurrent emblem used to convey the utter futility of this war is the molehill. York is mockingly crowned before his execution on a molehill, and King Henry retires from the mayhem at Towton to a molehill in order to meditate on the happy contemplative life he has been denied. The molehill suggests the ironic perversity of humanity's quest for worldly power, whereby those who possess power are incapable of exercising it wisely and those who burn with ambition are denied legitimate opportunity.

One sure sign of moral chaos throughout this play is the phenomenon of oath breaking. In the opening scene, Richard of York accepts under oath an obligation to honor Henry VI as his king in return for being named king after Henry's death, but he is soon talked out of his promise by his son Richard on the specious grounds that the oath was not made before "a true and lawful magistrate" (1.2.23). This masterful equivocation, anticipated in the perfidies of the Duke of Suffolk in *1* and *2 Henry VI*, prepares us for Richard of Gloucester's later perfidies in *Richard III*. (In Shakespeare's sources, especially Edward Hall, Parliament plays a major role in working out the compromise between York and Henry; Shakespeare shows us, instead, a personal agreement made between two contending leaders on the basis of private will and assertion of military power—an agreement that is easily broken on the same pragmatic grounds.) King Henry is no less forsworn in denying to his own son the crown bestowed on him as birthright by sacred law and custom. Lewis, the French King, excuses his shifting of alliance from King Henry to the Yorkists on the grounds of simple expediency. Clarence forswears his oaths made to his brother Edward and changes sides in the wars, offended at Edward's perfidy in having renounced his intent to marry the French King's sister-in-law. Soon Clarence is back again in the Yorkist camp, having now betrayed the promises he made to the Lancastrians. Warwick the kingmaker forswears his oaths to Edward because Edward has undermined Warwick's embassy to France. Where, in fact, do truth and justice reside, now that England is governed by two kings who are both forsworn? The common people sense this dilemma, as revealed in the attitudes of two gamekeepers; they capture Henry to whom they were once loyal, because they are now "sworn in all allegiance" to Edward but would be true subjects again to Henry "If he were seated as King Edward is" (3.1.70, 95). Political and military reality governs political ethics; the ruler to be acknowledged is he who can establish control.

Another sign of moral decay in this play is the dominance of vengeful purpose. *3 Henry VI*, indeed, can be viewed as a kind of revenge play in which Richard of Gloucester finally emerges as the consummate avenger in a society of avengers. In the opening confrontation between the Yorkists and the Lancastrians, Warwick taunts the Lancastrians with having lost many of their fathers in the recent military action at St. Albans; the fathers of Northumberland, Westmorland, and Clifford have all fallen in that one battle. (Historically, Westmorland and Clifford appear to be the same man with the same father, Old Clifford of *2 Henry VI*; Shakespeare gives us more fatherless sons by this division of one man into two.) The sons, of course, vow vengeance. Clifford, renowned as "the butcher" for his cruelty, exacts a terrible price for his father's death through the slaughter of the defenseless young Rutland and the mocking execution of Rutland's father, the Duke of York. York's surviving sons take vengeance, not only on Clifford, but also on King Henry, his son Edward, and many others. Warwick turns against Edward of York more to avenge an insult than to aid Henry and is himself cut down by the Yorkists at Barnet (4.2). The implacable pattern of an eye for an eye eventually takes on a providential meaning, especially as seen from the hindsight of *Richard III*, but, as we experience this play in the theater, the reality is chiefly one of much brutality and horror.

As in earlier plays of the series, the relationships between men and women echo the discord of the English nation and contribute, in turn, to further discord. Margaret of Anjou, the remorseless defender of her son Edward's claim to the throne, acts with increasingly masculine authority, while her ineffectual husband Henry VI abdicates responsibility. She is the Lancastrian general, resourceful in battle and often victorious, implacable in vengeance. This inversion of male and female roles is reflected on the Yorkist side by Edward IV's disastrous marriage with Lady Elizabeth Grey. She is a widow with no family position or political power to bring to the marriage—nothing, in fact, but her ambition on behalf of her kinsmen. Edward's attraction to her is fleshly and imprudent. To make matters worse, Warwick is at that very moment negotiating a highly favorable marriage treaty for Edward with the King of France. Edward IV thus unconsciously apes the earlier willfulness of his counterpart, Henry VI (whose choice of Margaret of Anjou in *1 Henry VI* was no less catastrophic). Edward IV's snubbing of Warwick leads to the defection of that powerful leader and through him to the defection of Edward's brother Clarence, who has succumbed to the charms of Warwick's daughter Isabel. And whereas *1 Henry VI* at least counterbalances the uxoriousness of Henry with the positive example of Lord Talbot, *3 Henry VI* fails to discover any such central noble character. (To be sure, we are briefly introduced to the young Earl of Richmond, who is to be Henry VII, but only as a glimpse of a hopeful future.) The almost total lack of any effectively virtuous character gives to *3 Henry VI* its predominantly dismaying and helpless mood. The heroes have been destroyed.

Richard of Gloucester alone seems to profit from England's decline. Like his father, York, his strategy has been to let England flay herself into anarchic vulnerability. Once the father York has disappeared from the scene, young Richard's malevolent character becomes increasingly apparent. No longer merely one of York's brave sons, Richard is the new genius of discord. As the youngest of three sons who will eventually supplant his older brothers and their rights of inheritance, Richard is a supreme example of inversion in a world turned upside down. His bravura soliloquy in 3.2 is often included in performances of *Richard III*, for it yields rich clues to his emerging character: he is ambitious, ruthless, deformed from birth, and, above all, a consummate deceiver. To the audience he boasts of his ability, claiming that as a hypocrite he will excel the combined talents of Nestor, Ulysses, Sinon, Proteus, and Machiavelli. The superb self-assurance is arresting, the heartless consistency admirable even though despicable. In a second soliloquy, virtually at the end of the play, having already dispatched

Henry VI and his son Edward, Richard confides to the audience that Clarence is to be his next victim. And, although Richard pledges fealty to his young nephew, Edward, the Yorkist crown prince, at the Yorkist victory celebration with which the play ends, we know that Richard's kiss of peace is no more trustworthy than Judas's kiss given to Christ (see 5.7.33–4). All those standing between Richard and the throne are to be eliminated. Clearly, the pious longings for peace expressed by King Edward IV are to be cruelly violated.

The Third Part of King Henry The Sixth

[Dramatis Personae

KING HENRY THE SIXTH
QUEEN MARGARET
PRINCE EDWARD, *their son*
DUKE OF EXETER,
EARL OF NORTHUMBERLAND,
EARL OF WESTMORLAND,   *supporters of*
EARL OF OXFORD,   *the house*
LORD CLIFFORD,   *of Lancaster*
SOMERVILLE,
A HUNTSMAN *guarding Edward*

DUKE OF YORK, *Richard Plantagenet*
EDWARD, *Earl of March, later Duke*
of York and KING EDWARD IV,
GEORGE, *later Duke of Clarence,*   *York's sons*
RICHARD, *later Duke of Gloucester,*
EARL OF RUTLAND,
LADY GREY, *later Edward IV's queen*
PRINCE EDWARD, *her infant son*
EARL RIVERS, *her brother*
SIR JOHN MORTIMER,   } *York's uncles*
SIR HUGH MORTIMER,
DUKE OF NORFOLK,
EARL OF PEMBROKE,
LORD HASTINGS,   *supporters of the*
LORD STAFFORD,   *house of York*
SIR WILLIAM STANLEY,
SIR JOHN MONTGOMERY,
A NOBLEMAN,

TUTOR *of the Earl of Rutland*
Two KEEPERS *or gamekeepers*
Three WATCHMEN *guarding Edward's tent*
A SOLDIER *in the Yorkist army*

EARL OF WARWICK,   *supporters of York*
MARQUESS MONTAGUE,   *and then of Lancaster*
DUKE OF SOMERSET,
HENRY, EARL OF RICHMOND
LIEUTENANT *of the Tower of London*
MAYOR OF YORK
MAYOR OF COVENTRY
A SON *that has killed his father*
A FATHER *that has killed his son*
MESSENGERS
POSTS

KING LEWIS *of France*
LADY BONA, *his sister-in-law*
LORD BOURBON, *French Admiral*

English and French Soldiers, Attendants, Aldermen, a Nurse
to Prince Edward

SCENE: *England and France*]

1.1

Alarum. Enter [Richard] Plantagenet [Duke of York], Edward, Richard, Norfolk, Montague, Warwick, [with drum] and soldiers, [wearing white roses in their hats. A chair of state is onstage.]

WARWICK
I wonder how the King escaped our hands.

YORK
While we pursued the horsemen of the north,
He slyly stole away and left his men;
Whereat the great lord of Northumberland,
Whose warlike ears could never brook retreat,   5
Cheered up the drooping army, and himself,
Lord Clifford, and Lord Stafford, all abreast,
Charged our main battle's front and, breaking in,   8
Were by the swords of common soldiers slain.   9

EDWARD
Lord Stafford's father, Duke of Buckingham,
Is either slain or wounded dangerous;   11
I cleft his beaver with a downright blow.   12
That this is true, father, behold his blood.
           [He shows his bloody weapon.]

MONTAGUE *[to York]*
And, brother, here's the Earl of Wiltshire's blood,   14
Whom I encountered as the battles joined.   15
           [He shows his weapon.]

RICHARD *[showing the Duke of Somerset's head]*
Speak thou for me and tell them what I did.   16

YORK
Richard hath best deserved of all my sons.
But is Your Grace dead, my lord of Somerset?   18

NORFOLK
Such hap have all the line of John of Gaunt!   19

RICHARD
Thus do I hope to shake King Henry's head.

WARWICK
And so do I. Victorious prince of York,
Before I see thee seated in that throne   22

Which now the house of Lancaster usurps,
I vow by heaven these eyes shall never close.
This is the palace of the fearful King,   25
And this the regal seat. Possess it, York,
For this is thine and not King Henry's heirs'.

YORK
Assist me, then, sweet Warwick, and I will,
For hither we have broken in by force.

NORFOLK
We'll all assist you. He that flies shall die.

YORK
Thanks, gentle Norfolk. Stay by me, my lords,   31
And soldiers, stay and lodge by me this night.   32
           They go up [to the chair of state].

WARWICK
And when the King comes, offer him no violence,
Unless he seek to thrust you out perforce.   34
           [The soldiers withdraw.]

YORK
The Queen this day here holds her Parliament,
But little thinks we shall be of her council.   36
By words or blows here let us win our right.

RICHARD
Armed as we are, let's stay within this house.

WARWICK
The Bloody Parliament shall this be called,
Unless Plantagenet, Duke of York, be king   40
And bashful Henry deposed, whose cowardice
Hath made us bywords to our enemies.   42

YORK
Then leave me not, my lords. Be resolute.
I mean to take possession of my right.

WARWICK
Neither the King, nor he that loves him best,
The proudest he that holds up Lancaster,   46
Dares stir a wing if Warwick shake his bells.   47
I'll plant Plantagenet, root him up who dares.
Resolve thee, Richard; claim the English crown.   49
           [York seats himself in the throne.]

*Flourish. Enter King Henry, Clifford,
Northumberland, Westmorland, Exeter, and the
rest. [All wear red roses.]*

KING HENRY
My lords, look where the sturdy rebel sits,   50
Even in the chair of state! Belike he means,   51
Backed by the power of Warwick, that false peer,
To aspire unto the crown and reign as king.

1.1. Location: London. The Parliament House (see lines 35–9, 71, etc.), also referred to as King Henry VI's palace, line 25, since in the fifteenth and sixteenth centuries the Parliament House and Westminster Palace were part of the same complex. The throne is onstage, seemingly on a raised platform.
0.1 Alarum trumpet call to arms. (York and his followers, in hot pursuit of King Henry, have just arrived from St. Albans.) **0.3 drum** drummer. **0.4 white roses** (The badge of the house of York.)
5 brook retreat endure the order to withdraw from the attack
8 battle's army's   **9 Were . . . slain** (In *2 Henry VI*, 5.2, it is York who kills old Clifford.)   **11 dangerous** dangerously   **12 beaver** face guard of a helmet, i.e., here the helmet itself   **14 brother** (Montague was actually brother to Warwick, but his father, Salisbury of *2 Henry VI*, was brother-in-law of York.)   **15 battles joined** armies joined in combat.   **16 s.d. the Duke . . . head** the head of Edmund Beaufort, second Duke of Somerset, who appears in *2 Henry VI*. See 5.1.73 n.
18 But . . . Somerset? i.e., Are you really dead, my lord of Somerset? (Like his son, York contemptuously addresses his slain enemy.)
19 Such . . . Gaunt! (Norfolk wishes ill luck to all the descendants of John of Gaunt, including King Henry VI, as well as Somerset, who is already dead.)   **22 Before** i.e., until

25 fearful timid   **31 gentle** noble   **32.1 They go up** i.e., Plantagenet, his sons, Norfolk, Montague, and Warwick, all seemingly go up onto the dais or raised platform supporting the throne. (The soldiers may withdraw at this point; they must reenter later at line 169.)   **34 perforce** by force.   **36 of her council** (1) taking part in the Privy Council meeting (2) serving as confidential advisers.   **40 be** become   **42 bywords** i.e., objects of scorn.   **our enemies** i.e., the French.
46 he . . . up person that supports   **47 shake his bells** (Bells were sometimes fastened to the legs of a falcon to incite it to greater ferocity and to terrify its victims.)   **49 Resolve thee** Be resolute
49.2 Flourish trumpet fanfare.   **49.4 red roses** (The badge of the house of Lancaster.)   **50 sturdy** self-assured   **51 chair of state** throne.   **Belike** Evidently

Earl of Northumberland, he slew thy father,
And thine, Lord Clifford, and you both have vowed
  revenge
On him, his sons, his favorites, and his friends.

NORTHUMBERLAND
Be Duke of Lancaster. Let him be king.

WARWICK [to King Henry]
Be Duke of Lancaster. Let him be king.

NORTHUMBERLAND
If I be not, heavens be revenged on me!   57

CLIFFORD
The hope thereof makes Clifford mourn in steel.   58

WESTMORLAND
What, shall we suffer this? Let's pluck him down.
My heart for anger burns. I cannot brook it.

KING HENRY
Be patient, gentle Earl of Westmorland.

CLIFFORD
Patience is for poltroons, such as he.   62
He durst not sit there, had your father lived.
My gracious lord, here in the Parliament
Let us assail the family of York.

NORTHUMBERLAND
Well hast thou spoken, cousin. Be it so.   66

KING HENRY
Ah, know you not the city favors them,   67
And they have troops of soldiers at their beck?

EXETER
But when the Duke is slain, they'll quickly fly.

KING HENRY
Far be the thought of this from Henry's heart,
To make a shambles of the Parliament House!   71
Cousin of Exeter, frowns, words, and threats
Shall be the war that Henry means to use.—
Thou factious Duke of York, descend my throne
And kneel for grace and mercy at my feet!
I am thy sovereign.

YORK   I am thine.

EXETER
For shame, come down. He made thee Duke of York.   77

YORK
It was my inheritance, as the earldom was.   78

EXETER
Thy father was a traitor to the crown.   79

WARWICK
Exeter, thou art a traitor to the crown
In following this usurping Henry.

CLIFFORD
Whom should he follow but his natural king?

WARWICK
True, Clifford. That's Richard, Duke of York.

KING HENRY [to York]
And shall I stand, and thou sit in my throne?

YORK
It must and shall be so. Content thyself.

WARWICK [to King Henry]
Be Duke of Lancaster. Let him be king.

WESTMORLAND
He is both King and Duke of Lancaster,
And that the lord of Westmorland shall maintain.

WARWICK
And Warwick shall disprove it. You forget
That we are those which chased you from the field
And slew your fathers, and with colors spread   91
Marched through the city to the palace gates.

NORTHUMBERLAND
Yes, Warwick, I remember it to my grief;
And, by his soul, thou and thy house shall rue it.   94

WESTMORLAND
Plantagenet, of thee and these thy sons,
Thy kinsmen and thy friends, I'll have more lives
Than drops of blood were in my father's veins.   97

CLIFFORD
Urge it no more, lest that, instead of words,   98
I send thee, Warwick, such a messenger
As shall revenge his death before I stir.   100

WARWICK
Poor Clifford, how I scorn his worthless threats!

YORK
Will you we show our title to the crown?   102
If not, our swords shall plead it in the field.

KING HENRY
What title hast thou, traitor, to the crown?
Thy father was, as thou art, Duke of York,   105
Thy grandfather, Roger Mortimer, Earl of March.
I am the son of Henry the Fifth,
Who made the Dauphin and the French to stoop
And seized upon their towns and provinces.

WARWICK
Talk not of France, sith thou hast lost it all.   110

KING HENRY
The Lord Protector lost it, and not I.   111
When I was crowned I was but nine months old.

RICHARD
You are old enough now, and yet, methinks, you lose.—
Father, tear the crown from the usurper's head.

EDWARD
Sweet father, do so. Set it on your head.

MONTAGUE [to York]
Good brother, as thou lov'st and honorest arms,
Let's fight it out and not stand caviling thus.

RICHARD
Sound drums and trumpets, and the King will fly.

---

57 be not i.e., be not avenged   58 in steel i.e., in armor, not in
mourning attire.   62 poltroons arrant cowards.   he i.e., York.
66 cousin kinsman. (Also in line 72.)   67 the city i.e., London
71 shambles slaughterhouse   77–8 He . . . was (Compare with *1
Henry VI*, 3.1.161–74, where the King restored to Richard the whole
inheritance of the house of York, which included the earldom of
March.)   79 Thy . . . crown (On the execution of Richard, Earl of
Cambridge, for treason by Henry V, see *Henry V*, 2.2, and *1 Henry VI*,
2.4.90–4, 2.5.84–91.)

91 colors battle flags   94 his i.e., the second Earl of Northumberland's, who fell at St. Albans on the Lancastrian side. (This event is
not shown in *2 Henry VI*.) The speaker is the third Earl.   97 my
father's (Three noble fathers died on the Lancastrian side at St.
Albans, according to Hall: Northumberland, old Clifford, and Somerset. Westmorland's father was not a casualty in that battle, but Shakespeare may be replacing Somerset here to keep the symmetry of
three.)   98 lest that lest   100 his i.e., old Clifford's; see note at line 97
102 Will you Do you desire   105 Thy . . . York (Shakespeare's historical inaccuracy; Richard's father was never Duke of York. That title
belonged to his oldest brother, Edward, who died at Agincourt; it was
given by Henry VI to Richard.)   110 sith since   111 Lord Protector
i.e., Humphrey, Duke of Gloucester

YORK   Sons, peace!

NORTHUMBERLAND
Peace, thou! And give King Henry leave to speak.

WARWICK
Plantagenet shall speak first. Hear him, lords,
And be you silent and attentive too,
For he that interrupts him shall not live.

KING HENRY
Think'st thou that I will leave my kingly throne,
Wherein my grandsire and my father sat?
No! First shall war unpeople this my realm;
Ay, and their colors, often borne in France,
And now in England to our heart's great sorrow,
Shall be my winding-sheet. Why faint you, lords?   129
My title's good, and better far than his.

WARWICK
Prove it, Henry, and thou shalt be king.

KING HENRY
Henry the Fourth by conquest got the crown.

YORK
'Twas by rebellion against his king.

KING HENRY [aside]
I know not what to say; my title's weak.—
Tell me, may not a king adopt an heir?

YORK   What then?

KING HENRY
An if he may, then am I lawful king;   137
For Richard, in the view of many lords,
Resigned the crown to Henry the Fourth,
Whose heir my father was, and I am his.

YORK
He rose against him, being his sovereign,   141
And made him to resign his crown perforce.

WARWICK
Suppose, my lords, he did it unconstrained,
Think you 'twere prejudicial to his crown?   144

EXETER
No, for he could not so resign his crown
But that the next heir should succeed and reign.

KING HENRY
Art thou against us, Duke of Exeter?

EXETER
His is the right, and therefore pardon me.   148

YORK
Why whisper you, my lords, and answer not?

EXETER
My conscience tells me he is lawful king.

KING HENRY [aside]
All will revolt from me and turn to him.

NORTHUMBERLAND
Plantagenet, for all the claim thou lay'st,
Think not that Henry shall be so deposed.

WARWICK
Deposed he shall be, in despite of all.   154

NORTHUMBERLAND
Thou art deceived. 'Tis not thy southern power   155
Of Essex, Norfolk, Suffolk, nor of Kent,
Which makes thee thus presumptuous and proud,
Can set the Duke up in despite of me.

CLIFFORD
King Henry, be thy title right or wrong,
Lord Clifford vows to fight in thy defense.
May that ground gape and swallow me alive
Where I shall kneel to him that slew my father!

KING HENRY
Oh, Clifford, how thy words revive my heart!

YORK
Henry of Lancaster, resign thy crown.
What mutter you, or what conspire you, lords?

WARWICK
Do right unto this princely Duke of York,
Or I will fill the house with armèd men
And over the chair of state, where now he sits,
Write up his title with usurping blood.   169
He stamps with his foot, and the soldiers show
themselves.

KING HENRY
My lord of Warwick, hear but one word:
Let me for this my lifetime reign as king.

YORK
Confirm the crown to me and to mine heirs,
And thou shalt reign in quiet while thou liv'st.

KING HENRY
I am content. Richard Plantagenet,
Enjoy the kingdom after my decease.

CLIFFORD
What wrong is this unto the Prince your son!

WARWICK
What good is this to England and himself!   177

WESTMORLAND
Base, fearful, and despairing Henry!

CLIFFORD
How hast thou injured both thyself and us!

WESTMORLAND
I cannot stay to hear these articles.   180

NORTHUMBERLAND   Nor I.

CLIFFORD
Come, cousin, let us tell the Queen these news.

WESTMORLAND
Farewell, fainthearted and degenerate King,
In whose cold blood no spark of honor bides.   184
[Exit with his men.]

NORTHUMBERLAND
Be thou a prey unto the house of York
And die in bonds for this unmanly deed!   186
[Exit with his men.]

CLIFFORD
In dreadful war mayst thou be overcome,
Or live in peace abandoned and despised!
[Exit with his men.]

---

129 **winding-sheet** sheet in which a corpse was wrapped.   **faint** lose
heart   137 **An if** If   141 **him, being** i.e., Richard, who was
144 **'twere . . . crown** it would invalidate his, Richard's, entitlement
to the throne and his heirs' right to inherit it.   148 **His** i.e., York's
154 **despite** spite. (Also in line 158.)

155 **deceived** mistaken.   169 **usurping blood** i.e., the blood of usurping Henry VI.   177 **What . . . to** i.e., What a good thing for. (Warwick
welcomes Henry's decision.)   180 **articles** terms of agreement.
184 **cold** listless, cowardly   186 **bonds** fetters

WARWICK
　　Turn this way, Henry, and regard them not.
EXETER
　　They seek revenge and therefore will not yield.　190
KING HENRY
　　Ah, Exeter!
WARWICK　　　　Why should you sigh, my lord?
KING HENRY
　　Not for myself, Lord Warwick, but my son,
　　Whom I unnaturally shall disinherit.
　　But be it as it may: [to York] I here entail　194
　　The crown to thee and to thine heirs forever,
　　Conditionally, that here thou take an oath
　　To cease this civil war, and whilst I live
　　To honor me as thy king and sovereign,
　　And neither by treason nor hostility
　　To seek to put me down and reign thyself.
YORK
　　This oath I willingly take and will perform.
WARWICK
　　Long live King Henry! Plantagenet, embrace him.
　　　　　　[York descends and embraces Henry.]
KING HENRY
　　And long live thou and these thy forward sons!　203
YORK
　　Now York and Lancaster are reconciled.
EXETER
　　Accursed be he that seeks to make them foes!　205
　　　　　　　　　　Sennet. Here they come down.
YORK
　　Farewell, my gracious lord. I'll to my castle.　206
　　　　　　[Exeunt York and his sons with their men.]
WARWICK
　　And I'll keep London with my soldiers.
　　　　　　　　　　[Exit Warwick with his men.]
NORFOLK
　　And I to Norfolk with my followers.
　　　　　　　　　　[Exit Norfolk with his men.]
MONTAGUE
　　And I unto the sea from whence I came.　209
　　　　　　　　　　[Exit Montague with his men.]
KING HENRY
　　And I, with grief and sorrow, to the court.

　　　　Enter the Queen [Margaret and Edward, Prince of
　　　　Wales].

EXETER
　　Here comes the Queen, whose looks bewray her anger.　211
　　I'll steal away.

KING HENRY　　Exeter, so will I.　　　　[They start to leave.]
QUEEN MARGARET
　　Nay, go not from me. I will follow thee.
KING HENRY
　　Be patient, gentle Queen, and I will stay.
QUEEN MARGARET
　　Who can be patient in such extremes?
　　Ah, wretched man! Would I had died a maid
　　And never seen thee, never borne thee son,
　　Seeing thou hast proved so unnatural a father!　218
　　Hath he deserved to lose his birthright thus?
　　Hadst thou but loved him half so well as I,
　　Or felt that pain which I did for him once,
　　Or nourished him as I did with my blood,
　　Thou wouldst have left thy dearest heart-blood
　　　　there,
　　Rather than have made that savage duke thine heir
　　And disinherited thine only son.
PRINCE
　　Father, you cannot disinherit me.
　　If you be king, why should not I succeed?
KING HENRY
　　Pardon me, Margaret. Pardon me, sweet son.
　　The Earl of Warwick and the Duke enforced me.
QUEEN MARGARET
　　Enforced thee? Art thou king, and wilt be forced?
　　I shame to hear thee speak. Ah, timorous wretch!
　　Thou hast undone thyself, thy son, and me,
　　And given unto the house of York such head　233
　　As thou shalt reign but by their sufferance.　234
　　To entail him and his heirs unto the crown,
　　What is it but to make thy sepulcher
　　And creep into it far before thy time?
　　Warwick is Chancellor and the lord of Calais;
　　Stern Falconbridge commands the narrow seas;　239
　　The Duke is made Protector of the realm;　240
　　And yet shalt thou be safe? Such safety finds
　　The trembling lamb environèd with wolves.　242
　　Had I been there, which am a silly woman,　243
　　The soldiers should have tossed me on their pikes　244
　　Before I would have granted to that act.　245
　　But thou prefer'st thy life before thine honor;
　　And seeing thou dost, I here divorce myself
　　Both from thy table, Henry, and thy bed,
　　Until that act of Parliament be repealed
　　Whereby my son is disinherited.
　　The northern lords that have forsworn thy colors　251
　　Will follow mine, if once they see them spread;
　　And spread they shall be, to thy foul disgrace
　　And utter ruin of the house of York.
　　Thus do I leave thee.—Come, son, let's away.
　　Our army is ready. Come, we'll after them.

190 revenge i.e., for their fathers' deaths   194 entail bequeath irrevocably   203 forward precocious, zealous, promising   205.1 Sennet trumpet notes signaling a procession.   Here they come down (York and his sons, together with Norfolk, Montague, and Warwick, have evidently been on the dais around the throne since line 32. Once York has descended and embraced Henry, formalizing their agreement, the rest of the York faction can descend and prepare to depart.)   206 castle i.e., Sandal Castle in Yorkshire. (See the next scene.)   209 unto the sea (Actually, Montague appears in scene 2 at Sandal Castle, not at the sea; possibly he is confused here with his uncle, William Neville, Baron Falconbridge. See line 239 below.)   211 bewray betray, reveal

218 unnatural i.e., showing no feeling for a son   233 head i.e., free rein   234 As that   239 Falconbridge i.e., William Neville or his son Thomas. (See line 209 above and note.)   narrow seas i.e., English Channel   240 Duke i.e., Duke of York   242 environèd surrounded   243 silly helpless   244 tossed impaled.   pikes long steel-pointed or axlike weapons   245 granted yielded   251 The northern lords i.e., Northumberland, Westmorland, and Clifford (as also in the three lords of line 270)

KING HENRY
Stay, gentle Margaret, and hear me speak.

QUEEN MARGARET
Thou hast spoke too much already. Get thee gone.

KING HENRY
Gentle son Edward, thou wilt stay with me?

QUEEN MARGARET
Ay, to be murdered by his enemies!

PRINCE
When I return with victory from the field,
I'll see Your Grace. Till then I'll follow her.

QUEEN MARGARET
Come, son, away. We may not linger thus.
    [*Exeunt Queen Margaret and the Prince.*]

KING HENRY
Poor Queen! How love to me and to her son
Hath made her break out into terms of rage!
Revenged may she be on that hateful duke,
Whose haughty spirit, wingèd with desire,
Will cost my crown, and like an empty eagle   268
Tire on the flesh of me and of my son!   269
The loss of those three lords torments my heart.   270
I'll write unto them and entreat them fair.   271
Come, cousin, you shall be the messenger.

EXETER
And I, I hope, shall reconcile them all.
                          Flourish. Exeunt.

❧

[1.2]

Enter Richard, Edward, and Montague.

RICHARD
Brother, though I be youngest, give me leave.   1

EDWARD
No, I can better play the orator.

MONTAGUE
But I have reasons strong and forcible.

Enter the Duke of York.

YORK
Why, how now, sons and brother, at a strife?   4
What is your quarrel? How began it first?

EDWARD
No quarrel, but a slight contention.

YORK   About what?

RICHARD
About that which concerns Your Grace and us:
The crown of England, Father, which is yours.

YORK
Mine, boy? Not till King Henry be dead.

RICHARD
Your right depends not on his life or death.

EDWARD
Now you are heir; therefore enjoy it now.
By giving the house of Lancaster leave to breathe, 13
It will outrun you, father, in the end.

YORK
I took an oath that he should quietly reign.

EDWARD
But for a kingdom any oath may be broken.
I would break a thousand oaths to reign one year.

RICHARD
No. God forbid Your Grace should be forsworn.

YORK
I shall be, if I claim by open war.

RICHARD
I'll prove the contrary, if you'll hear me speak.

YORK
Thou canst not, son. It is impossible.

RICHARD
An oath is of no moment, being not took   22
Before a true and lawful magistrate
That hath authority over him that swears.
Henry had none, but did usurp the place.
Then, seeing 'twas he that made you to depose,   26
Your oath, my lord, is vain and frivolous.
Therefore, to arms! And, father, do but think
How sweet a thing it is to wear a crown,
Within whose circuit is Elysium   30
And all that poets feign of bliss and joy.   31
Why do we linger thus? I cannot rest
Until the white rose that I wear be dyed
Even in the lukewarm blood of Henry's heart.

YORK
Richard, enough. I will be king, or die.
[*To Montague*] Brother, thou shalt to London presently 36
And whet on Warwick to this enterprise.
Thou, Richard, shalt to the Duke of Norfolk
And tell him privily of our intent.   39
You, Edward, shall unto my Lord Cobham,
With whom the Kentishmen will willingly rise.
In them I trust, for they are soldiers,
Witty, courteous, liberal, full of spirit.   43
While you are thus employed, what resteth more   44
But that I seek occasion how to rise,
And yet the King not privy to my drift,   46
Nor any of the house of Lancaster?

Enter a Messenger.

But stay, what news? Why com'st thou in such post? 48

MESSENGER
The Queen with all the northern earls and lords
Intend here to besiege you in your castle.

---

268 cost i.e., deprive me of. (With a pun on *coast*, "attack," "fly from the straight course," a metaphor that generates the image of the eagle.)   **empty** hungry   **269 Tire** feed ravenously   **270 those three lords** i.e., Westmorland, Northumberland, and Clifford; see lines 176–88   **271 fair** civilly, kindly.
1.2. Location: Sandal Castle (the Duke of York's castle) in Yorkshire.
1 give me leave permit me (to speak first).   **4 brother** (See the note for 1.1.14.)

13 to breathe i.e., to enjoy a respite   **22 moment** significance
26 depose take an oath   **30 Elysium** the classical abode after life of those beloved of the gods   **31 feign** portray imaginatively
36 presently immediately   **39 privily** secretly   **43 Witty** intelligent.
liberal large-minded   **44 what resteth more** what else remains
46 privy to aware of   **48 post** haste.

She is hard by with twenty thousand men,
And therefore fortify your hold, my lord.

YORK
Ay, with my sword. What, think'st thou that we fear
    them?
Edward and Richard, you shall stay with me;
My brother Montague shall post to London.
Let noble Warwick, Cobham, and the rest,
Whom we have left protectors of the King,
With powerful policy strengthen themselves
And trust not simple Henry nor his oaths.

MONTAGUE
Brother, I go. I'll win them, fear it not.
And thus most humbly I do take my leave.
                        Exit Montague.

    Enter [Sir John] Mortimer and [Sir Hugh,] his
    brother.

YORK
Sir John and Sir Hugh Mortimer, mine uncles,
You are come to Sandal in a happy hour.
The army of the Queen mean to besiege us.

SIR JOHN
She shall not need. We'll meet her in the field.

YORK   What, with five thousand men?

RICHARD
Ay, with five hundred, father, for a need.
A woman's general. What should we fear?
                        A march afar off.

EDWARD
I hear their drums. Let's set our men in order,
And issue forth and bid them battle straight.

YORK
Five men to twenty! Though the odds be great,
I doubt not, uncle, of our victory.
Many a battle have I won in France
Whenas the enemy hath been ten to one.
Why should I not now have the like success?
                        Alarum. Exeunt.

❧

[1.3]

    [Alarums.] Enter Rutland and his Tutor.

RUTLAND
Ah, whither shall I fly to scape their hands?
Ah, tutor, look where bloody Clifford comes!

    Enter Clifford [and soldiers].

CLIFFORD
Chaplain, away! Thy priesthood saves thy life.
As for the brat of this accursèd duke,

Whose father slew my father, he shall die.

TUTOR
And I, my lord, will bear him company.

CLIFFORD   Soldiers, away with him!

TUTOR
Ah, Clifford, murder not this innocent child,
Lest thou be hated both of God and man!
          Exit [dragged off by soldiers].

CLIFFORD
How now, is he dead already? Or is it fear
That makes him close his eyes? I'll open them.

RUTLAND
So looks the pent-up lion o'er the wretch
That trembles under his devouring paws;
And so he walks, insulting o'er his prey,
And so he comes, to rend his limbs asunder.
Ah, gentle Clifford, kill me with thy sword
And not with such a cruel threat'ning look!
Sweet Clifford, hear me speak before I die!
I am too mean a subject for thy wrath.
Be thou revenged on men, and let me live.

CLIFFORD
In vain thou speak'st, poor boy. My father's blood
Hath stopped the passage where thy words should
    enter.

RUTLAND
Then let my father's blood open it again.
He is a man, and, Clifford, cope with him.

CLIFFORD
Had I thy brethren here, their lives and thine
Were not revenge sufficient for me;
No, if I digged up thy forefathers' graves
And hung their rotten coffins up in chains,
It could not slake mine ire nor ease my heart.
The sight of any of the house of York
Is as a fury to torment my soul;
And till I root out their accursèd line
And leave not one alive, I live in hell.
Therefore—   *[Lifting his sword.]*

RUTLAND
Oh, let me pray before I take my death!
To thee I pray. Sweet Clifford, pity me!

CLIFFORD
Such pity as my rapier's point affords.

RUTLAND
I never did thee harm. Why wilt thou slay me?

CLIFFORD
Thy father hath.

RUTLAND   But 'twas ere I was born.
Thou hast one son. For his sake pity me,
Lest in revenge thereof, sith God is just,
He be as miserably slain as I.
Ah, let me live in prison all my days,

---

52 **hold** stronghold, castle   58 **policy** stratagem, cunning   63 **in a happy hour** opportunely.   67 **for a need** if necessary.   70 **straight** immediately.   74 **Whenas** when
1.3. Location: Field of battle between Sandal Castle and Wakefield. The action follows continuously from the previous scene.
0.1 *Alarums* calls to arms (signaling by sound effects a battle fought offstage)
4 duke i.e., Duke of York, who killed old Clifford in *2 Henry VI*, 5.2

12 **pent-up** caged, hence fierce and hungry   14 **insulting** gloating, exulting   16 **gentle** noble (with ironic suggestion of "free from harshness")   19 **mean** lowly. (Rutland appeals to the popular notion that, because the lion was a royal beast, it would show compassion to women and children. See 2.2.11–12.)   24 **cope with** engage in combat with   41 **sith** since

And when I give occasion of offense,   44
Then let me die, for now thou hast no cause.

CLIFFORD   No cause?
Thy father slew my father. Therefore, die.
                                            [*He stabs him.*]

RUTLAND
Di faciant laudis summa sit ista tuae!   [*He dies.*]   48

CLIFFORD
Plantagenet, I come, Plantagenet!
And this thy son's blood cleaving to my blade
Shall rust upon my weapon, till thy blood,
Congealed with this, do make me wipe off both.
            Exit [with soldiers, bearing off Rutland's body].

❧

[1.4]

Alarum. Enter Richard, Duke of York.

YORK
The army of the Queen hath got the field.   1
My uncles both are slain in rescuing me,   2
And all my followers to the eager foe
Turn back and fly, like ships before the wind   4
Or lambs pursued by hunger-starvèd wolves.
My sons—God knows what hath bechancèd them;
But this I know, they have demeaned themselves   7
Like men born to renown by life or death.
Three times did Richard make a lane to me,
And thrice cried, "Courage, father, fight it out!"
And full as oft came Edward to my side,
With purple falchion painted to the hilt   12
In blood of those that had encountered him.
And when the hardiest warriors did retire,
Richard cried, "Charge, and give no foot of ground!"
And cried, "A crown, or else a glorious tomb!   16
A scepter, or an earthly sepulcher!"
With this, we charged again, but, out, alas!   18
We budged again, as I have seen a swan   19
With bootless labor swim against the tide   20
And spend her strength with overmatching waves.   21
                            A short alarum within.
Ah, hark! The fatal followers do pursue,   22
And I am faint and cannot fly their fury;
And, were I strong, I would not shun their fury.
The sands are numbered that makes up my life.   25
Here must I stay, and here my life must end.

        *Enter the Queen [Margaret], Clifford,
        Northumberland, the young Prince, and soldiers.*

Come, bloody Clifford, rough Northumberland,
I dare your quenchless fury to more rage.   28
I am your butt, and I abide your shot.   29

NORTHUMBERLAND
Yield to our mercy, proud Plantagenet.   30

CLIFFORD
Ay, to such mercy as his ruthless arm,
With downright payment, showed unto my father.
Now Phaëthon hath tumbled from his car   33
And made an evening at the noontide prick.   34

YORK
My ashes, as the phoenix, may bring forth   35
A bird that will revenge upon you all;
And in that hope I throw mine eyes to heaven,
Scorning whate'er you can afflict me with.
Why come you not? What? Multitudes, and fear?

CLIFFORD
So cowards fight when they can fly no further;
So doves do peck the falcon's piercing talons;
So desperate thieves, all hopeless of their lives,
Breathe out invectives 'gainst the officers.

YORK
O Clifford, but bethink thee once again,   44
And in thy thought o'errun my former time;   45
And, if thou canst for blushing, view this face,   46
And bite thy tongue, that slanders him with cowardice 47
Whose frown hath made thee faint and fly ere this!

CLIFFORD
I will not bandy with thee word for word,   49
But buckler with thee blows, twice two for one.   50
                            [*He threatens with his sword.*]

QUEEN MARGARET
Hold, valiant Clifford! For a thousand causes
I would prolong awhile the traitor's life.—
Wrath makes him deaf.—Speak thou, Northumberland.   53

NORTHUMBERLAND
Hold, Clifford! Do not honor him so much
To prick thy finger, though to wound his heart.
What valor were it, when a cur doth grin,   56
For one to thrust his hand between his teeth,
When he might spurn him with his foot away?   58
It is war's prize to take all vantages,   59
And ten to one is no impeach of valor.   60
                            [*They capture York, who struggles.*]

CLIFFORD
Ay, ay, so strives the woodcock with the gin.   61

NORTHUMBERLAND
So doth the coney struggle in the net.   62

---

44 occasion of cause for   **48 Di . . . tuae!** The gods grant that this
may be the height of your glory, the deed for which you will be best
known! (Ovid, *Heroides*, 2.66.)
1.4. Location: The battle of Wakefield continues.
1 got the field won the battle.   **2 uncles** i.e., Sir John and Sir Hugh
Mortimer   **4 Turn back** turn their backs   **7 demeaned** conducted
12 purple falchion a curved sword made purple with blood
16 And cried (Some text may be missing here; the parallelism of lines
9–13 suggests that Edward is quoted as speaking after Richard.)
18 out (An expression of reproach.)   **19 budged** gave way
20 bootless fruitless   **21 with** against   **22 followers** pursuing troops
25 sands (of the hourglass)

28 dare defy, provoke.   **more** even more   **29 butt** target   **30 Yield . . .
mercy** Put yourself at our mercy   **33 Phaëthon** son of the sun god,
who begged his father to allow him to drive the chariot of the sun; he
drove it so near the earth that Zeus destroyed him with a thunderbolt
34 noontide prick exact point of noon on a sundial.   **35 phoenix** fabulous bird that was consumed through spontaneous combustion and
was reborn from its own ashes   **44 but bethink thee** only call to mind
45 o'errun review   **46 for** despite   **47 him** i.e., myself, York
49 bandy exchange   **50 buckler** join in close combat, grapple
53 him i.e., Clifford   **56 grin** show its teeth   **58 spurn** kick
59 prize reward, benefit   **60 impeach** calling in question   **61 woodcock** (A proverbially stupid bird.)   **gin** snare, trap   **62 coney** rabbit

YORK
So triumph thieves upon their conquered booty;
So true men yield, with robbers so o'ermatched. 64

NORTHUMBERLAND [to the Queen]
What would Your Grace have done unto him now?

QUEEN MARGARET
Brave warriors, Clifford and Northumberland,
Come, make him stand upon this molehill here,
That raught at mountains with outstrechèd arms 68
Yet parted but the shadow with his hand.— 69
What, was it you that would be England's king?
Was 't you that reveled in our Parliament 71
And made a preachment of your high descent? 72
Where are your mess of sons to back you now, 73
The wanton Edward and the lusty George?
And where's that valiant crookback prodigy, 75
Dicky, your boy, that with his grumbling voice
Was wont to cheer his dad in mutinies? 77
Or, with the rest, where is your darling Rutland?
Look, York, I stained this napkin with the blood 79
That valiant Clifford, with his rapier's point,
Made issue from the bosom of the boy;
And if thine eyes can water for his death,
I give thee this to dry thy cheeks withal. 83

[She gives him the bloodstained cloth.]

Alas, poor York, but that I hate thee deadly, 84
I should lament thy miserable state.
I prithee, grieve, to make me merry, York.
What, hath thy fiery heart so parched thine entrails
That not a tear can fall for Rutland's death?
Why art thou patient, man? Thou shouldst be mad;
And I, to make thee mad, do mock thee thus.
Stamp, rave, and fret, that I may sing and dance.
Thou wouldst be fee'd, I see, to make me sport. 92
York cannot speak, unless he wear a crown.—
A crown for York! And, lords, bow low to him.
Hold you his hands, whilst I do set it on.

[She puts a paper crown on his head.]

Ay, marry, sir, now looks he like a king! 96
Ay, this is he that took King Henry's chair, 97
And this is he was his adopted heir.
But how is it that great Plantagenet
Is crowned so soon, and broke his solemn oath?
As I bethink me, you should not be king
Till our King Henry had shook hands with death.
And will you pale your head in Henry's glory, 103
And rob his temples of the diadem,
Now, in his life, against your holy oath? 105
Oh, 'tis a fault too-too unpardonable!
Off with the crown, and, with the crown, his head!
And whilst we breathe, take time to do him dead. 108

CLIFFORD
That is my office, for my father's sake.

QUEEN MARGARET
Nay, stay. Let's hear the orisons he makes. 110

YORK
She-wolf of France, but worse than wolves of France,
Whose tongue more poisons than the adder's tooth!
How ill-beseeming is it in thy sex
To triumph like an Amazonian trull 114
Upon their woes whom fortune captivates! 115
But that thy face is, vizardlike, unchanging, 116
Made impudent with use of evil deeds,
I would essay, proud Queen, to make thee blush. 118
To tell thee whence thou cam'st, of whom derived,
Were shame enough to shame thee, wert thou not
   shameless.
Thy father bears the type of King of Naples, 121
Of both the Sicils and Jerusalem, 122
Yet not so wealthy as an English yeoman. 123
Hath that poor monarch taught thee to insult? 124
It needs not, nor it boots thee not, proud Queen, 125
Unless the adage must be verified
That beggars mounted run their horse to death.
'Tis beauty that doth oft make women proud;
But, God he knows, thy share thereof is small.
'Tis virtue that doth make them most admired;
The contrary doth make thee wondered at.
'Tis government that makes them seem divine; 132
The want thereof makes thee abominable. 133
Thou art as opposite to every good
As the Antipodes are unto us, 135
Or as the south to the Septentrion. 136
Oh, tiger's heart wrapped in a woman's hide!
How couldst thou drain the lifeblood of the child,
To bid the father wipe his eyes withal,
And yet be seen to bear a woman's face?
Women are soft, mild, pitiful, and flexible; 141
Thou stern, obdurate, flinty, rough, remorseless.
Bid'st thou me rage? Why, now thou hast thy wish.
Wouldst have me weep? Why, now thou hast thy will.
For raging wind blows up incessant showers,
And, when the rage allays, the rain begins. 146

[He weeps.]

These tears are my sweet Rutland's obsequies, 147
And every drop cries vengeance for his death
'Gainst thee, fell Clifford, and thee, false Frenchwoman. 149

NORTHUMBERLAND
Beshrew me, but his passions moves me so 150
That hardly can I check my eyes from tears. 151

---

64 **true** honest   68 **That raught** he that reached   69 **parted but** only divided. (The prize York reached for turned out to be illusory.) 71 **reveled** turned things upside down with your faction, as though in a riotous masquerade   72 **preachment of** sermon about   73 **mess** group of four   75 **prodigy** monster   77 **cheer** urge on. **mutinies** rebellions   79 **napkin** handkerchief   83 **withal** with.   84 **but** were it not   92 **fee'd** paid   96 **marry** i.e., indeed. (Originally an oath, "by the Virgin Mary.")   97 **chair** throne   103 **pale** encircle   105 **life** lifetime   108 **breathe** rest.   **do him dead** kill him.

110 **orisons** prayers   114–15 **To . . . captivates!** to exult over the woes of those whom fortune takes captive, like some slattern belonging to the race of legendary female warriors!   116 **But that** Were it not that. **vizardlike** masklike   118 **essay** attempt   121 **type** title   122 **both the Sicils** i.e., Sicily and Naples (known as the Kingdom of the Two Sicilies) 123 **yeoman** landowner below rank of gentleman.   124 **insult** triumph scornfully.   125 **needs not** is unnecessary. **boots** profits 132 **government** self-government   133 **want** lack   135 **Antipodes** people dwelling on the opposite side of the world   136 **Septentrion** the seven stars, i.e., the Big Dipper, representing the north.   141 **pitiful** capable of pity   146 **allays** abates   147 **obsequies** funeral observances   149 **fell** cruel   150 **Beshrew** Curse   151 **check** restrain

YORK
>   That face of his the hungry cannibals
>   Would not have touched, would not have stained with
>   blood.
>   But you are more inhuman, more inexorable,
>   Oh, ten times more, than tigers of Hyrcania.   155
>   See, ruthless Queen, a hapless father's tears!
>   This cloth thou dipped'st in blood of my sweet boy,
>   And I with tears do wash the blood away.
>   Keep thou the napkin, and go boast of this;
>   And if thou tell'st the heavy story right,   160
>   Upon my soul, the hearers will shed tears.
>   Yea, even my foes will shed fast-falling tears
>   And say, "Alas, it was a piteous deed!"
>   There, take the crown, and with the crown my curse;   164
>   And in thy need such comfort come to thee
>   As now I reap at thy too cruel hand!
>   Hardhearted Clifford, take me from the world.
>   My soul to heaven, my blood upon your heads!

NORTHUMBERLAND
>   Had he been slaughterman to all my kin,
>   I should not for my life but weep with him,   170
>   To see how inly sorrow gripes his soul.   171

QUEEN MARGARET
>   What, weeping-ripe, my Lord Northumberland?   172
>   Think but upon the wrong he did us all,
>   And that will quickly dry thy melting tears.

CLIFFORD [*stabbing him*]
>   Here's for my oath. Here's for my father's death.

QUEEN MARGARET [*stabbing him*]
>   And here's to right our gentlehearted king.

YORK
>   Open Thy gate of mercy, gracious God!
>   My soul flies through these wounds to seek out Thee.
>   [*He dies.*]

QUEEN MARGARET
>   Off with his head and set it on York gates,
>   So York may overlook the town of York.
>   *Flourish. Exeunt* [*with the body*].

[2.1]

> *A march. Enter Edward, Richard, and their*
> *power.*

EDWARD
>   I wonder how our princely father scaped,
>   Or whether he be scaped away or no
>   From Clifford's and Northumberland's pursuit.
>   Had he been ta'en, we should have heard the news;

>   Had he been slain, we should have heard the news;
>   Or had he scaped, methinks we should have heard
>   The happy tidings of his good escape.
>   How fares my brother? Why is he so sad?

RICHARD
>   I cannot joy until I be resolved   9
>   Where our right valiant father is become.   10
>   I saw him in the battle range about
>   And watched him how he singled Clifford forth.
>   Methought he bore him in the thickest troop   13
>   As doth a lion in a herd of neat,   14
>   Or as a bear encompassed round with dogs,
>   Who having pinched a few and made them cry,   16
>   The rest stand all aloof and bark at him.
>   So fared our father with his enemies;
>   So fled his enemies my warlike father.   19
>   Methinks 'tis prize enough to be his son.
>   See how the morning opes her golden gates
>   And takes her farewell of the glorious sun!   22
>   How well resembles it the prime of youth,
>   Trimmed like a younker prancing to his love!   24

EDWARD
>   Dazzle mine eyes, or do I see three suns?   25

RICHARD
>   Three glorious suns, each one a perfect sun,
>   Not separated with the racking clouds,   27
>   But severed in a pale clear-shining sky.
>   See, see! They join, embrace, and seem to kiss,
>   As if they vowed some league inviolable.
>   Now are they but one lamp, one light, one sun.   31
>   In this the heaven figures some event.   32

EDWARD
>   'Tis wondrous strange, the like yet never heard of.
>   I think it cites us, brother, to the field,   34
>   That we, the sons of brave Plantagenet,
>   Each one already blazing by our meeds,   36
>   Should notwithstanding join our lights together
>   And overshine the earth as this the world.   38
>   Whate'er it bodes, henceforward will I bear
>   Upon my target three fair-shining suns.   40

RICHARD
>   Nay, bear three daughters. By your leave I speak it,   41
>   You love the breeder better than the male.   42

> *Enter one* [*a Messenger*] *blowing.*

---

9 resolved informed   **10 Where . . . become** what is become of our very valiant father.   **13 bore him** conducted himself   **14 neat** cattle   **16 pinched** bit   **19 fled his enemies** his enemies fled from   **22 farewell** (The dawn is pictured as remaining behind while the sun ascends the sky.)   **24 Trimmed** dressed up.   **younker** young man   **25 three suns** (According to the chronicles, it was because Edward saw three suns as a favorable omen before the battle of Mortimer's Cross, in which he triumphed, that he chose the bright sun as his badge.)   **27 with** by.   **racking** driving, scudding   **31 Now . . . sun** i.e., The three suns now coalesce into one disk.   **32 figures** prefigures   **34 cites** incites, impels   **36 blazing . . . meeds** blazing brilliantly in our well-merited rewards   **38 overshine** (1) shine upon (2) surpass in shining.   **as . . . world** just as this celestial three-in-one sun we have seen shines on the world.   **40 target** shield   **41 daughters** i.e., instead of sons or *suns*.   **42 breeder** female. (Richard jokes about Edward's weakness for women, to be demonstrated in 3.2 and following.)   **42.1 *blowing*** either (1) blowing a horn, or (2) panting. (Holinshed characterizes the messenger as "puffing and blowing" as he arrives; Hall speaks of one who "came blowing to King Edward.")

---

155 Hyrcania region of the ancient Persian empire, reputed to abound in wild beasts. (See the *Aeneid*, 4.366–7.)   **160 heavy** sorrowful   **164 There . . . crown** (If York's hands are still restrained [see line 95], he may gesture here that his tormenters are to take his crown, and his handkerchief at line 159.)   **170 for my life** if my life depended on it   **171 inly** inward.   **gripes** grieves. (With suggestion also of *grips*, "seizes.")   **172 weeping-ripe** ready to weep
2.1. Location: Fields near the Welsh border or marches (line 140), historically identified as near Mortimer's Cross in Herefordshire, several days after the battle of Wakefield.
0.2 *power* army.

But what art thou, whose heavy looks foretell   43
Some dreadful story hanging on thy tongue?

MESSENGER
Ah, one that was a woeful looker-on
Whenas the noble Duke of York was slain,   46
Your princely father and my loving lord!

EDWARD
Oh, speak no more, for I have heard too much.

RICHARD
Say how he died, for I will hear it all.

MESSENGER
Environèd he was with many foes,   50
And stood against them, as the hope of Troy   51
Against the Greeks that would have entered Troy.
But Hercules himself must yield to odds;
And many strokes, though with a little ax,
Hews down and fells the hardest-timbered oak.
By many hands your father was subdued,
But only slaughtered by the ireful arm   57
Of unrelenting Clifford and the Queen,
Who crowned the gracious Duke in high despite,
Laughed in his face; and when with grief he wept,
The ruthless Queen gave him to dry his cheeks
A napkin steepèd in the harmless blood
Of sweet young Rutland, by rough Clifford slain.
And after many scorns, many foul taunts,
They took his head, and on the gates of York
They set the same; and there it doth remain,
The saddest spectacle that e'er I viewed.

EDWARD
Sweet Duke of York, our prop to lean upon,
Now thou art gone, we have no staff, no stay.   69
Oh, Clifford, boist'rous Clifford! Thou hast slain   70
The flower of Europe for his chivalry;
And treacherously hast thou vanquished him,
For hand to hand he would have vanquished thee.
Now my soul's palace is become a prison.   74
Ah, would she break from hence, that this my body
Might in the ground be closèd up in rest!
For never henceforth shall I joy again.
Never, oh, never, shall I see more joy!   78

RICHARD
I cannot weep, for all my body's moisture
Scarce serves to quench my furnace-burning heart;
Nor can my tongue unload my heart's great burden,
For selfsame wind that I should speak withal   82
Is kindling coals that fires all my breast,
And burns me up with flames that tears would quench.
To weep is to make less the depth of grief.
Tears, then, for babes; blows and revenge for me!
Richard, I bear thy name. I'll venge thy death,
Or die renownèd by attempting it.

EDWARD
His name that valiant duke hath left with thee;

His dukedom and his chair with me is left.   90

RICHARD
Nay, if thou be that princely eagle's bird,   91
Show thy descent by gazing 'gainst the sun;   92
For "chair" and "dukedom," "throne" and "kingdom" say;
Either that is thine, or else thou wert not his.   94

*March. Enter Warwick, Marquess Montague,
and their army.*

WARWICK
How now, fair lords? What fare? What news abroad?   95

RICHARD
Great lord of Warwick, if we should recount
Our baleful news, and at each word's deliverance   97
Stab poniards in our flesh till all were told,   98
The words would add more anguish than the wounds.
Oh, valiant lord, the Duke of York is slain!

EDWARD
Oh, Warwick, Warwick! That Plantagenet,
Which held thee dearly as his soul's redemption,
Is by the stern Lord Clifford done to death.

WARWICK
Ten days ago I drowned these news in tears;
And now, to add more measure to your woes,   105
I come to tell you things sith then befallen.   106
After the bloody fray at Wakefield fought,
Where your brave father breathed his latest gasp,   108
Tidings, as swiftly as the posts could run,   109
Were brought me of your loss and his depart.   110
I, then in London, keeper of the King,   111
Mustered my soldiers, gathered flocks of friends,
And very well appointed, as I thought,   113
Marched toward Saint Albans to intercept the Queen,
Bearing the King in my behalf along;   115
For by my scouts I was advertisèd   116
That she was coming with a full intent
To dash our late decree in Parliament   118
Touching King Henry's oath and your succession.   119
Short tale to make, we at Saint Albans met,
Our battles joined, and both sides fiercely fought.   121
But whether 'twas the coldness of the King,
Who looked full gently on his warlike queen,
That robbed my soldiers of their heated spleen,   124
Or whether 'twas report of her success,
Or more than common fear of Clifford's rigor,   126
Who thunders to his captives blood and death,
I cannot judge; but, to conclude with truth,

90 his chair i.e., his ducal seat, but also the claim to the throne
91 bird i.e., offspring   92 gazing . . . sun (According to Pliny and
other writers, eagles could gaze unblinkingly at the sun and would
test their young by forcing them to do so.)   94 that i.e., the throne,
symbolized by the sun.   his i.e., Plantagenet's son.   94.2 army (The
Octavo text specifies drum, i.e., drummer, and ensign along with soldiers.)   95 What fare? How are things faring?   97 at . . . deliverance
as we delivered each word   98 poniards daggers   105 measure
quantity   106 sith since   108 latest last   109 posts messengers
110 depart departure, i.e., death.   111 keeper jailer   113 appointed
equipped   115 Bearing . . . along taking the King along with me for my
own advantage   116 advertisèd informed   118 To . . . late to overturn
our recent   119 Touching regarding   121 battles armies   124 heated
spleen i.e., courage roused to a high pitch   126 rigor fierceness

43 heavy sorrowful   46 Whenas when   50 Environèd Surrounded
51 the hope of Troy i.e., Hector   57 ireful angry   69 stay support.
70 boist'rous savage   74 soul's palace i.e., body   78 see more joy
see joy any more.   82 For . . . withal since the very breath that I
should use in speaking

Their weapons like to lightning came and went;
Our soldiers', like the night owl's lazy flight,
Or like an idle thresher with a flail,   131
Fell gently down, as if they struck their friends.
I cheered them up with justice of our cause,
With promise of high pay and great rewards,
But all in vain. They had no heart to fight,
And we in them no hope to win the day,
So that we fled: the King unto the Queen;
Lord George your brother, Norfolk, and myself   138
In haste, posthaste, are come to join with you.
For in the marches here we heard you were,   140
Making another head to fight again.   141

EDWARD
Where is the Duke of Norfolk, gentle Warwick?   142
And when came George from Burgundy to England?

WARWICK
Some six miles off the Duke is with his soldiers;
And for your brother, he was lately sent   145
From your kind aunt, Duchess of Burgundy,   146
With aid of soldiers to this needful war.

RICHARD
'Twas odds, belike, when valiant Warwick fled.   148
Oft have I heard his praises in pursuit,   149
But ne'er till now his scandal of retire.   150

WARWICK
Nor now my scandal, Richard, dost thou hear;
For thou shalt know this strong right hand of mine
Can pluck the diadem from faint Henry's head
And wring the awful scepter from his fist,   154
Were he as famous and as bold in war
As he is famed for mildness, peace, and prayer.

RICHARD
I know it well, Lord Warwick. Blame me not.
'Tis love I bear thy glories make me speak.   158
But in this troublous time what's to be done?
Shall we go throw away our coats of steel
And wrap our bodies in black mourning gowns,
Numb'ring our Ave Marys with our beads?   162
Or shall we on the helmets of our foes
Tell our devotion with revengeful arms?   164
If for the last, say ay, and to it, lords.

WARWICK
Why, therefore Warwick came to seek you out,
And therefore comes my brother Montague.
Attend me, lords. The proud insulting Queen,   168
With Clifford and the haught Northumberland,   169

And of their feather many more proud birds,
Have wrought the easy-melting King like wax.   171
He swore consent to your succession,
His oath enrollèd in the Parliament,   173
And now to London all the crew are gone
To frustrate both his oath and what beside   175
May make against the house of Lancaster.   176
Their power, I think, is thirty thousand strong.
Now, if the help of Norfolk and myself,
With all the friends that thou, brave Earl of March, 179
Amongst the loving Welshmen canst procure,   180
Will but amount to five-and-twenty thousand,
Why, via! To London will we march,   182
And once again bestride our foaming steeds,
And once again cry "Charge!" upon our foes,
But never once again turn back and fly.   185

RICHARD
Ay, now methinks I hear great Warwick speak.
Ne'er may he live to see a sunshine day   187
That cries "Retire!" if Warwick bid him stay.   188

EDWARD
Lord Warwick, on thy shoulder will I lean;
And when thou fail'st—as God forbid the hour!—
Must Edward fall, which peril heaven forfend!   191

WARWICK
No longer Earl of March, but Duke of York;
The next degree is England's royal throne.   193
For King of England shalt thou be proclaimed
In every borough as we pass along;
And he that throws not up his cap for joy
Shall for the fault make forfeit of his head.
King Edward, valiant Richard, Montague,
Stay we no longer, dreaming of renown,   199
But sound the trumpets and about our task.

RICHARD
Then, Clifford, were thy heart as hard as steel,   201
As thou hast shown it flinty by thy deeds,
I come to pierce it or to give thee mine.

EDWARD
Then strike up drums. God and Saint George for us! 204

Enter a Messenger.

WARWICK   How now? What news?

MESSENGER
The Duke of Norfolk sends you word by me
The Queen is coming with a puissant host;   207
And craves your company for speedy counsel.

WARWICK
Why then it sorts. Brave warriors, let's away.   209
                                                                Exeunt omnes.

❖

131 **flail** threshing tool   138 **Lord George** i.e., George, later Duke of Clarence, brother to Edward and Richard   140 **marches** borders (of Wales)   141 **Making another head** raising another armed force   142 **gentle** noble   145 **for** as for   146 **Duchess of Burgundy** (A granddaughter of John of Gaunt and distant relative of Richard of York, to whom, according to the chroniclers, both George and Richard were sent for protection after York's execution.)   148 **'Twas odds, belike** i.e., No doubt the odds were very heavy   149 **in pursuit** i.e., for pursuing the enemy   150 **his . . . retire** i.e., condemnation of him for retreating.   154 **awful** awe-inspiring   158 **make** that makes   162 **beads** rosary beads (used in reciting *Ave Marys*, i.e., Ave Marias or Hail Marys).   164 **Tell our devotion** (1) count off our prayers (2) proclaim our love. (Said ironically.)   168 **Attend** Listen to.   **insulting** scornfully triumphing   169 **haught** haughty

171 **wrought** worked on, manipulated   173 **enrollèd** recorded on official rolls   175 **frustrate** annul.   **what beside** anything else   176 **make against** militate against   179 **Earl of March** i.e., Edward, who, at his father's death, inherited this with other titles   180 **loving** loyal, friendly   182 **via** forward   185 **turn back** turn our backs   187 **he** i.e., anyone   188 **stay** stand firm.   191 **forfend** forbid.   193 **degree** step, rank   199 **Stay we** let us remain   201 **Clifford** (Richard apostrophizes his absent enemy.)   204 **Saint George** patron saint of England   207 **puissant** powerful   209 **sorts** is fitting, is working out.

[2.2]

Flourish. Enter the King [Henry], the Queen [Margaret], Clifford, Northumberland, and young Prince, with drum and trumpets. [York's head is set above the gates.]

QUEEN MARGARET [*to King Henry*]
Welcome, my lord, to this brave town of York.   1
Yonder's the head of that archenemy
That sought to be encompassed with your crown.
Doth not the object cheer your heart, my lord?

KING HENRY
Ay, as the rocks cheer them that fear their wreck.   5
To see this sight, it irks my very soul.
Withhold revenge, dear God! 'Tis not my fault,
Nor wittingly have I infringed my vow.

CLIFFORD
My gracious liege, this too much lenity
And harmful pity must be laid aside.
To whom do lions cast their gentle looks?
Not to the beast that would usurp their den.
Whose hand is that the forest bear doth lick?
Not his that spoils her young before her face.   14
Who scapes the lurking serpent's mortal sting?
Not he that sets his foot upon her back.
The smallest worm will turn, being trodden on,
And doves will peck in safeguard of their brood.   18
Ambitious York did level at thy crown,   19
Thou smiling while he knit his angry brows.
He, but a duke, would have his son a king
And raise his issue, like a loving sire;   22
Thou, being a king, blest with a goodly son,
Didst yield consent to disinherit him,
Which argued thee a most unloving father.   25
Unreasonable creatures feed their young;   26
And though man's face be fearful to their eyes,
Yet, in protection of their tender ones,
Who hath not seen them, even with those wings
Which sometime they have used with fearful flight,
Make war with him that climbed unto their nest,
Offering their own lives in their young's defense?
For shame, my liege, make them your precedent!
Were it not pity that this goodly boy
Should lose his birthright by his father's fault,
And long hereafter say unto his child,
"What my great-grandfather and grandsire got,
My careless father fondly gave away"?   38
Ah, what a shame were this! Look on the boy,
And let his manly face, which promiseth

Successful fortune, steel thy melting heart
To hold thine own and leave thine own with him.

KING HENRY
Full well hath Clifford played the orator,
Inferring arguments of mighty force.   44
But, Clifford, tell me, didst thou never hear
That things ill got had ever bad success?   46
And happy always was it for that son   47
Whose father for his hoarding went to hell?   48
I'll leave my son my virtuous deeds behind;
And would my father had left me no more!
For all the rest is held at such a rate   51
As brings a thousandfold more care to keep
Than in possession any jot of pleasure.
Ah, cousin York, would thy best friends did know
How it doth grieve me that thy head is here!

QUEEN MARGARET
My lord, cheer up your spirits. Our foes are nigh,
And this soft courage makes your followers faint.   57
You promised knighthood to our forward son.   58
Unsheathe your sword and dub him presently.   59
Edward, kneel down.   [*The Prince kneels.*]

KING HENRY
Edward Plantagenet, arise a knight,
And learn this lesson: Draw thy sword in right.

PRINCE [*rising*]
My gracious father, by your kingly leave,
I'll draw it as apparent to the crown,   64
And in that quarrel use it to the death.

CLIFFORD
Why, that is spoken like a toward prince.   66

Enter a Messenger.

MESSENGER
Royal commanders, be in readiness,
For with a band of thirty thousand men
Comes Warwick, backing of the Duke of York,   69
And in the towns, as they do march along,
Proclaims him king, and many fly to him.
Darraign your battle, for they are at hand.   72

CLIFFORD
I would Your Highness would depart the field.
The Queen hath best success when you are absent.

QUEEN MARGARET
Ay, good my lord, and leave us to our fortune.

KING HENRY
Why, that's my fortune too. Therefore I'll stay.

NORTHUMBERLAND
Be it with resolution then to fight.

PRINCE
My royal father, cheer these noble lords
And hearten those that fight in your defense.

2.2. Location: Before the walls of York.
0.3. *drum and trumpets* drummer and trumpeters   0.3–4 *York's . . . gates* (We learn at 2.6.52–3 that York's head has been placed on the gates of York. Whether these gates and the head are actually visible in the theater is an option, in the Elizabethan or modern staging. Conceivably the head is carried at this point.)   1 **brave** fine   5 **wreck** shipwreck, destruction.   14 **spoils** destroys, seizes as prey   18 **safeguard of** safeguarding   19 **level** aim   22 **raise . . . sire** bring up and provide advancement for his children as a good father should   25 **argued thee** showed you to be   26 **Unreasonable** Not endowed with reason   38 **fondly** foolishly

44 **Inferring** alleging, adducing   46 **success** outcome.   47–8 **And . . . hell** i.e., The son may seem fortunate in inheriting wealth, but the father who obtained that wealth by hoarding and miserly grasping will go to hell.   51 **rate** cost   57 **faint** fainthearted.   58 **forward** promising   59 **presently** at once.   64 **apparent** heir   66 **toward** ready, bold, promising   69 **Duke of York** i.e., Edward   72 **Darraign your battle** Set your army in battle array

Unsheathe your sword, good father; cry "Saint George!"   80

March. Enter Edward, Warwick, Richard, [George
of] Clarence, Norfolk, Montague, and soldiers.

EDWARD
Now, perjured Henry, wilt thou kneel for grace   81
And set thy diadem upon my head,
Or bide the mortal fortune of the field?   83

QUEEN MARGARET
Go rate thy minions, proud insulting boy!   84
Becomes it thee to be thus bold in terms   85
Before thy sovereign and thy lawful king?

EDWARD
I am his king, and he should bow his knee.
I was adopted heir by his consent.
Since when, his oath is broke; for, as I hear,
You, that are king, though he do wear the crown,   90
Have caused him, by new act of Parliament,
To blot out me and put his own son in.

CLIFFORD   And reason too.
Who should succeed the father but the son?

RICHARD
Are you there, butcher? Oh, I cannot speak!   95

CLIFFORD
Ay, crookback, here I stand to answer thee,
Or any he the proudest of thy sort.   97

RICHARD
'Twas you that killed young Rutland, was it not?

CLIFFORD
Ay, and old York, and yet not satisfied.

RICHARD
For God's sake, lords, give signal to the fight.

WARWICK
What say'st thou, Henry, wilt thou yield the crown?

QUEEN MARGARET
Why, how now, long-tongued Warwick, dare you speak?
When you and I met at Saint Albans last,
Your legs did better service than your hands.

WARWICK
Then 'twas my turn to fly, and now 'tis thine.

CLIFFORD
You said so much before, and yet you fled.

WARWICK
'Twas not your valor, Clifford, drove me thence.

NORTHUMBERLAND
No, nor your manhood that durst make you stay.

RICHARD
Northumberland, I hold thee reverently.   109
Break off the parley, for scarce I can refrain   110
The execution of my big-swoll'n heart   111
Upon that Clifford, that cruel child-killer.

CLIFFORD
I slew thy father. Call'st thou him a child?

RICHARD
Ay, like a dastard and a treacherous coward,
As thou didst kill our tender brother Rutland;
But ere sunset I'll make thee curse the deed.

KING HENRY
Have done with words, my lords, and hear me speak.

QUEEN MARGARET
Defy them, then, or else hold close thy lips.

KING HENRY
I prithee, give no limits to my tongue.   119
I am a king, and privileged to speak.

CLIFFORD
My liege, the wound that bred this meeting here
Cannot be cured by words. Therefore be still.

RICHARD
Then, executioner, unsheathe thy sword.   123
By Him that made us all, I am resolved   124
That Clifford's manhood lies upon his tongue.   125

EDWARD
Say, Henry, shall I have my right or no?
A thousand men have broke their fasts today   127
That ne'er shall dine unless thou yield the crown.

WARWICK
If thou deny, their blood upon thy head,   129
For York in justice puts his armor on.

PRINCE
If that be right which Warwick says is right,
There is no wrong, but everything is right.

RICHARD
Whoever got thee, there thy mother stands;   133
For, well I wot, thou hast thy mother's tongue.   134

QUEEN MARGARET
But thou art neither like thy sire nor dam,
But like a foul misshapen stigmatic,   136
Marked by the destinies to be avoided
As venom toads or lizards' dreadful stings.   138

RICHARD
Iron of Naples hid with English gilt,   139
Whose father bears the title of a king—
As if a channel should be called the sea—   141
Sham'st thou not, knowing whence thou art extraught,   142
To let thy tongue detect thy baseborn heart?   143

EDWARD
A wisp of straw were worth a thousand crowns   144
To make this shameless callet know herself.   145

119 **give** set   123 **executioner** (Richard caustically addresses Clifford, bidding him to put his sword where his mouth is; or possibly Richard speaks to himself.)   124 **resolved** convinced   125 **lies . . . tongue** i.e., consists only in words.   127 **broke their fasts** i.e., had breakfast   129 **deny** refuse. **upon** be upon   133–4 **Whoever . . . tongue** (Richard implies that Prince Edward is both a bastard and a mother's boy, resembling his mother in all he does. *Got* means "begot, fathered"; *wot* means "know.")   136 **stigmatic** one branded with the mark of his crime or deformity. (See *2 Henry VI*, 5.1.215.)   138 **venom** venomous   139 **Iron . . . gilt** i.e., You cheap product of Naples (being daughter of the titular King of Naples), being gilded over by an English marriage   141 **As . . . sea** i.e., comparing your father to a king is like comparing a rivulet or gutter (*channel*) to the sea   142 **extraught** descended, extracted   143 **detect** expose   144 **wisp of straw** (A traditional way of marking or branding a scolding woman.)   145 **callet** lewd woman

80.1–2 *George of Clarence* (Actually, George is not made Duke of Clarence until 2.6.104.)   81 **grace** mercy, pardon   83 **bide** await.
mortal fatal   84 **rate thy minions** chide your followers or favorites
85 **terms** language   90 **You, that are king** i.e., you, Margaret, who, in fact, rule   95 **butcher** (Clifford was nicknamed "the butcher" for his cruelty.)   97 **any he** any man. **sort** gang.   109 **hold thee reverently** hold you in the greatest respect.   110–11 **scarce . . . heart** scarcely can I restrain myself from carrying into action the hatred of my greatly swollen heart

Helen of Greece was fairer far than thou,
Although thy husband may be Menelaus;   147
And ne'er was Agamemnon's brother wronged   148
By that false woman, as this king by thee.
His father reveled in the heart of France,   150
And tamed the King, and made the Dauphin stoop;
And had he matched according to his state,   152
He might have kept that glory to this day.
But when he took a beggar to his bed
And graced thy poor sire with his bridal day,   155
Even then that sunshine brewed a shower for him
That washed his father's fortunes forth of France   157
And heaped sedition on his crown at home.
For what hath broached this tumult but thy pride?   159
Hadst thou been meek, our title still had slept,   160
And we, in pity of the gentle King,
Had slipped our claim until another age.   162

GEORGE
But when we saw our sunshine made thy spring,   163
And that thy summer bred us no increase,   164
We set the ax to thy usurping root;
And though the edge hath something hit ourselves,   166
Yet know thou, since we have begun to strike,
We'll never leave till we have hewn thee down   168
Or bathed thy growing with our heated bloods.   169

EDWARD [to Queen Margaret]
And in this resolution I defy thee,
Not willing any longer conference,
Since thou denied'st the gentle King to speak.—
Sound trumpets! Let our bloody colors wave!
And either victory, or else a grave.

QUEEN MARGARET   Stay, Edward.

EDWARD
No, wrangling woman, we'll no longer stay.
These words will cost ten thousand lives this day.   177

Exeunt omnes.

❖

[2.3]

Alarum. Excursions. Enter Warwick.

WARWICK
Forspent with toil, as runners with a race,   1
I lay me down a little while to breathe;   2

For strokes received and many blows repaid
Have robbed my strong-knit sinews of their strength,
And, spite of spite, needs must I rest awhile.   5

Enter Edward, running.

EDWARD
Smile, gentle heaven, or strike, ungentle death!   6
For this world frowns, and Edward's sun is clouded.

WARWICK
How now, my lord, what hap? What hope of good?   8

Enter [George of] Clarence.

GEORGE
Our hap is loss, our hope but sad despair,
Our ranks are broke, and ruin follows us.
What counsel give you? Whither shall we fly?

EDWARD
Bootless is flight. They follow us with wings,   12
And weak we are and cannot shun pursuit.

Enter Richard.

RICHARD
Ah, Warwick, why hast thou withdrawn thyself?
Thy brother's blood the thirsty earth hath drunk,   15
Broached with the steely point of Clifford's lance;   16
And in the very pangs of death he cried,
Like to a dismal clangor heard from far,
"Warwick, revenge! Brother, revenge my death!"
So, underneath the belly of their steeds,
That stained their fetlocks in his smoking blood,   21
The noble gentleman gave up the ghost.

WARWICK
Then let the earth be drunken with our blood!
I'll kill my horse, because I will not fly.
Why stand we like softhearted women here,
Wailing our losses, whiles the foe doth rage,
And look upon, as if the tragedy   27
Were played in jest by counterfeiting actors?   28
Here on my knee I vow to God above   [kneeling]
I'll never pause again, never stand still,
Till either death hath closed these eyes of mine
Or fortune given me measure of revenge.   32

EDWARD [kneeling]
O Warwick, I do bend my knee with thine,
And in this vow do chain my soul to thine!
And, ere my knee rise from the earth's cold face,
I throw my hands, mine eyes, my heart to Thee,   36
Thou setter-up and plucker-down of kings,
Beseeching Thee, if with Thy will it stands   38
That to my foes this body must be prey,
Yet that Thy brazen gates of heaven may ope

---

147 **Menelaus** husband of Helen of Greece, whose abduction led to the Trojan War. (By implication, King Henry is the cuckolded husband, just as Menelaus was.)   148 **Agamemnon** brother of Menelaus and leader of the Greeks in the Trojan War   150 **His father** i.e., Henry V   152 **had . . . state** i.e., if Henry VI had married someone equal to him in social position   155 **graced** honored.   **thy poor sire** i.e., Reignier, King of Naples.   **his** i.e., Henry VI's   157 **of** out of   159 **broached** set flowing, started   160 **title** claim to the throne   162 **Had slipped** would have postponed   163 **But . . . spring** i.e., But when we saw you reaping all the benefit of what should be ours   164 **increase** harvest   166 **something** somewhat   168 **leave** leave off   169 **Or . . . bloods** i.e., or shed our angry blood in an (unsuccessful) attempt to hinder your baleful increase.   177.1 *omnes* all.
2.3. Location: The field of battle near York, immediately following the preceding scene. (Historically, the field of battle was between Towton and Saxton in Yorkshire.)
0.1 *Excursions* sorties, forays of armed soldiers   1 **Forspent** Exhausted   2 **breathe** rest

---

5 **And . . . must I** and come what may, I must   6 **ungentle** ignoble   8 **hap** fortune.   12 **Bootless** Useless   15 **Thy brother's blood** (Warwick's half-brother, the Bastard of Salisbury, not among the *Dramatis Personae* of this play, was killed at Ferrybridge shortly before the battle of Towton.)   16 **Broached with** set flowing by   21 **fetlocks** i.e., hooves. (Literally, the fetlock is the projection just above the hoof at the back of the leg.)   **smoking** steaming, giving out vapor   27 **upon** on   28 **counterfeiting actors** actors performing roles   32 **measure** full quantity   36 **Thee** i.e., God   38 **stands** agrees

And give sweet passage to my sinful soul!

[*They rise.*]

Now, lords, take leave until we meet again,
Where'er it be, in heaven or in earth.

RICHARD
Brother, give me thy hand; and, gentle Warwick,   44
Let me embrace thee in my weary arms.

[*They embrace.*]

I, that did never weep, now melt with woe
That winter should cut off our springtime so.

WARWICK
Away, away! Once more, sweet lords, farewell.

GEORGE
Yet let us all together to our troops,
And give them leave to fly that will not stay,
And call them pillars that will stand to us;   51
And, if we thrive, promise them such rewards
As victors wear at the Olympian games.
This may plant courage in their quailing breasts,
For yet is hope of life and victory.
Forslow no longer! Make we hence amain.   *Exeunt.* 56

❖

[2.4]

Excursions. Enter Richard and Clifford [*meeting*].

RICHARD
Now, Clifford, I have singled thee alone.   1
Suppose this arm is for the Duke of York,
And this for Rutland—both bound to revenge,
Wert thou environed with a brazen wall.   4

CLIFFORD
Now, Richard, I am with thee here alone.
This is the hand that stabbed thy father York,
And this the hand that slew thy brother Rutland,
And here's the heart that triumphs in their death
And cheers these hands that slew thy sire and brother   9
To execute the like upon thyself.
And so, have at thee!   *They fight.* 11

Warwick comes [*to the aid of Richard*]. *Clifford flies.*

RICHARD   Nay, Warwick, single out some other chase,   12
For I myself will hunt this wolf to death.   *Exeunt.*

❖

[2.5]

Alarum. Enter King Henry alone.

KING HENRY
This battle fares like to the morning's war,
When dying clouds contend with growing light,
What time the shepherd, blowing of his nails,   3

Can neither call it perfect day nor night.
Now sways it this way, like a mighty sea
Forced by the tide to combat with the wind;
Now sways it that way, like the selfsame sea
Forced to retire by fury of the wind.
Sometime the flood prevails, and then the wind;
Now one the better, then another best;
Both tugging to be victors, breast to breast,
Yet neither conqueror nor conquerèd.
So is the equal poise of this fell war.   13
Here on this molehill will I sit me down.   [*He sits.*]
To whom God will, there be the victory!
For Margaret my queen, and Clifford too,
Have chid me from the battle, swearing both
They prosper best of all when I am thence.
Would I were dead, if God's good will were so!
For what is in this world but grief and woe?
O God! Methinks it were a happy life
To be no better than a homely swain,   22
To sit upon a hill, as I do now,
To carve out dials quaintly, point by point,   24
Thereby to see the minutes how they run:
How many makes the hour full complete,
How many hours brings about the day,
How many days will finish up the year,
How many years a mortal man may live.
When this is known, then to divide the times:
So many hours must I tend my flock,
So many hours must I take my rest,
So many hours must I contemplate,
So many hours must I sport myself,   34
So many days my ewes have been with young,
So many weeks ere the poor fools will ean,   36
So many years ere I shall shear the fleece.
So minutes, hours, days, months, and years,
Passed over to the end they were created,   39
Would bring white hairs unto a quiet grave.
Ah, what a life were this, how sweet, how lovely!
Gives not the hawthorn bush a sweeter shade   42
To shepherds looking on their silly sheep   43
Than doth a rich embroidered canopy
To kings that fear their subjects' treachery?
Oh, yes, it doth, a thousandfold it doth.
And to conclude, the shepherd's homely curds,
His cold thin drink out of his leather bottle,
His wonted sleep under a fresh tree's shade,   49
All which secure and sweetly he enjoys,
Is far beyond a prince's delicates—   51
His viands sparkling in a golden cup,
His body couchèd in a curious bed—   53
When care, mistrust, and treason waits on him.   54

*Alarum. Enter a Son that hath killed his father, at
one door* [*bearing in the dead body*].

---

44 **gentle** noble 51 **stand to** stand by 56 **Forslow** Delay. **amain**
with full speed.
2.4. Location: Scene continues at the battlefield.
1 **singled** singled out 4 **environed** surrounded 9 **cheers** urges on
11 **have at thee!** i.e., on guard, here I come! 12 **chase** prey
2.5. Location: The battlefield, as before.
3 **What time** when. **of** on (to warm them)

13 **poise** balance. **fell** cruel 22 **homely swain** simple peasant
24 **dials** sundials. **quaintly** artfully, intricately 34 **sport myself** take
recreation 36 **ean** bring forth (lambs) 39 **end** they end for which they
42–54 **Gives . . . him** (Cf. *2 Henry IV*, 4.5.23–8, and *Henry V*, 4.1.234–82.)
43 **silly** innocent, helpless 49 **wonted** accustomed 51 **delicates** luxuries 53 **curious** skillfully and daintily made, decorated

SON
Ill blows the wind that profits nobody.
This man, whom hand to hand I slew in fight,
May be possessèd with some store of crowns; 57
And I, that haply take them from him now, 58
May yet ere night yield both my life and them
To some man else, as this dead man doth me.—
Who's this? O God! It is my father's face,
Whom in this conflict I unwares have killed.
Oh, heavy times, begetting such events! 63
From London by the King was I pressed forth; 64
My father, being the Earl of Warwick's man, 65
Came on the part of York, pressed by his master; 66
And I, who at his hands received my life, 67
Have by my hands of life bereavèd him.
Pardon me, God, I knew not what I did! 69
And pardon, father, for I knew not thee!
My tears shall wipe away these bloody marks;
And no more words till they have flowed their fill.
                                    [He weeps.]

KING HENRY
Oh, piteous spectacle! Oh, bloody times!
Whiles lions war and battle for their dens,
Poor harmless lambs abide their enmity.
Weep, wretched man. I'll aid thee tear for tear; 75
And let our hearts and eyes, like civil war,
Be blind with tears, and break o'ercharged with grief. 78
                                    [He weeps.]

Enter at another door, a Father that hath killed his
    son, bearing of his son.

FATHER
Thou that so stoutly hath resisted me, 79
Give me thy gold, if thou hast any gold;
For I have bought it with an hundred blows.
But let me see: is this our foeman's face?
Ah, no, no, no, it is mine only son!
Ah, boy, if any life be left in thee,
Throw up thine eye! See, see what showers arise,
Blown with the windy tempest of my heart,
Upon thy wounds, that kills mine eye and heart!
Oh, pity, God, this miserable age!   [He weeps.]
What stratagems, how fell, how butcherly, 89
Erroneous, mutinous, and unnatural, 90
This deadly quarrel daily doth beget!
O boy, thy father gave thee life too soon,
And hath bereft thee of thy life too late! 93
KING HENRY
Woe above woe, grief more than common grief! 94
Oh, that my death would stay these ruthful deeds! 95
Oh, pity, pity, gentle heaven, pity!

The red rose and the white are on his face,
The fatal colors of our striving houses.
The one his purple blood right well resembles;
The other his pale cheeks, methinks, presenteth. 100
Wither one rose, and let the other flourish;
If you contend, a thousand lives must wither.
SON
How will my mother for a father's death
Take on with me and ne'er be satisfied! 104
FATHER
How will my wife for slaughter of my son
Shed seas of tears and ne'er be satisfied!
KING HENRY
How will the country for these woeful chances 107
Misthink the King and not be satisfied! 108
SON
Was ever son so rued a father's death?
FATHER
Was ever father so bemoaned his son?
KING HENRY
Was ever king so grieved for subjects' woe?
Much is your sorrow; mine ten times so much.
SON
I'll bear thee hence, where I may weep my fill.
                                [Exit with the body.]
FATHER
These arms of mine shall be thy winding-sheet; 114
My heart, sweet boy, shall be thy sepulchre,
For from my heart thine image ne'er shall go.
My sighing breast shall be thy funeral bell;
And so obsequious will thy father be, 118
E'en for the loss of thee, having no more,
As Priam was for all his valiant sons. 120
I'll bear thee hence, and let them fight that will,
For I have murdered where I should not kill.
                                Exit [with the body].
KING HENRY
Sad-hearted men, much overgone with care, 123
Here sits a king more woeful than you are.

    Alarums. Excursions. Enter the Queen
        [Margaret], the Prince, and Exeter.

PRINCE
Fly, father, fly! For all your friends are fled,
And Warwick rages like a chafèd bull. 126
Away! For death doth hold us in pursuit.
QUEEN MARGARET
Mount you, my lord. Towards Berwick post amain. 128
Edward and Richard, like a brace of greyhounds 129
Having the fearful flying hare in sight,

---

57 crowns i.e., coins, money   58 haply by chance   63 heavy sorrowful   64 pressed forth impressed into military service   65 man retainer, servant   66 part party, side   67 his my father's   69 Pardon . . . did (An echo of Luke 23:34, "Father, forgive them, for they know not what they do.")   75 abide endure, pay for   78 o'ercharged overfilled   79 stoutly bravely   89 stratagems deeds of violence.   fell cruel   90 Erroneous criminal   93 late lately.   94 above piled on   95 stay put a halt to.   ruthful pitiful

100 presenteth represents.   104 Take on with cry out against.   satisfied (1) consoled (2) satisfied in the desire for revenge. (Also in line 106.)   107 chances happenings   108 Misthink think ill of   114 winding-sheet shroud, burial cloth   118 obsequious dutiful in performing funeral obsequies   120 Priam King of Troy, reputed to have had fifty sons   123 overgone overcome   126 chafèd enraged   128 Berwick Berwick-on-Tweed, on the Scottish border at the North Sea shore.   post amain hasten with full speed.   129 brace pair

With fiery eyes sparkling for very wrath,
And bloody steel grasped in their ireful hands,   132
Are at our backs; and therefore hence amain.   133

EXETER
Away! For vengeance comes along with them.
Nay, stay not to expostulate. Make speed!
Or else come after. I'll away before.

KING HENRY
Nay, take me with thee, good sweet Exeter.
Not that I fear to stay, but love to go
Whither the Queen intends. Forward! Away! *Exeut.*

❧

2.6

A loud alarum. Enter Clifford, wounded, [with an arrow in his neck].

CLIFFORD
Here burns my candle out; ay, here it dies,
Which, whiles it lasted, gave King Henry light.
O Lancaster, I fear thy overthrow
More than my body's parting with my soul!
My love and fear glued many friends to thee;   5
And, now I fall, thy tough commixture melts,   6
Impairing Henry, strength'ning misproud York.   7
The common people swarm like summer flies;
And whither fly the gnats but to the sun?   9
And who shines now but Henry's enemies?
O Phoebus, hadst thou never given consent
That Phaëthon should check thy fiery steeds,   12
Thy burning car never had scorched the earth!   13
And, Henry, hadst thou swayed as kings should do,   14
Or as thy father and his father did,
Giving no ground unto the house of York,
They never then had sprung like summer flies;
I and ten thousand in this luckless realm
Had left no mourning widows for our death,
And thou this day hadst kept thy chair in peace.   20
For what doth cherish weeds but gentle air?   21
And what makes robbers bold but too much lenity?
Bootless are plaints, and cureless are my wounds;   23
No way to fly, nor strength to hold out flight.   24
The foe is merciless, and will not pity,
For at their hands I have deserved no pity.
The air hath got into my deadly wounds,
And much effuse of blood doth make me faint.   28
Come, York and Richard, Warwick and the rest;

I stabbed your fathers' bosoms. Split my breast.   30
[He faints.]

*Alarum and retreat. Enter Edward, Warwick,
Richard, and soldiers, Montague, and [George of]
Clarence.*

EDWARD
Now breathe we, lords. Good fortune bids us pause   31
And smooth the frowns of war with peaceful looks.
Some troops pursue the bloody-minded Queen,
That led calm Henry, though he were a king,
As doth a sail, filled with a fretting gust,   35
Command an argosy to stem the waves.   36
But think you, lords, that Clifford fled with them?

WARWICK
No, 'tis impossible he should escape;
For, though before his face I speak the words,   39
Your brother Richard marked him for the grave,
And wheresoe'er he is, he's surely dead.   41
Clifford groans [and dies].

RICHARD
Whose soul is that which takes her heavy leave?
A deadly groan, like life and death's departing.   43
See who it is.

EDWARD   And, now the battle's ended,
If friend or foe, let him be gently used.   45

RICHARD
Revoke that doom of mercy, for 'tis Clifford,   46
Who not contented that he lopped the branch   47
In hewing Rutland when his leaves put forth,   48
But set his murdering knife unto the root
From whence that tender spray did sweetly spring—   50
I mean our princely father, Duke of York.

WARWICK
From off the gates of York fetch down the head,
Your father's head, which Clifford placèd there;
Instead whereof let this supply the room.   54
Measure for measure must be answerèd.   55

EDWARD
Bring forth that fatal screech owl to our house,   56
That nothing sung but death to us and ours.
[Soldiers drag Clifford's body in front of York gates.]
Now death shall stop his dismal threat'ning sound,
And his ill-boding tongue no more shall speak.

WARWICK
I think his understanding is bereft.—   60

---

132 **ireful** wrathful   133 **hence amain** (Repeats the idea of *post amain* in line 128.)
2.6. Location: The battlefield, as before.
5 **My love and fear** Love and fear of me   6 **now** now that.
commixture compound (in which many friends have been glued together)   7 **Impairing** weakening.   **misproud** falsely proud
9 **the sun** (Refers to Edward's emblem.)   12 **Phaëthon** (See the note for 1.4.33.)   **check** control, manage   13 **car** chariot   14 **swayed** reigned   20 **chair** throne   21 **For . . . air?** (The implication is that King Henry's excessively mild rule has encouraged the rapid growth of his enemies, just as weeds grow fast if allowed to flourish.)
23 **Bootless are plaints** Lamentations are of no avail   24 **hold out** sustain   28 **effuse** effusion

30.2 *retreat* signal to cease the attack.   **31 breathe we** let us pause for breath   **35 fretting** blowing in gusts. (With a suggestion also of "nagging.")   **36 Command . . . waves** drive forward a large merchant vessel through the waves.   **39 his** i.e., Richard's   **41.1** *and dies* The Octavo text of *The True Tragedy* specifies here that "Clifford groans and then dies," but stage deaths are less precise than such stage directions might seem to indicate. If Clifford were to groan again at lines 69ff., the dramatic effect would be considerable.   **43 departing** parting.   **45 If** whether.   **gently used** treated in death with dignity.
46 doom judgment   **47 Who not contented** who did not rest contented   **48 when . . . forth** i.e., in the flowering of Rutland's youth   **50 spray** small and tender twig   **54 let . . . room** let Clifford's head take its place.   **55 answerèd** given in return.   **56 screech owl** (A conventional omen of death, here likened to Clifford.)   **house** family   **60 bereft** taken from him.

Speak, Clifford, dost thou know who speaks to thee?—
Dark cloudy death o'ershades his beams of life,
And he nor sees nor hears us what we say.   63

RICHARD
Oh, would he did! And so perhaps he doth.
'Tis but his policy to counterfeit,   65
Because he would avoid such bitter taunts
Which in the time of death he gave our father.

GEORGE
If so thou think'st, vex him with eager words.   68

RICHARD
Clifford, ask mercy and obtain no grace.

EDWARD
Clifford, repent in bootless penitence.

WARWICK
Clifford, devise excuses for thy faults.

GEORGE
While we devise fell tortures for thy faults.   72

RICHARD
Thou didst love York, and I am son to York.   73

EDWARD
Thou pitied'st Rutland. I will pity thee.

GEORGE
Where's Captain Margaret to fence you now?   75

WARWICK
They mock thee, Clifford. Swear as thou wast wont.   76

RICHARD
What, not an oath? Nay, then the world goes hard
When Clifford cannot spare his friends an oath.
I know by that he's dead; and, by my soul,
If this right hand would buy two hours' life
That I in all despite might rail at him,   81
This hand should chop it off, and with the issuing blood   82
Stifle the villain whose unstanchèd thirst   83
York and young Rutland could not satisfy.

WARWICK
Ay, but he's dead. Off with the traitor's head,
And rear it in the place your father's stands.
And now to London with triumphant march,
There to be crownèd England's royal king;
From whence shall Warwick cut the sea to France
And ask the Lady Bona for thy queen.   90
So shalt thou sinew both these lands together,   91
And, having France thy friend, thou shalt not dread   92
The scattered foe that hopes to rise again;
For though they cannot greatly sting to hurt,
Yet look to have them buzz to offend thine ears.   95
First will I see the coronation,
And then to Brittany I'll cross the sea
To effect this marriage, so it please my lord.   98

EDWARD
Even as thou wilt, sweet Warwick, let it be;

For in thy shoulder do I build my seat,   100
And never will I undertake the thing
Wherein thy counsel and consent is wanting.
Richard, I will create thee Duke of Gloucester,
And George, of Clarence. Warwick, as ourself,
Shall do and undo as him pleaseth best.

RICHARD
Let me be Duke of Clarence, George of Gloucester;
For Gloucester's dukedom is too ominous.   107

WARWICK
Tut, that's a foolish observation.
Richard, be Duke of Gloucester. Now to London,
To see these honors in possession.   *Exeunt.* 110

❖

[3.1]

*Enter [two Keepers] with crossbows in their
hands.*

FIRST KEEPER
Under this thick-grown brake we'll shroud ourselves,   1
For through this laund anon the deer will come;   2
And in this covert will we make our stand,
Culling the principal of all the deer.   4

SECOND KEEPER
I'll stay above the hill, so both may shoot.

FIRST KEEPER
That cannot be. The noise of thy crossbow
Will scare the herd, and so my shoot is lost.
Here stand we both, and aim we at the best;   8
And, for the time shall not seem tedious,   9
I'll tell thee what befell me on a day
In this self place where now we mean to stand.   11

SECOND KEEPER
Here comes a man. Let's stay till he be past.
[*They remain concealed.*]

*Enter the King [Henry, disguised,] with a prayer
book.*

KING HENRY
From Scotland am I stol'n, even of pure love,   13
To greet mine own land with my wishful sight.   14
No, Harry, Harry, 'tis no land of thine!
Thy place is filled, thy scepter wrung from thee,
Thy balm washed off wherewith thou wast anointed.
No bending knee will call thee Caesar now,
No humble suitors press to speak for right,   19
No, not a man comes for redress of thee;   20

---

63 **nor sees** neither sees   65 **policy** stratagem   68 **eager** biting, bitter
72 **fell** cruel.   **faults** crimes.   73 **Thou . . . to York** (Said sardonically,
as also in line 74.)   75 **fence** defend   76 **wont** accustomed to.
81 **despite** spite, contempt   82 **This hand** i.e., this left hand
83 **unstanchèd** unquenchable   90 **Lady Bona** daughter of the Duke of
Savoy and sister to the Queen of France   91 **sinew** join (as with sinew)
92 **France** France and her king   95 **look** expect   98 **so** provided that

100 **in thy shoulder** i.e., with your support.   **seat** throne   107 **Gloucester's . . . ominous** (Three dukes or earls of Gloucester had met with
violent deaths: Hugh Spenser, a favorite of Edward II, Thomas of
Woodstock, youngest son of Edward III [see *Richard II*, 1.1], and
Humphrey, uncle of Henry VI [see *2 Henry VI*, 3.2].)   110 **in possession** i.e., in our possession.
**3.1. Location: A forest in the north of England, near the Scottish
border.**
0.1 **Keepers** gamekeepers   1 **brake** thicket   2 **laund** glade
4 **Culling . . . deer** selecting the best deer.   8 **at the best** as best we
can   9 **for** so that   11 **self** same, very   13 **of** out of   14 **wishful**
longing   19 **speak for right** plead for justice   20 **of** from

For how can I help them, and not myself?

FIRST KEEPER [*aside to Second Keeper*]
Ay, here's a deer whose skin's a keeper's fee:　　　22
This is the quondam king. Let's seize upon him.　　23

KING HENRY
Let me embrace thee, sour adversity,
For wise men say it is the wisest course.

SECOND KEEPER [*aside*]
Why linger we? Let us lay hands upon him.

FIRST KEEPER [*aside*]
Forbear awhile. We'll hear a little more.

KING HENRY
My queen and son are gone to France for aid;
And, as I hear, the great commanding Warwick
Is thither gone, to crave the French King's sister
To wife for Edward. If this news be true,　　　　31
Poor Queen and son, your labor is but lost,
For Warwick is a subtle orator,
And Lewis a prince soon won with moving words.
By this account, then, Margaret may win him,
For she's a woman to be pitied much.
Her sighs will make a batt'ry in his breast;　　　37
Her tears will pierce into a marble heart.
The tiger will be mild whiles she doth mourn,
And Nero will be tainted with remorse　　　　　40
To hear and see her plaints, her brinish tears.　　41
Ay, but she's come to beg, Warwick to give;
She, on his left side, craving aid for Henry,
He, on his right, asking a wife for Edward.
She weeps and says her Henry is deposed;
He smiles and says his Edward is installed;
That she, poor wretch, for grief can speak no more,　47
Whiles Warwick tells his title, smooths the wrong,　48
Inferreth arguments of mighty strength,　　　　　49
And in conclusion wins the King from her
With promise of his sister, and what else,　　　　51
To strengthen and support King Edward's place.　52
Oh, Margaret, thus 'twill be, and thou, poor soul,
Art then forsaken, as thou went'st forlorn!
　　　　　　　　　　　[*The Keepers come forward.*]

SECOND KEEPER
Say, what art thou that talk'st of kings and queens?　55

KING HENRY
More than I seem, and less than I was born to.
A man at least, for less I should not be;
And men may talk of kings, and why not I?

SECOND KEEPER
Ay, but thou talk'st as if thou wert a king.

KING HENRY
Why, so I am, in mind, and that's enough.

SECOND KEEPER
But, if thou be a king, where is thy crown?

KING HENRY
My crown is in my heart, not on my head;
Not decked with diamonds and Indian stones,　　63
Nor to be seen. My crown is called content;
A crown it is that seldom kings enjoy.

SECOND KEEPER
Well, if you be a king crowned with content,
Your crown content and you must be contented
To go along with us. For, as we think,
You are the king King Edward hath deposed;
And we his subjects sworn in all allegiance
Will apprehend you as his enemy.　　　　　　71

KING HENRY
But did you never swear, and break an oath?

SECOND KEEPER
No, never such an oath, nor will not now.

KING HENRY
Where did you dwell when I was King of England?

SECOND KEEPER
Here in this country where we now remain.　　75

KING HENRY
I was anointed king at nine months old;
My father and my grandfather were kings,
And you were sworn true subjects unto me.
And tell me, then, have you not broke your oaths?

FIRST KEEPER
No, for we were subjects but while you were king.　80

KING HENRY
Why, am I dead? Do I not breathe a man?
Ah, simple men, you know not what you swear!　82
Look, as I blow this feather from my face,　　　83
And as the air blows it to me again,
Obeying with my wind when I do blow,　　　　85
And yielding to another when it blows,
Commanded always by the greater gust—
Such is the lightness of you common men.
But do not break your oaths, for of that sin
My mild entreaty shall not make you guilty.
Go where you will, the King shall be commanded;
And be you kings, command, and I'll obey.

FIRST KEEPER
We are true subjects to the King, King Edward.

KING HENRY
So would you be again to Henry,
If he were seated as King Edward is.

FIRST KEEPER
We charge you, in God's name, and the King's,
To go with us unto the officers.

KING HENRY
In God's name, lead. Your king's name be obeyed,
And what God will, that let your king perform;
And what he will, I humbly yield unto.　　　*Exeunt.*

❖

22 **fee** perquisite. (The gamekeeper will get a reward for capturing the King, just as gamekeepers were customarily awarded the horn and skins of a slain deer.)　23 **quondam** onetime, former　31 **To** as a　37 **a batt'ry in** an assault upon　40 **Nero** Roman emperor famed for his cruelty.　**tainted** touched, affected　41 **brinish** salty　47 **That** so that　48 **his title** i.e., Edward's royal claim.　**smooths** explains away　49 **Inferreth** adduces　51 **what else** other things also　52 **place** position of authority.　55 **what** who

63 **Indian stones** gems　71 **apprehend** arrest　75 **country** region　80 **but** only　82 **simple** foolish　83 **this feather** (Henry may take a feather from his hat.)　85 **wind** breath

[3.2]

*Enter King Edward, Gloucester, Clarence, [and]
Lady Grey.*

KING EDWARD
Brother of Gloucester, at Saint Albans field
This lady's husband, Sir Richard Grey, was slain,   2
His land then seized on by the conqueror.
Her suit is now to repossess those lands,
Which we in justice cannot well deny,
Because in quarrel of the house of York
The worthy gentleman did lose his life.   6

GLOUCESTER
Your Highness shall do well to grant her suit.
It were dishonor to deny it her.

KING EDWARD
It were no less, but yet I'll make a pause.

GLOUCESTER [*aside to Clarence*]   Yea, is it so?
I see the lady hath a thing to grant   12
Before the King will grant her humble suit.

CLARENCE [*aside to Gloucester*]
He knows the game. How true he keeps the wind!   14

GLOUCESTER [*aside to Clarence*]   Silence!

KING EDWARD
Widow, we will consider of your suit;
And come some other time to know our mind.

LADY GREY
Right gracious lord, I cannot brook delay.   18
May it please Your Highness to resolve me now,   19
And what your pleasure is shall satisfy me.   20

GLOUCESTER [*aside to Clarence*]
Ay, widow? Then I'll warrant you all your lands,   21
An if what pleases him shall pleasure you.   22
Fight closer, or, good faith, you'll catch a blow.   23

CLARENCE [*aside to Gloucester*]
I fear her not, unless she chance to fall.   24

GLOUCESTER [*aside to Clarence*]
God forbid that! For he'll take vantages.

KING EDWARD
How many children hast thou, widow? Tell me.

CLARENCE [*aside to Gloucester*]
I think he means to beg a child of her.   27

GLOUCESTER [*aside to Clarence*]
Nay, whip me, then; he'll rather give her two.   28

LADY GREY Three, my most gracious lord.

GLOUCESTER [*aside to Clarence*]
You shall have four, if you'll be ruled by him.   30

KING EDWARD
'Twere pity they should lose their father's lands.

LADY GREY
Be pitiful, dread lord, and grant it then.

KING EDWARD [*to his brothers*]
Lords, give us leave. I'll try this widow's wit.   33

GLOUCESTER [*aside to Clarence*]
Ay, good leave have you; for you will have leave   34
Till youth take leave and leave you to the crutch.   35
          [*Gloucester and Clarence stand apart.*]

KING EDWARD
Now tell me, madam, do you love your children?

LADY GREY
Ay, full as dearly as I love myself.

KING EDWARD
And would you not do much to do them good?

LADY GREY
To do them good I would sustain some harm.

KING EDWARD
Then get your husband's lands, to do them good.

LADY GREY
Therefore I came unto Your Majesty.

KING EDWARD
I'll tell you how these lands are to be got.

LADY GREY
So shall you bind me to Your Highness' service.

KING EDWARD
What service wilt thou do me if I give them?

LADY GREY
What you command that rests in me to do.   45

KING EDWARD
But you will take exceptions to my boon.   46

LADY GREY
No, gracious lord, except I cannot do it.   47

KING EDWARD
Ay, but thou canst do what I mean to ask.

LADY GREY
Why, then, I will do what Your Grace commands.

GLOUCESTER [*aside to Clarence*]
He plies her hard; and much rain wears the marble.

CLARENCE [*aside to Gloucester*]
As red as fire! Nay then, her wax must melt.   51

3.2. Location: London. The royal court.
0.1 *Gloucester, Clarence* i.e., Richard and George, King Edward's brothers, made dukes in 2.6.103–4   **2 Sir Richard Grey** (An error for Sir John Grey, who fell at the second battle of St. Albans fighting on the Lancastrian side; compare with *Richard III*, 1.3.127–30.)
6 in quarrel . . . York supporting the Yorkist cause. (A factual error; see previous note.)   **12 a thing** (With a sexual double entendre that runs through much of this scene.)   **14 game** (1) quarry in hunting (2) game of seduction.   **keeps the wind** hunts downwind of his prey (to prevent the game from catching his scent).   **18 brook** tolerate   **19 resolve me** answer me, end my uncertainty   **20 And . . . me** and whatever you please to grant will content me. (Richard, in the next speech, plays on sexual meanings of *pleasure* and *satisfy*.)   **21 warrant** guarantee   **22 An if** if.   **pleasure** please   **23 Fight closer . . . catch a blow** (The dueling terms here are used with sexual double meaning, as also in *fall* and *vantages*, lines 24, 25. See also *a thing*, line 12, *beg a child*, line 27, *crutch*, i.e., crotch, line 35, *service*, line 43, *do*, line 48, and *shift*, i.e., a woman's smock, line 108, for other sexual double entendres.)   **24 fear** i.e., fear for   **27 beg a child** (1) seek a court order to obtain custody of a minor (2) persuade Lady Grey to bear his child

28 whip me i.e., I'll bet a whipping the King has other designs.   **give her two** make her pregnant twice.   **30 have four** (Her fourth child would be sired by Edward.)   **33 give us leave** pardon us, i.e., leave us to confer alone.   **wit** intelligence.   **34–5 Ay . . . crutch** (Speaking privately to Clarence about their brother, Gloucester jests that the amorous Edward can have *good leave*, i.e., the liberty to play around with women like Elizabeth Grey until he loses his youth through fleshly dissipation and ends up hobbling on a crutch. With wordplay on *crutch/crotch* suggesting that Edward will find himself between Elizabeth's thighs.)   **45 rests in me** lies in my power   **46 take . . . boon** object to the request I ask.   **47 except** unless   **51 As red as fire** i.e., Edward is hotly importunate.

LADY GREY
Why stops my lord? Shall I not hear my task?

KING EDWARD
An easy task. 'Tis but to love a king.

LADY GREY
That's soon performed, because I am a subject.

KING EDWARD
Why, then, thy husband's lands I freely give thee.

LADY GREY
I take my leave with many thousand thanks.
[She curtsies, preparing to go.]

GLOUCESTER [aside to Clarence]
The match is made; she seals it with a curtsy.   57

KING EDWARD
But stay thee. 'Tis the fruits of love I mean.

LADY GREY
The fruits of love I mean, my loving liege.   59

KING EDWARD
Ay, but, I fear me, in another sense.
What love, think'st thou, I sue so much to get?

LADY GREY
My love till death, my humble thanks, my prayers—
That love which virtue begs and virtue grants.

KING EDWARD
No, by my troth, I did not mean such love.   64

LADY GREY
Why then you mean not as I thought you did.

KING EDWARD
But now you partly may perceive my mind.

LADY GREY
My mind will never grant what I perceive
Your Highness aims at, if I aim aright.   68

KING EDWARD
To tell thee plain, I aim to lie with thee.

LADY GREY
To tell you plain, I had rather lie in prison.   70

KING EDWARD
Why, then, thou shalt not have thy husband's lands.

LADY GREY
Why, then, mine honesty shall be my dower,   72
For by that loss I will not purchase them.   73

KING EDWARD
Therein thou wrong'st thy children mightily.

LADY GREY
Herein Your Highness wrongs both them and me.
But, mighty lord, this merry inclination
Accords not with the sadness of my suit.   77
Please you dismiss me, either with ay or no.

KING EDWARD
Ay, if thou wilt say ay to my request;
No, if thou dost say no to my demand.

LADY GREY
Then, no, my lord. My suit is at an end.

GLOUCESTER [aside to Clarence]
The widow likes him not. She knits her brows.   82

CLARENCE [aside to Gloucester]
He is the bluntest wooer in Christendom.

KING EDWARD [aside]
Her looks doth argue her replete with modesty;   84
Her words doth show her wit incomparable;
All her perfections challenge sovereignty.   86
One way or other, she is for a king,
And she shall be my love, or else my queen.—
Say that King Edward take thee for his queen?

LADY GREY
'Tis better said than done, my gracious lord.
I am a subject fit to jest withal,   91
But far unfit to be a sovereign.

KING EDWARD
Sweet widow, by my state I swear to thee   93
I speak no more than what my soul intends,
And that is, to enjoy thee for my love.

LADY GREY
And that is more than I will yield unto.
I know I am too mean to be your queen,   97
And yet too good to be your concubine.

KING EDWARD
You cavil, widow. I did mean my queen.

LADY GREY
'Twill grieve Your Grace my sons should call you father.

KING EDWARD
No more than when my daughters call thee mother.
Thou art a widow, and thou hast some children;
And, by God's mother, I, being but a bachelor,
Have other some. Why, 'tis a happy thing   104
To be the father unto many sons.
Answer no more, for thou shalt be my queen.

GLOUCESTER [aside to Clarence]
The ghostly father now hath done his shrift.   107

CLARENCE [aside to Gloucester]
When he was made a shriver, 'twas for shift.   108

KING EDWARD
Brothers, you muse what chat we two have had.   109
[Gloucester and Clarence come forward.]

GLOUCESTER
The widow likes it not, for she looks very sad.

KING EDWARD
You'd think it strange if I should marry her.

CLARENCE
To who, my lord?

KING EDWARD   Why, Clarence, to myself.   112

GLOUCESTER
That would be ten days' wonder at the least.   113

---

82 **likes** (1) loves (2) pleases 84 **argue her** show her to be 86 **challenge** lay claim to 91 **jest** dally 93 **state** i.e., kingship 97 **mean** low in social rank 104 **other some** some others. **happy** fortunate 107 **ghostly father** spiritual father, confessor. **done his shrift** finished hearing confession. 108 **When ... shift** (Gloucester jests that Edward's role as confessor must have been hastily and duplicitously put on. With wordplay on *shift* meaning "petticoat.") 109 **muse** wonder 112 **To who** (Edward might *marry her* in the sense of giving her in marriage to a wealthy subject; he might then take her as his mistress.) 113 **ten days' wonder** (One day longer than the proverbial "nine days' wonder," i.e., an event of sudden notoriety. Clarence points out the exaggeration in the next line.)

---

57 **seals** confirms (as in affixing a seal to a document) 59 **fruits of love** (Lady Grey interprets the King's sexual phrase in the innocent sense of "loyal feelings of affection toward the monarch.") 64 **troth** faith 68 **aim** guess 70 **lie** be confined. (With a play on King Edward's *lie* in sexual embrace.) 72 **honesty** chastity, virtue 73 **that loss** loss of that 77 **sadness** seriousness

CLARENCE
That's a day longer than a wonder lasts.
GLOUCESTER
By so much is the wonder in extremes. 115
KING EDWARD
Well, jest on, brothers. I can tell you both
Her suit is granted for her husband's lands.

Enter a Nobleman.

NOBLEMAN
My gracious lord, Henry your foe is taken
And brought your prisoner to your palace gate.
KING EDWARD
See that he be conveyed unto the Tower.
And go we, brothers, to the man that took him,
To question of his apprehension.— 122
Widow, go you along.—Lords, use her honorably.
    Exeunt. Manet Richard [of Gloucester].
GLOUCESTER
Ay, Edward will use women honorably.
Would he were wasted, marrow, bones, and all,
That from his loins no hopeful branch may spring 125
To cross me from the golden time I look for! 127
And yet, between my soul's desire and me—
The lustful Edward's title burièd— 129
Is Clarence, Henry, and his son young Edward,
And all the unlooked-for issue of their bodies, 131
To take their rooms ere I can place myself. 132
A cold premeditation for my purpose! 133
Why, then, I do but dream on sovereignty,
Like one that stands upon a promontory
And spies a far-off shore where he would tread,
Wishing his foot were equal with his eye, 137
And chides the sea that sunders him from thence,
Saying he'll lade it dry to have his way. 139
So do I wish the crown, being so far off,
And so I chide the means that keeps me from it, 141
And so I say I'll cut the causes off, 142
Flattering me with impossibilities. 143
My eye's too quick, my heart o'erweens too much, 144
Unless my hand and strength could equal them.
Well, say there is no kingdom then for Richard;
What other pleasure can the world afford?
I'll make my heaven in a lady's lap,
And deck my body in gay ornaments,
And witch sweet ladies with my words and looks. 150
Oh, miserable thought, and more unlikely

Than to accomplish twenty golden crowns! 152
Why, love forswore me in my mother's womb;
And, for I should not deal in her soft laws, 154
She did corrupt frail nature with some bribe
To shrink mine arm up like a withered shrub;
To make an envious mountain on my back, 157
Where sits deformity to mock my body;
To shape my legs of an unequal size;
To disproportion me in every part,
Like to a chaos, or an unlicked bear whelp 161
That carries no impression like the dam. 162
And am I then a man to be beloved?
Oh, monstrous fault, to harbor such a thought!
Then, since this earth affords no joy to me
But to command, to check, to o'erbear such 166
As are of better person than myself, 167
I'll make my heaven to dream upon the crown,
And, whiles I live, t'account this world but hell,
Until my misshaped trunk that bears this head
Be round impalèd with a glorious crown. 171
And yet I know not how to get the crown,
For many lives stand between me and home; 173
And I—like one lost in a thorny wood,
That rends the thorns and is rent with the thorns,
Seeking a way and straying from the way,
Not knowing how to find the open air,
But toiling desperately to find it out—
Torment myself to catch the English crown;
And from that torment I will free myself
Or hew my way out with a bloody ax.
Why, I can smile, and murder whiles I smile,
And cry "Content" to that which grieves my heart,
And wet my cheeks with artificial tears,
And frame my face to all occasions.
I'll drown more sailors than the mermaid shall; 186
I'll slay more gazers than the basilisk; 187
I'll play the orator as well as Nestor, 188
Deceive more slyly than Ulysses could, 189
And, like a Sinon, take another Troy. 190
I can add colors to the chameleon,
Change shapes with Proteus for advantages, 192
And set the murderous Machiavel to school. 193
Can I do this, and cannot get a crown?
Tut, were it farther off, I'll pluck it down.   *Exit.*

♣

115 **in extremes** an unusual wonder indeed.   **122 of his apprehension** about his being taken.   **125 wasted** wasted with disease—syphilis, in particular   **127 cross** thwart, frustrate   **129 The . . . burièd** i.e., even after lustful Edward's title to the throne is eliminated by his death   **131 unlooked-for** unforeseeable and undesirable   **132 rooms** places   **133 cold premeditation** discouraging prospect   **137 equal with his eye** i.e., able to achieve what he views   **139 lade** empty (by ladling, scooping)   **141 means** obstacles   **142 causes** i.e., causes of my impatience   **143 Flattering . . . impossibilities** deceiving myself with vain hopes.   **144 o'erweens** presumes   **150 witch** bewitch

152 **accomplish** get possession of   **154 for** so that   **157 envious** spiteful, detested   **161 unlicked bear whelp** (It was a popular notion that bears licked their shapeless newly born cubs into a proper shape.)   **162 impression** shape   **166 check** control, rebuke. **o'erbear** dominate **167 better person** handsomer appearance   **171 impalèd** encircled **173 home** i.e., the goal   **186 mermaid** (Mermaids allegedly had the power to lure sailors to destruction by their singing or weeping.) **187 basilisk** fabulous reptile said to kill by its gaze   **188–9 Nestor, Ulysses** Greek leaders in the Trojan War, noted, respectively, for aged wisdom and cunning   **190 Sinon** Greek warrior who allowed himself to be taken captive by the Trojans and who then, feigning resentment toward his Greek companions, persuaded Priam to bring the wooden horse within the city walls, by which Troy was taken   **192 Proteus** old man of the sea, able to assume different shapes. **for advantages** to gain tactical advantage   **193 set . . . school** teach Machiavelli how to be ruthless. (In the popular imagination, Machiavelli was the archetype of ruthless political cunning and atheism.)

[3.3]

*Flourish. Enter Lewis the French King, his sister
Bona, his Admiral, called Bourbon, Prince
Edward, Queen Margaret, and the Earl of Oxford.
Lewis sits, and riseth up again.*

KING LEWIS
Fair Queen of England, worthy Margaret,
Sit down with us. It ill befits thy state   2
And birth that thou shouldst stand while Lewis doth sit.

QUEEN MARGARET
No, mighty King of France. Now Margaret
Must strike her sail and learn awhile to serve   5
Where kings command. I was, I must confess,
Great Albion's queen in former golden days.   7
But now mischance hath trod my title down
And with dishonor laid me on the ground,
Where I must take like seat unto my fortune,   10
And to my humble state conform myself.

KING LEWIS
Why, say, fair Queen, whence springs this deep despair?

QUEEN MARGARET
From such a cause as fills mine eyes with tears
And stops my tongue, while heart is drowned in cares.

KING LEWIS
Whate'er it be, be thou still like thyself,   15
And sit thee by our side.   *(Seats her by him.)*
Yield not thy neck
To fortune's yoke, but let thy dauntless mind
Still ride in triumph over all mischance.
Be plain, Queen Margaret, and tell thy grief.   19
It shall be eased, if France can yield relief.   20

QUEEN MARGARET
Those gracious words revive my drooping thoughts
And give my tongue-tied sorrows leave to speak.
Now, therefore, be it known to noble Lewis
That Henry, sole possessor of my love,
Is, of a king, become a banished man   25
And forced to live in Scotland a forlorn,   26
While proud, ambitious Edward, Duke of York,
Usurps the regal title and the seat
Of England's true-anointed lawful king.
This is the cause that I, poor Margaret,
With this my son, Prince Edward, Henry's heir,
Am come to crave thy just and lawful aid;
And if thou fail us, all our hope is done.
Scotland hath will to help, but cannot help;
Our people and our peers are both misled,
Our treasure seized, our soldiers put to flight,
And, as thou see'st, ourselves in heavy plight.   37

KING LEWIS
Renownèd Queen, with patience calm the storm,
While we bethink a means to break it off.   39

QUEEN MARGARET
The more we stay, the stronger grows our foe.   40

KING LEWIS
The more I stay, the more I'll succor thee.   41

QUEEN MARGARET
Oh, but impatience waiteth on true sorrow.   42
And see where comes the breeder of my sorrow!

Enter Warwick.

KING LEWIS
What's he approacheth boldly to our presence?   44

QUEEN MARGARET
Our Earl of Warwick, Edward's greatest friend.

KING LEWIS
Welcome, brave Warwick! What brings thee to
France?   *He descends. She ariseth.*   46

QUEEN MARGARET
Ay, now begins a second storm to rise,
For this is he that moves both wind and tide.

WARWICK
From worthy Edward, King of Albion,
My lord and sovereign, and thy vowèd friend,
I come in kindness and unfeignèd love,
First, to do greetings to thy royal person,
And then to crave a league of amity;
And lastly, to confirm that amity
With nuptial knot, if thou vouchsafe to grant
That virtuous Lady Bona, thy fair sister,   56
To England's king in lawful marriage.

QUEEN MARGARET [*aside*]
If that go forward, Henry's hope is done.

WARWICK (*speaking to Bona*)
And, gracious madam, in our king's behalf
I am commanded, with your leave and favor,   60
Humbly to kiss your hand, and with my tongue
To tell the passion of my sovereign's heart—
Where fame, late ent'ring at his heedful ears,   63
Hath placed thy beauty's image and thy virtue.

QUEEN MARGARET
King Lewis and Lady Bona, hear me speak
Before you answer Warwick. His demand   66
Springs not from Edward's well-meant honest love,
But from deceit bred by necessity.
For how can tyrants safely govern home
Unless abroad they purchase great alliance?
To prove him tyrant this reason may suffice,
That Henry liveth still; but were he dead,
Yet here Prince Edward stands, King Henry's son.
Look, therefore, Lewis, that by this league and marriage
Thou draw not on thy danger and dishonor.   75
For though usurpers sway the rule awhile,   76
Yet heavens are just, and time suppresseth wrongs.

3.3. Location: France. The royal court. A throne and a seat or seats
are provided.
2 state rank   **5 strike her sail** lower her sail, i.e., act deferentially, as
the captain of a sea vessel does to one of higher rank   **7 Albion's**
England's   **10 like seat unto** a place befitting   **15 like thyself** i.e., as
befits your title   **19 grief** grievances.   **20 France** France and her king
25 of from being   **26 forlorn** outcast   **37 heavy** sorrowful
39 break it off i.e., cease the storm of grief.

40 stay delay   **41 The . . . thee** i.e., The longer preparation I make,
the greater help I can give you.   **42 waiteth on** attends, accompanies
44 What's he Who is he that   **46.1 descends** descends from the royal
dais.   **56 sister** i.e., sister-in-law   **60 leave and favor** kind permission   **63 fame** report.   **late** lately   **66 demand** request   **75 draw not
on** do not bring about   **76 sway** exercise

WARWICK
Injurious Margaret!
PRINCE EDWARD   And why not "Queen"?
WARWICK
Because thy father Henry did usurp,
And thou no more art prince than she is queen.
OXFORD
Then Warwick disannuls great John of Gaunt,   81
Which did subdue the greatest part of Spain;   82
And after John of Gaunt, Henry the Fourth,
Whose wisdom was a mirror to the wisest;   84
And after that wise prince, Henry the Fifth,
Who by his prowess conquerèd all France.
From these our Henry lineally descends.
WARWICK
Oxford, how haps it in this smooth discourse
You told not how Henry the Sixth hath lost   88
All that which Henry the Fifth had gotten?
Methinks these peers of France should smile at that.
But for the rest: you tell a pedigree
Of threescore-and-two years—a silly time   93
To make prescription for a kingdom's worth.   94
OXFORD
Why, Warwick, canst thou speak against thy liege,
Whom thou obeyèd'st thirty-and-six years,
And not bewray thy treason with a blush?   97
WARWICK
Can Oxford, that did ever fence the right,   98
Now buckler falsehood with a pedigree?   99
For shame! Leave Henry, and call Edward king.
OXFORD
Call him my king by whose injurious doom   101
My elder brother, the Lord Aubrey Vere,   102
Was done to death? And more than so, my father,   103
Even in the downfall of his mellowed years,
When nature brought him to the door of death?
No, Warwick, no! While life upholds this arm,
This arm upholds the house of Lancaster.
WARWICK   And I the house of York.
KING LEWIS
Queen Margaret, Prince Edward, and Oxford,
Vouchsafe, at our request, to stand aside
While I use further conference with Warwick.   111
                                        They stand aloof.

QUEEN MARGARET
Heavens grant that Warwick's words bewitch him not!
KING LEWIS
Now, Warwick, tell me, even upon thy conscience,
Is Edward your true king? For I were loath
To link with him that were not lawful chosen.

WARWICK
Thereon I pawn my credit and mine honor.   116
KING LEWIS
But is he gracious in the people's eye?
WARWICK
The more that Henry was unfortunate.
KING LEWIS
Then further, all dissembling set aside,
Tell me for truth the measure of his love   120
Unto our sister Bona.
WARWICK   Such it seems
As may beseem a monarch like himself.   122
Myself have often heard him say and swear
That this his love was an eternal plant,
Whereof the root was fixed in virtue's ground,
The leaves and fruit maintained with beauty's sun,
Exempt from envy, but not from disdain,   127
Unless the Lady Bona quit his pain.   128
KING LEWIS [*to the Lady Bona*]
Now, sister, let us hear your firm resolve.
BONA
Your grant, or your denial, shall be mine.   130
(*Speaks to Warwick*) Yet I confess that often ere this
    day,
When I have heard your king's desert recounted,   132
Mine ear hath tempted judgment to desire.   133
KING LEWIS
Then, Warwick, thus: our sister shall be Edward's.
And now forthwith shall articles be drawn   135
Touching the jointure that your king must make,   136
Which with her dowry shall be counterpoised.—   137
Draw near, Queen Margaret, and be a witness
That Bona shall be wife to the English King.
        [*Margaret, Edward, and Oxford come forward.*]
PRINCE EDWARD
To Edward, but not to the English King.
QUEEN MARGARET
Deceitful Warwick! It was thy device   141
By this alliance to make void my suit.
Before thy coming, Lewis was Henry's friend.
KING LEWIS
And still is friend to him and Margaret.
But if your title to the crown be weak,
As may appear by Edward's good success,
Then 'tis but reason that I be released
From giving aid which late I promisèd   148
Yet shall you have all kindness at my hand
That your estate requires and mine can yield.   150
WARWICK [*to Queen Margaret*]
Henry now lives in Scotland at his ease,
Where, having nothing, nothing can he lose.

---

78 **Injurious** Insulting 81 **disannuls** cancels, takes no account of
82 **Which** who 84 **a mirror** a model for emulation 88 **haps it** does
it happen that 93 **threescore-and-two** i.e., from 1399, the date of
Henry IV's accession, to 1461, that of Edward's. **silly** i.e., ridiculously
short 94 **prescription** claim founded upon long use and de facto
possession 97 **bewray** reveal 98 **fence** defend 99 **buckler** shield,
protect 101 **doom** judgment 102 **Lord Aubrey Vere** the eldest son
of the twelfth Earl of Oxford, John de Vere. (Both he and his father
were attainted and executed for treason by the Yorkists in 1462.)
103 **more than so** even more than that 111 **use further conference**
hold further conversation. 111.1 *aloof* to one side.

116 **pawn my credit** stake my reputation 120 **for truth** truly.
measure extent 122 **beseem** befit 127 **envy** ill will, malice. **but
. . . disdain** i.e., his love will wither if the lady disdains him. (Warwick uses the stock hyperbole of Petrarchan devotion.) 128 **quit**
requite, alleviate 130 **grant** granting, agreeing 132 **desert** deserving 133 **Mine . . . desire** what I have heard has prompted my judgment to desire him. 135 **articles** i.e., articles of a marriage contract
136 **Touching the jointure** concerning the marriage settlement for
the bride 137 **counterpoised** matched, balanced in amount.
141 **device** stratagem 148 **late** lately 150 **estate** rank, condition

And as for you yourself, our quondam queen,   153
You have a father able to maintain you,
And better 'twere you troubled him than France.

QUEEN MARGARET
Peace, impudent and shameless Warwick,
Proud setter-up and puller-down of kings!
I will not hence till, with my talk and tears,
Both full of truth, I make King Lewis behold   160
Thy sly conveyance and thy lord's false love;   161
For both of you are birds of selfsame feather.
                    Post blowing a horn within.

KING LEWIS
Warwick, this is some post to us or thee.

Enter the Post.

POST (*speaks to Warwick*)
My Lord Ambassador, these letters are for you,
Sent from your brother, Marquess Montague.
(*To Lewis*) These from our king unto Your Majesty.
(*To Margaret*) And, madam, these for you; from
whom I know not.   *They all read their letters.*

OXFORD [*to Prince Edward*]
I like it well that our fair queen and mistress
Smiles at her news, while Warwick frowns at his.

PRINCE EDWARD [*to Oxford*]
Nay, mark how Lewis stamps, as he were nettled.   169
I hope all's for the best.

KING LEWIS
Warwick, what are thy news? And yours, fair Queen?

QUEEN MARGARET
Mine, such as fill my heart with unhoped joys.

WARWICK
Mine, full of sorrow and heart's discontent.

KING LEWIS
What, has your king married the Lady Grey?
And now, to soothe your forgery and his,   175
Sends me a paper to persuade me patience?
Is this th'alliance that he seeks with France?
Dare he presume to scorn us in this manner?

QUEEN MARGARET
I told Your Majesty as much before.
This proveth Edward's love and Warwick's honesty.

WARWICK
King Lewis, I here protest, in sight of heaven
And by the hope I have of heavenly bliss,
That I am clear from this misdeed of Edward's—   183
No more my king, for he dishonors me,
But most himself, if he could see his shame.
Did I forget that by the house of York   186
My father came untimely to his death?   187
Did I let pass th'abuse done to my niece?   188
Did I impale him with the regal crown?   189

Did I put Henry from his native right?
And am I guerdoned at the last with shame?   191
Shame on himself! For my desert is honor;   192
And to repair my honor lost for him,
I here renounce him and return to Henry.
My noble Queen, let former grudges pass,
And henceforth I am thy true servitor.   196
I will revenge his wrong to Lady Bona
And replant Henry in his former state.

QUEEN MARGARET
Warwick, these words have turned my hate to love;
And I forgive and quite forget old faults,
And joy that thou becom'st King Henry's friend.

WARWICK
So much his friend, ay, his unfeignèd friend,
That, if King Lewis vouchsafe to furnish us
With some few bands of chosen soldiers,
I'll undertake to land them on our coast
And force the tyrant from his seat by war.   206
'Tis not his new-made bride shall succor him.   207
And as for Clarence, as my letters tell me,
He's very likely now to fall from him,   209
For matching more for wanton lust than honor,   210
Or than for strength and safety of our country.

BONA
Dear brother, how shall Bona be revenged
But by thy help to this distressèd queen?

QUEEN MARGARET
Renownèd prince, how shall poor Henry live,
Unless thou rescue him from foul despair?

BONA
My quarrel and this English queen's are one.

WARWICK
And mine, fair Lady Bona, joins with yours.

KING LEWIS
And mine with hers, and thine, and Margaret's.
Therefore at last I firmly am resolved
You shall have aid.

QUEEN MARGARET
Let me give humble thanks for all at once.

KING LEWIS [*to the Post*]
Then, England's messenger, return in post   222
And tell false Edward, thy supposèd king,
That Lewis of France is sending over masquers   224
To revel it with him and his new bride.
Thou see'st what's passed. Go fear thy king withal.   226

BONA
Tell him, in hope he'll prove a widower shortly,
I'll wear the willow garland for his sake.   228

QUEEN MARGARET
Tell him my mourning weeds are laid aside   229

---

153 **quondam** former   160 **conveyance** underhand dealing
161.1 *Post* messenger   169 **as** as if   175 **to soothe your forgery** to
gloss over your deceit   183 **clear from** innocent of   186 **by** i.e., while
serving, in the cause of   187 **My father** i.e., Salisbury (who, according
to the chronicles, was captured at Wakefield and beheaded by the Lancastrians)   188 **th'abuse . . . niece** (The chronicles report that Edward
attempted to "deflower" Warwick's niece while she was a guest in his
house.)   189 **impale him** i.e., encircle his head

191 **guerdoned** rewarded   192 **my desert** what I deserve   196 **true
servitor** loyal servant   206 **tyrant** usurper   207 '**Tis . . . him** i.e., No
newly chosen bride like Lady Grey is going to be enough to save him
209 **fall from him** desert King Edward   210 **matching** marrying
222 **in post** in haste   224 **masquers** dancers in a masque or court revels. (Said ironically.)   226 **fear** frighten.   **withal** with this.   228 **willow garland** (Symbol of a forsaken lover; said here contemptuously.
The leaves are from the great willow herb, or loosestrife, not from the
willow tree.)   229 **weeds** garments

And I am ready to put armor on.

WARWICK
Tell him from me that he hath done me wrong,
And therefore I'll uncrown him ere 't be long.
There's thy reward. [*He gives money.*] Begone.

Exit Post.

KING LEWIS   But Warwick,
Thou and Oxford, with five thousand men,
Shall cross the seas and bid false Edward battle;
And, as occasion serves, this noble queen
And prince shall follow with a fresh supply.   237
Yet, ere thou go, but answer me one doubt: 238
What pledge have we of thy firm loyalty?

WARWICK
This shall assure my constant loyalty,
That, if our queen and this young prince agree,
I'll join mine eldest daughter and my joy
To him forthwith in holy wedlock bands.   242

QUEEN MARGARET
Yes, I agree, and thank you for your motion.—   244
Son Edward, she is fair and virtuous;
Therefore delay not. Give thy hand to Warwick,
And, with thy hand, thy faith irrevocable
That only Warwick's daughter shall be thine.

PRINCE EDWARD
Yes, I accept her, for she well deserves it;
And here, to pledge my vow, I give my hand.
He gives his hand to Warwick.

KING LEWIS
Why stay we now? These soldiers shall be levied,   251
And thou, Lord Bourbon, our high admiral,
Shall waft them over with our royal fleet.   253
I long till Edward fall by war's mischance
For mocking marriage with a dame of France.   255
Exeunt. Manet Warwick.

WARWICK
I came from Edward as ambassador,
But I return his sworn and mortal foe.
Matter of marriage was the charge he gave me,
But dreadful war shall answer his demand.
Had he none else to make a stale but me?   260
Then none but I shall turn his jest to sorrow.
I was the chief that raised him to the crown,
And I'll be chief to bring him down again—
Not that I pity Henry's misery,
But seek revenge on Edward's mockery.   *Exit.*

❖

[4.1]

*Enter Richard [Duke of Gloucester], Clarence,
Somerset, and Montague.*

GLOUCESTER
Now tell me, brother Clarence, what think you
Of this new marriage with the Lady Grey?
Hath not our brother made a worthy choice?

CLARENCE
Alas, you know, 'tis far from hence to France;
How could he stay till Warwick made return?   5

SOMERSET
My lords, forbear this talk. Here comes the King.   6

*Flourish. Enter King Edward, Lady Grey [as
Queen Elizabeth], Pembroke, Stafford, Hastings.
Four stand on one side and four on the other.*

GLOUCESTER   And his well-chosen bride.

CLARENCE
I mind to tell him plainly what I think.   8

KING EDWARD
Now, brother of Clarence, how like you our choice,
That you stand pensive, as half malcontent?   10

CLARENCE
As well as Lewis of France, or the Earl of Warwick,
Which are so weak of courage and in judgment   12
That they'll take no offense at our abuse.   13

KING EDWARD
Suppose they take offense without a cause;
They are but Lewis and Warwick, I am Edward,
Your king and Warwick's, and must have my will.   16

GLOUCESTER
And shall have your will, because our king.
Yet hasty marriage seldom proveth well.

KING EDWARD
Yea, brother Richard, are you offended too?

GLOUCESTER   Not I.
No, God forbid that I should wish them severed
Whom God hath joined together! Ay, and 'twere pity
To sunder them that yoke so well together.   23

KING EDWARD
Setting your scorns and your mislike aside,   24
Tell me some reason why the Lady Grey
Should not become my wife and England's queen.
And you too, Somerset and Montague,
Speak freely what you think.

CLARENCE
Then this is mine opinion: that King Lewis
Becomes your enemy for mocking him
About the marriage of the Lady Bona.

GLOUCESTER
And Warwick, doing what you gave in charge,   32
Is now dishonorèd by this new marriage.

---

237 supply reinforcements.   **238 but** only   **242 eldest daughter** (A
historical inaccuracy; Prince Edward was betrothed to a younger
daughter of Warwick, Anne, who later married Richard of Gloucester; the eldest daughter, Isabella, was already the wife of the Duke
of Clarence.)   **244 motion** proposal.   **251 stay** delay   **253 waft** convey by water   **255.1 Manet** He remains onstage   **260 stale** dupe,
laughingstock
4.1. Location: London. The royal court.
0.2 Somerset Historically, this is the third Duke of Somerset. See note
at 5.1.73.

5 stay wait. (Clarence speaks ironically.)   **6.3. Four stand** i.e., the four
already onstage. Edward is seemingly in the middle.   **8 mind** intend
10 malcontent discontented.   **12 Which** who   **13 abuse** insult. (Clarence
speaks with scornful irony, as does Gloucester in lines 20–3.)   **16 have
my will** (1) have my way (2) fulfill my lust.   **23 yoke** are bound in
marriage. (But Gloucester parodies the language of the marriage service in such a way as to suggest sexual coupling and the yoking of
oxen.)   **24 mislike** displeasure   **32 gave in charge** commissioned

KING EDWARD
    What if both Lewis and Warwick be appeased
    By such invention as I can devise?   35
MONTAGUE
    Yet, to have joined with France in such alliance
    Would more have strengthened this our commonwealth
    'Gainst foreign storms than any homebred marriage.
HASTINGS
    Why, knows not Montague that of itself
    England is safe, if true within itself?
MONTAGUE
    But the safer when 'tis backed with France.
HASTINGS
    'Tis better using France than trusting France.
    Let us be backed with God and with the seas
    Which He hath giv'n for fence impregnable,
    And with their helps only defend ourselves;   45
    In them and in ourselves our safety lies.
CLARENCE
    For this one speech Lord Hastings well deserves
    To have the heir of the Lord Hungerford.   48
KING EDWARD
    Ay, what of that? It was my will and grant,
    And for this once my will shall stand for law.
GLOUCESTER
    And yet methinks Your Grace hath not done well
    To give the heir and daughter of Lord Scales
    Unto the brother of your loving bride.   53
    She better would have fitted me or Clarence.
    But in your bride you bury brotherhood.
CLARENCE
    Or else you would not have bestowed the heir
    Of the Lord Bonville on your new wife's son,   57
    And leave your brothers to go speed elsewhere.   58
KING EDWARD
    Alas, poor Clarence! Is it for a wife
    That thou art malcontent? I will provide thee.
CLARENCE
    In choosing for yourself you showed your judgment,
    Which being shallow, you shall give me leave
    To play the broker in mine own behalf;   63
    And to that end I shortly mind to leave you.   64
KING EDWARD
    Leave me or tarry, Edward will be king,   65
    And not be tied unto his brothers' will.
QUEEN ELIZABETH
    My lords, before it pleased His Majesty
    To raise my state to title of a queen,
    Do me but right, and you must all confess
    That I was not ignoble of descent;

And meaner than myself have had like fortune.   71
But as this title honors me and mine,
So your dislikes, to whom I would be pleasing,   73
Doth cloud my joys with danger and with sorrow.   74
KING EDWARD
    My love, forbear to fawn upon their frowns.   75
    What danger or what sorrow can befall thee
    So long as Edward is thy constant friend
    And their true sovereign, whom they must obey?
    Nay, whom they shall obey, and love thee too,
    Unless they seek for hatred at my hands;
    Which if they do, yet will I keep thee safe,
    And they shall feel the vengeance of my wrath.
GLOUCESTER [aside]
    I hear, yet say not much, but think the more.

                    Enter a Post.

KING EDWARD
    Now, messenger, what letters or what news
    From France?
POST
    My sovereign liege, no letters, and few words,
    But such as I, without your special pardon,   87
    Dare not relate.
KING EDWARD
    Go to, we pardon thee. Therefore, in brief,   89
    Tell me their words as near as thou canst guess them. 90
    What answer makes King Lewis unto our letters?
POST
    At my depart, these were his very words: 92
    "Go tell false Edward, thy supposèd king,
    That Lewis of France is sending over masquers
    To revel it with him and his new bride."
KING EDWARD
    Is Lewis so brave? Belike he thinks me Henry.   96
    But what said Lady Bona to my marriage?
POST
    These were her words, uttered with mild disdain:
    "Tell him, in hope he'll prove a widower shortly,
    I'll wear the willow garland for his sake."
KING EDWARD
    I blame not her, she could say little less;
    She had the wrong. But what said Henry's queen?
    For I have heard that she was there in place.
POST
    "Tell him," quoth she, "my mourning weeds are
        done,   104
    And I am ready to put armor on."
KING EDWARD
    Belike she minds to play the Amazon.   106
    But what said Warwick to these injuries?   107
POST
    He, more incensed against Your Majesty

---

35 invention scheme, plan **45 only** alone **48 To . . . Hungerford**
(Clarence scornfully resents the way that King Edward has won Hastings's support by giving him a wealthy bride who is heir to a powerful nobleman.) **53 brother** i.e., Lord Anthony Rivers (whose
marriage to the daughter of Lord Scales was one of the advancements
of Queen Elizabeth's kindred so much resented by Edward's brothers
and other noble supporters) **57 son** i.e., Sir Thomas Grey, Marquess
Dorset, another of the Queen's upstart relatives advanced by Edward
58 speed prosper **63 broker** agent, go-between **64 mind** intend
65 Leave Whether you leave

71 meaner more lowly **73 would** wish to **74 danger** apprehension
75 forbear . . . frowns stop trying to overcome their disapproval by
ingratiating yourself. **87 pardon** i.e., permission **89 Go to** (An
expression of remonstrance.) **90 guess** recollect **92 depart** departure
96 Belike Perhaps **104 done** i.e., no longer needed **106 Amazon**
mythical female warrior. **107 injuries** insults.

Than all the rest, discharged me with these words: 109
"Tell him from me that he hath done me wrong,
And therefore I'll uncrown him ere 't be long."

KING EDWARD
Ha! Durst the traitor breathe out so proud words?
Well, I will arm me, being thus forewarned.
They shall have wars and pay for their presumption.
But say, is Warwick friends with Margaret?

POST
Ay, gracious sovereign, they are so linked in friendship
That young Prince Edward marries Warwick's daughter.

CLARENCE
Belike the elder; Clarence will have the younger.   118
Now, brother king, farewell, and sit you fast,   119
For I will hence to Warwick's other daughter,
That, though I want a kingdom, yet in marriage   121
I may not prove inferior to yourself.—
You that love me and Warwick, follow me.

Exit Clarence, and Somerset follows.

GLOUCESTER [aside] Not I.
My thoughts aim at a further matter. I
Stay not for the love of Edward, but the crown.

KING EDWARD
Clarence and Somerset both gone to Warwick?
Yet am I armed against the worst can happen;   128
And haste is needful in this desperate case.
Pembroke and Stafford, you in our behalf
Go levy men and make prepare for war.   131
They are already, or quickly will be, landed.
Myself in person will straight follow you.   133

Exeunt Pembroke and Stafford.

But ere I go, Hastings and Montague,
Resolve my doubt. You twain, of all the rest,
Are near to Warwick by blood and by alliance.
Tell me if you love Warwick more than me.
If it be so, then both depart to him;
I rather wish you foes than hollow friends.
But if you mind to hold your true obedience,
Give me assurance with some friendly vow,   140
That I may never have you in suspect.   142

MONTAGUE
So God help Montague as he proves true!

HASTINGS
And Hastings as he favors Edward's cause!

KING EDWARD
Now, brother Richard, will you stand by us?

GLOUCESTER
Ay, in despite of all that shall withstand you.   146

KING EDWARD
Why, so. Then am I sure of victory.
Now therefore let us hence, and lose no hour
Till we meet Warwick with his foreign power.

Exeunt.

❧

109 **discharged** dismissed   118 **the elder** (Compare with the note for
3.3.242.)   119 **sit you fast** hold on tight to your throne   121 **want**
lack   128 **can** that can   131 **prepare** preparation   133 **straight** immediately   140 **mind** intend   142 **suspect** suspicion.   146 **despite** spite

[4.2]

_Enter Warwick and Oxford in England, with
French soldiers._

WARWICK
Trust me, my lord, all hitherto goes well.
The common people by numbers swarm to us.

Enter Clarence and Somerset.

But see where Somerset and Clarence comes!
Speak suddenly, my lords, are we all friends?

CLARENCE   Fear not that, my lord.

WARWICK
Then, gentle Clarence, welcome unto Warwick;   6
And welcome, Somerset! I hold it cowardice
To rest mistrustful where a noble heart   8
Hath pawned an open hand in sign of love;   9
Else might I think that Clarence, Edward's brother,
Were but a feignèd friend to our proceedings.
But welcome, sweet Clarence. My daughter shall be thine.
And now what rests but, in night's coverture,   13
Thy brother being carelessly encamped,
His soldiers lurking in the towns about,   15
And but attended by a simple guard,   16
We may surprise and take him at our pleasure?   17
Our scouts have found the adventure very easy;   18
That as Ulysses and stout Diomed   19
With sleight and manhood stole to Rhesus' tents   20
And brought from thence the Thracian fatal steeds,   21
So we, well covered with the night's black mantle,
At unawares may beat down Edward's guard   23
And seize himself. I say not "slaughter him,"
For I intend but only to surprise him.   25
You that will follow me to this attempt,
Applaud the name of Henry with your leader.

They all cry, "Henry!"

Why, then, let's on our way in silent sort,   28
For Warwick and his friends, God and Saint George!

Exeunt.

❧

[4.3]

Enter three Watchmen to guard the King's tent.

FIRST WATCH
Come on, my masters, each man take his stand.   1

4.2. Location: Fields in Warwickshire.
6 gentle noble   **8 rest** remain   **9 pawned** pledged   **13 rests** remains.
in night's coverture under cover of night   **15 lurking** idling, lodging
16 simple mere   **17 at our pleasure** whenever we wish.   **18 adventure** venturing (into Edward's camp)   **19–21 Ulysses . . . steeds** (In
Book 10 of the _Iliad,_ Ulysses and Diomedes under cover of night
stealthily enter the camp of the Thracian leader Rhesus, slay him and
twelve of his men, and lead away his horses. The horses are called
fatal steeds because of a prophecy foretelling that Troy would not fall
if these horses drank from the River Xanthus and grazed on the Trojan plain. Ovid alludes to the story in his _Metamorphoses,_ Book 13.)
19 stout brave   **20 sleight** cunning   **23 At unawares** unexpectedly,
suddenly   **25 surprise** capture   **28 sort** fashion.
4.3. Location: Edward's camp near Warwick.
1 masters good sirs

The King by this is set him down to sleep.   2
SECOND WATCH   What, will he not to bed?
FIRST WATCH
　Why, no, for he hath made a solemn vow
　Never to lie and take his natural rest
　Till Warwick or himself be quite suppressed.
SECOND WATCH
　Tomorrow then belike shall be the day,
　If Warwick be so near as men report.
THIRD WATCH
　But say, I pray, what nobleman is that
　That with the King here resteth in his tent?
FIRST WATCH
　'Tis the Lord Hastings, the King's chiefest friend.
THIRD WATCH
　Oh, is it so? But why commands the King
　That his chief followers lodge in towns about him,   13
　While he himself keeps in the cold field?   14
SECOND WATCH
　'Tis the more honor, because more dangerous.
THIRD WATCH
　Ay, but give me worship and quietness;   16
　I like it better than a dangerous honor.
　If Warwick knew in what estate he stands,   18
　'Tis to be doubted he would waken him.   19
FIRST WATCH
　Unless our halberds did shut up his passage.   20
SECOND WATCH
　Ay. Wherefore else guard we his royal tent
　But to defend his person from night foes?

　　　Enter Warwick, Clarence, Oxford, Somerset, and
　　　French soldiers, silent all.

WARWICK
　This is his tent, and see where stand his guard.
　Courage, my masters! Honor now or never!
　But follow me, and Edward shall be ours.   25
FIRST WATCH   Who goes there?
SECOND WATCH   Stay, or thou diest!
　　　Warwick and the rest cry all, "Warwick!
　　　Warwick!" and set upon the guard, who
　　　fly, crying, "Arm! Arm!" Warwick and the
　　　rest following them.

　　　The drum playing and trumpet sounding, enter
　　　Warwick, Somerset, and the rest, bringing the King
　　　[Edward] out in his gown, sitting in a chair.
　　　Richard [of Gloucester] and Hastings fly over the
　　　stage.

SOMERSET   What are they that fly there?

WARWICK
　Richard and Hastings. Let them go. Here is
　The Duke.
KING EDWARD   "The Duke"? Why Warwick, when we
　　　parted
　Thou calledst me King.
WARWICK   Ay, but the case is altered.
　When you disgraced me in my embassade,   32
　Then I degraded you from being king,
　And come now to create you Duke of York.
　Alas, how should you govern any kingdom,
　That know not how to use ambassadors,
　Nor how to be contented with one wife,
　Nor how to use your brothers brotherly,
　Nor how to study for the people's welfare,
　Nor how to shroud yourself from enemies?   40
KING EDWARD
　Yea, brother of Clarence, art thou here too?
　Nay, then I see that Edward needs must down.   42
　Yet, Warwick, in despite of all mischance,
　Of thee thyself and all thy complices,   44
　Edward will always bear himself as king.
　Though Fortune's malice overthrow my state,
　My mind exceeds the compass of her wheel.   47
WARWICK
　Then, for his mind, be Edward England's king.   48
　　　　　　Takes off his [Edward's] crown.
　But Henry now shall wear the English crown
　And be true king indeed, thou but the shadow.
　My lord of Somerset, at my request
　See that forthwith Duke Edward be conveyed
　Unto my brother, Archbishop of York.   53
　When I have fought with Pembroke and his fellows,
　I'll follow you, and tell what answer
　Lewis and the Lady Bona send to him.
　Now, for a while farewell, good Duke of York.
　　　　They [begin to] lead him out forcibly.
KING EDWARD
　What fates impose, that men must needs abide.
　It boots not to resist both wind and tide.   59
　　　　Exeunt [Edward, Somerset, and soldiers].
OXFORD
　What now remains, my lords, for us to do
　But march to London with our soldiers?
WARWICK
　Ay, that's the first thing that we have to do,
　To free King Henry from imprisonment
　And see him seated in the regal throne.   Exeunt.

❧

4.4

　　　Enter Rivers and Lady Grey [Queen Elizabeth].

---

2 by this by this time.   is set him has settled himself   13 about
round about   14 keeps remains, lodges   16 worship ease and dignity   18–19 If . . . him If Warwick knew the King's situation, it is to
be feared he would come to waken the King (and rescue him).
20 Unless . . . passage i.e., He might indeed, unless we guardsmen,
armed with our longhandled weapons bearing axlike heads, prevent
Warwick's gaining access to His Majesty.   25 But Only

32 embassade ambassadorial mission   40 shroud conceal, shield
42 needs must down must fall of necessity.   44 complices accomplices   47 My . . . wheel my spirit rises above the misery of Fortune
and her wheel. (Compass means "range, circumference.")   48 for his
mind i.e., in his own thoughts   53 Archbishop of York i.e., George
Neville.   59 boots avails
4.4. Location: London. The royal court.

RIVERS
　Madam, what makes you in this sudden change?   1

QUEEN ELIZABETH
　Why, brother Rivers, are you yet to learn
　What late misfortune is befall'n King Edward?   3

RIVERS
　What? Loss of some pitched battle against Warwick?

QUEEN ELIZABETH
　No, but the loss of his own royal person.

RIVERS   Then is my sovereign slain?

QUEEN ELIZABETH
　Ay, almost slain, for he is taken prisoner,
　Either betrayed by falsehood of his guard
　Or by his foe surprised at unawares;
　And, as I further have to understand,
　Is new committed to the Bishop of York,   10
　Fell Warwick's brother, and by that our foe.   11
　　　　　　　　　　　　　　　　　　　　　　12

RIVERS
　These news I must confess are full of grief.
　Yet, gracious madam, bear it as you may.
　Warwick may lose, that now hath won the day.

QUEEN ELIZABETH
　Till then fair hope must hinder life's decay.   16
　And I the rather wean me from despair
　For love of Edward's offspring in my womb.
　This is it that makes me bridle passion   19
　And bear with mildness my misfortune's cross.
　Ay, ay, for this I draw in many a tear   21
　And stop the rising of bloodsucking sighs,   22
　Lest with my sighs or tears I blast or drown   23
　King Edward's fruit, true heir to th'English crown.

RIVERS
　But, madam, where is Warwick then become?

QUEEN ELIZABETH
　I am informed that he comes towards London,
　To set the crown once more on Henry's head.
　Guess thou the rest. King Edward's friends must
　　down.   28
　But, to prevent the tyrant's violence—   29
　For trust not him that hath once broken faith—
　I'll hence forthwith unto the sanctuary,   31
　To save at least the heir of Edward's right.   32
　There shall I rest secure from force and fraud.
　Come, therefore, let us fly while we may fly.
　If Warwick take us we are sure to die.   *Exeunt.*

❖

[4.5]

　　　Enter Richard [Duke of Gloucester], Lord
　　　Hastings, and Sir William Stanley.

GLOUCESTER
　Now, my Lord Hastings and Sir William Stanley,
　Leave off to wonder why I drew you hither   2
　Into this chiefest thicket of the park.   3
　Thus stands the case: you know our king, my brother,
　Is prisoner to the Bishop here, at whose hands
　He hath good usage and great liberty,
　And, often but attended with weak guard,   7
　Comes hunting this way to disport himself.   8
　I have advertised him by secret means   9
　That if about this hour he make this way   10
　Under the color of his usual game,   11
　He shall here find his friends with horse and men
　To set him free from his captivity.

　　　Enter King Edward and a Huntsman with him.

HUNTSMAN
　This way, my lord, for this way lies the game.   14

KING EDWARD
　Nay, this way, man. See where the huntsmen stand.—
　Now, brother of Gloucester, Lord Hastings, and the
　　rest,
　Stand you thus close to steal the Bishop's deer?   17

GLOUCESTER
　Brother, the time and case requireth haste.   18
　Your horse stands ready at the park corner.

KING EDWARD
　But whither shall we then?

HASTINGS   To Lynn, my lord—   20
　And shipped from thence to Flanders?

GLOUCESTER
　Well guessed, believe me, for that was my meaning.

KING EDWARD
　Stanley, I will requite thy forwardness.   23

GLOUCESTER
　But wherefore stay we? 'Tis no time to talk.

KING EDWARD
　Huntsman, what say'st thou? Wilt thou go along?   25

HUNTSMAN
　Better do so than tarry and be hanged.

GLOUCESTER
　Come then, away. Let's ha' no more ado.

KING EDWARD
　Bishop, farewell! Shield thee from Warwick's frown,
　And pray that I may repossess the crown.   *Exeunt.*

❖

---

1 makes . . . change causes this sudden change (of mood) in you.
3 late recent   **10 have to** am given to   **11 new** newly.   **Bishop** Archbishop   **12 Fell** cruel.   **by that** i.e., by that token   **16 hope . . . decay** i.e., only hope can hold off my downfall and death.   **19 bridle passion** control my grief   **21 draw in** hold back   **22 bloodsucking sighs** (Sighs were thought to cost the heart a drop of blood.)   **23 blast** wither, blight   **28 must down** are destined to fall.   **29 prevent** forestall   **31 the sanctuary** residence inside a church building, providing immunity from law   **32 right** royal claim.

4.5. Location: A park belonging to the Archbishop of York, historically identified as Middleham Castle in Yorkshire.
2 Leave off cease   **3 chiefest thicket** thickest copse   **7 but attended with** attended only by   **8 to disport himself** for recreation.   **9 advertised** notified   **10 make** come   **11 color** pretext.   **his usual game** his usual custom of the hunt   **14 game** quarry.   **17 close** concealed   **18 case** circumstance   **20 Lynn** King's Lynn, a seaport in Norfolk   **23 requite thy forwardness** reward your zeal.   **25 go along** come along with us.

[4.6]

*Flourish. Enter King Henry the Sixth, Clarence,
Warwick, Somerset, young Henry [Earl of
Richmond], Oxford, Montague, and Lieutenant [of
the Tower].*

KING HENRY
  Master Lieutenant, now that God and friends
  Have shaken Edward from the regal seat
  And turned my captive state to liberty,
  My fear to hope, my sorrows unto joys,
  At our enlargement what are thy due fees?   5

LIEUTENANT
  Subjects may challenge nothing of their sov'reigns; 6
  But if an humble prayer may prevail,
  I then crave pardon of Your Majesty.

KING HENRY
  For what, Lieutenant? For well using me?
  Nay, be thou sure I'll well requite thy kindness,
  For that it made my imprisonment a pleasure— 11
  Ay, such a pleasure as encagèd birds
  Conceive when, after many moody thoughts,
  At last by notes of household harmony   14
  They quite forget their loss of liberty.
  But, Warwick, after God, thou set'st me free,
  And chiefly therefore I thank God and thee.
  He was the author, thou the instrument.
  Therefore, that I may conquer fortune's spite
  By living low, where fortune cannot hurt me, 20
  And that the people of this blessèd land
  May not be punished with my thwarting stars, 22
  Warwick, although my head still wear the crown,
  I here resign my government to thee,
  For thou art fortunate in all thy deeds.

WARWICK
  Your Grace hath still been famed for virtuous, 26
  And now may seem as wise as virtuous
  By spying and avoiding fortune's malice, 28
  For few men rightly temper with the stars. 29
  Yet in this one thing let me blame Your Grace:
  For choosing me when Clarence is in place. 31

CLARENCE
  No, Warwick, thou art worthy of the sway, 32
  To whom the heavens in thy nativity
  Adjudged an olive branch and laurel crown, 34
  As likely to be blest in peace and war;
  And therefore I yield thee my free consent. 36

WARWICK
  And I choose Clarence only for Protector. 37

KING HENRY
  Warwick and Clarence, give me both your hands.
              [*The King joins their hands.*]
  Now join your hands, and with your hands your hearts,
  That no dissension hinder government.
  I make you both Protectors of this land,
  While I myself will lead a private life
  And in devotion spend my latter days, 43
  To sin's rebuke and my Creator's praise.

WARWICK
  What answers Clarence to his sovereign's will?

CLARENCE
  That he consents, if Warwick yield consent;
  For on thy fortune I repose myself. 47

WARWICK
  Why, then, though loath, yet must I be content.
  We'll yoke together, like a double shadow
  To Henry's body, and supply his place—
  I mean, in bearing weight of government
  While he enjoys the honor and his ease.
  And, Clarence, now then it is more than needful
  Forthwith that Edward be pronounced a traitor,
  And all his lands and goods be confiscate.

CLARENCE
  What else? And that succession be determined. 56

WARWICK
  Ay, therein Clarence shall not want his part. 57

KING HENRY
  But with the first of all your chief affairs,
  Let me entreat—for I command no more—
  That Margaret your queen and my son Edward
  Be sent for, to return from France with speed;
  For till I see them here, by doubtful fear
  My joy of liberty is half eclipsed.

CLARENCE
  It shall be done, my sovereign, with all speed.

KING HENRY
  My lord of Somerset, what youth is that
  Of whom you seem to have so tender care?

SOMERSET
  My liege, it is young Henry, Earl of Richmond. 67

KING HENRY
  Come hither, England's hope. (*Lays his hand on his
    head.*) If secret powers
  Suggest but truth to my divining thoughts, 69
  This pretty lad will prove our country's bliss.
  His looks are full of peaceful majesty,
  His head by nature framed to wear a crown,
  His hand to wield a scepter, and himself

4.6. Location: The Tower of London.
0.1–4 *Enter . . . Tower* (In the Octavo stage direction, Warwick and
Clarence enter first "with the crown," and then Henry, Oxford, Somerset, and "the young Earl of Richmond.") **5 enlargement** release
from confinement **6 challenge** claim as a right **11 For that** because
14 household harmony harmonious song suited to a domestic life
20 low humbly **22 thwarting** crossing (in their astrological influence) **26 still** always.   **famed for virtuous** reputed to be virtuous
28 spying spying out, foreseeing **29 temper . . . stars** i.e., blend or
accord with their destiny. **31 in place** present. **32 sway** rule
34 Adjudged . . . crown i.e., awarded to you the symbols both of
peace and of honor in war **36 free** freely given

37 only for as sole **43 latter** last **47 repose myself** rely. **56 What
else? . . . determined** i.e., Yes, certainly. And it is also needful that the
order of succession to the throne (in view of Edward's removal) be
definitely established. **57 want** lack. (Clarence would have an interest in the crown previously claimed by his brother and willed to the
Yorkists after Henry's death.) **67 Henry . . . Richmond** Henry Tudor,
later Henry VII and founder of the Tudor dynasty. **69 divining** foreseeing the future

Likely in time to bless a regal throne.
Make much of him, my lords, for this is he
Must help you more than you are hurt by me.

Enter a Post.

WARWICK   What news, my friend?
POST
That Edward is escapèd from your brother   78
And fled, as he hears since, to Burgundy.   79
WARWICK
Unsavory news! But how made he escape?
POST
He was conveyed by Richard, Duke of Gloucester, 81
And the Lord Hastings, who attended him   82
In secret ambush on the forest side
And from the Bishop's huntsmen rescued him;
For hunting was his daily exercise.
WARWICK
My brother was too careless of his charge.
But let us hence, my sovereign, to provide
A salve for any sore that may betide.   88
        Exeunt. Mane[n]t Somerset, Richmond, and Oxford.
SOMERSET *[to Oxford]*
My lord, I like not of this flight of Edward's; 89
For doubtless Burgundy will yield him help,
And we shall have more wars before't be long.
As Henry's late presaging prophecy
Did glad my heart with hope of this young
        Richmond,
So doth my heart misgive me, in these conflicts
What may befall him, to his harm and ours.
Therefore, Lord Oxford, to prevent the worst,
Forthwith we'll send him hence to Brittany,
Till storms be past of civil enmity.
OXFORD
Ay, for if Edward repossess the crown,
'Tis like that Richmond with the rest shall down. 100
SOMERSET
It shall be so. He shall to Brittany.
Come, therefore, let's about it speedily.   *Exeunt.*

❖

[4.7]

Flourish. Enter [King] Edward, Richard [Duke of Gloucester], Hastings, and soldiers, [a troop of Hollanders].

KING EDWARD
Now, brother Richard, Lord Hastings, and the rest,
Yet thus far fortune maketh us amends
And says that once more I shall interchange
My wanèd state for Henry's regal crown.
Well have we passed and now repassed the seas,
And brought desirèd help from Burgundy.

What then remains, we being thus arrived
From Ravenspurgh haven before the gates of York,
But that we enter, as into our dukedom?   8
        [One knocks.]
GLOUCESTER
The gates made fast? Brother, I like not this;
For many men that stumble at the threshold
Are well foretold that danger lurks within.
KING EDWARD
Tush, man, abodements must not now affright us.   13
By fair or foul means we must enter in,
For hither will our friends repair to us.   15
HASTINGS
My liege, I'll knock once more to summon them.   16
        [He knocks.]
Enter, on the walls, the Mayor of York and his brethren [the aldermen].
MAYOR
My lords, we were forewarnèd of your coming
And shut the gates for safety of ourselves;
For now we owe allegiance unto Henry.
KING EDWARD
But, Master Mayor, if Henry be your king,
Yet Edward at the least is Duke of York.
MAYOR
True, my good lord, I know you for no less.
KING EDWARD
Why, and I challenge nothing but my dukedom,   23
As being well content with that alone.
GLOUCESTER *[aside]*
But when the fox hath once got in his nose,
He'll soon find means to make the body follow.
HASTINGS
Why, Master Mayor, why stand you in a doubt?
Open the gates. We are King Henry's friends.
MAYOR
Ay, say you so? The gates shall then be opened.   29
        He descends [with the aldermen].
GLOUCESTER
A wise stout captain, and soon persuaded!   30
HASTINGS
The good old man would fain that all were well,   31
So 'twere not long of him; but being entered,   32
I doubt not, I, but we shall soon persuade
Both him and all his brothers unto reason.

Enter [below] the Mayor and two aldermen.

---

78 your brother i.e., the Archbishop of York   **79 he** i.e., your brother
81 conveyed spirited away   **82 attended** awaited   **88 betide** occur,
develop.   **88.1 *Manent*** They remain onstage   **89 like not of** am displeased by   **100 like** likely.   **down** fall.
4.7. Location: Before the walls of York.

8 Ravenspurgh former seaport on the Yorkshire coast, at the mouth
of the River Humber   **13 abodements** omens (such as stumbling at
the threshold, a conventional sign of bad luck)   **15 repair** make their
way, return   **16.1 *on the walls*** (In this scene, the back wall of the
stage, or tiring-house facade, is imagined to be the walls of York; a
door in the facade represents the gates; and persons in the rear
gallery above the stage are *on the walls*.)   **23 challenge** claim
29.1 *descends* (The Mayor and aldermen descend from the rear gallery
behind the scenes and then enter below through the door representing
the gates of York.)   **30 stout** brave. (Said ironically.)   **31 fain** be glad
32 So . . . him as long as he does not bear the responsibility

KING EDWARD
So, Master Mayor, these gates must not be shut
But in the night or in the time of war.
What, fear not, man, but yield me up the keys.
                                        Takes his keys.
For Edward will defend the town and thee,
And all those friends that deign to follow me.   39

        March. Enter Montgomery, with drum and
        soldiers.

GLOUCESTER
Brother, this is Sir John Montgomery,   40
Our trusty friend, unless I be deceived.

KING EDWARD
Welcome, Sir John! But why come you in arms?

MONTGOMERY
To help King Edward in his time of storm,
As every loyal subject ought to do.

KING EDWARD
Thanks, good Montgomery; but we now forget
Our title to the crown, and only claim
Our dukedom till God please to send the rest.

MONTGOMERY
Then fare you well, for I will hence again.
I came to serve a king and not a duke.—
Drummer, strike up, and let us march away.   50
                    The drum begins to march.

KING EDWARD
Nay, stay, Sir John, awhile, and we'll debate
By what safe means the crown may be recovered.

MONTGOMERY
What talk you of debating? In few words,
If you'll not here proclaim yourself our king,
I'll leave you to your fortune and be gone
To keep them back that come to succor you.
Why shall we fight, if you pretend no title?   57

GLOUCESTER
Why, brother, wherefore stand you on nice points?   58

KING EDWARD
When we grow stronger, then we'll make our claim;
Till then, 'tis wisdom to conceal our meaning.   60

HASTINGS
Away with scrupulous wit! Now arms must rule.   61

GLOUCESTER
And fearless minds climb soonest unto crowns.
Brother, we will proclaim you out of hand;   63
The bruit thereof will bring you many friends.   64

KING EDWARD
Then be it as you will. For 'tis my right,
And Henry but usurps the diadem.

MONTGOMERY
Ay, now my sovereign speaketh like himself,
And now will I be Edward's champion.

HASTINGS
Sound, trumpet! Edward shall be here proclaimed.—
Come, fellow soldier, make thou proclamation.
        [*He gives a soldier a paper.*] *Flourish. Sound.*

SOLDIER [*reads*]   "Edward the Fourth, by the grace of
God, King of England and France, and lord of
Ireland, etc."

MONTGOMERY
And whosoe'er gainsays King Edward's right,   74
By this I challenge him to single fight.
                        Throws down his gauntlet.

ALL   Long live Edward the Fourth!

KING EDWARD
Thanks, brave Montgomery, and thanks unto you all.
If fortune serve me, I'll requite this kindness.
Now, for this night, let's harbor here in York;
And when the morning sun shall raise his car   80
Above the border of this horizon,
We'll forward towards Warwick and his mates;
For well I wot that Henry is no soldier.   83
Ah, froward Clarence, how evil it beseems thee   84
To flatter Henry and forsake thy brother!
Yet, as we may, we'll meet both thee and Warwick.
Come on, brave soldiers. Doubt not of the day,   87
And, that once gotten, doubt not of large pay.
                                        Exeunt.

❖

[4.8]

        Flourish. Enter the King [Henry], Warwick,
        Montague, Clarence, Oxford, and Exeter.

WARWICK
What counsel, lords? Edward from Belgia,   1
With hasty Germans and blunt Hollanders,   2
Hath passed in safety through the narrow seas   3
And with his troops doth march amain to London,   4
And many giddy people flock to him.   5

KING HENRY
Let's levy men and beat him back again.

CLARENCE
A little fire is quickly trodden out
Which, being suffered, rivers cannot quench.   8

WARWICK
In Warwickshire I have truehearted friends,
Not mutinous in peace, yet bold in war.
Those will I muster up. And thou, son Clarence,   11
Shalt stir up in Suffolk, Norfolk, and in Kent,
The knights and gentlemen to come with thee.
Thou, brother Montague, in Buckingham,
Northampton, and in Leicestershire, shalt find
Men well inclined to hear what thou command'st.

---

39 deign are willing.   **39.1** *drum* drummer   **40 Sir John Montgomery**
(Called "Sir Thomas" in the chronicles.)   **50.1** *drum . . . march* drummer strikes up a marching beat   **57 pretend** claim   **58 nice points**
overscrupulous details.   **60 meaning** intentions.   **61 scrupulous wit**
cautious or prudent reasoning.   **63 out of hand** at once   **64 bruit**
rumor, report

74 gainsays denies   **80 his car** i.e., Phoebus's chariot   **83 wot** know
84 froward perverse.
evil ill   **87 the day** the day's outcome
4.8. Location: The Bishop of London's palace.
1 Belgia i.e., the Low Countries   **2 hasty** quick-tempered.   **blunt**
harsh, merciless   **3 narrow seas** English Channel   **4 amain** with full
speed   **5 giddy** fickle   **8 suffered** allowed   **11 son** i.e., son-in-law

And thou, brave Oxford, wondrous well beloved,
In Oxfordshire shalt muster up thy friends.
My sovereign, with the loving citizens,
Like to his island girt in with the ocean,
Or modest Dian circled with her nymphs,   21
Shall rest in London till we come to him.   22
Fair lords, take leave and stand not to reply.   23
Farewell, my sovereign.

KING HENRY
Farewell, my Hector, and my Troy's true hope.   25

CLARENCE [kissing the King's hand]
In sign of truth, I kiss Your Highness' hand.

KING HENRY
Well-minded Clarence, be thou fortunate!   27

MONTAGUE [kissing the King's hand]
Comfort, my lord; and so I take my leave.

OXFORD [kissing the King's hand]
And thus I seal my truth, and bid adieu.   29

KING HENRY
Sweet Oxford, and my loving Montague,
And all at once, once more a happy farewell.   31

WARWICK
Farewell, sweet lords. Let's meet at Coventry.
          Exeunt [all but King Henry and Exeter].

KING HENRY
Here at the palace will I rest awhile.   33
Cousin of Exeter, what thinks Your Lordship?   34
Methinks the power that Edward hath in field
Should not be able to encounter mine.

EXETER
The doubt is that he will seduce the rest.   37

KING HENRY
That's not my fear. My meed hath got me fame.   38
I have not stopped mine ears to their demands,   39
Nor posted off their suits with slow delays.   40
My pity hath been balm to heal their wounds,
My mildness hath allayed their swelling griefs,
My mercy dried their water-flowing tears.   43
I have not been desirous of their wealth,
Nor much oppressed them with great subsidies,   45
Nor forward of revenge, though they much erred.   46
Then why should they love Edward more than me?
No, Exeter, these graces challenge grace;   48
And when the lion fawns upon the lamb,
The lamb will never cease to follow him.   50
          Shout within, "A Lancaster!" "A York!"

EXETER
Hark, hark, my lord! What shouts are these?

          Enter [King] Edward and his soldiers [with
            Gloucester].

KING EDWARD
Seize on the shamefaced Henry, bear him hence,   52
And once again proclaim us king of England!—
You are the fount that makes small brooks to flow.
Now stops thy spring; my sea shall suck them dry   55
And swell so much the higher by their ebb.—
Hence with him to the Tower. Let him not speak.
          Exit [guard] with King Henry.
And, lords, towards Coventry bend we our course,
Where peremptory Warwick now remains.   59
The sun shines hot, and, if we use delay,   60
Cold biting winter mars our hoped-for hay.   61

GLOUCESTER
Away betimes, before his forces join,   62
And take the great-grown traitor unawares.
Brave warriors, march amain towards Coventry.
                              Exeunt.

                    ❖

[5.1]

          Enter Warwick, the Mayor of Coventry, two
            Messengers, and others upon the walls.

WARWICK
Where is the post that came from valiant Oxford?—   1
How far hence is thy lord, mine honest fellow?

FIRST MESSENGER
By this at Dunsmore, marching hitherward.   3

WARWICK
How far off is our brother Montague?
Where is the post that came from Montague?

SECOND MESSENGER
By this at Daintry, with a puissant troop.   6

          Enter Somerville [to them, aloft].

WARWICK
Say, Somerville, what says my loving son?   7
And, by thy guess, how nigh is Clarence now?

SOMERVILLE
At Southam I did leave him with his forces,
And do expect him here some two hours hence.
                              [A march afar off.]

WARWICK
Then Clarence is at hand. I hear his drum.

---

21 modest Dian chaste Diana, goddess of the moon and of chastity
22 rest remain   **23 stand** wait   **25 Hector** i.e., chief protector of Troy.
(England derived its legendary descent from Troy, through Brutus,
great-grandson of Aeneas, supposed founder of the English nation.)
27 Well-minded Virtuously inclined   **29 seal my truth** confirm my
loyalty (as though putting a seal to a document)   **31 at once** together
33 palace i.e., Bishop's palace   **34 Cousin** (Form of address from the
King to his peers.)   **37 doubt** fear, danger   **38 My . . . fame** My merits
(for dealing generously and justly) have established my reputation.
39 their the commons'   **40 posted off** put off   **43 water-flowing tears**
tears flowing like water.   **45 subsidies** taxes   **46 forward of** eager
for   **48 challenge grace** claim favor   **50.1 A Lancaster! A York!** (Conflicting rallying cries for both sides.)

52 shamefaced shy, shamefast   **55 thy spring** i.e., the source of your
power   **59 peremptory** overbearing   **60–1 The sun . . . hay** i.e.,
Make hay while the sun shines.   **62 betimes** quickly.   **join** unite
5.1. Location: Before the walls of Coventry.
0.2 upon the walls (As in 4.7, the walls of this town are the tiring-house
facade backstage, and those appearing on the walls are in the rear gallery
above the stage.)   **1 post** messenger. (Also at line 5.)   **3 By this** By
this time.   **Dunsmore** a town within a day's march of Coventry; the
same is true of Daintry (Daventry), Southam, and Warwick in lines
6–13.   **6 puissant** powerful   **7 son** i.e., son-in-law.

SOMERVILLE
   It is not his, my lord. Here Southam lies. [*He points.*]
   The drum Your Honor hears marcheth from Warwick.

WARWICK
   Who should that be? Belike unlooked-for friends.

SOMERVILLE
   They are at hand, and you shall quickly know.

   March. Flourish. Enter [*King*] *Edward, Richard*
   [*Duke of Gloucester*], *and soldiers* [*below*].

KING EDWARD
   Go, trumpet, to the walls and sound a parle.   16
                        [*A parley is sounded.*]

GLOUCESTER
   See how the surly Warwick mans the wall!

WARWICK
   Oh, unbid spite! Is sportful Edward come?   18
   Where slept our scouts, or how are they seduced,
   That we could hear no news of his repair?   20

KING EDWARD
   Now, Warwick, wilt thou ope the city gates,
   Speak gentle words, and humbly bend thy knee,
   Call Edward king, and at his hands beg mercy?
   And he shall pardon thee these outrages.

WARWICK
   Nay, rather, wilt thou draw thy forces hence,   25
   Confess who set thee up and plucked thee down,
   Call Warwick patron, and be penitent?
   And thou shalt still remain the Duke of York.

GLOUCESTER
   I thought at least he would have said "the King";
   Or did he make the jest against his will?

WARWICK
   Is not a dukedom, sir, a goodly gift?

GLOUCESTER
   Ay, by my faith, for a poor earl to give.
   I'll do thee service for so good a gift.   33

WARWICK
   'Twas I that gave the kingdom to thy brother.

KING EDWARD
   Why, then, 'tis mine, if but by Warwick's gift.

WARWICK
   Thou art no Atlas for so great a weight;   36
   And, weakling, Warwick takes his gift again,
   And Henry is my king, Warwick his subject.

KING EDWARD
   But Warwick's king is Edward's prisoner.
   And, gallant Warwick, do but answer this:
   What is the body when the head is off?

GLOUCESTER
   Alas, that Warwick had no more forecast,   42

But, whiles he thought to steal the single ten,   43
The King was slyly fingered from the deck!
You left poor Henry at the Bishop's palace,
And ten to one you'll meet him in the Tower.   46

KING EDWARD
   'Tis even so. Yet you are Warwick still.   47

GLOUCESTER
   Come, Warwick, take the time. Kneel down, kneel down. 48
   Nay, when? Strike now, or else the iron cools.   49

WARWICK
   I had rather chop this hand off at a blow,
   And with the other fling it at thy face,
   Than bear so low a sail to strike to thee.

KING EDWARD
   Sail how thou canst, have wind and tide thy friend,
   This hand, fast wound about thy coal-black hair,
   Shall, whiles thy head is warm and new cut off,
   Write in the dust this sentence with thy blood:
   "Wind-changing Warwick now can change no more."   57

   Enter Oxford, with drum and colors.

WARWICK
   Oh, cheerful colors! See where Oxford comes!

OXFORD
   Oxford, Oxford, for Lancaster!
                        [*He and his forces enter the city.*]

GLOUCESTER
   The gates are open. Let us enter too.

KING EDWARD
   So other foes may set upon our backs.   61
   Stand we in good array, for they no doubt
   Will issue out again and bid us battle.
   If not, the city being but of small defense,
   We'll quickly rouse the traitors in the same.   65
                        [*Oxford appears above, on the walls.*]

WARWICK
   Oh, welcome, Oxford, for we want thy help.

   Enter Montague, with drum and colors.

MONTAGUE
   Montague, Montague, for Lancaster!
                        [*He and his forces enter the city.*]

GLOUCESTER
   Thou and thy brother both shall buy this treason   68
   Even with the dearest blood your bodies bear.

---

16 **trumpet** trumpeter.   **parle** trumpet call for a parley.   18 **unbid spite** unwelcome and vexatious circumstance.   **sportful** lascivious   20 **repair** approach.   25 **draw** withdraw   33 **do thee service** i.e., pay feudal homage. (Said ironically.)   36 **Atlas** the Titan's son in classical myth who carried the world on his shoulders   42 **forecast** forethought

43 **single ten** mere ten card. (Less valuable than the king card. Gloucester sardonically remarks that, while Warwick has been desperately trying to shore up his defenses, he has left his prize card, King Henry, inadequately guarded; see 4.8.)   46 **you'll . . . Tower** i.e., you'll soon be imprisoned in the Tower with King Henry.   47 **Yet . . . still** i.e., You are still the Earl of Warwick and still have time to change before disaster strikes; or, You are being your predictable self.   48 **time** opportunity.   49 **when?** i.e., when are you going to act? (An expression of impatience.)   **Strike . . . cools** i.e., Strike while the iron is hot. (But *strike* also means to "lower sail," "yield"; hence, Warwick's refusal to *bear so low a sail*, i.e., offer tokens of submission, in line 52. Compare with the note for 3.3.5.)   57 **Wind-changing** i.e., shifting, like a weathervane   57.1 *drum and colors* a drummer and a bearer of his heraldic insignia on a banner   61 **So** In that case.   **set . . . backs** attack us from the rear.   65 **rouse** cause (an animal) to rise from its lair   68 **buy** pay dearly for

KING EDWARD

    The harder matched, the greater victory.   70
    My mind presageth happy gain and conquest.   71

    Enter Somerset, with drum and colors.

SOMERSET

    Somerset, Somerset, for Lancaster!
                    [*He and his forces enter the city.*]

GLOUCESTER

    Two of thy name, both Dukes of Somerset,   73
    Have sold their lives unto the house of York,
    And thou shalt be the third, if this sword hold.

    Enter Clarence, with drum and colors.

WARWICK

    And lo, where George of Clarence sweeps along,
    Of force enough to bid his brother battle;   77
    With whom an upright zeal to right prevails   78
    More than the nature of a brother's love!   79
            [*Gloucester and Clarence whisper together.*]
    Come, Clarence, come; thou wilt, if Warwick call.

CLARENCE

    Father of Warwick, know you what this means?   81
            [*He takes his red rose out of his hat
                        and throws it at Warwick.*]
    Look here, I throw my infamy at thee.
    I will not ruinate my father's house,
    Who gave his blood to lime the stones together,   83
    And set up Lancaster. Why, trowest thou, Warwick,   84
    That Clarence is so harsh, so blunt, unnatural,   85
    To bend the fatal instruments of war
    Against his brother and his lawful king?   87
    Perhaps thou wilt object my holy oath.
    To keep that oath were more impiety   89
    Than Jephthah when he sacrificed his daughter.   91
    I am so sorry for my trespass made
    That, to deserve well at my brother's hands,
    I here proclaim myself thy mortal foe,
    With resolution, wheresoe'er I meet thee—

    As I will meet thee, if thou stir abroad—   96
    To plague thee for thy foul misleading me.
    And so, proudhearted Warwick, I defy thee,
    And to my brother turn my blushing cheeks.
    Pardon me, Edward! I will make amends;
    And, Richard, do not frown upon my faults,
    For I will henceforth be no more unconstant.

KING EDWARD

    Now welcome more, and ten times more beloved
    Than if thou never hadst deserved our hate!

GLOUCESTER

    Welcome, good Clarence. This is brotherlike.

WARWICK

    Oh, passing traitor, perjured and unjust!   106

KING EDWARD

    What, Warwick, wilt thou leave the town and fight?
    Or shall we beat the stones about thine ears?

WARWICK

    Alas, I am not cooped here for defense!   109
    I will away towards Barnet presently,   110
    And bid thee battle, Edward, if thou dar'st.

KING EDWARD

    Yes, Warwick, Edward dares, and leads the way.
    Lords, to the field! Saint George and victory!

    Exeunt [*King Edward and his company*]. *March.*
    Warwick and his company follows [*out of the city*].

                        ❧

[5.2]

    Alarum and excursions. Enter [*King*] *Edward,*
    bringing forth Warwick wounded.

KING EDWARD

    So, lie thou there. Die thou, and die our fear,
    For Warwick was a bug that feared us all.   2
    Now, Montague, sit fast. I seek for thee,   3
    That Warwick's bones may keep thine company.
                                            Exit.

WARWICK

    Ah, who is nigh? Come to me, friend or foe,
    And tell me who is victor, York or Warwick?
    Why ask I that? My mangled body shows,
    My blood, my want of strength, my sick heart shows,
    That I must yield my body to the earth
    And, by my fall, the conquest to my foe.
    Thus yields the cedar to the ax's edge,

---

70 **The harder . . . victory** The more powerful the enemy, the greater the victory. (Proverbial.)   71 **happy** fortunate   73 **Two of thy name** i.e., Edmund Beaufort, second Duke of Somerset, killed at St. Albans in 1455, and his son Henry, beheaded in 1464 for his Lancastrian sympathies. The Duke addressed here is Henry's brother Edmund, fourth Duke. Historically, the third Duke Henry is probably represented by the character called "Somerset" who appears earlier in this play in 4.1 and 4.6, although the effect of the play is to conflate the two by not clearly distinguishing them and by omitting the battle (Hexham) at which the third Duke fought for Lancaster and was accordingly executed by the Yorkists.   77 **Of force enough** with a powerful enough army   78–9 **With . . . love** (Warwick praises Clarence for allowing an upright zeal for the right cause [the Lancastrian cause] to prevail over the promptings of brotherly love that previously prompted Clarence to side with Edward.)   79.1 *Gloucester . . . together* (This stage direction, and that at 81.1–2, are basically from the Octavo text.)   81 **Father** Father-in-law   83 **ruinate** bring into ruin   84 **lime** cement   85 **And . . . Lancaster** in order to build up the house of Lancaster instead. **trowest thou** do you think   87 **bend** direct   89 **object** urge   91 **Jephthah** Jephthah made a solemn vow that, if granted the victory, he would sacrifice the first living creature that came to meet him on his return from war. When his daughter came to greet him, he had to sacrifice her (Judges 11:30ff.).

96 **abroad** from home, i.e., outside the city walls   106 **passing** surpassing   109 **I am . . . defense** i.e., I am here to fight, not simply to provide a passive defense for the city.   110 **Barnet** a town in Hertfordshire, about ten miles north of London. (Warwick's illogical proposal that the armies meet at Barnet, some seventy-five miles from Coventry, is a result of Shakespeare's telescoping and rearranging of historical events.)   **presently** immediately
5.2. Location: A field of battle near Barnet. (Despite the distance from Coventry to Barnet, the sense here is of virtually continuous action.)
2 **bug** bugbear, goblin.   **feared** frightened   3 **sit fast** position yourself as securely as you can.

Whose arms gave shelter to the princely eagle, 12
Under whose shade the ramping lion slept, 13
Whose top branch overpeered Jove's spreading tree 14
And kept low shrubs from winter's powerful wind.
These eyes, that now are dimmed with death's black veil,
Have been as piercing as the midday sun
To search the secret treasons of the world.
The wrinkles in my brows, now filled with blood,
Were likened oft to kingly sepulchers;
For who lived king, but I could dig his grave?
And who durst smile when Warwick bent his brow? 22
Lo, now my glory smeared in dust and blood!
My parks, my walks, my manors that I had
Even now forsake me, and of all my lands
Is nothing left me but my body's length.
Why, what is pomp, rule, reign, but earth and dust?
And, live we how we can, yet die we must.

Enter Oxford and Somerset.

SOMERSET
Ah, Warwick, Warwick! Wert thou as we are,
We might recover all our loss again.
The Queen from France hath brought a puissant power; 31
Even now we heard the news. Ah, couldst thou fly!

WARWICK
Why, then I would not fly. Ah, Montague,
If thou be there, sweet brother, take my hand,
And with thy lips keep in my soul awhile! 35
Thou lov'st me not, for, brother, if thou didst,
Thy tears would wash this cold congealèd blood
That glues my lips and will not let me speak.
Come quickly, Montague, or I am dead.

SOMERSET
Ah, Warwick, Montague hath breathed his last,
And to the latest gasp cried out for Warwick 41
And said, "Commend me to my valiant brother."
And more he would have said, and more he spoke,
Which sounded like a cannon in a vault, 44
That mought not be distinguished; but at last 45
I well might hear, delivered with a groan,
"Oh, farewell, Warwick!"

WARWICK
Sweet rest his soul! Fly, lords, and save yourselves,
For Warwick bids you all farewell, to meet in heaven.
[*He dies.*]

OXFORD
Away, away, to meet the Queen's great power!
Here they bear away his body. Exeunt.

❖

[5.3]

Flourish. Enter King Edward in triumph, with Richard [Duke of Gloucester], Clarence, and the rest.

KING EDWARD
Thus far our fortune keeps an upward course,
And we are graced with wreaths of victory.
But in the midst of this bright-shining day
I spy a black, suspicious, threat'ning cloud
That will encounter with our glorious sun 5
Ere he attain his easeful western bed:
I mean, my lords, those powers that the Queen
Hath raised in Gallia have arrived our coast 8
And, as we hear, march on to fight with us.

CLARENCE
A little gale will soon disperse that cloud
And blow it to the source from whence it came.
The very beams will dry those vapors up,
For every cloud engenders not a storm.

GLOUCESTER
The Queen is valued thirty thousand strong,
And Somerset, with Oxford, fled to her.
If she have time to breathe, be well assured 16
Her faction will be full as strong as ours.

KING EDWARD
We are advertised by our loving friends 18
That they do hold their course toward Tewkesbury. 19
We, having now the best at Barnet field,
Will thither straight, for willingness rids way; 21
And, as we march, our strength will be augmented
In every county as we go along.
Strike up the drum, cry "Courage!" and away.
Exeunt.

❖

[5.4]

Flourish. March. Enter the Queen [Margaret], young [Prince] Edward, Somerset, Oxford, and soldiers.

QUEEN MARGARET
Great lords, wise men ne'er sit and wail their loss,
But cheerly seek how to redress their harms. 2
What though the mast be now blown overboard,
The cable broke, the holding-anchor lost,
And half our sailors swallowed in the flood? 5
Yet lives our pilot still. Is't meet that he 6
Should leave the helm and, like a fearful lad,
With tearful eyes add water to the sea

12, 13 eagle, lion (Royal emblems; Warwick, the lofty *cedar* in this metaphor, has at times given his protection to both Edward and Henry.) **13 ramping** rampant, upreared. (A heraldic term.) **14 Jove's spreading tree** i.e., the oak **22 bent his brow** frowned. **31 puissant** powerful **35 with thy lips** i.e., with a kiss. (The soul was thought to leave the body through the mouth at death.) **41 latest** last **44 a vault** a hollow, echoing space **45 mought** might

5.3. Location: The field of battle near Barnet, as before.
5 sun i.e., the heraldic sun on the Yorkist coat of arms **8 Gallia** France. **arrived** reached **16 breathe** i.e., pause and muster her strength **18 advertised** notified **19 they** the Queen's and Somerset's forces. **Tewkesbury** an abbey town in Gloucestershire. **21 rids way** annihilates distance, makes the way seem short
5.4. Location: Near Tewkesbury, in Gloucestershire.
2 cheerly cheerfully **5 flood** water, sea. **6 our pilot** i.e., King Henry. **meet** fitting

And give more strength to that which hath too much,
Whiles, in his moan, the ship splits on the rock,   10
Which industry and courage might have saved?
Ah, what a shame, ah, what a fault were this!
Say Warwick was our anchor. What of that?
And Montague our topmast. What of him?
Our slaughtered friends the tackles. What of these?   15
Why, is not Oxford here another anchor?
And Somerset another goodly mast?
The friends of France our shrouds and tacklings?   18
And, though unskillful, why not Ned and I
For once allowed the skillful pilot's charge?   20
We will not from the helm to sit and weep,   21
But keep our course, though the rough wind say no,
From shelves and rocks that threaten us with wreck.   23
As good to chide the waves as speak them fair.   24
And what is Edward but a ruthless sea?
What Clarence but a quicksand of deceit?
And Richard but a ragged fatal rock?
All these the enemies to our poor bark.
Say you can swim, alas, 'tis but a while;
Tread on the sand, why, there you quickly sink;
Bestride the rock, the tide will wash you off,
Or else you famish—that's a threefold death.
This speak I, lords, to let you understand,
If case some one of you would fly from us,   34
That there's no hoped-for mercy with the brothers
More than with ruthless waves, with sands and rocks.
Why, courage then! What cannot be avoided
'Twere childish weakness to lament or fear.

PRINCE EDWARD
Methinks a woman of this valiant spirit
Should, if a coward heard her speak these words,
Infuse his breast with magnanimity
And make him, naked, foil a man at arms.   42
I speak not this as doubting any here;
For did I but suspect a fearful man,
He should have leave to go away betimes,   45
Lest in our need he might infect another
And make him of like spirit to himself.
If any such be here—as God forbid!—
Let him depart before we need his help.

OXFORD
Women and children of so high a courage,
And warriors faint! Why, 'twere perpetual shame.   50
O brave young Prince! Thy famous grandfather   51
Doth live again in thee. Long mayst thou live   52
To bear his image and renew his glories!   54

SOMERSET
And he that will not fight for such a hope,

Go home to bed, and, like the owl by day,
If he arise, be mocked and wondered at.

QUEEN MARGARET
Thanks, gentle Somerset; sweet Oxford, thanks.

PRINCE EDWARD
And take his thanks that yet hath nothing else.   59

Enter a Messenger.

MESSENGER
Prepare you, lords, for Edward is at hand,
Ready to fight. Therefore be resolute.

OXFORD
I thought no less. It is his policy   62
To haste thus fast, to find us unprovided.   63

SOMERSET
But he's deceived. We are in readiness.

QUEEN MARGARET
This cheers my heart, to see your forwardness.   65

OXFORD
Here pitch our battle. Hence we will not budge.   66

*Flourish and march. Enter [King] Edward,
Richard [Duke of Gloucester], Clarence, and
soldiers.*

KING EDWARD
Brave followers, yonder stands the thorny wood
Which, by the heavens' assistance and your strength,
Must by the roots be hewn up yet ere night.
I need not add more fuel to your fire,
For well I wot ye blaze to burn them out.   71
Give signal to the fight, and to it, lords!

QUEEN MARGARET
Lords, knights, and gentlemen, what I should say
My tears gainsay; for every word I speak,   74
Ye see, I drink the water of mine eye.   75
Therefore, no more but this: Henry, your sovereign,
Is prisoner to the foe, his state usurped,   77
His realm a slaughterhouse, his subjects slain,
His statutes canceled, and his treasure spent;
And yonder is the wolf that makes this spoil.   80
You fight in justice. Then, in God's name, lords,
Be valiant, and give signal to the fight.   82

*Alarum. Retreat. Excursions [in which
Queen Margaret, Prince Edward, Oxford,
and Somerset are taken]. Exeunt.*

❖

---

10 **in his moan** as he makes lamentation   15 **tackles** rigging.
18 **shrouds** ropes or cables supporting the mast   20 **charge** responsibility.   21 **from** go away from   23 **shelves** sandbanks, shoals
24 **As good to** i.e., One might as well.   **speak them fair** address them
courteously.   34 **If** in   42 **And . . . arms** and inspire him, unarmed,
to take on and defeat a fully armed soldier.   45 **betimes** at once
50–1 **Women . . . faint!** Can warriors shrink in cowardly fashion when
women and children are so courageous?   52 **grandfather** i.e., Henry V
54 **image** likeness

59 **take . . . else** take my thanks, I who as yet have nothing else to give.
62 **policy** stratagem   63 **unprovided** unprepared.   65 **forwardness**
eagerness.   66 **pitch our battle** draw up our armies.   71 **I wot . . . out**
i.e., I know you're afire with enthusiasm to destroy our enemy (literally, to burn out a thorny wood).   74 **gainsay** forbid   74–5 **for . . . eye**
(Margaret's point is that this is no time for words; they will only distract her from the fury expressed in her tears.)   77 **state** royal status
as king   80 **spoil** plunder, destruction.   82.1 **Alarum** (The Octavo
version provides that *chambers*, or short cannon, are "discharged,"
after which King Edward and his brothers and allies enter with "a
great shout," and cry "For York! For York!" and take the Queen and
her son.)

[5.5]

Flourish. Enter [King] Edward, Richard [Duke of Gloucester]; Queen [Margaret, as prisoner]; Clarence; Oxford, Somerset [as prisoners].

KING EDWARD
Now here a period of tumultuous broils.   1
Away with Oxford to Hames Castle straight.   2
For Somerset, off with his guilty head.   3
Go, bear them hence. I will not hear them speak.

OXFORD
For my part, I'll not trouble thee with words.

SOMERSET
Nor I, but stoop with patience to my fortune.
                          Exeunt [Oxford and Somerset, guarded].

QUEEN MARGARET
So part we sadly in this troublous world,
To meet with joy in sweet Jerusalem.   8

KING EDWARD
Is proclamation made that who finds Edward   9
Shall have a high reward, and he his life?

GLOUCESTER
It is. And lo, where youthful Edward comes!

Enter [soldiers, with] the Prince [Edward].

KING EDWARD
Bring forth the gallant. Let us hear him speak.
What, can so young a thorn begin to prick?
Edward, what satisfaction canst thou make   14
For bearing arms, for stirring up my subjects,
And all the trouble thou hast turned me to?

PRINCE EDWARD
Speak like a subject, proud ambitious York!
Suppose that I am now my father's mouth;
Resign thy chair, and where I stand kneel thou,   19
Whilst I propose the selfsame words to thee,
Which, traitor, thou wouldst have me answer to.

QUEEN MARGARET
Ah, that thy father had been so resolved!

GLOUCESTER
That you might still have worn the petticoat
And ne'er have stol'n the breech from Lancaster.   24

PRINCE EDWARD
Let Aesop fable in a winter's night;   25
His currish riddles sorts not with this place.   26

GLOUCESTER
By heaven, brat, I'll plague ye for that word.

QUEEN MARGARET
Ay, thou wast born to be a plague to men.

GLOUCESTER
For God's sake, take away this captive scold.

PRINCE EDWARD
Nay, take away this scolding crookback rather.

KING EDWARD
Peace, willful boy, or I will charm your tongue.   31

CLARENCE
Untutored lad, thou art too malapert.   32

PRINCE EDWARD
I know my duty. You are all undutiful.
Lascivious Edward, and thou perjured George,
And thou misshapen Dick, I tell ye all
I am your better, traitors as ye are,
And thou usurp'st my father's right and mine.

KING EDWARD
Take that, thou likeness of this railer here!   38
                                              Stabs him.

GLOUCESTER
Sprawl'st thou? Take that, to end thy agony.   39
                                        Richard stabs him.

CLARENCE
And there's for twitting me with perjury.
                    Clarence stabs him. [Prince Edward dies.]

QUEEN MARGARET Oh, kill me too!

GLOUCESTER Marry, and shall.   *Offers to kill her.* 42

KING EDWARD
Hold, Richard, hold, for we have done too much.

GLOUCESTER
Why should she live, to fill the world with words?
                                      [Margaret swoons.]

KING EDWARD
What, doth she swoon? Use means for her recovery.

GLOUCESTER *[aside to Clarence]*
Clarence, excuse me to the King my brother;
I'll hence to London on a serious matter.
Ere ye come there, be sure to hear some news.   48

CLARENCE *[aside to Gloucester]* What? What?

GLOUCESTER *[aside to Clarence]* The Tower, the Tower.
                                              Exit.

QUEEN MARGARET *[reviving]*
O Ned, sweet Ned, speak to thy mother, boy!
Canst thou not speak? Oh, traitors, murderers!
They that stabbed Caesar shed no blood at all,
Did not offend, nor were not worthy blame,
If this foul deed were by to equal it.   55
He was a man; this, in respect, a child,   56
And men ne'er spend their fury on a child.
What's worse than murderer, that I may name it?
No, no, my heart will burst an if I speak;
And I will speak, that so my heart may burst.
Butchers and villains, bloody cannibals!

5.5. Location: Scene continues at the battlefield near Tewkesbury. **1 period** termination **2 Hames Castle** i.e., Hammes Castle near Calais (where Oxford was indeed confined, but not until his capture some three years after Tewkesbury) **3 For** As for **8 sweet Jerusalem** i.e., the heavenly Jerusalem. **9 who** anyone who **14 satisfaction** recompense **19 chair** throne **24 breech** breeches, symbol of male authority **25 Aesop** Greek teller of fables (who, like Gloucester, was reputed to have been deformed). **in . . . night** i.e., in a setting fitted for such childish tales **26 His . . . place** his mean riddles are inappropriate to this place. (Prince Edward is retorting to Gloucester's gibe, denying the allegation that his father was henpecked.)

31 charm cast a spell upon, i.e., silence **32 malapert** saucy. **38 this railer here** i.e., Queen Margaret. **39 Sprawl'st thou?** i.e., Are you twitching in the throes of death? **42 Marry, and shall** i.e., Indeed, I will. **s.d. Offers to** He is about to **48 be sure** expect **55 equal** compare with **56 respect** comparison

How sweet a plant have you untimely cropped!
You have no children, butchers; if you had,
The thought of them would have stirred up remorse.
But if you ever chance to have a child,
Look in his youth to have him so cut off
As, deathsmen, you have rid this sweet young prince!   67

KING EDWARD
Away with her. Go, bear her hence perforce.   68

QUEEN MARGARET
Nay, never bear me hence. Dispatch me here!
Here sheathe thy sword. I'll pardon thee my death.   70
What, wilt thou not? Then, Clarence, do it thou.

CLARENCE
By heaven, I will not do thee so much ease.   72

QUEEN MARGARET
Good Clarence, do. Sweet Clarence, do thou do it.

CLARENCE
Didst thou not hear me swear I would not do it?

QUEEN MARGARET
Ay, but thou usest to forswear thyself.
'Twas sin before, but now 'tis charity.   75
What, wilt thou not? Where is that devil's butcher,
Hard-favored Richard? Richard, where art thou?   78
Thou art not here. Murder is thy almsdeed;   79
Petitioners for blood thou ne'er put'st back.   80

KING EDWARD
Away, I say! I charge ye, bear her hence.

QUEEN MARGARET
So come to you and yours as to this prince!   82
                                    Exit Queen, [guarded].

KING EDWARD   Where's Richard gone?

CLARENCE
To London, all in post—[aside] and, as I guess,   84
To make a bloody supper in the Tower.

KING EDWARD
He's sudden, if a thing comes in his head.
Now march we hence. Discharge the common sort   87
With pay and thanks, and let's away to London
And see our gentle queen how well she fares.
By this, I hope, she hath a son for me.   Exeunt.   90

❖

[5.6]

Enter Henry the Sixth and Richard [Duke of
Gloucester], with the Lieutenant [of the Tower],
on the walls.

GLOUCESTER
Good day, my lord. What, at your book so hard?   1

KING HENRY
Ay, my good lord—"my lord," I should say rather.
'Tis sin to flatter. "Good" was little better.   3
"Good Gloucester" and "good devil" were alike,   4
And both preposterous; therefore, not "good lord."   5

GLOUCESTER [to the Lieutenant]
Sirrah, leave us to ourselves. We must confer.   6
                                    [Exit Lieutenant.]

KING HENRY
So flies the reckless shepherd from the wolf;   7
So first the harmless sheep doth yield his fleece
And next his throat unto the butcher's knife.
What scene of death hath Roscius now to act?   10

GLOUCESTER
Suspicion always haunts the guilty mind;
The thief doth fear each bush an officer.   12

KING HENRY
The bird that hath been limèd in a bush,   13
With trembling wings misdoubteth every bush;   14
And I, the hapless male to one sweet bird,   15
Have now the fatal object in my eye
Where my poor young was limed, was caught, and killed.

GLOUCESTER
Why, what a peevish fool was that of Crete,   18
That taught his son the office of a fowl!
And yet, for all his wings, the fool was drowned.

KING HENRY
I, Daedalus; my poor boy, Icarus;
Thy father, Minos, that denied our course;   22
The sun that seared the wings of my sweet boy,   23
Thy brother Edward; and thyself, the sea
Whose envious gulf did swallow up his life.   25
Ah, kill me with thy weapon, not with words!
My breast can better brook thy dagger's point   27
Than can my ears that tragic history.   28
But wherefore dost thou come? Is't for my life?

GLOUCESTER
Think'st thou I am an executioner?

KING HENRY
A persecutor I am sure thou art.
If murdering innocents be executing,
Why, then thou art an executioner.

GLOUCESTER
Thy son I killed for his presumption.

KING HENRY
Hadst thou been killed when first thou didst presume,

---

67 rid removed, killed   68 perforce by force.   70 I'll . . . death (Executioners customarily asked pardon of the persons being executed, and
were forgiven.)   72 ease i.e., easing of your grief in death.   75 thou
usest you are accustomed   78 Hard-favored ugly   79 almsdeed act
of charity   80 Petitioners . . . back you never turn away persons
asking for blood.   82 So come May it happen   84 post haste
87 common sort ordinary soldiers   90 this this time
5.6. Location: The Tower of London.
1 book i.e., book of devotion

3 little better i.e., little more than flattery.   4 were would be   5 preposterous unnatural   6 Sirrah (Customary form of address to inferiors.)   7 reckless heedless   10 Roscius celebrated Roman actor much
admired by Cicero and regarded by the Elizabethans as a model of
tragic acting   12 an officer to be an arresting officer.   13 limèd snared
with birdlime, a sticky substance smeared on branches   14 misdoubteth is mistrustful of   15 male father, begetter.   bird chick, offspring   18 peevish silly.   that of Crete (Daedalus escaped from Crete,
where he had fashioned for King Minos a labyrinth to contain the
Minotaur, by devising wings for himself and his son Icarus, but Icarus
flew too near the sun, which melted the wax in his wings, thus causing
him to fall into the sea.)   22 course i.e., departure   23 sun (With reference to the Yorkist heraldic badge, as at 2.1.25.)   25 envious gulf malicious whirlpool   27 brook endure   28 history story.

Thou hadst not lived to kill a son of mine.
And thus I prophesy, that many a thousand,
Which now mistrust no parcel of my fear,   38
And many an old man's sigh and many a widow's,
And many an orphan's water-standing eye—   40
Men for their sons', wives for their husbands',
Orphans for their parents' timeless death—   42
Shall rue the hour that ever thou wast born.
The owl shrieked at thy birth—an evil sign;
The night crow cried, aboding luckless time;   45
Dogs howled, and hideous tempest shook down trees;
The raven rooked her on the chimney's top;   47
And chatt'ring pies in dismal discords sung.   48
Thy mother felt more than a mother's pain,
And yet brought forth less than a mother's hope,
To wit, an indigested and deformèd lump,   51
Not like the fruit of such a goodly tree.
Teeth hadst thou in thy head when thou wast born,
To signify thou cam'st to bite the world;
And if the rest be true which I have heard,
Thou cam'st—

GLOUCESTER
I'll hear no more. Die, prophet, in thy speech.
                                        Stabs him.

For this, amongst the rest, was I ordained.
KING HENRY
Ay, and for much more slaughter after this.
Oh, God, forgive my sins, and pardon thee!   *Dies.*
GLOUCESTER
What, will the aspiring blood of Lancaster
Sink in the ground? I thought it would have mounted.
See how my sword weeps for the poor King's death!   63
Oh, may such purple tears be always shed   64
From those that wish the downfall of our house!
If any spark of life be yet remaining,
Down, down to hell, and say I sent thee thither,
                                        Stabs him again.
I, that have neither pity, love, nor fear.
Indeed, 'tis true that Henry told me of;   69
For I have often heard my mother say
I came into the world with my legs forward.
Had I not reason, think ye, to make haste
And seek their ruin that usurped our right?
The midwife wondered and the women cried,
"Oh, Jesus bless us, he is born with teeth!"
And so I was, which plainly signified
That I should snarl and bite and play the dog.
Then, since the heavens have shaped my body so,
Let hell make crook'd my mind to answer it.   79
I have no brother, I am like no brother;
And this word "love," which graybeards call divine,
Be resident in men like one another

And not in me. I am myself alone.
Clarence, beware. Thou keep'st me from the light;
But I will sort a pitchy day for thee;   85
For I will buzz abroad such prophecies
That Edward shall be fearful of his life,   87
And then, to purge his fear, I'll be thy death.   88
King Henry and the Prince his son are gone;
Clarence, thy turn is next, and then the rest,
Counting myself but bad till I be best.   91
I'll throw thy body in another room
And triumph, Henry, in thy day of doom.
                                Exit [with the body].

❖

[5.7]

*Flourish. Enter King [Edward], Queen [Elizabeth],
Clarence, Richard [Duke of Gloucester], Hastings,
Nurse [with the young Prince], and attendants.
[King Edward sits on his throne.]*

KING EDWARD
Once more we sit in England's royal throne,
Repurchased with the blood of enemies.
What valiant foemen, like to autumn's corn,   3
Have we mowed down in tops of all their pride!   4
Three Dukes of Somerset, threefold renowned   5
For hardy and undoubted champions;   6
Two Cliffords, as the father and the son;   7
And two Northumberlands—two braver men
Ne'er spurred their coursers at the trumpet's sound;   9
With them, the two brave bears, Warwick and Montague,   10
That in their chains fettered the kingly lion
And made the forest tremble when they roared.
Thus have we swept suspicion from our seat   13
And made our footstool of security.
Come hither, Bess, and let me kiss my boy.
                                [He kisses his son.]
Young Ned, for thee, thine uncles and myself
Have in our armors watched the winter's night,   17
Went all afoot in summer's scalding heat,
That thou mightst repossess the crown in peace;
And of our labors thou shalt reap the gain.
GLOUCESTER *[aside]*
I'll blast his harvest, if your head were laid;   21
For yet I am not looked on in the world.   22
This shoulder was ordained so thick to heave,

---

85 sort select.   **pitchy** black   **87 of** for   **88 thy** Clarence's   **91 bad**
unfortunate
**5.7. Location: London. The royal court. A throne is provided
onstage.**
3 corn grain   **4 in tops** at the height   **5 Three . . . Somerset** Historically,
the three are Edmund Beaufort, second Duke, whose head Richard dis-
plays at 1.1.16; his son Henry, third Duke, who appears briefly as a
Yorkist in 4.1 and 4.6; and Henry's brother Edmund, who appears in
5.1. Shakespeare appears to have conflated Henry and his brother in
this play; see 5.1.73 n.   **6 undoubted** (1) undeniable (2) fearless   **7 as** to
wit   **9 coursers** horses   **10 bears** (Refers to the Neville family emblem.)
13 seat throne   **17 watched** stayed awake throughout   **21 blast** blight.
were laid were laid out to rest in death. (With a suggestion also of
grain flattened out by a storm.)   **22 looked on** heeded, respected

---

38 mistrust . . . fear i.e., feel none of the mistrust that I feel   **40 water-
standing** i.e., filled with tears   **42 timeless** untimely   **45 night crow**
nightjar or owl.   **aboding** foreboding   **47 rooked her** couched, roosted
48 pies magpies   **51 indigested** shapeless, chaotic   **63 weeps** i.e., drips
blood   **64 purple** bloodred   **69 that** what   **79 answer** match

And heave it shall some weight, or break my back.
Work thou the way, and thou shalt execute.   25

KING EDWARD
   Clarence and Gloucester, love my lovely queen,
   And kiss your princely nephew, brothers both.

CLARENCE
   The duty that I owe unto Your Majesty
   I seal upon the lips of this sweet babe.
                                        [*He kisses the Prince.*]

QUEEN ELIZABETH
   Thanks, noble Clarence; worthy brother, thanks.   30

GLOUCESTER
   And, that I love the tree from whence thou sprang'st,
   Witness the loving kiss I give the fruit.
                                        [*He kisses the Prince.*]
   [*Aside*] To say the truth, so Judas kissed his master,
   And cried "All hail!" whenas he meant all harm.

KING EDWARD
   Now am I seated as my soul delights,
   Having my country's peace and brothers' loves.

CLARENCE
   What will Your Grace have done with Margaret?
   Reignier, her father, to the King of France
   Hath pawned the Sicils and Jerusalem,   39
   And hither have they sent it for her ransom.   40

KING EDWARD
   Away with her, and waft her hence to France.   41
   And now what rests but that we spend the time   42
   With stately triumphs, mirthful comic shows,   43
   Such as befits the pleasure of the court?
   Sound drums and trumpets! Farewell sour annoy!
   For here, I hope, begins our lasting joy.   46
                                        [*Flourish.*] *Exeunt omnes.*

---

25 Work thou (Addressed to himself, indicating his head.)   **thou shalt** (Addressed to his shoulder and arm.)   **30 brother** i.e., brother-in-law

39 the Sicils (See the note to 1.4.122.)   **40 it** i.e., the money raised by "pawn"   **41 waft** convey by water   **42 rests** remains   **43 triumphs** festivities   **46.1 *omnes*** all.

The Tragedy of King Richard the Third

The fascinating evil ruler for whom *Richard III* is named has already made his appearance in the third part of *Henry VI*, in the four-play sequence that makes up Shakespeare's first foray into English history. In the final installment in this tetralogy, Richard, Duke of Gloucester, stands fully revealed as the evil genius of England's prolonged crisis of civil war. With a bold stroke, Shakespeare opens *Richard III* with his arresting soliloquy; Richard takes over the stage in a way that has held audiences spellbound ever since Richard Burbage first performed the role. Richard announces his determination to "prove a villain," both defying and fulfilling Nature, which made his body deformed. In fact, he has already begun his treacherous course, and we see at once how his plot against Clarence, founded on something so trivial as the letter G, has manipulated the King and has ensnared Clarence. Then, with outrageous hypocrisy, he "comforts" Clarence. Within less than a hundred lines, Shakespeare makes us feel how brilliant, cynical, charming, and dangerous Richard of Gloucester is. Richard proceeds to dominate the other characters—and the whole play—to an extraordinary degree.

By organizing this play firmly around Richard, Shakespeare solved the problems of giving form to his drama and of concluding the series of plays about the dynastic rivalry of York and Lancaster. *Richard III* begins and ends with a peace, yet the recent peace of the Yorkist King Edward is scorned and sabotaged by Richard as soon as it is introduced. It is vulnerable to factions at court and is bitterly denounced by that living embodiment of the cruel and violent past, Queen Margaret. There can be no peace in England while Richard lives to undermine it. Still, as the plot moves through Richard's exhilarating rise to the throne and the events of his tragic fall—when his conscience, the spirits of those he murdered, and the Earl of Richmond punish and defeat him—we see that his career is part of a larger order, a seemingly providential plan of retribution for wickedness and injustice and for

reconciling England's divisions. For all its specific reminders of past warfare and atrocity on both Yorkist and Lancastrian sides, *Richard III* dramatizes an archetypal struggle between good and evil, personified in Richard the villain-hero and Richmond his opponent, who plays the role of the righteous agent of divine and poetic justice.

Dramatically, Richmond, like Queen Margaret, is more a symbol than a fully developed character. It is Richard who is the exciting figure as he deceives and manipulates others and finally faces the chillingly isolated condition into which he has brought himself by being so truly a villain. He climbs to power by deceit, and so he is constantly acting a part. Richard's ability as an actor is seemingly limitless. He has already boasted, in *3 Henry VI*, that he can deceive more slyly than Ulysses, Sinon, or Machiavelli and can put on more false shapes than Proteus. To us as audience, he is cynically candid and boastful, setting us up in advance to watch his unbelievable performances. In an instant, before our eyes, he is the concerned younger brother of Clarence, sharing a hatred of Queen Elizabeth and her kindred; he is the jocular uncle of the little princes; or he is the pious recluse studying divinity with his clerical teachers, reluctant to accept the responsibilities of state that are thrust upon him by his importunate subjects (i.e., by Catesby and Buckingham, who are also actors in this staged scene).

None of these bravura performances, however, matches the wooing of Lady Anne. Richard himself sees it as the great test of his powers and is suitably impressed by his victory. The wooing scene, to some critics, challenges credibility. One key to credibility must lie in superb acting. The actor who plays Richard must transform himself from the gloating villain we know in soliloquy to the grief-stricken lover. Richard's argument is, after all, speciously plausible: that he has killed Anne's husband and father-in-law out of desperate love for her. The argument appeals to vanity, that most fatal of human weaknesses.

What power Anne suddenly appears to have over Richard! She can kill him or spare his life. Richard shrewdly judges her as one who is not able to kill, and so he risks offering her his sword. As stage manager, he has altered her role from that of sincere mourner to the stereotype of the proud woman worshiped by her groveling servant in love. With superb irony, Richard has inverted the appearance and the reality of control in this struggle between man and woman, winning mastery by flattering Anne that she has such power over his emotions and his life. From his amazing success, Richard concludes that ordinary men and women can be made to believe anything and to betray their own instincts by "the plain devil and dissembling looks" (1.2.239). Richard is indeed devil-like; his role as actor stems in part from that of the Vice in the morality play, brilliantly comic and sinister. Yet even the devil can prevail over his victims only when they acquiesce in evil. The devil can deceive the senses, but acceptance of evil is still an act of the perverted will. Anne is guilty, however much we can appreciate the mesmerizing power of Richard's personality. By the end of the scene, she has violated everything she holds sacred.

The image of Richard as devil or Vice raises questions of motivation and of symbolic meaning, and suggests two seemingly disparate ways of reading the play, one psychological and the other providential. Is Richard a human character, propelled toward the throne by his insatiable ambition, like Macbeth? Is there a clue to his behavior in his ugliness and misanthropy? One might argue that he compensates for his ugliness and unlovability by resolving to domineer. Feeling unwanted, he despises all humans and undertakes to prove them weak and corrupt in order to affirm himself. He expresses a universal human penchant for cruelty and senseless domination. Yet the proposition that Richard is evil *because* he was born ugly logically can be reversed as well: he was born ugly *because* he is evil. In providential terms, Richard can be seen as the result of a divine plan in which evil ironically has a place in a larger scheme of things that is ultimately benign.

This latter concept, owing much to Renaissance notions of platonic correspondence between outer appearances and inner qualities, is grounded on the idea of a vast struggle in the cosmos between the forces of absolute good and the forces of absolute evil, one in which every event in human life has divine meaning and cause. Richard's birth is, according to this theory, a physical manifestation of that divine meaning. Providential destiny, having determined the need for a genius of evil at this point in English history, decrees that Richard shall be born. The teeth and hunched back merely give evidence of what is already predetermined. In the apt words of the choric Queen Margaret, Richard was "sealed in thy nativity / The slave of nature and the son of hell" (1.3.229–30). Though he devotes himself to selfish ambition and evildoing, Richard ultimately serves the righteous purpose of divine Providence in human affairs. He functions, in this interpretation, as a scourge of God, whose plots or tyranny are permitted in order to bring just retribution upon offenders of the moral law. He is fundamentally unlike Shakespeare's more human villains, such as Macbeth or Claudius, but belongs, instead, to a special group of villains, including Iago in *Othello* and Edmund in *King Lear*. Like them, Richard is driven both by human motivation and by his preexistent evil genius; he displays the "motiveless malignity" ascribed by Coleridge to Iago.

Such a reading is only one approach to an understanding of Richard's character and function; he is also a human being involved in a struggle for power, motivated by ambition and hatred. The two readings, one psychological and the other providential, are complementary and need not contradict each other. The psychological reading seems more intelligible to us today, based as it is on character and motivation. The providential reading, more traditional in its ideology, helps explain not only Richard's delight in evil but also the necessity for so much evil and suffering in England's civil wars. This theory of history owes much to Edward Hall's *Union of the Two Noble and Illustre Families of Lancaster and York* (1542), Shakespeare's chief source, along with Raphael Holinshed's *Chronicles* (1578), for his *Henry VI* plays. Shakespeare's treatment of Richard is ultimately indebted to Polydore Vergil's *Anglica Historia* (1534) and especially to *The History of King Richard the Third*, attributed to Sir Thomas More (published 1557). This latter work, adopted in turn by Edward Hall, Richard Grafton, and Raphael Holinshed, purposefully blackens Richard's character. He becomes a study in the nature of tyranny, an object lesson to future rulers and their subjects. He is, moreover, a result of the curse placed by God on the English people for their sinful disobedience.

Richmond, in this Tudor explanation, becomes God's minister, chosen to destroy the scourge and thereafter to fulfill a new and happy covenant between God and humanity as King Henry VII. Thus, the play hardly touches on the sensitive matter of his somewhat remote Lancastrian claim to the crown. His victory at Bosworth is not one more turn of Fortune's wheel raising or deposing Lancastrian or Yorkist kings, but the end of a long cycle of unnatural violence, and his marriage to the Yorkist Princess Elizabeth is the restoration and the symbol of unity and peace in England's fair land. Although modern historians more impartially regard the defeat of Richard III at Bosworth Field in 1485 as a political overthrow not unlike Henry IV's overthrow of Richard II and stress that Richard III was a talented administrator guilty of no worse political crimes than those of his more fortunate successor, Elizabethan audiences (under constant promptings of the Tudor state) could not have found sufficient meaning in such a neutral interpretation. They were taught to see history as revealing God's intention and to view Henry VII's accession not as a parallel to the deposing of Richard II by Henry IV but, instead, as a divinely sanctioned deliverance of the English nation, to which Elizabeth's subjects were the happy heirs. Accordingly, the Tudor myth stressed the tyrannical nature of Richard III's seizure of power and conversely minimized the political and Machiavellian elements in Henry VII's takeover. Bosworth Field was seen as an act of God, a rising up of some irresistible force, and under no circumstances as a precedent for future rebellion.

In the *Henry VI* plays, Shakespeare puts considerable distance between himself and the Tudor orthodox reading of history, allowing the grim realities of civil war to speak for themselves. In *Richard III*, however, the pattern shown in the chronicles provides Shakespeare with an essential structural device. Viewing the civil wars in retrospect, *Richard III* potentially manifests a cohesive sense in which England's suffering has fulfilled a necessary plan of fall from innocence, leading through sin and penitence to regeneration. Evil is seen at last as something through which good triumphs, in English history, as in the story of humankind's fall and a restoration by divine grace.

This providential scheme imposes a double irony on *Richard III*. In the short run, Richard appears to be complete master over his victims. "Your imprisonment shall not be long," Richard assures his brother Clarence. "I will deliver you, or else lie for you" (1.1.114–15). The audience, already let in on the secret, can shiver at the grisly humor of these double entendres. Clarence will indeed soon be delivered—to his death. Richard's henchmen are fond of such jokes, too. When Lord Hastings is on his way to the Tower, where he plans to stay for midday dinner, Buckingham observes aside, "And supper too, although thou know'st it not" (3.2.122). Buckingham, knowing that Hastings is about to be arrested in the Tower and executed for treason, chillingly suggests that Hastings will soon be a feast for worms. Shortly before, Catesby has assured Hastings of Richard's and Buckingham's favor: "The princes both make high account of you—/[*Aside*] For they account his head upon the Bridge" (3.2.69–70). That is to say, Hastings's severed head will soon be raised on a pole on London Bridge as a grim warning to those who run afoul of the new regime. Richard has a phrase for such wit: "Thus, like the formal Vice, Iniquity, /I moralize two meanings in one word" (3.1.82–3). The point of such ironies is always the same: the scheming villain is cleverer than his victims, deceiving them through equivocation and triumphing in their spriritual blindness.

The delayed irony of the play, however, ultimately offers another possible explanation for the seemingly nihilistic conclusions of the early scenes; that is, there may be a larger plan at work, of which Richard is unconscious and in which he plays a role quite unlike the one he creates for himself. In this interpretive view, Shakespeare's Richard fulfills a plan of which he is unaware, as in the chronicles of Edward Hall and others, even in the process of what he gloatingly regards as his own self-aggrandizement.

Providential plans are always complex, inscrutable to the minds of mortals, and understood least by those who unwittingly execute them. In attempting to prove his own contention that human nature is bestial and that a Machiavellian man of utter self-confidence can force his way to the top, flouting all conventions of morality, Richard succeeds in demonstrating the opposite. From the moment he takes the throne, he feels it insecure beneath him; opposition and betrayal spring up from every quarter, and, in his last moments, a mere horse is worth his whole kingdom. With sardonic comedy and poetic justice, Richard becomes the proverbial beguiler who is beguiled.

Even if this is not the only way to interpret Richard's character, the play does offer for our consideration a theory of divine causality in which virtually all of Richard's victims deserve their fate because they have offended God. Prophecies and dreams give structure to the sequence of retributive actions and keep grim score. As the choric Margaret observes, a York must pay for a Lancaster, eye for an eye: Edward IV for Henry VI, young Edward V for Henry VI's son Edward. Thus, the Yorkist princes, though guiltless, die for their family's sins. The Yorkist Queen Elizabeth, like the Lancastrian Margaret, must outlive her husband into impotent old age, bewailing her children's cruel deaths. Clarence sees his death as punishment for breaking his oath at the battle of Tewkesbury and for his part in murdering Henry VI's son, Prince Edward. The Queen's kindred have been guilty of ambition, and Lord Hastings, in turn, is vulnerable because he has been willing to plot with Richard against the Queen's kindred. Margaret's curses serve both to warn the characters of their fates (a warning they blindly ignore) and to invite each person to curse himself or herself unwittingly but with ironic appropriateness. Lady Anne wishes unhappiness on any woman so insane as to marry Richard. Buckingham protests in a most sacred oath that whenever he turns again on the Queen's kindred, he will deserve to be punished by the treachery of his dearest friend (i.e., Richard). Dreams serve the same purpose of divine warning, giving Clarence a grotesque intimation of his death by drowning (in a butt of malmsey wine) and warning Hastings (through Stanley's dream) that the boar, Richard, will cut off his head. Thus, the English court punishes itself through Richard. He is the essence of the courtiers' factionalism, able to succeed as he does only because they forswear their most holy vows and conspire to destroy one another. They deserve to be outwitted at their own dismal game. Yet their falls are curative as well; Richard's victims acknowledge the justice of their undoings and penitently implore divine forgiveness. Richard contrastingly finds conscience a torment, rather than a voice of comfort and wisdom.

Richard III is not without its ironies and historical anxieties. Richard's own successful career of evil through much of the play demonstrates how rhetoric and theater can be used to dupe and to corrupt. The political process seems endlessly prone to cynical manipulation, and triumph comes chiefly to those who know how to use rhetoric to calculated effect. The Lord Mayor and his London associates are as pliable as the aristocracy. For all the belated assurances of providential meaning in Richard's rise to power and overthrow, we are allowed to speculate uncomfortably about the pragmatic action of history and its seeming ability to thrust forward into prominence an evil king or a good one, as individual temperament happens to dictate. Finally, there is the question of how Richard is supplanted. Whatever the reasons for Richard's baleful emergence, the process of his overthrow requires human agency and a rebellion against established (even if tyrannical) royal authority. To thoughtful observers in the sixteenth century, including Queen Elizabeth, any such rebellion, no matter how seemingly necessary, established a disturbing precedent and a threat to Tudor monarchical stability. If *Richard III* finds reassuring answers in the victory of Henry Tudor, Earl of Richmond, it does so in the face of pressing and troublesome circumstances.

The pattern of reciprocity and retaliation is much more than a way of demonstrating an ultimate divine purpose in human affairs; it is also a theatrically effective way of structuring a drama so as to make it coherent and entertaining. Shakespeare strikes us as above all a man of the theater, an artist and entertainer who senses masterfully what his audiences want. The shape of *Richard III*, as it moves through the anxieties of Richard's seemingly unstoppable rise to power to an eventual affirmation that brings closure not only to this play but to the entire four-play cycle of the three parts of *Henry VI* and *Richard III*, is immensely satisfying as theatrical experience. Modern audiences, with no ideological commitment to the propagandistic view that God chose Henry VII as the savior of England, can respond warmly to the play's artistic and theatrical depiction of coherence and pattern. That pattern allows us to enjoy Richard's villainies as theatrical performance while perceiving that those villainies are contained and disarmed by a larger structure.

Good eventually triumphs over evil in *Richard III*, if only because some Englishmen have the patience and common sense to endure a presumably deserved punishment and wait for deliverance. As in *3 Henry VI*, the common people have little to do with the action of the play. They are choric spokesmen and bystanders, virtuous in their attitude (except for the two suborned murderers of Clarence). In their plain folk wisdom, they see the folly and evil their betters ignore: "Oh, full of danger is the Duke of Gloucester, / And the Queen's sons and brothers haught and proud" (2.3.28–9). And, although they accept Richard as ruler, they do so most reluctantly; Buckingham's first attempt to persuade the people to this course meets with apathy and silence. Their wisdom is to "leave it all to God" (line 46). In the fullness of time, this faith in goodness brings its just reward.

Richard III compresses historical time. It begins where *3 Henry VI* has left off, with the return of Edward IV to the throne in 1471, and ends with the defeat of Richard III, the last Yorkist king, at the battle of Bosworth (1485). Because of its close relation in subject to passages in *3 Henry VI* and its similar Senecan style, the play appears to have been written soon after its predecessors, sometime between 1591 and 1594. It greatly condenses events of fourteen years, particularly at the beginning, when King Henry VI's funeral rites (1471), Richard's courtship of Lady Anne (1472), Clarence's murder in the Tower (1478), and Edward's death (1483) are made to take place at the same time. Similarly, Buckingham's rebellion (1483), Richmond's thwarted sailing (1483), and his landing at Milford Haven (1485) are also compressed. Queen Margaret's role is a nonhistorical addition to the play, for the widowed Queen never left France after her ransom in 1475 by Louis XI.

Richard III is irresistible in performance. However much Richard reveals himself to be a conscienceless villain, his versatility as a performer and his taking us into his confidence invite a kind of complicity between actor and audience that is the stuff of dramatic excitement. These qualities are brilliantly on display in two film versions, that of Laurence Olivier in 1955 and that of Ian McKellan in 1995. The first shows Richard's protean skills in deception as he soliloquizes candidly to us as his confidants, then transforms himself into the devoted brother of George Clarence (John Gielgud) and then the heartstricken wooer of the Lady Anne (Claire Bloom), seemingly at the mercy of the lady he worships. Ian McKellan transfers the play to the era of an imagined English civil war in the 1930s in which the ruthless, Nazi-like Richard claws his way to the top. His thirst for mayhem is psychotic, but is not without its esthetic dimension as well; he murders with artistry and style, and savors the results by examining photographs of his dead victims. His teamwork with Buckingham (Jim Broadbent) in bamboozling the citizens of London is a thing of beauty. Closeups focus on McKellan's creased visage as he contemplates his next move. Al Pacino's *Looking for Richard* (1996) explores the play in rehearsal with an all-star cast including Winona Ryder, Kevin Spacey, Alec Baldwin, and Aidan Quinn. Many other great actors have excelled in the quintessentially theatrical role of Richard, including Marius Goring, Brian Bedford, Ian Holm, Antony Sher, Kevin Kline, and Simon Russell Beale.

The Tragedy of King Richard the Third

⌐⌐⌐

[*Dramatis Personae*

KING EDWARD THE FOURTH
QUEEN ELIZABETH, *wife of King Edward*
EDWARD, PRINCE OF WALES, ⎱ *sons of Edward and*
RICHARD, DUKE OF YORK, ⎰ *Elizabeth*
GEORGE, DUKE OF CLARENCE,
RICHARD, DUKE OF GLOUCESTER, ⎱ *brothers of the King*
   later King Richard III,
DUCHESS OF YORK, *mother of Edward IV,*
   Clarence, and Richard, Duke of Gloucester
LADY ANNE, *widow of Edward, Prince of Wales*
   (son of Henry VI); later wife of Richard, Duke of
   Gloucester
MARGARET, *widow of King Henry VI*
BOY, *son of Clarence (Edward Plantagenet, Earl of*
   Warwick)
GIRL, *daughter of Clarence (Margaret Plantagenet,*
   Countess of Salisbury)

ANTHONY WOODVILLE, EARL RIVERS, *brother of*
   Queen Elizabeth
MARQUESS OF DORSET, ⎱ *sons of Queen*
LORD GREY, ⎰ *Elizabeth*
SIR THOMAS VAUGHAN, *executed with Rivers and*
   Grey

WILLIAM, LORD HASTINGS, *the Lord Chamberlain*
DUKE OF BUCKINGHAM, *Richard's supporter, later*
   in opposition
SIR WILLIAM CATESBY,
SIR RICHARD RATCLIFFE, ⎱ *Richard's supporters*
LORD LOVELL, ⎰ *and henchmen*
SIR JAMES TYRREL,
DUKE OF NORFOLK, ⎱ *Richard's generals*
EARL OF SURREY, ⎰

HENRY, EARL OF RICHMOND, *later King Henry VII*

SCENE: *England.*]

LORD STANLEY, EARL OF DERBY, ⎫
EARL OF OXFORD, ⎥
SIR JAMES BLUNT, ⎬ *supporters of*
SIR WALTER HERBERT, ⎥ *Richmond*
SIR WILLIAM BRANDON, ⎥
CHRISTOPHER URSWICK, *a priest,* ⎭

CARDINAL BOURCHIER, *Archbishop of Canterbury*
ARCHBISHOP OF YORK (*Thomas Rotherham*)
BISHOP OF ELY (*John Morton*)
GHOSTS *of King Henry VI, Edward Prince of*
   Wales, and others murdered by Richard
   (Clarence, Rivers, Grey, Vaughan, Hastings, the
   two young princes, Anne, and Buckingham)
SIR ROBERT BRACKENBURY, *Lieutenant of the Tower*
TRESSEL, ⎫
BERKELEY, ⎥ *attending the*
HALBERDIER, ⎬ *Lady Anne*
GENTLEMAN, ⎭
Two MURDERERS
KEEPER *in the Tower*
Three CITIZENS
MESSENGER *to Queen Elizabeth*
LORD MAYOR OF LONDON
MESSENGER *to Lord Hastings*
PURSUIVANT
PRIEST
SCRIVENER
Two BISHOPS
PAGE *to Richard III*
Four MESSENGERS *to Richard III*
SHERIFF OF WILTSHIRE

Lords, Attendants, Aldermen, Citizens, Councilors,
   Soldiers

1.1

Enter Richard, Duke of Gloucester, solus.

RICHARD
Now is the winter of our discontent
Made glorious summer by this son of York,   2
And all the clouds that loured upon our house   3
In the deep bosom of the ocean buried.
Now are our brows bound with victorious wreaths,   5
Our bruisèd arms hung up for monuments,   6
Our stern alarums changed to merry meetings,   7
Our dreadful marches to delightful measures.   8
Grim-visaged War hath smoothed his wrinkled
    front;   9
And now, instead of mounting barbèd steeds   10
To fright the souls of fearful adversaries,   11
He capers nimbly in a lady's chamber
To the lascivious pleasing of a lute.
But I, that am not shaped for sportive tricks,   14
Nor made to court an amorous looking glass;
I, that am rudely stamped, and want love's majesty   16
To strut before a wanton ambling nymph;   17
I, that am curtailed of this fair proportion,   18
Cheated of feature by dissembling Nature,   19
Deformed, unfinished, sent before my time
Into this breathing world scarce half made up,
And that so lamely and unfashionable   22
That dogs bark at me as I halt by them—   23
Why, I, in this weak piping time of peace,   24
Have no delight to pass away the time,
Unless to see my shadow in the sun
And descant on mine own deformity.   27
And therefore, since I cannot prove a lover
To entertain these fair well-spoken days,   29
I am determinèd to prove a villain
And hate the idle pleasures of these days.
Plots have I laid, inductions dangerous,   32
By drunken prophecies, libels, and dreams,
To set my brother Clarence and the King
In deadly hate the one against the other;
And if King Edward be as true and just

As I am subtle, false, and treacherous,
This day should Clarence closely be mewed up   38
About a prophecy, which says that G   39
Of Edward's heirs the murderer shall be.
Dive, thoughts, down to my soul; here Clarence
    comes.

Enter Clarence, guarded, and Brackenbury,
[Lieutenant of the Tower].

Brother, good day. What means this armèd guard
That waits upon Your Grace?
CLARENCE   His Majesty,   43
Tend'ring my person's safety, hath appointed   44
This conduct to convey me to the Tower.   45
RICHARD
Upon what cause?
CLARENCE   Because my name is George.
RICHARD
Alack, my lord, that fault is none of yours.
He should, for that, commit your godfathers.
Oh, belike His Majesty hath some intent   49
That you should be new christened in the Tower.   50
But what's the matter, Clarence, may I know?   51
CLARENCE
Yea, Richard, when I know; for I protest
As yet I do not. But, as I can learn,
He hearkens after prophecies and dreams,
And from the crossrow plucks the letter G,   55
And says a wizard told him that by G
His issue disinherited should be;   57
And, for my name of George begins with G,   58
It follows in his thought that I am he.
These, as I learn, and suchlike toys as these   60
Hath moved His Highness to commit me now.   61
RICHARD
Why, this it is when men are ruled by women.
'Tis not the King that sends you to the Tower;
My Lady Grey his wife, Clarence, 'tis she   64
That tempers him to this extremity.   65
Was it not she, and that good man of worship,   66
Anthony Woodville, her brother there,   67

1.1. Location: London. Near the Tower.
0.1 *solus* alone.   **2 son** Edward IV was the son of Richard, Duke of York. (With a pun on "sun"; Edward IV used the sun on his badge.)
3 loured looked threateningly   **5 brows** foreheads   **6 arms** armor.
monuments trophies   **7 alarums** calls to arms, or assaults   **8 dreadful** formidable, awe-inspiring.   **measures** stately dances.   **9 wrinkled front** furrowed forehead   **10 barbèd** armored   **11 fearful** frightened
14 sportive amorous   **16 rudely stamped** roughly fashioned, coined.
want lack   **17 ambling** walking affectedly, i.e., wantonly   **18 curtailed** cut short, denied.   **proportion** shape   **19 feature** shapeliness of body   **22 unfashionable** badly fashioned   **23 halt** limp   **24 piping time** i.e., a time when the music heard is that of pipes and not fifes and drums   **27 descant** compose variations, comment on   **29 entertain** pass away pleasurably.   **well-spoken** refined, elegant   **32 inductions** preparations

38 mewed up confined (like a hawk)   **39 prophecy . . . G** (The prophecy is mentioned in the chronicles; the quibble is that *G* stands for *Gloucester* and not for *George*, the given name of the Duke of Clarence.)
43 waits attends   **44 Tend'ring** having care for   **45 conduct** escort
49 belike probably   **50 new christened** (Anticipates, ironically, Clarence's death by drowning in 1.4.)   **51 matter** reason, cause
55 crossrow Christ-crossrow, or alphabet (so called from the cross printed before the alphabet in the hornbook)   **57 issue** offspring
58 for because   **60 toys** trifles   **61 commit** arrest   **64 My Lady Grey** (A disrespectful reference to the Queen, whose maiden name was Elizabeth Woodville and who, when the King married her, was the widow of Sir John Grey.)   **65 tempers** governs, directs   **66 worship** honor. (Said ironically.)   **67 Woodville** i.e., Earl Rivers (whom Richard also disrespectfully refers to by his family name rather than by his recently acquired title)

That made him send Lord Hastings to the Tower,
From whence this present day he is delivered?
We are not safe, Clarence, we are not safe.

CLARENCE
By heaven, I think there is no man secure
But the Queen's kindred and night-walking heralds 72
That trudge betwixt the King and Mistress Shore. 73
Heard you not what an humble suppliant
Lord Hastings was to her for his delivery? 75

RICHARD
Humbly complaining to Her Deity 76
Got my Lord Chamberlain his liberty. 77
I'll tell you what: I think it is our way, 78
If we will keep in favor with the King,
To be her men and wear her livery. 80
The jealous, o'erworn widow and herself, 81
Since that our brother dubbed them gentlewomen, 82
Are mighty gossips in our monarchy. 83

BRACKENBURY
I beseech Your Graces both to pardon me:
His Majesty hath straitly given in charge 85
That no man shall have private conference,
Of what degree soever, with your brother. 87

RICHARD
Even so? An't please Your Worship, Brackenbury, 88
You may partake of anything we say.
We speak no treason, man. We say the King
Is wise and virtuous, and his noble queen
Well struck in years, fair, and not jealous. 92
We say that Shore's wife hath a pretty foot,
A cherry lip, a bonny eye, a passing pleasing tongue; 94
And that the Queen's kindred are made gentlefolks.
How say you, sir? Can you deny all this?

BRACKENBURY
With this, my lord, myself have naught to do.

RICHARD
Naught to do with Mistress Shore? I tell thee, fellow, 98
He that doth naught with her, excepting one,
Were best to do it secretly, alone.

BRACKENBURY   What one, my lord?

RICHARD
Her husband, knave. Wouldst thou betray me? 102

BRACKENBURY
I beseech Your Grace to pardon me, and withal 103
Forbear your conference with the noble Duke.

CLARENCE
We know thy charge, Brackenbury, and will obey.

RICHARD
We are the Queen's abjects, and must obey. 106
Brother, farewell. I will unto the King;
And whatsoe'er you will employ me in,
Were it to call King Edward's widow sister, 109
I will perform it to enfranchise you. 110
Meantime, this deep disgrace in brotherhood
Touches me deeper than you can imagine. 112

CLARENCE
I know it pleaseth neither of us well.

RICHARD
Well, your imprisonment shall not be long;
I will deliver you, or else lie for you. 115
Meantime, have patience.

CLARENCE   I must perforce. Farewell. 116
Exit Clarence [with Brackenbury and guard].

RICHARD
Go tread the path that thou shalt ne'er return.
Simple, plain Clarence, I do love thee so
That I will shortly send thy soul to heaven,
If heaven will take the present at our hands.
But who comes here? The new-delivered Hastings? 121

Enter Lord Hastings.

HASTINGS
Good time of day unto my gracious lord.

RICHARD
As much unto my good Lord Chamberlain.
Well are you welcome to the open air.
How hath Your Lordship brooked imprisonment? 125

HASTINGS
With patience, noble lord, as prisoners must.
But I shall live, my lord, to give them thanks 127
That were the cause of my imprisonment.

RICHARD
No doubt, no doubt; and so shall Clarence too,
For they that were your enemies are his,
And have prevailed as much on him as you.

HASTINGS
More pity that the eagles should be mewed,
Whiles kites and buzzards prey at liberty. 133

RICHARD   What news abroad? 134

HASTINGS
No news so bad abroad as this at home:

---

72 **night-walking heralds** i.e., secret messengers for an assignation
73 **Mistress Shore** Jane Shore, the King's mistress, and wife of a gold-smith in Lombard Street. (The title *Mistress* is a respectful form of address for any woman, married or unmarried.)   75 **her** i.e., Jane Shore   76 **Her Deity** (A mock title for Jane Shore, suggesting she is even more elevated than "Her Grace" or "Her Majesty.")   77 **Lord Chamberlain** i.e., Lord Hastings   78 **our way** i.e., our only way (to succeed)   80 **men** servants   81 **widow** i.e., Queen Elizabeth. (See the note for line 64.)   **herself** i.e., Jane Shore   82 **Since that** since.   **gentlewomen** (A sneer at the Queen's family, which was gentle but not noble until after her marriage with the King; Jane Shore was, of course, neither gentle nor noble.)   83 **mighty gossips** i.e., influential busybodies   85 **straitly . . . charge** strictly ordered   87 **degree** rank 88 **An't** If it   92 **Well struck** i.e., well along.   **not jealous** (Implies there are things she might be jealous about.)   94 **passing** surpass-ingly   98 **Naught** (Richard quibbles on the meanings "nothing" and "naughtiness," "the sexual act.")   102 **betray me** i.e., into naming the King as a person who does "naught" with Mistress Shore.

103 **withal** furthermore   106 **abjects** abjectly servile subjects 109 **King Edward's widow** i.e., the widow whom Edward has made queen   110 **enfranchise** release from imprisonment   112 **Touches . . . imagine** (1) distresses me more than can be imagined (2) concerns me (in my personal ambition) more than you could possibly guess. 115 **lie for you** (1) take your place in prison (2) tell lies about you. 116 **perforce** necessarily.   121 **new-delivered** recently released 125 **brooked** endured   127 **give them thanks** i.e., pay them back. (Said ironically.)   133 **kites** scavengers of the hawk family 134 **abroad** at large, circulating.

The King is sickly, weak, and melancholy,
And his physicians fear him mightily.   137

RICHARD
Now, by Saint John, that news is bad indeed!
Oh, he hath kept an evil diet long   139
And overmuch consumed his royal person.
'Tis very grievous to be thought upon.
Where is he, in his bed?

HASTINGS   He is.

RICHARD
Go you before, and I will follow you.   *Exit Hastings.*
He cannot live, I hope, and must not die
Till George be packed with post-horse up to heaven.   146
I'll in, to urge his hatred more to Clarence
With lies well steeled with weighty arguments;   148
And, if I fail not in my deep intent,
Clarence hath not another day to live.
Which done, God take King Edward to his mercy
And leave the world for me to bustle in!
For then I'll marry Warwick's youngest daughter.   153
What though I killed her husband and her father?   154
The readiest way to make the wench amends
Is to become her husband and her father,
The which will I; not all so much for love
As for another secret close intent   158
By marrying her which I must reach unto.
But yet I run before my horse to market.
Clarence still breathes, Edward still lives and reigns;
When they are gone, then must I count my gains.
                                                         Exit.

❖

1.2

*Enter the corpse of [King] Henry the Sixth, with
Halberds to guard it; Lady Anne being the
mourner [attended by Tressel and Berkeley].*

ANNE
Set down, set down your honorable load—
If honor may be shrouded in a hearse—   2
Whilst I awhile obsequiously lament   3
Th'untimely fall of virtuous Lancaster.
                    [*The bearers set down the coffin.*]
Poor key-cold figure of a holy king,   5
Pale ashes of the house of Lancaster,
Thou bloodless remnant of that royal blood,
Be it lawful that I invocate thy ghost   8
To hear the lamentations of poor Anne,

Wife to thy Edward, to thy slaughtered son,
Stabbed by the selfsame hand that made these wounds!
Lo, in these windows that let forth thy life   12
I pour the helpless balm of my poor eyes.   13
Oh, cursèd be the hand that made these holes!
Cursèd the heart that had the heart to do it!
Cursèd the blood that let this blood from hence!
More direful hap betide that hated wretch   17
That makes us wretched by the death of thee
Than I can wish to wolves, to spiders, toads,
Or any creeping venomed thing that lives!
If ever he have child, abortive be it,   21
Prodigious, and untimely brought to light,   22
Whose ugly and unnatural aspect   23
May fright the hopeful mother at the view,
And that be heir to his unhappiness!   25
If ever he have wife, let her be made
More miserable by the life of him
Than I am made by my young lord and thee!—   28
Come now towards Chertsey with your holy load,   29
Taken from Paul's to be interrèd there.   30
                    [*The bearers take up the hearse.*]
And still as you are weary of this weight,   31
Rest you, whiles I lament King Henry's corpse.

Enter Richard, Duke of Gloucester.

RICHARD
Stay, you that bear the corpse, and set it down.

ANNE
What black magician conjures up this fiend
To stop devoted charitable deeds?   35

RICHARD
Villains, set down the corpse, or, by Saint Paul,
I'll make a corpse of him that disobeys.

HALBERDIER [*advancing with his halberd lowered*]
My lord, stand back, and let the coffin pass.

RICHARD
Unmannered dog, stand thou when I command!   39
Advance thy halberd higher than my breast,   40
Or, by Saint Paul, I'll strike thee to my foot
And spurn upon thee, beggar, for thy boldness.   42
                    [*The bearers set down the hearse.*]

ANNE
What do you tremble? Are you all afraid?   43
Alas, I blame you not, for you are mortal,
And mortal eyes cannot endure the devil.—
Avaunt, thou dreadful minister of hell!   46
Thou hadst but power over his mortal body;
His soul thou canst not have. Therefore, begone.

---

137 **fear** fear for   139 **diet** course of life, regimen   146 **with post-
horse** by post-horses, i.e., by swiftest possible means   148 **steeled**
reinforced   153 **Warwick's youngest daughter** the Lady Anne
Neville, widow of Edward, Prince of Wales, son of King Henry VI.
154 **father** i.e., father-in-law (Henry VI).   158 **intent** design (i.e.,
Richard hopes to ally himself with the house of Lancaster to bolster
his claim to the throne)
1.2. Location: London. A street.
0.2 *Halberds* halberdiers, guards with halberds, or long poleaxes
2 **hearse** (Probably here an open coffin on a bier.)   3 **obsequiously** as
befits a funeral, mournfully   5 **key-cold** extremely cold, cold as a
metal key. (Proverbial.)   8 **Be it** Let it be.   **invocate** invoke

12 **windows** i.e., wounds   13 **helpless** useless, unavailing
17 **hap betide** fortune befall   21 **abortive** misshapen, premature
22 **Prodigious** monstrous, unnatural   23 **aspect** appearance
25 **unhappiness** evil nature, bad luck.   28 **by . . . thee** i.e., by the
deaths of Prince Edward and King Henry VI.   29 **Chertsey**
monastery in Surrey, near London, where King Henry's body is to be
buried   30 **Paul's** Saint Paul's Cathedral in London   31 **still as** as
often as   35 **devoted** holy   39 **stand** halt   40 **Advance . . . breast**
Raise your halberd upright   42 **spurn** trample   43 **What** Why
46 **Avaunt** Begone

RICHARD
Sweet saint, for charity, be not so curst.   49

ANNE
Foul devil, for God's sake hence and trouble us not,   50
For thou hast made the happy earth thy hell,
Filled it with cursing cries and deep exclaims.   52
If thou delight to view thy heinous deeds,
Behold this pattern of thy butcheries.   54
                              [She uncovers the corpse.]
Oh, gentlemen, see, see dead Henry's wounds
Open their congealed mouths and bleed afresh!   56
Blush, blush, thou lump of foul deformity!
For 'tis thy presence that exhales this blood   58
From cold and empty veins where no blood dwells.
Thy deeds inhuman and unnatural
Provokes this deluge most unnatural.
O God, which this blood mad'st, revenge his death!
O earth, which this blood drink'st, revenge his death!
Either heav'n with lightning strike the murd'rer dead,
Or earth gape open wide and eat him quick,   65
As thou dost swallow up this good king's blood,
Which his hell-governed arm hath butcherèd!

RICHARD
Lady, you know no rules of charity,
Which renders good for bad, blessings for curses.

ANNE
Villain, thou know'st nor law of God nor man.   70
No beast so fierce but knows some touch of pity.   71

RICHARD
But I know none, and therefore am no beast.

ANNE
Oh, wonderful, when devils tell the truth!   73

RICHARD
More wonderful, when angels are so angry.
Vouchsafe, divine perfection of a woman,   75
Of these supposèd crimes to give me leave
By circumstance but to acquit myself.   77

ANNE
Vouchsafe, defused infection of a man,   78
Of these known evils but to give me leave
By circumstance t'accuse thy cursèd self.

RICHARD
Fairer than tongue can name thee, let me have
Some patient leisure to excuse myself.

ANNE
Fouler than heart can think thee, thou canst make
No excuse current but to hang thyself.   84

RICHARD
By such despair I should accuse myself.

ANNE
And by despairing shalt thou stand excused
For doing worthy vengeance on thyself
That didst unworthy slaughter upon others.

RICHARD   Say that I slew them not?

ANNE   Then say they were not slain.
But dead they are, and, devilish slave, by thee.

RICHARD   I did not kill your husband.

ANNE   Why, then he is alive.

RICHARD
Nay, he is dead, and slain by Edward's hand.

ANNE
In thy foul throat thou liest! Queen Margaret saw
Thy murd'rous falchion smoking in his blood,   96
The which thou once didst bend against her breast,   97
But that thy brothers beat aside the point.

RICHARD
I was provokèd by her sland'rous tongue,
That laid their guilt upon my guiltless shoulders.   100

ANNE
Thou wast provokèd by thy bloody mind,
That never dream'st on aught but butcheries.   102
Didst thou not kill this king?

RICHARD   I grant ye.

ANNE
Dost grant me, hedgehog? Then God grant me too   104
Thou mayst be damnèd for that wicked deed!
Oh, he was gentle, mild, and virtuous!

RICHARD
The better for the King of Heaven that hath him.

ANNE
He is in heaven, where thou shalt never come.

RICHARD
Let him thank me that holp to send him thither;   109
For he was fitter for that place than earth.

ANNE
And thou unfit for any place but hell.

RICHARD
Yes, one place else, if you will hear me name it.

ANNE   Some dungeon.

RICHARD   Your bedchamber.

ANNE
Ill rest betide the chamber where thou liest!   115

RICHARD
So will it, madam, till I lie with you.

ANNE
I hope so.

RICHARD   I know so. But, gentle Lady Anne,
To leave this keen encounter of our wits
And fall something into a slower method,   119
Is not the causer of the timeless deaths   120
Of these Plantagenets, Henry and Edward,
As blameful as the executioner?

---

49 **curst** spiteful, shrewish.   50 **hence** go hence, depart   52 **exclaims** exclamations.   54 **pattern** example   56 **bleed afresh** (A phenomenon popularly supposed to occur in the presence of the murderer.)   58 **exhales** draws out   65 **quick** alive   70 **nor . . . nor** neither . . . nor   71 **so fierce but knows** is so savage that it has not   73 **Oh . . . truth** (Anne bitterly reinterprets Richard's *am no beast*, "am not beastly," to mean that he is neither man nor beast, but devil.)   75 **Vouchsafe** Deign, consent   77 **circumstance** detailed argument   78 **defused** diffused, disordered, shapeless; *defused infection* means "spreading plague"   84 **current** genuine, acceptable (as in coinage)

96 **falchion** curved sword   97 **bend** direct, aim   100 **their** my brothers'   102 **aught** anything   104 **hedgehog** (Richard's heraldic emblem featured a boar or wild hog.)   109 **holp** helped   115 **betide** befall   119 **something into a** into a somewhat   120 **timeless** untimely

ANNE
    Thou wast the cause and most accurst effect.   123
RICHARD
    Your beauty was the cause of that effect—   124
    Your beauty, that did haunt me in my sleep
    To undertake the death of all the world,
    So I might live one hour in your sweet bosom.
ANNE
    If I thought that, I tell thee, homicide,   128
    These nails should rend that beauty from my cheeks. 129
RICHARD
    These eyes could not endure that beauty's wrack;   130
    You should not blemish it, if I stood by.
    As all the world is cheerèd by the sun,
    So I by that. It is my day, my life.
ANNE
    Black night o'ershade thy day, and death thy life!
RICHARD
    Curse not thyself, fair creature—thou art both.
ANNE
    I would I were, to be revenged on thee.   136
RICHARD
    It is a quarrel most unnatural
    To be revenged on him that loveth thee.
ANNE
    It is a quarrel just and reasonable
    To be revenged on him that killed my husband.
RICHARD
    He that bereft thee, lady, of thy husband
    Did it to help thee to a better husband.
ANNE
    His better doth not breathe upon the earth.
RICHARD
    He lives that loves thee better than he could.   144
ANNE
    Name him.
RICHARD   Plantagenet.
ANNE   Why, that was he.   145
RICHARD
    The selfsame name, but one of better nature.
ANNE
    Where is he?
RICHARD   Here.   [She] spits at him.
            Why dost thou spit at me?
ANNE
    Would it were mortal poison for thy sake!
RICHARD
    Never came poison from so sweet a place.
ANNE
    Never hung poison on a fouler toad.   150

Out of my sight! Thou dost infect mine eyes.
RICHARD
    Thine eyes, sweet lady, have infected mine.   152
ANNE
    Would they were basilisks, to strike thee dead!   153
RICHARD
    I would they were, that I might die at once;
    For now they kill me with a living death.
    Those eyes of thine from mine have drawn salt tears,
    Shamed their aspects with store of childish drops;   157
    These eyes, which never shed remorseful tear—
    No, when my father York and Edward wept
    To hear the piteous moan that Rutland made   160
    When black-faced Clifford shook his sword at him;   161
    Nor when thy warlike father, like a child,   162
    Told the sad story of my father's death
    And twenty times made pause to sob and weep,
    That all the standers-by had wet their cheeks   165
    Like trees bedashed with rain—in that sad time
    My manly eyes did scorn an humble tear;
    And what these sorrows could not thence exhale,   168
    Thy beauty hath, and made them blind with weeping.
    I never sued to friend nor enemy;   170
    My tongue could never learn sweet smoothing words;   171
    But now thy beauty is proposed my fee,   172
    My proud heart sues and prompts my tongue to speak.
                            She looks scornfully at him.
    Teach not thy lip such scorn, for it was made
    For kissing, lady, not for such contempt.
    If thy revengeful heart cannot forgive,
    Lo, here I lend thee this sharp-pointed sword,
    Which if thou please to hide in this true breast
    And let the soul forth that adoreth thee,
    I lay it naked to the deadly stroke
    And humbly beg the death upon my knee.   181
            He [kneels and] lays his breast open; she offers at [it]
                                          with his sword.
    Nay, do not pause; for I did kill King Henry—
    But 'twas thy beauty that provokèd me.
    Nay, now dispatch; 'twas I that stabbed young Edward—
    But 'twas thy heavenly face that set me on.   185
                                    She falls the sword.
    Take up the sword again, or take up me.
ANNE
    Arise, dissembler. Though I wish thy death,
    I will not be thy executioner.
RICHARD [rising]
    Then bid me kill myself, and I will do it.

---

123 **effect** fulfillment.   124 **effect** result   128 **homicide** murderer
129 **rend** tear   130 **wrack** destruction   136 **I would I were** (If Anne
were truly both Richard's day and his life, she could terminate both.)
144 **He lives** i.e., There is a man.   **he** i.e., Prince Edward   145 **Plantagenet** (Richard's father, the Duke of York, adopted this name when
he made his claim to the English throne—see *1 Henry VI*, 2.4.36—but
the name had been in the family of England's Angevin rulers since
the time of Henry II and thus could also be claimed by Henry VI and
his son, Prince Edward.)   150 **poison . . . toad** (Toads were popularly
regarded as poisonous.)

152 **infected** i.e., with love (since love was thought to enter through
the eyes)   153 **basilisks** mythical reptiles reputed to kill by their
looks   157 **aspects** appearance   160 **Rutland** second son of Richard,
Duke of York. (See *3 Henry VI*, 1.3, for his death scene.)   161 **black-faced** i.e., foreboding in appearance   162 **thy warlike father** i.e., the
Earl of Warwick   165 **That** so that   168 **exhale** draw out   170 **sued**
supplicated, appealed   171 **smoothing** flattering   172 **now** now
that.   **proposed my fee** proposed as my reward   181 **the death**
death after sentencing.   181.1 **offers** aims   185.1 **falls** lets fall

ANNE
I have already.

RICHARD   That was in thy rage.
Speak it again, and even with the word
This hand, which for thy love did kill thy love,
Shall for thy love kill a far truer love.
To both their deaths shalt thou be accessory.

ANNE   I would I knew thy heart.   195

RICHARD   'Tis figured in my tongue.   196

ANNE   I fear me both are false.

RICHARD   Then never man was true.

ANNE   Well, well, put up your sword.

RICHARD   Say, then, my peace is made.

ANNE   That shalt thou know hereafter.

RICHARD   But shall I live in hope?

ANNE   All men, I hope, live so.

RICHARD   Vouchsafe to wear this ring.   204

ANNE   To take is not to give.   205

              [He slips the ring on her finger.]

RICHARD
Look how my ring encompasseth thy finger,   206
Even so thy breast encloseth my poor heart;
Wear both of them, for both of them are thine.
And if thy poor devoted servant may   209
But beg one favor at thy gracious hand,
Thou dost confirm his happiness forever.

ANNE   What is it?

RICHARD
That it may please you leave these sad designs
To him that hath most cause to be a mourner,
And presently repair to Crosby House,   215
Where, after I have solemnly interred
At Chertsey monast'ry this noble king
And wet his grave with my repentant tears,
I will with all expedient duty see you.   219
For divers unknown reasons, I beseech you,   220
Grant me this boon.

ANNE
With all my heart, and much it joys me, too,
To see you are become so penitent.—
Tressel and Berkeley, go along with me.

RICHARD
Bid me farewell.

ANNE   'Tis more than you deserve;
But since you teach me how to flatter you,
Imagine I have said farewell already.

              Exeunt two [Tressel and Berkeley] with Anne.

RICHARD
Sirs, take up the corpse.

GENTLEMAN   Towards Chertsey, noble lord?

RICHARD
No, to Whitefriars. There attend my coming.   229

              Exeunt [bearers with] corpse.

Was ever woman in this humor wooed?
Was ever woman in this humor won?
I'll have her, but I will not keep her long.
What? I, that killed her husband and his father,
To take her in her heart's extremest hate,
With curses in her mouth, tears in her eyes,
The bleeding witness of my hatred by,
Having God, her conscience, and these bars against me,   237
And I no friends to back my suit withal
But the plain devil and dissembling looks?
And yet to win her! All the world to nothing!   240
Ha!
Hath she forgot already that brave prince,
Edward, her lord, whom I, some three months since,
Stabbed in my angry mood at Tewkesbury?
A sweeter and a lovelier gentleman,
Framed in the prodigality of nature,   246
Young, valiant, wise, and, no doubt, right royal,
The spacious world cannot again afford.   248
And will she yet abase her eyes on me,   249
That cropped the golden prime of this sweet prince   250
And made her widow to a woeful bed?
On me, whose all not equals Edward's moiety?   252
On me, that halts and am misshapen thus?   253
My dukedom to a beggarly denier,   254
I do mistake my person all this while.
Upon my life, she finds, although I cannot,
Myself to be a marv'lous proper man.   257
I'll be at charges for a looking glass   258
And entertain a score or two of tailors   259
To study fashions to adorn my body.
Since I am crept in favor with myself,
I will maintain it with some little cost.
But first I'll turn yon fellow in his grave,   263
And then return lamenting to my love.
Shine out, fair sun, till I have bought a glass,   265
That I may see my shadow as I pass.   Exit.

                    ❖

1.3

Enter the Queen Mother [Elizabeth], Lord Rivers,
[Marquess of Dorset,] and Lord Grey.

RIVERS
Have patience, madam. There's no doubt His Majesty
Will soon recover his accustomed health.

GREY
In that you brook it ill, it makes him worse.   3
Therefore, for God's sake, entertain good comfort,   4
And cheer His Grace with quick and merry eyes.

---

195 **would** wish 196 **figured** portrayed 204 **Vouchsafe** Consent
205 **To take . . . give** i.e., I accept the ring but I make no promises.
206 **Look how** Just as 209 **servant** i.e., male admirer, one whom she
may command 215 **presently repair** go right away. **Crosby House**
(One of Richard's London dwellings; built originally by Sir John Crosby.)
219 **expedient** expeditious 220 **unknown** secret 229 **Whitefriars**
the Carmelite priory in London. **attend** await

237 **bars** obstacles 240 **All . . . nothing** i.e., Against infinite odds.
246 **Framed . . . nature** i.e., formed in nature's most lavish mood
248 **afford** (because Nature was so lavish). 249 **abase her eyes** degrade
herself by looking favorably 250 **cropped** cut short. **prime** springtime, early manhood 252 **Edward's moiety** half of Edward's worth.
253 **halts** limps 254 **denier** small copper coin, the twelfth part of a sou
257 **proper** handsome 258 **be . . . for** undertake the expense of
259 **entertain** retain, employ 263 **in** into 265 **glass** mirror
1.3. Location: London. The royal court.
3 **brook** endure 4 **entertain . . . comfort** cheer up

QUEEN ELIZABETH
If he were dead, what would betide on me?   6

GREY
No other harm but loss of such a lord.

QUEEN ELIZABETH
The loss of such a lord includes all harms.

GREY
The heavens have blessed you with a goodly son
To be your comforter when he is gone.

QUEEN ELIZABETH
Ah, he is young, and his minority
Is put unto the trust of Richard Gloucester,
A man that loves not me, nor none of you.

RIVERS
Is it concluded he shall be Protector?

QUEEN ELIZABETH
It is determined, not concluded yet;   15
But so it must be, if the King miscarry.   16

*Enter Buckingham and [*Lord Stanley Earl of*]
Derby.*

GREY
Here come the lords of Buckingham and Derby.

BUCKINGHAM
Good time of day unto Your Royal Grace!

STANLEY
God make Your Majesty joyful, as you have been!

QUEEN ELIZABETH
The Countess Richmond, good my lord of Derby,   20
To your good prayer will scarcely say amen.
Yet, Derby, notwithstanding she's your wife
And loves not me, be you, good lord, assured
I hate not you for her proud arrogance.   24

STANLEY
I do beseech you, either not believe
The envious slanders of her false accusers,   26
Or, if she be accused on true report,
Bear with her weakness, which I think proceeds
From wayward sickness and no grounded malice.   29

QUEEN ELIZABETH
Saw you the King today, my lord of Derby?

STANLEY
But now the Duke of Buckingham and I
Are come from visiting His Majesty.   31

QUEEN ELIZABETH
What likelihood of his amendment, lords?   33

BUCKINGHAM
Madam, good hope; His Grace speaks cheerfully.

QUEEN ELIZABETH
God grant him health! Did you confer with him?

BUCKINGHAM
Ay, madam. He desires to make atonement   36
Between the Duke of Gloucester and your brothers,   37
And between them and my Lord Chamberlain,   38
And sent to warn them to his royal presence.   39

QUEEN ELIZABETH
Would all were well! But that will never be.
I fear our happiness is at the height.

*Enter Richard [*Duke of Gloucester, and Lord
Hastings*].*

RICHARD
They do me wrong, and I will not endure it!
Who is it that complains unto the King
That I, forsooth, am stern and love them not?
By holy Paul, they love His Grace but lightly
That fill his ears with such dissentious rumors.   46
Because I cannot flatter and look fair,   47
Smile in men's faces, smooth, deceive, and cog,   48
Duck with French nods and apish courtesy,   49
I must be held a rancorous enemy.
Cannot a plain man live and think no harm,
But thus his simple truth must be abused
With silken, sly, insinuating Jacks?   53

GREY
To whom in all this presence speaks Your Grace?   54

RICHARD
To thee, that hast nor honesty nor grace.   55
When have I injured thee? When done thee wrong?
Or thee? Or thee? Or any of your faction?
A plague upon you all! His Royal Grace—
Whom God preserve better than you would wish!—
Cannot be quiet scarce a breathing while   60
But you must trouble him with lewd complaints.   61

QUEEN ELIZABETH
Brother of Gloucester, you mistake the matter.
The King, on his own royal disposition,   63
And not provoked by any suitor else,
Aiming, belike, at your interior hatred,   65
That in your outward action shows itself
Against my children, brothers, and myself,
Makes him to send, that he may learn the ground   68
Of your ill will, and thereby to remove it.

RICHARD
I cannot tell. The world is grown so bad   70
That wrens make prey where eagles dare not perch.

---

6 **betide on** become of   15 **determined, not concluded** i.e., decided though not officially passed   16 **miscarry** perish.   20 **The Countess Richmond** i.e., Margaret Beaufort (1443–1509), who married, successively, Edmund Tudor (Earl of Richmond), Lord Henry Stafford, and Thomas Lord Stanley (here called the Earl of Derby), to whom she is currently married. By the Earl of Richmond, she was mother of the future Henry VII.   24 **arrogance** i.e., ambition for her son.   26 **envious** malicious   29 **wayward** not yielding readily to treatment. **grounded** firmly fixed   31 **But now** Just now   33 **amendment** recovery

36 **atonement** reconciliation   37 **brothers** (Only one brother, Earl Rivers, is mentioned in the play, though historically Elizabeth had others; Shakespeare may be thinking of other kinsmen, including her sons, whom she helped to advance.)   38 **Lord Chamberlain** Hastings   39 **warn** summon   46 **dissentious** quarrelsome, discordant   47 **look fair** put on a pleasing appearance   48 **smooth** flatter. **cog** deceive   49 **Duck . . . nods** i.e., bow affectedly   53 **With silken** by smooth. **Jacks** lowbred persons.   54 **presence** company   55 **grace** sense of duty or propriety. (Playing upon *Your Grace* in the preceding line.)   60 **breathing while** i.e., brief time   61 **lewd** vile, base   63 **disposition** inclination   65 **Aiming** guessing. **belike** probably   68 **Makes him** causes him. (The implied subject is "The king's own disposition.")   **ground** cause   70 **I cannot tell** i.e., I don't know what to think. (Richard plays the role of the exasperated moralist.)

Since every Jack became a gentleman,
There's many a gentle person made a Jack.

QUEEN ELIZABETH
Come, come, we know your meaning, brother Gloucester;
You envy my advancement and my friends'.   75
God grant we never may have need of you!

RICHARD
Meantime, God grants that I have need of you.
Our brother is imprisoned by your means,   78
Myself disgraced, and the nobility
Held in contempt, while great promotions
Are daily given to ennoble those
That scarce some two days since were worth a noble.   82

QUEEN ELIZABETH
By Him that raised me to this careful height   83
From that contented hap which I enjoyed,   84
I never did incense His Majesty
Against the Duke of Clarence, but have been
An earnest advocate to plead for him.
My lord, you do me shameful injury
Falsely to draw me in these vile suspects.   89

RICHARD
You may deny that you were not the mean   90
Of my Lord Hastings' late imprisonment.

RIVERS   She may, my lord, for—

RICHARD
She may, Lord Rivers! Why, who knows not so?
She may do more, sir, than denying that:
She may help you to many fair preferments,   95
And then deny her aiding hand therein,
And lay those honors on your high desert.   97
What may she not? She may, ay, marry, may she—   98

RIVERS   What, marry, may she?

RICHARD
What, marry, may she? Marry with a king,   100
A bachelor, and a handsome stripling too!   101
Iwis your grandam had a worser match.   102

QUEEN ELIZABETH
My lord of Gloucester, I have too long borne
Your blunt upbraidings and your bitter scoffs.
By heaven, I will acquaint His Majesty
Of those gross taunts that oft I have endured.
I had rather be a country servant maid
Than a great queen with this condition,
To be so baited, scorned, and stormèd at.   109

Enter old Queen Margaret [behind].

Small joy have I in being England's queen.

QUEEN MARGARET [*aside*]
And lessened be that small, God I beseech him!
Thy honor, state, and seat is due to me.   112

RICHARD
What? Threat you me with telling of the King?   113
Tell him, and spare not. Look what I have said   114
I will avouch 't in presence of the King.
I dare adventure to be sent to the Tower.   116
'Tis time to speak; my pains are quite forgot.   117

QUEEN MARGARET [*aside*]
Out, devil! I do remember them too well: 118
Thou killed'st my husband Henry in the Tower,
And Edward, my poor son, at Tewkesbury.

RICHARD
Ere you were queen, ay, or your husband king,
I was a packhorse in his great affairs,   122
A weeder-out of his proud adversaries,
A liberal rewarder of his friends.
To royalize his blood I spent mine own.

QUEEN MARGARET [*aside*]
Ay, and much better blood than his or thine.

RICHARD
In all which time you and your husband Grey
Were factious for the house of Lancaster;   128
And, Rivers, so were you. Was not your husband   129
In Margaret's battle at Saint Albans slain?
Let me put in your minds, if you forget,
What you have been ere this, and what you are;
Withal, what I have been, and what I am.   133

QUEEN MARGARET [*aside*]
A murd'rous villain, and so still thou art.

RICHARD
Poor Clarence did forsake his father, Warwick,   135
Ay, and forswore himself—which Jesu pardon!—

QUEEN MARGARET [*aside*]   Which God revenge!

RICHARD
To fight on Edward's party for the crown;
And for his meed, poor lord, he is mewed up.   139
I would to God my heart were flint, like Edward's,
Or Edward's soft and pitiful, like mine.
I am too childish-foolish for this world.

QUEEN MARGARET [*aside*]
Hie thee to hell for shame, and leave this world,   143
Thou cacodemon! There thy kingdom is.   144

RIVERS
My lord of Gloucester, in those busy days
Which here you urge to prove us enemies,   146

75 friends' i.e., kinsmen's. **78 Our brother** i.e., Clarence **82 noble**
(1) gold coin worth six shillings eight pence (2) nobleman. **83 careful**
full of cares **84 hap** fortune **89 in** into. **suspects** suspicions.
90 mean means **95 preferments** advantages, promotions **97 lay . . .
desert** attribute these high honors to your rich deservings. **98 marry**
i.e., indeed. (A mild oath, literally, "by the Virgin Mary.") **100 Marry**
with Wed. (Punning on *marry,* indeed, in line 98.) **101 stripling**
young man **102 Iwis** (1) Certainly (2) *I wis,* I know **109 baited**
harassed, as in bearbaiting **109.1 Queen Margaret** (Historically, the
widow of Henry VI was held prisoner in England for five years following the battle of Tewkesbury in 1471 and then was sent to France;
see the note to line 167 below.)

112 state degree, high rank. **seat** throne **113 Threat** Threaten
114 Look what Whatever **116 adventure to be** risk being **117 pains**
efforts (in King Edward's behalf) **118 Out** (An exclamation of anger.)
122 packhorse workhorse, beast of burden **128 Were factious for**
fought factiously on the side of **129 husband** (Queen Elizabeth's
first husband, Sir John Grey, fell fighting on the Lancastrian side at
Saint Albans.) **133 Withal** in addition **135 father** i.e., father-in-law.
(See *3 Henry VI,* 4.1, when Clarence deserted his brothers to marry
Warwick's daughter Isabella and supported the Lancastrian cause for
a time; thereafter, he forswore his oath to Warwick by returning to
fight on Edward's *party* [line 138] or side.) **139 meed** reward.
mewed caged (like a hawk) **143 Hie** Hasten **144 cacodemon** evil
spirit. **146 urge** cite

We followed then our lord, our sovereign king.
So should we you, if you should be our king.

RICHARD
If I should be? I had rather be a peddler.
Far be it from my heart, the thought thereof!

QUEEN ELIZABETH
As little joy, my lord, as you suppose
You should enjoy were you this country's king,
As little joy you may suppose in me
That I enjoy, being the queen thereof.

QUEEN MARGARET [*aside*]
Ah, little joy enjoys the queen thereof,
For I am she, and altogether joyless.
I can no longer hold me patient.   [*Advancing.*]
Hear me, you wrangling pirates, that fall out
In sharing that which you have pilled from me!   159
Which of you trembles not that looks on me?
If not, that I am queen, you bow like subjects,   161
Yet that, by you deposed, you quake like rebels?   162
[*To Richard*] Ah, gentle villain, do not turn away!   163

RICHARD
Foul wrinkled witch, what mak'st thou in my sight?   164

QUEEN MARGARET
But repetition of what thou hast marred;   165
That will I make before I let thee go.   166

RICHARD
Wert thou not banishèd on pain of death?   167

QUEEN MARGARET
I was; but I do find more pain in banishment
Than death can yield me here by my abode.
A husband and a son thou ow'st to me,   170
And thou a kingdom; all of you allegiance.   171
This sorrow that I have by right is yours,
And all the pleasures you usurp are mine.

RICHARD
The curse my noble father laid on thee   174
When thou didst crown his warlike brows with paper
And with thy scorns drew'st rivers from his eyes,
And then, to dry them, gav'st the Duke a clout   177
Steeped in the faultless blood of pretty Rutland—   178
His curses then, from bitterness of soul
Denounced against thee, are all fall'n upon thee;   180
And God, not we, hath plagued thy bloody deed.

QUEEN ELIZABETH
So just is God, to right the innocent.

HASTINGS
Oh, 'twas the foulest deed to slay that babe,   183
And the most merciless, that e'er was heard of!

RIVERS
Tyrants themselves wept when it was reported.   185

DORSET
No man but prophesied revenge for it.   186

BUCKINGHAM
Northumberland, then present, wept to see it.

QUEEN MARGARET
What? Were you snarling all before I came,
Ready to catch each other by the throat,
And turn you all your hatred now on me?
Did York's dread curse prevail so much with heaven
That Henry's death, my lovely Edward's death,
Their kingdom's loss, my woeful banishment,
Should all but answer for that peevish brat?   194
Can curses pierce the clouds and enter heaven?
Why, then, give way, dull clouds, to my quick curses!   196
Though not by war, by surfeit die your king,   197
As ours by murder, to make him a king!
Edward thy son, that now is Prince of Wales,
For Edward our son, that was Prince of Wales,
Die in his youth by like untimely violence!
Thyself a queen, for me that was a queen,
Outlive thy glory, like my wretched self!
Long mayst thou live to wail thy children's death
And see another, as I see thee now,
Decked in thy rights, as thou art stalled in mine!   206
Long die thy happy days before thy death,
And, after many lengthened hours of grief,
Die neither mother, wife, nor England's queen!
Rivers and Dorset, you were standers-by,   210
And so wast thou, Lord Hastings, when my son   211
Was stabbed with bloody daggers: God, I pray him,
That none of you may live his natural age,   213
But by some unlooked accident cut off!   214

RICHARD
Have done thy charm, thou hateful withered hag!   215

QUEEN MARGARET
And leave out thee? Stay, dog, for thou shalt hear me.
If heaven have any grievous plague in store
Exceeding those that I can wish upon thee,
Oh, let them keep it till thy sins be ripe,   219
And then hurl down their indignation
On thee, the troubler of the poor world's peace!
The worm of conscience still begnaw thy soul!   222
Thy friends suspect for traitors while thou liv'st,
And take deep traitors for thy dearest friends!
No sleep close up that deadly eye of thine,
Unless it be while some tormenting dream
Affrights thee with a hell of ugly devils!
Thou elvish-marked, abortive, rooting hog,   228

---

159 pilled pillaged, robbed   **161–2 If . . . rebels** i.e., Even if you do not bow low to me as your queen, you quake as rebels who have deposed me.   **163 gentle** nobly born. *Gentle villain* is an oxymoron, since *villain* can mean "one ignobly born."   **164 mak'st thou** are you doing   **165 But . . . marred** Only reciting your crimes   **166 That** that repetition or recital   **167 banishèd** (Margaret was banished in 1464, returned to England in 1471, and after the Battle of Tewkesbury was confined in the Tower until 1476, when she returned to France, dying there in 1482, one year before the historical time of this scene.)   **170 thou** i.e., Richard   **171 thou** i.e., Elizabeth   **174 The curse** (See *3 Henry VI*, 1.4.164–6.)   **177 clout** cloth, handkerchief   **178 faultless** innocent   **180 Denounced** proclaimed vengefully   **183 that babe** i.e., Rutland (who historically was an older brother of Richard)

185 Tyrants Even pitiless men   **186 No . . . prophesied** There was no one who did not prophesy   **194 but answer for** merely atone for, equal.   **peevish** silly, senseless   **196 quick** lively, piercing   **197 surfeit** dissipated living   **206 Decked** dressed.   **stalled** installed   **210–11 Rivers, Dorset, Hastings** (Not present in Shakespeare's dramatization of the event in *3 Henry VI*, 5.5, but named in the chronicles as having been present.)   **213 natural age** full course of life   **214 unlooked** unexpected   **215 charm** magic curse, pronounced by a witch   **219 them** i.e., the heavens, heaven   **222 still begnaw** continually gnaw   **228 elvish-marked** marked by elves at birth.   **hog** (Alludes to Richard's badge, the wild boar.)

Thou that wast sealed in thy nativity   229
The slave of nature and the son of hell!   230
Thou slander of thy heavy mother's womb,   231
Thou loathèd issue of thy father's loins,
Thou rag of honor, thou detested—   233

RICHARD
Margaret.

QUEEN MARGARET   Richard!

RICHARD   Ha?

QUEEN MARGARET   I call thee not.

RICHARD
I cry thee mercy then, for I did think   235
That thou hadst called me all these bitter names.

QUEEN MARGARET
Why, so I did, but looked for no reply.
Oh, let me make the period to my curse!   238

RICHARD
'Tis done by me, and ends in "Margaret."

QUEEN ELIZABETH [to Queen Margaret]
Thus have you breathed your curse against yourself.

QUEEN MARGARET
Poor painted queen, vain flourish of my fortune!   241
Why strew'st thou sugar on that bottled spider,   242
Whose deadly web ensnareth thee about?
Fool, fool, thou whet'st a knife to kill thyself.
The day will come that thou shalt wish for me
To help thee curse this poisonous bunch-backed toad. 246

HASTINGS
False-boding woman, end thy frantic curse,   247
Lest to thy harm thou move our patience.

QUEEN MARGARET
Foul shame upon you! You have all moved mine.

RIVERS
Were you well served, you would be taught your duty. 250

QUEEN MARGARET
To serve me well, you all should do me duty,   251
Teach me to be your queen, and you my subjects.   252
Oh, serve me well, and teach yourselves that duty!

DORSET
Dispute not with her. She is lunatic.

QUEEN MARGARET
Peace, Master Marquess, you are malapert.   255
Your fire-new stamp of honor is scarce current.   256
Oh, that your young nobility could judge
What 'twere to lose it and be miserable!
They that stand high have many blasts to shake them, 259
And if they fall, they dash themselves to pieces.

RICHARD
Good counsel, marry! Learn it, learn it, Marquess.

DORSET
It touches you, my lord, as much as me.

RICHARD
Ay, and much more; but I was born so high.   263
Our aerie buildeth in the cedar's top,   264
And dallies with the wind and scorns the sun.

QUEEN MARGARET
And turns the sun to shade; alas, alas!   266
Witness my son, now in the shade of death,
Whose bright outshining beams thy cloudy wrath
Hath in eternal darkness folded up.
Your aerie buildeth in our aerie's nest.
O God, that see'st it, do not suffer it!
As it is won with blood, lost be it so!

BUCKINGHAM
Peace, peace, for shame, if not for charity!

QUEEN MARGARET
Urge neither charity nor shame to me.
                              [Turning to the others.]
Uncharitably with me have you dealt,
And shamefully my hopes by you are butchered.
My charity is outrage, life my shame,   277
And in that shame still live my sorrow's rage!

BUCKINGHAM   Have done, have done.

QUEEN MARGARET
O princely Buckingham, I'll kiss thy hand
In sign of league and amity with thee.
Now fair befall thee and thy noble house!   282
Thy garments are not spotted with our blood,
Nor thou within the compass of my curse.   284

BUCKINGHAM
Nor no one here; for curses never pass   285
The lips of those that breathe them in the air.

QUEEN MARGARET
I will not think but they ascend the sky   287
And there awake God's gentle-sleeping peace.
O Buckingham, take heed of yonder dog!
Look when he fawns, he bites; and when he bites,   290
His venom tooth will rankle to the death.   291
Have not to do with him, beware of him;
Sin, death, and hell have set their marks on him,
And all their ministers attend on him.

RICHARD
What doth she say, my lord of Buckingham?

BUCKINGHAM
Nothing that I respect, my gracious lord.   296

QUEEN MARGARET
What, dost thou scorn me for my gentle counsel?

---

229 sealed stamped   **230 slave of nature** i.e., wretch made by the malignancy of nature (as seen in his deformity)   **231 heavy** (1) sorrowful (2) weighted down in pregnancy   **233 rag** tattered remnant **235 cry thee mercy** beg your pardon. (Said sarcastically.)   **238 period** conclusion   **241 painted** counterfeit.   **vain . . . fortune** i.e., mere ornament of a position that is mine by right.   **242 bottled** bottle-shaped, swollen   **246 bunch-backed** hunch-backed   **247 False-boding** Falsely prophesying   **250 well served** treated as you deserve. (But Margaret turns the phrase around to mean "served as befitting one of royal rank.")   **your duty** your place (i.e., to be obedient).   **251 duty** reverence   **252 Teach me** i.e., show by your obedience what is my role   **255 Master** (A title for a boy of good family, used insultingly here.)   **malapert** impudent.   **256 fire-new** newly coined.   **current** genuine as legal tender.   **259 blasts** strong gusts of wind

263 born so high i.e., born noble—unlike you.   **264 aerie** eagle's brood   **266 sun** (With a play on *son* in the next line.)   **277 My . . . shame** i.e., Instead of charity I receive outrage, and the only life given me is one of shame; or, outrage is all the charity I feel, and shame is my only life   **282 fair befall** good luck to   **284 compass** scope, boundary   **285 pass** get any further than   **287 I . . . but** I must believe that   **290 Look when** (1) Whenever (2) Expect that when **291 venom** envenomed.   **rankle** cause a festering wound **296 respect** heed

And soothe the devil that I warn thee from?   298
Oh, but remember this another day,
When he shall split thy very heart with sorrow,
And say poor Margaret was a prophetess!
Live each of you the subjects to his hate,   302
And he to yours, and all of you to God's!   *Exit.*

BUCKINGHAM
My hair doth stand on end to hear her curses.

RIVERS
And so doth mine. I muse why she's at liberty.   305

RICHARD
I cannot blame her. By God's holy mother,
She hath had too much wrong, and I repent
My part thereof that I have done to her.

QUEEN ELIZABETH
I never did her any, to my knowledge.

RICHARD
Yet you have all the vantage of her wrong.   310
I was too hot to do somebody good   311
That is too cold in thinking of it now.   312
Marry, as for Clarence, he is well repaid;
He is franked up to fatting for his pains—   314
God pardon them that are the cause thereof!

RIVERS
A virtuous and a Christian-like conclusion,
To pray for them that have done scathe to us.   317

RICHARD
So do I ever—(*speaks to himself*) being well advised.   318
For had I cursed now, I had cursed myself.

Enter Catesby.

CATESBY
Madam, His Majesty doth call for you,
And for Your Grace, and yours, my gracious lord.

QUEEN ELIZABETH
Catesby, I come.—Lords, will you go with me?

RIVERS
We wait upon Your Grace.   323
Exeunt all but [Richard Duke of] Gloucester.

RICHARD
I do the wrong, and first begin to brawl.
The secret mischiefs that I set abroach   325
I lay unto the grievous charge of others.   326
Clarence, who I indeed have cast in darkness,
I do beweep to many simple gulls—   328
Namely, to Derby, Hastings, Buckingham—
And tell them 'tis the Queen and her allies
That stir the King against the Duke my brother.
Now they believe it, and withal whet me   332
To be revenged on Rivers, Dorset, Grey.
But then I sigh and, with a piece of Scripture,

Tell them that God bids us do good for evil.   335
And thus I clothe my naked villainy
With odd old ends stol'n forth of Holy Writ,   337
And seem a saint when most I play the devil.

Enter two Murderers.

But soft! Here come my executioners.—   339
How now, my hardy, stout, resolvèd mates,   340
Are you now going to dispatch this thing?

FIRST MURDERER
We are, my lord, and come to have the warrant
That we may be admitted where he is.

RICHARD
Well thought upon. I have it here about me.
                              [*He gives the warrant.*]
When you have done, repair to Crosby Place.   345
But sirs, be sudden in the execution,
Withal obdurate; do not hear him plead;   347
For Clarence is well-spoken, and perhaps
May move your hearts to pity if you mark him.   349

FIRST MURDERER
Tut, tut, my lord, we will not stand to prate;   350
Talkers are no good doers. Be assured
We go to use our hands and not our tongues.

RICHARD
Your eyes drop millstones when fools' eyes fall tears.   353
I like you, lads. About your business straight.
Go, go, dispatch.

FIRST MURDERER   We will, my noble lord.   [*Exeunt.*]

❖

1.4

Enter Clarence and Keeper.

KEEPER
Why looks Your Grace so heavily today?   1

CLARENCE
Oh, I have passed a miserable night,
So full of fearful dreams, of ugly sights,
That, as I am a Christian faithful man,
I would not spend another such a night
Though 'twere to buy a world of happy days,
So full of dismal terror was the time!

KEEPER
What was your dream, my lord? I pray you, tell me.

CLARENCE
Methoughts that I had broken from the Tower   9
And was embarked to cross to Burgundy,   10
And in my company my brother Gloucester,
Who from my cabin tempted me to walk

---

298 **soothe** flatter   302 **the subjects to** subjugated to   305 **muse** wonder   310 **vantage of her wrong** benefits derived from the wrongs she has suffered.   311 **too hot . . . good** i.e., too eager in helping Edward to the throne   312 **That . . . cold** who is too ungrateful   314 **franked . . . fatting** shut up in a frank or sty to be fattened for slaughter   317 **scathe** harm   318 **well advised** cautious.   323 **wait upon** attend   325 **set abroach** set flowing   326 **lay . . . of** impute as a serious accusation against   328 **gulls** credulous persons   332 **withal** furthermore.   **whet** urge, incite

335 **for** in return for   337 **ends** fragments, tags   339 **soft** gently; wait a minute.   340 **stout . . . mates** bold, resolute fellows   345 **repair** betake yourselves   347 **Withal** at the same time   349 **mark** pay attention to   350 **prate** prattle   353 **millstones** heavy stone disks used for grinding. (To *drop millstones* was proverbially to show signs of hardheartedness.)   **fall** let fall
1.4. Location: London. The Tower.
1 heavily sad   **9 Methoughts** It seemed to me   **10 Burgundy** (Clarence and Richard, according to the chronicles, had been sent to Burgundy for protection following their father's death.)

Upon the hatches. Thence we looked toward England 13
And cited up a thousand heavy times, 14
During the wars of York and Lancaster,
That had befall'n us. As we paced along
Upon the giddy footing of the hatches, 17
Methought that Gloucester stumbled, and in falling
Struck me, that thought to stay him, overboard 19
Into the tumbling billows of the main. 20
Oh, Lord, methought what pain it was to drown!
What dreadful noise of waters in my ears!
What sights of ugly death within my eyes!
Methought I saw a thousand fearful wracks; 24
Ten thousand men that fishes gnawed upon;
Wedges of gold, great anchors, heaps of pearl, 26
Inestimable stones, unvalued jewels, 27
All scattered in the bottom of the sea.
Some lay in dead men's skulls, and in the holes
Where eyes did once inhabit there were crept,
As 'twere in scorn of eyes, reflecting gems,
That wooed the slimy bottom of the deep 32
And mocked the dead bones that lay scattered by.

KEEPER
Had you such leisure in the time of death
To gaze upon these secrets of the deep?

CLARENCE
Methought I had, and often did I strive
To yield the ghost; but still the envious flood 37
Stopped in my soul and would not let it forth 38
To seek the empty, vast, and wand'ring air,
But smothered it within my panting bulk, 40
Which almost burst to belch it in the sea.

KEEPER
Awaked you not in this sore agony?

CLARENCE
No, no, my dream was lengthened after life.
Oh, then began the tempest to my soul!
I passed, methought, the melancholy flood, 45
With that sour ferryman which poets write of, 46
Unto the kingdom of perpetual night.
The first that there did greet my stranger soul 48
Was my great father-in-law, renownèd Warwick,
Who spake aloud, "What scourge for perjury
Can this dark monarchy afford false Clarence?"
And so he vanished. Then came wand'ring by
A shadow like an angel, with bright hair 53
Dabbled in blood, and he shrieked out aloud,
"Clarence is come—false, fleeting, perjured Clarence, 55
That stabbed me in the field by Tewkesbury.
Seize on him, Furies, take him unto torment!"
With that, methought, a legion of foul fiends

Environed me and howlèd in mine ears
Such hideous cries that with the very noise
I trembling waked, and for a season after 61
Could not believe but that I was in hell,
Such terrible impression made my dream.

KEEPER
No marvel, my lord, though it affrighted you.
I am afraid, methinks, to hear you tell it.

CLARENCE
Ah, keeper, keeper, I have done these things,
That now give evidence against my soul,
For Edward's sake, and see how he requites me! 68
O God! If my deep prayers cannot appease thee,
But thou wilt be avenged on my misdeeds,
Yet execute thy wrath in me alone!
Oh, spare my guiltless wife and my poor children!
Keeper, I prithee, sit by me awhile.
My soul is heavy, and I fain would sleep. 74

KEEPER
I will, my lord. God give Your Grace good rest!
[Clarence sleeps.]

Enter Brackenbury, the Lieutenant.

BRACKENBURY
Sorrow breaks seasons and reposing hours, 76
Makes the night morning and the noontide night.
Princes have but their titles for their glories,
An outward honor for an inward toil,
And, for unfelt imaginations, 80
They often feel a world of restless cares;
So that between their titles and low name 82
There's nothing differs but the outward fame. 83

Enter two Murderers.

FIRST MURDERER   Ho! Who's here?

BRACKENBURY
What would'st thou, fellow, and how cam'st thou hither?

SECOND MURDERER   I would speak with Clarence, and I
came hither on my legs.

BRACKENBURY   What, so brief?

FIRST MURDERER   'Tis better, sir, than to be tedious.—
Let him see our commission, and talk no more.
[Brackenbury] reads [it].

BRACKENBURY
I am in this commanded to deliver
The noble Duke of Clarence to your hands.
I will not reason what is meant hereby,
Because I will be guiltless from the meaning. 94
There lies the Duke asleep, and there the keys.
[He gives keys.]
I'll to the King and signify to him
That thus I have resigned to you my charge.

---

13 **hatches** movable planks forming a deck.   14 **cited up** recalled.
heavy difficult   17 **giddy** unsteady   19 **stay** hold, steady   20 **main**
ocean.   24 **wracks** shipwrecked vessels   26 **Wedges** ingots
27 **Inestimable** precious and innumerable.   **unvalued** priceless
32 **wooed** (These lifeless eyes have nothing to flirt with but the
murky depths.)   37 **envious flood** malicious water   38 **Stopped**
held   40 **bulk** body   45 **melancholy flood** i.e., River Styx   46 **ferryman** i.e., Charon, who ferried souls to Hades, *the kingdom of perpetual
night* (line 47)   48 **stranger** i.e., newly arrived   53 **shadow** i.e., ghost of
Edward, Prince of Wales, son of Henry VI   55 **fleeting** fickle, deceitful

61 **season** time   68 **requites** repays   74 **fain** willingly   76 **breaks . . .
hours** disrupts the normal rhythms of life and hours properly
devoted to sleep   80 **for unfelt imaginations** in return for glories
that are merely illusory   82 **low name** i.e., the lowly position of ordinary men   83 **fame** reputation.   94 **will be** wish to be

FIRST MURDERER   You may, sir; 'tis a point of wisdom.
Fare you well.   *Exit [Brackenbury with Keeper].*

SECOND MURDERER   What, shall I stab him as he
sleeps?

FIRST MURDERER   No. He'll say 'twas done cowardly,
when he wakes.

SECOND MURDERER   Why, he shall never wake until the
great Judgment Day.

FIRST MURDERER   Why, then he'll say we stabbed him
sleeping.

SECOND MURDERER   The urging of that word "judgment" hath bred a kind of remorse in me.

FIRST MURDERER   What, art thou afraid?

SECOND MURDERER   Not to kill him, having a warrant,
but to be damned for killing him, from the which no
warrant can defend me.

FIRST MURDERER   I thought thou hadst been resolute.

SECOND MURDERER   So I am—to let him live.

FIRST MURDERER   I'll back to the Duke of Gloucester
and tell him so.

SECOND MURDERER   Nay, I prithee, stay a little. I hope
this passionate humor of mine will change. It was 119
wont to hold me but while one tells twenty.   120

FIRST MURDERER   How dost thou feel thyself now?

SECOND MURDERER   Faith, some certain dregs of conscience are yet within me.

FIRST MURDERER   Remember our reward when the
deed 's done.

SECOND MURDERER   Zounds, he dies! I had forgot the 126
reward.

FIRST MURDERER   Where's thy conscience now?

SECOND MURDERER   Oh, in the Duke of Gloucester's
purse.

FIRST MURDERER   When he opens his purse to give us
our reward, thy conscience flies out.

SECOND MURDERER   'Tis no matter; let it go. There's few
or none will entertain it.   134

FIRST MURDERER   What if it come to thee again?

SECOND MURDERER   I'll not meddle with it; it makes a
man a coward. A man cannot steal but it accuseth him;
a man cannot swear but it checks him; a man cannot 138
lie with his neighbor's wife but it detects him. 'Tis a
blushing, shamefaced spirit that mutinies in a man's
bosom. It fills a man full of obstacles. It made me once
restore a purse of gold that by chance I found. It
beggars any man that keeps it. It is turned out of
towns and cities for a dangerous thing, and every man
that means to live well endeavors to trust to himself
and live without it.

FIRST MURDERER   Zounds, 'tis even now at my elbow,
persuading me not to kill the Duke.

SECOND MURDERER   Take the devil in thy mind, and 149
believe him not. He would insinuate with thee but to 150
make thee sigh.   151

FIRST MURDERER   Tut, I am strong-framed; he cannot
prevail with me.

SECOND MURDERER   Spoke like a tall man that respects 154
thy reputation. Come, shall we fall to work?

FIRST MURDERER   Take him on the costard with the hilts 156
of thy sword, and then throw him into the malmsey 157
butt in the next room.   158

SECOND MURDERER   Oh, excellent device! And make a sop 159
of him.

FIRST MURDERER   Soft, he wakes.

SECOND MURDERER   Strike!

FIRST MURDERER   No, we'll reason with him.   163

CLARENCE [*waking*]
    Where art thou, keeper? Give me a cup of wine.

SECOND MURDERER
    You shall have wine enough, my lord, anon.

CLARENCE   In God's name, what art thou?

FIRST MURDERER   A man, as you are.

CLARENCE   But not, as I am, royal.

FIRST MURDERER   Nor you, as we are, loyal.

CLARENCE
    Thy voice is thunder, but thy looks are humble.

FIRST MURDERER
    My voice is now the King's, my looks mine own.

CLARENCE
    How darkly and how deadly dost thou speak!   172
    Your eyes do menace me. Why look you pale?
    Who sent you hither? Wherefore do you come?

SECOND MURDERER   To, to, to—

CLARENCE   To murder me?

BOTH   Ay, ay.

CLARENCE
    You scarcely have the hearts to tell me so,
    And therefore cannot have the hearts to do it.
    Wherein, my friends, have I offended you?

FIRST MURDERER
    Offended us you have not, but the King.

CLARENCE
    I shall be reconciled to him again.

SECOND MURDERER
    Never, my lord; therefore prepare to die.

CLARENCE
    Are you drawn forth among a world of men   184
    To slay the innocent? What is my offense?
    Where is the evidence that doth accuse me?
    What lawful quest have given their verdict up   187
    Unto the frowning judge? Or who pronounced
    The bitter sentence of poor Clarence' death
    Before I be convict by course of law?   190
    To threaten me with death is most unlawful.
    I charge you, as you hope to have redemption
    By Christ's dear blood shed for our grievous sins,
    That you depart and lay no hands on me.
    The deed you undertake is damnable.

---

119 passionate humor compassionate mood   **120 wont** accustomed.
tells counts   **126 Zounds** i.e., By God's (Christ's) wounds   **134 entertain** it receive it, give it welcome.   **138 checks** reproves, stops
149–50 Take . . . not i.e., Listen to the devil and pay no heed to conscience.
150–1 He . . . sigh Your conscience would ingratiate itself with you merely
for the purpose of making you unhappy.

154 tall brave   **156 Take** Strike.   **costard** head. (Literally, a kind of
apple.)   **157–8 malmsey butt** wine barrel. (Malmsey is a sweet wine.)
159 sop bread or cake soaked in wine   **163 reason** talk   **172 darkly**
ominously   **184 drawn . . . men** especially selected from the whole
human race   **187 quest** inquest, i.e., jury   **190 convict** convicted

FIRST MURDERER
What we will do, we do upon command.

SECOND MURDERER
And he that hath commanded is our king.

CLARENCE
Erroneous vassals! The great King of kings   198
Hath in the table of His law commanded   199
That thou shalt do no murder. Will you then
Spurn at His edict and fulfill a man's?
Take heed; for He holds vengeance in His hand
To hurl upon their heads that break His law.

SECOND MURDERER
And that same vengeance doth He hurl on thee
For false forswearing and for murder, too.
Thou didst receive the Sacrament to fight   206
In quarrel of the house of Lancaster.

FIRST MURDERER
And, like a traitor to the name of God,
Didst break that vow, and with thy treacherous blade
Unripped'st the bowels of thy sovereign's son.   210

SECOND MURDERER
Whom thou wast sworn to cherish and defend.

FIRST MURDERER
How canst thou urge God's dreadful law to us
When thou hast broke it in such dear degree?   213

CLARENCE
Alas! For whose sake did I that ill deed?
For Edward, for my brother, for his sake.
He sends you not to murder me for this,
For in that sin he is as deep as I.
If God will be avengèd for the deed,
Oh, know you yet he doth it publicly!
Take not the quarrel from His powerful arm.
He needs no indirect or lawless course
To cut off those that have offended Him.

FIRST MURDERER
Who made thee, then, a bloody minister   223
When gallant-springing brave Plantagenet,   224
That princely novice, was struck dead by thee?   225

CLARENCE
My brother's love, the devil, and my rage.   226

FIRST MURDERER
Thy brother's love, our duty, and thy faults
Provoke us hither now to slaughter thee.

CLARENCE
If you do love my brother, hate not me!
I am his brother, and I love him well.
If you are hired for meed, go back again,   231
And I will send you to my brother Gloucester,
Who shall reward you better for my life
Than Edward will for tidings of my death.

SECOND MURDERER
You are deceived. Your brother Gloucester hates you.

CLARENCE
Oh, no, he loves me, and he holds me dear.
Go you to him from me.

FIRST MURDERER   Ay, so we will.

CLARENCE
Tell him, when that our princely father York
Blessed his three sons with his victorious arm
And charged us from his soul to love each other,
He little thought of this divided friendship.
Bid Gloucester think of this, and he will weep.

FIRST MURDERER
Ay, millstones, as he lessoned us to weep.   243

CLARENCE
Oh, do not slander him, for he is kind.

FIRST MURDERER
Right, as snow in harvest. Come, you deceive
   yourself.   245
'Tis he that sends us to destroy you here.

CLARENCE
It cannot be, for he bewept my fortune,
And hugged me in his arms, and swore with sobs
That he would labor my delivery.   249

FIRST MURDERER
Why, so he doth, when he delivers you
From this earth's thralldom to the joys of heaven. 251

SECOND MURDERER
Make peace with God, for you must die, my lord.

CLARENCE
Have you that holy feeling in your souls
To counsel me to make my peace with God,
And are you yet to your own souls so blind
That you will war with God by murd'ring me?
Oh, sirs, consider, they that set you on
To do this deed will hate you for the deed.

SECOND MURDERER [to First Murderer]
What shall we do?

CLARENCE   Relent, and save your souls.
Which of you, if you were a prince's son,
Being pent from liberty, as I am now,   261
If two such murderers as yourselves came to you,
Would not entreat for life?

FIRST MURDERER
Relent? No. 'Tis cowardly and womanish.

CLARENCE
Not to relent is beastly, savage, devilish.
[To Second Murderer] My friend, I spy some pity in thy looks..
Oh, if thine eye be not a flatterer,
Come thou on my side, and entreat for me,
As you would beg, were you in my distress.
A begging prince what beggar pities not?

SECOND MURDERER   Look behind you, my lord.

FIRST MURDERER
  Take that, and that! (*Stabs him.*) If all this will not do,
  I'll drown you in the malmsey butt within.
                         Exit [*with the body*].

SECOND MURDERER
  A bloody deed, and desperately dispatched!
  How fain, like Pilate, would I wash my hands   275
  Of this most grievous murder!

     Enter First Murderer.

FIRST MURDERER
  How now? What mean'st thou that thou help'st me not?
  By heaven, the Duke shall know how slack you
    have been.

SECOND MURDERER
  I would he knew that I had saved his brother!
  Take thou the fee, and tell him what I say,
  For I repent me that the Duke is slain.   *Exit.*

FIRST MURDERER
  So do not I. Go, coward as thou art.—
  Well, I'll go hide his body in some hole
  Till that the Duke give order for his burial;
  And when I have my meed, I will away,
  For this will out, and then I must not stay.   *Exit.* 286

             ❖

2.1

    Flourish. Enter the King [*Edward*], *sick, the*
    Queen [*Elizabeth*], *Lord Marquess Dorset,* [*Grey,*]
    Rivers, Hastings, Catesby, Buckingham, [*and*
    others].

KING EDWARD
  Why, so. Now have I done a good day's work.
  You peers, continue this united league.
  I every day expect an embassage
  From my Redeemer to redeem me hence;
  And more in peace my soul shall part to heaven,
  Since I have made my friends at peace on earth.
  Rivers and Hastings, take each other's hand;
  Dissemble not your hatred, swear your love.   8

RIVERS [*taking Hastings' hand*]
  By heaven, my soul is purged from grudging hate,
  And with my hand I seal my true heart's love.

HASTINGS
  So thrive I, as I truly swear the like!

KING EDWARD
  Take heed you dally not before your king,   12
  Lest he that is the supreme King of kings
  Confound your hidden falsehood, and award   14
  Either of you to be the other's end.   15

HASTINGS
  So prosper I, as I swear perfect love!

RIVERS
  And I, as I love Hastings with my heart!

KING EDWARD
  Madam, yourself is not exempt from this,
  Nor you, son Dorset, Buckingham, nor you;   19
  You have been factious one against the other.   20
  Wife, love Lord Hastings; let him kiss your hand;
  And what you do, do it unfeignedly.

QUEEN ELIZABETH
  There, Hastings, I will never more remember
  Our former hatred, so thrive I and mine!   24
              [*Hastings kisses her hand.*]

KING EDWARD
  Dorset, embrace him. Hastings, love Lord Marquess.

DORSET
  This interchange of love, I here protest,   26
  Upon my part shall be inviolable.

HASTINGS   And so swear I.   [*They embrace.*]

KING EDWARD
  Now, princely Buckingham, seal thou this league
  With thy embracements to my wife's allies,
  And make me happy in your unity.

BUCKINGHAM [*to the Queen*]
  Whenever Buckingham doth turn his hate
  Upon Your Grace, but with all duteous love   33
  Doth cherish you and yours, God punish me
  With hate in those where I expect most love!
  When I have most need to employ a friend,
  And most assurèd that he is a friend,
  Deep, hollow, treacherous, and full of guile   38
  Be he unto me! This do I beg of God,
  When I am cold in love to you or yours.
              [*They*] *embrace.*

KING EDWARD
  A pleasing cordial, princely Buckingham,   41
  Is this thy vow unto my sickly heart.
  There wanteth now our brother Gloucester here   43
  To make the blessèd period of this peace.   44

BUCKINGHAM   And, in good time,
  Here comes Sir Richard Ratcliffe and the Duke.

     Enter Ratcliffe and [*Richard Duke of*] *Gloucester.*

RICHARD
  Good morrow to my sovereign king and queen;
  And, princely peers, a happy time of day!

KING EDWARD
  Happy, indeed, as we have spent the day.
  Gloucester, we have done deeds of charity,
  Made peace of enmity, fair love of hate,
  Between these swelling wrong-incensèd peers.   52

---

275 fain gladly. **Pilate** The Roman governor of Judaea who ordered the crucifixion of Jesus at the behest of the chief priests but symbolically washed his hands of the business (Matthew 27:24). **286 this will out** ("Murder will out" was a proverbial saying.)
2.1. Location: London. The royal court.
0.1 *Flourish* Trumpet call to announce the arrival of a distinguished person. **8 Dissemble** conceal, disguise (under a false appearance of love) **12 dally** trifle **14 Confound** defeat **15 Either . . . end** each of you to be the agent of death of the other.

19 son stepson **20 factious** quarrelsome **24 mine** my family and children. **26 protest** declare **33 but** and does not **38 Deep** subtle, crafty **41 cordial** restorative **43 wanteth** is lacking **44 period** conclusion **52 swelling** i.e., with anger or rivalry

RICHARD
A blessèd labor, my most sovereign lord.
Among this princely heap, if any here,   54
By false intelligence, or wrong surmise,   55
Hold me a foe;
If I unwittingly, or in my rage,
Have aught committed that is hardly borne   58
By any in this presence, I desire
To reconcile me to his friendly peace.
'Tis death to me to be at enmity;
I hate it, and desire all good men's love.
First, madam, I entreat true peace of you,
Which I will purchase with my duteous service;
Of you, my noble cousin Buckingham,
If ever any grudge were lodged between us;
Of you and you, Lord Rivers, and of Dorset,
That all without desert have frowned on me;   68
Dukes, earls, lords, gentlemen—indeed, of all.
I do not know that Englishman alive
With whom my soul is any jot at odds
More than the infant that is born tonight.   72
I thank my God for my humility.

QUEEN ELIZABETH
A holy day shall this be kept hereafter.
I would to God all strifes were well compounded.   75
My sovereign lord, I do beseech Your Highness
To take our brother Clarence to your grace.

RICHARD
Why, madam, have I offered love for this,
To be so flouted in this royal presence?   79
Who knows not that the gentle Duke is dead?   80

                                        They all start.

You do him injury to scorn his corpse.

KING EDWARD
Who knows not he is dead? Who knows he is?

QUEEN ELIZABETH
All-seeing heaven, what a world is this!

BUCKINGHAM
Look I so pale, Lord Dorset, as the rest?

DORSET
Ay, my good lord, and no man in the presence   85
But his red color hath forsook his cheeks.

KING EDWARD
Is Clarence dead? The order was reversed.

RICHARD
But he, poor man, by your first order died,
And that a wingèd Mercury did bear;   89
Some tardy cripple bare the countermand,   90
That came too lag to see him buried.   91

God grant that some, less noble and less loyal,   92
Nearer in bloody thoughts but not in blood,   93
Deserve not worse than wretched Clarence did,   94
And yet go current from suspicion!   95

                Enter [Lord Stanley] Earl of Derby.

STANLEY [kneeling]
A boon, my sovereign, for my service done!   96

KING EDWARD
I prithee, peace. My soul is full of sorrow.

STANLEY
I will not rise unless Your Highness hear me.

KING EDWARD
Then say at once what is it thou requests.

STANLEY
The forfeit, sovereign, of my servant's life,   100
Who slew today a riotous gentleman
Lately attendant on the Duke of Norfolk.

KING EDWARD
Have I a tongue to doom my brother's death,   103
And shall that tongue give pardon to a slave?   104
My brother killed no man; his fault was thought,
And yet his punishment was bitter death.
Who sued to me for him? Who, in my wrath,
Kneeled at my feet, and bid me be advised?   108
Who spoke of brotherhood? Who spoke of love?
Who told me how the poor soul did forsake
The mighty Warwick and did fight for me?
Who told me, in the field at Tewkesbury,
When Oxford had me down, he rescued me   113
And said, "Dear brother, live, and be a king"?
Who told me, when we both lay in the field
Frozen almost to death, how he did lap me   116
Even in his garments, and did give himself,
All thin and naked, to the numb-cold night?   118
All this from my remembrance brutish wrath
Sinfully plucked, and not a man of you
Had so much grace to put it in my mind.
But when your carters or your waiting vassals   122
Have done a drunken slaughter and defaced   123
The precious image of our dear Redeemer,   124
You straight are on your knees for pardon, pardon;   125
And I, unjustly too, must grant it you.

                                        [Stanley rises.]

But for my brother not a man would speak,
Nor I, ungracious, speak unto myself
For him, poor soul. The proudest of you all
Have been beholding to him in his life;   130

92–5 God . . . suspicion! i.e., (ironically) Pray God there be not persons who deserve worse than Clarence got, persons less noble or related by blood to the King than he, although closely involved in bloody plots, who yet go undetected! (Richard means the Queen and her kindred.) **95 go current** are accepted at face value (like legal currency). **from** free from **96 A boon** (I crave) a favor **100 The forfeit** i.e., The remission of the forfeit **103 doom** decree **104 slave** servant, wretch. **108 advised** cautious. **113 Oxford** (See 3 Henry VI, 5.5.2; this episode has no historical basis.) **116 lap** wrap **118 thin** thinly clad **122 your carters . . . vassals** your cart drivers or your attendants **123–4 defaced . . . Redeemer** i.e., killed a man. (God made humanity in his own image; Genesis 1:27.) **125 straight** at once **130 beholding** beholden

54 heap assembly **55 false intelligence** being misinformed **58 hardly borne** taken amiss, deeply resented **68 all without desert** wholly without my having deserved it **72 More than the infant** i.e., more than is that infant's soul **75 compounded** settled. **79 flouted** mocked **80 gentle** noble **85 presence** i.e., royal presence **89 Mercury** messenger of the classical gods **90 tardy cripple** (Richard privately shares with the audience a jest on his own role in this.) **bare** bore **91 lag** late

Yet none of you would once beg for his life.
O God, I fear thy justice will take hold
On me and you, and mine and yours, for this!
Come, Hastings, help me to my closet. Ah, poor Clarence!   134
     Exeunt some with King and Queen.

RICHARD

This is the fruits of rashness. Marked you not
How that the guilty kindred of the Queen
Looked pale when they did hear of Clarence' death?
Oh, they did urge it still unto the King.
God will revenge it. Come, lords, will you go   138
To comfort Edward with our company?

BUCKINGHAM We wait upon Your Grace. *Exeunt.*

❖

2.2

*Enter the old Duchess of York, with the two
children of Clarence, [Edward and Margaret
Plantagenet].*

BOY

Good grandam, tell us, is our father dead?

DUCHESS No, boy.

GIRL

Why do you weep so oft, and beat your breast,
And cry, "O Clarence, my unhappy son"?

BOY

Why do you look on us, and shake your head,
And call us orphans, wretches, castaways,
If that our noble father were alive?   7

DUCHESS

My pretty cousins, you mistake me both.   8
I do lament the sickness of the King,
As loath to lose him, not your father's death;
It were lost sorrow to wail one that's lost.

BOY

Then, you conclude, my grandam, he is dead.
The King mine uncle is to blame for it.
God will revenge it, whom I will importune   14
With earnest prayers all to that effect.

GIRL And so will I.

DUCHESS

Peace, children, peace! The King doth love you well.
Incapable and shallow innocents,   18
You cannot guess who caused your father's death.

BOY

Grandam, we can; for my good uncle Gloucester
Told me the King, provoked to it by the Queen,
Devised impeachments to imprison him;   22
And when my uncle told me so, he wept,
And pitied me, and kindly kissed my cheek;
Bade me rely on him as on my father,
And he would love me dearly as his child.

DUCHESS

Ah, that deceit should steal such gentle shape,
And with a virtuous visor hide deep vice!   28
He is my son—ay, and therein my shame;
Yet from my dugs he drew not this deceit.   30

BOY

Think you my uncle did dissemble, grandam?

DUCHESS Ay, boy.

BOY

I cannot think it. Hark, what noise is this?   33

*Enter the Queen [Elizabeth], with her hair about
her ears; Rivers and Dorset after her.*

QUEEN ELIZABETH

Ah, who shall hinder me to wail and weep,
To chide my fortune and torment myself?
I'll join with black despair against my soul,
And to myself become an enemy.

DUCHESS

What means this scene of rude impatience?   38

QUEEN ELIZABETH

To make an act of tragic violence.   39
Edward, my lord, thy son, our king, is dead!   40
Why grow the branches when the root is gone?
Why wither not the leaves that want their sap?
If you will live, lament; if die, be brief,   43
That our swift-wingèd souls may catch the King's
Or, like obedient subjects, follow him
To his new kingdom of ne'er-changing night.

DUCHESS

Ah, so much interest have I in thy sorrow
As I had title in thy noble husband!   48
I have bewept a worthy husband's death
And lived with looking on his images;   50
But now two mirrors of his princely semblance   51
Are cracked in pieces by malignant death,
And I for comfort have but one false glass,   53
That grieves me when I see my shame in him.   54
Thou art a widow; yet thou art a mother,
And hast the comfort of thy children left;
But death hath snatched my husband from mine arms
And plucked two crutches from my feeble hands,
Clarence and Edward. Oh, what cause have I,   59
Thine being but a moiety of my moan,   60
To overgo thy woes and drown thy cries!   61

BOY

Ah, aunt! You wept not for our father's death.
How can we aid you with our kindred tears?   63

28 **visor** mask 30 **dugs** breasts 33.1–2 ***with her ... ears*** (A conventional sign of grief.) 38 **rude impatience** violent unwillingness to accept misfortune. 39 **make** perform. (Continues the theatrical metaphor in the previous line.) 40 **Edward ... dead** (Clarence's death, February 1478, and Edward IV's death, April 1483, are treated as if they had occurred nearly together.) 43 **brief** quick 48 **title** i.e., as mother of the King 50 **images** likenesses; here, children 51 **two mirrors** i.e., Edward and Clarence. (The Duchess does not count Rutland.) 53 **false glass** i.e., Richard 54 **my ... him** a son of whom to be ashamed. 59 **what ... I** what a cause I have 60 **moiety of my moan** half (the cause) of my grief 61 **overgo** exceed 63 **kindred tears** i.e., tears of kinfolks.

134 **closet** private chambers. 138 **still** continually
2.2. Location: London. The royal court.
7 **If that** if 8 **cousins** kinfolks 14 **importune** solicit, beg
18 **Incapable** Unable to understand 22 **impeachments** accusations

GIRL
Our fatherless distress was left unmoaned;
Your widow-dolor likewise be unwept!   65

QUEEN ELIZABETH
Give me no help in lamentation;
I am not barren to bring forth complaints.   67
All springs reduce their currents to mine eyes,   68
That I, being governed by the watery moon,   69
May send forth plenteous tears to drown the world!
Ah for my husband, for my dear lord Edward!

CHILDREN
Ah for our father, for our dear lord Clarence!

DUCHESS
Alas for both, both mine, Edward and Clarence!

QUEEN ELIZABETH
What stay had I but Edward? And he's gone.   74

CHILDREN
What stay had we but Clarence? And he's gone.

DUCHESS
What stays had I but they? And they are gone.

QUEEN ELIZABETH
Was never widow had so dear a loss!   77

CHILDREN
Were never orphans had so dear a loss!

DUCHESS
Was never mother had so dear a loss!
Alas, I am the mother of these griefs;
Their woes are parceled, mine is general.   81
She for an Edward weeps, and so do I;
I for a Clarence weep, so doth not she.
These babes for Clarence weep, and so do I;
I for an Edward weep, so do not they.
Alas, you three, on me, threefold distressed,
Pour all your tears! I am your sorrow's nurse,   87
And I will pamper it with lamentation.   88

DORSET [to Queen Elizabeth]
Comfort, dear mother. God is much displeased
That you take with unthankfulness his doing.
In common worldly things 'tis called ungrateful
With dull unwillingness to repay a debt   92
Which with a bounteous hand was kindly lent;
Much more to be thus opposite with heaven   94
For it requires the royal debt it lent you.   95

RIVERS
Madam, bethink you like a careful mother
Of the young Prince your son. Send straight for him;
Let him be crowned. In him your comfort lives.
Drown desperate sorrow in dead Edward's grave

And plant your joys in living Edward's throne.

Enter Richard [Duke of Gloucester], Buckingham,
[Lord Stanley Earl of] Derby, Hastings, and
Ratcliffe.

RICHARD [to Queen Elizabeth]
Sister, have comfort. All of us have cause
To wail the dimming of our shining star,
But none can help our harms by wailing them.—
Madam, my mother, I do cry you mercy;   104
I did not see Your Grace. Humbly on my knee
I crave your blessing.   [He kneels.]

DUCHESS
God bless thee, and put meekness in thy breast,
Love, charity, obedience, and true duty!

RICHARD
Amen! [Aside] And make me die a good old man!
That is the butt end of a mother's blessing;   110
I marvel that Her Grace did leave it out.

BUCKINGHAM
You cloudy princes and heart-sorrowing peers,   112
That bear this heavy mutual load of moan,   113
Now cheer each other in each other's love.
Though we have spent our harvest of this king,
We are to reap the harvest of his son.
The broken rancor of your high-swoll'n hates,
But lately splintered, knit, and joined together,   118
Must gently be preserved, cherished, and kept.   119
Me seemeth good that with some little train   120
Forthwith from Ludlow the young Prince be fet   121
Hither to London, to be crowned our king.

RIVERS
Why with some little train, my lord of Buckingham?

BUCKINGHAM
Marry, my lord, lest by a multitude   124
The new-healed wound of malice should break out,
Which would be so much the more dangerous
By how much the estate is green and yet ungoverned.   127
Where every horse bears his commanding rein   128
And may direct his course as please himself,   129
As well the fear of harm, as harm apparent,   130
In my opinion, ought to be prevented.

RICHARD
I hope the King made peace with all of us;
And the compact is firm and true in me.

RIVERS
And so in me, and so, I think, in all.
Yet since it is but green, it should be put
To no apparent likelihood of breach,

65 widow-dolor widow's grief   67 barren to i.e., unable to. (She is pregnant with grief.)   68 All . . . eyes Let all springs be concentrated in my eyes   69 I . . . moon (Her grief is now a sea, fed by springs and her tides governed by the moon.)   74 stay support   77 dear costly, grievous   81 Their . . . general the woes of Queen Elizabeth and these children are particular to each of them, mine is all-embracing. 87 nurse source of sustenance   88 pamper feed luxuriously, nourish 92 dull sluggish   94 opposite with contrary toward   95 For it requires because it calls back

104 cry you mercy beg your pardon   110 butt end concluding portion. (The butt is the end of a spear shaft.)   112 cloudy clouded with grief   113 moan lamentation   118 But lately splintered only recently bound together (as with a splint)   119 Must . . . preserved i.e., the recent mending of differences must be preserved   120 Me seemeth It seems to me.   train entourage   121 Ludlow royal castle in Shropshire, near the Welsh border.   fet fetched   124 multitude i.e., large train or entourage   127 estate state, government.   green unripe, i.e., newly established   128 bears . . . rein controls the reins that ought to control him   129 as please as it pleases   130 As . . . apparent both the fear of trouble and the actual manifestation of it

Which haply by much company might be urged.   137
Therefore I say with noble Buckingham
That it is meet so few should fetch the Prince.   139

HASTINGS   And so say I.

RICHARD

Then be it so; and go we to determine
Who they shall be that straight shall post to Ludlow.   142
Madam, and you, my sister, will you go
To give your censures in this business?   144

QUEEN ELIZABETH, DUCHESS   With all our hearts.   145

Exeunt. Manent Buckingham and Richard.

BUCKINGHAM

My lord, whoever journeys to the Prince,
For God's sake let not us two stay at home;
For by the way I'll sort occasion,   148
As index to the story we late talked of,   149
To part the Queen's proud kindred from the Prince.

RICHARD

My other self, my counsel's consistory,   151
My oracle, my prophet! My dear cousin,
I, as a child, will go by thy direction,
Toward Ludlow then, for we'll not stay behind.

Exeunt.

❖

2.3

*Enter one Citizen at one door, and another at the
other.*

FIRST CITIZEN

Good morrow, neighbor. Whither away so fast?

SECOND CITIZEN

I promise you, I scarcely know myself.   2
Hear you the news abroad?

FIRST CITIZEN   Yes, that the King is dead.

SECOND CITIZEN

Ill news, by'r Lady; seldom comes the better.   5
I fear, I fear 'twill prove a giddy world.   6

Enter another Citizen.

THIRD CITIZEN

Neighbors, God speed!

FIRST CITIZEN   Give you good morrow, sir.

THIRD CITIZEN

Doth the news hold of good King Edward's death?   8

SECOND CITIZEN

Ay, sir, it is too true, God help the while!

THIRD CITIZEN

Then, masters, look to see a troublous world.   10

FIRST CITIZEN

No, no; by God's good grace his son shall reign.

THIRD CITIZEN

Woe to that land that's governed by a child!   12

SECOND CITIZEN

In him there is a hope of government,
Which in his nonage, council under him,   14
And in his full and ripened years, himself,
No doubt shall then, and till then, govern well.

FIRST CITIZEN

So stood the state when Henry the Sixth
Was crowned in Paris but at nine months old.

THIRD CITIZEN

Stood the state so? No, no, good friends, God wot,   19
For then this land was famously enriched
With politic, grave counsel; then the King   21
Had virtuous uncles to protect His Grace.

FIRST CITIZEN

Why, so hath this, both by his father and mother.

THIRD CITIZEN

Better it were they all came by his father,
Or by his father there were none at all;
For emulation who shall now be nearest
Will touch us all too near, if God prevent not.   26
Oh, full of danger is the Duke of Gloucester,
And the Queen's sons and brothers haught and proud!   29
And were they to be ruled, and not to rule,
This sickly land might solace as before.   31

FIRST CITIZEN

Come, come, we fear the worst. All will be well.

THIRD CITIZEN

When clouds are seen, wise men put on their cloaks;
When great leaves fall, then winter is at hand;
When the sun sets, who doth not look for night?
Untimely storms makes men expect a dearth.
All may be well; but if God sort it so,   37
'Tis more than we deserve or I expect.

SECOND CITIZEN

Truly, the hearts of men are full of fear.
You cannot reason almost with a man   40
That looks not heavily and full of dread.   41

THIRD CITIZEN

Before the days of change, still is it so.   42
By a divine instinct men's minds mistrust   43
Ensuing danger; as, by proof, we see   44
The water swell before a boist'rous storm.
But leave it all to God. Whither away?

SECOND CITIZEN

Marry, we were sent for to the justices.

THIRD CITIZEN

And so was I. I'll bear you company.   *Exeunt.*

❖

---

137 haply perhaps.   **urged** encouraged, provoked.   **139 meet** fitting
142 post hasten   **144 censures** judgments   **145.1 *Manent*** They
remain onstage   **148 by** on.   **sort** find, contrive   **149 index** prologue.   **late** lately   **151 consistory** council chamber
2.3. Location: London. A street.
2 promise assure   **5 Ill . . . better** Ill news, by Our Lady. Good news
comes seldom; most news is bad news.   **6 giddy** mad   **8 Doth the
news hold** Is the news true   **10 masters** good sirs.   **troublous** troubled, disorderly

12 Woe . . . child! (Compare with Ecclesiastes 10:16: "Woe to thee, O
land, when thy king is a child.")   **14 nonage** minority.   **council
under him** i.e., with the Privy Council governing in his name
19 wot knows   **21 politic** sagacious   **26 emulation** ambitious rivalry
29 haught haughty   **31 solace** be happy, have comfort   **37 sort** dispose   **40 You . . . man** There is scarcely anyone with whom you can
talk   **41 heavily** sad   **42 still** ever   **43 mistrust** suspect, fear
44 proof experience

2.4

Enter [the] Archbishop [of York], [the] young
[Duke of] York, the Queen [Elizabeth], and the
Duchess [of York].

ARCHBISHOP
　Last night, I hear, they lay at Stony Stratford,　　　　1
　And at Northampton they do rest tonight.　　　　　　2
　Tomorrow, or next day, they will be here.

DUCHESS
　I long with all my heart to see the Prince.
　I hope he is much grown since last I saw him.

QUEEN ELIZABETH
　But I hear, no; they say my son of York
　Has almost overta'en him in his growth.

YORK
　Ay, mother, but I would not have it so.

DUCHESS
　Why, my young cousin? It is good to grow.

YORK
　Grandam, one night as we did sit at supper,
　My uncle Rivers talked how I did grow
　More than my brother. "Ay," quoth my uncle Gloucester,
　"Small herbs have grace; great weeds do grow apace."　13
　And since, methinks, I would not grow so fast,　　　14
　Because sweet flow'rs are slow and weeds make haste.

DUCHESS
　Good faith, good faith, the saying did not hold　　　16
　In him that did object the same to thee.　　　　　　17
　He was the wretched'st thing when he was young,
　So long a-growing and so leisurely,
　That, if his rule were true, he should be gracious.

ARCHBISHOP
　And so no doubt he is, my gracious madam.

DUCHESS
　I hope he is, but yet let mothers doubt.

YORK
　Now, by my troth, if I had been remembered,　　　23
　I could have given my uncle's Grace a flout　　　　24
　To touch his growth nearer than he touched mine.　25

DUCHESS
　How, my young York? I prithee, let me hear it.

YORK
　Marry, they say my uncle grew so fast
　That he could gnaw a crust at two hours old;
　'Twas full two years ere I could get a tooth.
　Grandam, this would have been a biting jest.　　　30

DUCHESS
　I prithee, pretty York, who told thee this?

YORK　Grandam, his nurse.

DUCHESS
　His nurse? Why, she was dead ere thou wast born.

YORK
　If 'twere not she, I cannot tell who told me.

QUEEN ELIZABETH
　A parlous boy! Go to, you are too shrewd.　　　　35

DUCHESS
　Good madam, be not angry with the child.

QUEEN ELIZABETH　Pitchers have ears.　　　　　　37

Enter a Messenger.

ARCHBISHOP
　Here comes a messenger.—What news?

MESSENGER
　Such news, my lord, as grieves me to report.

QUEEN ELIZABETH
　How doth the Prince?

MESSENGER　　　　　　Well, madam, and in health.

DUCHESS　What is thy news?

MESSENGER
　Lord Rivers and Lord Grey are sent to Pomfret,　42
　And with them Sir Thomas Vaughan, prisoners.

DUCHESS
　Who hath committed them?

MESSENGER　　　　　　　　The mighty dukes
　Gloucester and Buckingham.

ARCHBISHOP　　　　　　　　For what offense?

MESSENGER
　The sum of all I can, I have disclosed.
　Why or for what the nobles were committed
　Is all unknown to me, my gracious lord.

QUEEN ELIZABETH
　Ay me, I see the ruin of my house!
　The tiger now hath seized the gentle hind;　　　　50
　Insulting tyranny begins to jut　　　　　　　　　51
　Upon the innocent and aweless throne.　　　　　52
　Welcome, destruction, blood, and massacre!
　I see, as in a map, the end of all.　　　　　　　54

DUCHESS
　Accursèd and unquiet wrangling days,
　How many of you have mine eyes beheld!
　My husband lost his life to get the crown,
　And often up and down my sons were tossed　　　58
　For me to joy and weep their gain and loss;
　And being seated, and domestic broils　　　　　60
　Clean overblown, themselves the conquerors　　61
　Make war upon themselves, brother to brother,
　Blood to blood, self against self. O preposterous　63

2.4. **Location: London. The royal court.**
1 **Stony Stratford** village in Buckinghamshire　2 **Northampton** town
in Northamptonshire and hence farther from London than Stony
Stratford. The Prince was taken back to Northampton after the arrest
of Rivers, Grey, and Vaughan. The Archbishop does not yet know of
that arrest, but the Folio version of his speech, followed here, is based
misleadingly on historical information of subsequent events. (The quartos reverse the order in which the two towns are named.) **13 grace**
virtuous qualities. **apace** rapidly. **14 since** ever since **16–17 the
saying . . . thee** the saying did not at all apply to the person who
applied it to you, i.e., Richard. **23 troth** truth, faith. **had been
remembered** had recollected **24 my . . . flout** His Grace, my uncle, a
mocking gibe **25 touch . . . nearer** i.e., taunt him about his growth
more tellingly **30 biting** (With a play on the idea of teething.)

35 **parlous** cunning, precocious. **Go to** (An expression of remonstrance.) **shrewd** sharp-tongued. **37 Pitchers have ears** Little
pitchers have large ears. (Proverbial.) **42 Pomfret** the castle at Pontefract in Yorkshire **50 hind** doe **51 Insulting** scornfully triumphing. **jut** encroach **52 aweless** inspiring no awe (because of the
youth of the King) **54 map** i.e., of future events **58 up . . . tossed**
i.e., my sons were raised and then lowered on fortune's wheel
60 seated i.e., on the throne **61 Clean overblown** entirely finished
63 preposterous monstrous, perverse

And frantic outrage, end thy damnèd spleen,
Or let me die, to look on death no more!

QUEEN ELIZABETH
Come, come, my boy, we will to sanctuary.
Madam, farewell.

DUCHESS   Stay, I will go with you.

QUEEN ELIZABETH
You have no cause.

ARCHBISHOP [to the Queen]   My gracious lady, go,
And thither bear your treasure and your goods.
For my part, I'll resign unto Your Grace
The seal I keep; and so betide to me   71
As well I tender you and all of yours!   72
Go, I'll conduct you to the sanctuary.   Exeunt.

❖

3.1

*The trumpets sound. Enter [the] young Prince
[Edward], the Dukes of Gloucester and
Buckingham, [Lord] Cardinal [Bourchier, Catesby],
etc.*

BUCKINGHAM
Welcome, sweet Prince, to London, to your chamber.   1

RICHARD
Welcome, dear cousin, my thoughts' sovereign!
The weary way hath made you melancholy.

PRINCE EDWARD
No, uncle, but our crosses on the way   4
Have made it tedious, wearisome, and heavy.
I want more uncles here to welcome me.   6

RICHARD
Sweet Prince, the untainted virtue of your years
Hath not yet dived into the world's deceit.
Nor more can you distinguish of a man
Than of his outward show—which, God he knows,
Seldom or never jumpeth with the heart.
Those uncles which you want were dangerous.   11
Your Grace attended to their sugared words
But looked not on the poison of their hearts.
God keep you from them, and from such false
    friends!

PRINCE EDWARD
God keep me from false friends! But they were none.

RICHARD
My lord, the Mayor of London comes to greet you.

Enter [the] Lord Mayor [and his train].

MAYOR   64
God bless Your Grace with health and happy days!

PRINCE EDWARD
I thank you, good my lord, and thank you all.   66
        [The Mayor and his train stand aside.]
I thought my mother and my brother York
Would long ere this have met us on the way.
Fie, what a slug is Hastings, that he comes not   22
To tell us whether they will come or no!

Enter Lord Hastings.

BUCKINGHAM
And, in good time, here comes the sweating lord.

PRINCE EDWARD
Welcome, my lord. What, will our mother come?

HASTINGS
On what occasion God he knows, not I,   26
The Queen your mother and your brother York
Have taken sanctuary. The tender Prince
Would fain have come with me to meet Your Grace,
But by his mother was perforce withheld.   30

BUCKINGHAM
Fie, what an indirect and peevish course   31
Is this of hers!—Lord Cardinal, will Your Grace
Persuade the Queen to send the Duke of York
Unto his princely brother presently?   34
If she deny, Lord Hastings, go with him,
And from her jealous arms pluck him perforce.   36

CARDINAL
My lord of Buckingham, if my weak oratory
Can from his mother win the Duke of York,
Anon expect him here; but if she be obdurate   39
To mild entreaties, God in heaven forbid
We should infringe the holy privilege
Of blessèd sanctuary! Not for all this land
Would I be guilty of so deep a sin.

BUCKINGHAM
You are too senseless-obstinate, my lord,
Too ceremonious and traditional.   45
Weigh it but with the grossness of this age,   46
You break not sanctuary in seizing him.
The benefit thereof is always granted
To those whose dealings have deserved the place
And those who have the wit to claim the place.
This prince hath neither claimed it nor deserved it,
And therefore, in mine opinion, cannot have it.
Then, taking him from thence that is not there,   53
You break no privilege nor charter there.
Oft have I heard of sanctuary men,
But sanctuary children never till now.

CARDINAL
My lord, you shall o'errule my mind for once.
Come on, Lord Hastings, will you go with me?

HASTINGS   I go, my lord.

PRINCE EDWARD
Good lords, make all the speedy haste you may.
                              [*Exeunt Cardinal and Hastings.*]
Say, uncle Gloucester, if our brother come,
Where shall we sojourn till our coronation?   62

RICHARD
Where it seems best unto your royal self.
If I may counsel you, some day or two
Your Highness shall repose you at the Tower;   65
Then where you please, and shall be thought most fit
For your best health and recreation.

PRINCE EDWARD
I do not like the Tower, of any place.   68
Did Julius Caesar build that place, my lord?

BUCKINGHAM
He did, my gracious lord, begin that place,
Which, since, succeeding ages have re-edified.   71

PRINCE EDWARD
Is it upon record, or else reported   72
Successively from age to age, he built it?

BUCKINGHAM   Upon record, my gracious lord.

PRINCE EDWARD
But say, my lord, it were not registered,   75
Methinks the truth should live from age to age,
As 'twere retailed to all posterity,   77
Even to the general all-ending day.   78

RICHARD [*aside*]
So wise so young, they say, do never live long.

PRINCE EDWARD   What say you, uncle?

RICHARD
I say, without characters fame lives long.   81
[*Aside*] Thus, like the formal Vice, Iniquity,   82
I moralize two meanings in one word.   83

PRINCE EDWARD
That Julius Caesar was a famous man;
With what his valor did enrich his wit,   85
His wit set down to make his valor live.   86
Death makes no conquest of this conqueror,
For now he lives in fame, though not in life.
I'll tell you what, my cousin Buckingham—

BUCKINGHAM   What, my gracious lord?

PRINCE EDWARD
An if I live until I be a man,   91
I'll win our ancient right in France again
Or die a soldier, as I lived a king.

RICHARD [*aside*]
Short summers lightly have a forward spring.   94

        Enter young York, Hastings, [and the] Cardinal.

BUCKINGHAM
Now, in good time, here comes the Duke of York.

PRINCE EDWARD
Richard of York, how fares our loving brother?   96

YORK
Well, my dread lord—so must I call you now.   97

PRINCE EDWARD
Ay, brother, to our grief, as it is yours.
Too late he died that might have kept that title,   99
Which by his death hath lost much majesty.

RICHARD
How fares our cousin, noble lord of York?

YORK
I thank you, gentle uncle. Oh, my lord,   102
You said that idle weeds are fast in growth;   103
The Prince my brother hath outgrown me far.

RICHARD
He hath, my lord.

YORK   And therefore is he idle?

RICHARD
Oh, my fair cousin, I must not say so.

YORK
Then he is more beholding to you than I.   107

RICHARD
He may command me as my sovereign,
But you have power in me as in a kinsman.

YORK
I pray you, uncle, give me this dagger.

RICHARD
My dagger, little cousin? With all my heart.   111

PRINCE EDWARD   A beggar, brother?

YORK
Of my kind uncle, that I know will give;   113
And being but a toy, which is no grief to give.   114

RICHARD
A greater gift than that I'll give my cousin.

YORK
A greater gift? Oh, that's the sword to it.

RICHARD
Ay, gentle cousin, were it light enough.

YORK
Oh, then I see you will part but with light gifts.   118
In weightier things you'll say a beggar nay.

RICHARD
It is too heavy for Your Grace to wear.

YORK
I weigh it lightly, were it heavier.   121

---

62 sojourn reside   **65 Tower** (Although in the fifteenth century—the historical time this play represents—the Tower of London was a royal palace, by Shakespeare's day it had acquired a sinister reputation.) **68 of any place** of all places.   **71 re-edified** rebuilt.   **72 upon record** in the written record.   **reported** i.e., by oral tradition   **75 say** suppose.   **registered** written down   **77 retailed** repeated, handed down from one to another   **78 general . . . day** Day of Judgment.   **81 without characters** even lacking written records   **82 formal Vice** i.e., the conventional Vice figure of the morality play, a comic tempter to evil, who would habitually *moralize two meanings in one word*, that is, play on double meanings in a single phrase, as Richard does in the phrase *live long*.   **83 moralize** interpret, illustrate   **85–6 With . . . live** having improved his understanding through his military achievements, he used his understanding to set down in writing an account (the *Gallic Wars*) that would make his valor immortal.   **91 An if** If

94 lightly commonly, often.   **forward** early. (Alludes to Edward's precociousness.)   **96 our** i.e., my. (The royal "we.")   **97 dread** inspiring reverential fear (as King)   **99 late** lately   **102 gentle** noble   **103 idle** worthless   **107 beholding** beholden   **111 With . . . heart** Willingly. (Richard combines in one phrase an overt generosity and a hidden threat.)   **113 that** who   **114 toy** trifle   **118 light** trivial   **121 I weigh . . . heavier** I consider it a trifle (playing on the literal meanings of "light" and "heavy") and would do so even if it were heavier.

RICHARD
    What, would you have my weapon, little lord?
YORK
    I would, that I might thank you as you call me.
RICHARD   How?
YORK   Little.   125
PRINCE EDWARD
    My lord of York will still be cross in talk.   126
    Uncle, Your Grace knows how to bear with him.
YORK
    You mean, to bear me, not to bear with me.
    Uncle, my brother mocks both you and me:
    Because that I am little, like an ape,
    He thinks that you should bear me on your shoulders.   131
BUCKINGHAM [aside to Hastings]
    With what a sharp-provided wit he reasons!   132
    To mitigate the scorn he gives his uncle,
    He prettily and aptly taunts himself.
    So cunning and so young is wonderful.
RICHARD [to the Prince]
    My lord, will't please you pass along?
    Myself and my good cousin Buckingham
    Will to your mother, to entreat of her
    To meet you at the Tower and welcome you.
YORK [to the Prince]
    What, will you go unto the Tower, my lord?
PRINCE EDWARD
    My Lord Protector needs will have it so.
YORK
    I shall not sleep in quiet at the Tower.
RICHARD   Why, what should you fear?
YORK
    Marry, my uncle Clarence' angry ghost.
    My grandam told me he was murdered there.
PRINCE EDWARD   I fear no uncles dead.
RICHARD   Nor none that live, I hope.
PRINCE EDWARD
    An if they live, I hope I need not fear.   148
    But come, my lord; with a heavy heart,
    Thinking on them, go I unto the Tower.   150
                    [A sennet.] Exeunt Prince, York,
                Hastings, [Cardinal, and others]. Manent
                    Richard, Buckingham, [and Catesby].
BUCKINGHAM
    Think you, my lord, this little prating York   151
    Was not incensèd by his subtle mother   152
    To taunt and scorn you thus opprobriously?

RICHARD
    No doubt, no doubt. Oh, 'tis a parlous boy,   154
    Bold, quick, ingenious, forward, capable.
    He is all the mother's, from the top to toe.
BUCKINGHAM
    Well, let them rest.—Come hither, Catesby.   157
    Thou art sworn as deeply to effect what we intend
    As closely to conceal what we impart.
    Thou know'st our reasons urged upon the way.   160
    What think'st thou? Is it not an easy matter
    To make William Lord Hastings of our mind
    For the installment of this noble Duke
    In the seat royal of this famous isle?
CATESBY
    He for his father's sake so loves the Prince   165
    That he will not be won to aught against him.
BUCKINGHAM
    What think'st thou, then, of Stanley? Will not he?
CATESBY
    He will do all in all as Hastings doth.
BUCKINGHAM
    Well, then, no more but this: go, gentle Catesby,
    And, as it were far off, sound thou Lord Hastings   170
    How he doth stand affected to our purpose,   171
    And summon him tomorrow to the Tower
    To sit about the coronation.   173
    If thou dost find him tractable to us,
    Encourage him, and tell him all our reasons.
    If he be leaden, icy, cold, unwilling,
    Be thou so too; and so break off the talk,
    And give us notice of his inclination.
    For we tomorrow hold divided councils,   179
    Wherein thyself shalt highly be employed.
RICHARD
    Commend me to Lord William. Tell him, Catesby,   181
    His ancient knot of dangerous adversaries   182
    Tomorrow are let blood at Pomfret Castle;   183
    And bid my lord, for joy of this good news,
    Give Mistress Shore one gentle kiss the more.   185
BUCKINGHAM
    Good Catesby, go, effect this business soundly.   186
CATESBY
    My good lords both, with all the heed I can.   187
RICHARD
    Shall we hear from you, Catesby, ere we sleep?
CATESBY   You shall, my lord.
RICHARD
    At Crosby House, there shall you find us both.
                                        Exit Catesby.

---

125 **Little** (York saucily suggests that he would give little thanks for such a "light" gift.)   126 **My . . . talk** i.e., My younger brother is always twisting words in his wittily perverse but annoying way.   131 **bear me . . . shoulders** (At fairs, the bear commonly carried an ape on his back. The speech is doubtless an allusion to Richard's hump and puns triply on *bear with*, "put up with," *bear*, "carry," and *bear*, "an animal.")   132 **sharp-provided** nimble and ready   148 **An if** If.   **they** i.e., Rivers and Grey. (Grey was, in fact, Edward's stepbrother, not his uncle. See the note to 1.3.37.)   150.1 **sennet** trumpet call to announce the approach or departure of processions.   150.2 *Manent* They remain onstage   151 **prating** chattering, prattling   152 **incensèd** incited

154 **parlous** clever, but also dangerous   157 **let them rest** leave them for the moment.   160 **the way** i.e., the journey to London from Ludlow.   165 **He . . . sake** i.e., Hastings for King Edward IV's sake   170 **sound** sound out   171 **doth stand affected** is disposed   173 **sit** sit in council   179 **divided councils** (While the regular Council meets about the coronation, Richard plans also to have his own private consultation at Crosby House.)   181 **Lord William** i.e., Hastings.   182 **knot** group   183 **are let blood** will be bled, i.e., executed   185 **Mistress Shore** (According to Thomas More, Jane Shore had become the mistress of Hastings after the death of Edward IV.)   186 **soundly** thoroughly.   187 **heed** attention, care

BUCKINGHAM
Now, my lord, what shall we do if we perceive
Lord Hastings will not yield to our complots?   192

RICHARD
Chop off his head. Something we will determine.
And look when I am king, claim thou of me   194
The earldom of Hereford and all the movables   195
Whereof the King my brother was possessed.

BUCKINGHAM
I'll claim that promise at Your Grace's hand.

RICHARD
And look to have it yielded with all kindness.
Come, let us sup betimes, that afterwards   199
We may digest our complots in some form.   *Exeunt.*   200

❖

3.2

Enter a Messenger to the door of Hastings.

MESSENGER   My lord! My lord!
HASTINGS [*within*]   Who knocks?
MESSENGER   One from the Lord Stanley.
HASTINGS [*within*]   What is 't o'clock?   4
MESSENGER   Upon the stroke of four.

Enter Lord Hastings.

HASTINGS
Cannot my Lord Stanley sleep these tedious nights?

MESSENGER
So it appears by that I have to say.
First, he commends him to your noble self.

HASTINGS   What then?

MESSENGER
Then certifies Your Lordship that this night   10
He dreamt the boar had razèd off his helm.   11
Besides, he says there are two councils kept,
And that may be determined at the one
Which may make you and him to rue at th'other.   14
Therefore he sends to know Your Lordship's pleasure,
If you will presently take horse with him   16
And with all speed post with him toward the north,
To shun the danger that his soul divines.

HASTINGS
Go, fellow, go, return unto thy lord.
Bid him not fear the separated councils.
His Honor and myself are at the one,   21
And at the other is my good friend Catesby,
Where nothing can proceed that toucheth us
Whereof I shall not have intelligence.   24
Tell him his fears are shallow, without instance.   25

And for his dreams, I wonder he's so simple   26
To trust the mock'ry of unquiet slumbers.
To fly the boar before the boar pursues   28
Were to incense the boar to follow us,
And make pursuit where he did mean no chase.
Go, bid thy master rise and come to me,
And we will both together to the Tower,
Where he shall see the boar will use us kindly.

MESSENGER
I'll go, my lord, and tell him what you say.   *Exit.*

Enter Catesby.

CATESBY
Many good morrows to my noble lord!

HASTINGS
Good morrow, Catesby. You are early stirring.
What news, what news, in this our tott'ring state?

CATESBY
It is a reeling world, indeed, my lord,
And I believe will never stand upright
Till Richard wear the garland of the realm.

HASTINGS
How? Wear the garland? Dost thou mean the crown?

CATESBY   Ay, my good lord.

HASTINGS
I'll have this crown of mine cut from my shoulders   43
Before I'll see the crown so foul misplaced.
But canst thou guess that he doth aim at it?

CATESBY
Ay, on my life, and hopes to find you forward   46
Upon his party for the gain thereof;   47
And thereupon he sends you this good news,
That this same very day your enemies,
The kindred of the Queen, must die at Pomfret.

HASTINGS
Indeed, I am no mourner for that news,
Because they have been still my adversaries.   52
But that I'll give my voice on Richard's side
To bar my master's heirs in true descent,
God knows I will not do it, to the death.   55

CATESBY
God keep Your Lordship in that gracious mind!

HASTINGS
But I shall laugh at this a twelvemonth hence,
That they which brought me in my master's hate,   58
I live to look upon their tragedy.   59
Well, Catesby, ere a fortnight make me older,
I'll send some packing that yet think not on 't.

CATESBY
'Tis a vile thing to die, my gracious lord,
When men are unprepared and look not for it.

---

192 complots conspiracies.   **194 look when** as soon as   **195 movables**
personal property, other than real estate   **199 betimes** early, soon
200 digest arrange, perfect.   **form** good order.
3.2. Location: Before Lord Hastings' house.
4 What is 't o'clock? What time is it?   **10 certifies** informs   **11 boar**
i.e., Richard.   **razèd** torn, slashed   **14 th'other** i.e., the regular Council meeting in the Tower, in which Hastings and Stanley will participate.   **16 presently** immediately   **21 His Honor** Lord Stanley
24 intelligence information.   **25 instance** grounds.

26 for as for.   **simple** simpleminded (as)   **28 fly** flee   **43 crown** i.e.,
head. (Recalls Stanley's dream in line 11 and anticipates Hastings'
execution by beheading.)   **46 forward** inclined   **47 Upon his party**
on his side   **52 still** always   **55 to the death** i.e., though I lose my
life. (A common asseveration, but here with ironic meaning.)
58–9 That . . . tragedy that I will live to see the fatal end of those who
brought me out of favor with King Edward IV.

HASTINGS

Oh, monstrous, monstrous! And so falls it out   64
With Rivers, Vaughan, Grey; and so 'twill do
With some men else, that think themselves as safe
As thou and I—who, as thou know'st, are dear
To princely Richard and to Buckingham.

CATESBY

The princes both make high account of you—   69
[Aside] For they account his head upon the Bridge.   70

HASTINGS

I know they do, and I have well deserved it.

Enter Lord Stanley [Earl of Derby].

Come on, come on, where is your boar spear, man?
Fear you the boar, and go so unprovided?

STANLEY

My lord, good morrow. Good morrow, Catesby.
You may jest on, but, by the Holy Rood,   75
I do not like these several councils, I.   76

HASTINGS   My lord,
I hold my life as dear as you do yours,
And never in my days, I do protest,
Was it so precious to me as 'tis now.
Think you, but that I know our state secure,   81
I would be so triumphant as I am?

STANLEY

The lords at Pomfret, when they rode from London,   83
Were jocund and supposed their states were sure,   84
And they indeed had no cause to mistrust;
But yet you see how soon the day o'ercast.   86
This sudden stab of rancor I misdoubt.   87
Pray God, I say, I prove a needless coward!
What, shall we toward the Tower? The day is spent.   89

HASTINGS

Come, come, have with you. Wot you what, my lord?   90
Today the lords you talk of are beheaded.

STANLEY

They, for their truth, might better wear their heads   92
Than some that have accused them wear their hats.   93
But come, my lord, let's away.   94

Enter a Pursuivant.

HASTINGS

Go on before. I'll talk with this good fellow.
Exit Lord Stanley [Earl of Derby] and Catesby.

How now, sirrah? How goes the world with thee?   96

PURSUIVANT

The better that Your Lordship please to ask.

HASTINGS

I tell thee, man, 'tis better with me now
Than when thou met'st me last where now we meet.
Then was I going prisoner to the Tower,
By the suggestion of the Queen's allies;   101
But now, I tell thee—keep it to thyself—
This day those enemies are put to death,
And I in better state than e'er I was.

PURSUIVANT

God hold it, to Your Honor's good content!   105

HASTINGS

Gramercy, fellow. There, drink that for me.   106

Throws him his purse.

PURSUIVANT   I thank Your Honor.   *Exit Pursuivant.*

Enter a Priest.

PRIEST

Well met, my lord. I am glad to see Your Honor.

HASTINGS

I thank thee, good Sir John, with all my heart.   109
I am in your debt for your last exercise;   110
Come the next Sabbath, and I will content you.   111

[He whispers in his ear.]

PRIEST   I'll wait upon Your Lordship.

Enter Buckingham.

BUCKINGHAM

What, talking with a priest, Lord Chamberlain?
Your friends at Pomfret, they do need the priest;
Your Honor hath no shriving work in hand.   115

HASTINGS

Good faith, and when I met this holy man,
The men you talk of came into my mind.
What, go you toward the Tower?

BUCKINGHAM

I do, my lord, but long I cannot stay there.
I shall return before Your Lordship thence.

HASTINGS

Nay, like enough, for I stay dinner there.   121

BUCKINGHAM   [aside]

And supper too, although thou know'st it not.—   122
Come, will you go?

HASTINGS   I'll wait upon Your Lordship.

Exeunt.

❧

---

64 so . . . out so it has happened   **69 high account** great estimation.
(The quibble on *high* appears in the next line.)   **70 account** expect,
reckon. (Punning on *account* in the previous line.)   **the Bridge** London Bridge, on a tower of which the heads of traitors were exposed.
75 Rood cross   **76 several** separate   **81 our state** the positions we
(Stanley and Hastings) occupy   **83 London** (An error for "Ludlow"?)
84 jocund merry   **86 o'ercast** became overcast.   **87 This . . . misdoubt**
This sudden rancorous vengeance (against Rivers, Vaughan, and Grey)
makes me uneasy.   **89 spent** i.e., well advanced (although the scene
began at 4:00 A.M.).   **90 have with you** let's go together.   **Wot** Know
92-3 They . . . hats They, for their honest loyalty (to King Edward and
now his son), might more justly be allowed to keep their heads than
some of their accusers wear their hats of office.   **94.1 Pursuivant**
attendant on a herald with authority to serve warrants.

96 sirrah (Form of address to inferiors.)   **101 suggestion** instigation
105 hold it continue it (i.e., the better state)   **106 Gramercy** Many
thanks   **109 Sir** (Common title for addressing any priest.)
110 exercise sermon or devotional exercise   **111 content** compensate
115 shriving work confession and absolution   **121 stay** stay for
122 And supper . . . not i.e., You won't be leaving as soon as you
think. (Also suggesting that Hastings will be a feast for worms.)

3.3

Enter Sir Richard Ratcliffe, with Halberds, carrying
the nobles [Rivers, Grey, and Vaughan] to death
at Pomfret.

RATCLIFFE   Come, bring forth the prisoners.

RIVERS
Sir Richard Ratcliffe, let me tell thee this:
Today shalt thou behold a subject die
For truth, for duty, and for loyalty.

GREY
God bless the Prince from all the pack of you!   5
A knot you are of damnèd bloodsuckers.   6

VAUGHAN
You live that shall cry woe for this hereafter.

RATCLIFFE
Dispatch. The limit of your lives is out.   8

RIVERS
O Pomfret, Pomfret! O thou bloody prison,
Fatal and ominous to noble peers!
Within the guilty closure of thy walls   11
Richard the Second here was hacked to death;
And, for more slander to thy dismal seat,   13
We give to thee our guiltless blood to drink.

GREY
Now Margaret's curse is fall'n upon our heads,
When she exclaimed on Hastings, you, and I,
For standing by when Richard stabbed her son.

RIVERS
Then cursed she Richard, then cursed she Buckingham,
Then cursed she Hastings. Oh, remember, God,
To hear her prayer for them, as now for us!
And for my sister and her princely sons,
Be satisfied, dear God, with our true blood,
Which, as thou know'st, unjustly must be spilt.

RATCLIFFE
Make haste. The hour of death is expiate.   24

RIVERS
Come, Grey, come, Vaughan, let us here embrace.
                                        [*They embrace.*]
Farewell, until we meet again in heaven.   *Exeunt.*

❧

3.4

Enter Buckingham, [Lord Stanley Earl of] Derby,
Hastings, Bishop of Ely, Norfolk, Ratcliffe, Lovell,
with others, at a table.

HASTINGS
Now, noble peers, the cause why we are met
Is to determine of the coronation.   2
In God's name, speak. When is the royal day?

BUCKINGHAM
Is all things ready for the royal time?

STANLEY
It is, and wants but nomination.   5

ELY
Tomorrow, then, I judge a happy day.   6

BUCKINGHAM
Who knows the Lord Protector's mind herein?
Who is most inward with the noble Duke?   8

ELY
Your Grace, methinks, should soonest know his mind.

BUCKINGHAM
We know each other's faces; for our hearts,   10
He knows no more of mine than I of yours,
Or I of his, my lord, than you of mine.
Lord Hastings, you and he are near in love.

HASTINGS
I thank His Grace, I know he loves me well;
But, for his purpose in the coronation,
I have not sounded him, nor he delivered
His gracious pleasure any way therein.
But you, my honorable lords, may name the time,
And in the Duke's behalf I'll give my voice,   19
Which I presume he'll take in gentle part.   20

Enter [Richard Duke of] Gloucester.

ELY
In happy time, here comes the Duke himself.

RICHARD
My noble lords and cousins all, good morrow.   22
I have been long a sleeper; but I trust
My absence doth neglect no great design   24
Which by my presence might have been concluded.

BUCKINGHAM
Had you not come upon your cue, my lord,
William Lord Hastings had pronounced your part,
I mean your voice for crowning of the King.

RICHARD
Than my Lord Hastings no man might be bolder.
His Lordship knows me well, and loves me well.—
My lord of Ely, when I was last in Holborn,   31
I saw good strawberries in your garden there.
I do beseech you send for some of them.

ELY
Marry, and will, my lord, with all my heart.
                                        Exit Bishop.

RICHARD
Cousin of Buckingham, a word with you.
                                  [*Drawing him aside.*]
Catesby hath sounded Hastings in our business,
And finds the testy gentleman so hot
That he will lose his head ere give consent
His master's child, as worshipfully he terms it,   39
Shall lose the royalty of England's throne.

3.3. Location: Pomfret (Pontefract) Castle.
5 pack gang   **6 knot** group   **8 Dispatch** Hurry.   **is out** has been
reached.   **11 closure** enclosure   **13 for . . . seat** i.e., to add further to
the evil reputation of this place   **24 expiate** fully come.
3.4. Location: London. The Tower.
2 determine of decide upon

5 wants but nomination lacks only naming of the day.   **6 happy**
favorable   **8 inward** intimate   **10 for** as for   **19 voice** vote
20 in gentle part with gracious acceptance.   **22 cousins** i.e., peers
24 neglect cause the neglect of   **31 Holborn** (location of the Bishop's
London palace)   **39 worshipfully** reverently. (Said contemptuously.)

BUCKINGHAM
Withdraw yourself awhile. I'll go with you.
Exeunt [Richard and Buckingham].
STANLEY
We have not yet set down this day of triumph.
Tomorrow, in my judgment, is too sudden,
For I myself am not so well provided   44
As else I would be, were the day prolonged.   45

Enter the Bishop of Ely.

ELY
Where is my lord the Duke of Gloucester?
I have sent for these strawberries.
HASTINGS
His Grace looks cheerfully and smooth this morning;   48
There's some conceit or other likes him well   49
When that he bids good morrow with such spirit.
I think there's never a man in Christendom
Can lesser hide his love or hate than he,
For by his face straight shall you know his heart.
STANLEY
What of his heart perceive you in his face
By any likelihood he showed today?
HASTINGS
Marry, that with no man here he is offended;
For, were he, he had shown it in his looks.
STANLEY   I pray God he be not, I say.

Enter Richard and Buckingham.

RICHARD
I pray you all, tell me what they deserve
That do conspire my death with devilish plots
Of damnèd witchcraft, and that have prevailed
Upon my body with their hellish charms?
HASTINGS
The tender love I bear Your Grace, my lord,   63
Makes me most forward in this princely presence
To doom th'offenders, whosoe'er they be:
I say, my lord, they have deservèd death.
RICHARD
Then be your eyes the witness of their evil.
                                        [He bares his arm.]
Look how I am bewitched! Behold, mine arm
Is like a blasted sapling withered up.   69
And this is Edward's wife, that monstrous witch,
Consorted with that harlot strumpet Shore,   71
That by their witchcraft thus have markèd me.
HASTINGS
If they have done this deed, my noble lord—
RICHARD
If? Thou protector of this damnèd strumpet,
Talk'st thou to me of "ifs"? Thou art a traitor.—
Off with his head! Now, by Saint Paul I swear,
I will not dine until I see the same.
Lovell and Ratcliffe, look that it be done.   78

The rest that love me, rise and follow me.   79
        *Exeunt. Manent Lovell and Ratcliffe, with the Lord
                                                Hastings.*
HASTINGS
Woe, woe for England! Not a whit for me,
For I, too fond, might have prevented this.   81
Stanley did dream the boar did raze our helms,
And I did scorn it and disdain to fly.
Three times today my footcloth horse did stumble,   84
And started, when he looked upon the Tower,
As loath to bear me to the slaughterhouse.
Oh, now I need the priest that spake to me!
I now repent I told the pursuivant,
As too triumphing, how mine enemies
Today at Pomfret bloodily were butchered,
And I myself secure in grace and favor.
O Margaret, Margaret, now thy heavy curse
Is lighted on poor Hastings' wretched head!
RATCLIFFE
Come, come, dispatch. The Duke would be at
    dinner.
Make a short shrift. He longs to see your head.   95
HASTINGS
Oh, momentary grace of mortal men,   96
Which we more hunt for than the grace of God!
Who builds his hope in air of your good looks   98
Lives like a drunken sailor on a mast,
Ready with every nod to tumble down
Into the fatal bowels of the deep.
LOVELL
Come, come, dispatch. 'Tis bootless to exclaim.   102
HASTINGS
Oh, bloody Richard! Miserable England!
I prophesy the fearful'st time to thee
That ever wretched age hath looked upon.
Come, lead me to the block; bear him my head.
They smile at me who shortly shall be dead.
                                            Exeunt.

❖

[3.5]

*Enter Richard [Duke of Gloucester] and
Buckingham in rotten armor, marvelous
ill-favored.*

RICHARD
Come, cousin, canst thou quake and change thy color,
Murder thy breath in middle of a word,   2
And then again begin, and stop again,
As if thou wert distraught and mad with terror?

79.1 *Manent* They remain onstage   **81 fond** foolish   **84 footcloth**
large, richly ornamented cloth laid over the back of a horse and hanging to the ground on each side.   **stumble** (An omen of misfortune.)
95 shrift confession.   **96 grace** favor, fortune   **98 Who** Anyone who.
in . . . looks on the insubstantial foundation of your favor   **102 bootless** useless
3.5. Location: London. The Tower.
0.2 *rotten* rusty   **0.2–3 *marvelous ill-favored*** remarkably unattractive.   **2 Murder** i.e., stop, catch

---

44 provided equipped   **45 prolonged** postponed.   **48 smooth** pleasant   **49 conceit** fancy, idea.   **likes** pleases   **63 tender** dear
69 blasted shriveled   **71 Consorted** associated   **78 look** see to it

BUCKINGHAM
Tut, I can counterfeit the deep tragedian,
Speak and look back, and pry on every side,   6
Tremble and start at wagging of a straw;
Intending deep suspicion, ghastly looks   8
Are at my service, like enforcèd smiles;
And both are ready in their offices,   10
At any time, to grace my stratagems.
But what, is Catesby gone?

RICHARD
He is; and, see, he brings the Mayor along.

        Enter the Mayor and Catesby.

BUCKINGHAM   Lord Mayor—
RICHARD   Look to the drawbridge there!
BUCKINGHAM   Hark, a drum!
RICHARD   Catesby, o'erlook the walls.   [*Exit Catesby.*]   17
BUCKINGHAM
Lord Mayor, the reason we have sent—
RICHARD
Look back, defend thee, here are enemies!
BUCKINGHAM
God and our innocence defend and guard us!

        Enter Lovell and Ratcliffe, with Hastings' head.

RICHARD
Be patient. They are friends, Ratcliffe and Lovell.
LOVELL
Here is the head of that ignoble traitor,
The dangerous and unsuspected Hastings.
RICHARD
So dear I loved the man that I must weep.
I took him for the plainest harmless creature
That breathed upon the earth a Christian,
Made him my book wherein my soul recorded   27
The history of all her secret thoughts.
So smooth he daubed his vice with show of virtue
That, his apparent open guilt omitted—   30
I mean, his conversation with Shore's wife—   31
He lived from all attainder of suspects.   32
BUCKINGHAM
Well, well, he was the covert'st sheltered traitor   33
That ever lived. Look ye, my Lord Mayor,
Would you imagine, or almost believe,   35
Were't not that by great preservation   36
We live to tell it, that the subtle traitor
This day had plotted, in the Council House,
To murder me and my good lord of Gloucester?
MAYOR   Had he done so?   39
RICHARD
What, think you we are Turks or infidels?
Or that we would, against the form of law,

Proceed thus rashly in the villain's death,
But that the extreme peril of the case,
The peace of England, and our persons' safety,
Enforced us to this execution?
MAYOR
Now fair befall you! He deserved his death,   47
And Your good Graces both have well proceeded   48
To warn false traitors from the like attempts.
BUCKINGHAM
I never looked for better at his hands
After he once fell in with Mistress Shore.
Yet had we not determined he should die   52
Until Your Lordship came to see his end,
Which now the loving haste of these our friends,
Something against our meanings, have prevented;   55
Because, my lord, we would have had you hear   56
The traitor speak and timorously confess
The manner and the purpose of his treasons,
That you might well have signified the same
Unto the citizens, who haply may   60
Misconster us in him and wail his death.   61
MAYOR
But, my good lord, Your Grace's words shall serve
As well as I had seen and heard him speak.   63
And do not doubt, right noble princes both,
But I'll acquaint our duteous citizens
With all your just proceedings in this cause.
RICHARD
And to that end we wished Your Lordship here,
T'avoid the censures of the carping world.
BUCKINGHAM
Which, since you come too late of our intent,   69
Yet witness what you hear we did intend.   70
And so, my good Lord Mayor, we bid farewell.
                                Exit Mayor.
RICHARD
Go, after, after, cousin Buckingham.
The Mayor towards Guildhall hies him in all post.   73
There, at your meet'st advantage of the time,   74
Infer the bastardy of Edward's children.   75
Tell them how Edward put to death a citizen
Only for saying he would make his son
Heir to the Crown—meaning indeed his house,   78
Which, by the sign thereof, was termèd so.   79
Moreover, urge his hateful luxury   80

And bestial appetite in change of lust,   81
Which stretched unto their servants, daughters, wives,   82
Even where his raging eye or savage heart,
Without control, lusted to make a prey.
Nay, for a need, thus far come near my person: 85
Tell them, when that my mother went with child   86
Of that insatiate Edward, noble York   87
My princely father then had wars in France,
And by true computation of the time
Found that the issue was not his begot—
Which well appearèd in his lineaments,   91
Being nothing like the noble duke my father.
Yet touch this sparingly, as 'twere far off,
Because, my lord, you know my mother lives.

BUCKINGHAM
Doubt not, my lord, I'll play the orator
As if the golden fee for which I plead
Were for myself. And so, my lord, adieu.   96

RICHARD
If you thrive well, bring them to Baynard's Castle,   98
Where you shall find me well accompanied
With reverend fathers and well-learnèd bishops.

BUCKINGHAM
I go; and towards three or four o'clock
Look for the news that the Guildhall affords.
                                        Exit Buckingham.

RICHARD
Go, Lovell, with all speed to Doctor Shaw.   103
[*To Ratcliffe*] Go thou to Friar Penker. Bid them both   104
Meet me within this hour at Baynard's Castle.
                                        Exeunt [all but Richard].
Now will I go to take some privy order   106
To draw the brats of Clarence out of sight,
And to give order that no manner person   108
Have any time recourse unto the princes.   *Exit.* 109

❖

[3.6]

Enter a Scrivener [with a paper in his hand].

SCRIVENER
Here is the indictment of the good Lord Hastings,
Which in a set hand fairly is engrossed   2
That it may be today read o'er in Paul's.   3
And mark how well the sequel hangs together: 4

Eleven hours I have spent to write it over,
For yesternight by Catesby was it sent me;
The precedent was full as long a-doing.   7
And yet within these five hours Hastings lived,
Untainted, unexamined, free, at liberty.   9
Here's a good world the while! Who is so gross   10
That cannot see this palpable device?
Yet who so bold but says he sees it not?
Bad is the world, and all will come to naught
When such ill dealing must be seen in thought.   14
                                                    Exit.

❖

[3.7]

*Enter Richard [Duke of Gloucester] and
Buckingham, at several doors.*

RICHARD
How now, how now, what say the citizens?

BUCKINGHAM
Now, by the holy mother of our Lord,
The citizens are mum, say not a word.

RICHARD
Touched you the bastardy of Edward's children?   4

BUCKINGHAM
I did; with his contract with Lady Lucy   5
And his contract by deputy in France;   6
Th'insatiate greediness of his desire   7
And his enforcement of the city wives;   8
His tyranny for trifles; his own bastardy,   9
As being got, your father then in France,   10
And his resemblance, being not like the Duke.
Withal I did infer your lineaments,   12
Being the right idea of your father   13
Both in your form and nobleness of mind;
Laid open all your victories in Scotland,   15
Your discipline in war, wisdom in peace,   16
Your bounty, virtue, fair humility;
Indeed, left nothing fitting for your purpose
Untouched or slightly handled in discourse.
And when mine oratory drew toward end,
I bid them that did love their country's good
Cry, "God save Richard, England's royal king!"

RICHARD   And did they so?

81 in . . . lust i.e., constantly desiring new mistresses   **82 their** i.e., the citizens'   **85 for a need** if necessary   **86–7 when . . . Of** when my mother was pregnant with   **91 his lineaments** Edward's features   **96 golden fee** i.e., crown   **98 Baynard's Castle** Richard's residence on the north bank of the Thames. It was founded by Baynard, a nobleman in the time of the Conquest, and had belonged to Richard's father.   **103, 104 Doctor Shaw, Friar Penker** (Well-known divines who delivered sermons in Richard's favor.)   **106 take . . . order** give some secret instruction   **108 no manner person** no one at all   **109 Have . . . recourse** have access at any time
3.6. Location: London. A street.
2 in . . . engrossed is written out in a style of script used for legal documents   **3 read . . . Paul's** posted and read publicly in St. Paul's Cathedral.   **4 the sequel** what follows

7 precedent prepared indictment serving as a first draft   **9 Untainted, unexamined** not yet accused or interrogated   **10 Here's . . . while!** Here's a fine state of affairs!   **gross** dull, stupid   **14 seen in thought** i.e., perceived in silence.
3.7. Location: The courtyard of Baynard's Castle.
0.2 several separate   **4 Touched you** Did you deal with, touch upon, discuss   **5 contract** betrothal   **Lady Lucy** Elizabeth Lucy (by whom Edward had a child, though there was no formal contract of betrothal)   **6 deputy** (See *3 Henry VI*, 3.3.49 ff., where Warwick, as deputy, contracts with Louis XI of France for the marriage of King Edward to Lady Bona, sister of the French queen.)   **7 Th'insatiate** the insatiable   **8 enforcement** forcible seduction   **9 tyranny for trifles** harsh punishment of minor offenses, or cruel behavior over trifles   **10 got begot**   **12 Withal . . . lineaments** Besides that, I pointed to your features   **13 right idea** true image   **15 Laid . . . Scotland** I elaborated on your successful expedition against Scotland in 1482   **16 discipline** skill, training

BUCKINGHAM
    No, so God help me, they spake not a word,
    But, like dumb statues or breathing stones,
    Stared each on other and looked deadly pale.
    Which when I saw, I reprehended them,
    And asked the Mayor what meant this willful silence.
    His answer was, the people were not used
    To be spoke to but by the Recorder.   30
    Then he was urged to tell my tale again:
    "Thus saith the Duke, thus hath the Duke inferred"—   32
    But nothing spake in warrant from himself.   33
    When he had done, some followers of mine own,
    At lower end of the hall, hurled up their caps,
    And some ten voices cried, "God save King Richard!"
    And thus I took the vantage of those few: 37
    "Thanks, gentle citizens and friends," quoth I,
    "This general applause and cheerful shout
    Argues your wisdoms and your love to Richard"—
    And even here brake off and came away.   41

RICHARD
    What tongueless blocks were they! Would they not speak?

BUCKINGHAM   No, by my troth, my lord.

RICHARD
    Will not the Mayor, then, and his brethren come?   44

BUCKINGHAM
    The Mayor is here at hand. Intend some fear;   45
    Be not you spoke with but by mighty suit.   46
    And look you get a prayer book in your hand,
    And stand between two churchmen, good my lord,
    For on that ground I'll make a holy descant;   49
    And be not easily won to our requests.
    Play the maid's part: still answer nay and take it.

RICHARD
    I go; and if you plead as well for them
    As I can say nay to thee for myself,
    No doubt we'll bring it to a happy issue.   54

BUCKINGHAM
    Go, go, up to the leads. The Lord Mayor knocks.   55
                                            [Exit Richard.]

    Enter the Mayor, [aldermen,] and citizens.

    Welcome, my lord. I dance attendance here;   56
    I think the Duke will not be spoke withal.   57

    Enter Catesby.

    Now, Catesby, what says your lord to my request?

CATESBY
    He doth entreat Your Grace, my noble lord,
    To visit him tomorrow or next day.
    He is within, with two right reverend fathers,
    Divinely bent to meditation,

    And in no worldly suits would he be moved
    To draw him from his holy exercise.

BUCKINGHAM
    Return, good Catesby, to the gracious Duke.
    Tell him myself, the Mayor and aldermen,
    In deep designs, in matter of great moment,
    No less importing than our general good,   68
    Are come to have some conference with His Grace.

CATESBY
    I'll signify so much unto him straight.   Exit.

BUCKINGHAM
    Aha, my lord, this prince is not an Edward!
    He is not lolling on a lewd love bed
    But on his knees at meditation;
    Not dallying with a brace of courtesans   74
    But meditating with two deep divines;   75
    Not sleeping, to engross his idle body,   76
    But praying, to enrich his watchful soul.
    Happy were England, would this virtuous prince
    Take on His Grace the sovereignty thereof;
    But sure I fear we shall not win him to it.

MAYOR
    Marry, God defend His Grace should say us nay!   81

BUCKINGHAM
    I fear he will.—Here Catesby comes again.

    Enter Catesby.

    Now, Catesby, what says His Grace?

CATESBY   My lord,
    He wonders to what end you have assembled
    Such troops of citizens to come to him,
    His Grace not being warned thereof before.
    He fears, my lord, you mean no good to him.

BUCKINGHAM
    Sorry I am my noble cousin should
    Suspect me that I mean no good to him.
    By heaven, we come to him in perfect love,
    And so once more return and tell His Grace.
                                        Exit [Catesby].

    When holy and devout religious men
    Are at their beads, 'tis much to draw them thence,   93
    So sweet is zealous contemplation.   94

    Enter Richard aloft, between two bishops. [Catesby
    returns to the main stage.]

MAYOR
    See where His Grace stands, 'tween two clergymen!

BUCKINGHAM
    Two props of virtue for a Christian prince,
    To stay him from the fall of vanity.   97
    And, see, a book of prayer in his hand,
    True ornaments to know a holy man.—   99
    Famous Plantagenet, most gracious prince,

---

30 the Recorder London's chief legal officer.   **32 inferred** alleged,
asserted   **33 in . . . himself** on his own authority.   **37 vantage**
advantage   **41 brake** broke   **44 brethren** fellow aldermen
45 Intend Pretend   **46 mighty suit** importunate entreaty.
49 ground the plainsong or melody on which a *descant* or melodious
accompaniment is raised   **54 issue** outcome.   **55 leads** flat lead coverings for roof; hence, the roof itself.   **56 dance attendance** i.e., am
kept waiting   **57 withal** with.

68 No less importing concerned with nothing less   **74 brace** pair
75 deep learned   **76 engross** fatten   **81 defend** forbid   **93 beads** i.e.,
prayers beads.   **much** hard.   **94.1 aloft** i.e., on the gallery above the
stage, rear. (The tiring-house facade in this scene is imagined to be the
facade of Baynard's Castle.)   **97 stay** steady or keep   **99 ornaments**
i.e., the bishops as well as the prayer book

Lend favorable ear to our requests,
And pardon us the interruption
Of thy devotion and right Christian zeal.

RICHARD

My lord, there needs no such apology.
I do beseech Your Grace to pardon me,
Who, earnest in the service of my God,
Deferred the visitation of my friends.
But, leaving this, what is Your Grace's pleasure?

BUCKINGHAM

Even that, I hope, which pleaseth God above,
And all good men of this ungoverned isle.

RICHARD

I do suspect I have done some offense
That seems disgracious in the city's eye,   112
And that you come to reprehend my ignorance.

BUCKINGHAM

You have, my lord. Would it might please Your Grace,
On our entreaties, to amend your fault!

RICHARD

Else wherefore breathe I in a Christian land?   116

BUCKINGHAM

Know then, it is your fault that you resign
The supreme seat, the throne majestical,
The sceptered office of your ancestors,
Your state of fortune and your due of birth,   120
The lineal glory of your royal house,
To the corruption of a blemished stock;   122
While, in the mildness of your sleepy thoughts,   123
Which here we waken to our country's good,
The noble isle doth want her proper limbs;   125
Her face defaced with scars of infamy,
Her royal stock graft with ignoble plants,   127
And almost shouldered in the swallowing gulf   128
Of dark forgetfulness and deep oblivion.
Which to recure, we heartily solicit   130
Your gracious self to take on you the charge
And kingly government of this your land—
Not as protector, steward, substitute,
Or lowly factor for another's gain,   134
But as successively from blood to blood,   135
Your right of birth, your empery, your own.   136
For this, consorted with the citizens,   137
Your very worshipful and loving friends,   138
And by their vehement instigation,
In this just cause come I to move Your Grace.

RICHARD

I cannot tell if to depart in silence
Or bitterly to speak in your reproof

Best fitteth my degree or your condition.   143
If not to answer, you might haply think   144
Tongue-tied ambition, not replying, yielded   145
To bear the golden yoke of sovereignty,
Which fondly you would here impose on me.   147
If to reprove you for this suit of yours,
So seasoned with your faithful love to me,   149
Then on the other side I checked my friends.   150
Therefore, to speak, and to avoid the first,
And then, in speaking, not to incur the last,
Definitively thus I answer you.   153
Your love deserves my thanks, but my desert   154
Unmeritable shuns your high request.   155
First, if all obstacles were cut away,
And that my path were even to the crown   157
As the ripe revenue and due of birth,   158
Yet so much is my poverty of spirit,
So mighty and so many my defects,
That I would rather hide me from my greatness—   161
Being a bark to brook no mighty sea—   162
Than in my greatness covet to be hid   163
And in the vapor of my glory smothered.
But, God be thanked, there is no need of me,
And much I need to help you, were there need.   166
The royal tree hath left us royal fruit,
Which, mellowed by the stealing hours of time,   168
Will well become the seat of majesty
And make, no doubt, us happy by his reign.
On him I lay that you would lay on me,   171
The right and fortune of his happy stars,
Which God defend that I should wring from him!   173

BUCKINGHAM

My lord, this argues conscience in Your Grace;
But the respects thereof are nice and trivial,   175
All circumstances well consideréd.
You say that Edward is your brother's son.
So say we too, but not by Edward's wife;
For first was he contract to Lady Lucy—   179
Your mother lives a witness to his vow—   180
And afterward by substitute betrothed   181
To Bona, sister to the King of France.   182
These both put off, a poor petitioner,
A care-crazed mother to a many sons,

143 degree rank. **condition** social status. **144 haply** perhaps
145 Tongue-tied silent. (Silence gives consent.) **yielded** consented
147 fondly foolishly **149 seasoned** i.e., made agreeable or palatable
150 checked rebuked, i.e., would have rebuked **153 Definitively**
once and for all **154–5 my desert Unmeritable** my unworthiness
157 even smooth **158 ripe revenue** possession ready to be inherited
161 my greatness i.e., my claim to the throne **162 bark** ship. **brook**
endure **163 Than . . . hid** than wish to be enveloped in and overwhelmed by my greatness, i.e., the throne. **166 I need** I lack the requisite ability **168 stealing** stealthily moving **171 that** what
173 defend forbid **175 respects thereof** considerations by which
you support your argument. **nice** overscrupulous **179 contract**
contracted **180 Your . . . vow** (According to the chronicles, Richard's
mother, in opposing Edward's intention of marrying Lady Grey because
it was interfering with the negotiations for his marriage to Lady Bona
of Savoy, asserted that Lady Elizabeth Lucy was already Edward's
trothplight wife. Compare with 3.5.75 and 3.7.6.) **181 substitute**
proxy **182 sister** i.e., sister-in-law, the Queen's sister

112 disgracious unbecoming, displeasing **116 Else . . . land?** i.e.,
How could I call myself a Christian if I am not prepared to amend my
faults? **120 state of fortune** position to which fortune entitles you
122 blemished i.e., through bastardy; see lines 177–91 below
123 sleepy passive **125 want her proper limbs** lack its own limbs, is
crippled **127 graft** engrafted **128 shouldered in** jostled into, or
immersed up to the shoulders in **130 recure** restore, make whole
134 factor agent **135 successively** in order of succession **136 empery**
empire **137 consorted** associated, leagued **138 worshipful** respectful

A beauty-waning and distressèd widow,
Even in the afternoon of her best days,
Made prize and purchase of his wanton eye,   187
Seduced the pitch and height of his degree   188
To base declension and loathed bigamy.   189
By her, in his unlawful bed, he got
This Edward, whom our manners call the Prince.   191
More bitterly could I expostulate,   192
Save that, for reverence to some alive,   193
I give a sparing limit to my tongue.
Then, good my lord, take to your royal self   195
This proffered benefit of dignity,
If not to bless us and the land withal,
Yet to draw forth your noble ancestry   198
From the corruption of abusing times
Unto a lineal true-derivèd course.

MAYOR
Do, good my lord. Your citizens entreat you.

BUCKINGHAM
Refuse not, mighty lord, this proffered love.

CATESBY
Oh, make them joyful. Grant their lawful suit!

RICHARD
Alas, why would you heap this care on me?
I am unfit for state and majesty.
I do beseech you, take it not amiss;
I cannot nor I will not yield to you.

BUCKINGHAM
If you refuse it—as, in love and zeal,   208
Loath to depose the child, your brother's son,
As well we know your tenderness of heart   210
And gentle, kind, effeminate remorse,   211
Which we have noted in you to your kindred
And equally indeed to all estates—   213
Yet know, whe'er you accept our suit or no,   214
Your brother's son shall never reign our king,
But we will plant some other in the throne
To the disgrace and downfall of your house.
And in this resolution here we leave you.—
Come, citizens. Zounds! I'll entreat no more.   219

RICHARD
Oh, do not swear, my lord of Buckingham.
                                    Exeunt [Buckingham,
                                    Mayor, aldermen, and the citizens].

CATESBY
Call him again, sweet prince. Accept their suit.
If you deny them, all the land will rue it.

RICHARD
Will you enforce me to a world of cares?
Call them again. I am not made of stone,
But penetrable to your kind entreaties,
Albeit against my conscience and my soul.

                    Enter Buckingham and the rest.

Cousin of Buckingham, and sage, grave men,
Since you will buckle fortune on my back,
To bear her burden, whe'er I will or no,
I must have patience to endure the load.
But if black scandal or foul-faced reproach
Attend the sequel of your imposition,   232
Your mere enforcement shall acquittance me   233
From all the impure blots and stains thereof;
For God doth know, and you may partly see,
How far I am from the desire of this.

MAYOR
God bless Your Grace! We see it and will say it.

RICHARD
In saying so, you shall but say the truth.

BUCKINGHAM
Then I salute you with this royal title:
Long live Richard, England's worthy king!

MAYOR AND CITIZENS   Amen.

BUCKINGHAM
Tomorrow may it please you to be crowned?

RICHARD
Even when you please, for you will have it so.

BUCKINGHAM
Tomorrow, then, we will attend Your Grace.
And so most joyfully we take our leave.

RICHARD [*to the Bishops*]
Come, let us to our holy work again.—
Farewell, my cousin. Farewell, gentle friends. *Exeunt.*

                              ❧

4.1

                    *Enter [at one door] the Queen [Elizabeth], the
                    Duchess of York, and Marquess [of] Dorset; [at
                    another door] Anne, Duchess of Gloucester,
                    [leading Lady Margaret Plantagenet, Clarence's
                    young daughter].*

DUCHESS
Who meets us here? My niece Plantagenet   1
Led in the hand of her kind aunt of Gloucester?
Now, for my life, she's wand'ring to the Tower,   3
On pure heart's love to greet the tender Prince.   4
Daughter, well met.

ANNE   God give Your Graces both   5
A happy and a joyful time of day!

QUEEN ELIZABETH
As much to you, good sister. Whither away?   7

187 purchase booty   **188–9 Seduced . . . declension** i.e., seduced him
away from his high rank to ignoble decline. (*Pitch* is the highest point
in a falcon's flight.)   **189 bigamy** (Edward was not only bound by
previous contracts, as indicated in lines 178–82 above, but also, by
marrying a widow, entered into a union that was widely regarded as
bigamous.)   **191 manners** sense of politeness   **192 expostulate** discuss, dilate   **193 some alive** i.e., the Duchess of York. (See 3.5.93–4.)
195 good my lord my good lord   **198 draw forth** rescue, extract
208 as from being   **210 As . . . know** since we know well   **211 kind,
effeminate remorse** natural, tender pity   **213 estates** ranks. (Buckingham argues that this virtue of pity is found in Richard's treatment
of everyone.)   **214 whe'er** whether   **219 Zounds!** By His (God's)
wounds!

232 your imposition the duty that you lay upon me   **233 Your . . .
acquittance me** the mere fact of your insistence will exonerate me
4.1. Location: London. Before the Tower.
1 niece i.e., granddaughter   **3 for** on   **4 On** out of.   **tender** young
5 Daughter i.e., Daughter-in-law   **7 sister** i.e., sister-in-law.

ANNE
No farther than the Tower, and, as I guess,
Upon the like devotion as yourselves,
To gratulate the gentle princes there.   9
                                                                    10
QUEEN ELIZABETH
Kind sister, thanks. We'll enter all together.

Enter [Brackenbury] the Lieutenant.

And, in good time, here the Lieutenant comes.—
Master Lieutenant, pray you, by your leave,
How doth the Prince and my young son of York?
BRACKENBURY
Right well, dear madam. By your patience,
I may not suffer you to visit them;
The King hath strictly charged the contrary.   16
QUEEN ELIZABETH
The King! Who's that?
BRACKENBURY   I mean the Lord Protector.
QUEEN ELIZABETH
The Lord protect him from that kingly title!
Hath he set bounds between their love and me?
I am their mother; who shall bar me from them?   20
DUCHESS
I am their father's mother; I will see them.
ANNE
Their aunt I am in law, in love their mother;
Then bring me to their sights. I'll bear thy blame
And take thy office from thee, on my peril.   25
BRACKENBURY
No, madam, no; I may not leave it so.
I am bound by oath, and therefore pardon me.
                                                Exit Lieutenant.

Enter [Lord] Stanley [Earl of Derby].

STANLEY
Let me but meet you, ladies, one hour hence,
And I'll salute Your Grace of York as mother,   29
And reverend looker-on, of two fair queens.   30
[To Anne] Come, madam, you must straight to
    Westminster,
There to be crownèd Richard's royal queen.
QUEEN ELIZABETH   Ah, cut my lace asunder,   33
That my pent heart may have some scope to beat,
Or else I swoon with this dead-killing news!
ANNE
Despiteful tidings! Oh, unpleasing news!
DORSET
Be of good cheer. Mother, how fares Your Grace?
QUEEN ELIZABETH
Oh, Dorset, speak not to me. Get thee gone!
Death and destruction dogs thee at thy heels;
Thy mother's name is ominous to children.
If thou wilt outstrip death, go cross the seas

And live with Richmond, from the reach of hell.   42
Go, hie thee, hie thee from this slaughterhouse,   43
Lest thou increase the number of the dead
And make me die the thrall of Margaret's curse,   45
Nor mother, wife, nor England's counted queen.   46
STANLEY
Full of wise care is this your counsel, madam.
[To Dorset] Take all the swift advantage of the hours.
You shall have letters from me to my son   49
In your behalf, to meet you on the way.   50
Be not ta'en tardy by unwise delay.   51
DUCHESS
Oh, ill-dispersing wind of misery!   52
Oh, my accursèd womb, the bed of death!
A cockatrice hast thou hatched to the world,   54
Whose unavoided eye is murderous.
STANLEY *[to Anne]*
Come, madam, come. I in all haste was sent.
ANNE
And I with all unwillingness will go.
Oh, would to God that the inclusive verge   58
Of golden metal that must round my brow
Were red-hot steel, to sear me to the brains!
Anointed let me be with deadly venom   61
And die ere men can say, "God save the Queen!"
QUEEN ELIZABETH
Go, go, poor soul. I envy not thy glory.
To feed my humor, wish thyself no harm.   64
ANNE
No? Why? When he that is my husband now
Came to me, as I followed Henry's corpse,
When scarce the blood was well washed from his hands
Which issued from my other angel husband   68
And that dear saint which then I weeping followed— 69
Oh, when, I say, I looked on Richard's face,
This was my wish: "Be thou," quoth I, "accurst
For making me, so young, so old a widow!   72
And, when thou wed'st, let sorrow haunt thy bed;
And be thy wife—if any be so mad—
More miserable by the life of thee
Than thou hast made me by my dear lord's death!"
Lo, ere I can repeat this curse again,
Within so small a time, my woman's heart
Grossly grew captive to his honey words   79
And proved the subject of mine own soul's curse,

---

9 **like devotion** same devout errand   10 **gratulate** greet, salute
16 **suffer** permit   20 **bounds** barriers   25 **take . . . thee** i.e., relieve
you of the responsibility   29 **mother** i.e., mother-in-law (of Elizabeth
as widow of Edward and of Anne as wife of King Richard)
30 **looker-on** beholder.   **two fair queens** i.e., Elizabeth and Anne,
since Anne's husband, Richard, is about to be crowned.   33 **lace** cord
used to lace the bodice

42 **with Richmond** i.e., with Henry Tudor, Earl of Richmond, at this
time in Brittany   43 **hie** hasten   45 **thrall** subject, victim   46 **Nor**
neither.   **counted** accepted, esteemed   49–50 **You . . . way** i.e., I will
arrange to have a letter catch up with you on your journey, recom-
mending you to my stepson, the Earl of Richmond. (Lord Stanley's
own son, George Stanley, may also be involved in this rapid negotiation; see 4.4.494–6 ff. below.)   51 **ta'en** taken, caught   52 **ill-dispersing**
evil-spreading   54 **cockatrice** basilisk. (See the note for 1.2.153.)
58 **inclusive verge** enclosing circle, i.e., the crown, here likened to an
instrument of torture used to punish regicides or other criminals
61 **Anointed** (Anne desires to be anointed with poison rather than
with holy oil, as in the ceremony of coronation.)   64 **To . . . harm** Do
not curse yourself (or, possibly, I do not wish you harm) just to satisfy
my vengeful mood.   68 **angel husband** Edward, son of Henry VI
69 **saint** Henry VI   72 **so old a widow** i.e., destined to live so long as
a widow.   79 **Grossly** stupidly

Which hitherto hath held mine eyes from rest;   81
For never yet one hour in his bed
Did I enjoy the golden dew of sleep,
But with his timorous dreams was still awaked.   84
Besides, he hates me for my father Warwick,
And will, no doubt, shortly be rid of me.

QUEEN ELIZABETH
    Poor heart, adieu! I pity thy complaining.

ANNE
    No more than with my soul I mourn for yours.

DORSET
    Farewell, thou woeful welcomer of glory!   89

ANNE
    Adieu, poor soul, that tak'st thy leave of it!

DUCHESS [to Dorset]
    Go thou to Richmond, and good fortune guide thee!
    [To Anne] Go thou to Richard, and good angels tend thee!
    [To Queen Elizabeth] Go thou to sanctuary, and good
        thoughts possess thee!
    I to my grave, where peace and rest lie with me!
    Eighty-odd years of sorrow have I seen,
    And each hour's joy wracked with a week of teen.   96
                                        [They start to go.]

QUEEN ELIZABETH
    Stay, yet look back with me unto the Tower.
    Pity, you ancient stones, those tender babes
    Whom envy hath immured within your walls—   99
    Rough cradle for such little pretty ones!
    Rude ragged nurse, old sullen playfellow   101
    For tender princes, use my babies well!
    So foolish sorrows bids your stones farewell.   *Exeunt.*

❖

4.2

*Sound a sennet. Enter Richard, in pomp;
Buckingham, Catesby, Ratcliffe, Lovell, [a Page,
and others].*

KING RICHARD
    Stand all apart. Cousin of Buckingham!   1
                [The others stand aside, out of earshot.]

BUCKINGHAM   My gracious sovereign?

KING RICHARD
    Give me thy hand.
                Sound [trumpets. Here he ascends the throne.]
                        Thus high, by thy advice
    And thy assistance, is King Richard seated.
    But shall we wear these glories for a day?
    Or shall they last, and we rejoice in them?

BUCKINGHAM
    Still live they, and forever let them last!

KING RICHARD
    Ah, Buckingham, now do I play the touch,   8
    To try if thou be current gold indeed: 9
    Young Edward lives. Think now what I would speak.

BUCKINGHAM   Say on, my loving lord.

KING RICHARD
    Why, Buckingham, I say I would be king.

BUCKINGHAM
    Why, so you are, my thrice-renownèd lord.

KING RICHARD
    Ha! Am I king? 'Tis so. But Edward lives.

BUCKINGHAM
    True, noble prince.

KING RICHARD   Oh, bitter consequence,   15
    That Edward still should live "true, noble prince"!   16
    Cousin, thou wast not wont to be so dull.   17
    Shall I be plain? I wish the bastards dead,
    And I would have it suddenly performed.   19
    What say'st thou now? Speak suddenly; be brief.

BUCKINGHAM   Your Grace may do your pleasure.

KING RICHARD
    Tut, tut, thou art all ice; thy kindness freezes.
    Say, have I thy consent that they shall die?

BUCKINGHAM
    Give me some little breath, some pause, dear lord,
    Before I positively speak in this.
    I will resolve you herein presently.   *Exit Buckingham.* 26

CATESBY [to those standing aside]
    The King is angry. See, he gnaws his lip.

KING RICHARD [aside]
    I will converse with iron-witted fools   28
    And unrespective boys. None are for me   29
    That look into me with considerate eyes.   30
    High-reaching Buckingham grows circumspect.—   31
    Boy!

PAGE [approaching]   My lord?

KING RICHARD
    Know'st thou not any whom corrupting gold
    Will tempt unto a close exploit of death?   35

PAGE
    My lord, I know a discontented gentleman
    Whose humble means match not his haughty spirit.
    Gold were as good as twenty orators,
    And will, no doubt, tempt him to anything.

KING RICHARD
    What is his name?

PAGE   His name, my lord, is Tyrrel.

KING RICHARD
    I partly know the man. Go call him hither, boy.
                                        Exit [Page].

---

81 **hitherto** until now   84 **timorous** full of fears.   **still** continually
89 **glory** i.e., the rank of queen—*woeful* because it involves marriage
to Richard.   96 **wracked** destroyed, or, *racked*, tortured.   **teen** woe.
99 **envy** malice.   **immured** walled up   101 **Rude** Rough
4.2. Location: London. The royal court.
1 **apart** aside.

8 **play the touch** play the part of a touchstone (to test the quality of
gold)   9 **current** sterling, genuine   15 **bitter consequence** i.e., intolerable answer to my words, and an intolerable fact   16 **"true, noble
prince"** (Richard mockingly repeats Buckingham's evasive reply in
line 15 and applies it to the irritating fact that young Edward still
lives and is a noble prince.)   17 **wast not wont** used not   19 **suddenly** swiftly   26 **resolve** answer   28–31 **I will . . . circumspect** i.e.,
Apparently I have no choice but to communicate my intentions to
dim-witted fools and inattentive boys. I will have nothing more to do
with men who look into my thoughts too searchingly. Ambitious
Buckingham grows wary.   35 **close** secret

[*Aside*] The deep-revolving, witty Buckingham
No more shall be the neighbor to my counsels.
Hath he so long held out with me untired,
And stops he now for breath? Well, be it so.

Enter [Lord] Stanley [Earl of Derby].

How now, Lord Stanley? What's the news?
STANLEY   Know, my loving lord,
The Marquess Dorset, as I hear, is fled
To Richmond, in the parts where he abides.
                                         [*He stands apart.*]
KING RICHARD
Come hither, Catesby. Rumor it abroad
That Anne my wife is very grievous sick;
I will take order for her keeping close.   52
Inquire me out some mean poor gentleman,   53
Whom I will marry straight to Clarence' daughter.
The boy is foolish, and I fear not him.   55
Look how thou dream'st! I say again, give out
That Anne my queen is sick and like to die.   57
About it, for it stands me much upon   58
To stop all hopes whose growth may damage me.
                                              [*Exit Catesby.*]
I must be married to my brother's daughter,   60
Or else my kingdom stands on brittle glass.
Murder her brothers, and then marry her—
Uncertain way of gain! But I am in
So far in blood that sin will pluck on sin.   64
Tear-falling pity dwells not in this eye.   65

Enter [Page, with] Tyrrel.

Is thy name Tyrrel?
TYRREL
James Tyrrel, and your most obedient subject.
KING RICHARD
Art thou, indeed?
TYRREL   Prove me, my gracious lord.   68
KING RICHARD
Dar'st thou resolve to kill a friend of mine?
TYRREL   Please you;   70
But I had rather kill two enemies.
KING RICHARD
Why, there thou hast it: two deep enemies,
Foes to my rest and my sweet sleep's disturbers
Are they that I would have thee deal upon—   74
Tyrrel, I mean those bastards in the Tower.
TYRREL
Let me have open means to come to them,   76
And soon I'll rid you from the fear of them.

KING RICHARD   42
Thou sing'st sweet music. Hark, come hither, Tyrrel.
Go, by this token. [*He gives him a token.*] Rise, and lend
   thine ear.   *Whispers.*
There is no more but so. Say it is done,
And I will love thee and prefer thee for it.   81
TYRREL   I will dispatch it straight.   *Exit.*

Enter Buckingham.

BUCKINGHAM
My lord, I have considered in my mind
The late request that you did sound me in.   84
KING RICHARD
Well, let that rest. Dorset is fled to Richmond.
BUCKINGHAM   I hear the news, my lord.
KING RICHARD
Stanley, he is your wife's son. Well, look to it.   87
BUCKINGHAM
My lord, I claim the gift, my due by promise,
For which your honor and your faith is pawned: 89
Th'earldom of Hereford and the movables
Which you have promisèd I shall possess.
KING RICHARD
Stanley, look to your wife. If she convey
Letters to Richmond, you shall answer it.   93
BUCKINGHAM
What says Your Highness to my just request?
KING RICHARD
I do remember me, Henry the Sixth
Did prophesy that Richmond should be king,
When Richmond was a little peevish boy.
A king! Perhaps, perhaps—
BUCKINGHAM   My lord!
KING RICHARD
How chance the prophet could not at that time   100
Have told me, I being by, that I should kill him?   101
BUCKINGHAM
My lord, your promise for the earldom!
KING RICHARD
Richmond! When last I was at Exeter,
The Mayor in courtesy showed me the castle
And called it Rougemont, at which name I started, 105
Because a bard of Ireland told me once
I should not live long after I saw Richmond.
BUCKINGHAM   My lord!
KING RICHARD   Ay, what's o'clock?   109
BUCKINGHAM
I am thus bold to put Your Grace in mind
Of what you promised me.
KING RICHARD   Well, but what's o'clock?
BUCKINGHAM   Upon the stroke of ten.
KING RICHARD   Well, let it strike.
BUCKINGHAM   Why let it strike?

---

42 **deep-revolving** deeply scheming.   **witty** cunning   52 **I will . . .
close** I will give orders for her close confinement.   53 **mean** of humble station   55 **boy** i.e., Clarence's eldest son, Edward Plantagenet,
Earl of Warwick   57 **like** likely   58 **stands . . . upon** is a matter of the
utmost importance to me   60 **brother's daughter** i.e., Elizabeth of
York, daughter to Edward IV, who will, in fact, later become the
queen of Henry VII; see 4.5.7–9 and 5.5.29–31   64 **pluck on** draw on
65 **Tear-falling** Tear-dropping   68 **Prove** Test   70 **Please** If it please
74 **deal upon** proceed against   76 **open** unhampered

81 **prefer** promote, advance   84 **late** recent.   **sound me in** ask me
about.   87 **he** i.e., Richmond   89 **pawned** pledged   93 **it** for it.
100 **the prophet** i.e., Henry VI   101 **by** nearby.   **him** (The word
applies to Richmond and Henry VI.)   105 **Rougemont** i.e., Red Hill.
(With a play on "Richmond.")   109 **what's o'clock?** what time is it?

KING RICHARD
Because that, like a jack, thou keep'st the stroke   116
Betwixt thy begging and my meditation.
I am not in the giving vein today.   118

BUCKINGHAM
May it please you to resolve me in my suit.   119

KING RICHARD
Thou troublest me. I am not in the vein.
                    Exit [*with all but Buckingham*].

BUCKINGHAM
And is it thus? Repays he my deep service
With such contempt? Made I him king for this?
O, let me think on Hastings, and be gone
To Brecknock, while my fearful head is on!   *Exit.* 124

❖

[4.3]

Enter Tyrrel.

TYRREL
The tyrannous and bloody act is done,
The most arch deed of piteous massacre   2
That ever yet this land was guilty of.
Dighton and Forrest, whom I did suborn   4
To do this piece of ruthless butchery,
Albeit they were fleshed villains, bloody dogs,   6
Melted with tenderness and mild compassion,
Wept like to children in their deaths' sad story.   8
"Oh, thus," quoth Dighton, "lay the gentle babes."
"Thus, thus," quoth Forrest, "girdling one another
Within their alabaster innocent arms.
Their lips were four red roses on a stalk,
Which in their summer beauty kissed each other.
A book of prayers on their pillow lay,
Which once," quoth Forrest, "almost changed my mind;
But oh, the devil!"—there the villain stopped;
When Dighton thus told on: "We smotherèd
The most replenishèd sweet work of Nature   18
That from the prime creation e'er she framed."   19
Hence both are gone; with conscience and remorse   20
They could not speak; and so I left them both,
To bear this tidings to the bloody king.

Enter [King] Richard.

And here he comes.—All health, my sovereign lord!
KING RICHARD
Kind Tyrrel, am I happy in thy news?

TYRREL
If to have done the thing you gave in charge   25
Beget your happiness, be happy then,
For it is done.
KING RICHARD   But didst thou see them dead?
TYRREL
I did, my lord.
KING RICHARD   And buried, gentle Tyrrel?
TYRREL
The chaplain of the Tower hath buried them;
But where, to say the truth, I do not know.
KING RICHARD
Come to me, Tyrrel, soon at after-supper,   31
When thou shalt tell the process of their death.   32
Meantime, but think how I may do thee good,
And be inheritor of thy desire.   34
Farewell till then.
TYRREL   I humbly take my leave.   [*Exit.*]
KING RICHARD
The son of Clarence have I pent up close,   36
His daughter meanly have I matched in marriage,   37
The sons of Edward sleep in Abraham's bosom,   38
And Anne my wife hath bid this world good night.
Now, for I know the Breton Richmond aims   40
At young Elizabeth, my brother's daughter,   41
And by that knot looks proudly on the crown,   42
To her go I, a jolly thriving wooer.

Enter Ratcliffe.

RATCLIFFE   My lord!
KING RICHARD
Good or bad news, that thou com'st in so bluntly?
RATCLIFFE
Bad news, my lord. Morton is fled to Richmond,   46
And Buckingham, backed with the hardy Welshmen,
Is in the field, and still his power increaseth.   48
KING RICHARD
Ely with Richmond troubles me more near   49
Than Buckingham and his rash-levied strength.   50
Come, I have learned that fearful commenting   51
Is leaden servitor to dull delay;   52
Delay leads impotent and snail-paced beggary.   53
Then fiery expedition be my wing,   54
Jove's Mercury, and herald for a king!   55

25 gave in charge ordered, commanded   **31 after-supper** dessert after supper   **32 process** story   **34 be . . . desire** expect to get what you ask.   **36 pent up close** strictly confined   **37 His . . . marriage** (Margaret Plantagenet was about twelve years old when Richard died. Shakespeare may have confused her with Lady Cicely, a daughter of Edward IV, whom Richard, according to Holinshed, intended to marry to "a man found in a cloud, and of an unknown lineage and family.")   **38 Abraham's bosom** (See Luke 16:22.)   **40 for** because. **Breton** located in Brittany   **41 my brother's** Edward's   **42 by that knot** by virtue of that alliance   **46 Morton** i.e., John Morton, Bishop of Ely, who had been kept prisoner at Brecknock (or Brecon) Castle; he is the Ely of 3.4   **48 power** army   **49 near** deeply   **50 rash-levied** hastily recruited   **51 fearful commenting** timorous talk   **52 leaden servitor** sluggish attendant   **53 leads** leads to.   **beggary** ruin. **54 expedition** speed   **55 Mercury** messenger of the gods

116 jack the figure of a man that strikes the bell on the outside of a clock. (With a play on the meaning "lowbred fellow." Richard's complaint is that Buckingham, like the jack of a clock, being on the point of striking the hour—i.e., speaking his request—breaks the continuity of Richard's reflections.)   **118 vein** mood   **119 resolve me** give me a final answer   **124 Brecknock** i.e., Brecon, Buckingham's family seat in Wales.   **fearful** full of fears
4.3. Location: London. The royal court.
2 arch deed i.e., chief or notorious act   **4 suborn** bribe   **6 fleshed** experienced in bloodshed   **8 in their . . . story** in telling the story of their deaths.   **18 replenishèd** complete, perfect   **19 prime** first
20 gone undone, unnerved

Go muster men. My counsel is my shield;   56
We must be brief when traitors brave the field.   57

Exeunt.

❖

4.[4]

Enter old Queen Margaret.

QUEEN MARGARET
So now prosperity begins to mellow   1
And drop into the rotten mouth of death.
Here in these confines slyly have I lurked   3
To watch the waning of mine enemies.
A dire induction am I witness to,   5
And will to France, hoping the consequence   6
Will prove as bitter, black, and tragical.
Withdraw thee, wretched Margaret. Who comes here?
[*She steps aside.*]

Enter Duchess [of York] and Queen [Elizabeth].

QUEEN ELIZABETH
Ah, my poor princes! Ah, my tender babes!
My unblown flowers, new-appearing sweets!   10
If yet your gentle souls fly in the air
And be not fixed in doom perpetual,   12
Hover about me with your airy wings
And hear your mother's lamentation!

QUEEN MARGARET [*aside*]
Hover about her; say that right for right   15
Hath dimmed your infant morn to agèd night.   16

DUCHESS
So many miseries have crazed my voice   17
That my woe-wearied tongue is still and mute.
Edward Plantagenet, why art thou dead?   19

QUEEN MARGARET [*aside*]
Plantagenet doth quit Plantagenet.   20
Edward for Edward pays a dying debt.   21

QUEEN ELIZABETH
Wilt thou, O God, fly from such gentle lambs   22
And throw them in the entrails of the wolf?
When didst thou sleep when such a deed was done?   24

QUEEN MARGARET [*aside*]
When holy Harry died, and my sweet son.   25

DUCHESS
Dead life, blind sight, poor mortal-living ghost,   26

Woe's scene, world's shame, grave's due by life usurped,   27
Brief abstract and record of tedious days,   28
Rest thy unrest on England's lawful earth,
[*sitting down*]
Unlawfully made drunk with innocent blood!   30

QUEEN ELIZABETH
Ah, that thou wouldst as soon afford a grave   31
As thou canst yield a melancholy seat!
Then would I hide my bones, not rest them here.
Ah, who hath any cause to mourn but we?
[*Sitting down by her.*]

QUEEN MARGARET [*coming forward*]
If ancient sorrow be most reverend,   35
Give mine the benefit of seniory   36
And let my griefs frown on the upper hand.   37
If sorrow can admit society,   [*sitting down with them*]
Tell o'er your woes again by viewing mine:
I had an Edward, till a Richard killed him;   40
I had a Harry, till a Richard killed him: 41
Thou hadst an Edward, till a Richard killed him;   42
Thou hadst a Richard, till a Richard killed him.   43

DUCHESS
I had a Richard too, and thou didst kill him;   44
I had a Rutland too, thou holp'st to kill him.   45

QUEEN MARGARET
Thou hadst a Clarence too, and Richard killed him.
From forth the kennel of thy womb hath crept
A hellhound that doth hunt us all to death.
That dog, that had his teeth before his eyes   49
To worry lambs and lap their gentle blood,   50
That foul defacer of God's handiwork,
That excellent grand tyrant of the earth   52
That reigns in gallèd eyes of weeping souls,   53
Thy womb let loose, to chase us to our graves.
O upright, just, and true-disposing God,
How do I thank thee that this carnal cur   56
Preys on the issue of his mother's body   57
And makes her pew-fellow with others' moan!   58

DUCHESS
O Harry's wife, triumph not in my woes!
God witness with me, I have wept for thine.

QUEEN MARGARET
Bear with me. I am hungry for revenge,
And now I cloy me with beholding it.   62

---

56 **My . . . shield** i.e., I will take counsel by arming myself and trust no adviser other than my own weapons   57 **brave** challenge
4.4. Location: London. Near the royal court.
1 **mellow** mature   3 **confines** regions.   **slyly** stealthily   5 **induction** beginning (as of a play)   6 **will** will go.   **the consequence** what follows, the sequel and conclusion (as in a play)   10 **unblown** unopened.   **sweets** flowers.   12 **doom perpetual** eternal destiny   15 **right for right** i.e., a just punishment for an offense against justice   16 **dimmed . . . night** i.e., brought the youthful promise of your children to ruin and death.   17 **crazed** cracked   19 **Edward Plantagenet** the Duchess's son, the dead King Edward IV; or, his son Edward V   20 **quit** requite   21 **Edward . . . debt** Edward IV (or else Edward V) for Edward, the son of Margaret and Henry VI.   **dying debt** debt paid through death.   22 **fly . . . lambs** i.e., abandon my two sons   24 **When** i.e., Whenever till now   25 **Harry** i.e., Henry VI   26 **mortal-living ghost** i.e., a dead person still among the living

27 **grave's . . . usurped** i.e., one who, by living too long, deprives the grave of its due   28 **abstract** epitome   30 **Unlawfully . . . drunk** i.e., England's earth, which is unlawfully made drunk   31 **that thou** would that you, England's earth   35 **reverend** worthy of respect   36 **seniory** seniority of claim   37 **on . . . hand** i.e., from a place of precedence.   40 **Edward** i.e., my son, the former Prince of Wales   41 **Harry** i.e., my husband, King Henry VI   42 **Thou** i.e., Queen Elizabeth.   **Edward** i.e., Edward V   43 **Thou . . . Richard** Thou, Queen Elizabeth, had a son, the young Duke of York   44 **Richard** i.e., Duke of York, the Duchess's husband and father of Richard III, killed by Margaret's army at the Battle of Wakefield in 1460   45 **Rutland** i.e., Edmund, son of the Duke of York, also killed at Wakefield   49 **teeth** (Richard was supposedly born with teeth.)   50 **worry** bite on the throat, tear to pieces   52 **excellent** unparalleled   53 **gallèd** sore with weeping   56 **carnal** flesh-eating   57 **issue** offspring   58 **pew-fellow** i.e., intimate associate   62 **cloy me** gorge myself

Thy Edward he is dead that killed my Edward;   63
Thy other Edward dead, to quit my Edward;   64
Young York he is but boot, because both they   65
Matched not the high perfection of my loss.
Thy Clarence he is dead that stabbed my Edward;
And the beholders of this frantic play,   68
Th'adulterate Hastings, Rivers, Vaughan, Grey,   69
Untimely smothered in their dusky graves.   70
Richard yet lives, hell's black intelligencer,   71
Only reserved their factor to buy souls   72
And send them thither; but at hand, at hand
Ensues his piteous and unpitied end.   74
Earth gapes, hell burns, fiends roar, saints pray,
To have him suddenly conveyed from hence.
Cancel his bond of life, dear God, I pray,
That I may live and say, "The dog is dead!"

QUEEN ELIZABETH
Oh, thou didst prophesy the time would come
That I should wish for thee to help me curse
That bottled spider, that foul bunch-backed toad!   81

QUEEN MARGARET
I called thee then vain flourish of my fortune;   82
I called thee then poor shadow, painted queen,
The presentation of but what I was,   84
The flattering index of a direful pageant,   85
One heaved a-high to be hurled down below,
A mother only mocked with two fair babes,
A dream of what thou wast, a garish flag   88
To be the aim of every dangerous shot;   89
A sign of dignity, a breath, a bubble,   90
A queen in jest, only to fill the scene.
Where is thy husband now? Where be thy brothers?
Where be thy two sons? Wherein dost thou joy?
Who sues and kneels and says, "God save the Queen"
Where be the bending peers that flattered thee?   95
Where be the thronging troops that followed thee?   96
Decline all this, and see what now thou art: 97
For happy wife, a most distressèd widow;
For joyful mother, one that wails the name;
For one being sued to, one that humbly sues;
For queen, a very caitiff crowned with care;   101
For she that scorned at me, now scorned of me;   102
For she being feared of all, now fearing one;
For she commanding all, obeyed of none.
Thus hath the course of justice whirled about

And left thee but a very prey to time,
Having no more but thought of what thou wast   107
To torture thee the more, being what thou art.
Thou didst usurp my place, and dost thou not
Usurp the just proportion of my sorrow?
Now thy proud neck bears half my burdened yoke,   111
From which even here I slip my weary head
And leave the burden of it all on thee.
Farewell, York's wife, and queen of sad mischance!
These English woes shall make me smile in France.
                                        [She starts to leave.]
QUEEN ELIZABETH
O thou well skilled in curses, stay awhile,
And teach me how to curse mine enemies!
QUEEN MARGARET
Forbear to sleep the nights, and fast the days;
Compare dead happiness with living woe;
Think that thy babes were sweeter than they were
And he that slew them fouler than he is.
Bett'ring thy loss makes the bad causer worse;   122
Revolving this will teach thee how to curse.   123
QUEEN ELIZABETH
My words are dull. Oh, quicken them with thine!   124
QUEEN MARGARET
Thy woes will make them sharp, and pierce like mine.
                                        Exit Margaret.
DUCHESS
Why should calamity be full of words?
QUEEN ELIZABETH
Windy attorneys to their client's woes,   127
Airy succeeders of intestate joys,   128
Poor breathing orators of miseries,   129
Let them have scope! Though what they will impart
Help nothing else, yet do they ease the heart.
DUCHESS
If so, then be not tongue-tied. Go with me,
And in the breath of bitter words let's smother
My damnèd son that thy two sweet sons smothered.
                                        [Sound trumpet.]
The trumpet sounds. Be copious in exclaims.   135

Enter King Richard and his train [marching, with
drums and trumpets].

KING RICHARD
Who intercepts me in my expedition?   136
DUCHESS
Oh, she that might have intercepted thee,
By strangling thee in her accursèd womb,
From all the slaughters, wretch, that thou hast done!
QUEEN ELIZABETH
Hid'st thou that forehead with a golden crown
Where should be branded, if that right were right,

---

63 Thy Edward Edward IV.   **my Edward** the son of Henry VI   **64 other Edward** Edward V.   **quit** requite   **65 Young York** Richard, Duke of York, the younger of the princes murdered in the Tower.   **but boot** merely into the bargain   **68 frantic** frenzied, insane   **69 Th'adulterate** the adulterous   **70 smothered** buried   **71 intelligencer** agent, go-between, spy   **72 Only . . . factor** chosen above all others as their (hell's) agent, and sent to earth for no other purpose   **74 piteous** deplorable   **81 bottled** bottle-shaped, swollen (as at 1.3.242).   **bunch-backed** hunchbacked   **82 flourish** mere ornament, embellishment. (See 1.3.241.)   **84 presentation** representation, semblance   **85 index** argument, preface, prologue.   **pageant** spectacular entertainment   **88–9 garish . . . shot** i.e., standard-bearer, conspicuous in appearance, and thus the target of enemy fire   **90 sign** mere token   **95 bending** bowing   **96 troops** supporters, followers   **97 Decline** Go through in order. (A grammatical metaphor.)   **101 caitiff** wretch, slave   **102 of** by. (Also in lines 103 and 104.)

107 no . . . thought only the memory   **111 burdened** burdensome   **122 Bett'ring** Magnifying   **123 Revolving** meditating on   **124 quicken** put life into   **127 Windy . . . woes** i.e., Words, which are airy pleaders on behalf of one who is suffering   **128 Airy . . . joys** insubstantial words, all that is left of joys that died unfulfilled. (Literally, having died without anything to bequeath.)   **129 breathing** speaking   **135 exclaims** exclamations.   **136 expedition** (1) haste (2) military undertaking.

The slaughter of the prince that owed that crown   142
And the dire death of my poor sons and brothers?
Tell me, thou villain slave, where are my children?

DUCHESS
Thou toad, thou toad, where is thy brother Clarence?
And little Ned Plantagenet, his son?   146

QUEEN ELIZABETH
Where is the gentle Rivers, Vaughan, Grey?

DUCHESS   Where is kind Hastings?

KING RICHARD
A flourish, trumpets! Strike alarum, drums!   149
Let not the heavens hear these telltale women   150
Rail on the Lord's anointed. Strike, I say!
                    Flourish. Alarums.
Either be patient and entreat me fair,   152
Or with the clamorous report of war   153
Thus will I drown your exclamations.

DUCHESS   Art thou my son?

KING RICHARD
Ay, I thank God, my father, and yourself.

DUCHESS
Then patiently hear my impatience.

KING RICHARD
Madam, I have a touch of your condition,   158
That cannot brook the accent of reproof.

DUCHESS
Oh, let me speak!

KING RICHARD   Do then, but I'll not hear.

DUCHESS
I will be mild and gentle in my words.

KING RICHARD
And brief, good mother, for I am in haste.

DUCHESS
Art thou so hasty? I have stayed for thee,   163
God knows, in torment and in agony.   164

KING RICHARD
And came I not at last to comfort you?

DUCHESS
No, by the Holy Rood, thou know'st it well,   166
Thou cam'st on earth to make the earth my hell.
A grievous burden was thy birth to me;
Tetchy and wayward was thy infancy;   169
Thy schooldays frightful, desp'rate, wild, and furious;
Thy prime of manhood daring, bold, and venturous;
Thy age confirmed, proud, subtle, sly, and bloody,   172
More mild, but yet more harmful—kind in hatred.   173
What comfortable hour canst thou name
That ever graced me with thy company?

KING RICHARD
Faith, none, but Humphrey Hour, that called Your Grace   176

To breakfast once forth of my company.   177
If I be so disgracious in your eye,   178
Let me march on and not offend you, madam.—
Strike up the drum.

DUCHESS   I prithee, hear me speak.

KING RICHARD
You speak too bitterly.

DUCHESS   Hear me a word,
For I shall never speak to thee again.

KING RICHARD   So.

DUCHESS
Either thou wilt die by God's just ordinance
Ere from this war thou turn a conqueror,   185
Or I with grief and extreme age shall perish
And nevermore behold thy face again.
Therefore take with thee my most grievous curse,
Which in the day of battle tire thee more
Than all the complete armor that thou wear'st!
My prayers on the adverse party fight,   191
And there the little souls of Edward's children
Whisper the spirits of thine enemies   193
And promise them success and victory!
Bloody thou art, bloody will be thy end;
Shame serves thy life and doth thy death attend.   196
                        Exit.

QUEEN ELIZABETH
Though far more cause, yet much less spirit to curse
Abides in me; I say amen to her.

KING RICHARD
Stay, madam. I must talk a word with you.

QUEEN ELIZABETH
I have no more sons of the royal blood
For thee to slaughter. For my daughters, Richard,   201
They shall be praying nuns, not weeping queens,
And therefore level not to hit their lives.   203

KING RICHARD
You have a daughter called Elizabeth,
Virtuous and fair, royal and gracious.

QUEEN ELIZABETH
And must she die for this? Oh, let her live,
And I'll corrupt her manners, stain her beauty,   207
Slander myself as false to Edward's bed,
Throw over her the veil of infamy;
So she may live unscarred of bleeding slaughter,   210
I will confess she was not Edward's daughter.

KING RICHARD
Wrong not her birth. She is a royal princess.

QUEEN ELIZABETH
To save her life, I'll say she is not so.

KING RICHARD
Her life is safest only in her birth.   214

QUEEN ELIZABETH
And only in that safety died her brothers.

---

142 **owed** owned   146 **Ned Plantagenet** (See 4.3.36.)   149 **flourish** fanfare.   **alarum** call to arms   150 **telltale** tattling, gabbling   152 **entreat me fair** treat me with courtesy   153 **report** noise   158 **condition** disposition   163 **stayed** waited   164 **in agony** i.e., in childbirth.
166 **Holy Rood** Christ's cross   169 **Tetchy** fretful, peevish   172 **age confirmed** riper manhood   173 **kind in hatred** concealing hatred under pretense of kindness.   176 **Humphrey Hour** (To "dine with Duke Humphrey" was to go hungry; hence, Richard flippantly suggests he was saved from a spare breakfast. The passage is obscure.)

177 **forth of** away from   178 **disgracious** unpleasing, disliked
185 **turn** return   191 **party** side   193 **Whisper** whisper to   196 **serves** accompanies   201 **For my** As for my   203 **level** aim   207 **manners** morals   210 **So** provided.   **of** by   214 **Her . . . birth** Her best guarantee of personal safety is her high birth.

KING RICHARD
　Lo, at their birth good stars were opposite.　216

QUEEN ELIZABETH
　No, to their lives ill friends were contrary.　217

KING RICHARD
　All unavoided is the doom of destiny.　218

QUEEN ELIZABETH
　True, when avoided grace makes destiny.　219
　My babes were destined to a fairer death,
　If grace had blessed thee with a fairer life.

KING RICHARD
　You speak as if that I had slain my cousins.　222

QUEEN ELIZABETH
　Cousins, indeed, and by their uncle cozened　223
　Of comfort, kingdom, kindred, freedom, life.
　Whose hand soever lanced their tender hearts,　225
　Thy head, all indirectly, gave direction.　226
　No doubt the murd'rous knife was dull and blunt
　Till it was whetted on thy stone-hard heart,
　To revel in the entrails of my lambs.
　But that still use of grief makes wild grief tame,　230
　My tongue should to thy ears not name my boys
　Till that my nails were anchored in thine eyes;
　And I, in such a desp'rate bay of death,　233
　Like a poor bark of sails and tackling reft,　234
　Rush all to pieces on thy rocky bosom.

KING RICHARD
　Madam, so thrive I in my enterprise　236
　And dangerous success of bloody wars　237
　As I intend more good to you and yours
　Than ever you or yours by me were harmed!

QUEEN ELIZABETH
　What good is covered with the face of heaven,　240
　To be discovered, that can do me good?

KING RICHARD
　Th'advancement of your children, gentle lady.

QUEEN ELIZABETH
　Up to some scaffold, there to lose their heads.

KING RICHARD
　Unto the dignity and height of fortune,
　The high imperial type of this earth's glory.　245

QUEEN ELIZABETH
　Flatter my sorrow with report of it;
　Tell me what state, what dignity, what honor,
　Canst thou demise to any child of mine?　248

KING RICHARD
　Even all I have—ay, and myself and all—
　Will I withal endow a child of thine,
　So in the Lethe of thy angry soul　251

Thou drown the sad remembrance of those wrongs
Which thou supposest I have done to thee.

QUEEN ELIZABETH
　Be brief, lest that the process of thy kindness　254
　Last longer telling than thy kindness' date.　255

KING RICHARD
　Then know that from my soul I love thy daughter.　256

QUEEN ELIZABETH
　My daughter's mother thinks it with her soul.

KING RICHARD　What do you think?

QUEEN ELIZABETH
　That thou dost love my daughter from thy soul.
　So from thy soul's love didst thou love her brothers,　260
　And from my heart's love I do thank thee for it.

KING RICHARD
　Be not so hasty to confound my meaning.　262
　I mean that with my soul I love thy daughter
　And do intend to make her Queen of England.

QUEEN ELIZABETH
　Well then, who dost thou mean shall be her king?

KING RICHARD
　Even he that makes her queen. Who else should be?

QUEEN ELIZABETH
　What, thou?

KING RICHARD　Even so. How think you of it?

QUEEN ELIZABETH
　How canst thou woo her?

KING RICHARD　　　　　　That would I learn of you,
　As one being best acquainted with her humor.　269

QUEEN ELIZABETH
　And wilt thou learn of me?

KING RICHARD　　　　　　Madam, with all my heart.

QUEEN ELIZABETH
　Send to her, by the man that slew her brothers,
　A pair of bleeding hearts; thereon engrave
　"Edward" and "York"; then haply will she weep.　273
　Therefore present to her—as sometime Margaret　274
　Did to thy father, steeped in Rutland's blood—　275
　A handkerchief, which, say to her, did drain
　The purple sap from her sweet brother's body;
　And bid her wipe her weeping eyes withal.
　If this inducement move her not to love,
　Send her a letter of thy noble deeds.
　Tell her thou mad'st away her uncle Clarence,
　Her uncle Rivers, ay, and for her sake
　Mad'st quick conveyance with her good aunt Anne.　283

KING RICHARD
　You mock me, madam. This is not the way
　To win your daughter.

QUEEN ELIZABETH　　　　　There is no other way,
　Unless thou couldst put on some other shape
　And not be Richard that hath done all this.

216 **opposite** hostile.　217 **contrary** opposed.　218 **unavoided**
unavoidable　219 **avoided grace** i.e., Richard, in whom grace is void
or lacking　222 **as if that** as if　223 **cozened** cheated　225 **Whose
hand soever** Whoever it was whose hand　226 **all indirectly** by indirect means, and wrongly　230 **But . . . grief** Were it not that constant
grieving　233 **bay** (1) inlet (2) position of a hunted animal turning to
face the hounds　234 **bark** sailing vessel.　**reft** bereft　236 **so thrive
I** may I so thrive　237 **success** sequel, result　240 **covered with** hidden by (and therefore not yet revealed to humanity)　245 **imperial
type** symbol of rule　248 **demise** convey, transmit, lease　251 **So**
provided that.　**Lethe** river in the underworld, the waters of which
produce forgetfulness

254 **process** story　255 **date** duration.　256 **from** with. (But Queen
Elizabeth, in lines 259–61, sarcastically uses the word in the sense
"apart from," "at variance with.")　260 **So** Just so. (Said ironically.)
262 **confound** deliberately misconstrue　269 **humor** temperament.
273 **haply** perhaps　274 **sometime** once　275 **Rutland's** (See *3 Henry
VI*, 1.4.79–83.)　283 **conveyance with** disposal of

KING RICHARD
Say that I did all this for love of her.
QUEEN ELIZABETH
Nay, then indeed she cannot choose but hate thee,
Having bought love with such a bloody spoil.   290
KING RICHARD
Look what is done cannot be now amended.   291
Men shall deal unadvisedly sometimes,   292
Which after-hours gives leisure to repent.
If I did take the kingdom from your sons,
To make amends I'll give it to your daughter.
If I have killed the issue of your womb,
To quicken your increase I will beget   297
Mine issue of your blood upon your daughter.
A grandam's name is little less in love
Than is the doting title of a mother;
They are as children but one step below,
Even of your metal, of your very blood,   302
Of all one pain, save for a night of groans   303
Endured of her for whom you bid like sorrow.   304
Your children were vexation to your youth,
But mine shall be a comfort to your age.
The loss you have is but a son being king,
And by that loss your daughter is made queen.
I cannot make you what amends I would;
Therefore accept such kindness as I can.   310
Dorset your son, that with a fearful soul
Leads discontented steps in foreign soil,
This fair alliance quickly shall call home
To high promotions and great dignity.
The king that calls your beauteous daughter wife
Familiarly shall call thy Dorset brother;   316
Again shall you be mother to a king,
And all the ruins of distressful times
Repaired with double riches of content.
What? We have many goodly days to see.
The liquid drops of tears that you have shed
Shall come again, transformed to orient pearl,   322
Advantaging their love with interest   323
Of ten times double gain of happiness.
Go then, my mother, to thy daughter go.
Make bold her bashful years with your experience;
Prepare her ears to hear a wooer's tale;
Put in her tender heart th'aspiring flame
Of golden sovereignty; acquaint the Princess
With the sweet silent hours of marriage joys.
And when this arm of mine hath chastisèd
The petty rebel, dull-brained Buckingham,
Bound with triumphant garlands will I come
And lead thy daughter to a conqueror's bed;
To whom I will retail my conquest won,
And she shall be sole victoress, Caesar's Caesar.   335

QUEEN ELIZABETH
What were I best to say? Her father's brother
Would be her lord? Or shall I say her uncle?
Or, he that slew her brothers and her uncles?
Under what title shall I woo for thee
That God, the law, my honor, and her love
Can make seem pleasing to her tender years?
KING RICHARD
Infer fair England's peace by this alliance.   343
QUEEN ELIZABETH
Which she shall purchase with still-lasting war.   344
KING RICHARD
Tell her the King, that may command, entreats.
QUEEN ELIZABETH
That at her hands which the King's King forbids.   346
KING RICHARD
Say she shall be a high and mighty queen.
QUEEN ELIZABETH
To vail the title, as her mother doth.   348
KING RICHARD
Say I will love her everlastingly.
QUEEN ELIZABETH
But how long shall that title "ever" last?
KING RICHARD
Sweetly in force unto her fair life's end.
QUEEN ELIZABETH
But how long fairly shall her sweet life last?   352
KING RICHARD
As long as heaven and nature lengthens it.
QUEEN ELIZABETH
As long as hell and Richard likes of it.
KING RICHARD
Say I, her sovereign, am her subject low.
QUEEN ELIZABETH
But she, your subject, loathes such sovereignty.
KING RICHARD
Be eloquent in my behalf to her.
QUEEN ELIZABETH
An honest tale speeds best being plainly told.   358
KING RICHARD
Then plainly to her tell my loving tale.
QUEEN ELIZABETH
Plain and not honest is too harsh a style.
KING RICHARD
Your reasons are too shallow and too quick.   361
QUEEN ELIZABETH
Oh, no, my reasons are too deep and dead—
Too deep and dead, poor infants, in their graves.
KING RICHARD
Harp not on that string, madam. That is past.
QUEEN ELIZABETH
Harp on it still shall I till heartstrings break.

---

290 spoil slaughter. (A hunting term.)   291 Look what Whatever
292 shall deal cannot but act   297 quicken your increase give new
life to your progeny   302 metal substance. (With a suggestion also of
mettle, "spirit." The Folio reads "mettall.")   303 pain labor, effort   304
of by.   bid endured, bided   310 can am able (to give).   316 Familiarly familiarly   322 orient bright, shining   323 Advantaging their
love augmenting the love that prompted tears   335 retail relate

343 Infer Allege, adduce (as a reason)   344 still-lasting war i.e., perpetual domestic strife.   346 forbids (The Book of Common Prayer,
echoing the injunctions of Leviticus 18, prohibits the marriage of a
man with his brother's daughter.)   348 vail yield; lower or abase as a
sign of submission   352 fairly without foul play   358 speeds succeeds   361 quick hasty. (With a pun on the meaning "alive," contrasted with dead in the next line, just as shallow is punningly
contrasted with deep.)

KING RICHARD
   Now, by my George, my Garter, and my crown—   366
QUEEN ELIZABETH
   Profaned, dishonored, and the third usurped.
KING RICHARD
   I swear—
QUEEN ELIZABETH   By nothing, for this is no oath.
   Thy George, profaned, hath lost his lordly honor;   369
   Thy Garter, blemished, pawned his knightly virtue;
   Thy crown, usurped, disgraced his kingly glory.
   If something thou wouldst swear to be believed,
   Swear then by something that thou hast not wronged.
KING RICHARD
   Then, by myself—
QUEEN ELIZABETH   Thyself is self-misused.
KING RICHARD
   Now, by the world—
QUEEN ELIZABETH   'Tis full of thy foul wrongs.
KING RICHARD
   My father's death—
QUEEN ELIZABETH   Thy life hath it dishonored.
KING RICHARD
   Why then, by God—
QUEEN ELIZABETH   God's wrong is most of all.
   If thou didst fear to break an oath with Him,
   The unity the King my husband made   379
   Thou hadst not broken, nor my brothers died.
   If thou hadst feared to break an oath by Him,
   Th'imperial metal circling now thy head
   Had graced the tender temples of my child,
   And both the princes had been breathing here,
   Which now, two tender bedfellows for dust,
   Thy broken faith hath made the prey for worms.
   What canst thou swear by now?
KING RICHARD   The time to come.
QUEEN ELIZABETH
   That thou hast wrongèd in the time o'erpast;
   For I myself have many tears to wash
   Hereafter time, for time past wronged by thee.   390
   The children live whose fathers thou hast slaughtered,
   Ungoverned youth, to wail it in their age;   392
   The parents live whose children thou hast butchered,
   Old barren plants, to wail it with their age.
   Swear not by time to come, for that thou hast
   Misused ere used, by times ill-used o'erpast.   396
KING RICHARD
   As I intend to prosper and repent,   397
   So thrive I in my dangerous affairs
   Of hostile arms! Myself myself confound!   399

Heaven and fortune bar me happy hours!
Day, yield me not thy light, nor, night, thy rest!
Be opposite all planets of good luck   402
To my proceeding if, with dear heart's love,
Immaculate devotion, holy thoughts,
I tender not thy beauteous, princely daughter!   405
In her consists my happiness and thine;
Without her follows to myself and thee,
Herself, the land, and many a Christian soul,
Death, desolation, ruin, and decay.
It cannot be avoided but by this;
It will not be avoided but by this.
Therefore, dear mother—I must call you so—
Be the attorney of my love to her.
Plead what I will be, not what I have been,
Not my deserts, but what I will deserve.
Urge the necessity and state of times,   416
And be not peevish-fond in great designs.   417
QUEEN ELIZABETH
   Shall I be tempted of the devil thus?
KING RICHARD
   Ay, if the devil tempt you to do good.
QUEEN ELIZABETH
   Shall I forget myself to be myself?   420
KING RICHARD
   Ay, if yourself's remembrance wrong yourself.   421
QUEEN ELIZABETH
   Yet thou didst kill my children.
KING RICHARD
   But in your daughter's womb I bury them,
   Where in that nest of spicery they will breed   424
   Selves of themselves, to your recomforture.   425
QUEEN ELIZABETH
   Shall I go win my daughter to thy will?
KING RICHARD
   And be a happy mother by the deed.
QUEEN ELIZABETH
   I go. Write to me very shortly,
   And you shall understand from me her mind.
KING RICHARD
   Bear her my true love's kiss; and so, farewell.
                Exit Queen [*Elizabeth*].

Relenting fool, and shallow, changing woman!

    Enter Ratcliffe; [*Catesby following*].

How now, what news?
RATCLIFFE
   Most mighty sovereign, on the western coast
   Rideth a puissant navy; to our shores   434
   Throng many doubtful, hollow-hearted friends,   435

---

366 **George . . . Garter** (The George, a badge showing Saint George slaying the dragon, was not added to the insignia of the Order of the Garter until the reign of Henry VII or Henry VIII.) 369 **his** its (as also in lines 370, 371) 379 **The unity** i.e., the reconciliation between Queen Elizabeth and her enemies 390 **Hereafter time** in the future 392 **Ungoverned** i.e., without a father's guidance or rule 396 **Misused . . . o'erpast** misused even before it came time to be used, by your ill use of past times. 397 **As . . . repent** i.e., I swear that as I hope to thrive and intend to repent 399 **Myself . . . confound!** May I destroy myself!

402 **opposite** opposed, adverse 405 **I tender not** I fail to show a tender regard for 416 **state of times** urgent political need 417 **And . . . designs** and do not stand by, childishly foolish as great plans are afoot. 420 **Shall . . . myself?** i.e., Shall I, in order to be queen mother, forget that I am the person you have wronged? 421 **wrong yourself** i.e., interferes with what is to your advantage. 424 **nest of spicery** (The fabled phoenix arose anew from the nest of spices, its funeral pyre.) 425 **recomforture** comfort, consolation. 434 **puissant** powerful 435 **doubtful** apprehensive

Unarmed and unresolved to beat them back.
'Tis thought that Richmond is their admiral;
And there they hull, expecting but the aid   437
Of Buckingham to welcome them ashore.   438

KING RICHARD
Some light-foot friend post to the Duke of Norfolk: 440
Ratcliffe, thyself, or Catesby; where is he?

CATESBY
Here, my good lord.

KING RICHARD   Catesby, fly to the Duke.

CATESBY
I will, my lord, with all convenient haste.   443

KING RICHARD
Ratcliffe, come hither. Post to Salisbury.
When thou com'st thither—[To Catesby] Dull, unmindful
    villain,
Why stay'st thou here, and go'st not to the Duke?

CATESBY
First, mighty liege, tell me Your Highness' pleasure,
What from Your Grace I shall deliver to him.

KING RICHARD
Oh, true, good Catesby. Bid him levy straight
The greatest strength and power that he can make,   450
And meet me suddenly at Salisbury.   451

CATESBY   I go.   Exit.

RATCLIFFE
What, may it please you, shall I do at Salisbury?

KING RICHARD
Why, what wouldst thou do there before I go?

RATCLIFFE
Your Highness told me I should post before.   455

KING RICHARD
My mind is changed.

    Enter Lord Stanley [Earl of Derby].

                    Stanley, what news with you?

STANLEY
None good, my liege, to please you with the hearing,
Nor none so bad but well may be reported.

KING RICHARD
Hoyday, a riddle! Neither good nor bad!
What need'st thou run so many miles about,   459
When thou mayst tell thy tale the nearest way?   461
Once more, what news?

STANLEY   Richmond is on the seas.

KING RICHARD
There let him sink, and be the seas on him!
White-livered runagate, what doth he there?   464

STANLEY
I know not, mighty sovereign, but by guess.

KING RICHARD   Well, as you guess?

STANLEY
Stirred up by Dorset, Buckingham, and Morton,

He makes for England, here to claim the crown.

KING RICHARD
Is the chair empty? Is the sword unswayed?   469
Is the King dead? The empire unpossessed?   470
What heir of York is there alive but we?
And who is England's king but great York's heir?
Then tell me, what makes he upon the seas?   473

STANLEY
Unless for that, my liege, I cannot guess.

KING RICHARD
Unless for that he comes to be your liege,
You cannot guess wherefore the Welshman comes.   476
Thou wilt revolt and fly to him, I fear.

STANLEY
No, my good lord; therefore mistrust me not.

KING RICHARD
Where is thy power, then, to beat him back?   479
Where be thy tenants and thy followers?
Are they not now upon the western shore,
Safe-conducting the rebels from their ships?

STANLEY
No, my good lord, my friends are in the north.

KING RICHARD
Cold friends to me! What do they in the north
When they should serve their sovereign in the west?

STANLEY
They have not been commanded, mighty King.
Pleaseth Your Majesty to give me leave,   487
I'll muster up my friends and meet Your Grace
Where and what time Your Majesty shall please.

KING RICHARD
Ay, thou wouldst be gone to join with Richmond.
But I'll not trust thee.

STANLEY   Most mighty sovereign,
You have no cause to hold my friendship doubtful.
I never was nor never will be false.

KING RICHARD
Go then and muster men, but leave behind
Your son, George Stanley. Look your heart be firm,
Or else his head's assurance is but frail.   496

STANLEY
So deal with him as I prove true to you.

                    Exit Stanley [Earl of Derby].

    Enter a Messenger.

FIRST MESSENGER
My gracious sovereign, now in Devonshire,
As I by friends am well advisèd,
Sir Edward Courtney and the haughty prelate,   499
Bishop of Exeter, his elder brother,
With many more confederates, are in arms.   501

    Enter another Messenger.

437 their admiral i.e., of the puissant navy named three lines earlier
438 hull drift with the sails furled   440 light-foot swift-footed.   post
hasten   443 convenient appropriate, suitable   450 make raise
451 suddenly swiftly   455 post hasten   459 Hoyday Heyday.
(Expressing mock wonderment.)   461 the nearest way directly, simply.   464 White-livered runagate Cowardly renegade, vagabond

469 chair throne   470 empire kingdom   473 makes he is he doing
476 Welshman (Richmond was the grandson of Owen Tudor, a
Welshman of Anglesea, who fathered three sons and a daughter by
Katharine of Valois, widow of Henry V.)   479 power army
487 Pleaseth May it please   496 assurance safety   499 advisèd
informed   501 brother (Actually, a cousin.)

SECOND MESSENGER
In Kent, my liege, the Guildfords are in arms,
And every hour more competitors   504
Flock to the rebels, and their power grows strong.

Enter another Messenger.

THIRD MESSENGER
My lord, the army of great Buckingham—
KING RICHARD
Out on ye, owls! Nothing but songs of death?   507
                                        He striketh him.
There, take thou that, till thou bring better news.
THIRD MESSENGER
The news I have to tell Your Majesty
Is that by sudden floods and fall of waters
Buckingham's army is dispersed and scattered,
And he himself wandered away alone,
No man knows whither.
KING RICHARD   I cry thee mercy.   513
There is my purse to cure that blow of thine.
                                        [*He gives money.*]
Hath any well-advisèd friend proclaimed   515
Reward to him that brings the traitor in?
THIRD MESSENGER
Such proclamation hath been made, my lord.

Enter another Messenger.

FOURTH MESSENGER
Sir Thomas Lovell and Lord Marquess Dorset,   518
'Tis said, my liege, in Yorkshire are in arms.
But this good comfort bring I to Your Highness:
The Breton navy is dispersed by tempest.
Richmond, in Dorsetshire, sent out a boat
Unto the shore, to ask those on the banks
If they were his assistants, yea or no,
Who answered him they came from Buckingham
Upon his party. He, mistrusting them,
Hoised sail and made his course again for Brittany. 527
KING RICHARD
March on, march on, since we are up in arms,
If not to fight with foreign enemies,
Yet to beat down these rebels here at home.

Enter Catesby.

CATESBY
My liege, the Duke of Buckingham is taken!
That is the best news. That the Earl of Richmond
Is with a mighty power landed at Milford   533
Is colder tidings, yet they must be told.
KING RICHARD
Away towards Salisbury! While we reason here,   535

A royal battle might be won and lost.
Someone take order Buckingham be brought
To Salisbury. The rest march on with me.
                                        Flourish. Exeunt.

❧

4.[5]

*Enter [Lord Stanley Earl of] Derby and Sir
Christopher [Urswick, a priest].*

STANLEY
Sir Christopher, tell Richmond this from me:
That in the sty of the most deadly boar
My son George Stanley is franked up in hold.   3
If I revolt, off goes young George's head;
The fear of that holds off my present aid.
So get thee gone; commend me to thy lord.
Withal say that the Queen hath heartily consented   7
He should espouse Elizabeth her daughter.
But tell me, where is princely Richmond now?
CHRISTOPHER
At Pembroke, or at Ha'rfordwest, in Wales.   10
STANLEY   What men of name resort to him?   11
CHRISTOPHER
Sir Walter Herbert, a renownèd soldier,
Sir Gilbert Talbot, Sir William Stanley,
Oxford, redoubted Pembroke, Sir James Blunt,   14
And Rice ap Thomas, with a valiant crew,
And many other of great name and worth;
And towards London do they bend their power,   17
If by the way they be not fought withal.
STANLEY
Well, hie thee to thy lord; I kiss his hand.   19
My letter will resolve him of my mind.   20
                                        [*He gives a letter.*]
Farewell.   *Exeunt.*

❧

5.1

*Enter Buckingham, with [Sheriff and] halberds, led
to execution.*

BUCKINGHAM
Will not King Richard let me speak with him?
SHERIFF
No, my good lord. Therefore be patient.
BUCKINGHAM
Hastings, and Edward's children, Grey, and Rivers,
Holy King Henry, and thy fair son Edward,   4
Vaughan, and all that have miscarried   5

---

504 **competitors** confederates   507 **owls** (The cry of the owl was thought to portend death.)   513 **I cry thee mercy** I beg your pardon. 515 **well-advisèd** judicious   518 **Sir Thomas Lovell** (Not the Lovell of 3.4 and 3.5, who was historically Sir Francis Lovell, Richard's Lord Chamberlain, but perhaps related to him.)   527 **Hoised** hoisted 533 **Milford** Milford Haven on the coast of Wales in the county of Pembroke. (A gap of two years is bridged here. Richmond's first fruitless expedition was in October 1483; his landing at Milford was in August 1485.)   535 **reason** talk

4.5. Location: London. The house of Lord Stanley, Earl of Derby. 0.1 *Sir* (Honorific title for a clergyman.)   **3 franked up in hold** shut up in custody, as in a pigpen.   **7 Withal** In addition   **10 Ha'rfordwest** Haverfordwest, in Wales   **11 name** rank   **14 redoubted Pembroke** awe-inspiring Jasper Tudor, Earl of Pembroke (uncle to Richmond)   **17 bend their power** direct their forces   **19 hie** hasten **20 resolve him of** inform him concerning
5.1. Location: Salisbury. An open place.
4 thy i.e., Henry VI's   **5 miscarrièd** perished

By underhand corrupted foul injustice:
If that your moody, discontented souls
Do through the clouds behold this present hour,   7
Even for revenge mock my destruction!
This is All Souls' Day, fellow, is it not?   10
SHERIFF   It is, my lord.

BUCKINGHAM
Why, then All Souls' Day is my body's doomsday.
This is the day which, in King Edward's time,
I wished might fall on me when I was found
False to his children and his wife's allies;
This is the day wherein I wished to fall
By the false faith of him whom most I trusted;
This, this All Souls' Day to my fearful soul
Is the determined respite of my wrongs.   19
That high All-Seer which I dallied with
Hath turned my feignèd prayer on my head
And given in earnest what I begged in jest.
Thus doth he force the swords of wicked men
To turn their own points in their masters' bosoms.
Thus Margaret's curse falls heavy on my neck:
"When he," quoth she, "shall split thy heart with sorrow,   26
Remember Margaret was a prophetess."
Come lead me, officers, to the block of shame.
Wrong hath but wrong, and blame the due of blame.
       Exeunt Buckingham with officers.

❧

5.2

*Enter Richmond, Oxford, [Sir James] Blunt, [Sir
Walter] Herbert, and others, with drum and
colors.*

RICHMOND
Fellows in arms, and my most loving friends
Bruised underneath the yoke of tyranny,
Thus far into the bowels of the land   3
Have we marchèd on without impediment;
And here receive we from our father Stanley   5
Lines of fair comfort and encouragement.
The wretched, bloody, and usurping boar,
That spoiled your summer fields and fruitful vines,   8
Swills your warm blood like wash, and makes his trough   9
In your emboweled bosoms, this foul swine   10
Is now even in the center of this isle,
Near to the town of Leicester, as we learn.
From Tamworth thither is but one day's march.
In God's name, cheerly on, courageous friends,   14
To reap the harvest of perpetual peace
By this one bloody trial of sharp war.

OXFORD
Every man's conscience is a thousand swords
To fight against this guilty homicide.

HERBERT
I doubt not but his friends will turn to us.

BLUNT
He hath no friends but what are friends for fear,   20
Which in his dearest need will fly from him.   21

RICHMOND
All for our vantage. Then, in God's name, march!
True hope is swift and flies with swallow's wings;
Kings it makes gods and meaner creatures kings.   24
       Exeunt omnes.

❧

[5.3]

*Enter King Richard in arms, with Norfolk,
Ratcliffe, and the Earl of Surrey [and others].*

KING RICHARD
Here pitch our tent, even here in Bosworth Field.
My lord of Surrey, why look you so sad?

SURREY
My heart is ten times lighter than my looks.

KING RICHARD
My lord of Norfolk—

NORFOLK   Here, most gracious liege.

KING RICHARD
Norfolk, we must have knocks; ha! Must we not?   5

NORFOLK
We must both give and take, my loving lord.

KING RICHARD
Up with my tent! Here will I lie tonight.
     [*Soldiers begin to set up King Richard's tent.*]
But where tomorrow? Well, all's one for that.   8
Who hath descried the number of the traitors?   9

NORFOLK
Six or seven thousand is their utmost power.

KING RICHARD
Why, our battalia trebles that account.   11
Besides, the King's name is a tower of strength,
Which they upon the adverse faction want.   13
Up with the tent! Come, noble gentlemen,
Let us survey the vantage of the ground.   15
Call for some men of sound direction.   16
Let's lack no discipline, make no delay,
For, lords, tomorrow is a busy day.   *Exeunt.*

*Enter [on the other side of the stage] Richmond,
Sir William Brandon, Oxford, and Dorset, [Blunt,
Herbert, and others. Some of the soldiers pitch
Richmond's tent.]*

---

7 moody, discontented angry, vengeance-seeking   **10 All Souls' Day**
November 2, the day on which the Church intercedes for all Christian
souls   **19 the determined . . . wrongs** the ordained date to which
the punishment of my evil practices was respited or postponed.
26 he Richard
5.2. Location: A camp near Tamworth.
3 bowels interior   **5 father** stepfather, Lord Stanley, Earl of Derby
8 spoiled despoiled   **9 Swills** gulps.   **wash** hogwash, swill
10 emboweled disemboweled   **14 cheerly** cheerily, heartily

20 for fear i.e., out of fearing Richard   **21 dearest** direst   **24 meaner**
of lower degree.   **24.1 omnes** all.
5.3. Location: Bosworth Field.
5 knocks blows   **8 all's . . . that** be that as it may.   **9 descried** recon-
noitred   **11 battalia** army   **13 want** lack.   **15 vantage of the ground**
i.e., way in which the field can best be used for tactical advantage.
16 direction judgment, military skill.

RICHMOND
 The weary sun hath made a golden set,
 And, by the bright track of his fiery car,   20
 Gives token of a goodly day tomorrow.
 Sir William Brandon, you shall bear my standard.   22
 Give me some ink and paper in my tent.
 I'll draw the form and model of our battle,
 Limit each leader to his several charge,   25
 And part in just proportion our small power.   26
 My lord of Oxford, you, Sir William Brandon,
 And you, Sir Walter Herbert, stay with me.
 The Earl of Pembroke keeps his regiment;   29
 Good Captain Blunt, bear my good-night to him,
 And by the second hour in the morning
 Desire the Earl to see me in my tent.
 Yet one thing more, good Captain, do for me:
 Where is Lord Stanley quartered, do you know?

BLUNT
 Unless I have mista'en his colors much,
 Which well I am assured I have not done,
 His regiment lies half a mile at least
 South from the mighty power of the King.   38

RICHMOND
 If without peril it be possible,
 Sweet Blunt, make some good means to speak with him,
 And give him from me this most needful note.
                                   [He gives a letter.]

BLUNT
 Upon my life, my lord, I'll undertake it.
 And so, God give you quiet rest tonight!

RICHMOND
 Good night, good Captain Blunt.   [Exit Blunt.]
                                   Come, gentlemen,
 Let us consult upon tomorrow's business.
 Into my tent; the dew is raw and cold.
                                   They withdraw into the tent.

 Enter [to his tent, King] Richard, Ratcliffe,
 Norfolk, and Catesby.

KING RICHARD
 What is't o'clock?
CATESBY   It's suppertime, my lord;
 It's nine o'clock.
KING RICHARD   I will not sup tonight.
 Give me some ink and paper.
 What, is my beaver easier than it was,   50
 And all my armor laid into my tent?
CATESBY
 It is, my liege, and all things are in readiness.
KING RICHARD
 Good Norfolk, hie thee to thy charge.
 Use careful watch; choose trusty sentinels.
NORFOLK   I go, my lord.

KING RICHARD
 Stir with the lark tomorrow, gentle Norfolk.
NORFOLK   I warrant you, my lord.   [Exit.] 57
KING RICHARD   Catesby!
CATESBY
 My lord?
KING RICHARD   Send out a pursuivant at arms   59
 To Stanley's regiment. Bid him bring his power   60
 Before sunrising, lest his son George fall
 Into the blind cave of eternal night.   [Exit Catesby.]
 Fill me a bowl of wine. Give me a watch.   63
 Saddle white Surrey for the field tomorrow.   64
 Look that my staves be sound and not too heavy.   65
 Ratcliffe!
RATCLIFFE   My lord?
KING RICHARD
 Saw'st thou the melancholy Lord Northumberland?
RATCLIFFE
 Thomas the Earl of Surrey and himself,
 Much about cockshut time, from troop to troop   70
 Went through the army, cheering up the soldiers.
KING RICHARD
 So, I am satisfied. Give me a bowl of wine.
 I have not that alacrity of spirit
 Nor cheer of mind that I was wont to have.   74
                                   [Wine is brought.]
 Set it down. Is ink and paper ready?
RATCLIFFE
 It is, my lord.
KING RICHARD   Bid my guard watch. Leave me.
 Ratcliffe, about the mid of night come to my tent
 And help to arm me. Leave me, I say.
                            Exit Ratcliffe. [Richard sleeps.]

 Enter [Lord Stanley Earl of] Derby, to Richmond
 in his tent, [lords and others attending].

STANLEY
 Fortune and victory sit on thy helm!   79
RICHMOND
 All comfort that the dark night can afford
 Be to thy person, noble father-in-law!   81
 Tell me, how fares our loving mother?
STANLEY
 I, by attorney, bless thee from thy mother,   83
 Who prays continually for Richmond's good.
 So much for that. The silent hours steal on,
 And flaky darkness breaks within the east.   86
 In brief—for so the season bids us be—   87
 Prepare thy battle early in the morning,   88
 And put thy fortune to the arbitrament   89

---

20 car chariot (of Phoebus)   22 standard flag.   25 Limit appoint.
several charge individual command   26 And . . . power and divide
proportionately our small army.   29 keeps i.e., is with   38 power
army   50 beaver face-guard or visor of helmet.   easier looser, better
fitting

57 warrant guarantee   59 pursuivant at arms junior officer acting as
messenger   60 power forces   63 watch watch light, candle marked
into equal divisions to show time; or, perhaps, sentinel.   64 white
Surrey (The name seems to be Shakespeare's invention. The chroniclers say that Richard was mounted on a "great white courser.")
65 staves lance shafts   70 cockshut time evening twilight; possibly,
the time at which the poultry are shut up   74 was wont used   79 helm
helmet.   81 father-in-law stepfather.   83 by attorney as proxy
86 flaky streaked with light   87 season time   88 battle troops
89 arbitrament arbitration

Of bloody strokes and mortal-staring war.   90
I, as I may—that which I would I cannot—   91
With best advantage will deceive the time   92
And aid thee in this doubtful shock of arms.   93
But on thy side I may not be too forward,   94
Lest, being seen, thy brother, tender George,   95
Be executed in his father's sight.
Farewell. The leisure and the fearful time   97
Cuts off the ceremonious vows of love
And ample interchange of sweet discourse
Which so long sundered friends should dwell upon.
God give us leisure for these rites of love!
Once more, adieu. Be valiant, and speed well!   102

RICHMOND
Good lords, conduct him to his regiment.
I'll strive with troubled thoughts to take a nap,
Lest leaden slumber peise me down tomorrow,   105
When I should mount with wings of victory.
Once more, good night, kind lords and gentlemen.
                    Exeunt. [Richmond remains.]
O Thou whose captain I account myself,
Look on my forces with a gracious eye;
Put in their hands thy bruising irons of wrath,
That they may crush down with a heavy fall
The usurping helmets of our adversaries!
Make us thy ministers of chastisement,
That we may praise thee in the victory!
To thee I do commend my watchful soul
Ere I let fall the windows of mine eyes.   116
Sleeping and waking, oh, defend me still!   117
                                    [He sleeps.]

Enter the Ghost of young Prince Edward, son [of]
Harry the Sixth, to Richard.

GHOST (*to Richard*)
Let me sit heavy on thy soul tomorrow!   118
Think, how thou stabbed'st me in my prime of youth
At Tewkesbury. Despair therefore and die!
(*To Richmond*) Be cheerful, Richmond, for the wrongèd souls
Of butchered princes fight in thy behalf.
King Henry's issue, Richmond, comforts thee. [*Exit.*]

Enter the Ghost of Henry the Sixth.

GHOST (*to Richard*)
When I was mortal, my anointed body   124
By thee was punchèd full of deadly holes.
Think on the Tower and me. Despair and die!   126
Harry the Sixth bids thee despair and die!
(*To Richmond*) Virtuous and holy, be thou conqueror!

Harry, that prophesied thou shouldst be king,   129
Doth comfort thee in thy sleep. Live and flourish!
                                        [Exit.]

Enter the Ghost of Clarence.

GHOST [*to Richard*]
Let me sit heavy in thy soul tomorrow,
I, that was washed to death with fulsome wine,   132
Poor Clarence, by thy guile betrayed to death!
Tomorrow in the battle think on me,
And fall thy edgeless sword. Despair and die!   135
(*To Richmond*) Thou offspring of the house of Lancaster,
The wrongèd heirs of York do pray for thee.
Good angels guard thy battle! Live and flourish!   138
                                        [Exit.]

Enter the Ghosts of Rivers, Grey, [and] Vaughan.

GHOST OF RIVERS [*to Richard*]
Let me sit heavy in thy soul tomorrow,
Rivers that died at Pomfret! Despair and die!
GHOST OF GREY [*to Richard*]
Think upon Grey, and let thy soul despair!
GHOST OF VAUGHAN [*to Richard*]
Think upon Vaughan, and, with guilty fear,
Let fall thy lance. Despair and die!
ALL (*to Richmond*)
Awake, and think our wrongs in Richard's bosom
Will conquer him! Awake, and win the day!
                                    [Exeunt Ghosts.]

Enter the Ghost of Hastings.

GHOST [*to Richard*]
Bloody and guilty, guiltily awake
And in a bloody battle end thy days!
Think on Lord Hastings. Despair and die!
(*To Richmond*) Quiet untroubled soul, awake, awake!
Arm, fight, and conquer for fair England's sake!
                                        [Exit.]

Enter the Ghosts of the two young Princes.

GHOSTS (*to Richard*)
Dream on thy cousins smothered in the Tower.   151
Let us be lead within thy bosom, Richard,
And weigh thee down to ruin, shame, and death!
Thy nephews' souls bid thee despair and die!
(*To Richmond*) Sleep, Richmond, sleep in peace, and
    wake in joy.
Good angels guard thee from the boar's annoy!   156
Live, and beget a happy race of kings!
Edward's unhappy sons do bid thee flourish.
                                    [Exeunt Ghosts.]

Enter the Ghost of Lady Anne, his wife.

GHOST [*to Richard*]
Richard, thy wife, that wretched Anne thy wife,
That never slept a quiet hour with thee,

---

90 mortal-staring fatal-visaged   **91 that . . . cannot** i.e., I cannot fight
openly on your side, though I want to   **92 With . . . time** as best I can
I will work for your side without seeming to do so   **93 shock**
encounter   **94 forward** zealous   **95 brother** i.e., stepbrother.   **tender**
young, of tender years   **97 leisure** i.e., brief time allowed   **102 speed
well** may you succeed.   **105 peise** weigh   **116 windows** i.e., eyelids
117 still continually.   **118 sit heavy on** be oppressive to   **124 anointed**
i.e., with the sacred oil used in the coronation ceremony; compare
with 4.4.151   **126 Tower** (Where Henry VI was supposed to have
been murdered.)

129 prophesied (See *3 Henry VI*, 4.6.68 ff.)   **132 washed to death** i.e.,
drowned in a butt of malmsey.   **fulsome** cloying   **135 fall** let fall.
edgeless blunt, useless   **138 battle** troops.   **151 cousins** i.e.,
nephews   **156 the boar's annoy** i.e., Richard's attack.

Now fills thy sleep with perturbations.
Tomorrow in the battle think on me,
And fall thy edgeless sword. Despair and die!
(*To Richmond*) Thou quiet soul, sleep thou a quiet sleep;
Dream of success and happy victory!
Thy adversary's wife doth pray for thee.   [*Exit.*]

Enter the Ghost of Buckingham.

GHOST [*to Richard*]
    The first was I that helped thee to the crown;
    The last was I that felt thy tyranny.
    Oh, in the battle think on Buckingham,
    And die in terror of thy guiltiness!
    Dream on, dream on of bloody deeds and death;
    Fainting, despair; despairing, yield thy breath!   172
    (*To Richmond*) I died for hope ere I could lend thee aid,   173
    But cheer thy heart, and be thou not dismayed.
    God and good angels fight on Richmond's side,
    And Richard fall in height of all his pride!   [*Exit.*] 176
                            Richard starteth up out of a dream.

KING RICHARD
    Give me another horse! Bind up my wounds!
    Have mercy, Jesu!—Soft, I did but dream.
    O coward conscience, how dost thou afflict me!
    The lights burn blue. It is now dead midnight.   180
    Cold fearful drops stand on my trembling flesh.
    What do I fear? Myself? There's none else by.
    Richard loves Richard; that is, I am I.   183
    Is there a murderer here? No. Yes, I am.
    Then fly. What, from myself? Great reason why: 185
    Lest I revenge. What, myself upon myself?
    Alack, I love myself. Wherefore? For any good   187
    That I myself have done unto myself?
    Oh, no! Alas, I rather hate myself
    For hateful deeds committed by myself!
    I am a villain. Yet I lie, I am not.
    Fool, of thyself speak well. Fool, do not flatter.
    My conscience hath a thousand several tongues,   193
    And every tongue brings in a several tale,
    And every tale condemns me for a villain.
    Perjury, perjury, in the highest degree,
    Murder, stern murder, in the direst degree,
    All several sins, all used in each degree,   198
    Throng to the bar, crying all, "Guilty! Guilty!"   199
    I shall despair. There is no creature loves me,   200
    And if I die no soul will pity me.
    And wherefore should they, since that I myself
    Find in myself no pity to myself?
    Methought the souls of all that I had murdered

Came to my tent, and every one did threat
Tomorrow's vengeance on the head of Richard.

    Enter Ratcliffe.

RATCLIFFE   My lord!
KING RICHARD   Zounds! Who is there?
RATCLIFFE
    My lord, 'tis I. The early village cock
    Hath twice done salutation to the morn.
    Your friends are up and buckle on their armor.
KING RICHARD
    Oh, Ratcliffe, I have dreamed a fearful dream!
    What think'st thou, will our friends prove all true?
RATCLIFFE
    No doubt, my lord.
KING RICHARD   Oh, Ratcliffe, I fear, I fear!
RATCLIFFE
    Nay, good my lord, be not afraid of shadows.
KING RICHARD
    By the apostle Paul, shadows tonight
    Have struck more terror to the soul of Richard
    Than can the substance of ten thousand soldiers
    Armèd in proof and led by shallow Richmond.   219
    'Tis not yet near day. Come, go with me;
    Under our tents I'll play the eavesdropper,
    To see if any mean to shrink from me.
                    Exeunt [*Richard and Ratcliffe*].

    Enter the Lords to Richmond, [*sitting in his tent*].

LORDS   Good morrow, Richmond!
RICHMOND
    Cry mercy, lords and watchful gentlemen,   224
    That you have ta'en a tardy sluggard here.
A LORD   How have you slept, my lord?
RICHMOND
    The sweetest sleep and fairest-boding dreams
    That ever entered in a drowsy head
    Have I since your departure had, my lords.
    Methought their souls whose bodies Richard murdered
    Came to my tent and cried on victory.   231
    I promise you, my soul is very jocund   232
    In the remembrance of so fair a dream.
    How far into the morning is it, lords?
A LORD   Upon the stroke of four.
RICHMOND
    Why, then 'tis time to arm and give direction.

    His oration to his soldiers.

    More than I have said, loving countrymen,   237
    The leisure and enforcement of the time   238
    Forbids to dwell upon. Yet remember this:
    God and our good cause fight upon our side.
    The prayers of holy saints and wrongèd souls,
    Like high-reared bulwarks, stand before our faces.

---

172 Fainting losing heart   **173 for hope** i.e., for hoping to support you, or for want of hope, hoping in vain to help   **176 Richard fall** may Richard fall   **180 lights burn blue** (Superstitiously regarded as evidence of the presence of ghosts.)   **183 I am I** (A blasphemy of God's "*ego sum*.")   **185 fly** flee.   **187 Wherefore?** Why?   **193 several** different, separate   **198 used . . . degree** committed in every degree of infamy, from bad to worst   **199 bar** i.e., bar of justice   **200 despair** (Considered the only unforgivable sin.)

219 proof armor   **224 Cry mercy** I beg your pardon   **231 cried on victory** invoked victory, cried out to it.   **232 promise** assure. **jocund** cheerful   **237 have said** have already said before **238 leisure** i.e., brief time allowed

Richard except, those whom we fight against   243
Had rather have us win than him they follow.
For what is he they follow? Truly, gentlemen,
A bloody tyrant and a homicide;
One raised in blood, and one in blood established;   247
One that made means to come by what he hath,   248
And slaughtered those that were the means to help him;
A base, foul stone, made precious by the foil   250
Of England's chair, where he is falsely set;   251
One that hath ever been God's enemy.
Then if you fight against God's enemy,
God will in justice ward you as his soldiers;   254
If you do sweat to put a tyrant down,
You sleep in peace, the tyrant being slain;
If you do fight against your country's foes,
Your country's fat shall pay your pains the hire;   258
If you do fight in safeguard of your wives,
Your wives shall welcome home the conquerors;
If you do free your children from the sword,
Your children's children quits it in your age.   262
Then, in the name of God and all these rights,
Advance your standards! Draw your willing swords!   264
For me, the ransom of my bold attempt   265
Shall be this cold corpse on the earth's cold face;   266
But if I thrive, the gain of my attempt
The least of you shall share his part thereof.
Sound drums and trumpets boldly and cheerfully;
God and Saint George! Richmond and victory!
                                                        [Exeunt.]

*Enter King Richard, Ratcliffe, [attendants and
forces].*

KING RICHARD
What said Northumberland as touching Richmond?
RATCLIFFE
That he was never trainèd up in arms.
KING RICHARD
He said the truth. And what said Surrey then?
RATCLIFFE
He smiled and said, "The better for our purpose."
KING RICHARD
He was in the right, and so indeed it is.
                                        The clock striketh.
Tell the clock there. Give me a calendar.   276
Who saw the sun today?   *[He takes an almanac.]*
RATCLIFFE   Not I, my lord.
KING RICHARD
Then he disdains to shine, for by the book   278
He should have braved the east an hour ago.   279
A black day will it be to somebody.

Ratcliffe!
RATCLIFFE
My lord?
KING RICHARD   The sun will not be seen today;
The sky doth frown and lour upon our army.   283
I would these dewy tears were from the ground.
Not shine today? Why, what is that to me
More than to Richmond? For the selfsame heaven
That frowns on me looks sadly upon him.

Enter Norfolk.

NORFOLK
Arm, arm, my lord, the foe vaunts in the field!   288
KING RICHARD
Come, bustle, bustle! Caparison my horse.   289
Call up Lord Stanley; bid him bring his power.
I will lead forth my soldiers to the plain,
And thus my battle shall be orderèd: 292
My foreward shall be drawn out all in length,   293
Consisting equally of horse and foot;
Our archers shall be placèd in the midst.
John Duke of Norfolk, Thomas Earl of Surrey,
Shall have the leading of this foot and horse.
They thus directed, we will follow   298
In the main battle, whose puissance on either side   299
Shall be well wingèd with our chiefest horse.   300
This, and Saint George to boot! What think'st thou,
Norfolk?   301
NORFOLK
A good direction, warlike sovereign.
This found I on my tent this morning.
                                        He showeth him a paper.
KING RICHARD *[reads]*
"Jockey of Norfolk, be not so bold,   304
For Dickon thy master is bought and sold."   305
A thing devisèd by the enemy.
Go, gentlemen, every man unto his charge.
Let not our babbling dreams affright our souls;
Conscience is but a word that cowards use,
Devised at first to keep the strong in awe.
Our strong arms be our conscience, swords our law!
March on, join bravely! Let us to it pell-mell;   312
If not to heaven, then hand in hand to hell.

His oration to his army.

What shall I say more than I have inferred?   314
Remember whom you are to cope withal:
A sort of vagabonds, rascals, and runaways,   316
A scum of Bretons and base lackey peasants,   317
Whom their o'ercloyèd country vomits forth   318
To desperate adventures and assured destruction.

---

243 **except** excepted   247 **in blood** by bloodshed   248 **made means**
i.e., has taken advantage, created opportunity   250 **foil** a thin leaf of
metal placed under a gem to set it off to advantage   251 **chair** throne.
set (1) seated (2) set like a jewel   254 **ward** protect   258 **Your . . . hire**
England's prosperity will reward your efforts   262 **Your . . . age** your
grandchildren will requite it when you are old.   264 **Advance** raise
265–6 **the ransom . . . face** i.e., if I fail, there will be no question of
ransom, but only death   276 **Tell** Count the strokes of.   **calendar**
almanac.   278 **the book** i.e., the almanac   279 **braved** made splendid

283 **lour** look threateningly   288 **vaunts** boasts his strength
289 **Caparison** Put on the battle trappings of   292 **battle** troops
293 **foreward** vanguard   298 **directed** deployed   299 **main battle**
main body of troops.   **puissance** strength   300 **wingèd** flanked.
horse cavalry.   301 **to boot** i.e., to give us aid in addition.   304 **Jockey**
i.e., Jack, John   305 **Dickon** i.e., Dick, Richard.   **bought and sold**
done for, finished.   312 **join** join battle.   **pell-mell** headlong, hand
to hand   314 **inferred** alleged.   316 **sort** gang   317 **lackey** servile
318 **o'ercloyèd** satiated, glutted

You sleeping safe, they bring to you unrest;
You having lands, and blest with beauteous wives,
They would restrain the one, distain the other.   322
And who doth lead them but a paltry fellow,
Long kept in Brittany at our mother's cost?   324
A milksop, one that never in his life
Felt so much cold as over shoes in snow?   326
Let's whip these stragglers o'er the seas again.
Lash hence these overweening rags of France,   328
These famished beggars, weary of their lives,
Who, but for dreaming on this fond exploit,   330
For want of means, poor rats, had hanged themselves.   331
If we be conquered, let men conquer us,
And not these bastard Bretons, whom our fathers
Have in their own land beaten, bobbed, and thumped,   334
And in record left them the heirs of shame.   335
Shall these enjoy our lands? Lie with our wives?
Ravish our daughters? [*Drum afar off.*] Hark! I hear
    their drum.
Fight, gentlemen of England! Fight, bold yeomen!
Draw, archers, draw your arrows to the head!   339
Spur your proud horses hard, and ride in blood;
Amaze the welkin with your broken staves!   341

        [*Enter a Messenger.*]

What says Lord Stanley? Will he bring his power?
MESSENGER   My lord, he doth deny to come.
KING RICHARD   Off with his son George's head!
NORFOLK
My lord, the enemy is past the marsh.
After the battle let George Stanley die.

KING RICHARD
A thousand hearts are great within my bosom.
Advance our standards! Set upon our foes!   348
Our ancient word of courage, fair Saint George,   349
Inspire us with the spleen of fiery dragons!   350
Upon them! Victory sits on our helms!   *Exeunt.*

[5.4]

    *Alarum. Excursions. [Norfolk and forces continue
    to make forays, entering and exiting.] Enter [in the
    melee] Catesby.*

CATESBY
Rescue, my lord of Norfolk, rescue, rescue!
The King enacts more wonders than a man,   2
Daring an opposite to every danger.   3
His horse is slain, and all on foot he fights,
Seeking for Richmond in the throat of death.
Rescue, fair lord, or else the day is lost!

        [*Alarums.*] Enter [*King*] Richard.

KING RICHARD
A horse! A horse! My kingdom for a horse!
CATESBY
Withdraw, my lord. I'll help you to a horse.
KING RICHARD
Slave, I have set my life upon a cast,   9
And I will stand the hazard of the die.   10
I think there be six Richmonds in the field;   11
Five have I slain today instead of him.
A horse! A horse! My kingdom for a horse! [*Exeunt.*]

        ❖

[5.5]

    *Alarum. Enter Richard and Richmond; they fight.
    Richard is slain. [Exit Richmond.] Then, retreat
    being sounded, [flourish, and] enter Richmond,
    [Lord Stanley Earl of] Derby bearing the crown,
    with other lords, etc.*

RICHMOND
God and your arms be praised, victorious friends!
The day is ours; the bloody dog is dead.
STANLEY [*offering him the crown*]
Courageous Richmond, well hast thou acquit thee.
Lo, here this long-usurpèd royalty
From the dead temples of this bloody wretch
Have I plucked off, to grace thy brows withal.   6
Wear it, enjoy it, and make much of it.
RICHMOND
Great God of heaven, say amen to all!
But, tell me, is young George Stanley living?
STANLEY
He is, my lord, and safe in Leicester town,
Whither, if it please you, we may now withdraw us.
RICHMOND
What men of name are slain on either side?   12
STANLEY
John Duke of Norfolk, Walter Lord Ferrers,
Sir Robert Brackenbury, and Sir William Brandon.
RICHMOND
Inter their bodies as becomes their births.
Proclaim a pardon to the soldiers fled

322 restrain deprive you of. **distain** defile, sully **324 our mother's** (Richmond's mother was not Richard's. This error occurs in the second edition of Holinshed's *Chronicles*. The first edition reads "brothers," the reference being to the fact that Richmond had been supported at the court of the Duke of Brittany at the cost of Charles, Duke of Burgundy, Richard's brother-in-law.) **326 over shoes** i.e., over his shoe-tops
328 rags ragged fellows **330 fond** foolish **331 want of means** poverty
334 bobbed thrashed **335 And . . . shame** and left them with nothing but the promise of a shameful record in history. **339 to the head** to the head of the arrow. **341 Amaze the welkin** Frighten the skies
348 Advance our standards! Raise our flags! **349 word of courage** battle cry **350 dragons** (Richard ironically identifies with the dragon slain by Saint George.)
5.4. Location: Bosworth Field, as before; the action is continuous.
0.1 *Excursions* Sorties

2 than a man than seems possible for a human being **3 Daring . . . danger** boldly facing every danger in battle. **9 cast** throw of the dice
10 stand the hazard accept the fortune. **die** (Singular of *dice*.)
11 six Richmonds i.e., Richmond himself and five men dressed like him as a safety precaution
5.5. Location: Action continues at Bosworth Field.
0.2 *retreat* trumpet signal to withdraw, cease the attack **6 withal** with. **12 of name** of title

That in submission will return to us,
And then, as we have ta'en the Sacrament,   18
We will unite the white rose and the red.
Smile heaven upon this fair conjunction,   20
That long have frowned upon their enmity!
What traitor hears me and says not amen?
England hath long been mad, and scarred herself;
The brother blindly shed the brother's blood,
The father rashly slaughtered his own son,
The son, compelled, been butcher to the sire.
All this divided York and Lancaster,
Divided in their dire division.

18 **ta'en the Sacrament** sworn a sacred oath on the Sacrament (to marry Princess Elizabeth, daughter of Edward IV, thereby uniting the houses of York and of Lancaster, white rose and red rose)   **20 conjunction** union. (An astrological metaphor.)

Oh, now let Richmond and Elizabeth,
The true succeeders of each royal house,
By God's fair ordinance conjoin together!   31
And let their heirs, God, if thy will be so,
Enrich the time to come with smooth-faced peace,
With smiling plenty, and fair prosperous days!
Abate the edge of traitors, gracious Lord,   35
That would reduce these bloody days again   36
And make poor England weep in streams of blood!
Let them not live to taste this land's increase
That would with treason wound this fair land's peace!
Now civil wounds are stopped, peace lives again.   40
That she may long live here, God say amen! [*Exeunt.*]

31 **ordinance** decree   35 **Abate** Blunt, render ineffective   **36 reduce** bring back   **40 stopped** closed up

The Life and Death of King John

The Life and Death of King John is usually dated on grounds of style between Shakespeare's two historical tetralogies, perhaps shortly before *Richard II* in 1594 or 1595. In structure and characterization, it is also transitional from the episodic first series (*Henry VI* through *Richard III*) to the more tightly organized second series (*Richard II* through *Henry V*). It stands alone among Shakespeare's history plays of the 1590s in choosing the early thirteenth century for its subject, rather than the fifteenth century. Yet the political problems are familiar.

Foremost is the uncertainty of John's claim to the English throne. He occupies that throne by "strong possession" and also seemingly by the last will and testament of his deceased eldest brother, King Richard I. But could such a will disinherit Arthur, the son of John's older brother Geoffrey? English primogeniture specified that property must descend to the eldest son; after Richard's death, without direct heirs, his next brother, Geoffrey, would inherit and then Geoffrey's son, Arthur. Significantly, even John's mother, Queen Eleanor, who publicly supports John's claim, privately admits that "strong possession" is much more on their side than "right" (1.1.39–40). All parties concede, then, that young Arthur's claim is legally superior.

Yet such a claim raises serious practical questions, because it challenges the status quo. John is de facto king, and Arthur a child. To make the dilemma complete, Arthur has no ambitions to rule and seemingly no talent for leadership. Without the unremitting zeal of his widowed mother, Constance, Arthur would retire into the private world of kindness and love, where his virtues shine. Moreover, Constance's uncompromising defense of her son's true claim requires her to seek alliance with the French for an invasion of England. Such an appalling prospect of invasion and civil war inevitably poses the question: is the replacement of John by Arthur worth the price? Which is better—an ongoing regime flawed by uncertain claim and political compromises or restitution of the "right" by violent and potentially self-destructive means?

Shakespeare refuses to simplify the issues. John is neither a monstrous tyrant nor a martyred hero, although both interpretations were available to Shakespeare in sixteenth-century historical writings. Catholic historians of the late Middle Ages, such as Polydore Vergil, had uniformly condemned John, partly, at least, because of his interference with the Church. The English Reformation brought about a conscious rewriting of history, and, in John Bale's play *King Johan* (1538, with later revisions), the protagonist is unassailably a champion of the right. Centuries ahead of his time, this King John comprehends the true interests of the state in fending off the encroachments of the international Church. He fails only because his people are superstitious and his aristocrats are the dupes of Catholic meddling. Bale's play is transparently a warning to Tudor England. This portrait of John as a martyr continues unabated in John Foxe's *Acts and Monuments* and in the chronicles of Richard Grafton and Raphael Holinshed, which were based on Foxe. Most virulent of all is the play called *The Troublesome Reign of King John* (c. 1587–1591), once thought to be by Shakespeare and analyzed by some recent editors an unauthorized quarto of Shakespeare's text but now generally regarded as the work of some more chauvinistic playwright, most probably George Peele. Although generally close to Shakespeare's play in its narrative of events, it also contains scenes of the most degraded anti-Catholic humor, featuring gross abbots who conceal nuns in their private rooms, and the like. Against such a corrupt institution, the plundering undertaken by King John's loyal follower, Philip the Bastard (also known as Sir Richard Plantagenet), is wholly justifiable. John and the Bastard would be invincible, were it not for the base Catholic loyalties of the nobility.

Shakespeare consciously declines to endorse either the Catholic or the Protestant interpretation of the reign of King John. (Interestingly, neither side showed any interest in Magna Carta; not until the seventeenth century was that event interpreted as a famous precedent for constitutional restraints imposed on the monarchy.) To be sure, some anticlericalism still remains in the play. John grandly proclaims that "no Italian priest/Shall tithe or toll in our dominions." John is "supreme head" of Church and State (the actual title claimed by Henry VIII), defending his people against "this meddling priest" with his "juggling witchcraft" (3.1.153–69). Yet Shakespeare's King John is not vindictive against the Church. He seizes some of its wealth, not as a reprisal, but to support his costly military campaigns; when he is poisoned by a monk, neither John nor anyone else assumes that a Catholic conspiracy is responsible—as it is in *Troublesome Reign*. Similarly, the baronial opposition to John is motivated not by secret leanings toward Rome but by understandable revulsion at the apparent murder of Arthur.

Shakespeare's balanced treatment need not merely reflect his own political allegiances, whatever they were. Artistically, *King John* is a study of impasse, of tortured political dilemmas to which there can be no clear answer. How do people behave under such trying circumstances? Shakespeare's play is remarkable for its sensitivity and compassion toward all sides. His most completely sympathetic characters are those innocently caught in the political cross fire, such as Arthur and the Lady Blanche. Among the major contenders for power, all except the ruthless Dauphin Lewis are guided by worthy intentions and yet are forced to make unfortunate and self-contradictory compromises. Constance, for all her virtuous singleness of mind, must seek a French invasion of England. King Philip of France, bound to Constance's cause by all the holy vows of heaven, changes his purpose when England offers a profitable marriage alliance and then shifts quickly back again when the papacy demands in the name of the Church that Philip punish King John for heresy. Philip's conscience is troubled about both decisions, but what is a king to do when faced with practical choices affecting his people's welfare and his own political safety?

Even Pandulph, the papal legate, can be viewed as a well-intentioned statesman caught in the web of political compromise. Presumably, he is sincere in his belief that King John's defiance of the papacy—in particular, his refusal to accept the Pope's choice, Stephen Langton, as Archbishop of Canterbury—represents a grave threat to Catholic Christendom. Yet Pandulph reveals an unprincipled cunning when he teaches King Philip how to equivocate a sacred vow, or instructs the apt young Lewis in Machiavellian intrigue. As Pandulph explains, the French can exploit King John's capture of Arthur by invading England in Arthur's name, thereby forcing John to murder his nephew in order to terminate the rival claim to the throne. Arthur's death will, in turn, drive the English nobility over to the French side. By this stratagem, the seemingly bad luck of Arthur's capture can neatly be turned to the advantage of France and the international Church (3.4.126–81). Lewis learns his lesson only too well. What Pandulph has failed to take into account is the insincerity of Lewis's alliance with papal power. When the legate has achieved through the invasion what he wants—the submission of John—and then tries to call off Lewis's army, Pandulph discovers too late that the young Frenchman cares only for war on his own terms. Pandulph's cunning becomes a weapon turned against himself.

John is, like his enemies, a talented man justly punished by his own perjuries. His failings are serious, but they are also understandable. Given the fact that he is king, his desire to maintain rule serves both his own interests and those of political order generally. The deal by which John bargains away his French territories of Angiers, Touraine, Maine, Poitiers, and the rest, in order to win peace with France, is prudent under the circumstances but a blow to those English dreams of greatness that John professes to uphold. When France immediately repudiates this treaty, John merely gets what he deserves for entering such a deal. His surrender of the crown to the papacy is again the canny result of yielding to the least dangerous of the alternatives available but diminishes John's already shaky authority nonetheless.

Most heinous is John's determination to be rid of Arthur. He has compelling reasons, to be sure. As Pandulph predicts, the French invasion of England, using Arthur's claim as its pretext, forces John to consider Arthur as an immediate threat to himself. (Queen Elizabeth had long agonized over a similar problem with her captive, Mary, Queen of Scots; so long as Mary lived, a Catholic and claimant to the throne, English Catholics had a perennial rallying point.) What is a ruling king to do with a rival claimant in his captivity? As Henry IV also discovers once he has captured Richard II, the logic demanding death is inexorable. Yet such a deed is not only murder but also murder of one's close kinsman and murder of the Lord's anointed in the eyes of those believing the captive, in this case Arthur, to be rightful king. Furthermore, it is sure to backfire and punish the doer by arousing national resentment and rebellion. John quickly regrets Arthur's death, but we suspect that the regret is, in part, motivated by fear of the consequences. The same ironic predicament that protects John against his own worst instincts, momentarily saving the boy from Hubert's instruments of torture, also justly prevents John from obtaining any political benefit from this brief reprieve; Hubert is too late, Arthur dies in a fall, and the lords are convinced of John's guilt. With fitting irony, John is punished for his crime after he has decided not to do it and after the murder itself has failed to take place.

The word used to sum up the universal political scheming and oath breaking in this play is *commodity*, or self-interest (2.1.574). The word is introduced by the Bastard, the fascinating choric figure of *King John*, whose reactions to the events of the play are so important in shaping our own. The Bastard is an outsider from birth and so not beholden to society for its usual tawdry benefits. As the natural son of the great King Richard Coeur de Lion, the Bastard is a kind of folk hero: he is instinctively royal and yet a commoner, a projection of the Elizabethan audience's sentimental fondness for monarchy and at the same time a hero representing a cross section of society. He is a fictional character in a largely historical world. His quarrel with his effete brother Robert over the inheritance of their father's property comically mirrors the futility of the dynastic quarrel between King John and Arthur. In both contentions, a will left by the deceased confuses the issue of genealogical priority. Thus John, who defends the Bastard's unconventional claim to his inheritance, discovers a natural ally.

The Bastard is strangely drawn to commodity at first. He finds it exhilarating to trust his fortune to war and royal favor, rather than to the easy comfort of a landed estate. The wars enable him to pursue a quest for self-identity. After learning from his reluctant mother who his real father was, the Bastard must venge himself upon the Duke of Austria, who (unhistorically) killed his father. When first confronted with the moral ambiguity of the war, the Bastard's response is mischievous, almost Vicelike. He makes the cunning suggestion, for example, that France and England join against the city of Angiers until it surrenders, after which they may resume fighting one another. Clearly, this Machiavellian proposal embodies, even satirizes, the spirit of commodity. Yet the Bastard is not motivated by self-interest or a cynical delight in duping people, as is the bastard Edmund in *King Lear*. This Bastard's illegitimacy has no such ominous cosmic import. Instead, he is at first the detached witty observer, wryly amused at the seemingly inherent absurdity of politics. Although he does protest also that he will worship commodity for his own gain, we never see him doing so. Despite his philosophic detachment, he remains loyal to England and to John. In fact, he is the play's greatest patriot.

The supreme test for the Bastard, as for all well-meaning characters and for the audience as well, is the death of Arthur. The Bastard must experience disaffection and even revulsion if he is to retain our sympathy as choric interpreter. Yet his chief function is to triumph over that revulsion and, in so doing, to act as counterpart to the more rash English lords. They have come hastily to the conclusion that John is guilty of Arthur's death. This is, of course, true in the main, but they do not know all the circumstances, and truth, as usual is more complicated than they suppose. Only the Bastard consistently phrases his condemnation in qualified terms: "It is a damnèd and a bloody work . . . If that it be the work of any hand" (4.3.57–9). Moreover, the lords have concluded that John's guilt justifies their rebellion. Yet they stoop to commodity of the very sort they condemn. They fight for the supposed good of England by allying themselves with Lewis of France. Once again, the ironies of cosmic justice demand that such commodity be repaid by treachery. The lords are luckily saved just in time by Lord Melun's revelation of Lewis's plan, just as John had been saved from his own headstrong folly by the kindness of Hubert. The Bastard's decision to remain loyal to John thus proves not only prudent but also right-minded. He has led our sympathies through disaffection to acceptance. Rebellion only worsens matters by playing into the hands of opportunists. Loyalty to John is still, in a sense, a kind of commodity, for it involves compromise and acceptance of politics as morally a world unto itself. Nevertheless, loyalty is a conscientious choice and is rewarded finally by the accession of young Henry III, who at last combines political legitimacy and the will to act.

The ending of *King John* is not without its ironies. England, having suffered through the dynastic uncertainties of a child claimant to the throne (as also in the *Henry VI* plays, *Richard III, Richard II*, and Christopher Marlowe's *Edward II*), must now face a new destiny under the young and unproven Henry III. The irony is often underscored, in some modern productions at least, by doubling the parts of Arthur and Henry III for the same juvenile actor. Is there sufficient reason to suppose that the problem will not recur? The Bastard's role in seeking affirmation is a crucial one, and yet he does so from his vantage point as the play's most visibly unhistorical personage. As a fictional character, the Bastard is free to invent fictions around him, to instruct King John in the playing of a part that will benefit England, and to fashion a concluding speech in which there can be hope for the future. What sort of consolation does this fiction provide? To dwell on the conflict between history and fiction is not to subvert all hope by labeling fiction as mere fantasy, but it does call attention to the fruitfully ambiguous relation between Shakespeare's stubbornly historical subject matter and his function as creative artist.

The Life and Death of King John

[*Dramatis Personae*

KING JOHN
QUEEN ELEANOR, *his mother*
PRINCE HENRY, *his son, afterward King Henry III*
ARTHUR, *Duke of Brittaine (Brittany), King John's nephew*
CONSTANCE, *Arthur's mother, widow of King John's elder brother, Geoffrey*
BLANCHE *of Spain, niece of King John*

LADY FAULCONBRIDGE, *widow of Sir Robert Faulconbridge*
Philip the BASTARD, *afterward knighted as Sir Richard Plantagenet, her illegitimate son by Richard I (Richard Coeur de Lion)*
ROBERT FAULCONBRIDGE, *her legitimate son*
JAMES GURNEY, *her attendant*

EARL OF PEMBROKE
EARL OF ESSEX
EARL OF SALISBURY

LORD BIGOT
HUBERT DE BURGH, *in the service of King John*
PETER OF POMFRET, *a prophet*
An English HERALD
Two MESSENGERS *to King John*
FIRST EXECUTIONER

KING PHILIP *of France (Philip II)*
LEWIS, *the Dauphin*
DUKE OF AUSTRIA *(Limoges)*
MELUN, *a French lord*
CHATILLON, *ambassador from France to King John*
A French HERALD
A MESSENGER *to the Dauphin*
CITIZEN *of Angiers*

CARDINAL PANDULPH, *the Pope's legate*

Lords, a Sheriff, Soldiers, Citizens of Angiers, Executioners, and Attendants

scene: *Partly in England and partly in France*]

1.1

Enter King John, Queen Eleanor, Pembroke, Essex, and Salisbury, with the[m] Chatillon of France.

KING JOHN
Now, say, Chatillon, what would France with us? 1
CHATILLON
Thus, after greeting, speaks the King of France,
In my behavior, to the majesty— 3
The borrowed majesty—of England here. 4
ELEANOR
A strange beginning: "borrowed majesty"!

KING JOHN
Silence, good mother. Hear the embassy. 6
CHATILLON
Philip of France, in right and true behalf
Of thy deceasèd brother Geoffrey's son,
Arthur Plantagenet, lays most lawful claim
To this fair island and the territories,
To Ireland, Poitiers, Anjou, Touraine, Maine,
Desiring thee to lay aside the sword
Which sways usurpingly these several titles, 13
And put the same into young Arthur's hand,
Thy nephew and right royal sovereign.
KING JOHN
What follows if we disallow of this? 16

1.1. Location: England. The court of King John.
1 **what . . . us?** what does the King of France want with us? **3 In my behavior** in my person and conduct, through me **4 borrowed** i.e., not belonging by true right

6 **embassy** message. 13 **sways** manages, directs. **several titles** distinct possessions 16 **disallow of** reject

CHATILLON
The proud control of fierce and bloody war,   17
To enforce these rights so forcibly withheld.

KING JOHN
Here have we war for war and blood for blood,
Controlment for controlment. So answer France.

CHATILLON
Then take my king's defiance from my mouth,
The farthest limit of my embassy.

KING JOHN
Bear mine to him, and so depart in peace.
Be thou as lightning in the eyes of France;
For ere thou canst report I will be there,   25
The thunder of my cannon shall be heard.   26
So, hence! Be thou the trumpet of our wrath
And sullen presage of your own decay.—   28
An honorable conduct let him have.   29
Pembroke, look to't.—Farewell, Chatillon.
                    Exeunt Chatillon and Pembroke.

ELEANOR
What now, my son? Have I not ever said
How that ambitious Constance would not cease
Till she had kindled France and all the world
Upon the right and party of her son?   34
This might have been prevented and made whole   35
With very easy arguments of love,   36
Which now the manage of two kingdoms must   37
With fearful bloody issue arbitrate.   38

KING JOHN
Our strong possession and our right for us.

ELEANOR *[aside to King John]*
Your strong possession much more than your right,
Or else it must go wrong with you and me—
So much my conscience whispers in your ear,
Which none but heaven and you and I shall hear.

          Enter a Sheriff, [who whispers to Essex].

ESSEX
My liege, here is the strangest controversy,   44
Come from the country to be judged by you,
That e'er I heard. Shall I produce the men?

KING JOHN   Let them approach.
          [The Sheriff goes to summon the men.]
Our abbeys and our priories shall pay
This expedition's charge.

          *Enter Robert Faulconbridge and Philip, [his
          bastard brother].*

                    What men are you?

BASTARD
Your faithful subject I, a gentleman,
Born in Northamptonshire, and eldest son,
As I suppose, to Robert Faulconbridge,
A soldier, by the honor-giving hand
Of Coeur de Lion knighted in the field.   54

KING JOHN *[to Robert]*   What art thou?

ROBERT
The son and heir to that same Faulconbridge.

KING JOHN
Is that the elder, and art thou the heir?
You came not of one mother then, it seems.

BASTARD
Most certain of one mother, mighty King—
That is well known—and, as I think, one father.
But for the certain knowledge of that truth
I put you o'er to heaven and to my mother.   62
Of that I doubt, as all men's children may.

ELEANOR
Out on thee, rude man! Thou dost shame thy mother   64
And wound her honor with this diffidence.   65

BASTARD
I, madam? No, I have no reason for it.
That is my brother's plea and none of mine—
The which if he can prove, 'a pops me out   68
At least from fair five hundred pound a year.
Heaven guard my mother's honor and my land!

KING JOHN
A good blunt fellow.—Why, being younger born,
Doth he lay claim to thine inheritance?

BASTARD
I know not why, except to get the land.
But once he slandered me with bastardy.   74
But whe'er I be as true begot or no,   75
That still I lay upon my mother's head;   76
But that I am as well begot, my liege—
Fair fall the bones that took the pains for me!—   78
Compare our faces and be judge yourself.
If old Sir Robert did beget us both
And were our father, and this son like him,
O old Sir Robert, father, on my knee
I give heaven thanks I was not like to thee!

KING JOHN
Why, what a madcap hath heaven lent us here!

ELEANOR
He hath a trick of Coeur de Lion's face;   85
The accent of his tongue affecteth him.   86
Do you not read some tokens of my son
In the large composition of this man?   88

KING JOHN
Mine eye hath well examinèd his parts

---

17 control compulsion   **25 report** (1) deliver your message (2) sound
like thundering cannon   **26 cannon** (An anachronism, since gunpowder was not employed in Europe until the fourteenth century.)
28 sullen presage dismal portent, omen.   **decay** ruin.   **29 conduct**
escort, guard   **34 Upon** in behalf of.   **party** cause   **35 prevented . . .
whole** foreseen and set right   **36 arguments of love** amicable negotiation   **37 manage** management, leadership. (With suggestion of
manège, the controlling of horses.)   **38 issue** consequence   **44 liege**
feudal master, lord

54 Coeur de Lion Lion-heart, i.e., Richard I   **62 put you o'er** refer
you   **64 Out on thee** (An expression of reproach.)   **65 diffidence**
distrust, suspicion.   **68 'a** he   **74 once** (1) at one time (2) in short
75 whe'er whether   **76 lay . . . head** leave to my mother to give
account   **78 Fair . . . bones** may good come to the bones of him. (May
he rest in peace.)   **85 trick** characteristic look   **86 affecteth** resembles   **88 large composition** (1) general constitution (2) big build

And finds them perfect Richard. [*To Robert*] Sirrah,   90
  speak.
What doth move you to claim your brother's land?

BASTARD
  Because he hath a half-face like my father.   92
  With half that face would he have all my land—   93
  A half-faced groat five hundred pound a year!   94

ROBERT
  My gracious liege, when that my father lived,   95
  Your brother did employ my father much—   96

BASTARD
  Well, sir, by this you cannot get my land.
  Your tale must be how he employed my mother.

ROBERT
  —And once dispatched him in an embassy
  To Germany, there with the Emperor
  To treat of high affairs touching that time.   101
  Th'advantage of his absence took the King   102
  And in the meantime sojourned at my father's;
  Where how he did prevail I shame to speak,
  But truth is truth. Large lengths of seas and shores
  Between my father and my mother lay,
  As I have heard my father speak himself,
  When this same lusty gentleman was got.   108
  Upon his deathbed he by will bequeathed
  His lands to me, and took it on his death   110
  That this my mother's son was none of his;
  And if he were, he came into the world
  Full fourteen weeks before the course of time.
  Then, good my liege, let me have what is mine,
  My father's land, as was my father's will.

KING JOHN
  Sirrah, your brother is legitimate.
  Your father's wife did after wedlock bear him,
  And if she did play false, the fault was hers—
  Which fault lies on the hazards of all husbands   119
  That marry wives. Tell me, how if my brother,
  Who, as you say, took pains to get this son,
  Had of your father claimed this son for his?
  In sooth, good friend, your father might have kept
  This calf, bred from his cow, from all the world;
  In sooth he might. Then, if he were my brother's,   125
  My brother might not claim him, nor your father,   126
  Being none of his, refuse him. This concludes: 127
  My mother's son did get your father's heir;
  Your father's heir must have your father's land.

ROBERT
  Shall then my father's will be of no force
  To dispossess that child which is not his?

BASTARD
  Of no more force to dispossess me, sir,
  Than was his will to get me, as I think.

ELEANOR [*to the Bastard*]
  Whether hadst thou rather be: a Faulconbridge   134
  And like thy brother, to enjoy thy land,
  Or the reputed son of Coeur de Lion,
  Lord of thy presence, and no land beside?   137

BASTARD
  Madam, an if my brother had my shape   138
  And I had his, Sir Robert's his, like him,   139
  And if my legs were two such riding-rods,   140
  My arms such eel skins stuffed, my face so thin
  That in mine ear I durst not stick a rose   142
  Lest men should say "Look, where three-farthings goes!"
  And, to his shape, were heir to all this land,   144
  Would I might never stir from off this place,   145
  I would give it every foot to have this face;   146
  I would not be Sir Nob in any case.   147

ELEANOR
  I like thee well. Wilt thou forsake thy fortune,
  Bequeath thy land to him, and follow me?
  I am a soldier and now bound to France.

BASTARD [*to Robert*]
  Brother, take you my land. I'll take my chance.
  Your face hath got five hundred pound a year,
  Yet sell your face for five pence and 'tis dear.—   153
  Madam, I'll follow you unto the death.

ELEANOR
  Nay, I would have you go before me thither.   155

BASTARD
  Our country manners give our betters way.   156

KING JOHN   What is thy name?

BASTARD
  Philip, my liege, so is my name begun;
  Philip, good old Sir Robert's wife's eldest son.

90 Sirrah (Customary form of address to inferiors.)   92 half-face (1) profile (2) thin face   93 With . . . face i.e., With only half his father's thin face (but with plenty of cheek)   94 A half-faced . . . year! i.e., The very idea, a scrawny fellow like him enjoying an annual income of £500! (*A groat*, featuring the monarch's likeness in profile, was a very thin coin worth four pence.)   95 when that when   96 Your brother i.e., Richard Coeur de Lion   101 To . . . time i.e., to discuss matters that were currently of first importance.   102 Th'advantage . . . King The King (Richard) took advantage of his (Sir Robert's) absence   108 lusty vigorous, merry.   got begotten.   110 took . . . death i.e., swore solemnly (the most solemn oath being an oath on one's deathbed)   119 lies on the hazards is one of the risks   125 if . . . brother's i.e., even if Richard Coeur de Lion did beget Philip the Bastard   126–7 nor . . . concludes nor could Sir Robert Falconbridge disclaim Philip as his heir, even if Philip was not of his begetting. This settles the case

134 Whether Which of the two   137 Lord of thy presence i.e., royal-blooded master of your own person   138 an if if   139 I had . . . him i.e., if I had Sir Robert's shape as my brother now has. (*Sir Robert's his* means "Sir Robert's.")   140 riding-rods switches. (Probably with a suggestion of sexual emaciation and insufficiency, as also in *eel skins stuffed*, line 141, and *Sir Nob in any case*, line 147.)   142 stick a rose (The Queen's likeness on the three-farthing coin was distinguished from that on the three-halfpence by a rose behind her head. The Bastard's taunt is based on the thinness of the coin.)   144 to his shape in addition to (inheriting) his physical characteristics   145 Would . . . place i.e., may I never stir from this spot if I am not speaking the truth   146 it every foot every foot of it.   this face my own appearance   147 Nob (Diminutive of "Robert"; with a possible play on "knob," "head" in a sexual sense and as head of the family.)   153 'tis dear would be overpriced (since a *groat* is worth fourpence). 155 Nay . . . thither Nay, if we are talking about going to our deaths, I'd just as soon you went first. (Eleanor plays with the Bastard's conventional vow *unto the death*, "as long as I live.")   156 give . . . way yield precedence to our superiors. (The Bastard jokes that he will not upset social precedence to rush before Queen Eleanor to death.)

KING JOHN

From henceforth bear his name whose form thou bearest.
Kneel thou down Philip, but rise more great:

[*The Bastard kneels and is knighted.*]

Arise Sir Richard, and Plantagenet.

[*The Bastard rises.*]

BASTARD

Brother by th' mother's side, give me your hand.
My father gave me honor; yours gave land.
Now blessèd be the hour, by night or day,   165
When I was got, Sir Robert was away!   166

ELEANOR

The very spirit of Plantagenet!
I am thy grandam, Richard. Call me so.

BASTARD

Madam, by chance but not by truth; what though?   169
Something about, a little from the right,   170
In at the window, or else o'er the hatch.   171
Who dares not stir by day must walk by night,   172
And have is have, however men do catch.   173
Near or far off, well won is still well shot,   174
And I am I, howe'er I was begot.

KING JOHN [*to Robert*]

Go, Faulconbridge. Now hast thou thy desire:
A landless knight makes thee a landed squire.—   177
Come, madam, and come, Richard, we must speed
For France, for France, for it is more than need.

BASTARD [*to Robert*]

Brother, adieu. Good fortune come to thee!
For thou wast got i'th'way of honesty.   181

Exeunt all but [*the*] *Bastard.*

A foot of honor better than I was,   182
But many a many foot of land the worse!
Well, now can I make any Joan a lady.   184
"Good e'en, Sir Richard!"—"God-a-mercy, fellow!"—   185
And if his name be George, I'll call him Peter,
For new-made honor doth forget men's names;
'Tis too respective and too sociable   188
For your conversion. Now your traveler,   189

He and his toothpick at My Worship's mess,   190
And when my knightly stomach is sufficed,
Why then I suck my teeth and catechize   192
My pickèd man of countries: "My dear sir,"   193
Thus, leaning on mine elbow, I begin,
"I shall beseech you"—that is Question now;
And then comes Answer like an Absey book: 196
"Oh, sir," says Answer, "at your best command;
At your employment; at your service, sir."
"No sir," says Question, "I, sweet sir, at yours";
And so, ere Answer knows what Question would,   200
Saving in dialogue of compliment,   201
And talking of the Alps and Apennines,
The Pyrenean and the river Po,
It draws toward supper in conclusion so.
But this is worshipful society   205
And fits the mounting spirit like myself,
For he is but a bastard to the time   207
That doth not smack of observation.   208
And so am I—whether I smack or no,   209
And not alone in habit and device,   210
Exterior form, outward accoutrement,   211
But from the inward motion—to deliver   212
Sweet, sweet, sweet poison for the age's tooth;   213
Which, though I will not practice to deceive,   214
Yet, to avoid deceit, I mean to learn;   215
For it shall strew the footsteps of my rising.   216
But who comes in such haste in riding robes?
What woman-post is this? Hath she no husband   218
That will take pains to blow a horn before her?   219

Enter Lady Faulconbridge and James Gurney.

Oh, me! 'Tis my mother.—How now, good lady?
What brings you here to court so hastily?

LADY FAULCONBRIDGE

Where is that slave, thy brother? Where is he,   222
That holds in chase mine honor up and down?   223

BASTARD

My brother Robert, old Sir Robert's son?
Colbrand the Giant, that same mighty man?   225
Is it Sir Robert's son that you seek so?

165–6 Now . . . away i.e., I thank God that, at the blessed time when I was conceived, whether by night or day, Sir Robert was absent.   **169 not by truth** not honorably, not chastely.   **what though?** what of that?   **170 Something about** Somewhat roundabout, clandestinely   **171 In . . . hatch** i.e., something done clandestinely, out of wedlock. A *hatch* is the lower half of a door, separate from the top half. Ordinary business at the pantry or storeroom would be done through the upper half door. (With this witticism, the Bastard launches into a medley of proverbs.)   **172 Who . . . night** (In another proverb, the Bastard refers to the irregular way in which he was conceived and through which he can now claim his ancestry.)   **173 And . . . catch** and possession is what matters, however it is achieved.   **174 Near . . . shot** i.e., In archery, hitting the target is what matters, whatever the distance. (With sexual suggestion.)   **177 A landless knight** i.e., the Bastard, who is willing to trade his inheritance for a knighthood   **181 For . . . honesty** For you were conceived in wedlock. (With a condescending suggestion that Robert is a "good honest fellow.")   **182 foot** degree   **184 Joan** (Frequently used to designate any girl, usually of the lower class.)   **185 Good e'en** Good evening, good afternoon. (The Bastard imagines himself, in his new title, encountering a lower-class person.)   **God-a-mercy** Thanks, God reward you   **188–9 'Tis . . . conversion** remembering names shows more courteous respect for persons of lower social status than a newly made knight has to concern himself with.

190 toothpick (An affection associated with foreign travel and the latest courtly fashion.)   **My Worship's mess** i.e., my dinner table. (A knight was formally addressed as "Your Worship.")   **192 suck my teeth** (i.e., in contrast to the use of toothpick by the *traveler*)   **193 pickèd** (1) refined (2) having picked his teeth   **196 Absey** ABC, primer   **200 would** intends, asks   **201 Saving . . . compliment** except in polite but inane conversation   **205 worshipful society** polite society, high society   **207–8 but a bastard . . . observation** i.e., not a true son of the times unless he observes and practices the art of courtly obsequiousness.   **209–13 And so . . . tooth** i.e., And indeed (being a bastard), I am not a true child of the time, whether or not I seem to behave like a flatterer, not merely in my attire and knightly insignia and other outward forms and accoutrements, but from a secret desire to deliver the sweet poison of flattery to satisfy the age's sweet tooth for it   **214–16 Which . . . rising** which, though I do it not to deceive others, yet, to avoid being deceived myself, I mean to learn the art of ingratiating myself; for it will facilitate and smooth my rise in importance, like rushes strewn as a floor covering.   **218 woman-post** female messenger   **219 blow a horn** (The ordinary signal of approach; with a punning reference to the horn of cuckoldry.)   **222 slave** wretch   **223 holds in chase** pursues   **225 Colbrand the Giant** legendary Danish giant slain by Guy of Warwick in a popular romance named after its hero. (Said mockingly.)

LADY FAULCONBRIDGE
Sir Robert's son, ay, thou unreverent boy,
Sir Robert's son. Why scorn'st thou at Sir Robert?
He is Sir Robert's son, and so art thou.

BASTARD
James Gurney, wilt thou give us leave awhile?   230

GURNEY
Good leave, good Philip.

BASTARD
                    Philip? Sparrow! James,   231
There's toys abroad. Anon I'll tell thee more.   232

Exit James.

Madam, I was not old Sir Robert's son;
Sir Robert might have eat his part in me   234
Upon Good Friday and ne'er broke his fast.
Sir Robert could do well—marry, to confess—   236
Could he get me! Sir Robert could not do it;   237
We know his handiwork. Therefore, good mother,
To whom am I beholding for these limbs?   239
Sir Robert never holp to make this leg.   240

LADY FAULCONBRIDGE
Hast thou conspirèd with thy brother too,
That for thine own gain shouldst defend mine honor?
What means this scorn, thou most untoward knave?   243

BASTARD
Knight, knight, good mother, Basilisco-like.   244
What! I am dubbed; I have it on my shoulder.   245
But, mother, I am not Sir Robert's son.
I have disclaimed Sir Robert and my land;
Legitimation, name, and all is gone.
Then, good my mother, let me know my father;
Some proper man, I hope. Who was it, mother?   250

LADY FAULCONBRIDGE
Hast thou denied thyself a Faulconbridge?

BASTARD
As faithfully as I deny the devil.

LADY FAULCONBRIDGE
King Richard Coeur de Lion was thy father.
By long and vehement suit I was seduced
To make room for him in my husband's bed.
Heaven lay not my transgression to my charge!
Thou art the issue of my dear offense,   257
Which was so strongly urged past my defense.

BASTARD
Now, by this light, were I to get again,   259
Madam, I would not wish a better father.
Some sins do bear their privilege on earth,   261

And so doth yours. Your fault was not your folly.   262
Needs must you lay your heart at his dispose,   263
Subjected tribute to commanding love,
Against whose fury and unmatchèd force
The aweless lion could not wage the fight,   266
Nor keep his princely heart from Richard's hand.
He that perforce robs lions of their hearts   268
May easily win a woman's. Ay, my mother,
With all my heart I thank thee for my father!
Who lives and dares but say thou didst not well   271
When I was got, I'll send his soul to hell.
Come, lady, I will show thee to my kin;   273
    And they shall say, when Richard me begot,
If thou hadst said him nay, it had been sin.   275
    Who says it was, he lies; I say 'twas not.   *Exeunt.* 276

❧

[2.1]

*Enter, before Angiers, Philip King of France,
Lewis [the] Dauphin, Austria, Constance, Arthur,
[and soldiers].*

KING PHILIP
Before Angiers well met, brave Austria.—
Arthur, that great forerunner of thy blood,   2
Richard, that robbed the lion of his heart
And fought the holy wars in Palestine,   4
By this brave duke came early to his grave;   5
And, for amends to his posterity,
At our importance hither is he come   7
To spread his colors, boy, in thy behalf,   8
And to rebuke the usurpation   9
Of thy unnatural uncle, English John.
Embrace him, love him, give him welcome hither.

ARTHUR [*to Austria*]
God shall forgive you Coeur de Lion's death
The rather that you give his offspring life,
Shadowing their right under your wings of war.   14

262 **Your . . . folly** You were morally at fault but not foolish (in whom you yielded to).   263 **dispose** disposal   266 **aweless lion** (During his imprisonment by the Duke of Austria, according to legend, Coeur de Lion slew the Duke's son and as punishment was given to a hungry lion. When the lion attacked him, he slew it by thrusting his hand down its throat and tearing out its heart, which he is supposed to have eaten.)   268 **perforce** forcibly   271 **Who** Whoever   273 **my kin** i.e., my newly discovered royal family   275 **said him nay** refused him   276 **Who . . . was** Whoever says it was a sin for you to say yes to Richard

2.1. **Location:** France. Before Angiers. (The French and Austrian forces enter from opposite sides before the "gates" of Angiers seen backstage.)

0.1 *Angiers* Angers, on the Loire River   0.2 *Austria* (The Duke of Austria wears a lion skin that he supposedly took from Coeur de Lion; see note 5.)   2 **forerunner** ancestor. (Richard was actually not a direct ancestor of Arthur, but his uncle.)   4 **fought . . . Palestine** (Richard took part in the third Crusade in 1191–1192.)   5 **By . . . duke** (A confusion of the Duke of Austria with Viscount Limoges, before whose castle Richard was mortally wounded. The roles of the two were combined in *The Troublesome Reign of King John*, as they are in this play.)   7 **importance** importunity   8 **spread his colors** display his military colors, his battle ensigns   9 **rebuke** put down   14 **Shadowing their right** sheltering the cause of Arthur and his supporters

230 **give us leave** leave us alone   231 **Philip? Sparrow!** i.e., Call me Philip no more; it's too common a name for me now, as slight in value as the name "sparrow" for the tiny songbird. (Compare John Skelton's mock elegy on "Philip Sparrow.")   232 **There's toys abroad** There's a trifling business going on. (A suggestive understatement.)   234 **eat** eaten. (Pronounced "et.")   236–7 **Sir . . . get me!** To tell the truth, Sir Robert would have had his hands full attempting to beget me! (*Marry* was originally an oath, "by the Virgin Mary.")   239 **beholding** beholden   240 **holp** helped   243 **untoward** unmannerly   244 **Basilisco-like** (The character Basilisco in the play *Solyman and Perseda*, presumably by Thomas Kyd, insists braggartlike on his knighthood but nevertheless is called "Knave" by his servant.)   245 **dubbed** made a knight by a touch of the sword on the shoulder   250 **proper** handsome, fine   257 **dear** (1) precious, costly (2) loving   259 **get** be conceived   261 **do . . . earth** i.e., are excusable, venial

I give you welcome with a powerless hand,
But with a heart full of unstainèd love.
Welcome before the gates of Angiers, Duke.

KING PHILIP
A noble boy! Who would not do thee right?

AUSTRIA [*kissing Arthur*]
Upon thy cheek lay I this zealous kiss,
As seal to this indenture of my love: 20
That to my home I will no more return
Till Angiers and the right thou hast in France,
Together with that pale, that white-faced shore,   23
Whose foot spurns back the ocean's roaring tides
And coops from other lands her islanders,   25
Even till that England, hedged in with the main,   26
That water-wallèd bulwark, still secure   27
And confident from foreign purposes,
Even till that utmost corner of the west
Salute thee for her king. Till then, fair boy,
Will I not think of home, but follow arms.

CONSTANCE
Oh, take his mother's thanks, a widow's thanks,
Till your strong hand shall help to give him strength
To make a more requital to your love!   34

AUSTRIA
The peace of heaven is theirs that lift their swords
In such a just and charitable war.

KING PHILIP
Well then, to work. Our cannon shall be bent   37
Against the brows of this resisting town.
Call for our chiefest men of discipline,   39
To cull the plots of best advantages.   40
We'll lay before this town our royal bones,
Wade to the marketplace in Frenchmen's blood,
But we will make it subject to this boy.   43

CONSTANCE
Stay for an answer to your embassy,
Lest unadvised you stain your swords with blood. 45
My Lord Chatillon may from England bring
That right in peace which here we urge in war,
And then we shall repent each drop of blood
That hot rash haste so indirectly shed.   49

Enter Chatillon.

KING PHILIP
A wonder, lady! Lo, upon thy wish,
Our messenger Chatillon is arrived.—
What England says, say briefly, gentle lord;   52
We coldly pause for thee. Chatillon, speak.   53

CHATILLON
Then turn your forces from this paltry siege
And stir them up against a mightier task.

England, impatient of your just demands,
Hath put himself in arms. The adverse winds,
Whose leisure I have stayed, have given him time 58
To land his legions all as soon as I.
His marches are expedient to this town,   60
His forces strong, his soldiers confident.
With him along is come the Mother-Queen,
An Ate, stirring him to blood and strife;   63
With her her niece, the Lady Blanche of Spain;   64
With them a bastard of the King's deceased;   65
And all th'unsettled humors of the land—   66
Rash, inconsiderate, fiery voluntaries,   67
With ladies' faces and fierce dragons' spleens—   68
Have sold their fortunes at their native homes,
Bearing their birthrights proudly on their backs, 70
To make a hazard of new fortunes here.
In brief, a braver choice of dauntless spirits   72
Than now the English bottoms have waft o'er   73
Did never float upon the swelling tide
To do offense and scathe in Christendom.   75

                              Drum beats.

The interruption of their churlish drums   76
Cuts off more circumstance. They are at hand,   77
To parley or to fight. Therefore prepare.

KING PHILIP
How much unlooked-for is this expedition!   79

AUSTRIA
By how much unexpected, by so much
We must awake endeavor for defense,
For courage mounteth with occasion.   82
Let them be welcome, then. We are prepared.

*Enter King [John] of England, [the] Bastard,
Queen [Eleanor], Blanche, Pembroke, and others.*

KING JOHN
Peace be to France, if France in peace permit
Our just and lineal entrance to our own.   85
If not, bleed France, and peace ascend to heaven,
Whiles we, God's wrathful agent, do correct   87
Their proud contempt that beats His peace to heaven. 88

KING PHILIP
Peace be to England, if that war return
From France to England, there to live in peace.
England we love, and for that England's sake   91
With burden of our armor here we sweat.

---

20 **indenture** contract   23 **pale . . . shore** i.e., the chalk cliffs at Dover
25 **coops** encloses for defense   26 **main** ocean   27 **still** perpetually
34 **more** greater   37 **bent** directed   39 **men of discipline** men
trained in military strategy   40 **To . . . advantages** to select positions
that are most favorable for attack.   43 **But we will** i.e., if necessary
to, or, if we do not   45 **unadvised** rashly   49 **indirectly** wrongfully,
misdirectedly   52 **England** the King of England. (Also in line 56 and
perhaps line 46.)   **gentle** noble   53 **coldly** calmly

58 **leisure** convenience.   **stayed** waited for   60 **expedient** speedy
63 **Ate** Greek goddess of discord   64 **her niece** i.e., Eleanor's granddaughter and John's niece   65 **of . . . deceased** of the deceased King,
i.e., Richard   66 **th'unsettled humors** i.e., the disgruntled individuals   67 **inconsiderate** reckless, heedless.   **voluntaries** volunteers
68 **With . . . spleens** i.e., young and beardless and with hot tempers.
(The spleen was thought to be the seat of the passions.)   70 **Bearing . . .
backs** i.e., having sold everything to obtain armor   72 **choice**
picked company   73 **bottoms** i.e., ships.   **waft** wafted   75 **scathe**
harm   76 **churlish** uncouth, rude   77 **circumstance** detailed reporting.   79 **expedition** (1) speed (2) military force.   82 **occasion** emergency.   85 **lineal** by right of birth   87 **correct** chastise   88 **Their . . .
heaven** the proud contempt of those who banish the peace of God.
91 **England's** i.e., Arthur's, whose claim to England the French King
is supporting

This toil of ours should be a work of thine;   93
But thou from loving England art so far
That thou hast underwrought his lawful king,   95
Cut off the sequence of posterity,   96
Outfacèd infant state, and done a rape   97
Upon the maiden virtue of the crown.
Look here upon thy brother Geoffrey's face:
These eyes, these brows, were molded out of his;
This little abstract doth contain that large   101
Which died in Geoffrey, and the hand of time   102
Shall draw this brief into as huge a volume.   103
That Geoffrey was thy elder brother born,
And this his son. England was Geoffrey's right,
And this is Geoffrey's. In the name of God,   106
How comes it then that thou art called a king,
When living blood doth in these temples beat
Which owe the crown that thou o'ermasterest?   109

KING JOHN
From whom hast thou this great commission, France,
To draw my answer from thy articles?   111

KING PHILIP
From that supernal judge that stirs good thoughts   112
In any breast of strong authority
To look into the blots and stains of right.
That judge hath made me guardian to this boy,
Under whose warrant I impeach thy wrong   116
And by whose help I mean to chastise it.

KING JOHN
Alack, thou dost usurp authority.

KING PHILIP
Excuse it is to beat usurping down.   119

ELEANOR
Who is it thou dost call usurper, France?

CONSTANCE
Let me make answer: thy usurping son.

ELEANOR
Out, insolent! Thy bastard shall be king,   122
That thou mayst be a queen and check the world!   123

CONSTANCE
My bed was ever to thy son as true   124
As thine was to thy husband, and this boy
Liker in feature to his father Geoffrey
Than thou and John in manners—being as like
As rain to water, or devil to his dam.   128

My boy a bastard? By my soul, I think
His father never was so true begot.   130
It cannot be, an if thou wert his mother.   131

ELEANOR [to Arthur]
There's a good grandam, boy, that blots thy father.   132

CONSTANCE [to Arthur]
There's a good grandam, boy, that would blot thee.   133

AUSTRIA
Peace!

BASTARD   Hear the crier!

AUSTRIA   What the devil art thou?   134

BASTARD
One that will play the devil, sir, with you,
An 'a may catch your hide and you alone.   136
You are the hare of whom the proverb goes,   137
Whose valor plucks dead lions by the beard.
I'll smoke your skin coat an I catch you right.   139
Sirrah, look to't. I'faith I will, i'faith.

BLANCHE
Oh, well did he become that lion's robe   141
That did disrobe the lion of that robe!

BASTARD
It lies as sightly on the back of him   143
As great Alcides' shows upon an ass.—   144
But, ass, I'll take that burden from your back,
Or lay on that shall make your shoulders crack.   146

AUSTRIA
What cracker is this same that deafs our ears   147
With this abundance of superfluous breath?—
King Philip, determine what we shall do straight.   149

KING PHILIP
Women and fools, break off your conference.—
King John, this is the very sum of all:
England and Ireland, Anjou, Touraine, Maine,
In right of Arthur do I claim of thee.
Wilt thou resign them and lay down thy arms?

KING JOHN
My life as soon. I do defy thee, France.—
Arthur of Brittaine, yield thee to my hand,   156
And out of my dear love I'll give thee more
Than e'er the coward hand of France can win.
Submit thee, boy.

ELEANOR   Come to thy grandam, child.

CONSTANCE
Do, child, go to it grandam, child;   160
Give grandam kingdom, and it grandam will

---

93 This . . . thine i.e., You should be supporting our cause also, since it is your duty   **95 underwrought his** undermined its   **96 sequence of posterity** lawful succession   **97 Outfacèd infant state** defied the majesty of a boy king   **101–2 This . . . Geoffrey** this little epitome or abridgment contains that which, in its complete form, died in Geoffrey. (The legal metaphor continues in the next line.)   **103 draw this brief** enlarge this epitome   **106 this** i.e., Arthur himself, or Angiers, or the English crown   **109 owe** own   **111 To draw . . . articles** to demand of me an answer to the items in your indictment.   **112 supernal** celestial, supreme   **116 whose** i.e., the supreme judge's, God's. (Also in line 117.)   **impeach** accuse   **119 Excuse . . . down** i.e., The excuse for what you call my usurping of authority is that I am, in fact, resisting and defeating usurpation.   **122 Out** (An exclamation of remonstrance.)   **Thy bastard** i.e., Arthur, who, if illegitimate as alleged here, would have no claim to the throne. (See note 130–1.)   **123 check** control   **124 thy son** Geoffrey   **128 dam** mother.

130–1 His father . . . mother (If Geoffrey were illegitimate, as charged here, then Arthur's claim to the throne would be invalid; see note 122.)   **131 an if** if   **132 blots** slanders   **133 blot** (With a pun on "obliterate, efface.")   **134 Hear the crier!** (Austria is mockingly compared to the town crier, whose function in courts of justice was to call for silence.)   **136 An 'a** if he.   **hide** i.e., the lion's skin Austria wears in celebration of his triumph over Richard Coeur de Lion   **137 the proverb** i.e., "Even hares may insult the dead lion." (This proverb occurs in Erasmus's *Adages*.)   **139 I'll . . . coat** i.e., I'll thrash your own skin   **141 he** i.e., Richard Coeur de Lion   **143 sightly** suitably. (Said ironically.)   **him** i.e., the Duke of Austria   **144 Alcides'** Hercules slew the Nemean lion as one of his twelve labors and thereafter wore its pelt.   **146 lay on that** i.e., beat you with a club that   **147 cracker** i.e., boaster. (With a play on *crack*, line 146.)   **149 straight** at once.   **156 Brittaine** Brittany   **160 Do . . . grandam** (Contemptuous baby talk; *it* means "its," referring to the child in the neuter. Also in line 161.)

Give it a plum, a cherry, and a fig.
There's a good grandam.

ARTHUR   Good my mother, peace!
I would that I were low laid in my grave.
I am not worth this coil that's made for me.   165

[He weeps.]

ELEANOR
His mother shames him so, poor boy, he weeps.

CONSTANCE
Now shame upon you, whe'er she does or no!   167
His grandam's wrongs, and not his mother's shames,   168
Draws those heaven-moving pearls from his poor eyes,
Which heaven shall take in nature of a fee.   170
Ay, with these crystal beads heaven shall be bribed   171
To do him justice and revenge on you.

ELEANOR
Thou monstrous slanderer of heaven and earth!

CONSTANCE
Thou monstrous injurer of heaven and earth!
Call not me slanderer. Thou and thine usurp
The dominations; royalties, and rights   176
Of this oppressèd boy. This is thy eldest son's son,   177
Infortunate in nothing but in thee.   178
Thy sins are visited in this poor child;   179
The canon of the law is laid on him,   180
Being but the second generation
Removèd from thy sin-conceiving womb.

KING JOHN
Bedlam, have done.

CONSTANCE   I have but this to say,   183
That he is not only plaguèd for her sin,   184
But God hath made her sin and her the plague   185
On this removèd issue, plagued for her   186
And with her plague; her sin his injury,   187
Her injury the beadle to her sin,   188
All punished in the person of this child,
And all for her. A plague upon her!

ELEANOR
Thou unadvisèd scold, I can produce   191
A will that bars the title of thy son.   192

CONSTANCE
Ay, who doubts that? A will, a wicked will,
A woman's will, a cankered grandam's will!

KING PHILIP
Peace, lady! Pause, or be more temperate.
It ill beseems this presence to cry aim   196
To these ill-tunèd repetitions.—   197
Some trumpet summon hither to the walls   198
These men of Angiers. Let us hear them speak
Whose title they admit, Arthur's or John's.   200

*Trumpet sounds. Enter a Citizen upon the
walls.*

CITIZEN
Who is it that hath warned us to the walls?   201

KING PHILIP
'Tis France, for England.

KING JOHN   England, for itself.   202
You men of Angiers, and my loving subjects—

KING PHILIP
You loving men of Angiers, Arthur's subjects,
Our trumpet called you to this gentle parle—   205

KING JOHN
For our advantage; therefore hear us first.
These flags of France, that are advancèd here   207
Before the eye and prospect of your town,
Have hither marched to your endamagement.
The cannons have their bowels full of wrath,
And ready mounted are they to spit forth
Their iron indignation 'gainst your walls.
All preparation for a bloody siege
And merciless proceeding by these French
Confronts your city's eyes, your winking gates;   215
And but for our approach those sleeping stones,   216
That as a waist doth girdle you about,   217
By the compulsion of their ordinance   218
By this time from their fixèd beds of lime   219
Had been dishabited, and wide havoc made   220
For bloody power to rush upon your peace.
But on the sight of us your lawful king,
Who painfully, with much expedient march,   223
Have brought a countercheck before your gates
To save unscratched your city's threatened cheeks,   225
Behold, the French, amazed, vouchsafe a parle;   226

---

165 coil disturbance, fuss **167 whe'er** whether **168 wrongs** wrongdo-ings. **shames** insults **170 a fee** i.e., the fee paid to heaven in return for being Arthur's advocate. **171 beads** i.e., tears, here as gifts used to curry favor, or prayer beads **176 dominations, royalties** territories, royal prerogatives **177 eldest son's son** i.e., eldest grandchild, not son of the eldest son **178 Infortunate** unfortunate **179 visited** punished **180 canon . . . law** i.e., that the sins of parents shall be visited upon their children to the third and fourth generation; see Exodus 20:5 **183 Bed-lam** Lunatic **184–8 That . . . sin** not only that Arthur is cursed because of Eleanor's adultery (see lines 124 ff.), but that God has made use of sinful Eleanor and her son John to be the plague of Arthur in the third generation, plagued as he is on her account and through the agency of her son John; her sin becomes Arthur's affliction, and her wrongdoing the beadle or punishing parish officer necessitated by her sin. **186 removèd issue** descendant at one remove, i.e., Arthur. **for her** on her account **187 with her plague** i.e., by the offspring, John, with whom she was cursed. **his injury** i.e., the wrong done to Arthur **188 Her injury** Eleanor's wrong deeds, which act as the officer (*beadle*) to incite her son John (*her sin*) on to further wrongs **191 unadvised** rash **192 A will** i.e., according to Holinshed and other chroniclers, the final testament of Richard Coeur de Lion, naming John as his heir and disinheriting Arthur, who had been named heir in a previous will. (But Constance deliberately takes *will* to mean "willfulness.")

196–7 It . . . repetitions It is not proper in my royal presence to encourage or abet these unharmonious recitals of accusation. (*Cry aim* is a term of encouragement to archers as they are about to shoot.) **197 repetitions** recitals. **198 trumpet** trumpeter **200.1-2 upon the walls** i.e., in the upper gallery rearstage. (Throughout this scene, the tiring-house facade is visualized as the walls of Angiers.) **201 warned** summoned **202 'Tis France, for England** i.e., It is the French King, on behalf of Arthur, true King of England. **205 parle** parley **207 advanced** raised **215 your city's . . . gates** (The gates of the city, now closed, are its eyes, able to open and shut and look out upon the outer world.) **216 but . . . approach** were it not for the timely arrival of us English **217 waist** belt **218 their ordinance** the French artillery **219 lime** i.e., mortar **220 dishabited** (1) dislodged (2) undressed **223 painfully** having taken great pains or care. **expedient** swift **225 cheeks** i.e., walls **226 amazed** stunned with fear. **vouchsafe a parle** agree to a parley

And now, instead of bullets wrapped in fire
To make a shaking fever in your walls,
They shoot but calm words folded up in smoke
To make a faithless error in your ears.
Which trust accordingly, kind citizens,
And let us in, your king, whose labored spirits,
Forwearied in this action of swift speed,
Craves harborage within your city walls.

KING PHILIP
When I have said, make answer to us both.
Lo, in this right hand, whose protection
Is most divinely vowed upon the right
Of him it holds, stands young Plantagenet,
Son to the elder brother of this man
And king o'er him and all that he enjoys.
For this downtrodden equity we tread
In warlike march these greens before your town,
Being no further enemy to you
Than the constraint of hospitable zeal
In the relief of this oppressèd child
Religiously provokes. Be pleasèd then
To pay that duty which you truly owe
To him that owes it, namely this young prince;
And then our arms, like to a muzzled bear,
Save in aspect, hath all offense sealed up.
Our cannons' malice vainly shall be spent
Against th'invulnerable clouds of heaven;
And with a blessèd and unvexed retire,
With unhacked swords and helmets all unbruised,
We will bear home that lusty blood again
Which here we came to spout against your town,
And leave your children, wives, and you in peace.
But if you fondly pass our proffered offer,
'Tis not the roundure of your old-faced walls
Can hide you from our messengers of war,
Though all these English and their discipline
Were harbored in their rude circumference.
Then tell us, shall your city call us lord
In that behalf which we have challenged it,
Or shall we give the signal to our rage
And stalk in blood to our possession?

227 CITIZEN
In brief, we are the King of England's subjects.
229 For him, and in his right, we hold this town.
230 KING JOHN
231 Acknowledge then the King, and let me in.
232 CITIZEN
233 That can we not. But he that proves the King,   270
To him will we prove loyal. Till that time
Have we rammed up our gates against the world.
235 KING JOHN
236 Doth not the crown of England prove the King?
237 And if not that, I bring you witnesses,
238 Twice fifteen thousand hearts of England's breed—
BASTARD   Bastards, and else.   276
240 KING JOHN
241 To verify our title with their lives.
KING PHILIP
As many and as wellborn bloods as those—   278
244 BASTARD   Some bastards too.
KING PHILIP
246 Stand in his face to contradict his claim.   280
CITIZEN
248 Till you compound whose right is worthiest,   281
We for the worthiest hold the right from both.   282
250 KING JOHN
251 Then God forgive the sin of all those souls
252 That to their everlasting residence,
253 Before the dew of evening fall, shall fleet,   285
In dreadful trial of our kingdom's king!   286
255 KING PHILIP
Amen, amen! Mount, chevaliers! To arms!   287
BASTARD
258 Saint George, that swinged the dragon, and e'er since   288
259 Sits on 's horseback at mine hostess' door,   289
260 Teach us some fence! [To Austria] Sirrah, were I at home,   290
261 At your den, sirrah, with your lioness,   291
262 I would set an ox head to your lion's hide,   292
And make a monster of you.
264 AUSTRIA   Peace! No more.
BASTARD [to the others]
Oh, tremble, for you hear the lion roar.
KING JOHN
Up higher to the plain, where we'll set forth
In best appointment all our regiments.   296
BASTARD
Speed then, to take advantage of the field.   297

227 bullets cannon-balls   229 folded up in smoke i.e., using the deceptive concealment of rhetoric   230 faithless error perfidious lie   231 trust accordingly trust as such lies deserve, i.e., not at all   232 labored oppressed with labor   233 Forwearied in exhausted by   235 said finished speaking   236–8 in . . . holds i.e., being held by my right hand, which hand is most sacredly committed to defend the right of the person (Arthur) whose hand it now holds   240 enjoys possesses, rules over.   241 For On behalf of.   equity justice, right   244 constraint necessity   246 Religiously enjoined by sacred oath   248 owes owns, has a right to   250 Save . . . up except in appearance, will see to it that all capacity for injury to you is sealed up   251–2 Our . . . heaven i.e., Our cannons will be fired off harmlessly into the air   253 blessèd and unvexed retire peaceful and unhindered withdrawal   255 lusty vigorous, sturdy   258 fondly pass foolishly pass up   259 roundure roundness, enclosure, circumference   260 messengers i.e., cannonballs   261 discipline military skill   262 in . . . circumference inside the walls' rugged fortifications   264 In . . . which on behalf of him for whom

270 proves i.e., proves himself, proves to be   276 else others, such-like.   278 bloods men of mettle and of good breeding   280 in his face opposite to him   281 compound settle, agree   282 for in the interests of.   hold withhold   285 fleet fly, leave (their bodies)   286 In . . . king in fearful encounter to determine who is ruler of our kingdom. (With a suggestion, too, of the soul's *dreadful trial* before God.)   287 chevaliers knights.   288 swinged whipped, thrashed   289 Sits . . . door (One of the most common signs at tavern doors was that of Saint George and the dragon.)   290 fence skill in swordsmanship.   291 lioness (With a suggestion of "whore.")   292 set an ox head i.e., give you the horns of a cuckold   296 appointment order, readiness   297 take . . . field gain tactical position.

KING PHILIP

It shall be so; and at the other hill
Command the rest to stand. God and our right! 299
Exeunt [separately. The citizens remain above, on the
walls.]

Here after excursions, enter the Herald of
France, with trumpets, to the gates.

FRENCH HERALD

You men of Angiers, open wide your gates,
And let young Arthur, Duke of Brittaine, in,
Who by the hand of France this day hath made 302
Much work for tears in many an English mother, 303
Whose sons lie scattered on the bleeding ground.
Many a widow's husband groveling lies,
Coldly embracing the discolored earth,
And victory, with little loss, doth play
Upon the dancing banners of the French,
Who are at hand, triumphantly displayed, 309
To enter conquerors and to proclaim
Arthur of Brittaine England's king and yours. 311

Enter English Herald, with trumpet.

ENGLISH HERALD

Rejoice, you men of Angiers, ring your bells!
King John, your king and England's, doth approach,
Commander of this hot malicious day. 314
Their armors, that marched hence so silver bright,
Hither return all gilt with Frenchmen's blood. 316
There stuck no plume in any English crest 317
That is removèd by a staff of France. 318
Our colors do return in those same hands 319
That did display them when we first marched forth; 320
And like a jolly troop of huntsmen come
Our lusty English, all with purpled hands 322
Dyed in the dying slaughter of their foes. 323
Open your gates and give the victors way.

CITIZEN

Heralds, from off our towers we might behold,
From first to last, the onset and retire 326
Of both your armies, whose equality 327
By our best eyes cannot be censurèd. 328
Blood hath bought blood, and blows have answered
blows,
Strength matched with strength, and power
confronted power.
Both are alike, and both alike we like.

One must prove greatest. While they weigh so even,
We hold our town for neither, yet for both. 333

Enter the two Kings, with their powers, at several
doors: [King John with Queen Eleanor, Blanche,
the Bastard, and forces at one door, King Philip
with Lewis, Austria, and forces at the other].

KING JOHN

France, hast thou yet more blood to cast away?
Say, shall the current of our right run on,
Whose passage, vexed with thy impediment,
Shall leave his native channel and o'erswell 337
With course disturbed even thy confining shores, 338
Unless thou let his silver water keep
A peaceful progress to the ocean?

KING PHILIP

England, thou hast not saved one drop of blood
In this hot trial more than we of France;
Rather, lost more. And by this hand I swear, 343
That sways the earth this climate overlooks, 344
Before we will lay down our just-borne arms,
We'll put thee down, 'gainst whom these arms we bear,
Or add a royal number to the dead, 347
Gracing the scroll that tells of this war's loss
With slaughter coupled to the name of kings.

BASTARD

Ha, majesty! How high thy glory towers 350
When the rich blood of kings is set on fire!
Oh, now doth Death line his dead chaps with steel; 352
The swords of soldiers are his teeth, his fangs;
And now he feasts, mousing the flesh of men 354
In undetermined differences of kings. 355
Why stand these royal fronts amazèd thus? 356
Cry havoc, Kings! Back to the stainèd field, 367
You equal potents, fiery-kindled spirits! 368
Then let confusion of one part confirm 359
The other's peace. Till then, blows, blood, and death! 360

KING JOHN

Whose party do the townsmen yet admit? 361

KING PHILIP

Speak, citizens, for England. Who's your king?

CITIZEN

The King of England, when we know the king.

KING PHILIP

Know him in us, that here hold up his right. 364

---

299 **the rest** i.e., our reserve forces   299.3 *excursions* skirmishes, sorties   302 **by . . . France** with the aid of the French King   303 **work** cause   309 **displayed** (1) deployed in a column (2) unfurled, as a banner   311.1 *trumpet* trumpeter.   314 **Commander** victor.   **hot malicious day** a day hotly and violently contested.   316 **gilt** gilded in red   317–8 **There . . . France** i.e., No English helmet was so dishonored as to have the plume of its crest struck off by a French spear.   319–20 **Our . . . forth** i.e., We have not been obliged to strike our colors; we hold them bravely aloft as we did at the start of the battle, since no English standard-bearer has been struck down   322 **lusty** vigorous   323 **Dyed . . . foes** (Huntsmen dipped their hands in the blood of a slain deer to celebrate the slaughter.)   326 **onset and retire** attack and withdrawal   327–8 **whose . . . censurèd** which are so evenly matched that our keenest observations cannot determine any difference.

333.1 *powers* armies.   *several* separate   337 **his native** its normal   337–8 **and . . . shores** (John hints that his might, fully roused in defense of what he claims for his own right, will spill over into new French territory.)   343 **this hand** i.e., my own royal hand   344 **climate** portion of the sky   347 **a royal number** i.e., a king's name. (King Philip will win or die in the attempt and perhaps take other kings with him.)   350 **How . . . towers** To what height the glory-seeking spirit of majesty soars. (An image from hawking.)   352 **chaps** jaws   354 **mousing** tearing, gnawing   355 **undetermined differences** unsettled quarrels   356 **royal fronts** kings' faces   357 **Cry havoc** Proclaim a general slaughter with no taking of prisoners.   **stainèd** bloodstained   358 **potents** potentates   359–60 **Then . . . peace** Then let the destruction of one side (and nothing short of that) award victory and peace to the other side.   361 **yet** now   364 **hold up his right** support his (Arthur's) claim.

KING JOHN

In us, that are our own great deputy
And bear possession of our person here,
Lord of our presence, Angiers, and of you.   366
                                              367

CITIZEN

A greater power than we denies all this,
And, till it be undoubted, we do lock
Our former scruple in our strong-barred gates,
Kinged of our fear, until our fears, resolved,   371
Be by some certain king purged and deposed.   372

BASTARD

By heaven, these scroyles of Angiers flout you, kings,   373
And stand securely on their battlements
As in a theater, whence they gape and point
At your industrious scenes and acts of death.
Your royal presences be ruled by me: 377
Do like the mutines of Jerusalem,   378
Be friends awhile, and both conjointly bend   379
Your sharpest deeds of malice on this town.
By east and west let France and England mount
Their battering cannon, chargèd to the mouths,   382
Till their soul-fearing clamors have brawled down   383
The flinty ribs of this contemptuous city.
I'd play incessantly upon these jades,   385
Even till unfencèd desolation   386
Leave them as naked as the vulgar air.   387
That done, dissever your united strengths,
And part your mingled colors once again;
Turn face to face and bloody point to point.
Then, in a moment, Fortune shall cull forth
Out of one side her happy minion,   392
To whom in favor she shall give the day,   393
And kiss him with a glorious victory.
How like you this wild counsel, mighty states?   395
Smacks it not something of the policy?   396

KING JOHN

Now, by the sky that hangs above our heads,
I like it well. France, shall we knit our powers
And lay this Angiers even with the ground,
Then after fight who shall be king of it?

BASTARD [to King Philip]

An if thou hast the mettle of a king,
Being wronged as we are by this peevish town,   402
Turn thou the mouth of thy artillery,
As we will ours, against these saucy walls;
And when that we have dashed them to the ground,   405

Why, then defy each other, and pell-mell   406
Make work upon ourselves, for heaven or hell.

KING PHILIP

Let it be so. Say, where will you assault?

KING JOHN

We from the west will send destruction
Into this city's bosom.

AUSTRIA   I from the north.

KING PHILIP   Our thunder from the south
Shall rain their drift of bullets on this town.   413

BASTARD [to King John]

Oh, prudent discipline! From north to south   414
Austria and France shoot in each other's mouth.
I'll stir them to it.—Come, away, away!

[The armies start to move.]

CITIZEN

Hear us, great kings! Vouchsafe awhile to stay,
And I shall show you peace and fair-faced league,
Win you this city without stroke or wound,
Rescue those breathing lives to die in beds
That here come sacrifices for the field.
Persever not, but hear me, mighty kings.   422

KING JOHN

Speak on with favor. We are bent to hear.   423

CITIZEN

That daughter there of Spain, the Lady Blanche,
Is near to England. Look upon the years   425
Of Lewis the Dauphin and that lovely maid.
If lusty love should go in quest of beauty,   427
Where should he find it fairer than in Blanche?
If zealous love should go in search of virtue,   429
Where should he find it purer than in Blanche?
If love ambitious sought a match of birth,   431
Whose veins bound richer blood than Lady Blanche?   432
Such as she is, in beauty, virtue, birth,
Is the young Dauphin every way complete.   434
If not complete of, say he is not she,   435
And she again wants nothing, to name want,   436
If want it be not that she is not he.   437
He is the half part of a blessèd man,
Left to be finishèd by such as she,
And she a fair divided excellence,
Whose fullness of perfection lies in him.
Oh, two such silver currents, when they join,
Do glorify the banks that bound them in;
And two such shores to two such streams made one,
Two such controlling bounds, shall you be, kings,
To these two princes, if you marry them.
This union shall do more than battery can   447
To our fast-closèd gates; for at this match,   448

---

366 bear . . . person embody the claims of sovereignty in my own person, needing no deputy   367 Lord of our presence my own master   371 Kinged of ruled by   372 by . . . king by one king or the other   373 scroyles scoundrels   377 Your royal presences May Your Majesties   378 mutines mutineers.   Jerusalem (During the siege of Jerusalem by Titus, A.D. 70, rival Jewish factions united to resist the Romans.)   379 conjointly bend together aim   382 chargèd to the mouths filled to the brim with shot   383 soul-fearing inspiring fear in the soul.   brawled down i.e., noisily leveled   385 play . . . jades i.e., (1) fire cannon repeatedly upon these wretches (2) torment these nags. (Jades are ill-conditioned horses.)   386 unfencèd defenseless   387 vulgar common   392 minion favorite   393 give the day award the victory   395 states kings.   396 something somewhat.   the policy the art of politics, a canny maneuver.   402 peevish stubborn   405 when that when

406 pell-mell headlong, hand to hand   413 drift of bullets shower of cannonballs   414 prudent discipline fine military skill. (Said sardonically.)   422 Persever Persevere   423 favor permission.   bent inclined   425 near to England a near relative of King John, i.e., his niece.   427 lusty amorous   429 zealous virtue-loving   431 of birth i.e., of high royal rank   432 bound contain   434 complete accomplished, perfect in.   435–7 If . . . he i.e., The two young people lack only each other's qualities to be complete in themselves.   436 wants lacks   437 If . . . he unless it is called a lack that she is not he.   447 battery artillery   448 match (1) marriage (2) fire used to ignite gunpowder

With swifter spleen than powder can enforce,   449
The mouth of passage shall we fling wide ope
And give you entrance. But without this match,
The sea enragèd is not half so deaf,
Lions more confident, mountains and rocks
More free from motion, no, not Death himself
In mortal fury half so peremptory,   455
As we to keep this city.

BASTARD   Here's a stay   456
That shakes the rotten carcass of old Death   457
Out of his rags! Here's a large mouth, indeed,   458
That spits forth Death and mountains, rocks and seas,
Talks as familiarly of roaring lions
As maids of thirteen do of puppy dogs.
What cannoneer begot this lusty blood?   462
He speaks plain cannon: fire and smoke and bounce.   463
He gives the bastinado with his tongue.   464
Our ears are cudgeled; not a word of his
But buffets better than a fist of France.
Zounds! I was never so bethumped with words   467
Since I first called my brother's father Dad.   468
                            [The French confer apart.]

ELEANOR [to King John]
Son, list to this conjunction; make this match.   469
Give with our niece a dowry large enough,
For by this knot thou shalt so surely tie
Thy now unsured assurance to the crown
That yon green boy shall have no sun to ripe   473
The bloom that promiseth a mighty fruit.
I see a yielding in the looks of France;
Mark how they whisper. Urge them while their souls
Are capable of this ambition,   477
Lest zeal, now melted by the windy breath   478
Of soft petitions, pity, and remorse,   479
Cool and congeal again to what it was.

CITIZEN
Why answer not the double majesties
This friendly treaty of our threatened town?   482

KING PHILIP
Speak England first, that hath been forward first
To speak unto this city. What say you?

KING JOHN
If that the Dauphin there, they princely son,   485
Can in this book of beauty read "I love,"   486

Her dowry shall weigh equal with a queen;   487
For Anjou and fair Touraine, Maine, Poitiers,
And all that we upon this side the sea—
Except this city now by us besieged—
Find liable to our crown and dignity,   491
Shall gild her bridal bed and make her rich
In titles, honors, and promotions,   493
As she in beauty, education, blood,
Holds hand with any princess of the world.   495

KING PHILIP
What say'st thou, boy? Look in the lady's face.

LEWIS
I do, my lord, and in her eye I find
A wonder, or a wondrous miracle,
The shadow of myself formed in her eye,   499
Which, being but the shadow of your son,   500
Becomes a sun and makes your son a shadow.   501
I do protest I never loved myself
Till now infixèd I beheld myself
Drawn in the flattering table of her eye.   504
                            Whispers with Blanche.

BASTARD
Drawn in the flattering table of her eye!   505
    Hanged in the frowning wrinkle of her brow
And quartered in her heart! He doth espy   507
    Himself love's traitor. This is pity now,
That, hanged and drawn and quartered, there should be
In such a love so vile a lout as he.   510

BLANCHE [to Lewis]
My uncle's will in this respect is mine.
If he see aught in you that makes him like,
That anything he sees which moves his liking   513
I can with ease translate it to my will;   514
Or if you will, to speak more properly,   515
I will enforce it easily to my love.
Further I will not flatter you, my lord,
That all I see in you is worthy love,
Than this: that nothing do I see in you,
Though churlish thoughts themselves should be your
    judge,   520
That I can find should merit any hate.

KING JOHN
What say these young ones? What say you, my niece?

BLANCHE
That she is bound in honor still to do

449 **spleen** i.e., eager, violent energy   455 **peremptory** determined
456–8 **Here's . . . rags!** i.e., Here's a pause for consideration, one that
shakes things up so that the skeleton of Death itself is shaken out of
its rags and tatters!   456 **stay** hindrance, obstacle   458 **mouth** i.e.,
like the mouth of a cannon but spewing forth rhetoric   462 **lusty blood**
hot-blooded chap. (Said sardonically.)   463 **bounce** i.e., the noise of the
cannon.   464 **bastinado** beating with a cudgel   467 **Zounds!** By God's
(Christ's) wounds!   468 **Since . . . Dad** i.e., since I learned to speak.
(Colloquial, but here with particular fitness to the Bastard's illegitimacy.)   469 **list** listen   473 **green** youthful, hence unripe.   **boy** i.e.,
Arthur. (Seemingly not onstage.)   477 **capable of** susceptible to.
ambition i.e., scheme that might seem to their advantage   478 **zeal** i.e.,
the French King's zeal in Arthur's behalf. (The metaphor is one of
melting and hardening wax.)   479 **remorse** compassion   482 **treaty**
proposal   485 **If that** If   486 **book . . . "I love"** (An allusion to
William Lilly's famous Latin grammar, in which the verb *amo*, "I
love," was used as a paradigm.)

487 **dowry** (What John offers as a wedding dowry is precisely
Arthur's inheritance, none of his own.)   491 **Find liable** regard as
subject   493 **promotions** advancements in courtly degree   495 **Holds
hand with** equals   499 **shadow** image, reflection   500 **being** from
being.   **shadow** pale and substanceless imitation   501 **Becomes . . .
shadow** i.e., becomes the bright image of my new self discovered by
gazing into her eyes, an image that casts into the shade my former
self.   504 **Drawn** pictured.   **table** tablet or flat surface on which the
picture is painted   505 **Drawn** (With a pun on the meaning "disemboweled." The pun is continued in the next two lines in *Hanged* and
quartered; Elizabethan punishment for traitors specified that they be
hanged, taken down while still alive, *drawn*, or disemboweled, and
quartered, or cut up.)   507 **quartered** (With a pun on the meaning
"lodged" and, in heraldry, "placed quarterly on a shield or coat of
arms.")   510 **love** (1) profession of love (2) lover   513 **That anything**
whatever   514 **will** desire   515 **properly** exactly   520 **churlish** sparing of praise

What you in wisdom still vouchsafe to say.

KING JOHN
Speak then, Prince Dauphin. Can you love this lady?

LEWIS
Nay, ask me if I can refrain from love,
For I do love her most unfeignedly.

KING JOHN
Then do I give Volquessen, Touraine, Maine,
Poitiers, and Anjou, these five provinces,
With her to thee, and this addition more,
Full thirty thousand marks of English coin.   531
Philip of France, if thou be pleased withal,   532
Command thy son and daughter to join hands.   533

KING PHILIP
It likes us well. Young princes, close your hands.   534
[Lewis and Blanche exchange pledges of love.]

AUSTRIA
And your lips too, for I am well assured
That I did so when I was first assured.   [They kiss.]   536

KING PHILIP
Now, citizens of Angiers, ope your gates.
Let in that amity which you have made,
For at Saint Mary's chapel presently   539
The rites of marriage shall be solemnized.
Is not the Lady Constance in this troop?
I know she is not, for this match made up   542
Her presence would have interrupted much.
Where is she and her son? Tell me, who knows.   544

LEWIS
She is sad and passionate at Your Highness' tent.   545

KING PHILIP
And, by my faith, this league that we have made
Will give her sadness very little cure.
Brother of England, how may we content
This widow lady? In her right we came,
Which we, God knows, have turned another way,
To our own vantage.

KING JOHN   We will heal up all,
For we'll create young Arthur Duke of Brittaine
And Earl of Richmond, and this rich, fair town
We make him lord of. Call the Lady Constance.
Some speedy messenger bid her repair   555
To our solemnity. I trust we shall,   556
If not fill up the measure of her will,   557
Yet in some measure satisfy her so   558
That we shall stop her exclamation.   559
Go we, as well as haste will suffer us,   560
To this unlooked-for, unprepared pomp.
                     Exeunt [all but the Bastard].

BASTARD
Mad world, mad kings, mad composition!   562

John, to stop Arthur's title in the whole,
Hath willingly departed with a part;   564
And France, whose armor conscience buckled on,
Whom zeal and charity brought to the field
As God's own soldier, rounded in the ear   567
With that same purpose-changer, that sly devil,   568
That broker that still breaks the pate of faith,   569
That daily break-vow, he that wins of all,   570
Of kings, of beggars, old men, young men, maids—
Who, having no external thing to lose   572
But the word "maid," cheats the poor maid of that—   573
That smooth-faced gentleman, tickling Commodity,   574
Commodity, the bias of the world—   575
The world, who of itself is peisèd well,   576
Made to run even upon even ground,
Till this advantage, this vile-drawing bias,   578
This sway of motion, this Commodity,   579
Makes it take head from all indifferency,   580
From all direction, purpose, course, intent.
And this same bias, this Commodity,
This bawd, this broker, this all-changing word,   583
Clapped on the outward eye of fickle France,   584
Hath drawn him from his own determined aid,   585
From a resolved and honorable war,   586
To a most base and vile-concluded peace.
And why rail I on this Commodity?
But for because he hath not wooed me yet.   589
Not that I have the power to clutch my hand   590
When his fair angels would salute my palm,   591
But for my hand, as unattempted yet,   592
Like a poor beggar, raileth on the rich.
Well, whiles I am a beggar, I will rail
And say there is no sin but to be rich;
And being rich, my virtue then shall be
To say there is no vice but beggary.
Since kings break faith upon Commodity,   598
Gain, be my lord, for I will worship thee.   Exit.

❧

564 **departed with** given up   567 **rounded** whispered to
568 **With** by   569 **broker** go-between. (With a pun on "one who
breaks.")   **still . . . faith** continually knocks loyalty and truth over
the head   570 **wins of** gets the better of   572 **Who** i.e., the maids
573 **cheats** i.e., he, Commodity, cheats   574 **smooth-faced** smiling,
bland.   **tickling Commodity** the itch to promote one's self-interest at
the expense of one's honor and the general welfare   575 **bias** swaying influence. (From the game of bowls, in which a weight in the side
of a bowl causes it to curve.)   576 **peisèd** balanced, in equilibrium
578–80 **Till . . . indifferency** till this advantage-seeking mania, this
leading astray toward moral degradation, this swaying of things
from their proper course, this Commodity, induces the world to strip
away the moral force of all impartiality   583 **all-changing** causing
change in everything   584 **Clapped . . . France** put before the
impressionable eye of the King of France. (The eye is *outward* as contrasted with the inward eye of reason and conscience.)   585 **his . . .
aid** the aid he had determined to give Arthur   586 **resolved**
resolved upon   589 **But for** Merely   590 **clutch** clench (in a gesture
of refusal)   591 **angels** coins bearing the figure of an angel, worth
ten shillings.   **salute** kiss. (With a pun on the idea of an angelic salutation.)   592 **for** because.   **unattempted** untempted   598 **upon**
because of

531 **marks** (A mark was the equivalent of thirteen shillings four pence.)
532 **withal** with this   533 **daughter** i.e., future daughter-in-law
534 **likes** pleases.   **close** clasp   536 **assured** betrothed. (With a play on
assured, "certain," in line 535.)   539 **presently** at once   542 **made up**
arranged, concluded   544 **who** whoever   545 **passionate** filled with passionate sorrow   555 **repair** come   556 **our solemnity** i.e., the wedding.
557 **the measure** the full measure and extent   558 **so** in such a way
559 **exclamation** complaint.   560 **suffer** allow   562 **composition**
agreement, compromise.

3.1

Enter Constance, Arthur, and Salisbury.

CONSTANCE
Gone to be married? Gone to swear a peace?
False blood to false blood joined! Gone to be friends?
Shall Lewis have Blanche, and Blanche those provinces?
It is not so; thou hast misspoke, misheard.
Be well advised; tell o'er thy tale again.   5
It cannot be; thou dost but say 'tis so.
I trust I may not trust thee, for thy word
Is but the vain breath of a common man.   8
Believe me, I do not believe thee, man;
I have a king's oath to the contrary.
Thou shalt be punished for thus frighting me,
For I am sick and capable of fears,   12
Oppressed with wrongs, and therefore full of fears,
A widow, husbandless, subject to fears,
A woman, naturally born to fears;
And though thou now confess thou didst but jest,   16
With my vexed spirits I cannot take a truce,   17
But they will quake and tremble all this day.
What dost thou mean by shaking of thy head?
Why dost thou look so sadly on my son?
What means that hand upon that breast of thine?
Why holds thine eye that lamentable rheum,   22
Like a proud river peering o'er his bounds?   23
Be these sad signs confirmers of thy words?
Then speak again—not all thy former tale,
But this one word: whether thy tale be true.

SALISBURY
As true as I believe you think them false   27
That give you cause to prove my saying true.

CONSTANCE
Oh, if thou teach me to believe this sorrow,
Teach thou this sorrow how to make me die!
And let belief and life encounter so
As doth the fury of two desperate men
Which in the very meeting fall and die.
Lewis marry Blanche? [*To Arthur*] Oh, boy, then where
    art thou?
France friend with England, what becomes of me?
[*To Salisbury*] Fellow, begone! I cannot brook thy sight.   36
This news hath made thee a most ugly man.

SALISBURY
What other harm have I, good lady, done,
But spoke the harm that is by others done?

CONSTANCE
Which harm within itself so heinous is
As it makes harmful all that speak of it.

ARTHUR
I do beseech you, madam, be content.   42

CONSTANCE
If thou that bid'st me be content wert grim,
Ugly, and slanderous to thy mother's womb,   44
Full of unpleasing blots and sightless stains,   45
Lame, foolish, crooked, swart, prodigious,   46
Patched with foul moles and eye-offending marks,   47
I would not care, I then would be content,
For then I should not love thee, no, nor thou
Become thy great birth nor deserve a crown.   50
But thou art fair, and at thy birth, dear boy,
Nature and Fortune joined to make thee great.
Of Nature's gifts thou mayst with lilies boast,
And with the half-blown rose. But Fortune, oh,   54
She is corrupted, changed, and won from thee.
Sh' adulterates hourly with thine uncle John,   56
And with her golden hand hath plucked on France   57
To tread down fair respect of sovereignty,   58
And made his majesty the bawd to theirs.   59
France is a bawd to Fortune and King John,
That strumpet Fortune, that usurping John!
[*To Salisbury*] Tell me, thou fellow, is not France forsworn?   62
Envenom him with words, or get thee gone   63
And leave those woes alone which I alone   64
Am bound to underbear.

SALISBURY   Pardon me, madam,   65
I may not go without you to the kings.

CONSTANCE
Thou mayst, thou shalt. I will not go with thee.
I will instruct my sorrows to be proud,
For grief is proud and makes his owner stoop.
                              [*She sits on the ground.*]
To me and to the state of my great grief   70
Let kings assemble, for my grief's so great
That no supporter but the huge, firm earth
Can hold it up. Here I and sorrows sit.
Here is my throne; bid kings come bow to it.

    *Enter King John, [King Philip of] France, [Lewis
    the] Dauphin, Blanche, Eleanor, Philip [the
    Bastard], Austria, [and attendants]. [The two
    kings are arm in arm.]*

KING PHILIP [*to Blanche*]
'Tis true, fair daughter, and this blessèd day   75
Ever in France shall be kept festival.
To solemnize this day the glorious sun
Stays in his course and plays the alchemist,   78
Turning with splendor of his precious eye
The meager cloddy earth to glittering gold.

3.1. **Location: France. The French King's quarters.**
5 **Be well advised** Be sure of what you are saying   **8 a common man**
i.e., a subject, not a king.   **12 capable of** susceptible to   **16 though . . .**
confess even if you were now to confess   **17 take a truce** make peace
22 lamentable rheum sad moisture, i.e., tears   **23 peering o'er his**
i.e., overflowing its   **27 them** the French and English kings
36 brook endure   **42 content** calm.

44 **slanderous** disgraceful   **45 sightless** unsightly   **46 swart**
swarthy.   **prodigious** monstrous, an evil omen   **47 Patched** blotched
50 Become befit   **54 half-blown** only partly opened, still young
56 adulterates commits adultery   **57–9 And . . . theirs** and with
tempting gold has incited the King of France to tread underfoot
Arthur's rights of sovereignty, and has made the King the pander to
Fortune in furthering the designs of King John.   **57 golden** i.e., offering gold   **62 is not France forsworn?** hasn't the French King broken
his oath?   **63 Envenom . . . words** Vituperate upon him with poisonous curses   **64 leave . . . woes alone** stop trying to assuage those
woes   **65 underbear** endure.   **70 state** majesty, as in a chair of state
75 'Tis true (King Philip is in mid-conversation with Blanche.)
78 Stays in his course stands still.   **his** its

The yearly course that brings this day about
Shall never see it but a holy day.
CONSTANCE [*rising*]
A wicked day, and not a holy day!
What hath this day deserved? What hath it done,
That it in golden letters should be set   85
Among the high tides in the calendar?   86
Nay, rather turn this day out of the week,
This day of shame, oppression, perjury.
Or if it must stand still, let wives with child   89
Pray that their burdens may not fall this day,
Lest that their hopes prodigiously be crossed.   91
But on this day let seamen fear no wreck;   92
No bargains break that are not this day made.   93
This day, all things begun come to ill end,
Yea, faith itself to hollow falsehood change!
KING PHILIP
By heaven, lady, you shall have no cause
To curse the fair proceedings of this day.
Have I not pawned to you my majesty?   98
CONSTANCE
You have beguiled me with a counterfeit
Resembling majesty, which, being touched and tried, 100
Proves valueless. You are forsworn, forsworn!
You came in arms to spill mine enemies' blood,   102
But now in arms you strengthen it with yours.   103
The grappling vigor and rough frown of war   104
Is cold in amity and painted peace,   105
And our oppression hath made up this league.   106
Arm, arm, you heavens, against these perjured kings!
A widow cries; be husband to me, heavens!   108
Let not the hours of this ungodly day   109
Wear out the day in peace, but ere sunset   110
Set armèd discord twixt these perjured kings!
Hear me, oh, hear me!
AUSTRIA   Lady Constance, peace!
CONSTANCE
War, war, no peace! Peace is to me a war.
O Limoges, O Austria, thou dost shame   114
That bloody spoil. Thou slave, thou wretch, thou coward! 115
Thou little valiant, great in villainy!
Thou ever strong upon the stronger side!
Thou Fortune's champion, that dost never fight
But when Her humorous Ladyship is by   119

To teach thee safety! Thou art perjured too,   120
And sooth'st up greatness. What a fool art thou,   121
A ramping fool, to brag and stamp and swear   122
Upon my party! Thou cold-blooded slave,   123
Hast thou not spoke like thunder on my side,
Been sworn my soldier, bidding me depend
Upon thy stars, thy fortune, and thy strength?
And dost thou now fall over to my foes?   127
Thou wear a lion's hide! Doff it for shame,   128
And hang a calfskin on those recreant limbs.   129
AUSTRIA
Oh, that a man should speak those words to me!
BASTARD
And hang a calfskin on those recreant limbs.
AUSTRIA
Thou dar'st not say so, villain, for thy life.
BASTARD
And hang a calfskin on those recreant limbs.
KING JOHN [*to the Bastard*]
We like not this. Thou dost forget thyself.   134

                    Enter Pandulph.

KING PHILIP
Here comes the holy legate of the Pope.
PANDULPH
Hail, you anointed deputies of heaven!
To thee, King John, my holy errand is.
I Pandulph, of fair Milan cardinal,
And from Pope Innocent the legate here,
Do in his name religiously demand
Why thou against the Church, our holy mother,
So willfully dost spurn, and force perforce   142
Keep Stephen Langton, chosen Archbishop   143
Of Canterbury, from that Holy See.
This, in our foresaid Holy Father's name,
Pope Innocent, I do demand of thee.
KING JOHN
What earthy name to interrogatories   147
Can task the free breath of a sacred king?   148
Thou canst not, Cardinal, devise a name
So slight, unworthy, and ridiculous,
To charge me to an answer, as the Pope.   151
Tell him this tale, and from the mouth of England
Add thus much more: that no Italian priest

---

85 golden i.e., red   **86 high tides** i.e., great festivals   **89 stand still** remain   **91 prodigiously be crossed** be thwarted by some monstrous birth defect.   **92 But** Except, other than (since this is the most evil of days).   **wreck** shipwreck   **93 No . . . made** break only agreements made on this day.   **98 pawned** pledged.   **my majesty** i.e., my kingly word.   **100 touched** tested (as one tests gold by rubbing it on a touchstone)   **102 in arms** in armor   **103 But . . . yours** but now by this embrace you strengthen the King of England's blood (i.e., dynastic claim) with a marriage with your own blood (i.e., Lewis). **104–6 The grappling . . . league** The vigorous sternness of a war that should have been fought on my behalf has turned cold in the false amity of this pretended friendship; only a joint wish to oppress Arthur and me could have brought about this alliance.   **106 our oppression** our being oppressed   **108 A widow cries** It is a widow that cries   **109–10 Let . . . peace** Do not let this wicked day pass by peaceably   **114 Limoges** (Compare with the note for 2.1.5.) **115 spoil** booty, i.e., the lion's pelt that Austria wears.   **119 humorous** capricious

120 safety i.e., how to choose the safe side.   **121 sooth'st up greatness** you flatter the influential.   **122 ramping** roaring, making a fierce show   **123 Upon my party** in my behalf.   **127 fall over** go over, desert   **128 Thou . . . hide!** To think that you presume to wear a lion's hide!   **129 calfskin** (Customarily used to make coats for the fools kept to amuse great families.)   **recreant** cowardly, having deserted the cause   **134 Thou . . . thyself** i.e., Remember your place, and be silent.   **142 spurn** oppose scornfully. (Literally, "kick.") **force perforce** by compulsion   **143 Stephen Langton** Pope Innocent's choice to be Archbishop of Canterbury, whose rejection by King John led to a papal bull of deposition and eventual resolution only after John had been forced to pay tribute and acknowledge England to be a papal fiefdom   **147–8 What . . . king?** What earth-born official can take to task the free breath of a sacred king by asking him to submit to formal questioning? (John denies any divine authority in the Pope's office.)   **151 charge . . . answer** command me to answer

Shall tithe or toll in our dominions;   154
But as we, under God, are supreme head,   155
So, under Him, that great supremacy
Where we do reign we will alone uphold
Without th'assistance of a mortal hand.
So tell the Pope, all reverence set apart   159
To him and his usurped authority.   160

KING PHILIP
Brother of England, you blaspheme in this.

KING JOHN
Though you and all the kings of Christendom
Are led so grossly by this meddling priest,   163
Dreading the curse that money may buy out,   164
And by the merit of vile gold, dross, dust,
Purchase corrupted pardon of a man
Who in that sale sells pardon from himself,   167
Though you and all the rest, so grossly led,
This juggling witchcraft with revenue cherish,   169
Yet I alone, alone do me oppose
Against the Pope, and count his friends my foes.

PANDULPH
Then, by the lawful power that I have,
Thou shalt stand cursed and excommunicate;
And blessèd shall he be that doth revolt
From his allegiance to an heretic;
And meritorious shall that hand be called,
Canonizèd and worshiped as a saint,
That takes away by any secret course
Thy hateful life.

CONSTANCE   Oh, lawful let it be
That I have room with Rome to curse awhile!   180
Good father Cardinal, cry thou "Amen"
To my keen curses, for without my wrong   182
There is no tongue hath power to curse him right.

PANDULPH
There's law and warrant, lady, for my curse.

CONSTANCE
And for mine too. When law can do no right,   185
Let it be lawful that law bar no wrong.   186
Law cannot give my child his kingdom here,
For he that holds his kingdom holds the law;
Therefore, since law itself is perfect wrong,   188
How can the law forbid my tongue to curse?

PANDULPH
Philip of France, on peril of a curse,   191

Let go the hand of that arch-heretic,
And raise the power of France upon his head   193
Unless he do submit himself to Rome.

ELEANOR
Look'st thou pale, France? Do not let go thy hand.

CONSTANCE [to Eleanor]
Look to it, devil, lest that France repent,   196
And by disjoining hands, hell lose a soul.   197

AUSTRIA
King Philip, listen to the Cardinal.

BASTARD
And hang a calfskin on his recreant limbs.

AUSTRIA
Well, ruffian, I must pocket up these wrongs,   200
Because—

BASTARD   Your breeches best may carry them.

KING JOHN
Philip, what say'st thou to the Cardinal?

CONSTANCE
What should he say, but as the Cardinal?   203

LEWIS
Bethink you, father, for the difference   204
Is purchase of a heavy curse from Rome
Or the light loss of England for a friend.
Forgo the easier.

BLANCHE   That's the curse of Rome.

CONSTANCE
Oh, Lewis, stand fast! The devil tempts thee here
In likeness of a new, untrimmèd bride.   209

BLANCHE
The Lady Constance speaks not from her faith   210
But from her need.   211

CONSTANCE [to King Philip]   Oh, if thou grant my need,
Which only lives but by the death of faith,   212
That need must needs infer this principle: 213
That faith would live again by death of need.   214
Oh, then tread down my need, and faith mounts up,   215
Keep my need up, and faith is trodden down!   216

KING JOHN
The King is moved, and answers not to this.

CONSTANCE [to King Philip]
Oh, be removed from him, and answer well!   218

---

154 **tithe** impose tithes, a tenth of one's income given to the Church.
toll collect taxes   155 **supreme head** (The title assumed by Henry VIII
at the time of the Reformation.)   159–60 **all . . . To** Ambiguous: (1)
offering no offense to (2) refuting all obedience to   163 **led** led astray.
this meddling priest i.e., the Pope   164 **the curse . . . out** i.e., excommunication, which a bribe to Rome can fix   167 **sells . . . himself** (1)
damns himself irretrievably by such sale of indulgences (2) sells pardons that, stemming only from him, can have no divine efficacy
169 **juggling** cheating, deceiving.   **cherish** maintain   180 **room,
Rome** (An obvious pun, pronounced alike in Elizabethan England.)
182 **without my wrong** i.e., (1) without recognition of the wrong done
to me (2) without the motive of suffering wrongs as I have suffered
185–6 **When . . . wrong** i.e., When the law itself is powerless to remedy evils, people must be free to pursue wrongful remedies (such as
cursing).   188 **holds the law** i.e., holds the law hostage   191 **a curse**
excommunication

193 **And . . . head** and raise a French army against him   196–7 **Look . . .
soul** (To Constance, Eleanor's advice is a diabolical attempt to prevent the salvation that the King of France would obtain by obeying
the Pope.)   200 **pocket up** submit to. (But the Bastard plays on the
literal sense of putting in one's breeches pocket, perhaps suggesting
further that Austria will get a swift kick in the breeches.)   203 **but . . .
Cardinal** except as the Cardinal instructs.   204 **difference** choice
209 **untrimmèd** i.e., freshly married, unshorn (suggesting she is still a
virgin). (This alludes to the temptation of Saint Anthony by the devil
in the form of a naked woman.)   210–11 **not . . . need** not from what
she really believes (and what her Catholic faith teaches her) but out of
political and military necessity.   212 **Which . . . faith** i.e., which need
is so strong only because I have lost faith in your broken promise
213 **needs infer** necessarily imply   214 **That . . . need** i.e., my faith
will be rekindled once my prior and compelling necessity, Arthur's
claim, has been satisfied.   215 **tread down** i.e., put down by satisfying, subdue   216 **trodden down** i.e., no longer needed.   218 **removed**
separated. (Playing on *moved* in line 217.)

AUSTRIA

   Do so, King Philip. Hang no more in doubt.

BASTARD

   Hang nothing but a calfskin, most sweet lout.   220

KING PHILIP

   I am perplexed and know not what to say.

PANDULPH

   What canst thou say but will perplex thee more,
   If thou stand excommunicate and cursed?

KING PHILIP

   Good Reverend Father, make my person yours,   224
   And tell me how you would bestow yourself.   225
   This royal hand and mine are newly knit,
   And the conjunction of our inward souls
   Married in league, coupled and linked together
   With all religious strength of sacred vows.
   The latest breath that gave the sound of words   230
   Was deep-sworn faith, peace, amity, true love
   Between our kingdoms and our royal selves;
   And even before this truce, but new before,   233
   No longer than we well could wash our hands
   To clap this royal bargain up of peace,   235
   Heaven knows, they were besmeared and overstained
   With slaughter's pencil, where revenge did paint   237
   The fearful difference of incensèd kings.   238
   And shall these hands, so lately purged of blood,
   So newly joined in love, so strong in both,   240
   Unyoke this seizure and this kind regreet?   241
   Play fast and loose with faith? So jest with heaven,
   Make such unconstant children of ourselves
   As now again to snatch our palm from palm,
   Unswear faith sworn, and on the marriage bed
   Of smiling peace to march a bloody host,
   And make a riot on the gentle brow   247
   Of true sincerity? Oh, holy sir,
   My Reverend Father, let it not be so!
   Out of your grace, devise, ordain, impose
   Some gentle order; and then we shall be blest
   To do your pleasure and continue friends.

PANDULPH

   All form is formless, order orderless,
   Save what is opposite to England's love.
   Therefore to arms! Be champion of our Church,
   Or let the Church, our mother, breathe her curse,
   A mother's curse, on her revolting son.   257
   France, thou mayst hold a serpent by the tongue,   258
   A chafèd lion by the mortal paw,   259
   A fasting tiger safer by the tooth,
   Than keep in peace that hand which thou dost hold.

KING PHILIP

   I may disjoin my hand, but not my faith.

PANDULPH

   So mak'st thou faith an enemy to faith,   263
   And like a civil war set'st oath to oath,
   Thy tongue against thy tongue. Oh, let thy vow
   First made to heaven, first be to heaven performed,
   That is, to be the champion of our Church!
   What since thou swor'st is sworn against thyself   268
   And may not be performèd by thyself,
   For that which thou hast sworn to do amiss
   Is not amiss when it is truly done;   271
   And being not done where doing tends to ill,
   The truth is then most done not doing it.
   The better act of purposes mistook   274
   Is to mistake again; though indirect,   275
   Yet indirection thereby grows direct,
   And falsehood falsehood cures, as fire cools fire   277
   Within the scorchèd veins of one new-burned.   278
   It is religion that doth make vows kept,
   But thou hast sworn against religion;
   By what thou swear'st against the thing thou swear'st,   281
   And mak'st an oath the surety for thy truth
   Against an oath. The truth thou art unsure   283
   To swear, swears only not to be forsworn,   284
   Else what a mockery should it be to swear!
   But thou dost swear only to be forsworn,   286
   And most forsworn to keep what thou dost swear.
   Therefore thy later vows against thy first
   Is in thyself rebellion to thyself;
   And better conquest never canst thou make
   Than arm thy constant and thy nobler parts
   Against these giddy loose suggestions,   292
   Upon which better part our prayers come in,   293
   If thou vouchsafe them. But if not, then know   294
   The peril of our curses light on thee
   So heavy as thou shalt not shake them off,   296
   But in despair die under their black weight.

AUSTRIA

   Rebellion, flat rebellion!

BASTARD   Will't not be?   298
   Will not a calfskin stop that mouth of thine?

---

220 Hang i.e., Wear. (Playing on *Hang*, "hesitate," in line 219.)
224 make . . . yours put yourself in my place   **225 bestow** conduct
230 latest most recent   **233 even before** just before.   **but new** immediately   **235 clap . . . up** i.e., conclude with a grasping of hands
237 pencil paintbrush.   **paint** picture, represent   **238 difference** dissension   **240 both** i.e., blood and love   **241 Unyoke this seizure** disjoin this handclasp.   **regreet** returned salutation, counterclasp.
247 And . . . brow and assault the gentle countenance   **257 revolting** rebellious   **258 mayst hold** may sooner hold   **259 mortal** deadly

263 So . . . to faith i.e., You are trying to set your promise to John against your religious vow to the Church   **268 since** since then
271 truly done i.e., not done at all (since, as Pandulph explains two lines later, an ill-considered vow is best performed by not performing it. This is an example of equivocation, much deplored by many Elizabethans and regarded as typical of Catholic duplicity.)   **274–5 The better . . . again** i.e., The best thing to do when one has made a wrong turn is to turn again   **277–8 as fire . . . new-burned** (Burns were commonly treated with heat, on the proverbial theory that one fire drives out another.)   **281 By . . . thing thou swear'st** you swear against the very thing by which you swear; i.e., by your oath of allegiance to John you directly violate your prior vows given to the Church
283–4 The truth . . . forsworn i.e., Your oath of allegiance to the true faith, which you are now hesitant to affirm, is above all a promise not to break your oath   **286 But . . . forsworn** i.e., But you are now proposing an oath to John in which you will indeed break your prior oath   **292 suggestions** temptations   **293 Upon . . . part** in support of which better side   **294 vouchsafe** accept, agree to   **296 as** that
298 Rebellion i.e., You, King Philip, are rebelling against the Church.
Will't not be? i.e., Will nothing serve to keep you quiet?

LEWIS
Father, to arms!

BLANCHE   Upon thy wedding day?
Against the blood that thou hast marrièd?   301
What, shall our feast be kept with slaughtered men?
Shall braying trumpets and loud churlish drums,
Clamors of hell, be measures to our pomp?   304
[Kneeling] Oh, husband, hear me! Ay, alack, how new
Is "husband" in my mouth! Even for that name,
Which till this time my tongue did ne'er pronounce,
Upon my knee I beg, go not to arms
Against mine uncle.

CONSTANCE [kneeling] Oh, upon my knee,
Made hard with kneeling, I do pray to thee,
Thou virtuous Dauphin: alter not the doom
Forethought by heaven!   312

BLANCHE [to Lewis]
Now shall I see thy love. What motive may
Be stronger with thee than the name of wife?

CONSTANCE
That which upholdeth him that thee upholds: 315
His honor.—Oh, thine honor, Lewis, thine honor!

LEWIS [to King Philip]
I muse Your Majesty doth seem so cold,   317
When such profound respects do pull you on.   318

PANDULPH
I will denounce a curse upon his head.   319

KING PHILIP [letting go of King John's hand]
Thou shalt not need. England, I will fall from thee.

CONSTANCE [rising]
Oh, fair return of banished majesty!

ELEANOR
Oh, foul revolt of French inconstancy!

KING JOHN
France, thou shalt rue this hour within this hour.

BASTARD
Old Time the clock setter, that bald sexton Time,
Is it as he will? Well then, France shall rue.   325

BLANCHE [rising]
The sun's o'ercast with blood. Fair day, adieu!
Which is the side that I must go withal?   327
I am with both: each army hath a hand,
And in their rage, I having hold of both,
They whirl asunder and dismember me.
Husband, I cannot pray that thou mayst win;
Uncle, I needs must pray that thou mayst lose;
Father, I may not wish the fortune thine;   333
Grandam, I will not wish thy wishes thrive.
Whoever wins, on that side shall I lose;
Assurèd loss before the match be played.

LEWIS
Lady, with me, with me thy fortune lies.

BLANCHE
There where my fortune lives, there my life dies.

KING JOHN [to the Bastard]
Cousin, go draw our puissance together.   339
                                        [Exit the Bastard.]
France, I am burned up with inflaming wrath,
A rage whose heat hath this condition,
That nothing can allay, nothing but blood—
The blood, and dearest-valued blood, of France.

KING PHILIP
Thy rage shall burn thee up, and thou shalt turn
To ashes, ere our blood shall quench that fire.
Look to thyself. Thou art in jeopardy.

KING JOHN
No more than he that threats. To arms let's hie!   347
                                        Exeunt [separately].

❖

3.2

Alarums, excursions. Enter [the] Bastard, with
Austria's head.

BASTARD
Now, by my life, this day grows wondrous hot.
Some airy devil hovers in the sky   2
And pours down mischief. Austria's head lie there,
While Philip breathes.   [He puts down the head.]   4

Enter [King] John, Arthur, [and] Hubert.

KING JOHN
Hubert, keep this boy. Philip, make up!   5
My mother is assailèd in our tent,
And ta'en, I fear.

BASTARD   My lord, I rescued her;
Her Highness is in safety, fear you not.
But on, my liege! For very little pains
Will bring this labor to an happy end.
                                        Exeunt [with Austria's head].

❖

3.3

Alarums, excursions, retreat. Enter [King] John,
Eleanor, Arthur, [the] Bastard, Hubert, [and]
lords.

KING JOHN [to Eleanor]
So shall it be; Your Grace shall stay behind   1
So strongly guarded. [To Arthur] Cousin, look not sad.   2

301 blood (Blanche is related by blood to King John.)   304 measures
musical accompaniment.   pomp i.e., wedding ceremony.   312 Forethought destined   315 that thee upholds who supports you
317 muse wonder   318 respects considerations   319 denounce proclaim, call down   325 France shall rue i.e., if Time is to decide,
France will rue sooner or later.   327 withal with.   333 Father i.e.,
Father-in-law, King Philip

339 Cousin Kinsman.   puissance armed force   347 hie hasten.
3.2. Location: France. Plains near Angiers. The battle is seen as following immediately upon the previous scene.
0.1 Alarums Calls to arms.   excursions sorties   2 airy devil (Aerial
spirits or devils were thought to be the cause of tempests, thunder,
lightning, etc.)   4 breathes catches his breath.   5 make up advance,
press on.
3.3. Location: Scene continues on the plains near Angiers.
0.1 retreat signal for withdrawal of forces.   1 stay behind i.e., remain
here in charge of the English territories   2 So thus.   Cousin Nephew

Thy grandam loves thee, and thy uncle will
As dear be to thee as thy father was.

ARTHUR
Oh, this will make my mother die with grief!

KING JOHN [*to the Bastard*]
Cousin, away for England! Haste before,
And, ere our coming, see thou shake the bags
Of hoarding abbots; imprisoned angels   8
Set at liberty. The fat ribs of peace   9
Must by the hungry now be fed upon.
Use our commission in his utmost force.   11

BASTARD
Bell, book, and candle shall not drive me back   12
When gold and silver becks me to come on.   13
I leave Your Highness.—Grandam, I will pray,
If ever I remember to be holy,
For your fair safety. So I kiss your hand.

ELEANOR
Farewell, gentle cousin.

KING JOHN   Coz, farewell.   17
                    [*Exit the Bastard.*]

ELEANOR
Come hither, little kinsman. Hark, a word.
                    [*She takes Arthur aside.*]

KING JOHN
Come hither, Hubert. O my gentle Hubert,
We owe thee much! Within this wall of flesh   20
There is a soul counts thee her creditor   21
And with advantage means to pay thy love;   22
And, my good friend, thy voluntary oath   23
Lives in this bosom, dearly cherishèd.   24
Give me thy hand. I had a thing to say,
But I will fit it with some better tune.
By heaven, Hubert, I am almost ashamed
To say what good respect I have of thee.   28

HUBERT
I am much bounden to Your Majesty.   29

KING JOHN
Good friend, thou hast no cause to say so yet,
But thou shalt have; and, creep time ne'er so slow,
Yet it shall come for me to do thee good.   32
I had a thing to say—but let it go.
The sun is in the heaven, and the proud day,
Attended with the pleasures of the world,
Is all too wanton and too full of gauds   36
To give me audience. If the midnight bell   37
Did with his iron tongue and brazen mouth
Sound on into the drowsy race of night;   39

If this same were a churchyard where we stand,
And thou possessèd with a thousand wrongs;   41
Or if that surly spirit, melancholy,
Had baked thy blood and made it heavy, thick,
Which else runs tickling up and down the veins,
Making that idiot, laughter, keep men's eyes   45
And strain their cheeks to idle merriment,   46
A passion hateful to my purposes;   47
Or if that thou couldst see me without eyes,
Hear me without thine ears, and make reply
Without a tongue, using conceit alone,   50
Without eyes, ears, and harmful sound of words—   51
Then, in despite of brooded watchful day,   52
I would into thy bosom pour my thoughts.
But, ah, I will not! Yet I love thee well,
And, by my troth, I think thou lov'st me well.

HUBERT
So well that what you bid me undertake,   56
Though that my death were adjunct to my act,   57
By heaven, I would do it.

KING JOHN   Do not I know thou wouldst?
Good Hubert, Hubert, Hubert, throw thine eye
On yon young boy. I'll tell thee what, my friend,
He is a very serpent in my way,
And wheresoe'er this foot of mine doth tread
He lies before me. Dost thou understand me?
Thou art his keeper.

HUBERT   And I'll keep him so
That he shall not offend Your Majesty.

KING JOHN   Death.

HUBERT
My lord?

KING JOHN   A grave.

HUBERT   He shall not live.

KING JOHN   Enough.
I could be merry now. Hubert, I love thee.
Well, I'll not say what I intend for thee.
Remember.—Madam, fare you well.
I'll send those powers o'er to Your Majesty.   70

ELEANOR
My blessing go with thee!

KING JOHN   For England, cousin, go. 71
Hubert shall be your man, attend on you
With all true duty.—On toward Calais, ho!   *Exeunt.*

❧

---

8 angels gold coins. (With a common pun on God's angels.)   **9 fat
ribs of peace** (i.e., in contrast to the skeleton of war, the *bare-ribbed
Death* of 5.2.177)   **11 his** its   **12 Bell, book, and candle** (Articles used
in the office of excommunication.)   **13 becks** beckon   **17 Coz**
Cousin, i.e., kinsman   **20 Within . . . flesh** i.e., Within me   **21 counts
. . . creditor** acknowledges a debt to you   **22 advantage** interest
23–4 thy . . . bosom your freely given allegiance warms my heart
28 respect opinion   **29 bounden** obligated   **32 it . . . for me** time will
provide me an opportunity   **36 gauds** showy ornaments, trifles
37 To . . . audience to hear what I have to say, i.e., to provide the suitable occasion.   **39 race** running, course. ("Face" and "ear" have been
suggested as emendations.)

41 And . . . wrongs i.e., and if you were a hardened villain, having
committed a thousand crimes. (*Possessed* means "obsessed by, and
possessed by devils.")   **45 idiot** jester.   **keep** hold captive, possess
46 strain stretch (in laughter)   **47 passion** emotion   **50 conceit**
thought   **51 harmful** (Because it is dangerous to speak of such
matters.)   **52 brooded** brooding, and hence vigilant in defense
of its young. (Sometimes emended to *broad-eyed*.)   **56 what** whatever
57 adjunct to consequent upon   **70 those powers** i.e., the troops
already agreed upon for the defense of England's French territories;
see lines 1–2.   **o'er** i.e., from England to France   **71 cousin** i.e.,
Arthur

[3.4]

Enter [King Philip of] France, [Lewis the]
Dauphin, Pandulph, [and] attendants.

KING PHILIP
So, by a roaring tempest on the flood,   1
A whole armada of convicted sail   2
Is scattered and disjoined from fellowship.

PANDULPH
Courage and comfort! All shall yet go well.

KING PHILIP
What can go well when we have run so ill?
Are we not beaten? Is not Angiers lost?
Arthur ta'en prisoner? Divers dear friends slain?
And bloody England into England gone,   8
O'erbearing interruption, spite of France?   9

LEWIS
What he hath won, that hath he fortified.
So hot a speed, with such advice disposed,   11
Such temperate order in so fierce a cause,
Doth want example. Who hath read or heard   13
Of any kindred action like to this?   14

KING PHILIP
Well could I bear that England had this praise,
So we could find some pattern of our shame.   16

Enter Constance, [with her hair about her ears].

Look who comes here! A grave unto a soul,   17
Holding th'eternal spirit, against her will,
In the vile prison of afflicted breath.—   19
I prithee, lady, go away with me.

CONSTANCE
Lo, now! Now see the issue of your peace.   21

KING PHILIP
Patience, good lady. Comfort, gentle Constance.

CONSTANCE
No, I defy all counsel, all redress,   23
But that which ends all counsel, true redress:
Death. Death, O amiable, lovely Death!
Thou odoriferous stench! Sound rottenness!   26
Arise forth from the couch of lasting night,   27
Thou hate and terror to prosperity,
And I will kiss thy detestable bones,
And put my eyeballs in thy vaulty brows,   30
And ring these fingers with thy household worms,   31
And stop this gap of breath with fulsome dust,   32

And be a carrion monster like thyself.
Come, grin on me, and I will think thou smil'st,
And buss thee as thy wife. Misery's love,   35
Oh, come to me!

KING PHILIP   O fair affliction, peace!   36

CONSTANCE
No, no, I will not, having breath to cry.   37
Oh, that my tongue were in the thunder's mouth!
Then with a passion would I shake the world,
And rouse from sleep that fell anatomy   40
Which cannot hear a lady's feeble voice,
Which scorns a modern invocation.   42

PANDULPH
Lady, you utter madness and not sorrow.

CONSTANCE
Thou art not holy to belie me so.
I am not mad. This hair I tear is mine;
My name is Constance; I was Geoffrey's wife;
Young Arthur is my son; and he is lost.
I am not mad; I would to heaven I were,
For then 'tis like I should forget myself!   49
Oh, if I could, what grief should I forget?
Preach some philosophy to make me mad,
And thou shalt be canonized, Cardinal;
For, being not mad but sensible of grief,   53
My reasonable part produces reason   54
How I may be delivered of these woes,   55
And teaches me to kill or hang myself.
If I were mad, I should forget my son,
Or madly think a babe of clouts were he.   58
I am not mad. Too well, too well I feel
The different plague of each calamity.   60

KING PHILIP
Bind up those tresses. Oh, what love I note
In the fair multitude of those her hairs!
Where but by chance a silver drop hath fallen,   63
Even to that drop ten thousand wiry friends   64
Do glue themselves in sociable grief,   65
Like true, inseparable, faithful loves,
Sticking together in calamity.

CONSTANCE
To England, if you will.

KING PHILIP   Bind up your hairs.   68

CONSTANCE
Yes, that I will. And wherefore will I do it?
I tore them from their bonds and cried aloud,
"Oh, that these hands could so redeem my son,   71

3.4. Location: France. The French King's quarters.
1 flood seas   **2 armada** (With probable allusion to the scattering of the Spanish Armada in 1588.)   **convicted** doomed   **8 bloody England** the blood-stained King of England   **9 O'erbearing interruption** overcoming all resistance.   **spite** in spite   **11 with . . . disposed** directed with such judgment   **13 Doth want example** lacks parallel instance.   **14 kindred** comparable   **16 So** provided.   **pattern** precedent   **17 A grave . . . soul** i.e., A mere shell of a body without the will to live   **19 prison . . . breath** (The soul was thought to leave the body from the mouth with the last expiring breath.)   **21 issue** outcome   **23 defy all counsel** reject all comfort (i.e., all attempts to calm me)   **26 odoriferous** sweet-smelling.   **Sound** Wholesome   **27 lasting** everlasting   **30 vaulty** arched and hollow   **31 these** i.e., my.   **thy household worms** the worms of your retinue   **32 this gap of breath** i.e., my mouth.   **fulsome** loathsome

35 buss kiss.   **Misery's love** You whom those in misery love (as a way of ending their misery)   **36 affliction** afflicted one   **37 having** so long as I have   **40 fell anatomy** fierce skeleton (the usual figure of Death in pictorial representations)   **42 modern** everyday, commonplace.   **invocation** entreaty.   **49 like** likely   **53 sensible of** capable of feeling   **54 reasonable part** brain   **55 delivered of** (1) freed from (2) delivered of, as in childbirth   **58 babe of clouts** rag doll   **60 different plague** distinct affliction   **63 silver drop** i.e., tear   **64 wiry friends** i.e., hairs   **65 Do . . . grief** i.e., cling together in sympathy of grief, bound to one another by the tears falling on them   **68 To England** (Constance answers Philip's invitation at line 20, saying, in effect, "If you love me and wish to assuage my grief, attack England on Arthur's behalf.")   **71 redeem** free from imprisonment

As they have given these hairs their liberty!"
But now I envy at their liberty,
And will again commit them to their bonds,
Because my poor child is a prisoner.

[*She binds up her hair.*]

And, father Cardinal, I have heard you say
That we shall see and know our friends in heaven.
If that be true, I shall see my boy again;
For since the birth of Cain, the first male child,   79
To him that did but yesterday suspire,   80
There was not such a gracious creature born.
But now will canker sorrow eat my bud   82
And chase the native beauty from his cheek,   83
And he will look as hollow as a ghost,
As dim and meager as an ague's fit,
And so he'll die; and, rising so again,
When I shall meet him in the court of heaven
I shall not know him. Therefore never, never
Must I behold my pretty Arthur more.

PANDULPH
You hold too heinous a respect of grief.   90

CONSTANCE
He talks to me that never had a son.

KING PHILIP
You are as fond of grief as of your child.   92

CONSTANCE
Grief fills the room up of my absent child,   93
Lies in his bed, walks up and down with me,
Puts on his pretty looks, repeats his words,
Remembers me of all his gracious parts,   96
Stuffs out his vacant garments with his form;
Then, have I reason to be fond of grief?
Fare you well! Had you such a loss as I,
I could give better comfort than you do.

[*She unbinds her hair again.*]

I will not keep this form upon my head   101
When there is such disorder in my wit.
O Lord! My boy, my Arthur, my fair son!
My life, my joy, my food, my all the world!
My widow-comfort, and my sorrows' cure!   *Exit.*

KING PHILIP
I fear some outrage, and I'll follow her.   106
                                            Exit [*attended*].

LEWIS
There's nothing in this world can make me joy.
Life is as tedious as a twice-told tale
Vexing the dull ear of a drowsy man;   109
And bitter shame hath spoiled the sweet world's taste,
That it yields naught but shame and bitterness.   111

PANDULPH
Before the curing of a strong disease,
Even in the instant of repair and health,
The fit is strongest. Evils that take leave,   114
On their departure most of all show evil.
What have you lost by losing of this day?   116

LEWIS
All days of glory, joy, and happiness.

PANDULPH
If you had won it, certainly you had.
No, no. When Fortune means to men most good,   119
She looks upon them with a threat'ning eye.
'Tis strange to think how much King John hath lost
In this which he accounts so clearly won.
Are not you grieved that Arthur is his prisoner?

LEWIS
As heartily as he is glad he hath him.

PANDULPH
Your mind is all as youthful as your blood.   125
Now hear me speak with a prophetic spirit;
For even the breath of what I mean to speak
Shall blow each dust, each straw, each little rub,   128
Out of the path which shall directly lead
Thy foot to England's throne. And therefore mark.
John hath seized Arthur, and it cannot be
That, whiles warm life plays in that infant's veins,   132
The misplaced John should entertain an hour,   133
One minute, nay, one quiet breath of rest.
A scepter snatched with an unruly hand   135
Must be as boisterously maintained as gained;   136
And he that stands upon a slipp'ry place
Makes nice of no vile hold to stay him up.   138
That John may stand, then Arthur needs must fall;
So be it, for it cannot be but so.

LEWIS
But what shall I gain by young Arthur's fall?

PANDULPH
You, in the right of Lady Blanche your wife,
May then make all the claim that Arthur did.

LEWIS
And lose it, life and all, as Arthur did.

PANDULPH
How green you are and fresh in this old world!
John lays you plots; the times conspire with you,   146
For he that steeps his safety in true blood   147
Shall find but bloody safety, and untrue.   148
This act so evilly borne shall cool the hearts   149
Of all his people and freeze up their zeal,
That none so small advantage shall step forth   151

To check his reign but they will cherish it;
No natural exhalation in the sky,   153
No scope of nature, no distempered day,   154
No common wind, no customèd event,   155
But they will pluck away his natural cause   156
And call them meteors, prodigies, and signs,
Abortives, presages, and tongues of heaven   158
Plainly denouncing vengeance upon John.   159

LEWIS
Maybe he will not touch young Arthur's life,
But hold himself safe in his prisonment.   161

PANDULPH
Oh, sir, when he shall hear of your approach,
If that young Arthur be not gone already,
Even at that news he dies; and then the hearts
Of all his people shall revolt from him,   165
And kiss the lips of unacquainted change,   166
And pick strong matter of revolt and wrath   167
Out of the bloody fingers' ends of John.
Methinks I see this hurly all on foot;   169
And, oh, what better matter breeds for you   170
Than I have named! The bastard Faulconbridge
Is now in England, ransacking the Church,
Offending charity. If but a dozen French
Were there in arms, they would be as a call   174
To train ten thousand English to their side,   175
Or as a little snow, tumbled about,
Anon becomes a mountain. O noble Dauphin,
Go with me to the King. 'Tis wonderful
What may be wrought out of their discontent,
Now that their souls are topful of offense.   180
For England go. I will whet on the King.

LEWIS
Strong reasons make strange actions. Let us go.   182
If you say ay, the King will not say no.   *Exeunt.*

❖

4.1

*Enter Hubert and Executioners [with irons and
rope].*

HUBERT
Heat me these irons hot, and look thou stand   1
Within the arras. When I strike my foot   2

Upon the bosom of the ground, rush forth
And bind the boy which you shall find with me
Fast to the chair. Be heedful. Hence, and watch.

FIRST EXECUTIONER
I hope your warrant will bear out the deed.   6

HUBERT
Uncleanly scruples! Fear not you. Look to't.   7
                    [The Executioners withdraw.]
Young lad, come forth. I have to say with you.   8

Enter Arthur.

ARTHUR
Good morrow, Hubert.

HUBERT   Good morrow, little prince.

ARTHUR
As little prince, having so great a title   10
To be more prince, as may be. You are sad.   11

HUBERT
Indeed, I have been merrier.

ARTHUR   Mercy on me!
Methinks nobody should be sad but I.
Yet I remember, when I was in France,
Young gentlemen would be as sad as night,
Only for wantonness. By my christendom,   16
So I were out of prison and kept sheep,   17
I should be as merry as the day is long;
And so I would be here, but that I doubt   19
My uncle practices more harm to me.   20
He is afraid of me, and I of him.
Is it my fault that I was Geoffrey's son?
No, indeed, is't not; and I would to heaven
I were your son, so you would love me, Hubert.   24

HUBERT *[aside]*
If I talk to him, with his innocent prate   25
He will awake my mercy, which lies dead.
Therefore I will be sudden, and dispatch.

ARTHUR
Are you sick, Hubert? You look pale today.
In sooth, I would you were a little sick,   29
That I might sit all night and watch with you.   30
I warrant I love you more than you do me.

HUBERT *[aside]*
His words do take possession of my bosom.—
Read here, young Arthur.   *[Showing a paper.]*
                    [Aside] How now, foolish rheum?   33
Turning dispiteous torture out of door?   34
I must be brief, lest resolution drop
Out at mine eyes in tender womanish tears.—
Can you not read it? Is it not fair writ?   37

153 **exhalation** fiery vapor or meteor   154 **scope of nature** irregular phenomenon showing nature's extraordinary range. **distempered** stormy   155 **customèd** customary   156 **pluck away his** discard its. **cause** explanation   158 **Abortives** untimely or monstrous births   159 **denouncing** calling down   161 **But . . . prisonment** but regard himself as safe so long as Arthur is imprisoned.   165 **his** John's   166 **kiss . . . change** i.e., welcome any unfamiliar change   167 **strong matter** (1) compelling evidence (2) festering pus   169 **hurly** commotion. **on foot** in motion   170 **breeds** is ripening   174 **call** (1) decoy or call-bird (2) call to arms   175 **train** attract   180 **topful of offense** brimful of grievance and sated with John's offenses.   182 **make strange actions** call for unusual or heretofore unthought-of actions (such as an invasion of England).
4.1. Location: England. A room in a castle. A chair is provided.
1 look take care   **2 Within the arras** behind the wall hangings. (Evidently, the Executioners go out as though to heat their irons and then conceal themselves behind the arras, ready at line 71 to come forth.)

6 **bear out** provide sufficient authority for   7 **Uncleanly** Improper, impure   8 **to say** something to speak about   10–11 **As . . . be** I am as little a prince, despite my being entitled to be greater, as is possible.   16 **for wantonness** out of affected behavior. **By my christendom** As I am a Christian   17 **So** provided   19 **doubt** fear   20 **practices** plots   24 **so** provided   25 **prate** prattle   29 **sooth** truth   30 **watch with** stay awake tending to   33 **rheum** i.e., tears. (Literally, a fluid discharge.)   34 **Turning . . . door?** Banishing pitiless torture?   37 **fair** handsomely, legibly

ARTHUR
Too fairly, Hubert, for so foul effect.   38
Must you with hot irons burn out both mine eyes?

HUBERT
Young boy, I must.

ARTHUR   And will you?

HUBERT   And I will.

ARTHUR
Have you the heart? When your head did but ache,
I knit my handkerchief about your brows—   42
The best I had, a princess wrought it me—   43
And I did never ask it you again;   44
And with my hand at midnight held your head,
And like the watchful minutes to the hour   46
Still and anon cheered up the heavy time,   47
Saying, "What lack you?" and "Where lies your grief?"
Or "What good love may I perform for you?"   49
Many a poor man's son would have lain still
And ne'er have spoke a loving word to you,
But you at your sick service had a prince.   52
Nay, you may think my love was crafty love,
And call it cunning. Do, an if you will.   54
If heaven be pleased that you must use me ill,
Why then you must. Will you put out mine eyes?
These eyes that never did nor never shall
So much as frown on you?

HUBERT   I have sworn to do it,
And with hot irons must I burn them out.

ARTHUR
Ah, none but in this iron age would do it!   60
The iron of itself, though heat red-hot,   61
Approaching near these eyes, would drink my tears
And quench his fiery indignation   63
Even in the matter of mine innocence;   64
Nay, after that, consume away in rust
But for containing fire to harm mine eye.   66
Are you more stubborn-hard than hammered iron?
An if an angel should have come to me   68
And told me Hubert should put out mine eyes,
I would not have believed him—no tongue but Hubert's.

HUBERT [calling]
Come forth!   [He stamps his foot.]

[Executioners come forth, with a cord, irons, etc.]

           Do as I bid you do.

ARTHUR
Oh, save me, Hubert, save me! My eyes are out
Even with the fierce looks of these bloody men.

HUBERT
Give me the iron, I say, and bind him here.
                  [They start to bind Arthur to a chair.]

ARTHUR
Alas, what need you be so boisterous-rough?   75
I will not struggle; I will stand stone-still.
For heaven sake, Hubert, let me not be bound!
Nay, hear me, Hubert: drive these men away,
And I will sit as quiet as a lamb;
I will not stir, nor wince, nor speak a word,
Nor look upon the iron angerly.   81
Thrust but these men away, and I'll forgive you,
Whatever torment you do put me to.

HUBERT [to the men]
Go stand within. Let me alone with him.

FIRST EXECUTIONER
I am best pleased to be from such a deed.   85
                              [Exeunt Executioners.]

ARTHUR
Alas, I then have chid away my friend!
He hath a stern look, but a gentle heart.
Let him come back, that his compassion may
Give life to yours.

HUBERT   Come, boy, prepare yourself.

ARTHUR
Is there no remedy?

HUBERT   None but to lose your eyes.

ARTHUR
Oh, heaven, that there were but a mote in yours,   91
A grain, a dust, a gnat, a wandering hair,
Any annoyance in that precious sense!   93
Then feeling what small things are boisterous there,   94
Your vile intent must needs seem horrible.

HUBERT
Is this your promise? Go to, hold your tongue.   96

ARTHUR
Hubert, the utterance of a brace of tongues   97
Must needs want pleading for a pair of eyes.   98
Let me not hold my tongue. Let me not, Hubert!   99
Or, Hubert, if you will, cut out my tongue,
So I may keep mine eyes. Oh, spare mine eyes,   101
Though to no use but still to look on you!   102
Lo, by my troth, the instrument is cold   103
And would not harm me.

HUBERT   I can heat it, boy.

ARTHUR
No, in good sooth. The fire is dead with grief,   105
Being create for comfort, to be used   106
In undeserved extremes. See else yourself.   107
There is no malice in this burning coal;
The breath of heaven hath blown his spirit out   109
And strewed repentant ashes on his head.   110

HUBERT
But with my breath I can revive it, boy.

ARTHUR
An if you do, you will but make it blush
And glow with shame of your proceedings, Hubert.
Nay, it perchance will sparkle in your eyes, 114
And, like a dog that is compelled to fight,
Snatch at his master that doth tarre him on. 116
All things that you should use to do me wrong
Deny their office. Only you do lack 118
That mercy which fierce fire and iron extends, 119
Creatures of note for mercy-lacking uses. 120

HUBERT
Well, see to live. I will not touch thine eye 121
For all the treasure that thine uncle owes. 122
Yet am I sworn, and I did purpose, boy,
With this same very iron to burn them out.

ARTHUR
Oh, now you look like Hubert! All this while
You were disguisèd.

HUBERT   Peace! No more. Adieu.
Your uncle must not know but you are dead. 127
I'll fill these doggèd spies with false reports. 128
And, pretty child, sleep doubtless and secure 129
That Hubert, for the wealth of all the world,
Will not offend thee.

ARTHUR   Oh, heaven! I thank you, Hubert. 131
HUBERT
Silence! No more. Go closely in with me. 132
Much danger do I undergo for thee.   Exeunt.

❧

4.2

*Enter [King] John, Pembroke, Salisbury, and other
lords. [The King sits on his throne.]*

KING JOHN
Here once again we sit, once again crowned,
And looked upon, I hope, with cheerful eyes.

PEMBROKE
This "once again," but that Your Highness pleased,
Was once superfluous. You were crowned before,
And that high royalty was ne'er plucked off,
The faiths of men ne'er stainèd with revolt.
Fresh expectation troubled not the land
With any longed-for change or better state.

SALISBURY
Therefore, to be possessed with double pomp, 9
To guard a title that was rich before, 10
To gild refinèd gold, to paint the lily,

To throw a perfume on the violet,
To smooth the ice, or add another hue
Unto the rainbow, or with taper light
To seek the beauteous eye of heaven to garnish, 15
Is wasteful and ridiculous excess.

PEMBROKE
But that your royal pleasure must be done, 17
This act is as an ancient tale new told,
And in the last repeating troublesome,
Being urgèd at a time unseasonable.

SALISBURY
In this the antique and well-noted face 21
Of plain old form is much disfigurèd; 22
And, like a shifted wind unto a sail, 23
It makes the course of thoughts to fetch about, 24
Startles and frights consideration, 25
Makes sound opinion sick and truth suspected, 26
For putting on so new a fashioned robe. 27

PEMBROKE
When workmen strive to do better than well,
They do confound their skill in covetousness; 29
And oftentimes excusing of a fault
Doth make the fault the worse by th'excuse,
As patches set upon a little breach 32
Discredit more in hiding of the fault
Than did the fault before it was so patched.

SALISBURY
To this effect, before you were new-crowned,
We breathed our counsel. But it pleased Your Highness 36
To overbear it, and we are all well pleased, 37
Since all and every part of what we would
Doth make a stand at what Your Highness will. 39

KING JOHN
Some reasons of this double coronation
I have possessed you with, and think them strong; 41
And more, more strong, when lesser is my fear, 42
I shall endue you with. Meantime but ask 43
What you would have reformed that is not well,
And well shall you perceive how willingly
I will both hear and grant you your requests.

PEMBROKE
Then I—as one that am the tongue of these 47
To sound the purposes of all their hearts, 48
Both for myself and them, but chief of all
Your safety, for the which myself and them 50
Bend their best studies—heartily request 51

114 **sparkle in** scatter sparks into   116 **Snatch** snap.   **tarre** provoke, incite   118 **Deny their office** renounce their natural function.   119 **extends** proffer   120 **Creatures . . . uses** things (i.e, fire and iron) noted for unmerciful uses.   121 **see to live** i.e., live, and continue to see.   122 **owes** owns.   127 **but** other than that   128 **I'll . . . spies** I'll mislead the spies who are doggedly and maliciously watching us   129 **doubtless** fearless   131 **offend** harm   132 **closely** secretly   **4.2. Location:** England. The court of King John.   9 **to be . . . pomp** to be given possession (of the crown) with a spurious second ceremony   10 **guard** trim, ornament; also, protect

15 **eye of heaven** i.e., the sun (much too fair and bright to be enhanced by a *taper light* or candle)   17 **But that** Were it not that   21 **well-noted** familiar   22 **form** custom   23 **a shifted wind** a wind that shifts direction   24 **fetch about** change direction, tack   25 **frights consideration** i.e., frightens everyone into anxious reflection   26–7 **Makes . . . robe** causes the soundness of your judgment and the truth of your claims to be suspected when you dress the English throne in this strange new ceremony.   29 **confound** destroy, disrupt.   **in covetousness** i.e., by their greedy desire to do better   32 **breach** hole   36 **breathed** spoke   37 **overbear** overrule   39 **Doth . . . at** (1) may go no further than (2) makes a stand of resistance opposing   41 **possessed you with** informed you of   42–3 **And . . . with** i.e., and I shall provide you with even more and stronger reasons when the emergency is past and can be talked about.   47 **tongue** spokesman   48 **sound** express   50 **them** i.e., they   51 **Bend** direct.   **studies** efforts

Th'enfranchisement of Arthur, whose restraint
Doth move the murmuring lips of discontent
To break into this dangerous argument:
If what in rest you have in right you hold,   55
Why then your fears—which, as they say, attend   56
The steps of wrong—should move you to mew up   57
Your tender kinsman and to choke his days   58
With barbarous ignorance and deny his youth
The rich advantage of good exercise?   60
That the time's enemies may not have this   61
To grace occasions, let it be our suit   62
That you have bid us ask his liberty,   63
Which for our goods we do no further ask   64
Than whereupon our weal, on you depending,   65
Counts it your weal he have his liberty.   66

Enter Hubert.

KING JOHN
Let it be so. I do commit his youth
To your direction.—Hubert, what news with you?
                              [*He takes Hubert aside.*]
PEMBROKE
This is the man should do the bloody deed;
He showed his warrant to a friend of mine.
The image of a wicked heinous fault
Lives in his eye; that close aspect of his   72
Doth show the mood of a much troubled breast,
And I do fearfully believe 'tis done
What we so feared he had a charge to do.   75
SALISBURY
The color of the King doth come and go
Between his purpose and his conscience,
Like heralds twixt two dreadful battles set.   78
His passion is so ripe it needs must break.   79
PEMBROKE
And when it breaks, I fear will issue thence
The foul corruption of a sweet child's death.
KING JOHN [*coming forward*]
We cannot hold mortality's strong hand.
Good lords, although my will to give is living,   83
The suit which you demand is gone and dead.
He tells us Arthur is deceased tonight.   85
SALISBURY
Indeed we feared his sickness was past cure.

PEMBROKE   52
Indeed we heard how near his death he was
Before the child himself felt he was sick.
This must be answered, either here or hence.   89
KING JOHN
Why do you bend such solemn brows on me?
Think you I bear the shears of destiny?
Have I commandment on the pulse of life?
SALISBURY
It is apparent foul play, and 'tis shame   93
That greatness should so grossly offer it.   94
So thrive it in your game! And so, farewell.   95
PEMBROKE
Stay yet, Lord Salisbury. I'll go with thee,
And find th'inheritance of this poor child,
His little kingdom of a forcèd grave.   98
That blood which owed the breadth of all this isle, 99
Three foot of it doth hold; bad world the while!   100
This must not be thus borne. This will break out
To all our sorrows, and ere long, I doubt.   102
                              Exeunt [*lords*].
KING JOHN
They burn in indignation. I repent.
There is no sure foundation set on blood,
No certain life achieved by others' death.

Enter Messenger.

A fearful eye thou hast. Where is that blood   106
That I have seen inhabit in those cheeks?
So foul a sky clears not without a storm.
Pour down thy weather: how goes all in France? 109
MESSENGER
From France to England. Never such a power
For any foreign preparation
Was levied in the body of a land.   111
The copy of your speed is learned by them;   112
For when you should be told they do prepare,   113
The tidings comes that they are all arrived.
KING JOHN
Oh, where hath our intelligence been drunk?   116
Where hath it slept? Where is my mother's care,
That such an army could be drawn in France   118
And she not hear of it?
MESSENGER   My liege, her ear
Is stopped with dust. The first of April died
Your noble mother; and, as I hear, my lord,
The Lady Constance in a frenzy died

52 Th'enfranchisement the freeing from imprisonment   **55–8 If . . .
kinsman** If you have a just and right claim to the kingdom you hold
in quiet possession, why is it that your fears—which, the murmurers
say, stem from your wrongdoing—should move you to incarcerate
young Arthur   **60 exercise** exercise in arms and other gentlemanly
accomplishments.   **61–3 That . . . liberty** In order that the enemies of
the present state of affairs may not have this matter to lend support to
their criticisms, let the concession that you invited us to ask for (lines
43–6) be Arthur's liberty   **64–6 Which . . . liberty** which we ask on
our own behalf only to the (considerable) extent that our welfare,
depending on you, reckons it a matter of your own welfare as well
that Arthur be set at liberty.   **72 Lives in his eye** shows itself in the
look of his eye.   **close aspect** furtive appearance   **75 charge** commission   **78 battles** armies in battle order   **79 ripe** (like a boil full of
pus, the *foul corruption* of line 81)   **83 give** i.e., grant your suit   **85
tonight** last night.

89 answered atoned for.   **hence** i.e., on the field of battle, or perhaps
in heaven.   **93 apparent** evident, blatant   **94 That . . . it** i.e., that a
king should flaunt foul play so flagrantly   **95 So . . . game!** May your
schemes lead to the same (bad) end!   **98 forcèd** imposed by violence
99 owed owned   **100 bad . . . while!** these are bad times!
102 doubt fear.   **106 fearful** full of fear and prompting fear in others
109 weather storm, tempest.   **goes all** is it all going. (But the Messenger replies literally in the sense that everything is physically going
from France to England in an invasion.)   **111 preparation** expedition
112 body i.e., length and breadth   **113 The copy . . . speed** i.e., The
example of your speed, when you proceed to Angiers (see 2.1.56 ff.)
116 our intelligence our spies, spy network   **118 drawn** mustered,
assembled

Three days before. But this from rumor's tongue
I idly heard; if true or false I know not.   124

KING JOHN
Withhold thy speed, dreadful Occasion!   125
Oh, make a league with me till I have pleased   126
My discontented peers! What, mother dead?
How wildly then walks my estate in France!   128
Under whose conduct came those powers of France   129
That thou for truth giv'st out are landed here?   130

MESSENGER
Under the Dauphin.

Enter [the] Bastard and Peter of Pomfret.

KING JOHN   Thou hast made me giddy
With these ill tidings. [*To the Bastard*] Now, what says
      the world
To your proceedings? Do not seek to stuff   133
My head with more ill news, for it is full.

BASTARD
But if you be afeard to hear the worst,   135
Then let the worst unheard fall on your head.   136

KING JOHN
Bear with me, cousin, for I was amazed   137
Under the tide; but now I breathe again
Aloft the flood, and can give audience   139
To any tongue, speak it of what it will.

BASTARD
How I have sped among the clergymen,   141
The sums I have collected shall express.
But as I traveled hither through the land,
I find the people strangely fantasied,   144
Possessed with rumors, full of idle dreams,
Not knowing what they fear, but full of fear.
And here's a prophet that I brought with me
From forth the streets of Pomfret, whom I found   148
With many hundreds treading on his heels,   149
To whom he sung, in rude harsh-sounding rhymes,
That ere the next Ascension Day at noon   151
Your Highness should deliver up your crown.

KING JOHN [*to Peter*]
Thou idle dreamer, wherefore didst thou so?

PETER
Foreknowing that the truth will fall out so.

KING JOHN
Hubert, away with him! Imprison him,
And on that day at noon, whereon he says
I shall yield up my crown, let him be hanged.
Deliver him to safety, and return,   158

For I must use thee. [*Exit Hubert with Peter of Pomfret.*]
                    Oh, my gentle cousin,   159
Hear'st thou the news abroad, who are arrived?

BASTARD
The French, my lord. Men's mouths are full of it.
Besides, I met Lord Bigot and Lord Salisbury,
With eyes as red as new-enkindled fire,
And others more, going to seek the grave
Of Arthur, whom they say is killed tonight   165
On your suggestion.

KING JOHN   Gentle kinsman, go   166
And thrust thyself into their companies.
I have a way to win their loves again.
Bring them before me.

BASTARD   I will seek them out.

KING JOHN
Nay, but make haste, the better foot before.   170
Oh, let me have no subject enemies
When adverse foreigners affright my towns   172
With dreadful pomp of stout invasion!   173
Be Mercury, set feathers to thy heels,   174
And fly like thought from them to me again.   175

BASTARD
The spirit of the time shall teach me speed.   *Exit.*

KING JOHN
Spoke like a sprightful noble gentleman!   177
[*To the Messenger*] Go after him, for he perhaps shall
      need
Some messenger betwixt me and the peers;
And be thou he.

MESSENGER   With all my heart, my liege.   [*Exit.*]

KING JOHN   My mother dead!

Enter Hubert.

HUBERT
My lord, they say five moons were seen tonight:
Four fixèd, and the fifth did whirl about
The other four in wondrous motion.

KING JOHN
Five moons!

HUBERT   Old men and beldams in the streets   186
Do prophesy upon it dangerously.   187
Young Arthur's death is common in their mouths,
And, when they talk of him, they shake their heads
And whisper one another in the ear;
And he that speaks doth grip the hearer's wrist,
Whilst he that hears makes fearful action,   192
With wrinkled brows, with nods, with rolling eyes.
I saw a smith stand with his hammer, thus,
The whilst his iron did on the anvil cool,
With open mouth swallowing a tailor's news;

---

124 idly by chance   **125 Occasion** course of events.   **126 make . . .
me** i.e., give me a respite, a truce   **128 walks my estate** goes my state
of affairs, my holdings   **129 conduct** command   **130 for . . . out**
report as a truth   **133 proceedings** i.e., mission against the monasteries; see 3.3.6 ff.   **135–6 But . . . head** But if you are afraid to listen to
bad news, misfortune will come upon you unawares (and be much
more dangerous).   **137 amazed** bewildered   **139 Aloft the flood**
above the waves, with my head above water. (Continuing the
metaphor of the *tide*, line 138.)   **141 sped** succeeded   **144 strangely
fantasied** full of strange fancies   **148 Pomfret** Pontefract, in Yorkshire   **149 treading on** following him at   **151 Ascension Day** the
Thursday forty days after Easter, celebrating the ascent of Christ into
heaven   **158 safety** safekeeping

159 gentle noble   **165 is killed tonight** was killed last night
166 suggestion instigation.   **170 the better foot before** i.e., as quickly
as you can.   **172 adverse** hostile   **173 stout** bold   **174 feathers** (Mercury, messenger of the gods, had winged sandals.)   **175 like thought**
as swift as thought   **177 sprightful** spirited   **186 beldams** old
women   **187 prophesy upon it** make predictions from it, expound its
meaning for the future.   **dangerously** in terms of future danger, or
threateningly to public order.   **192 action** gestures

Who, with his shears and measure in his hand,
Standing on slippers, which his nimble haste
Had falsely thrust upon contrary feet,   199
Told of a many thousand warlike French   200
That were embattlèd and ranked in Kent.   201
Another lean unwashed artificer   202
Cuts off his tale and talks of Arthur's death.

KING JOHN
Why seek'st thou to possess me with these fears?   204
Why urgest thou so oft young Arthur's death?
Thy hand hath murdered him. I had a mighty cause
To wish him dead, but thou hadst none to kill him.

HUBERT
No had, my lord? Why, did you not provoke me?   208

KING JOHN
It is the curse of kings to be attended
By slaves that take their humors for a warrant   210
To break within the bloody house of life,   211
And on the winking of authority   212
To understand a law, to know the meaning   213
Of dangerous majesty, when perchance it frowns
More upon humor than advised respect.   215

HUBERT [showing his warrant]
Here is your hand and seal for what I did.

KING JOHN
Oh, when the last account twixt heaven and earth
Is to be made, then shall this hand and seal
Witness against us to damnation!
How oft the sight of means to do ill deeds   220
Make deeds ill done! Hadst not thou been by,   221
A fellow by the hand of nature marked,
Quoted, and signed to do a deed of shame,   223
This murder had not come into my mind.
But, taking note of thy abhorred aspect,
Finding thee fit for bloody villainy,
Apt, liable to be employed in danger,   227
I faintly broke with thee of Arthur's death,   228
And thou, to be endearèd to a king,
Made it no conscience to destroy a prince.   230

HUBERT   My lord—

KING JOHN
Hadst thou but shook thy head or made a pause
When I spake darkly what I purposèd,   233
Or turned an eye of doubt upon my face,

As bid me tell my tale in express words,   235
Deep shame had struck me dumb, made me break off,
And those thy fears might have wrought fears in me.
But thou didst understand me by my signs
And didst in signs again parley with sin,
Yea, without stop didst let thy heart consent,
And consequently thy rude hand to act
The deed which both our tongues held vile to name.
Out of my sight, and never see me more!
My nobles leave me, and my state is braved,   244
Even at my gates, with ranks of foreign powers.
Nay, in the body of this fleshly land,   246
This kingdom, this confine of blood and breath,   247
Hostility and civil tumult reigns
Between my conscience and my cousin's death.

HUBERT
Arm you against your other enemies;
I'll make a peace between your soul and you.
Young Arthur is alive. This hand of mine
Is yet a maiden and an innocent hand,
Not painted with the crimson spots of blood.
Within this bosom never entered yet
The dreadful motion of a murderous thought;   256
And you have slandered nature in my form,   257
Which, howsoever rude exteriorly,   258
Is yet the cover of a fairer mind
Than to be butcher of an innocent child.

KING JOHN
Doth Arthur live? Oh, haste thee to the peers!
Throw this report on their incensèd rage,   262
And make them tame to their obedience.
Forgive the comment that my passion made
Upon thy feature, for my rage was blind,   265
And foul imaginary eyes of blood   266
Presented thee more hideous than thou art.
Oh, answer not, but to my closet bring   268
The angry lords with all expedient haste.
I conjure thee but slowly; run more fast!   270

                              Exeunt [separately].

✽

4.3

Enter Arthur, on the walls, [disguised as a shipboy].

ARTHUR
The wall is high, and yet will I leap down.
Good ground, be pitiful and hurt me not!

---

199 **upon contrary feet** the left slipper on the right foot and vice versa
200 **a many thousand** many thousands of   201 **embattlèd and ranked** drawn up in orderly battle array   202 **artificer** artisan
204 **possess . . . fears** (1) frighten me with these tidings (2) bewitch me with these fearful tidings.   208 **No had** Had I not.   **provoke** incite
210 **humors** whims   211 **To break . . . life** to assault bloodily the temple of the soul, i.e., commit a murder   212 **the winking of authority** the giving of a wink or knowing glance of command   213 **understand a law** i.e., infer what is being commanded   215 **upon humor** through whim.   **advised respect** careful consideration.   220–1 **How . . . done!** How often seeing a way to do ill deeds prompts us to go sinfully ahead!   223 **Quoted, and signed** particularly designated and marked out   227 **liable** alacritous, well suited.   228 **faintly broke with** hesitatingly and almost inaudibly broached the subject with   230 **Made . . . destroy** had no scruples against killing   233 **darkly** indirectly, ambiguously

235 **As** as though to.   **express** explicit   244 **my state is braved** my authority is challenged   246 **in . . . land** i.e., in my own body, the microcosm of my kingdom   247 **confine** (1) territorial limit (2) prison
256 **motion** impulse   257 **slandered . . . form** i.e., slandered my nature by judging me harshly in terms of my unattractive appearance
258 **rude** rough   262 **Throw . . . rage** i.e., Tell them this news as though throwing water on their burning rage   265 **feature** outward appearance   266 **imaginary . . . blood** your eyes, which I imagined to be bloody in thought, or, more probably, my eyes made bloodshot with rage at imagined wrong   268 **closet** private chamber   270 **conjure** adjure, urge
4.3. Location: England. Before the walls of a castle.
0.1 on the walls in the gallery rearstage

There's few or none do know me; if they did,
This shipboy's semblance hath disguised me quite. 4
I am afraid, and yet I'll venture it.
If I get down, and do not break my limbs,
I'll find a thousand shifts to get away. 7
As good to die and go as die and stay.
                                          [*He leaps down.*]
Oh, me! My uncle's spirit is in these stones.
Heaven take my soul, and England keep my bones!
                                          Dies.

*Enter Pembroke, Salisbury [with a letter], and
Bigot.*

SALISBURY
Lords, I will meet him at Saint Edmundsbury. 11
It is our safety, and we must embrace 12
This gentle offer of the perilous time. 13
PEMBROKE
Who brought that letter from the Cardinal?
SALISBURY
The Count Melun, a noble lord of France,
Whose private with me of the Dauphin's love 16
Is much more general than these lines import. 17
BIGOT
Tomorrow morning let us meet him then.
SALISBURY
Or rather, then set forward, for 'twill be
Two long days' journey, lords, or ere we meet. 20

Enter [the] Bastard.

BASTARD
Once more today well met, distempered lords! 21
The King by me requests your presence straight. 22
SALISBURY
The King hath dispossessed himself of us.
We will not line his thin bestainèd cloak 24
With our pure honors, nor attend the foot 25
That leaves the print of blood where'er it walks.
Return and tell him so. We know the worst.
BASTARD
Whate'er you think, good words, I think, were best.
SALISBURY
Our griefs, and not our manners, reason now. 29
BASTARD
But there is little reason in your grief.
Therefore 'twere reason you had manners now.
PEMBROKE
Sir, sir, impatience hath his privilege. 32
BASTARD
'Tis true—to hurt his master, no man else. 33

SALISBURY
This is the prison. [*He sees Arthur's body.*] What is he lies here?
PEMBROKE
O death, made proud with pure and princely beauty!
The earth had not a hole to hide this deed.
SALISBURY
Murder, as hating what himself hath done, 37
Doth lay it open to urge on revenge. 38
BIGOT
Or, when he doomed this beauty to a grave, 39
Found it too precious-princely for a grave.
SALISBURY [*to the Bastard*]
Sir Richard, what think you? You have beheld.
Or have you read or heard, or could you think, 42
Or do you almost think, although you see, 43
That you do see? Could thought, without this object, 44
Form such another? This is the very top, 45
The height, the crest, or crest unto the crest,
Of murder's arms. This is the bloodiest shame, 47
The wildest savagery, the vilest stroke
That ever walleyed wrath or staring rage 49
Presented to the tears of soft remorse. 50
PEMBROKE
All murders past do stand excused in this; 51
And this, so sole and so unmatchable, 52
Shall give a holiness, a purity,
To the yet unbegotten sin of times, 54
And prove a deadly bloodshed but a jest, 55
Exampled by this heinous spectacle. 56
BASTARD
It is a damnèd and a bloody work,
The graceless action of a heavy hand— 58
If that it be the work of any hand.
SALISBURY
If that it be the work of any hand?
We had a kind of light what would ensue. 61
It is the shameful work of Hubert's hand,
The practice and the purpose of the King, 63
From whose obedience I forbid my soul,
Kneeling before this ruin of sweet life,   [*he kneels*]
And breathing to his breathless excellence
The incense of a vow, a holy vow, 67
Never to taste the pleasures of the world,
Never to be infected with delight, 69
Nor conversant with ease and idleness,
Till I have set a glory to this hand 71
By giving it the worship of revenge. 72

---

4 semblance disguise **7 shifts** (1) stratagems (2) changes of costume
11 him i.e., the Dauphin. **Saint Edmundsbury** Bury St. Edmunds, in
Suffolk **12 our safety** our only means of safety **13 gentle** gracious.
of the i.e., made in such a **16 private** private communication
17 general all-embracing **20 or ere** before **21 distempered** disaffected **22 straight** at once. **24 line** provide a lining for, reinforce
25 attend the foot follow in the footsteps of one, serve one **29 griefs**
grievances. **reason** speak. (But the Bastard answers in the sense of
"rationality," line 30, and "common sense," line 31.) **32 his** its.
(Also in line 33.) **33 'Tis . . . else** i.e., Anger punishes itself. (A
proverbial idea.)

37 as as if **38 lay it open** proclaim the deed **39 he** i.e., Murder
42–3 Or . . . think Have you either read or heard (of anything like
this), or could you believe or even begin to believe **44 That** that
which **44–5 Could . . . another?** Could one possibly imagine another
sight like this without its actually being seen? **47 arms** coat of arms.
(This deed is the crest on top of the crest of Murder's coat of arms.)
49 walleyed glaring fiercely **50 tears** i.e., tearful view. **remorse**
pity. **51 in this** in comparison to this **52 sole** unique **54 times** i.e.,
future times **55 but** to be only **56 Exampled by** compared with
58 graceless unholy. **heavy** wicked **61 light** premonition **63 practice** plot, treachery **67 The incense of a vow** i.e., a vow that ascends
to heaven, like incense **69 infected** tainted; imbued **71 this hand**
i.e., either Arthur's hand or Salisbury's own hand, which he raises in
taking an oath **72 worship** honor, sacred function

PEMBROKE, BIGOT [*kneeling*]
  Our souls religiously confirm thy words.

        Enter Hubert.

HUBERT
  Lords, I am hot with haste in seeking you.
  Arthur doth live. The King hath sent for you.
SALISBURY [*to the others*]
  Oh, he is bold and blushes not at death.—
  Avaunt, thou hateful villain! Get thee gone!   77
HUBERT
  I am no villain.
SALISBURY [*drawing his sword*]   Must I rob the law?   78
BASTARD
  Your sword is bright, sir. Put it up again.   79
SALISBURY
  Not till I sheathe it in a murderer's skin.
HUBERT [*drawing*]
  Stand back, Lord Salisbury, stand back, I say!
  By heaven, I think my sword's as sharp as yours.
  I would not have you, lord, forget yourself,
  Nor tempt the danger of my true defense,   84
  Lest I, by marking of your rage, forget   85
  Your worth, your greatness, and nobility.
BIGOT
  Out, dunghill! Dar'st thou brave a nobleman?   87
HUBERT
  Not for my life. But yet I dare defend
  My innocent life against an emperor.
SALISBURY
  Thou art a murderer.
HUBERT   Do not prove me so;   90
  Yet I am none. Whose tongue soe'er speaks false,
  Not truly speaks; who speaks not truly, lies.
PEMBROKE
  Cut him to pieces!
BASTARD [*drawing*]   Keep the peace, I say!
SALISBURY
  Stand by, or I shall gall you, Faulconbridge.   94
BASTARD
  Thou wert better gall the devil, Salisbury.
  If thou but frown on me, or stir thy foot,
  Or teach thy hasty spleen to do me shame,   97
  I'll strike thee dead. Put up thy sword betime,   98
  Or I'll so maul you and your toasting iron   99
  That you shall think the devil is come from hell.
BIGOT
  What wilt thou do, renownèd Faulconbridge?
  Second a villain and a murderer?
HUBERT
  Lord Bigot, I am none.
BIGOT   Who killed this prince?

HUBERT
  'Tis not an hour since I left him well.
  I honored him, I loved him, and will weep
  My date of life out for his sweet life's loss. [*He weeps.*]   106
SALISBURY
  Trust not those cunning waters of his eyes,
  For villainy is not without such rheum,   108
  And he, long traded in it, makes it seem   109
  Like rivers of remorse and innocency.
  Away with me, all you whose souls abhor
  Th'uncleanly savors of a slaughterhouse!   112
  For I am stifled with this smell of sin.
BIGOT
  Away toward Bury, to the Dauphin there!
PEMBROKE
  There, tell the King, he may inquire us out.
                                    Exeunt lords.
BASTARD
  Here's a good world! Knew you of this fair work?
  Beyond the infinite and boundless reach
  Of mercy, if thou didst this deed of death,
  Art thou damned, Hubert.
HUBERT   Do but hear me, sir.
BASTARD   Ha! I'll tell thee what;
  Thou'rt damned as black—nay, nothing is so black;
  Thou art more deep damned than Prince Lucifer.
  There is not yet so ugly a fiend of hell
  As thou shalt be, if thou didst kill this child.
HUBERT
  Upon my soul—
BASTARD   If thou didst but consent
  To this most cruel act, do but despair;   126
  And if thou want'st a cord, the smallest thread
  That ever spider twisted from her womb
  Will serve to strangle thee; a rush will be a beam   129
  To hang thee on; or wouldst thou drown thyself,
  Put but a little water in a spoon
  And it shall be as all the ocean,
  Enough to stifle such a villain up.
  I do suspect thee very grievously.
HUBERT
  If I in act, consent, or sin of thought
  Be guilty of the stealing that sweet breath
  Which was embounded in this beauteous clay,   137
  Let hell want pains enough to torture me.   138
  I left him well.
BASTARD   Go, bear him in thine arms.
  I am amazed, methinks, and lose my way   140
  Among the thorns and dangers of this world.
                        [*Hubert picks up Arthur.*]
  How easy dost thou take all England up!
  From forth this morsel of dead royalty,
  The life, the right, and truth of all this realm
  Is fled to heaven; and England now is left
  To tug and scamble and to part by th' teeth   146

---

77 Avaunt Begone **78 Must . . . law?** Must I deprive the law of its intended victim by killing you myself? **79 bright** i.e., unused **84 tempt** risk, test **85 by marking of your rage** paying attention only to your wrath **87 brave** insult **90 prove me so** i.e., make me a murderer by tempting me to kill you **94 Stand by** Stand aside. **gall** wound **97 spleen** i.e., wrath **98 betime** promptly **99 toasting iron** sword. (Used contemptuously.)

106 date duration **108 rheum** watery discharge, i.e., tears **109 traded** experienced **112 savors** odors **126 but** nothing but **129 rush** reed **137 clay** i.e., Arthur's body **138 want** lack **140 amazed** stunned **146 scamble** scramble. **part by th' teeth** tear apart by the teeth, as a ravenous animal would do

The unowed interest of proud-swelling state.   147
Now for the bare-picked bone of majesty   148
Doth dogged war bristle his angry crest,   149
And snarleth in the gentle eyes of peace.
Now powers from home and discontents at home   151
Meet in one line; and vast confusion waits,   152
As doth a raven on a sick-fall'n beast,
The imminent decay of wrested pomp.   154
Now happy he whose cloak and cincture can   155
Hold out this tempest! Bear away that child,
And follow me with speed. I'll to the King.
A thousand businesses are brief in hand,   158
And heaven itself doth frown upon the land.

Exeunt.

❖

[5].1

Enter King John and Pandulph, [with] attendants.

KING JOHN *[giving Pandulph the crown]*
Thus have I yielded up into your hand
The circle of my glory.
PANDULPH *[giving back the crown]*   Take again
From this my hand, as holding of the Pope   3
Your sovereign greatness and authority.
KING JOHN
Now keep your holy word. Go meet the French,
And from His Holiness use all your power
To stop their marches 'fore we are inflamed.
Our discontented counties do revolt;   8
Our people quarrel with obedience,
Swearing allegiance and the love of soul   10
To stranger blood, to foreign royalty.   11
This inundation of mistempered humor   12
Rests by you only to be qualified.   13
Then pause not, for the present time's so sick
That present med'cine must be ministered,   15
Or overthrow incurable ensues.
PANDULPH
It was my breath that blew this tempest up,
Upon your stubborn usage of the Pope;
But since you are a gentle convertite,   19
My tongue shall hush again this storm of war

And make fair weather in your blust'ring land.
On this Ascension Day, remember well,
Upon your oath of service to the Pope,
Go I to make the French lay down their arms.
Exit [with attendants].
KING JOHN
Is this Ascension Day? Did not the prophet
Say that before Ascension Day at noon
My crown I should get off? Even so I have.
I did suppose it should be on constraint;
But, heav'n be thanked, it is but voluntary.

Enter [the] Bastard.

BASTARD
All Kent hath yielded. Nothing there holds out
But Dover Castle. London hath received,
Like a kind host, the Dauphin and his powers.   32
Your nobles will not hear you, but are gone
To offer service to your enemy,
And wild amazement hurries up and down
The little number of your doubtful friends.   36
KING JOHN
Would not my lords return to me again
After they heard young Arthur was alive?
BASTARD
They found him dead and cast into the streets,
An empty casket, where the jewel of life
By some damned hand was robbed and ta'en away.
KING JOHN
That villain Hubert told me he did live.
BASTARD
So, on my soul, he did, for aught he knew.
But wherefore do you droop? Why look you sad?
Be great in act, as you have been in thought.
Let not the world see fear and sad distrust   46
Govern the motion of a kingly eye.
Be stirring as the time; be fire with fire;   48
Threaten the threat'ner, and outface the brow
Of bragging horror. So shall inferior eyes,   50
That borrow their behaviors from the great,
Grow great by your example and put on
The dauntless spirit of resolution.
Away, and glister like the god of war
When he intendeth to become the field!   55
Show boldness and aspiring confidence.
What, shall they seek the lion in his den,
And fright him there? And make him tremble there?
Oh, let it not be said! Forage, and run   59
To meet displeasure farther from the doors,
And grapple with him ere he come so nigh.
KING JOHN
The legate of the Pope hath been with me,
And I have made a happy peace with him;

---

147 **unowed interest** disputed ownership or control   148–9 **Now . . . crest** Now implacable war, like a dog fighting over royal majesty as though it were a carcass already picked to the bone, angrily bristles its mane   151–2 **Now . . . waits** Now armies from abroad and discontented subjects here in England meet in united purpose; and limitless chaos hungrily awaits   154 **wrested pomp** usurped majesty.
155 **cincture** belt   158 **are brief in hand** demand immediate action
5.1 Location: England. The court of King John.
3 **as . . . Pope** as signifying that you receive the crown from the Pope
8 **counties** shires; possibly, nobles   10 **love of soul** most sincere love
11 **stranger** foreign   12–13 **This . . . qualified** This distempered behavior (thought to be caused by the excess of one of the bodily humors) can be brought back to normal only by you.   15 **present** prompt   19 **convertite** convert

32 **powers** army.   36 **doubtful** not to be relied on; fearful
46 **distrust** lack of confidence, fainting courage   48 **as the time** as the state of affairs demands   50 **inferior eyes** the eyes of humble subjects
55 **become** grace, adorn   59 **Forage** Seek out the enemy as prey

And he hath promised to dismiss the powers
Led by the Dauphin.
BASTARD   Oh inglorious league!
Shall we, upon the footing of our land,   66
Send fair-play orders and make compromise,   67
Insinuation, parley, and base truce
To arms invasive? Shall a beardless boy,   69
A cockered silken wanton, brave our fields   70
And flesh his spirit in a warlike soil,   71
Mocking the air with colors idly spread,   72
And find no check? Let us, my liege, to arms!   73
Perchance the Cardinal cannot make your peace;
Or if he do, let it at least be said
They saw we had a purpose of defense.   76

KING JOHN
Have thou the ordering of this present time.

BASTARD
Away, then, with good courage! [*Aside*] Yet I know   78
Our party may well meet a prouder foe.   *Exeunt.*   79

❧

[5].2

*Enter, in arms, [Lewis the] Dauphin, Salisbury,
Melun, Pembroke, Bigot, soldiers.*

LEWIS
My Lord Melun, let this be copied out,   1
And keep it safe for our remembrance.
                        [*He gives a document.*]
Return the precedent to these lords again,   3
That, having our fair order written down,   4
Both they and we, perusing o'er these notes,
May know wherefore we took the Sacrament,   6
And keep our faiths firm and inviolable.

SALISBURY
Upon our sides it never shall be broken.
And, noble Dauphin, albeit we swear
A voluntary zeal and an unurged faith   10
To your proceedings, yet believe me, Prince,
I am not glad that such a sore of time   12
Should seek a plaster by contemned revolt,   13
And heal the inveterate canker of one wound   14

By making many. Oh, it grieves my soul
That I must draw this metal from my side   16
To be a widow maker! Oh, and there
Where honorable rescue and defense   18
Cries out upon the name of Salisbury!   19
But such is the infection of the time
That, for the health and physic of our right,   21
We cannot deal but with the very hand   22
Of stern injustice and confusèd wrong.
And is't not pity, O my grievèd friends,
That we, the sons and children of this isle,
Were born to see so sad an hour as this,
Wherein we step after a stranger, march   27
Upon her gentle bosom, and fill up
Her enemies' ranks—I must withdraw and weep
Upon the spot of this enforcèd cause—   30
To grace the gentry of a land remote   31
And follow unacquainted colors here?   [*He weeps.*] 32
What, here? O nation, that thou couldst remove!   33
That Neptune's arms, who clippeth thee about,   34
Would bear thee from the knowledge of thyself,
And grapple thee unto a pagan shore,
Where these two Christian armies might combine   37
The blood of malice in a vein of league,   38
And not to spend it so unneighborly!

LEWIS
A noble temper dost thou show in this,
And great affections wrestling in thy bosom   41
Doth make an earthquake of nobility.   42
Oh, what a noble combat hast thou fought
Between compulsion and a brave respect!   44
Let me wipe off this honorable dew,
That silverly doth progress on thy cheeks.
                     [*He wipes away Salisbury's tears.*]
My heart hath melted at a lady's tears,
Being an ordinary inundation;
But this effusion of such manly drops,
This shower, blown up by tempest of the soul,
Startles mine eyes and makes me more amazed
Than had I seen the vaulty top of heaven   52
Figured quite o'er with burning meteors.   53
Lift up thy brow, renownèd Salisbury,

---

66 upon . . . land standing on our native soil   67 fair-play orders
chivalric conditions   69 To arms invasive to an invading army.
70 cockered . . . wanton spoiled, dandified youngster.   brave
(1) arrogantly display his splendor in (2) defy   71 flesh initiate in
bloodshed or inure to bloodshed   72 idly carelessly, insolently
73 check restraint.   76 of defense to defend ourselves.   78–9 Yet . . .
foe i.e., Yet, considering the poor morale on our side, we may very
well find ourselves up against a proud and formidable force. (If this
is not an aside, the Bastard could mean "our side is ready to take on a
more spirited and fierce foe than this one.")
5.2. Location: England. The Dauphin's camp at St. Edmundsbury.
1 this i.e., the agreement with the English lords. (See lines 33–4 of the
preceding scene.)   3 precedent original document, first draft
4 order agreement   6 took the Sacrament i.e., received communion
to confirm the sacredness of our vows   10 unurged uncompelled
12–13 that . . . revolt that the ills of this troublesome time should seek
out the despised remedy of rebellion. (A *plaster* is a dressing for a
wound.)   14 inveterate canker chronic and deep-seated ulcer

16 metal i.e., sword   18–19 Where . . . Salisbury where the patriotic
cause of rescuing and defending my country from her enemies calls
out upon me, Salisbury, to be its champion.   21 physic medical cure
22 We . . . hand i.e., we are obliged to use the very means (which we
otherwise deplore). The nobles must fight fire with fire.   27 step . . .
stranger serve a foreign invader   30 spot (1) stain (2) place.   enforcèd cause cause into which I am forced   31 grace . . . remote honor
the aristocracy of a foreign land (France)   32 unacquainted colors
the banners of a foreign power   33 remove depart, change location,
i.e., go from this scene of civil carnage to a crusade against pagan
enemies.   34 That . . . about i.e., Would that the sea, which encircles
and embraces you   37–8 combine . . . league i.e., unite the malice
they now expend on one another in a league of hostility, a crusade,
against a pagan foe   41 affections passions   42 Doth . . . nobility
i.e., produces tumult in your noble nature.   44 compulsion what you
are compelled to do (by the hard necessities of the times).   brave
respect gallant consideration (of your country's need).   52 had I
seen if I had seen   53 Figured adorned

And with a great heart heave away this storm.
Commend these waters to those baby eyes   56
That never saw the giant world enraged,
Nor met with fortune other than at feasts,
Full warm of blood, of mirth, of gossiping.
Come, come, for thou shalt thrust thy hand as deep
Into the purse of rich prosperity
As Lewis himself. So, nobles, shall you all,
That knit your sinews to the strength of mine.

            Enter Pandulph.

And even there, methinks, an angel spake.   64
Look where the holy legate comes apace,
To give us warrant from the hand of heaven,
And on our actions set the name of right
With holy breath.
PANDULPH   Hail, noble prince of France!
The next is this: King John hath reconciled
Himself to Rome. His spirit is come in   70
That so stood out against the holy Church,
The great metropolis and see of Rome.
Therefore thy threat'ning colors now wind up,   73
And tame the savage spirit of wild war,
That, like a lion fostered up at hand,   75
It may lie gently at the foot of peace
And be no further harmful than in show.
LEWIS
Your Grace shall pardon me; I will not back.   78
I am too highborn to be propertied,   79
To be a secondary at control,   80
Or useful servingman and instrument
To any sovereign state throughout the world.
Your breath first kindled the dead coal of wars
Between this chastised kingdom and myself,
And brought in matter that should feed this fire;
And now 'tis far too huge to be blown out
With that same weak wind which enkindled it.
You taught me how to know the face of right,   88
Acquainted me with interest to this land,   89
Yea, thrust this enterprise into my heart.
And come ye now to tell me John hath made
His peace with Rome? What is that peace to me?
I, by the honor of my marriage bed,   93
After young Arthur, claim this land for mine;
And, now it is half conquered, must I back
Because that John hath made his peace with Rome?
Am I Rome's slave? What penny hath Rome borne,
What men provided, what munition sent,
To underprop this action? Is't not I   99

That undergo this charge? Who else but I,   100
And such as to my claim are liable,   101
Sweat in this business and maintain this war?
Have I not heard these islanders shout out
"*Vive le Roi!*" as I have banked their towns?   104
Have I not here the best cards for the game
To win this easy match played for a crown?   106
And shall I now give o'er the yielded set?   107
No, no, on my soul, it never shall be said.
PANDULPH
You look but on the outside of this work.
LEWIS
Outside or inside, I will not return
Till my attempt so much be glorified
As to my ample hope was promisèd
Before I drew this gallant head of war,   113
And culled these fiery spirits from the world
To outlook conquest and to win renown   115
Even in the jaws of danger and of death.
            [*A trumpet sounds.*]
What lusty trumpet thus doth summon us?   117

            Enter [*the*] *Bastard.*

BASTARD
According to the fair play of the world,   118
Let me have audience. I am sent to speak.
My holy lord of Milan, from the King
I come, to learn how you have dealt for him;
And, as you answer, I do know the scope
And warrant limited unto my tongue.
PANDULPH
The Dauphin is too willful-opposite,   124
And will not temporize with my entreaties.   125
He flatly says he'll not lay down his arms.
BASTARD
By all the blood that ever fury breathed,   127
The youth says well. Now hear our English king,
For thus his royalty doth speak in me.
He is prepared, and reason too he should.   130
This apish and unmannerly approach,
This harnessed masque and unadvisèd revel,   132
This unhaired sauciness and boyish troops,   133
The King doth smile at, and is well prepared
To whip this dwarfish war, these pygmy arms,
From out the circle of his territories.   136
That hand which had the strength, even at your door,

---

56 **Commend** Entrust, bequeath. (Leave tears to babies, says the
Dauphin, that have never known the fury of the world at large and
have had no worse fortune than to be well fed and entertained.)
64 **an angel spake** (1) i.e., Pandulph comes with warrant from "the
hand of heaven" (2) a pun on *angel* meaning a coin, in "the purse of
rich prosperity." A trumpet may sound at this point.   70 **is come in**
has submitted   73 **wind up** furl   75 **at hand** by hand (and hence
tame)   78 **shall** must.   **back** go back.   79 **propertied** made a tool of
80 **secondary at control** subordinate under someone else's command
88 **right** my true claim   89 **interest** title, right   93 **by the . . . bed** i.e.,
in the name of Blanche, my wife   99 **underprop** support

100 **charge** expense.   101 **And . . . liable** and those who are subject
to my demands for service   104 "*Vive le Roi!*" Long live the King!
(Also a term in card playing; the metaphor continues in *banked*, "won
by putting in the bank," *game, match, crown*, "a five-shilling stake," *set*,
"round in a game," etc.)   **banked** coasted, skirted   106 **crown**
(1) symbol of monarchy (2) stake in a game.   107 **give . . . set** abandon the hand or round already won.   113 **drew** assembled.   **head of
war** army   115 **outlook** stare down   117 **lusty** vigorous   118 **fair
play** i.e., rules of chivalry   124 **willful-opposite** stubbornly opposed
125 **temporize** come to an agreement   127 **By . . . breathed** By all the
bloodthirsty passion that fury ever breathed forth   130 **reason . . .
should** with good reason.   132 **This . . . revel** this masque in armor
and ill-considered festive entertainment   133 **unhaired** beardless,
youthful   136 **circle** confines

To cudgel you and make you take the hatch,   138
To dive like buckets in concealèd wells,   139
To crouch in litter of your stable planks,   140
To lie like pawns locked up in chests and trunks,   141
To hug with swine, to seek sweet safety out   142
In vaults and prisons, and to thrill and shake   143
Even at the crying of your nation's crow,   144
Thinking his voice an armèd Englishman—
Shall that victorious hand be feebled here
That in your chambers gave you chastisement?   147
No! Know the gallant monarch is in arms,
And like an eagle o'er his aerie towers   149
To souse annoyance that comes near his nest.   150
And you degenerate, you ingrate revolts,   151
You bloody Neroes, ripping up the womb   152
Of your dear mother England, blush for shame!
For your own ladies and pale-visaged maids
Like Amazons come tripping after drums,   155
Their thimbles into armèd gauntlets change,   156
Their needles to lances, and their gentle hearts
To fierce and bloody inclination.

LEWIS
There end thy brave, and turn thy face in peace.   159
We grant thou canst outscold us. Fare thee well.
We hold our time too precious to be spent
With such a brabbler.

PANDULPH   Give me leave to speak.   162

BASTARD
No, I will speak.

LEWIS   We will attend to neither.   163
Strike up the drums, and let the tongue of war
Plead for our interest and our being here.

BASTARD
Indeed, your drums, being beaten, will cry out;
And so shall you, being beaten. Do but start
An echo with the clamor of thy drum,
And even at hand a drum is ready braced   169
That shall reverberate all as loud as thine.
Sound but another, and another shall,
As loud as thine, rattle the welkin's ear   172
And mock the deep-mouthed thunder. For at hand—
Not trusting to this halting legate here,   174
Whom he hath used rather for sport than need—
Is warlike John; and in his forehead sits

A bare-ribbed Death, whose office is this day   177
To feast upon whole thousands of the French.
LEWIS
Strike up our drums, to find this danger out.
BASTARD
And thou shalt find it, Dauphin, do not doubt.
                    [Drums beat.] Exeunt [separately].

❧

[5].3

Alarums. Enter [King] John and Hubert.

KING JOHN
How goes the day with us? Oh, tell me, Hubert.
HUBERT
Badly, I fear. How fares Your Majesty?
KING JOHN
This fever that hath troubled me so long
Lies heavy on me. Oh, my heart is sick!

Enter a Messenger.

MESSENGER
My lord, your valiant kinsman, Faulconbridge,
Desires Your Majesty to leave the field
And send him word by me which way you go.
KING JOHN
Tell him, toward Swinstead, to the abbey there.   8
MESSENGER
Be of good comfort, for the great supply   9
That was expected by the Dauphin here
Are wrecked three nights ago on Goodwin Sands.   11
This news was brought to Richard but even now.   12
The French fight coldly and retire themselves.   13
KING JOHN
Ay me, this tyrant fever burns me up
And will not let me welcome this good news.
Set on toward Swinstead. To my litter straight;
Weakness possesseth me, and I am faint.   *Exeunt.*

❧

[5].4

Enter Salisbury, Pembroke, and Bigot.

SALISBURY
I did not think the King so stored with friends.   1
PEMBROKE
Up once again! Put spirit in the French.
If they miscarry, we miscarry too.
SALISBURY
That misbegotten devil, Faulconbridge,
In spite of spite, alone upholds the day.   5

---

138 **take the hatch** leap over the lower-half door; i.e., make a hasty and undignified retreat   139 **concealèd wells** wells offering a place to hide   140 **crouch** i.e., hide.   **litter** straw bedding for animals. **planks** floors   141 **pawns** articles in pawn   142 **hug** i.e., bed down   143 **thrill** shiver   144 **crying . . . crow** i.e., crowing of the rooster, a French national symbol   147 **your chambers** i.e., your own terrain   149 **o'er . . . towers** soaring over his nest   150 **souse** swoop down upon   151 **revolts** rebels   152 **Neroes** (The Roman emperor Nero allegedly ripped open the womb of his mother after having murdered her.)   155 **Amazons** female warriors of ancient mythology   156 **armèd gauntlets** steel-plated gloves worn as part of the armor   159 **brave** defiant boast.   **turn thy face** go back the way you came   162 **brabbler** noisy, quarrelsome person.   163 **attend to** (1) listen to (2) wait for   169 **ready braced** i.e., tightened, ready to be struck   172 **welkin's** heaven's, sky's   174 **this . . . here** i.e., Pandulph. (John will not hesitate or waver like this indecisive cleric, says the Bastard.)

177 **bare-ribbed Death** i.e., Death envisaged as a skeleton.   **office** function
5.3. Location: England. The field of battle.
8 **Swinstead** i.e., Swineshead in Lincolnshire   9 **supply** reinforcement   11 **Goodwin Sands** dangerous shoals off Kent.   12 **Richard** i.e., the Bastard   13 **retire themselves** retreat.
5.4. Location: The field of battle, as before.
1 **stored** supplied   5 **In spite of spite** i.e., despite anything we do

PEMBROKE
　They say King John, sore sick, hath left the field.

　　　Enter Melun, wounded, [led by a soldier].

MELUN
　Lead me to the revolts of England here.　　　　　　7
SALISBURY
　When we were happy we had other names.
PEMBROKE
　It is the Count Melun.
SALISBURY　　　　　　　　Wounded to death.
MELUN
　Fly, noble English, you are bought and sold!　　　10
　Unthread the rude eye of rebellion　　　　　　　11
　And welcome home again discarded faith.
　Seek out King John and fall before his feet;
　For if the French be lords of this loud day,
　He means to recompense the pains you take　　　15
　By cutting off your heads. Thus hath he sworn,
　And I with him, and many more with me,
　Upon the altar at Saint Edmundsbury,
　Even on that altar where we swore to you
　Dear amity and everlasting love.
SALISBURY
　May this be possible? May this be true?
MELUN
　Have I not hideous death within my view,
　Retaining but a quantity of life,　　　　　　　　23
　Which bleeds away, even as a form of wax
　Resolveth from his figure 'gainst the fire?　　　25
　What in the world should make me now deceive,
　Since I must lose the use of all deceit?　　　　27
　Why should I then be false, since it is true
　That I must die here and live hence by truth?　29
　I say again, if Lewis do win the day,
　He is forsworn if e'er those eyes of yours
　Behold another day break in the east.
　But even this night, whose black contagious breath　33
　Already smokes about the burning crest　　　　34
　Of the old, feeble, and day-wearied sun,
　Even this ill night, your breathing shall expire,
　Paying the fine of rated treachery　　　　　　37
　Even with a treacherous fine of all your lives,　38
　If Lewis by your assistance win the day.
　Commend me to one Hubert with your king;
　The love of him, and this respect besides,　　41
　For that my grandsire was an Englishman,　　42
　Awakes my conscience to confess all this.
　In lieu whereof, I pray you, bear me hence　　44
　From forth the noise and rumor of the field,　45

Where I may think the remnant of my thoughts
In peace, and part this body and my soul
With contemplation and devout desires.
SALISBURY
　We do believe thee, and beshrew my soul　　　49
　But I do love the favor and the form　　　　　　50
　Of this most fair occasion, by the which
　We will untread the steps of damnèd flight,　　52
　And like a bated and retirèd flood,　　　　　　53
　Leaving our rankness and irregular course,　　54
　Stoop low within those bounds we have o'erlooked　55
　And calmly run on in obedience
　Even to our ocean, to our great King John.
　My arm shall give thee help to bear thee hence,
　For I do see the cruel pangs of death
　Right in thine eye. Away, my friends! New flight,　60
　And happy newness, that intends old right!　　61

　　　　　　　　Exeunt [leading off Melun].

❖

[5.]5

　　　Enter [Lewis the] Dauphin and his train.

LEWIS
　The sun of heaven, methought, was loath to set,
　But stayed and made the western welkin blush,
　When English measure backward their own ground　3
　In faint retire. Oh, bravely came we off,　　　4
　When with a volley of our needless shot,　　　5
　After such bloody toil, we bid good night,
　And wound our tatt'ring colors clearly up,　　7
　Last in the field, and almost lords of it!

　　　Enter a Messenger.

MESSENGER
　Where is my prince, the Dauphin?
LEWIS　　　　　　　　　　　　Here. What news?
MESSENGER
　The Count Melun is slain. The English lords
　By his persuasion are again fall'n off,　　　　11
　And your supply, which you have wished so long,
　Are cast away and sunk on Goodwin Sands.
LEWIS
　Ah, foul shrewd news! Beshrew thy very heart!　14
　I did not think to be so sad tonight

---

7 **revolts** rebels　**10 bought and sold** i.e., betrayed.　**11 Unthread . . . rebellion** Pull back from the hazards of rebellion, just as you would withdraw thread from a needle's eye　**15 He** i.e., the French Dauphin　**23 quantity** small quantity　**25 Resolveth from his figure** melts and loses its shape　**27 use** profit　**29 hence** in the next world　**33 contagious** (Night air was thought to be noxious.)　**34 smokes** grows misty　**37 fine** penalty.　**rated** (1) assessed, evaluated (2) rebuked, chided　**38 fine** end. (With a pun on *fine* of the previous line.)　**41 respect** consideration　**42 For that** because, in that　**44 In lieu whereof** In payment for which (information)　**45 rumor** noise

49–50 beshrew . . . form curses on my soul if I do not love the attractive appearance　**52 untread** retrace.　**damnèd flight** cursed breaking away from proper obedience　**53–4 And . . . course** and like a river that has abated and receded, ceasing to flood beyond its proper bounds　**55 Stoop low** (1) subside, like a river (2) kneel.　**o'erlooked** (1) overflowed (2) disregarded　**60 Right** unmistakably　**60–1 New . . . right!** Welcome our new flight (as contrasted with our *damnèd flight* from proper obedience, line 52), and a happy change for the better, that proceeds toward the old right of loyalty to King John!
5.5 Location: England. The French camp.
3 measure traverse　**4 faint retire** fainthearted retreat.　**bravely . . . off** we left the field of battle in fine fettle　**5 needless** i.e., fired toward a disappearing enemy that needed no encouragement to flee　**7 tatt'ring** flying in tatters (because of the day's fierce engagement).　**clearly** free from entanglement, without enemy interference　**11 are again fall'n off** have withdrawn allegiance once again　**14 shrewd** of evil import

As this hath made me. Who was he that said
King John did fly an hour or two before
The stumbling night did part our weary powers?   18
MESSENGER
Whoever spoke it, it is true, my lord.
LEWIS
Well, keep good quarter and good care tonight.   20
The day shall not be up so soon as I,
To try the fair adventure of tomorrow.   *Exeunt.*   22

❖

[5].6

Enter [the] Bastard and Hubert, severally.

HUBERT
Who's there? Speak, ho! Speak quickly, or I shoot.
BASTARD
A friend. What art thou?
HUBERT   Of the part of England.   2
BASTARD
Whither dost thou go?
HUBERT   What's that to thee?
Why may not I demand of thine affairs
As well as thou of mine?
BASTARD   Hubert, I think?
HUBERT   Thou hast a perfect thought.   7
I will upon all hazards well believe   8
Thou art my friend, that know'st my tongue so well.
Who art thou?
BASTARD   Who thou wilt. And if thou please,
Thou mayst befriend me so much as to think
I come one way of the Plantagenets.
HUBERT
Unkind remembrance! Thou and eyeless night   13
Have done me shame. Brave soldier, pardon me,
That any accent breaking from thy tongue   15
Should scape the true acquaintance of mine ear.
BASTARD
Come, come; sans compliment, what news abroad?   17
HUBERT
Why, here walk I in the black brow of night,
To find you out.
BASTARD   Brief, then; and what's the news?
HUBERT
Oh, my sweet sir, news fitting to the night,
Black, fearful, comfortless, and horrible.
BASTARD
Show me the very wound of this ill news.
I am no woman; I'll not swoon at it.

HUBERT
The King, I fear, is poisoned by a monk.
I left him almost speechless, and broke out   25
To acquaint you with this evil, that you might
The better arm you to the sudden time   27
Than if you had at leisure known of this.   28
BASTARD
How did he take it? Who did taste to him?   29
HUBERT
A monk, I tell you, a resolvèd villain,
Whose bowels suddenly burst out. The King
Yet speaks and peradventure may recover.
BASTARD
Who didst thou leave to tend His Majesty?
HUBERT
Why, know you not? The lords are all come back,
And brought Prince Henry in their company,
At whose request the King hath pardoned them,   35
And they are all about His Majesty.
BASTARD
Withhold thine indignation, mighty heaven,
And tempt us not to bear above our power!   39
I'll tell thee, Hubert, half my power this night,   40
Passing these flats, are taken by the tide;   41
These Lincoln Washes have devourèd them.
Myself, well mounted, hardly have escaped.
Away before! Conduct me to the King.   44
I doubt he will be dead or ere I come.   *Exeunt.*   45

❖

[5].7

Enter Prince Henry, Salisbury, and Bigot.

PRINCE HENRY
It is too late. The life of all his blood   1
Is touched corruptibly, and his pure brain,   2
Which some suppose the soul's frail dwelling-house,
Doth by the idle comments that it makes   4
Foretell the ending of mortality.   5

Enter Pembroke.

PEMBROKE
His Highness yet doth speak, and holds belief
That, being brought into the open air,

18 **stumbling** causing one to stumble   20 **quarter** watch   22 **adventure** hazard, fortune
5.6. Location: England. An open place in the neighborhood of Swinstead, i.e., Swineshead Abbey.
0.1 *severally* at separate doors.   **2 Of the part** On the side
7 perfect correct   **8 upon all hazards** against any odds   **13 Unkind remembrance** (Hubert chides his own faulty memory.)   **Thou** i.e., My memory   **15 accent** speech   **17 sans compliment** without the usual civilities

25 **out** away   27 **to the sudden time** for this emergency   28 **at leisure** i.e., later, because of a leisurely report   29 **it** i.e., the poison. **Who . . . him?** (A "taster" was supposed to eat a portion of everything the King was to eat in order to protect him from poisoning. The monk who did so here took the poison knowingly—as a *resolvèd villain*—to ensure the King's death.)   35 **Prince Henry** i.e., John's son, the future Henry III   39 **tempt . . . power** don't try us beyond our power of endurance.   40 **power** army   41 **Passing** traversing. **flats** tidal flatlands in the large inlet called the Wash, between Lincolnshire and Norfolk   44 **Away before!** Lead the way!   45 **doubt** fear.   **or ere** before
5.7. Location: England. The orchard of Swinstead, i.e., Swineshead Abbey.
1 The life . . . blood His vital spirits (thought to be made in the heart and circulated to the veins)   **2 touched** infected.   **corruptibly** leading to corruption and death.   **pure** clear   **4 idle comments** babble   **5 mortality** life.

It would allay the burning quality
Of that fell poison which assaileth him.   9

PRINCE HENRY
Let him be brought into the orchard here.

                                                          [*Exit Bigot.*]

Doth he still rage?

PEMBROKE   He is more patient
Than when you left him. Even now he sung.

PRINCE HENRY
Oh, vanity of sickness! Fierce extremes   13
In their continuance will not feel themselves.   14
Death, having preyed upon the outward parts,   15
Leaves them insensible, and his siege is now   16
Against the mind, the which he pricks and wounds
With many legions of strange fantasies,   18
Which, in their throng and press to that last hold,   19
Confound themselves. 'Tis strange that Death should sing. 20
I am the cygnet to this pale faint swan,   21
Who chants a doleful hymn to his own death,
And from the organ pipe of frailty sings
His soul and body to their lasting rest.

SALISBURY
Be of good comfort, Prince, for you are born
To set a form upon that indigest   26
Which he hath left so shapeless and so rude.   27

          [*King*] *John brought in* [*in a chair, attended by*
          Bigot].

KING JOHN
Ay, marry, now my soul hath elbowroom;
It would not out at windows nor at doors.
There is so hot a summer in my bosom
That all my bowels crumble up to dust.
I am a scribbled form, drawn with a pen   32
Upon a parchment, and against this fire
Do I shrink up.

PRINCE HENRY   How fares Your Majesty?

KING JOHN
Poisoned—ill fare! Dead, forsook, cast off;   35
And none of you will bid the winter come
To thrust his icy fingers in my maw,
Nor let my kingdom's rivers take their course
Through my burned bosom, nor entreat the north
To make his bleak winds kiss my parchèd lips
And comfort me with cold. I do not ask you much—
I beg cold comfort; and you are so strait   42
And so ingrateful, you deny me that.

PRINCE HENRY
Oh, that there were some virtue in my tears   44
That might relieve you!

KING JOHN   The salt in them is hot.
Within me is a hell, and there the poison
Is as a fiend confined to tyrannize
On unreprievable condemnèd blood.

          Enter [*the*] *Bastard.*

BASTARD
Oh, I am scalded with my violent motion
And spleen of speed to see Your Majesty!   50

KING JOHN
Oh, cousin, thou art come to set mine eye.   51
The tackle of my heart is cracked and burnt,   52
And all the shrouds wherewith my life should sail   53
Are turnèd to one thread, one little hair.
My heart hath one poor string to stay it by,   55
Which holds but till thy news be utterèd,
And then all this thou see'st is but a clod
And module of confounded royalty.   58

BASTARD
The Dauphin is preparing hitherward,   59
Where God He knows how we shall answer him!   60
For in a night the best part of my power,   61
As I upon advantage did remove,   62
Were in the Washes all unwarily
Devourèd by the unexpected flood.   [*The King dies.*] 64

SALISBURY
You breathe these dead news in as dead an ear.—
My liege! My lord!—But now a king, now thus.

PRINCE HENRY
Even so must I run on, and even so stop.
What surety of the world, what hope, what stay,   68
When this was now a king and now is clay?

BASTARD [*to the King*]
Art thou gone so? I do but stay behind
To do the office for thee of revenge,
And then my soul shall wait on thee to heaven,   72
As it on earth hath been thy servant still.—   73
Now, now, you stars that move in your right spheres,   74
Where be your powers? Show now your mended faiths,   75
And instantly return with me again
To push destruction and perpetual shame
Out of the weak door of our fainting land.
Straight let us seek, or straight we shall be sought;   79
The Dauphin rages at our very heels.

---

9 **fell** cruel   13 **vanity** absurdity   13–14 **Fierce . . . themselves** Intense
agonies overwhelm the senses, producing numbness.   15–16 **Death . . .
insensible** i.e., Death's approach begins with the limbs, leaving them
without pulse or sensation   18 **legions** (1) vast numbers (2) armies
19 **hold** stronghold (the mind)   20 **Confound themselves** destroy
themselves, becoming incoherent and senseless.   21 **cygnet** young
swan. (It was a popular belief that the swan sang only once in its life,
just before it died, as its spirit attempted to pass through its long
neck, the *organ pipe of frailty*, of line 23.)   26 **indigest** shapeless
mass, i.e., the confused state   27 **rude** shapeless, i.e., ungoverned.
32 **a scribbled form** a hastily drafted document, i.e., a perishable
being   35 **fare** (1) food (2) fortune.   42 **cold comfort** (1) the comfort
of cold to my burning (2) empty consolation (since real consolation is
no longer possible).   **strait** niggardly

44 **virtue** healing power   50 **spleen** i.e., eagerness   51 **set mine eye**
close my eyes (in death).   52 **tackle** rigging of a ship   53 **shrouds**
ropes giving support to masts. (With a suggestion also of burial garments.)   55 **string** (1) heartstring (2) rope, as in lines 53–4.   **stay it**
support itself   58 **module** counterfeit, mere image.   **confounded**
destroyed   59 **preparing** repairing, coming   60 **answer** meet and
oppose   61 **in a night** during the night.   **power** army   62 **upon . . .
remove** shifted position to gain tactical advantage   64 **flood** i.e., tide.
68 **stay** support   72 **wait on** attend   73 **still** always.   74 **stars** i.e.,
nobles.   **right spheres** proper orbits (around the throne, like heavenly bodies around the earth)   75 **faiths** loyalties (to the crown)
79 **Straight . . . seek** Let us seek out and engage the enemy at once

SALISBURY
It seems you know not, then, so much as we.
The Cardinal Pandulph is within at rest,
Who half an hour since came from the Dauphin,
And brings from him such offers of our peace
As we with honor and respect may take,   85
With purpose presently to leave this war.

BASTARD
He will the rather do it when he sees
Ourselves well sinewèd to our defense.   88

SALISBURY
Nay, 'tis in a manner done already,
For many carriages he hath dispatched   90
To the seaside, and put his cause and quarrel
To the disposing of the Cardinal,
With whom yourself, myself, and other lords,
If you think meet, this afternoon will post   94
To consummate this business happily.

BASTARD
Let it be so. And you, my noble Prince,
With other princes that may best be spared,
Shall wait upon your father's funeral.   98

PRINCE HENRY
At Worcester must his body be interred,
For so he willed it.

BASTARD   Thither shall it, then.
And happily may your sweet self put on   101

The lineal state and glory of the land,   102
To whom, with all submission, on my knee
I do bequeath my faithful services   104
And true subjection everlastingly.   [*He kneels.*]

SALISBURY
And the like tender of our love we make,   106
To rest without a spot for evermore.   107
                [*All kneel to Prince Henry, and then rise.*]

PRINCE HENRY
I have a kind soul that would give you thanks
And knows not how to do it but with tears.

BASTARD
Oh, let us pay the time but needful woe,   110
Since it hath been beforehand with our griefs.   111
This England never did, nor never shall,
Lie at the proud foot of a conqueror
But when it first did help to wound itself.
Now these her princes are come home again,   115
Come the three corners of the world in arms   116
And we shall shock them. Naught shall make us rue,   117
If England to itself do rest but true.
                    Exeunt [*with the King's body*].

---

85 respect self-respect   **88 well sinewèd to our** well strengthened in
our own   **90 carriages** baggage vehicles   **94 post** hasten   **98 wait
upon** act as escorts and pallbearers in   **101 happily** propitiously

102 lineal state crown by right of succession   **104 bequeath** give
106 tender offer   **107 rest** remain.   **spot** stain   **110 but needful woe**
no more weeping than necessary   **111 Since . . . griefs** since the troubled time in which we find ourselves has anticipated our sorrows.
115 Now Now that.   **home** i.e., back to true faith and allegiance
116 three . . . world i.e., all the world except England, the fourth corner   **117 shock** meet with force

The Tragedy of King Richard the Second

❧❧❧

Richard II (c. 1595–1596) is the first play in Shakespeare's great four-play historical saga, or tetralogy, that continues with the two parts of Henry IV (c. 1596–1598) and concludes with Henry V (1599). In this, his second, tetralogy, Shakespeare dramatizes the beginnings of the great conflict called the Wars of the Roses, having already dramatized the conclusion of that civil war in his earlier tetralogy on Henry VI and Richard III (c. 1589–1594). Both sequences move from an outbreak of civil faction to the eventual triumph of political stability. Together, they comprise the story of England's long century of political turmoil from the 1390s until Henry Tudor's victory over Richard III in 1485. Yet Shakespeare chose to tell the two halves of this chronicle in reverse order. His culminating statement about kingship in Henry V focuses on the earlier historical period, on the education and kingly success of Prince Hal.

With Richard II, then, Shakespeare turns to the events that had launched England's century of crisis. These events were still fresh and relevant to Elizabethan minds. Richard and Bolingbroke's contest for the English crown provided a sobering example of political wrongdoing and, at least by implication, a rule for political right conduct. One prominent reason for studying history, to an Elizabethan, was to avoid the errors of the past. The relevance of such historical analogy was, in fact, vividly underscored some six years after Shakespeare wrote the play: in 1601, followers of the Earl of Essex commissioned Shakespeare's acting company to perform a revived play about Richard II on the eve of what was to be an abortive rebellion, perhaps with the intention of inciting a riot. Whether the play was Shakespeare's is not certain, but it seems likely. The acting company was ultimately exonerated, but not before Queen Elizabeth concluded that she was being compared to Richard II. When he wrote the play, Shakespeare presumably did not know that it would be used for such a purpose, but he must have known that the overthrow of Richard II was, in any case,

a controversial subject because of its potential use as a precedent for rebellion. The scene of Richard's deposition (4.1) was considered so provocative by Elizabeth's government that it was censored in the printed quartos of Shakespeare's play during the Queen's lifetime.

In view of the startling relevance of this piece of history to Shakespeare's own times, then, what are the rights and wrongs of Richard's deposition, and to what extent can political lessons be drawn from Shakespeare's presentation?

To begin with, we should not underestimate Richard's attractive qualities, as a man and even as a king. Throughout the play, Richard is consistently more impressive and majestic in appearance than his rival, Bolingbroke. Richard fascinates us with his verbal sensitivity, his poetic insight, and his dramatic self-consciousness. He eloquently expounds a sacramental view of kingship, according to which "Not all the water in the rough rude sea / Can wash the balm off from an anointed king" (3.2.54–5). Bolingbroke can depose Richard but can never capture the aura of majesty Richard possesses; Bolingbroke may succeed politically but only at the expense of desecrating an idea. Richard is much more interesting to us as a man than Bolingbroke, more capable of grief, more tender in his personal relationships, and more in need of being understood. Indeed, a major factor in Richard's tragedy is the conflict between his public role (wherein he sees himself as divinely appointed, almost superhuman) and his private role (wherein he is emotionally dependent and easily hurt). He confuses what the medieval and Renaissance world knew as the king's "two bodies," the sacramental body of kingship, which is eternal, and the human body of a single occupant of the throne, whose frail mortal condition is subject to time and fortune. Richard's failure to perceive and to act wisely on this difference is part of his tragic predicament, but his increasing insight, through suffering, into the truth of the distinction is also part of his spiritual growth. His dilemma, however poignantly individual, lies at the heart of kingship. Richard is thus very much a king. Although he sometimes indulges in childish sentimentality, at his best he is superbly refined, perceptive, and poetic.

These qualities notwithstanding, Richard is an incompetent ruler, compared with the man who supplants him. Richard himself confesses to the prodigal expense of "too great a court." In order to raise funds, he has been obliged to "farm our royal realm"; that is, to sell for ready cash the right of collecting taxes to individual courtiers, who are then free to extort what the market will bear (1.4.43–5). Similarly, Richard proposes to issue "blank charters" (line 48) to his minions, who will then be authorized to fill in the amount of tax to be paid by any hapless subject. These abuses were infamous to Elizabethan audiences as symbols of autocratic misgovernment. No less heinous is Richard's seizure of the dukedom of Lancaster from his cousin Bolingbroke. Although Richard does receive the consent of his Council to banish Bolingbroke because of the divisiveness of the quarrel between him and Mowbray, the King violates the very idea of inheritance of property when he takes away Bolingbroke's title and lands. And, as his uncle the Duke of York remonstrates, Richard's own right to the throne depends on that idea of due inheritance. By offending against the most sacred concepts of order and degree, he teaches others to rebel.

Richard's behavior even prior to the commencement of the play arouses suspicion. The nature of his complicity in the death of his uncle Thomas of Woodstock, Duke of Gloucester, is perhaps never entirely clear, and Gloucester may have given provocation. Indeed, one can sympathize with the predicament of a young ruler prematurely thrust into the center of power by the untimely death of his father, the crown prince, now having to cope with an array of worldly-wise, advice-giving uncles. Nevertheless, Richard is unambiguously guilty of murder in the eyes of Gloucester's widow, while her brother-in-law John of Gaunt, Duke of Lancaster, assumes that Richard has caused Gloucester's death, "the which if wrongfully / Let heaven revenge" (1.2.39–40). Apparently, too, Gaunt's son Bolingbroke believes Richard to be a murderer, and he brings accusation against Thomas Mowbray, Duke of Norfolk, partly as a means of embarrassing the King, whom he cannot accuse directly. Mowbray's lot is an unenviable one: he was in command at Calais when Gloucester was executed there, and he hints that Richard ordered the execution (even though Mowbray alleges that he himself did not carry out the order). For his part, Richard is only too glad to banish the man suspected of having been his agent in murder. Mowbray is a convenient scapegoat.

The polished, ceremonial tone of the play's opening is vitiated, then, by our growing awareness of hidden violence and factionalism going on behind the scene. Our first impression of Richard is of a king devoted to the public display of conciliatory even-handedness. He listens to the rival claims of Bolingbroke and Mowbray, and, when he cannot reconcile them peacefully, he orders a trial by combat. This trial (1.3) is replete with ceremonial repetition and ritual. The combatants are duly sworn in the justice of their cause, and God is to decide the quarrel by awarding victory to the champion who speaks the truth. Richard, the presiding officer, assumes the role of God's anointed deputy on earth. Yet it becomes evident in due course that Richard is a major perpetrator of injustice rather than an impartial judge, that Bolingbroke is after greater objectives than he acknowledges even to himself, and that Richard's refusal to let the trial by combat take place and his banishment of the two contenders are his desperate ways of burying a problem he cannot deal with forthrightly. His uncles reluctantly consent to the banishment only because they, too, see that disaffection has reached alarming proportions.

Bolingbroke's motivation in these opening scenes is perhaps even more obscure than Richard's. Our first impression of Bolingbroke is of forthrightness, moral indignation, and patriotic zeal. In fact, we never really question the earnestness of his outrage at Richard's misgovernance, his longing to avenge a family murder (for Gloucester was his uncle, too), or his bitter disappointment at being banished. Yet we are prompted to ask further: what is the essential cause of the enmity between Bolingbroke and Richard? If Mowbray is only a stalking-horse, is not Gloucester's death also the excuse for pursuing a preexistent animosity? Richard, for one, appears to think so. His portrayal of Bolingbroke as a scheming politician, who curries favor with the populace in order to build a widely based alliance against the King himself, is telling and prophetic. Bolingbroke, says Richard, acts "As were our England in reversion his, / And he our subjects' next degree in hope" (1.4.35–6). This unflattering appraisal might be ascribed to malicious envy on Richard's part, were it not proved by subsequent events to be wholly accurate.

Paradoxically, Richard is far the more prescient of the two contenders for the English throne. It is he, in fact, who perceives from the start that the conflict between them is irreconcilable. He banishes Bolingbroke as his chief rival and does not doubt what motives will call Bolingbroke home again. Meanwhile, Bolingbroke disclaims any motive for his return other than love of country and hatred of injustice. Although born with a political canniness that Richard lacks, Bolingbroke does not reflect (out loud, at least) upon the consequences of his own acts. As a man of action, he lives in the present. Richard, conversely, a person of exquisite contemplative powers and poetic imagination, does not deign to cope with the practical. He both envies and despises Bolingbroke's easy way with the commoners. Richard cherishes kingship for the majesty and the royal prerogative it confers, not for the power to govern wisely. Thus it is that, despite his perception of what will follow, Richard habitually indulges his worst instincts, buying a moment of giddy pleasure at the expense of future disaster.

Granted Richard's incompetence as a ruler, is Bolingbroke justified in armed rebellion against him? According to Bolingbroke's uncle, the Duke of York (who later, to be sure, shifts his allegiance), and to the Bishop of Carlisle, Bolingbroke is not justified in the rebellion. The attitude of these men can be summed up by the phrase "passive obedience." And, although Bolingbroke's own father, John of Gaunt, dies before his son returns to England to seize power, Gaunt, too, is opposed to such human defiances of the sacred institution of kingship. "God's is the quarrel," he insists (1.2.37). Because Richard is God's anointed deputy on earth, as Gaunt sees the matter, only God may punish the King's wrongdoing. Gaunt may not question Richard's guilt, but neither does he question God's ability to avenge. Gaunt sees human intervention in God's affair as blasphemous: "for I may never lift / An angry arm against His minister" (1.2.40–1). To be sure, Gaunt does acknowledge a solemn duty to offer frank advice to extremists of both sides, and he does so unsparingly. He consents to the banishment of his son, and he rebukes Richard with his dying breath.

This doctrine of passive obedience was familiar to Elizabethans, for they heard it in church periodically in official homilies against rebellion. It was the Tudor state's answer to those who asserted a right to overthrow reputedly evil kings. The argument was logically ingenious. Why are evil rulers permitted to govern from time to time? Presumably, because God wishes to test a people or to punish them for waywardness. Any king performing such chastisement is a divine scourge. Accordingly, the worst thing a people can do is to rebel against God's scourge, thereby manifesting more waywardness. Instead, they must attempt to remedy the insolence in their hearts, advise the King to mend his ways, and patiently await God's pardon. If they do so, they will not long be disappointed. The doctrine is essentially conservative, defending the status quo. It is reinforced in this play by the Bishop of Carlisle's prophecy that God will avenge through civil war the deposition of his anointed (4.1.126–50); an Elizabethan audience would have appreciated the irony of the prophecy's having come true and having been the subject of Shakespeare's first historical tetralogy. Moreover, in *Richard II* the doctrine of passive obedience is a moderate position between the extremes of tyranny and rebellion, and is expressed by thoughtful, selfless characters. We might be tempted to label it Shakespeare's view if we did not also perceive that the doctrine is continually placed in ironic conflict with harsh political realities. The character who most reflects

the ironies and even ludicrous incongruities of the position is the Duke of York.

York is to an extent a choric character, that is, one who helps direct our viewpoint, because his transfer of loyalties from Richard to Bolingbroke structurally delineates the decline of Richard's fortunes and the concurrent rise of Bolingbroke's. At first York shares his brother Gaunt's unwillingness to act, despite their dismay at Richard's willfulness. It is only when Richard seizes the dukedom of Lancaster that York can no longer hold his tongue. His condemnation is as bitter as that of Gaunt, hinting even at loss of allegiance (2.1.200–8). Still, he accepts the responsibility, so cavalierly bestowed by Richard, of governing England in the King's absence. He musters what force he can to oppose Bolingbroke's advance and lectures against this rebellion with the same vehemence he had used against Richard's despotism. Yet, when faced with Bolingbroke's overwhelming military superiority, he accedes rather than fights in behalf of a lost cause. However much this may resemble cowardice or mere expediency, it also displays a pragmatic logic. Once Bolingbroke has become de facto king, in York's view, he must be acknowledged and obeyed. By a kind of analogy to the doctrine of passive obedience (which more rigorous theorists would never allow), York accepts the status quo as inevitable. He is vigorously ready to defend the new regime, just as he earlier defended Richard's de jure rule. York's inconsistent loyalty helps define the structure of the play.

When, however, this conclusion brings York to the point of turning in his own son, Aumerle, for a traitor and quarreling with his wife as to whether their son shall live, the ironic absurdity is apparent. Bolingbroke, now King Henry, himself is amused, in one of the play's rare light-hearted moments (5.3.79–80). At the same time, the comedy deals with serious issues, especially the conflict between public responsibility urged by York and private or emotional satisfaction urged by his Duchess—a conflict seen earlier, for example, in the debate between Gaunt and his sister-in-law, the widowed Duchess of Gloucester (1.2). When a family and a kingdom are divided against one another, there can be no really satisfactory resolution.

We are never entirely convinced that all the fine old medieval theories surrounding kingship—divine right, passive obedience, trial by combat, and the like—can ever wholly explain or remedy the complex and nasty political situation afflicting England. The one man capable of decisive action, in fact, is he who never theorizes at all: Bolingbroke. As we have seen, his avowed motive for opposing Mowbray—simple patriotic indignation—is uttered with such earnestness that we wonder if indeed Bolingbroke has examined those political ambitions in himself that are so plainly visible to Richard and others. This same discrepancy between surface and depth applies to Bolingbroke's motives in returning to England. We cannot be sure at what time he begins to plot that return; the conspiracy announced by Northumberland (2.1.224–300) follows so closely after Richard's violation of Bolingbroke's hereditary rights and is already so well advanced that we gain the impression of an already existing plot, though some of this impression may be simply owing to Shakespeare's characteristic compression of historic time. When Bolingbroke arrives in England, in any case, he protests to York with seemingly passionate sincerity that he comes only for his dukedom of Lancaster (2.3.113–36). If so, why does he set about executing Richard's followers without legal authority and otherwise establishing his own claim to power? Why does he indulge in homophobic slurs against Richard, insinuating that Richard's favorites have "Broke the possession of a royal bed" (3.1.13), when, as far as we can see from the devotion Richard shows to his queen, the charges are trumped up and untrue? Does Bolingbroke seriously think he can reclaim his dukedom by force and then yield to Richard without either maintaining Richard as a puppet king or placing himself in intolerable jeopardy? And can he suppose that his allies, Northumberland and the rest, who have now openly defied the King, will countenance the return to power of one who would never trust them again? It is in this context that York protests, "Well, well, I see the issue of these arms" (2.3.152). The deposition of Richard and then Richard's death are unavoidable conclusions once Bolingbroke has succeeded in an armed rebellion. There can be no turning back. Yet Bolingbroke simply will not think in these terms. He permits Northumberland to proceed with almost sadistic harshness in the arrest and impeachment of Richard and then admonishes Northumberland in public for acting so harshly; the dirty work goes forward, with Northumberland taking the blame, while Bolingbroke assumes a statesmanlike pose. When the new King Henry discovers—to his surprise, evidently—that Richard's life is now a burden to the state, he ponders aloud, "Have I no friend will rid me of this living fear?" (5.4.2) and then rebukes Exton for proceeding on cue.

Bolingbroke's pragmatic spirit and new mode of governing are the embodiment of de facto rule. Ultimately, the justification for his authority is the very fact of its existence, its functioning. Bolingbroke is the man of the hour. To apply William Butler Yeats's striking contrast, the Lancastrian usurpers, Bolingbroke and his son, are vessels of clay, whereas Richard is a vessel of porcelain. One is durable and utilitarian, yet unattractive; the other is exquisite, fragile, and impractical. The comparison does not force us to prefer one to the other, even though Yeats himself characteristically sided with beauty against politics. Rather, Shakespeare gives us our choice, allowing us to see in ourselves an inclination toward political and social stability or toward artistic temperament.

The paradox may suggest that the qualities of a good administrator are not those of a sensitive, thoughtful man. However hopeless as a king, Richard stands before us increasingly as an introspective and fascinating person. The contradictions of his character are aptly focused in the business of breaking a mirror during his deposition: it is at once symbolic of a narcissistic, shallow concern for appearances and a quest for a deeper, inward truth, so that the smashing of the mirror is an act both of self-destruction and of self-discovery. When Richard's power crumbles, his spirit is enhanced, as though loss of power and royal identity were necessary for the discovery of true values.

In this there is a faint anticipation of King Lear's self-learning, fearfully and preciously bought. The trace is only slight here, because in good part *Richard II* is a political history play rather than a tragedy and because Richard's self-realization is imperfect. Nevertheless, when Richard faces deposition and separation from his queen, and especially when he is alone in prison expecting to die, he strives to understand his life and through it the general condition of humanity. He gains our sympathy in the wonderfully humane interchange between this deposed king and the poor groom of his stable, who once took care of Richard's horse, roan Barbary, now the possession of the new monarch (5.5.67–94). Richard perceives a contradiction in heaven's assurances about salvation: Christ promises to receive all God's children, and yet He also warns that it is as hard for a rich man to enter heaven as for a camel to be thread through a needle's eye (5.5.16–17). The paradox echoes the Beatitudes: the last shall be first, the meek shall inherit the earth. Richard, now one of the downtrodden, gropes for an understanding of the vanity of human achievement whereby he can aspire to the victory Christ promised. At his death, that victory seems to him assured: his soul will mount to its seat on high "Whilst my gross flesh sinks downward, here to die" (line 112).

In this triumph of spirit over flesh, the long downward motion of Richard's worldly fortune is crucially reversed. By the same token, the worldly success of Bolingbroke is shown to be no more than that: worldly success. His archetype is Cain, the primal murderer of a brother. To the extent that the play is a history, Bolingbroke's de facto success is a matter of political relevance; but, in the belated movement toward Richard's personal tragedy, we experience a profound countermovement that partly achieves a purgative sense of atonement and reassurance. Whatever Richard may have lost, his gain is also great.

Balance and symmetry are unusually important in *Richard II*. The play begins and ends with elaborate ritual obeisance to the concept of social and monarchic order, and yet, in both cases, a note of personal disorder refuses to be subdued by the public ceremonial. Shakespeare keeps our response to both Richard and Bolingbroke ambivalent by clouding their respective responsibilities for murder. Just as Richard's role in Gloucester's death remains unclear, so Bolingbroke's role in the assassination of Richard remains equally unclear. Mowbray and Exton, as scapegoats, are in some respects parallel. Because Richard and Bolingbroke are both implicated in the deaths of near kinsmen, both are associated with Cain's murder of Abel. As Bolingbroke rises in worldly fortune, Richard falls; as Richard finds insight and release through suffering, Bolingbroke finds guilt and remorse through distasteful political necessity. Verbally and structurally, the play explores the rhetorical figure of chiasmus, or the pairing of opposites in an inverted and diagonal pattern whereby one goes down as the other goes up and vice versa. Again and again, the ritual effects of staging and style draw our attention to the balanced conflicts between the two men and within Richard. Symmetry helps to focus these conflicts in visual and aural ways. In particular, the deposition scene, with its spectacle of a coronation in reverse, brings the sacramental and human sides of the central figure into poignant dramatic relationship.

Women play a subsidiary role in this play about male struggles for power, and yet the brief scenes in which women take part—the Duchess of Gloucester with Gaunt (1.2), Richard's queen with his courtiers and gardeners and then with Richard himself (2.2, 3.4, 5.1), the Duchess of York with her husband and son and King Henry (5.2–5.3)—highlight for us important thematic contrasts between the public and private spheres, power and powerlessness, political struggle and humane sensitivity, the state and the family. The women, excluded from roles of practical authority, offer, nonetheless, an invaluable critical perspective on the fateful and often self-consuming political games that men play among themselves. As in *Julius Caesar* and *Troilus and Cressida*, the men of *Richard II* ignore women's warnings and insights to their own peril and to the discomfiting of the body politic.

The imagery of *Richard II* reinforces structure and meaning. The play is unlike the history plays that follow in its extensive use of blank verse and rhyme and in its interwoven sets of recurring images; *Richard II* is, in this respect, more typical of the so-called lyric period (c. 1594–1596) that also produced *Romeo and Juliet* and *A Midsummer Night's Dream*. Image patterns locate the play in our imaginations as a kind of lost Eden. England is a garden mismanaged by her royal gardener, so that weeds and caterpillars (e.g., Bushy, Bagot, and Green) flourish. The "garden" scene (3.4), located near the center of the play, offering a momentary haven of allegorical reflection on the play's hectic events, is central in the development of the garden metaphor. England is also a sick body, ill-tended by her royal physician, and a family divided against itself, yielding abortive and sterile progeny. Her political ills are attested to by disorders in the cosmos: comets, shooting stars, withered bay trees, and weeping rains. Night owls, associated with death, prevail over the larks of morning. The sun, royally associated at first with Richard, deserts him for Bolingbroke and leaves Richard as the Phaëthon who has mishandled the sun-god's chariot and so scorched the earth. Linked to the sun image is the prevalent leitmotif of ascent and descent. And, touching on all these, a cluster of Biblical images sees England as a despoiled garden of Eden witnessing a second fall of humanity. Richard repeatedly brands his enemies and deserters as Judases and Pilates—not always fairly; nonetheless, in his last agony, he finds genuine consolation in Christ's example. For a man so self-absorbed in the drama of his existence, this poetic method is intensely suitable. Language and stage action have combined perfectly to express the conflict between a sensitive but flawed king and his efficient but unlovable successor.

In performance, the play belongs to Richard. However much he ends up the loser, his role calls for a kind of royal charisma that Bolingbroke never achieves. Such was the effect, at any rate, in Brian Bedford's enactment of the role at Stratford, Canada, in 1983; his appearance on the walls of Flint Castle in 3.3, splendidly attired in white robes with gold trim, embodied a regal image of kingship that was then forced to humble itself before Bolingbroke's brute might. John Gielgud, Alec Guinness, Michael Redgrave, Paul Scofield, John Neville, Ian McKellan, Ian Richardson, Richard Pasco, Ian Richardson, Derek Jacobi, Alan Howard, Jeremy Irons, Ralph Fiennes, the actress Fiona Shaw, and still other leading performers of their day have found the role one in which they could enthrall audiences with the nuanced cadences of Richard's speeches. The role has also afforded a wide range of interpretations; Guinness saw him as unhappily neurotic, Gielgud as kindly, Redgrave as effeminate, Scofield as cerebral and remote, McKellan as one who is convinced of his semi-divine nature. The play has also become a vehicle for spectacle and striking visual effects emphasizing the symmetries of the text's attention to poetic symbolism and social ritual; glittering pageantry and fading splendor vie for our interest and our loyalties.

The Tragedy of King Richard the Second

[*Dramatis Personae*

KING RICHARD THE SECOND
QUEEN, *Richard's wife*
JOHN OF GAUNT, *Duke of Lancaster, King Richard's uncle*
HENRY BOLINGBROKE, *John of Gaunt's son, Duke of Hereford and claimant to his father's dukedom of Lancaster, later King Henry IV*
DUKE OF YORK, *Edmund of Langley, King Richard's uncle*
DUCHESS OF YORK
DUKE OF AUMERLE, *York's son and the Earl of Rutland*
DUCHESS OF GLOUCESTER, *widow of Thomas of Woodstock, Duke of Gloucester (King Richard's uncle)*

THOMAS MOWBRAY, *Duke of Norfolk,*
EARL OF SALISBURY,
LORD BERKELEY,
DUKE OF SURREY,
BISHOP OF CARLISLE,
SIR STEPHEN SCROOP,
ABBOT OF WESTMINSTER,
BUSHY,
BAGOT,
GREEN,
CAPTAIN *of the Welsh Army,*
} *supporters of King Richard*
} *favorites of King Richard,*

EARL OF NORTHUMBERLAND,
HARRY PERCY, *Northumberland's son,*
LORD ROSS,
LORD WILLOUGHBY,
LORD FITZWATER,
SIR PIERCE OF EXTON,
Another LORD,
} *supporters of Bolingbroke*

LORD MARSHAL
Two HERALDS
GARDENER
GARDENER'S MAN
LADY *attending the Queen*
KEEPER *of the prison*
A MAN *attending Exton*

SERVINGMAN *to York*
GROOM *of the stable*

Lords, Officers, Soldiers, Attendants, Ladies attending the Queen

scene: England and Wales]

[1.1]

Enter King Richard, John of Gaunt, with other nobles and attendants.

KING RICHARD
Old John of Gaunt, time-honored Lancaster,   1
Hast thou according to thy oath and bond
Brought hither Henry Hereford, thy bold son,
Here to make good the boist'rous late appeal,   4
Which then our leisure would not let us hear,   5
Against the Duke of Norfolk, Thomas Mowbray?
GAUNT   I have, my liege.   7
KING RICHARD
Tell me, moreover, hast thou sounded him   8

1.1 Location: A room of state. (Holinshed's *Chronicles* places this scene at Windsor, in 1398.)
1 Old John of Gaunt (Born in 1340 at Ghent; hence the surname *Gaunt*. In 1398 he was fifty-eight years old.)

4 late recent.   **appeal** accusation, formal challenge or impeachment that the accuser was obliged to maintain in combat   **5 our, us** (The royal plural.)   **leisure** i.e., lack of leisure   **7 liege** i.e., sovereign.
8 sounded inquired of

If he appeal the Duke on ancient malice,   9
Or worthily, as a good subject should,
On some known ground of treachery in him?

GAUNT
As near as I could sift him on that argument,   12
On some apparent danger seen in him   13
Aimed at Your Highness, no inveterate malice.

KING RICHARD
Then call them to our presence.   [*Exit an attendant.*]
                                       Face to face,
And frowning brow to brow, ourselves will hear   16
The accuser and the accuséd freely speak.
High-stomached are they both, and full of ire;   18
In rage, deaf as the sea, hasty as fire.

Enter Bolingbroke and Mowbray.

BOLINGBROKE
Many years of happy days befall
My gracious sovereign, my most loving liege!

MOWBRAY
Each day still better others' happiness,   22
Until the heavens, envying earth's good hap,   23
Add an immortal title to your crown!

KING RICHARD
We thank you both. Yet one but flatters us,
As well appeareth by the cause you come: 26
Namely, to appeal each other of high treason.
Cousin of Hereford, what dost thou object   38
Against the Duke of Norfolk, Thomas Mowbray?

BOLINGBROKE
First—heaven be the record to my speech!—   30
In the devotion of a subject's love,
Tend'ring the precious safety of my prince,   32
And free from other misbegotten hate,
Come I appellant to this princely presence.   34
Now, Thomas Mowbray, do I turn to thee;
And mark my greeting well, for what I speak
My body shall make good upon this earth
Or my divine soul answer it in heaven.   38
Thou art a traitor and a miscreant,   39
Too good to be so and too bad to live,   40
Since the more fair and crystal is the sky,   41
The uglier seem the clouds that in it fly.
Once more, the more to aggravate the note,   43
With a foul traitor's name stuff I thy throat,
And wish, so please my sovereign, ere I move,   45
What my tongue speaks my right-drawn sword may prove.   46

MOWBRAY
Let not my cold words here accuse my zeal.   47
'Tis not the trial of a woman's war,   48
The bitter clamor of two eager tongues,   49
Can arbitrate this cause betwixt us twain;   50
The blood is hot that must be cooled for this.
Yet can I not of such tame patience boast
As to be hushed and naught at all to say.
First, the fair reverence of Your Highness curbs me
From giving reins and spurs to my free speech,
Which else would post until it had returned   56
These terms of treason doubled down his throat.
Setting aside his high blood's royalty,   58
And let him be no kinsman to my liege,   59
I do defy him, and I spit at him,
Call him a slanderous coward and a villain;
Which to maintain I would allow him odds
And meet him, were I tied to run afoot   63
Even to the frozen ridges of the Alps
Or any other ground inhabitable   65
Wherever Englishman durst set his foot.
Meantime, let this defend my loyalty:
By all my hopes, most falsely doth he lie.

BOLINGBROKE [*throwing down his gage*]
Pale trembling coward, there I throw my gage,   69
Disclaiming here the kindred of the King,   70
And lay aside my high blood's royalty,
Which fear, not reverence, makes thee to except.   72
If guilty dread have left thee so much strength
As to take up mine honor's pawn, then stoop.   74
By that, and all the rites of knighthood else,
Will I make good against thee, arm to arm,
What I have spoke or thou canst worse devise.   77

MOWBRAY [*taking up the gage*]
I take it up; and by that sword I swear
Which gently laid my knighthood on my shoulder,
I'll answer thee in any fair degree
Or chivalrous design of knightly trial;
And when I mount, alive may I not light   82
If I be traitor or unjustly fight!

KING RICHARD
What doth our cousin lay to Mowbray's charge?
It must be great that can inherit us   85
So much as of a thought of ill in him.

BOLINGBROKE
Look what I speak, my life shall prove it true: 87
That Mowbray hath received eight thousand nobles   88
In name of lendings for Your Highness' soldiers,   89

---

9 **appeal** accuse. **on . . . malice** on the grounds of a long-standing enmity **12 sift** discover by questioning. **argument** subject **13 apparent** obvious, manifest **16 ourselves** I myself. (The royal plural.) **18 High-stomached** Haughty **22 Each . . . happiness** May each day improve on the happiness of other past days **23 hap** fortune **26 you come** for which you come **28 what . . . object** what accusation do you bring **30 record** witness **32 Tend'ring** watching over, holding dear **34 appellant** as the accuser **38 answer** answer for **39 miscreant** irreligious villain **40 good** i.e., noble, high-born **41 crystal** clear. (The image alludes to the crystal spheres in which, according to the Ptolemaic conception of the universe, the heavenly bodies were fixed.) **43 aggravate the note** emphasize the stigma, i.e., the charge of treason **45 so please** if it please **46 right-drawn** justly drawn

47 accuse my zeal cast doubt on my zeal or loyalty. **48 woman's war** i.e., war of words **49 eager** sharp, biting **50 Can** that can **56 post** ride at high speed (like a messenger riding relays of horses) **58 Setting . . . royalty** Disregarding Bolingbroke's royal blood (as grandson of Edward III) **59 let him be** suppose him to be **63 tied** obliged **65 inhabitable** uninhabitable **69 gage** a pledge to combat (usually a glove or gauntlet, i.e., a mailed or armored glove) **70 Disclaiming** relinquishing. **kindred** kinship **72 except** exempt, set aside. **74 pawn** i.e., the gage **77 or . . . devise** or anything worse you can imagine to have been said about you. **82 light** alight, dismount **85 inherit us** put me in possession of, make me have **87 Look what** Whatever **88 nobles** gold coins worth six shillings eight pence **89 lendings** advances on pay

The which he hath detained for lewd employments, 90
Like a false traitor and injurious villain.
Besides I say, and will in battle prove
Or here or elsewhere to the furthest verge 93
That ever was surveyed by English eye,
That all the treasons for these eighteen years 95
Complotted and contrivèd in this land 96
Fetch from false Mowbray their first head and
    spring. 97
Further I say, and further will maintain
Upon his bad life to make all this good,
That he did plot the Duke of Gloucester's death, 100
Suggest his soon-believing adversaries, 101
And consequently, like a traitor coward, 102
Sluiced out his innocent soul through streams of
    blood— 103
Which blood, like sacrificing Abel's, cries 104
Even from the tongueless caverns of the earth 105
To me for justice and rough chastisement.
And, by the glorious worth of my descent,
This arm shall do it or this life be spent.

KING RICHARD
How high a pitch his resolution soars! 109
Thomas of Norfolk, what say'st thou to this?

MOWBRAY
Oh, let my sovereign turn away his face
And bid his ears a little while be deaf,
Till I have told this slander of his blood 113
How God and good men hate so foul a liar!

KING RICHARD
Mowbray, impartial are our eyes and ears.
Were he my brother, nay, my kingdom's heir,
As he is but my father's brother's son,
Now, by my scepter's awe I make a vow, 118
Such neighbor nearness to our sacred blood
Should nothing privilege him nor partialize 120
The unstooping firmness of my upright soul.
He is our subject, Mowbray; so art thou.
Free speech and fearless I to thee allow.

MOWBRAY
Then, Bolingbroke, as low as to thy heart
Through the false passage of thy throat thou liest!
Three parts of that receipt I had for Calais 126
Disbursed I duly to His Highness' soldiers;

The other part reserved I by consent,
For that my sovereign liege was in my debt 129
Upon remainder of a dear account 130
Since last I went to France to fetch his queen. 131
Now swallow down that lie. For Gloucester's death, 132
I slew him not, but to my own disgrace 133
Neglected my sworn duty in that case. 134
[To Gaunt] For you, my noble lord of Lancaster,
The honorable father to my foe,
Once did I lay an ambush for your life,
A trespass that doth vex my grievèd soul;
But ere I last received the Sacrament
I did confess it, and exactly begged 140
Your Grace's pardon, and I hope I had it.
This is my fault. As for the rest appealed, 142
It issues from the rancor of a villain,
A recreant and most degenerate traitor, 144
Which in myself I boldly will defend, 145
And interchangeably hurl down my gage 146
Upon this overweening traitor's foot, 147
To prove myself a loyal gentleman
Even in the best blood chambered in his bosom. 149
    [He throws down his gage. Bolingbroke picks it up.]
In haste whereof most heartily I pray 150
Your Highness to assign our trial day.

KING RICHARD
Wrath-kindled gentlemen, be ruled by me;
Let's purge this choler without letting blood. 153
This we prescribe, though no physician;
Deep malice makes too deep incision.
Forget, forgive; conclude and be agreed; 156
Our doctors say this is no month to bleed.— 157
Good uncle, let this end where it begun;
We'll calm the Duke of Norfolk, you your son.

GAUNT
To be a make-peace shall become my age.
Throw down, my son, the Duke of Norfolk's gage.

KING RICHARD
And Norfolk, throw down his.

GAUNT   When, Harry, when?
Obedience bids I should not bid again.

KING RICHARD
Norfolk, throw down, we bid; there is no boot. 164

---

90 **lewd** vile, base 93 **Or** either 95 **these eighteen years** i.e., ever since the Peasants' Revolt of 1381 96 **Complotted** plotted in a conspiracy 97 **Fetch** derive. **head and spring** (Synonymous words meaning "origin.") 100 **Duke of Gloucester's death** (Thomas of Woodstock, Duke of Gloucester, a younger son of Edward III and brother of John of Gaunt, was murdered at Calais in September 1397, while in Mowbray's custody.) 101 **Suggest . . . adversaries** did prompt Gloucester's easily persuaded enemies (to believe him guilty of treason) 102 **consequently** afterward 103 **Sluiced out** let flow (as by the opening of a sluice, or valve) 104 **Abel's** (For the story of Cain's murder of his brother Abel, the first such murder on earth and the archetype of the killing of a kinsman, see Genesis 4:3–12.) 105 **tongueless** resonant but without articulate speech; echoing 109 **pitch** highest reach of a falcon's flight 113 **this slander . . . blood** this disgrace to the royal family 118 **my scepter's awe** the reverence due my scepter 120 **nothing** not at all. **partialize** make partial, bias 126 **receipt** money received

129 **For that** because 130 **Upon . . . account** for the balance of a heavy debt 131 **Since . . . queen** (Mowbray went in 1395 to France to negotiate the King's marriage to Isabella, daughter of the French King Charles VI, but Richard himself escorted her to England.) 132 **For** As for 132–4 **For . . . case** (Mowbray speaks guardedly but seems to imply that he postponed the execution of Gloucester that he was ordered by Richard to carry out.) 140 **exactly** (1) explicitly (2) fully 142 **appealed** of which I am charged 144 **recreant** cowardly; or, coward (used as a noun) 145 **Which** which charge. **in myself** in my own person 146 **interchangeably** in exchange, reciprocally 147 **overweening** arrogant, proud 149 **Even in** by shedding 150 **In haste whereof** To hasten which proof of my innocence 153 **Let's . . . blood** let's treat this wrath (caused by an excess of bile or choler) by purging (vomiting or evacuation) rather than by medical bloodletting. (With a play on "bloodshed in combat.") 156 **conclude** come to a final agreement 157 **no month to bleed** (Learned authorities often differed as to which months or seasons were best for medicinal bloodletting.) 164 **boot** help for it.

MOWBRAY [*kneeling*]
Myself I throw, dread sovereign, at thy foot.   165
My life thou shalt command, but not my shame.
The one my duty owes; but my fair name,
Despite of death that lives upon my grave,   168
To dark dishonor's use thou shalt not have.
I am disgraced, impeached, and baffled here,   170
Pierced to the soul with slander's venomed spear,
The which no balm can cure but his heart-blood
Which breathed this poison.

KING RICHARD   Rage must be withstood.   173
Give me his gage. Lions make leopards tame.   174

MOWBRAY
Yea, but not change his spots. Take but my shame,   175
And I resign my gage. My dear dear lord,
The purest treasure mortal times afford   177
Is spotless reputation; that away,
Men are but gilded loam or painted clay.
A jewel in a ten-times-barred-up chest
Is a bold spirit in a loyal breast.
Mine honor is my life; both grow in one;   182
Take honor from me, and my life is done.
Then, dear my liege, mine honor let me try;   184
In that I live, and for that will I die.

KING RICHARD [*to Bolingbroke*]
Cousin, throw up your gage; do you begin.   186

BOLINGBROKE
Oh, God defend my soul from such deep sin!
Shall I seem crestfallen in my father's sight?
Or with pale beggar-fear impeach my height   189
Before this out-dared dastard? Ere my tongue   190
Shall wound my honor with such feeble wrong,   191
Or sound so base a parle, my teeth shall tear   192
The slavish motive of recanting fear   193
And spit it bleeding in his high disgrace,   194
Where shame doth harbor, even in Mowbray's face.   195
[*Exit Gaunt.*]

KING RICHARD
We were not born to sue but to command;
Which since we cannot do to make you friends,
Be ready, as your lives shall answer it,
At Coventry upon Saint Lambert's day.   199

There shall your swords and lances arbitrate
The swelling difference of your settled hate.
Since we cannot atone you, we shall see   202
Justice design the victor's chivalry.   203
Lord Marshal, command our officers at arms
Be ready to direct these home alarms.   205
Exeunt.

❦

[1.2]

Enter John of Gaunt with the Duchess of Gloucester.

GAUNT
Alas, the part I had in Woodstock's blood   1
Doth more solicit me than your exclaims   2
To stir against the butchers of his life!   3
But since correction lieth in those hands   4
Which made the fault that we cannot correct,
Put we our quarrel to the will of heaven,
Who, when they see the hours ripe on earth,
Will rain hot vengeance on offenders' heads.

DUCHESS
Finds brotherhood in thee no sharper spur?
Hath love in thy old blood no living fire?
Edward's seven sons, whereof thyself art one,   11
Were as seven vials of his sacred blood
Or seven fair branches springing from one root.
Some of those seven are dried by nature's course,
Some of those branches by the Destinies cut;
But Thomas, my dear lord, my life, my Gloucester,
One vial full of Edward's sacred blood,
One flourishing branch of his most royal root,
Is cracked, and all the precious liquor spilt,
Is hacked down, and his summer leaves all faded,
By envy's hand and murder's bloody ax.   21
Ah, Gaunt, his blood was thine! That bed, that womb,
That metal, that self mold that fashioned thee,   23
Made him a man; and though thou livest and breathest,
Yet art thou slain in him. Thou dost consent   25
In some large measure to thy father's death
In that thou see'st thy wretched brother die,
Who was the model of thy father's life.   28
Call it not patience, Gaunt; it is despair.
In suff'ring thus thy brother to be slaughtered,
Thou showest the naked pathway to thy life,   31

165 **Myself I throw** i.e., I throw myself, instead of my gage
168 **Despite . . . grave** that will live in the epitaph on my grave in spite of devouring Death   170 **impeached** accused.   **baffled** publicly dishonored   173 **Which . . . poison** of him who uttered this slander.   174 **Lions . . . tame** (The royal arms showed a lion rampant; Mowbray's emblem was a leopard.)   175 **spots** (1) leopard spots (2) stains of dishonor.   177 **mortal times** our earthly lives   182 **in one** inseparably   184 **try** put to the test   186 **throw . . . gage** i.e., surrender your gage up to me, thereby ending the quarrel. (Richard is probably seated on a raised throne, as in scene 3.)   189 **impeach my height** discredit my high rank   190 **out-dared** dared down, cowed. **dastard** coward.   191 **feeble wrong** dishonorable submission   192 **sound . . . parle** trumpet so shameful a negotiation, i.e., consent to ask a truce   192–5 **my teeth . . . face** my teeth will bite off my tongue as a craven instrument of cowardly capitulation and spit it out bleeding, to its (the tongue's) great disgrace, into Mowbray's face, where shame abides perpetually.   195.1 *Exit Gaunt* (A stage direction from the Folio, adopted by most editors so that Gaunt will not be required to exit at the end of scene 1 and then immediately reenter.)   199 **Saint Lambert's day** September 17.

202 **atone** reconcile   203 **design . . . chivalry** designate who is the true chivalric victor.   205 **home alarms** domestic conflicts.
1.2. Location: John of Gaunt's house (? No place is specified, and the scene is not in Holinshed.)
1 **the part . . . blood** my kinship with Thomas of Woodstock, the Duke of Gloucester (i.e., as his older brother)   2 **exclaims** exclamations   3 **stir** take action   4 **those hands** i.e., Richard's (whom Gaunt charges with responsibility for Gloucester's death)   11 **Edward's** Edward III's   21 **envy's** malice's   23 **metal** substance out of which a person or a thing is made. (With a sense too of *mettle*, "temperament, disposition.")   **self** selfsame   25 **consent** acquiesce   28 **model** likeness, copy   31 **naked** i.e., undefended

Teaching stern murder how to butcher thee.
That which in mean men we entitle patience   33
Is pale cold cowardice in noble breasts.
What shall I say? To safeguard thine own life
The best way is to venge my Gloucester's death.

GAUNT
God's is the quarrel; for God's substitute,   37
His deputy anointed in His sight,
Hath caused his death; the which if wrongfully   39
Let heaven revenge, for I may never lift
An angry arm against His minister.

DUCHESS
Where then, alas, may I complain myself?   42

GAUNT
To God, the widow's champion and defense.

DUCHESS
Why, then, I will. Farewell, old Gaunt.
Thou goest to Coventry, there to behold
Our cousin Hereford and fell Mowbray fight.   46
Oh, sit my husband's wrongs on Hereford's spear,   47
That it may enter butcher Mowbray's breast!
Or if misfortune miss the first career,   49
Be Mowbray's sins so heavy in his bosom
That they may break his foaming courser's back
And throw the rider headlong in the lists,   52
A caitiff recreant to my cousin Hereford!   53
Farewell, old Gaunt. Thy sometimes brother's wife   54
With her companion, Grief, must end her life.

GAUNT
Sister, farewell. I must to Coventry.
As much good stay with thee as go with me!

DUCHESS
Yet one word more. Grief boundeth where it falls,   58
Not with the empty hollowness, but weight.   59
I take my leave before I have begun,   60
For sorrow ends not when it seemeth done.
Commend me to thy brother, Edmund York.   62
Lo, this is all. Nay, yet depart not so!
Though this be all, do not so quickly go;
I shall remember more. Bid him—ah, what?—
With all good speed at Pleshey visit me.   66
Alack, and what shall good old York there see
But empty lodgings and unfurnished walls,   68
Unpeopled offices, untrodden stones,   69
And what hear there for welcome but my groans?
Therefore commend me; let him not come there

To seek out sorrow that dwells everywhere.
Desolate, desolate, will I hence and die.   33
The last leave of thee takes my weeping eye.   *Exeunt.*

❖

[1.3]   37

Enter Lord Marshal and the Duke [of] Aumerle.

MARSHAL
My Lord Aumerle, is Harry Hereford armed?

AUMERLE
Yea, at all points, and longs to enter in.   2

MARSHAL
The Duke of Norfolk, sprightfully and bold,   3
Stays but the summons of the appellant's trumpet.   4

AUMERLE
Why then the champions are prepared, and stay
For nothing but His Majesty's approach.

*The trumpets sound, and the King enters with his
nobles [Gaunt, Bushy, Bagot, Green, and others].
When they are set, enter [Mowbray] the Duke of
Norfolk in arms, defendant, [with a herald].*

KING RICHARD   52
Marshal, demand of yonder champion   53
The cause of his arrival here in arms.   54
Ask him his name, and orderly proceed
To swear him in the justice of his cause.   9

MARSHAL [*to Mowbray*]
In God's name and the King's, say who thou art
And why thou comest thus knightly clad in arms,
Against what man thou com'st, and what thy quarrel.   13
Speak truly on thy knighthood and thy oath,
As so defend thee heaven and thy valor!

MOWBRAY
My name is Thomas Mowbray, Duke of Norfolk,
Who hither come engagèd by my oath—
Which God defend a knight should violate!—   18
Both to defend my loyalty and truth
To God, my king, and my succeeding issue
Against the Duke of Hereford that appeals me,   21
And by the grace of God and this mine arm
To prove him, in defending of myself,
A traitor to my God, my king, and me;
And as I truly fight, defend me heaven!

*The trumpets sound. Enter [Bolingbroke,] Duke of
Hereford, appellant, in armor, [with a herald].*

KING RICHARD
Marshal, ask yonder knight in arms

---

33 **mean** lowly   37 **God's substitute** i.e., the King, God's deputy on
earth   39 **his** i.e., Gloucester's   42 **complain myself** lodge a complaint on my own behalf.   46 **cousin** kinsman.   **fell** fierce   47 **sit . . .
wrongs** may my husband's wrongs sit   49 **misfortune** i.e., Mowbray's downfall.   **career** charge of the horse in a tourney or combat
52 **lists** barriers enclosing the tournament area   53 **caitiff** base, cowardly   54 **sometimes** late   58 **boundeth** bounces, rebounds, returns.
(The Duchess apologizes for speaking yet again; her grief, she says,
continues on and on, like a bouncing tennis ball.)   59 **Not . . . weight**
(Grief is not hollow, like a tennis ball, but continues to move because
of its heaviness.)   60 **begun** i.e., begun to grieve   62 **Edmund York**
Edmund of Langley, fifth son of Edward III.   66 **Pleshey** Gloucester's country seat, in Essex   68 **unfurnished** bare   69 **offices** service
quarters, workrooms

1.3. **Location:** The lists at Coventry. Scaffolds or raised seats are provided for the King and his nobles, and chairs are provided for the
combatants.
2 **at all points** completely.   **in** i.e., into the lists, the space designed
for combat.   3 **sprightfully** with high spirit   4 **Stays** awaits
9 **orderly** according to the rules   13 **quarrel** complaint.   18 **defend**
forbid   21 **appeals** accuses

Both who he is and why he cometh hither
Thus plated in habiliments of war;   28
And formally, according to our law,
Depose him in the justice of his cause.   30

MARSHAL [to Bolingbroke]
What is thy name? And wherefore com'st thou hither,
Before King Richard in his royal lists?
Against whom comest thou? And what's thy quarrel?
Speak like a true knight, so defend thee heaven!

BOLINGBROKE
Harry of Hereford, Lancaster, and Derby
Am I, who ready here do stand in arms
To prove, by God's grace and my body's valor,
In lists, on Thomas Mowbray, Duke of Norfolk,
That he is a traitor foul and dangerous
To God of heaven, King Richard, and to me;
And as I truly fight, defend me heaven!

MARSHAL
On pain of death, no person be so bold
Or daring-hardy as to touch the lists,   43
Except the Marshal and such officers
Appointed to direct these fair designs.

BOLINGBROKE
Lord Marshal, let me kiss my sovereign's hand
And bow my knee before His Majesty;   47
For Mowbray and myself are like two men
That vow a long and weary pilgrimage.
Then let us take a ceremonious leave
And loving farewell of our several friends.   51

MARSHAL [to King Richard]
The appellant in all duty greets Your Highness
And craves to kiss your hand and take his leave.

KING RICHARD [coming down]
We will descend and fold him in our arms.
                            [He embraces Bolingbroke.]
Cousin of Hereford, as thy cause is right,   55
So be thy fortune in this royal fight!   56
Farewell, my blood—which if today thou shed,
Lament we may, but not revenge thee dead.

BOLINGBROKE
Oh, let no noble eye profane a tear   59
For me if I be gored with Mowbray's spear.   60
As confident as is the falcon's flight
Against a bird do I with Mowbray fight.
[To the King] My loving lord, I take my leave of you;
[To Aumerle] Of you, my noble cousin, Lord Aumerle;
Not sick, although I have to do with death,
But lusty, young, and cheerly drawing breath.   66
Lo, as at English feasts, so I regreet   67
The daintiest last, to make the end most sweet.   68

[To Gaunt] O thou, the earthly author of my blood,
Whose youthful spirit, in me regenerate,   70
Doth with a twofold vigor lift me up   71
To reach at victory above my head,
Add proof unto mine armor with thy prayers,   73
And with thy blessings steel my lance's point
That it may enter Mowbray's waxen coat   75
And furbish new the name of John o' Gaunt   76
Even in the lusty havior of his son.   77

GAUNT
God in thy good cause make thee prosperous!
Be swift like lightning in the execution,
And let thy blows, doubly redoubled,
Fall like amazing thunder on the casque   81
Of thy adverse pernicious enemy.
Rouse up thy youthful blood, be valiant, and live.

BOLINGBROKE
Mine innocence and Saint George to thrive!   84

MOWBRAY
However God or fortune cast my lot,
There lives or dies, true to King Richard's throne,
A loyal, just, and upright gentleman.
Never did captive with a freer heart
Cast off his chains of bondage and embrace
His golden uncontrolled enfranchisement   90
More than my dancing soul doth celebrate
This feast of battle with mine adversary.
Most mighty liege, and my companion peers,
Take from my mouth the wish of happy years.   94
As gentle and as jocund as to jest   95
Go I to fight. Truth hath a quiet breast.   96

KING RICHARD
Farewell, my lord. Securely I espy   97
Virtue with valor couchèd in thine eye.—   98
Order the trial, Marshal, and begin.

MARSHAL
Harry of Hereford, Lancaster, and Derby,
Receive thy lance; and God defend the right!
                        [A lance is given to Bolingbroke.]

BOLINGBROKE
Strong as a tower in hope, I cry "Amen!"   102

MARSHAL [to an officer]
Go bear this lance to Thomas, Duke of Norfolk.
                        [A lance is given to Norfolk.]

FIRST HERALD
Harry of Hereford, Lancaster, and Derby
Stands here for God, his sovereign, and himself,
On pain to be found false and recreant,
To prove the Duke of Norfolk, Thomas Mowbray,

---

28 plated armored.   habiliments the attire   30 Depose him take his sworn deposition   43 daring-hardy daringly bold, reckless.   touch i.e., interfere in   47 bow my knee (Presumably Bolingbroke kneels to Richard and, at about line 69, to Gaunt.)   51 several various   55 as insofar as   56 royal fight i.e., a fight taking place in the presence of the King.   59–60 profane . . . For me misuse tears by weeping for me   66 lusty full of vigor.   cheerly cheerfully   67 regreet greet, salute   68 The daintiest i.e., the most tasty, the finest. (Bolingbroke refers to the custom of ending banquets with a sweet dessert.)

70 regenerate born anew   71 twofold i.e., of father and son   73 proof invulnerability   75 enter . . . coat pierce Mowbray's armor as though it were made of wax   76 furbish polish   77 lusty havior vigorous behavior, deportment   81 amazing bewildering.   casque helmet   84 Mine . . . thrive! May my innocence and the protectorship of Saint George bring me victory!   90 enfranchisement freedom   94 Take . . . years take from me the wish that you may enjoy many happy years.   95 gentle unperturbed in spirit.   to jest i.e., to a play or entertainment   96 quiet calm   97 Securely Confidently   98 couchèd lodged, expressed, leveled in readiness (as with a lance)   102 Strong . . . hope (Alludes to Psalm 61:3: "for thou hast been my hope, and a strong tower for me against the face of the enemy.")

A traitor to his God, his king, and him,   108
And dares him to set forward to the fight.

SECOND HERALD

Here standeth Thomas Mowbray, Duke of Norfolk,
On pain to be found false and recreant,
Both to defend himself and to approve   112
Henry of Hereford, Lancaster, and Derby,
To God, his sovereign, and to him disloyal,   114
Courageously and with a free desire
Attending but the signal to begin.   116

MARSHAL

Sound, trumpets, and set forward, combatants!
                    [*A charge is sounded. Richard throws
                                    down his baton.*]
Stay! The King hath thrown his warder down.   118

KING RICHARD

Let them lay by their helmets and their spears,
And both return back to their chairs again.
[*To his counselors*] Withdraw with us, and let the trumpets
    sound
While we return these dukes what we decree.   122
                    [*A long flourish. Richard consults apart with
                                    Gaunt and others.*]
Draw near,
And list what with our council we have done.   124
For that our kingdom's earth should not be soiled   125
With that dear blood which it hath fosterèd;
And for our eyes do hate the dire aspect   127
Of civil wounds plowed up with neighbors' sword;
And for we think the eagle-wingèd pride
Of sky-aspiring and ambitious thoughts,
With rival-hating envy, set on you   131
To wake our peace, which in our country's cradle
Draws the sweet infant breath of gentle sleep,
Which, so roused up with boist'rous untuned drums, 134
With harsh-resounding trumpets' dreadful bray
And grating shock of wrathful iron arms,
Might from our quiet confines fright fair peace
And make us wade even in our kindred's blood:
Therefore we banish you our territories.
You, cousin Hereford, upon pain of life,   140
Till twice five summers have enriched our fields,
Shall not regreet our fair dominions,
But tread the stranger paths of banishment.   143

BOLINGBROKE

Your will be done. This must my comfort be:
That sun that warms you here shall shine on me,
And those his golden beams to you here lent
Shall point on me and gild my banishment.

KING RICHARD

Norfolk, for thee remains a heavier doom,

Which I with some unwillingness pronounce:
The sly slow hours shall not determinate   150
The dateless limit of thy dear exile.   151
The hopeless word of "never to return"
Breathe I against thee, upon pain of life.

MOWBRAY

A heavy sentence, my most sovereign liege,
And all unlooked-for from Your Highness' mouth.
A dearer merit, not so deep a maim   156
As to be cast forth in the common air,
Have I deservèd at Your Highness' hands.
The language I have learned these forty years,
My native English, now I must forgo;
And now my tongue's use is to me no more
Than an unstringèd viol or a harp,   162
Or like a cunning instrument cased up,   163
Or, being open, put into his hands   164
That knows no touch to tune the harmony.
Within my mouth you have enjailed my tongue,
Doubly portcullised with my teeth and lips,   167
And dull unfeeling barren ignorance
Is made my jailer to attend on me.
I am too old to fawn upon a nurse,
Too far in years to be a pupil now.
What is thy sentence then but speechless death,
Which robs my tongue from breathing native breath? 173

KING RICHARD

It boots thee not to be compassionate.   174
After our sentence plaining comes too late.   175

MOWBRAY

Then thus I turn me from my country's light,
To dwell in solemn shades of endless night.
                                    [*He starts to leave.*]

KING RICHARD

Return again, and take an oath with thee.
Lay on our royal sword your banished hands.
                    [*They place their hands on Richard's sword.*]
Swear by the duty that you owe to God—
Our part therein we banish with yourselves—   181
To keep the oath that we administer:
You never shall, so help you truth and God,
Embrace each other's love in banishment,
Nor never look upon each other's face,
Nor never write, regreet, nor reconcile
This louring tempest of your homebred hate;   187
Nor never by advisèd purpose meet   188
To plot, contrive, or complot any ill   189
'Gainst us, our state, our subjects, or our land.

BOLINGBROKE   I swear.

---

108 **him** himself, Bolingbroke. (See line 40.)   112 **approve** prove
114 **him** i.e., Mowbray. (See line 24.)   116 **Attending** awaiting
118 **warder** staff or truncheon borne by the King when presiding over
a trial by combat   122 **While we return** until I inform   122.1 *flourish*
fanfare.   124 **list** hear   125 **For that** In order that   127 **for** because
(also in line 129)   131 **envy** enmity.   **set on you** set you on
134 **Which** i.e., which enmity, disturbance of the peace. (Although, in
literal terms, the antecedent of *Which* is *peace* in line 132.)   140 **life**
i.e., loss of life   143 **stranger** alien

150 **sly** stealthy.   **determinate** put to an end   151 **dateless limit**
unlimited term.   **dear** grievous   156 **dearer merit** better reward.
maim injury   162 **viol** a six-stringed instrument, related to the modern violin, played with a curved bow   163 **cunning** skillfully made
164 **open** taken from its case.   **his** that person's   167 **portcullised**
shut in by a portcullis, an iron grating over a gateway that can be
raised and lowered   173 **breathing . . . breath** speaking English.
174 **boots** avails.   **compassionate** full of laments.   175 **plaining**
complaining   181 **Our part therein** i.e., the duty you owe me as King
187 **louring** threatening, scowling   188 **advisèd** deliberate, premeditated   189 **complot** plot together

MOWBRAY   And I, to keep all this.

BOLINGBROKE

Norfolk, so far as to mine enemy: 193
By this time, had the King permitted us,
One of our souls had wandered in the air,
Banished this frail sepulchre of our flesh,   196
As now our flesh is banished from this land.
Confess thy treasons ere thou fly the realm.
Since thou hast far to go, bear not along
The clogging burden of a guilty soul.   200

MOWBRAY

No, Bolingbroke. If ever I were traitor,
My name be blotted from the book of life,
And I from heaven banished as from hence!
But what thou art, God, thou, and I do know,
And all too soon, I fear, the King shall rue.—
Farewell, my liege. Now no way can I stray;   206
Save back to England, all the world's my way.   *Exit.*

KING RICHARD [*to Gaunt*]

Uncle, even in the glasses of thine eyes   208
I see thy grievèd heart. Thy sad aspect
Hath from the number of his banished years
Plucked four away. [*To Bolingbroke*] Six frozen winters
    spent,
Return with welcome home from banishment.

BOLINGBROKE

How long a time lies in one little word!
Four lagging winters and four wanton springs   214
End in a word; such is the breath of kings.

GAUNT

I thank my liege that in regard of me
He shortens four years of my son's exile.
But little vantage shall I reap thereby;
For, ere the six years that he hath to spend
Can change their moons and bring their times about,
My oil-dried lamp and time-bewasted light   221
Shall be extinct with age and endless night;
My inch of taper will be burnt and done,   223
And blindfold Death not let me see my son.   224

KING RICHARD

Why, uncle, thou hast many years to live.

GAUNT

But not a minute, King, that thou canst give.
Shorten my days thou canst with sullen sorrow,
And pluck nights from me, but not lend a morrow;
Thou canst help Time to furrow me with age,
But stop no wrinkle in his pilgrimage;   230
Thy word is current with him for my death,   231
But dead, thy kingdom cannot buy my breath.   232

KING RICHARD

Thy son is banished upon good advice,
Whereto thy tongue a party verdict gave.   234
Why at our justice seem'st thou then to lour?

GAUNT

Things sweet to taste prove in digestion sour.
You urged me as a judge, but I had rather
You would have bid me argue like a father.
Oh, had it been a stranger, not my child,
To smooth his fault I should have been more mild.   240
A partial slander sought I to avoid   241
And in the sentence my own life destroyed.
Alas, I looked when some of you should say   243
I was too strict, to make mine own away;   244
But you gave leave to my unwilling tongue
Against my will to do myself this wrong.

KING RICHARD

Cousin, farewell; and, uncle, bid him so.
Six years we banish him, and he shall go.
            [*Flourish. Exit King Richard with his train.*]

AUMERLE [*to Bolingbroke*]

Cousin, farewell. What presence must not know,   249
From where you do remain let paper show.   [*Exit.*] 250

MARSHAL [*to Bolingbroke*]

My lord, no leave take I, for I will ride,   251
As far as land will let me, by your side.
            [*Bolingbroke makes no answer. The Lord Marshal
                                        stands aside.*]

GAUNT [*to Bolingbroke*]

Oh, to what purpose dost thou hoard thy words,
That thou returnest no greeting to thy friends?

BOLINGBROKE

I have too few to take my leave of you,
When the tongue's office should be prodigal   256
To breathe the abundant dolor of the heart.   257

GAUNT

Thy grief is but thy absence for a time.   258

BOLINGBROKE

Joy absent, grief is present for that time.   259

GAUNT

What is six winters? They are quickly gone.

BOLINGBROKE

To men in joy; but grief makes one hour ten.

GAUNT

Call it a travel that thou tak'st for pleasure.   262

BOLINGBROKE

My heart will sigh when I miscall it so,
Which finds it an enforcèd pilgrimage.

GAUNT

The sullen passage of thy weary steps   265

---

193 so far let me say this much   **196 sepulchre of our flesh** i.e., body, the temple or tomb of the soul   **200 clogging** (A clog was a wooden block attached to the leg to hinder movement.)   **206 stray** take the wrong road   **208 glasses** mirrors (here glistening with tears)   **214 wanton** luxuriant   **221 oil-dried** empty of oil   **223 taper** candle   **224 blindfold Death** i.e., *blindfold* because *Death* deprives its victims of their sight and because it is often pictured as an eyeless skull   **230 in his pilgrimage** brought about in time's journey   **231 current** i.e., as good as current coin, valid   **232 dead** i.e., once I am dead. **buy** i.e., restore with a payment

234 a party verdict one person's share in a joint verdict   **240 smooth** extenuate   **241 partial slander** accusation of partiality (on behalf of my son)   **243 looked when** expected that, awaited the point at which   **244 to . . . away** in making away with my own (son)   **249 What . . . know** What I cannot learn from you in person   **250 s.d. Exit** (The exit is uncertain; see 1.4.1–4.)   **251 no leave take I** i.e., I will not take my leave of you, my lord; I will not say good-bye   **256 office** function. **prodigal** lavish   **257 To breathe** in uttering   **258 grief** grievance   **259 grief** unhappiness   **262 travel** (The Quarto spelling, "trauaile," suggests an interchangeable meaning of "travel" and "labor.")   **265 sullen** (1) melancholy (2) dull

Esteem as foil wherein thou art to set
The precious jewel of thy home return.

BOLINGBROKE
Nay, rather every tedious stride I make
Will but remember me what a deal of world   269
I wander from the jewels that I love.
Must I not serve a long apprenticehood
To foreign passages, and in the end,   272
Having my freedom, boast of nothing else   273
But that I was a journeyman to grief?   274

GAUNT
All places that the eye of heaven visits   275
Are to a wise man ports and happy havens.
Teach thy necessity to reason thus:
There is no virtue like necessity.
Think not the King did banish thee,
But thou the King. Woe doth the heavier sit   280
Where it perceives it is but faintly borne.   281
Go, say I sent thee forth to purchase honor,   282
And not the King exiled thee; or suppose
Devouring pestilence hangs in our air
And thou art flying to a fresher clime.
Look what thy soul holds dear, imagine it   286
To lie that way thou goest, not whence thou com'st.
Suppose the singing birds musicians,
The grass whereon thou tread'st the presence strewed,   289
The flowers fair ladies, and thy steps no more
Than a delightful measure or a dance;   291
For gnarling sorrow hath less power to bite   292
The man that mocks at it and sets it light.   293

BOLINGBROKE
Oh, who can hold a fire in his hand
By thinking on the frosty Caucasus?   295
Or cloy the hungry edge of appetite
By bare imagination of a feast?
Or wallow naked in December snow
By thinking on fantastic summer's heat?   299
Oh, no, the apprehension of the good
Gives but the greater feeling to the worse.
Fell Sorrow's tooth doth never rankle more   302
Than when he bites but lanceth not the sore.   303

GAUNT   266
Come, come, my son, I'll bring thee on thy way.   304
Had I thy youth and cause, I would not stay.   305

BOLINGBROKE
Then, England's ground, farewell. Sweet soil, adieu,   269
My mother and my nurse that bears me yet!
Where'er I wander, boast of this I can:
Though banished, yet a trueborn Englishman.

Exeunt.

❀

[1.4]

*Enter the King, with Bagot, [Green,] etc. at one
door, and the Lord Aumerle at another.*

KING RICHARD
We did observe.—Cousin Aumerle,
How far brought you high Hereford on his way?   1

AUMERLE
I brought high Hereford, if you call him so,
But to the next highway, and there I left him.   4

KING RICHARD
And say, what store of parting tears were shed?

AUMERLE
Faith, none for me, except the northeast wind,   6
Which then blew bitterly against our faces,
Awaked the sleeping rheum and so by chance   8
Did grace our hollow parting with a tear.   9

KING RICHARD
What said our cousin when you parted with him?

AUMERLE   "Farewell!"
And, for my heart disdainèd that my tongue   12
Should so profane the word, that taught me craft   13
To counterfeit oppression of such grief
That words seemed buried in my sorrow's grave.
Marry, would the word "farewell" have lengthened   16
  hours
And added years to his short banishment,
He should have had a volume of farewells;
But since it would not, he had none of me.   19

KING RICHARD
He is our cousin, cousin; but 'tis doubt,
When time shall call him home from banishment,
Whether our kinsman come to see his friends.   22
Ourself and Bushy, Bagot here, and Green
Observed his courtship to the common people,
How he did seem to dive into their hearts
With humble and familiar courtesy,
What reverence he did throw away on slaves,
Wooing poor craftsmen with the craft of smiles

---

266 foil thin metal leaf set behind gems to show off their luster;
hence, that which sets something off to advantage   **269 remember**
remind.   **a deal of world** a great distance   **272 passages** wanderings, experiences   **273 Having my freedom** (1) having completed my
apprenticeship (2) having been allowed to return home   **274 journeyman** (Literally, one who labors for day wages as a fully qualified
craftsman—with a hint also of one who makes a journey. Bolingbroke
will be proficient only in grief.)   **275 the eye of heaven** the sun
280 But . . . King i.e., but suppose that you are banishing the King to
the moral wilderness his crimes deserve.   **280–1 Woe . . . borne** Woe
is all the more oppressive when it perceives that the sufferer is fainthearted.   **282 purchase** acquire, win   **286 Look what** Whatever
289 the presence strewed the royal presence chamber strewn with
rushes   **291 measure** stately, formal dance   **292 gnarling** snarling,
growling   **293 sets it light** regards it lightly.   **295 Caucasus** mountain range between the Black and Caspian seas.   **299 fantastic** imagined   **302 Fell** Fierce.   **rankle** cause irritation and festering
303 lanceth not does not open the wound (to permit the release of the
infection; Bolingbroke's point is that sorrow should be openly confronted, not rationalized or covered over and thus allowed to fester)

304 bring escort   **305 stay** linger.
1.4 Location: The court.
1 We did observe (The scene begins in the midst of a conversation.)
4 next nearest   **6 for me** on my part.   **except** except that   **8 rheum**
watery discharge (i.e., tears)   **9 hollow** insincere   **12 for** because
13 that i.e., my disdain. (Aumerle says he pretended to be overcome
by grief in order to avoid saying an insincere "Farewell" to Bolingbroke.)   **16 Marry** Indeed. (From the oath, "by the Virgin Mary.")
19 of from   **22 friends** kinsmen, i.e., us, his cousins.

And patient underbearing of his fortune,   29
As 'twere to banish their affects with him.   30
Off goes his bonnet to an oyster wench;
A brace of draymen bid God speed him well   32
And had the tribute of his supple knee,
With "Thanks, my countrymen, my loving friends,"
As were our England in reversion his,   35
And he our subjects' next degree in hope.   36

GREEN
Well, he is gone, and with him go these thoughts.   37
Now for the rebels which stand out in Ireland,   38
Expedient manage must be made, my liege,   39
Ere further leisure yield them further means
For their advantage and Your Highness' loss.

KING RICHARD
We will ourself in person to this war.
And, for our coffers with too great a court   43
And liberal largess are grown somewhat light,   44
We are enforced to farm our royal realm,   45
The revenue whereof shall furnish us
For our affairs in hand. If that come short,
Our substitutes at home shall have blank charters,   48
Whereto, when they shall know what men are rich,
They shall subscribe them for large sums of gold   50
And send them after to supply our wants;   51
For we will make for Ireland presently.   52

Enter Bushy.

Bushy, what news?

BUSHY
Old John of Gaunt is grievous sick, my lord,
Suddenly taken, and hath sent posthaste
To entreat Your Majesty to visit him.

KING RICHARD   Where lies he?

BUSHY   At Ely House.   58

KING RICHARD
Now put it, God, in the physician's mind
To help him to his grave immediately!
The lining of his coffers shall make coats   61
To deck our soldiers for these Irish wars.
Come, gentlemen, let's all go visit him.
Pray God we may make haste and come too late!

ALL   Amen.   *Exeunt.*

❖

[2.1]

Enter John of Gaunt sick, with the Duke of York,
etc.

GAUNT
Will the King come, that I may breathe my last
In wholesome counsel to his unstaid youth?   2

YORK
Vex not yourself, nor strive not with your breath,   3
For all in vain comes counsel to his ear.

GAUNT
Oh, but they say the tongues of dying men
Enforce attention like deep harmony.
Where words are scarce, they are seldom spent in vain,
For they breathe truth that breathe their words in pain.   8
He that no more must say is listened more   9
    Than they whom youth and ease have taught to glose.   10
More are men's ends marked than their lives before.   11
    The setting sun, and music at the close,
As the last taste of sweets, is sweetest last,   13
Writ in remembrance more than things long past.   14
Though Richard my life's counsel would not hear,   15
My death's sad tale may yet undeaf his ear.   16

YORK
No, it is stopped with other, flattering sounds,
As praises, of whose taste the wise are fond;   18
Lascivious meters, to whose venom sound   19
The open ear of youth doth always listen;
Report of fashions in proud Italy,   21
Whose manners still our tardy-apish nation   22
Limps after in base imitation.
Where doth the world thrust forth a vanity—
So it be new, there's no respect how vile—   25
That is not quickly buzzed into his ears?
Then all too late comes counsel to be heard
Where will doth mutiny with wit's regard.   28
Direct not him whose way himself will choose.   29
'Tis breath thou lack'st, and that breath wilt thou lose.

GAUNT
Methinks I am a prophet new inspired,
And thus expiring do foretell of him:
His rash fierce blaze of riot cannot last,   33
For violent fires soon burn out themselves;
Small showers last long, but sudden storms are short;

---

29 underbearing bearing, endurance   **30 banish . . . him** take their
affections with him into banishment.   **32 brace of draymen** pair of
cart drivers   **35 As . . . his** i.e., as if my England were to revert to him
as true owner after my death   **36 our . . . hope** i.e., the heir presumptive to the throne and favorite choice of the people.   **37 go** let go
38 for as for.   **stand out** hold out, resist   **39 Expedient manage**
speedy arrangements   **43 for** because.   **too great a court** i.e., too
great an extravagance at court   **44 liberal largess** extravagant generosity (to courtiers)   **45 farm** lease the right of collecting taxes, for a
present cash payment, to the highest bidder   **48 substitutes** deputies.
blank charters writs authorizing the collection of revenues or forced
loans to the crown, blank spaces being left for the names of the parties and the sums they were to provide   **50 subscribe them** put
down their names   **51 them** i.e., the sums collected   **52 presently** at
once.   **58 Ely House** (Palace of the Bishop of Ely in Holborn, a London district.)   **61 lining** contents. (With pun on lining for coats.)
coats coats of mail, armor

2.1 Location: Ely House.
0.1 Enter John of Gaunt sick (Presumably he is carried in by servants in
a chair.)   **2 unstaid** uncontrolled   **3 strive . . . breath** i.e., don't waste
your breath   **8 they** those persons   **9 He . . . listened more** He who
will soon be silenced by death is listened to more   **10 glose** flatter,
deceive in speech.   **11 marked** noticed   **13 is sweetest last** is longest
remembered as sweet   **14 Writ in remembrance** written down in the
memory   **15 my life's counsel** my advice while I lived   **16 My . . . tale**
my grave dying speech   **18 As . . . fond** such as praises, which even
wise men are foolishly inclined to hear   **19 meters** verses. **venom** poisonous   **21 proud Italy** (Roger Ascham, John Lyly, and other sixteenth-century writers complained of the growing influence of Italian
luxury.)   **22 still** always.   **tardy-apish** imitative but behind the times
25 So so long as.   **there's no respect** it makes no difference   **28 Where
. . . regard** where natural inclination rebels against what reason
esteems.   **29 Direct . . . choose** Don't try to offer advice to one who
insists on going his own way.   **33 riot** profligacy

He tires betimes that spurs too fast betimes; 36
With eager feeding food doth choke the feeder;
Light vanity, insatiate cormorant, 38
Consuming means, soon preys upon itself. 39
This royal throne of kings, this sceptered isle,
This earth of majesty, this seat of Mars, 41
This other Eden, demi-paradise,
This fortress built by Nature for herself
Against infection and the hand of war, 44
This happy breed of men, this little world, 45
This precious stone set in the silver sea,
Which serves it in the office of a wall 47
Or as a moat defensive to a house,
Against the envy of less happier lands,
This blessed plot, this earth, this realm, this England,
This nurse, this teeming womb of royal kings, 51
Feared by their breed and famous by their birth, 52
Renownèd for their deeds as far from home
For Christian service and true chivalry
As is the sepulcher in stubborn Jewry 55
Of the world's ransom, blessèd Mary's son,
This land of such dear souls, this dear dear land,
Dear for her reputation through the world,
Is now leased out—I die pronouncing it—
Like to a tenement or pelting farm. 60
England, bound in with the triumphant sea, 61
Whose rocky shore beats back the envious siege
Of wat'ry Neptune, is now bound in with shame, 63
With inky blots and rotten parchment bonds. 64
That England that was wont to conquer others
Hath made a shameful conquest of itself.
Ah, would the scandal vanish with my life,
How happy then were my ensuing death! 68

Enter King [Richard] and Queen, [Aumerle,
Bushy, Green, Bagot, Ross, and Willoughby,] etc.

YORK
The King is come. Deal mildly with his youth,
For young hot colts being reined do rage the more.
QUEEN
How fares our noble uncle Lancaster?
KING RICHARD
What comfort, man? How is't with agèd Gaunt?
GAUNT
Oh, how that name befits my composition! 73
Old Gaunt indeed, and gaunt in being old.
Within me grief hath kept a tedious fast,
And who abstains from meat that is not gaunt? 76
For sleeping England long time have I watched; 77

Watching breeds leanness, leanness is all gaunt.
The pleasure that some fathers feed upon
Is my strict fast—I mean, my children's looks— 80
And, therein fasting, hast thou made me gaunt. 81
Gaunt am I for the grave, gaunt as a grave,
Whose hollow womb inherits naught but bones. 83
KING RICHARD
Can sick men play so nicely with their names? 84
GAUNT
No, misery makes sport to mock itself. 85
Since thou dost seek to kill my name in me, 86
I mock my name, great King, to flatter thee. 87
KING RICHARD
Should dying men flatter with those that live? 88
GAUNT
No, no, men living flatter those that die. 89
KING RICHARD
Thou, now a-dying, sayest thou flatterest me.
GAUNT
Oh, no, thou diest, though I the sicker be.
KING RICHARD
I am in health, I breathe, and see thee ill.
GAUNT
Now He that made me knows I see thee ill;
Ill in myself to see, and in thee seeing ill. 94
Thy deathbed is no lesser than thy land,
Wherein thou liest in reputation sick;
And thou, too careless patient as thou art,
Commit'st thy anointed body to the cure
Of those physicians that first wounded thee. 99
A thousand flatterers sit within thy crown,
Whose compass is no bigger than thy head, 101
And yet, encagèd in so small a verge, 102
The waste is no whit lesser than thy land. 103
Oh, had thy grandsire with a prophet's eye 104
Seen how his son's son should destroy his sons, 105
From forth thy reach he would have laid thy shame, 106
Deposing thee before thou wert possessed, 107
Which art possessed now to depose thyself. 108
Why, cousin, wert thou regent of the world, 109
It were a shame to let this land by lease;

---

36 **betimes** soon, early   38 **Light vanity** frivolous dissipation. **cormorant** glutton. (Literally, a voracious seabird.)   39 **means** i.e., means of sustenance   41 **earth of majesty** land fit for kings.   **seat of Mars** residence of the god of war   44 **infection** (1) plague (2) moral pollution   45 **happy breed** fortunate race   47 **office** function   51 **teeming** fruitful   52 **by their breed** for their ancestral reputation for prowess   55 **stubborn Jewry** i.e., Judea, called stubborn because it resisted Christianity   60 **tenement** land or property held by a tenant.   **pelting** paltry   61 **bound in** bordered, surrounded   63 **bound in** legally constrained   64 **blots . . . bonds** i.e., the blank charters.   68 **ensuing** approaching   73 **composition** constitution.   76 **meat** food   77 **watched** kept watch at night, been vigilant

80 **Is . . . fast** is something I must forgo   81 **therein fasting** i.e., since I am starved of that pleasure   83 **inherits** possesses, will receive   84 **nicely** (1) ingeniously (2) triflingly   85 **to mock** of mocking   86–7 **Since . . . thee** Since you seek to destroy my family name (by banishing my son), I mock my name to please you and flatter your greatness.   88 **flatter with** try to please   89 **flatter** i.e., are attentive to, offer comfort to   94 **Ill . . . ill** seeing myself to be physically ill, and seeing the illness in you of abusing your royal authority.   99 **physicians** i.e., the King's favorites   101 **compass** circle, circumference   102 **verge** (1) circle, ring (2) the compass about the King's court, which extended for twelve miles   103 **waste** (1) waist, circumference (2) that which is destroyed. (With a quibble on the legal meaning of *waste*, "damage done to property by a tenant.")   **whit** bit, speck   104 **grandsire** i.e., Edward III   105 **destroy his sons** (1) destroy Edward III's sons, Richard's uncles (2) destroy Richard's own heritage   106 **From . . . shame** he would have put the matter you have shamefully handled out of your reach   107 **Deposing** dispossessing. **possessed** put in possession of the crown   108 **Which . . . thyself** you who are now seized with an obsessive desire to give away your authority (by leasing the realm to favorites).   109 **cousin** kinsman, nephew.   **regent** ruler

But, for thy world enjoying but this land,   111
Is it not more than shame to shame it so?
Landlord of England art thou now, not king.   113
Thy state of law is bondslave to the law,   114
And thou—

KING RICHARD   A lunatic lean-witted fool,
Presuming on an ague's privilege,   116
Darest with thy frozen admonition   117
Make pale our cheek, chasing the royal blood
With fury from his native residence.   119
Now, by my seat's right royal majesty,   120
Wert thou not brother to great Edward's son,   121
This tongue that runs so roundly in thy head   122
Should run thy head from thy unreverent shoulders.   123

GAUNT
Oh, spare me not, my brother Edward's son,
For that I was his father Edward's son!   125
That blood already, like the pelican,   126
Hast thou tapped out and drunkenly caroused.   127
My brother Gloucester, plain well-meaning soul—
Whom fair befall in heaven 'mongst happy souls!—   129
May be a precedent and witness good
That thou respect'st not spilling Edward's blood.   131
Join with the present sickness that I have,   132
And thy unkindness be like crooked age   133
To crop at once a too-long-withered flower!—   134
Live in thy shame, but die not shame with thee!   135
These words hereafter thy tormentors be!—
Convey me to my bed, then to my grave.
Love they to live that love and honor have.   138

       Exit [borne off by his attendants].

KING RICHARD
And let them die that age and sullens have,   139
For both hast thou, and both become the grave.   140

YORK
I do beseech Your Majesty, impute his words
To wayward sickliness and age in him.
He loves you, on my life, and holds you dear
As Harry Duke of Hereford, were he here.   144

KING RICHARD
Right, you say true. As Hereford's love, so his;   145
As theirs, so mine; and all be as it is.

       [*Enter Northumberland.*]

NORTHUMBERLAND
My liege, old Gaunt commends him to Your Majesty.

KING RICHARD
What says he?

NORTHUMBERLAND   Nay, nothing, all is said.
His tongue is now a stringless instrument;
Words, life, and all, old Lancaster hath spent.

YORK
Be York the next that must be bankrupt so!
Though death be poor, it ends a mortal woe.   152

KING RICHARD
The ripest fruit first falls, and so doth he;
His time is spent, our pilgrimage must be.   154
So much for that. Now for our Irish wars:
We must supplant those rough rug-headed kerns,   156
Which live like venom where no venom else   157
But only they have privilege to live.   158
And, for these great affairs do ask some charge,   159
Towards our assistance we do seize to us
The plate, coin, revenues, and movables   161
Whereof our uncle Gaunt did stand possessed.

YORK
How long shall I be patient? Ah, how long
Shall tender duty make me suffer wrong?
Not Gloucester's death, nor Hereford's banishment,
Nor Gaunt's rebukes, nor England's private wrongs,   166
Nor the prevention of poor Bolingbroke   167
About his marriage, nor my own disgrace,   168
Have ever made me sour my patient cheek
Or bend one wrinkle on my sovereign's face.   170
I am the last of noble Edward's sons,
Of whom thy father, Prince of Wales, was first.
In war was never lion raged more fierce,   173
In peace was never gentle lamb more mild,
Than was that young and princely gentleman.
His face thou hast, for even so looked he,
Accomplished with the number of thy hours;   177
But when he frowned, it was against the French
And not against his friends. His noble hand

---

111 But . . . land i.e., but since you enjoy as your domain only this land of England (rather than the whole world)   **113 Landlord** i.e., One who leases out property   **114 Thy . . . the law** i.e., Your legal status as King is now subservient to and at the mercy of the law governing contracts, such as blank charters   **116 an ague's privilege** i.e., a sick person's right to be testy   **117 frozen** (1) chilly (2) caused by a chill   **119 his** its   **120 seat's throne's**   **121 great Edward's son** Edward the Black Prince, Richard's father **122–3 runs . . . run** runs on, talks . . . drive, chase   **122 roundly** unceremoniously, bluntly   **123 unreverent** irreverent, disrespectful **125 For that** simply because   **126 pelican** (The pelican was thought to feed its ingrateful and murderous young with its own blood.) **127 tapped out** drawn as from a tapped barrel.   **caroused** gulped, quaffed.   **129 Whom fair befall** to whom may good come   **131 thou respect'st not** you care nothing about   **132–4 Join . . . flower!** May your unnatural behavior act in concert with my present illness and my advanced years to cut down my life like a too-long-withered flower! (*Unkindness* means both cruelty and behavior contrary to the natural bond that should exist in blood ties.)   **135 die . . . thee** i.e., may your shame live after you.   **138 Love they** Let them desire **139 sullens** sullenness, melancholy   **140 become** suit   **144 As** i.e., as he would love. (But see the next note.)

145 Right . . . his (Richard deliberately takes the opposite of what York had intended to say; Richard gibes that Gaunt is as little fond of the King as is Hereford.)   **152 Though . . . woe** Though death is the privation of life, it does end the misery of human existence which is itself a kind of death in life.   **154 our . . . be** i.e., our journey through life is yet to be completed but will also end.   **156–8 We . . . live** We must expel these shaggy-haired light-armed Irish foot soldiers, who live there like poisonous snakes where no others are allowed to exist. (Richard alludes to the freedom of Ireland from snakes, traditionally ascribed to Saint Patrick.)   **159 for** because.   **ask some charge** require some expenditure   **161 movables** personal property   **166 Nor . . . wrongs** nor the rebukes given to Gaunt, nor wrongs inflicted on private English subjects   **167–8 prevention . . . marriage** (Holinshed's *Chronicles* report that Richard had forestalled Bolingbroke's intended marriage with the Duke de Berri's daughter.)   **170 bend . . . on** once frown at   **173 was . . . fierce** never was there a lion more fiercely enraged   **177 Accomplished . . . hours** i.e., when he was your age

Did win what he did spend, and spent not that
Which his triumphant father's hand had won.
His hands were guilty of no kindred blood,   182
But bloody with the enemies of his kin.
Oh, Richard! York is too far gone with grief,
Or else he never would compare between.   185

KING RICHARD
Why, uncle, what's the matter?

YORK   O my liege,
Pardon me, if you please; if not, I, pleased   187
Not to be pardoned, am content withal.   188
Seek you to seize and grip into your hands
The royalties and rights of banished Hereford?   190
Is not Gaunt dead? And doth not Hereford live?
Was not Gaunt just? And is not Harry true?
Did not the one deserve to have an heir?
Is not his heir a well-deserving son?
Take Hereford's rights away, and take from Time   195
His charters and his customary rights;   196
Let not tomorrow then ensue today;   197
Be not thyself; for how art thou a king
But by fair sequence and succession?
Now, afore God—God forbid I say true!—
If you do wrongfully seize Hereford's rights,
Call in the letters patents that he hath   202
By his attorneys general to sue   203
His livery, and deny his offered homage,   204
You pluck a thousand dangers on your head,
You lose a thousand well-disposèd hearts,
And prick my tender patience to those thoughts   207
Which honor and allegiance cannot think.

KING RICHARD
Think what you will, we seize into our hands
His plate, his goods, his money, and his lands.

YORK
I'll not be by the while. My liege, farewell.   211
What will ensue hereof there's none can tell;
But by bad courses may be understood   213
That their events can never fall out good.   *Exit.*   214

KING RICHARD
Go, Bushy, to the Earl of Wiltshire straight.   215
Bid him repair to us to Ely House   216
To see this business. Tomorrow next   217
We will for Ireland, and 'tis time, I trow.   218
And we create, in absence of ourself,
Our uncle York Lord Governor of England,
For he is just and always loved us well.—

Come on, our queen. Tomorrow must we part.
Be merry, for our time of stay is short.   223
    [*Flourish.*] *Exeunt King and Queen* [*with attendants*].
    Manet Northumberland [*with Willoughby and Ross*].

NORTHUMBERLAND
Well, lords, the Duke of Lancaster is dead.

ROSS
And living too, for now his son is duke.

WILLOUGHBY
Barely in title, not in revenues.

NORTHUMBERLAND
Richly in both, if justice had her right.

ROSS
My heart is great, but it must break with silence,   228
Ere 't be disburdened with a liberal tongue.   229

NORTHUMBERLAND
Nay, speak thy mind; and let him ne'er speak more   230
That speaks thy words again to do thee harm!

WILLOUGHBY
Tends that thou wouldst speak to the Duke of
    Hereford?   232
If it be so, out with it boldly, man.
Quick is mine ear to hear of good towards him.

ROSS
No good at all that I can do for him,
Unless you call it good to pity him,
Bereft and gelded of his patrimony.   237

NORTHUMBERLAND
Now, afore God, 'tis shame such wrongs are borne
In him, a royal prince, and many more   239
Of noble blood in this declining land.
The King is not himself, but basely led
By flatterers; and what they will inform   242
Merely in hate 'gainst any of us all,   243
That will the King severely prosecute
'Gainst us, our lives, our children, and our heirs.

ROSS
The commons hath he pilled with grievous taxes,   246
And quite lost their hearts; the nobles hath he fined
For ancient quarrels, and quite lost their hearts.

WILLOUGHBY
And daily new exactions are devised,
As blanks, benevolences, and I wot not what.   250
But what i' God's name doth become of this?   251

NORTHUMBERLAND
Wars hath not wasted it, for warred he hath not,
But basely yielded upon compromise
That which his noble ancestors achieved with blows.
More hath he spent in peace than they in wars.

ROSS
The Earl of Wiltshire hath the realm in farm.   256

---

182 kindred blood blood of one's relatives **185 compare between**
draw comparisons. **187 pleased** satisfied **188 withal** with that,
nonetheless. **190 royalties** privileges granted through the King and
belonging, in this case, to a member of the royal family **195 Take . . .
and take** i.e., If you take . . . you take **196 His** Time's **197 ensue** follow **202–4 Call . . . livery** i.e., revoke the royal grant giving him the
privilege to sue through his attorneys for possession of his inheritance
204 deny refuse. **homage** avowal of allegiance (by which ceremony
Bolingbroke would be able legally to secure his inheritance) **207 prick**
i.e., incite **211 by** nearby, present **213 by** concerning. **may** it may
214 events outcomes **215 Earl of Wiltshire** (The King's Lord Treasurer and one of his notorious favorites.) **216 repair** come **217 see**
see to. **Tomorrow next** Tomorrow **218 trow** believe.

223.2 *Manet* He remains onstage **228 great** i.e., great with sorrow
229 liberal unrestrained, freely speaking **230 ne'er speak more** i.e.,
die **232 Tends . . . to** Does what you wish to say concern
237 gelded i.e., deprived. (Literally, castrated.) **239 In him** in his
case, or, by him **242 inform** charge, report as spies **243 Merely in
hate** out of pure hatred **246 pilled** plundered **250 blanks** blank
charters. **benevolences** forced loans to the crown (not actually
employed until considerably later, in 1473). **wot** know **251 this** i.e.,
this unjustly collected revenue. **256 in farm** on lease.

WILLOUGHBY
  The King's grown bankrupt, like a broken man.   257
NORTHUMBERLAND
  Reproach and dissolution hangeth over him.
ROSS
  He hath not money for these Irish wars,
  His burdenous taxations notwithstanding,
  But by the robbing of the banished Duke.
NORTHUMBERLAND
  His noble kinsman. Most degenerate king!
  But, lords, we hear this fearful tempest sing,
  Yet seek no shelter to avoid the storm;
  We see the wind sit sore upon our sails,   265
  And yet we strike not, but securely perish.   266
ROSS
  We see the very wrack that we must suffer,   267
  And unavoided is the danger now   268
  For suffering so the causes of our wrack.   269
NORTHUMBERLAND
  Not so. Even through the hollow eyes of death   270
  I spy life peering; but I dare not say
  How near the tidings of our comfort is.
WILLOUGHBY
  Nay, let us share thy thoughts, as thou dost ours.
ROSS
  Be confident to speak, Northumberland.
  We three are but thyself, and speaking so
  Thy words are but as thoughts. Therefore be bold.
NORTHUMBERLAND
  Then thus: I have from Port le Blanc,
  A bay in Brittany, received intelligence
  That Harry Duke of Hereford, Rainold Lord Cobham,
    280
  That late broke from the Duke of Exeter,   281
  His brother, Archbishop late of Canterbury,   282
  Sir Thomas Erpingham, Sir John Ramston,
  Sir John Norbery, Sir Robert Waterton, and Francis
     Coint,
  All these well furnished by the Duke of Brittany
  With eight tall ships, three thousand men of war,   286
  Are making hither with all due expedience   287
  And shortly mean to touch our northern shore.
  Perhaps they had ere this, but that they stay   289
  The first departing of the King for Ireland.   290
  If then we shall shake off our slavish yoke,

  Imp out our drooping country's broken wing,   292
  Redeem from broking pawn the blemished crown,   293
  Wipe off the dust that hides our scepter's gilt,   294
  And make high majesty look like itself,
  Away with me in post to Ravenspurgh;   296
  But if you faint, as fearing to do so,   297
  Stay and be secret, and myself will go.
ROSS
  To horse, to horse! Urge doubts to them that fear.
WILLOUGHBY
  Hold out my horse, and I will first be there.   *Exeunt.* 300

✿

[2.2]

Enter the Queen, Bushy, [and] Bagot.

BUSHY
  Madam, Your Majesty is too much sad.
  You promised, when you parted with the King,   2
  To lay aside life-harming heaviness   3
  And entertain a cheerful disposition.   4
QUEEN
  To please the King I did; to please myself
  I cannot do it. Yet I know no cause
  Why I should welcome such a guest as grief,
  Save bidding farewell to so sweet a guest
  As my sweet Richard. Yet again methinks
  Some unborn sorrow ripe in Fortune's womb
  Is coming towards me, and my inward soul
  With nothing trembles. At something it grieves
  More than with parting from my lord the King.
BUSHY
  Each substance of a grief hath twenty shadows,   14
  Which shows like grief itself but is not so;
  For sorrow's eyes, glazèd with blinding tears,
  Divides one thing entire to many objects,   17
  Like perspectives, which rightly gazed upon   18
  Show nothing but confusion, eyed awry   19
  Distinguish form. So your sweet Majesty,   20
  Looking awry upon your lord's departure,   21
  Find shapes of grief more than himself to wail,   22
  Which, looked on as it is, is naught but shadows
  Of what it is not. Then, thrice-gracious Queen,

---

292 **Imp out** piece out. (A term from falconry, meaning to attach new
feathers to a disabled wing of a bird.)   293 **from broking pawn** from
being pledged to pawnbrokers   294 **gilt** gold (with pun on *guilt*)
296 **past** haste.   **Ravenspurgh** on the Yorkshire coast, at the mouth
of the Humber River   297 **faint** are fainthearted   300 **Hold . . . and** If
my horse holds out
2.2 Location: The court. According to Holinshed, the Queen
remained at Windsor Castle when Richard left for Ireland.
2 **with** from   3 **heaviness** melancholy   4 **entertain** put on   14 **Each . . .
shadows** i.e., For every real grief there exist twenty imagined ones
17 **thing entire to** complete thing into   18 **perspectives** (In lines
16–17, Bushy seems to have in mind a glass with a multifaceted
lens, multiplying images of the object being viewed; in lines 18–20,
perspectives are pictures of figures made to appear distorted or confused, except when viewed obliquely, *eyed awry.*)   **rightly** directly,
straight   19 **awry** obliquely   20 **Distinguish form** make the form
distinct and normal.   21 **awry** i.e., mistakenly, distortedly   22 **himself** i.e., the grief itself.   **wail** bewail

---

257 **broken** financially ruined   265 **sore** sorely, grievously   266 **strike**
(1) furl the sails (2) strike blows.   **securely** heedlessly, overconfidently
267 **wrack** ruin   268 **unavoided** unavoidable   269 **suffering** permitting   270 **eyes** eye sockets   280 . . . (A line is probably missing here,
perhaps because of censorship. From information contained in Holinshed, it may have read something like "Thomas, son and heir to the
Earl of Arundel" or "The son of Richard, Earl of Arundel.")   281 **late
broke from** lately escaped from the custody of. (Holinshed records
that "the Earl of Arundel's son, named Thomas, which was kept in
the Duke of Exeter's house, escaped out of the realm . . . and went
to his uncle Thomas Arundel, late Archbishop of Canterbury.")
282 **His** i.e., the Earl of Arundel's.   **late** until recently   286 **tall** stately.
men of war troops   287 **expedience** expedition, speed   289–90 **stay . . .
King** wait until the King departs

More than your lord's departure weep not. More is not
    seen,
Or if it be, 'tis with false sorrow's eye,
Which for things true weeps things imaginary.   27

QUEEN
It may be so, but yet my inward soul
Persuades me it is otherwise. Howe'er it be,
I cannot but be sad—so heavy sad
As, though on thinking on no thought I think,   31
Makes me with heavy nothing faint and shrink.   32

BUSHY
'Tis nothing but conceit, my gracious lady.   33

QUEEN
'Tis nothing less. Conceit is still derived   34
From some forefather grief. Mine is not so,
For nothing hath begot my something grief,   36
Or something hath the nothing that I grieve.   37
'Tis in reversion that I do possess;   38
But what it is, that is not yet known what,   39
I cannot name. 'Tis nameless woe, I wot.   40

[Enter Green.]

GREEN
God save Your Majesty! And well met, gentlemen.
I hope the King is not yet shipped for Ireland.

QUEEN
Why hopest thou so? 'Tis better hope he is,
For his designs crave haste, his haste good hope.   44
Then wherefore dost thou hope he is not shipped?

GREEN
That he, our hope, might have retired his power,   46
And driven into despair an enemy's hope,
Who strongly hath set footing in this land.
The banished Bolingbroke repeals himself   49
And with uplifted arms is safe arrived   50
At Ravenspurgh.

QUEEN   Now God in heaven forbid!

GREEN
Ah, madam, 'tis too true; and that is worse,   52
The lord Northumberland, his son young Harry
    Percy,
The lords of Ross, Beaumont, and Willoughby,
With all their powerful friends, are fled to him.

BUSHY
Why have you not proclaimed Northumberland
And all the rest revolted faction traitors?   57

GREEN
We have, whereupon the Earl of Worcester
Hath broken his staff, resigned his stewardship,   59
And all the household servants fled with him
To Bolingbroke.

QUEEN
So, Green, thou art the midwife to my woe,
And Bolingbroke my sorrow's dismal heir.   63
Now hath my soul brought forth her prodigy,   64
And I, a gasping new-delivered mother,
Have woe to woe, sorrow to sorrow joined.

BUSHY
Despair not, madam.

QUEEN   Who shall hinder me?
I will despair, and be at enmity
With cozening hope. He is a flatterer,   69
A parasite, a keeper-back of death
Who gently would dissolve the bonds of life   71
Which false hope lingers in extremity.   72

[Enter York.]

GREEN   Here comes the Duke of York.

QUEEN
With signs of war about his agèd neck.   74
Oh, full of careful business are his looks!   75
Uncle, for God's sake, speak comfortable words.   76

YORK
Should I do so, I should belie my thoughts.
Comfort's in heaven, and we are on the earth,
Where nothing lives but crosses, cares, and grief.   79
Your husband, he is gone to save far off,   80
Whilst others come to make him lose at home.
Here am I left to underprop his land,   82
Who, weak with age, cannot support myself.
Now comes the sick hour that his surfeit made;
Now shall he try his friends that flattered him.   85

[Enter a Servingman.]

SERVINGMAN
My lord, your son was gone before I came.   86

YORK
He was? Why, so. Go all which way it will!
The nobles they are fled, the commons they are cold,
And will, I fear, revolt on Hereford's side.
Sirrah, get thee to Pleshey, to my sister Gloucester;   90
Bid her send me presently a thousand pound.   91
Hold, take my ring.   92

---

27 for in place of. **weeps** weeps for   **31–2 As . . . shrink** that, though I seem to be thinking of nothing, my "nothing" is so *heavy* or saddening that I faint and fall back under the weight. **33 conceit** fancy   **34 'Tis nothing less** i.e., It is anything but that. **still** always   **36 something** i.e., substantial   **37 something . . . grieve** the unsubstantial grief, the nothing, that I grieve about has something to it, some substance.   **38–40 'Tis . . . name** i.e., My grief is like a legacy that will come to me at some future time, but I cannot tell its nature yet. **40 wot** know, assume. **44 For . . . hope** for his plans require that he proceed expeditiously to Ireland, and with our hopes that his haste bring success. **46 retired his power** held back his army (in order to be able to repulse Bolingbroke's landing) **49 repeals** recalls (from exile) **50 uplifted arms** brandished weapons **52 that** what **57 rest** rest of the

59 broken his staff broken his badge of office (in token of resignation as Lord High Steward. Worcester is brother of the Earl of Northumberland.) **63 dismal heir** ill-omened offspring. **64 prodigy** monstrous birth **69 cozening** cheating. **He** i.e., False hope **71 Who** i.e., death **72 lingers** causes to linger **74 signs of war** i.e., a piece of armor called the gorget, an iron collar that could be worn with ordinary clothes **75 careful business** worried preoccupation **76 comfortable** affording comfort **79 crosses** obstacles, obstructions **80 save far off** i.e., defend his rule in Ireland **82 underprop** prop up, support **85 try** test **86 your son** i.e., the Duke of Aumerle **90 Sirrah** (Said to inferiors.) **sister** sister-in-law **91 presently** immediately **92 ring** (By which the Duchess will know that the request is sent by York himself.)

SERVINGMAN
    My lord, I had forgot to tell Your Lordship:
    Today, as I came by, I callèd there—
    But I shall grieve you to report the rest.
YORK   What is't, knave?   96
SERVINGMAN
    An hour before I came, the Duchess died.
YORK
    God for his mercy, what a tide of woes
    Comes rushing on this woeful land at once!
    I know not what to do. I would to God,
    So my untruth had not provoked him to it,   101
    The King had cut off my head with my brother's.   102
    What, are there no posts dispatched for Ireland?
    How shall we do for money for these wars?
    Come, sister—cousin, I would say—pray pardon
        me.—
    Go, fellow, get thee home. Provide some carts
    And bring away the armor that is there.
                           [*Exit Servingman.*]
    Gentlemen, will you go muster men?
    If I know how or which way to order these affairs
    Thus disorderly thrust into my hands,
    Never believe me. Both are my kinsmen:
    Th'one is my sovereign, whom both my oath
    And duty bids defend; t'other again
    Is my kinsman, whom the King hath wronged,
    Whom conscience and my kindred bids to right.   115
    Well, somewhat we must do.—Come, cousin,   116
    I'll dispose of you.—Gentlemen,   117
    Go, muster up your men, and meet me presently
    At Berkeley. I should to Pleshey too,   119
    But time will not permit. All is uneven,
    And everything is left at six and seven.   121
                    Exeunt Duke [*of York*], *Queen.*
                    Manent Bushy, [*Bagot,*] *Green.*
BUSHY
    The wind sits fair for news to go to Ireland,
    But none returns. For us to levy power
    Proportionable to the enemy
    Is all unpossible.
GREEN
    Besides, our nearness to the King in love
    Is near the hate of those love not the King.   127
BAGOT
    And that is the wavering commons, for their love
    Lies in their purses, and whoso empties them
    By so much fills their hearts with deadly hate.
BUSHY
    Wherein the King stands generally condemned.

BAGOT
    If judgment lie in them, then so do we,   132
    Because we ever have been near the King.   133
GREEN
    Well, I will for refuge straight to Bristol Castle.
    The Earl of Wiltshire is already there.
BUSHY
    Thither will I with you, for little office   136
    Will the hateful commons perform for us,   137
    Except like curs to tear us all to pieces.
    [*To Bagot*] Will you go along with us?
BAGOT
    No, I will to Ireland to His Majesty.
    Farewell. If heart's presages be not vain,   141
    We three here part that ne'er shall meet again.
BUSHY
    That's as York thrives to beat back Bolingbroke.   143
GREEN
    Alas, poor duke! The task he undertakes
    Is numbering sands and drinking oceans dry.
    Where one on his side fights, thousands will fly.
    Farewell at once, for once, for all, and ever.
BUSHY
    Well, we may meet again.
BAGOT   I fear me, never.
                               [*Exeunt.*]

❖

[2.3]

    Enter [*Bolingbroke, Duke of*] *Hereford,* [*and*]
    Northumberland [*with forces*].

BOLINGBROKE
    How far is it, my lord, to Berkeley now?
NORTHUMBERLAND   Believe me, noble lord,
    I am a stranger here in Gloucestershire.
    These high wild hills and rough uneven ways
    Draws out our miles and makes them wearisome;
    And yet your fair discourse hath been as sugar,
    Making the hard way sweet and delectable.
    But I bethink me what a weary way
    From Ravenspurgh to Cotswold will be found   9
    In Ross and Willoughby, wanting your company,   10
    Which, I protest, hath very much beguiled   11
    The tediousness and process of my travel.   12
    But theirs is sweetened with the hope to have
    The present benefit which I possess;
    And hope to joy is little less in joy   15
    Than hope enjoyed. By this the weary lords   16

---

132 If . . . we i.e., If the power to pass judgment is given to the wavering commons, then we, too, stand condemned   **133 ever** always   **136 office** service   **137 hateful** full of hate, angry   **141 vain** in vain   **143 That's . . . thrives** i.e., That depends upon York's efforts and success
2.3 Location: In Gloucestershire, near Berkeley Castle.
9 Cotswold hilly district in Gloucestershire   **10 In** by.   **wanting** lacking   **11 protest** declare   **12 tediousness and process** tedious process   **15–16 And hope . . . enjoyed** and the hope of future happiness is only slightly less joyous than happiness already enjoyed.   **16 this** this expectation

---

96 knave i.e., fellow.   **101 So my untruth** provided that my disloyalty   **102 brother's** i.e., the Duke of Gloucester's.   **115 my . . . right** my kinship to him bids that I right his wrong.   **116 somewhat** something.   **cousin** i.e., the Queen   **117 dispose of** make arrangements for   **119 Berkeley** a castle near Bristol.   **121 at six and seven** i.e., in confusion.   **121.2 Manent** They remain onstage   **127 Is . . . King** makes us enemies of those who oppose the King.

Shall make their way seem short, as mine hath done
By sight of what I have: your noble company.

BOLINGBROKE
Of much less value is my company
Than your good words. But who comes here?

Enter Harry Percy.

NORTHUMBERLAND
It is my son, young Harry Percy,
Sent from my brother Worcester whencesoever.—   22
Harry, how fares your uncle?   23

PERCY
I had thought, my lord, to have learned his health of
     you.

NORTHUMBERLAND   Why, is he not with the Queen?

PERCY
No, my good lord. He hath forsook the court,
Broken his staff of office, and dispersed
The household of the King.

NORTHUMBERLAND   What was his reason?
He was not so resolved when last we spake together.

PERCY
Because Your Lordship was proclaimèd traitor.
But he, my lord, is gone to Ravenspurgh
To offer service to the Duke of Hereford,
And sent me over by Berkeley to discover
What power the Duke of York had levied there,   34
Then with directions to repair to Ravenspurgh.   35

NORTHUMBERLAND
Have you forgot the Duke of Hereford, boy?   36

PERCY
No, my good lord, for that is not forgot
Which ne'er I did remember. To my knowledge
I never in my life did look on him.

NORTHUMBERLAND
Then learn to know him now. This is the Duke.

PERCY
My gracious lord, I tender you my service,   41
Such as it is, being tender, raw, and young,
Which elder days shall ripen and confirm
To more approvèd service and desert.   44

BOLINGBROKE
I thank thee, gentle Percy, and be sure
I count myself in nothing else so happy
As in a soul rememb'ring my good friends;   47
And as my fortune ripens with thy love,   48
It shall be still thy true love's recompense.   49
My heart this covenant makes, my hand thus seals it.
     [He offers Percy his hand.]

NORTHUMBERLAND
How far is it to Berkeley? And what stir   51
Keeps good old York there with his men of war?

PERCY
There stands the castle by yon tuft of trees,
Manned with three hundred men, as I have heard,
And in it are the lords of York, Berkeley, and Seymour,
None else of name and noble estimate.   56

[Enter Ross and Willoughby.]

NORTHUMBERLAND
Here come the lords of Ross and Willoughby,
Bloody with spurring, fiery red with haste.   58

BOLINGBROKE
Welcome, my lords. I wot your love pursues   59
A banished traitor. All my treasury
Is yet but unfelt thanks, which, more enriched,   61
Shall be your love and labor's recompense.

ROSS
Your presence makes us rich, most noble lord.

WILLOUGHBY
And far surmounts our labor to attain it.

BOLINGBROKE
Evermore thank's the exchequer of the poor,   65
Which, till my infant fortune comes to years,   66
Stands for my bounty. But who comes here?   67

[Enter Berkeley.]

NORTHUMBERLAND
It is my lord of Berkeley, as I guess.

BERKELEY
My lord of Hereford, my message is to you.

BOLINGBROKE
My lord, my answer is—to "Lancaster";   70
And I am come to seek that name in England,
And I must find that title in your tongue
Before I make reply to aught you say.

BERKELEY
Mistake me not, my lord, 'tis not my meaning
To raze one title of your honor out.   75
To you, my lord, I come, what lord you will,   76
From the most gracious regent of this land,
The Duke of York, to know what pricks you on   78
To take advantage of the absent time   79
And fright our native peace with self-borne arms.   80

[Enter York.]

---

22 **whencesoever** from wherever he is.   23 **your uncle** i.e., the Earl of Worcester.   34 **power** troops   35 **directions** instructions.   **repair** go   36 **boy** (A rebuke for not respectfully greeting Bolingbroke, though historically Percy was two years Bolingbroke's senior.)   41 **tender** offer. (With a pun in the next line on the meaning "inexperienced.")   **my service** (Presumably Percy kneels to Bolingbroke, and so do Ross and Willoughby when they enter.)   44 **approvèd** proven, demonstrated   47 **in a** in my   48–9 **And . . . recompense** and as my fortunes improve, assisted by your loyalty to me, I will be increasingly enabled to reward you for that loyalty.

51 **stir** action   56 **estimate** rank.   58 **spurring** i.e., hard riding   59 **wot** am aware that. (Bolingbroke graciously indicates his awareness of the risk they are taking in supporting him.)   61 **unfelt** impalpable, expressed in words, not gifts.   **which** i.e., which treasury. **more enriched** i.e., with still more thanks added, or, with substantial gifts at a later date   65 **Evermore . . . poor** "Thank you" is always the exchequer of the poor, i.e., the only means they have to repay favors   66 **comes to years** reaches maturity   67 **Stands for** serves in place of   70 **"Lancaster"** (Bolingbroke will enter into no negotiations unless his proper title, taken away by Richard, is given him.)   75 **raze** scrape (or perhaps *rase*, "erase")   76 **what . . . will** whatever title you prefer to be addressed by. (Said sardonically.)   78 **pricks** spurs   79 **the absent time** i.e., the time of the King's absence   80 **self-borne** borne in your own private cause, not the country's welfare. (Also suggesting *self-born*, "originating in the self.")

BOLINGBROKE
I shall not need transport my words by you;
Here comes His Grace in person.—My noble uncle!

[He kneels.]

YORK
Show me thy humble heart, and not thy knee,
Whose duty is deceivable and false.   84

BOLINGBROKE   My gracious uncle—

YORK   Tut, tut!
Grace me no grace, nor uncle me no uncle.
I am no traitor's uncle; and that word "grace"
In an ungracious mouth is but profane.
Why have those banished and forbidden legs
Dared once to touch a dust of England's ground?   91
But then more "why?" Why have they dared to march
So many miles upon her peaceful bosom,
Frighting her pale-faced villages with war
And ostentation of despisèd arms?   95
Com'st thou because the anointed King is hence?
Why, foolish boy, the King is left behind,
And in my loyal bosom lies his power.
Were I but now the lord of such hot youth
As when brave Gaunt, thy father, and myself
Rescued the Black Prince, that young Mars of men,   101
From forth the ranks of many thousand French,
Oh, then how quickly should this arm of mine,
Now prisoner to the palsy, chastise thee
And minister correction to thy fault!   105

BOLINGBROKE
My gracious uncle, let me know my fault.
On what condition stands it and wherein?   107

YORK
Even in condition of the worst degree:
In gross rebellion and detested treason.
Thou art a banished man, and here art come
Before the expiration of thy time
In braving arms against thy sovereign.   112

BOLINGBROKE [standing]
As I was banished, I was banished Hereford;
But as I come, I come for Lancaster.   114
And, noble uncle, I beseech Your Grace
Look on my wrongs with an indifferent eye.   116
You are my father, for methinks in you
I see old Gaunt alive. Oh, then, my father,
Will you permit that I shall stand condemned   119
A wandering vagabond, my rights and royalties   120
Plucked from my arms perforce and given away
To upstart unthrifts? Wherefore was I born?   122
If that my cousin king be King in England,
It must be granted I am Duke of Lancaster.
You have a son, Aumerle, my noble cousin;

Had you first died, and he been thus trod down,   126
He should have found his uncle Gaunt a father
To rouse his wrongs and chase them to the bay.   128
I am denied to sue my livery here,   129
And yet my letters patents give me leave.   130
My father's goods are all distrained and sold,   131
And these, and all, are all amiss employed.
What would you have me do? I am a subject,
And I challenge law. Attorneys are denied me,   134
And therefore personally I lay my claim
To my inheritance of free descent.   136

NORTHUMBERLAND
The noble Duke hath been too much abused.

ROSS
It stands Your Grace upon to do him right.   138

WILLOUGHBY
Base men by his endowments are made great.   139

YORK
My lords of England, let me tell you this:
I have had feeling of my cousin's wrongs   141
And labored all I could to do him right;
But in this kind to come, in braving arms,   143
Be his own carver, and cut out his way   144
To find out right with wrong—it may not be;
And you that do abet him in this kind
Cherish rebellion and are rebels all.

NORTHUMBERLAND
The noble Duke hath sworn his coming is
But for his own, and for the right of that
We all have strongly sworn to give him aid;
And let him never see joy that breaks that oath!   151

YORK
Well, well, I see the issue of these arms.   152
I cannot mend it, I must needs confess,
Because my power is weak and all ill-left;   154
But if I could, by Him that gave me life,
I would attach you all and make you stoop   156
Unto the sovereign mercy of the King.
But since I cannot, be it known unto you
I do remain as neuter. So fare you well—   159
Unless you please to enter in the castle
And there repose you for this night.

BOLINGBROKE
An offer, uncle, that we will accept.
But we must win Your Grace to go with us   163
To Bristol Castle, which they say is held
By Bushy, Bagot, and their complices,   165

---

84 duty gesture of obeisance.   deceivable deceitful, deceptive
91 dust particle of dust   95 ostentation display.   despisèd despicable   101 the Black Prince i.e., Edward, the eldest son of Edward III
and King Richard's father   105 minister administer   107 condition
defect in me, or provision of the law.   wherein in what does it consist.   112 braving defiant (also at line 143)   114 for Lancaster i.e.,
under the title of Lancaster and in order to claim it.   116 indifferent
impartial   119 condemned condemned as   120 royalties privileges
granted by the King   122 unthrifts spendthrifts.

126 first i.e., before Gaunt   128 rouse chase from cover, expose.   the
bay the extremity where the hunted animal turns on its pursuers.
129 I am . . . here I am denied the right to sue for possession of hereditary rights in England. (See 2.1.202–4 and note.)   130 letters patents
i.e., letters from the King indicating a subject's legal rights
131 distrained seized officially   134 challenge law claim my legal
rights.   136 of free descent by legal succession.   138 stands . . .
upon is incumbent upon Your Grace   139 his endowments i.e., the
properties that rightly belong to Bolingbroke   141 cousin's nephew's
143 kind fashion   144 Be . . . carver i.e., act on his own authority,
help himself   151 joy i.e., the joy of heaven   152 issue outcome
154 power army.   ill-left left in dismay and with inadequate means
156 attach arrest   159 as neuter neutral.   163 win persuade
165 Bagot (According to 2.2.140, Bagot had gone to Ireland.)

The caterpillars of the commonwealth,
Which I have sworn to weed and pluck away.

YORK
It may be I will go with you; but yet I'll pause,
For I am loath to break our country's laws.
Nor friends nor foes, to me welcome you are.   170
Things past redress are now with me past care.
                                                          Exeunt.

❧

[2.4]

Enter Earl of Salisbury and a Welsh Captain.

WELSH CAPTAIN
My lord of Salisbury, we have stayed ten days   1
And hardly kept our countrymen together,   2
And yet we hear no tidings from the King.   3
Therefore we will disperse ourselves. Farewell.

SALISBURY
Stay yet another day, thou trusty Welshman.
The King reposeth all his confidence in thee.

WELSH CAPTAIN
'Tis thought the King is dead. We will not stay.
The bay trees in our country are all withered,
And meteors fright the fixèd stars of heaven;
The pale-faced moon looks bloody on the earth,
And lean-looked prophets whisper fearful change;   11
Rich men look sad, and ruffians dance and leap,
The one in fear to lose what they enjoy,
The other to enjoy by rage and war.   14
These signs forerun the death or fall of kings.   15
Farewell. Our countrymen are gone and fled,
As well assured Richard their king is dead.   [*Exit.*] 17

SALISBURY
Ah, Richard! With the eyes of heavy mind
I see thy glory like a shooting star
Fall to the base earth from the firmament.
Thy sun sets weeping in the lowly west,
Witnessing storms to come, woe, and unrest.   22
Thy friends are fled to wait upon thy foes,   23
And crossly to thy good all fortune goes.   [*Exit.*] 24

❧

[3.1]

*Enter [Bolingbroke,] Duke of Hereford, York,
Northumberland, [with] Bushy and Green,
prisoners.*

BOLINGBROKE   Bring forth these men.
Bushy and Green, I will not vex your souls—
Since presently your souls must part your bodies—   3
With too much urging your pernicious lives,   4

For 'twere no charity; yet, to wash your blood
From off my hands, here in the view of men
I will unfold some causes of your deaths.   7
You have misled a prince, a royal king,
A happy gentleman in blood and lineaments,   9
By you unhappied and disfigured clean.   10
You have in manner with your sinful hours   11
Made a divorce betwixt his queen and him,
Broke the possession of a royal bed,
And stained the beauty of a fair queen's cheeks
With tears drawn from her eyes by your foul wrongs.
Myself—a prince by fortune of my birth,
Near to the King in blood, and near in love
Till you did make him misinterpret me—
Have stooped my neck under your injuries
And sighed my English breath in foreign clouds,   20
Eating the bitter bread of banishment,
Whilst you have fed upon my seigniories,   22
Disparked my parks and felled my forest woods,   23
From my own windows torn my household coat,   24
Razed out my imprese, leaving me no sign,   25
Save men's opinions and my living blood,
To show the world I am a gentleman.
This and much more, much more than twice all this,
Condemns you to the death.—See them delivered
    over
To execution and the hand of death.

BUSHY
More welcome is the stroke of death to me
Than Bolingbroke to England. Lords, farewell.

GREEN
My comfort is that heaven will take our souls
And plague injustice with the pains of hell.

BOLINGBROKE
My lord Northumberland, see them dispatched.
    [*Exeunt Northumberland with the prisoners, guarded.*]
Uncle, you say the Queen is at your house.
For God's sake, fairly let her be entreated.   37
Tell her I send to her my kind commends.   38
Take special care my greetings be delivered.

YORK
A gentleman of mine I have dispatched
With letters of your love to her at large.   41

BOLINGBROKE
Thanks, gentle uncle. Come, lords, away,
To fight with Glendower and his complices.   43
Awhile to work, and after holiday.   *Exeunt.* 44

❧

---

170 **Nor** Neither as
2.4 Location: A camp in Wales.
1 **stayed** waited   2 **hardly** with difficulty   3 **yet** still   11 **lean-looked**
lean-looking   14 **to . . . rage** in hopes of possessing by violence
15 **forerun** anticipate   17 **As** as being   22 **Witnessing** betokening
23 **wait upon** attend, offer allegiance to   24 **crossly** adversely
3.1 Location: Bristol. The castle.
3 **presently** immediately   4 **urging** emphasizing as reasons (for your
executions)

7 **unfold** reveal   9 **happy** fortunate.   **blood and lineaments** birth
and natural characteristics   10 **By . . . clean** by you made wretched
and wholly marred in reputation.   11 **in manner** as it were   20 **foreign clouds** i.e., the air of foreign lands (and adding to the clouds
with sighs)   22 **seigniories** estates   23 **Disparked** thrown open to
uses other than hunting and forestry   24 **household coat** coat of
arms (frequently emblazoned on stained or painted windows)
25 **Razed** scraped (or perhaps *rased*, "erased").   **imprese** heraldic
device, emblematic design   37 **entreated** treated.   38 **commends**
regards, compliments.   41 **at large** conveyed in full.   43 **Glendower**
(Owen Glendower was not, according to Holinshed's *Chronicles*, at this
time in arms against Bolingbroke. Possibly he is to be identified here
with the Welsh captain of the preceding scene.)   44 **after** afterwards

[3.2]

[Drums. Flourish and colors.] Enter the King, Aumerle, [the Bishop of] Carlisle, etc. [with soldiers].

KING RICHARD
Barkloughly Castle call they this at hand?   1

AUMERLE
Yea, my lord. How brooks Your Grace the air   2
After your late tossing on the breaking seas?   3

KING RICHARD
Needs must I like it well. I weep for joy   4
To stand upon my kingdom once again.
Dear earth, I do salute thee with my hand,
                [He bends and touches the ground.]
Though rebels wound thee with their horses' hoofs.
As a long-parted mother with her child   8
Plays fondly with her tears and smiles in meeting,
So, weeping, smiling, greet I thee, my earth,
And do thee favors with my royal hands.
Feed not thy sovereign's foe, my gentle earth,
Nor with thy sweets comfort his ravenous sense,   13
But let thy spiders, that suck up thy venom,   14
And heavy-gaited toads lie in their way,   15
Doing annoyance to the treacherous feet
Which with usurping steps do trample thee.
Yield stinging nettles to mine enemies;
And when they from thy bosom pluck a flower,
Guard it, I pray thee, with a lurking adder,
Whose double tongue may with a mortal touch   21
Throw death upon thy sovereign's enemies.—
Mock not my senseless conjuration, lords.   23
This earth shall have a feeling, and these stones
Prove armèd soldiers, ere her native king   25
Shall falter under foul rebellion's arms.

CARLISLE
Fear not, my lord. That Power that made you king
Hath power to keep you king in spite of all.
The means that heavens yield must be embraced
And not neglected; else heaven would,   30
And we will not. Heaven's offer we refuse,   31
The proffered means of succor and redress.   32

AUMERLE
He means, my lord, that we are too remiss,
Whilst Bolingbroke through our security   34
Grows strong and great in substance and in power.

KING RICHARD
Discomfortable cousin, know'st thou not   36

That when the searching eye of heaven is hid   37
Behind the globe that lights the lower world,   38
Then thieves and robbers range abroad unseen
In murders and in outrage boldly here;
But when from under this terrestrial ball   41
He fires the proud tops of the eastern pines   42
And darts his light through every guilty hole,
Then murders, treasons, and detested sins,
The cloak of night being plucked from off their backs,
Stand bare and naked, trembling at themselves?   46
So when this thief, this traitor, Bolingbroke,
Who all this while hath reveled in the night
Whilst we were wand'ring with the Antipodes,   49
Shall see us rising in our throne, the east,
His treasons will sit blushing in his face,
Not able to endure the sight of day,
But, self-affrighted, tremble at his sin.
Not all the water in the rough rude sea
Can wash the balm off from an anointed king;   55
The breath of worldly men cannot depose   56
The deputy elected by the Lord.   57
For every man that Bolingbroke hath pressed   58
To lift shrewd steel against our golden crown,   59
God for his Richard hath in heavenly pay
A glorious angel. Then, if angels fight,
Weak men must fall, for heaven still guards the right. 62

Enter Salisbury.

Welcome, my lord. How far off lies your power?

SALISBURY
Nor near nor farther off, my gracious lord,   64
Than this weak arm. Discomfort guides my tongue   65
And bids me speak of nothing but despair.
One day too late, I fear me, noble lord,
Hath clouded all thy happy days on earth.
Oh, call back yesterday, bid time return,
And thou shalt have twelve thousand fighting men!
Today, today, unhappy day too late,
O'erthrows thy joys, friends, fortune, and thy state;   72
For all the Welshmen, hearing thou wert dead,
Are gone to Bolingbroke, dispersed, and fled.

AUMERLE
Comfort, my liege. Why looks Your Grace so pale?

KING RICHARD
But now the blood of twenty thousand men   76
   Did triumph in my face, and they are fled;   77
And till so much blood thither come again,
   Have I not reason to look pale and dead?   79

3.2. Location: The coast of Wales, near Harlech Castle.
1 Barkloughly i.e., Harlech   **2 brooks** enjoys   **3 late** recent   **4 Needs must** Necessarily   **8 a long-parted mother with** a mother long parted from   **13 sweets** i.e., bounty.   **sense** appetite   **14 suck . . . venom** (Alludes to the belief that spiders drew their poison from the earth.)   **15 heavy-gaited** lumbering, clumsy   **21 double** forked.   **mortal** deadly   **23 senseless conjuration** solemn entreaty of senseless things; or, one that makes no sense to you, being so fanciful   **25 native** entitled (to the crown) by birth, rightful. (Richard was born at Bordeaux.)   **30–1 else . . . not** i.e., otherwise, we spurn heaven's will.   **32 succor and redress** help and remedy.   **34 security** overconfidence   **36 Discomfortable** Disheartening, discouraging

37–8 when . . . world i.e., when the sun is hid behind the earth, lighting its lower side   **41 this terrestrial ball** the earth   **42 He fires** the sun lights up. (Literally, "sets on fire.")   **46 at themselves** i.e., at being caught in their crimes.   **49 Antipodes** people on the other side of the world; here, the Irish. (A geographical hyperbole.)   **55 balm** consecrated oil used in anointing a king   **56 worldly** earthly   **57 elected** chosen   **58 pressed** impressed, forced into the ranks   **59 shrewd** keen, biting   **62 still** always   **64 Nor near** Neither nearer   **65 Discomfort** Discouragement   **72 state** royal power   **76 But now** Even now.   **twenty** (A seeming discrepancy with *twelve* in line 70; perhaps the result of Richard's hyperbole.)   **77 triumph** i.e., shine forth   **79 pale and dead** deathly pale.

All souls that will be safe, fly from my side,
For time hath set a blot upon my pride. 81

AUMERLE
Comfort, my liege. Remember who you are.

KING RICHARD
I had forgot myself. Am I not king?
Awake, thou coward majesty, thou sleepest!
Is not the king's name twenty thousand names?
Arm, arm, my name! A puny subject strikes
At thy great glory. Look not to the ground,
Ye favorites of a king. Are we not high?
High be our thoughts. I know my uncle York
Hath power enough to serve our turn. But who comes
here?

Enter Scroop.

SCROOP
More health and happiness betide my liege 91
Than can my care-tuned tongue deliver him! 92

KING RICHARD
Mine ear is open and my heart prepared.
The worst is worldly loss thou canst unfold. 94
Say, is my kingdom lost? Why, 'twas my care, 95
And what loss is it to be rid of care?
Strives Bolingbroke to be as great as we?
Greater he shall not be; if he serve God,
We'll serve Him too, and be his fellow so. 99
Revolt our subjects? That we cannot mend;
They break their faith to God as well as us.
Cry woe, destruction, ruin, and decay;
The worst is death, and death will have his day.

SCROOP
Glad am I that Your Highness is so armed 104
To bear the tidings of calamity.
Like an unseasonable stormy day,
Which makes the silver rivers drown their shores
As if the world were all dissolved to tears,
So high above his limits swells the rage 109
Of Bolingbroke, covering your fearful land 110
With hard bright steel and hearts harder than steel.
Whitebeards have armed their thin and hairless scalps 112
Against Thy Majesty; boys with women's voices
Strive to speak big, and clap their female joints 114
In stiff unwieldy arms against thy crown. 115
Thy very beadsmen learn to bend their bows 116
Of double-fatal yew against thy state; 117

Yea, distaff-women manage rusty bills 118
Against thy seat. Both young and old rebel, 119
And all goes worse than I have power to tell.

KING RICHARD
Too well, too well thou tell'st a tale so ill.
Where is the Earl of Wiltshire? Where is Bagot? 122
What is become of Bushy? Where is Green,
That they have let the dangerous enemy
Measure our confines with such peaceful steps? 125
If we prevail, their heads shall pay for it.
I warrant they have made peace with Bolingbroke.

SCROOP
Peace have they made with him indeed, my lord.

KING RICHARD
Oh, villains, vipers, damned without redemption!
Dogs easily won to fawn on any man!
Snakes in my heart-blood warmed, that sting my
heart!
Three Judases, each one thrice worse than Judas!
Would they make peace? Terrible hell
Make war upon their spotted souls for this! 134

SCROOP
Sweet love, I see, changing his property, 135
Turns to the sourest and most deadly hate.
Again uncurse their souls. Their peace is made
With heads and not with hands. Those whom you
curse 138
Have felt the worst of death's destroying wound
And lie full low, graved in the hollow ground. 140

AUMERLE
Is Bushy, Green, and the Earl of Wiltshire dead?

SCROOP
Ay, all of them at Bristol lost their heads.

AUMERLE
Where is the Duke my father with his power?

KING RICHARD
No matter where. Of comfort no man speak!
Let's talk of graves, of worms, and epitaphs,
Make dust our paper, and with rainy eyes
Write sorrow on the bosom of the earth.
Let's choose executors and talk of wills.
And yet not so, for what can we bequeath
Save our deposèd bodies to the ground? 150
Our lands, our lives, and all are Bolingbroke's,
And nothing can we call our own but death
And that small model of the barren earth 153
Which serves as paste and cover to our bones. 154
For God's sake, let us sit upon the ground

---

81 **blot** stain   91 **More . . . betide** May more health and happiness
befall   92 **care-tuned** i.e., tuned by sorrow and to the key of sorrow.
deliver deliver to   94 **unfold** reveal.   95 **care** trouble   99 **his fellow** his (Bolingbroke's) equal   104 **armed** prepared   109 **his limits**
(1) its banks (2) the limits properly allowed to Bolingbroke's rage
110 **fearful** full of fears   112 **Whitebeards** Old men.   **thin** sparsely
haired   114 **Strive . . . joints** strive to speak with deep manlike
voices, and thrust their adolescent limbs   115 **arms** armor
116 **beadsmen** old almsmen or pensioners whose duty it was to pray
for a benefactor; here, for the King   117 **double-fatal** doubly fatal
(since the wood of the yew was used for bows and since its foliage
and berries are poisonous; yews were also commonly planted in
graveyards)

118–19 **distaff-women . . . seat** spinning women wield unused and
hence rusty pikes (long-handled ax-like weapons) against your throne.
122 **Bagot** (Although the King names Bagot here, he mentions only *three*
Judases in line 132 and Aumerle does not ask about Bagot in line 141; in
3.4 we learn that Bagot is not executed along with the other three but
reappears instead in 4.1.)   125 **Measure our confines** travel over my
kingdom.   **peaceful** unopposed   134 **spotted** stained with treason
135 **his property** its distinctive quality   138 **hands** (Used in swearing
oaths, surrendering, etc.)   140 **graved** buried   150 **deposèd**
(1) dethroned, as in 4.1 (2) deprived of those functions carried out by
the body in this transitory life (3) deposited   153 **model** microcosm or
mold, i.e., the body   154 **paste** pastry, pie crust

And tell sad stories of the death of kings—
How some have been deposed, some slain in war,
Some haunted by the ghosts they have deposed,   158
Some poisoned by their wives, some sleeping killed,
All murdered. For within the hollow crown
That rounds the mortal temples of a king   161
Keeps Death his court, and there the antic sits,   162
Scoffing his state and grinning at his pomp,   163
Allowing him a breath, a little scene,   164
To monarchize, be feared, and kill with looks,   165
Infusing him with self and vain conceit,   166
As if this flesh which walls about our life
Were brass impregnable; and humored thus,   168
Comes at the last and with a little pin
Bores through his castle wall, and—farewell, king!
Cover your heads, and mock not flesh and blood   171
With solemn reverence. Throw away respect,
Tradition, form, and ceremonious duty,
For you have but mistook me all this while.
I live with bread like you, feel want,
Taste grief, need friends. Subjected thus,   176
How can you say to me I am a king?

CARLISLE
My lord, wise men ne'er sit and wail their woes,
But presently prevent the ways to wail.   179
To fear the foe, since fear oppresseth strength,   180
Gives in your weakness strength unto your foe,   181
And so your follies fight against yourself.
Fear, and be slain. No worse can come to fight;   183
And fight and die is death destroying death,   184
Where fearing dying pays death servile breath.   185

AUMERLE
My father hath a power. Inquire of him,   186
And learn to make a body of a limb.   187

KING RICHARD
Thou chid'st me well. Proud Bolingbroke, I come
To change blows with thee for our day of doom.   189
This ague fit of fear is overblown;   190
An easy task it is to win our own.   191

Say, Scroop, where lies our uncle with his power?
Speak sweetly, man, although thy looks be sour.

SCROOP
Men judge by the complexion of the sky   194
    The state and inclination of the day.
So may you by my dull and heavy eye;
    My tongue hath but a heavier tale to say.
I play the torturer, by small and small   198
To lengthen out the worst that must be spoken:
Your uncle York is joined with Bolingbroke,
And all your northern castles yielded up,
And all your southern gentlemen in arms   202
Upon his party.

KING RICHARD   Thou hast said enough.   203
[To Aumerle] Beshrew thee, cousin, which didst lead
me forth   204
Of that sweet way I was in to despair.
What say you now? What comfort have we now?
By heaven, I'll hate him everlastingly
That bids me be of comfort any more.
Go to Flint Castle. There I'll pine away;   209
A king, woe's slave, shall kingly woe obey.
That power I have, discharge, and let them go
To ear the land that hath some hope to grow,   212
For I have none. Let no man speak again
To alter this, for counsel is but vain.

AUMERLE
My liege, one word.

KING RICHARD   He does me double wrong   215
That wounds me with the flatteries of his tongue.
Discharge my followers. Let them hence away,
From Richard's night to Bolingbroke's fair day.
                                    [Exeunt.]

❖

[3.3]

Enter [with drum and colors] Bolingbroke, York,
Northumberland, [attendants, and forces].

BOLINGBROKE
So that by this intelligence we learn   1
The Welshmen are dispersed, and Salisbury
Is gone to meet the King, who lately landed
With some few private friends upon this coast.

NORTHUMBERLAND
The news is very fair and good, my lord:
Richard not far from hence hath hid his head.

YORK
It would beseem the Lord Northumberland   7
To say "King Richard." Alack the heavy day
When such a sacred king should hide his head!

---

158 deposed deprived of life **161 rounds** encircles **162 antic**
grotesque figure, jester **163 Scoffing his state** scoffing at the King's
regality **164 breath** breathing space, moment **165 monarchize** play
the monarch. **kill with looks** i.e., order someone's death with a mere
glance **166 self and vain conceit** vain conceit of himself **168 and
humored thus** and Death, having amused himself at the King's
expense, having led the King on in this humor **171 Cover your heads**
Replace your hats (which have been removed out of respect for the
King) **176 Subjected** Made subject to grief, want, etc. (With pun on
"being treated like a subject.") **179 But . . . wail** but promptly
anticipate and thus prevent the courses that result in lamentation.
180–1 To fear . . . foe i.e., To be afraid of the foe is merely a weakness
that, by oppressing your own resolve, gives advantage to the foe
183 Fear . . . fight i.e., If you fear, you are sure to be slain, and no
worse fate can come to you if you fight **184–5 fight . . . breath** to
die fighting is to conquer death in the very act of dying, whereas to
die fearfully pays to death the tribute of servility. **186 power** army
(as also in line 192). **of** about, or from **187 learn . . . limb** i.e., discover how to make a partial force substitute for a complete one.
189 change exchange. **for . . . doom** i.e., in order to settle our fates,
which of us is to die now. **190 This ague . . . overblown** This parox-
ysm of shivering in fear has blown over **191 our own** i.e., my own
kingdom.

194 complexion appearance **198 by small and small** little by little
202–3 And . . . party and all your men of rank in southern England
are also in arms on Bolingbroke's side. **204 Beshrew** Confound. (Literally, *curse.*) **forth** out **209 Flint Castle** (Near Chester.) **212 ear**
plow **215 double wrong** i.e., in deceiving me and in leading me into
false hope once again
3.3 Location: Wales. Before Flint Castle.
1 intelligence information **7 beseem** be appropriate for, be seemly
behavior in

NORTHUMBERLAND
Your Grace mistakes. Only to be brief
Left I his title out.
YORK   The time hath been,
Would you have been so brief with him, he would
Have been so brief with you to shorten you,   13
For taking so the head, your whole head's length.   14
BOLINGBROKE
Mistake not, uncle, further than you should.
YORK
Take not, good cousin, further than you should,
Lest you mistake the heavens are over our heads.   17
BOLINGBROKE
I know it, uncle, and oppose not myself
Against their will. But who comes here?

            Enter Percy.

Welcome, Harry. What, will not this castle yield?
PERCY
The castle royally is manned, my lord,
Against thy entrance.
BOLINGBROKE
Royally? Why, it contains no king?
PERCY   Yes, my good lord,
It doth contain a king. King Richard lies   25
Within the limits of yon lime and stone,
And with him are the Lord Aumerle, Lord Salisbury,
Sir Stephen Scroop, besides a clergyman
Of holy reverence—who, I cannot learn.
NORTHUMBERLAND
Oh, belike it is the Bishop of Carlisle.   30
BOLINGBROKE [to Northumberland]   Noble lord,
Go to the rude ribs of that ancient castle;   32
Through brazen trumpet send the breath of parley   33
Into his ruined ears, and thus deliver: 34
Henry Bolingbroke
On both his knees doth kiss King Richard's hand
And sends allegiance and true faith of heart
To his most royal person, hither come
Even at his feet to lay my arms and power,
Provided that my banishment repealed   40
And lands restored again be freely granted.   41
If not, I'll use the advantage of my power,   42
And lay the summer's dust with showers of blood
Rained from the wounds of slaughtered Englishmen—
The which how far off from the mind of Bolingbroke
It is such crimson tempest should bedrench   46
The fresh green lap of fair King Richard's land,
My stooping duty tenderly shall show.   48

Go, signify as much while here we march
Upon the grassy carpet of this plain.
    [Northumberland and attendants advance to the castle.]
Let's march without the noise of threat'ning drum,
That from this castle's tottered battlements   52
Our fair appointments may be well perused.   53
Methinks King Richard and myself should meet
With no less terror than the elements
Of fire and water, when their thund'ring shock   56
At meeting tears the cloudy cheeks of heaven.
Be he the fire, I'll be the yielding water;
The rage be his, whilst on the earth I rain   59
My waters—on the earth, and not on him.   60
March on, and mark King Richard how he looks.   61

    [Bolingbroke's forces march about the stage.] The
    trumpets sound [a parley without and answer
    within, then a flourish. King] Richard appeareth
    on the walls [with the Bishop of Carlisle, Aumerle,
    Scroop, and Salisbury].

See, see, King Richard doth himself appear,
As doth the blushing discontented sun   63
From out the fiery portal of the east
When he perceives the envious clouds are bent   65
To dim his glory and to stain the track
Of his bright passage to the occident.   67
YORK
Yet looks he like a king. Behold, his eye,   68
As bright as is the eagle's, lightens forth   69
Controlling majesty. Alack, alack, for woe,
That any harm should stain so fair a show!
KING RICHARD [to Northumberland]
We are amazed; and thus long have we stood
To watch the fearful bending of thy knee,   73
Because we thought ourself thy lawful king.
And if we be, how dare thy joints forget
To pay their awful duty to our presence?   76
If we be not, show us the hand of God   77
That hath dismissed us from our stewardship;
For well we know, no hand of blood and bone   79
Can grip the sacred handle of our scepter,
Unless he do profane, steal, or usurp.   81
And though you think that all, as you have done,
Have torn their souls by turning them from us,   83
And we are barren and bereft of friends,   84
Yet know, my master, God omnipotent,   85
Is mustering in his clouds on our behalf

13 to as to   14 taking so the head i.e., (1) presumptuously omitting
thus his title (2) being headstrong   17 mistake fail to perceive that.
(Plays on Bolingbroke's use of mistake, just as York has punned on
brief and head.)   25 lies resides   30 belike probably   32 rude ribs
i.e., rugged walls   33 brazen (1) brass (2) bold.   breath of parley i.e.,
call for a conference   34 his ruined ears i.e., its (the castle's) ancient
and battered loopholes   40 my banishment repealed the revocation
of my banishment   41 lands restored again the restoration of my
lands   42 advantage of my power superiority of my army   46 is is
that   48 stooping duty submissive kneeling

52 tottered in tottering condition, or dilapidated   53 fair appointments handsome show of military preparedness   56 fire and water
i.e., lightning and rain   59–60 whilst . . . waters while I moisten the
earth with my tears   61.2 parley trumpet summons to a negotiation.
61.4 on the walls i.e., in the gallery of the tiring-house, above, to the
rear of the stage   63 blushing i.e., turning red with anger   65 he i.e.,
the sun.   envious hostile   67 occident west.   68 Yet Still, or nevertheless.   he i.e., King Richard   69 lightens forth flashes out, like
lightning   73 watch wait for   76 awful reverential, full of awe
77 hand signature   79 no . . . bone no human hand   81 Unless he do
profane without committing sacrilege   83 Have . . . us have imper-
iled their souls by turning traitor to me   84 And and that
85 know know that

Armies of pestilence; and they shall strike
Your children yet unborn and unbegot,
That lift your vassal hands against my head   89
And threat the glory of my precious crown.   90
Tell Bolingbroke—for yon methinks he stands—
That every stride he makes upon my land
Is dangerous treason. He is come to open   93
The purple testament of bleeding war;   94
But ere the crown he looks for live in peace,
Ten thousand bloody crowns of mothers' sons   96
Shall ill become the flower of England's face,   97
Change the complexion of her maid-pale peace   98
To scarlet indignation, and bedew
Her pastures' grass with faithful English blood.

NORTHUMBERLAND
The King of heaven forbid our lord the King
Should so with civil and uncivil arms   102
Be rushed upon! Thy thrice-noble cousin
Harry Bolingbroke doth humbly kiss thy hand;
And by the honorable tomb he swears
That stands upon your royal grandsire's bones,
And by the royalties of both your bloods,
Currents that spring from one most gracious head,   108
And by the buried hand of warlike Gaunt,
And by the worth and honor of himself,
Comprising all that may be sworn or said,
His coming hither hath no further scope   112
Than for his lineal royalties, and to beg   113
Enfranchisement immediate on his knees;   114
Which on thy royal party granted once,   115
His glittering arms he will commend to rust,   116
His barbèd steeds to stables, and his heart   117
To faithful service of Your Majesty.
This swears he, as he is a prince and just,
And as I am a gentleman I credit him.

KING RICHARD
Northumberland, say thus the King returns: 121
His noble cousin is right welcome hither,
And all the number of his fair demands
Shall be accomplished without contradiction.   124
With all the gracious utterance thou hast
Speak to his gentle hearing kind commends.   126
        [*Northumberland and attendants retire to Bolingbroke
                                        and York.*]

[*To Aumerle*] We do debase ourself, cousin, do we not,
To look so poorly and to speak so fair?   128
Shall we call back Northumberland, and send
Defiance to the traitor, and so die?

AUMERLE
No, good my lord. Let's fight with gentle words
Till time lend friends, and friends their helpful swords.

KING RICHARD
Oh, God, oh, God, that e'er this tongue of mine,
That laid the sentence of dread banishment
On yon proud man, should take it off again
With words of sooth! Oh, that I were as great   136
As is my grief, or lesser than my name!
Or that I could forget what I have been,
Or not remember what I must be now!
Swell'st thou, proud heart? I'll give thee scope to beat, 140
Since foes have scope to beat both thee and me.   141
        [*Northumberland returns to the castle walls.*]

AUMERLE
Northumberland comes back from Bolingbroke.

KING RICHARD
What must the King do now? Must he submit?
The King shall do it. Must he be deposed?
The King shall be contented. Must he lose
The name of king? I' God's name, let it go.
I'll give my jewels for a set of beads,   147
My gorgeous palace for a hermitage,
My gay apparel for an almsman's gown,   149
My figured goblets for a dish of wood,   150
My scepter for a palmer's walking-staff,   151
My subjects for a pair of carvèd saints,
And my large kingdom for a little grave,
A little, little grave, an obscure grave;
Or I'll be buried in the King's highway,
Some way of common trade, where subjects' feet   156
May hourly trample on their sovereign's head;
For on my heart they tread now whilst I live,
And, buried once, why not upon my head?   159
Aumerle, thou weep'st, my tenderhearted cousin.
We'll make foul weather with despisèd tears;
Our sighs and they shall lodge the summer corn   162
And make a dearth in this revolting land.   163
Or shall we play the wantons with our woes   164
And make some pretty match with shedding tears?   165
As thus, to drop them still upon one place,   166
Till they have fretted us a pair of graves   167
Within the earth; and, therein laid, there lies
Two kinsmen digged their graves with weeping eyes.   169
Would not this ill do well? Well, well, I see
I talk but idly, and you laugh at me.—
Most mighty prince, my lord Northumberland,
What says King Bolingbroke? Will His Majesty
Give Richard leave to live till Richard die?
You make a leg, and Bolingbroke says ay.   175

---

89 That of you that.   **vassal** subject   **90 threat** threaten   **93–4 open
. . . testament** initiate a bloodstained legacy. (Blood was often said to
be purple.)   **96–7 Ten . . . face** the bloody heads of 10,000 young men
(the flower of England) will disfigure the blossoming face of our
country   **98 maid-pale** i.e., pale like the complexion of a young English maid   **102 civil** used in civil strife.   **uncivil** barbarous, violent
108 head source   **112 scope** purpose, aim   **113 lineal royalties**
hereditary rights as one of royal blood   **114 Enfranchisement** freedom (from banishment)   **115 party** part   **116 commend** give over
117 barbèd armored   **121 returns** answers   **124 accomplished** fulfilled   **126 commends** regards.   **128 poorly** abject.   **fair** courteously.

136 sooth cajolery, flattery.   **140 scope** freedom, space   **141 scope**
capacity, opportunity   **147 set of beads** rosary   **149 almsman's
gown** plain attire of one who lives on alms or charity   **150 figured**
ornamented, embossed   **151 palmer's** pilgrim's   **156 trade** passage
159 buried once once I am buried   **162 Our . . . corn** our sighs and
tears will beat down the summer grain fields   **163 revolting**
rebelling   **164 play the wantons** sport, frolic   **165 match** game, contest   **166 still** continually   **167 fretted us** eaten away for us, worn.
(With a play on "complained.")   **169 digged** who dug   **175 a leg** an
obeisance

NORTHUMBERLAND
My lord, in the base court he doth attend   176
To speak with you, may it please you to come down.   177
KING RICHARD
Down, down I come, like glistering Phaëton,   178
Wanting the manage of unruly jades.   179
In the base court? Base court, where kings grow base,
To come at traitors' calls and do them grace.   181
In the base court? Come down? Down, court! Down,
    king!
For night owls shriek where mounting larks should
    sing.   [*Exeunt from above.*]

        [*Northumberland rejoins Bolingbroke.*]

BOLINGBROKE
What says His Majesty?
NORTHUMBERLAND   Sorrow and grief of heart
Makes him speak fondly, like a frantic man.   185
Yet he is come.

        [*Enter King Richard and his attendants below.*]

BOLINGBROKE   Stand all apart,   187
And show fair duty to His Majesty.   *He kneels down.*   188
My gracious lord!
KING RICHARD
Fair cousin, you debase your princely knee   190
To make the base earth proud with kissing it.   191
Me rather had my heart might feel your love   192
Than my unpleased eye see your courtesy.
Up, cousin, up. Your heart is up, I know,
Thus high at least [*touching his crown*], although your
    knee be low.
BOLINGBROKE [*rising*]
My gracious lord, I come but for mine own.
KING RICHARD
Your own is yours, and I am yours, and all.
BOLINGBROKE
So far be mine, my most redoubted lord,   198
As my true service shall deserve your love.
KING RICHARD
Well you deserve. They well deserve to have
That know the strong'st and surest way to get.
[*To York, who weeps*] Uncle, give me your hands. Nay,
    dry your eyes;
Tears show their love, but want their remedies.   203
[*To Bolingbroke*] Cousin, I am too young to be your
    father,   204

Though you are old enough to be my heir.
What you will have, I'll give, and willing too,
For do we must what force will have us do.
Set on towards London, cousin, is it so?
BOLINGBROKE
Yea, my good lord.
KING RICHARD   Then I must not say no.
                              [*Flourish. Exeunt.*]

                              ❧

[3.4]

        Enter the Queen with [two Ladies,] her attendants.

QUEEN
What sport shall we devise here in this garden,
To drive away the heavy thought of care?
LADY   Madam, we'll play at bowls.   3
QUEEN
'Twill make me think the world is full of rubs,   4
And that my fortune runs against the bias.   5
LADY   Madam, we'll dance.
QUEEN
My legs can keep no measure in delight   7
When my poor heart no measure keeps in grief.   8
Therefore, no dancing, girl; some other sport.
LADY   Madam, we'll tell tales.
QUEEN
Of sorrow or of joy?
LADY   Of either, madam.
QUEEN   Of neither, girl;
For if of joy, being altogether wanting,   13
It doth remember me the more of sorrow;   14
Or if of grief, being altogether had,
It adds more sorrow to my want of joy.
For what I have I need not to repeat,
And what I want it boots not to complain.   18
LADY
Madam, I'll sing.
QUEEN   'Tis well that thou hast cause,
But thou shouldst please me better wouldst thou
    weep.   20
LADY
I could weep, madam, would it do you good.
QUEEN
And I could sing, would weeping do me good,   22
And never borrow any tear of thee.   23

        Enter Gardeners [a Master and two Men].

But stay, here come the gardeners.
Let's step into the shadow of these trees.

---

176 **base court** outer or lower court of a castle   177 **may it please you**
if you please   178 **glistering** glistening, glittering. **Phaëton** son of
the sun-god, whose chariot he attempted to steer across the sky;
unable to control the horses of the sun, he was hurled from the chariot by Jupiter   179 **Wanting . . . jades** lacking the skill in horsemanship to control unruly nags.   181 **do them grace** (1) bow to them
(2) treat them graciously.   185 **fondly** foolishly. **frantic** mad
187 **apart** aside   188 **fair duty** respect   190–91 **debase . . . base** (Continues the wordplay on *base* in line 180.)   192 **Me rather had** I had
rather   198 **mine** i.e., my loved lord (changing Richard's meaning of
yours in the previous line).   **redoubted** dread   203 **want their remedies** lack remedies for what caused them.   204 **too young** (Historically, Richard and Bolingbroke were both thirty-three.)

3.4 Location: The Duke of York's garden.
3 **bowls**, lawn bowling. (A common Elizabethan game.)   4 **rubs**
impediments (in the game of bowls)   5 **against the bias** i.e., contrary,
athwart. (Literally, not following the naturally curved path of a bowl,
which was weighted on one side.)   7 **measure** a stately slow dance
8 **measure** moderation   13 **wanting** lacking   14 **remember** remind
18 **boots** helps   20 **wouldst thou** if you would   22 **would . . . good**
i.e., if weeping would make me any less unhappy   23 **never borrow**
never need to borrow

My wretchedness unto a row of pins,   26
They will talk of state, for everyone doth so   27
Against a change; woe is forerun with woe.   28
                          [*The Queen and Ladies stand apart.*]
GARDENER [*to one Man*]
Go bind thou up young dangling apricots
Which, like unruly children, make their sire
Stoop with oppression of their prodigal weight.   31
Give some supportance to the bending twigs.
[*To the other*] Go thou, and like an executioner
Cut off the heads of too-fast-growing sprays
That look too lofty in our commonwealth.
All must be even in our government.   36
You thus employed, I will go root away
The noisome weeds which without profit suck   38
The soil's fertility from wholesome flowers.
MAN
Why should we in the compass of a pale   40
Keep law and form and due proportion,
Showing as in a model our firm estate,   42
When our sea-wallèd garden, the whole land,
Is full of weeds, her fairest flowers choked up,
Her fruit trees all unpruned, her hedges ruined,
Her knots disordered, and her wholesome herbs   46
Swarming with caterpillars?
GARDENER   Hold thy peace.
He that hath suffered this disordered spring   48
Hath now himself met with the fall of leaf.   49
The weeds which his broad-spreading leaves did
     shelter,
That seemed in eating him to hold him up,   51
Are plucked up root and all by Bolingbroke:
I mean the Earl of Wiltshire, Bushy, Green.
MAN
What, are they dead?
GARDENER   They are; and Bolingbroke
Hath seized the wasteful King. Oh, what pity is it
That he had not so trimmed and dressed his land   56
As we this garden! We at time of year   57
Do wound the bark, the skin of our fruit trees,
Lest being overproud in sap and blood   59
With too much riches it confound itself;
Had he done so to great and growing men,
They might have lived to bear and he to taste
Their fruits of duty. Superfluous branches
We lop away, that bearing boughs may live;   64
Had he done so, himself had borne the crown   65
Which waste of idle hours hath quite thrown down.
MAN
What, think you the King shall be deposed?

GARDENER
Depressed he is already, and deposed   68
'Tis doubt he will be. Letters came last night   69
To a dear friend of the good Duke of York's,
That tell black tidings.
QUEEN [*coming forward*] Oh, I am pressed to death   71
Through want of speaking! Thou, old Adam's likeness,72
Set to dress this garden, how dares   73
Thy harsh rude tongue sound this unpleasing news?
What Eve, what serpent, hath suggested thee   75
To make a second fall of cursèd man?
Why dost thou say King Richard is deposed?
Dar'st thou, thou little better thing than earth,
Divine his downfall? Say where, when, and how   79
Cam'st thou by this ill tidings? Speak, thou wretch.
GARDENER
Pardon me, madam. Little joy have I
To breathe this news, yet what I say is true.
King Richard, he is in the mighty hold
Of Bolingbroke. Their fortunes both are weighed:
In your lord's scale is nothing but himself
And some few vanities that make him light;
But in the balance of great Bolingbroke,
Besides himself, are all the English peers,
And with their odds he weighs King Richard down.
Post you to London and you will find it so;   90
I speak no more than everyone doth know.
QUEEN
Nimble mischance, that art so light of foot,
Doth not thy embassage belong to me,   93
And am I last that knows it? Oh, thou thinkest
To serve me last, that I may longest keep
Thy sorrow in my breast.—Come, ladies, go   96
To meet at London London's king in woe.
What, was I born to this, that my sad look
Should grace the triumph of great Bolingbroke?   99
Gard'ner, for telling me these news of woe,
Pray God the plants thou graft'st may never grow.
                                    Exit [*with Ladies*].
GARDENER
Poor queen! So that thy state might be no worse,   102
I would my skill were subject to thy curse.
Here did she fall a tear; here in this place   104
I'll set a bank of rue, sour herb of grace.   105
Rue even for ruth here shortly shall be seen,   106
In the remembrance of a weeping queen.   *Exeunt.*

❖

26 **My . . . pins** i.e., I'd bet my immeasurable grief against the merest trifle   **27 state** statecraft, politics   **28 Against . . . woe** when change is imminent; sad times are heralded by gloomy predictions. **31 prodigal** excessive   **36 even** equal   **38 noisome** harmful   **40 pale** enclosure, enclosed garden   **42 firm** stable   **46 knots** flower beds laid out in intricate designs   **48 suffered** allowed   **49 fall of leaf** i.e., autumn.   **51 in eating him** i.e., while they were really eating his sustenance   **56 dressed** put in order   **57 at . . . year** in the appropriate season   **59 overproud in** swollen with   **64 bearing** fruit-bearing **65 crown** (1) royal crown (2) crown of a tree

68 **Depressed** Brought low   **69 'Tis doubt** there is fear   **71 pressed to death** (Allusion to the *peine forte et dure*, inflicted by pressure of heavy weights upon the chests of indicted persons who refused to plead and remained silent.)   **72 old Adam** (In his role as the first gardener.)   **73 dress** cultivate   **75 suggested** tempted   **79 Divine** prophesy   **90 Post** Hasten. (See the note at 1.1.56.)   **93 embassage** message.   **belong to** concern   **96 Thy sorrow** the sorrow that you (mischance) report   **99 triumph** triumphal procession.   **Bolingbroke** (The original spelling, "Bullingbrooke," indicates the rhyme with *look* in the previous line, pronounced something like "bruke" and "luke.")   **102 So that** Provided that   **104 fall** let fall   **105 rue** "herb of grace," a plant symbolical of repentance, ruth, or sorrow for another's misery   **106 ruth** pity

[4.1]

Enter Bolingbroke with the Lords [Aumerle,
Northumberland, Harry Percy, Fitzwater, Surrey,
the Bishop of Carlisle, the Abbot of Westminster,
and another Lord, Herald, officers] to Parliament.
[The throne is provided on stage.]

BOLINGBROKE
Call forth Bagot.

Enter [officers with] Bagot.

Now, Bagot, freely speak thy mind,
What thou dost know of noble Gloucester's death,
Who wrought it with the King, and who performed   4
The bloody office of his timeless end.   5

BAGOT
Then set before my face the Lord Aumerle.

BOLINGBROKE [*to Aumerle*]
Cousin, stand forth, and look upon that man.
                    [*Aumerle comes forward.*]

BAGOT
My lord Aumerle, I know your daring tongue
Scorns to unsay what once it hath delivered.   9
In that dead time when Gloucester's death was plotted, 10
I heard you say, "Is not my arm of length,   11
That reacheth from the restful English court   12
As far as Calais, to mine uncle's head?"
Amongst much other talk that very time   14
I heard you say that you had rather refuse
The offer of an hundred thousand crowns
Than Bolingbroke's return to England—   17
Adding withal how blest this land would be   18
In this your cousin's death.

AUMERLE   Princes and noble lords,
What answer shall I make to this base man?
Shall I so much dishonor my fair stars   22
On equal terms to give him chastisement?   23
Either I must, or have mine honor soiled
With the attainder of his slanderous lips.   25
                    [*He throws down his gage.*]
There is my gage, the manual seal of death,   26
That marks thee out for hell. I say thou liest,
And will maintain what thou hast said is false
In thy heart-blood, though being all too base
To stain the temper of my knightly sword.

BOLINGBROKE
Bagot, forbear. Thou shalt not take it up.

AUMERLE
Excepting one, I would he were the best   32
In all this presence that hath moved me so.

FITZWATER [*throwing down a gage*]
If that thy valor stand on sympathy,   34
There is my gage, Aumerle, in gage to thine.   35
By that fair sun which shows me where thou stand'st,
I heard thee say, and vauntingly thou spak'st it, 37
That thou wert cause of noble Gloucester's death.
If thou deny'st it twenty times, thou liest,
And I will turn thy falsehood to the heart,   40
Where it was forgèd, with my rapier's point.

AUMERLE [*taking up the gage*]
Thou dar'st not, coward, live to see that day.

FITZWATER
Now, by my soul, I would it were this hour.

AUMERLE
Fitzwater, thou art damned to hell for this.

PERCY
Aumerle, thou liest. His honor is as true
In this appeal as thou art all unjust;   46
And that thou art so, there I throw my gage
                    [*throwing down a gage*]
To prove it on thee to the extremest point   48
Of mortal breathing. Seize it if thou dar'st.   49

AUMERLE [*taking up the gage*]
An if I do not, may my hands rot off   50
And never brandish more revengeful steel   51
Over the glittering helmet of my foe!

ANOTHER LORD [*throwing down a gage*]
I task the earth to the like, forsworn Aumerle,   53
And spur thee on with full as many lies   54
As may be holloed in thy treacherous ear
From sun to sun. There is my honor's pawn;   56
Engage it to the trial, if thou darest.   57

AUMERLE [*taking up the gage*]
Who sets me else? By heaven, I'll throw at all!   58
I have a thousand spirits in one breast
To answer twenty thousand such as you.

SURREY
My lord Fitzwater, I do remember well
The very time Aumerle and you did talk.

FITZWATER
'Tis very true. You were in presence then,   63
And you can witness with me this is true.

SURREY   As false, by heaven, as heaven itself is true.

FITZWATER
Surrey, thou liest.

SURREY   Dishonorable boy!
That lie shall lie so heavy on my sword

4.1 Location: Westminster Hall.
4 Who . . . King who prevailed upon the King to have the murder
performed **5 office** function. **timeless** untimely **9 unsay** deny,
take back. **delivered** reported. **10 dead** (1) deadly (2) dark, silent
11 of length long **12 restful** i.e., untroubled by Gloucester **14 that
very time** (An inconsistency; Gloucester's death occurred before Bolingbroke left England.) **17 Than . . . return** than have Bolingbroke
return **18 withal** in addition **22 stars** i.e., fortune, rank **23 On . . .
chastisement** as to challenge him as my equal. **25 attainder** dishonoring accusation **25.1 gage** usually a glove or a gauntlet (a mailed or
armored glove), as at 1.1.69 ff. **26 manual . . . death** death warrant
sealed by my hand

32 one i.e., Bolingbroke. **best** highest in rank **34 stand on sympathy** i.e., insists on correspondence of rank in your opponent **35 in gage**
engaged **37 vauntingly** boastfully **40 turn** turn back **46 appeal**
accusation. (As also in line 80.) **all unjust** totally false **48–9 to . . .
breathing** to the point of death. **50 An if** If **51 more** any more,
ever again **53 I . . . like** I burden the ground in the same way
54 lies accusations of lying **56 sun to sun** sunrise to sunset. **honor's
pawn** pledge of honor. (Also in line 71.) **57 Engage . . . trial** take it
up as a pledge to combat **58 Who . . . else?** Who else puts up stakes
against me or challenges me to a game? **throw** (1) throw dice (2)
throw down gages **63 in presence** present

That it shall render vengeance and revenge,   68
Till thou the lie-giver and that lie do lie
In earth as quiet as thy father's skull.
In proof whereof, there is my honor's pawn.
                                    [*He throws down a gage.*]
Engage it to the trial if thou dar'st.

FITZWATER [*taking up the gage*]
  How fondly dost thou spur a forward horse!   73
  If I dare eat, or drink, or breathe, or live,
  I dare meet Surrey in a wilderness   75
  And spit upon him whilst I say he lies,
  And lies, and lies. There is my bond of faith,
  To tie thee to my strong correction.
                                    [*He throws down a gage.*]
  As I intend to thrive in this new world,   79
  Aumerle is guilty of my true appeal.   80
  Besides, I heard the banished Norfolk say
  That thou, Aumerle, didst send two of thy men
  To execute the noble Duke at Calais.

AUMERLE
  Some honest Christian trust me with a gage.
                    [*He borrows a gage and throws it down.*]
  That Norfolk lies, here do I throw down this,
  If he may be repealed, to try his honor.   86

BOLINGBROKE
  These differences shall all rest under gage   87
  Till Norfolk be repealed. Repealed he shall be,
  And, though mine enemy, restored again
  To all his lands and seigniories. When he is returned,
  Against Aumerle we will enforce his trial.

CARLISLE
  That honorable day shall never be seen.
  Many a time hath banished Norfolk fought
  For Jesu Christ in glorious Christian field,
  Streaming the ensign of the Christian cross   95
  Against black pagans, Turks, and Saracens;
  And, toiled with works of war, retired himself   97
  To Italy, and there at Venice gave
  His body to that pleasant country's earth
  And his pure soul unto his captain, Christ,
  Under whose colors he had fought so long.

BOLINGBROKE   Why, Bishop, is Norfolk dead?
CARLISLE   As surely as I live, my lord.
BOLINGBROKE
  Sweet peace conduct his sweet soul to the bosom   104
  Of good old Abraham! Lords appellants,   105
  Your differences shall all rest under gage
  Till we assign you to your days of trial.   107

          Enter York.

YORK
  Great Duke of Lancaster, I come to thee
  From plume-plucked Richard, who with willing soul
  Adopts thee heir, and his high scepter yields
  To the possession of thy royal hand.
  Ascend his throne, descending now from him,
  And long live Henry, fourth of that name!

BOLINGBROKE
  In God's name, I'll ascend the regal throne.

CARLISLE   Marry, God forbid!
  Worst in this royal presence may I speak,   116
  Yet best beseeming me to speak the truth.   117
  Would God that any in this noble presence
  Were enough noble to be upright judge
  Of noble Richard! Then true noblesse would   120
  Learn him forbearance from so foul a wrong.   121
  What subject can give sentence on his king?
  And who sits here that is not Richard's subject?
  Thieves are not judged but they are by to hear,   124
  Although apparent guilt be seen in them;   125
  And shall the figure of God's majesty,   126
  His captain, steward, deputy elect,
  Anointed, crownèd, planted many years,
  Be judged by subject and inferior breath,
  And he himself not present? Oh, forfend it God   130
  That in a Christian climate souls refined   131
  Should show so heinous, black, obscene a deed!   132
  I speak to subjects, and a subject speaks,
  Stirred up by God thus boldly for his king.
  My lord of Hereford here, whom you call king,   135
  Is a foul traitor to proud Hereford's king.
  And if you crown him, let me prophesy:
  The blood of English shall manure the ground
  And future ages groan for this foul act;
  Peace shall go sleep with Turks and infidels,
  And in this seat of peace tumultuous wars
  Shall kin with kin and kind with kind confound;   142
  Disorder, horror, fear, and mutiny
  Shall here inhabit, and this land be called
  The field of Golgotha and dead men's skulls.   145
  Oh, if you raise this house against this house,   146
  It will the woefullest division prove
  That ever fell upon this cursèd earth.
  Prevent it, resist it, let it not be so,
  Lest child, child's children, cry against you woe!

NORTHUMBERLAND
  Well have you argued, sir, and for your pains
  Of capital treason we arrest you here.—   152

---

68 **it** i.e., my sword   73 **fondly** foolishly.   **forward** willing   75 **in a wilderness** i.e., where fighting might go on uninterrupted to the death   79 **in . . . world** i.e., under the new king   80 **appeal** accusation.   86 **repealed** recalled from exile.   **try** test   87 **under gage** as challenges   95 **Streaming** flying   97 **toiled** wearied   104–5 **bosom . . . Abraham** i.e., heaven. (See Luke 16:22.)   105 **Lords appellants** Lords who appear as formal accusers   107.1 *Enter York* (Probably Richard's scepter, etc., are brought in at line 162, but York here invites Bolingbroke to ascend the throne with the surrendered scepter, and so perhaps the regalia are brought on here.)

116 **Worst** Least in rank   117 **best beseeming me** i.e., most befitting to me as a clergyman   120 **noblesse** nobleness   121 **Learn him forbearance** teach him to forbear   124 **judged . . . by** condemned unless they are present   125 **apparent** manifest   126 **figure** image   130 **forfend** forbid   131 **souls refined** civilized people   132 **obscene** odious, repulsive   135 **My . . . Hereford** (Carlisle refuses to refer to Bolingbroke as king or even as Duke of Lancaster, since he lost the latter title at the time of his banishment.)   142 **Shall . . . confound** shall destroy kinsmen by means of kinsmen and fellow countrymen by means of fellow countrymen   145 **Golgotha** Calvary, the hill outside of Jerusalem called "the place of dead men's skulls" (see Mark 15:22 and John 19:17) where Jesus was crucified   146 **this house . . . this house** i.e., Lancaster against York. (See Mark 3:25.)   152 **Of** on a charge of

My lord of Westminster, be it your charge
To keep him safely till his day of trial.

[*Carlisle is taken into custody.*]

May it please you, lords, to grant the commons' suit? 155

BOLINGBROKE

Fetch hither Richard, that in common view
He may surrender; so we shall proceed   157
Without suspicion.

YORK   I will be his conduct.   *Exit.* 158

BOLINGBROKE

Lords, you that here are under our arrest,
Procure your sureties for your days of answer.   160
Little are we beholding to your love,   161
And little looked for at your helping hands.   162

*Enter Richard and York [with Officers bearing
the crown and regalia].*

KING RICHARD

Alack, why am I sent for to a king,
Before I have shook off the regal thoughts
Wherewith I reigned? I hardly yet have learned
To insinuate, flatter, bow, and bend my knee.
Give sorrow leave awhile to tutor me
To this submission. Yet I well remember
The favors of these men. Were they not mine?   169
Did they not sometime cry, "All hail!" to me?
So Judas did to Christ. But he, in twelve,
Found truth in all but one; I, in twelve thousand, none.
God save the King! Will no man say amen?
Am I both priest and clerk? Well then, amen.   174
God save the King, although I be not he;
And yet, amen, if heaven do think him me.
To do what service am I sent for hither?

YORK

To do that office of thine own good will
Which tired majesty did make thee offer:
The resignation of thy state and crown
To Henry Bolingbroke.

KING RICHARD

Give me the crown. [*He takes the crown.*] Here, cousin,
    seize the crown.
Here, cousin,
On this side my hand, and on that side thine.
Now is this golden crown like a deep well
That owes two buckets, filling one another,   186
The emptier ever dancing in the air,
The other down, unseen, and full of water.

That bucket down and full of tears am I,
Drinking my griefs, whilst you mount up on high.

BOLINGBROKE

I thought you had been willing to resign.

KING RICHARD

My crown I am, but still my griefs are mine.
You may my glories and my state depose,
But not my griefs; still am I king of those.

BOLINGBROKE

Part of your cares you give me with your crown.

KING RICHARD

Your cares set up do not pluck my cares down.   196
My care is loss of care, by old care done;   197
Your care is gain of care, by new care won.   198
The cares I give I have, though given away;   199
They 'tend the crown, yet still with me they stay. 200

BOLINGBROKE

Are you contented to resign the crown?

KING RICHARD

Ay, no; no, ay; for I must nothing be;   202
Therefore no, no, for I resign to thee.   203
Now mark me how I will undo myself: 204

[*He yields his crown and scepter.*]

I give this heavy weight from off my head
And this unwieldy scepter from my hand,
The pride of kingly sway from out my heart;
With mine own tears I wash away my balm,
With mine own hands I give away my crown,
With mine own tongue deny my sacred state,
With mine own breath release all duteous oaths. 211
All pomp and majesty I do forswear;
My manors, rents, revenues I forgo;
My acts, decrees, and statutes I deny.
God pardon all oaths that are broke to me!
God keep all vows unbroke are made to thee!   216
Make me, that nothing have, with nothing grieved, 217
And thou with all pleased, that hast all achieved!
Long mayst thou live in Richard's seat to sit,
And soon lie Richard in an earthy pit!
God save King Henry, unkinged Richard says,
And send him many years of sunshine days!—
What more remains?

NORTHUMBERLAND [*presenting a paper*]

                No more but that you read   223
These accusations and these grievous crimes
Committed by your person and your followers
Against the state and profit of this land;

---

155 **the commons' suit** request of the commons (i.e., that Richard be formally tried and the causes of his deposition made public. This line begins the abdication passage omitted in early quartos of the play.) 157 **surrender** i.e., surrender the crown, abdicate 158 **conduct** escort. 160 **sureties** persons who will guarantee your appearance. **your days of answer** the time when you must appear to stand trial. 161 **beholding** beholden, indebted 162 **little . . . hands** i.e., I did not expect this from you, thinking you were on our side. 169 **favors** (1) faces (2) support, good will 174 **priest and clerk** (In religious services, the clerk or assistant would say "Amen" to the priest's prayers.) 186 **owes** owns, has. **filling one another** (The raising of the full bucket lowers the other to be filled in turn.)

196–200 **Your . . . stay** i.e., Your assuming the cares of office does not assuage my griefs. My grief is loss of kingly responsibility, destroyed by a failure in diligence; your concern is gaining of kingly responsibility, won by zealous effort. The anxieties I transfer to you I also keep for myself, despite my giving them to you; they accompany the crown and yet still remain with me. 202 **Ay** (1) Yes (2) I. (But, says Richard, I am nothing, and therefore "Ay" is "I" or "nothing," that is, "no.") 203 **no, no . . . thee** (Richard plays on the logic that a double negative equals a positive; with an aural pun on *no/know*.) 204 **undo** (1) divest (2) unmake 211 **release . . . oaths** release my subjects from their oaths of duty. 216 **are** that are 217 **Make** i.e., May God make. **with nothing grieved** (1) grieved at nothing (2) grieved at having nothing 223 **read** i.e., read aloud

That, by confessing them, the souls of men
May deem that you are worthily deposed.

KING RICHARD
Must I do so? And must I ravel out   229
My weaved-up follies? Gentle Northumberland,
If thy offenses were upon record,
Would it not shame thee in so fair a troop   232
To read a lecture of them? If thou wouldst,   233
There shouldst thou find one heinous article
Containing the deposing of a king
And cracking the strong warrant of an oath,
Marked with a blot, damned in the book of heaven.   237
Nay, all of you that stand and look upon me,
Whilst that my wretchedness doth bait myself,   239
Though some of you, with Pilate, wash your hands,   240
Showing an outward pity, yet you Pilates
Have here delivered me to my sour cross,   242
And water cannot wash away your sin.

NORTHUMBERLAND
My lord, dispatch. Read o'er these articles.   244

KING RICHARD
Mine eyes are full of tears; I cannot see.
And yet salt water blinds them not so much
But they can see a sort of traitors here.   247
Nay, if I turn mine eyes upon myself,
I find myself a traitor with the rest;
For I have given here my soul's consent
T'undeck the pompous body of a king,   251
Made glory base and sovereignty a slave,
Proud majesty a subject, state a peasant.   253

NORTHUMBERLAND   My lord—

KING RICHARD
No lord of thine, thou haught insulting man,   255
Nor no man's lord. I have no name, no title,
No, not that name was given me at the font,
But 'tis usurped. Alack the heavy day,
That I have worn so many winters out
And know not now what name to call myself!
Oh, that I were a mockery king of snow,
Standing before the sun of Bolingbroke,
To melt myself away in water drops!
Good king, great king, and yet not greatly good,
An if my word be sterling yet in England,   265
Let it command a mirror hither straight,   266
That it may show me what a face I have,
Since it is bankrupt of his majesty.   268

BOLINGBROKE
Go some of you and fetch a looking glass.   269
                          [Exit an Attendant.]

NORTHUMBERLAND
Read o'er this paper while the glass doth come.

KING RICHARD
Fiend, thou torments me ere I come to hell!

BOLINGBROKE
Urge it no more, my lord Northumberland.

NORTHUMBERLAND
The commons will not then be satisfied.

KING RICHARD
They shall be satisfied. I'll read enough
When I do see the very book indeed
Where all my sins are writ, and that's myself.   276

          Enter one with a glass.

Give me that glass, and therein will I read.
                          [He takes the mirror.]
No deeper wrinkles yet? Hath sorrow struck
So many blows upon this face of mine,
And made no deeper wounds? O flattering glass,
Like to my followers in prosperity,   281
Thou dost beguile me! Was this face the face   282
That every day under his household roof
Did keep ten thousand men? Was this the face
That, like the sun, did make beholders wink?   285
Is this the face which faced so many follies,   286
That was at last outfaced by Bolingbroke?   287
A brittle glory shineth in this face—
As brittle as the glory is the face,
                          [He throws down the mirror.]
For there it is, cracked in an hundred shivers.
Mark, silent king, the moral of this sport:
How soon my sorrow hath destroyed my face.

BOLINGBROKE
The shadow of your sorrow hath destroyed   293
The shadow of your face.

KING RICHARD   Say that again.   294
The shadow of my sorrow? Ha! Let's see.
'Tis very true, my grief lies all within;
And these external manners of laments   297
Are merely shadows to the unseen grief   298
That swells with silence in the tortured soul.
There lies the substance; and I thank thee, King,   300
For thy great bounty, that not only giv'st   301
Me cause to wail, but teachest me the way
How to lament the cause. I'll beg one boon,   303
And then be gone and trouble you no more.
Shall I obtain it?

BOLINGBROKE   Name it, fair cousin.

KING RICHARD
"Fair cousin"? I am greater than a king.
For when I was a king, my flatterers
Were then but subjects; being now a subject,

---

229 **ravel out** unravel   232 **troop** company   233 **read a lecture** give a public reading (as a warning)   237 **Marked . . . damned** (Modifying *article* in line 234)   239 **bait** torment, harass (as in bearbaiting)   240 **wash your hands** (See Matthew 27:24. Richard persistently compares himself to Christ; see also 3.2.132; 4.1.171.)   242 **sour** bitter   244 **dispatch** conclude, be done.   247 **sort** gang   251 **pompous** stately, splendid   253 **state** high rank, stateliness   255 **haught** haughty   265 **An if** if.   **sterling** valid currency   266 **straight** immediately   268 **his** its   269 **some** i.e., someone

276.1 *glass* mirror.   281 **in prosperity** i.e., in my prosperity   282 **Was this face** (An echo of Christopher Marlowe's *Doctor Faustus*, 5.1, in which the protagonist addresses Helen of Troy.)   285 **wink** close the eyes, blink.   286 **faced** countenanced   287 **outfaced** stared down, discountenanced   293 **shadow** outward show, or, overshadowing nature   294 **shadow** reflection (in the mirror)   297 **manners** forms, manifestations   298 **shadows to** shadowings forth or embodiments of   300 **There** i.e., In my soul   301 **that** you who   303 **boon** favor

I have a king here to my flatterer.   309
Being so great, I have no need to beg.
BOLINGBROKE   Yet ask.
KING RICHARD   And shall I have?
BOLINGBROKE   You shall.
KING RICHARD   Then give me leave to go.
BOLINGBROKE   Whither?
KING RICHARD
Whither you will, so I were from your sights.
BOLINGBROKE
Go some of you, convey him to the Tower.   317
KING RICHARD
Oh, good! "Convey"? Conveyers are you all,   318
That rise thus nimbly by a true king's fall.
        [*Exeunt King Richard, some lords, and a guard.*]
BOLINGBROKE
On Wednesday next we solemnly set down
Our coronation. Lords, prepare yourselves.   321
        Exeunt. Manent [*the Abbot of*] *Westminster,* [*the*
                Bishop of] *Carlisle, Aumerle.*
ABBOT
A woeful pageant have we here beheld.
CARLISLE
The woe's to come, the children yet unborn
Shall feel this day as sharp to them as thorn.   324
AUMERLE
You holy clergymen, is there no plot
To rid the realm of this pernicious blot?
ABBOT   My lord,
Before I freely speak my mind herein,
You shall not only take the Sacrament
To bury mine intents, but also to effect   330
Whatever I shall happen to devise.
I see your brows are full of discontent,
Your hearts of sorrow, and your eyes of tears.
Come home with me to supper; I'll lay
A plot shall show us all a merry day.   *Exeunt.* 335

                        ❧

[5.1]

        Enter the Queen with [*Ladies,*] *her attendants.*

QUEEN
This way the King will come. This is the way
To Julius Caesar's ill-erected tower,   2
To whose flint bosom my condemnèd lord
Is doomed a prisoner by proud Bolingbroke.
Here let us rest, if this rebellious earth
Have any resting for her true king's queen.

        Enter Richard [*and guard*].

But soft, but see, or rather do not see
My fair rose wither. Yet look up, behold,

That you in pity may dissolve to dew,
And wash him fresh again with true-love tears.—
Ah, thou, the model where old Troy did stand,   11
Thou map of honor, thou King Richard's tomb,   12
And not King Richard! Thou most beauteous inn,   13
Why should hard-favored grief be lodged in thee   14
When triumph is become an alehouse guest?   15
KING RICHARD
Join not with grief, fair woman, do not so,
To make my end too sudden. Learn, good soul,   17
To think our former state a happy dream,
From which awaked, the truth of what we are
Shows us but this. I am sworn brother, sweet,
To grim Necessity, and he and I
Will keep a league till death. Hie thee to France,   22
And cloister thee in some religious house.   23
Our holy lives must win a new world's crown,   24
Which our profane hours here have thrown down.
QUEEN
What, is my Richard both in shape and mind
Transformed and weakened? Hath Bolingbroke
Deposed thine intellect? Hath he been in thy heart?
The lion dying thrusteth forth his paw
And wounds the earth, if nothing else, with rage
To be o'erpowered; and wilt thou, pupil-like,   31
Take the correction, mildly kiss the rod,
And fawn on rage with base humility,
Which art a lion and the king of beasts?   34
KING RICHARD
A king of beasts, indeed! If aught but beasts,   35
I had been still a happy king of men.
Good sometimes queen, prepare thee hence for France.   37
Think I am dead and that even here thou takest,
As from my deathbed, thy last living leave.
In winter's tedious nights sit by the fire
With good old folks, and let them tell thee tales
Of woeful ages long ago betid;   42
And ere thou bid good night, to quit their griefs   43
Tell thou the lamentable tale of me
And send the hearers weeping to their beds;
Forwhy the senseless brands will sympathize   46
The heavy accent of thy moving tongue,   47
And in compassion weep the fire out;
And some will mourn in ashes, some coal-black,   49
For the deposing of a rightful king.

        Enter Northumberland [*attended*].

---

309 **to** as   317 **convey** escort   318 **Convey** Steal.   321.1 *Manent*
They remain onstage   324 **Shall** who will   330 **To . . . intents** to conceal my plans   335 **shall** that shall
5.1 Location: London. A street leading to the Tower.
2 **Julius . . . tower** (The Tower of London, ascribed by tradition to
Julius Caesar, was built by William the Conqueror to hold the city in
subordination.)   **ill-erected** erected for evil ends or with evil results

11 **thou . . . stand** i.e., you ruined majesty, pattern of fallen greatness
like the desolate waste where Troy once stood   12 **map of honor** i.e.,
the mere outline of a once-glorious honor   13 **inn** residence, house
14 **hard-favored** unpleasant-looking   15 **is . . . guest** lodges in such a
vulgar tavern (i.e., in Bolingbroke).   17 **To . . . sudden** to kill me
quickly with grief.   22 **Hie** Hasten   23 **religious house** convent.
24 **new world's** heaven's   31 **To be** at being   34 **Which art** you who
are   35 **king of beasts** (1) lion (2) ruler over beastly men   37 **sometimes** former   42 **Of . . . betid** of woe that happened ages ago
43 **quit their griefs** requite their tales of woe   46–7 **Forwhy . . .
tongue** because even the inanimate and unfeeling firebrands will
respond to the doleful tone of your affecting tale   49 **And . . . coal-
black** and some of the brands will heap ashes on themselves like
grieving mourners and turn black with charring as though dressing
themselves in the black of mourning

NORTHUMBERLAND
My lord, the mind of Bolingbroke is changed;
You must to Pomfret, not unto the Tower.   52
And, madam, there is order ta'en for you: 53
With all swift speed you must away to France.

KING RICHARD
Northumberland, thou ladder wherewithal
The mounting Bolingbroke ascends my throne,
The time shall not be many hours of age
More than it is ere foul sin, gathering head,   58
Shall break into corruption. Thou shalt think,   59
Though he divide the realm and give thee half,
It is too little, helping him to all;   61
He shall think that thou, which knowest the way
To plant unrightful kings, wilt know again,
Being ne'er so little urged another way,   64
To pluck him headlong from the usurpèd throne.   65
The love of wicked men converts to fear,   66
That fear to hate, and hate turns one or both   67
To worthy danger and deservèd death.   68

NORTHUMBERLAND
My guilt be on my head, and there an end.   69
Take leave and part, for you must part forthwith.   70

KING RICHARD
Doubly divorced! Bad men, you violate
A twofold marriage, twixt my crown and me,
And then betwixt me and my married wife.
[To Queen] Let me unkiss the oath twixt thee and me;   74
And yet not so, for with a kiss 'twas made.—
Part us, Northumberland: I towards the north,
Where shivering cold and sickness pines the clime;   77
My wife to France, from whence, set forth in pomp,
She came adornèd hither like sweet May,
Sent back like Hallowmas or short'st of day.   80

QUEEN
And must we be divided? Must we part?

KING RICHARD
Ay, hand from hand, my love, and heart from heart.

QUEEN [to Northumberland]
Banish us both and send the King with me.

NORTHUMBERLAND
That were some love, but little policy.   84

QUEEN
Then whither he goes, thither let me go.

KING RICHARD
So two, together weeping, make one woe.
Weep thou for me in France, I for thee here;
Better far off than, near, be ne'er the near.   88

Go count thy way with sighs, I mine with groans.

QUEEN
So longest way shall have the longest moans.   90

KING RICHARD
Twice for one step I'll groan, the way being short,
And piece the way out with a heavy heart.   92
Come, come, in wooing sorrow let's be brief,
Since, wedding it, there is such length in grief.   94
One kiss shall stop our mouths, and dumbly part;   95
Thus give I mine, and thus take I thy heart.
[They kiss.]

QUEEN
Give me mine own again. 'Twere no good part   97
To take on me to keep and kill thy heart.   [They kiss.]   98
So, now I have mine own again, begone,
That I may strive to kill it with a groan.

KING RICHARD
We make woe wanton with this fond delay.   101
Once more, adieu! The rest let sorrow say.
Exeunt [in two separate groups].

❧

[5.2]

Enter Duke of York and the Duchess.

DUCHESS
My lord, you told me you would tell the rest,
When weeping made you break the story off,
Of our two cousins coming into London.   3

YORK
Where did I leave?

DUCHESS   At that sad stop, my lord,   4
Where rude misgoverned hands from windows' tops   5
Threw dust and rubbish on King Richard's head.

YORK
Then, as I said, the Duke, great Bolingbroke,
Mounted upon a hot and fiery steed
Which his aspiring rider seemed to know,   9
With slow but stately pace kept on his course,
Whilst all tongues cried, "God save thee, Bolingbroke!"
You would have thought the very windows spake,
So many greedy looks of young and old
Through casements darted their desiring eyes
Upon his visage, and that all the walls
With painted imagery had said at once,   16
"Jesu preserve thee! Welcome, Bolingbroke!"

---

52 **Pomfret** Pontefract Castle in Yorkshire   53 **order ta'en** arrangement made   58 **gathering head** gathering to a head   59 **corruption** putrid matter, pus.   61 **helping** since you helped   64 **Being . . . way** though scarcely urged at all   65 **To** how to   66 **converts** changes   67 **That fear** i.e., that fear changes.   **one or both** i.e., the new king or his partner, or both   68 **worthy** well-merited   69 **and . . . end** and let the topic be closed on that note.   70 **part . . . part** separate . . . depart   74 **unkiss** annul with a kiss (regarded as the seal of a ceremonial bond)   77 **pines the clime** afflicts the climate   80 **Hallowmas** All Saints' Day (November 1), regarded as the beginning of winter.   **short'st of day** the winter solstice.   84 **policy** political practicality.   88 **better . . . the near** i.e., better to be far apart than near and yet unable to meet. (The second *near* means "nearer.")

90 **So . . . moans** i.e., Then I will have to sigh and groan more than you, since my journey is longer.   92 **piece . . . out** make the journey seem longer   94 **Since . . . grief** i.e., since wedding ourselves to grief, we embark on a sadness that is only beginning. (A wry joke on the commonplace that a brief and romantic courtship is often the prelude to an interminable marriage.)   95 **and dumbly part** and then let us part in silence   97–8 **'Twere . . . me** It would not be wise of me to take it upon myself   101 **We . . . wanton** We sport with our grief.   **fond** (1) loving (2) pointless, foolish
5.2 Location: The Duke of York's house.
3 **cousins** kinsmen, i.e., nephews (Richard and Bolingbroke)   4 **leave** leave off.   5 **misgoverned** unruly.   **windows' tops** upper windows   9 **Which . . . know** which seemed to know its ambitious rider
16 **With painted imagery** i.e., showing crowds of people, as on a tapestry or painted cloth, depicting a procession.   **at once** all together

Whilst he, from the one side to the other turning,
Bareheaded, lower than his proud steed's neck,   19
Bespake them thus: "I thank you, countrymen."   20
And thus still doing, thus he passed along.   21

DUCHESS
Alack, poor Richard! Where rode he the whilst?

YORK
As in a theater the eyes of men,
After a well-graced actor leaves the stage,
Are idly bent on him that enters next,   25
Thinking his prattle to be tedious,
Even so, or with much more contempt, men's eyes
Did scowl on gentle Richard. No man cried, "God
  save him!"
No joyful tongue gave him his welcome home,
But dust was thrown upon his sacred head—
Which with such gentle sorrow he shook off,
His face still combating with tears and smiles,
The badges of his grief and patience,   33
That had not God for some strong purpose steeled
The hearts of men, they must perforce have melted,   35
And barbarism itself have pitied him.
But heaven hath a hand in these events,
To whose high will we bound our calm contents.   38
To Bolingbroke are we sworn subjects now,
Whose state and honor I for aye allow.   40

    [Enter Aumerle.]

DUCHESS
Here comes my son Aumerle.

YORK   Aumerle that was;   41
But that is lost for being Richard's friend,
And, madam, you must call him Rutland now.
I am in Parliament pledge for his truth   44
And lasting fealty to the new-made king.

DUCHESS
Welcome, my son. Who are the violets now   46
That strew the green lap of the new-come spring?   47

AUMERLE
Madam, I know not, nor I greatly care not.
God knows I had as lief be none as one.   49

YORK
Well, bear you well in this new spring of time,   50
Lest you be cropped before you come to prime.   51
What news from Oxford? Do these jousts and triumphs
  hold?   52

AUMERLE   For aught I know, my lord, they do.

YORK   You will be there, I know.

AUMERLE
If God prevent not, I purpose so.

YORK
What seal is that, that hangs without thy bosom?   56
Yea, look'st thou pale? Let me see the writing.

AUMERLE
My lord, 'tis nothing.

YORK   No matter, then, who see it.
I will be satisfied. Let me see the writing.

AUMERLE
I do beseech Your Grace to pardon me.   60
It is a matter of small consequence,
Which for some reasons I would not have seen.   62

YORK
Which for some reasons, sir, I mean to see.
I fear, I fear—

DUCHESS   What should you fear?
'Tis nothing but some bond that he is entered into
For gay apparel 'gainst the triumph day.   66

YORK
Bound to himself? What doth he with a bond   67
That he is bound to? Wife, thou art a fool.—   68
Boy, let me see the writing.

AUMERLE
I do beseech you, pardon me. I may not show it.

YORK
I will be satisfied. Let me see it, I say.
          He plucks it out of his bosom and reads it.
Treason! Foul treason! Villain! Traitor! Slave!

DUCHESS   What is the matter, my lord?

YORK [*calling offstage*]   Ho! Who is within there?

    [*Enter a Servingman.*]

                                        Saddle my horse!—
God for his mercy, what treachery is here?   75

DUCHESS   Why, what is it, my lord?

YORK [*to the Servingman*]
Give me my boots, I say! Saddle my horse!—
                                        [*Exit Servingman.*]
Now, by mine honor, by my life, my troth,   78
I will appeach the villain.

DUCHESS   What is the matter?   79

YORK
Peace, foolish woman.

DUCHESS
I will not peace. What is the matter, Aumerle?

AUMERLE
Good mother, be content. It is no more
Than my poor life must answer.

DUCHESS   Thy life answer?

---

19 lower bowing lower   **20 Bespake** addressed   **21 still** continually
25 idly indifferently   **33 badges** insignia, outward signs   **35 perforce** necessarily   **38 we . . . contents** i.e., we bind ourselves to be
calmly content.   **40 state** i.e., royal title.   **allow** acknowledge.
41 Aumerle that was (Aumerle, as a member of Richard's party, lost
his dukedom, though he remained Earl of Rutland.)   **44 pledge** the
guarantor.   **truth** loyalty   **46–7 Who . . . spring** i.e., Who are the
favorites of the new king?   **49 I had . . . one** I'd be just as glad to be
left out as to be a favorite at court.   **50 bear you** bear yourself
51 cropped plucked, i.e., beheaded   **52 Do . . . hold?** Are those tourneys and pageants going forward? (According to Holinshed, these
tourneys at Oxford were part of a conspiracy against Bolingbroke by
the Abbot of Westminster and others; the new king was to be invited
to attend and there be assassinated.)

56 seal i.e., seal attached to the border of a document   **60 pardon me**
i.e., excuse me if I don't comply.   **62 have seen** wish to be seen.
66 'gainst in anticipation of   **67–8 What . . . bound to?** i.e., Why
should *he* have the bond instead of the creditor to whom the debt is
owed?   **75 God** i.e., I pray God   **78 troth** faith, allegiance
79 appeach inform against, publicly accuse

YORK [*calling*]
Bring me my boots! I will unto the King.

His [Serving]man enters with his boots.

DUCHESS
Strike him, Aumerle. Poor boy, thou art amazed. 85
[*To the Servingman*] Hence, villain! Never more come
in my sight.
YORK   Give me my boots, I say.
[*The Servingman helps him on with his boots, and exit.*]
DUCHESS   Why, York, what wilt thou do?
Wilt thou not hide the trespass of thine own?
Have we more sons? Or are we like to have? 90
Is not my teeming date drunk up with time? 91
And wilt thou pluck my fair son from mine age
And rob me of a happy mother's name?
Is he not like thee? Is he not thine own?
YORK   Thou fond mad woman, 95
Wilt thou conceal this dark conspiracy?
A dozen of them here have ta'en the Sacrament, 97
And interchangeably set down their hands, 98
To kill the King at Oxford.
DUCHESS   He shall be none; 99
We'll keep him here. Then what is that to him? 100
YORK
Away, fond woman! Were he twenty times my son
I would appeach him.
DUCHESS   Hadst thou groaned for him 102
As I have done, thou wouldst be more pitiful. 103
But now I know thy mind. Thou dost suspect
That I have been disloyal to thy bed,
And that he is a bastard, not thy son.
Sweet York, sweet husband, be not of that mind!
He is as like thee as a man may be,
Not like to me, or any of my kin,
And yet I love him.
YORK   Make way, unruly woman! *Exit.*
DUCHESS
After, Aumerle! Mount thee upon his horse, 111
Spur post, and get before him to the King, 112
And beg thy pardon ere he do accuse thee.
I'll not be long behind. Though I be old,
I doubt not but to ride as fast as York.
And never will I rise up from the ground
Till Bolingbroke have pardoned thee. Away, begone!
[*Exeunt separately.*]

❖

[5.3]

*Enter [Bolingbroke, now] King [Henry], with his
nobles [Harry Percy and others].*

KING HENRY
Can no man tell me of my unthrifty son? 1
'Tis full three months since I did see him last.
If any plague hang over us, 'tis he.
I would to God, my lords, he might be found.
Inquire at London, 'mongst the taverns there,
For there, they say, he daily doth frequent
With unrestrainèd loose companions,
Even such, they say, as stand in narrow lanes
And beat our watch, and rob our passengers— 9
While he, young wanton and effeminate boy, 10
Takes on the point of honor to support 11
So dissolute a crew.
PERCY
My lord, some two days since I saw the Prince,
And told him of those triumphs held at Oxford. 14
KING HENRY   And what said the gallant?
PERCY
His answer was, he would unto the stews, 16
And from the common'st creature pluck a glove, 17
And wear it as a favor, and with that 18
He would unhorse the lustiest challenger. 19
KING HENRY
As dissolute as desperate! Yet through both
I see some sparks of better hope, which elder years
May happily bring forth. But who comes here? 22

Enter Aumerle, amazed.

AUMERLE   Where is the King?
KING HENRY
What means our cousin, that he stares and looks
So wildly?
AUMERLE
God save Your Grace! I do beseech Your Majesty
To have some conference with Your Grace alone.
KING HENRY [*to his nobles*]
Withdraw yourselves, and leave us here alone.
[*Exeunt Percy and lords.*]
What is the matter with our cousin now?
AUMERLE [*kneeling*]
Forever may my knees grow to the earth,
My tongue cleave to the roof within my mouth, 31
Unless a pardon ere I rise or speak.
KING HENRY
Intended or committed was this fault?
If on the first, how heinous e'er it be, 34

85 **Strike him** i.e., Strike the servant.   **amazed** confused, bewildered.
90 **Have we more sons?** (Historically, this Duchess of York was the
Duke's second wife and was not Aumerle's mother; she was, however, the mother of another son, Richard, subsequently Earl of Cambridge.)   91 **teeming date** period of childbearing   95 **fond** foolish
97–9 **A dozen . . . Oxford** ("Hereupon was an indenture sextipartite
made, sealed with their seals and signed with their hands, in the
which each stood bound to other, to do their whole endeavor for the
accomplishing of their purposed exploit." [Holinshed])
100 **that** i.e., the plot   102 **groaned for** i.e., given birth to. (But see
note, line 90.)   103 **pitiful** pitying.   111 **After** Go after him.   **his
horse** i.e., one of York's horses   112 **Spur post** ride as fast as possible

5.3 Location: The court (i.e., Windsor Castle).
1 **unthrifty** profligate   9 **watch** night watchmen.   **passengers**
passers-by, wayfarers   10 **wanton** pampered youth.   **effeminate**
self-indulgent   11 **Takes on** i.e., makes it a   14 **held** i.e., to be
held   16 **stews** brothels   17 **common'st** most promiscuous   18 **with
that** i.e., wearing that as a favor   19 **lustiest** most vigorous and brave
22 **happily** with good fortune.   **22.1** *amazed* distraught.   31 **My . . .
mouth** (See Psalm 137:6: "If I do not remember thee, let my tongue
cleave to the roof of my mouth.")   34 **If on the first** i.e., If intended
only

To win thy after-love I pardon thee.

AUMERLE [*rising*]
Then give me leave that I may turn the key,
That no man enter till my tale be done.

KING HENRY　Have thy desire.

　　　　　[*Aumerle locks the door.*] *The Duke of York*
　　　　　　　　　knocks at the door and crieth.

YORK [*within*]
My liege, beware! Look to thyself.
Thou hast a traitor in thy presence there.

KING HENRY [*drawing*]　Villain, I'll make thee safe.　41

AUMERLE
Stay thy revengeful hand. Thou hast no cause to fear.

YORK [*within*]
Open the door, secure, foolhardy King!　43
Shall I for love speak treason to thy face?　44
Open the door, or I will break it open.

　　　　　　　[*King Henry unlocks the door.*]

　　　　[*Enter York.*]

KING HENRY
What is the matter, uncle? Speak.
Recover breath; tell us how near is danger,
That we may arm us to encounter it.

YORK [*giving letter*]
Peruse this writing here, and thou shalt know
The treason that my haste forbids me show.　50

AUMERLE
Remember, as thou read'st, thy promise passed.
I do repent me. Read not my name there;
My heart is not confederate with my hand.　53

YORK
It was, villain, ere thy hand did set it down.
I tore it from the traitor's bosom, King;
Fear, and not love, begets his penitence.
Forget to pity him, lest thy pity prove　57
A serpent that will sting thee to the heart.

KING HENRY
Oh, heinous, strong, and bold conspiracy!
O loyal father of a treacherous son,
Thou sheer, immaculate, and silver fountain,　61
From whence this stream through muddy passages
Hath held his current and defiled himself,　63
Thy overflow of good converts to bad,　64
And thy abundant goodness shall excuse
This deadly blot in thy digressing son.　66

YORK
So shall my virtue be his vice's bawd,
And he shall spend mine honor with his shame,
As thriftless sons their scraping fathers' gold.　69

Mine honor lives when his dishonor dies,
Or my shamed life in his dishonor lies.　71
Thou kill'st me in his life; giving him breath,　72
The traitor lives, the true man's put to death.

DUCHESS [*within*]
What ho, my liege! For God's sake, let me in.

KING HENRY
What shrill-voiced suppliant makes this eager cry?

DUCHESS [*within*]
A woman, and thy aunt, great King. 'Tis I.
Speak with me, pity me, open the door!
A beggar begs that never begged before.

KING HENRY
Our scene is altered from a serious thing,
And now changed to "The Beggar and the King."　80
My dangerous cousin, let your mother in.
I know she is come to pray for your foul sin.

　　　[*Aumerle opens the door. Enter the Duchess. She
　　　kneels.*]

YORK
If thou do pardon whosoever pray,　83
More sins for this forgiveness prosper may.　84
This festered joint cut off, the rest rest sound;
This let alone will all the rest confound.　86

DUCHESS
O King, believe not this hardhearted man.
Love loving not itself, none other can.　88

YORK
Thou frantic woman, what dost thou make here?　89
Shall thy old dugs once more a traitor rear?　90

DUCHESS
Sweet York, be patient.—Hear me, gentle liege.

KING HENRY
Rise up, good aunt.

DUCHESS　　　　　　　Not yet, I thee beseech.
Forever will I walk upon my knees,
And never see day that the happy sees,　94
Till thou give joy, until thou bid me joy,
By pardoning Rutland, my transgressing boy.

AUMERLE [*kneeling*]
Unto my mother's prayers I bend my knee.　97

YORK [*kneeling*]
Against them both my true joints bended be.
Ill mayst thou thrive, if thou grant any grace!

DUCHESS
Pleads he in earnest? Look upon his face.
His eyes do drop no tears, his prayers are in jest;
His words come from his mouth, ours from our breast.
He prays but faintly and would be denied;

---

41 I'll . . . safe I'll make you harmless (by running you through).
43 secure unsuspecting, heedless　**44 speak . . . face** i.e., speak so disrespectfully as to call you *secure* and *foolhardy*.　**50 haste . . . show** i.e., breathlessness prevents me from revealing.　**53 hand** signature.
57 Forget Forget your promise　**61 sheer** clear, pure　**63 himself** (1) itself (2) himself, Aumerle　**64 Thy . . . bad** your excess of goodness changes to bad (in Aumerle)　**66 digressing** deviating from his proper course, transgressing　**69 scraping** parsimonious

71 in . . . lies will be hostage to his dishonorable conduct.　**72 in his life** if you permit him to live　**80 "The Beggar . . . King"** (Probably one of Shakespeare's many allusions to the ballad of King Cophetua and the Beggar Maid.)　**83 whosoever pray** anyone who presents a petition　**84 for** because of　**86 alone** untreated.　**confound** ruin.
88 Love . . . can i.e., He who does not love himself in his own son can love no one else, not even the King.　**89 make** do　**90 once . . . rear** i.e., give life again to a traitor by now redeeming Aumerle from death.　**94 And . . . sees** and never enjoy the happiness that those who are happy experience　**97 Unto** In support of

We pray with heart and soul and all beside.   104
His weary joints would gladly rise, I know;
Our knees still kneel till to the ground they grow.   106
His prayers are full of false hypocrisy,
Ours of true zeal and deep integrity.
Our prayers do outpray his; then let them have
That mercy which true prayer ought to have.

KING HENRY
Good aunt, stand up.

DUCHESS   Nay, do not say "stand up."
Say "pardon" first, and afterwards "stand up."
An if I were thy nurse, thy tongue to teach,   113
"Pardon" should be the first word of thy speech.
I never longed to hear a word till now;
Say "pardon," King; let pity teach thee how.
The word is short, but not so short as sweet;
No word like "pardon" for kings' mouths so meet.

YORK
Speak it in French, King: say "pardonne moy."   119

DUCHESS
Dost thou teach pardon pardon to destroy?
Ah, my sour husband, my hardhearted lord,
That sets the word itself against the word!
Speak "pardon" as 'tis current in our land;
The chopping French we do not understand.   124
Thine eye begins to speak; set thy tongue there,
Or in thy piteous heart plant thou thine ear,
That hearing how our plaints and prayers do pierce,
Pity may move thee "pardon" to rehearse.   128

KING HENRY
Good aunt, stand up.

DUCHESS   I do not sue to stand.
Pardon is all the suit I have in hand.

KING HENRY
I pardon him, as God shall pardon me.

DUCHESS
Oh, happy vantage of a kneeling knee!   132
Yet am I sick for fear. Speak it again;
Twice saying "pardon" doth not pardon twain
But makes one pardon strong.

KING HENRY   With all my heart
I pardon him.   [All rise.]

DUCHESS   A god on earth thou art.

KING HENRY
But for our trusty brother-in-law and the Abbot,   137
With all the rest of that consorted crew,   138
Destruction straight shall dog them at the heels.
Good uncle, help to order several powers   140
To Oxford, or where'er these traitors are.
They shall not live within this world, I swear,
But I will have them, if I once know where.
Uncle, farewell, and, cousin, adieu.

Your mother well hath prayed; and prove you true.   145

DUCHESS
Come, my old son. I pray God make thee new.   146
           Exeunt [in two groups].

❖

[5.4]

Enter Sir Pierce [of] Exton [and his Men].

EXTON
Didst thou not mark the King, what words he spake,
"Have I no friend will rid me of this living fear?"   2
Was it not so?

MAN   These were his very words.

EXTON
"Have I no friend?" quoth he. He spake it twice,
And urged it twice together, did he not?

MAN   He did.

EXTON
And speaking it, he wishtly looked on me,   7
As who should say, "I would thou wert the man   8
That would divorce this terror from my heart"—
Meaning the King at Pomfret. Come, let's go.
I am the King's friend, and will rid his foe.   11
           [*Exeunt.*]

❖

[5.5]

Enter Richard alone.

KING RICHARD
I have been studying how I may compare
This prison where I live unto the world;
And, for because the world is populous,   3
And here is not a creature but myself,
I cannot do it. Yet I'll hammer it out.   5
My brain I'll prove the female to my soul,
My soul the father, and these two beget
A generation of still-breeding thoughts;   8
And these same thoughts people this little world,   9
In humors like the people of this world,   10
For no thought is contented. The better sort,
As thoughts of things divine, are intermixed   12
With scruples and do set the word itself   13
Against the word, as thus, "Come, little ones,"   14
And then again,
"It is as hard to come as for a camel
To thread the postern of a small needle's eye."   17

---

145 prove you true may you prove loyal.   **146 old** unregenerate
**5.4 Location: The court. The opening stage direction in the Quarto
reads** *Manet Sir Pierce Exton, etc.,* **suggesting continuity of action
with the preceding scene.**
2 will who will   **7 wishtly** intently   **8 As . . . say** as if to say   **11 rid**
rid him of
5.5 Location: Pomfret Castle. A dungeon.
3 for because because   **5 hammer** i.e., work, puzzle   **8 still-breeding**
constantly breeding   **9 this little world** myself and this prison as a
microcosm of the world   **10 humors** temperaments, peculiar fancies
12 As such as   **13 scruples** doubts   **13–14 do set . . . word** i.e., oppose
one scriptural passage against its apparent opposite   **14–17 Come . . .
eye** (See Matthew 19:14, 24.)   **17 postern** narrow gate

104 beside besides.   **106 still** continually   **113 An if** If   **119 pardonne moy** *pardonnez-moi,* excuse me. (An affectedly polite refusal.)
124 chopping logic chopping, changing the sense   **128 rehearse** pronounce.   **132 happy vantage** fortunate gain   **137 But for** But as for.
brother-in-law i.e., John Holland, Earl of Huntingdon and Duke of
Exeter, who had married Bolingbroke's sister (see 2.1.281 and note).
Abbot Abbot of Westminster; see 4.1.321–34   **138 consorted** conspiring, confederate   **140 powers** forces

Thoughts tending to ambition, they do plot
Unlikely wonders—how these vain weak nails
May tear a passage through the flinty ribs
Of this hard world, my ragged prison walls, 21
And, for they cannot, die in their own pride. 22
Thoughts tending to content flatter themselves 23
That they are not the first of fortune's slaves,
Nor shall not be the last—like seely beggars 25
Who, sitting in the stocks, refuge their shame 26
That many have and others must sit there;
And in this thought they find a kind of ease,
Bearing their own misfortunes on the back
Of such as have before endured the like.
Thus play I in one person many people,
And none contented. Sometimes am I king;
Then treason makes me wish myself a beggar, 33
And so I am. Then crushing penury 34
Persuades me I was better when a king;
Then am I kinged again, and by and by
Think that I am unkinged by Bolingbroke,
And straight am nothing. But whate'er I be,
Nor I, nor any man that but man is, 39
With nothing shall be pleased till he be eased 40
With being nothing. (*The music plays.*) Music do I
　hear? 41
Ha, ha, keep time! How sour sweet music is,
When time is broke and no proportion kept!
So is it in the music of men's lives.
And here have I the daintiness of ear
To check time broke in a disordered string, 46
But for the concord of my state and time
Had not an ear to hear my true time broke.
I wasted time, and now doth time waste me;
For now hath Time made me his numb'ring clock. 50
My thoughts are minutes, and with sighs they jar 51
Their watches on unto mine eyes, the outward watch 52
Whereto my finger, like a dial's point, 53
Is pointing still in cleansing them from tears.
Now sir, the sounds that tell what hour it is
Are clamorous groans that strike upon my heart,
Which is the bell. So sighs and tears and groans
Show minutes, hours, and times. But my time 58
Runs posting on in Bolingbroke's proud joy, 59
While I stand fooling here, his jack of the clock. 60
This music mads me. Let it sound no more, 61
For though it have holp madmen to their wits, 62

In me it seems it will make wise men mad.
　　　　　　　　　　　　[*The music ceases.*]
Yet blessing on his heart that gives it me!
For 'tis a sign of love; and love to Richard
Is a strange brooch in this all-hating world. 66

Enter a Groom of the stable.

GROOM
Hail, royal prince!
KING RICHARD　　　　Thanks, noble peer.
The cheapest of us is ten groats too dear. 68
What art thou, and how comest thou hither,
Where no man never comes but that sad dog
That brings me food to make misfortune live?
GROOM
I was a poor groom of thy stable, King,
When thou wert king; who, traveling towards York,
With much ado at length have gotten leave
To look upon my sometimes royal master's face. 75
Oh, how it earned my heart when I beheld 76
In London streets, that coronation day,
When Bolingbroke rode on roan Barbary,
That horse that thou so often hast bestrid,
That horse that I so carefully have dressed! 80
KING RICHARD
Rode he on Barbary? Tell me, gentle friend,
How went he under him?
GROOM
So proudly as if he disdained the ground.
KING RICHARD
So proud that Bolingbroke was on his back!
That jade hath eat bread from my royal hand; 85
This hand hath made him proud with clapping him. 86
Would he not stumble? Would he not fall down,
Since pride must have a fall, and break the neck
Of that proud man that did usurp his back?
Forgiveness, horse! Why do I rail on thee,
Since thou, created to be awed by man,
Wast born to bear? I was not made a horse,
And yet I bear a burden like an ass,
Spurred, galled, and tired by jauncing Bolingbroke. 94

Enter one [a Keeper] to Richard with meat.

KEEPER [*to Groom*]
Fellow, give place. Here is no longer stay.
KING RICHARD [*to Groom*]
If thou love me, 'tis time thou wert away.
GROOM
What my tongue dares not, that my heart shall say.
　　　　　　　　　　　　　Exit Groom.

21 **ragged** rugged　22 **for** because.　**pride** prime.　23 **content** contentment　25 **seely** simpleminded　26 **refuge their shame** i.e., seek refuge from their disgrace by reflecting　33 **treason** i.e., the thought of treason　34 **penury** poverty　39–41 **Nor . . . nothing** neither I nor any person alive can be fully satisfied with the things of this life until he or she is released by death.　46 **check** rebuke.　**string** stringed instrument　50 **numb'ring clock** i.e., a clock that numbers hours and minutes (not an hourglass).　51–2 **My . . . watch** My sad thoughts, occurring every minute, are parts of an inner clock that, by means of the sighs they provoke, transfer their cares to my eyes, the face of the clock　53 **dial's point** clock hand　58 **times** quarters and halves.　59 **posting** hastening　60 **jack of the clock** manikin that struck the bell on a clock.　61 **mads** maddens　62 **holp** helped

66 **strange brooch** rare jewel　68 **ten groats too dear** (There is a pun on *royal* and *noble* in the preceding lines. A royal (ten shillings) is worth ten groats (ten times four pence) more than a noble (six shillings, eight pence) is; hence, Richard is saying that he, "the cheapest of us" because he is a prisoner, is worth no more than the groom, whom he greets as his "noble peer.")　75 **sometimes** former　76 **earned** grieved　80 **dressed** tended, groomed.　85 **eat** eaten. (Pronounced "et.")　86 **clapping** patting, stroking　94 **galled** made sore.　**jauncing** prancing, hard-riding.　94.1 *meat* food.

KEEPER
My lord, will't please you to fall to?

KING RICHARD
Taste of it first, as thou art wont to do.   99

KEEPER
My lord, I dare not. Sir Pierce of Exton, who
Lately came from the King, commands the contrary.

KING RICHARD
The devil take Henry of Lancaster and thee!
Patience is stale, and I am weary of it.
                              [*He beats the Keeper.*]

KEEPER   Help, help, help!

                The murderers [Exton and his men] rush in.

KING RICHARD
How now, what means death in this rude assault?
Villain, thy own hand yields thy death's instrument.
          [*He snatches a weapon from a man and kills him.*]
Go thou, and fill another room in hell.   107
          [*He kills another.*] *Here Exton strikes him down.*
That hand shall burn in never-quenching fire
That staggers thus my person. Exton, thy fierce hand   109
Hath with the King's blood stained the King's own
     land.
Mount, mount, my soul! Thy seat is up on high,
Whilst my gross flesh sinks downward, here to die.
                              [*He dies.*]

EXTON
As full of valor as of royal blood.
Both have I spilled. Oh, would the deed were good!
For now the devil, that told me I did well,
Says that this deed is chronicled in hell.
This dead king to the living king I'll bear.
Take hence the rest, and give them burial here.
                              [*Exeunt, with the bodies.*]

                                ❖

[5.6]

          [*Flourish.*] *Enter Bolingbroke [as King], with the
          Duke of York, [other lords, and attendants].*

KING HENRY
Kind uncle York, the latest news we hear
Is that the rebels have consumed with fire
Our town of Ci'cester in Gloucestershire,   3
But whether they be ta'en or slain we hear not.

                Enter Northumberland.

Wecome, my lord. What is the news?

NORTHUMBERLAND
First, to thy sacred state wish I all happiness.
The next news is, I have to London sent

The heads of Salisbury, Spencer, Blunt, and Kent.
The manner of their taking may appear   9
At large discoursèd in this paper here.   10
                              [*He gives a paper.*]

KING HENRY
We thank thee, gentle Percy, for thy pains,
And to thy worth will add right worthy gains.   12

                Enter Lord Fitzwater.

FITZWATER
My lord, I have from Oxford sent to London
The heads of Brocas and Sir Bennet Seely,
Two of the dangerous consorted traitors   15
That sought at Oxford thy dire overthrow.

KING HENRY
Thy pains, Fitzwater, shall not be forgot;
Right noble is thy merit, well I wot.   18

          *Enter Henry Percy [with the Bishop of Carlisle,
          guarded].*

PERCY
The grand conspirator, Abbot of Westminster,   19
With clog of conscience and sour melancholy   20
Hath yielded up his body to the grave;
But here is Carlisle living, to abide   22
Thy kingly doom and sentence of his pride.   23

KING HENRY   Carlisle, this is your doom:
Choose out some secret place, some reverent room,   25
More than thou hast, and with it joy thy life.   26
So as thou liv'st in peace, die free from strife;   27
For though mine enemy thou hast ever been,
High sparks of honor in thee have I seen.

          Enter Exton, with [attendants bearing] the coffin.

EXTON
Great King, within this coffin I present
Thy buried fear. Herein all breathless lies
The mightiest of thy greatest enemies,
Richard of Bordeaux, by me hither brought.

KING HENRY
Exton, I thank thee not, for thou hast wrought
A deed of slander with thy fatal hand   35
Upon my head and all this famous land.

EXTON
From your own mouth, my lord, did I this deed.

KING HENRY
They love not poison that do poison need,
Nor do I thee. Though I did wish him dead,
I hate the murderer, love him murderèd.

---

99 **Taste . . . first** i.e., to ensure that it isn't poisoned   **107 room** place
109 **staggers** causes to stagger
5.6 Location: The court.
3 **Ci'cester** Cirencester

9 **taking** capture   10 **At large discoursèd** related in full   **12 worth**
(1) deserving (2) present wealth   **15 consorted** conspiring   **18 wot**
know.   **19 grand** chief   **20 clog** burden   **22 abide** await   **23 doom**
judgment   **25 reverent room** place suitable for religious retirement
26 More than thou hast i.e., larger than your present cell, or more
worthy of reverence.   **joy** enjoy, have the benefit of   **27 So as** Provided that   **35 deed of slander** i.e., a deed sure to arouse slanderous
talk about the new King

The guilt of conscience take thou for thy labor,
But neither my good word nor princely favor.
With Cain go wander through the shades of night,   43
And never show thy head by day nor light.
                    [*Exeunt Exton and attendants.*]
Lords, I protest my soul is full of woe
That blood should sprinkle me to make me grow.

Come mourn with me for what I do lament,
And put on sullen black incontinent.   48
I'll make a voyage to the Holy Land
To wash this blood off from my guilty hand.
March sadly after. Grace my mournings here   51
In weeping after this untimely bier.
                    [*Exeunt in procession, following the coffin.*]

---

43 Cain murderer of his brother Abel; see 1.1.104

48 incontinent immediately.   **51 Grace** Dignify

The First Part of King Henry the Fourth

❧

The opening of *1 Henry IV* is taut and grave in tone. England is "shaken" and "wan with care." The troubles of *Richard II,* to which this play (c. 1596–1597) is a close sequel, have not been left behind. However much King Henry would prefer to unite his countrymen against a common foreign enemy in a crusade to the Holy Lands, he is prevented from doing so by continuing civil war. The impassioned rhetoric of his opening speech can only end in anticlimax, for the actual purpose of this meeting in council is to receive and assess reports of military action against the throne.

Henry's current troubles are in the far reaches of his kingdom: Scots in the north, Welsh in the west. Fighting for Henry on these two fronts are the nobles of the Percy family who helped him to power: Harry Percy ("Hotspur"), his father (Henry Percy) the Earl of Northumberland, his uncle the Earl of Worcester, and his brother-in-law Edmund Mortimer, the Earl of March. Apparently, they have fought bravely. Yet we soon sense that all is not well between the new King and those who rebelled with him against Richard II. A quarrel breaks out because Hotspur refuses to deliver to Henry some prisoners as required by feudal obedience. The matter of the ransom money is only a technicality; what is really at issue? In part, it is Henry's insistence on being obeyed on principle. Admiring Hotspur inordinately, the King feels he must discipline affectionately this fine young warrior as a father would discipline his son. Even more deeply, however, the issue of the prisoners galls Henry because of the proviso that he ransom Mortimer, captured by the Welsh. Henry does not forget that Mortimer is his chief rival for the English crown, being descended from the Duke of Clarence (elder brother to Henry's father, Gaunt) and having been proclaimed by Richard as heir to the throne. (Shakespeare accentuates the dynastic threat by combining two Edmund Mortimers from his historical sources: one who married Glendower's daughter and another who claimed the English throne; see 1.3.80–5 and

note.) Mortimer is the last person Henry would wish ransomed. Moreover, the King suspects Mortimer of having fought with something less than total zeal against the Welsh Glendower. Mortimer's marriage to Glendower's daughter confirms the King's worst fears. Henry knows Northumberland and Worcester to be expert in treasonous plotting, since they conspired with him to overthrow Richard. Now, Henry believes, these Percys are extending their alliance by a series of calculated marriages in order to seize power once again. This time their claimant is Mortimer.

Shakespeare's sympathies are many sided. The Percy clan is, in fact, organizing against Henry, but not without cause. As they see it, the man they helped to the throne has done little for them since. His manner of disciplining them sounds too much like hostility and ingratitude. Other counselors attend the King constantly while Worcester is banished from court. In such an atmosphere of distrust, suspicion breeds still more suspicion. The situation has deteriorated, surely more than either party originally intended.

Hotspur is the most attractive of the rebels—to us as well as to King Henry. He is outspoken, courageous, witty, and domineering in conversation. Above all, he is a disciple of manliness, loyalty, chivalry, bravery in battle—the attributes of an upstanding and somewhat old-fashioned sense of honor. Yet a fatal defect dwells even in these attractive qualities. Hotspur is impatient, proud, unwilling to tolerate a rival—be it Glendower or Prince Hal (Henry, Prince of Wales). In his first speech, purporting to explain his refusal to deliver the prisoners, he brilliantly satirizes an effete courtier who had come to him from King Henry in the midst of a battle. The satire betrays many harsh qualities in Hotspur: the self-indulgent wrath that returns fully to him even in recollection of the encounter, the pride in his own stoical indifference to suffering, and especially the obsessive nature (revealed in the repetitive pattern of the rhetoric) of his contempt for courtiers generally. Surely his scorn for stay-at-home politicians is directed in part at King Henry himself. To Hotspur, all courtiers are effeminate, perfume-wearing, affected in mannerism and speech, and scarcely masculine. This preoccupation of Hotspur's makes him extraordinarily prone to one-sided judgments. Like most excessive devotees of chivalry, he divides humanity into two categories: those who are gentlemen, like himself, and those who are beneath contempt. The "vile politician" Bolingbroke and his son, the "sword-and-buckler Prince of Wales" (1.3.240, 229) fall into the latter category.

Prone as he is to such an overly simple view of political behavior, Hotspur can see no good in the King's cause and no evil in his own. He is a poor listener because of his obsession and yet an easy prey to his uncle and father, who require his leadership for their cause. They need only implant the suggestion that King Henry is acting from a political motive in his refusal to ransom Mortimer, and Hotspur is ready to leap incautiously to the defense of their cause. The great irony is that Hotspur fails to see political motives in the machinations of his own relatives. While he fights for bright honor, they maneuver cautiously for position and prove to be uncertain allies when the hour of battle approaches. Most crucially, they betray Hotspur in the prebattle negotiations, at which he is not present. As Worcester explains to Vernon during their return to rebel headquarters (5.2.3–25), they cannot let Hotspur know of the King's offer to settle matters by a general pardon. Although, as they realize, the King could pardon Hotspur's youth, there can be no turning back for themselves. Thus, the honor for which Hotspur fights is at bottom a lie, and the mutual esteem that might have grown between him and a much-reformed Prince of Wales is thwarted by the polarization of attitudes in the two camps. Hotspur's brand of honor is the victim of its own excess and lends some credence to Falstaff's wry conclusion that honor "is a mere scutcheon" (5.1.139–40).

The contrasting of Falstaff and Hotspur on the theme of honor suggests that they are dramatic foils for each other, representing extremes between which Hal must choose. Shakespeare uses this foil device structurally and consciously; for example, he has considerably reduced the age of the Hotspur he found in Raphael Holinshed's *Chronicles* (1578) in order to stress the similarity between Hotspur and Prince Hal. Conversely, to emphasize the contrast between Falstaff and Hotspur, Shakespeare envisages Falstaff as old (nearly sixty, by his own admission), fat, humorous, and without honor. Falstaff's vices are Hotspur's virtues, and the reverse. Whereas Hotspur offers to Hal a model of chivalric striving and attention to duty, Falstaff is a highwayman and a liar. On the other hand, Hotspur is a fanatic, unbending and self-absorbed even in the company of his sprightly wife, Kate, and irritated by music and poetry; Falstaff is the epitome of merriment and joie de vivre. We excuse much in him because

he lusts after life with such an appetite and ingratiates himself to others by inviting them to laugh at his expense.

Despite the nearly irresistible attractiveness of Falstaff as a jolly companion and butt of humorous joking, he and Prince Hal are perennially caught up in witty debate as to the importance of Falstaff in Hal's life and whether the young man will have to get rid of Falstaff once Hal is king. The bantering raillery of their first scene (1.2) seems designed to provide diverting entertainment for the Prince and for us, and yet, beneath the word games and oneupmanship, we perceive that Hal and Falstaff are talking about the hanging of thieves and the question of whether or not Hal should give in to sinful temptation. Can the relationship of Hal and Falstaff continue unchanged into the reign of Henry V? Will there be gallows standing and justice for highwaymen? Will "Monsieur Remorse," as Poins calls Falstaff, ever sincerely repent? Will the Prince, for that matter? To allay our fears, Hal soliloquizes at scene's end, vowing his determination to use these scapegrace companions as mere foils for his triumphal reformation at the appropriate time. But this explanation raises an opposite danger in our sympathies: is he callously using his companions merely to create a self-serving myth of Prince Hal, the Politician with the Common Touch? Is Francis the drawer no more to Hal than a butt for his raillery? Since the rejection of Falstaff is, by Hal's own words, already determined, can we credit him with a serious friendship? Where do Shakespeare's sympathies lie—with the need for political order or with the hedonistic spirit of youth? One possible interpretation is that he recognizes the validity of both, and accordingly shows us a prince who is genuinely fond of Falstaff's exuberant company but who also knows that he is a king's son and must sooner or later accept the consequences of that unsought role. Falstaff's gift to him is youthful irresponsibility, which must be cherished (by all of us), even though it cannot last.

This compassionate interpretation is, to be sure, only one of many possibilities. Recent theater history has demonstrated how supple the play is, allowing directors and actors to choose among an array of possibilities. At one extreme, Hal can be played as a matter-of-fact and even cynical young man who knows from the very start exactly where he is going and what use he can make of Falstaff and company—as played, for example, by Richard Burton at Stratford-upon-Avon in 1951 (directed by Anthony Quayle and John Kidd). At the opposite extreme, Hal can be seen as a defiant rebel whose hatred for his unsympathetically cold father makes him reluctant to grow up and accept adult responsibility; this was the line taken, for example, by Gerard Murphy in Trevor Nunn's 1982 production for the Royal Shakespeare Company. Murphy's Hal was an unruly child for whom Falstaff was a nurturing substitute parent. Between these polarities, Hal can be variously seen as an alcoholic or a prudish snob or a playboy or simply a young man who wants to enjoy life. Correspondingly, the role of Falstaff offers widely varying possibilities as a kind of jolly scapegrace older friend, a calculating con artist and jokester who knows how to play for sympathy through self-effacing humor, or a dangerously irresponsible hedonist. King Henry as father can be seen as a sorely tested father burdened with heavy responsibilities and an ungrateful son, a guilt-ridden monarch who fears remorsefully that Hal's waywardness is heaven's punishment for the King's sins, or a hard-bitten politician engaged in a life-and-death struggle for power with aristocrats as Machiavellian as he. An important reason for the play's great success is its openness to interpretation.

In the Gad's Hill robbery, Falstaff reveals that his "cowardice" differs from the natural craven fear of Bardolph and Peto. He fights no longer than he sees "reason," that is, not against unfair odds such as two athletic young men in the dark (or later, at Shrewsbury, against the burly Scots giant, the Douglas). A man could get killed that way. Falstaff's cowardice, then, is philosophic, seen by himself in a humorous perspective. The same is true of his lying about the robbery. However much Hal exults in exposing Falstaff as a fraud, we cannot dismiss the possibility that Falstaff may see through the Prince's scheme, and may then feed Hal the expectedly outlandish lie (two men in buckram become eleven men) as a means of begging for affection. Falstaff's only way of pleading his cause is to tickle the Prince's fancy, in his role as a kind of court fool. What Falstaff most wants is to be loved and retained for what he is, and that, poignantly enough, is the one thing the mature Henry V cannot grant.

Throughout 1 Henry IV, Shakespeare seems interested in the relationships between fathers and sons. These relationships help structure the comparisons and contrasts among foil characters. Falstaff is a foil, not only for Hotspur, but also for Henry IV; that is, despite all his insistence on youthful irresponsibility, Falstaff acts as a kind of parental figure to Hal. In the tavern scene (2.4), Falstaff and Hal take turns playing king and crown prince, and in both roles Falstaff wittily argues his case as companion and guide to the heir to the throne. Is it better to be old and merry, fat and loved, or to be hated like Pharaoh's lean kine? Falstaff argues against the gravity of council meetings with the same amused fervor that he later directs at the grinning honor of a dead hero. Hal, in his turn as king, questions the propriety of a "devil" haunting the crown prince "in the likeness of an old fat man," a "reverend Vice," a "gray Iniquity," a "father ruffian" (2.4.442–9). For all the good humor in this exchange, both men are asking whether Falstaff or King Henry serves Hal as the better model. Hal anticipates some of the very arguments his father will use against him next day at court, and, indeed, the insistent presence of that sober adult world makes itself felt even in the tavern. When, under the pressure of that looming responsibility, Falstaff's merrymaking turns to something like urgent self-

justification in his moving litany of appeals that Hal "banish not him thy Harry's company—banish plump Jack, and banish all the world," the Prince seems aware that he must face the consequences of his destiny. "I do, I will," he answers (lines 472–6), in a tone that can vary onstage (depending on the actor) from sober resolution to fond regret to awakening as from a dream.

Hotspur, too, is regarded as a son by more than one father. King Henry only half-jokingly wishes it could be proved that some night-tripping fairy had exchanged his Harry in the cradle for Harry Percy (1.1.85–9). Paradoxically, the King admires Hotspur all the more for standing up to him, just as another imperious father figure, Owen Glendower, bestows grudging but real admiration on Hotspur for his outspokenness (3.1.1–185). Hotspur's rebellious ways are cherished because they seem to promise manliness and fame; Hal's rebellious ways are feared and despised because they seem to reject the values of duty and leadership on which King Henry bases his self-respect. In these terms, the play must resolve Hal's coming of age, his acceptance of his role as true son of the King, and his proving his worth to the King. Hal must find his adult self—a self that differs greatly from that of King Henry—but must do so in a way that preserves the integrity of their relationship and the real debt he owes his father.

Prince Hal's uncertain journey toward maturity does not involve him in any significant relationships with women. His task is to fulfill what is expected of him as his father's son in a world of political and military conflict. Women stand on the periphery of affairs, as in Richard II, and yet the scenes in which they appear offer important perspectives on male competitiveness and ambition. Hotspur's wife, Kate, must put up with being condescended to and told little about men's doings; yet Hotspur's genuine fondness for her shows the best side of his personality, and her worries about his obsessive ways indicate that she understands him better than he understands himself. Morton's Welsh wife, too, introduces into this play an element of tenderness and anxious concern that is notably lacking in the earlier part of 3.1, when Hotspur cannot stop himself from quarreling pointlessly with his senior ally, Glendower. Hotspur's insensitivity to the Welsh lady's beautiful song is perhaps a key to his impending tragedy, for he is never a good listener. On a lower social scale, Mistress Quickly devotedly looks after Falstaff, only to be repaid with misogynistic insults that she does not appear to understand and with mooching that she recognizes all too well. Prince Hal, meantime, plays the role of intelligent observer of the battle of the sexes, even while he postpones his own engagement in that merry war. He must first sort out who he is in terms of male goals of career and success.

These conflicts surrounding Hal reach their climax and resolution at the field of Shrewsbury in Act 5. Hal's worth must be proven at Hotspur's expense. The rivalry between the two has been intense throughout the play, as seen for example in Hal's brilliant mimicking of Hotspur's devotion to bloodshed (2.4.101–8). Aware that his tarnished reputation puts him at a disadvantage, Hal speaks nobly of his rival and impresses even the adversarial camp with his regal bearing (5.1.83–100, 5.2.51–68). He rescues his father in the battle, thereby proving to King Henry that his son does not wish to supplant him, as he had feared. After the battle, Hal frees his Scottish adversary the Douglas in a display of princely magnificence, doing so with a more generous motive than Hotspur had displayed in his earlier release of the Douglas as his prisoner (1.3.259–62). Meantime, Hal has put considerable distance between himself and Falstaff, though sensitive still to the warmth of old memories. When he sees Hotspur and Falstaff on the ground together, both seemingly dead, Hal views as in a tableau the contrasting models between which he has shaped his own identity. Yet Falstaff is not dead. He rises to mutilate Hotspur's body and to claim the honor due Hal for Hotspur's death. For all Falstaff's witty commentary at the expense of honor, his own opposite course is unsuited to a time of war or to Hal's new public role. Falstaff's abuse of military conscription, his carrying a bottle of sack in place of a pistol, show him at his wittiest still, but in a world that may not tolerate such pranks. The merry games are out of place and childish. With characteristic generosity and imprudence, Hal gives the credit for Hotspur's death to Falstaff, who claims it so cravenly. Even so, the magic of their association has vanished. The time of adulthood is upon Hal.

The First Part of King Henry The Fourth

[Dramatis Personae

KING HENRY THE FOURTH
PRINCE HENRY, *Prince of Wales,*
PRINCE JOHN OF LANCASTER, } *sons of the King*
EARL OF WESTMORLAND
SIR WALTER BLUNT

EARL OF NORTHUMBERLAND, *Henry Percy,*
HARRY PERCY (HOTSPUR), *his son,*
EARL OF WORCESTER, *Northumberland's*
  younger brother,
LORD MORTIMER, *Edmund Mortimer*
  also referred to as the Earl of March,   *rebels*
OWEN GLENDOWER,   *against*
EARL OF DOUGLAS, *Archibald Douglas,*   *the King*
SIR RICHARD VERNON,
ARCHBISHOP OF YORK, *Richard Scroop,*
SIR MICHAEL, *a member of the*
  Archbishop's household,

LADY PERCY, *Hotspur's wife and Mortimer's sister*
LADY MORTIMER, *Mortimer's wife and Glendower's*
  daughter

SIR JOHN FALSTAFF
NED POINS
BARDOLPH
PETO
GADSHILL, *arranger of the highway robbery*
HOSTESS OF THE TAVERN, *Mistress Quickly*
FRANCIS, *a drawer, or tapster*
VINTNER, *or tavern keeper*

FIRST CARRIER
SECOND CARRIER
HOSTLER
CHAMBERLAIN
FIRST TRAVELER
SHERIFF
SERVANT *to Hotspur*
MESSENGER
SECOND MESSENGER

Soldiers, Travelers, Lords, Attendants

SCENE: *England and Wales*]

[1.1]

Enter the King, Lord John of Lancaster, [the] Earl of Westmorland, [Sir Walter Blunt,] with others.

KING

So shaken as we are, so wan with care,
Find we a time for frighted peace to pant, 2
And breathe short-winded accents of new broils 3
To be commenced in strands afar remote. 4
No more the thirsty entrance of this soil 5
Shall daub her lips with her own children's blood; 6
No more shall trenching war channel her fields 7
Nor bruise her flowerets with the armèd hoofs
Of hostile paces. Those opposèd eyes, 9
Which, like the meteors of a troubled heaven,
All of one nature, of one substance bred,
Did lately meet in the intestine shock 12
And furious close of civil butchery, 13
Shall now in mutual well-beseeming ranks
March all one way and be no more opposed
Against acquaintance, kindred, and allies.
The edge of war, like an ill-sheathèd knife,
No more shall cut his master. Therefore, friends, 18
As far as to the sepulcher of Christ—
Whose soldier now, under whose blessèd cross
We are impressèd and engaged to fight— 21
Forthwith a power of English shall we levy, 22
Whose arms were molded in their mothers' womb 23
To chase these pagans in those holy fields
Over whose acres walked those blessèd feet
Which fourteen hundred years ago were nailed
For our advantage on the bitter cross.
But this our purpose now is twelve month old,
And bootless 'tis to tell you we will go. 29
Therefore we meet not now. Then let me hear 30
Of you, my gentle cousin Westmorland, 31
What yesternight our council did decree
In forwarding this dear expedience. 33

WESTMORLAND

My liege, this haste was hot in question, 34
And many limits of the charge set down 35
But yesternight, when all athwart there came 36
A post from Wales loaden with heavy news, 37
Whose worst was that the noble Mortimer,
Leading the men of Herefordshire to fight
Against the irregular and wild Glendower,

Was by the rude hands of that Welshman taken,
A thousand of his people butcherèd—
Upon whose dead corpse there was such misuse, 43
Such beastly shameless transformation, 44
By those Welshwomen done as may not be
Without much shame retold or spoken of.

KING

It seems then that the tidings of this broil
Brake off our business for the Holy Land.

WESTMORLAND

This matched with other did, my gracious lord; 49
For more uneven and unwelcome news 50
Came from the north, and thus it did import:
On Holy Rood Day, the gallant Hotspur there, 52
Young Harry Percy, and brave Archibald,
That ever-valiant and approvèd Scot, 54
At Holmedon met, where they did spend 55
A sad and bloody hour,
As by discharge of their artillery 57
And shape of likelihood the news was told; 58
For he that brought them, in the very heat 59
And pride of their contention did take horse, 60
Uncertain of the issue any way.

KING

Here is a dear, a true industrious friend, 62
Sir Walter Blunt, new lighted from his horse, 63
Stained with the variation of each soil
Betwixt that Holmedon and this seat of ours;
And he hath brought us smooth and welcome news. 66
The Earl of Douglas is discomfited; 67
Ten thousand bold Scots, two-and-twenty knights,
Balked in their own blood, did Sir Walter see 69
On Holmedon's plains. Of prisoners, Hotspur took
Mordake, Earl of Fife and eldest son 71
To beaten Douglas, and the Earl of Atholl,
Of Murray, Angus, and Menteith.
And is not this an honorable spoil?
A gallant prize? Ha, cousin, is it not?

WESTMORLAND

In faith, it is a conquest for a prince to boast of.

KING

Yea, there thou mak'st me sad, and mak'st me sin
In envy that my lord Northumberland
Should be the father to so blest a son—
A son who is the theme of honor's tongue,
Amongst a grove the very straightest plant, 81
Who is sweet Fortune's minion and her pride, 82
Whilst I, by looking on the praise of him,
See riot and dishonor stain the brow 84
Of my young Harry. Oh, that it could be proved

1.1. Location: The royal court.
2 Find we let us find. **frighted** frightened **3 breathe short-winded accents** speak, even though we are out of breath. **accents** words. **broils** battles **4 strands afar remote** far-off shores, i.e., of the Holy Land (to which, at the end of *Richard II*, Henry has pledged himself to a crusade). **5 thirsty entrance** i.e., parched mouth **6 daub** coat, smear **7 trenching** cutting, plowing **9 paces** horses' tread. **12 intestine** internal **13 close** hand-to-hand encounter. **civil** (as in "civil war") **18 his** its **21 impressèd** conscripted **22 power** army **23 their mother's** i.e., England's, but also suggesting *their mothers'* **29 bootless** useless **30 Therefore . . . now** That is not the reason for our present meeting. **31 Of** from. **gentle cousin** noble kinsman **33 dear expedience** urgent expedition. **34 hot in question** being hotly debated **35 limits . . . charge** particulars of military responsibility **36 athwart** at cross purposes, contrarily **37 post** messenger. **loaden** laden

43 corpse corpses **44 transformation** mutilation **49 other** other news **50 uneven** disconcerting, distressing **52 Holy Rood Day** September 14 **54 approvèd** proved by experience **55 Holmedon** Humbleton in Northumberland **57 by** judging from **58 shape of likelihood** likely outcome **59 them** the news **60 pride** height **62–3 Here . . . Blunt** (Whether Blunt enters at the start of the scene, or now, or possibly not at all, is not certain in the original text.) **66 smooth** pleasant **67 discomfited** defeated **69 Balked** heaped up in balks, or ridges **71 Mordake** i.e., Murdoch, son of the Earl of Albany **81 plant** young tree **82 minion** favorite **84 riot** debauchery

That some night-tripping fairy had exchanged   86
In cradle clothes our children where they lay,
And called mine Percy, his Plantagenet!   88
Then would I have his Harry, and he mine.
But let him from my thoughts. What think you, coz,   90
Of this young Percy's pride? The prisoners
Which he in this adventure hath surprised   92
To his own use he keeps, and sends me word   93
I shall have none but Mordake, Earl of Fife.   94

WESTMORLAND
This is his uncle's teaching. This is Worcester,
Malevolent to you in all aspects,
Which makes him prune himself and bristle up   96
The crest of youth against your dignity.   97

KING
But I have sent for him to answer this;
And for this cause awhile we must neglect
Our holy purpose to Jerusalem.
Cousin, on Wednesday next our council we
Will hold at Windsor. So inform the lords.
But come yourself with speed to us again,
For more is to be said and to be done
Than out of anger can be utterèd.

WESTMORLAND   I will, my liege.   *Exeunt.*

❧

[1.2]

Enter Prince of Wales and Sir John Falstaff.

FALSTAFF
Now, Hal, what time of day is it, lad?

PRINCE   Thou art so fat-witted with drinking of old sack,   2
and unbuttoning thee after supper, and sleeping upon
benches after noon, that thou hast forgotten to de-   4
mand that truly which thou wouldst truly know. What
a devil hast thou to do with the time of the day? Unless   6
hours were cups of sack, and minutes capons, and
clocks the tongues of bawds, and dials the signs of   8
leaping houses, and the blessed sun himself a fair hot   9
wench in flame-colored taffeta, I see no reason why   10
thou shouldst be so superfluous to demand the time   11
of the day.

FALSTAFF   Indeed, you come near me now, Hal, for we   13
that take purses go by the moon and the seven stars,   14

and not by Phoebus, "he, that wandering knight so   15
fair." And I prithee, sweet wag, when thou art king,   16
as, God save Thy Grace—Majesty I should say, for   17
grace thou wilt have none—

PRINCE   What, none?

FALSTAFF   No, by my troth, not so much as will serve to   20
be prologue to an egg and butter.   21

PRINCE   Well, how then? Come, roundly, roundly.   22

FALSTAFF   Marry, then, sweet wag, when thou art   23
king, let not us that are squires of the night's body be   24
called thieves of the day's beauty. Let us be Diana' for-   25
esters, gentlemen of the shade, minions of the moon;   26
and let men say we be men of good government,   27
being governed, as the sea is, by our noble and chaste
mistress the moon, under whose countenance we steal.   29

PRINCE   Thou sayest well, and it holds well too, for the   30
fortune of us that are the moon's men doth ebb and
flow like the sea, being governed, as the sea is, by the
moon. As, for proof, now: a purse of gold most
resolutely snatched on Monday night and most dissolutely spent on Tuesday morning, got with swearing
"Lay by" and spent with crying "Bring in," now in as   36
low an ebb as the foot of the ladder and by and by in   37
as high a flow as the ridge of the gallows.   38

FALSTAFF   By the Lord, thou say'st true, lad. And is not
my hostess of the tavern a most sweet wench?

PRINCE   As the honey of Hybla, my old lad of the castle.   41
And is not a buff jerkin a most sweet robe of durance?   42

FALSTAFF   How now, how now, mad wag, what, in thy
quips and thy quiddities? What a plague have I to do   44
with a buff jerkin?

PRINCE   Why, what a pox have I to do with my hostess   46
of the tavern?

FALSTAFF   Well, thou hast called her to a reckoning many   48
a time and oft.

PRINCE   Did I ever call for thee to pay thy part?

FALSTAFF   No, I'll give thee thy due, thou hast paid all
there.

PRINCE   Yea, and elsewhere, so far as my coin would
stretch, and where it would not I have used my credit.

15–16 Phoebus . . . fair (Phoebus, god of the sun, is here equated with the wandering knight of a ballad or popular romance.)   **17 Grace** royal highness. (With pun on spiritual *grace* and also on the *grace* or blessing before a meal.)   **20 troth** faith   **21 prologue . . . butter** i.e., grace before a brief meal.   **22 roundly** i.e., out with it.   **23 Marry** Indeed. (Literally, "by the Virgin Mary.")   **wag** joker   **24–5 let . . . beauty** i.e., let not us who are attendants on the goddess of night, members of her household, be blamed for stealing daylight by sleeping in the daytime.   **25–6 Diana's foresters** (An elegant name for thieves by night; Diana is goddess of the moon and the hunt.)   **26 minions** favorites   **27 government** (1) conduct (2) commonwealth   **29 countenance** (1) face (2) patronage, approval.   **steal** (1) move stealthily (2) rob.   **30 it holds well** the comparison is apt   **36 Lay by** (A cry of highwaymen, like "Hands up!")   **Bring in** (An order given to a waiter in a tavern.)   **37 ladder** (1) pier ladder (2) gallows ladder   **38 ridge** crossbar   **41 Hybla** (A town, famed for its honey, in Sicily near Syracuse.)   **old . . . castle** (1) a roisterer (2) the name, Sir John Oldcastle, borne by Falstaff in an earlier version of this play.   **42 buff jerkin** a leather jacket worn by officers of the law.   **durance** (1) imprisonment (2) durability, durable cloth.   **44 quiddities** subtleties of speech.   **46 pox** syphilis. (Here, *what a pox* is used as an expletive, like "what the devil.")   **48 reckoning** settlement of the bill. (With bawdy suggestion that is continued in *pay thy part* and *my coin would stretch*.)

---

86 night-tripping i.e., moving nimbly in the night   **88 Plantagenet** (Family name of English royalty since Henry II.)   **90 let him** let him go.   **coz** cousin, i.e., kinsman   **92 surprised** ambushed, captured   **93 To . . . use** i.e., to collect ransom for them   **94 none but Mordake** (Since Mordake was of royal blood, being grandson to Robert II of Scotland, Hotspur could not claim him as his prisoner according to the law of arms.)   **96 Malevolent . . . aspects** (1) implacably hostile to you (2) in astrological terms, a planet in a disobedient orbit, ominous as seen from every angle   **97 Which . . . himself** i.e., which teaching makes Hotspur preen himself (as a falcon preens its feathers)   **1.2. Location: London, perhaps in an apartment of the Prince's.**   **2 sack** a Spanish white wine   **4 forgotten** forgotten how   **6 a devil** in the devil   **8 dials** clocks   **9 leaping houses** houses of prostitution   **10 taffeta** (Commonly worn by prostitutes.)   **11 superfluous** (1) unnecessarily concerned (2) self-indulgent   **13 you . . . now** i.e., you've scored a point on me   **14 go by** (1) travel by the light of (2) tell time by.   **the seven stars** the Pleiades

FALSTAFF   Yea, and so used it that, were it not here apparent that thou art heir apparent—But I prithee, sweet wag, shall there be gallows standing in England when thou art king? And resolution thus fubbed as it 58 is with the rusty curb of old father Antic the law? Do 59 not thou, when thou art king, hang a thief.

PRINCE   No, thou shalt.

FALSTAFF   Shall I? Oh, rare! By the Lord, I'll be a brave 62 judge.

PRINCE   Thou judgest false already. I mean, thou shalt have the hanging of the thieves, and so become a rare 65 hangman.

FALSTAFF   Well, Hal, well; and in some sort it jumps 67 with my humor as well as waiting in the court, I can 68 tell you.

PRINCE   For obtaining of suits? 70

FALSTAFF   Yea, for obtaining of suits, whereof the hangman hath no lean wardrobe. 'Sblood, I am as 72 melancholy as a gib cat or a lugged bear. 73

PRINCE   Or an old lion, or a lover's lute.

FALSTAFF   Yea, or the drone of a Lincolnshire bagpipe.

PRINCE   What sayest thou to a hare, or the melancholy 76 of Moorditch? 77

FALSTAFF   Thou hast the most unsavory similes, and art indeed the most comparative, rascalliest, sweet young 79 prince. But Hal, I prithee, trouble me no more with vanity. I would to God thou and I knew where a com- 81 modity of good names were to be bought. An old lord 82 of the council rated me the other day in the street 83 about you, sir, but I marked him not; and yet he talked very wisely, but I regarded him not; and yet he talked wisely, and in the street too.

PRINCE   Thou didst well, for wisdom cries out in the 87 streets and no man regards it. 88

FALSTAFF   Oh, thou hast damnable iteration, and art 89 indeed able to corrupt a saint. Thou hast done much harm upon me, Hal, God forgive thee for it. Before I knew thee, Hal, I knew nothing; and now am I, if a 92 man should speak truly, little better than one of the wicked. I must give over this life, and I will give it over. By the Lord, an I do not I am a villain. I'll be 95 damned for never a king's son in Christendom.

PRINCE   Where shall we take a purse tomorrow, Jack?

FALSTAFF   Zounds, where thou wilt, lad, I'll make one. 98 An I do not, call me villain and baffle me. 99

PRINCE   I see a good amendment of life in thee—from praying to purse taking.

FALSTAFF   Why, Hal, 'tis my vocation, Hal. 'Tis no sin for a man to labor in his vocation. 102

Enter Poins.

Poins! Now shall we know if Gadshill have set a 104 match. Oh, if men were to be saved by merit, what 105 hole in hell were hot enough for him? This is the most omnipotent villain that ever cried "Stand!" to a 107 true man. 108

PRINCE   Good morrow, Ned.

POINS   Good morrow, sweet Hal.—What says Monsieur Remorse? What says Sir John, Sack-and-Sugar Jack? How agrees the devil and thee about thy soul that thou soldest him on Good Friday last for a cup of Madeira and a cold capon's leg?

PRINCE   Sir John stands to his word; the devil shall have 115 his bargain, for he was never yet a breaker of proverbs. He will give the devil his due.

POINS   Then art thou damned for keeping thy word with the devil.

PRINCE   Else he had been damned for cozening the 120 devil.

POINS   But my lads, my lads, tomorrow morning, by four o'clock early, at Gad's Hill, there are pilgrims 123 going to Canterbury with rich offerings and traders riding to London with fat purses. I have vizards for 125 you all; you have horses for yourselves. Gadshill lies 126 tonight in Rochester. I have bespoke supper tomorrow 127 night in Eastcheap. We may do it as secure as sleep. If 128 you will go, I will stuff your purses full of crowns; if 129 you will not, tarry at home and be hanged.

FALSTAFF   Hear ye, Yedward, if I tarry at home and go 131 not, I'll hang you for going. 132

POINS   You will, chops? 133

FALSTAFF   Hal, wilt thou make one?

PRINCE   Who, I rob? I a thief? Not I, by my faith.

FALSTAFF   There's neither honesty, manhood, nor good fellowship in thee, nor thou cam'st not of the blood royal, if thou darest not stand for ten shillings. 138

---

58 **resolution** courage (of a highwayman).   **fubbed** cheated
59 **Antic** buffoon   62 **rare** splendid.   **brave** excellent   65 **have . . . thieves** (1) be in charge of hanging thieves (or protecting them from hanging) (2) hang like other thieves.   **rare** (1) rarely used (2) excellent   67–8 **jumps . . . humor** suits my temperament   68 **waiting in the court** being in attendance at the royal court   70 **suits** petitions. (But Falstaff uses the word to mean suits of clothes; clothes belonging to an executed man were given to the executioner.)   72 **'Sblood** By his (Christ's) blood   73 **gib cat** tomcat.   **lugged bear** bear led by a chain and baited by dogs.   76 **hare** (A proverbially melancholy animal.)   77 **Moorditch** (A foul ditch draining Moorfields, outside London walls.)   79 **comparative** given to abusive comparisons   81 **vanity** worldliness.   81–2 **commodity** supply   82 **names** reputations   83 **rated** chastised   87–8 **wisdom . . . regards it** (Hal paraphrases Proverbs 1:20–4, "Wisdom crieth without, and putteth forth her voice in the streets . . . and no man regarded," in jocose reply to Falstaff's mock sanctimoniousness.)   89 **iteration** repetition (of biblical texts, with a neat twist)   92 **nothing** i.e., no evil   95 **an** if

98 **Zounds** By his (Christ's) wounds.   **make one** be one of the party.
99 **baffle** publicly disgrace   102 **vocation** (A favorite term of the reforming Protestant ministers to describe the function or station to which one is called by God. Falstaff comically misapplies it to justify highway robbing.)   104 **Gadshill** (The name of one of the highwaymen.)   104–5 **set a match** arranged a robbery.   105 **by merit** i.e., according to their deservings rather than by God's grace   107 **omnipotent** unparalleled, utter.   **"Stand!"** "Stand and deliver!" i.e., Hand over your money.   108 **true man** honest citizen.   115 **stands to** keeps   120 **Else** Otherwise.   **cozening** cheating   123 **Gad's Hill** (Location near Rochester on the road from London to Canterbury; one of the highwaymen is called Gadshill.)   125 **vizards** masks   126 **lies** lodges   127 **bespoke** ordered   128 **Eastcheap** market district in London, with many taverns.   129 **crowns** gold coins   131 **Yedward** (Nickname for *Edward*, Poins's first name.)   131–2 **if I . . . going** i.e., there's no chance of my not going; sooner than that, I'd have you hanged instead for going in my place.   133 **chops** i.e., fat jaws or cheeks.   138 **stand . . . shillings** (1) stand up and fight for booty (2) be worth ten shillings, the value of the *royal*, the gold coin alluded to in *blood royal* (line 138).

PRINCE   Well then, once in my days I'll be a madcap.

FALSTAFF   Why, that's well said.

PRINCE   Well, come what will, I'll tarry at home.

FALSTAFF   By the Lord, I'll be a traitor then, when thou art king.

PRINCE   I care not.

POINS   Sir John, I prithee leave the Prince and me alone. I will lay him down such reasons for this adventure that he shall go.

FALSTAFF   Well, God give thee the spirit of persuasion and him the ears of profiting, that what thou speakest may move and what he hears may be believed, that the true prince may, for recreation sake, prove a false thief; for the poor abuses of the time want counte- 152 nance. Farewell. You shall find me in Eastcheap.   153

PRINCE   Farewell, thou latter spring! Farewell, All- 154 hallown summer!   [Exit Falstaff.] 155

POINS   Now, my good sweet honey lord, ride with us tomorrow. I have a jest to execute that I cannot manage alone. Falstaff, Peto, Bardolph, and Gadshill shall rob those men that we have already waylaid— 159 yourself and I will not be there—and when they have the booty, if you and I do not rob them, cut this head off from my shoulders.

PRINCE   How shall we part with them in setting forth?

POINS   Why, we will set forth before or after them and appoint them a place of meeting, wherein it is at our pleasure to fail; and then will they adventure upon the 166 exploit themselves, which they shall have no sooner achieved but we'll set upon them.

PRINCE   Yea, but 'tis like that they will know us by our 169 horses, by our habits, and by every other appoint- 170 ment, to be ourselves.   171

POINS   Tut, our horses they shall not see—I'll tie them in the wood; our vizards we will change after we leave them; and, sirrah, I have cases of buckram for the 174 nonce, to immask our noted outward garments.   175

PRINCE   Yea, but I doubt they will be too hard for us.   176

POINS   Well, for two of them, I know them to be as true-bred cowards as ever turned back; and for the 178 third, if he fight longer than he sees reason, I'll for-swear arms. The virtue of this jest will be the incompre- 180 hensible lies that this same fat rogue will tell us when 181 we meet at supper—how thirty at least he fought with, what wards, what blows, what extremities he 183 endured; and in the reproof of this lives the jest.   184

PRINCE   Well, I'll go with thee. Provide us all things nec-essary and meet me tomorrow night in Eastcheap. There I'll sup. Farewell.

POINS   Farewell, my lord.   Exit Poins.

PRINCE

I know you all, and will awhile uphold
The unyoked humor of your idleness.   190
Yet herein will I imitate the sun,
Who doth permit the base contagious clouds   192
To smother up his beauty from the world,
That when he please again to be himself,   194
Being wanted he may be more wondered at   195
By breaking through the foul and ugly mists
Of vapors that did seem to strangle him.
If all the year were playing holidays,
To sport would be as tedious as to work;
But when they seldom come, they wished-for come,
And nothing pleaseth but rare accidents.   201
So when this loose behavior I throw off
And pay the debt I never promisèd,
By how much better than my word I am,
By so much shall I falsify men's hopes;   205
And like bright metal on a sullen ground,   206
My reformation, glitt'ring o'er my fault,
Shall show more goodly and attract more eyes
Than that which hath no foil to set it off.   209
I'll so offend to make offense a skill,   210
Redeeming time when men think least I will.   Exit. 211

❖

[1.3]

*Enter the King, Northumberland, Worcester,
Hotspur, Sir Walter Blunt, with others.*

KING

My blood hath been too cold and temperate,
Unapt to stir at these indignities,
And you have found me, for accordingly   3
You tread upon my patience. But be sure
I will from henceforth rather be myself,   5
Mighty and to be feared, than my condition,   6
Which hath been smooth as oil, soft as young down,
And therefore lost that title of respect
Which the proud soul ne'er pays but to the proud.

WORCESTER

Our house, my sovereign liege, little deserves   10
The scourge of greatness to be used on it—
And that same greatness too which our own hands
Have holp to make so portly.   13

NORTHUMBERLAND [*to the King*]   My lord—

KING

Worcester, get thee gone, for I do see

152–3 **want countenance** lack sponsorship (from men of rank).
154–5 **All-hallown summer** a season of clement weather around All Saints' Day, November 1; the *latter spring* or "Indian summer" of Fal-staff's old age.   159 **waylaid** set an ambush for   166 **pleasure** choice, discretion   169 **like** likely   170 **habits** garments   170–1 **appoint-ment** accoutrement   174 **sirrah** (Usually addressed to an inferior; here, a sign of intimacy.)   174–5 **cases . . . nonce** suits of buckram, a stiff-finished heavily sized fabric, for the purpose   175 **immask** hide, disguise.   **noted** known   176 **doubt** fear.   **too hard** too formidable   178 **turned back** turned their backs and ran away   180–1 **incompre-hensible** boundless   183 **wards** parries   184 **reproof** disproof

190 **unyoked . . . idleness** unbridled inclination of your frivolity.
192 **contagious** noxious   194 **That** so that   195 **wanted** missed, lacked   201 **accidents** events.   205 **hopes** expectations   206 **sullen ground** dark background, like a *foil*. (See line 209.)   209 **foil** metal sheet laid contrastingly behind a jewel to set off its luster   210 **to** as to.   **skill** i.e., clever tactic, piece of good policy   211 **Redeeming time** i.e., making amends for lost time
1.3. Location: London. The court (historically at Windsor).
3 **found me** found me so   5 **myself** i.e., my royal self   6 **my condi-tion** my natural (mild) disposition   10 **Our house** i.e., The Percy family   13 **holp** helped.   **portly** majestic, prosperous.

Danger and disobedience in thine eye.
Oh, sir, your presence is too bold and peremptory,
And majesty might never yet endure
The moody frontier of a servant brow. 19
You have good leave to leave us. When we need 20
Your use and counsel, we shall send for you.

Exit Worcester.

[*To Northumberland*] You were about to speak.

NORTHUMBERLAND   Yea, my good lord.
Those prisoners in Your Highness' name demanded,
Which Harry Percy here at Holmedon took,
Were, as he says, not with such strength denied
As is delivered to Your Majesty. 26
Either envy, therefore, or misprision 27
Is guilty of this fault, and not my son.

HOTSPUR [*to the King*]
My liege, I did deny no prisoners.
But I remember when the fight was done,
When I was dry with rage and extreme toil,
Breathless and faint, leaning upon my sword,
Came there a certain lord, neat and trimly dressed,
Fresh as a bridegroom, and his chin new reaped 34
Showed like a stubble land at harvest home. 35
He was perfumèd like a milliner, 36
And twixt his finger and his thumb he held
A pouncet box, which ever and anon 38
He gave his nose and took't away again,
Who therewith angry, when it next came there, 40
Took it in snuff; and still he smiled and talked, 41
And as the soldiers bore dead bodies by
He called them untaught knaves, unmannerly,
To bring a slovenly unhandsome corpse
Betwixt the wind and his nobility.
With many holiday and lady terms 46
He questioned me, amongst the rest demanded
My prisoners in Your Majesty's behalf.
I then, all smarting with my wounds being cold,
To be so pestered with a popinjay, 50
Out of my grief and my impatience 51
Answered neglectingly I know not what,
He should, or he should not; for he made me mad
To see him shine so brisk, and smell so sweet,
And talk so like a waiting-gentlewoman
Of guns and drums and wounds—God save the
     mark!— 56
And telling me the sovereignest thing on earth 57
Was parmacety for an inward bruise, 58

And that it was great pity, so it was,
This villainous saltpeter should be digged 60
Out of the bowels of the harmless earth,
Which many a good tall fellow had destroyed 62
So cowardly, and but for these vile guns
He would himself have been a soldier.
This bald unjointed chat of his, my lord, 65
I answered indirectly, as I said, 66
And I beseech you, let not his report
Come current for an accusation 68
Betwixt my love and your high majesty.

BLUNT [*to the King*]
The circumstance considered, good my lord,
Whate'er Lord Harry Percy then had said
To such a person and in such a place,
At such a time, with all the rest retold,
May reasonably die, and never rise
To do him wrong or any way impeach 75
What then he said, so he unsay it now. 76

KING
Why, yet he doth deny his prisoners, 77
But with proviso and exception 78
That we at our own charge shall ransom straight 79
His brother-in-law, the foolish Mortimer, 80
Who, on my soul, hath willfully betrayed
The lives of those that he did lead to fight
Against that great magician, damned Glendower,
Whose daughter, as we hear, that Earl of March 84
Hath lately married. Shall our coffers then
Be emptied to redeem a traitor home?
Shall we buy treason and indent with fears 87
When they have lost and forfeited themselves?
No, on the barren mountains let him starve!
For I shall never hold that man my friend
Whose tongue shall ask me for one penny cost
To ransom home revolted Mortimer. 92

HOTSPUR   Revolted Mortimer?
He never did fall off, my sovereign liege, 94
But by the chance of war. To prove that true
Needs no more but one tongue for all those wounds,
Those mouthèd wounds, which valiantly he took, 97
When on the gentle Severn's sedgy bank, 98
In single opposition, hand to hand,

---

19 **moody frontier** i.e., angry brow, frown. (*Frontier* literally means "outwork" or "fortification.")   20 **good leave** full permission   26 **delivered** reported   27 **envy** malice.   **misprision** misunderstanding   34 **chin new reaped** i.e., with beard freshly barbered according to the latest fashion, not like a soldier's beard   35 **Showed** looked.   **harvest home** end of harvest, fields being cut back to stubble.   36 **milliner** dealer in fancy articles, such as gloves and hats   38 **pouncet box** perfume box with perforated lid   40 **Who** i.e., his nose   41 **Took it in snuff** (1) inhaled it (2) took offense.   **still** continually   46 **holiday and lady** dainty and effeminate   50 **popinjay** parrot   51 **grief** pain   56 **God . . . mark** (Probably originally a formula to avert evil omen; here, an expression of impatience.)   57 **sovereignest** most efficacious   58 **parmacety** spermaceti, a fatty substance taken from the head of the sperm whale, used as a medicinal ointment

60 **saltpeter** potassium nitrate, used to make gunpowder and also used medicinally   62 **tall** brave   65 **bald** trivial   66 **indirectly** inattentively, offhandedly   68 **Come current** (1) be taken at face value (2) come rushing in   75 **impeach** discredit   76 **so** provided that   77 **yet** (emphatic) i.e., even now.   **deny** refuse to surrender   78 **proviso and exception** (synonymous terms)   79 **straight** straightway, at once   80 **Mortimer** (There were two Edmund Mortimers; Shakespeare confuses them and combines their stories. It was the uncle [1376–1409?] who was captured by Glendower and married Glendower's daughter; it was the nephew [1391–1425], fifth Earl of March, who was proclaimed heir presumptive to King Richard II after the death of his father, the fourth earl, whom Richard had named as his heir. The uncle was brother to the fourth earl and to Hotspur's wife, Elizabeth, called Kate in this play.)   84 **Earl of March** (The "Mortimer" of line 80; see note there.)   87 **indent with fears** i.e., make a bargain or come to terms with traitors whom we have reason to fear   92 **revolted** rebellious   94 **fall off** change his allegiance   97 **mouthèd** gaping and eloquent   98 **Severn's** (The Severn River flows from northern Wales and western England into the Bristol Channel.)   **sedgy** bordered with reeds

He did confound the best part of an hour   100
In changing hardiment with great Glendower.   101
Three times they breathed, and three times did they
    drink,
Upon agreement, of swift Severn's flood,   102
Who then, affrighted with their bloody looks,   103
Ran fearfully among the trembling reeds   104
And hid his crisp head in the hollow bank,   106
Bloodstainèd with these valiant combatants.
Never did bare and rotten policy   108
Color her working with such deadly wounds,   109
Nor never could the noble Mortimer
Receive so many, and all willingly.
Then let not him be slandered with revolt.   112

KING
Thou dost belie him, Percy, thou dost belie him.
He never did encounter with Glendower.
I tell thee,
He durst as well have met the devil alone
As Owen Glendower for an enemy.
Art thou not ashamed? But, sirrah, henceforth
Let me not hear you speak of Mortimer.
Send me your prisoners with the speediest means,
Or you shall hear in such a kind from me   121
As will displease you.—My lord Northumberland,
We license your departure with your son.
Send us your prisoners, or you will hear of it.
            Exit King [with Blunt, and train].

HOTSPUR
An if the devil come and roar for them   125
I will not send them. I will after straight   126
And tell him so, for I will ease my heart,
Albeit I make a hazard of my head.   128

NORTHUMBERLAND
What, drunk with choler? Stay and pause awhile.   129
Here comes your uncle.

            Enter Worcester.

HOTSPUR   Speak of Mortimer?
Zounds, I will speak of him, and let my soul
Want mercy if I do not join with him!
Yea, on his part I'll empty all these veins,   132
And shed my dear blood drop by drop in the dust,   133
But I will lift the downtrod Mortimer
As high in the air as this unthankful king,
As this ingrate and cankered Bolingbroke.   137

NORTHUMBERLAND
Brother, the King hath made your nephew mad.

WORCESTER
Who struck this heat up after I was gone?

HOTSPUR
He will forsooth have all my prisoners;
And when I urged the ransom once again
Of my wife's brother, then his cheek looked pale,
And on my face he turned an eye of death,   143
Trembling even at the name of Mortimer.

WORCESTER
I cannot blame him. Was not he proclaimed   145
By Richard, that dead is, the next of blood?   146

NORTHUMBERLAND
He was; I heard the proclamation.
And then it was when the unhappy king—   148
Whose wrongs in us God pardon!—did set forth   149
Upon his Irish expedition;   150
From whence he, intercepted, did return   151
To be deposed and shortly murderèd.

WORCESTER
And for whose death we in the world's wide mouth
Live scandalized and foully spoken of.

HOTSPUR
But, soft, I pray you, did King Richard then   155
Proclaim my brother Edmund Mortimer   156
Heir to the crown?

NORTHUMBERLAND   He did; myself did hear it.

HOTSPUR
Nay, then I cannot blame his cousin king,   158
That wished him on the barren mountains starve.
But shall it be that you that set the crown
Upon the head of this forgetful man,
And for his sake wear the detested blot
Of murderous subornation—shall it be   163
That you a world of curses undergo,
Being the agents, or base second means,   165
The cords, the ladder, or the hangman rather?
Oh, pardon me that I descend so low
To show the line and the predicament   168
Wherein you range under this subtle king!   169
Shall it for shame be spoken in these days,
Or fill up chronicles in time to come,
That men of your nobility and power
Did gage them both in an unjust behalf,   173
As both of you—God pardon it!—have done,
To put down Richard, that sweet lovely rose,
And plant this thorn, this canker, Bolingbroke?   176
And shall it in more shame be further spoken
That you are fooled, discarded, and shook off
By him for whom these shames ye underwent?
No! Yet time serves wherein you may redeem   180
Your banished honors and restore yourselves

---

100 confound consume **101 changing hardiment** exchanging blows, matching valor **102 breathed** paused for breath **103 flood** river **104 Who** i.e., the river **106 crisp** curly, i.e., rippled **108 bare** paltry. **policy** cunning **109 Color** disguise **112 revolt** i.e., the accusation of rebellion. **121 kind** manner **125 An if** If **126 will after straight** will go after him immediately **128 Albeit . . . head** even if I risk being beheaded. **129 choler** anger. **132 Want mercy** lack mercy, be damned **133 on his part** i.e., fighting on Mortimer's side **137 cankered** spoiled, malignant. **Bolingbroke** i.e., King Henry IV. (Hotspur pointedly refuses to acknowledge his royalty.)

143 an eye of death a fearful look **145 he** i.e., Mortimer **146 next of blood** heir to the throne. **148 unhappy** unfortunate **149 in us** caused by our doings **150 Irish expedition** (Richard II was putting down a rebellion in Ireland when Bolingbroke returned to England from exile.) **151 intercepted** interrupted **155 soft** i.e., wait a minute **156 brother** brother-in-law **158 cousin** (With a pun on cozen, "cheat.") **163 murderous subornation** the suborning of, or inciting to, murder **165 second means** agents **168 To . . . predicament** to show the direction things are moving and the danger to you **169 range** (1) are ranked; (2) stray **173 gage them** engage, pledge themselves **176 canker** (1) canker rose or dog rose, wild and unfragrant (2) ulcer **180 Yet** Still

Into the good thoughts of the world again;
Revenge the jeering and disdained contempt   183
Of this proud king, who studies day and night
To answer all the debt he owes to you   185
Even with the bloody payment of your deaths.
Therefore, I say—
WORCESTER   Peace, cousin, say no more.   187
And now I will unclasp a secret book,
And to your quick-conceiving discontents   189
I'll read you matter deep and dangerous,
As full of peril and adventurous spirit
As to o'erwalk a current roaring loud
On the unsteadfast footing of a spear.   193
HOTSPUR
If he fall in, good night, or sink or swim!   194
Send danger from the east unto the west,
So honor cross it from the north to south,   196
And let them grapple. Oh, the blood more stirs
To rouse a lion than to start a hare!
NORTHUMBERLAND [*to Worcester*]
Imagination of some great exploit
Drives him beyond the bounds of patience.
HOTSPUR
By heaven, methinks it were an easy leap
To pluck bright honor from the pale-faced moon,
Or dive into the bottom of the deep,
Where fathom line could never touch the ground,   204
And pluck up drownèd honor by the locks,
So he that doth redeem her thence might wear
Without corrival all her dignities;   207
But out upon this half-faced fellowship!   208
WORCESTER [*to Northumberland*]
He apprehends a world of figures here,   209
But not the form of what he should attend.—   210
Good cousin, give me audience for a while.
HOTSPUR
I cry you mercy.
WORCESTER   Those same noble Scots   212
That are your prisoners—
HOTSPUR   I'll keep them all.
By God, he shall not have a Scot of them,   214
No, if a scot would save his soul, he shall not!   215
I'll keep them, by this hand.
WORCESTER   You start away
And lend no ear unto my purposes.
Those prisoners you shall keep.
HOTSPUR   Nay, I will, that's flat.   218

He said he would not ransom Mortimer,
Forbade my tongue to speak of Mortimer,
But I will find him when he lies asleep,
And in his ear I'll holler "Mortimer!"
Nay, I'll have a starling shall be taught to speak
Nothing but "Mortimer," and give it him
To keep his anger still in motion.   225
WORCESTER   Hear you, cousin, a word.
HOTSPUR
All studies here I solemnly defy,   227
Save how to gall and pinch this Bolingbroke,
And that same sword-and-buckler Prince of Wales.   229
But that I think his father loves him not
And would be glad he met with some mischance,
I would have him poisoned with a pot of ale.
WORCESTER
Farewell, kinsman. I'll talk to you
When you are better tempered to attend.
NORTHUMBERLAND [*to Hotspur*]
Why, what a wasp-stung and impatient fool
Art thou to break into this woman's mood,
Tying thine ear to no tongue but thine own!
HOTSPUR
Why, look you, I am whipped and scourged with rods,
Nettled and stung with pismires, when I hear   239
Of this vile politician, Bolingbroke.   240
In Richard's time—what do you call the place?—
A plague upon it, it is in Gloucestershire;
'Twas where the madcap duke his uncle kept,   243
His uncle York; where I first bowed my knee
Unto this king of smiles, this Bolingbroke—
'Sblood, when you and he came back from
Ravenspurgh.   246
NORTHUMBERLAND   At Berkeley Castle.   247
HOTSPUR   You say true.
Why, what a candy deal of courtesy   249
This fawning greyhound then did proffer me!
"Look when his infant fortune came to age,"   251
And "gentle Harry Percy," and "kind cousin"—
Oh, the devil take such cozeners!—God forgive me!   253
Good uncle, tell your tale; I have done.
WORCESTER
Nay, if you have not, to it again;
We will stay your leisure.
HOTSPUR   I have done, i'faith.   256
WORCESTER
Then once more to your Scottish prisoners.
Deliver them up without their ransom straight,   258
And make the Douglas' son your only mean   259

---

183 **Revenge** and wherein you may revenge yourself against.
disdained disdainful   185 **answer** satisfy, discharge   187 **cousin**
nephew   189 **quick-conceiving** comprehending quickly   193 **spear**
i.e., spear laid across a stream as a narrow bridge.   194 **If . . . swim** i.e.,
Anyone daring such a thing will face a life-or-death challenge. (Hotspur's imagination is fired by the thought of risking everything on such
an attempt.)   196 **So** provided that. (Also at line 206.)   204 **fathom
line** a weighted line marked at fathom intervals (six feet), used for
measuring the depth of water   207 **corrival** rival, competitor
208 **out . . . fellowship!** down with this paltry business of sharing glory
with others!   209 **apprehends** snatches at.   **figures** figures of the
imagination, or figures of speech   210 **form** essential nature.   **attend**
give attention to.   212 **cry you mercy** beg your pardon.   214–15 **Scot
. . . scot** Scotsman . . . trifling amount   218 **that's flat** that's for sure.

225 **still** continually   227 **studies** pursuits.   **defy** renounce
229 **sword-and-buckler** swashbuckling. (Gentlemen generally preferred
to wear the rapier and the dagger.)   239 **Nettled** stung with nettles.
pismires ants. (From the urinous smell of an anthill.)   240 **politician**
deceitful schemer   243 **kept** dwelled   246 **Ravenspurgh** on the
Yorkshire coast, at the mouth of the Humber River, where Bolingbroke
landed on his return from exile (*Richard II*, 2.1.296).   247 **Berkeley
Castle** castle near Bristol.   249 **candy** sugared, flattering   251 **Look
when** When, as soon as   253 **cozeners** cheats. (With pun on *cousins*.)
256 **stay** await   258 **Deliver them up** Free them   259 **the Douglas' son**
i.e., Mordake. (See 1.1.71 and note.)   **mean** i.e., agent

For powers in Scotland, which, for divers reasons   260
Which I shall send you written, be assured
Will easily be granted. [*To Northumberland*] You, my
        lord,
Your son in Scotland being thus employed,
Shall secretly into the bosom creep   264
Of that same noble prelate well beloved,
The Archbishop.

HOTSPUR   Of York, is it not?

WORCESTER   True, who bears hard   268
His brother's death at Bristol, the Lord Scroop.
I speak not this in estimation,   270
As what I think might be, but what I know
Is ruminated, plotted, and set down,
And only stays but to behold the face
Of that occasion that shall bring it on.

HOTSPUR
I smell it. Upon my life, it will do well.

NORTHUMBERLAND
Before the game is afoot thou still let'st slip.   276

HOTSPUR
Why, it cannot choose but be a noble plot.   277
And then the power of Scotland and of York   278
To join with Mortimer, ha?

WORCESTER   And so they shall.

HOTSPUR
In faith, it is exceedingly well aimed.   280

WORCESTER
And 'tis no little reason bids us speed,
To save our heads by raising of a head;   282
For, bear ourselves as even as we can,   283
The King will always think him in our debt,   284
And think we think ourselves unsatisfied
Till he hath found a time to pay us home.   286
And see already how he doth begin
To make us strangers to his looks of love.

HOTSPUR
He does, he does. We'll be revenged on him.

WORCESTER
Cousin, farewell. No further go in this
Than I by letters shall direct your course.
When time is ripe, which will be suddenly,   292
I'll steal to Glendower and Lord Mortimer,
Where you and Douglas and our powers at once,   294
As I will fashion it, shall happily meet   295
To bear our fortunes in our own strong arms,   296
Which now we hold at much uncertainty.

NORTHUMBERLAND
Farewell, good brother. We shall thrive, I trust.

HOTSPUR
Uncle, adieu. Oh, let the hours be short
Till fields and blows and groans applaud our sport!   300
        Exeunt [in separate groups].

❖

[2.1]

Enter a Carrier with a lantern in his hand.

FIRST CARRIER   Heigh-ho! An it be not four by the day,   1
I'll be hanged. Charles's Wain is over the new   2
chimney, and yet our horse not packed. What, hostler!   3

HOSTLER [*within*]   Anon, anon.   4

FIRST CARRIER   I prithee, Tom, beat Cut's saddle, put a   5
few flocks in the point. Poor jade is wrung in the   6
withers out of all cess.   7

Enter another Carrier.

SECOND CARRIER   Peas and beans are as dank here as a   8
dog, and that is the next way to give poor jades the   9
bots. This house is turned upside down since Robin   10
Hostler died.

FIRST CARRIER   Poor fellow never joyed since the price
of oats rose. It was the death of him.

SECOND CARRIER   I think this be the most villainous
house in all London road for fleas. I am stung like a
tench.   16

FIRST CARRIER   Like a tench? By the Mass, there is ne'er
a king Christian could be better bit than I have been   18
since the first cock.   19

SECOND CARRIER   Why, they will allow us ne'er a jordan,   20
and then we leak in your chimney, and your chamber-   21
lye breeds fleas like a loach.   22

FIRST CARRIER [*calling*]   What, Hostler! Come away and   23
be hanged! Come away.

SECOND CARRIER   I have a gammon of bacon and two   25
races of ginger, to be delivered as far as Charing Cross.   26

FIRST CARRIER   God's body, the turkeys in my pannier   27
are quite starved. What, hostler! A plague on thee!
Hast thou never an eye in thy head? Canst not hear?
An 'twere not as good deed as drink to break the pate   30
on thee, I am a very villain. Come, and be hanged!   31
Hast no faith in thee?   32

Enter Gadshill.

2.1. Location: An innyard on the London-Canterbury road.
0.1 *Carrier* one whose trade was conveying goods, usually by packhorses   **1 An** If.   **by the day** in the morning   **2 Charles's Wain**
i.e., Charlemagne's wagon; the constellation Ursa Major (the Big
Dipper)   **3 horse** horses.   **hostler** groom.   **4 Anon** Right away,
coming   **5 beat** soften.   **Cut's saddle** packsaddle of the horse
named *Cut*, meaning "bobtailed"   **6 flocks** tufts of wool.   **point**
pommel of the saddle.   **jade** nag   **6–7 wrung . . . withers** chafed
(by his saddle) on the ridge between his shoulder-blades   **7 cess**
measure, estimate.   **8 Peas and beans** i.e., Horse fodder   **8–9 dank
. . . dog** i.e., damp as can be   **9 next** nearest, quickest   **10 bots**
intestinal maggots.   **house** inn   **16 tench** a spotted fish, whose
spots may have been likened to flea bites.   **18 king Christian**
Christian king, accustomed to have the best of everything   **19 first
cock** i.e., midnight.   **20 jordan** chamberpot   **21 chimney** fireplace
21–2 chamber-lye urine   **22 loach** a small freshwater fish, thought
to harbor parasites.   **23 Come away** Come along   **25 gammon of
bacon** ham   **26 races** roots.   **Charing Cross** a market town lying
between London and Westminster.   **27 pannier** basket   **30 An** If
30–1 An . . . hanged! i.e., I'll be hanged if it wouldn't be a good
idea to smack you on the head. Come along, damn you!   **32 faith**
trustworthiness

---

260 For powers for raising an army   **264 secretly . . . creep** win the confidence   **268 bears hard** resents   **270 estimation** guesswork   **276 still
let'st slip** always let loose the dogs.   **277 cannot choose but be** cannot
help being   **278 power** army   **280 aimed** designed.   **282 head** army
283 even carefully   **284 him** himself   **286 home** (1) fully (2) with a
thrust to the heart.   **292 suddenly** soon   **294 at once** all together
295 happily fortunately   **296 arms** (1) limbs (2) military might
300 fields battlefields

GADSHILL   Good morrow, carriers. What's o'clock?

FIRST CARRIER   I think it be two o'clock.   34

GADSHILL   I prithee, lend me thy lantern to see my
gelding in the stable.   36

FIRST CARRIER   Nay, by God, soft, I know a trick worth   37
two of that, i'faith.

GADSHILL   [to the Second Carrier]   I pray thee, lend me thine.

SECOND CARRIER   Ay, when, canst tell? Lend me thy   40
lantern, quoth he! Marry, I'll see thee hanged first.   41

GADSHILL   Sirrah carrier, what time do you mean to
come to London?

SECOND CARRIER   Time enough to go to bed with a   44
candle, I warrant thee.—Come, neighbor Mugs, we'll   45
call up the gentlemen. They will along with company,   46
for they have great charge.   Exeunt [Carriers].   47

GADSHILL   What, ho! Chamberlain!   48

Enter Chamberlain.

CHAMBERLAIN   At hand, quoth pickpurse.   49

GADSHILL   That's even as fair as—at hand, quoth the   50
chamberlain; for thou variest no more from picking of   51
purses than giving direction doth from laboring; thou   52
layest the plot how.   53

CHAMBERLAIN   Good morrow, Master Gadshill. It holds   54
current that I told you yesternight: there's a franklin in   55
the Weald of Kent hath brought three hundred marks   56
with him in gold. I heard him tell it to one of his company last night at supper—a kind of auditor, one that
hath abundance of charge too, God knows what. They
are up already, and call for eggs and butter. They will
away presently.   61

GADSHILL   Sirrah, if they meet not with Saint Nicholas'   62
clerks, I'll give thee this neck.   63

CHAMBERLAIN   No, I'll none of it. I pray thee, keep that   64
for the hangman, for I know thou worshipest Saint
Nicholas as truly as a man of falsehood may.

GADSHILL   What talkest thou to me of the hangman? If   67
I hang, I'll make a fat pair of gallows; for if I hang, old
Sir John hangs with me, and thou knowest he is no
starveling. Tut, there are other Trojans that thou   70
dream'st not of, the which for sport sake are content
to do the profession some grace, that would, if matters   72

should be looked into, for their own credit sake   73
make all whole. I am joined with no foot-landrakers,   74
no long-staff sixpenny strikers, none of these mad   75
mustachio purple-hued malt-worms, but with nobility   76
and tranquillity, burgomasters and great oneyers, such   77
as can hold in, such as will strike sooner than speak,   78
and speak sooner than drink, and drink sooner than
pray. And yet, zounds, I lie, for they pray continually
to their saint, the commonwealth, or rather not pray to
her but prey on her, for they ride up and down on her
and make her their boots.   83

CHAMBERLAIN   What, the commonwealth their boots?
Will she hold out water in foul way?   85

GADSHILL   She will, she will. Justice hath liquored her.   86
We steal as in a castle, cocksure. We have the receipt   87
of fern seed; we walk invisible.   88

CHAMBERLAIN   Nay, by my faith, I think you are more
beholding to the night than to fern seed for your   90
walking invisible.

GADSHILL   Give me thy hand. Thou shalt have a share
in our purchase, as I am a true man.   93

CHAMBERLAIN   Nay, rather let me have it as you are a
false thief.

GADSHILL   Go to; *homo* is a common name to all men.   96
Bid the hostler bring my gelding out of the stable. Farewell, you muddy knave.   [Exeunt separately.]   98

❖

[2.2]

Enter Prince, Poins, Peto, and [Bardolph].

POINS   Come, shelter, shelter! I have removed Falstaff's
horse, and he frets like a gummed velvet.   2

PRINCE   Stand close.   [They step aside.]   3

Enter Falstaff.

FALSTAFF   Poins! Poins, and be hanged! Poins!

PRINCE   [coming forward]   Peace, ye fat-kidneyed rascal!
What a brawling dost thou keep!   6

FALSTAFF   Where's Poins, Hal?

---

34 two o'clock (An evasive answer; the First Carrier knows that it is
at least four o'clock; see line 1.)   36 gelding castrated male horse
37 soft i.e., wait a minute   40 Ay . . . tell? i.e., You must be joking.
41 quoth he forsooth, indeed.   44–5 Time . . . candle i.e., Soon
enough. (Another evasive answer.)   46–7 They . . . charge i.e., They
wish to travel in company, because they have lots of valuable cargo.
48 Chamberlain (Male equivalent of a chambermaid. His entrance in
the Quarto at line 47 may suggest that he is visible before Gadshill
calls for him, giving point to his remark about being "At hand.")
49 At . . . pickpurse i.e., I am right beside you, as the pickpurse said.
50 fair good, apt   51–3 thou variest . . . how i.e., you don't actually
do the stealing, but you give directions, like a master workman to his
apprentices.   54–5 holds current that holds true what   55 a franklin
a yeoman owning his own land   56 Weald wooded region.   marks
coins of the value of thirteen shillings four pence   61 presently
immediately.   62–3 Saint Nicholas' clerks highwaymen. (Saint
Nicholas was popularly supposed to be the patron of thieves.)   64 I'll
none I want none   67 What Why   70 Trojans i.e., jolly fellows,
roisterers   72 profession i.e., robbery.   grace credit, favor

73–4 for . . . whole for the sake of their own reputation will make sure
that all goes well. (Gadshill hints that they may be joined by some
persons of social importance, such as the Prince.)   74 foot-landrakers
thieves who travel on foot   75 long-staff six-penny strikers robbers
with long staves who would knock down their victims for sixpence
76 mustachio . . . malt-worms purple-faced drunkards with huge
mustaches   77 tranquillity those who lead easy lives.   oneyers
ones, persons (?)   78 hold in keep a secret; hold fast   83 boots booty.
(With pun on *boots*, "shoes.")   85 Will . . . way? Will she let you go
dry in muddy roads? i.e., Will she protect you in tight places?
86 liquored (1) made waterproof by oiling (2) bribed (3) made drunk
87 as in a castle i.e., in complete security.   receipt recipe, formula
88 of fern seed i.e., of becoming invisible (since fern seed, almost
invisible itself, was popularly supposed to render its possessor invisible)   90 beholding beholden   93 purchase booty   96 Go to (An
expression of impatience.   *homo* . . . men the Latin name for man
applies to all types; the phrase "true man" applies to me as well as
the next man.   98 muddy stupid
2.2. Location: The highway, near Gad's Hill.
2 frets (1) is vexed (2) rubs and frays like *gummed velvet*, velvet made
glossy with a stiffening gum   3 close concealed.   6 keep keep up.

PRINCE   He is walked up to the top of the hill. I'll go seek him.   [*He steps aside.*]

FALSTAFF   I am accursed to rob in that thief's company. The rascal hath removed my horse and tied him I know not where. If I travel but four foot by the square 12 further afoot, I shall break my wind. Well, I doubt not but to die a fair death for all this, if I scape hanging for 14 killing that rogue. I have forsworn his company hourly any time this two-and-twenty years, and yet I am bewitched with the rogue's company. If the rascal have not given me medicines to make me love him, I'll be 18 hanged; it could not be else—I have drunk medicines. Poins! Hal! A plague upon you both! Bardolph! Peto! I'll starve ere I'll rob a foot further. An 'twere not as 21 good a deed as drink to turn true man and to leave 22 these rogues, I am the veriest varlet that ever chewed 23 with a tooth. Eight yards of uneven ground is three- 24 score-and-ten miles afoot with me, and the stony- hearted villains know it well enough. A plague upon it when thieves cannot be true one to another! (*They whistle.*) Whew! A plague upon you all! Give me my 28 horse, you rogues, give me my horse, and be hanged!

PRINCE   [*coming forward*]   Peace, ye fat-guts! Lie down. Lay thine ear close to the ground and list if thou 31 canst hear the tread of travelers.

FALSTAFF   Have you any levers to lift me up again, being down? 'Sblood, I'll not bear mine own flesh so far afoot again for all the coin in thy father's Exchequer. What a plague mean ye to colt me thus?   36

PRINCE   Thou liest. Thou art not colted, thou art uncolted.

FALSTAFF   I prithee, good Prince Hal, help me to my 39 horse, good king's son.   40

PRINCE   Out, ye rogue! Shall I be your hostler?

FALSTAFF   Go hang thyself in thine own heir-apparent garters! If I be ta'en, I'll peach for this. An I have not 43 ballads made on you all and sung to filthy tunes, let a cup of sack be my poison. When a jest is so forward, 45 and afoot too! I hate it.   46

Enter Gadshill.

GADSHILL   Stand!   47

FALSTAFF   So I do, against my will.

POINS   [*coming forward with Bardolph and Peto*]   Oh, 'tis our setter. I know his voice.   50

BARDOLPH   What news?

GADSHILL   Case ye, case ye, on with your vizards! 52

There's money of the King's coming down the hill; 'tis going to the King's Exchequer.

FALSTAFF   You lie, ye rogue, 'tis going to the King's Tavern.

GADSHILL   There's enough to make us all.   57

FALSTAFF   To be hanged.

PRINCE   Sirs, you four shall front them in the narrow 59 lane; Ned Poins and I will walk lower. If they scape 60 from your encounter, then they light on us.

PETO   How many be there of them?

GADSHILL   Some eight or ten.

FALSTAFF   Zounds, will they not rob us?

PRINCE   What, a coward, Sir John Paunch?

FALSTAFF   Indeed, I am not John of Gaunt, your 66 grandfather, but yet no coward, Hal.

PRINCE   Well, we leave that to the proof.   68

POINS   Sirrah Jack, thy horse stands behind the hedge. When thou need'st him, there thou shalt find him. Farewell, and stand fast.

FALSTAFF   Now cannot I strike him, if I should be 72 hanged.   73

PRINCE   [*to Poins*]   Ned, where are our disguises?

POINS   [*to Prince*]   Here, hard by. Stand close.
    [*Exeunt Prince and Poins.*]

FALSTAFF   Now, my masters, happy man be his dole, 76 say I. Every man to his business.   [*They stand aside.*]

Enter the Travelers.

FIRST TRAVELER   Come, neighbor. The boy shall lead our horses down the hill; we'll walk afoot awhile, and ease our legs.

THIEVES   [*coming forward*]   Stand!

TRAVELERS   Jesus bless us!

FALSTAFF   Strike! Down with them! Cut the villains' throats! Ah, whoreson caterpillars, bacon-fed knaves! 84 They hate us youth. Down with them, fleece them!

TRAVELERS   Oh, we are undone, both we and ours forever!

FALSTAFF   Hang ye, gorbellied knaves, are ye undone? 88 No, ye fat chuffs; I would your store were here. On, 89 bacons, on! What, ye knaves, young men must live. 90 You are grandjurors, are ye? We'll jure ye, 'faith. 91
    Here they rob them and bind them. Exeunt.

Enter the Prince and Poins [in buckram].

PRINCE   The thieves have bound the true men. Now could thou and I rob the thieves and go merrily to London, it would be argument for a week, laughter 94 for a month, and a good jest forever.

---

12 **square** a measuring tool   14 **fair** exemplary.   **for all** despite all   18 **medicines** love potions   21–4 **An . . . tooth** i.e., If it don't think it's a good idea to reform and turn informer, I'm the damnedest scoundrel that ever lived. (Cf. 2.1.30–1 and n.)   28 **Whew** (Perhaps Falstaff tries to answer the whistling he hears or mocks it.)   31 **list** listen   36 **colt** trick, cheat. (In lines 37–8, Prince Hal puns on the common meaning.)   39–40 **help . . . horse** help me to find my horse. (But in line 41, the Prince comically retorts as though having been asked to hold the stirrup while Falstaff mounted, as a hostler would do.)   43 **peach** inform on you   45 **so forward** so far advanced   46 **afoot** (1) in progress (2) on foot, i.e., not on horseback   47 **Stand!** Don't move! (But Falstaff answers in the sense of "stand on one's feet.")   50 **setter** arranger of the robbery. (See 1.2.104–5 and note.)   52 **Case ye** Put on your masks

57 **make us all** make our fortunes (or, as Falstaff sees it, make us be hanged).   59 **front** confront   60 **lower** further downhill.   66 **John of Gaunt** Henry IV's father, born at Ghent (and hence giving Falstaff a chance to pun on *gaunt* as the opposite of his fatness)   68 **proof** test.   72–3 **Now . . . hanged** (Falstaff wishes he could hit Poins, who is too quick for him.)   76 **happy . . . dole** may happiness be every man's portion or lot   84 **Ah . . . knaves!** i.e., Ah, you abominable parasites, you over-fed rascals!   88 **gorbellied** big-bellied   89 **chuffs** churls, rich but miserly.   **store** total wealth   90 **bacons** fat men   91 **grandjurors** i.e., men of wealth, able to serve on juries   94 **argument** a subject for conversation

POINS   Stand close. I hear them coming.

           [They stand aside.]

    Enter the thieves again.

FALSTAFF   Come, my masters, let us share, and then to   97
horse before day. An the Prince and Poins be not two
arrant cowards, there's no equity stirring. There's no   99
more valor in that Poins than in a wild duck.

           [The thieves begin to share the booty.]

PRINCE   Your money!

POINS   Villains!

    *As they are sharing, the Prince and Poins set upon
them. They all run away, and Falstaff, after a blow
or two, runs away too, leaving the booty behind
them.*

PRINCE
Got with much ease. Now merrily to horse.
The thieves are all scattered and possessed with fear
So strongly that they dare not meet each other;
Each takes his fellow for an officer.
Away, good Ned. Falstaff sweats to death
And lards the lean earth as he walks along.   108
Were't not for laughing, I should pity him.

POINS   How the fat rogue roared!   *Exeunt.*

[2.3]

    Enter Hotspur, solus, reading a letter.

HOTSPUR   "But, for mine own part, my lord, I could be
well contented to be there, in respect of the love I bear
your house." He could be contented; why is he not,   3
then? In respect of the love he bears our house! He
shows in this he loves his own barn better than he
loves our house. Let me see some more. "The purpose
you undertake is dangerous"—why, that's certain.
'Tis dangerous to take a cold, to sleep, to drink; but I
tell you, my lord fool, out of this nettle, danger, we
pluck this flower, safety. "The purpose you undertake
is dangerous, the friends you have named uncertain,
the time itself unsorted, and your whole plot too light   12
for the counterpoise of so great an opposition." Say   13
you so, say you so? I say unto you again, you are a
shallow, cowardly hind, and you lie. What a lack-brain   15
is this! By the Lord, our plot is a good plot as
ever was laid, our friends true and constant; a good
plot, good friends, and full of expectation; an excellent   18
plot, very good friends. What a frosty-spirited rogue is
this! Why, my lord of York commends the plot and   20

the general course of the action. Zounds, an I were   21
now by this rascal, I could brain him with his lady's   22
fan. Is there not my father, my uncle, and myself? Lord   23
Edmund Mortimer, my lord of York, and Owen Glendower? Is there not besides the Douglas? Have I not all
their letters to meet me in arms by the ninth of the next
month, and are they not some of them set forward
already? What a pagan rascal is this, an infidel! Ha,   28
you shall see now in very sincerity of fear and
cold heart will he to the King and lay open all our
proceedings. Oh, I could divide myself and go to buf-   31
fets for moving such a dish of skim milk with so hon-   32
orable an action! Hang him, let him tell the King, we
are prepared. I will set forward tonight.

    Enter his Lady.

How now, Kate? I must leave you within these two
hours.

LADY PERCY
Oh, my good lord, why are you thus alone?
For what offense have I this fortnight been
A banished woman from my Harry's bed?
Tell me, sweet lord, what is't that takes from thee
Thy stomach, pleasure, and thy golden sleep?   41
Why dost thou bend thine eyes upon the earth
And start so often when thou sit'st alone?
Why hast thou lost the fresh blood in thy cheeks
And given my treasures and my rights of thee   45
To thick-eyed musing and curst melancholy?   46
In thy faint slumbers I by thee have watched   47
And heard thee murmur tales of iron wars,
Speak terms of manage to thy bounding steed,   49
Cry, "Courage! To the field!" And thou hast talked
Of sallies and retires, of trenches, tents,   51
Of palisadoes, frontiers, parapets,   52
Of basilisks, of cannon, culverin,   53
Of prisoners' ransom, and of soldiers slain,
And all the currents of a heady fight.   55
Thy spirit within thee hath been so at war,
And thus hath so bestirred thee in thy sleep,
That beads of sweat have stood upon thy brow
Like bubbles in a late-disturbèd stream,   59
And in thy face strange motions have appeared,
Such as we see when men restrain their breath
On some great sudden hest. Oh, what portents are   62
    these?
Some heavy business hath my lord in hand,
And I must know it, else he loves me not.

---

97 **masters** good sirs   99 **arrant** notorious, unmitigated.   **equity**
judgment, discernment   108 **lards** drips fat on, bastes
**2.3. Location: Hotspur's estate (identified historically as Warkworth
Castle in Northumberland).**
0.1 *solus* alone   3 **house** family. (But Hotspur replies derisively in
lines 4–6 as though to the literal sense of a building that one might
compare to a barn.)   12 **unsorted** unsuitable   13 **for . . . of** to counterbalance   15 **hind** menial, peasant   18 **expectation** promise
20 **lord of York** i.e., Archbishop Scroop. (Also in line 24.)

21–2 **an . . . rascal** if I were face to face with this rascal, instead of
reading his letter   22–3 **his lady's fan** his wife's fan—a suitable light
weapon with which to chastise such a milktoast.   28 **pagan** unbelieving   31–2 **divide . . . buffets** i.e., fight with myself   32 **moving** urging   41 **stomach** appetite   45 **And . . . thee** and given the precious
right I have as wife to share your thoughts   46 **thick-eyed** dull-
sighted, vacant, abstracted.   **curst** ill-tempered   47 **faint** restless.
watched lain awake   49 **manage** horsemanship   51 **retires** retreats
52–3 **Of . . . culverin** of stakes set in the ground for defense, of ram-
parts, protective walls, of large and smaller cannon   55 **heady** headlong   59 **late-disturbèd** recently stirred up   62 **hest** command;
endeavor.

HOTSPUR [*calling*]
What, ho!

[*Enter a Servant.*]

Is Gilliams with the packet gone?
SERVANT   He is, my lord, an hour ago.
HOTSPUR
Hath Butler brought those horses from the sheriff?   67
SERVANT
One horse, my lord, he brought even now.   68
HOTSPUR
What horse? A roan, a crop-ear, is it not?   69
SERVANT
It is, my lord.
HOTSPUR   That roan shall be my throne.
Well, I will back him straight. Oh, *Esperance!*   71
Bid Butler lead him forth into the park.

[*Exit Servant.*]

LADY PERCY   But hear you, my lord.
HOTSPUR   What say'st thou, my lady?
LADY PERCY   What is it carries you away?   75
HOTSPUR   Why, my horse, my love, my horse.
LADY PERCY   Out, you mad-headed ape!   77
A weasel hath not such a deal of spleen   78
As you are tossed with. In faith,   79
I'll know your business, Harry, that I will.
I fear my brother Mortimer doth stir
About his title, and hath sent for you   82
To line his enterprise; but if you go—   83
HOTSPUR
So far afoot, I shall be weary, love.
LADY PERCY
Come, come, you paraquito, answer me   85
Directly unto this question that I ask.
In faith, I'll break thy little finger, Harry,
An if thou wilt not tell me all things true.   88
HOTSPUR   Away,
Away, you trifler! Love? I love thee not;
I care not for thee, Kate. This is no world
To play with mammets and to tilt with lips.   92
We must have bloody noses and cracked crowns,   93
And pass them current too. Gods me, my horse!   94
What say'st thou, Kate? What wouldst thou have with
me?
LADY PERCY
Do you not love me? Do you not, indeed?
Well, do not, then, for since you love me not

I will not love myself. Do you not love me?
Nay, tell me if you speak in jest or no.
HOTSPUR   Come, wilt thou see me ride?
And when I am a-horseback I will swear
I love thee infinitely. But hark you, Kate,
I must not have you henceforth question me
Whither I go, nor reason whereabout.   104
Whither I must, I must; and, to conclude,
This evening must I leave you, gentle Kate.
I know you wise, but yet no farther wise
Than Harry Percy's wife; constant you are,
But yet a woman; and for secrecy,
No lady closer, for I well believe   110
Thou wilt not utter what thou dost not know,
And so far will I trust thee, gentle Kate.
LADY PERCY   How, so far?
HOTSPUR
Not an inch further. But hark you, Kate:
Whither I go, thither shall you go too.
Today will I set forth, tomorrow you.
Will this content you, Kate?
LADY PERCY   It must, of force. *Exeunt.*   117

❖

[2.4]

Enter Prince and Poins.

PRINCE   Ned, prithee, come out of that fat room, and   1
lend me thy hand to laugh a little.
POINS   Where hast been, Hal?
PRINCE   With three or four loggerheads amongst three   4
or four score hogsheads. I have sounded the very bass   5
string of humility. Sirrah, I am sworn brother to a
leash of drawers, and can call them all by their Christian   7
names, as Tom, Dick, and Francis. They take it already   8
upon their salvation that, though I be but Prince of   9
Wales, yet I am the king of courtesy, and tell me flatly
I am no proud Jack like Falstaff, but a Corinthian, a lad   11
of mettle, a good boy—by the Lord, so they call me!—
and when I am King of England I shall command all
the good lads in Eastcheap. They call drinking deep   14
"dyeing scarlet"; and when you breathe in your water-   15
ing they cry "hem!" and bid you "play it off." To con-   16
clude, I am so good a proficient in one quarter of an
hour that I can drink with any tinker in his own language during my life. I tell thee, Ned, thou hast lost
much honor that thou wert not with me in this action.

67 **sheriff** i.e., bailiff.   68 **even** just   69 **roan** roan-colored, i.e., with white or grey interspersed in the overall color of the coat   71 **back** mount.   *Esperance* Hope. (The motto of the Percy family.)   75 **carries you away** carries you beyond the bounds of reason and judgment. (But Hotspur puns on the literal meaning.)   77 **Out** (An expression of impatience.)   78 **spleen** (The spleen was thought to be the source of impulsive and irritable behavior.)   79 **tossed** tossed about, agitated   82 **title** claim to the throne   83 **line** strengthen   85 **paraquito** little parrot. (A term of endearment.)   88 **An if** if   92 **mammets** dolls. (With a quibble on the Latin *mamma* meaning "breast.")   93 **crowns** (1) heads (2) coins worth five shillings. (Cracked coins would not "pass current," as Hotspur jokes in the next line.)   94 **Gods me** God save me

104 **reason whereabout** ask about what.   110 **closer** more close-mouthed   117 **of force** perforce, of necessity.
2.4. Location: A tavern in Eastcheap, London, usually identified as the Boar's Head. Some tavern furniture, including stools, is provided onstage.
1 **fat** stuffy, or, a vat room   4 **loggerheads** blockheads   5 **hogsheads** wine barrels.   **bass** (With a pun on *base*.)   7 **leash of drawers** three waiters   8–9 **take . . . salvation** already maintain it as they hope to be saved   11 **Jack** (1) Jack Falstaff (2) fellow.   **Corinthian** i.e., gay blade, good sport. (Corinth was reputed to be licentious.)
14–15 **They . . . scarlet** (Either because excessive drinking causes a red complexion or because urine, produced by *drinking deep*, was sometimes used for fixing dyes.)   15–16 **breathe . . . watering** pause for breath in your drinking   16 **play it off** drink it up.

But, sweet Ned—to sweeten which name of Ned, I
give thee this pennyworth of sugar, clapped even now   22
into my hand by an underskinker, one that never   23
spake other English in his life than "Eight shillings
and sixpence," and "You are welcome," with this
shrill addition, "Anon, anon, sir! Score a pint of bas-   26
tard in the Half-Moon," or so. But, Ned, to drive away   27
the time till Falstaff come, I prithee do thou stand in
some by-room while I question my puny drawer to   29
what end he gave me the sugar; and do thou never
leave calling "Francis," that his tale to me may be
nothing but "Anon." Step aside, and I'll show thee a
precedent.   [*Exit Poins.*]   33

POINS [*within*] Francis!
PRINCE Thou art perfect.
POINS [*within*] Francis!

Enter [Francis, a] drawer.

FRANCIS Anon, anon, sir.—Look down into the Pom-   37
garnet, Ralph.   38
PRINCE Come hither, Francis.
FRANCIS My lord?
PRINCE How long hast thou to serve, Francis?   41
FRANCIS Forsooth, five years, and as much as to—
POINS [*within*] Francis!
FRANCIS [*calling*] Anon, anon, sir.
PRINCE Five year! By'r Lady, a long lease for the   45
clinking of pewter. But Francis, darest thou be so
valiant as to play the coward with thy indenture and   47
show it a fair pair of heels and run from it?
FRANCIS Oh, Lord, sir, I'll be sworn upon all the books in   49
England, I could find in my heart—
POINS [*within*] Francis!
FRANCIS [*calling*] Anon, sir.
PRINCE How old art thou, Francis?
FRANCIS Let me see, about Michaelmas next I shall   54
be—
POINS [*within*] Francis!
FRANCIS [*calling*] Anon, sir. Pray, stay a little, my lord.
PRINCE Nay, but hark you, Francis: for the sugar thou
gavest me, 'twas a pennyworth, was 't not?
FRANCIS Oh, Lord, I would it had been two!
PRINCE I will give thee for it a thousand pound. Ask
me when thou wilt, and thou shalt have it.
POINS [*within*] Francis!
FRANCIS [*calling*] Anon, anon.
PRINCE Anon, Francis? No, Francis; but tomorrow,
Francis, or, Francis, o'Thursday, or indeed, Francis,
when thou wilt. But, Francis—
FRANCIS My lord?

PRINCE Wilt thou rob this leathern-jerkin, crystal-
button, not-pated, agate-ring, puke-stocking, caddis-   69
garter, smooth-tongue, Spanish-pouch—   70
FRANCIS Oh, Lord, sir, who do you mean?   71
PRINCE Why, then, your brown bastard is your only
drink; for look you, Francis, your white canvas   73
doublet will sully. In Barbary, sir, it cannot come to so   74
much.   75
FRANCIS What, sir?   76
POINS [*within*] Francis!
PRINCE Away, you rogue! Dost thou not hear them call?
Here they both call him; the drawer stands   79
amazed, not knowing which way to go.

Enter Vintner.

VINTNER What stand'st thou still and hear'st such a
calling? Look to the guests within.   [*Exit Francis.*]   80
My lord, old Sir John, with half a dozen more, are at the
door. Shall I let them in?
PRINCE Let them alone awhile, and then open the door.
[*Exit Vintner.*]

[*Calling*] Poins!

Enter Poins.

POINS Anon, anon, sir.
PRINCE Sirrah, Falstaff and the rest of the thieves are at
the door. Shall we be merry?
POINS As merry as crickets, my lad. But hark ye, what
cunning match have you made with this jest of the
drawer? Come, what's the issue?   90
PRINCE I am now of all humors that have showed   91
themselves humors since the old days of Goodman   92
Adam to the pupil age of this present twelve o'clock at   93
midnight.   94
                                                   95

[*Enter Francis, hurrying across the stage with
wine.*]

What's o'clock, Francis?
FRANCIS Anon, anon, sir.   [*Exit.*]
PRINCE That ever this fellow should have fewer words
than a parrot, and yet the son of a woman! His industry is upstairs and downstairs, his eloquence the parcel
of a reckoning. I am not yet of Percy's mind, the Hot-   100
spur of the north, he that kills me some six or seven   101
dozen of Scots at a breakfast, washes his hands, and   102
says to his wife, "Fie upon this quiet life! I want
work." "Oh, my sweet Harry," says she, "how many

22 sugar (Used to sweeten wine.) **23 underskinker** assistant to a
waiter or bartender **26–7 Anon . . . Half-Moon** Coming, sir!—
Charge a pint of a sweet Spanish wine to the customers in the room
of the inn called "the Half-Moon." **29 by-room** side-room. **puny
drawer** inexperienced tapster or bartender **33 precedent** example.
37–8 Pomgarnet Pomegranate. (Another room in the inn.) **41 serve**
i.e., serve out your apprenticeship **45 By'r Lady** By Our Lady
47 indenture contract of apprenticeship **49 books** i.e., Bibles
54 Michaelmas September 29

69–71 Wilt . . . Spanish-pouch i.e., Will you rob your master of your
services by running away, this man with his leather jacket, transparent buttons, cropped hair, a ring with small figures in an agate stone
for a seal, dark woolen stockings, worsted garters, an ingratiating
flattering manner of speech, wallet of Spanish leather **73–6 Why . . .
much** (The Prince talks seeming nonsense in order to bewilder Francis, but he also implies that Francis should stick to his trade, since he
will not cut much of a figure in the world.) **75 it** i.e., sugar
79.3 Vintner i.e., Innkeeper. **80 What** Why **90 match** game, contest
91 issue outcome, point. **92–5 I . . . midnight** i.e., I'm now in a
mood for anything that has happened in the whole history of the
world. **93 Goodman** (Title for a yeoman.) **94 pupil** youthful
100–1 parcel . . . reckoning items of a bill. **102 kills me** i.e., kills.
(*Me* is used colloquially.)

hast thou killed today?" "Give my roan horse a drench," says he, and answers, "Some fourteen," an hour after, "a trifle, a trifle." I prithee, call in Falstaff. 107 I'll play Percy, and that damned brawn shall play Dame Mortimer his wife. "Rivo!" says the drunkard. Call in 109 ribs, call in tallow. 110

Enter Falstaff, [Gadshill, Bardolph, and Peto; 111 *Francis following with wine].*

POINS　Welcome, Jack. Where hast thou been?

FALSTAFF　A plague of all cowards, I say, and a vengeance too! Marry and amen! Give me a cup of 113 sack, boy. Ere I lead this life long, I'll sew nether-stocks, and mend them and foot them too. A plague 115 of all cowards! Give me a cup of sack, rogue. Is there 116 no virtue extant? *He drinketh.*

PRINCE　Didst thou never see Titan kiss a dish of butter, pitiful-hearted Titan, that melted at the sweet tale of 119 the sun's? If thou didst, then behold that compound. 120

FALSTAFF　You rogue, here's lime in this sack too. There 121 is nothing but roguery to be found in villainous man, 122 yet a coward is worse than a cup of sack with lime in it. A villainous coward! Go thy ways, old Jack, die when thou wilt. If manhood, good manhood, be not forgot upon the face of the earth, then am I a shotten herring. There lives not three good men unhanged in 127 England, and one of them is fat and grows old, God 128 help the while! A bad world, I say. I would I were a weaver; I could sing psalms or anything. A plague of 130 all cowards, I say still. 131

PRINCE　How now, woolsack, what mutter you?

FALSTAFF　A king's son! If I do not beat thee out of thy 133 kingdom with a dagger of lath, and drive all thy subjects afore thee like a flock of wild geese, I'll never 135 wear hair on my face more. You, Prince of Wales!

PRINCE　Why, you whoreson round man, what's the matter?

FALSTAFF　Are not you a coward? Answer me to that. And Poins there?

POINS　Zounds, ye fat paunch, an ye call me coward, by the Lord, I'll stab thee.

FALSTAFF　I call thee coward? I'll see thee damned ere I call thee coward, but I would give a thousand pound I could run as fast as thou canst. You are straight enough in the shoulders; you care not who sees your back. Call you that backing of your friends? A plague upon such backing! Give me them that will face me.

Give me a cup of sack. I am a rogue if I drunk today.

PRINCE　Oh, villain, thy lips are scarce wiped since thou drunk'st last.

FALSTAFF　All is one for that. (*He drinketh.*) A plague of 153 all cowards, still say I.

PRINCE　What's the matter?

FALSTAFF　What's the matter? There be four of us here have ta'en a thousand pound this day morning. 157

PRINCE　Where is it, Jack, where is it?

FALSTAFF　Where is it? Taken from us it is. A hundred upon poor four of us.

PRINCE　What, a hundred, man?

FALSTAFF　I am a rogue if I were not at half-sword with 162 a dozen of them two hours together. I have scaped by 163 miracle. I am eight times thrust through the doublet, 164 four through the hose, my buckler cut through and 165 through, my sword hacked like a handsaw—*ecce* 166 *signum!* I never dealt better since I was a man. All 167 would not do. A plague of all cowards! Let them 168 speak. If they speak more or less than truth, they are villains and the sons of darkness.

PRINCE　Speak, sirs, how was it?

GADSHILL　We four set upon some dozen—

FALSTAFF　Sixteen at least, my lord.

GADSHILL　And bound them.

PETO　No, no, they were not bound.

FALSTAFF　You rogue, they were bound, every man of them, or I am a Jew else, an Hebrew Jew.

GADSHILL　As we were sharing, some six or seven fresh men set upon us—

FALSTAFF　And unbound the rest, and then come in the other. 181

PRINCE　What, fought you with them all?

FALSTAFF　All? I know not what you call all, but if I fought not with fifty of them, I am a bunch of radish. If there were not two- or three-and-fifty upon poor old Jack, then am I no two-legged creature.

PRINCE　Pray God you have not murdered some of them.

FALSTAFF　Nay, that's past praying for. I have peppered two of them. Two I am sure I have paid, two rogues in buckram suits. I tell thee what, Hal, if I tell thee a lie, spit in my face, call me horse. Thou knowest my old ward. Here I lay, and thus I bore my point. [*He* 192 *demonstrates his stance.*] Four rogues in buckram let drive at me—

PRINCE　What, four? Thou said'st but two even now. 195

FALSTAFF　Four, Hal, I told thee four.

POINS　Ay, ay, he said four.

FALSTAFF　These four came all afront, and mainly thrust 198 at me. I made me no more ado but took all their seven 199 points in my target, thus. 200

---

107 **drench** draft (sometimes of medicine). **says he** i.e., he tells a servant 109 **brawn** fat boar 110 **Rivo** (An exclamation of uncertain meaning, but related to drinking.) 111 **ribs** rib roast. **tallow** fat drippings. 113 **of** on 115–16 **netherstocks** stockings (the sewing or mending of which is a menial occupation) 116 **foot** make a new foot for 119 **Titan** i.e., the sun 120 **that** i.e., the butter 121 **compound** melting butter, i.e., Falstaff. 122 **lime in this sack** i.e., lime added to make the wine sparkle 127–8 **a shotten herring** a herring that has cast its roe and is consequently thin. 130 **the while** i.e., in these bad times. 131 **weaver** (Many psalm-singing Protestant immigrants from the Low Countries were weavers.) 133 **woolsack** bale of wool 135 **dagger of lath** (The Vice, a stock comic figure in morality plays, was so armed.)

153 **All . . . that** No matter. 157 **this day morning** this morning. 162 **at half-sword** fighting at close quarters 163 **scaped** escaped 164 **doublet** Elizabethan upper garment like a jacket 165 **hose** close-fitting breeches. **buckler** shield 166–7 *ecce signum* behold the proof. (Familiar words from the Mass.) 167–8 **All . . . do** All that I did was of no use. 181 **other** others. 192 **ward** defensive stance, parry. **lay** stood 195 **even** just 198 **afront** abreast. **mainly** powerfully 199 **made me** made. (*Me* is used colloquially.) 200 **target** shield

PRINCE   Seven? Why, there were but four even now.

FALSTAFF   In buckram?

POINS   Ay, four, in buckram suits.

FALSTAFF   Seven, by these hilts, or I am a villain else.   204

PRINCE [*aside to Poins*]   Prithee, let him alone. We shall have more anon.

FALSTAFF   Dost thou hear me, Hal?

PRINCE   Ay, and mark thee too, Jack.   208

FALSTAFF   Do so, for it is worth the listening to. These nine in buckram that I told thee of—

PRINCE   So, two more already.

FALSTAFF   Their points being broken—   212

POINS   Down fell their hose.

FALSTAFF   Began to give me ground; but I followed me   214
close, came in foot and hand; and with a thought   215
seven of the eleven I paid.

PRINCE   Oh, monstrous! Eleven buckram men grown out of two!

FALSTAFF   But, as the devil would have it, three misbegotten knaves in Kendal green came at my back   220
and let drive at me; for it was so dark, Hal, that thou
couldst not see thy hand.

PRINCE   These lies are like their father that begets them,   223
gross as a mountain, open, palpable. Why, thou
claybrained guts, thou knotty-pated fool, thou whore-   225
son, obscene, greasy tallow-keech—   226

FALSTAFF   What, art thou mad? Art thou mad? Is not the truth the truth?

PRINCE   Why, how couldst thou know these men in
Kendal green when it was so dark thou couldst not see
thy hand? Come, tell us your reason. What sayest
thou to this?

POINS   Come, your reason, Jack, your reason.

FALSTAFF   What, upon compulsion? Zounds, an I were
at the strappado, or all the racks in the world, I would   235
not tell you on compulsion. Give you a reason on compulsion? If reasons were as plentiful as blackberries,   237
I would give no man a reason upon compulsion, I.

PRINCE   I'll be no longer guilty of this sin. This sanguine   239
coward, this bed-presser, this horse-backbreaker, this
huge hill of flesh—

FALSTAFF   'Sblood, you starveling, you eel-skin, you
dried neat's tongue, you bull's pizzle, you stockfish!   243
Oh, for breath to utter what is like thee! You tailor's
yard, you sheath, you bowcase, you vile standing   245
tuck—   246

PRINCE   Well, breathe awhile, and then to it again, and
when thou hast tired thyself in base comparisons,
hear me speak but this.

POINS   Mark, Jack.

PRINCE   We two saw you four set on four and bound
them, and were masters of their wealth. Mark now
how a plain tale shall put you down. Then did we two
set on you four, and, with a word, outfaced you from   254
your prize, and have it, yea, and can show it you here
in the house. And, Falstaff, you carried your guts
away as nimbly, with as quick dexterity, and roared
for mercy, and still run and roared, as ever I heard bull
calf. What a slave art thou, to hack thy sword as thou
hast done, and then say it was in fight! What trick,
what device, what starting-hole canst thou now find   261
out to hide thee from this open and apparent shame?

POINS   Come, let's hear, Jack. What trick hast thou now?

FALSTAFF   By the Lord, I knew ye as well as he that
made ye. Why, hear you, my masters, was it for me to
kill the heir apparent? Should I turn upon the true
prince? Why, thou knowest I am as valiant as Hercules, but beware instinct. The lion will not touch the
true prince. Instinct is a great matter; I was now a
coward on instinct. I shall think the better of myself
and thee during my life—I for a valiant lion, and thou
for a true prince. But by the Lord, lads, I am glad you
have the money. Hostess, clap to the doors! Watch   273
tonight, pray tomorrow. Gallants, lads, boys, hearts   274
of gold, all the titles of good fellowship come to you!
What, shall we be merry? Shall we have a play
extempore?

PRINCE   Content; and the argument shall be thy run-   278
ning away.

FALSTAFF   Ah, no more of that, Hal, an thou lovest me!

Enter Hostess.

HOSTESS
Oh, Jesu, my lord the Prince!

PRINCE   How now, my lady the hostess, what say'st
thou to me?

HOSTESS   Marry, my lord, there is a nobleman of the
court at door would speak with you. He says he
comes from your father.

PRINCE   Give him as much as will make him a royal   287
man, and send him back again to my mother.   288

FALSTAFF   What manner of man is he?

HOSTESS   An old man.

FALSTAFF   What doth Gravity out of his bed at mid-   291
night? Shall I give him his answer?

PRINCE   Prithee, do, Jack.

FALSTAFF   Faith, and I'll send him packing.   *Exit.*

PRINCE   Now, sirs. By'r Lady, you fought fair; so did
you, Peto; so did you, Bardolph. You are lions too,
you ran away upon instinct, you will not touch the
true prince; no, fie!

BARDOLPH   Faith, I ran when I saw others run.

---

204 by these hilts by my sword hilt.   **208 mark** (1) pay heed (2) keep
count   **212 points** sword points. (But Poins puns on the sense of laces,
by which the hose were attached to the doublet.)   **214 followed me**
followed   **215 with a thought** quick as a thought   **220 Kendal** a
town known for its textiles   **223 their father** (1) Falstaff (2) the devil,
proverbially the father of lies   **225 knotty-pated** thickheaded
226 tallow-keech lump of tallow   **235 strappado** a kind of torture
237 reasons . . . blackberries (Falstaff puns on *raisins*, pronounced
nearly like *reasons*.)   **239 sanguine** ruddy   **243 neat's** ox's.   **pizzle**
penis.   **stockfish** dried cod.   **245 yard** yardstick   **245–6 standing
tuck** rapier standing on its point, or no longer pliant

254 with a word (1) in a word (2) with a minimum of speech.
outfaced frightened   **261 starting-hole** point of shelter (like a rabbit's hole)   **273 Watch** (1) Keep watchful vigil. (See Matthew 26:41.)
(2) Carouse   **274 pray** (1) pray to God (2) prey   **278 argument** plot of
the play   **287–8 Give . . . man** (Prince Hal puns on the value of coins:
a *noble* was worth six shillings eight pence; a *royal* was worth ten
shillings.)   **291 What doth** Why is

PRINCE   Faith, tell me now in earnest, how came Falstaff's sword so hacked?

PETO   Why, he hacked it with his dagger, and said he would swear truth out of England but he would make 303 you believe it was done in fight, and persuaded us to do the like.

BARDOLPH   Yea, and to tickle our noses with spear grass to make them bleed, and then to beslubber our gar- 307 ments with it and swear it was the blood of true men. I did that I did not this seven year before: I blushed to 309 hear his monstrous devices.

PRINCE   Oh, villain, thou stolest a cup of sack eighteen years ago and wert taken with the manner, and ever 312 since thou hast blushed extempore. Thou hadst fire 313 and sword on thy side, and yet thou ran'st away. What instinct hadst thou for it?

BARDOLPH   My lord, do you see these meteors? Do you 316 behold these exhalations?   [Pointing to his own face.] 317

PRINCE   I do.

BARDOLPH   What think you they portend?   319

PRINCE   Hot livers and cold purses.   320

BARDOLPH   Choler, my lord, if rightly taken.   321

PRINCE   No, if rightly taken, halter.   322

Enter Falstaff.

Here comes lean Jack, here comes bare-bone.—How now, my sweet creature of bombast? How long is't 324 ago, Jack, since thou sawest thine own knee?

FALSTAFF   My own knee? When I was about thy years, Hal, I was not an eagle's talon in the waist; I could have crept into any alderman's thumb ring. A plague of sighing and grief! It blows a man up like a bladder. There's villainous news abroad. Here was Sir John Bracy from your father. You must to the court in the morning. That same mad fellow of the north, Percy, and he of Wales that gave Amamon the bastinado and 333 made Lucifer cuckold and swore the devil his true 334 liegeman upon the cross of a Welsh hook—what a 335 plague call you him?

POINS   Owen Glendower.

FALSTAFF   Owen, Owen, the same; and his son-in-law Mortimer, and old Northumberland, and that

sprightly Scot of Scots, Douglas, that runs a-horseback up a hill perpendicular—

PRINCE   He that rides at high speed, and with his pistol kills a sparrow flying.

FALSTAFF   You have hit it.   344

PRINCE   So did he never the sparrow.

FALSTAFF   Well, that rascal hath good mettle in him; he will not run.   347

PRINCE   Why, what a rascal art thou then to praise him so for running!

FALSTAFF   A-horseback, ye cuckoo; but afoot he will not budge a foot.

PRINCE   Yes, Jack, upon instinct.

FALSTAFF   I grant ye, upon instinct. Well, he is there too, and one Mordake, and a thousand blue-caps more. 354 Worcester is stolen away tonight. Thy father's beard is turned white with the news. You may buy land now as cheap as stinking mackerel.

PRINCE   Why, then, it is like, if there come a hot June 358 and this civil buffeting hold, we shall buy maiden- 359 heads as they buy hobnails, by the hundreds.

FALSTAFF   By the mass, lad, thou sayest true; it is like we shall have good trading that way. But tell me, Hal, art not thou horrible afeard? Thou being heir appar- ent, could the world pick thee out three such enemies again as that fiend Douglas, that spirit Percy, and that devil Glendower? Art thou not horribly afraid? Doth not thy blood thrill at it?

PRINCE   Not a whit, i'faith. I lack some of thy instinct.

FALSTAFF   Well, thou wilt be horribly chid tomorrow 369 when thou comest to thy father. If thou love me, practice an answer.

PRINCE   Do thou stand for my father, and examine me upon the particulars of my life.

FALSTAFF   Shall I? Content. This chair shall be my state, 374 this dagger my scepter, and this cushion my crown.
                   [Falstaff establishes himself on his "throne."]

PRINCE   Thy state is taken for a joint stool, thy golden 376 scepter for a leaden dagger, and thy precious rich 377 crown for a pitiful bald crown.

FALSTAFF   Well, an the fire of grace be not quite out of thee, now shalt thou be moved. Give me a cup of sack to make my eyes look red, that it may be thought I have wept; for I must speak in passion, and I will do it in King Cambyses' vein.   383

PRINCE   Well, here is my leg.   [He bows.]

FALSTAFF   And here is my speech. Stand aside, nobil- ity.

HOSTESS   Oh, Jesu, this is excellent sport, i'faith!

FALSTAFF
Weep not, sweet queen, for trickling tears are vain.

HOSTESS   Oh, the Father, how he holds his countenance! 389

303 **swear . . . would** swear oaths until they go out of fashion if he did not   307 **beslubber** smear, cover   309 **that** something   312 **taken . . . manner** caught with the goods   313 **extempore** without needing any occasion. (Bardolph is red-faced whether he blushes or not.) **fire** i.e., a red nose and complexion caused by heavy drinking 316, 317 **meteors, exhalations** i.e., the red blotches on Bardolph's face. 319 **portend** signify. (Meteors, comets, and other meteorological phe- nomena were widely regarded as omens of disaster.)   320 **Hot . . . purses** i.e., Livers inflamed by drink and purses made empty by spending.   321 **Choler** A choleric or combative temperament. **taken** understood. (But the Prince, in his next speech, uses the word to mean "arrested.")   322 **halter** hangman's noose. (The Prince plays on Bardolph's *choler*, which he takes as *collar*.)   322.1 (Falstaff's entry in the Quarto after line 321 suggests he is visible to the audience while the Prince talks of a hangman's halter.)   324 **bombast** (1) cotton padding (2) fustian speech.   333 **Amamon** (The name of a demon.) **bastinado** beating on the soles of the feet   334 **made . . . cuckold** i.e., gave Lucifer his horns, the sign of cuckoldry   334–5 **and swore . . . liegeman** and made the devil take an oath of allegiance as a true sub- ject   335 **Welsh hook** curved-bladed pike lacking the cross shape of the sword on which such oaths were usually sworn

344 **hit it** described it exactly. (But the Prince takes *hit* literally in the next line.)   347 **run** flee. (But the Prince answers punningly in the sense of "ride at high speed.")   354 **blue-caps** Scottish soldiers 358 **like** likely   359 **hold** continues   369 **chid** chided   374 **state** chair of state, throne   376 **joint stool** a stool made by a joiner or furniture maker   377 **leaden** of soft metal, hence inferior   383 **in . . . vein** i.e., in the ranting and (by Shakespeare's time) old-fashioned style of Thomas Preston's *Cambyses*, an early Elizabethan tragedy.   389 **the Father** i.e., in God's name.   **holds his countenance** keeps a straight face.

FALSTAFF
For God's sake, lords, convey my tristful queen,   390
For tears do stop the floodgates of her eyes.   391
HOSTESS   Oh, Jesu, he doth it as like one of these harlotry 392
players as ever I see!   393
FALSTAFF
Peace, good pint pot; peace, good tickle-brain.—   394
Harry, I do not only marvel where thou spendest thy
time, but also how thou art accompanied; for though 396
the camomile, the more it is trodden on the faster it 397
grows, yet youth, the more it is wasted the sooner it 398
wears. That thou art my son I have partly thy mother's 399
word, partly my own opinion, but chiefly a villainous
trick of thine eye and a foolish hanging of thy nether 401
lip that doth warrant me. If then thou be son to me, 402
here lies the point: why, being son to me, art thou so
pointed at? Shall the blessed sun of heaven prove a
micher and eat blackberries? A question not to be 405
asked. Shall the son of England prove a thief and take
purses? A question to be asked. There is a thing, Harry,
which thou hast often heard of, and it is known
to many in our land by the name of pitch. This pitch, 409
as ancient writers do report, doth defile; so doth the 410
company thou keepest. For, Harry, now I do not speak
to thee in drink but in tears, not in pleasure but in
passion, not in words only but in woes also. And yet 413
there is a virtuous man whom I have often noted in
thy company, but I know not his name.
PRINCE   What manner of man, an it like Your Majesty? 416
FALSTAFF   A goodly portly man, i'faith, and a corpulent; 417
of a cheerful look, a pleasing eye, and a most noble
carriage; and, as I think, his age some fifty, or, by'r
Lady, inclining to threescore; and now I remember me,
his name is Falstaff. If that man should be lewdly 421
given, he deceiveth me; for, Harry, I see virtue in his
looks. If then the tree may be known by the fruit, as the 423
fruit by the tree, then peremptorily I speak it, there is 424
virtue in that Falstaff. Him keep with, the rest banish.
And tell me now, thou naughty varlet, tell me, where
hast thou been this month?
PRINCE   Dost thou speak like a king? Do thou stand for
me, and I'll play my father.
FALSTAFF   Depose me? If thou dost it half so gravely, so
majestically, both in word and matter, hang me up by
the heels for a rabbit-sucker or a poulter's hare.   432
[Hal takes Falstaff's place on the "throne."]

PRINCE   Well, here I am set.   433
FALSTAFF   And here I stand. Judge, my masters.
PRINCE   Now, Harry, whence come you?
FALSTAFF   My noble lord, from Eastcheap.
PRINCE   The complaints I hear of thee are grievous.
FALSTAFF   'Sblood, my lord, they are false.—Nay, I'll 438
tickle ye for a young prince, i'faith.   439
PRINCE   Swearest thou, ungracious boy? Henceforth
ne'er look on me. Thou art violently carried away from
grace. There is a devil haunts thee in the likeness of an
old fat man; a tun of man is thy companion. Why dost 443
thou converse with that trunk of humors, that bolting- 444
hutch of beastliness, that swollen parcel of dropsies, 445
that huge bombard of sack, that stuffed cloak-bag of 446
guts, that roasted Manningtree ox with the pudding in 447
his belly, that reverend Vice, that gray Iniquity, that 448
father ruffian, that vanity in years? Wherein is he good 449
but to taste sack and drink it? Wherein neat and
cleanly but to carve a capon and eat it? Wherein 451
cunning but in craft? Wherein crafty but in villainy? 452
Wherein villainous but in all things? Wherein worthy
but in nothing?
FALSTAFF   I would Your Grace would take me with 455
you. Whom means Your Grace?   456
PRINCE   That villainous abominable misleader of youth,
Falstaff, that old white-bearded Satan.
FALSTAFF   My lord, the man I know.
PRINCE   I know thou dost.
FALSTAFF   But to say I know more harm in him than in
myself were to say more than I know. That he is old,
the more the pity, his white hairs do witness it; but
that he is, saving your reverence, a whoremaster, that 464
I utterly deny. If sack and sugar be a fault, God help
the wicked! If to be old and merry be a sin, then many
an old host that I know is damned. If to be fat be to be 467
hated, then Pharaoh's lean kine are to be loved. No, 468
my good lord, banish Peto, banish Bardolph, banish
Poins; but for sweet Jack Falstaff, kind Jack Falstaff,
true Jack Falstaff, valiant Jack Falstaff, and therefore
more valiant being as he is old Jack Falstaff, banish not
him thy Harry's company, banish not him thy Harry's
company—banish plump Jack, and banish all the
world.

---

390 convey escort away.   tristful sorrowing   391 stop fill   392 harlotry scurvy, vagabond   393 players actors   394 tickle-brain (A slang
term for strong liquor, here applied as a nickname for the tavern hostess.)   396–9 for though . . . wears (Falstaff parodies the style of John
Lyly's Euphues, with its elaborate balanced antitheses, alliterative
effects, and illustrations drawn from fanciful natural history. Camomile
is an aromatic creeping herb whose flowers and leaves are used medicinally.)   401 trick trait   402 warrant assure   405 micher truant
409–10 This . . . defile (An allusion to the familiar proverb from
Ecclesiasticus 13:1 about the defilement of touching pitch.)   pitch a
sticky, black residue from the distillation of tar, used to seal wood
from moisture   413 passion sorrow   416 an it like if it please
417 portly (1) stately (2) corpulent   421 lewdly wickedly   423 If . . .
by the fruit (See Matthew 12:33.)   424 peremptorily decisively
432 rabbit-sucker unweaned rabbit.   poulter's poulterer's

433 set seated.   438 'Sblood i.e., By Christ's blood   439 tickle ye for
amuse you in the role of   443 tun (1) large barrel (2) ton   444 converse associate.   humors body fluids, diseases   444–5 bolting-hutch
large bin   445 dropsies accumulations of fluids causing swelling
446 bombard leathern drinking vessel.   cloak-bag portmanteau
447 Manningtree ox (Manningtree, a town in Essex, had noted fairs
where, no doubt, oxen were roasted whole.)   pudding sausage-like
entrails   448 Vice, Iniquity (Allegorical names for the chief comic
character and tempter in morality plays.)   449 vanity person given
to worldly desires   451 cleanly (1) pure (2) deft.   a capon a castrated
rooster for the table   452 cunning (1) skillful (2) crafty   455–6 take
me with you let me catch up with your meaning.   464 saving your
reverence i.e., with my apology for using offensive language
467 host innkeeper   468 Pharaoh's lean kine (See Genesis 41, where
Pharaoh's dream of seven well-fattened cattle being devoured by
seven lean ones is interpreted by Joseph as a prophecy of seven years'
famine to come.)

PRINCE   I do, I will.   [*A knocking.*
                               Exeunt Hostess, Francis, and Bardolph.]

Enter Bardolph, running.

BARDOLPH   Oh, my lord, my lord! The sheriff with a
most monstrous watch is at the door.   478
FALSTAFF   Out, ye rogue! Play out the play. I have
much to say in the behalf of that Falstaff.

Enter the Hostess.

HOSTESS   Oh, Jesu, my lord, my lord!
PRINCE   Heigh, heigh! The devil rides upon a fiddle-   482
stick. What's the matter?   483
HOSTESS   The sheriff and all the watch are at the door.
They are come to search the house. Shall I let them in?
FALSTAFF   Dost thou hear, Hal? Never call a true piece 486
of gold a counterfeit. Thou art essentially made   487
without seeming so.   488
PRINCE   And thou a natural coward without instinct.
FALSTAFF   I deny your major. If you will deny the   490
sheriff, so; if not, let him enter. If I become not a cart 491
as well as another man, a plague on my bringing up!   492
I hope I shall as soon be strangled with a halter as
another.
PRINCE   Go hide thee behind the arras. The rest walk   495
up above. Now, my masters, for a true face and good   496
conscience.
FALSTAFF   Both which I have had, but their date is out, 498
and therefore I'll hide me.   [*He hides behind the arras.*]
PRINCE   Call in the sheriff.
                      [*Exeunt all except the Prince and Peto.*]

Enter Sheriff and the Carrier.

Now, Master Sheriff, what is your will with me?
SHERIFF
First, pardon me, my lord. A hue and cry   502
Hath followed certain men unto this house.
PRINCE   What men?
SHERIFF
One of them is well known, my gracious lord,
A gross, fat man.
CARRIER   As fat as butter.
PRINCE
The man, I do assure you, is not here,
For I myself at this time have employed him.
And, Sheriff, I will engage my word to thee   509
That I will, by tomorrow dinnertime,   510
Send him to answer thee, or any man,

For anything he shall be charged withal;
And so let me entreat you leave the house.
SHERIFF
I will, my lord. There are two gentlemen
Have in this robbery lost three hundred marks.
PRINCE
It may be so. If he have robbed these men,
He shall be answerable; and so farewell.
SHERIFF   Good night, my noble lord.
PRINCE
I think it is good morrow, is it not?   519
SHERIFF
Indeed, my lord, I think it be two o'clock.
                                   Exit [*with Carrier*].
PRINCE   This oily rascal is known as well as Paul's. Go 521
call him forth.
PETO   [*discovering Falstaff*]   Falstaff—Fast asleep behind
the arras, and snorting like a horse.
PRINCE   Hark, how hard he fetches breath. Search his
pockets. (*He searcheth his pockets, and findeth certain
papers.*) What hast thou found?
PETO   Nothing but papers, my lord.
PRINCE   Let's see what they be. Read them.
PETO [*reads*]
     Item, A capon,...2s. 2d.
     Item, Sauce,...4d.
     Item, Sack, two gallons, ...5s. 8d.
     Item, Anchovies and sack after
          supper,..2s. 6d.
     Item, Bread, ...ob. 534
PRINCE   Oh, monstrous! But one halfpennyworth of
bread to this intolerable deal of sack? What there is
else, keep close; we'll read it at more advantage. There 537
let him sleep till day. I'll to the court in the morning.
We must all to the wars, and thy place shall be
honorable. I'll procure this fat rogue a charge of foot, 540
and I know his death will be a march of twelve score.   541
The money shall be paid back again with advantage.   542
Be with me betimes in the morning; and so, good   543
morrow, Peto.
PETO   Good morrow, good my lord.   545
               Exeunt [*separately. Falstaff is concealed
                            once more behind the arras.*]

❧

[3.1]

*Enter Hotspur, Worcester, Lord Mortimer,
[and] Owen Glendower.*

478 watch posse of constables   **482–3 The . . . fiddlestick** i.e., Here's
much ado about nothing.   **486–8 Dost . . . seeming so** (In this difficult passage, Falstaff seems to suggest that he is true gold, not counterfeit, and so should not be betrayed to the watch by the Prince,
who, he hopes, is not merely playacting at the tavern but is truly one
of its madcap members.)   **490 deny your major** reject your major
premise.   **deny** refuse entrance to   **491 become** befit, adorn.   **cart**
i.e., hangman's cart   **492 bringing up** (1) upbringing (2) being
brought before the authorities to be hanged.   **495 arras** wall hanging
or tapestry.   **496 up above** upstairs.   **498 date is out** lease has run
out   **502 hue and cry** outcry calling for the pursuit of a felon   **509
engage** pledge   **510 dinnertime** i.e., about noon

519 morrow morning   **521 Paul's** Saint Paul's Cathedral.   **534 ob.**
obolus, i.e., halfpenny   **537 close** hidden.   **advantage** favorable
opportunity.   **540 charge of foot** command of a company of infantry
541 twelve score i.e., two hundred and forty yards.   **542 advantage**
interest.   **543 betimes** early   **545.1–2 Exeunt . . . arras** (Onstage, the
arras is evidently arranged so that Falstaff can exit behind it once the
scene is over.)
3.1 Location: Wales. Glendower's residence. (Holinshed places a
meeting of the rebel deputies at Bangor in the Archdeacon's house,
but in this present "unhistorical" scene, as invented by Shakespeare, Glendower is host throughout.) Seats are provided onstage.

MORTIMER
    These promises are fair, the parties sure,
    And our induction full of prosperous hope.   2
HOTSPUR
    Lord Mortimer, and cousin Glendower,
    Will you sit down? And uncle Worcester—
    A plague upon it, I have forgot the map.
GLENDOWER [producing a map]
    No, here it is. Sit, cousin Percy,
    Sit, good cousin Hotspur—for by that name
    As oft as Lancaster doth speak of you   8
    His cheek looks pale, and with a rising sigh
    He wisheth you in heaven.
HOTSPUR   And you in hell,
    As oft as he hears Owen Glendower spoke of.
GLENDOWER
    I cannot blame him. At my nativity
    The front of heaven was full of fiery shapes,   13
    Of burning cressets, and at my birth   14
    The frame and huge foundation of the earth
    Shaked like a coward.
HOTSPUR   Why, so it would have done
    At the same season, if your mother's cat
    Had but kittened, though yourself had never been
        born.
GLENDOWER
    I say the earth did shake when I was born.
HOTSPUR
    And I say the earth was not of my mind,
    If you suppose as fearing you it shook.
GLENDOWER
    The heavens were all on fire; the earth did tremble.
HOTSPUR
    Oh, then the earth shook to see the heavens on fire,
    And not in fear of your nativity.
    Diseasèd nature oftentimes breaks forth
    In strange eruptions; oft the teeming earth
    Is with a kind of colic pinched and vexed
    By the imprisoning of unruly wind
    Within her womb, which, for enlargement striving,   29
    Shakes the old beldam earth and topples down   30
    Steeples and moss-grown towers. At your birth
    Our grandam earth, having this distemp'rature,   32
    In passion shook.
GLENDOWER   Cousin, of many men   33
    I do not bear these crossings. Give me leave   34
    To tell you once again that at my birth
    The front of heaven was full of fiery shapes,
    The goats ran from the mountains, and the herds
    Were strangely clamorous to the frighted fields.
    These signs have marked me extraordinary,
    And all the courses of my life do show
    I am not in the roll of common men.

Where is he living, clipped in with the sea   42
That chides the banks of England, Scotland, Wales,   43
Which calls me pupil or hath read to me?   44
And bring him out that is but woman's son   45
Can trace me in the tedious ways of art   46
And hold me pace in deep experiments.   47
HOTSPUR
    I think there's no man speaks better Welsh.   48
    I'll to dinner.
MORTIMER
    Peace, cousin Percy; you will make him mad.
GLENDOWER
    I can call spirits from the vasty deep.   51
HOTSPUR
    Why, so can I, or so can any man;
    But will they come when you do call for them?
GLENDOWER
    Why, I can teach you, cousin, to command the devil.
HOTSPUR
    And I can teach thee, coz, to shame the devil
    By telling truth. Tell truth and shame the devil.
    If thou have power to raise him, bring him hither,
    And I'll be sworn I have power to shame him hence.
    Oh, while you live, tell truth and shame the devil!
MORTIMER
    Come, come, no more of this unprofitable chat.
GLENDOWER
    Three times hath Henry Bolingbroke made head   61
    Against my power; thrice from the banks of Wye   62
    And sandy-bottomed Severn have I sent him
    Bootless home and weather-beaten back.   64
HOTSPUR
    Home without boots, and in foul weather too!
    How scapes he agues, in the devil's name?   66
GLENDOWER
    Come, here is the map. Shall we divide our right
    According to our threefold order ta'en?   68
MORTIMER
    The Archdeacon hath divided it   69
    Into three limits very equally: 70
    England, from Trent and Severn hitherto,   71
    By south and east is to my part assigned;
    All westward, Wales beyond the Severn shore,
    And all the fertile land within that bound,
    To Owen Glendower; and, dear coz, to you   75
    The remnant northward, lying off from Trent.

2 induction beginning.   **prosperous hope** hope of prospering.
8 Lancaster i.e., King Henry, here demoted to Duke of Lancaster
13 front brow, face. (As also at line 36.)   **14 cressets** lights burning in
metal baskets suspended from the ends of long poles or ceilings;
hence, meteors   **29 enlargement** release   **30 beldam** grandmother
32 distemp'rature disorder   **33 passion** suffering.   **of** from
34 crossings contradictions.

42–4 Where . . . to me? i.e., Where is there anyone in all of sea-walled
Great Britain who can claim to have been my instructor?   **45–7 And . . .
experiments** And I challenge you to produce a single human being
who can follow my tracks in the arcane craft of magic or keep up with
me in occult experiments.   **48 speaks better Welsh** (Hotspur hides
an insult behind the literal meaning, since "to speak Welsh" meant
colloquially both "to boast" and "to speak nonsense.")   **51 call** summon. (but Hotspur sardonically replies in the sense of "call out to,"
whether or not there is any response.)   **vasty deep** lower world.
61 made head raised a force   **62 power** army   **64 Bootless** without
advantage. (But Hotspur quibbles on the sense of "barefoot.")
66 agues fevers   **68 order ta'en** arrangements made.   **69 Archdeacon** i.e., the Archdeacon of Bangor, in whose house, according to
Holinshed, a meeting took place between deputies of the rebel leaders   **70 limits** regions   **71 hitherto** to this point   **75 coz** cousin, i.e.,
brother-in-law

And our indentures tripartite are drawn,
Which being sealèd interchangeably—
A business that this night may execute—   79
Tomorrow, cousin Percy, you and I
And my good lord of Worcester will set forth
To meet your father and the Scottish power,
As is appointed us, at Shrewsbury.
My father Glendower is not ready yet,   84
Nor shall we need his help these fourteen days.
[*To Glendower*] Within that space you may have drawn
    together   86
Your tenants, friends, and neighboring gentlemen.

GLENDOWER
A shorter time shall send me to you, lords;
And in my conduct shall your ladies come,   89
From whom you now must steal and take no leave,
For there will be a world of water shed
Upon the parting of your wives and you.

HOTSPUR [*consulting the map*]
Methinks my moiety, north from Burton here,   93
In quantity equals not one of yours.
See how this river comes me cranking in   95
And cuts me from the best of all my land
A huge half-moon, a monstrous cantle, out.   97
I'll have the current in this place dammed up,
And here the smug and silver Trent shall run   99
In a new channel, fair and evenly.
It shall not wind with such a deep indent
To rob me of so rich a bottom here.   102

GLENDOWER
Not wind? It shall, it must. You see it doth.

MORTIMER
Yea, but mark how he bears his course and runs me up   104
With like advantage on the other side,
Gelding the opposèd continent as much   106
As on the other side it takes from you.

WORCESTER
Yea, but a little charge will trench him here   108
And on this north side win this cape of land;
And then he runs straight and even.

HOTSPUR
I'll have it so. A little charge will do it.

GLENDOWER   I'll not have it altered.

HOTSPUR   Will not you?

GLENDOWER   No, nor you shall not.

HOTSPUR   Who shall say me nay?

GLENDOWER   Why, that will I.

HOTSPUR   77
Let me not understand you, then; speak it in Welsh.

GLENDOWER
I can speak English, lord, as well as you;
For I was trained up in the English court,
Where, being but young, I framèd to the harp   120
Many an English ditty lovely well,
And gave the tongue a helpful ornament—   122
A virtue that was never seen in you.

HOTSPUR
Marry, and I am glad of it with all my heart!
I had rather be a kitten and cry "mew"
Than one of these same meter balladmongers.
I had rather hear a brazen can'stick turned   127
Or a dry wheel grate on the axletree,   128
And that would set my teeth nothing on edge,   129
Nothing so much as mincing poetry.
'Tis like the forced gait of a shuffling nag.   131

GLENDOWER   Come, you shall have Trent turned.

HOTSPUR
I do not care. I'll give thrice so much land
To any well-deserving friend;
But in the way of bargain, mark ye me,
I'll cavil on the ninth part of a hair.
Are the indentures drawn? Shall we be gone?   136
                                                                137

GLENDOWER
The moon shines fair; you may away by night.
I'll haste the writer and withal   139
Break with your wives of your departure hence.   140
I am afraid my daughter will run mad,
So much she doteth on her Mortimer.   *Exit.*

MORTIMER
Fie, cousin Percy, how you cross my father!

HOTSPUR
I cannot choose. Sometimes he angers me
With telling me of the moldwarp and the ant,   145
Of the dreamer Merlin and his prophecies,   146
And of a dragon and a finless fish,
A clip-winged griffin and a moulten raven,   148
A couching lion and a ramping cat,   149
And such a deal of skimble-skamble stuff   150
As puts me from my faith. I tell you what: 151
He held me last night at least nine hours
In reckoning up the several devils' names   153

77 **tripartite** i.e., drawn up in triplicate, each document *sealèd interchangeably* (line 78) with the seal of all signatories.   **drawn** drawn up   79 **this night may execute** may be carried out tonight   84 **father** father-in-law   86 **may** will be able to   89 **conduct** escort   93 **moiety** share   95 **comes me cranking in** comes bending in on my share. (The Trent, by turning northward to the North Sea instead of continuing eastward into the Wash, cuts Hotspur off from rich land in Lincolnshire and its vicinity.)   97 **cantle** piece   99 **smug** smooth   102 **bottom** valley   104 **runs me** runs. (*Me* is used colloquially.)   106 **Gelding . . . continent** cutting off from the land which it bounds on the opposite side. (The Trent's southerly loop from Stoke to Burton deprives Mortimer of a piece of land, just as its later northerly course deprives Hotspur.)   108 **charge** expenditure.   **trench** provide a new channel

120 **framèd to the harp** set to harp accompaniment   122 **gave . . . ornament** i.e., added to the words a pleasing ornament of music; also, gave to the English tongue the ornament of music and poetry   127 **can'stick turned** candlestick turned on a lathe   128 **axletree** axle   129 **nothing** not at all   131 **shuffling** hobbled   136 **cavil . . . hair** argue about the most trivial detail.   137 **drawn** drawn up.   139 **writer** i.e., scrivener who would be drawing the indentures.   **withal** also   140 **Break with** inform   145 **moldwarp** mole. (Holinshed tells us that the division was arranged because of a prophecy that represented King Henry as the mole and the others as the dragon, the lion, and the wolf, who should divide the land among them.)   146 **Merlin** the bard, prophet, and magician of Arthurian story, Welsh in origin   148 **griffin** a fabulous beast, half lion, half eagle.   **moulten** having molted   149 **couching** couchant, crouching. (Heraldic term.)   **ramping** rampant, advancing on its hind legs. (Hotspur is ridiculing the heraldic emblems that Glendower holds so dear.)   150 **skimble-skamble** foolish, nonsensical   151 **puts . . . faith** drives me from my (Christian) faith.   153 **several** various

That were his lackeys. I cried "Hum," and "Well, go to," 154
But marked him not a word. Oh, he is as tedious
As a tirèd horse, a railing wife,
Worse than a smoky house. I had rather live
With cheese and garlic in a windmill, far,
Than feed on cates and have him talk to me   159
In any summer house in Christendom.

MORTIMER
In faith, he is a worthy gentleman,
Exceedingly well read, and profited   162
In strange concealments, valiant as a lion   163
And wondrous affable, and as bountiful
As mines of India. Shall I tell you, cousin?
He holds your temper in a high respect   166
And curbs himself even of his natural scope   167
When you come 'cross his humor. Faith, he does.   168
I warrant you that man is not alive
Might so have tempted him as you have done   170
Without the taste of danger and reproof.
But do not use it oft, let me entreat you.

WORCESTER [to Hotspur]
In faith, my lord, you are too willful-blame,   173
And since your coming hither have done enough
To put him quite besides his patience.   175
You must needs learn, lord, to amend this fault.
Though sometimes it show greatness, courage,
    blood—   177
And that's the dearest grace it renders you—   178
Yet oftentimes it doth present harsh rage,   179
Defect of manners, want of government,   180
Pride, haughtiness, opinion, and disdain,   181
The least of which haunting a nobleman
Loseth men's hearts and leaves behind a stain
Upon the beauty of all parts besides,   184
Beguiling them of commendation.   185

HOTSPUR
Well, I am schooled. Good manners be your speed!   186
Here come our wives, and let us take our leave.

Enter Glendower with the ladies.

MORTIMER
This is the deadly spite that angers me: 188
My wife can speak no English, I no Welsh.

GLENDOWER
My daughter weeps she'll not part with you;
She'll be a soldier too, she'll to the wars.

MORTIMER
Good father, tell her that she and my aunt Percy   192

Shall follow in your conduct speedily.   193
    Glendower speaks to her in Welsh, and she answers
                                him in the same.

GLENDOWER
She is desperate here; a peevish self-willed harlotry, 194
One that no persuasion can do good upon.
                        The lady speaks in Welsh.

MORTIMER [to her]
I understand thy looks. That pretty Welsh   196
Which thou pourest down from these swelling heavens 197
I am too perfect in; and, but for shame,   198
In such a parley should I answer thee.   199
                        The lady again in Welsh.
I understand thy kisses and thou mine,
And that's a feeling disputation.   201
But I will never be a truant, love,
Till I have learned thy language; for thy tongue
Makes Welsh as sweet as ditties highly penned,   204
Sung by a fair queen in a summer's bower,
With ravishing division, to her lute.   206

GLENDOWER
Nay, if you melt, then will she run mad.   207
                The lady speaks again in Welsh.

MORTIMER
Oh, I am ignorance itself in this!

GLENDOWER
She bids you on the wanton rushes lay you down   209
And rest your gentle head upon her lap,
And she will sing the song that pleaseth you
And on your eyelids crown the god of sleep,   212
Charming your blood with pleasing heaviness,   213
Making such difference twixt wake and sleep   214
As is the difference betwixt day and night
The hour before the heavenly-harnessed team   216
Begins his golden progress in the east.

MORTIMER
With all my heart I'll sit and hear her sing.
By that time will our book, I think, be drawn.   219

GLENDOWER   Do so;
And those musicians that shall play to you
Hang in the air a thousand leagues from hence,
And straight they shall be here. Sit, and attend.
            [Mortimer reclines with his head
                        in his wife's lap.]

HOTSPUR   Come, Kate, thou art perfect in lying down;
    come, quick, quick, that I may lay my head in thy lap.

LADY PERCY   Go, ye giddy goose.
                    [Hotspur lies with his head
                in Kate's lap.] The music plays.

---

154 **go to** i.e., you don't say   159 **cates** delicacies   162 **profited** proficient   163 **concealments** occult practices   166 **temper** temperament
167 **scope** freedom of speech   168 **come 'cross** contradict   170 **Might**
who could   173 **too willful-blame** blameworthy for too much self-will
175 **besides** out of   177 **blood** spirit   178 **dearest grace** best (and costli-
est) credit   179 **present** represent   180 **want of government** lack of
self-control   181 **opinion** vanity, arrogance   184 **all parts besides** all
other abilities   185 **Beguiling** depriving   186 **Good . . . speed!** i.e., May
these good manners you praise so bring you success! (Said wryly; Hotspur doubts that good manners count for much in a time of war.)   188
spite vexation   192 **aunt** (Percy's wife, here called Kate, was aunt of
Edmund Mortimer, the fifth Earl of March, but was sister-in-law to the
Sir Edward Mortimer who married Glendower's daughter.)

193 **conduct** safe-conduct, escort   194 **desperate here** adamant on this
point (i.e., her decision to accompany Mortimer).   **peevish self-willed
harlotry** childish, willful, silly wench   196 **That pretty Welsh** i.e., Your
eloquent tears   197 **heavens** i.e., eyes   198 **perfect** proficient
199 **such a parley** i.e., the same language (of weeping)   201 **disputation** conversation, debate.   204 **highly penned** eloquently composed,
in high style   206 **division** variation, passage in which rapid short
notes vary a theme   207 **melt** i.e., weep   209 **wanton rushes** i.e., soft
floor covering   212 **crown . . . sleep** make sleep supreme ruler
213 **heaviness** drowsiness   214 **difference** nearly indistinguishable
difference   216 **the heavenly-harnessed team** i.e., the team of horses
drawing the chariot of the sun   219 **book** document, indentures

HOTSPUR

Now I perceive the devil understands Welsh;
And 'tis no marvel he is so humorous.   228
By'r Lady, he is a good musician.

LADY PERCY   Then should you be nothing but musical,
for you are altogether governed by humors. Lie still,
ye thief, and hear the lady sing in Welsh.   232

HOTSPUR   I had rather hear Lady, my brach, howl in   233
Irish.

LADY PERCY   Wouldst thou have thy head broken?   235

HOTSPUR   No.

LADY PERCY   Then be still.

HOTSPUR   Neither, 'tis a woman's fault.   238

LADY PERCY   Now God help thee!   239

HOTSPUR   To the Welsh lady's bed.

LADY PERCY   What's that?

HOTSPUR   Peace, she sings.

Here the lady sings a Welsh song.

HOTSPUR

Come, Kate, I'll have your song too.

LADY PERCY

Not mine, in good sooth.

HOTSPUR   Not yours, in good sooth! Heart, you swear   245
like a comfit maker's wife. "Not you, in good sooth,"   246
and "as true as I live," and "as God shall mend me,"
and "as sure as day,"
And givest such sarcenet surety for thy oaths   249
As if thou never walk'st further than Finsbury.   250
Swear me, Kate, like a lady as thou art,
A good mouth-filling oath, and leave "in sooth,"
And such protest of pepper-gingerbread,   253
To velvet-guards and Sunday citizens.   254
Come, sing.

LADY PERCY   I will not sing.

HOTSPUR   'Tis the next way to turn tailor, or be redbreast 257
teacher. An the indentures be drawn, I'll away within   258
these two hours; and so, come in when ye will.   *Exit.*

GLENDOWER

Come, come, Lord Mortimer. You are as slow
As hot Lord Percy is on fire to go.
By this our book is drawn; we'll but seal,   262
And then to horse immediately.

MORTIMER   With all my heart.   *Exeunt.*

❦

[3.2]

Enter the King, Prince of Wales, and others.

KING

Lords, give us leave. The Prince of Wales and I
Must have some private conference; but be near at
  hand,
For we shall presently have need of you.

Exeunt Lords.

I know not whether God will have it so
For some displeasing service I have done,
That in his secret doom out of my blood   6
He'll breed revengement and a scourge for me;
But thou dost in thy passages of life   8
Make me believe that thou art only marked   9
For the hot vengeance and the rod of heaven   10
To punish my mistreadings. Tell me else,   11
Could such inordinate and low desires,   12
Such poor, such bare, such lewd, such mean attempts,   13
Such barren pleasures, rude society,
As thou art matched withal and grafted to,   15
Accompany the greatness of thy blood
And hold their level with thy princely heart?   17

PRINCE

So please Your Majesty, I would I could
Quit all offenses with as clear excuse   19
As well as I am doubtless I can purge   20
Myself of many I am charged withal.
Yet such extenuation let me beg
As, in reproof of many tales devised,   23
Which oft the ear of greatness needs must hear
By smiling pickthanks and base newsmongers,   25
I may, for some things true, wherein my youth
Hath faulty wandered and irregular,
Find pardon on my true submission.

KING

God pardon thee! Yet let me wonder, Harry,
At thy affections, which do hold a wing   30
Quite from the flight of all thy ancestors.   31
Thy place in Council thou hast rudely lost,   32
Which by thy younger brother is supplied,
And art almost an alien to the hearts
Of all the court and princes of my blood.
The hope and expectation of thy time   36
Is ruined, and the soul of every man
Prophetically do forethink thy fall.

---

228 **humorous** whimsical, capricious.   232 **thief** i.e., rascal
233 **brach** bitch hound   235 **broken** i.e., struck so as to break the
skin.   238 **Neither . . . fault** i.e., I won't do that either; it's womanish
to be submissive.   239 **help** amend. (But Hotspur answers in the
sense of "assist with an amour.")   245 **Heart** i.e., By Christ's heart
246 **comfit maker's** confectioner's   249 **sarcenet** soft, flimsy. (From
the soft silken material known as *sarcenet*.)   250 **Finsbury** a field just
outside London frequented by the London citizenry. (Hotspur jokes
with Kate as though she were a citizen's wife, using the pious and
modest oaths of such people.)   253 **protest . . . gingerbread** i.e.,
mealy-mouthed protestations   254 **velvet-guards** i.e., wives who
wear velvet trimming   257–8 **'Tis . . . teacher** i.e., The only use one
might put singing to is to become a tailor (since tailors were noted for
effeminacy and singing at their work) or an instructor to caged song-
birds before they are sold. (Hotspur airily dismisses singing, as he
does poetry.)   262 **By this** By this time.   **but** just

3.2 **Location:** The royal court (historically, Westminster).
6 **doom** judgment.   **blood** offspring   8 **passages** course, conduct
9–11 **thou . . . mistreadings** (1) you are marked as the means of heaven's
vengeance against me, or (2) you are marked to suffer heaven's
vengeance because of my sins.   11 **else** how otherwise   12 **inordinate** (1) immoderate (2) unworthy of your rank   13 **lewd** low, base.
attempts undertakings   15 **withal** with   17 **hold their level** claim
equality   19 **Quit** acquit myself of   20 **doubtless** certain   23 **in
reproof** upon disproof   25 **By . . . newsmongers** from smiling flatterers and ignoble talebearers   30 **affections** inclinations.   **hold a wing**
fly a course   31 **from** at variance with   32 **rudely** by violence.
(According to an apocryphal story, Prince Hal boxed the ears of the
Lord Chief Justice and was sent to prison for it; see *2 Henry IV*,
1.2.54–5, 192, and 5.2.70–1.)   36 **The hope . . . time** The hopes that
people had for you

Had I so lavish of my presence been,
So common-hackneyed in the eyes of men, 40
So stale and cheap to vulgar company,
Opinion, that did help me to the crown, 42
Had still kept loyal to possession 43
And left me in reputeless banishment,
A fellow of no mark nor likelihood. 45
By being seldom seen, I could not stir
But like a comet I was wondered at,
That men would tell their children, "This is he!"
Others would say, "Where, which is Bolingbroke?"
And then I stole all courtesy from heaven, 50
And dressed myself in such humility
That I did pluck allegiance from men's hearts,
Loud shouts and salutations from their mouths,
Even in the presence of the crownèd King.
Thus did I keep my person fresh and new,
My presence, like a robe pontifical, 56
Ne'er seen but wondered at; and so my state, 57
Seldom but sumptuous, showed like a feast 58
And won by rareness such solemnity. 59
The skipping King, he ambled up and down
With shallow jesters and rash bavin wits, 61
Soon kindled and soon burnt; carded his state, 62
Mingled his royalty with cap'ring fools,
Had his great name profanèd with their scorns, 64
And gave his countenance, against his name, 65
To laugh at gibing boys and stand the push 66
Of every beardless vain comparative; 67
Grew a companion to the common streets,
Enfeoffed himself to popularity, 69
That, being daily swallowed by men's eyes,
They surfeited with honey and began
To loathe the taste of sweetness, whereof a little
More than a little is by much too much.
So when he had occasion to be seen,
He was but as the cuckoo is in June,
Heard, not regarded—seen, but with such eyes
As, sick and blunted with community, 77
Afford no extraordinary gaze,
Such as is bent on sunlike majesty
When it shines seldom in admiring eyes;
But rather drowsed and hung their eyelids down,
Slept in his face, and rendered such aspect 82
As cloudy men use to their adversaries, 83

Being with his presence glutted, gorged, and full.
And in that very line, Harry, standest thou; 85
For thou hast lost thy princely privilege
With vile participation. Not an eye 87
But is aweary of thy common sight,
Save mine, which hath desired to see thee more—
Which now doth that I would not have it do, 90
Make blind itself with foolish tenderness. 91

PRINCE
   I shall hereafter, my thrice gracious lord,
   Be more myself.
KING   For all the world 93
   As thou art to this hour was Richard then
   When I from France set foot at Ravenspurgh,
   And even as I was then is Percy now.
   Now, by my scepter, and my soul to boot, 97
   He hath more worthy interest to the state 98
   Than thou the shadow of succession. 99
   For of no right, nor color like to right, 100
   He doth fill fields with harness in the realm, 101
   Turns head against the lion's armèd jaws, 102
   And, being no more in debt to years than thou, 103
   Leads ancient lords and reverend bishops on
   To bloody battles and to bruising arms.
   What never-dying honor hath he got
   Against renownèd Douglas! Whose high deeds, 107
   Whose hot incursions and great name in arms
   Holds from all soldiers chief majority 109
   And military title capital 110
   Through all the kingdoms that acknowledge Christ.
   Thrice hath this Hotspur, Mars in swaddling clothes,
   This infant warrior, in his enterprises
   Discomfited great Douglas, ta'en him once, 114
   Enlargèd him and made a friend of him, 115
   To fill the mouth of deep defiance up 116
   And shake the peace and safety of our throne.
   And what say you to this? Percy, Northumberland,
   The Archbishop's Grace of York, Douglas, Mortimer, 119
   Capitulate against us and are up. 120
   But wherefore do I tell these news to thee?
   Why, Harry, do I tell thee of my foes,
   Which art my nearest and dearest enemy? 123
   Thou that art like enough, through vassal fear, 124
   Base inclination, and the start of spleen, 125
   To fight against me under Percy's pay,

To dog his heels and curtsy at his frowns,
To show how much thou art degenerate.

PRINCE
Do not think so. You shall not find it so.
And God forgive them that so much have swayed
Your Majesty's good thoughts away from me!
I will redeem all this on Percy's head
And in the closing of some glorious day
Be bold to tell you that I am your son,
When I will wear a garment all of blood
And stain my favors in a bloody mask,   136
Which, washed away, shall scour my shame with it.
And that shall be the day, whene'er it lights,   138
That this same child of honor and renown,
This gallant Hotspur, this all-praisèd knight,
And your unthought-of Harry chance to meet.   141
For every honor sitting on his helm,   142
Would they were multitudes, and on my head
My shames redoubled! For the time will come
That I shall make this northern youth exchange
His glorious deeds for my indignities.
Percy is but my factor, good my lord,   147
To engross up glorious deeds on my behalf;   148
And I will call him to so strict account
That he shall render every glory up,
Yea, even the slightest worship of his time,   151
Or I will tear the reckoning from his heart.
This in the name of God I promise here,
The which if He be pleased I shall perform,
I do beseech Your Majesty may salve   155
The long-grown wounds of my intemperance.   156
If not, the end of life cancels all bonds,
And I will die a hundred thousand deaths
Ere break the smallest parcel of this vow.

KING
A hundred thousand rebels die in this!
Thou shalt have charge and sovereign trust herein.   161

Enter Blunt.

How now, good Blunt? Thy looks are full of speed.

BLUNT
So hath the business that I come to speak of.
Lord Mortimer of Scotland hath sent word
That Douglas and the English rebels met   164
The eleventh of this month at Shrewsbury.
A mighty and a fearful head they are,
If promises be kept on every hand,   167
As ever offered foul play in a state.

KING
The Earl of Westmorland set forth today,
With him my son, Lord John of Lancaster;
For this advertisement is five days old.
On Wednesday next, Harry, you shall set forward;   172

On Thursday we ourselves will march. Our meeting   174
Is Bridgnorth. And, Harry, you shall march   175
Through Gloucestershire; by which account,
Our business valuèd, some twelve days hence   177
Our general forces at Bridgnorth shall meet.
Our hands are full of business. Let's away!
Advantage feeds him fat while men delay.   *Exeunt.*   180

❖

[3.3]

Enter Falstaff and Bardolph.

FALSTAFF   Bardolph, am I not fallen away vilely since   1
this last action? Do I not bate? Do I not dwindle? Why,   2
my skin hangs about me like an old lady's loose gown;
I am withered like an old applejohn. Well, I'll repent,   4
and that suddenly, while I am in some liking. I shall be   5
out of heart shortly, and then I shall have no strength   6
to repent. An I have not forgotten what the inside of a
church is made of, I am a peppercorn, a brewer's   8
horse. The inside of a church! Company, villainous   9
company, hath been the spoil of me.
BARDOLPH   Sir John, you are so fretful you cannot live 11
long.
FALSTAFF   Why, there is it. Come sing me a bawdy
song; make me merry. I was as virtuously given as a   14
gentleman need to be, virtuous enough: swore little,
diced not above seven times—a week, went to a
bawdy house not above once in a quarter—of an
hour, paid money that I borrowed—three or four
times, lived well and in good compass; and now I live   19
out of all order, out of all compass.
BARDOLPH   Why, you are so fat, Sir John, that you must
needs be out of all compass, out of all reasonable
compass, Sir John.
FALSTAFF   Do thou amend thy face, and I'll amend my
life. Thou art our admiral, thou bearest the lantern in   25
the poop, but 'tis in the nose of thee. Thou art the
Knight of the Burning Lamp.   27
BARDOLPH   Why, Sir John, my face does you no harm.
FALSTAFF   No, I'll be sworn, I make as good use of it as
many a man doth of a death's-head or a *memento mori.*   30
I never see thy face but I think upon hellfire and

---

136 **favors** features   138 **lights** dawns   141 **unthought-of** lightly valued, disregarded   142 **For** As for   147 **factor** agent   148 **engross up** amass, buy up   151 **even . . . time** every smallest honor he has ever won   155 **salve** soothe, heal   156 **intemperance** dissolute living.
161 **charge** command (of troops)   164 **Lord Mortimer of Scotland** (A Scottish nobleman, unrelated to Glendower's son-in-law.)   167 **head** armed force   172 **advertisement** tidings, news

174 **meeting** place of rendezvous   175 **Bridgnorth** a town near Shrewsbury.   177 **Our business valuèd** estimating how long our business will take   180 **Advantage . . . fat** Opportunity (for rebellion) prospers.   **him** himself
3.3. Location: A tavern in Eastcheap, as in 2.4.
1 **fallen away** shrunk   2 **action** i.e., the robbery at Gad's Hill.   **bate** lose weight.   4 **applejohn** a kind of apple still in good eating condition when shriveled.   5 **liking** (1) good bodily condition (2) inclination.   6 **out of heart** (1) disinclined, disheartened (2) out of condition
8 **peppercorn** unground dried pepper berry   8–9 **brewer's horse** i.e., one that is old, withered, and decrepit.   11 **fretful** (1) anxious (2) fretted, frayed   14 **given** inclined   19 **good compass** reasonable limits; also, in Bardolph's speech, girth, circumference   25 **admiral** flagship. **lantern** i.e., a light for the rest of the fleet to follow; here applied to Bardolph's inflamed nose, red from overdrinking   27 **Knight . . . Lamp** Falstaff parodies the names of heroes in popular chivalric romances.   30 *memento mori* reminder of death, such as a death's head or a skull engraved on a seal ring.

Dives that lived in purple; for there he is in his robes, 32
burning, burning. If thou wert any way given to
virtue, I would swear by thy face; my oath should be
"By this fire, that's God's angel." But thou art 35
altogether given over, and wert indeed, but for the 36
light in thy face, the son of utter darkness. When thou
ran'st up Gad's Hill in the night to catch my horse, if
I did not think thou hadst been an *ignis fatuus* or a ball 39
of wildfire, there's no purchase in money. Oh, thou art 40
a perpetual triumph, an everlasting bonfire light! 41
Thou hast saved me a thousand marks in links and 42
torches, walking with thee in the night betwixt tavern
and tavern; but the sack that thou hast drunk me
would have bought me lights as good cheap at the 45
dearest chandler's in Europe. I have maintained that 46
salamander of yours with fire any time this two-and- 47
thirty years. God reward me for it!

BARDOLPH   'Sblood, I would my face were in your belly! 49

FALSTAFF   God-a-mercy! So should I be sure to be
heartburned.

Enter Hostess.

How now, Dame Partlet the hen? Have you inquired 52
yet who picked my pocket?

HOSTESS   Why, Sir John, what do you think, Sir John?
Do you think I keep thieves in my house? I have
searched, I have inquired, so has my husband, man
by man, boy by boy, servant by servant. The tithe of a 57
hair was never lost in my house before.

FALSTAFF   Ye lie, hostess. Bardolph was shaved and 59
lost many a hair; and I'll be sworn my pocket was 60
picked. Go to, you are a woman, go.

HOSTESS   Who, I? No, I defy thee! God's light, I was 62
never called so in mine own house before.

FALSTAFF   Go to, I know you well enough.

HOSTESS   No, Sir John, you do not know me, Sir John.
I know you, Sir John. You owe me money, Sir John,
and now you pick a quarrel to beguile me of it. I
bought you a dozen of shirts to your back.

FALSTAFF   Dowlas, filthy dowlas. I have given them 69
away to bakers' wives; they have made bolters of 70
them.

HOSTESS   Now, as I am a true woman, holland of eight 72
shillings an ell. You owe money here besides, Sir 73
John, for your diet and by-drinkings, and money lent 74
you, four-and-twenty pound.

FALSTAFF   He had his part of it. Let him pay. 76

HOSTESS   He? Alas, he is poor, he hath nothing.

FALSTAFF   How, poor? Look upon his face. What call
you rich? Let them coin his nose, let them coin his
cheeks. I'll not pay a denier. What, will you make a 80
younker of me? Shall I not take mine ease in mine inn 81
but I shall have my pocket picked? I have lost a seal
ring of my grandfather's worth forty mark.

HOSTESS   Oh, Jesu, I have heard the Prince tell him, I
know not how oft, that that ring was copper.

FALSTAFF   How? The Prince is a Jack, a sneak-up. 86
'Sblood, an he were here, I would cudgel him like a
dog if he would say so. 88

*Enter the Prince [with Peto], marching, and
Falstaff meets him playing upon his truncheon like
a fife.*

How now, lad, is the wind in that door, i'faith? Must 89
we all march?

BARDOLPH   Yea, two and two, Newgate fashion. 91

HOSTESS   My lord, I pray you, hear me.

PRINCE   What say'st thou, Mistress Quickly? How doth
thy husband? I love him well; he is an honest man.

HOSTESS   Good my lord, hear me.

FALSTAFF   Prithee, let her alone and list to me.

PRINCE   What say'st thou, Jack?

FALSTAFF   The other night I fell asleep here behind the
arras and had my pocket picked. This house is turned 99
bawdy house; they pick pockets.

PRINCE   What didst thou lose, Jack?

FALSTAFF   Wilt thou believe me, Hal? Three or four
bonds of forty pound apiece and a seal ring of my
grandfather's.

PRINCE   A trifle, some eightpenny matter.

HOSTESS   So I told him, my lord, and I said I heard Your
Grace say so; and, my lord, he speaks most vilely of
you, like a foulmouthed man as he is, and said he
would cudgel you.

PRINCE   What, he did not!

HOSTESS   There's neither faith, truth, nor womanhood
in me else.

FALSTAFF   There's no more faith in thee than in a stewed 113
prune, nor no more truth in thee than in a drawn fox; 114
and for womanhood, Maid Marian may be the dep- 115
uty's wife of the ward to thee. Go, you thing, go. 116

HOSTESS   Say, what thing, what thing?

FALSTAFF   What thing? Why, a thing to thank God on. 118

HOSTESS   I am no thing to thank God on, I would thou 119
shouldst know it! I am an honest man's wife, and,

---

32 **Dives** the rich man who went to hell, referred to in Luke 16:19–31
35 **"By . . . angel"** (Psalms 104:4, Hebrews 1:7, and Exodus 3:2
describe angels that appear in flames of fire.)   36 **given over** abandoned to wickedness   39 *ignis fatuus* will-o'-the-wisp   40 **wildfire**
fireworks; lightning; will-o'-the-wisp   41 **triumph** procession led by
torches   42 **links** torches, flares   45 **good cheap** cheap   46 **dearest
chandler's** most expensive candle maker's   47 **salamander** lizard
reputed to be able to live in fire   49 **I . . . belly** (A colloquial way of
objecting to an insult. Falstaff responds in the literal sense: A face like
yours would give me massive indigestion.)   52 **Partlet** (Traditional
name of a hen.)   57 **tithe** tenth part   59 **was shaved** (1) had his
beard cut (2) was cheated and robbed   60 **lost many a hair** (1) was
shaved (2) was made bald by syphilis   62 **God's light** (A mild oath.)
69 **Dowlas** a coarse kind of linen   70 **bolters** cloths for sifting flour
72 **holland** fine linen   73 **an ell** a measure of forty-five inches.
74 **diet** meals.   **by-drinkings** drinks between meals

76 **He** Bardolph   80 **denier** one-twelfth of a French sou; type of very
small coin.   81 **younker** greenhorn   86 **Jack** knave, rascal.   **sneak-
up** sneak.   88.2 **truncheon** officer's staff   89 **is . . . door** i.e., is that the
way the wind is blowing   91 **Newgate** a famous city prison in London.
(Prisoners marched two by two.)   99 **arras** curtain   113–14 **stewed
prune** (Customarily associated with bawdy houses.)   114 **drawn fox**
fox driven from cover and wily in getting back   115–16 **Maid . . .
thee** i.e., Maid Marian, a disreputable woman in Robin Hood ballads,
morris dances, and the like, was a model of respectability compared
with you.   118–19 **What thing . . . no thing** (With sexual quibbles.)

setting thy knighthood aside, thou art a knave to call 121
me so.

FALSTAFF   Setting thy womanhood aside, thou art a
beast to say otherwise.

HOSTESS   Say, what beast, thou knave, thou?

FALSTAFF   What beast? Why, an otter.

PRINCE   An otter, Sir John! Why an otter?

FALSTAFF   Why? She's neither fish nor flesh; a man
knows not where to have her.   129

HOSTESS   Thou art an unjust man in saying so. Thou or
any man knows where to have me, thou knave, thou.

PRINCE   Thou sayst true, hostess, and he slanders thee
most grossly.

HOSTESS   So he doth you, my lord, and said this other
day you owed him a thousand pound.

PRINCE   Sirrah, do I owe you a thousand pound?

FALSTAFF   A thousand pound, Hal? A million. Thy love
is worth a million; thou owest me thy love.

HOSTESS   Nay, my lord, he called you Jack and said he
would cudgel you.

FALSTAFF   Did I, Bardolph?

BARDOLPH   Indeed, Sir John, you said so.

FALSTAFF   Yea, if he said my ring was copper.

PRINCE   I say 'tis copper. Darest thou be as good as thy
word now?

FALSTAFF   Why, Hal, thou knowest, as thou art but
man, I dare; but as thou art prince, I fear thee as I fear
the roaring of the lion's whelp.   148

PRINCE   And why not as the lion?

FALSTAFF   The King himself is to be feared as the lion.
Dost thou think I'll fear thee as I fear thy father? Nay,
an I do, I pray God my girdle break.

PRINCE   Oh, if it should, how would thy guts fall about
thy knees! But, sirrah, there's no room for faith, truth,
nor honesty in this bosom of thine; it is all filled up
with guts and midriff. Charge an honest woman with
picking thy pocket? Why, thou whoreson, impudent,
embossed rascal, if there were anything in thy pocket 158
but tavern reckonings, memorandums of bawdy 159
houses, and one poor pennyworth of sugar candy to
make thee long-winded, if thy pocket were enriched
with any other injuries but these, I am a villain. And 162
yet you will stand to it; you will not pocket up wrong! 163
Art thou not ashamed?

FALSTAFF   Dost thou hear, Hal? Thou knowest in the
state of innocency Adam fell; and what should poor
Jack Falstaff do in the days of villainy? Thou see'st I
have more flesh than another man, and therefore
more frailty. You confess then you picked my pocket.

PRINCE   It appears so by the story.

FALSTAFF   Hostess, I forgive thee. Go make ready breakfast. Love thy husband, look to thy servants, cherish
thy guests. Thou shalt find me tractable to any honest
reason; thou see'st I am pacified still. Nay, prithee, 174
begone.   *Exit Hostess.*
Now, Hal, to the news at court: for the robbery, lad,
how is that answered?

PRINCE   Oh, my sweet beef, I must still be good angel to
thee. The money is paid back again.

FALSTAFF   Oh, I do not like that paying back. 'Tis a
double labor.   180

PRINCE   I am good friends with my father and may do
anything.

FALSTAFF   Rob me the exchequer the first thing thou
dost, and do it with unwashed hands too.   184

BARDOLPH   Do, my lord.

PRINCE   I have procured thee, Jack, a charge of foot.   186

FALSTAFF   I would it had been of horse. Where shall I
find one that can steal well? Oh, for a fine thief, of the 188
age of two-and-twenty or thereabouts! I am heinously
unprovided. Well, God be thanked for these rebels; 190
they offend none but the virtuous. I laud them, I 191
praise them.

PRINCE   Bardolph!

BARDOLPH   My lord?

PRINCE   [*giving letters*]
Go bear this letter to Lord John of Lancaster,
To my brother John; this to my lord of Westmorland.
                                                    [*Exit Bardolph.*]
Go, Peto, to horse, to horse, for thou and I
Have thirty miles to ride yet ere dinnertime.
                                                    [*Exit Peto.*]
Jack, meet me tomorrow in the Temple Hall   199
At two o'clock in the afternoon.
There shalt thou know thy charge, and there receive
Money and order for their furniture.   202
The land is burning. Percy stands on high,
And either we or they must lower lie.   [*Exit.*]

FALSTAFF
Rare words! Brave world! Hostess, my breakfast, come! 205
Oh, I could wish this tavern were my drum!   [*Exit.*] 206

❖

[4.1]

[*Enter Hotspur, Worcester, and Douglas.*]

HOTSPUR
Well said, my noble Scot. If speaking truth

---

121 **setting ... aside** (Mistress Quickly means, "without wishing to offend your rank of knighthood," but Falstaff replies in line 123 with the meaning, "setting aside your womanhood as of no value or pertinence.")   129 **have** understand. (With a sly suggestion of sexual possession—a meaning that eludes Mistress Quickly.)   148 **whelp** cub.
158 **embossed** (1) swollen with fat (2) foaming at the mouth and exhausted, like a hunted animal.   **rascal** (1) scoundrel (2) immature and inferior deer   159 **memorandums** souvenirs   162 **injuries** i.e., those things you claim to have lost, thereby suffering harm   163 **stand to it** make a stand, insist on your supposed rights.   **pocket up** endure silently

174 **still** always.   180 **double labor** i.e., the taking and the returning.
184 **with unwashed hands** without further ado   186 **charge of foot** command of a company of infantry.   188 **one** i.e., a companion in thievery. (Falstaff sees war as the opportunity for stealing and conning.)   190 **unprovided** ill-equipped.   191 **they ... virtuous** i.e., the rebels, by providing the occasion of war, give dishonest men a chance to profiteer and hence offend only those who are honest.   199 **Temple Hall** i.e., at the Inner Temple, one of the Inns of Court   202 **furniture** equipment, furnishing.   205 **Brave** Splendid   206 **drum** (Possibly Falstaff means that he wishes he could continue to enjoy this tavern instead of risking his life in battle. He may also be punning on *tavern/taborn*, i.e., *taborin*, a kind of drum.)
4.1. Location: The rebel camp near Shrewsbury.

In this fine age were not thought flattery,
Such attribution should the Douglas have   3
As not a soldier of this season's stamp   4
Should go so general current through the world.   5
By God, I cannot flatter; I do defy   6
The tongues of soothers! But a braver place   7
In my heart's love hath no man than yourself.
Nay, task me to my word; approve me, lord.   9

DOUGLAS   Thou art the king of honor.
No man so potent breathes upon the ground   11
But I will beard him.

Enter one [a Messenger] with letters.

HOTSPUR   Do so, and 'tis well.—   12
What letters hast thou there?—I can but thank you.   13

MESSENGER
These letters come from your father.

HOTSPUR
Letters from him? Why comes he not himself?

MESSENGER
He cannot come, my lord. He is grievous sick.

HOTSPUR
Zounds, how has he the leisure to be sick
In such a jostling time? Who leads his power?   18
Under whose government come they along?   19

MESSENGER
His letters bears his mind, not I, my lord.
[Hotspur reads the letter.]

WORCESTER
I prithee, tell me, doth he keep his bed?   21

MESSENGER
He did, my lord, four days ere I set forth,
And at the time of my departure thence
He was much feared by his physicians.   24

WORCESTER
I would the state of time had first been whole   25
Ere he by sickness had been visited.
His health was never better worth than now.

HOTSPUR
Sick now? Droop now? This sickness doth infect
The very life-blood of our enterprise;
'Tis catching hither, even to our camp.
He writes me here that inward sickness—
And that his friends by deputation   32
Could not so soon be drawn, nor did he think it meet   33
To lay so dangerous and dear a trust
On any soul removed but on his own.   35
Yet doth he give us bold advertisement   36

That with our small conjunction we should on,   37
To see how fortune is disposed to us;
For, as he writes, there is no quailing now,   39
Because the King is certainly possessed   40
Of all our purposes. What say you to it?

WORCESTER
Your father's sickness is a maim to us.   42

HOTSPUR
A perilous gash, a very limb lopped off.
And yet, in faith, it is not! His present want   44
Seems more than we shall find it. Were it good   45
To set the exact wealth of all our states   46
All at one cast? To set so rich a main   47
On the nice hazard of one doubtful hour?   48
It were not good, for therein should we read   49
The very bottom and the soul of hope,   50
The very list, the very utmost bound   51
Of all our fortunes.

DOUGLAS   Faith, and so we should;
Where now remains a sweet reversion,   53
We may boldly spend upon the hope
Of what is to come in.
A comfort of retirement lives in this.   56

HOTSPUR
A rendezvous, a home to fly unto,
If that the devil and mischance look big   58
Upon the maidenhead of our affairs.   59

WORCESTER
But yet I would your father had been here.
The quality and hair of our attempt   61
Brooks no division. It will be thought   62
By some that know not why he is away
That wisdom, loyalty, and mere dislike   64
Of our proceedings kept the Earl from hence.
And think how such an apprehension   66
May turn the tide of fearful faction   67
And breed a kind of question in our cause.
For well you know we of the off'ring side   69
Must keep aloof from strict arbitrament,   70
And stop all sight-holes, every loop from whence   71
The eye of reason may pry in upon us.
This absence of your father's draws a curtain   73
That shows the ignorant a kind of fear
Before not dreamt of.

HOTSPUR   You strain too far.   75
I rather of his absence make this use:

---

3 **attribution** praise, tribute 4–5 **As . . . world** that no one coined as a soldier in this current campaign should enjoy such a current reputation. (To *go . . . current* is to be put into circulation, continuing the image of coining in line 4.) 6 **defy** proclaim against 7 **soothers** flatterers. **braver** better, dearer 9 **task . . . word** challenge me to make good my word. **approve** test 11–12 **No . . . him** i.e., I am ready to defy anyone alive. 13 **I can . . . you** (Said to Douglas.) 18 **jostling** contending, clashing 19 **government** command 21 **keep** keep to 24 **feared** feared for 25 **time** the times 32–3 **And that . . . drawn** and that his allies could not so soon be assembled by anyone other than himself, any deputy 33 **meet** appropriate 35 **On . . . own** on anyone other than himself. 36 **advertisement** counsel, advice

37 **conjunction** joint force. **on** go on 39 **quailing** losing heart 40 **possessed** informed 42 **maim** injury 44 **want** absence 45 **more** more serious 46 **To . . . states** to stake the absolute total of our resources 47 **cast** throw of the dice. **main** stake in gambling; also, an army 48 **nice** precarious, delicate. **hazard** (1) game at dice (2) venture 49–50 **should . . . hope** we should discover the utmost foundation and basis of our hopes, the most we could rely on 51 **list** limit 53 **Where . . . reversion** since as things stand we can expect reinforcements. (A *reversion* is literally part of an estate yet to be inherited.) 56 **retirement** something to fall back on 58 **big** threatening 59 **maidenhead** i.e., commencement 61 **hair** kind, nature 62 **Brooks** tolerates 64 **loyalty** i.e., to the crown 66 **apprehension** (1) perception (2) apprehensiveness 67 **fearful faction** timid support 69 **off'ring side** side that attacks 70 **strict arbitrament** just inquiry or investigation 71 **sight-holes** peep-holes. (*Loop* or *loophole* has the same meaning.) 73 **draws** draws aside, opens 75 **strain too far** exaggerate.

It lends a luster and more great opinion,
A larger dare to our great enterprise,
Than if the Earl were here; for men must think,
If we without his help can make a head
To push against a kingdom, with his help
We shall o'erturn it topsy-turvy down.
Yet all goes well, yet all our joints are whole.

DOUGLAS
As heart can think. There is not such a word
Spoke of in Scotland as this term of fear.

Enter Sir Richard Vernon.

HOTSPUR
My cousin Vernon, welcome, by my soul.

VERNON
Pray God my news be worth a welcome, lord.
The Earl of Westmorland, seven thousand strong,
Is marching hitherwards; with him Prince John.

HOTSPUR
No harm. What more?

VERNON   And further I have learned
The King himself in person is set forth,
Or hitherwards intended speedily,
With strong and mighty preparation.

HOTSPUR
He shall be welcome too. Where is his son,
The nimble-footed madcap Prince of Wales,
And his comrades, that doffed the world aside
And bid it pass?

VERNON   All furnished, all in arms
All plumed like estridges, that with the wind
Bated like eagles having lately bathed,
Glittering in golden coats, like images,
As full of spirit as the month of May
And gorgeous as the sun at midsummer,
Wanton as youthful goats, wild as young bulls.
I saw young Harry, with his beaver on,
His cuisses on his thighs, gallantly armed,
Rise from the ground like feathered Mercury,
And vaulted with such ease into his seat
As if an angel dropped down from the clouds
To turn and wind a fiery Pegasus
And witch the world with noble horsemanship.

HOTSPUR
No more, no more! Worse than the sun in March
This praise doth nourish agues. Let them come.
They come like sacrifices in their trim,

And to the fire-eyed maid of smoky war   114
All hot and bleeding will we offer them.
The mailèd Mars shall on his altar sit   116
Up to the ears in blood. I am on fire
To hear this rich reprisal is so nigh,   118
And yet not ours. Come, let me taste my horse,   119
Who is to bear me like a thunderbolt
Against the bosom of the Prince of Wales.
Harry to Harry shall, hot horse to horse,
Meet and ne'er part till one drop down a corse.   123
Oh, that Glendower were come!

VERNON   There is more news:
I learned in Worcester, as I rode along,
He cannot draw his power this fourteen days.   126

DOUGLAS
That's the worst tidings that I hear of yet.

WORCESTER
Ay, by my faith, that bears a frosty sound.

HOTSPUR
What may the King's whole battle reach unto?   129

VERNON
To thirty thousand.

HOTSPUR   Forty let it be!
My father and Glendower being both away,
The powers of us may serve so great a day.   132
Come, let us take a muster speedily.
Doomsday is near; die all, die merrily.

DOUGLAS
Talk not of dying. I am out of fear   135
Of death or death's hand for this one half year.

                              Exeunt.

                    ❖

[4.2]

Enter Falstaff, [and] Bardolph.

FALSTAFF   Bardolph, get thee before to Coventry; fill me
a bottle of sack. Our soldiers shall march through; we'll
to Sutton Coldfield tonight.   3

BARDOLPH   Will you give me money, Captain?

FALSTAFF   Lay out, lay out.   5

BARDOLPH   This bottle makes an angel.   6

FALSTAFF   An if it do, take it for thy labor; an if it make
twenty, take them all; I'll answer the coinage. Bid my   8
lieutenant Peto meet me at town's end.

BARDOLPH   I will, Captain. Farewell.   *Exit.*

FALSTAFF   If I be not ashamed of my soldiers, I am a
soused gurnet. I have misused the King's press dam-   12
nably. I have got, in exchange of a hundred and fifty

77 **opinion** renown   78 **dare** daring   80 **make a head** raise an armed
force   83 **Yet** Still.   **joints** limbs   92 **intended** on the verge of departure   96–7 **that doffed . . . pass?** i.e., that thumbed their noses at
responsibilities, telling the world to mind its own business?   97 **furnished** equipped   98–9 **All . . . bathed** i.e., all plumed with ostrich
feathers, fluttering their wings in the wind like eagles having just
bathed. (The text may be defective.)   100 **coats** (1) coats of mail
(2) heraldic coats of arms.   **images** gilded statues   103 **Wanton**
sportive, frolicsome   104 **beaver** visor; hence, helmet   105 **cuisses**
armor for the thighs   107 **seat** saddle   109 **wind** wheel about.
Pegasus winged horse of Greek mythology   110 **witch** bewitch
111–12 **Worse . . . agues** (The spring sun was believed to give impetus
to chills and fevers, by drawing up vapors. Vernon's speech, says
Hotspur, gives one the shudders.)   113 **sacrifices** beasts for sacrifice.
trim fine apparel, trappings

114 **maid** i.e., Bellona, goddess of war   116 **mailèd** dressed in mail,
armor   118 **reprisal** prize   119 **taste** try, feel under me   123 **corse**
corpse.   126 **draw his power** muster his army   129 **battle** army
132 **The . . . us** our forces   135 **out of** free from
4.2. Location: A public road near Coventry.
3 **Sutton Coldfield** (In Warwickshire near Coventry.)   5 **Lay out** Pay
for it yourself   6 **makes an angel** i.e., makes ten shillings I've spent
for you. (But Falstaff answers as though *makes* means "produces,"
implying that Bardolph can profit from the transaction.)   8 **I'll . . .
coinage** I'll take responsibility for any proceeds.   12 **soused gurnet** a
kind of pickled fish.   **King's press** royal warrant for the impressment of troops

soldiers, three hundred and odd pounds. I press me 14
none but good householders, yeomen's sons, inquire 15
me out contracted bachelors, such as had been asked 16
twice on the banns—such a commodity of warm 17
slaves as had as lief hear the devil as a drum, such as 18
fear the report of a caliver worse than a struck fowl or 19
a hurt wild duck. I pressed me none but such toasts- 20
and-butter, with hearts in their bellies no bigger than 21
pins' heads, and they have bought out their services; 22
and now my whole charge consists of ancients, cor- 23
porals, lieutenants, gentlemen of companies—slaves 24
as ragged as Lazarus in the painted cloth, where the 25
glutton's dogs licked his sores, and such as indeed
were never soldiers, but discarded unjust servingmen, 27
younger sons to younger brothers, revolted tapsters, 28
and hostlers trade-fallen, the cankers of a calm world 29
and a long peace, ten times more dishonorable-ragged
than an old feazed ancient. And such have I, to fill up 31
the rooms of them as have bought out their services,
that you would think that I had a hundred and fifty tattered prodigals lately come from swine keeping, from 34
eating draff and husks. A mad fellow met me on the way 35
and told me I had unloaded all the gibbets and pressed 36
the dead bodies. No eye hath seen such scarecrows. I'll
not march through Coventry with them, that's flat. 38
Nay, and the villains march wide betwixt the legs as if
they had gyves on, for indeed I had the most of them 40
out of prison. There's not a shirt and a half in all my
company, and the half shirt is two napkins tacked together and thrown over the shoulders like a herald's
coat without sleeves; and the shirt, to say the truth,
stolen from my host at Saint Albans, or the red-nose 45
innkeeper of Daventry. But that's all one; they'll find 46
linen enough on every hedge. 47

Enter the Prince [and the] Lord of Westmorland.

PRINCE   How now, blown Jack? How now, quilt? 48
FALSTAFF   What, Hal? How now, mad wag? What a
devil dost thou in Warwickshire?—My good lord of

Westmorland, I cry you mercy. I thought Your Honor 51
had already been at Shrewsbury.
WESTMORLAND   Faith, Sir John, 'tis more than time that
I were there, and you too; but my powers are there 54
already. The King, I can tell you, looks for us all. We
must away all night. 56
FALSTAFF   Tut, never fear me. I am as vigilant as a cat to 57
steal cream.
PRINCE   I think, to steal cream indeed, for thy theft hath 59
already made thee butter. But tell me, Jack, whose 60
fellows are these that come after?
FALSTAFF   Mine, Hal, mine.
PRINCE   I did never see such pitiful rascals.
FALSTAFF   Tut, tut, good enough to toss; food for 64
powder, food for powder. They'll fill a pit as well as 65
better. Tush, man, mortal men, mortal men.
WESTMORLAND   Ay, but, Sir John, methinks they are
exceeding poor and bare, too beggarly. 68
FALSTAFF   Faith, for their poverty, I know not where 69
they had that, and for their bareness, I am sure they
never learned that of me.
PRINCE   No, I'll be sworn, unless you call three fingers 72
in the ribs bare. But, sirrah, make haste. Percy is 73
already in the field.   *Exit.*
FALSTAFF   What, is the King encamped?
WESTMORLAND   He is, Sir John. I fear we shall stay too
long.   *[Exit.]*
FALSTAFF   Well,
To the latter end of a fray and the beginning of a feast 79
Fits a dull fighter and a keen guest.   *Exit.* 80

❖

[4.3]

*Enter Hotspur, Worcester, Douglas, [and]
Vernon.*

HOTSPUR
We'll fight with him tonight.
WORCESTER   It may not be.
DOUGLAS
You give him then advantage.
VERNON   Not a whit. 2
HOTSPUR
Why say you so? Looks he not for supply? 3
VERNON
So do we.
HOTSPUR   His is certain; ours is doubtful.

14 press me draft, conscript   **15 good** i.e., wealthy.   **yeomen's** small
freeholders'   **16 contracted** engaged to be married   **17 banns** public
announcements, declared on three Sundays in succession, of an intent
to marry.   **warm** i.e., loving their comfort   **18 lief** willingly   **19 caliver**
musket.   **struck** wounded   **20–1 toasts-and-butter** weaklings
22 bought . . . services i.e., paid, bribed, to be released from military
duty   **23 charge** company, troop.   **ancients** ensigns, standard-bear-
ers. (By appointing a disproportionate number of junior officers, Falstaff has made it possible to collect for himself their more substantial
pay.)   **24 gentlemen of companies** a kind of junior officer
25 painted cloth cheap hangings for a room. (For the story of Lazarus
the beggar and Dives the rich man, see Luke 16:19–31.)   **27 unjust**
dishonest   **28 younger . . . brothers** (i.e., with no possibility of inheritance).   **revolted** runaway   **29 trade-fallen** whose business has
fallen away.   **cankers** cankerworms that destroy leaves and buds.
(Used figuratively.)   **31 feazed ancient** frayed flag.   **34 prodigals**
spendthrifts (See Luke 15:15–16.)   **35 draff** hogwash.   **mad** madcap
36 gibbets gallows   **38 that's flat** that's for sure.   **40 gyves** fetters
45 my host the innkeeper   **45, 46 Saint Albans, Daventry** (Towns
north and west of London, on the road to Coventry.)   **46 that's all
one** no matter   **47 hedge** (where wet linen was spread out to dry and
could be easily stolen.)   **48 blown** swollen, inflated; also, short of
wind.   **quilt** thickly padded.

51 cry you mercy beg your pardon.   **54 powers** soldiers   **56 must
away** must march   **57 fear** worry about   **59–60 thy . . . butter** i.e., all
the cream (rich things) you have stolen has been churned into butter-
fat in your barrel-like belly.   **64 toss** toss on a pike   **64–5 food for
powder** cannon fodder   **68 poor and bare** inferior and threadbare.
(But Falstaff puns on the sense of "financially strapped and lean.")
69 for as for   **72–3 three . . . ribs** i.e., Falstaff's fat-covered ribs. (A
finger was a measure of three-fourths of an inch.)   **79–80 To . . . guest**
i.e., Better to be late to a battle and early to a feast. (*Keen* means "with
keen appetite.")
4.3. Location: The rebel camp near Shrewsbury.
2 then i.e., if you wait. (Addressed to Worcester, not Hotspur.)   **3 supply** reinforcements.

WORCESTER
   Good cousin, be advised, stir not tonight.

VERNON
   Do not, my lord.

DOUGLAS   You do not counsel well.
   You speak it out of fear and cold heart.

VERNON
   Do me no slander, Douglas. By my life,
   And I dare well maintain it with my life,
   If well-respected honor bid me on,   10
   I hold as little counsel with weak fear   11
   As you, my lord, or any Scot that this day lives.
   Let it be seen tomorrow in the battle
   Which of us fears.

DOUGLAS   Yea, or tonight.

VERNON   Content.

HOTSPUR   Tonight, say I.

VERNON
   Come, come, it may not be. I wonder much,
   Being men of such great leading as you are,
   That you foresee not what impediments   19
   Drag back our expedition. Certain horse   21
   Of my cousin Vernon's are not yet come up.
   Your uncle Worcester's horse came but today,
   And now their pride and mettle is asleep,   24
   Their courage with hard labor tame and dull,
   That not a horse is half the half of himself.

HOTSPUR
   So are the horses of the enemy
   In general journey-bated and brought low.   28
   The better part of ours are full of rest.

WORCESTER
   The number of the King exceedeth our.
   For God's sake, cousin, stay till all come in.   31
                   The trumpet sounds a parley.

     Enter Sir Walter Blunt.

BLUNT
   I come with gracious offers from the King,
   If you vouchsafe me hearing and respect.   33

HOTSPUR
   Welcome, Sir Walter Blunt; and would to God
   You were of our determination!   35
   Some of us love you well; and even those some   36
   Envy your great deservings and good name
   Because you are not of our quality   38
   But stand against us like an enemy.

BLUNT
   And God defend but still I should stand so,   40
   So long as out of limit and true rule   41
   You stand against anointed majesty.
   But to my charge. The King hath sent to know   43

   The nature of your griefs and whereupon   44
   You conjure from the breast of civil peace
   Such bold hostility, teaching his duteous land
   Audacious cruelty. If that the King   47
   Have any way your good deserts forgot,
   Which he confesseth to be manifold,
   He bids you name your griefs, and with all speed
   You shall have your desires with interest
   And pardon absolute for yourself and these
   Herein misled by your suggestion.   53

HOTSPUR
   The King is kind; and well we know the King
   Knows at what time to promise, when to pay.
   My father and my uncle and myself
   Did give him that same royalty he wears,
   And when he was not six-and-twenty strong,
   Sick in the world's regard, wretched and low,
   A poor unminded outlaw sneaking home,   60
   My father gave him welcome to the shore;
   And when he heard him swear and vow to God
   He came but to be Duke of Lancaster,
   To sue his livery and beg his peace   64
   With tears of innocency and terms of zeal,
   My father, in kind heart and pity moved,
   Swore him assistance, and performed it too.
   Now when the lords and barons of the realm
   Perceived Northumberland did lean to him,
   The more and less came in with cap and knee,   70
   Met him in boroughs, cities, villages,
   Attended him on bridges, stood in lanes,   72
   Laid gifts before him, proffered him their oaths,
   Gave him their heirs as pages, followed him   74
   Even at the heels in golden multitudes.   75
   He presently, as greatness knows itself,   76
   Steps me a little higher than his vow   77
   Made to my father while his blood was poor   78
   Upon the naked shore at Ravenspurgh,
   And now, forsooth, takes on him to reform
   Some certain edicts and some strait decrees   81
   That lie too heavy on the commonwealth,
   Cries out upon abuses, seems to weep
   Over his country's wrongs; and by this face,   84
   This seeming brow of justice, did he win
   The hearts of all that he did angle for;
   Proceeded further—cut me off the heads   87
   Of all the favorites that the absent King
   In deputation left behind him here
   When he was personal in the Irish war.   90

---

44 griefs grievances **47 If that** If **53 suggestion** instigation.
60 unminded disregarded **64 To sue . . . peace** to petition to take
possession of his rightful inheritance and be reconciled with King
Richard II **70 The more . . . knee** persons of all ranks came to him with
cap in hand and with bended knee **72 Attended** waited for. **stood
in lanes** stood row-deep along the roads **74 Gave . . . pages** i.e.,
brought him their heirs to serve as pages and also as hostages to the
fathers' loyalty **75 golden** (1) auspicious, celebrating (2) majestically
attired **76 knows itself** perceives its own strength **77 Steps me** i.e.,
steps. (*Me* is used colloquially.) **vow** i.e., Bolingbroke's vow to seek
no more than his inheritance **78 while . . . poor** i.e., while Bolingbroke's spirits were still humbled and his dynastic claim in question
81 strait strict **84 face** show, pretense **87 cut me** i.e., cut **90 personal** in person

---

10 well-respected well weighed or considered **11 I hold . . . counsel**
I have as little to do **19 leading** leadership **21 expedition** speedy
progress. **horse** cavalry. (As also at line 23.) **24 pride and mettle**
spirit **28 journey-bated** tired from the journey **31.1 parley** trumpet
summons to a conference. **33 respect** attention. **35 determination**
persuasion (in the fight). **36 even those some** those same persons
38 Because only because. **quality** party **40 defend** forbid. **still**
always **41 limit** bounds of allegiance **43 charge** commission.

BLUNT
Tut, I came not to hear this.

HOTSPUR   Then to the point.
In short time after, he deposed the King,
Soon after that, deprived him of his life,
And in the neck of that tasked the whole state;   94
To make that worse, suffered his kinsman March—
Who is, if every owner were well placed,   96
Indeed his king—to be engaged in Wales,   97
There without ransom to lie forfeited;   98
Disgraced me in my happy victories,   99
Sought to entrap me by intelligence;   100
Rated mine uncle from the Council board;   101
In rage dismissed my father from the court;
Broke oath on oath, committed wrong on wrong,
And in conclusion drove us to seek out
This head of safety, and withal to pry   105
Into his title, the which we find
Too indirect for long continuance.

BLUNT
Shall I return this answer to the King?

HOTSPUR
Not so, Sir Walter. We'll withdraw awhile.
Go to the King; and let there be impawned   110
Some surety for a safe return again,
And in the morning early shall mine uncle
Bring him our purposes. And so farewell.   113

BLUNT
I would you would accept of grace and love.

HOTSPUR
And maybe so we shall.

BLUNT
                              Pray God you do. [Exeunt.]

❖

[4.4]

Enter [the] Archbishop of York, [and] Sir Michael.

ARCHBISHOP [*giving letters*]
Hie, good Sir Michael, bear this sealèd brief   1
With wingèd haste to the Lord Marshal,   2
This to my cousin Scroop, and all the rest   3
To whom they are directed. If you knew
How much they do import, you would make haste.

SIR MICHAEL   My good lord, I guess their tenor.

ARCHBISHOP   Like enough you do.   7
Tomorrow, good Sir Michael, is a day

Wherein the fortune of ten thousand men
Must bide the touch; for, sir, at Shrewsbury,   10
As I am truly given to understand,
The King with mighty and quick-raisèd power
Meets with Lord Harry. And I fear, Sir Michael,
What with the sickness of Northumberland,
Whose power was in the first proportion,   15
And what with Owen Glendower's absence thence,
Who with them was a rated sinew too   17
And comes not in, o'erruled by prophecies,
I fear the power of Percy is too weak
To wage an instant trial with the King.   20

SIR MICHAEL
Why, my good lord, you need not fear;
There is Douglas and Lord Mortimer.

ARCHBISHOP   No, Mortimer is not there.

SIR MICHAEL
But there is Mordake, Vernon, Lord Harry Percy,
And there is my lord of Worcester, and a head   25
Of gallant warriors, noble gentlemen.

ARCHBISHOP
And so there is. But yet the King hath drawn
The special head of all the land together: 28
The Prince of Wales, Lord John of Lancaster,
The noble Westmorland, and warlike Blunt,
And many more corrivals and dear men   31
Of estimation and command in arms.   32

SIR MICHAEL
Doubt not, my lord, they shall be well opposed.

ARCHBISHOP
I hope no less, yet needful 'tis to fear;
And, to prevent the worst, Sir Michael, speed.
For if Lord Percy thrive not, ere the King
Dismiss his power he means to visit us,   37
For he hath heard of our confederacy,
And 'tis but wisdom to make strong against him.
Therefore make haste. I must go write again
To other friends; and so farewell, Sir Michael.
                              Exeunt [separately].

❖

[5.1]

*Enter the King, Prince of Wales, Lord John of
Lancaster, Sir Walter Blunt, [and] Falstaff.*

KING
How bloodily the sun begins to peer
Above yon bosky hill! The day looks pale   2
At his distemperature.   3

PRINCE   The southern wind   4
Doth play the trumpet to his purposes,

---

94 in . . . that next, immediately after.   **tasked** laid taxes upon   **96 if
. . . placed** if every claimant were given his proper place   **97 engaged**
held as hostage   **98 lie forfeited** remain prisoner, unreclaimed
99 Disgraced me (by demanding the prisoners; see 1.3.23 ff.)   **happy**
fortunate   **100 intelligence** secret information, i.e., from spies
101 Rated scolded   **105 head of safety** armed force for our protection.
withal also   **110 impawned** pledged   **113 purposes** proposals.
4.4. Location: York. The Archbishop's palace.
1 brief letter, dispatch   **2 Lord Marshal** i.e., Thomas Mowbray, son
of the Duke of Norfolk who is exiled in *Richard II*, and a longtime
enemy of the new King   **3 Scroop** i.e., perhaps Sir Stephen Scroop
of *Richard II*, 3.2.91–218, or Lord Scroop of Masham of *Henry* V, 2.2
7 Like Likely

10 bide the touch be put to the test (like gold)   **15 in . . . proportion**
of the largest size   **17 rated sinew** main strength or support reckoned upon   **20 instant** immediate   **25 head** troop   **28 special head**
notable leaders   **31 corrivals** partners in the enterprise   **32 estimation** reputation, importance   **37 he** i.e., the King
5.1. Location: The King's camp near Shrewsbury.
2 bosky bushy   **3 his distemperature** i.e., the sun's unhealthy
appearance.   **4 trumpet** trumpeter.   **his** its, the sun's

And by his hollow whistling in the leaves
Foretells a tempest and a blust'ring day.

KING

Then with the losers let it sympathize,
For nothing can seem foul to those that win.

The trumpet sounds.

Enter Worcester [and Vernon].

How now, my lord of Worcester? 'Tis not well
That you and I should meet upon such terms
As now we meet. You have deceived our trust
And made us doff our easy robes of peace   12
To crush our old limbs in ungentle steel.
This is not well, my lord, this is not well.
What say you to it? Will you again unknit
This churlish knot of all-abhorrèd war
And move in that obedient orb again   17
Where you did give a fair and natural light,
And be no more an exhaled meteor,   19
A prodigy of fear, and a portent   20
Of broachèd mischief to the unborn times?   21

WORCESTER   Hear me, my liege:
For mine own part, I could be well content
To entertain the lag end of my life
With quiet hours, for I protest   24
I have not sought the day of this dislike.   26

KING

You have not sought it? How comes it, then?

FALSTAFF   Rebellion lay in his way, and he found it.

PRINCE   Peace, chewet, peace!

WORCESTER   29

It pleased Your Majesty to turn your looks
Of favor from myself and all our house;
And yet I must remember you, my lord,
We were the first and dearest of your friends.   32
For you my staff of office did I break
In Richard's time, and posted day and night   35
To meet you on the way, and kiss your hand,
When yet you were in place and in account
Nothing so strong and fortunate as I.   38
It was myself, my brother, and his son
That brought you home and boldly did outdare   40
The dangers of the time. You swore to us,
And you did swear that oath at Doncaster,
That you did nothing purpose 'gainst the state,
Nor claim no further than your new-fall'n right, 44
The seat of Gaunt, dukedom of Lancaster.
To this we swore our aid. But in short space
It rained down fortune show'ring on your head,
And such a flood of greatness fell on you—

What with our help, what with the absent King,
What with the injuries of a wanton time,   50
The seeming sufferances that you had borne,   51
And the contrarious winds that held the King
So long in his unlucky Irish wars
That all in England did repute him dead—
And from this swarm of fair advantages
You took occasion to be quickly wooed   56
To grip the general sway into your hand;
Forgot your oath to us at Doncaster;
And being fed by us, you used us so
As that ungentle gull, the cuckoo's bird,   60
Useth the sparrow; did oppress our nest,
Grew by our feeding to so great a bulk
That even our love durst not come near your sight 63
For fear of swallowing; but with nimble wing
We were enforced, for safety sake, to fly
Out of your sight and raise this present head,   66
Whereby we stand opposèd by such means   67
As you yourself have forged against yourself
By unkind usage, dangerous countenance,   69
And violation of all faith and troth
Sworn to us in your younger enterprise.

KING

These things indeed you have articulate,   72
Proclaimed at market crosses, read in churches,   73
To face the garment of rebellion   74
With some fine color that may please the eye   75
Of fickle changelings and poor discontents,   76
Which gape and rub the elbow at the news   77
Of hurly-burly innovation.   78
And never yet did insurrection want   79
Such water-colors to impaint his cause,   80
Nor moody beggars, starving for a time   81
Of pell-mell havoc and confusion.   82

PRINCE

In both your armies there is many a soul   83
Shall pay full dearly for this encounter,
If once they join in trial. Tell your nephew
The Prince of Wales doth join with all the world
In praise of Henry Percy. By my hopes—   87
This present enterprise set off his head—   88
I do not think a braver gentleman,
More active-valiant or more valiant-young,
More daring or more bold, is now alive
To grace this latter age with noble deeds.

---

12 easy comfortable   **17 orb** orbit, sphere of action. (The King's subjects, like planets and stars in the Ptolemaic cosmos, were supposed to revolve around the kingly center, comparable to the earth, in fixed courses.)   **19 exhaled meteor** (Meteors were believed to be vapors drawn up or *exhaled* by the sun and visible as streaks of light; they were regarded as ill omens.)   **20 prodigy of fear** fearful omen   **21 broachèd** set flowing, already begun   **24 entertain** occupy   **26 the . . . dislike** this time of discord.   **29 chewet** chough, jackdaw. (Here, a chatterer.)   **32 remember** remind   **35 posted** rode swiftly   **38 Nothing** not at all   **40 home** back to England from exile   **44 new-fall'n** recently inherited (by the death of John of Gaunt)

50 injuries abuses.   **wanton** ill-managed   **51 sufferances** suffering, distress   **56 occasion** the opportunity   **60 ungentle . . . bird** rude nestling, the cuckoo's young offspring. (The cuckoo lays its eggs in other birds' nests.)   **63 our love** we who loved you   **66 head** armed force   **67 opposèd . . . means** goaded into opposition by such factors   **69 dangerous countenance** threatening behavior   **72 articulate** set forth, specified   **73 market crosses** (Christian crosses were often erected in the centers of marketplaces—a good place for public announcements.)   **74 face** trim, adorn   **75 color** (1) hue (2) specious appearance   **76 changelings** turncoats   **77 rub the elbow** i.e., hug themselves with delight   **78 innovation** rebellion.   **79 want** lack   **80 water-colors** i.e., thin excuses. (See *color*, line 75.)   **his** its   **81 moody** sullen, angry   **82 havoc** plundering   **83 both your** i.e., your and our   **87 hopes** i.e., hopes of salvation   **88 This . . . head** i.e., if this present rebellion is taken from his account, not held against him

For my part, I may speak it to my shame,
I have a truant been to chivalry;
And so I hear he doth account me too.
Yet this before my father's majesty:
I am content that he shall take the odds
Of his great name and estimation,   98
And will, to save the blood on either side,
Try fortune with him in a single fight.

KING
And, Prince of Wales, so dare we venture thee,   101
Albeit considerations infinite   102
Do make against it.—No, good Worcester, no.
We love our people well; even those we love
That are misled upon your cousin's part;   105
And, will they take the offer of our grace,   106
Both he and they and you, yea, every man
Shall be my friend again, and I'll be his.
So tell your cousin, and bring me word
What he will do. But if he will not yield,
Rebuke and dread correction wait on us,   111
And they shall do their office. So, begone.
We will not now be troubled with reply.
We offer fair; take it advisedly.
                            Exit Worcester [with Vernon].

PRINCE
It will not be accepted, on my life.
The Douglas and the Hotspur both together
Are confident against the world in arms.

KING
Hence, therefore, every leader to his charge;
For on their answer will we set on them,
And God befriend us as our cause is just!   120
                    Exeunt. Manent Prince, Falstaff.

FALSTAFF   Hal, if thou see me down in the battle and
bestride me, so; 'tis a point of friendship.   122

PRINCE   Nothing but a colossus can do thee that friendship. Say thy prayers, and farewell.

FALSTAFF   I would 'twere bedtime, Hal, and all well.

PRINCE   Why, thou owest God a death.   *[Exit.]* 126

FALSTAFF   'Tis not due yet; I would be loath to pay him
before his day. What need I be so forward with him
that calls not on me? Well, 'tis no matter; honor pricks 129
me on. Yea, but how if honor prick me off when I   130
come on? How then? Can honor set to a leg? No. Or   131
an arm? No. Or take away the grief of a wound? No.   132
Honor hath no skill in surgery, then? No. What is
honor? A word. What is in that word "honor"? What is
that "honor"? Air. A trim reckoning! Who hath it? He
that died o' Wednesday. Doth he feel it? No. Doth he
hear it? No. 'Tis insensible, then? Yea, to the dead. But
will it not live with the living? No. Why? Detraction 138

will not suffer it. Therefore I'll none of it. Honor is a 139
mere scutcheon. And so ends my catechism.   140
                                                            Exit.

❖

[5.2]

Enter Worcester [and] Sir Richard Vernon.

WORCESTER
Oh, no, my nephew must not know, Sir Richard,
The liberal and kind offer of the King.

VERNON
'Twere best he did.

WORCESTER   Then are we all undone.
It is not possible, it cannot be,
The King should keep his word in loving us;
He will suspect us still and find a time
To punish this offense in other faults.   7
Suspicion all our lives shall be stuck full of eyes;   8
For treason is but trusted like the fox,
Who, never so tame, so cherished, and locked up,   10
Will have a wild trick of his ancestors.   11
Look how we can, or sad or merrily,   12
Interpretation will misquote our looks,
And we shall feed like oxen at a stall,
The better cherished still the nearer death.
My nephew's trespass may be well forgot;
It hath the excuse of youth and heat of blood,
And an adopted name of privilege—   18
A harebrained Hotspur, governed by a spleen.   19
All his offenses live upon my head
And on his father's. We did train him on,   21
And, his corruption being ta'en from us,   22
We as the spring of all shall pay for all.   23
Therefore, good cousin, let not Harry know
In any case the offer of the King.

Enter Hotspur [and Douglas, with soldiers].

VERNON
Deliver what you will; I'll say 'tis so.   26
Here comes your cousin.

HOTSPUR   My uncle is returned.
Deliver up my lord of Westmorland.   28
Uncle, what news?

WORCESTER
The King will bid you battle presently.

DOUGLAS
Defy him by the lord of Westmorland.   31

---

98 **estimation** reputation   101 **venture** hazard, risk   102 **Albeit**
although it be that. (The subjunctive has the force of "were it not
that.")   105 **cousin's** i.e., nephew's   106 **will they** if they will.
grace pardon   111 **wait on us** are awaiting my royal command
120.1 *Manent* They remain onstage   122 **bestride** stand over in order
to defend.   **so** well and good   126 **thou . . . death** (Proverbial, with a
pun on *debt*.)   129 **pricks** spurs   130 **prick me off** mark me off (as
one dead)   131 **set to** rejoin or set   132 **grief** pain   138 **Detraction**
Slander

139 **suffer** allow   140 **scutcheon** heraldic emblem carried in funerals,
displayed on coaches, etc.; it was the lowest form of symbol, having
no pennon or other insignia.   **catechism** the principles of faith given
in the form of question and answer.
5.2. Location: Near the rebel camp.
7 **To . . . faults** to find other faults in us to punish (as a way of getting
back at us for defying him militarily).   8 **stuck . . . eyes** i.e., provided
with many eyes, suspiciously inquisitive   10 **never so** be he never so
11 **trick** trait   12 **or sad** either sad   18 **an adopted . . . privilege** i.e., a
nickname, "Hotspur," to justify his rashness   19 **spleen** intemperate
impulse.   21 **train** incite, draw   22 **his . . . us** i.e., since his guilt originated in us   23 **spring** source   26 **Deliver** Report   28 **Deliver up**
Release (as hostage; see 4.3.110–11)   31 **Defy him by** Send back your
defiance with

HOTSPUR

Lord Douglas, go you and tell him so.

DOUGLAS

Marry, and shall, and very willingly.   *Exit Douglas.*

WORCESTER

There is no seeming mercy in the King.

HOTSPUR

Did you beg any? God forbid!

WORCESTER

I told him gently of our grievances,
Of his oathbreaking, which he mended thus,
By now forswearing that he is forsworn.
He calls us rebels, traitors, and will scourge
With haughty arms this hateful name in us.

Enter Douglas.

DOUGLAS

Arm, gentlemen, to arms! For I have thrown
A brave defiance in King Henry's teeth,
And Westmorland, that was engaged, did bear it;   42
Which cannot choose but bring him quickly on.   43

WORCESTER

The Prince of Wales stepped forth before the King,
And, nephew, challenged you to single fight.

HOTSPUR

Oh, would the quarrel lay upon our heads,
And that no man might draw short breath today
But I and Harry Monmouth! Tell me, tell me,   49
How showed his tasking? Seemed it in contempt?   50

VERNON

No, by my soul. I never in my life
Did hear a challenge urged more modestly,   52
Unless a brother should a brother dare
To gentle exercise and proof of arms.   54
He gave you all the duties of a man,   55
Trimmed up your praises with a princely tongue,   56
Spoke your deservings like a chronicle,
Making you ever better than his praise
By still dispraising praise valued with you;   59
And, which became him like a prince indeed,
He made a blushing cital of himself,   61
And chid his truant youth with such a grace
As if he mastered there a double spirit
Of teaching and of learning instantly.   64
There did he pause. But let me tell the world,
If he outlive the envy of this day,   66
England did never owe so sweet a hope,   67
So much misconstrued in his wantonness.   68

HOTSPUR

Cousin, I think thou art enamorèd
On his follies. Never did I hear
Of any prince so wild a liberty.   71

But be he as he will, yet once ere night
I will embrace him with a soldier's arm,
That he shall shrink under my courtesy.   74
Arm, arm with speed! And, fellows, soldiers, friends,
Better consider what you have to do
Than I, that have not well the gift of tongue,
Can lift your blood up with persuasion.

Enter a Messenger.

FIRST MESSENGER   My lord, here are letters for you.

HOTSPUR   I cannot read them now.

Oh, gentlemen, the time of life is short!
To spend that shortness basely were too long   82
If life did ride upon a dial's point,   83
Still ending at the arrival of an hour.   84
An if we live, we live to tread on kings;
If die, brave death, when princes die with us!   86
Now, for our consciences, the arms are fair   87
When the intent of bearing them is just.

Enter another [Messenger].

SECOND MESSENGER

My lord, prepare. The King comes on apace.

HOTSPUR

I thank him that he cuts me from my tale,
For I profess not talking. Only this—   91
Let each man do his best. And here draw I
A sword, whose temper I intend to stain
With the best blood that I can meet withal
In the adventure of this perilous day.
Now, *Esperance!* Percy! And set on.   96
Sound all the lofty instruments of war,
And by that music let us all embrace;
For, heaven to earth, some of us never shall   99
A second time do such a courtesy.

Here they embrace. The trumpets sound. [Exeunt.]

❧

[5.3]

The King enters with his power [and passes over the stage]. Alarum to the battle. Then enter Douglas, and Sir Walter Blunt [dressed like King Henry].

BLUNT

What is thy name, that in the battle thus
Thou crossest me? What honor dost thou seek
Upon my head?

DOUGLAS   Know then my name is Douglas,
And I do haunt thee in the battle thus
Because some tell me that thou art a king.

---

42 brave proud   **43 engaged** held as hostage   **49 Monmouth** (A name for the Prince, taken from the Welsh town where he was born.)
50 showed his tasking appeared his giving the challenge.   **52 urged** put forward   **54 gentle** befitting noble birth.   **proof of arms** test of martial skill.   **55 duties** due merits   **56 Trimmed . . . praises** adorned his praise of you   **59 By . . . you** by consistently disparaging praise itself as not sufficient to measure your true worth   **61 cital** account, recital   **64 instantly** simultaneously.   **66 envy** hostility   **67 owe** own   **68 wantonness** playful sportiveness.   **71 liberty** licentiousness.

74 shrink under my courtesy (1) be daunted by my greater courtesy (2) fall back before my attack.   **82–4 To . . . hour** Life is too short to spend it basely, even if life were to last only the time needed for the dial (or sundial) to advance a single hour, ending when that hour is up.   **86 brave** glorious   **87 for** as for.   **fair** just   **91 I . . . talking** I have no calling as an orator.   **96 Esperance** (The motto of the Percy family.)   **99 heaven to earth** i.e., I'll wager heaven against earth   **5.3. Location: Shrewsbury field. The scene is virtually continuous.**   **0.1** *power* army.   **0.2** *Alarum* Trumpet signal to advance

BLUNT   They tell thee true.

DOUGLAS
The lord of Stafford dear today hath bought   7
Thy likeness, for instead of thee, King Harry,   8
This sword hath ended him. So shall it thee,
Unless thou yield thee as my prisoner.

BLUNT
I was not born a yielder, thou proud Scot,
And thou shalt find a king that will revenge
Lord Stafford's death.   *They fight. Douglas kills Blunt.*

Then enter Hotspur.

HOTSPUR
Oh, Douglas, hadst thou fought at Holmedon thus,
I never had triumphed upon a Scot.

DOUGLAS
All's done, all's won; here breathless lies the King.   16

HOTSPUR   Where?

DOUGLAS   Here.

HOTSPUR
This, Douglas? No. I know this face full well.
A gallant knight he was; his name was Blunt,
Semblably furnished like the King himself.   21

DOUGLAS
A fool go with thy soul, whither it goes!   22
A borrowed title hast thou bought too dear.
Why didst thou tell me that thou wert a king?

HOTSPUR
The King hath many marching in his coats.   25

DOUGLAS
Now, by my sword, I will kill all his coats!
I'll murder all his wardrobe, piece by piece,
Until I meet the King.

HOTSPUR   Up, and away!
Our soldiers stand full fairly for the day.   *[Exeunt.]* 29

Alarum. Enter Falstaff, solus.

FALSTAFF   Though I could scape shot-free at London, I   30
fear the shot here; here's no scoring but upon the pate.   31
Soft, who are you? Sir Walter Blunt. There's honor for
you. Here's no vanity! I am as hot as molten lead, and   33
as heavy too. God keep lead out of me! I need no more
weight than mine own bowels. I have led my ragamuffins where they are peppered. There's not three of
my hundred and fifty left alive, and they are for the
town's end, to beg during life. But who comes here?   38

Enter the Prince.

PRINCE
What, stands thou idle here? Lend me thy sword.

7 **dear** dearly   7–8 **bought Thy likeness** paid for his resemblance to
you   16 **breathless** i.e., dead   21 **Semblably furnished** similarly
accoutered   22 **A . . . soul** i.e., May the stigma of "fool" accompany
your soul (for having dressed as a decoy of King Henry)   25 **coats**
vests worn over armor embroidered with a coat of arms.   29 **stand . . .
day** i.e., seem in an auspicious position, likely to win the victory.
30 **shot-free** without paying the tavern bill   31 **scoring** (1) cutting
(2) marking up of charges, by notches on a stick or on the inn door
33 **Here's no vanity!** i.e. (ironically), If this doesn't show what I was
saying about honor, then nothing does!   38 **town's end** i.e., city gate,
frequented by beggars

Many a nobleman lies stark and stiff
Under the hoofs of vaunting enemies,
Whose deaths are yet unrevenged. I prithee,
Lend me thy sword.

FALSTAFF   Oh, Hal, I prithee, give me leave to breathe
awhile. Turk Gregory never did such deeds in arms as   45
I have done this day. I have paid Percy, I have made   46
him sure.   47

PRINCE
He is, indeed, and living to kill thee.
I prithee, lend me thy sword.

FALSTAFF   Nay, before God, Hal, if Percy be alive, thou
gets not my sword; but take my pistol, if thou wilt.

PRINCE
Give it me. What, is it in the case?

FALSTAFF   Ay, Hal, 'tis hot, 'tis hot. There's that will   53
sack a city.
*The Prince draws it out and finds it to be a bottle
of sack.*

PRINCE
What, is it a time to jest and dally now?
He throws the bottle at him. Exit.

FALSTAFF   Well, if Percy be alive, I'll pierce him. If he do   56
come in my way, so; if he do not, if I come in his   57
willingly, let him make a carbonado of me. I like not in   58
such grinning honor as Sir Walter hath. Give me life,
which if I can save, so; if not, honor comes unlooked
for, and there's an end.   *[Exit.]* 61

❧

[5.4]

*Alarum. Excursions. Enter the King, the Prince,
Lord John of Lancaster, [and the] Earl of
Westmorland.*

KING   I prithee,
Harry, withdraw thyself; thou bleedest too much.
Lord John of Lancaster, go you with him.

LANCASTER
Not I, my lord, unless I did bleed too.

PRINCE
I beseech Your Majesty, make up,   5
Lest your retirement do amaze your friends.   6

KING
I will do so. My lord of Westmorland,
Lead him to his tent.

45 **Turk Gregory** (*Turk* is an abusive term signifying a tyrant, and
Gregory refers probably to Pope Gregory XIII, who was assumed to
have encouraged the Massacre of Saint Bartholomew [1572], in which
many French Protestants were slain, and to have encouraged plots
against Elizabeth.)   46–7 **made him sure** made sure of him. (But
Prince Hal takes *sure* in a different sense, meaning "safe.")   53 **hot**
(Falstaff implies he has been firing at the enemy.)   56 **Percy . . .
pierce** (Elizabethan pronunciation rendered the pun more obvious
than it is now.)   57 **so** well and good   58 **carbonado** meat scored
across for broiling   61 **there's an end** (1) that concludes the subject of
my catechism (see 5.1.129–40) (2) thus life ends.
5.4 Location: Scene continues at Shrewsbury field.
0.1 *Excursions* Sorties. (The fallen body of Blunt may be removed at
some point or may be onstage still at 5.4.77 when Hal kills Hotspur.)
5 make up go forward   **6 retirement** retreat.   **amaze** alarm

WESTMORLAND
Come, my lord, I'll lead you to your tent.
PRINCE
Lead me, my lord? I do not need your help.
And God forbid a shallow scratch should drive
The Prince of Wales from such a field as this,
Where stained nobility lies trodden on
And rebels' arms triumph in massacres!
LANCASTER
We breathe too long. Come, cousin Westmorland,   15
Our duty this way lies. For God's sake, come.
        [*Exeunt Prince John and Westmorland.*]
PRINCE
By God, thou hast deceived me, Lancaster!
I did not think thee lord of such a spirit.
Before, I loved thee as a brother, John,
But now I do respect thee as my soul.
KING
I saw him hold Lord Percy at the point   21
With lustier maintenance than I did look for   22
Of such an ungrown warrior.
PRINCE
Oh, this boy lends mettle to us all!   *Exit.*

    [*Enter Douglas.*]

DOUGLAS
Another king? They grow like Hydra's heads.   25
I am the Douglas, fatal to all those
That wear those colors on them. What art thou   27
That counterfeit'st the person of a king?
KING
The King himself, who, Douglas, grieves at heart
So many of his shadows thou hast met   30
And not the very King. I have two boys
Seek Percy and thyself about the field;   32
But, seeing thou fall'st on me so luckily,
I will assay thee; and defend thyself.   34
DOUGLAS
I fear thou art another counterfeit;
And yet, in faith, thou bearest thee like a king.
But mine I am sure thou art, whoe'er thou be,
And thus I win thee.
        They fight; the King being in danger,
                enter Prince of Wales.
PRINCE
Hold up thy head, vile Scot, or thou art like   39
Never to hold it up again! The spirits
Of valiant Shirley, Stafford, Blunt, are in my arms.
It is the Prince of Wales that threatens thee,
Who never promiseth but he means to pay.   43
        They fight. Douglas flieth.
Cheerly, my lord. How fares Your Grace?

Sir Nicholas Gawsey hath for succor sent,
And so hath Clifton. I'll to Clifton straight.
KING   Stay and breathe awhile.
Thou hast redeemed thy lost opinion,   48
And showed thou mak'st some tender of my life   49
In this fair rescue thou hast brought to me.
PRINCE
Oh, God, they did me too much injury
That ever said I hearkened for your death.   52
If it were so, I might have let alone
The insulting hand of Douglas over you,   54
Which would have been as speedy in your end
As all the poisonous potions in the world,
And saved the treacherous labor of your son.
KING
Make up to Clifton; I'll to Sir Nicholas Gawsey.   58
        Exit King.

    Enter Hotspur.

HOTSPUR
If I mistake not, thou art Harry Monmouth.
PRINCE
Thou speak'st as if I would deny my name.
HOTSPUR
My name is Harry Percy.
PRINCE   Why then, I see
A very valiant rebel of the name.
I am the Prince of Wales; and think not, Percy,
To share with me in glory any more.
Two stars keep not their motion in one sphere,
Nor can one England brook a double reign   66
Of Harry Percy and the Prince of Wales.
HOTSPUR
Nor shall it, Harry, for the hour is come
To end the one of us; and would to God
Thy name in arms were now as great as mine!
PRINCE
I'll make it greater ere I part from thee,
And all the budding honors on thy crest
I'll crop to make a garland for my head.   73
HOTSPUR
I can no longer brook thy vanities.   *They fight.*   74

    Enter Falstaff.

FALSTAFF   Well said, Hal! To it, Hal! Nay, you shall find   75
no boy's play here, I can tell you.   76

    *Enter Douglas. He fighteth with Falstaff, who falls
    down as if he were dead.*   [*Exit Douglas.*]
    The Prince killeth Percy.

HOTSPUR
Oh, Harry, thou hast robbed me of my youth!
I better brook the loss of brittle life
Than those proud titles thou hast won of me;

15 **breathe** rest, pause for breath (as also at line 47)   **21 at the point**
at sword's point   **22 lustier maintenance** more vigorous bearing
25 Hydra's heads (The heads of the Lernaean Hydra grew again as
fast as they were cut off.)   **27 colors** i.e., the colors of the King's
insignia   **30 shadows** having form without substance   **32 Seek** who
seek   **34 assay thee** put you to the test   **39 like** likely   **43 pay**
(1) settle a debt (2) kill.

48 **opinion** reputation   49 **thou . . . of** you have some care for
52 **hearkened** listened (as for welcome news)   54 **insulting** exulting
58 **Make up** Advance   66 **brook** endure   73 **crop** pluck   74 **vanities**
empty boasts.   75 **Well said** Well done   76.3 *killeth* mortally
wounds

They wound my thoughts worse than thy sword my
    flesh.
But thoughts, the slaves of life, and life, time's fool,   81
And time, that takes survey of all the world,
Must have a stop. Oh, I could prophesy,
But that the earthy and cold hand of death
Lies on my tongue. No, Percy, thou art dust,
And food for—   [*He dies.*]

PRINCE
For worms, brave Percy. Fare thee well, great heart.
Ill-weaved ambition, how much art thou shrunk!
When that this body did contain a spirit,
A kingdom for it was too small a bound;
But now two paces of the vilest earth
Is room enough. This earth that bears thee dead
Bears not alive so stout a gentleman.   93
If thou wert sensible of courtesy,   94
I should not make so dear a show of zeal;   95
But let my favors hide thy mangled face,   96
And, even in thy behalf, I'll thank myself
For doing these fair rites of tenderness.
          [*He covers Hotspur's face with a scarf
                          or other favor.*]
Adieu, and take thy praise with thee to heaven!
Thy ignominy sleep with thee in the grave,
But not remembered in thy epitaph!
          He spieth Falstaff on the ground.
What, old acquaintance, could not all this flesh
Keep in a little life? Poor Jack, farewell!
I could have better spared a better man.
Oh, I should have a heavy miss of thee   105
If I were much in love with vanity.   106
Death hath not struck so fat a deer today,
Though many dearer, in this bloody fray.
Emboweled will I see thee by and by.   109
Till then in blood by noble Percy lie.   *Exit.*
                   Falstaff riseth up.

FALSTAFF   Emboweled? If thou embowel me today, I'll
give you leave to powder me and eat me too tomor- 112
row. 'Sblood, 'twas time to counterfeit, or that hot ter- 113
magant Scot had paid me, scot and lot too. Counterfeit? 114
I lie, I am no counterfeit. To die is to be a counterfeit,
for he is but the counterfeit of a man who hath not the
life of a man; but to counterfeit dying, when a man
thereby liveth, is to be no counterfeit but the true and
perfect image of life indeed. The better part of valor is 119
discretion, in the which better part I have saved my
life. Zounds, I am afraid of this gunpowder Percy,
though he be dead. How if he should counterfeit too
and rise? By my faith, I am afraid he would prove the

better counterfeit. Therefore I'll make him sure; yea,
and I'll swear I killed him. Why may not he rise as well
as I? Nothing confutes me but eyes, and nobody sees 126
me. Therefore, sirrah [*stabbing him*], with a new
wound in your thigh, come you along with me.
          He takes up Hotspur on his back.

    Enter Prince [and] John of Lancaster.

PRINCE
Come, brother John; full bravely hast thou fleshed   129
Thy maiden sword.
LANCASTER   But soft, whom have we here?
Did you not tell me this fat man was dead?
PRINCE   I did; I saw him dead,
Breathless and bleeding on the ground.—Art thou
    alive?
Or is it fantasy that plays upon our eyesight?
I prithee, speak. We will not trust our eyes
Without our ears. Thou art not what thou seem'st.
FALSTAFF   No, that's certain, I am not a double man; but 137
if I be not Jack Falstaff, then am I a Jack. There is Percy 138
[*throwing the body down*]. If your father will do me
any honor, so; if not, let him kill the next Percy himself. I look to be either earl or duke, I can assure you.
PRINCE
Why, Percy I killed myself and saw thee dead.
FALSTAFF   Didst thou? Lord, Lord, how this world is
given to lying! I grant you I was down and out of
breath, and so was he; but we rose both at an instant 145
and fought a long hour by Shrewsbury clock. If I may
be believed, so; if not, let them that should reward
valor bear the sin upon their own heads. I'll take it 148
upon my death I gave him this wound in the thigh. 149
If the man were alive and would deny it, zounds, I
would make him eat a piece of my sword.
LANCASTER
This is the strangest tale that ever I heard.
PRINCE
This is the strangest fellow, brother John.—
Come, bring your luggage nobly on your back.
For my part, if a lie may do thee grace,   155
I'll gild it with the happiest terms I have.   156
          A retreat is sounded.
The trumpet sounds retreat; the day is our.
Come, brother, let us to the highest of the field, 158
To see what friends are living, who are dead.
          Exeunt [Prince of Wales and Lancaster].
FALSTAFF   I'll follow, as they say, for reward. He that re-
wards me, God reward him! If I do grow great, I'll
grow less; for I'll purge, and leave sack, and live 162
cleanly as a nobleman should do.
          Exit [bearing off the body].

          ❧

---

81 thoughts . . . fool i.e., our mental consciousness, which is dependent on physical existence, and our life itself, which is subject to time
93 stout valiant   **94 sensible of courtesy** able to hear my praise
95 dear handsome, heartfelt.   **zeal** admiration   **96 favors** plume,
scarf, glove, or similar article   **105 heavy** (1) serious (2) corpulent
106 vanity frivolity.   **109 Emboweled** Disemboweled, i.e., for
embalming and burial   **112 powder** salt   **113–14 termagant** violent
and blustering, like the heathen god of the Saracens in medieval and
Renaissance lore   **114 paid** i.e., killed.   **scot and lot** i.e., in full.
(Originally the phrase was the term for a parish tax.)   **119 part** con-
stituent part, quality, role

126 Nothing . . . eyes i.e., Nothing can contradict me but an eyewitness   **129 fleshed** initiated (in battle)   **137 double man** (1) specter
(2) two men   **138 Jack** knave.   **145 at an instant** simultaneously
148–9 take . . . death i.e., swear with my eternal soul at risk   **155 a lie**
i.e., this lie of yours.   **grace** credit   **156 happiest** most felicitous
158 highest highest vantage point   **162 purge** (1) reduce in weight,
using laxatives (2) repent

[5.5]

The trumpets sound. Enter the King, Prince of Wales, Lord John of Lancaster, Earl of Westmorland, with Worcester and Vernon prisoners.

KING
Thus ever did rebellion find rebuke.
Ill-spirited Worcester! Did not we send grace,
Pardon, and terms of love to all of you?
And wouldst thou turn our offers contrary?
Misuse the tenor of thy kinsman's trust?   5
Three knights upon our party slain today,
A noble earl, and many a creature else
Had been alive this hour,
If like a Christian thou hadst truly borne
Betwixt our armies true intelligence.   10

WORCESTER
What I have done my safety urged me to;
And I embrace this fortune patiently,
Since not to be avoided it falls on me.

KING
Bear Worcester to the death, and Vernon too.
Other offenders we will pause upon.
               [Exeunt Worcester and Vernon, guarded.]
How goes the field?

PRINCE
The noble Scot, Lord Douglas, when he saw
The fortune of the day quite turned from him,
The noble Percy slain, and all his men

Upon the foot of fear, fled with the rest;   20
And falling from a hill, he was so bruised
That the pursuers took him. At my tent
The Douglas is; and I beseech Your Grace
I may dispose of him.

KING   With all my heart.

PRINCE
Then, brother John of Lancaster,
To you this honorable bounty shall belong.   26
Go to the Douglas, and deliver him
Up to his pleasure, ransomless and free.
His valors shown upon our crests today   29
Have taught us how to cherish such high deeds
Even in the bosom of our adversaries.

LANCASTER
I thank Your Grace for this high courtesy,
Which I shall give away immediately.   33

KING
Then this remains, that we divide our power.
You, son John, and my cousin Westmorland
Towards York shall bend you with your dearest speed   36
To meet Northumberland and the prelate Scroop,
Who, as we hear, are busily in arms.
Myself and you, son Harry, will towards Wales,
To fight with Glendower and the Earl of March.
Rebellion in this land shall lose his sway,   41
Meeting the check of such another day;   42
And since this business so fair is done,   43
Let us not leave till all our own be won.   *Exeunt.*   44

5.5 **Location:** The battlefield.
5 **Misuse . . . trust?** i.e., Would you abuse Hotspur's confidence in you (by concealing the generosity of my offer, in your role as emissary)?   10 **intelligence** information, report.

20 **Upon . . . fear** fleeing in panic   26 **this honorable bounty** the honor of this bounteous act   29 **crests** i.e., helmets   33 **give away** pass along, confer on Douglas   36 **bend you** direct your course. **dearest** most urgent   41 **his** its   42 **Meeting . . . day** i.e., when the rebellion is entirely repulsed at one more battlefield   43 **fair** successfully   44 **leave** leave off

The Second Part of King Henry the Fourth

Shakespeare wrote *2 Henry IV* quite soon after *1 Henry IV*, perhaps in 1597, partly, no doubt, to capitalize on the enormous theatrical success of Falstaff and partly to finish the story of Falstaff's rejection. In writing *2 Henry IV*, Shakespeare drew on materials similar to those used for *1 Henry IV*, notably Raphael Holinshed's *Chronicles* (1587) and the anonymous play *The Famous Victories of Henry V* (1583–1588). Moreover, he undertook to write a play that structurally is much like its predecessor, revealing more similarity between these plays than one can find elsewhere in Shakespeare. Even the three *Henry VI* plays do not reiterate structural patterns to the same degree. Is Shakespeare repeating himself, rewriting the earlier play, and, if so, why? Is *2 Henry IV* essentially a way of giving audiences more of what they had found so entertaining in the earlier play, or is it a way of reflecting on new and troublesome issues only partially raised in *1 Henry IV*? The similarities are indeed marked, though, as we shall see, their chief function may be to highlight the important contrasts that arise through a consideration of the surface resemblances.

The structural pattern runs as follows. In both plays, Shakespeare alternates between scenes of political seriousness and scenes of comic irresponsibility, juxtaposing a rebellion in the land with a rebellion in the King's own family. In *1 Henry IV*, we move from a council of war (1.1) to a planning of the robbery at Gad's Hill (1.2). The scenes comment on each other by their nearness and by their mutual concern with lawlessness. Similarly, in *2 Henry IV*, we are at first introduced to a political rebellion in the north of England, after which we encounter Falstaff and Prince Hal's page. In both plays, 2.2 shows us Hal with Poins, setting up a future meeting to embarrass Falstaff by means of a plot, and, in both plays, 2.4 is a long, centrally located scene at the tavern, involving Hal and Falstaff in a contest of wits devised to expose Falstaff as a resourceful liar. The festivities in both scenes are brought to an end by a knocking at the door. (The act-scene divisions may not be Shakespeare's, for they do not appear in the early quartos of either play; nevertheless, the structural location of these scenes is similar.) Between these linked scenes of comic action, we turn in both plays to the rebel camp of the Percys for a discussion of military planning against King Henry (2.3). In both plays, Falstaff goes off supposedly to fight against the rebels, but instead manages to abuse his authority as recruiting officer and to garner undeserved honors, either through wounding the dead Hotspur in the leg or through capturing Coleville of the Dale with the aid of an inflated reputation. The battle scenes are punctuated by Falstaff's wry soliloquies; his disputation on wine in *2 Henry IV* (4.3.88–123) serves a function like that of his better-known catechism on honor in *1 Henry IV* (5.1.129–40). Both plays introduce a confrontation between Hal and his father: the son is penitent for his waywardness, the father lectures on statecraft, and the prodigal son is recovered into kingly grace. Prince Hal goes on thereafter to win public honor and to prove himself his father's true son. Even the rejection of Falstaff, with which the second play ends, finds its counterpart in *1 Henry IV* in Hal's impatience with Falstaff during the battle of Shrewsbury, his elegy over the seemingly dead body of his onetime companion, and his resolve to be henceforth a prince.

These resemblances, and still others, are further highlighted when we realize that Shakespeare continues to use in his second play the structural device of foils, or paired characters, around Hal, who help define alternative models of conduct. The father is, as before, an awesome figure of authority—one whose sternness Hal never fully adopts and yet one whose public role as king Hal must inherit. Falstaff, as before, offers himself as a companion in revelry, dissipation, and joie de vivre, and must be rejected, even though much of what he says offers insight into the coldness of King Henry and especially of Hal's dutiful brother Prince John. Yet the chief purpose of these recapitulations is to suggest profound differences.

2 Henry IV does not simply go over familiar material. Even the resemblances noted so far embody significant changes: the opening scene of the first play takes place at court, the second in the country; the second scene of the first play sets up the trick to be played on Falstaff, whereas in the second play this event takes place in 2.2; this same second scene of the first play is chiefly a battle of wits between Hal and Falstaff, whereas in the second play Falstaff has to cope with the pointed questioning of the Lord Chief Justice; and so on. Repeatedly, the similarities of situations reveal how much Hal has still to learn, how much Falstaff has changed, and how much more complicated the political process is than it first appeared. The foil relationships in this play focus less on honor, as in *1 Henry IV*, than on two related matters: rumor or reputation, and justice.

Rumor begins the play—quite literally, since Rumor is presented to us in allegorized form as portrayed by Virgil, painted full of tongues, spreading false information about the battle of Shrewsbury just ended. Rumor takes particular delight in its most cruel trick of all—raising false hopes and then dashing them. In the scene following at the Percys' household, we see Rumor as it manifests itself in the real world of men, beguiling Northumberland with the "news" of his son Hotspur's triumph, only to disappoint him afterward with the stark truth of defeat and death. What is the function of the uncharacteristic allegory at the start of this play? It serves first to establish a new dispiriting tone. The rebels are in disarray, and their cause is in jeopardy. Hotspur is dead, and with him has died the bright honor of his cause. His kinsmen, always more Machiavellian than he, are now warier than ever. Northumberland is persuaded, in a later scene, to prevaricate to his allies and to withdraw to Scotland when they most need his support, waiting to come in on their side only when he can be sure of success. The atmosphere of realpolitik and of dealing in false appearances is a consequence of a world governed by rumor. The rebels' case is never as attractive in this play as in *1 Henry IV*; Hotspur's idealism and chivalry are sorely missed.

Rumor has profound consequences for the King's side as well, and for Falstaff and Prince Hal. Falstaff rides on false reputation through the early scenes of *2 Henry IV*. He evades arrest at the hands of the Lord Chief Justice because of his presumed deeds at Shrewsbury, which we know to be illusory. His day's service at Shrewsbury "hath a little gilded over" his "night's exploit on Gad's Hill," as the Lord Chief Justice reluctantly concedes (1.2.147–8). His reputation makes possible his capture of Coleville of the Dale at Gaultree Forest, even though, by this time, Falstaff's reputation is clearly beginning to wear thin.

Conversely, Hal discovers that his reputation for prodigality will not leave him. Despite his having lost track of Falstaff, not even knowing of the old man's whereabouts until he agrees to revisit his onetime companion in the tavern for old times' sake, Hal realizes that everyone assumes the worst of him. All expect his future reign to be one of continual riot. He himself characterizes his visit to the tavern, in order to see Falstaff again, as a base "transformation" like those Ovidian portrayals of Jove in lowly human disguise. Talking with Poins in 2.2.1–44, Hal professes to be "exceeding weary" of the "disgrace" it is in him to remember all his vile companions, including Poins, and he sardonically congratulates his companion on thinking like everyone else when Poins assumes that any weeping on Hal's part for his father's death would be no more than princely hypocrisy. "Let the end try the man," says Hal, in what should be a plain notice of his reformation, but no one credits him with sincerity. When his father does take to his deathbed, surrounded by hushed courtiers, Hal, until now notably absent from court, enters with exaggerated offhandedness, as though eschewing the show of mourning he knows cannot be believed in him. His taking the crown from the pillow of his seemingly dead father strikes King Henry and his courtiers as one last confirmation of Hal's desire to supplant his father, and indeed we, too, are forced to wonder at Hal's imprudence. (The patricidal overtones in one of Shakespeare's sources, *The Famous Victories of Henry V*, are much more overt than those in Shakespeare's play.)

The structural recapitulations of *2 Henry IV*, then, in which Hal first jests with Falstaff at the tavern and afterward confronts his father at court, are no mere repetitions; they stress the dreary fact that a reputation for riotous conduct persists, that the father's embracing of his son has lapsed into renewed distrust, and that "reformation" is not the simple process Hal once supposed. Reformation is first a matter of improving one's own conduct, but it is also a matter of improving one's image. Hal has been aware of the need for attending to one's image, even as early as his famous "I know you all" soliloquy (1.2.189–211) in *1 Henry IV*, but he has grossly underestimated the difficulty of overcoming an unsavory reputation. This is not a happy revelation to a young man who is impatient of ceremony and public display, but it is the way of the world and an integral part of any successful kingship. King Henry's last advice to Hal, in fact, once they have been reconciled anew, concerns the manipulations of appearances in the name of statecraft; the father urges the son to resolve civil strife by going to war against some foreign enemy. He must "busy giddy minds / With foreign quarrels" (4.5.212–13). Hal will adopt this stratagem in *Henry V* by warring against the French. Meantime, in *2 Henry IV*, he must overcome his reputation, not only with his father, but also with the Lord Chief Justice, the nobles of the court, and his brothers. Not until the play's end do they believe other than that Hal will turn riot loose in his kingdom. The intransigent nature of false "rumor" or reputation does much to explain why the new King must reject Falstaff so publicly and so sharply. He has, in fact, already rejected Falstaff in the sense of leaving him, but no one has taken the point—least of all Falstaff, who now presses in upon the new King with hopes of reward and license to act as he pleases. "The laws of England are at my commandment," he exults (5.3.138–9). Only a public repudiation can meet the demands of kingship by making full use of the act's symbolic value. Hal must reject Falstaff, not only in his heart, but also in the view of his nation. It is a distasteful act, perhaps as much to him as to us, but it is made necessary by the political exigencies of the moment.

The play's concern with justice emerges in the first confrontation between the Lord Chief Justice and Falstaff (1.2.54–226). The one represents law; the other, license. Who is to represent and administer the law during Henry V's reign? The Lord Chief Justice is a firm and austere figure, a deputy or substitute for the father-king—one who has presumed to imprison Hal for resisting his authority. This Lord Chief Justice does not expect to remain in office once the new King is crowned; like other serious characters in the play, he longs for reassurance in the troubled times of civil war and of change of administration under a monarchy. In contrast to this somewhat awesome parental figure, Falstaff offers hedonism and irresponsibility. His wit is, in a sense, no less engaging than in *1 Henry IV*. His scenes with Shallow and Silence, as they choose soldiers for the upcoming campaign or prepare for the golden time they anticipate, are as funny as the best of Falstaff. The pairing of the Lord Chief Justice and Falstaff as foils might suggest at first that one is lacking where the other is strong and that Hal must steer between extremes.

Yet this play does not give us a genuine debate on justice, like that on honor in *1 Henry IV*, in which Falstaff's comments on honor strike home because of Hotspur's fanaticism. The Lord Chief Justice of this play is essentially in the right, however austere, and Falstaff is essentially in the wrong, however funny. The Lord Chief Justice sees through Falstaff and patiently bides his time. Falstaff's excesses are more pronounced than in the earlier play. We see him with Doll Tearsheet, a whore, in maudlin, drunken conversation. He is associated with images of disease—gout, the pox, or syphilis, consumption, lameness—and of purging. His lying is not as consistently clever as before. Hal recalls the brilliant lie about the Gad's Hill robbery and credits Falstaff (perhaps ironically) with having seen through the Prince's trick on that occasion (2.4.305–7), but, in the second tavern scene, Falstaff can only stammer uninventively that he had no idea that Hal was behind him in disguise, listening to his foulmouthed reproaches. Falstaff's rioting with Pistol disturbs the peace, and in such brawls homicides occur, necessitating arrest and punishment (5.4). When Falstaff appears with the diminutive page, as in 1.2, we are forcefully reminded of the grossness of his body, even if he,

too, laughs at this. His mooching off Mistress Quickly and his breach of promise of marriage to her, though hinted at in the earlier play, are much more open here; the humor is keen, but we cannot forget that Falstaff is victimizing a gullible woman. Lawsuits and arrests are more prominent in this play than in its predecessor. Falstaff's abuse of authority to recruit soldiers, about which he discourses wittily in the earlier play, is here fully shown, both in its hilarity and in its lawless consequences.

Falstaff's new companions, Pistol, Doll, and then Justice Shallow and Justice Silence, sharpen our perception of Falstaff's increasingly flagrant lawlessness. Shallow and Silence are, by their very profession, counterparts to the Lord Chief Justice. In their complacent interest in their own prosperity ("How a good yoke of bullocks at Stamford fair?" 3.2.39), in their countenancing of influence peddling by their subordinates (5.1.37–52), and in Shallow's foxy aspirations to deceive Falstaff before Falstaff can deceive him, these pillars of rural respectability reveal how far injustice has permeated the English countryside. They are fit companions for Falstaff when he hears the news of his rejection and are suitably victimized by Falstaff's inability to repay a loan that Justice Shallow has advanced to him from motives of self-interest. These old men, myopically recollecting the jolly days of their youth, accentuate Falstaff's physical frailty and aging. Falstaff mocks the stories of their escapades, but he, too, as he confesses to Doll over his drink, is old. The necessary course of justice is made plain by the structural configurations of the play. Falstaff and his companions seek lawlessness and must be rebuked; the Lord Chief Justice, who fears rejection, must instead be embraced by Hal explicitly as a father figure ("You shall be as a father to my youth," 5.2.118) in order to reaffirm public decency. The Lord Chief Justice is to bear "the balance and the sword" (line 103) as emblems of justice and its stern role in maintaining order; Falstaff is dismissed as "The tutor and the feeder of my riots" (5.5.62). These necessities are plain, even though they do not answer the emotionally complicated issue of Hal's (and our) fondness for the companion of his youth.

Hal's brother, Prince John of Lancaster, is another opposite to Falstaff. Here the contrast is less prejudicial to Falstaff. Prince John takes charge of his ailing father's wars and engineers a surrender of the rebels at Gaultree Forest that is a triumph of equivocation and double-dealing. It also saves the nation from further civil conflict, at least for the time being, and establishes the peace that Hal inherits and turns to his advantage against France. It seems all too much in keeping with the realpolitik that has characterized the conduct of both sides heretofore and may thus be said to be a suitable conclusion. The dismaying "revolution of the times" (3.1.46) brings with it the cooling of friendships and the recollection of dire prophecies from the days of Richard II. The only justification possible for what John does is that it succeeds. It surely lacks the glory and honor attendant on the conflict of Hal and Hotspur in *1 Henry IV*. Not coincidentally, Hal is far away from Gaultree Forest when this dismal surrender is brought about. Prince John is a master at knowing how to "construe the times to their necessities" (4.1.104). His acts scarcely represent justice any more than honor. "Is this proceeding just and honorable?" ask the betrayed rebels and are answered merely "Is your assembly so?" (4.2.110–11). The end justifies the means. Falstaff's observations at Prince John's expense therefore have point. John is, as Falstaff characterizes him, "soberblooded"; he drinks no wine and relies not on valor but on sagacity. Falstaff hopes that Hal will prove more valiant, tempering "the cold blood he did naturally inherit of his father" (4.3.87–117) with the imbibing of sherry and other pleasures learned from Falstaff. Whatever the merits of drinking as an inducement to courage, we do perceive that Prince John is too much his father's son and that Hal will avoid this chilly extreme in his quest for a kingly identity that is both symbol and substance.

Hal has thus learned something from Falstaff, if only as a caution against extremes, and partly for this reason his rejection of Falstaff must come as a shock no matter how inevitable it is. Hal may well appear to dwindle in the process, for he has given up a good deal of his private self to adopt the public role thrust upon him. In performance, this dwindling can turn out to be more than the prize of maturity is worth: Orson Welles's film called *Chimes at Midnight* (1965–1966) memorably focuses on Welles's own role as Falstaff in the two *Henry IV* plays, and, in the second play in particular, as the victim of a series of farewells in which Falstaff's touching bid for affection deserves more than a heartless rejection. This Falstaff's jollity and wit never quite conceal the look of hurt in the eye of a fat man who fears to be unloved. A simultaneous darkening of Hal's character is a common feature of other recent productions. Michael Pennington, in a modern-dress production directed by Michael Bogadnov for the new English Shakespeare company in 1986–1987, interpreted Hal as shrewd and self-confident in his ostentatious snubbing of Falstaff in the play's final scene, as though to underscore the new king's view of Falstaff as irrelevant to the political world over which Hal must now rule. A production at Stratford-upon-Avon in 1964 under the joint direction of John Barton, Peter Hall, and Clifford Williams gave an iconoclastic and distinctly unpatriotic reading to the contrast between a calculatedly Machiavellian Prince John and a thoroughly debauched Falstaff (Hugh Griffith), with Hal as the canny politician making his successful way in a world of realpolitik.

Perhaps, then, Prince Hal accepts the public role thrust upon him in this play not unwillingly but at the same time with an awareness that he does so at some cost to himself—and to Falstaff. His terms of rejection are not wholly ungenerous—he allows the possibility of Falstaff's returning to court if he reforms, and makes financial allowance so that Falstaff will have no need to continue in crime—but the finality of the action remains stunning. We are left with a broken Falstaff, on his way to the Fleet prison by order of the Lord Chief Justice, trying to deceive himself into believing that all will be well. Hal and England have turned in a new direction; a war against the French is clearly in prospect already, which will absorb the energies of the new King and of his father's erstwhile political enemies as well. For better and for worse, the emergence of Hal into his public role is complete.

The Second Part of King Henry the Fourth

The Actors' Names

RUMOR, *the Presenter*
KING HENRY THE FOURTH
PRINCE HENRY, *afterwards crowned* KING HENRY THE
    FIFTH
PRINCE JOHN OF LANCASTER   *sons to Henry IV*
HUMPHREY [DUKE] OF GLOUCESTER   *and brethren*
THOMAS [DUKE] OF CLARENCE   *to Henry V*

[EARL OF] NORTHUMBERLAND
[SCROOP,] THE ARCHBISHOP
    OF YORK
[LORD] MOWBRAY   *opposites against King*
[LORD] HASTING   *Henry IV*
LORD BARDOLPH
TRAVERS
MORTON
[SIR JOHN]COLEVILLE

[EARL OF] WARWICK
[EARL OF] WESTMORLAND
[EARL OF] SURREY
GOWER   *of the King's party*
HARCOURT
[BLUNT]
LORD CHIEF JUSTICE
[*His* SERVANT]

POINS
[SIR JOHN] FALSTAFF
BARDOLPH
PISTOL   *irregular humorists*
PETO
[FALSTAFF'S] PAGE

SHALLOW   *both country justices*
SILENCE
DAVY, *servant to Shallow*
FANG *and* SNARE, *two sergeants*
MOLDY, SHADOW, WART, FEEBLE, [*and*]
    BULLCALF, *country soldiers*
[FRANCIS, *a drawer*]

NORTHUMBERLAND'S WIFE
PERCY'S WIDOW [LADY PERCY]
HOSTESS QUICKLY
DOLL TEARSHEET
DRAWERS
BEADLES
GROOMS
[PORTER]

EPILOGUE

[*Lords, Attendants, Messengers, Pages, Musicians,*
    Officers, etc.]

[SCENE: *England*]

Induction

Enter Rumor, painted full of tongues.

Induction. Location: Although the allegory of Rumor, based ultimately on Virgil's depiction of Fama as full of eyes, ears, and
tongues in the *Aeneid* (4.179–90), is timeless, Rumor is here represented as standing in front of Northumberland's castle, Warkworth.
The play is supposed to open immediately after the battle of
Shrewsbury, in which Henry Percy, or Hotspur, and the Scottish
Earl of Douglas have been overthrown. We are concerned first of all
with the news of the battle with which *1 Henry IV* ended.

RUMOR
  Open your ears, for which of you will stop
  The vent of hearing when loud Rumor speaks?
  I, from the orient to the drooping west,
  Making the wind my post-horse, still unfold   4
  The acts commencèd on this ball of earth.
  Upon my tongues continual slanders ride,
  The which in every language I pronounce,

4 post-horse horse kept at an inn or post-house for the use of travelers. **still** continually

Stuffing the ears of men with false reports.
I speak of peace while covert enmity,
Under the smile of safety, wounds the world.
And who but Rumor, who but only I,
Make fearful musters and prepared defense, 12
Whiles the big year, swoll'n with some other grief, 13
Is thought with child by the stern tyrant War,
And no such matter? Rumor is a pipe 15
Blown by surmises, jealousies, conjectures, 16
And of so easy and so plain a stop 17
That the blunt monster with uncounted heads, 18
The still-discordant wav'ring multitude,
Can play upon it. But what need I thus 20
My well-known body to anatomize 21
Among my household? Why is Rumor here? 22
I run before King Harry's victory,
Who in a bloody field by Shrewsbury
Hath beaten down young Hotspur and his troops,
Quenching the flame of bold rebellion
Even with the rebels' blood. But what mean I
To speak so true at first? My office is
To noise abroad that Harry Monmouth fell 29
Under the wrath of noble Hotspur's sword,
And that the King before the Douglas' rage
Stooped his anointed head as low as death.
This have I rumored through the peasant towns 33
Between that royal field of Shrewsbury
And this worm-eaten hold of ragged stone, 35
Where Hotspur's father, old Northumberland,
Lies crafty-sick. The posts come tiring on, 37
And not a man of them brings other news
Than they have learned of me. From Rumor's tongues
They bring smooth comforts false, worse than true
　wrongs.　　　　　　　　　　　　　　*Exit Rumor.* 40

❧

[1.1]

Enter the Lord Bardolph at one door.

LORD BARDOLPH
Who keeps the gate here, ho?

　　　[Enter the Porter.]

　　　　　　　　　　　Where is the Earl? 1

PORTER
　What shall I say you are?
LORD BARDOLPH　　　　　　Tell thou the Earl
　That the Lord Bardolph doth attend him here. 3
PORTER
　His Lordship is walked forth into the orchard.
　Please it Your Honor knock but at the gate,
　And he himself will answer.

　　　Enter the Earl [of] Northumberland [in a nightcap,
　　　supporting himself with a crutch].

LORD BARDOLPH　　　　　　Here comes the Earl
　　　　　　　　　　　　　　[Exit Porter.]
NORTHUMBERLAND
　What news, Lord Bardolph? Every minute now
　Should be the father of some stratagem. 8
　The times are wild. Contention, like a horse
　Full of high feeding, madly hath broke loose 10
　And bears down all before him.
LORD BARDOLPH　　　　　　Noble Earl,
　I bring you certain news from Shrewsbury.
NORTHUMBERLAND
　Good, an God will!
LORD BARDOLPH　　　As good as heart can wish. 13
　The King is almost wounded to the death,
　And, in the fortune of my lord your son,
　Prince Harry slain outright; and both the Blunts
　Killed by the hand of Douglas. Young Prince John
　And Westmorland and Stafford fled the field,
　And Harry Monmouth's brawn, the hulk Sir John, 19
　Is prisoner to your son. Oh, such a day,
　So fought, so followed, and so fairly won, 21
　Came not till now to dignify the times
　Since Caesar's fortunes!
NORTHUMBERLAND　　　How is this derived? 23
　Saw you the field? Came you from Shrewsbury?
LORD BARDOLPH
　I spake with one, my lord, that came from thence,
　A gentleman well bred and of good name,
　That freely rendered me these news for true.

　　　Enter Travers.

NORTHUMBERLAND
　Here comes my servant Travers, who I sent
　On Tuesday last to listen after news.
LORD BARDOLPH
　My lord, I overrode him on the way, 30
　And he is furnished with no certainties
　More than he haply may retail from me. 32
NORTHUMBERLAND
　Now, Travers, what good tidings comes with you?

---

12 **musters** assemblies of soldiers　13 **big** swollen, pregnant with disaster　15 **And no such matter** and yet there is no substance in such rumors.　**pipe** recorder (a wind instrument)　16 **jealousies** suspicions
17 **of . . . stop** whose stops or openings are so easily played on
18 **blunt** stupid, dull-witted.　**uncounted** countless　20 **what** why
21 **anatomize** lay open minutely, explain　22 **household** retinue, i.e., the audience.　29 **Harry Monmouth** Prince Hal (who was born at Monmouth in Wales)　33 **peasant** rural, provincial　35 **hold** stronghold, fortress　37 **crafty-sick** feigning sickness.　**The . . . on** The messengers gallop hard, exhausting their horses　40 **smooth . . . wrongs** i.e., false good news that is ultimately worse than hurtful truth.
1.1. Location: Warkworth. Before Northumberland's castle.
0.1 *Lord Bardolph* (An ally of the Percys; not to be confused with Bardolph, Falstaff's red-faced companion.)　**1 keeps** guards

3 **attend** await　8 **stratagem** violent deed.　10 **high feeding** too-rich fodder　13 **an** if　19 **brawn** fat boar　21 **followed** carried through
23 **Since Caesar's fortunes** i.e., since Julius Caesar defeated Pharnaces at Zela in 47 B.C., proclaiming *Veni, vidi, vici* ("I came, I saw, I overcame"). The alliteration in line 21 (*fought, followed, fairly*) recalls that famous message.　**derived** learned, obtained.　**30 overrode** overtook　**32 haply** perhaps.　**retail** relate

TRAVERS
My lord, Sir John Umfrevill turned me back   34
With joyful tidings and, being better horsed,
Outrode me. After him came spurring hard
A gentleman almost forspent with speed   37
That stopped by me to breathe his bloodied horse.   38
He asked the way to Chester, and of him
I did demand what news from Shrewsbury.   40
He told me that rebellion had bad luck
And that young Harry Percy's spur was cold.
With that, he gave his able horse the head,   43
And bending forward struck his armèd heels
Against the panting sides of his poor jade   45
Up to the rowel head, and starting so   46
He seemed in running to devour the way,
Staying no longer question.

NORTHUMBERLAND   Ha? Again: 48
Said he young Harry Percy's spur was cold?
Of Hotspur, Coldspur? That rebellion
Had met ill luck?

LORD BARDOLPH   My lord, I'll tell you what:
If my young lord your son have not the day,   52
Upon mine honor, for a silken point   53
I'll give my barony. Never talk of it.

NORTHUMBERLAND
Why should that gentleman that rode by Travers
Give then such instances of loss?

LORD BARDOLPH   Who, he?
He was some hilding fellow that had stol'n   57
The horse he rode on and, upon my life,
Spoke at a venture. Look, here comes more news.   59

Enter Morton.

NORTHUMBERLAND
Yea, this man's brow, like to a title leaf,   60
Foretells the nature of a tragic volume.
So looks the strand whereon the imperious flood   62
Hath left a witnessed usurpation.   63
Say, Morton, didst thou come from Shrewsbury?

MORTON
I ran from Shrewsbury, my noble lord,
Where hateful death put on his ugliest mask
To fright our party.

NORTHUMBERLAND   How doth my son and brother?
Thou tremblest, and the whiteness in thy cheek
Is apter than thy tongue to tell thy errand.
Even such a man, so faint, so spiritless,
So dull, so dead in look, so woebegone,
Drew Priam's curtain in the dead of night   72

And would have told him half his Troy was burnt;
But Priam found the fire ere he his tongue,   74
And I my Percy's death ere thou report'st it.
This thou wouldst say, "Your son did thus and thus;
Your brother thus; so fought the noble Douglas"—
Stopping my greedy ear with their bold deeds.   78
But in the end, to stop my ear indeed,   79
Thou hast a sigh to blow away this praise,
Ending with "Brother, son, and all are dead."

MORTON
Douglas is living, and your brother, yet;
But for my lord your son—

NORTHUMBERLAND   Why, he is dead.
See what a ready tongue suspicion hath!
He that but fears the thing he would not know   85
Hath by instinct knowledge from others' eyes
That what he feared is chancèd. Yet speak, Morton.   87
Tell thou an earl his divination lies,   88
And I will take it as a sweet disgrace
And make thee rich for doing me such wrong.

MORTON
You are too great to be by me gainsaid.   91
Your spirit is too true, your fears too certain.   92

NORTHUMBERLAND
Yet, for all this, say not that Percy's dead.   93
I see a strange confession in thine eye.
Thou shak'st thy head and hold'st it fear or sin
To speak a truth. If he be slain, say so.
The tongue offends not that reports his death;
And he doth sin that doth belie the dead,   98
Not he which says the dead is not alive.
Yet the first bringer of unwelcome news
Hath but a losing office, and his tongue   101
Sounds ever after as a sullen bell   102
Remembered tolling a departing friend.   103

LORD BARDOLPH
I cannot think, my lord, your son is dead.

MORTON
I am sorry I should force you to believe
That which I would to God I had not seen;
But these mine eyes saw him in bloody state,
Rend'ring faint quittance, wearied and outbreathed,   108
To Harry Monmouth, whose swift wrath beat down
The never-daunted Percy to the earth,
From whence with life he never more sprung up.
In few, his death, whose spirit lent a fire   112
Even to the dullest peasant in his camp,
Being bruited once, took fire and heat away   114
From the best-tempered courage in his troops;   115
For from his metal was his party steeled,   116

---

34 Sir John Umfrevill i.e., perhaps the *gentleman* mentioned in line 26
37 forspent exhausted   **38 breathe** rest.   **bloodied** i.e., with spurring
40 demand ask   **43 gave . . . head** loosened the reins with which he
had reined in his powerful horse   **45 jade** nag   **46 rowel head** the
end of the spur, in which the barbed wheel turns.   **starting** springing
forward   **48 Staying** waiting for   **52 day** victory   **53 point** tag for
fastening clothes (i.e., something of very small value)   **57 hilding**
good-for-nothing   **59 at a venture** at random, recklessly.   **60 title
leaf** title page   **62–3 So . . . usurpation** So looks the shore whereon
the invading ocean has left behind the evidence of its encroachment.
(Morton's brow is furrowed like wrinkled sand.)   **72 Priam's curtain**
the bedcurtains of Priam, King of Troy

74 ere . . . tongue before the messenger had time to speak   **78 Stopping** filling   **79 stop . . . indeed** prevent my ever hearing again
85 He The person   **87 is chancèd** has occurred.   **88 divination**
prophecy   **91 gainsaid** contradicted.   **92 spirit** intuition, powers of
perception   **93 for** in spite of   **98 belie** slander, misreport   **101 losing office** i.e., thankless task   **102 sullen** mournful   **103 tolling** ringing the funeral bell for   **108 quittance** requital, i.e., resistance.
outbreathed out of breath   **112 In few** In few words   **114 bruited**
rumored, reported   **115 best-tempered** i.e., like the highest quality
steel   **116 metal** (1) steel, continuing the metaphor of line 115
(2) mettle, courage

Which once in him abated, all the rest   117
Turned on themselves, like dull and heavy lead.   118
And as the thing that's heavy in itself
Upon enforcement flies with greatest speed,   120
So did our men, heavy in Hotspur's loss,
Lend to this weight such lightness with their fear
That arrows fled not swifter toward their aim
Than did our soldiers, aiming at their safety,
Fly from the field. Then was that noble Worcester
Too soon ta'en prisoner; and that furious Scot,
The bloody Douglas, whose well-laboring sword
Had three times slain th'appearance of the King,   128
'Gan vail his stomach and did grace the shame   129
Of those that turned their backs, and in his flight,
Stumbling in fear, was took. The sum of all
Is that the King hath won and hath sent out
A speedy power to encounter you, my lord,   133
Under the conduct of young Lancaster   134
And Westmorland. This is the news at full.

NORTHUMBERLAND
For this I shall have time enough to mourn.
In poison there is physic; and these news,   137
Having been well, that would have made me sick,   138
Being sick, have in some measure made me well.   139
And as the wretch whose fever-weakened joints
Like strengthless hinges buckle under life,   141
Impatient of his fit, breaks like a fire   142
Out of his keeper's arms, even so my limbs,   143
Weakened with grief, being now enraged with grief,   144
Are thrice themselves. Hence, therefore, thou nice
    crutch!   [He throws away his crutch.]   145
A scaly gauntlet now with joints of steel   146
Must glove this hand. And hence, thou sickly coif!   147
    [He takes off his nightcap.]
Thou art a guard too wanton for the head   148
Which princes, fleshed with conquest, aim to hit.   149
Now bind my brows with iron, and approach   150
The ragged'st hour that time and spite dare bring   151
To frown upon th'enragèd Northumberland!
Let heaven kiss earth! Now let not Nature's hand
Keep the wild flood confined! Let order die,   154
And let this world no longer be a stage
To feed contention in a ling'ring act;   156
But let one spirit of the firstborn Cain   157

Reign in all bosoms, that, each heart being set   158
On bloody courses, the rude scene may end,   159
And darkness be the burier of the dead!

LORD BARDOLPH
This strainèd passion doth you wrong, my lord.   161

MORTON
Sweet Earl, divorce not wisdom from your honor.
The lives of all your loving complices   163
Lean on your health, the which, if you give o'er
To stormy passion, must perforce decay.   165
You cast th'event of war, my noble lord,   166
And summed the account of chance, before you said   167
"Let us make head." It was your presurmise   168
That in the dole of blows your son might drop.   169
You knew he walked o'er perils, on an edge,
More likely to fall in than to get o'er;
You were advised his flesh was capable   172
Of wounds and scars, and that his forward spirit   173
Would lift him where most trade of danger ranged.   174
Yet did you say, "Go forth." And none of this,   175
Though strongly apprehended, could restrain   176
The stiff-borne action. What hath then befall'n,   177
Or what hath this bold enterprise brought forth,
More than that being which was like to be?   179

LORD BARDOLPH
We all that are engagèd to this loss   180
Knew that we ventured on such dangerous seas
That if we wrought out life 'twas ten to one.   182
And yet we ventured, for the gain proposed
Choked the respect of likely peril feared;   184
And since we are o'erset, venture again.   185
Come, we will all put forth, body and goods.   186

MORTON
'Tis more than time. And, my most noble lord,
I hear for certain, and dare speak the truth,
The gentle Archbishop of York is up   189
With well-appointed powers. He is a man   190
Who with a double surety binds his followers.   191
My lord your son had only but the corpse,   192
But shadows and the shows of men, to fight.   193
For that same word "rebellion" did divide
The action of their bodies from their souls,
And they did fight with queasiness, constrained,

---

117 abated (1) blunted (2) slackened   **118 Turned on themselves** (1) bent backwards (2) turned and ran   **120 Upon enforcement** when set forcibly in motion   **128 th'appearance of the King** i.e., warriors dressed like the King. (See *1 Henry IV*, 5.3 and 5.4.25–38.)   **129 'Gan ... stomach** began to abate or lower his courage.   **grace** sanction (by his own running away)   **133 power** armed force   **134 conduct** command   **137 physic** medicine   **138 Having ... sick** that would have made me sick if I had been well   **139 Being sick, have** I being sick, this same news has   **141 buckle under life** bend under the weight of the living man   **142 fit** attack of illness   **143 keeper's** nurse's   **144 grief ... grief** pain and sickness ... sorrow   **145 nice** delicate, effeminate   **146 scaly gauntlet** armored glove   **147 sickly coif** close-fitting cap worn by an invalid.   **148 wanton** effeminate, luxurious   **149 fleshed** inflamed by the taste of blood and success   **150 approach** let approach   **151 ragged'st** roughest   **154 flood** river, ocean   **156 in ... act** in a drawn-out act (as of a play). (Northumberland wishes for an end to the lingering dissolution of a world in conflict.)   **157 of ... Cain** i.e., of murder

158 that so that   **159 rude scene** (1) violent action (2) crude play. (See line 156 and n.)   **161 strainèd** excessive   **163 complices** allies   **165 perforce** necessarily   **166 cast th'event** calculated the outcome   **167 summed ... chance** summed up and weighed the risks   **168 make head** raise an army.   **presurmise** presupposition   **169 dole** dealing out, distribution. (With a possible punning suggestion of "grief, sorrow.")   **172 advised** aware   **173 Of** of receiving.   **forward** eager, ardent   **174 trade** trafficking   **175–7 And none ... action** And yet none of these potential dangers, though strongly understood to be possible, could hold back a military action that was resolutely carried out.   **179 that ... be** what was likely to occur.   **180 engagèd to** involved in   **182 if ... one** if we came out alive, we survived ten-to-one odds.   **184 Choked the respect** suppressed the consideration   **185 o'erset** defeated, overthrown   **186 all put forth** (1) all set out, as though putting out to sea (2) stake everything   **189–90 The gentle ... powers** the nobly born Archbishop Scroop is ready with well-equipped troops.   **191 a double surety** both temporal and spiritual authority   **192 only** but only.   **corpse** the bodies without the souls   **193 But** only.   **to fight** to use for fighting.

As men drink potions, that their weapons only   197
Seemed on our side; but, for their spirits and souls,   198
This word "rebellion," it had froze them up
As fish are in a pond. But now the Bishop
Turns insurrection to religion.   201
Supposed sincere and holy in his thoughts,   202
He's followed both with body and with mind,
And doth enlarge his rising with the blood   204
Of fair King Richard, scraped from Pomfret stones;   205
Derives from heaven his quarrel and his cause;
Tells them he doth bestride a bleeding land   207
Gasping for life under great Bolingbroke;   208
And more and less do flock to follow him.   209

NORTHUMBERLAND
I knew of this before, but, to speak truth,
This present grief had wiped it from my mind.
Go in with me, and counsel every man   212
The aptest way for safety and revenge.
Get posts and letters, and make friends with speed—   214
Never so few, and never yet more need.   *Exeunt.*

❦

[1.2]

*Enter Sir John [Falstaff] alone, with his Page
bearing his sword and buckler.*

FALSTAFF   Sirrah, you giant, what says the doctor to my   1
water?   2
PAGE   He said, sir, the water itself was a good healthy
water, but, for the party that owed it, he might have   4
more diseases than he knew for.   5
FALSTAFF   Men of all sorts take a pride to gird at me.   6
The brain of this foolish-compounded clay, man, is   7
not able to invent anything that tends to laughter
more than I invent or is invented on me. I am not only
witty in myself, but the cause that wit is in other men.
I do here walk before thee like a sow that hath
overwhelmed all her litter but one. If the Prince put
thee into my service for any other reason than to set   13
me off, why then I have no judgment. Thou whoreson   14
mandrake, thou art fitter to be worn in my cap than to   15
wait at my heels. I was never manned with an agate   16

till now; but I will inset you neither in gold nor silver,
but in vile apparel, and send you back again to your
master for a jewel—the juvenal, the Prince your   19
master, whose chin is not yet fledge. I will sooner   20
have a beard grow in the palm of my hand than he
shall get one of his cheek, and yet he will not stick to   22
say his face is a face royal. God may finish it when he   23
will; 'tis not a hair amiss yet. He may keep it still at a   24
face royal, for a barber shall never earn sixpence out of
it; and yet he'll be crowing as if he had writ man ever   26
since his father was a bachelor. He may keep his own
grace, but he's almost out of mine, I can assure him.   28
What said Master Dommelton about the satin for my
short cloak and my slops?   30
PAGE   He said, sir, you should procure him better
assurance than Bardolph. He would not take his bond   32
and yours; he liked not the security.
FALSTAFF   Let him be damned, like the glutton! Pray   34
God his tongue be hotter! A whoreson Achitophel, a   35
rascally yea-forsooth knave, to bear a gentleman in   36
hand and then stand upon security! The whoreson   37
smoothy-pates do now wear nothing but high shoes   38
and bunches of keys at their girdles; and if a man is   39
through with them in honest taking up, then they   40
must stand upon security. I had as lief they would put   41
ratsbane in my mouth as offer to stop it with security.   42
I looked 'a should have sent me two-and-twenty   43
yards of satin, as I am a true knight, and he sends me
"security"! Well, he may sleep in security, for he hath   45
the horn of abundance, and the lightness of his wife   46
shines through it. And yet cannot he see, though he   47
have his own lantern to light him. Where's Bardolph?   48
PAGE   He's gone into Smithfield to buy Your Worship a   49
horse.

197 **As . . . potions** the way people drink distasteful medicines, queasily **198 for** as for **201 to religion** into a sacred cause. **202 Supposed** i.e., Rightly thought to be **204–5 And doth . . . stones** and attracts new supporters and allies to the cause of rebellion by sanctifying as a holy relic the blood of Richard II, scraped from the stones of Pontefract Castle where the King was murdered. **207 bestride** stand over to protect **208 Bolingbroke** i.e., King Henry IV, here deprived of his title by the Archbishop **209 more and less** all classes **212 counsel every man** let every man give advice as to **214 posts** messengers. **make** collect
1.2. Location: London. A street.
0.2 *buckler* shield. **1 Sirrah** (Form of address to a social inferior.) **1–2 to my water** about my urine sample. **4 owed** owned **5 knew for** was aware of. **6 gird** jeer **7 foolish-compounded** composed of folly **13–14 set me off** be a foil to me, show me to the best advantage **14 whoreson** (A generalized term of abuse meaning "vile" or "detestable.") **15 mandrake** plant with a forked, man-shaped root. **fitter . . . cap** i.e., as small and decorous as a brooch worn in my cap **16 wait at my heels** i.e., wait in attendance on me, follow me about. **manned . . . agate** i.e., provided with a servant as small as the little figures cut in agate stone for jewelry and seal rings

19 **juvenal** youth   20 **fledge** covered with down.   22 **stick** hesitate 23 **face royal** (Punning on the *royal*, a coin with the King's face stamped on it.)   24 **a hair** (1) a single hair of the beard (2) a jot.   **at** at the value of   26 **writ man** called himself man   28 **grace** (1) title suited to his royal rank (2) favor   30 **slops** loose breeches.   32 **assurance** guarantee.   **Bardolph** (One of Falstaff's followers, not the Lord Bardolph of scene 1.)   34 **the glutton** (A reference to the parable of Dives the rich man, who, sent to hell for his covetousness, cried out imploringly that Lazarus, the poor leper, might dip his finger in water to cool Dives's burning tongue, Luke 16:19–31.)   35 **hotter** i.e., than Dives's tongue in hell.   **Achitophel** abettor of Absalom's treason against David (2 Samuel 15–17)   36 **yea-forsooth knave** i.e., Puritan tradesman who uses mild oaths but is a rascal for all that   36–7 **bear . . . in hand** delude a gentleman with false hopes   37 **stand upon security** insist upon guarantee of payment. (As also at line 41.)   38 **smoothy-pates** (Alludes to the short hair of Puritan tradesmen.)   38–9 **high shoes . . . keys** (Indications of their financial prosperity and putting on airs.)   39–40 **is . . . taking up** has agreed with them straightforwardly on credit terms   41 **lief** willingly   42 **ratsbane** rat poison 43 **looked 'a** expected that he   45 **in security** i.e., in a false and complacent sense of security   46 **horn of abundance** (1) cornucopia (2) cuckold's horn, a sign of his wife's infidelity.   **lightness** (1) wantonness (2) light showing through a lantern (which would have windows of *horn*, thereby giving the cuckold a lantern in his own forehead)   47 **cannot he see** i.e., he cannot see his own wife's infidelity   48 **lantern** (The Quarto spelling "lanthorne" preserves Falstaff's continued joke about cuckold's horns.)   49 **Smithfield** district near Saint Paul's Cathedral, famous as a livestock market

FALSTAFF   I bought him in Paul's, and he'll buy me a 51
horse in Smithfield. An I could get me but a wife in the 52
stews, I were manned, horsed, and wived. 53

Enter [the] Lord Chief Justice [and his Servant].

PAGE   Sir, here comes the nobleman that committed the 54
Prince for striking him about Bardolph.

FALSTAFF   Wait close; I will not see him. 56

[He tries to slip away.]

CHIEF JUSTICE   What's he that goes there?

SERVANT   Falstaff, an't please Your Lordship.

CHIEF JUSTICE   He that was in question for the robbery? 59

SERVANT   He, my lord. But he hath since done good service at Shrewsbury, and, as I hear, is now going with
some charge to the Lord John of Lancaster. 62

CHIEF JUSTICE   What, to York? Call him back again.

SERVANT   Sir John Falstaff!

FALSTAFF   Boy, tell him I am deaf.

PAGE   You must speak louder; my master is deaf.

CHIEF JUSTICE   I am sure he is, to the hearing of
anything good.—Go pluck him by the elbow; I must
speak with him.

SERVANT   Sir John!

FALSTAFF   What, a young knave, and begging? Is there
not wars? Is there not employment? Doth not the King
lack subjects? Do not the rebels need soldiers? Though
it be a shame to be on any side but one, it is worse
shame to beg than to be on the worst side, were it 75
worse than the name of rebellion can tell how to 76
make it. 77

SERVANT   You mistake me, sir.

FALSTAFF   Why, sir, did I say you were an honest man?
Setting my knighthood and my soldiership aside, I 80
had lied in my throat if I had said so. 81

SERVANT   I pray you, sir, then set your knighthood and
your soldiership aside, and give me leave to tell you 83
you lie in your throat if you say I am any other than
an honest man.

FALSTAFF   I give thee leave to tell me so? I lay aside that
which grows to me? If thou get'st any leave of me, 87
hang me; if thou tak'st leave, thou wert better be
hanged. You hunt counter. Hence! Avaunt! 89

SERVANT   Sir, my lord would speak with you.

CHIEF JUSTICE   Sir John Falstaff, a word with you.

FALSTAFF   My good lord! God give Your Lordship good
time of day. I am glad to see Your Lordship abroad. I 93
heard say Your Lordship was sick. I hope Your Lordship

goes abroad by advice. Your Lordship, though not 95
clean past your youth, have yet some smack of age
in you, some relish of the saltness of time in you, and 97
I most humbly beseech Your Lordship to have a reverent care of your health.

CHIEF JUSTICE   Sir John, I sent for you before your
expedition to Shrewsbury.

FALSTAFF   An't please Your Lordship, I hear His Majesty is returned with some discomfort from Wales.

CHIEF JUSTICE   I talk not of His Majesty. You would not
come when I sent for you.

FALSTAFF   And I hear, moreover, His Highness is fallen
into this same whoreson apoplexy.

CHIEF JUSTICE   Well, God mend him! I pray you, let me
speak with you.

FALSTAFF   This apoplexy, as I take it, is a kind of
lethargy, an't please Your Lordship, a kind of sleeping
in the blood, a whoreson tingling.

CHIEF JUSTICE   What tell you me of it? Be it as it is. 113

FALSTAFF   It hath it original from much grief, from 114
study, and perturbation of the brain. I have read the
cause of his effects in Galen. It is a kind of deafness. 116

CHIEF JUSTICE   I think you are fallen into the disease,
for you hear not what I say to you.

FALSTAFF   Very well, my lord, very well. Rather, an't
please you, it is the disease of not listening, the
malady of not marking, that I am troubled withal.

CHIEF JUSTICE   To punish you by the heels would 122
amend the attention of your ears, and I care not if I do
become your physician.

FALSTAFF   I am as poor as Job, my lord, but not so 125
patient. Your Lordship may minister the potion of
imprisonment to me in respect of poverty; but how I 127
should be your patient to follow your prescriptions,
the wise may make some dram of a scruple, or indeed 129
a scruple itself.

CHIEF JUSTICE   I sent for you, when there were matters
against you for your life, to come speak with me. 132

FALSTAFF   As I was then advised by my learned counsel
in the laws of this land service, I did not come. 134

CHIEF JUSTICE   Well, the truth is, Sir John, you live in
great infamy.

FALSTAFF   He that buckles himself in my belt cannot
live in less.

CHIEF JUSTICE   Your means are very slender, and your 139
waste is great.

FALSTAFF   I would it were otherwise; I would my
means were greater, and my waist slenderer.

CHIEF JUSTICE   You have misled the youthful Prince.

51 **Paul's** i.e., Saint Paul's Cathedral nave, resort of servingmen seeking employment 52 **An** If 53 **stews** brothels. **I . . . wived** (Proverbially, to be thus provided with a servant, a horse, and a wife at Saint
Paul's, Smithfield, and Westminster, respectively, was to be taken for
a sucker.) 54 **committed** i.e., to prison. (According to an apocryphal
story, Prince Hal boxed the ears of the Lord Chief Justice; see 1 *Henry
IV*, 3.2.32 and note, and 2 *Henry IV*, 5.2.70–1.) 56 **close** concealed
59 **in question** under judicial examination 62 **charge** command of
soldiers 75–7 **were it . . . make it** even if that side were worse than
the hated name of "rebellion" it can teach us to understand what it is.
80–1 **Setting . . . so** Granted that true knights and soldiers do not tell
lies, I would have lied outrageously if I had called you an honest
man. 83 **leave** permission 87 **grows to** is an integral part of
89 **hunt counter** run the wrong way on the trail. (A hunting term.)
93 **abroad** out of doors.

95 **by advice** by medical advice. 97 **saltness** flavor, relish 113 **What
Why** 114 **it original** its origin 116 **his** its. **Galen** the famous
Greek authority on medicine. 122 **punish . . . heels** set you in the
stocks or fetters 125 **Job** the long-suffering protagonist of the Book
of Job 127 **in . . . poverty** by reason of my being too poor to pay a
fine 129 **make . . . scruple** entertain some small portion of doubt.
(*Dram* and *scruple* are small apothecaries' weights.) 132 **for your life**
i.e., carrying the death penalty 134 **land service** military service.
(With a pun on avoiding the "service" of a legal summons and also
on Falstaff's *land service* at Gad's Hill. Falstaff points to his sword
and shield as his *learned counsel*, his legal counsel.) 139 **means** financial resources

FALSTAFF   The young Prince hath misled me. I am the 144
fellow with the great belly, and he my dog. 145

CHIEF JUSTICE   Well, I am loath to gall a new-healed
wound. Your day's service at Shrewsbury hath a little
gilded over your night's exploit on Gad's Hill. You 148
may thank th'unquiet time for your quiet o'erposting 149
that action.

FALSTAFF   My lord?

CHIEF JUSTICE   But since all is well, keep it so. Wake not
a sleeping wolf.

FALSTAFF   To wake a wolf is as bad as smell a fox. 154

CHIEF JUSTICE   What, you are as a candle, the better
part burnt out.

FALSTAFF   A wassail candle, my lord, all tallow. If I did 157
say of wax, my growth would approve the truth. 158

CHIEF JUSTICE   There is not a white hair on your face
but should have his effect of gravity. 160

FALSTAFF   His effect of gravy, gravy, gravy. 161

CHIEF JUSTICE   You follow the young Prince up and
down, like his ill angel. 163

FALSTAFF   Not so, my lord. Your ill angel is light, but I 164
hope he that looks upon me will take me without 165
weighing. And yet in some respects I grant I cannot 166
go. I cannot tell. Virtue is of so little regard in these 167
costermongers' times that true valor is turned bear- 168
ward; pregnancy is made a tapster, and his quick wit 169
wasted in giving reckonings. All the other gifts appur- 170
tenant to man, as the malice of this age shapes them, 171
are not worth a gooseberry. You that are old consider
not the capacities of us that are young; you do measure
the heat of our livers with the bitterness of your galls. 174
And we that are in the vaward of our youth, I must 175
confess, are wags too. 176

CHIEF JUSTICE   Do you set down your name in the
scroll of youth, that are written down old with all the

characters of age? Have you not a moist eye, a dry 179
hand, a yellow cheek, a white beard, a decreasing leg,
an increasing belly? Is not your voice broken, your
wind short, your chin double, your wit single, and 182
every part about you blasted with antiquity? And will 183
you yet call yourself young? Fie, fie, fie, Sir John!

FALSTAFF   My lord, I was born about three of the clock
in the afternoon, with a white head and something a 186
round belly. For my voice, I have lost it with halloing 187
and singing of anthems. To approve my youth further, 188
I will not. The truth is, I am only old in judgment and
understanding; and he that will caper with me for a 190
thousand marks, let him lend me the money, and have 191
at him! For the box of the ear that the Prince gave you, 192
he gave it like a rude prince, and you took it like a
sensible lord. I have checked him for it, and the young 194
lion repents—[aside] marry, not in ashes and sack- 195
cloth, but in new silk and old sack. 196

CHIEF JUSTICE   Well, God send the Prince a better
companion!

FALSTAFF   God send the companion a better prince! I
cannot rid my hands of him.

CHIEF JUSTICE   Well, the King hath severed you and
Prince Harry. I hear you are going with Lord John of
Lancaster against the Archbishop and the Earl of
Northumberland.

FALSTAFF   Yea, I thank your pretty sweet wit for it. But
look you pray, all you that kiss my lady Peace at home, 206
that our armies join not in a hot day; for, by the Lord,
I take but two shirts out with me, and I mean not to
sweat extraordinarily. If it be a hot day, and I brandish
anything but a bottle, I would I might never spit white 210
again. There is not a dangerous action can peep
out his head but I am thrust upon it. Well, I cannot last 212
ever. But it was alway yet the trick of our English 213
nation, if they have a good thing, to make it too
common. If ye will needs say I am an old man, you
should give me rest. I would to God my name were
not so terrible to the enemy as it is. I were better to be
eaten to death with a rust than to be scoured to
nothing with perpetual motion.

CHIEF JUSTICE   Well, be honest, be honest; and God
bless your expedition!

FALSTAFF   Will Your Lordship lend me a thousand
pound to furnish me forth? 223

CHIEF JUSTICE   Not a penny, not a penny. You are too
impatient to bear crosses. Fare you well. Commend 225

144–5 I am . . . dog (Falstaff seems to compare himself to the man in
the moon with his dog; the *great belly* is the full moon.)   148 exploit
i.e., the famous robbery in *1 Henry IV*, 2.2   149 o'erposting escaping
the consequences of   154 smell a fox suspect something. (Compare
with "smell a rat." Falstaff implies that the Justice is not to be trusted.)
157 wassail candle large candle lighted up at a feast.   tallow a mixture of animal fats (as contrasted with bees' wax).   158 wax beeswax.
(With a pun on "growth.")   approve the truth confirm the statement.
160 but . . . gravity but should testify to the gravity and wisdom of
age.   161 gravy grease, sweat. Falstaff jests that the huge bulk of his
advanced years produces not gravity but sweat, which was thought
to be an exuding of fat from the body.   163 ill angel evil attendant
spirit. (But Falstaff quibbles on the meaning "a clipped angel,"
a coin worth six shillings eight pence.)   164 light i.e., underweight
(because the coin is "clipped." Refers also to Satan, "an angel of
light," 2 Corinthians 11:14.)   165–6 take . . . weighing accept me
at face value without putting me on the scales or considering the
matter further.   167 go (1) walk (2) pass current.   cannot tell
(1) don't know what to think (2) don't count as good money.
168 costermongers' i.e., materialistic. (A costermonger is a hawker of
fruits or vegetables.)   168–9 bearward one who handles tame bears
169 pregnancy quickness (of wit), intellectual capacity   170 reckonings tavern bills.   170–1 appurtenant belonging   174 heat . . . galls
(The liver was thought to be the source of passion and to be active in
youth; the gall was thought to be the seat of melancholy and rancor,
and to become prevalent with age.)   175 vaward vanguard leading
into middle age   176 wags high-spirited youths

179 characters (1) characteristics (2) letters   182 single feeble
183 blasted withered, blighted   186 something a a somewhat
187 For As for. (Also in line 192.)   halloing shouting to hounds
188 approve prove   190 caper with me compete with me in dancing
191 marks coins worth thirteen shillings four pence   191–2 have at
him! i.e., I challenge him to dance more nimbly than I!   192 box of
the ear (See the note to line 54, above.)   194 sensible (1) intelligent
(2) capable of receiving physical sensations.   checked rebuked
195 marry indeed. (Literally, "by the Virgin Mary.")   195–6 ashes and
sackcloth penitent's garb   196 sack a white Spanish wine.   206 look
be sure, take care that   210 spit white i.e., from thirst   212 his its,
the dangerous military action   213 alway yet always.   trick habit
223 furnish equip   225 crosses (1) afflictions (2) silver coins stamped
with the figure of the cross.

me to my cousin Westmorland.

[Exeunt Chief Justice and his Servant.]

FALSTAFF   If I do, fillip me with a three-man beetle. A   227
man can no more separate age and covetousness than
'a can part young limbs and lechery; but the gout galls
the one, and the pox pinches the other, and so both   230
the degrees prevent my curses. Boy!   231

PAGE   Sir?

FALSTAFF   What money is in my purse?

PAGE   Seven groats and two pence.   234

FALSTAFF   I can get no remedy against this consumption
of the purse; borrowing only lingers and lingers it out,   236
but the disease is incurable. [*He gives letters.*] Go bear
this letter to my lord of Lancaster, this to the Prince,
this to the Earl of Westmorland, and this to old Mistress Ursula, whom I have weekly sworn to marry   240
since I perceived the first white hair of my chin. About
it. You know where to find me.   [*Exit Page.*]
A pox of this gout! Or, a gout of this pox! For the one or
the other plays the rogue with my great toe. 'Tis no matter if I do halt; I have the wars for my color, and my   245
pension shall seem the more reasonable. A good wit
will make use of anything. I will turn diseases to
commodity.   [*Exit.*] 248

✤

[1.3]

*Enter the Archbishop [of York], Thomas Mowbray
(Earl Marshal), the Lord Hastings, and [Lord]
Bardolph.*

ARCHBISHOP
Thus have you heard our cause and known our
   means;
And, my most noble friends, I pray you all,
Speak plainly your opinions of our hopes.
And first, Lord Marshal, what say you to it?

MOWBRAY
I well allow the occasion of our arms,   5
But gladly would be better satisfied
How in our means we should advance ourselves   7
To look with forehead bold and big enough   8
Upon the power and puissance of the King.   9

HASTINGS
Our present musters grow upon the file   10
To five-and-twenty thousand men of choice;   11
And our supplies live largely in the hope   12

Of great Northumberland; whose bosom burns
With an incensèd fire of injuries.

LORD BARDOLPH
The question then, Lord Hastings, standeth thus:
Whether our present five-and-twenty thousand
May hold up head without Northumberland?   17

HASTINGS
With him, we may.

LORD BARDOLPH   Yea, marry, there's the point.
But if without him we be thought too feeble,
My judgment is we should not step too far
Till we had his assistance by the hand;
For in a theme so bloody-faced as this
Conjecture, expectation, and surmise   22
Of aids incertain should not be admitted.

ARCHBISHOP
'Tis very true, Lord Bardolph, for indeed
It was young Hotspur's case at Shrewsbury.

LORD BARDOLPH
It was, my lord; who lined himself with hope,   27
Eating the air on promise of supply,   28
Flatt'ring himself with project of a power   29
Much smaller than the smallest of his thoughts,   30
And so, with great imagination
Proper to madmen, led his powers to death   32
And winking leapt into destruction.   33

HASTINGS
But, by your leave, it never yet did hurt
To lay down likelihoods and forms of hope.

LORD BARDOLPH
Yes, if this present quality of war—   36
Indeed the instant action, a cause on foot—   37
Lives so in hope, as in an early spring   38
We see th'appearing buds, which to prove fruit   39
Hope gives not so much warrant as despair   40
That frosts will bite them. When we mean to build,   41
We first survey the plot, then draw the model;   42
And when we see the figure of the house,   43
Then must we rate the cost of the erection,   44
Which if we find outweighs ability,   45
What do we then but draw anew the model
In fewer offices, or at least desist   47
To build at all? Much more, in this great work,
Which is almost to pluck a kingdom down
And set another up, should we survey
The plot of situation and the model,
Consent upon a sure foundation,   52
Question surveyors, know our own estate,   53

---

227 fillip knock.   **three-man beetle** a huge pile-driving mallet requiring three men to wield it.   **230–1 both . . . curses** i.e., both age and youth, the one afflicted with gout and the other with *pox*, or syphilis, have their own curses which anticipate mine.   **234 groats** coins worth four pence   **236 lingers** prolongs, draws   **240 Ursula** (Mistress Quickly's first name? or else another woman to whom Falstaff has made empty promises)   **245 halt** limp.   **color** excuse   **248 commodity** profit.
1.3. Location: York. The Archbishop's palace.
0.1 *Thomas Mowbray* son of Thomas Mowbray, Duke of Norfolk, who was banished by Richard II   **5 allow . . . arms** concede the justice of our arming   **7 in** with   **8 forehead** i.e., assurance, defiant gaze   **9 puissance** strength   **10 upon the file** according to our records   **11 men of choice** choice men   **12 And . . . hope** and our chance of getting reinforcements depends largely on our hopes

17 hold up head be a sufficient military power   **22 theme** business   **27 lined** fortified   **28 Eating . . . supply** i.e., living in false hopes of reinforcement   **29 project . . . power** anticipation of the arrival of an armed force   **30 Much smaller** i.e., that proved in fact to be much smaller   **32 Proper to** characteristic of   **33 winking** shutting his eyes   **36–41 Yes . . . them** i.e., Yes, it's all right to hope, so long as we bear in mind that our hopes, given the present situation of war already on foot, may turn out to be like hopes for the first-appearing buds of spring—buds that too often are frost-bitten. (The text may be corrupt here.)   **42 model** plan   **43 figure** design   **44 rate** estimate   **45 ability** i.e., ability to pay   **47 offices** rooms.   **at least** at the worst   **52 Consent** agree   **53 surveyors** architects.   **estate** wealth

How able such a work to undergo,
To weigh against his opposite; or else   55
We fortify in paper and in figures,   56
Using the names of men instead of men,
Like one that draws the model of an house
Beyond his power to build it, who, half through,
Gives o'er and leaves his part-created cost   60
A naked subject to the weeping clouds   61
And waste for churlish winter's tyranny.

HASTINGS
Grant that our hopes, yet likely of fair birth, 63
Should be stillborn, and that we now possessed
The utmost man of expectation,   65
I think we are a body strong enough,
Even as we are, to equal with the King.

LORD BARDOLPH
What, is the King but five-and-twenty thousand?

HASTINGS
To us no more, nay, not so much, Lord Bardolph.
For his divisions, as the times do brawl,   70
Are in three heads: one power against the French, 71
And one against Glendower; perforce a third   72
Must take up us. So is the unfirm King   73
In three divided, and his coffers sound   74
With hollow poverty and emptiness.

ARCHBISHOP
That he should draw his several strengths together 76
And come against us in full puissance
Need not be dreaded.

HASTINGS   If he should do so,
To French and Welsh he leaves his back unarmed,   80
They baying him at the heels. Never fear that.

LORD BARDOLPH
Who is it like should lead his forces hither?   81

HASTINGS
The Duke of Lancaster and Westmorland;
Against the Welsh, himself and Harry Monmouth.
But who is substituted 'gainst the French,   84
I have no certain notice.

ARCHBISHOP   Let us on,
And publish the occasion of our arms.   86
The commonwealth is sick of their own choice;
Their overgreedy love hath surfeited.
An habitation giddy and unsure   89
Hath he that buildeth on the vulgar heart.   90
O thou fond many, with what loud applause   91
Didst thou beat heaven with blessing Bolingbroke, 92
Before he was what thou wouldst have him be!

And being now trimmed in thine own desires,   94
Thou, beastly feeder, art so full of him
That thou provok'st thyself to cast him up.   96
So, so, thou common dog, didst thou disgorge   97
Thy glutton bosom of the royal Richard;
And now thou wouldst eat thy dead vomit up,
And howl'st to find it. What trust is in these times?
They that, when Richard lived, would have him die,
Are now become enamored on his grave.
Thou, that threw'st dust upon his goodly head
When through proud London he came sighing on
After th'admirèd heels of Bolingbroke,
Criest now, "O earth, yield us that king again,
And take thou this!" Oh, thoughts of men accurst!
Past and to come seems best; things present, worst.

MOWBRAY
Shall we go draw our numbers and set on?   109

HASTINGS
We are time's subjects, and time bids begone.
                                   Exeunt.

♣

[2.1]

*Enter Hostess [Quickly] of the tavern and two
officers: [Fang, followed by Snare].*

HOSTESS   Master Fang, have you entered the action?   1
FANG   It is entered.
HOSTESS   Where's your yeoman? Is't a lusty yeoman?   3
    Will 'a stand to't?   4
FANG   [*looking around him*]   Sirrah—where's Snare?
HOSTESS   Oh, Lord, ay, good Master Snare.
SNARE   [*from behind them*]   Here, here.
FANG   Snare, we must arrest Sir John Falstaff.
HOSTESS   Yea, good Master Snare, I have entered him 9
    and all.
SNARE   It may chance cost some of us our lives, for he 11
    will stab.
HOSTESS   Alas the day, take heed of him! He stabbed
    me in mine own house, most beastly, in good faith. 'A
    cares not what mischief he does; if his weapon be out,
    he will foin like any devil; he will spare neither man, 16
    woman, nor child.
FANG   If I can close with him, I care not for his thrust. 18
HOSTESS   No, nor I neither. I'll be at your elbow.
FANG   An I but fist him once, and 'a come but within 20
    my vice—   21

HOSTESS I am undone by his going, I warrant you; he's 22
an infinitive thing upon my score. Good Master Fang, 23
hold him sure. Good Master Snare, let him not scape.
'A comes continually to Pie Corner—saving your 25
manhoods—to buy a saddle; and he is indited to dinner 26
to the Lubber's Head in Lumbert street, to Master 27
Smooth's the silkman. I pray you, since my exion is en- 28
tered and my case so openly known to the world, let
him be brought in to his answer. A hundred mark is a 30
long one for a poor lone woman to bear; and I have 31
borne, and borne, and borne, and have been fubbed 32
off, and fubbed off, and fubbed off, from this day to 33
that day, that it is a shame to be thought on. There is
no honesty in such dealing, unless a woman should
be made an ass and a beast, to bear every knave's
wrong. Yonder he comes, and that arrant malmsey- 37
nose knave, Bardolph, with him. Do your offices, do 38
your offices. Master Fang and Master Snare, do me, do 39
me, do me your offices.

Enter Sir John [Falstaff], and Bardolph, and the
Boy [Page].

FALSTAFF How now, whose mare's dead? What's the 41
matter?

FANG Sir John, I arrest you at the suit of Mistress
Quickly.

FALSTAFF Away, varlets!—Draw, Bardolph. Cut me off
the villain's head. Throw the quean in the channel. 46

[They draw.]

HOSTESS Throw me in the channel? I'll throw thee in the
channel. Wilt thou? Wilt thou? Thou bastardly rogue!
Murder, murder! Ah, thou honeysuckle villain! Wilt 49
thou kill God's officers and the King's? Ah, thou hon- 50
eyseed rogue! Thou art a honeyseed, a man-queller, 51
and a woman-queller. 52

FALSTAFF Keep them off, Bardolph.

OFFICERS A rescue! A rescue! 54

HOSTESS Good people, bring a rescue or two. Thou
woo't, woo't thou? Thou woo't, woo't ta? Do, do, thou 56
rogue! Do, thou hempseed! 57

PAGE Away, you scullion, you rampallian, you fus- 58
tilarian! I'll tickle your catastrophe. 59

Enter [the] Lord Chief Justice and his men.

CHIEF JUSTICE
What is the matter? Keep the peace here, ho!

HOSTESS Good my lord, be good to me. I beseech you,
stand to me. 62

CHIEF JUSTICE
How now, Sir John? What are you brawling here? 63
Doth this become your place, your time, and business?
You should have been well on your way to York.—
Stand from him, fellow. Wherefore hang'st thou
upon him?

HOSTESS Oh, my most worshipful lord, an't please Your
Grace, I am a poor widow of Eastcheap, and he is
arrested at my suit.

CHIEF JUSTICE For what sum?

HOSTESS It is more than for some, my lord, it is for all,
all I have. He hath eaten me out of house and home;
he hath put all my substance into that fat belly of his.
But I will have some of it out again, or I will ride thee
o'nights like the mare. 75

FALSTAFF I think I am as like to ride the mare, if I have
any vantage of ground to get up. 77

CHIEF JUSTICE How comes this, Sir John? Fie, what 78
man of good temper would endure this tempest of 79
exclamation? Are you not ashamed to enforce a poor 80
widow to so rough a course to come by her own? 81

FALSTAFF What is the gross sum that I owe thee?

HOSTESS Marry, if thou wert an honest man, thyself and
the money too. Thou didst swear to me upon a parcel- 84
gilt goblet, sitting in my Dolphin chamber, at the 85
round table, by a seacoal fire, upon Wednesday in 86
Wheeson week, when the Prince broke thy head for 87
liking his father to a singing-man of Windsor, thou 88
didst swear to me then, as I was washing thy wound,
to marry me and make me my lady thy wife. Canst
thou deny it? Did not goodwife Keech, the butcher's 91
wife, come in then and call me gossip Quickly? 92
Coming in to borrow a mess of vinegar, telling us she 93
had a good dish of prawns, whereby thou didst desire 94
to eat some, whereby I told thee they were ill for a
green wound? And didst thou not, when she was 96
gone downstairs, desire me to be no more so familiar- 97
ity with such poor people, saying that ere long they 98

22 **going** i.e., going without paying 23 **infinitive** (Hostess Quickly's malapropism for "infinite," endless.) **score** accounts. 25 **continuantly** (Perhaps a mixup of "continually" and "incontinently," immediately.) **Pie Corner** a corner in the Smithfield district of London, known for its cooks' shops 25–6 **saving your manhoods** i.e., with apologies for mentioning anything so indelicate 26 **indited** (For "invited.") 27 **Lubber's Head** i.e., Libbard's Head, Leopard's Head Inn. **Lumbert** i.e., Lombard 28 **exion** action, lawsuit 30 **mark** (Worth thirteen shillings four pence.) 31 **long one** huge reckoning. (With unconscious sexual suggestion.) 32–3 **fubbed off** put off with excuses. (Probably with unintended sexual meaning, continued from *borne, and borne* and then carried forward in *bear* [36], *do me* [39–40], *stand to me* [62], etc.) 37–8 **malmsey-nose** red-nosed (from drinking malmsey, a sweet red wine) 39 **do me** i.e., do your duty for me. (With unintended sexual suggestion.) 41 **whose mare's dead?** i.e., what's all the fuss about? 46 **quean** slut, hussy. **channel** street gutter. 49 **honeysuckle** (For "homicidal.") 50–1 **honeyseed** (For "homicide.") 51 **man-queller** murderer 52 **woman-queller** destroyer of women. (But with suggestion also of "seducer.") 54 **A rescue!** i.e., Come help the officers in their rescue of the hostess! (Said to anyone within earshot.) 56 **woo't thou** wilt thou. **ta** thou. 57 **hempseed** (Alludes perhaps to the Page and his diminutive size. Hangman's rope was made of hemp. Mistress Quickly may mean "homicide"; cf. *honeyseed* in line 50–1.)

58 **scullion** kitchen wench. **rampallian** scoundrel, ruffian 58–9 **fustilarian** fat, frowsy woman. 59 **catastrophe** i.e., backside. 62 **stand to** stand by. (With bawdy suggestion.) 63 **What** Why 75 **o'nights** by night. **mare** nightmare. 77 **vantage of ground** superior position. **get up** mount. (With intended sexual suggestion, continued from *ride the mare* in line 76.) 78–80 **what . . . exclamation?** what man of good disposition would have behaved so as to invite such vituperation? 81 **come by her own** get what is hers. 84–5 **parcel-gilt** partly gilded 85 **Dolphin chamber** (The name of a room in her inn.) 86 **seacoal** bituminous coal, brought in by sea 87 **Wheeson** Whitsun (Pentecost). **broke** hit, made a cut on 88 **liking** comparing. **singing-man** chorister 91 **goodwife** (Title of a married woman.) **Keech** (Literally, "a lump of tallow.") 92 **gossip** (Literally, a fellow godparent; hence, a female friend.) 93 **mess** small quantity 94 **prawns** shrimps. **whereby** whereupon 96 **green** fresh, raw 97–8 **familiarity** (The Hostess's word for "familiar.")

should call me madam? And didst thou not kiss me
and bid me fetch thee thirty shillings? I put thee now
to thy book oath. Deny it if thou canst.   101

FALSTAFF   My lord, this is a poor mad soul, and she
says up and down the town that her eldest son is like
you. She hath been in good case, and the truth is,   104
poverty hath distracted her. But for these foolish of-   105
ficers, I beseech you I may have redress against them.

CHIEF JUSTICE   Sir John, Sir John, I am well acquainted
with your manner of wrenching the true case the
false way. It is not a confident brow, nor the throng of
words that come with such more than impudent
sauciness from you, can thrust me from a level   111
consideration. You have, as it appears to me, practiced
upon the easy-yielding spirit of this woman and made
her serve your uses both in purse and in person.   114

HOSTESS   Yea, in truth, my lord.

CHIEF JUSTICE   Pray thee, peace.—Pay her the debt
you owe her, and unpay the villainy you have done
her. The one you may do with sterling money, and
the other with current repentance.   119

FALSTAFF   My lord, I will not undergo this sneap   120
without reply. You call honorable boldness impudent
sauciness. If a man will make curtsy and say nothing,   122
he is virtuous. No, my lord, my humble duty remem-   123
bered, I will not be your suitor. I say to you, I do desire   124
deliverance from these officers, being upon hasty
employment in the King's affairs.

CHIEF JUSTICE   You speak as having power to do wrong.   127
But answer in th'effect of your reputation, and satisfy   128
the poor woman.

FALSTAFF   Come hither, hostess.   [He takes her aside.]

Enter a messenger [Gower].

CHIEF JUSTICE   Now, Master Gower, what news?

GOWER
The King, my lord, and Harry Prince of Wales
Are near at hand. The rest the paper tells.
                    [He gives a letter. The Chief Justice reads.]

FALSTAFF [to Mistress Quickly]   As I am a gentleman.

HOSTESS   Faith, you said so before.

FALSTAFF   As I am a gentleman. Come, no more words
of it.

HOSTESS   By this heavenly ground I tread on, I must be
fain to pawn both my plate and the tapestry of my   139
dining chambers.

FALSTAFF   Glasses, glasses, is the only drinking. And for   141

thy walls, a pretty slight drollery, or the story of the   142
Prodigal, or the German hunting in water work, is   143
worth a thousand of these bed-hangers and these   144
fly-bitten tapestries. Let it be ten pound, if thou canst.
Come, an 'twere not for thy humors, there's not a   146
better wench in England. Go wash thy face, and draw   147
the action. Come, thou must not be in this humor
with me. Dost not know me? Come, come, I know
thou wast set on to this.

HOSTESS   Pray thee, Sir John, let it be but twenty
nobles. I'faith, I am loath to pawn my plate, so God   152
save me, la!

FALSTAFF   Let it alone; I'll make other shift. You'll be a   154
fool still.

HOSTESS   Well, you shall have it, though I pawn my
gown. I hope you'll come to supper. You'll pay me all
together?

FALSTAFF   Will I live? [To Bardolph] Go with her, with   159
her; hook on, hook on.   160

HOSTESS   Will you have Doll Tearsheet meet you at
supper?

FALSTAFF   No more words. Let's have her.
                *Exeunt Hostess and Sergeant [Fang, Bardolph, and
                                                                    others].*

CHIEF JUSTICE [to Gower]   I have heard better news.

FALSTAFF   What's the news, my lord?

CHIEF JUSTICE [to Gower]   Where lay the King tonight?   166

GOWER   At Basingstoke, my lord.   167

FALSTAFF   I hope, my lord, all's well. What is the news,
my lord?

CHIEF JUSTICE [to Gower]   Come all his forces back?

GOWER
No, fifteen hundred foot, five hundred horse   171
Are marched up to my lord of Lancaster,   172
Against Northumberland and the Archbishop.

FALSTAFF   Comes the King back from Wales, my noble
lord?

CHIEF JUSTICE [to Gower]
You shall have letters of me presently.   176
Come, go along with me, good Master Gower.
                                                        [They start to go.]

FALSTAFF   My lord!

CHIEF JUSTICE   What's the matter?

FALSTAFF   Master Gower, shall I entreat you with me to
dinner?   181

GOWER   I must wait upon my good lord here, I thank   182
you, good Sir John.

---

101 **book oath** oath on a Bible.   104 **in good case** well-to-do. (Perhaps with bawdy suggestion.)   105 **distracted her** driven her mad. **for** as for   111 **level** fair-minded, evenhanded   114 **serve your uses** (With erotic suggestion.)   119 **current** genuine. (With an allusion to current, or lawful, coin, the *sterling* of line 118.)   120 **sneap** reproof   122 **curtsy** bow   123–4 **my . . . remembered** i.e., with all due consideration of the respect I owe to your position   127 **as . . . wrong** as if you had the license to do whatever wrong you wish to do.   128 **in . . . reputation** i.e., in a manner becoming a man of your reputation   139 **fain** obliged, content.   **plate** platters, etc., of silver or gold plate   141 **Glasses . . . drinking** i.e., Glasses are all the fashion now for drinking, instead of metal tankards.

142 **drollery** e.g., a Dutch comic genre painting   142–3 **the Prodigal** the Prodigal Son. (See Luke 15:11–32.)   143 **German . . . work** hunting scene painted by a German or Dutch artist as imitation tapestry   144 **bed-hangers** (Falstaff implies that the Hostess's tapestries are only good enough to serve as curtains around a four-poster bed.)   146 **an 'twere** if it were.   **humors** whims, vagaries   147 **draw** withdraw   152 **nobles** coins current at six shillings eight pence.   154 **shift** expedient.   159 **Will I live?** i.e., As sure as I live.   160 **hook on** i.e., follow her   166 **tonight** this past night.   167 **Basingstoke** a town in Hampshire   171 **foot** foot soldiers.   **horse** cavalry troops   172 **to** to be led by   176 **presently** immediately.   181 **dinner** midday meal.   182 **wait upon** accompany

CHIEF JUSTICE   Sir John, you loiter here too long, being 184
you are to take soldiers up in counties as you go. 185

FALSTAFF   Will you sup with me, Master Gower? 186

CHIEF JUSTICE   What foolish master taught you these
manners, Sir John?

FALSTAFF   Master Gower, if they become me not, he was
a fool that taught them me.—This is the right fencing
grace, my lord: tap for tap, and so part fair. 191

CHIEF JUSTICE   Now the Lord lighten thee! Thou art a 192
great fool.

                               [Exeunt separately.]

❧

[2.2]

Enter the Prince [Henry, and] Poins.

PRINCE   Before God, I am exceeding weary.

POINS   Is't come to that? I had thought weariness durst
not have attached one of so high blood. 3

PRINCE   Faith, it does me, though it discolors the 4
complexion of my greatness to acknowledge it. Doth it 5
not show vilely in me to desire small beer? 6

POINS   Why, a prince should not be so loosely studied 7
as to remember so weak a composition. 8

PRINCE   Belike then my appetite was not princely got, 9
for, by my troth, I do now remember the poor
creature, small beer. But indeed these humble considerations make me out of love with my greatness. What
a disgrace is it to me to remember thy name! Or to
know thy face tomorrow! Or to take note how many
pair of silk stockings thou hast, viz., these, and those 15
that were thy peach-colored ones! Or to bear the in- 16
ventory of thy shirts, as, one for superfluity and an- 17
other for use! But that the tennis-court keeper knows 18
better than I; for it is a low ebb of linen with thee 19
when thou keepest not racket there, as thou hast not 20
done a great while, because the rest of the low coun- 21
tries have made a shift to eat up thy holland. And God 22
knows whether those that bawl out the ruins of thy 23
linen shall inherit His kingdom. But the midwives say 24
the children are not in the fault, whereupon the world 25
increases and kindreds are mightily strengthened. 26

POINS   How ill it follows, after you have labored so hard,
you should talk so idly! Tell me, how many good 28
young princes would do so, their fathers being so sick
as yours at this time is?

PRINCE   Shall I tell thee one thing, Poins?

POINS   Yes, faith, and let it be an excellent good thing.

PRINCE   It shall serve among wits of no higher breeding
than thine.

POINS   Go to. I stand the push of your one thing that 35
you will tell.

PRINCE   Marry, I tell thee it is not meet that I should be 37
sad, now my father is sick. Albeit I could tell to thee, 38
as to one it pleases me, for fault of a better, to call my
friend, I could be sad, and sad indeed too.

POINS   Very hardly upon such a subject. 41

PRINCE   By this hand, thou thinkest me as far in the
devil's book as thou and Falstaff for obduracy and
persistency. Let the end try the man. But I tell thee,
my heart bleeds inwardly that my father is so sick.
And keeping such vile company as thou art hath in
reason taken from me all ostentation of sorrow. 47

POINS   The reason?

PRINCE   What wouldst thou think of me if I should
weep?

POINS   I would think thee a most princely hypocrite.

PRINCE   It would be every man's thought, and thou art
a blessed fellow to think as every man thinks. Never a
man's thought in the world keeps the roadway better 54
than thine. Every man would think me an hypocrite
indeed. And what accites your most worshipful 56
thought to think so?

POINS   Why, because you have been so lewd and so 58
much engraffed to Falstaff. 59

PRINCE   And to thee.

POINS   By this light, I am well spoke on; I can hear it
with mine own ears. The worst that they can say of me
is that I am a second brother and that I am a proper 63
fellow of my hands, and those two things I confess I 64
cannot help. By the Mass, here comes Bardolph.

Enter Bardolph and Boy [Page].

184–5 being . . . up seeing that you are to levy soldiers   **186 sup** come to supper   **191 grace** form, style. (Falstaff is saying that, by refusing to answer the Chief Justice's questions in lines 180 ff., Falstaff is only paying him back tit for tat for ignoring Falstaff's questions, lines 165–77.)   **fair** on good terms.   **192 lighten** (1) enlighten (2) reduce in weight
2.2. Location: London. Prince Henry's dwelling.
3 attached seized   **4–5 discolors . . . greatness** puts a blush on the cheek of my high rank   **6 show** appear.   **small beer** weak kind of beer, hence inferior.   **7 studied** versed, inclined   **8 so . . . composition** i.e., weak beer, trifles.   **9 Belike** Probably.   **got** begotten   **15 viz.** namely. (An abbreviation of the Latin *videlicet*.)   **16 bear** bear in mind   **17 for superfluity** in reserve as a clean change (of shirt)   **18–22 But . . . holland** i.e., The keeper of the tennis court knows that your inventory of shirts is at a low ebb and that you do not have a clean shirt to shift into, because you have not been seen at the tennis court lately, the reason being that you have sold or pawned your best shirt to pay for your visits to brothels. (With wordplay on *rest* as meaning "repose" and "remainder," on *the low countries* as meaning "the Netherlands" and "the lower members, the sexual organs," on *shift* as meaning "contrivance" and "change of clothes," and on *holland* as meaning "fine linen from Holland" and "the Netherlands," as before.)

23–4 those . . . linen i.e., your bastards, who cry out from your cast-off shirts made into swaddling clothes   **24 inherit His kingdom** i.e., go to heaven. (See Matthew 5:10, 25:34, or 19:14: "Suffer the little children . . . to come to me, for of such is the kingdom of heaven.")   **25 in the fault** to be blamed (for being illegitimate)   **26 kindreds** families   **28 talk so idly** manage to say so little.   **35 Go to** (An expression of impatience.)   **push** attack, thrust   **37–8 it is . . . sad** it would seem very inappropriate if I were to appear sad (given my reputation as a prodigal son)   **41 Very hardly** Not very likely   **47 ostentation** outward manifestation   **54 keeps the roadway** i.e., follows the common way of thinking   **56 accites** induces (with a quibble on "summons")   **58 lewd** base   **59 engraffed** closely attached   **63 second brother** i.e., a younger son, without inheritance   **63–4 proper . . . hands** i.e., good fighter

PRINCE And the boy that I gave Falstaff. 'A had him from me Christian, and look if the fat villain have not 67 transformed him ape. 68

BARDOLPH God save Your Grace!

PRINCE And yours, most noble Bardolph!

POINS [to Bardolph] Come, you virtuous ass, you bashful fool, must you be blushing? Wherefore blush you 72 now? What a maidenly man-at-arms are you become! Is't such a matter to get a pottle pot's maidenhead? 74

PAGE 'A calls me e'en now, my lord, through a red 75 lattice, and I could discern no part of his face from the 76 window. At last I spied his eyes, and methought he had made two holes in the alewife's petticoat and so 78 peeped through.

PRINCE [to Poins] Has not the boy profited?

BARDOLPH Away, you whoreson upright rabbit, away! 81

PAGE Away, you rascally Althaea's dream, away! 82

PRINCE Instruct us, boy. What dream, boy?

PAGE Marry, my lord, Althaea dreamt she was delivered of a firebrand, and therefore I call him her dream.

PRINCE A crown's worth of good interpretation. There 86 'tis, boy.   [He gives money.]

POINS Oh, that this blossom could be kept from cankers! 88 Well, there is sixpence to preserve thee. 89
[He gives money.]

BARDOLPH An you do not make him be hanged among 90 you, the gallows shall have wrong.

PRINCE And how doth thy master, Bardolph?

BARDOLPH Well, my lord. He heard of Your Grace's coming to town. There's a letter for you.
[He gives a letter.]

POINS Delivered with good respect. And how doth the 95 martlemas, your master? 96

BARDOLPH In bodily health, sir.

POINS Marry, the immortal part needs a physician, but that moves not him. Though that be sick, it dies not.

PRINCE I do allow this wen to be as familiar with me as 100 my dog, and he holds his place, for look you how he 101 writes.   [He shows the letter to Poins.]

POINS [reading the superscription] "John Falstaff, knight."—Every man must know that, as oft as he 104 has occasion to name himself, even like those that are kin to the King, for they never prick their finger but they say, "There's some of the King's blood spilt."

"How comes that?" says he that takes upon 108 him not to conceive. The answer is as ready as a 109 borrower's cap: "I am the King's poor cousin, sir." 110

PRINCE Nay, they will be kin to us, or they will fetch it 111 from Japheth. But the letter. [He reads.] "Sir John 112 Falstaff knight, to the son of the King nearest his father, Harry Prince of Wales, greeting."

POINS Why, this is a certificate. 115

PRINCE Peace! [He reads.] "I will imitate the honorable Romans in brevity."

POINS Sure he means brevity in breath, short-winded.

PRINCE [reads] "I commend me to thee, I commend 119 thee, and I leave thee. Be not too familiar with 120 Poins, for he misuses thy favors so much that he swears thou art to marry his sister Nell. Repent at idle times as thou mayst, and so farewell.

"Thine, by yea and no, which is as much as to 124 say, as thou usest him, Jack Falstaff with my familiars, John with my brothers and sisters, 126 and Sir John with all Europe."

POINS My lord, I'll steep this letter in sack and make 128 him eat it.

PRINCE That's to make him eat twenty of his words. But 130 do you use me thus, Ned? Must I marry your sister?

POINS God send the wench no worse fortune! But I never said so.

PRINCE Well, thus we play the fools with the time, and the spirits of the wise sit in the clouds and mock us.—Is your master here in London?

BARDOLPH Yea, my lord.

PRINCE Where sups he? Doth the old boar feed in the old frank? 139

BARDOLPH At the old place, my lord, in Eastcheap.

PRINCE What company?

PAGE Ephesians, my lord, of the old church. 142

PRINCE Sup any women with him?

PAGE None, my lord, but old Mistress Quickly and Mistress Doll Tearsheet.

PRINCE What pagan may that be? 146

PAGE A proper gentlewoman, sir, and a kinswoman of my master's.

PRINCE Even such kin as the parish heifers are to the town bull. Shall we steal upon them, Ned, at supper? 150

POINS I am your shadow, my lord; I'll follow you.

67–8 have . . . ape i.e., has not dressed him fantastically. 72 blushing i.e., red-faced (from drink). Wherefore Why 74 get . . . maidenhead i.e., knock off a two-quart tankard of ale. 75 e'en now just now, a moment ago 75–6 red lattice (Red lattices identified taverns.) 76 discern distinguish 78 petticoat i.e., red petticoat—a sign of disreputability 81 upright standing on two legs 82 Althaea's dream (Althaea dreamed that her newborn son would live only so long as a brand on the fire lasted. The Page mistakenly relates Hecuba's dream: when pregnant with Paris, Hecuba dreamed she would be delivered of a firebrand that would destroy Troy.) 86 A crown's Five shillings' 88 cankers cankerworms, worms that destroy buds and leaves. 89 to preserve thee (Allusion to the cross on the sixpence.) 90 An If 95 good respect proper ceremony. (Said ironically.) 96 martlemas i.e., Martinmas beef, beef slaughtered on November 11 (and fattened beforehand) 100 wen swelling 101 holds his place keeps up his familiarity with me 104 Every . . . that i.e., Falstaff wants to make sure that everyone is aware of his knightly rank

108–9 takes . . . conceive pretends not to understand. 109–10 as ready . . . cap i.e., as quick in coming forth as a cap is doffed by one seeking aid 111–12 Nay . . . Japheth i.e., Such petitioners insistently claim that they are connected to us of the royal family, if not in fact able to trace their ancestry all the way back to Japheth, the third son of Noah and the ancestor of all gentiles, hence of all Europeans (Genesis 10:2–5). 115 certificate (By putting his own name before that of the Prince as addressee, Falstaff has misappropriated a style normally reserved for sovereigns addressing subjects.) 119–20 I commend . . . leave thee (Falstaff self-importantly adopts the brief style of Julius Caesar's famous veni, vidi, vici; see 1.1.23 and note.) 124 by yea and no (A mild Puritan oath.) 126 familiars intimate friends 128 steep soak 130 twenty i.e., a considerable number 139 frank sty, pen. (Often thought to refer to the Boar's Head Tavern.) 142 Ephesians . . . church i.e., Good fellows of the usual, disreputable fellowship. 146 pagan i.e., harlot 150 town bull a communally owned bull that local farmers could mate with their heifers.

PRINCE Sirrah, you boy, and Bardolph, no word to
your master that I am yet come to town. There's for
your silence.   [He gives money.]

BARDOLPH I have no tongue, sir.

PAGE And for mine, sir, I will govern it.

PRINCE Fare you well; go. [Exeunt Bardolph and Page.]
This Doll Tearsheet should be some road.   158

POINS I warrant you, as common as the way between
Saint Albans and London.

PRINCE How might we see Falstaff bestow himself 161
tonight in his true colors, and not ourselves be seen?

POINS Put on two leathern jerkins and aprons, and wait 163
upon him at his table as drawers.   164

PRINCE From a God to a bull? A heavy descension! It 165
was Jove's case. From a prince to a prentice? A low 166
transformation! That shall be mine, for in everything
the purpose must weigh with the folly. Follow me, 168
Ned.   Exeunt.

✦

[2.3]

*Enter Northumberland, his wife [Lady
Northumberland], and the wife to Harry Percy
[Lady Percy].*

NORTHUMBERLAND
I pray thee, loving wife and gentle daughter,   1
Give even way unto my rough affairs.   2
Put not you on the visage of the times   3
And be like them to Percy troublesome.   4

LADY NORTHUMBERLAND
I have given over; I will speak no more.
Do what you will; your wisdom be your guide.

NORTHUMBERLAND
Alas, sweet wife, my honor is at pawn,
And, but my going, nothing can redeem it.   8

LADY PERCY
Oh, yet, for God's sake, go not to these wars!
The time was, father, that you broke your word,
When you were more endeared to it than now,   11
When your own Percy, when my heart's dear Harry,
Threw many a northward look to see his father
Bring up his powers; but he did long in vain.
Who then persuaded you to stay at home?
There were two honors lost, yours and your son's.
For yours, the God of heaven brighten it!   17
For his, it stuck upon him as the sun
In the gray vault of heaven, and by his light   19
Did all the chivalry of England move   20

To do brave acts. He was indeed the glass   21
Wherein the noble youth did dress themselves.
He had no legs that practiced not his gait;   23
And speaking thick, which nature made his blemish, 24
Became the accents of the valiant,
For those that could speak low and tardily
Would turn their own perfection to abuse   27
To seem like him. So that in speech, in gait,   28
In diet, in affections of delight,   29
In military rules, humors of blood,   30
He was the mark and glass, copy and book,   31
That fashioned others. And him—oh, wondrous
him!—
Oh, miracle of men!—him did you leave,
Second to none, unseconded by you,   34
To look upon the hideous god of war
In disadvantage, to abide a field   36
Where nothing but the sound of Hotspur's name
Did seem defensible. So you left him.   38
Never, oh, never do his ghost the wrong
To hold your honor more precise and nice   40
With others than with him! Let them alone.
The Marshal and the Archbishop are strong.
Had my sweet Harry had but half their numbers,
Today might I, hanging on Hotspur's neck,
Have talked of Monmouth's grave.

NORTHUMBERLAND   Beshrew your heart, 45
Fair daughter, you do draw my spirits from me
With new lamenting ancient oversights.   47
But I must go and meet with danger there,
Or it will seek me in another place
And find me worse provided.

LADY NORTHUMBERLAND   Oh, fly to Scotland,   50
Till that the nobles and the armèd commons
Have of their puissance made a little taste.   52

LADY PERCY
If they get ground and vantage of the King,   53
Then join you with them like a rib of steel,
To make strength stronger; but, for all our loves,
First let them try themselves. So did your son;
He was so suffered. So came I a widow,   57
And never shall have length of life enough
To rain upon remembrance with mine eyes,   59
That it may grow and sprout as high as heaven
For recordation to my noble husband.   61

---

158 should must. road i.e., common whore. 161 bestow behave
163 jerkins jackets 164 drawers tapsters, tavern waiters. 165 heavy
descension grievous descent or degradation. 166 Jove's case
(Jupiter, for the love of Europa, transformed himself into a bull.)
168 weigh with match; counterbalance
2.3. Location: Warkworth. Before Northumberland's castle.
1 daughter i.e., daughter-in-law 2 Give . . . affairs i.e., Make things
as easy for me as you can at this difficult time. 3 Put . . . times i.e.,
Don't look as bleak or troubled as are the times 4 to Percy i.e., to me
8 but except for 11 endeared pledged, bound by affection 17 For
As for. (Also in line 18.) 19 gray sky-blue 20 chivalry men-at-arms

21 glass mirror 23 He . . . gait i.e., There was no man alive and able
to walk who did not imitate Hotspur's stride 24 thick impulsively,
impetuously 27–8 turn . . . him i.e., debase their own manner of
speech and adopt his. 29 affections of delight tastes for pleasure
30 humors of blood temperament 31 mark mark to aim at 34 Second . . . you this man who was second to none. unseconded unsupported 36 In disadvantage i.e., outnumbered. abide a field face a
battle 38 defensible able to make defense. 40 To . . . nice to be
more punctilious in honoring your commitments 45 Monmouth's
i.e., Prince Hal's (since he was born at Monmouth). Beshrew your
heart (A reproachful oath.) 47 new lamenting lamenting anew
50 provided prepared. 52 Have . . . taste have put their strength to
some test. 53 get . . . of achieve a military advantage over 57 suffered allowed to proceed. came became 59 To rain . . . eyes to
water remembrance with my tears, as though it were a plant like
rosemary 61 recordation remembrance, memorial

NORTHUMBERLAND
Come, come, go in with me. 'Tis with my mind
As with the tide swelled up unto his height,
That makes a still-stand, running neither way. 64
Fain would I go to meet the Archbishop, 65
But many thousand reasons hold me back.
I will resolve for Scotland. There am I, 67
Till time and vantage crave my company. *Exeunt.* 68

❧

[2.4]

Enter a Drawer, [Francis, and another].

FRANCIS What the devil hast thou brought there?
Applejohns? Thou knowest Sir John cannot endure 2
an applejohn.
SECOND DRAWER Mass, thou sayst true. The Prince 4
once set a dish of applejohns before him, and told
him there were five more Sir Johns, and, putting off
his hat, said, "I will now take my leave of these six
dry, round, old, withered knights." It angered him to
the heart. But he hath forgot that.
FRANCIS Why, then, cover, and set them down. And 10
see if thou canst find out Sneak's noise; Mistress Tear- 11
sheet would fain hear some music.

Enter Will [a third Drawer].

THIRD DRAWER Dispatch! The room where they 13
supped is too hot; they'll come in straight. 14
FRANCIS Sirrah, here will be the Prince and Master
Poins anon, and they will put on two of our jerkins
and aprons, and Sir John must not know of it.
Bardolph hath brought word.
THIRD DRAWER By the Mass, here will be old utas. It 19
will be an excellent stratagem.
SECOND DRAWER I'll see if I can find out Sneak. *Exit.* 21

*Enter Mistress Quickly [the Hostess] and Doll
Tearsheet.*

HOSTESS I'faith, sweetheart, methinks now you are in
an excellent good temperality. Your pulsidge beats as 23
extraordinarily as heart would desire, and your color, 24
I warrant you, is as red as any rose, in good truth, la!
But, i'faith, you have drunk too much canaries, and 26
that's a marvelous searching wine, and it perfumes 27
the blood ere one can say, "What's this?" How do you
now?
DOLL Better than I was. Hem!

HOSTESS Why, that's well said. A good heart's worth
gold. Lo, here comes Sir John.

Enter Sir John [Falstaff].

FALSTAFF [*singing*] "When Arthur first in court"— 33
Empty the jordan. [*Exit a Drawer.*] 34
[*Singing*] "And was a worthy king"—
How now, Mistress Doll?
HOSTESS Sick of a calm, yea, good faith. 37
FALSTAFF So is all her sect. An they be once in a calm, 38
they are sick.
DOLL A pox damn you, you muddy rascal, is that all
the comfort you give me?
FALSTAFF You make fat rascals, Mistress Doll. 42
DOLL I make them? Gluttony and diseases make them;
I make them not.
FALSTAFF If the cook help to make the gluttony, you
help to make the diseases, Doll. We catch of you, Doll,
we catch of you. Grant that, my poor virtue, grant that.
DOLL Yea, joy, our chains and our jewels. 48
FALSTAFF "Your brooches, pearls, and ouches." For to 49
serve bravely is to come halting off, you know; to
come off the breach with his pike bent bravely, and to
surgery bravely; to venture upon the charged cham- 52
bers bravely— 53
DOLL Hang yourself, you muddy conger, hang yourself!
HOSTESS By my troth, this is the old fashion. You two
never meet but you fall to some discord. You are both,
i' good truth, as rheumatic as two dry toasts; you 58
cannot one bear with another's confirmities. What the 59
goodyear! One must bear, and that [*to Doll*] must be 60
you. You are the weaker vessel, as they say, the
emptier vessel.
DOLL Can a weak empty vessel bear such a huge full
hogshead? There's a whole merchant's venture of Bor- 64
deaux stuff in him; you have not seen a hulk better 65
stuffed in the hold. Come, I'll be friends with thee,
Jack. Thou art going to the wars, and whether I shall
ever see thee again or no there is nobody cares. 68

Enter Drawer.

DRAWER Sir, Ancient Pistol's below, and would speak 69
with you.
DOLL Hang him, swaggering rascal! Let him not come
hither. It is the foul-mouthed'st rogue in England.

---

64 **still-stand** point of balance, standstill 65 **Fain** Gladly 67 **resolve
for** decide to go to 68 **vantage** opportunity
2.4. Location: London. A tavern in Eastcheap, usually identified as
the Boar's Head. Some tavern furniture is provided.
2 **Applejohns** a kind of apple eaten when shriveled and withered.
4 **Mass** i.e., By the Mass 10 **cover** spread the cloth, set the table
11 **noise** band of musicians 13 **Dispatch** Hurry up 14 **straight** very
soon. 19 **old utas** i.e., rare fun. 21 s.d. *Exit* (Will may exit too, and
perhaps Francis exits at 34. The *drawers* or tapsters presumably come
and go, serving the customers.) 23 **temperality** i.e., temper. **pulsidge**
i.e., pulse 24 **extraordinarily** i.e., ordinarily, regularly 26 **canaries**
Canary. (A light, sweet wine from the Canary Islands.) 27 **searching**
penetrating. **perfumes** i.e., permeates

33 **"When . . . court"** (A fragment from the ballad "Sir Launcelot du
Lake.") 34 **jordan** chamber pot. 37 **calm** i.e., qualm 38 **sect** sex.
42 **rascals** (1) lean deer (2) good-for-nothings 48 **Yea . . . jewels** i.e.,
Yea, indeed, you *catch* or steal our valuables. 49 **"Your brooches . . .
ouches"** (A line from a ballad, but also referring to venereal scabs and
sores.) 52–3 **charged chambers** small cannon; with bawdy double
meaning, as in *breach* and *pike* (51), *surgery* (venereal treatment, 52),
conger (eel, with sexual connotation, 54), *bear* (63) etc. 58 **rheumatic**
(Blunder for "choleric" or "splenetic"?) 59 **confirmities** (For "infirmities.") 59–60 **What the goodyear!** (An expletive, meaning something like "What the devil.") 60 **bear** (1) put up with another's
infirmities (2) bear the weight of a lover (3) bear children 64 **hogshead**
large cask. **venture** cargo 64–5 **Bordeaux stuff** i.e., wine 65 **hulk**
large, unwieldy cargo ship 68.1 *Drawer* (perhaps Francis)
69 **Ancient** ensign, standard-bearer

HOSTESS   If he swagger, let him not come here. No, by
my faith, I must live among my neighbors. I'll no 74
swaggerers. I am in good name and fame with the 75
very best. Shut the door; there comes no swaggerers
here. I have not lived all this while to have swaggering
now. Shut the door, I pray you.

FALSTAFF   Dost thou hear, Hostess?

HOSTESS   Pray ye, pacify yourself, Sir John. There comes
no swaggerers here.

FALSTAFF   Dost thou hear? It is mine ancient.

HOSTESS   Tilly-fally, Sir John, ne'er tell me. And your ancient 83
swaggerer comes not in my doors. I was before Master
Tisick, the debuty, t'other day, and, as he said to me, 85
'twas no longer ago than Wednesday last, i'good faith,
"Neighbor Quickly," says he—Master Dumbe, our
minister, was by then—"Neighbor Quickly," says he,
"receive those that are civil, for," said he, "you are in 89
an ill name." Now 'a said so, I can tell whereupon. 90
"For," says he, "you are an honest woman, and well
thought on; therefore take heed what guests you receive. Receive," says he, "no swaggering companions." There comes none here. You would bless you 93
to hear what he said. No, I'll no swaggerers. 94

FALSTAFF   He's no swaggerer, hostess; a tame cheater, 96
i'faith; you may stroke him as gently as a puppy
greyhound. He'll not swagger with a Barbary hen, if 98
her feathers turn back in any show of resistance.—
Call him up, drawer.   [Exit Drawer.]

HOSTESS   Cheater, call you him? I will bar no honest 101
man my house, nor no cheater, but I do not love
swaggering, by my troth. I am the worse when one
says "swagger." Feel, masters, how I shake; look you,
I warrant you.

DOLL   So you do, hostess.

HOSTESS   Do I? Yea, in very truth, do I, an 'twere an 107
aspen leaf. I cannot abide swaggerers.

Enter Ancient Pistol, [Bardolph,] and Boy [Page].

PISTOL   God save you, Sir John!

FALSTAFF   Welcome, Ancient Pistol. Here, Pistol, I
charge you with a cup of sack. Do you discharge upon 111
mine hostess.

PISTOL   I will discharge upon her, Sir John, with two
bullets.

FALSTAFF   She is pistol-proof, sir; you shall not hardly 115
offend her.   116

HOSTESS   Come, I'll drink no proofs nor no bullets. I'll
drink no more than will do me good, for no man's
pleasure, I.

PISTOL   Then to you, Mistress Dorothy; I will charge
you.

DOLL   Charge me? I scorn you, scurvy companion.
What, you poor, base, rascally, cheating, lack-linen 123
mate? Away, you moldy rogue, away! I am meat for 124
your master.

PISTOL   I know you, Mistress Dorothy.

DOLL   Away, you cutpurse rascal! You filthy bung, 127
away! By this wine, I'll thrust my knife in your moldy
chops an you play the saucy cuttle with me. Away, 129
you bottle-ale rascal! You basket-hilt stale juggler, you! 130
Since when, I pray you, sir? God's light, with two 131
points on your shoulder? Much! 132

PISTOL   God let me not live, but I will murder your ruff 133
for this.

FALSTAFF   No more, Pistol, I would not have you go off
here. Discharge yourself of our company, Pistol.

HOSTESS   No, good Captain Pistol, not here, sweet
Captain.

DOLL   Captain? Thou abominable damned cheater, art
thou not ashamed to be called captain? An captains
were of my mind, they would truncheon you out for 141
taking their names upon you before you have earned
them. You a captain? You slave, for what? For tearing
a poor whore's ruff in a bawdy house? He a captain?
Hang him, rogue! He lives upon moldy stewed 145
prunes and dried cakes. A captain? God's light, these 146
villains will make the word as odious as the word
"occupy," which was an excellent good word before it 148
was ill sorted. Therefore captains had need look to't. 149

BARDOLPH   Pray thee, go down, good Ancient. 150

FALSTAFF   Hark thee hither, Mistress Doll.

PISTOL   Not I. I tell thee what, Corporal Bardolph, I
could tear her. I'll be revenged of her.

PAGE   Pray thee, go down.

PISTOL   I'll see her damned first, to Pluto's damned 155
lake, by this hand, to th'infernal deep, 156
With Erebus and tortures vile also. 157
Hold hook and line, say I.
Down, down, dogs! Down, faitors! 159

---

74 **I'll no** I'll have no   75 **fame** reputation   83 **Tilly-fally** i.e., Fiddle-
sticks   85 **Tisick** (Literally, phthisic, a cough or consumption.)
debuty deputy, deputy alderman   89–90 **are . . . name** have a bad
reputation.   90 **whereupon** upon what grounds.   93–4 **companions**
fellows.   94 **You . . . bless you** i.e., You'd be surprised   96 **tame
cheater** harmless card sharper   98 **Barbary hen** guinea hen. (Slang
term for a prostitute.)   101 **Cheater** (Mistress Quickly may understand the word as *escheator*, "an officer of the King's exchequer.")
107 **an 'twere** i.e., as if I were   111 **charge** pledge, drink to (2) load
(as in loading a pistol).   **discharge upon** toast; with bawdy double
meaning; see also *charge, Pistol, bullets* (testicles), *meat* (slang for
"whore"), etc.   115 **pistol-proof** (1) invulnerable to the charms of
Pistol (2) sexually impregnable to the *discharge of bullets* (testicles).
shall not hardly i.e., shall scarcely. (A colloquial expression.)
116 **offend her** do her any harm. (With sexual suggestion.)

123 **lack-linen** i.e., without a shirt to your name   124 **mate** low fellow.   **meat** (with a pun on "mate"; pronounced alike)   127 **bung**
(1) pickpocket (2) something that fills a hole   129 **chops** jaws.   **an . . .
cuttle** if you try any of your tricks. (*Cuttle* was a slang term for a pickpocket's cutting knife.)   130 **You basket-hilt . . . juggler** (Doll compares Pistol to a cheap entertainer who shows off his prowess
in fencing with cudgels that are equipped with basketwork hilts.)
131 **Since when** i.e., Since when do you claim to be so brave and military?   132 **points** lace tags, probably used here to hold together Pistol's tattered linen.   **Much!** (An exclamation of scornful incredulity.)
133 **murder your ruff** tear your pleated, starched collar (such as prostitutes wore)   141 **truncheon you out** cudgel you out of here
145–6 **stewed prunes** (Associated with brothels.)   148 **occupy** fornicate   149 **ill sorted** corrupted, put in such bad company.   **had need**
would do well to   150 **go down** calm down, or, go downstairs and
leave   155–6 **Pluto's damned lake** a river of the underworld
157 **Erebus** the underworld   159 **faitors** imposters, cheats.

Have we not Hiren here?   160

HOSTESS   Good Captain Peesel, be quiet; 'tis very late,
i'faith. I beseek you now, aggravate your choler.   162

PISTOL

These be good humors, indeed! Shall packhorses   163
And hollow pampered jades of Asia,
Which cannot go but thirty mile a day,
Compare with Caesars, and with cannibals,   166
And Troiant Greeks? Nay, rather damn them with   167
King Cerberus, and let the welkin roar.   168
Shall we fall foul for toys?   169

HOSTESS   By my troth, Captain, these are very bitter
words.

BARDOLPH   Begone, good Ancient. This will grow to a
brawl anon.

PISTOL

Die men like dogs! Give crowns like pins! Have we
not Hiren here?   174

HOSTESS   O' my word, Captain, there's none such   175
here. What the goodyear, do you think I would deny   176
her? For God's sake, be quiet.   177

PISTOL

Then feed and be fat, my fair Calipolis.   178
Come, give's some sack.
Si fortune me tormente, sperato me contento.   180
Fear we broadsides? No, let the fiend give fire.   181
Give me some sack, and, sweetheart, lie thou there.
                        [*He lays down his sword.*]
Come we to full points here, and are etceteras
nothings?   183

FALSTAFF   Pistol, I would be quiet.

PISTOL

Sweet knight, I kiss thy neaf.   185
What, we have seen the seven stars.   186

DOLL   For God's sake, thrust him downstairs. I cannot
endure such a fustian rascal.   188

PISTOL

"Thrust him downstairs?" Know we not Galloway
nags?   189

FALSTAFF   Quoit him down, Bardolph, like a shove-   190
groat shilling. Nay, an 'a do nothing but speak   191
nothing, 'a shall be nothing here.   192

BARDOLPH   Come, get you downstairs.

PISTOL [*snatching up his sword*]

What, shall we have incision? Shall we imbrue?   194
Then death rock me asleep, abridge my doleful days!   195
Why then, let grievous, ghastly, gaping wounds
Untwine the Sisters Three. Come, Atropos, I say!   197

HOSTESS   Here's goodly stuff toward!   198

FALSTAFF   Give me my rapier, boy.

DOLL   I pray thee, Jack, I pray thee, do not draw.

FALSTAFF [*to Pistol*]   Get you downstairs.   [*They fight.*]

HOSTESS   Here's a goodly tumult! I'll forswear keeping
house afore I'll be in these tirrits and frights. So,   203
murder, I warrant now. Alas, alas, put up your naked
weapons, put up your naked weapons.
                [*Exit Bardolph, driving Pistol out.*]

DOLL   I pray thee, Jack, be quiet; the rascal's gone. Ah,
you whoreson little valiant villain, you!

HOSTESS   Are you not hurt i'th' groin? Methought 'a
made a shrewd thrust at your belly.   209

[*Enter Bardolph.*]

FALSTAFF   Have you turned him out o'doors?

BARDOLPH   Yea, sir. The rascal's drunk. You have hurt
him, sir, i'th' shoulder.

FALSTAFF   A rascal! To brave me?   213

DOLL   Ah, you sweet little rogue, you! Alas, poor ape,
how thou sweat'st! Come, let me wipe thy face. Come
on, you whoreson chops. Ah, rogue, i'faith, I love   216
thee. Thou art as valorous as Hector of Troy, worth   217
five of Agamemnon, and ten times better than the   218
Nine Worthies. Ah, villain!   219

FALSTAFF   A rascally slave! I will toss the rogue in a   220
blanket.   221

DOLL   Do, an thou dar'st for thy heart. An thou dost, I'll 222
canvass thee between a pair of sheets.   223

Enter Music.

---

160 **Hiren** i.e., Pistol's fanciful name for his sword, with a seeming allusion to a lost play by Peele, *The Turkish Mahomet and Hiren the Fair Greek. Hiren* means "Irene," "Peace." (Throughout, Pistol's colorful speech is full of echoes of the contemporary theater.)   162 **beseek** beseech.   **aggravate** (For "moderate.")   163 **good humors** i.e., fine goings-on   163–7 **Shall ... Greeks** (Misquotation from Marlowe's *2 Tamburlaine*, 4.4.1–2.)   166 **cannibals** (The association here with Caesar would seem to suggest "Hannibals," but *cannibals* appears in the apparent source for this passage, John Eliot's *Orthoepia Gallica*, 1593. Pistol is ready to take on cannibals, Trojan Greeks, or anybody.)   167 **Troiant** Trojan   168 **Cerberus** three-headed dog guarding the entrance to Hades.   **welkin** heavens   169 **fall ... toys** fall out over trifles.   174 **Give crowns like pins!** Pass out kingdoms as if they were of the value of a pin! (As Tamburlaine does to his followers.)   175–6 **there's none such here** (The hostess seems to think that Pistol is asking after Hiren or Irene as though she were a whore living in the tavern.)   176–7 **deny her** keep her from you; deny that she was here, if she were.   178 **Then ... Calipolis** (Garbled version of a line in Peele's *The Battle of Alcazar*, 2.3.70.)   180 *Si ... contento* If fortune torments me, hope contents me. (An ignorant medley of Spanish and Italian.)   181 **broadsides** volleys fired from one side of a ship.   **give fire** shoot.   183 **full points** full stops, periods; also, swords' points.   **etceteras nothings** (Both words suggest the female sexual anatomy.)   185 **neaf** fist.   186 **the seven stars** the Pleiades, or Big Dipper. (Pistol means they have shared many night adventures.)   188 **fustian** bombastic, worthless

189 **Galloway nags** an Irish breed of small but swift horses (here used abusively to mean "harlots")   190 **Quoit** Throw   190–1 **shove-groat shilling** an Edward VI shilling used in shove-groat, a game in which the coins were shoved toward a mark   191–2 **an 'a ... here** if he spouts nonsense he must get out of here.   194 **incision** bloodshed.   **imbrue** dye with blood.   195 **death ... asleep** (Quotation from a poem written by Anne Boleyn or her brother as they awaited execution.)   197 **the Sisters Three** the three Fates: Clotho (who spun or *untwined* the thread of life), Lachesis (who unwound it), and Atropos (who severed it).   198 **toward** about to happen.   203 **tirrits** agitations, fits   209 **shrewd** vicious   213 **brave** defy   216 **chops** fat cheeks.   217 **Hector of Troy** leader of the Trojans; the type of valor   218 **Agamemnon** leader of the Greeks at Troy   219 **Nine Worthies** Hector, Alexander, Julius Caesar; Joshua, David, Judas Maccabaeus; Arthur, Charlemagne, Godfrey of Boulogne.   220–1 **toss ... blanket** (A humiliating punishment for cowards and rascals.)   222 **an ... heart** i.e., if your heart tells you to.   223 **canvass ... sheets** (Doll's more sexual version of tossing in a blanket.)   223.1 *Music* Musicians.

PAGE   The music is come, sir.

FALSTAFF   Let them play. Play, sirs. Sit on my knee, Doll. A rascal bragging slave! The rogue fled from me like quicksilver.

DOLL   [*sitting on his knee*]   I'faith, and thou followed'st him like a church. Thou whoreson little tidy Bartholo- 229 mew boar-pig, when wilt thou leave fighting o'days 230 and foining o'nights, and begin to patch up thine old 231 body for heaven?

Enter [behind] Prince and Poins [disguised as drawers].

FALSTAFF   Peace, good Doll, do not speak like a death's-head; do not bid me remember mine end.   234

DOLL   Sirrah, what humor's the Prince of?   235

FALSTAFF   A good shallow young fellow. 'A would have made a good pantler, 'a would ha' chipped bread well.   237

DOLL   They say Poins has a good wit.

FALSTAFF   He a good wit? Hang him, baboon! His wit's as thick as Tewkesbury mustard. There's no more con- 240 ceit in him than is in a mallet.   241

DOLL   Why does the Prince love him so, then?

FALSTAFF   Because their legs are both of a bigness, and 243 'a plays at quoits well, and eats conger and fennel, and 244 drinks off candles' ends for flapdragons, and rides the 245 wild mare with the boys, and jumps upon joint 246 stools, and swears with a good grace, and wears his 247 boots very smooth like unto the sign of the Leg, and 248 breeds no bate with telling of discreet stories; and such 249 other gambol faculties 'a has that show a weak mind 250 and an able body, for the which the Prince admits him. For the Prince himself is such another; the weight of a hair will turn the scales between their avoirdupois.   254

PRINCE   [*to Poins*]   Would not this nave of a wheel 255 have his ears cut off?   256

POINS   Let's beat him before his whore.   257

PRINCE   Look whe'er the withered elder hath not his 258 poll clawed like a parrot.   259

POINS   Is it not strange that desire should so many years outlive performance?

FALSTAFF   Kiss me, Doll.

PRINCE   [*to Poins*]   Saturn and Venus this year in 263 conjunction? What says th'almanac to that?   264

POINS   And look whether the fiery Trigon, his man, be 265 not lisping to his master's old tables, his notebook, his 266 counsel keeper.

FALSTAFF   [*to Doll*]   Thou dost give me flattering busses.   268

DOLL   By my troth, I kiss thee with a most constant heart.

FALSTAFF   I am old, I am old.

DOLL   I love thee better than I love e'er a scurvy young boy of them all.

FALSTAFF   What stuff wilt have a kirtle of? I shall 274 receive money o' Thursday; shalt have a cap tomorrow. A merry song. Come, it grows late; we'll to bed. Thou'lt forget me when I am gone.

DOLL   By my troth, thou'lt set me a-weeping an thou say'st so. Prove that ever I dress myself handsome till thy return—well, hearken a'th'end.   280

FALSTAFF   Some sack, Francis.

PRINCE, POINS   [*coming forward*]   Anon, anon, sir.   282

FALSTAFF   Ha? A bastard son of the King's? And art not thou Poins his brother?

PRINCE   Why, thou globe of sinful continents, what a 285 life dost thou lead!

FALSTAFF   A better than thou. I am a gentleman; thou art a drawer.

PRINCE   Very true, sir, and I come to draw you out by 289 the ears.   290

HOSTESS   Oh, the Lord preserve Thy Grace! By my troth, welcome to London. Now, the Lord bless that sweet face of thine! Oh, Jesu, are you come from Wales?

FALSTAFF   Thou whoreson mad compound of majesty, 294 by this light flesh and corrupt blood, thou art wel- 295 come.

DOLL   How, you fat fool! I scorn you.

POINS   My lord, he will drive you out of your revenge and turn all to a merriment, if you take not the heat.   299

---

229 like a church (implying perhaps that Falstaff has borne down on Pistol with his impressive bulk).   **tidy** plump, tender   **229–30 Bartholo-mew boar-pig** (Allusion to the serving of roast pig at Bartholomew Fair, August 24, in Smithfield.)   **231 foining** thrusting, fornicating   **234 death's-head** skull, used emblematically as a reminder of the inevitability of death   **235 what . . . of?** what is the Prince's disposition, temperament, mood?   **237 pantler** pantry worker.   **chipped bread** cut off the hard bread crusts   **240 Tewkesbury mustard** (Tewkesbury in Gloucestershire was famous for mustard.)   **240–1 con-ceit** wit   **241 mallet** wooden hammer, heavy and not at all sharp.   **243 of a bigness** of equal size   **244 quoits** a throwing game played across a net like badminton, but with a flat ring that is caught and thrown back.   **conger and fennel** conger eel seasoned with a yellow-flowered herb. (Rich fare, likely to dull the wits.)   **245 drinks . . . flapdragons** i.e., drinks liquor with a lighted candle floating in it, or extinguishes the candle with his mouth. (A tavern sport.)   **246 wild mare** leapfrog, or a game in which boys pile on top of one another until the *mare* collapses   **246–7 joint stools** stools made by a joiner or crafts-man   **248 smooth** i.e., well-fitting.   **sign . . . Leg** sign over a bootmaker's shop   **249 breeds . . . stories** creates no ill will by tattling secrets   **250 gambol** sportive   **254 avoirdupois** weight.   **255 nave** hub. (Refers to Falstaff's rotundity; with a pun on "knave.")   **256 have . . . off** i.e., as the punishment for slandering royalty.   **257 before** in front of   **258 elder** (1) elder tree (2) old man   **259 poll . . . parrot** (Doll is prob-ably rumpling the hair on Falstaff's head, his *poll*.)

263–4 Saturn . . . conjunction i.e., Will the planets that govern satur-nine old age and love be near one another in the heavens?   **265 fiery Trigon** (The twelve signs of the zodiac were divided into four *trigons* or triangles, one of which, consisting of Aries, Leo, and Sagittarius, was characterized as fiery. These three form a triangle because they are not contiguous on the circle of the zodiac but occur at points equivalent roughly to April, August, and December, at 120-degree intervals. The other three *trigons* were characterized as watery, airy, and earthy. The joke here is directed against Bardolph's fiery face.)   **266 lisping . . . notebook** whispering lovingly to Falstaff's old confi-dante, i.e., Mistress Quickly.   **tables** notebook (for assignations)   **268 busses** kisses.   **274 stuff** material.   **kirtle** skirt   **280 hearken a'th'end** i.e., wait and see.   **282 Anon, anon** (The cry of the drawer, or tapster, in answering his customers' demands for service, as in *1 Henry IV*, 2.4.21 ff.)   **285 globe . . . continents** (1) spherical person made up entirely of sinful contents (2) terrestrial globe of continents in which sin is omnipresent   **289–90 draw . . . ears** (as one might grab by the ears a naughty child caught in some mischief)   **294 com-pound** lump, mass   **295 by . . . blood** (An extension of the oath, "by this light," here reworded to apply to Doll.)   **299 if . . . heat** if you don't strike while the iron is hot.

PRINCE   You whoreson candle-mine you, how vilely 300
did you speak of me even now before this honest,
virtuous, civil gentlewoman!

HOSTESS   God's blessing of your good heart! And so
she is, by my troth.

FALSTAFF   Didst thou hear me?

PRINCE   Yea, and you knew me, as you did when you 306
ran away by Gad's Hill. You knew I was at your back, 307
and spoke it on purpose to try my patience.

FALSTAFF   No, no, no, not so, I did not think thou wast
within hearing.

PRINCE   I shall drive you then to confess the willful 311
abuse, and then I know how to handle you. 312

FALSTAFF   No abuse, Hal, o' mine honor, no abuse.

PRINCE   Not? To dispraise me, and call me pantler and
bread-chipper and I know not what?

FALSTAFF   No abuse, Hal.

POINS   No abuse?

FALSTAFF   No abuse, Ned, i'th' world, honest Ned,
none. I dispraised him before the wicked, that the
wicked might not fall in love with thee [to Hal]; in
which doing, I have done the part of a careful friend
and a true subject, and thy father is to give me thanks
for it. No abuse, Hal. None, Ned, none. No, faith,
boys, none.

PRINCE   See now whether pure fear and entire coward- 325
ice doth not make thee wrong this virtuous gentlewoman to close with us. Is she of the wicked? Is thine 327
hostess here of the wicked? Or is thy boy of the
wicked? Or honest Bardolph, whose zeal burns in his
nose, of the wicked?

POINS   Answer, thou dead elm, answer.

FALSTAFF   The fiend hath pricked down Bardolph irre- 332
coverable, and his face is Lucifer's privy kitchen, 333
where he doth nothing but roast maltworms. For the 334
boy, there is a good angel about him, but the devil
blinds him too. 336

PRINCE   For the women?

FALSTAFF   For one of them, she's in hell already and
burns poor souls. For th'other, I owe her money, and 339
whether she be damned for that I know not. 340

HOSTESS   No, I warrant you.

FALSTAFF   No, I think thou art not; I think thou art quit 342
for that. Marry, there is another indictment upon thee, 343
for suffering flesh to be eaten in thy house, contrary to 344
the law, for the which I think thou wilt howl. 345

HOSTESS   All victuallers do so. What's a joint of mutton 346
or two in a whole Lent?

PRINCE   You, gentlewoman—

DOLL   What says Your Grace?

FALSTAFF   His Grace says that which his flesh rebels 350
against.   Peto knocks at door. 351

HOSTESS   Who knocks so loud at door? Look to th'
door there, Francis.

[Francis goes to the door. Enter Peto.]

PRINCE   Peto, how now, what news?

PETO
The King your father is at Westminster,
And there are twenty weak and wearied posts   356
Come from the north. And as I came along
I met and overtook a dozen captains,
Bareheaded, sweating, knocking at the taverns,
And asking everyone for Sir John Falstaff.

PRINCE
By heaven, Poins, I feel me much to blame,
So idly to profane the precious time
When tempest of commotion, like the south   363
Borne with black vapor, doth begin to melt   364
And drop upon our bare unarmèd heads.
Give me my sword and cloak. Falstaff, good night.
                    Exeunt Prince and Poins, [and Peto].

FALSTAFF   Now comes in the sweetest morsel of the
night, and we must hence and leave it unpicked.
            [Knocking within. Bardolph goes to the door.]
More knocking at the door!

[Bardolph returns.]

How now, what's the matter?

BARDOLPH
You must away to court, sir, presently.   372
A dozen captains stay at door for you.

FALSTAFF   [to the Page]   Pay the musicians, sirrah. Farewell, hostess; farewell, Doll. You see, my good
wenches, how men of merit are sought after. The undeserver may sleep, when the man of action is called
on. Farewell, good wenches. If I be not sent away post, 378
I will see you again ere I go.

DOLL   I cannot speak. If my heart be not ready to
burst—well, sweet Jack, have a care of thyself.

FALSTAFF   Farewell, farewell.
                            Exit [with Bardolph and Page].

HOSTESS   Well, fare thee well. I have known thee these
twenty-nine years come peascod time, but an honester 384
and truer-hearted man—well, fare thee well.

BARDOLPH   [at the door]   Mistress Tearsheet!

HOSTESS   What's the matter?

BARDOLPH   Bid Mistress Tearsheet come to my
master.

300 candle-mine magazine or storehouse of tallow   306–7 Yea . . .
Gad's Hill (See 1 Henry IV, 2.4.)   311–12 to confess . . . abuse to confess that you slandered me intentionally   325 entire sheer   327 to
close with in order to appease and come to terms with.   she Doll
332 pricked down marked, or designated   333 privy private
334 maltworms topers, drunkards.   For As for. (Also in lines 337 and
338.)   336 blinds (so that he cannot see his Good Angel)   339 burns
i.e., infects with venereal disease   340 damned (since usury was condemned by the church as well as the state)   342–3 quit for that
(1) acquitted of that charge (2) repaid (as much as you are ever likely
to be).   344 flesh to be eaten (Allusion to enactments to prevent the
sale of meat in Lent; with sexual double entendre on mutton,
"whore.")   345 howl (in hell).   346 victuallers i.e., innkeepers

350–1 His . . . against (Falstaff wryly observes that sexual arousal and
feelings of revulsion are often linked; with wordplay on Grace as both
an honorific form of address for a prince and a spiritual quality.)
356 posts messengers   363 commotion insurrection. south south
wind (regarded as a breeder of tempests)   364 Borne laden
372 presently immediately.   378 post immediately   384 peascod
time i.e., early summer, when peas are still unripe

HOSTESS   Oh, run, Doll, run; run, good Doll. Come.—
She comes blubbered.—Yea, will you come, Doll?   391
Exeunt.

❖

[3.1]

Enter the King in his nightgown, alone [with a Page].

KING
Go call the Earls of Surrey and of Warwick;
But ere they come, bid them o'erread these letters   2
And well consider of them. Make good speed.
                    [He gives letters. Exit Page.]
How many thousand of my poorest subjects
Are at this hour asleep! O sleep, O gentle sleep,
Nature's soft nurse, how have I frighted thee,
That thou no more wilt weigh my eyelids down
And steep my senses in forgetfulness?
Why rather, sleep, liest thou in smoky cribs,   9
Upon uneasy pallets stretching thee,   10
And hushed with buzzing night-flies to thy slumber,
Than in the perfumed chambers of the great,
Under the canopies of costly state,   13
And lulled with sound of sweetest melody?
O thou dull god, why liest thou with the vile   15
In loathsome beds, and leavest the kingly couch
A watch-case or a common 'larum bell?   17
Wilt thou upon the high and giddy mast
Seal up the shipboy's eyes, and rock his brains
In cradle of the rude imperious surge   20
And in the visitation of the winds,   21
Who take the ruffian billows by the top,   22
Curling their monstrous heads and hanging them
With deafing clamor in the slippery clouds,   24
That, with the hurly, death itself awakes?   25
Canst thou, O partial sleep, give thy repose
To the wet sea-boy in an hour so rude,
And, in the calmest and most stillest night,
With all appliances and means to boot,   29
Deny it to a king? Then happy low, lie down!   30
Uneasy lies the head that wears a crown.   31

Enter Warwick, Surrey, and Sir John Blunt.

WARWICK
Many good morrows to Your Majesty!
KING   Is it good morrow, lords?
WARWICK   'Tis one o'clock, and past.

KING
Why, then, good morrow to you all, my lords.
Have you read o'er the letters that I sent you?
WARWICK   We have, my liege.
KING
Then you perceive the body of our kingdom,
How foul it is, what rank diseases grow,   39
And with what danger near the heart of it.
WARWICK
It is but as a body yet distempered,   41
Which to his former strength may be restored   42
With good advice and little medicine.   43
My Lord Northumberland will soon be cooled.
KING
O God, that one might read the book of fate,
And see the revolution of the times   46
Make mountains level, and the continent,   47
Weary of solid firmness, melt itself
Into the sea, and other times to see
The beachy girdle of the ocean   50
Too wide for Neptune's hips, how chance's mocks   51
And changes fill the cup of alteration
With divers liquors! Oh, if this were seen,
The happiest youth, viewing his progress through,   54
What perils past, what crosses to ensue,   55
Would shut the book and sit him down and die.
'Tis not ten years gone
Since Richard and Northumberland, great friends,
Did feast together, and in two years after
Were they at wars. It is but eight years since
This Percy was the man nearest my soul,   61
Who like a brother toiled in my affairs
And laid his love and life under my foot,   63
Yea, for my sake, even to the eyes of Richard   64
Gave him defiance. But which of you was by—
[To Warwick] You, cousin Nevil, as I may remember—   66
When Richard, with his eye brimful of tears,
Then checked and rated by Northumberland,   68
Did speak these words, now proved a prophecy:
"Northumberland, thou ladder by the which   70
My cousin Bolingbroke ascends my throne"?—
Though then, God knows, I had no such intent,
But that necessity so bowed the state
That I and greatness were compelled to kiss—
"The time shall come," thus did he follow it,
"The time will come, that foul sin, gathering head,
Shall break into corruption"—so went on,   77
Foretelling this same time's condition   78
And the division of our amity.

---

391 **blubbered** disfigured with weeping.
3.1. Location: Westminster. The royal court.
0.1 *nightgown* dressing gown   2 **o'erread** read over   9 **cribs** hovels
10 **uneasy** uncomfortable.   **thee** thyself   13 **state** magnificence
15 **dull** drowsy.   **vile** low in rank   17 **watch-case** sentry box, or a
space in which the occupant is restlessly aware of the passage of time
20 **rude** turbulent   21 **visitation** violent onset   22 **Who** which, i.e.,
the winds   24 **deafing** deafening.   **slippery** quickly slipping by
25 **That** so that.   **hurly** tumult   29 **appliances** aids to induce sleep.
to boot as well, besides   30 **low** humble persons   31.1 *Sir John
Blunt* (Since he says nothing and is omitted from the Folio, his presence may be unnecessary, but see line 35, "to you all.")

39 **rank** festering   41 **distempered** sick   42 **his** its   43 **little** a little
46 **revolution of the times** changes brought by the passage of time
47 **continent** dry land   50–1 **The beachy . . . hips** (The King compares the sea to a girdle around the waist of the sea god Neptune, *too wide* because the sea has receded, leaving a dry strand.)   51 **chance's mocks** the mockeries of Fortune   54 **progress through** life's progress from beginning to end   55 **crosses** afflictions   61 **This Percy** i.e., Northumberland   63 **under my foot** at my service   64 **to the eyes of** i.e., face to face with   66 **Nevil** (An error; this Earl of Warwick's surname is Beauchamp.)   68 **checked and rated** rebuked   70–7 **Northumberland . . . corruption** (See *Richard II*, 5.1.55 ff.)   78 **same** present

WARWICK
There is a history in all men's lives,
Figuring the nature of the times deceased,   81
The which observed, a man may prophesy,
With a near aim, of the main chance of things   83
As yet not come to life, who in their seeds   84
And weak beginnings lie intreasurèd.   85
Such things become the hatch and brood of time,   86
And by the necessary form of this   87
King Richard might create a perfect guess
That great Northumberland, then false to him,
Would of that seed grow to a greater falseness,
Which should not find a ground to root upon
Unless on you.
KING   Are these things then necessities?
Then let us meet them like necessities;
And that same word even now cries out on us.   94
They say the Bishop and Northumberland
Are fifty thousand strong.
WARWICK   It cannot be, my lord.
Rumor doth double, like the voice and echo,
The numbers of the feared. Please it Your Grace
To go to bed. Upon my soul, my lord,
The powers that you already have sent forth
Shall bring this prize in very easily.
To comfort you the more, I have received
A certain instance that Glendower is dead.   103
Your Majesty hath been this fortnight ill,
And these unseasoned hours perforce must add   105
Unto your sickness.
KING   I will take your counsel.
And were these inward wars once out of hand,   107
We would, dear lords, unto the Holy Land.   *Exeunt.* 108

❧

[3.2]

Enter Justice Shallow and Justice Silence.

SHALLOW   Come on, come on, come on, give me your
hand, sir, give me your hand, sir. An early stirrer, by
the rood! And how doth my good cousin Silence?   3
SILENCE   Good morrow, good cousin Shallow.
SHALLOW   And how doth my cousin your bedfellow?
And your fairest daughter and mine, my goddaughter
Ellen?
SILENCE   Alas, a black ouzel, cousin Shallow!   8
SHALLOW   By yea and no, sir. I dare say my cousin
William is become a good scholar. He is at Oxford still,
is he not?

SILENCE   Indeed, sir, to my cost.
SHALLOW   'A must then to the Inns o' Court shortly. I   13
was once of Clement's Inn, where I think they will talk   14
of mad Shallow yet.
SILENCE   You were called "lusty Shallow" then, cousin.   16
SHALLOW   By the Mass, I was called anything, and I
would have done anything indeed too, and roundly   18
too. There was I, and Little John Doit of Staffordshire,
and black George Barnes, and Francis Pickbone, and
Will Squele, a Cotswold man. You had not four such   21
swinge-bucklers in all the Inns o' Court again. And I   22
may say to you, we knew where the bona-robas were   23
and had the best of them all at commandment. Then   24
was Jack Falstaff, now Sir John, a boy, and page to
Thomas Mowbray, Duke of Norfolk.   26
SILENCE   This Sir John, cousin, that comes hither anon
about soldiers?
SHALLOW   The same Sir John, the very same. I see him   29
break Scoggin's head at the court gate, when 'a was a   30
crack not thus high. And the very same day did I fight   31
with one Sampson Stockfish, a fruiterer, behind
Gray's Inn. Jesu, Jesu, the mad days that I have spent!   33
And to see how many of my old acquaintance are
dead!
SILENCE   We shall all follow, cousin.
SHALLOW   Certain, 'tis certain, very sure, very sure.
Death, as the Psalmist saith, is certain to all, all shall 38
die. How a good yoke of bullocks at Stamford fair?   39
SILENCE   By my troth, I was not there.
SHALLOW   Death is certain. Is old Double of your town
living yet?
SILENCE   Dead, sir.
SHALLOW   Jesu, Jesu, dead! 'A drew a good bow; and
dead? 'A shot a fine shoot. John o' Gaunt loved him   45
well, and betted much money on his head. Dead? 'A
would have clapped i'th' clout at twelve score, and   47
carried you a forehand shaft a fourteen and fourteen   48
and a half, that it would have done a man's heart good   49
to see. How a score of ewes now?
SILENCE   Thereafter as they be; a score of good ewes   51
may be worth ten pounds.
SHALLOW   And is old Double dead?
SILENCE   Here come two of Sir John Falstaff's men, as I
think.

Enter Bardolph and one with him.

---

81 **Figuring** depicting, reproducing.   **deceased** past   83 **main chance**
probable outcome   84 **who** which   85 **intreasurèd** stored up.
86 **hatch and brood** offspring, consequence   87 **necessary form**
inevitable pattern   94 **cries . . . us** calls us to action; reproves us for
inaction.   103 **certain instance** unquestionable proof   105 **unseasoned** unseasonable, late   107 **inward** civil.   **out of hand** done with
108 **We . . . Land** (Compare the last four lines of *Richard II* and lines
18–27 of scene 1 of *1 Henry IV*.)
**3.2. Location: Gloucestershire. Before Justice Shallow's house. A
table and chairs must be provided onstage.**
3 **rood** cross.   **cousin** kinsman. (As also at lines 4, 5, and 9.)   8 **ouzel**
blackbird. (Ellen is dark-complexioned, not fair.)

13 **Inns o' Court** legal societies of London   14 **Clement's Inn** one of
the Inns of Chancery; in Shallow's time, these institutions prepared
one for the Inns of Court   16 **lusty** merry, lascivious   18 **roundly**
robustly, without ceremony   21 **Cotswold** from the Cotswold Hills
in Gloucestershire   22 **swinge-bucklers** swashbucklers, roisterers
23 **bona-robas** good-looking wenches, smart-looking prostitutes
24 **at commandment** at our beck and call.   26 **Thomas Mowbray**
(rival to Bolingbroke in *Richard II*)   29 **see** saw   30 **Scoggin** (Perhaps John Scogan, court jester to Edward IV and protagonist of an
Elizabethan jestbook known as "Scogan's Jests.")   31 **crack** pert little
boy   33 **Gray's Inn** one of the Inns of Court.   38–9 **Death . . . die**
(See Psalm 89:48.)   39 **How** How much (is the asking price for)
45 **John o' Gaunt** (Father of Henry IV.)   47 **clapped . . . score** hit the
bull's-eye at 240 yards   48–9 **carried . . . half** i.e., could shoot a heavy
arrow in a straight line rather than in a curved trajectory for a distance
of 280 to 290 yards. (*You* is used colloquially.)   51 **Thereafter . . . be**
According to their quality

SHALLOW Good morrow, honest gentlemen.

BARDOLPH I beseech you, which is Justice Shallow?

SHALLOW I am Robert Shallow, sir, a poor esquire of 58
this county, and one of the King's justices of the
peace. What is your good pleasure with me?

BARDOLPH My captain, sir, commends him to you, my 61
captain, Sir John Falstaff, a tall gentleman, by heaven, 62
and a most gallant leader.

SHALLOW He greets me well, sir. I knew him a good
backsword man. How doth the good knight? May I 65
ask how my lady his wife doth?

BARDOLPH Sir, pardon; a soldier is better accommo- 67
dated than with a wife. 68

SHALLOW It is well said, in faith, sir, and it is well said
indeed too. "Better accommodated"! It is good, yea,
indeed is it. Good phrases are surely, and ever were,
very commendable. "Accommodated"! It comes of
"accommodo." Very good, a good phrase.

BARDOLPH Pardon sir, I have heard the word.
"Phrase" call you it? By this day, I know not the
phrase. But I will maintain the word with my sword to
be a soldierlike word, and a word of exceeding good 77
command, by heaven. "Accommodated"; that is, 78
when a man is, as they say, accommodated; or when
a man is being whereby 'a may be thought to be
accommodated, which is an excellent thing.

Enter Falstaff.

SHALLOW It is very just.—Look, here comes good Sir 82
John.—Give me your good hand, give me Your
Worship's good hand. By my troth, you like well and 84
bear your years very well. Welcome, good Sir John.

FALSTAFF I am glad to see you well, good Master Robert
Shallow.—Master Surecard, as I think?

SHALLOW No, Sir John, it is my cousin Silence, in 88
commission with me. 89

FALSTAFF Good Master Silence, it well befits you should
be of the peace. 91

SILENCE Your good Worship is welcome.

FALSTAFF Fie, this is hot weather, gentlemen. Have you
provided me here half a dozen sufficient men? 94

SHALLOW Marry, have we, sir. Will you sit?

[They sit at a table.]

FALSTAFF Let me see them, I beseech you.

SHALLOW Where's the roll? Where's the roll? Where's
the roll? Let me see, let me see, let me see. So, so, so,
so, so, so, so; yea, marry, sir. Ralph Moldy! Let them
appear as I call; let them do so, let them do so. Let me
see, where is Moldy? 101

[Enter Moldy.]

MOLDY Here, an't please you. 102

SHALLOW What think you, Sir John? A good-limbed
fellow, young, strong, and of good friends. 104

FALSTAFF Is thy name Moldy?

MOLDY Yea, an't please you.

FALSTAFF 'Tis the more time thou wert used.

SHALLOW Ha, ha, ha! Most excellent, i'faith! Things
that are moldy lack use. Very singular good, in faith,
well said, Sir John, very well said.

FALSTAFF Prick him. [*Shallow writes on the muster roll.*] 111

MOLDY I was pricked well enough before, an you could 112
have let me alone. My old dame will be undone now 113
for one to do her husbandry and her drudgery. You 114
need not to have pricked me. There are other men
fitter to go out than I.

FALSTAFF Go to. Peace, Moldy, you shall go, Moldy, it
is time you were spent. 118

MOLDY Spent?

SHALLOW Peace, fellow, peace. Stand aside. Know you
where you are? For th'other, Sir John, let me see: 121
Simon Shadow!

[Enter Shadow.]

FALSTAFF Yea, marry, let me have him to sit under.
He's like to be a cold soldier. 124

SHALLOW Where's Shadow?

SHADOW Here, sir.

FALSTAFF Shadow, whose son art thou?

SHADOW My mother's son, sir.

FALSTAFF Thy mother's son! Like enough, and thy 129
father's shadow. So the son of the female is the 130
shadow of the male. It is often so, indeed; but much of
the father's substance.

SHALLOW Do you like him, Sir John?

FALSTAFF Shadow will serve for summer. Prick him 134
[*aside*], for we have a number of shadows fill up the 135
muster book.

SHALLOW Thomas Wart!

[Enter Wart.]

FALSTAFF Where's he?

WART Here, sir.

FALSTAFF Is thy name Wart?

WART Yea, sir.

FALSTAFF Thou art a very ragged wart.

SHALLOW Shall I prick him, Sir John?

---

58 **esquire** (A social rank between gentleman and knight.) 61 **commends him** sends his respects 62 **tall** valiant 65 **backsword** cudgel
with a basket hilt used for fencing practice. (See the note for 2.4.130.)
67–8 **accommodated** furnished, equipped. (A bit of fine language on
Bardolph's part, perhaps with sexual innuendo.) 77–8 **a word . . .
command** a perfectly good military term 82 **just** true. 84 **like well**
are in good condition, thrive 88–9 **in . . . me** serving as a fellow justice of the peace. 91 **of the peace** i.e., a magistrate. (With a play on
the name *Silence*, "peace.") 94 **sufficient** fit for service 101.1 *Enter
Moldy* (The recruits may be brought on all at once.)

102 **an't** if it. (Also in line 106.) 104 **of good friends** well connected
by family. 111 **Prick him** Mark him down on the list. 112 **pricked**
i.e., (1) vexed, grieved (2) turning sour or moldy. (With sexual suggestion also, continued in *undone, husbandry, drudgery,* and *spent,* "sexually used up.") 113 **dame** wife (rather than "mother," in view of the
sexual punning) 114 **husbandry** farm work. (But see the note at line
112.) 118 **spent** used up. (But see the note at line 112.) 121 **other**
others 124 **like** likely. **cold** (1) cool, deliberate (2) cowardly
129 **son** (With play on "sun," continuing in the following lines.)
130 **shadow** i.e., image and namesake. (But, Falstaff jests, the father is
only uncertainly copied in his son, since no man can ever be sure of
his paternity the way a mother is sure that a child is truly hers. Yet
the child consumes much of the father's *substance.*) 134 **serve**
(1) suffice (2) be inducted. **for summer** (when shade is desirable)
135 **shadows** i.e., fictitious names for which the officer in charge
receives pay. **fill** to fill

FALSTAFF   It were superfluous, for his apparel is built upon his back and the whole frame stands upon pins. 145 Prick him no more.

SHALLOW   Ha, ha, ha! You can do it, sir, you can do it. 147 I commend you well.—Francis Feeble!

[Enter Feeble.]

FEEBLE   Here, sir.

SHALLOW   What trade art thou, Feeble?

FEEBLE   A woman's tailor, sir.

SHALLOW   Shall I prick him, sir?

FALSTAFF   You may. But if he had been a man's tailor, he'd a' pricked you.—Wilt thou make as many holes 154 in an enemy's battle as thou hast done in a woman's 155 petticoat?

FEEBLE   I will do my good will, sir. You can have no more.

FALSTAFF   Well said, good woman's tailor! Well said, courageous Feeble! Thou wilt be as valiant as the wrathful dove or most magnanimous mouse. Prick the 161 woman's tailor. Well, Master Shallow, deep, Master Shallow.

FEEBLE   I would Wart might have gone, sir.

FALSTAFF   I would thou wert a man's tailor, that thou mightst mend him and make him fit to go. I cannot put him to a private soldier that is the leader of so 167 many thousands. Let that suffice, most forcible Feeble. 168

FEEBLE   It shall suffice, sir.

FALSTAFF   I am bound to thee, reverend Feeble. Who is 170 next?

SHALLOW   Peter Bullcalf o'th' green!

[Enter Bullcalf.]

FALSTAFF   Yea, marry, let's see Bullcalf.

BULLCALF   Here, sir.

FALSTAFF   'Fore God, a likely fellow! Come, prick me 175 Bullcalf till he roar again.

BULLCALF   Oh, Lord! Good my lord Captain—

FALSTAFF   What, dost thou roar before thou art pricked?

BULLCALF   Oh, Lord, sir! I am a diseased man.

FALSTAFF   What disease hast thou?

BULLCALF   A whoreson cold, sir, a cough, sir, which I caught with ringing in the King's affairs upon his 182 coronation day, sir. 183

FALSTAFF   Come, thou shalt go to the wars in a gown. 184 We will have away thy cold, and I will take such order 185 that thy friends shall ring for thee.—Is here all? 186

SHALLOW   Here is two more called than your number; you must have but four here, sir. And so, I pray you, go in with me to dinner.

FALSTAFF   Come, I will go drink with you, but I cannot tarry dinner. I am glad to see you, by my troth, Master 191 Shallow.

SHALLOW   Oh, Sir John, do you remember since we lay 193 all night in the Windmill in Saint George's Field? 194

FALSTAFF   No more of that, good Master Shallow, no more of that.

SHALLOW   Ha! 'Twas a merry night. And is Jane Nightwork alive?

FALSTAFF   She lives, Master Shallow.

SHALLOW   She never could away with me. 200

FALSTAFF   Never, never; she would always say she could not abide Master Shallow.

SHALLOW   By the Mass, I could anger her to the heart. She was then a bona-roba. Doth she hold her own well?

FALSTAFF   Old, old, Master Shallow.

SHALLOW   Nay, she must be old. She cannot choose but be old. Certain she's old, and had Robin Nightwork by old Nightwork before I came to Clement's Inn.

SILENCE   That's fifty-five year ago.

SHALLOW   Ha, cousin Silence, that thou hadst seen that that this knight and I have seen! Ha, Sir John, said I well?

FALSTAFF   We have heard the chimes at midnight, Master Shallow.

SHALLOW   That we have, that we have, that we have, in faith, Sir John, we have. Our watchword was "Hem, 217 boys!" Come, let's to dinner, come, let's to dinner. 218 Jesus, the days that we have seen! Come, come.

Exeunt [Falstaff and the Justices].

BULLCALF   Good Master Corporate Bardolph, stand my 220 friend, and here's four Harry ten shillings in French 221 crowns for you. *[He gives money.]* In very truth, sir, I had as lief be hanged, sir, as go. And yet for mine own 223 part, sir, I do not care, but rather because I am unwilling, and for mine own part have a desire to stay with my friends. Else, sir, I did not care, for mine own part, so much.

BARDOLPH   Go to, stand aside.

MOLDY   And, good Master Corporal Captain, for my old 229 dame's sake, stand my friend. She has nobody to do 230 anything about her when I am gone, and she is old 231 and cannot help herself. *[He gives money.]* You shall have forty, sir. 233

BARDOLPH   Go to, stand aside.

---

145 **the whole . . . pins** i.e., he's pinned together, badly made physically, and therefore needs no more pinpricks. (In a carpentry metaphor, the *pins* are also pegs for joining timber.)   147 **can do it** know how to make a joke.   154 **a' pricked** (1) have attired (2) have thrust you through. (With suggestion of male sexual penetration of the male; tailors were often considered effeminate.)   155 **battle** army   161 **magnanimous** stouthearted   167 **put him to** enlist him as   168 **thousands** i.e., of vermin, lice.   170 **bound** obliged   175 **likely** able-bodied   182–3 **ringing . . . day** i.e., ringing the church bells to celebrate the anniversary of the King's coronation   184 **gown** dressing gown.   185 **have away** do away with.   **take such order** provide   186 **for thee** (1) in your place (2) at your death.

191 **tarry** spare the time for   193 **since** when   194 **the Windmill** a brothel, or an inn in a brothel district.   **Saint George's Field** a popular place of resort on the south bank of the Thames   200 **away with** tolerate   217–18 **Hem, boys!** i.e., Down the hatch!   220 **Corporate** (For "Corporal.")   **stand** be, act as   221 **Harry ten shillings** i.e., money coined in the reign of Henry VII, current in late Elizabethan times at half the face value. (The reference is anachronistic. Four such coins would be worth twenty shillings, or one pound. Bullcalf gives his bribe in *French crowns*, worth four shillings each; presumably he gives five such coins.)   223 **lief** willingly   229–31 **old dame's . . . do anything** (With a sexually equivocal suggestion of mother or wife; see similar innuendo at line 113 above.)   233 **forty** i.e., forty shillings

FEEBLE   By my troth, I care not. A man can die but once. We owe God a death. I'll ne'er bear a base mind. An't be my destiny, so; an't be not, so. No man's too good to serve 's prince. And let it go which way it will, he that dies this year is quit for the next.   239

BARDOLPH   Well said. Thou'rt a good fellow.

FEEBLE   Faith, I'll bear no base mind.   241

Enter Falstaff and the Justices.

FALSTAFF   Come, sir, which men shall I have?

SHALLOW   Four of which you please.

BARDOLPH   [*to Falstaff*] Sir, a word with you. [*Aside*] I have three pound to free Moldy and Bullcalf.

FALSTAFF   Go to, well.   246

SHALLOW   Come, Sir John, which four will you have?

FALSTAFF   Do you choose for me.

SHALLOW   Marry, then, Moldy, Bullcalf, Feeble, and Shadow.

FALSTAFF   Moldy and Bullcalf: for you, Moldy, stay at   251
home till you are past service; and for your part, Bull-   252
calf, grow till you come unto it. I will none of you.   253

SHALLOW   Sir John, Sir John, do not yourself wrong. They are your likeliest men, and I would have you served with the best.

FALSTAFF   Will you tell me, Master Shallow, how to choose a man? Care I for the limb, the thews, the   258
stature, bulk, and big assemblance of a man? Give me   259
the spirit, Master Shallow. Here's Wart; you see what a ragged appearance it is. 'A shall charge you and   261
discharge you with the motion of a pewterer's ham-   262
mer, come off and on swifter than he that gibbets on   263
the brewer's bucket. And this same half-faced fellow,   264
Shadow; give me this man. He presents no mark to the enemy; the foeman may with as great aim level at   266
the edge of a penknife. And for a retreat, how swiftly will this Feeble the woman's tailor run off! Oh, give me the spare men, and spare me the great ones.—Put me a caliver into Wart's hand, Bardolph.   270

BARDOLPH   [*giving Wart a musket*] Hold, Wart, traverse.   271
Thus, thus, thus.

FALSTAFF   Come, manage me your caliver. So. [*Wart performs maneuvers with the musket.*] Very well. Go to. Very good, exceeding good. Oh, give me always a little, lean, old, chapped, bald shot. Well said, i'faith, Wart,   276
thou'rt a good scab. Hold, there's a tester for thee.   277

[*He gives sixpence.*]

SHALLOW   He is not his craft's master; he doth not do it right. I remember at Mile End Green, when I lay at   279
Clement's Inn—I was then Sir Dagonet in Arthur's   280
show—there was a little quiver fellow, and 'a would   281
manage you his piece thus [*Shallow demonstrates*], and   282
'a would about and about, and come you in and come   283
you in. "Ra-ta-ta!" would 'a say, "Bounce," would 'a   284
say, and away again would 'a go, and again would 'a come. I shall ne'er see such a fellow.

FALSTAFF   These fellows will do well, Master Shallow. God keep you, Master Silence. I will not use many words with you. Fare you well, gentlemen both. I thank you. I must a dozen mile tonight. Bardolph, give the soldiers coats.

SHALLOW   Sir John, the Lord bless you! God prosper your affairs! God send us peace! At your return, visit our house; let our old acquaintance be renewed. Peradventure I will with ye to the court.

FALSTAFF   'Fore God, would you would.

SHALLOW   Go to; I have spoke at a word. God keep you.   297

FALSTAFF   Fare you well, gentle gentlemen.

Exit [*Shallow with Silence*].

On, Bardolph; lead the men away.

[*Exeunt Bardolph, recruits, etc.*]

As I return, I will fetch off these justices. I do see   300
the bottom of Justice Shallow. Lord, Lord, how subject we old men are to this vice of lying! This same starved justice hath done nothing but prate to me of the wildness of his youth and the feats he hath done about Turnbull Street, and every third   305
word a lie, duer paid to the hearer than the Turk's   306
tribute. I do remember him at Clement's Inn like a   307
man made after supper of a cheese paring. When 'a was naked, he was, for all the world, like a forked rad-ish, with a head fantastically carved upon it with a knife. 'A was so forlorn that his dimensions to any   311
thick sight were invisible. 'A was the very genius of   312
famine, yet lecherous as a monkey, and the whores called him mandrake. 'A came ever in the rearward of   314
the fashion, and sung those tunes to the overscutched   315
huswives that he heard the carmen whistle, and sware   316
they were his fancies or his good-nights. And now is   317

---

239 **quit** free, clear   241 **bear** have   246 **Go to, well** i.e., All right, fine, say no more.   251 **for** as for   252 **past service** (1) too old to serve militarily (2) too old for sexual functioning   253 **come unto it** (1) are a man old enough to fight (2) have arrived at sexual maturity.   258 **thews** strength   259 **assemblance** appearance, frame   261–2 **charge . . . discharge you** load and fire   262–3 **motion . . . hammer** i.e., precise, quick motion   263–4 **come . . . bucket** raise and lower his musket quicker than a brewer's man raises and lowers the beam (*bucket*) of the brewer's yoke across his shoulders.   264 **half-faced** thin-faced. (Alludes to the profile portraits on coins.)   266 **as great aim** as much likelihood of hitting the target.   **level** aim   270 **caliver** light musket   271 **traverse** march, or, perhaps, perform the manual of arms, an exercise drill with a musket.   276 **shot** marksman.   **Well said** Well done   277 **scab** rascal. (Punning on the name *Wart*.)   **tester** sixpence

279 **Mile End Green** a drilling ground for citizen soldiers, to the east of London.   **lay** lodged   280–1 **Sir . . . show** (An exhibition of archery was held annually at Mile End Green, called "Arthur's show," in which each archer took the name of one of King Arthur's knights; Shallow played the part of Sir Dagonet, Arthur's fool.)   281 **quiver** nimble   282 **piece** firearm   283–4 **'a would . . . you in** i.e., he was skillful at firing and then running around to the rear rank of muske-teers to reload while the next rank fired, and so on.   284 **Bounce** bang   297 **I have . . . word** I mean what I say.   300 **fetch off** get the better of   305 **Turnbull Street** a street in Clerkenwell, ill-reputed   306 **duer** more promptly   306–7 **Turk's tribute** tribute money paid annually to the Sultan of Turkey by merchants and others.   311 **forlorn** meager, thin   312 **thick** imperfect.   **invisible** (Some edi-tors retain the reading of the Quarto and the Folio, "invincible," as meaning "invisible" or "indeterminable.")   **genius** spirit, personifi-cation   314 **mandrake** root of a plant, said to resemble the body of a man.   315–16 **overscutched huswives** outworn and often-whipped prostitutes   316 **carmen** wagoners   317 **fancies . . . good-nights** impromptu love songs and serenades (of which he claimed authorship).

this Vice's dagger become a squire, and talks as 318
familiarly of John o' Gaunt as if he had been sworn 319
brother to him, and I'll be sworn 'a ne'er saw him but 320
once in the tilt-yard, and then he burst his head for 321
crowding among the marshal's men. I saw it, and told
John o' Gaunt he beat his own name, for you might 323
have thrust him and all his apparel into an eelskin; the 324
case of a treble hautboy was a mansion for him, a 325
court. And now has he land and beefs. Well, I'll be 326
acquainted with him if I return, and 't shall go hard 327
but I'll make him a philosopher's two stones to me. If 328
the young dace be a bait for the old pike, I see no 329
reason in the law of nature but I may snap at him. Let
time shape, and there an end.   [*Exit.*]

[4.1]

*Enter the Archbishop [of York], Mowbray, [Lord]
Bardolph, Hastings, [and others,] within the Forest
of Gaultree.*

ARCHBISHOP   What is this forest called?
HASTINGS
'Tis Gaultree Forest, an't shall please Your Grace.   2
ARCHBISHOP
Here stand, my lords, and send discoverers forth   3
To know the numbers of our enemies.   4
HASTINGS
We have sent forth already.
ARCHBISHOP   'Tis well done.
My friends and brethren in these great affairs,
I must acquaint you that I have received
New-dated letters from Northumberland,
Their cold intent, tenor, and substance, thus: 9
Here doth he wish his person, with such powers   10
As might hold sortance with his quality,   11
The which he could not levy. Whereupon
He is retired, to ripe his growing fortunes,   13
To Scotland, and concludes in hearty prayers
That your attempts may overlive the hazard   15
And fearful meeting of their opposite.   16

MOWBRAY
Thus do the hopes we have in him touch ground   17
And dash themselves to pieces.

Enter Messenger.

HASTINGS   Now, what news?
MESSENGER
West of this forest, scarcely off a mile,
In goodly form comes on the enemy,
And, by the ground they hide, I judge their number
Upon or near the rate of thirty thousand.   22
MOWBRAY
The just proportion that we gave them out.   23
Let us sway on and face them in the field.   24
ARCHBISHOP
What well-appointed leader fronts us here?   25

Enter Westmorland.

MOWBRAY
I think it is my lord of Westmorland.
WESTMORLAND
Health and fair greeting from our general,
The Prince, Lord John and Duke of Lancaster.
ARCHBISHOP
Say on, my lord of Westmorland, in peace,
What doth concern your coming.
WESTMORLAND   Then, my lord,   30
Unto Your Grace do I in chief address
The substance of my speech. If that rebellion   32
Came like itself, in base and abject routs,   33
Led on by bloody youth, guarded with rags,   34
And countenanced by boys and beggary,   35
I say, if damned commotion so appeared   36
In his true, native, and most proper shape,
You, reverend father, and these noble lords
Had not been here to dress the ugly form
Of base and bloody insurrection
With your fair honors. You, Lord Archbishop,
Whose see is by a civil peace maintained,   42
Whose beard the silver hand of peace hath touched,
Whose learning and good letters peace hath tutored,   44
Whose white investments figure innocence,   45
The dove and very blessèd spirit of peace,
Wherefore do you so ill translate yourself   47
Out of the speech of peace that bears such grace
Into the harsh and boist'rous tongue of war,   49
Turning your books to graves, your ink to blood,
Your pens to lances, and your tongue divine
To a loud trumpet and a point of war?   52

---

318 Vice's dagger (The Vice, or comic character of the morality plays, was sometimes armed with a wooden dagger.)   **319–20 sworn brother** companion in arms who has taken a chivalric oath to share his fortunes   **321 tilt-yard** tournament ground at Westminster.   **he burst his head** he, Shallow, had his head beaten so that he bled   **323 beat his own name** i.e., was thrashing a gaunt person   **324 him** Shallow   **325 case** instrument case.   **hautboy** ancestor of the oboe. (The *treble hautboy* was the smallest and narrowest of this family of instruments.)   **326 beefs** oxen.   **327–8 and 't . . . to me** and with any kind of luck I'll be able to turn Shallow into my philosopher's stone, supposedly able to change ordinary metal into gold and preserved youth and health. (*Two stones* also suggests "testicles.")   **329 dace** small fish used for live bait
4.1. Location: Yorkshire. Gaultree Forest.
2 an't if it   **3 discoverers** scouts   **4 know** learn   **9 cold** dispiriting, gloomy   **10 powers** forces   **11 hold sortance** accord.   **quality** rank   **13 ripe . . . fortunes** let his fortunes grow and ripen   **15 overlive** survive   **16 opposite** adversary.

17 touch ground hit bottom   **22 rate** total   **23 The just . . . out** The precise number that we estimated.   **24 sway on** advance   **25 well-appointed** well-armed.   **fronts** confronts   **30 What . . . coming** what your coming means.   **32 If that** If   **33 routs** mobs   **34 bloody** passionate.   **guarded** adorned, trimmed   **35 countenanced** supported.   **beggary** beggars   **36 commotion** tumult, sedition   **42 see** diocese.   **civil** orderly, law-abiding   **44 good letters** scholarship   **45 investments figure** vestments symbolize   **47 translate** (1) change from one language to another (2) transform   **49 tongue** language   **52 point of war** signal of war.

ARCHBISHOP
Wherefore do I this? So the question stands.
Briefly to this end: we are all diseased,   54
And with our surfeiting and wanton hours   55
Have brought ourselves into a burning fever,
And we must bleed for it; of which disease   57
Our late King Richard, being infected, died.
But, my most noble lord of Westmorland,
I take not on me here as a physician,   60
Nor do I as an enemy to peace
Troop in the throngs of military men,
But rather show awhile like fearful war   63
To diet rank minds, sick of happiness,   64
And purge th'obstructions which begin to stop
Our very veins of life. Hear me more plainly.
I have in equal balance justly weighed   67
What wrongs our arms may do, what wrongs we
    suffer,
And find our griefs heavier than our offenses.   69
We see which way the stream of time doth run,
And are enforced from our most quiet there   71
By the rough torrent of occasion,   72
And have the summary of all our griefs,
When time shall serve, to show in articles;   74
Which long ere this we offered to the King,
And might by no suit gain our audience.
When we are wronged and would unfold our griefs,
We are denied access unto his person
Even by those men that most have done us wrong.
The dangers of the days but newly gone,
Whose memory is written on the earth
With yet-appearing blood, and the examples
Of every minute's instance, present now,   83
Hath put us in these ill-beseeming arms,   84
Not to break peace, or any branch of it,
But to establish here a peace indeed,
Concurring both in name and quality.   87
WESTMORLAND
Whenever yet was your appeal denied?
Wherein have you been gallèd by the King?   89
What peer hath been suborned to grate on you,   90
That you should seal this lawless bloody book   91
Of forged rebellion with a seal divine   92
And consecrate commotion's bitter edge?   93

ARCHBISHOP
My brother general, the commonwealth;   94
To brother born unhouseled cruelty   95
I make my quarrel in particular.   96
WESTMORLAND
There is no need of any such redress;
Or if there were, it not belongs to you.
MOWBRAY
Why not to him in part, and to us all   99
That feel the bruises of the days before,
And suffer the condition of these times
To lay a heavy and unequal hand   102
Upon our honors?
WESTMORLAND   O my good Lord Mowbray,
Construe the times to their necessities,   104
And you shall say indeed it is the time,
And not the King, that doth you injuries.
Yet for your part, it not appears to me
Either from the King or in the present time
That you should have an inch of any ground
To build a grief on. Were you not restored
To all the Duke of Norfolk's seigniories,   111
Your noble and right well remembered father's?
MOWBRAY
What thing, in honor, had my father lost,
That need to be revived and breathed in me?   114
The King that loved him, as the state stood then,   115
Was force perforce compelled to banish him;   116
And then that Henry Bolingbroke and he,
Being mounted and both rousèd in their seats,   118
Their neighing coursers daring of the spur,   119
Their armèd staves in charge, their beavers down,   120
Their eyes of fire sparkling through sights of steel,   121
And the loud trumpet blowing them together,
Then, then, when there was nothing could have stayed
My father from the breast of Bolingbroke,
Oh, when the King did throw his warder down—   125
His own life hung upon the staff he threw—
Then threw he down himself and all their lives
That by indictment and by dint of sword   128
Have since miscarried under Bolingbroke.
WESTMORLAND
You speak, Lord Mowbray, now you know not what.
The Earl of Hereford was reputed then   131

---

54 **we** the whole commonwealth   55–79 **And . . . wrong** (Omitted from the Quarto probably because of censorship, since these lines plead the cause of rebellion; also lines 103–39.)   55 **wanton** self-indulgent   57 **bleed** (1) be bled by a doctor (2) bleed in war   60 **take . . . as** do not now undertake the role of   63 **show** appear   64 **To . . . happiness** to deny excess to those who are bloated with indolent luxury   67 **equal balance** balanced scales.   **justly** exactly   69 **griefs** grievances   71 **our . . . there** our greatest quiet therein, i.e., in the stream of time   72 **occasion** circumstances   74 **articles** specified items   83 **Of . . . instance** presented every minute   84 **ill-beseeming** unsuitable, inappropriate   87 **Concurring . . . quality** i.e., a peace that will be both in name and in fact.   89 **gallèd** injured, made sore with chafing   90 **suborned . . . on** induced to annoy, harass   91–2 **That . . . divine** i.e., that you should put your seal of approval on this lawless and forged rebellion, much as if a bishop were to license a seditious book   93 **And . . . edge** and sanctify the cruel sword-edge of sedition.

94–6 **My brother . . . particular** (The text is corrupt here, but the general sense seems to be: the grievances of my brother-Englishmen and the cruelty shown to my blood brother Scroop [who was executed at Bristol by Henry IV; see *1 Henry IV*, 1.3.269] provoke me to make this cause my own. *Unhouseled* means "denied extreme unction.")   99 **Why . . . part** Why shouldn't redress belong in some measure to the Archbishop for the killing of his brother, Scroop   102 **unequal** unjust   104 **to** according to.   **their necessities** i.e., that which is necessary in a time of disorder and civil strife   111 **seigniories** properties, estates   114 **breathed** given the breath of life   115 **state** condition of things   116 **force perforce** willy-nilly. (For the banishment of Mowbray by Richard II, see *Richard II*, 1.1 and 1.3.)   118 **rousèd . . . seats** raised in their saddles   119 **daring of the spur**, eager to be urged on   120 **armèd . . . charge** lances ready for the charge.   **beavers** movable visors of helmets   121 **sights** eye slits   125 **warder** staff of command   128 **That . . . sword** that either through the miscarriage of justice or by the brute force of the sword   131 **Earl of Hereford** i.e., Bolingbroke, later King Henry IV

In England the most valiant gentleman.
Who knows on whom fortune would then have
    smiled?
But if your father had been victor there,
He ne'er had borne it out of Coventry;   135
For all the country in a general voice
Cried hate upon him, and all their prayers and love
Were set on Hereford, whom they doted on,
And blessed, and graced, indeed more than the King.
But this is mere digression from my purpose.
Here come I from our princely general
To know your griefs, to tell you from His Grace
That he will give you audience; and wherein   143
It shall appear that your demands are just,
You shall enjoy them, everything set off   145
That might so much as think you enemies.   146

MOWBRAY
But he hath forced us to compel this offer,
And it proceeds from policy, not love.

WESTMORLAND
Mowbray, you overween to take it so.   149
This offer comes from mercy, not from fear.
For, lo, within a ken our army lies,   151
Upon mine honor, all too confident
To give admittance to a thought of fear.
Our battle is more full of names than yours,   154
Our men more perfect in the use of arms,
Our armor all as strong, our cause the best.
Then reason will our hearts should be as good.   157
Say you not then our offer is compelled.

MOWBRAY
Well, by my will we shall admit no parley.   159

WESTMORLAND
That argues but the shame of your offense.
A rotten case abides no handling.   161

HASTINGS
Hath the Prince John a full commission,
In very ample virtue of his father,   163
To hear and absolutely to determine   164
Of what conditions we shall stand upon?   165

WESTMORLAND
That is intended in the General's name.   166
I muse you make so slight a question.   167

ARCHBISHOP [giving a document]
Then take, my lord of Westmorland, this schedule,
For this contains our general grievances.

Each several article herein redressed,   170
All members of our cause, both here and hence,   171
That are insinewed to this action,   172
Acquitted by a true substantial form   173
And present execution of our wills   174
To us and to our purposes confined,   175
We come within our awful banks again   176
And knit our powers to the arm of peace.

WESTMORLAND
This will I show the General. Please you, lords,
In sight of both our battles we may meet,   179
And either end in peace—which God so frame!— 180
Or to the place of difference call the swords   181
Which must decide it.

ARCHBISHOP   My lord, we will do so.
                                                    Exit Westmorland.

MOWBRAY
There is a thing within my bosom tells me
That no conditions of our peace can stand.

HASTINGS
Fear you not that. If we can make our peace
Upon such large terms and so absolute   186
As our conditions shall consist upon,   187
Our peace shall stand as firm as rocky mountains.

MOWBRAY
Yea, but our valuation shall be such   189
That every slight and false-derivèd cause,
Yea, every idle, nice, and wanton reason,   191
Shall to the King taste of this action,
That, were our royal faiths martyrs in love,   193
We shall be winnowed with so rough a wind
That even our corn shall seem as light as chaff   195
And good from bad find no partition.   196

ARCHBISHOP
No, no, my lord. Note this: the King is weary
Of dainty and such picking grievances;   198
For he hath found to end one doubt by death   199
Revives two greater in the heirs of life,   200
And therefore will he wipe his tables clean   201
And keep no telltale to his memory
That may repeat and history his loss   203
To new remembrance. For full well he knows
He cannot so precisely weed this land   205
As his misdoubts present occasion.   206
His foes are so enrooted with his friends
That, plucking to unfix an enemy,

170–6 **Each . . . again** Provided that each separate article herein is
redressed, and that all members who are joined together in this action
are pardoned, both here and henceforward, by a formal agreement
and by immediate satisfaction of our demands as regards us and our
intents, we will return into the bounds of respect imposed by our reverence for royal authority   179 **battles** armies   180 **frame** bring
about   181 **difference** conflict   186 **large** liberal   187 **consist** insist
189 **our valuation** i.e., the King's estimation of us   191 **idle . . .
wanton** foolish, petty, and frivolous   193 **That . . . love** i.e., so that
even if our allegiance to the King were as strong as the devotion of
martyrs   195 **corn** grain, wheat   196 **partition** distinction.
198 **picking** fastidious, trivial   199 **doubt** danger, source of fear
200 **heirs of life** those who survive   201 **tables** tablets, notebooks
203 **history** record, chronicle   205 **precisely** thoroughly   206 **misdoubts** suspicions

---

135 **borne . . . Coventry** i.e., carried away the prize from Coventry,
where the trial by combat was to have been held   143 **wherein** wherever   145 **set off** set aside   146 **think you** make you seem
149 **overween** are arrogant or presumptuous   151 **a ken** sight
154 **battle** army.   **names** noble names   157 **reason will** i.e., it stands
to reason that   159 **by my will** as far as I'm concerned.   **admit no
parley** agree to no conference.   161 **case** (1) container (2) cause.
abides tolerates   163 **very ample virtue** full authority   164–5 **To
hear . . . upon?** to hear our grievances and be able to make a final
decision regarding the terms we insist upon?   166 **intended** understood, implied.   **name** i.e., title.   167 **muse** wonder

He doth unfasten so and shake a friend.
So that this land, like an offensive wife
That hath enraged him on to offer strokes,
As he is striking, holds his infant up
And hangs resolved correction in the arm   213
That was upreared to execution.

HASTINGS
Besides, the King hath wasted all his rods   215
On late offenders, that he now doth lack   216
The very instruments of chastisement,
So that his power, like to a fangless lion,
May offer, but not hold.

ARCHBISHOP   'Tis very true.   219
And therefore be assured, my good Lord Marshal,
If we do now make our atonement well,   221
Our peace will, like a broken limb united,
Grow stronger for the breaking.

MOWBRAY   Be it so.
Here is returned my lord of Westmorland.

Enter Westmorland.

WESTMORLAND
The Prince is here at hand. Pleaseth Your Lordship   225
To meet His Grace just distance 'tween our armies.   226

MOWBRAY
Your Grace of York, in God's name then set forward.

ARCHBISHOP
Before, and greet His Grace.—My lord, we come.   228

❧

[4.2]

Enter Prince John [of Lancaster] and his army.

PRINCE JOHN
You are well encountered here, my cousin Mowbray.   1
Good day to you, gentle Lord Archbishop,   2
And so to you, Lord Hastings, and to all.
My lord of York, it better showed with you   4
When that your flock, assembled by the bell,
Encircled you to hear with reverence
Your exposition on the holy text
Than now to see you here an iron man,   8
Cheering a rout of rebels with your drum,   9
Turning the word to sword and life to death.   10
That man that sits within a monarch's heart
And ripens in the sunshine of his favor,
Would he abuse the countenance of the King,   13

Alack, what mischiefs might he set abroach   14
In shadow of such greatness! With you, Lord Bishop,   15
It is even so. Who hath not heard it spoken   16
How deep you were within the books of God,   17
To us the speaker in his parliament,   18
To us th'imagined voice of God himself,
The very opener and intelligencer   20
Between the grace, the sanctities, of heaven
And our dull workings? Oh, who shall believe   22
But you misuse the reverence of your place,
Employ the countenance and grace of heav'n
As a false favorite doth his prince's name,
In deeds dishonorable? You have ta'en up,   26
Under the counterfeited zeal of God,
The subjects of His substitute, my father,   28
And both against the peace of heaven and him
Have here up-swarmed them.

ARCHBISHOP   Good my lord of Lancaster,   30
I am not here against your father's peace;
But, as I told my lord of Westmorland,
The time misordered doth, in common sense,   33
Crowd us and crush us to this monstrous form
To hold our safety up. I sent Your Grace
The parcels and particulars of our grief,   36
The which hath been with scorn shoved from the
    court,
Whereon this Hydra son of war is born,   38
Whose dangerous eyes may well be charmed asleep   39
With grant of our most just and right desires,
And true obedience, of this madness cured,
Stoop tamely to the foot of majesty.

MOWBRAY
If not, we ready are to try our fortunes
To the last man.

HASTINGS   And though we here fall down,   44
We have supplies to second our attempt;   45
If they miscarry, theirs shall second them,   46
And so success of mischief shall be born,   47
And heir from heir shall hold this quarrel up
Whiles England shall have generation.   49

PRINCE JOHN
You are too shallow, Hastings, much too shallow,
To sound the bottom of the aftertimes.   51

---

213 **hangs resolved correction** interrupts in mid-action the punishment that was intended   215 **wasted . . . rods** exhausted the supply of whipping rods, i.e., spent all his punishments   216 **late** other recent   219 **offer . . . hold** threaten violence but not hold fast.
221 **atonement** reconciliation   225 **Pleaseth** May it please   226 **just distance** halfway   228 **Before** i.e., Go before
4.2. Location: This scene is apparently continuous with the previous scene. In the Quarto, Prince John and his army enter before the last two lines of 4.1.
1 **cousin** (Normal address of royal family to a duke.)   2 **gentle** noble   4 **it . . . you** it showed you to better advantage   8 **iron man** (1) warrior clad in armor (2) merciless fighter   9 **rout** mob   10 **the word** i.e., the word of God, the Scriptures   13 **Would he** if he should choose to. **countenance** favor

14 **set abroach** set aflowing, begin   15 **In shadow . . . greatness** i.e., furtively, not in the open *sunshine* of the King's favor (line 12).
16 **even** just   17 **within . . . God** (1) versed in works of divinity (2) in God's good graces   18 **speaker** i.e., spokesman for God, just as the Speaker of Parliament spoke in the name of the King   20 **opener and intelligencer** interpreter and messenger   22 **dull workings** imperfect human perceptions.   26 **ta'en up** enlisted   28 **His substitute** God's deputy   30 **up-swarmed** raised up in swarms   33 **time misordered** disorders of the time.   **in common sense** i.e., as anyone can see   36 **parcels** items, details.   **grief** grievances   38 **Hydra** (The Lernaean Hydra was a fabulous monster with several heads; when one was cut off, others grew in its place.)   39 **eyes** (The image here conflates Hydra with Argus, Juno's watchful guard with one hundred eyes, who was charmed asleep by Mercury's music.)   44 **though** even if   45 **supplies** forces in reserve   46 **miscarry** come to grief.   **theirs** their reinforcements   47 **success** succession   49 **generation** issue, offspring.   51 **sound . . . aftertimes** i.e., predict what the future will bring. (*Sound the bottom* means "plumb the depths.")

WESTMORLAND
  Pleaseth Your Grace to answer them directly   52
  How far forth you do like their articles.
PRINCE JOHN
  I like them all, and do allow them well,   54
  And swear here, by the honor of my blood,
  My father's purposes have been mistook,
  And some about him have too lavishly   57
  Wrested his meaning and authority.
  My lord, these griefs shall be with speed redressed,
  Upon my soul, they shall. If this may please you,
  Discharge your powers unto their several counties,   61
  As we will ours; and here between the armies
  Let's drink together friendly and embrace,
  That all their eyes may bear those tokens home
  Of our restorèd love and amity.
ARCHBISHOP
  I take your princely word for these redresses.
PRINCE JOHN
  I give it you, and will maintain my word,
  And thereupon I drink unto Your Grace.
              [They drink together, and embrace.]
HASTINGS
  Go, Captain, and deliver to the army
  This news of peace. Let them have pay, and part.   70
  I know it will well please them. Hie thee, Captain.
                        [Exit a Captain.]
ARCHBISHOP
  To you, my noble lord of Westmorland.
WESTMORLAND
  I pledge Your Grace; and, if you knew what pains
  I have bestowed to breed this present peace,
  You would drink freely. But my love to ye
  Shall show itself more openly hereafter.
ARCHBISHOP
  I do not doubt you.
WESTMORLAND   I am glad of it.
  Health to my lord and gentle cousin, Mowbray.
MOWBRAY
  You wish me health in very happy season,   79
  For I am on the sudden something ill.   80
ARCHBISHOP
  Against ill chances men are ever merry,   81
  But heaviness foreruns the good event.   82
WESTMORLAND
  Therefore be merry, coz, since sudden sorrow   83
  Serves to say thus, "Some good thing comes
      tomorrow."
ARCHBISHOP
  Believe me, I am passing light in spirit.   85
MOWBRAY
  So much the worse, if your own rule be true.
                        Shout [within].

PRINCE JOHN
  The word of peace is rendered. Hark, how they shout! 87
MOWBRAY
  This had been cheerful after victory.   88
ARCHBISHOP
  A peace is of the nature of a conquest,
  For then both parties nobly are subdued,
  And neither party loser.
PRINCE JOHN [to Westmorland]   Go, my lord,
  And let our army be dischargèd too.
                    [Exit Westmorland.]
  And, good my lord, so please you, let our trains   93
  March by us, that we may peruse the men
  We should have coped withal.
ARCHBISHOP   Go, good Lord Hastings,   95
  And ere they be dismissed, let them march by.
                    [Exit Hastings.]
PRINCE JOHN
  I trust, lords, we shall lie tonight together.   97

              Enter Westmorland.

  Now cousin, wherefore stands our army still?   98
WESTMORLAND
  The leaders, having charge from you to stand,   99
  Will not go off until they hear you speak.
PRINCE JOHN   They know their duties.

              Enter Hastings.

HASTINGS [to the Archbishop]
  My lord, our army is dispersed already.
  Like youthful steers unyoked, they take their courses
  East, west, north, south, or, like a school broke up,
  Each hurries toward his home and sporting-place.
WESTMORLAND
  Good tidings, my lord Hastings, for the which
  I do arrest thee, traitor, of high treason.
  And you, Lord Archbishop, and you, Lord Mowbray,
  Of capital treason I attach you both.   109
MOWBRAY
  Is this proceeding just and honorable?
WESTMORLAND   Is your assembly so?
ARCHBISHOP
  Will you thus break your faith?
PRINCE JOHN   I pawned thee none.   112
  I promised you redress of these same grievances
  Whereof you did complain, which, by mine honor,
  I will perform with a most Christian care.
  But for you rebels, look to taste the due   116
  Meet for rebellion and such acts as yours.   117
  Most shallowly did you these arms commence,   118
  Fondly brought here and foolishly sent hence.—   119
  Strike up our drums; pursue the scattered stray.   120

52 Pleaseth May it please   54 allow approve, sanction   57 lavishly loosely, negligently   61 powers forces.   several respective   70 part depart.   79 in . . . season at an opportune moment   80 something somewhat   81 Against When about to face   82 heaviness . . . event sadness comes over men prior to a happy outcome.   83 coz cousin, kinsman   85 passing surpassingly

87 rendered proclaimed.   88 had been would have been   93 trains followers, armies   95 coped withal encountered, fought with. 97 lie lodge. (With perhaps a hidden suggestion of "tell untruths.") 98 wherefore why   99 charge command   109 capital punishable by death.   attach arrest   112 pawned pledged   116 for as for.   look expect   117 Meet fitting   118 shallowly without due consideration. arms hostilities   119 Fondly foolishly   120 stray stragglers.

God, and not we, hath safely fought today.
Some guard these traitors to the block of death,
Treason's true bed and yielder-up of breath.

                                 [Exeunt.]

❖

[4.3]

*Alarum. Excursions. Enter Falstaff [and Sir John
Coleville, meeting].*

FALSTAFF   What's your name, sir? Of what condition   1
are you, and of what place?

COLEVILLE   I am a knight, sir, and my name is Coleville
of the Dale.

FALSTAFF   Well, then, Coleville is your name, a knight is
your degree, and your place the Dale. Coleville shall be
still your name, a traitor your degree, and the dungeon   7
your place, a place deep enough; so shall you be still   8
Coleville of the Dale.   9

COLEVILLE   Are not you Sir John Falstaff?

FALSTAFF   As good a man as he, sir, whoe'er I am. Do
ye yield, sir, or shall I sweat for you? If I do sweat,
they are the drops of thy lovers, and they weep for thy   13
death. Therefore rouse up fear and trembling, and do
observance to my mercy.   15

COLEVILLE   I think you are Sir John Falstaff, and in that
thought yield me.

FALSTAFF   I have a whole school of tongues in this belly   18
of mine, and not a tongue of them all speaks any other   19
word but my name. An I had but a belly of any indif-   20
ferency, I were simply the most active fellow in Eu-   21
rope. My womb, my womb, my womb undoes me.   22
Here comes our general.

*Enter [Prince] John [of Lancaster], Westmorland,
[Blunt,] and the rest.*

PRINCE JOHN
The heat is past; follow no further now.   24
Call in the powers, good cousin Westmorland.

                    [Exit Westmorland. Sound] retreat.

Now, Falstaff, where have you been all this while?
When everything is ended, then you come.
These tardy tricks of yours will, on my life,
One time or other break some gallows' back.

FALSTAFF   I would be sorry, my lord, but it should be   30
thus. I never knew yet but rebuke and check was the   31
reward of valor. Do you think me a swallow, an arrow,
or a bullet? Have I, in my poor and old motion, the

expedition of thought? I have speeded hither with the   34
very extremest inch of possibility. I have foundered   35
nine score and odd posts, and here, travel-tainted as I   36
am, have in my pure and immaculate valor taken Sir
John Coleville of the Dale, a most furious knight and
valorous enemy. But what of that? He saw me and
yielded, that I may justly say, with the hook-nosed fel-   40
low of Rome, "I came, saw, and overcame."   41

PRINCE JOHN   It was more of his courtesy than your
deserving.

FALSTAFF   I know not. Here he is, and here I yield him.
And I beseech Your Grace, let it be booked with the   45
rest of this day's deeds, or, by the Lord, I will have it
in a particular ballad else, with mine own picture on   47
the top on't, Coleville kissing my foot. To the which
course if I be enforced, if you do not all show like gilt   49
twopences to me, and I in the clear sky of fame   50
o'ershine you as much as the full moon doth the cin-   51
ders of the element, which show like pins' heads to   52
her, believe not the word of the noble. Therefore let
me have right, and let desert mount.   54

PRINCE JOHN   Thine's too heavy to mount.

FALSTAFF   Let it shine, then.

PRINCE JOHN   Thine's too thick to shine.   57

FALSTAFF   Let it do something, my good lord, that may
do me good, and call it what you will.

PRINCE JOHN   Is thy name Coleville?

COLEVILLE   It is, my lord.

PRINCE JOHN   A famous rebel art thou, Coleville.

FALSTAFF   And a famous true subject took him.

COLEVILLE
I am, my lord, but as my betters are
That led me hither. Had they been ruled by me,   65
You should have won them dearer than you have.   66

FALSTAFF   I know not how they sold themselves. But
thou, like a kind fellow, gavest thyself away gratis, and
I thank thee for thee.

Enter Westmorland.

PRINCE JOHN   Now, have you left pursuit?

WESTMORLAND
Retreat is made and execution stayed.   71

PRINCE JOHN
Send Coleville with his confederates
To York, to present execution.   73
Blunt, lead him hence, and see you guard him sure.

                    [Exit Blunt with Coleville.]

And now dispatch we toward the court, my lords.   75

**4.3. Location: Gaultree Forest, as before. The scene is continuous.
0.1** *Alarum. Excursions* trumpet call and sallies of troops (here
engaged in pursuing the scattered stragglers [4.2.120] in the wake of
the arrest of the rebel leaders.) **1 condition** rank   **7–9 dungeon . . .
Dale** (Falstaff jests that a deep dungeon can be thought of as a kind of
dale or pit.)   **13 drops** tears.   **lovers** friends   **15 observance** reverence,
homage   **18–20 I have . . . name** (Falstaff jests that his belly eloquently identifies him. *School* means "large number.")   **20–1 indifferency** moderate size   **21 were** would be   **22 womb** belly   **24 heat**
hot pursuit   **30–1 but . . . thus** if it were otherwise. (It is fitting, Falstaff wryly says, that valor is never properly recognized, because that
is how the world goes.)   **31 check** reprimand

34 expedition speed   **35 very extremest inch** fullest extent
35–6 foundered . . . posts lamed at least 180 post-horses   **40–1 hook-
nosed . . . Rome** i.e., Julius Caesar   **45 booked** recorded by the
chroniclers   **47 a particular ballad** a broadside ballad written and
published on this particular episode.   **else** otherwise   **49–50 if . . . to
me** if you do not all look like counterfeit coins (literally, twopenny
pieces gilded to resemble half-crowns worth thirty pence each) in
comparison with me   **51–2 cinders . . . element** i.e., stars   **52 to compared with   **54 desert mount** merit ascend, be promoted.   **57 thick**
(1) opaque, dim (2) heavy   **65 been ruled by me** listened to my
advice   **66 dearer** i.e., at greater military cost   **71 Retreat . . . stayed**
The order for withdrawal has been sounded, and the slaughter has
been stopped.   **73 present** immediate   **75 dispatch we** let us hasten

I hear the King my father is sore sick.
Our news shall go before us to His Majesty,
Which, cousin, you shall bear to comfort him,   78
And we with sober speed will follow you.   79

FALSTAFF   My lord, I beseech you give me leave to go
through Gloucestershire, and, when you come to
court, stand my good lord in your good report.   82

PRINCE JOHN
Fare you well, Falstaff. I, in my condition,   83
Shall better speak of you than you deserve.
[*Exeunt all but Falstaff.*]

FALSTAFF   I would you had but the wit; 'twere better
than your dukedom. Good faith, this same young
sober-blooded boy doth not love me, nor a man cannot make him laugh. But that's no marvel; he drinks
no wine. There's never none of these demure boys
come to any proof, for thin drink doth so overcool   90
their blood, and making many fish meals, that they
fall into a kind of male greensickness, and then, when   92
they marry, they get wenches. They are generally fools   93
and cowards, which some of us should be too, but for
inflammation. A good sherris sack hath a twofold op-   95
eration in it. It ascends me into the brain, dries me   96
there all the foolish and dull and crudy vapors which   97
environ it, makes it apprehensive, quick, forgetive,   98
full of nimble, fiery, and delectable shapes, which, delivered o'er to the voice, the tongue, which is the birth,
becomes excellent wit. The second property of your   101
excellent sherris is the warming of the blood, which,
before cold and settled, left the liver white and pale,   103
which is the badge of pusillanimity and cowardice.
But the sherris warms it and makes it course from the   105
innards to the parts' extremes. It illumineth the face,   106
which as a beacon gives warning to all the rest of this
little kingdom, man, to arm; and then the vital com-   108
moners and inland petty spirits muster me all to their   109
captain, the heart, who, great and puffed up with this   110
retinue, doth any deed of courage; and this valor
comes of sherris. So that skill in the weapon is nothing
without sack, for that sets it a-work, and learning a   113
mere hoard of gold kept by a devil till sack com-   114
mences and sets it in act and use. Hereof comes it   115
that Prince Harry is valiant, for the cold blood he did
naturally inherit of his father, he hath, like lean, ster-   117

ile, and bare land, manured, husbanded, and tilled   118
with excellent endeavor of drinking good and good   119
store of fertile sherris, that he is become very hot and   120
valiant. If I had a thousand sons, the first human   121
principle I would teach them should be to forswear
thin potations and to addict themselves to sack.   123

Enter Bardolph.

How now, Bardolph?
BARDOLPH   The army is discharged all and gone.
FALSTAFF   Let them go. I'll through Gloucestershire, and
there will I visit Master Robert Shallow, Esquire. I have
him already tempering between my finger and my   128
thumb, and shortly will I seal with him. Come away.   129
[*Exeunt.*]

❧

[4.4]

*Enter the King, Warwick, Thomas Duke of
Clarence, Humphrey [Duke] of Gloucester, [and
others].*

KING
Now, lords, if God doth give successful end
To this debate that bleedeth at our doors,   2
We will our youth lead on to higher fields   3
And draw no swords but what are sanctified.   4
Our navy is addressed, our power collected,   5
Our substitutes in absence well invested,   6
And everything lies level to our wish.   7
Only we want a little personal strength,   8
And pause us till these rebels now afoot
Come underneath the yoke of government.
WARWICK
Both which we doubt not but Your Majesty
Shall soon enjoy.
KING   Humphrey, my son of Gloucester,
Where is the Prince your brother?
GLOUCESTER
I think he's gone to hunt, my lord, at Windsor.
KING
And how accompanied?
GLOUCESTER   I do not know, my lord.
KING
Is not his brother Thomas of Clarence with him?
GLOUCESTER
No, my good lord, he is in presence here.
CLARENCE   What would my lord and father?

78 cousin i.e., Westmorland   **79 sober** deliberate   **82 stand my good
lord** act as my patron   **83 condition** i.e., function as commander
90 come to any proof stand up well under testing, turn out well
92 greensickness a kind of anemia thought to affect young women
93 get wenches beget girls.   **95 inflammation** spirits inflamed by
liquor.   **sherris sack** sherry   **96 ascends me** i.e., ascends. (*Me* is used
colloquially, as also in line 109.)   **97 crudy vapors** curdled exhalations (ascending from the body to the brain, thereby obstructing it)
98 apprehensive quick to perceive.   **forgetive** inventive   **101 wit**
verbal dexterity.   **103 liver** (Thought to be the seat of courage.)
105 course run   **106 the parts' extremes** the body's various extremities.   **108–10 and then . . . heart** and then the vital spirits that function in the body's interior, like troops of commoners all rally to the
support of their leader, the heart   **113–15 and learning . . . use** i.e.,
and learning is a mere heap of uselessly acquired knowledge, a secret
horde guarded over by some evil spirit, until wine releases its potential (as at a university commencement) and transforms that potential
into intellectual adventurousness.   **117 lean** barren

118 husbanded cultivated   **119–20 good and good store** good quality
and plenty   **121 human** (1) mundane, worldly (2) manly (3) humane
(so spelled in the Quarto)   **123 potations** drinks   **128 tempering**
softening (like a piece of wax)   **129 seal with** i.e., shape him to my
purposes; seal a bargain with (continuing the metaphor of sealing wax)
4.4. Location: King Henry's court at Westminster. The Jerusalem
Chamber (adjoining Westminster Abbey), so called for its various
inscriptions concerning Jerusalem.
2 debate strife   **3 our youth** our young men.   **higher fields** i.e., a
crusade to Palestine   **4 what** those that   **5 addressed** ready, prepared   **6 substitutes** deputies.   **invested** appointed, empowered
7 level conformable   **8 want** lack

KING
Nothing but well to thee, Thomas of Clarence.
How chance thou art not with the Prince thy brother?
He loves thee, and thou dost neglect him, Thomas;
Thou hast a better place in his affection
Than all thy brothers. Cherish it, my boy,
And noble offices thou mayst effect   24
Of mediation, after I am dead,
Between his greatness and thy other brethren.
Therefore omit him not, blunt not his love,   27
Nor lose the good advantage of his grace   28
By seeming cold or careless of his will.
For he is gracious, if he be observed.   30
He hath a tear for pity and a hand
Open as day for meting charity.   32
Yet notwithstanding, being incensed, he is flint,   33
As humorous as winter, and as sudden   34
As flaws congealèd in the spring of day.   35
His temper, therefore, must be well observed.   36
Chide him for faults, and do it reverently,
When you perceive his blood inclined to mirth;
But, being moody, give him time and scope,
Till that his passions, like a whale on ground,   39
Confound themselves with working. Learn this,
    Thomas,
                                                                       41
And thou shalt prove a shelter to thy friends,
A hoop of gold to bind thy brothers in,   43
That the united vessel of their blood,   44
Mingled with venom of suggestion—   45
As, force perforce, the age will pour it in—   46
Shall never leak, though it do work as strong   47
As aconitum or rash gunpowder.   48

CLARENCE
I shall observe him with all care and love.

KING
Why art thou not at Windsor with him, Thomas?

CLARENCE
He is not there today; he dines in London.

KING
And how accompanied? Canst thou tell that?

CLARENCE
With Poins and other his continual followers.

KING
Most subject is the fattest soil to weeds,   54
And he, the noble image of my youth,
Is overspread with them. Therefore my grief
Stretches itself beyond the hour of death.
The blood weeps from my heart when I do shape

In forms imaginary th'unguided days
And rotten times that you shall look upon
When I am sleeping with my ancestors.
For when his headstrong riot hath no curb,
When rage and hot blood are his counselors,
When means and lavish manners meet together,   64
Oh, with what wings shall his affections fly   65
Towards fronting peril and opposed decay!   66

WARWICK
My gracious lord, you look beyond him quite.   67
The Prince but studies his companions
Like a strange tongue, wherein, to gain the language,   69
'Tis needful that the most immodest word
Be looked upon and learned, which, once attained,
Your Highness knows, comes to no further use
But to be known and hated. So, like gross terms,   73
The Prince will in the perfectness of time
Cast off his followers, and their memory
Shall as a pattern or a measure live
By which His Grace must mete the lives of other,   77
Turning past evils to advantages.

KING
'Tis seldom when the bee doth leave her comb   79
In the dead carrion.

Enter Westmorland.

                    Who's here? Westmorland?   80

WESTMORLAND
Health to my sovereign, and new happiness
Added to that that I am to deliver!
Prince John your son doth kiss Your Grace's hand.
Mowbray, the Bishop Scroop, Hastings, and all
Are brought to the correction of your law.
There is not now a rebel's sword unsheathed,
But Peace puts forth her olive everywhere.
The manner how this action hath been borne
Here at more leisure may Your Highness read,
With every course in his particular.   90

                    [*He gives a document.*]

KING
Oh, Westmorland, thou art a summer bird,
Which ever in the haunch of winter sings   92
The lifting up of day.

Enter Harcourt.

                    Look, here's more news.   93

HARCOURT
From enemies heaven keep Your Majesty,
And, when they stand against you, may they fall
As those that I am come to tell you of!
The Earl Northumberland and the Lord Bardolph,

---

24 **offices** functions. **effect** perform, accomplish   27 **omit** neglect
28 **grace** favor   30 **observed** paid proper respect, humored.   32 **meting** meting out, distributing   33 **flint** i.e., both in hardness and in
giving off sparks   34 **humorous** capable of change in mood
35 **flaws congealèd** snow squalls.   **spring of day** early morning.
36 **temper** disposition   39 **moody** angry   41 **Confound** exhaust,
consume.   **working** exertion.   43–8 **A hoop . . . gunpowder** (The
King urges Thomas to act like a hoop of gold binding his brothers one
to another, so that the chalice of kinship in which their bloods are
combined may never leak, even when their enemies will attempt to
pour into it the poison of mistrust. *Suggestion* means "suspicion";
aconitum is a strong poison extracted from monkshood; *rash* means
"quick-acting.")   54 **fattest** richest

64 **lavish** unrestrained, licentious   65 **affections** inclinations
66 **fronting . . . decay** danger and ruin that confront him.   67 **look
beyond** go too far in judging   69 **strange** foreign   73 **like gross
terms** just as with coarse expressions   77 **mete** measure, appraise.
other others   79–80 **'Tis . . . carrion** Rarely does the bee that has
made a honeycomb in dead carrion abandon that honeycomb; i.e.,
the Prince will not forsake his corrupt delights.   90 **course . . . particular** event or phase set forth in detail.   **his** its   92 **haunch** latter end
93 **lifting up** dawn

With a great power of English and of Scots,
Are by the sheriff of Yorkshire overthrown.
The manner and true order of the fight
This packet, please it you, contains at large.   101
                                [*He gives letters.*]

KING
And wherefore should these good news make
    me sick?
Will Fortune never come with both hands full,
But write her fair words still in foulest letters?   104
She either gives a stomach and no food—   105
Such are the poor, in health; or else a feast
And takes away the stomach—such are the rich
That have abundance and enjoy it not.
I should rejoice now at this happy news,
And now my sight fails and my brain is giddy.
Oh, me! Come near me. Now I am much ill.
            [*The King swoons. Several come to his aid.*]

GLOUCESTER
Comfort, Your Majesty!
CLARENCE   O my royal father!
WESTMORLAND
My sovereign lord, cheer up yourself, look up.
WARWICK
Be patient, princes. You do know these fits
Are with His Highness very ordinary.
Stand from him, give him air; he'll straight be well.
CLARENCE
No, no, he cannot long hold out these pangs.
Th'incessant care and labor of his mind
Hath wrought the mure that should confine it in   119
So thin that life looks through and will break out.
GLOUCESTER
The people fear me, for they do observe   121
Unfathered heirs and loathly births of nature.   122
The seasons change their manners, as the year   123
Had found some months asleep and leapt them over.
CLARENCE
The river hath thrice flowed, no ebb between,   125
And the old folk, time's doting chronicles,
Say it did so a little time before
That our great-grandsire, Edward, sicked and died.   128
WARWICK
Speak lower, princes, for the King recovers.
GLOUCESTER
This apoplexy will certain be his end.
KING
I pray you, take me up and bear me hence
Into some other chamber. Softly, pray.

                          ❖

[4.5]

[*The King is borne to another part of the stage, to bed.*]

KING
Let there be no noise made, my gentle friends,
Unless some dull and favorable hand   2
Will whisper music to my weary spirit.
WARWICK
Call for the music in the other room.
KING
Set me the crown upon my pillow here.
CLARENCE
His eye is hollow, and he changes much.
WARWICK
Less noise, less noise!
            [*The crown is placed on the King's pillow.*]
        Enter [*Prince*] Harry.
PRINCE   Who saw the Duke of Clarence?
CLARENCE
I am here, brother, full of heaviness.   8
PRINCE
How now, rain within doors, and none abroad?   9
How doth the King?
GLOUCESTER   Exceeding ill.
PRINCE
Heard he the good news yet? Tell it him.
GLOUCESTER
He altered much upon the hearing it.
PRINCE   If he be sick with joy, he'll recover without
    physic.   15
WARWICK
Not so much noise, my lords. Sweet Prince, speak low.
The King your father is disposed to sleep.
CLARENCE
Let us withdraw into the other room.
WARWICK
Will't please Your Grace to go along with us?
PRINCE
No, I will sit and watch here by the King.
        [*Exeunt all but the Prince and the King.*]
Why doth the crown lie there upon his pillow,
Being so troublesome a bedfellow?
O polished perturbation, golden care,   23
That keep'st the ports of slumber open wide   24
To many a watchful night! Sleep with it now;   25
Yet not so sound and half so deeply sweet   26
As he whose brow with homely biggen bound   27
Snores out the watch of night. O majesty,   28
When thou dost pinch thy bearer, thou dost sit
Like a rich armor worn in heat of day,

---

101 at large in full.   **104 still** always   **105 stomach** appetite
119 wrought the mure worn the wall   **121 fear** frighten   **121–2 they
. . . nature** they take note of ominous signs, such as parthenogenic
and other unnatural births.   **123 as** as if   **125 river** i.e., Thames.
(Holinshed records this event as having happened on October 12,
1412.)   **128 Edward** Edward III.   **sicked** fell sick

4.5. Location: The scene is continuous.
2 dull and favorable soothing and kindly   **8 heaviness** sadness.
9 rain i.e., tears   **15 physic** medicine.   **23 perturbation** cause of perturbation   **24 ports** gates   **25 watchful** wakeful.   **Sleep with it** i.e.,
May you (King Henry) sleep even with this symbol of care beside
you   **26 Yet not** i.e., yet your sleep will nonetheless not be
27 biggen nightcap   **28 Snores . . . night** i.e., snores the night through.

That scald'st with safety. By his gates of breath   31
There lies a downy feather which stirs not.
Did he suspire, that light and weightless down   33
Perforce must move.—My gracious lord! My father!—
This sleep is sound indeed. This is a sleep
That from this golden rigol hath divorced   36
So many English kings. Thy due from me
Is tears and heavy sorrows of the blood,   38
Which nature, love, and filial tenderness
Shall, O dear father, pay thee plenteously.
My due from thee is this imperial crown,
Which, as immediate from thy place and blood,   42
Derives itself to me. [*He puts on the crown.*] Lo, where
it sits,   43
Which God shall guard. And put the world's whole
strength   44
Into one giant arm, it shall not force
This lineal honor from me. This from thee   46
Will I to mine leave, as 'tis left to me.   *Exit.*
KING [*awakening*]   Warwick! Gloucester! Clarence!

Enter Warwick, Gloucester, Clarence, [and others].

CLARENCE
Doth the King call?
WARWICK   What would Your Majesty?
KING
Why did you leave me here alone, my lords?
CLARENCE
We left the Prince my brother here, my liege,
Who undertook to sit and watch by you.
KING
The Prince of Wales? Where is he? Let me see him.
He is not here.
WARWICK
This door is open; he is gone this way.
GLOUCESTER
He came not through the chamber where we stayed.
KING
Where is the crown? Who took it from my pillow?
WARWICK
When we withdrew, my liege, we left it here.
KING
The Prince hath ta'en it hence. Go seek him out.
Is he so hasty that he doth suppose
My sleep my death?
Find him, my lord of Warwick; chide him hither.
[*Exit Warwick.*]
This part of his conjoins with my disease   63
And helps to end me. See, sons, what things you are!
How quickly Nature falls into revolt
When gold becomes her object!
For this the foolish overcareful fathers
Have broke their sleep with thoughts,   68
Their brains with care, their bones with industry;

For this they have engrossèd and piled up   70
The cankered heaps of strange-achievèd gold;   71
For this they have been thoughtful to invest   72
Their sons with arts and martial exercises—
When, like the bee, tolling from every flower,   74
Our thighs packed with wax, our mouths with honey,
We bring it to the hive, and like the bees   76
Are murdered for our pains. This bitter taste   77
Yields his engrossments to the ending father.   78

Enter Warwick.

Now, where is he that will not stay so long
Till his friend sickness have determined me?   80
WARWICK
My lord, I found the Prince in the next room,
Washing with kindly tears his gentle cheeks,   82
With such a deep demeanor in great sorrow   83
That Tyranny, which never quaffed but blood,   84
Would, by beholding him, have washed his knife   85
With gentle eyedrops. He is coming hither.
KING
But wherefore did he take away the crown?

Enter [Prince] Harry [with the crown].

Lo, where he comes. Come hither to me, Harry.—
Depart the chamber; leave us here alone.
Exeunt [Warwick and the rest].
PRINCE
I never thought to hear you speak again.
KING
Thy wish was father, Harry, to that thought.
I stay too long by thee; I weary thee.
Dost thou so hunger for mine empty chair   93
That thou wilt needs invest thee with my honors   94
Before thy hour be ripe? Oh, foolish youth,
Thou seek'st the greatness that will overwhelm thee.
Stay but a little, for my cloud of dignity   97
Is held from falling with so weak a wind   98
That it will quickly drop. My day is dim.
Thou hast stol'n that which after some few hours
Were thine without offense, and at my death   101
Thou hast sealed up my expectation.   102
Thy life did manifest thou loved'st me not;
And thou wilt have me die assured of it.
Thou hid'st a thousand daggers in thy thoughts,

---

31 scald'st with safety burns while providing safety.   **gates of breath** lips and nose   **33 suspire** breathe   **36 rigol** circle, i.e., crown **38 blood** (1) heart (2) kinship   **42 as immediate from** as I am next in line to   **43 Derives itself** descends   **44 put . . . strength** if all the strength in the world were put   **46 lineal** inherited   **63 part** act. **conjoins** unites, joins   **68 thoughts** cares

70 engrossèd amassed   **71 cankered** rusting and malignant. **strange-achievèd** won by unusual effort or means, or in distant lands **72 thoughtful** careful   **74 tolling** taking as toll, collecting   **76–7 and like . . . pains** (Compare Bartholomew, *De Proprietatibus Rerum:* "Bees that are unobedient to the king, they deem themselves by their own doom for to die by the wound of their own sting.")   **77–8 This . . . father** His stored-up treasures yield this bitter taste to the dying father.   **80 Till . . . me?** till sickness, befriending him, has put an end to me?   **82 kindly** natural, filial   **83 deep intense   84 That . . . blood** that even the personified spirit of Cruelty, despite its insatiable thirst for blood   **85 his knife** (A conventional attribute of personifications like Revenge and Wrath.)   **93 chair** throne   **94 wilt needs** must **97 cloud of dignity** earthly greatness, as evanescent as a cloud   **98 so weak a wind** i.e., the King's failing breath, compared to the wind that was thought to hold up the clouds   **101–2 and at . . . expectation** and now that I am dying you have confirmed my worst fears.

Which thou hast whetted on thy stony heart,
To stab at half an hour of my life.
What, canst thou not forbear me half an hour?   108
Then get thee gone and dig my grave thyself,
And bid the merry bells ring to thine ear
That thou art crownèd, not that I am dead.
Let all the tears that should bedew my hearse
Be drops of balm to sanctify thy head.   113
Only compound me with forgotten dust;   114
Give that which gave thee life unto the worms.
Pluck down my officers, break my decrees,
For now a time is come to mock at form.   117
Harry the Fifth is crowned. Up, vanity!   118
Down, royal state! All you sage counselors, hence!   119
And to the English court assemble now,
From every region, apes of idleness!   121
Now, neighbor confines, purge you of your scum.   122
Have you a ruffian that will swear, drink, dance,
Revel the night, rob, murder, and commit
The oldest sins the newest kind of ways?
Be happy; he will trouble you no more.
England shall double gild his treble guilt;
England shall give him office, honor, might;
For the fifth Harry from curbed license plucks   129
The muzzle of restraint, and the wild dog   130
Shall flesh his tooth on every innocent.   131
O my poor kingdom, sick with civil blows!
When that my care could not withhold thy riots,   133
What wilt thou do when riot is thy care?   134
Oh, thou wilt be a wilderness again,
Peopled with wolves, thy old inhabitants!

PRINCE [*kneeling and returning the crown*]
Oh, pardon me, my liege! But for my tears,   137
The moist impediments unto my speech,
I had forestalled this dear and deep rebuke   139
Ere you with grief had spoke and I had heard
The course of it so far. There is your crown;
And He that wears the crown immortally
Long guard it yours! If I affect it more   143
Than as your honor and as your renown,
Let me no more from this obedience rise,   145
Which my most inward true and duteous spirit
Teacheth this prostrate and exterior bending.
God witness with me, when I here came in,
And found no course of breath within Your Majesty,   149
How cold it struck my heart! If I do feign,
Oh, let me in my present wildness die

And never live to show th'incredulous world
The noble change that I have purposèd!
Coming to look on you, thinking you dead,
And dead almost, my liege, to think you were,
I spake unto this crown as having sense,   156
And thus upbraided it: "The care on thee depending   157
Hath fed upon the body of my father;
Therefore, thou best of gold art worst of gold.
Other, less fine in carat, is more precious,
Preserving life in med'cine potable;   161
But thou, most fine, most honored, most renowned,
Hast eat thy bearer up." Thus, my most royal liege,   163
Accusing it, I put it on my head,
To try with it, as with an enemy   165
That had before my face murdered my father,
The quarrel of a true inheritor.   167
But if it did infect my blood with joy
Or swell my thoughts to any strain of pride,   169
If any rebel or vain spirit of mine
Did with the least affection of a welcome   171
Give entertainment to the might of it,   172
Let God forever keep it from my head
And make me as the poorest vassal is
That doth with awe and terror kneel to it!

KING Oh, my son,
God put it in thy mind to take it hence,
That thou mightst win the more thy father's love,
Pleading so wisely in excuse of it!
Come hither, Harry, sit thou by my bed,
    [*The Prince rises and sits by the bed.*]
And hear, I think, the very latest counsel   181
That ever I shall breathe. God knows, my son,
By what bypaths and indirect crook'd ways
I met this crown, and I myself know well
How troublesome it sat upon my head.
To thee it shall descend with better quiet,
Better opinion, better confirmation,   187
For all the soil of the achievement goes   188
With me into the earth. It seemed in me
But as an honor snatched with boist'rous hand,   190
And I had many living to upbraid
My gain of it by their assistances,
Which daily grew to quarrel and to bloodshed,
Wounding supposèd peace. All these bold fears   194
Thou see'st with peril I have answerèd,
For all my reign hath been but as a scene   196
Acting that argument. And now my death   197

---

108 **forbear** spare   113 **balm** consecrated oil used in anointing the King at his coronation   114 **compound** mix   117 **form** ceremony, orderly usages.   118 **vanity** folly.   119 **state** ceremony.   121 **apes of idleness** foolishly idle hangers-on.   122 **neighbor confines** neighboring countries   129–30 **For . . . restraint** for Harry the Fifth unmuzzles the unlawful licentiousness and vice that have hitherto been restrained (*curbed*).   131 **flesh his tooth on** i.e., plunge his teeth into the flesh of. (To *flesh* means "to initiate into bloodshed," "to make an animal eager for prey by the taste of blood.")   133 **When . . . riots** When even the care I took to maintain discipline could not rein in your disorders of civil strife   134 **care** inclination, concern.   137 **But for** Were it not for   139 **had** would have.   **dear** severe, grievous (because deeply felt emotionally)   143 **affect** desire   145 **obeisance** kneeling posture   149 **course** current

156 **as having sense** as if it were capable of sense impressions   157 **The care . . . depending** The worry that comes from maintaining you   161 **med'cine potable** potable gold, an elixir, thought from Galen's time to possess magical powers to cure   163 **eat** eaten. (Pronounced "et.")   165 **To try with it** to dispute with it. (Also suggesting "try it on.")   167 **The quarrel . . . inheritor** (The Prince, as the son and heir of a murdered man, has a quarrel to settle with the murderer, i.e., the crown.)   169 **strain** feeling, tendency   171 **affection** inclination   172 **Give . . . of it** show appreciation or desire for the power it represents   181 **latest** last   187 **opinion** public support, reputation   188 **soil** stain   190 **boist'rous** violent   194 **fears** objects of fear   196–7 **hath been . . . argument** has seemed like a drama enacting that theme (of rebellion).

Changes the mood, for what in me was purchased   198
Falls upon thee in a more fairer sort;   199
So thou the garland wear'st successively.   200
Yet, though thou stand'st more sure than I could do,
Thou art not firm enough, since griefs are green,   202
And all my friends, which thou must make thy
    friends,   203
Have but their stings and teeth newly ta'en out,
By whose fell working I was first advanced   205
And by whose power I well might lodge a fear   206
To be again displaced. Which to avoid,
I cut them off, and had a purpose now
To lead out many to the Holy Land,
Lest rest and lying still might make them look   210
Too near unto my state. Therefore, my Harry,   211
Be it thy course to busy giddy minds
With foreign quarrels, that action, hence borne out,   213
May waste the memory of the former days.   214
More would I, but my lungs are wasted so
That strength of speech is utterly denied me.
How I came by the crown, O God forgive,
And grant it may with thee in true peace live!
PRINCE   My gracious liege,
    You won it, wore it, kept it, gave it me.
    Then plain and right must my possession be,
    Which I with more than with a common pain   222
    'Gainst all the world will rightfully maintain.

Enter [Prince John of] Lancaster, [Warwick, and
others].

KING
    Look, look, here comes my John of Lancaster.
PRINCE JOHN
    Health, peace, and happiness to my royal father!
KING
    Thou bring'st me happiness and peace, son John;
    But health, alack, with youthful wings is flown
    From this bare withered trunk. Upon thy sight   228
    My worldly business makes a period.   229
    Where is my lord of Warwick?
PRINCE   My lord of Warwick!

[Warwick comes forward.]

KING
    Doth any name particular belong
    Unto the lodging where I first did swoon?   232
WARWICK
    'Tis called Jerusalem, my noble lord.
KING
    Laud be to God! Even there my life must end.
    It hath been prophesied to me many years

    I should not die but in Jerusalem,
    Which vainly I supposed the Holy Land.
    But bear me to that chamber; there I'll lie.
    In that Jerusalem shall Harry die.
              [Exeunt, bearing the King in his bed.]

❧

[5.1]

Enter Shallow, Falstaff, and Bardolph [and Page].

SHALLOW   By Cock and pie, sir, you shall not away   1
  tonight.—What, Davy, I say!
FALSTAFF   You must excuse me, Master Robert Shallow.
SHALLOW   I will not excuse you, you shall not be excused, excuses shall not be admitted, there is no excuse
  shall serve, you shall not be excused.—Why, Davy!

    [Enter Davy.]

DAVY   Here, sir.
SHALLOW   Davy, Davy, Davy, Davy, let me see, Davy,
  let me see, Davy, let me see. Yea, marry, William cook, 9
  bid him come hither.—Sir John, you shall not be
  excused.
DAVY   Marry, sir, thus: those precepts cannot be   12
  served. And, again, sir: shall we sow the headland   13
  with wheat?
SHALLOW   With red wheat, Davy. But for William   15
  cook—are there no young pigeons?
DAVY   Yes, sir. Here is now the smith's note for shoeing 17
  and plow irons.   *[He gives a paper.]*
SHALLOW   Let it be cast and paid.—Sir John, you shall   19
  not be excused.
DAVY   Now, sir, a new link to the bucket must needs be   21
  had. And sir, do you mean to stop any of William's
  wages about the sack he lost at Hinckley fair?   23
SHALLOW   'A shall answer it. Some pigeons, Davy, a   24
  couple of short-legged hens, a joint of mutton, and
  any pretty little tiny kickshaws, tell William cook.   26
      [Davy and Shallow confer privately.]
DAVY   Doth the man of war stay all night, sir?
SHALLOW   Yea, Davy. I will use him well. A friend i'th'
  court is better than a penny in purse. Use his men
  well, Davy, for they are arrant knaves, and will
  backbite.
DAVY   No worse than they are backbitten, sir, for they   32
  have marvelous foul linen.   33
SHALLOW   Well conceited, Davy. About thy business,   34
  Davy.

---

198 **mood** state of mind; mode, musical key. **purchased** acquired
rather than inherited **199 sort** manner, way **200 So** thus. **garland**
crown. **successively** by right of succession. **202 griefs are green**
grievances are fresh. **203 friends** former allies **205 fell working**
ruthless efforts **206 lodge** harbor **210–11 look . . . state** examine
too skeptically my regal claim. **213 action . . . out** military action,
conducted in other lands **214 waste** efface, obliterate **222 pain**
effort **228 Upon thy sight** At the very moment of my seeing you
229 makes a period comes to an end. **232 lodging** room, chamber

5.1. Location: Gloucestershire. Shallow's house.
1 By Cock and pie (A mild oath, meaning "By God and the ordinal or
book of services for the Church.") **9 William cook** William the cook
12 precepts writs, summonses **13 headland** strip of unplowed land
at the edge of a field to allow for the turning of the plow **15 red
wheat** a variety of red-tinged wheat planted late in the summer
17 note bill **19 cast** added up **21 link** chain. **bucket** yoke or pail
23 Hinckley market town not far from Coventry, famous for its fairs
24 answer pay for **26 kickshaws** fancy dishes. (From the French
quelque chose.) **32 backbitten** (With pun on "bitten by vermin.")
33 marvelous marvelously **34 Well conceited** Ingeniously punned

DAVY   I beseech you, sir, to countenance William Visor   36
of Wo'ncot against Clement Perkes o'th' Hill.

SHALLOW   There is many complaints, Davy, against that
Visor. That Visor is an arrant knave, on my knowledge.

DAVY   I grant Your Worship that he is a knave, sir; but
yet, God forbid, sir, but a knave should have some
countenance at his friend's request. An honest man,
sir, is able to speak for himself, when a knave is not.
I have served Your Worship truly, sir, this eight years;
an I cannot once or twice in a quarter bear out a knave   46
against an honest man, I have little credit with Your
Worship. The knave is mine honest friend, sir; therefore, I beseech you, let him be countenanced.

SHALLOW   Go to, I say he shall have no wrong. Look   50
about, Davy.   [Exit Davy.]   51
Where are you, Sir John? Come, come, come, off with
your boots.—Give me your hand, Master Bardolph.

BARDOLPH   I am glad to see Your Worship.

SHALLOW   I thank thee with all my heart, kind Master
Bardolph. [To the Page] And welcome, my tall fellow.   56
—Come, Sir John.

FALSTAFF   I'll follow you, good Master Robert Shallow.
                                    [Exit Shallow.]
Bardolph, look to our horses.
                        [Exeunt Bardolph and Page.]
If I were sawed into quantities, I should make four   60
dozen of such bearded hermits' staves as Master Shal-   61
low. It is a wonderful thing to see the semblable   62
coherence of his men's spirits and his. They, by   63
observing of him, do bear themselves like foolish justices; he, by conversing with them, is turned into a   65
justice-like servingman. Their spirits are so mar-   66
ried in conjunction with the participation of society   67
that they flock together in consent, like so many wild
geese. If I had a suit to Master Shallow, I would humor
his men with the imputation of being near their mas-   70
ter; if to his men, I would curry with Master Shallow   71
that no man could better command his servants. It is
certain that either wise bearing or ignorant carriage is   73
caught, as men take diseases, one of another. Therefore let men take heed of their company. I will devise
matter enough out of this Shallow to keep Prince
Harry in continual laughter the wearing out of six   77
fashions, which is four terms, or two actions, and 'a   78
shall laugh without intervallums. Oh, it is much that a   79

lie with a slight oath and a jest with a sad brow will   80
do with a fellow that never had the ache in his shoul-   81
ders! Oh, you shall see him laugh till his face be like a   82
wet cloak ill laid up.   83

SHALLOW [within]   Sir John!

FALSTAFF   I come, Master Shallow, I come, Master
Shallow.   [Exit.]

❖

[5.2]

*Enter Warwick [and the] Lord Chief Justice
[meeting].*

WARWICK
How now, my Lord Chief Justice, whither away?   1

CHIEF JUSTICE   How doth the King?

WARWICK
Exceeding well. His cares are now all ended.   3

CHIEF JUSTICE
I hope, not dead.

WARWICK   He's walked the way of nature,   4
And to our purposes he lives no more.

CHIEF JUSTICE
I would His Majesty had called me with him.
The service that I truly did his life   7
Hath left me open to all injuries.

WARWICK
Indeed I think the young King loves you not.

CHIEF JUSTICE
I know he doth not, and do arm myself
To welcome the condition of the time,
Which cannot look more hideously upon me
Than I have drawn it in my fantasy.

*Enter [Prince] John [of Lancaster], Thomas [of
Clarence], and Humphrey [of Gloucester, with]
Westmorland, [and others].*

WARWICK
Here come the heavy issue of dead Harry.   14
Oh, that the living Harry had the temper   15
Of he, the worst of these three gentlemen!   16
How many nobles then should hold their places
That must strike sail to spirits of vile sort!   18

CHIEF JUSTICE
O God, I fear all will be overturned.

PRINCE JOHN
Good morrow, cousin Warwick, good morrow.

GLOUCESTER, CLARENCE   Good morrow, cousin.

PRINCE JOHN
We meet like men that had forgot to speak.   22

---

36 **countenance** favor   46 **bear out** support   50 **Go to** (An expression of remonstrance.)   50–1 **Look about** Get busy   56 **tall** brave.
(But also with an ironic witticism about the Page's small stature.)
60 **quantities** pieces   61 **hermits' staves** staffs or canes belonging to
hermits and, like them, thin as a rail   62 **semblable coherence** close
correspondence   65 **conversing** associating   66–7 **married . . . society** united by close association   70 **with . . . near** by implying that I
am friendly with, or that they enjoy the confidence of. (Probably the
latter.)   71 **curry with** flatter   73 **carriage** demeanor, behavior
77–8 **six . . . actions** six changes in the fashion of clothing, which
occupies the same time as the four terms of court (Michaelmas,
Hilary, Easter, and Trinity, all in all comprising one legal year), or two
lawsuits (which proceed slowly at the rate of only two a year)
79 **intervallums** intervals between terms of court

80 **sad** serious   81–2 **a fellow . . . shoulders** i.e., someone who is
youthfully inexperienced in the troubles and complexities of this
world and hence gullible.   82 **him** Prince Hal   83 **ill laid up** carelessly put away wet so that it wrinkles.
5.2. Location: Westminster. The royal court.
1 **whither away?** where are you going?   3 **well** i.e., at peace.
4 **walked . . . nature** i.e., died   7 **truly** loyally   14 **heavy issue** grieving sons   15 **temper** disposition   16 **he, the worst** the least worthy
18 **That . . . sort** who now must humble themselves before despicable
people, like ships lowering their sails in token of submission.   22 **forgot** forgotten how

WARWICK   We do remember, but our argument   23
    Is all too heavy to admit much talk.

PRINCE JOHN
    Well, peace be with him that hath made us heavy!

CHIEF JUSTICE
    Peace be with us, lest we be heavier!

GLOUCESTER
    O good my lord, you have lost a friend indeed,
    And I dare swear you borrow not that face
    Of seeming sorrow; it is sure your own.

PRINCE JOHN
    Though no man be assured what grace to find,   30
    You stand in coldest expectation.   31
    I am the sorrier; would 'twere otherwise.

CLARENCE
    Well, you must now speak Sir John Falstaff fair,   33
    Which swims against your stream of quality.   34

CHIEF JUSTICE
    Sweet princes, what I did I did in honor,
    Led by th'impartial conduct of my soul,
    And never shall you see that I will beg
    A ragged and forestalled remission.   38
    If truth and upright innocency fail me,
    I'll to the King my master that is dead
    And tell him who hath sent me after him.

WARWICK   Here comes the Prince.

     Enter the Prince [as King Henry the Fifth] and
     Blunt.

CHIEF JUSTICE
    Good morrow, and God save Your Majesty!

KING
    This new and gorgeous garment, majesty,
    Sits not so easy on me as you think.
    Brothers, you mix your sadness with some fear.
    This is the English, not the Turkish court;
    Not Amurath an Amurath succeeds,   48
    But Harry Harry. Yet be sad, good brothers,
    For, by my faith, it very well becomes you.
    Sorrow so royally in you appears
    That I will deeply put the fashion on
    And wear it in my heart. Why then, be sad,
    But entertain no more of it, good brothers,
    Than a joint burden laid upon us all.
    For me, by heaven, I bid you be assured,   56
    I'll be your father and your brother too.
    Let me but bear your love, I'll bear your cares.
    Yet weep that Harry's dead, and so will I;
    But Harry lives that shall convert those tears
    By number into hours of happiness.   61

PRINCES
    We hope no otherwise from Your Majesty.

KING
    You all look strangely on me. [*To the Chief Justice*] And
       you most.
    You are, I think, assured I love you not.

CHIEF JUSTICE
    I am assured, if I be measured rightly,
    Your Majesty hath no just cause to hate me.

KING   No?
    How might a prince of my great hopes forget
    So great indignities you laid upon me?
    What? Rate, rebuke, and roughly send to prison   70
    Th'immediate heir of England? Was this easy?   71
    May this be washed in Lethe and forgotten?   72

CHIEF JUSTICE
    I then did use the person of your father;   73
    The image of his power lay then in me.
    And in th'administration of his law,
    Whiles I was busy for the commonwealth,
    Your Highness pleasèd to forget my place,
    The majesty and power of law and justice,
    The image of the King whom I presented,   79
    And struck me in my very seat of judgment;
    Whereon, as an offender to your father,
    I gave bold way to my authority
    And did commit you. If the deed were ill,   83
    Be you contented, wearing now the garland,   84
    To have a son set your decrees at naught,
    To pluck down justice from your awful bench,   86
    To trip the course of law and blunt the sword
    That guards the peace and safety of your person,
    Nay, more, to spurn at your most royal image
    And mock your workings in a second body?   90
    Question your royal thoughts, make the case yours;
    Be now the father and propose a son,   92
    Hear your own dignity so much profaned,
    See your most dreadful laws so loosely slighted,
    Behold yourself so by a son disdained,
    And then imagine me taking your part
    And in your power soft silencing your son.   97
    After this cold considerance sentence me,   98
    And, as you are a king, speak in your state   99
    What I have done that misbecame my place,
    My person, or my liege's sovereignty.

KING
    You are right justice, and you weigh this well.   102
    Therefore still bear the balance and the sword;   103
    And I do wish your honors may increase,
    Till you do live to see a son of mine
    Offend you and obey you, as I did.
    So shall I live to speak my father's words:
    "Happy am I, that have a man so bold
    That dares do justice on my proper son;   109

---

23 argument subject   **30 grace to find** favor he will find   **31 coldest** most comfortless   **33 speak . . . fair** speak courteously to Sir John Falstaff   **34 swims . . . quality** runs counter to your natural inclination and position.   **38 A . . . remission** a half-hearted (beggarly) pardon, which is sure to be refused or whose effect is gone before it is granted. **48 Amurath** a Turkish sultan who, upon succeeding his father, had his brothers strangled   **56 For** As for   **61 By . . . happiness** i.e., for each of our many tears, there will be an hour of happiness.

70 Rate Chide   **71 easy** of small importance, easily forgotten. **72 Lethe** the river of forgetfulness in Hades   **73 use** represent **79 presented** represented   **83 commit** i.e., to prison   **84 garland** crown   **86 awful** awe-inspiring   **90 And . . . body** and ridicule your justice as administered by your representative or deputy.   **92 propose** imagine, suppose   **97 soft** gently   **98 cold considerance** calm reflection   **99 state** royal capacity   **102 right** true, ideal   **103 balance** scales (which, along with the sword, were emblematic of justice) **109 proper** own

And not less happy, having such a son
That would deliver up his greatness so
Into the hands of justice." You did commit me;
For which I do commit into your hand
Th'unstainèd sword that you have used to bear,   114
With this remembrance, that you use the same   115
With the like bold, just, and impartial spirit
As you have done 'gainst me. There is my hand.
You shall be as a father to my youth.
My voice shall sound as you do prompt mine ear,   119
And I will stoop and humble my intents
To your well-practiced wise directions.
And, princes all, believe me, I beseech you:
My father is gone wild into his grave,   123
For in his tomb lie my affections,   124
And with his spirits sadly I survive,   125
To mock the expectation of the world,
To frustrate prophecies, and to raze out
Rotten opinion, who hath writ me down   128
After my seeming. The tide of blood in me   129
Hath proudly flowed in vanity till now;   130
Now doth it turn and ebb back to the sea,
Where it shall mingle with the state of floods   132
And flow henceforth in formal majesty.
Now call we our high court of Parliament.
And let us choose such limbs of noble counsel
That the great body of our state may go   136
In equal rank with the best-governed nation;   137
That war, or peace, or both at once, may be
As things acquainted and familiar to us,
[*To Chief Justice*] In which you, father, shall have
    foremost hand.
Our coronation done, we will accite,   141
As I before remembered, all our state.   142
And, God consigning to my good intents,   143
No prince nor peer shall have just cause to say,
God shorten Harry's happy life one day!   *Exeunt.*

❖

[5.3]

*[A table and chairs are set out.] Enter Sir John
[Falstaff], Shallow, Silence, Davy, Bardolph,
[and the] Page. [Davy provides food and wine.]*

SHALLOW   Nay, you shall see my orchard, where, in an
arbor, we will eat a last year's pippin of mine own   2
grafting, with a dish of caraways, and so forth. Come,   3
cousin Silence. And then to bed.

FALSTAFF   'Fore God, you have here a goodly dwelling
and a rich.
SHALLOW   Barren, barren, barren. Beggars all, beggars
all, Sir John. Marry, good air. Spread, Davy, spread,   8
Davy. Well said, Davy.   9
FALSTAFF   This Davy serves you for good uses. He is
your servingman and your husband.   11
SHALLOW   A good varlet, a good varlet, a very good   12
varlet, Sir John. By the Mass, I have drunk too much
sack at supper. A good varlet. Now sit down, now sit
down. Come, cousin.
SILENCE   Ah, sirrah, quoth 'a, we shall   16
[*sings*] "Do nothing but eat, and make good cheer,
    And praise God for the merry year,
    When flesh is cheap and females dear,   19
    And lusty lads roam here and there
    So merrily,
    And ever among so merrily."   22
FALSTAFF   There's a merry heart, good Master Silence!
I'll give you a health for that anon.   24
SHALLOW   Give Master Bardolph some wine, Davy.
DAVY [*to the guests*]   Sweet sir, sit.—I'll be with you
anon.—Most sweet sir, sit. Master Page, good
master Page, sit. Proface! What you want in meat,   28
we'll have in drink. But you must bear. The heart's all.   29
    [*They sit. Exit Davy.*]
SHALLOW   Be merry, Master Bardolph, and, my little
soldier there, be merry.
SILENCE   [*sings*]
    "Be merry, be merry, my wife has all,
    For women are shrews, both short and tall.
    'Tis merry in hall when beards wags all,   34
    And welcome merry Shrovetide.   35
    Be merry, be merry."
FALSTAFF   I did not think Master Silence had been a
man of this mettle.   38
SILENCE   Who, I? I have been merry twice and once   39
ere now.

Enter Davy.

DAVY [*to the guests*]   There's a dish of leather-coats for   41
you.
SHALLOW   Davy!
DAVY   Your Worship? I'll be with you straight. [*To
Falstaff*] A cup of wine, sir?
SILENCE [*sings*]
    "A cup of wine that's brisk and fine,

---

114 have used have been accustomed   **115 remembrance** reminder,
admonition   **119 sound** speak   **123–4 My . . . affections** i.e., my
wildness, having disappeared with my father's death, is buried along
with my father   **125 spirits** soul, spiritual heritage.   **sadly** soberly
128 who which   **129 After my seeming** according to what I appeared
to be.   **blood** passion   **130 proudly** overbearingly.   **vanity** folly
132 state of floods majesty of the ocean   **136–7 go . . . rank** march
side by side   **141 accite** summon   **142 remembered** mentioned.
state peers, nobility.   **143 consigning** to sanctioning
5.3. Location: Gloucestershire. Shallow's orchard.
2 pippin a kind of apple   **3 caraways** (Pastries made with caraway
seeds were often eaten with apples.)

8 Spread Spread the cloth   **9 Well said** Well done. (Also in line 49.)
11 husband steward.   **12 varlet** (1) servant (2) rascal   **16 quoth'a**
said he   **19 flesh** meat. (With sexual suggestion.)   **22 ever among** all
the while   **24 give you a health** drink you a toast   **28 Proface** (Formula of welcome to a meal, meaning "May it do you good.")   **want**
lack.   **meat** food   **29 bear** be patient.   **The heart's all** i.e., A spirit
of hospitality is what counts; don't judge us by the lavishness of the
entertainment but by our good will.   **34 beards wags all** all the
beards wag up and down (as men talk and laugh)   **35 Shrovetide**
three-day period of merrymaking before Ash Wednesday and Lent
38 mettle spirit.   **39 twice and once** i.e., now and again   **41 leather-
coats** russet apples

> And drink unto thee, leman mine,   47
> And a merry heart lives long-a."

FALSTAFF   Well said, Master Silence.

SILENCE   And we shall be merry; now comes in the sweet o'th' night.

FALSTAFF   Health and long life to you, Master Silence.

SILENCE [*sings*]

> "Fill the cup, and let it come,   53
> I'll pledge you a mile to th' bottom."   54

SHALLOW   Honest Bardolph, welcome. If thou want'st   55 anything, and wilt not call, beshrew thy heart. [*To the*   56 *Page*] Welcome, my little tiny thief, and welcome indeed, too. I'll drink to Master Bardolph, and to all the cabileros about London.   59

DAVY   I hope to see London once ere I die.

BARDOLPH   An I might see you there, Davy!

SHALLOW   By the Mass, you'll crack a quart together,   62 ha, will you not, Master Bardolph?

BARDOLPH   Yea, sir, in a pottle pot.   64

SHALLOW   By God's liggens, I thank thee. The knave   65 will stick by thee, I can assure thee that. 'A will not out, ' a; 'tis true bred.   67

BARDOLPH   And I'll stick by him, sir.

SHALLOW   Why, there spoke a king. Lack nothing; be merry. (*One knocks at door.*) Look who's at door there, ho! Who knocks?   [*Davy goes to the door.*]

FALSTAFF [*to Silence*]   Why, now you have done me right.   73

SILENCE [*sings*]

> "Do me right,
> And dub me knight,
>   Samingo."   76

Is't not so?

FALSTAFF   'Tis so.

SILENCE   Is't so? Why then, say an old man can do somewhat.   80

DAVY [*returning*]   An't please Your Worship, there's one Pistol come from the court with news.

FALSTAFF   From the court? Let him come in.

     Enter Pistol.

How now, Pistol?

PISTOL   Sir John, God save you!

FALSTAFF   What wind blew you hither, Pistol?

PISTOL   Not the ill wind which blows no man to good. Sweet knight, thou art now one of the greatest men in this realm.

SILENCE   By'r Lady, I think 'a be, but goodman Puff of   90 Bar'son.

PISTOL   Puff?

> Puff i'thy teeth, most recreant coward base!—   93
> Sir John, I am thy Pistol and thy friend,
> And helter-skelter have I rode to thee,
> And tidings do I bring, and lucky joys,
> And golden times, and happy news of price.   97

FALSTAFF   I pray thee now, deliver them like a man of   98 this world.   99

PISTOL

> A foutre for the world and worldlings base!   100
> I speak of Africa and golden joys.   101

FALSTAFF

> O base Assyrian knight, what is thy news?   102
> Let King Cophetua know the truth thereof.   103

SILENCE [*sings*]

> "And Robin Hood, Scarlet, and John."   104

PISTOL

> Shall dunghill curs confront the Helicons?   105
> And shall good news be baffled?   106
> Then, Pistol, lay thy head in Furies' lap.   107

SHALLOW   Honest gentleman, I know not your breed-   108 ing.   109

PISTOL   Why then, lament therefor.   110

SHALLOW   Give me pardon, sir. If, sir, you come with news from the court, I take it there's but two ways: either to utter them or conceal them. I am, sir, under the King, in some authority.

PISTOL   Under which king, Besonian? Speak, or die.   115

SHALLOW   Under King Harry.

PISTOL   Harry the Fourth, or Fifth?

SHALLOW   Harry the Fourth.

PISTOL   A foutre for thine office!—

> Sir John, thy tender lambkin now is king;
> Harry the Fifth's the man. I speak the truth.
> When Pistol lies, do this, and fig me like   120
> The bragging Spaniard.

FALSTAFF   What, is the old King dead?

PISTOL

> As nail in door. The things I speak are just.

FALSTAFF   Away, Bardolph, saddle my horse! Master Robert Shallow, choose what office thou wilt in the land, 'tis thine. Pistol, I will double-charge thee with   126 dignities.

---

47 leman sweetheart   **53 let it come** i.e., pass it around   **54 a mile to th' bottom** i.e., even if the cup were a mile deep.   **55–6 If . . . heart** If you want something and don't ask for it, you deserve a mild curse. **59 cabileros** cavaliers, gallants   **62 crack** consume   **64 pottle pot** two-quart tankard.   **65 By God's liggens** (An oath, perhaps "By God's little eyelid.")   **67 out** drop out   **72–3 done me right** i.e., kept up with me in drinking.   **76 Samingo** (A corruption of "Sir Mingo," the titular knight of a French drinking song; derived from the Latin *mingo*, "I urinate"—a result of much drinking.)   **80 somewhat** something.   **90 but** except. (Silence interprets *greatest* in the sense of "heaviest.")   **goodman** yeoman

93 recreant faithless, base   **97 price** great value.   **98–9 a man . . . world** an ordinary man using plain ordinary speech.   **100 foutre** (From the French *foutre*, "fornicate"; a scornful phrase.)   **101 Africa** (Fabled for its wealth.)   **102 Assyrian** (Falstaff adopts Pistol's high-flown style and metrics.)   **103 Cophetua** (King Cophetua married a beggar maid, according to the popular ballad "King Cophetua and the Beggar Maid." More inflated rhetoric.)   **104 "And . . . John"** (A scrap from another ballad.)   **105 Helicons** i.e., poets. (Mount Helicon was the abode of the Muses.) Pistol takes umbrage at the drunken interruption of his poetically phrased announcement.   **106 baffled** confounded, foiled.   **107 lay . . . lap** (Pistol appeals his wrong to the avenging goddesses of classical mythology.)   **108–9 breeding** parentage, rank   **110 therefor** for that.   **115 Besonian** low, beggarly rascal. (From Italian *bisogno*, "need.")   **120 fig** insult with a vulgar gesture, consisting of thrusting the thumb between the index and middle fingers. (The gesture was thought to originate in Spain, as line 121 suggests. It means much the same as *foutre*, lines 100 and 117.)   **126 double-charge** (With a play on Pistol's name.)

BARDOLPH   Oh, joyful day! I would not take a knighthood for my fortune.

PISTOL   What, I do bring good news?

FALSTAFF   Carry Master Silence to bed.

[*Silence is carried off.*]

Master Shallow, my lord Shallow—be what thou wilt, I am fortune's steward—get on thy boots. We'll ride all night.—Oh, sweet Pistol!—Away, Bardolph!   [*Exit Bardolph.*]

Come, Pistol, utter more to me, and withal devise something to do thyself good. Boot, boot, Master 137 Shallow! I know the young King is sick for me. Let us take any man's horses; the laws of England are at my commandment. Blessed are they that have been my friends, and woe to my Lord Chief Justice!

PISTOL

Let vultures vile seize on his lungs also!
"Where is the life that late I led?" say they.   143
Why, here it is. Welcome these pleasant days!

Exeunt.

❧

[5.4]

Enter Beadle and three or four officers [dragging in Hostess Quickly and Doll Tearsheet].

HOSTESS   No, thou arrant knave! I would to God that I might die, that I might have thee hanged. Thou hast drawn my shoulder out of joint.

BEADLE   The constables have delivered her over to me, and she shall have whipping cheer, I warrant her. 5 There hath been a man or two killed about her.   6

DOLL   Nuthook, nuthook, you lie! Come on, I'll tell thee 7 what, thou damned tripe-visaged rascal, an the child I 8 go with do miscarry, thou wert better thou hadst 9 struck thy mother, thou paper-faced villain!   10

HOSTESS   Oh, the Lord, that Sir John were come! He would make this a bloody day to somebody. But I pray God the fruit of her womb miscarry!   13

BEADLE   If it do, you shall have a dozen of cushions again; you have but eleven now. Come, I charge you 15 both, go with me, for the man is dead that you and Pistol beat amongst you.

DOLL   I'll tell you what, you thin man in a censer, I will 18 have you as soundly swinged for this—you bluebottle 19 rogue, you filthy famished correctioner, if you be not swinged, I'll forswear half-kirtles.   21

BEADLE   Come, come, you she knight-errant, come.   22

HOSTESS   Oh, God, that right should thus overcome 23 might! Well, of sufferance comes ease.   24

DOLL   Come, you rogue, come, bring me to a justice.

HOSTESS   Ay, come, you starved bloodhound.

DOLL   Goodman death, goodman bones!

HOSTESS   Thou atomy, thou!   28

DOLL   Come, you thin thing, come, you rascal!   29

BEADLE   Very well.   [*Exeunt.*]

❧

[5.5]

Enter [Grooms as] strewers of rushes.

FIRST GROOM   More rushes, more rushes!

SECOND GROOM   The trumpets have sounded twice.

THIRD GROOM   'Twill be two o'clock ere they come from the coronation. Dispatch, dispatch.   [*Exeunt.*]   4

Trumpets sound, and the King and his train pass over the stage. After them enter Falstaff, Shallow, Pistol, Bardolph, and the Boy [Page].

FALSTAFF   Stand here by me, Master Shallow; I will make the King do you grace. I will leer upon him as 6 'a comes by, and do but mark the countenance that he will give me.

PISTOL   God bless thy lungs, good knight!

FALSTAFF   Come here, Pistol, stand behind me.—Oh, if I had had time to have made new liveries, I would 11 have bestowed the thousand pound I borrowed of 12 you. But 'tis no matter; this poor show doth better. 13 This doth infer the zeal I had to see him.   14

SHALLOW   It doth so.

FALSTAFF   It shows my earnestness of affection—

SHALLOW   It doth so.

FALSTAFF   My devotion—

SHALLOW   It doth, it doth, it doth.

FALSTAFF   As it were, to ride day and night, and not to deliberate, not to remember, not to have patience to shift me—   22

SHALLOW   It is best, certain.

FALSTAFF   But to stand stained with travel and sweating with desire to see him, thinking of nothing else, putting all affairs else in oblivion, as if there were nothing else to be done but to see him.

---

137 **Boot, boot** Put on your riding boots   143 **"Where . . . led"** (Fragment of a poem or ballad.)
5.4. Location: London. A street.
5 **whipping cheer** i.e., a whipping for supper   6 **about her** (1) in her company (2) on her account.   7 **Nuthook** Hook for pulling down branches in nutting; here, a constable   8 **tripe-visaged** sausage-faced   9 **go with** am pregnant with. (Doll implies that the father of the child, perhaps Falstaff, will retaliate if the child is aborted by rough handling.)   10 **paper-faced** pale   13 **miscarry** (The Hostess must mean just the opposite of this.)   15 **eleven now** (The Beadle accuses Doll of using one of the cushions to make her appear pregnant; pregnant women were spared execution.)   18 **thin . . . censer** i.e., figure of a man on the lid of a censer or incense burner, embossed in low relief   19 **swinged** thrashed.   **bluebottle** (An allusion to the Beadle's blue coat.)   21 **half-kirtles** skirts.

22 **she knight-errant** i.e., a streetwalker working at night. (With a mocking comparison to some heroine of a romance.)   23–4 **right . . . might** (The Hostess gets this backward.)   24 **sufferance** suffering. (Suffering now promises a better future, since one's luck is bound to change.)   28 **atomy** (For "anatomy," skeleton; an *atomy* is an "atom," "speck.")   29 **rascal** (1) lean deer (2) scoundrel.
5.5. Location: A public place near Westminster Abbey.
0.1 *rushes* straw often used as floor covering.
4 **Dispatch** Hurry   6 **grace** honor.   **leer** glance invitingly   11 **new liveries** new outfits bearing the King's insignia   12 **bestowed** spent   13 **you** i.e., Justice Shallow.   **poor show** appearing in inferior garments   14 **infer** imply   22 **shift me** change my apparel

PISTOL   'Tis *semper idem*, for *obsque hoc nihil est*. 'Tis all in   28
every part.   29

SHALLOW   'Tis so, indeed.

PISTOL
My knight, I will inflame thy noble liver   31
And make thee rage.
Thy Doll, and Helen of thy noble thoughts,   33
Is in base durance and contagious prison,   34
Haled thither   35
By most mechanical and dirty hand.   36
Rouse up Revenge from ebon den with fell Alecto's
snake,   37
For Doll is in. Pistol speaks naught but truth.   38

FALSTAFF   I will deliver her.

[Shouts within, and the trumpets sound.]

PISTOL
There roared the sea, and trumpet-clangor sounds.

*Enter the King and his train, [the Lord Chief
Justice among them].*

FALSTAFF
God save Thy Grace, King Hal, my royal Hal!

PISTOL
The heavens thee guard and keep, most royal imp of
fame!   42

FALSTAFF   God save thee, my sweet boy!

KING
My Lord Chief Justice, speak to that vain man.   44

CHIEF JUSTICE *[to Falstaff]*
Have you your wits? Know you what 'tis you speak?

FALSTAFF
My King! My Jove! I speak to thee, my heart!

KING
I know thee not, old man. Fall to thy prayers.
How ill white hairs becomes a fool and jester!
I have long dreamt of such a kind of man,
So surfeit-swelled, so old, and so profane,   50
But being awaked I do despise my dream.
Make less thy body hence, and more thy grace;   52
Leave gormandizing. Know the grave doth gape   53
For thee thrice wider than for other men.
Reply not to me with a fool-born jest.
Presume not that I am the thing I was,
For God doth know, so shall the world perceive,
That I have turned away my former self;
So will I those that kept me company.
When thou dost hear I am as I have been,
Approach me, and thou shalt be as thou wast,
The tutor and the feeder of my riots.

Till then, I banish thee, on pain of death,
As I have done the rest of my misleaders,
Not to come near our person by ten mile.
For competence of life I will allow you,   66
That lack of means enforce you not to evils.
And, as we hear you do reform yourselves,
We will, according to your strengths and qualities,
Give you advancement.—Be it your charge, my lord,
To see performed the tenor of my word.
Set on.   *[Exeunt King and his train.]*

FALSTAFF   Master Shallow, I owe you a thousand
pound.

SHALLOW   Yea, marry, Sir John, which I beseech you to
let me have home with me.

FALSTAFF   That can hardly be, Master Shallow. Do not
you grieve at this. I shall be sent for in private to him.
Look you, he must seem thus to the world. Fear not
your advancements; I will be the man yet that shall
make you great.

SHALLOW   I cannot perceive how, unless you give me
your doublet and stuff me out with straw. I beseech
you, good Sir John, let me have five hundred of my
thousand.

FALSTAFF   Sir, I will be as good as my word. This that
you heard was but a color.   87

SHALLOW   A color that I fear you will die in, Sir John.   88

FALSTAFF   Fear no colors. Go with me to dinner. Come,   89
Lieutenant Pistol, come, Bardolph. I shall be sent for
soon at night.   91

*Enter [the Lord Chief] Justice and Prince John [of
Lancaster, with officers].*

CHIEF JUSTICE
Go carry Sir John Falstaff to the Fleet.   92
Take all his company along with him.

FALSTAFF   My lord, my lord—

CHIEF JUSTICE
I cannot now speak. I will hear you soon.—
Take them away.

PISTOL
Si fortuna me tormenta, spero me contenta.   97

*Exeunt [all but Prince John
and the Chief Justice].*

PRINCE JOHN
I like this fair proceeding of the King's.
He hath intent his wonted followers   99
Shall all be very well provided for,
But all are banished till their conversations   101
Appear more wise and modest to the world.

CHIEF JUSTICE   And so they are.

PRINCE JOHN
The King hath called his parliament, my lord.

---

28 *semper ... est* "always the same," for "apart from this there is
nothing." (Pistol approvingly rephrases Falstaff's dedication to put
his loyalty to the Prince above all else.) *Obsque* is an error for *absque*.
28–9 'Tis ... part (A very free translation of the Latin.)   31 liver (The
seat of the passions.)   33 Helen i.e., Helen of Troy, the type of womanly beauty   34 durance imprisonment.   contagious pestilential
35 Haled dragged   36 mechanical menial, base   37 ebon black.
Alecto one of the Furies, who were depicted with snakes twined in
their hair   38 in i.e., in prison.   42 imp scion   44 vain foolish
50 surfeit-swelled swollen from gluttony   52 hence henceforth
53 gormandizing gluttonous feeding.

66 competence of life modest allowance   87 color pretense. (But
Shallow uses the word to mean *collar*, "hangman's noose.")   88 die
(1) be hanged (2) be dyed   89 colors standards or flags (of the
enemy). "Fear not," says Falstaff.   91 soon at night early in the
evening.   92 Fleet a famous London prison   97 Si ... contenta (See
the note for 2.4.180, above.)   99 wonted accustomed   101 conversations conduct

CHIEF JUSTICE   He hath.

PRINCE JOHN

I will lay odds that, ere this year expire,
We bear our civil swords and native fire   107
As far as France. I heard a bird so sing,
Whose music, to my thinking, pleased the King.
Come, will you hence?   [*Exeunt.*]

❖

Epilogue

[*Enter Epilogue.*]

EPILOGUE

First, my fear; then, my curtsy; last, my speech. My   1
fear is your displeasure; my curtsy, my duty; and my
speech, to beg your pardons. If you look for a good
speech now, you undo me, for what I have to say is of
mine own making, and what indeed I should say will,
I doubt, prove mine own marring. But to the purpose,   6
and so to the venture. Be it known to you, as it is very
well, I was lately here in the end of a displeasing play,   8
to pray your patience for it and to promise you a better. I meant indeed to pay you with this, which, if like
an ill venture it come unluckily home, I break, and   11
you, my gentle creditors, lose. Here I promised you I
would be, and here I commit my body to your mer-

cies. Bate me some and I will pay you some and, as   14
most debtors do, promise you infinitely.

If my tongue cannot entreat you to acquit me, will   17
you command me to use my legs? And yet that were
but light payment, to dance out of your debt. But a
good conscience will make any possible satisfaction,
and so would I. All the gentlewomen here have forgiven me. If the gentlemen will not, then the gentlemen do not agree with the gentlewomen, which was
never seen before in such an assembly   .

One word more, I beseech you. If you be not too
much cloyed with fat meat, our humble author will
continue the story, with Sir John in it, and make you   26
merry with fair Katharine of France. Where, for anything I know, Falstaff shall die of a sweat, unless al-   28
ready 'a be killed with your hard opinions; for Oldcas-   29
tle died a martyr, and this is not the man. My tongue   30
is weary; when my legs are too, I will bid you good   31
night; and so I kneel down before you, but, indeed, to
pray for the Queen.   [*Exit Epilogue.*]

---

107 civil . . . fire i.e., our weapons used recently in civil war
Epilogue
1 curtsy bow, obeisance   **6 doubt** fear   **8 displeasing play** (Identification is uncertain.)   **11 ill venture** unlucky sending out of merchant
vessels.   **break** (1) break my promise (2) become bankrupt

14 Bate me some Let me off from some portion of the debt   **17 use
my legs** i.e., perform the jig that normally concluded performances in
the public theaters.   **26 Sir John in it** (Shakespeare evidently originally intended to introduce Falstaff into *Henry V*; instead, only his
death is reported there in 2.1 and 2.3.)   **28 sweat** i.e., plague, fever, or
venereal disease   **29–30 Oldcastle . . . man** i.e., Falstaff was not
intended to resemble Sir John Oldcastle, the Lollard venerated by sixteenth-century Puritans as a martyr for their beliefs. (This statement
may have been intended to placate Lord Cobham, descendant of Oldcastle, whose resentment of Shakespeare's use of the Oldcastle name
in an earlier version of the *Henry IV* plays may have led to the change
of the name to Falstaff.)   **31 when . . . too** when my legs are tired
from dancing the jig

The Life of King Henry the Fifth

❧

Henry V (1599) is Shakespeare's culminating statement in the genre of the English history play. Unlike the late and atypical *Henry VIII* (1613), which is separated from the rest of Shakespeare's history plays by some fourteen years, *Henry V* sums up the historical themes with which Shakespeare had been fascinated for an entire decade. The play, first published in a memorially reconstructed and abridged quarto in 1600, must have been written not long after *2 Henry IV*, perhaps as an opening production for the Chamberlain's Men's new Bankside theater, the Globe, in 1599. To be sure, the play does not entirely fulfill the promise made in *2 Henry IV* to "continue the story, with Sir John in it, and make you merry with fair Katharine of France." Falstaff is missing. As before, Shakespeare apparently saw a grand design to his four-play sequence (which had started with *Richard II*) but improvised when he came to the writing of each part. Despite these minor adjustments in the overall plan, however, *Henry V* is clearly intended to bring to fulfillment the education of a politician-prince and to illustrate the arts of political kingship that Prince Hal had derived from his experiences in the earlier plays.

In a sense, too, *Henry V* sums up the achievement of the English history play, not only for Shakespeare, but also for other popular playwrights. The patriotic history play, born in the excitement of the Armada era immediately after 1588, had nearly run its course by 1599 and was soon to be supplanted by other dramatic genres, such as satire and revenge tragedy. Dark and complex political realities were already changing the buoyant mood in which the history play had been born: the aging Queen Elizabeth was near death and without a Protestant heir, while fear of another invasion threatened. In *Henry V*, we sense the approaching end of an era, for the play both celebrates the achievements of the English monarchy and examines its limits.

Henry V has become a controversial play, chiefly because our recent experiences with war have led us to be wary of political leaders who, in the name of patriotism, lay claim to and invade another country. George Bernard Shaw is prominent among those who have deplored Henry as a priggish and complacent warmonger and imperialist. Many historically minded critics, on the other hand, warn of the dangers of reading anachronistically from a modern perspective, and they argue that Henry is an admirable model of conduct according to Renaissance notions of statecraft and military leadership. What is Shakespeare's attitude toward his war hero? Does he sympathize with Henry's condescension toward the French and his order to every soldier to kill his French prisoners? Or is Shakespeare's admiration qualified by ironic reservations? As is usual in Shakespeare's work, the perspective is complex and balanced. The play pulls us in two directions. Although the Chorus, which interprets the play for us, approves of Henry's military posture, the grandiose rhetoric of war is consistently undercut by matter-of-fact revelations of people's self-interested motives. This contrast between rhetorical illusion and political reality extends from the justification of Henry's French campaign to his state marriage with Katharine of France. On the ethical issue of killing the French prisoners, for example, the play offers us contradictory and seemingly irreconcilable impressions. At the end of 4.6, Henry orders that "every soldier" is to "kill his prisoners," evidently because the English are under attack and cannot spare men to guard those who have been captured. In 4.7 (lines 1–10 and 54–5), however, we are told by Gower that the King gave the order in retaliation for the massacre by the cowardly French of the boys guarding the English luggage. Similarly, on the eve of the battle of Agincourt, we are left to draw our own conclusions about King Henry's conversation with his soldiers (4.1. 98–227). Is he evading the question of whether his cause is just by turning to a really very different matter of responsibility for someone else's sins, or is he simply testing his men with hard questions to prepare them for battle? Ironic puzzles such as these probably never amount to open disillusionment in this play, although some modern critics and directors would argue otherwise; the ironies are perhaps, instead, the acknowledgment of a special kind of morality pertaining to kingship.

Skill in rhetoric is a key to Henry's success—in defying the French Dauphin, in preparing troops for battle, or in wooing the French princess for his queen. As the Archbishop of Canterbury notes approvingly, King Henry's versatility as a rhetorician applies to all the vital disciplines of kingship: Henry can "reason in divinity," "debate of commonwealth affairs," "discourse of war," handle "any cause of policy," and in all such matters speak in "sweet and honeyed sentences" (1.1.39–51). Through the arts of language, Henry displays piety, learning, administrative sagacity, political cunning, and military intrepidity. Like the contemporary play *Julius Caesar* (1599), *Henry V* is concerned with techniques of persuasion. (The earlier *Richard III* is also a highly rhetorical play, though chiefly through the negative example of tyrannical behavior.) Yet, however much we may be swayed emotionally by the rhetoric, we realize that the public figure of Henry V is a mask behind which we can perceive little. Only rarely do we glimpse the affable young companion of the *Henry IV* plays. King Henry has accepted the responsibility of playing a political role. It denies him a private and separate identity, even—or especially—in choosing a wife. And it complicates our task of assessing the sincerity of his utterances. Is he genuinely pious, or has he merely learned the usefulness of pious utterance in swaying people's hearts? What especially are his motives for going to war against France?

Shakespeare could have begun this play with the stirring scene (1.2) in which Henry, urged on by his advisers, issues a defiant challenge to the French ambassadors. Instead, Shakespeare treats us to a prior glimpse beneath the patriotic surface. It seems that the Archbishop of Canterbury, threatened with a bill in Parliament designed to take away the better half of the Church's possessions, has resolved to parry with a counterproposal, whereby the Church will give Henry a very substantial sum for his French campaign, provided the offensive tax bill can be conveniently forgotten. The Archbishop has already been negotiating with Henry and surmises that the plan will work. This revelation is not shocking to us; it merely reveals the political process at work. The faint undercurrent of anticlericalism suggests that Henry is to be admired for putting pressure on his clergy with such success; they are rich and can afford to support the war. In any case, the dramatic effect is to show how men's practical motives affect their rhetoric. When, in the subsequent scene, the Archbishop delivers a public lecture on the English claim to France, we know that this learned prelate has a prior and self-interested commitment to the war. His intricate dynastic argument, which he proclaims

to be "as clear as is the summer's sun" (1.2.86), gives to the war a much-needed public justification. Henry's questions indicate not only his genuine concern about the legitimacy of his claim but also his political need for the Church's endorsement of his cause; he has already claimed certain French dukedoms and must have the Church's official approval of those claims before he can proceed. He similarly needs the backing of his nobles, who also have their own reasons for approving the campaign. Henry skillfully orchestrates the scene to produce the desired effect of unanimous and patriotic consent.

Although never directly stated, Henry's own motives for going to war must also combine sincere zeal with calculated self-interest. As king, he longs to recover the French territory that England governed in the great days of Poitiers and Crécy. As a man, he bristles at the contemptuous challenge of the Dauphin; Henry must still strive to overcome his reputation as a wastrel and must prove himself worthy of honorable comparison with his great ancestors. Politically (and this motive remains most hidden), Henry has absorbed his father's sage advice to "busy giddy minds / With foreign quarrels" (2 *Henry IV*, 4.5.213–14), to blunt political opposition at home by uniting English resentment against a foreign scapegoat.

The exigencies of war do indeed provide Henry with an opportunity for proceeding against his political enemies. He arrests the Earl of Cambridge, Lord Scroop, and Sir Thomas Grey at Southampton on charges of conspiring with France. The scene (2.2) is, for Shakespeare, uncharacteristically one-sided. We are never even told that Cambridge is the chief pretender to the English throne, son of the Duke of York, married to Anne Mortimer, and founder of the Yorkist claim in the York-Lancastrian wars—the sort of rival whom Shakespeare elsewhere portrays with understanding. Instead, the rhetoric of the Chorus to Act 2 blatantly warns us to expect "hell and treason" (line 29). These three conspirators, like Judases, says the Chorus, have bargained away their king for gold. (In fact, Cambridge insists that his motive was not financial, though he is not permitted to say what it was.) The playwright does not give them complex motives; they are sinners, so horrified by their own intents that they are actually grateful to be caught. The scene serves, by such rhetorical devices, to strengthen Henry's claim to the English throne as well as to the territories in France. Opposition to his rule during wartime is, in the view of the Chorus, simply treasonous; all persuasive evidences of dynastic rival claims are hidden from our view.

Comedy also contributes to the rhetorical image-making of the hero in *Henry V*. The tavern crew is on hand, though deprived of the now-deceased Falstaff's beguiling company and more distant from Henry than in the earlier history plays. Only briefly and in disguise, on the night before the battle, does the King encounter Pistol. The name of Bardolph comes to Henry as though in recollection of a distant past, when he hears that Bardolph is about to be executed for stealing from French churches. Henry confirms the sentence: "We would have all such offenders so cut off" (3.6.107). Whatever momentary pang Henry may feel, he remains constant to his banishment of Falstaff. And, although Shakespeare pleads for our sympathies in the seriocomic account of Falstaff's death, seen through the childlike naiveté of Mistress Quickly, there is no hope of reconciliation between Henry and his former mates. Pistol, despite his ornamental language, is little more than a boaster, coward, and thief. The tavern revelers are now the opportunists of war, troublemakers such as are found in every army, engaging rascals deserving to be cudgeled by more honorable men.

Pistol gets his comeuppance from Captain Fluellen, who replaces Falstaff as the chief comic figure, both in prominence (his role is second in length to that of Henry) and in proximity to the King. Fluellen is a Welshman, like King Henry, who was born at Monmouth in what was then Wales (hence the appropriateness of his former title as Prince of Wales). Fluellen is proud of this kinship. Because he is loyal and valiant, he is a person worthy to be seen in Henry's company. Yet there is none of the brilliant duel of wits previously linking Henry and Falstaff. Fluellen is a humorous character, identified at once by such comically exaggerated features as his Welsh accent and mannerisms of speech, his old-fashioned and somewhat fanatical sense of military propriety, and his devotion to the ancient rules of military discipline. Fluellen is a caricature, subject to mild satirical laughter, and there is a note of condescension in Henry's habit of playing practical jokes on the captain. We tend to laugh at, rather than with, him. (Henry makes practical jokes at others' expense as well, such as the soldier named Williams, with whom he exchanges gloves.) Unlike Falstaff, Fluellen lacks perspective on his own pomposity. He is a zealot for duty, and one feels Henry is taking unfair advantage when he picks on one who is such an easy mark for laughter. We suspect that Henry is using people again, bolstering his public image as the king with the common touch, borrowing a little Welsh color for myth-making purposes. At the same time, Fluellen is steadfast, upright, and a credit to his countryman Henry. With his fellow captains from Scotland, Ireland, and England, he demonstrates that Britishers can fight together, even if they do antagonize one another with their proud regional customs. Those customs are to be cherished as part of the British character; because Pistol offers gratuitous insult to the Welsh tradition of wearing a leek in the cap on Saint Davy's Day, he must be thrashed.

As with the comic characters and Henry's political enemies, *Henry V* is rhetorically one-sided in its presentation of the French. Patriotism is a raw emotion, and Henry cannot appeal to it without awakening hostility toward the enemy. (Ironically enough, the great film version of *Henry*

V by Laurence Olivier was created in 1944 during World War II to arouse national feelings against the Germans rather than against the French, and with complete success. Any enemy will do in such patriotic moods.) The French are portrayed as haughty, vastly superior in numbers, envious of one another, contemptuous of their own leadership (especially the Dauphin), treacherous (attacking the boys with the luggage), and craven. Even their joking is characterized by an unattractively bestial kind of bawdry (3.7.48–68). The British—"we few, we happy few" (4.3.60)—are tired and outnumbered but invincible and seemingly protected by God. Henry's order to kill the French prisoners and his description of the rapes and pillages his soldiers will commit if Harfleur fails to surrender (3.3.1–27) do, to be sure, raise serious questions about the morality of war under the best of kings; the play may be caustic toward the French nobility but does not necessarily exonerate the English. Even here, however, we are led to believe that, because the French are so execrably governed, France will suffer less under English rule. Henry takes care that his soldiers will not despoil the French countryside except under conditions of military "necessity." Only in Montjoy, the Duke of Burgundy, and Katharine of France does Shakespeare offer redeeming portraits of the French character, and in these instances the terms of hierarchical ascendancy seem clear: masculine English dominance, gentle French submissiveness. Katharine becomes "la belle France," depicted in Burgundy's eloquent peacemaking speech as being so much in need of competent management.

Women exist only on the margins of this war play, as in Shakespeare's other historical plays. Mistress Quickly's role is chiefly as a reminder to us that men fight with one another for the possession of women; the ludicrous quarrel of Pistol and Nym over Mistress Quickly anticipates the way in which Katharine of France will be one of the chief spoils of the war itself. Women also wait patiently at home while their men fight, and tend them when they are sick. Mistress Quickly's recollection of the death of Falstaff (2.3.9–25) is masterful in its evocation of tender solicitude, illiterate piety, and unwitting eroticism. Later, in France, Pistol pauses with momentary regret over news of the death of his wife from venereal disease (5.1.80–1). Katharine of France, though vastly better born, finds her role as a woman no less circumscribed. We first see her learning English from Alice, her lady in waiting (3.4). Why is she learning English? The obvious political reason, never explicitly stated, emerges with a kind of violence: the scene of the English lesson follows immediately after King Henry's ultimatum to the citizens of Harfleur to surrender or see their women raped and their children impaled by English weapons (3.3.27–41). Katharine accepts her lot with good grace, as though she had any other choice but to do so. We gather from her scene with Alice that she is a woman of spirit who can be imperious, vain, and curious about sex. Because she also is very French, the wooing scene in Act 5 can play comically on the differences of temperament between her and Henry, who is as English as she is French. These differences make Henry and Katharine potentially compatible through complementarity—male and female, soldier and lady, English and French—but the compact is patently a hierarchical one of conqueror and conquered. (Emma Thompson, in Kenneth Branagh's film version of 1989, brings to the role of Katharine a gracefully and persuasively feminist interpretation of an independent-minded woman who is decidedly skeptical about the courtship to which she is subjected, but even she discovers that she has no choice other than to capitulate to Henry's—i.e., Branagh's—charm and the imperatives of international diplomacy.) Historically, we know that the product of their sexual union, Henry VI, will bring to a dismal end the harmony of discords that presides uncertainly over the end of *Henry V*.

Henry woos Katharine with real flair, despite their unstated mutual recognition that their courtship is, above all, a matter of state, in which they must play predetermined roles. The individual within Henry V gives way to the public personality, but he never loses his style. He manages always to be true to himself, as a wooer or as a soldier. We see him in disguise, hobnobbing with common soldiers of his camp on the eve of battle, earnestly discussing with them the morality of war. We see him, with endearing human inconsistency, coveting all the glory of victory over the French and then adjuring his soldiers to give credit for that victory to God alone. Even if we are at times less attracted to this successful warrior and politician than to the carefree young man of *1 Henry IV*, we can still honor Henry's choice of responsible maturity and see that it is even compassionately self-denying. A king cannot be like other men, and Henry is willing to accept this price of leadership.

The Chorus presents *Henry V* to us as if it were an epic poem as well as a drama. Henry is an epic hero, defined in terms of mythic allusions and abstractions. He is compared to Mars, the god of war, with Famine, Sword, and Fire leashed at his heels, crouched and ready for employment. He is the "mirror of all Christian kings," and his followers are "English Mercurys" (2.0.6–7) with winged heels. Personified Expectation sits in the air, promising crowns and crownets to Henry and his followers. Henry's fleet of ships in the English Channel becomes "A city on th'inconstant billows dancing" (3.0.15). On the eve of battle, amidst his brothers, friends, and countrymen, Henry warms every heart with "cheerful semblance and sweet majesty" and with his "largest universal like the sun" (4.0.40–3). He forbids vainglorious pride and gives credit for his victory "Quite from himself to God" (5.0.22).

The action the Chorus describes is comparably epic, as it moves from England to France and back again, leaping over time, surveying all levels of society in the English nation, portraying famous military encounters seemingly more suited to epic narration (or to film, as both Laurence Olivier's 1944 film and Kenneth Branagh's more recent film version brilliantly demonstrate) than to the stage. The stage's limitation forms, indeed, a major burden of the Chorus's argument. He apologizes to the spectators for the "flat unraisèd spirits" that have dared to bring forth so vast an object "On this unworthy scaffold," in this "cockpit" or "wooden O" (Prologue). The play confines "mighty men" "In little room," "Mangling by starts the full course of their glory" (Epilogue).

This apology sounds like becoming modesty on Shakespeare's part, in conceding the truth of Ben Jonson's objection that a few hired actors with rusty swords can scarcely do justice to England's great wars of the past. *Henry V* is not a Jonsonian neoclassical play. Paradoxically, however, Shakespeare's acknowledgment of the limited means at his disposal to create mimetic spectacle amounts to a defense of his own theater of the imagination. Through the Chorus's repeated urgings that we use our "imaginary forces" to supply what the actors and the theater necessarily lack, Shakespeare invites us as spectators and partners into his world of art. The play becomes a journey of thought, of making "imaginary puissance." When Shakespeare and his acting company talk of horses, we are to "see them / Printing their proud hoofs i'th' receiving earth" (Prologue). This is not to minimize the importance of the theatrical experience but, indeed, quite the opposite, since we are instructed to liberate ourselves through that theatrical experience and to re-create by means of Shakespeare's script an epic vision. Shakespeare's stage, bare of scenery, relying on good actors and the words they speak, becomes through its very flexibility more versatile in creating that vision than the most ornate and mechanically sophisticated illusionistic theater.

Nothing illustrates better the controversial and timely nature of this play than the history of recent productions, on stage and in film and television. Once viewed as a stalwart defense of England's national greatness, so much so that Winston Churchill could invoke Henry's famous speech before the Battle of Agincourt ("We few, we happy few") in celebration of Britain's "finest hour" of defending England against Nazi Germany, *Henry V* was destined to become, in the years of disillusionment following World War II and especially during the Vietnam era, a vehicle for a satirical and dismaying view of war. Directors have sometimes chosen to have the Boy who accompanies Pistol, Bardolph, and Nym to France brutally killed in open view of the audience by French soldiers. (The script does not specify such action.) A production by the Royal Shakespeare Company in 1964, directed by Peter Hall, showed the influence of Bertolt Brecht and Jan Kott (author of *Shakespeare Our Contemporary*) by staging the Battle of Agincourt in terrifying darkness, with reminiscences of the Guernica atrocity of the Spanish Civil War celebrated by Pablo Picasso's famous painting on the subject. In a number of productions, King Henry has been presented as a brazen devotee of imperialistic war, or a calculating politician for whom even the business of wooing is a matter of wearisome diplomatic necessity (as in Ian Holm's portrayal at Stratford-upon-Avon in 1964).

Alternatively, Henry has sometimes been seen as a self-doubting hero, keenly attuned to the absurdity of what it is that destiny has thrust upon him. Some of these remarkable contrasts can be discerned in the differences between Olivier's World War II film production and that of Branagh in 1989, in the wake of Vietnam and the Falklands episode.

The Life of King Henry the Fifth

[Dramatis Personae

CHORUS

KING HENRY THE FIFTH
HUMPHREY, DUKE OF GLOUCESTER,
JOHN, DUKE OF BEDFORD, } *the King's brothers*
DUKE OF CLARENCE,
DUKE OF EXETER, *the King's uncle*
DUKE OF YORK, *the King's cousin*
EARL OF SALISBURY
EARL OF WESTMORLAND
EARL OF WARWICK
EARL OF HUNTINGDON

ARCHBISHOP OF CANTERBURY
BISHOP OF ELY

RICHARD, EARL OF CAMBRIDGE, } *conspirators*
HENRY, LORD SCROOP OF MASHAM, } *against the King*
SIR THOMAS GREY,

SIR THOMAS ERPINGHAM,
CAPTAIN GOWER,
CAPTAIN FLUELLEN, } *officers in the King's army*
CAPTAIN MACMORRIS,
CAPTAIN JAMY,
JOHN BATES,
ALEXANDER COURT, } *soldiers in the King's army*
MICHAEL WILLIAMS,
An English HERALD

PISTOL,
NYM, } *Falstaff's former tavern-mates*
BARDOLPH,
BOY, *formerly Falstaff's page*
HOSTESS, *formerly Mistress Quickly, now married
    to Pistol*

DUKE OF BURGUNDY

FRENCH KING, *Charles the Sixth*
QUEEN ISABEL *of France*
DAUPHIN, *Lewis*
KATHARINE, *Princess of France*
ALICE, *a lady attending Katharine*
DUKE OF ORLEANS
DUKE OF BERRI
DUKE OF BOURBON
DUKE OF BRITTANY
CONSTABLE OF FRANCE
LORD RAMBURES
LORD GRANDPRÉ
GOVERNOR OF HARFLEUR
MONSIEUR LE FER, *a French soldier*
MONTJOY, *the French herald*
French AMBASSADORS *to England*

Lords, Ladies, Officers, Soldiers, Citizens, Messengers, and Attendants

SCENE: *England, afterwards France*]

Prologue

Enter [Chorus as] Prologue.

CHORUS

Oh, for a Muse of fire, that would ascend 1
The brightest heaven of invention! 2
A kingdom for a stage, princes to act,
And monarchs to behold the swelling scene! 4
Then should the warlike Harry, like himself, 5
Assume the port of Mars; and at his heels, 6
Leashed in like hounds, should famine, sword, and
   fire
Crouch for employment. But pardon, gentles all, 8
The flat unraisèd spirits that hath dared 9
On this unworthy scaffold to bring forth 10
So great an object. Can this cockpit hold 11
The vasty fields of France? Or may we cram 12
Within this wooden O the very casques 13
That did affright the air at Agincourt?
Oh, pardon! Since a crooked figure may 15
Attest in little place a million; 16
And let us, ciphers to this great account, 17
On your imaginary forces work. 18
Suppose within the girdle of these walls
Are now confined two mighty monarchies,
Whose high uprearèd and abutting fronts 21
The perilous narrow ocean parts asunder. 22
Piece out our imperfections with your thoughts:
Into a thousand parts divide one man,
And make imaginary puissance. 25
Think, when we talk of horses, that you see them
Printing their proud hoofs i'th' receiving earth.
For 'tis your thoughts that now must deck our kings, 28
Carry them here and there, jumping o'er times,
Turning th'accomplishment of many years
Into an hourglass—for the which supply, 31
Admit me Chorus to this history,
Who, Prologue-like, your humble patience pray
Gently to hear, kindly to judge, our play.   *Exit.*

Prologue.
1 Muse of fire (Of the four elements—earth, air, fire, and water—fire
is the most sublime and mounting.)   **2 invention** poetic imagination.
4 swelling splendid, magnificent   **5 like himself** i.e., presented in a
fashion worthy of so great a king.   **6 port** bearing   **8 gentles** gentlemen and gentlewomen   **9 flat unraisèd** uninspired, lifeless.   **spirits**
i.e., actors and playwright.   **hath** (Elizabethan usage often pairs a
plural subject with a singular verb.)   **10 scaffold** stage   **11 cockpit**
(Elizabethan theaters were shaped rather like arenas for animal fighting.)   **12 vasty** vast, spacious   **13 O** (Refers to a round theater such
as the Globe; the play may have been performed at the Curtain Theater.)   **casques** helmets   **15 crooked figure** cipher or zero (which,
added to a number, will multiply its value tenfold)   **16 Attest** stand
for   **17 account** (1) sum total (continuing the metaphor of *crooked figure*) (2) story   **18 imaginary forces** forces of imagination   **21 abutting** touching, bordering.   **fronts** (1) frontiers, i.e., the cliffs of Dover
and Calais (2) foreheads   **22 perilous . . . ocean** i.e., English Channel
25 puissance armed might, army.   **28 deck** dress, adorn   **31 the
which supply** which service

1.1

Enter the two bishops, [the Archbishop] of
Canterbury and [the Bishop of] Ely.

CANTERBURY

My lord, I'll tell you. That self bill is urged 1
Which in th'eleventh year of the last king's reign
Was like, and had indeed against us passed, 3
But that the scambling and unquiet time 4
Did push it out of farther question. 5

ELY

But how, my lord, shall we resist it now?

CANTERBURY

It must be thought on. If it pass against us,
We lose the better half of our possession.
For all the temporal lands which men devout 9
By testament have given to the Church
Would they strip from us, being valued thus:
As much as would maintain, to the King's honor,
Full fifteen earls and fifteen hundred knights,
Six thousand and two hundred good esquires, 14
And, to relief of lazars and weak age 15
Of indigent faint souls past corporal toil, 16
A hundred almshouses right well supplied;
And to the coffers of the King beside
A thousand pounds by th' year. Thus runs the bill.

ELY   This would drink deep.

CANTERBURY   'Twould drink the cup and all.

ELY   But what prevention?

CANTERBURY

The King is full of grace and fair regard.

ELY

And a true lover of the holy Church.

CANTERBURY

The courses of his youth promised it not.
The breath no sooner left his father's body
But that his wildness, mortified in him, 27
Seemed to die too; yea, at that very moment
Consideration like an angel came 29
And whipped th'offending Adam out of him, 30
Leaving his body as a paradise
T'envelop and contain celestial spirits.
Never was such a sudden scholar made;
Never came reformation in a flood
With such a heady currance, scouring faults; 35
Nor never Hydra-headed willfulness 36
So soon did lose his seat, and all at once, 37
As in this king.

ELY   We are blessed in the change.

CANTERBURY

Hear him but reason in divinity,

1.1. Location: England. The royal court.
1 self same   **3 like** likely (to have passed)   **4 scambling** unsettled
5 question consideration.   **9 temporal** used for secular purposes
14 esquires members of the gentry, ranking just below knights
15 lazars lepers   **16 corporal** physical   **27 mortified** killed   **29 Consideration** meditation, reflection   **30 offending Adam** original sin
35 heady currance headlong current   **36 Hydra-headed** i.e., many-
headed. (Alludes to the Lernaean Hydra, a monster of many heads
overcome by Hercules.)   **37 his seat** its throne

And, all-admiring, with an inward wish
You would desire the King were made a prelate.
Hear him debate of commonwealth affairs,
You would say it hath been all in all his study.
List his discourse of war, and you shall hear   44
A fearful battle rendered you in music.   45
Turn him to any cause of policy,   46
The Gordian knot of it he will unloose,   47
Familiar as his garter, that, when he speaks,   48
The air, a chartered libertine, is still,   49
And the mute wonder lurketh in men's ears   50
To steal his sweet and honeyed sentences;   51
So that the art and practic part of life   52
Must be the mistress to this theoric.   53
Which is a wonder how His Grace should glean it,
Since his addiction was to courses vain,   55
His companies unlettered, rude, and shallow,   56
His hours filled up with riots, banquets, sports,   57
And never noted in him any study,
Any retirement, any sequestration
From open haunts and popularity.   60

ELY
The strawberry grows underneath the nettle,
And wholesome berries thrive and ripen best
Neighbored by fruit of baser quality;
And so the Prince obscured his contemplation
Under the veil of wildness, which, no doubt,
Grew like the summer grass, fastest by night,
Unseen, yet crescive in his faculty.   67

CANTERBURY
It must be so, for miracles are ceased.   68
And therefore we must needs admit the means   69
How things are perfected.

ELY   But, my good lord,
How now for mitigation of this bill
Urged by the Commons? Doth His Majesty
Incline to it, or no?

CANTERBURY   He seems indifferent,   73
Or rather swaying more upon our part
Than cherishing th'exhibiters against us;   75
For I have made an offer to His Majesty,
Upon our spiritual convocation   77
And in regard of causes now in hand,   78
Which I have opened to His Grace at large,   79

As touching France, to give a greater sum
Than ever at one time the clergy yet
Did to his predecessors part withal.   82

ELY
How did this offer seem received, my lord?

CANTERBURY
With good acceptance of His Majesty,
Save that there was not time enough to hear,
As I perceived His Grace would fain have done,   86
The severals and unhidden passages   87
Of his true titles to some certain dukedoms,
And generally to the crown and seat of France,   89
Derived from Edward, his great-grandfather.   90

ELY
What was th'impediment that broke this off?

CANTERBURY
The French ambassador upon that instant
Craved audience; and the hour I think is come
To give him hearing. Is it four o'clock?

ELY   It is.

CANTERBURY
Then go we in to know his embassy,   96
Which I could with a ready guess declare
Before the Frenchman speak a word of it.

ELY
I'll wait upon you, and I long to hear it.   *Exeunt.*

❧

[1.2]

*Enter the King, Humphrey [Duke of Gloucester],
Bedford, Clarence, Warwick, Westmorland, and
Exeter [with attendants].*

KING
Where is my gracious lord of Canterbury?

EXETER
Not here in presence.

KING   Send for him, good uncle.

WESTMORLAND
Shall we call in th'ambassador, my liege?

KING
Not yet, my cousin. We would be resolved,   4
Before we hear him, of some things of weight
That task our thoughts, concerning us and France.   6

*Enter two bishops, [the Archbishop of Canter-
bury and the Bishop of Ely].*

CANTERBURY
God and his angels guard your sacred throne,
And make you long become it!

KING   Sure we thank you.   8
My learnèd lord, we pray you to proceed,

44 List Listen to   **45 rendered . . . music** i.e., eloquently narrated.
46 cause of policy matter of statecraft   **47 Gordian knot** i.e., great
difficulty resolved forcefully. (It was foretold that whoever should
untie the Gordian knot would rule Asia. Alexander solved the problem by cutting the knot.)   **48 Familiar** as offhandedly or routinely.
that so that   **49 chartered libertine** free spirit, licensed to roam at
will   **50–1 the mute . . . sentences** i.e., wonder makes men silent,
eagerly listening to hear more of his sweetly profitable wise sayings
52–3 So . . . theoric so that experience in practical life must have been
the teacher by which he acquired his theoretical conception.
55 addiction inclination   **56 companies** companions.   **rude** coarse
57 riots reveling.   **sports** amusements   **60 open . . . popularity**
places of public resort and low company.   **67 crescive . . . faculty** naturally inclined to grow.   **68 miracles are ceased** (Protestants generally believed that no miracles occurred after the revelation of Christ.)
69 means i.e., natural causes   **73 indifferent** impartial   **75 exhibiters** those who introduce bills in Parliament   **77 Upon** on behalf of.
convocation formal assembly of the clergy   **78 in hand** under consideration   **79 opened** expounded.   **at large** in full

82 withal with.   **86 fain** gladly   **87 severals** details.   **unhidden passages** clear lines of descent   **89 seat** throne   **90 Edward** Edward III
96 embassy message
1.2. Location: England. The royal court.
4 cousin (A form of address customarily used by royalty in addressing their nobles. In this case, Westmorland is in fact related to the
King by marriage.)   **be resolved** come to a decision   **6 task** engage,
occupy   **8 become** adorn, grace

And justly and religiously unfold
Why the law Salic that they have in France   11
Or should or should not bar us in our claim.   12
And God forbid, my dear and faithful lord,
That you should fashion, wrest, or bow your reading,
Or nicely charge your understanding soul   15
With opening titles miscreate, whose right   16
Suits not in native colors with the truth;   17
For God doth know how many now in health
Shall drop their blood in approbation   19
Of what your reverence shall incite us to.   20
Therefore take heed how you impawn our person,   21
How you awake our sleeping sword of war.
We charge you in the name of God take heed;
For never two such kingdoms did contend
Without much fall of blood, whose guiltless drops
Are every one a woe, a sore complaint   26
'Gainst him whose wrongs gives edge unto the
    swords   27
That makes such waste in brief mortality.   28
Under this conjuration speak, my lord;   29
For we will hear, note, and believe in heart
That what you speak is in your conscience washed
As pure as sin with baptism.

CANTERBURY
Then hear me, gracious sovereign, and you peers,
That owe yourselves, your lives, and services
To this imperial throne. There is no bar
To make against Your Highness' claim to France
But this, which they produce from Pharamond: 37
"In terram Salicam mulieres ne succedant,"
"No woman shall succeed in Salic land."
Which Salic land the French unjustly gloze   40
To be the realm of France, and Pharamond
The founder of this law and female bar.
Yet their own authors faithfully affirm
That the land Salic is in Germany,
Between the floods of Saale and of Elbe;   45
Where, Charles the Great having subdued the Saxons,   46
There left behind and settled certain French,
Who, holding in disdain the German women
For some dishonest manners of their life,   49
Established then this law: to wit, no female
Should be inheritrix in Salic land—
Which Salic, as I said, twixt Elbe and Saale,
Is at this day in Germany called Meissen.
Then doth it well appear the Salic law
Was not devisèd for the realm of France;
Nor did the French possess the Salic land

Until four hundred one-and-twenty years
After defunction of King Pharamond,   58
Idly supposed the founder of this law,   59
Who died within the year of our redemption
Four hundred twenty-six; and Charles the Great
Subdued the Saxons, and did seat the French
Beyond the River Saale, in the year
Eight hundred five. Besides, their writers say,
King Pepin, which deposèd Childeric,   65
Did, as heir general, being descended   66
Of Blithild, which was daughter to King Clothair,
Make claim and title to the crown of France.
Hugh Capet also, who usurped the crown
Of Charles the Duke of Lorraine, sole heir male
Of the true line and stock of Charles the Great,
To find his title with some shows of truth,   72
Though, in pure truth, it was corrupt and naught,
Conveyed himself as th'heir to th' Lady Lingard,   74
Daughter to Charlemagne, who was the son   75
To Lewis the Emperor, and Lewis the son
Of Charles the Great. Also King Lewis the Tenth,   77
Who was sole heir to the usurper Capet,
Could not keep quiet in his conscience,
Wearing the crown of France, till satisfied
That fair Queen Isabel, his grandmother,
Was lineal of the Lady Ermengard,   82
Daughter to Charles the foresaid Duke of Lorraine;
By the which marriage the line of Charles the Great
Was reunited to the crown of France.
So that, as clear as is the summer's sun,
King Pepin's title and Hugh Capet's claim,
King Lewis his satisfaction, all appear   88
To hold in right and title of the female;
So do the kings of France unto this day,
Howbeit they would hold up this Salic law   91
To bar Your Highness claiming from the female,
And rather choose to hide them in a net   93
Than amply to imbar their crooked titles   94
Usurped from you and your progenitors.

KING
May I with right and conscience make this claim?
CANTERBURY
The sin upon my head, dread sovereign!
For in the Book of Numbers is it writ,
When the man dies, let the inheritance   99
Descend unto the daughter. Gracious lord,   100
Stand for your own; unwind your bloody flag!   101
Look back into your mighty ancestors:

11 **Salic** (See explanation at lines 39–45.)   **12 Or** either   **15 nicely charge** subtly and foolishly burden   **16 opening titles miscreate** expounding spurious claims   **17 Suits . . . colors** i.e., does not naturally harmonize   **19 approbation** support, proof   **20 your reverence** (1) an honorific title for an archbishop, Your Reverence (2) your sacred authority   **21 impawn** put under an obligation   **26 woe** grievance.   **sore** severe, grievous   **27 wrongs** wrongdoings   **28 in brief mortality** i.e., among mortal, short-lived men.   **29 conjuration** solemn adjuration   **37 Pharamond** legendary Frankish king   **40 gloze** gloss   **45 floods** rivers   **46 Charles the Great** Charlemagne   **49 dishonest** unchaste

58 defunction death   **59 Idly** foolishly   **65 which** who. (As also in line 67.)   **66 heir general** heir through male or female line   **72 find** provide   **74 Conveyed himself** passed himself off   **75 Charlemagne** (Holinshed's and Hall's error, followed by Shakespeare, for Charles the Bald or Charles II, emperor of the West; Luitgard [Shakespeare's Lingard] became Charlemagne's wife after the death of Fastrada in 794.)   **77 Lewis the Tenth** (Actually, Louis IX; an error copied from Holinshed.)   **82 lineal of** descended from   **88 Lewis his satisfaction** Lewis's conviction   **91 Howbeit** notwithstanding   **93 hide . . . net** i.e., conceal the weakness of their case in a tangle of contradictions   **94 amply to imbar** frankly to bar claim to   **99–100 When . . . daughter** (This paraphrase leaves out an important phrase. Numbers 27:8 reads, "When a man dies leaving no son, his patrimony shall pass to his daughter.")   **101 unwind** unfurl

Go, my dread lord, to your great-grandsire's tomb, 103
From whom you claim! Invoke his warlike spirit,
And your great-uncle's, Edward the Black Prince,
Who on the French ground played a tragedy, 106
Making defeat on the full power of France, 107
Whiles his most mighty father on a hill
Stood smiling to behold his lion's whelp
Forage in blood of French nobility.
O noble English, that could entertain 111
With half their forces the full pride of France
And let another half stand laughing by,
All out of work and cold for action! 114

ELY
Awake remembrance of these valiant dead,
And with your puissant arm renew their feats!
You are their heir; you sit upon their throne;
The blood and courage that renownèd them 118
Runs in your veins; and my thrice-puissant liege
Is in the very May morn of his youth,
Ripe for exploits and mighty enterprises.

EXETER
Your brother kings and monarchs of the earth
Do all expect that you should rouse yourself
As did the former lions of your blood.

WESTMORLAND
They know Your Grace hath cause, and means, and
    might;
So hath Your Highness. Never king of England 126
Had nobles richer and more loyal subjects,
Whose hearts have left their bodies here in England
And lie pavilioned in the fields of France. 129

CANTERBURY
Oh, let their bodies follow, my dear liege,
With blood, and sword, and fire to win your right!
In aid whereof we of the spirituality 132
Will raise Your Highness such a mighty sum
As never did the clergy at one time
Bring in to any of your ancestors.

KING
We must not only arm t'invade the French,
But lay down our proportions to defend 137
Against the Scot, who will make road upon us 138
With all advantages. 139

CANTERBURY
They of those marches, gracious sovereign, 140
Shall be a wall sufficient to defend
Our inland from the pilfering borderers.

KING
We do not mean the coursing snatchers only, 143

But fear the main intendment of the Scot, 144
Who hath been still a giddy neighbor to us. 145
For you shall read that my great-grandfather
Never went with his forces into France
But that the Scot on his unfurnished kingdom 148
Came pouring like the tide into a breach
With ample and brim fullness of his force, 150
Galling the gleanèd land with hot assays, 151
Girding with grievous siege castles and towns;
That England, being empty of defense,
Hath shook and trembled at th'ill neighborhood. 154

CANTERBURY
She hath been then more feared than harmed, my
    liege. 155
For hear her but exampled by herself: 156
When all her chivalry hath been in France 157
And she a mourning widow of her nobles, 158
She hath herself not only well defended
But taken and impounded as a stray 160
The King of Scots, whom she did send to France 161
To fill King Edward's fame with prisoner kings
And make her chronicle as rich with praise
As is the ooze and bottom of the sea
With sunken wrack and sumless treasuries. 165

A LORD
But there's a saying very old and true:
    "If that you will France win,
    Then with Scotland first begin."
For once the eagle England being in prey, 169
To her unguarded nest the weasel Scot
Comes sneaking, and so sucks her princely eggs,
Playing the mouse in absence of the cat,
To 'tame and havoc more than she can eat. 173

EXETER
It follows then the cat must stay at home;
Yet that is but a crushed necessity, 175
Since we have locks to safeguard necessaries
And pretty traps to catch the petty thieves. 177
While that the armèd hand doth fight abroad, 178
Th'advisèd head defends itself at home; 179
For government, though high, and low, and lower, 180
Put into parts, doth keep in one consent, 181

---

103 **great-grandsire's** i.e., Edward III's. His descent through his
mother Isabella from the French King Philip IV is the basis of English
claims to the French kingdom—a claim through female inheritance.
Hence the importance of lines 39–55.   106 **tragedy** i.e., the Battle of
Crécy, 1346, a major defeat for the French   107 **power** army
111 **entertain** engage, encounter   114 **for action** for want of action.
118 **renownèd** brought renown to   126 **So** so indeed   129 **pavilioned**
tented, encamped   132 **spirituality** clergy   137 **lay . . . proportions**
allocate our forces   138 **road** inroad, raid   139 **With all advantages**
whenever a good opportunity presents itself.   140 **They . . . marches**
Our English forces in the territories bordering Scotland   143 **coursing snatchers** hit-and-run Scottish raiders on fast-galloping horses

144 **intendment** plan, hostile intent   145 **still** always.   **giddy** unstable, fickle   148 **unfurnished** unprovided with defense   150 **brim**
absolute, complete   151 **Galling . . . assays** harassing the land stripped
of defenders with hot attacks   154 **th'ill neighborhood** the unneigh-
borliness.   155 **feared** frightened   156 **hear . . . herself** i.e., only listen
how England can be instructed by an example from her own history
157 **chivalry** knights   158 **And she . . . nobles** and she, England, wid-
owlike in being deprived of her nobility while they fight in France
160–1 **impounded . . . Scots** (King David II of Scotland was captured
and imprisoned in 1346 while Edward III was in France.)   161 **to
France** (Historically, David II was imprisoned in London, not sent to
France.)   165 **wrack** wreckage.   **sumless** inestimable   169 **in prey**
absent in search of prey   173 **to 'tame and havoc** to attame (i.e., break
into) and ravage   175 **crushed necessity** distorted conclusion
177 **pretty** ingenious   178 **While that** While   179 **advisèd** wise, prudent   180 **though . . . lower** i.e., though composed of three broad
social ranks (corresponding also to three singing voices from treble to
bass)   181 **Put into parts** separated into different functions (and into
different parts in part-music).   **one consent** mutual harmony

Congreeing in a full and natural close,   182
Like music.
CANTERBURY   Therefore doth heaven divide
The state of man in divers functions,
Setting endeavor in continual motion,
To which is fixèd, as an aim or butt,   186
Obedience; for so work the honeybees,
Creatures that by a rule in nature teach
The act of order to a peopled kingdom,
They have a king, and officers of sorts,   190
Where some, like magistrates, correct at home;   191
Others, like merchants, venture trade abroad;
Others, like soldiers, armèd in their stings,
Make boot upon the summer's velvet buds,   194
Which pillage they with merry march bring home
To the tent royal of their emperor,
Who, busied in his majesty, surveys
The singing masons building roofs of gold,
The civil citizens kneading up the honey,
The poor mechanic porters crowding in   200
Their heavy burdens at his narrow gate,
The sad-eyed justice with his surly hum   202
Delivering o'er to executors pale   203
The lazy yawning drone. I this infer,
That many things, having full reference   205
To one consent, may work contrariously.   206
As many arrows loosèd several ways   207
Come to one mark, as many ways meet in one town,   208
As many fresh streams meet in one salt sea,
As many lines close in the dial's center,   210
So may a thousand actions once afoot
End in one purpose, and be all well borne   212
Without defeat. Therefore to France, my liege!
Divide your happy England into four,
Whereof take you one quarter into France,
And you withal shall make all Gallia shake.   216
If we with thrice such powers left at home
Cannot defend our own doors from the dog,
Let us be worried, and our nation lose   219
The name of hardiness and policy.   220
KING
Call in the messengers sent from the Dauphin.   221
                                        [*Exeunt some.*]
Now are we well resolved, and by God's help
And yours, the noble sinews of our power,
France being ours, we'll bend it to our awe,   224

Or break it all to pieces. Or there we'll sit,   225
Ruling in large and ample empery   226
O'er France and all her almost kingly dukedoms,
Or lay these bones in an unworthy urn,
Tombless, with no remembrance over them.
Either our history shall with full mouth
Speak freely of our acts, or else our grave,
Like Turkish mute, shall have a tongueless mouth,
Not worshiped with a waxen epitaph.   233

                    Enter Ambassadors of France.

Now are we well prepared to know the pleasure
Of our fair cousin Dauphin; for we hear   235
Your greeting is from him, not from the King.
FIRST AMBASSADOR
May't please Your Majesty to give us leave
Freely to render what we have in charge,
Or shall we sparingly show you far off
The Dauphin's meaning and our embassy?
KING
We are no tyrant, but a Christian king,
Unto whose grace our passion is as subject
As is our wretches fettered in our prisons.
Therefore with frank and with uncurbèd plainness
Tell us the Dauphin's mind.
FIRST AMBASSADOR   Thus, then, in few:
Your Highness, lately sending into France,
Did claim some certain dukedoms, in the right
Of your great predecessor, King Edward the Third.
In answer of which claim, the Prince our master
Says that you savor too much of your youth,
And bids you be advised there's naught in France
That can be with a nimble galliard won;   252
You cannot revel into dukedoms there.
He therefore sends you, meeter for your spirit,   254
This tun of treasure, and in lieu of this   255
Desires you let the dukedoms that you claim
Hear no more of you. This the Dauphin speaks.
                    [*A casket is presented;
                    Exeter examines its contents.*]
KING
What treasure, uncle?
EXETER   Tennis balls, my liege.
KING
We are glad the Dauphin is so pleasant with us.   259
His present and your pains we thank you for.
When we have matched our rackets to these balls,   261
We will in France, by God's grace, play a set
Shall strike his father's crown into the hazard.   263

---

182 Congreeing agreeing together.   **close** musical cadence   **186 aim
or butt** target. (All endeavor is to direct itself toward obedience.)
190 They . . . king (A common error of early natural history, derived
from Aristotle. The simile of the bees appears in Virgil, Sir Thomas
Elyot, John Lyly, and others.)   **of sorts** various kinds   **191 correct**
administer justice   **194 Make boot** prey   **200 mechanic** engaged in
manual labor   **202 sad-eyed** grave-eyed   **203 executors pale** executioners, pale in their terrible sternness   **205–6 having . . . consent**
united by a common understanding   **207 As** Just as.   **loosèd several
ways** shot from different directions   **208 ways** roads   **210 close**
come together.   **dial's** sundial's   **212 borne** carried out, sustained
216 Gallia France. (Latin name.)   **219 worried** (1) torn apart or harried, as by dogs (2) made anxious   **220 hardiness and policy** bravery
and statesmanship.   **221 Dauphin** heir apparent to the French
throne.   **224 ours** i.e., ours by right.   **our awe** submission to us

225 Or there Either there   **226 empery** dominion   **233 Not . . . epitaph** i.e., with not even so much as a wax (as opposed to bronze) epitaph; one easily effaced.   **235 cousin** fellow prince (though Henry
does also claim a line of descent in the French royal family)   **252 galliard** a lively dance   **254 meeter** more fitting   **255 tun** cask
259 pleasant jocular. (Also in line 281.)   **261 rackets** (1) tennis rackets
(2) noisy military assaults   **263 crown** (1) royal crown (2) final point
scored, or a coin (worth five shillings in English coinage) staked in
the game.   **hazard** (1) in "royal" tennis, an opening in one of the
high walls enclosing the court; hitting the ball into such a "hazard"
scored a winning point (2) jeopardy.

Tell him he hath made a match with such a wrangler 264
That all the courts of France will be disturbed 265
With chases. And we understand him well, 266
How he comes o'er us with our wilder days, 267
Not measuring what use we made of them.
We never valued this poor seat of England, 269
And therefore, living hence, did give ourself 270
To barbarous license—as 'tis ever common
That men are merriest when they are from home. 272
But tell the Dauphin I will keep my state, 273
Be like a king, and show my sail of greatness 274
When I do rouse me in my throne of France.
For that I have laid by my majesty 276
And plodded like a man for working days, 277
But I will rise there with so full a glory
That I will dazzle all the eyes of France,
Yea, strike the Dauphin blind to look on us.
And tell the pleasant Prince this mock of his
Hath turned his balls to gunstones, and his soul 282
Shall stand sore chargèd for the wasteful vengeance 283
That shall fly with them; for many a thousand
    widows
Shall this his mock mock out of their dear husbands,
Mock mothers from their sons, mock castles down,
And some are yet ungotten and unborn 287
That shall have cause to curse the Dauphin's scorn.
But this lies all within the will of God,
To whom I do appeal, and in whose name
Tell you the Dauphin I am coming on
To venge me as I may, and to put forth
My rightful hand in a well-hallowed cause.
So get you hence in peace; and tell the Dauphin
His jest will savor but of shallow wit
When thousands weep more than did laugh at it.—
Convey them with safe conduct.—Fare you well. 297
                              Exeunt Ambassadors.

EXETER   This was a merry message.
KING
We hope to make the sender blush at it.
Therefore, my lords, omit no happy hour 300
That may give furth'rance to our expedition; 301
For we have now no thought in us but France,
Save those to God, that run before our business. 303
Therefore let our proportions for these wars 304
Be soon collected, and all things thought upon
That may with reasonable swiftness add
More feathers to our wings; for, God before, 307

We'll chide this Dauphin at his father's door.
Therefore let every man now task his thought, 309
That this fair action may on foot be brought.
                              Flourish. Exeunt.

✤

2.0

Enter Chorus.

CHORUS
Now all the youth of England are on fire,
And silken dalliance in the wardrobe lies. 2
Now thrive the armorers, and honor's thought
Reigns solely in the breast of every man.
They sell the pasture now to buy the horse,
Following the mirror of all Christian kings, 6
With wingèd heels, as English Mercurys. 7
For now sits Expectation in the air
And hides a sword from hilts unto the point 9
With crowns imperial, crowns and coronets, 10
Promised to Harry and his followers.
The French, advised by good intelligence 12
Of this most dreadful preparation,
Shake in their fear, and with pale policy 14
Seek to divert the English purposes.
O England! Model to thy inward greatness, 16
Like little body with a mighty heart,
What mightst thou do, that honor would thee do, 18
Were all thy children kind and natural?
But see, thy fault France hath in thee found out,
A nest of hollow bosoms, which he fills
With treacherous crowns; and three corrupted men, 22
One, Richard Earl of Cambridge, and the second,
Henry Lord Scroop of Masham, and the third,
Sir Thomas Grey, knight, of Northumberland,
Have, for the gilt of France—oh, guilt indeed!— 26
Confirmed conspiracy with fearful France, 27
And by their hands this grace of kings must die,
If hell and treason hold their promises,
Ere he take ship for France, and in Southampton.
Linger your patience on, and we'll digest 31
Th'abuse of distance, force a play. 32
The sum is paid, the traitors are agreed,
The King is set from London, and the scene
Is now transported, gentles, to Southampton.
There is the playhouse now, there must you sit,
And thence to France shall we convey you safe,

---

264 **wrangler** adversary, disputant 265 **courts** (1) tennis courts (2)
royal courts 266 **chases** (1) returns of the ball (2) chasing after game
(3) chasing the enemy. 267 **comes o'er us** taunts me. (*Us* is the royal
plural.) 269 **seat** throne 270 **living hence** not frequenting the royal
court 272 **from** away from 273 **keep my state** i.e., fulfill the role of
king 274 **sail** full swell. (Henry says he has not yet revealed his full
majesty in laying claim to France.) 276 **For that** i.e., In anticipation
of that great event 277 **for** suited and ready for 282 **gunstones**
cannonballs 283 **sore chargèd** sorely burdened with responsibility.
wasteful destructive 287 **yet ungotten** not yet conceived 297 **Convey** Escort 300 **omit . . . hour** lose no favorable opportunity
301 **expedition** (1) invasion of France (2) haste 303 **that . . . business**
that properly come first. 304 **proportions** levies of men 307 **God
before** with God leading, helping

309 **task** tax, exercise
2.0 Chorus.
2 **silken . . . lies** i.e., silken apparel and idle pleasure are packed
away. 6 **the mirror . . . kings** i.e., the ideal or model to which all
other kings should compare themselves 7 **Mercurys** (Mercury, classical messenger of the gods, always wears winged heels.) 9 **hides a
sword** i.e., holds up a sword completely impaled with the prizes of
war 10 **With . . . coronets** with the crowns of emperors, kings, and
nobles 12 **intelligence** information gathering 14 **pale policy** fainthearted stratagems 16 **Model to** Outward manifestation of
18 **would** would have 22 **crowns** coins, money (as a bribe) 26 **gilt**
gold 27 **fearful** frightened, cowardly 31–2 **digest . . . play** com-
press long distance (and time) into what can be encompassed in a
play, an *abuse* of the unities of time and place.

And bring you back, charming the narrow seas
To give you gentle pass; for, if we may,   39
We'll not offend one stomach with our play.   40
But, when the King come forth, and not till then,   41
Unto Southampton do we shift our scene.   *Exit.*   42

❦

2.1

Enter Corporal Nym and Lieutenant Bardolph.

BARDOLPH   Well met, Corporal Nym.

NYM   Good morrow, Lieutenant Bardolph.

BARDOLPH   What, are Ancient Pistol and you friends   3
yet?

NYM   For my part, I care not. I say little; but when time
shall serve, there shall be smiles—but that shall be as
it may. I dare not fight, but I will wink and hold out   7
mine iron. It is a simple one, but what though? It will   8
toast cheese, and it will endure cold as another man's   9
sword will—and there's an end.   10

BARDOLPH   I will bestow a breakfast to make you
friends, and we'll be all three sworn brothers to
France. Let 't be so, good Corporal Nym.

NYM   Faith, I will live so long as I may, that's the certain
of it; and when I cannot live any longer, I will do as I
may. That is my rest; that is the rendezvous of it.   16

BARDOLPH   It is certain, Corporal, that he is married to
Nell Quickly, and certainly she did you wrong, for
you were trothplight to her.   19

NYM   I cannot tell. Things must be as they may. Men
may sleep, and they may have their throats about
them at that time, and some say knives have edges. It
must be as it may. Though Patience be a tired mare,   23
yet she will plod. There must be conclusions. Well, I   24
cannot tell.

Enter Pistol and [Hostess] Quickly.

BARDOLPH   Here comes Ancient Pistol and his wife.
Good Corporal, be patient here.

NYM   How now, mine host Pistol?

PISTOL
Base tike, call'st thou me host?   29
Now, by this hand, I swear, I scorn the term!
Nor shall my Nell keep lodgers.

HOSTESS   No, by my troth, not long; for we cannot lodge
and board a dozen or fourteen gentlewomen that live

honestly by the prick of their needles, but it will be   34
thought we keep a bawdy house straight. [*Nym and
Pistol draw.*] Oh, welladay, Lady! If he be not hewn   36
now, we shall see willful adultery and murder com-   37
itted.

BARDOLPH   Good Lieutenant! Good Corporal! Offer   39
nothing here.   40

NYM   Pish!

PISTOL
Pish for thee, Iceland dog!   42
Thou prick-eared cur of Iceland!

HOSTESS   Good Corporal Nym, show thy valor, and   44
put up your sword.   [*They sheathe their swords.*]

NYM   Will you shog off? I would have you solus.   46

PISTOL
Solus, egregious dog? O viper vile!
The solus in thy most mervailous face!   48
The solus in thy teeth, and in thy throat,   49
And in thy hateful lungs, yea, in thy maw, pardie,   50
And, which is worse, within thy nasty mouth!
I do retort the solus in thy bowels;
For I can take, and Pistol's cock is up,   53
And flashing fire will follow.

NYM   I am not Barbason; you cannot conjure me. I have   55
an humor to knock you indifferently well. If you grow   56
foul with me, Pistol, I will scour you with my rapier, as   57
I may, in fair terms. If you would walk off, I would   58
prick your guts a little, in good terms, as I may, and
that's the humor of it.   60

PISTOL
O braggart vile and damnèd furious wight!   61
The grave doth gape, and doting death is near.
Therefore exhale!   [*They draw their swords.*]   63

BARDOLPH   [*drawing his sword*]   Hear me, hear me what
I say. He that strikes the first stroke, I'll run him up to
the hilts, as I am a soldier.

PISTOL
An oath of mickle might, and fury shall abate.   67
[*Pistol and Nym sheathe their swords.*]
[*To Nym*] Give me thy fist, thy forefoot to me give.
Thy spirits are most tall.   69

---

34 prick (With a bawdy double meaning, probably unintended, as also
in *Pistol's cock,* line 53.)   **36 welladay** wellaway, alas.   **Lady** i.e., by
Our Lady. (An oath.)   **hewn** struck down   **37 adultery** (Blunder for
"battery"?)   **39–40 Offer nothing** Attempt no violence   **42 Iceland
dog** a small, shaggy dog often kept as a house pet. (Pistol's humor is
to use extravagant epithets, like this one, tags from current plays, and
scraps of foreign languages.)   **44 valor** (She means "calm," "forbearance.")   **46 shog off** move along.   **solus** alone. (Nym proposes a duel;
see *walk off* in line 58.)   **48 mervailous** marvelous, astonishing
49–50 The solus . . . thy lungs (The most offensive insult possible, as
in *Hamlet's* "the lie i'th' throat / As deep as to the lungs," 2.2.574–5.)
50 maw belly.   **pardie** *par Dieu,* by God   **53 take** catch fire.   **cock is
up** trigger is cocked. (With bawdy pun.)   **55 Barbason** (The name of
a fiend.)   **conjure** exorcise. (Nym mocks Pistol's hyperbolic rant as
though it were a conjuration.)   **55–6 I have an humor** I'm in the mood.
(*Humor* is a favorite word with Nym, as in lines 60, 71, 97, 116, 121, and
126.)   **57 foul** (1) foulmouthed (2) fouled from firing and in need of
scouring   **58 in fair terms** i.e., make no mistake about it. (*In good terms*
at line 59 means the same.)   **walk off** walk aside (to fight)   **60 that's
. . . it** that's my mood.   **61 wight** person.   **63 exhale** draw (sword, much
as the sun draws forth vapors).   **67 mickle** great   **69 tall** valiant.

---

39 pass passage   **40 offend one stomach** (1) offend anyone's taste by
sudden shifts in scene (2) make anyone seasick   **41–2 But . . . scene**
i.e., The scene will be shifted to Southampton after a scene in London.
(These lines sound as though they were added as an afterthought, to
accommodate the inclusion of the comic scene in 2.1.)
2.1. Location: London. A street.
3 Ancient ensign, standard-bearer   **7 wink** shut the eyes   **8 iron**
sword.   **though** of that.   **9 endure cold** i.e., doesn't mind being
drawn from its sheath   **10 there's an end** that's all there is to it.
16 rest last stake (in the gambling game of primero).   **rendezvous**
last resort   **19 trothplight** betrothed   **23–4 Though . . . plod** i.e.,
Patient persistence will ultimately achieve its goal. (Nym hints, as
he does elsewhere, at violence toward Pistol.)   **24 conclusions** an
end to matters. (Nym hints darkly that the end must come soon.)
29 tike cur

NYM   I will cut thy throat, one time or other, in fair
terms. That is the humor of it.

PISTOL   *Couple a gorge!*   72
That is the word. I thee defy again.
O hound of Crete, think'st thou my spouse to get?   74
No, to the spital go,   75
And from the powdering tub of infamy   76
Fetch forth the lazar kite of Cressid's kind,   77
Doll Tearsheet she by name, and her espouse.
I have, and I will hold, the quondam Quickly   79
For the only she; and—*pauca!* There's enough.   80
Go to.

Enter the Boy.

BOY   Mine host Pistol, you must come to my master,
and you, hostess. He is very sick and would to bed.
Good Bardolph, put thy face between his sheets, and   84
do the office of a warming pan. Faith, he's very ill.

BARDOLPH   Away, you rogue!

HOSTESS   By my troth, he'll yield the crow a pudding   87
one of these days. The King has killed his heart. Good   88
husband, come home presently.   *Exit [with Boy].*   89

BARDOLPH   Come, shall I make you two friends? We
must to France together. Why the devil should we
keep knives to cut one another's throats?

PISTOL
Let floods o'erswell, and fiends for food howl on!

NYM   You'll pay me the eight shillings I won of you at
betting?

PISTOL   Base is the slave that pays.

NYM   That now I will have. That's the humor of it.

PISTOL   As manhood shall compound. Push home.   98
[They] draw.

BARDOLPH   *[drawing]*   By this sword, he that makes
the first thrust, I'll kill him! By this sword, I will.

PISTOL
Sword is an oath, and oaths must have their course.   101
[He sheathes his sword.]

BARDOLPH   Corporal Nym, an thou wilt be friends, be   102
friends; an thou wilt not, why, then, be enemies with
me too. Prithee, put up.   104

NYM   I shall have my eight shillings I won of you at
betting?

PISTOL
A noble shalt thou have, and present pay;   107
And liquor likewise will I give to thee,

And friendship shall combine, and brotherhood.
I'll live by Nym, and Nym shall live by me.   110
Is not this just? For I shall sutler be   111
Unto the camp, and profits will accrue.
Give me thy hand.

NYM   I shall have my noble?

PISTOL   In cash most justly paid.

NYM   Well, then, that's the humor of 't.
[Nym and Bardolph sheathe their swords.]

Enter Hostess.

HOSTESS   As ever you come of women, come in quickly 117
to Sir John. Ah, poor heart, he is so shaked of a burning quotidian tertian that it is most lamentable to be- 119
hold. Sweet men, come to him.   *[Exit.]*

NYM   The King hath run bad humors on the knight,   121
that's the even of it.   122

PISTOL   Nym, thou hast spoke the right.
His heart is fracted and corroborate.   124

NYM   The King is a good king, but it must be as it may;
he passes some humors and careers.   126

PISTOL
Let us condole the knight, for, lambkins, we will live.   127
[Exeunt.]

❖

[2.2]

Enter Exeter, Bedford, and Westmorland.

BEDFORD
'Fore God, His Grace is bold to trust these traitors.

EXETER
They shall be apprehended by and by.

WESTMORLAND
How smooth and even they do bear themselves!   3
As if allegiance in their bosoms sat,
Crownèd with faith and constant loyalty.

BEDFORD
The King hath note of all that they intend,
By interception which they dream not of.

EXETER
Nay, but the man that was his bedfellow,   8
Whom he hath dulled and cloyed with gracious
favors—   9

---

72 *Couple a gorge! Couper la gorge!*, "Cut the throat!"   74 **hound of
Crete** (Parallel to *Iceland dog*, line 42.)   75 **spital** hospital   76 **powdering tub** (Originally a tub used for salting beef; here, alluding to a
method of curing venereal disease by sweating.)   77 **lazar . . . kind**
i.e., diseased, leprous whore (a *kite* is a bird of prey) like Cressida,
the fallen woman, who, in Robert Henryson's *Testament of Cresseid*, is
shown as being rejected by Diomede and infected with leprosy
79 **quondam** former   80 **only she** i.e., only woman in the world.
pauca i.e., in brief   84 **face** (Bardolph's face is fiery with drinking.)
87 **he'll** (Refers to the Boy or Falstaff.)   **yield . . . pudding** i.e., be
hanged on the gallows and eaten by carrion birds   88 **his** i.e., Falstaff's   89 **presently** immediately.   98 **As . . . compound** As valor
shall settle the matter (in fight).   101 **Sword is an oath** (Quibbling on
sword as *'s word*, i.e., "God's word.")   102 **an if**   104 **put up** i.e., put
up your sword.   107 **A noble . . . pay** i.e., I'll settle for paying you six
shillings eight pence ready money

110 **Nym** (Quibbles on *nim*, meaning "thief.")   111 **sutler** seller of
liquor and provisions to the soldiers   117 **come of** were born of
119 **quotidian tertian** (A *quotidian* fever was one that came daily; a
tertian fever, one that came on alternate days, though some authorities believed that different fevers might mix and intensify their
effects.)   121 **run bad humors** i.e., vented his displeasure   122 **even**
level truth   124 **fracted** broken.   **corroborate** (Blunder for "broken
to pieces" or "corrupted"? The word means "strengthened, confirmed.")   126 **passes . . . careers** lets pass (i.e., indulges in) some
idiosyncrasies and capers. (A *career* is a full gallop.)   127 **condole**
express our commiseration of or sympathy with.   **lambkins** (A term
of endearment.)
2.2. Location: Southampton, a seaport on England's southern coast.
3 **smooth and even** pleasant and calm   8 **bedfellow** i.e., constant
companion. (Refers to Scroop.)   9 **dulled** dulled the appetite of

That he should, for a foreign purse, so sell
His sovereign's life to death and treachery!

Sound trumpets. Enter the King, Scroop, Cam-
bridge, and Grey, [and attendants].

KING
Now sits the wind fair, and we will aboard.   12
My lord of Cambridge, and my kind lord of Masham,
And you, my gentle knight, give me your thoughts.
Think you not that the pow'rs we bear with us   15
Will cut their passage through the force of France,
Doing the execution and the act
For which we have in head assembled them?   18

SCROOP
No doubt, my liege, if each man do his best.

KING
I doubt not that, since we are well persuaded
We carry not a heart with us from hence
That grows not in a fair consent with ours,   22
Nor leave not one behind that doth not wish
Success and conquest to attend on us.

CAMBRIDGE
Never was monarch better feared and loved
Than is Your Majesty. There's not, I think, a subject
That sits in heart-grief and uneasiness
Under the sweet shade of your government.

GREY
True. Those that were your father's enemies
Have steeped their galls in honey, and do serve you   30
With hearts create of duty and of zeal.   31

KING
We therefore have great cause of thankfulness,
And shall forget the office of our hand   33
Sooner than quittance of desert and merit   34
According to the weight and worthiness.

SCROOP
So service shall with steelèd sinews toil,
And labor shall refresh itself with hope,
To do Your Grace incessant services.

KING
We judge no less.—Uncle of Exeter,
Enlarge the man committed yesterday   40
That railed against our person. We consider
It was excess of wine that set him on,
And on his more advice we pardon him.   43

SCROOP
That's mercy, but too much security.   44
Let him be punished, sovereign, lest example
Breed, by his sufferance, more of such a kind.   46

KING   Oh, let us yet be merciful.

CAMBRIDGE
So may Your Highness, and yet punish too.

GREY
Sir, you show great mercy if you give him life   50
After the taste of much correction.   51

KING
Alas, your too much love and care of me
Are heavy orisons 'gainst this poor wretch!   53
If little faults proceeding on distemper   54
Shall not be winked at, how shall we stretch our eye 55
When capital crimes, chewed, swallowed, and
digested,   56
Appear before us? We'll yet enlarge that man,   57
Though Cambridge, Scroop, and Grey, in their dear
care
And tender preservation of our person,
Would have him punished. And now to our French
causes.
Who are the late commissioners?   61

CAMBRIDGE   I one, my lord.
Your Highness bade me ask for it today.   63

SCROOP   So did you me, my liege.

GREY   And I, my royal sovereign.

KING [*giving them papers*]
Then, Richard Earl of Cambridge, there is yours;
There yours, Lord Scroop of Masham; and sir knight,
Grey of Northumberland, this same is yours.
Read them, and know I know your worthiness.—
My lord of Westmorland, and uncle Exeter,
We will aboard tonight.—Why, how now, gentlemen?
What see you in those papers, that you lose
So much complexion?—Look ye how they change!   73
Their cheeks are paper.—Why, what read you there   74
That have so cowarded and chased your blood
Out of appearance?

CAMBRIDGE   I do confess my fault,   76
And do submit me to Your Highness' mercy.

GREY, SCROOP   To which we all appeal.

KING
The mercy that was quick in us but late   79
By your own counsel is suppressed and killed.
You must not dare, for shame, to talk of mercy,
For your own reasons turn into your bosoms,
As dogs upon their masters, worrying you.—   83
See you, my princes and my noble peers,
These English monsters! My lord of Cambridge here,
You know how apt our love was to accord   86
To furnish him with all appurtenants   87
Belonging to his honor; and this man
Hath for a few light crowns lightly conspired   89
And sworn unto the practices of France   90

---

12 **sits . . . fair** the wind blows from a favorable quarter   **15 pow'rs**
armed forces   **18 in head** as an army   **22 grows . . . consent** does not
act in harmony   **30 galls** i.e., resentment   **31 create** composed
33 office use, function   **34 quittance** requital   **40 Enlarge** set free
43 more advice explaining and apologizing for what happened
44 security overconfidence.   **46 sufferance** being pardoned

50 **give him life** allow him to live   51 **correction** punishment.
53 **heavy orisons** weighty prayers, pleas   54 **proceeding on distem-**
per resulting from unstable condition (caused by excessive drinking)
55 **stretch** open wide, not wink   56 **capital** punishable by death.
chewed . . . digested i.e., premeditated   57 **yet** in spite of what you
say   61 **late** recently appointed (to serve while Henry is in France)
63 **it** i.e., my commission   73 **complexion** color.   74 **paper** i.e., white
as a sheet.   76 **appearance** (1) sight (2) your faces. (Presumably
the traitors kneel at this point.)   79 **quick** alive   83 **worrying you**
tearing at your throat.   86 **accord** consent   87 **appurtenants** appurtenances   89 **light** insignificant.   **lightly** readily, casually
90 **practices** plots

To kill us here in Hampton. To the which
This knight, no less for bounty bound to us   92
Than Cambridge is, hath likewise sworn. But oh,
What shall I say to thee, Lord Scroop, thou cruel,
Ingrateful, savage, and inhuman creature?
Thou that didst bear the key of all my counsels,
That knew'st the very bottom of my soul,
That almost mightst have coined me into gold,
Wouldst thou have practiced on me for thy use?   99
May it be possible that foreign hire
Could out of thee extract one spark of evil
That might annoy my finger? 'Tis so strange   102
That though the truth of it stands off as gross   103
As black and white, my eye will scarcely see it.
Treason and murder ever kept together,
As two yoke-devils sworn to either's purpose,   106
Working so grossly in a natural cause   107
That admiration did not whoop at them.   108
But thou, 'gainst all proportion, didst bring in   109
Wonder to wait on treason and on murder;   110
And whatsoever cunning fiend it was
That wrought upon thee so preposterously   112
Hath got the voice in hell for excellence.   113
All other devils that suggest by treasons   114
Do botch and bungle up damnation   115
With patches, colors, and with forms being fetched   116
From glist'ring semblances of piety;   117
But he that tempered thee bade thee stand up,   118
Gave thee no instance why thou shouldst do treason,   119
Unless to dub thee with the name of traitor.   120
If that same demon that hath gulled thee thus
Should with his lion gait walk the whole world,   122
He might return to vasty Tartar back   123
And tell the legions, "I can never win
A soul so easy as that Englishman's."
Oh, how hast thou with jealousy infected   126
The sweetness of affiance! Show men dutiful?   127
Why, so didst thou. Seem they grave and learnèd?
Why, so didst thou. Come they of noble family?
Why, so didst thou. Seem they religious?
Why, so didst thou. Or are they spare in diet,
Free from gross passion or of mirth or anger,   132
Constant in spirit, not swerving with the blood,   133

Garnished and decked in modest complement,   134
Not working with the eye without the ear,   135
And but in purgèd judgment trusting neither?   136
Such and so finely bolted didst thou seem.   137
And thus thy fall hath left a kind of blot   138
To mark the full-fraught man and best endued   139
With some suspicion. I will weep for thee;   140
For this revolt of thine, methinks, is like
Another fall of man.—Their faults are open.   142
Arrest them to the answer of the law;   143
And God acquit them of their practices!
EXETER   I arrest thee of high treason, by the name of
    Richard Earl of Cambridge.
    I arrest thee of high treason, by the name of Henry Lord
    Scroop of Masham.
    I arrest thee of high treason, by the name of Thomas
    Grey, knight, of Northumberland.
SCROOP
    Our purposes God justly hath discovered,   151
    And I repent my fault more than my death,
    Which I beseech Your Highness to forgive,
    Although my body pay the price of it.
CAMBRIDGE
    For me, the gold of France did not seduce,
    Although I did admit it as a motive   156
    The sooner to effect what I intended.   157
    But God be thankèd for prevention,
    Which I in sufferance heartily will rejoice,   159
    Beseeching God and you to pardon me.
GREY
    Never did faithful subject more rejoice
    At the discovery of most dangerous treason
    Than I do at this hour joy o'er myself,
    Prevented from a damnèd enterprise.
    My fault, but not my body, pardon, sovereign.
KING
    God quit you in his mercy! Hear your sentence.   166
    You have conspired against our royal person,
    Joined with an enemy proclaimed, and from his
        coffers
    Received the golden earnest of our death,   169
    Wherein you would have sold your king to slaughter,
    His princes and his peers to servitude,
    His subjects to oppression and contempt,
    And his whole kingdom into desolation.
    Touching our person seek we no revenge,   174

92 This knight i.e., Grey **99 practiced on** plotted against. **use** profit. (With play on the meaning "interest derived from usury"; Scroop had served as Lord Treasurer.) **102 annoy** injure **103 stands . . . gross** appears as obvious **106 yoke-devils** partners in a diabolical cause **107–8 Working . . . them** working together so manifestly toward a purpose suited to their evil natures that they provoked no outcry of wonder. **109 proportion** fitness of things **110 Wonder** astonishment (that Scroop should be a murderer). **wait on** attend, accompany **112 wrought** worked. **preposterously** unnaturally **113 voice** vote **114–17 All . . . piety** All other devils that tempt make at least some effort to dress damnation up in a plausible semblance of piety **118–20 But . . . traitor** but the devil that tempted you to treason simply ordered you to stand up an unabashed rebel, and gave you no specious justification to do treason other than for the sheer sake of having the name of traitor. **122 lion gait** (The devil, according to 1 Peter 5:8, strides about the world like a roaring lion, "seeking whom he may devour.") **123 vasty** vast. **Tartar** Tartarus, the hell of classical mythology **126 jealousy** suspicion **127 affiance** trust. **Show** Appear **132 or of** either of **133 swerving with the blood** sinning through passion

134 decked . . . complement wearing the look of modesty **135–6 Not . . . neither** trusting neither eye nor ear alone, and not trusting either one except when refined by wisdom and judgment. **138–40 And . . . suspicion** And thus your fall into sin has been such as to cast some suspicion on even those who seem fully and richly endowed with virtuous qualities. **142 fall of man** humankind's original disobedience to God in the Garden of Eden. **open** apparent, obvious. **143 to the answer of** so that they will be answerable to **151 discovered** revealed **156 did . . . motive** i.e., accepted money from France as a means **157 The . . . intended** (Cambridge's real motive, barely hinted at here, was to assist his brother-in-law Edmund Mortimer, fifth Earl of March, to the throne as the standard-bearer of the Yorkist claim against the Lancastrian Henry.) **159 sufferance** my suffering and patient endurance **166 quit** (1) pardon (2) requite, punish **169 golden earnest** advance payment **174 Touching our person** As regards my own personal safety

But we our kingdom's safety must so tender,　175
Whose ruin you have sought, that to her laws
We do deliver you. Get you therefore hence,
Poor miserable wretches, to your death,
The taste whereof God of his mercy give
You patience to endure, and true repentance
Of all your dear offenses!—Bear them hence.　181

> *Exeunt [Cambridge, Scroop, and Grey, guarded].*

Now, lords, for France, the enterprise whereof
Shall be to you, as us, like glorious.　183
We doubt not of a fair and lucky war,
Since God so graciously hath brought to light
This dangerous treason lurking in our way
To hinder our beginnings. We doubt not now
But every rub is smoothèd on our way.　188
Then forth, dear countrymen! Let us deliver
Our puissance into the hand of God,　190
Putting it straight in expedition.　191
Cheerly to sea! The signs of war advance!　192
No king of England, if not king of France!

> *Flourish. [Exeunt.]*

❖

[2.3]

> *Enter Pistol, Nym, Bardolph, Boy, and Hostess.*

HOSTESS　Prithee, honey-sweet husband, let me bring
thee to Staines.　2

PISTOL　No, for my manly heart doth earn. Bardolph, be　3
blithe; Nym, rouse thy vaunting veins; Boy, bristle thy
courage up; for Falstaff he is dead, and we must earn
therefore.

BARDOLPH　Would I were with him, wheresome'er he is,
either in heaven or in hell!

HOSTESS　Nay, sure he's not in hell. He's in Arthur's　9
bosom, if ever man went to Arthur's bosom. 'A made　10
a finer end, and went away an it had been any　11
christom child. 'A parted ev'n just between twelve　12
and one, ev'n at the turning o'th' tide. For after I saw
him fumble with the sheets, and play with flowers,
and smile upon his finger's end, I knew there was but
one way; for his nose was as sharp as a pen, and 'a　16
babbled of green fields. "How now, Sir John?" quoth I.　17
"What, man? Be o' good cheer." So 'a cried out, "God,
God, God!" three or four times. Now I, to comfort him,
bid him 'a should not think of God; I hoped there was

no need to trouble himself with any such thoughts yet.
So 'a bade me lay more clothes on his feet. I put my
hand into the bed and felt them, and they were as cold
as any stone; then I felt to his knees, and so upward　24
and upward, and all was as cold as any stone.　25

NYM　They say he cried out of sack.　26

HOSTESS　Ay, that 'a did.

BARDOLPH　And of women.

HOSTESS　Nay, that 'a did not.

BOY　Yes, that 'a did, and said they were devils incarnate.

HOSTESS　'A could never abide carnation; 'twas a color
he never liked.

BOY　'A said once the devil would have him about
women.

HOSTESS　'A did in some sort, indeed, handle women;　36
but then he was rheumatic, and talked of the Whore of　37
Babylon.

BOY　Do you not remember, 'a saw a flea stick upon
Bardolph's nose, and 'a said it was a black soul
burning in hell?

BARDOLPH　Well, the fuel is gone that maintained that　42
fire. That's all the riches I got in his service.

NYM　Shall we shog? The King will be gone from South-　44
ampton.

PISTOL
Come, let's away.—My love, give me thy lips.

> *[He kisses the Hostess.]*

Look to my chattels and my movables.　47
Let senses rule. The word is "Pitch and pay."　48
Trust none,
For oaths are straws, men's faiths are wafer cakes,　50
And Holdfast is the only dog, my duck.　51
Therefore, *caveto* be thy counselor.　52
Go, clear thy crystals.—Yokefellows in arms,　53
Let us to France, like horseleeches, my boys,
To suck, to suck, the very blood to suck!

BOY　And that's but unwholesome food, they say.

PISTOL　Touch her soft mouth, and march.

BARDOLPH　Farewell, hostess.　　　*[Kissing her.]*

NYM　I cannot kiss, that is the humor of it; but adieu.

PISTOL
Let huswifery appear. Keep close, I thee command.　60

HOSTESS　Farewell! Adieu!　　　*Exeunt [separately].*

---

175 tender regard, hold dear　**181 dear** grievous, dire　**183 like**
alike, equally　**188 But** but that.　**rub** obstacle. (A bowling term.)
190 puissance armed might　**191 straight in expedition** immediately
in action.　**192 The signs . . . advance!** Lift high our banners!
2.3. London. A street.
2 Staines town on the road from London to Southampton.　**3 earn**
grieve. (But in line 5 there may also be a play on the sense of "find
other employment," since Pistol and the others are now on their
own.)　**9–10 Arthur's bosom** (Malapropism for "Abraham's bosom";
see Luke 16:22.)　**10 'A** He　**11 an** as if　**12 christom** (Mistress Quickly
means "new christened." A *chrisom* is a white robe put on a child at
baptism to betoken innocence. Christenings were performed soon
after birth because of the high rate of infant mortality.)　**16–17 'a babbled of green fields** (This line contains Theobald's famous emendation. The Folio has "and a Table of greene fields." Mistress Quickly
seems unaware that Falstaff was reciting the Twenty-third Psalm.)

24–5 upward . . . stone (The Hostess seems unaware of the sexual implications of her speech. *Stone* can mean "testicle.")　**26 of sack** against
sack (a Spanish wine).　**36 handle** discuss. (Though an unintended literal sense is also comically present.)　**37 rheumatic** feverish, or perhaps
an error for "lunatic." (Because "Rome" was pronounced "room,"
rheumatic also prepares for the allusion to the Whore of Babylon, i.e., the
Church of Rome. See also Revelation 17:4–5.)　**42 fuel** i.e., liquor, supplied by Falstaff, that has given Bardolph his red face　**44 shog** be off.
47 chattels . . . movables personal property.　**48 Let . . . pay** i.e., Keep
your eyes and ears open, and let your motto as hostess be "cash down."
50 wafer cakes i.e., easily broken　**51 Holdfast . . . dog** i.e., a large
clamp or *holdfast* is best at holding things tight, like a tenacious dog.
(Compare the proverb, "Brag is a good dog, but Holdfast is better.")
Mistress Quickly is bidden to keep a tight hold on things.　**52 *caveto***
beware. (The correct imperative plural of the Latin is *cavete*.)　**53 clear
thy crystals** wipe your eyes.　**Yokefellows** Companions　**60 Let . . .
close** i.e., Be a thrifty housekeeper and stay at home

2.4

Flourish. Enter the French King, the Dauphin, the Dukes of Berri and Brittany, [the Constable, and others].

FRENCH KING
Thus comes the English with full power upon us,
And more than carefully it us concerns
To answer royally in our defenses.
Therefore the Dukes of Berri and of Brittany,
Of Brabant and of Orleans, shall make forth,   5
And you, Prince Dauphin, with all swift dispatch,
To line and new-repair our towns of war   7
With men of courage and with means defendant;   8
For England his approaches makes as fierce   9
As waters to the sucking of a gulf.   10
It fits us then to be as provident
As fear may teach us, out of late examples   12
Left by the fatal and neglected English   13
Upon our fields.
DAUPHIN   My most redoubted father,   14
It is most meet we arm us 'gainst the foe;   15
For peace itself should not so dull a kingdom,
Though war nor no known quarrel were in question,
But that defenses, musters, preparations,
Should be maintained, assembled, and collected
As were a war in expectation.   20
Therefore, I say 'tis meet we all go forth
To view the sick and feeble parts of France.
And let us do it with no show of fear—
No, with no more than if we heard that England
Were busied with a Whitsun morris dance.   25
For, my good liege, she is so idly kinged,   26
Her scepter so fantastically borne
By a vain, giddy, shallow, humorous youth,   28
That fear attends her not.
CONSTABLE   Oh, peace, Prince Dauphin!
You are too much mistaken in this king.
Question Your Grace the late ambassadors,
With what great state he heard their embassy,   32
How well supplied with noble counselors,
How modest in exception, and withal   34
How terrible in constant resolution,   35
And you shall find his vanities forespent   36
Were but the outside of the Roman Brutus,   37
Covering discretion with a coat of folly,
As gardeners do with ordure hide those roots   39

That shall first spring and be most delicate.
DAUPHIN
Well, 'tis not so, my Lord High Constable;
But though we think it so, it is no matter.
In cases of defense 'tis best to weigh
The enemy more mighty than he seems.
So the proportions of defense are filled,   45
Which of a weak and niggardly projection   46
Doth, like a miser, spoil his coat with scanting
A little cloth.
FRENCH KING   Think we King Harry strong;
And, princes, look you strongly arm to meet him.   49
The kindred of him hath been fleshed upon us;   50
And he is bred out of that bloody strain
That haunted us in our familiar paths.
Witness our too-much-memorable shame
When Crécy battle fatally was struck,   54
And all our princes captived by the hand
Of that black name, Edward, Black Prince of Wales;
Whiles that his mountain sire, on mountain standing, 57
Up in the air, crowned with the golden sun,
Saw his heroical seed and smiled to see him   59
Mangle the work of nature and deface   60
The patterns that by God and by French fathers   61
Had twenty years been made. This is a stem   62
Of that victorious stock; and let us fear
The native mightiness and fate of him.   64

Enter a Messenger.

MESSENGER
Ambassadors from Harry King of England
Do crave admittance to Your Majesty.
FRENCH KING
We'll give them present audience. Go and bring them.
                          [*Exit Messenger.*]
You see this chase is hotly followed, friends.
DAUPHIN
Turn head and stop pursuit; for coward dogs   69
Most spend their mouths when what they seem to
    threaten   70
Runs far before them. Good my sovereign,
Take up the English short, and let them know
Of what a monarchy you are the head.
Self-love, my liege, is not so vile a sin
As self-neglecting.

Enter Exeter [and others].

FRENCH KING   From our brother of England?   75

2.4. Location: France. The royal court.
5 make forth set forth 7 line reinforce 8 defendant defensive
9 England the King of England 10 gulf whirlpool. 12 late recent
13 fatal and neglected fatally underestimated 14 redoubted reverenced 15 meet appropriate 20 As were as if there were 25 Whitsun morris dance folk dance often performed during Whitsuntide, in early summer, by persons in fancy costumes and decked with bells.
26 idly frivolously 28 humorous capricious 32 state dignity
34 exception making objections. withal in addition 35 terrible awesome, terrifying 36 vanities forespent follies used up and now a thing of the past 37 Brutus i.e., the elder Brutus, Lucius Junius Brutus, who pretended to be stupid (brutus) as a ruse to allay the suspicions of the tyrant Tarquin until the time for overthrow was ripe
39 ordure manure, mulch

45 So . . . filled In that way an adequate and full defense is provided
46 Which . . . projection which defense, if designed on too small and miserly a scale 49 look be sure 50 kindred i.e., his great-grandfather Edward III and great-uncle Edward the Black Prince. fleshed initiated in the shedding of blood, with foretaste of further success
54 Crécy French defeat in 1346. struck waged 57 mountain sire i.e., Edward III, born in mountainous Wales, and of sturdy proportions 59–62 Saw . . . made Beheld his heroical son (the Black Prince) and smiled to see him mangle Nature's handiwork in the shape of young Frenchmen, whom, some twenty or so years earlier, God and their French fathers had created and begotten. 64 fate what he is destined to do 69 Turn . . . pursuit Turn and face the pursuing hounds. (Hunting terms.) 70 Most . . . mouths bay the loudest
75 brother fellow monarch

EXETER
From him, and thus he greets Your Majesty:
He wills you, in the name of God Almighty,
That you divest yourself and lay apart   78
The borrowed glories that by gift of heaven,
By law of nature and of nations, 'longs   80
To him and to his heirs, namely, the crown
And all wide-stretchèd honors that pertain   82
By custom and the ordinance of times   83
Unto the crown of France. That you may know
'Tis no sinister nor no awkward claim,   85
Picked from the wormholes of long-vanished days,
Nor from the dust of old oblivion raked,
He sends you this most memorable line,   88
                                        [*giving a paper*]
In every branch truly demonstrative,
Willing you overlook this pedigree.   90
And when you find him evenly derived   91
From his most famed of famous ancestors,
Edward the Third, he bids you then resign
Your crown and kingdom, indirectly held   94
From him the native and true challenger.   95
FRENCH KING   Or else what follows?
EXETER
Bloody constraint; for if you hide the crown   97
Even in your hearts, there will he rake for it.
Therefore in fierce tempest is he coming,
In thunder and in earthquake, like a Jove,
That if requiring fail, he will compel;   101
And bids you, in the bowels of the Lord,   102
Deliver up the crown, and to take mercy
On the poor souls for whom this hungry war
Opens his vasty jaws, and on your head   105
Turning the widows' tears, the orphans' cries,   106
The dead men's blood, the privèd maidens' groans,   107
For husbands, fathers, and betrothèd lovers
That shall be swallowed in this controversy.
This is his claim, his threat'ning, and my message—
Unless the Dauphin be in presence here,
To whom expressly I bring greeting too.
FRENCH KING
For us, we will consider of this further.
Tomorrow shall you bear our full intent
Back to our brother of England.
DAUPHIN   For the Dauphin,
I stand here for him. What to him from England?
EXETER
Scorn and defiance, slight regard, contempt,
And anything that may not misbecome   118
The mighty sender, doth he prize you at.   119

Thus says my king, and if your father's Highness
Do not, in grant of all demands at large,   121
Sweeten the bitter mock you sent His Majesty,
He'll call you to so hot an answer of it   123
That caves and womby vaultages of France   124
Shall chide your trespass and return your mock
In second accent of his ordinance.   126
DAUPHIN
Say if my father render fair return   127
It is against my will, for I desire
Nothing but odds with England. To that end,   129
As matching to his youth and vanity,
I did present him with the Paris balls.   131
EXETER
He'll make your Paris Louvre shake for it,   132
Were it the mistress court of mighty Europe.
And be assured, you'll find a diff'rence,
As we his subjects have in wonder found,
Between the promise of his greener days   136
And these he masters now. Now he weighs time
Even to the utmost grain. That you shall read   138
In your own losses, if he stay in France.
FRENCH KING
Tomorrow shall you know our mind at full.   140
                                        Flourish.
EXETER
Dispatch us with all speed, lest that our king
Come here himself to question our delay;
For he is footed in this land already.
FRENCH KING
You shall be soon dispatched with fair conditions.
A night is but small breath and little pause
To answer matters of this consequence.
                                Flourish. Exeunt.

                                ✤

[3.0]

Enter Chorus.

CHORUS
Thus with imagined wing our swift scene flies   1
In motion of no less celerity
Than that of thought. Suppose that you have seen
The well-appointed King at Dover pier   4
Embark his royalty, and his brave fleet   5
With silken streamers the young Phoebus fanning.   6
Play with your fancies, and in them behold

---

78 **apart** aside   80 **'longs** belongs   82 **wide-stretchèd** stretching far and wide   83 **ordinance of times** decrees of tradition   85 **sinister** illegitimate.   **awkward** oblique   88 **line** pedigree   90 **Willing you overlook** desiring that you look over   91 **evenly** directly   94 **indirectly** wrongfully   95 **native** natural (by birthright).   **challenger** claimant.   97 **constraint** coercion, compulsion   101 **requiring** requesting   102 **in . . . Lord** in the name of God's compassion. (See Philippians 1:8.)   105–6 **and on . . . tears** and who, poor souls, are pouring on your head their widows' tears   107 **privèd** deprived (by loss of loved ones)   118 **misbecome** be inappropriate for   119 **prize** value, appraise

121 **in grant of** in assenting to.   **at large** in full   123 **of it** for it   124 **womby vaultages** hollow recesses   126 **In . . . ordinance** in loud echoing of the sound of King Henry's ordnance (cannon).   127 **fair return** courteous reply   129 **odds** (1) strife (2) betting odds, as in tennis   131 **Paris balls** tennis balls.   132 **Louvre** the French royal palace   136 **greener** younger   138 **grain** grain of sand (in an hourglass).   **That . . . read** i.e., You will see this new seriousness manifested   140.1 *Flourish* (This trumpet call is sounded as the French King arises from his throne, thereby dismissing the embassy, but Exeter boldly insists on speaking further.)
3.0. Chorus.
1 **imagined wing** wings of imagination   4 **well-appointed** well-equipped.   **Dover** (Seemingly an error for Hampton, i.e., Southampton.)   5 **brave** handsome   6 **the . . . fanning** i.e., fluttering in the rising sun.

Upon the hempen tackle shipboys climbing; 8
Hear the shrill whistle, which doth order give
To sounds confused; behold the threaden sails, 10
Borne with th'invisible and creeping wind,
Draw the huge bottoms through the furrowed sea, 12
Breasting the lofty surge. Oh, do but think 13
You stand upon the rivage and behold 14
A city on th'inconstant billows dancing;
For so appears this fleet majestical,
Holding due course to Harfleur. Follow, follow!
Grapple your minds to sternage of this navy, 18
And leave your England as dead midnight still,
Guarded with grandsires, babies, and old women,
Either past or not arrived to pith and puissance; 21
For who is he whose chin is but enriched
With one appearing hair that will not follow
These culled and choice-drawn cavaliers to France? 24
Work, work your thoughts, and therein see a siege;
Behold the ordnance on their carriages,
With fatal mouths gaping on girded Harfleur. 27
Suppose th'ambassador from the French comes back,
Tells Harry that the King doth offer him
Katharine his daughter, and with her, to dowry,
Some petty and unprofitable dukedoms.
The offer likes not; and the nimble gunner 32
With linstock now the devilish cannon touches, 33
Alarum, and chambers go off.
And down goes all before them. Still be kind,
And eke out our performance with your mind.

Exit.

❧

[3.1]

Enter the King, Exeter, Bedford, and Gloucester.
Alarum, [with soldiers carrying] scaling ladders at
Harfleur.

KING
Once more unto the breach, dear friends, once more,
Or close the wall up with our English dead!
In peace there's nothing so becomes a man
As modest stillness and humility.
But when the blast of war blows in our ears,
Then imitate the action of the tiger:
Stiffen the sinews, conjure up the blood,
Disguise fair nature with hard-favored rage. 8
Then lend the eye a terrible aspect: 9
Let it pry through the portage of the head 10
Like the brass cannon; let the brow o'erwhelm it 11

As fearfully as doth a gallèd rock 12
O'erhang and jutty his confounded base, 13
Swilled with the wild and wasteful ocean. 14
Now set the teeth and stretch the nostril wide,
Hold hard the breath, and bend up every spirit
To his full height. On, on, you noblest English,
Whose blood is fet from fathers of war-proof, 18
Fathers that, like so many Alexanders, 19
Have in these parts from morn till even fought, 20
And sheathed their swords for lack of argument. 21
Dishonor not your mothers; now attest
That those whom you called fathers did beget you.
Be copy now to men of grosser blood, 24
And teach them how to war. And you, good yeomen,
Whose limbs were made in England, show us here
The mettle of your pasture. Let us swear 27
That you are worth your breeding, which I doubt not,
For there is none of you so mean and base
That hath not noble luster in your eyes.
I see you stand like greyhounds in the slips, 31
Straining upon the start. The game's afoot. 32
Follow your spirit, and upon this charge 33
Cry, "God for Harry! England and Saint George!" 34
Alarum, and chambers go off. [Exeunt.]

❧

[3.2]

Enter Nym, Bardolph, Pistol, and Boy.

BARDOLPH   On, on, on, on, on! To the breach, to the
breach!
NYM   Pray thee, Corporal, stay. The knocks are too hot,
and for mine own part I have not a case of lives. The 4
humor of it is too hot, that is the very plainsong of it. 5
PISTOL
"The plainsong" is most just; for humors do abound.
Knocks go and come; God's vassals drop and die; 7
[*He sings*] "And sword and shield
    In bloody field
      Doth win immortal fame."
BOY   Would I were in an alehouse in London! I would
give all my fame for a pot of ale and safety.
PISTOL   And I:
[*He sings*] "If wishes would prevail with me, 14
My purpose should not fail with me,
      But thither would I hie." 16

8 hempen rope   **10 threaden** stitched   **12 bottoms** hulls of ships
13 surge swell of the sea.   **14 rivage** shore   **18 Grapple** Attach, hook.
to sternage to the sterns   **21 pith** strength   **24 choice-drawn** carefully
selected   **27 fatal** deadly.   **girded** besieged   **32 likes** pleases
33 linstock staff holding a gunner's match.   **33.1 *Alarum*** Call to arms.
chambers small cannon (fired off backstage, or "within")
3.1. Location: France. Before Harfleur.
0.2 *scaling ladders* (Presumably these are set up against the facade
of the tiring-house, upstage, which is perceived to be the walls of
Harfleur.)   **8 hard-favored** unsightly, ugly   **9 terrible aspect** terrifying appearance   **10 portage** portholes, eyes   **11 o'erwhelm** project
over

12 fearfully frighteningly.   **gallèd** washed away, eroded   **13 O'erhang . . . base** hang and project over its worn-away base   **14 Swilled**
washed.   **wasteful** destructive   **18 fet** fetched, derived.   **of war-
proof** tested in war   **19 Alexanders** (Alexander grieved that there
were no new worlds for him to conquer.)   **20 even** evening
21 argument opposition.   **24 copy** models   **27 mettle . . . pasture**
quality of your breeding. (Literally, *pasture* means "feeding.")
31 slips leashes   **32 The game's afoot** The quarry is out of its lair and
running.   **33 Follow your spirit** i.e., Obey the impulse of your vital
powers   **34 Saint George** patron saint of England.
**3.2. Location: Before Harfleur, as in the previous scene; the action is
essentially continuous.**
4 case set   **5 plainsong** simple melody, simple truth   **7 God's vassals** i.e., mortal men   **14 with me** in my case   **16 hie** hasten.

BOY [sings]
"As duly, but not as truly,
    As bird doth sing on bough."

Enter Fluellen.

FLUELLEN   Up to the breach, you dogs! Avaunt, you cul- 19
lions!   [*Driving them forward.*] 20
PISTOL
Be merciful, great duke, to men of mold.   21
Abate thy rage, abate thy manly rage,
Abate thy rage, great duke!
Good bawcock, bate thy rage! Use lenity, sweet chuck! 24
NYM   These be good humors! Your Honor runs bad   25
humors.   *Exit* [*with all but Boy*]. 26
BOY   As young as I am, I have observed these three
swashers. I am boy to them all three, but all they three, 28
though they would serve me, could not be man to me; 29
for indeed three such antics do not amount to a man. 30
For Bardolph, he is white-livered and red-faced, by the 31
means whereof 'a faces it out but fights not. For Pistol, 32
he hath a killing tongue and a quiet sword, by the
means whereof 'a breaks words and keeps whole 34
weapons. For Nym, he hath heard that men of few
words are the best men, and therefore he scorns to say
his prayers, lest 'a should be thought a coward; but
his few bad words are matched with as few good
deeds, for 'a never broke any man's head but his own,
and that was against a post when he was drunk. They
will steal anything and call it purchase. Bardolph 41
stole a lute case, bore it twelve leagues, and sold it for 42
three halfpence. Nym and Bardolph are sworn brothers in filching, and in Calais they stole a fire shovel. I
knew by that piece of service the men would carry 45
coals. They would have me as familiar with men's 46
pockets as their gloves or their handkerchiefs, which
makes much against my manhood, if I should take 48
from another's pocket to put into mine, for it is plain
pocketing up of wrongs. I must leave them and seek 50
some better service. Their villainy goes against my 51
weak stomach, and therefore I must cast it up.   *Exit.* 52

Enter Gower [*and Fluellen, meeting*].

GOWER   Captain Fluellen, you must come presently to
the mines. The Duke of Gloucester would speak with 54
you.
FLUELLEN   To the mines? Tell you the Duke it is not so
good to come to the mines; for look you, the mines is
not according to the disciplines of the war. The 58
concavities of it is not sufficient. For look you, th'athver- 59
sary, you may discuss unto the Duke, look you, 60
is digt himself four yard under the countermines. By 61
Cheshu, I think 'a will plow up all, if there is not better 62
directions.
GOWER   The Duke of Gloucester, to whom the order of
the siege is given, is altogether directed by an Irishman, a very valiant gentleman, i'faith.
FLUELLEN   It is Captain Macmorris, is it not?
GOWER   I think it be.
FLUELLEN   By Cheshu, he is an ass, as in the world! I
will verify as much in his beard. He has no more di- 70
rections in the true disciplines of the wars, look you,
of the Roman disciplines, than is a puppy dog.

Enter Macmorris and Captain Jamy.

GOWER   Here 'a comes, and the Scots captain, Captain
Jamy, with him.
FLUELLEN   Captain Jamy is a marvelous falorous gen-
tleman, that is certain, and of great expedition and 76
knowledge in th'aunchient wars, upon my particular
knowledge of his directions. By Cheshu, he will
maintain his argument as well as any military man in
the world, in the disciplines of the pristine wars of the 80
Romans.
JAMY   I say gud day, Captain Fluellen.
FLUELLEN   Good e'en to Your Worship, good Captain 83
James.
GOWER   How now, Captain Macmorris, have you quit
the mines? Have the pioneers given o'er? 86
MACMORRIS   By Chrish, la, 'tish ill done! The work ish
give over, the trompet sound the retreat. By my hand
I swear, and my father's soul, the work ish ill done; it
ish give over. I would have blowed up the town, so
Chrish save me, la, in an hour. Oh, 'tish ill done, 'tish
ill done! By my hand, 'tish ill done!
FLUELLEN   Captain Macmorris, I beseech you now, will
you voutsafe me, look you, a few disputations with 94
you, as partly touching or concerning the disciplines
of the war, the Roman wars, in the way of argument,

19 **Avaunt** Begone   **19–20 cullions** rascals. (The original meaning
was "testicles.")   **21 duke** leader, commander. (Latin *dux*.) A flattering title for a captain.   **men of mold** mere mortals.   **24 bawcock**
fine fellow. (French *beau coq*.)   **chuck** (A term of endearment.)
25–6 Your . . . humors i.e., (1) You are behaving very idiosyncratically,
Your Honor (2) Your fury is out of control. (Addressed to Fluellen,
who is doubtless threatening or beating Nym, Bardolph, and Pistol to
make them go forward.)   **28 swashers** swashbucklers.   **29 man**
(1) servant (2) a manly, brave person   **30 antics** buffoons, zanies
31 For As for. (Also in lines 32 and 35.)   **white-livered** i.e., cowardly.
(In extreme fear, the blood was thought to sink below the liver, leaving it bloodless.)   **32 'a faces it out** he has the martial-looking face
for it, puts on a brave front   **34 breaks words** (1) misuses language
and fails to keep his word (2) uses words as weapons   **41 purchase**
(1) something paid for (2) thieves' cant for stolen goods.   **42 leagues**
(about three miles each)   **45–6 carry coals** (1) do dirty, hard work,
such as hauling coal (2) put up with insults.   **48 makes** goes
50 pocketing . . . wrongs (1) putting up with insults (2) receiving
stolen goods.   **51–2 goes . . . stomach** (1) goes against my inclination
(2) makes me sick   **52 cast it up** (1) cast it aside (2) vomit it.   **s.d.**
Exit (A scene break may occur here, though it is not marked as such
in most editions. Possibly Fluellen did not leave the stage at line 26.)

54 mines tunnels dug under the walls of the beseiged city to plant
explosives.   **58 disciplines of the war** science of warfare (about
which there were many books from Greek and Roman times down to
the Renaissance; Fluellen's humor involves an obsession with this
study and a preference for traditional methods).   **59 concavities** i.e.,
depth   **59–60 athversary** (Fluellen's pronunciation of *adversary*.)
60 discuss explain   **61 is digt . . . countermines** has dug himself
countermines four yards beneath our mines.   **62 Cheshu** Jesu, Jesus.
plow blow. (In Fluellen's Welsh dialect, *p* is regularly substituted for *b*
and *f* for *v*.)   **70 in his beard** i.e., to his face.   **76 expedition** readiness of argument, quickness of wit   **80 pristine** ancient   **83 Good
e'en** Good afternoon or evening   **86 pioneers** sappers, diggers
94 voutsafe vouchsafe, permit

look you, and friendly communication—partly to satisfy my opinion, and partly for the satisfaction, look
you, of my mind, as touching the direction of the military discipline, that is the point.

JAMY   It sall be vary gud, gud feith, gud captens bath, 101
and I sall quite you with gud leve, as I may pick 102
occasion. That sall I, marry.   103

MACMORRIS   It is no time to discourse, so Chrish save
me! The day is hot, and the weather, and the wars,
and the King, and the dukes. It is no time to discourse.
The town is beseeched, and the trumpet call us to the 107
breach, and we talk, and, be Chrish, do nothing. 'Tis 108
shame for us all. So God sa' me, 'tis shame to stand
still, it is shame, by my hand! And there is throats to
be cut, and works to be done, and there ish nothing
done, so Chrish sa' me, la!   112

JAMY   By the Mess, ere theise eyes of mine take 113
themselves to slomber, ay'll de gud service, or I'll lig i'th' 114
grund for it, ay, or go to death! And I'll pay't as
valorously as I may, that sall I suerly do, that is the
breff and the long. Marry, I wad full fain heard some 117
question 'tween you twae.   118

FLUELLEN   Captain Macmorris, I think, look you, under
your correction, there is not many of your nation—

MACMORRIS   Of my nation? What ish my nation? Ish a 121
villain, and a bastard, and a knave, and a rascal? What 122
ish my nation? Who talks of my nation?

FLUELLEN   Look you, if you take the matter otherwise
than is meant, Captain Macmorris, peradventure I
shall think you do not use me with that affability as in
discretion you ought to use me, look you, being as
good a man as yourself, both in the disciplines of war
and in the derivation of my birth, and in other particularities.

MACMORRIS   I do not know you so good a man as myself. So Chrish save me, I will cut off your head!

GOWER   Gentlemen both, you will mistake each other. 133

JAMY   Ah, that's a foul fault!   *A parley [is sounded].* 134

GOWER   The town sounds a parley.

FLUELLEN   Captain Macmorris, when there is more better opportunity to be required, look you, I will be so 137
bold as to tell you I know the disciplines of war; and
there is an end.   *Exit [with others].*

❖

[3.3]

*[Enter the Governor and some citizens on the
walls.] Enter the King [Henry] and all his train
before the gates.*

KING
How yet resolves the Governor of the town?
This is the latest parle we will admit.   2
Therefore to our best mercy give yourselves,
Or, like to men proud of destruction,   4
Defy us to our worst; for as I am a soldier,
A name that in my thoughts becomes me best,
If I begin the batt'ry once again   7
I will not leave the half-achievèd Harfleur
Till in her ashes she lie burièd.
The gates of mercy shall be all shut up,
And the fleshed soldier, rough and hard of heart,   11
In liberty of bloody hand shall range   12
With conscience wide as hell, mowing like grass   13
Your fresh fair virgins and your flow'ring infants.
What is it then to me if impious War,
Arrayed in flames like to the prince of fiends,
Do with his smirched complexion all fell feats   17
Enlinked to waste and desolation?
What is't to me, when you yourselves are cause,
If your pure maidens fall into the hand
Of hot and forcing violation?
What rein can hold licentious Wickedness
When down the hill he holds his fierce career?   23
We may as bootless spend our vain command   24
Upon th'enragèd soldiers in their spoil
As send precepts to the leviathan   26
To come ashore. Therefore, you men of Harfleur,
Take pity of your town and of your people
Whiles yet my soldiers are in my command,
Whiles yet the cool and temperate wind of grace   30
O'erblows the filthy and contagious clouds   31
Of heady murder, spoil, and villainy.   32
If not, why, in a moment look to see   33
The blind and bloody soldier with foul hand   34
Defile the locks of your shrill-shrieking daughters;
Your fathers taken by the silver beards,
And their most reverend heads dashed to the walls;
Your naked infants spitted upon pikes,

**3.3. Location: Before the gates of Harfleur, as in the previous scene.
The action is essentially continuous, as it is usually in battle
sequences; possibly some of the captains in 3.2 do not need to exit
here. The gates are represented by the tiring-house facade. Those
who appear *on the walls* are seen in the gallery backstage.**
2 latest parle last parley   **4 like . . . destruction** i.e., like men elated
at the prospect of slaughter and glorying in destruction   **7 batt'ry**
attack   **11 fleshed** made fierce with the taste of blood   **12–13 In liberty . . . as hell** will range with free license to shed blood and with a
conscience wide and loose enough to sanction anything that hell itself
would justify   **17 smirched** blackened, covered with grime.   **fell**
savage   **23 career** gallop.   **24 bootless** fruitlessly   **26 precepts** written summons.   **leviathan** whale   **30 grace** mercy   **31 O'er blows**
blows away. (Contagion was thought to reside in clouds and mists.)
32 heady violent; headstrong   **33 look** expect   **34 blind** i.e., blinded
with lust and rage

101 bath both   **102 quite** requite, answer.   **with gud leve** with good
leave, with your kind permission   **103 marry** indeed. (Originally, "by
the Virgin Mary.")   **107 beseeched** besieged   **108 be** by   **112 Chrish
sa' me** Christ save me   **113 Mess** Mass   **114 ay'll de** I'll do.   **lig** lie
117 breff brief.   **wad full fain heard** would very willingly have
heard   **118 question** discussion   **121 What ish** i.e., What about
121–2 Ish a villain i.e., Is my nation a villain (etc.)?, or Macmorris
may be making a declarative statement, saying that anyone who says
anything against my nation is a villain, etc.   **133 will mistake** (Two
possible meanings: [1] insist on misunderstanding [2] are going to
misunderstand.)   **134 s.d. *parley*** trumpet summons to a negotiation
137 required found

Whiles the mad mothers with their howls confused
Do break the clouds, as did the wives of Jewry 40
At Herod's bloody-hunting slaughtermen. 41
What say you? Will you yield, and this avoid,
Or, guilty in defense, be thus destroyed? 43

GOVERNOR
Our expectation hath this day an end.
The Dauphin, whom of succors we entreated, 45
Returns us that his powers are yet not ready 46
To raise so great a siege. Therefore, great King,
We yield our town and lives to thy soft mercy.
Enter our gates, dispose of us and ours,
For we no longer are defensible.

KING
Open your gates.   [*Exit Governor.*]
                    Come, uncle Exeter,
Go you and enter Harfleur; there remain,
And fortify it strongly 'gainst the French.
Use mercy to them all. For us, dear uncle, 54
The winter coming on and sickness growing
Upon our soldiers, we will retire to Calais.
Tonight in Harfleur will we be your guest;
Tomorrow for the march are we addressed. 58

                    Flourish, and enter the town.

❖

[3.4]

Enter Katharine and [Alice,] an old gentlewoman.

KATHARINE   Alice, tu as été en Angleterre, et tu bien 1
parles le langage.
ALICE   Un peu, madame.
KATHARINE   Je te prie, m'enseignez; il faut que
j'apprenne à parler. Comment appelez-vous la main
en anglais?
ALICE   La main? Elle est appelée de hand.
KATHARINE   De hand. Et les doigts?
ALICE   Les doigts? Ma foi, j'oublie les doigts; mais je me
souviendrai. Les doigts? Je pense qu'ils sont appelés 10
de fingres; oui, de fingres.
KATHARINE   La main, de hand; les doigts, de fingres. Je
pense que je suis le bon écolier; j'ai gagné deux
mots d'anglais vîtement. Comment appelez-vous les
ongles?

ALICE   Les ongles? Nous les appelons de nailes.
KATHARINE   De nailes. Écoutez, dites-moi si je parle
bien: de hand, de fingres, et de nailes.
ALICE   C'est bien dit, madame; il est fort bon anglais.
KATHARINE   Dites-moi l'anglais pour le bras. 20
ALICE   De arm, madame.
KATHARINE   Et le coude?
ALICE   D' elbow.
KATHARINE   D' elbow. Je m'en fais la répétition de tous
les mots que vous m'avez appris dès à présent.
ALICE   Il est trop difficile, madame, comme je pense.
KATHARINE   Excusez-moi, Alice; écoutez: d' hand, de
fingre, de nailes, d' arma, de bilbow.
ALICE   D' elbow, madame.
KATHARINE   Oh, Seigneur Dieu, je m'en oublie! D' elbow. 30
Comment appelez-vous le col?
ALICE   De nick, madame.
KATHARINE   De nick. Et le menton?
ALICE   De chin.
KATHARINE   De sin. Le col, de nick; le menton, de sin.
ALICE   Oui. Sauf votre honneur, en vérité, vous pro-
noncez les mots aussi droit que les natifs d'Angleterre.
KATHARINE   Je ne doute point d'apprendre, par la grâce
de Dieu, et en peu de temps.
ALICE   N'avez-vous pas déjà oublié ce que je vous ai 40
enseigné?
KATHARINE   Non, je réciterai à vous promptement: d'
hand, de fingre, de mailes—
ALICE   De nailes, madame.
KATHARINE   De nailes, de arm, de ilbow.
ALICE   Sauf votre honneur, d' elbow.
KATHARINE   Ainsi dis-je; d' elbow, de nick, et de sin.
Comment appelez-vous le pied et la robe?

40 **Jewry** Judaea   41 **Herod's . . . slaughtermen** (For the account of
Herod's slaughter of the innocent children in his attempt to murder
the infant Jesus, see Matthew 2:16–18.)   43 **in defense** i.e., by not surrendering   45 **of succors** for help   46 **Returns** replies to   54 **For** As
for   58 **addressed** prepared.
3.4. Location: The French court at Rouen.

Translation:
KATHARINE   Alice, you have been in England and speak the language
well.
ALICE   A little, my lady.
KATHARINE   I pray you teach me; I have to learn to speak it. What do
you call *la main* in English?
ALICE   *La main?* It is called de hand.
KATHARINE   De hand. And *les doigts?*
ALICE   *Les doigts?* Dear me, I forget *les doigts;* but I shall remember. I
think that they are called de fingres; yes, de fingres.
KATHARINE   *La main,* de hand; *les doigts,* de fingres. I think that I am a
clever scholar; I have learned two English words in no time. What
do you call *les ongles?*

ALICE   *Les ongles?* We call them de nailes.
KATHARINE   De nailes. Listen; tell me whether or not I speak correctly:
de hand, de fingres, and de nailes.
ALICE   That is correct, my lady; it is very good English.
KATHARINE   Tell me the English for *le bras.*
ALICE   De arm, my lady.
KATHARINE   And *le coude?*
ALICE   D' elbow.
KATHARINE   D' elbow. I am going to repeat all the words you have
taught me so far.
ALICE   It is too hard, my lady, I fear.
KATHARINE   Pardon me, Alice; listen: d' hand, de fingre, de nailes, d'
arma, de bilbow.
ALICE   D' elbow, my lady.
KATHARINE   Oh, Lord, I can't remember! D' elbow. What do you call *le
col?*
ALICE   De nick, my lady.
KATHARINE   De nick. And *le menton?*
ALICE   De chin.
KATHARINE   De sin. *Le col,* de nick; *le menton,* de sin.
ALICE   Yes. If I may say so, really you pronounce the words just as cor-
rectly as native Englishmen.
KATHARINE   I have no doubt that I shall learn, with God's help, in a
very short time.
ALICE   Haven't you already forgotten what I have taught you?
KATHARINE   No. I shall recite to you at once: d' hand, de fingre, de
mailes—
ALICE   De nailes, my lady.
KATHARINE   De nailes, de arm, de ilbow.
ALICE   By your leave, d' elbow.
KATHARINE   That's what I said; d' elbow, de nick, and de sin. What do
you call *le pied* and *la robe?*

ALICE   Le foot, madame, et le count.

KATHARINE   Le foot et le count! Oh, Seigneur Dieu! Ils   50
sont les mots de son mauvais, corruptible, gros, et
impudique, et non pour les dames d'honneur d'user.
Je ne voudrais prononcer ces mots devant les seig-
neurs de France pour tout le monde. Foh! Le foot et le
count! Néanmoins, je réciterai une autre fois ma leçon
ensemble: d' hand, de fingre, de nailes, de arm,
d' elbow, de nick, de sin, de foot, le count.

ALICE   Excellent, madame!

KATHARINE   C'est assez pour une fois. Allons-nous à
dîner.   Exit [with Alice].

❦

[3.5]

*Enter the King of France, the Dauphin, [the Duke
of Brittany,] the Constable of France, and others.*

FRENCH KING
'Tis certain he hath passed the River Somme.

CONSTABLE
And if he be not fought withal, my lord,   2
Let us not live in France; let us quit all
And give our vineyards to a barbarous people.

DAUPHIN
O Dieu vivant! Shall a few sprays of us,   5
The emptying of our fathers' luxury,   6
Our scions, put in wild and savage stock,   7
Spurt up so suddenly into the clouds   8
And overlook their grafters?   9

BRITTANY
Normans, but bastard Normans, Norman bastards!
Mort de ma vie, if they march along   11
Unfought withal, but I will sell my dukedom   12
To buy a slobbery and a dirty farm   13
In that nook-shotten isle of Albion.   14

CONSTABLE
Dieu de batailles, where have they this mettle?   15
Is not their climate foggy, raw, and dull,

On whom as in despite the sun looks pale,   17
Killing their fruit with frowns? Can sodden water,   18
A drench for sur-reined jades, their barley broth,   19
Decoct their cold blood to such valiant heat?   20
And shall our quick blood, spirited with wine,   21
Seem frosty? Oh, for honor of our land,
Let us not hang like roping icicles   23
Upon our houses' thatch, whiles a more frosty people
Sweat drops of gallant youth in our rich fields!
"Poor" may we call them in their native lords.   26

DAUPHIN   By faith and honor,
Our madams mock at us and plainly say   28
Our mettle is bred out, and they will give   29
Their bodies to the lust of English youth
To new-store France with bastard warriors.   31

BRITTANY
They bid us to the English dancing schools   32
And teach lavoltas high and swift corantos,   33
Saying our grace is only in our heels   34
And that we are most lofty runaways.   35

FRENCH KING
Where is Montjoy the herald? Speed him hence.   36
Let him greet England with our sharp defiance.
Up, princes, and with spirit of honor edged   38
More sharper than your swords, hie to the field!   39
Charles Delabreth, High Constable of France,
You Dukes of Orleans, Bourbon, and of Berri,
Alençon, Brabant, Bar, and Burgundy,
Jaques Chatillion, Rambures, Vaudemont,
Beaumont, Grandpré, Roussi, and Faulconbridge,
Foix, Lestrelles, Boucicault, and Charolais,
High dukes, great princes, barons, lords, and knights,
For your great seats now quit you of great shames.   47
Bar Harry England, that sweeps through our land   48
With pennons painted in the blood of Harfleur.   49
Rush on his host, as doth the melted snow   50
Upon the valleys, whose low vassal seat
The Alps doth spit and void his rheum upon.   52
Go down upon him—you have power enough—
And in a captive chariot into Rouen
Bring him our prisoner.

CONSTABLE   This becomes the great.   55
Sorry am I his numbers are so few,
His soldiers sick and famished in their march,
For I am sure, when he shall see our army,

ALICE   Le foot, my lady, and le count. [As she pronounces them, *foot*
sounds to Katharine like *foutre*, fornicate, and *count* (for *gown*) sounds
like French for the female sexual organ, *cunt* in English.]

KATHARINE   Le foot and le count! Oh, Lord! Those are naughty words,
wicked, coarse, and immodest, and are not fit to be used by ladies. I
wouldn't say those words before French gentlemen for the whole
world. Bah! Le foot and le count! Nevertheless, I shall recite my
whole lesson once more: d' hand, de fingre, de nailes, de arm, d'
elbow, de nick, de sin, de foot, le count.

ALICE   Excellent, my lady.

KATHARINE   That's enough for one time. Let's go to dinner.

3.5. Location: The French court at Rouen.
2 withal with. (As also in line 12).   **5–9** *O . . . grafters?* O living God,
shall a few sprigs derived from native French stock, from the pouring
out of our forefathers' lust (during and after the Norman Conquest)
being grafted onto the wild and savage stock (of English Saxons),
sprout up suddenly to lofty heights and domineer over the plants or
trees from which the grafts were taken, i.e., us native French?
11 *Mort de ma vie* Death to my life   **12 but I will** i.e., if I do not
13 slobbery wet and slimy   **14 nook-shotten** full of nooks and
angles. (Refers to the coastline.)   **isle of Albion** island of England,
Scotland, and Wales.   **15** *Dieu de batailles* God of battles.   **where**
from where

17 as in despite as if despising them, the English   **18 sodden water**
boiled water   **19 A drench . . . jades** i.e., stuff no better than what
they give their overridden horses to drink.   **barley broth** ale
20 Decoct warm up   **21 quick** lively   **23 roping** hanging down
like a rope   **26 "Poor" . . . lords** i.e., Our fields, though rich in themselves, may be called poor in that they are owned by a spiritless
aristocracy.   **28 madams** wives, ladies   **29 bred out** exhausted by
breeding   **31 new-store** newly supply   **32 bid us** bid us go
33 lavoltas, corantos fashionable dances   **34 in our heels** (1) in dancing gracefully (2) in running away   **35 lofty** (1) noble (2) leaping.
runaways cowards. (But referring also to the movements of the
dances.)   **36 Montjoy** title of the chief herald of France   **38 edged**
given a sharp edge   **39 hie** hasten   **47 For** in the name of, in defense
of.   **seats** positions.   **quit you** rid, free yourselves   **48 Bar** Stop; bar
the claim of   **49 pennons** banners, streamers   **50 host** army
52 rheum watery discharge, i.e., streams or avalanches   **55 becomes
the great** befits greatness.

He'll drop his heart into the sink of fear 59
And for achievement offer us his ransom. 60

FRENCH KING
Therefore, Lord Constable, haste on Montjoy,
And let him say to England that we send
To know what willing ransom he will give.
Prince Dauphin, you shall stay with us in Rouen.

DAUPHIN
Not so, I do beseech Your Majesty.

FRENCH KING
Be patient, for you shall remain with us.
Now forth, Lord Constable and princes all,
And quickly bring us word of England's fall. *Exeunt.*

❖

[3.6]

*Enter Captains, English and Welsh: Gower and
Fluellen, [meeting].*

GOWER   How now, Captain Fluellen? Come you from
the bridge? 2
FLUELLEN   I assure you, there is very excellent services 3
committed at the bridge.
GOWER   Is the Duke of Exeter safe?
FLUELLEN   The Duke of Exeter is as magnanimous as
Agamemnon, and a man that I love and honor with 7
my soul, and my heart, and my duty, and my live, 8
and my living, and my uttermost power. He is not—
God be praised and blessed!—any hurt in the world,
but keeps the bridge most valiantly, with excellent discipline. There is an aunchient lieutenant there at the 12
pridge, I think in my very conscience he is as valiant
a man as Mark Antony, and he is a man of no esti- 14
mation in the world, but I did see him do as gallant 15
service.
GOWER   What do you call him?
FLUELLEN   He is called Aunchient Pistol.
GOWER   I know him not.

Enter Pistol.

FLUELLEN   Here is the man.
PISTOL
Captain, I thee beseech to do me favors.
The Duke of Exeter doth love thee well.
FLUELLEN   Ay, I praise God, and I have merited some
love at his hands.
PISTOL
Bardolph, a soldier, firm and sound of heart,
And of buxom valor, hath, by cruel fate 26
And giddy Fortune's furious fickle wheel,

That goddess blind
That stands upon the rolling restless stone—
FLUELLEN   By your patience, Aunchient Pistol. Fortune
is painted blind, with a muffler afore her eyes, to sig- 31
nify to you that Fortune is blind; and she is painted
also with a wheel, to signify to you, which is the moral
of it, that she is turning, and inconstant, and mutabil-
ity, and variation; and her foot, look you, is fixed upon
a spherical stone, which rolls, and rolls, and rolls. In
good truth, the poet is make a most excellent descrip- 37
tion of it. Fortune is an excellent moral. 38
PISTOL
Fortune is Bardolph's foe, and frowns on him; 39
For he hath stol'n a pax, 40
And hangèd must 'a be—a damnèd death!
Let gallows gape for dog; let man go free,
And let not hemp his windpipe suffocate.
But Exeter hath given the doom of death 44
For pax of little price.
Therefore, go speak—the Duke will hear thy voice—
And let not Bardolph's vital thread be cut
With edge of penny cord and vile reproach. 48
Speak, Captain, for his life, and I will thee requite. 49
FLUELLEN   Aunchient Pistol, I do partly understand
your meaning.
PISTOL   Why then rejoice therefor.
FLUELLEN   Certainly, Aunchient, it is not a thing to re-
joice at. For if, look you, he were my brother, I would
desire the Duke to use his good pleasure and put him
to execution; for discipline ought to be used.
PISTOL
Die and be damned! And *figo* for thy friendship! 57
FLUELLEN   It is well.
PISTOL   The fig of Spain! *Exit.*
FLUELLEN   Very good.
GOWER   Why, this is an arrant counterfeit rascal! I
remember him now; a bawd, a cutpurse.
FLUELLEN   I'll assure you, 'a uttered as prave words at
the pridge as you shall see in a summer's day. But it is
very well. What he has spoke to me, that is well, I
warrant you, when time is serve.
GOWER   Why, 'tis a gull, a fool, a rogue, that now and 67
then goes to the wars, to grace himself at his return
into London under the form of a soldier. And such
fellows are perfect in the great commanders' names, 70
and they will learn you by rote where services were 71
done—at such and such a sconce, at such a breach, at 72
such a convoy; who came off bravely, who was shot,
who disgraced, what terms the enemy stood on—and 74
this they con perfectly in the phrase of war, which 75

---

59 **sink** pit   60 **for achievement** instead of achieving victory, as his
sole accomplishment
3.6 Location: The English camp in northern France.
2 **bridge** (According to Holinshed, the French were beaten in their
attempt to break down the bridge over the Ternoise. The audience is
not told this, however, and might assume the river to be the Somme,
mentioned in 3.5.1.)   3 **services** exploits. (As also in line 71.)
7 **Agamemnon** leader of the Greeks against Troy   8 **live** life
12 **aunchient lieutenant** (Pistol is elsewhere given the rank of
ancient, or ensign.)   14–15 **estimation** fame   26 **buxom** (1) vigorous
(2) compliant, meek

31 **muffler** blindfold   37 **is make** has made   38 **moral** emblem.
39 **Fortune . . . foe** (Probably alludes to the ballad "Fortune, my foe!")
40 **pax** metal disk with a crucifix stamped on it, kissed by the priest
and communicants during Mass. (But Holinshed describes an incident in which the object stolen is a *pyx*, the vessel containing the consecrated host.)   44 **doom** judgment, sentence   48 **cord** rope
49 **requite** repay.   57 *figo* gesture of contempt made by thrusting the
thumb between the index and middle fingers   67 **gull** simpleton
70 **are perfect in** i.e., can recite perfectly   71 **learn** teach, recite
72 **sconce** fortification   74 **terms . . . stood on** conditions the enemy
insisted on   75 **con** learn by heart

they trick up with new-tuned oaths. And what a 76
beard of the General's cut and a horrid suit of the 77
camp will do among foaming bottles and ale-washed 78
wits is wonderful to be thought on. But you must
learn to know such slanders of the age, or else you 80
may be marvelously mistook. 81

FLUELLEN I tell you what, Captain Gower, I do perceive
he is not the man that he would gladly make show
to the world he is. If I find a hole in his coat, I will tell 84
him my mind. [*Drum heard.*] Hark you, the King is
coming, and I must speak with him from the pridge. 86

*Drum and colors. Enter the King and his poor
soldiers [and Gloucester].*

God pless Your Majesty!

KING How now, Fluellen, cam'st thou from the bridge?

FLUELLEN Ay, so please Your Majesty. The Duke of
Exeter has very gallantly maintained the pridge. The
French is gone off, look you, and there is gallant and
most prave passages. Marry, th'athversary was have 93
possession of the pridge, but he is enforced to retire,
and the Duke of Exeter is master of the pridge. I can
tell Your Majesty, the Duke is a prave man.

KING What men have you lost, Fluellen?

FLUELLEN The perdition of th'athversary hath been very 98
great, reasonable great. Marry, for my part, I think the
Duke hath lost never a man, but one that is like to be ex- 100
ecuted for robbing a church, one Bardolph, if Your Majesty know the man. His face is all bubukles, and whelks, 102
and knobs, and flames o' fire, and his lips blows at his
nose, and it is like a coal of fire, sometimes plue and
sometimes red; but his nose is executed, and his fire's
out.

KING We would have all such offenders so cut off. And we
give express charge that, in our marches through the 108
country, there be nothing compelled from the villages,
nothing taken but paid for, none of the French upbraided or abused in disdainful language; for when lenity and cruelty play for a kingdom, the gentler gamester 112
is the soonest winner. 113

Tucket. Enter Montjoy.

MONTJOY You know me by my habit. 114

KING Well then, I know thee. What shall I know of thee?

MONTJOY My master's mind.

KING Unfold it.

MONTJOY Thus says my King: "Say thou to Harry of
England, though we seemed dead, we did but sleep.
Advantage is a better soldier than rashness. Tell him 120
we could have rebuked him at Harfleur, but that we

thought not good to bruise an injury till it were full 122
ripe. Now we speak upon our cue, and our voice is
imperial. England shall repent his folly, see his 124
weakness, and admire our sufferance. Bid him there- 125
fore consider of his ransom, which must proportion 126
the losses we have borne, the subjects we have lost,
the disgrace we have digested; which in weight to re- 128
answer, his pettiness would bow under. For our losses, 129
his exchequer is too poor; for th'effusion of our blood, 130
the muster of his kingdom too faint a number; and for 131
our disgrace, his own person kneeling at our feet but
a weak and worthless satisfaction. To this add defiance; and tell him, for conclusion, he hath betrayed his
followers, whose condemnation is pronounced." So far 135
my King and master; so much my office.

KING
What is thy name? I know thy quality. 137

MONTJOY Montjoy.

KING
Thou dost thy office fairly. Turn thee back
And tell thy King I do not seek him now,
But could be willing to march on to Calais
Without impeachment. For, to say the sooth, 142
Though 'tis no wisdom to confess so much
Unto an enemy of craft and vantage, 144
My people are with sickness much enfeebled,
My numbers lessened, and those few I have
Almost no better than so many French,
Who when they were in health, I tell thee, herald,
I thought upon one pair of English legs 149
Did march three Frenchmen. Yet, forgive me, God, 150
That I do brag thus! This your air of France
Hath blown that vice in me. I must repent. 152
Go, therefore, tell thy master here I am;
My ransom is this frail and worthless trunk, 154
My army but a weak and sickly guard.
Yet, God before, tell him we will come on,
Though France himself and such another neighbor
Stand in our way. There's for thy labor, Montjoy.
   [*He gives a purse.*]
Go bid thy master well advise himself. 159
If we may pass, we will; if we be hindered,
We shall your tawny ground with your red blood
Discolor. And so, Montjoy, fare you well.
The sum of all our answer is but this:
We would not seek a battle as we are,
Nor, as we are, we say we will not shun it. 165
So tell your master.

76 trick dress.   **new-tuned** i.e., of the latest fashion   **77–8 horrid . . .
camp** fierce battle outfit   **80 slanders of the age** persons who are a
disgrace to the times   **81 mistook** mistaken, deluded.   **84 a hole . . .
coat** i.e., a weak spot in him. (Proverbial.)   **86 from the pridge** with
news concerning the bridge.   **86.1** *poor* bedraggled   **93 passages**
deeds of arms.   **was** did   **98 perdition** losses   **100 like** likely
102 bubukles carbuncles.   **whelks** boils, pimples   **108 express
charge** explicit orders   **112 gamester** player   **113.1** *Tucket* Trumpet
signal, fanfare.   **114 habit** i.e., tabard, herald's coat.   **120 Advantage**
Knowing how to wait for favorable circumstance and position

122 bruise an injury squeeze a boil or pimple   **124 England** i.e.,
King Henry   **125 admire our sufferance** wonder at our patience.
126 proportion be proportional to   **128–9 which . . . under** i.e., to
compensate for which his means are too slender.   **130 exchequer**
treasury   **131 muster** roll call   **135 condemnation** death sentence
137 quality rank and profession; ability.   **142 impeachment** impediment.   **sooth** truth   **144 vantage** superiority in resources
149–50 upon . . . Frenchman i.e., an English soldier is worth three
Frenchmen.   **152 blown** swelled; caused to blossom   **154 trunk**
body   **159 advise himself** consider.   **165 as we are** being who we
are. (Playing on the meaning "in the condition we are" in the previous line.)

MONTJOY
    I shall deliver so. Thanks to Your Highness.   [*Exit.*]
GLOUCESTER
    I hope they will not come upon us now.
KING
    We are in God's hand, brother, not in theirs.
    March to the bridge. It now draws toward night.
    Beyond the river we'll encamp ourselves,
    And on tomorrow bid them march away.   *Exeunt.* 172

❧

[3.7]

*Enter the Constable of France, the Lord Rambures,
Orleans, Dauphin, with others.*

CONSTABLE   Tut, I have the best armor of the world.
    Would it were day!
ORLEANS   You have an excellent armor; but let my
    horse have his due.
CONSTABLE   It is the best horse of Europe.
ORLEANS   Will it never be morning?
DAUPHIN   My lord of Orleans and my Lord High
    Constable, you talk of horse and armor?
ORLEANS   You are as well provided of both as any
    prince in the world.
DAUPHIN   What a long night is this! I will not change
    my horse with any that treads but on four pasterns. 12
    Ça, ha! He bounds from the earth as if his entrails 13
    were hairs; *le cheval volant,* the Pegasus, *qui a les narines* 14
    de feu! When I bestride him, I soar, I am a hawk. He 15
    trots the air. The earth sings when he touches it. The
    basest horn of his hoof is more musical than the pipe 17
    of Hermes. 18
ORLEANS   He's of the color of the nutmeg.
DAUPHIN   And of the heat of the ginger. It is a beast for
    Perseus. He is pure air and fire; and the dull elements 21
    of earth and water never appear in him, but only in 22
    patient stillness while his rider mounts him. He is in-
    deed a horse, and all other jades you may call beasts.
CONSTABLE   Indeed, my lord, it is a most absolute and 25
    excellent horse.
DAUPHIN   It is the prince of palfreys. His neigh is like 27
    the bidding of a monarch, and his countenance
    enforces homage.
ORLEANS   No more, cousin.
DAUPHIN   Nay, the man hath no wit that cannot, from
    the rising of the lark to the lodging of the lamb, vary 32

deserved praise on my palfrey. It is a theme as fluent
as the sea; turn the sands into eloquent tongues, and
my horse is argument for them all. 'Tis a subject for a 35
sovereign to reason on, and for a sovereign's sovereign 36
to ride on, and for the world, familiar to us and un- 37
known, to lay apart their particular functions and 38
wonder at him. I once writ a sonnet in his praise, and 39
began thus: "Wonder of nature—"
ORLEANS   I have heard a sonnet begin so to one's
    mistress.
DAUPHIN   Then did they imitate that which I composed
    to my courser, for my horse is my mistress. 44
ORLEANS   Your mistress bears well.
DAUPHIN   Me well, which is the prescript praise and 46
    perfection of a good and particular mistress. 47
CONSTABLE   Nay, for methought yesterday your mis-
    tress shrewdly shook your back. 49
DAUPHIN   So perhaps did yours.
CONSTABLE   Mine was not bridled. 51
DAUPHIN   Oh, then belike she was old and gentle, and 52
    you rode like a kern of Ireland, your French hose off, 53
    and in your strait strossers. 54
CONSTABLE   You have good judgment in horsemanship.
DAUPHIN   Be warned by me, then: they that ride so,
    and ride not warily, fall into foul bogs. I had rather
    have my horse to my mistress. 58
CONSTABLE   I had as lief have my mistress a jade. 59
DAUPHIN   I tell thee, Constable, my mistress wears his 60
    own hair. 61
CONSTABLE   I could make as true a boast as that, if I had
    a sow to my mistress.
DAUPHIN   *"Le chien est retourné à son propre vomissement,* 64
    et la truie lavée au bourbier." Thou mak'st use of 65
    anything.
CONSTABLE   Yet do I not use my horse for my mistress,
    or any such proverb so little kin to the purpose. 68
RAMBURES   My Lord Constable, the armor that I saw in
    your tent tonight, are those stars or suns upon it?
CONSTABLE   Stars, my lord.
DAUPHIN   Some of them will fall tomorrow, I hope.
CONSTABLE   And yet my sky shall not want. 73
DAUPHIN   That may be, for you bear a many superflu- 74
    ously, and 'twere more honor some were away. 75

---

172 bid . . . away bid our army march toward Calais.
3.7. Location: The French camp, near Agincourt.
12 pasterns i.e., hooves. (The *pastern* literally is the part of the horse's
leg just above the hoof.)   **13–14 as . . . hairs** i.e., as if he were a tennis
ball. (Tennis balls were stuffed with hair. Or perhaps *hairs* should
read *hares*.)   **14–15 le cheval . . . feu** the flying horse, Pegasus, with
nostrils breathing fire.   **17 basest horn** (1) lowest part (2) hoofbeat
17–18 pipe of Hermes (Hermes, messenger of the gods, charmed
Argus of the hundred eyes asleep with playing on his pipe.)
21 Perseus (According to some Greek legends and to Ovid, Perseus
rode Pegasus when he rescued Andromeda from the dragon.)
21–2 air . . . water (Of the four elements supposed to make up all matter, water and earth are the heavier, while fire and air ascend.)
25 absolute perfect   **27 palfreys** saddle horses.   **32 lodging** lying
down.   **vary** produce variations of

35 argument subject   **36 reason** discourse   **37–9 for . . . him** for both
the known and unknown worlds to put aside their differences and
join in wondering at him.   **44 horse is my mistress** (Here begins a
series of bawdy double entendres involving human and animal sexuality: *bears, shook your back, rode, foul bogs, doing,* etc.)   **46 prescript**
prescribed   **47 particular** acknowledging only one master
49 shrewdly viciously   **51 Mine . . . bridled** i.e., At least my mistress
was not a horse.   **52 belike** probably   **53 kern** Irish foot soldier.
(Here it is used to mean "rustic" or "boor.")   **French hose** wide
breeches   **54 strait strossers** tight trousers, i.e., bare-legged.   **58 to** as
59 lief happily.   **jade** (1) worn-out horse (2) slut.   **60–1 wears . . .
hair** i.e., is not artificially wigged, like an elegant court lady, and perhaps bald from syphilis.   **64–5 "Le chien . . . bourbier"** The dog is
returned to his own vomit, and the washed sow to the mire. (See 2
Peter 2:22.)   **68 kin** related   **73 sky** i.e., sky of honor.   **want** be lacking (in honor).   **74 a many** many. (Parallel to "a few.")   **75 'twere . . .
away** i.e., it would be more honest and proper if some of your stars
were done away with.

CONSTABLE   Even as your horse bears your praises, who would trot as well, were some of your brags dismounted.

DAUPHIN   Would I were able to load him with his desert! Will it never be day? I will trot tomorrow a mile, and my way shall be paved with English faces. 79 80

CONSTABLE   I will not say so, for fear I should be faced out of my way. But I would it were morning, for I would fain be about the ears of the English. 82 83 84

RAMBURES   Who will go to hazard with me for twenty prisoners? 85

CONSTABLE   You must first go yourself to hazard, ere you have them.

DAUPHIN   'Tis midnight. I'll go arm myself.   *Exit.*

ORLEANS   The Dauphin longs for morning.

RAMBURES   He longs to eat the English.

CONSTABLE   I think he will eat all he kills.

ORLEANS   By the white hand of my lady, he's a gallant prince.

CONSTABLE   Swear by her foot, that she may tread out the oath. 95 96

ORLEANS   He is simply the most active gentleman of France.

CONSTABLE   Doing is activity, and he will still be doing. 99

ORLEANS   He never did harm, that I heard of. 100

CONSTABLE   Nor will do none tomorrow. He will keep that good name still.

ORLEANS   I know him to be valiant.

CONSTABLE   I was told that by one that knows him better than you.

ORLEANS   What's he?

CONSTABLE   Marry, he told me so himself, and he said he cared not who knew it.

ORLEANS   He needs not; it is no hidden virtue in him. 109

CONSTABLE   By my faith, sir, but it is. Never anybody saw it but his lackey. 'Tis a hooded valor, and when it appears it will bate. 110 111 112

ORLEANS   Ill will never said well.

CONSTABLE   I will cap that proverb with "There is flattery in friendship."

ORLEANS   And I will take up that with "Give the devil his due." 116 117

CONSTABLE   Well placed. There stands your friend for the devil. Have at the very eye of that proverb with "A pox of the devil." 118 119

ORLEANS   You are the better at proverbs by how much "A fool's bolt is soon shot." 122

CONSTABLE   You have shot over. 123

ORLEANS   'Tis not the first time you were overshot. 124

Enter a Messenger.

MESSENGER   My Lord High Constable, the English lie within fifteen hundred paces of your tents.

CONSTABLE   Who hath measured the ground?

MESSENGER   The Lord Grandpré.

CONSTABLE   A valiant and most expert gentleman.
    [*Exit Messenger.*]
Would it were day! Alas, poor Harry of England! He longs not for the dawning as we do.

ORLEANS   What a wretched and peevish fellow is this King of England, to mope with his fat-brained followers so far out of his knowledge! 133

CONSTABLE   If the English had any apprehension, they would run away. 135

ORLEANS   That they lack; for if their heads had any intellectual armor, they could never wear such heavy headpieces.

RAMBURES   That island of England breeds very valiant creatures; their mastiffs are of unmatchable courage.

ORLEANS   Foolish curs, that run winking into the mouth of a Russian bear and have their heads crushed like rotten apples. You may as well say "That's a valiant flea that dare eat his breakfast on the lip of a lion." 142

CONSTABLE   Just, just! And the men do sympathize with the mastiffs in robustious and rough coming on, leaving their wits with their wives; and then give them great meals of beef and iron and steel, they will eat like wolves and fight like devils. 146 147

ORLEANS   Ay, but these English are shrewdly out of beef. 151

CONSTABLE   Then shall we find tomorrow they have only stomachs to eat and none to fight. Now is it time to arm. Come, shall we about it? 154

ORLEANS
It is now two o'clock; but let me see, by ten
We shall have each a hundred Englishmen.   *Exeunt.*

❖

[4.0]

[*Enter*] Chorus.

CHORUS
Now entertain conjecture of a time 1
When creeping murmur and the poring dark 2
Fills the wide vessel of the universe.
From camp to camp, through the foul womb of night,
The hum of either army stilly sounds, 5

79–80 Would . . . desert! I wish I could find words to equal his deserving! **82–3 faced . . . way** braved out of my way, put to shame. **84 fain** gladly. **about the ears** buffeting the heads **85 go to hazard** bet, play at dice. (But the Constable replies in the sense of "encounter danger.") **95–6 tread . . . oath** (1) fulfill the oath by dancing (2) stamp on, spurn the oath. **99 Doing** (1) Acting, pretending (2) Copulating. **still** continually **100 did harm** i.e., offended. (But the Constable uses it to mean "hurt any enemy.") **109 He needs not** i.e., There is no need for him to proclaim it himself. **it** i.e., valor. **110–11 Never . . . lackey** i.e., He shows "valor" only in beating his servant. **111 hooded valor** (The hawk was kept hooded to prevent it from beating its wings, or "bating.") **112 bate** (1) beat its wings (2) abate, be downcast. **116–17 Give . . . due** Give even the devil his due; everyone deserves some praise. (But the Constable uses this proverb against the Dauphin by likening him to the devil.) **118–19 There . . . devil** i.e., You just called the Dauphin the devil. **119 Have . . . eye** Shoot straight at the mark. (A sporting term appropriate to this verbal contest of "capping proverbs.")

122 bolt short, blunt arrow **123 shot over** i.e., shot over the mark. **124 overshot** i.e., outshot, defeated. **133 mope** (1) wander about (2) be downcast **135 apprehension** (1) sense (2) sense of danger **142 winking** shutting their eyes **146 Just** Exactly. **sympathize with** resemble **147 robustious** violent, boisterous **151 shrewdly out of** devilishly short of **154 stomachs** appetites
4.0. Chorus.
1 entertain conjecture of imagine **2 poring** in which one must strain the eyes to see **5 stilly** softly

That the fixed sentinels almost receive
The secret whispers of each other's watch.
Fire answers fire, and through their paly flames   8
Each battle sees the other's umbered face.   9
Steed threatens steed, in high and boastful neighs
Piercing the night's dull ear; and from the tents
The armorers, accomplishing the knights,   12
With busy hammers closing rivets up,
Give dreadful note of preparation.
The country cocks do crow, the clocks do toll,
And the third hour of drowsy morning name.
Proud of their numbers and secure in soul,   17
The confident and overlusty French   18
Do the low-rated English play at dice,   19
And chide the cripple tardy-gaited night,
Who like a foul and ugly witch doth limp
So tediously away. The poor condemnèd English,
Like sacrifices, by their watchful fires
Sit patiently and inly ruminate   24
The morning's danger; and their gesture sad,   25
Investing lank-lean cheeks and war-worn coats,   26
Presenteth them unto the gazing moon
So many horrid ghosts. Oh, now, who will behold
The royal captain of this ruined band
Walking from watch to watch, from tent to tent,
Let him cry, "Praise and glory on his head!"
For forth he goes and visits all his host,   32
Bids them good morrow with a modest smile,
And calls them brothers, friends, and countrymen.
Upon his royal face there is no note
How dread an army hath enrounded him.   36
Nor doth he dedicate one jot of color   37
Unto the weary and all-watchèd night,   38
But freshly looks and overbears attaint   39
With cheerful semblance and sweet majesty;
That every wretch, pining and pale before,
Beholding him, plucks comfort from his looks.
A largess universal like the sun
His liberal eye doth give to everyone,
Thawing cold fear, that mean and gentle all   45
Behold, as may unworthiness define,   46
A little touch of Harry in the night.
And so our scene must to the battle fly;
Where—oh, for pity!—we shall much disgrace
With four or five most vile and ragged foils,   50
Right ill-disposed in brawl ridiculous,
The name of Agincourt. Yet sit and see,
Minding true things by what their mockeries be.   53

                                                    Exit.

❖

8 paly pale   9 battle army.   umbered shadowed   12 accomplishing
equipping   17 secure overconfident   18 overlusty overly merry
19 play gamble for   24 inly inwardly   25 gesture sad serious bearing
26 Investing clothing   32 host army   36 enrounded surrounded
37 dedicate yield up.   color i.e., bright color of complexion   38 all-
watchèd spent entirely in wakefulness and waiting   39 overbears
attaint overcomes the effects of weariness and depression   45 mean
and gentle those of low and of high birth   46 unworthiness I, who am
unworthy of praising so great an object   50 foils blunted fencing swords
53 Minding bearing in mind.   mockeries inadequate imitations

[4.1]

Enter the King, Bedford, and Gloucester.

KING
Gloucester, 'tis true that we are in great danger;
The greater therefore should our courage be.
Good morrow, brother Bedford. God Almighty!
There is some soul of goodness in things evil,
Would men observingly distill it out;   5
For our bad neighbor makes us early stirrers,
Which is both healthful and good husbandry.   7
Besides, they are our outward consciences,
And preachers to us all, admonishing
That we should dress us fairly for our end.   10
Thus may we gather honey from the weed
And make a moral of the devil himself.

        Enter Erpingham.

Good morrow, old Sir Thomas Erpingham.
A good soft pillow for that good white head
Were better than a churlish turf of France.   15
ERPINGHAM
Not so, my liege. This lodging likes me better,   16
Since I may say, "Now lie I like a king."
KING
'Tis good for men to love their present pains
Upon example; so the spirit is eased.   19
And when the mind is quickened, out of doubt
The organs, though defunct and dead before,
Break up their drowsy grave and newly move   22
With casted slough and fresh legerity.   23
Lend me thy cloak, Sir Thomas. [*The King puts on
    Erpingham's cloak.*] Brothers both,   24
Commend me to the princes in our camp;   25
Do my good morrow to them, and anon
Desire them all to my pavilion.
GLOUCESTER   We shall, my liege.
ERPINGHAM   Shall I attend Your Grace?
KING   No, my good knight,
Go with my brothers to my lords of England.
I and my bosom must debate awhile,
And then I would no other company.
ERPINGHAM
The Lord in heaven bless thee, noble Harry!
                        Exeunt [all but the King].
KING
God-a-mercy, old heart! Thou speak'st cheerfully.

        Enter Pistol.

PISTOL   *Che vous là?*   36

4.1. Location: The English camp at Agincourt.
5 Would men if one could   7 husbandry economy, thrift.   10 dress
us fairly prepare ourselves well   15 churlish rough, hard   16 likes
pleases   19 Upon example i.e., following or considering the example
of persons such as King Henry and Erpingham   22–3 Break . . . legerity break out of their lethargy and move more nimbly, like a snake having cast off its old skin.   24 Brothers both i.e., Bedford and
Gloucester   25 Commend me convey my greetings   36 *Che vous là?*
i.e., *Qui va là?* ("Who goes there?") or *Qui vous là?* ("Who are you
there?"). (Pistol's imperfect French.)

KING A friend.

PISTOL
Discuss unto me: art thou officer,
Or art thou base, common, and popular?

KING I am a gentleman of a company.

PISTOL Trail'st thou the puissant pike?

KING Even so. What are you?

PISTOL
As good a gentleman as the Emperor.

KING Then you are a better than the King.

PISTOL
The King's a bawcock and a heart of gold,
A lad of life, an imp of fame,
Of parents good, of fist most valiant.
I kiss his dirty shoe, and from heartstring
I love the lovely bully. What is thy name?

KING Harry le Roy.

PISTOL
Le Roy? A Cornish name. Art thou of Cornish crew?

KING No, I am a Welshman.

PISTOL Know'st thou Fluellen?

KING Yes.

PISTOL
Tell him I'll knock his leek about his pate
Upon Saint Davy's Day.

KING Do not you wear your dagger in your cap that day, lest he knock that about yours.

PISTOL Art thou his friend?

KING And his kinsman too.

PISTOL The *figo* for thee, then!

KING I thank you. God be with you!

PISTOL My name is Pistol called. *Exit.*

KING It sorts well with your fierceness.

Manet King [*standing apart*].

Enter Fluellen and Gower [*meeting*].

GOWER Captain Fluellen!

FLUELLEN So, in the name of Jesu Christ, speak fewer. It is the greatest admiration in the universal world, when the true and aunchient prerogatifes and laws of the wars is not kept. If you would take the pains but to examine the wars of Pompey the Great, you shall find, I warrant you, that there is no tiddle-taddle nor pibble-pabble in Pompey's camp. I warrant you, you shall find the ceremonies of the wars, and the cares of it, and the forms of it, and the sobriety of it, and the modesty of it, to be otherwise.

GOWER Why, the enemy is loud; you hear him all night.

FLUELLEN If the enemy is an ass and a fool and a prating coxcomb, is it meet, think you, that we should also, look you, be an ass and a fool and a prating coxcomb? In your own conscience, now?

GOWER I will speak lower.

FLUELLEN I pray you and beseech you that you will.

Exit [*with Gower*].

KING
Though it appear a little out of fashion,
There is much care and valor in this Welshman.

Enter three soldiers, John Bates, Alexander Court, and Michael Williams.

COURT Brother John Bates, is not that the morning which breaks yonder?

BATES I think it be. But we have no great cause to desire the approach of day.

WILLIAMS We see yonder the beginning of the day, but I think we shall never see the end of it.—Who goes there?

KING A friend.

WILLIAMS Under what captain serve you?

KING Under Sir Thomas Erpingham.

WILLIAMS A good old commander and a most kind gentleman. I pray you, what thinks he of our estate?

KING Even as men wrecked upon a sand, that look to be washed off the next tide.

BATES He hath not told his thought to the King?

KING No, nor it is not meet he should. For, though I speak it to you, I think the King is but a man, as I am. The violet smells to him as it doth to me; the element shows to him as it doth to me; all his senses have but human conditions. His ceremonies laid by, in his nakedness he appears but a man; and though his affections are higher mounted than ours, yet when they stoop, they stoop with the like wing. Therefore when he sees reason of fears, as we do, his fears, out of doubt, be of the same relish as ours are. Yet, in reason, no man should possess him with any appearance of fear, lest he, by showing it, should dishearten his army.

BATES He may show what outward courage he will; but I believe, as cold a night as 'tis, he could wish himself in Thames up to the neck; and so I would he were, and I by him, at all adventures, so we were quit here.

KING By my troth, I will speak my conscience of the King: I think he would not wish himself anywhere but where he is.

38 Discuss Declare **39 popular** of low birth. **40 gentleman of a company** gentleman serving as a volunteer. **41 Trail'st . . . pike?** i.e., Are you in the infantry? **45 bawcock** fine fellow. (From the French *beau coq.*) **46 imp of fame** child or scion of renown **49 bully** (A term of endearment meaning "fine fellow.") **52 Welshman** (Henry was born at Monmouth, then considered part of Wales.) **55–6 leek . . . Day** (On Saint David's Day, March 1, the leek was worn in memory of a Welsh victory over the Saxons in 540 A.D., since Saint David, the Welsh leader, had commanded his followers to wear leeks in their caps on that occasion.) **61 *figo*** (A provoking gesture of contempt; see the note for 3.6.57.) **64 sorts** fits, agrees **64.1 *Manet King*** The King remains. **66 fewer** i.e., calmly, more quietly. **67 admiration** wonder **70 Pompey the Great** Roman general defeated by Julius Caesar **71–2 tiddle-taddle nor pibble-pabble** tittle-tattle nor bibble-babble **74 sobriety** orderliness, decorum **75 modesty** propriety

78–9 prating coxcomb chattering fool **97 estate** situation. **98 wrecked** shipwrecked **101 meet** fitting **103–4 element shows** sky appears **105 ceremonies** symbols of royalty **107 affections . . . mounted** desires soar higher. (A falconry metaphor continued in *stoop,* "descend," "swoop down," and *with the like wing,* "similarly.") **110 relish** taste **111 possess him with** induce in him **117 at all adventures** at all events (since the Thames would be less risky under any circumstances than the impending battle). **quit here** out of this situation.

BATES   Then I would he were here alone. So should he be sure to be ransomed, and a many poor men's lives saved.

KING   I dare say you love him not so ill to wish him here alone, howsoever you speak this to feel other men's 125 minds. Methinks I could not die anywhere so contented as in the King's company, his cause being just and his quarrel honorable.

WILLIAMS   That's more than we know.

BATES   Ay, or more than we should seek after; for we know enough if we know we are the King's subjects. If his cause be wrong, our obedience to the King wipes the crime of it out of us.

WILLIAMS   But if the cause be not good, the King himself hath a heavy reckoning to make, when all those legs and arms and heads, chopped off in a battle, shall join together at the Latter Day and cry all, 137 "We died at such a place"—some swearing, some crying for a surgeon, some upon their wives left poor behind them, some upon the debts they owe, some upon their children rawly left. I am afeard there are 141 few die well that die in a battle; for how can they charitably dispose of anything, when blood is their argument? Now, if these men do not die well, it will be a black matter for the King that led them to it; who 145 to disobey were against all proportion of subjection. 146

KING   So, if a son that is by his father sent about merchandise do sinfully miscarry upon the sea, the 148 imputation of his wickedness, by your rule, should be 149 imposed upon his father that sent him; or if a servant, under his master's command transporting a sum of money, be assailed by robbers and die in many 152 irreconciled iniquities, you may call the business of the 153 master the author of the servant's damnation. But this is not so. The King is not bound to answer the par- 155 ticular endings of his soldiers, the father of his son, nor the master of his servant; for they purpose not their 157 deaths when they propose their services. Besides, there is no king, be his cause never so spotless, if it 159 come to the arbitrament of swords, can try it out with 160 all unspotted soldiers. Some, peradventure, have on 161 them the guilt of premeditated and contrived murder; some, of beguiling virgins with the broken seals of 163 perjury; some, making the wars their bulwark, that 164 have before gored the gentle bosom of peace with pillage and robbery. Now, if these men have defeated 166 the law and outrun native punishment, though they 167 can outstrip men, they have no wings to fly from God. War is his beadle, war is his vengeance; so that here 169

men are punished for before-breach of the King's laws 170 in now the King's quarrel. Where they feared the 171 death, they have borne life away; and where they 172 would be safe, they perish. Then if they die unpro- 173 vided, no more is the King guilty of their damnation 174 than he was before guilty of those impieties for the which they are now visited. Every subject's duty is the 176 King's; but every subject's soul is his own. Therefore should every soldier in the wars do as every sick man in his bed, wash every mote out of his conscience; and 179 dying so, death is to him advantage, or not dying, the time was blessedly lost wherein such preparation was gained. And in him that escapes, it were not sin to think that, making God so free an offer, He let him outlive that day to see His greatness and to teach others how they should prepare.

WILLIAMS   'Tis certain, every man that dies ill, the ill 186 upon his own head, the King is not to answer it.

BATES   I do not desire he should answer for me, and yet I determine to fight lustily for him.

KING   I myself heard the King say he would not be ransomed.

WILLIAMS   Ay, he said so, to make us fight cheerfully; but when our throats are cut, he may be ransomed and we ne'er the wiser.

KING   If I live to see it, I will never trust his word after.

WILLIAMS   You pay him then! That's a perilous shot out 196 of an elder-gun, that a poor and a private displeasure 197 can do against a monarch. You may as well go about to turn the sun to ice with fanning in his face with a peacock's feather. You'll never trust his word after! Come, 'tis a foolish saying.

KING   Your reproof is something too round. I should be 202 angry with you, if the time were convenient.

WILLIAMS   Let it be a quarrel between us, if you live.

KING   I embrace it.

WILLIAMS   How shall I know thee again?

KING   Give me any gage of thine, and I will wear it in 207 my bonnet. Then if ever thou dar'st acknowledge it, I will make it my quarrel.

WILLIAMS   Here's my glove. Give me another of thine.

KING   There.   [*They exchange gloves.*]

WILLIAMS   This will I also wear in my cap. If ever thou come to me and say, after tomorrow, "This is my glove," by this hand, I will take thee a box on the ear. 214

KING   If ever I live to see it, I will challenge it.

WILLIAMS   Thou dar'st as well be hanged.

KING   Well, I will do it, though I take thee in the King's company.

WILLIAMS   Keep thy word. Fare thee well.

---

125 **feel** feel out   137 **Latter Day** last day, Christian Day of Judgment
141 **rawly** without provision   145 **who** whom   146 **proportion of
subjection** proper duty of a subject.   148 **sinfully miscarry** die in his
sins   149 **imputation . . . wickedness** wickedness imputed to him
152–3 **in . . . iniquities** with his wicked deeds unabsolved   155
answer answer for   157 **purpose** intend   159–60 **if . . . swords** if a
dispute can be settled only by swords   161 **unspotted** innocent
163 **broken seals** (1) broken promises (2) violated maidenheads
164 **bulwark** refuge from punishment (for offenses committed)
166 **defeated** broken   167 **native** at home   169 **beadle** parish officer
responsible for punishing petty offenders

170 **before-breach** prior violation   171–3 **Where . . . perish** i.e.,
Whereas before they feared execution but escaped punishment, here
where they look for safety they die in battle.   173–4 **unprovided**
spiritually unprepared   176 **visited** i.e., by punishment.   179 **mote**
small impurity   186 **dies ill** dies in sin   196 **You pay him then!** i.e.,
That will really pay him back for his perfidy, won't it? (Said sarcastically.)   197 **elder-gun** popgun made from a branch of elder with the
pith hollowed out   202 **round** direct, brusque.   207 **gage** pledge
214 **take** give, strike

BATES Be friends, you English fools, be friends. We
have French quarrels enough, if you could tell how to 221
reckon.
KING Indeed, the French may lay twenty French crowns 223
to one they will beat us, for they bear them on their
shoulders; but it is no English treason to cut French 225
crowns, and tomorrow the King himself will be a
clipper.   *Exeunt soldiers.*
Upon the King! Let us our lives, our souls,
Our debts, our careful wives,   229
Our children, and our sins lay on the King!
We must bear all. Oh, hard condition,
Twin-born with greatness, subject to the breath   232
Of every fool, whose sense no more can feel   233
But his own wringing! What infinite heartsease   234
Must kings neglect that private men enjoy!
And what have kings that privates have not too,   236
Save ceremony, save general ceremony?
And what art thou, thou idol ceremony?
What kind of god art thou, that suffer'st more
Of mortal griefs than do thy worshipers?
What are thy rents? What are thy comings-in?   241
O ceremony, show me but thy worth!
What is thy soul of adoration?   243
Art thou aught else but place, degree, and form,   244
Creating awe and fear in other men?
Wherein thou art less happy, being feared,
Than they in fearing.
What drink'st thou oft, instead of homage sweet,
But poisoned flattery? Oh, be sick, great greatness,   249
And bid thy ceremony give thee cure!   250
Thinks thou the fiery fever will go out   251
With titles blown from adulation?   252
Will it give place to flexure and low bending?   253
Canst thou, when thou command'st the beggar's
    knee,
Command the health of it? No, thou proud dream,
That play'st so subtly with a king's repose.
I am a king that find thee, and I know   257
'Tis not the balm, the scepter, and the ball,   258
The sword, the mace, the crown imperial,   259

The intertissued robe of gold and pearl,   260
The farcèd title running 'fore the king,   261
The throne he sits on, nor the tide of pomp
That beats upon the high shore of this world—
No, not all these, thrice-gorgeous ceremony,
Not all these, laid in bed majestical,
Can sleep so soundly as the wretched slave
Who, with a body filled and vacant mind,
Gets him to rest, crammed with distressful bread;   268
Never sees horrid night, the child of hell,
But like a lackey from the rise to set   270
Sweats in the eye of Phoebus, and all night   271
Sleeps in Elysium; next day after dawn   272
Doth rise and help Hyperion to his horse,   273
And follows so the ever-running year
With profitable labor to his grave.
And but for ceremony, such a wretch,
Winding up days with toil and nights with sleep,
Had the forehand and vantage of a king.   278
The slave, a member of the country's peace,   279
Enjoys it, but in gross brain little wots   280
What watch the King keeps to maintain the peace,   281
Whose hours the peasant best advantages.   282

    Enter Erpingham.

ERPINGHAM
My lord, your nobles, jealous of your absence,   283
Seek through your camp to find you.
KING   Good old knight,
Collect them all together at my tent.
I'll be before thee.
ERPINGHAM   I shall do't, my lord.   *Exit.* 286
KING
O God of battles, steel my soldiers' hearts;
Possess them not with fear! Take from them now
The sense of reck'ning, ere th'opposèd numbers   289
Pluck their hearts from them. Not today, O Lord,
Oh, not today, think not upon the fault   291
My father made in compassing the crown!   292
I Richard's body have interrèd new,   293
And on it have bestowed more contrite tears
Than from it issued forcèd drops of blood.
Five hundred poor I have in yearly pay
Who twice a day their withered hands hold up
Toward heaven, to pardon blood; and I have built
Two chantries, where the sad and solemn priests   299
Sing still for Richard's soul. More will I do;   300

---

221 **could tell** knew   223 **lay** bet. (But also anticipating the meaning
"lay down or lose in battle.")   **crowns** (1) coins (2) heads   225 **English treason** (It was a treasonable offense to clip or "cut" English coins;
it obviously is no offense to slash French heads, and even King Henry
will be such a "clipper.")   229 **careful** full of cares   232–4 **Twin-born
. . . wringing** i.e., inseparable from the condition of being born of
royal rank, a condition that makes a king the subject of the idle gossip
of every fool, even those whose sensibilities pay attention to nothing
other than the rumbling of their own stomachs.   236 **privates** private
persons   241 **comings-in** revenues.   243 **thy soul of adoration** the
essential quality that makes you so much admired.   244 **place** rank
249–50 **Oh . . . cure!** Learn to cure yourself by being sick, by treating
poisoned flattery and ceremoniousness as a medicine that will purge
you of being in love with your own great greatness.   251–2 **Thinks . . .
adulation?** Do you really think that the fever of vain pride will be
extinguished by speeches breathed by flatterers? (*Blown* also suggests
"inflated.")   253 **Will . . . bending?** i.e., Will the sickness yield to
bowing and scraping?   257 **find thee** i.e., experience greatness and
am able to appraise its worth and limitations   258 **balm** consecrating
oil used to anoint a king in his coronation.   **ball** orb of sovereignty
259 **mace** ceremonial staff

260 **intertissued** interwoven   261 **farcèd** stuffed (with pompous
phrases)   268 **distressful** earned by hard work   270 **lackey** (1) footman running alongside the chariot of the sun (2) peasant.   **rise to set**
sunrise to sunset   271 **Phoebus** the sun god   272 **Elysium** in Greek
mythology, the abode of the blessed   273 **Hyperion** the father of the
sun, or the sun itself. (The peasant is up before the sun.)   278 **Had**
would have.   **forehand** upper hand   279 **member** sharer   280 **it** i.e.,
peace.   **wots** knows   281 **watch** wakeful guard   282 **the peasant
best advantages** most benefit the peasant.   283 **jealous of** apprehensive because of   286 **be there** 289 **sense of reck'ning** ability to
reckon up the odds   291 **the fault** i.e., the deposition and murder of
Richard II   292 **compassing** obtaining   293 **new** anew   299 **chantries**
chapels in which masses for the dead were celebrated.   **sad** grave
300 **still** continually

Though all that I can do is nothing worth,
Since that my penitence comes after all,   302
Imploring pardon.

Enter Gloucester.

GLOUCESTER My liege!
KING   My brother Gloucester's voice? Ay;
    I know thy errand. I will go with thee.
    The day, my friends, and all things stay for me.
                                        Exeunt.

❖

[4.2]

*Enter the Dauphin, Orleans, Rambures, and
Beaumont.*

ORLEANS
    The sun doth gild our armor. Up, my lords!
DAUPHIN   *Monte à cheval! My horse! Varlet! Lacquais!* Ha!   2
ORLEANS   Oh, brave spirit!
DAUPHIN   *Via, les eaux et terre!*   4
ORLEANS   *Rien puis? L'air et feu?*   5
DAUPHIN   *Cieux*, cousin Orleans.   6

Enter Constable.

    Now, my Lord Constable?
CONSTABLE
    Hark, how our steeds for present service neigh!   8
DAUPHIN
    Mount them, and make incision in their hides,   9
    That their hot blood may spin in English eyes   10
    And dout them with superfluous courage. Ha!   11
RAMBURES
    What, will you have them weep our horses' blood?
    How shall we then behold their natural tears?

Enter Messenger.

MESSENGER
    The English are embattled, you French peers.   14
CONSTABLE
    To horse, you gallant princes, straight to horse!
    Do but behold yond poor and starvèd band,
    And your fair show shall suck away their souls,   17
    Leaving them but the shales and husks of men.   18
    There is not work enough for all our hands,
    Scarce blood enough in all their sickly veins
    To give each naked curtal ax a stain   21

That our French gallants shall today draw out
And sheathe for lack of sport. Let us but blow on
    them,
The vapor of our valor will o'erturn them.
'Tis positive against all exceptions, lords,   25
That our superfluous lackeys and our peasants,
Who in unnecessary action swarm
About our squares of battle, were enough   28
To purge this field of such a hilding foe,   29
Though we upon this mountain's basis by   30
Took stand for idle speculation—   31
But that our honors must not. What's to say?   32
A very little little let us do
And all is done. Then let the trumpets sound
The tucket sonance and the note to mount;   35
For our approach shall so much dare the field   36
That England shall couch down in fear and yield.

Enter Grandpré.

GRANDPRÉ
    Why do you stay so long, my lords of France?
    Yond island carrions, desperate of their bones,   39
    Ill-favoredly become the morning field.   40
    Their ragged curtains poorly are let loose,   41
    And our air shakes them passing scornfully.   42
    Big Mars seems bankrupt in their beggared host   43
    And faintly through a rusty beaver peeps.   44
    The horsemen sit like fixèd candlesticks,
    With torch staves in their hand, and their poor jades   46
    Lob down their heads, drooping the hides and hips,   47
    The gum down-roping from their pale-dead eyes,   48
    And in their pale dull mouths the gimmaled bit   49
    Lies foul with chewed grass, still and motionless;
    And their executors, the knavish crows,   51
    Fly o'er them all impatient for their hour.
    Description cannot suit itself in words
    To demonstrate the life of such a battle   54
    In life so lifeless as it shows itself.
CONSTABLE
    They have said their prayers, and they stay for death.   56
DAUPHIN
    Shall we go send them dinners and fresh suits,
    And give their fasting horses provender,   58
    And after fight with them?
CONSTABLE
    I stay but for my guard. On to the field!   60
    I will the banner from a trumpet take,   61

---

302 Since that necessitating that
4.2. Location: The French camp.
0.2 *Beaumont* (The Folio text mentions Lord Beaumont but does not
give him a speaking part.) **2** *Monte à cheval!* To horse! **4** *Via . . .
terre!* Begone, waters and earth! (The Dauphin imagines himself riding through and over rivers and solid ground.) **5** *Rien . . . feu?*
Nothing more? What about air and fire? (i.e., Why not soar above all
four elements, not just water and earth?) **6** *Cieux* The heavens. (The
Dauphin carries the metaphor one step further to its ultimate height.)
8 present service immediate action **9 incision** i.e., with spurs
10 spin gush, spatter **11 And . . . courage** i.e., and put out the English eyes with the horses' superfluous blood, the proof of their excessive courage. **dout** put out **14 embattled** arranged in battle order
17 fair show impressive appearance **18 shales** shells **21 curtal ax**
cutlass, short sword

25 exceptions objections **28 squares of battle** four-sided military
formations **29 hilding** worthless, base **30 basis** foot. **by** nearby
31 speculation looking on **32 But that** except for the fact that
35 tucket sonance trumpet call. **mount** mount our horses **36 dare**
(1) defy (2) stupify with fear **39 carrions** cadavers for the scavenger
birds. **desperate of** without hope of saving **40 Ill-favoredly
become** i.e., are an eyesore to **41 curtains** colors, banners **42 passing** exceedingly **43 Mars** the god of war **44 beaver** visor **46 torch
staves** i.e., tapers in place of lances. (The horsemen themselves look
like carved candleholders.) **47 Lob down** hang down. **drooping**
letting droop **48 gum** watery discharge. **down-roping** hanging
down ropelike **49 gimmaled** jointed **51 their executors** the disposers of their remains **54 battle** army **56 stay for** await
58 provender fodder **60 guard** (Including a standard-bearer.)
61 trumpet trumpeter

And use it for my haste. Come, come, away!
The sun is high, and we outwear the day.   *Exeunt.*   63

❖

[4.3]

*Enter Gloucester, Bedford, Exeter, Erpingham,
with all his host, Salisbury, and Westmorland.*

GLOUCESTER   Where is the King?

BEDFORD
The King himself is rode to view their battle.   2

WESTMORLAND
Of fighting men they have full threescore thousand.

EXETER
There's five to one. Besides, they all are fresh.

SALISBURY
God's arm strike with us! 'Tis a fearful odds.
God b'wi' you, princes all; I'll to my charge.   6
If we no more meet till we meet in heaven,
Then, joyfully, my noble lord of Bedford,
My dear lord Gloucester, and my good lord Exeter,
And my kind kinsman, warriors all, adieu!   10

BEDFORD
Farewell, good Salisbury, and good luck go with thee!

EXETER
Farewell, kind lord. Fight valiantly today!
And yet I do thee wrong to mind thee of it,   13
For thou art framed of the firm truth of valor.   14
                               [Exit Salisbury.]

BEDFORD
He is as full of valor as of kindness,
Princely in both.

Enter the King.

WESTMORLAND   Oh, that we now had here
But one ten thousand of those men in England
That do no work today!

KING   What's he that wishes so?   18
My cousin Westmorland? No, my fair cousin.
If we are marked to die, we are enough   20
To do our country loss; and if to live,   21
The fewer men, the greater share of honor.
God's will, I pray thee, wish not one man more.
By Jove, I am not covetous for gold,
Nor care I who doth feed upon my cost;   25
It yearns me not if men my garments wear;   26
Such outward things dwell not in my desires.
But if it be a sin to covet honor
I am the most offending soul alive.
No, faith, my coz, wish not a man from England.   30
God's peace, I would not lose so great an honor
As one man more, methinks, would share from me   32
For the best hope I have. Oh, do not wish one more!   33

Rather proclaim it, Westmorland, through my host   34
That he which hath no stomach to this fight,   35
Let him depart; his passport shall be made
And crowns for convoy put into his purse.   37
We would not die in that man's company
That fears his fellowship to die with us.   39
This day is called the Feast of Crispian.   40
He that outlives this day and comes safe home
Will stand a-tiptoe when this day is named
And rouse him at the name of Crispian.
He that shall see this day and live old age   44
Will yearly on the vigil feast his neighbors   45
And say, "Tomorrow is Saint Crispian."
Then will he strip his sleeve and show his scars,
And say, "These wounds I had on Crispin's Day."
Old men forget; yet all shall be forgot,   49
But he'll remember with advantages   50
What feats he did that day. Then shall our names,
Familiar in his mouth as household words—
Harry the King, Bedford and Exeter,
Warwick and Talbot, Salisbury and Gloucester—
Be in their flowing cups freshly remembered.
This story shall the good man teach his son;
And Crispin Crispian shall ne'er go by,
From this day to the ending of the world,
But we in it shall be rememberèd—
We few, we happy few, we band of brothers.
For he today that sheds his blood with me
Shall be my brother; be he ne'er so vile,   62
This day shall gentle his condition.   63
And gentlemen in England now abed
Shall think themselves accurst they were not here,
And hold their manhoods cheap whiles any speaks
That fought with us upon Saint Crispin's Day.

Enter Salisbury.

SALISBURY
My sovereign lord, bestow yourself with speed.   68
The French are bravely in their battles set,   69
And will with all expedience charge on us.   70

KING
All things are ready, if our minds be so.

WESTMORLAND
Perish the man whose mind is backward now!   72

KING
Thou dost not wish more help from England, coz?

WESTMORLAND
God's will, my liege, would you and I alone,
Without more help, could fight this royal battle!

---

63 **outwear** waste
4.3. Location: The English camp.
2 battle army.   **6 charge** post, command.   **10 kinsman** i.e., Westmorland, whose son had married Salisbury's daughter   **13 mind** remind
14 framed made, built   **18 What's** Who is   **20–1 enough . . . loss**
enough loss for our country to suffer   **25 upon my cost** at my
expense   **26 yearns** grieves   **30 coz** cousin, kinsman   **32 share from
me** take from me as his share   **33 For . . . have** i.e., in exchange for
my hope of eternal life.

34 host army   **35 stomach to** appetite for   **37 crowns for convoy**
travel money   **39 That . . . us** who is afraid to risk his life in my company.   **40 Feast of Crispian** Saint Crispin's Day, October 25. (Crispinus and Crispianus were martyrs who fled from Rome in the third
century; according to legend, they disguised themselves as shoemakers and afterward became the patron saints of that craft.)   **44 live**
live to see   **45 vigil** evening before a feast day   **49 yet** in time
50 advantages additions of his own   **62 vile** lowly   **63 gentle his
condition** i.e., raise his social status to the equivalent of gentleman
in that he is my "brother."   **68 bestow yourself** take up your battle
position   **69 bravely . . . set** finely arrayed in their battalions
70 expedience speed   **72 backward** reluctant

KING
Why, now thou hast unwished five thousand men,
Which likes me better than to wish us one.—
You know your places. God be with you all!   77

Tucket. Enter Montjoy.

MONTJOY
Once more I come to know of thee, King Harry,
If for thy ransom thou wilt now compound   80
Before thy most assurèd overthrow;
For certainly thou art so near the gulf   82
Thou needs must be englutted. Besides, in mercy   83
The Constable desires thee thou wilt mind   84
Thy followers of repentance, that their souls
May make a peaceful and a sweet retire   86
From off these fields where, wretches, their poor
     bodies
Must lie and fester.

KING   Who hath sent thee now?
MONTJOY   The Constable of France.
KING
I pray thee, bear my former answer back:
Bid them achieve me, and then sell my bones.
Good God, why should they mock poor fellows thus?   91
The man that once did sell the lion's skin
While the beast lived was killed with hunting him.
A many of our bodies shall no doubt   95
Find native graves, upon the which, I trust,   96
Shall witness live in brass of this day's work.
And those that leave their valiant bones in France,
Dying like men, though buried in your dunghills,
They shall be famed; for there the sun shall greet them
And draw their honors reeking up to heaven,   101
Leaving their earthly parts to choke your clime,
The smell whereof shall breed a plague in France.
Mark then abounding valor in our English,   104
That, being dead, like to the bullets crazing   105
Break out into a second course of mischief,
Killing in relapse of mortality.   107
Let me speak proudly. Tell the Constable
We are but warriors for the working day.   109
Our gayness and our gilt are all besmirched
With rainy marching in the painful field.
There's not a piece of feather in our host—
Good argument, I hope, we will not fly—
And time hath worn us into slovenry.   114
But, by the Mass, our hearts are in the trim!   115
And my poor soldiers tell me, yet ere night

They'll be in fresher robes, or they will pluck   117
The gay new coats o'er the French soldiers' heads   118
And turn them out of service. If they do this—   119
As, if God please, they shall—my ransom then
Will soon be levied. Herald, save thou thy labor.   121
Come thou no more for ransom, gentle herald.   122
They shall have none, I swear, but these my joints,
Which if they have as I will leave 'em them,
Shall yield them little, tell the Constable.
MONTJOY
I shall, King Harry. And so fare thee well.
Thou never shalt hear herald any more.   *Exit.*
KING
I fear thou wilt once more come again for a ransom.

Enter York [and kneels].

YORK
My lord, most humbly on my knee I beg
The leading of the vaward.   130
KING
Take it, brave York. Now, soldiers, march away.
And how thou pleasest, God, dispose the day!
                                            Exeunt.

❖

[4.4]

*Alarum. Excursions. Enter Pistol, French Soldier,
[and] Boy.*

PISTOL Yield, cur!
FRENCH SOLDIER *Je pense que vous êtes le gentilhomme de*   2
bonne qualité.   3
PISTOL
Qualtitie calmie custure me!   4
Art thou a gentleman? What is thy name? Discuss.   5
FRENCH SOLDIER *O Seigneur Dieu!*   6
PISTOL
Oh, Signieur Dew should be a gentleman.
Perpend my words, O Signieur Dew, and mark: 8
O Signieur Dew, thou diest on point of fox,   9
Except, O signieur, thou do give to me   10
Egregious ransom.   [*He threatens him with his sword.*]   11
FRENCH SOLDIER *Oh, prenez miséricorde! Ayez pitié de*   12
moi!   13
PISTOL
"Moy" shall not serve. I will have forty moys,   14
Or I will fetch thy rim out at thy throat   15

77 **likes** pleases   80 **compound** make terms   82 **gulf** whirlpool
83 **englutted** swallowed up.   84 **mind** remind   86 **retire** retreat
91 **achieve** capture   95 **A many** Many. (The phrase is an exact parallel to "a few.")   96 **native** in our own land (i.e., England)   101 **reeking** (1) breathing (2) smelling   104 **abounding** overflowing,
abundant   105 **crazing** shattering, with a suggestion also of *grazing*,
"ricocheting"   107 **Killing . . . mortality** killing (their foes) as they
(the English) fall back (decompose) into their elements; also, like the
bullet, with a deadly ricochet.   109 **for the working day** to do serious work, not take a holiday.   114 **slovenry** slovenliness, untidiness.
115 **in the trim** fully rigged, ready for action.

117–19 **They'll . . . service** they will be more freshly dressed by nightfall, if no other way than by defrocking the French soldiers like incapable servants being dismissed and stripped of their livery. (Soldiers
got to keep such spoils of war from their victims.)   121 **levied** collected.   122 **gentle** noble   130 **vaward** vanguard.
4.4. Location: The field of battle.
0.1 *Excursions* Sorties.   2–3 *Je . . . qualité* I think that you are a gentleman of high rank.   4 *calmie custure me* (These words are perhaps
derived from the refrain of a popular song, supposed to be Irish, "Calen
o custure me.")   5 **Discuss** Speak.   6 *O Seigneur Dieu!* O Lord God!
8 **Perpend** Attend to, consider   9 **fox** sword   10 **Except** unless
11 **Egregious** huge   12–13 **Oh . . . moi!** Oh, have mercy! Take pity on me!
14 **Moy** (Pistol, not understanding, takes *moi* for the name of a coin or
a sum of money, a moiety or half.)   15 **rim** midriff, diaphragm

In drops of crimson blood.

FRENCH SOLDIER   *Est-il impossible d'échapper la force de ton* 17
  bras? 18

PISTOL   Brass, cur?
  Thou damnèd and luxurious mountain goat, 20
  Offer'st me brass?

FRENCH SOLDIER   *Oh, pardonnez-moi!*

PISTOL
  Say'st thou me so? Is that a ton of moys?— 23
  Come hither, boy. Ask me this slave in French
  What is his name.

BOY   *Écoutez: comment êtes-vous appelé?* 26

FRENCH SOLDIER   *Monsieur Le Fer.*

BOY   He says his name is Master Fer.

PISTOL   Master Fer? I'll fer him, and firk him, and ferret 29
  him. Discuss the same in French unto him.

BOY   I do not know the French for fer, and ferret, and
  firk.

PISTOL
  Bid him prepare, for I will cut his throat.

FRENCH SOLDIER   *Que dit-il, monsieur?* 34

BOY   *Il me commande à vous dire que vous faites vous* 35
  prêt; car ce soldat ici est disposé tout à cette heure de 36
  couper votre gorge. 37

PISTOL
  Owy, cuppele gorge, permafoy, 38
  Peasant, unless thou give me crowns, brave crowns,
  Or mangled shalt thou be by this my sword.

FRENCH SOLDIER   *Oh, je vous supplie, pour l'amour de* 41
  Dieu, me pardonner! Je suis le gentilhomme de bonne 42
  maison. Gardez ma vie, et je vous donnerai deux cents 43
  écus. 44

PISTOL   What are his words?

BOY   He prays you to save his life. He is a gentleman of
  a good house, and for his ransom he will give you two 47
  hundred crowns.

PISTOL
  Tell him my fury shall abate, and I
  The crowns will take.

FRENCH SOLDIER   *Petit monsieur, que dit-il?* 51

BOY   *Encore qu'il est contre son jurement de pardonner* 52
  aucun prisonnier, néanmoins, pour les écus que vous 53
  l'avez promis, il est content à vous donner la liberté, 54
  le franchisement. 55

FRENCH SOLDIER *[kneeling]*   *Sur mes genoux je vous* 56
  donne mille remercîments; et je m'estime heureux que 57
  j'ai tombé entre les mains d'un chevalier, je pense, 58
  le plus brave, vaillant, et très-distingué seigneur 59
  d'Angleterre. 60

PISTOL   Expound unto me, boy.

BOY   He gives you, upon his knees, a thousand thanks,
  and he esteems himself happy that he hath fallen into
  the hands of one, as he thinks, the most brave, valorous, and thrice-worthy signieur of England.

PISTOL
  As I suck blood, I will some mercy show.
  Follow me!

BOY   *Suivez-vous le grand capitaine.* 68
      [Exeunt Pistol and French Soldier.]
  I did never know so full a voice issue
  from so empty a heart! But the saying is true, "The
  empty vessel makes the greatest sound." Bardolph and
  Nym had ten times more valor than this roaring devil 72
  i'th'old play, that everyone may pare his nails with 73
  a wooden dagger, and they are both hanged; and so 74
  would this be, if he durst steal anything adventur-
  ously. I must stay with the lackeys, with the luggage
  of our camp. The French might have a good prey of 77
  us, if he knew of it, for there is none to guard it but
  boys.   *Exit.*

✦

[4.5]

*Enter Constable, Orleans, Bourbon, Dauphin, and
Rambures.*

CONSTABLE   *Oh, diable!* 1

ORLEANS   *Oh, Seigneur! Le jour est perdu, tout est perdu!* 2

DAUPHIN
  Mort de ma vie! All is confounded, all. 3
  Reproach and everlasting shame
  Sits mocking in our plumes.   *A short alarum.*
  Oh, méchante fortune! Do not run away. 6

CONSTABLE   Why, all our ranks are broke.

DAUPHIN
  Oh, perdurable shame! Let's stab ourselves. 8
  Be these the wretches that we played at dice for?

ORLEANS
  Is this the king we sent to for his ransom?

BOURBON
  Shame and eternal shame, nothing but shame!
  Let us die! In once more! Back again!

17–18 *Est-il . . . bras?* Is it impossible to escape the strength of your arm? (But Pistol takes *bras*, "arm," for *brass*.)   **20 luxurious** lecherous   **23 a ton of moys** (This is what Pistol phonetically makes out of *pardonnez-moi*.)   **26 *Écoutez . . . appelé?*** Listen: what is your name?   **29 firk** trounce.   **ferret** worry (like a ferret)   **34–7 *Que . . . gorge*** What does he say, sir? BOY He bids me tell you that you must prepare yourself, because this soldier intends to cut your throat immediately.   **38 *Owy* Oui,** "yes."   **permafoy** *per ma foi,* by my faith   **41–4 *Oh . . . écus*** Oh, I pray you, for the love of God, to pardon! I am a gentleman of a good house; preserve my life, and I shall give you two hundred crowns.   **47 house** family   **51–5 *Petit . . . franchisement*** What does he say, little sir? BOY Although it is against his oath to pardon any prisoner, nevertheless, for the sake of the crowns you have promised, he is willing to give you your liberty, your freedom.

56–60 *Sur . . . d'Angleterre* On my knees, I give you a thousand thanks, and I consider myself happy that I have fallen into the hands of a knight, as I think, the bravest, most valiant, and very distinguished gentleman in England.   **68 *Suivez-vous . . . capitaine*** Follow the great captain.   **72–4 this roaring . . . dagger** Shakespeare refers several times to the devil in the morality play with his dagger of lath; see *2H6*, 4.2.2 and *Twelfth Night*, 4.2.126. The paring of the devil's nails was a proverbial act of bravado.   **77 a good prey** i.e., easy pickings   **4.5. Location: The field of battle still.**
1 *Oh, diable!* Oh, the devil!   **2 *Oh . . . perdu!*** Oh, Lord, the day is lost, all is lost!   **3 *Mort . . . vie!*** Death to my life!   **confounded** lost
6 *Oh, méchante fortune!* Oh, malicious fortune!   **8 perdurable** everlasting

And he that will not follow Bourbon now,
Let him go hence, and with his cap in hand,
Like a base pander, hold the chamber door
Whilst by a slave, no gentler than my dog,   16
His fairest daughter is contaminated.

CONSTABLE
Disorder, that hath spoiled us, friend us now!   18
Let us on heaps go offer up our lives.   19

ORLEANS
We are enough yet living in the field
To smother up the English in our throngs,
If any order might be thought upon.

BOURBON
The devil take order now! I'll to the throng.
Let life be short, else shame will be too long.

                                              Exeunt.

[4.6]

*Alarum. Enter the King and his train, [Exeter,
and others,] with prisoners.*

KING
Well have we done, thrice valiant countrymen!
But all's not done; yet keep the French the field.   2

EXETER
The Duke of York commends him to Your Majesty.

KING
Lives he, good uncle? Thrice within this hour
I saw him down, thrice up again and fighting.
From helmet to the spur all blood he was.

EXETER
In which array, brave soldier, doth he lie,
Larding the plain; and by his bloody side,   8
Yokefellow to his honor-owing wounds,   9
The noble Earl of Suffolk also lies.
Suffolk first died; and York, all haggled over,   11
Comes to him, where in gore he lay insteeped,   12
And takes him by the beard, kisses the gashes
That bloodily did yawn upon his face.   14
He cries aloud, "Tarry, my cousin Suffolk!
My soul shall thine keep company to heaven;
Tarry, sweet soul, for mine, then fly abreast,
As in this glorious and well-foughten field
We kept together in our chivalry!"
Upon these words I came and cheered him up.
He smiled me in the face, raught me his hand,   21
And with a feeble grip says, "Dear my lord,
Commend my service to my sovereign."
So did he turn, and over Suffolk's neck
He threw his wounded arm, and kissed his lips,
And so, espoused to death, with blood he sealed

A testament of noble-ending love.
The pretty and sweet manner of it forced
Those waters from me which I would have stopped;   29
But I had not so much of man in me,
And all my mother came into mine eyes   31
And gave me up to tears.

KING   I blame you not;
For, hearing this, I must perforce compound   33
With mistful eyes, or they will issue too.   *Alarum.*   34
But, hark, what new alarum is this same?
The French have reinforced their scattered men.
Then every soldier kill his prisoners!   37
Give the word through.   *Exeunt.*

[4.7]

Enter Fluellen and Gower.

FLUELLEN   Kill the poys and the luggage? 'Tis expressly   1
against the law of arms. 'Tis as arrant a piece of
knavery, mark you now, as can be offert; in your
conscience, now, is it not?

GOWER   'Tis certain there's not a boy left alive; and the
cowardly rascals that ran from the battle ha' done this
slaughter. Besides, they have burned and carried
away all that was in the King's tent, wherefore the
King most worthily hath caused every soldier to cut
his prisoner's throat. Oh, 'tis a gallant king!

FLUELLEN   Ay, he was porn at Monmouth, Captain   11
Gower. What call you the town's name where Alexander the Pig was born?

GOWER   Alexander the Great.

FLUELLEN   Why, I pray you, is not "pig" great? The pig,
or the great, or the mighty, or the huge, or the
magnanimous, are all one reckonings, save the phrase 17
is a little variations.

GOWER   I think Alexander the Great was born in
Macedon. His father was called Philip of Macedon, as
I take it.

FLUELLEN   I think it is e'en Macedon where Alexander is
born. I tell you, Captain, if you look in the maps of the
'orld, I warrant you sall find, in the comparisons between Macedon and Monmouth, that the situations,
look you, is both alike. There is a river in Macedon,
and there is also moreover a river at Monmouth. It is
called Wye at Monmouth, but it is out of my prains
what is the name of the other river; but 'tis all one, 'tis
alike as my fingers is to my fingers, and there is sal-
mons in both. If you mark Alexander's life well, Harry
of Monmouth's life is come after it indifferent well, for 32
there is figures in all things. Alexander, God knows,   33

---

16 **gentler** (1) more nobly born (2) tenderer   18 **friend** befriend
19 **on** in
4.6. Location: The field of battle still.
2 **yet . . . field** the French are in the field of battle still.   8 **Larding**
fattening, enriching (with his blood)   9 **honor-owing** honor-owning,
honorable   11 **haggled over** mangled, hacked   12 **insteeped**
steeped, soaked   14 **yawn** gape   21 **me in the** in my.   **raught**
reached

29 **waters** i.e., tears   31 **my mother** i.e., the tenderer part of me
33 **perforce** necessarily.   **compound** come to terms   34 **issue** issue
forth tears   37 **kill his prisoners** (This follows Holinshed, who says
that Henry, alarmed by the outcry of the lackeys and boys of the
camp, feared a new attack and ordered the prisoners killed as a precaution. Gower, 4.7.8–10, attributes the King's action to revenge.)
4.7. Location: The field of battle still.
1 **luggage** i.e., lackeys guarding the luggage.   11 **Monmouth** (i.e., in
Wales)   17 **are . . . reckonings** come to the same thing   32 **is . . . well**
resembles it fairly well   33 **figures** comparisons, similes

and you know, in his rages, and his furies, and his
wraths, and his cholers, and his moods, and his displeasures, and his indignations, and also being a little
intoxicates in his prains, did, in his ales and his angers,　37
look you, kill his best friend, Cleitus.　38

GOWER　Our King is not like him in that. He never killed
any of his friends.

FLUELLEN　It is not well done, mark you now, to take
the tales out of my mouth ere it is made and finished.
I speak but in the figures and comparisons of it. As
Alexander killed his friend Cleitus, being in his ales
and his cups, so also Harry Monmouth, being in his
right wits and his good judgments, turned away the
fat knight with the great-belly doublet. He was full of　47
jests, and gipes, and knaveries, and mocks. I have　48
forgot his name.

GOWER　Sir John Falstaff.

FLUELLEN　That is he. I'll tell you there is good men
porn at Monmouth.

GOWER　Here comes His Majesty.

Alarum. Enter King Harry, [Warwick, Gloucester,
Exeter, and others,] and Bourbon, with [other]
prisoners. Flourish.

KING
I was not angry since I came to France
Until this instant. Take a trumpet, herald;　55
Ride thou unto the horsemen on yond hill.
If they will fight with us, bid them come down,
Or void the field. They do offend our sight.　58
If they'll do neither, we will come to them,
And make them skirr away as swift as stones　60
Enforcèd from the old Assyrian slings.　61
Besides, we'll cut the throats of those we have,
And not a man of them that we shall take
Shall taste our mercy. Go and tell them so.

Enter Montjoy.

EXETER
Here comes the herald of the French, my liege.

GLOUCESTER
His eyes are humbler than they used to be.

KING
How now, what means this, herald? Know'st thou
　not
That I have fined these bones of mine for ransom?　68
Com'st thou again for ransom?

MONTJOY　　　　　　　　　No, great King.
I come to thee for charitable license,
That we may wander o'er this bloody field
To book our dead and then to bury them,　72
To sort our nobles from our common men.

For many of our princes—woe the while!—
Lie drowned and soaked in mercenary blood;　75
So do our vulgar drench their peasant limbs　76
In blood of princes; and the wounded steeds
Fret fetlock-deep in gore and with wild rage　78
Yerk out their armèd heels at their dead masters,　79
Killing them twice. Oh, give us leave, great King,
To view the field in safety, and dispose
Of their dead bodies!

KING　　　　　　　　　　I tell thee truly, herald,
I know not if the day be ours or no,
For yet a many of your horsemen peer　84
And gallop o'er the field.

MONTJOY　　　　　　　　　The day is yours.

KING
Praisèd be God, and not our strength, for it!
What is this castle called that stands hard by?

MONTJOY　They call it Agincourt.

KING
Then call we this the field of Agincourt,
Fought on the day of Crispin Crispianus.

FLUELLEN　Your grandfather of famous memory, an't　91
please Your Majesty, and your great-uncle Edward the
Plack Prince of Wales, as I have read in the chronicles,
fought a most prave pattle here in France.

KING　They did, Fluellen.

FLUELLEN　Your Majesty says very true. If Your Majesties is remembered of it, the Welshmen did good
service in a garden where leeks did grow, wearing
leeks in their Monmouth caps, which, Your Majesty　99
know, to this hour is an honorable badge of the
service; and I do believe Your Majesty takes no scorn
to wear the leek upon Saint Tavy's Day.　102

KING
I wear it for a memorable honor,
For I am Welsh, you know, good countryman.

FLUELLEN　All the water in Wye cannot wash Your
Majesty's Welsh plood out of your pody, I can tell you
that. God pless it and preserve it, as long as it pleases
His Grace, and His Majesty too!

KING　Thanks, good my countryman.

FLUELLEN　By Jeshu, I am Your Majesty's countryman.
I care not who know it. I will confess it to all the 'orld.
I need not to be ashamed of Your Majesty, praised be
God, so long as Your Majesty is an honest man.

KING
God keep me so!

Enter Williams [with a glove in his cap].

　　　　　　　　　Our heralds go with him.
Bring me just notice of the numbers dead　115

---

37 **in his ales** i.e., under the influence of ale　38 **Cleitus** a general
and close associate of Alexander, whom Alexander killed in a drinking bout.　47 **great-belly doublet** a man's close-fitting jacket, in
which the lower part was stuffed out with bombast or padding.
48 **gipes** gibes, jokes　55 **trumpet** trumpeter　58 **void** leave
60 **skirr** scurry　61 **Enforcèd** discharged　68 **fined . . . ransom** i.e.,
agreed to pay as a fine or ransom only these bones of mine and no
more.　72 **book** record

75 **mercenary** i.e., of common soldiers, who fought for pay　76 **vulgar** commoners　78 **fetlock-deep** (The *fetlock* is above the hoof, at the
back of the leg.)　79 **Yerk** kick　84 **peer** (1) look bout anxiously
(2) appear　91 **grandfather** i.e., great-grandfather, Edward III.　**an't**
if it　99 **Monmouth caps** round and rimless caps with a tapering
crown, commonly worn by the Welsh　102 **Saint Tavy's Day** the festival of Saint David, patron saint of Wales, March 1—an occasion for
the celebration of Welsh traditions, though the wearing of leeks to
commemorate the great victory in 540 against the Saxons did not
begin until well after the setting of this play.　115 **just** exact

On both our parts.
                    [*Exeunt Heralds and Gower with Montjoy.*]
                    Call yonder fellow hither.
EXETER [*to Williams*]   Soldier, you must come to the King.
KING   Soldier, why wear'st thou that glove in thy cap?
WILLIAMS   An't please Your Majesty, 'tis the gage of
one that I should fight withal, if he be alive.
KING   An Englishman?
WILLIAMS   An't please Your Majesty, a rascal that swag-
gered with me last night, who, if 'a live and ever dare
to challenge this glove, I have sworn to take him a box
o'th'ear; or if I can see my glove in his cap, which he
swore, as he was a soldier, he would wear if 'a lived, I
will strike it out soundly.
KING   What think you, Captain Fluellen, is it fit this
soldier keep his oath?
FLUELLEN   He is a craven and a villain else, an't please   130
Your Majesty, in my conscience.
KING   It may be his enemy is a gentleman of great sort,   132
quite from the answer of his degree.   133
FLUELLEN   Though he be as good a gentleman as the
devil is, as Lucifer and Beelzebub himself, it is
necessary, look Your Grace, that he keep his vow and
his oath. If he be perjured, see you now, his reputation
is as arrant a villain and a Jack-sauce as ever his   138
black shoe trod upon God's ground and His earth, in
my conscience, la!
KING [*to Williams*]   Then keep thy vow, sirrah, when
thou meet'st the fellow.
WILLIAMS   So I will, my liege, as I live.
KING   Who serv'st thou under?
WILLIAMS   Under Captain Gower, my liege.
FLUELLEN   Gower is a good captain, and is good
knowledge and literatured in the wars.   147
KING   Call him hither to me, soldier.
WILLIAMS   I will, my liege.   *Exit.*
KING   Here, Fluellen, wear thou this favor for me and
stick it in thy cap. [*He gives Fluellen Williams' glove.*]
When Alençon and myself were down together, I
plucked this glove from his helm. If any man challenge   153
this, he is a friend to Alençon and an enemy to our
person. If thou encounter any such, apprehend him,
an thou dost me love.   156
FLUELLEN [*putting the glove in his cap*]   Your Grace doo's   157
me as great honors as can be desired in the hearts of
his subjects. I would fain see the man that   159
has but two legs that shall find himself aggriefed at
this glove, that is all. But I would fain see it once, an't   161
please God of his grace that I might see.
KING   Know'st thou Gower?
FLUELLEN   He is my dear friend, an't please you.
KING   Pray thee, go seek him and bring him to my tent.
FLUELLEN   I will fetch him.   *Exit.*

KING
My lord of Warwick, and my brother Gloucester,
Follow Fluellen closely at the heels.
The glove which I have given him for a favor
May haply purchase him a box o'th'ear.   170
It is the soldier's; I by bargain should
Wear it myself. Follow, good cousin Warwick.
If that the soldier strike him, as I judge
By his blunt bearing he will keep his word,
Some sudden mischief may arise of it;
For I do know Fluellen valiant
And touched with choler, hot as gunpowder,   177
And quickly will return an injury.   178
Follow, and see there be no harm between them.
Go you with me, uncle of Exeter.   *Exeunt [separately].*

❖

[4.8]

Enter Gower and Williams.

WILLIAMS   I warrant it is to knight you, Captain.

Enter Fluellen.

FLUELLEN   God's will and his pleasure, Captain, I
beseech you now, come apace to the King. There is
more good toward you, peradventure, than is in your
knowledge to dream of.
WILLIAMS   Sir, know you this glove?
FLUELLEN   Know the glove? I know the glove is a glove.
WILLIAMS   I know this, and thus I challenge it.
                                            Strikes him.
FLUELLEN   'Sblood, an arrant traitor as any 's in the   9
universal world, or in France, or in England!
GOWER [*to Williams*]   How now, sir? You villain!
WILLIAMS   Do you think I'll be forsworn?
FLUELLEN   Stand away, Captain Gower. I will give
treason his payment into plows, I warrant you.   14
WILLIAMS   I am no traitor.
FLUELLEN   That's a lie in thy throat.—I charge you in His   16
Majesty's name, apprehend him. He's a friend of the
Duke Alençon's.

Enter Warwick and Gloucester.

WARWICK   How now, how now, what's the matter?
FLUELLEN   My lord of Warwick, here is—praised be
God for it!—a most contagious treason come to light,   21
look you, as you shall desire in a summer's day.—
Here is His Majesty.

Enter King [Henry] and Exeter.

KING   How now, what's the matter?
FLUELLEN   My liege, here is a villain and a traitor that,
look Your Grace, has struck the glove which Your
Majesty is take out of the helmet of Alençon.

---

130 **craven** coward   132 **sort** rank   133 **quite . . . degree** i.e., too high
in rank to answer the challenge of one so low.   138 **Jack-sauce** saucy
knave   147 **literatured** well read   153 **helm** helmet.   156 **an** if
157 **doo's** does   159 **fain** willingly   161 **an't** if it. (Also in line 164.)

170 **haply** perhaps   177 **touched with choler** hot-tempered
178 **return an injury** repay an insult.
4.8. Location: The English camp.
9 **'Sblood** By His (Christ's) blood   14 **his** its.   **into plows** in blows
16 **lie in thy throat** i.e., inexcusable lie.   21 **contagious** noxious

WILLIAMS   My liege, this was my glove; here is the fellow of it. [*Showing his other glove.*] And he that I gave it to in change promised to wear it in his cap. I promised 30
to strike him, if he did. I met this man with my glove in his cap, and I have been as good as my word.

FLUELLEN   Your Majesty hear now, saving Your Majesty's manhood, what an arrant, rascally, beggarly, lousy knave it is. I hope Your Majesty is pear me 35
testimony and witness, and will avouchment, that this 36
is the glove of Alençon that Your Majesty is give me, in your conscience, now.

KING   Give me thy glove, soldier. Look, here is the fellow of it.   [*He shows his other glove.*]
'Twas I indeed thou promisèd'st to strike,
And thou hast given me most bitter terms. 42

FLUELLEN   An't please Your Majesty, let his neck answer for it, if there is any martial law in the world.

KING
How canst thou make me satisfaction?

WILLIAMS   All offenses, my lord, come from the heart. Never came any from mine that might offend Your Majesty.

KING   It was ourself thou didst abuse.

WILLIAMS   Your Majesty came not like yourself. You appeared to me but as a common man—witness the night, your garments, your lowliness. And what Your 52
Highness suffered under that shape, I beseech you take it for your own fault and not mine; for had you been as I took you for, I made no offense. Therefore I beseech Your Highness pardon me.

KING
Here, uncle Exeter, fill this glove with crowns,
And give it to this fellow.—Keep it, fellow,
And wear it for an honor in thy cap
Till I do challenge it.—Give him the crowns.
          [*Exeter gives the glove and gold to Williams.*]
And Captain, you must needs be friends with him.

FLUELLEN   By this day and this light, the fellow has mettle enough in his belly.—Hold, there is twelvepence for you. [*He offers Williams a coin.*] And I pray you to serve God, and keep you out of prawls, and prabbles, and quarrels, and dissensions, and I warrant 66
you it is the better for you.

WILLIAMS   I will none of your money.

FLUELLEN   It is with a good will. I can tell you, it will serve you to mend your shoes. Come, wherefore should you be so pashful? Your shoes is not so good. 'Tis a good silling, I warrant you, or I will change it.

          Enter [an English] Herald.

KING   Now, herald, are the dead numbered?

HERALD [*giving a paper*]
Here is the number of the slaughtered French.

KING
What prisoners of good sort are taken, uncle? 75

EXETER [*reading*]
Charles Duke of Orlean
John Duke of Bourbon,
Of other lords and baron
Full fifteen hundred, bes

KING
This note doth tell me of te
That in the field lie slain. C
And nobles bearing banner
One hundred twenty-six; ad
Of knights, esquires, and ga
Eight thousand and four hun
Five hundred were but yester
So that in these ten thousand t
There are but sixteen hundred
The rest are princes, barons, lor
And gentlemen of blood and qu
The names of those their nobles
Charles Delabreth, High Constab
Jaques of Chatillion, Admiral of F
The Master of the Crossbows, Lor
Great-Master of France, the brave S
    Dauphin
John, Duke of Alençon; Anthony, Du
The brother to the Duke of Burgundy
And Edward, Duke of Bar; of lusty ea
Grandpré and Roussi, Faulconbridge a
Beaumont and Marle, Vaudemont and Le
Here was a royal fellowship of death!
Where is the number of our English dead?
          [*He is given another pape.*]
Edward the Duke of York, the Earl of Suffolk,
Sir Richard Keighley, Davy Gam, esquire;
None else of name, and of all other men 105
But five-and-twenty. O God, thy arm was here!
And not to us, but to thy arm alone,
Ascribe we all. When, without stratagem,
But in plain shock and even play of battle, 109
Was ever known so great and little loss
On one part and on th'other? Take it, God,
For it is none but thine.

EXETER   'Tis wonderful. 112

KING
Come, go we in procession to the village.
And be it death proclaimèd through our host
To boast of this or take that praise from God
Which is his only.

FLUELLEN   Is it not lawful, an't please Your Majesty, to tell how many is killed?

KING
Yes, Captain, but with this acknowledgment,
That God fought for us.

---

30 change exchange   **35 is pear** will bear   **36 avouchment** avouch
42 terms words.   **52 lowliness** humble mien.
66 prabbles i.e., brabbles, scuffles   **75 good sort** high rank

76–112 Charles . . . thine (The catalogue of the captured and slain is from Holinshed.)   **82 bearing banners** i.e., with coats of arms
95 Great-Master grandmaster, i.e., the chief officer of the royal household   **98 lusty** vigorous   **105 name** rank, social importance
109 even equal

THE LIFE OF KING HENRY TH...

912 : 4.8

...science, he did us great good.

...s.

FLUELLEN Yes, ... *nobis* and *Te Deum*, 123
...y enclosed in clay;
KING Do we ...y and to England then,
Let the... France arrived more happy men. 126
The ...
An...

Exeunt.

❧

...*er Chorus.*

...safe to those that have not read the story 1
...I may prompt them; and of such as have,
...mbly pray them to admit th'excuse 3
...time, of numbers, and due course of things,
...hich cannot in their huge and proper life
...e here presented. Now we bear the King
Toward Calais. Grant him there. There seen,
Heave him away upon your wingèd thoughts
Athwart the sea. Behold, the English beach 9
Pales in the flood with men, wives, and boys, 10
Whose shouts and claps outvoice the deep-mouthed
  sea,
Which like a mighty whiffler 'fore the King 12
Seems to prepare his way. So let him land,
And solemnly see him set on to London.
So swift a pace hath thought that even now
You may imagine him upon Blackheath, 16
Where that his lords desire him to have borne 17
His bruisèd helmet and his bended sword
Before him through the city. He forbids it,
Being free from vainness and self-glorious pride,
Giving full trophy, signal, and ostent 21
Quite from himself to God. But now behold,
In the quick forge and working-house of thought,
How London doth pour out her citizens!
The Mayor and all his brethren, in best sort, 25
Like to the senators of th'antique Rome
With the plebeians swarming at their heels,
Go forth and fetch their conquering Caesar in;

As by a lower but loving likelihood, 29
Were now the General of our gracious Empress, 30
As in good time he may, from Ireland coming,
Bringing rebellion broachèd on his sword, 32
How many would the peaceful city quit
To welcome him! Much more, and much more cause, 34
Did they this Harry. Now in London place him;
As yet the lamentation of the French 36
Invites the King of England's stay at home; 37
The Emperor's coming in behalf of France, 38
To order peace between them . . . and omit 39
All the occurrences, whatever chanced,
Till Harry's back-return again to France. 41
There must we bring him; and myself have played
The interim by rememb'ring you 'tis past. 43
Then brook abridgment, and your eyes advance, 44
After your thoughts, straight back again to France.

Exit.

❧

[5.1]

Enter Fluellen [with a leek in his cap, and a cudgel], and Gower.

GOWER Nay, that's right. But why wear you your leek today? Saint Davy's Day is past.

FLUELLEN There is occasions and causes why and wherefore in all things. I will tell you asse my friend, 4
Captain Gower. The rascally, scald, beggarly, lousy, 5
pragging knave, Pistol, which you and yourself and all the world know to be no petter than a fellow, look you now, of no merits, he is come to me and prings me pread and salt yesterday, look you, and bid me eat my leek. It was in a place where I could not breed no contention with him; but I will be so bold as to wear it in my cap till I see him once again, and then I will tell him a little piece of my desires.

Enter Pistol.

GOWER Why, here he comes, swelling like a turkey-cock.

FLUELLEN 'Tis no matter for his swellings nor his turkey-cocks.—God pless you, Aunchient Pistol! You scurvy, lousy knave, God pless you!

PISTOL
Ha, art thou bedlam? Dost thou thirst, base Trojan, 19

---

123 *Non nobis* i.e., Psalm 115, beginning, "Not unto us, O Lord, not unto us, but unto thy name give glory." *Te Deum* a hymn of thanksgiving, beginning, "We praise thee O God" 126 **happy** fortunate
5.0. (Between Acts 4 and 5, there is historically an interval of about five years during which Henry made a second campaign in France that brought the French to terms in the Treaty of Troyes, with which the play ends.)
1 **Vouchsafe** Permit it 3 **admit th'excuse** excuse our handling
9 **Athwart** across 10 **Pales in** hems in, surrounds. **flood** sea
12 **whiffler** an usher heading the procession to clear the way
16 **Blackheath** open area just outside London, to the southeast
17 **Where that** where 21 **Giving . . . ostent** giving every memorial, token, and display of victory 25 **sort** array

29–34 **As . . . him** (Seemingly, an allusion to the Earl of Essex, who left London on his Irish expedition on March 27, 1599, in an attempt to put down Tyrone's rebellion; he returned unsuccessful and under a cloud on September 28 of the same year. These lines, therefore, were probably written between the dates mentioned.) 29 **a . . . likelihood** a less exalted comparison but one that shows much love 30 **Empress** i.e., Elizabeth 32 **broachèd** transfixed, spitted 36–7 **As . . . home** i.e., the French are so dejected that Henry can stay in England without fear of loss in France 38 **Emperor's coming** (The Holy Roman Emperor, Sigismund, came to England on behalf of France in May 1416.) 39 **them . . . and omit** (Something appears to be left out here. Possibly it should read, "them, and the death / O' the Dauphin, leap we over, and omit . . .") 41 **Harry's back-return** i.e., Henry's second campaign, commencing in 1417 43 **rememb'ring** reminding
44 **brook** tolerate, excuse
5.1. Location: France. The English camp.
4 **asse** as 5 **scald** scurvy 19 **bedlam** crazy. **Trojan** i.e., rascal

To have me fold up Parca's fatal web?   20
Hence, I am qualmish at the smell of leek.   21

FLUELLEN   I peseech you heartily, scurvy, lousy knave,
at my desires, and my requests, and my petitions, to
eat, look you, this leek. [*He offers the leek.*] Because,
look you, you do not love it, nor your affections and
your appetites and your disgestions doo's not agree
with it, I would desire you to eat it.

PISTOL
Not for Cadwallader and all his goats.   28

FLUELLEN   There is one goat for you. (*Strikes him.*) Will
you be so good, scald knave, as eat it?

PISTOL   Base Trojan, thou shalt die.

FLUELLEN   You say very true, scald knave, when God's
will is. I will desire you to live in the meantime and
eat your victuals. Come, there is sauce for it. [*He strikes
him.*] You called me yesterday mountain squire, but I   35
will make you today a squire of low degree. I pray   36
you, fall to. If you can mock a leek, you can eat a leek.

GOWER   Enough, Captain, you have astonished him.   38

FLUELLEN   By Jesu, I will make him eat some part of my
leek, or I will peat his pate four days. Bite, I pray you; 40
it is good for your green wound and your ploody   41
coxcomb.   42

PISTOL   Must I bite?

FLUELLEN   Yes, certainly, and out of doubt and out of
question too, and ambiguities.

PISTOL
By this leek, I will most horribly revenge—
                          [*Fluellen threatens him.*]
I eat and eat—I swear—

FLUELLEN   Eat, I pray you. Will you have some more
sauce to your leek? There is not enough leek to
swear by.

PISTOL
Quiet thy cudgel; thou dost see I eat.

FLUELLEN   Much good do you, scald knave, heartily.
Nay, pray you, throw none away; the skin is good for
your broken coxcomb. When you take occasions to see   54
leeks hereafter, I pray you, mock at 'em, that is all.

PISTOL   Good.

FLUELLEN   Ay, leeks is good. Hold you, there is a groat 57
to heal your pate.   [*He offers a coin.*]

PISTOL   Me, a groat?

FLUELLEN   Yes, verily, and in truth you shall take it, or
I have another leek in my pocket which you shall eat.

PISTOL
I take thy groat in earnest of revenge.   62

FLUELLEN   If I owe you anything, I will pay you in
cudgels. You shall be a woodmonger and buy nothing
of me but cudgels. God b'wi'you, and keep you, and
heal your pate.   *Exit.*

PISTOL   All hell shall stir for this.

GOWER   Go, go, you are a counterfeit cowardly knave.
Will you mock at an ancient tradition, begun upon an
honorable respect and worn as a memorable trophy of   70
predeceased valor, and dare not avouch in your deeds   71
any of your words? I have seen you gleeking and   72
galling at this gentleman twice or thrice. You thought   73
because he could not speak English in the native garb
he could not therefore handle an English cudgel. You
find it otherwise; and henceforth let a Welsh correction teach you a good English condition. Fare
ye well.   *Exit.*

PISTOL
Doth Fortune play the huswife with me now?   79
News have I that my Doll is dead   80
I'th' spital of a malady of France,   81
And there my rendezvous is quite cut off.
Old I do wax, and from my weary limbs   83
Honor is cudgeled. Well, bawd I'll turn,
And something lean to cutpurse of quick hand.   85
To England will I steal, and there I'll steal;
And patches will I get unto these cudgeled scars,
And swear I got them in the Gallia wars.   *Exit.*   88

❖

[5.2]

*Enter, at one door, King Henry, Exeter, Bedford,
[Gloucester, Clarence,] Warwick, [Westmorland,]
and other lords; at another, Queen Isabel, the
[French] King, the Duke of Burgundy, [the
Princess Katharine, Alice,] and other French.*

KING HENRY
Peace to this meeting, wherefor we are met!
Unto our brother France and to our sister,
Health and fair time of day; joy and good wishes
To our most fair and princely cousin Katharine;
And, as a branch and member of this royalty,   5
By whom this great assembly is contrived,
We do salute you, Duke of Burgundy;
And princes French, and peers, health to you all!

FRENCH KING
Right joyous are we to behold your face,
Most worthy brother England. Fairly met!
So are you, princes English, every one.

---

20 **Parca's** (The Parcae, or Fates, spun, drew out, and cut the thread of
destiny.)   21 **qualmish** squeamish, nauseated   28 **Cadwallader** sev-
enth-century Welsh warrior king.   **goats** (Pistol makes the customary
taunt that the Welsh were goatherds.)   35 **mountain squire** i.e., a
squire owning mountainous, poor land   36 **squire of low degree**
(Allusion to a popular medieval romance, *The Squire of Low Degree.*
Fluellen threatens to make Pistol into a lowly, contemptible figure,
towered over by a mountain squire.)   38 **astonished** dazed, terrified
40 **pate** head   41 **green** raw   42 **coxcomb** fool's cap; here, the scalp.
54 **broken** bleeding (not "fractured")   57 **groat** fourpenny coin
62 **in earnest of** as a down payment for

70 **respect** consideration   71 **predeceased valor** valor of those now
dead   72–3 **gleeking and galling** mocking and scoffing   79 **huswife**
hussy, fickle jade   80 **Doll** (At 2.1.17–18 we learn that Pistol was married to Nell Quickly. The similarity of *Doll* and *Nell* could suggest a
textual error here, or authorial forgetfulness, or a change in the characters' fortunes.)   81 **spital** hospital.   **malady of France** venereal
disease   83 **wax** grow   85 **something lean to** I'll incline somewhat
to   88 **Gallia** French
5.2. Location: The French court.
5 **royalty** royal family

QUEEN ISABEL

So happy be the issue, brother England,   12
Of this good day and of this gracious meeting,
As we are now glad to behold your eyes—
Your eyes, which hitherto have borne in them
Against the French that met them in their bent   16
The fatal balls of murdering basilisks.   17
The venom of such looks, we fairly hope,
Have lost their quality, and that this day
Shall change all griefs and quarrels into love.   20

KING HENRY

To cry amen to that, thus we appear.

QUEEN ISABEL

You English princes all, I do salute you.

BURGUNDY

My duty to you both, on equal love,
Great Kings of France and England! That I have
     labored
With all my wits, my pains, and strong endeavors
To bring your most imperial Majesties
Unto this bar and royal interview,
Your mightiness on both parts best can witness.   27
Since, then, my office hath so far prevailed
That, face to face and royal eye to eye,
You have congreeted, let it not disgrace me   31
If I demand, before this royal view,   32
What rub or what impediment there is   33
Why that the naked, poor, and mangled Peace,
Dear nurse of arts, plenties, and joyful births,
Should not in this best garden of the world,
Our fertile France, put up her lovely visage?   37
Alas, she hath from France too long been chased,
And all her husbandry doth lie on heaps,   39
Corrupting in it own fertility.   40
Her vine, the merry cheerer of the heart,
Unprunèd dies; her hedges even-pleached,   42
Like prisoners wildly overgrown with hair,
Put forth disordered twigs; her fallow leas   44
The darnel, hemlock, and rank fumitory   45
Doth root upon, while that the coulter rusts   46
That should deracinate such savagery.   47
The even mead, that erst brought sweetly forth   48
The freckled cowslip, burnet, and green clover,   49
Wanting the scythe, all uncorrected, rank,   50
Conceives by idleness, and nothing teems   51
But hateful docks, rough thistles, kecksies, burrs,   52
Losing both beauty and utility.
And all our vineyards, fallows, meads, and hedges,   54

Defective in their natures, grow to wildness;   55
Even so our houses and ourselves and children   56
Have lost, or do not learn for want of time,
The sciences that should become our country,   58
But grow like savages—as soldiers will
That nothing do but meditate on blood—
To swearing and stern looks, diffused attire,   61
And everything that seems unnatural.
Which to reduce into our former favor   63
You are assembled, and my speech entreats
That I may know the let why gentle Peace   65
Should not expel these inconveniences
And bless us with her former qualities.

KING HENRY

If, Duke of Burgundy, you would the peace,   68
Whose want gives growth to th'imperfections   69
Which you have cited, you must buy that peace
With full accord to all our just demands,
Whose tenors and particular effects   72
You have enscheduled briefly in your hands.   73

BURGUNDY

The King hath heard them, to the which as yet
There is no answer made.

KING HENRY   Well then, the peace,
Which you before so urged, lies in his answer.

FRENCH KING

I have but with a cursitory eye   77
O'erglanced the articles. Pleaseth Your Grace   78
To appoint some of your council presently
To sit with us once more, with better heed
To re-survey them, we will suddenly   81
Pass our accept and peremptory answer.   82

KING HENRY

Brother, we shall.—Go, uncle Exeter,
And brother Clarence, and you, brother Gloucester,
Warwick, and Huntingdon, go with the King,
And take with you free power to ratify,
Augment, or alter, as your wisdoms best
Shall see advantageable for our dignity,   88
Anything in or out of our demands,
And we'll consign thereto.—Will you, fair sister,   90
Go with the princes, or stay here with us?

QUEEN ISABEL

Our gracious brother, I will go with them.
Haply a woman's voice may do some good   93
When articles too nicely urged be stood on.   94

KING HENRY

Yet leave our cousin Katharine here with us.
She is our capital demand, comprised   96
Within the fore-rank of our articles.   97

---

12 issue outcome   **16 in their bent** (1) as they were directed (2) in their glance   **17 fatal balls** (1) cannonballs (2) eyeballs.   **basilisks** (1) large cannon (2) monsters supposed to kill with their gaze. **20 griefs** grievances   **27 bar** tribunal   **31 congreeted** greeted each other   **32 demand** ask   **33 rub** obstacle. (A term from bowls.) **37 put up** show, lift up   **39 husbandry** harvest, foison   **40 it** its **42 even-pleached** smoothly intertwined   **44 fallow leas** uncultivated open fields   **45 darnel . . . fumitory** i.e., weeds that grow in cultivated land   **46 coulter** plow blade   **47 deracinate** root out   **48 even mead** level meadow.   **erst** formerly   **49 burnet** a herb   **50 Wanting** lacking   **51 Conceives** gives birth (to weeds).   **teems** flourishes **52 kecksies** dry stalks   **54 fallows** land plowed and left lying

55 Defective . . . natures naturally inclined to wildness   **56 houses** households   **58 sciences** skills   **61 diffused** disordered   **63 reduce . . . favor** return to our former good appearance and good graces **65 let** hindrance   **68 would** wish   **69 want** lack   **72 tenors . . . effects** general purport and specific details   **73 enscheduled** drawn up in writing   **77 cursitory** cursory, hasty   **78 Pleaseth** May it please **81 suddenly** speedily   **82 Pass . . . answer** deliver our agreed-to and final answer.   **88 advantageable** advantageous   **90 consign** agree, subscribe   **93 Haply** Perhaps   **94 nicely** punctiliously, with insistence on detail.   **stood on** insisted on.   **96 capital** chief   **97 fore-rank** first row

QUEEN ISABEL
She hath good leave.

Exeunt omnes. Manent King [Henry]
and Katharine [with Alice].

KING HENRY   Fair Katharine, and most fair,   98
Will you vouchsafe to teach a soldier terms
Such as will enter at a lady's ear
And plead his love suit to her gentle heart?

KATHARINE   Your Majesty shall mock at me. I cannot
speak your England.

KING HENRY   O fair Katharine, if you will love me
soundly with your French heart, I will be glad to hear
you confess it brokenly with your English tongue. Do
you like me, Kate?

KATHARINE   *Pardonnez-moi,* I cannot tell wat is "like
me."

KING HENRY   An angel is like you, Kate, and you are
like an angel.

KATHARINE   [*to Alice*]   *Que dit-il? Que je suis semblable à*   112
les anges?   113

ALICE   *Oui, vraiment, sauf Votre Grâce, ainsi dit-il.*   114

KING HENRY   I said so, dear Katharine, and I must not
blush to affirm it.

KATHARINE   *Oh, bon Dieu! Les langues des hommes sont*
pleines de tromperies.

KING HENRY   What says she, fair one? That the tongues
of men are full of deceits?

ALICE   *Oui,* dat de tongues of de mans is be full of
deceits. Dat is de Princess.

KING HENRY   The Princess is the better Englishwoman.   123
I'faith, Kate, my wooing is fit for thy understanding.
I am glad thou canst speak no better English, for if
thou couldst, thou wouldst find me such a plain king
that thou wouldst think I had sold my farm to buy my
crown. I know no ways to mince it in love, but directly   128
to say, "I love you." Then if you urge me farther than
to say, "Do you, in faith?" I wear out my suit. Give me   130
your answer, i'faith, do, and so clap hands and a   131
bargain. How say you, lady?

KATHARINE   *Sauf votre honneur,* me understand well.

KING HENRY   Marry, if you would put me to verses or
to dance for your sake, Kate, why, you undid me. For
the one I have neither words nor measure, and for the   136
other I have no strength in measure, yet a reasonable   137
measure in strength. If I could win a lady at leapfrog,   138
or by vaulting into my saddle with my armor on my
back, under the correction of bragging be it spoken, I
should quickly leap into a wife. Or if I might buffet for   141
my love, or bound my horse for her favors, I could lay   142
on like a butcher and sit like a jackanapes, never off.   143
But before God, Kate, I cannot look greenly, nor gasp   144
out my eloquence, nor I have no cunning in protesta-

tion—only downright oaths, which I never use till   146
urged, nor never break for urging. If thou canst love a
fellow of this temper, Kate, whose face is not worth   148
sunburning, that never looks in his glass for love of   149
anything he sees there, let thine eye be thy cook. I   150
speak to thee plain soldier. If thou canst love me for
this, take me. If not, to say to thee that I shall die is
true; but for thy love, by the Lord, no. Yet I love thee
too. And while thou liv'st, dear Kate, take a fellow of
plain and uncoined constancy, for he perforce must   155
do thee right, because he hath not the gift to woo in
other places. For these fellows of infinite tongue that
can rhyme themselves into ladies' favors, they do
always reason themselves out again. What? A speaker
is but a prater, a rhyme is but a ballad. A good leg will
fall, a straight back will stoop, a black beard will turn   161
white, a curled pate will grow bald, a fair face will
wither, a full eye will wax hollow; but a good heart,
Kate, is the sun and the moon—or rather the sun and
not the moon, for it shines bright and never changes,
but keeps his course truly. If thou would have such a
one, take me. And take me, take a soldier; take a
soldier, take a king. And what say'st thou then to my
love? Speak, my fair, and fairly, I pray thee.

KATHARINE   Is it possible dat I sould love de *ennemi* of
France?

KING HENRY   No, it is not possible you should love the
enemy of France, Kate; but in loving me you should
love the friend of France, for I love France so well that
I will not part with a village of it. I will have it all mine.
And, Kate, when France is mine and I am yours, then
yours is France and you are mine.

KATHARINE   I cannot tell wat is dat.

KING HENRY   No, Kate? I will tell thee in French, which
I am sure will hang upon my tongue like a new-
married wife about her husband's neck, hardly to be
shook off. *Je quand sur le possession de France, et quand*   182
vous avez le possession de moi—let me see, what ?   183
Saint Denis be my speed!—*donc vôtre est France et vous*   184
êtes mienne. It is as easy for me, Kate, to conquer the   185
kingdom as to speak so much more French. I shall
never move thee in French, unless it be to laugh at
me.

KATHARINE   *Sauf votre honneur, le français que vous parlez,*   189
il est meilleur que l' anglais lequel je parle.   190

KING HENRY   No, faith, is't not, Kate. But thy speaking
of my tongue, and I thine, most truly-falsely, must   192
needs be granted to be much at one. But, Kate, dost   193
thou understand thus much English: Canst thou
love me?

---

98 s.d. *omnes* all.   *Manent* They remain onstage   112–14 *Que . . .*
ainsi dit-il? What does he say? That I am like the angels? ALICE Yes,
truly, save Your Grace, he says so.   123 is . . . Englishwoman i.e., is
the better for preferring honesty.   128 mince it speak coyly
130 wear out my suit expend all my resources as a wooer.   131 clap
clasp   136 measure (skill in) meter   137 measure dance
138 measure amount, aptitude   141 buffet box   142 bound make
prance   143 jackanapes ape, monkey   144 greenly like a lovesick
youth

146 downright straightforward   148–9 not . . . sunburning i.e.,
already so tanned that more sun could make it worse. (Tanned and
dark complexions were generally considered unhandsome.)
149 glass mirror   150 be thy cook dress up and garnish my plain
looks.   155 uncoined (1) not put into circulation (2) unalloyed, fixed,
steady   161 fall shrink, lose its shapeliness   182–5 *Je . . . mienne*
(Henry haltingly translates into French the last sentence of his previous speech.)   184 Saint Denis patron saint of France.   be my speed
help me.   189–90 *Sauf . . . parle* Saving your honor, the French that
you speak is better than the English that I speak.   192 truly-falsely
true-heartedly but incorrectly   193 at one alike.

KATHARINE   I cannot tell.

KING HENRY   Can any of your neighbors tell, Kate? I'll ask them. Come, I know thou lovest me. And at night, when you come into your closet, you'll question 199 this gentlewoman about me; and I know, Kate, you will to her dispraise those parts in me that you love with your heart. But, good Kate, mock me mercifully, the rather, gentle Princess, because I love thee cruelly. If ever thou be'st mine, Kate, as I have a saving faith within me tells me thou shalt, I get thee with scambling, and thou must therefore needs prove a 206 good soldier-breeder. Shall not thou and I, between Saint Denis and Saint George, compound a boy, half French, half English, that shall go to Constantinople and take the Turk by the beard? Shall we not? What say'st thou, my fair flower-de-luce?   211

KATHARINE   I do not know dat.

KING HENRY   No; 'tis hereafter to know, but now to promise. Do but now promise, Kate, you will endeavor for your French part of such a boy, and for my English moiety take the word of a king and a bachelor. 216 How answer you, *la plus belle Katharine du monde, mon* 217 *très cher et devin déesse?*   218

KATHARINE   Your Majestee 'ave *fausse* French enough 219 to deceive de most *sage demoiselle* dat is *en France.*

KING HENRY   Now, fie upon my false French! By mine honor, in true English, I love thee, Kate; by which honor I dare not swear thou lovest me, yet my blood begins to flatter me that thou dost, notwithstanding the poor and untempering effect of my visage. Now 225 beshrew my father's ambition! He was thinking of civil 226 wars when he got me; therefore was I created with a stubborn outside, with an aspect of iron, that when I 228 come to woo ladies I fright them. But in faith, Kate, the elder I wax the better I shall appear. My comfort is that old age, that ill layer-up of beauty, can do no more spoil upon my face. Thou hast me, if thou hast me, at the worst; and thou shalt wear me, if thou wear me, better and better. And therefore tell me, most fair Katharine, will you have me? Put off your maiden blushes; avouch the thoughts of your heart with the 236 looks of an empress; take me by the hand, and say, "Harry of England, I am thine." Which word thou shalt no sooner bless mine ear withal, but I will tell thee aloud, "England is thine, Ireland is thine, France is thine, and Henry Plantagenet is thine"—who, though I speak it before his face, if he be not fellow with the best king, thou shalt find the best king 243 of good fellows. Come, your answer in broken music! 244 For thy voice is music, and thy English broken. Therefore, queen of all, Katharine, break thy mind to 246 me in broken English. Wilt thou have me?

KATHARINE   Dat is as it shall please de *roi mon père.*   248

KING HENRY   Nay, it will please him well, Kate. It shall please him, Kate.

KATHARINE   Den it sall also content me.

KING HENRY   Upon that I kiss your hand, and I call you my queen.   [*He attempts to kiss her hand.*]

KATHARINE   *Laissez, mon seigneur, laissez, laissez! Ma* 254 *foi, je ne veux point que vous abaissiez votre grandeur* 255 *en baisant la main d'une—Notre Seigneur!—indigne* 256 *serviteur. Excusez-moi, je vous supplie, mon très-puissant* 257 *seigneur.*   258

KING HENRY   Then I will kiss your lips, Kate.

KATHARINE   *Les dames et demoiselles pour être baisées* 260 *devant leur noces, il n'est pas la coutume de France.*   261

KING HENRY   [*to Alice*]   Madam my interpreter, what says she?

ALICE   Dat it is not be de fashion *pour les* ladies of France—I cannot tell wat is *baiser* en Anglish.

KING HENRY   To kiss.

ALICE   Your Majestee *entend* bettre *que moi.*   267

KING HENRY   It is not a fashion for the maids in France to kiss before they are married, would she say?

ALICE   *Oui, vraiment.*   270

KING HENRY   O Kate, nice customs curtsy to great kings. 271 Dear Kate, you and I cannot be confined within the weak list of a country's fashion. We are the makers of 273 manners, Kate; and the liberty that follows our places 274 stops the mouth of all find-faults, as I will do yours, for upholding the nice fashion of your country in denying me a kiss. Therefore, patiently and yielding. [*He kisses her.*] You have witchcraft in your lips, Kate. There is more eloquence in a sugar touch of them than in the tongues of the French council, and they should sooner persuade Harry of England than a general petition of monarchs.—Here comes your father.

Enter the French power and the English lords.

BURGUNDY   God save Your Majesty! My royal cousin, teach you our princess English?

KING HENRY   I would have her learn, my fair cousin, how perfectly I love her, and that is good English.

BURGUNDY   Is she not apt?

KING HENRY   Our tongue is rough, coz, and my condi- 288 tion is not smooth; so that, having neither the voice 289 nor the heart of flattery about me, I cannot so conjure up the spirit of love in her that he will appear in his true likeness.

---

199 **closet** private chamber   206 **scambling** the scuffles of war 211 **flower-de-luce** fleur-de-lis, the emblem of France.   216 **moiety** half   217–18 **la plus . . . déesse** the most beautiful Katharine in the world, my very dear and divine goddess.   219 **fausse** i.e., false (both "incorrect" and "deceptive")   225 **untempering** unsettling, unsoftening   226 **beshrew** curses on   228 **aspect** appearance   236 **avouch** vouch for, confirm   243 **fellow with** on equal terms with   244 **broken music** (Henry quibbles on the term for music composed in parts for different instruments.)   246 **break** open

248 **de roi mon père** the King my father.   254–8 **Laissez . . . seigneur** Don't, my lord, don't, don't! By my faith, I do not wish you to lower your greatness by kissing the hand of an—our dear Lord!— unworthy servant; excuse me, I beg you, my most powerful lord. (*Serviteur* is masculine and not appropriately applied to a lady, but the error may be Shakespeare's.)   260–1 **Les dames . . . France** It is not customary in France for ladies and young girls to be kissed before their marriage.   267 **entend . . . moi** understands better than I. 270 **Oui, vraiment** Yes, truly.   271 **nice** fastidious   273 **list** limit, barrier   274 **follows our places** attends our (high) rank   288 **Our tongue** (1) Our English language (2) My soldierly speech   288–9 **condition** soldierly manner

BURGUNDY Pardon the frankness of my mirth, if I answer you for that. If you would conjure in her, you must make a circle; if conjure up love in her in his true likeness, he must appear naked and blind. Can you blame her then, being a maid yet rosed over with the virgin crimson of modesty, if she deny the appearance of a naked blind boy in her naked seeing self? It were, my lord, a hard condition for a maid to consign to.

KING HENRY Yet they do wink and yield, as love is blind and enforces.

BURGUNDY They are then excused, my lord, when they see not what they do.

KING HENRY Then, good my lord, teach your cousin to consent winking.

BURGUNDY I will wink on her to consent, my lord, if you will teach her to know my meaning; for maids, well summered and warm kept, are like flies at Bartholomew-tide: blind, though they have their eyes, and then they will endure handling, which before would not abide looking on.

KING HENRY This moral ties me over to time and a hot summer; and so I shall catch the fly, your cousin, in the latter end, and she must be blind too.

BURGUNDY As love is, my lord, before it loves.

KING HENRY It is so; and you may, some of you, thank love for my blindness, who cannot see many a fair French city for one fair French maid that stands in my way.

FRENCH KING Yes, my lord, you see them perspectively, the cities turned into a maid; for they are all girdled with maiden walls that war hath never entered.

KING HENRY Shall Kate be my wife?

FRENCH KING So please you.

KING HENRY I am content, so the maiden cities you talk of may wait on her. So the maid that stood in the way for my wish shall show me the way to my will.

FRENCH KING We have consented to all terms of reason.

KING HENRY Is't so, my lords of England?

WESTMORLAND
The King hath granted every article:
His daughter first, and then in sequel all
According to their firm proposèd natures.

EXETER
Only he hath not yet subscribèd this:
Where Your Majesty demands that the King of France,
having any occasion to write for matter of grant, shall
name Your Highness in this form and with this addition, in French, *Notre très cher fils Henri, Roi d'Angleterre, Héritier de France*; and thus in Latin, *Praeclarissimus filius noster Henricus, Rex Angliae et Haeres Franciae.*

FRENCH KING
Nor this I have not, brother, so denied
But your request shall make me let it pass.

KING HENRY
I pray you then, in love and dear alliance,
Let that one article rank with the rest,
And thereupon give me your daughter.

FRENCH KING
Take her, fair son, and from her blood raise up
Issue to me, that the contending kingdoms
Of France and England, whose very shores look pale
With envy of each other's happiness,
May cease their hatred, and this dear conjunction
Plant neighborhood and Christian-like accord
In their sweet bosoms, that never war advance
His bleeding sword twixt England and fair France.

LORDS Amen!

KING HENRY
Now, welcome, Kate; and bear me witness all,
That here I kiss her as my sovereign queen.
                         [*He kisses her.*] *Flourish.*

QUEEN ISABEL
God, the best maker of all marriages,
Combine your hearts in one, your realms in one!
As man and wife, being two, are one in love,
So be there twixt your kingdoms such a spousal
That never may ill office, or fell jealousy,
Which troubles oft the bed of blessèd marriage,
Thrust in between the paction of these kingdoms
To make divorce of their incorporate league;
That English may as French, French Englishmen,
Receive each other. God speak this "Amen"!

ALL Amen!

KING HENRY
Prepare we for our marriage, on which day,
My lord of Burgundy, we'll take your oath,
And all the peers', for surety of our leagues.
Then shall I swear to Kate, and you to me;

---

294 **conjure in her** (with bawdy double meaning of raising up something within her *circle*, line 295) 296 **naked and blind** (as Cupid is conventionally portrayed) 297 **yet rosed over** still blushing 298–9 **if . . . self** if she refuses to admit the entry of a naked boy in her sight, or herself being naked? 300 **a hard condition** (Suggesting erection.) **consign** agree 301–2 **Yet . . . enforces** Yet young maidens do close their eyes and say yes, prompted to do so by their own bashfulness and male importunity. 307 **wink on her** give her an encouraging wink 309 **summered** nurtured 309–10 **Bartholomew-tide** August 24 (when flies, bees, etc., are sluggish) 311 **handling** (1) handling of the beehive (2) sexual handling 313–14 **This moral . . . summer** The lesson of your fable would oblige me to wait for the heat of summer 316 **As . . . loves** (Love is blind before it loves, because it cannot yet see the beloved and because love has not yet opened the lover's eyes.) 318–20 **who . . . my way** i.e., since I am so preoccupied with Katharine that I have forgotten for the moment about all those French towns I want. (He is joking; he gets the French towns, along with her.) 321 **perspectively** i.e., as in an optical device that presents different images when viewed from different angles 323 **maiden** unbreached. (With a sexual metaphor, continued in *entered*.) 326 **so** provided that 327 **wait on her** attend her, go along with her (as part of her dowry). 328 **will** (1) intention of ruling France (2) sexual desire.

333 **According . . . natures** exactly as specified in the proposals. 334 **subscribèd** agreed to, signed to 336 **for . . . grant** in official deeds, granting title to land and the like 337–8 **addition** title 338–9 *Notre . . . France* i.e., Our very dear son Henry, King of England, Heir of France. 340 *Praeclarissimus* most famous. (Presumably an error for "*Praecarissimus*" or "*Praecarissimi*," "most dear." Shakespeare is following Holinshed, who took the error from Hall.) 342 **so** so firmly 343 **But** but that 361 **spousal** marriage 362 **ill office** unfriendly dealings. **fell** cruel 364 **paction** alliance, compact

And may our oaths well kept and prosperous be!

Sennet.   Exeunt.

❖

[Epilogue]

Enter Chorus.

CHORUS
Thus far, with rough and all-unable pen,
   Our bending author hath pursued the story,   2
In little room confining mighty men,
   Mangling by starts the full course of their glory.   4

Epilogue.
2 bending i.e., under the weight of his task   **4 by starts** in fits and
starts, in fragments

Small time, but in that small most greatly lived   5
   This star of England. Fortune made his sword,
By which the world's best garden he achieved,   7
   And of it left his son imperial lord.
Henry the Sixth, in infant bands crowned King   9
   Of France and England, did this king succeed;
Whose state so many had the managing,
   That they lost France and made his England bleed,
Which oft our stage hath shown; and, for their sake,   13
In your fair minds let this acceptance take.   [*Exit.*]   14

5 Small time (Henry V ruled for only nine years, dying at the age of
thirty-five.)   **7 best garden** i.e., France   **9 infant bands** swaddling
clothes   **13 Which . . . shown** (Refers to the three parts of *King Henry
VI.*)   **their** i.e., the actors and the author, the presenters on *our stage*
(line 13)   **14 let . . . take** let this play meet with your approval.

The Life of King Henry the Eighth

However much we may like to think of *The Tempest* (c. 1610–1611) as Shakespeare's farewell to his art, celebrating his retirement to Stratford in 1611 or 1612, his career was, in fact, not quite finished. *The Famous History of the Life of King Henry the Eighth* was performed by the King's men, Shakespeare's acting company, at the Globe playhouse on June 29, 1613, as a "new" play, though perhaps it had also been performed earlier that spring at the indoors Blackfriars playhouse. During the Globe performance, small cannon (called "chambers") were discharged to welcome Henry VIII and his fellow-masquers to Cardinal Wolsey's house (1.4.64 ff.), accidentally setting fire to the thatch roof and burning the Globe to the ground in less than an hour. (The theater was subsequently rebuilt.) The letter reporting this incident refers to the play by the title *All Is True*, but its identification with the extant play of *Henry VIII* is virtually certain.

The letter, written by Henry Wotton to Sir Edmund Bacon on June 29, 1613, is worth quoting in full:

Now, to let matters of state sleep, I will entertain you at the present with what has happened this week at the Bank's side. The King's players had a new play, called *All Is True*, representing some principal pieces of the reign of Henry VIII, which was set forth with many extraordinary circumstances of pomp and majesty, even to the matting of the stage; the Knights of the Order with their Georges and garters, the Guard with their embroidered coats, and the like: sufficient in truth within a while to make greatness very familiar, if not ridiculous. Now, King Henry making a masque at the Cardinal Wolsey's house, and certain chambers being shot off at his entry, some of the paper, or other stuff, wherewith one of them was stopped, did light on the thatch, where being thought at first but an idle smoke, and their eyes more attentive to the show, it kindled inwardly, and ran round like a train, consuming within less than an hour the whole house to the very grounds. This was the fatal period of that virtuous fabric, wherein yet nothing did perish but wood and straw, and a few forsaken cloaks; only one man had his breeches set on fire, that would perhaps have broiled them, if he had no by the benefit of a provident wit put it out with bottle ale.

Shakespeare, then, did not fully retire once he had written *The Tempest*. Instead, he seems to have chosen to collaborate with the man who was to be his successor as chief playwright for the King's Men, John Fletcher. This considerably younger writer had already achieved a fine success with a number of plays in 1607 and afterwards, some of them written in collaboration with Francis Beaumont. He then moved on to still other collaborations, including that with his senior and now retiring colleague, Shakespeare. *Henry VIII* appears to have been one of their joint efforts, along with *The Two Noble Kinsmen*. (The lost *Cardenio* may have been another.) The case for joint authorship remains uncertain, but is attractive. To be sure, *Henry VIII* was included in the First Folio of 1623 by Shakespeare's former colleagues (Heminges and Condell) who had agreed to edit his works, whereas *The Two Noble Kinsmen* was not included. Perhaps they felt that Fletcher's presence was more dominant in *The Two Noble Kinsmen* and Shakespeare's more dominant in *Henry VIII*, or they may have held to the view that *Henry VIII* was entirely Shakespeare's. Yet the likelihood of some degree of collaboration is by no means ruled out by these circumstances.

A tentative division of writing assignments, based on the analyses of James Spedding, Cyrus Hoy, and the editors of the Oxford Shakespeare, gives the following to Shakespeare: 1.1–2, 2.3–4, 3.2 (through line 204), and 5.1. In addition Shakespeare may have been primarily responsible for 2.1–2, the remainder of 3.2, and 4.1–2, with some touching up by Fletcher. These assignments leaves to Fletcher the primary responsibility for 1.3–4, 3.1, and 5.2–4. The Prologue and Epilogue are tentatively assigned to Fletcher.

Whatever the facts of the case, Shakespeare certainly knew the work of the younger man who became his heir as chief writer for the King's Men. In his own work, Shakespeare was moving toward the kind of dramaturgy practiced by Fletcher. Unquestionably, Shakespeare's style did change in his later years under the influence of an audience that was becoming increasingly courtly and sophisticated—the very sort of audience for whom Fletcher knew how to write. The Prologue to *Henry VIII* suggests that the play was written with the more exclusive audience of Blackfriars theater ("The first and happiest hearers of the town") particularly in mind. Such changing circumstances may help explain why *Henry VIII*, though nominally an English history play in the genre Shakespeare had helped make famous, is so very different in kind from the *Henry IV* plays and *Henry V*. *Henry VIII* is stylistically close to Shakespeare's late romances, where an artistic kinship with Fletcher is also marked. In some ways, *Henry VIII* is better understood in the context of the late romances than in relation to the English history plays.

What was the purpose in this unexpected return to the English history play? Shakespeare had set it aside fourteen years earlier, in 1599, bringing to completion in *Henry V* a series of eight plays on England's civil wars of the fifteenth century and another on the reign of King John. Why turn in 1613 to a historical subject so separated in time from that of Shakespeare's earlier interest and potentially so controversial because of its relation to the religious battle between Catholics and Protestants? A common critical view throughout much of the twentieth century held *Henry VIII* to be the product of Shakespeare's presumed dotage, especially Act 5, with its apparent anticlimax following the deaths of the play's central characters, Wolsey and Katharine. More recent efforts to understand the whole of *Henry VIII* regard it as an experimental work, blending conventional genres (history, tragedy, and romance) and stressing masquelike stage effects in the opulent manner of court entertainment. Since its thematic focus is also one of courtly celebration, expressing gratitude for Queen Elizabeth's Protestant rule and wary hopes that her successor James will follow suit, the play may best be seen as a reworking of the English history play to meet the new mood of 1613. This return to a type of drama long since abandoned by Shakespeare resembles his similar fascination during his late years with the once-forgotten genre of romance.

In some ways, *Henry VIII* is deliberately unlike Shakespeare's earlier history plays, and so should not be judged by their standards. The Prologue is at pains to stress that the play will contain no merriment or bawdry, no "fellow / In a long motley coat." And, indeed, the play is unusually lacking in a comic subplot devoted to the endearing antics of a tavern crew. To be sure, the views of the citizens are not ignored, for Queen Katharine champions their hatred of Wolsey's taxes. In Act 5, in scenes now generally ascribed to Fletcher, the people put in a brief appearance, crowding bumptiously forward at the christening of the Princess Elizabeth (5.4). Even here, however, the tone is one of condescending amusement at their childish eagerness to see their future queen. The common people do not provide choric commentary, as they do in *Richard III* or *Richard II*.

These factors may well reflect the increasing influence of the court on Shakespeare and the King's men. Ever since they had become the King's men in 1603, when James I came to the throne, Shakespeare's company had enjoyed a closer relationship with the throne than before. *Measure for Measure* and *Macbeth*, among other of Shakespeare's plays, seem to contain flattering allusions to the new monarch. Moreover, Shakespeare's company acquired the lease of Blackfriars in 1608 and henceforth used this "private" theater as their winter playhouse in which to perform their plays for a courtly and sophisticated clientele. Such well-to-do theater-goers, who had patronized the boys' acting companies in the early 1600s (as noted in *Hamlet*), increasingly turned their attention to those adult companies of the late 1600s, such as the King's Men, who were ready to cater to courtly tastes in theater. Shakespeare's late plays are staged with public, private, and courtly conditions of performance in mind. The late romances show the influence of Inigo Jones's lavish designs for court masques, as in *Cymbeline's* use of machinery for celestial ascents and descents. *Henry VIII* reflects similar conditions of staging in its masquing scene (1.4), in the pageantlike trial of Katharine and the baptism of Elizabeth, and in the vision of white-robed figures dancing before the dying Katharine (4.2). This affinity to courtly entertainment should not be overstressed, for Shakespeare's company remained a public company throughout his career, and its stage was always fluidly bare of scenery when compared with Jones's ingenious devices and use of scenic perspective. Nonetheless, *Henry VIII* should be viewed as a history play for a somewhat more select audience than that of his earlier histories. The play's ornate compliments to Elizabeth have a courtly flavor. The year 1613 saw the politically important marriage of the Elector Palatine to James's daughter Elizabeth, who was often flatteringly compared with her namesake Queen Elizabeth, and, although *Henry VIII* is not among the plays known to have been performed for this occasion, the marriage itself would have given added significance to the play.

Shakespeare's earlier histories also honor, as well as examine critically, the institution of monarchy, but even here *Henry VIII* provides a different emphasis. Shakespeare's earlier histories had focused on such issues as the education of a prince and the dilemmas of power a ruler faces. *Henry VIII* is less a study of kingship and more a dramatic expression of gratitude. *Henry VIII* is not a patriotic play in a broadly popular sense. It lacks battles and triumphant oratory. It voices thanksgiving for a particular ruling family. *Henry VIII* is, above all, the remarkable story of Queen Elizabeth's birth. The story is certainly not without its ironies, for history unfolds in mysterious ways, and Elizabeth's parents were complex persons. Shakespeare's play reveals an increasing psychological interest in analysis of motive, as do other later history plays such as John Ford's *Perkin Warbeck*. Yet the unifying impulse of the play remains the celebration of the birth of Elizabeth.

This rising action in the play is counterpointed by a series of tragic falls, which indeed seem at first to be the play's chief concern. These falls proceed in remorseless succession—Buckingham, Katharine, Wolsey. In the edifying manner of that staple of medieval tragedy, the "Fall of Princes," these deaths offer useful lessons on statecraft and personal conduct. All these characters stoically exemplify the art of holy dying. One after another, they forgive their enemies and regret such sins as they have committed, and yet they also prophesy that God's retribution will light on offenders' heads. The prevailing mood in the falls of Buckingham and Katharine is one of pity, for both are victims of the ruthless Wolsey.

Cardinal Wolsey is the most interesting character of the three and best illustrates another convention of medieval tragedy, the Wheel of Fortune. Even as he topples one victim after another, dispatching Surrey to Ireland, wheedling his way into the King's favor, reversing England's foreign policy with bewildering speed from pro-French to pro-Empire and back again, all the while amassing a vast personal fortune and negotiating for supreme power within the Roman church, we sense that he is preparing his own catastrophe. Fortune raises insolent worldly persons of this sort, but an overseeing power is at work and will manifest itself through the King. Wolsey, in a nobly contrite farewell, sees the moral of his fall: had he served God zealously, God would not "Have left me naked to mine enemies" (3.2.458). Wolsey knows he has ventured beyond his depth in scheming, "Like little wanton boys that swim on bladders" (line 360). Shakespeare's appraisal of this controversial man is mixed, partly because his chief source, Raphael Holinshed's *Chronicles* (second edition, 1587), incorporated both anti-Wolseyan diatribes and George Cavendish's appreciative account of Wolsey's last days. Still, the portraiture remains consistent throughout, for Wolsey is always intelligent and munificent (as in his founding of Cardinal College, later Christ Church, at Oxford) even though he

employs his talents for worldly ends. His chief wrongdoing is his meddling on behalf of Rome, his finagling to gain the papacy, and most of all his sending of England's wealth overseas for reasons of private gain. Yet even this corrupt behavior has a function in the rising action of the story, for, had not Wolsey schemed against Queen Katharine in his plot to marry King Henry to the French Duchess of Alençon, Katharine might never have fallen to make way for Anne Bullen, and had not Wolsey given a sumptuous party to impress the court with his magnificence (1.4), Henry might never have met Queen Elizabeth's mother. Wolsey's fate is to introduce Henry to the woman whose rise will mean Wolsey's fall and the birth of a future queen. An overriding cosmic irony converts the worst intents of schemers to beneficent ends.

King Henry and Anne Bullen, who, as Elizabeth's parents, play the roles essential to England's bright future, are largely unaware of the great destiny they are performing. Henry especially, like Wolsey, is examined with some skepticism. His pious insistence that "conscience" alone banishes him from Katharine's bed elicits a wry observation, sotto voce, from the Duke of Suffolk: "No, his conscience / Has crept too near another lady" (2.2.17–18). As Henry neglectfully condones Wolsey's abuse of authority and credulously accepts perjured testimony against Buckingham, we catch glimpses of the whimsical tyrant whom history has revealed to us. These criticisms are muted, however, for Henry is, after all, Elizabeth's father. He is not only exonerated from most wrongdoing but steps boldly forward at the play's end as champion of religious reform. Anne, too, is ambivalently treated. In her scene with the Old Lady (2.3), we are reminded of the all-too-apparent reasons there are for suspecting that Anne is a schemer, a high-class auctioneer of her beauty who knows that Henry will pay handsomely. An Elizabethan audience would be bound to recall her grim fate at the hands of the public executioner. Yet, in her own person, Anne resists these ironies. All the characters of the play, whether they stand to profit or lose by Anne's marriage, speak admiringly of her beauty and honor. Although her speeches are few, her appearances are sumptuously staged, with Anne at the center of a meaningful pageant.

The religious issue is presented with a similar tact and ambiguity, for it, too, is both controversial and of significance to England's future. Our sympathies are charitably disposed toward Katharine, whose innocent fall is a sad price for England's larger happiness. Shakespeare refuses to associate her with the decaying order of Catholicism, as he might have done. On the other hand, Bishop Gardiner, the villain of Act 5, is undeniably a Catholic and persecutor of heretics, a dangerous man whose overthrow by Henry and the Protestant Cranmer signals the beginning of a new era in religion. Though Shakespeare tactfully omits the relationship between Katharine's divorce and the Reformation, his audience would have had little difficulty making the connection in Act 5 between Cranmer's Protestant victory and the birth of Elizabeth. These two rising actions coalesce and give perspective to the pitiable falls from greatness that have necessarily contributed to a happy and even miraculous conclusion. History and tragicomic romance fulfill a common purpose in *Henry VIII*.

Act 5 is thus central to the play's thematic concerns, despite the apparently episodic way in which it introduces new characters (notably Archbishop Cranmer) and new issues. The ending confirms a pattern seen earlier in the sad stories of Buckingham and especially Wolsey, in which we mortals "outrun / By violent swiftness that which we run at, / And lose by overrunning" (1.1.141–3). Vain human striving after fame overreaches itself and brings itself down. The process is, in *Henry VIII*, not primarily a punishment for villainy, for there are no real villains here, but a curative process by which frail, proud men ascend on Fortune's wheel, only to discover how illusory are her rewards and how comforting are Fortune's losses that bring us to ourselves. Not a moment of ease does Wolsey enjoy until he is ruined in worldly terms. He assures Thomas Cromwell, at the moment of his fall, that "I know myself now, and I feel within me / A peace above all earthly dignities" (3.2.379–80). His fall is thus a happy fall, an instructive one for himself and others: "Mark but my fall, and that that ruined me" (line 440). Even Katharine and her gentleman usher, Griffith, perceive a happiness in Wolsey's decline, not because it satisfies a desire for vengeance, but because it offers a comforting precedent of self-discovery through suffering: "His overthrow heaped happiness upon him; / For then, and not till then, he felt himself" (4.2.64–5). To know oneself in these terms, *nosce teipsum*, is to enjoy the inestimable gift of penance and the laying aside of worldly striving. Cranmer is a suitable protagonist in Act 5 and a substitute for Wolsey as the King's adviser because he cares so little for himself in a worldly sense. He is the instrument of a higher power that, having imposed various trials on members of the court for their individual and collective betterment, at last reveals a meaning in that suffering and a future happiness arising out of humanity's imperfect attempts to know itself. As Buckingham says earlier (2.1.124), "Heaven has an end in all."

As history play, *Henry VIII* encompasses a lot. In relating the rise and fall of Buckingham, Wolsey, Queen Katharine, and the rest, the play touches on several weighty historical themes: the uneasy tenure of people in high places, the emergence of a powerful monarchy, the loss of authority of the old nobility (exemplified by Buckingham) during a time when persons of no hereditary pretensions (such as Wolsey and Cromwell) are coming into new prominence, the victory of Protestantism over Catholicism, the bitter factionalism accompanying such historical transitions (which must have seemed acutely relevant to observers of King James's court in 1613), and still more. To compare *Henry VIII* with Holinshed's chronicles is to see how expertly Shakespeare has selected and causally linked his materials from those voluminous pages of history without distorting the overall import of those materials. Among the myriad historical events chronicled are the Treaty of the Field of the Cloth of Gold (1520), the enmity between Wolsey and Buckingham ending in the latter's arrest and execution (1520–1521), French abrogation of the treaty (1523), Wolsey's illegal tax (1525), Henry's meeting Anne Bullen (1525), the arrival of Cardinal Campeius (1528), Queen Katharine's being brought to court (1528), the rise to favor of Gardiner (1529) and then of Cranmer (1533), Wolsey's being found out by Henry (1529) and his death (1530), the naming of Sir Thomas More as Lord Chancellor (1529), Anne's being made Marchioness of Pembroke (1532), her marriage to Henry, coronation, and giving birth to Elizabeth (1533), the christening of Elizabeth (1533), the death of Katharine (1536), the indictment and trial of Cranmer (1544), and much more. Yet, for all its manifold historical content, the play is also illustrative of a pattern of events found in Shakespeare's late romances: that of the providential rise and fall and of eventual restoration of divine promises of happiness.

The play when staged offers a visual contrast between ceremonial pomp and worldly loss leading to renunciation and death. The processions and public events, conveyed by unusually full stage directions, celebrate the ordered arrangement of a hierarchical society. Yet among the most powerful scenes are those of Wolsey bidding farewell to his wealth and power, and Katharine in her isolation and approaching death. The Prologue promises to give us noble scenes, "Sad, high, and working, full of state and woe," and in this we are not disappointed. The Prologue also promises that the audience "May here find truth too"; and, despite the necessary omission of much bloodshed (we are never told directly what will become of Anne Bullen and Sir Thomas More), the play does give a vivid account of Henry VIII's time. We "see / The very persons of our noble story / As they were living." Our impression is of great political and religious change, of splendor and richness, above all of the insecurity of worldly felicity under such a king. Theatrically, the play is sumptuous, pageantlike; though it chooses not to amuse us with comedy, and eschews battle scenes, it abounds in personages from history. In *Henry VIII*, the history play is adapted to the world of romance.

Henry VIII was a very "big" play on stage in the Restoration period, the eighteenth century, and the nineteenth century. It afforded choice roles of operatic grandeur for leading actors and actresses who regarded such plays as vehicles for their star appearances. Thomas Betterton, John Philip Kemble, Sarah Siddons, and Charles Kean, among others, were famous in their roles; Cardinal Wolsey and Queen Katharine both are given speeches of high passion and sorrow designed to bring down the house. Increasingly large theaters encouraged elaborate sets in expensive historical reconstruction for which *Henry VIII* offered ample excuse. Even into the twentieth century, the play was a favorite for such actors and actresses as Charles Laughton, Sibyl Thorndike, and Flora Robson. More recently, large productions in a traditional theatrical idiom have given way to presentational staging on minimalist sets, requiring a very different approach to a play like *Henry VIII*. One notable effect has been to see the play as more ambiguous than it was formerly perceived to be, more intent on grasping the impossibility of recovering historical "truth" in any full sense, more inclined to question and subvert its own nominal premises of patriotism and monarchical hierarchy. The text offers ample material for skeptical readings of this sort, most of all in the notably unstable character of King Henry himself. *Henry VIII* speaks to many today as a chronicle of historical duplicity and discontinuity, in which the element of improbable romance is no longer an incongruity but an inescapable facet of the illusory nature of history itself.

The Life of King Henry the Eighth

[Dramatis Personae

KING HENRY THE EIGHTH

DUKE OF BUCKINGHAM
DUKE OF NORFOLK
DUKE OF SUFFOLK
EARL OF SURREY, *son-in-law of the Duke of Buckingham*
LORD ABERGAVENNY, *son-in-law of the Duke of Buckingham*
LORD SANDYS *(Sir Walter Sandys)*
LORD CHAMBERLAIN
LORD CHANCELLOR *(Sir Thomas More)*
SIR HENRY GUILDFORD
SIR THOMAS LOVELL
SIR ANTHONY DENNY
SIR NICHOLAS VAUX

CARDINAL WOLSEY
THOMAS CROMWELL, *Wolsey's secretary, later secretary to the Privy Council*
SECRETARY *of Wolsey*
SERVANT *of Wolsey*
CARDINAL CAMPEIUS
CAPUCHIUS, *Ambassador from the Emperor Charles the Fifth*
GARDINER, *King Henry's secretary, later Bishop of Winchester*
PAGE *to Gardiner*
THOMAS CRANMER, *Archbishop of Canterbury*
Bishop of Lincoln

QUEEN KATHARINE, *King Henry's wife, later divorced*
PATIENCE, *her attendant*
GRIFFITH, *her gentleman usher*
GENTLEWOMAN,⎫ *attending*
GENTLEMAN, ⎭ *Queen Katharine*

ANNE BULLEN, *Queen Katharine's Maid of Honor, later Queen*
OLD LADY, *friend of Anne Bullen*

BRANDON
SERGEANT AT ARMS
SURVEYOR *to the Duke of Buckingham*
Three GENTLEMEN
CRIER
SCRIBE
MESSENGER *to Queen Katharine*
DOCTOR BUTTS, *the King's physician*
KEEPER *of the Council Chamber*
PORTER
Porter's MAN
GARTER KING AT ARMS

Silent characters in the coronation procession of 4.1 and the christening procession of 5.3:
MARQUESS DORSET
THE MARCHIONESS DORSET
THE DUCHESS OF NORFOLK
THE LORD MAYOR OF LONDON
THE BISHOP OF LONDON

Speaker of the PROLOGUE *and* EPILOGUE

Lords, Ladies, Gentlemen, Judges, Bishops, Priests, Vergers, Lord Mayor of London and Aldermen, Common People, Attendants, Guards, Tipstaves, Halberdiers, Scribes, Secretaries, Officers, Pursuivants, Pages, Guards, Queen Katharine's Women, Musicians, Choristers, and Dancers as spirits

SCENE: *London; Westminster; Kimbolton]*

Dramatis Personae
LORD CHANCELLOR **(Sir Thomas More)** More was named Lord Chancellor in 1529; hence the character appearing in 4.1 and 5.3 as *Lord Chancellor* is Thomas More. Earlier in Henry VIII's reign, Wolsey had served as Lord Chancellor, but he is not identified as such in the speech headings of this play.

MARQUESS DORSET (See note at 4.1.36[6].)   THE DUCHESS OF NORFOLK (See note at 4.1.36[9].)

Prologue

[Enter Prologue.]

PROLOGUE

I come no more to make you laugh. Things now
That bear a weighty and a serious brow,
Sad, high, and working, full of state and woe,   3
Such noble scenes as draw the eye to flow,
We now present. Those that can pity here
May, if they think it well, let fall a tear;
The subject will deserve it. Such as give
Their money out of hope they may believe
May here find truth too. Those that come to see
Only a show or two, and so agree   10
The play may pass, if they be still and willing,
I'll undertake may see away their shilling   12
Richly in two short hours. Only they   13
That come to hear a merry, bawdy play,
A noise of targets, or to see a fellow   15
In a long motley coat guarded with yellow,   16
Will be deceived. For, gentle hearers, know   17
To rank our chosen truth with such a show
As fool and fight is, beside forfeiting
Our own brains and the opinion that we bring   20
To make that only true we now intend,   21
Will leave us never an understanding friend.
Therefore, for goodness' sake, and as you are known
The first and happiest hearers of the town,   24
Be sad, as we would make you. Think ye see   25
The very persons of our noble story
As they were living. Think you see them great,   27
And followed with the general throng and sweat
Of thousand friends; then, in a moment, see
How soon this mightiness meets misery.
And if you can be merry then, I'll say
A man may weep upon his wedding day.   *[Exit.]*

1.1

*Enter the Duke of Norfolk at one door; at the
other, the Duke of Buckingham and the Lord
Abergavenny.*

BUCKINGHAM
Good morrow, and well met. How have ye done
Since last we saw in France?
NORFOLK   I thank Your Grace,   2
Healthful, and ever since a fresh admirer   3
Of what I saw there.
BUCKINGHAM   An untimely ague   4
Stayed me a prisoner in my chamber when   5
Those suns of glory, those two lights of men,
Met in the vale of Andren.
NORFOLK   Twixt Guynes and Arde.   7
I was then present, saw them salute on horseback,
Beheld them when they lighted, how they clung   9
In their embracement, as they grew together;   10
Which had they, what four throned ones could have
weighed
Such a compounded one?   11
BUCKINGHAM   All the whole time
I was my chamber's prisoner.
NORFOLK   Then you lost
The view of earthly glory. Men might say
Till this time pomp was single, but now married
To one above itself. Each following day   16
Became the next day's master, till the last   17
Made former wonders its. Today the French,   18
All clinquant, all in gold, like heathen gods,   19
Shone down the English; and tomorrow they   20
Made Britain India—every man that stood   21
Showed like a mine. Their dwarfish pages were
As cherubins, all gilt. The madams too,   23
Not used to toil, did almost sweat to bear
The pride upon them, that their very labor   25
Was to them as a painting. Now this masque   26
Was cried incomparable; and th'ensuing night   27
Made it a fool and beggar. The two kings,   28
Equal in luster, were now best, now worst,
As presence did present them; him in eye   30
Still him in praise; and being present both,   31
'Twas said they saw but one, and no discerner   32
Durst wag his tongue in censure. When these suns—   33
For so they phrase 'em—by their heralds challenged
The noble spirits to arms, they did perform

Prologue.
3 Sad . . . working serious, lofty, and exciting the emotions.   **state** dignity   **10 show** spectacle   **12 shilling** twelve pence. (The standard price for admission to standing room in the Globe Theater was a penny.)   **13 two short hours** (A conventional period of time for a play.)   **15 targets** shields   **16 motley coat** pied costume of the fool. (Probably a slighting reference to Will Summers, Henry VIII's fool, as portrayed in Samuel Rowley's *When You See Me You Know Me*, 1605, reprinted 1613. The play also features Patch, Wolsey's fool.)   **guarded** trimmed   **17 deceived** disappointed.   **know** i.e., it must be acknowledged that   **20 Our own brains** i.e., the labor of our brains   **20–1 the opinion . . . intend** the reputation we have for presenting truthfully what we intend to play   **24 The first . . . hearers** the foremost and best-qualified audience   **25 sad** serious   **27 As** as if.   **great** in high position
1.1. Location: London. The royal court.

2 saw saw each other   **3 fresh** untired   **4 what I saw there** (Norfolk's description is of the famous meeting of Henry VIII and Francis I of France in 1520. It was near Calais, at the Field of the Cloth of Gold, so called because of the magnificence of the display.)   **ague** fever   **5 Stayed** kept   **7 vale of Andren** (The name, more properly *Ardres*, appears as *Andren* in Holinshed.)   **Arde** Ardres   **9 lighted** alighted, dismounted   **10 as** as if   **11 Which had they** i.e., if they had grown together.   **weighed** equaled in weight   **16 following** succeeding   **17 master** teacher, model   **18 its** its own.   **19 clinquant** glittering   **20 they** the English   **21 India** i.e., seem as wealthy as the West Indies or India   **23 gilt** (Carved statues of cherubim in churches were often gilded.)   **madams** ladies   **25 pride** finery.   **that so that   26 Was . . . painting** i.e., gave them a flushed appearance through their exertions, creating the appearance of wearing cosmetics.   **27 cried** declared, extolled as   **28 Made . . . beggar** made it seem cheap by comparison.   **30 As . . . them** as each came into view   **30–1 him . . . praise** the one in view at the moment received the praise   **32–3 'Twas . . . censure** observers avowed that the two kings were indistinguishable in splendor, and no beholder dared prattle in judging one above the other.

Beyond thought's compass, that former fabulous story,   36
Being now seen possible enough, got credit,   37
That *Bevis* was believed.
BUCKINGHAM   Oh, you go far.   38
NORFOLK
As I belong to worship and affect   39
In honor honesty, the tract of everything   40
Would by a good discourser lose some life
Which action's self was tongue to. All was royal;   42
To the disposing of it naught rebelled.   43
Order gave each thing view; the office did   44
Distinctly his full function.
BUCKINGHAM   Who did guide—   45
I mean, who set the body and the limbs
Of this great sport together, as you guess?   47
NORFOLK
One, certes, that promises no element   48
In such a business.
BUCKINGHAM   I pray you, who, my lord?
NORFOLK
All this was ordered by the good discretion
Of the right reverend Cardinal of York.   51
BUCKINGHAM
The devil speed him! No man's pie is freed   52
From his ambitious finger. What had he
To do in these fierce vanities? I wonder   54
That such a keech can with his very bulk   55
Take up the rays o'th' beneficial sun   56
And keep it from the earth.
NORFOLK   Surely, sir,
There's in him stuff that puts him to these ends;   58
For being not propped by ancestry, whose grace
Chalks successors their way, nor called upon   60
For high feats done to th' crown, neither allied   61
To eminent assistants, but spiderlike,   62
Out of his self-drawing web, 'a gives us note   63
The force of his own merit makes his way—
A gift that heaven gives for him, which buys
A place next to the King.
ABERGAVENNY   I cannot tell
What heaven hath given him—let some graver eye
Pierce into that—but I can see his pride
Peep through each part of him. Whence has he that?
If not from hell, the devil is a niggard,

Or has given all before, and he begins   71
A new hell in himself.
BUCKINGHAM   Why the devil,
Upon this French going-out, took he upon him,   73
Without the privity o'th' King, t'appoint   74
Who should attend on him? He makes up the file   75
Of all the gentry, for the most part such
To whom as great a charge as little honor   77
He meant to lay upon; and his own letter,   78
The honorable board of council out,   79
Must fetch him in he papers.
ABERGAVENNY   I do know   80
Kinsmen of mine, three at the least, that have
By this so sickened their estates that never   82
They shall abound as formerly.
BUCKINGHAM   Oh, many   83
Have broke their backs with laying manors on 'em   84
For this great journey. What did this vanity   85
But minister communication of   86
A most poor issue?
NORFOLK   Grievingly I think   87
The peace between the French and us not values   88
The cost that did conclude it.
BUCKINGHAM   Every man,
After the hideous storm that followed, was   90
A thing inspired, and, not consulting, broke   91
Into a general prophecy: that this tempest,
Dashing the garment of this peace, aboded   93
The sudden breach on't.
NORFOLK   Which is budded out;   94
For France hath flawed the league and hath attached   95
Our merchants' goods at Bordeaux.
ABERGAVENNY   Is it therefore
Th'ambassador is silenced?
NORFOLK   Marry, is't.   97
ABERGAVENNY
A proper title of a peace, and purchased   98
At a superfluous rate!
BUCKINGHAM   Why, all this business   99
Our reverend Cardinal carried.
NORFOLK   Like it Your Grace,   100
The state takes notice of the private difference

36 **that . . . story** so that stories previously thought fabulous   37 **got credit** gained credibility   38 ***Bevis*** the fourteenth-century romance *Bevis of Hampton*   39–40 **belong . . . honesty** am of noble rank and love truth with honorable regard   40 **tract** telling; course   42 **Which . . . to** which would be best described by the event itself.   43 **To . . . rebelled** nothing jarred or was out of place in the execution of the event.   44–5 **Order . . . function** Everything appeared in its proper place, and every official performed his function without confusion.   47 **sport** entertainment   48 **certes** certainly.   **promises no element** i.e., is out of his element   51 **Cardinal of York** Cardinal Wolsey.   52 **speed** prosper   54 **fierce** extravagant   55 **keech** (Literally, fat of a slaughtered animal rolled into a lump; applied to Wolsey, who was reputed to be a butcher's son.)   56 **sun** i.e., King Henry   58 **stuff . . . him** traits that whet him on   60 **Chalks . . . way** indicates the path noble descendants are to follow   61 **high feats** great services   61–2 **allied . . . assistants** connected with high officials of the crown   63 **self-drawing** spun out of his own entrails.   **'a . . . note** he lets us know

71 **he** Wolsey   73 **going-out** expedition, display   74 **Without . . . King** without the King's being privy (to his plan)   75 **file** list   77–8 **To . . . upon** (i.e., the Cardinal imposed charges for defraying the expenses of the costly interview on those noblemen to whom he gave places of little honor)   78 **letter** i.e., summons   79 **out** not consulted   80 **Must . . . papers** compels the cooperation of every person he cites. (*He papers* means "whomever he lists.")   82 **sickened** i.e., depleted   83 **abound** thrive   84 **Have . . . 'em** i.e., have ruined themselves financially by pawning their estates for expensive wardrobes to adorn their own backs   85–7 **What . . . issue?** What did this extravagance accomplish other than to provide occasion for a conference that yielded meager results?   88 **not values** is not worth   90 **hideous storm** (Holinshed reports such a storm that interrupted the festivities and was taken as a prognostication.)   91 **not consulting** without consulting one another beforehand   93 **Dashing the garment** shattering the fabric.   **aboded** foretold   94 **on't** of it.   **is budded out** i.e., has come to pass   95 **flawed** broken.   **attached** seized   97 **silenced** confined to house arrest.   **Marry** (An oath, originally "by the Virgin Mary.")   98 **A proper . . . peace** A fine business to give the name of peace to   99 **superfluous rate** excessive price.   100 **carried** supervised.   **Like it** May it please

Betwixt you and the Cardinal. I advise you—
And take it from a heart that wishes towards you
Honor and plenteous safety—that you read   104
The Cardinal's malice and his potency
Together; to consider further that   106
What his high hatred would effect wants not   107
A minister in his power. You know his nature,   108
That he's revengeful, and I know his sword
Hath a sharp edge; it's long, and 't may be said
It reaches far, and where 'twill not extend,
Thither he darts it. Bosom up my counsel;   112
You'll find it wholesome. Lo, where comes that rock   113
That I advise your shunning.   114

Enter Cardinal Wolsey, the purse borne before him,
certain of the guard, and two Secretaries with
papers. The Cardinal in his passage fixeth his eye
on Buckingham, and Buckingham on him, both
full of disdain.

WOLSEY [*to a secretary*]
The Duke of Buckingham's surveyor, ha?   115
Where's his examination?

SECRETARY   Here, so please you.   116
[*He gives a paper.*]

WOLSEY
Is he in person ready?

SECRETARY   Ay, please Your Grace.

WOLSEY
Well, we shall then know more, and Buckingham
Shall lessen this big look.   119
Exeunt Cardinal and his train.

BUCKINGHAM
This butcher's cur is venom-mouthed, and I   120
Have not the power to muzzle him; therefore best
Not wake him in his slumber. A beggar's book   122
Outworths a noble's blood.

NORFOLK   What, are you chafed?   123
Ask God for temp'rance; that's th'appliance only   124
Which your disease requires.

BUCKINGHAM   I read in 's looks
Matter against me, and his eye reviled   126
Me as his abject object. At this instant   127
He bores me with some trick. He's gone to th' King;   128
I'll follow and outstare him.

NORFOLK   Stay, my lord,
And let your reason with your choler question   130
What 'tis you go about. To climb steep hills
Requires slow pace at first. Anger is like
A full hot horse who, being allowed his way,   133

Self-mettle tires him. Not a man in England   134
Can advise me like you. Be to yourself
As you would to your friend.

BUCKINGHAM   I'll to the King,
And from a mouth of honor quite cry down   137
This Ipswich fellow's insolence, or proclaim   138
There's difference in no persons.

NORFOLK   Be advised;   139
Heat not a furnace for your foe so hot
That it do singe yourself. We may outrun
By violent swiftness that which we run at,
And lose by overrunning. Know you not
The fire that mounts the liquor till 't run o'er   144
In seeming to augment it wastes it? Be advised.
I say again there is no English soul
More stronger to direct you than yourself,
If with the sap of reason you would quench
Or but allay the fire of passion.

BUCKINGHAM   Sir,   149
I am thankful to you, and I'll go along
By your prescription. But this top-proud fellow,   151
Whom from the flow of gall I name not, but   152
From sincere motions, by intelligence,   153
And proofs as clear as founts in July when   154
We see each grain of gravel, I do know
To be corrupt and treasonous.

NORFOLK   Say not "treasonous."

BUCKINGHAM
To th' King I'll say't, and make my vouch as strong   157
As shore of rock. Attend. This holy fox,
Or wolf, or both—for he is equal ravenous   159
As he is subtle, and as prone to mischief
As able to perform't—his mind and place   161
Infecting one another, yea, reciprocally,
Only to show his pomp as well in France
As here at home, suggests the King our master   164
To this last costly treaty, th'interview   165
That swallowed so much treasure and like a glass
Did break i'th' wrenching.

NORFOLK   Faith, and so it did.   167

BUCKINGHAM
Pray, give me favor, sir. This cunning cardinal   168
The articles o'th' combination drew   169
As himself pleased; and they were ratified
As he cried "Thus let be," to as much end   171
As give a crutch to th' dead. But our count-cardinal   172
Has done this, and 'tis well; for worthy Wolsey,
Who cannot err, he did it. Now this follows,

---

104 read estimate, interpret **106 Together** i.e., as equally strong
107–8 wants . . . power is not without an agency under his control.
112 Bosom up Take to heart and shut up in your bosom **113 whole-**
some beneficial. **114.1** *purse* i.e., containing the great seal, pertaining to Wolsey as Lord Chancellor **115 surveyor** overseer of a
household or estate **116 examination** deposition. **119 big** haughty
120 butcher's cur (Another dig at Wolsey's reputed lowly origin.)
122 book book learning **123 blood** noble descent. **chafed** angry.
124 appliance only only remedy **126 Matter against** quarrel with
127 abject cast-off, rejected **128 bores** undermines, cheats **130 with**
. . . question debate with your anger **133 full hot** high-spirited

134 Self-mettle his own ardent spirits **137 of honor** i.e., of a gentleman **138 Ipswich** (Wolsey's birthplace) **139 difference** distinctions
in rank. **Be advised** Take care **144 mounts** causes (by boiling) to
rise **149 allay** temper, moderate **151 top-proud** supremely proud
152 from . . . gall i.e., from promptings of anger **153 motions**
motives. **intelligence** secret information **154 founts** springs
157 vouch assertion, allegation **159 equal** equally **161 place** office,
rank **164 suggests** incites **165 last** latest, recent. **interview** i.e.,
Field of the Cloth of Gold **167 wrenching** rough handling, rinsing.
168 favor attention **169 articles o'th' combination** terms of the
peace treaty **171–2 to . . . dead** to just about as useful a purpose as a
crutch is to a dead person. **172 count-cardinal** i.e., cardinal putting
on the airs of an aristocrat

Which, as I take it, is a kind of puppy
To th'old dam, treason: Charles the Emperor, 176
Under pretense to see the Queen his aunt—
For 'twas indeed his color, but he came 178
To whisper Wolsey—here makes visitation; 179
His fears were that the interview betwixt
England and France might through their amity
Breed him some prejudice, for from this league
Peeped harms that menaced him; privily 183
Deals with our cardinal, and, as I trow— 184
Which I do well, for I am sure the Emperor
Paid ere he promised, whereby his suit was granted
Ere it was asked—but when the way was made
And paved with gold, the Emperor thus desired
That he would please to alter the King's course 189
And break the foresaid peace. Let the King know,
As soon he shall by me, that thus the Cardinal
Does buy and sell his honor as he pleases, 192
And for his own advantage.
NORFOLK   I am sorry
To hear this of him, and could wish he were
Something mistaken in't.
BUCKINGHAM   No, not a syllable. 195
I do pronounce him in that very shape
He shall appear in proof. 197

Enter Brandon, a Sergeant at Arms before him,
and two or three of the guard.

BRANDON
Your office, Sergeant: execute it.
SERGEANT   Sir,
My lord the Duke of Buckingham, and Earl
Of Hereford, Stafford, and Northampton, I
Arrest thee of high treason, in the name
Of our most sovereign king.
BUCKINGHAM [*to Norfolk*]   Lo, you, my lord,
The net has fall'n upon me! I shall perish
Under device and practice.
BRANDON   I am sorry 204
To see you ta'en from liberty, to look on 205
The business present. 'Tis His Highness' pleasure
You shall to th' Tower.
BUCKINGHAM   It will help me nothing 207
To plead mine innocence, for that dye is on me
Which makes my whit'st part black. The will of
heav'n
Be done in this and all things! I obey.
O my Lord Aberga'nny, fare you well.
BRANDON
Nay, he must bear you company. [*To Abergavenny*]
The King
Is pleased you shall to the Tower, till you know

How he determines further.
ABERGAVENNY   As the Duke said,
The will of heaven be done and the King's pleasure
By me obeyed!
BRANDON   Here is a warrant from
The King t'attach Lord Montacute and the bodies 217
Of the Duke's confessor, John de la Car, 218
One Gilbert Perk, his chancellor—
BUCKINGHAM   So, so; 219
These are the limbs o'th' plot. No more, I hope?
BRANDON
A monk o'th' Chartreux.
BUCKINGHAM   Oh, Nicholas Hopkins?
BRANDON   He. 221
BUCKINGHAM
My surveyor is false. The o'er-great Cardinal
Hath showed him gold; my life is spanned already. 223
I am the shadow of poor Buckingham, 224
Whose figure even this instant cloud puts on, 225
By dark'ning my clear sun. My lord, farewell. 226
                                        Exeunt.

❖

1.2

Cornets. Enter King Henry, leaning on the
Cardinal's shoulder, the nobles, and Sir Thomas
Lovell. The Cardinal places himself under the
King's feet on his right side. [The Cardinal's
Secretary attends him.]

KING [*to Wolsey*]
My life itself, and the best heart of it, 1
Thanks you for this great care. I stood i'th' level 2
Of a full-charged confederacy, and give thanks 3
To you that choked it. Let be called before us
That gentleman of Buckingham's. In person 5
I'll hear him his confessions justify, 6
And point by point the treasons of his master
He shall again relate. 8

A noise within, crying "Room for the Queen!"
Enter the Queen [Katharine], ushered by the Duke
of Norfolk, and [the Duke of] Suffolk. She kneels.
[The] King riseth from his state, takes her up,
kisses and placeth her by him.

KATHARINE
Nay, we must longer kneel. I am a suitor.

---

176 dam mother (used especially of animals).   **Charles** i.e., Charles V, Holy Roman Emperor, nephew of Queen Katharine. (Charles had much to fear from an English-French alliance.)   **178 color** pretext   **179 whisper** whisper to   **183 privily** secretly   **184 trow** believe   **189 he** Wolsey   **192 his** King Henry's.   **he** Wolsey   **195 Something mistaken** somewhat misrepresented   **197 in proof** in experience.   **204 device and practice** stratagems and plots.   **205 to look on** i.e., and am sorry to witness   **207 nothing** not at all

217 attach arrest   **218–19 John de la Car, Gilbert Perk** (The names are from Holinshed's account: "Master John de la Car, alias de la Court, the Duke's confessor, and Sir Gilbert Perke, priest, the Duke's chancellor.")   **221 Chartreux** Carthusian order.   **223 spanned** measured   **224–6 I am . . . sun** I am the mere semblance of my former self, whose form and future hopes are obscured in this sudden cloud of affliction by the darkening of my king's favor.
1.2. Location: London. The council chamber.
0.1 *Cornets* Trumpet-like wind instruments   **0.3–4** *under . . . feet* i.e., at the foot of the royal dais   **1 best heart** most essential part   **2 level** aim, line of fire   **3 full-charged confederacy** fully loaded conspiracy   **5 That . . . Buckingham's** i.e., Buckingham's surveyor (1.1.115), whom Wolsey has induced to testify against his master   **6 justify** prove, confirm   **8.4** *state* chair of state, raised seat with a canopy

KING
Arise, and take place by us. Half your suit
Never name to us; you have half our power.
The other moiety ere you ask is given.   12
Repeat your will and take it.

KATHARINE   Thank Your Majesty.   13
That you would love yourself, and in that love
Not unconsidered leave your honor nor
The dignity of your office, is the point
Of my petition.

KING   Lady mine, proceed.

KATHARINE
I am solicited, not by a few,
And those of true condition, that your subjects
Are in great grievance. There have been commissions   19
Sent down among 'em which hath flawed the heart   20
Of all their loyalties; wherein, although,   21
My good lord Cardinal, they vent reproaches
Most bitterly on you, as putter-on   24
Of these exactions, yet the King our master—
Whose honor heaven shield from soil!—even he
escapes not   26
Language unmannerly, yea, such which breaks
The sides of loyalty and almost appears
In loud rebellion.

NORFOLK   Not "almost appears,"
It doth appear; for, upon these taxations,
The clothiers all, not able to maintain
The many to them 'longing, have put off   32
The spinsters, carders, fullers, weavers, who,   33
Unfit for other life, compelled by hunger
And lack of other means, in desperate manner
Daring th'event to th' teeth, are all in uproar,   36
And danger serves among them.

KING   Taxation?   37
Wherein? And what taxation? My lord Cardinal,
You that are blamed for it alike with us,
Know you of this taxation?

WOLSEY   Please you, sir,
I know but of a single part in aught   41
Pertains to th' state, and front but in that file   42
Where others tell steps with me.

KATHARINE   No, my lord?   43
You know no more than others? But you frame   44
Things that are known alike, which are not whole-
some   45
To those which would not know them and yet must   46
Perforce be their acquaintance. These exactions,   47

Whereof my sovereign would have note, they are   48
Most pestilent to th' hearing, and to bear 'em
The back is sacrifice to the load. They say   50
They are devised by you, or else you suffer
Too hard an exclamation.

KING   Still "exaction"!   52
The nature of it? In what kind, let's know,
Is this exaction?

KATHARINE   I am much too venturous
In tempting of your patience, but am boldened   55
Under your promised pardon. The subjects' grief   56
Comes through commissions, which compels from
each
The sixth part of his substance, to be levied   58
Without delay; and the pretense for this   59
Is named your wars in France. This makes bold
mouths:
Tongues spit their duties out, and cold hearts freeze
Allegiance in them. Their curses now   62
Live where their prayers did, and it's come to pass   63
This tractable obedience is a slave   64
To each incensèd will. I would Your Highness   65
Would give it quick consideration, for
There is no primer business.

KING   By my life,   67
This is against our pleasure.

WOLSEY   And for me,
I have no further gone in this than by   69
A single voice, and that not passed me but   70
By learnèd approbation of the judges. If I am   71
Traduced by ignorant tongues, which neither know   72
My faculties nor person, yet will be   73
The chronicles of my doing, let me say
'Tis but the fate of place, and the rough brake   75
That virtue must go through. We must not stint   76
Our necessary actions in the fear
To cope malicious censurers, which ever,   78
As ravenous fishes, do a vessel follow
That is new trimmed, but benefit no further   80
Than vainly longing. What we oft do best,   81
By sick interpreters, once weak ones, is   82
Not ours, or not allowed; what worst, as oft   83
Hitting a grosser quality, is cried up   84
For our best act. If we shall stand still,   85
In fear our motion will be mocked or carped at,   86

---

12 **moiety** half   13 **Repeat your will** Express your desire   19 **true
condition** disposition to loyalty   20 **grievance** distress.   **commissions**
writs authorizing a tax levy, and the agents to carry them out
21 **flawed** damaged, cracked   24 **putter-on** instigator   26 **soil** moral
stain   32 **to them 'longing** in their employ.   **put off** laid off
33 **The spinsters . . . fullers** the spinners, those who comb wool for
impurities, those who beat wool to clean it   36 **Daring . . . teeth** defiantly challenging the outcome   37 **danger . . . them** mischief has
joined in their unrest.   41–3 **I know . . . me** I am acquainted with a
single share only in state affairs, and merely march in the front rank
with others who march with me.   44–7 **you frame . . . acquaintance**
you devise measures known to all (the Council) which are harmful to
those who would much prefer not to be acquainted with them and
yet must perforce put up with them.

48 **note** knowledge   50 **is sacrifice to** i.e., is bowed down under
52 **exclamation** accusation.   55 **boldened** made bold   56 **grief** grievance   58 **substance** wealth   59 **pretense** pretext   62–5 **Their . . . will**
They curse now whereas before they prayed, with the result that
once-docile obedience is overmastered by angry defiance.   67 **primer**
more urgent   69–71 **I have . . . judges** i.e., my part in this was only to
cast one vote in accord with the unanimous wise judgment of the
Privy Council.   72 **Traduced** defamed   73 **faculties** qualities
75 **place** high office.   **brake** thicket   76 **stint** stop   78 **To cope** of
encountering.   **ever** always   80 **new trimmed** newly fitted out
81 **longing** i.e., that the vessel will sink. (Wolsey is confident that his
enemies will not soon profit from any fall from power on his part.)
81–5 **What . . . act** Often our best deeds are, by malicous or sometimes
weak-witted critics, either not credited to us or else disapproved of;
our worst efforts, meantime, appealing to vulgar natures, are called
the best things we've done.   86 **In fear** for fear that

We should take root here where we sit,
Or sit, state-statues only.

KING   Things done well,   88
And with a care, exempt themselves from fear;
Things done without example, in their issue   90
Are to be feared. Have you a precedent   92
Of this commission? I believe, not any.
We must not rend our subjects from our laws   93
And stick them in our will. Sixth part of each?   94
A trembling contribution! Why, we take   95
From every tree lop, bark, and part o'th' timber,   96
And though we leave it with a root, thus hacked,
The air will drink the sap. To every county   98
Where this is questioned send our letters with   99
Free pardon to each man that has denied
The force of this commission. Pray look to't;   101
I put it to your care.

WOLSEY [*aside to his Secretary*]   A word with you.
Let there be letters writ to every shire
Of the King's grace and pardon. The grieved commons 104
Hardly conceive of me; let it be noised   105
That through our intercession this revokement
And pardon comes. I shall anon advise you   107
Further in the proceeding.   *Exit Secretary.*

         Enter Surveyor.

KATHARINE
I am sorry that the Duke of Buckingham
Is run in your displeasure.

KING   It grieves many.   110
The gentleman is learned, and a most rare speaker,   111
To nature none more bound; his training such   112
That he may furnish and instruct great teachers
And never seek for aid out of himself. Yet see,   114
When these so noble benefits shall prove
Not well disposed, the mind growing once corrupt,   116
They turn to vicious forms, ten times more ugly
Than ever they were fair. This man so complete,   118
Who was enrolled 'mongst wonders, and when we,
Almost with ravished list'ning, could not find
His hour of speech a minute—he, my lady,
Hath into monstrous habits put the graces   122
That once were his, and is become as black
As if besmeared in hell. Sit by us. You shall hear—
This was his gentleman in trust—of him
Things to strike honor sad.—Bid him recount
The fore-recited practices, whereof   127
We cannot feel too little, hear too much.   128

WOLSEY [*to the Surveyor*]
Stand forth, and with bold spirit relate what you,
Most like a careful subject, have collected   130
Out of the Duke of Buckingham.

KING   Speak freely.

SURVEYOR
First, it was usual with him—every day
It would infect his speech—that if the King
Should without issue die, he'll carry it so   134
To make the scepter his. These very words
I've heard him utter to his son-in-law,
Lord Aberga'nny, to whom by oath he menaced
Revenge upon the Cardinal.

WOLSEY   Please Your Highness, note
This dangerous conception in this point.
Not friended by his wish to your high person,   140
His will is most malignant, and it stretches
Beyond you to your friends.

KATHARINE   My learned lord Cardinal,
Deliver all with charity.

KING   Speak on.   143
How grounded he his title to the crown
Upon our fail? To this point hast thou heard him   145
At any time speak aught?

SURVEYOR   He was brought to this
By a vain prophecy of Nicholas Henton.   147

KING
What was that Henton?

SURVEYOR   Sir, a Chartreux friar,
His confessor, who fed him every minute
With words of sovereignty.

KING   How know'st thou this?   150

SURVEYOR
Not long before Your Highness sped to France,
The Duke being at the Rose, within the parish   152
Saint Lawrence Poultney, did of me demand
What was the speech among the Londoners   154
Concerning the French journey. I replied,
Men feared the French would prove perfidious,   157
To the King's danger. Presently the Duke
Said, 'twas the fear indeed, and that he doubted   158
'Twould prove the verity of certain words
Spoke by a holy monk, "that oft," says he,
"Hath sent to me, wishing me to permit
John de la Car, my chaplain, a choice hour
To hear from him a matter of some moment;   163
Whom after under the confession's seal
He solemnly had sworn that what he spoke
My chaplain to no creature living but
To me should utter, with demure confidence   167
This pausingly ensued: 'Neither the King nor 's heirs,

---

88 **state-statues** mere statues of statesmen   90 **example** precedent.
issue consequences   92 **Of** for   93 **rend** tear   94 **stick . . . will** make
them the victims of our caprice.   95 **trembling** fearful, causing to
tremble   96 **lop** branch   98 **The air . . . sap** i.e., the tree will dry up
and die.   99 **questioned** disputed, resisted   101 **force** validity
104 **grace** mercy.   **grieved** aggrieved   105 **Hardly conceive** have a
bad opinion.   **noised** reported, rumored   107 **anon** soon   110 **Is
run in** has incurred   111 **rare** excellent   112 **To . . . bound** none more
indebted to nature for talents   114 **out of** beyond   116 **disposed**
applied   118 **complete** accomplished   122 **habits** garments, i.e.,
shapes   127 **practices** intrigues   127–8 **whereof . . . much** i.e., of
which it behooves us to hear for our own safety, however painful it is
to feel.

130 **collected** i.e., learned by spying   134 **issue** offspring.   **carry it so**
manage affairs so as   140 **Not . . . person** Not being aided by the fulfillment of his wish regarding Your Majesty (that you should die
without an heir)   143 **Deliver** tell   145 **fail** i.e., dying without an
heir.   147 **Henton** (According to Holinshed, an alias for Nicholas
Hopkins; see 1.1.221.)   150 **of sovereignty** about gaining sovereign
power.   152 **the Rose** (A manor house belonging to Buckingham.)
154 **speech** talk   157 **Presently** Immediately   158 **doubted** feared,
suspected   163 **moment** importance   167 **demure** grave, solemn

Tell you the Duke, shall prosper. Bid him strive
To gain the love o'th' commonalty; the Duke
Shall govern England.' "
KATHARINE   If I know you well,
You were the Duke's surveyor, and lost your office
On the complaint o'th' tenants. Take good heed
You charge not in your spleen a noble person   174
And spoil your nobler soul. I say, take heed;
Yes, heartily beseech you.
KING   Let him on.—   176
Go forward.
SURVEYOR   On my soul, I'll speak but truth.
I told my lord the Duke, by th' devil's illusions
The monk might be deceived, and that 'twas
    dangerous
To ruminate on this so far until
It forged him some design, which, being believed,   181
It was much like to do. He answered, "Tush,   182
It can do me no damage," adding further
That, had the King in his last sickness failed,   184
The Cardinal's and Sir Thomas Lovell's heads
Should have gone off.
KING   Ha? What, so rank? Aha,
There's mischief in this man.—Canst thou say further?
SURVEYOR
I can, my liege.
KING   Proceed.
SURVEYOR   Being at Greenwich,
After Your Highness had reproved the Duke
About Sir William Bulmer—
KING   I remember
Of such a time. Being my sworn servant,
The Duke retained him his. But on; what hence?   192
SURVEYOR
"If," quoth he, "I for this had been committed,
As to the Tower I thought, I would have played
The part my father meant to act upon   195
Th'usurper Richard, who, being at Salisbury,
Made suit to come in 's presence, which if granted,
As he made semblance of his duty, would   198
Have put his knife into him."
KING   A giant traitor!
WOLSEY
Now, madam, may His Highness live in freedom,   200
And this man out of prison?
KATHARINE   God mend all!
KING [to the Surveyor]
There's something more would out of thee. What
    say't?
SURVEYOR
After "the Duke his father," with "the knife,"
He stretched him, and, with one hand on his dagger,   204
Another spread on 's breast, mounting his eyes,   205

He did discharge a horrible oath, whose tenor
Was, were he evil used, he would outgo   207
His father by as much as a performance
Does an irresolute purpose.
KING   There's his period,   209
To sheathe his knife in us. He is attached;   210
Call him to present trial. If he may   211
Find mercy in the law, 'tis his; if none,
Let him not seek't of us. By day and night,
He's traitor to th' height.   Exeunt. 214

❖

1.3

Enter Lord Chamberlain and Lord Sandys.

CHAMBERLAIN
Is't possible the spells of France should juggle   1
Men into such strange mysteries?
SANDYS   New customs,
Though they be never so ridiculous,   2
Nay, let 'em be unmanly, yet are followed.
CHAMBERLAIN
As far as I see, all the good our English
Have got by the late voyage is but merely   6
A fit or two o'th' face; but they are shrewd ones,   7
For when they hold 'em, you would swear directly   8
Their very noses had been counselors
To Pepin or Clotharius, they keep state so.   10
SANDYS
They have all new legs, and lame ones. One would
    take it,   11
That never see 'em pace before, the spavin   12
Or springhalt reigned among 'em.
CHAMBERLAIN   Death, my lord!   13
Their clothes are after such a pagan cut to't   14
That sure they've worn out Christendom.

Enter Sir Thomas Lovell.

                                  How now?   15
What news, Sir Thomas Lovell?
LOVELL   Faith, my lord,
I hear of none but the new proclamation
That's clapped upon the court gate.
CHAMBERLAIN   What is't for?   18

174 **spleen** malice   176 **on** go on.   181 **forged him** caused him to
fashion.   **being believed** i.e., if the Duke put faith in what the monk
was telling him   182 **much like** very likely   184 **failed** died
192 **his** as his own.   195 **my father** i.e., the Duke of Buckingham of
Richard III's time   198 **semblance of his duty** a show of dutiful
kneeling   200 **may** can   204 **stretched him** raised himself to his full
height   205 **mounting** raising

207 **evil used** badly treated   209 **irresolute** unaccomplished.
period aim, goal   210 **attached** arrested   211 **present** immediate
214 **to the height** in the highest degree.
1.3. Location: London. The royal court.
1 **juggle** beguile, bewitch   2 **mysteries** artificial fashions.   6 **the late
voyage** i.e., to the Field of the Cloth of Gold   7 **fit . . . face** affected
ways of screwing up the face into a grimace   8 **hold 'em** i.e., maintain the grimaces   10 **Pepin or Clotharius** kings of ancient France in
the sixth and eighth centuries.   **keep state** i.e., behave with an
affected dignity   11 **legs** mannerisms of walking and making obeisances   12 **see 'em pace** saw them walk.   **spavin** lameness in horses
caused by swelling of the joints   13 **springhalt** nervous twitching in
a horse's hind legs.   **Death** By God's death. (An oath.)   14–15 **Their
. . . Christendom** Their clothes are fashioned in such an ungodly style
that one might suppose they have exhausted the repertory of fashions
available in Christian society.   18 **clapped** posted

LOVELL
The reformation of our traveled gallants,
That fill the court with quarrels, talk, and tailors.

CHAMBERLAIN
I'm glad 'tis there. Now I would pray our monsieurs
To think an English courtier may be wise
And never see the Louvre.

LOVELL   They must either—   23
For so run the conditions—leave those remnants
Of fool and feather that they got in France,   25
With all their honorable points of ignorance   26
Pertaining thereunto, as fights and fireworks,   27
Abusing better men than they can be
Out of a foreign wisdom, renouncing clean   29
The faith they have in tennis and tall stockings,
Short blistered breeches, and those types of travel,   31
And understand again like honest men,   32
Or pack to their old playfellows. There, I take it,   33
They may, *cum privilegio*, "oui" away   34
The lag end of their lewdness and be laughed at.   35

SANDYS
'Tis time to give 'em physic, their diseases   36
Are grown so catching.

CHAMBERLAIN   What a loss our ladies
Will have of these trim vanities!

LOVELL   Ay, marry,   38
There will be woe indeed, lords. The sly whoresons
Have got a speeding trick to lay down ladies;   40
A French song and a fiddle has no fellow.   41

SANDYS
The devil fiddle 'em! I am glad they are going,
For sure there's no converting of 'em. Now
An honest country lord, as I am, beaten
A long time out of play, may bring his plainsong   45
And have an hour of hearing, and, by'r Lady,
Held current music too.

CHAMBERLAIN   Well said, Lord Sands.   47
Your colt's tooth is not cast yet?

SANDYS   No, my lord,   48
Nor shall not while I have a stump.

CHAMBERLAIN   Sir Thomas,   49
Whither were you a-going?

LOVELL   To the Cardinal's.
Your Lordship is a guest too.

CHAMBERLAIN   Oh, 'tis true.
This night he makes a supper, and a great one,   52

To many lords and ladies. There will be
The beauty of this kingdom, I'll assure you.

LOVELL
That churchman bears a bounteous mind indeed,
A hand as fruitful as the land that feeds us;   56
His dews fall everywhere.

CHAMBERLAIN   No doubt he's noble;
He had a black mouth that said other of him.   58

SANDYS
He may, my lord. H'as wherewithal: in him   59
Sparing would show a worse sin than ill doctrine.   60
Men of his way should be most liberal;   61
They are set here for examples.

CHAMBERLAIN   True, they are so;
But few now give so great ones. My barge stays;   63
Your Lordship shall along. Come, good Sir Thomas,   64
We shall be late else, which I would not be,   65
For I was spoke to, with Sir Henry Guildford,   66
This night to be comptrollers.

SANDYS   I am Your Lordship's.   67
                                          Exeunt.

❖

1.4

*Hautboys. A small table under a state for the
Cardinal, a longer table for the guests. Then enter
Anne Bullen and divers other ladies and gentlemen
as guests, at one door; at another door enter Sir
Henry Guildford.*

GUILDFORD
Ladies, a general welcome from His Grace
Salutes ye all. This night he dedicates
To fair content and you. None here, he hopes,
In all this noble bevy, has brought with her   4
One care abroad. He would have all as merry   5
As, first, good company, good wine, good welcome
Can make good people.

*Enter Lord Chamberlain, Lord Sandys, and [Sir
Thomas] Lovell.*

                                          Oh, my lord, you're tardy.
The very thought of this fair company
Clapped wings to me.

CHAMBERLAIN   You are young, Sir Harry Guildford.
SANDYS
Sir Thomas Lovell, had the Cardinal
But half my lay thoughts in him, some of these   11

23 **Louvre** royal palace in France, seat of the French court.   **25 fool
and feather** i.e., folly and fashion   **26 honorable . . . ignorance** i.e.,
what they ignorantly regard as honorable   **27 as** such as.   **fireworks**
(With added suggestion of "whores.")   **29 renouncing** i.e., as a way
of leaving their folly   **31 blistered** puffed.   **types** badges, marks
32 understand (1) comprehend (2) use their legs to "stand under"
them   **33 pack** be off   **34 cum privilegio** with exclusive right, immunity   **34–5 "oui" . . . lewdness** i.e., in French manner pass the remainder of their worthless lives   **36 physic** purging medicine   **38 trim
vanities** finely dressed but worthless dandies.   **40 speeding** successful.   **lay down** seduce   **41 fiddle** (With sexual suggestion of something to fiddle with.)   **fellow** equal.   **45 play** (1) playing the role of
wooer (2) performing music.   **plainsong** (1) simple melody or air
(2) plain, simple wooing   **47 Held current** regarded as fashionable
48 colt's tooth i.e., lecherousness of youth.   **cast** shed, cast aside
49 stump i.e., of a tooth. (With a bawdy pun.)   **52 makes** gives

56 fruitful generous   **58 He . . . mouth** a person must have an evil
habit of speech   **59 H'as wherewithal** He has the necessary means
60 Sparing . . . doctrine frugality would look more sinful than heresy.
61 way way of life   **63 ones** examples.   **stays** waits for me
64 along come along.   **65 else** otherwise   **66 spoke to** asked
67 comptrollers stewards, masters of ceremonies.
1.4. Location: Westminster. A hall in York Place.
0.1 Hautboys Reed instruments related to the modern oboe.   **state**
canopy   **4 bevy** company   **5 abroad** away from home.   **11 lay
thoughts** (1) thoughts not suited to a clergyman (2) thoughts of sexual pleasure

Should find a running banquet ere they rested,   12
I think would better please 'em. By my life,   13
They are a sweet society of fair ones.

LOVELL
Oh, that Your Lordship were but now confessor
To one or two of these!

SANDYS   I would I were;
They should find easy penance.

LOVELL   Faith, how easy?   17

SANDYS
As easy as a down bed would afford it.

CHAMBERLAIN
Sweet ladies, will it please you sit? Sir Harry,
Place you that side; I'll take the charge of this.   20
[The guests are shown their places at table.]
His Grace is ent'ring. Nay, you must not freeze;
Two women placed together makes cold weather.
My Lord Sandys, you are one will keep 'em waking;   23
Pray, sit between these ladies.

SANDYS   By my faith,
And thank Your Lordship. By your leave, sweet ladies.
[He takes a place between Anne Bullen
and another lady.]
If I chance to talk a little wild, forgive me;
I had it from my father.

ANNE   Was he mad, sir?

SANDYS
Oh, very mad, exceeding mad, in love too.
But he would bite none; just as I do now,
He would kiss you twenty with a breath.   30
[He kisses her.]

CHAMBERLAIN   Well said, my lord.   31
So, now you're fairly seated. Gentlemen,
The penance lies on you if these fair ladies
Pass away frowning.

SANDYS   For my little cure,   34
Let me alone.   35

Hautboys. Enter Cardinal Wolsey and takes his
state.

WOLSEY
You're welcome, my fair guests. That noble lady
Or gentleman that is not freely merry
Is not my friend. This, to confirm my welcome;
And to you all, good health!   [He drinks.]

SANDYS   Your Grace is noble.
Let me have such a bowl may hold my thanks   40
And save me so much talking.

WOLSEY   My Lord Sandys,
I am beholding to you. Cheer your neighbors.   42

Ladies, you are not merry. Gentlemen,
Whose fault is this?

SANDYS   The red wine first must rise
In their fair cheeks, my lord; then we shall have 'em
Talk us to silence.

ANNE   You are a merry gamester,   46
My Lord Sandys.

SANDYS   Yes, if I make my play.   47
Here's to Your Ladyship; and pledge it, madam,   48
For 'tis to such a thing—

ANNE   You cannot show me.   49

SANDYS [to Wolsey]
I told Your Grace they would talk anon.
Drum and trumpet. Chambers discharged.

WOLSEY   What's that?   50

CHAMBERLAIN
Look out there, some of ye.   [Exit a Servant.]

WOLSEY   What warlike voice,
And to what end, is this? Nay, ladies, fear not;
By all the laws of war you're privileged.   53

Enter a Servant.

CHAMBERLAIN
How now? What is't?

SERVANT   A noble troop of strangers,   54
For so they seem. They've left their barge and landed,
And hither make, as great ambassadors   56
From foreign princes.

WOLSEY   Good Lord Chamberlain,
Go give 'em welcome; you can speak the French
tongue;
And pray receive 'em nobly and conduct 'em
Into our presence, where this heaven of beauty   60
Shall shine at full upon them. Some attend him.
[Exit Chamberlain, attended.]
All rise, and tables removed.
You have now a broken banquet, but we'll mend it.
A good digestion to you all! And once more
I shower a welcome on ye. Welcome all!   64

Hautboys. Enter King and others, as masquers,
habited like shepherds, ushered by the Lord
Chamberlain. They pass directly before the
Cardinal and gracefully salute him.

A noble company! What are their pleasures?

CHAMBERLAIN
Because they speak no English, thus they prayed
To tell Your Grace that, having heard by fame   67

---

12 **running banquet** hasty meal. (With amorous suggestion of pursuit and sensuous indulgence, found also in *lay, confessor, easy penance*, etc.) 13 **I think** i.e., which I think 17 **Faith** In faith 20 **Place you** assign places on 23 **waking** lively. (With sexual innuendo.) 30 **He . . . breath** he would kiss twenty women at one breath. (*You* is used colloquially.) 31 **said** done 34 **For** As for. **cure** (1) remedy to prevent frowning (2) cure of souls (continuing the ecclesiastical metaphor of lines 15 and 33) 35 **Let me alone** leave it to me. 35.2 **state** chair of state. 40 **may** as may 42 **beholding** beholden. **Cheer** Entertain

46 **gamester** sportful, frolicsome person. (But Sandys, in his reply, plays on the sense of "gambler.") 47 **make my play** score, in cards and in the game of love. 48 **pledge it** drink in response to my toast 49 **'tis . . . thing** (Sandys proposes his toast in an unfinished sentence that is erotically suggestive.) **You . . . me** i.e., You can't teach me a lesson in how to drink a toast. (Anne parries the erotic suggestion of Sandys by drinking to him.) 50 s.d. *Chambers* small cannon (the firing of which in 1613 probably started the fire that burned down the Globe playhouse) 53 **privileged** i.e., entitled to immunity in the event of conflict. 54 **strangers** foreigners 56 **make** come 60 **this . . . beauty** this assemblage of beautiful ladies 64.1 *masquers* participants in a masque or masked festivities—*the revels* referred to in line 73 64.2 *habited* dressed 67 **fame** report

Of this so noble and so fair assembly
This night to meet here, they could do no less,
Out of the great respect they bear to beauty,
But leave their flocks, and, under your fair conduct,   71
Crave leave to view these ladies and entreat
An hour of revels with 'em.

WOLSEY   Say, Lord Chamberlain,   73
They have done my poor house grace, for which I pay
    'em
A thousand thanks, and pray 'em take their pleasures.
                        Choose ladies; King and Anne Bullen.

KING
The fairest hand I ever touched! O beauty,
Till now I never knew thee!   *Music. Dance.*

WOLSEY [*to the Chamberlain*]
My lord!

CHAMBERLAIN   Your Grace?

WOLSEY   Pray tell 'em thus much from me:
There should be one amongst 'em by his person
More worthy this place than myself, to whom,   80
If I but knew him, with my love and duty
I would surrender it.

CHAMBERLAIN   I will, my lord.
                        Whisper [*with the masquers*].

WOLSEY
What say they?

CHAMBERLAIN   Such a one, they all confess,
There is indeed, which they would have Your Grace
Find out, and he will take it.

WOLSEY   Let me see, then.   85
                        [*He comes from his chair of state.*]
By all your good leaves, gentlemen; here I'll make
My royal choice.   [*He bows before the King.*]

KING [*unmasking*]   Ye have found him, Cardinal.
You hold a fair assembly; you do well, lord.
You are a churchman, or I'll tell you, Cardinal,
I should judge now unhappily.

WOLSEY   I am glad   90
Your Grace is grown so pleasant.

KING   My Lord Chamberlain,   91
Prithee, come hither. What fair lady's that?

CHAMBERLAIN
An't please Your Grace, Sir Thomas Bullen's
    daughter—   93
The Viscount Rochford—one of Her Highness'
    women.

KING
By heaven, she is a dainty one.—Sweetheart,
I were unmannerly to take you out   96
And not to kiss you. [*He kisses Anne.*] A health,
    gentlemen!   97
Let it go round.   [*He offers a toast.*]

WOLSEY
Sir Thomas Lovell, is the banquet ready

I'th' privy chamber?

LOVELL   Yes, my lord.

WOLSEY [*to the King*]   Your Grace,
I fear, with dancing is a little heated.

KING
I fear, too much.

WOLSEY   There's fresher air, my lord,
In the next chamber.

KING
Lead in your ladies every one.—Sweet partner,
I must not yet forsake you.—Let's be merry,
Good my lord Cardinal. I have half a dozen healths
To drink to these fair ladies, and a measure   107
To lead 'em once again; and then let's dream
Who's best in favor. Let the music knock it.   109
                        Exeunt, with trumpets.

❖

2.1

Enter two Gentlemen, at several doors.

FIRST GENTLEMAN
Whither away so fast?

SECOND GENTLEMAN   Oh, God save ye!
Ev'n to the hall, to hear what shall become   2
Of the great Duke of Buckingham.

FIRST GENTLEMAN   I'll save you
That labor, sir. All's now done but the ceremony
Of bringing back the prisoner.

SECOND GENTLEMAN   Were you there?

FIRST GENTLEMAN
Yes, indeed was I.

SECOND GENTLEMAN   Pray, speak what has happened.

FIRST GENTLEMAN
You may guess quickly what.

SECOND GENTLEMAN   Is he found guilty?

FIRST GENTLEMAN
Yes, truly is he, and condemned upon't.

SECOND GENTLEMAN
I am sorry for't.

FIRST GENTLEMAN   So are a number more.

SECOND GENTLEMAN   But pray, how passed it?   10

FIRST GENTLEMAN
I'll tell you in a little. The great Duke   11
Came to the bar, where to his accusations
He pleaded still not guilty and alleged   13
Many sharp reasons to defeat the law.   14
The King's attorney on the contrary
Urged on the examinations, proofs, confessions   16
Of divers witnesses, which the Duke desired
To have brought viva voce to his face;   18

---

107 measure stately dance   **109 best in favor** best-looking, or, most
in favor with the ladies.   **knock it** strike up.
2.1. Location: Westminster.
0.1 *several* separate   **2 the hall** i.e., Westminster Hall, where the trial
was held   **10 passed it** did it proceed.   **11 in a little** in brief.
13 alleged brought forward   **14 law** i.e., case against him.   **16 examinations** depositions.   **proofs** testimonies   **18 viva voce** in person

---

71 under . . . conduct with your kind permission   **73 revels** festive
dancing and masking   **80 this place** i.e., this chair of state   **85 it** i.e.,
the chair of state.   **90 unhappily** unfavorably (at such a display of
wealth).   **91 pleasant** merry.   **93 An't** If it   **96 take you out** lead you
out for a dance   **97 health** toast

At which appeared against him his surveyor,
Sir Gilbert Perk his chancellor, and John Car,   20
Confessor to him, with that devil monk,
Hopkins, that made this mischief.

SECOND GENTLEMAN   That was he
That fed him with his prophecies?

FIRST GENTLEMAN   The same.
All these accused him strongly, which he fain   24
Would have flung from him, but indeed he could not;
And so his peers, upon this evidence,
Have found him guilty of high treason. Much
He spoke, and learnedly, for life; but all
Was either pitied in him or forgotten.   29

SECOND GENTLEMAN
After all this, how did he bear himself?

FIRST GENTLEMAN
When he was brought again to th' bar, to hear
His knell rung out, his judgment, he was stirred   32
With such an agony he sweat extremely,
And something spoke in choler, ill and hasty.   34
But he fell to himself again, and sweetly   35
In all the rest showed a most noble patience.

SECOND GENTLEMAN
I do not think he fears death.

FIRST GENTLEMAN   Sure he does not;
He never was so womanish. The cause
He may a little grieve at.

SECOND GENTLEMAN   Certainly
The Cardinal is the end of this.

FIRST GENTLEMAN   'Tis likely,   40
By all conjectures: first, Kildare's attainder,   41
Then deputy of Ireland, who removed,   42
Earl Surrey was sent thither, and in haste too,
Lest he should help his father.

SECOND GENTLEMAN   That trick of state   44
Was a deep envious one.

FIRST GENTLEMAN   At his return   45
No doubt he will requite it. This is noted,   46
And generally: whoever the King favors,   47
The Cardinal instantly will find employment,
And far enough from court too.

SECOND GENTLEMAN   All the commons
Hate him perniciously and, o' my conscience,   50
Wish him ten fathom deep. This duke as much
They love and dote on, call him bounteous
Buckingham,

The mirror of all courtesy—   53

*Enter Buckingham from his arraignment, tipstaves
before him, the ax with the edge towards him,
halberds on each side, accompanied with Sir
Thomas Lovell, Sir Nicholas Vaux, Sir Walter
Sandys, and common people, etc.*

FIRST GENTLEMAN   Stay there, sir,
And see the noble ruined man you speak of.

SECOND GENTLEMAN
Let's stand close and behold him.

BUCKINGHAM   All good people,   55
You that thus far have come to pity me,
Hear what I say, and then go home and lose me.   57
I have this day received a traitor's judgment,
And by that name must die. Yet, heaven bear witness,
And if I have a conscience, let it sink me,   60
Even as the ax falls, if I be not faithful!
The law I bear no malice for my death;
'T has done, upon the premises, but justice;   63
But those that sought it I could wish more Christians.   64
Be what they will, I heartily forgive 'em.
Yet let 'em look they glory not in mischief,
Nor build their evils on the graves of great men,   67
For then my guiltless blood must cry against 'em.
For further life in this world I ne'er hope,
Nor will I sue, although the King have mercies   70
More than I dare make faults. You few that loved me   71
And dare be bold to weep for Buckingham,
His noble friends and fellows, whom to leave   73
Is only bitter to him, only dying,   74
Go with me like good angels to my end,
And as the long divorce of steel falls on me   76
Make of your prayers one sweet sacrifice,   77
And lift my soul to heaven.—Lead on, i' God's name!

LOVELL
I do beseech Your Grace, for charity,
If ever any malice in your heart
Were hid against me, now to forgive me frankly.

BUCKINGHAM
Sir Thomas Lovell, I as free forgive you
As I would be forgiven. I forgive all.
There cannot be those numberless offenses
'Gainst me that I cannot take peace with; no black
    envy   85
Shall mark my grave. Commend me to His Grace,
And if he speak of Buckingham, pray tell him
You met him half in heaven. My vows and prayers
Yet are the King's and, till my soul forsake,   89
Shall cry for blessings on him. May he live

---

20 Sir (A common courtesy title for a priest.)   24 which i.e., which
accusations.   fain gladly   29 Was . . . forgotten either produced no
effect or produced only ineffectual pity.   32 judgment sentence
34 choler anger.   ill malevolent   35 fell to recovered   40 end cause
41 Kildare's attainder i.e., the confiscation of estates and sentencing
to death of the Earl of Kildare, Lord Lieutenant of Ireland (whom
Wolsey, according to Holinshed, removed to make room for Thomas
Howard, Earl of Surrey, son-in-law to Buckingham, and thereby to
keep Surrey in effective exile)   42 who removed i.e., Kildare having
been removed   44 father i.e., father-in-law.   trick of state political
stratagem   45 envious malicious   46 requite repay   47 generally
by everybody   50 perniciously with deadly hatred

53 mirror i.e., paragon   53.1 *tipstaves* bailiffs   53.3 *halberds* halberdiers, with long-handled weapons   53.4 *Walter* ("William" in
Holinshed)   55 close as close as possible and silently out of view
57 lose forget   60 sink ruin, damn   63 premises evidence   64 more
better   67 Nor . . . men i.e., nor extend their own evil careers by extinguishing the lives of noblemen. (*Evils* may suggest "hovels" or "privies.")   70 sue petition   71 make faults commit offenses.   73–4 whom
. . . dying the loss of whose dear company is the only cause of bitterness in dying alone   76 divorce of steel i.e., separation of body and
soul effected by the executioner's ax   77 sacrifice offering   85 take
make.   envy malice   89 Yet still.   forsake leave my body

Longer than I have time to tell his years!   91
Ever beloved and loving may his rule be!
And when old Time shall lead him to his end,
Goodness and he fill up one monument!   94

LOVELL
To th' waterside I must conduct Your Grace,
Then give my charge up to Sir Nicholas Vaux,
Who undertakes you to your end.

VAUX   Prepare there;   97
The Duke is coming. See the barge be ready,
And fit it with such furniture as suits   99
The greatness of his person.

BUCKINGHAM   Nay, Sir Nicholas,
Let it alone; my state now will but mock me.   101
When I came hither, I was Lord High Constable
And Duke of Buckingham; now, poor Edward Bohun.   103
Yet I am richer than my base accusers,
That never knew what truth meant. I now seal it,   105
And with that blood will make 'em one day groan
    for't.   106
My noble father, Henry of Buckingham,
Who first raised head against usurping Richard,   108
Flying for succor to his servant Banister,
Being distressed, was by that wretch betrayed,
And without trial fell; God's peace be with him!
Henry the Seventh succeeding, truly pitying
My father's loss, like a most royal prince
Restored me to my honors, and out of ruins
Made my name once more noble. Now his son,
Henry the Eighth, life, honor, name, and all
That made me happy, at one stroke has taken
Forever from the world. I had my trial,
And must needs say a noble one; which makes me
A little happier than my wretched father.   120
Yet thus far we are one in fortunes: both
Fell by our servants, by those men we loved most—
A most unnatural and faithless service!
Heaven has an end in all. Yet, you that hear me,   124
This from a dying man receive as certain:
Where you are liberal of your loves and counsels
Be sure you be not loose; for those you make friends   127
And give your hearts to, when they once perceive
The least rub in your fortunes, fall away   129
Like water from ye, never found again
But where they mean to sink ye. All good people,
Pray for me! I must now forsake ye. The last hour
Of my long weary life is come upon me.
Farewell! And when you would say something that is
    sad,
Speak how I fell. I have done; and God forgive me!
                                        Exeunt Duke and train.

FIRST GENTLEMAN
Oh, this is full of pity! Sir, it calls,
I fear, too many curses on their heads
That were the authors.

SECOND GENTLEMAN   If the Duke be guiltless,
'Tis full of woe. Yet I can give you inkling
Of an ensuing evil, if it fall,
Greater than this.

FIRST GENTLEMAN   Good angels keep it from us!
What may it be? You do not doubt my faith, sir?   142

SECOND GENTLEMAN
This secret is so weighty, 'twill require
A strong faith to conceal it.

FIRST GENTLEMAN   Let me have it;
I do not talk much.

SECOND GENTLEMAN   I am confident;   145
You shall, sir. Did you not of late days hear   146
A buzzing of a separation   147
Between the King and Katharine?

FIRST GENTLEMAN   Yes, but it held not; 148
For when the King once heard it, out of anger
He sent command to the Lord Mayor straight
To stop the rumor and allay those tongues   151
That durst disperse it.

SECOND GENTLEMAN   But that slander, sir,
Is found a truth now, for it grows again
Fresher than e'er it was, and held for certain
The King will venture at it. Either the Cardinal,
Or some about him near, have, out of malice   156
To the good Queen, possessed him with a scruple   157
That will undo her. To confirm this too,
Cardinal Campeius is arrived, and lately,   159
As all think, for this business.

FIRST GENTLEMAN   'Tis the Cardinal;
And merely to revenge him on the Emperor   161
For not bestowing on him at his asking
The archbishopric of Toledo, this is purposed.   163

SECOND GENTLEMAN
I think you have hit the mark. But is't not cruel
That she should feel the smart of this? The Cardinal   165
Will have his will, and she must fall.

FIRST GENTLEMAN   'Tis woeful.
We are too open here to argue this;   167
Let's think in private more.   *Exeunt.*

❧

91 **tell** count   94 **monument** tomb.   97 **undertakes** takes charge of
99 **furniture** furnishings   101 **state** rank   103 **Bohun** (The Duke's
family name was actually Stafford; Shakespeare follows the error in
Holinshed.)   105 **seal** ratify, attest to the truth of   106 **will** that will.
(Buckingham's shed blood will cry out from the grave for
vengeance.)   108 **raised head** gathered an army.   **Richard** Richard
III   120 **happier** more fortunate   124 **end** aim   127 **loose** wanting in
restraint, careless   129 **rub** impediment. (A term from bowls.)

142 **faith** i.e., ability to keep a secret   145 **am confident** i.e., trust your
discretion   146 **shall** i.e., shall hear it.   **late** recent   147 **buzzing**
rumor   148 **held not** ceased; or perhaps was not believed   151 **allay**
subdue, confute   156 **about him near** close to him   157 **possessed . . .
scruple** put into Henry's mind a doubt. (Katharine had been married
to Henry's older brother, Prince Arthur, who died, still in his early
teens, a year after the marriage. Such a precontract would normally
invalidate a subsequent marriage with any close relative of Arthur's,
but Henry's marriage to Katharine had been made possible by a
papal dispensation.)   159 **Cardinal Campeius** Cardinal Lorenzo
Campeggio, sent from Rome to confer on the legality of the King's
marriage   161 **Emperor** (The Queen was the aunt of Charles V, Holy
Roman Emperor and King of Spain; see 1.1.176 and note.)   163 **purposed** intended.   165 **smart** pain   167 **open** public

2.2

Enter Lord Chamberlain, reading this letter.

CHAMBERLAIN   "My lord, the horses Your Lordship sent
for, with all the care I had, I saw well chosen, ridden,   2
and furnished. They were young and handsome, and   3
of the best breed in the north. When they were ready
to set out for London, a man of my lord Cardinal's,
by commission and main power, took 'em from me   6
with this reason: his master would be served before a
subject, if not before the King; which stopped our
mouths, sir."
I fear he will indeed. Well, let him have them.
He will have all, I think.

*Enter to the Lord Chamberlain the Dukes of
Norfolk and Suffolk.*

NORFOLK   Well met, my Lord Chamberlain.

CHAMBERLAIN   Good day to both Your Graces.

SUFFOLK
How is the King employed?

CHAMBERLAIN   I left him private,   14
Full of sad thoughts and troubles.

NORFOLK   What's the cause?   15

CHAMBERLAIN
It seems the marriage with his brother's wife
Has crept too near his conscience.

SUFFOLK   No, his conscience
Has crept too near another lady.

NORFOLK   'Tis so.
This is the Cardinal's doing. The king-cardinal,
That blind priest, like the eldest son of Fortune,   20
Turns what he list. The King will know him one day.   21

SUFFOLK
Pray God he do! He'll never know himself else.

NORFOLK
How holily he works in all his business,   23
And with what zeal! For, now he has cracked the
    league
Between us and the Emperor, the Queen's great-
    nephew,
He dives into the King's soul and there scatters
Dangers, doubts, wringing of the conscience,
Fears, and despairs, and all these for his marriage.
And out of all these to restore the King,
He counsels a divorce, a loss of her
That, like a jewel, has hung twenty years
About his neck, yet never lost her luster;
Of her that loves him with that excellence
That angels love good men with; even of her
That, when the greatest stroke of fortune falls,
Will bless the King. And is not this course pious?   36

CHAMBERLAIN
Heaven keep me from such counsel! 'Tis most true
These news are everywhere; every tongue speaks 'em,   38
And every true heart weeps for 't. All that dare
Look into these affairs see this main end,
The French King's sister. Heaven will one day open   41
The King's eyes, that so long have slept upon   42
This bold bad man.

SUFFOLK   And free us from his slavery.

NORFOLK   We had need pray,
And heartily, for our deliverance,
Or this imperious man will work us all
From princes into pages. All men's honors   47
Lie like one lump before him, to be fashioned   48
Into what pitch he please.

SUFFOLK   For me, my lords,   49
I love him not, nor fear him; there's my creed.
As I am made without him, so I'll stand,   51
If the King please. His curses and his blessings
Touch me alike; they're breath I not believe in.
I knew him, and I know him; so I leave him
To him that made him proud, the Pope.

NORFOLK   Let's in,
And with some other business put the King
From these sad thoughts that work too much upon
    him.—
My lord, you'll bear us company?

CHAMBERLAIN   Excuse me;
The King has sent me otherwhere. Besides,   59
You'll find a most unfit time to disturb him.
Health to Your Lordships!

NORFOLK   Thanks, my good Lord Chamberlain.   61

*Exit Lord Chamberlain; and the King draws
the curtain and sits reading pensively.*

SUFFOLK
How sad he looks! Sure he is much afflicted.   62

KING
Who's there, ha?

NORFOLK   Pray God he be not angry.

KING
Who's there, I say? How dare you thrust yourselves
Into my private meditations?
Who am I? Ha?

NORFOLK
A gracious king that pardons all offenses
Malice ne'er meant. Our breach of duty this way   68
Is business of estate, in which we come   69
To know your royal pleasure.

KING   Ye are too bold.
Go to! I'll make ye know your times of business.   71

2.2. Location: London. The royal court.
2 ridden broken in, trained   3 furnished equipped.   6 commission
and main power warrant and sheer force   14 private alone   15 sad
serious   20–1 blind . . . list (Wolsey is the favored son of Fortune,
conventionally depicted as blind and turning her wheel.)   21 list
wishes.   23 he i.e., Wolsey   36 Will bless the King (Katharine does,
in fact, bless the King who has brought about her misfortune, at
4.2.163.)

38 news are (*News* was commonly considered a plural noun.)
41 The . . . sister i.e., the Duchess of Alençon; see 3.2.86–7.   42 slept
upon been blind to   47 pages attendants.   48 lump i.e., lump of
clay   49 pitch shape, height (literally, of a falcon's flight), i.e., degree
of dignity.   For As for   51 As . . . stand i.e., Inasmuch as my rank
was conferred on me by the King, not by Wolsey, I'll stand firm
59 otherwhere elsewhere.   61.2 *curtain* (The King is probably in a
"discovery space" rear stage.)   62 afflicted troubled.   68 this way in
this respect   69 estate public weal   71 Go to! (An exclamation of
impatience.)

Is this an hour for temporal affairs, ha?

Enter Wolsey and Campeius, with a commission.

Who's there? My good lord Cardinal? O my Wolsey,
The quiet of my wounded conscience,
Thou art a cure fit for a king. [*To Campeius*] You're
   welcome,
Most learnèd reverend sir, into our kingdom.
Use us and it. [*To Wolsey*] My good lord, have great
   care
I be not found a talker.

WOLSEY   Sir, you cannot.   78
I would Your Grace would give us but an hour
Of private conference.

KING [*to Norfolk and Suffolk*]   We are busy; go.

NORFOLK [*aside to Suffolk*]
This priest has no pride in him?

SUFFOLK [*aside to Norfolk*]   Not to speak of.
I would not be so sick, though, for his place.   82
But this cannot continue.

NORFOLK [*aside to Suffolk*]   If it do,
I'll venture one have-at-him.

SUFFOLK [*aside to Norfolk*]   I another.   84

Exeunt Norfolk and Suffolk.

WOLSEY
Your Grace has given a precedent of wisdom   85
Above all princes, in committing freely
Your scruple to the voice of Christendom.   87
Who can be angry now? What envy reach you?   88
The Spaniard, tied by blood and favor to her,   89
Must now confess, if they have any goodness,   90
The trial just and noble. All the clerks—   91
I mean the learnèd ones in Christian kingdoms—
Have their free voices. Rome, the nurse of judgment,   93
Invited by your noble self, hath sent
One general tongue unto us: this good man,   95
This just and learnèd priest, Card'nal Campeius,
Whom once more I present unto Your Highness.

KING [*embracing Campeius*]
And once more in mine arms I bid him welcome,
And thank the holy conclave for their loves.   99
They have sent me such a man I would have wished
   for.

CAMPEIUS
Your Grace must needs deserve all strangers' loves,   101
You are so noble. To Your Highness' hand
I tender my commission, by whose virtue,   103
The court of Rome commanding, you, my lord

Cardinal of York, are joined with me their servant
In the unpartial judging of this business.
               [*He gives the King a document.*]

KING
Two equal men. The Queen shall be acquainted   107
Forthwith for what you come. Where's Gardiner?   108

WOLSEY
I know Your Majesty has always loved her
So dear in heart not to deny her that   110
A woman of less place might ask by law: 111
Scholars allowed freely to argue for her.

KING
Ay, and the best she shall have, and my favor
To him that does best; God forbid else.—Cardinal,
Prithee, call Gardiner to me, my new secretary.
I find him a fit fellow.   [*Wolsey goes to the door.*] 116

Enter Gardiner.

WOLSEY [*aside to Gardiner*]
Give me your hand. Much joy and favor to you;
You are the King's now.

GARDINER [*aside to Wolsey*]   But to be commanded
Forever by Your Grace, whose hand has raised me.

KING   Come hither, Gardiner.   *Walks and whispers.*

CAMPEIUS
My lord of York, was not one Doctor Pace   121
In this man's place before him?

WOLSEY   Yes, he was.

CAMPEIUS
Was he not held a learnèd man?

WOLSEY   Yes, surely.

CAMPEIUS
Believe me, there's an ill opinion spread then
Even of yourself, Lord Cardinal.

WOLSEY   How? Of me?

CAMPEIUS
They will not stick to say you envied him,   126
And, fearing he would rise, he was so virtuous,
Kept him a foreign man still, which so grieved him   128
That he ran mad and died.

WOLSEY   Heaven's peace be with him! 129
That's Christian care enough. For living murmurers 130
There's places of rebuke. He was a fool,
For he would needs be virtuous. That good fellow,
               [*indicating Gardiner*]
If I command him, follows my appointment;   133
I will have none so near else. Learn this, brother: 134
We live not to be gripped by meaner persons.   135

78 I . . . talker i.e., lest my offer of hospitality be only talk, not deeds.
82 sick i.e., sick with pride.   **for his place** even to gain his high
office.   **84 have-at-him** i.e., thrust at him (Wolsey) in fencing.
85 precedent example   **87 scruple** doubt.   **the voice of Christendom** i.e., the Pope, through his representative Campeius, and the clerics and scholars of various Continental universities to whom Henry
submitted his problem of "conscience."   **88 envy** malice   **89 The
Spaniard** i.e., Charles V and his court.   **her** Katharine   **90 confess**
concede   **91 clerks** clerics, scholars   **93 Have their free voices** may
vote as they choose.   **95 One general tongue** i.e., a spokesman
99 conclave College of Cardinals   **101 needs** necessarily.   **strangers'**
foreigners'   **103 tender** submit

107 equal equally impartial.   **acquainted** informed   **108 Gardiner**
i.e., Stephen Gardiner, Wolsey's secretary; he later becomes one of the
most influential members of the King's Council.   **110 that** that which
111 of less place even of lower rank   **116 fit** apt   **121 Doctor Pace**
i.e., Richard Pace, Dean of Saint Paul's and Secretary of State, who
served King Henry and Wolsey on diplomatic missions   **126 stick**
hesitate.   **envied him** i.e., were hostile toward Pace   **128 Kept . . .
still** kept him constantly abroad on diplomatic missions   **129 died**
(Pace actually died in 1536, six years after Wolsey's death.)   **130 murmurers** grumblers, troublemakers   **133 appointment** bidding
134 none . . . else i.e., no one besides him so close to the King.
135 gripped clutched at, grasped by the hand.   **meaner** of lower
social rank

KING [*to Gardiner*]
    Deliver this with modesty to th' Queen.   136
                         Exit Gardiner.
    The most convenient place that I can think of
    For such receipt of learning is Blackfriars;   138
    There ye shall meet about this weighty business.
    My Wolsey, see it furnished. O my lord,
    Would it not grieve an able man to leave   141
    So sweet a bedfellow? But conscience, conscience!
    Oh, 'tis a tender place, and I must leave her.   *Exeunt.*

❧

2.3

Enter Anne Bullen and an Old Lady.

ANNE
    Not for that neither. Here's the pang that pinches: 1
    His Highness having lived so long with her, and she
    So good a lady that no tongue could ever
    Pronounce dishonor of her—by my life,   4
    She never knew harm-doing—oh, now, after
    So many courses of the sun enthroned,   6
    Still growing in a majesty and pomp, the which   7
    To leave a thousandfold more bitter than
    'Tis sweet at first t'acquire—after this process,   9
    To give her the avaunt! It is a pity   10
    Would move a monster.
OLD LADY   Hearts of most hard temper
    Melt and lament for her.
ANNE   Oh, God's will, much better
    She ne'er had known pomp. Though 't be temporal,   13
    Yet, if that quarrel, Fortune, do divorce   14
    It from the bearer, 'tis a sufferance panging   15
    As soul and body's severing.
OLD LADY   Alas, poor lady!
    She's a stranger now again.
ANNE   So much the more   17
    Must pity drop upon her. Verily,
    I swear, 'tis better to be lowly born
    And range with humble livers in content   20
    Than to be perked up in a glist'ring grief   21
    And wear a golden sorrow.
OLD LADY   Our content
    Is our best having.
ANNE   By my troth and maidenhead,   23

    I would not be a queen.
OLD LADY   Beshrew me, I would,
    And venture maidenhead for't; and so would you,
    For all this spice of your hypocrisy.   26
    You that have so fair parts of woman on you   27
    Have too a woman's heart, which ever yet
    Affected eminence, wealth, sovereignty;   29
    Which, to say sooth, are blessings; and which gifts,   30
    Saving your mincing, the capacity   31
    Of your soft cheveril conscience would receive   32
    If you might please to stretch it.
ANNE   Nay, good troth.
OLD LADY
    Yes, troth, and troth. You would not be a queen?
ANNE
    No, not for all the riches under heaven.
OLD LADY
    'Tis strange. A threepence bowed would hire me,   36
    Old as I am, to queen it. But I pray you,
    What think you of a duchess? Have you limbs
    To bear that load of title?
ANNE   No, in truth.
OLD LADY
    Then you are weakly made. Pluck off a little;   40
    I would not be a young count in your way   41
    For more than blushing comes to. If your back
    Cannot vouchsafe this burden, 'tis too weak   43
    Ever to get a boy.
ANNE   How you do talk!   44
    I swear again, I would not be a queen
    For all the world.
OLD LADY   In faith, for little England
    You'd venture an emballing. I myself   47
    Would for Carnarvonshire, although there 'longed   48
    No more to th' crown but that. Lo, who comes here?

Enter Lord Chamberlain.

CHAMBERLAIN
    Good morrow, ladies. What were't worth to know
    The secret of your conference?
OLD LADY   My good lord,   51
    Not your demand; it values not your asking.   52
    Our mistress' sorrows we were pitying.
CHAMBERLAIN
    It was a gentle business, and becoming
    The action of good women. There is hope
    All will be well.
ANNE   Now I pray God, amen!

---

136 Deliver . . . modesty Make this known gently   **138 receipt of learning** reception of learned opinion, or of learned men. **Blackfriars** monastic buildings in London surrendered to the crown in Henry VIII's time   **141 able** vigorous
2.3. Location: London. The Queen's apartments.
1 Not . . . neither (Anne and the Old Lady are understood to be in mid conversation about the Queen's plight.)   **4 Pronounce** speak   **6 So . . . sun** so many years   **7 Still** always   **9 process** course of events   **10 give . . . avaunt** bid her begone.   **pity** pitiful situation   **13 temporal** merely worldly prosperity, not heavenly   **14 quarrel** quarreler, troublemaker   **15 sufferance panging** suffering as painful   **17 stranger** foreigner   **20 range** rank.   **livers** persons   **21 perked up** trimmed out   **23 having** possession.   **troth** good faith

26 For . . . spice in spite of this dash or touch   **27 parts** qualities   **29 Affected** loved, aspired to   **30 sooth** truth   **31 Saving your mincing** with all due respect to your affected coyness   **32 cheveril** kid leather. (Used as a type of flexibility.)   **36 bowed** crooked and therefore worthless; with sexual pun on "bawd," continued in *queen* ("quean," "whore"), *bear, count* (female pudenda), *way, emballing*   **40 Pluck off** Come lower   **41 count** (A rank below that of duke.)   **43 vouchsafe this burden** i.e., accept this load of honors. (With sexual suggestion of bearing a man.)   **44 get** beget   **47 emballing** investiture with the ball as a royal emblem. (With sexual suggestion of fornicating.)   **48 Carnarvonshire** an especially impoverished and barren Welsh county.   **'longed** belonged   **51 conference** conversation.   **52 Not your demand** i.e., it is not even worth your inquiring. **values not** is not worth

CHAMBERLAIN
You bear a gentle mind, and heav'nly blessings
Follow such creatures. That you may, fair lady,
Perceive I speak sincerely, and high note's
Ta'en of your many virtues, the King's Majesty
Commends his good opinion of you, and   61
Does purpose honor to you no less flowing   62
Than Marchioness of Pembroke; to which title
A thousand pound a year, annual support,
Out of his grace he adds.
ANNE   I do not know   65
What kind of my obedience I should tender.
More than my all is nothing; nor my prayers   67
Are not words duly hallowed, nor my wishes   68
More worth than empty vanities; yet prayers and
   wishes   69
Are all I can return. Beseech Your Lordship,
Vouchsafe to speak my thanks and my obedience,   71
As from a blushing handmaid, to His Highness,
Whose health and royalty I pray for.
CHAMBERLAIN   Lady,
I shall not fail t'approve the fair conceit   74
The King hath of you. [*Aside*] I have perused her well;
Beauty and honor in her are so mingled
That they have caught the King. And who knows yet
But from this lady may proceed a gem
To lighten all this isle? [*To Anne*] I'll to the King,   79
And say I spoke with you.
ANNE   My honored lord!   *Exit Lord Chamberlain.*
OLD LADY   Why, this it is! See, see,
I have been begging sixteen years in court,
Am yet a courtier beggarly, nor could   84
Come pat betwixt too early and too late   85
For any suit of pounds; and you—O fate!—   86
A very fresh fish here—fie, fie, fie upon
This compelled fortune!—have your mouth filled up   88
Before you open it.
ANNE   This is strange to me.
OLD LADY
How tastes it? Is it bitter? Forty pence, no.   90
There was a lady once—'tis an old story—
That would not be a queen, that would she not,
For all the mud in Egypt. Have you heard it?   93
ANNE
Come, you are pleasant.
OLD LADY   With your theme, I could   94
O'ermount the lark. The Marchioness of Pembroke?
A thousand pounds a year for pure respect?
No other obligation? By my life,   96

That promises more thousands. Honor's train   98
Is longer than his foreskirt. By this time   99
I know your back will bear a duchess. Say,
Are you not stronger than you were?
ANNE   Good lady,
Make yourself mirth with your particular fancy,   102
And leave me out on't. Would I had no being   103
If this salute my blood a jot. It faints me   104
To think what follows.
The Queen is comfortless, and we forgetful
In our long absence. Pray, do not deliver   107
What here you've have heard to her.
OLD LADY   What do you think me? *Exeunt.*

❧

2.4

Trumpets, sennet, and cornets. Enter two Vergers,
with short silver wands; next them two Scribes, in
the habit of doctors; after them the [Arch]bishop
of Canterbury alone; after him the Bishops of
Lincoln, Ely, Rochester, and Saint Asaph; next
them, with some small distance, follows a
Gentleman bearing the purse, with the great seal,
and a cardinal's hat; then two Priests, bearing each
a silver cross; then [Griffith,] a Gentleman Usher,
bareheaded, accompanied with a Sergeant at Arms
bearing a silver mace; then two Gentlemen bearing
two great silver pillars; after them, side by side, the
two Cardinals; two Noblemen with the sword and
mace. The King takes place under the cloth of state;
the two Cardinals sit under him as judges. The
Queen takes place some distance from the King.
The Bishops place themselves on each side the
court, in manner of a consistory; below them the
Scribes. The Lords sit next the Bishops. The rest of
the attendants stand in convenient order about the
stage.

WOLSEY
Whilst our commission from Rome is read,
Let silence be commanded.
KING   What's the need?
It hath already publicly been read,
And on all sides th'authority allowed;   4
You may then spare that time.
WOLSEY   Be't so. Proceed.
SCRIBE
Say, "Henry King of England, come into the court."

---

61 **Commends** expresses   62 **purpose** intend.   **flowing** abundant
65 **grace** favor   67–9 **More . . . vanities** Even more than I can possibly
offer (in the way of thankful obedience) would be as nothing; my
prayers aren't holy enough, and my good wishes (for the King) are
mere vain and worthless things   71 **Vouchsafe** be so kind as
74 **approve . . . conceit** confirm the good opinion   79 **lighten** give
light to. (A prophecy of the birth of Queen Elizabeth.)   84 **beggarly**
still in need   85 **pat** precisely at the opportune time   86 **suit of
pounds** request for money   88 **compelled** unsought, forced upon
one   90 **Forty pence, no** i.e., I'll venture a small sum that it isn't bitter to you.   93 **the mud in Egypt** i.e., the wealth of Egypt resulting
from its fecund land.   94 **pleasant** merry.   96 **pure** mere

98–9 **Honor's . . . foreskirt** i.e., Honors to come will exceed this present gift, just as an elongated robe trailing behind is longer than the
front of a skirt.   102 **your . . . fancy** your own private imaginings
103 **on't** of it.   103–4 **Would . . . jot** May I cease to live if this excites
me in the slightest.   104 **faints me** makes me faint   107 **deliver**
report
2.4. Location: London. A hall in Blackfriars.
0.1 *sennet* trumpet call announcing a procession.   *Vergers* those who
carry the verge or emblem of office; particularly, attendants on a church
dignitary   0.3 *habit of doctors* furred black gowns and flat caps worn
by doctors of law   0.14 *cloth of state* canopy   0.18 *consistory* ecclesiastical court   4 **allowed** conceded

CRIER
Henry King of England, come into the court.
KING   Here.
SCRIBE
Say, "Katharine Queen of England, come into the court."
CRIER
Katharine Queen of England, come into the court.
The Queen makes no answer, rises out of her chair,
goes about the court, comes to the King, and kneels at
his feet; then speaks.

KATHARINE
Sir, I desire you do me right and justice,
And to bestow your pity on me; for
I am a most poor woman, and a stranger,   13
Born out of your dominions, having here
No judge indifferent, nor no more assurance   15
Of equal friendship and proceeding. Alas, sir,   16
In what have I offended you? What cause
Hath my behavior given to your displeasure
That thus you should proceed to put me off   19
And take your good grace from me? Heaven witness,
I have been to you a true and humble wife,
At all times to your will conformable,
Ever in fear to kindle your dislike,   23
Yea, subject to your countenance—glad or sorry
As I saw it inclined. When was the hour
I ever contradicted your desire,
Or made it not mine too? Or which of your friends
Have I not strove to love, although I knew
He were mine enemy? What friend of mine
That had to him derived your anger did I   30
Continue in my liking, nay, gave notice
He was from thence discharged? Sir, call to mind
That I have been your wife in this obedience
Upward of twenty years, and have been blessed
With many children by you. If, in the course   35
And process of this time, you can report,
And prove it too, against mine honor aught—   37
My bond to wedlock, or my love and duty
Against your sacred person—in God's name   39
Turn me away, and let the foul'st contempt
Shut door upon me, and so give me up
To the sharp'st kind of justice. Please you, sir,
The King your father was reputed for
A prince most prudent, of an excellent
And unmatched wit and judgment. Ferdinand   45
My father, King of Spain, was reckoned one   46
The wisest prince that there had reigned by many   47
A year before. It is not to be questioned
That they had gathered a wise council to them
Of every realm, that did debate this business,
Who deemed our marriage lawful. Wherefore I
    humbly
Beseech you, sir, to spare me till I may

Be by my friends in Spain advised, whose counsel
I will implore. If not, i'th' name of God,
Your pleasure be fulfilled!
WOLSEY   You have here, lady,
And of your choice, these reverend fathers, men
Of singular integrity and learning,
Yea, the elect o'th' land, who are assembled
To plead your cause. It shall be therefore bootless   59
That longer you desire the court, as well   60
For your own quiet as to rectify   61
What is unsettled in the King.
CAMPEIUS   His Grace
Hath spoken well and justly. Therefore, madam,
It's fit this royal session do proceed,
And that without delay their arguments
Be now produced and heard.
KATHARINE   Lord Cardinal,
To you I speak.
WOLSEY   Your pleasure, madam?
KATHARINE   Sir,
I am about to weep; but, thinking that
We are a queen, or long have dreamed so, certain   69
The daughter of a king, my drops of tears
I'll turn to sparks of fire.
WOLSEY   Be patient yet.
KATHARINE
I will when you are humble; nay, before,   72
Or God will punish me. I do believe,
Induced by potent circumstances, that   74
You are mine enemy, and make my challenge   75
You shall not be my judge. For it is you
Have blown this coal betwixt my lord and me—   77
Which God's dew quench! Therefore I say again,
I utterly abhor, yea, from my soul   79
Refuse you for my judge, whom yet once more
I hold my most malicious foe, and think not
At all a friend to truth.
WOLSEY   I do profess   82
You speak not like yourself, who ever yet   83
Have stood to charity and displayed th'effects   84
Of disposition gentle and of wisdom
O'ertopping woman's pow'r. Madam, you do me
    wrong.
I have no spleen against you, nor injustice   87
For you or any. How far I have proceeded,
Or how far further shall, is warranted   89
By a commission from the consistory,
Yea, the whole consistory of Rome. You charge me
That I have blown this coal. I do deny it.
The King is present. If it be known to him
That I gainsay my deed, how may he wound,   94

13 **stranger** foreigner   15 **indifferent** impartial   16 **equal** fair
19 **put me off** discard me   23 **dislike** displeasure   30 **to him derived**
drawn upon himself   35 **many children** (The Queen gave birth to
five children, only one of whom, later Queen Mary, survived infancy.)
37 **honor** chaste reputation.   **aught** anything   39 **Against** toward
45 **wit** intelligence   46–7 **one The wisest** the very wisest

59 **bootless** profitless   60 **That . . . court** that you entreat the court to
postpone its work   61 **quiet** peace of mind   69 **certain** certainly
72 **before** i.e., sooner than that (which will never be)   74 **Induced**
persuaded   75 **make my challenge** I raise my formal objection (that)
77 **Have blown this coal** i.e., who have stirred up this trouble
79 **abhor** protest against. (A technical term of canon law.)   82 **profess**
declare   83 **ever yet** always   84 **stood to** upheld   87 **spleen** malice
89 **warranted** justified   94 **gainsay my deed** deny my acts

And worthily, my falsehood, yea, as much   95
As you have done my truth! If he know
That I am free of your report, he knows   97
I am not of your wrong. Therefore in him   98
It lies to cure me, and the cure is to   99
Remove these thoughts from you; the which before   100
His Highness shall speak in, I do beseech   101
You, gracious madam, to unthink your speaking
And to say so no more.

KATHARINE   My lord, my lord,
I am a simple woman, much too weak
T'oppose your cunning. You're meek and humble-
   mouthed;
You sign your place and calling, in full seeming,   106
With meekness and humility; but your heart
Is crammed with arrogancy, spleen, and pride.
You have, by fortune and His Highness' favors,
Gone slightly o'er low steps and now are mounted   110
Where pow'rs are your retainers, and your words,   111
Domestics to you, serve your will as't please   112
Yourself pronounce their office. I must tell you,   113
You tender more your person's honor than   114
Your high profession spiritual; that again
I do refuse you for my judge; and here
Before you all appeal unto the Pope,
To bring my whole cause 'fore His Holiness,
And to be judged by him.
                She curtsies to the King and offers to depart.
CAMPEIUS   The Queen is obstinate,
Stubborn to justice, apt to accuse it, and   120
Disdainful to be tried by't. 'Tis not well.
She's going away.
KING   Call her again.
CRIER
Katharine Queen of England, come into the court.
GRIFFITH   Madam, you are called back.
KATHARINE
What need you note it? Pray you, keep your way;   126
When you are called, return. Now, the Lord help!
They vex me past my patience. Pray you, pass on.
I will not tarry; no, nor ever more
Upon this business my appearance make
In any of their courts.
                Exeunt Queen and her attendants.
KING   Go thy ways, Kate.
That man i'th' world who shall report he has
A better wife, let him in naught be trusted
For speaking false in that. Thou art alone—
If thy rare qualities, sweet gentleness,

Thy meekness saintlike, wifelike government,   136
Obeying in commanding, and thy parts   137
Sovereign and pious else, could speak thee out—   138
The queen of earthly queens.—She's noble born,
And like her true nobility she has
Carried herself towards me.
WOLSEY   Most gracious sir,   141
In humblest manner I require Your Highness   142
That it shall please you to declare, in hearing
Of all these ears—for where I am robbed and bound,
There must I be unloosed, although not there
At once and fully satisfied—whether ever I   146
Did broach this business to Your Highness, or
Laid any scruple in your way, which might
Induce you to the question on't? Or ever
Have to you, but with thanks to God for such
A royal lady, spake one the least word that might   151
Be to the prejudice of her present state,
Or touch of her good person?
KING   My lord Cardinal,   153
I do excuse you; yea, upon mine honor,   154
I free you from't. You are not to be taught   155
That you have many enemies that know not
Why they are so, but, like to village curs,
Bark when their fellows do. By some of these
The Queen is put in anger. You're excused.
But will you be more justified? You ever   160
Have wished the sleeping of this business, never
   desired
It to be stirred, but oft have hindered, oft,
The passages made toward it. On my honor,   163
I speak my good lord Cardinal to this point,   164
And thus far clear him. Now, what moved me to't,
I will be bold with time and your attention;
Then mark th'inducement. Thus it came; give heed
   to't:
My conscience first received a tenderness,
Scruple, and prick, on certain speeches uttered
By th' Bishop of Bayonne, then French ambassador,
Who had been hither sent on the debating
A marriage twixt the Duke of Orleans and
Our daughter Mary. I'th' progress of this business,
Ere a determinate resolution, he—   174
I mean the Bishop—did require a respite   175
Wherein he might the King his lord advertise   176
Whether our daughter were legitimate,
Respecting this our marriage with the dowager,   178
Sometimes our brother's wife. This respite shook   179
The bosom of my conscience, entered me,
Yea, with a spitting power, and made to tremble   181

---

95 worthily deservedly   **97 free** innocent.   **report** accusation
98 am . . . wrong am not free from being slandered by you.   **99 cure
me** i.e., make me better, not by rectifying my behavior, which is
blameless, but by removing the distress you cause me   **100–1 before
. . . in** before the King rebukes you for this   **106 sign** signify, show
marks of.   **in full seeming** with great ostentation   **110 slightly** easily   **111–13 Where . . . office** where persons of rank serve your will,
and your very words are servants to carry out your wishes in any
way you choose; they are immediately acted on.   **114 tender more**
are more concerned for   **120 Stubborn** resistant.   **apt to accuse it**
ready to find fault with it   **126 What** Why.   **keep your way** move on

136 government self-control, behavior   **137 Obeying in commanding** the combined qualities of obedient wife and regal queen
137–8 and thy . . . out and if your noble virtues both royal and devotional could adequately describe you   **141 Carried** borne, behaved
142 require request   **146 At . . . satisfied** given full restitution
151 one the least a single   **153 touch** sullying   **154 excuse** exonerate
155 are not do not need   **160 justified** vindicated.   **163 passages**
proceedings   **164 speak** bear witness for   **174 determinate resolution** final decision   **175 require** request   **176 advertise** inform,
confer with   **178 dowager** widow   **179 Sometimes** formerly
181 spitting piercing

The region of my breast, which forced such way
That many mazed considerings did throng   183
And pressed in with this caution. First, methought 184
I stood not in the smile of heaven, who had   185
Commanded nature that my lady's womb,
If it conceived a male child by me, should
Do no more offices of life to't than   188
The grave does to th' dead; for her male issue
Or died where they were made, or shortly after   190
This world had aired them. Hence I took a thought 191
This was a judgment on me that my kingdom,
Well worthy the best heir o'th' world, should not
Be gladded in't by me. Then follows that   194
I weighed the danger which my realms stood in
By this my issue's fail, and that gave to me   196
Many a groaning throe. Thus hulling in   197
The wild sea of my conscience, I did steer
Toward this remedy, whereupon we are
Now present here together; that's to say,
I meant to rectify my conscience—which
I then did feel full sick, and yet not well—   202
By all the reverend fathers of the land
And doctors learned. First I began in private   204
With you, my lord of Lincoln. You remember
How under my oppression I did reek   206
When I first moved you.

LINCOLN   Very well, my liege. 207

KING
I have spoke long. Be pleased yourself to say
How far you satisfied me.

LINCOLN   So please Your Highness,
The question did at first so stagger me—
Bearing a state of mighty moment in't   211
And consequence of dread—that I committed   212
The daring'st counsel which I had to doubt   213
And did entreat Your Highness to this course
Which you are running here.

KING [to Canterbury]   I then moved you,
My lord of Canterbury, and got your leave
To make this present summons. Unsolicited
I left no reverend person in this court,
But by particular consent proceeded
Under your hands and seals. Therefore, go on,   220
For no dislike i'th' world against the person
Of the good Queen, but the sharp thorny points
Of my allegèd reasons, drives this forward.
Prove but our marriage lawful, by my life   224
And kingly dignity, we are contented

To wear our mortal state to come with her,   226
Katharine our queen, before the primest creature 227
That's paragoned o'th' world.

CAMPEIUS   So please Your Highness, 228
The Queen being absent, 'tis a needful fitness   229
That we adjourn this court till further day.   230
Meanwhile must be an earnest motion   231
Made to the Queen to call back her appeal
She intends unto His Holiness.

KING [aside]   I may perceive
These cardinals trifle with me. I abhor
This dilatory sloth and tricks of Rome.
My learned and well-belovèd servant, Cranmer,
Prithee, return. With thy approach, I know,   237
My comfort comes along.—Break up the court!
I say, set on.   Exeunt in manner as they entered. 239

❖

3.1

Enter Queen and her women, as at work.

KATHARINE
Take thy lute, wench. My soul grows sad with
    troubles;
Sing, and disperse 'em if thou canst. Leave working. 2
              Song.

GENTLEWOMAN [*sings*]
    Orpheus with his lute made trees,   3
    And the mountain tops that freeze,
        Bow themselves when he did sing.
    To his music plants and flowers
    Ever sprung, as sun and showers   7
        There had made a lasting spring.

    Everything that heard him play,
    Even the billows of the sea,
        Hung their heads, and then lay by.   11
    In sweet music is such art,
    Killing care and grief of heart
        Fall asleep, or hearing, die.

Enter a Gentleman.

KATHARINE   How now?

GENTLEMAN
An't please Your Grace, the two great cardinals
Wait in the presence.

KATHARINE   Would they speak with me? 17

---

183 mazed considerings conflicting and confused thoughts   **184 caution** warning.   **185 smile** i.e., favor   **188 offices** services   **190 Or** either   **191 aired them** given them air to breathe.   **194 gladded** made happy   **196 By . . . fail** by my lacking a son   **197 throe** pang, pain.   **hulling** drifting with sails furled   **202 yet** still, even now   **204 doctors** scholars, divines   **206 oppression** distress.   **reek** sweat   **207 moved** mentioned the business to   **211–12 Bearing . . . dread** relating to matters of the greatest consequence to the state and an outcome too fearful to contemplate   **212–13 I committed . . . doubt** i.e., I screwed up my courage   **220 Under . . . seals** i.e., with your signed agreement.   **224 Prove but** If you can only prove

226 wear . . . her (1) share the state of human existence with her till we die (2) share royal pomp with her   **227 primest** most excellent   **228 paragoned** set forth as a perfect model   **229 needful fitness** necessary and proper action   **230 further** future   **231 motion** appeal, request   **237 Prithee, return** (Henry apostrophizes the Protestant churchman, Thomas Cranmer, who at this time, though the play doesn't say so directly, is on the Continent collecting opinions on the King's marriage question. His return is mentioned at 3.2.401.)   **239 set on** do it, proceed.
3.1. Location: London. The Queen's apartments.
2 Leave Stop   **3 Orpheus** legendary musician in Greek mythology. **made trees** i.e., caused trees to bow   **7 as** as if   **11 lay by** subsided.   **17 presence** reception room.

GENTLEMAN
They willed me say so, madam.
KATHARINE   Pray Their Graces   18
To come near.   [*The Gentleman goes to the door.*]
What can be their business
With me, a poor weak woman, fall'n from favor?
I do not like their coming. Now I think on't,
They should be good men, their affairs as righteous.   22
But all hoods make not monks.

Enter the two cardinals, Wolsey and Campeius.

WOLSEY   Peace to Your Highness!
KATHARINE
Your Graces find me here part of a huswife—   24
I would be all—against the worst may happen.   25
What are your pleasures with me, reverend lords?
WOLSEY
May it please you, noble madam, to withdraw
Into your private chamber, we shall give you
The full cause of our coming.
KATHARINE   Speak it here.
There's nothing I have done yet, o'my conscience,
Deserves a corner. Would all other women   31
Could speak this with as free a soul as I do!   32
My lords, I care not, so much I am happy   33
Above a number, if my actions   34
Were tried by ev'ry tongue, ev'ry eye saw 'em,
Envy and base opinion set against 'em,   36
I know my life so even. If your business   37
Seek me out, and that way I am wife in,   38
Out with it boldly. Truth loves open dealing.
WOLSEY   *Tanta est erga te mentis integritas, regina ser-*   40
enissima—   41
KATHARINE   Oh, good my lord, no Latin!
I am not such a truant since my coming
As not to know the language I have lived in.
A strange tongue makes my cause more strange,
suspicious;   45
Pray, speak in English. Here are some will thank you,
If you speak truth, for their poor mistress' sake.
Believe me, she has had much wrong. Lord Cardinal,
The willing'st sin I ever yet committed
May be absolved in English.
WOLSEY   Noble lady,
I am sorry my integrity should breed—
And service to His Majesty and you—
So deep suspicion, where all faith was meant.
We come not by the way of accusation,   54
To taint that honor every good tongue blesses,
Nor to betray you any way to sorrow—
You have too much, good lady—but to know

How you stand minded in the weighty difference   58
Between the King and you, and to deliver,   59
Like free and honest men, our just opinions   60
And comforts to your cause.
CAMPEIUS   Most honored madam,
My lord of York, out of his noble nature,
Zeal, and obedience he still bore Your Grace,   63
Forgetting, like a good man, your late censure
Both of his truth and him—which was too far—   65
Offers, as I do, in a sign of peace,   66
His service and his counsel.
KATHARINE [*aside*]   To betray me.—
My lords, I thank you both for your good wills.
Ye speak like honest men; pray God ye prove so!
But how to make ye suddenly an answer
In such a point of weight, so near mine honor—
More near my life, I fear—with my weak wit,   72
And to such men of gravity and learning,
In truth, I know not. I was set at work   74
Among my maids, full little, God knows, looking
Either for such men or such business.
For her sake that I have been—for I feel   77
The last fit of my greatness—good Your Graces,   78
Let me have time and counsel for my cause.
Alas, I am a woman, friendless, hopeless!
WOLSEY
Madam, you wrong the King's love with these fears.
Your hopes and friends are infinite.
KATHARINE   In England
But little for my profit. Can you think, lords,   83
That any Englishman dare give me counsel,
Or be a known friend, 'gainst His Highness' pleasure,
Though he be grown so desperate to be honest,   86
And live a subject? Nay, forsooth, my friends,   87
They that must weigh out my afflictions,   88
They that my trust must grow to, live not here.
They are, as all my other comforts, far hence
In mine own country, lords.
CAMPEIUS   I would Your Grace
Would leave your griefs and take my counsel.
KATHARINE   How, sir?
CAMPEIUS
Put your main cause into the King's protection;
He's loving and most gracious. 'Twill be much
Both for your honor better and your cause;
For if the trial of the law o'ertake ye,
You'll part away disgraced.
WOLSEY   He tells you rightly.   97
KATHARINE
Ye tell me what ye wish for both—my ruin.
Is this your Christian counsel? Out upon ye!

---

18 **willed** bade   22 **as righteous** i.e., as righteous as they are good.
24 **part of a huswife** i.e., in some measure tending to household
duties   25 **I ... all** i.e., I wish to be a complete housewife, in case I
am divorced and forced to live alone.   **against** in anticipation of
31 **a corner** i.e., secrecy.   32 **free** innocent   33 **happy** fortunate (in
virtue)   34 **a number** many   36 **Envy ... opinion** every sort of envy
and malicious rumor   37 **even** constant, upright.   38 **Seek ... in**
concerns me regarding my conduct as a wife   40–1 *Tanta ... serenis-
sima* So great is the integrity of our intentions toward you, most royal
queen   45 **strange** foreign   54 **by the way** for the purpose

58 **minded** inclined, disposed.   **difference** quarrel   59 **deliver**
declare   60 **free** frank, honorable   63 **still bore** has always borne
65 **far** severe   66 **in** as   72 **wit** understanding   74 **set** seated   77 **For
... been** For the sake of the queenly person I once was   78 **fit** brief
space, short spell   83 **profit** benefit.   86 **so desperate** i.e., reckless
enough as   87 **live a subject** be allowed to continue unpunished in
this realm.   88 **weigh out** compensate for, counterbalance   97 **part
away** depart

Heaven is above all yet; there sits a judge
That no king can corrupt.
CAMPEIUS   Your rage mistakes us.   101
KATHARINE
The more shame for ye! Holy men I thought ye,
Upon my soul, two reverend cardinal virtues;   103
But cardinal sins and hollow hearts I fear ye.   104
Mend 'em, for shame, my lords. Is this your comfort?
The cordial that ye bring a wretched lady,   106
A woman lost among ye, laughed at, scorned?
I will not wish ye half my miseries;
I have more charity. But say I warned ye;
Take heed, for heaven's sake take heed, lest at once   110
The burden of my sorrows fall upon ye.
WOLSEY
Madam, this is a mere distraction.   112
You turn the good we offer into envy.   113
KATHARINE
Ye turn me into nothing. Woe upon ye
And all such false professors! Would you have me—
If you have any justice, any pity,
If ye be anything but churchmen's habits—   117
Put my sick cause into his hands that hates me?
Alas, he's banished me his bed already,
His love too long ago! I am old, my lords,
And all the fellowship I hold now with him
Is only my obedience. What can happen
To me above this wretchedness? All your studies   123
Make me a curse like this!
CAMPEIUS   Your fears are worse.   124
KATHARINE
Have I lived thus long—let me speak myself,   125
Since virtue finds no friends—a wife, a true one?
A woman, I dare say without vainglory,
Never yet branded with suspicion?
Have I with all my full affections
Still met the King, loved him next heav'n, obeyed him, 130
Been out of fondness superstitious to him,   131
Almost forgot my prayers to content him,
And am I thus rewarded? 'Tis not well, lords.
Bring me a constant woman to her husband,
One that ne'er dreamed a joy beyond his pleasure,
And to that woman, when she has done most,
Yet will I add an honor: a great patience.
WOLSEY
Madam, you wander from the good we aim at.   138
KATHARINE
My lord, I dare not make myself so guilty
To give up willingly that noble title

Your master wed me to. Nothing but death
Shall e'er divorce my dignities.
WOLSEY   Pray, hear me.
KATHARINE
Would I had never trod this English earth
Or felt the flatteries that grow upon it!
Ye have angels' faces, but heaven knows your hearts.
What will become of me now, wretched lady?
I am the most unhappy woman living.
[*To her women*] Alas, poor wenches, where are now
    your fortunes?
Shipwrecked upon a kingdom where no pity,
No friends, no hope, no kindred weep for me?
Almost no grave allowed me? Like the lily,
That once was mistress of the field and flourished,
I'll hang my head and perish.
WOLSEY   If Your Grace
Could but be brought to know our ends are honest,   154
You'd feel more comfort. Why should we, good lady,
Upon what cause, wrong you? Alas, our places,   156
The way of our profession, is against it;
We are to cure such sorrows, not to sow 'em.
For goodness' sake, consider what you do,
How you may hurt yourself, ay, utterly
Grow from the King's acquaintance, by this carriage.   161
The hearts of princes kiss obedience,
So much they love it, but to stubborn spirits
They swell and grow as terrible as storms.
I know you have a gentle, noble temper,   165
A soul as even as a calm. Pray, think us   166
Those we profess, peacemakers, friends, and servants.
CAMPEIUS
Madam, you'll find it so. You wrong your virtues
With these weak women's fears. A noble spirit,
As yours was put into you, ever casts   170
Such doubts as false coin from it. The King loves you; 171
Beware you lose it not. For us, if you please   172
To trust us in your business, we are ready
To use our utmost studies in your service.   174
KATHARINE
Do what ye will, my lords, and pray forgive me
If I have used myself unmannerly;   176
You know I am a woman, lacking wit
To make a seemly answer to such persons.
Pray, do my service to His Majesty.   179
He has my heart yet, and shall have my prayers
While I shall have my life. Come, reverend fathers,
Bestow your counsels on me. She now begs
That little thought when she set footing here   183
She should have bought her dignities so dear.
                                   Exeunt.

---

101 mistakes misjudges   **103 cardinal virtues** (The Cardinal Virtues are justice, temperance, fortitude, and prudence, constituting four of the seven virtues opposing the seven Deadly Sins.)   **104 cardinal sins** i.e., the seven Deadly Sins   **106 cordial** restorative medicine   **110 at once** all at once   **112 mere distraction** sheer frenzy.   **113 envy** ill will, malice.   **117 habits** garments   **123 above** more than   **123–4 All . . . this!** i.e., I challenge you, in your clerical exertions, to devise a worse fate than I already have!   **124 worse** i.e., than the reality.   **125 speak** describe, speak for   **130 Still** always.   **next** next to   **131 superstitious** i.e., to the point of idolatry   **138 wander from** mistake

154 ends are honest intentions are honorable   **156 places** official positions   **161 Grow from** become estranged from.   **carriage** conduct.   **165 temper** disposition   **166 even** steadfast   **170–1 As . . . from** it such as was given to you, always rejects such doubts as if they were counterfeit coins.   **172 For** As for   **174 studies** efforts   **176 used myself** conducted myself   **179 do my service** pay my respects   **183 That** who.   **set footing here** landed in England

3.2

Enter the Duke of Norfolk, Duke of Suffolk, Lord
Surrey, and Lord Chamberlain.

NORFOLK
If you will now unite in your complaints,
And force them with a constancy, the Cardinal   2
Cannot stand under them. If you omit   3
The offer of this time, I cannot promise   4
But that you shall sustain more new disgraces
With these you bear already.

SURREY   I am joyful
To meet the least occasion that may give me
Remembrance of my father-in-law, the Duke,   8
To be revenged on him.

SUFFOLK   Which of the peers   9
Have uncontemned gone by him, or at least   10
Strangely neglected? When did he regard   11
The stamp of nobleness in any person
Out of himself?

CHAMBERLAIN   My lords, you speak your pleasures. 13
What he deserves of you and me I know;
What we can do to him, though now the time
Gives way to us, I much fear. If you cannot   16
Bar his access to th' King, never attempt
Anything on him, for he hath a witchcraft
Over the King in 's tongue.

NORFOLK   Oh, fear him not;
His spell in that is out. The King hath found   20
Matter against him that forever mars
The honey of his language. No, he's settled,   22
Not to come off, in his displeasure.

SURREY   Sir,   23
I should be glad to hear such news as this
Once every hour.

NORFOLK   Believe it, this is true.
In the divorce his contrary proceedings   26
Are all unfolded, wherein he appears   27
As I would wish mine enemy.

SURREY   How came
His practices to light?

SUFFOLK   Most strangely.

SURREY   Oh, how, how?   29

SUFFOLK
The Cardinal's letters to the Pope miscarried,   30
And came to th'eye o'th' King, wherein was read
How that the Cardinal did entreat His Holiness
To stay the judgment o'th' divorce; for if   33
It did take place, "I do," quoth he, "perceive
My king is tangled in affection to
A creature of the Queen's, Lady Anne Bullen."   36

SURREY
Has the King this?

SUFFOLK   Believe it.

SURREY   Will this work?

CHAMBERLAIN
The King in this perceives him, how he coasts   38
And hedges his own way. But in this point   39
All his tricks founder, and he brings his physic   40
After his patient's death. The King already
Hath married the fair lady.

SURREY   Would he had!

SUFFOLK
May you be happy in your wish, my lord,
For I profess you have it.

SURREY   Now, all my joy
Trace the conjunction!

SUFFOLK   My amen to't.

NORFOLK   All men's.   45

SUFFOLK
There's order given for her coronation.
Marry, this is yet but young, and may be left   47
To some ears unrecounted. But, my lords,
She is a gallant creature, and complete   49
In mind and feature. I persuade me, from her   50
Will fall some blessing to this land which shall
In it be memorized.

SURREY   But will the King   52
Digest this letter of the Cardinal's?   53
The Lord forbid!

NORFOLK   Marry, amen!

SUFFOLK   No, no;
There be more wasps that buzz about his nose
Will make this sting the sooner. Cardinal Campeius
Is stol'n away to Rome, hath ta'en no leave,
Has left the cause o'th' King unhandled, and
Is posted, as the agent of our cardinal,   59
To second all his plot. I do assure you
The King cried "Ha!" at this.

CHAMBERLAIN   Now, God incense him,
And let him cry "Ha!" louder!

NORFOLK   But, my lord,
When returns Cranmer?

SUFFOLK
He is returned in his opinions, which   64
Have satisfied the King for his divorce,
Together with all famous colleges,
Almost, in Christendom. Shortly, I believe,
His second marriage shall be published, and   68
Her coronation. Katharine no more
Shall be called Queen, but Princess Dowager
And widow to Prince Arthur.

NORFOLK   This same Cranmer's

3.2. Location: London. Antechamber to the King's apartments.
2 force urge   **3–4 If . . . time** If you let this opportunity pass
8 father-in-law i.e., Buckingham. (See 2.1.41–4 and notes.)   **9 him**
Wolsey.   **10 uncontemned** unscorned   **11 Strangely neglected** negligently disregarded.   **13 Out of** excepting   **16 Gives way to** favors
20 out finished.   **22 settled** fixed   **23 come off** escape.   **his** i.e., the
King's   **26 contrary** contradictory, divisive   **27 unfolded** exposed
29 practices plots   **30 miscarried** went astray   **33 stay** stop, delay
36 creature dependent

38–9 coasts And hedges goes a roundabout way, as by coast and
hedgerow   **40 physic** medicine, cure   **45 Trace** follow   **47 young**
recent, new   **49 complete** perfect, excellent   **50 persuade me** am
confident   **52 memorized** caused to be remembered. (Refers
prophetically to Queen Elizabeth.)   **53 Digest** put up with, "swallow"   **59 Is posted** has gone in haste   **64 in his opinions** having
sent ahead his written opinions   **68 published** proclaimed

A worthy fellow, and hath ta'en much pain
In the King's business.

SUFFOLK   He has, and we shall see him
For it an archbishop.

NORFOLK   So I hear.

SUFFOLK   'Tis so.

Enter Wolsey and Cromwell.

The Cardinal!

NORFOLK   Observe, observe, he's moody.
                    [The nobles stand aside and observe.]

WOLSEY
The packet, Cromwell, gave't you the King?   76

CROMWELL
To his own hand, in 's bedchamber.

WOLSEY   Looked he
O'th'inside of the paper?

CROMWELL   Presently   78
He did unseal them, and the first he viewed
He did it with a serious mind; a heed   80
Was in his countenance. You he bade
Attend him here this morning.

WOLSEY   Is he ready
To come abroad?   83

CROMWELL   I think by this he is.   84

WOLSEY   Leave me awhile.   *Exit Cromwell.*
[To himself] It shall be to the Duchess of Alençon,
The French King's sister; he shall marry her.
Anne Bullen? No, I'll no Anne Bullens for him;
There's more in't than fair visage. Bullen?
No, we'll no Bullens. Speedily I wish
To hear from Rome. The Marchioness of Pembroke?

NORFOLK
He's discontented.

SUFFOLK   Maybe he hears the King
Does whet his anger to him.

SURREY   Sharp enough,
Lord, for thy justice!

WOLSEY *[to himself]*
The late Queen's gentlewoman, a knight's daughter,   95
To be her mistress' mistress? The Queen's queen?
This candle burns not clear; 'tis I must snuff it,   97
Then out it goes. What though I know her virtuous
And well deserving? Yet I know her
A spleeny Lutheran, and not wholesome to   100
Our cause, that she should lie i'th' bosom of
Our hard-ruled king. Again, there is sprung up   102
An heretic, an arch one, Cranmer, one
Hath crawled into the favor of the King   104
And is his oracle.

NORFOLK   He is vexed at something.   105

*Enter King, reading of a schedule, [and Lovell.
Wolsey stands apart, not observing the King.]*

SURREY
I would 'twere something that would fret the string,   106
The master cord on 's heart.

SUFFOLK   The King, the King!   107

KING *[to himself]*
What piles of wealth hath he accumulated
To his own portion! And what expense by th'hour
Seems to flow from him! How i'th' name of thrift
Does he rake this together?—Now, my lords,
Saw you the Cardinal?

NORFOLK   My lord, we have
Stood here observing him. Some strange commotion
Is in his brain. He bites his lip, and starts,
Stops on a sudden, looks upon the ground,
Then lays his finger on his temple; straight   116
Springs out into fast gait, then stops again,
Strikes his breast hard, and anon he casts
His eye against the moon. In most strange postures
We have seen him set himself.

KING   It may well be
There is a mutiny in 's mind. This morning
Papers of state he sent me to peruse,
As I required; and wot you what I found   123
There—on my conscience, put unwittingly?
Forsooth, an inventory, thus importing   125
The several parcels of his plate, his treasure,   126
Rich stuffs and ornaments of household, which
I find at such proud rate that it outspeaks   128
Possession of a subject.

NORFOLK   It's heaven's will.   129
Some spirit put this paper in the packet
To bless your eye withal.

KING   If we did think   131
His contemplation were above the earth
And fixed on spiritual object, he should still   133
Dwell in his musings; but I am afraid   134
His thinkings are below the moon, not worth   135
His serious considering.

*King takes his seat; whispers [to] Lovell,
who goes to the Cardinal [Wolsey].*

WOLSEY   Heaven forgive me!
Ever God bless Your Highness!

KING   Good my lord,
You are full of heavenly stuff and bear the inventory   138
Of your best graces in your mind, the which
You were now running o'er. You have scarce time
To steal from spiritual leisure a brief span
To keep your earthly audit. Sure in that

---

106 **fret** gnaw through. (With a pun on the musical sense of pressing
the string of a musical instrument against a "fret" or bar, continued in
the play on *cord/chord*.)   107 **on 's** of his   116 **straight** at once
123 **wot** know   125 **importing** signifying   126 **several parcels** various items.   **plate** precious metal in the form of household plate
128–9 **outspeaks . . . subject** describes possessions exceeding what a
subject should have.   131 **withal** with.   133–4 **he . . . musings** I
would allow him to continue in those holy meditations   135 **below
the moon** i.e., in the mortal sphere   138 **stuff . . . inventory** (The
King chooses his words with sardonic irony to apply both to spiritual
contemplation and to the accumulation of wealth. The joke continues
in *steal* and *audit*.)

---

76 **packet** parcel of dispatches   78 **Presently** Immediately   80 **heed**
concern   83 **abroad** out of his private rooms.   84 **by this** by this time
95 **late** former   97 **clear** bright.   **snuff it** trim its wick   100 **spleeny**
hot-headed, contentious   102 **hard-ruled** hard to manage   104 **Hath**
who has   105.1 *schedule* scroll

I deem you an ill husband, and am glad   143
To have you therein my companion.
WOLSEY   Sir,   144
For holy offices I have a time; a time
To think upon the part of business which
I bear i'th' state; and nature does require
Her times of preservation, which perforce
I, her frail son, amongst my brethren mortal,
Must give my tendance to.
KING   You have said well.   150
WOLSEY
And ever may Your Highness yoke together,
As I will lend you cause, my doing well
With my well saying!
KING   'Tis well said again,
And 'tis a kind of good deed to say well;
And yet words are no deeds. My father loved you;
He said he did, and with his deed did crown   156
His word upon you. Since I had my office,
I have kept you next my heart, have not alone
Employed you where high profits might come home,
But pared my present havings, to bestow   160
My bounties upon you.
WOLSEY [aside]   What should this mean?
SURREY [aside]
The Lord increase this business!
KING   Have I not made you
The prime man of the state? I pray you, tell me   163
If what I now pronounce you have found true;   164
And if you may confess it, say withal
If you are bound to us or no. What say you?
WOLSEY
My sovereign, I confess your royal graces,   167
Show'red on me daily, have been more than could   168
My studied purposes requite, which went   169
Beyond all man's endeavors. My endeavors
Have ever come too short of my desires,
Yet filed with my abilities. Mine own ends   172
Have been mine so that evermore they pointed   173
To th' good of your most sacred person and
The profit of the state. For your great graces
Heaped upon me, poor undeserver, I
Can nothing render but allegiant thanks;   177
My prayers to heaven for you; my loyalty,
Which ever has and ever shall be growing,
Till death, that winter, kill it.
KING   Fairly answered.
A loyal and obedient subject is

Therein illustrated. The honor of it   182
Does pay the act of it, as, i'th' contrary,   183
The foulness is the punishment. I presume   184
That, as my hand has opened bounty to you,   185
My heart dropped love, my pow'r rained honor, more
On you than any, so your hand and heart,
Your brain, and every function of your power,
Should, notwithstanding that your bond of duty,   189
As 'twere in love's particular, be more   190
To me, your friend, than any.
WOLSEY   I do profess
That for Your Highness' good I ever labored
More than mine own; that am, have, and will be—   193
Though all the world should crack their duty to you 194
And throw it from their soul, though perils did
Abound as thick as thought could make 'em and
Appear in forms more horrid—yet my duty,
As doth a rock against the chiding flood,   198
Should the approach of this wild river break,   199
And stand unshaken yours.
KING   'Tis nobly spoken.
Take notice, lords, he has a loyal breast,
For you have seen him open't.—Read o'er this,
              [giving him papers]
And after, this, and then to breakfast with
What appetite you have.
              Exit King, frowning upon the Cardinal
              [Wolsey]; the nobles throng after him [the King],
              smiling and whispering, [and so exeunt].
WOLSEY   What should this mean?
What sudden anger's this? How have I reaped it?   205
He parted frowning from me, as if ruin
Leaped from his eyes. So looks the chafèd lion   207
Upon the daring huntsman that has galled him,   208
Then makes him nothing. I must read this paper—   209
I fear, the story of his anger. [He reads.] 'Tis so!
This paper has undone me. 'Tis th'account
Of all that world of wealth I have drawn together
For mine own ends—indeed, to gain the popedom
And fee my friends in Rome. Oh, negligence,   214
Fit for a fool to fall by! What cross devil   215
Made me put this main secret in the packet   216
I sent the King? Is there no way to cure this?
No new device to beat this from his brains?
I know 'twill stir him strongly; yet I know
A way, if it take right, in spite of fortune   220
Will bring me off again. [He reads again.] What's this?
   "To th' Pope"?   221
The letter, as I live, with all the business
I writ to 's Holiness. Nay then, farewell!

I have touched the highest point of all my greatness,
And, from that full meridian of my glory   225
I haste now to my setting. I shall fall
Like a bright exhalation in the evening,   227
And no man see me more.

Enter to Wolsey the Dukes of Norfolk and Suffolk,
the Earl of Surrey, and the Lord Chamberlain.

NORFOLK
Hear the King's pleasure, Cardinal, who commands
    you
To render up the great seal presently   230
Into our hands, and to confine yourself
To Asher House, my lord of Winchester's,   232
Till you hear further from His Highness.

WOLSEY   Stay,
Where's your commission, lords? Words cannot carry 234
Authority so weighty.

SUFFOLK   Who dare cross 'em,   235
Bearing the King's will from his mouth expressly?

WOLSEY
Till I find more than will or words to do it—   237
I mean your malice—know, officious lords,   238
I dare and must deny it. Now I feel
Of what coarse metal ye are molded—envy;   240
How eagerly ye follow my disgraces
As if it fed ye, and how sleek and wanton   242
Ye appear in everything may bring my ruin!
Follow your envious courses, men of malice!
You have Christian warrant for 'em, and no doubt   245
In time will find their fit rewards. That seal
You ask with such a violence, the King,
Mine and your master, with his own hand gave me;
Bade me enjoy it, with the place and honors,
During my life; and, to confirm his goodness,
Tied it by letters patents. Now, who'll take it?   251

SURREY
The King that gave it.

WOLSEY   It must be himself, then.

SURREY
Thou art a proud traitor, priest.

WOLSEY   Proud lord, thou liest!
Within these forty hours Surrey durst better
Have burnt that tongue than said so.

SURREY   Thy ambition,
Thou scarlet sin, robbed this bewailing land   256
Of noble Buckingham, my father-in-law.

The heads of all thy brother cardinals,
With thee and all thy best parts bound together,   259
Weighed not a hair of his. Plague of your policy!   260
You sent me deputy for Ireland,
Far from his succor, from the King, from all   262
That might have mercy on the fault thou gav'st him;   263
Whilst your great goodness, out of holy pity,   264
Absolved him with an ax.

WOLSEY   This, and all else   265
This talking lord can lay upon my credit,   266
I answer is most false. The Duke by law
Found his deserts. How innocent I was
From any private malice in his end   269
His noble jury and foul cause can witness.
If I loved many words, lord, I should tell you
You have as little honesty as honor,
That in the way of loyalty and truth   273
Toward the King, my ever royal master,
Dare mate a sounder man than Surrey can be,   275
And all that love his follies.

SURREY   By my soul,
Your long coat, priest, protects you; thou shouldst feel
My sword i'th' lifeblood of thee else.—My lords,
Can ye endure to hear this arrogance?
And from this fellow? If we live thus tamely,
To be thus jaded by a piece of scarlet,   281
Farewell nobility! Let His Grace go forward
And dare us with his cap, like larks.

WOLSEY   All goodness   283
Is poison to thy stomach.

SURREY   Yes, that goodness
Of gleaning all the land's wealth into one,
Into your own hands, Card'nal, by extortion;
The goodness of your intercepted packets
You writ to th' Pope against the King. Your goodness,
Since you provoke me, shall be most notorious.—
My lord of Norfolk, as you are truly noble,
As you respect the common good, the state
Of our despised nobility, our issues,   292
Who, if he live, will scarce be gentlemen,   293
Produce the grand sum of his sins, the articles   294
Collected from his life. [*To Wolsey*] I'll startle you
Worse than the sacring bell, when the brown wench   296
Lay kissing in your arms, Lord Cardinal.

WOLSEY
How much, methinks, I could despise this man,
But that I am bound in charity against it!

---

225 **meridian** a star's highest point of altitude   227 **exhalation** any astronomical phenomenon, such as a meteor or a falling star   230 **presently** immediately   232 **To Asher . . . Winchester's** Esher House (as it is spelled today), in Surrey, belonged to Wolsey, who was Bishop of Winchester at the time of his arrest, though the wording here may anticipate the ascendancy of Stephen Gardiner to the bishopric after Wolsey's fall.   234 **commission** authorizing warrant   235 **cross** oppose   237–8 **Till . . . malice** Until I find better reason than your professed verbal statement of the King's will—which is really your own malice—to do as you say   240 **metal** (1) substance (2) mettle, temperament.   **envy** malice   242 **sleek and wanton** oily and merciless   245 **Christian warrant** i.e., the example of other uncharitable Christians   251 **letters patents** formal and public bestowing of rights or powers.   256 **Thou scarlet sin** (Refers to his cardinal's cassock, described as scarlet; see 3.1.103–4. See also Isaiah 1:18.)

259 **parts** qualities   260 **Weighed** equaled in weight.   **Plague . . . policy!** A plague on your scheming!   262 **his succor** any attempt to save Buckingham   263 **fault . . . him** offense you charged him (Buckingham) with   264–5 **Whilst . . . ax** while you demonstrated your holiness and pity by administering last rites to Buckingham in the form of a beheading.   266 **lay . . . credit** charge against my good name   269 **From** of   273 **That** I who   275 **mate** vie with   281 **jaded** intimidated, made fools of   283 **dare . . . larks** dazzle us with his cardinal's hat as birds with a mirror or a piece of scarlet cloth.   292 **issues** sons   293 **he** Wolsey   294 **articles** items of the indictment   296 **sacring bell** bell rung at the most solemn portions of the Mass. (Surrey imagines a scene in which Wolsey is in bed with a wench instead of officiating at Mass.)

NORFOLK
Those articles, my lord, are in the King's hand;   300
But thus much, they are foul ones.

WOLSEY   So much fairer   301
And spotless shall mine innocence arise
When the King knows my truth.

SURREY   This cannot save you.   303
I thank my memory, I yet remember
Some of these articles, and out they shall.   305
Now, if you can blush and cry "guilty," Cardinal,
You'll show a little honesty.

WOLSEY   Speak on, sir;
I dare your worst objections. If I blush,   308
It is to see a nobleman want manners.   309

SURREY
I had rather want those than my head. Have at you!   310
First, that without the King's assent or knowledge
You wrought to be a legate, by which power   312
You maimed the jurisdiction of all bishops.

NORFOLK
Then, that in all you writ to Rome, or else
To foreign princes, "Ego et Rex meus"   315
Was still inscribed, in which you brought the King   316
To be your servant.

SUFFOLK   Then that, without the knowledge
Either of King or Council, when you went
Ambassador to the Emperor, you made bold
To carry into Flanders the great seal.   320

SURREY
Item, you sent a large commission   321
To Gregory de Cassado, to conclude,
Without the King's will or the state's allowance,   323
A league between His Highness and Ferrara.

SUFFOLK
That out of mere ambition you have caused   325
Your holy hat to be stamped on the King's coin.

SURREY
Then, that you have sent innumerable substance—   327
By what means got, I leave to your own conscience—
To furnish Rome, and to prepare the ways   329
You have for dignities, to the mere undoing   330
Of all the kingdom. Many more there are,
Which since they are of you, and odious,
I will not taint my mouth with.

CHAMBERLAIN   O my lord,
Press not a falling man too far! 'Tis virtue.   334

His faults lie open to the laws; let them,
Not you, correct him. My heart weeps to see him
So little of his great self.

SURREY   I forgive him.

SUFFOLK
Lord Cardinal, the King's further pleasure is—
Because all those things you have done of late
By your power legative within this kingdom   340
Fall into th' compass of a praemunire—   341
That therefore such a writ be sued against you   342
To forfeit all your goods, lands, tenements,   343
Chattels, and whatsoever, and to be   344
Out of the King's protection. This is my charge.

NORFOLK
And so we'll leave you to your meditations
How to live better. For your stubborn answer   347
About the giving back the great seal to us,
The King shall know it and, no doubt, shall thank you.
So fare you well, my little good lord Cardinal.

                         Exeunt all but Wolsey.

WOLSEY
So farewell to the little good you bear me.
Farewell? A long farewell, to all my greatness!
This is the state of man: today he puts forth
The tender leaves of hopes; tomorrow blossoms,
And bears his blushing honors thick upon him;   355
The third day comes a frost, a killing frost,
And when he thinks, good easy man, full surely   357
His greatness is a-ripening, nips his root,
And then he falls as I do. I have ventured,
Like little wanton boys that swim on bladders,   360
This many summers in a sea of glory,
But far beyond my depth. My high-blown pride
At length broke under me and now has left me,
Weary and old with service, to the mercy
Of a rude stream that must forever hide me.   365
Vain pomp and glory of this world, I hate ye!
I feel my heart new opened. Oh, how wretched
Is that poor man that hangs on princes' favors!
There is betwixt that smile we would aspire to,
That sweet aspect of princes, and their ruin,   370
More pangs and fears than wars or women have;
And when he falls, he falls like Lucifer,   372
Never to hope again.

                 Enter Cromwell, standing amazed.

                         Why, how now, Cromwell?   373

---

300 hand (1) handwriting (2) possession   **301 thus much** (I can say) this much   **303 truth** loyalty.   **305 out they shall** out they come, here they are.   **308 dare** defy.   **objections** accusations.   **309 want** lack   **310 Have at you!** Here goes!   **312 wrought** connived, worked.   **legate** representative of the Pope   **315 "Ego et Rex meus"** my king and I. (Literally, "I and my king"; Norfolk accuses Wolsey of using the phrase in such a way as to make the King his "servant" by naming himself first, but the Latin construction requires that "ego" precede any nouns parallel with it.)   **316 still** always   **320 To . . . seal** (Taking the great seal out of the country was illegal, owing to the danger of its falling into the hands of foreign powers.)   **321 Item** i.e., Another item is.   **large** with full power to act   **323 allowance** assent   **325 mere** sheer   **327 innumerable substance** uncountable wealth   **329 To furnish Rome** (Implies that Wolsey made gifts to Rome as bribes to obtain his own advancement.)   **330 mere** utter   **334 'Tis virtue** i.e., It's virtuous not to do so.

340 legative as a papal legate   **341 Fall . . . praemunire** fall within the penalties for violating a writ of praemunire, i.e., a writ by which one could be charged with appealing to a foreign court (especially a papal court) in an action involving an English subject and hence relevant to the King's court   **342 sued** moved, issued   **343 tenements** properties not owned outright but held for some set term   **344 Chattels** personal possessions   **347 For** As for   **355 blushing honors** honors that cause a glow of pleasure in the face, and that are rosy of color like the blossom   **357 easy** complacent, credulous   **360 wanton** sportful   **365 rude stream** rough torrent   **370 their ruin** the ruin that reliance on princes' uncertain favors can bring about, or the ruin of those who thus rely   **372 he** the *poor man* of line 368, here imagined to fall into endless despair like Lucifer or Satan, chief of the angels who rebelled against God and was thrown out of heaven into hell   **373 s.d. amazed** stunned.

CROMWELL
I have no power to speak, sir.
WOLSEY   What, amazed
At my misfortunes? Can thy spirit wonder
A great man should decline? Nay, an you weep,   376
I am fall'n indeed.
CROMWELL   How does Your Grace?
WOLSEY   Why, well;
Never so truly happy, my good Cromwell.
I know myself now, and I feel within me
A peace above all earthly dignities,
A still and quiet conscience. The King has cured me,
I humbly thank His Grace, and from these shoulders,
These ruined pillars, out of pity, taken
A load would sink a navy: too much honor.
Oh, 'tis a burden, Cromwell, 'tis a burden
Too heavy for a man that hopes for heaven.
CROMWELL
I am glad Your Grace has made that right use of it.
WOLSEY
I hope I have. I am able now, methinks,
Out of a fortitude of soul I feel,
To endure more miseries and greater far
Than my weakhearted enemies dare offer.
What news abroad?
CROMWELL   The heaviest and the worst
Is your displeasure with the King.
WOLSEY   God bless him!   393
CROMWELL
The next is that Sir Thomas More is chosen
Lord Chancellor in your place.
WOLSEY   That's somewhat sudden.
But he's a learnèd man. May he continue
Long in His Highness' favor and do justice
For truth's sake and his conscience, that his bones,
When he has run his course and sleeps in blessings,
May have a tomb of orphans' tears wept on him!   400
What more?
CROMWELL   That Cranmer is returned with welcome,
Installed Lord Archbishop of Canterbury.
WOLSEY
That's news indeed.
CROMWELL   Last, that the Lady Anne,
Whom the King hath in secrecy long married,
This day was viewed in open as his queen,
Going to chapel, and the voice is now   406
Only about her coronation.
WOLSEY
There was the weight that pulled me down. Oh,
    Cromwell,
The King has gone beyond me. All my glories   409
In that one woman I have lost forever.
No sun shall ever usher forth mine honors,
Or gild again the noble troops that waited   412
Upon my smiles. Go get thee from me, Cromwell!
I am a poor fall'n man, unworthy now

To be thy lord and master. Seek the King;
That sun, I pray, may never set! I have told him
What and how true thou art. He will advance thee;
Some little memory of me will stir him—
I know his noble nature—not to let
Thy hopeful service perish too. Good Cromwell,
Neglect him not; make use now, and provide   421
For thine own future safety.
CROMWELL   O my lord,
Must I then leave you? Must I needs forgo
So good, so noble, and so true a master?
Bear witness, all that have not hearts of iron,
With what a sorrow Cromwell leaves his lord.
The King shall have my service, but my prayers
Forever and forever shall be yours.
WOLSEY
Cromwell, I did not think to shed a tear
In all my miseries, but thou hast forced me,
Out of thy honest truth, to play the woman.   431
Let's dry our eyes. And thus far hear me, Cromwell,
And when I am forgotten, as I shall be,
And sleep in dull cold marble, where no mention
Of me more must be heard of, say I taught thee;
Say Wolsey, that once trod the ways of glory,
And sounded all the depths and shoals of honor,   437
Found thee a way, out of his wreck, to rise in,   438
A sure and safe one, though thy master missed it.
Mark but my fall, and that that ruined me.
Cromwell, I charge thee, fling away ambition!   441
By that sin fell the angels; how can man, then,
The image of his Maker, hope to win by it?
Love thyself last; cherish those hearts that hate thee.
Corruption wins not more than honesty.
Still in thy right hand carry gentle peace   446
To silence envious tongues. Be just, and fear not.
Let all the ends thou aim'st at be thy country's,
Thy God's, and truth's; then if thou fall'st, O Cromwell,
Thou fall'st a blessed martyr.
Serve the King, and—prithee, lead me in.
There take an inventory of all I have,
To the last penny; 'tis the King's. My robe,   453
And my integrity to heaven, is all
I dare now call mine own. O Cromwell, Cromwell,
Had I but served my God with half the zeal
I served my king, he would not in mine age
Have left me naked to mine enemies.
CROMWELL
Good sir, have patience.
WOLSEY   So I have. Farewell
The hopes of court! My hopes in heaven do dwell.
                                        Exeunt.

❧

---

376 an if   393 displeasure disgrace   400 orphans' i.e., such as would
be under the legal guardianship of the Lord Chancellor   406 voice
talk   409 gone beyond overreached   412 troops i.e., of retainers

421 make use take advantage   431 play the woman i.e., shed tears.
437 sounded explored, fathomed   438 wreck shipwreck   441 fling
away ambition (Audiences were probably aware that Cromwell
failed to heed this advice and was beheaded in 1540.)   446 Still
Always   453 robe i.e., clerical robe

4.1

Enter two Gentlemen, meeting one another.

FIRST GENTLEMAN
You're well met once again.
SECOND GENTLEMAN   So are you.   1
FIRST GENTLEMAN
You come to take your stand here and behold
The Lady Anne pass from her coronation?
SECOND GENTLEMAN
'Tis all my business. At our last encounter
The Duke of Buckingham came from his trial.
FIRST GENTLEMAN
'Tis very true. But that time offered sorrow;
This, general joy.
SECOND GENTLEMAN   'Tis well. The citizens,
I am sure, have shown at full their royal minds—   8
As, let 'em have their rights, they are ever forward—   9
In celebration of this day with shows,
Pageants, and sights of honor.
FIRST GENTLEMAN   Never greater,
Nor, I'll assure you, better taken, sir.   12
SECOND GENTLEMAN
May I be bold to ask what that contains,
That paper in your hand?
FIRST GENTLEMAN   Yes, 'tis the list
Of those that claim their offices this day
By custom of the coronation.
The Duke of Suffolk is the first, and claims
To be High Steward; next, the Duke of Norfolk,
He to be Earl Marshal. You may read the rest.
                              [*He offers a paper.*]
SECOND GENTLEMAN
I thank you, sir. Had I not known those customs,
I should have been beholding to your paper.   21
But, I beseech you, what's become of Katharine,
The Princess Dowager? How goes her business?
FIRST GENTLEMAN
That I can tell you too. The Archbishop
Of Canterbury, accompanied with other
Learnèd and reverend fathers of his order,
Held a late court at Dunstable, six miles off   27
From Ampthill, where the Princess lay, to which   28
She was often cited by them, but appeared not;   29
And, to be short, for not-appearance and   30
The King's late scruple, by the main assent   31
Of all these learnèd men she was divorced,
And the late marriage made of none effect;   33
Since which she was removed to Kimbolton,   34
Where she remains now sick.
SECOND GENTLEMAN   Alas, good lady!
                              [*Trumpets.*]

4.1. Location: A street in Westminster.
1 You're well met I am happy to see you   **8 royal minds** hearts and minds loyal to the crown. (Said with a certain condescension.)   **9 let . . . rights** to give them due credit.   **forward** i.e., eager to do   **12 taken** received   **21 beholding** beholden   **27 late** recent. (As also in lines 31 and 33.)   **Dunstable** a town northwest of London in Bedfordshire   **28 lay** lodged   **29 cited** summoned   **30 short** brief   **31 main assent** general agreement   **33 of none effect** null and void   **34 Kimbolton** in Huntingtonshire

The trumpets sound. Stand close, the Queen is
    coming.   *Hautboys.*   36

          The Order of the Coronation.

1. *A lively flourish of Trumpets.*
2. *Then, two* Judges.
3. Lord Chancellor, *with purse and mace before him.*
4. Choristers, *singing. Music.*
5. Mayor of London, *bearing the mace. Then* Garter, *in his coat of arms, and on his head he wore a gilt copper crown.*
6. Marquess Dorset, *bearing a scepter of gold, on his head a demi-coronal of gold. With him, the* Earl of Surrey, *bearing the rod of silver with the dove, crowned with an earl's coronet. Collars of S's.*
7. Duke of Suffolk, *in his robe of estate, his coronet on his head, bearing a long white wand, as High Steward. With him, the* Duke of Norfolk, *with the rod of marshalship, a coronet on his head. Collars of S's.*
8. A canopy borne by four of the Cinque Ports; *under it, the* Queen *in her robe, in her hair, richly adorned with pearl, crowned. On each side her, the* Bishops of London *and* Winchester.
9. *The old* Duchess of Norfolk, *in a coronal of gold wrought with flowers, bearing the Queen's train.*
10. *Certain* Ladies *or* Countesses, *with plain circlets of gold without flowers.*
          Exeunt, first passing over the stage in order and state, and then a great flourish of trumpets.

SECOND GENTLEMAN
A royal train, believe me. These I know.   37
Who's that that bears the scepter?
FIRST GENTLEMAN   Marquess Dorset,
And that the Earl of Surrey, with the rod.
SECOND GENTLEMAN
A bold brave gentleman. That should be
The Duke of Suffolk?
FIRST GENTLEMAN   'Tis the same: High Steward.
SECOND GENTLEMAN
And that my Lord of Norfolk?
FIRST GENTLEMAN   Yes.
SECOND GENTLEMAN [*looking at the Queen*]
          Heaven bless thee!

36 close aside.   **36.1–28** *The Order of the Coronation:* (3) **Lord Chancellor** Sir Thomas More. (See note at 5.3.0.2.)   (4) *Music* Musicians (as also in line 91).   (5) **Garter** i.e., Garter King at Arms, a chief herald of the College of Arms.   (6) **Marquess Dorset** Henry Grey, brother-in-law of Henry VIII and father of Lady Jane Grey (who, as a granddaughter of Henry VII, became a claimant for the throne in 1553 and was executed). *Collars of S's* golden chains of office made of flat, broad S-shaped links, ornately decorated.   (8) **Cinque Ports** barons of the Cinque Ports, a group of seaport towns (originally Dover, Hastings, Sandwich, Hythe, and Romney) situated on the southeast coast of England, in ancient times furnishing the chief parts of the English navy, in return for which they had many privileges and franchises.   *in her hair* with hair loosely hanging (customary for brides)   (9) **Duchess of Norfolk** The once-mighty family (including the Duke, named in 36[9]) lost power more devastatingly than any other noble family under Henry VIII, though the Duchess survived to be godmother (along with the Marchioness Dorset) to the young Elizabeth who was to become Elizabeth I. The family regained much of its ascendancy by the time this play was staged.   **37 train** procession

Thou hast the sweetest face I ever looked on.
Sir, as I have a soul, she is an angel;
Our King has all the Indies in his arms,
And more, and richer, when he strains that lady.   46
I cannot blame his conscience.

FIRST GENTLEMAN   They that bear
The cloth of honor over her are four barons   48
Of the Cinque Ports.   49

SECOND GENTLEMAN
Those men are happy, and so are all are near her.   50
I take it she that carries up the train
Is that old noble lady, Duchess of Norfolk.

FIRST GENTLEMAN
It is, and all the rest are countesses.

SECOND GENTLEMAN
Their coronets say so. These are stars indeed.

FIRST GENTLEMAN
And sometimes falling ones.

SECOND GENTLEMAN   No more of that.   55

[*Exit the last of the procession.*]

Enter a third Gentleman.

FIRST GENTLEMAN
God save you, sir! Where have you been broiling?   56

THIRD GENTLEMAN
Among the crowd i'th'Abbey, where a finger   57
Could not be wedged in more. I am stifled
With the mere rankness of their joy.

SECOND GENTLEMAN   You saw   59
The ceremony?

THIRD GENTLEMAN   That I did.

FIRST GENTLEMAN   How was it?

THIRD GENTLEMAN
Well worth the seeing.

SECOND GENTLEMAN   Good sir, speak it to us.   61

THIRD GENTLEMAN
As well as I am able. The rich stream
Of lords and ladies, having brought the Queen
To a prepared place in the choir, fell off   64
A distance from her, while Her Grace sat down
To rest awhile, some half an hour or so,
In a rich chair of state, opposing freely   67
The beauty of her person to the people.
Believe me, sir, she is the goodliest woman
That ever lay by man; which when the people
Had the full view of, such a noise arose
As the shrouds make at sea in a stiff tempest,   72
As loud, and to as many tunes. Hats, cloaks—
Doublets, I think—flew up; and had their faces   74
Been loose, this day they had been lost. Such joy
I never saw before. Great-bellied women,
That had not half a week to go, like rams   77

In the old time of war, would shake the press   78
And make 'em reel before 'em. No man living
Could say "This is my wife" there, all were woven
So strangely in one piece.

SECOND GENTLEMAN   But what followed?

THIRD GENTLEMAN
At length Her Grace rose and with modest paces
Came to the altar, where she kneeled, and saintlike
Cast her fair eyes to heaven and prayed devoutly,
Then rose again and bowed her to the people;
When by the Archbishop of Canterbury
She had all the royal makings of a queen,
As holy oil, Edward Confessor's crown,   88
The rod, and bird of peace, and all such emblems
Laid nobly on her; which performed, the choir,
With all the choicest music of the kingdom,   91
Together sung *Te Deum*. So she parted,   92
And with the same full state paced back again   93
To York Place, where the feast is held.

FIRST GENTLEMAN   Sir,
You must no more call it York Place; that's past,
For since the Cardinal fell that title's lost.
'Tis now the King's, and called Whitehall.

THIRD GENTLEMAN   I know it,
But 'tis so lately altered that the old name   98
Is fresh about me.

SECOND GENTLEMAN   What two reverend bishops
Were those that went on each side of the Queen?

THIRD GENTLEMAN
Stokesley and Gardiner, the one of Winchester,   101
Newly preferred from the King's secretary,   102
The other, London.

SECOND GENTLEMAN   He of Winchester   103
Is held no great good lover of the Archbishop's,
The virtuous Cranmer.

THIRD GENTLEMAN   All the land knows that.
However, yet there is no great breach; when it comes,
Cranmer will find a friend will not shrink from him.   107

SECOND GENTLEMAN
Who may that be, I pray you?

THIRD GENTLEMAN   Thomas Cromwell,
A man in much esteem with th' King, and truly
A worthy friend. The King has made him Master
O'th' Jewel House,
And one already of the Privy Council.

SECOND GENTLEMAN
He will deserve more.

THIRD GENTLEMAN   Yes, without all doubt.
Come, gentlemen, ye shall go my way, which
Is to th' court, and there ye shall be my guests.

---

46 **strains** embraces   48 **cloth of honor** canopy   49 **Cinque Ports**
(See above at 36.1–28 [8].)   50 **all** all who   55 **falling** (With a sexual
pun.)   56 **broiling** sweating.   57 **i'th'Abbey** in Westminster Abbey,
traditional site of English coronations for centuries   59 **mere rankness** (1) sheer exuberance (2) smelliness   61 **speak** describe   64 **fell
off** withdrew   67 **opposing** presenting in full view   72 **shrouds** sail
ropes   74 **Doublets** close-fitting jackets   77 **rams** battering rams

78 **press** crowd   88 **As** namely   91 **music** musicians   92 *Te Deum*
(A hymn of thanksgiving, the opening words of which are, *Te Deum
laudamus*, "Thee, God, we praise.")   **parted** departed   93 **state** dignity   98 **lately** recently   101–2 **Gardiner . . . secretary** (Gardiner,
secretary to the King, was made Bishop of Winchester at the fall of
Wolsey; he continued to act as secretary for several years.)   102 **preferred** promoted   103 **London** i.e., Bishop of London.   107 **will not**
who will not

Something I can command. As I walk thither,   116
I'll tell ye more.

BOTH   You may command us, sir.   *Exeunt.*

❖

4.2

*Enter Katharine, Dowager, sick, led between
Griffith, her gentleman usher, and Patience, her
woman.*

GRIFFITH
How does Your Grace?

KATHARINE   Oh, Griffith, sick to death!
My legs like loaden branches bow to th'earth,   2
Willing to leave their burden. Reach a chair. [*She sits.*]
So; now, methinks, I feel a little ease.
Didst thou not tell me, Griffith, as thou led'st me,
That the great child of honor, Cardinal Wolsey,
Was dead?

GRIFFITH   Yes, madam; but I think Your Grace,
Out of the pain you suffered, gave no ear to't.

KATHARINE
Prithee, good Griffith, tell me how he died.
If well, he stepped before me happily   10
For my example.

GRIFFITH   Well, the voice goes, madam;   11
For after the stout Earl Northumberland   12
Arrested him at York, and brought him forward,
As a man sorely tainted, to his answer,   14
He fell sick suddenly and grew so ill
He could not sit his mule.

KATHARINE   Alas, poor man!

GRIFFITH
At last, with easy roads, he came to Leicester,   17
Lodged in the abbey, where the reverend abbot,
With all his convent, honorably received him,   19
To whom he gave these words: "O father Abbot,
An old man, broken with the storms of state,
Is come to lay his weary bones among ye.
Give him a little earth for charity!"
So went to bed, where eagerly his sickness
Pursued him still; and three nights after this,
About the hour of eight, which he himself
Foretold should be his last, full of repentance,
Continual meditations, tears, and sorrows,
He gave his honors to the world again,
His blessèd part to heaven, and slept in peace.

KATHARINE
So may he rest; his faults lie gently on him!
Yet thus far, Griffith, give me leave to speak him,   32
And yet with charity. He was a man
Of an unbounded stomach, ever ranking   34

Himself with princes; one that by suggestion   35
Tied all the kingdom. Simony was fair play.   36
His own opinion was his law. I'th' presence   37
He would say untruths, and be ever double   38
Both in his words and meaning. He was never,
But where he meant to ruin, pitiful.   40
His promises were, as he then was, mighty;
But his performance, as he is now, nothing.
Of his own body he was ill, and gave   43
The clergy ill example.

GRIFFITH   Noble madam,
Men's evil manners live in brass; their virtues
We write in water. May it please Your Highness
To hear me speak his good now?

KATHARINE   Yes, good Griffith;
I were malicious else.

GRIFFITH   This cardinal,
Though from an humble stock, undoubtedly
Was fashioned to much honor. From his cradle
He was a scholar, and a ripe and good one,
Exceeding wise, fair-spoken, and persuading;
Lofty and sour to them that loved him not,
But, to those men that sought him, sweet as summer.
And though he were unsatisfied in getting,   55
Which was a sin, yet in bestowing, madam,
He was most princely. Ever witness for him
Those twins of learning that he raised in you,   58
Ipswich and Oxford, one of which fell with him,   59
Unwilling to outlive the good that did it;   60
The other, though unfinished, yet so famous,
So excellent in art, and still so rising,   62
That Christendom shall ever speak his virtue.
His overthrow heaped happiness upon him;
For then, and not till then, he felt himself,   65
And found the blessedness of being little.   66
And, to add greater honors to his age
Than man could give him, he died fearing God.

KATHARINE
After my death I wish no other herald,
No other speaker of my living actions,   70
To keep mine honor from corruption
But such an honest chronicler as Griffith.
Whom I most hated living, thou hast made me,   73
With thy religious truth and modesty,   74
Now in his ashes honor. Peace be with him!
Patience, be near me still, and set me lower.
I have not long to trouble thee. Good Griffith,
Cause the musicians play me that sad note   78
I named my knell, whilst I sit meditating   79

---

116 **Something . . . command** I have a certain amount of influence.
4.2. Location: Kimbolton Castle in Huntingtonshire. The Queen's apartments.
2 loaden laden, weighted down   **10 well** i.e., spiritually prepared.
happily fittingly   **11 the voice goes** people say   **12 stout** brave
14 sorely tainted grievously corrupted.   **to his answer** to answer the
charges against him   **17 roads** stages (of a journey)   **19 convent**
monastery   **32 speak** describe   **34 stomach** ambition

35 **suggestion** crafty dealing   36 **Tied** fettered, controlled.   **Simony**
The selling of ecclesiastical offices   37 **I'th' presence** In the presence
chamber, where the King conducted state business   38 **double**
duplicitous   40 **pitiful** pitying, compassionate   43 **ill** lax, unchaste
55 **unsatisfied in getting** insatiable in acquiring wealth   58–9 **Those
. . . Oxford** Griffith apostrophizes the places where Wolsey founded
two institutions of learning: a college (no longer extant) at Ipswich,
where he was born, and a college at Oxford that is now Christ
Church.   60 **good that did** goodness that founded   62 **art** learning
65 **felt** knew   66 **little** of humble station.   70 **living** while alive   73
Whom He whom   74 **modesty** moderation   78 **note** tune   79 **knell**
dirge. (Literally, the stroke or sound of a bell slowly rung for a death.)

On that celestial harmony I go to.
                Sad and solemn music. [Katharine sleeps.]

GRIFFITH
She is asleep. Good wench, let's sit down quiet,
For fear we wake her. Softly, gentle Patience.   82
                              [They sit.]

*The vision. Enter, solemnly tripping one after
another, six personages, clad in white robes,
wearing on their heads garlands of bays, and
golden vizards on their faces, branches of bays or
palm in their hands. They first congee unto her,
then dance; and, at certain changes, the first two
hold a spare garland over her head, at which the
other four make reverent curtsies. Then the two
that held the garland deliver the same to the
other next two, who observe the same order in their
changes, and holding the garland over her head;
which done, they deliver the same garland to the
last two, who likewise observe the same order; at
which, as it were by inspiration, she makes in her
sleep signs of rejoicing, and holdeth up her hands
to heaven; and so in their dancing vanish, carrying
the garland with them. The music continues.*

KATHARINE *[waking]*
Spirits of peace, where are ye? Are ye all gone,
And leave me here in wretchedness behind ye?
GRIFFITH
Madam, we are here.
KATHARINE   It is not you I call for.
Saw ye none enter since I slept?
GRIFFITH   None, madam.
KATHARINE
No? Saw you not, even now, a blessèd troop
Invite me to a banquet, whose bright faces
Cast thousand beams upon me, like the sun?
They promised me eternal happiness,
And brought me garlands, Griffith, which I feel
I am not worthy yet to wear. I shall, assuredly.
GRIFFITH
I am most joyful, madam, such good dreams
Possess your fancy.
KATHARINE   Bid the music leave;   94
They are harsh and heavy to me.   *Music ceases.*
PATIENCE *[to Griffith]*   Do you note
How much Her Grace is altered on the sudden?
How long her face is drawn? How pale she looks,
And of an earthy cold? Mark her eyes!
GRIFFITH
She is going, wench. Pray, pray.
PATIENCE   Heaven comfort her!

          Enter a Messenger.

MESSENGER
An't like Your Grace—
KATHARINE   You are a saucy fellow.   100

Deserve we no more reverence?
GRIFFITH *[to the Messenger]*   You are to blame,
Knowing she will not lose her wonted greatness,   102
To use so rude behavior. Go to, kneel.
MESSENGER *[kneeling]*
I humbly do entreat Your Highness' pardon;
My haste made me unmannerly. There is staying   105
A gentleman, sent from the King, to see you.
KATHARINE
Admit him entrance, Griffith. But this fellow
Let me ne'er see again.   *Exit Messenger.*

     Enter Lord Capuchius [admitted by Griffith].

                    If my sight fail not,
You should be Lord Ambassador from the Emperor,   109
My royal nephew, and your name Capuchius.
CAPUCHIUS
Madam, the same; your servant.
KATHARINE   Oh, my lord,
The times and titles now are altered strangely
With me since first you knew me. But I pray you,
What is your pleasure with me?
CAPUCHIUS   Noble lady,
First, mine own service to Your Grace; the next,   115
The King's request that I would visit you,
Who grieves much for your weakness, and by me
Sends you his princely commendations,
And heartily entreats you take good comfort.
KATHARINE
O my good lord, that comfort comes too late;
'Tis like a pardon after execution.
That gentle physic, given in time, had cured me,   122
But now I am past all comforts here but prayers.
How does His Highness?
CAPUCHIUS   Madam, in good health.
KATHARINE
So may he ever do, and ever flourish,
When I shall dwell with worms, and my poor name
Banished the kingdom!—Patience, is that letter
I caused you write yet sent away?
PATIENCE   No, madam.
KATHARINE
Sir, I most humbly pray you to deliver
This to my lord the King.
          [The letter is given to Capuchius.]
CAPUCHIUS   Most willing, madam.
KATHARINE
In which I have commended to his goodness
The model of our chaste loves, his young daughter—   132
The dews of heaven fall thick in blessings on her!—
Beseeching him to give her virtuous breeding—   134
She is young, and of a noble modest nature;
I hope she will deserve well—and a little

82.4 *bays* laurel (indicating celebration)   82.5 *vizards* masks
82.6 *congee* make a congé, a ceremonious bow   82.7 *changes* figures
in the dance   94 *fancy* imagination.   **music leave** musicians cease
100 **An't like** If it please

102 **lose** forgo.   **wonted** accustomed   105 **staying** waiting
109 **Emperor** i.e., Charles V   115 **service** dutiful greetings   122 **physic**
remedy.   **had** would have   132 **model** image.   **young daughter** i.e.,
Mary, the only one of Katharine's many children to live to maturity;
she became Queen of England (1553–1558) before her half-sister Elizabeth (1558–1603)   134 **breeding** upbringing

To love her for her mother's sake, that loved him,
Heaven knows how dearly. My next poor petition
Is that His Noble Grace would have some pity
Upon my wretched women, that so long
Have followed both my fortunes faithfully;   141
Of which there is not one, I dare avow—
And now I should not lie—but will deserve,   143
For virtue and true beauty of the soul,
For honesty and decent carriage,   145
A right good husband. Let him be a noble;
And sure those men are happy that shall have 'em.
The last is for my men—they are the poorest,
But poverty could never draw 'em from me—
That they may have their wages duly paid 'em,
And something over to remember me by.   151
If heaven had pleased to have given me longer life
And able means, we had not parted thus.   153
These are the whole contents. And, good my lord,
By that you love the dearest in this world,
As you wish Christian peace to souls departed,
Stand these poor people's friend, and urge the King
To do me this last right.

CAPUCHIUS   By heaven, I will,
Or let me lose the fashion of a man!   159

KATHARINE
I thank you, honest lord. Remember me
In all humility unto His Highness.
Say his long trouble now is passing
Out of this world. Tell him in death I blessed him,
For so I will. Mine eyes grow dim. Farewell,
My lord. Griffith, farewell. Nay, Patience,
You must not leave me yet. I must to bed;
Call in more women. When I am dead, good wench,
Let me be used with honor. Strew me over
With maiden flowers, that all the world may know   169
I was a chaste wife to my grave. Embalm me,
Then lay me forth; although unqueened, yet like   171
A queen, and daughter to a king, inter me.
I can no more.   *Exeunt, leading Katharine.* 173

❖

5.1

*Enter Gardiner, Bishop of Winchester, a Page with
a torch before him, met by Sir Thomas Lovell.*

GARDINER
It's one o'clock, boy, is't not?
PAGE   It hath struck.
GARDINER
These should be hours for necessities,

Not for delights; times to repair our nature
With comforting repose, and not for us
To waste these times.—Good hour of night, Sir Thomas!
Whither so late?
LOVELL   Came you from the King, my lord?
GARDINER
I did, Sir Thomas, and left him at primero   7
With the Duke of Suffolk.
LOVELL   I must to him too,
Before he go to bed. I'll take my leave.
GARDINER
Not yet, Sir Thomas Lovell. What's the matter?
It seems you are in haste. An if there be   11
No great offense belongs to't, give your friend
Some touch of your late business. Affairs that walk,   13
As they say spirits do, at midnight, have
In them a wilder nature than the business
That seeks dispatch by day.
LOVELL   My lord, I love you,   16
And durst commend a secret to your ear   17
Much weightier than this work. The Queen's in labor,   18
They say, in great extremity, and feared   19
She'll with the labor end.
GARDINER   The fruit she goes with
I pray for heartily, that it may find
Good time, and live; but for the stock, Sir Thomas,   22
I wish it grubbed up now.
LOVELL   Methinks I could   23
Cry the amen; and yet my conscience says   24
She's a good creature and, sweet lady, does
Deserve our better wishes.
GARDINER   But, sir, sir,
Hear me, Sir Thomas. You're a gentleman
Of mine own way. I know you wise, religious;   28
And, let me tell you, it will ne'er be well—
'Twill not, Sir Thomas Lovell, take't of me—
Till Cranmer, Cromwell—her two hands—and she
Sleep in their graves.
LOVELL   Now, sir, you speak of two
The most remarked i'th' kingdom. As for Cromwell,   33
Beside that of the Jewel House, is made Master   34
O'th' Rolls, and the King's secretary; further, sir,   35
Stands in the gap and trade of more preferments   36
With which the time will load him. Th'Archbishop   37
Is the King's hand and tongue, and who dare speak
One syllable against him?
GARDINER   Yes, yes, Sir Thomas,
There are that dare, and I myself have ventured
To speak my mind of him; and indeed this day,
Sir, I may tell it you, I think—I have

---

141 **both my fortunes** i.e., good and ill **143 now** i.e., on my
deathbed, when true speaking is of utmost spiritual importance
145 honesty . . . carriage chastity and proper behavior **151 over** in
addition **153 able** sufficient **159 fashion** title, character **169
maiden flowers** spring flowers, symbolic of chastity. (Compare *The
Winter's Tale*, 4.4.113–29.) **171 lay me forth** lay me out for burial
173 can can do
5.1. Location: London. A gallery in the palace.

7 **primero** gambling card game **11 An if** If **13 touch** hint. **late**
recent **16 dispatch** accomplishment **17 commend** entrust **18 this
work** i.e., what I have been involved in. **19 feared** i.e., it is feared
that **22 Good time** good fortune, a good delivery. **stock** trunk or
main stem (i.e., Queen Anne herself) **23 grubbed up** rooted up
24 Cry the amen give assent **28 way** religious faith (opposed to
Protestant reform). **33 remarked** under the public eye **34–5 Master
O'th' Rolls** keeper of rolls, patents, and grants made under the great
seal, and records of the Court of Chancery **36 gap and trade** opening and beaten path **37 time** course of events

Incensed the lords o'th' Council that he is— 43
For so I know he is, they know he is—
A most arch heretic, a pestilence
That does infect the land; with which they, moved, 46
Have broken with the King, who hath so far 47
Given ear to our complaint, of his great grace
And princely care foreseeing those fell mischiefs 49
Our reasons laid before him, hath commanded 50
Tomorrow morning to the Council board
He be convented. He's a rank weed, Sir Thomas, 52
And we must root him out. From your affairs
I hinder you too long. Good night, Sir Thomas.

LOVELL
Many good nights, my lord. I rest your servant. 55

                 Exeunt Gardiner and Page.

     Enter King and Suffolk.

KING [*to Suffolk*]
Charles, I will play no more tonight.
My mind's not on't; you are too hard for me. 57

SUFFOLK
Sir, I did never win of you before.

KING   But little, Charles,
Nor shall not, when my fancy's on my play.— 60
Now, Lovell, from the Queen what is the news?

LOVELL
I could not personally deliver to her
What you commanded me, but by her woman
I sent your message, who returned her thanks
In the great'st humbleness and desired Your Highness
Most heartily to pray for her.

KING   What say'st thou, ha?
To pray for her? What, is she crying out?

LOVELL
So said her woman, and that her suff'rance made 68
Almost each pang a death.

KING   Alas, good lady!

SUFFOLK
God safely quit her of her burden, and 70
With gentle travail, to the gladding of
Your Highness with an heir!

KING   'Tis midnight, Charles.
Prithee, to bed, and in thy prayers remember
Th'estate of my poor queen. Leave me alone, 74
For I must think of that which company
Would not be friendly to.

SUFFOLK   I wish Your Highness
A quiet night, and my good mistress will 77
Remember in my prayers.

KING   Charles, good night. 78

                    Exit Suffolk.

     Enter Sir Anthony Denny.

Well, sir, what follows?

DENNY
Sir, I have brought my lord the Archbishop,
As you commanded me.

KING   Ha? Canterbury?

DENNY
Ay, my good lord.

KING   'Tis true. Where is he, Denny?

DENNY
He attends Your Highness' pleasure.

KING   Bring him to us.

                       [Exit Denny.]

LOVELL [*aside*]
This is about that which the Bishop spake. 84
I am happily come hither. 85

     Enter Cranmer and Denny.

KING
Avoid the gallery. (*Lovell seems to stay.*) Ha? I have said.
Begone. 86
What?   *Exeunt Lovell and Denny.*

CRANMER [*aside*]   I am fearful. Wherefore frowns he thus?
'Tis his aspect of terror. All's not well. 88

KING
How now, my lord? You do desire to know
Wherefore I sent for you.

CRANMER [*kneeling*]   It is my duty 90
T'attend Your Highness' pleasure.

KING   Pray you, arise,
My good and gracious lord of Canterbury.
Come, you and I must walk a turn together;
I have news to tell you. Come, come, give me your
   hand.   *[Cranmer rises.]*
Ah, my good lord, I grieve at what I speak
And am right sorry to repeat what follows.
I have, and most unwillingly, of late
Heard many grievous—I do say, my lord,
Grievous—complaints of you, which, being
   considered,
Have moved us and our Council that you shall
This morning come before us, where I know
You cannot with such freedom purge yourself 102
But that, till further trial in those charges
Which will require your answer, you must take
Your patience to you and be well contented
To make your house our Tow'r. You a brother of us, 106
It fits we thus proceed, or else no witness 107
Would come against you.

CRANMER [*kneeling*]   I humbly thank Your Highness,
And am right glad to catch this good occasion
Most throughly to be winnowed, where my chaff 110
And corn shall fly asunder. For I know 111

---

43 Incensed stirred up   **46–7 with . . . King** which they, moved to anger at the idea, have disclosed to the King   **49 fell** terrible, cruel **50 hath** (that) he has   **52 convented** summoned.   **55 rest** remain **57 hard** good a player   **60 fancy's** mind's   **68 suff'rance** suffering **70 God** May God.   **quit** release   **74 estate** condition   **77–8 and my . . . Remember** and I will remember my good mistress, the Queen

84 the Bishop i.e., Gardiner   **85 happily** luckily   **86 Avoid** Vacate **88 'Tis . . . terror** This is his expression when he is angry. **90 Wherefore** why   **102 freedom** ease and completeness.   **purge** excuse, clear   **106 You . . . of us** i.e., Since you are a member of the Privy Council and therefore very close to me   **107 fits** is appropriate **110–11 Most . . . asunder** i.e., most thoroughly to be sifted and tested, so that what is good in me (the *corn*, or grain) can be separated from what is worthless (the *chaff*).

There's none stands under more calumnious tongues 112
Than I myself, poor man.
KING   Stand up, good Canterbury!
Thy truth and thy integrity is rooted
In us, thy friend. Give me thy hand, stand up.
                              [Cranmer rises.]
Prithee, let's walk. Now, by my halidom,   116
What manner of man are you? My lord, I looked   117
You would have given me your petition that
I should have ta'en some pains to bring together
Yourself and your accusers and to have heard you
Without endurance further.
CRANMER   Most dread liege,   121
The good I stand on is my truth and honesty.
If they shall fail, I, with mine enemies,   123
Will triumph o'er my person, which I weigh not,   124
Being of those virtues vacant. I fear nothing   125
What can be said against me.
KING   Know you not
How your state stands i'th' world, with the whole
  world?
Your enemies are many, and not small; their practices 128
Must bear the same proportion, and not ever   129
The justice and the truth o'th' question carries   130
The due o'th' verdict with it. At what ease   131
Might corrupt minds procure knaves as corrupt   132
To swear against you? Such things have been done.
You are potently opposed, and with a malice
Of as great size. Ween you of better luck,   135
I mean in perjured witness, than your master,   136
Whose minister you are, whiles here he lived
Upon this naughty earth? Go to, go to,   138
You take a precipice for no leap of danger
And woo your own destruction.
CRANMER   God and Your Majesty
Protect mine innocence! Or I fall into
The trap is laid for me.
KING   Be of good cheer;   142
They shall no more prevail than we give way to.   143
Keep comfort to you, and this morning see
You do appear before them. If they shall chance,
In charging you with matters, to commit you,   146
The best persuasions to the contrary
Fail not to use, and with what vehemency
Th'occasion shall instruct you. If entreaties
Will render you no remedy, this ring
Deliver them, and your appeal to us

There make before them. [He gives a ring.] Look, the
  good man weeps!
He's honest, on mine honor. God's blest mother,
I swear he is truehearted, and a soul
None better in my kingdom. Get you gone,
And do as I have bid you.   Exit Cranmer.
                        He has strangled
His language in his tears.

            Enter Old Lady [followed by Lovell].

LOVELL [as he enters]   Come back! What mean you?
OLD LADY
I'll not come back. The tidings that I bring
Will make my boldness manners.—Now, good angels 159
Fly o'er thy royal head, and shade thy person
Under their blessèd wings!
KING   Now, by thy looks
I guess thy message. Is the Queen delivered?
Say ay, and of a boy.
OLD LADY   Ay, ay, my liege,
And of a lovely boy. The God of heaven
Both now and ever bless her! 'Tis a girl
Promises boys hereafter. Sir, your queen
Desires your visitation, and to be
Acquainted with this stranger. 'Tis as like you
As cherry is to cherry.
KING   Lovell!
LOVELL   Sir?
KING
Give her an hundred marks. I'll to the Queen.   170
            Exit King. [Lovell gives the money to
                        the Old Lady and exits.]
OLD LADY
An hundred marks? By this light, I'll ha' more.
An ordinary groom is for such payment.   172
I will have more, or scold it out of him.
Said I for this the girl was like to him?
I'll have more, or else unsay't; and now,
While 'tis hot, I'll put it to the issue.   176
                              Exit Lady.

                        ❖

5.2

      Enter Cranmer, Archbishop of Canterbury,
      [pursuivants, pages, etc. attending at the door].

CRANMER
I hope I am not too late, and yet the gentleman
That was sent to me from the Council prayed me
To make great haste. [He tries the door.] All fast?
What means this? [Calling] Ho!   3

---

112 There's . . . tongues no one is more the object of slander
116 by my halidom i.e., by all that is holy   117 looked expected
121 endurance imprisonment   123–5 I . . . vacant I will join with my
enemies in condemning my fallen self, which I do not value at all if it
is void of truth and honesty.   125 nothing not at all   128 small
insignificant   128–31 their . . . with it their schemes must be correspondingly numerous and mighty, and it is not always the case that
having justice and truth on your side will ensure an innocent verdict.
131 At what ease How easily   132 procure suborn
135 Ween you of Do you expect to have   136 master i.e., Christ
138 naughty wicked   138 naughty wicked.   Go to (An expression
of impatience.)   142 is that is   143 than . . . way to than I allow.
146 commit i.e., to prison in the Tower

159 good angels may good angels   170 an hundred marks i.e., about
sixty-seven pounds.   172 for suited for   176 put it to force
5.2. Location: London. Adjacent to the council chamber.
0.2 pursuivants messengers, subordinates. (As also in line 24.)
at the door i.e., at a stage door, as though guarding the entrance to
the Council chamber   3 fast locked.

Who waits there?

Enter [Door-] keeper.

Sure you know me?

KEEPER   Yes, my lord,
But yet I cannot help you.

CRANMER   Why?

KEEPER
Your Grace must wait till you be called for.

Enter Doctor Butts.

CRANMER   So.

BUTTS *[aside]*
This is a piece of malice. I am glad
I came this way so happily. The King   9
Shall understand it presently.   *Exit Butts.*

CRANMER *[aside]*   'Tis Butts,   10
The King's physician. As he passed along,
How earnestly he cast his eyes upon me!
Pray heaven he sound not my disgrace! For certain   13
This is of purpose laid by some that hate me—   14
God turn their hearts! I never sought their malice—
To quench mine honor. They would shame to make
    me   16
Wait else at door, a fellow councillor,
'Mong boys, grooms, and lackeys. But their pleasures
Must be fulfilled, and I attend with patience.   19

Enter the King and Butts at a window above.

BUTTS
I'll show Your Grace the strangest sight—

KING   What's that, Butts?

BUTTS
I think Your Highness saw this many a day.

KING
Body o' me, where is it?

BUTTS   There, my lord:
The high promotion of His Grace of Canterbury,
Who holds his state at door, 'mongst pursuivants,   24
Pages, and footboys.

KING   Ha? 'Tis he, indeed.
Is this the honor they do one another?
'Tis well there's one above 'em yet. I had thought   27
They had parted so much honesty among 'em—   28
At least good manners—as not thus to suffer
A man of his place, and so near our favor,   30
To dance attendance on Their Lordships' pleasures,   31
And at the door too, like a post with packets.   32

By holy Mary, Butts, there's knavery!
Let 'em alone, and draw the curtain close.
We shall hear more anon.
          [They conceal themselves behind the curtain.
          Cranmer remains waiting at the door, below.]

❖

[5.3]

*A council table brought in with chairs and stools,
and placed under the state. Enter Lord Chancellor;
places himself at the upper end of the table on the
left hand, a seat being left void above him, as for
Canterbury's seat. Duke of Suffolk, Duke of
Norfolk, Surrey, Lord Chamberlain, Gardiner, seat
themselves in order on each side. Cromwell at
lower end, as secretary. [Keeper at the door.]*

CHANCELLOR
Speak to the business, Master Secretary.
Why are we met in council?

CROMWELL   Please Your Honors,
The chief cause concerns His Grace of Canterbury.

GARDINER
Has he had knowledge of it?

CROMWELL   Yes.

NORFOLK   Who waits there?

KEEPER
Without, my noble lords?

GARDINER   Yes.

KEEPER   My lord Archbishop,   5
And has done half an hour, to know your pleasures.

CHANCELLOR
Let him come in.

KEEPER   Your Grace may enter now.
                  Cranmer approaches the council table.

CHANCELLOR
My good Lord Archbishop, I'm very sorry
To sit here at this present and behold   9
That chair stand empty. But we all are men,
In our own natures frail, and capable   11
Of our flesh—few are angels—out of which frailty   12
And want of wisdom, you, that best should teach us,
Have misdemeaned yourself, and not a little,   14
Toward the King first, then his laws, in filling
The whole realm, by your teaching and your
    chaplains'—
For so we are informed—with new opinions,
Divers and dangerous, which are heresies
And, not reformed, may prove pernicious.   19

---

9 **happily** fortunately.   10 **presently** at once.   13 **sound** fathom; or
proclaim   14 **laid** contrived as a trap   16 **quench mine honor**
destroy my reputation.   **19.1 *at a window above*** (The gallery over
the stage, representing a peephole through which the Council could
be spied upon. The Folio text makes no scene division between this
and the following scene, so that the Council would assemble under
the view and in the hearing of the King, and the main stage, imagined
in scene 2 to be adjacent to the Council chamber, becomes in scene 3
the chamber itself.)   24 **holds his state** maintains his dignity   27 **one
above** (Suggests Henry's role as a godlike figure.)   28 **parted . . . honesty** shared sufficient respect   30 **place** official position   31 **dance
attendance** stand waiting around   32 **post with packets** a messenger
with letters.

5.3. Location: The Council chamber. Scene is continuous with the
previous.
0.2 *state* canopy.   ***Lord Chancellor*** Thomas More was appointed
Lord Chancellor in 1529. His execution in 1535 on order of Henry VIII
for refusing to assent to the King's divorce of Katharine of Aragon is
not mentioned in this play, but presumably an Elizabethan audience
would have this fact well in mind.   5 **Without** Outside the door.
(Although Cranmer seemingly has never exited, the stage has now
become the room into which he has been waiting to be admitted.)
9 **present** present time   11–12 **capable . . . flesh** susceptible to the
weaknesses of the flesh   14 **misdemeaned yourself** been guilty of
misconduct   19 **pernicious** deadly.

GARDINER
　　Which reformation must be sudden too,
　　My noble lords; for those that tame wild horses
　　Pace 'em not in their hands to make 'em gentle,　　22
　　But stop their mouths with stubborn bits and spur 'em
　　Till they obey the manage. If we suffer,　　24
　　Out of our easiness and childish pity　　25
　　To one man's honor, this contagious sickness,
　　Farewell all physic! And what follows then?　　27
　　Commotions, uproars, with a general taint
　　Of the whole state, as of late days our neighbors,
　　The upper Germany, can dearly witness,　　30
　　Yet freshly pitied in our memories.

CRANMER
　　My good lords, hitherto, in all the progress
　　Both of my life and office, I have labored,
　　And with no little study, that my teaching
　　And the strong course of my authority
　　Might go one way, and safely; and the end
　　Was ever to do well. Nor is there living—
　　I speak it with a single heart, my lords—　　38
　　A man that more detests, more stirs against,　　39
　　Both in his private conscience and his place,　　40
　　Defacers of a public peace than I do.
　　Pray heaven the King may never find a heart
　　With less allegiance in it! Men that make　　43
　　Envy and crooked malice nourishment　　44
　　Dare bite the best. I do beseech Your Lordships　　45
　　That in this case of justice, my accusers,
　　Be what they will, may stand forth face to face
　　And freely urge against me.

SUFFOLK　　　　　　　　　　Nay, my lord,　　48
　　That cannot be. You are a councillor,
　　And by that virtue no man dare accuse you.　　50

GARDINER
　　My lord, because we have business of more moment,
　　We will be short with you. 'Tis His Highness' pleasure,
　　And our consent, for better trial of you,
　　From hence you be committed to the Tower,
　　Where, being but a private man again,
　　You shall know many dare accuse you boldly—
　　More than, I fear, you are provided for.　　57

CRANMER
　　Ah, my good lord of Winchester, I thank you;
　　You are always my good friend. If your will pass,　　59
　　I shall both find Your Lordship judge and juror,
　　You are so merciful. I see your end;
　　'Tis my undoing. Love and meekness, lord,
　　Become a churchman better than ambition.
　　Win straying souls with modesty again;　　64
　　Cast none away. That I shall clear myself,

Lay all the weight ye can upon my patience,
I make as little doubt as you do conscience　　67
In doing daily wrongs. I could say more,　　68
But reverence to your calling makes me modest.

GARDINER
　　My lord, my lord, you are a sectary,　　70
　　That's the plain truth. Your painted gloss discovers,　　71
　　To men that understand you, words and weakness.　　72

CROMWELL
　　My lord of Winchester, you're a little,
　　By your good favor, too sharp. Men so noble,　　74
　　However faulty, yet should find respect　　75
　　For what they have been. 'Tis a cruelty
　　To load a falling man.

GARDINER　　　　　　　　Good Master Secretary,　　77
　　I cry Your Honor mercy; you may worst　　78
　　Of all this table say so.

CROMWELL　　　　　　　　Why, my lord?

GARDINER
　　Do not I know you for a favorer
　　Of this new sect? Ye are not sound.

CROMWELL　　　　　　　　　　　　Not sound?　　81

GARDINER
　　Not sound, I say.

CROMWELL　　　　Would you were half so honest!
　　Men's prayers then would seek you, not their fears.

GARDINER
　　I shall remember this bold language.

CROMWELL　　　　　　　　　　　　Do.
　　Remember your bold life too.

CHANCELLOR　　　　　　This is too much.
　　Forbear, for shame, my lords.

GARDINER　　　　　　　　I have done.

CROMWELL　　　　　　　　　　And I.

CHANCELLOR [to Cranmer]
　　Then thus for you, my lord: it stands agreed,
　　I take it, by all voices, that forthwith
　　You be conveyed to th' Tower a prisoner,
　　There to remain till the King's further pleasure
　　Be known unto us. Are you all agreed, lords?

ALL
　　We are.

CRANMER　　Is there no other way of mercy,
　　But I must needs to th' Tower, my lords?

GARDINER　　　　　　　　　What other　　93
　　Would you expect? You are strangely troublesome.　　94
　　Let some o'th' guard be ready there.

　　　　　　　Enter the Guard.

CRANMER　　　　　　　　　For me?

---

22 **Pace . . . hands** don't lead them gently by hand through their paces
24 **manage** training, handling.　**suffer** allow　25 **easiness** laxness
27 **physic** medicine, cure.　30 **upper Germany** (Refers to the Peasants' Wars, 1524; possibly refers to the massacre of the Anabaptists in 1535.)　38 **single** honest; not given to double-dealing　39 **stirs** is active　40 **place** official capacity　43–5 **Men . . . best** Men who feed constantly on envy and malice are the most accomplished at accusing the virtuous.　48 **urge** make accusation　50 **by that virtue** by virtue of that　57 **provided** prepared　59 **pass** prevail　64 **Win . . . again** Win back erring sinners with restraint and moderation

67–8 **I make . . . wrongs** no matter how hard you try my powers of endurance, I have as little doubt (that I can clear myself) as you have scruples against doing daily wrongs.　70 **sectary** follower of a heretical Protestant sect　71 **painted gloss discovers** false exterior (in speech and acts) reveals　72 **words** i.e., mere words　74 **By . . . favor** if you don't mind my saying so　75 **find** be accorded　77 **load** burden　78 **I cry . . . mercy** I beg your pardon. (Said ironically.)　**worst** with least justification　81 **sound** orthodox.　93 **must needs to** must necessarily go to　94 **strangely** uncommonly

Must I go like a traitor thither?
GARDINER [to the Guard]   Receive him,
And see him safe i'th' Tower.
CRANMER   Stay, good my lords,
I have a little yet to say. Look there, my lords.
                              [He shows the King's ring.]
By virtue of that ring, I take my cause
Out of the grips of cruel men and give it   100
To a most noble judge, the King my master.
CHAMBERLAIN
This is the King's ring.
SURREY   'Tis no counterfeit.
SUFFOLK
'Tis the right ring, by heaven! I told ye all,
When we first put this dangerous stone a-rolling,
'Twould fall upon ourselves.
NORFOLK   Do you think, my lords,
The King will suffer but the little finger
Of this man to be vexed?
CHAMBERLAIN   'Tis now too certain.
How much more is his life in value with him!   108
Would I were fairly out on't!
CROMWELL   My mind gave me,   109
In seeking tales and informations
Against this man, whose honesty the devil
And his disciples only envy at,   112
Ye blew the fire that burns ye. Now have at ye!   113

Enter King, frowning on them; takes his seat.

GARDINER
Dread sovereign, how much are we bound to heaven
In daily thanks, that gave us such a prince,
Not only good and wise, but most religious;
One that in all obedience makes the Church
The chief aim of his honor, and, to strengthen
That holy duty out of dear respect,   119
His royal self in judgment comes to hear
The cause betwixt her and this great offender.
KING
You were ever good at sudden commendations,   122
Bishop of Winchester. But know I come not
To hear such flattery now, and in my presence
They are too thin and base to hide offenses.
To me you cannot reach, you play the spaniel,   126
And think with wagging of your tongue to win me;
But whatsoe'er thou tak'st me for, I'm sure
Thou hast a cruel nature and a bloody.
[To Cranmer] Good man, sit down. [Cranmer sits.] Now
    let me see the proudest
He, that dares most, but wag his finger at thee.   131
By all that's holy, he had better starve   132
Than but once think this place becomes thee not.   133

SURREY
May it please Your Grace—
KING   No, sir, it does not please me.
I had thought I had had men of some understanding
And wisdom of my Council, but I find none.
Was it discretion, lords, to let this man,
This good man—few of you deserve that title—
This honest man, wait like a lousy footboy
At chamber door? And one as great as you are?
Why, what a shame was this! Did my commission
Bid ye so far forget yourselves? I gave ye
Power as he was a councillor to try him,
Not as a groom. There's some of ye, I see,
More out of malice than integrity,
Would try him to the utmost, had ye mean,   146
Which ye shall never have while I live.
CHANCELLOR   Thus far,
My most dread sovereign, may it like Your Grace   148
To let my tongue excuse all. What was purposed
Concerning his imprisonment was rather,
If there be faith in men, meant for his trial
And fair purgation to the world than malice,   152
I'm sure, in me.
KING   Well, well, my lords, respect him.
Take him, and use him well; he's worthy of it.
I will say thus much for him: if a prince
May be beholding to a subject, I   156
Am, for his love and service, so to him.
Make me no more ado, but all embrace him.
Be friends, for shame, my lords! [They all embrace
    Cranmer.] My lord of Canterbury,
I have a suit which you must not deny me:
That is, a fair young maid that yet wants baptism;
You must be godfather and answer for her.
CRANMER
The greatest monarch now alive may glory
In such an honor. How may I deserve it,
That am a poor and humble subject to you?
KING
Come, come, my lord, you'd spare your spoons. You
    shall have   166
Two noble partners with you: the old Duchess of
    Norfolk
And Lady Marquess Dorset. Will these please you?—
Once more, my lord of Winchester, I charge you,
Embrace and love this man.
GARDINER   With a true heart
And brother-love I do it.   [He embraces Cranmer.]
CRANMER   And let heaven
Witness how dear I hold this confirmation.
KING
Good man, those joyful tears show thy true heart.
The common voice, I see, is verified   174
Of thee, which says thus, "Do my lord of Canterbury
A shrewd turn, and he's your friend forever."   176
Come, lords, we trifle time away; I long

---

100 grips clutches   **108 in value with him** valued by the King.
109 on't of it (this trouble).   **gave** told   **112 envy at** hate   **113 have
at ye!** i.e., on guard, watch out!   **113.1 Enter King** (The King has presumably come down behind the scene from above. He enters on the
main stage.)   **119 dear respect** heartfelt piety   **122 sudden commendations** improvised compliments   **126 To me** To me whom   **131 He**
the person   **132 starve** die   **133 this place** this council chamber, or
this high office

146 mean means   **148 like** please   **152 purgation** clearing of himself
156 beholding beholden   **166 you'd . . . spoons** (Said jestingly;
spoons were a common christening gift.)   **174 voice** report, opinion
176 shrewd malicious

To have this young one made a Christian.
As I have made ye one, lords, one remain;   179
So I grow stronger, you more honor gain.   *Exeunt*

❖

5.[4]

Noise and tumult within. Enter Porter and his
Man.

PORTER   You'll leave your noise anon, ye rascals! Do   1
you take the court for Paris Garden? Ye rude slaves,   2
leave your gaping.   3
ONE (*within*)   Good master porter, I belong to th' larder.   4
PORTER   Belong to th' gallows, and be hanged, ye rogue!
Is this a place to roar in?—Fetch me a dozen crab tree
staves, and strong ones; these are but switches to   7
'em.—I'll scratch your heads. You must be seeing   8
christenings? Do you look for ale and cakes here, you   9
rude rascals?
MAN
Pray, sir, be patient. 'Tis as much impossible—
Unless we sweep 'em from the door with cannons—
To scatter 'em as 'tis to make 'em sleep
On May Day morning, which will never be.   14
We may as well push against Paul's as stir 'em.   15
PORTER   How got they in, and be hanged?   16
MAN
Alas, I know not. How gets the tide in?
As much as one sound cudgel of four foot—   18
You see the poor remainder—could distribute,
I made no spare, sir.
PORTER   You did nothing, sir.   20
MAN
I am not Samson, nor Sir Guy, nor Colbrand,   21
To mow 'em down before me; but if I spared any
That had a head to hit, either young or old,
He or she, cuckold or cuckold maker,
Let me ne'er hope to see a chine again;   25
And that I would not for a cow, God save her!   26
ONE (*within*)   Do you hear, master porter?
PORTER   I shall be with you presently, good master
puppy.—Keep the door close, sirrah.
MAN   What would you have me do?
PORTER   What should you do, but knock 'em down by
th' dozens? Is this Moorfields to muster in? Or have   32

we some strange Indian with the great tool come to   33
court, the women so besiege us? Bless me, what a fry   34
of fornication is at door! On my Christian conscience,   35
this one christening will beget a thousand; here will
be father, godfather, and all together.
MAN   The spoons will be the bigger, sir. There is a fel-   38
low somewhat near the door—he should be a brazier   39
by his face, for, o' my conscience, twenty of the dog   40
days now reign in 's nose; all that stand about him are   41
under the line, they need no other penance. That fire-   42
drake did I hit three times on the head, and three   43
times was his nose discharged against me; he stands
there like a mortar-piece to blow us. There was a   45
haberdasher's wife of small wit near him that railed
upon me till her pinked porringer fell off her head for   47
kindling such a combustion in the state. I missed the   48
meteor once and hit that woman, who cried out   49
"Clubs!" when I might see from far some forty trun-   50
cheoners draw to her succor, which were the hope o'th'   51
Strand, where she was quartered. They fell on; I   52
made good my place. At length they came to th'   53
broomstaff to me. I defied 'em still, when suddenly a   54
file of boys behind 'em, loose shot, delivered such a   55
shower of pebbles that I was fain to draw mine honor   56
in and let 'em win the work. The devil was amongst   57
'em, I think, surely.
PORTER   These are the youths that thunder at a playhouse and fight for bitten apples, that no audience but
the tribulation of Tower Hill or the limbs of Lime-   61
house, their dear brothers, are able to endure. I have   62
some of 'em in *Limbo Patrum*, and there they are like   63
to dance these three days, besides the running ban-   64
quet of two beadles that is to come.   65

Enter Lord Chamberlain.

CHAMBERLAIN
Mercy o' me, what a multitude are here!

---

179 **ye one** you united in spirit
5.4. Location: London. The palace yard.
0.2 *Man* servant, assistant.   **1 leave** stop.   **anon** immediately   **2 Paris**
Garden a bear-baiting arena on the Bankside.   **3 gaping** shouting.
4 I . . . larder i.e., I am a servant of the palace household, in the pantry.
7–8 to 'em compared to them, i.e., to cudgels made of crab tree.   **9 ale**
and cakes (Refreshments appropriate to christenings and other festivals.)   **14 May Day morning** (Allusion to the custom of rising before
dawn on May Day for early morning festivities.)   **15 Paul's** Saint Paul's
Cathedral   **16 and be hanged** (An oath: I'll be hanged if I know.)
18 cudgel club   **20 made no spare** exercised no frugality   **21 Samson**
biblical character of great strength.   **Sir Guy, Colbrand** (Colbrand was
a legendary Danish giant slain by Guy of Warwick in the popular English romance named after its hero.)   **25 chine** backbone; hence, a joint
of beef or other meat   **26 for a cow** i.e., for anything (*cow* perhaps being
suggested by *chine*)   **32 Moorfields** an open space outside London
walls, used, among other things, as a training ground for the militia

33 tool genitals. (This sentence alludes to the Jacobean excitement
over exhibited Indians.)   **34–5 fry of fornication** swarm of would-be
fornicators   **38 spoons** i.e., as christening presents. (See 5.3.166.)
39 brazier worker in brass   **40–1 dog days** i.e., midsummer, when Sir-
ius, the Dog Star, rises at about the same time as the sun   **42 under**
the line on the equator   **42–3 firedrake** fiery dragon   **45 mortar-piece**
short cannon.   **blow us** (1) blow us up (2) blow his nose at us.
47 pinked porringer small close-fitting cap ornamented with perfora-
tions   **48 combustion** tumult.   **in the state** (1) in the commonwealth
(2) in the brazier, whose inflamed complexion, comically likened here
to a miniature cosmos, seems made up of meteors and discharging
cannons.   **48–9 the meteor** i.e., the red-faced brazier   **50 Clubs** (The
rallying cry for London apprentices to join in or stop a brawl.)
50–1 truncheoners men armed with cudgels   **51 hope** pride and joy
51–2 th' Strand a prosperous street of shops and residences   **52 fell**
on made their assault   **53 made . . . place** stood my ground.   **53–4**
came . . . me i.e., began fighting at close quarters with me.   **55 file**
row.   **loose shot** throwers or marksmen not attached to a particular
company   **56 fain** obliged   **56–7 draw . . . in** i.e., withdraw from the
fight   **57 work** earthwork, fort.   **61 tribulation** troublemakers, gang.
limbs lads; here, rowdies   **61–2 Limehouse** a dockyard area east of
Tower Hill, a rough neighborhood   **63** *Limbo Patrum* resting place
for the souls of those who died before Christ's coming or not having
been baptized; hence, prison.   **like** likely   **64 dance** kick their heels
64–5 running banquet whipping through the streets following
imprisonment (like a *banquet* or "dessert" after a meal)   **65 beadles**
minor officials charged with punishing petty offenses

They grow still too; from all parts they are coming,
As if we kept a fair here. Where are these porters,
These lazy knaves? You've made a fine hand, fellows! 69
There's a trim rabble let in. Are all these 70
Your faithful friends o'th' suburbs? We shall have 71
Great store of room, no doubt, left for the ladies, 72
When they pass back from the christening.

PORTER   An't please Your Honor, 73
We are but men, and what so many may do,
Not being torn a-pieces, we have done.
An army cannot rule 'em.

CHAMBERLAIN   As I live, 76
If the King blame me for't, I'll lay ye all 77
By th' heels, and suddenly, and on your heads 78
Clap round fines for neglect. You're lazy knaves, 79
And here ye lie baiting of bombards, when 80
Ye should do service. [*A trumpet.*] Hark, the trumpets
    sound.
They're come already from the christening.
Go break among the press, and find a way out 83
To let the troop pass fairly, or I'll find 84
A Marshalsea shall hold ye play these two months. 85

PORTER
Make way there for the Princess!

MAN [*to a spectator*]   You great fellow,
Stand close up, or I'll make your head ache.

PORTER [*to another*]
You i'th' camlet, get up o'th' rail! 88
I'll peck you o'er the pales else.   *Exeunt.* 89

❧

5.[5]

> *Enter trumpets, sounding; then two Aldermen, Lord*
> *Mayor, Garter, Cranmer, Duke of Norfolk with his*
> *marshal's staff, Duke of Suffolk, two noblemen*
> *bearing great standing bowls for the christening*
> *gifts; then four noblemen bearing a canopy, under*
> *which the Duchess of Norfolk, godmother, bearing*
> *the child richly habited in a mantle, etc., train*
> *borne by a lady; then follows the Marchioness*
> *Dorset, the other godmother, and ladies. The troop*
> *pass once about the stage, and Garter speaks.*

GARTER   Heaven, from thy endless goodness, send
prosperous life, long, and ever happy, to the high and
mighty Princess of England, Elizabeth!

> *Flourish. Enter King and guard.*

CRANMER [*kneeling*]
And to your royal Grace and the good Queen,
My noble partners and myself thus pray 5
All comfort, joy, in this most gracious lady
Heaven ever laid up to make parents happy 7
May hourly fall upon ye!

KING
Thank you, good Lord Archbishop.
What is her name?

CRANMER   Elizabeth.

KING   Stand up, lord.
    [*Cranmer rises. The King kisses the child.*]
With this kiss take my blessing. God protect thee,
Into whose hand I give thy life.

CRANMER   Amen.

KING
My noble gossips, you've been too prodigal. 13
I thank ye heartily; so shall this lady,
When she has so much English.

CRANMER   Let me speak, sir,
For heaven now bids me; and the words I utter
Let none think flattery, for they'll find 'em truth.
This royal infant—heaven still move about her!— 18
Though in her cradle, yet now promises
Upon this land a thousand thousand blessings,
Which time shall bring to ripeness. She shall be—
But few now living can behold that goodness—
A pattern to all princes living with her,
And all that shall succeed. Saba was never 24
More covetous of wisdom and fair virtue
Than this pure soul shall be. All princely graces
That mold up such a mighty piece as this is, 27
With all the virtues that attend the good,
Shall still be doubled on her. Truth shall nurse her,
Holy and heavenly thoughts still counsel her.
She shall be loved and feared. Her own shall bless her; 31
Her foes shake like a field of beaten corn, 32
And hang their heads with sorrow. Good grows with
    her.
In her days every man shall eat in safety
Under his own vine what he plants, and sing
The merry songs of peace to all his neighbors.
God shall be truly known, and those about her 37
From her shall read the perfect ways of honor 38
And by those claim their greatness, not by blood. 39
Nor shall this peace sleep with her; but as when 40
The bird of wonder dies, the maiden phoenix, 41
Her ashes new-create another heir
As great in admiration as herself, 43
So shall she leave her blessedness to one, 44
When heaven shall call her from this cloud of
    darkness, 45

---

69 **fine hand** fine job. (Said ironically.)   70 **trim** fine. (Said ironically.)
71 **suburbs** areas outside London walls and hence outside its legal
jurisdiction.   72 **store** plenty   73 **An't** If it   76 **rule** control   77–8 **lay
. . . heels** put you in the stocks or in chains   79 **round** heavy   80 **baiting of bombards** drinking from leathern bottles   83 **press** crowd
84 **troop** royal retinue   85 **Marshalsea** prison in Southwark.   **hold
ye play** keep you from your sports and amusements   88 **camlet** a kind
of fabric made of silk and goat's hair. (Since no "crowd" is onstage,
the Porter may be speaking to his audience here as though it were
crowding to see the christening.)   89 **peck** pitch.   **pales** railings
5.5. Location: London. The royal court.
0.2 *Garter* Garter King at Arms, a chief herald of the College of Arms

5 **partners** co-sponsors   7 **laid up** provided   13 **gossips** godparents
18 **still** ever   24 **Saba** the Queen of Sheba, who visited Solomon to
discover wisdom from him; see 1 Kings 10:1–10   27 **mighty piece**
princely person   31 **own** own people   32 **beaten corn** wind-beaten
grain   37 **God . . . known** i.e., True religion shall prevail   38 **read**
learn   39 **greatness** nobility   40 **sleep** i.e., die   41 **phoenix** mythical
bird believed to rise from its own ashes; a symbol of regeneration
43 **great in admiration** greatly wondered at   44 **she** i.e., Elizabeth.
one i.e., King James I   45 **cloud of darkness** i.e., mortal life

Who from the sacred ashes of her honor
Shall starlike rise, as great in fame as she was,
And so stand fixed. Peace, plenty, love, truth, terror,   48
That were the servants to this chosen infant,
Shall then be his, and like a vine grow to him.
Wherever the bright sun of heaven shall shine,
His honor and the greatness of his name
Shall be, and make new nations. He shall flourish,
And like a mountain cedar reach his branches
To all the plains about him. Our children's children
Shall see this and bless heaven.

KING   Thou speakest wonders.

CRANMER
She shall be, to the happiness of England,
An agèd princess; many days shall see her,
And yet no day without a deed to crown it.   59
Would I had known no more! But she must die,
She must, the saints must have her; yet a virgin,
A most unspotted lily shall she pass
To th' ground, and all the world shall mourn her.

KING   Oh, Lord Archbishop,
Thou hast made me now a man! Never, before
This happy child, did I get anything.   66
This oracle of comfort has so pleased me
That when I am in heaven I shall desire
To see what this child does, and praise my Maker.
I thank ye all. To you, my good Lord Mayor,
And you, good brethren, I am much beholding;   71
I have received much honor by your presence,

---

48 **terror** quality inspiring awe   59 **deed** good deed   66 **get** beget;
achieve   71 **beholding** beholden

And ye shall find me thankful. Lead the way, lords.
Ye must all see the Queen, and she must thank ye;
She will be sick else. This day, no man think   75
H'as business at his house; for all shall stay.   76
This little one shall make it holiday.   *Exeunt.*

The Epilogue

[Enter the Epilogue.]

EPILOGUE
'Tis ten to one this play can never please
All that are here. Some come to take their ease,
And sleep an act or two; but those, we fear,
We've frighted with our trumpets; so, 'tis clear,
They'll say 'tis naught. Others to hear the city   5
Abused extremely, and to cry "That's witty!"
Which we have not done neither; that I fear   7
All the expected good we're like to hear   8
For this play at this time is only in
The merciful construction of good women,   10
For such a one we showed 'em. If they smile   11
And say 'twill do, I know, within a while
All the best men are ours; for 'tis ill hap   13
If they hold when their ladies bid 'em clap.   *[Exit.]* 14

---

75 sick unhappy **76 H'as** (that) he has. **stay** i.e., cease work.
Epilogue.
5 naught worthless. **the city** i.e., London and its citizens, the satirical objects of "city comedy" by Ben Jonson, Thomas Middleton, and others **7 that** so that **8 expected good** anticipated approval, applause **10 construction** interpretation **11 such a one** (ambiguously referring to Katharine, Anne, or Elizabeth, or to all three) **13 are ours** will be on our side. **ill hap** bad luck **14 hold** hold back

The Tragedies

Titus Andronicus

Although *Titus Andronicus* has been singled out by some critics as unworthy of Shakespeare's genius—T. S. Eliot called it "one of the stupidest and most uninspired plays ever written"—recent performance history has shown that *Titus* can succeed brilliantly before audiences. In his memorable production at Stratford-upon-Avon in 1959, Peter Brook chose to stage the entrance of the ravished and mutilated Lavinia (Vivien Leigh) with scarlet ribbons trailing from her wrists and mouth, in a visual stylizing that gave to the violence an emotional seriousness even while it avoided gory realism. The long ribbons translated the text into visual symbols. Titus (Laurence Olivier) was a battered veteran from the start of the play, war-wearied, Lear-like in his suffering and agonies of disillusionment. Deborah Warner's more realistic production, at the Swan Theatre, Stratford-upon-Avon in 1987 with Sonia Ritter as Lavinia, stressed the horror of rape and its painful relevance to a late-twentieth-century world deeply concerned with human rights and especially the victimization of women. Interpretations of Tamora in this and other productions have variously seen her as exotic, sexually magnetic, cunning, playful, and deeply sadistic. Most recently, an innovative film version by Julie Taymor, with Anthony Hopkins as Titus, has intrigued a larger audience with this relatively little-known play about wanton violence. Hopkins shows how grim black humor can ironize the effects of gross cruelty and turn our laughter into an attempt to comprehend humanity's apparently fathomless penchant for inhumanity. Recent criticism, too, has taken *Titus* seriously as a study in violence that is painfully relevant to our modern experience.

Titus Andronicus is unmistakably an early play. First published in quarto in 1594 "as it was played by the Right Honorable the Earl of Derby, Earl of Pembroke, and Earl of Sussex Their Servants," it could have been written as early as 1590–1591 or even before. The allusion in theater owner and manager Philip Henslowe's *Diary* for January 24, 1594, to a new production by Sussex's men of "Titus & Ondronicus" could refer to a new play or one newly revised or newly acquired by the company. Shakespeare's *Titus Andronicus* was thus widely separated in time from the great tragedies; *Romeo and Juliet* is the only other tragedy (excluding the English history plays) of the decade preceding 1599. Moreover, the play may not be entirely Shakespeare's. The first three scenes (Act 1 together with scenes 1 and 2 of Act 2) and the first scene of Act 4 have been plausibly attributed to George Peele. The two dramatists seem to have worked on their separate stints independently, with some resulting discrepancies. Shakespeare was apparently responsible for the play's overall design. Even so, *Titus Andronicus* was thus widely separated in time and in collaborative authorship from the great tragedies that Shakespeare would produce, most of them a decade or more later. How are we to respond to and appraise an apprenticeship in tragedy that is so isolated in terms of artistic career from the mature tragedies that we reckon among his greatest achievements?

Titus Andronicus is studded with bookish references to classical authors—another likely indication of an early date. No other tragedy, and perhaps no other Shakespearean play, reveals such direct evidence of youthful learning. Some of its many untranslated Latin phrases are school children's favorites, such as the *"Integer vitae"* of Horace that is immediately recognized by Chiron. "I read it in the grammar long ago," he says (4.2.23). Classical allusions compare the chief characters of the play with Aeneas and Dido, Queen of Carthage; Hector, King Priam, and Queen Hecuba of Troy; Ajax and Odysseus among the Greeks; Hercules, Prometheus, Orpheus, Coriolanus, Semiramis the siren Queen of Assyria, Pyramus, Cornelia the mother of the Gracchi, Actaeon; and others. Yet these learned references are far from being a mere display of youthful learning; through a controlled and self-conscious artistry, they enable us to explore a tragic world whose moral dimensions are defined in terms of classical literary models. Especially significant are the references to victims of rape and vengeance: Virginia the Roman, killed by her father Virginius to save her from rape; the chaste Lucrece, ravished by Tarquin; Philomel, raped and deprived of her tongue by Tereus, whose name she then reveals by weaving the information into a tapestry; and Procne, her sister and the wife of Tereus, who avenges Philomel by serving Tereus's son ltys to him in a meal.

Titus Andronicus does not record actual historical events. Shakespeare, assisted by Peele, seems to have put it together from a medley of sources, none of which provided a complete narrative model. An eighteenth-century chapbook called *The History of Titus Andronicus*, once thought to give a reliable version of an original to which the dramatists has access, has now been shown to be an expansion of the story based on a ballad of 1594 which in turn was modeled on the extant play, so that this play stands first in the line of succession. The dramatists drew from varied materials. Ovid's *Metamorphoses* gave them a number of legends, especially that of Tereus, Philomel, and Procne. Seneca's *Thyestes* offered in dramatic form a similar tale of vengeance, in which two sons are slain and served to their parent in a grisly banquet. One or even two plays about Titus may have existed prior to the text we have. Even if Shakespeare used such prose and dramatic sources in writing his major portion of the play, however, some scholars believe that one or even two plays about Titus may have existed prior to Shakespeare's and that we can deduce their contributions to his work by examining two later continental plays derived from them: *Tragaedia van Tito Andronico* (German, 1620) and *Aran en Titus* (Dutch, 1641). Possibly one of these earlier plays was the "Titus & Vespacia" entered in Henslowe's *Diary* for April 11, 1592, as acted by Lord Strange's men. Even if the dramatists used such prose and dramatic sources, however, they also knew well the Ovidian and Senecan originals that had inspired them. Elizabethan revenge tragedy, containing some Senecan influences (though those Senecan elements should not be over-stressed), was a strongly formative influence, especially Kyd's *The Spanish Tragedy* (c. 1587). The phenomenal recent stage successes of Marlowe had left their mark: Titus's killing of his son Mutius recalls *Tamburlaine Part II*, and Aaron's Vice-like boasting of wanton villainy recalls *The Jew of Malta*. The dramatists' reading of Virgil is evident not only in repeated references to the tragic love story of Dido and Aeneas but also in his choice of the name Lavinia (*The Aeneid*, Book 7 ff.)

As this sizable list of influences suggests, *Titus Andronicus* remains close to its models, however original it may be in its narrative outline. Although the play anticipates several motifs in Shakespeare's later tragedies—the ingratitude of Rome toward its honored general as in *Coriolanus*, Roman political factionalism as in *Julius Caesar*, infirm old age confronted by human bestiality as in *King Lear*—*Titus Andronicus* is the kind of revenge play one might expect of a gifted young playwright and collaborator in the early 1590s. The successful models for tragic writing in those years were Kyd and Marlowe; Greene, Peele, and others paid these two the flattery of imitation. So, to an extent, did Shakespeare. We can best understand *Titus Andronicus* if we view it as a revenge play in the sensational vein of Shakespeare's immediate predecessors, with substantial assistance by Peele and with generous additions of Ovidian pathos. We should not look to *Titus Andronicus* for that poetic density and complexity of vision we find in later Shakespearean tragedy; as a revenge play, *Titus Andronicus* focuses on violence and horror, and its mood is one of revulsion. The style, too, requires some adjustment in our expectations. Owing much to Kyd, Marlowe, and Ovid, it is replete with rhetorical figures and classical allusions in the manner of Shakespeare's Ovidian poems from the early 1590s, *Venus and Adonis* and *The Rape of Lucrece*. Even if its "early" features are manifest, the style works to good dramatic effect in highly wrought scenes, as when Titus pleads for justice to the unresponsive senators (3.1.1–47) or lays a trap for Tamora and her sons under the guise of his supposed madness (5.2). The seeming incongruity of violent action and elaborately refined metaphor, as in Titus's florid lament for Lavinia's mutilation (3.1.65 ff.), is not, as Eugene Waith has shown (*Shakespeare Survey*, 1957, 39–49), without its purpose, for it evokes pathos on behalf of gruesome suffering in a deliberately Ovidian manner, abstracting and generalizing human torment. As in Ovid, the interest is not in moralizing lessons but in the "transforming power of intense states of emotion."

Violence is an enduring feature of *Titus Andronicus*, and its function must be understood if the play is not to be dismissed as merely hyperbolical in its bloodshed. We are constantly aware of ritual human sacrifice, murder, and maiming, as in Titus's sentencing of Tamora's son Alarbus and his slaying of his own son Mutius, the massacre by Tamora's sons of Bassianus and their ravishing of Lavinia, the subsequent execution of two of Titus's sons wrongfully accused of Bassianus's murder, the cutting off of Titus's hand, the feeding to Tamora of her sons' bodies ground into a fine paste, and still more. Savage mutilation is characteristic of many of these atrocities, especially in the lopping off of hands and tongue. The play's climax is, in the manner of revenge tragedy, a spectacle of blood, with the deaths in rapid succession of Lavinia, Tamora, Titus, and Saturninus. These multiple slaughters cause revulsion in some viewers, such as T. S. Eliot, but to others the violence reveals a pattern and offers its own ethical stance on vengeance. Although we do not sense in this early play the same controlled perspective on human evil as in *Hamlet*, for example, we see that Shakespeare is intensely aware of the conflict between order and disorder. In the final scenes, Aaron the Moor is caught and sentenced to execution, Tamora and Saturninus are slain, Titus's brother Marcus appeals to Roman justice for vindication on the grounds that his family had no alternative, and Titus's last remaining son Lucius vows as the new emperor to "heal Rome's harms and wipe away her woe" (5.3.148). Even if this resolution does not fully satisfy the ethical dilemmas with which the play began, it reveals Shakespeare's disinclination to allow the fulfillment of private vengeance to be the play's ultimate concern. Shakespeare is interested throughout in the ethical problems generated by revenge, and the play's relentless horror may be a commentary on the self-defeating nature of a revenge code. Violence is also integral to the theatrical design of the play; its pattern of vengeance and counter-vengeance seems strikingly modern to us, attuned as we are to the twentieth-century "theater of cruelty" championed by Antonin Artaud.

The first part of *Titus Andronicus* functions to give the avenger a motive for his bloody course of action. Ironically, Titus is himself responsible for setting in motion the events that will overwhelm him. His family, the Andronici, are the first to practice vengeance, a fact that diminishes the sympathy they might later have been able to enjoy as victims and exiles. In fact, it is Lucius, ultimately to become the restorer of political stability, who first demands the ritual slaying of a captive Goth, Tamora's son Alarbus, to appease the spirits of the Andronici slain in battle. Such a demand is understandable in terms of family honor, but it is also vengeful and pagan. Despite the Romans' claim to be superior to the barbarians they fight (see 1.1.379, for example), their acts too often do not justify that claim to moral superiority. This irony is complete when the Gothic Queen Tamora and her sons become the spokespersons for godlike mercy. As Tamora's son Chiron bitterly observes, "Was never Scythia half so barbarous" (1.1.131).

Equally violent and unnatural is Titus's slaying of his own son Mutius for assisting in the abduction of Titus's daughter, Lavinia. This tragic error stems, like the first, from Titus's narrow sense of family honor. Titus has unwisely refused the imperial crown, bestowing it instead on the treacherous Saturninus, and has promised Lavinia as bride to the new emperor, despite her prior betrothal to Saturninus's virtuous rival and brother, Bassianus. Titus's reasons for these actions are never satisfactorily explained, but presumably arise from a misguided if honorable impulse to let others exercise political power while he, the valiant defender of Rome, plays the role of senior statesman. He is also, like King Lear, imperious and paternalistic in his own family, insisting on having his way. When Titus's sons and Bassianus are driven to the expedient of abducting the lady, Titus cannot endure the shame of his violated promise and so kills Mutius in the ensuing melee. Yet, for this sacrifice on

behalf of the Emperor, Titus receives only ingratitude and hostility. Moreover, he has taught Tamora and her sons to seek vengeance.

Once the Andronici become the victims of Tamora and her supporters, they gain in sympathy. They suffer unspeakable atrocities. Hunted down by jeering sadists who amuse themselves through rape and mutilation, the Andronici band together in mutual tribulation and selflessly attempt to ease one another's agony. They discover Rome to be a "wilderness of tigers" (3.1.54) in which the law blindly condemns Titus's innocent sons for the murder of Bassianus. Still, Titus has committed the first barbarism and turns increasingly to barbarism in his desire for vengeance. Because the Andronici are too much like their enemies, the prevailing mood, as in most revenge plays, is more ironic than tragic. There is no strong sense (despite the capture of Aaron) that moral order is restored along with political order. The Andronici are vindicated, and they have gained some wisdom through suffering, but they are still the avengers who gave the first offense.

Equally unsettling is the play's depiction of gender relations. Titus is a patriarchal figure who responds with violence toward his own son when that son challenges his authority to give away his daughter Lavinia to Saturninus. In the play's bloody conclusion, Titus is the slayer of his own daughter as well, lest she "survive her shame" and by her presence continually remind Titus of the disgrace he has suffered by her rape (5.3.41–2). The archaic code of male domination insists that a father's honor is paramount and that his daughter's death is preferable to shameful life even if, as in Lavinia's case, she is wholly innocent and victimized in losing her chastity. (In *The Rape of Lucrece*, an innocent wife must pay the same terrible price to vindicate her husband's honor.) At the opposite end of the spectrum, Tamora personifies a masculine fantasy of the fearsome transgressing female. Because she is both wanton and domineering, her sexuality is intolerable to most noble Romans; she captivates Saturninus and Aaron with her sensual beauty, but ultimately in this play such a dangerous woman must be tricked into the gruesomely appropriate crime of eating her own sons. Roman order is reestablished at last. Even so, its patriarchal ascendancy has been responsible for the carnage to no less an extent than has the more overtly erotic violence of the non-Roman "barbarians" like Tamora, her sons, and Aaron.

Titus Andronicus displays many conventions of the revenge play found earlier in *The Spanish Tragedy*. The avenger, Titus, is a man of high position conscientiously serving the state, like Kyd's Hieronimo, who discovers that the state itself is too corrupt to give him justice for the wrongs done to his family. The evildoers are members of the Emperor's family, protected by their royal connection. Private and public interests clash, and public welfare is the loser. The avenger has difficulty proving the identity of the villains but finds an ingenious way at last (through Lavinia's writing in the sand). Once he becomes the avenger, like Hieronimo, Titus grows as remorseless and canny as his enemies. He becomes a menace to public order, uttering enigmatic threats and blazoning forth the injustices of the state. Verging on true madness, he also employs madness as a cloak for his Machiavellian intrigues. His plotting succeeds in duping Queen Tamora into allowing him to arrange his gruesome banquet. The drama ends, like *The Spanish Tragedy*, in a kind of play-within-the-play, as Tamora's two sons take the roles of Rape and Murder, Tamora, Revenge, and Titus the cook. Playacting turns deadly earnest with a rapid succession of slaughters. Titus and Lavinia, like Hieronimo and Bel-Imperia, do not outlive their act of vengeance.

This conventional pattern accepts revenge as inevitable and consistent according to its own code. As in *The Spanish Tragedy*, where the choric Revenge controls the action for his own sinister purposes and welcomes the suffering of innocents or the collapse of governments as grist for his mill, *Titus Andronicus* portrays a world in which the avenger can act seemingly only through violence. Even Lavinia and Titus's young grandson endorse plotting and murder. Titus practices cunning toward his enemies, vowing to "o'erreach them in their own devices" (5.2.143). Our attention is increasingly drawn to the artistry of the "devices" on both sides. The machinations of Aaron and Tamora demand ingenuity in return. An eye must pay for an eye; the punishment must fit the crime. To be sure, Titus and his family do struggle to understand the moral nature of their universe. "If any power pities wretched tears, / To that I call," prays Titus, lifting his mangled hand toward heaven and imploring divine assistance (3.1.208–9). Repeatedly, the Andronici ask if a divine justice exists, if it cares about savagery among humans, and if that justice will assist the defenseless. "O heavens," asks Marcus, "can you hear a good man groan / And not relent, or not compassion him?" (4.1.124–5). Why should such terrible evils afflict the human race "Unless the gods delight in tragedies?" (line 61). Marcus seeks the identities of his niece's ravishers, hoping that Lavinia will be able to "display at last / What God will have discovered for revenge" (lines 74–5). Is revenge to be God's or humanity's? In part, at least, Marcus sees himself and his family as agents of divine justice, like Hamlet, though Titus's own errors will also require his own destruction. Yet even these questionings about the cosmos are a part of the revenge tradition, for Hieronimo in *The Spanish Tragedy* implores the gods in similar terms. Titus, for all his pleas to the heavens, is ultimately the avenger in a revenge play. He does not, like Hamlet, submit himself to what he takes to be the will of Providence and wait for whatever opportunity heaven will provide. Titus swears an oath of revenge and proceeds with the most gruesome acts imaginable. In his death there is no talk of reconcili-

ation between divine and human will. As the moment of climax approaches, revenge is seen to be a force from hell, from the "infernal kingdom," while true justice is employed "with Jove in heaven" (5.2.30; 4.3.40). Titus is a protagonist suited to a play in which revenge proceeds by its own pitiless rules, in which brutality is the dominant fact of life, and in which violence is the only apparent means of redress. Divine ideas of justice mock humanity's blind attempts at self-governance without offering reassurance and direction.

Titus Andronicus illuminates the nature of evil more than it attempts to transcend evil through human nobility, as in the later tragedies. This distinctive quality is made especially manifest by the play's outward resemblance to *King Lear*. Titus is old, infirm of judgment, and victimized by his own decision to relinquish power to a person whose villainy he does not comprehend. He is, as Lear says of himself, certainly more sinned against than sinning. Titus approaches madness and generalizes in his grief about the omnipresence of murder and ingratitude in nature (3.2.52–78). His reflections on human injustice suggest the immense difficulty of distinguishing illusion from true substance ("Grief has so wrought on him / He takes false shadows for true substances," lines 79–80), a motif of illusion that reappears in the allegorical play-within-the-play. Queen Tamora reveals an innate viciousness and sexual depravity like that of Goneril and Regan. Aaron the Moor, perhaps the first of Shakespeare's gloating Vice-like villains, resembles Edmund in *King Lear* as well as Richard III, Don John (in *Much Ado About Nothing*), and Iago (in *Othello*). *Titus Andronicus* shows us, in embryonic form and close to their sources, many of Shakespeare's later tragic themes and methods.

Aaron the Moor is the most vital character in this early play. Like the Vice of the morality play or like Marlowe's stage Machiavel, Aaron takes delight in pure evil and displays his cunning for the admiration of the audience. Evil to him is "sport," "wit," "stratagem," and, above all, "policy" (5.1.96; 2.3.1; 2.1.104). His malice encompasses all humanity and proceeds from no motive other than the sinister pleasure he takes in devising plots. When he is finally captured, Aaron boasts triumphantly of the extent and variety of his cruel accomplishments:

> Even now I curse the day—and yet, I think,
> Few come within the compass of my curse—
> Wherein I did not some notorious ill,
> As kill a man, or else devise his death,
> Ravish a maid, or plot the way to do it,
> Accuse some innocent and forswear myself,
> Set deadly enmity between two friends,
> Make poor men's cattle break their necks,
> Set fire on barns and haystacks in the night
> And bid the owners quench them with their tears.
> Oft have I digged up dead men from their graves
> And set them upright at their dear friends' door,
> Even when their sorrows almost was forgot. (5.1.125–37)

Through its depiction of evil as both comic and diabolical, this portrait gives us a vivid insight into the origins of a particular type of remorseless, gloating villain that Shakespeare was to develop in his later history plays and tragedies.

The seemingly attractive side to Aaron, his fiercely protective instincts toward his bastard son born of Tamora, is part of the central evil of this play: pride of family turning to violent revenge. Aaron and his son in their blackness of complexion are equated with barbarism, pagan atheism (Aaron scoffs at those who believe in God), and diabolism. Racial issues are thus as painfully explicit as those of gender in this play: Rome claims superiority over black peoples as over the Scythians, and yet the play sees Rome as fatally violent in its patriarchal, sexist, and racist assumptions. Aaron and Tamora are not the moral opposites of Saturninus and his Roman subjects but are, instead, symbolic of the inner darkness and carnality shared by all sorts of people.

As a revenge play, *Titus Andronicus* is theatrically effective. To be appreciated properly, it should be seen or read in these terms, rather than with the expectations we bring to *King Lear*. Shakespeare here presents barbarism and civilization as polar opposites, but he refuses to equate Rome with civilization, and he allows Titus at last no escape from the barbarism that he himself sets in motion. No tragic self-awareness grows out of Titus's humiliation, as it does in *King Lear*, no regret other than for having relinquished power to Saturninus. Instead of tragic self-awareness, we are left with an overpowering impression of the human potential for brutality. This vision is unameliorated. The constant reminder of a better world of justice and compassion merely serves to heighten the play's ironic and futile sense of wasted goodness.

Titus Andronicus

[*Dramatis Personae*

SATURNINUS, *son of the late Emperor of Rome, and afterward declared Emperor*
BASSIANUS, *his brother*

TITUS ANDRONICUS, *a noble Roman, general against the Goths*
LUCIUS,
QUINTUS,
MARTIUS, } *his sons*
MUTIUS,
LAVINIA, *his daughter*
YOUNG LUCIUS, *a* BOY, *Lucius's son*
MARCUS ANDRONICUS, *tribune of the people, and Titus's brother*
PUBLIUS, *Marcus's son*
SEMPRONIUS,
CAIUS, } *Titus's kinsmen*
VALENTINE,

TAMORA, *Queen of the Goths, afterward Empress of Rome*
ALARBUS,
DEMETRIUS, } *her sons*
CHIRON,
AARON, *a Moor, her lover*
NURSE

A Roman CAPTAIN
MESSENGER *to Titus*
CLOWN
AEMILIUS, *a noble Roman*
GOTHS
A Roman LORD
A ROMAN

Senators, Tribunes, Judges, Goths, Soldiers, Attendants, a Child of Aaron and Tamora

SCENE: *Rome, and the country near it*]

[1.1]

[Flourish.] Enter the tribunes and senators aloft; and then enter [below] Saturninus and his followers at one door, and Bassianus and his followers [at the other,] with drums and trumpets.

SATURNINUS

Noble patricians, patrons of my right,
Defend the justice of my cause with arms;
And, countrymen, my loving followers,
Plead my successive title with your swords. 4
I am his firstborn son that was the last 5
That ware the imperial diadem of Rome. 6
Then let my father's honors live in me,
Nor wrong mine age with this indignity. 8

BASSIANUS

Romans, friends, followers, favorers of my right,
If ever Bassianus, Caesar's son,
Were gracious in the eyes of royal Rome, 11
Keep then this passage to the Capitol, 12
And suffer not dishonor to approach
The imperial seat, to virtue consecrate, 14
To justice, continence, and nobility; 15
But let desert in pure election shine, 16
And, Romans, fight for freedom in your choice.

[Enter] Marcus Andronicus, with the crown.

MARCUS

Princes, that strive by factions and by friends
Ambitiously for rule and empery, 19
Know that the people of Rome, for whom we stand
A special party, have by common voice 21
In election for the Roman empery
Chosen Andronicus, surnamèd Pius 23
For many good and great deserts to Rome.
A nobler man, a braver warrior,
Lives not this day within the city walls.
He by the Senate is accited home 27
From weary wars against the barbarous Goths,

That with his sons, a terror to our foes, 29
Hath yoked a nation strong, trained up in arms. 30
Ten years are spent since first he undertook
This cause of Rome, and chastisèd with arms
Our enemies' pride. Five times he hath returned
Bleeding to Rome, bearing his valiant sons
In coffins from the field. 35
And now at last, laden with honor's spoils,
Returns the good Andronicus to Rome,
Renownèd Titus, flourishing in arms. 38
Let us entreat, by honor of his name 39
Whom worthily you would have now succeed, 40
And in the Capitol and Senate's right,
Whom you pretend to honor and adore, 42
That you withdraw you and abate your strength,
Dismiss your followers, and, as suitors should,
Plead your deserts in peace and humbleness.

SATURNINUS

How fair the tribune speaks to calm my thoughts! 46

BASSIANUS

Marcus Andronicus, so I do affy 47
In thy uprightness and integrity,
And so I love and honor thee and thine,
Thy noble brother Titus and his sons,
And her to whom my thoughts are humbled all, 51
Gracious Lavinia, Rome's rich ornament,
That I will here dismiss my loving friends,
And to my fortunes and the people's favor
Commit my cause in balance to be weighed.
Exeunt soldiers [of Bassianus].

SATURNINUS

Friends that have been thus forward in my right,
I thank you all and here dismiss you all,
And to the love and favor of my country
Commit myself, my person, and the cause.
[Exeunt the soldiers of Saturninus.]
Rome, be as just and gracious unto me
As I am confident and kind to thee. 61
Open the gates and let me in.

BASSIANUS

Tribunes, and me, a poor competitor. 63
*[Flourish.] They [Saturninus and Bassianus]
go up into the Senate House.*

Enter a Captain.

1.1. Location: Rome. Before the Capitol. The tomb of the Andronici is provided onstage, possibly as a large property backstage or at a trapdoor.
0.1 *Flourish* trumpet call. **0.2** *aloft* i.e., probably in the gallery, rearstage above the tiring-house, looking down on the main stage. **0.3** *followers* (including soldiers; see *Exeunt soldiers* at lines 55.1 and 59.1) **0.4** *drums and trumpets* drummers and trumpeters. **4 successive title** hereditary title to the succession **5 his . . . that** the firstborn son of him who **6 ware** wore **8 age** seniority. **this indignity** i.e., the challenge of my right by a younger brother. **11 Were gracious** found favor and acceptance **14 consecrate** consecrated **15 continence** self-restraint **16 pure election** free choice, i.e., of the Roman citizens. (Bassianus urges the Romans to let merit, or *desert*, prevail, rather than inherited right.) **17.1 [Enter] . . . crown** (In the Folio text, Marcus enters aloft, but the Quarto version, which makes no mention of this, may have been staged differently. When Marcus awards to Titus a white cloak at lines 185–6 below, the action is more suited to Marcus's being on the main stage, and he could well stay there throughout.) **19 empery** rule (as emperor) **21 A special party** i.e., a representative group specially chosen. (As a tribune, Marcus Andronicus has been elected by the *people of Rome*, line 20, the plebeians, to represent their rights.) **23 Chosen** i.e., nominated. **surnamèd** given the honorary epithet of. **Pius** dutiful, patriotic **27 accited** summoned

29 That who, i.e., Titus **30 yoked** subdued **35 field** (The Quarto follows with three and one-half lines deleted from the Second and Third Quartos and the Folio because they are inconsistent with lines 96–147 below and probably represent a canceled first draft that the printer of the Quarto mistakenly included: "and at this day / To the monument of the Andronici, / Done sacrifice of expiation, / And slain the noblest prisoner of the Goths.") **38 flourishing** eminent **39–40 by . . . succeed** i.e., by the honorable name of him you choose as worthy candidate **42 Whom** which (referring to the right of the Capitol and Senate). **pretend** assert, profess **46 fair** courteously, gently **47 affy** trust **51 all** entirely **61 confident** without suspicion **63 poor competitor** rival of lower rank. (Bassianus is younger brother and thus not in the direct line of inheritance.) **63.2 go up** (The *gates* mentioned in line 62 are presumably a door in the facade of the tiring-house, rearstage, below the gallery. Saturninus and Bassianus presumably exit through this door and ascend inside the tiring-house to the gallery or Senate House, where they reappear with the tribunes and senators.)

CAPTAIN

Romans, make way! The good Andronicus,
Patron of virtue, Rome's best champion,   65
Successful in the battles that he fights,
With honor and with fortune is returned
From where he circumscribèd with his sword   68
And brought to yoke the enemies of Rome.   69

> *Sound drums and trumpets, and then enter two*
> *of Titus' sons, [Martius and Mutius]; and then*
> *two men bearing a coffin covered with black;*
> *then two other sons [Lucius and Quintus]; then*
> *Titus Andronicus; and then Tamora, the Queen*
> *of Goths, and her three sons [Alarbus,] Chiron,*
> *and Demetrius, with Aaron the Moor, and oth-*
> *ers as many as can be. Then set down the coffin,*
> *and Titus speaks.*

TITUS

Hail, Rome, victorious in thy mourning weeds!   70
Lo, as the bark that hath discharged his freight   71
Returns with precious lading to the bay
From whence at first she weighed her anchorage,   73
Cometh Andronicus, bound with laurel boughs,
To re-salute his country with his tears,
Tears of true joy for his return to Rome.
Thou great defender of this Capitol,   77
Stand gracious to the rites that we intend!
Romans, of five-and-twenty valiant sons,
Half of the number that King Priam had,   80
Behold the poor remains, alive and dead.
These that survive let Rome reward with love;
These that I bring unto their latest home,   83
With burial amongst their ancestors.   84
Here Goths have given me leave to sheathe my sword. 85
Titus, unkind and careless of thine own,   86
Why suffer'st thou thy sons, unburied yet,
To hover on the dreadful shore of Styx?   88
Make way to lay them by their brethren.
                                         They open the tomb.
There greet in silence, as the dead are wont,
And sleep in peace, slain in your country's wars!
O sacred receptacle of my joys,
Sweet cell of virtue and nobility,
How many sons hast thou of mine in store
That thou wilt never render to me more!   95

LUCIUS

Give us the proudest prisoner of the Goths,
That we may hew his limbs, and on a pile
Ad manes fratrum sacrifice his flesh   98
Before this earthy prison of their bones,

That so the shadows be not unappeased,   100
Nor we disturbed with prodigies on earth.   101

TITUS

I give him you, the noblest that survives,
The eldest son of this distressèd queen.

TAMORA [*kneeling*]

Stay, Roman brethren! Gracious conqueror,   104
Victorious Titus, rue the tears I shed,
A mother's tears in passion for her son;   106
And if thy sons were ever dear to thee,
Oh, think my son to be as dear to me!
Sufficeth not that we are brought to Rome   109
To beautify thy triumphs, and return   110
Captive to thee and to thy Roman yoke,
But must my sons be slaughtered in the streets
For valiant doings in their country's cause?
Oh, if to fight for king and commonweal
Were piety in thine, it is in these.
Andronicus, stain not thy tomb with blood!   116
Wilt thou draw near the nature of the gods?
Draw near them then in being merciful.
Sweet mercy is nobility's true badge.
Thrice noble Titus, spare my firstborn son.

TITUS [*raising her*]

Patient yourself, madam, and pardon me.   121
These are their brethren, whom your Goths beheld   122
Alive and dead, and for their brethren slain
Religiously they ask a sacrifice.
To this your son is marked, and die he must
T'appease their groaning shadows that are gone.

LUCIUS

Away with him! And make a fire straight,   127
And with our swords, upon a pile of wood,
Let's hew his limbs till they be clean consumed.   129
                    Exeunt Titus' sons with Alarbus.

TAMORA

Oh, cruel, irreligious piety!

CHIRON

Was never Scythia half so barbarous.   131

DEMETRIUS

Oppose not Scythia to ambitious Rome.   132
Alarbus goes to rest, and we survive
To tremble under Titus' threat'ning look.
Then, madam, stand resolved, but hope withal   135
The selfsame gods that armed the Queen of Troy   136
With opportunity of sharp revenge
Upon the Thracian tyrant in his tent
May favor Tamora, the Queen of Goths—

---

100 shadows shades, ghosts   **101 prodigies** omens, portents of ill
104 s.d. kneeling (In a drawing of Act 1 of *Titus,* done in about 1595
by Henry Peacham, Tamora's sons are also shown kneeling.)
106 passion grief   **109 Sufficeth not** Doesn't it suffice   **110 triumphs**
(1) successes (2) entry procession in honor of victory.   **return** i.e.,
accompany your return   **116 tomb** family tomb   **121 Patient** Calm
122 their brethren i.e., the brothers of those who have been slain
127 straight at once   **129 clean** wholly   **131 Scythia** a region north
of the Black Sea; its people were notorious for their savagery
132 Oppose Contrast   **135 withal** besides   **136 Queen of Troy**
Hecuba, wife of Priam, who after the fall of Troy was carried to
Greece as a slave; there she found occasion to avenge the death of her
son Polydorus by killing the two sons of the murderer, Polymnestor,
King of Thrace

---

65 Patron sponsor and pattern   **68 circumscribèd** restrained, confined
69.5 *Titus Andronicus* (Titus may enter drawn in a chariot; he refers to
his chariot in line 250.)   **70 weeds** garments.   **71 bark** sailing vessel.
his its   **73 anchorage** anchors   **77 Thou** i.e., Jupiter Capitolinus
80 King Priam King of Troy at the time of its fall; he had fifty sons
83 latest final   **84 With** i.e., let Rome reward with   **85 Here . . . sword**
i.e., The defeated Goths have been so good as to let me put up my
weapon. (Said ironically; the Goths had no choice.)   **86 unkind** deficient in natural feeling   **88 Styx** river surrounding Hades across which
souls might not cross until they had received proper burial.   **95 more**
again.   **98 *Ad manes fratrum*** to the departed spirits of (our) brothers

When Goths were Goths and Tamora was queen—
To quit the bloody wrongs upon her foes.   141

*Enter the sons of Andronicus again [with their
swords bloody].*

LUCIUS
See, lord and father, how we have performed
Our Roman rites. Alarbus' limbs are lopped,
And entrails feed the sacrificing fire,
Whose smoke, like incense, doth perfume the sky.
Remaineth naught but to inter our brethren
And with loud 'larums welcome them to Rome.   147

TITUS
Let it be so, and let Andronicus
Make this his latest farewell to their souls.   149

Sound trumpets, and lay the coffin in the tomb.

In peace and honor rest you here, my sons;
Rome's readiest champions, repose you here in rest,
Secure from worldly chances and mishaps!
Here lurks no treason, here no envy swells,
Here grow no damnèd drugs; here are no storms,   154
No noise, but silence and eternal sleep.
In peace and honor rest you here, my sons!

Enter Lavinia.

LAVINIA
In peace and honor live Lord Titus long;
My noble lord and father, live in fame!
Lo, at this tomb my tributary tears   159
I render for my brethren's obsequies,   160
And at thy feet I kneel, with tears of joy   *[kneeling]*
Shed on this earth for thy return to Rome.
Oh, bless me here with thy victorious hand,
Whose fortunes Rome's best citizens applaud!

TITUS
Kind Rome, that hast thus lovingly reserved
The cordial of mine age to glad my heart!   166
Lavinia, live; outlive thy father's days
And fame's eternal date, for virtue's praise!   168
                                           [She rises.]

MARCUS
Long live Lord Titus, my belovèd brother,   169
Gracious triumpher in the eyes of Rome!

TITUS
Thanks, gentle tribune, noble brother Marcus.

MARCUS
And welcome, nephews, from successful wars,
You that survive, and you that sleep in fame!
Fair lords, your fortunes are alike in all,   174

That in your country's service drew your swords;
But safer triumph is this funeral pomp
That hath aspired to Solon's happiness,   177
And triumphs over chance in honor's bed.   178
Titus Andronicus, the people of Rome,
Whose friend in justice thou hast ever been,
Send thee by me, their tribune and their trust,   181
This palliament of white and spotless hue,   182
And name thee in election for the empire   183
With these our late-deceasèd emperor's sons.
Be *candidatus* then, and put it on,   185
And help to set a head on headless Rome.
                          [He offers Titus a white robe.]

TITUS
A better head her glorious body fits
Than his that shakes for age and feebleness.
What, should I don this robe and trouble you?
Be chosen with proclamations today,
Tomorrow yield up rule, resign my life,
And set abroad new business for you all?   192
Rome, I have been thy soldier forty years,
And led my country's strength successfully,
And buried one-and-twenty valiant sons,
Knighted in field, slain manfully in arms,
In right and service of their noble country.   197
Give me a staff of honor for mine age,
But not a scepter to control the world.
Upright he held it, lords, that held it last.

MARCUS
Titus, thou shalt obtain and ask the empery.   201

SATURNINUS
Proud and ambitious tribune, canst thou tell?   202

TITUS   Patience, Prince Saturninus.

SATURNINUS   Romans, do me right.
Patricians, draw your swords, and sheathe them not
Till Saturninus be Rome's emperor.
Andronicus, would thou were shipped to hell
Rather than rob me of the people's hearts!

LUCIUS
Proud Saturnine, interrupter of the good
That noble-minded Titus means to thee!

TITUS *[to Saturninus]*
Content thee, prince. I will restore to thee
The people's hearts, and wean them from
    themselves.   212

BASSIANUS
Andronicus, I do not flatter thee,
But honor thee, and will do till I die.
My faction if thou strengthen with thy friends,
I will most thankful be; and thanks to men
Of noble minds is honorable meed.   217

---

141 **quit** requite   147 **'larums** trumpet calls   149.1 *the coffin*
(Although there is presumably more than one dead son, the staging
may have relied on one coffin for the sake of economy.)   154 **drugs**
poisonous plants   159 **tributary** paid in tribute   160 **obsequies** acts
performed in honor of the dead   166 **cordial** restorative; or comfort,
pleasure   168 **And . . . praise!** and, as a tribute to your virtue, may
you outlive fame itself!   169 MARCUS (Many editors have Marcus
speak from above, since the Folio stage direction earlier at line 17.1–2
specifies that he is to enter *"aloft,"* but the Quarto version makes no
mention of this. The present edition keeps him on the main stage
throughout.)   174 **Fair . . . all** You noble lords who have survived,
you share a common good fortune in having been victorious

177 **Solon's happiness** i.e., the happiness defined by Solon (a Greek
sage and lawgiver): that no man may be called happy until after his
death   178 **And . . . bed** and triumphs over the vicissitudes of fortune in an honorable grave.   181 **trust** trusted representative
182 **palliament** candidate's gown or cloak   183 **in election** i.e., as a
candidate   185 ***candidatus*** a candidate. (Literally, one clad in white.)
192 **abroad** i.e., on foot   197 **In . . . of** serving the just cause of
201 **obtain and ask** obtain simply by asking   202 **canst thou tell?** i.e.,
that's what you think.   212 **from themselves** i.e., from their present
intention.   217 **meed** reward.

TITUS
    People of Rome, and people's tribunes here,
    I ask your voices and your suffrages.   219
    Will ye bestow them friendly on Andronicus?

TRIBUNES
    To gratify the good Andronicus
    And gratulate his safe return to Rome,   222
    The people will accept whom he admits.

TITUS
    Tribunes, I thank you, and this suit I make:
    That you create our emperor's eldest son,   225
    Lord Saturnine, whose virtues will, I hope,
    Reflect on Rome as Titan's rays on earth,   227
    And ripen justice in this commonweal.
    Then, if you will elect by my advice,
    Crown him and say, "Long live our emperor!"

MARCUS
    With voices and applause of every sort,
    Patricians and plebeians, we create
    Lord Saturninus Rome's great emperor,
    And say, "Long live our Emperor Saturnine!"   234
          [*Saturninus is crowned. A long flourish till they*
                           come down.]

SATURNINUS
    Titus Andronicus, for thy favors done
    To us in our election this day,
    I give thee thanks in part of thy deserts,   237
    And will with deeds requite thy gentleness.   238
    And, for an onset, Titus, to advance   239
    Thy name and honorable family,
    Lavinia will I make my empress,
    Rome's royal mistress, mistress of my heart,
    And in the sacred Pantheon her espouse.   243
    Tell me, Andronicus, doth this motion please thee? 244

TITUS
    It doth, my worthy lord, and in this match
    I hold me highly honored of Your Grace.   246
    And here in sight of Rome to Saturnine,
    King and commander of our commonweal,
    The wide world's emperor, do I consecrate
    My sword, my chariot, and my prisoners,
    Presents well worthy Rome's imperious lord.   251
    Receive them, then, the tribute that I owe,
    Mine honor's ensigns humbled at thy feet.   253
               [*A tribute is laid at Saturninus' feet.*]

SATURNINUS
    Thanks, noble Titus, father of my life!
    How proud I am of thee and of thy gifts
    Rome shall record, and when I do forget
    The least of these unspeakable deserts,   257
    Romans, forget your fealty to me.

TITUS [*to Tamora*]
    Now, madam, are you prisoner to an emperor,
    To him that for your honor and your state
    Will use you nobly and your followers.

SATURNINUS [*aside*]
    A goodly lady, trust me, of the hue
    That I would choose, were I to choose anew.—
    Clear up, fair queen, that cloudy countenance.
    Though chance of war hath wrought this change of
        cheer,   265
    Thou com'st not to be made a scorn in Rome.
    Princely shall be thy usage every way.
    Rest on my word, and let not discontent   268
    Daunt all your hopes. Madam, he comforts you
    Can make you greater than the Queen of Goths. 270
    Lavinia, you are not displeased with this?

LAVINIA
    Not I, my lord, sith true nobility   272
    Warrants these words in princely courtesy.   273

SATURNINUS
    Thanks, sweet Lavinia.—Romans, let us go.
    Ransomless here we set our prisoners free.
    Proclaim our honors, lords, with trump and drum.
          [*Tamora, Chiron, Demetrius, and Aaron are*
        released. Sound drums and trumpets. Saturninus
                     starts to leave, attended.]

BASSIANUS [*seizing Lavinia*]
    Lord Titus, by your leave, this maid is mine.

TITUS
    How, sir? Are you in earnest then, my lord?

BASSIANUS
    Ay, noble Titus, and resolved withal
    To do myself this reason and this right.

MARCUS
    Suum cuique is our Roman justice.   281
    This prince in justice seizeth but his own.

LUCIUS [*joining Bassianus*]
    And that he will and shall, if Lucius live.

TITUS
    Traitors, avaunt! Where is the Emperor's guard? 284
    Treason, my lord! Lavinia is surprised!   285

SATURNINUS
    Surprised? By whom?

BASSIANUS   By him that justly may
    Bear his betrothed from all the world away.

MUTIUS
    Brothers, help to convey her hence away,
    And with my sword I'll keep this door safe.
          [*Exeunt Bassianus, Marcus, Lucius, Quintus,*
                    and Martius, with Lavinia.]

TITUS [*to Saturninus*]
    Follow, my lord, and I'll soon bring her back.

219 voices votes.   **suffrages** votes.   **222 gratulate** salute, rejoice in   **225 create** i.e., elect   **227 Titan's** (Helios, the sun god, was a descendant of the Titans.)   **234.2** *come down* (This stage direction is in the Folio.)   **237 in** as   **238 gentleness** nobleness.   **239 onset** beginning   **243 Pantheon** Roman temple dedicated to all the gods   **244 motion** proposal   **246 hold me** consider myself.   **of** by   **251 imperious** imperial   **253 ensigns** tokens   **257 unspeakable** inexpressible

265 cheer countenance   **268 Rest** Rely   **270 Can** who can   **272 sith** since   **273 Warrants** justifies   **281** *Suum cuique* To each his own   **284–5 Traitors . . . surprised!** (Evidently, Saturninus, starting to leave, has not quite realized what has happened, and his guard, accompanying him, has been caught napping. *Surprised* means "taken, seized.")

MUTIUS [*guarding the door*]
    My lord, you pass not here.
TITUS   What, villain boy?
    Barr'st me my way in Rome?   [*He stabs Mutius.*]
MUTIUS   Help, Lucius, help!   292
                                [*He dies.*]
    [*During the fray, exeunt Saturninus, Tamora,*
          Demetrius, Chiron, and Aaron.]

    [*Enter Lucius.*]

LUCIUS [*to Titus*]
    My lord, you are unjust; and more than so,
    In wrongful quarrel you have slain your son.
TITUS
    Nor thou nor he are any sons of mine.   295
    My sons would never so dishonor me.
    Traitor, restore Lavinia to the Emperor.
LUCIUS
    Dead, if you will, but not to be his wife
    That is another's lawful promised love.   [*Exit.*] 299

    Enter aloft the Emperor [*Saturninus*] *with*
    Tamora and her two sons and Aaron the Moor.

SATURNINUS
    No, Titus, no. The Emperor needs her not,
    Nor her, nor thee, nor any of thy stock.
    I'll trust by leisure him that mocks me once;   302
    Thee never, nor thy traitorous haughty sons,
    Confederates all thus to dishonor me.
    Was none in Rome to make a stale   305
    But Saturnine? Full well, Andronicus,
    Agree these deeds with that proud brag of thine
    That said'st I begged the empire at thy hands.
TITUS
    Oh, monstrous! What reproachful words are these?
SATURNINUS
    But go thy ways; go, give that changing piece   310
    To him that flourished for her with his sword.   311
    A valiant son-in-law thou shalt enjoy,
    One fit to bandy with thy lawless sons,   313
    To ruffle in the commonwealth of Rome.   314
TITUS
    These words are razors to my wounded heart.
SATURNINUS
    And therefore, lovely Tamora, Queen of Goths,
    That like the stately Phoebe 'mongst her nymphs   317
    Dost overshine the gallant'st dames of Rome,

If thou be pleased with this my sudden choice,
Behold, I choose thee, Tamora, for my bride,
And will create thee Empress of Rome.
Speak, Queen of Goths, dost thou applaud my choice?
And here I swear by all the Roman gods,
Sith priest and holy water are so near,
And tapers burn so bright, and everything
In readiness for Hymenaeus stand,   326
I will not re-salute the streets of Rome,
Or climb my palace, till from forth this place   328
I lead espoused my bride along with me.
TAMORA
    And here in sight of heaven to Rome I swear,
    If Saturnine advance the Queen of Goths,
    She will a handmaid be to his desires,
    A loving nurse, a mother to his youth.
SATURNINUS
    Ascend, fair queen, Pantheon. Lords, accompany
    Your noble emperor and his lovely bride,
    Sent by the heavens for Prince Saturnine,
    Whose wisdom hath her fortune conquerèd.   337
    There shall we consummate our spousal rites.   338
                Exeunt omnes [*except Titus*].
TITUS
    I am not bid to wait upon this bride.   339
    Titus, when wert thou wont to walk alone,
    Dishonored thus and challengèd of wrongs?   341

    Enter Marcus and Titus' sons [*Lucius,*
    Quintus, and Martius].

MARCUS
    Oh, Titus, see, oh, see what thou hast done!
    In a bad quarrel slain a virtuous son.
TITUS
    No, foolish tribune, no; no son of mine,
    Nor thou, nor these, confederates in the deed
    That hath dishonored all our family—
    Unworthy brother and unworthy sons!
LUCIUS
    But let us give him burial as becomes;   348
    Give Mutius burial with our brethren.
TITUS
    Traitors, away! He rests not in this tomb.
    This monument five hundred years hath stood,
    Which I have sumptuously re-edified.   352
    Here none but soldiers and Rome's servitors   353
    Repose in fame, none basely slain in brawls.
    Bury him where you can, he comes not here.
MARCUS
    My lord, this is impiety in you.
    My nephew Mutius' deeds do plead for him;
    He must be buried with his brethren.

292.2–3 During . . . Aaron (Evidently Saturninus, realizing he has been dishonored by the seizure of Lavinia and having decided in any case that he prefers Tamora, lines 262–3, decides to ascend to the Capitol and proclaim forthwith his choice of Tamora and repudiation of Lavinia.)   **295 Nor** Neither. (Also in line 301.)   **299 s.d. Exit** (Lucius may take Mutius's body with him and return with it at line 341, but the presence of the dead body onstage from lines 299 to 341 would not be an inappropriate horror.)   **302 by leisure** not any time soon, barely   **305 Was . . . stale** Was there no one in Rome to be made a laughing-stock   **310 changing piece** fickle wench   **311 flourished . . . sword** brandished his sword to obtain her.   **313 bandy** brawl   **314 ruffle** swagger   **317 Phoebe** Diana, goddess of the hunt and of chastity, and associated with the moon. The irony of linking chastity with Tamora soon becomes apparent in the play.

326 Hymenaeus Roman god of marriage   **328 climb** ascend the stairs to   **337 Whose . . . conquerèd** i.e., whose wise choice to be my queen has overcome her ill fortune of being conquered in battle.   **338.1 omnes** all.   **339 bid** invited   **341 challengèd** accused   **348 becomes** is fitting   **352 re-edified** rebuilt.   **353 servitors** armed defenders

MARTIUS
And shall.
QUINTUS   Or him we will accompany.
TITUS
"And shall"? What villain was it spake that word?
MARTIUS
He that would vouch it in any place but here.   361
TITUS
What, would you bury him in my despite?
MARCUS
No, noble Titus, but entreat of thee
To pardon Mutius and to bury him.
TITUS
Marcus, even thou hast struck upon my crest,   365
And, with these boys, mine honor thou hast wounded.
My foes I do repute you every one.
So trouble me no more, but get you gone.
QUINTUS
He is not with himself. Let us withdraw.   369
MARTIUS
Not I, till Mutius' bones be buried.
          The brother [Marcus] and the sons kneel.
MARCUS
Brother, for in that name doth nature plead—
MARTIUS
Father, and in that name doth nature speak—
TITUS
Speak thou no more, if all the rest will speed.   373
MARCUS
Renownèd Titus, more than half my soul—
LUCIUS
Dear father, soul and substance of us all—
MARCUS
Suffer thy brother Marcus to inter   376
His noble nephew here in virtue's nest,
That died in honor and Lavinia's cause.
Thou art a Roman; be not barbarous.
The Greeks upon advice did bury Ajax,   380
That slew himself, and wise Laertes' son
Did graciously plead for his funerals.   382
Let not young Mutius, then, that was thy joy,
Be barred his entrance here.
TITUS   Rise, Marcus, rise.
          [They rise.]
The dismal'st day is this that e'er I saw,
To be dishonored by my sons in Rome!
Well, bury him, and bury me the next.
          They put him [Mutius] in the tomb.

LUCIUS
There lie thy bones, sweet Mutius, with thy friends,
Till we with trophies do adorn thy tomb.   389
          They all kneel.
ALL
No man shed tears for noble Mutius;
He lives in fame that died in virtue's cause.   391
          [They rise.] Exeunt all but Marcus and Titus.
MARCUS
My lord, to step out of these dreary dumps,   392
How comes it that the subtle Queen of Goths
Is of a sudden thus advanced in Rome?
TITUS
I know not, Marcus, but I know it is—
Whether by device or no, the heavens can tell.   396
Is she not then beholding to the man   397
That brought her for this high good turn so far?
MARCUS
Yes, and will nobly him remunerate.   399

          [Flourish.] Enter the Emperor [Saturninus],
          Tamora, and her two sons, with [Aaron] the
          Moor, at one door. Enter at the other door
          Bassianus and Lavinia, with others, [Lucius,
          Martius, and Quintus].

SATURNINUS
So, Bassianus, you have played your prize.   400
God give you joy, sir, of your gallant bride!
BASSIANUS
And you of yours, my lord! I say no more,
Nor wish no less; and so I take my leave.
SATURNINUS
Traitor, if Rome have law or we have power,   404
Thou and thy faction shall repent this rape.   405
BASSIANUS
"Rape" call you it, my lord, to seize my own,
My true-betrothèd love and now my wife?
But let the laws of Rome determine all;
Meanwhile am I possessed of that is mine.   409
SATURNINUS
'Tis good, sir. You are very short with us,
But if we live we'll be as sharp with you.
BASSIANUS
My lord, what I have done, as best I may
Answer I must, and shall do with my life.
Only thus much I give Your Grace to know:
By all the duties that I owe to Rome,
This noble gentleman, Lord Titus here,
Is in opinion and in honor wronged,   417

---

361 vouch . . . here maintain what I said anywhere but in this sacred place.   365 my crest the crest of my helmet (symbolizing the honor of my name)   369 not with himself distracted.   373 if . . . speed if all is to succeed, or, possibly, if you remaining sons do not wish to be slain like Mutius.   376 Suffer Permit   380 advice deliberation. Ajax Greek hero of the Trojan War who went mad because the armor of Achilles was awarded to Odysseus, slew a flock of sheep deludedly thinking them Greeks, and later committed suicide in shame; he was refused burial until *Laertes' son*, line 381, Odysseus, successfully pleaded for his funeral rites   382 funerals funeral obsequies. (Compare French *funerailles*.)

389 trophies memorials   389.1 *They all kneel* (Some editors think it unlikely that Titus joins his sons in kneeling or in saying lines 390–1, but Titus has relented and is not without feeling for the son he has slain.)   391.1 *Exeunt* (Perhaps the sons go off in order to accompany Bassianus' entry at line 399, or they may simply stand aside.)   392 dumps melancholy   396 device scheming   397 beholding beholden   399 Yes . . . remunerate (Said sarcastically; Tamora will show her gratitude in physical ways.)   400 played your prize played and won your bout (as in fencing).   404 we I. (The royal plural; also at lines 410–11, etc.)   405 rape forcible seizure.   409 that that which   417 opinion reputation

That, in the rescue of Lavinia,
With his own hand did slay his youngest son
In zeal to you, and highly moved to wrath
To be controlled in that he frankly gave.   421
Receive him, then, to favor, Saturnine,
That hath expressed himself in all his deeds
A father and a friend to thee and Rome.

TITUS
Prince Bassianus, leave to plead my deeds.   425
'Tis thou, and those, that have dishonored me.   426
Rome and the righteous heavens be my judge
How I have loved and honored Saturnine!
                                    [*He kneels.*]

TAMORA [*to Saturninus*]
My worthy lord, if ever Tamora
Were gracious in those princely eyes of thine,
Then hear me speak indifferently for all;   431
And at my suit, sweet, pardon what is past.

SATURNINUS
What, madam? Be dishonored openly,
And basely put it up without revenge?   434

TAMORA
Not so, my lord. The gods of Rome forfend   435
I should be author to dishonor you!   436
But on mine honor dare I undertake   437
For good Lord Titus' innocence in all,
Whose fury not dissembled speaks his griefs.   439
Then at my suit look graciously on him;
Lose not so noble a friend on vain suppose,   441
Nor with sour looks afflict his gentle heart.
[*Aside to Saturninus*] My lord, be ruled by me, be won
    at last;
Dissemble all your griefs and discontents.
You are but newly planted in your throne;
Lest then the people, and patricians too,
Upon a just survey take Titus' part   447
And so supplant you for ingratitude,
Which Rome reputes to be a heinous sin,
Yield at entreats; and then let me alone.   450
I'll find a day to massacre them all
And raze their faction and their family,
The cruel father and his traitorous sons
To whom I suèd for my dear son's life,
And make them know what 'tis to let a queen
Kneel in the streets and beg for grace in vain.—
[*Aloud*] Come, come, sweet Emperor; come,
    Andronicus;
Take up this good old man, and cheer the heart   458
That dies in tempest of thy angry frown.

SATURNINUS
Rise, Titus, rise. My empress hath prevailed.

TITUS [*rising*]
I thank Your Majesty and her, my lord.
These words, these looks, infuse new life in me.

TAMORA
Titus, I am incorporate in Rome,   463
A Roman now adopted happily,   464
And must advise the Emperor for his good.
This day all quarrels die, Andronicus.   466
And let it be mine honor, good my lord,
That I have reconciled your friends and you.
For you, Prince Bassianus, I have passed
My word and promise to the Emperor
That you will be more mild and tractable.
And fear not, lords, and you, Lavinia:
By my advice, all humbled on your knees,
You shall ask pardon of His Majesty.   474
        [*Lucius, Martius, Quintus, and Lavinia kneel.*]

LUCIUS
We do, and vow to heaven and to His Highness
That what we did was mildly as we might,   476
Tend'ring our sister's honor and our own.   477

MARCUS [*kneeling*]
That, on mine honor, here do I protest.   478

SATURNINUS [*turning away*]
Away, and talk not! Trouble us no more.

TAMORA
Nay, nay, sweet Emperor, we must all be friends.
The tribune and his nephews kneel for grace;
I will not be denied. Sweetheart, look back.

SATURNINUS
Marcus, for thy sake and thy brother's here,
And at my lovely Tamora's entreats,
I do remit these young men's heinous faults.
Stand up.   [*The Andronici rise.*]
Lavinia, though you left me like a churl,
I found a friend, and sure as death I swore
I would not part a bachelor from the priest.
Come; if the Emperor's court can feast two brides,
You are my guest, Lavinia, and your friends.
This day shall be a love-day, Tamora.   492

TITUS
Tomorrow, an it please Your Majesty   493
To hunt the panther and the hart with me,
With horn and hound we'll give Your Grace *bonjour*.   495

SATURNINUS
Be it so, Titus, and gramercy too.   496
        Exeunt. Sound trumpets. Manet [Aaron the] Moor.

❖

421 To . . . gave i.e., to be restrained from freely bestowing Lavinia
on you, Saturninus.   425 leave to plead cease pleading on behalf
of   426 those those sons of mine   431 indifferently impartially
434 put it up put up with it   435 forfend forbid   436 be author
propose a way   437 undertake assert, vouch   439 Whose . . .
griefs whose unconcealed anger gives testimonial to his grievances.   441 vain suppose idle supposition   447 survey examination   450 at entreats to entreaty.   let me alone leave it to me.
458 Take up raise from kneeling

463 am incorporate in have been admitted to the fellowship of
464 happily (1) fortunately (2) opportunely   466 all let all
474.1 Lucius . . . kneel (Perhaps Bassianus kneels also, though his pardon seems to have been assured at line 469.)   476–7 was mildly . . .
Tend'ring was done as mildly as we could manage, taking into
account the need to defend   478 That . . . protest I acted on the same
honorable impulse.   492 love-day (1) day appointed to settle
disputes (2) day for love   493 an if   495 bonjour good day.
496 gramercy great thanks.   496.1 Manet He remains onstage. (The
Folio has Aaron exiting with the rest and reentering. The tomb of Act
1 is possibly concealed by a curtain backstage.)

[2.1]

AARON
>Now climbeth Tamora Olympus' top,   1
>Safe out of fortune's shot, and sits aloft,
>Secure of thunder's crack or lightning flash,   3
>Advanced above pale envy's threatening reach.
>As when the golden sun salutes the morn
>And, having gilt the ocean with his beams,
>Gallops the zodiac in his glistering coach   7
>And overlooks the highest-peering hills,   8
>So Tamora.
>Upon her wit doth earthly honor wait,   10
>And virtue stoops and trembles at her frown.   11
>Then, Aaron, arm thy heart and fit thy thoughts
>To mount aloft with thy imperial mistress,
>And mount her pitch whom thou in triumph long   14
>Hast prisoner held, fettered in amorous chains
>And faster bound to Aaron's charming eyes   16
>Than is Prometheus tied to Caucasus.   17
>Away with slavish weeds and servile thoughts!   18
>I will be bright, and shine in pearl and gold,
>To wait upon this new-made empress.
>To wait, said I? To wanton with this queen,
>This goddess, this Semiramis, this nymph,   22
>This siren that will charm Rome's Saturnine
>And see his shipwreck and his commonweal's.
>Holla! What storm is this?   25

Enter Chiron and Demetrius, braving.

DEMETRIUS
>Chiron, thy years wants wit, thy wits wants edge   26
>And manners, to intrude where I am graced   27
>And may, for aught thou knowest, affected be.   28
CHIRON
>Demetrius, thou dost overween in all,   29
>And so in this, to bear me down with braves.   30
>'Tis not the difference of a year or two
>Makes me less gracious or thee more fortunate;
>I am as able and as fit as thou
>To serve, and to deserve my mistress' grace,
>And that my sword upon thee shall approve,   35
>And plead my passions for Lavinia's love.
AARON [*aside*]
>Clubs, clubs! These lovers will not keep the peace.   37

DEMETRIUS
>Why, boy, although our mother, unadvised,   38
>Gave you a dancing-rapier by your side,   39
>Are you so desperate grown to threat your friends?   40
>Go to! Have your lath glued within your sheath   41
>Till you know better how to handle it.
CHIRON
>Meanwhile, sir, with the little skill I have,
>Full well shalt thou perceive how much I dare.
DEMETRIUS
>Ay, boy, grow ye so brave?   *They draw.*
AARON [*coming forward*]   Why, how now, lords?
>So near the Emperor's palace dare ye draw   46
>And maintain such a quarrel openly?
>Full well I wot the ground of all this grudge.   48
>I would not for a million of gold
>The cause were known to them it most concerns,
>Nor would your noble mother for much more
>Be so dishonored in the court of Rome.
>For shame, put up.
DEMETRIUS   Not I, till I have sheathed   53
>My rapier in his bosom, and withal   54
>Thrust those reproachful speeches down his throat
>That he hath breathed in my dishonor here.
CHIRON
>For that I am prepared and full resolved,
>Foul-spoken coward, that thund'rest with thy tongue
>And with thy weapon nothing dar'st perform!
AARON   Away, I say!
>Now, by the gods that warlike Goths adore,
>This petty brabble will undo us all.   62
>Why, lords, and think you not how dangerous
>It is to jet upon a prince's right?   64
>What, is Lavinia then become so loose,
>Or Bassianus so degenerate,
>That for her love such quarrels may be broached   67
>Without controlment, justice, or revenge?   68
>Young lords, beware! And should the Empress know
>This discord's ground, the music would not please.   70
CHIRON
>I care not, I, knew she and all the world.   71
>I love Lavinia more than all the world.
DEMETRIUS
>Youngling, learn thou to make some meaner choice.   73
>Lavinia is thine elder brother's hope.
AARON
>Why, are ye mad? Or know ye not in Rome
>How furious and impatient they be,
>And cannot brook competitors in love?   77

2.1. Location: Scene continues. Aaron remains onstage.
1 Olympus home of the Greek gods   **3 of** from   **7 Gallops** gallops through   **8 overlooks** looks down on from on high   **10 wit** intelligence. **wait** attend   **11 virtue . . . frown** her displeasure makes even virtue (or, the virtuous) afraid.   **14 pitch** height to which a falcon soars before descending on its prey. (The image of *mounting* has sexual connotations also.)   **16 charming** exerting a magic spell   **17 Prometheus** Titan who stole fire from the chariot of the sun and gave it to humanity; as punishment, Zeus fastened him to a mountain in the Caucasus and sent a vulture to feast on his liver   **18 weeds** garments   **22 Semiramis** mythical Queen of Assyria, famous for her cruelty and lust   **25.1 *braving*** defying (each other).   **26 wants** lack. **edge** sharpness, incisiveness   **27 graced** favored   **28 affected** loved   **29 overween** arrogantly presume   **30 braves** threats   **35 approve** prove   **37 Clubs, clubs!** (A cry summoning the apprentices of London to join in or to suppress a riot or rebellion.)

38 unadvised ill-advisedly   **39 a dancing-rapier** an ornamental weapon worn in dancing   **40 to** as to   **41 Go to** (An expression of impatience.) **lath** counterfeit stage weapon of wood   **46 So . . . palace** (It was usually against the law to draw a sword in the presence of the King or near his royal residence. See also line 64.)   **48 wot** know   **53 put up** sheathe your swords.   **54 withal** besides   **62 brabble** quarrel, brawl   **64 jet** encroach   **67 broached** begun, set flowing   **68 controlment** restraint   **70 ground** basis. (With a pun on the musical meaning "bass upon which a melody is constructed.")   **71 knew she** if she knew   **73 meaner** of lower degree   **77 brook** endure

I tell you, lords, you do but plot your deaths
By this device.
CHIRON   Aaron, a thousand deaths
Would I propose to achieve her whom I love.   80
AARON
To achieve her? How?
DEMETRIUS   Why makes thou it so strange?   81
She is a woman, therefore may be wooed;
She is a woman, therefore may be won;
She is Lavinia, therefore must be loved.
What, man, more water glideth by the mill
Than wots the miller of, and easy it is   86
Of a cut loaf to steal a shive, we know.   87
Though Bassianus be the Emperor's brother,
Better than he have worn Vulcan's badge.   89
AARON [*aside*]
Ay, and as good as Saturninus may.
DEMETRIUS
Then why should he despair that knows to court it   91
With words, fair looks, and liberality?
What, hast not thou full often struck a doe
And borne her cleanly by the keeper's nose?   94
AARON
Why then, it seems some certain snatch or so   95
Would serve your turns.
CHIRON   Ay, so the turn were served.   96
DEMETRIUS
Aaron, thou hast hit it.
AARON   Would you had hit it too!   97
Then should not we be tired with this ado.
Why, hark ye, hark ye, and are you such fools
To square for this? Would it offend you then   100
That both should speed?   101
CHIRON
Faith, not me.
DEMETRIUS   Nor me, so I were one.   102
AARON
For shame, be friends, and join for that you jar.   103
'Tis policy and stratagem must do   104
That you affect, and so must you resolve   105
That what you cannot as you would achieve,   106
You must perforce accomplish as you may.   107
Take this of me: Lucrece was not more chaste   108
Than this Lavinia, Bassianus' love.
A speedier course than lingering languishment   110

Must we pursue, and I have found the path.
My lords, a solemn hunting is in hand;   112
There will the lovely Roman ladies troop.
The forest walks are wide and spacious,
And many unfrequented plots there are,   115
Fitted by kind for rape and villainy.   116
Single you thither then this dainty doe,   117
And strike her home by force, if not by words;   118
This way, or not at all, stand you in hope.
Come, come, our empress, with her sacred wit   120
To villainy and vengeance consecrate,   121
Will we acquaint withal what we intend;   122
And she shall file our engines with advice   123
That will not suffer you to square yourselves,   124
But to your wishes' height advance you both.
The Emperor's court is like the house of Fame,   126
The palace full of tongues, of eyes, and ears;
The woods are ruthless, dreadful, deaf, and dull.
There speak and strike, brave boys, and take your turns;
There serve your lust, shadowed from heaven's eye,
And revel in Lavinia's treasury.
CHIRON
Thy counsel, lad, smells of no cowardice.
DEMETRIUS
Sit fas aut nefas, till I find the stream   133
To cool this heat, a charm to calm these fits,
Per Stygia, per manes vehor.   *Exeunt.* 135

❖

[2.2]

*Enter Titus Andronicus and his three sons [and
Marcus], making a noise with hounds and horns.*

TITUS
The hunt is up, the morn is bright and gray,   1
The fields are fragrant, and the woods are green.
Uncouple here, and let us make a bay   3
And wake the Emperor and his lovely bride,
And rouse the Prince, and ring a hunter's peal,   5
That all the court may echo with the noise.
Sons, let it be your charge, as it is ours,   7
To attend the Emperor's person carefully.

---

80 propose be ready to meet   **81 Why . . . strange?** Why do you act
so surprised?   **86 wots** knows   **87 shive** slice   **89 Vulcan's badge**
i.e., cuckold's horns, alluding to the public shame to which Vulcan
was exposed by his wife Venus's affair with Mars.   **91 knows to
court it** knows how to play the wooer   **94 cleanly by** clean past,
without being observed   **95 snatch** sudden or quick catch. (With a
bawdy pun: "a quickie.")   **96 serve your turns** answer your purposes. (With sexual suggestion of a turn in the bed that is underscored in Chiron's reply.)   **97 hit it . . . hit it** hit the nail on the head
. . . scored sexually   **100 square** quarrel   **101 speed** succeed.   **102 so**
so long as   **103 join . . . jar** conspire to obtain what you're quarreling
over.   **104 policy** contrivance, craft   **105 That you affect** that which
you desire   **106–7 That . . . may** that if you can't do this in the way
you'd prefer, you must necessarily accomplish it as best you can, by
whatever means.   **108 Lucrece** a chaste Roman lady ravished by Tarquin, as told in Shakespeare's poem *The Rape of Lucrece*   **110 languishment** love distress

112 solemn ceremonial   **115 plots** i.e., plots of ground   **116 by kind**
by nature   **117 Single** Single out (as in hunting)   **118 home** effectually, thoroughly, to the desired place. (With sexual suggestion.)
120 sacred i.e., consecrated (to villainy)   **121 consecrate** dedicated
122 withal with   **123 file our engines** sharpen our devices
124 That . . . yourselves that will make it possible for you not to quarrel with each other over this   **126 house of Fame** residence of rumor.
(Described in Ovid's *Metamorphoses*, Book 12, and in Chaucer's *Hous
of Fame*; see also Virgil, *Aeneid*, 4.179–90.)   **133 Sit fas aut nefas** Be it
right or wrong   **135 Per . . . vehor** I am carried through the Stygian
regions, through the realm of the shades. (Adapted from Seneca's
Hippolytus, line 1180.)
2.2. Location: The grounds of the Emperor's palace.
1 gray cold, sunless light of early morning   **3 Uncouple . . . bay**
Unleash the hounds, and incite them to keep up a deep, prolonged
barking   **5 ring a hunter's peal** blow a peal on the hunting horns (to
set the dogs going)   **7 ours** mine

I have been troubled in my sleep this night,
But dawning day new comfort hath inspired.   10

Here a cry of hounds, and wind horns in a peal.
Then enter Saturninus, Tamora, Bassianus,
Lavinia, Chiron, Demetrius, and their attendants.

Many good morrows to Your Majesty;
Madam, to you as many and as good.
I promisèd Your Grace a hunter's peal.

SATURNINUS
And you have rung it lustily, my lords—   14
Somewhat too early for new-married ladies.

BASSIANUS
Lavinia, how say you?

LAVINIA   I say no;
I have been broad awake two hours and more.

SATURNINUS
Come on, then, horse and chariots let us have,
And to our sport. [*To Tamora*] Madam, now shall ye see
Our Roman hunting.

MARCUS   I have dogs, my lord,
Will rouse the proudest panther in the chase   21
And climb the highest promontory top.

TITUS
And I have horse will follow where the game   23
Makes way and run like swallows o'er the plain.   24

DEMETRIUS [*aside to Chiron*]
Chiron, we hunt not, we, with horse nor hound,
But hope to pluck a dainty doe to ground.   *Exeunt.*

[2.3]

Enter Aaron alone [with a bag of gold].

AARON
He that had wit would think that I had none,
To bury so much gold under a tree
And never after to inherit it.   3
Let him that thinks of me so abjectly
Know that this gold must coin a stratagem   5
Which, cunningly effected, will beget
A very excellent piece of villainy.
And so repose, sweet gold, for their unrest   8
That have their alms out of the Empress' chest.   9
[*He hides the gold.*]

Enter Tamora alone to the Moor.

TAMORA
My lovely Aaron, wherefore look'st thou sad,
When everything doth make a gleeful boast?   11
The birds chant melody on every bush,
The snake lies rollèd in the cheerful sun,   13
The green leaves quiver with the cooling wind
And make a checkered shadow on the ground.
Under their sweet shade, Aaron, let us sit,
And whilst the babbling echo mocks the hounds,
Replying shrilly to the well-tuned horns,
As if a double hunt were heard at once,
Let us sit down and mark their yellowing noise;   20
And after conflict such as was supposed
The wand'ring prince and Dido once enjoyed   22
When with a happy storm they were surprised   23
And curtained with a counsel-keeping cave,   24
We may, each wreathèd in the other's arms,
Our pastimes done, possess a golden slumber,
Whiles hounds and horns and sweet melodious birds
Be unto us as is a nurse's song
Of lullaby to bring her babe asleep.

AARON
Madam, though Venus govern your desires,
Saturn is dominator over mine.   31
What signifies my deadly-standing eye,   32
My silence, and my cloudy melancholy,   33
My fleece of woolly hair that now uncurls
Even as an adder when she doth unroll
To do some fatal execution?
No, madam, these are no venereal signs.   37
Vengeance is in my heart, death in my hand,
Blood and revenge are hammering in my head.
Hark, Tamora, the empress of my soul,
Which never hopes more heaven than rests in thee,   41
This is the day of doom for Bassianus:
His Philomel must lose her tongue today,   43
Thy sons make pillage of her chastity
And wash their hands in Bassianus' blood.
See'st thou this letter? Take it up, I pray thee,   46
[*giving her a letter*]
And give the King this fatal-plotted scroll.
Now question me no more; we are espied.
Here comes a parcel of our hopeful booty,   49
Which dreads not yet their lives' destruction.

Enter Bassianus and Lavinia.

TAMORA
Ah, my sweet Moor, sweeter to me than life!

10.1 *cry* deep barking. *wind* blow   14 **lustily** heartily   21 **Will** that
will.   **chase** royal hunting ground   23 **horse will** horses that will
24 **run** (The First Quarto's "runnes" is possible, in parallel to *Makes,*
but the verb probably applies to the *horse* rather than to the *game*.)
2.3. Location: A forest near Rome. A pit is provided in the stage,
presumably at a trapdoor, and near it some representation of an
elder tree.
3 **inherit** possess   5 **coin** fabricate. (With a pun on the literal meaning.)
8–9 **for . . . chest** i.e., to discomfit those who will find this gold taken
from Tamora's treasure chest.

11 **boast** display.   13 **rollèd** coiled   20 **yellowing** yelling, baying
22 **prince** i.e., Aeneas, who, taking shelter from a storm with Dido in a
cave during a hunt, made love to her   23 **happy** fortuitous   24 **And . . .**
cave and were concealed by a secret-keeping cave   31 **Saturn . . . mine**
i.e., Saturn, as the dominant planet in my horoscope, governs my temperament and makes it cold and sullen (unlike Venus's effect, which is
amorous).   32 **deadly-standing** fixed with a death-dealing stare
33 **cloudy** gloomy   37 **venereal** erotic, Venus-like   41 **Which . . .**
thee which hopes for no greater bliss than may be found in you
43 **Philomel** (An allusion to the story in Ovid's *Metamorphoses* of
Philomela, raped by her brother-in-law, Tereus; compare with 2.4.26
below. He cut out her tongue so that she could not disclose his villainy. She succeeded in weaving the account of her misfortune in a
tapestry.)   46 **Take it up** Take it   49 **parcel** part.   **hopeful** hoped-for

AARON

No more, great Empress. Bassianus comes.
Be cross with him, and I'll go fetch thy sons   53
To back thy quarrels, whatsoe'er they be.   [*Exit.*]

BASSIANUS

Who have we here? Rome's royal empress,
Unfurnished of her well-beseeming troop?   56
Or is it Dian, habited like her,   57
Who hath abandonèd her holy groves
To see the general hunting in this forest?

TAMORA

Saucy controller of my private steps!   60
Had I the power that some say Dian had,
Thy temples should be planted presently   62
With horns, as was Actaeon's, and the hounds   63
Should drive upon thy new-transformèd limbs,   64
Unmannerly intruder as thou art!

LAVINIA

Under your patience, gentle Empress,   66
'Tis thought you have a goodly gift in horning,   67
And to be doubted that your Moor and you   68
Are singled forth to try experiments.   69
Jove shield your husband from his hounds today!
'Tis pity they should take him for a stag.

BASSIANUS

Believe me, Queen, your swart Cimmerian   72
Doth make your honor of his body's hue,
Spotted, detested, and abominable.
Why are you sequestered from all your train,
Dismounted from your snow-white goodly steed,
And wandered hither to an obscure plot,
Accompanied but with a barbarous Moor,
If foul desire had not conducted you?

LAVINIA

And, being intercepted in your sport,
Great reason that my noble lord be rated   81
For sauciness. [*To Bassianus*] I pray you, let us hence,
And let her joy her raven-colored love;   83
This valley fits the purpose passing well.   84

BASSIANUS

The King my brother shall have note of this.

LAVINIA

Ay, for these slips have made him noted long.   86
Good king, to be so mightily abused!   87

TAMORA

Why have I patience to endure all this?

Enter Chiron and Demetrius.

53 **Be cross** Pick a quarrel   56 **Unfurnished . . . troop** unprovided with a suitable escort.   57 **Dian** Diana, huntress and goddess of chastity. (Here used sarcastically.)   **habited** dressed   60 **Saucy controller** Impudent critic, censurer   62 **presently** immediately   63 **Actaeon's** (An allusion to the story of Actaeon, who was transformed into a stag by Diana and killed by his own hounds as punishment for having watched her and her nymphs at their bath. The horns signify cuckoldry.)   64 **drive** rush   66 **Under . . . Empress** If you will allow my saying so, noble and kind Empress. (Said with ironic politeness.)   67 **horning** cuckolding   68 **doubted** suspected, feared   69 **Are . . . experiments** i.e., are alone together to experiment with each other.   72 **Cimmerian** i.e., of black complexion. (The Cimmerii in the *Odyssey* live in perpetual darkness.)   81 **my noble lord** i.e., Bassianus.   **rated** berated   83 **joy** enjoy   84 **passing** surpassingly   86 **slips** offenses.   **noted** notorious, stigmatized   87 **abused** deceived.

DEMETRIUS

How now, dear sovereign, and our gracious mother,
Why doth Your Highness look so pale and wan?

TAMORA

Have I not reason, think you, to look pale?
These two have 'ticed me hither to this place.   92
A barren detested vale you see it is;
The trees, though summer, yet forlorn and lean,
Overcome with moss and baleful mistletoe;   95
Here never shines the sun; here nothing breeds,
Unless the nightly owl or fatal raven.   97
And when they showed me this abhorrèd pit,
They told me here at dead time of the night
A thousand fiends, a thousand hissing snakes,
Ten thousand swelling toads, as many urchins,   101
Would make such fearful and confusèd cries
As any mortal body hearing it
Should straight fall mad or else die suddenly.
No sooner had they told this hellish tale
But straight they told me they would bind me here
Unto the body of a dismal yew
And leave me to this miserable death.
And then they called me foul adulteress,
Lascivious Goth, and all the bitterest terms   110
That ever ear did hear to such effect;
And had you not by wondrous fortune come,
This vengeance on me had they executed.
Revenge it, as you love your mother's life,
Or be ye not henceforth called my children.

DEMETRIUS

This is a witness that I am thy son.
                    Stab him [*Bassianus*].

CHIRON

And this for me, struck home to show my strength.
                    [*He also stabs Bassianus, who dies.*]

LAVINIA

Ay, come, Semiramis, nay, barbarous Tamora,   118
For no name fits thy nature but thy own!

TAMORA [*to Chiron*]

Give me the poniard. You shall know, my boys,   120
Your mother's hand shall right your mother's wrong.

DEMETRIUS

Stay, madam, here is more belongs to her.   122
First thresh the corn, then after burn the straw.   123
This minion stood upon her chastity,   124
Upon her nuptial vow, her loyalty,
And with that painted hope braves your mightiness;   126
And shall she carry this unto her grave?

CHIRON

An if she do, I would I were an eunuch.   128
Drag hence her husband to some secret hole
And make his dead trunk pillow to our lust.

92 **'ticed** enticed   95 **Overcome** overgrown.   **baleful** i.e., parasitic   97 **fatal** ominous   101 **urchins** (1) hedgehogs (2) goblins, elves   110 **Goth** (A quibble; pronounced somewhat like "goat," symbolic of lechery.)   118 **Semiramis** (See the note to 2.1.22.)   120 **poniard** dagger.   122 **belongs to her** that is to be her portion.   123 **First . . . straw** (The proverbial phrase "to thrash in a woman's barn" means to have sex with her. *Corn* is grain.)   124 **minion** hussy, wench   126 **painted** specious, unreal   128 **An if** If

TAMORA
    But when ye have the honey ye desire,
    Let not this wasp outlive, us both to sting.   132

CHIRON
    I warrant you, madam, we will make that sure.—
    Come, mistress, now perforce we will enjoy
    That nice-preservèd honesty of yours.   135

LAVINIA
    O Tamora! Thou bearest a woman's face—

TAMORA
    I will not hear her speak. Away with her!

LAVINIA
    Sweet lords, entreat her hear me but a word.

DEMETRIUS [to Tamora]
    Listen, fair madam. Let it be your glory
    To see her tears, but be your heart to them
    As unrelenting flint to drops of rain.

LAVINIA
    When did the tiger's young ones teach the dam?
    Oh, do not learn her wrath; she taught it thee!   143
    The milk thou suck'st from her did turn to marble;   144
    Even at thy teat thou hadst thy tyranny.   145
    Yet every mother breeds not sons alike;
    [To Chiron]   Do thou entreat her show a woman's pity.

CHIRON
    What, wouldst thou have me prove myself a bastard?   148

LAVINIA
    'Tis true, the raven doth not hatch a lark.
    Yet have I heard—Oh, could I find it now!—   150
    The lion, moved with pity, did endure   151
    To have his princely paws pared all away.   152
    Some say that ravens foster forlorn children   153
    The whilst their own birds famish in their nests.   154
    Oh, be to me, though thy hard heart say no,
    Nothing so kind, but something pitiful!   156

TAMORA
    I know not what it means.—Away with her!   157

LAVINIA
    Oh, let me teach thee! For my father's sake,
    That gave thee life when well he might have slain thee,
    Be not obdurate; open thy deaf ears.

TAMORA
    Hadst thou in person ne'er offended me,
    Even for his sake am I pitiless.
    Remember, boys, I poured forth tears in vain
    To save your brother from the sacrifice,
    But fierce Andronicus would not relent.
    Therefore away with her, and use her as you will—
    The worse to her, the better loved of me.

LAVINIA
    O Tamora, be called a gentle queen,
    And with thine own hands kill me in this place!

---

132 **outlive** live longer   135 **nice-preservèd honesty** fastidiously preserved chastity   143 **learn** teach   144 **thou suck'st** that you sucked   145 **hadst thy tyranny** gained your cruelty.   148 **a bastard** i.e., false to my parentage, an unnatural son.   150 **find it** find it true   151–2 **The lion . . . away** (In their unnatural cruelty, Tamora and her sons stand out in contrast to the grateful lion of proverbial lore that refuses to attack the person who once removed a thorn from its paw.)   153 **forlorn** abandoned (by other birds)   154 **birds** chicks   156 **Nothing . . . pitiful!** if not as kind as the raven, do show at least some pity!   157 **it** i.e., pity

    For 'tis not life that I have begged so long;
    Poor I was slain when Bassianus died.
        [She clutches Tamora imploringly.]

TAMORA
    What beg'st thou, then? Fond woman, let me go.   172

LAVINIA
    'Tis present death I beg, and one thing more   173
    That womanhood denies my tongue to tell: 174
    Oh, keep me from their worse-than-killing lust,
    And tumble me into some loathsome pit,
    Where never man's eye may behold my body!
    Do this, and be a charitable murderer.

TAMORA
    So should I rob my sweet sons of their fee.
    No, let them satisfy their lust on thee.

DEMETRIUS [to Lavinia]
    Away! For thou hast stayed us here too long.

LAVINIA
    No grace, no womanhood? Ah, beastly creature!
    The blot and enemy to our general name!   183
    Confusion fall—   184

CHIRON
    Nay, then I'll stop your mouth. [To Demetrius] Bring
        thou her husband.
    This is the hole where Aaron bid us hide him.
    [Demetrius and Chiron throw the body of Bassianus
        into the pit, then exeunt, dragging off Lavinia.]

TAMORA
    Farewell, my sons. See that you make her sure.   187
    Ne'er let my heart know merry cheer indeed
    Till all the Andronici be made away.   189
    Now will I hence to seek my lovely Moor,
    And let my spleenful sons this trull deflower.   [Exit.] 191

    Enter Aaron, with two of Titus' sons [Quintus
    and Martius].

AARON
    Come on, my lords, the better foot before.   192
    Straight will I bring you to the loathsome pit
    Where I espied the panther fast asleep.

QUINTUS
    My sight is very dull, whate'er it bodes.

MARTIUS
    And mine, I promise you. Were it not for shame,
    Well could I leave our sport to sleep awhile.
        [He falls into the pit.]

QUINTUS
    What, art thou fallen? What subtle hole is this,
    Whose mouth is covered with rude-growing briers
    Upon whose leaves are drops of new-shed blood
    As fresh as morning dew distilled on flowers?
    A very fatal place it seems to me.
    Speak, brother. Hast thou hurt thee with the fall?

---

172 **Fond** Foolish   173 **present** immediate   174 **denies** forbids   183 **our general name** i.e., women's reputation.   184 **Confusion** Destruction   187 **sure** safe, incapable of revenge.   189 **made away** murdered.   191 **spleenful** lustful.   **trull** whore, slut   192 **better foot before** best foot forward.

MARTIUS
    Oh, brother, with the dismal'st object hurt   204
    That ever eye with sight made heart lament!   205
AARON [aside]
    Now will I fetch the King to find them here,
    That he thereby may have a likely guess
    How these were they that made away his brother.
                                                            Exit.
MARTIUS
    Why dost not comfort me and help me out
    From this unhallowed and bloodstainèd hole?
QUINTUS
    I am surprisèd with an uncouth fear.   211
    A chilling sweat o'erruns my trembling joints;
    My heart suspects more than mine eye can see.
MARTIUS
    To prove thou hast a true-divining heart,
    Aaron and thou look down into this den
    And see a fearful sight of blood and death.
QUINTUS
    Aaron is gone, and my compassionate heart
    Will not permit mine eyes once to behold
    The thing whereat it trembles by surmise.   219
    Oh, tell me who it is! For ne'er till now
    Was I a child to fear I know not what.
MARTIUS
    Lord Bassianus lies berayed in blood,   222
    All on a heap, like to a slaughtered lamb,
    In this detested, dark, blood-drinking pit.
QUINTUS
    If it be dark, how dost thou know 'tis he?
MARTIUS
    Upon his bloody finger he doth wear
    A precious ring that lightens all this hole,   227
    Which like a taper in some monument   228
    Doth shine upon the dead man's earthy cheeks   229
    And shows the ragged entrails of this pit.   230
    So pale did shine the moon on Pyramus   231
    When he by night lay bathed in maiden blood.   232
    Oh, brother, help me with thy fainting hand—
    If fear hath made thee faint, as me it hath—
    Out of this fell devouring receptacle,   235
    As hateful as Cocytus' misty mouth.   236
QUINTUS [offering to help]
    Reach me thy hand, that I may help thee out,
    Or, wanting strength to do thee so much good,   238
    I may be plucked into the swallowing womb
    Of this deep pit, poor Bassianus' grave.
    I have no strength to pluck thee to the brink.

MARTIUS
    Nor I no strength to climb without thy help.
QUINTUS
    Thy hand once more; I will not loose again
    Till thou art here aloft or I below.
    Thou canst not come to me—I come to thee.
                                            [He falls in.]

    Enter the Emperor [Saturninus, with atten-
    dants], and Aaron the Moor.

SATURNINUS
    Along with me! I'll see what hole is here,   246
    And what he is that now is leapt into it.
                                    [He speaks into the pit.]
    Say, who art thou that lately didst descend
    Into this gaping hollow of the earth?
MARTIUS [from within the pit]
    The unhappy sons of old Andronicus,
    Brought hither in a most unlucky hour
    To find thy brother Bassianus dead.
SATURNINUS
    My brother dead! I know thou dost but jest.
    He and his lady both are at the lodge
    Upon the north side of this pleasant chase;   255
    'Tis not an hour since I left them there.
MARTIUS
    We know not where you left them all alive,
    But, out alas! Here have we found him dead.   258

    Enter Tamora, [Titus] Andronicus, and Lucius.

TAMORA   Where is my lord the King?
SATURNINUS
    Here, Tamora, though gripped with killing grief.
TAMORA
    Where is thy brother Bassianus?
SATURNINUS
    Now to the bottom dost thou search my wound: 262
    Poor Bassianus here lies murderèd.
TAMORA
    Then all too late I bring this fatal writ,
    The complot of this timeless tragedy,   265
    And wonder greatly that man's face can fold   266
    In pleasing smiles such murderous tyranny.
                            She giveth Saturnine a letter.
SATURNINUS (reads the letter)
    "An if we miss to meet him handsomely,   268
    Sweet huntsman—Bassianus 'tis we mean—
    Do thou so much as dig the grave for him.   270
    Thou know'st our meaning. Look for thy reward
    Among the nettles at the elder tree   272
    Which overshades the mouth of that same pit
    Where we decreed to bury Bassianus.   274
    Do this, and purchase us thy lasting friends."   275

204–5 with . . . lament! I am hurt with the most dismal sight that ever
made the heart lament!   211 surprisèd overcome.   uncouth strange
219 by surmise even to imagine.   222 berayed in defiled by
227 ring (Presumably the carbuncle, which was believed to emit
light.)   228 monument tomb   229 earthy clay-colored, pale
230 ragged entrails rough interior   231 Pyramus the lover of Thisbe,
who killed himself in the mistaken supposition that she was dead.
(See *A Midsummer Night's Dream*, 1.2, 3.1, and 5.1.)   232 maiden
blood (Although Pyramus dies first, Thisbe then plunges his sword
into her bosom, so that they are bathed in the blood of both.)
235 fell savage   236 Cocytus' misty mouth i.e., the mouth of hell.
Cocytus is the river of lamentations in Hades.   238 wanting lacking

246 Along Come along   255 chase hunting ground   258 out alas! alas!
(*Out* intensifies the interjection.)   262 search probe   265 complot plot,
conspiracy.   timeless untimely   266 fold hide, enfold   268 An if If.
handsomely conveniently   270 Do . . . as be so good as to. (Said with
mock ceremoniousness.)   272 elder tree (An ominous sign; traditionally, Judas hanged himself from an elder tree after having betrayed
Jesus.)   274 decreed decided   275 purchase win

Oh, Tamora, was ever heard the like?
This is the pit, and this the elder tree.
Look, sirs, if you can find the huntsman out
That should have murdered Bassianus here.   279
AARON [*finding the gold*]
My gracious lord, here is the bag of gold.
SATURNINUS [*to Titus*]
Two of thy whelps, fell curs of bloody kind,   281
Have here bereft my brother of his life.—
Sirs, drag them from the pit unto the prison!
There let them bide until we have devised
Some never-heard-of torturing pain for them.
            [*Martius and Quintus are dragged out of the pit,
                    and Bassianus's body is raised.*]
TAMORA
What, are they in this pit? Oh, wondrous thing!
How easily murder is discoverèd!
TITUS [*kneeling*]
High Emperor, upon my feeble knee
I beg this boon, with tears not lightly shed,
That this fell fault of my accursèd sons—
Accursèd if the fault be proved in them—
SATURNINUS
If it be proved? You see it is apparent.   292
Who found this letter? Tamora, was it you?
TAMORA
Andronicus himself did take it up.   294
TITUS
I did, my lord, yet let me be their bail.
For, by my fathers' reverend tomb, I vow   296
They shall be ready at Your Highness' will
To answer their suspicion with their lives.   298
SATURNINUS
Thou shalt not bail them. See thou follow me.
Some bring the murdered body, some the murderers.
Let them not speak a word. The guilt is plain;
For, by my soul, were there worse end than death,
That end upon them should be executed.
TAMORA
Andronicus, I will entreat the King.
Fear not thy sons; they shall do well enough.   305
TITUS [*rising*]
Come, Lucius, come. Stay not to talk with them.   306
            [*Exeunt bearing the dead body of Bassianus;
                    Martius and Quintus under guard.*]

❖

[2.4]

*Enter the Empress' sons with Lavinia, her hands
cut off, and her tongue cut out, and ravished.*

DEMETRIUS
So, now go tell, an if thy tongue can speak,
Who 'twas that cut thy tongue and ravished thee.

CHIRON
Write down thy mind, bewray thy meaning so,   3
An if thy stumps will let thee play the scribe.
DEMETRIUS
See how with signs and tokens she can scrawl.   5
CHIRON [*to Lavinia*]
Go home, call for sweet water, wash thy hands.   6
DEMETRIUS
She hath no tongue to call, nor hands to wash;
And so let's leave her to her silent walks.
CHIRON
An 'twere my cause, I should go hang myself.   9
DEMETRIUS
If thou hadst hands to help thee knit the cord.   10
            Exeunt [Chiron and Demetrius].

*[Wind horns.] Enter Marcus from hunting.
[Lavinia flees from him.]*

MARCUS
Who is this? My niece, that flies away so fast?
Cousin, a word. Where is your husband?   12
            [*He see her injuries.*]
If I do dream, would all my wealth would wake me!   13
If I do wake, some planet strike me down,   14
That I may slumber an eternal sleep!
Speak, gentle niece, what stern ungentle hands   16
Hath lopped and hewed and made thy body bare
Of her two branches, those sweet ornaments
Whose circling shadows kings have sought to sleep in,   19
And might not gain so great a happiness   20
As half thy love? Why dost not speak to me?   21
Alas, a crimson river of warm blood,
Like to a bubbling fountain stirred with wind,
Doth rise and fall between thy rosèd lips,
Coming and going with thy honey breath.
But, sure, some Tereus hath deflowered thee   26
And, lest thou shouldst detect him, cut thy tongue.   27
Ah, now thou turn'st away thy face for shame!
And notwithstanding all this loss of blood,
As from a conduit with three issuing spouts,
Yet do thy cheeks look red as Titan's face   31
Blushing to be encountered with a cloud.   32
Shall I speak for thee? Shall I say 'tis so?
Oh, that I knew thy heart, and knew the beast,
That I might rail at him to ease my mind!
Sorrow concealèd, like an oven stopped,   36
Doth burn the heart to cinders where it is.
Fair Philomela, why, she but lost her tongue,

3 **bewray** reveal   5 **scrawl** gesticulate. (But also anticipating her writing in 4.1.70-9.)   6 **sweet** perfumed   9 **cause** case   10 **knit** tie the knot in 10.2 **Wind horns** Blow hunting horns (offstage. The stage direction is from the Folio.)   12 **Cousin** Kinswoman   13 **would . . . me** I would give all my wealth to have this be only a bad dream.   14 **strike me down** exert its baleful influence on me   16 **stern** cruel   19 **shadows** i.e., protection, shelter   20-1 **And . . . thy love** and could find nowhere any happiness half so great as having your love.   26 **Tereus** i.e., the ravisher of Philomela; see the note to 2.3.43   27 **detect** expose 31 **Titan's** the sun god's   32 **Blushing . . . cloud** (The sun blushes for shame at being covered by a cloud, as if in concealment of some secret sorrow or shame; see lines 36–7.)   36 **stopped** closed too long, plugged up

279 **should** was to   281 **fell** cruel, fierce.   **kind** nature   292 **apparent** evident.   294 **take** pick   296 **fathers'** forefathers'   298 **their suspicion** the suspicion they are under   305 **Fear not** Fear not for   306 **them** i.e., Martius and Quintus.
2.4. Location: The forest still.

And in a tedious sampler sewed her mind;   39
But, lovely niece, that mean is cut from thee.
A craftier Tereus, cousin, hast thou met,
And he hath cut those pretty fingers off
That could have better sewed than Philomel.
Oh, had the monster seen those lily hands
Tremble like aspen leaves upon a lute
And make the silken strings delight to kiss them,
He would not then have touched them for his life!   47
Or had he heard the heavenly harmony
Which that sweet tongue hath made,
He would have dropped his knife and fell asleep,
As Cerberus at the Thracian poet's feet.   51
Come, let us go and make thy father blind,
For such a sight will blind a father's eye.
One hour's storm will drown the fragrant meads;   54
What will whole months of tears thy father's eyes?
Do not draw back, for we will mourn with thee.
Oh, could our mourning ease thy misery!   *Exeunt.*

❦

[3.1]

*Enter the judges and senators [and tribunes]
with Titus' two sons bound, passing over the
stage to the place of execution, and Titus going
before, pleading.*

TITUS
Hear me, grave fathers! Noble tribunes, stay!
For pity of mine age, whose youth was spent
In dangerous wars whilst you securely slept;
For all my blood in Rome's great quarrel shed,   4
For all the frosty nights that I have watched,   5
And for these bitter tears which now you see
Filling the agèd wrinkles in my cheeks,
Be pitiful to my condemnèd sons,
Whose souls is not corrupted as 'tis thought.
For two-and-twenty sons I never wept,   10
Because they died in honor's lofty bed.
          *[Titus] Andronicus lieth down and the judges
                    pass by him. [Titus weeps.]*
For these, tribunes, in the dust I write
My heart's deep languor and my soul's sad tears.
Let my tears stanch the earth's dry appetite;   14
My sons' sweet blood will make it shame and blush.   15
                    [Exeunt all but Titus.]
O earth, I will befriend thee more with rain
That shall distill from these two ancient urns   17

Than youthful April shall with all his showers.
In summer's drought I'll drop upon thee still;   19
In winter with warm tears I'll melt the snow,
And keep eternal springtime on thy face,
So thou refuse to drink my dear sons' blood.   22

          Enter Lucius, with his weapon drawn.

O reverend tribunes! O gentle, agèd men!
Unbind my sons, reverse the doom of death,   24
And let me say, that never wept before,
My tears are now prevailing orators.
LUCIUS
O noble father, you lament in vain.
The tribunes hear you not. No man is by,
And you recount your sorrows to a stone.
TITUS
Ah, Lucius, for thy brothers let me plead.—
Grave tribunes, once more I entreat of you—
LUCIUS
My gracious lord, no tribune hears you speak.
TITUS
Why, 'tis no matter, man. If they did hear,
They would not mark me; if they did mark,
They would not pity me; yet plead I must,
And bootless unto them.   36
Therefore I tell my sorrows to the stones,
Who, though they cannot answer my distress,
Yet in some sort they are better than the tribunes,
For that they will not intercept my tale.   40
When I do weep, they humbly at my feet
Receive my tears and seem to weep with me;
And, were they but attirèd in grave weeds,   43
Rome could afford no tribunes like to these.   44
A stone is soft as wax, tribunes more hard than stones;
A stone is silent and offendeth not,
And tribunes with their tongues doom men to death.
                              [He rises.]
But wherefore stand'st thou with thy weapon drawn?
LUCIUS
To rescue my two brothers from their death,
For which attempt the judges have pronounced
My everlasting doom of banishment.
TITUS
O happy man! They have befriended thee.
Why, foolish Lucius, dost thou not perceive
That Rome is but a wilderness of tigers?
Tigers must prey, and Rome affords no prey
But me and mine. How happy art thou then
From these devourers to be banishèd!
But who comes with our brother Marcus here?

          Enter Marcus with Lavinia.

MARCUS
Titus, prepare thy agèd eyes to weep,
Or if not so, thy noble heart to break.
I bring consuming sorrow to thine age.

---

39 **tedious sampler** laboriously contrived embroidered cloth or tapestry. (See the note to 2.3.43.) **sewed her mind** put her story down in embroidery 47 **for his life** to save his life. 51 **Cerberus . . . feet** (According to legend, Orpheus's sweet singing charmed even Cerberus, the three-headed dog guarding the entrance to Hades.)
54 **meads** meadows
3.1. Location: Rome. A street.
4 **my** i.e., my and my sons' 5 **watched** stayed awake 10 **two-and-twenty** (At 1.1.79 and 195, we are told that twenty-one of Titus's twenty-five sons died fighting. Mutius is the twenty-second to die, though scarcely "in honor's lofty bed," as Titus sees it.) 14 **stanch** satisfy 15 **shame** be ashamed 17 **urns** i.e., tear-filled eyes

19 **still** continually 22 **So** on condition that 24 **doom** sentence
36 **bootless** in vain 40 **For that** in that. **intercept** interrupt
43 **grave weeds** sober garments 44 **afford** provide

TITUS
Will it consume me? Let me see it, then.
MARCUS
This was thy daughter.
TITUS   Why, Marcus, so she is.
LUCIUS   Ay me, this object kills me!   64
TITUS
Fainthearted boy, arise, and look upon her.   65
Speak, Lavinia, what accursèd hand
Hath made thee handless in thy father's sight?
What fool hath added water to the sea,
Or brought a faggot to bright-burning Troy?
My grief was at the height before thou cam'st,
And now, like Nilus, it disdaineth bounds.   71
Give me a sword, I'll chop off my hands too,
For they have fought for Rome, and all in vain;
And they have nursed this woe in feeding life;   74
In bootless prayer have they been held up,
And they have served me to effectless use.   76
Now all the service I require of them
Is that the one will help to cut the other.
'Tis well, Lavinia, that thou hast no hands,
For hands to do Rome service is but vain.
LUCIUS
Speak, gentle sister, who hath martyred thee?   81
MARCUS
Oh, that delightful engine of her thoughts,   82
That blabbed them with such pleasing eloquence,   83
Is torn from forth that pretty hollow cage
Where, like a sweet melodious bird, it sung
Sweet varied notes, enchanting every ear.
LUCIUS
Oh, say thou for her: who hath done this deed?
MARCUS
Oh, thus I found her, straying in the park,
Seeking to hide herself, as doth the deer
That hath received some unrecuring wound.   90
TITUS
It was my dear, and he that wounded her   91
Hath hurt me more than had he killed me dead;
For now I stand as one upon a rock
Environed with a wilderness of sea,
Who marks the waxing tide grow wave by wave,
Expecting ever when some envious surge   96
Will in his brinish bowels swallow him.   97
This way to death my wretched sons are gone;
Here stands my other son, a banished man,
And here my brother, weeping at my woes;
But that which gives my soul the greatest spurn   101
Is dear Lavinia, dearer than my soul.

Had I but seen thy picture in this plight,
It would have madded me; what shall I do
Now I behold thy lively body so?   105
Thou hast no hands to wipe away thy tears,
Nor tongue to tell me who hath martyred thee.
Thy husband he is dead, and for his death   108
Thy brothers are condemned, and dead by this.   109
Look, Marcus! Ah, son Lucius, look on her!
When I did name her brothers, then fresh tears
Stood on her cheeks, as doth the honey-dew   112
Upon a gathered lily almost withered.
MARCUS
Perchance she weeps because they killed her husband;
Perchance because she knows them innocent.
TITUS
If they did kill thy husband, then be joyful,
Because the law hath ta'en revenge on them.
No, no, they would not do so foul a deed;
Witness the sorrow that their sister makes.
Gentle Lavinia, let me kiss thy lips;
Or make some sign how I may do thee ease.
Shall thy good uncle, and thy brother Lucius,
And thou, and I, sit round about some fountain,   123
Looking all downwards to behold our cheeks
How they are stained, like meadows yet not dry
With miry slime left on them by a flood?
And in the fountain shall we gaze so long
Till the fresh taste be taken from that clearness,
And made a brine pit with our bitter tears?
Or shall we cut away our hands, like thine?
Or shall we bite our tongues, and in dumb shows   131
Pass the remainder of our hateful days?
What shall we do? Let us that have our tongues
Plot some device of further misery,   134
To make us wondered at in time to come.
LUCIUS
Sweet father, cease your tears, for at your grief
See how my wretched sister sobs and weeps.
MARCUS
Patience, dear niece. Good Titus, dry thine eyes.
TITUS
Ah, Marcus, Marcus! Brother, well I wot   139
Thy napkin cannot drink a tear of mine,   140
For thou, poor man, hast drowned it with thine own.
LUCIUS
Ah, my Lavinia, I will wipe thy cheeks.
TITUS
Mark, Marcus, mark! I understand her signs.
Had she a tongue to speak, now would she say
That to her brother which I said to thee.
His napkin, with his true tears all bewet,

---

64 **object** object of sight   65 **arise** (Evidently, Lucius has collapsed or
fallen to his knees in grief.)   71 **Nilus** the Nile   74 **they . . . life** i.e.,
in sustaining Rome, my hands have merely prolonged the misery of
the Andronici   76 **effectless** fruitless   81 **martyred** mutilated
82 **engine** instrument   83 **blabbed** uttered   90 **unrecuring** incurable
91 **dear** (With a familiar pun on *deer*, line 89.)   96 **Expecting ever
when** continually awaiting the moment when.   **envious** spiteful
97 **his** its   101 **spurn** stroke, kick

105 **lively** living, actual (as contrasted with her picture)   108 **husband
he** husband   109 **by this** by this time.   112 **honey-dew** sweet dew-
like substance, or the dew itself   123 **fountain** spring   131 **bite** bite
out.   **dumb shows** mute pageants   134 **device** (1) strategy (2) dramatic representation   139 **wot** know   140 **napkin** handkerchief

Can do no service on her sorrowful cheeks.
Oh, what a sympathy of woe is this,
As far from help as Limbo is from bliss!   149

Enter Aaron the Moor alone.

AARON
Titus Andronicus, my lord the Emperor
Sends thee this word: that if thou love thy sons,
Let Marcus, Lucius, or thyself, old Titus,
Or any one of you, chop off your hand
And send it to the King. He for the same
Will send thee hither both thy sons alive,   155
And that shall be the ransom for their fault.   156

TITUS
O gracious Emperor! O gentle Aaron!
Did ever raven sing so like a lark,
That gives sweet tidings of the sun's uprise?
With all my heart I'll send the Emperor my hand.
Good Aaron, wilt thou help to chop it off?

LUCIUS
Stay, father, for that noble hand of thine,
That hath thrown down so many enemies,
Shall not be sent. My hand will serve the turn.
My youth can better spare my blood than you,
And therefore mine shall save my brothers' lives.

MARCUS
Which of your hands hath not defended Rome
And reared aloft the bloody battle-ax,
Writing destruction on the enemy's castle?
Oh, none of both but are of high desert.
My hand hath been but idle; let it serve
To ransom my two nephews from their death.
Then have I kept it to a worthy end.

AARON
Nay, come, agree whose hand shall go along,
For fear they die before their pardon come.

MARCUS
My hand shall go.

LUCIUS   By heaven, it shall not go!

TITUS
Sirs, strive no more. Such withered herbs as these
Are meet for plucking up, and therefore mine.   178

LUCIUS
Sweet father, if I shall be thought thy son,
Let me redeem my brothers both from death.

MARCUS
And for our father's sake and mother's care,
Now let me show a brother's love to thee.

TITUS
Agree between you. I will spare my hand.   183

LUCIUS   Then I'll go fetch an ax.
MARCUS   But I will use the ax.
                              Exeunt [Lucius and Marcus].
TITUS
Come hither, Aaron. I'll deceive them both.
Lend me thy hand, and I will give thee mine.   187
AARON *[aside]*
If that be called deceit, I will be honest,
And never whilst I live deceive men so;
But I'll deceive you in another sort,
And that you'll say, ere half an hour pass.
                              He cuts off Titus' hand.

Enter Lucius and Marcus again.

TITUS
Now stay your strife. What shall be is dispatched.
Good Aaron, give His Majesty my hand.
Tell him it was a hand that warded him   194
From thousand dangers. Bid him bury it.
More hath it merited; that let it have.   196
As for my sons, say I account of them
As jewels purchased at an easy price,
And yet dear too, because I bought mine own.   199
AARON
I go, Andronicus, and for thy hand
Look by and by to have thy sons with thee.   201
[Aside] Their heads, I mean. Oh, how this villainy
Doth fat me with the very thoughts of it!   203
Let fools do good, and fair men call for grace;   204
Aaron will have his soul black like his face.   *Exit.*
TITUS *[kneeling]*
Oh, here I lift this one hand up to heaven
And bow this feeble ruin to the earth.
If any power pities wretched tears,
To that I call! *[To Lavinia, who kneels]* What, wouldst
    thou kneel with me?
Do, then, dear heart, for heaven shall hear our prayers,
Or with our sighs we'll breathe the welkin dim   211
And stain the sun with fog, as sometime clouds
When they do hug him in their melting bosoms.   213
MARCUS
O brother, speak with possibility,   214
And do not break into these deep extremes.
TITUS
Is not my sorrow deep, having no bottom?
Then be my passions bottomless with them.   217
MARCUS
But yet let reason govern thy lament.
TITUS
If there were reason for these miseries,
Then into limits could I bind my woes.   219

---

149 **Limbo** region bordering hell, where were confined the souls of
those barred from heaven through no fault of their own, such as good
persons who lived before the Christian era or who died unbaptized
155 **Will . . . alive** (Aaron's secret double meaning may be, "will send
to you here, you being alive, both your sons.")   156 **that** (Secretly,
that may refer to the sons being sent here—dead.)   178 **meet** fit
183 **spare** (In a virtuous deception, Titus uses a double meaning for
spare; ostensibly he means "save from being cut off," but secretly he
means "do without.")

187 **Lend . . . mine** (Another pun, on *hand:* "Give me your assistance,
and I'll give you my hand.")   194 **warded** guarded   196 **that** i.e.,
burial   199 **dear** (1) expensive (2) precious.   **because . . . own**
because I am buying back what was mine to begin with, my own
dear sons.   201 **Look** expect   203 **fat** fatten, feed   204 **fair** (1) fair-
complexioned (2) fair-minded.   **grace** virtue   211 **Or . . . dim** or
make cloudy the sky with our sighs   213 **melting** i.e., dissolving into
teardroplike rain   214 **with** within the bounds of   217 **Then . . .
them** Then let my passionate outbursts be ceaseless (*bottomless*), like
my sorrows.   219 **reason** explanation. (Playing on *reason*, rational
behavior, in line 218.)

When heaven doth weep, doth not the earth o'erflow? 221
If the winds rage, doth not the sea wax mad,
Threat'ning the welkin with his big-swoll'n face?
And wilt thou have a reason for this coil? 224
I am the sea. Hark how her sighs doth blow! 225
She is the weeping welkin, I the earth.
Then must my sea be movèd with her sighs,
Then must my earth with her continual tears
Become a deluge overflowed and drowned,
Forwhy my bowels cannot hide her woes, 230
But like a drunkard must I vomit them. 231
Then give me leave, for losers will have leave
To ease their stomachs with their bitter tongues. 233

Enter a Messenger, with two heads and a hand.

MESSENGER
Worthy Andronicus, ill art thou repaid
For that good hand thou sent'st the Emperor.
Here are the heads of thy two noble sons,
And here's thy hand in scorn to thee sent back—
Thy grief their sports, thy resolution mocked, 238
That woe is me to think upon thy woes 239
More than remembrance of my father's death.
[He sets down the heads and hand, and exit.]

MARCUS
Now let hot Etna cool in Sicily, 241
And be my heart an ever-burning hell!
These miseries are more than may be borne.
To weep with them that weep doth ease somedeal, 244
But sorrow flouted at is double death. 245

LUCIUS
Ah, that this sight should make so deep a wound,
And yet detested life not shrink thereat! 247
That ever death should let life bear his name, 248
Where life hath no more interest but to breathe! 249
[Lavinia kisses Titus.]

MARCUS
Alas, poor heart, that kiss is comfortless
As frozen water to a starvèd snake. 251

TITUS
When will this fearful slumber have an end? 252

MARCUS
Now, farewell, flatt'ry! Die, Andronicus. 253
Thou dost not slumber. See thy two sons' heads,

Thy warlike hand, thy mangled daughter here,
Thy other banished son with this dear sight 256
Struck pale and bloodless, and thy brother, I,
Even like a stony image, cold and numb.
Ah, now no more will I control thy griefs! 259
Rend off thy silver hair, thy other hand
Gnawing with thy teeth, and be this dismal sight
The closing up of our most wretched eyes. 262
Now is a time to storm. Why art thou still?

TITUS   Ha, ha, ha!

MARCUS
Why dost thou laugh? It fits not with this hour.

TITUS
Why, I have not another tear to shed.
Besides, this sorrow is an enemy,
And would usurp upon my wat'ry eyes
And make them blind with tributary tears. 269
Then which way shall I find Revenge's cave?
For these two heads do seem to speak to me
And threat me I shall never come to bliss
Till all these mischiefs be returned again 273
Even in their throats that hath committed them.
Come, let me see what task I have to do.
You heavy people, circle me about, 276
That I may turn me to each one of you
And swear unto my soul to right your wrongs.
*[They form a circle about Titus,
and he pledges each.]*
The vow is made. Come, brother, take a head,
And in this hand the other will I bear.
*[They pick up the two heads, and give the hand
to Lavinia.]*
And, Lavinia, thou shalt be employed:
Bear thou my hand, sweet wench, between thy teeth.
As for thee, boy, [to Lucius] go get thee from my sight;
Thou art an exile, and thou must not stay.
Hie to the Goths and raise an army there.
And if ye love me, as I think you do,
Let's kiss and part, for we have much to do.
[They kiss.] Exeunt [Titus, Marcus, and Lavinia].

LUCIUS
Farewell, Andronicus, my noble father,
The woefull'st man that ever lived in Rome.
Farewell, proud Rome, till Lucius come again!
He loves his pledges dearer than his life. 291
Farewell, Lavinia, my noble sister.
Oh, would thou wert as thou tofore hast been! 293
But now nor Lucius nor Lavinia lives 294
But in oblivion and hateful griefs.
If Lucius live, he will requite your wrongs
And make proud Saturnine and his empress

---

221 weep i.e., rain (as though in tears).   **o'erflow** become flooded.
224 coil noise, fuss.   **225 her** i.e., Lavinia's, personifying the winds'
rage   **230 Forwhy** because.   **bowels** (Supposed to be the seat of
compassion; also, the bowels of the earth.)   **231 vomit** (The double
image is of vomiting and of volcanic eruption. Grief is like a conflict
of the four elements of fire, air, water, and earth—anger, sighs, tears,
and bowels.)   **233 ease their stomachs** relieve their resentments.
(With a play on *vomit*.)   **238 sports** entertainment   **239 That . . . me**
so that I am woeful   **241 Etna** volcanic mountain on the island of
Sicily (which will, compared to Marcus's burning heart, seem cool.
Compare with the note to line 231.)   **244 doth ease somedeal** eases
the heart somewhat   **245 But . . . death** i.e., but to mock and deny
sorrow is to experience it again and again.   **247 shrink** wither away
248 bear his name i.e., still be called life   **249 Where . . . breathe** i.e.,
where virtually nothing remains of life except the drawing of breath.
251 starvèd benumbed with cold   **252 fearful slumber** dreadful
nightmare   **253 flatt'ry** comforting deception.

256 dear grievous   **259 control** try to restrain   **262 closing up** closing
in death   **269 tributary tears** tears paid as tribute (to sorrow, the
usurping enemy).   **273 mischiefs** evils, injuries   **276 heavy** sorrowing
291 He . . . life His vows are more important to him than his life; or,
he loves his family, left behind in Rome as hostages to fortune, more
than his life.   **293 tofore** heretofore, formerly   **294 nor Lucius** neither Lucius

Beg at the gates, like Tarquin and his queen.   298
Now will I to the Goths and raise a power   299
To be revenged on Rome and Saturnine.   *Exit Lucius.*

❖

[3.2]

A banquet [set out]. Enter [Titus] Andronicus,
Marcus, Lavinia, and the boy [young Lucius].

TITUS
So, so. Now sit, and look you eat no more
Than will preserve just so much strength in us
As will revenge these bitter woes of ours.
Marcus, unknit that sorrow-wreathen knot.   4
Thy niece and I, poor creatures, want our hands   5
And cannot passionate our tenfold grief   6
With folded arms. This poor right hand of mine
Is left to tyrannize upon my breast,   8
Who, when my heart, all mad with misery,   9
Beats in this hollow prison of my flesh,
Then thus I thump it down.   [*He beats his breast.*]
[*To Lavinia*] Thou map of woe, that thus dost talk in
    signs,   12
When thy poor heart beats with outrageous beating,
Thou canst not strike it thus to make it still.
Wound it with sighing, girl, kill it with groans;   15
Or get some little knife between thy teeth
And just against thy heart make thou a hole,
That all the tears that thy poor eyes let fall
May run into that sink and, soaking in,   19
Drown the lamenting fool in sea-salt tears.   20

MARCUS
Fie, brother, fie! Teach her not thus to lay
Such violent hands upon her tender life.

TITUS
How now, has sorrow made thee dote already?   23
Why, Marcus, no man should be mad but I.
What violent hands can she lay on her life?
Ah, wherefore dost thou urge the name of hands,
To bid Aeneas tell the tale twice o'er   27
How Troy was burnt and he made miserable?
Oh, handle not the theme, to talk of hands,
Lest we remember still that we have none.   30
Fie, fie, how franticly I square my talk,   31
As if we should forget we had no hands
If Marcus did not name the word of hands!
Come, let's fall to; and, gentle girl, eat this.
Here is no drink! Hark, Marcus, what she says;

I can interpret all her martyred signs.
She says she drinks no other drink but tears,
Brewed with her sorrow, mashed upon her cheeks.   38
Speechless complainer, I will learn thy thought;
In thy dumb action will I be as perfect   40
As begging hermits in their holy prayers.
Thou shalt not sigh, nor hold thy stumps to heaven,
Nor wink, nor nod, nor kneel, nor make a sign,
But I of these will wrest an alphabet
And by still practice learn to know thy meaning.   45

BOY [*weeping*]
Good grandsire, leave these bitter deep laments!
Make my aunt merry with some pleasing tale.

MARCUS
Alas, the tender boy, in passion moved,   48
Doth weep to see his grandsire's heaviness.

TITUS
Peace, tender sapling! Thou art made of tears,
And tears will quickly melt thy life away.
                Marcus strikes the dish with a knife.
What dost thou strike at, Marcus, with thy knife?

MARCUS
At that that I have killed, my lord: a fly.

TITUS
Out on thee, murderer! Thou kill'st my heart.
Mine eyes are cloyed with view of tyranny.
A deed of death done on the innocent
Becomes not Titus' brother. Get thee gone!
I see thou art not for my company.

MARCUS
Alas, my lord, I have but killed a fly.

TITUS
"But"? How if that fly had a father and mother?
How would he hang his slender gilded wings   61
And buzz lamenting doings in the air!   62
Poor harmless fly,
That, with his pretty buzzing melody,
Came here to make us merry! And thou hast killed
    him.

MARCUS
Pardon me, sir. It was a black ill-favored fly,   66
Like to the Empress' Moor. Therefore I killed him.

TITUS   Oh, oh, oh!
Then pardon me for reprehending thee,
For thou hast done a charitable deed.
Give me thy knife. I will insult on him,   71
Flattering myself as if it were the Moor   72
Come hither purposely to poison me.—
There's for thyself, and that's for Tamora!
                [*He takes the knife and strikes.*]
Ah, sirrah!   75
Yet I think we are not brought so low   76

298 **Tarquin** Tarquinius Superbus, seventh king of Rome, who, because his son had raped a Roman lady, Lucretia, was banished and his kingdom overthrown; a republic was then established   299 **power** army
3.2. Location: Rome. Titus's house.
0.1 *banquet* (A table with chairs and dishes is brought on.)   4 **sorrow-wreathen knot** arms folded in a conventional expression of grief.
5 **want** lack   6 **passionate** express passionately   8 **tyrannize** i.e., by beating   9 **Who** which   12 **map** picture   15 **Wound it with sighing** (Each sigh was believed to cost the heart a drop of blood.)   19 **sink** receptacle   20 **fool** (Here a term of pity or endearment.)   23 **dote** be deranged   27 **Aeneas** (Aeneas tells of the fall of Troy in Book 2 of Virgil's *Aeneid.*)   30 **still** continually   31 **square** shape, regulate

38 **mashed** mixed with hot water in a mash, as for brewing   40 **action** gesture.   **perfect** thoroughly acquainted   45 **still** continual   48 **passion** sorrow   61 **he** i.e., the father   62 **And . . . air** i.e., and tell sad stories, expressing his sorrow by buzzing about.   66 **ill-favored** ugly   71 **insult on** exult over   72 **Flattering . . . if** deluding myself into believing   75 **sirrah** (Ordinary term of address to inferiors.)   76 **Yet . . . not** I do not think we are yet

But that between us we can kill a fly
That comes in likeness of a coal black Moor.

MARCUS
Alas, poor man! Grief has so wrought on him
He takes false shadows for true substances.

TITUS
Come, take away. Lavinia, go with me.   81
I'll to thy closet and go read with thee   82
Sad stories chancèd in the times of old.   83
Come, boy, and go with me. Thy sight is young,
And thou shalt read when mine begin to dazzle.   85

Exeunt.

❖

[4.1]

*Enter Lucius's son, and Lavinia running after
him, and the boy flies from her, with his books
under his arm. Enter Titus and Marcus.*

BOY
Help, grandsire, help! My aunt Lavinia
Follows me everywhere, I know not why.
Good uncle Marcus, see how swift she comes.
Alas, sweet aunt, I know not what you mean.

[He drops his books.]

MARCUS
Stand by me, Lucius. Do not fear thine aunt.

TITUS
She loves thee, boy, too well to do thee harm.

BOY
Ay, when my father was in Rome she did.   7

MARCUS
What means my niece Lavinia by these signs?

TITUS
Fear her not, Lucius. Somewhat doth she mean.   9

MARCUS
See, Lucius, see how much she makes of thee;
Somewhither would she have thee go with her.
Ah, boy, Cornelia never with more care   12
Read to her sons than she hath read to thee   13
Sweet poetry and Tully's *Orator*.   14
Canst thou not guess wherefore she plies thee thus?   15

BOY
My lord, I know not, I, nor can I guess,
Unless some fit or frenzy do possess her;
For I have heard my grandsire say full oft,
Extremity of griefs would make men mad,
And I have read that Hecuba of Troy   20
Ran mad for sorrow. That made me to fear,
Although, my lord, I know my noble aunt

Loves me as dear as e'er my mother did,
And would not but in fury fright my youth—   24
Which made me down to throw my books and fly,
Causeless, perhaps. But pardon me, sweet aunt,
And, madam, if my uncle Marcus go,   27
I will most willingly attend Your Ladyship.

MARCUS   Lucius, I will.   29

*[Lavinia turns over with her stumps the book
that young Lucius has let fall.]*

TITUS
How now, Lavinia? Marcus, what means this?
Some book there is that she desires to see.
Which is it, girl, of these?—Open them, boy.
[To Lavinia] But thou art deeper read and better skilled;
Come and take choice of all my library,
And so beguile thy sorrow till the heavens
Reveal the damned contriver of this deed.—
Why lifts she up her arms in sequence thus?   37

MARCUS
I think she means that there were more than one
Confederate in the fact. Ay, more there was;   39
Or else to heaven she heaves them for revenge.

TITUS
Lucius, what book is that she tosseth so?   41

BOY
Grandsire, 'tis Ovid's *Metamorphoses*.
My mother gave it me.

MARCUS   For love of her that's gone,
Perhaps, she culled it from among the rest.

TITUS
Soft, so busily she turns the leaves!   (*Help her.*)
What would she find? Lavinia, shall I read?
This is the tragic tale of Philomel,   48
And treats of Tereus' treason and his rape;   49
And rape, I fear, was root of thy annoy.   50

MARCUS
See, brother, see! Note how she quotes the leaves.   51

TITUS
Lavinia, wert thou thus surprised, sweet girl,
Ravished and wronged as Philomela was,
Forced in the ruthless, vast, and gloomy woods?   54
See, see!
Ay, such a place there is, where we did hunt—
Oh, had we never, never hunted there!—
Patterned by that the poet here describes,
By nature made for murders and for rapes.

MARCUS
Oh, why should nature build so foul a den,
Unless the gods delight in tragedies?

TITUS
Give signs, sweet girl—for here are none but friends—
What Roman lord it was durst do the deed.
Or slunk not Saturnine, as Tarquin erst,   64

---

81 **take away** clear the table. (The "banquet" and furniture are
removed from the stage as the scene ends.)   82 **closet** private room
83 **chancèd** that occurred   85 **dazzle** become dazzled, unable to see.
4.1. Location: Rome. Titus's garden.
7 **Ay . . . did** i.e., Yes, she loved me back in those happy days when my
father was still here, before our troubles began.   9 **Somewhat** Something   12 **Cornelia** the mother of the Gracchi brothers, the two most
famous tribunes in Roman history. (Her success in educating her sons
was highly regarded.)   13 **Read** gave instruction   14 **Tully's *Orator*** a
treatise on rhetoric by Cicero, either *De Oratore* or *ad M. Brutum Orator*.
15 **plies** importunes   20 **Hecuba** (See 1.1.136 and note.)

24 **but in fury** except in madness   27 **go** i.e., come with us. (See line
11.) The boy doesn't want to be alone with his mad aunt.   29 **Lucius**
young Lucius, the boy   37 **in sequence** one after the other   39 **fact**
deed, crime.   41 **tosseth** turns the pages of   48–9 **Philomel, Tereus**
(Compare with the note for 2.3.43.)   50 **annoy** injury.   51 **quotes**
examines   54 **vast** desolate   64 **Or . . . erst** Or was it Saturnine who
slunk, like Tarquin of old. (See 3.1.298 and note.)

That left the camp to sin in Lucrece' bed?

MARCUS
Sit down, sweet niece. Brother, sit down by me.

[*They sit.*]

Apollo, Pallas, Jove, or Mercury   67
Inspire me, that I may this treason find!
My lord, look here. Look here, Lavinia.

He writes his name with his staff, and guides it
with feet and mouth.

This sandy plot is plain; guide, if thou canst,   70
This after me. I have writ my name
Without the help of any hand at all.
Cursed be that heart that forced us to this shift!   73
Write thou, good niece, and here display at last
What God will have discovered for revenge.   75
Heaven guide thy pen to print thy sorrows plain,
That we may know the traitors and the truth!

She takes the staff in her mouth, and guides
it with her stumps, and writes.

Oh, do ye read, my lord, what she hath writ?

TITUS   "Stuprum. Chiron. Demetrius."   79

MARCUS
What, what! The lustful sons of Tamora
Performers of this heinous, bloody deed?

TITUS
Magni Dominator poli,   82
Tam lentus audis scelera, tam lentus vides?   83

MARCUS
Oh, calm thee, gentle lord, although I know
There is enough written upon this earth
To stir a mutiny in the mildest thoughts
And arm the minds of infants to exclaims.   87
My lord, kneel down with me; Lavinia, kneel;
And kneel, sweet boy, the Roman Hector's hope.   89

[*All kneel.*]

And swear with me—as, with the woeful fere   90
And father of that chaste dishonored dame,   91
Lord Junius Brutus sware for Lucrece' rape—   92
That we will prosecute by good advice   93
Mortal revenge upon these traitorous Goths,
And see their blood or die with this reproach.

[*They rise.*]

TITUS
'Tis sure enough, an you knew how.   96
But if you hunt these bear whelps, then beware:
The dam will wake an if she wind ye once.   98
She's with the lion deeply still in league,   99

And lulls him whilst she playeth on her back,   100
And when he sleeps will she do what she list.   101
You are a young huntsman, Marcus. Let alone,   102
And come, I will go get a leaf of brass,   103
And with a gad of steel will write these words,   104
And lay it by. The angry northern wind   105
Will blow these sands like Sibyl's leaves abroad,   106
And where's our lesson then? Boy, what say you?   107

BOY
I say, my lord, that if I were a man,
Their mother's bedchamber should not be safe   109
For these base bondmen to the yoke of Rome.   110

MARCUS
Ay, that's my boy! Thy father hath full oft
For his ungrateful country done the like.   112

BOY
And, uncle, so will I, an if I live.

TITUS
Come, go with me into mine armory.
Lucius, I'll fit thee, and withal my boy   115
Shall carry from me to the Empress' sons
Presents that I intend to send them both.
Come, come. Thou'lt do my message, wilt thou not?

BOY
Ay, with my dagger in their bosoms, grandsire.

TITUS
No, boy, not so. I'll teach thee another course.
Lavinia, come. Marcus, look to my house.
Lucius and I'll go brave it at the court.   122
Ay, marry, will we, sir, and we'll be waited on.   123

Exeunt [*Titus, Lavinia, and young Lucius*].

MARCUS
O heavens, can you hear a good man groan
And not relent, or not compassion him?   125
Marcus, attend him in his ecstasy,   126
That hath more scars of sorrow in his heart   127
Than foemen's marks upon his battered shield,
But yet so just that he will not revenge.
Revenge the heavens for old Andronicus!   *Exit.* 130

❧

---

67 **Pallas** Pallas Athene, Minerva   70 **plain** level, smooth   73 **shift** expedient.   75 **will have discovered** wishes to have uncovered 79 *Stuprum* **Rape.**   82–3 *Magni . . . vides?* Ruler of the mighty heavens, are you so slow to hear crimes, so slow to see? (Derived from Seneca, *Hippolytus*, 671–2, and the *Moral Epistles*, 107.)   87 **exclaims** exclamations, outcries.   89 **the Roman . . . hope** i.e., you who are the hope of your father, just as Astyanax was the hope of the great Hector of Troy.   90–2 **as . . . rape** just as both Lucius Junius Brutus, the woeful husband (*fere*, spouse), and the father of that chaste dishonored lady, Lucrece, swore to avenge her rape. (See 2.1.108 and note.)   93 **prosecute . . . advice** pursue by well-considered means   96 **an** if   98 **dam** mother.   **wind** scent   99 **the lion** the royal beast, i.e., Saturninus.   **still** always

100 **playeth on her back** (1) sports playfully like a wild animal (2) provides sex to Saturninus   101 **list** choose, please. (With a suggestion of sexual infidelity.)   102–5 **You . . . by** i.e., You are inexperienced in dealing with such cunning enemies, Marcus. Leave off your useless oaths vowing frontal attack, and I will devise something that will give permanence to our outcries, like words etched on a sheet of brass with a steel stylus, by means of which I shall store our vengeance up (*lay it by*) until the time is ripe.   105–7 **The angry . . . then?** Your oaths are like sands too easily scattered (like the prophecies of the Cumaean Sibyl, posted at the windswept entrance to her cave), and where will we be then with what we intend?
109–10 **Their . . . Rome** no place of hiding would be spared in my seeking to destroy these slaves who, rightly considered (i.e., setting aside their having been freed by Saturninus), are captives of Rome.   112 **done the like** i.e., fought against tyranny   115 **fit thee** provide you with arms.   **withal** in addition   122 **brave it** put on a good show, cut a bold figure   123 **marry** (A mild interjection, equivalent to "Indeed!"; originally an oath, "by the Virgin Mary.")   **be waited on** i.e., demand attention.   125 **compassion** have compassion for 126 **ecstasy** madness   127 **That** he who   130 **Revenge the heavens** May the heavens take revenge (since Andronicus will not)

[4.2]

*Enter Aaron, Chiron, and Demetrius, at one
door, and at the other door young Lucius and
another, with a bundle of weapons and verses
writ upon them.*

CHIRON
Demetrius, here's the son of Lucius.
He hath some message to deliver us.
AARON
Ay, some mad message from his mad grandfather.
BOY
My lords, with all the humbleness I may,
I greet your honors from Andronicus—
[*Aside*] And pray the Roman gods confound you both!   6
DEMETRIUS
Gramercy, lovely Lucius. What's the news?   7
BOY [*aside*]
That you are both deciphered, that's the news,   8
For villains marked with rape.—May it please you,
My grandsire, well advised, hath sent by me   10
The goodliest weapons of his armory
To gratify your honorable youth,   12
The hope of Rome; for so he bid me say.
And so I do, and with his gifts present
Your Lordships, that, whenever you have need,
You may be armèd and appointed well.   16
            [*His attendant presents the bundle.*]
And so I leave you both—[*aside*] like bloody villains.
            Exit [*with attendant*].
DEMETRIUS
What's here? A scroll, and written round about?   19
Let's see:
[*He reads.*] "Integer vitae, scelerisque purus,   20
        Non eget Mauri iaculis, nec arcu."   21
CHIRON
Oh, 'tis a verse in Horace; I know it well.
I read it in the grammar long ago.   23
AARON
Ay, just; a verse in Horace; right, you have it.   24
[*Aside*] Now, what a thing it is to be an ass!
Here's no sound jest! The old man hath found their
    guilt,   26
And sends them weapons wrapped about with lines
That wound, beyond their feeling, to the quick.   28
But were our witty empress well afoot,   29
She would applaud Andronicus' conceit.   30

4.2. Location: Rome. The Emperor's palace.
0.3 *another* (Presumably an attendant of Lucius, bearing the weapons
and verses; see line 16.1.)   **6 confound** destroy   **7 Gramercy** Many
thanks   **8 deciphered** detected   **10 well advised** having considered
carefully   **12 gratify** grace, please   **16 appointed** equipped   **19 round
about** all around.   **20–1** *Integer . . . arcu* (The opening lines of perhaps
the best known of the Odes of Horace, 22: "He who is spotless in life
and free of crime needs not the Moorish javelin or bow.")   **23 grammar**
i.e., Latin grammar book. (William Lilly's grammar book, containing
this passage, was widely used in Elizabethan England.)   **24 just** precisely   **26 Here's no sound jest!** (Said ironically to mean its opposite:
Here's a splendid joke indeed!)   **28 beyond . . . quick** i.e., far beyond
the capacity of Demetrius and Chiron to be sensitive to the injury, yet to
the very heart of the matter.   **29 witty** clever.   **afoot** up and about, i.e.,
not in childbed (as we soon learn she is)   **30 conceit** design.

But let her rest in her unrest awhile.—   31
And now, young lords, was 't not a happy star   32
Led us to Rome, strangers, and, more than so,
Captives, to be advancèd to this height?
It did me good, before the palace gate
To brave the tribune in his brother's hearing.   36
DEMETRIUS
But me more good to see so great a lord
Basely insinuate and send us gifts.   38
AARON
Had he not reason, Lord Demetrius?
Did you not use his daughter very friendly?
DEMETRIUS
I would we had a thousand Roman dames
At such a bay, by turn to serve our lust.   42
CHIRON
A charitable wish, and full of love!
AARON
Here lacks but your mother for to say amen.
CHIRON
And that would she, for twenty thousand more.   45
DEMETRIUS
Come, let us go and pray to all the gods
For our belovèd mother in her pains.   47
AARON
Pray to the devils. The gods have given us over.
            Trumpets sound [*within*].
DEMETRIUS
Why do the Emperor's trumpets flourish thus?
CHIRON
Belike for joy the Emperor hath a son.   50
DEMETRIUS
Soft, who comes here?

    *Enter Nurse, with a blackamoor child
    [in her arms].*

NURSE   Good morrow, lords.   51
Oh, tell me, did you see Aaron the Moor?
AARON
Well, more or less, or ne'er a whit at all,   53
Here Aaron is; and what with Aaron now?   54
NURSE
O gentle Aaron, we are all undone.
Now help, or woe betide thee evermore!
AARON
Why, what a caterwauling dost thou keep!   57
What dost thou wrap and fumble in thy arms?
NURSE
Oh, that which I would hide from heaven's eye,
Our empress' shame and stately Rome's disgrace!
She is delivered, lords, she is delivered.

31 her unrest i.e., her labor of delivery   **32 happy** fortunate
36 To . . . hearing i.e., to taunt Marcus in Titus's presence.   **38 insinu-**
ate ingratiate himself by flattery   **42 At such a bay** cornered thus (as
in hunting).   **by turn** (1) one after the other (2) doing a sexual "turn"
45 more more such occasions.   **47 pains** labor pains. (Tamora is
being delivered of a child sired by Aaron; see lines 29–31 above.)
50 Belike Probably   **51 Soft** i.e., Wait a minute   **53 more** (Punning
on *Moor*.)   **54 what** what's your business   **57 keep** keep up.

AARON   To whom?   62

NURSE   I mean she is brought abed.

AARON

Well, God give her good rest. What hath he sent her?   64

NURSE   A devil.

AARON

Why, then she is the devil's dam. A joyful issue!   66

NURSE

A joyless, dismal, black, and sorrowful issue!   67

Here is the babe, as loathsome as a toad

Amongst the fair-faced breeders of our clime.

The Empress sends it thee, thy stamp, thy seal,   70

And bids thee christen it with thy dagger's point.

AARON

Zounds, ye whore, is black so base a hue?   72

[To the child] Sweet blowze, you are a beauteous

   blossom, sure.   73

DEMETRIUS   Villain, what hast thou done?

AARON   That which thou canst not undo.

CHIRON   Thou hast undone our mother.

AARON   Villain, I have done thy mother.   77

DEMETRIUS

And therein, hellish dog, thou hast undone her.

Woe to her chance, and damned her loathèd choice!   79

Accurst the offspring of so foul a fiend!   80

CHIRON   It shall not live.

AARON   It shall not die.

NURSE

Aaron, it must. The mother wills it so.

AARON

What, must it, Nurse? Then let no man but I

Do execution on my flesh and blood.

DEMETRIUS

I'll broach the tadpole on my rapier's point.   86

Nurse, give it me. My sword shall soon dispatch it.

AARON   [taking the child and drawing his sword]

Sooner this sword shall plow thy bowels up.

Stay, murderous villains, will you kill your brother?

Now, by the burning tapers of the sky

That shone so brightly when this boy was got,   91

He dies upon my scimitar's sharp point

That touches this my firstborn son and heir!

I tell you, younglings, not Enceladus   94

With all his threat'ning band of Typhon's brood,   95

Nor great Alcides, nor the god of war   96

Shall seize this prey out of his father's hands.

What, what, ye sanguine, shallow-hearted boys!   98

Ye white-limed walls! Ye alehouse painted signs!   99

Coal black is better than another hue

In that it scorns to bear another hue;

For all the water in the ocean

Can never turn the swan's black legs to white,

Although she lave them hourly in the flood.   104

Tell the Empress from me, I am of age

To keep mine own, excuse it how she can.   106

DEMETRIUS

Wilt thou betray thy noble mistress thus?

AARON

My mistress is my mistress, this myself,   108

The vigor and the picture of my youth.

This before all the world do I prefer;

This maugre all the world will I keep safe,   111

Or some of you shall smoke for it in Rome.   112

DEMETRIUS

By this our mother is forever shamed.

CHIRON

Rome will despise her for this foul escape.   114

NURSE

The Emperor in his rage will doom her death.

CHIRON

I blush to think upon this ignomy.   116

AARON

Why, there's the privilege your beauty bears.   117

Fie, treacherous hue, that will betray with blushing

The close enacts and counsels of thy heart!   119

Here's a young lad framed of another leer.   120

Look how the black slave smiles upon the father,

As who should say, "Old lad, I am thine own."   122

He is your brother, lords, sensibly fed   123

Of that self blood that first gave life to you,   124

And from that womb where you imprisoned were

He is enfranchisèd and come to light.

Nay, he is your brother by the surer side,   127

Although my seal be stampèd in his face.   128

NURSE

Aaron, what shall I say unto the Empress?

DEMETRIUS

Advise thee, Aaron, what is to be done,   130

And we will all subscribe to thy advice.   131

Save thou the child, so we may all be safe.   132

---

62 **To whom** (Aaron plays on *delivered*, line 61, in the sense of "handed over or transferred to another person," though he, of course, knows that the Nurse means "delivered of a child.") **64 God . . . rest** (Again, Aaron jestingly pretends to misinterpret *brought abed*, line 63, in its literal sense.) **66 dam** mother. **issue** result. **67 issue** offspring. **70 thy stamp, thy seal** i.e., bearing your imprint **72 Zounds** By His (Christ's) wounds **73 blowze** red-cheeked one. (Usually addressed to a wench or slattern; here, an affectionately abusive term for the child.) **77 done** i.e., had sexual intercourse with. (Playing on *undone* in the previous line.) **79 chance** luck. **damned** damned be **80 Accurst** Accursed be **86 broach** impale **91 got** begotten **94 Enceladus** one of the giants who rose against the gods and were defeated by them; Enceladus was buried under Mount Etna in Sicily **95 Typhon** a terrible giant-monster who attacked the gods and was flung into Tartarus **96 Alcides** Hercules, a descendant of Alcaeus

98 **sanguine** red-cheeked (as distinguished from black-complexioned). **shallow-hearted** cowardly **99 white-limed** whitewashed. (The image is of a fair exterior hiding darkness within.) **alehouse painted signs** i.e., cheap painted imitations of men. **104 lave** wash. **flood** stream. **106 excuse . . . can** let her explain her situation as well as she can. **108 this myself** i.e., this child is a part of myself **111 maugre** in spite of **112 smoke** i.e., suffer. (The metaphor is from burning at the stake.) **114 escape** escapade, outrageous transgression. **116 ignomy** ignominy, shame. **117 Why . . . bears** i.e., Blushing is one of the benefits of your fair complexion. (Said ironically; Aaron prefers a hue that cannot incriminate itself.) **119 close enacts** secret purposes **120 framed** made. **leer** countenance, complexion. **122 As . . . say** as if saying, as if one might say **123–4 sensibly . . . blood** given corporeal sustenance by that same blood **127 surer** i.e., mother's **128 seal be stampèd** (See line 70 above; the child bears the imprint of the father in his looks.) **130 Advise thee** Consider **131 subscribe** agree **132 so** so long as

AARON
>   Then sit we down, and let us all consult.
>   My son and I will have the wind of you;   134
>   Keep there. Now talk at pleasure of your safety.
> > *[They sit.]*

DEMETRIUS *[to the Nurse]*
>   How many women saw this child of his?

AARON
>   Why, so, brave lords! When we join in league,
>   I am a lamb; but if you brave the Moor,   138
>   The chafèd boar, the mountain lioness,   139
>   The ocean swells not so as Aaron storms.
>   *[To the Nurse]* But say again, how many saw the child?

NURSE
>   Cornelia the midwife and myself,
>   And no one else but the delivered Empress.

AARON
>   The Empress, the midwife, and yourself.
>   Two may keep counsel when the third's away.
>   Go to the Empress, tell her this I said.   *He kills her.*
>   Wheak, wheak!—   147
>   So cries a pig preparèd to the spit.   148
> > *[They all stand up.]*

DEMETRIUS
>   What mean'st thou, Aaron? Wherefore didst thou
>   this?

AARON
>   Oh, Lord, sir, 'tis a deed of policy.   150
>   Shall she live to betray this guilt of ours,
>   A long-tongued, babbling gossip? No, lords, no.
>   And now be it known to you my full intent.
>   Not far, one Muly lives, my countryman:
>   His wife but yesternight was brought to bed;
>   His child is like to her, fair as you are.
>   Go pack with him, and give the mother gold,   157
>   And tell them both the circumstance of all,
>   And how by this their child shall be advanced
>   And be receivèd for the Emperor's heir,
>   And substituted in the place of mine,
>   To calm this tempest whirling in the court;
>   And let the Emperor dandle him for his own.
>   Hark ye, lords, you see I have given her physic,   164
> > *[pointing to the Nurse]*
>   And you must needs bestow her funeral.   165
>   The fields are near, and you are gallant grooms.   166
>   This done, see that you take no longer days,   167
>   But send the midwife presently to me.   168
>   The midwife and the nurse well made away,
>   Then let the ladies tattle what they please.

CHIRON
>   Aaron, I see thou wilt not trust the air
>   With secrets.

DEMETRIUS   For this care of Tamora,
>   Herself and hers are highly bound to thee.
> > *Exeunt [Demetrius and Chiron,*
> > *bearing off the Nurse's body].*

AARON
>   Now to the Goths, as swift as swallow flies,
>   There to dispose this treasure in mine arms   175
>   And secretly to greet the Empress' friends.   176
>   Come on, you thick-lipped slave, I'll bear you hence,
>   For it is you that puts us to our shifts.   178
>   I'll make you feed on berries and on roots,
>   And feed on curds and whey, and suck the goat,
>   And cabin in a cave, and bring you up   181
>   To be a warrior and command a camp.
> > *Exit [with the child].*

❖

[4.3]

> *Enter Titus, old Marcus, [his son Publius,]*
> *young Lucius, and other gentlemen*
> *[Sempronius, Caius], with bows; and Titus*
> *bears the arrows with letters on the ends of*
> *them.*

TITUS
>   Come, Marcus, come. Kinsmen, this is the way.
>   Sir boy, let me see your archery.
>   Look ye draw home enough, and 'tis there straight.   3
>   *Terras Astraea reliquit;*   4
>   Be you remembered, Marcus, she's gone, she's fled.   5
>   Sirs, take you to your tools. You, cousins, shall
>   Go sound the ocean, and cast your nets;
>   Happily you may catch her in the sea;   8
>   Yet there's as little justice as at land.
>   No; Publius and Sempronius, you must do it;
>   'Tis you must dig with mattock and with spade,
>   And pierce the inmost center of the earth.
>   Then, when you come to Pluto's region,   13
>   I pray you, deliver him this petition.
>   Tell him it is for justice and for aid,
>   And that it comes from old Andronicus,
>   Shaken with sorrows in ungrateful Rome.
>   Ah, Rome! Well, well, I made thee miserable
>   What time I threw the people's suffrages   19
>   On him that thus doth tyrannize o'er me.
>   Go, get you gone, and pray be careful all,
>   And leave you not a man-of-war unsearched.

---

134 **have . . . you** take the position of advantage (as in hunting, where to be downwind is to be where one will not be scented by the game) **138 brave** taunt, defy. (Playing on *brave*, gallant, well-dressed, in line 137.) **139 chafèd** enraged **147 Wheak** (Aaron mimics her dying cry.) **148 prepared to the spit** being spitted for roasting. **150 policy** prudent action. **157 pack** make a deal **164 physic** medicine **165 bestow** provide, furnish **166 grooms** fellows. **167 days** time **168 presently** at once

175 **dispose** dispose of   176 **greet . . . friends** i.e., join forces with the Goths, who presumably will defend Tamora's interests in Rome. **178 shifts** stratagems, tricks. **181 cabin** lodge **4.3. Location: Rome. A public place.** **3 home** to the full extent (of the bow).   **'tis there straight** it will reach the point aimed at forthwith. **4 Terras Astraea reliquit** Astraea (the goddess of justice) has abandoned the earth. (From Ovid, *Metamorphoses*, 1.150.) **5 Be you remembered** remember.   **she's** Justice is **8 Happily** haply, perhaps **13 Pluto's region** the underworld, ruled over by Pluto **19 What time** when.   **suffrages** assent, votes

This wicked emperor may have shipped her hence,   23
And, kinsmen, then we may go pipe for justice.   24
MARCUS
Oh, Publius, is not this a heavy case,   25
To see thy noble uncle thus distract?   26
PUBLIUS
Therefore, my lords, it highly us concerns
By day and night t'attend him carefully,
And feed his humor kindly as we may,   29
Till time beget some careful remedy.   30
MARCUS
Kinsmen, his sorrows are past remedy.   31
Join with the Goths and with revengeful war
Take wreak on Rome for this ingratitude,   33
And vengeance on the traitor Saturnine.
TITUS
Publius, how now? How now, my masters?   35
What, have you met with her?   36
PUBLIUS
No, my good lord, but Pluto sends you word,
If you will have Revenge from hell, you shall.
Marry, for Justice, she is so employed,   39
He thinks, with Jove in heaven, or somewhere else,
So that perforce you must needs stay a time.   41
TITUS
He doth me wrong to feed me with delays.
I'll dive into the burning lake below   43
And pull her out of Acheron by the heels.   44
Marcus, we are but shrubs, no cedars we,
No big-boned men framed of the Cyclops' size,   46
But metal, Marcus, steel to the very back,
Yet wrung with wrongs more than our backs can bear.
And sith there's no justice in earth nor hell,   49
We will solicit heaven and move the gods
To send down Justice for to wreak our wrongs.   51
Come, to this gear. You are a good archer, Marcus.   52
    He gives them the arrows.
"Ad Jovem," that's for you; here, "Ad Apollinem";   53
"Ad Martem," that's for myself;   54
Here, boy, "to Pallas"; here, "to Mercury";   55
"To Saturn," Caius—not "to Saturnine"!
You were as good to shoot against the wind.   57
To it, boy! Marcus, loose when I bid.   58
Of my word, I have written to effect;   59
There's not a god left unsolicited.

MARCUS
Kinsmen, shoot all your shafts into the court.
We will afflict the Emperor in his pride.
TITUS
Now, masters, draw. [*They shoot.*] Oh, well said,
    Lucius!   63
Good boy, in Virgo's lap! Give it Pallas.   64
MARCUS
My lord, I aim a mile beyond the moon;   65
Your letter is with Jupiter by this.
TITUS   Ha, ha!
Publius, Publius, what hast thou done?
See, see, thou hast shot off one of Taurus' horns.   69
MARCUS
This was the sport, my lord: when Publius shot,
The Bull, being galled, gave Aries such a knock   71
That down fell both the Ram's horns in the court;   72
And who should find them but the Empress' villain?   73
She laughed, and told the Moor he should not choose   74
But give them to his master for a present.   75
TITUS
Why, there it goes. God give His Lordship joy!   76

    *Enter the Clown, with a basket, and two
    pigeons in it.*

News, news from heaven! Marcus, the post is come.—
Sirrah, what tidings? Have you any letters?
Shall I have justice? What says Jupiter?
CLOWN   Ho, the gibbet maker? He says that he hath   80
taken them down again, for the man must not be   81
hanged till the next week.
TITUS   But what says Jupiter, I ask thee?
CLOWN   Alas, sir, I know not Jupiter. I never drank
with him in all my life.
TITUS   Why, villain, art not thou the carrier?   86
CLOWN   Ay, of my pigeons, sir; nothing else.
TITUS   Why, didst thou not come from heaven?
CLOWN   From heaven! Alas, sir, I never came there.
God forbid I should be so bold to press to heaven in
my young days. Why, I am going with my pigeons to
the tribunal plebs, to take up a matter of brawl betwixt   92
my uncle and one of the Emperal's men.   93
MARCUS   [*to Titus*]   Why, sir, that is as fit as can be to
serve for your oration; and let him deliver the
pigeons to the Emperor from you.

---

23 **her** i.e., Justice, the goddess Astraea. (In his madness, Titus imagines that Saturninus may ship Astraea out of the country in an armed naval vessel, a *man-of-war*.)   24 **pipe** whistle, i.e., look in vain   25 **heavy case** sad situation   26 **distract** distracted, crazed   29 **feed his humor** humor him   30 **careful** showing and requiring care   31 **remedy** (In the Quarto, this word is followed by a catchword *But* at the foot of the page that is not repeated in the first line of the next page, possibly suggesting an omission in the text, something like "But let us live in hope that Lucius will.")   33 **wreak** vengeance   35 **masters** good sirs. 36 **her** i.e., Justice.   39 **for** as for   41 **stay a time** wait awhile. 43 **burning lake** i.e., Phlegethon, the burning river of the underworld 44 **Acheron** a river in the underworld   46 **Cyclops** one-eyed giants in Homer's *Odyssey* (9)   49 **sith** since   51 **for to wreak** to avenge 52 **gear** business.   53–4 ***Ad Jovem, Ad Apollinem, Ad Martem*** to Jove, to Apollo, to Mars   55 **Pallas** Pallas Athene   57 **You ... wind** You might as well shoot against the wind (as appeal to Saturninus). 58 **loose** let fly   59 **Of** On

63 **well said** well done   64 **in Virgo's lap** in the constellation of the Virgin (the zodiacal sign representing Astraea, having fled from earth).   **Give it Pallas** i.e., Shoot the arrow labeled "Pallas" there.   65 **a mile ... moon** (Marcus' literal meaning is intended to humor Titus' madness, but his expression also means "wild conjecture, far wide of the mark," thus commenting on the madness of their proceedings.)   69 **Taurus** the Bull; a zodiacal sign   71 **galled** slightly wounded.   **Ares** the horned Ram; a zodiacal sign   72 **horns** i.e., signs of being a cuckold, bestowed by Aaron on the Emperor 73 **villain** i.e., Aaron, both servant and villain in the modern sense. 74–5 **should ... But** must   76 **there it goes** (A hunting cry of encouragement.)   76.1 **Clown** rustic   80 **gibbet maker** (The Clown seems to have heard "Jupiter" as "gibbeter.")   81 **them** i.e., the gallows. **must not be** is not to be   86 **carrier** postman. (But the Clown answers in the sense of "one who carries things.")   92 **tribunal plebs** i.e., *tribuni plebs*, tribunes charged to look after the interests of the plebeians   93 **Emperal's** (Malapropism for "Emperor's.")

TITUS [*to Clown*]
    Sirrah, come hither. Make no more ado,   97
    But give your pigeons to the Emperor.
    By me thou shalt have justice at his hands.
    Hold, hold; meanwhile here's money for thy charges. 100
                        [*He gives money.*]
    Give me pen and ink.
    Sirrah, can you with a grace deliver up a supplication?
CLOWN   Ay, sir.
TITUS [*writing and handing him a supplication*]   Then
    here is a supplication for you. And when you come to
    him, at the first approach you must kneel, then kiss
    his foot, then deliver up your pigeons, and then look
    for your reward. I'll be at hand, sir; see you do it
    bravely.   109
CLOWN   I warrant you, sir. Let me alone.   110
TITUS
    Sirrah, hast thou a knife? Come let me see it.
         [*He takes the knife and gives it to Marcus.*]
    Here, Marcus, fold it in the oration;
    [*To the Clown*] For thou must hold it like an humble
    supplicant.—
    And when thou hast given it to the Emperor,
    Knock at my door and tell me what he says.
CLOWN   God be with you, sir. I will.   *Exit.*
TITUS   Come, Marcus, let us go. Publius, follow me.
                                 Exeunt.

❖

[4.4]

*Enter Emperor [Saturninus] and Empress
[Tamora] and her two sons [and others, including guards]. The Emperor brings the arrows in
his hand that Titus shot at him. [The Emperor
and Empress sit.]*

SATURNINUS
    Why, lords, what wrongs are these! Was ever seen
    An emperor in Rome thus overborne,   2
    Troubled, confronted thus, and, for the extent   3
    Of equal justice, used in such contempt?   4
    My lords, you know, as know the mightful gods,
    However these disturbers of our peace
    Buzz in the people's ears, there naught hath passed
    But even with law against the willful sons   8
    Of old Andronicus. And what an if
    His sorrows have so overwhelmed his wits?
    Shall we be thus afflicted in his wreaks,   11
    His fits, his frenzy, and his bitterness?
    And now he writes to heaven for his redress.
    See, here's "to Jove," and this "to Mercury,"
    This "to Apollo," this to the god of war—

    Sweet scrolls to fly about the streets of Rome!
    What's this but libeling against the Senate
    And blazoning our unjustice everywhere?   18
    A goodly humor, is it not, my lords?   19
    As who would say, in Rome no justice were.
    But if I live, his feignèd ecstasies   21
    Shall be no shelter to these outrages;
    But he and his shall know that justice lives   23
    In Saturninus' health, whom, if he sleep,   24
    He'll so awake as he in fury shall   25
    Cut off the proud'st conspirator that lives.   26
TAMORA
    My gracious lord, my lovely Saturnine,
    Lord of my life, commander of my thoughts,
    Calm thee, and bear the faults of Titus' age,
    Th'effects of sorrow for his valiant sons,
    Whose loss hath pierced him deep and scarred his
       heart;
    And rather comfort his distressèd plight
    Than prosecute the meanest or the best   33
    For these contempts. [*Aside*] Why, thus it shall become
    High-witted Tamora to gloze withal.   35
    But, Titus, I have touched thee to the quick;
    Thy lifeblood out, if Aaron now be wise,   37
    Then is all safe, the anchor in the port.

              Enter Clown.

    How now, good fellow, wouldst thou speak with us?
CLOWN   Yea, forsooth, an your mistress-ship be emperial.
TAMORA   Empress I am, but yonder sits the Emperor.
CLOWN   'Tis he. [*He kneels.*] God and Saint Stephen give
    you good e'en. I have brought you a letter and a   43
    couple of pigeons here.
             He [Saturninus] reads the letter.
SATURNINUS
    Go, take him away, and hang him presently.   45
CLOWN   How much money must I have?   46
TAMORA   Come, sirrah, you must be hanged.
CLOWN   Hanged! By'r Lady, then I have brought up a 48
    neck to a fair end.   *Exit [guarded].*
SATURNINUS
    Despiteful and intolerable wrongs!
    Shall I endure this monstrous villainy?
    I know from whence this same device proceeds.
    May this be borne?—as if his traitorous sons,
    That died by law for murder of our brother,
    Have by my means been butchered wrongfully!
    Go, drag the villain hither by the hair.
    Nor age nor honor shall shape privilege.   57

---

97 Sirrah (In the early texts, this line is preceded by four lines that appear to be a first draft of lines 102–3: "TITUS Tell me, can you deliver an oration to the Emperor with a grace? CLOWN Nay, truly, sir, I could never say grace in all my life.")   **100 charges** expenses.   **109 bravely** handsomely, stylishly.   **110 Let me alone** Leave it to me.
4.4. Location: Rome. Before or in the palace.
2 overborne oppressed   **3 for the extent** as his reward for the exercising   **4 equal** evenhanded   **8 even** conformable   **11 wreaks** revengeful acts

18 blazoning proclaiming   **19 humor** whim, caprice   **21 ecstasies** fits of madness   **23–6 But . . . lives** but Titus and the Andronici will learn (to their sorrow) that justice is alive and well in me, Saturninus, whose fury, once awakened, will punish even the proudest of conspirators. (Some editors emend "he" in lines 24 and 25 to "she," supposing that the reference is to the goddess of Justice.)   **33 the meanest or the best** those of low or high station   **35 High-witted** clever.   **to gloze withal** to deceive in this way.   **37 Thy lifeblood out** once your lifeblood is spilled.   **wise** i.e., wise enough to keep silent about the baby   **43 good e'en** good afternoon or evening.   **45 presently** at once.   **46 must** I am I to   **48 By'r Lady** By Our Lady, the Virgin Mary   **57 Nor** neither.   **shape privilege** make for exemption.

For this proud mock I'll be thy slaughterman,
Sly frantic wretch, that holp'st to make me great   59
In hope thyself should govern Rome and me.   60

Enter nuntius, Aemilius.

What news with thee, Aemilius?

AEMILIUS
Arm, my lords! Rome never had more cause.
The Goths have gathered head, and with a power   63
Of high-resolvèd men bent to the spoil   64
They hither march amain under conduct   65
Of Lucius, son to old Andronicus,
Who threats in course of this revenge to do
As much as ever Coriolanus did.   68

SATURNINUS
Is warlike Lucius general of the Goths?
These tidings nip me, and I hang the head
As flowers with frost or grass beat down with storms.
Ay, now begins our sorrows to approach.
'Tis he the common people love so much;
Myself hath often heard them say,
When I have walkèd like a private man,   75
That Lucius' banishment was wrongfully,   76
And they have wished that Lucius were their emperor.

TAMORA
Why should you fear? Is not your city strong?

SATURNINUS
Ay, but the citizens favor Lucius
And will revolt from me to succor him.

TAMORA
King, be thy thoughts imperious, like thy name.   81
Is the sun dimmed, that gnats do fly in it?   82
The eagle suffers little birds to sing
And is not careful what they mean thereby,   84
Knowing that with the shadow of his wings
He can at pleasure stint their melody;   86
Even so mayst thou the giddy men of Rome.   87
Then cheer thy spirit, for know, thou Emperor,
I will enchant the old Andronicus
With words more sweet and yet more dangerous
Than baits to fish or honey-stalks to sheep,   91
Whenas the one is wounded with the bait,   92
The other rotted with delicious feed.   93

SATURNINUS
But he will not entreat his son for us.   94

TAMORA
If Tamora entreat him, then he will;
For I can smooth and fill his agèd ears   96
With golden promises, that were his heart

Almost impregnable, his old ears deaf,
Yet should both ear and heart obey my tongue.
[*To Aemilius*] Go thou before to be our ambassador.
Say that the Emperor requests a parley
Of warlike Lucius, and appoint the meeting   102
Even at his father's house, the old Andronicus.

SATURNINUS
Aemilius, do this message honorably,
And if he stand on hostage for his safety,   105
Bid him demand what pledge will please him best.   106

AEMILIUS
Your bidding shall I do effectually.   *Exit.*

TAMORA
Now will I to that old Andronicus
And temper him with all the art I have   109
To pluck proud Lucius from the warlike Goths.
And now, sweet Emperor, be blithe again
And bury all thy fear in my devices.

SATURNINUS
Then go successantly, and plead to him.   *Exeunt.* 113

❖

[5.1]

[*Flourish.*] *Enter Lucius with an army
of Goths, with drums and soldiers.*

LUCIUS
Approvèd warriors and my faithful friends,   1
I have receivèd letters from great Rome   2
Which signifies what hate they bear their emperor
And how desirous of our sight they are.
Therefore, great lords, be as your titles witness,   5
Imperious, and impatient of your wrongs,
And wherein Rome hath done you any scath   7
Let him make treble satisfaction.   8

A GOTH
Brave slip, sprung from the great Andronicus,   9
Whose name was once our terror, now our comfort,
Whose high exploits and honorable deeds
Ingrateful Rome requites with foul contempt,
Be bold in us. We'll follow where thou lead'st,   13
Like stinging bees in hottest summer's day
Led by their master to the flowered fields,   15
And be avenged on cursèd Tamora.

ALL THE GOTHS
And as he saith, so say we all with him.

LUCIUS
I humbly thank him, and I thank you all.
But who comes here, led by a lusty Goth?   19

*Enter a Goth, leading of Aaron with his child in
his arms.*

---

59 **holp'st** helped   60.1 *nuntius* messenger   63 **gathered head** raised
an army.   **power** armed force   64 **bent to the spoil** intent on plunder
65 **amain** forcefully, swiftly.   **conduct** command   68 **Coriolanus** an
early Roman hero turned enemy of Rome, about whom Shakespeare
wrote one of his later tragedies   75 **walkèd . . . man** i.e., gone in disguise among the commoners, like Henry V or the Duke in *Measure for
Measure*   76 **wrongfully** wrongfully imposed   81 **imperious** imperial   82 **that** merely because   84 **careful** full of concern   86 **stint** stop
87 **giddy** changeable in opinion and allegiance   91 **honey-stalks**
clover. (Too much clover can make sheep ill.)   92 **Whenas** when
93 **rotted** afflicted by the rot, a liver disease in sheep   94 **entreat his
son** i.e., entreat Lucius not to attack Rome   96 **smooth** flatter

102 **Of** with   105 **stand** insist   106 **demand** request   109 **temper**
work upon   113 **successantly** at once
5.1. Location: Near Rome.
0.2 *drums* drummers   1 **Approvèd** Put to proof, tried   2 **letters** a
letter   5 **be . . . witness** live up to the greatness your noble titles
proclaim   7 **scath** injury   8 **him** Saturninus (who is to pay for all
the wrongs Rome has done the Goths)   9 **slip** offspring, scion
13 **bold** confident   15 **their master** (Bees were thought to be led by
a king bee.)   19 **lusty** valiant

ANOTHER GOTH

Renownèd Lucius, from our troops I strayed
To gaze upon a ruinous monastery,   21
And as I earnestly did fix mine eye
Upon the wasted building, suddenly   23
I heard a child cry underneath a wall.
I made unto the noise, when soon I heard   25
The crying babe controlled with this discourse: 26
"Peace, tawny slave, half me and half thy dam!   27
Did not thy hue bewray whose brat thou art,   28
Had nature lent thee but thy mother's look,
Villain, thou mightst have been an emperor.
But where the bull and cow are both milk white,
They never do beget a coal black calf.
Peace, villain, peace!"—even thus he rates the babe—   33
"For I must bear thee to a trusty Goth,
Who, when he knows thou art the Empress' babe,
Will hold thee dearly for thy mother's sake."
With this, my weapon drawn, I rushed upon him,
Surprised him suddenly, and brought him hither
To use as you think needful of the man.   39

LUCIUS

O worthy Goth, this is the incarnate devil
That robbed Andronicus of his good hand!
This is the pearl that pleased your empress' eye,
And here's the base fruit of her burning lust.—   43
Say, walleyed slave, whither wouldst thou convey   44
This growing image of thy fiendlike face?   45
Why dost not speak? What, deaf? Not a word?—
A halter, soldiers! Hang him on this tree,
And by his side his fruit of bastardy.

AARON

Touch not the boy. He is of royal blood.

LUCIUS

Too like the sire for ever being good.   50
First hang the child, that he may see it sprawl—   51
A sight to vex the father's soul withal.
Get me a ladder.

[*A ladder is brought, which Aaron
is made to ascend.*]

AARON   Lucius, save the child,
And bear it from me to the Empress.
If thou do this, I'll show thee wondrous things
That highly may advantage thee to hear.
If thou wilt not, befall what may befall,
I'll speak no more but "Vengeance rot you all!"

LUCIUS

Say on. An if it please me which thou speak'st,   59
Thy child shall live, and I will see it nourished.   60

AARON

An if it please thee! Why, assure thee, Lucius,
'Twill vex thy soul to hear what I shall speak;
For I must talk of murders, rapes, and massacres,

Acts of black night, abominable deeds,
Complots of mischief, treason, villainies,   65
Ruthful to hear, yet piteously performed.   66
And this shall all be buried in my death,
Unless thou swear to me my child shall live.

LUCIUS

Tell on thy mind. I say thy child shall live.

AARON

Swear that he shall, and then I will begin.

LUCIUS

Who should I swear by? Thou believest no god.
That granted, how canst thou believe an oath?

AARON

What if I do not? As, indeed, I do not.
Yet, for I know thou art religious   74
And hast a thing within thee callèd conscience,
With twenty popish tricks and ceremonies
Which I have seen thee careful to observe,
Therefore I urge thy oath. For that I know   78
An idiot holds his bauble for a god   79
And keeps the oath which by that god he swears,
To that I'll urge him. Therefore thou shalt vow
By that same god, what god soe'er it be
That thou adorest and hast in reverence,
To save my boy, to nourish and bring him up,
Or else I will discover naught to thee.

LUCIUS

Even by my god I swear to thee I will.

AARON

First know thou, I begot him on the Empress.

LUCIUS

O most insatiate and luxurious woman!   88

AARON

Tut, Lucius, this was but a deed of charity
To that which thou shalt hear of me anon.   90
'Twas her two sons that murdered Bassianus;
They cut thy sister's tongue, and ravished her,
And cut her hands, and trimmed her as thou sawest.   93

LUCIUS

O detestable villain! Call'st thou that trimming?

AARON

Why, she was washed and cut and trimmed, and 'twas
Trim sport for them which had the doing of it.   96

LUCIUS

O barbarous, beastly villains, like thyself!

AARON

Indeed, I was their tutor to instruct them.
That codding spirit had they from their mother,   99
As sure a card as ever won the set;   100
That bloody mind I think they learned of me,
As true a dog as ever fought at head.   102
Well, let my deeds be witness of my worth.
I trained thy brethren to that guileful hole   104

---

21 ruinous decayed   **23 wasted** ruined   **25 made unto** approached
26 controlled calmed   **27 slave** (Used affectionately, as also in *brat,*
line 28, and *villain,* lines 30 and 33.)   **dam** mother.   **28 bewray** reveal
33 rates chides   **39 use . . . man** deal with the man as you think fit.
43 fruit i.e., the baby   **44 walleyed** glaring   **45 image** likeness
50 for ever being ever to be   **51 sprawl** twitch convulsively in the
death agony   **59 An if** If   **60 nourished** cared for.

65 Complots conspiracies   **66 Ruthful** lamentable, pitiable.
piteously in a way to excite pity   **74 for** because   **78 urge** insist on.
For that Because   **79 bauble** fool's stick   **88 luxurious** lecherous
90 To compared to   **93 trimmed** (1) decked out, made ready (2) cut off
the excrescences (3) ravished   **96 Trim** fine. (With a play on *trimmed,*
lines 93–5.)   **99 codding** lustful   **100 set** game   **102 as . . . head** as
ever went for the bear's head (in bearbaiting).   **104 trained** lured

Where the dead corpse of Bassianus lay;
I wrote the letter that thy father found,
And hid the gold within that letter mentioned,
Confederate with the Queen and her two sons;
And what not done, that thou hast cause to rue,
Wherein I had no stroke of mischief in it?
I played the cheater for thy father's hand,   111
And when I had it, drew myself apart
And almost broke my heart with extreme laughter.
I pried me through the crevice of a wall   114
When, for his hand, he had his two sons' heads,
Beheld his tears, and laughed so heartily
That both mine eyes were rainy like to his;
And when I told the Empress of this sport,
She swoonèd almost at my pleasing tale,
And for my tidings gave me twenty kisses.

A GOTH
What, canst thou say all this and never blush?

AARON
Ay, like a black dog, as the saying is.   122

LUCIUS
Art thou not sorry for these heinous deeds?

AARON
Ay, that I had not done a thousand more.
Even now I curse the day—and yet, I think,
Few come within the compass of my curse—
Wherein I did not some notorious ill,
As kill a man, or else devise his death,
Ravish a maid, or plot the way to do it,
Accuse some innocent and forswear myself,
Set deadly enmity between two friends,
Make poor men's cattle break their necks,
Set fire on barns and haystacks in the night
And bid the owners quench them with their tears.
Oft have I digged up dead men from their graves
And set them upright at their dear friends' door,
Even when their sorrows almost was forgot,
And on their skins, as on the bark of trees,
Have with my knife carvèd in Roman letters,
"Let not your sorrow die, though I am dead."
But I have done a thousand dreadful things   141
As willingly as one would kill a fly,
And nothing grieves me heartily indeed
But that I cannot do ten thousand more.

LUCIUS [to his soldiers]
Bring down the devil, for he must not die
So sweet a death as hanging presently.   146
        [Aaron is brought down.]

AARON
If there be devils, would I were a devil,
To live and burn in everlasting fire,

So I might have your company in hell
But to torment you with my bitter tongue!

LUCIUS
Sirs, stop his mouth, and let him speak no more.
        [Aaron is gagged.]

        Enter Aemilius.

A GOTH
My lord, there is a messenger from Rome
Desires to be admitted to your presence.   153

LUCIUS   Let him come near.
Welcome, Aemilius. What's the news from Rome?

AEMILIUS
Lord Lucius, and you princes of the Goths,
The Roman Emperor greets you all by me;
And, for he understands you are in arms,   158
He craves a parley at your father's house,
Willing you to demand your hostages,
And they shall be immediately delivered.

A GOTH   What says our general?

LUCIUS
Aemilius, let the Emperor give his pledges   163
Unto my father and my uncle Marcus,
And we will come. March away.   [Flourish. Exeunt.]

❖

[5.2]

        Enter Tamora and her two sons, disguised.

TAMORA
Thus, in this strange and sad habiliment,   1
I will encounter with Andronicus
And say I am Revenge, sent from below
To join with him and right his heinous wrongs.
Knock at his study, where they say he keeps   5
To ruminate strange plots of dire revenge.
Tell him Revenge is come to join with him
And work confusion on his enemies.   8

        They knock, and Titus [above] opens his
        study door.

TITUS
Who doth molest my contemplation?
Is it your trick to make me ope the door,
That so my sad decrees may fly away   11
And all my study be to no effect?
You are deceived, for what I mean to do,
See here, in bloody lines I have set down,
And what is written shall be executed.
        [He shows a paper.]

TAMORA
Titus, I am come to talk with thee.

---

111 **cheater** (1) deceiver (2) escheater, one designated to take care of property forfeited to the crown   114 **pried me** peered. (*Me* is used colloquially.)   122 **like a black dog** ("To blush like a black dog" is a proverb with ironic meaning, as here; at 4.2.117–19, Aaron is proud that, being black, he cannot blush.)   141 **But** i.e., But why go on with this recital. (Sometimes emended to *Tut*, as in the Second Quarto.)   146 **presently** immediately.

153 **Desires** who desires   158 **for** since   163 **pledges** hostages. (Both sides to the parley are to send hostages to the opposite camp while the talks continue, to ensure against any treacherous dealing.)   **5.2. Location: Rome. The court of Titus' house.**   1 **sad habiliment** somber garments   5 **keeps** keeps himself   8 **confusion** destruction   11 **sad decrees** solemn resolutions

TITUS
No, not a word. How can I grace my talk,
Wanting a hand to give it action?   18
Thou hast the odds of me; therefore no more.   19

TAMORA
If thou didst know me, thou wouldst talk with me.

TITUS
I am not mad; I know thee well enough.
Witness this wretched stump, witness these crimson
  lines,   22
Witness these trenches made by grief and care,   23
Witness the tiring day and heavy night,
Witness all sorrow, that I know thee well
For our proud empress, mighty Tamora.
Is not thy coming for my other hand?

TAMORA
Know, thou sad man, I am not Tamora;
She is thy enemy, and I thy friend.
I am Revenge, sent from th'infernal kingdom
To ease the gnawing vulture of thy mind
By working wreakful vengeance on thy foes.   32
Come down and welcome me to this world's light;
Confer with me of murder and of death.
There's not a hollow cave or lurking-place,
No vast obscurity or misty vale   36
Where bloody murder or detested rape
Can couch for fear, but I will find them out,   38
And in their ears tell them my dreadful name,
Revenge, which makes the foul offender quake.

TITUS
Art thou Revenge? And art thou sent to me
To be a torment to mine enemies?

TAMORA
I am. Therefore come down and welcome me.

TITUS
Do me some service ere I come to thee.
Lo, by thy side where Rape and Murder stands.
Now give some surance that thou art Revenge: 46
Stab them, or tear them on thy chariot wheels,
And then I'll come and be thy wagoner,
And whirl along with thee about the globe.
Provide thee two proper palfreys, black as jet,   50
To hale thy vengeful wagon swift away   51
And find out murderers in their guilty caves;
And when thy car is loaden with their heads,   53
I will dismount, and by thy wagon wheel
Trot like a servile footman all day long,
Even from Hyperion's rising in the east   56
Until his very downfall in the sea;
And day by day I'll do this heavy task,
So thou destroy Rapine and Murder there.   59

TAMORA
These are my ministers, and come with me.

TITUS
Are they thy ministers? What are they called?

TAMORA
Rape and Murder, therefore callèd so
'Cause they take vengeance of such kind of men.   63

TITUS
Good Lord, how like the Empress' sons they are,
And you the Empress! But we worldly men   65
Have miserable, mad, mistaking eyes.
O sweet Revenge, now do I come to thee,
And if one arm's embracement will content thee,
I will embrace thee in it by and by.   [Exit above.]

TAMORA
This closing with him fits his lunacy.   70
Whate'er I forge to feed his brainsick humors   71
Do you uphold and maintain in your speeches,
For now he firmly takes me for Revenge;
And being credulous in this mad thought,
I'll make him send for Lucius his son,
And whilst I at a banquet hold him sure,   76
I'll find some cunning practice out of hand   77
To scatter and disperse the giddy Goths
Or at the least make them his enemies.
See, here he comes, and I must ply my theme.   80

[Enter Titus below.]

TITUS
Long have I been forlorn, and all for thee.
Welcome, dread Fury, to my woeful house.   82
Rapine and Murder, you are welcome too.
How like the Empress and her sons you are!
Well are you fitted, had you but a Moor.   85
Could not all hell afford you such a devil?
For well I wot the Empress never wags   87
But in her company there is a Moor;
And, would you represent our queen aright,
It were convenient you had such a devil.   90
But welcome as you are. What shall we do?

TAMORA
What wouldst thou have us do, Andronicus?

DEMETRIUS
Show me a murderer, I'll deal with him.

CHIRON
Show me a villain that hath done a rape,
And I am sent to be revenged on him.

TAMORA
Show me a thousand that hath done thee wrong,
And I will be revengèd on them all.

TITUS [to Demetrius]
Look round about the wicked streets of Rome,
And when thou find'st a man that's like thyself,
Good Murder, stab him; he's a murderer.

18 Wanting . . . action lacking a hand to provide suitable gesture by way of support.   19 odds of advantage over   22 crimson i.e., bloody (as in line 14)   23 trenches i.e., wrinkles   32 wreakful vengeful   36 obscurity place of darkness and desolation   38 couch lie hidden   46 surance assurance   50 proper excellent, handsome.   palfreys horses   51 hale pull   53 car chariot   56 Hyperion's the sun god's   59 So provided that

63 of . . . men i.e., upon rapists and murderers.   65 worldly mortal   70 closing agreeing   71 forge invent.   humors moods, whims   76 hold him sure detain Lucius where he can do no harm   77 practice plot.   out of hand on the spur of the moment   80 ply my theme apply myself to my plan.   82 Fury (The Furies were primeval beings devoted to avenging certain crimes, especially against the ties of kinship.)   85 fitted i.e., fitted out to resemble the Empress   87 wags moves about   90 were convenient would be fitting

[*To Chiron*] Go thou with him, and when it is thy hap   101
To find another that is like to thee,
Good Rapine, stab him; he is a ravisher.
[*To Tamora*] Go thou with them, and in the Emperor's
   court
There is a queen, attended by a Moor;
Well shalt thou know her by thine own proportion,
For up and down she doth resemble thee.   107
I pray thee, do on them some violent death;
They have been violent to me and mine.

TAMORA
Well hast thou lessoned us; this shall we do.
But would it please thee, good Andronicus,
To send for Lucius, thy thrice-valiant son,
Who leads towards Rome a band of warlike Goths,
And bid him come and banquet at thy house,
When he is here, even at thy solemn feast,   115
I will bring in the Empress and her sons,
The Emperor himself, and all thy foes,
And at thy mercy shall they stoop and kneel,
And on them shalt thou ease thy angry heart.
What says Andronicus to this device?

TITUS [*calling*]
Marcus, my brother! 'Tis sad Titus calls.

   Enter Marcus.

Go, gentle Marcus, to thy nephew Lucius;
Thou shalt inquire him out among the Goths.
Bid him repair to me and bring with him   124
Some of the chiefest princes of the Goths.
Bid him encamp his soldiers where they are.
Tell him the Emperor and the Empress too
Feast at my house, and he shall feast with them.
This do thou for my love; and so let him,
As he regards his agèd father's life.

MARCUS
This will I do, and soon return again.   [*Exit.*]

TAMORA
Now will I hence about thy business
And take my ministers along with me.

TITUS
Nay, nay, let Rape and Murder stay with me,
Or else I'll call my brother back again
And cleave to no revenge but Lucius.   136

TAMORA [*aside to her sons*]
What say you, boys? Will you abide with him
Whiles I go tell my lord the Emperor
How I have governed our determined jest?   139
Yield to his humor, smooth and speak him fair,   140
And tarry with him till I turn again.   141

TITUS [*aside*]
I knew them all, though they supposed me mad,
And will o'erreach them in their own devices—
A pair of cursèd hellhounds and their dam!

DEMETRIUS
Madam, depart at pleasure. Leave us here.

TAMORA
Farewell, Andronicus. Revenge now goes
To lay a complot to betray thy foes.   147

TITUS
I know thou dost; and, sweet Revenge, farewell.
                                    [*Exit Tamora.*]

CHIRON
Tell us, old man, how shall we be employed?

TITUS
Tut, I have work enough for you to do.   [*He calls.*]
   Publius, come hither! Caius, and Valentine!

   [*Enter Publius, Caius, and Valentine.*]

PUBLIUS   What is your will?
TITUS   Know you these two?
PUBLIUS
   The Empress' sons, I take them: Chiron, Demetrius.   154

TITUS
Fie, Publius, fie! Thou art too much deceived.
The one is Murder, and Rape is the other's name;
And therefore bind them, gentle Publius.
Caius and Valentine, lay hands on them.
Oft have you heard me wish for such an hour,
And now I find it. Therefore bind them sure,   160
And stop their mouths if they begin to cry.   [*Exit.*] 161
                [*Publius, Caius, and Valentine lay hold
                            on Chiron and Demetrius.*]

CHIRON
Villains, forbear! We are the Empress' sons.

PUBLIUS
And therefore do we what we are commanded.—   163
Stop close their mouths; let them not speak a word.
                [*They gag and bind the two sons.*]
Is he sure bound? Look that you bind them fast.

   *Enter Titus Andronicus with a knife,
   and Lavinia with a basin.*

TITUS
Come, come, Lavinia. Look, thy foes are bound.—
Sirs, stop their mouths. Let them not speak to me,
But let them hear what fearful words I utter.—
O villains, Chiron and Demetrius!
Here stands the spring whom you have stained with
   mud,   170
This goodly summer with your winter mixed.
You killed her husband, and for that vile fault
Two of her brothers were condemned to death,
My hand cut off and made a merry jest;
Both her sweet hands, her tongue, and that more dear
Than hands or tongue, her spotless chastity,
Inhuman traitors, you constrained and forced.
What would you say if I should let you speak?
Villains, for shame you could not beg for grace.   179

101 **hap** chance   107 **up and down** from top to toe   115 **solemn**
stately   124 **repair** come   136 **but Lucius** i.e., but that which Lucius
and his army can provide.   139 **governed . . . jest** managed the
exploit we determined on.   140 **smooth . . . fair** flatter and humor
him   141 **turn** return

147 **complot** conspiracy   154 **take them** take them to be   160 **sure**
securely   161 **cry** cry out.   163 **therefore** for that very reason
170 **spring** i.e., Lavinia   179 **for shame . . . grace** i.e., your colossal
shame would not let you beg for mercy, would choke your plea.

Hark, wretches, how I mean to martyr you.   180
This one hand yet is left to cut your throats,
Whiles that Lavinia 'tween her stumps doth hold   182
The basin that receives your guilty blood.
You know your mother means to feast with me,
And calls herself Revenge, and thinks me mad.
Hark, villains, I will grind your bones to dust,
And with your blood and it I'll make a paste,   187
And of the paste a coffin I will rear,   188
And make two pasties of your shameful heads,   189
And bid that strumpet, your unhallowed dam,
Like to the earth swallow her own increase.   191
This is the feast that I have bid her to,
And this the banquet she shall surfeit on;
For worse than Philomel you used my daughter,
And worse than Procne I will be revenged.   195
And now prepare your throats. Lavinia, come.
                              He cuts their throats.
Receive the blood, and when that they are dead,
Let me go grind their bones to powder small,
And with this hateful liquor temper it,   199
And in that paste let their vile heads be baked.
Come, come, be everyone officious   201
To make this banquet, which I wish may prove
More stern and bloody than the Centaurs' feast.   203
So, now bring them in, for I'll play the cook,
And see them ready against their mother comes.   205
                     Exeunt [bearing the dead bodies].

❖

[5.3]

Enter Lucius, Marcus, and the Goths [with
Aaron prisoner, and an attendant bearing
his child].

LUCIUS
Uncle Marcus, since 'tis my father's mind
That I repair to Rome, I am content.   2
A GOTH
And ours with thine, befall what fortune will.   3
LUCIUS
Good uncle, take you in this barbarous Moor,   4
This ravenous tiger, this accursed devil.
Let him receive no sust'nance. Fetter him

---

180 martyr torture, kill cruelly   **182 Whiles that** while   **187 paste**
dough   **188 coffin** pie crust. (Also suggesting the container in which
they will be buried.)   **189 pasties** meat pies   **191 Like ... increase**
swallow her offspring, just as the earth devours all her children when
they have died.   **195 worse than Procne** (An allusion to Procne's
revenge on Tereus for raping her sister Philomel; compare with the
note for 2.3.43. She killed her son Itys and served his flesh to Tereus, his
father. In Seneca's *Thyestes*, Atreus similarly sets before Thyestes a dish
of his own children's flesh.)   **199 temper** moisten, mix   **201 officious**
busy   **203 Centaurs' feast** i.e., the wedding feast of Pirithous and Hippodamia to which the Lapithae invited the Centaurs, fabulous creatures, half-men and half-horses. (The Centaurs attempted to carry off
the women but were slaughtered by their hosts.)   **205 against** by the
time that
5.3. Location: The scene appears to take place in a court in Titus's
house; in the opening lines, Lucius speaks as if he and his soldiers
have just arrived in Rome.
2 repair return   **3 ours with thine** i.e., our intentions are in agreement with yours   **4 in** i.e., into Titus's house; see line 123

Till he be brought unto the Empress' face   7
For testimony of her foul proceedings.   8
And see the ambush of our friends be strong;   9
I fear the Emperor means no good to us.
AARON
Some devil whisper curses in my ear
And prompt me that my tongue may utter forth
The venomous malice of my swelling heart!
LUCIUS
Away, inhuman dog, unhallowed slave!
Sirs, help our uncle to convey him in.
                    [Exeunt Goths, with Aaron.]
                        Sound trumpets [within].
The trumpets show the Emperor is at hand.

         Enter Emperor [Saturninus] and Empress
         [Tamora], with [Aemilius,] tribunes, [senators],
         and others.

SATURNINUS
What, hath the firmament more suns than one?   17
LUCIUS
What boots it thee to call thyself a sun?   18
MARCUS
Rome's emperor, and nephew, break the parle.   19
These quarrels must be quietly debated.
The feast is ready which the careful Titus   21
Hath ordained to an honorable end,
For peace, for love, for league, and good to Rome.
Please you therefore draw nigh and take your places.
SATURNINUS   Marcus, we will.
         [A table is brought in. The company sit down.]

         Trumpets sounding, enter Titus like a cook,
         placing the dishes, and Lavinia with a veil over
         her face, [young Lucius, and others].

TITUS
Welcome, my gracious lord; welcome, dread Queen;
Welcome, ye warlike Goths; welcome, Lucius;
And welcome, all. Although the cheer be poor,   28
'Twill fill your stomachs. Please you eat of it.
SATURNINUS
Why art thou thus attired, Andronicus?
TITUS
Because I would be sure to have all well
To entertain Your Highness and your empress.
TAMORA
We are beholding to you, good Andronicus.   33
TITUS
An if Your Highness knew my heart, you were.—   34
My lord the Emperor, resolve me this: 35
Was it well done of rash Virginius   36

---

7 unto before   **8 For testimony of** to testify regarding   **9 ambush**
forces lying in wait to attack   **17 What ... than one** i.e., Two suns cannot occupy the same heavenly sphere, and Rome cannot have two
kings at once.   **18 boots** avails   **19 break the parle** cease the dispute.
21 careful (1) full of sorrows (2) assiduous   **28 cheer** fare   **33 behold-**
ing beholden   **34 were** would be.   **35 resolve** answer   **36 Virginius**
(According to Livy, the Roman centurion Virginius killed his daughter
to prevent her from being raped. Shakespeare chooses, instead, an
alternate version that was also current in the Renaissance: Virginius
kills his daughter after her rape to preserve her honor. This version is
closer to the action of Shakespeare's play.)

To slay his daughter with his own right hand
Because she was enforced, stained, and deflowered?

SATURNINUS   It was, Andronicus.

TITUS   Your reason, mighty lord?

SATURNINUS

Because the girl should not survive her shame,   41
And by her presence still renew his sorrows.   42

TITUS

A reason mighty, strong, and effectual;
A pattern, precedent, and lively warrant
For me, most wretched, to perform the like.
Die, die, Lavinia, and thy shame with thee,
And with thy shame thy father's sorrow die!

                                                           [*He kills Lavinia.*]

SATURNINUS

What hast thou done, unnatural and unkind?   48

TITUS

Killed her for whom my tears have made me blind.
I am as woeful as Virginius was,
And have a thousand times more cause than he
To do this outrage, and it now is done.

SATURNINUS

What, was she ravished? Tell who did the deed.

TITUS

Will't please you eat? Will't please Your Highness
feed?

TAMORA

Why hast thou slain thine only daughter thus?

TITUS

Not I; 'twas Chiron and Demetrius.
They ravished her and cut away her tongue,
And they, 'twas they that did her all this wrong.

SATURNINUS

Go fetch them hither to us presently.   59

TITUS

Why, there they are, both bakèd in this pie,
Whereof their mother daintily hath fed,
Eating the flesh that she herself hath bred.
'Tis true, 'tis true; witness my knife's sharp point.

                                                          He stabs the Empress.

SATURNINUS

Die, frantic wretch, for this accursèd deed!

                                                             [*He kills Titus.*]

LUCIUS

Can the son's eye behold his father bleed?
There's meed for meed, death for a deadly deed!   66

                    [*He kills Saturninus. A great tumult, during
                     which Marcus, Lucius, and others go aloft.*]

MARCUS

You sad-faced men, people and sons of Rome,
By uproars severed, as a flight of fowl   68
Scattered by winds and high tempestuous gusts,
Oh, let me teach you how to knit again
This scattered corn into one mutual sheaf,   71
These broken limbs again into one body.

A ROMAN LORD

Let Rome herself be bane unto herself,   73
And she whom mighty kingdoms curtsy to,   74
Like a forlorn and desperate castaway   75
Do shameful execution on herself!   76
But if my frosty signs and chaps of age,   77
Grave witnesses of true experience,
Cannot induce you to attend my words,   79
[*To Lucius*] Speak, Rome's dear friend, as erst our
ancestor,   80
When with his solemn tongue he did discourse
To lovesick Dido's sad-attending ear   82
The story of that baleful burning night
When subtle Greeks surprised King Priam's Troy.
Tell us what Sinon hath bewitched our ears,   85
Or who hath brought the fatal engine in
That gives our Troy, our Rome, the civil wound.   87
My heart is not compact of flint nor steel,   88
Nor can I utter all our bitter grief,
But floods of tears will drown my oratory
And break my utt'rance, even in the time
When it should move ye to attend me most
And force you to commiseration.
Here's Rome's young captain. Let him tell the tale,
While I stand by and weep to hear him speak.

LUCIUS

Then, gracious auditory, be it known to you
That Chiron and the damned Demetrius
Were they that murderèd our emperor's brother,
And they it were that ravishèd our sister.
For their fell faults our brothers were beheaded,   100
Our father's tears despised and basely cozened   101
Of that true hand that fought Rome's quarrel out   102
And sent her enemies unto the grave;
Lastly, myself unkindly banishèd,   104
The gates shut on me, and turned weeping out
To beg relief among Rome's enemies,
Who drowned their enmity in my true tears
And oped their arms to embrace me as a friend.
I am the turned-forth, be it known to you,   109
That have preserved her welfare in my blood   110
And from her bosom took the enemy's point,   111
Sheathing the steel in my adventurous body.   112
Alas, you know I am no vaunter, I;
My scars can witness, dumb although they are,   114
That my report is just and full of truth.

---

41 **Because** In order that   42 **still** continually   48 **unkind** (1) unnatural
(2) cruel.   59 **presently** at once.   66 **meed for meed** measure for measure.   66.1–2 *A great . . . aloft* (In lines 130–4, Marcus and Lucius offer
to throw themselves down from where they are speaking.)   68 **severed**
disunited   71 **corn** grain

73–6 **Let . . . herself!** (This Roman lord's first reaction to the horror he
has witnessed is to foresee apocalyptically a downfall of the Roman
Empire and of civilization itself. Both Emperor Saturninus and Rome's
great general, Titus, lie dead, along with other casualties. *Bane* is poison.
The speaker may be Aemilius, but not necessarily so.)   77 **if . . . age** if
my white hairs and wrinkles   79 **attend** listen to   80 **as . . . ancestor**
just as formerly our founder, Aeneas, spoke   82 **sad-attending** seriously listening   85 **Sinon** the crafty Greek who persuaded the Trojans
to take the wooden horse (the *fatal engine*) into their city   87 **civil**
incurred in civil strife   88 **compact** composed   100 **For . . . faults** For
the savage deeds of Chiron and Demetrius   101 **cozened** cheated
102 **fought . . . out** fought to the finish on behalf of Rome   104
unkindly unnaturally   109 **turned-forth** exile   110 **in** by   111 **from . . .
point** took in my own bosom the sword's point aimed at her, Rome's,
bosom   112 **adventurous** willing to incur risk   114 **dumb . . . are** (The
scars are dumb mouths, giving mute testimony.)

But soft, methinks I do digress too much,
Citing my worthless praise. Oh, pardon me,
For when no friends are by, men praise themselves.

MARCUS
Now is my turn to speak. Behold the child:
                    [pointing to the child in the arms of an attendant]
Of this was Tamora deliverèd,
The issue of an irreligious Moor,
Chief architect and plotter of these woes.
The villain is alive in Titus' house,
And as he is to witness, this is true.
Now judge what cause had Titus to revenge
These wrongs unspeakable, past patience,
Or more than any living man could bear.
Now have you heard the truth. What say you,
        Romans?
Have we done aught amiss, show us wherein,   129
And from the place where you behold us pleading,
The poor remainder of Andronici
Will hand in hand all headlong hurl ourselves
And on the ragged stones beat forth our souls
And make a mutual closure of our house.   134
Speak, Romans, speak, and if you say we shall,
Lo, hand in hand, Lucius and I will fall.

AEMILIUS
Come, come, thou reverend man of Rome,
And bring our emperor gently in thy hand,
Lucius our emperor; for well I know
The common voice do cry it shall be so.

ALL
Lucius, all hail, Rome's royal emperor!

MARCUS [to attendants]
Go, go into old Titus' sorrowful house
And hither hale that misbelieving Moor
To be adjudged some direful slaughtering death
As punishment for his most wicked life.
                    [Exeunt attendants. Marcus, Lucius,
                        and the others come down.]

ALL
Lucius, all hail, Rome's gracious governor!

LUCIUS
Thanks, gentle Romans. May I govern so
To heal Rome's harms and wipe away her woe!
But, gentle people, give me aim awhile,   149
For nature puts me to a heavy task.
Stand all aloof, but, uncle, draw you near
To shed obsequious tears upon this trunk.—   152
Oh, take this warm kiss on thy pale cold lips,
                                        [kissing Titus]
These sorrowful drops upon thy bloodstained face,
The last true duties of thy noble son!

MARCUS [kissing Titus]
Tear for tear, and loving kiss for kiss,
Thy brother Marcus tenders on thy lips.
Oh, were the sum of these that I should pay
Countless and infinite, yet would I pay them!

LUCIUS [to young Lucius]
Come hither, boy. Come, come, and learn of us
To melt in showers. Thy grandsire loved thee well.
Many a time he danced thee on his knee,
Sung thee asleep, his loving breast thy pillow;
Many a story hath he told to thee,
And bid thee bear his pretty tales in mind
And talk of them when he was dead and gone.

MARCUS
How many thousand times hath these poor lips,
When they were living, warmed themselves on thine!
Oh, now, sweet boy, give them their latest kiss.   169
Bid him farewell; commit him to the grave.
Do them that kindness, and take leave of them.   171

BOY [kissing Titus]
Oh, grandsire, grandsire! Ev'n with all my heart
Would I were dead, so you did live again!
Oh, Lord, I cannot speak to him for weeping.
My tears will choke me if I ope my mouth.

                    [Enter attendants with Aaron.]

A ROMAN
You sad Andronici, have done with woes.   176
Give sentence on this execrable wretch
That hath been breeder of these dire events.

LUCIUS
Set him breast-deep in earth and famish him;
There let him stand and rave and cry for food.
If anyone relieves or pities him,
For the offense he dies. This is our doom.   182
Some stay to see him fastened in the earth.

AARON
Ah, why should wrath be mute and fury dumb?
I am no baby, I, that with base prayers
I should repent the evils I have done.
Ten thousand worse than ever yet I did
Would I perform, if I might have my will.
If one good deed in all my life I did,
I do repent it from my very soul.

LUCIUS
Some loving friends convey the Emperor hence,
And give him burial in his fathers' grave.   192
My father and Lavinia shall forthwith
Be closèd in our household's monument.
As for that ravenous tiger, Tamora,
No funeral rite, nor man in mourning weed,
No mournful bell shall ring her burial;
But throw her forth to beasts and birds to prey.   198
Her life was beastly and devoid of pity,
And being dead, let birds on her take pity.   200
                    Exeunt, [bearing the dead bodies].

---

129 **Have we** If we have   134 **closure** conclusion, death   149 **give me aim** bear with me, give me encouragement. (An archery metaphor: to give aim is to stand near the target and help direct the shooter's aim by observing the results.)   152 **obsequious** dutiful, mourning

169 **latest** last   171 **them** i.e., the lips.   176 A ROMAN (The speech is sometimes assigned to Aemilius.)   182 **doom** judgment.
192 **fathers'** (The original text's "fathers" could signify singular or plural. Probably Lucius means the ancestral tomb.)   198 **prey** prey upon.   200 **pity** (The First Quarto text closes the play with this line. The Second Quarto and subsequent texts add the following four lines: "See justice done on Aaron, that damned Moor, By whom our heavy haps had their beginning. Then, afterwards, to order well the state, That like events may ne'er it ruinate.")

Romeo and Juliet

Though a tragedy, *Romeo and Juliet* is, in some ways, more closely comparable to Shakespeare's romantic comedies and early writings than to his later tragedies. Stylistically belonging to the years 1594–1596, it is in the lyric vein of the sonnets, *A Midsummer Night's Dream, The Merchant of Venice*, and *Richard II*, all of which are from the mid 1590s. Like them, it uses a variety of rhyme schemes (couplets, quatrains, octets, and even sonnets) and revels in punning, metaphor, and wit combat. It is separated in tone and in time from the earliest of the great tragedies, *Julius Caesar* and *Hamlet*, by almost half a decade, and, except for the experimental *Titus Andronicus*, it is the only tragedy (that is not also a history) that Shakespeare wrote in the first decade of his career—a period devoted otherwise to romantic comedy and English history.

Like many comedies, *Romeo and Juliet* is a love story, celebrating the exquisite, brief joy of youthful passion. Even its tragic ending stresses the poignancy of that brief beauty, not the bitter futility of love, as in *Troilus and Cressida* or *Othello*. The tragic ending of *Romeo and Juliet* underscores the observation made by a vexed lover in *A Midsummer Night's Dream* that "The course of true love never did run smooth" (1.1.134). True love in *Romeo and Juliet*, as in *A Midsummer Night's Dream*, is destined to be crossed by differences in blood or family background, differences in age, arbitrary choices of family or friends, or uncontrollable catastrophes, such as war, death, and sickness. Love is thus, as in *A Midsummer Night's Dream*, "momentary as a sound, / Swift as a shadow, short as any dream," swallowed up by darkness; "So quick bright things come to confusion" (1.1.143–9). A dominant pattern of imagery in *Romeo and Juliet* evokes a corresponding sense of suddenness and violence: fire, gunpowder, hot blood, lightning, the inconstant wind, the storm-tossed or shipwrecked vessel. The beauty of a love that is so threatened and so fragile is intensified by the brevity of the experience. A tragic outcome therefore affirms the uniqueness and pristine quality of youthful ecstasy. The flowering and fading of a joy "too rich for use, for earth too dear" (1.5.48), does not so much condemn the unfeeling world as welcome the martyrdom of literally dying for love.

As protagonists, Romeo and Juliet lack tragic stature by any classical definition or in terms of the medieval convention of the Fall of Princes. The lovers are not extraordinary except in their passionate attachment to one another. They belong to prominent merchant families rather than to the nobility. They (especially Juliet) are very young, more so than any other of Shakespeare's tragic protagonists, and are indeed younger than most couples marrying in England at the time the play was written; Juliet is not yet fourteen (1.2.9, 1.3.13). Romeo and Juliet's dilemma of parental opposition is of the domestic sort often found in comedy. In fact, several characters in the play partly resemble the conventional character types of the Latin comic playwright Plautus or of Italian neoclassical comedy: the domineering father who insists that his daughter marry according to his choice, the unwelcome rival wooer, the garrulous and bawdy nurse, and, of course, the lovers. The Italian *novella*, to which Shakespeare often turned for his plots, made use of these same types and paid little attention to the classical precept that protagonists in a tragic story ought to be persons of high rank who are humbled through some inner flaw, or hamartia.

The story of Romeo and Juliet goes back ultimately to the fifth-century A.D. Greek romance of *Ephesiaca*, in which we find the motif of the sleeping potion as a means of escaping an unwelcome marriage. Masuccio of Salerno, in his *Il Novellino*, in 1476, combined the narrative of the heroine's deathlike trance and seeming burial alive with that of the hero's tragic failure to receive news from the friar that she is still alive. Luigi da Porto, in his *novella* (c. 1530), set the scene at Verona, provided the names of Romeo and Giulietta for the hero and heroine, added the account of their feuding families, the Montecchi and Cappelletti, introduced the killing of Tybalt (Theobaldo), and provided other important details. Luigi's version was followed by Matteo Bandello's famous *Novelle* of 1554, which was translated into French by Pierre Boaistuau (1559). The French version became the source for Arthur Brooke's long narrative poem in English, *The Tragical History of Romeus and Juliet* (1562). Brooke mentions having seen a play on the subject, but it is doubtful that Shakespeare knew this old play or, if he did know it, made use of it. Brooke's poem was his chief and probably only source. Shakespeare has condensed Brooke's action from nine months to less than a week, has greatly expanded the role of Mercutio, and has given to the Nurse a warmth and humorous richness not found in the usual Italian duenna, or *balia*. He has also tidied up the Friar's immorality and deleted the antipapal tone. Inheriting from Brooke a cautionary narrative against unruly yielding to sexual passion, in the homiletic vein of Puritan preachers, Shakespeare instead sympathizes with the perils of young lovers whose desires are unappreciated by an unfeeling world. Throughout all these changes, Shakespeare retains Brooke's romantic (rather than classically tragic) conception of love overwhelmed by external obstacles.

Like the romantic comedies, *Romeo and Juliet* is often funny and bawdy. Samson and Gregory in the first scene are slapstick cowards, hiding behind the law and daring to quarrel only when reinforcements arrive. The Nurse delights us with her earthy recollections of the day she weaned Juliet: the child tasting "the wormwood on the nipple / Of my dug" (1.3.31–2), the warm Italian sun, an earthquake, the Nurse's husband telling his lame but often-repeated bawdy joke about women falling on their backs. Mercutio employs his inventive and sardonic humor to twit Romeo for lovesickness and the Nurse for her pomposity. She, in turn, scolds Peter and plagues Juliet (who is breathlessly awaiting news from Romeo) with a history of her back ailments. Mercutio and the Nurse are among Shakespeare's bawdiest characters. Their wry and salacious view of love contrasts with the nobly innocent and yet physically passionate love of Romeo and Juliet. Mercutio and the Nurse cannot take part in the play's denouement; one dies, misinterpreting Romeo's appeasement of Tybalt, and the other proves insensitive to Juliet's depth of feeling. Yet the disappearance of these engaging companions takes from the play some of its vitality and most of its funniness. The death of Tybalt turns the play from comedy to tragedy.

The lovers, too, are at first well suited to Shakespearean romantic comedy. When we meet Romeo, he is not in love with Juliet at all, despite the play's title, but is mooning over a "hardhearted wench" (in Mercutio's words) named Rosaline. This "goddess" appropriately never appears in the play; she is almost a disembodied idea in Romeo's mind, a scornful beauty like Phoebe in *As You Like It*. Romeo's love for her is tedious and self-pitying, like that of the conventional wooer in a sonnet sequence by Francesco Petrarch or one of his imitators. Juliet, although not yet fourteen, must change all this by teaching Romeo the nature of true love. She will have none of his shopworn clichés learned in the service of Rosaline, his flowery protestations and swearing by the moon, lest they prove to be love's perjuries. With her innocent candor, she insists (like many heroines of the romantic comedies) on dispelling the mask of pretense that lovers too often show one another. "Capulet" and "Montague" are mere labels, not the inner self. Although Juliet would have been more coy, she confesses, had she known that Romeo was overhearing her, she will now "prove more true / Than those that have more cunning to be strange" (2.2.100–1). She is more practical than he in assessing danger and making plans. Later she also proves herself remarkably able to bear misfortune.

The comedy of the play's first half is, to be sure, overshadowed by the certainty of disaster. The opening chorus plainly warns us that the lovers will die. They are "star-crossed," and they speak of themselves as such. Romeo fears "Some consequence yet hanging in the stars" when he reluctantly goes to the Capulets' feast (1.4.107); after he has slain Tybalt, he cries "Oh, I am fortune's fool!" (3.1.135); and, at the news of Juliet's supposed death, he proclaims "Then I defy you, stars!" (5.1.24). Yet in what sense are Romeo and Juliet "star-crossed"? The concept is deliberately broad in this play, encompassing many factors, such as hatred, bumbling, bad luck, and simple lack of awareness.

The first scene presents feuding as a major cause in the tragedy. The quarrel between the two families is so ancient that the original motives are no longer even discussed. Inspired by the "fiery" Tybalt, factionalism pursues its mindless course, despite the efforts of the Prince to end it. Although the elders of both families talk of peace, they call for their swords quickly enough when a fray begins. Still, this senseless hatred does not lead to tragedy until its effects are fatally complicated through misunderstanding. With poignant irony, good intentions are repeatedly undermined by lack of knowledge. We can see why Juliet does not tell her family of her secret marriage with a presumably hated Montague, but, in fact, Capulet has accepted Romeo as a guest in his house under the terms of chivalric hospitality, praising him as a "virtuous and well governed youth" (1.5.69). For all his dictatorial ways, and the manifest advantages he may see in marrying his daughter to an aristocrat like Paris, Capulet would, of course, never propose the match if he knew his daughter to be married already. Not knowing of Juliet's marriage, he and his wife can only interpret her refusal to marry Paris as caprice. Count Paris himself is victim of this tragedy of unawareness. He is an eminently suitable wooer for Juliet, rich and nobly born, considerate, peace-loving, and deeply fond of Juliet (as he shows by his private and sincere grief at her tomb). Certainly, he would never intentionally woo a married woman. Not knowing, he plays the unattractive role of the rival wooer and dies for it. Similarly, Mercutio cannot understand Romeo's seemingly craven behavior toward Tybalt and so begins the duel that leads to Romeo's banishment. The final scene, with Friar Laurence's retelling of the story, allows us to see the survivors confronted with what they have all unknowingly done.

Chance, or accident, plays a role of importance equal to that of hatred and unawareness. An outbreak of the plague prevents Friar John from conveying Friar Laurence's letter to Romeo at Mantua. Friar Laurence, going hurriedly to the Capulets' tomb, arrives in time for Juliet's awakening but some minutes after Romeo has killed Paris and taken poison. Juliet awakens only moments later. The Watch comes just too late to prevent her suicide. Friar Laurence expresses well the sense of frustration at plans gone awry by such narrow margins: "what an unkind hour / Is guilty of this lamentable chance!" (5.3.145–6). Earlier, Capulet's decision to move the wedding date up one day has crucially affected the timing. Human miscalculation contributes also to the catastrophe: Mercutio is killed under Romeo's arm, and Friar Laurence wonders unhappily if any of his complicated plans "Miscarried by my fault" (5.3.267). Character and human decision play a part in this tragedy, for Romeo should not have dueled with Tybalt, no matter what the provocation. In choosing to kill Tybalt, he has deliberately cast aside as "effeminate" the gentle and forgiving qualities he has learned from his love of Juliet (3.1.113) and thus is guilty of a rash and self-destructive action. To ascribe the cause of the tragedy in Aristotelian fashion to his and Juliet's impulsiveness is, however, to ignore much of the rest of the play.

Instead, the ending of the play brings a pattern out of the seeming welter of mistakes and animosities. "A greater power than we can contradict / Hath thwarted our intents," says Friar Laurence, suggesting that the seeming bad luck of the delayed letter was, in fact, the intent of a mysterious higher intelligence (5.3.153–4). Prince Escalus, too, finds a necessary meaning in the tragic event. "See what a scourge is laid upon your hate," he admonishes the Montagues and Capulets, "That heaven finds means to kill your joys with love." Romeo and Juliet are "Poor sacrifices of our enmity" (lines 292–304). As the Prologue had foretold, their deaths will "bury their parents' strife"; the families' feud is a stub-

born evil force "Which, but their children's end, naught could remove." Order is preciously restored; the price is great, but the sacrifice nonetheless confirms a sense of a larger intention in what had appeared to be simply hatred and misfortune. Throughout the play, love and hate are interrelated opposites, yoked through the rhetorical device of oxymoron, or inherent contradiction. Romeo apostrophizes "O brawling love, O loving hate" (1.1.176), and Juliet later echoes his words: "My only love sprung from my only hate" (1.5.139). This paradox expresses a conflict in humankind, as in the universe itself. "Two such opposèd kings encamp them still / In man as well as herbs," says Friar Laurence, "grace and rude will" (2.3.27–8). Hatred is a condition of our corrupted wills, of our fall from grace, and it attempts to destroy what is gracious in human beings. In this cosmic strife, love must pay the sacrifice, as Romeo and Juliet do with their lives, but, because their deaths are finally perceived as the cost of so much hatred, the two families come to terms with their collective guilt and resolve henceforth to be worthy of the sacrifice.

Structurally, *Romeo and Juliet* gives considerable prominence to the feuding of the two families. Public scenes occur at key points—at beginning, middle, and end (1.1, 3.1, and 5.3)—and each such scene concerns violence and its consequences. The play begins with a brawl. Tybalt is a baleful presence in 1.1 and 3.1, implacably bent on vengeance. The three public scenes are alike, too, in that they bring into confrontation the entire families of Capulets and Montagues, who call for swords and demand reprisal from the state for what they themselves have set in motion. Prince Escalus dominates these three public scenes. He must offer judgment in each, giving the families fair warning, then exiling Romeo for Tybalt's death, and finally counseling the families on the meaning of their collective tragedy. He is a spokesman for public order and security ("Mercy but murders, pardoning those that kill," 3.1.196), even though he is also unable to prevent the tragedy. He stands above the conflict and yet is affected by it; his own kinsman, Mercutio, is one of the casualties. For all his dignity and impartiality, Escalus's official function is somehow tangential to the central emotional experience of the play. The law does not provide a remedy. Still, it can preside and arbitrate. To Escalus is given the final speech promising both punishment and pardon, and it is he who sums up the paradoxical interdependence of love and hate. Although the morning after the catastrophe brings with it sorrow, it also brings peace, however "glooming." Escalus is master of ceremonies for a restored order through which the families and we are reconciled to what has occurred.

In good part, the public scenes of the play serve to frame the love plot and the increasing isolation of the separated lovers, but these public scenes have a function of their own to the extent that the tragedy has touched and altered everyone. The final tableau is not the kiss of the dying lovers but the handclasp of the reconciled fathers. The long, last public ceremonial is important because, although the private catastrophe of the lovers is unalterably complete, recognition occurs only when the Friar recounts at great length to all the community the story we already know. As we watch the bereaved families responding with shock to the story of Romeo and Juliet's tragedy, we understand the reason for its length: only when it is too late do the families begin to comprehend their own complicity in the disaster that has occurred. This recognition is not that of the protagonists, as in the Aristotelian conception of recognition, nor does it accompany a reversal in the love tragedy; that reversal already has taken place in Romeo's banishment and the lovers' deaths. This lack of correspondence with an Aristotelian definition of tragedy is not, however, a structural flaw; rather, it is a manifestation of the dual focus of the tragedy on the lovers and on all Verona. The city itself is a kind of protagonist, suffering through its own violence and coming at last to the sad comfort that wisdom brings.

The timeless nature of a tragic story about young lovers has resulted in its being an irresistible vehicle for modern updatings in the theater and in film, many of them highly successful in bringing the play into the lives of modern and young audiences. Productions in this vein have raised important questions about the protagonists' attitudes toward love and the nature of the social environment in which their tragedy occurs. The play's vivid bawdry invites an atmosphere of hedonism that can be understood, implicitly at least, in terms of the sexual revolution of the 1960s and afterwards. The boy actor who originally played Juliet on Shakespeare's stage has been replaced by Olivia Hussey, for example, in Franco Zeffirelli's popular film of 1968; Hussey is so gorgeously appealing in her first long night-time conversation with Romeo that his insistent "Oh, wilt thou leave me so unsatisfied?" takes on new urgency. Subsequently, the film briefly shows the lovers in bed, unclothed. Mercutio is sometimes portrayed as homosexual: mutedly so in the Zeffirelli film, aggressively so in Terry Hands's 1973 production at Stratford-upon-Avon, and flamboyantly so in Baz Luhrmann's immensely successful film, *Romeo + Juliet*, of 1996. In this last version, Mercutio is an African American drag queen, while Friar Laurence is a New Age priest. Juliet's mother in this same film is hilarious as a pill-popping, chain-smoking, and hard-drinking society dame slithering her ectomorphically slim body into a Cleopatra outfit for the huge masked ball that she and her nouveau riche husband are putting on in their tastelessly expensive block-long mansion—just the sort of parents whom one can count on not to understand their daughter. Luhrmann's Nurse is an Hispanic woman bellowing "Huliet! Huliet!" to remind us that the film is set in a southern United States city like Los Angeles or Miami. (It was actually filmed in Mexico City.) The street violence is also Hispanic, with rival gangs setting fire to gas stations and shooting automatic weapons during high-speed car chases. This updating of the violence with which the play begins owes some of its inspiration, presumably, to Leonard Bernstein's *West Side Story* (1957), set in Spanish Harlem.

Such innovations are at their best when they point to the play's insistent dramatization of violence and love in conflict. What responsibility does society bear for youthful tragedy when the models for behavior available to young people are what they are in today's world? How can a young man like Romeo escape the peer pressures of gang loyalties and macho stereotypes? Romeo struggles against these pressures in his crucial moment of decision; knowing that Juliet has taught him a better way, he yet succumbs to the mores of his tribe and to his own need to revenge on Tybalt the death of Mercutio. In these modern productions, as in the play itself, the violent response is too believable. As Friar Laurence says, "grace and rude will" do battle within the human psyche, too often with tragic outcome, and young love must pay the price.

Romeo and Juliet

[*Dramatis Personae*

CHORUS

ESCALUS, *Prince of Verona*
MERCUTIO, *the Prince's kinsman and Romeo's friend*
PARIS, *a young count and kinsman of the Prince*
PAGE *to Count Paris*

MONTAGUE
MONTAGUE'S WIFE
ROMEO, *son of the Montagues*
BENVOLIO, *Montague's nephew and Romeo's friend*
ABRAHAM, *a servant of the Montague household*
BALTHASAR, *a servant of the Montague household attending Romeo*

CAPULET
CAPULET'S WIFE
JULIET, *daughter of the Capulets*
NURSE
TYBALT, *nephew of Capulet's Wife*

PETRUCHIO, *Capulet's kinsman*
SECOND CAPULET, *an old man, Capulet's kinsman*
PETER, *a servant of the Capulet household attending the Nurse*
SAMSON ⎫
GREGORY ⎪
ANTHONY ⎬ *servants of the Capulet household*
POTPAN ⎪
CLOWN *or* SERVANT ⎪
Other SERVANTS ⎭

FRIAR LAURENCE ⎫ *Franciscan friars*
FRIAR JOHN ⎭

APOTHECARY
Three MUSICIANS (*Simon Catling, Hugh Rebeck, and James Soundpost*)
Three WATCHMEN

Citizens, Maskers, Torchbearers, Guards, Servants, and Attendants

SCENE: *Verona; Mantua*]

The Prologue

[*Enter Chorus.*]

CHORUS
  Two households, both alike in dignity,   1
    In fair Verona, where we lay our scene,
  From ancient grudge break to new mutiny,   3
    Where civil blood makes civil hands unclean.   4
  From forth the fatal loins of these two foes.
    A pair of star-crossed lovers take their life;   6
  Whose misadventured piteous overthrows   7
  Doth with their death bury their parents' strife.
  The fearful passage of their death-marked love,   9
    And the continuance of their parents' rage,
  Which, but their children's end, naught could remove,
    Is now the two hours' traffic of our stage;   12
  The which if you with patient ears attend,
  What here shall miss, our toil shall strive to mend.   14
                                   [*Exit.*]

♣

Prologue.
1–14 (The Prologue is in the form of a sonnet.)
1 dignity rank, status   **3 mutiny** strife, discord   **4 Where . . . unclean** where citizens' hands uncivilly are stained in civil strife with their fellow citizens' blood.   **6 star-crossed** thwarted by destiny, by adverse stars   **7 misadventured** unlucky

9 passage progress   **12 two hours' traffic** A conventional way of referring to the length of stage performances in the early modern period, not to be taken too literally, but indicative of a brisk pace   **14 What . . . mend** what is defective or inadequate in the short summary I have given you here, the actors' efforts in the following two hours will amply and fully make clear.

[1.1]

Enter Samson and Gregory, with swords
and bucklers, of the house of Capulet.

SAMSON   Gregory, on my word, we'll not carry coals.   1
GREGORY   No, for then we should be colliers.   2
SAMSON   I mean, an we be in choler, we'll draw.   3
GREGORY   Ay, while you live, draw your neck out of   4
collar.   5
SAMSON   I strike quickly, being moved.   6
GREGORY   But thou art not quickly moved to strike.
SAMSON   A dog of the house of Montague moves me.   8
GREGORY   To move is to stir, and to be valiant is to
stand. Therefore, if thou art moved, thou run'st away.   10
SAMSON   A dog of that house shall move me to stand. I
will take the wall of any man or maid of Montague's.   12
GREGORY   That shows thee a weak slave, for the   13
weakest goes to the wall.   14
SAMSON   'Tis true, and therefore women, being the
weaker vessels, are ever thrust to the wall. Therefore I   16
will push Montague's men from the wall and thrust
his maids to the wall.
GREGORY   The quarrel is between our masters and us   19
their men.   20
SAMSON   'Tis all one. I will show myself a tyrant: when   21
I have fought with the men, I will be civil with the
maids—I will cut off their heads.
GREGORY   The heads of the maids?
SAMSON   Ay, the heads of the maids, or their maidenheads. Take it in what sense thou wilt.   26
GREGORY   They must take it in sense that feel it.   27
SAMSON   Me they shall feel while I am able to stand,   28
and 'tis known I am a pretty piece of flesh.   29
GREGORY   'Tis well thou art not fish; if thou hadst, thou   30
hadst been Poor John. Draw thy tool. Here comes of   31
the house of Montagues.

Enter two other Servingmen
[Abraham and another].

SAMSON   My naked weapon is out. Quarrel, I will back
thee.
GREGORY   How, turn thy back and run?
SAMSON   Fear me not.   36
GREGORY   No, marry. I fear thee!   37
SAMSON   Let us take the law of our side. Let them   38
begin.
GREGORY   I will frown as I pass by, and let them take it
as they list.   41
SAMSON   Nay, as they dare. I will bite my thumb at   42
them, which is disgrace to them if they bear it.
            [Samson makes taunting gestures.]
ABRAHAM   Do you bite your thumb at us, sir?
SAMSON   I do bite my thumb, sir.
ABRAHAM   Do you bite your thumb at us, sir?
SAMSON *[aside to Gregory]*   Is the law of our side if I
say ay?
GREGORY *[aside to Samson]*   No.
SAMSON *[to Abraham]*   No, sir, I do not bite my thumb
at you, sir, but I bite my thumb, sir.
GREGORY   Do you quarrel, sir?
ABRAHAM   Quarrel, sir? No, sir.
SAMSON   But if you do, sir, I am for you. I serve as good
a man as you.
ABRAHAM   No better.
SAMSON   Well, sir.

Enter Benvolio.

GREGORY *[to Samson]*   Say "better." Here comes one of   58
my master's kinsmen.   59
SAMSON *[to Abraham]*   Yes, better, sir.
ABRAHAM   You lie.
SAMSON   Draw, if you be men. Gregory, remember thy
washing blow.   *They fight.*   63
BENVOLIO   Part, fools!
Put up your swords. You know not what you do.

Enter Tybalt [with sword drawn].

TYBALT
What, art thou drawn among these heartless hinds?   66
Turn thee, Benvolio. Look upon thy death.
BENVOLIO
I do but keep the peace. Put up thy sword,
Or manage it to part these men with me.   69
TYBALT
What, drawn and talk of peace? I hate the word
As I hate hell, all Montagues, and thee.
Have at thee, coward!   *[They fight.]*   72

Enter three or four Citizens with clubs
or partisans.

1.1. Location: Verona. A public place.
0.2 *bucklers* small shields   **1 carry coals** i.e., endure insults.   **2 colliers**
(Coal carriers were regarded as dirty and of evil repute.)   **3 an** if.
choler anger (produced by one of the four humors).   **draw** draw
swords.   **5 collar** i.e., hangman's noose. (With pun on *colliers* and
choler.)   **6 moved** i.e., to anger. (With pun in next line.)   **8 moves**
incites   **10 stand** i.e., stand one's ground.   **12 take the wall** take the
cleaner side of the walk nearest the wall, thus forcing others out into
the gutter   **13–14 the weakest . . . wall** (A proverb expressing the
idea that the weakest are always forced to give way.)   **16 weaker**
vessels (Saint Paul bids husbands give honor to their wives "as unto
the weaker vessel," 1 Peter 3:7.)   **thrust to the wall** (With suggestion
of amorous assault.)   **19–20 between . . . men** i.e., between the males
of one household and the males of the other household; we have no
quarrel with the women.   **21 one** the same.   **26 what sense** whatever
ever meaning   **27 They . . . feel it** i.e., It is the maids who must
receive by way of physical sensation (*sense*) what I have to offer,
because they are the ones who can feel it.   **28 stand** (With suggestion
of "have an erection," continued in the next few lines in *draw thy tool*
and *my naked weapon is out*.)   **29–30 flesh . . . fish** (Refers to the
proverbial phrase, "neither fish nor flesh.")   **31 Poor John** hake
salted and dried—a poor Lenten kind of food. (Probably with a
bawdy suggestion of sexual insufficiency.)   **comes of** i.e., come
members of

36 Fear Mistrust. (But Gregory deliberately misunderstands in the
next line, saying, in effect, "No indeed, do you think I'd be afraid of
you?")   **37 marry** i.e., indeed. (Originally an oath, "by the Virgin
Mary.")   **38 take the law of** have the law on   **41 list** please.   **42 bite**
my thumb i.e., make an insulting and probably obscene gesture
58–9 one . . . kinsmen i.e., Tybalt, who is approaching. (Not Benvolio,
who has just entered unobserved by the servingmen.)   **63 washing**
slashing with great force   **66 heartless hinds** cowardly menials.
69 manage use   **72 Have at thee** i.e., On guard, here I come
72.2 *partisans* long-handled spears.

CITIZENS
>Clubs, bills, and partisans! Strike! Beat them down! 73
>Down with the Capulets! Down with the Montagues! 74

Enter old Capulet in his gown, and his Wife.

CAPULET
>What noise is this? Give me my long sword, ho! 75

CAPULET'S WIFE
>A crutch, a crutch! Why call you for a sword?

CAPULET
>My sword, I say! Old Montague is come
>And flourishes his blade in spite of me. 78

Enter old Montague and his Wife.

MONTAGUE
>Thou villain Capulet!—Hold me not; let me go.

MONTAGUE'S WIFE
>Thou shalt not stir one foot to seek a foe. 80

Enter Prince Escalus, with his train.

PRINCE
>Rebellious subjects, enemies to peace,
>Profaners of this neighbor-stainèd steel— 82
>Will they not hear? What, ho! You men, you beasts,
>That quench the fire of your pernicious rage
>With purple fountains issuing from your veins, 85
>On pain of torture, from those bloody hands
>Throw your mistempered weapons to the ground 87
>And hear the sentence of your movèd prince. 88
>Three civil brawls, bred of an airy word, 89
>By thee, old Capulet, and Montague,
>Have thrice disturbed the quiet of our streets
>And made Verona's ancient citizens
>Cast by their grave-beseeming ornaments 93
>To wield old partisans in hands as old,
>Cankered with peace, to part your cankered hate. 95
>If ever you disturb our streets again
>Your lives shall pay the forfeit of the peace. 97
>For this time all the rest depart away.
>You, Capulet, shall go along with me,
>And Montague, come you this afternoon,
>To know our farther pleasure in this case,
>To old Freetown, our common judgment-place. 102
>Once more, on pain of death, all men depart.
>>*Exeunt [all but Montague, Montague's Wife,*
>>*and Benvolio].*

MONTAGUE
>Who set this ancient quarrel new abroach? 104
>Speak, nephew, were you by when it began? 105

BENVOLIO
>Here were the servants of your adversary,
>And yours, close fighting ere I did approach.
>I drew to part them. In the instant came
>The fiery Tybalt with his sword prepared, 109
>Which, as he breathed defiance to my ears,
>He swung about his head and cut the winds
>Who, nothing hurt withal, hissed him in scorn. 112
>While we were interchanging thrusts and blows,
>Came more and more, and fought on part and part 114
>Till the Prince came, who parted either part. 115

MONTAGUE'S WIFE
>Oh, where is Romeo? Saw you him today?
>Right glad I am he was not at this fray.

BENVOLIO
>Madam, an hour before the worshiped sun
>Peered forth the golden window of the east, 119
>A troubled mind drave me to walk abroad, 120
>Where, underneath the grove of sycamore
>That westward rooteth from this city side, 122
>So early walking did I see your son.
>Towards him I made, but he was ware of me 124
>And stole into the covert of the wood. 125
>I, measuring his affections by my own, 126
>Which then most sought where most might not be
>>found, 127
>Being one too many by my weary self,
>Pursued my humor, not pursuing his, 129
>And gladly shunned who gladly fled from me. 130

MONTAGUE
>Many a morning hath he there been seen,
>With tears augmenting the fresh morning's dew,
>Adding to clouds more clouds with his deep sighs;
>But all so soon as the all-cheering sun
>Should in the farthest east begin to draw
>The shady curtains from Aurora's bed, 136
>Away from light steals home my heavy son 137
>And private in his chamber pens himself,
>Shuts up his windows, locks fair daylight out,
>And makes himself an artificial night.
>Black and portentous must this humor prove
>Unless good counsel may the cause remove.

BENVOLIO
>My noble uncle, do you know the cause?

MONTAGUE
>I neither know it nor can learn of him.

---

73 Clubs rallying cry, summoning apprentices with their clubs. **bills** long-handled spears with hooked blades **74.1 gown** nightgown, dressing gown **75 long sword** heavy, old-fashioned sword **78 spite** defiance, despite **80.1 train** retinue. **82 Profaners . . . steel** you who profane your weapons by staining them with neighbors' blood **85 purple** bloody, dark red **87 mistempered** (1) having been tempered, or hardened, in hot blood rather than cold water (2) malignant, ill-tempered **88 movèd** angry **89 airy** flippant, saucy **93 grave-beseeming ornaments** i.e., staffs and other appurtenances suited to wise old age **95 Cankered . . . cankered** corroded (from disuse) . . . malignant **97 Your . . . peace** death will be the penalty for breaking the peace. **102 Freetown** (Brooke's translation, in his poem *Romeus and Juliet*, of *Villa Franca*, as found in the Italian story.) **common** public

104 set . . . abroach reopened this old quarrel, set it flowing. **105 by** near **109 prepared** drawn, ready **112 Who . . . withal** which winds, not at all injured thereby **114 on part and part** on one side and the other **115 either part** both parties. **119 forth** from forth **120 drave . . . abroad** drove me to take a walk **122 That . . . side** that grows on the west side of this city **124 made** moved. **ware** wary, aware **125 covert** cover, hiding place **126 affections** wishes, inclination **127 Which . . . found** which then chiefly desired a place where I might be alone **129 humor** mood **130 who** him who **136 Aurora** goddess of dawn **137 heavy** (1) sad (2) the opposite of *light*. **son** (punning on *sun*, line 134)

BENVOLIO
  Have you importuned him by any means?   145
MONTAGUE
  Both by myself and many other friends.
  But he, his own affections' counselor,
  Is to himself—I will not say how true,   148
  But to himself so secret and so close,   149
  So far from sounding and discovery,   150
  As is the bud bit with an envious worm   151
  Ere he can spread his sweet leaves to the air
  Or dedicate his beauty to the sun.
  Could we but learn from whence his sorrows grow,
  We would as willingly give cure as know.

              Enter Romeo.

BENVOLIO
  See where he comes. So please you, step aside.   156
  I'll know his grievance or be much denied.
MONTAGUE
  I would thou wert so happy by thy stay   158
  To hear true shrift.—Come, madam, let's away.   159
              Exeunt [Montague and his Wife].
BENVOLIO
  Good morrow, cousin.
ROMEO   Is the day so young?   160
BENVOLIO
  But new struck nine.
ROMEO   Ay me! Sad hours seem long.
  Was that my father that went hence so fast?
BENVOLIO
  It was. What sadness lengthens Romeo's hours?
ROMEO
  Not having that which, having, makes them short.
BENVOLIO In love?
ROMEO Out—
BENVOLIO Of love?
ROMEO
  Out of her favor where I am in love.
BENVOLIO
  Alas, that Love, so gentle in his view,   169
  Should be so tyrannous and rough in proof!   170
ROMEO
  Alas, that Love, whose view is muffled still,   171
  Should without eyes see pathways to his will!   172
  Where shall we dine?—Oh, me! What fray was here?
  Yet tell me not, for I have heard it all.
  Here's much to do with hate, but more with love.
  Why, then, O brawling love, O loving hate,
  O anything of nothing first create,   177
  O heavy lightness, serious vanity,
  Misshapen chaos of well-seeming forms,
  Feather of lead, bright smoke, cold fire, sick health,

Still-waking sleep, that is not what it is!   181
  This love feel I, that feel no love in this.
  Dost thou not laugh?
BENVOLIO   No, coz, I rather weep.   183
ROMEO
  Good heart, at what?
BENVOLIO   At thy good heart's oppression.
ROMEO
  Why, such is love's transgression.
  Griefs of mine own lie heavy in my breast,
  Which thou wilt propagate, to have it pressed   187
  With more of thine. This love that thou hast shown   188
  Doth add more grief to too much of mine own.
  Love is a smoke made with the fume of sighs;
  Being purged, a fire sparkling in lovers' eyes;   191
  Being vexed, a sea nourished with lovers' tears.
  What is it else? A madness most discreet,   193
  A choking gall, and a preserving sweet.
  Farewell, my coz.
BENVOLIO   Soft! I will go along.   195
  An if you leave me so, you do me wrong.   196
ROMEO
  Tut, I have lost myself. I am not here.
  This is not Romeo; he's some other where.
BENVOLIO
  Tell me in sadness, who is that you love?   199
ROMEO   What, shall I groan and tell thee?
BENVOLIO
  Groan? Why, no, but sadly tell me who.   201
ROMEO
  Bid a sick man in sadness make his will—
  A word ill urged to one that is so ill!   203
  In sadness, cousin, I do love a woman.
BENVOLIO
  I aimed so near when I supposed you loved.
ROMEO
  A right good markman! And she's fair I love.   206
BENVOLIO
  A right fair mark, fair coz, is soonest hit.   207
ROMEO
  Well, in that hit you miss. She'll not be hit
  With Cupid's arrow. She hath Dian's wit,   209
  And, in strong proof of chastity well armed,   210
  From love's weak childish bow she lives unharmed.
  She will not stay the siege of loving terms,   212
  Nor bide th'encounter of assailing eyes,   213
  Nor ope her lap to saint-seducing gold.
  Oh, she is rich in beauty, only poor
  That when she dies, with beauty dies her store.   216

145 **any means** every means possible. **148 true** i.e., wise in counseling himself **149 close** secretive **150 sounding** being fathomed (to discover deep or inner secrets) **151 envious** malicious **156 So please you** If you please **158 happy** fortunate, successful **159 To** as to. **shrift** confession. **160 cousin** kinsman. **169 Love** Cupid. **view** appearance **170 in proof** in reality, in experience. **171 view . . . still** sight is blindfolded always. (Love is blind.) **172 to his will** to what he wants. **177 create** created

181 **Still-waking** continually awake **183 coz** cousin, kinsman **187–8 propagate . . . thine** increase by having it, i.e., my own grief, oppressed or made still heavier with your grief on my account. (The image of propagating and pressing is appropriately sexual.) **191 purged** i.e., of smoke **193 discreet** judicious, prudent **195 Soft!** i.e., Wait a moment! **196 An if** If **199 sadness** seriousness. **is that** is it that **201 sadly** seriously. (But Romeo plays on the word, and on *in sadness*, in the sense of "sorrowfully.") **203 A word** i.e., *sadly* or *in sadness*—too sad a word, says Romeo, for a melancholy lover **206 fair** beautiful **207 fair mark** clear, distinct target **209 Dian** Diana, huntress and goddess of chastity **210 proof** armor **212 stay** submit to **213 bide** abide, endure **216 store** wealth. (She will die without children, and therefore her beauty will die with her.)

BENVOLIO

Then she hath sworn that she will still live chaste?   217

ROMEO

She hath, and in that sparing makes huge waste,   218
For beauty starved with her severity   219
Cuts beauty off from all posterity.
She is too fair, too wise, wisely too fair,
To merit bliss by making me despair.   222
She hath forsworn to love, and in that vow   223
Do I live dead, that live to tell it now.

BENVOLIO

Be ruled by me. Forget to think of her.

ROMEO

Oh, teach me how I should forget to think!

BENVOLIO

By giving liberty unto thine eyes:
Examine other beauties.

ROMEO   'Tis the way

To call hers, exquisite, in question more.   229
These happy masks that kiss fair ladies' brows,
Being black, puts us in mind they hide the fair.
He that is strucken blind cannot forget
The precious treasure of his eyesight lost.
Show me a mistress that is passing fair: 234
What doth her beauty serve but as a note
Where I may read who passed that passing fair?   236
Farewell. Thou canst not teach me to forget.

BENVOLIO

I'll pay that doctrine, or else die in debt.   *Exeunt.* 238

❧

[1.2]

*Enter Capulet, County Paris, and the Clown
[a Servingman].*

CAPULET

But Montague is bound as well as I,   1
In penalty alike, and 'tis not hard, I think,
For men so old as we to keep the peace.

PARIS

Of honorable reckoning are you both,   4
And pity 'tis you lived at odds so long.
But now, my lord, what say you to my suit?

CAPULET

But saying o'er what I have said before: 7
My child is yet a stranger in the world;
She hath not seen the change of fourteen years.
Let two more summers wither in their pride
Ere we may think her ripe to be a bride.

PARIS

Younger than she are happy mothers made.

CAPULET

And too soon marred are those so early made.
The earth hath swallowed all my hopes but she;
She is the hopeful lady of my earth.   15
But woo her, gentle Paris, get her heart;
My will to her consent is but a part;
And, she agreed, within her scope of choice   18
Lies my consent and fair-according voice.   19
This night I hold an old accustomed feast,   20
Whereto I have invited many a guest
Such as I love; and you among the store,   22
One more, most welcome, makes my number more.
At my poor house look to behold this night
Earth-treading stars that make dark heaven light.
Such comfort as do lusty young men feel   26
When well-appareled April on the heel   27
Of limping winter treads, even such delight
Among fresh fennel buds shall you this night   29
Inherit at my house. Hear all, all see,   30
And like her most whose merit most shall be;
Which on more view of many, mine, being one,   32
May stand in number, though in reck'ning none.   33
Come, go with me. [*To the Servingman, giving a paper*]
    Go, sirrah, trudge about   34
Through fair Verona; find those persons out
Whose names are written there, and to them say,
My house and welcome on their pleasure stay.   37
    Exit [*with Paris*].

SERVINGMAN   Find them out whose names are written
here! It is written that the shoemaker should meddle   39
with his yard and the tailor with his last, the fisher   40
with his pencil, and the painter with his nets; but I am   41
sent to find those persons whose names are here writ,   42
and can never find what names the writing person   43
hath here writ. I must to the learned.—In good time!   44

Enter Benvolio and Romeo.

---

217 **still** always   218 **sparing** miserliness   219 **starved with** killed by
222 **To . . . despair** to achieve her own salvation through chaste living
while driving me to the spiritually dangerous state of despair.
223 **forsworn to** renounced, repudiated   229 **in question more** even
more keenly to mind, into consideration.   234 **mistress** i.e., eligible
young woman.   **passing** surpassingly   236 **passed** surpassed
238 **I'll . . . debt** i.e., I'll fulfill my obligation to do that, or feel I have
failed as a friend.
1.2. Location: Verona.
0.1 *County* Count   1 **bound** legally obligated (to keep the peace)
4 **reckoning** estimation, repute   7 **o'er** again

15 **the hopeful . . . earth** i.e., my heir and hope for posterity. (*Earth*
includes property and lands.)   18 **she** if she be   19 **according** agreeing   20 **old accustomed** traditional   22 **store** group   26 **lusty** lively
27 **well-appareled** newly clothed in green   29 **fennel** flowering herb
thought to have the power of awakening passion   30 **Inherit** possess
32–3 **Which . . . none** i.e., when you have looked over many ladies,
my daughter, being one of them, may be numerically counted among
the lot, but you will not think her worth your notice. (Capulet refers
to the proverbial saying, "one is no number.")   34 **sirrah** (Customary
form of address to servants.)   37 **on . . . stay** wait to serve their pleasure.   39–41 **It is . . . nets** i.e., If a shoemaker cannot be expected to
have any skill with a *yard* (a tailor's yardstick) and conversely a tailor
with a *last* (a shoemaker's form), and similarly with a painter's *pencil*
(a paintbrush) in a fisherman's hands or a net in a painter's hands,
why should I, an illiterate servant, be expected to be able to read a
written note of invitation? (*Meddle, yard,* and *pencil* are often slang
expressions for sexual activity and the male sexual organ, but since
last and *nets* don't seem to convey sexual meaning here, the humor is
more directed at comic inappropriateness.)   42 **find** locate   43 **find**
figure out   44 **In good time** i.e., Here comes help.

BENVOLIO
Tut, man, one fire burns out another's burning,
One pain is lessened by another's anguish; 46
Turn giddy, and be holp by backward turning; 47
One desperate grief cures with another's languish. 48
Take thou some new infection to thy eye,
And the rank poison of the old will die. 50
ROMEO
Your plaintain leaf is excellent for that. 51
BENVOLIO
For what, I pray thee?
ROMEO   For your broken shin.
BENVOLIO   Why, Romeo, art thou mad?
ROMEO
Not mad, but bound more than a madman is; 54
Shut up in prison, kept without my food,
Whipped and tormented and—Good e'en, good
  fellow. 56
SERVINGMAN   God gi' good e'en. I pray, sir, can you read? 57
ROMEO
Ay, mine own fortune in my misery.
SERVINGMAN   Perhaps you have learned it without 59
book. But, I pray, can you read anything you see? 60
ROMEO
Ay, if I know the letters and the language.
SERVINGMAN   Ye say honestly. Rest you merry! 62
                                        [Going.]
ROMEO   Stay, fellow, I can read.   He reads the letter.
"Signor Martino and his wife and daughters,
County Anselme and his beauteous sisters,
The lady widow of Vitruvio,
Signor Placentio and his lovely nieces,
Mercutio and his brother Valentine,
Mine uncle Capulet, his wife, and daughters,
My fair niece Rosaline, and Livia,
Signor Valentio and his cousin Tybalt,
Lucio and the lively Helena."
A fair assembly. Whither should they come?
SERVINGMAN   Up.
ROMEO   Whither? To supper?
SERVINGMAN   To our house.
ROMEO   Whose house?
SERVINGMAN   My master's.
ROMEO
Indeed, I should have asked thee that before.
SERVINGMAN   Now I'll tell you without asking. My
master is the great rich Capulet; and if you be not of
the house of Montagues, I pray, come and crush a cup 82
of wine. Rest you merry!   [Exit.]

BENVOLIO
At this same ancient feast of Capulet's 84
Sups the fair Rosaline whom thou so loves,
With all the admirèd beauties of Verona.
Go thither, and with unattainted eye 87
Compare her face with some that I shall show,
And I will make thee think thy swan a crow.
ROMEO
When the devout religion of mine eye 90
Maintains such falsehood, then turn tears to fires; 91
And these who, often drowned, could never die, 92
Transparent heretics, be burnt for liars! 93
One fairer than my love? The all-seeing sun
Ne'er saw her match since first the world begun.
BENVOLIO
Tut, you saw her fair, none else being by,
Herself poised with herself in either eye; 97
But in that crystal scales let there be weighed 98
Your lady's love against some other maid
That I will show you shining at this feast,
And she shall scant show well that now seems best. 101
ROMEO
I'll go along, no such sight to be shown,
But to rejoice in splendor of mine own.   [Exeunt.] 103

❖

[1.3]

Enter Capulet's Wife and Nurse.

WIFE
Nurse, where's my daughter? Call her forth to me.
NURSE
Now, by my maidenhead at twelve year old,
I bade her come. What, lamb! What, ladybird! 3
God forbid, where's this girl? What, Juliet! 4

Enter Juliet.

JULIET   How now? Who calls?
NURSE   Your mother.
JULIET
Madam, I am here. What is your will?
WIFE
This is the matter.—Nurse, give leave awhile, 8
We must talk in secret.—Nurse, come back again;
I have remembered me, thou's hear our counsel. 10
Thou knowest my daughter's of a pretty age.

---

46 **another's anguish** the anguish of another pain   47 **holp . . . turn-ing** helped by turning in the reverse direction   48 **cures . . . languish** is cured by the suffering of a second *grief* or pain.   50 **rank** foul
51 **Your . . . that** i.e., (sardonically) Your proverbial nostrums are about as useful in curing my real grief as is a folk remedy for minor abrasions such as a *broken shin* (line 52) or surface wound on the leg—that is, no use at all.   54 **bound** (The usual treatment for madness.)
56 **Good e'en** Good evening. (Used after noon.)   57 **gi'** give you
59–60 **Perhaps . . . book** (1) Perhaps that's some sort of book that you've committed to memory (2) Misery is something one can learn without knowing how to read.   62 **Rest you merry** i.e., Farewell. (The servingman can see he is getting nowhere.)   82 **crush** i.e., drink

84 **ancient** customary   87 **unattainted** unbiased   90–3 **When . . . liars!** (Romeo, recalling that persons suspected of witchcraft were sometimes thrown into water to see if they would drown or float, and that those who did not drown were declared witches and burned at the stake, protests that whenever he is a heretic in love by looking at some woman other than Rosaline he should be similarly burned by having his own tears turn into flames, since he will have shown that his flood of tears could not drown him, i.e., was insufficient. *Transparent* means "manifest," "clear.")   97 **poised** weighed, balanced   98 **crystal scales** i.e., Romeo's eyes   101 **scant** scarcely
103 **mine own** i.e., the sight of my own Rosaline.
1.3. Location: Verona. Capulet's house.
3 **ladybird** (A term of affection.)   4 **God forbid** (A mild oath.)
8 **give leave** leave us   10 **thou's** thou shalt

NURSE
Faith, I can tell her age unto an hour.
WIFE
She's not fourteen.
NURSE   I'll lay fourteen of my teeth—
And yet, to my teen be it spoken, I have but four—   14
She's not fourteen. How long is it now
To Lammastide?
WIFE   A fortnight and odd days.   16
NURSE
Even or odd, of all days in the year,
Come Lammas Eve at night shall she be fourteen.
Susan and she—God rest all Christian souls!—   19
Were of an age. Well, Susan is with God;
She was too good for me. But, as I said,
On Lammas Eve at night shall she be fourteen,
That shall she, marry, I remember it well.   23
'Tis since the earthquake now eleven years,
And she was weaned—I never shall forget it—
Of all the days of the year, upon that day;
For I had then laid wormwood to my dug,   27
Sitting in the sun under the dovehouse wall.
My lord and you were then at Mantua—
Nay, I do bear a brain! But, as I said,   30
When it did taste the wormwood on the nipple
Of my dug and felt it bitter, pretty fool,   32
To see it tetchy and fall out wi'th' dug!   33
"Shake" quoth the dovehouse. 'Twas no need, I trow,   34
To bid me trudge!   35
And since that time it is eleven years,
For then she could stand high-lone; nay, by the rood,   37
She could have run and waddled all about.
For even the day before, she broke her brow,   39
And then my husband—God be with his soul!
'A was a merry man—took up the child.   41
"Yea," quoth he, "dost thou fall upon thy face?
Thou wilt fall backward when thou hast more wit,   43
Wilt thou not, Jule?" and, by my halidom,   44
The pretty wretch left crying and said "Ay."
To see now how a jest shall come about!   46
I warrant, an I should live a thousand years,
I never should forget it. "Wilt thou not, Jule?" quoth
    he,
And, pretty fool, it stinted and said "Ay."   49
WIFE
Enough of this. I pray thee, hold thy peace.

NURSE
Yes, madam. Yet I cannot choose but laugh
To think it should leave crying and say "Ay."
And yet, I warrant, it had upon it brow   53
A bump as big as a young cockerel's stone—   54
A perilous knock—and it cried bitterly.
"Yea," quoth my husband, "fall'st upon thy face?
Thou wilt fall backward when thou comest to age,
Wilt thou not, Jule?" It stinted and said "Ay."
JULIET
And stint thou too, I pray thee, Nurse, say I.   59
NURSE
Peace, I have done. God mark thee to his grace!
Thou wast the prettiest babe that e'er I nursed.
An I might live to see thee married once,   62
I have my wish.
WIFE
Marry, that "marry" is the very theme
I came to talk of. Tell me, daughter Juliet,
How stands your disposition to be married?   66
JULIET
It is an honor that I dream not of.
NURSE
An honor? Were not I thine only nurse,
I would say thou hadst sucked wisdom from thy teat.   69
WIFE
Well, think of marriage now. Younger than you
Here in Verona, ladies of esteem,
Are made already mothers. By my count
I was your mother much upon these years   73
That you are now a maid. Thus then in brief:
The valiant Paris seeks you for his love.
NURSE
A man, young lady! Lady, such a man
As all the world—why, he's a man of wax.   77
WIFE
Verona's summer hath not such a flower.
NURSE
Nay, he's a flower, in faith, a very flower.   79
WIFE
What say you? Can you love the gentleman?
This night you shall behold him at our feast.
Read o'er the volume of young Paris' face,
And find delight writ there with beauty's pen;
Examine every married lineament,   84
And see how one another lends content;   85
And what obscured in this fair volume lies   86
Find written in the margent of his eyes.   87
This precious book of love, this unbound lover,   88

To beautify him, only lacks a cover.   89
The fish lives in the sea, and 'tis much pride   90
For fair without the fair within to hide.   91
That book in many's eyes doth share the glory,   92
That in gold clasps locks in the golden story;   93
So shall you share all that he doth possess
By having him, making yourself no less.

NURSE
No less? Nay, bigger. Women grow by men.   96

WIFE
Speak briefly, can you like of Paris' love?   97

JULIET
I'll look to like, if looking liking move;   98
But no more deep will I endart mine eye
Than your consent gives strength to make it fly.

Enter Servingman.

SERVINGMAN   Madam, the guests are come, supper
served up, you called, my young lady asked for, the
Nurse cursed in the pantry, and everything in extremity. I must hence to wait. I beseech you, follow straight.   104
WIFE   We follow thee.   [*Exit Servingman.*]
                     Juliet, the County stays.   105

NURSE
Go, girl, seek happy nights to happy days.   *Exeunt.*

❖

[1.4]

*Enter Romeo, Mercutio, Benvolio, with five or
six other masquers; torchbearers.*

ROMEO
What, shall this speech be spoke for our excuse?   1
Or shall we on without apology?   2

BENVOLIO
The date is out of such prolixity.   3
We'll have no Cupid hoodwinked with a scarf,   4
Bearing a Tartar's painted bow of lath,   5
Scaring the ladies like a crowkeeper,   6
Nor no without-book prologue, faintly spoke   7
After the prompter, for our entrance;
But let them measure us by what they will,   9
We'll measure them a measure, and be gone.   10

ROMEO
Give me a torch. I am not for this ambling.
Being but heavy, I will bear the light.   12

MERCUTIO
Nay, gentle Romeo, we must have you dance.

ROMEO
Not I, believe me. You have dancing shoes
With nimble soles; I have a soul of lead   15
So stakes me to the ground I cannot move.

MERCUTIO
You are a lover; borrow Cupid's wings,
And soar with them above a common bound.   18

ROMEO
I am too sore enpiercèd with his shaft   19
To soar with his light feathers, and so bound
I cannot bound a pitch above dull woe.   21
Under love's heavy burden do I sink.

MERCUTIO
And, to sink in it, should you burden love—   23
Too great oppression for a tender thing.

ROMEO
Is love a tender thing? It is too rough,
Too rude, too boisterous, and it pricks like thorn.

MERCUTIO
If love be rough with you, be rough with love;
Prick love for pricking, and you beat love down.   28
Give me a case to put my visage in.   29
                                   [*He puts on a mask.*]
A visor for a visor! What care I   30
What curious eye doth quote deformities?   31
Here are the beetle brows shall blush for me.

BENVOLIO
Come, knock and enter, and no sooner in
But every man betake him to his legs.   34

ROMEO
A torch for me. Let wantons light of heart
Tickle the senseless rushes with their heels,   36
For I am proverbed with a grandsire phrase: 37
I'll be a candle-holder and look on.   38
The game was ne'er so fair, and I am done.   39

---

89 a cover i.e., marriage, an embracing wife.   **90–1 The fish . . . hide**
i.e., The fish has its own suitable environment, and similarly in marriage the fair Juliet is imagined as a beautiful book cover "binding" Paris) would suitably enhance Paris's worth.   **92–3 That book
. . . story** i.e., In many persons' eyes, a good story is all the more
admirable for being handsomely bound. (*Clasps* means [1] book fas-
tenings [2] embraces.)   **96 bigger** i.e., by pregnancy.   **97 like of** be
pleased with   **98 liking move** may provoke affection   **104 straight**
at once.   **105 County stays** Count (Paris) waits for you.
1.4. Location: Verona. A street.
1 speech (Masquers were customarily preceded by a messenger or
"presenter" with a set speech of compliment.)   **2 on** go on, approach
3 The date . . . prolixity Such windy rhetoric is out of fashion.
4 Cupid i.e., messenger or "presenter," probably a boy, disguised as
Cupid.   **hoodwinked** blindfolded   **5 Tartar's . . . bow** (Tartars'
bows, shorter and more curved than the English longbow, were
thought to have resembled the old Roman bow with which Cupid
was pictured.)   **lath** flimsy wood   **6 crowkeeper** scarecrow
7 without-book memorized   **9 measure** judge   **10 measure . . .
measure** tread a dance for them

12 heavy (1) sad (2) the opposite of *light* (as at 1.1.137)   **15 soul** (Punning on *sole*.)   **18 common bound** (1) ordinary limit (2) normal
dance leap.   **19 sore** sorely. (With pun on *soar*.)   **21 bound** leap.
(With wordplay on *bound*, "confined," in the previous line.)   **pitch**
height. (A term from falconry for the highest point of a hawk's flight.)
23 And . . . love i.e., You wouldn't just sink *under* love's heavy burden, you'd sink *into* it and burden it. (Suggesting sexual penetration.)
28 Prick . . . down i.e., If love gets rough, fight back. (But with bawdy
suggestion of *pricking* as a way to satisfy desire and cause detumescence.)   **29 case** mask   **30 A visor . . . visor** i.e., A mask for an ugly
masklike face.   **31 quote** take notice of   **34 to his legs** to dancing.
36 senseless rushes reeds used as floor covering, or insensate green
rushes   **37 proverbed . . . phrase** furnished with an old proverb
38 candle-holder i.e., bystander. (Referring to the proverbial idea that
one who lacks ability himself can hold the candle and thus provide
light for one who is able to act.)   **39 The game . . . done** (Another
proverbial truism, that it is best to quit when one is ahead.)

MERCUTIO
   Tut, dun's the mouse, the constable's own word.   40
   If thou art dun, we'll draw thee from the mire   41
   Of—save your reverence—love, wherein thou stickest   42
   Up to the ears. Come, we burn daylight, ho!   43
ROMEO
   Nay, that's not so.
MERCUTIO   I mean, sir, in delay
   We waste our lights in vain, like lamps by day.
   Take our good meaning, for our judgment sits   46
   Five times in that ere once in our five wits.   47
ROMEO
   And we mean well in going to this masque,
   But 'tis no wit to go.
MERCUTIO   Why, may one ask?   49
ROMEO
   I dreamt a dream tonight.
MERCUTIO   And so did I.   50
ROMEO
   Well, what was yours?
MERCUTIO   That dreamers often lie.   51
ROMEO
   In bed asleep, while they do dream things true.
MERCUTIO
   Oh, then, I see Queen Mab hath been with you.   53
   She is the fairies' midwife, and she comes
   In shape no bigger than an agate stone   55
   On the forefinger of an alderman,   56
   Drawn with a team of little atomi   57
   Over men's noses as they lie asleep.
   Her chariot is an empty hazelnut,
   Made by the joiner squirrel or old grub,   60
   Time out o' mind the fairies' coachmakers.
   Her wagon spokes made of long spinners' legs,   62
   The cover of the wings of grasshoppers,
   Her traces of the smallest spider web,
   Her collars of the moonshine's wat'ry beams,
   Her whip of cricket's bone, the lash of film,   66
   Her wagoner a small gray-coated gnat,   67

Not half so big as a round little worm   68
Pricked from the lazy finger of a maid.   69
And in this state she gallops night by night
Through lovers' brains, and then they dream of love;
O'er courtiers' knees, that dream on curtsies straight;   72
O'er lawyers' fingers, who straight dream on fees;
O'er ladies' lips, who straight on kisses dream,
Which oft the angry Mab with blisters plagues
Because their breaths with sweetmeats tainted are.   76
Sometime she gallops o'er a courtier's nose,
And then dreams he of smelling out a suit.   78
And sometime comes she with a tithe-pig's tail   79
Tickling a parson's nose as 'a lies asleep;
Then dreams he of another benefice.   81
Sometime she driveth o'er a soldier's neck,
And then dreams he of cutting foreign throats,
Of breaches, ambuscadoes, Spanish blades,   84
Of healths five fathom deep, and then anon   85
Drums in his ear, at which he starts and wakes,
And being thus frighted swears a prayer or two
And sleeps again. This is that very Mab
That plats the manes of horses in the night,   89
And bakes the elflocks in foul sluttish hairs,   90
Which once untangled much misfortune bodes.   91
This is the hag, when maids lie on their backs,
That presses them and learns them first to bear,   93
Making them women of good carriage.   94
This is she—
ROMEO   Peace, peace, Mercutio, peace!
   Thou talk'st of nothing.
MERCUTIO   True, I talk of dreams,
   Which are the children of an idle brain,
   Begot of nothing but vain fantasy,   98
   Which is as thin of substance as the air,
   And more inconstant than the wind, who woos
   Even now the frozen bosom of the north,
   And being angered, puffs away from thence,
   Turning his side to the dew-dropping south.
BENVOLIO
   This wind you talk of blows us from ourselves.   104
   Supper is done, and we shall come too late.
ROMEO
   I fear, too early; for my mind misgives   106
   Some consequence yet hanging in the stars

---

40 dun's . . . word i.e., "keep still"—just the sort of thing a constable might say. (Matching proverb with proverb, Mercutio answers Romeo's "I am done" by twitting him for being mousy. Constables were much laughed at for inappropriately pompous speech.) **41–3 If . . . ears** (To Mercutio, Romeo's love melancholy recalls the Christmas game called "Dun is in the mire," in which a heavy log, representing a horse named Dun, was hauled out of an imaginary mire by the players. *Save your reverence* is Mercutio's mock apology for speaking of so improper an expression as being mired up to the ears in love.) **43 burn daylight** i.e., waste time. (But Romeo quibbles, protesting that it is not literally daytime.) **46–7 Take . . . wits** Try to understand what I am trying to say (rather than quibbling with phrases like "burn daylight"), for wise judgment is five times more pleased with good meaning than with the ingenious wit of our frail senses. **49 wit** wisdom (playing on *wits* in line 47; *mean* in line 48 plays on *meaning* in line 46) **50 tonight** last night. **51 lie** tell falsehoods. (But Mercutio answers in the sense of "lie down in bed.") **53 Queen Mab** (Possibly a name of Celtic origin for the Fairy Queen.) **55 agate stone** (Precious stone often carved with diminutive figures and set in a ring.) **56 alderman** member of the municipal council **57 atomi** tiny creatures (atoms) **60 joiner** furniture maker. **grub** insect larva (which bores holes in nuts) **62 spinners'** spiders' **66 film** gossamer thread **67 wagoner** chariot driver

68–9 a round . . . maid (Worms proverbially breed in the fingers of the idle.) **72 curtsies** bows, obeisances. **straight** immediately **76 sweetmeats** candies or candied preserves **78 smelling . . . suit** i.e., finding a petitioner who will pay for the use of his influence at court. **79 tithe-pig** pig given to the parson in lieu of money as the parishioner's tithing, or granting of a tenth **81 benefice** ecclesiastical living. **84 Of breaches . . . blades** of opening up gaps in fortifications, of ambushes, of swords from Toledo in Spain, where the best swords were made **85 Of healths . . . deep** of toasts drunk deep **89 That plats . . . night** (According to popular superstition, the tangles that persistently turn up in the manes of horses were "witches' stirrups," i.e., footholds for witches as they rode.) **90–1 And bakes . . . bodes** (*Elflocks* or clumps of matted hair were so named because they were imagined to be the work of elves, who would torment anyone so presumptuous as to untangle the elflocks.) **93 learns** teaches **94 good carriage** (1) commendable deportment (2) skill in bearing the weight of men in sexual intercourse (3) able subsequently to carry a child. **98 vain fantasy** delusive imagination **104 from ourselves** from our plans. **106 misgives** fears

Shall bitterly begin his fearful date   108
With this night's revels, and expire the term   109
Of a despisèd life closed in my breast
By some vile forfeit of untimely death.
But He that hath the steerage of my course
Direct my suit! On, lusty gentlemen.   113

BENVOLIO   Strike, drum.   *They march about the stage,* 114
                           and [retire to one side].

❖

[1.5]

Servingmen come forth with napkins.

FIRST SERVINGMAN   Where's Potpan, that he helps not
to take away? He shift a trencher? He scrape a trencher?   2

SECOND SERVINGMAN   When good manners shall lie all
in one or two men's hands, and they unwashed too,
'tis a foul thing.

FIRST SERVINGMAN   Away with the joint stools, remove   6
the court cupboard, look to the plate. Good thou, save   7
me a piece of marchpane, and, as thou loves me, let   8
the porter let in Susan Grindstone and Nell.
                            [*Exit Second Servingman.*]
Anthony and Potpan!

                   [*Enter two more Servingmen.*]

THIRD SERVINGMAN   Ay, boy, ready.

FIRST SERVINGMAN   You are looked for and called for,
asked for and sought for, in the great chamber.

FOURTH SERVINGMAN   We cannot be here and there
too. Cheerly, boys! Be brisk awhile, and the longest   15
liver take all.   *Exeunt.*   16

         Enter [Capulet and family and] all the guests
         and gentlewomen to the masquers.

CAPULET   [*to the masquers*]
Welcome, gentlemen! Ladies that have their toes
Unplagued with corns will walk a bout with you.   18
Ah, my mistresses, which of you all
Will now deny to dance? She that makes dainty,   20
She, I'll swear, hath corns. Am I come near ye now?   21
Welcome, gentlemen! I have seen the day
That I have worn a visor and could tell
A whispering tale in a fair lady's ear
Such as would please. 'Tis gone, 'tis gone, 'tis gone.
You are welcome, gentlemen! Come, musicians, play.
                   Music plays, and they dance.

A hall, a hall! Give room! And foot, it, girls.   27
[*To Servingmen*]   More light, you knaves, and turn the
   tables up,   28
And quench the fire; the room is grown too hot.
[*To his cousin*]   Ah, sirrah, this unlooked-for sport
   comes well.   30
Nay, sit, nay, sit, good cousin Capulet,   31
For you and I are past our dancing days.
How long is't now since last yourself and I
Were in a mask?

SECOND CAPULET   By'r Lady, thirty years.

CAPULET
What, man? 'Tis not so much, 'tis not so much;
'Tis since the nuptial of Lucentio,
Come Pentecost as quickly as it will,   37
Some five-and-twenty years, and then we masked.

SECOND CAPULET
'Tis more, 'tis more. His son is elder, sir;
His son is thirty.

CAPULET   Will you tell me that?
His son was but a ward two years ago.   41

ROMEO   [*to a Servingman*]
What lady's that which doth enrich the hand
Of yonder knight?

SERVINGMAN   I know not, sir.

ROMEO
Oh, she doth teach the torches to burn bright!
It seems she hangs upon the cheek of night
As a rich jewel in an Ethiop's ear—
Beauty too rich for use, for earth too dear!   48
So shows a snowy dove trooping with crows   49
As yonder lady o'er her fellows shows.
The measure done, I'll watch her place of stand,   51
And, touching hers, make blessèd my rude hand.   52
Did my heart love till now? Forswear it, sight!   53
For I ne'er saw true beauty till this night.

TYBALT
This, by his voice, should be a Montague.
Fetch me my rapier, boy. What dares the slave   56
Come hither, covered with an antic face,   57
To fleer and scorn at our solemnity?   58
Now, by the stock and honor of my kin,
To strike him dead I hold it not a sin.

CAPULET
Why, how now, kinsman? Wherefore storm you so?

---

27 **A hall** i.e., Clear the hall for dancing   28 **turn . . . up** move the
tables out of the way for the dancing (by taking up the boards and
then removing the supporting trestles)   30 **sirrah** (Normally used in
addressing social inferiors. Perhaps Capulet uses a jesting tone
toward his kinsman or possibly addresses himself.)   **unlooked-for
sport** i.e., arrival of the masquers, providing more men for the dancing   31 **cousin** (*Cousin* often means "kinsman"; at 1.2.69, "Mine
uncle Capulet" is named on the invitation list.)   37 **Pentecost** seventh Sunday after Easter (and never as late as mid-July, two weeks
before Lammas or August 1, when according to 1.3.16, the play takes
place; a seeming inconsistency).   41 **a ward** a minor under guardianship   48 **dear** precious.   49 **shows** appears   51 **The measure done**
When this dance is over.   **her place of stand** where she stands
52 **hers** her hand.   **rude** rough   53 **Forswear it** Deny any previous
oath   56 **What** How   57 **antic face** grotesque mask   58 **fleer** jeer.
solemnity time-honored festivity.

---

108 **date** appointed time   109 **expire** bring to an end   113 **lusty**
lively   114 **drum** drummer.
**1.5. Location: The action, continuous from the previous scene, is
now imaginatively transferred to a hall in Capulet's house.**
2 **take away** clear the table.   6 **joint
stools** stools of which the parts are fitted by a joiner or furniture
maker   7 **court cupboard** sideboard.   **plate** silverware.   8 **marchpane** cake made from sugar and almonds, marzipan   15–16 **the
longest . . . all** (A proverb in defense of merriment.)   18 **walk a bout**
dance a turn   20 **makes dainty** seems coyly reluctant (to dance)
21 **Am . . . now?** Have I hit a sensitive point, struck home?

TYBALT
Uncle, this is a Montague, our foe,
A villain that is hither come in spite
To scorn at our solemnity this night.   63
CAPULET
Young Romeo is it?
TYBALT   'Tis he, that villain Romeo.
CAPULET
Content thee, gentle coz, let him alone.
'A bears him like a portly gentleman,   67
And, to say truth, Verona brags of him
To be a virtuous and well governed youth.
I would not for the wealth of all this town
Here in my house do him disparagement.
Therefore be patient; take no note of him.
It is my will, the which if thou respect,
Show a fair presence and put off these frowns,   74
An ill-beseeming semblance for a feast.   75
TYBALT
It fits when such a villain is a guest.
I'll not endure him.
CAPULET   He shall be endured.
What, goodman boy? I say he shall. Go to!   78
Am I the master here, or you? Go to.
You'll not endure him! God shall mend my soul,
You'll make a mutiny among my guests!   81
You will set cock-a-hoop! You'll be the man!   82
TYBALT
Why, uncle, 'tis a shame.
CAPULET   Go to, go to,
You are a saucy boy. Is't so, indeed?
This trick may chance to scathe you. I know what,   85
You must contrary me. Marry, 'tis time.—   86
Well said, my hearts!—You are a princox, go.   87
Be quiet, or—More light, more light!—For shame!
I'll make you quiet.—What, cheerly, my hearts!
TYBALT
Patience perforce with willful choler meeting   90
Makes my flesh tremble in their different greeting.   91
I will withdraw. But this intrusion shall,
Now seeming sweet, convert to bitt'rest gall.   *Exit.*
ROMEO [*to Juliet*]
If I profane with my unworthiest hand   94
This holy shrine, the gentle sin is this: 95
My lips, two blushing pilgrims, ready stand
To smooth that rough touch with a tender kiss.
JULIET
Good pilgrim, you do wrong your hand too much,

Which mannerly devotion shows in this;
For saints have hands that pilgrims' hands do touch,   100
And palm to palm is holy palmers' kiss.   101
ROMEO
Have not saints lips, and holy palmers too?
JULIET
Ay, pilgrim, lips that they must use in prayer.
ROMEO
Oh, then, dear saint, let lips do what hands do.   104
They pray; grant thou, lest faith turn to despair.
JULIET
Saints do not move, though grant for prayers' sake.   106
ROMEO
Then move not, while my prayer's effect I take.   107
                         [*He kisses her.*]
Thus from my lips, by thine, my sin is purged.
JULIET
Then have my lips the sin that they have took.
ROMEO
Sin from my lips? Oh, trespass sweetly urged!
Give me my sin again.   [*He kisses her.*]
JULIET   You kiss by th' book.   111
NURSE [*approaching*]
Madam, your mother craves a word with you.
                         [*Juliet retires.*]
ROMEO
What is her mother?
NURSE   Marry, bachelor,   113
Her mother is the lady of the house,
And a good lady, and a wise and virtuous.
I nursed her daughter that you talked withal.   116
I tell you, he that can lay hold of her
Shall have the chinks.
ROMEO [*aside*]   Is she a Capulet?   118
Oh, dear account! My life is my foe's debt.   119
BENVOLIO [*approaching*]
Away, begone! The sport is at the best.   120
ROMEO
Ay, so I fear; the more is my unrest.
                         [*The masquers prepare to leave.*]
CAPULET
Nay, gentlemen, prepare not to be gone.
We have a trifling foolish banquet towards.   123
                         [*One whispers in his ear.*]
Is it e'en so? Why, then, I thank you all.
I thank you, honest gentlemen. Good night.   125

63 spite malice   **67 portly** of good deportment   **74 presence**
demeanor   **75 semblance** facial expression   **78 goodman boy** (A
belittling term for Tybalt; *Goodman* applied to one below the rank of
gentleman but still of some substance, like a wealthy farmer.)   **Go to**
(An expression of irritation.)   **81 mutiny** disturbance   **82 You . . .
man!** i.e., You'll set mischief abroach (literally, turn the tap and let the
liquor flow)! You'll be the big shot!   **85 scathe** harm   **86 contrary**
oppose, thwart.   **'tis time** i.e., it's time you were taught a lesson.
87 Well said Well done. (Said to the dancers.)   **princox** saucy boy
90–1 Patience . . . greeting The attempt to be patient under duress
when I am so angry causes me to tremble at the contrary meeting of
these two opposite impulses.   **94–107** (These lines are in the form of
a Shakespearean sonnet; they are followed by a quatrain.)   **95 shrine**
i.e., Juliet's hand

100 saints i.e., images of saints that are venerated by pilgrims
101 palmers pilgrims who have been to the Holy Land and have
brought back a palm. (With a pun on the palm of the hand.)   **104 let . . .
do** let lips touch, just as hands touch.   **106 Saints . . . sake** Venerated
images and statues of saints remain motionless but nonetheless intercede on behalf of praying pilgrims.   **107 move** (Romeo quibbles on
Juliet's metaphorical use of the word *move* to urge that she remain
motionless while he kisses her.)   **111 by th' book** by the rules, like
an expert.   **113 What** Who   **116 withal** with.   **118 the chinks** plenty
of coins, money. (A slang expression.)   **119 dear account** heavy reckoning.   **my foe's debt** due to my foe, at his mercy.   **120 The sport . . .
best** i.e., It is time to leave. (Refers to the proverb, "When play is at
the best, it is time to leave"; compare at 1.4.39.)   **123 foolish banquet
towards** insignificant light refreshment just ready.   **125 honest**
honorable

More torches here! Come on then, let's to bed.   126
[*To his cousin*] Ah, sirrah, by my fay, it waxes late.   127
I'll to my rest.
                    [*All proceed to leave but Juliet and the Nurse.*]

JULIET
Come hither, Nurse. What is yond gentleman?

NURSE
The son and heir of old Tiberio.

JULIET
What's he that now is going out of door?

NURSE
Marry, that, I think, be young Petruchio.

JULIET
What's he that follows here, that would not dance?

NURSE   I know not.

JULIET
Go ask his name. [*The Nurse goes.*] If he be marrièd,
My grave is like to be my wedding bed.   136

NURSE [*returning*]
His name is Romeo, and a Montague,
The only son of your great enemy.

JULIET
My only love sprung from my only hate!
Too early seen unknown, and known too late!
Prodigious birth of love it is to me   141
That I must love a loathèd enemy.

NURSE
What's tis? What's tis?

JULIET   A rhyme I learned even now   143
Of one I danced withal.   *One calls within* "Juliet."

NURSE   Anon, anon!   144
Come, let's away. The strangers all are gone.   *Exeunt.*

❧

[2.0]

        [*Enter*] *Chorus.*

CHORUS
Now old desire doth in his deathbed lie,   1
    And young affection gapes to be his heir;   2
That fair for which love groaned for and would die,   3
    With tender Juliet matched, is now not fair.   4
Now Romeo is beloved and loves again,
    Alike bewitchèd by the charm of looks;   6
But to his foe supposed he must complain,   7
    And she steal love's sweet bait from fearful hooks.   8
Being held a foe, he may not have access
    To breathe such vows as lovers use to swear;   10
And she as much in love, her means much less
    To meet her new-belovèd anywhere.

126 **torches** i.e., to light the guests as they leave   127 **fay** faith
136 **like** likely   141 **Prodigious** Ominous   143 **tis** this. (Dialect pronunciation.)   144 **Anon** i.e., We're coming
2.0. Chorus.
1–14 (This chorus is a sonnet.)   **2 gapes** waits open-mouthed   **3 fair** beauty, i.e., Rosaline   **4 matched** compared   **6 Alike** i.e., equally with Juliet   **7 foe supposed** i.e., Juliet, a Capulet; also, his opposite number in the war of love.   **complain** offer his love plaint   **8 And she . . . hooks** and she must steal moments of happy love from frightening circumstances designed to catch her unawares.   **10 use** are accustomed

But passion lends them power, time means, to meet,   13
Temp'ring extremities with extreme sweet.   [*Exit.*]   14

❧

[2.1]

        Enter Romeo alone.

ROMEO
Can I go forward when my heart is here?   1
Turn back, dull earth, and find thy center out.   2
                            [*Romeo retires.*]

        Enter Benvolio with Mercutio.

BENVOLIO
Romeo! My cousin Romeo! Romeo!

MERCUTIO   He is wise
And, on my life, hath stol'n him home to bed.

BENVOLIO
He ran this way and leapt this orchard wall.
Call, good Mercutio.

MERCUTIO   Nay, I'll conjure too.   7
Romeo! Humors! Madman! Passion! Lover!   8
Appear thou in the likeness of a sigh.
Speak but one rhyme, and I am satisfied;
Cry but "Ay me!" Pronounce but "love" and "dove."
Speak to my gossip Venus one fair word,   12
One nickname for her purblind son and heir,   13
Young Abraham Cupid, he that shot so trim   14
When King Cophetua loved the beggar maid.—   15
He heareth not, he stirreth not, he moveth not;
The ape is dead, and I must conjure him.—   17
I conjure thee by Rosaline's bright eyes,
By her high forehead and her scarlet lip,
By her fine foot, straight leg, and quivering thigh,
And the demesnes that there adjacent lie,   21
That in thy likeness thou appear to us.

BENVOLIO
An if he hear thee, thou wilt anger him.   23

MERCUTIO
This cannot anger him. 'Twould anger him
To raise a spirit in his mistress' circle   25
Of some strange nature, letting it there stand   26

13 **time means** time lends them means   14 **Temp'ring extremities** mitigating the hardships.   **sweet** sweetness, pleasure.
2.1. Location: Verona. Outside of Capulet's walled orchard.
1 forward i.e., away   **2 Turn . . . out** (Romeo bids his own earthbound body find out its *center*, its soul or heart (i.e., Juliet), much as in the Ptolemaic system all earthly things seek out their center, the earth, standing at the center of the universe. His body is *dull* in that, like earth, it is the lowest and heaviest of the four elements, associated with melancholy.)   **7 conjure** raise him with magical incantation   **8 Humors** Moods.   **12 gossip** crony   **13 purblind** dim-sighted   **14 Young Abraham** i.e., one who is young and yet, like the Biblical Abraham, old; Cupid was paradoxically the youngest and the oldest of the gods   **15 King Cophetua** (In an old ballad, the King falls in love with a beggar maid and makes her his queen.)   **17 ape** (Used as a term of endearment.)   **21 demesnes** regions. (With bawdy suggestion as to what is adjacent to the thighs; bawdy puns on terms of conjuration continue in *raise, spirit*, i.e., "phallus" or "semen," *circle, stand, laid it, raise up*.)   **23 An if** If   **25 circle** (1) conjuring circle (2) vagina   **26 strange** belonging to another person. (With suggestion of a rival possessing Rosaline sexually.)

Till she had laid it and conjured it down;   27
That were some spite. My invocation   28
Is fair and honest; in his mistress' name
I conjure only but to raise up him.

BENVOLIO
Come, he hath hid himself among these trees
To be consorted with the humorous night.   32
Blind is his love, and best befits the dark.

MERCUTIO
If love be blind, love cannot hit the mark.
Now will he sit under a medlar tree   35
And wish his mistress were that kind of fruit
As maids call medlars when they laugh alone.
Oh, Romeo, that she were, oh, that she were
An open-arse, and thou a pop'ring pear!   39
Romeo, good night. I'll to my truckle bed;   40
This field bed is too cold for me to sleep.   41
Come, shall we go?

BENVOLIO   Go, then, for 'tis in vain
To seek him here that means not to be found.
                                    Exit [*with Mercutio*].

❧

[2.2]

ROMEO [*coming forward*]
He jests at scars that never felt a wound.   1
            [*A light appears above, as at Juliet's window.*]
But soft, what light through yonder window breaks?
It is the east, and Juliet is the sun.
Arise, fair sun, and kill the envious moon,
Who is already sick and pale with grief
That thou her maid art far more fair than she.   6
Be not her maid, since she is envious;   7
Her vestal livery is but sick and green   8
And none but fools do wear it. Cast it off.
            [*Juliet appears aloft as at her window.*]
It is my lady, oh, it is my love.
Oh, that she knew she were!
She speaks, yet she says nothing. What of that?

Her eye discourses. I will answer it.
I am too bold. 'Tis not to me she speaks.
Two of the fairest stars in all the heaven,
Having some business, do entreat her eyes
To twinkle in their spheres till they return.   17
What if her eyes were there, they in her head?   18
The brightness of her cheek would shame those stars
As daylight doth a lamp; her eyes in heaven
Would through the airy region stream so bright   21
That birds would sing and think it were not night.
See how she leans her cheek upon her hand!
Oh, that I were a glove upon that hand,
That I might touch that cheek!

JULIET   Ay me!

ROMEO [*aside*]   She speaks.
Oh, speak again, bright angel, for thou art
As glorious to this night, being o'er my head,
As is a wingèd messenger of heaven
Unto the white-upturnèd wond'ring eyes   29
Of mortals that fall back to gaze on him
When he bestrides the lazy puffing clouds
And sails upon the bosom of the air.

JULIET [*to herself*]
Oh, Romeo, Romeo, wherefore art thou Romeo?   33
Deny thy father and refuse thy name!
Or, if thou wilt not, be but sworn my love,
And I'll no longer be a Capulet.

ROMEO [*aside*]
Shall I hear more, or shall I speak at this?

JULIET
'Tis but thy name that is my enemy;
Thou art thyself, though not a Montague.   39
What's Montague? It is nor hand, nor foot,   40
Nor arm, nor face, nor any other part
Belonging to a man. Oh, be some other name!
What's in a name? That which we call a rose
By any other word would smell as sweet;
So Romeo would, were he not Romeo called,
Retain that dear perfection which he owes   46
Without that title. Romeo, doff thy name,   47
And for thy name, which is no part of thee,   48
Take all myself.

ROMEO   I take thee at thy word!
Call me but love, and I'll be new baptized;
Henceforth I never will be Romeo.

JULIET
What man art thou that, thus bescreened in night,   52
So stumblest on my counsel?

ROMEO   By a name   53
I know not how to tell thee who I am.
My name, dear saint, is hateful to myself,
Because it is an enemy to thee;
Had I it written, I would tear the word.

---

27 laid it (1) laid the spirit to rest (2) provided sexual satisfaction leading to detumescence   **28 were some spite** would be vexing.
32 consorted associated.   **humorous** (1) moist, damp (2) well suited to the *humor* of melancholy   **35 medlar** a fruit that was edible only when partly decayed, used as a slang term for women's sexual organs   **39 open-arse** (Another name for the *medlar*, making explicit the sexual metaphor.)   **pop'ring pear** poppering pear (named after Poperinghe in Flanders). A fruit with phallic associations because of its shape and its suggestive name ("pop 'er in").   **40 truckle bed** a bed on casters to be rolled under a standing bed when not in use
41 field bed i.e., the ground
2.2. Location: The action, continuous from the previous scene, is now imaginatively transferred to inside Capulet's orchard. A rhymed couplet links the two scenes. Romeo has been hiding from his friends as though concealed by the orchard wall. He speaks at once and then turns to observe Juliet's window, which is probably in the gallery above, rearstage.
1.1 *A light appears* (Some editors assume that Juliet is visible at line 1.)
6 maid i.e., votary of Diana, goddess of the moon and patroness of virgins   **7 her** the moon's, Diana's, as the goddess of chastity. (Addressed to Juliet as the sun; Romeo hopes that she will not be a devotee of chastity.)   **8 Her vestal livery** the uniform of Diana's chaste votaries.
sick and green (Suggesting the pallor of moonlight, as well as anemia or *greensickness* [see 3.5.156], to which teenage girls were susceptible.)

17 spheres transparent concentric shells supposed to carry the heavenly bodies with them in their revolution around the earth   **18 there** i.e., in the spheres   **21 stream** shine   **29 white-upturnèd** looking upward so that the whites of the eyes are visible   **33 wherefore** why   **39 though not** (1) even if you were not (2) though not in anything essential
40 nor hand neither hand   **46 owes** owns   **47 doff** cast off   **48 for** in exchange for   **52 bescreened** concealed   **53 counsel** secret thought.

JULIET
  My ears have yet not drunk a hundred words
  Of thy tongue's uttering, yet I know the sound:
  Art thou not Romeo and a Montague?

ROMEO
  Neither, fair maid, if either thee dislike.   61

JULIET
  How camest thou hither, tell me, and wherefore?
  The orchard walls are high and hard to climb,
  And the place death, considering who thou art,
  If any of my kinsmen find thee here.

ROMEO
  With love's light wings did I o'erperch these walls, 66
  For stony limits cannot hold love out,
  And what love can do, that dares love attempt;
  Therefore thy kinsmen are no stop to me.

JULIET
  If they do see thee, they will murder thee.

ROMEO
  Alack, there lies more peril in thine eye
  Than twenty of their swords. Look thou but sweet,
  And I am proof against their enmity.   73

JULIET
  I would not for the world they saw thee here.

ROMEO
  I have night's cloak to hide me from their eyes;
  And but thou love me, let them find me here. 76
  My life were better ended by their hate
  Than death prorogued, wanting of thy love. 78

JULIET
  By whose direction found'st thou out this place?

ROMEO
  By love, that first did prompt me to inquire.
  He lent me counsel, and I lent him eyes.
  I am no pilot; yet, wert thou as far
  As that vast shore washed with the farthest sea,
  I should adventure for such merchandise.

JULIET
  Thou knowest the mask of night is on my face,
  Else would a maiden blush bepaint my cheek
  For that which thou hast heard me speak tonight.
  Fain would I dwell on form—fain, fain deny 88
  What I have spoke; but farewell compliment! 89
  Dost thou love me? I know thou wilt say "Ay,"
  And I will take thy word. Yet if thou swear'st
  Thou mayst prove false. At lovers' perjuries,
  They say, Jove laughs. O gentle Romeo,
  If thou dost love, pronounce it faithfully.
  Or if thou thinkest I am too quickly won,
  I'll frown and be perverse and say thee nay,
  So thou wilt woo, but else not for the world.
  In truth, fair Montague, I am too fond, 98
  And therefore thou mayst think my havior light. 99
  But trust me, gentleman, I'll prove more true
  Than those that have more cunning to be strange. 101

  I should have been more strange, I must confess,
  But that thou overheard'st, ere I was ware, 103
  My true-love passion. Therefore pardon me,
  And not impute this yielding to light love,
  Which the dark night hath so discovered. 106

ROMEO
  Lady, by yonder blessèd moon I vow,
  That tips with silver all these fruit-tree tops—

JULIET
  Oh, swear not by the moon, th'inconstant moon,
  That monthly changes in her circled orb, 110
  Lest that thy love prove likewise variable.

ROMEO
  What shall I swear by?

JULIET   Do not swear at all;
  Or, if thou wilt, swear by thy gracious self,
  Which is the god of my idolatry,
  And I'll believe thee.

ROMEO   If my heart's dear love—

JULIET
  Well, do not swear. Although I joy in thee,
  I have no joy of this contract tonight. 117
  It is too rash, too unadvised, too sudden, 118
  Too like the lightning, which doth cease to be
  Ere one can say it lightens. Sweet, good night!
  This bud of love, by summer's ripening breath,
  May prove a beauteous flower when next we meet.
  Good night, good night! As sweet repose and rest 123
  Come to thy heart as that within my breast!

ROMEO
  Oh, wilt thou leave me so unsatisfied?

JULIET
  What satisfaction canst thou have tonight?

ROMEO
  Th'exchange of thy love's faithful vow for mine.

JULIET
  I gave thee mine before thou didst request it;
  And yet I would it were to give again.

ROMEO
  Wouldst thou withdraw it? For what purpose, love?

JULIET
  But to be frank and give it thee again. 131
  And yet I wish but for the thing I have.
  My bounty is as boundless as the sea,
  My love as deep; the more I give to thee,
  The more I have, for both are infinite.
                [*The Nurse calls within.*]
  I hear some noise within. Dear love, adieu!—
  Anon, good Nurse!—Sweet Montague, be true.
  Stay but a little; I will come again.   [*Exit, above.*]

ROMEO
  Oh, blessèd, blessèd night! I am afeard,
  Being in night, all this is but a dream,
  Too flattering-sweet to be substantial.

     [*Enter Juliet, above.*]

---

61 thee dislike displeases you. **66 o'erperch** fly over **73 proof** protected **76 but** unless **78 prorogued** postponed. **wanting of** lacking **88 Fain** Gladly. **dwell on form** preserve the proper formalities **89 compliment** etiquette, convention. **98 fond** infatuated **99 havior light** behavior frivolous. **101 strange** reserved, aloof, modest.

103 ware aware **106 Which** i.e., which yielding. **discovered** revealed. **110 orb** orbit, sphere **117 contract** exchanging of vows **118 unadvised** unconsidered **123 As** May just as **131 frank** liberal, bounteous

JULIET
Three words, dear Romeo, and good night indeed.
If that thy bent of love be honorable,
Thy purpose marriage, send me word tomorrow,   143
By one that I'll procure to come to thee,
Where and what time thou wilt perform the rite,
And all my fortunes at thy foot I'll lay
And follow thee my lord throughout the world.
NURSE [within]   Madam!
JULIET
I come, anon.—But if thou meanest not well,
I do beseech thee—
NURSE [within]   Madam!
JULIET   By and by, I come—   151
To cease thy strife and leave me to my grief.   152
Tomorrow will I send.
ROMEO   So thrive my soul—
JULIET   A thousand times good night!   [Exit, above.]
ROMEO
A thousand times the worse, to want thy light.
Love goes toward love as schoolboys from their
    books,
But love from love, toward school with heavy looks.
                    [He starts to leave.]

    Enter Juliet [above] again.

JULIET
Hist! Romeo, hist! Oh, for a falconer's voice,
To lure this tassel-gentle back again!   160
Bondage is hoarse and may not speak aloud,   161
Else would I tear the cave where Echo lies   162
And make her airy tongue more hoarse than mine
With repetition of "My Romeo!"
ROMEO
It is my soul that calls upon my name.
How silver-sweet sound lovers' tongues by night,
Like softest music to attending ears!
JULIET
Romeo!
ROMEO   My nyas?
JULIET   What o'clock tomorrow   168
Shall I send to thee?
ROMEO   By the hour of nine.
JULIET
I will not fail. 'Tis twenty year till then.—
I have forgot why I did call thee back.
ROMEO
Let me stand here till thou remember it.
JULIET
I shall forget, to have thee still stand there,   173
Remembering how I love thy company.

ROMEO
And I'll still stay, to have thee still forget,
Forgetting any other home but this.
JULIET
'Tis almost morning. I would have thee gone—
And yet no farther than a wanton's bird,   178
That lets it hop a little from his hand,
Like a poor prisoner in his twisted gyves,   180
And with a silken thread plucks it back again,
So loving-jealous of his liberty.   182
ROMEO
I would I were thy bird.
JULIET   Sweet, so would I.
Yet I should kill thee with much cherishing.
Good night, good night! Parting is such sweet sorrow
That I shall say good night till it be morrow.
                    [Exit, above.]
ROMEO
Sleep dwell upon thine eyes, peace in thy breast!
Would I were sleep and peace, so sweet to rest!
Hence will I to my ghostly friar's close cell,   189
His help to crave, and my dear hap to tell.   Exit. 190

❖

[2.3]

    Enter Friar [Laurence] alone, with a basket.

FRIAR LAURENCE
The gray-eyed morn smiles on the frowning night,
Check'ring the eastern clouds with streaks of light,
And fleckled darkness like a drunkard reels   3
From forth day's path and Titan's fiery wheels.   4
Now, ere the sun advance his burning eye,   5
The day to cheer and night's dank dew to dry,
I must up-fill this osier cage of ours   7
With baleful weeds and precious-juicèd flowers.   8
The earth that's nature's mother is her tomb;
What is her burying grave, that is her womb;
And from her womb children of divers kind
We sucking on her natural bosom find,
Many for many virtues excellent,
None but for some, and yet all different.   14
Oh, mickle is the powerful grace that lies   15
In plants, herbs, stones, and their true qualities.   16
For naught so vile that on the earth doth live   17
But to the earth some special good doth give;
Nor aught so good but, strained from that fair use,   19
Revolts from true birth, stumbling on abuse.
Virtue itself turns vice, being misapplied,
And vice sometime by action dignified.

    Enter Romeo.

143 bent purpose, inclination   151 By and by Immediately
152 strife striving   160 tassel-gentle tercel gentle, the male of the
goshawk   161 Bondage is hoarse i.e., In confinement one can speak
only in a loud whisper   162 tear pierce (with noise).   Echo (In Book
3 of Ovid's Metamorphoses, Echo, rejected by Narcissus, pines away in
lonely caves until only her voice is left.)   168 nyas eyas, fledgling
173 still always

178 wanton's spoiled child's   180 gyves fetters   182 his its
189 ghostly spiritual.   close narrow   190 dear hap good fortune
2.3. Location: Verona. Friar Laurence's monastery garden.
3 fleckled dappled   4 From forth out of the way of.   Titan's (Helios,
the sun god, was a descendant of the race of Titans.)   5 advance raise
7 osier cage willow basket   8 baleful harmful   14 None but for some
there are none that are not useful for something   15 mickle great.
grace beneficent virtue   16 true proper, inherent   17 For naught so
vile For there is nothing so vile   19 strained forced, perverted

Within the infant rind of this weak flower
Poison hath residence and medicine power:
For this, being smelt, with that part cheers each part;   25
Being tasted, stays all senses with the heart.   26
Two such opposèd kings encamp them still   27
In man as well as herbs—grace and rude will;
And where the worser is predominant,
Full soon the canker death eats up that plant.   30

ROMEO
Good morrow, Father.

FRIAR LAURENCE   Benedicite!   31
What early tongue so sweet saluteth me?
Young son, it argues a distempered head   33
So soon to bid good morrow to thy bed.
Care keeps his watch in every old man's eye,
And where care lodges sleep will never lie;
But where unbruisèd youth with unstuffed brain   37
Doth couch his limbs, there golden sleep doth reign.
Therefore thy earliness doth me assure
Thou art uproused with some distemp'rature;
Or if not so, then here I hit it right:
Our Romeo hath not been in bed tonight.

ROMEO
That last is true. The sweeter rest was mine.

FRIAR LAURENCE
God pardon sin! Wast thou with Rosaline?

ROMEO
With Rosaline, my ghostly father? No.
I have forgot that name, and that name's woe.

FRIAR LAURENCE
That's my good son. But where hast thou been, then?

ROMEO
I'll tell thee ere thou ask it me again.
I have been feasting with mine enemy,
Where on a sudden one hath wounded me
That's by me wounded. Both our remedies   51
Within thy help and holy physic lies.   52
I bear no hatred, blessèd man, for, lo,
My intercession likewise steads my foe.   54

FRIAR LAURENCE
Be plain, good son, and homely in thy drift.   55
Riddling confession finds but riddling shrift.   56

ROMEO
Then plainly know my heart's dear love is set
On the fair daughter of rich Capulet.
As mine on hers, so hers is set on mine,
And all combined, save what thou must combine
By holy marriage. When and where and how
We met, we wooed, and made exchange of vow
I'll tell thee as we pass; but this I pray,
That thou consent to marry us today.

FRIAR LAURENCE
Holy Saint Francis, what a change is here!
Is Rosaline, that thou didst love so dear,

So soon forsaken? Young men's love then lies
Not truly in their hearts, but in their eyes.
Jesu Maria, what a deal of brine
Hath washed thy sallow cheeks for Rosaline!
How much salt water thrown away in waste
To season love, that of it doth not taste!
The sun not yet thy sighs from heaven clears,
Thy old groans yet ringing in mine ancient ears.
Lo, here upon thy cheek the stain doth sit
Of an old tear that is not washed off yet.
If e'er thou wast thyself and these woes thine,   77
Thou and these woes were all for Rosaline.
And art thou changed? Pronounce this sentence then: 79
Women may fall, when there's no strength in men.

ROMEO
Thou chid'st me oft for loving Rosaline.

FRIAR LAURENCE
For doting, not for loving, pupil mine.

ROMEO
And bad'st me bury love.

FRIAR LAURENCE   Not in a grave
To lay one in, another out to have.

ROMEO
I pray thee, chide not. She whom I love now
Doth grace for grace and love for love allow.   86
The other did not so.

FRIAR LAURENCE   Oh, she knew well
Thy love did read by rote, that could not spell.   88
But come, young waverer, come, go with me,
In one respect I'll thy assistant be;   90
For this alliance may so happy prove
To turn your households' rancor to pure love.   92

ROMEO
Oh, let us hence! I stand on sudden haste.   93

FRIAR LAURENCE
Wisely and slow. They stumble that run fast.

                                            Exeunt.

❖

[2.4]

Enter Benvolio and Mercutio.

MERCUTIO
Where the devil should this Romeo be?   1
Came he not home tonight?   2

BENVOLIO
Not to his father's. I spoke with his man.

MERCUTIO
Why, that same pale hardhearted wench, that
    Rosaline,
Torments him so that he will sure run mad.

BENVOLIO
Tybalt, the kinsman to old Capulet,
Hath sent a letter to his father's house.

---

25 that part i.e., the odor   **26 stays** halts.   **with** together with   **27 them still** themselves always   **30 canker** cankerworm   **31 Benedicite!** A blessing on you!   **33 argues** demonstrates, provides evidence of.   **distempered** disturbed, disordered   **37 unstuffed** not overcharged, carefree   **51 Both our remedies** The remedy for both of us   **52 physic** medicine, healing property   **54 intercession** petition.   **steads** helps   **55 homely** simple   **56 shrift** absolution.

77 If . . . thine If ever you had any proper sense of self and understanding of your love sorrows   **79 sentence** maxim   **86 grace** favor,   **88 did read . . . spell** i.e., was like a schoolboy's exercise, repeating words without understanding.   **90 In one respect** for one reason (at least)   **92 To** as to   **93 stand on** am in need of, insist on
2.4. Location: Verona. A street.
1 should can   **2 tonight** last night.

MERCUTIO A challenge, on my life.

BENVOLIO Romeo will answer it. 9

MERCUTIO Any man that can write may answer a letter.

BENVOLIO Nay, he will answer the letter's master, how he dares, being dared.

MERCUTIO Alas poor Romeo! He is already dead, stabbed with a white wench's black eye, run through the ear with a love song, the very pin of his heart cleft 15 with the blind bow-boy's butt shaft. And is he a man 16 to encounter Tybalt?

BENVOLIO Why, what is Tybalt?

MERCUTIO More than prince of cats. Oh, he's the 19 courageous captain of compliments. He fights as you 20 sing prick song, keeps time, distance, and proportion; 21 he rests his minim rests, one, two, and the third in 22 your bosom. The very butcher of a silk button, a 23 duellist, a duellist, a gentleman of the very first house, 24 of the first and second cause. Ah, the immortal 25 *passado!* The *punto reverso!* The *hay!* 26

BENVOLIO The what?

MERCUTIO The pox of such antic, lisping, affecting phan- 28 tasimes, these new tuners of accent! "By Jesu, a very 29 good blade! A very tall man! A very good whore!" 30 Why, is not this a lamentable thing, grandsire, that we 31 should be thus afflicted with these strange flies, these 32 fashionmongers, these pardon-me's, who stand so 33 much on the new form that they cannot sit at ease on 34 the old bench? Oh, their bones, their bones! 35

Enter Romeo.

BENVOLIO Here comes Romeo, here comes Romeo.

MERCUTIO Without his roe, like a dried herring. Oh, 37 flesh, flesh, how art thou fishified! Now is he for the numbers that Petrarch flowed in. Laura to his lady 39 was but a kitchen wench—marry, she had a better love to berhyme her—Dido a dowdy, Cleopatra a 41 gypsy, Helen and Hero hildings and harlots, Thisbe a 42 gray eye or so, but not to the purpose. Signor Romeo, 43 *bonjour!* There's a French salutation to your French 44 slop. You gave us the counterfeit fairly last night. 45

ROMEO Good morrow to you both. What counterfeit did I give you?

MERCUTIO The slip, sir, the slip. Can you not conceive? 48

ROMEO Pardon, good Mercutio. My business was great, and in such a case as mine a man may strain courtesy.

MERCUTIO That's as much as to say, such a case as yours 51 constrains a man to bow in the hams. 52

ROMEO Meaning, to curtsy. 53

MERCUTIO Thou hast most kindly hit it. 54

ROMEO A most courteous exposition.

MERCUTIO Nay, I am the very pink of courtesy. 56

ROMEO Pink for flower.

MERCUTIO Right.

ROMEO Why then is my pump well flowered. 59

MERCUTIO Sure wit, follow me this jest now till thou hast worn out thy pump, that when the single sole of it is worn, the jest may remain, after the wearing, solely singular. 63

ROMEO Oh, single-soled jest, solely singular for the 64 singleness! 65

MERCUTIO Come between us, good Benvolio. My wits faints.

ROMEO Switch and spurs, switch and spurs! Or I'll cry 68 a match. 69

MERCUTIO Nay, if our wits run the wild-goose chase, I 70 am done, for thou hast more of the wild goose in one of thy wits than, I am sure, I have in my whole five. Was I with you there for the goose? 73

ROMEO Thou wast never with me for anything when thou wast not there for the goose. 75

MERCUTIO I will bite thee by the ear for that jest. 76

ROMEO Nay, good goose, bite not.

MERCUTIO Thy wit is a very bitter sweeting; it is a most 78 sharp sauce. 79

ROMEO And is it not, then, well served in to a sweet goose?

---

9 answer it accept the challenge. (But Mercutio replies in the sense of "write in reply.") **15 pin** peg in the center of a target **16 butt shaft** unbarbed arrow, allotted to children and thus to Cupid. **19 prince of cats** (The name of the king of cats in *Reynard the Fox* was Tybalt or Tybert.) **20 captain of compliments** master of ceremony and dueling etiquette. **21 prick song** music written out. **proportion** rhythm **22 minim rests** short rests in musical notation **23 butcher . . . button** i.e., one able to strike a specific button on his adversary's person **24 first house** best school of fencing **25 first and second cause** causes according to the code of dueling that would oblige one to seek the satisfaction of one's honor. **26 *passado*** forward thrust. ***punto reverso*** backhanded stroke. ***hay*** thrust through. (From the Italian *hai*, meaning "you have [it].") **28 The pox of** Plague take. **antic** grotesque **28–9 phantasimes** coxcombs, fantastically dressed or mannered **29 new tuners of accent** those who introduce new foreign words and slang phrases into their speech. **30 tall** valiant **31 grandsire** i.e., one who disapproves of the new fashion and prefers old custom **32 flies** parasites **33 pardon-me's** i.e., those who affect overly polite manners. **stand** (1) insist (2) the opposite of *sit*, line 34 **34–5 form . . . bench** (*Form* means both "fashion" or "code of manners" and "bench.") **35 bones** French *bon*, "good" (with play on English *bone*) **37 Without his roe** i.e., Looking thin and emaciated, sexually spent. (With a pun on the first syllable of Romeo's name; the remaining syllables, *me-oh*, sound like the expression of a melancholy lover. *Roe* also suggests a female deer or "dear.") **39 numbers** verses. **Laura** the lady to whom the Italian Renaissance poet Petrarch addressed his love poems. (Other romantic heroines are named in the following passage: Dido, Queen of Carthage; Cleopatra; Helen of Troy; Hero, beloved of Leander; and Thisbe, beloved of Pyramus.) **to** in comparison with

41 dowdy homely woman **42 gypsy** Egyptian; whore. **hildings** good-for-nothings **43 not** i.e., that is not **44 to** to match **44–5 French slop** loose trousers of French fashion. **45 fairly** handsomely, effectively **48 slip** (Counterfeit coins were called "slips.") **conceive** i.e., get the joke. **51 case** (1) situation (2) physical condition. (Mercutio also bawdily suggests that Romeo has been in a *case*, i.e., the female genitalia.) **52 bow in the hams** (1) make a low bow (2) show the effects of venereal disease. **53 curtsy** bow, make obeisance. **54 kindly** graciously. (But also suggesting natural and physical explanations.) **56 pink** embodied perfection. (But suggesting also the flower called *pink*, the color, and *pinking* of a shoe; see next note.) **59 pump well flowered** shoe expertly pinked or perforated in ornamental figures suggesting flowers. **63 solely singular** unique. **64 single-soled** i.e., thin, contemptible **65 singleness** feebleness. **68 Switch and spurs** i.e., Keep up the rapid pace of the hunt (in the game of wits) **68–9 cry a match** claim the victory. **70 wild-goose chase** a horse race in which the leading rider dares his competitors to follow him wherever he goes **73 Was . . . goose?** Did I score a point in calling you a goose? **75 for the goose** (1) behaving like a goose (2) looking for a prostitute. **76 bite . . . ear** i.e., give you an affectionate nibble on the ear. (Said ironically, however, and Romeo parries.) **78 sweeting** sweet-flavored variety of apple **79 sharp sauce** (1) "biting" retort (2) tart sauce, of the sort that should be served with cooked goose (as Romeo points out).

MERCUTIO   Oh, here's a wit of cheveril, that stretches   82
from an inch narrow to an ell broad!   83
ROMEO   I stretch it out for that word "broad," which,
added to the goose, proves thee far and wide a broad   85
goose.
MERCUTIO   Why, is not this better now than groaning for
love? Now art thou sociable, now art thou Romeo;
now art thou what thou art, by art as well as by nature.
For this driveling love is like a great natural that runs   90
lolling up and down to hide his bauble in a hole.   91
BENVOLIO   Stop there, stop there.
MERCUTIO   Thou desirest me to stop in my tale against   93
the hair.   94
BENVOLIO   Thou wouldst else have made thy tale large.
MERCUTIO   Oh, thou art deceived; I would have made it
short, for I was come to the whole depth of my tale
and meant indeed to occupy the argument no longer.
ROMEO   Here's goodly gear!   99

Enter Nurse and her man [Peter].

A sail, a sail!   100
MERCUTIO   Two, two: a shirt and a smock.   101
NURSE   Peter!
PETER   Anon!
NURSE   My fan, Peter.
MERCUTIO   Good Peter, to hide her face, for her fan's
the fairer face.
NURSE   God gi' good morrow, gentlemen.
MERCUTIO   God gi' good e'en, fair gentlewoman.
NURSE   Is it good e'en?   109
MERCUTIO   'Tis no less, I tell ye, for the bawdy hand of
the dial is now upon the prick of noon.   111
NURSE   Out upon you! What a man are you?   112
ROMEO   One, gentlewoman, that God hath made for
himself to mar.   114
NURSE   By my troth, it is well said. "For himself to mar,"   115
quoth 'a? Gentlemen, can any of you tell me where I   116
may find the young Romeo?
ROMEO   I can tell you; but young Romeo will be older
when you have found him than he was when you
sought him. I am the youngest of that name, for fault   120
of a worse.
NURSE   You say well.

MERCUTIO   Yea, is the worst well? Very well took, i' faith,   123
wisely, wisely.
NURSE   If you be he, sir, I desire some confidence with   125
you.
BENVOLIO   She will indite him to some supper.   127
MERCUTIO   A bawd, a bawd, a bawd! So ho!   128
ROMEO   What hast thou found?
MERCUTIO   No hare, sir, unless a hare, sir, in a lenten   130
pie, that is something stale and hoar ere it be spent.   131
[*He sings.*]
An old hare hoar,
And an old hare hoar,
Is very good meat in Lent.
But a hare that is hoar
Is too much for a score,   136
When it hoars ere it be spent.
Romeo, will you come to your father's? We'll to din-
ner thither.
ROMEO   I will follow you.
MERCUTIO   Farewell, ancient lady. Farewell, [*singing*]
"Lady, lady, lady." *Exeunt [Mercutio and Benvolio].*   142
NURSE   I pray you, sir, what saucy merchant was this   143
that was so full of his ropery?   144
ROMEO   A gentleman, Nurse, that loves to hear himself
talk, and will speak more in a minute than he will
stand to in a month.   147
NURSE   An 'a speak anything against me, I'll take him   148
down, an 'a were lustier than he is, and twenty such   149
Jacks; and if I cannot, I'll find those that shall. Scurvy   150
knave! I am none of his flirt-gills. I am none of his   151
skains-mates. [*To Peter*] And thou must stand by, too,   152
and suffer every knave to use me at his pleasure!
PETER   I saw no man use you at his pleasure. If I had,
my weapon should quickly have been out; I warrant   155
you, I dare draw as soon as another man, if I see
occasion in a good quarrel, and the law on my side.
NURSE   Now, afore God, I am so vexed that every part   158
about me quivers. Scurvy knave! Pray you, sir, a   159
word; and as I told you, my young lady bid me
inquire you out. What she bid me say, I will keep to
myself. But first let me tell ye, if ye should lead her
in a fool's paradise, as they say, it were a very gross
kind of behavior, as they say. For the gentlewoman
is young; and therefore if you should deal double

---

82 cheveril kid leather, easily stretched   **83 ell** (forty-five inches)
85 broad large, complete; perhaps also wanton   **90 natural** idiot
91 lolling with his tongue (or bauble) hanging out.   **bauble** (1) jester's
wand (2) phallus   **93 stop in my tale** (1) stop short in my story (2) stuff
in my penis   **93–4 against the hair** against the grain, against my wish.
(With bawdy suggestion of pubic hair. The sexual punning continues
in *large* [erect], *short* [detumescent], *come to the depth of my tale, occupy,*
etc.)   **99 goodly gear** matter for mockery. (With suggestion of "ample
sexual apparatus.")   **100 A sail** (To Romeo, the Nurse is an imposing
galleon in full sail.)   **101 a shirt and a smock** i.e., a man and a woman.
109 Is it good e'en? Is it afternoon already?   **111 prick** point on the
dial of a clock. (With bawdy suggestion.)   **112 Out upon you** (Expression of indignation.)   **What** What kind of   **114 mar** i.e., disfigure
morally through sin. (Humankind, made in God's image, mars that
image sinfully.)   **115 troth** faith   **116 quoth 'a** said he. (A sarcastic
interjection, meaning "forsooth" or "indeed.")   **120 fault** lack

123 took understood   **125 confidence** (The Nurse's mistake for "conference.")   **127 indite** (Benvolio's deliberate malapropism for
"invite.")   **128 So ho** (Cry of hunter sighting game.)   **130 hare**
(Slang word for "prostitute"; similarly, with *stale* and *meat* in the following lines.)   **130–1 a lenten pie** a pie that should contain no meat,
in observance of Lent   **131 hoar** moldy. (With pun on "whore"; *stale*
also can mean "whore.")   **spent** consumed.   **136 for a score** for a
reckoning, to pay good money for   **142 "Lady, lady, lady"** (Refrain
from the ballad *Chaste Susanna*.)   **143 merchant** i.e., fellow   **144 ropery** vulgar humor, knavery.   **147 stand to** carry out, stand in support
of   **148 An 'a** If he   **148–9 take him down** cut him down to size.
(With unintended bawdy suggestion.)   **150 Jacks** knaves   **151 flirt-
gills** loose women.   **152 skains-mates** (Perhaps daggermates, outlaws, or gangster molls.)   **155 weapon** (With bawdy suggestion,
perhaps unrecognized by the speaker, as also in *at his pleasure*.)
158–9 every part . . . quivers (More bawdy suggestion, unrecognized
by the Nurse.)

with her, truly it were an ill thing to be offered to any
gentlewoman, and very weak dealing.   167

ROMEO   Nurse, commend me to thy lady and mistress.
I protest unto thee—   169

NURSE   Good heart, and i'faith I will tell her as much.
Lord, Lord, she will be a joyful woman.

ROMEO   What wilt thou tell her, Nurse? Thou dost not
mark me.   173

NURSE   I will tell her, sir, that you do protest, which, as
I take it, is a gentlemanlike offer.

ROMEO   Bid her devise
Some means to come to shrift this afternoon,   177
And there she shall at Friar Laurence' cell
Be shrived and married. Here is for thy pains.   179
                                    [He offers money.]

NURSE   No, truly, sir, not a penny.

ROMEO   Go to, I say you shall.

NURSE
This afternoon, sir? Well, she shall be there.

ROMEO
And stay, good Nurse, behind the abbey wall.
Within this hour my man shall be with thee
And bring thee cords made like a tackled stair,   185
Which to the high topgallant of my joy   186
Must be my convoy in the secret night.   187
Farewell. Be trusty, and I'll quit thy pains.   188
Farewell. Commend me to thy mistress.
                                [Romeo starts to leave.]

NURSE
Now God in heaven bless thee! Hark you, sir.

ROMEO   What say'st thou, my dear Nurse?

NURSE
Is your man secret? Did you ne'er hear say,   192
"Two may keep counsel, putting one away"?   193

ROMEO
'Warrant thee, my man's as true as steel.

NURSE   Well, sir, my mistress is the sweetest lady—
Lord, Lord! When 'twas a little prating thing—Oh,
there is a nobleman in town, one Paris, that would
fain lay knife aboard; but she, good soul, had as lief   198
see a toad, a very toad, as see him. I anger her
sometimes and tell her that Paris is the properer man,   200
but I'll warrant you, when I say so, she looks as pale
as any clout in the versal world. Doth not rosemary   202
and Romeo begin both with a letter?   203

ROMEO   Ay, Nurse, what of that? Both with an R.

NURSE   Ah, mocker! That's the dog's name; R is for   205
the—No; I know it begins with some other letter; and   206
she hath the prettiest sententious of it, of you and   207
rosemary, that it would do you good to hear it.

ROMEO   Commend me to thy lady.

NURSE   Ay, a thousand times.   [Exit Romeo.]
Peter!

PETER   Anon!

NURSE   Before, and apace.   Exeunt. 212

❧

[2.5]

Enter Juliet.

JULIET
The clock struck nine when I did send the Nurse;
In half an hour she promised to return.
Perchance she cannot meet him. That's not so.
Oh, she is lame! Love's heralds should be thoughts,
Which ten times faster glides than the sun's beams
Driving back shadows over louring hills.   6
Therefore do nimble-pinioned doves draw Love,   7
And therefore hath the wind-swift Cupid wings.
Now is the sun upon the highmost hill
Of this day's journey, and from nine till twelve
Is three long hours, yet she is not come.
Had she affections and warm youthful blood,   12
She would be as swift in motion as a ball;
My words would bandy her to my sweet love,   14
And his to me.
But old folks, many feign as they were dead—   16
Unwieldy, slow, heavy, and pale as lead.

Enter Nurse [and Peter].

Oh, God, she comes!—O honey Nurse, what news?
Hast thou met with him? Send thy man away.

NURSE   Peter, stay at the gate.   [Exit Peter.]

JULIET
Now, good sweet Nurse—Oh, Lord, why lookest thou
sad?
Though news be sad, yet tell them merrily;
If good, thou shamest the music of sweet news
By playing it to me with so sour a face.

NURSE
I am aweary. Give me leave awhile.   25
Fie, how my bones ache! What a jaunce have I had!   26

JULIET
I would thou hadst my bones and I thy news.
Nay, come, I pray thee, speak. Good, good Nurse,
speak.

167 weak contemptible   **169 protest** vow. (Romeo may intend only
to protest his good intentions, but the Nurse seemingly takes the
word to mean "propose," as if Romeo is making a *gentlemanlike offer*
[line 175] of marriage that would ensure against Juliet's being led into
a *fool's paradise* [line 163]—i.e., being seduced.)   **173 mark** attend to
177 shrift confession and absolution   **179 shrived** absolved
185 tackled stair rope ladder   **186 topgallant** highest mast and sail of
a ship, the summit   **187 convoy** conveyance, means of passage
188 quit reward, requite   **192 secret** trustworthy.   **193 keep counsel**
keep a secret   **198 fain lay knife aboard** like to assert his claim (just
as a guest at an inn did by bringing his knife to the dinner table; with
sexual suggestion also).   **lief** willingly   **200 properer** handsomer
202 clout faded rag.   **versal** universal.   **rosemary** (Associated with
weddings and funerals.)   **203 a letter** one and the same letter.

205 the dog's name (The letter *R* was thought to resemble the dog's
growl.)   **205–6 R is for . . . letter** (Perhaps the Nurse is about to say
"arse," but has a notion that it begins with some other letter. In any case,
she decides against saying such an indelicate word.)   **207 sententious**
(The Nurse probably means "sentences," maxims.)   **212 Before, and
apace** Go before me quickly.
2.5. Location: Verona. Outside Capulet's house, perhaps in the
orchard or garden.
6 louring dark, threatening   **7 Love** i.e., Venus, whose chariot was
drawn by swift-winged doves   **12 affections** desires   **14 bandy** toss
to and fro, as in tennis   **16 feign as** act as though   **25 Give me leave**
Let me alone   **26 jaunce** jouncing, jolting

NURSE
Jesu, what haste! Can you not stay awhile?   29
Do you not see that I am out of breath?

JULIET
How art thou out of breath, when thou hast breath
To say to me that thou art out of breath?
The excuse that thou dost make in this delay
Is longer than the tale thou dost excuse.   34
Is thy news good or bad? Answer to that;
Say either, and I'll stay the circumstance.   36
Let me be satisfied: is't good or bad?

NURSE   Well, you have made a simple choice. You know   38
not how to choose a man. Romeo? No, not he. Though
his face be better than any man's, yet his leg excels all
men's; and for a hand, and a foot, and a body, though
they be not to be talked on, yet they are past compare.   42
He is not the flower of courtesy, but, I'll warrant him,
as gentle as a lamb. Go thy ways, wench. Serve God.
What, have you dined at home?

JULIET
No, no; but all this did I know before.
What says he of our marriage? What of that?

NURSE
Lord, how my head aches! What a head have I!
It beats as it would fall in twenty pieces.
My back o' t'other side—ah, my back, my back!   50
Beshrew your heart for sending me about   51
To catch my death with jauncing up and down!

JULIET
I'faith, I am sorry that thou art not well.
Sweet, sweet, sweet Nurse, tell me, what says my
love?

NURSE
Your love says, like an honest gentleman,
And a courteous, and a kind, and a handsome,
And, I warrant, a virtuous—Where is your mother?

JULIET
Where is my mother? Why, she is within,
Where should she be? How oddly thou repliest!
"Your love says, like an honest gentleman,   60
'Where is your mother?' "

NURSE   O God's Lady dear!
Are you so hot? Marry, come up, I trow.   62
Is this the poultice for my aching bones?
Henceforward do your messages yourself.

JULIET
Here's such a coil! Come, what says Romeo?   65

NURSE
Have you got leave to go to shrift today?

JULIET   I have.

NURSE
Then hie you hence to Friar Laurence' cell;
There stays a husband to make you a wife.   68

Now comes the wanton blood up in your cheeks;
They'll be in scarlet straight at any news.   71
Hie you to church. I must another way,
To fetch a ladder, by the which your love
Must climb a bird's nest soon when it is dark.   74
I am the drudge, and toil in your delight,
But you shall bear the burden soon at night.
Go. I'll to dinner. Hie you to the cell.

JULIET
Hie to high fortune! Honest Nurse, farewell.
                         Exeunt [*separately*].

❖

[2.6]

Enter Friar [*Laurence*] *and Romeo.*

FRIAR LAURENCE
So smile the heavens upon this holy act   1
That after-hours with sorrow chide us not!

ROMEO
Amen, amen! But come what sorrow can,
It cannot countervail the exchange of joy   4
That one short minute gives me in her sight.
Do thou but close our hands with holy words,   6
Then love-devouring death do what he dare;
It is enough I may but call her mine.

FRIAR LAURENCE
These violent delights have violent ends
And in their triumph die, like fire and powder,   10
Which as they kiss consume. The sweetest honey
Is loathsome in his own deliciousness,   12
And in the taste confounds the appetite.   13
Therefore love moderately. Long love doth so;
Too swift arrives as tardy as too slow.

Enter Juliet.

Here comes the lady. Oh, so light a foot
Will ne'er wear out the everlasting flint.
A lover may bestride the gossamers   18
That idles in the wanton summer air,   19
And yet not fall, so light is vanity.   20

JULIET
Good even to my ghostly confessor.   21

FRIAR LAURENCE
Romeo shall thank thee, daughter, for us both.   22

JULIET
As much to him, else is his thanks too much.   23

ROMEO
Ah, Juliet, if the measure of thy joy
Be heaped like mine, and that thy skill be more   25
To blazon it, then sweeten with thy breath   26
This neighbor air, and let rich music's tongue
Unfold the imagined happiness that both   28
Receive in either by this dear encounter.   29

JULIET
Conceit, more rich in matter than in words,   30
Brags of his substance, not of ornament.   31
They are but beggars that can count their worth.
But my true love is grown to such excess
I cannot sum up sum of half my wealth.   34

FRIAR LAURENCE
Come, come with me, and we will make short work;
For, by your leaves, you shall not stay alone
Till Holy Church incorporate two in one.   [*Exeunt.*]

[3.1]

Enter Mercutio, Benvolio, and men.

BENVOLIO
I pray thee, good Mercutio, let's retire.
The day is hot, the Capels are abroad,   2
And if we meet we shall not scape a brawl,
For now, these hot days, is the mad blood stirring.

MERCUTIO   Thou art like one of these fellows that when
he enters the confines of a tavern, claps me his sword   6
upon the table and says, "God send me no need of
thee!" and by the operation of the second cup draws   8
him on the drawer, when indeed there is no need.   9

BENVOLIO   Am I like such a fellow?

MERCUTIO   Come, come, thou art as hot a Jack in thy   11
mood as any in Italy, and as soon moved to be moody,   12
and as soon moody to be moved.   13

BENVOLIO   And what to?

MERCUTIO   Nay, an there were two such, we should   15
have none shortly, for one would kill the other. Thou!
Why, thou wilt quarrel with a man that hath a hair
more or a hair less in his beard than thou hast. Thou
wilt quarrel with a man for cracking nuts, having no
other reason but because thou hast hazel eyes. What
eye but such an eye would spy out such a quarrel? Thy
head is as full of quarrels as an egg is full of meat, and   22
yet thy head hath been beaten as addle as an egg for   23
quarreling. Thou hast quarreled with a man for coughing in the street, because he hath wakened thy dog that

hath lain asleep in the sun. Didst thou not fall out
with a tailor for wearing his new doublet before   27
Easter? With another, for tying his new shoes with old
ribbon? And yet thou wilt tutor me from quarreling!

BENVOLIO   An I were so apt to quarrel as thou art, any
man should buy the fee simple of my life for an hour   31
and a quarter.   32

MERCUTIO   The fee simple! Oh, simple!   33

Enter Tybalt, Petruchio, and others.

BENVOLIO   By my head, here comes the Capulets.

MERCUTIO   By my heel, I care not.

TYBALT [*to his companions*]
Follow me close, for I will speak to them.—
Gentlemen, good e'en. A word with one of you.

MERCUTIO   And but one word with one of us? Couple it
with something: make it a word and a blow.

TYBALT   You shall find me apt enough to that, sir, an
you will give me occasion.

MERCUTIO   Could you not take some occasion without
giving?

TYBALT   Mercutio, thou consortest with Romeo.   44

MERCUTIO   "Consort"? What, dost thou make us minstrels? An thou make minstrels of us, look to hear
nothing but discords. Here's my fiddlestick; here's   47
that shall make you dance. Zounds, "consort"!   48

BENVOLIO
We talk here in the public haunt of men.
Either withdraw unto some private place,
Or reason coldly of your grievances,   51
Or else depart; here all eyes gaze on us.   52

MERCUTIO
Men's eyes were made to look, and let them gaze.
I will not budge for no man's pleasure, I.

Enter Romeo.

TYBALT
Well, peace be with you, sir. Here comes my man.

MERCUTIO
But I'll be hanged, sir, if he wear your livery.   56
Marry, go before to field, he'll be your follower;   57
Your Worship in that sense may call him "man."   58

TYBALT
Romeo, the love I bear thee can afford
No better term than this: thou art a villain.

ROMEO
Tybalt, the reason that I have to love thee
Doth much excuse the appertaining rage   62
To such a greeting. Villain am I none.

---

25 **that** if   26 **blazon** describe, set forth. (A heraldic term.)
28 **Unfold** make known.   **imagined** i.e., unexpressed   29 **in either**
from each other   30–1 **Conceit . . . ornament** True understanding,
more enriched by the actual reality (of love) than by mere words, finds
more worth in the substance of that reality than in outward show.
34 **sum up sum** add up the total
3.1. Location: Verona. A public place.
2 **Capels** Capulets   6 **claps me** claps. (*Me* is a now-archaic dative of
reference, used colloquially.)   8–9 **draws . . . drawer** draws his sword
against the tapster or waiter   9 **there is no need** i.e., of his sword.
11 **as hot a Jack** as hot-tempered a fellow   12 **moody** angry   13 **to be**
moved at being provoked.   15 **an** if   22 **meat** i.e., edible matter
23 **addle** addled, confused

27 **doublet** man's jacket   31 **fee simple** outright possession   31–2 **an**
hour . . . quarter i.e., my life would last no longer in such circumstances.
33 **Oh, simple!** Oh, how stupid!   44 **consortest** keep company with.
(But Mercutio quibbles on its musical sense of "accompany" or "play
together.")   47 **fiddlestick** (Mercutio means his sword.)   48 **that** that
which.   **Zounds** By God's (Christ's) wounds   51 **coldly** calmly
52 **depart** go away separately   56 **livery** servant's uniform. (Mercutio
deliberately mistakes Tybalt's phrase *my man* to mean "my servant.")
57 **field** field where a duel might occur   58 **Your Worship** (A title of
honor used here with mock politeness.)   62 **the appertaining rage** the
rage that would ordinarily be appropriate to

Therefore, farewell. I see thou knowest me not.

TYBALT
Boy, this shall not excuse the injuries   65
That thou hast done me. Therefore turn and draw.

ROMEO
I do protest I never injured thee,
But love thee better than thou canst devise   68
Till thou shalt know the reason of my love.
And so, good Capulet—which name I tender   70
As dearly as mine own—be satisfied.

MERCUTIO
Oh, calm, dishonorable, vile submission!
Alla stoccata carries it away.   [*He draws.*]   73
Tybalt, you ratcatcher, will you walk?   74

TYBALT   What wouldst thou have with me?

MERCUTIO   Good king of cats, nothing but one of your
nine lives, that I mean to make bold withal, and, as   77
you shall use me hereafter, dry-beat the rest of the   78
eight. Will you pluck your sword out of his pilcher by   79
the ears? Make haste, lest mine be about your ears ere   80
it be out.

TYBALT   I am for you.   [*He draws.*]

ROMEO
Gentle Mercutio, put thy rapier up.

MERCUTIO   Come, sir, your *passado*.   [*They fight.*]   84

ROMEO
Draw, Benvolio, beat down their weapons.
Gentlemen, for shame, forbear this outrage!
Tybalt, Mercutio, the Prince expressly hath
Forbid this bandying in Verona streets.
Hold, Tybalt! Good Mercutio!
     [*Tybalt under Romeo's arm stabs Mercutio.*] *Away*
          Tybalt [*with his followers*].

MERCUTIO   I am hurt.   89
A plague o' both your houses! I am sped.   90
Is he gone, and hath nothing?

BENVOLIO   What, art thou hurt?

MERCUTIO
Ay, ay, a scratch, a scratch; marry, 'tis enough.
Where is my page? Go, villain, fetch a surgeon.
     [*Exit Page.*]

ROMEO
Courage, man, the hurt cannot be much.

MERCUTIO   No, 'tis not so deep as a well, nor so wide as
a church door, but 'tis enough, 'twill serve. Ask for me
tomorrow, and you shall find me a grave man. I am   97
peppered, I warrant, for this world. A plague o' both   98
your houses! Zounds, a dog, a rat, a mouse, a cat, to
scratch a man to death! A braggart, a rogue, a villain,
that fights by the book of arithmetic! Why the devil   101
came you between us? I was hurt under your arm.

ROMEO   I thought all for the best.

MERCUTIO
Help me into some house, Benvolio,
Or I shall faint. A plague o' both your houses!
They have made worm's meat of me. I have it,
And soundly too. Your houses!
               Exit [*supported by Benvolio*].

ROMEO
This gentleman, the Prince's near ally,   108
My very friend, hath got this mortal hurt   109
In my behalf; my reputation stained
With Tybalt's slander—Tybalt, that an hour
Hath been my cousin! O sweet Juliet,   112
Thy beauty hath made me effeminate,   113
And in my temper softened valor's steel.   114

     Enter Benvolio.

BENVOLIO
O Romeo, Romeo, brave Mercutio is dead!
That gallant spirit hath aspired the clouds,   116
Which too untimely here did scorn the earth.

ROMEO
This day's black fate on more days doth depend;   118
This but begins the woe others must end.   119

     [*Enter Tybalt.*]

BENVOLIO
Here comes the furious Tybalt back again.

ROMEO
Alive in triumph, and Mercutio slain!
Away to heaven, respective lenity,   122
And fire-eyed fury be my conduct now!   123
Now, Tybalt, take the "villain" back again
That late thou gavest me, for Mercutio's soul
Is but a little way above our heads,
Staying for thine to keep him company.
Either thou or I, or both, must go with him.

TYBALT
Thou, wretched boy, that didst consort him here,
Shalt with him hence.

ROMEO   This shall determine that.
               They fight. Tybalt falls.

BENVOLIO   Romeo, away, begone!
The citizens are up, and Tybalt slain.

---

65 Boy (A deliberate and grave insult when addressed to a grown
man. Tybalt's use of *thee* and *thou* in lines 59–60 and following is similarly insulting; Romeo's use of this personal form in lines 61–4 and
67–9, on the other hand, is appropriate to a close family tie that he
privately acknowledges but is of course misunderstood by Tybalt and
the bystanders.)   **68 devise** imagine   **70 tender** value   **73 *Alla stoccata . . . away** i.e. (scornfully), This elegant Italian way of fencing,
and the fancy terminology to go with it, will win the day, I suppose.
(*Alla stoccata* means "at the thrust.")   **74 ratcatcher** (An allusion to
Tybalt as king of cats; see 2.4.19.)   **77 make bold withal** make free
with   **78 dry-beat** beat soundly (without drawing blood)   **79–80 out
. . . ears** out of its scabbard by the handle or hilt.   **84 *passado*** forward thrust. (Another fancy Italian fencing term of the sort Mercutio
despises.)   **89 s.d. *Away Tybalt*** (Because the phrase is unusual for an
exit stage direction, some editors plausibly assign this as a speech to
Petruchio, who enters at line 33.1 and is otherwise silent.)   **90 sped**
done for.

97 grave (Mercutio thus puns with his last breath.)   **98 peppered** finished, done for   **101 by . . . arithmetic** by the numbers, as in a text-
book on fencing (as at 2.4.20–3).   **108 ally** kinsman   **109 very** true
112 cousin kinsman.   **113 effeminate** weak   **114 temper** disposition.
(But with a play on the tempering of a steel sword.)   **116 aspired**
ascended to   **118 This day's . . . depend** This day hangs threateningly over the time to come   **119 others** other days to come
122 respective lenity considerate gentleness   **123 conduct** guide

Stand not amazed. The Prince will doom thee death   133
If thou art taken. Hence, begone, away!

ROMEO
Oh, I am fortune's fool!

BENVOLIO   Why dost thou stay?   135

Exit Romeo.

Enter Citizens.

FIRST CITIZEN
Which way ran he that killed Mercutio?
Tybalt, that murderer, which way ran he?

BENVOLIO
There lies that Tybalt.

FIRST CITIZEN   Up, sir, go with me.
I charge thee in the Prince's name, obey.

*Enter Prince [attended], old Montague,
Capulet, their Wives, and all.*

PRINCE
Where are the vile beginners of this fray?

BENVOLIO
O noble Prince, I can discover all   141
The unlucky manage of this fatal brawl.   142
There lies the man, slain by young Romeo,
That slew thy kinsman, brave Mercutio.

CAPULET'S WIFE
Tybalt, my cousin! O my brother's child!
O Prince! O cousin! Husband! Oh, the blood is spilled
Of my dear kinsman! Prince, as thou art true,
For blood of ours shed blood of Montague.
O cousin, cousin!

PRINCE
Benvolio, who began this bloody fray?

BENVOLIO
Tybalt, here slain, whom Romeo's hand did slay.
Romeo, that spoke him fair, bid him bethink   152
How nice the quarrel was, and urged withal   153
Your high displeasure. All this—utterèd
With gentle breath, calm look, knees humbly bowed—
Could not take truce with the unruly spleen   156
Of Tybalt deaf to peace, but that he tilts
With piercing steel at bold Mercutio's breast,
Who, all as hot, turns deadly point to point,
And, with a martial scorn, with one hand beats
Cold death aside and with the other sends
It back to Tybalt, whose dexterity
Retorts it. Romeo he cries aloud,   163
"Hold, friends! Friends, part!" and swifter than his
    tongue
His agile arm beats down their fatal points,
And twixt them rushes; underneath whose arm
An envious thrust from Tybalt hit the life   167
Of stout Mercutio, and then Tybalt fled;   168
But by and by comes back to Romeo,
Who had but newly entertained revenge,   170

And to't they go like lightning, for, ere I
Could draw to part them was stout Tybalt slain,
And, as he fell, did Romeo turn and fly.
This is the truth, or let Benvolio die.

CAPULET'S WIFE
He is a kinsman to the Montague.
Affection makes him false; he speaks not true.   176
Some twenty of them fought in this black strife,
And all those twenty could but kill one life.
I beg for justice, which thou, Prince, must give.
Romeo slew Tybalt; Romeo must not live.

PRINCE
Romeo slew him, he slew Mercutio.
Who now the price of his dear blood doth owe?

MONTAGUE
Not Romeo, Prince, he was Mercutio's friend;
His fault concludes but what the law should end,   184
The life of Tybalt.

PRINCE   And for that offense
Immediately we do exile him hence.
I have an interest in your hate's proceeding;
My blood for your rude brawls doth lie a-bleeding;   188
But I'll amerce you with so strong a fine   189
That you shall all repent the loss of mine.
I will be deaf to pleading and excuses;
Nor tears nor prayers shall purchase out abuses.   192
Therefore use none. Let Romeo hence in haste,   193
Else, when he is found, that hour is his last.   194
Bear hence this body and attend our will.   195
Mercy but murders, pardoning those that kill.   196

Exeunt, [some carrying Tybalt's body].

❧

[3.2]

Enter Juliet alone.

JULIET
Gallop apace, you fiery-footed steeds,   1
Towards Phoebus' lodging! Such a wagoner   2
As Phaëthon would whip you to the west   3
And bring in cloudy night immediately.   4
Spread thy close curtain, love-performing night,   5

---

133 amazed dazed.   **doom thee death** sentence you to death
135 fool dupe.   **141 discover** reveal   **142 manage** conduct   **152 fair**
civilly.   **bethink** consider   **153 nice** trivial.   **withal** besides
156 take truce make peace   **163 Retorts** returns   **167 envious** malicious   **168 stout** brave   **170 entertained** harbored thoughts of

176 Affection Partiality   **184 concludes but** only finishes   **188 My blood** i.e., blood of my kinsman. (Here we learn that Mercutio is kin to the Prince.)   **189 amerce** penalize   **192 Nor** neither.   **purchase out abuses** redeem misdeeds.   **193 hence** depart   **194 Else** Otherwise   **195 attend our will** be on hand to hear further judgment.
196 but murders merely encourages murder by excessive leniency
3.2. Location: Verona. Capulet's house.
1 apace quickly.   **steeds** i.e., the horses of the sun god's chariot
2 Phoebus (Often equated with Helios, the sun god.)   **lodging** i.e., in the west, below the horizon.   **2–4 Such . . . immediately** i.e., One who is impetuously young, as we are, would understand the need to make the day as short as possible and would quickly bring it to an end. (The mythical allusion is sadly ironic, for Phaëthon drove the chariot of the sun so badly that he had to be destroyed by Zeus.)
5 close enclosing

That runaways' eyes may wink, and Romeo   6
Leap to these arms, untalked of and unseen.   7
Lovers can see to do their amorous rites
By their own beauties; or, if love be blind,
It best agrees with night. Come, civil night,   10
Thou sober-suited matron all in black,
And learn me how to lose a winning match   12
Played for a pair of stainless maidenhoods.
Hood my unmanned blood, bating in my cheeks,   14
With thy black mantle till strange love grown bold   15
Think true love acted simple modesty.
Come, night. Come, Romeo. Come, thou day in night;
For thou wilt lie upon the wings of night
Whiter than new snow upon a raven's back.
Come, gentle night, come, loving, black-browed night,
Give me my Romeo, and when I shall die   21
Take him and cut him out in little stars,
And he will make the face of heaven so fine
That all the world will be in love with night
And pay no worship to the garish sun.   25
Oh, I have bought the mansion of a love
But not possessed it, and though I am sold,
Not yet enjoyed. So tedious is this day
As is the night before some festival
To an impatient child that hath new robes
And may not wear them. Oh, here comes my nurse,   31

      Enter Nurse, with cords.

And she brings news, and every tongue that speaks
But Romeo's name speaks heavenly eloquence.
Now, Nurse, what news? What hast thou there? The
    cords
That Romeo bid thee fetch?
NURSE   Ay, ay, the cords.
                     [*She throws them down.*]
JULIET
Ay me, what news? Why dost thou wring thy hands?
NURSE
Ah, weraday! He's dead, he's dead, he's dead!   37
We are undone, lady, we are undone!
Alack the day, he's gone, he's killed, he's dead!
JULIET
Can heaven be so envious?
NURSE   Romeo can,   40
Though heaven cannot. Oh, Romeo, Romeo!
Who ever would have thought it? Romeo!

JULIET
What devil art thou that dost torment me thus?
This torture should be roared in dismal hell.
Hath Romeo slain himself? Say thou but "Ay,"
And that bare vowel "I" shall poison more   46
Than the death-darting eye of cockatrice.   47
I am not I, if there be such an "Ay,"
Or those eyes shut, that makes thee answer "Ay."   49
If he be slain, say "Ay," or if not, "No."
Brief sounds determine of my weal or woe.   51
NURSE
I saw the wound. I saw it with mine eyes—
God save the mark!—here on his manly breast.   53
A piteous corpse, a bloody piteous corpse;
Pale, pale as ashes, all bedaubed in blood,
All in gore-blood. I swoonèd at the sight.   56
JULIET
Oh, break, my heart! Poor bankrupt, break at once!
To prison, eyes; ne'er look on liberty!
Vile earth, to earth resign; end motion here,   59
And thou and Romeo press one heavy bier!   60
NURSE
O Tybalt, Tybalt, the best friend I had!
O courteous Tybalt! Honest gentleman!   62
That ever I should live to see thee dead!
JULIET
What storm is this that blows so contrary?
Is Romeo slaughtered, and is Tybalt dead?
My dearest cousin, and my dearer lord?
Then, dreadful trumpet, sound the general doom!   67
For who is living, if those two are gone?
NURSE
Tybalt is gone, and Romeo banishèd;
Romeo that killed him, he is banishèd.
JULIET
Oh, God! Did Romeo's hand shed Tybalt's blood?
NURSE
It did, it did. Alas the day it did!
JULIET
O serpent heart, hid with a flow'ring face!   73
Did ever dragon keep so fair a cave?   74
Beautiful tyrant! Fiend angelical!
Dove-feathered raven! Wolvish-ravening lamb!
Despisèd substance of divinest show!   77
Just opposite to what thou justly seem'st,
A damnèd saint, an honorable villain!
O nature, what hadst thou to do in hell
When thou didst bower the spirit of a fiend   81
In mortal paradise of such sweet flesh?
Was ever book containing such vile matter

6–7 That runaways' . . . unseen (Perhaps Juliet is thinking of the elopement that will surely be necessary once she and Romeo secretly marry; they will embrace in the dark of *love-performing night,* untalked of and unseen by others and by each other. A difficult passage that is sometimes interpreted, uncertainly, as referring to the sun's horses as the *runaways. Wink* means "close, be shut.") **10 civil** circumspect, somberly attired **12 learn** teach **14 Hood** Cover. (A term in falconry; the hawk's eyes were covered so that it would not *bate* or beat its wings.) **unmanned** untamed (in falconry; with a pun on "not yet sexually possessed") **15 strange** diffident **21 I** (Often emended to *he,* following the Fourth Quarto, but Juliet may mean that when she is dead she will share Romeo's beauty with the world. Dying may also hint at sexual climax.) **25 garish** dazzling **31.1 cords** ropes (for the ladder). **37 weraday!** welladay, alas! **40 envious** malicious.

46 "I" (Pronounced identically with "Ay.") **47 cockatrice** basilisk, a mythical serpent that could kill by its look. **49 those eyes shut** if Romeo's eyes are shut (in death) **51 weal** welfare, happiness **53 God . . . mark** (An oath registering shock and horror.) **56 goreblood** clotted blood. **59 Vile . . . here** May my vile body resign itself to burial, ending life itself **60 press** weigh down. **bier** litter for carrying corpses. **62 Honest** Honorable **67 trumpet** i.e., the last trumpet. **general doom** Day of Judgment. **73 hid . . . face** concealed beneath a beautiful face. **74 keep** occupy, guard. **cave** i.e., one with treasure in it. **77 show** appearance. **81 bower** give lodging to

So fairly bound? Oh, that deceit should dwell
In such a gorgeous palace!
NURSE   There's no trust,
No faith, no honesty in men; all perjured,
All forsworn, all naught, all dissemblers.   87
Ah, where's my man? Give me some aqua vitae.   88
These griefs, these woes, these sorrows make me old.
Shame come to Romeo!
JULIET   Blistered be thy tongue
For such a wish! He was not born to shame.
Upon his brow shame is ashamed to sit,
For 'tis a throne where honor may be crowned
Sole monarch of the universal earth.
Oh, what a beast was I to chide at him!
NURSE
Will you speak well of him that killed your cousin?
JULIET
Shall I speak ill of him that is my husband?
Ah, poor my lord, what tongue shall smooth thy name   98
When I, thy three-hours wife, have mangled it?
But wherefore, villain, didst thou kill my cousin?
That villain cousin would have killed my husband.
Back, foolish tears, back to your native spring!
Your tributary drops belong to woe,   103
Which you, mistaking, offer up to joy.
My husband lives, that Tybalt would have slain,   105
And Tybalt's dead, that would have slain my
    husband.
All this is comfort. Wherefore weep I then?
Some word there was, worser than Tybalt's death,
That murdered me. I would forget it fain,   109
But oh, it presses to my memory
Like damnèd guilty deeds to sinners' minds!
"Tybalt is dead, and Romeo—banishèd."
That "banishèd," that one word "banishèd"
Hath slain ten thousand Tybalts. Tybalt's death
Was woe enough, if it had ended there;
Or, if sour woe delights in fellowship
And needly will be ranked with other griefs,   117
Why followed not, when she said "Tybalt's dead,"
"Thy father," or "thy mother," nay, or both,
Which modern lamentation might have moved?   120
But with a rearward following Tybalt's death,   121
"Romeo is banishèd"—to speak that word
Is father, mother, Tybalt, Romeo, Juliet,
All slain, all dead. "Romeo is banishèd!"
There is no end, no limit, measure, bound,
In that word's death; no words can that woe sound.   126
Where is my father and my mother, Nurse?
NURSE
Weeping and wailing over Tybalt's corpse.
Will you go to them? I will bring you thither.

JULIET
Wash they his wounds with tears? Mine shall be spent,
When theirs are dry, for Romeo's banishment.
Take up those cords.—Poor ropes, you are beguiled,
Both you and I, for Romeo is exiled.
He made you for a highway to my bed,
But I, a maid, die maiden-widowèd.
Come, cords, come, Nurse. I'll to my wedding bed,
And death, not Romeo, take my maidenhead.
NURSE [taking up the cords]
Hie to your chamber. I'll find Romeo
To comfort you. I wot well where he is.   139
Hark ye, your Romeo will be here at night.
I'll to him. He is hid at Laurence' cell.
JULIET [giving a ring]
Oh, find him! Give this ring to my true knight,
And bid him come to take his last farewell.
                              Exeunt [separately].

[3.3]

Enter Friar [Laurence].

FRIAR LAURENCE
Romeo, come forth; come forth, thou fearful man.   1
Affliction is enamored of thy parts,   2
And thou art wedded to calamity.

        [*Enter*] *Romeo.*

ROMEO
Father, what news? What is the Prince's doom?   4
What sorrow craves acquaintance at my hand
That I yet know not?
FRIAR LAURENCE   Too familiar
Is my dear son with such sour company.
I bring thee tidings of the Prince's doom.
ROMEO
What less than doomsday is the Prince's doom?   9
FRIAR LAURENCE
A gentler judgment vanished from his lips: 10
Not body's death, but body's banishment.
ROMEO
Ha, banishment? Be merciful, say "death";
For exile hath more terror in his look,
Much more than death. Do not say "banishment."
FRIAR LAURENCE
Here from Verona art thou banishèd.
Be patient, for the world is broad and wide.
ROMEO
There is no world without Verona walls   17
But purgatory, torture, hell itself.
Hence "banishèd" is banished from the world,
And world's exile is death. Then "banishèd,"   20
Is death mistermed. Calling death "banishèd,"

---

87 naught worthless, evil   **88 man** servant.   **aqua vitae** alcoholic
spirits.   **98 poor my lord** my poor lord.   **smooth thy name** speak
your name kindly   **103 Your . . . woe** You should be shed, offered as
a tribute, on some occasion of real woe   **105 that** whom   **109 fain**
gladly   **117 needly** of necessity.   **ranked with** accompanied by
120 Which . . . moved which might have prompted a normal grief-
stricken response.   **121 rearward** rearguard, following afterward
126 sound (1) fathom (2) express.

139 wot know
3.3. Location: Verona. Friar Laurence's cell.
1 fearful full of fear   **2 parts** qualities   **4 doom** judgment.
9 doomsday the Day of judgment, i.e., end of the world
10 vanished issued (into air)   **17 without** outside of   **20 world's
exile** exile from the world

Thou cut'st my head off with a golden ax
And smilest upon the stroke that murders me.

FRIAR LAURENCE
Oh, deadly sin! Oh, rude unthankfulness!
Thy fault our law calls death, but the kind Prince,   25
Taking thy part, hath rushed aside the law   26
And turned that black word "death" to "banishment."
This is dear mercy, and thou see'st it not.

ROMEO
'Tis torture, and not mercy. Heaven is here
Where Juliet lives, and every cat and dog
And little mouse, every unworthy thing,
Live here in heaven and may look on her,
But Romeo may not. More validity,   33
More honorable state, more courtship lives   34
In carrion flies than Romeo. They may seize
On the white wonder of dear Juliet's hand
And steal immortal blessing from her lips,
Who even in pure and vestal modesty   38
Still blush, as thinking their own kisses sin;   39
But Romeo may not, he is banishèd.
Flies may do this, but I from this must fly.
They are free men, but I am banishèd.
And sayest thou yet that exile is not death?
Hadst thou no poison mixed, no sharp-ground knife,
No sudden mean of death, though ne'er so mean,   45
But "banishèd" to kill me? "Banishèd"?
Oh, Friar, the damnèd use that word in hell;
Howling attends it. How hast thou the heart,
Being a divine, a ghostly confessor,
A sin absolver, and my friend professed,
To mangle me with that word "banishèd"?

FRIAR LAURENCE
Thou fond mad man, hear me a little speak.   52

ROMEO
Oh, thou wilt speak again of banishment.

FRIAR LAURENCE
I'll give thee armor to keep off that word,
Adversity's sweet milk, philosophy,
To comfort thee, though thou art banishèd.

ROMEO
Yet "banishèd"? Hang up philosophy!   57
Unless philosophy can make a Juliet,
Displant a town, reverse a prince's doom,   59
It helps not, it prevails not. Talk no more.

FRIAR LAURENCE
Oh, then I see that madmen have no ears.

ROMEO
How should they, when that wise men have no eyes?

FRIAR LAURENCE
Let me dispute with thee of thy estate.   63

ROMEO
Thou canst not speak of that thou dost not feel.   64
Wert thou as young as I, Juliet thy love,
An hour but married, Tybalt murderèd,
Doting like me, and like me banishèd,
Then mightst thou speak, then mightst thou tear thy
    hair,
And fall upon the ground, as I do now,
Taking the measure of an unmade grave.
            [He falls upon the ground.] Knock [within].

FRIAR LAURENCE
Arise. One knocks. Good Romeo, hide thyself.

ROMEO
Not I, unless the breath of heartsick groans,
Mistlike, infold me from the search of eyes.   Knock.

FRIAR LAURENCE
Hark, how they knock!—Who's there?—Romeo, arise.
Thou wilt be taken.—Stay awhile!—Stand up.
                                    Knock.
Run to my study.—By and by!—God's will,
What simpleness is this?—I come, I come!   Knock. 77
Who knocks so hard? Whence come you? What's your
    will?   [Going to the door.]

NURSE [within]
Let me come in, and you shall know my errand.
I come from Lady Juliet.

FRIAR LAURENCE   Welcome, then.
                        [He opens the door.]

        Enter Nurse.

NURSE
O holy Friar, oh, tell me, holy Friar,
Where's my lady's lord, where's Romeo?

FRIAR LAURENCE
There on the ground, with his own tears made drunk.

NURSE
Oh, he is even in my mistress' case,   84
Just in her case! Oh, woeful sympathy!   85
Piteous predicament! Even so lies she,
Blubb'ring and weeping, weeping and blubb'ring.—
Stand up, stand up! Stand, an you be a man.
For Juliet's sake, for her sake, rise and stand!
Why should you fall into so deep an O?   90

ROMEO Nurse!   [He rises.]

NURSE
Ah sir, ah sir! Death's the end of all.

ROMEO
Spakest thou of Juliet? How is it with her?
Doth not she think me an old murderer,   94
Now I have stained the childhood of our joy
With blood removed but little from her own?
Where is she? And how doth she? And what says
My concealed lady to our canceled love?   98

---

25 Thy fault . . . death For your crime, the law demands a death sentence **26 rushed** thrust **33 validity** true worth **34 courtship** (1) courtliness (2) occasion for wooing **38 vestal** maidenly **39 Still . . . sin** continually look red, as though blushing to think that their touching each other is sin **45 mean . . . mean** means . . . base **52 fond** foolish, frantic **57 Yet** Still **59 Displant** uproot **63 dispute** reason. **estate** situation.

64 that that which **77 simpleness** foolishness **84 even** exactly. **case** situation **85 woeful sympathy** mutuality of grief. **90 an O** a fit of groaning. (A sexual meaning, unrecognized by the speaker, is suggested by *rise and stand* in the previous line.) **94 old** hardened **98 concealed** secret. **canceled** nullified (by the impending exile)

NURSE
    Oh, she says nothing, sir, but weeps and weeps,
    And now falls on her bed, and then starts up,
    And "Tybalt" calls, and then on Romeo cries,
    And then down falls again.
ROMEO   As if that name,
    Shot from the deadly level of a gun,   103
    Did murder her, as that name's cursèd hand
    Murdered her kinsman. Oh, tell me, Friar, tell me,
    In what vile part of this anatomy
    Doth my name lodge? Tell me, that I may sack   107
    The hateful mansion.
             [He draws a weapon, but is restrained.]
FRIAR LAURENCE   Hold thy desperate hand!
    Art thou a man? Thy form cries out thou art;
    Thy tears are womanish, thy wild acts denote
    The unreasonable fury of a beast.
    Unseemly woman in a seeming man,
    And ill-beseeming beast in seeming both!
    Thou hast amazed me. By my holy order,
    I thought thy disposition better tempered.   115
    Hast thou slain Tybalt? Wilt thou slay thyself,
    And slay thy lady, that in thy life lives,
    By doing damnèd hate upon thyself?
    Why railest thou on thy birth, the heaven, and earth,
    Since birth, and heaven, and earth, all three do meet 120
    In thee at once, which thou at once wouldst lose?
    Fie, fie, thou shamest thy shape, thy love, thy wit, 122
    Which, like a usurer, abound'st in all,   123
    And usest none in that true use indeed   124
    Which should bedeck thy shape, thy love, thy wit. 125
    Thy noble shape is but a form of wax,   126
    Digressing from the valor of a man;
    Thy dear love sworn but hollow perjury,
    Killing that love which thou hast vowed to cherish;
    Thy wit, that ornament to shape and love,
    Misshapen in the conduct of them both,   131
    Like powder in a skilless soldier's flask   132
    Is set afire by thine own ignorance,
    And thou dismembered with thine own defense. 134
    What, rouse thee, man! Thy Juliet is alive,
    For whose dear sake thou wast but lately dead; 136
    There art thou happy. Tybalt would kill thee, 137
    But thou slewest Tybalt; there art thou happy.
    The law that threatened death becomes thy friend
    And turns it to exile; there art thou happy.
    A pack of blessings light upon thy back,
    Happiness courts thee in her best array,
    But like a mishavèd and sullen wench   143
    Thou pout'st upon thy fortune and thy love.

Take heed, take heed, for such die miserable.
    Go, get thee to thy love, as was decreed.   146
    Ascend her chamber; hence and comfort her.
    But look thou stay not till the watch be set,   148
    For then thou canst not pass to Mantua,
    Where thou shalt live till we can find a time
    To blaze your marriage, reconcile your friends, 151
    Beg pardon of the Prince, and call thee back
    With twenty hundred thousand times more joy
    Than thou went'st forth in lamentation.
    Go before, Nurse. Commend me to thy lady,
    And bid her hasten all the house to bed,
    Which heavy sorrow makes them apt unto.
    Romeo is coming.
NURSE
    Oh, Lord, I could have stayed here all the night
    To hear good counsel. Oh, what learning is!—
    My lord, I'll tell my lady you will come.
ROMEO
    Do so, and bid my sweet prepare to chide.
NURSE *[giving a ring]*
    Here, sir, a ring she bid me give you, sir.
    Hie you, make haste, for it grows very late.   *[Exit.]*
ROMEO
    How well my comfort is revived by this!
FRIAR LAURENCE
    Go hence. Good night. And here stands all your state: 166
    Either be gone before the watch be set,
    Or by the break of day disguised from hence.
    Sojourn in Mantua. I'll find out your man,
    And he shall signify from time to time
    Every good hap to you that chances here.   171
    Give me thy hand. 'Tis late. Farewell, good night.
ROMEO
    But that a joy past joy calls out on me,
    It were a grief so brief to part with thee.   174
    Farewell.   *Exeunt [separately].*

❖

[3.4]

Enter old Capulet, his Wife, and Paris.

CAPULET
    Things have fall'n out, sir, so unluckily,   1
    That we have had no time to move our daughter. 2
    Look you, she loved her kinsman Tybalt dearly,
    And so did I. Well, we were born to die.
    'Tis very late. She'll not come down tonight.
    I promise you, but for your company   6
    I would have been abed an hour ago.
PARIS
    These times of woe afford no times to woo.
    Madam, good night. Commend me to your daughter.

---

103 **level** aim   107 **sack** destroy   115 **tempered** harmonized, balanced.   120 **birth . . . earth** life, soul, and body   122–5 **thou shamest . . . wit** you shame your physical form, love, and mind (corresponding to life, soul, and body), all of which you have in abundance but which you misuse as a usurer misuses wealth, using improperly the treasure that you should put to proper use.   126 **form of wax** waxwork, mere outer form   131 **conduct** guidance   132 **powder** gunpowder. **flask** powder horn   134 **dismembered . . . defense** blown to pieces by that which should defend you, i.e., your *wit*, or intellect.   136 **wast . . . dead** i.e., only recently were wishing yourself dead. (See line 70.)   137 **happy** fortunate.   143 **mishavèd** misbehaved

146 **decreed** (1) arranged earlier (2) decreed by heaven for those who have married.   148 **the watch be set** guards are posted (at the city gates) 151 **blaze** publish, divulge. **friends** relations   166 **here . . . state** your fortune depends on what follows 171 **good hap** fortunate event 174 **brief** quickly
3.4. Location: Verona. Capulet's house.
1 **fall'n out** happened 2 **move** persuade 6 **promise** assure

WIFE
    I will, and know her mind early tomorrow.
    Tonight she's mewed up to her heaviness.   11

CAPULET
    Sir Paris, I will make a desperate tender   12
    Of my child's love. I think she will be ruled
    In all respects by me; nay, more, I doubt it not.
    Wife, go you to her ere you go to bed.
    Acquaint her here of my son Paris' love,
    And bid her, mark you me, on Wednesday next—   17
    But soft, what day is this?

PARIS   Monday, my lord.   18

CAPULET
    Monday! Ha, ha! Well, Wednesday is too soon;
    O' Thursday let it be. O'Thursday, tell her,
    She shall be married to this noble earl.
    Will you be ready? Do you like this haste?
    We'll keep no great ado—a friend or two;
    For hark you, Tybalt being slain so late,   24
    It may be thought we held him carelessly,   25
    Being our kinsman, if we revel much.
    Therefore we'll have some half a dozen friends,
    And there an end. But what say you to Thursday?

PARIS
    My lord, I would that Thursday were tomorrow.

CAPULET
    Well, get you gone. O' Thursday be it, then.
    [*To his Wife*] Go you to Juliet ere you go to bed;
    Prepare her, wife, against this wedding day.—   32
    Farewell, my lord.—Light to my chamber, ho!—
    Afore me, it is so very late   34
    That we may call it early by and by.
    Good night.   *Exeunt.*

❧

[3.5]

Enter Romeo and Juliet aloft [at the window].

JULIET
    Wilt thou be gone? It is not yet near day.
    It was the nightingale, and not the lark,
    That pierced the fearful hollow of thine ear;   3
    Nightly she sings on yond pomegranate tree.
    Believe me, love, it was the nightingale.

ROMEO
    It was the lark, the herald of the morn,
    No nightingale. Look, love, what envious streaks
    Do lace the severing clouds in yonder east.   8
    Night's candles are burnt out, and jocund day   9
    Stands tiptoe on the misty mountain tops.
    I must be gone and live, or stay and die.

JULIET
    Yond light is not daylight, I know it, I.
    It is some meteor that the sun exhaled   13
    To be to thee this night a torchbearer
    And light thee on thy way to Mantua.
    Therefore stay yet. Thou need'st not to be gone.

ROMEO
    Let me be ta'en; let me be put to death.
    I am content, so thou wilt have it so.   18
    I'll say yon gray is not the morning's eye;
    'Tis but the pale reflex of Cynthia's brow.   20
    Nor that is not the lark whose notes do beat
    The vaulty heaven so high above our heads.
    I have more care to stay than will to go.   23
    Come, death, and welcome! Juliet wills it so.
    How is't, my soul? Let's talk. It is not day.

JULIET
    It is, it is. Hie hence, begone, away!   26
    It is the lark that sings so out of tune,
    Straining harsh discords and unpleasing sharps.   28
    Some say the lark makes sweet division;   29
    This doth not so, for she divideth us.
    Some say the lark and loathèd toad changed eyes;   31
    Oh, now I would they had changed voices too,
    Since arm from arm that voice doth us affray,   33
    Hunting thee hence with hunt's-up to the day.   34
    Oh, now begone! More light and light it grows.

ROMEO
    More light and light, more dark and dark our woes!

Enter Nurse [hastily].

NURSE   Madam!
JULIET   Nurse?

NURSE
    Your lady mother is coming to your chamber.
    The day is broke; be wary, look about.   [*Exit.*]

JULIET
    Then window, let day in, and let life out.

ROMEO
    Farewell, farewell! One kiss, and I'll descend.
    [*They kiss. He climbs down from the window.*]

JULIET
    Art thou gone so? Love, lord, ay, husband, friend!   43
    I must hear from thee every day in the hour,
    For in a minute there are many days.
    Oh, by this count I shall be much in years   46
    Ere I again behold my Romeo!

ROMEO [*from below her window*]   Farewell!

---

11 mewed up to cooped up with. (A term from falconry, reminiscent of 2.2.159–68.) **heaviness** sorrow. **12 desperate tender** bold offer **17 mark you me** listen to this **18 soft** wait a minute **24 late** recently **25 held him carelessly** did not regard him highly **32 against** in anticipation of **34 Afore me** i.e., By my life. (A mild oath.)
3.5. Location: Verona. Capulet's orchard with Juliet's chamber window above, and, at lines 68 ff., the interior of Juliet's chamber.
3 fearful apprehensive, anxious **8 severing** separating **9 jocund** cheerful

13 exhaled i.e., has drawn out of the ground. (Meteors were thought to be vapors of luminous gas drawn up by the sun.) **18 so** as long as, since **20 reflex** reflection. **Cynthia's** the moon's **23 care** desire, concern **26 Hie hence** Hasten away **28 sharps** notes relatively high in pitch and hence discordant. **29 division** variations on a melody, made by dividing each note into notes of briefer duration **31 changed** exchanged. (A popular saying, to account for the observation that the lark has very ordinary eyes and the toad remarkable ones.) **33 arm from arm** from one another's arms. **affray** frighten **34 hunt's-up** a song or tune originally designed to awaken huntsmen; later, used also to serenade a newly married couple **43 friend** lover. **46 much in years** much older

I will omit no opportunity
That may convey my greetings, love, to thee.

JULIET
Oh, think'st thou we shall ever meet again?

ROMEO
I doubt it not, and all these woes shall serve
For sweet discourses in our times to come.

JULIET
Oh, God, I have an ill-divining soul!   54
Methinks I see thee, now thou art so low,
As one dead in the bottom of a tomb.
Either my eyesight fails or thou lookest pale.

ROMEO
And trust me, love, in my eye so do you.
Dry sorrow drinks our blood. Adieu, adieu!   *Exit.*   59

JULIET
O Fortune, Fortune! All men call thee fickle.
If thou art fickle, what dost thou with him
That is renowned for faith? Be fickle, Fortune!
For then, I hope, thou wilt not keep him long,
But send him back.

Enter Mother [Capulet's Wife].

WIFE   Ho, daughter, are you up?

JULIET
Who is't that calls? It is my lady mother.
Is she not down so late, or up so early?   66
What unaccustomed cause procures her hither?   67
                    [*She goeth down from the window.*]

WIFE
Why, how now, Juliet?

JULIET   Madam, I am not well.

WIFE
Evermore weeping for your cousin's death?
What, wilt thou wash him from his grave with tears?
An if thou couldst, thou couldst not make him live;
Therefore, have done. Some grief shows much of love,   72
But much of grief shows still some want of wit.   73

JULIET
Yet let me weep for such a feeling loss.   74

WIFE
So shall you feel the loss, but not the friend
Which you weep for.

JULIET   Feeling so the loss,
I cannot choose but ever weep the friend.   77

WIFE
Well, girl, thou weep'st not so much for his death
As that the villain lives which slaughtered him.

JULIET
What villain, madam?

WIFE   That same villain, Romeo.

JULIET [*aside*]
Villain and he be many miles asunder.—
God pardon him! I do, with all my heart;
And yet no man like he doth grieve my heart.   83

WIFE
That is because the traitor murderer lives.

JULIET
Ay, madam, from the reach of these my hands.
Would none but I might venge my cousin's death!

WIFE
We will have vengeance for it, fear thou not.
Then weep no more. I'll send to one in Mantua,
Where that same banished runagate doth live,   89
Shall give him such an unaccustomed dram   90
That he shall soon keep Tybalt company.
And then, I hope, thou wilt be satisfied.

JULIET
Indeed, I never shall be satisfied
With Romeo till I behold him—dead—
Is my poor heart so for a kinsman vexed.
Madam, if you could find out but a man
To bear a poison, I would temper it,   97
That Romeo should, upon receipt thereof,
Soon sleep in quiet. Oh, how my heart abhors
To hear him named, and cannot come to him
To wreak the love I bore my cousin   101
Upon his body that hath slaughtered him!   102

WIFE
Find thou the means, and I'll find such a man.
But now I'll tell thee joyful tidings, girl.

JULIET
And joy comes well in such a needy time.
What are they, beseech Your Ladyship?

WIFE
Well, well, thou hast a careful father, child,   107
One who, to put thee from thy heaviness,   108
Hath sorted out a sudden day of joy   109
That thou expects not, nor I looked not for.

JULIET
Madam, in happy time, what day is that?

WIFE
Marry, my child, early next Thursday morn,   112
The gallant, young, and noble gentleman,
The County Paris, at Saint Peter's Church
Shall happily make thee there a joyful bride.

JULIET
Now, by Saint Peter's Church, and Peter too,
He shall not make me there a joyful bride!

---

54 ill-divining prophesying of evil **59 Dry sorrow** (The heat of the body in sorrow and despair was thought to descend into the bowels and dry up the blood.) **66 down** in bed **67 procures** induces to come. **67.1** (As indicated by the bracketed stage direction, which is from the First Quarto, Juliet, who has appeared until now at her "window" above the stage, evidently descends quickly to the main stage and joins her mother for the remainder of the scene. The stage, which before was to have been imagined as Capulet's orchard, is now Juliet's chamber. Juliet's mother has entered onto the main stage four lines earlier.) **72 have done** cease. **73 want of wit** lack of intelligence. **74 feeling** deeply felt **77 the friend** (Juliet secretly means "my lover," as at line 43, but, of course, her mother hears it as "Tybalt.")

83 no man like he no man so much as he. **grieve** (1) anger (2) grieve with longing. (Juliet speaks to her mother throughout in intentional ambiguities, at lines 85, 86, 99, 100–2, etc.) **89 runagate** renegade, fugitive **90 Shall** who will. **dram** dose. (Literally, one-eighth of a fluid ounce.) **97 temper** (1) mix, concoct (2) alloy, dilute. (In her intended double meanings about Romeo dead, poisoned, and sleeping in quiet, Juliet is, of course, unaware of an ironic anticipation of how these things will be fulfilled.) **101 wreak** (1) avenge (2) bestow **102 his body that** the body of him who **107 careful** full of care (for you) **108 heaviness** sorrow **109 sorted** chosen **112 Marry** i.e., By the Virgin Mary

I wonder at this haste, that I must wed
Ere he that should be husband comes to woo.
I pray you, tell my lord and father, madam,
I will not marry yet, and when I do I swear
It shall be Romeo, whom you know I hate,
Rather than Paris. These are news indeed!

WIFE
Here comes your father. Tell him so yourself,
And see how he will take it at your hands.

Enter Capulet and Nurse.

CAPULET
When the sun sets, the earth doth drizzle dew,
But for the sunset of my brother's son
It rains downright.—
How now, a conduit, girl? What, still in tears?   129
Evermore show'ring? In one little body
Thou counterfeits a bark, a sea, a wind;   131
For still thy eyes, which I may call the sea,
Do ebb and flow with tears; the bark thy body is,
Sailing in this salt flood; the winds, thy sighs,
Who, raging with thy tears, and they with them,
Without a sudden calm, will overset   136
Thy tempest-tossèd body.—How now, wife?
Have you delivered to her our decree?

WIFE
Ay, sir, but she will none, she gives you thanks.   139
I would the fool were married to her grave!

CAPULET
Soft, take me with you, take me with you, wife.   141
How? Will she none? Doth she not give us thanks?
Is she not proud? Doth she not count her blest,   143
Unworthy as she is, that we have wrought   144
So worthy a gentleman to be her bride?   145

JULIET
Not proud you have, but thankful that you have.
Proud can I never be of what I hate,
But thankful even for hate that is meant love.   148

CAPULET
How, how, how, how, chopped logic? What is this?
"Proud," and "I thank you," and "I thank you not,"
And yet "not proud"? Mistress minion, you,   151
Thank me no thankings, nor proud me no prouds,
But fettle your fine joints 'gainst Thursday next   153
To go with Paris to Saint Peter's Church,
Or I will drag thee on a hurdle thither.   155
Out, you greensickness carrion! Out, you baggage!   156
You tallow-face!

WIFE [*to Capulet*]   Fie, fie! What, are you mad?   157

JULIET [*kneeling*]
Good father, I beseech you on my knees,
Hear me with patience but to speak a word.

CAPULET
Hang thee, young baggage, disobedient wretch!
I tell thee what: get thee to church o' Thursday
Or never after look me in the face.
Speak not, reply not, do not answer me!
My fingers itch. Wife, we scarce thought us blest
That God had lent us but this only child;
But now I see this one is one too much,
And that we have a curse in having her.
Out on her, hilding!

NURSE   God in heaven bless her!   168
You are to blame, my lord, to rate her so.   169

CAPULET
And why, my Lady Wisdom? Hold your tongue,
Good Prudence. Smatter with your gossips, go.   171

NURSE
I speak no treason.

CAPULET   Oh, God-i'-good-e'en!   172

NURSE
May not one speak?

CAPULET   Peace, you mumbling fool!
Utter your gravity o'er a gossip's bowl,   174
For here we need it not.

WIFE   You are too hot.

CAPULET   God's bread, it makes me mad!   176
Day, night, hour, tide, time, work, play,   177
Alone, in company, still my care hath been
To have her matched. And having now provided
A gentleman of noble parentage,
Of fair demesnes, youthful, and nobly liened,   181
Stuffed, as they say, with honorable parts,   182
Proportioned as one's thought would wish a man—
And then to have a wretched puling fool,   184
A whining mammet, in her fortune's tender,   185
To answer, "I'll not wed, I cannot love,
I am too young; I pray you, pardon me."
But, an you will not wed, I'll pardon you.   188
Graze where you will, you shall not house with me.
Look to't, think on't. I do not use to jest.   190
Thursday is near. Lay hand on heart; advise.   191
An you be mine, I'll give you to my friend;
An you be not, hang, beg, starve, die in the streets,
For, by my soul, I'll ne'er acknowledge thee,
Nor what is mine shall never do thee good.
Trust to't, bethink you. I'll not be forsworn.   *Exit.*   196

JULIET
Is there no pity sitting in the clouds
That sees into the bottom of my grief?

---

129 conduit water pipe, fountain **131 bark** sailing vessel **136 Without** unless there is **139 will . . . thanks** says "no thank you," she'll have no part of it. **141 take . . . you** let me understand you **143 count her** consider herself **144 wrought** arranged for **145 bride** bridegroom. **148 hate . . . love** that which is hateful but which was meant lovingly. **151 minion** spoiled darling, minx **153 fettle** make ready. **'gainst** in anticipation of **155 a hurdle** a conveyance on which criminals were dragged to execution **156 greensickness** (An anemic ailment of young unmarried women; it suggests Juliet's paleness.) **baggage** hussy. **157 tallow-face** paleface.

168 hilding jade, baggage. **169 rate** berate, scold **171 Smatter** Chatter. **gossips** gossiping women friends **172 God-i'-good-e'en** i.e., For God's sake. (Literally, God give you good evening.) **174 gravity** wisdom. (Said contemptuously.) **176 God's bread** i.e., By God's (Christ's) Sacrament **177 tide** season **181 demesnes** estates. **liened** descended **182 parts** qualities **184 puling** whining **185 mammet** doll. **in . . . tender** when an offer of good fortune is made to her **188 pardon you** i.e., allow you to depart. (Said caustically.) **190 do not use** am not accustomed **191 advise** consider carefully. **196 be forsworn** i.e., go back on my word.

O sweet my mother, cast me not away!
Delay this marriage for a month, a week;
Or if you do not, make the bridal bed
In that dim monument where Tybalt lies.

WIFE
Talk not to me, for I'll not speak a word.
Do as thou wilt, for I have done with thee.   *Exit.*

JULIET [*rising*]
Oh, God!—O Nurse, how shall this be prevented?
My husband is on earth, my faith in heaven.   206
How shall that faith return again to earth,   207
Unless that husband send it me from heaven   208
By leaving earth? Comfort me, counsel me.   209
Alack, alack, that heaven should practice stratagems
Upon so soft a subject as myself!
What say'st thou? Hast thou not a word of joy?
Some comfort, Nurse.

NURSE   Faith, here it is.
Romeo is banished, and all the world to nothing   214
That he dares ne'er come back to challenge you,   215
Or if he do, it needs must be by stealth.
Then, since the case so stands as now it doth,
I think it best you married with the County.
Oh, he's a lovely gentleman!
Romeo's a dishclout to him. An eagle, madam,   220
Hath not so green, so quick, so fair an eye
As Paris hath. Beshrew my very heart,   222
I think you are happy in this second match,
For it excels your first; or if it did not,
Your first is dead—or 'twere as good he were,
As living here and you no use of him.

JULIET   Speak'st thou from thy heart?

NURSE
And from my soul too. Else beshrew them both.

JULIET   Amen!   229

NURSE   What?

JULIET
Well, thou hast comforted me marvelous much.
Go in, and tell my lady I am gone,
Having displeased my father, to Laurence' cell
To make confession and to be absolved.

NURSE
Marry, I will; and this is wisely done.   [*Exit.*]

JULIET
Ancient damnation! Oh, most wicked fiend!   236
Is it more sin to wish me thus forsworn,   237
Or to dispraise my lord with that same tongue
Which she hath praised him with above compare
So many thousand times? Go, counselor,
Thou and my bosom henceforth shall be twain.   241

I'll to the Friar to know his remedy.
If all else fail, myself have power to die.   *Exit.*

❖

[4.1]

Enter Friar [Laurence] and County Paris.

FRIAR LAURENCE
On Thursday, sir? The time is very short.

PARIS
My father Capulet will have it so,
And I am nothing slow to slack his haste.   3

FRIAR LAURENCE
You say you do not know the lady's mind?
Uneven is the course. I like it not.

PARIS
Immoderately she weeps for Tybalt's death,
And therefore have I little talked of love,
For Venus smiles not in a house of tears.   8
Now, sir, her father counts it dangerous
That she do give her sorrow so much sway,
And in his wisdom hastes our marriage
To stop the inundation of her tears,
Which, too much minded by herself alone,   13
May be put from her by society.   14
Now do you know the reason of this haste.

FRIAR LAURENCE [*aside*]
I would I knew not why it should be slowed.—
Look, sir, here comes the lady toward my cell.

Enter Juliet.

PARIS
Happily met, my lady and my wife!

JULIET
That may be, sir, when I may be a wife.

PARIS
That "may be" must be, love, on Thursday next.

JULIET
What must be shall be.

FRIAR LAURENCE   That's a certain text.

PARIS
Come you to make confession to this father?

JULIET
To answer that, I should confess to you.

PARIS
Do not deny to him that you love me.

JULIET
I will confess to you that I love him.

PARIS
So will ye, I am sure, that you love me.

JULIET
If I do so, it will be of more price,   27
Being spoke behind your back, than to your face.

---

206 **my faith in heaven** i.e., I am married to Romeo in the sight of
heaven.   207–9 **How . . . leaving earth?** i.e., How can I remarry while
Romeo is still alive?   214 **all . . . nothing** the odds are overwhelming
215 **challenge** lay claim to   220 **dishclout** dishrag   222 **Beshrew** (A
mild oath. Also in line 228.)   229 **Amen** (Juliet says "Amen" as
though to answer the Nurse's prayer that her heart and soul be
cursed. The Nurse does not get the point.)   236 **Ancient damnation!**
Damnable old woman!   237 **forsworn** i.e., false to my marriage vows
241 **bosom** secret thoughts.   **twain** separated.

4.1. Location: Verona. Friar Laurence's cell.
3 **nothing . . . haste** not at all reluctant to lessen his haste, i.e., willing to
speed matters along.   8 **Venus . . . tears** (1) amorousness is not appropriate in a house of mourning (2) the planet Venus does not exert a
favorable influence when it is in an inauspicious *house* or constellation
of the zodiac.   13 **too . . . alone** too mind-consuming when she is alone
14 **society** companionship.   27 **more price** greater worth

PARIS

Poor soul, thy face is much abused with tears.

JULIET

The tears have got small victory by that,
For it was bad enough before their spite.   31

PARIS

Thou wrong'st it more than tears with that report.   32

JULIET

That is no slander, sir, which is a truth;
And what I spake, I spake it to my face.   34

PARIS

Thy face is mine, and thou hast slandered it.

JULIET

It may be so, for it is not mine own.—   36
Are you at leisure, holy Father, now,
Or shall I come to you at evening Mass?

FRIAR LAURENCE

My leisure serves me, pensive daughter, now.—   39
My lord, we must entreat the time alone.   40

PARIS

God shield I should disturb devotion!   41
Juliet, on Thursday early will I rouse ye.
Till then, adieu, and keep this holy kiss.   *Exit.*

JULIET

Oh, shut the door! And when thou hast done so,
Come weep with me—past hope, past cure, past help!

FRIAR LAURENCE

Ah, Juliet, I already know thy grief;
It strains me past the compass of my wits.   47
I hear thou must, and nothing may prorogue it,   48
On Thursday next be married to this county.

JULIET

Tell me not, Friar, that thou hearest of this,
Unless thou tell me how I may prevent it.
If in thy wisdom thou canst give no help,
Do thou but call my resolution wise
And with this knife I'll help it presently.   54

                          [She shows a knife.]

God joined my heart and Romeo's, thou our hands;
And ere this hand, by thee to Romeo sealed,
Shall be the label to another deed,   57
Or my true heart with treacherous revolt
Turn to another, this shall slay them both.   59
Therefore, out of thy long-experienced time,   60
Give me some present counsel, or, behold,
Twixt my extremes and me this bloody knife   62
Shall play the umpire, arbitrating that
Which the commission of thy years and art   64
Could to no issue of true honor bring.
Be not so long to speak; I long to die   66
If what thou speak'st speak not of remedy.

FRIAR LAURENCE

Hold, daughter. I do spy a kind of hope,
Which craves as desperate an execution
As that is desperate which we would prevent.
If, rather than to marry County Paris,
Thou hast the strength of will to slay thyself,
Then is it likely thou wilt undertake
A thing like death to chide away this shame,
That cop'st with Death himself to scape from it;   75
And if thou darest, I'll give thee remedy.

JULIET

Oh, bid me leap, rather than marry Paris,
From off the battlements of any tower,
Or walk in thievish ways, or bid me lurk   79
Where serpents are; chain me with roaring bears,
Or hide me nightly in a charnel house,   81
O'ercovered quite with dead men's rattling bones,
With reeky shanks and yellow chopless skulls;   83
Or bid me go into a new-made grave
And hide me with a dead man in his tomb—
Things that, to hear them told, have made me
    tremble—
And I will do it without fear or doubt,
To live an unstained wife to my sweet love.

FRIAR LAURENCE

Hold, then. Go home, be merry, give consent
To marry Paris. Wednesday is tomorrow.
Tomorrow night look that thou lie alone;
Let not the Nurse lie with thee in thy chamber.
Take thou this vial, being then in bed,
                          [showing her a vial]
And this distilling liquor drink thou off,   94
When presently through all thy veins shall run
A cold and drowsy humor; for no pulse   96
Shall keep his native progress, but surcease;   97
No warmth, no breath shall testify thou livest;
The roses in thy lips and cheeks shall fade
To wanny ashes, thy eyes' windows fall   100
Like death when he shuts up the day of life;
Each part, deprived of supple government,   102
Shall, stiff and stark and cold, appear like death.
And in this borrowed likeness of shrunk death
Thou shalt continue two-and-forty hours,
And then awake as from a pleasant sleep.
Now, when the bridegroom in the morning comes
To rouse thee from thy bed, there art thou dead.
Then, as the manner of our country is,
In thy best robes uncovered on the bier
Thou shalt be borne to that same ancient vault
Where all the kindred of the Capulets lie.
In the meantime, against thou shalt awake,   113
Shall Romeo by my letters know our drift,   114

---

31 spite malice.   **32 Thou . . . report** Your apology for your face slanders it more than your tears do.   **34 to my face** (1) openly (2) about my face.   **36 is not mine own** (1) is beyond my control, does not reveal me truly (2) belongs to Romeo.   **39 pensive** sorrowful   **40 entreat . . . alone** ask you to leave us alone.   **41 God shield** God forbid   **47 compass** bounds   **48 prorogue** delay   **54 presently** at once.   **57 label** strip attached to a deed to carry the seal; hence, confirmation, seal   **59 both** i.e., hand and heart.   **60 time** age   **62 extremes** extreme difficulties   **64 commission** authority.   **art** skill   **66 so long** so slow. (With wordplay on *long,* "yearn," later in this same line.)

75 That . . . himself either (1) you who are willing to encounter Death by killing yourself, or (2) that simulates Death itself.   **it** this shame   **79 thievish ways** roads frequented by thieves   **81 charnel house** vault for human bones   **83 reeky** reeking, malodorous.   **chopless** without the lower jaw   **94 distilling** infusing the body, or distilled   **96 humor** fluid   **97 his native** its natural.   **surcease** cease   **100 wanny** wan, pale   **102 supple government** control of motion   **113 against** anticipating when   **114 drift** plan

And hither shall he come; and he and I
Will watch thy waking, and that very night   116
Shall Romeo bear thee hence to Mantua.
And this shall free thee from this present shame,
If no inconstant toy nor womanish fear   119
Abate thy valor in the acting it.

JULIET [taking the vial]
Give me, give me! Oh, tell not me of fear!

FRIAR LAURENCE
Hold, get you gone. Be strong and prosperous   122
In this resolve. I'll send a friar with speed
To Mantua, with my letters to thy lord.

JULIET
Love give me strength, and strength shall help afford.   125
Farewell, dear Father!   Exeunt [separately].

❖

[4.2]

Enter Father Capulet, Mother [Capulet's Wife],
Nurse, and Servingmen, two or three.

CAPULET
So many guests invite as here are writ.
                         [Exit one or two servingmen.]
Sirrah, go hire me twenty cunning cooks.   2
SERVINGMAN   You shall have none ill, sir, for I'll try if   3
they can lick their fingers.
CAPULET   How canst thou try them so?
SERVINGMAN   Marry, sir, 'tis an ill cook that cannot lick
his own fingers; therefore he that cannot lick his
fingers goes not with me.
CAPULET   Go, begone.   [Exit Servingman.]
We shall be much unfurnished for this time.   10
What, is my daughter gone to Friar Laurence?
NURSE   Ay, forsooth.
CAPULET
Well, he may chance to do some good on her.
A peevish self-willed harlotry it is.   14

        Enter Juliet.

NURSE
See where she comes from shrift with merry look.
CAPULET
How now, my headstrong, where have you been
    gadding?
JULIET
Where I have learned me to repent the sin
Of disobedient opposition
To you and your behests, and am enjoined   19
By holy Laurence to fall prostrate here,   [kneeling]
To beg your pardon. Pardon, I beseech you!
Henceforward I am ever ruled by you.
CAPULET
Send for the County! Go tell him of this.
I'll have this knot knit up tomorrow morning.

JULIET
I met the youthful lord at Laurence' cell
And gave him what becomèd love I might,   26
Not stepping o'er the bounds of modesty.
CAPULET
Why, I am glad on 't. This is well. Stand up.
                                     [Juliet rises.]
This is as 't should be. Let me see the County;
Ay, marry, go, I say, and fetch him hither.
Now, afore God, this reverend holy friar,
All our whole city is much bound to him.   32
JULIET
Nurse, will you go with me into my closet   33
To help me sort such needful ornaments   34
As you think fit to furnish me tomorrow?
WIFE
No, not till Thursday. There is time enough.
CAPULET
Go, Nurse, go with her. We'll to church tomorrow.
                         Exeunt [Juliet and Nurse].
WIFE
We shall be short in our provision.
'Tis now near night.
CAPULET   Tush, I will stir about,
And all things shall be well, I warrant thee, wife.
Go thou to Juliet, help to deck up her.
I'll not to bed tonight. Let me alone.   42
I'll play the huswife for this once.—What, ho!—   43
They are all forth. Well, I will walk myself
To County Paris, to prepare up him
Against tomorrow. My heart is wondrous light,
Since this same wayward girl is so reclaimed.
                                          Exeunt.

❖

[4.3]

Enter Juliet and Nurse.

JULIET
Ay, those attires are best. But, gentle Nurse,
I pray thee, leave me to myself tonight;
For I have need of many orisons   3
To move the heavens to smile upon my state,
Which, well thou knowest, is cross and full of sin.   5

        Enter Mother [Capulet's Wife].

WIFE
What, are you busy, ho? Need you my help?
JULIET
No, madam, we have culled such necessaries   7
As are behooveful for our state tomorrow.   8
So please you, let me now be left alone,
And let the Nurse this night sit up with you,

---

116 **watch** keep a watch over, be on hand for   119 **toy** idle fancy
122 **prosperous** successful   125 **help afford** provide help.
4.2. Location: Verona. Capulet's house.
2 **cunning** skilled   3 **none ill** no bad ones.   **try** test   10 **unfurnished** unprovided   14 **A peevish . . . is** i.e., She's a silly good-for-
nothing.   19 **behests** commands

26 **becomèd** befitting   32 **bound** indebted   33 **closet** chamber
34 **sort** choose   42 **Let me alone** Leave things to me.   43 **huswife**
housewife
4.3. Location: Verona. Capulet's house; Juliet's bed, enclosed by
bedcurtains, is set up in the discovery space.
3 **orisons** prayers   5 **cross** perverse   7 **culled** picked out
8 **behooveful** needful.   **state** ceremony

For I am sure you have your hands full all
In this so sudden business.
WIFE   Good night.
Get thee to bed and rest, for thou hast need.
                    Exeunt [Capulet's Wife and Nurse].

JULIET
Farewell! God knows when we shall meet again.
I have a faint cold fear thrills through my veins   15
That almost freezes up the heat of life.
I'll call them back again to comfort me.—
Nurse!—What should she do here?
My dismal scene I needs must act alone.
Come, vial.   [*She takes out the vial.*]
What if this mixture do not work at all?
Shall I be married then tomorrow morning?
No, no, this shall forbid it. Lie thou there.
                    [*She lays down a dagger.*]
What if it be a poison, which the Friar
Subtly hath ministered to have me dead,
Lest in this marriage he should be dishonored
Because he married me before to Romeo?
I fear it is; and yet methinks it should not,
For he hath still been tried a holy man.   29
How if, when I am laid into the tomb,
I wake before the time that Romeo
Come to redeem me? There's a fearful point!
Shall I not then be stifled in the vault,
To whose foul mouth no healthsome air breathes in,
And there die strangled ere my Romeo comes?
Or, if I live, is it not very like   36
The horrible conceit of death and night,   37
Together with the terror of the place—
As in a vault, an ancient receptacle,   39
Where for this many hundred years the bones
Of all my buried ancestors are packed;
Where bloody Tybalt, yet but green in earth,   42
Lies fest'ring in his shroud; where, as they say,
At some hours in the night spirits resort—
Alack, alack, is it not like that I,
So early waking, what with loathsome smells,
And shrieks like mandrakes torn out of the earth,   47
That living mortals, hearing them, run mad—   48
Oh, if I wake, shall I not be distraught,
Environèd with all these hideous fears,   50
And madly play with my forefathers' joints,
And pluck the mangled Tybalt from his shroud,
And in this rage, with some great kinsman's bone   53
As with a club dash out my desp'rate brains?
Oh, look! Methinks I see my cousin's ghost
Seeking out Romeo, that did spit his body   56

Upon a rapier's point. Stay, Tybalt, stay!   57
Romeo, Romeo, Romeo! Here's drink—I drink to thee.
                    [*She drinks and falls upon her bed,
                        within the curtains.*]

[4.4]

*Enter Lady of the House [Capulet's Wife]
and Nurse.*

WIFE
Hold, take these keys, and fetch more spices, Nurse.
NURSE
They call for dates and quinces in the pastry.   2

Enter old Capulet.

CAPULET
Come, stir, stir, stir! The second cock hath crowed.
The curfew bell hath rung; 'tis three o'clock.
Look to the baked meats, good Angelica.   5
Spare not for cost.
NURSE   Go, you cotquean, go,   6
Get you to bed. Faith, you'll be sick tomorrow
For this night's watching.   8
CAPULET
No, not a whit. What, I have watched ere now
All night for lesser cause, and ne'er been sick.
WIFE
Ay, you have been a mouse-hunt in your time,   11
But I will watch you from such watching now.   12
                    Exeunt Lady and Nurse.
CAPULET   A jealous hood, a jealous hood!   13

*Enter three or four [Servingmen] with spits and
logs, and baskets.*

Now, fellow, what is there?
FIRST SERVINGMAN
Things for the cook, sir, but I know not what.
CAPULET   Make haste, make haste. [*Exit First Servingman.*]
[*To Second Servingman*]   Sirrah, fetch drier logs.
Call Peter. He will show thee where they are.
SECOND SERVINGMAN
I have a head, sir, that will find out logs   18
And never trouble Peter for the matter.
CAPULET
Mass, and well said. A merry whoreson, ha!   20

---

57 Stay Stop, wait
4.4. Location: Scene continues. Juliet's bed remains visible.
2 pastry room in which pastry was made.   **5 baked meats** pies, pastry   **6 cotquean** i.e., a man who acts the housewife. (Literally, a cottage housewife.)   **8 watching** being awake.   **11 mouse-hunt** i.e., hunter of women. (Literally, a weasel.)   **12 watch . . . watching** i.e., keep an eye on you to prevent such nighttime activity. (Playing on *watching* in line 8.)   **13 A jealous hood** i.e., You wear the cap of jealousy   **18 I . . . logs** i.e., (1) I have a good head for finding things (2) My wooden head knows all about logs   **20 Mass** By the Mass. **whoreson** i.e., fellow. (An abusive term used familiarly.)

---

15 faint producing faintness.   **thrills** that pierces, shivers   **29 still been tried** always been tried and proven to be   **36 like** likely. (Also at line 45.)   **37 conceit** idea   **39 As** namely   **42 green** new, freshly **47 mandrakes** (The root of the mandragora or mandrake resembled the human form; the plant was fabled to utter a shriek when torn from the ground.)   **48 That** so that   **50 fears** objects of fear   **53 rage** madness.   **great** i.e., of an earlier generation, as in *great*-grandfather **56 spit** impale

Thou shalt be loggerhead.   [*Exit Servingman.*]
                              Good faith, 'tis day.   21
The County will be here with music straight,   22
For so he said he would.   *Play music* [*within*].
                    I hear him near.
Nurse! Wife! What, ho! What, Nurse, I say!

          Enter Nurse.

Go waken Juliet, go and trim her up.
I'll go and chat with Paris. Hie, make haste,
Make haste. The bridegroom he is come already.
Make haste, I say.   [*Exit Capulet.*]

                    ❧

[4.5]

          [*The Nurse goes to the bed.*]

NURSE
    Mistress! What, mistress! Juliet!—Fast, I warrant her,
        she.   1
    Why, lamb, why, lady! Fie, you slugabed!
    Why, love, I say! Madam! Sweetheart! Why, bride!
    What, not a word? You take your pennyworths now.   4
    Sleep for a week; for the next night, I warrant,
    The County Paris hath set up his rest   6
    That you shall rest but little. God forgive me,   7
    Marry, and amen! How sound is she asleep!   8
    I needs must wake her.—Madam, madam, madam!
    Ay, let the County take you in your bed;   10
    He'll fright you up, i'faith.—Will it not be?
                    [*She opens the bedcurtains.*]
    What, dressed, and in your clothes, and down again?
    I must needs wake you. Lady, lady, lady!
    Alas, alas! Help, help! My lady's dead!
    Oh, weraday, that ever I was born!
    Some aqua vitae, ho! My lord! My lady!   15
                                                        16

          [*Enter Capulet's Wife.*]

WIFE
    What noise is here?
NURSE
                    Oh, lamentable day!
WIFE
    What is the matter?
NURSE
                    Look, look! Oh, heavy day!   18
WIFE
    Oh, me, oh, me! My child, my only life!
    Revive, look up, or I will die with thee!
    Help, help! Call help.

          Enter Father [*Capulet*].

CAPULET
    For shame, bring Juliet forth. Her lord is come.

NURSE
    She's dead, deceased. She's dead, alack the day!
WIFE
    Alack the day, she's dead, she's dead, she's dead!
CAPULET
    Ha! Let me see her. Out, alas! She's cold.
    Her blood is settled, and her joints are stiff;   26
    Life and these lips have long been separated.
    Death lies on her like an untimely frost
    Upon the sweetest flower of all the field.
NURSE
    Oh, lamentable day!
WIFE
                    Oh, woeful time!
CAPULET
    Death, that hath ta'en her hence to make me wail,
    Ties up my tongue and will not let me speak.

          Enter Friar [*Laurence*] *and the County* [*Paris,
          with Musicians*].

FRIAR LAURENCE
    Come, is the bride ready to go to church?
CAPULET
    Ready to go, but never to return.
    Oh, son, the night before thy wedding day
    Hath Death lain with thy wife. There she lies,
    Flower as she was, deflowered by him.
    Death is my son-in-law, Death is my heir;
    My daughter he hath wedded. I will die,
    And leave him all; life, living, all is Death's.   40
PARIS
    Have I thought long to see this morning's face,   41
    And doth it give me such a sight as this?
WIFE
    Accurst, unhappy, wretched, hateful day!
    Most miserable hour that e'er time saw
    In lasting labor of his pilgrimage!   45
    But one, poor one, one poor and loving child,
    But one thing to rejoice and solace in,
    And cruel Death hath catched it from my sight!
NURSE
    O woe! O woeful, woeful, woeful day!
    Most lamentable day, most woeful day
    That ever, ever I did yet behold!
    O day, O day, O day! O hateful day!
    Never was seen so black a day as this.
    O woeful day, O woeful day!
PARIS
    Beguiled, divorcèd, wrongèd, spited, slain!
    Most detestable Death, by thee beguiled,
    By cruel, cruel thee quite overthrown!
    O love! O life! Not life, but love in death!
CAPULET
    Despised, distressèd, hated, martyred, killed!
    Uncomfortable time, why cam'st thou now   60

---

21 loggerhead (1) put in charge of getting logs (2) a blockhead.
22 straight straightway, immediately
4.5. Location: Scene continues. Juliet's bed remains visible.
1 Fast Fast asleep   **4 pennyworths** small portions (of sleep)   **6 set . . .
rest** staked his all, resolved to play all out. (From the card game of
primero, here with obviously bawdy meaning.)   **7–8 God . . . amen!**
(The Nurse apologizes amiably for her bawdy talk.)   **10 take . . . bed**
(1) find you still abed (2) possess you sexually   **15 weraday** wellaway,
alas   **16 aqua vitae** strong alcoholic spirits   **18 heavy** sorrowful

26 settled congealed   **40 living** means of living, property
41–64 Have . . . buried (A stage direction in the First Quarto, "*All at
once cry out and wring their hands,*" may suggest that the four mourners are to speak simultaneously, a possibility since all have six lines of
text.)   **45 lasting** unceasing   **60 Uncomfortable** Comfortless

To murder, murder our solemnity?   61
O child! O child! My soul, and not my child!
Dead art thou! Alack, my child is dead,
And with my child my joys are burièd.

FRIAR LAURENCE
Peace, ho, for shame! Confusion's cure lives not   65
In these confusions. Heaven and yourself
Had part in this fair maid; now heaven hath all,
And all the better is it for the maid.
Your part in her you could not keep from death,   69
But heaven keeps his part in eternal life.
The most you sought was her promotion,   71
For 'twas your heaven she should be advanced;   72
And weep ye now, seeing she is advanced
Above the clouds, as high as heaven itself?
Oh, in this love you love your child so ill
That you run mad, seeing that she is well.
She's not well married that lives married long,
But she's best married that dies married young.
Dry up your tears, and stick your rosemary   79
On this fair corpse, and, as the custom is,
And in her best array, bear her to church;
For though fond nature bids us all lament,   82
Yet nature's tears are reason's merriment.   83

CAPULET
All things that we ordainèd festival   84
Turn from their office to black funeral: 85
Our instruments to melancholy bells,
Our wedding cheer to a sad burial feast,
Our solemn hymns to sullen dirges change,   88
Our bridal flowers serve for a buried corpse,
And all things change them to the contrary.   90

FRIAR LAURENCE
Sir, go you in, and, madam, go with him,
And go, Sir Paris. Everyone prepare
To follow this fair corpse unto her grave.
The heavens do lour upon you for some ill;   94
Move them no more by crossing their high will.   95
                    Exeunt. Manet [Nurse with Musicians].

FIRST MUSICIAN
Faith, we may put up our pipes and be gone.

NURSE
Honest good fellows, ah, put up, put up!
For well you know this is a pitiful case.   [*Exit.*]

FIRST MUSICIAN
Ay, by my troth, the case may be amended.   99

        Enter Peter.

PETER   Musicians, oh, musicians, "Heart's ease,"   100
"Heart's ease." Oh, an you will have me live, play
"Heart's ease."
FIRST MUSICIAN   Why "Heart's ease"?   64
PETER   Oh, musicians, because my heart itself plays "My
heart is full." Oh, play me some merry dump to   105
comfort me.
FIRST MUSICIAN   Not a dump we! 'Tis no time to play
now.
PETER   You will not, then?
FIRST MUSICIAN   No.
PETER   I will then give it you soundly.
FIRST MUSICIAN   What will you give us?
PETER   No money, on my faith, but the gleek; I will give   113
you the minstrel.   114
FIRST MUSICIAN   Then will I give you the serving-   115
creature.   116
PETER   Then will I lay the serving-creature's dagger on   117
your pate. I will carry no crotchets. I'll re you, I'll fa   118
you. Do you note me?   119
FIRST MUSICIAN   An you re us and fa us, you note us.
SECOND MUSICIAN   Pray you, put up your dagger and   121
put out your wit.   122
PETER   Then have at you with my wit! I will dry-beat   123
you with an iron wit, and put up my iron dagger.
Answer me like men:
        "When griping griefs the heart doth wound,   126
            And doleful dumps the mind oppress,
        Then music with her silver sound—"   128
Why "silver sound"? Why "music with her silver
sound"? What say you, Simon Catling?   130
FIRST MUSICIAN   Marry, sir, because silver hath a sweet
sound.
PETER   Pretty! What say you, Hugh Rebeck?   133
SECOND MUSICIAN   I say "silver sound" because musi-
cians sound for silver.   135
PETER   Pretty too! What say you, James Soundpost?   136
THIRD MUSICIAN   Faith, I know not what to say.

---

61 **solemnity** ceremony, festivity. 65 **Confusion's** Calamity's 69 **Your part** i.e., The mortal part you begot 71 **promotion** social advancement 72 **your heaven** i.e., your idea of the greatest good 79 **rosemary** symbol of immortality and enduring love; therefore used at both funerals and weddings 82 **fond nature** foolish human nature 83 **nature's... merriment** that which causes human nature to weep is an occasion of joy to reason. 84 **ordainèd festival** intended to be festive 85 **office** function 88 **sullen** mournful 90 **them** themselves 94 **lour...ill** frown upon you because of some sinfulness 95 **Move** anger.
95.1 **Manet** She remains onstage 99 **the case...amended** things generally could be much better. (With a punning suggestion of an instrument case that is in need of repair.) 99.1 **Peter** (The Second Quarto has *Enter Will Kemp*, the actor for whom Shakespeare or perhaps the bookkeeper intended this role.)

100 **"Heart's ease"** (A popular ballad; so too with "My heart is full" in lines 104–5.) 105 **dump** mournful tune or dance 113 **gleek** scornful rebuke 113–14 **I will... minstrel** I will insult you by calling you what you are, a minstrel. (Minstrels were widely regarded as vagabonds.) 115–16 **Then... serving-creature** Then I'll insult you right back by calling you what you are, a servant. 117–18 **Then... crotchets** Then I'll knock you about the head with my dagger. I'll not put up with your whims. (*Crotchets* are also quarter notes, appropriate to the musicians' trade.) 118–19 **I'll re... me?** i.e., I'll give you a thrashing, do you hear? (Again using musical terms: *re* and *fa* are the names of notes, and *note* can mean "set to music.") 121–2 **put up... wit** sheathe your dagger and stop being a smart aleck. (But *put up* and *put out* can also mean "display." Peter chooses to answer to this meaning.) 123 **have at you** here I come. **dry-beat** thrash (without drawing blood) 126–8 **"When... sound"** (From Richard Edwards's song, "In Commendation of Music," published in *The Paradise of Dainty Devices*, 1576.) 130 **Catling** (A catling was a small lute-string made of catgut.) 133 **Rebeck** (A rebeck was a fiddle with three strings.) 135 **sound** make music 136 **Soundpost** (A soundpost is the pillar or peg that supports the sounding board of a stringed instrument.)

PETER Oh, I cry you mercy, you are the singer. I will say 138
for you. It is "music with her silver sound" because
musicians have no gold for sounding: 140
          "Then music with her silver sound
              With speedy help doth lend redress."   *Exit.*
FIRST MUSICIAN   What a pestilent knave is this same!
SECOND MUSICIAN   Hang him, Jack! Come, we'll in here,
tarry for the mourners, and stay dinner.   *Exeunt.* 145

❧

[5.1]

Enter Romeo.

ROMEO
If I may trust the flattering truth of sleep,   1
My dreams presage some joyful news at hand.
My bosom's lord sits lightly in his throne,   3
And all this day an unaccustomed spirit
Lifts me above the ground with cheerful thoughts.
I dreamt my lady came and found me dead—
Strange dream, that gives a dead man leave to
    think!—
And breathed such life with kisses in my lips
That I revived and was an emperor.
Ah me, how sweet is love itself possessed   10
When but love's shadows are so rich in joy!   11

Enter Romeo's man [Balthasar, booted].

News from Verona! How now, Balthasar,
Dost thou not bring me letters from the Friar?
How doth my lady? Is my father well?
How fares my Juliet? That I ask again,
For nothing can be ill if she be well.
BALTHASAR
Then she is well, and nothing can be ill.
Her body sleeps in Capels' monument,
And her immortal part with angels lives.
I saw her laid low in her kindred's vault,
And presently took post to tell it you.   21
Oh, pardon me for bringing these ill news,
Since you did leave it for my office, sir.   23
ROMEO
Is it e'en so? Then I defy you, stars!—
Thou knowest my lodging. Get me ink and paper,
And hire post-horses. I will hence tonight.
BALTHASAR
I do beseech you, sir, have patience.
Your looks are pale and wild, and do import   28
Some misadventure.
ROMEO   Tush, thou art deceived.
Leave me, and do the thing I bid thee do.
Hast thou no letters to me from the Friar?

BALTHASAR
No, my good lord.
ROMEO   No matter. Get thee gone,
And hire those horses. I'll be with thee straight.
                            Exit [Balthasar].
Well, Juliet, I will lie with thee tonight.
Let's see for means. O mischief, thou art swift   35
To enter in the thoughts of desperate men!
I do remember an apothecary—   37
And hereabouts 'a dwells—which late I noted   38
In tattered weeds, with overwhelming brows,   39
Culling of simples. Meager were his looks;   40
Sharp misery had worn him to the bones;
And in his needy shop a tortoise hung,
An alligator stuffed, and other skins
Of ill-shaped fishes; and about his shelves
A beggarly account of empty boxes,   45
Green earthen pots, bladders, and musty seeds,
Remnants of packthread, and old cakes of roses   47
Were thinly scattered to make up a show.
Noting this penury, to myself I said,
"An if a man did need a poison now,   50
Whose sale is present death in Mantua,   51
Here lives a caitiff wretch would sell it him."   52
Oh, this same thought did but forerun my need,
And this same needy man must sell it me.
As I remember, this should be the house.
Being holiday, the beggar's shop is shut.—
What, ho! Apothecary!

[Enter Apothecary.]

APOTHECARY   Who calls so loud?
ROMEO
Come hither, man. I see that thou art poor.
Hold, there is forty ducats. [*He shows gold.*] Let me
    have   59
A dram of poison, such soon-speeding gear   60
As will disperse itself through all the veins
That the life-weary taker may fall dead,
And that the trunk may be discharged of breath   63
As violently as hasty powder fired
Doth hurry from the fatal cannon's womb.
APOTHECARY
Such mortal drugs I have, but Mantua's law   66
Is death to any he that utters them.   67
ROMEO
Art thou so bare and full of wretchedness,
And fearest to die? Famine is in thy cheeks,

---

138 cry you mercy beg your pardon **140 have . . . sounding** i.e., (1)
are paid only silver for playing (2) have no gold to jingle in their
pockets **145 stay** await
5.1. Location: Mantua. A street.
1 flattering i.e., telling me what I want to believe **3 bosom's lord**
i.e., heart **10 itself possessed** actually enjoyed **11 love's shadows**
dreams of love **11.1 *booted*** wearing riding boots—a conventional
stage sign of traveling **21 presently took post** at once started off
with post-horses **23 for my office** as my duty **28 import** denote

35 for means by what means. **37 apothecary** druggist **38 which . . .
noted** whom lately I noticed **39 weeds** garments. **overwhelming
brows** forehead and eyebrows jutting out over his eyes **40 simples**
medicinal herbs. **Meager** Impoverished **45 beggarly account** poor
array **47 cakes of roses** petals pressed into cakes to be used as perfume **50 An if** If **51 present** immediate **52 caitiff** miserable.
would who would **59 ducats** gold coins. **60 soon-speeding gear**
quickly effective stuff **63 trunk** body **66 mortal** deadly **67 any he**
anyone. **utters** issues, sells

Need and oppression starveth in thy eyes,   70
Contempt and beggary hangs upon thy back.
The world is not thy friend, nor the world's law;
The world affords no law to make thee rich.
Then be not poor, but break it, and take this.

APOTHECARY
My poverty but not my will consents.

ROMEO
I pay thy poverty and not thy will.

APOTHECARY [*giving poison*]
Put this in any liquid thing you will
And drink it off, and if you had the strength
Of twenty men it would dispatch you straight.

ROMEO [*giving gold*]
There is thy gold—worse poison to men's souls,
Doing more murder in this loathsome world
Than these poor compounds that thou mayst not sell.
I sell thee poison; thou hast sold me none.
Farewell. Buy food, and get thyself in flesh.
                                   [*Exit Apothecary.*]
Come, cordial and not poison, go with me   85
To Juliet's grave, for there must I use thee.   *Exit.*

❧

[5.2]

Enter Friar John to Friar Laurence.

FRIAR JOHN
Holy Franciscan friar! Brother, ho!

Enter [Friar] Laurence.

FRIAR LAURENCE
This same should be the voice of Friar John.
Welcome from Mantua! What says Romeo?
Or if his mind be writ, give me his letter.

FRIAR JOHN
Going to find a barefoot brother out—
One of our order—to associate me   6
Here in this city visiting the sick,
And finding him, the searchers of the town,   8
Suspecting that we both were in a house
Where the infectious pestilence did reign,
Sealed up the doors and would not let us forth,
So that my speed to Mantua there was stayed.   12

FRIAR LAURENCE
Who bare my letter, then, to Romeo?

FRIAR JOHN
I could not send it—here it is again—
Nor get a messenger to bring it thee,
So fearful were they of infection.   [*He gives a letter.*]

FRIAR LAURENCE
Unhappy fortune! By my brotherhood,
The letter was not nice but full of charge,   18
Of dear import, and the neglecting it   19
May do much danger. Friar John, go hence.
Get me an iron crow and bring it straight   21
Unto my cell.

FRIAR JOHN   Brother, I'll go and bring it thee.   *Exit.*

FRIAR LAURENCE
Now must I to the monument alone.
Within this three hours will fair Juliet wake.
She will beshrew me much that Romeo   26
Hath had no notice of these accidents;   27
But I will write again to Mantua,
And keep her at my cell till Romeo come—
Poor living corpse, closed in a dead man's tomb!
                                              Exit.

❧

[5.3]

*Enter Paris, and his Page [bearing flowers, per-
fumed water, and a torch. Juliet, lying in seeming death atop her bier and perhaps concealed at
first from the audience's view, is understood to
be in the Capulets' burial vault, with Tybalt's
body also there.]*

PARIS
Give me thy torch, boy. Hence, and stand aloof.   1
Yet put it out, for I would not be seen.
Under yond yew trees lay thee all along,   3
Holding thy ear close to the hollow ground.
So shall no foot upon the churchyard tread,
Being loose, unfirm, with digging up of graves,   6
But thou shalt hear it. Whistle then to me
As signal that thou hearest something approach.
Give me those flowers. Do as I bid thee. Go.

PAGE [*aside*]
I am almost afraid to stand alone   10
Here in the churchyard, yet I will adventure.
                                       [*He retires.*]

PARIS [*strewing flowers and perfumed water*]
Sweet flower, with flowers thy bridal bed I strew— 12
    Oh, woe! Thy canopy is dust and stones—   13
Which with sweet water nightly I will dew,   14
    Or wanting that, with tears distilled by moans. 15
The obsequies that I for thee will keep   16
Nightly shall be to strew thy grave and weep.
                                     Whistle Boy.

The boy gives warning something doth approach.
What cursèd foot wanders this way tonight

---

18 **nice** trivial.   **charge** importance   19 **dear** precious, urgent   21 **crow** crowbar   26 **beshrew** i.e., reprove   27 **accidents** events
5.3. **Location:** Verona. A churchyard and the vault or tomb belong- ing to the Capulets. Juliet's bier may be thrust onstage from the "discovery" space or may be concealed until the tomb is "opened" by Romeo at 83.1, perhaps by the drawing back of curtains.
1 **aloof** to one side, at a distance.   3 **all along** at full length   6 **Being** i.e., the soil being   10 **stand** stay   12 **Sweet flower** i.e., Juliet
13 **canopy** covering   14 **sweet** perfumed.   **dew** moisten   15 **wanting** lacking   16 **obsequies** ceremonies in memory of the dead

---

70 **starveth** are revealed by the starving look   85 **cordial** restorative for the heart
5.2. **Location:** Verona. Friar Laurence's cell.
6 **associate** accompany   8 **searchers of the town** town officials charged with public health (and especially concerned about the *pestilence* or plague)   12 **speed** successful journey, progress.   **stayed** stopped.

To cross my obsequies and true love's rite? 20
What, with a torch? Muffle me, night, awhile. 21

[He retires.]

Enter Romeo and Balthasar, [with a torch, a
mattock, and a crowbar].

ROMEO
Give me that mattock and the wrenching iron. 22

[He takes the tools.]

Hold, take this letter. Early in the morning
See thou deliver it to my lord and father.

[He gives a letter and takes a torch.]

Give me the light. Upon thy life I charge thee,
Whate'er thou hearest or see'st, stand all aloof
And do not interrupt me in my course. 27
Why I descend into this bed of death
Is partly to behold my lady's face,
But chiefly to take thence from her dead finger
A precious ring—a ring that I must use
In dear employment. Therefore hence, begone. 32
But if thou, jealous, dost return to pry 33
In what I farther shall intend to do,
By heaven, I will tear thee joint by joint
And strew this hungry churchyard with thy limbs. 36
The time and my intents are savage-wild,
More fierce and more inexorable far
Than empty tigers or the roaring sea. 39

BALTHASAR
I will be gone, sir, and not trouble ye.

ROMEO
So shalt thou show me friendship. Take thou that.

[He gives him money.]

Live, and be prosperous; and farewell, good fellow.

BALTHASAR *[aside]*
For all this same, I'll hide me hereabout. 43
His looks I fear, and his intents I doubt. *[He retires.]* 44

ROMEO
Thou detestable maw, thou womb of death, 45
Gorged with the dearest morsel of the earth,
Thus I enforce thy rotten jaws to open,
And in despite I'll cram thee with more food. 48

[He begins to open the tomb.]

PARIS
This is that banished haughty Montague
That murdered my love's cousin, with which grief
It is supposèd the fair creature died,
And here is come to do some villainous shame
To the dead bodies. I will apprehend him.

[He comes forward.]

Stop thy unhallowed toil, vile Montague!
Can vengeance be pursued further than death?

Condemnèd villain, I do apprehend thee.
Obey and go with me, for thou must die.

ROMEO
I must indeed, and therefore came I hither.
Good gentle youth, tempt not a desperate man.
Fly hence and leave me. Think upon these gone; 60
Let them affright thee. I beseech thee, youth,
Put not another sin upon my head
By urging me to fury. Oh, begone!
By heaven, I love thee better than myself,
For I come hither armed against myself.
Stay not, begone. Live, and hereafter say
A madman's mercy bid thee run away.

PARIS
I do defy thy conjuration, 68
And apprehend thee for a felon here.

ROMEO
Wilt thou provoke me? Then have at thee, boy!

[They fight.]

PAGE
Oh, Lord, they fight! I will go call the watch. *[Exit.]*

PARIS
Oh, I am slain! *[He falls.]* If thou be merciful,
Open the tomb, lay me with Juliet. *[He dies.]*

ROMEO
In faith, I will. Let me peruse this face.
Mercutio's kinsman, noble County Paris!
What said my man when my betossèd soul
Did not attend him as we rode? I think
He told me Paris should have married Juliet. 78
Said he not so? Or did I dream it so?
Or am I mad, hearing him talk of Juliet,
To think it was so? Oh, give me thy hand,
One writ with me in sour misfortune's book.
I'll bury thee in a triumphant grave.

[He opens the tomb.]

A grave? Oh, no! A lantern, slaughtered youth, 84
For here lies Juliet, and her beauty makes
This vault a feasting presence full of light. 86
Death, lie thou there, by a dead man interred.

[He lays Paris in the tomb.]

How oft when men are at the point of death
Have they been merry, which their keepers call 89
A lightening before death! Oh, how may I 90
Call this a lightening? O my love, my wife!
Death, that hath sucked the honey of thy breath,
Hath had no power yet upon thy beauty.
Thou art not conquered; beauty's ensign yet 94
Is crimson in thy lips and in thy cheeks,
And death's pale flag is not advancèd there. 96
Tybalt, liest thou there in thy bloody sheet? 97
Oh, what more favor can I do to thee
Than with that hand that cut thy youth in twain
To sunder his that was thine enemy? 100

---

20 cross interrupt   **21 Muffle** Conceal.   **22 wrenching iron** crowbar.
27 course intended action.   **32 dear employment** important business.
33 jealous suspicious   **36 hungry** hungry for corpses   **39 empty**
hungry   **43 For all this same** All the same   **44 fear** distrust.   **doubt**
suspect.   **45 womb** belly   **48 in despite** defiantly   **48.1 He . . . tomb**
Whether the tomb is represented by a bier thrust onstage or by a curtained recess (see indication of scene location above at the start of
5.3), Romeo may mime the action here and at line 83.1 of using tools
to open it.

60 gone dead   **68 conjuration** solemn entreaty   **78 should have** was
to have   **84 lantern** turret room full of windows   **86 feasting pres-**
ence reception chamber for feasting   **89 keepers** attendants, jailers
90 lightening exhilaration (supposed to occur just before death)
94 ensign banner   **96 advancèd** raised   **97 sheet** shroud.   **100 his**
i.e., my (Romeo's) own

Forgive me, cousin!—Ah, dear Juliet,
Why art thou yet so fair? Shall I believe
That unsubstantial Death is amorous,   103
And that the lean abhorrèd monster keeps
Thee here in dark to be his paramour?
For fear of that I still will stay with thee   106
And never from this palace of dim night
Depart again. Here, here will I remain
With worms that are thy chambermaids. Oh, here
Will I set up my everlasting rest   110
And shake the yoke of inauspicious stars
From this world-wearied flesh. Eyes, look your last!
Arms, take your last embrace! And lips, O you
The doors of breath, seal with a righteous kiss
A dateless bargain to engrossing death!   115
                              [*He kisses Juliet.*]
Come, bitter conduct, come, unsavory guide,   116
Thou desperate pilot, now at once run on   117
The dashing rocks thy seasick weary bark!
Here's to my love. [*He drinks.*] O true apothecary!
Thy drugs are quick. Thus with a kiss I die. [*He dies.*]

> *Enter Friar [Laurence] with lantern, crow,*
> *and spade.*

FRIAR LAURENCE
Saint Francis be my speed! How oft tonight   121
Have my old feet stumbled at graves! Who's there?
BALTHASAR
Here's one, a friend, and one that knows you well.
FRIAR LAURENCE
Bliss be upon you. Tell me, good my friend,
What torch is yond that vainly lends his light   125
To grubs and eyeless skulls? As I discern,   126
It burneth in the Capels' monument.
BALTHASAR
It doth so, holy sir, and there's my master,
One that you love.
FRIAR LAURENCE   Who is it?
BALTHASAR   Romeo.
FRIAR LAURENCE
How long hath he been there?
BALTHASAR   Full half an hour.
FRIAR LAURENCE
Go with me to the vault.
BALTHASAR   I dare not, sir.
My master knows not but I am gone hence,
And fearfully did menace me with death
If I did stay to look on his intents.
FRIAR LAURENCE
Stay, then, I'll go alone. Fear comes upon me.
Oh, much I fear some ill unthrifty thing.   136

BALTHASAR
As I did sleep under this yew tree here
I dreamt my master and another fought,
And that my master slew him.
FRIAR LAURENCE [*advancing to the tomb*]   Romeo!
Alack, alack, what blood is this which stains
The stony entrance of this sepulcher?
What mean these masterless and gory swords
To lie discolored by this place of peace?   143
                              [*He looks in the tomb.*]
Romeo! Oh, pale! Who else? What, Paris too?
And steeped in blood? Ah, what an unkind hour   145
Is guilty of this lamentable chance!
The lady stirs.   [*Juliet wakes.*]
JULIET
O comfortable Friar, where is my lord?   148
I do remember well where I should be,
And there I am. Where is my Romeo?
                              [*A noise within.*]
FRIAR LAURENCE
I hear some noise. Lady, come from that nest
Of death, contagion, and unnatural sleep.
A greater power than we can contradict
Hath thwarted our intents. Come, come away.
Thy husband in thy bosom there lies dead,
And Paris, too. Come, I'll dispose of thee
Among a sisterhood of holy nuns.
Stay not to question, for the watch is coming.
Come, go, good Juliet. [*A noise again.*] I dare no longer
     stay.   *Exit [Friar Laurence]*.
JULIET
Go, get thee hence, for I will not away.
What's here? A cup, closed in my true love's hand?
Poison, I see, hath been his timeless end.   162
O churl, drunk all, and left no friendly drop   163
To help me after? I will kiss thy lips;
Haply some poison yet doth hang on them,   165
To make me die with a restorative.   [*She kisses him.*]
Thy lips are warm.

> *Enter [Paris's] Boy and Watch.*

FIRST WATCH   Lead, boy. Which way?
JULIET
Yea, noise? Then I'll be brief. O happy dagger!   169
                              [*She takes Romeo's dagger.*]
This is thy sheath. There rust, and let me die.
                              [*She stabs herself and dies.*]
PAGE
This is the place, there where the torch doth burn.
FIRST WATCH
The ground is bloody. Search about the churchyard.
Go, some of you, whoe'er you find attach.   173
                              [*Exeunt some.*]
Pitiful sight! Here lies the County slain,

---

103 unsubstantial lacking material existence   **106 still** always
110 set . . . rest (See 4.5.6. The meaning is, "make my final determination," with allusion to the idea of repose.)   **115 dateless bargain**
everlasting contract.   **engrossing** monopolizing, taking all; also,
drawing up the contract   **116 conduct** guide (i.e., the poison)
117 desperate reckless, despairing   **121 be my speed** prosper me and
let me arrive in time.   **125 vainly** uselessly   **126 grubs** insect larvae
136 unthrifty unfortunate.

143.1 He looks . . . tomb Whether the Friar is to enter the tomb
depends on staging arrangements.   **145 unkind** unnatural
148 comfortable comforting   **162 timeless** (1) untimely (2) everlasting   **163 churl** miser   **165 Haply** perhaps   **169 happy** opportune
173 attach arrest, detain.

And Juliet bleeding, warm, and newly dead,
Who here hath lain these two days burièd.
Go tell the Prince. Run to the Capulets.
Raise up the Montagues. Some others search.
                          [Exeunt others.]
We see the ground whereon these woes do lie,
But the true ground of all these piteous woes   180
We cannot without circumstance descry.   181

        Enter [some of the Watch, with] Romeo's
        man [Balthasar].

SECOND WATCH
Here's Romeo's man. We found him in the
churchyard.
FIRST WATCH
Hold him in safety till the Prince come hither.   183

        Enter Friar [Laurence], and another Watchman
        [with tools].

THIRD WATCH
Here is a friar, that trembles, sighs, and weeps.
We took this mattock and this spade from him
As he was coming from this churchyard's side.
FIRST WATCH
A great suspicion. Stay the Friar, too.   187

        Enter the Prince [and attendants].

PRINCE
What misadventure is so early up
That calls our person from our morning rest?   189

        Enter Capels [Capulet and his Wife].

CAPULET
What should it be that is so shrieked abroad?
CAPULET'S WIFE
Oh, the people in the street cry "Romeo,"
Some "Juliet," and some "Paris," and all run
With open outcry toward our monument.
PRINCE
What fear is this which startles in our ears?   194
FIRST WATCH
Sovereign, here lies the County Paris slain,
And Romeo dead, and Juliet, dead before,
Warm and new killed.
PRINCE
Search, seek, and know how this foul murder comes.   198
FIRST WATCH
Here is a friar, and slaughtered Romeo's man,
With instruments upon them fit to open   200
These dead men's tombs.
CAPULET
O heavens! O wife, look how our daughter bleeds!
This dagger hath mista'en, for lo, his house   203
Is empty on the back of Montague,
And it mis-sheathèd in my daughter's bosom!

CAPULET'S WIFE
Oh, me! This sight of death is as a bell
That warns my old age to a sepulcher.

        Enter Montague.

PRINCE
Come, Montague, for thou art early up
To see thy son and heir more early down.
MONTAGUE
Alas, my liege, my wife is dead tonight;
Grief of my son's exile hath stopped her breath.
What further woe conspires against mine age?
PRINCE   Look, and thou shalt see.
MONTAGUE [seeing Romeo's body]
O thou untaught! What manners is in this,   214
To press before thy father to a grave?   215
PRINCE
Seal up the mouth of outrage for a while,   216
Till we can clear these ambiguities
And know their spring, their head, their true descent; 218
And then will I be general of your woes   219
And lead you even to death. Meantime, forbear,   220
And let mischance be slave to patience.   221
Bring forth the parties of suspicion.   222
FRIAR LAURENCE
I am the greatest, able to do least,
Yet most suspected, as the time and place
Doth make against me, of this direful murder;   225
And here I stand, both to impeach and purge   226
Myself condemnèd and myself excused.   227
PRINCE
Then say at once what thou dost know in this.
FRIAR LAURENCE
I will be brief, for my short date of breath   229
Is not so long as is a tedious tale.
Romeo, there dead, was husband to that Juliet,
And she, there dead, that Romeo's faithful wife.
I married them, and their stol'n marriage day
Was Tybalt's doomsday, whose untimely death
Banished the new-made bridegroom from this city,
For whom, and not for Tybalt, Juliet pined.
You, to remove that siege of grief from her,
Betrothed and would have married her perforce   238
To County Paris. Then comes she to me,
And with wild looks bid me devise some means
To rid her from this second marriage,
Or in my cell there would she kill herself.
Then gave I her—so tutored by my art—
A sleeping potion, which so took effect
As I intended, for it wrought on her   245
The form of death. Meantime I writ to Romeo   246

180 **ground** basis. (Playing on the meaning "earth" in line 179.) 181
circumstance details 183 **in safety** under guard 187 **Stay** Detain
189 **our person** (The royal "we.") 194 **startles** cries alarmingly
198 **know** learn 200 **instruments** tools 203 **his house** its scabbard

214 **untaught** ill-mannered youth. (Said with affectionate irony.)
215 **press** hasten, go 216 **mouth of outrage** (1) popular outcry (2)
entrance to the tomb 218 **spring, head** (Both words mean "source.")
219 **be . . . woes** be leader in lamentation 220 **even to death** in
lamentation for the dead. 221 **let . . . patience** i.e., let us bear our
misfortune patiently. 222 **of** under 225 **make** conspire, tell
226–7 **to . . . excused** to accuse myself of what is to be condemned in
me and to exonerate myself where I ought to be excused. 229 **date
of breath** time left to live 238 **perforce** by compulsion 245 **wrought**
fashioned 246 **form** appearance

That he should hither come as this dire night   247
To help to take her from her borrowed grave,
Being the time the potion's force should cease.
But he which bore my letter, Friar John,
Was stayed by accident, and yesternight   251
Returned my letter back. Then all alone
At the prefixèd hour of her waking
Came I to take her from her kindred's vault,
Meaning to keep her closely at my cell   255
Till I conveniently could send to Romeo.
But when I came, some minute ere the time
Of her awakening, here untimely lay
The noble Paris and true Romeo dead.
She wakes, and I entreated her come forth
And bear this work of heaven with patience.
But then a noise did scare me from the tomb,
And she, too desperate, would not go with me,
But, as it seems, did violence on herself.
All this I know, and to the marriage
Her nurse is privy; and if aught in this   266
Miscarried by my fault, let my old life
Be sacrificed some hour before his time   268
Unto the rigor of severest law.

PRINCE
We still have known thee for a holy man.   270
Where's Romeo's man? What can he say to this?

BALTHASAR
I brought my master news of Juliet's death,
And then in post he came from Mantua   273
To this same place, to this same monument.
This letter he early bid me give his father,   275
                    [*showing a letter*]
And threatened me with death, going in the vault,
If I departed not and left him there.

PRINCE [*taking the letter*]
Give me the letter. I will look on it.
Where is the County's page, that raised the watch?
Sirrah, what made your master in this place?   280

PAGE   247
He came with flowers to strew his lady's grave,
And bid me stand aloof, and so I did.
Anon comes one with light to ope the tomb,
And by and by my master drew on him,   251
And then I ran away to call the watch.

PRINCE
This letter doth make good the Friar's words,
Their course of love, the tidings of her death;
And here he writes that he did buy a poison
Of a poor 'pothecary, and therewithal   289
Came to this vault to die, and lie with Juliet.
Where be these enemies? Capulet, Montague,
See what a scourge is laid upon your hate,
That heaven finds means to kill your joys with love.   293
And I, for winking at your discords, too   294
Have lost a brace of kinsmen. All are punished.   295

CAPULET
O brother Montague, give me thy hand.
This is my daughter's jointure, for no more   297
Can I demand.

MONTAGUE   But I can give thee more,
For I will raise her statue in pure gold,   299
That whiles Verona by that name is known
There shall no figure at such rate be set   301
As that of true and faithful Juliet.

CAPULET
As rich shall Romeo's by his lady's lie;
Poor sacrifices of our enmity!

PRINCE
A glooming peace this morning with it brings;
    The sun, for sorrow, will not show his head.
Go hence to have more talk of these sad things.
    Some shall be pardoned, and some punishèd;
For never was a story of more woe
Than this of Juliet and her Romeo.   [*Exeunt.*]

247 as this this very   **251 stayed** stopped   **255 closely** secretly
266 privy in on the secret   **268 his** its   **270 still** always   **273 post**
haste   **275 This . . . father** He bade me give this letter to his father
early in the morning (5.3.23–4)   **280 made** did

289 therewithal with the poison   **293 kill your joys** (1) destroy your
happiness (2) kill your children.   **with** by means of   **294 winking at**
shutting my eyes to   **295 a brace** of two   **297 jointure** marriage
settlement   **299 raise** (The Second Quarto reading, "raie," is defended
by some editors in the sense of "array," make ready.)   **301 rate** value

Julius Caesar

Julius Caesar stands midway in Shakespeare's dramatic career, at a critical juncture. In some ways, it is an epilogue to his English history plays of the 1590s; in other ways, it introduces the period of the great tragedies. The play evidently was first performed at the new Globe playhouse in the fall of 1599, shortly after *Henry V* (the last of Shakespeare's history plays about medieval England) and around the time of *As You Like It* (one of the last of Shakespeare's happy romantic comedies). It shortly preceded *Hamlet.* It is placed among the tragedies in the Folio of 1623, where it was first published, and is entitled *The Tragedy of Julius Caesar,* but in the table of contents it is listed as *The Life and Death of Julius Caesar* as though it were a history.

Julius Caesar shares with Shakespeare's history plays an absorption in the problems of civil war and popular unrest. Rome, like England, suffers an internal division that is reflected in the perturbed state of the heavens themselves. The commoners, or plebeians, are easily swayed by demagogues. Opportunists prosper in this atmosphere of crisis, although fittingly even they are sometimes undone by their own scheming. Politics seems to require a morality quite apart from that of personal life, posing a tragic dilemma for Brutus, as it did for Richard II or Henry VI. The blending of history and tragedy in *Julius Caesar,* then, is not unlike that found in several English history plays. Rome was a natural subject to which Shakespeare might turn in his continuing depiction of political behavior. Roman culture had recently been elevated to new importance by the classical orientation of the Renaissance. As a model of political organization, it loomed larger in Elizabethan consciousness than it does in ours, because so few other models were available and because Greek culture was less accessible in language and tradition. According to a widely accepted mythology, Elizabethans considered themselves descended from the Romans through another Brutus, the great-grandson of Aeneas.

Yet the differences between Roman and English history are as important as the similarities. Rome's choice during her civil wars lay between a senatorial republican form of government and a strong single ruler. Although the monarchical English might be inclined to be suspicious of republicanism, they had no experience to compare with it—certainly not their various peasants' revolts, such as Jack Cade's rebellion (in *2 Henry VI*). On the other hand, Roman one-man rule as it flourished under Octavius Caesar lacked the English sanctions of divine right. Rome was, after all, a pagan culture, and Shakespeare carefully preserves this non-Christian frame of reference. The gods are frequently invoked and appear to respond with prophetic dreams and auguries, but their ultimate intentions are baffling. Human beings strive blindly; the will of the gods is inscrutable. The outcome of *Julius Caesar* is far different from the restoration of providentially ordained order at the end of *Richard III*. Calm is restored and political authority reestablished, but we are by no means sure that a divine morality has been served. Roman history for Shakespeare is history divested of its divine imperatives and located in a distant political setting, making dispassionate appraisal less difficult. In Plutarch's *Lives of the Noble Grecians and Romans,* as translated by Sir Thomas North, Shakespeare discovered a rich opportunity for pursuing the ironies of political life to which he had been increasingly attracted in the English histories. In fact, he was drawn throughout his career to Plutarch: to the portrait of Portia in "The Life of Marcus Brutus," not only for Portia in *Julius Caesar,* but also for Lucrece in *The Rape of Lucrece,* Kate in *1 Henry IV,* and Portia in *The Merchant of Venice;* to "The Life of Theseus" for the Duke of *A Midsummer Night's Dream;* and to various lives for *Julius Caesar, Coriolanus, Antony and Cleopatra,* and *Timon of Athens.* Freed from the orthodoxies of the Elizabethan worldview, Shakespeare turned in the Roman or classical plays toward irony or outright satire (as in *Troilus and Cressida*) and toward the personal tragedy of political dilemma (as in *Coriolanus* and *Julius Caesar*). These are to be the dominant motifs of the Roman or classical plays, as distinguished from both the English histories and the great tragedies of evil, in which politics plays a lesser part (*Hamlet, Othello, King Lear, Macbeth*).

Julius Caesar is an ambivalent study of civil conflict. As in *Richard II*, the play is structured around two protagonists rather than one. Caesar and Brutus, men of extraordinary abilities and debilitating weaknesses, are more like one another than either would care to admit. This antithetical balance reflects a dual tradition: the medieval view of Dante and of Geoffrey Chaucer, condemning Brutus and Cassius as conspirators, and the Renaissance view of Sir Philip Sidney and Ben Jonson, condemning Caesar as a tyrant. These opposing views still live on in various twentieth-century productions that seek to enlist the play on the side of conservatism or liberalism. In one famous production by Orson Welles for the Mercury Theatre in 1937, Caesar was made out to resemble Benito Mussolini, Italy's fascist dictator, with reference also to Franco's fascists in Spain when that civil war was at its peak. Welles's subtitle for his production, "Death of a Dictator," left no doubt as to the intended statement. The film version of 1953 by John Houseman and Joseph Maniewicz dyed its khaki military uniforms green to suggest the German Wehrmacht; the music adopted for the production deliberately aped the music that accompanied Nazi marching columns in newsreels in the 1930s. Trevor Nunn, at Stratford-upon-Avon in 1972, similarly drew overt parallels to German fascism. At Stratford, Connecticut, in 1979, director Gerald Freedman presented Caesar as a Latin American dictator; at Ashland, Oregon, in 1982, Jerry Turner likened Caesar to Che Guevara. Such interpretations reflect what the conspirators themselves believe, as they cry "Liberty! Freedom! Tyranny is dead!" but the play itself invites widely varying interpretations. Caesar has sometimes appeared as a great leader and a man of great natural authority despite his manifest weaknesses, involved in a struggle to the death with conspirators whose motives and personalities are as complex as his. Anthony Quayle and Michael Langham sought such a balance in their 1950 production at Stratford-upon-Avon; so did Glen Byam Shaw in 1957. The film version of 1953 by John Houseman and Joseph Maniewicz achieved a kind of balance, despite its antifascist leanings, by evenly distributing its major roles among various well-known actors and actresses—John Gielgud as Cassius, Marlon Brando as Antony, James Mason as Brutus, Louis Calhern as Caesar, Greer Garson as Calpurnia, Deborah Kerr as Portia—instead of allowing one actor to dominate the play. Most recent criticism similarly has abandoned the fruitless debate as to whether Brutus or Caesar is the tragic protagonist, and whether one or the other of them is to be seen as morally superior, in favor of a multiple perspective.

Caesar is a study in paradox. He is unquestionably a great general, astute in politics, decisive in his judgments, and sharp in his evaluation of men, as, for example, in his distrust of Cassius with his "lean and hungry look" (1.2.194). Yet this mightiest of men, who in Cassius's phrase bestrides the narrow world "like a Colossus" (line 136), is also deaf in one ear, prone to fevers and epilepsy, unable to compete with Cassius by swimming the Tiber fully armed, and afflicted with a sterile marriage. Physical limitations of this sort are common enough, but in Caesar they are constantly juxtaposed with his aspirations to be above mortal weakness. He dies boasting that he is like the "northern star," constant, unique, "Unshaked of motion" (3.1.61–71). He professes to fear nothing and yet is notoriously superstitious. He calmly reflects that "death, a necessary end, / Will come when it will come," and then arrogantly boasts in the next moment that "Danger knows full well / That Caesar is more dangerous than he" (2.2.36–45). As his wife puts it, Caesar's "wisdom is consumed in confidence" (line 49). He willfully betrays his own best instincts and ignores plain warnings through self-deception. He stops a procession to hear a soothsayer and then dismisses the man as "a dreamer" (1.2.24). He commissions his augurers to determine whether he should stay at home on the ides of March and then persuades himself that acting on their advice would be a sign of weakness. Most fatally, he thinks himself above flattery and so is especially vulnerable to it. So wise and powerful a man as this cannot stop the process of his own fate, because his fate and character are interwoven: he is the victim of his own hubris. His insatiable desire for the crown overbalances his judgment; no warnings of the gods can save him. Even his virtues conspire against him, for he regards himself as one who puts public interest ahead of personal affairs, and so he brushes aside the letter of Artemidorus that would have told him of the conspiracy.

Brutus, for all his opposition to Caesar, is also a paradoxical figure. His strengths are quite unlike those of Caesar, but his weaknesses are surprisingly similar. Brutus is a noble Roman from an ancient family whose glory it has been to defend the personal liberties of Rome, the republican tradition. Brutus's virtues are personal virtues. He enjoys an admirable rapport with his courageous and intelligent wife, and is genuinely kind to his servants. In friendship he is trustworthy. He deplores oaths in the conspiracy because his word is his bond. He finds Caesar's ambition for power distasteful and vulgar; his opposition to Caesar is both idealistic and patrician. Brutus's hubris is a pride of family, and on this score he is vulnerable to flattery. As Cassius reminds him, alluding to Brutus's ancestor Lucius Junius Brutus, who founded the Roman Republic in 509 B.C.: "There was a Brutus once that would have brooked / Th'eternal devil to keep his state in Rome / As easily as a king" (1.2.159–61). Should not Marcus Brutus be the savior of his country from a return to tyranny? Is not he a more fit leader for Rome than Caesar? " 'Brutus' and 'Caesar.' What should be in that 'Caesar'? / Why should that name be sounded more than yours?" (lines 142–3). Cassius's strategy is to present to Brutus numerous testimonials "all tending to the great opinion / That Rome holds of his name" (lines 318–19). Cassius plays the role of tempter here, but the notion he suggests is not new to Brutus.

The parallelism of Brutus's pride and Caesar's ambition is strongly underscored by the way in which these great figures appear to us in two adjoining scenes: 2.1 and 2.2. In these two scenes, the protagonists enter alone during the troubled night, call for a servant, receive the conspirators, and dispute the wise caution of their wives. Both men are predisposed to the temptations that are placed before them. Brutus has often thought of himself as the indispensable man for the preservation of Rome's liberties. Despite his good breeding and coolly rational manner, he is as dominating a personality as Caesar and as hard to move once his mind is made up. Indeed, the conspiracy founders on Brutus's repeated insistence on having his own way. He allows no oaths among the conspirators and will not kill Antony along with Caesar. He permits Antony to speak after him at Caesar's funeral. He vetoes Cicero as a fellow conspirator. In each instance, the other conspirators are unanimously opposed to Brutus's choice but yield to him. Brutus cuts off Cassius's objections before hearing them fully, being accustomed to having his way without dispute. His motives are in part noble and idealistic: Brutus wishes to have the conspirators behave generously and openly, as heroes rather than as henchmen. Yet there is something loftily patrician in his desire to have the fruits of conspiracy without any of the dirty work. His willingness to have Antony speak after him betrays a vain confidence in his own oratory and an unjustified faith in the plebeian mob. Moreover, when Brutus overrides Cassius once more in the decision to fight at Philippi and is proved wrong by the event, no idealistic motive can excuse Brutus's insistence on being obeyed; Cassius is the more experienced soldier. Still, Brutus's fatal limitations as leader of a coup d'état are inseparable from his virtues as a private man. The truth is that such a noble man is, by his very nature, unsuited for the stern exigencies of assassination and civil war. Brutus is strong-minded about his ideals, but he cannot be ruthless. The means and the end of revolution drift further and further apart. He cannot supply his troops at Philippi because he will not forage among the peasants of the countryside and will not countenance among his allies the routine corruptions of an army in time of war, though at the same time that he upbraids Cassius for not sending him gold he does not stop to ask where the gold would come from. Even suicide is distasteful for Brutus, obliging him to embarrass his friends by asking their help. Brutus is too high-minded and genteel a man for the troubled times in which he lives.

The times indeed seem to demand ruthless action of the sort Antony and Octavius are all too ready to provide. The greatest irony of Brutus's fall is that the coup he undertakes for Roman liberty yields only further diminutions of that liberty. The plebeians are not ready for the commonwealth Brutus envisages. From the first, they are portrayed as amiable but "saucy" (even in the opinion of their tribunes, Flavius and Marullus). They adulate Caesar at the expense of their previous idol, Pompey. When Brutus successfully appeals for a moment to their changeable loyalties, they cry "Let him be Caesar," and "Caesar's better parts / Shall be crowned in Brutus" (3.2.51–2). If Brutus were not swayed by this hero-worship, he would have good cause to be disillusioned. To his credit, he is not the demogogue the plebeians take him for and so cannot continue to bend them to his will. Cassius, too, for all his villainlike role as tempter to Brutus, his envious motive, and his Epicurean skepticism, reveals a finer nature as the play progresses. Inspired perhaps by Brutus's philosophic idealism, Cassius turns philosopher also and accepts defeat in a noble but ineffectual cause. Yet even his death is futile; Cassius is misinformed about the fate of his friend Titinius and so stabs himself just when the battle is going well for the conspirators.

The ultimate victors are Antony and Octavius. Antony, whatever finer nature he may possess, becomes under the stress of circumstance a cunning bargainer with the conspirators and a masterful rhetorician who characterizes himself to the plebeians as a "plain blunt man" (3.2.219). In sardonic soliloquy at the end of his funeral oration, he observes, "Now let it work. Mischief, thou art afoot. / Take thou what course thou wilt" (lines 261–2). He is, to be sure, stirred by loyalty to Caesar's memory, but to the end of avenging Caesar's death he is prepared to unleash violence at whatever risk to the state. He regards Lepidus contemptuously as a mere creature under his command. Antony is older than Octavius and teaches the younger man about political realities, but an Elizabethan audience would probably savor the irony that Octavius will subsequently beat Antony at his own game. At Philippi, Octavius's refusal to accept Antony's directions in the battle (5.1.16–20) gives us a glimpse of the peremptory manner for which he is to become famous, like his predecessor. Antony and Octavius together are, in any case, a fearsome pair, matter-of-factly noting down the names of those who must die, including their own kinsmen. They cut off the bequests left to the populace in Caesar's will, by which Antony had won the hearts of the plebeians (4.1). Many innocent persons are sacrificed in the new reign of terror, including Cicero and the poet unluckily named Cinna. In such deaths, art and civilization yield to expediency. Rationality gives way to frenzied rhetoric and to a struggle for power in which

Rome's republican tradition is buried forever. Such is the achievement of Brutus's noble revolution.

Appropriately for such a depiction of ambivalent political strife, *Julius Caesar* is written chiefly in the oratorical mode. It resembles its near contemporary, *Henry V*, in devoting so much attention to speeches of public persuasion. The famous orations following Caesar's assassination—one by Brutus in the so-called Laconic style (that is, concise and sententious) and one by Antony in the Asiatic style (that is, more florid, anecdotal, and literary)—are only the most prominent of many public utterances. In the first scene, Marullus rebukes the plebeians for their disloyalty to Pompey and for the moment dissuades them from idolizing Caesar. Decius Brutus changes Caesar's presumably unalterable mind about staying home on the ides of March (2.2). Caesar lectures the Senate on the virtues of constancy. Before Philippi, the contending armies clash with verbal taunts. Antony and Octavius end the play with tributes to the dead Brutus. In less public scenes as well, oratory serves to win Brutus over to the conspirators, to urge unavailingly that Brutus confide in his wife, or to warn the unheeding Caesar of his danger. The decline of the conspirators' cause shows in their descent from rational discourse to private bickering (4.3). The play gives us a range of rhetorical styles, from the deliberative (having to do with careful consideration of choices) to the forensic (analogous to pleading at law, maintaining one side or the other of a given question), to the epideictic (for display, as in set orations). The imagery, suitably public and rhetorical in its function, is of a fixed star in the firmament, a Colossus bestriding the petty world of humans, a tide of fortune in the affairs of humankind, a statue spouting fountains of blood. The city of Rome is a vivid presence in the play, conveyed at times through Elizabethan anachronisms, such as striking clocks, sweaty nightcaps, "towers and windows, yea, . . . chimney tops" (1.1.39), but in an eclectic fusion of native and classical traditions wherein anachronisms become functionally purposeful. Style affords us one more way of considering *Julius Caesar* as a Janus play, looking back to Shakespeare's history plays and forward to his tragedies.

Women are marginalized in *Julius Caesar,* much as in Shakespeare's English history plays. Portia and Calpurnia are alike, not only in their concern for their husbands' welfare, but also in their inability to do anything to ensure their husbands' safety and prosperity. Fittingly in such an unremittingly patriarchal play, Portia and Calpurnia are noble Roman matrons of the type we also see earlier in *The Rape of Lucrece* or *Titus Andronicus* and later in Octavia (*Antony and Cleopatra*) and Volumnia (*Coriolanus*): unassailably virtuous, descended from patrician stock, and submissive to the essentially male values of unflinching duty and stoical reserve. Portia, daughter of the great Cato of Utica who committed suicide rather than submit to Caesar's tyranny, emulates her father's example by taking her own life rather than outlive her husband's shame in defeat. Calpurnia expounds her prophetic dream of Caesar's bleeding statue (2.2.76–9) only to be rebuked for womanly cowardice. These women do what they can to offer their men an alternative perspective on political ambition—one in which caution and attentiveness to family values stand in opposition to the competitive mores of the male-dominated world—but the women are doomed, like Cassandra and Andromache (in *Troilus and Cressida*), to see their quiet wisdom ignored or misinterpreted. Most touching of all is the scene of marital mutuality between Portia and Brutus (2.1.234–310), in which we realize that Portia's concern and sympathy for her husband cannot save Brutus from himself.

A structural pattern to be found in *Julius Caesar,* as noted by John Velz (see bibliography), is the replicating action of rise and fall by which the great men of ancient Rome succeed one another. The process antedates the play itself, for Pompey's faded glory mentioned in Act 1 is a reminder—or should be a reminder—that good fortune lasts but a day. We behold Caesar at the point of his greatest triumph and his imminent decline to death. "O mighty Caesar! Dost thou lie so low?" asks Antony when he sees the prostrate body of the once most powerful man alive. "Are all thy conquests, glories, triumphs, spoils, / Shrunk to this little measure?" (3.1.150–2). Brutus and Cassius step forward into prominence only to be supplanted by Antony and Octavius. Antony is unaware, though presumably the audience is aware, that Antony is to fall at the hands of Octavius. The process of incessant change, reinforced by such metaphors as the tide in the affairs of humans (already noted), offering its mocking comment on Caesar's self-comparison to the fixed northern star, is not simply a meaningless descent on the grand staircase of history, for Octavius's *Pax Romana* lies at the end of the cycle from republic to empire. Still, that resting place is beyond the conclusion of this open-ended play. What we see here again and again is a human blindness to history, through which a succession of protagonists repeat one another's errors without intending to do so. Cassius, like Caesar, goes to his death in the face of unpropitious omens that he now partly believes to be true. The eagles that accompanied Cassius and his army to Philippi desert him as the moment of battle approaches. These omens suggest a balance between character and fate, for, though the leaders of Rome have one by one fallen through their own acts and choices, they have also, it seems, fulfilled a prearranged destiny. Brutus, confronted by the Ghost of Caesar and assured that he will see this spirit of Caesar at Philippi, answers resolutely, "Why, I will see thee at Philippi, then" (4.3.288). Defeated in battle, as he sensed he would be, Brutus takes his own life. Cassius dies on his birthday. *Sic transit gloria mundi.*

Julius Caesar

[Dramatis Personae

JULIUS CAESAR
CALPURNIA, *Caesar's wife*
MARK ANTONY,
OCTAVIUS CAESAR, } *triumvirs after Caesar's death*
LEPIDUS,

MARCUS BRUTUS
PORTIA, *Brutus's wife*
CAIUS CASSIUS,
CASCA,
DECIUS BRUTUS,
CINNA, } *conspirators with Brutus*
METELLUS CIMBER,
TREBONIUS,
CAIUS LIGARIUS,

CICERO,
PUBLIUS, } *senators*
POPILIUS LENA,
FLAVIUS, } *tribunes of the people*
MARULLUS,

SOOTHSAYER
ARTEMIDORUS, *a teacher of rhetoric*
CINNA, *a poet*
Another POET

LUCILIUS,
TITINIUS,
MESSALA,
YOUNG CATO,
VOLUMNIUS,
VARRO, } *officers and soldiers in the army*
CLAUDIUS, *of Brutus and Cassius*
CLITUS,
DARDANIUS,
LABEO,
FLAVIUS,

PINDARUS, *Cassius's servant*
LUCIUS, } *Brutus's servants*
STRATO,
Caesar's SERVANT
Antony's SERVANT
Octavius's SERVANT

CARPENTER
COBBLER
Five PLEBEIANS
Three SOLDIERS *in Brutus' army*
Two SOLDIERS *in Antony's army*
MESSENGER

GHOST *of Caesar*

Senators, Plebeians, Officers, Soldiers, and Attendants

SCENE: *Rome; the neighborhood of Sardis; the neighborhood of Philippi*]

1.1

*Enter Flavius, Marullus, and certain commoners
over the stage.*

FLAVIUS
Hence! Home, you idle creatures, get you home!

Is this a holiday? What, know you not,
Being mechanical, you ought not walk   3
Upon a laboring day without the sign   4
Of your profession?—Speak, what trade art thou?
CARPENTER   Why, sir, a carpenter.
MARULLUS
Where is thy leather apron and thy rule?

1.1 Location: Rome. A street.

3 mechanical of the artisan class   **4 sign** garb and implements

1055

What dost thou with thy best apparel on?—
You, sir, what trade are you?
COBBLER   Truly, sir, in respect of a fine workman, I am   10
but, as you would say, a cobbler.   11
MARULLUS
But what trade art thou? Answer me directly.
COBBLER   A trade, sir, that I hope I may use with a safe
conscience, which is indeed, sir, a mender of bad soles.   14
FLAVIUS
What trade, thou knave? Thou naughty knave, what
trade?   15
COBBLER   Nay, I beseech you, sir, be not out with me.   16
Yet if you be out, sir, I can mend you.   17
FLAVIUS
What mean'st thou by that? Mend me, thou saucy
fellow?
COBBLER   Why, sir, cobble you.   19
FLAVIUS   Thou art a cobbler, art thou?
COBBLER   Truly, sir, all that I live by is with the awl. I   21
meddle with no tradesman's matters nor women's   22
matters, but withal I am indeed, sir, a surgeon to old   23
shoes. When they are in great danger, I recover them.   24
As proper men as ever trod upon neat's leather have   25
gone upon my handiwork.
FLAVIUS
But wherefore art not in thy shop today?
Why dost thou lead these men about the streets?
COBBLER   Truly, sir, to wear out their shoes, to get myself
into more work. But indeed, sir, we make holiday
to see Caesar and to rejoice in his triumph.   31
MARULLUS
Wherefore rejoice? What conquest brings he home?
What tributaries follow him to Rome   33
To grace in captive bonds his chariot wheels?
You blocks, you stones, you worse than senseless
things!   35
O you hard hearts, you cruel men of Rome,
Knew you not Pompey? Many a time and oft   37
Have you climbed up to walls and battlements,   38
To towers and windows, yea, to chimney tops,   39
Your infants in your arms, and there have sat
The livelong day, with patient expectation,

To see great Pompey pass the streets of Rome.   42
And when you saw his chariot but appear,
Have you not made an universal shout,
That Tiber trembled underneath her banks   45
To hear the replication of your sounds   46
Made in her concave shores?   47
And do you now put on your best attire?
And do you now cull out a holiday?   49
And do you now strew flowers in his way
That comes in triumph over Pompey's blood?   51
Begone!
Run to your houses, fall upon your knees,
Pray to the gods to intermit the plague   54
That needs must light on this ingratitude.   55
FLAVIUS
Go, go, good countrymen, and for this fault
Assemble all the poor men of your sort;   57
Draw them to Tiber banks, and weep your tears
Into the channel, till the lowest stream   59
Do kiss the most exalted shores of all.   60
                              Exeunt all the commoners.
See whe'er their basest mettle be not moved.   61
They vanish tongue-tied in their guiltiness.
Go you down that way towards the Capitol;
This way will I. Disrobe the images   64
If you do find them decked with ceremonies.   65
MARULLUS   May we do so?
You know it is the Feast of Lupercal.   67
FLAVIUS
It is no matter. Let no images
Be hung with Caesar's trophies. I'll about   69
And drive away the vulgar from the streets;   70
So do you too, where you perceive them thick.
These growing feathers plucked from Caesar's wing
Will make him fly an ordinary pitch,   73
Who else would soar above the view of men   74
And keep us all in servile fearfulness.   *Exeunt.*

10 **in . . . workman** (1) as far as skilled work is concerned (2) compared with a skilled worker   **11 cobbler** (1) one who works with shoes (2) bungler.   **14 soles** (With pun on "souls.")   **15 naughty** good-for-nothing   **16 out** out of temper   **17 out** having worn-out shoes.   **mend you** (1) cure your bad temper (2) repair your shoes.   **19 cobble you** mend your shoes. (The meaning "to pelt with stones" also suggests itself here, though perhaps it was not in general use until later in the seventeenth century.)   **21 awl** (Punning on *all*.)   **22 meddle with** (1) have to do with (2) have sexual intercourse with   **23 withal** yet. (With pun on *with awl*.)   **24 recover** (1) resole (2) cure   **25 proper** fine, handsome.   **as . . . leather** (Proverbial. *Neat's leather* is cowhide.)   **31 triumph** triumphal procession. (Caesar had overthrown the sons of Pompey the Great in Spain at the Battle of Munda, March 17, 45 B.C. The triumph was held that October.)   **33 tributaries** captives who will pay ransom (tribute)   **35 senseless** insensible like stone (hence, unfeeling)   **37 Pompey** (Caesar had overthrown the great soldier and onetime triumvir at the Battle of Pharsalus in 48 B.C. Pompey fled to Egypt, where he was murdered.)   **38–9 battlements . . . chimney tops** (The details are appropriate to an Elizabethan cityscape.)

42 great (Alludes to Pompey's epithet, *Magnus*, "great.")   **pass** pass through   **45 Tiber** the Tiber River   **46 replication** echo   **47 concave** hollowed out, overhanging   **49 cull** pick   **51 Pompey's blood** (1) Pompey's offspring (2) the blood of the Pompeys.   **54 intermit** suspend   **55 needs must** must necessarily   **57 sort** rank   **59–60 till . . . all** until even at its lowest reach the river is filled to the brim.   **61 See . . . moved** See how even their ignoble natures can be appealed to. (*Mettle* and *metal* are interchangeable, meaning both "temperament" and the natural substance. A base *metal* is one that is easily changed or *moved*, unlike gold; compare 1.2.308–10.)   **64 images** statues (of Caesar in royal regalia, set up by his followers)   **65 ceremonies** ceremonial trappings.   **67 Feast of Lupercal** a feast of purification (*Februa*, whence *February*) in honor of Pan, celebrated from ancient times in Rome on February 15 of each year. (Historically, this celebration came some months after Caesar's triumph in October of 45 B.C. The celebrants, called *Luperci*, raced around the Palatine Hill and the Circus carrying thongs of goatskin, with which they lightly struck those who came in their way. Women so touched were suppposed to be cured of barrenness; hence Caesar's wish that Antony would strike Calpurnia, 1.2.6–9.)   **69 trophies** spoils of war hung up as memorials of victory.   **about** go around the other way   **70 vulgar** commoners, plebeians   **73 pitch** highest point in flight. (A term from falconry.)   **74 else** otherwise

[1.2]

Enter Caesar, Antony for the course, Calpurnia,
Portia, Decius, Cicero, Brutus, Cassius, Casca, a
Soothsayer; after them, Marullus and Flavius;
[citizens following].

CAESAR
Calpurnia!

CASCA   Peace, ho! Caesar speaks.

CAESAR   Calpurnia!

CALPURNIA   Here, my lord.

CAESAR
Stand you directly in Antonio's way   3
When he doth run his course. Antonio!

ANTONY   Caesar, my lord?

CAESAR
Forget not, in your speed, Antonio,
To touch Calpurnia; for our elders say
The barren, touchèd in this holy chase,
Shake off their sterile curse.

ANTONY   I shall remember.   9
When Caesar says "Do this," it is performed.

CAESAR
Set on, and leave no ceremony out.   [*Flourish.*]   11

SOOTHSAYER   Caesar!

CAESAR   Ha? Who calls?

CASCA
Bid every noise be still. Peace yet again!
[*The music ceases.*]

CAESAR
Who is it in the press that calls on me?   15
I hear a tongue shriller than all the music
Cry "Caesar!" Speak. Caesar is turned to hear.

SOOTHSAYER
Beware the ides of March.

CAESAR   What man is that?   18

BRUTUS
A soothsayer bids you beware the ides of March.

CAESAR
Set him before me. Let me see his face.

CASSIUS
Fellow, come from the throng. [*The Soothsayer comes*
forward.] Look upon Caesar.

CAESAR
What say'st thou to me now? Speak once again.

SOOTHSAYER   Beware the ides of March.

CAESAR
He is a dreamer. Let us leave him. Pass.   24
Sennet. Exeunt. Manent Brutus and Cassius.

CASSIUS
Will you go see the order of the course?   25

BRUTUS   Not I.

CASSIUS   I pray you, do.

BRUTUS
I am not gamesome. I do lack some part   28
Of that quick spirit that is in Antony.
Let me not hinder, Cassius, your desires;
I'll leave you.

CASSIUS
Brutus, I do observe you now of late.
I have not from your eyes that gentleness
And show of love as I was wont to have.   34
You bear too stubborn and too strange a hand   35
Over your friend that loves you.

BRUTUS   Cassius,
Be not deceived. If I have veiled my look,   37
I turn the trouble of my countenance
Merely upon myself. Vexèd I am   39
Of late with passions of some difference,   40
Conceptions only proper to myself,   41
Which give some soil, perhaps, to my behaviors.   42
But let not therefore my good friends be grieved—
Among which number, Cassius, be you one—
Nor construe any further my neglect
Than that poor Brutus, with himself at war,
Forgets the shows of love to other men.

CASSIUS
Then, Brutus, I have much mistook your passion,
By means whereof this breast of mine hath buried   49
Thoughts of great value, worthy cogitations.   50
Tell me, good Brutus, can you see your face?

BRUTUS
No, Cassius, for the eye sees not itself
But by reflection, by some other things.

CASSIUS   'Tis just.   54
And it is very much lamented, Brutus,
That you have no such mirrors as will turn
Your hidden worthiness into your eye,
That you might see your shadow. I have heard   58
Where many of the best respect in Rome,   59
Except immortal Caesar, speaking of Brutus
And groaning underneath this age's yoke,
Have wished that noble Brutus had his eyes.   62

BRUTUS
Into what dangers would you lead me, Cassius,
That you would have me seek into myself
For that which is not in me?

CASSIUS
Therefore, good Brutus, be prepared to hear;
And since you know you cannot see yourself

1.2. Location: A public place or street, perhaps as in the previous scene.
0.1 *for the course* i.e., stripped for the race, carrying a goatskin thong
3 Antonio (Here and occasionally elsewhere Shakespeare employs Italian forms of Latin proper names, perhaps for metrical reasons.)
9 sterile curse curse of barrenness.   **11 Set on** Proceed   **15 press** throng   **18 ides of March** March 15.   **24.1 *Sennet*** trumpet call signaling the arrival or departure of a dignitary   **Manent** They remain onstage   **25 order of the course** ritual and progress of the race.

---

28 gamesome fond of sports, merry.   **34 wont** accustomed   **35 You . . . hand** You behave too stubbornly and in too unfriendly a manner. (The metaphor is from horsemanship.)   **37 veiled my look** i.e., been introverted, seemed less friendly   **39 Merely** entirely   **40 passions of some difference** conflicting emotions   **41 only proper to** relating only to   **42 soil** blemish   **49–50 By . . . value** because of which misunderstanding (my assuming you were displeased with me) I have kept to myself important thoughts   **54 just** true.   **58 shadow** image, reflection.   **59 best respect** highest repute and station   **62 had his eyes** (1) could see things from the perspective of Caesar's critics, or (2) could see better with his own eyes.

So well as by reflection, I, your glass,   68
Will modestly discover to yourself   69
That of yourself which you yet know not of.
And be not jealous on me, gentle Brutus.   71
Were I a common laughter, or did use   72
To stale with ordinary oaths my love   73
To every new protester; if you know   74
That I do fawn on men and hug them hard
And after scandal them, or if you know   76
That I profess myself in banqueting   77
To all the rout, then hold me dangerous.   78
                           Flourish, and shout.

BRUTUS
What means this shouting? I do fear the people
Choose Caesar for their king.
CASSIUS   Ay, do you fear it?
Then must I think you would not have it so.
BRUTUS
I would not, Cassius, yet I love him well.
But wherefore do you hold me here so long?
What is it that you would impart to me?
If it be aught toward the general good,
Set honor in one eye and death i'th'other
And I will look on both indifferently;   87
For let the gods so speed me as I love   88
The name of honor more than I fear death.
CASSIUS
I know that virtue to be in you, Brutus,
As well as I do know your outward favor.   91
Well, honor is the subject of my story.
I cannot tell what you and other men
Think of this life; but, for my single self,
I had as lief not be as live to be   95
In awe of such a thing as I myself.   96
I was born free as Caesar, so were you;
We both have fed as well, and we can both
Endure the winter's cold as well as he.
For once, upon a raw and gusty day,
The troubled Tiber chafing with her shores,
Caesar said to me, "Dar'st thou, Cassius, now
Leap in with me into this angry flood
And swim to yonder point?" Upon the word,
Accoutred as I was, I plungèd in   105
And bade him follow; so indeed he did.
The torrent roared, and we did buffet it
With lusty sinews, throwing it aside   108
And stemming it, with hearts of controversy.   109

But ere we could arrive the point proposed,
Caesar cried, "Help me, Cassius, or I sink!"
Ay, as Aeneas, our great ancestor,   112
Did from the flames of Troy upon his shoulder
The old Anchises bear, so from the waves of Tiber
Did I the tirèd Caesar. And this man
Is now become a god, and Cassius is
A wretched creature and must bend his body   117
If Caesar carelessly but nod on him.
He had a fever when he was in Spain,
And when the fit was on him I did mark
How he did shake. 'Tis true, this god did shake.
His coward lips did from their color fly,   122
And that same eye whose bend doth awe the world   123
Did lose his luster. I did hear him groan.   124
Ay, and that tongue of his that bade the Romans
Mark him and write his speeches in their books,
Alas, it cried, "Give me some drink, Titinius,"
As a sick girl. Ye gods, it doth amaze me
A man of such a feeble temper should   129
So get the start of the majestic world   130
And bear the palm alone.   *Shout. Flourish.*   131
BRUTUS   Another general shout!
I do believe that these applauses are
For some new honors that are heaped on Caesar.
CASSIUS
Why, man, he doth bestride the narrow world
Like a Colossus, and we petty men   136
Walk under his huge legs and peep about
To find ourselves dishonorable graves.
Men at some time are masters of their fates.
The fault, dear Brutus, is not in our stars,
But in ourselves, that we are underlings.
"Brutus" and "Caesar." What should be in that
     "Caesar"?
Why should that name be sounded more than yours?   143
Write them together, yours is as fair a name;
Sound them, it doth become the mouth as well;
Weigh them, it is as heavy; conjure with 'em,
"Brutus" will start a spirit as soon as "Caesar."   147
Now, in the names of all the gods at once,
Upon what meat doth this our Caesar feed
That he is grown so great? Age, thou art shamed!
Rome, thou hast lost the breed of noble bloods!   151
When went there by an age since the great flood   152

---

68 glass mirror   **69 modestly discover** reveal without exaggeration   **71 jealous on** suspicious of.   **gentle** noble   **72 laughter** laughing-stock, as at 4.3.114; or perhaps *laugher*, a shallow fellow who laughs at every jest.   **did use** were accustomed   **73 stale** cheapen, make common.   **ordinary** (1) commonplace (2) customary (3) tavern   **74 protester** one who protests or declares friendship   **76 after scandal** afterwards slander   **77 profess myself** make declarations of friendship   **78 rout** mob   **78.1** *Flourish* Fanfare for a dignitary   **87 indifferently** impartially   **88 speed me** make me prosper   **91 favor** appearance.   **95 as lief not be** just as soon not exist   **96 such ... myself** i.e., a fellow mortal.   **105 Accoutred** fully dressed in armor   **108 lusty sinews** vigorous might. (Literally, tendons.)   **109 stemming** making headway against.   **hearts of controversy** hearts fired up by rivalry.

112 Aeneas hero of Virgil's *Aeneid*, the legendary founder of Rome (hence *our great ancestor*), who bore his aged father Anchises out of burning Troy as it was falling to the Greeks   **117 bend his body** bow   **122 color** (1) i.e., normal healthy hue (2) military colors, flag. (The lips are personified as deserters.)   **123 bend** glance, gaze   **124 his** its   **129 temper** constitution   **130 get ... of** gain ascendancy over   **131 palm** victor's prize   **136 Colossus** (A 100-foot-high bronze statue of Helios, the sun god, one of the seven wonders of the ancient world, was commonly supposed to have stood astride the entrance to the harbor of Rhodes.)   **143 be sounded** (1) be spoken and celebrated (2) resound   **147 start** raise. (Perhaps the crowd is heard to shout a third time at this point, or somewhere else in this conversation. At line 226 below, we are told that "They shouted thrice.")   **151 the breed ... bloods** the bloodline of men of noble stock and valiant spirit.   **152 flood** i.e., the classical analogue of Noah's flood, in which all humanity was destroyed except for Deucalion and his wife Pyrrha

But it was famed with more than with one man?   153
When could they say, till now, that talked of Rome,
That her wide walks encompassed but one man?
Now is it Rome indeed, and room enough,   156
When there is in it but one only man.
Oh, you and I have heard our fathers say
There was a Brutus once that would have brooked   159
Th'eternal devil to keep his state in Rome   160
As easily as a king.   161

BRUTUS
That you do love me, I am nothing jealous.   162
What you would work me to, I have some aim.   163
How I have thought of this and of these times
I shall recount hereafter. For this present,
I would not, so with love I might entreat you,   166
Be any further moved. What you have said   167
I will consider; what you have to say
I will with patience hear and find a time
Both meet to hear and answer such high things.   170
Till then, my noble friend, chew upon this:
Brutus had rather be a villager
Than to repute himself a son of Rome
Under these hard conditions as this time
Is like to lay upon us.   175

CASSIUS   I am glad that my weak words
Have struck but thus much show of fire from Brutus.   177

Enter Caesar and his train. [Brutus and
Cassius continue to confer privately.]

BRUTUS
The games are done, and Caesar is returning.

CASSIUS
As they pass by, pluck Casca by the sleeve,
And he will, after his sour fashion, tell you
What hath proceeded worthy note today.

BRUTUS
I will do so. But look you, Cassius,
The angry spot doth glow on Caesar's brow,
And all the rest look like a chidden train.   184
Calpurnia's cheek is pale, and Cicero
Looks with such ferret and such fiery eyes   186
As we have seen him in the Capitol,
Being crossed in conference by some senators.   188

CASSIUS
Casca will tell us what the matter is.

CAESAR   Antonio!

ANTONY   Caesar?

CAESAR
Let me have men about me that are fat,

Sleek-headed men, and such as sleep o' nights.
Yond Cassius has a lean and hungry look.
He thinks too much. Such men are dangerous.

ANTONY
Fear him not, Caesar, he's not dangerous.
He is a noble Roman, and well given.   197

CAESAR
Would he were fatter! But I fear him not.
Yet if my name were liable to fear,
I do not know the man I should avoid
So soon as that spare Cassius. He reads much,
He is a great observer, and he looks
Quite through the deeds of men. He loves no plays,   203
As thou dost, Antony; he hears no music.   204
Seldom he smiles, and smiles in such a sort   205
As if he mocked himself and scorned his spirit
That could be moved to smile at anything.
Such men as he be never at heart's ease
Whiles they behold a greater than themselves,
And therefore are they very dangerous.
I rather tell thee what is to be feared
Than what I fear, for always I am Caesar.
Come on my right hand, for this ear is deaf,
And tell me truly what thou think'st of him.
Sennet. Exeunt Caesar and his train. [Casca remains
with Brutus and Cassius.]

CASCA   You pulled me by the cloak. Would you speak   215
with me?

BRUTUS
Ay, Casca. Tell us what hath chanced today,   217
That Caesar looks so sad.   218

CASCA   Why, you were with him, were you not?

BRUTUS
I should not then ask Casca what had chanced.

CASCA   Why, there was a crown offered him; and, being
offered him, he put it by with the back of his hand,
thus, and then the people fell a-shouting.

BRUTUS   What was the second noise for?

CASCA   Why, for that too.

CASSIUS
They shouted thrice. What was the last cry for?   226

CASCA   Why, for that too.

BRUTUS   Was the crown offered him thrice?

CASCA   Ay, marry, was't, and he put it by thrice, every   229
time gentler than other, and at every putting-by mine
honest neighbors shouted.   231

CASSIUS   Who offered him the crown?

CASCA   Why, Antony.

BRUTUS
Tell us the manner of it, gentle Casca.   234

CASCA   I can as well be hanged as tell the manner of it.
It was mere foolery; I did not mark it. I saw Mark An-

---

153 **famed with** famous for   156 **Rome, room** (Pronounced alike.)
159 **Brutus** i.e., Lucius Junius Brutus, who expelled the Tarquins and
founded the Roman republic (c. 509 B.C.).   **brooked** tolerated
160 **keep his state** set himself up in majesty   161 **As . . . king** as readily as he would tolerate a king.   162 **nothing jealous** not at all doubtful.   163 **work** persuade.   **aim** inkling.   166 **so . . . you** if I might
entreat you in the name of friendship   167 **moved** urged.   170 **meet**
fitting   175 **like** likely   177.1 *train* retinue. (See 1.2.0.1–4 for the
names of those in the procession.)   184 **a chidden train** scolded followers.   186 **ferret** ferretlike, i.e., small and red   188 **crossed in conference** opposed in debate

197 **given** disposed.   203 **through** i.e., into the motives of   204 **hears
no music** (Regarded as a sign of a morose and treacherous character.)
205 **sort** manner   215 **cloak** (Elizabethan costume; see also *sleeve,* line
179, and *doublet,* line 265. The Roman toga was sleeveless.)
217 **chanced** happened   218 **sad** serious.   226 **thrice** (See note at
1.2.147.)   229 **marry** i.e., indeed. (Originally, "by the Virgin Mary.")
231 **honest** worthy. (Said contemptuously.)   234 **gentle** noble

tony offer him a crown—yet 'twas not a crown neither, 'twas one of these coronets—and, as I told you, 238 he put it by once; but for all that, to my thinking, he would fain have had it. Then he offered it to him again; 240 then he put it by again; but to my thinking he was very loath to lay his fingers off it. And then he offered it the third time. He put it the third time by, and still 243 as he refused it the rabblement hooted and clapped 244 their chapped hands, and threw up their sweaty night- 245 caps, and uttered such a deal of stinking breath be- 246 cause Caesar refused the crown that it had almost choked Caesar, for he swooned and fell down at it. And for mine own part I durst not laugh for fear of opening my lips and receiving the bad air.

CASSIUS
But soft, I pray you. What, did Caesar swoon?   251

CASCA   He fell down in the marketplace, and foamed at mouth, and was speechless.

BRUTUS
'Tis very like. He hath the falling sickness.   254

CASSIUS
No, Caesar hath it not, but you and I,
And honest Casca, we have the falling sickness.

CASCA   I know not what you mean by that, but I am sure Caesar fell down. If the tag-rag people did not 258 clap him and hiss him, according as he pleased and displeased them, as they use to do the players in the 260 theater, I am no true man.   261

BRUTUS
What said he when he came unto himself?

CASCA   Marry, before he fell down, when he perceived the common herd was glad he refused the crown, he plucked me ope his doublet and offered them his throat 265 to cut. An I had been a man of any occupation, if I 266 would not have taken him at a word, I would I might go to hell among the rogues. And so he fell. When he came to himself again, he said if he had done or said anything amiss, he desired Their Worships to think it was his infirmity. Three or four wenches where I stood cried, "Alas, good soul!" and forgave him with all their hearts. But there's no heed to be taken of them; if Caesar had stabbed their mothers they would have done no less.

BRUTUS
And after that, he came thus sad away?   276

CASCA   Ay.

CASSIUS   Did Cicero say anything?

CASCA   Ay, he spoke Greek.

CASSIUS   To what effect?

CASCA   Nay, an I tell you that, I'll ne'er look you i'th' face again. But those that understood him smiled at one another and shook their heads; but, for mine own part, it was Greek to me. I could tell you more news too. Marullus and Flavius, for pulling scarves off Cae- 285 sar's images, are put to silence. Fare you well. There 286 was more foolery yet, if I could remember it.

CASSIUS   Will you sup with me tonight, Casca?

CASCA   No, I am promised forth.   289

CASSIUS   Will you dine with me tomorrow?

CASCA   Ay, if I be alive, and your mind hold, and your dinner worth the eating.

CASSIUS   Good. I will expect you.

CASCA   Do so. Farewell both.   *Exit.*

BRUTUS
What a blunt fellow is this grown to be!
He was quick mettle when he went to school.   296

CASSIUS
So is he now in execution
Of any bold or noble enterprise,
However he puts on this tardy form.   299
This rudeness is a sauce to his good wit,   300
Which gives men stomach to digest his words   301
With better appetite.

BRUTUS
And so it is. For this time I will leave you.
Tomorrow, if you please to speak with me,
I will come home to you; or, if you will,
Come home to me, and I will wait for you.

CASSIUS
I will do so. Till then, think of the world.   307
                                          Exit Brutus.

Well, Brutus, thou art noble. Yet I see
Thy honorable mettle may be wrought   309
From that it is disposed. Therefore it is meet   310
That noble minds keep ever with their likes;
For who so firm that cannot be seduced?
Caesar doth bear me hard, but he loves Brutus.   313
If I were Brutus now, and he were Cassius,
He should not humor me. I will this night   315
In several hands in at his windows throw,   316
As if they came from several citizens,
Writings, all tending to the great opinion

285 **scarves** decorations, festoons   286 **put to silence** dismissed from office. (So reported in Plutarch. Shakespeare's wording ominously suggests that they were executed.)   289 **promised forth** engaged to dine out.   296 **quick mettle** of a lively temperament   299 **However** however much.   **tardy form** air of ennui and disengagement. 300 **rudeness** rough manner.   **wit** intellect   301 **stomach** appetite, inclination   307 **the world** i.e., the state of the world.   309 **mettle** (As often, the word combines the senses of *mettle*, "temperament," and *metal*, "substance." The latter meaning continues here in the chemical metaphor of metal that is *wrought* or transmuted. As *honorable mettle* [or noble metal], gold cannot be transmuted into base substances, and yet Cassius proposes to do just that with Brutus. Compare this with 1.1.61.)   309–10 **wrought . . . disposed** turned away from its natural disposition.   310 **meet** fitting   313 **doth . . . hard** bears me a grudge and keeps me on a short rein.   315 **He . . . humor me** i.e., I wouldn't put up with being cajoled or humored. (*He* could refer to Caesar or Brutus.)   316 **several hands** different handwritings

238 **coronets** chaplets, garlands   240 **fain** gladly   243–4 **still as** whenever   245–6 **nightcaps** (Scornful allusion to the *pilleus*, a felt cap worn by the plebeians on festival days.)   251 **soft** i.e., wait a minute 254 **like** likely.   **falling sickness** epilepsy. (But Cassius takes it to mean "falling into servitude.")   258 **tag-rag** ragtag, riffraff   260 **use** are accustomed   261 **true** honest   265 **plucked me ope** pulled open. (*Me* is used colloquially.)   **doublet** Elizabethan upper garment, like a jacket   266 **An** If.   **man . . . occupation** (1) working man (2) man of action   276 **sad** somberly

That Rome holds of his name, wherein obscurely
Caesar's ambition shall be glancèd at.   320
And after this let Caesar seat him sure,   321
For we will shake him, or worse days endure.   *Exit.*

❖

[1.3]

Thunder and lightning. Enter, [meeting,] Casca
[with his sword drawn] and Cicero.

CICERO
Good even, Casca. Brought you Caesar home?   1
Why are you breathless? And why stare you so?

CASCA
Are not you moved, when all the sway of earth
Shakes like a thing unfirm? Oh, Cicero,   3
I have seen tempests when the scolding winds
Have rived the knotty oaks, and I have seen   6
Th'ambitious ocean swell and rage and foam
To be exalted with the threat'ning clouds;   8
But never till tonight, never till now,
Did I go through a tempest dropping fire.
Either there is a civil strife in heaven,
Or else the world, too saucy with the gods,   12
Incenses them to send destruction.

CICERO
Why, saw you anything more wonderful?   14

CASCA
A common slave—you know him well by sight—
Held up his left hand, which did flame and burn
Like twenty torches joined, and yet his hand,
Not sensible of fire, remained unscorched.   18
Besides—I ha' not since put up my sword—   19
Against the Capitol I met a lion,   20
Who glazed upon me and went surly by   21
Without annoying me. And there were drawn   22
Upon a heap a hundred ghastly women,   23
Transformèd with their fear, who swore they saw
Men all in fire walk up and down the streets.
And yesterday the bird of night did sit   26
Even at noonday upon the marketplace,
Hooting and shrieking. When these prodigies   28
Do so conjointly meet, let not men say,   29
"These are their reasons, they are natural,"
For I believe they are portentous things
Unto the climate that they point upon.   32

CICERO
Indeed, it is a strange-disposèd time.
But men may construe things after their fashion,   34

Clean from the purpose of the things themselves.   35
Comes Caesar to the Capitol tomorrow?

CASCA
He doth; for he did bid Antonio
Send word to you he would be there tomorrow.

CICERO
Good night then, Casca. This disturbèd sky
Is not to walk in.

CASCA   Farewell, Cicero.   *Exit Cicero.*

Enter Cassius.

CASSIUS
Who's there?

CASCA   A Roman.

CASSIUS   Casca, by your voice.

CASCA
Your ear is good. Cassius, what night is this!   42

CASSIUS
A very pleasing night to honest men.

CASCA
Who ever knew the heavens menace so?

CASSIUS
Those that have known the earth so full of faults.
For my part, I have walked about the streets,
Submitting me unto the perilous night,
And thus unbracèd, Casca, as you see,   48
Have bared my bosom to the thunder-stone;   49
And when the cross blue lightning seemed to open   50
The breast of heaven, I did present myself
Even in the aim and very flash of it.

CASCA
But wherefore did you so much tempt the heavens?
It is the part of men to fear and tremble   54
When the most mighty gods by tokens send   55
Such dreadful heralds to astonish us.   56

CASSIUS
You are dull, Casca, and those sparks of life
That should be in a Roman you do want,   58
Or else you use not. You look pale, and gaze,
And put on fear, and cast yourself in wonder,   60
To see the strange impatience of the heavens.
But if you would consider the true cause
Why all these fires, why all these gliding ghosts,
Why birds and beasts from quality and kind,   64
Why old men, fools, and children calculate,   65
Why all these things change from their ordinance,   66
Their natures, and preformèd faculties,   67
To monstrous quality—why, you shall find   68
That heaven hath infused them with these spirits
To make them instruments of fear and warning
Unto some monstrous state.   71

320 **glancèd** hinted   321 **seat him sure** seat himself securely in
power (i.e., watch out)
1.3 Location: A street.
1 **Brought** Escorted   3 **sway** established order   6 **rived** split
8 **exalted with** raised to the level of   12 **saucy** insolent   14 **more
wonderful** else that was wondrous.   18 **Not sensible of** not feeling
19 **put up** sheathed   20 **Against** in front of, opposite   21 **glazed**
stared glassily   22 **annoying** harming   22–3 **drawn . . . heap** huddled together   23 **ghastly** pallid   26 **bird of night** owl, a bird of evil
omen   28 **prodigies** abnormalities, wonders   29 **conjointly meet**
coincide   32 **climate** region   34 **construe** interpret.   **after their
fashion** in their own way

35 **Clean . . . purpose** contrary to the actual import or meaning
42 **what night** what a night   48 **unbracèd** with doublet unfastened
49 **thunder-stone** thunderbolt   50 **cross** forked, jagged   54 **part**
appropriate role   55 **tokens** signs   56 **astonish** stun, terrify
58 **want** lack   60 **put on** adopt, show signs of.   **in wonder** into a
state of wonder   64 **from . . . kind** (behaving) contrary to their true
nature   65 **calculate** reckon, prophesy   66 **ordinance** established
nature   67 **preformèd** innate, congenital   68 **monstrous** unnatural
71 **Unto . . . state** pointing to some disorder in the commonwealth or
state of affairs.

Now could I, Casca, name to thee a man
Most like this dreadful night,
That thunders, lightens, opens graves, and roars
As doth the lion in the Capitol—
A man no mightier than thyself or me
In personal action, yet prodigious grown   77
And fearful, as these strange eruptions are.   78

CASCA
'Tis Caesar that you mean, is it not, Cassius?

CASSIUS
Let it be who it is. For Romans now
Have thews and limbs like to their ancestors';   81
But, woe the while, our fathers' minds are dead,   82
And we are governed with our mothers' spirits.
Our yoke and sufferance show us womanish.   84

CASCA
Indeed, they say the senators tomorrow
Mean to establish Caesar as a king,
And he shall wear his crown by sea and land
In every place save here in Italy.

CASSIUS
I know where I will wear this dagger then;
Cassius from bondage will deliver Cassius.
Therein, ye gods, you make the weak most strong;   91
Therein, ye gods, you tyrants do defeat.
Nor stony tower, nor walls of beaten brass,   93
Nor airless dungeon, nor strong links of iron,
Can be retentive to the strength of spirit;   95
But life, being weary of these worldly bars,   96
Never lacks power to dismiss itself.
If I know this, know all the world besides,   98
That part of tyranny that I do bear
I can shake off at pleasure.   *Thunder still.*   99

CASCA   So can I.
So every bondman in his own hand bears
The power to cancel his captivity.

CASSIUS
And why should Caesar be a tyrant then?
Poor man, I know he would not be a wolf
But that he sees the Romans are but sheep;
He were no lion, were not Romans hinds.   106
Those that with haste will make a mighty fire
Begin it with weak straws. What trash is Rome,
What rubbish and what offal, when it serves   109
For the base matter to illuminate   110
So vile a thing as Caesar! But, O grief,
Where hast thou led me? I perhaps speak this
Before a willing bondman; then I know
My answer must be made. But I am armed,   114
And dangers are to me indifferent.   115

CASCA
You speak to Casca, and to such a man
That is no fleering telltale. Hold. My hand.   117
Be factious for redress of all these griefs,   118
And I will set this foot of mine as far
As who goes farthest.   [*They shake hands.*]
CASSIUS   There's a bargain made.   120
Now know you, Casca, I have moved already   121
Some certain of the noblest-minded Romans
To undergo with me an enterprise
Of honorable dangerous consequence;
And I do know by this they stay for me   125
In Pompey's porch. For now, this fearful night,   126
There is no stir or walking in the streets,
And the complexion of the element   128
In favor 's like the work we have in hand,   129
Most bloody, fiery, and most terrible.

Enter Cinna.

CASCA
Stand close awhile, for here comes one in haste.   131
CASSIUS
'Tis Cinna; I do know him by his gait.
He is a friend.—Cinna, where haste you so?
CINNA
To find out you. Who's that? Metellus Cimber?
CASSIUS
No, it is Casca, one incorporate   135
To our attempts. Am I not stayed for, Cinna?
CINNA
I am glad on't. What a fearful night is this!   137
There's two or three of us have seen strange sights.
CASSIUS   Am I not stayed for? Tell me.
CINNA
Yes, you are. Oh, Cassius, if you could
But win the noble Brutus to our party—
CASSIUS
Be you content. Good Cinna, take this paper,   142
                              [*giving papers*]
And look you lay it in the praetor's chair,   143
Where Brutus may but find it. And throw this   144
In at his window. Set this up with wax
Upon old Brutus' statue. All this done,   146
Repair to Pompey's porch, where you shall find us.   147
Is Decius Brutus and Trebonius there?
CINNA
All but Metellus Cimber, and he's gone

---

77 **prodigious** ominous   78 **fearful** inspiring fear   81 **thews** sinews, muscles   82 **woe the while** alas for the age   84 **yoke and sufferance** patience under the yoke   91 **Therein** i.e., In the ability to commit suicide   93 **Nor** Neither   95 **Can . . . spirit** can confine a resolute spirit   96 **bars** (1) prison bars (2) burdens (such as tyranny)   98 **know . . . besides** let the rest of the world know   99 s.d. *Thunder still* Continuous thunder.   106 **were** would be.   **hinds** (1) female of the red deer (2) servants, menials.   109 **offal** refuse, wood shavings   110 **matter** i.e., fuel   114 **My answer . . . made** I will have to answer (to Caesar) for what I have said.   **armed** (1) provided with weapons (2) morally fortified   115 **indifferent** unimportant.

117 **fleering** fawning; scornful.   **Hold. My hand** Enough; here is my hand.   118 **factious** active as a partisan.   **griefs** grievances   120 **who** whoever   121 **moved** urged   125 **by this** by this time.   **stay** wait   126 **Pompey's porch** the colonnade of Pompey's great open theater, dedicated in 55 B.C. (Caesar was assassinated there, though Shakespeare has the assassination take place in the Capitol [i.e., the Senate chamber].)   128 **element** sky   129 **favor 's** appearance is   131 **close** concealed, still   135 **incorporate** admitted as a member   137 **on't** of it.   142 **Be you content** Set your mind at rest.   143 **praetor's chair** official seat of a praetor, Roman magistrate ranking next below the consul. (Brutus was praetor, one of sixteen.)   144 **Where . . . it** where Brutus cannot help finding it.   146 **old Brutus** (Lucius Junius Brutus; Brutus was reputed to be his descendant.)   147 **Repair** proceed. (Also in line 152.)

To seek you at your house. Well, I will hie,   150
And so bestow these papers as you bade me.

CASSIUS
That done, repair to Pompey's theater.   *Exit Cinna.*
Come, Casca, you and I will yet ere day
See Brutus at his house. Three parts of him   154
Is ours already, and the man entire
Upon the next encounter yields him ours.

CASCA
Oh, he sits high in all the people's hearts;
And that which would appear offense in us,   158
His countenance, like richest alchemy,   159
Will change to virtue and to worthiness.   160

CASSIUS
Him and his worth, and our great need of him,
You have right well conceited. Let us go,   162
For it is after midnight, and ere day
We will awake him and be sure of him.   *Exeunt.*

❖

2.1

Enter Brutus in his orchard.

BRUTUS   What, Lucius, ho!—
I cannot by the progress of the stars
Give guess how near to day.—Lucius, I say!—
I would it were my fault to sleep so soundly.—
When, Lucius, when? Awake, I say! What, Lucius!   5

Enter Lucius.

LUCIUS   Called you, my lord?

BRUTUS
Get me a taper in my study, Lucius.   7
When it is lighted, come and call me here.

LUCIUS   I will, my lord.   *Exit.*

BRUTUS
It must be by his death. And for my part
I know no personal cause to spurn at him,   11
But for the general. He would be crowned.   12
How that might change his nature, there's the
    question.
It is the bright day that brings forth the adder,
And that craves wary walking. Crown him—that—   15
And then I grant we put a sting in him
That at his will he may do danger with.
Th'abuse of greatness is when it disjoins
Remorse from power. And to speak truth of Caesar, 19

I have not known when his affections swayed   20
More than his reason. But 'tis a common proof   21
That lowliness is young ambition's ladder,   22
Whereto the climber-upward turns his face;
But when he once attains the upmost round   24
He then unto the ladder turns his back,
Looks in the clouds, scorning the base degrees   26
By which he did ascend. So Caesar may.
Then, lest he may, prevent. And since the quarrel
Will bear no color for the thing he is,   29
Fashion it thus: that what he is, augmented,   30
Would run to these and these extremities;
And therefore think him as a serpent's egg
Which, hatched, would, as his kind, grow
    mischievous;   33
And kill him in the shell.

Enter Lucius.

LUCIUS
The taper burneth in your closet, sir.   35
Searching the window for a flint, I found
This paper, thus sealed up, and I am sure
It did not lie there when I went to bed.
                        Gives him the letter.

BRUTUS
Get you to bed again. It is not day.
Is not tomorrow, boy, the ides of March?   40

LUCIUS   I know not, sir.

BRUTUS
Look in the calendar and bring me word.

LUCIUS   I will, sir.   *Exit.*

BRUTUS
The exhalations whizzing in the air   44
Give so much light that I may read by them.
                        Opens the letter and reads.
"Brutus, thou sleep'st. Awake, and see thyself!
Shall Rome, etc. Speak, strike, redress!"
"Brutus, thou sleep'st. Awake!"
Such instigations have been often dropped
Where I have took them up.
"Shall Rome, etc." Thus must I piece it out:
Shall Rome stand under one man's awe? What, Rome?
My ancestors did from the streets of Rome
The Tarquin drive, when he was called a king.
"Speak, strike, redress!" Am I entreated
To speak and strike? O Rome, I make thee promise,
If the redress will follow, thou receivest   57
Thy full petition at the hand of Brutus.   58

Enter Lucius.

LUCIUS   Sir, March is wasted fifteen days.
                        Knock within.

---

150 **hie** go quickly   154 **parts** i.e., quarters   158–60 **that which . . .
worthiness** his endorsement and honorable name will convert into
virtue and worthiness those things in our conspiracy that would otherwise seem offensive, just as alchemy is supposed to transform base
metals into richest gold.   162 **conceited** (1) conceived, grasped (2)
expressed in a figure.
2.1. Location: Rome. Brutus' orchard, or garden.
5 **When** (An exclamation of impatience.)   7 **Get . . . taper** Put a candle for me   11 **spurn** kick   12 **general** general cause, common good.
15 **craves** requires.   **that** that is the issue   19 **Remorse** scruple, compassion

20 **affections swayed** passions ruled   21 **proof** experience   22 **lowliness** pretended humbleness   24 **round** rung   26 **base degrees** (1)
lower rungs (2) persons of lower social station   29 **Will . . . is** can
carry no appearance of justice so far as his conduct to date is concerned   30 **Fashion it** put the matter   33 **as his kind** according to its
nature.   **mischievous** harmful   35 **closet** private chamber, study
40 **ides** fifteenth day   44 **exhalations** meteors   57 **If . . . follow** i.e., if
striking Caesar will lead to the reform of grievances   58 **at** from

BRUTUS

'Tis good. Go to the gate; somebody knocks.

[*Exit Lucius.*]

Since Cassius first did whet me against Caesar,

I have not slept.

Between the acting of a dreadful thing

And the first motion, all the interim is   64

Like a phantasma or a hideous dream.   65

The genius and the mortal instruments   66

Are then in council; and the state of man,   67

Like to a little kingdom, suffers then

The nature of an insurrection.   69

Enter Lucius.

LUCIUS

Sir, 'tis your brother Cassius at the door,   70

Who doth desire to see you.

BRUTUS   Is he alone?

LUCIUS

No, sir. There are more with him.

BRUTUS   Do you know them?

LUCIUS

No, sir. Their hats are plucked about their ears,

And half their faces buried in their cloaks,

That by no means I may discover them   75

By any mark of favor.

BRUTUS   Let 'em enter.   [*Exit Lucius.*]   76

They are the faction. O conspiracy,

Sham'st thou to show thy dangerous brow by night,

When evils are most free? Oh, then, by day   79

Where wilt thou find a cavern dark enough

To mask thy monstrous visage? Seek none,

conspiracy!

Hide it in smiles and affability;

For if thou put thy native semblance on,

Not Erebus itself were dim enough   84

To hide thee from prevention.   85

Enter the conspirators, Cassius, Casca, Decius,
Cinna, Metellus [Cimber] , and Trebonius.

CASSIUS

I think we are too bold upon your rest.   86

Good morrow, Brutus. Do we trouble you?

BRUTUS

I have been up this hour, awake all night.

Know I these men that come along with you?

CASSIUS

Yes, every man of them, and no man here

But honors you; and every one doth wish

You had but that opinion of yourself

Which every noble Roman bears of you.

This is Trebonius.

BRUTUS   He is welcome hither.

CASSIUS

This, Decius Brutus.

BRUTUS   He is welcome too.

CASSIUS

This, Casca; this, Cinna; and this, Metellus Cimber.

BRUTUS   They are all welcome.

What watchful cares do interpose themselves   98

Betwixt your eyes and night?

CASSIUS   Shall I entreat a word?

They [Brutus and Cassius] whisper.

DECIUS

Here lies the east. Doth not the day break here?   101

CASCA   No.

CINNA

Oh, pardon, sir, it doth; and yon gray lines

That fret the clouds are messengers of day.   104

CASCA

You shall confess that you are both deceived.   105

Here, as I point my sword, the sun arises,

Which is a great way growing on the south,   107

Weighing the youthful season of the year.   108

Some two months hence, up higher toward the north

He first presents his fire; and the high east   110

Stands, as the Capitol, directly here.

BRUTUS [*coming forward*]

Give me your hands all over, one by one.   112

CASSIUS

And let us swear our resolution.

BRUTUS

No, not an oath. If not the face of men,   114

The sufferance of our souls, the time's abuse—   115

If these be motives weak, break off betimes,   116

And every man hence to his idle bed;   117

So let high-sighted tyranny range on   118

Till each man drop by lottery. But if these,   119

As I am sure they do, bear fire enough

To kindle cowards and to steel with valor   121

The melting spirits of women, then, countrymen,

What need we any spur but our own cause

To prick us to redress? What other bond   124

Than secret Romans that have spoke the word   125

And will not palter? And what other oath   126

Than honesty to honesty engaged   127

That this shall be or we will fall for it?

64 motion proposal or impulse   65 phantasma hallucination
66–7 The genius . . . council The tutelary god or attendant spirit allotted to every person at birth is then intensely at debate with the person's physical faculties and passionate nature   69 The nature of an a
kind of   70 brother i.e., brother-in-law. (Cassius had married a sister
of Brutus.)   75 discover identify   76 favor appearance   79 free free
to roam at will.   84 Erebus primeval Darkness (sprung, according to
Hesiod, from Chaos and his sister Night)   85 prevention detection
and being forestalled.   86 upon in intruding upon

98 watchful cares sleep-preventing worries   101 Here (Decius points
eastward.)   104 fret mark with interlacing lines   105 deceived mistaken.   107 growing encroaching   108 Weighing considering, in
consequence of   110 high due   112 all over one and all   114–16 If . . .
betimes If the gravely serious faces of Romans, the suffering we feel,
the corruptions of the present day are insufficient to move us, we
should break off at once   117 idle (1) unused (2) in which men are
idle   118 high-sighted upward-gazing (compare with 2.1.26); or
haughty, looking down from on high   119 by lottery i.e., as the capricious tyrant chances to pick on them.   these i.e., these injustices just
cited   121 cowards even cowards.   steel harden   124 prick spur
125 Than . . . word than the word of Romans who, having given their
word of honor, will remain secret   126 palter shift position evasively.
127 honesty personal honor

Swear priests and cowards and men cautelous,   129
Old feeble carrions, and such suffering souls   130
That welcome wrongs; unto bad causes swear   131
Such creatures as men doubt. But do not stain   132
The even virtue of our enterprise,   133
Nor th'insuppressive mettle of our spirits,   134
To think that or our cause or our performance   135
Did need an oath, when every drop of blood
That every Roman bears—and nobly bears—
Is guilty of a several bastardy   138
If he do break the smallest particle
Of any promise that hath passed from him.

CASSIUS
But what of Cicero? Shall we sound him?   141
I think he will stand very strong with us.

CASCA
Let us not leave him out.

CINNA   No, by no means.

METELLUS
Oh, let us have him, for his silver hairs
Will purchase us a good opinion   145
And buy men's voices to commend our deeds.
It shall be said his judgment ruled our hands;
Our youths and wildness shall no whit appear,
But all be buried in his gravity.

BRUTUS
Oh, name him not. Let us not break with him,   150
For he will never follow anything
That other men begin.

CASSIUS   Then leave him out.

CASCA   Indeed he is not fit.

DECIUS
Shall no man else be touched but only Caesar?

CASSIUS
Decius, well urged. I think it is not meet   156
Mark Antony, so well beloved of Caesar,
Should outlive Caesar. We shall find of him   158
A shrewd contriver; and you know his means,   159
If he improve them, may well stretch so far   160
As to annoy us all. Which to prevent,   161
Let Antony and Caesar fall together.

BRUTUS
Our course will seem too bloody, Caius Cassius,
To cut the head off and then hack the limbs,
Like wrath in death and envy afterwards;   165
For Antony is but a limb of Caesar.
Let's be sacrificers, but not butchers, Caius.
We all stand up against the spirit of Caesar,
And in the spirit of men there is no blood.

Oh, that we then could come by Caesar's spirit
And not dismember Caesar! But, alas,
Caesar must bleed for it. And, gentle friends,   172
Let's kill him boldly, but not wrathfully;
Let's carve him as a dish fit for the gods,
Not hew him as a carcass fit for hounds.
And let our hearts, as subtle masters do,
Stir up their servants to an act of rage   177
And after seem to chide 'em. This shall make
Our purpose necessary, and not envious;   179
Which so appearing to the common eyes,
We shall be called purgers, not murderers.   181
And for Mark Antony, think not of him;   182
For he can do no more than Caesar's arm
When Caesar's head is off.

CASSIUS   Yet I fear him,
For in the engrafted love he bears to Caesar—   185

BRUTUS
Alas, good Cassius, do not think of him.
If he love Caesar, all that he can do
Is to himself—take thought and die for Caesar.   188
And that were much he should, for he is given   189
To sports, to wildness, and much company.

TREBONIUS
There is no fear in him. Let him not die,   191
For he will live, and laugh at this hereafter.   192

                                        Clock strikes.

BRUTUS
Peace! Count the clock.

CASSIUS   The clock hath stricken three.

TREBONIUS
'Tis time to part.

CASSIUS   But it is doubtful yet
Whether Caesar will come forth today or no;
For he is superstitious grown of late,
Quite from the main opinion he held once
Of fantasy, of dreams, and ceremonies.   198
It may be these apparent prodigies,   199
The unaccustomed terror of this night,
And the persuasion of his augurers   201
May hold him from the Capitol today.

DECIUS
Never fear that. If he be so resolved,
I can o'ersway him; for he loves to hear
That unicorns may be betrayed with trees,   205
And bears with glasses, elephants with holes,   206
Lions with toils, and men with flatterers;   207

129–32 **Swear . . . doubt** Let priests and cowards and shifty old men tottering on the brink of the grave swear oaths, and long-suffering souls that submit supinely to wrongs; it is contemptible, untrustworthy persons like these who swear oaths to bad causes.   133 **even** steadfast, consistent   134 **insuppressive** indomitable   135 **or . . . or** either . . . or   138 **a several bastardy** an individual act unworthy of his parentage   141 **sound him** sound him out.   145 **purchase** procure. (Playing on the financial sense of *silver*, line 144.)   150 **break with** confide in   156 **meet** fitting   158 **of** in   159 **shrewd** malicious; artful   160 **improve** exploit, make good use of   161 **annoy** injure   165 **envy** malice

172 **gentle** noble   177 **their servants** i.e., our hands   179 **envious** malicious   181 **purgers** those who heal by bleeding the patient   182 **for** as for   185 **engrafted** firmly implanted   188 **take thought** give way to melancholy   189 **much he should** more than is to be expected of him, hence unlikely; or, eminently desirable   191 **no fear** nothing to fear   192.1 *Clock strikes* (An anachronism much commented upon; the mechanical clock was not invented until c. 1300.)   198 **fantasy** imaginings.   **ceremonies** omens drawn from the performance of some rite.   199 **apparent** manifest, both visible and obvious   201 **augurers** augurs, official interpreters of omens   205 **unicorns . . . trees** i.e., by having the unicorn imprison itself by driving its horn into a tree as it charges at the hunter   206 **glasses** mirrors (enabling the hunter to approach the bear while it dazzles itself in the mirror).   **holes** pitfalls   207 **toils** nets, snares

But when I tell him he hates flatterers,
He says he does, being then most flattered.
Let me work;
For I can give his humor the true bent,   211
And I will bring him to the Capitol.

CASSIUS
Nay, we will all of us be there to fetch him.

BRUTUS
By the eighth hour. Is that the uttermost?   214

CINNA
Be that the uttermost, and fail not then.

METELLUS
Caius Ligarius doth bear Caesar hard,   216
Who rated him for speaking well of Pompey.   217
I wonder none of you have thought of him.

BRUTUS
Now, good Metellus, go along by him.   219
He loves me well, and I have given him reasons;
Send him but hither, and I'll fashion him.   221

CASSIUS
The morning comes upon 's. We'll leave you, Brutus.
And, friends, disperse yourselves; but all remember
What you have said, and show yourselves true
    Romans.

BRUTUS
Good gentlemen, look fresh and merrily;
Let not our looks put on our purposes,   226
But bear it as our Roman actors do,
With untired spirits and formal constancy.   228
And so good morrow to you every one.   229
                      Exeunt. Manet Brutus.
Boy! Lucius!—Fast asleep? It is no matter.   230
Enjoy the honey-heavy dew of slumber.
Thou hast no figures nor no fantasies   232
Which busy care draws in the brains of men;   233
Therefore thou sleep'st so sound.

    Enter Portia.

PORTIA   Brutus, my lord!

BRUTUS
Portia, what mean you? Wherefore rise you now?
It is not for your health thus to commit
Your weak condition to the raw cold morning.

PORTIA
Nor for yours neither. You've ungently, Brutus,   238
Stole from my bed. And yesternight, at supper,
You suddenly arose, and walked about
Musing and sighing, with your arms across,   241

And when I asked you what the matter was,
You stared upon me with ungentle looks.
I urged you further; then you scratched your head
And too impatiently stamped with your foot.
Yet I insisted, yet you answered not,   246
But with an angry wafture of your hand   247
Gave sign for me to leave you. So I did,
Fearing to strengthen that impatience
Which seemed too much enkindled, and withal   250
Hoping it was but an effect of humor,   251
Which sometime hath his hour with every man.   252
It will not let you eat, nor talk, nor sleep,
And could it work so much upon your shape
As it hath much prevailed on your condition,   255
I should not know you, Brutus. Dear my lord,   256
Make me acquainted with your cause of grief.

BRUTUS
I am not well in health, and that is all.

PORTIA
Brutus is wise, and were he not in health
He would embrace the means to come by it.

BRUTUS
Why, so I do. Good Portia, go to bed.   261

PORTIA
Is Brutus sick? And is it physical   262
To walk unbracèd and suck up the humors   263
Of the dank morning? What, is Brutus sick,
And will he steal out of his wholesome bed
To dare the vile contagion of the night,
And tempt the rheumy and unpurgèd air   267
To add unto his sickness? No, my Brutus,
You have some sick offense within your mind,
Which by the right and virtue of my place
I ought to know of. [*She kneels.*] And upon my knees
I charm you, by my once-commended beauty,   272
By all your vows of love, and that great vow
Which did incorporate and make us one,
That you unfold to me, your self, your half,
Why you are heavy, and what men tonight   276
Have had resort to you; for here have been
Some six or seven, who did hide their faces
Even from darkness.

BRUTUS   Kneel not, gentle Portia.
                                [*He raises her.*]

PORTIA
I should not need if you were gentle Brutus.
Within the bond of marriage, tell me, Brutus,
Is it excepted I should know no secrets   282
That appertain to you? Am I your self
But as it were in sort or limitation,   284

---

211 humor disposition   **214 the eighth hour** i.e., 8 A.M. (The Elizabethan way of reckoning time. By Roman reckoning, the day began at 6 A.M., so that *the eighth hour* would be 2 P.M.) **uttermost** latest. **216 bear Caesar hard** bear a grudge toward Caesar. (See 1.2.313n.) **217 rated** rebuked **219 by him** by way of his house. **221 fashion** shape (to our purposes) **226 put on** display, wear in open view **228 formal constancy** steadfast appearance, decorum. **229.1 Manet** He remains onstage **230 Lucius** (Brutus calls to his servant, who is evidently within, asleep, after having admitted the conspirators at line 85; later, at line 310, he is still within when Brutus calls to him.) **232 figures** imaginings **233 care** anxiety **238 ungently** discourteously, unkindly **241 across** folded. (A sign of melancholy.)

246 Yet . . . yet Still . . . still **247 wafture** waving **250 withal** moreover **251 humor** imbalance of temperament **252 his** its **255 condition** inner state of mind **256 know you** recognize you as **261 so I do** (Said with a double meaning not perceived by Portia: I seek through Caesar's death the means to better the health of the state.) **262 physical** healthful **263 unbracèd** with loosened clothing. **humors** damps, mists **267 rheumy and unpurgèd** conducive to illness and not cleansed of its impurities (which night air was thought to contain) **272 charm** conjure, entreat **276 heavy** sad **282 excepted** made an exception that **284 in . . . limitation** only up to a point. (A legal phrase.)

To keep with you at meals, comfort your bed, 285
And talk to you sometimes? Dwell I but in the suburbs 286
Of your good pleasure? If it be no more,
Portia is Brutus' harlot, not his wife.

BRUTUS
You are my true and honorable wife,
As dear to me as are the ruddy drops
That visit my sad heart.

PORTIA
If this were true, then should I know this secret.
I grant I am a woman, but withal 293
A woman that Lord Brutus took to wife.
I grant I am a woman, but withal
A woman well reputed, Cato's daughter. 296
Think you I am no stronger than my sex,
Being so fathered and so husbanded?
Tell me your counsels, I will not disclose 'em. 299
I have made strong proof of my constancy,
Giving myself a voluntary wound
Here, in the thigh. Can I bear that with patience,
And not my husband's secrets?

BRUTUS   O ye gods,
Render me worthy of this noble wife!
                                    Knock [within].
Hark, hark, one knocks. Portia, go in awhile,
And by and by thy bosom shall partake
The secrets of my heart.
All my engagements I will construe to thee, 308
All the charactery of my sad brows. 309
Leave me with haste.   Exit Portia.
      [Calling]   Lucius, who's that knocks?

      Enter Lucius and [Caius] Ligarius [wearing a
      kerchief].

LUCIUS
Here is a sick man that would speak with you. 311
BRUTUS
Caius Ligarius, that Metellus spake of.
Boy, stand aside.   [Exit Lucius.]
                    Caius Ligarius, how? 313
LIGARIUS
Vouchsafe good morrow from a feeble tongue. 314
BRUTUS
Oh, what a time have you chose out, brave Caius, 315
To wear a kerchief! Would you were not sick!
LIGARIUS
I am not sick, if Brutus have in hand
Any exploit worthy the name of honor.
BRUTUS
Such an exploit have I in hand, Ligarius,

Had you a healthful ear to hear of it.
LIGARIUS
By all the gods that Romans bow before,
I here discard my sickness! [He throws off his kerchief.]
                    Soul of Rome!
Brave son, derived from honorable loins!
Thou like an exorcist hast conjured up
My mortifièd spirit. Now bid me run, 325
And I will strive with things impossible,
Yea, get the better of them. What's to do?
BRUTUS
A piece of work that will make sick men whole. 328
LIGARIUS
But are not some whole that we must make sick?
BRUTUS
That must we also. What it is, my Caius,
I shall unfold to thee as we are going
To whom it must be done.
LIGARIUS   Set on your foot, 332
And with a heart new-fired I follow you
To do I know not what; but it sufficeth
That Brutus leads me on.   Thunder.
BRUTUS   Follow me, then.   Exeunt.

❖

[2.2]

      Thunder and lightning. Enter Julius Caesar, in his
      nightgown.

CAESAR
Nor heaven nor earth have been at peace tonight. 1
Thrice hath Calpurnia in her sleep cried out,
"Help, ho, they murder Caesar!"—Who's within?

      Enter a Servant.

SERVANT   My lord?
CAESAR
Go bid the priests do present sacrifice 5
And bring me their opinions of success. 6
SERVANT   I will, my lord.   Exit.

      Enter Calpurnia.

CALPURNIA
What mean you, Caesar? Think you to walk forth?
You shall not stir out of your house today.
CAESAR
Caesar shall forth. The things that threatened me
Ne'er looked but on my back. When they shall see
The face of Caesar, they are vanishèd.
CALPURNIA
Caesar, I never stood on ceremonies, 13

285 **keep** stay, be   286 **suburbs** periphery. (In Elizabethan London, prostitutes frequented the suburbs.)   293 **withal** in addition
296 **Cato's daughter** (Cato the Younger of Utica was famous for his integrity; he sided with Pompey against Caesar in 48 B.C. and later killed himself rather than submit to Caesar's tyranny. He was Brutus's uncle as well as his father-in-law.)   299 **counsels** secrets   308 **construe** explain fully   309 **charactery** handwriting, i.e., what is figured there
311 **sick man** (In Elizabethan medicine, a poultice was often applied to the forehead of a patient and wrapped in a handkerchief; hence the kerchief in line 316.)   313 **how?** i.e., how are you?   314 **Vouchsafe** Deign (to accept)   315 **brave** noble

325 **mortifièd** deadened   328 **whole** healthy, i.e., free of the disease of tyranny.   332 **To whom** i.e., to him to whom
2.2 Location: Caesar's house.
0.2 nightgown housecoat.   **1 Nor** Neither   **5 present sacrifice** immediate examination of the entrails of sacrificed animals for omens
6 success the result, what will follow.   **13 stood on ceremonies** attached importance to omens

Yet now they fright me. There is one within,
Besides the things that we have heard and seen,
Recounts most horrid sights seen by the watch.   16
A lioness hath whelpèd in the streets,   17
And graves have yawned and yielded up their dead.   18
Fierce fiery warriors fight upon the clouds
In ranks and squadrons and right form of war,   20
Which drizzled blood upon the Capitol.
The noise of battle hurtled in the air;   22
Horses did neigh, and dying men did groan,
And ghosts did shriek and squeal about the streets.
Oh, Caesar, these things are beyond all use,   25
And I do fear them.

CAESAR   What can be avoided
Whose end is purposed by the mighty gods?
Yet Caesar shall go forth; for these predictions
Are to the world in general as to Caesar.

CALPURNIA
When beggars die there are no comets seen;
The heavens themselves blaze forth the death of
    princes.   31

CAESAR
Cowards die many times before their deaths;
The valiant never taste of death but once.
Of all the wonders that I yet have heard,
It seems to me most strange that men should fear,
Seeing that death, a necessary end,
Will come when it will come.

            Enter a Servant.

                    What say the augurers?

SERVANT
They would not have you to stir forth today.
Plucking the entrails of an offering forth,
They could not find a heart within the beast.

CAESAR
The gods do this in shame of cowardice.
Caesar should be a beast without a heart
If he should stay at home today for fear.
No, Caesar shall not. Danger knows full well
That Caesar is more dangerous than he.
We are two lions littered in one day,
And I the elder and more terrible;
And Caesar shall go forth.

CALPURNIA   Alas, my lord,
Your wisdom is consumed in confidence.   49
Do not go forth today! Call it my fear
That keeps you in the house, and not your own.
We'll send Mark Antony to the Senate House,
And he shall say you are not well today.
Let me, upon my knee, prevail in this.   [*She kneels.*]

CAESAR
Mark Antony shall say I am not well,

And for thy humor I will stay at home.   56
                    [*He raises her.*]

            Enter Decius.

Here's Decius Brutus. He shall tell them so.

DECIUS
Caesar, all hail! Good morrow, worthy Caesar.
I come to fetch you to the Senate House.

CAESAR
And you are come in very happy time   60
To bear my greeting to the senators
And tell them that I will not come today.
Cannot is false, and that I dare not, falser;
I will not come today. Tell them so, Decius.

CALPURNIA
Say he is sick.

CAESAR   Shall Caesar send a lie?
Have I in conquest stretched mine arm so far
To be afeard to tell graybeards the truth?
Decius, go tell them Caesar will not come.

DECIUS
Most mighty Caesar, let me know some cause,
Lest I be laughed at when I tell them so.

CAESAR
The cause is in my will: I will not come.
That is enough to satisfy the Senate.
But for your private satisfaction,
Because I love you, I will let you know.
Calpurnia here, my wife, stays me at home.   75
She dreamt tonight she saw my statue,   76
Which like a fountain with an hundred spouts
Did run pure blood; and many lusty Romans   78
Came smiling and did bathe their hands in it.
And these does she apply for warnings and portents   80
Of evils imminent, and on her knee
Hath begged that I will stay at home today.

DECIUS
This dream is all amiss interpreted;
It was a vision fair and fortunate.
Your statue spouting blood in many pipes,
In which so many smiling Romans bathed,
Signifies that from you great Rome shall suck
Reviving blood, and that great men shall press   88
For tinctures, stains, relics, and cognizance.   89
This by Calpurnia's dream is signified.

CAESAR
And this way have you well expounded it.

DECIUS
I have, when you have heard what I can say;
And know it now. The Senate have concluded
To give this day a crown to mighty Caesar.
If you shall send them word you will not come,

16 **watch** (An anachronism, since there was no *watch,* or "body of
night watchmen," in Caesar's Rome.)   17 **whelpèd** given birth
18 **yawned** gaped   20 **right form** regular formation   22 **hurtled**
clashed   25 **use** normal experience   31 **blaze forth** proclaim (in
a blaze of light)   49 **consumed in confidence** destroyed by overconfidence.

56 **humor** whim   60 **happy** opportune   75 **stays** detains
76 **tonight** last night   78 **lusty** lively, merry   80 **apply for** interpret
as   88 **press** crowd around   89 **tinctures** handkerchiefs dipped in
the blood of martyrs, with healing powers; or colors in a coat of
arms. (*Tinctures, stains,* and *relics* are all venerated properties, as
though Caesar were a saint.)   **cognizance** heraldic emblems worn
by a nobleman's followers.

Their minds may change. Besides, it were a mock   96
Apt to be rendered for someone to say   97
"Break up the Senate till another time
When Caesar's wife shall meet with better dreams."
If Caesar hide himself, shall they not whisper
"Lo, Caesar is afraid"?
Pardon me, Caesar, for my dear dear love
To your proceeding bids me tell you this,   103
And reason to my love is liable.   104

CAESAR
How foolish do your fears seem now, Calpurnia!
I am ashamèd I did yield to them.
Give me my robe, for I will go.

*Enter Brutus, Ligarius, Metellus, Casca,
Trebonius, Cinna, and Publius.*

And look where Publius is come to fetch me.

PUBLIUS
Good morrow, Caesar.

CAESAR   Welcome, Publius.
What, Brutus, are you stirred so early too?
Good morrow, Casca. Caius Ligarius,
Caesar was ne'er so much your enemy
As that same ague which hath made you lean.   113
What is't o'clock?

BRUTUS   Caesar, 'tis strucken eight.   114

CAESAR
I thank you for your pains and courtesy.

Enter Antony.

See, Antony, that revels long o' nights,
Is notwithstanding up. Good morrow, Antony.

ANTONY   So to most noble Caesar.

CAESAR *[to a Servant]*   Bid them prepare within.   119
                                    [Exit Servant.]
I am to blame to be thus waited for.
Now, Cinna. Now, Metellus. What, Trebonius,
I have an hour's talk in store for you;
Remember that you call on me today.
Be near me, that I may remember you.

TREBONIUS
Caesar, I will. *[Aside]* And so near will I be
That your best friends shall wish I had been further.

CAESAR
Good friends, go in and taste some wine with me,
And we, like friends, will straightway go together.

BRUTUS *[aside]*
That every like is not the same, O Caesar,   129
The heart of Brutus earns to think upon!   *Exeunt.* 130

❧

[2.3]

Enter Artemidorus [reading a paper].

ARTEMIDORUS   "Caesar, beware of Brutus; take heed of
Cassius; come not near Casca; have an eye to Cinna;
trust not Trebonius; mark well Metellus Cimber; De-
cius Brutus loves thee not; thou hast wronged Caius
Ligarius. There is but one mind in all these men, and
it is bent against Caesar. If thou be'st not immortal,
look about you. Security gives way to conspiracy. The   7
mighty gods defend thee! Thy lover,   8
                                    Artemidorus."
Here will I stand till Caesar pass along,
And as a suitor will I give him this.
My heart laments that virtue cannot live
Out of the teeth of emulation.   13
If thou read this, O Caesar, thou mayest live;
If not, the Fates with traitors do contrive.   *Exit.* 15

[2.4]

Enter Portia and Lucius.

PORTIA
I prithee, boy, run to the Senate House.
Stay not to answer me, but get thee gone.—
Why dost thou stay?

LUCIUS   To know my errand, madam.

PORTIA
I would have had thee there and here again
Ere I can tell thee what thou shouldst do there.
[Aside] O constancy, be strong upon my side;   6
Set a huge mountain 'tween my heart and tongue!
I have a man's mind, but a woman's might.
How hard it is for women to keep counsel!—   9
Art thou here yet?

LUCIUS   Madam, what should I do?
Run to the Capitol, and nothing else?
And so return to you, and nothing else?

PORTIA
Yes, bring me word, boy, if thy lord look well,
For he went sickly forth; and take good note
What Caesar doth, what suitors press to him.
Hark, boy, what noise is that?

LUCIUS   I hear none, madam.

PORTIA   Prithee, listen well.
I heard a bustling rumor, like a fray,   19
And the wind brings it from the Capitol.

LUCIUS   Sooth, madam, I hear nothing.   21

Enter the Soothsayer.

96–7 **mock . . . rendered** sarcastic remark apt to be made   **103 proceeding** advantage   **104 reason . . . liable** my reasoning is swayed by
my affection.   **113 ague** fever   **114 eight** 8 A.M. (See 2.1.214n on
Roman time.)   **119 prepare within** i.e., set out wine in the other room
and prepare to leave. (Perhaps addressed to the servant who entered
at line 37, or to Calpurnia.) The ritual drinking of wine is a pledge of
friendship that should preclude violence; see lines 127–8.
129 That . . . same i.e., That not all those who behave "like friends"
(line 128) are actually so. (Proverbial.)   **130 earns** grieves

2.3 **Location: A street near the Capitol.**
7 Security gives way Overconfidence opens a path   **8 lover** friend
13 Out . . . emulation beyond the bite of grudging envy.   **15 contrive**
conspire.
2.4 **Location: Before the house of Brutus.**
6 constancy resolution   **9 counsel** a secret.   **19 bustling rumor** confused sound.   **fray** fight   **21 Sooth** Truly

PORTIA
  Come hither, fellow. Which way hast thou been?
SOOTHSAYER   At mine own house, good lady.
PORTIA
  What is't o'clock?
SOOTHSAYER   About the ninth hour, lady.   24
PORTIA
  Is Caesar yet gone to the Capitol?
SOOTHSAYER
  Madam, not yet. I go to take my stand,
  To see him pass on to the Capitol.
PORTIA
  Thou hast some suit to Caesar, hast thou not?
SOOTHSAYER
  That I have, lady, if it will please Caesar
  To be so good to Caesar as to hear me:
  I shall beseech him to befriend himself.
PORTIA
  Why, know'st thou any harm 's intended towards him?
SOOTHSAYER
  None that I know will be, much that I fear may chance.
  Good morrow to you. Here the street is narrow.
  The throng that follows Caesar at the heels,
  Of senators, of praetors, common suitors,   36
  Will crowd a feeble man almost to death.
  I'll get me to a place more void, and there   38
  Speak to great Caesar as he comes along.   *Exit.*
PORTIA
  I must go in. Ay me, how weak a thing
  The heart of woman is! O Brutus,
  The heavens speed thee in thine enterprise!—
  Sure, the boy heard me.—Brutus hath a suit
  That Caesar will not grant.—Oh, I grow faint.—
  Run, Lucius, and commend me to my lord;
  Say I am merry. Come to me again   46
  And bring me word what he doth say to thee.
                          Exeunt [separately].

❖

3.1

  Flourish. Enter Caesar, Brutus, Cassius, Casca,
  Decius, Metellus [Cimber], Trebonius, Cinna,
  Antony, Lepidus, Artemidorus, Publius, [Popilius
  Lena], and the Soothsayer; [others following].

CAESAR [*to the Soothsayer*]   The ides of March are come.
SOOTHSAYER   Ay, Caesar, but not gone.
ARTEMIDORUS   Hail, Caesar! Read this schedule.   3
DECIUS
  Trebonius doth desire you to o'erread,

At your best leisure, this his humble suit.
ARTEMIDORUS
  O Caesar, read mine first, for mine's a suit
  That touches Caesar nearer. Read it, great Caesar.
CAESAR
  What touches us ourself shall be last served.
ARTEMIDORUS
  Delay not, Caesar, read it instantly.
CAESAR
  What, is the fellow mad?
PUBLIUS   Sirrah, give place.   10
CASSIUS
  What, urge you your petitions in the street?
  Come to the Capitol.

        [*Caesar goes to the Capitol and takes his place, the*
        rest following.]

POPILIUS [*to Cassius*]
  I wish your enterprise today may thrive.
CASSIUS   What enterprise, Popilius?
POPILIUS [*to Cassius*]   Fare you well.
                          [*He advances to Caesar.*]
BRUTUS   What said Popilius Lena?
CASSIUS
  He wished today our enterprise might thrive.
  I fear our purpose is discoverèd.
BRUTUS
  Look how he makes to Caesar. Mark him.   19
             [*Popilius speaks apart to Caesar.*]
CASSIUS
  Casca, be sudden, for we fear prevention.
  Brutus, what shall be done? If this be known,
  Cassius or Caesar never shall turn back,   22
  For I will slay myself.
BRUTUS   Cassius, be constant.   23
  Popilius Lena speaks not of our purposes;
  For look, he smiles, and Caesar doth not change.   25
CASSIUS
  Trebonius knows his time, for look you, Brutus,
  He draws Mark Antony out of the way.
                  [*Exit Trebonius with Antony.*]
DECIUS
  Where is Metellus Cimber? Let him go
  And presently prefer his suit to Caesar.   29
BRUTUS
  He is addressed. Press near and second him.   30
CINNA
  Casca, you are the first that rears your hand.
                          [*They press near Caesar.*]
CAESAR
  Are we all ready? What is now amiss
  That Caesar and his Senate must redress?

---

24 **the ninth hour** i.e., 9 A.M. (In Roman reckoning, the ninth hour
would be 3 P.M.)   36 **praetors** judges   38 **void** empty, uncrowded
46 **merry** cheerful. (Not "mirthful.")
3.1 **Location: Before the Capitol, and, following line 12, within the
Capitol.**
0.4. *others following* (Citizens may be present, though not certainly
so; see lines 83 and 93–4.)   3 **schedule** document.

10 **Sirrah** Fellow. (A form of address to a social inferior.)   **place** way.
19 **makes to** advances toward   22–3 **Cassius . . . myself** Either Cassius or Caesar will never return from the Capitol alive, for I will commit suicide if this attempt fails.   23 **be constant** hold steady.
25 **change** change expression.   29 **presently prefer** immediately urge
30 **addressed** ready.

METELLUS [*kneeling*]
  Most high, most mighty, and most puissant Caesar,   34
  Metellus Cimber throws before thy seat
  An humble heart—
CAESAR   I must prevent thee, Cimber.   36
  These couchings and these lowly courtesies   37
  Might fire the blood of ordinary men,   38
  And turn preordinance and first decree   39
  Into the law of children. Be not fond   40
  To think that Caesar bears such rebel blood   41
  That will be thawed from the true quality   42
  With that which melteth fools—I mean, sweet words,
  Low-crookèd curtsies, and base spaniel fawning.   44
  Thy brother by decree is banishèd.
  If thou dost bend and pray and fawn for him,   46
  I spurn thee like a cur out of my way.   47
  Know, Caesar doth not wrong, nor without cause
  Will he be satisfied.
METELLUS
  Is there no voice more worthy than my own
  To sound more sweetly in great Caesar's ear
  For the repealing of my banished brother?   52
BRUTUS [*kneeling*]
  I kiss thy hand, but not in flattery, Caesar,
  Desiring thee that Publius Cimber may
  Have an immediate freedom of repeal.   55
CAESAR
  What, Brutus?
CASSIUS [*kneeling*]   Pardon, Caesar! Caesar, pardon!
  As low as to thy foot doth Cassius fall,
  To beg enfranchisement for Publius Cimber.   58
CAESAR
  I could be well moved, if I were as you;
  If I could pray to move, prayers would move me.   60
  But I am constant as the northern star,   61
  Of whose true-fixed and resting quality   62
  There is no fellow in the firmament.   63
  The skies are painted with unnumbered sparks;
  They are all fire and every one doth shine;
  But there's but one in all doth hold his place.
  So in the world: 'tis furnished well with men,
  And men are flesh and blood, and apprehensive;   68
  Yet in the number I do know but one
  That unassailable holds on his rank,   70
  Unshaked of motion. And that I am he,   71
  Let me a little show it even in this:

That I was constant Cimber should be banished,
And constant do remain to keep him so.
CINNA [*kneeling*]
  O Caesar—
CAESAR   Hence! Wilt thou lift up Olympus?   75
DECIUS [*kneeling*]
  Great Caesar—
CAESAR   Doth not Brutus bootless kneel?   76
CASCA Speak hands for me!
          They stab Caesar, [Casca first, Brutus last].
CAESAR *Et tu, Brutè?* Then fall, Caesar!   *Dies.*   78
CINNA
  Liberty! Freedom! Tyranny is dead!
  Run hence, proclaim, cry it about the streets.
CASSIUS
  Some to the common pulpits, and cry out   81
  "Liberty, freedom, and enfranchisement!"   82
BRUTUS
  People and senators, be not affrighted.
  Fly not; stand still. Ambition's debt is paid.   84
CASCA
  Go to the pulpit, Brutus.
DECIUS   And Cassius too.
BRUTUS Where's Publius?   86
CINNA
  Here, quite confounded with this mutiny.   87
METELLUS
  Stand fast together, lest some friend of Caesar's
  Should chance—
BRUTUS
  Talk not of standing. Publius, good cheer.   90
  There is no harm intended to your person,
  Nor to no Roman else. So tell them, Publius.
CASSIUS
  And leave us, Publius, lest that the people,
  Rushing on us, should do your age some mischief.
BRUTUS
  Do so, and let no man abide this deed   95
  But we the doers.   [*Exeunt all but the conspirators.*]

          Enter Trebonius.

CASSIUS
  Where is Antony?
TREBONIUS   Fled to his house amazed.   97
  Men, wives, and children stare, cry out, and run
  As it were doomsday.
BRUTUS   Fates, we will know your pleasures.   99
  That we shall die, we know; 'tis but the time,   100
  And drawing days out, that men stand upon.   101

34 **puissant** powerful 36 **prevent** forestall 37 **couchings . . . courtesies** kneelings and submissive bows 38 **fire the blood of** incite 39–40 **And turn . . . children** and turn preordained law into the kinds of childish and flexible rules that children use in their games. 40 **fond** so foolish as 41 **rebel** rebellious against reason 42 **true quality** proper firmness and stability. (The metaphor is from alchemy.) 44 **Low-crookèd curtsies** obsequious bows 46 **bend** bow 47 **spurn** kick 52 **repealing** recall 55 **freedom of repeal** permission to return. 58 **enfranchisement** i.e., restoration of citizenship 60 **pray to move** make petition (as you do) 61 **northern star** polestar 62 **resting** remaining stationary 63 **fellow** equal 68 **apprehensive** capable of perception 70 **rank** place in line or file, position 71 **Unshaked of motion** (1) unswayed by petitions (2) with perfect steadiness.

75 **Olympus** mountain dwelling of the Greek gods 76 **bootless** in vain 78 *Et tu, Brutè?* You too, Brutus? (Literally, "Even thou.") 81 **common pulpits** public platforms or rostra 82 **enfranchisement** restoration of civil rights. (Cf. line 58 above.) 84 **Ambition's debt** What Caesar's ambition deserved 86 **Publius** (An old senator, too confused to flee.) 87 **mutiny** uprising, discord. 90 **standing** making a stand. 95 **abide** (1) suffer the consequences of (2) remain here with 97 **amazed** stupified. 99 **As** as if 100–1 **'tis . . . upon** i.e., it is only the time of our deaths, and how long we have to live, that we are uncertain about, make a question of.

CASCA
　　Why, he that cuts off twenty years of life
　　Cuts off so many years of fearing death.
BRUTUS
　　Grant that, and then is death a benefit.
　　So are we Caesar's friends, that have abridged
　　His time of fearing death. Stoop, Romans, stoop,
　　And let us bathe our hands in Caesar's blood
　　Up to the elbows and besmear our swords.
　　Then walk we forth even to the marketplace,   109
　　And, waving our red weapons o'er our heads,
　　Let's all cry "Peace, freedom, and liberty!"
CASSIUS
　　Stoop, then, and wash. [*They bathe their hands and
　　　　weapons.*] How many ages hence
　　Shall this our lofty scene be acted over
　　In states unborn and accents yet unknown!   114
BRUTUS
　　How many times shall Caesar bleed in sport,   115
　　That now on Pompey's basis lies along   116
　　No worthier than the dust!
CASSIUS   So oft as that shall be,
　　So often shall the knot of us be called   119
　　The men that gave their country liberty.
DECIUS
　　What, shall we forth?
CASSIUS   Ay, every man away.
　　Brutus shall lead, and we will grace his heels   122
　　With the most boldest and best hearts of Rome.

　　　　Enter a Servant.

BRUTUS
　　Soft, who comes here? A friend of Antony's.
SERVANT [*kneeling*]
　　Thus, Brutus, did my master bid me kneel;
　　Thus did Mark Antony bid me fall down,
　　And, being prostrate, thus he bade me say:
　　"Brutus is noble, wise, valiant, and honest;   128
　　Caesar was mighty, bold, royal, and loving.
　　Say I love Brutus and I honor him;
　　Say I feared Caesar, honored him, and loved him.
　　If Brutus will vouchsafe that Antony
　　May safely come to him and be resolved   133
　　How Caesar hath deserved to lie in death,
　　Mark Antony shall not love Caesar dead
　　So well as Brutus living, but will follow
　　The fortunes and affairs of noble Brutus
　　Thorough the hazards of this untrod state   138
　　With all true faith." So says my master Antony.
BRUTUS
　　Thy master is a wise and valiant Roman;
　　I never thought him worse.

Tell him, so please him come unto this place,   142
He shall be satisfied and, by my honor,
Depart untouched.
SERVANT   I'll fetch him presently.   144
　　　　　　　　　　Exit Servant.
BRUTUS
　　I know that we shall have him well to friend.   145
CASSIUS
　　I wish we may. But yet have I a mind
　　That fears him much, and my misgiving still   147
　　Falls shrewdly to the purpose.   148

　　　　Enter Antony.

BRUTUS
　　But here comes Antony.—Welcome, Mark Antony.
ANTONY
　　O mighty Caesar! Dost thou lie so low?
　　Are all thy conquests, glories, triumphs, spoils,
　　Shrunk to this little measure? Fare thee well.—
　　I know not, gentlemen, what you intend,
　　Who else must be let blood, who else is rank;   154
　　If I myself, there is no hour so fit
　　As Caesar's death's hour, nor no instrument
　　Of half that worth as those your swords, made rich
　　With the most noble blood of all this world.
　　I do beseech ye, if you bear me hard,   159
　　Now, whilst your purpled hands do reek and smoke,   160
　　Fulfill your pleasure. Live a thousand years,   161
　　I shall not find myself so apt to die;   162
　　No place will please me so, no mean of death,
　　As here by Caesar, and by you cut off,
　　The choice and master spirits of this age.
BRUTUS
　　Oh, Antony, beg not your death of us.
　　Though now we must appear bloody and cruel,
　　As by our hands and this our present act
　　You see we do, yet see you but our hands
　　And this the bleeding business they have done.
　　Our hearts you see not. They are pitiful;   171
　　And pity to the general wrong of Rome—
　　As fire drives out fire, so pity pity—   173
　　Hath done this deed on Caesar. For your part,
　　To you our swords have leaden points, Mark Antony.   175
　　Our arms in strength of malice, and our hearts   176
　　Of brothers' temper, do receive you in   177
　　With all kind love, good thoughts, and reverence.
CASSIUS
　　Your voice shall be as strong as any man's   179
　　In the disposing of new dignities.   180

---

109 the marketplace i.e., the Forum   **114 accents** languages   **115 in sport** for entertainment   **116 on Pompey's . . . along** lies prostrate on the pedestal of Pompey's statue   **119 knot** group   **122 grace his heels** follow him close at heels (in a triumphal procession; cf. 1.1.34)   **128 honest** honorable   **133 be resolved** receive an explanation   **138 Thorough** through.   **untrod state** still unexplored state of affairs

142 so if it should   **144 presently** immediately.   **145 to friend** for a friend.   **147 fears** distrusts   **148 Falls . . . purpose** is intensely to the point.   **154 let blood** bled (a medical term), i.e., killed.   **rank** swollen, diseased (and hence in need of bleeding)   **159 bear me hard** bear ill will to me   **160 purpled** bloody.   **reek** steam   **161 Live** If I should live   **162 apt** ready   **171 pitiful** full of pity   **173 pity pity** i.e., pity for the general wrong of Rome has driven out pity for Caesar   **175 leaden** i.e., blunt   **176–7 Our . . . temper** i.e., Both our arms, though seeming strong in enmity, and our hearts, full of brotherly feeling   **179 voice** vote, authority   **180 dignities** offices of state.

BRUTUS

Only be patient till we have appeased
The multitude, beside themselves with fear,
And then we will deliver you the cause   183
Why I, that did love Caesar when I struck him,
Have thus proceeded.

ANTONY   I doubt not of your wisdom.
Let each man render me his bloody hand.

[*He shakes hands with the conspirators.*]

First, Marcus Brutus, will I shake with you;
Next, Caius Cassius, do I take your hand;
Now, Decius Brutus, yours; now yours, Metellus;
Yours, Cinna; and, my valiant Casca, yours;
Though last, not least in love, yours, good Trebonius.
Gentlemen all—alas, what shall I say?
My credit now stands on such slippery ground   193
That one of two bad ways you must conceit me,   194
Either a coward or a flatterer.
That I did love thee, Caesar, oh, 'tis true!
If then thy spirit look upon us now,
Shall it not grieve thee dearer than thy death   198
To see thy Antony making his peace,
Shaking the bloody fingers of thy foes—
Most noble—in the presence of thy corpse?
Had I as many eyes as thou hast wounds,
Weeping as fast as they stream forth thy blood,
It would become me better than to close   204
In terms of friendship with thine enemies.
Pardon me, Julius! Here wast thou bayed, brave hart,   206
Here didst thou fall, and here thy hunters stand,
Signed in thy spoil and crimsoned in thy lethe.   208
O world, thou wast the forest to this hart,
And this indeed, O world, the heart of thee!
How like a deer, strucken by many princes,
Dost thou here lie!

CASSIUS

Mark Antony—

ANTONY   Pardon me, Caius Cassius.
The enemies of Caesar shall say this;   214
Then in a friend it is cold modesty.   215

CASSIUS

I blame you not for praising Caesar so,
But what compact mean you to have with us?
Will you be pricked in number of our friends,   218
Or shall we on and not depend on you?

ANTONY

Therefore I took your hands, but was indeed
Swayed from the point by looking down on Caesar.
Friends am I with you all, and love you all,

Upon this hope, that you shall give me reasons
Why and wherein Caesar was dangerous.

BRUTUS

Or else were this a savage spectacle.   225
Our reasons are so full of good regard   226
That were you, Antony, the son of Caesar,
You should be satisfied.

ANTONY   That's all I seek,
And am moreover suitor that I may
Produce his body to the marketplace,   230
And in the pulpit, as becomes a friend,   231
Speak in the order of his funeral.   232

BRUTUS

You shall, Mark Antony.

CASSIUS   Brutus, a word with you.
[*Aside to Brutus*] You know not what you do. Do not
   consent
That Antony speak in his funeral.
Know you how much the people may be moved
By that which he will utter?

BRUTUS [*aside to Cassius*]   By your pardon:
I will myself into the pulpit first
And show the reason of our Caesar's death.
What Antony shall speak, I will protest   240
He speaks by leave and by permission,
And that we are contented Caesar shall
Have all true rites and lawful ceremonies.
It shall advantage more than do us wrong.

CASSIUS [*aside to Brutus*]

I know not what may fall. I like it not.   245

BRUTUS

Mark Antony, here, take you Caesar's body.
You shall not in your funeral speech blame us,
But speak all good you can devise of Caesar,
And say you do't by our permission.
Else shall you not have any hand at all
About his funeral. And you shall speak
In the same pulpit whereto I am going,
After my speech is ended.

ANTONY   Be it so.
I do desire no more.

BRUTUS

Prepare the body then, and follow us.   255

Exeunt. Manet Antony.

ANTONY

Oh, pardon me, thou bleeding piece of earth,
That I am meek and gentle with these butchers!
Thou art the ruins of the noblest man
That ever livèd in the tide of times.   259
Woe to the hand that shed this costly blood!   260
Over thy wounds now do I prophesy—
Which, like dumb mouths, do ope their ruby lips

---

183 deliver report to   **193 credit** credibility   **194 conceit** think, judge
198 dearer more deeply   **204 close** come to an agreement
206 bayed brought to bay.   **hart** stag. (With pun on *heart*.)
208 Signed . . . spoil marked with the tokens of your slaughter.
(The *spoil* in hunting is the cutting up of the quarry and distribution
of reward to the hounds.)   **lethe** river of oblivion in the underworld,
here associated with death and blood. (Perhaps fused with Cocytus,
river of blood in the underworld.)   **214 The enemies** Even the
enemies   **215 cold modesty** sober moderation.   **218 pricked** marked
down

225 else were this otherwise this would be   **226 regard** account, consideration   **230 Produce** bring forth.   **marketplace** Forum
231 pulpit public platform   **232 order** ceremony   **240 protest**
announce, insist   **245 fall** befall, happen.   **255.1 Manet** He remains
onstage   **259 tide of times** course of all history.   **260 costly** (1) valuable (2) fraught with dire consequences

To beg the voice and utterance of my tongue—
A curse shall light upon the limbs of men;
Domestic fury and fierce civil strife
Shall cumber all the parts of Italy;   266
Blood and destruction shall be so in use
And dreadful objects so familiar   268
That mothers shall but smile when they behold
Their infants quartered with the hands of war,   270
All pity choked with custom of fell deeds;   271
And Caesar's spirit, ranging for revenge,   272
With Ate by his side come hot from hell,   273
Shall in these confines with a monarch's voice   274
Cry havoc and let slip the dogs of war,   275
That this foul deed shall smell above the earth
With carrion men, groaning for burial.

Enter Octavius' Servant.

You serve Octavius Caesar, do you not?
SERVANT   I do, Mark Antony.
ANTONY
Caesar did write for him to come to Rome.
SERVANT
He did receive his letters, and is coming,   281
And bid me say to you by word of mouth—
O Caesar!—   [*Seeing the body.*]
ANTONY
Thy heart is big. Get thee apart and weep.
Passion, I see, is catching, for mine eyes,   285
Seeing those beads of sorrow stand in thine,
Began to water. Is thy master coming?
SERVANT
He lies tonight within seven leagues of Rome.   288
ANTONY
Post back with speed and tell him what hath chanced.   289
Here is a mourning Rome, a dangerous Rome,
No Rome of safety for Octavius yet;   291
Hie hence and tell him so. Yet stay awhile;
Thou shalt not back till I have borne this corpse
Into the marketplace. There shall I try,   294
In my oration, how the people take
The cruel issue of these bloody men,   296
According to the which thou shalt discourse   297
To young Octavius of the state of things.   298
Lend me your hand.   *Exeunt [with Caesar's body].*

❖

[3.2]

*Enter Brutus and [presently] goes into the pulpit,
and Cassius, with the Plebeians.*

PLEBEIANS
We will be satisfied! Let us be satisfied!   1
BRUTUS
Then follow me, and give me audience, friends.—
Cassius, go you into the other street
And part the numbers.   4
Those that will hear me speak, let 'em stay here;
Those that will follow Cassius, go with him;
And public reasons shall be renderèd
Of Caesar's death.
FIRST PLEBEIAN   I will hear Brutus speak.
SECOND PLEBEIAN
I will hear Cassius, and compare their reasons
When severally we hear them renderèd.   10
        [*Exit Cassius, with some of the Plebeians.*]
THIRD PLEBEIAN
The noble Brutus is ascended. Silence!
BRUTUS   Be patient till the last.
Romans, countrymen, and lovers, hear me for my   13
cause, and be silent that you may hear. Believe me for
mine honor, and have respect to mine honor, that you
may believe. Censure me in your wisdom, and awake   16
your senses, that you may the better judge. If there be 17
any in this assembly, any dear friend of Caesar's, to
him I say that Brutus' love to Caesar was no less than
his. If then that friend demand why Brutus rose
against Caesar, this is my answer: not that I loved Caesar less, but that I loved Rome more. Had you rather
Caesar were living and die all slaves, than that Caesar
were dead, to live all free men? As Caesar loved me, I
weep for him; as he was fortunate, I rejoice at it; as he
was valiant, I honor him; but, as he was ambitious, I
slew him. There is tears for his love; joy for his fortune;
honor for his valor; and death for his ambition.
Who is here so base that would be a bondman? If any,
speak, for him have I offended. Who is here so rude   30
that would not be a Roman? If any, speak, for him
have I offended. Who is here so vile that will not love
his country? If any, speak, for him have I offended. I
pause for a reply.
ALL   None, Brutus, none!
BRUTUS   Then none have I offended. I have done no
more to Caesar than you shall do to Brutus. The ques-   37
tion of his death is enrolled in the Capitol, his glory   38
not extenuated wherein he was worthy, nor his   39

---

266 **cumber** overwhelm; entangle, burden 268 **objects** sights
270 **quartered** cut to pieces 271 **custom . . . deeds** the familiarity of
cruel deeds 272 **ranging** roaming up and down in search of prey
273 **Ate** goddess of discord and moral chaos 274 **confines** regions.
monarch's i.e., authoritative 275 **Cry havoc** give the signal for sack,
pillage, and slaughter, taking no prisoners. **let slip** unleash
281 **letters** (Not necessarily plural. The Latin word for letter, *litterae*,
has a plural form.) 285 **Passion** Sorrow 288 **lies** lodges. **seven
leagues** about twenty miles 289 **Post** Ride. **chanced** happened.
291 **Rome** (With pun on "room," as at 1.2.156.) 294 **try** test
296 **cruel issue** outcome of the cruelty 297 **the which** the outcome of which 298 **young Octavius** (He was eighteen in March
of 44 B.C.)

3.2 **Location:** The Forum.
1 **be satisfied** have an explanation. 4 **part** divide 10 **severally** separately 13 **lovers** friends. (This speech by Brutus is in what Plutarch
calls the Lacedemonian or Spartan style, brief and sententious. Its
content is original with Shakespeare.) 16 **Censure** Judge 17 **senses**
intellectual powers 30 **rude** barbarous 37 **than . . . Brutus** (In lines
45–7 below, Brutus offers to die for Rome if his country should ask.)
37–8 **The question . . . enrolled** The considerations that necessitated
his death are recorded 39 **extenuated** minimized

offenses enforced for which he suffered death.   40

*Enter Mark Antony [and others] with Caesar's
body.*

Here comes his body, mourned by Mark Antony, who,
though he had no hand in his death, shall receive the
benefit of his dying, a place in the commonwealth, as
which of you shall not? With this I depart, that, as I
slew my best lover for the good of Rome, I have the   45
same dagger for myself when it shall please my country to need my death.

ALL   Live, Brutus, live, live!   [*Brutus comes down.*]

FIRST PLEBEIAN
Bring him with triumph home unto his house.

SECOND PLEBEIAN
Give him a statue with his ancestors.   50

THIRD PLEBEIAN
Let him be Caesar.

FOURTH PLEBEIAN   Caesar's better parts
Shall be crowned in Brutus.

FIRST PLEBEIAN
We'll bring him to his house with shouts and clamors.

BRUTUS
My countrymen—

SECOND PLEBEIAN   Peace, silence! Brutus speaks.

FIRST PLEBEIAN   Peace, ho!

BRUTUS
Good countrymen, let me depart alone,
And, for my sake, stay here with Antony.
Do grace to Caesar's corpse, and grace his speech   58
Tending to Caesar's glories, which Mark Antony,   59
By our permission, is allowed to make.
I do entreat you, not a man depart,
Save I alone, till Antony have spoke.   *Exit.*

FIRST PLEBEIAN
Stay, ho, and let us hear Mark Antony.

THIRD PLEBEIAN
Let him go up into the public chair.
We'll hear him. Noble Antony, go up.

ANTONY
For Brutus' sake I am beholding to you.   66
    [*He goes into the pulpit.*]

FOURTH PLEBEIAN   What does he say of Brutus?

THIRD PLEBEIAN   He says, for Brutus' sake
He finds himself beholding to us all.

FOURTH PLEBEIAN
'Twere best he speak no harm of Brutus here.

FIRST PLEBEIAN
This Caesar was a tyrant.

THIRD PLEBEIAN   Nay, that's certain.
We are blest that Rome is rid of him.

SECOND PLEBEIAN
Peace! Let us hear what Antony can say.

ANTONY
You gentle Romans—

ALL   Peace, ho! Let us hear him.

ANTONY
Friends, Romans, countrymen, lend me your ears.   75
I come to bury Caesar, not to praise him.
The evil that men do lives after them;
The good is oft interrèd with their bones.
So let it be with Caesar. The noble Brutus
Hath told you Caesar was ambitious.
If it were so, it was a grievous fault,
And grievously hath Caesar answered it.   82
Here, under leave of Brutus and the rest—   83
For Brutus is an honorable man,
So are they all, all honorable men—
Come I to speak in Caesar's funeral.
He was my friend, faithful and just to me;
But Brutus says he was ambitious,
And Brutus is an honorable man.
He hath brought many captives home to Rome,
Whose ransoms did the general coffers fill.
Did this in Caesar seem ambitious?
When that the poor have cried, Caesar hath wept;   93
Ambition should be made of sterner stuff.
Yet Brutus says he was ambitious,
And Brutus is an honorable man.
You all did see that on the Lupercal   97
I thrice presented him a kingly crown,
Which he did thrice refuse. Was this ambition?
Yet Brutus says he was ambitious,
And sure he is an honorable man.
I speak not to disprove what Brutus spoke,
But here I am to speak what I do know.
You all did love him once, not without cause.
What cause withholds you then to mourn for him?
O judgment! Thou art fled to brutish beasts,
And men have lost their reason. Bear with me;
My heart is in the coffin there with Caesar,
And I must pause till it come back to me.

FIRST PLEBEIAN
Methinks there is much reason in his sayings.

SECOND PLEBEIAN
If thou consider rightly of the matter,
Caesar has had great wrong.

THIRD PLEBEIAN   Has he, masters?   112
I fear there will a worse come in his place.

FOURTH PLEBEIAN
Marked ye his words? He would not take the crown,
Therefore 'tis certain he was not ambitious.

FIRST PLEBEIAN
If it be found so, some will dear abide it.   116

---

40 enforced exaggerated, insisted upon   **45 lover** friend   **50 SECOND
PLEBEIAN** (Not the same person who exited at line 10; the numbering
here refers to those who stay to hear Brutus.)   **58 Do grace** Show
respect.   **grace his speech** listen courteously to Antony's speech
59 Tending to relating to, dealing with   **66 beholding** beholden

75 Friends (This speech by Antony is thought to illustrate the Asiatic
or "florid" style of speaking. In it Shakespeare gathers various hints
from Plutarch ("Marcus Antonius" and "Dion") and Appian, but the
speech is Shakespeare's invention.)   **82 answered** paid the penalty
for   **83 under leave** by permission   **93 When that** When   **97 Lupercal** (See 1.1.67 and note.)   **112 masters** good sirs.   **116 dear abide it**
pay a heavy penalty for it.

SECOND PLEBEIAN
Poor soul, his eyes are red as fire with weeping.
THIRD PLEBEIAN
There's not a nobler man in Rome than Antony.
FOURTH PLEBEIAN
Now mark him. He begins again to speak.
ANTONY
But yesterday the word of Caesar might
Have stood against the world. Now lies he there,
And none so poor to do him reverence.   122
Oh, masters, if I were disposed to stir
Your hearts and minds to mutiny and rage,   124
I should do Brutus wrong, and Cassius wrong,
Who, you all know, are honorable men.
I will not do them wrong; I rather choose
To wrong the dead, to wrong myself and you,
Than I will wrong such honorable men.
But here's a parchment with the seal of Caesar.
I found it in his closet; 'tis his will.   131
                              [He shows the will.]
Let but the commons hear this testament—   132
Which, pardon me, I do not mean to read—
And they would go and kiss dead Caesar's wounds
And dip their napkins in his sacred blood,   135
Yea, beg a hair of him for memory,
And dying, mention it within their wills,
Bequeathing it as a rich legacy
Unto their issue.
FOURTH PLEBEIAN
We'll hear the will! Read it, Mark Antony.
ALL
The will, the will! We will hear Caesar's will.
ANTONY
Have patience, gentle friends: I must not read it.
It is not meet you know how Caesar loved you.   143
You are not wood, you are not stones, but men;
And being men, hearing the will of Caesar,
It will inflame you, it will make you mad.
'Tis good you know not that you are his heirs,
For if you should, oh, what would come of it?
FOURTH PLEBEIAN
Read the will! We'll hear it, Antony.
You shall read us the will, Caesar's will.
ANTONY
Will you be patient? Will you stay awhile?
I have o'ershot myself to tell you of it.   152
I fear I wrong the honorable men
Whose daggers have stabbed Caesar; I do fear it.
FOURTH PLEBEIAN
They were traitors. "Honorable men"!
ALL   The will! The testament!
SECOND PLEBEIAN
They were villains, murderers. The will! Read the will!

ANTONY
You will compel me then to read the will?
Then make a ring about the corpse of Caesar
And let me show you him that made the will.
Shall I descend? And will you give me leave?
ALL   Come down.
SECOND PLEBEIAN   Descend.
THIRD PLEBEIAN   You shall have leave.
             [Antony comes down. They gather around Caesar.]
FOURTH PLEBEIAN   A ring; stand round.
FIRST PLEBEIAN
Stand from the hearse. Stand from the body.   166
SECOND PLEBEIAN
Room for Antony, most noble Antony!
ANTONY
Nay, press not so upon me. Stand farre off.   168
ALL   Stand back! Room! Bear back!
ANTONY
If you have tears, prepare to shed them now.
You all do know this mantle. I remember   171
The first time ever Caesar put it on;
'Twas on a summer's evening in his tent,
That day he overcame the Nervii.   174
Look, in this place ran Cassius' dagger through.
See what a rent the envious Casca made.   176
Through this the well-belovèd Brutus stabbed,
And as he plucked his cursèd steel away,
Mark how the blood of Caesar followed it,
As rushing out of doors to be resolved   180
If Brutus so unkindly knocked or no;   181
For Brutus, as you know, was Caesar's angel.   182
Judge, O you gods, how dearly Caesar loved him!
This was the most unkindest cut of all;   184
For when the noble Caesar saw him stab,
Ingratitude, more strong than traitors' arms,
Quite vanquished him. Then burst his mighty heart,
And in his mantle muffling up his face,
Even at the base of Pompey's statue,
Which all the while ran blood, great Caesar fell.
Oh, what a fall was there, my countrymen!
Then I, and you, and all of us fell down,
Whilst bloody treason flourished over us.   193
Oh, now you weep, and I perceive you feel
The dint of pity. These are gracious drops.   195
Kind souls, what weep you when you but behold   196
Our Caesar's vesture wounded? Look you here,   197
Here is himself, marred as you see with traitors.
                              [He lifts Caesar's mantle.]
FIRST PLEBEIAN   Oh, piteous spectacle!
SECOND PLEBEIAN   O noble Caesar!

---

122 And none . . . reverence i.e., and yet no one is below him in fortune now, no one of even the lowest social station to look up to and
revere him.   124 mutiny riot, tumult   131 closet private chamber,
study   132 commons common people   135 napkins handkerchiefs
143 meet fitting that   152 o'ershot myself gone further than I should

166 hearse bier.   168 farre farther   171 mantle cloak, toga.   174 the
Nervii the Belgian tribe whose defeat in 57 B.C. is described in Caesar's Gallic Wars, 2.15–28   176 rent tear, hole   envious malicious,
spiteful   180 be resolved learn for certain   181 unkindly cruelly
and unnaturally   182 angel (1) daimon or genius, guardian angel (2)
best beloved.   184 unkindest (1) most cruel (2) most unnatural. (The
double superlative was grammatically acceptable in Shakespeare's
day.)   193 flourished (1) triumphed insolently (2) brandished its
sword   195 dint impression   196 what why, or how much
197 vesture clothing

THIRD PLEBEIAN   Oh, woeful day!

FOURTH PLEBEIAN   Oh, traitors, villains!

FIRST PLEBEIAN   Oh, most bloody sight!

SECOND PLEBEIAN   We will be revenged.

ALL   Revenge! About! Seek! Burn! Fire! Kill! Slay! Let   205
not a traitor live!

ANTONY   Stay, countrymen.

FIRST PLEBEIAN   Peace there! Hear the noble Antony.

SECOND PLEBEIAN   We'll hear him, we'll follow him,
we'll die with him!

ANTONY
Good friends, sweet friends, let me not stir you up
To such a sudden flood of mutiny.
They that have done this deed are honorable.
What private griefs they have, alas, I know not,   214
That made them do it. They are wise and honorable,
And will no doubt with reasons answer you.
I come not, friends, to steal away your hearts.
I am no orator, as Brutus is,
But, as you know me all, a plain blunt man
That love my friend, and that they know full well
That gave me public leave to speak of him.   221
For I have neither wit, nor words, nor worth,   222
Action, nor utterance, nor the power of speech   223
To stir men's blood. I only speak right on.
I tell you that which you yourselves do know,
Show you sweet Caesar's wounds, poor poor dumb
   mouths,
And bid them speak for me. But were I Brutus,
And Brutus Antony, there were an Antony
Would ruffle up your spirits and put a tongue   229
In every wound of Caesar that should move
The stones of Rome to rise and mutiny.

ALL
We'll mutiny!

FIRST PLEBEIAN   We'll burn the house of Brutus!

THIRD PLEBEIAN
Away, then! Come, seek the conspirators.

ANTONY
Yet hear me, countrymen. Yet hear me speak.

ALL
Peace, ho! Hear Antony, most noble Antony!

ANTONY
Why, friends, you go to do you know not what.
Wherein hath Caesar thus deserved your loves?
Alas, you know not. I must tell you then:
You have forgot the will I told you of.

ALL
Most true. The will! Let's stay and hear the will.

ANTONY
Here is the will, and under Caesar's seal.
To every Roman citizen he gives,
To every several man, seventy-five drachmas.   243

SECOND PLEBEIAN   Most noble Caesar! We'll revenge his death.

THIRD PLEBEIAN   O royal Caesar!

ANTONY   Hear me with patience.

ALL   Peace, ho!

ANTONY
Moreover, he hath left you all his walks,
His private arbors, and new-planted orchards,
On this side Tiber; he hath left them you,
And to your heirs forever—common pleasures,   251
To walk abroad and recreate yourselves.
Here was a Caesar! When comes such another?

FIRST PLEBEIAN
Never, never! Come, away, away!
We'll burn his body in the holy place
And with the brands fire the traitors' houses.
Take up the body.

SECOND PLEBEIAN   Go fetch fire!

THIRD PLEBEIAN   Pluck down benches!

FOURTH PLEBEIAN   Pluck down forms, windows, any-   259
thing!   *Exeunt Plebeians [with the body].*

ANTONY
Now let it work. Mischief, thou art afoot.
Take thou what course thou wilt.

Enter [Octavius'] Servant.

How now, fellow?

SERVANT
Sir, Octavius is already come to Rome.

ANTONY   Where is he?

SERVANT
He and Lepidus are at Caesar's house.

ANTONY
And thither will I straight to visit him.   266
He comes upon a wish. Fortune is merry,   267
And in this mood will give us anything.

SERVANT
I heard him say Brutus and Cassius
Are rid like madmen through the gates of Rome.   270

ANTONY
Belike they had some notice of the people,   271
How I had moved them. Bring me to Octavius.

Exeunt.

❖

[3.3]

*Enter Cinna the poet, and after him the Ple-
beians.*

CINNA
I dreamt tonight that I did feast with Caesar,   1

---

205 **About!** To work!   214 **griefs** grievances   221 **public leave** permission to speak publicly   222–3 **neither . . . speech** neither intelligence, vocabulary, moral authority, gesture, rhetorical skill, nor
polished delivery   229 **ruffle up** stir to anger   243 **several** individual.   **drachmas** coins. (This is a substantial bequest.)

251 **common pleasures** public pleasure gardens (in which)
259 **forms, windows** benches, window frames and shutters
266 **straight** straightway, at once   267 **upon a wish** just when
wanted.   **merry** favorably disposed   270 **Are rid** have ridden
271 **Belike** Likely enough.   **of** about; or, from
3.3. Location: A street.
1 **tonight** last night

And things unluckily charge my fantasy.   2
I have no will to wander forth of doors,
Yet something leads me forth.
FIRST PLEBEIAN   What is your name?
SECOND PLEBEIAN   Whither are you going?
THIRD PLEBEIAN   Where do you dwell?
FOURTH PLEBEIAN   Are you a married man or a
    bachelor?
SECOND PLEBEIAN   Answer every man directly.
FIRST PLEBEIAN   Ay, and briefly.
FOURTH PLEBEIAN   Ay, and wisely.
THIRD PLEBEIAN   Ay, and truly, you were best.   13
CINNA   What is my name? Whither am I going? Where
    do I dwell? Am I a married man or a bachelor? Then
    to answer every man directly and briefly, wisely and
    truly: wisely I say, I am a bachelor.
SECOND PLEBEIAN   That's as much as to say they are
    fools that marry. You'll bear me a bang for that, I fear.   19
    Proceed directly.   20
CINNA   Directly, I am going to Caesar's funeral.   21
FIRST PLEBEIAN   As a friend or an enemy?
CINNA   As a friend.
SECOND PLEBEIAN   That matter is answered directly.
FOURTH PLEBEIAN   For your dwelling—briefly.
CINNA   Briefly, I dwell by the Capitol.
THIRD PLEBEIAN   Your name, sir, truly.
CINNA   Truly, my name is Cinna.
FIRST PLEBEIAN   Tear him to pieces! He's a conspirator!
CINNA   I am Cinna the poet, I am Cinna the poet!
FOURTH PLEBEIAN   Tear him for his bad verses, tear him
    for his bad verses!
CINNA   I am not Cinna the conspirator.
FOURTH PLEBEIAN   It is no matter, his name's Cinna.
    Pluck but his name out of his heart, and turn him   35
    going.   36
THIRD PLEBEIAN   Tear him, tear him! Come, brands, ho,
    firebrands! To Brutus', to Cassius'; burn all! Some to
    Decius' house, and some to Casca's; some to Ligarius'.
    Away, go!
    Exeunt all the Plebeians, [dragging off Cinna].

❖

4.1

Enter Antony [with a list], Octavius, and Lepidus.

ANTONY
    These many, then, shall die. Their names are pricked.   1
OCTAVIUS
    Your brother too must die. Consent you, Lepidus?
LEPIDUS
    I do consent—
OCTAVIUS   Prick him down, Antony.

LEPIDUS
    Upon condition Publius shall not live,
    Who is your sister's son, Mark Antony.
ANTONY
    He shall not live. Look, with a spot I damn him.   6
    But Lepidus, go you to Caesar's house.
    Fetch the will hither, and we shall determine   8
    How to cut off some charge in legacies.   9
LEPIDUS   What, shall I find you here?
OCTAVIUS   Or here or at the Capitol.   *Exit Lepidus.* 11
ANTONY
    This is a slight, unmeritable man,   12
    Meet to be sent on errands. Is it fit,
    The threefold world divided, he should stand   14
    One of the three to share it?
OCTAVIUS   So you thought him,
    And took his voice who should be pricked to die   16
    In our black sentence and proscription.   17
ANTONY
    Octavius, I have seen more days than you;
    And though we lay these honors on this man
    To ease ourselves of divers sland'rous loads,   20
    He shall but bear them as the ass bears gold,
    To groan and sweat under the business,
    Either led or driven as we point the way;
    And having brought our treasure where we will,
    Then take we down his load, and turn him off,
    Like to the empty ass, to shake his ears   26
    And graze in commons.
OCTAVIUS   You may do your will;   27
    But he's a tried and valiant soldier.
ANTONY
    So is my horse, Octavius, and for that
    I do appoint him store of provender.   30
    It is a creature that I teach to fight,
    To wind, to stop, to run directly on,   32
    His corporal motion governed by my spirit.   33
    And in some taste is Lepidus but so.   34
    He must be taught, and trained, and bid go forth—
    A barren-spirited fellow, one that feeds
    On objects, arts, and imitations,   37
    Which, out of use and staled by other men,   38
    Begin his fashion. Do not talk of him   39
    But as a property. And now, Octavius,   40

2 **unluckily . . . fantasy** oppress my imagination with foreboding.
13 **you were best** you'd better.   19 **bear . . . bang** get a beating from
me   20 **directly** without evasion.   21 **Directly** (1) Straight there
(2) At once   35–6 **turn him going** send him packing.
4.1. Location: Rome. A table is perhaps set out.
1 **pricked** marked down on a list (with a stylus making an impression
on a wax tablet, or piercing a sheet of paper).

6 **spot** mark (on the list).   **damn** condemn   8–9 **determine . . . legacies** find a way to reduce the outlay of Caesar's estate, by altering the
will.   11 **Or** Either   12 **slight, unmeritable** insignificant and undeserving   14 **threefold** i.e., consisting of Europe, Africa, and Asia. The
Roman world was divided among the triumvirate, with most of Gaul
on both sides of the Alps to Antony, Spain and Old Gaul to Lepidus,
and Africa, Sardinia, and Sicily to Octavius.   16 **took his voice** acceded
to his opinion (i.e., about Publius)   17 **black sentence** death sentence.
proscription (Proscription branded a man as an outlaw, confiscated
his property, offered a reward for his murder, and prohibited his sons
and grandsons from holding public office.)   20 **sland'rous** giving
cause for slander   26 **empty** unloaded   27 **commons** public pasture.
30 **appoint** assign, provide.   **provender** fodder.   32 **wind** turn.
(Horse trainer's term.)   **directly on** straight ahead   33 **corporal**
bodily   34 **taste** degree, sense   37 **On . . . imitations** on curiosities,
artificial things, and the following of fashion—copied things merely,
taken up secondhand   38 **staled** made common or cheap
39 **Begin his fashion** are for him the ultimate in fashion.   40 **property** tool.

Listen great things. Brutus and Cassius   41
Are levying powers. We must straight make head.   42
Therefore let our alliance be combined,   43
Our best friends made, our means stretched;   44
And let us presently go sit in council
How covert matters may be best disclosed   46
And open perils surest answerèd.   47

OCTAVIUS
Let us do so, for we are at the stake   48
And bayed about with many enemies;   49
And some that smile have in their hearts, I fear,
Millions of mischiefs.   *Exeunt.* 51

❧

[4.2]

Drum. Enter Brutus, Lucilius, [Lucius,] and the
army. Titinius and Pindarus meet them.

BRUTUS   Stand, ho!   1
LUCILIUS   Give the word, ho, and stand!   2
BRUTUS
What now, Lucilius, is Cassius near?
LUCILIUS
He is at hand, and Pindarus is come
To do you salutation from his master.
BRUTUS
He greets me well. Your master, Pindarus,   6
In his own change, or by ill officers,   7
Hath given me some worthy cause to wish   8
Things done, undone; but if he be at hand
I shall be satisfied.
PINDARUS   I do not doubt   10
But that my noble master will appear
Such as he is, full of regard and honor.   12
BRUTUS
He is not doubted.—A word, Lucilius.
              [Brutus and Lucilius speak apart.]
How he received you let me be resolved.   14
LUCILIUS
With courtesy and with respect enough,
But not with such familiar instances   16
Nor with such free and friendly conference   17
As he hath used of old.
BRUTUS   Thou hast described

A hot friend cooling. Ever note, Lucilius:
When love begins to sicken and decay
It useth an enforcèd ceremony.   21
There are no tricks in plain and simple faith.
But hollow men, like horses hot at hand,   23
Make gallant show and promise of their mettle;   24
                        Low march within.
But when they should endure the bloody spur,
They fall their crests and like deceitful jades   26
Sink in the trial. Comes his army on?   27
LUCILIUS
They mean this night in Sardis to be quartered.   28
The greater part, the horse in general,   29
Are come with Cassius.

Enter Cassius and his powers.

BRUTUS   Hark, he is arrived.
March gently on to meet him.   31
CASSIUS   Stand, ho!
BRUTUS   Stand, ho! Speak the word along.
FIRST SOLDIER   Stand!
SECOND SOLDIER   Stand!
THIRD SOLDIER   Stand!
CASSIUS
Most noble brother, you have done me wrong.
BRUTUS
Judge me, you gods! Wrong I mine enemies?
And if not so, how should I wrong a brother?
CASSIUS
Brutus, this sober form of yours hides wrongs;   40
And when you do them—
BRUTUS   Cassius, be content;   41
Speak your griefs softly. I do know you well.   42
Before the eyes of both our armies here,
Which should perceive nothing but love from us,
Let us not wrangle. Bid them move away.
Then in my tent, Cassius, enlarge your griefs,   46
And I will give you audience.
CASSIUS   Pindarus,
Bid our commanders lead their charges off   48
A little from this ground.
BRUTUS
Lucius, do you the like, and let no man
Come to our tent till we have done our conference.
Let Lucilius and Titinius guard our door.   52
         Exeunt. Manent Brutus and Cassius.
      [Lucilius and Titinius stand guard at the door.]

❧

41 **Listen** hear   42 **powers** armies.   **straight make head** immediately raise an army.   43 **let . . . combined** let us work as one
44 **made** mustered, made certain.   **stretched** used to fullest advantage, extended to the utmost   46 **How . . . disclosed** (to determine)
how hidden dangers may best be discovered   47 **surest answerèd**
most safely met.   48 **at the stake** i.e., like a bear in the sport of bearbaiting   49 **bayed about** surrounded as by baying dogs   51 **mischiefs** harms, evils.
4.2. Location: Camp near Sardis, in Asia Minor. Before Brutus's
tent. 1–2 **Stand . . . stand!** Halt! Pass the word!   6 **He . . . well** His
greetings are welcome.   7 **In . . . officers** whether from an alteration
in his feelings toward me or through the acts of unworthy subordinates   8 **worthy** justifiable   10 **be satisfied** have things explained to
my satisfaction.   12 **full . . . honor** deserving all respect and honor.
14 **resolved** informed, put out of doubt.   16 **familiar instances**
proofs of intimate friendship   17 **conference** conversation

21 **enforcèd** constrained   23 **hollow** insincere.   **hot at hand** restless
and full of spirit when held in, at the start   24 **mettle** spirit   26 **fall
their crests** lower their necks (literally, the ridge or mane of the neck),
hang their heads.   **jades** worthless horses   27 **Sink** give way, fail
28 **Sardis** (The capital city of Lydia in Asia Minor.)   29 **the horse in
general** all the cavalry   31 **gently** mildly, not hostilely   40 **sober
form** dignified manner, appearance   41 **be content** keep calm
42 **griefs** grievances.   **I . . . well** i.e., We've known one another long
and can proceed calmly.   46 **enlarge** speak freely   48 **charges** troops
52 **Lucilius** (The Folio reads *Lucius* here and *Lucillius* in line 50, but,
when Shakespeare interpolated a passage in the next scene at lines
124–66, he evidently intended to have Lucilius guarding the door.)

[4.3]

CASSIUS
That you have wronged me doth appear in this:
You have condemned and noted Lucius Pella 2
For taking bribes here of the Sardians,
Wherein my letters, praying on his side, 4
Because I knew the man, was slighted off. 5

BRUTUS
You wronged yourself to write in such a case.

CASSIUS
In such a time as this it is not meet 7
That every nice offense should bear his comment. 8

BRUTUS
Let me tell you, Cassius, you yourself
Are much condemned to have an itching palm, 10
To sell and mart your offices for gold 11
To undeservers.

CASSIUS   I an itching palm?
You know that you are Brutus that speaks this,
Or, by the gods, this speech were else your last. 14

BRUTUS
The name of Cassius honors this corruption, 15
And chastisement doth therefore hide his head. 16

CASSIUS   Chastisement?

BRUTUS
Remember March, the ides of March remember.
Did not great Julius bleed for justice' sake?
What villain touched his body that did stab 20
And not for justice? What, shall one of us, 21
That struck the foremost man of all this world
But for supporting robbers, shall we now 23
Contaminate our fingers with base bribes,
And sell the mighty space of our large honors 25
For so much trash as may be graspèd thus? 26
I had rather be a dog and bay the moon 27
Than such a Roman.

CASSIUS   Brutus, bait not me. 28
I'll not endure it. You forget yourself
To hedge me in. I am a soldier, I, 30
Older in practice, abler than yourself
To make conditions. 32

BRUTUS   Go to! You are not, Cassius.

CASSIUS   I am.

BRUTUS   I say you are not.

CASSIUS
Urge me no more; I shall forget myself. 36
Have mind upon your health. Tempt me no farther. 37

BRUTUS   Away, slight man! 38

CASSIUS
Is't possible?

BRUTUS   Hear me, for I will speak.
Must I give way and room to your rash choler? 40
Shall I be frighted when a madman stares? 41

CASSIUS
O ye gods, ye gods! Must I endure all this?

BRUTUS
All this? Ay, more. Fret till your proud heart break.
Go show your slaves how choleric you are,
And make your bondmen tremble. Must I budge? 45
Must I observe you? Must I stand and crouch 46
Under your testy humor? By the gods, 47
You shall digest the venom of your spleen 48
Though it do split you; for, from this day forth,
I'll use you for my mirth, yea, for my laughter,
When you are waspish.

CASSIUS   Is it come to this? 51

BRUTUS
You say you are a better soldier.
Let it appear so; make your vaunting true, 53
And it shall please me well. For mine own part,
I shall be glad to learn of noble men. 55

CASSIUS
You wrong me every way! You wrong me, Brutus.
I said an elder soldier, not a better.
Did I say "better"?

BRUTUS   If you did, I care not.

CASSIUS
When Caesar lived he durst not thus have moved me. 59

BRUTUS
Peace, peace! You durst not so have tempted him. 60

CASSIUS   I durst not?

BRUTUS   No.

CASSIUS
What, durst not tempt him?

BRUTUS   For your life you durst not.

CASSIUS
Do not presume too much upon my love.
I may do that I shall be sorry for.

BRUTUS
You have done that you should be sorry for.
There is no terror, Cassius, in your threats,
For I am armed so strong in honesty
That they pass by me as the idle wind,

4.3. Location: The scene is continuous. Brutus and Cassius remain onstage, which now represents the interior of Brutus's tent.
2 noted publicly disgraced.   **Lucius Pella** a Roman praetor in Sardis
4 letters i.e., letter. (See 3.1.281n.)   **praying** entreating   **5 slighted off** slightingly dismissed.   **7 meet** fitting   **8 nice** trivial.   **bear his comment** be taken note of. (*His* means "its.")   **10 condemned to have** accused of having   **11 mart** traffic in   **14 else** otherwise
15 honors lends the appearance of honor to, countenances   **16 And . . . head** and for that reason those who might rebuke such corruption are reluctant to speak out.   **20–1 What . . . justice?** Which of us was villain enough to stab for any cause other than justice?
23 But only.   **robbers** (According to Plutarch, Caesar "was a favorer and suborner of all of them that did rob and spoil by his countenance and authority.")   **25 the mighty . . . honors** the greatness of our honorable reputations and the high offices we have power to confer   **26 trash** i.e., money (despised in Brutus's stoic philosophy)
27 bay howl at   **28 bait** harass   **30 hedge me in** crowd me, limit my authority.   **32 make conditions** i.e., manage affairs, make decisions about Lucius Pella and other officers.

36 Urge Provoke   **37 Tempt** Provoke   **38 slight** insignificant
40 way and room free course and scope.   **choler** wrathful temperament.   **41 stares** looks wildly at me.   **45 bondmen** (Probably not distinguished from "slaves" in line 44.)   **budge** flinch.   **46 observe** defer to.   **crouch** cringe   **47 humor** temperament.   **48 digest** swallow.   **spleen** i.e., irascibility   **51 waspish** hotheaded.   **53 vaunting** boasting   **55 I shall . . . men** (Said sarcastically: "Wouldn't it be a nice surprise to learn that some men can be noble after all?", or, "I am glad to be corrected by such a noble person as yourself.")   **59 moved** angered   **60 tempted** provoked

Which I respect not. I did send to you   70
For certain sums of gold, which you denied me;
For I can raise no money by vile means.   72
By heaven, I had rather coin my heart
And drop my blood for drachmas than to wring
From the hard hands of peasants their vile trash
By any indirection. I did send   76
To you for gold to pay my legions,
Which you denied me. Was that done like Cassius?
Should I have answered Caius Cassius so?
When Marcus Brutus grows so covetous
To lock such rascal counters from his friends,   81
Be ready, gods, with all your thunderbolts,
Dash him to pieces!

CASSIUS   I denied you not.

BRUTUS
You did.

CASSIUS   I did not. He was but a fool
That brought my answer back. Brutus hath rived my
    heart.   85
A friend should bear his friend's infirmities,
But Brutus makes mine greater than they are.

BRUTUS
I do not, till you practice them on me.

CASSIUS
You love me not.

BRUTUS   I do not like your faults.

CASSIUS
A friendly eye could never see such faults.

BRUTUS
A flatterer's would not, though they do appear
As huge as high Olympus.

CASSIUS
Come, Antony, and young Octavius, come,
Revenge yourselves alone on Cassius;
For Cassius is aweary of the world,
Hated by one he loves, braved by his brother,   96
Checked like a bondman, all his faults observed,   97
Set in a notebook, learned and conned by rote   98
To cast into my teeth. Oh, I could weep
My spirit from mine eyes! There is my dagger,
    [offering his unsheathed dagger]
And here my naked breast; within, a heart
Dearer than Pluto's mine, richer than gold.   102
If that thou be'st a Roman, take it forth.
I, that denied thee gold, will give my heart.   104
Strike, as thou didst at Caesar; for I know,
When thou didst hate him worst, thou loved'st him
    better
Than ever thou loved'st Cassius.

BRUTUS   Sheathe your dagger.
Be angry when you will, it shall have scope;   108

Do what you will, dishonor shall be humor.   109
Oh, Cassius, you are yokèd with a lamb   110
That carries anger as the flint bears fire,
Who, much enforcèd, shows a hasty spark   112
And straight is cold again.

CASSIUS   Hath Cassius lived   113
To be but mirth and laughter to his Brutus
When grief and blood ill-tempered vexeth him?   115

BRUTUS
When I spoke that, I was ill-tempered too.

CASSIUS
Do you confess so much? Give me your hand.

BRUTUS
And my heart too.   [They embrace.]

CASSIUS   Oh, Brutus!

BRUTUS   What's the matter?

CASSIUS
Have not you love enough to bear with me,
When that rash humor which my mother gave me   120
Makes me forgetful?

BRUTUS   Yes, Cassius, and from henceforth,
When you are overearnest with your Brutus,
He'll think your mother chides, and leave you so.   123

    Enter a Poet [followed by Lucilius and Titinius,
    who have been standing guard at the door].

POET
Let me go in to see the generals!
There is some grudge between 'em; 'tis not meet
They be alone.

LUCILIUS   You shall not come to them.

POET   Nothing but death shall stay me.

CASSIUS   How now? What's the matter?

POET
For shame, you generals! What do you mean?
Love and be friends, as two such men should be;
For I have seen more years, I'm sure, than ye.

CASSIUS
Ha, ha, how vilely doth this cynic rhyme!   132

BRUTUS
Get you hence, sirrah. Saucy fellow, hence!

CASSIUS
Bear with him, Brutus. 'Tis his fashion.

BRUTUS
I'll know his humor when he knows his time.   135
What should the wars do with these jigging fools?   136
Companion, hence!

CASSIUS   Away, away, begone!   Exit Poet.   137

BRUTUS
Lucilius and Titinius, bid the commanders

---

70 **respect not** pay no attention to.   72 **can raise no money** i.e., refuse to raise money   76 **indirection** devious or unjust means.   81 **rascal counters** i.e., paltry sums. (*Counters* were uncurrent coins or disks used by shopkeepers as tokens in making reckonings.)   85 **rived** cleft, split   96 **braved** defied   97 **Checked** rebuked   98 **conned by rote** memorized   102 **Dearer** richer.   **Pluto** god of the underworld (fused with Plutus, god of riches)   104 **that denied** i.e., who you insist denied   108 **scope** free rein

109 **dishonor . . . humor** i.e., I'll regard your dishonorable conduct and self-righteous anger as the effects of temperament, something to be humored.   110 **yokèd with** allied with   112 **enforcèd** provoked, struck upon   113 **straight** at once   115 **blood ill-tempered** disposition imbalanced by the humors of the body   120 **that rash humor** i.e., choler, anger   123 **leave you so** let it go at that.   132 **cynic** i.e., rude fellow; also one claiming to be a Cynic philosopher, hence outspoken   135 **I'll . . . time** I'll indulge his eccentric behavior when he knows the proper time for it.   136 **jigging** rhyming in jerky doggerel   137 **Companion** Fellow

Prepare to lodge their companies tonight.

CASSIUS
And come yourselves, and bring Messala with you
Immediately to us.   [*Exeunt Lucilius and Titinius.*]

BRUTUS [*to Lucius within*]   Lucius, a bowl of wine.

CASSIUS
I did not think you could have been so angry.

BRUTUS
Oh, Cassius, I am sick of many griefs.

CASSIUS
Of your philosophy you make no use
If you give place to accidental evils.   145

BRUTUS
No man bears sorrow better. Portia is dead.

CASSIUS   Ha? Portia?

BRUTUS   She is dead.

CASSIUS
How scaped I killing when I crossed you so?   149
Oh, insupportable and touching loss!
Upon what sickness?

BRUTUS   Impatient of my absence,
And grief that young Octavius with Mark Antony
Have made themselves so strong—for with her death 153
That tidings came—with this she fell distract
And, her attendants absent, swallowed fire.   155

CASSIUS
And died so?

BRUTUS   Even so.

CASSIUS   O ye immortal gods!

Enter Boy [Lucius] with wine and tapers.

BRUTUS
Speak no more of her.—Give me a bowl of wine.—
In this I bury all unkindness, Cassius.   *Drinks.*

CASSIUS
My heart is thirsty for that noble pledge.
Fill, Lucius, till the wine o'erswell the cup;
I cannot drink too much of Brutus' love.   161
                    [*He drinks. Exit Lucius.*]

Enter Titinius and Messala.

BRUTUS
Come in, Titinius. Welcome, good Messala.
Now sit we close about this taper here
And call in question our necessities.   [*They sit.*] 164

CASSIUS
Portia, art thou gone?

BRUTUS   No more, I pray you.
Messala, I have here receivèd letters   166

That young Octavius and Mark Antony
Come down upon us with a mighty power,   168
Bending their expedition toward Philippi.   169
                    [*He shows a letter.*]

MESSALA
Myself have letters of the selfsame tenor.

BRUTUS   With what addition?

MESSALA
That by proscription and bills of outlawry   172
Octavius, Antony, and Lepidus
Have put to death an hundred senators.

BRUTUS
Therein our letters do not well agree;
Mine speak of seventy senators that died
By their proscriptions, Cicero being one.

CASSIUS
Cicero one?

MESSALA   Cicero is dead,
And by that order of proscription.
Had you your letters from your wife, my lord?   180

BRUTUS   No, Messala.

MESSALA
Nor nothing in your letters writ of her?   182

BRUTUS
Nothing, Messala.

MESSALA   That, methinks, is strange.

BRUTUS
Why ask you? Hear you aught of her in yours?

MESSALA   No, my lord.

BRUTUS
Now, as you are a Roman, tell me true.

MESSALA
Then like a Roman bear the truth I tell,
For certain she is dead, and by strange manner.

BRUTUS
Why, farewell, Portia. We must die, Messala.
With meditating that she must die once,   190
I have the patience to endure it now.

MESSALA
Even so great men great losses should endure.   192

CASSIUS
I have as much of this in art as you,   193
But yet my nature could not bear it so.   194

BRUTUS
Well, to our work alive. What do you think   195
Of marching to Philippi presently?

---

145 **place** way.   **accidental evils** misfortunes caused by chance
(which should be a matter of indifference to a philosopher like Brutus).   149 **scaped I killing** did I escape being killed   153 **her death**
i.e., news of her death   155 **swallowed fire** (According to Plutarch,
as translated by Thomas North, Portia "took hot burning coals and
cast them in her mouth, and kept her mouth so close that she choked
herself.")   161.2 *Titinius* (Lucilius does not return with Titinius, as he
was ordered to do at lines 140–1, probably because he was not in Shakespeare's original version of this scene.)   164 **call in question** consider,
discuss   166 **letters** (Probably a single letter. See 3.1.281n and 4.3.4n.)

168 **power** army   169 **Bending** directing.   **expedition** rapid march;
warlike enterprise   172 **proscription** (See the note at 4.1.17.)
180–94 **Had . . . so** (This passage is sometimes regarded as contradictory to lines 142–65 and redundant. Perhaps it is the original account of
Portia's death, and lines 142–65 are part of a later interpolation, but it is
also possible that both are intended, the first being Brutus's intimate
revelation of the news to his friend and the second being Brutus's
recovery of his stoic reserve now on display for Messala and Titinius.)
182 **nothing . . . her** nothing written about her in the letter or letters
you've received.   190 **once** at some time   192 **Even so** In just such a
way   193 **art** i.e., the acquired theoretical wisdom of stoical fortitude
(as contrasted with the gifts of *nature* in line 194)   195 **alive** concerning
us who are alive and dealing with present and future realities.

CASSIUS
 I do not think it good.
BRUTUS   Your reason?
CASSIUS   This it is:
 'Tis better that the enemy seek us.
 So shall he waste his means, weary his soldiers,
 Doing himself offense, whilst we, lying still,   200
 Are full of rest, defense, and nimbleness.
BRUTUS
 Good reasons must of force give place to better.   202
 The people twixt Philippi and this ground
 Do stand but in a forced affection,
 For they have grudged us contribution.
 The enemy, marching along by them,
 By them shall make a fuller number up,
 Come on refreshed, new-added, and encouraged;
 From which advantage shall we cut him off
 If at Philippi we do face him there,
 These people at our back.
CASSIUS   Hear me, good brother—   211
BRUTUS
 Under your pardon. You must note beside   212
 That we have tried the utmost of our friends;
 Our legions are brim full, our cause is ripe.
 The enemy increaseth every day;
 We, at the height, are ready to decline.
 There is a tide in the affairs of men
 Which, taken at the flood, leads on to fortune;
 Omitted, all the voyage of their life
 Is bound in shallows and in miseries.   220
 On such a full sea are we now afloat,
 And we must take the current when it serves
 Or lose our ventures.
CASSIUS   Then, with your will, go on.   223
 We'll along ourselves and meet them at Philippi.
BRUTUS
 The deep of night is crept upon our talk,
 And nature must obey necessity,
 Which we will niggard with a little rest.   227
 There is no more to say.
CASSIUS   No more. Good night.
 Early tomorrow will we rise and hence.   229
BRUTUS
 Lucius!

 Enter Lucius.

 My gown.   [*Exit Lucius.*]
                    Farewell, good Messala.   230
 Good night, Titinius. Noble, noble Cassius,
 Good night and good repose.
CASSIUS   Oh, my dear brother!

 This was an ill beginning of the night.
 Never come such division 'tween our souls!
 Let it not, Brutus.

 Enter Lucius with the gown.

BRUTUS   Everything is well.
CASSIUS   Good night, my lord.
BRUTUS   Good night, good brother.
TITINIUS, MESSALA   Good night, Lord Brutus.
BRUTUS   Farewell, everyone.
                    Exeunt [*all but Brutus and Lucius*].
 Give me the gown. Where is thy instrument?   241
LUCIUS
 Here in the tent.
BRUTUS   What, thou speak'st drowsily!
 Poor knave, I blame thee not; thou art o'erwatched.   243
 Call Claudius and some other of my men;
 I'll have them sleep on cushions in my tent.
LUCIUS [*calling*]   Varro and Claudius!

 Enter Varro and Claudius.

VARRO   Calls my lord?
BRUTUS
 I pray you, sirs, lie in my tent and sleep.
 It may be I shall raise you by and by   249
 On business to my brother Cassius.
VARRO
 So please you, we will stand and watch your pleasure. 251
BRUTUS
 I will not have it so. Lie down, good sirs.
 It may be I shall otherwise bethink me.   253
                    [*Varro and Claudius lie down.*]
 Look, Lucius, here's the book I sought for so;
 I put it in the pocket of my gown.
LUCIUS
 I was sure Your Lordship did not give it me.
BRUTUS
 Bear with me, good boy, I am much forgetful.
 Canst thou hold up thy heavy eyes awhile
 And touch thy instrument a strain or two?   259
LUCIUS
 Ay, my lord, an't please you.
BRUTUS   It does, my boy.   260
 I trouble thee too much, but thou art willing.
LUCIUS   It is my duty, sir.
BRUTUS
 I should not urge thy duty past thy might;
 I know young bloods look for a time of rest.   264
LUCIUS   I have slept, my lord, already.
BRUTUS
 It was well done, and thou shalt sleep again;
 I will not hold thee long. If I do live,

---

200 offense harm   202 of force necessarily   211 These . . . back i.e.,
with the people our enemy would otherwise recruit being instead in
territory we control.   212 Under your pardon i.e., Excuse me, let me
continue.   220 bound in confined to   223 ventures investments (of
enterprise at sea).   with your will as you wish   227 niggard stint
(by sleeping only briefly)   229 hence depart.   230 gown housecoat.

241 instrument i.e., perhaps a lute or cithern.   243 knave boy.
o'erwatched tired from lack of sleep.   249 raise rouse   251 watch
your pleasure wakefully await your commands.   253 otherwise
bethink me change my mind.   259 touch i.e., play on.   strain
tune, musical phrase   260 an't if it   264 young bloods youthful
constitutions

I will be good to thee.
                    Music, and a song. [Lucius falls asleep.]
This is a sleepy tune. O murd'rous slumber,   269
Layest thou thy leaden mace upon my boy,   270
That plays thee music? Gentle knave, good night;
I will not do thee so much wrong to wake thee.
If thou dost nod, thou break'st thy instrument;
I'll take it from thee. And, good boy, good night.
                    [He removes Lucius' instrument,
                              and begins to read.]
Let me see, let me see; is not the leaf turned down
Where I left reading? Here it is, I think.

          Enter the Ghost of Caesar.

How ill this taper burns! Ha! Who comes here?   277
I think it is the weakness of mine eyes
That shapes this monstrous apparition.
It comes upon me.—Art thou any thing?   280
Art thou some god, some angel, or some devil,
That mak'st my blood cold and my hair to stare?   282
Speak to me what thou art.
GHOST
    Thy evil spirit, Brutus.
BRUTUS   Why com'st thou?
GHOST
    To tell thee thou shalt see me at Philippi.
BRUTUS   Well; then I shall see thee again?
GHOST   Ay, at Philippi.
BRUTUS
    Why, I will see thee at Philippi, then.   *[Exit Ghost.]*
    Now I have taken heart, thou vanishest.
    Ill spirit, I would hold more talk with thee.—
    Boy, Lucius! Varro! Claudius! Sirs, awake!
    Claudius!
LUCIUS   The strings, my lord, are false.   292
BRUTUS
    He thinks he still is at his instrument.—
    Lucius, awake!
LUCIUS   My lord?
BRUTUS
    Didst thou dream, Lucius, that thou so cried'st out?
LUCIUS
    My lord, I do not know that I did cry.
BRUTUS
    Yes, that thou didst. Didst thou see anything?
LUCIUS   Nothing, my lord.
BRUTUS
    Sleep again, Lucius. Sirrah Claudius!
    [To Varro] Fellow thou, awake!
VARRO   My lord?
CLAUDIUS   My lord?
                              [They get up.]

BRUTUS
    Why did you so cry out, sirs, in your sleep?
VARRO, CLAUDIUS
    Did we, my lord?
BRUTUS   Ay. Saw you anything?
VARRO
    No, my lord, I saw nothing.
CLAUDIUS   Nor I, my lord.
BRUTUS
    Go and commend me to my brother Cassius.   305
    Bid him set on his powers betimes before,   306
    And we will follow.
VARRO, CLAUDIUS   It shall be done, my lord.
                                        Exeunt.

                         ❧

5.1

          Enter Octavius, Antony, and their army.

OCTAVIUS
    Now, Antony, our hopes are answerèd.
    You said the enemy would not come down,
    But keep the hills and upper regions.   3
    It proves not so. Their battles are at hand;   4
    They mean to warn us at Philippi here,   5
    Answering before we do demand of them.
ANTONY
    Tut, I am in their bosoms, and I know   7
    Wherefore they do it. They could be content
    To visit other places, and come down   9
    With fearful bravery, thinking by this face   10
    To fasten in our thoughts that they have courage;
    But 'tis not so.   12

          Enter a Messenger.

MESSENGER   Prepare you, generals.
    The enemy comes on in gallant show.
    Their bloody sign of battle is hung out,   14
    And something to be done immediately.   15
ANTONY
    Octavius, lead your battle softly on   16
    Upon the left hand of the even field.
OCTAVIUS
    Upon the right hand, I. Keep thou the left.
ANTONY
    Why do you cross me in this exigent?   19

---

305 commend me deliver my greetings   **306 set . . . before** march
away with his troops early in the morning, before me
5.1 Location: The plains of Philippi, in Macedonia.
3 keep remain in   **4 battles** armies   **5 warm** challenge   **7 bosoms**
secret councils   **9 visit other places** i.e., be elsewhere   **10 fearful**
bravery (1) awesome ostentation (2) a show of bravery to conceal
their fear.   **face** pretense (of courage)   **12 'tis not so** (1) their plan
cannot deceive us (2) they have no courage.   **14 bloody sign** red
flag or crimson coat of arms as battle signal   **15 to be** is to be
16 softly warily, with restraint   **19 cross** contradict.   **exigent** critical
moment.

---

269 murd'rous producing the likeness of death   **270 leaden mace**
heavy staff of office (used by a sheriff to touch the shoulder of one
being placed under arrest)   **277 How . . . burns!** (Ghostly apparitions
were thought to be accompanied by such effects as lights burning low
and blue.)   **280 upon** toward   **282 stare** stand on end.   **292 false** out
of tune.

OCTAVIUS
    I do not cross you, but I will do so.   *March.*   20

        Drum. Enter Brutus, Cassius, and their army;
        [*Lucilius, Titinius, Messala, and others*].

BRUTUS   They stand and would have parley.

CASSIUS
    Stand fast, Titinius. We must out and talk.   22

OCTAVIUS
    Mark Antony, shall we give sign of battle?

ANTONY
    No, Caesar, we will answer on their charge.   24
    Make forth. The generals would have some words.   25

OCTAVIUS [*to his officers*]   Stir not until the signal.
        [*The two sides advance toward one another.*]

BRUTUS
    Words before blows. Is it so, countrymen?

OCTAVIUS
    Not that we love words better, as you do.

BRUTUS
    Good words are better than bad strokes, Octavius.

ANTONY
    In your bad strokes, Brutus, you give good words.   30
    Witness the hole you made in Caesar's heart,
    Crying "Long live! Hail, Caesar!"

CASSIUS   Antony,
    The posture of your blows are yet unknown;   33
    But for your words, they rob the Hybla bees,   34
    And leave them honeyless.

ANTONY   Not stingless too?

BRUTUS   Oh, yes, and soundless too.
    For you have stol'n their buzzing, Antony,
    And very wisely threat before you sting.   39

ANTONY
    Villains! You did not so when your vile daggers   40
    Hacked one another in the sides of Caesar.
    You showed your teeth like apes, and fawned like
        hounds,
    And bowed like bondmen, kissing Caesar's feet,   42
    Whilst damnèd Casca, like a cur, behind,
    Struck Caesar on the neck. Oh, you flatterers!

CASSIUS
    Flatterers? Now, Brutus, thank yourself!
    This tongue had not offended so today
    If Cassius might have ruled.   48

OCTAVIUS
    Come, come, the cause. If arguing make us sweat,   49
    The proof of it will turn to redder drops.   50
    Look,   [*He draws.*]

    I draw a sword against conspirators.
    When think you that the sword goes up again?   53
    Never, till Caesar's three-and-thirty wounds   54
    Be well avenged, or till another Caesar   55
    Have added slaughter to the sword of traitors.   56

BRUTUS
    Caesar, thou canst not die by traitors' hands,   57
    Unless thou bring'st them with thee.

OCTAVIUS   So I hope.   58
    I was not born to die on Brutus' sword.   59

BRUTUS
    Oh, if thou wert the noblest of thy strain,   60
    Young man, thou couldst not die more honorable.

CASSIUS
    A peevish schoolboy, worthless of such honor,   62
    Joined with a masker and a reveler!   63

ANTONY
    Old Cassius still.

OCTAVIUS   Come, Antony, away!—   64
    Defiance, traitors, hurl we in your teeth.
    If you dare fight today, come to the field;
    If not, when you have stomachs.   67
        Exeunt Octavius, Antony, and army.

CASSIUS
    Why, now, blow wind, swell billow, and swim bark!   68
    The storm is up, and all is on the hazard.   69

BRUTUS
    Ho, Lucilius! Hark, a word with you.

LUCILIUS (*stands forth*)   My lord?
        [*Brutus and Lucilius converse apart.*]

CASSIUS   Messala!

MESSALA (*stands forth*)   What says my general?

CASSIUS   Messala,
    This is my birthday, as this very day   75
    Was Cassius born. Give me thy hand, Messala.
    Be thou my witness that against my will,
    As Pompey was, am I compelled to set   78
    Upon one battle all our liberties.
    You know that I held Epicurus strong   80
    And his opinion. Now I change my mind
    And partly credit things that do presage.   82
    Coming from Sardis, on our former ensign   83

20 **cross you** contradict you perversely. **do so** do as I said. **22 out** go out **24 answer on their charge** respond when they attack. **25 Make forth** March forward. **30 In . . . words** i.e., As you deliver cruel blows, Brutus, you use deceiving flattery. **33 The posture . . . are** how you will strike your blows is **34 for** as for. **Hybla** a mountain and a town in ancient Sicily, famous for honey **39 very wisely** (Said ironically; Brutus suggests that Antony is all bluster and no action.) **threat** threaten **40 so** i.e., give warning **42 showed your teeth** i.e., in smiles **48 ruled** prevailed (in urging that Antony be killed). **49 the cause** to our business. **50 proof** trial

53 **up** in its sheath **54 three-and-thirty** (Plutarch has it three-and-twenty.) **55 another Caesar** i.e., myself, Octavius **56 Have . . . to** has also been slaughtered by **57–8 thou . . . thee** i.e., the only traitors here are in your own army. **58–9 So . . . sword** i.e. (sardonically), I'm glad to hear that, since you are the traitor I mean, and since you are not in my army, I cannot, according to your assertion, die at your hands. **60 if** even if. **strain** lineage **62 peevish** silly, childish. **schoolboy** (Octavius was eighteen at the time of Caesar's assassination.) **worthless** unworthy **63 a masker . . . reveler** i.e., Antony, noted for his dissipation **64 Old . . . still** i.e., Cassius, as envious and ill-willed as ever. (Said sardonically.) **67 stomachs** appetites (for fighting), courage. **68 billow** wave. **swim bark** let the sailing vessel swim for its life. **69 on the hazard** at stake. **75 as** inasmuch as **78 Pompey** (The reference is to the battle of Pharsalus, where Pompey was persuaded to fight Caesar against his own judgment.) **set** stake **80 Epicurus** Greek philosopher (341–270 B.C.) who, because he held the gods to be indifferent to human affairs, spurned belief in omens or superstitions **82 presage** foretell events. **83 former ensign** foremost standard, the legion's *aquila*, a tall standard surmounted by the image of an eagle

Two mighty eagles fell, and there they perched,   84
Gorging and feeding from our soldiers' hands,
Who to Philippi here consorted us.   86
This morning are they fled away and gone,
And in their steads do ravens, crows, and kites   88
Fly o'er our heads and downward look on us
As we were sickly prey. Their shadows seem   90
A canopy most fatal, under which   91
Our army lies, ready to give up the ghost.

MESSALA
Believe not so.

CASSIUS   I but believe it partly,   93
For I am fresh of spirit and resolved
To meet all perils very constantly.   95

BRUTUS
Even so, Lucilius.   [*He rejoins Cassius.*]

CASSIUS   Now, most noble Brutus,   96
The gods today stand friendly, that we may,   97
Lovers in peace, lead on our days to age!   98
But since the affairs of men rest still incertain,   99
Let's reason with the worst that may befall.   100
If we do lose this battle, then is this
The very last time we shall speak together.
What are you then determinèd to do?

BRUTUS
Even by the rule of that philosophy
By which I did blame Cato for the death   105
Which he did give himself—I know not how,
But I do find it cowardly and vile,
For fear of what might fall, so to prevent   108
The time of life—arming myself with patience   109
To stay the providence of some high powers   110
That govern us below.

CASSIUS   Then, if we lose this battle,
You are contented to be led in triumph
Thorough the streets of Rome?   113

BRUTUS
No, Cassius, no. Think not, thou noble Roman,
That ever Brutus will go bound to Rome;
He bears too great a mind. But this same day
Must end that work the ides of March begun.
And whether we shall meet again I know not;
Therefore our everlasting farewell take.
Forever and forever farewell, Cassius!
If we do meet again, why, we shall smile;
If not, why then this parting was well made.

CASSIUS   84
Forever and forever farewell, Brutus!
If we do meet again, we'll smile indeed;
If not, 'tis true this parting was well made.

BRUTUS
Why, then, lead on. Oh, that a man might know
The end of this day's business ere it come!   127
But it sufficeth that the day will end,
And then the end is known.—Come, ho, away!
                                        Exeunt.

❖

[5.2]

Alarum. Enter Brutus and Messala.

BRUTUS
Ride, ride, Messala, ride, and give these bills   1
Unto the legions on the other side.   2
                [*He hands him written orders.*]
                                    Loud alarum.

Let them set on at once; for I perceive   3
But cold demeanor in Octavio's wing,   4
And sudden push gives them the overthrow.
Ride, ride, Messala! Let them all come down.   6
                            Exeunt [*separately*].

❖

[5.3]

Alarums. Enter Cassius [*carrying a standard*], *and
Titinius.*

CASSIUS
Oh, look, Titinius, look, the villains fly!   1
Myself have to mine own turned enemy.   2
This ensign here of mine was turning back;   3
I slew the coward and did take it from him.   4

TITINIUS
Oh, Cassius, Brutus gave the word too early,
Who, having some advantage on Octavius,
Took it too eagerly. His soldiers fell to spoil,   7
Whilst we by Antony are all enclosed.   8

Enter Pindarus.

---

84 **fell** swooped down   86 **consorted** accompanied   88 **kites** scavenger birds (also raptors)   90 **As** as if   91 **fatal** presaging death   93 **but** only   95 **constantly** resolutely.   96 **Even so, Lucilius** (This phrase marks the end of Brutus's private conversation apart with Lucilius.)   97 **The gods** May the gods   98 **Lovers** friends.   **age** old age.   99 **still** always   100 **reason** reckon   105 **Cato** i.e., Marcus Porcius Cato, Brutus' father-in-law, who killed himself to avoid submission to Caesar in 46 B.C. (See 2.1.296 and note.) Brutus's condemnation of Cato's suicide out of fear of failure can perhaps be reconciled with lines 114–17 below and with Brutus's own later suicide (5.5.50), since on that occasion Brutus is responding to certain defeat and disgrace. The seeming contradiction may also be owing to an ambiguity in North's Plutarch.   108 **fall** befall.   **prevent** anticipate the end, cut short   109 **time** term, extent   110 **stay** await   113 **Thorough** through

127 ere before
5.2 Location: The plains of Philippi. The field of battle.
0.1 *Alarum* (This is seemingly an anticipatory stage direction; the battle actually begins with the *Loud alarum* at line 2. An *alarum* is off stage sounds, signifying a battle.)   **1 bills** orders   **2 side** wing (i.e., Cassius's wing).   **3 set on** attack   **4 cold demeanor** faintheartedness   **6 come down** i.e., from the hills, where the Republican army has been awaiting the signal to attack. (See 5.1.2–3.)
5.3 Location: The field of battle still.
1 the villains i.e., my own troops   **2 mine own** my own men   **3 ensign** bearer of the standard. (A legion's *aquila*, or "eagle standard," had great significance and needed to be guarded.)   **4 it** i.e., the standard   **7 spoil** looting   **8 enclosed** surrounded.

PINDARUS

Fly further off, my lord, fly further off!
Mark Antony is in your tents, my lord.
Fly therefore, noble Cassius, fly far off.

CASSIUS

This hill is far enough. Look, look, Titinius:
Are those my tents where I perceive the fire?

TITINIUS

They are, my lord.

CASSIUS   Titinius, if thou lovest me,
Mount thou my horse, and hide thy spurs in him
Till he have brought thee up to yonder troops
And here again, that I may rest assured
Whether yond troops are friend or enemy.

TITINIUS

I will be here again even with a thought.   *Exit.* 19

CASSIUS

Go, Pindarus, get higher on that hill.
My sight was ever thick. Regard Titinius,   21
And tell me what thou not'st about the field.   22
                    [*Pindarus goes up.*]
This day I breathèd first. Time is come round,   23
And where I did begin, there shall I end.
My life is run his compass.—Sirrah, what news?   25

PINDARUS (*above*) Oh, my lord!

CASSIUS What news?

PINDARUS [*above*]

Titinius is enclosèd round about
With horsemen, that make to him on the spur,   29
Yet he spurs on. Now they are almost on him.
Now, Titinius! Now some light. Oh, he   31
Lights too. He's ta'en. (*Shout.*) And hark! They shout
  for joy.

CASSIUS   Come down, behold no more.
Oh, coward that I am, to live so long
To see my best friend ta'en before my face!   35

          Enter Pindarus [from above].

Come hither, sirrah.
In Parthia did I take thee prisoner,   37
And then I swore thee, saving of thy life,   38
That whatsoever I did bid thee do
Thou shouldst attempt it. Come now, keep thine oath;
Now be a freeman, and with this good sword,
That ran through Caesar's bowels, search this bosom.   42
Stand not to answer. Here, take thou the hilts,   43
And when my face is covered, as 'tis now,
Guide thou the sword. [*Pindarus does so.*] Caesar, thou
  art revengèd,
Even with the sword that killed thee.   [*He dies.*]

PINDARUS

So, I am free, yet would not so have been,   47
Durst I have done my will. Oh, Cassius!   48
Far from this country Pindarus shall run,
Where never Roman shall take note of him.   [*Exit.*]

          *Enter Titinius [wearing a garland of laurel] and
          Messala.*

MESSALA

It is but change, Titinius; for Octavius   51
Is overthrown by noble Brutus' power,
As Cassius' legions are by Antony.

TITINIUS

These tidings will well comfort Cassius.

MESSALA

Where did you leave him?

TITINIUS   All disconsolate,
With Pindarus his bondman, on this hill.

MESSALA

Is not that he that lies upon the ground?

TITINIUS

He lies not like the living. Oh, my heart!

MESSALA

Is not that he?

TITINIUS   No, this was he, Messala,
But Cassius is no more. O setting sun,
As in thy red rays thou dost sink to night,
So in his red blood Cassius' day is set.
The sun of Rome is set. Our day is gone;   63
Clouds, dews, and dangers come; our deeds are done.
Mistrust of my success hath done this deed.   65

MESSALA

Mistrust of good success hath done this deed.
O hateful Error, Melancholy's child,   67
Why dost thou show to the apt thoughts of men   68
The things that are not? O Error, soon conceived,
Thou never com'st unto a happy birth,
But kill'st the mother that engendered thee.   71

TITINIUS

What, Pindarus! Where art thou, Pindarus?

MESSALA

Seek him, Titinius, whilst I go to meet
The noble Brutus, thrusting this report
Into his ears. I may say "thrusting" it,
For piercing steel and darts envenomèd
Shall be as welcome to the ears of Brutus
As tidings of this sight.

TITINIUS   Hie you, Messala,
And I will seek for Pindarus the while.
                              [*Exit Messala.*]
Why didst thou send me forth, brave Cassius?
Did I not meet thy friends? And did not they
Put on my brows this wreath of victory

---

19 **even . . . thought** as quick as thought.   21 **thick** imperfect, dim.
Regard Observe   22.1 *Pindarus goes up* (Pindarus may climb to the
gallery, or may exit and ascend behind the scenes; see line 35.1 and
note.)   23 **I breathèd first** i.e., it is my birthday.   25 **his compass** its
circuit, circle (as drawn by a geometer's compass).   29 **make . . . spur**
approach him riding rapidly   31 **light** alight, dismount.   35.1 *Enter*
(Pindarus may descend in full view of the audience; see note at 22.1.)
37 **Parthia** (What is now northern Iran.)   38 **swore . . . of** made you
swear, when I spared   42 **search** probe, penetrate   43 **Stand** Delay.
hilts sword hilt

47 **so** in this manner   48 **Durst . . . will** if I had dared do what I
wished.   51 **change** exchange of advantage, quid pro quo   63 **sun**
(With pun on *son.*)   65 **Mistrust** i.e., Cassius's doubt   67 **Melancholy's child** i.e., bred of pessimism   68 **apt** impressionable   71 **the
mother** i.e., the melancholy person who too readily believes the worst

And bid me give it thee? Didst thou not hear their
   shouts?
Alas, thou hast misconstrued everything.
But, hold thee, take this garland on thy brow.   85
         [*He places the garland on Cassius's brow.*]
Thy Brutus bid me give it thee, and I
Will do his bidding. Brutus, come apace   87
And see how I regarded Caius Cassius.
By your leave, gods! This is a Roman's part.
Come, Cassius' sword, and find Titinius' heart.
                        [*He stabs himself and*] *dies.*

      Alarum. Enter Brutus, Messala, young Cato,
      Strato, Volumnius, and Lucilius, [Labeo, and
      Flavius].

BRUTUS
   Where, where, Messala, doth his body lie?
MESSALA
   Lo, yonder, and Titinius mourning it.
BRUTUS
   Titinius' face is upward.
CATO   He is slain.
BRUTUS
   O Julius Caesar, thou art mighty yet!
   Thy spirit walks abroad and turns our swords
   In our own proper entrails.   *Low alarums.*
CATO   Brave Titinius!   96
   Look whe'er he have not crowned dead Cassius.   97
BRUTUS
   Are yet two Romans living such as these?
   The last of all the Romans, fare thee well!
   It is impossible that ever Rome
   Should breed thy fellow. Friends, I owe more tears
   To this dead man than you shall see me pay.—
   I shall find time, Cassius, I shall find time.—
   Come, therefore, and to Thasos send his body.   104
   His funerals shall not be in our camp,   105
   Lest it discomfort us. Lucilius, come,   106
   And come, young Cato, let us to the field.
   Labeo and Flavius, set our battles on.   108
   'Tis three o'clock, and, Romans, yet ere night   109
   We shall try fortune in a second fight.
                        Exeunt [with the bodies].

❖

[5.4]

      Alarum. Enter Brutus, Messala, [young] Cato,
      Lucilius, and Flavius.

BRUTUS
   Yet, countrymen, oh, yet hold up your heads!
            [*Exit, followed by Messala and Flavius.*]
CATO
   What bastard doth not? Who will go with me?   2
   I will proclaim my name about the field:
   I am the son of Marcus Cato, ho!
   A foe to tyrants, and my country's friend.
   I am the son of Marcus Cato, ho!

            Enter soldiers, and fight.

LUCILIUS
   And I am Brutus, Marcus Brutus I!
   Brutus, my country's friend! Know me for Brutus!
            [*Young Cato is slain by Antony's men.*]
   O young and noble Cato, art thou down?
   Why, now thou diest as bravely as Titinius,
   And mayst be honored, being Cato's son.
FIRST SOLDIER [*capturing Lucilius*]
   Yield, or thou diest.
LUCILIUS [*offering money*]   Only I yield to die.   12
   There is so much that thou wilt kill me straight;   13
   Kill Brutus, and be honored in his death.
FIRST SOLDIER
   We must not. A noble prisoner!
SECOND SOLDIER
   Room, ho! Tell Antony, Brutus is ta'en.

            Enter Antony.

FIRST SOLDIER
   I'll tell the news. Here comes the General.—
   Brutus is ta'en, Brutus is ta'en, my lord.
ANTONY   Where is he?
LUCILIUS
   Safe, Antony, Brutus is safe enough.
   I dare assure thee that no enemy
   Shall ever take alive the noble Brutus.
   The gods defend him from so great a shame!
   When you do find him, or alive or dead,   24
   He will be found like Brutus, like himself.
ANTONY [*to First Soldier*]
   This is not Brutus, friend, but, I assure you,
   A prize no less in worth. Keep this man safe;
   Give him all kindness. I had rather have
   Such men my friends than enemies.—Go on,
   And see whe'er Brutus be alive or dead;   30
   And bring us word unto Octavius' tent
   How everything is chanced.   32
            Exeunt [separately, some bearing Cato's body].

❖

85 **hold thee** wait   87 **apace** quickly   96 **own proper** very own
96 s.d. *Low alarums* Offstage sound effects suggesting the activity
of distant battle.   97 **whe'er** whether   104 **Thasos** an island off
the coast of Thrace, near Philippi   105 **funerals** funeral obsequies
106 **discomfort us** discourage our troops.   108 **battles** armies
109 **yet ere might** (The historical battles fought at Philippi were
actually weeks apart.)
5.4. Location: Scene continues at the field of battle.

2 **What ... not?** Who is so base that he would not do so?   12 **Only ...**
die I surrender only on condition that I die at your hands.   13 **There**
... straight Here is money if you will kill me at once   24 **or alive**
either alive   30 **whe'er** whether   32 **is chanced** has fallen out.

[5.5]

Enter Brutus, Dardanius, Clitus, Strato, and Volumnius.

BRUTUS
Come, poor remains of friends, rest on this rock.
                                    [*He sits.*]

CLITUS
Statilius showed the torchlight, but, my lord,   2
He came not back. He is or ta'en or slain.   3

BRUTUS
Sit thee down, Clitus. Slaying is the word.
It is a deed in fashion. Hark thee, Clitus.
                                    [*He whispers.*]

CLITUS
What, I, my lord? No, not for all the world.

BRUTUS
Peace then. No words.

CLITUS   I'll rather kill myself.

BRUTUS
Hark thee, Dardanius.   [*He whispers.*]

DARDANIUS   Shall I do such a deed?
    [*Dardanius and Clitus move away from Brutus.*]

CLITUS   Oh, Dardanius!

DARDANIUS   Oh, Clitus!

CLITUS
What ill request did Brutus make to thee?

DARDANIUS
To kill him, Clitus. Look, he meditates.

CLITUS
Now is that noble vessel full of grief,
That it runs over even at his eyes.

BRUTUS
Come hither, good Volumnius. List a word.   15

VOLUMNIUS
What says my lord?

BRUTUS   Why, this, Volumnius:
The ghost of Caesar hath appeared to me
Two several times by night—at Sardis once,   18
And this last night here in Philippi fields.
I know my hour is come.

VOLUMNIUS   Not so, my lord.

BRUTUS
Nay, I am sure it is, Volumnius.
Thou see'st the world, Volumnius, how it goes;
Our enemies have beat us to the pit.   *Low alarums.* 23
It is more worthy to leap in ourselves
Than tarry till they push us. Good Volumnius,
Thou know'st that we two went to school together.
Even for that our love of old, I prithee,   27

BRUTUS
Hold thou my sword hilts whilst I run on it.   28

VOLUMNIUS
That's not an office for a friend, my lord.
                                    Alarum still.

CLITUS
Fly, fly, my lord! There is no tarrying here.

BRUTUS
Farewell to you, and you, and you, Volumnius.
Strato, thou hast been all this while asleep;
Farewell to thee too, Strato. Countrymen,
My heart doth joy that yet in all my life
I found no man but he was true to me.
I shall have glory by this losing day
More than Octavius and Mark Antony
By this vile conquest shall attain unto.
So fare you well at once, for Brutus' tongue   39
Hath almost ended his life's history.
Night hangs upon mine eyes; my bones would rest,
That have but labored to attain this hour.   42
                Alarum. Cry within, "Fly, fly, fly!"

CLITUS
Fly, my lord, fly!

BRUTUS   Hence, I will follow.
        [*Exeunt Clitus, Dardanius, and Volumnius.*]
I prithee, Strato, stay thou by thy lord.
Thou art a fellow of a good respect;   45
Thy life hath had some smatch of honor in it.   46
Hold then my sword, and turn away thy face,
While I do run upon it. Wilt thou, Strato?

STRATO
Give me your hand first. Fare you well, my lord.

BRUTUS
Farewell, good Strato. [*He runs on his sword.*] Caesar,
    now be still.
I killed not thee with half so good a will.   *Dies.* 51

        Alarum. Retreat. Enter Antony, Octavius;
        Messala, Lucilius [as prisoners]; and the army.

OCTAVIUS   What man is that?

MESSALA
My master's man. Strato, where is thy master?

STRATO
Free from the bondage you are in, Messala.
The conquerors can but make a fire of him,
For Brutus only overcame himself,   56
And no man else hath honor by his death.

LUCILIUS
So Brutus should be found. I thank thee, Brutus,
That thou hast proved Lucilius' saying true.   59

OCTAVIUS
All that served Brutus, I will entertain them.   60

5.5. Location: The field of battle still.
2–3 Statilius . . . slain (According to Plutarch, a scout named Statilius has gone through the enemy lines to reconnoitre and to hold up a torch if all is well at Cassius's camp; he signals back but is then captured and slain.)   **3 or ta'en** either taken   **15 List** Listen to   **18 several** separate   **23 beat** driven.   **pit** trap for wild animals; also, a grave.   **27 that our love** that friendship of ours

28 hilts hilt   **39 at once** all together, or without further ado   **42 That . . . hour** that have striven all life long only to achieve this moment of death.   **45 respect** reputation   **46 some smatch** some flavor, a touch   **51.1 *Retreat*** signal to retire.   **56 Brutus . . . himself** only Brutus conquered Brutus   **59 saying** (See 5.4.21–5.)   **60 entertain** take into service

Fellow, wilt thou bestow thy time with me?

STRATO

Ay, if Messala will prefer me to you.   62

OCTAVIUS   Do so, good Messala.

MESSALA   How died my master, Strato?

STRATO

I held the sword, and he did run on it.

MESSALA

Octavius, then take him to follow thee,   66

That did the latest service to my master.   67

ANTONY

This was the noblest Roman of them all.

All the conspirators save only he

Did that they did in envy of great Caesar;

He only in a general honest thought   71

And common good to all made one of them.

His life was gentle, and the elements   73

So mixed in him that Nature might stand up

And say to all the world, "This was a man!"

OCTAVIUS

According to his virtue let us use him,

With all respect and rites of burial.

Within my tent his bones tonight shall lie,

Most like a soldier, ordered honorably.   79

So call the field to rest, and let's away   80

To part the glories of this happy day.   81

Exeunt omnes [*with Brutus's body*].

---

62 prefer recommend   **66 follow** serve   **67 latest** last   **71 general**
i.e., selfless. (Cf. 2.1.2 n.)

73 gentle noble.   **elements** (Humankind as a microcosm is made up
of earth, air, fire, and water, formed into the four humors of phlegm,
blood, yellow bile [or choler], and black bile [or melancholy], whose
qualities were mingled in Brutus in due proportions.)   **79 ordered**
treated, arranged for; accorded solemn rites. (Cf. 1.2.25 n.)   **80 field**
army in the field   **81 part** share.   **happy** fortunate   **81.1** *omnes* all

Hamlet, Prince of Denmark

⮂

A recurring motif in *Hamlet* is of a seemingly healthy exterior concealing an interior sickness. Mere pretense of virtue, as Hamlet warns his mother, "will but skin and film the ulcerous place, / Whiles rank corruption, mining all within, / Infects unseen" (3.4.154–6). Polonius confesses, when he is about to use his daughter as a decoy for Hamlet, that "with devotion's visage / And pious action we do sugar o'er / The devil himself"; and his observation elicits a more anguished mea culpa from Claudius in an aside: "How smart a lash that speech doth give my conscience! / The harlot's cheek, beautied with plast'ring art, / Is not more ugly to the thing that helps it / Than is my deed to my most painted word" (3.1.47–54).

This motif of concealed evil and disease continually reminds us that, in both a specific and a broader sense, "Something is rotten in the state of Denmark" (1.4.90). The specific source of contamination is a poison: the poison with which Claudius has killed Hamlet's father, the poison in the players' enactment of "The Murder of Gonzago," and the two poisons (envenomed sword and poisoned drink) with which Claudius and Laertes plot to rid themselves of young Hamlet. More generally, the poison is an evil nature seeking to destroy humanity's better self, as in the archetypal murder of Abel by Cain. "Oh, my offense is rank! It smells to heaven," laments Claudius, "It hath the primal eldest curse upon 't, / A brother's murder" (3.3.36–8). To Hamlet, his father and Claudius typify what is best and worst in humanity; one is the sungod Hyperion and the other, a satyr. Claudius is a "serpent" and a "mildewed ear, / Blasting his wholesome brother" (1.5.40; 3.4.65–6). Many a person, in Hamlet's view, is tragically destined to behold his or her better qualities corrupted by "some vicious mole of nature" over which the individual seems to have no control. "His virtues else, be they as pure as grace, / As infinite as man may undergo, / Shall in the general censure take corruption / From that particular fault." The "dram of evil" pol-lutes "all the noble substance" (1.4.24–37). Thus, poison spreads outward to infect the whole individual, just as bad individuals can infect an entire court or nation.

Hamlet, his mind attuned to philosophical matters, is keenly and poetically aware of humanity's fallen condition. He is, moreover, a shrewd observer of the Danish court, familiar with its ways and at the same time newly returned from abroad, looking at Denmark with a stranger's eyes. What particularly darkens his view of humanity, however, is not the general fact of corrupted human nature but rather Hamlet's knowledge of a dreadful secret. Even before he learns of his father's murder, Hamlet senses that there is something more deeply amiss than his mother's overhasty marriage to her deceased husband's brother. This is serious enough, to be sure, for it violates a taboo (parallel to the marriage of a widower to his deceased wife's sister, long regarded as incestuous by the English) and is thus understandably referred to as "incest" by Hamlet and his father's ghost. The appalling spectacle of Gertrude's "wicked speed, to post / With such dexterity to incestuous sheets" (1.2.156–7) overwhelms Hamlet with revulsion at carnal appetite and intensifies the emotional crisis any son would go through when forced to contemplate his father's death and his mother's remarriage. Still, the Ghost's revelation is of something far worse, something Hamlet has subconsciously feared and suspected. "Oh, my prophetic soul! My uncle!" (1.5.42). Now Hamlet believes he has confirming evidence for his intuition that the world itself is "an unweeded garden / That grows to seed. Things rank and gross in nature / Possess it merely" (1.2.135–7).

Something is indeed rotten in the state of Denmark. The monarch on whom the health and safety of the kingdom depend is a murderer. Yet few persons know his secret: Hamlet, Horatio only belatedly, Claudius himself, and ourselves as audience. Many ironies and misunderstandings within the play cannot be understood without a proper awareness of this gap between Hamlet's knowledge and most others' ignorance of the murder. For, according to their own lights, Polonius and the rest behave as courtiers normally behave, obeying and flattering a king whom they acknowledge as their legitimate ruler who has been chosen by a constitutional process of "election" and is therefore their legitimate ruler. They do not know that he is a murderer. Hamlet, for his part, is so obsessed with the secret murder that he overreacts to those around him, rejecting overtures of friendship and becoming embittered, callous, brutal, and even violent. His antisocial behavior gives the others good reason to fear him as a menace to the state. Nevertheless, we share with Hamlet a knowledge of the truth and know that he is right, whereas the others are at best unhappily deceived by their own blind complicity in evil.

Rosencrantz and Guildenstern, for instance, are boyhood friends of Hamlet but are now dependent on the favor of King Claudius. Despite their seeming concern for their one-time comrade and Hamlet's initial pleasure in receiving them, they are faceless courtiers whose very names, like their personalities, are virtually interchangeable. "Thanks, Rosencrantz and gentle Guildenstern," says the King, and "Thanks, Guildenstern and gentle Rosencrantz," echoes the Queen (2.2.33–4). They cannot understand why Hamlet increasingly mocks their overtures of friendship, whereas Hamlet cannot stomach their subservience to the King. The secret murder divides Hamlet from them, since only he knows of it. As the confrontation between Hamlet and Claudius grows more deadly, Rosencrantz and Guildenstern, not knowing the true cause, can only interpret Hamlet's behavior as dangerous madness. The wild display he puts on during the performance of "The Murder of Gonzago" and then the killing of Polonius are evidence of a treasonous threat to the crown, eliciting from them staunch assertions of the divine right of kings. "Most holy and religious fear it is / To keep those many many bodies safe / That live and feed upon Your Majesty," professes Guildenstern, and Rosencrantz reiterates the theme: "The cess of majesty / Dies not alone, but like a gulf doth draw / What's near it with it" (3.3.8–17). These sentiments of Elizabethan orthodoxy, similar to ones frequently heard in Shakespeare's history plays, are here undercut by a devastating irony, since they are spoken unwittingly in defense of a murderer. This irony pursues Rosencrantz and Guildenstern to their graves, for they are killed performing what they see as their duty to convey Hamlet safely to England. They are as ignorant of Claudius's secret orders for the murder of Hamlet in England as they are of Claudius's real reason for wishing to be rid of his stepson. That Hamlet should ingeniously remove the secret commission from Rosencrantz and Guildenstern's packet and substitute an order for their execution is ironically fitting, even though they are guiltless of having plotted Hamlet's death. "Why, man, they did make love to this employment," says Hamlet to Horatio. "They are not

near my conscience. Their defeat / Does by their own insinuation grow" (5.2.57–9). They have condemned themselves, in Hamlet's eyes, by interceding officiously in deadly affairs of which they had no comprehension. Hamlet's judgment of them is harsh, and he himself appears hardened and pitiless in his role as agent in their deaths, but he is right that they have courted their own destiny.

Polonius, too, dies for meddling. It seems an unfair fate, since he wishes no physical harm to Hamlet and is only trying to ingratiate himself with Claudius. Yet Polonius's complicity in jaded court politics is deeper than his fatuous parental sententiousness might lead one to suppose. His famous advice to his son, often quoted out of context as though it were wise counsel, is, in fact, a worldly gospel of self-interest and concern for appearances. Like his son, Laertes, he cynically presumes that Hamlet's affection for Ophelia cannot be serious, since princes are not free to marry ladies of the court; accordingly, Polonius obliges his daughter to return the love letters she so cherishes. Polonius's spies are everywhere, seeking to entrap Polonius's own son in fleshly sin or to discover symptoms of Hamlet's presumed lovesickness. Polonius may cut a ridiculous figure as a prattling busybody, but he is wily and even menacing in his intent. He has actually helped Claudius to the throne and is an essential instrument of royal policy. His ineffectuality and ignorance of the murder do not really excuse his guilty involvement.

Ophelia is more innocent than her father and brother, and more truly affectionate toward Hamlet. She earns our sympathy because she is caught between the conflicting wills of the men who are supremely important to her—her lover, her father, and her brother. Obedient by instinct and training to patriarchal instruction, she is unprepared to cope with divided authority and so takes refuge in passivity. Nevertheless, her pitiable story suggests that weak-willed acquiescence is poisoned by the evil to which it surrenders. However passively, Ophelia becomes an instrument through which Claudius attempts to spy on Hamlet. She is much like Gertrude, for the Queen has yielded to Claudius's importunity without ever knowing fully what awful price Claudius has paid for her and for the throne. The resemblance between Ophelia and Gertrude confirms Hamlet's tendency to generalize about feminine weakness—"frailty, thy name is woman" (1.2.146)—and prompts his misogynistic outburst against Ophelia when he concludes she, too, is spying on him. His rejection of love and friendship (except for Horatio's) seems paranoid in character and yet is at least partially justified by the fact that so many of the court are in fact conspiring to learn what he is up to.

Their oversimplification of his dilemma and their facile analyses vex Hamlet as much as their meddling. When they presume to diagnose his malady, the courtiers actually reveal more about themselves than about Hamlet—something we as readers and viewers might well bear in mind. Rosencrantz and Guildenstern think in political terms, reflecting their own ambitious natures, and Hamlet takes mordant delight in leading them on. "Sir, I lack advancement," he mockingly answers Rosencrantz's questioning as to the cause of his distemper. Rosencrantz is immediately taken in: "How can that be, when you have the voice of the King himself for your succession in Denmark?" (3.2.338–41). Actually, Hamlet does hold a grudge against Claudius for having "Popped in between th'election and my hopes" (5.2.65), using the Danish custom of "election" by the chief lords of the realm to deprive young Hamlet of the succession that would normally have been his. Nevertheless, it is a gross oversimplification to suppose that political frustration is the key to Hamlet's sorrow, and to speculate thus is presumptuous. "Why, look you now, how unworthy a thing you make of me!" Hamlet protests to Rosencrantz and Guildenstern. "You would play upon me, you would seem to know my stops, you would pluck out the heart of my mystery" (3.2.362–5). An even worse offender in the distortion of complex truth is Polonius, whose facile diagnosis of lovesickness appears to have been inspired by recollections of Polonius's own far-off youth. ("Truly in my youth I suffered much extremity for love, very near this," 2.2.189–91). Polonius's fatuous complacency in his own powers of analysis—"If circumstances lead me, I will find / Where truth is hid, though it were hid indeed / Within the center" (2.2.157–9)—reads like a parody of Hamlet's struggle to discover what is true and what is not.

Thus, although Hamlet may seem to react with excessive bitterness toward those who are set to watch over him, the corruption he decries in Denmark is both real and universal. "The time is out of joint," he laments. "Oh, cursèd spite / That ever I was born to set it right!" (1.5.197–8). How is he to proceed in setting things right? Ever since the nineteenth century, it has been fashionable to discover reasons for Hamlet's delaying his revenge. The basic Romantic approach is to find a defect, or tragic flaw, in Hamlet himself. In Coleridge's words, Hamlet suffers from "an overbalance in the contemplative faculty" and is "one who vacillates from sensibility and procrastinates from thought, and loses the power of action in the energy of resolve." More recent psychological critics, such as Freud's disciple Ernest Jones, still seek answers to the Romantics' question by explaining Hamlet's failure of will. In Jones' interpretation, Hamlet is the victim of an Oedipal trauma: he has longed unconsciously to possess his mother and for that very reason cannot bring himself to punish the hated uncle who has supplanted him in his incestuous and forbidden desire. Such interpretations suggest, among other things, that Hamlet continues to serve as a mirror in which analysts who would pluck out the heart of his mystery see an image of their own concerns— just as Rosencrantz and Guildenstern read politics, and Polonius reads lovesickness, into Hamlet's distress.

We can ask, however, not only whether the explanations for Hamlet's supposed delay are valid but also whether the question they seek to answer is itself valid. Is the delay unnecessary or excessive? The question did not even arise until the nineteenth century. Earlier audiences were evidently satisfied that Hamlet must test the Ghost's credibility, since apparitions can tell half-truths to deceive people, and that, once Hamlet has confirmed the Ghost's word, he proceeds as resolutely as his canny adversary allows. More recent criticism, perhaps reflecting a modern absorption in existentialist philosophy, has proposed that Hamlet's dilemma is a matter, not of personal failure, but of the absurdity of action itself in a corrupt world. Does what Hamlet is asked to do make any sense, given the bestial nature of humanity and the impossibility of knowing what is right? In part, it is a matter of style: Claudius's Denmark is crassly vulgar, and to combat this vulgarity on its own terms seems to require the sort of bad histrionics Hamlet derides in actors who mouth their lines or tear a passion to tatters. Hamlet's dilemma of action can best be studied in the play by comparing him with various characters who are obliged to act in situations similar to his own and who respond in meaningfully different ways.

Three young men—Hamlet, Laertes, and Fortinbras— are called upon to avenge their fathers' violent deaths. Ophelia, too, has lost a father by violent means, and her madness and death are another kind of reaction to such a loss. The responses of Laertes and Fortinbras offer rich parallels to Hamlet, in both cases implying the futility of positive and forceful action. Laertes thinks he has received an unambiguous mandate to take revenge, since Hamlet has undoubtedly slain Polonius and helped to deprive Ophelia of her sanity. Accordingly, Laertes comes back to Denmark in a fury, stirring the rabble with his demagoguery and spouting Senecan rant about dismissing conscience "to the profoundest pit" in his quest for vengeance (4.5.135). When Claudius asks what Laertes would do to Hamlet "To show yourself in deed your father's son / More than in words," Laertes fires back: "To cut his throat i'th' church" (4.7.126–7). This resolution is understandable. The pity is, however, that Laertes has only superficially identified the murderer in the case. He is too easily deceived by Claudius, because he has jumped to easy and fallacious conclusions, and so is doomed to become a pawn in Claudius's sly maneuverings. Too late he sees his error and must die for it, begging and receiving Hamlet's forgiveness. Before we accuse Hamlet of thinking too deliberately before acting, we must consider that Laertes does not think enough.

Fortinbras of Norway, as his name implies ("strong in arms"), is one who believes in decisive action. At the beginning of the play, we learn that his father has been slain in battle by old Hamlet and that Fortinbras has collected an army to win back by force the territory fairly won by the Danes in that encounter. Like Hamlet, young Fortinbras does not succeed his father to the throne but must now contend with an uncle-king. When this uncle, at Claudius's instigation, forbids Fortinbras to march against the Danes and rewards him for his restraint with a huge annual income and a commission to fight the Poles instead, Fortinbras sagaciously welcomes the new opportunity. He pockets the money, marches against Poland, and waits for occasion to deliver Denmark as well into his hands. Clearly this is more of a success story than that of Laertes, and Hamlet does, after all, give his blessing to the "election" of Fortinbras to the Danish throne. Fortinbras is the man of the hour, the representative of a restored political stability. Yet Hamlet's admiration for this man on horseback is qualified by a profound reservation. Hamlet's dying prophecy that the election will light on Fortinbras (5.2.357–8) is suffused with ironies, so much so that the incongruity is sometimes made conscious and deliberate in performance. Earlier in the play, the spectacle of Fortinbras marching against Poland "to gain a little patch of ground / That hath in it no profit but the name" prompts Hamlet to berate himself for inaction, but he cannot ignore the absurdity of the effort. "Two thousand souls and twenty thousand ducats / Will not debate the question of this straw." The soldiers will risk their very lives "Even for an eggshell" (4.4.19–54). It is only one step from this view of the vanity of ambitious striving to the speculation that great Caesar or Alexander, dead and turned to dust, may one day produce the loam or clay with which to stop the bunghole of a beer barrel. Fortinbras epitomizes the ongoing political order after Hamlet's death, but is that order of any consequence to us after we have imagined with Hamlet the futility of most human endeavor?

To ask such a question is to seek passive or self-abnegating answers to the riddle of life, and Hamlet is attuned to such inquiries. Even before he learns of his father's murder, he contemplates suicide, wishing "that the Everlasting had not fixed / His canon 'gainst self-slaughter" (1.2.131–2). As with the alternative of action, other characters serve as foils to Hamlet, revealing both the attractions and perils of withdrawal. Ophelia is destroyed by meekly acquiescing in others' desires. Whether she commits suicide is uncertain, but the very possibility reminds us that Hamlet has twice considered and reluctantly rejected this despairing path as forbidden by Christian teaching—the second such occasion being his "To be, or not to be" soliloquy in 3.1. He has also playacted at the madness to which Ophelia succumbs. Gertrude identifies herself with Ophelia and like her has surrendered her will to male aggressiveness. We suspect she knows little of the actual murder (see 3.4.31) but dares not think how deeply she may be implicated. Although her death is evidently not a suicide (see 5.2.291–7), it is passive and expiatory.

A more attractive alternative to decisive action for Hamlet is acting in the theater, and he is full of exuberant advice to the visiting players. The play they perform before Claudius at Hamlet's request and with some lines added by him—a play consciously archaic in style—offers to the Danish court a kind of heightened reflection of itself, a homiletic artifact, rendering in conventional terms the taut anxieties and terrors of murder for the sake of noble passion. Structurally, the play within the play becomes not an escape for Hamlet into inaction but rather the point on which the whole drama pivots and the scene in which contemplation of past events is largely replaced with stirrings toward action. When Lucianus in the Mousetrap play turns out to be nephew rather than brother to the dead king, the audience finds itself face to face, not with history, but with prophecy. We are not surprised when, in his conversations with the players, Hamlet openly professes his admiration for the way in which art holds "the mirror up to nature, to show virtue her feature, scorn her own image, and the very age and body of the time his form and pressure" (3.2.22–4). Hamlet admires the dramatist's ability to transmute raw human feeling into tragic art, depicting and ordering reality as Shakespeare's play of *Hamlet* does for us. Yet playacting can also be, Hamlet recognizes, a self-indulgent escape for him, a way of unpacking his heart with words and of verbalizing his situation without doing something to remedy it. Acting and talking remind him too much of Polonius, who was an actor in his youth and who continues to be, like Hamlet, an inveterate punster.

Of the passive responses in the play, the stoicism of Hortatio is by far the most attractive to Hamlet. "More an antique Roman than a Dane" (5.2.343), Horatio is, as Hamlet praises him, immune to flattering or to opportunities for cheap self-advancement. He is "As one, in suffering all, that suffers nothing, / A man that Fortune's buffets and rewards / Hast ta'en with equal thanks" (3.2.65–7). Such a person has a sure defense against the worst that life can offer. Hamlet can trust and love Horatio as he can no one else. Yet even here there are limits, for Horatio's skeptical and Roman philosophy cuts him off from a Christian and metaphysical overview. "There are more things in heaven and earth, Horatio, / Than are dreamt of in your philosophy" (1.5.175–6). After they have beheld together the skulls of Yorick's graveyard, Horatio seemingly does not share with Hamlet the exulting Christian perception that, although human life is indeed vain, Providence will reveal a pattern transcending human sorrow.

Hamlet's path must lie somewhere between the rash suddenness of Laertes or the canny resoluteness of Fortinbras on the one hand, and the passivity of Ophelia or Gertrude and the stoic resignation of Horatio on the other. At first he alternates between action and inaction, finding neither satisfactory. The Ghost has commanded Hamlet to revenge but has not explained how this is to be done; indeed, Gertrude is to be left passively to heaven and her conscience. If this method will suffice for her (and Christian wisdom taught that such a purgation was as thorough as it was sure), why not for Claudius? If Claudius must be killed, should it be while he is at his sin rather than at his prayers? The play is full of questions, stemming chiefly from the enigmatic commands of the Ghost. "Say, why is this? Wherefore? What should we do?" (1.4.57). Hamlet is not incapable of action. He shows unusual strength and cunning on the pirate ship, in his duel with Laertes ("I shall win at the odds"; 5.2.209), and especially in his slaying of Polonius—an action hardly characterized by "thinking too precisely on th'event" (4.4.42). Here is forthright action of the sort Laertes espouses. Yet, when the corpse behind his mother's arras turns out to be Polonius rather than Claudius, Hamlet concludes from the mistake that he has offended heaven. Even if Polonius deserves what he got, Hamlet believes he has made himself into a cruel "scourge" of Providence who must himself suffer retribution as well as deal it out. Swift action has not accomplished what the Ghost commanded.

The Ghost does not appear to speak for Providence in any case. His message is of revenge, a pagan concept deeply embedded in most societies but at odds with Christian teaching. His wish that Claudius be sent to hell and that Gertrude be more gently treated might, in fact, be the judgment of an impartial deity but here comes wrapped in the passionate involvement of a murdered man's restless spirit. This is not to say that Hamlet is being tempted to perform a damnable act, as he fears is possible, but that the Ghost's command cannot readily be reconciled with a complex and balanced view of justice. If Hamlet were to spring on Claudius in the fullness of his vice and cut his throat, we would pronounce Hamlet a murderer. What Hamlet believes he has learned instead is that he must become the instrument of Providence according to *its* plans, not his own. After his return from England, he senses triumphantly that all will be for the best if he allows an unseen power to decide the time and place for his final act. Under these conditions, rash action will be right. "Rashly, / And praised be rashness for it— let us know / Our indiscretion sometime serves us well / When our deep plots do pall, and that should learn us / There's a divinity that shapes our ends, / Rough-hew them how we will" (5.2.6–11). Passivity, too, is now a proper course, for Hamlet puts himself wholly at the disposal of Providence. What had seemed so impossible when Hamlet tried to formulate his own design proves elementary once he trusts to a divine justice in which he now firmly believes. Rashness and passivity are perfectly fused. Hamlet is revenged without having to commit premeditated murder and is relieved of his painful existence without having to commit suicide.

The circumstances of *Hamlet'*s catastrophe do indeed seem to accomplish all that Hamlet desires, by a route so circuitous that no one could ever have foreseen or devised it. Polonius's death, as it turns out, was instrumental after all, for it led to Laertes's angry return to Denmark and the challenge to a duel. Every seemingly unrelated event has its place; "There is special providence in the fall of a sparrow" (5.2.217–18). Repeatedly, the characters stress the role of seeming accident leading to just retribution. Even Horatio, for whom the events of the play suggest a pattern of randomness and violence, of "accidental judgments" and "casual slaughters," can see at last, "in this upshot, purposes mistook / Fall'n on th'inventors' heads" (5.2.384–7). In a similar vein, Laertes confesses himself "a woodcock to mine own springe" (line 309). As Hamlet had said earlier, of Rosencrantz and Guildenstern, " 'tis the sport to have the engineer / Hoist with his own petard" (3.4.213–14). Thus, too, Claudius's poisoned cup, intended for Hamlet, kills the Queen for whom Claudius had done such evil in order to acquire her and the throne. The destiny of evil in this play is to overreach itself.

In its final resolution, *Hamlet* incorporates a broader conception of justice than its revenge formula seemed at first to make possible. Yet, in its origins, *Hamlet* is a revenge story, and these traditions have left some residual savagery in the play. In the *Historia Danica* of Saxo Grammaticus, 1180–1208, and in the rather free translation of Saxo into French by François de Belleforest, *Histoires Tragiques* (1576), Hamlet is cunning and bloodily resolute throughout. He kills an eavesdropper without a qualm during the interview with his mother and exchanges letters on his way to England with characteristic shrewdness. Ultimately, he returns to Denmark, sets fire to his uncle's hall, slays its courtly inhabitants, and claims his rightful throne from a grateful people. The Ghost, absent in this account, may well have been supplied by Thomas Kyd, author of *The Spanish Tragedy* (c. 1587) and seemingly of a lost *Hamlet* play in existence by 1589. *The Spanish Tragedy* bears many resemblances to our *Hamlet* and suggests what the lost *Hamlet* may well have contained: a sensational murder, a Senecan Ghost demanding revenge, the avenger hampered by court intrigue, his resort to a feigned madness, and his difficulty in authenticating the ghostly vision. A German version of *Hamlet,* called *Der bestrafte Brudermord* (1710), based seemingly on the older *Hamlet,* includes such details as the play within the play, the sparing of the King at his prayers in order to damn his soul, Ophelia's madness, the fencing match with poisoned swords and poisoned drink, and the final catastrophe of vengeance and death. Similarly, the early unauthorized First Quarto of *Hamlet* (1603) offers some passages seemingly based on the older play by Kyd.

Although this evidence suggests that Shakespeare received most of the material for the plot intact, his transformation of that material was nonetheless immeasurable. To be sure, Kyd's *The Spanish Tragedy* contains many rhetorical passages on the inadequacy of human justice, but the overall effect is still sensational and the outcome is a triumph for the pagan spirit of revenge. So, too, with the many revenge plays of the 1590s and 1600s that Kyd's dramatic genius had inspired, including Shakespeare's own *Titus Andronicus* (c. 1589–1592). *Hamlet,* written in about 1599–1601 (it is not mentioned by Frances Meres in his *Palladis Tamia: Wit's Treasury,* in 1598, and was entered in the Stationers' Register, the official record book of the London Company of Stationers [booksellers and printers], in 1602), is unparalleled in its philosophical richness. Its ending is truly cathartic, for Hamlet dies, not as a bloodied avenger, but as one who has affirmed the tragic dignity of the human race. His courage and faith, maintained in the face of great odds, atone for the dismal corruption in which Denmark has festered. His resolutely honest inquiries have taken him beyond the revulsion and doubt that express so eloquently, among other matters, the fearful response of Shakespeare's own generation to a seeming breakdown of established political, theological, and cosmological beliefs. Hamlet finally perceives that "if it be not now, yet it will come," and that "The readiness is all" (5.2.219–20). This discovery, this revelation of necessity and meaning in Hamlet's great reversal of fortune, enables him to confront the tragic circumstance of his life with understanding and heroism and to demonstrate the triumph of the human spirit even in the moment of his catastrophe.

Such an assertion of the individual will does not lessen the tragic waste with which *Hamlet* ends. Hamlet is dead, and the great promise of his life is forever lost. Few others have survived. Justice has seemingly been fulfilled in the deaths of Claudius, Gertrude, Rosencrantz and Guildenstern, Polonius, Laertes, and perhaps even Ophelia, but in a wild and extravagant way, as though Justice herself, more vengeful than providential, were unceasingly hungry for victims. Hamlet, the minister of that justice, has likewise grown indifferent to the spilling of blood, even if he submits himself at last to the will of a force he recognizes as providential. Denmark faces the kind of political uncertainty with which the play began. However much Hamlet may admire Fortinbras's resolution, the prince of Norway seems an alien choice for Denmark—even an ironic one. Horatio sees so little point in outliving the catastrophe of this play that he would choose death, were it not that he must draw his breath in pain to ensure that Hamlet's story is truly told. Still, that truth has been rescued from oblivion. Amid the ruin of the final scene, we share the artist's vision, through which we struggle to interpret and give order to the tragedy that proves inseparable from human existence.

The performance history of *Hamlet* is extraordinarily rich. It also attests to a variety of interpetations that is equally textured. Eighteenth-century versions by David Garrick and others often took out or severely reduced the Fortinbras plot; indeed, the play is so long that it almost certainly was not acted in its entirety even in Shake-

speare's day. Garrick also deleted the Gravediggers' scene and much besides in Act 5. Pictorial scenery in the nineteenth century tended to favor opulent renditions of the play-within-the-play and Ophelia's mad scenes. Hamlet was portrayed in 1864, at the Lyceum Theater, as a Viking in a primitive medieval decor. Henry Irving, undertaking the role of Hamlet from 1864 to 1885, chose a decor of the fifth or sixth century, with castle battlements set among massive rocks glimmering under the soft light of the moon in the first act. John Gielgud became famous as a leading Hamlet of his day, beginning in 1930 at the Old Vic, emphasizing the pale, introspective, sonorous-voiced Hamlet that Coleridge had imagined. More recently, *Hamlet* has been seen from an existential vantage (by Tyrone Guthrie, 1938, at the Old Vic) in the modern-dress context of a Europe precariously trapped between the first World War and a second about to begin. Laurence Olivier, in his film version of 1948, explored the Freudian dimensions of "a man who could not make up his mind"; influenced by Ernest Jones's *Hamlet and Oedipus,* Olivier allowed the camera eye to linger on the Queen's bedchamber and its bed, where Hamlet encountered his mother in a scene (3.4) heavy with incestuous overtones.

Recent productions on stage, in film, and on television amply demonstrate how Shakespeare's best-known play can lend itself to other kinds of relevance to our modern world. Political interpretations sometimes focus on Claudius as a Machiavel in the school of modern spin-doctoring. At the Wisdom Bridge Theater's Chicago production in the 1970s, for example, directed by Robert Falls with Aiden Quinn as Hamlet, Claudius was the Great Communicator in the style of Ronald Reagan. His first scene (1.2) featured the new king on an array of television sets, blandly explaining to the Danish public the reasons for his rapid assumption of power and marriage with the widow of his dead brother. Claudius and Gertrude never appeared onstage in this scene; the audience saw the king on television, while the stage itself was given over to his zealous public relations team, nattily dressed, preparing a reception for the press representatives, making sure the event went smoothly. Fading posters of the dead king offered contrasting reminders of the regime which Claudius had so astutely supplanted.

More recently, in Michael Almereyda's low-budget film of 2000, the setting throughout is the New York world of privilege and high finance. Claudius (Kyle MacLachlan) is a chief executive officer of a superconglomerate financial empire. Gertrude (Diane Venora) is a suburban wife utterly seduced by the expensive privileges she now enjoys, of stretch limosines, private bathing pools in their high-rise empire, and the surroundings of obsequious flattery that immense wealth can command. Hamlet (Ethan Hawke), conversely, is a rebel with a cause, ostentatiously out of step in his moth-eaten ski cap, his scruffy clothes, his mania for the latest film and computer technology, and his disdain for corrupting privilege. The ghost of Hamlet's father (Sam Shepard) eerily appears on the swank penthouse battlements of New York's concrete skyscrapers, berattling the television monitors of up-to-date security systems. The overall effect is indeed strikingly modern and plausible. Another popular film version is that of Franco Zeffirelli (1990), with Mel Gibson as a matinee idol Hamlet, Alan Bates as a believably sexy Claudius, Glenn Close as a Gertrude who is erotically infatuated with her new husband, and some compellingly handsome scenery. Grigori Kozintsev's Russian film version of 1964, based on a script by Boris Pasternak, is visually eloquent in its recurring images of stone, iron, fire, sea, and earth. Kenneth Branagh's four-hour *Hamlet* (1996) is notable for its intrepedity in offering an essentially uncut version and for some superb performances, especially that of Derek Jacobi as Claudius. Jacobi had starred earlier as Hamlet onstage (Old Vic, 1979) and in the BBC television series of all the plays beginning in 1979. Richard Burton's memorable stage performance (1964, at New York's Lunt-Fontanne Theater) is available on video. This play is especially fortunate in a rich archive of filmed or televised versions that make possible a comparative study in production by some of the greatest Shakespearean actors of the twentieth and twenty-first centuries. These varied interpretations abundantly show how *Hamlet* and its fascinating protagonist can be satirical, rebellious, mordant, funny, disillusioned, melancholic, introspective, and much more. The play that puzzles and fascinates readers is also immensely disturbing in performance.

Hamlet, Prince of Denmark

[*Dramatis Personae*

GHOST *of Hamlet, the former King of Denmark*
CLAUDIUS, *King of Denmark, the former King's brother*
GERTRUDE, *Queen of Denmark, widow of the former King and now wife of Claudius*
HAMLET, *Prince of Denmark, son of the late King and of Gertrude*

POLONIUS, *councillor to the King*
LAERTES, *his son*
OPHELIA, *his daughter*
REYNALDO, *his servant*

HORATIO, *Hamlet's friend and fellow student*

VOLTIMAND,
CORNELIUS,
ROSENCRANTZ,
GUILDENSTERN, } *members of the Danish court*
OSRIC,
A GENTLEMAN,
A LORD,

BERNARDO,
FRANCISCO, } *officers and soldiers on watch*
MARCELLUS,

FORTINBRAS, *Prince of Norway*
CAPTAIN *in his army*

Three or Four PLAYERS, *taking the roles of* PROLOGUE, PLAYER KING, PLAYER QUEEN, *and* LUCIANUS
Two MESSENGERS
FIRST SAILOR
Two CLOWNS, *a gravedigger and his companion*
PRIEST
FIRST AMBASSADOR *from England*

Lords, Soldiers, Attendants, Guards, other Players, Followers of Laertes, other Sailors, another Ambassador or Ambassadors from England

SCENE: *Denmark*]

[1.1]

Enter Bernardo and Francisco, two sentinels,
[meeting].

BERNARDO   Who's there?

FRANCISCO
Nay, answer me. Stand and unfold yourself.   2

BERNARDO   Long live the King!

FRANCISCO   Bernardo?

BERNARDO   He.

FRANCISCO
You come most carefully upon your hour.

BERNARDO
'Tis now struck twelve. Get thee to bed, Francisco.

FRANCISCO
For this relief much thanks. 'Tis bitter cold,
And I am sick at heart.

BERNARDO   Have you had quiet guard?

FRANCISCO   Not a mouse stirring.

BERNARDO   Well, good night.
If you do meet Horatio and Marcellus,
The rivals of my watch, bid them make haste.   14

Enter Horatio and Marcellus.

FRANCISCO
I think I hear them.—Stand, ho! Who is there?

HORATIO   Friends to this ground.   16

MARCELLUS   And liegemen to the Dane.   17

FRANCISCO   Give you good night.   18

MARCELLUS
Oh, farewell, honest soldier. Who hath relieved you?

FRANCISCO
Bernardo hath my place. Give you good night.
Exit Francisco.

MARCELLUS   Holla! Bernardo!

BERNARDO   Say, what, is Horatio there?

HORATIO   A piece of him.

BERNARDO
Welcome, Horatio. Welcome, good Marcellus.

HORATIO
What, has this thing appeared again tonight?

BERNARDO   I have seen nothing.

MARCELLUS
Horatio says 'tis but our fantasy,   27
And will not let belief take hold of him
Touching this dreaded sight twice seen of us.
Therefore I have entreated him along   30
With us to watch the minutes of this night,   31
That if again this apparition come
He may approve our eyes and speak to it.   33

HORATIO
Tush, tush, 'twill not appear.

BERNARDO   Sit down awhile

1.1 **Location: Elsinore castle. A guard platform.**
2 me (Francisco emphasizes that *he* is the sentry currently on watch.)
unfold yourself reveal your identity.   **14 rivals** partners   **16 ground**
country, land.   **17 liegemen to the Dane** men sworn to serve the
Danish king.   **18 Give** May God give   **27 fantasy** imagination
30 along to come along   **31 watch** keep watch during   **33 approve**
corroborate

And let us once again assail your ears,
That are so fortified against our story,
What we have two nights seen.

HORATIO   Well, sit we down,
And let us hear Bernardo speak of this.

BERNARDO   Last night of all,   39
When yond same star that's westward from the pole   40
Had made his course t'illume that part of heaven   41
Where now it burns, Marcellus and myself,
The bell then beating one—

Enter Ghost.

MARCELLUS
Peace, break thee off! Look where it comes again!

BERNARDO
In the same figure like the King that's dead.

MARCELLUS
Thou art a scholar. Speak to it, Horatio.   46

BERNARDO
Looks 'a not like the King? Mark it, Horatio.   47

HORATIO
Most like. It harrows me with fear and wonder.

BERNARDO
It would be spoke to.

MARCELLUS   Speak to it, Horatio.   49

HORATIO
What art thou that usurp'st this time of night,   50
Together with that fair and warlike form
In which the majesty of buried Denmark   52
Did sometimes march? By heaven, I charge thee, speak!   53

MARCELLUS
It is offended.

BERNARDO   See, it stalks away.

HORATIO
Stay! Speak, speak! I charge thee, speak!   *Exit Ghost.*

MARCELLUS   'Tis gone and will not answer.

BERNARDO
How now, Horatio? You tremble and look pale.
Is not this something more than fantasy?
What think you on't?   59

HORATIO
Before my God, I might not this believe
Without the sensible and true avouch   61
Of mine own eyes.

MARCELLUS   Is it not like the King?

HORATIO   As thou art to thyself.
Such was the very armor he had on
When he the ambitious Norway combated.   65
So frowned he once when, in an angry parle,   66
He smote the sledded Polacks on the ice.   67
'Tis strange.

---

39 Last . . . all i.e., This *very* last night. (Emphatic.)   **40 pole** polestar,
north star   **41 his** its.   **t'illume** to illuminate   **46 scholar** one
learned enough to know how to question a ghost properly.   **47 'a** he
49 It . . . to (It was commonly believed that a ghost could not speak
until spoken to.)   **50 usurp'st** wrongfully takes over   **52 buried**
Denmark the buried King of Denmark   **53 sometimes** formerly
59 on't of it.   **61 sensible** confirmed by the senses.   **avouch** warrant,
evidence   **65 Norway** King of Norway   **66 parle** parley   **67 sledded**
traveling on sleds.   **Polacks** Poles

MARCELLUS

Thus twice before, and jump at this dead hour,   69
With martial stalk hath he gone by our watch.   70

HORATIO

In what particular thought to work I know not,   71
But in the gross and scope of mine opinion   72
This bodes some strange eruption to our state.

MARCELLUS

Good now, sit down, and tell me, he that knows,   74
Why this same strict and most observant watch
So nightly toils the subject of the land,   76
And why such daily cast of brazen cannon   77
And foreign mart for implements of war,   78
Why such impress of shipwrights, whose sore task   79
Does not divide the Sunday from the week.
What might be toward, that this sweaty haste   81
Doth make the night joint-laborer with the day?
Who is't that can inform me?

HORATIO   That can I;
At least, the whisper goes so. Our last king,
Whose image even but now appeared to us,
Was, as you know, by Fortinbras of Norway,
Thereto pricked on by a most emulate pride,   87
Dared to the combat; in which our valiant Hamlet—
For so this side of our known world esteemed him—   89
Did slay this Fortinbras; who by a sealed compact   90
Well ratified by law and heraldry   91
Did forfeit, with his life, all those his lands
Which he stood seized of, to the conqueror;   93
Against the which a moiety competent   94
Was gagèd by our king, which had returned   95
To the inheritance of Fortinbras   96
Had he been vanquisher, as, by the same cov'nant   97
And carriage of the article designed,   98
His fell to Hamlet. Now, sir, young Fortinbras,
Of unimprovèd mettle hot and full,   100
Hath in the skirts of Norway here and there   101
Sharked up a list of lawless resolutes   102
For food and diet to some enterprise   103
That hath a stomach in't, which is no other—   104
As it doth well appear unto our state—
But to recover of us, by strong hand
And terms compulsatory, those foresaid lands
So by his father lost. And this, I take it,
Is the main motive of our preparations,

The source of this our watch, and the chief head   110
Of this posthaste and rummage in the land.   111

BERNARDO

I think it be no other but e'en so.
Well may it sort that this portentous figure   113
Comes armèd through our watch so like the King
That was and is the question of these wars.   115

HORATIO

A mote it is to trouble the mind's eye.   116
In the most high and palmy state of Rome,   117
A little ere the mightiest Julius fell,   118
The graves stood tenantless, and the sheeted dead   119
Did squeak and gibber in the Roman streets;
As stars with trains of fire and dews of blood,   121
Disasters in the sun; and the moist star   122
Upon whose influence Neptune's empire stands   123
Was sick almost to doomsday with eclipse.   124
And even the like precurse of feared events,   125
As harbingers preceding still the fates   126
And prologue to the omen coming on,   127
Have heaven and earth together demonstrated
Unto our climatures and countrymen.   129

Enter Ghost.

But soft, behold! Lo, where it comes again!   130
I'll cross it, though it blast me. (*It spreads his arms.*) Stay,
illusion!   131
If thou hast any sound or use of voice,
Speak to me!
If there be any good thing to be done
That may to thee do ease and grace to me,
Speak to me!
If thou art privy to thy country's fate,   137
Which, happily, foreknowing may avoid,   138
Oh, speak!
Or if thou hast uphoarded in thy life
Extorted treasure in the womb of earth,
For which, they say, you spirits oft walk in death,
Speak of it! (*The cock crows.*) Stay and speak!—Stop it,
Marcellus.

MARCELLUS

Shall I strike at it with my partisan?   144

HORATIO   Do, if it will not stand.   [*They strike at it.*]

BERNARDO   'Tis here!   146

HORATIO   'Tis here!   [*Exit Ghost.*] 147

69 **jump** exactly 70 **stalk** stride 71 **to work** i.e., to collect my thoughts and try to understand this 72 **gross and scope** general drift 74 **Good now** (An expression denoting entreaty or expostulation.) 76 **toils** causes to toil. **subject** subjects 77 **cast** casting 78 **mart** shopping 79 **impress** impressment, conscription 81 **toward** in preparation 87 **Thereto . . . pride** (Refers to old Fortinbras, not the Danish King.) **pricked on** incited. **emulate** emulous, ambitious 89 **this . . . world** i.e., all Europe, the Western world 90 **sealed** certified, confirmed 91 **heraldry** chivalry 93 **seized** possessed 94 **Against the** in return for. **moiety competent** corresponding portion 95 **gagèd** engaged, pledged. **had returned** would have passed 96 **inheritance** possession 97 **cov'nant** i.e., the *sealed compact* of line 90 98 **carriage . . . designed** purport of the article referred to 100 **unimprovèd mettle** untried, undisciplined spirits 101 **skirts** outlying regions, outskirts 102–4 **Sharked . . . in't** rounded up (as a shark scoops up fish) a troop of lawless desperadoes to feed and supply an enterprise of considerable daring

110 **head** source 111 **posthaste and rummage** frenetic activity and bustle 113 **Well . . . sort** That would explain why 115 **question** focus of contention 116 **mote** speck of dust 117 **palmy** flourishing 118 **Julius** Julius Caesar 119 **sheeted** shrouded 121 **As** (This abrupt transition suggests that matter is possibly omitted between lines 120 and 121.) **trains** trails 122 **Disasters** unfavorable signs or aspects. **moist star** i.e., moon, governing tides 123 **Neptune's . . . stands** the sea depends 124 **Was . . . eclipse** was eclipsed nearly to the cosmic darkness predicted for the second coming of Christ and the ending of the world. (See Matthew 24:29 and Revelation 6:12.) 125 **precurse** heralding, foreshadowing 126 **harbingers** forerunners. **still** always 127 **omen** calamitous event 129 **climatures** climes, regions 130 **soft** i.e., enough, break off 131 **cross** stand in its path, confront. **blast** wither, strike with a curse. 131 **s.d.** *his* its 137 **privy to** in on the secret of 138 **happily** haply, perchance 144 **partisan** long-handled spear. 146–7 **'Tis Here! / 'Tis here!** (Perhaps they attempt to strike at the Ghost, but are baffled by its seeming ability to be here and there and nowhere.)

MARCELLUS 'Tis gone.
    We do it wrong, being so majestical,
    To offer it the show of violence,
    For it is as the air invulnerable,
    And our vain blows malicious mockery.

BERNARDO
    It was about to speak when the cock crew.

HORATIO
    And then it started like a guilty thing
    Upon a fearful summons. I have heard
    The cock, that is the trumpet to the morn,   156
    Doth with his lofty and shrill-sounding throat
    Awake the god of day, and at his warning,
    Whether in sea or fire, in earth or air,
    Th'extravagant and erring spirit hies   160
    To his confine; and of the truth herein
    This present object made probation.   162

MARCELLUS
    It faded on the crowing of the cock.
    Some say that ever 'gainst that season comes   164
    Wherein our Savior's birth is celebrated,
    This bird of dawning singeth all night long,
    And then, they say, no spirit dare stir abroad;
    The nights are wholesome, then no planets strike,   168
    No fairy takes, nor witch hath power to charm,   169
    So hallowed and so gracious is that time.   170

HORATIO
    So have I heard and do in part believe it.
    But, look, the morn in russet mantle clad   172
    Walks o'er the dew of yon high eastward hill.
    Break we our watch up, and by my advice
    Let us impart what we have seen tonight
    Unto young Hamlet; for upon my life,
    This spirit, dumb to us, will speak to him.
    Do you consent we shall acquaint him with it,
    As needful in our loves, fitting our duty?

MARCELLUS
    Let's do't, I pray, and I this morning know
    Where we shall find him most conveniently.
                                    Exeunt.

[1.2]

*Flourish. Enter Claudius, King of Denmark,
Gertrude the Queen, [the] Council, as Polonius
and his son Laertes, Hamlet, cum aliis [including
Voltimand and Cornelius].*

KING
    Though yet of Hamlet our dear brother's death   1
    The memory be green, and that it us befitted
    To bear our hearts in grief and our whole kingdom

    To be contracted in one brow of woe,
    Yet so far hath discretion fought with nature
    That we with wisest sorrow think on him
    Together with remembrance of ourselves.
    Therefore our sometime sister, now our queen,   8
    Th'imperial jointress to this warlike state,   9
    Have we, as 'twere with a defeated joy—
    With an auspicious and a dropping eye,   11
    With mirth in funeral and with dirge in marriage,
    In equal scale weighing delight and dole—   13
    Taken to wife. Nor have we herein barred
    Your better wisdoms, which have freely gone
    With this affair along. For all, our thanks.
    Now follows that you know young Fortinbras,   17
    Holding a weak supposal of our worth,   18
    Or thinking by our late dear brother's death
    Our state to be disjoint and out of frame,   20
    Co-leaguèd with this dream of his advantage,   21
    He hath not failed to pester us with message
    Importing the surrender of those lands   23
    Lost by his father, with all bonds of law,   24
    To our most valiant brother. So much for him.
    Now for ourself and for this time of meeting.
    Thus much the business is: we have here writ
    To Norway, uncle of young Fortinbras—
    Who, impotent and bed-rid, scarcely hears   29
    Of this his nephew's purpose—to suppress
    His further gait herein, in that the levies,   31
    The lists, and full proportions are all made   32
    Out of his subject; and we here dispatch   33
    You, good Cornelius, and you, Voltimand,
    For bearers of this greeting to old Norway,
    Giving to you no further personal power
    To business with the King more than the scope
    Of these dilated articles allow.   *[He gives a paper.]*   38
    Farewell, and let your haste commend your duty.   39

CORNELIUS, VOLTIMAND
    In that, and all things, will we show our duty.

KING
    We doubt it nothing. Heartily farewell.   41
               [Exeunt Voltimand and Cornelius.]
    And now, Laertes, what's the news with you?
    You told us of some suit; what is't, Laertes?
    You cannot speak of reason to the Dane   44
    And lose your voice. What wouldst thou beg, Laertes,   45
    That shall not be my offer, not thy asking?
    The head is not more native to the heart,   47

---

156 trumpet trumpeter   **160 extravagant and erring** wandering beyond bounds. (The words have similar meaning.)   **hies** hastens **162 probation** proof.   **164 'gainst** just before   **168 strike** destroy by evil influence   **169 takes** bewitches.   **charm** cast a spell, control by enchantment   **170 gracious** full of grace   **172 russet** reddish brown **1.2 Location: The castle.**
0.2 as i.e., such as, including.   **0.3 cum aliis** with others   **1 our** my. (The royal "we"; also in the following lines.)

8 sometime former   **9 jointress** woman possessing property with her husband   **11 With . . . eye** with one eye smiling and the other weeping   **13 dole** grief   **17 Now . . . know** Next, you need to be informed that   **18 weak supposal** low estimate   **20 disjoint . . . frame** in a state of total disorder   **21 Co-leaguèd . . . advantage** joined to his illusory sense of having the advantage over us and to his vision of future success   **23 Importing** having for its substance **24 with . . . law** (See 1.1.91, "Well ratified by law and heraldry.") **29 impotent** helpless   **31 His** i.e., Fortinbras'.   **gait** proceeding **31–3 in that . . . subject** since the levying of troops and supplies is drawn entirely from the King of Norway's own subjects   **38 dilated** set out at length   **39 let . . . duty** let your swift obeying of orders, rather than mere words, express your dutifulness.   **41 nothing** not at all.   **44 the Dane** the Danish king   **45 lose your voice** waste your speech.   **47 native** closely connected, related

The hand more instrumental to the mouth,   48
Than is the throne of Denmark to thy father.
What wouldst thou have, Laertes?

LAERTES   My dread lord,
Your leave and favor to return to France,   51
From whence though willingly I came to Denmark
To show my duty in your coronation,
Yet now I must confess, that duty done,
My thoughts and wishes bend again toward France
And bow them to your gracious leave and pardon.   56

KING
Have you your father's leave? What says Polonius?

POLONIUS
H'ath, my lord, wrung from me my slow leave   58
By laborsome petition, and at last
Upon his will I sealed my hard consent.   60
I do beseech you, give him leave to go.

KING
Take thy fair hour, Laertes. Time be thine,   62
And thy best graces spend it at thy will.   63
But now, my cousin Hamlet, and my son—   64

HAMLET
A little more than kin, and less than kind.   65

KING
How is it that the clouds still hang on you?

HAMLET
Not so, my lord. I am too much in the sun.   67

QUEEN
Good Hamlet, cast thy nighted colo⊥ off,   68
And let thine eye look like a friend on Denmark.   69
Do not forever with thy vailèd lids   70
Seek for thy noble father in the dust.
Thou know'st 'tis common, all that lives must die,   72
Passing through nature to eternity.

HAMLET
Ay, madam, it is common.

QUEEN   If it be,
Why seems it so particular with thee?   75

HAMLET
Seems, madam? Nay, it is. I know not "seems."
'Tis not alone my inky cloak, good mother,
Nor customary suits of solemn black,   78
Nor windy suspiration of forced breath,   79

No, nor the fruitful river in the eye,   80
Nor the dejected havior of the visage,   81
Together with all forms, moods, shapes of grief,   82
That can denote me truly. These indeed seem,
For they are actions that a man might play.
But I have that within which passes show;
These but the trappings and the suits of woe.

KING
'Tis sweet and commendable in your nature, Hamlet,
To give these mourning duties to your father.
But you must know your father lost a father,
That father lost, lost his, and the survivor bound
In filial obligation for some term
To do obsequious sorrow. But to persever   92
In obstinate condolement is a course   93
Of impious stubbornness. 'Tis unmanly grief.
It shows a will most incorrect to heaven,
A heart unfortified, a mind impatient,   96
An understanding simple and unschooled.   97
For what we know must be and is as common
As any the most vulgar thing to sense,   99
Why should we in our peevish opposition
Take it to heart? Fie, 'tis a fault to heaven,
A fault against the dead, a fault to nature,
To reason most absurd, whose common theme
Is death of fathers, and who still hath cried,   104
From the first corpse till he that died today,   105
"This must be so." We pray you, throw to earth
This unprevailing woe and think of us   107
As of a father; for let the world take note,
You are the most immediate to our throne,   109
And with no less nobility of love
Than that which dearest father bears his son
Do I impart toward you. For your intent   112
In going back to school in Wittenberg,   113
It is most retrograde to our desire,   114
And we beseech you bend you to remain   115
Here in the cheer and comfort of our eye,
Our chiefest courtier, cousin, and our son.

QUEEN
Let not thy mother lose her prayers, Hamlet.
I pray thee, stay with us, go not to Wittenberg.

HAMLET
I shall in all my best obey you, madam.   120

KING
Why, 'tis a loving and a fair reply.
Be as ourself in Denmark. Madam, come.
This gentle and unforced accord of Hamlet
Sits smiling to my heart, in grace whereof   124
No jocund health that Denmark drinks today   125

---

48 instrumental serviceable   **51 leave and favor** kind permission
56 bow . . . pardon entreatingly make a deep bow, asking your permission to depart.   **58 H'ath** He has   **60 sealed** (as if sealing a legal
document).   **hard** reluctant   **62 Take thy fair hour** Enjoy your time
of youth   **63 And . . . will** and may your time be spent in exercising
your best qualities.   **64 cousin** any kin not of the immediate family
65 A little . . . kind Too close a blood relation, and yet we are less
than kinsmen in that our relationship lacks affection and is indeed
unnatural. (Hamlet plays on *kind* as [1] kindly [2] belonging to
nature, suggesting that Claudius is not the same kind of being as the
rest of humanity. The line is often delivered as an aside, though it
need not be.)   **67 the sun** i.e., the sunshine of the King's royal favor.
(With pun on *son*.)   **68 nighted color** (1) mourning garments of black
(2) dark melancholy   **69 Denmark** the King of Denmark.   **70 vailèd
lids** lowered eyes   **72 common** of universal occurrence. (But Hamlet
plays on the sense of "vulgar" in line 74.)   **75 particular** personal
78 customary customary to mourning   **79 suspiration** sighing

80 fruitful abundant   **81 havior** expression   **82 moods** outward
expression of feeling   **92 obsequious** suited to obsequies or funerals.
93 condolement sorrowing   **96 unfortified** i.e., against adversity
97 simple ignorant   **99 As . . . sense** as the most ordinary experience
104 still always   **105 the first corpse** (Abel's)   **107 unprevailing**
unavailing, useless   **109 most immediate** next in succession
112 impart toward liberally bestow on.   **For** As for   **113 to school**
i.e., to your studies.   **Wittenberg** famous German university
founded in 1502   **114 retrograde** contrary   **115 bend you** incline
yourself   **120 in all my best** to the best of my ability   **124 to** i.e., at.
grace thanksgiving   **125 jocund** merry

But the great cannon to the clouds shall tell,
And the King's rouse the heaven shall bruit again,   127
Respeaking earthly thunder. Come away.   128
                    Flourish. Exeunt all but Hamlet.

HAMLET
Oh, that this too too sullied flesh would melt,   129
Thaw, and resolve itself into a dew!
Or that the Everlasting had not fixed
His canon 'gainst self-slaughter! Oh, God, God,   132
How weary, stale, flat, and unprofitable
Seem to me all the uses of this world!
Fie on't, ah fie! 'Tis an unweeded garden
That grows to seed. Things rank and gross in nature
Possess it merely. That it should come to this!   137
But two months dead—nay, not so much, not two.
So excellent a king, that was to this   139
Hyperion to a satyr, so loving to my mother   140
That he might not beteem the winds of heaven   141
Visit her face too roughly. Heaven and earth,
Must I remember? Why, she would hang on him
As if increase of appetite had grown
By what it fed on, and yet within a month—
Let me not think on't; frailty, thy name is woman!—
A little month, or ere those shoes were old   147
With which she followed my poor father's body,
Like Niobe, all tears, why she, even she—   149
Oh, God, a beast, that wants discourse of reason,   150
Would have mourned longer—married with my
    uncle,
My father's brother, but no more like my father
Than I to Hercules. Within a month,
Ere yet the salt of most unrighteous tears
Had left the flushing in her gallèd eyes,   155
She married. Oh, most wicked speed, to post   156
With such dexterity to incestuous sheets!   157
It is not, nor it cannot come to good.
But break, my heart, for I must hold my tongue.

        Enter Horatio, Marcellus, and Bernardo.

HORATIO
Hail to Your Lordship!
HAMLET   I am glad to see you well.
    Horatio!—or I do forget myself.
HORATIO
The same, my lord, and your poor servant ever.

HAMLET
Sir, my good friend; I'll change that name with you.   163
And what make you from Wittenberg, Horatio?—   164
Marcellus.
MARCELLUS   My good lord.
HAMLET
I am very glad to see you. [*To Bernardo*] Good even,
    sir.—
But what in faith make you from Wittenberg?
HORATIO
A truant disposition, good my lord.
HAMLET
I would not hear your enemy say so,
Nor shall you do my ear that violence
To make it truster of your own report   171
Against yourself. I know you are no truant.
But what is your affair in Elsinore?
We'll teach you to drink deep ere you depart.
HORATIO
My lord, I came to see your father's funeral.
HAMLET
I prithee, do not mock me, fellow student;
I think it was to see my mother's wedding.
HORATIO
Indeed, my lord, it followed hard upon.   179
HAMLET
Thrift, thrift, Horatio! The funeral baked meats   180
Did coldly furnish forth the marriage tables.   181
Would I had met my dearest foe in heaven   182
Or ever I had seen that day, Horatio!   183
My father!—Methinks I see my father.
HORATIO
Where, my lord?
HAMLET   In my mind's eye, Horatio.
HORATIO
I saw him once. 'A was a goodly king.   186
HAMLET
'A was a man. Take him for all in all,
I shall not look upon his like again.
HORATIO
My lord, I think I saw him yesternight.
HAMLET   Saw? Who?
HORATIO   My lord, the King your father.
HAMLET   The King my father?
HORATIO
Season your admiration for a while   193
With an attent ear till I may deliver,   194
Upon the witness of these gentlemen,
This marvel to you.
HAMLET   For God's love, let me hear!
HORATIO
Two nights together had these gentlemen,

---

127 rouse drinking of a draft of liquor.   **bruit again** loudly echo
128 thunder i.e., of trumpet and kettledrum, sounded when the King
drinks; see 1.4.8–12.   **129 sullied** defiled. (The early quartos read
"sallied"; the Folio, "solid.")   **132 canon** law   **137 merely** completely.   **139 to** in comparison to   **140 Hyperion** Titan sun-god,
father of Helios.   **satyr** a lecherous creature of classical mythology,
half-human but with a goat's legs, tail, ears, and horns   **141 beteem**
allow   **147 or ere** even before   **149 Niobes** Tantalus's daughter,
Queen of Thebes, who boasted that she had more sons and daughters
than Leto; for this, Apollo and Artemis, children of Leto, slew her
fourteen children. She was turned by Zeus into a stone that continually dropped tears.   **150 wants . . . reason** lacks the faculty of reason
155 gallèd irritated, inflamed   **156 post** hasten   **157 incestuous** (In
Shakespeare's day, the marriage of a man like Claudius to his
deceased brother's wife was considered incestuous.)

163 change that name i.e., give and receive reciprocally the name of
"friend" rather than talk of "servant." Or Hamlet may be saying,
"No, I am *your* servant."   **164 make you from** are you doing away
from   **171 To . . . of** to make it trust   **179 hard** close   **180 baked
meats** meat pies   **181 coldly** i.e., as cold leftovers   **182 dearest** closest (and therefore deadliest)   **183 Or ever** ere, before   **186 'A** He
193 Season your admiration Moderate your astonishment
194 attent attentive

Marcellus and Bernardo, on their watch,
In the dead waste and middle of the night,   199
Been thus encountered. A figure like your father,
Armèd at point exactly, cap-à-pie,   201
Appears before them, and with solemn march
Goes slow and stately by them. Thrice he walked
By their oppressed and fear-surprisèd eyes
Within his truncheon's length, whilst they, distilled   205
Almost to jelly with the act of fear,   206
Stand dumb and speak not to him. This to me
In dreadful secrecy impart they did,   208
And I with them the third night kept the watch,
Where, as they had delivered, both in time,
Form of the thing, each word made true and good,
The apparition comes. I knew your father;
These hands are not more like.

HAMLET   But where was this?

MARCELLUS
My lord, upon the platform where we watch.

HAMLET
Did you not speak to it?

HORATIO   My lord, I did,
But answer made it none. Yet once methought
It lifted up it head and did address   217
Itself to motion, like as it would speak;   218
But even then the morning cock crew loud,   219
And at the sound it shrunk in haste away
And vanished from our sight.

HAMLET   'Tis very strange.

HORATIO
As I do live, my honored lord, 'tis true,
And we did think it writ down in our duty
To let you know of it.

HAMLET
Indeed, indeed, sirs. But this troubles me.
Hold you the watch tonight?

ALL   We do, my lord.

HAMLET   Armed, say you?

ALL   Armed, my lord.

HAMLET   From top to toe?

ALL   My lord, from head to foot.

HAMLET   Then saw you not his face?

HORATIO
Oh, yes, my lord, he wore his beaver up.   232

HAMLET   What looked he, frowningly?   233

HORATIO
A countenance more in sorrow than in anger.

HAMLET   Pale or red?

HORATIO   Nay, very pale.

HAMLET   And fixed his eyes upon you?

HORATIO   Most constantly.

HAMLET   I would I had been there.

HORATIO   It would have much amazed you.

HAMLET   Very like, very like. Stayed it long?

HORATIO
While one with moderate haste might tell a hundred.   242

MARCELLUS, BERNARDO   Longer, longer.

HORATIO   Not when I saw't.

HAMLET   His beard was grizzled—no?

HORATIO
It was, as I have seen it in his life,
A sable silvered.

HAMLET   I will watch tonight.
Perchance 'twill walk again.

HORATIO   I warr'nt it will.

HAMLET
If it assume my noble father's person,
I'll speak to it though hell itself should gape
And bid me hold my peace. I pray you all,
If you have hitherto concealed this sight,
Let it be tenable in your silence still,   253
And whatsomever else shall hap tonight,
Give it an understanding but no tongue.
I will requite your loves. So, fare you well.
Upon the platform twixt eleven and twelve
I'll visit you.

ALL   Our duty to Your Honor.

HAMLET
Your loves, as mine to you. Farewell.   259

                          Exeunt [all but Hamlet].
My father's spirit in arms! All is not well.
I doubt some foul play. Would the night were come!   261
Till then sit still, my soul. Foul deeds will rise,
Though all the earth o'erwhelm them, to men's eyes.

                                              Exit.

❖

[1.3]

Enter Laertes and Ophelia, his sister.

LAERTES
My necessaries are embarked. Farewell.
And, sister, as the winds give benefit
And convoy is assistant, do not sleep   3
But let me hear from you.

OPHELIA   Do you doubt that?

LAERTES
For Hamlet, and the trifling of his favor,   5
Hold it a fashion and a toy in blood,   6
A violet in the youth of primy nature,   7
Forward, not permanent, sweet, not lasting,   8
The perfume and suppliance of a minute—   9
No more.

OPHELIA   No more but so?

LAERTES   Think it no more.

---

199 dead waste desolate stillness   **201 at point** correctly in every detail.   **cap-à-pie** from head to foot   **205 truncheon** officer's staff. **distilled** dissolved   **206 act** action, operation   **208 dreadful** full of dread   **217 it** its   **217–18 did . . . speak** prepared to move as though it was about to speak   **219 even then** at that very instant **232 beaver** visor on the helmet   **233 What** How

242 tell count   **253 tenable** held   **259 Your loves** i.e., Say "Your loves" to me, not just your "duty."   **261 doubt** suspect **1.3. Location:** Polonius's chambers. **3 convoy is assistant** means of conveyance are available   **5 For** As for   **6 toy in blood** passing amorous fancy   **7 primy** in its prime, springtime   **8 Forward** precocious   **9 suppliance** pastime, something to fill the time

For nature crescent does not grow alone 11
In thews and bulk, but as this temple waxes 12
The inward service of the mind and soul
Grows wide withal. Perhaps he loves you now, 14
And now no soil nor cautel doth besmirch 15
The virtue of his will; but you must fear, 16
His greatness weighed, his will is not his own. 17
For he himself is subject to his birth.
He may not, as unvalued persons do,
Carve for himself, for on his choice depends 20
The safety and health of this whole state,
And therefore must his choice be circumscribed
Unto the voice and yielding of that body 23
Whereof he is the head. Then if he says he loves you,
It fits your wisdom so far to believe it
As he in his particular act and place 26
May give his saying deed, which is no further
Than the main voice of Denmark goes withal. 28
Then weigh what loss your honor may sustain
If with too credent ear you list his songs, 30
Or lose your heart, or your chaste treasure open
To his unmastered importunity. 32
Fear it, Ophelia, fear it, my dear sister,
And keep you in the rear of your affection, 34
Out of the shot and danger of desire.
The chariest maid is prodigal enough 36
If she unmask her beauty to the moon. 37
Virtue itself scapes not calumnious strokes.
The canker galls the infants of the spring 39
Too oft before their buttons be disclosed, 40
And in the morn and liquid dew of youth 41
Contagious blastments are most imminent. 42
Be wary then; best safety lies in fear.
Youth to itself rebels, though none else near. 44

OPHELIA
I shall the effect of this good lesson keep
As watchman to my heart. But, good my brother,
Do not, as some ungracious pastors do, 47
Show me the steep and thorny way to heaven,
Whiles like a puffed and reckless libertine 49
Himself the primrose path of dalliance treads,
And recks not his own rede.

Enter Polonius.

LAERTES   Oh, fear me not. 51

11–14 For nature . . . withal For nature, as it ripens, does not grow only in physical strength, but as the body matures the inner qualities of mind and soul grow along with it. (Laertes warns Ophelia that the mature Hamlet may not cling to his youthful interests.) **15 soil nor cautel** blemish nor deceit **16 The . . . will** the purity of his desire **17 His greatness weighed** taking into account his high fortune **20 Carve** i.e., choose **23 voice and yielding** assent, approval **26 in . . . place** in his particular restricted circumstances **28 main voice** general assent. **withal** along with. **30 credent** credulous. **list** listen to **32 unmastered** uncontrolled **34 keep . . . affection** don't advance as far as your affection might lead you. (A military metaphor.) **36 chariest** most scrupulously modest **37 If she unmask** if she does no more than show her beauty. **moon** (Symbol of chastity.) **39 canker galls** cankerworm destroys **40 buttons be disclosed** buds be opened **41 liquid dew** i.e., time when dew is fresh and bright **42 blastments** blights **44 Youth . . . rebels** Youth yields to the rebellion of the flesh **47 ungracious** ungodly **49 puffed** bloated, or swollen with pride **51 recks** heeds. **rede** counsel. **fear me not** don't worry on my account.

I stay too long. But here my father comes.
A double blessing is a double grace; 53
Occasion smiles upon a second leave. 54

POLONIUS
Yet here, Laertes? Aboard, aboard, for shame!
The wind sits in the shoulder of your sail,
And you are stayed for. There—my blessing with thee!
And these few precepts in thy memory
Look thou character. Give thy thoughts no tongue, 59
Nor any unproportioned thought his act. 60
Be thou familiar, but by no means vulgar. 61
Those friends thou hast, and their adoption tried, 62
Grapple them unto thy soul with hoops of steel,
But do not dull thy palm with entertainment 64
Of each new-hatched, unfledged courage. Beware 65
Of entrance to a quarrel, but being in,
Bear't that th'opposèd may beware of thee. 67
Give every man thy ear, but few thy voice;
Take each man's censure, but reserve thy judgment. 69
Costly thy habit as thy purse can buy, 70
But not expressed in fancy; rich, not gaudy, 71
For the apparel oft proclaims the man,
And they in France of the best rank and station
Are of a most select and generous chief in that. 74
Neither a borrower nor a lender be,
For loan oft loses both itself and friend,
And borrowing dulleth edge of husbandry. 77
This above all: to thine own self be true,
And it must follow, as the night the day,
Thou canst not then be false to any man.
Farewell. My blessing season this in thee! 81

LAERTES
Most humbly do I take my leave, my lord.

POLONIUS
The time invests you. Go, your servants tend. 83

LAERTES
Farewell, Ophelia, and remember well
What I have said to you.

OPHELIA   'Tis in my memory locked,
And you yourself shall keep the key of it.

LAERTES   Farewell.   *Exit Laertes.*

POLONIUS
What is't, Ophelia, he hath said to you?

OPHELIA
So please you, something touching the Lord Hamlet.

POLONIUS   Marry, well bethought. 91
'Tis told me he hath very oft of late
Given private time to you, and you yourself

53–4 A double . . . leave The goddess Occasion or Opportunity smiles on the happy circumstance of being able to say good-bye twice and thus receive a second blessing. **59 Look thou character** see to it that you inscribe. **60 unproportioned** badly calculated, intemperate. **his** its **61 familiar** sociable. **vulgar** common. **62 and . . . tried** and their suitability to be your friends having been put to the test **64 dull thy palm** i.e., shake hands so often as to make the gesture meaningless **65 courage** swashbuckler. **67 Bear't that** manage it so that **69 censure** opinion, judgment **70 habit** clothing **71 fancy** excessive ornament, decadent fashion **74 Are . . . that** are of a most refined and well-bred preeminence in choosing what to wear. **77 husbandry** thrift. **81 season** mature **83 invests** besieges, presses upon. **tend** attend, wait. **91 Marry** i.e., By the Virgin Mary. (A mild oath.)

Have of your audience been most free and bounteous.
If it be so—as so 'tis put on me,   95
And that in way of caution—I must tell you
You do not understand yourself so clearly
As it behooves my daughter and your honor.   98
What is between you? Give me up the truth.

OPHELIA
He hath, my lord, of late made many tenders   100
Of his affection to me.

POLONIUS
Affection? Pooh! You speak like a green girl,
Unsifted in such perilous circumstance.   103
Do you believe his tenders, as you call them?

OPHELIA
I do not know, my lord, what I should think.

POLONIUS
Marry, I will teach you. Think yourself a baby
That you have ta'en these tenders for true pay
Which are not sterling. Tender yourself more dearly,   108
Or—not to crack the wind of the poor phrase,   109
Running it thus—you'll tender me a fool.   110

OPHELIA
My lord, he hath importuned me with love
In honorable fashion.

POLONIUS
Ay, fashion you may call it. Go to, go to.   113

OPHELIA
And hath given countenance to his speech, my lord,   114
With almost all the holy vows of heaven.

POLONIUS
Ay, springes to catch woodcocks. I do know,   116
When the blood burns, how prodigal the soul   117
Lends the tongue vows. These blazes, daughter,
Giving more light than heat, extinct in both
Even in their promise as it is a-making,   120
You must not take for fire. From this time
Be something scanter of your maiden presence.   122
Set your entreatments at a higher rate   123
Than a command to parle. For Lord Hamlet,   124
Believe so much in him that he is young,   125
And with a larger tether may he walk
Than may be given you. In few, Ophelia,   127
Do not believe his vows, for they are brokers,   128
Not of that dye which their investments show,   129
But mere implorators of unholy suits,   130

Breathing like sanctified and pious bawds,   131
The better to beguile. This is for all: 132
I would not, in plain terms, from this time forth
Have you so slander any moment leisure   134
As to give words or talk with the Lord Hamlet.
Look to't, I charge you. Come your ways.   136

OPHELIA   I shall obey, my lord.   *Exeunt.*

❖

[1.4]

Enter Hamlet, Horatio, and Marcellus.

HAMLET
The air bites shrewdly; it is very cold.   1

HORATIO
It is a nipping and an eager air.   2

HAMLET
What hour now?

HORATIO   I think it lacks of twelve.   3

MARCELLUS
No, it is struck.

HORATIO   Indeed? I heard it not.
It then draws near the season   5
Wherein the spirit held his wont to walk.   6
   A flourish of trumpets, and two pieces go off
   [within].
What does this mean, my lord?

HAMLET
The King doth wake tonight and takes his rouse,   8
Keeps wassail, and the swagg'ring upspring reels;   9
And as he drains his drafts of Rhenish down,   10
The kettledrum and trumpet thus bray out
The triumph of his pledge.

HORATIO   Is it a custom?   12

HAMLET   Ay, marry, is't,
But to my mind, though I am native here
And to the manner born, it is a custom   15
More honored in the breach than the observance.   16
This heavy-headed revel east and west   17
Makes us traduced and taxed of other nations.   18
They clepe us drunkards, and with swinish phrase   19
Soil our addition; and indeed it takes   20
From our achievements, though performed at height,   21
The pith and marrow of our attribute.   22

So, oft it chances in particular men,
That for some vicious mole of nature in them, 24
As in their birth—wherein they are not guilty,
Since nature cannot choose his origin— 26
By their o'ergrowth of some complexion, 27
Oft breaking down the pales and forts of reason, 28
Or by some habit that too much o'erleavens 29
The form of plausive manners, that these men, 30
Carrying, I say, the stamp of one defect,
Being nature's livery or fortune's star, 32
His virtues else, be they as pure as grace, 33
As infinite as man may undergo, 34
Shall in the general censure take corruption 35
From that particular fault. The dram of evil 36
Doth all the noble substance often dout 37
To his own scandal.

> *Enter Ghost.*

HORATIO   Look, my lord, it comes! 38
HAMLET
Angels and ministers of grace defend us! 39
Be thou a spirit of health or goblin damned, 40
Bring with thee airs from heaven or blasts from hell, 41
Be thy intents wicked or charitable, 42
Thou com'st in such a questionable shape 43
That I will speak to thee. I'll call thee Hamlet,
King, father, royal Dane. Oh, answer me!
Let me not burst in ignorance, but tell
Why thy canonized bones, hearsèd in death, 47
Have burst their cerements; why the sepulcher 48
Wherein we saw thee quietly inurned 49
Hath oped his ponderous and marble jaws
To cast thee up again. What may this mean,
That thou, dead corpse, again in complete steel, 52
Revisits thus the glimpses of the moon, 53
Making night hideous, and we fools of nature 54
So horridly to shake our disposition 55
With thoughts beyond the reaches of our souls?
Say, why is this? Wherefore? What should we do?
            [*The Ghost*] *beckons* [*Hamlet*].

HORATIO
It beckons you to go away with it,
As if it some impartment did desire 59
To you alone.
MARCELLUS   Look with what courteous action
It wafts you to a more removèd ground.
But do not go with it.
HORATIO   No, by no means.
HAMLET
It will not speak. Then I will follow it.
HORATIO
Do not, my lord!
HAMLET   Why, what should be the fear?
I do not set my life at a pin's fee, 65
And for my soul, what can it do to that, 66
Being a thing immortal as itself?
It waves me forth again. I'll follow it.
HORATIO
What if it tempt you toward the flood, my lord, 69
Or to the dreadful summit of the cliff
That beetles o'er his base into the sea, 71
And there assume some other horrible form
Which might deprive your sovereignty of reason 73
And draw you into madness? Think of it.
The very place puts toys of desperation, 75
Without more motive, into every brain
That looks so many fathoms to the sea
And hears it roar beneath.
HAMLET
It wafts me still.—Go on, I'll follow thee.
MARCELLUS
You shall not go, my lord.   [*They try to stop him.*]
HAMLET   Hold off your hands!
HORATIO
Be ruled. You shall not go.
HAMLET   My fate cries out, 81
And makes each petty artery in this body 82
As hardy as the Nemean lion's nerve. 83
Still am I called. Unhand me, gentlemen.
By heaven, I'll make a ghost of him that lets me! 85
I say, away!—Go on, I'll follow thee.
                    Exeunt Ghost and Hamlet.
HORATIO
He waxes desperate with imagination.
MARCELLUS
Let's follow. 'Tis not fit thus to obey him.
HORATIO
Have after. To what issue will this come? 89
MARCELLUS
Something is rotten in the state of Denmark.

---

24 for . . . mole on account of some natural defect in their constitutions   26 his its   27 their o'ergrowth . . . complexion the excessive growth in individuals of some natural trait   28 pales palings, fences (as of a fortification)   29–30 o'erleavens . . . manners i.e., infects the way we should behave (much as bad yeast spoils the dough). *Plausive* means "pleasing."   32 Being . . . star (that stamp of defect) being a sign identifying one as wearing the livery of, and hence being the servant to, nature (unfortunate inherited qualities) or fortune (mischance)   33 His virtues else i.e., the other qualities of *these men* (line 30)   34 may undergo can sustain   35 in . . . censure in overall appraisal, in people's opinion generally   36-8 The dram . . . scandal i.e., The small drop of evil blots out or works against the noble substance of the whole and brings it into disrepute. (To *dout* is to blot out. A famous crux.)   39 ministers of grace messengers of God   40 Be . . . health Whether you are a good angel   41 Bring whether you bring   42 Be thy intents whether your intentions are   43 questionable inviting question   47 canonized buried according to the canons of the church.   hearsèd coffined   48 cerements grave clothes   49 inurned entombed   52 complete steel full armor   53 the glimpses . . . moon i.e., the sublunary world, all that is beneath the moon   54 fools of nature mere mortals, limited to natural knowledge and subject to nature   55 So . . . disposition to distress our mental composure so violently

59 impartment communication   65 fee value   66 for as for   69 flood sea   71 beetles o'er overhangs threateningly (like bushy eyebrows).   his its   73 deprive . . . reason take away the rule of reason over your mind   75 toys of desperation fancies of desperate acts, i.e., suicide   81 My fate cries out My destiny summons me   82 petty weak.   artery blood vessel system through which the vital spirits were thought to have been conveyed   83 Nemean lion's nerve as a sinew of the huge lion slain by Hercules as the first of his twelve labors.   85 lets hinders   89 Have after Let's go after him.   issue outcome

HORATIO
Heaven will direct it.

MARCELLUS   Nay, let's follow him.   *Exeunt.* 91

❧

[1.5]

Enter Ghost and Hamlet.

HAMLET
Whither wilt thou lead me? Speak. I'll go no further.

GHOST
Mark me.

HAMLET   I will.

GHOST   My hour is almost come,
When I to sulf'rous and tormenting flames
Must render up myself.

HAMLET   Alas, poor ghost!

GHOST
Pity me not, but lend thy serious hearing
To what I shall unfold.

HAMLET   Speak. I am bound to hear.   7

GHOST
So art thou to revenge, when thou shalt hear.

HAMLET   What?

GHOST   I am thy father's spirit,
Doomed for a certain term to walk the night,
And for the day confined to fast in fires,   12
Till the foul crimes done in my days of nature   13
Are burnt and purged away. But that I am forbid   14
To tell the secrets of my prison house,
I could a tale unfold whose lightest word
Would harrow up thy soul, freeze thy young blood,   17
Make thy two eyes like stars start from their spheres, 18
Thy knotted and combinèd locks to part,   19
And each particular hair to stand on end
Like quills upon the fretful porcupine.
But this eternal blazon must not be   22
To ears of flesh and blood. List, list, oh, list!
If thou didst ever thy dear father love—

HAMLET   Oh, God!

GHOST
Revenge his foul and most unnatural murder.

HAMLET   Murder?

GHOST
Murder most foul, as in the best it is,   28
But this most foul, strange, and unnatural.

HAMLET
Haste me to know't, that I, with wings as swift
As meditation or the thoughts of love,
May sweep to my revenge.

GHOST   I find thee apt;

And duller shouldst thou be than the fat weed   33
That roots itself in ease on Lethe wharf,   34
Wouldst thou not stir in this. Now, Hamlet, hear.
'Tis given out that, sleeping in my orchard,   36
A serpent stung me. So the whole ear of Denmark
Is by a forgèd process of my death   38
Rankly abused. But know, thou noble youth,   39
The serpent that did sting thy father's life
Now wears his crown.

HAMLET   Oh, my prophetic soul! My uncle!

GHOST
Ay, that incestuous, that adulterate beast,   43
With witchcraft of his wit, with traitorous gifts— 44
Oh, wicked wit and gifts, that have the power
So to seduce!—won to his shameful lust
The will of my most seeming-virtuous queen.
Oh, Hamlet, what a falling off was there!
From me, whose love was of that dignity
That it went hand in hand even with the vow   50
I made to her in marriage, and to decline
Upon a wretch whose natural gifts were poor
To those of mine!   53
But virtue, as it never will be moved,   54
Though lewdness court it in a shape of heaven,   55
So lust, though to a radiant angel linked,
Will sate itself in a celestial bed   57
And prey on garbage.
But soft, methinks I scent the morning air.
Brief let me be. Sleeping within my orchard,
My custom always of the afternoon,
Upon my secure hour thy uncle stole,   62
With juice of cursèd hebona in a vial,   63
And in the porches of my ears did pour   64
The leprous distillment, whose effect   65
Holds such an enmity with blood of man
That swift as quicksilver it courses through
The natural gates and alleys of the body,   68
And with a sudden vigor it doth posset   69
And curd, like eager droppings into milk,   70
The thin and wholesome blood. So did it mine,
And a most instant tetter barked about,   72
Most lazar-like, with vile and loathsome crust,   73
All my smooth body.
Thus was I, sleeping, by a brother's hand
Of life, of crown, of queen at once dispatched,   76

91 it i.e., the outcome.
1.5 Location: The battlements of the castle.
7 bound (1) ready (2) obligated by duty and fate. (The Ghost, in line 8, answers in the second sense.)   **12 fast** do penance by fasting   **13 crimes** sins.   **of nature** as a mortal   **14 But that** Were it not that   **17 harrow up** lacerate, tear   **18 spheres** i.e., eye-sockets, here compared to the orbits or transparent revolving spheres in which, according to Ptolemaic astronomy, the heavenly bodies were fixed   **19 knotted . . . locks** hair neatly arranged and confined   **22 eternal blazon** revelation of the secrets of eternity   **28 in the best** even at best

33 shouldst thou be you would have to be.   **fat** torpid, lethargic   **34 Lethe** the river of forgetfulness in Hades   **36 orchard** garden   **38 forgèd process** falsified account   **39 abused** deceived.   **43 adulterate** adulterous   **44 gifts** (1) talents (2) presents   **50 even with the vow** with the very vow   **53 To** compared with   **54 virtue, as it** just as virtue   **55 shape of heaven** heavenly form   **57 sate . . . bed** gratify its lustful appetite to the point of revulsion or ennui, even in a virtuously lawful marriage   **62 secure hour** time of being free from worries   **63 hebona** a poison. (The word seems to be a form of *ebony*, though it is thought perhaps to be related to *henbane*, a poison, or to *ebenus*, "yew.")   **64 porches** gateways   **65 leprous distillment** distillation causing leprosylike disfigurement   **68 gates** entry ways   **69–70 posset . . . curd** coagulate and curdle   **70 eager** sour, acid   **72 tetter** eruption of scabs.   **barked** covered with a rough covering, like bark on a tree   **73 lazar-like** leperlike   **76 dispatched** suddenly deprived

Cut off even in the blossoms of my sin,
Unhouseled, disappointed, unaneled,   78
No reck'ning made, but sent to my account   79
With all my imperfections on my head.
Oh, horrible! Oh, horrible, most horrible!
If thou hast nature in thee, bear it not.   82
Let not the royal bed of Denmark be
A couch for luxury and damnèd incest.   84
But, howsomever thou pursues this act,
Taint not thy mind nor let thy soul contrive
Against thy mother aught. Leave her to heaven
And to those thorns that in her bosom lodge,
To prick and sting her. Fare thee well at once.
The glowworm shows the matin to be near,   90
And 'gins to pale his uneffectual fire.   91
Adieu, adieu, adieu! Remember me.   [*Exit.*]

HAMLET
O all you host of heaven! O earth! What else?
And shall I couple hell? Oh, fie! Hold, hold, my heart,   94
And you, my sinews, grow not instant old,   95
But bear me stiffly up. Remember thee?
Ay, thou poor ghost, whiles memory holds a seat
In this distracted globe. Remember thee?   98
Yea, from the table of my memory   99
I'll wipe away all trivial fond records,   100
All saws of books, all forms, all pressures past   101
That youth and observation copied there,
And thy commandment all alone shall live
Within the book and volume of my brain,
Unmixed with baser matter. Yes, by heaven!
Oh, most pernicious woman!
Oh, villain, villain, smiling, damnèd villain!
My tables—meet it is I set it down   108
That one may smile, and smile, and be a villain.
At least I am sure it may be so in Denmark.
So, uncle, there you are. Now to my word: 111
It is "Adieu, adieu! Remember me."
I have sworn't.

Enter Horatio and Marcellus.

HORATIO   My lord, my lord!
MARCELLUS   Lord Hamlet!
HORATIO   Heavens secure him!   116
HAMLET   So be it.
MARCELLUS   Hillo, ho, ho, my lord!
HAMLET   Hillo, ho, ho, boy! Come, bird, come.   119
MARCELLUS   How is't, my noble lord?

HORATIO   What news, my lord?
HAMLET   Oh, wonderful!
HORATIO   Good my lord, tell it.
HAMLET   No, you will reveal it.
HORATIO   Not I, my lord, by heaven.
MARCELLUS   Nor I, my lord
HAMLET
How say you, then, would heart of man once think it?   127
But you'll be secret?
HORATIO, MARCELLUS   Ay, by heaven, my lord.
HAMLET
There's never a villain dwelling in all Denmark
But he's an arrant knave.   130
HORATIO
There needs no ghost, my lord, come from the grave
To tell us this.
HAMLET   Why, right, you are in the right.
And so, without more circumstance at all,   133
I hold it fit that we shake hands and part,
You as your business and desire shall point you—
For every man hath business and desire,
Such as it is—and for my own poor part,
Look you, I'll go pray.
HORATIO
These are but wild and whirling words, my lord.
HAMLET
I am sorry they offend you, heartily;
Yes, faith, heartily.
HORATIO   There's no offense, my lord.
HAMLET
Yes, by Saint Patrick, but there is, Horatio,   142
And much offense too. Touching this vision here,   143
It is an honest ghost, that let me tell you.   144
For your desire to know what is between us,
O'ermaster't as you may. And now, good friends,
As you are friends, scholars, and soldiers,
Give me one poor request.
HORATIO   What is't, my lord? We will.
HAMLET
Never make known what you have seen tonight.
HORATIO, MARCELLUS   My lord, we will not.
HAMLET   Nay, but swear't.
HORATIO   In faith, my lord, not I.   153
MARCELLUS   Nor I, my lord, in faith.
HAMLET   Upon my sword.   [*He holds out his sword.*]   155
MARCELLUS   We have sworn, my lord, already.   156
HAMLET   Indeed, upon my sword, indeed.
GHOST (*cries under the stage*)   Swear.
HAMLET
Ha, ha, boy, say'st thou so? Art thou there, truepenny?   159

---

78 Unhouseled . . . unaneled without having received the Sacrament
or other last rites including confession, absolution, and the holy oil of
extreme unction   **79 reck'ning** settling of accounts   **82 nature** i.e.,
the promptings of a son   **84 luxury** lechery   **90 matin** morning   **91
his** its   **94 couple** add.   **Hold** Hold together   **95 instant** instantly
98 globe (1) head (2) world (3) Globe Theater.   **99 table** tablet, slate
100 fond foolish   **101 All . . . past** all wise sayings, all shapes or
images imprinted on the tablets of my memory, all past impressions
108 My tables . . . down (Editors often specify that Hamlet makes a
note in his writing tablet, but he may simply mean that he is making
a mental observation of lasting impression.)   **111 there you are** i.e.,
there, I've noted that against you.   **116 secure him** keep him safe.
119 Hillo . . . come (A falconer's call to a hawk in air. Hamlet mocks
the hallooing as though it were a part of hawking.)

127 once ever   **130 But . . . knave** (Hamlet jokingly gives a self-evident answer: every villain is a thoroughgoing knave.)   **133 circumstance** ceremony, elaboration   **142 Saint Patrick** the keeper of
Purgatory   **143 offense** (Hamlet deliberately changes Horatio's "no
offense taken" to "an offense against all decency.")   **144 honest** genuine   **153 In faith . . . I** i.e., I swear not to tell what I have seen. (Horatio is not refusing to swear.)   **155 sword** i.e., the hilt in the form of a
cross.   **156 We . . . already** i.e., We swore *in faith*.   **159 truepenny**
honest old fellow.

Come on, you hear this fellow in the cellarage.
Consent to swear.

HORATIO   Propose the oath, my lord.

HAMLET
Never to speak of this that you have seen,
Swear by my sword.

GHOST [*beneath*] Swear.   [*They swear.*] 164

HAMLET
Hic et ubique? Then we'll shift our ground.   165
                    [*He moves to another spot.*]
Come hither, gentlemen,
And lay your hands again upon my sword.
Swear by my sword
Never to speak of this that you have heard.

GHOST [*beneath*] Swear by his sword.   [*They swear.*]

HAMLET
Well said, old mole. Canst work i'th'earth so fast?
A worthy pioneer!—Once more remove, good friends. 172
                    [*He moves again.*]

HORATIO
Oh, day and night, but this is wondrous strange!

HAMLET
And therefore as a stranger give it welcome.   174
There are more things in heaven and earth, Horatio,
Than are dreamt of in your philosophy.   176
But come;
Here, as before, never, so help you mercy,   178
How strange or odd some'er I bear myself—
As I perchance hereafter shall think meet
To put an antic disposition on—   181
That you, at such times seeing me, never shall,
With arms encumbered thus, or this headshake,   183
Or by pronouncing of some doubtful phrase
As "Well, we know," or "We could, an if we would,"   185
Or "If we list to speak," or "There be, an if they
    might,"   186
Or such ambiguous giving out, to note   187
That you know aught of me—this do swear,   188
So grace and mercy at your most need help you.

GHOST [*beneath*] Swear.   [*They swear.*]

HAMLET
Rest, rest, perturbèd spirit!—So, gentlemen,
With all my love I do commend me to you;   192
And what so poor a man as Hamlet is
May do t'express his love and friending to you,   194
God willing, shall not lack. Let us go in together,   195
And still your fingers on your lips, I pray.   196

The time is out of joint. Oh, cursèd spite   197
That ever I was born to set it right!
                    [*They wait for him to leave first.*]
Nay, come, let's go together.   *Exeunt.* 199

❖

[2.1]

Enter old Polonius with his man [Reynaldo].

POLONIUS
Give him this money and these notes, Reynaldo.
                    [*He gives money and papers.*]

REYNALDO   I will, my lord.

POLONIUS
You shall do marvelous wisely, good Reynaldo,   3
Before you visit him, to make inquire   4
Of his behavior.

REYNALDO   My lord, I did intend it.

POLONIUS
Marry, well said, very well said. Look you, sir,
Inquire me first what Danskers are in Paris,   7
And how, and who, what means, and where they
    keep,   8
What company, at what expense; and finding
By this encompassment and drift of question   10
That they do know my son, come you more nearer   11
Than your particular demands will touch it.   12
Take you, as 'twere, some distant knowledge of him,   13
As thus, "I know his father and his friends,
And in part him." Do you mark this, Reynaldo?

REYNALDO   Ay, very well, my lord.

POLONIUS
"And in part him, but," you may say, "not well.
But if't be he I mean, he's very wild,
Addicted so and so," and there put on him   19
What forgeries you please—marry, none so rank   20
As may dishonor him, take heed of that,
But, sir, such wanton, wild, and usual slips   22
As are companions noted and most known
To youth and liberty.

REYNALDO   As gaming, my lord.

POLONIUS   Ay, or drinking, fencing, swearing,
Quarreling, drabbing—you may go so far.   27

REYNALDO   My lord, that would dishonor him.

POLONIUS
Faith, no, as you may season it in the charge.   29
You must not put another scandal on him
That he is open to incontinency;   31

---

164 s.d. *They swear* (Seemingly they swear here, and at lines 170 and
190, as they lay their hands on Hamlet's sword. Triple oaths would
have particular force; these three oaths deal with what they have
seen, what they have heard, and what they promise about Hamlet's
antic disposition.) **165 *Hic et ubique?*** Here and everywhere? (Latin.)
172 pioneer foot soldier assigned to dig tunnels and excavations.
174 as a stranger i.e., needing your hospitality **176 your philosophy**
this subject that is called "natural philosophy" or "science." (*Your* is
not personal.) **178 so help you mercy** as you hope for God's mercy
when you are judged **181 antic** grotesque, strange **183 encumbered** folded **185 an if** if **186 list** wished. **There . . . might** There
are those who could talk if they were at liberty to do so **187 note**
indicate **188 aught** anything **192 commend . . . you** give you my
best wishes **194 friending** friendliness **195 lack** be lacking.
196 still always

197 out of joint in utter disorder. **199 let's go together** (Probably
they wait for him to leave first, but he refuses this ceremoniousness.)
2.1 Location: Polonius's chambers.
3 marvelous marvelously **4 inquire** inquiry **7 Danskers** Danes
8 what means what wealth (they have). **keep** dwell **10 encompassment . . . question** roundabout way of questioning **11-12 come . . .
it** you will find out more this way than by asking pointed questions
(*particular demands*). **13 Take you** Assume, pretend **19 put on**
impute to **20 forgeries** invented tales. **rank** gross **22 wanton**
sportive, unrestrained **27 drabbing** whoring **29 season** temper,
soften **31 incontinency** habitual sexual excess

That's not my meaning. But breathe his faults so
   quaintly   32
That they may seem the taints of liberty,   33
The flash and outbreak of a fiery mind,
A savageness in unreclaimèd blood,   35
Of general assault.   36
REYNALDO   But, my good lord—
POLONIUS   Wherefore should you do this?
REYNALDO   Ay, my lord, I would know that.
POLONIUS   Marry, sir, here's my drift,
And I believe it is a fetch of warrant.   41
You laying these slight sullies on my son,
As 'twere a thing a little soiled wi'th' working,   43
Mark you,
Your party in converse, him you would sound,   45
Having ever seen in the prenominate crimes   46
The youth you breathe of guilty, be assured   47
He closes with you in this consequence: 48
"Good sir," or so, or "friend," or "gentleman,"
According to the phrase or the addition   50
Of man and country.
REYNALDO   Very good, my lord.
POLONIUS   And then, sir, does 'a this—'a does—what
was I about to say? By the Mass, I was about to say
something. Where did I leave?
REYNALDO   At "closes in the consequence."
POLONIUS
At "closes in the consequence," ay, marry.
He closes thus: "I know the gentleman,
I saw him yesterday," or "th'other day,"
Or then, or then, with such or such, "and as you say,
There was 'a gaming," "there o'ertook in 's rouse,"   60
"There falling out at tennis," or perchance   61
"I saw him enter such a house of sale,"
Videlicet a brothel, or so forth. See you now,   63
Your bait of falsehood takes this carp of truth;   64
And thus do we of wisdom and of reach,   65
With windlasses and with assays of bias,   66
By indirections find directions out.   67
So by my former lecture and advice   68
Shall you my son. You have me, have you not?   69
REYNALDO
My lord, I have.
POLONIUS   God b'wi'ye; fare ye well.
REYNALDO   Good my lord.

POLONIUS
Observe his inclination in yourself.   72
REYNALDO   I shall, my lord.
POLONIUS   And let him ply his music.
REYNALDO   Well, my lord.
POLONIUS
Farewell.   *Exit Reynaldo.*

   Enter Ophelia.

         How now, Ophelia, what's the matter?
OPHELIA
Oh, my lord, my lord, I have been so affrighted!
POLONIUS   With what, i'th' name of God?
OPHELIA
My lord, as I was sewing in my closet,   79
Lord Hamlet, with his doublet all unbraced,   80
No hat upon his head, his stockings fouled,
Ungartered, and down-gyvèd to his ankle,   82
Pale as his shirt, his knees knocking each other,
And with a look so piteous in purport   84
As if he had been loosèd out of hell
To speak of horrors—he comes before me.
POLONIUS
Mad for thy love?
OPHELIA   My lord, I do not know,
But truly I do fear it.
POLONIUS   What said he?
OPHELIA
He took me by the wrist and held me hard.
Then goes he to the length of all his arm,
And, with his other hand thus o'er his brow
He falls to such perusal of my face
As 'a would draw it. Long stayed he so.   93
At last, a little shaking of mine arm
And thrice his head thus waving up and down,
He raised a sigh so piteous and profound
As it did seem to shatter all his bulk   97
And end his being. That done, he lets me go,
And with his head over his shoulder turned
He seemed to find his way without his eyes,
For out o' doors he went without their helps,
And to the last bended their light on me.
POLONIUS
Come, go with me. I will go seek the King.
This is the very ecstasy of love,   104
Whose violent property fordoes itself   105
And leads the will to desperate undertakings
As oft as any passion under heaven
That does afflict our natures. I am sorry.
What, have you given him any hard words of late?
OPHELIA
No, my good lord, but as you did command
I did repel his letters and denied

---

32 quaintly artfully, subtly   **33 taints of liberty** faults resulting from
free living   **35-6 A savageness . . . assault** a wildness in untamed
youth that assails all indiscriminately.   **41 fetch of warrant** legitimate
trick.   **43 wi'th' working** in the process of being made, i.e., in everyday experience   **45 Your . . . converse** the person you are conversing
with.   **sound** sound out   **46 Having ever** if he has ever.   **prenominate
crimes** aforenamed offenses   **47 breathe** speak   **48 closes . . . consequence** takes you into his confidence as follows   **50 addition** title
60 o'ertook in 's rouse overcome by drink   **61 falling out** quarreling
63 Videlicet namely   **64 carp** a fish   **65 reach** capacity, ability
66 windlasses i.e., circuitous paths. (Literally, circuits made to head
off the game in hunting.)   **assays of bias** attempts through indirection (like the curving path of the bowling ball, which is biased or
weighted to one side)   **67 directions** i.e., the way things really are
68 former lecture just-ended set of instructions   **69 have** understand

72 in yourself in your own person (as well as by asking questions of
others).   **79 closet** private chamber   **80 doublet** close-fitting jacket.
unbraced unfastened   **82 down-gyvèd** fallen to the ankles (like
gyves or fetters)   **84 in purport** in what it expressed   **93 As** as if
97 As that.   **bulk** body   **104 ecstasy** madness   **105 property fordoes** nature destroys

His access to me.

POLONIUS   That hath made him mad.
I am sorry that with better heed and judgment
I had not quoted him. I feared he did but trifle   114
And meant to wrack thee. But beshrew my jealousy!   115
By heaven, it is as proper to our age   116
To cast beyond ourselves in our opinions   117
As it is common for the younger sort
To lack discretion. Come, go we to the King.
This must be known, which, being kept close, might
     move   120
More grief to hide than hate to utter love.   121
Come.   *Exeunt.*

❧

[2.2]

*Flourish. Enter King and Queen, Rosencrantz,
and Guildenstern [with others].*

KING
Welcome, dear Rosencrantz and Guildenstern.
Moreover that we much did long to see you,   2
The need we have to use you did provoke
Our hasty sending. Something have you heard
Of Hamlet's transformation—so call it,
Sith nor th'exterior nor the inward man   6
Resembles that it was. What it should be,   7
More than his father's death, that thus hath put him
So much from th'understanding of himself,
I cannot dream of. I entreat you both
That, being of so young days brought up with him,   11
And sith so neighbored to his youth and havior,   12
That you vouchsafe your rest here in our court   13
Some little time, so by your companies
To draw him on to pleasures, and to gather
So much as from occasion you may glean,   16
Whether aught to us unknown afflicts him thus
That, opened, lies within our remedy.   18

QUEEN
Good gentlemen, he hath much talked of you,
And sure I am two men there is not living
To whom he more adheres. If it will please you
To show us so much gentry and good will   22
As to expend your time with us awhile
For the supply and profit of our hope,   24

Your visitation shall receive such thanks
As fits a kings's remembrance.

ROSENCRANTZ   Both Your Majesties   26
Might, by the sovereign power you have of us,   27
Put your dread pleasures more into command   28
Than to entreaty.

GUILDENSTERN   But we both obey,
And here give up ourselves in the full bent   30
To lay our service freely at your feet,
To be commanded.

KING
Thanks, Rosencrantz and gentle Guildenstern.

QUEEN
Thanks, Guildenstern and gentle Rosencrantz.
And I beseech you instantly to visit
My too much changèd son.—Go, some of you,
And bring these gentlemen where Hamlet is.

GUILDENSTERN
Heavens make our presence and our practices   38
Pleasant and helpful to him!

QUEEN   Ay, amen!
*Exeunt Rosencrantz and Guildenstern [with some
                                       attendants].*

Enter Polonius.

POLONIUS
Th'ambassadors from Norway, my good lord,
Are joyfully returned.

KING
Thou still hast been the father of good news.   42

POLONIUS
Have I, my lord? I assure my good liege
I hold my duty, as I hold my soul,
Both to my God and to my gracious king;
And I do think, or else this brain of mine
Hunts not the trail of policy so sure   47
As it hath used to do, that I have found
The very cause of Hamlet's lunacy.

KING
Oh, speak of that! That do I long to hear.

POLONIUS
Give first admittance to th'ambassadors.
My news shall be the fruit to that great feast.   52

KING
Thyself do grace to them and bring them in.   53
                                  [Exit Polonius.]
He tells me, my dear Gertrude, he hath found
The head and source of all your son's distemper.

QUEEN
I doubt it is no other but the main,   56
His father's death and our o'erhasty marriage.

*Enter Ambassadors [Voltimand and Cornelius,
with Polonius].*

---

114 **quoted** observed   115 **wrack** ruin, seduce.   **beshrew my jealousy!** a plague upon my suspicious nature!   116 **proper . . . age** characteristic of us (old) men   117 **cast beyond** overshoot, miscalculate.
(A metaphor from hunting.)   120 **known** made known (to the King).
close secret   120-1 **might . . . love** i.e., might cause more grief
(because of what Hamlet might do) by hiding the knowledge of Hamlet's strange behavior to Ophelia than unpleasantness by telling it.
2.2 Location: The castle.
2 **Moreover that** Besides the fact that   6 **Sith nor** since neither   7 **that**
what   11–12 **That . . . havior** that, seeing as you were brought up
with him from early youth (see 3.4.209, where Hamlet refers to
Rosencrantz and Guildenstern as "my two schoolfellows"), and since
you have been intimately acquainted with his youthful ways
13 **vouchsafe your rest** consent to stay   16 **occasion** opportunity
18 **opened** being revealed   22 **gentry** courtesy   24 **supply . . . hope**
aid and furtherance of what we hope for

26 **As fits . . . remembrance** as would be a fitting gift of a king who
rewards true service.   27 **of** over   28 **dread** inspiring awe   30 **in . . .
bent** to the utmost degree of our capacity. (An archery metaphor.)
38 **practices** doings   42 **still** always   47 **policy** statecraft   52 **fruit**
dessert   53 **grace** honor. (Punning on *grace* said before a *feast*, line
52.)   56 **doubt** fear, suspect.

KING

Well, we shall sift him.—Welcome, my good friends!   58
Say, Voltimand, what from our brother Norway?   59

VOLTIMAND

Most fair return of greetings and desires.   60
Upon our first, he sent out to suppress   61
His nephew's levies, which to him appeared
To be a preparation 'gainst the Polack,
But, better looked into, he truly found
It was against Your Highness. Whereat grieved
That so his sickness, age, and impotence   66
Was falsely borne in hand, sends out arrests   67
On Fortinbras, which he, in brief, obeys,
Receives rebuke from Norway, and in fine   69
Makes vow before his uncle never more
To give th'assay of arms against Your Majesty.   71
Whereon old Norway, overcome with joy,
Gives him three thousand crowns in annual fee
And his commission to employ those soldiers,
So levied as before, against the Polack,
With an entreaty, herein further shown,
                                        [giving a paper]
That it might please you to give quiet pass
Through your dominions for this enterprise
On such regards of safety and allowance   79
As therein are set down.

KING   It likes us well,   80
And at our more considered time we'll read,   81
Answer, and think upon this business.
Meantime we thank you for your well-took labor.
Go to your rest; at night we'll feast together.
Most welcome home!   Exeunt Ambassadors.

POLONIUS   This business is well ended.
My liege, and madam, to expostulate   86
What majesty should be, what duty is,
Why day is day, night night, and time is time,
Were nothing but to waste night, day, and time.
Therefore, since brevity is the soul of wit,   90
And tediousness the limbs and outward flourishes,
I will be brief. Your noble son is mad.
Mad call I it, for, to define true madness,
What is't but to be nothing else but mad?
But let that go.

QUEEN   More matter, with less art.

POLONIUS

Madam, I swear I use no art at all.
That he's mad, 'tis true; 'tis true 'tis pity,
And pity 'tis 'tis true—a foolish figure,   98
But farewell it, for I will use no art.
Mad let us grant him, then, and now remains
That we find out the cause of this effect,

Or rather say, the cause of this defect,
For this effect defective comes by cause.   103
Thus it remains, and the remainder thus.
Perpend.   105
I have a daughter—have while she is mine—
Who, in her duty and obedience, mark,
Hath given me this. Now gather and surmise.   108
[He reads the letter.] "To the celestial and my soul's
idol, the most beautified Ophelia"—
That's an ill phrase, a vile phrase; "beautified" is a
vile phrase. But you shall hear. Thus: [He reads.]
"In her excellent white bosom, these, etc."   113

QUEEN   Came this from Hamlet to her?

POLONIUS

Good madam, stay awhile, I will be faithful.   115
                                    [He reads.]
      "Doubt thou the stars are fire,
          Doubt that the sun doth move,
      Doubt truth to be a liar,   118
          But never doubt I love.
O dear Ophelia, I am ill at these numbers. I have not   120
art to reckon my groans. But that I love thee best, O   121
most best, believe it. Adieu.
                Thine evermore, most dear lady, whilst this
                      machine is to him, Hamlet."   124
This in obedience hath my daughter shown me,
And, more above, hath his solicitings,   126
As they fell out by time, by means, and place,   127
All given to mine ear.

KING   But how hath she   128
Received his love?

POLONIUS   What do you think of me?

KING

As of a man faithful and honorable.

POLONIUS

I would fain prove so. But what might you think,   131
When I had seen this hot love on the wing—
As I perceived it, I must tell you that,
Before my daughter told me—what might you,
Or my dear Majesty your queen here, think,
If I had played the desk or table book,   136
Or given my heart a winking, mute and dumb,   137
Or looked upon this love with idle sight?   138
What might you think? No, I went round to work,   139
And my young mistress thus I did bespeak: 140
"Lord Hamlet is a prince out of thy star;   141
This must not be." And then I prescripts gave her,   142

---

58 **sift him** question Polonius (or Hamlet closely).   59 **brother** fellow king   60 **desires** good wishes.   61 **Upon our first** At our first words on the business   66 **impotence** weakness   67 **borne in hand** deluded, taken advantage of.   **arrests** orders to desist   69 **in fine** in conclusion   71 **give th'assay** make trial of strength, challenge   79 **On . . . allowance** i.e., with such considerations for the safety of Denmark and permission for Fortinbras   80 **likes** pleases   81 **considered** suitable for deliberation   86 **expostulate** expound, inquire into   90 **wit** sense or judgment   98 **figure** figure of speech

103 **For . . . cause** i.e., for this defective behavior, this madness, must have a cause.   105 **Perpend** Consider.   108 **gather and surmise** draw your own conclusions.   113 **"In . . . etc."** (The letter is poetically addressed to her heart, where a letter would be kept by a young lady.)   115 **stay . . . faithful** i.e., hold on, I will do as you wish.   118 **Doubt** suspect   120 **ill . . . numbers** unskilled at writing verses.   121 **reckon** (1) count (2) number metrically, scan   124 **machine** i.e., body   126–8 **And . . . ear** and moreover she has told me when, how, and where his solicitings of her occurred.   131 **fain** gladly   136–7 **If . . . dumb** if I had acted as go-between, passing love notes, or if I had refused to let my heart acknowledge what my eyes could see   138 **with idle sight** complacently or incomprehendingly.   139 **round** roundly, plainly   140 **bespeak** address   141 **out of thy star** above your sphere, position   142 **prescripts** orders

That she should lock herself from his resort,
Admit no messengers, receive no tokens.
Which done, she took the fruits of my advice;
And he, repellèd—a short tale to make—
Fell into a sadness, then into a fast,
Thence to a watch, thence into a weakness,　　148
Thence to a lightness, and by this declension　　149
Into the madness wherein now he raves,
And all we mourn for.

KING [*to the Queen*]　　　　Do you think 'tis this?

QUEEN　It may be, very like.

POLONIUS
Hath there been such a time—I would fain know
　　that—
That I have positively said "'Tis so,"
When it proved otherwise?

KING　　　　　　　　Not that I know.

POLONIUS
Take this from this, if this be otherwise.　　156
If circumstances lead me, I will find
Where truth is hid, though it were hid indeed
Within the center.

KING　　　　　　How may we try it further?　　159

POLONIUS
You know sometimes he walks four hours together
Here in the lobby.

QUEEN　　　　　So he does indeed.

POLONIUS
At such a time I'll loose my daughter to him.　　162
Be you and I behind an arras then.　　163
Mark the encounter. If he love her not
And be not from his reason fall'n thereon,　　165
Let me be no assistant for a state,
But keep a farm and carters.

KING　　　　　　　　We will try it.　　167

Enter Hamlet [reading on a book].

QUEEN
But look where sadly the poor wretch comes reading.

POLONIUS
Away, I do beseech you both, away.
I'll board him presently. Oh, give me leave.　　170
　　　　Exeunt King and Queen [with attendants].
How does my good Lord Hamlet?

HAMLET　Well, God-a-mercy.　　172

POLONIUS　Do you know me, my lord?

HAMLET　Excellent well. You are a fishmonger.　　174

POLONIUS　Not I, my lord.

HAMLET　Then I would you were so honest a man.

POLONIUS　Honest, my lord?

HAMLET　Ay, sir. To be honest, as this world goes, is to
be one man picked out of ten thousand.

POLONIUS　That's very true, my lord.

HAMLET　For if the sun breed maggots in a dead dog,
being a good kissing carrion—Have you a daughter?　　182

POLONIUS　I have, my lord.

HAMLET　Let her not walk i'th' sun. Conception is a　　184
blessing, but as your daughter may conceive, friend,
look to't.

POLONIUS [*aside*]　How say you by that? Still harping
on my daughter. Yet he knew me not at first; 'a said
I was a fishmonger. 'A is far gone. And truly in my
youth I suffered much extremity for love, very near
this. I'll speak to him again.—What do you read,
my lord?

HAMLET　Words, words, words.

POLONIUS　What is the matter, my lord?　　194

HAMLET　Between who?

POLONIUS　I mean, the matter that you read, my lord.

HAMLET　Slanders, sir; for the satirical rogue says here
that old men have gray beards, that their faces are wrinkled, their eyes purging thick amber and plum-tree　　199
gum, and that they have a plentiful lack of wit, to-　　200
gether with most weak hams. All which, sir, though I
most powerfully and potently believe, yet I hold it not
honesty to have it thus set down, for yourself, sir, shall　　203
grow old as I am, if like a crab you could go backward.　　204

POLONIUS [*aside*]　Though this be madness, yet there is
method in't.—Will you walk out of the air, my lord?　　206

HAMLET　Into my grave.

POLONIUS　Indeed, that's out of the air. [*Aside*] How
pregnant sometimes his replies are! A happiness that　　209
often madness hits on, which reason and sanity could
not so prosperously be delivered of. I will leave him　　211
and suddenly contrive the means of meeting between　　212
him and my daughter.—My honorable lord, I will
most humbly take my leave of you.

HAMLET　You cannot, sir, take from me anything that I
will more willingly part withal—except my life, except　　216
my life, except my life.

Enter Guildenstern and Rosencrantz.

POLONIUS　Fare you well, my lord.

HAMLET　These tedious old fools!

POLONIUS　You go to seek the Lord Hamlet. There he is.

ROSENCRANTZ [*to Polonius*]　God save you, sir!
　　　　　　　　　　　　　　　[*Exit Polonius.*]

GUILDENSTERN　My honored lord!

---

148 **watch** state of sleeplessness　149 **lightness** lightheadedness.
declension decline, deterioration. (With a pun on the grammatical
sense.)　156 **Take this from this** (The actor probably gestures, indicating that he means his head from his shoulders, or his staff of office
or chain from his hands or neck, or something similar.)　159 **center**
center of the earth, traditionally an extraordinarily inaccessible place.
try test　162 **loose** (As one might release an animal that is being
mated.)　163 **arras** hanging, tapestry　165 **thereon** on that account
167 **carters** wagon drivers.　170 **I'll . . . leave** I'll accost him at once.
Please leave us alone; leave him to me.　172 **God-a-mercy** God have
mercy, i.e., thank you.　174 **fishmonger** fish merchant.

182 **a good kissing carrion** i.e., a good piece of flesh for kissing, or for
the sun to kiss　184 **i'th' sun** in public. (With additional implication
of the sunshine of princely favors.)　**Conception** (1) Understanding
(2) Pregnancy　194 **matter** substance. (But Hamlet plays on the sense
of "basis for a dispute.")　199 **purging** discharging.　**amber** i.e.,
resin, like the resinous *plum-tree gum*　200 **wit** understanding
203 **honesty** decency, decorum　204 **old** as old　206 **out of the air**
(The open air was considered dangerous for sick people.)　209 **pregnant** quick-witted, full of meaning.　**happiness** felicity of expression
211 **prosperously** successfully　212 **suddenly** immediately
216 **withal** with

ROSENCRANTZ   My most dear lord!

HAMLET   My excellent good friends! How dost thou,
Guildenstern? Ah, Rosencrantz! Good lads, how do
you both?

ROSENCRANTZ
As the indifferent children of the earth.   227

GUILDENSTERN
Happy in that we are not overhappy.
On Fortune's cap we are not the very button.

HAMLET   Nor the soles of her shoe?

ROSENCRANTZ   Neither, my lord.

HAMLET   Then you live about her waist, or in the mid-   232
dle of her favors?   233

GUILDENSTERN   Faith, her privates we.   234

HAMLET   In the secret parts of Fortune? Oh, most true,
she is a strumpet. What news?   236

ROSENCRANTZ   None, my lord, but the world's grown
honest.

HAMLET   Then is doomsday near. But your news is not
true. Let me question more in particular. What have
you, my good friends, deserved at the hands of
Fortune that she sends you to prison hither?

GUILDENSTERN   Prison, my lord?

HAMLET   Denmark's a prison.

ROSENCRANTZ   Then is the world one.

HAMLET   A goodly one, in which there are many
confines, wards, and dungeons, Denmark being one   247
o'th' worst.

ROSENCRANTZ   We think not so, my lord.

HAMLET   Why then 'tis none to you, for there is nothing
either good or bad but thinking makes it so. To me it
is a prison.

ROSENCRANTZ   Why then, your ambition makes it one.
'Tis too narrow for your mind.

HAMLET   Oh, God, I could be bounded in a nutshell and
count myself a king of infinite space, were it not that
I have bad dreams.

GUILDENSTERN   Which dreams indeed are ambition, for
the very substance of the ambitious is merely the   259
shadow of a dream.

HAMLET   A dream itself is but a shadow.

ROSENCRANTZ   Truly, and I hold ambition of so airy
and light a quality that it is but a shadow's shadow.

HAMLET   Then are our beggars bodies, and our mon-   264
archs and outstretched heroes the beggars' shadows.   265
Shall we to th' court? For, by my fay, I cannot reason.   266

ROSENCRANTZ, GUILDENSTERN   We'll wait upon you.   267

HAMLET   No such matter. I will not sort you with the   268
rest of my servants, for, to speak to you like an honest
man, I am most dreadfully attended. But, in the   270
beaten way of friendship, what make you at Elsinore?   271

ROSENCRANTZ   To visit you, my lord, no other occasion.

HAMLET   Beggar that I am, I am even poor in thanks;
but I thank you, and sure, dear friends, my thanks are
too dear a halfpenny. Were you not sent for? Is it your   275
own inclining? Is it a free visitation? Come, come, deal   276
justly with me. Come, come. Nay, speak.

GUILDENSTERN   What should we say, my lord?

HAMLET   Anything but to th' purpose. You were sent   279
for, and there is a kind of confession in your looks
which your modesties have not craft enough to color.   281
I know the good King and Queen have sent for you.

ROSENCRANTZ   To what end, my lord?

HAMLET   That you must teach me. But let me conjure   284
you, by the rights of our fellowship, by the consonancy   285
of our youth, by the obligation of our ever-preserved   286
love, and by what more dear a better proposer   287
could charge you withal, be even and direct with me   288
whether you were sent for or no.

ROSENCRANTZ   [aside to Guildenstern]   What say you?

HAMLET   [aside]   Nay, then, I have an eye of you.—If   291
you love me, hold not off.   292

GUILDENSTERN   My lord, we were sent for.

HAMLET   I will tell you why; so shall my anticipation   294
prevent your discovery, and your secrecy to the King   295
and Queen molt no feather. I have of late—but   296
wherefore I know not—lost all my mirth, forgone all
custom of exercises; and indeed it goes so heavily with
my disposition that this goodly frame, the earth,
seems to me a sterile promontory; this most excellent
canopy, the air, look you, this brave o'erhanging   301
firmament, this majestical roof fretted with golden   302
fire, why, it appeareth nothing to me but a foul and
pestilent congregation of vapors. What a piece of work   304
is a man! How noble in reason, how infinite in faculties,
in form and moving how express and admirable, in   306
action how like an angel, in apprehension how like a   307
god! The beauty of the world, the paragon of animals!
And yet, to me, what is this quintessence of dust?   309
Man delights not me—no, nor woman neither,
though by your smiling you seem to say so.

---

227 indifferent ordinary, at neither extreme of fortune or misfortune
232–3 the middle . . . favors i.e., her genitals.   **234 her privates we**
(1) we dwell in her privates, her genitals, in the middle of her favors
(2) we are her ordinary footsoldiers.   **236 strumpet** (Fortune was
proverbially thought of as fickle.)   **247 confines** places of confinement   **259 the very . . . ambitious** that seemingly very substantial
thing that the ambitious pursue   **264–5 Then . . . shadows** (Hamlet
pursues their argument about ambition to its absurd extreme: if ambition is only a shadow of a shadow, then beggars (who are presumably
without ambition) must be real, whereas monarchs and heroes are
only their shadows—*outstretched* like elongated shadows, made to
look bigger than they are.)   **266 fay** faith   **267 wait upon** accompany, attend. (But Hamlet uses the phrase in the sense of providing
menial service.)

268 sort class, categorize   **270 dreadfully attended** waited upon in
slovenly fashion.   **271 beaten way** familiar path, tried-and-true
course.   **make** do   **275 too dear a halfpenny** (1) too expensive at
even a halfpenny, i.e., of little worth (2) too expensive *by* a halfpenny
in return for worthless kindness.   **276 free** voluntary   **279 Anything
but to th' purpose** Anything except a straightforward answer. (Said
ironically.)   **281 color** disguise.   **284 conjure** adjure, entreat
285–6 the consonancy of our youth our closeness in our younger
days   **287 better** more skillful   **288 charge** urge.   **even** straight,
honest   **291 of** on   **292 hold not off** don't hold back.   **294–5 so . . .
discovery** in that way my saying it first will spare you from having to
reveal the truth   **296 molt no feather** i.e., not diminish in the least.
301 brave splendid   **302 fretted** adorned (with fretwork, as in a
vaulted ceiling)   **304 congregation** mass.   **piece of work** masterpiece   **306 express** well-framed, exact, expressive   **307 apprehension** power of comprehending   **309 quintessence** very essence.
(Literally, the fifth essence beyond earth, water, air, and fire, supposed to be extractable from them.)

ROSENCRANTZ   My lord, there was no such stuff in my thoughts.

HAMLET   Why did you laugh, then, when I said man delights not me?

ROSENCRANTZ   To think, my lord, if you delight not in man, what Lenten entertainment the players shall 317 receive from you. We coted them on the way, and 318 hither are they coming to offer you service.

HAMLET   He that plays the king shall be welcome; His Majesty shall have tribute of me. The adventurous 321 knight shall use his foil and target, the lover shall not 322 sigh gratis, the humorous man shall end his part in 323 peace, the clown shall make those laugh whose lungs 324 are tickle o'th' sear, and the lady shall say her mind 325 freely, or the blank verse shall halt for't. What players 326 are they?

ROSENCRANTZ   Even those you were wont to take such delight in, the tragedians of the city. 329

HAMLET   How chances it they travel? Their residence, 330 both in reputation and profit, was better both ways.

ROSENCRANTZ   I think their inhibition comes by the 332 means of the late innovation. 333

HAMLET   Do they hold the same estimation they did when I was in the city? Are they so followed?

ROSENCRANTZ   No, indeed are they not.

HAMLET   How comes it? Do they grow rusty? 337

ROSENCRANTZ   Nay, their endeavor keeps in the wonted 338 pace. But there is, sir, an aerie of children, little eyases, 339 that cry out on the top of question and are most tyran- 340 nically clapped for't. These are now the fashion, and 341 so berattle the common stages—so they call them— 342 that many wearing rapiers are afraid of goose quills 343 and dare scarce come thither.

HAMLET   What, are they children? Who maintains 'em? How are they escotted? Will they pursue the quality no 346 longer than they can sing? Will they not say after- 347

wards, if they should grow themselves to common 348 players—as it is most like, if their means are no 349 better—their writers do them wrong to make them 350 exclaim against their own succession? 351

ROSENCRANTZ   Faith, there has been much to-do on 352 both sides, and the nation holds it no sin to tar them to 353 controversy. There was for a while no money bid for 354 argument unless the poet and the player went to cuffs 355 in the question. 356

HAMLET   Is't possible?

GUILDENSTERN   Oh, there has been much throwing about of brains.

HAMLET   Do the boys carry it away? 360

ROSENCRANTZ   Ay, that they do, my lord—Hercules 361 and his load too. 362

HAMLET   It is not very strange; for my uncle is King of Denmark, and those that would make mouths at him 364 while my father lived give twenty, forty, a hundred ducats apiece for his picture in little. 'Sblood, 366 there is something in this more than natural, if philos- ophy could find it out.

A flourish [*of trumpets within*].

GUILDENSTERN   There are the players.

HAMLET   Gentlemen, you are welcome to Elsinore. Your hands, come then. Th'appurtenance of welcome is 371 fashion and ceremony. Let me comply with you in this 372 garb, lest my extent to the players, which, I tell you, 373 must show fairly outwards, should more appear like 374 entertainment than yours. You are welcome. But my 375 uncle-father and aunt-mother are deceived.

GUILDENSTERN   In what, my dear lord?

HAMLET   I am but mad north-north-west. When the 378 wind is southerly I know a hawk from a handsaw. 379

Enter Polonius.

POLONIUS   Well be with you, gentlemen!

HAMLET   Hark you, Guildenstern, and you too; at each ear a hearer. That great baby you see there is not yet out of his swaddling clouts. 383

ROSENCRANTZ   Haply he is the second time come to 384 them, for they say an old man is twice a child.

---

317 Lenten entertainment meager reception (appropriate to Lent) **318 coted** overtook and passed by   **321 tribute** (1) applause (2) homage paid in money.   **of** from   **322 foil and target** sword and shield   **323 gratis** for nothing.   **humorous man** eccentric character, dominated by one trait or "humor"   **323–4 in peace** i.e., with full license   **325 tickle o'th' sear** hair trigger, ready to laugh easily. (A *sear* is part of a gun-lock.)   **326 halt** limp   **329 tragedians** actors **330 residence** remaining in their usual place, i.e., in the city **332 inhibition** formal prohibition (from acting plays in the city) **333 late innovation** i.e., recent new fashion in satirical plays per- formed by boy actors in the "private" theaters; or the Earl of Essex's abortive rebellion in 1601 against Elizabeth's government. (A much debated passage of seemingly topical reference.)   **337 How . . . rusty?** Have they lost their polish, gone out of fashion? (This passage, through line 362, alludes to the rivalry between the children's compa- nies and the adult actors, given strong impetus by the reopening of the Children of the Chapel at the Blackfriars Theater in late 1600.) **338 keeps . . . wonted** continues in the usual   **339 aerie** nest.   **eyases** young hawks   **340 cry . . . question** speak shrilly, dominating the controversy (in decrying the public theaters)   **340–1 tyrannically** vehemently   **342 berattle . . . stages** clamor against the public the- aters   **343 many wearing rapiers** i.e., many men of fashion, afraid to patronize the common players for fear of being satirized by the poets writing for the boy actors.   **goose quills** i.e., pens of satirists **346 escotted** maintained.   **quality** (acting) profession   **346–7 no longer . . . sing** i.e., only until their voices change.

348 common regular, adult   **349 like** likely   **349–50 if . . . better** if they find no better way to support themselves   **351 succession** i.e., future careers.   **352 to-do** ado   **353 tar** incite (as in inciting dogs to attack a chained bear)   **354–6 There . . . question** i.e., For a while, no money was offered by the acting companies to playwrights for the plot to a play unless the satirical poets who wrote for the boys and the adult actors came to blows in the play itself.   **360 carry it away** i.e., win the day.   **361–2 Hercules . . . load** (Thought to be an allusion to the sign of the Globe Theatre, which allegedly was Hercules bear- ing the world on his shoulders.)   **364 mouths** faces   **366 ducats** gold coins.   **in little** in miniature.   **'Sblood** By God's (Christ's) blood **371 Th'appurtenance** The proper accompaniment   **372 comply** observe the formalities of courtesy   **373 garb** i.e., manner.   **my extent** that which I extend, i.e., my polite behavior   **374 show fairly outwards** show every evidence of cordiality   **375 entertainment** a (warm) reception   **378 north-north-west** just off true north, only partly.   **379 I . . . handsaw** (Speaking in his mad guise, Hamlet per- haps suggests that he can tell true from false. A *handsaw* may be a *hernshaw* or heron. Still, a supposedly mad disposition might com- pare hawks and handsaws.)   **383 swaddling clouts** cloths in which to wrap a newborn baby.   **384 Haply** Perhaps

HAMLET   I will prophesy he comes to tell me of the
players. Mark it.—You say right, sir, o' Monday 387
morning, 'twas then indeed. 388

POLONIUS   My lord, I have news to tell you.

HAMLET   My lord, I have news to tell you. When Roscius 390
was an actor in Rome—

POLONIUS   The actors are come hither, my lord.

HAMLET   Buzz, buzz! 393

POLONIUS   Upon my honor—

HAMLET   Then came each actor on his ass.

POLONIUS   The best actors in the world, either for
tragedy, comedy, history, pastoral, pastoral-comical,
historical-pastoral, tragical-historical, tragical-comical-
historical-pastoral, scene individable, or poem unlim- 399
ited. Seneca cannot be too heavy, nor Plautus too 400
light. For the law of writ and the liberty, these are the 401
only men.

HAMLET   O Jephthah, judge of Israel, what a treasure 403
hadst thou!

POLONIUS   What a treasure had he, my lord?

HAMLET   Why,
    "One fair daughter, and no more,
    The which he lovèd passing well." 408

POLONIUS   [aside]   Still on my daughter.

HAMLET   Am I not i'th' right, old Jephthah?

POLONIUS   If you call me Jephthah, my lord, I have a
daughter that I love passing well.

HAMLET   Nay, that follows not. 413

POLONIUS   What follows then, my lord? 414

HAMLET   Why,
    "As by lot, God wot," 416
and then, you know,
    "It came to pass, as most like it was"— 418
the first row of the pious chanson will show you more, 419
for look where my abridgment comes. 420

Enter the Players.

You are welcome, masters; welcome, all. I am glad to 421
see thee well. Welcome, good friends. Oh, old friend!
Why, thy face is valanced since I saw thee last. Com'st 423
thou to beard me in Denmark? What, my young lady 424

and mistress! By'r Lady, Your Ladyship is nearer to 425
heaven than when I saw you last, by the altitude of a 426
chopine. Pray God your voice, like a piece of uncur- 427
rent gold, be not cracked within the ring. Masters, you 428
are all welcome. We'll e'en to't like French falconers, 429
fly at anything we see. We'll have a speech straight. 430
Come, give us a taste of your quality. Come, a 431
passionate speech.

FIRST PLAYER   What speech, my good lord?

HAMLET   I heard thee speak me a speech once, but it
was never acted, or if it was, not above once, for the
play, I remember, pleased not the million; 'twas cav- 436
iar to the general. But it was—as I received it, and 437
others, whose judgments in such matters cried in the 438
top of mine—an excellent play, well digested in the 439
scenes, set down with as much modesty as cunning. I 440
remember one said there were no sallets in the lines to 441
make the matter savory, nor no matter in the phrase
that might indict the author of affectation, but called it 443
an honest method, as wholesome as sweet, and by very
much more handsome than fine. One speech in't I 445
chiefly loved: 'twas Aeneas' tale to Dido, and there-
about of it especially when he speaks of Priam's 447
slaughter. If it live in your memory, begin at this line: 448
let me see, let me see—
    "The rugged Pyrrhus, like th' Hyrcanian beast"— 450
'Tis not so. It begins with Pyrrhus:
    "The rugged Pyrrhus, he whose sable arms, 452
    Black as his purpose, did the night resemble
    When he lay couchèd in th' ominous horse, 454
    Hath now this dread and black complexion
        smeared
    With heraldry more dismal. Head to foot 456
    Now is he total gules, horridly tricked 457
    With blood of fathers, mothers, daughters, sons,
    Baked and impasted with the parching streets, 459
    That lend a tyrannous and a damnèd light 460

387–8 You say . . . then indeed (Said to impress upon Polonius the idea
that Hamlet is in serious conversation with his friends.)   390 Roscius a
famous Roman actor who died in 62 B.C.   393 Buzz (An interjection
used to denote stale news.)   399–400 scene . . . unlimited plays that
are unclassifiable and all-inclusive. (An absurdly catchall conclusion to
Polonius's pompous list of categories.)   400 Seneca writer of Latin
tragedies.   Plautus writer of Latin comedies   401 law . . . liberty dramatic composition both according to the rules and disregarding the
rules.   these i.e., the actors   403 Jephthah . . . Israel (Jephthah had to
sacrifice his daughter; see Judges 11. Hamlet goes on to quote from a
ballad on the theme.)   408 passing surpassingly   413 that follows not
i.e., just because you resemble Jephthah in having a daughter does not
logically prove that you love her.   414 What . . . lord? What does follow logically? (But Hamlet, pretending madness, answers with a fragment of a ballad, as if Polonius had asked, "What comes next?" See
419n.)   416 lot chance.   wot knows   418 like likely, probable
419 the first . . . more the first stanza of this biblically based ballad will
satisfy your stated desire to know *what follows* (line 414).   420 my
abridgment something that cuts short my conversation; also, a diversion   421 masters good sirs   423 valanced fringed (with a beard)
424 beard confront, challenge. (With obvious pun.)   young lady i.e.,
boy playing women's parts

425 By'r Lady By Our Lady   425–6 nearer to heaven i.e., taller
427 chopine thick-soled shoe of Italian fashion.   427–8 uncurrent not
passable as lawful coinage   428 cracked . . . ring i.e., changed from
adolescent to male voice, no longer suitable for women's roles. (Coins
featured rings enclosing the sovereign's head; if the coin was sufficiently clipped to invade within this ring, it was unfit for currency.)
429 e'en to't go at it   430 straight at once.   431 quality professional
skill.   436–7 caviar to the general i.e., an expensive delicacy not generally palatable to uneducated tastes.   438–9 cried in the top of i.e.,
spoke with greater authority than   439 digested arranged, ordered
440 modesty moderation, restraint.   cunning skill.   441 sallets i.e.,
something savory, spicy improprieties   443 indict convict
445 handsome well-proportioned.   fine elaborately ornamented,
showy.   447–8 Priam's slaughter the slaying of the ruler of Troy,
when the Greeks finally took the city   450 Pyrrhus a Greek hero in
the Trojan War, also known as Neoptolemus, son of Achilles—another
avenging son.   th' Hyrcanian beast i.e., the tiger. (On the death of
Priam, see Virgil, *Aeneid*, 2.506 ff.; compare the whole speech with
Marlowe's *Dido Queen of Carthage*, 2.1.214 ff. On the *Hyrcanian* tiger,
see *Aeneid*, 4.366–7. Hyrcania is on the Caspian Sea.)   452 rugged
shaggy, savage.   sable black (for reasons of camouflage during the
episode of the Trojan horse)   454 couchèd concealed.   ominous
horse fateful Trojan horse, by which the Greeks gained access to Troy
456 dismal calamitous.   457 total gules entirely red. (A heraldic
term.)   tricked spotted and smeared. (Heraldic.)   459 Baked . . .
streets roasted and encrusted, like a thick paste, by the parching heat
of the streets (because of the fires everywhere)   460 tyrannous cruel

To their lord's murder. Roasted in wrath and fire, 461
And thus o'ersizèd with coagulate gore, 462
With eyes like carbuncles, the hellish Pyrrhus 463
Old grandsire Priam seeks."
So proceed you.

POLONIUS   'Fore God, my lord, well spoken, with good
accent and good discretion.

FIRST PLAYER   "Anon he finds him
Striking too short at Greeks. His antique sword, 469
Rebellious to his arm, lies where it falls,
Repugnant to command. Unequal matched, 471
Pyrrhus at Priam drives, in rage strikes wide,
But with the whiff and wind of his fell sword 473
Th'unnervèd father falls. Then senseless Ilium, 474
Seeming to feel this blow, with flaming top
Stoops to his base, and with a hideous crash 476
Takes prisoner Pyrrhus' ear. For, lo! His sword,
Which was declining on the milky head 478
Of reverend Priam, seemed i'th'air to stick.
So as a painted tyrant Pyrrhus stood, 480
And, like a neutral to his will and matter, 481
Did nothing.
But as we often see against some storm 483
A silence in the heavens, the rack stand still, 484
The bold winds speechless, and the orb below 485
As hush as death, anon the dreadful thunder
Doth rend the region, so, after Pyrrhus' pause, 487
A rousèd vengeance sets him new a-work,
And never did the Cyclops' hammers fall 489
On Mars's armor forged for proof eterne 490
With less remorse than Pyrrhus' bleeding sword 491
Now falls on Priam.
Out, out, thou strumpet Fortune! All you gods
In general synod take away her power! 494
Break all the spokes and fellies from her wheel, 495
And bowl the round nave down the hill of heaven 496
As low as to the fiends!"

POLONIUS   This is too long.

HAMLET   It shall to the barber's with your beard.—Prithee, say on. He's for a jig or a tale of bawdry, or he 500
sleeps. Say on; come to Hecuba. 501

FIRST PLAYER
"But who, ah woe! had seen the moblèd queen"— 502

HAMLET   "The moblèd queen?"

POLONIUS   That's good. "Moblèd queen" is good.

FIRST PLAYER
"Run barefoot up and down, threat'ning the flames 505
With bisson rheum, a clout upon that head 506
Where late the diadem stood, and, for a robe, 507
About her lank and all o'erteemèd loins 508
A blanket, in the alarm of fear caught up—
Who this had seen, with tongue in venom steeped,
'Gainst Fortune's state would treason have
pronounced. 511
But if the gods themselves did see her then
When she saw Pyrrhus make malicious sport
In mincing with his sword her husband's limbs,
The instant burst of clamor that she made,
Unless things mortal move them not at all,
Would have made milch the burning eyes of heaven, 517
And passion in the gods." 518

POLONIUS   Look whe'er he has not turned his color and 519
has tears in 's eyes. Prithee, no more.

HAMLET   'Tis well; I'll have thee speak out the rest of
this soon.—Good my lord, will you see the players well
bestowed? Do you hear, let them be well used, for they 523
are the abstract and brief chronicles of the time. After 524
your death you were better have a bad epitaph than
their ill report while you live.

POLONIUS   My lord, I will use them according to their
desert.

HAMLET   God's bodikin, man, much better. Use every 529
man after his desert, and who shall scape whipping?
Use them after your own honor and dignity. The less 531
they deserve, the more merit is in your bounty. Take
them in.

POLONIUS   Come, sirs.   [Exit.]

HAMLET   Follow him, friends. We'll hear a play tomor-
row. [As they start to leave, Hamlet detains the First
Player.] Dost thou hear me, old friend? Can you play
The Murder of Gonzago?

FIRST PLAYER   Ay, my lord.

HAMLET   We'll ha 't tomorrow night. You could, for a 540
need, study a speech of some dozen or sixteen lines 541
which I would set down and insert in't, could you not?

FIRST PLAYER   Ay, my lord.

HAMLET   Very well. Follow that lord, and look you mock
him not.   Exeunt players.
My good friends, I'll leave you till night. You are welcome to Elsinore.

ROSENCRANTZ   Good my lord!
                    Exeunt [Rosencrantz and Guildenstern].

HAMLET
Ay, so, goodbye to you.—Now I am alone.
Oh, what a rogue and peasant slave am I!

---

461 **their lord's** i.e., Priam's   462 **o'ersizèd** covered as with size or glue   463 **carbuncles** large fiery-red precious stones thought to emit their own light   469 **antique** ancient, long-used   471 **Repugnant** disobedient, resistant   473 **fell** cruel   474 **Th' unnervèd** strengthless.   **senseless Ilium** inanimate citadel of Troy   476 **his** its   478 **declining** descending.   **milky** white-haired   480 **painted** motionless, as in a painting   481 **like . . . matter** i.e., as though suspended between his intention and its fulfillment   483 **against** just before   484 **rack** mass of clouds   485 **orb** globe, earth   487 **region** sky   489 **Cyclops** giant armor makers in the smithy of Vulcan   490 **proof** proven or tested resistance to assault   491 **remorse** pity   494 **synod** assembly   495 **fellies** pieces of wood forming the rim of a wheel   496 **nave** hub.   **hill of heaven** Mount Olympus   500 **jig** comic song and dance often given at the end of a play   501 **Hecuba** wife of Priam.   502 **who . . . had** anyone who had. (Also in line 510.)   **moblèd** muffled

505 **threat'ning the flames** i.e., weeping hard enough to dampen the flames   506 **bisson rheum** blinding tears.   **clout** cloth   507 **late** lately   508 **all o'erteemèd** utterly worn out with bearing children   511 **state** rule, managing.   **pronounced** proclaimed.   517 **milch** milky, moist with tears.   **burning eyes of heaven** i.e., stars, heavenly bodies   518 **passion** overpowering emotion   519 **whe'er** whether   523 **bestowed** lodged.   524 **abstract** summary account   529 **God's bodikin** By God's (Christ's) little body, bodykin. (Not to be confused with bodkin, "dagger.")   531 **after** according to   540 **ha 't** have it   541 **study** memorize

Is it not monstrous that this player here,
But in a fiction, in a dream of passion,   552
Could force his soul so to his own conceit   553
That from her working all his visage wanned,   554
Tears in his eyes, distraction in his aspect,   555
A broken voice, and his whole function suiting   556
With forms to his conceit? And all for nothing!   557
For Hecuba!
What's Hecuba to him, or he to Hecuba,
That he should weep for her? What would he do
Had he the motive and the cue for passion
That I have? He would drown the stage with tears
And cleave the general ear with horrid speech,   563
Make mad the guilty and appall the free,   564
Confound the ignorant, and amaze indeed   565
The very faculties of eyes and ears. Yet I,
A dull and muddy-mettled rascal, peak   567
Like John-a-dreams, unpregnant of my cause,   568
And can say nothing—no, not for a king
Upon whose property and most dear life   570
A damned defeat was made. Am I a coward?   571
Who calls me villain? Breaks my pate across?   572
Plucks off my beard and blows it in my face?
Tweaks me by the nose? Gives me the lie i'th' throat   574
As deep as to the lungs? Who does me this?
Ha, 'swounds, I should take it; for it cannot be   576
But I am pigeon-livered and lack gall   577
To make oppression bitter, or ere this   578
I should ha' fatted all the region kites   579
With this slave's offal. Bloody, bawdy villain!   580
Remorseless, treacherous, lecherous, kindless villain!   581
Oh, vengeance!
Why, what an ass am I! This is most brave,   583
That I, the son of a dear father murdered,
Prompted to my revenge by heaven and hell,
Must like a whore unpack my heart with words
And fall a-cursing, like a very drab,   587
A scullion! Fie upon't, foh! About, my brains!   588
Hum, I have heard
That guilty creatures sitting at a play
Have by the very cunning of the scene   591
Been struck so to the soul that presently   592

They have proclaimed their malefactions;
For murder, though it have no tongue, will speak
With most miraculous organ. I'll have these players
Play something like the murder of my father
Before mine uncle. I'll observe his looks;
I'll tent him to the quick. If 'a do blench,   598
I know my course. The spirit that I have seen
May be the devil, and the devil hath power
T'assume a pleasing shape; yea, and perhaps,
Out of my weakness and my melancholy,
As he is very potent with such spirits,   603
Abuses me to damn me. I'll have grounds   604
More relative than this. The play's the thing   605
Wherein I'll catch the conscience of the King.   *Exit.*

❖

[3.1]

Enter King, Queen, Polonius, Ophelia,
Rosencrantz, Guildenstern, lords.

KING
    And can you by no drift of conference   1
    Get from him why he puts on this confusion,
    Grating so harshly all his days of quiet
    With turbulent and dangerous lunacy?
ROSENCRANTZ
    He does confess he feels himself distracted,
    But from what cause 'a will by no means speak.
GUILDENSTERN
    Nor do we find him forward to be sounded,   7
    But with a crafty madness keeps aloof
    When we would bring him on to some confession
    Of his true state.
QUEEN   Did he receive you well?
ROSENCRANTZ   Most like a gentleman.
GUILDENSTERN
    But with much forcing of his disposition.   12
ROSENCRANTZ
    Niggard of question, but of our demands   13
    Most free in his reply.
QUEEN   Did you assay him   14
    To any pastime?
ROSENCRANTZ
    Madam, it so fell out that certain players
    We o'erraught on the way. Of these we told him,   17
    And there did seem in him a kind of joy
    To hear of it. They are here about the court,
    And, as I think, they have already order
    This night to play before him.
POLONIUS   'Tis most true,
    And he beseeched me to entreat Your Majesties
    To hear and see the matter.

---

552 But merely   **553 force . . . conceit** bring his innermost being so entirely into accord with his conception (of the role)   **554 from her working** as a result of, or in response to, his soul's activity.   **wanned** grew pale   **555 aspect** look, glance   **556–7 his whole . . . conceit** all his bodily powers responding with actions to suit his thought. **563 the general ear** everyone's ear.   **horrid** horrible   **564 appall** (Literally, make pale.)   **free** innocent   **565 Confound the ignorant** i.e., dumbfound those who know nothing of the crime that has been committed.   **amaze** stun   **567 muddy-mettled** dull-spirited **567–8 peak . . . cause** mope, like a dreaming idler, not quickened by my cause   **570 property** person and function   **571 damned defeat** damnable act of destruction   **572 pate** head   **574 Gives . . . throat** Calls me an out-and-out liar   **576 'swounds** by his (Christ's) wounds **577 pigeon-livered** (The pigeon or dove was popularly supposed to be mild because it secreted no gall.)   **578 To . . . bitter** to make things bitter for oppressors   **579 region kites** kites (birds of prey) of the air **580 offal** entrails.   **581 Remorseless** Pitiless.   **kindless** unnatural **583 brave** fine, admirable. (Said ironically.)   **587 drab** whore **588 scullion** menial kitchen servant. (Apt to be foul-mouthed.) **About** About it, to work   **591 cunning** art, skill.   **scene** dramatic presentation   **592 presently** at once

598 tent probe.   **the quick** the tender part of a wound, the core. **blench** quail, flinch   **603 spirits** humors (of melancholy) **604 Abuses** deludes   **605 relative** cogent, pertinent **3.1 Location:** The castle. **1 drift of conference** course of talk   **7 forward** willing.   **sounded** questioned   **12 disposition** inclination.   **13 Niggard of question** Laconic.   **demands** questions   **14 assay** try to win   **17 o'erraught** overtook

KING
        With all my heart, and it doth much content me
        To hear him so inclined.
        Good gentlemen, give him a further edge   26
        And drive his purpose into these delights.

ROSENCRANTZ
        We shall, my lord.

                        Exeunt Rosencrantz and Guildenstern.

KING   Sweet Gertrude, leave us too,
        For we have closely sent for Hamlet hither,   29
        That he, as 'twere by accident, may here
        Affront Ophelia.   31
        Her father and myself, lawful espials,   32
        Will so bestow ourselves that seeing, unseen,
        We may of their encounter frankly judge,
        And gather by him, as he is behaved,
        If 't be th'affliction of his love or no
        That thus he suffers for.

QUEEN   I shall obey you.
        And for your part, Ophelia, I do wish
        That your good beauties be the happy cause
        Of Hamlet's wildness. So shall I hope your virtues
        Will bring him to his wonted way again,
        To both your honors.

OPHELIA   Madam, I wish it may.

                                [Exit Queen.]

POLONIUS
        Ophelia, walk you here.—Gracious, so please you,   43
        We will bestow ourselves. *[To Ophelia]* Read on this
            book,   *[giving her a book]*   44
        That show of such an exercise may color   45
        Your loneliness. We are oft to blame in this—   46
        'Tis too much proved—that with devotion's visage   47
        And pious action we do sugar o'er
        The devil himself.

KING *[aside]*   Oh, 'tis too true!
        How smart a lash that speech doth give my
            conscience!
        The harlot's cheek, beautied with plast'ring art,
        Is not more ugly to the thing that helps it   53
        Than is my deed to my most painted word.   54
        Oh, heavy burden!

POLONIUS
        I hear him coming. Let's withdraw, my lord.   56

                        [The King and Polonius withdraw.]

            Enter Hamlet. [Ophelia pretends to read a book.]

HAMLET
        To be, or not to be, that is the question:
        Whether 'tis nobler in the mind to suffer
        The slings and arrows of outrageous fortune,

        Or to take arms against a sea of troubles
        And by opposing end them. To die, to sleep—
        No more—and by a sleep to say we end
        The heartache and the thousand natural shocks
        That flesh is heir to. 'Tis a consummation
        Devoutly to be wished. To die, to sleep;
        To sleep, perchance to dream. Ay, there's the rub,   66
        For in that sleep of death what dreams may come,
        When we have shuffled off this mortal coil,   68
        Must give us pause. There's the respect   69
        That makes calamity of so long life.   70
        For who would bear the whips and scorns of time,
        Th'oppressor's wrong, the proud man's contumely,   72
        The pangs of disprized love, the law's delay,   73
        The insolence of office, and the spurns   74
        That patient merit of th'unworthy takes,   75
        When he himself might his quietus make   76
        With a bare bodkin? Who would fardels bear,   77
        To grunt and sweat under a weary life,
        But that the dread of something after death,
        The undiscovered country from whose bourn   80
        No traveler returns, puzzles the will,
        And makes us rather bear those ills we have
        Than fly to others that we know not of?
        Thus conscience does make cowards of us all;
        And thus the native hue of resolution   85
        Is sicklied o'er with the pale cast of thought,   86
        And enterprises of great pitch and moment   87
        With this regard their currents turn awry   88
        And lose the name of action.—Soft you now,   89
        The fair Ophelia.—Nymph, in thy orisons   90
        Be all my sins remembered.

OPHELIA   Good my lord,   91
        How does Your Honor for this many a day?

HAMLET
        I humbly thank you; well, well, well.

OPHELIA
        My lord, I have remembrances of yours,
        That I have longèd long to redeliver.
        I pray you, now receive them.   *[She offers tokens.]*

HAMLET
        No, not I, I never gave you aught.

OPHELIA
        My honored lord, you know right well you did,
        And with them words of so sweet breath composed
        As made the things more rich. Their perfume lost,
        Take these again, for to the noble mind

---

26 **edge** incitement   29 **closely** privately   31 **Affront** confront, meet
32 **espials** spies   43 **Gracious** Your Grace (i.e., the King)
44 **bestow** conceal   45 **exercise** religious exercise. (The book she
reads is one of devotion.)   **color** give a plausible appearance to
46 **loneliness** being alone.   47 **too much proved** too often shown to
be true, too often practiced   53 **to . . . helps it** in comparison with the
cosmetic that fashions the cheek's false beauty   54 **painted word**
deceptive utterances.   56.1 *withdraw* (The King and Polonius may
retire behind an arras. The stage directions specify that they "enter"
again near the end of the scene.)

66 **rub** (Literally, an obstacle in the game of bowls.)   68 **shuffled**
sloughed, cast.   **coil** turmoil   69 **respect** consideration   70 **of . . .
life** so long-lived, something we willingly endure for so long. (Also
suggesting that long life is itself a calamity.)   72 **contumely** insolent
abuse   73 **disprized** unvalued   74 **office** officialdom.   **spurns**
insults   75 **of . . . takes** receives from unworthy persons   76 **quietus**
acquittance; here, death   77 **a bare bodkin** a mere dagger,
unsheathed.   **fardels** burdens   80 **bourn** frontier, boundary
85 **native hue** natural color, complexion   86 **cast** tinge, shade of color
87 **pitch** height (as of a falcon's flight).   **moment** importance
88 **regard** respect, consideration.   **currents** courses   89 **Soft you** i.e.,
Wait a minute, gently   90–1 **in . . . remembered** i.e., pray for me, sinner that I am.

Rich gifts wax poor when givers prove unkind.
There, my lord.   [*She gives tokens.*]
HAMLET   Ha, ha! Are you honest?   104
OPHELIA   My lord?
HAMLET   Are you fair?   106
OPHELIA   What means Your Lordship?
HAMLET   That if you be honest and fair, your honesty   108
should admit no discourse to your beauty.   109
OPHELIA   Could beauty, my lord, have better commerce   110
than with honesty?
HAMLET   Ay, truly, for the power of beauty will sooner
transform honesty from what it is to a bawd than the
force of honesty can translate beauty into his likeness.   114
This was sometime a paradox, but now the time gives   115
it proof. I did love you once.   116
OPHELIA   Indeed, my lord, you made me believe so.
HAMLET   You should not have believed me, for virtue   118
cannot so inoculate our old stock but we shall relish of   119
it. I loved you not.   120
OPHELIA   I was the more deceived.
HAMLET   Get thee to a nunnery. Why wouldst thou be a   122
breeder of sinners? I am myself indifferent honest, but   123
yet I could accuse me of such things that it were better
my mother had not borne me: I am very proud,
revengeful, ambitious, with more offenses at my beck   126
than I have thoughts to put them in, imagination to
give them shape, or time to act them in. What should
such fellows as I do crawling between earth and
heaven? We are arrant knaves all; believe none of us.
Go thy ways to a nunnery. Where's your father?
OPHELIA   At home, my lord.
HAMLET   Let the doors be shut upon him, that he may
play the fool nowhere but in 's own house. Farewell.
OPHELIA   Oh, help him, you sweet heavens!
HAMLET   If thou dost marry, I'll give thee this plague for
thy dowry: be thou as chaste as ice, as pure as snow,
thou shalt not escape calumny. Get thee to a nunnery,
farewell. Or, if thou wilt needs marry, marry a fool, for
wise men know well enough what monsters you   140
make of them. To a nunnery, go, and quickly too.
Farewell.
OPHELIA   Heavenly powers, restore him!
HAMLET   I have heard of your paintings too, well   144
enough. God hath given you one face, and you make
yourselves another. You jig, you amble, and you   146
lisp, you nickname God's creatures, and make your   147
wantonness your ignorance. Go to, I'll no more on't;   148

it hath made me mad. I say we will have no more
marriage. Those that are married already—all but
one—shall live. The rest shall keep as they are. To a
nunnery, go.   *Exit.*
OPHELIA
Oh, what a noble mind is here o'erthrown!
The courtier's, soldier's, scholar's, eye, tongue, sword,
Th'expectancy and rose of the fair state,   155
The glass of fashion and the mold of form,   156
Th'observed of all observers, quite, quite down!   157
And I, of ladies most deject and wretched,
That sucked the honey of his music vows,   159
Now see that noble and most sovereign reason
Like sweet bells jangled out of tune and harsh,
That unmatched form and feature of blown youth   162
Blasted with ecstasy. Oh, woe is me,   163
T'have seen what I have seen, see what I see!

Enter King and Polonius.

KING
Love? His affections do not that way tend;   165
Nor what he spake, though it lacked form a little,
Was not like madness. There's something in his soul
O'er which his melancholy sits on brood,   168
And I do doubt the hatch and the disclose   169
Will be some danger; which for to prevent,
I have in quick determination
Thus set it down: he shall with speed to England   172
For the demand of our neglected tribute.
Haply the seas and countries different
With variable objects shall expel   175
This something-settled matter in his heart,   176
Whereon his brains still beating puts him thus   177
From fashion of himself. What think you on't?   178
POLONIUS
It shall do well. But yet do I believe
The origin and commencement of his grief
Sprung from neglected love.—How now, Ophelia?
You need not tell us what Lord Hamlet said;
We heard it all.—My lord, do as you please,
But, if you hold it fit, after the play
Let his queen-mother all alone entreat him
To show his grief. Let her be round with him;   186
And I'll be placed, so please you, in the ear
Of all their conference. If you find him not,   188
To England send him, or confine him where

---

104 **honest** (1) truthful (2) chaste.   106 **fair** (1) beautiful (2) just, honorable.   108 **your honesty** your chastity   109 **discourse to** familiar dealings with   110 **commerce** dealings, intercourse   114 **his** its   115–16 **This . . . proof** This was formerly an unfashionable view, but now the present age confirms how true it is.   118–20 **virtue . . . of it** virtue cannot be grafted onto our sinful condition without our retaining some taste of the old stock.   122 **nunnery** convent. (With an awareness that the word was also used derisively to denote a brothel.)   123 **indifferent honest** reasonably virtuous   126 **beck** command   140 **monsters** (An illusion to the horns of a cuckold.) **you** i.e., you women   144 **paintings** use of cosmetics   146–8 **You jig . . . ignorance** i.e., You prance derisively and speak with affected coyness, you put new labels on God's creatures (by your use of cosmetics), and you excuse your affectations on the grounds of pretended ignorance.   148 **on't** of it

155 **Th'expectancy and rose** the hope and ornament   156 **The glass . . . form** the mirror of true self-fashioning and the pattern of courtly behavior   157 **Th'observed . . . observers** i.e., the center of attention and honor in the court   159 **music** musical, sweetly uttered   162 **blown** blossoming   163 **Blasted with ecstasy** blighted with madness.   165 **affections** emotions, feelings   168 **sits on brood** sits like a bird on a nest, about to *hatch* mischief (line 169)   169 **doubt** suspect, fear.   **disclose** disclosure, hatching   172 **set it down** resolved   175 **variable objects** various sights and surroundings to divert him   176 **This something . . . heart** the strange matter settled in his heart   177 **still** continually   178 **From . . . himself** out of his natural manner.   186 **round** blunt   188 **find him not** fails to discover what is troubling him

Your wisdom best shall think.

KING   It shall be so.
Madness in great ones must not unwatched go.

Exeunt.

❧

[3.2]

Enter Hamlet and three of the Players.

HAMLET   Speak the speech, I pray you, as I pronounced
it to you, trippingly on the tongue. But if you mouth
it, as many of our players do, I had as lief the town crier   3
spoke my lines. Nor do not saw the air too much with
your hand, thus, but use all gently; for in the very
torrent, tempest, and, as I may say, whirlwind of your
passion, you must acquire and beget a temperance
that may give it smoothness. Oh, it offends me to the
soul to hear a robustious periwig-pated fellow tear a   9
passion to tatters, to very rags, to split the ears of the
groundlings, who for the most part are capable of   11
nothing but inexplicable dumb shows and noise. I   12
would have such a fellow whipped for o'erdoing Ter-   13
magant. It out-Herods Herod. Pray you, avoid it.   14

FIRST PLAYER   I warrant Your Honor.

HAMLET   Be not too tame neither, but let your own
discretion be your tutor. Suit the action to the word,
the word to the action, with this special observance,
that you o'erstep not the modesty of nature. For   19
anything so o'erdone is from the purpose of playing,   20
whose end, both at the first and now, was and is to
hold as 'twere the mirror up to nature, to show virtue
her feature, scorn her own image, and the very age   23
and body of the time his form and pressure. Now this   24
overdone or come tardy off, though it makes the   25
unskillful laugh, cannot but make the judicious grieve,   26
the censure of the which one must in your allowance   27
o'erweigh a whole theater of others. Oh, there be players that I have seen play, and heard others praise, and
that highly, not to speak it profanely, that, neither   30
having th'accent of Christians nor the gait of Chris-   31
tian, pagan, nor man, have so strutted and bellowed   32
that I have thought some of nature's journeymen had   33

made men and not made them well, they imitated
humanity so abominably.   35

FIRST PLAYER   I hope we have reformed that indifferently   36
with us, sir.

HAMLET   Oh, reform it altogether. And let those that play
your clowns speak no more than is set down for them;
for there be of them that will themselves laugh, to set   40
on some quantity of barren spectators to laugh too,   41
though in the meantime some necessary question of
the play be then to be considered. That's villainous,
and shows a most pitiful ambition in the fool that uses
it. Go make you ready.   [*Exeunt Players.*]

Enter Polonius, Guildenstern, and Rosencrantz.

How now, my lord, will the King hear this piece of
work?

POLONIUS   And the Queen too, and that presently.   48

HAMLET   Bid the players make haste.   [*Exit Polonius.*]
Will you two help to hasten them?

ROSENCRANTZ
Ay, my lord.   *Exeunt they two.*

HAMLET   What ho, Horatio!

Enter Horatio.

HORATIO   Here, sweet lord, at your service.

HAMLET
Horatio, thou art e'en as just a man
As e'er my conversation coped withal.   54

HORATIO
Oh, my dear lord—

HAMLET   Nay, do not think I flatter,
For what advancement may I hope from thee
That no revenue hast but thy good spirits
To feed and clothe thee? Why should the poor be
    flattered?
No, let the candied tongue lick absurd pomp,   59
And crook the pregnant hinges of the knee   60
Where thrift may follow fawning. Dost thou hear?   61
Since my dear soul was mistress of her choice
And could of men distinguish her election,   63
Sh' hath sealed thee for herself, for thou hast been   64
As one, in suffering all, that suffers nothing,
A man that Fortune's buffets and rewards
Hast ta'en with equal thanks; and blest are those
Whose blood and judgment are so well commeddled   68
That they are not a pipe for Fortune's finger
To sound what stop she please. Give me that man   70
That is not passion's slave, and I will wear him
In my heart's core, ay, in my heart of heart,
As I do thee.—Something too much of this.—
There is a play tonight before the King.
One scene of it comes near the circumstance
Which I have told thee of my father's death.

3.2 **Location:** The castle.
3 **our players** players nowadays.   **I had as lief** I would just as soon
9 **robustious** violent, boisterous.   **periwig-pated** wearing a wig
11 **groundlings** spectators who paid least and stood in the yard of the
theater.   **capable of** able to understand   12 **dumb shows and noise**
noisy spectacle (rather than thoughtful drama)   13–14 **Termagant** a
supposed deity of the Mohammedans, not found in any English
medieval play but elsewhere portrayed as violent and blustering
14 **Herod** Herod of Jewry. (A character in *The Slaughter of the Innocents*
and other cycle plays. The part was played with great noise and fury.)
19 **modesty** restraint, moderation   20 **from** contrary to   23 **scorn** i.e.,
something foolish and deserving of scorn   23–4 **and the . . . pressure**
and the present state of affairs its likeness as seen in an impression,
such as wax.   25 **come tardy off** falling short   25–6 **the unskillful**
those lacking in judgment   27 **the censure . . . one** the judgment of
even one of whom.   **your allowance** your scale of values   30 **not . . .
profanely** (Hamlet anticipates his idea in lines 33–4 that some men
were not made by God at all.)   31-2 **Christians** i.e., ordinary decent
folk   32 **nor man** i.e., nor any human being at all   33 **journeymen**
common workmen

35 **abominably** (Shakespeare's usual spelling, "abhominably," suggests a literal though etymologically incorrect meaning, "removed
from human nature.")   36 **indifferently** tolerably   40 **of them** some
among them   41 **barren** i.e., of wit   48 **presently** at once.   54 **my . . .
withal** my dealings encountered.   59 **candied** sugared, flattering
60 **pregnant** compliant   61 **thrift** profit   63 **could . . . election** could
make distinguishing choices among persons   64 **sealed thee** (Literally, as one would seal a legal document to mark possession.)
68 **blood** passion.   **commeddled** commingled   70 **stop** hole in a
wind instrument for controlling the sound

I prithee, when thou see'st that act afoot,
Even with the very comment of thy soul   78
Observe my uncle. If his occulted guilt   79
Do not itself unkennel in one speech,   80
It is a damnèd ghost that we have seen,
And my imaginations are as foul
As Vulcan's stithy. Give him heedful note,   83
For I mine eyes will rivet to his face,
And after we will both our judgments join
In censure of his seeming.
HORATIO   Well, my lord.   86
If 'a steal aught the whilst this play is playing 87
And scape detecting, I will pay the theft.

[*Flourish.*] *Enter trumpets and kettledrums, King,*
Queen, Polonius, Ophelia, [Rosencrantz,
Guildenstern, and other lords, with guards
carrying torches].

HAMLET   They are coming to the play. I must be idle. 89
Get you a place.   [*The King, Queen, and courtiers sit.*]
KING   How fares our cousin Hamlet?   91
HAMLET   Excellent, i'faith, of the chameleon's dish: I eat 92
the air, promise-crammed. You cannot feed capons so. 93
KING   I have nothing with this answer, Hamlet. These 94
words are not mine.   95
HAMLET   No, nor mine now. [*To Polonius*] My lord, you 96
played once i'th'university, you say?
POLONIUS   That did I, my lord, and was accounted a
good actor.
HAMLET   What did you enact?
POLONIUS   I did enact Julius Caesar. I was killed i'th' 101
Capitol; Brutus killed me.   102
HAMLET   It was a brute part of him to kill so capital a 103
calf there.—Be the players ready?   104
ROSENCRANTZ   Ay, my lord. They stay upon your 105
patience.
QUEEN   Come hither, my dear Hamlet, sit by me.
HAMLET   No, good mother, here's metal more attractive. 108
POLONIUS [*to the King*]   Oho, do you mark that?
HAMLET   Lady, shall I lie in your lap?   110
[*Lying down at Ophelia's feet.*]

OPHELIA   No, my lord.
HAMLET   I mean, my head upon your lap?
OPHELIA   Ay, my lord.
HAMLET   Do you think I meant country matters? 114
OPHELIA   I think nothing, my lord.
HAMLET   That's a fair thought to lie between maids'
legs.
OPHELIA   What is, my lord?
HAMLET   Nothing.   119
OPHELIA   You are merry, my lord.
HAMLET   Who, I?
OPHELIA   Ay, my lord.
HAMLET   Oh, God, your only jig maker. What should a 123
man do but be merry? For look you how cheerfully my
mother looks, and my father died within 's two hours. 125
OPHELIA   Nay, 'tis twice two months, my lord.
HAMLET   So long? Nay then, let the devil wear black, for
I'll have a suit of sables. O heavens! Die two months 128
ago, and not forgotten yet? Then there's hope a great
man's memory may outlive his life half a year. But, by'r
Lady, 'a must build churches, then, or else shall 'a
suffer not thinking on, with the hobbyhorse, whose 132
epitaph is "For oh, for oh, the hobbyhorse is forgot." 133

The trumpets sound. Dumb show follows.

Enter a King and a Queen [very lovingly]; the
Queen embracing him, and he her. [She kneels,
and makes show of protestation unto him.] He
takes her up, and declines his head upon her neck.
He lies him down upon a bank of flowers. She,
seeing him asleep, leaves him. Anon comes in
another man, takes off his crown, kisses it, pours
poison in the sleeper's ears, and leaves him. The
Queen returns, finds the King dead, makes
passionate action. The Poisoner with some three or
four come in again, seem to condole with her. The
dead body is carried away. The Poisoner woos the
Queen with gifts; she seems harsh awhile, but in
the end accepts love.

[*Exeunt players.*]

OPHELIA   What means this, my lord?
HAMLET   Marry, this' miching mallico; it means mis- 135
chief.

---

78 very . . . soul your most penetrating observation and consideration **79 occulted** hidden **80 unkennel** (As one would say of a fox driven from its lair.) **83 Vulcan's stithy** the smithy, the place of stiths (anvils) of the Roman god of fire and metalworking. **86 censure of his seeming** judgment of his appearance or behavior. **87 If 'a steal aught** If he gets away with anything **89 idle** (1) unoccupied (2) mad. **91 cousin** i.e., close relative **92 chameleon's dish** (Chameleons were supposed to feed on air. Hamlet deliberately misinterprets the King's *fares* as "feeds." By his phrase *eat the air* he also plays on the idea of feeding himself with the promise of succession, of being the *heir.*) **93 capons** roosters castrated and *crammed* with feed to make them succulent **94 have . . . with** make nothing of, or gain nothing from **95 are not mine** do not respond to what I asked. **96 nor mine now** (Once spoken, words are proverbially no longer the speaker's own—and hence should be uttered warily.) **101–2 i'th' Capitol** (where Caesar was assassinated, according to *Julius Caesar*, 3.1, but see 1.3.126n in that play) **103 brute** (The Latin meaning of *brutus*, "stupid," was often used punningly with the name Brutus.) **part** (1) deed (2) role **104 calf** fool **105 stay upon** await **108 metal** substance that is *attractive*, i.e., magnetic, but with suggestion also of *mettle*, "disposition" **110 Lady . . . lap?** Onstage, Hamlet often lies at Ophelia's feet, but he could instead offer to do this and continue to stand.

114 country matters sexual intercourse. (With a bawdy pun on the first syllable of *country*.) **119 Nothing** The figure zero or naught, suggesting the female sexual anatomy. (*Thing* not infrequently has a bawdy connotation of male or female anatomy, and the reference here could be male.) **123 only jig maker** very best composer of jigs, i.e., pointless merriment. (Hamlet replies sardonically to Ophelia's observation that he is merry by saying, "If you're looking for someone who is really merry, you've come to the right person.") **125 within 's** within this (i.e., these) **128 suit of sables** garments trimmed with the dark fur of the sable and hence suited for a person in mourning. **132 suffer . . . on** undergo oblivion **133 "For . . . forgot"** (Verse of a song occurring also in *Love's Labor's Lost*, 3.1.27–8. The hobbyhorse was a character made up to resemble a horse and rider, appearing in the morris dance and such May-game sports. This song laments the disappearance of such customs under pressure from the Puritans.) **133.12 condole with** offer sympathy to **135 this' miching mallico** this is sneaking mischief

OPHELIA   Belike this show imports the argument of the 137
play.

Enter Prologue.

HAMLET   We shall know by this fellow. The players cannot keep counsel; they'll tell all.   140

OPHELIA   Will 'a tell us what this show meant?

HAMLET   Ay, or any show that you will show him. Be 142
not you ashamed to show, he'll not shame to tell you 143
what it means.

OPHELIA   You are naught, you are naught. I'll mark the 145
play.

PROLOGUE   For us, and for our tragedy,
Here stooping to your clemency,
We beg your hearing patiently.   [*Exit.*]   148

HAMLET   Is this a prologue, or the posy of a ring?   150

OPHELIA   'Tis brief, my lord.

HAMLET   As woman's love.

Enter [two Players as] King and Queen.

PLAYER KING
Full thirty times hath Phoebus' cart gone round   153
Neptune's salt wash and Tellus' orbèd ground,   154
And thirty dozen moons with borrowed sheen   155
About the world have times twelve thirties been,
Since love our hearts and Hymen did our hands   157
Unite commutual in most sacred bands.   158

PLAYER QUEEN
So many journeys may the sun and moon
Make us again count o'er ere love be done!
But, woe is me, you are so sick of late,
So far from cheer and from your former state,
That I distrust you. Yet, though I distrust,   163
Discomfort you, my lord, it nothing must.   164
For women's fear and love hold quantity;   165
In neither aught, or in extremity.   166
Now, what my love is, proof hath made you know,   167
And as my love is sized, my fear is so.
Where love is great, the littlest doubts are fear;   169
Where little fears grow great, great love grows there.

PLAYER KING
Faith, I must leave thee, love, and shortly too;
My operant powers their functions leave to do.   172
And thou shalt live in this fair world behind,   173
Honored, beloved; and haply one as kind
For husband shalt thou—

PLAYER QUEEN   Oh, confound the rest!

Such love must needs be treason in my breast.
In second husband let me be accurst!
None wed the second but who killed the first.   178

HAMLET   Wormwood, wormwood.   179

PLAYER QUEEN
The instances that second marriage move   180
Are base respects of thrift, but none of love.   181
A second time I kill my husband dead
When second husband kisses me in bed.

PLAYER KING
I do believe you think what now you speak,
But what we do determine oft we break.
Purpose is but the slave to memory,   186
Of violent birth, but poor validity,   187
Which now, like fruit unripe, sticks on the tree,   188
But fall unshaken when they mellow be.
Most necessary 'tis that we forget   190
To pay ourselves what to ourselves is debt.   191
What to ourselves in passion we propose,
The passion ending, doth the purpose lose.
The violence of either grief or joy
Their own enactures with themselves destroy.   195
Where joy most revels, grief doth most lament;   196
Grief joys, joy grieves, on slender accident.   197
This world is not for aye, nor 'tis not strange   198
That even our loves should with our fortunes change;
For 'tis a question left us yet to prove,
Whether love lead fortune, or else fortune love.
The great man down, you mark his favorite flies;   202
The poor advanced makes friends of enemies.   203
And hitherto doth love on fortune tend;   204
For who not needs shall never lack a friend,   205
And who in want a hollow friend doth try   206
Directly seasons him his enemy.   207
But, orderly to end where I begun,
Our wills and fates do so contrary run   209
That our devices still are overthrown;   210
Our thoughts are ours, their ends none of our own.   211
So think thou wilt no second husband wed,
But die thy thoughts when thy first lord is dead.

PLAYER QUEEN
Nor earth to me give food, nor heaven light,   214
Sport and repose lock from me day and night,   215

137 **Belike** Probably.   **argument** plot   140 **counsel** secret   142–3 **Be not you** Provided you are not   145 **naught** indecent. (Ophelia is reacting to Hamlet's pointed remarks about not being ashamed to show all.)   148 **stooping** bowing   150 **posy . . . ring** brief motto in verse inscribed in a ring.   153 **Phoebus' cart** the sun-god's chariot, making its yearly cycle   154 **salt** wash the sea.   **Tellus** goddess of the earth, of the *orbèd* ground   155 **borrowed** i.e., reflected   157 **Hymen** god of matrimony   158 **commutual** mutually.   **bands** bonds.   163 **distrust** am anxious about   164 **Discomfort . . . must it** must not distress you at all.   165 **hold quantity** keep proportion with one another   166 **In . . . extremity** (women feel) either no anxiety if they do not love or extreme anxiety if they do love.   167 **proof** experience   169 **the littlest** even the littlest   172 **My . . . to do** my vital functions are shutting down.   173 **behind** after I have gone

178 **None** (1) Let no woman; or (2) No woman does.   **but who** except the one who   179 **Wormwood** i.e., How bitter. (Literally, a bitter-tasting plant.)   180 **instances** motives.   **move** motivate   181 **base . . . thrift** ignoble considerations of material prosperity   186 **Purpose . . . memory** Our good intentions are subject to forgetfulness   187 **validity** strength, durability   188 **Which** i.e., purpose   190–1 **Most . . . debt** It's inevitable that in time we forget the obligations we have imposed on ourselves.   195 **enactures** fulfillments   196–7 **Where . . . accident** The capacity for extreme joy and grief go together, and often one extreme is instantly changed into its opposite on the slightest provocation.   198 **aye** ever   202 **down** fallen in fortune   203 **The poor . . . enemies** when one of humble station is promoted, you see his enemies suddenly becoming his friends.   204 **hitherto** up to this point in the argument, or, to this extent.   **tend** attend   205 **who not needs** he who is not in need (of wealth)   206 **who in want** he who, being in need.   **try** test (his generosity)   207 **seasons him** ripens him into   209 **Our . . . run** what we want and what we get go so contrarily   210 **devices** intentions.   **still** continually   211 **ends** results   214 **Nor** Let neither   215 **Sport . . . night** may day deny me its pastimes and night its repose

To desperation turn my trust and hope,
An anchor's cheer in prison be my scope!   217
Each opposite that blanks the face of joy   218
Meet what I would have well and it destroy!   219
Both here and hence pursue me lasting strife   220
If, once a widow, ever I be wife!

HAMLET   If she should break it now!

PLAYER KING
'Tis deeply sworn. Sweet, leave me here awhile;
My spirits grow dull, and fain I would beguile   224
The tedious day with sleep.

PLAYER QUEEN   Sleep rock thy brain,
And never come mischance between us twain!
                 [*He sleeps.*] *Exit* [*Player Queen*].

HAMLET   Madam, how like you this play?

QUEEN   The lady doth protest too much, methinks.   228

HAMLET   Oh, but she'll keep her word.

KING   Have you heard the argument? Is there no   230
offense in't?

HAMLET   No, no, they do but jest, poison in jest. No of-   232
fense i'th' world.   233

KING   What do you call the play?

HAMLET   *The Mousetrap.* Marry, how? Tropically.   235
This play is the image of a murder done in Vienna.
Gonzago is the Duke's name, his wife, Baptista. You   237
shall see anon. 'Tis a knavish piece of work, but what
of that? Your Majesty, and we that have free souls, it   239
touches us not. Let the galled jade wince, our withers   240
are unwrung.   241

            Enter Lucianus.

This is one Lucianus, nephew to the King.

OPHELIA   You are as good as a chorus, my lord.   243

HAMLET   I could interpret between you and your love,   244
if I could see the puppets dallying   245

OPHELIA   You are keen, my lord, you are keen.   246

HAMLET   It would cost you a groaning to take off mine
edge.

OPHELIA   Still better, and worse   249

HAMLET   So you mis-take your husbands.—Begin, mur-   250
derer; leave thy damnable faces and begin. Come, the
croaking raven doth bellow for revenge.

LUCIANUS
Thoughts black, hands apt, drugs fit, and time
     agreeing,
Confederate season, else no creature seeing,   254
Thou mixture rank, of midnight weeds collected,
With Hecate's ban thrice blasted, thrice infected,   256
Thy natural magic and dire property   257
On wholesome life usurp immediately.
       [*He pours the poison into the sleeper's ear.*]

HAMLET   'A poisons him i'th' garden for his estate. His   259
name's Gonzago. The story is extant, and written in
very choice Italian. You shall see anon how the
murderer gets the love of Gonzago's wife.
                    [*Claudius rises.*]

OPHELIA   The King rises.

HAMLET   What, frighted with false fire?   264

QUEEN   How fares my lord?

POLONIUS   Give o'er the play.

KING   Give me some light. Away!

POLONIUS   Lights, lights, lights!
           Exeunt all but Hamlet and Horatio.

HAMLET
"Why, let the strucken deer go weep,   269
     The hart ungallèd play.   270
For some must watch, while some must sleep;   271
     Thus runs the world away."   272
Would not this, sir, and a forest of feathers—if the   273
rest of my fortunes turn Turk with me—with two   274
Provincial roses on my razed shoes, get me a fellow-   275
ship in a cry of players?   276

HORATIO   Half a share.

HAMLET   A whole one, I.
"For thou dost know, O Damon dear,   279
     This realm dismantled was   280
Of Jove himself, and now reigns here   281
     A very, very—pajock."   282

---

217 anchor's cheer anchorite's or hermit's fare. **my scope** the extent of my happiness. **218–19 Each . . . destroy!** May every adverse thing that causes the face of joy to turn pale meet and destroy everything that I desire to see prosper! **220 hence** in the life hereafter **224 spirits** vital spirits **228 doth . . . much** makes too many promises and protestations **230 argument** plot. **232 jest** make believe. **232–3 offense** crime, injury. (Hamlet playfully alters the King's use of the word in line 231 to mean "cause for objection.") **235 Tropically** Figuratively. (The First Quarto reading, "trapically," suggests a pun on *trap* in *Mousetrap*.) **237 Duke's** i.e., King's. (An inconsistency that may be due to Shakespeare's possible acquaintance with a historical incident, the alleged murder of the Duke of Urbino by Luigi Gonzaga in 1538.) **239 free** guiltless **240 galled jade** horse whose hide is rubbed by saddle or harness. **withers** the part between the horse's shoulder blades **241 unwrung** not rubbed sore. **243 chorus** (In many Elizabethan plays, the forthcoming action was explained by an actor known as the "chorus"; at a puppet show, the actor who spoke the dialogue was known as an "interpreter," as indicated by the lines following.) **244 interpret** (1) ventriloquize the dialogue, as in puppet show (2) act as pander **245 puppets dallying** (With suggestion of sexual play, continued in *keen*, "sexually aroused," *groaning*, "moaning in pregnancy," and *edge*, "sexual desire" or "impetuosity.") **246 keen** sharp, bitter **249 Still . . . worse** More keen, always *bettering* what other people say with witty wordplay, but at the same time more offensive.

250 So Even thus (in marriage). **mis-take** take falseheartedly and cheat on. (The marriage vows say "for better, for worse.") **254 Confederate . . . seeing** the time and occasion conspiring (to assist me), and also no one seeing me **256 Hecate's ban** the curse of Hecate, the goddess of witchcraft **257 dire property** baleful quality **259 estate** i.e., the kingship. **His** i.e., the King's **264 false fire** the blank discharge of a gun loaded with powder but no shot. **269–72 Why . . . away** (Perhaps from an old ballad, with allusion to the popular belief that a wounded deer retires to weep and die; compare with *As You Like It*, 2.1.33–66.) **270 ungallèd** unafflicted **271 watch** remain awake **272 Thus . . . away** Thus the world goes. **273 this** i.e., this success with the play I have just presented. **feathers** (Allusion to the plumes that Elizabethan actors were fond of wearing.) **274 turn Turk with** turn renegade against, go back on **275 Provincial roses** rosettes of ribbon, named for roses grown in a part of France. **razed** with ornamental slashing **275–6 fellowship . . . players** partnership in a theatrical company. **276 cry** pack (of hounds, etc.) **279 Damon** the friend of Pythias, as Horatio is friend of Hamlet; or, a traditional pastoral name **280–2 This realm . . . pajock** i.e., Jove, representing divine authority and justice, has abandoned this realm to its own devices, leaving in his stead only a peacock or vain pretender to virtue (though the rhyme-word expected in place of *pajock* or "peacock" suggests that the realm is now ruled over by an "ass"). **280 dismantled** stripped, divested

HORATIO   You might have rhymed.

HAMLET   Oh, good Horatio, I'll take the ghost's word for a thousand pound. Didst perceive?

HORATIO   Very well, my lord.

HAMLET   Upon the talk of the poisoning?

HORATIO   I did very well note him.

Enter Rosencrantz and Guildenstern.

HAMLET   Aha! Come, some music! Come, the recorders.
"For if the King like not the comedy,
Why then, belike, he likes it not, perdy."   292
Come, some music.

GUILDENSTERN   Good my lord, vouchsafe me a word with you.

HAMLET   Sir, a whole history.

GUILDENSTERN   The King, sir—

HAMLET   Ay, sir, what of him?

GUILDENSTERN   Is in his retirement marvelous distempered.   299 / 300

HAMLET   With drink, sir?

GUILDENSTERN   No, my lord, with choler.   302

HAMLET   Your wisdom should show itself more richer to signify this to the doctor, for for me to put him to his purgation would perhaps plunge him into more choler.   305

GUILDENSTERN   Good my lord, put your discourse into some frame and start not so wildly from my affair.   308

HAMLET   I am tame, sir. Pronounce.

GUILDENSTERN   The Queen, your mother, in most great affliction of spirit, hath sent me to you.

HAMLET   You are welcome.

GUILDENSTERN   Nay, good my lord, this courtesy is not of the right breed. If it shall please you to make me a wholesome answer, I will do your mother's commandment; if not, your pardon and my return shall be the end of my business.   314 / 316

HAMLET   Sir, I cannot.

ROSENCRANTZ   What, my lord?

HAMLET   Make you a wholesome answer; my wit's diseased. But, sir, such answer as I can make, you shall command, or rather, as you say, my mother. Therefore no more, but to the matter. My mother, you say—

ROSENCRANTZ   Then thus she says: your behavior hath struck her into amazement and admiration.   325

HAMLET   Oh, wonderful son, that can so 'stonish a mother! But is there no sequel at the heels of this mother's admiration? Impart.

ROSENCRANTZ   She desires to speak with you in her closet ere you go to bed.   330

HAMLET   We shall obey, were she ten times our mother. Have you any further trade with us?

ROSENCRANTZ   My lord, you once did love me.

HAMLET   And do still, by these pickers and stealers.   334

ROSENCRANTZ   Good my lord, what is your cause of distemper? You do surely bar the door upon your own liberty if you deny your griefs to your friend.   337

HAMLET   Sir, I lack advancement.

ROSENCRANTZ   How can that be, when you have the voice of the King himself for your succession in Denmark?

HAMLET   Ay, sir, but "While the grass grows"—the proverb is something musty.   342 / 343

Enter the Players with recorders.

Oh, the recorders. Let me see one. [*He takes a recorder.*] To withdraw with you: why do you go about to recover the wind of me, as if you would drive me into a toil?   345 / 346

GUILDENSTERN   Oh, my lord, if my duty be too bold, my love is too unmannerly.   347 / 348

HAMLET   I do not well understand that. Will you play upon this pipe?   349

GUILDENSTERN   My lord, I cannot.

HAMLET   I pray you.

GUILDENSTERN   Believe me, I cannot.

HAMLET   I do beseech you.

GUILDENSTERN   I know no touch of it, my lord.

HAMLET   It is as easy as lying. Govern these ventages with your fingers and thumb, give it breath with your mouth, and it will discourse most eloquent music. Look you, these are the stops.   356

GUILDENSTERN   But these cannot I command to any utterance of harmony. I have not the skill.

HAMLET   Why, look you now, how unworthy a thing you make of me! You would play upon me, you would seem to know my stops, you would pluck out the heart of my mystery, you would sound me from my lowest note to the top of my compass, and there is much music, excellent voice, in this little organ, yet cannot you make it speak. 'Sblood, do you think I am easier to be played on than a pipe? Call me what instrument you will, though you can fret me, you cannot play upon me.   365 / 366 / 367 / 370

Enter Polonius.

God bless you, sir!

---

292 perdy (A corruption of the French *par dieu*, "by God.") **299 retirement** withdrawal to his chambers **299–300 distempered** out of humor. (But Hamlet deliberately plays on the wider application to any illness of mind or body, as in lines 335–6, especially to drunkenness.) **302 choler** anger. (But Hamlet takes the word in its more basic humoral sense of "bilious disorder.") **305 purgation** (Hamlet hints at something going beyond medical treatment to bloodletting and the extraction of confession.) **308 frame** order. **start** shy or jump away (like a horse; the opposite of *tame* in line 309) **314 breed** (1) kind (2) breeding, manners. **316 pardon** permission to depart **325 admiration** bewilderment. **330 closet** private chamber

334 pickers and stealers i.e., hands. (So called from the catechism, "to keep my hands from picking and stealing.") **337 liberty** i.e., being freed from *distemper*, line 336; but perhaps with a veiled threat as well. **deny** refuse to share **342 "While . . . grows"** (The rest of the proverb is "the silly horse starves"; Hamlet implies that his hopes of succession are distant in time at best.) **343 something** somewhat **343.1 Players** actors **345 withdraw** speak privately **345–6 recover the wind** get to the windward side (thus allowing the game to scent the hunter and thereby be driven in the opposite direction into the *toil* or net) **346 toil** snare. **347–8 if . . . unmannerly** if I am using an unmannerly boldness, it is my love that occasions it. **349 I . . . that** i.e., I don't understand how genuine love can be unmannerly. **356 ventages** finger-holes or *stops* (line 359) of the recorder **365 sound** (1) fathom (2) produce sound in **366 compass** range (of voice) **367 organ** musical instrument **370 fret** irritate. (With a quibble on the *frets* or ridges on the fingerboard of some stringed instruments to regulate the fingering.)

POLONIUS   My lord, the Queen would speak with you,
and presently.   374

HAMLET   Do you see yonder cloud that's almost in
shape of a camel?

POLONIUS   By th' Mass and 'tis, like a camel indeed.

HAMLET   Methinks it is like a weasel.

POLONIUS   It is backed like a weasel.

HAMLET   Or like a whale.

POLONIUS   Very like a whale.

HAMLET   Then I will come to my mother by and by.
[*Aside*] They fool me to the top of my bent.—I will   383
come by and by.

POLONIUS   I will say so.   [*Exit.*]

HAMLET   "By and by" is easily said. Leave me, friends.
                          [*Exeunt all but Hamlet.*]

'Tis now the very witching time of night,   387
When churchyards yawn and hell itself breathes out
Contagion to this world. Now could I drink hot
   blood
And do such bitter business as the day
Would quake to look on. Soft, now to my mother.
O heart, lose not thy nature! Let not ever   392
The soul of Nero enter this firm bosom.   393
Let me be cruel, not unnatural;
I will speak daggers to her, but use none.
My tongue and soul in this be hypocrites:
How in my words somever she be shent,   397
To give them seals never my soul consent!   *Exit.* 398

                ❖

[3.3]

Enter King, Rosencrantz, and Guildenstern.

KING

I like him not, nor stands it safe with us   1
To let his madness range. Therefore prepare you.
I your commission will forthwith dispatch,   3
And he to England shall along with you.
The terms of our estate may not endure   5
Hazard so near 's as doth hourly grow
Out of his brows.

GUILDENSTERN   We will ourselves provide.   7
Most holy and religious fear it is   8
To keep those many many bodies safe
That live and feed upon Your Majesty.

ROSENCRANTZ

The single and peculiar life is bound   11

With all the strength and armor of the mind
To keep itself from noyance, but much more   13
That spirit upon whose weal depends and rests   14
The lives of many. The cess of majesty   15
Dies not alone, but like a gulf doth draw   16
What's near it with it; or it is a massy wheel   17
Fixed on the summit of the highest mount,
To whose huge spokes ten thousand lesser things
Are mortised and adjoined, which, when it falls,   20
Each small annexment, petty consequence,   21
Attends the boist'rous ruin. Never alone   22
Did the King sigh, but with a general groan.

KING

Arm you, I pray you, to this speedy voyage,   24
For we will fetters put about this fear,
Which now goes too free-footed.

ROSENCRANTZ   We will haste us.

Exeunt gentlemen [Rosencrantz and Guildenstern].

Enter Polonius.

POLONIUS

My lord, he's going to his mother's closet.
Behind the arras I'll convey myself   28
To hear the process. I'll warrant she'll tax him home,   29
And, as you said—and wisely was it said—
'Tis meet that some more audience than a mother,   31
Since nature makes them partial, should o'erhear
The speech of vantage. Fare you well, my liege.   33
I'll call upon you ere you go to bed
And tell you what I know.

KING   Thanks, dear my lord.
                         Exit [Polonius].
Oh, my offense is rank! It smells to heaven.
It hath the primal eldest curse upon't,   37
A brother's murder. Pray can I not,
Though inclination be as sharp as will;   39
My stronger guilt defeats my strong intent,
And like a man to double business bound   41
I stand in pause where I shall first begin,
And both neglect. What if this cursèd hand
Were thicker than itself with brother's blood,
Is there not rain enough in the sweet heavens
To wash it white as snow? Whereto serves mercy   46
But to confront the visage of offense?   47
And what's in prayer but this twofold force,

---

13 noyance harm   **14 weal** well-being   **15 cess** decease, cessation   **16 gulf** whirlpool   **17 massy** massive   **20 mortised** fastened (as with a fitted joint).   **when it falls** i.e., when it descends, like the wheel of Fortune, bringing a king down with it   **21 Each . . . consequence** i.e., every hanger-on and unimportant person or thing connected with the King   **22 Attends** participates in   **24 Arm** Provide, prepare   **28 arras** screen of tapestry placed around the walls of household apartments. (On the Elizabethan stage, the arras was presumably over a door or aperture in the tiring-house facade.)   **29 process** proceedings.   **tax him home** reprove him severely   **31 meet** fitting   **33 of vantage** from an advantageous place, or, in addition.   **37 the primal eldest curse** the curse of Cain, the first murderer; he killed his brother Abel   **39 Though . . . will** though my desire is as strong as my determination   **41 bound** (1) destined (2) obliged. (The King wants to repent and still enjoy what he has gained.)   **46–7 Whereto . . . offense?** What function does mercy serve other than to meet sin face to face?

---

374 presently at once.   **383 They fool . . . bent** They humor my odd behavior to the limit of my ability or endurance. (Literally, the extent to which a bow may be bent.)   **387 witching time** time when spells are cast and evil is abroad   **392 nature** natural feeling.   **393 Nero** (This infamous Roman emperor put to death his mother, Agrippina, who had murdered her husband, Claudius.)   **397–8 How . . . consent!** however much she is to be rebuked by my words, may my soul never consent to ratify those words with deeds of violence!
3.3. Location: The castle.
1 him i.e., his behavior   **3 dispatch** prepare, cause to be drawn up   **5 terms of our estate** circumstances of my royal position   **7 Out . . . brows** i.e., from his brain, in the form of plots and threats.   **We . . . provide** We'll put ourselves in readiness.   **8 religious fear** sacred concern   **11 single and peculiar** individual and private

To be forestallèd ere we come to fall,   49
Or pardoned being down? Then I'll look up.
My fault is past. But oh, what form of prayer
Can serve my turn? "Forgive me my foul murder"?
That cannot be, since I am still possessed
Of those effects for which I did the murder:
My crown, mine own ambition, and my queen.
May one be pardoned and retain th'offense?   56
In the corrupted currents of this world   57
Offense's gilded hand may shove by justice,   58
And oft 'tis seen the wicked prize itself   59
Buys out the law. But 'tis not so above.
There is no shuffling, there the action lies   61
In his true nature, and we ourselves compelled,   62
Even to the teeth and forehead of our faults,   63
To give in evidence. What then? What rests?   64
Try what repentance can. What can it not?
Yet what can it, when one cannot repent?
O wretched state, O bosom black as death,
O limèd soul that, struggling to be free,   68
Art more engaged! Help, angels! Make assay.   69
Bow, stubborn knees, and heart with strings of steel,
Be soft as sinews of the newborn babe!
All may be well.   *[He kneels.]*

   Enter Hamlet.

HAMLET
Now might I do it pat, now 'a is a-praying;
And now I'll do't. *[He draws his sword.]* And so 'a goes   73
  to heaven,
And so am I revenged. That would be scanned: 75
A villain kills my father, and for that,
I, his sole son, do this same villain send
To heaven.
Why, this is hire and salary, not revenge.
'A took my father grossly, full of bread,   80
With all his crimes broad blown, as flush as May;   81
And how his audit stands who knows save heaven?   82
But in our circumstance and course of thought   83
'Tis heavy with him. And am I then revenged,
To take him in the purging of his soul,
When he is fit and seasoned for his passage?   86
No!
Up, sword, and know thou a more horrid hent.   88
                    [He puts up his sword.]

When he is drunk asleep, or in his rage,   89
Or in th'incestuous pleasure of his bed,
At game, a-swearing, or about some act   91
That has no relish of salvation in't—   92
Then trip him, that his heels may kick at heaven,
And that his soul may be as damned and black
As hell, whereto it goes. My mother stays.   95
This physic but prolongs thy sickly days.   *Exit.*   96
KING
My words fly up, my thoughts remain below.
Words without thoughts never to heaven go.   *Exit.*

                        ❖

[3.4]

   Enter [Queen] Gertrude and Polonius.

POLONIUS
'A will come straight. Look you lay home to him.   1
Tell him his pranks have been too broad to bear with,   2
And that Your Grace hath screened and stood
  between
Much heat and him. I'll silence me even here.   4
Pray you, be round with him.   5
HAMLET *(within)* Mother, mother, mother!
QUEEN I'll warrant you, fear me not.
Withdraw, I hear him coming.
       [Polonius hides behind the arras.]

   Enter Hamlet.

HAMLET Now, mother, what's the matter?
QUEEN
Hamlet, thou hast thy father much offended.   10
HAMLET
Mother, you have my father much offended.
QUEEN
Come, come, you answer with an idle tongue.   12
HAMLET
Go, go, you question with a wicked tongue.
QUEEN
Why, how now, Hamlet?
HAMLET   What's the matter now?
QUEEN
Have you forgot me?
HAMLET   No, by the rood, not so: 15
You are the Queen, your husband's brother's wife,
And—would it were not so!—you are my mother.
QUEEN
Nay, then, I'll set those to you that can speak.   18

49 **forestallèd** prevented (from sinning) 56 **th'offense** the thing for which one offended 57 **currents** courses of events 58 **gilded hand** hand offering gold as a bribe. **shove by** thrust aside 59 **wicked prize** prize won by wickedness 61 **There . . . lies** There in heaven can be no evasion, there the deed lies exposed to view 62 **his** its 63 **to the teeth and forehead** face to face, concealing nothing 64 **give in** provide. **rests** remains. 68 **limèd** caught as with birdlime, a sticky substance used to ensnare birds 69 **engaged** entangled. **assay** trial. (Said to himself, or to the angels to try him.) 73 **pat** opportunely 75 **would be scanned** needs to be looked into, or, would be interpreted as follows 80 **grossly, full of bread** i.e., enjoying his worldly pleasures rather than fasting. (See Ezekiel 16:49.) 81 **crimes broad blown** sins in full bloom. **flush** vigorous 82 **audit** account. **save** except for 83 **in . . . thought** as we see it from our mortal perspective 86 **seasoned** matured, readied 88 **know . . . hent** await to be grasped by me on a more horrid occasion. (*Hent* means "act of seizing.")

89 **drunk . . . rage** dead drunk, or in a fit of sexual passion 91 **game** gambling 92 **relish** trace, savor 95 **stays** awaits (me). 96 **physic** purging (by prayer), or, Hamlet's postponement of the killing **3.4. Location: The Queen's private chamber.**
1 **lay home** reprove him soundly 2 **broad** unrestrained 4 **Much heat** i.e., the King's anger. **I'll silence me** I'll quietly conceal myself. (Ironic, since it is his crying out at line 24 that leads to his death. Some editors emend *silence* to "sconce." The First Quarto's reading, "shroud," is attractive.) 5 **round** blunt 10 **thy father** i.e., your step-father, Claudius 12 **idle** foolish 15 **forgot me** i.e., forgotten that I am your mother. **rood** cross of Christ 18 **speak** i.e., speak to someone so rude.

HAMLET

Come, come, and sit you down; you shall not budge.
You go not till I set you up a glass
Where you may see the inmost part of you.

QUEEN

What wilt thou do? Thou wilt not murder me?
Help, ho!

POLONIUS [behind the arras]   What ho! Help!

HAMLET [drawing]

How now? A rat? Dead for a ducat, dead!   25

[He thrusts his rapier through the arras.]

POLONIUS [behind the arras]

Oh, I am slain!   [He falls and dies.]

QUEEN   Oh, me, what hast thou done?

HAMLET   Nay, I know not. Is it the King?

QUEEN

Oh, what a rash and bloody deed is this!

HAMLET

A bloody deed—almost as bad, good mother,
As kill a king, and marry with his brother.

QUEEN

As kill a king!

HAMLET   Ay, lady, it was my word.

[He parts the arras and discovers Polonius.]

Thou wretched, rash, intruding fool, farewell!
I took thee for thy better. Take thy fortune.
Thou find'st to be too busy is some danger.—   34
Leave wringing of your hands. Peace, sit you down,
And let me wring your heart, for so I shall,
If it be made of penetrable stuff,
If damnèd custom have not brazed it so   38
That it be proof and bulwark against sense.   39

QUEEN

What have I done, that thou dar'st wag thy tongue
In noise so rude against me?

HAMLET   Such an act
That blurs the grace and blush of modesty,
Calls virtue hypocrite, takes off the rose
From the fair forehead of an innocent love
And sets a blister there, makes marriage vows   45
As false as dicers' oaths. Oh, such a deed
As from the body of contraction plucks   47
The very soul, and sweet religion makes   48
A rhapsody of words. Heaven's face does glow   49
O'er this solidity and compound mass   50
With tristful visage, as against the doom,   51
Is thought-sick at the act.

QUEEN   Ay me, what act,   52
That roars so loud and thunders in the index?   53

HAMLET [showing her two likenesses]

Look here upon this picture, and on this,

The counterfeit presentment of two brothers.   55
See what a grace was seated on this brow:
Hyperion's curls, the front of Jove himself,   57
An eye like Mars to threaten and command,   58
A station like the herald Mercury   59
New-lighted on a heaven-kissing hill—   60
A combination and a form indeed
Where every god did seem to set his seal   62
To give the world assurance of a man.
This was your husband. Look you now what follows:
Here is your husband, like a mildewed ear,   65
Blasting his wholesome brother. Have you eyes?   66
Could you on this fair mountain leave to feed   67
And batten on this moor? Ha, have you eyes?   68
You cannot call it love, for at your age
The heyday in the blood is tame, it's humble,   70
And waits upon the judgment, and what judgment
Would step from this to this? Sense, sure, you have,   72
Else could you not have motion, but sure that sense
Is apoplexed, for madness would not err,   74
Nor sense to ecstasy was ne'er so thralled,   75
But it reserved some quantity of choice   76
To serve in such a difference. What devil was't   77
That thus hath cozened you at hoodman-blind?   78
Eyes without feeling, feeling without sight,
Ears without hands or eyes, smelling sans all,   80
Or but a sickly part of one true sense
Could not so mope. O shame, where is thy blush?   82
Rebellious hell,
If thou canst mutine in a matron's bones,   84
To flaming youth let virtue be as wax   85
And melt in her own fire. Proclaim no shame   86
When the compulsive ardor gives the charge,   87
Since frost itself as actively doth burn,   88
And reason panders will.   89

QUEEN   Oh, Hamlet, speak no more!
Thou turn'st mine eyes into my very soul,
And there I see such black and grainèd spots   92

---

25 Dead for a ducat i.e., I bet a ducat he's dead; or, a ducat is his life's fee.   34 busy nosey   38 damnèd custom habitual wickedness. brazed brazened, hardened   39 proof impenetrable, like *proof* or tested armor.   sense feeling.   45 sets a blister i.e., brands as a harlot   47 contraction the marriage contract   48 sweet religion makes i.e., makes marriage vows   49 rhapsody senseless string   49–52 Heaven's . . . act Heaven's face blushes at this solid world compounded of the various elements, with sorrowful face as though the day of doom were near, and is sick with horror at the deed (i.e., Gertrude's marriage).   53 index table of contents, prelude or preface.

55 counterfeit presentment representation in portraiture   57 Hyperion's the sun-god's.   front brow   58 Mars god of war   59 station manner of standing.   Mercury winged messenger of the gods   60 New-lighted newly alighted.   heaven-kissing reaching to the sky   62 set his seal i.e., affix his approval   65 ear i.e., of grain   66 Blasting blighting   67 leave cease   68 batten gorge.   moor barren or marshy ground. (Suggesting also "dark-skinned.")   70 The heyday . . . blood (The blood was thought to be the source of sexual desire.)   72 Sense Perception through the five senses (the functions of the middle or sensible soul)   74 apoplexed paralyzed.   err so err   75–7 Nor . . . difference nor could your physical senses ever have been so enthralled to *ecstasy* or lunacy that they could not distinguish to some degree between Hamlet Senior and Claudius.   78 cozened cheated. hoodman-blind blindman's buff. (In this game, says Hamlet, the devil must have pushed Claudius toward Gertrude while she was blindfolded.)   80 sans without   82 mope be dazed, act aimlessly.   84 mutine mutiny   85–6 To . . . fire when it comes to sexually passionate youth, let virtue melt like a candle or stick of sealing wax held over a candle flame. (There's no point in hoping for self-restraint among young people when matronly women set such a bad example.)   86–9 Proclaim . . . will Call it no shameful business when the compelling ardor of youth delivers the attack, i.e., commits lechery, since the *frost* of advanced age burns with as active a fire of lust and reason perverts itself by fomenting lust rather than restraining it.   92 grainèd ingrained, indelible

As will not leave their tinct.

HAMLET   Nay, but to live   93
In the rank sweat of an enseamèd bed,   94
Stewed in corruption, honeying and making love   95
Over the nasty sty!   96

QUEEN   Oh, speak to me no more!
These words like daggers enter in my ears.
No more, sweet Hamlet!

HAMLET   A murderer and a villain,
A slave that is not twentieth part the tithe   100
Of your precedent lord, a vice of kings,   101
A cutpurse of the empire and the rule,
That from a shelf the precious diadem stole
And put it in his pocket!

QUEEN   No more!   105

Enter Ghost [*in his nightgown*].

HAMLET   A king of shreds and patches—   106
Save me, and hover o'er me with your wings,
You heavenly guards! What would your gracious
    figure?

QUEEN   Alas, he's mad!

HAMLET
Do you not come your tardy son to chide,
That, lapsed in time and passion, lets go by   111
Th'important acting of your dread command?   112
Oh, say!

GHOST
Do not forget. This visitation
Is but to whet thy almost blunted purpose.   115
But look, amazement on thy mother sits.   116
Oh, step between her and her fighting soul!
Conceit in weakest bodies strongest works.   118
Speak to her, Hamlet.

HAMLET   How is it with you, lady?

QUEEN   Alas, how is't with you,
That you do bend your eye on vacancy,
And with th'incorporal air do hold discourse?   122
Forth at your eyes your spirits wildly peep,
And, as the sleeping soldiers in th'alarm,   124
Your bedded hair, like life in excrements,   125
Start up and stand on end. O gentle son,
Upon the heat and flame of thy distemper   127
Sprinkle cool patience. Whereon do you look?

HAMLET
On him, on him! Look you how pale he glares!
His form and cause conjoined, preaching to stones,   130
Would make them capable.—Do not look upon me,   131
Lest with this piteous action you convert   132
My stern effects. Then what I have to do   133
Will want true color—tears perchance for blood.   134

QUEEN   To whom do you speak this?

HAMLET   Do you see nothing there?

QUEEN
Nothing at all, yet all that is I see.

HAMLET   Nor did you nothing hear?

QUEEN   No, nothing but ourselves.

HAMLET
Why, look you there, look how it steals away!
My father, in his habit as he lived!   141
Look where he goes even now out at the portal!

Exit Ghost.

QUEEN
This is the very coinage of your brain.   143
This bodiless creation ecstasy   144
Is very cunning in.   145

HAMLET   Ecstasy?
My pulse as yours doth temperately keep time,
And makes as healthful music. It is not madness
That I have uttered. Bring me to the test,
And I the matter will reword, which madness   150
Would gambol from. Mother, for love of grace,   151
Lay not that flattering unction to your soul   152
That not your trespass but my madness speaks.
It will but skin and film the ulcerous place,   154
Whiles rank corruption, mining all within,   155
Infects unseen. Confess yourself to heaven,
Repent what's past, avoid what is to come,
And do not spread the compost on the weeds   158
To make them ranker. Forgive me this my virtue;   159
For in the fatness of these pursy times   160
Virtue itself of vice must pardon beg,
Yea, curb and woo for leave to do him good.   162

QUEEN
Oh, Hamlet, thou hast cleft my heart in twain.

HAMLET
Oh, throw away the worser part of it,
And live the purer with the other half.
Good night. But go not to my uncle's bed;
Assume a virtue, if you have it not.
That monster, custom, who all sense doth eat,   168
Of habits devil, is angel yet in this,   169

---

93 **leave their tinct** surrender their dark stain.   94 **enseamèd** saturated in the grease and filth of passionate lovemaking   95 **Stewed** soaked, bathed. (With a suggestion of "stew," brothel.)   96 **Over . . . sty** (Like barnyard animals.)   100 **tithe** tenth part   101 **precedent lord** former husband.   **vice** (From the morality plays, a model of iniquity and a buffoon.)   105.1 **nightgown** a robe for indoor wear   106 **A king . . . patches** i.e., a king whose splendor is all sham; a clown or fool dressed in motley   111 **lapsed . . . passion** having let time and passion slip away   112 **Th'important** the importunate, urgent   115 **whet** sharpen   116 **amazement** distraction   118 **Conceit** Imagination   122 **th'incorporal** the immaterial   124 **as . . . th'alarm** like soldiers called out of sleep by an alarum   125 **bedded** laid flat. **like life in excrements** i.e., as though hair, an outgrowth of the body, had a life of its own. (Hair was thought to be lifeless because it lacks sensation, and so its standing on end would be unnatural and ominous.)   127 **distemper** disorder

130 **His . . . conjoined** His appearance joined to his cause for speaking   131 **capable** capable of feeling, receptive.   132–3 **convert . . . effects** divert me from my stern duty.   134 **want . . . blood** lack plausibility so that (with a play on the normal sense of *color*) I shall shed colorless tears instead of blood.   141 **habit** clothes.   **as** as when   143 **very mere   144–5 This . . . in** Madness is skillful in creating this kind of hallucination.   150 **reword** repeat word for word   151 **gambol** skip away   152 **unction** ointment   154 **skin** grow a skin over   155 **mining** working under the surface   158 **compost** manure   159 **this my virtue** my virtuous talk in reproving you   160 **fatness** grossness. **pursy** flabby, out of shape   162 **curb** bow, bend the knee.   **leave** permission   168 **who . . . eat** which consumes and overwhelms the physical senses   169 **Of habits devil** devil-like in prompting evil habits

That to the use of actions fair and good
He likewise gives a frock or livery   171
That aptly is put on. Refrain tonight,   172
And that shall lend a kind of easiness
To the next abstinence; the next more easy;
For use almost can change the stamp of nature,   175
And either . . . the devil, or throw him out   176
With wondrous potency. Once more, good night;
And when you are desirous to be blest,   178
I'll blessing beg of you. For this same lord,   179
             [pointing to Polonius]
I do repent; but heaven hath pleased it so
To punish me with this, and this with me,   181
That I must be their scourge and minister.   182
I will bestow him, and will answer well   183
The death I gave him. So, again, good night.
I must be cruel only to be kind.
This bad begins, and worse remains behind.   186
One word more, good lady.

QUEEN   What shall I do?

HAMLET
Not this by no means that I bid you do:
Let the bloat king tempt you again to bed,   189
Pinch wanton on your cheek, call you his mouse,   190
And let him, for a pair of reechy kisses,   191
Or paddling in your neck with his damned fingers,   192
Make you to ravel all this matter out   193
That I essentially am not in madness,
But mad in craft. 'Twere good you let him know,   195
For who that's but a queen, fair, sober, wise,
Would from a paddock, from a bat, a gib,   197
Such dear concernings hide? Who would do so?   198
No, in despite of sense and secrecy,   199
Unpeg the basket on the house's top,   200
Let the birds fly, and like the famous ape,   201
To try conclusions, in the basket creep   202
And break your own neck down.   203

QUEEN
Be thou assured, if words be made of breath,
And breath of life, I have no life to breathe
What thou hast said to me.

HAMLET
I must to England. You know that?

QUEEN   Alack,
I had forgot. 'Tis so concluded on.

HAMLET
There's letters sealed, and my two schoolfellows,
Whom I will trust as I will adders fanged,
They bear the mandate; they must sweep my way   211
And marshal me to knavery. Let it work.   212
For 'tis the sport to have the engineer   213
Hoist with his own petard, and 't shall go hard   214
But I will delve one yard below their mines   215
And blow them at the moon. Oh, 'tis most sweet
When in one line two crafts directly meet.   217
This man shall set me packing.   218
I'll lug the guts into the neighbor room.
Mother, good night indeed. This counselor
Is now most still, most secret, and most grave,
Who was in life a foolish prating knave.—
Come, sir, to draw toward an end with you.—   223
Good night, mother.
    Exeunt [separately, Hamlet dragging in Polonius].

[4.1]

*Enter King and Queen, with Rosencrantz and
Guildenstern.*

KING
There's matter in these sighs, these profound heaves.   1
You must translate; 'tis fit we understand them.
Where is your son?

QUEEN
Bestow this place on us a little while.
    [Exeunt Rosencrantz and Guildenstern.]
Ah, mine own lord, what have I seen tonight!

---

171 livery an outer appearance, a customary garb (and hence a predisposition easily assumed in time of stress)   **172 aptly** readily   **175 use** habit.   **the stamp of nature** our inborn traits   **176 And either** (A defective line, often emended by inserting the word "master" after *either*, following the Third Quarto and early editors, or some other word such as "shame," "lodge," "curb," or "house.")   **178–9 when . . . you** i.e., when you are ready to be penitent and seek God's blessing, I will ask your blessing as a dutiful son should.   **181 To punish . . . with me** to seek retribution from me for killing Polonius, and from him through my means   **182 their scourge and minister** i.e., agent of heavenly retribution.   **183 bestow** stow, dispose of.   **answer** account or pay for   **186 This** i.e., The killing of Polonius.   **behind** to come. **189 bloat** bloated   **190 Pinch wanton** i.e., leave his love pinches on your cheeks, branding you as wanton   **191 reechy** dirty, filthy **192 paddling** fingering amorously   **193 ravel . . . out** unravel, disclose   **195 in craft** by cunning.   **good** (Said sarcastically; also the following eight lines.)   **197 paddock** toad.   **gib** tomcat   **198 dear concernings** important affairs   **199 sense and secrecy** secrecy that common sense requires   **200 Unpeg the basket** open the cage, i.e., let out the secret   **201 famous ape** (In a story now lost.)   **202 try conclusions** test the outcome (in which the ape apparently enters a cage from which birds have been released and then tries to fly out of the cage as they have done, falling to its death)   **203 down** in the fall.

211–12 sweep . . . knavery sweep a path before me and conduct me to some *knavery* or treachery prepared for me.   **212 work** proceed. **213 engineer** maker of *engines* of war   **214 Hoist with** blown up by. **petard** an explosive used to blow in a door or make a breach **214–15 't shall . . . will** unless luck is against me, I will   **215 mines** tunnels used in warfare to undermine the enemy's emplacements; Hamlet will countermine by going under their mines   **217 in one line** i.e., mines and countermines on a collision course, or the countermines directly below the mines.   **crafts** acts of guile, plots **218 set me packing** set me to making schemes, and set me to lugging (him); and, also, send me off in a hurry.   **223 draw . . . end** finish up. (With a pun on *draw*, "pull.")
4.1 Location: The castle.
0.1 Enter . . . Queen (Some editors argue that Gertrude does not in fact exit at the end of 3.4 and that the scene is continuous here. It is true that the Folio ends 3.4 with "*Exit Hamlet tugging in Polonius,*" not naming Gertrude, and opens 4.1 with "*Enter King.*" Yet the Second Quarto concludes 3.4 with a simple "*Exit,*" which often stands ambiguously for a single exit or an exeunt in early modern texts, and then starts 4.1 with "*Enter King, and Queene, with Rosencraus and Guyldensterne.*" The King's opening lines in 4.1 suggest that he has had time, during a brief intervening pause, to become aware of Gertrude's highly wrought emotional state. In line 35, the King refers to Gertrude's *closet* as though it were elsewhere. The differences between the Second Quarto and the Folio offer an alternative staging. In either case, 4.1 follows swiftly upon 3.4.)   **1 matter** significance. **heaves** heavy sighs.

KING
    What, Gertrude? How does Hamlet?

QUEEN
    Mad as the sea and wind when both contend
    Which is the mightier. In his lawless fit,
    Behind the arras hearing something stir,
    Whips out his rapier, cries, "A rat, a rat!"
    And in this brainish apprehension kills   11
    The unseen good old man.

KING   Oh, heavy deed!   12
    It had been so with us, had we been there.   13
    His liberty is full of threats to all—
    To you yourself, to us, to everyone.
    Alas, how shall this bloody deed be answered?   16
    It will be laid to us, whose providence   17
    Should have kept short, restrained, and out of haunt   18
    This mad young man. But so much was our love,
    We would not understand what was most fit,
    But, like the owner of a foul disease,
    To keep it from divulging, let it feed
    Even on the pith of life. Where is he gone?   22

QUEEN
    To draw apart the body he hath killed,
    O'er whom his very madness, like some ore   25
    Among a mineral of metals base,   26
    Shows itself pure: 'a weeps for what is done.

KING   Oh, Gertrude, come away!
    The sun no sooner shall the mountains touch
    But we will ship him hence, and this vile deed
    We must with all our majesty and skill
    Both countenance and excuse.—Ho, Guildenstern!   32

Enter Rosencrantz and Guildenstern.

    Friends both, go join you with some further aid.
    Hamlet in madness hath Polonius slain,
    And from his mother's closet hath he dragged him.
    Go seek him out, speak fair, and bring the body   36
    Into the chapel. I pray you, haste in this.

        [Exeunt Rosencrantz and Guildenstern.]
    Come, Gertrude, we'll call up our wisest friends
    And let them know both what we mean to do
    And what's untimely done   40
    Whose whisper o'er the world's diameter,   41
    As level as the cannon to his blank,   42
    Transports his poisoned shot, may miss our name
    And hit the woundless air. Oh, come away!   44
    My soul is full of discord and dismay.   *Exeunt.*

❧

11 brainish apprehension frenzied misapprehension   **12 heavy** grievous   **13 us** i.e., me. (The royal "we"; also in line 15.)   **16 answered** explained.   **17 providence** foresight   **18 short** i.e., on a short tether.   **out of haunt** secluded   **22 from divulging** from becoming publicly known   **25 ore** vein of gold   **26 mineral** mine   **32 countenance** put the best face on   **36 fair** gently, courteously   **40 And . . . done** (A defective line; conjectures as to the missing words include "So, haply, slander" [Capell and others]; "For, haply, slander" [Theobald and others]; and "So envious slander" [Jenkins].)   **41 diameter** extent from side to side   **42 As level** with as direct aim.   **his blank** its target at point-blank range   **44 woundless** invulnerable

[4.2]

Enter Hamlet.

HAMLET   Safely stowed.

ROSENCRANTZ, GUILDENSTERN (*within*)   Hamlet! Lord
    Hamlet!

HAMLET   But soft, what noise? Who calls on Hamlet? Oh,
    here they come.

Enter Rosencrantz and Guildenstern.

ROSENCRANTZ
    What have you done, my lord, with the dead body?

HAMLET
    Compounded it with dust, whereto 'tis kin.

ROSENCRANTZ
    Tell us where 'tis, that we may take it thence
    And bear it to the chapel.

HAMLET   Do not believe it.

ROSENCRANTZ   Believe what?

HAMLET   That I can keep your counsel and not mine   12
    own. Besides, to be demanded of a sponge, what rep-   13
    lication should be made by the son of a king?   14

ROSENCRANTZ   Take you me for a sponge, my lord?

HAMLET   Ay, sir, that soaks up the King's countenance,   16
    his rewards, his authorities. But such officers do the   17
    King best service in the end. He keeps them, like an
    ape, an apple, in the corner of his jaw, first mouthed
    to be last swallowed. When he needs what you have
    gleaned, it is but squeezing you, and, sponge, you
    shall be dry again.

ROSENCRANTZ   I understand you not, my lord.

HAMLET   I am glad of it. A knavish speech sleeps in a   24
    foolish ear.

ROSENCRANTZ   My lord, you must tell us where the
    body is and go with us to the King.

HAMLET   The body is with the King, but the King is not   28
    with the body. The King is a thing—   29

GUILDENSTERN   A thing, my lord?

HAMLET   Of nothing. Bring me to him. Hide fox, and all   31
    after!   *Exeunt [running].*   32

❧

[4.3]

Enter King, and two or three.

4.2 Location: The castle.
12–13 That . . . own i.e., Don't expect me to do as you bid me and not follow my own counsel.   **13 demanded of** questioned by   **13–14 replication** reply   **16 countenance** favor   **17 authorities** delegated power, influence.   **24 sleeps in** has no meaning to   **28–9 The . . . body** (Perhaps alludes to the legal commonplace of "the king's two bodies," which drew a distinction between the sacred office of kingship and the particular mortal who possessed it at any given time. Hence, although Claudius's body is necessarily a part of him, true kingship is not contained in it. Similarly, Claudius will have Polonius's body when it is found, but there is no kingship in this business either.)   **31 Of nothing** (1) of no account (2) lacking the essence of kingship, as in lines 28–9 and note.   **31–2 Hide . . . after** (An old signal cry in the game of hide-and-seek, suggesting that Hamlet now runs away from them.)
4.3. Location: The castle.

KING

I have sent to seek him, and to find the body.
How dangerous is it that this man goes loose!
Yet must not we put the strong law on him.
He's loved of the distracted multitude,   4
Who like not in their judgment, but their eyes,   5
And where 'tis so, th'offender's scourge is weighed,   6
But never the offense. To bear all smooth and even,   7
This sudden sending him away must seem
Deliberate pause. Diseases desperate grown   9
By desperate appliance are relieved,   10
Or not at all.

Enter Rosencrantz, [Guildenstern,]
and all the rest.

How now, what hath befall'n?

ROSENCRANTZ

Where the dead body is bestowed, my lord,
We cannot get from him.

KING   But where is he?

ROSENCRANTZ

Without, my lord; guarded, to know your pleasure.   14

KING

Bring him before us.

ROSENCRANTZ [*calling*]   Ho! Bring in the lord.

They enter [with Hamlet].

KING   Now, Hamlet, where's Polonius?

HAMLET   At supper.

KING   At supper? Where?

HAMLET   Not where he eats, but where 'a is eaten. A
certain convocation of politic worms are e'en at him.   20
Your worm is your only emperor for diet. We fat all   21
creatures else to fat us, and we fat ourselves for maggots. Your fat king and your lean beggar is but
variable service—two dishes, but to one table. That's   24
the end.

KING   Alas, alas!

HAMLET   A man may fish with the worm that hath eat   27
of a king, and eat of the fish that hath fed of that
worm.

KING   What dost thou mean by this?

HAMLET   Nothing but to show you how a king may go
a progress through the guts of a beggar.   32

KING   Where is Polonius?

HAMLET   In heaven. Send thither to see. If your messenger find him not there, seek him i'th'other place yourself. But if indeed you find him not within this month,

you shall nose him as you go up the stairs into the   37
lobby.

KING [*to some attendants*]   Go seek him there.

HAMLET   'A will stay till you come. [*Exeunt attendants.*]

KING

Hamlet, this deed, for thine especial safety—
Which we do tender, as we dearly grieve   42
For that which thou hast done—must send thee hence
With fiery quickness. Therefore prepare thyself.
The bark is ready, and the wind at help,   45
Th'associates tend, and everything is bent   46
For England.

HAMLET   For England!

KING   Ay, Hamlet.

HAMLET   Good.

KING

So is it, if thou knew'st our purposes.

HAMLET   I see a cherub that sees them. But come, for   52
England! Farewell, dear mother.

KING   Thy loving father, Hamlet.

HAMLET   My mother. Father and mother is man and
wife, man and wife is one flesh, and so, my mother.
Come, for England!   *Exit.*

KING

Follow him at foot; tempt him with speed aboard.   58
Delay it not. I'll have him hence tonight.
Away! For everything is sealed and done
That else leans on th'affair. Pray you, make haste.   61
                        [*Exeunt all but the King.*]
And, England, if my love thou hold'st at aught—   62
As my great power thereof may give thee sense,   63
Since yet thy cicatrice looks raw and red   64
After the Danish sword, and thy free awe   65
Pays homage to us—thou mayst not coldly set   66
Our sovereign process, which imports at full,   67
By letters congruing to that effect,   68
The present death of Hamlet. Do it, England,   69
For like the hectic in my blood he rages,   70
And thou must cure me. Till I know 'tis done,
Howe'er my haps, my joys were ne'er begun.   *Exit.*   72

❖

[4.4]

Enter Fortinbras with his army over the stage.

FORTINBRAS

Go, Captain, from me greet the Danish king.

---

4 **of** by.   **distracted** fickle, unstable   5 **Who . . . eyes** who choose not
by judgment but by appearance   6–7 **th'offender's . . . offense** i.e.,
the populace often takes umbrage at the severity of a punishment
without taking into account the gravity of the crime   7 **To . . . even**
To manage the business in an unprovocative way   9 **Deliberate**
pause carefully considered action.   10 **appliance** remedies   14 **With-**
out Outside   20 **politic worms** crafty worms (suited to a master spy
like Polonius)   **e'en** even now   21 **Your worm** Your average worm.
(Compare *your fat king and your lean beggar* in line 23.)   **diet** food, eating. (With a punning reference to the Diet of Worms, a famous
convocation held in 1521.)   24 **service** food served at table. (Worms
feed on kings and beggars alike.)   27 **eat** eaten. (Pronounced *et*.)
32 **progress** royal journey of state

37 **nose** smell   42 **tender** regard, hold dear.   **dearly** intensely
45 **bark** sailing vessel   46 **tend** wait.   **bent** in readiness   52 **cherub**
(Cherubim are angels of knowledge. Hamlet hints that both he and
heaven are onto Claudius's tricks.)   58 **at foot** close behind, at heel
61 **leans on** bears upon, is related to   62 **England** i.e., King of England.   **at aught** at any value   63 **As . . . sense** for so my great power
may give you a just appreciation of the importance of valuing my
love   64 **cicatrice** scar   65 **free awe** unconstrained show of respect
66 **coldly set** regard with indifference   67 **process** command.
imports at full conveys specific directions for   68 **congruing** agreeing   69 **present** immediate   70 **hectic** persistent fever   72 **Howe'er**
. . . begun whatever else happens, I cannot begin to be happy.
4.4 Location: The coast of Denmark.

Tell him that by his license Fortinbras   2
Craves the conveyance of a promised march   3
Over his kingdom. You know the rendezvous.
If that His Majesty would aught with us,
We shall express our duty in his eye;   6
And let him know so.
CAPTAIN   I will do't, my lord.
FORTINBRAS   Go softly on.   [*Exeunt all but the Captain.*]   9

Enter Hamlet, Rosencrantz, [Guildenstern,] etc.

HAMLET   Good sir, whose powers are these?   10
CAPTAIN   They are of Norway, sir.
HAMLET   How purposed, sir, I pray you?
CAPTAIN   Against some part of Poland.
HAMLET   Who commands them, sir?
CAPTAIN
    The nephew to old Norway, Fortinbras.
HAMLET
    Goes it against the main of Poland, sir,   16
    Or for some frontier?
CAPTAIN
    Truly to speak, and with no addition,   18
    We go to gain a little patch of ground
    That hath in it no profit but the name.
    To pay five ducats, five, I would not farm it;   21
    Nor will it yield to Norway or the Pole
    A ranker rate, should it be sold in fee.   23
HAMLET
    Why, then the Polack never will defend it.
CAPTAIN
    Yes, it is already garrisoned.
HAMLET
    Two thousand souls and twenty thousand ducats
    Will not debate the question of this straw.   27
    This is th'impostume of much wealth and peace,   28
    That inward breaks, and shows no cause without   29
    Why the man dies. I humbly thank you, sir.
CAPTAIN
    God b'wi'you, sir.   [*Exit.*]
ROSENCRANTZ   Will't please you go, my lord?
HAMLET
    I'll be with you straight. Go a little before.
        [*Exeunt all except Hamlet.*]
    How all occasions do inform against me   33
    And spur my dull revenge! What is a man,
    If his chief good and market of his time   35
    Be but to sleep and feed? A beast, no more.
    Sure he that made us with such large discourse,   37
    Looking before and after, gave us not   38
    That capability and godlike reason

To fust in us unused. Now, whether it be   40
Bestial oblivion, or some craven scruple   41
Of thinking too precisely on th'event—   42
A thought which, quartered, hath but one part
    wisdom
And ever three parts coward—I do not know
Why yet I live to say "This thing's to do,"
Sith I have cause, and will, and strength, and means   46
To do't. Examples gross as earth exhort me: 47
Witness this army of such mass and charge,   48
Led by a delicate and tender prince,   49
Whose spirit with divine ambition puffed
Makes mouths at the invisible event,   51
Exposing what is mortal and unsure
To all that fortune, death, and danger dare,   53
Even for an eggshell. Rightly to be great   54
Is not to stir without great argument,   55
But greatly to find quarrel in a straw   56
When honor's at the stake. How stand I, then,   57
That have a father killed, a mother stained,
Excitements of my reason and my blood,   59
And let all sleep, while to my shame I see
The imminent death of twenty thousand men
That for a fantasy and trick of fame   62
Go to their graves like beds, fight for a plot   63
Whereon the numbers cannot try the cause,   64
Which is not tomb enough and continent   65
To hide the slain? Oh, from this time forth
My thoughts be bloody or be nothing worth!   *Exit.*

❖

[4.5]

*Enter Horatio, [Queen] Gertrude, and a Gentle-
man.*

QUEEN
    I will not speak with her.
GENTLEMAN   She is importunate,
    Indeed distract. Her mood will needs be pitied.   2
QUEEN   What would she have?
GENTLEMAN
    She speaks much of her father, says she hears
    There's tricks i'th' world, and hems, and beats her
        heart,   5
    Spurns enviously at straws, speaks things in doubt   6

---

2 license permission **3 conveyance** unhindered passage **6 We . . .
eye** I will come pay my respects in person **9 softly** slowly, circum-
spectly **10 powers** forces **16 main** main part **18 addition** exaggeration **21 To pay** i.e., For a yearly rental of. **farm it** take a lease
of it **23 ranker** higher. **in fee** fee simple, outright. **27 debate . . .
straw** argue about this trifling matter. **28 th'impostume** the abscess
29 inward breaks festers within. **without** externally **33 inform
against** denounce; take shape against **35 market of** profit of
37 discourse power of reasoning **38 Looking before and after** able
to review past events and anticipate the future

40 fust grow moldy **41 oblivion** forgetfulness. **craven** cowardly
42 precisely scrupulously. **th'event** the outcome **46 Sith** since
47 gross obvious **48 charge** expense **49 delicate and tender** of fine
and youthful qualities **51 Makes mouths** makes scornful faces.
invisible event unforeseeable outcome **53 dare** could do (to him)
54–7 Rightly . . . stake True greatness is not a matter of being moved
to action solely by a great cause; rather, it is to respond greatly to an
apparently trivial cause when honor is at the stake. **59 blood** (The
supposed seat of the passions.) **62 fantasy** fanciful caprice, illusion.
trick trifle, deceit **63 plot** plot of ground **64 Whereon . . . cause** on
which there is insufficient room for the soldiers needed to fight for it
65 continent receptacle, container
4.5 Location: The castle.
2 distract out of her mind. **5 tricks** deceptions. **hems** clears her
throat, makes "hmm" sounds. **heart** i.e., breast **6 Spurns . . .
straws** kicks spitefully, takes offense at trifles. **in doubt** of obscure
meaning

That carry but half sense. Her speech is nothing,
Yet the unshapèd use of it doth move   8
The hearers to collection; they yawn at it,   9
And botch the words up fit to their own thoughts,   10
Which, as her winks and nods and gestures yield
    them,   11
Indeed would make one think there might be thought,   12
Though nothing sure, yet much unhappily.   13

HORATIO
'Twere good she were spoken with, for she may strew
Dangerous conjectures in ill-breeding minds.   15

QUEEN   Let her come in.   [Exit Gentleman.]
[Aside] To my sick soul, as sin's true nature is,
Each toy seems prologue to some great amiss.   18
So full of artless jealousy is guilt,   19
It spills itself in fearing to be spilt.   20

        Enter Ophelia [distracted].

OPHELIA
Where is the beauteous majesty of Denmark?
QUEEN   How now, Ophelia?
OPHELIA (she sings)
    "How should I your true love know
        From another one?
    By his cockle hat and staff,   25
        And his sandal shoon."   26
QUEEN   Alas, sweet lady, what imports this song?
OPHELIA   Say you? Nay, pray you, mark.
    "He is dead and gone, lady,   (Song.)
        He is dead and gone;
    At his head a grass-green turf,
        At his heels a stone."
Oho!   33
QUEEN   Nay, but Ophelia—
OPHELIA   Pray you, mark.
[Sings] "White his shroud as the mountain snow"—

        Enter King.

QUEEN   Alas, look here, my lord.
OPHELIA
    "Larded with sweet flowers;   (Song.) 38
    Which bewept to the ground did not go
        With true-love showers."   40
KING   How do you, pretty lady?
OPHELIA   Well, God 'ild you! They say the owl was a   42

baker's daughter. Lord, we know what we are, but
know not what we may be. God be at your table!
KING   Conceit upon her father.   45
OPHELIA   Pray let's have no words of this; but when
they ask you what it means, say you this:
    "Tomorrow is Saint Valentine's day,   (Song.)
        All in the morning betime,   49
    And I a maid at your window,
        To be your Valentine.
    Then up he rose, and donned his clothes,
        And dupped the chamber door,   53
    Let in the maid, that out a maid
        Never departed more."
KING   Pretty Ophelia—
OPHELIA   Indeed, la, without an oath, I'll make an end
on't:
[Sings]   "By Gis and by Saint Charity,   59
        Alack, and fie for shame!
    Young men will do't, if they come to't;
        By Cock, they are to blame.   62
    Quoth she, 'Before you tumbled me,
        You promised me to wed.'"
He answers:
    "'So would I ha' done, by yonder sun,
        An thou hadst not come to my bed.'"   67
KING   How long hath she been thus?
OPHELIA   I hope all will be well. We must be patient,
but I cannot choose but weep to think they would lay
him i'th' cold ground. My brother shall know of it.
And so I thank you for your good counsel. Come, my
coach! Good night, ladies, good night, sweet ladies,
good night, good night.   [Exit.]
KING [to Horatio]
Follow her close. Give her good watch, I pray you.
                                        [Exit Horatio.]
Oh, this is the poison of deep grief; it springs
All from her father's death—and now behold!
Oh, Gertrude, Gertrude,
When sorrows come, they come not single spies,   79
But in battalions. First, her father slain;
Next, your son gone, and he most violent author
Of his own just remove; the people muddied,   82
Thick and unwholesome in their thoughts and
    whispers
For good Polonius' death—and we have done but
    greenly,   84
In hugger-mugger to inter him; poor Ophelia   85
Divided from herself and her fair judgment,
Without the which we are pictures or mere beasts;
Last, and as much containing as all these,   88
Her brother is in secret come from France,

8 unshapèd use incoherent manner   9 collection inference, a guess
at some sort of meaning.   yawn gape, wonder; grasp. (The Folio
reading, "aim," is possible.)   10 botch patch   11 Which which
words.   yield deliver, represent   12–13 there might . . . unhappily
that a great deal could be guessed at of a most unfortunate nature,
even if one couldn't be at all sure.   15 ill-breeding prone to suspect
the worst and to make mischief   18 toy trifle.   amiss calamity.
19–20 So . . . spilt Guilt is so burdened with conscience and guileless
fear of detection that it reveals itself through apprehension of disaster.   20.1 Enter Ophelia (In the First Quarto, Ophelia enters, "playing
on a lute, and her hair down, singing.")   25 cockle hat hat with cockleshell stuck in it as a sign that the wearer had been a pilgrim to the
shrine of Saint James of Compostella in Spain   26 shoon shoes.
33 Oho! (Perhaps a sigh.)   38 Larded strewn, bedecked   40 showers
i.e., tears   42 God 'ild God yield or reward.   owl (Refers to a legend
about a baker's daughter who was turned into an owl for being
ungenerous when Jesus begged a loaf of bread.)

45 Conceit Fancy, brooding   49 betime early   53 dupped did up,
opened   59 Gis Jesus   62 Cock (A perversion of "God" in oaths;
here also with a quibble on the slang word for penis.)   67 An if
79 spies scouts sent in advance of the main force   82 remove
removal.   muddied stirred up, confused   84 greenly foolishly
85 hugger-mugger secret haste   88 as much containing as full of
serious matter

Feeds on this wonder, keeps himself in clouds, 90
And wants not buzzers to infect his ear 91
With pestilent speeches of his father's death,
Wherein necessity, of matter beggared, 93
Will nothing stick our person to arraign 94
In ear and ear. Oh, my dear Gertrude, this, 95
Like to a murd'ring piece, in many places 96
Gives me superfluous death.   *A noise within.* 97

QUEEN   Alack, what noise is this?

KING   Attend!
Where is my Switzers? Let them guard the door. 100

Enter a Messenger.

What is the matter?

MESSENGER   Save yourself, my lord!
The ocean, overpeering of his list, 102
Eats not the flats with more impetuous haste 103
Than young Laertes, in a riotous head, 104
O'erbears your officers. The rabble call him lord,
And, as the world were now but to begin, 106
Antiquity forgot, custom not known, 107
The ratifiers and props of every word, 108
They cry, "Choose we! Laertes shall be king!"
Caps, hands, and tongues applaud it to the clouds, 110
"Laertes shall be king, Laertes king!"

QUEEN
How cheerfully on the false trail they cry!
                              A noise within.
Oh, this is counter, you false Danish dogs! 113

Enter Laertes with others.

KING   The doors are broke.

LAERTES
Where is this King?—Sirs, stand you all without.

ALL   No, let's come in.

LAERTES   I pray you, give me leave.

ALL   We will, we will.

LAERTES   I thank you. Keep the door. [*Exeunt followers.*]
                              Oh, thou vile king,
Give me my father!

QUEEN [*restraining him*]   Calmly, good Laertes.

LAERTES
That drop of blood that's calm proclaims me bastard,

Cries cuckold to my father, brands the harlot
Even here between the chaste unsmirchèd brow 123
Of my true mother.

KING   What is the cause, Laertes,
That thy rebellion looks so giantlike? 125
Let him go, Gertrude. Do not fear our person. 126
There's such divinity doth hedge a king 127
That treason can but peep to what it would, 128
Acts little of his will. Tell me, Laertes, 129
Why thou art thus incensed. Let him go, Gertrude.
Speak, man.

LAERTES   Where is my father?

KING   Dead.

QUEEN
But not by him.

KING   Let him demand his fill.

LAERTES
How came he dead? I'll not be juggled with. 133
To hell, allegiance! Vows, to the blackest devil!
Conscience and grace, to the profoundest pit!
I dare damnation. To this point I stand, 136
That both the worlds I give to negligence, 137
Let come what comes, only I'll be revenged
Most throughly for my father. 139

KING   Who shall stay you?

LAERTES   My will, not all the world's. 141
And for my means, I'll husband them so well 142
They shall go far with little.

KING   Good Laertes,
If you desire to know the certainty
Of your dear father, is't writ in your revenge
That, swoopstake, you will draw both friend and foe, 146
Winner and loser?

LAERTES   None but his enemies.

KING   Will you know them, then?

LAERTES
To his good friends thus wide I'll ope my arms,
And like the kind life-rendering pelican 151
Repast them with my blood.

KING   Why, now you speak 152
Like a good child and a true gentleman.
That I am guiltless of your father's death,
And am most sensibly in grief for it, 155
It shall as level to your judgment 'pear 156
As day does to your eye.   *A noise within.*

---

90 **Feeds . . . clouds** feeds his resentment on this whole shocking turn of events, keeps himself aloof and mysterious   91 **wants** lacks. **buzzers** gossipers, informers   93 **necessity** i.e., the need to invent some plausible explanation.   **of matter beggared** unprovided with facts   94–5 **Will . . . ear** will not hesitate to accuse my (royal) person in everybody's ears.   96 **murd'ring piece** cannon loaded so as to scatter its shot   97 **Gives . . . death** kills me over and over. 99 **Attend!** Guard me!   100 **Switzers** Swiss guards, mercenaries 102 **overpeering of his list** overflowing its shore, boundary   103 **flats** i.e., flatlands near shore.   **impetuous** violent (perhaps also with the meaning of *impiteous* ["impitious," Q2], "pitiless")   104 **riotous head** insurrectionary advance   106–8 **And . . . word** and, as if the world were to be started all over afresh, utterly setting aside all ancient traditional customs that should confirm and underprop our every word and promise   110 **Caps** (The caps are thrown in the air.) 113 **counter** (A hunting term, meaning to follow the trail in a direction opposite to that which the game has taken.)

123 **between** amidst   125 **giantlike** (Recalling the rising of the giants of Greek mythology against Olympus.)   126 **fear our** fear for my 127 **hedge** protect, as with a surrounding barrier   128 **can . . . would** can only peep furtively, as through a barrier, at what it would intend 129 **Acts . . . will** (but) performs little of what it intends.   133 **juggled with** cheated, deceived.   136 **To . . . stand** I am resolved in this 137 **both . . . negligence** i.e., both this world and the next are of no consequence to me   139 **throughly** thoroughly   141 **My will . . . world's** I'll stop (*stay*) when my will is accomplished, not for anyone else's.   142 **for** as for   146 **swoopstake** i.e., indiscriminately. (Literally, taking all stakes on the gambling table at once. *Draw* is also a gambling term, meaning "take from.")   151 **pelican** (Refers to the belief that the female pelican fed its young with its own blood.) 152 **Repast** feed   155 **sensibly** feelingly   156 **level** plain

LAERTES
How now, what noise is that?

Enter Ophelia.

KING   Let her come in.
LAERTES
O heat, dry up my brains! Tears seven times salt
Burn out the sense and virtue of mine eye!   160
By heaven, thy madness shall be paid with weight   161
Till our scale turn the beam. O rose of May!   162
Dear maid, kind sister, sweet Ophelia!
O heavens, is't possible a young maid's wits
Should be as mortal as an old man's life?
Nature is fine in love, and where 'tis fine   166
It sends some precious instance of itself   167
After the thing it loves.   168
OPHELIA
    "They bore him barefaced on the bier,   (*Song.*)
        Hey non nonny, nonny, hey nonny,
        And in his grave rained many a tear—"
Fare you well, my dove!
LAERTES
Hadst thou thy wits and didst persuade revenge,
It could not move thus.
OPHELIA   You must sing "A-down a-down," and you 175
"call him a-down-a." Oh, how the wheel becomes it! It   176
is the false steward that stole his master's daughter.   177
LAERTES   This nothing's more than matter.   178
OPHELIA   There's rosemary, that's for remembrance;   179
pray you, love, remember. And there is pansies; that's   180
for thoughts.
LAERTES   A document in madness, thoughts and re-   182
membrance fitted.
OPHELIA   There's fennel for you, and columbines.   184
There's rue for you, and here's some for me; we may   185
call it herb of grace o' Sundays. You must wear your
rue with a difference. There's a daisy. I would give   187
you some violets, but they withered all when my   188
father died. They say 'a made a good end—

[*Sings*] "For bonny sweet Robin is all my joy."
LAERTES
Thought and affliction, passion, hell itself,   191
She turns to favor and to prettiness.   192
OPHELIA
    "And will 'a not come again?   (*Song.*)
    And will 'a not come again?
        No, no, he is dead.
        Go to thy deathbed,
    He never will come again.

    "His beard was as white as snow,
    All flaxen was his poll.   199
        He is gone, he is gone,
        And we cast away moan.
    God ha' mercy on his soul!"
And of all Christian souls, I pray God. God b'wi'you.
                    [*Exit, followed by Gertrude.*]
LAERTES   Do you see this, O God?
KING
Laertes, I must commune with your grief,
Or you deny me right. Go but apart,
Make choice of whom your wisest friends you will,   207
And they shall hear and judge twixt you and me.
If by direct or by collateral hand   209
They find us touched, we will our kingdom give,   210
Our crown, our life, and all that we call ours
To you in satisfaction; but if not,
Be you content to lend your patience to us,
And we shall jointly labor with your soul
To give it due content.
LAERTES   Let this be so.
His means of death, his obscure funeral—
No trophy, sword, nor hatchment o'er his bones,   217
No noble rite, nor formal ostentation—   218
Cry to be heard, as 'twere from heaven to earth,
That I must call't in question.
KING   So you shall,   220
And where th'offense is, let the great ax fall.
I pray you, go with me.   *Exeunt.*

[4.6]

Enter Horatio and others.

HORATIO
What are they that would speak with me?
GENTLEMAN   Seafaring men, sir. They say they have
letters for you.   3
HORATIO   Let them come in.   [*Exit Gentleman.*]
I do not know from what part of the world

160 **virtue** faculty, power   161 **paid with weight** repaid, avenged
equally or more   162 **beam** crossbar of a balance.   166–8 **Nature . . .
loves** Human nature is exquisitely sensitive in matters of love, and in
cases of sudden loss it sends some precious part of itself after the lost
object of that love. (In this case, Ophelia's sanity deserts her out of
sorrow for her lost father and perhaps too out of her love for Hamlet.)
175–6 **You . . . a-down-a** (Ophelia assigns the singing of refrains, like
her own "Hey non nonny," to others present.)   176 **wheel** spinning
wheel as accompaniment to the song, or refrain   177 **false steward**
(The story is unknown.)   178 **This . . . matter** This seeming nonsense
is more eloquent than sane utterance.   179 **rosemary** (Used as a symbol of remembrance both at weddings and at funerals.)   180 **pansies**
(Emblems of love and courtship; perhaps from French *pensèes*,
"thoughts.")   182 **document** instruction, lesson   184 **There's fennel
. . . columbines** (*Fennel* betokens flattery; *columbines*, unchastity or
ingratitude. Throughout, Ophelia addresses her various listeners,
giving one flower to one and another to another, perhaps with particular symbolic significance in each case.)   185 **rue** (Emblem of repentance—a signification that is evident in its popular name, *herb of
grace.*)   187 **with a difference** (A device used in heraldry to distinguish one family from another on the coat of arms, here suggesting
that Ophelia and the others have different causes of sorrow and
repentance; perhaps with a play on *rue* in the sense of "ruth," "pity.")
daisy (Emblem of love's victims and of faithlessness.)   188 **violets**
(Emblems of faithfulness.)

191 **Thought** Melancholy.   **passion** suffering   192 **favor** grace,
beauty   199 **poll** head.   207 **whom** whichever of   209 **collateral
hand** indirect agency   210 **us touched** me implicated   217 **trophy**
memorial.   **hatchment** tablet displaying the armorial bearings of a
deceased person   218 **ostentation** ceremony   220 **That** so that.
call't in question demand an explanation.
4.6. Location: The castle.
3 letters a letter

I should be greeted, if not from Lord Hamlet.

Enter Sailors.

FIRST SAILOR   God bless you, sir.

HORATIO   Let him bless thee too.

FIRST SAILOR   'A shall, sir, an't please him. There's a   9
letter for you, sir—it came from th'ambassador that   10
was bound for England—if your name be Horatio, as
I am let to know it is.   [*He gives a letter.*]

HORATIO [*reads*]   "Horatio, when thou shalt have over-   13
looked this, give these fellows some means to the King;   14
they have letters for him. Ere we were two days old at
sea, a pirate of very warlike appointment gave us   16
chase. Finding ourselves too slow of sail, we put on a
compelled valor, and in the grapple I boarded them.
On the instant they got clear of our ship, so I alone
became their prisoner. They have dealt with me like
thieves of mercy, but they knew what they did: I am to   21
do a good turn for them. Let the King have the letters
I have sent, and repair thou to me with as much speed   23
as thou wouldest fly death. I have words to speak in
thine ear will make thee dumb, yet are they much too
light for the bore of the matter. These good fellows will   26
bring thee where I am. Rosencrantz and Guildenstern
hold their course for England. Of them I have much to
tell thee. Farewell.

He that thou knowest thine, Hamlet."

Come, I will give you way for these your letters,   31
And do't the speedier that you may direct me
To him from whom you brought them.   *Exeunt.*

❖

[4.7]

Enter King and Laertes.

KING
Now must your conscience my acquittance seal,   1
And you must put me in your heart for friend,
Sith you have heard, and with a knowing ear,   3
That he which hath your noble father slain
Pursued my life.

LAERTES   It well appears. But tell me
Why you proceeded not against these feats   6
So crimeful and so capital in nature,   7
As by your safety, greatness, wisdom, all things else,
You mainly were stirred up.   9

KING   Oh, for two special reasons,
Which may to you perhaps seem much unsinewed,   11
But yet to me they're strong. The Queen his mother
Lives almost by his looks, and for myself—
My virtue or my plague, be it either which—

She is so conjunctive to my life and soul   15
That, as the star moves not but in his sphere,   16
I could not but by her. The other motive
Why to a public count I might not go   18
Is the great love the general gender bear him,   19
Who, dipping all his faults in their affection,
Work like the spring that turneth wood to stone,   21
Convert his gyves to graces, so that my arrows,   22
Too slightly timbered for so loud a wind,   23
Would have reverted to my bow again
But not where I had aimed them.

LAERTES
And so have I a noble father lost,
A sister driven into desp'rate terms,
Whose worth, if praises may go back again,   27
Stood challenger on mount of all the age   28
For her perfections. But my revenge will come.   29

KING
Break not your sleeps for that. You must not think
That we are made of stuff so flat and dull
That we can let our beard be shook with danger
And think it pastime. You shortly shall hear more.
I loved your father, and we love ourself;
And that, I hope, will teach you to imagine—

Enter a Messenger with letters.

How now? What news?

MESSENGER   Letters, my lord, from Hamlet:
This to Your Majesty, this to the Queen.

[*He gives letters.*]

KING   From Hamlet? Who brought them?

MESSENGER
Sailors, my lord, they say. I saw them not.
They were given me by Claudio. He received them
Of him that brought them.

KING   Laertes, you shall hear them.—
Leave us.   [*Exit Messenger.*]
[*He reads.*] "High and mighty, you shall know I am set
naked on your kingdom. Tomorrow shall I beg leave   45
to see your kingly eyes, when I shall, first asking your
pardon, thereunto recount the occasion of my sudden   47
and more strange return.   Hamlet."
What should this mean? Are all the rest come back?
Or is it some abuse, and no such thing?   50

LAERTES
Know you the hand?

KING   'Tis Hamlet's character. "Naked!"   51
And in a postscript here he says "alone."

---

9 **an't** if it   10 **th'ambassador** (Hamlet's ostensible role; see 3.2.172-3.)
13–14 **overlooked** looked over   14 **means** means of access
16 **appointment** equipage   21 **thieves of mercy** merciful thieves
23 **repair** come   26 **bore** caliber, i.e., importance   31 **way** means of
access
4.7. Location: The castle.
1 **my acquittance seal** confirm or acknowledge my innocence   3 **Sith**
since   6 **feats** acts   7 **capital** punishable by death   9 **mainly** greatly
11 **unsinewed** weak

15 **conjunctive** closely united. (An astronomical metaphor.)   16 **his**
its.   **sphere** one of the hollow spheres in which, according to Ptolemaic astronomy, the planets were supposed to move   18 **count**
account, reckoning, indictment   19 **general gender** common people
21 **Work** operate, act.   **spring** i.e., a spring with such a concentration
of lime that it coats a piece of wood with limestone, in effect gilding
and petrifying it   22 **gyves** fetters (which, gilded by the people's
praise, would look like badges of honor)   23 **Too . . . wind** with too
light a shaft for so powerful a gust (of popular sentiment)   27 **terms**
state, condition   28 **go back** recall what she was   29 **on mount** set
up on high   45 **naked** destitute, unarmed, without following
47 **pardon** (for returning without authorization)   50 **abuse** deceit.
no such thing not what the letter says.   51 **character** handwriting.

Can you devise me?

LAERTES
I am lost in it, my lord. But let him come.
It warms the very sickness in my heart
That I shall live and tell him to his teeth,
"Thus didst thou."

KING   If it be so, Laertes— 57
As how should it be so? How otherwise?— 58
Will you be ruled by me?

LAERTES   Ay, my lord,
So you will not o'errule me to a peace. 60

KING
To thine own peace. If he be now returned,
As checking at his voyage, and that he means 62
No more to undertake it, I will work him
To an exploit, now ripe in my device, 64
Under the which he shall not choose but fall;
And for his death no wind of blame shall breathe,
But even his mother shall uncharge the practice 67
And call it accident.

LAERTES   My lord, I will be ruled,
The rather if you could devise it so
That I might be the organ.

KING   It falls right. 70
You have been talked of since your travel much,
And that in Hamlet's hearing, for a quality
Wherein they say you shine. Your sum of parts 73
Did not together pluck such envy from him
As did that one, and that, in my regard,
Of the unworthiest siege. 76

LAERTES   What part is that, my lord?

KING
A very ribbon in the cap of youth,
Yet needful too, for youth no less becomes 79
The light and careless livery that it wears
Than settled age his sables and his weeds 81
Importing health and graveness. Two months since 82
Here was a gentleman of Normandy.
I have seen myself, and served against, the French,
And they can well on horseback, but this gallant 85
Had witchcraft in't; he grew unto his seat,
And to such wondrous doing brought his horse
As had he been incorpsed and demi-natured 88
With the brave beast. So far he topped my thought 89
That I in forgery of shapes and tricks
Come short of what he did. 90

LAERTES   A Norman was't?

KING   A Norman. 53

LAERTES
Upon my life, Lamord.

KING   The very same.

LAERTES
I know him well. He is the brooch indeed 94
And gem of all the nation.

KING   He made confession of you, 96
And gave you such a masterly report
For art and exercise in your defense, 98
And for your rapier most especial,
That he cried out 'twould be a sight indeed
If one could match you. Th'escrimers of their nation, 101
He swore, had neither motion, guard, nor eye
If you opposed them. Sir, this report of his
Did Hamlet so envenom with his envy
That he could nothing do but wish and beg
Your sudden coming o'er, to play with you. 106
Now, out of this—

LAERTES   What out of this, my lord?

KING
Laertes, was your father dear to you?
Or are you like the painting of a sorrow,
A face without a heart?

LAERTES   Why ask you this?

KING
Not that I think you did not love your father,
But that I know love is begun by time, 112
And that I see, in passages of proof, 113
Time qualifies the spark and fire of it. 114
There lives within the very flame of love
A kind of wick or snuff that will abate it, 116
And nothing is at a like goodness still, 117
For goodness, growing to a pleurisy, 118
Dies in his own too much. That we would do, 119
We should do when we would; for this "would"
    changes
And hath abatements and delays as many 121
As there are tongues, are hands, are accidents, 122
And then this "should" is like a spendthrift sigh, 123
That hurts by easing. But, to the quick o'th'ulcer: 124
Hamlet comes back. What would you undertake
To show yourself in deed your father's son
More than in words?

LAERTES   To cut his throat i'th' church.

---

53 devise explain to   **57 Thus didst thou** i.e., Here's for what you did to my father.   **58 As . . . otherwise?** how can this (Hamlet's return) be true? Yet how otherwise than true (since we have the evidence of his letter)?   **60 So** provided that   **62 checking at** i.e., turning aside from (like a falcon leaving the quarry to fly at a chance bird).   **that** if   **64 device** devising, invention   **67 uncharge the practice** acquit the stratagem of being a plot   **70 organ** agent, instrument.   **73 Your . . . parts** All your other virtues   **76 unworthiest siege** least important rank.   **79 no less becomes** is no less adorned by   **81–2 his sables . . . graveness** its rich robes furred with sable and its garments denoting dignified well-being and seriousness.   **85 can well** are skilled   **88–9 As . . . beast** as if, centaurlike, he had been made into one body with the horse, possessing half its nature.   **89 topped** surpassed   **90 forgery** fabrication

94 brooch ornament   **96 confession** testimonial, admission of superiority   **98 For . . . defense** with respect to your skill and practice with your weapon   **101 Th'escrimers** The fencers   **106 sudden** immediate.   **play** fence   **112 begun by time** i.e., created by the right circumstance and hence subject to change   **113 passages of proof** actual well-attested instances   **114 qualifies** weakens, moderates   **116 snuff** the charred part of a candlewick   **117 nothing . . . still** nothing remains at a constant level of perfection   **118 pleurisy** excess, plethora. (Literally, a chest inflammation.)   **119 in . . . much** of its own excess.   **That** That which   **121 abatements** diminutions   **122 As . . . accidents** as there are tongues to dissuade, hands to prevent, and chance events to intervene   **123 spendthrift sigh** (An allusion to the belief that sighs draw blood from the heart.)   **124 hurts by easing** i.e., costs the heart blood and wastes precious opportunity even while it affords emotional relief.   **quick o'th'ulcer** i.e., heart of the matter

KING
No place, indeed, should murder sanctuarize;   128
Revenge should have no bounds. But good Laertes,
Will you do this, keep close within your chamber.   130
Hamlet returned shall know you are come home.
We'll put on those shall praise your excellence   132
And set a double varnish on the fame
The Frenchman gave you, bring you in fine together,   134
And wager on your heads. He, being remiss,   135
Most generous, and free from all contriving,   136
Will not peruse the foils, so that with ease,
Or with a little shuffling, you may choose
A sword unbated, and in a pass of practice   139
Requite him for your father.
LAERTES   I will do't,
And for that purpose I'll anoint my sword.
I bought an unction of a mountebank   142
So mortal that, but dip a knife in it,
Where it draws blood no cataplasm so rare,   144
Collected from all simples that have virtue   145
Under the moon, can save the thing from death   146
That is but scratched withal. I'll touch my point
With this contagion, that if I gall him slightly,   148
It may be death.
KING   Let's further think of this,
Weigh what convenience both of time and means
May fit us to our shape. If this should fail,   151
And that our drift look through our bad performance,   152
'Twere better not assayed. Therefore this project
Should have a back or second, that might hold
If this did blast in proof. Soft, let me see.   155
We'll make a solemn wager on your cunnings—   156
I ha 't!
When in your motion you are hot and dry—
As make your bouts more violent to that end—   159
And that he calls for drink, I'll have prepared him
A chalice for the nonce, whereon but sipping,   161
If he by chance escape your venomed stuck,   162
Our purpose may hold there. [*A cry within.*] But stay,
what noise?

Enter Queen.

QUEEN
One woe doth tread upon another's heel,
So fast they follow. Your sister's drowned, Laertes.
LAERTES   Drowned! Oh, where?

QUEEN
There is a willow grows askant the brook,   167
That shows his hoar leaves in the glassy stream;   168
Therewith fantastic garlands did she make
Of crowflowers, nettles, daisies, and long purples,   170
That liberal shepherds give a grosser name,   171
But our cold maids do dead men's fingers call them.   172
There on the pendent boughs her crownet weeds   173
Clamb'ring to hang, an envious sliver broke,   174
When down her weedy trophies and herself   175
Fell in the weeping brook. Her clothes spread wide,
And mermaidlike awhile they bore her up,
Which time she chanted snatches of old lauds,   178
As one incapable of her own distress,   179
Or like a creature native and endued   180
Unto that element. But long it could not be
Till that her garments, heavy with their drink,
Pulled the poor wretch from her melodious lay   183
To muddy death.
LAERTES   Alas, then she is drowned?
QUEEN   Drowned, drowned.
LAERTES
Too much of water hast thou, poor Ophelia,
And therefore I forbid my tears. But yet
It is our trick; nature her custom holds,   188
Let shame say what it will. [*He weeps.*] When these
are gone,
The woman will be out. Adieu, my lord.   189
I have a speech of fire that fain would blaze,   190
But that this folly douts it.   *Exit.*
KING   Let's follow, Gertrude.   192
How much I had to do to calm his rage!
Now fear I this will give it start again;
Therefore let's follow.   *Exeunt.*

❧

[5.1]

Enter two Clowns [with spades and mattocks].

FIRST CLOWN   Is she to be buried in Christian burial,
when she willfully seeks her own salvation?   2

---

128 **sanctuarize** protect from punishment. (Alludes to the right of
sanctuary with which certain religious places were invested.)
130 **Will you do this** if you wish to do this   132 **put on those shall**
arrange for some to   134 **in fine** finally   135 **remiss** negligently
unsuspicious   136 **generous** noble-minded   139 **unbated** not
blunted, having no button.   **pass of practice** treacherous thrust in an
arranged bout   142 **unction** ointment.   **mountebank** quack doctor
144 **cataplasm** plaster or poultice   145 **simples** herbs.   **virtue**
potency   146 **Under the moon** i.e., anywhere (with reference perhaps
to the belief that herbs gathered at night had a special power)
148 **gall** graze, wound   151 **shape** part we propose to act.   152 **drift**
. . . **performance** intention should be made visible by our bungling
155 **blast in proof** come to grief when put to the test.   156 **cunnings**
respective skills   159 **As** i.e., and you should   161 **nonce** occasion
162 **stuck** thrust. (From *stoccado*, a fencing term.)

167 **askant** aslant   168 **hoar leaves** white or gray undersides of the
leaves   170 **long purples** early purple orchids   171 **liberal** free-spo-
ken.   **a grosser name** (The testicle-resembling tubers of the orchid,
which also in some cases resemble *dead men's fingers*, have earned various slang names like "dogstones" and "cullions.")   172 **cold** chaste
173 **pendent** overhanging.   **crownet** made into a chaplet or coronet
174 **envious sliver** malicious branch   175 **weedy** i.e., of plants
178 **lauds** hymns   179 **incapable of** lacking capacity to apprehend
180 **endued** adapted by nature   183 **lay** ballad, song   188 **It is our
trick** i.e., weeping is our natural way (when sad)   189–90 **When . . .
out** When my tears are all shed, the woman in me will be expended,
satisfied.   192 **douts** extinguishes. (The Second Quarto reads
"drownes.")
5.1 **Location:** A churchyard.
0.1 *Clowns* rustics   2 **salvation** (A blunder for "damnation," or perhaps a suggestion that Ophelia was taking her own shortcut to
heaven.)

SECOND CLOWN   I tell thee she is; therefore make her grave straight. The crowner hath sat on her, and finds it Christian burial.   4 5

FIRST CLOWN   How can that be, unless she drowned herself in her own defense?

SECOND CLOWN   Why, 'tis found so.   8

FIRST CLOWN   It must be *se offendendo,* it cannot be else. For here lies the point: if I drown myself wittingly, it argues an act, and an act hath three branches—it is to act, to do, and to perform. Argal, she drowned herself wittingly.   9 12

SECOND CLOWN   Nay, but hear you, goodman delve—   14

FIRST CLOWN   Give me leave. Here lies the water; good. Here stands the man; good. If the man go to this water and drown himself, it is, will he, nill he, he goes, mark you that. But if the water come to him and drown him, he drowns not himself. Argal, he that is not guilty of his own death shortens not his own life.   17

SECOND CLOWN   But is this law?

FIRST CLOWN   Ay, marry, is't—crowner's quest law.   22

SECOND CLOWN   Will you ha' the truth on't? If this had not been a gentlewoman, she should have been buried out o' Christian burial.

FIRST CLOWN   Why, there thou say'st. And the more pity that great folk should have countenance in this world to drown or hang themselves, more than their even-Christian. Come, my spade. There is no ancient gentlemen but gardeners, ditchers, and grave makers. They hold up Adam's profession.   26 27 29 31

SECOND CLOWN   Was he a gentleman?

FIRST CLOWN   'A was the first that ever bore arms.   33

SECOND CLOWN   Why, he had none.

FIRST CLOWN   What, art a heathen? How dost thou understand the Scripture? The Scripture says Adam digged. Could he dig without arms? I'll put another question to thee. If thou answerest me not to the purpose, confess thyself—   37 39

SECOND CLOWN   Go to.

FIRST CLOWN   What is he that builds stronger than either the mason, the shipwright, or the carpenter?

SECOND CLOWN   The gallows maker, for that frame outlives a thousand tenants.   43

FIRST CLOWN   I like thy wit well, in good faith. The gallows does well. But how does it well? It does well to those that do ill. Now thou dost ill to say the gallows   46

is built stronger than the church. Argal, the gallows may do well to thee. To't again, come.

SECOND CLOWN   "Who builds stronger than a mason, a shipwright, or a carpenter?"

FIRST CLOWN   Ay, tell me that, and unyoke.   52

SECOND CLOWN   Marry, now I can tell.

FIRST CLOWN   To't.

SECOND CLOWN   Mass, I cannot tell.   55

Enter Hamlet and Horatio [at a distance].

FIRST CLOWN   Cudgel thy brains no more about it, for your dull ass will not mend his pace with beating; and when you are asked this question next, say "a grave maker." The houses he makes lasts till doomsday. Go get thee in and fetch me a stoup of liquor.   60
[Exit Second Clown. First Clown digs.]
Song.

"In youth, when I did love, did love,   61
   Methought it was very sweet,
To contract—oh—the time for—a—my behove,   63
Oh, methought there—a—was nothing—a—
   meet."   64

HAMLET   Has this fellow no feeling of his business, 'a sings in grave-making?   65

HORATIO   Custom hath made it in him a property of easiness.   67 68

HAMLET   'Tis e'en so. The hand of little employment hath the daintier sense.   70

FIRST CLOWN   *Song.*
"But age with his stealing steps
   Hath clawed me in his clutch,
And hath shipped me into the land,   73
   As if I had never been such."

[He throws up a skull.]

HAMLET   That skull had a tongue in it and could sing once. How the knave jowls it to the ground, as if 'twere Cain's jawbone, that did the first murder! This might be the pate of a politician, which this ass now o'erreaches, one that would circumvent God, might it not?   76 78 79

HORATIO   It might, my lord.

HAMLET   Or of a courtier, which could say, "Good morrow, sweet lord! How dost thou, sweet lord?" This might be my Lord Such-a-one, that praised my Lord Such-a-one's horse when 'a meant to beg it, might it not?

HORATIO   Ay, my lord.

4 straight straightway, immediately. (But with a pun on strait, "narrow.")   crowner coroner.   sat on her conducted an inquest on her case   4–5 finds it gives his official verdict that her means of death was consistent with   8 found so determined so in the coroner's verdict.   9 se offendendo (A comic mistake for se defendendo, a term used in verdicts of self-defense.)   12 Argal (Corruption of ergo, "therefore.")   14 goodman (An honorific title often used with the name of a profession or craft.)   17 will he, nill he whether he will or no, willy-nilly   22 quest inquest   26 there thou say'st i.e., that's right.   27 countenance privilege   29 even-Christian fellow Christians. ancient going back to ancient times   31 hold up maintain   33 bore arms (To be entitled to bear a coat of arms would make Adam a gentleman, but as one who bore a spade, our common ancestor was an ordinary delver in the earth.)   37 arms i.e., the arms of the body. 39 confess thyself (The saying continues, "and be hanged.") 43 frame (1) gallows (2) structure   46 does well (1) is an apt answer (2) does a good turn.

52 unyoke i.e., after this great effort, you may unharness the team of your wits.   55 Mass By the Mass   60 stoup two-quart measure 61 In . . . love (This and the two following stanzas, with nonsensical variations, are from a poem attributed to Lord Vaux and printed in Tottel's Miscellany, 1557. The oh and a [for "ah"] seemingly are the grunts of the digger.)   63 To contract . . . behove i.e., to shorten the time for my own advantage. (Perhaps he means to prolong it.) 64 meet suitable, i.e., more suitable.   65 'a that he   67–8 property of easiness something he can do easily and indifferently.   70 daintier sense more delicate sense of feeling.   73 into the land i.e., toward my grave (?) (But note the lack of rhyme in steps, land.)   76 jowls dashes. (With a pun on jowl, "jawbone.")   78 politician schemer, plotter   79 o'erreaches circumvents, gets the better of

HAMLET   Why, e'en so, and now my Lady Worm's, chapless, and knocked about the mazard with a sexton's spade. Here's fine revolution, an we had the trick to see't. Did these bones cost no more the breeding but to play at loggets with them? Mine ache to think on't. [89][90][91][92]

FIRST CLOWN   *Song.*

"A pickax and a spade, a spade,
    For and a shrouding sheet;
Oh, a pit of clay for to be made   [95]
    For such a guest is meet."

                                    [*He throws up another skull.*]

HAMLET   There's another. Why may not that be the skull of a lawyer? Where be his quiddities now, his quillities, his cases, his tenures, and his tricks? Why does he suffer this mad knave now to knock him about the sconce with a dirty shovel, and will not tell him of his action of battery? Hum, this fellow might be in 's time a great buyer of land, with his statutes, his recognizances, his fines, his double vouchers, his recoveries. Is this the fine of his fines and the recovery of his recoveries, to have his fine pate full of fine dirt? Will his vouchers vouch him no more of his purchases, and double ones too, than the length and breadth of a pair of indentures? The very conveyances of his lands will scarcely lie in this box, and must th'inheritor himself have no more, ha? [99][100][102][103][104][105][106][107][108][109][110][111]

HORATIO   Not a jot more, my lord.

HAMLET   Is not parchment made of sheepskins?

HORATIO   Ay, my lord, and of calves' skins too.

HAMLET   They are sheep and calves which seek out assurance in that. I will speak to this fellow.—Whose grave's this, sirrah? [116][117][118]

FIRST CLOWN   Mine, sir.

[*Sings*] "Oh, pit of clay for to be made
    For such a guest is meet."

HAMLET   I think it be thine, indeed, for thou liest in't.

FIRST CLOWN   You lie out on't, sir, and therefore 'tis not yours. For my part, I do not lie in't, yet it is mine.

HAMLET   Thou dost lie in't, to be in't and say it is thine. 'Tis for the dead, not for the quick; therefore thou liest. [126]

FIRST CLOWN   'Tis a quick lie, sir; 'twill away again from me to you.

HAMLET   What man dost thou dig it for?

FIRST CLOWN   For no man, sir.

HAMLET   What woman, then?

FIRST CLOWN   For none, neither.

HAMLET   Who is to be buried in't?

FIRST CLOWN   One that was a woman, sir, but, rest her soul, she's dead.

HAMLET   How absolute the knave is! We must speak by the card, or equivocation will undo us. By the Lord, Horatio, this three years I have took note of it: the age is grown so picked that the toe of the peasant comes so near the heel of the courtier he galls his kibe.—How long hast thou been grave maker? [137][138][139][140][141]

FIRST CLOWN   Of all the days i'th' year, I came to't that day that our last king Hamlet overcame Fortinbras.

HAMLET   How long is that since?

FIRST CLOWN   Cannot you tell that? Every fool can tell that. It was that very day that young Hamlet was born—he that is mad and sent into England.

HAMLET   Ay, marry, why was he sent into England?

FIRST CLOWN   Why, because 'a was mad. 'A shall recover his wits there, or if 'a do not, 'tis no great matter there.

HAMLET   Why?

FIRST CLOWN   'Twill not be seen in him there. There the men are as mad as he.

HAMLET   How came he mad?

FIRST CLOWN   Very strangely, they say.

HAMLET   How strangely?

FIRST CLOWN   Faith, e'en with losing his wits.

HAMLET   Upon what ground? [160]

FIRST CLOWN   Why, here in Denmark. I have been sexton here, man and boy, thirty years.

HAMLET   How long will a man lie i'th'earth ere he rot?

FIRST CLOWN   Faith, if 'a be not rotten before 'a die—as we have many pocky corpses nowadays, that will scarce hold the laying in—'a will last you some eight year or nine year. A tanner will last you nine year. [165][166]

HAMLET   Why he more than another?

FIRST CLOWN   Why, sir, his hide is so tanned with his trade that 'a will keep out water a great while, and

---

89 chapless having no lower jaw.   **mazard** i.e., head. (Literally, a drinking vessel.)   **90 revolution** turn of Fortune's wheel, change.   **trick** knack   **91–2 cost . . . but** involve so little expense and care in upbringing that we may   **92 loggets** a game in which pieces of hard wood shaped like Indian clubs or bowling pins are thrown to lie as near as possible to a stake   **95 For and** and moreover   **99–100 his quiddities . . . quillities** his subtleties, his legal niceties   **100 tenures** the holding of a piece of property or office, or the conditions or period of such holding   **102 sconce** head   **103 action of battery** lawsuit about physical assault.   **104 his statutes** his legal documents acknowledging obligation of a debt   **104–5 recognizances** bonds undertaking to repay debts   **105 fines** procedures for converting entailed estates into "fee simple" or freehold.   **double vouchers** vouchers signed by two signatories guaranteeing the legality of real estate titles.   **recoveries** suits to obtain the authority of a court judgment for the holding of land.   **106–7 Is this . . . dirt?** Is this the end of his legal maneuvers and profitable land deals, to have the skull of his elegant head filled full of minutely sifted dirt? (With multiple wordplay on *fine* and *fines*.)   **107–10 Will . . . indentures?** Will his vouchers, even double ones, guarantee him no more land than is needed to bury him in, being no bigger than the deed of conveyance? (An *indenture* is literally a legal document drawn up in duplicate on a single sheet and then cut apart on a zigzag line so that each pair was uniquely matched.)   **111 box** (1) deed box (2) coffin.   **th'inheritor** the acquirer, owner   **116–17 assurance in that** safety in legal parchments.   **118 sirrah** (A term of address to inferiors.)

126 quick living   **137 absolute** strict, precise   **137–8 by the card** i.e., with precision. (Literally, by the mariner's compass-card, on which the points of the compass were marked.)   **138 equivocation** ambiguity in the use of terms   **139 took** taken   **139–41 the age . . . kibe** i.e., the age has grown so finical and mannered that the lower classes ape their social betters, chafing at their heels. (*Kibes* are chilblains on the heels.)   **160 ground** cause. (But, in the next line, the gravedigger takes the word in the sense of "land," "country.")   **165 pocky** rotten, diseased. (Literally, with the pox, or syphilis.)   **166 hold the laying in** hold together long enough to be interred.   **last you** last. (*You* is used colloquially here and in the following lines.)

your water is a sore decayer of your whoreson dead 171
body. [*He picks up a skull.*] Here's a skull now hath
lien you i'th'earth three-and-twenty years. 173

HAMLET   Whose was it?

FIRST CLOWN   A whoreson mad fellow's it was. Whose
do you think it was?

HAMLET   Nay, I know not.

FIRST CLOWN   A pestilence on him for a mad rogue! 'A
poured a flagon of Rhenish on my head once. This 179
same skull, sir, was, sir, Yorick's skull, the King's jester.

HAMLET   This?

FIRST CLOWN   E'en that.

HAMLET   Let me see. [*He takes the skull.*] Alas, poor
Yorick! I knew him, Horatio, a fellow of infinite jest, of
most excellent fancy. He hath bore me on his back a 185
thousand times, and now how abhorred in my
imagination it is! My gorge rises at it. Here hung those 187
lips that I have kissed I know not how oft. Where be
your gibes now? Your gambols, your songs, your 189
flashes of merriment that were wont to set the table on
a roar? Not one now, to mock your own grinning?
Quite chopfallen? Now get you to my lady's chamber 192
and tell her, let her paint an inch thick, to this favor 193
she must come. Make her laugh at that. Prithee,
Horatio, tell me one thing.

HORATIO   What's that, my lord?

HAMLET   Dost thou think Alexander looked o' this
fashion i'th'earth?

HORATIO   E'en so.

HAMLET   And smelt so? Pah! [*He throws down the skull.*]

HORATIO   E'en so, my lord.

HAMLET   To what base uses we may return, Horatio!
Why may not imagination trace the noble dust of
Alexander till 'a find it stopping a bunghole? 204

HORATIO   'Twere to consider too curiously to consider 205
so.

HAMLET   No, faith, not a jot, but to follow him thither
with modesty enough, and likelihood to lead it. As 208
thus: Alexander died, Alexander was buried, Alexander returneth to dust, the dust is earth, of earth we
make loam, and why of that loam whereto he was 211
converted might they not stop a beer barrel?
Imperious Caesar, dead and turned to clay, 213
Might stop a hole to keep the wind away.
Oh, that that earth which kept the world in awe
Should patch a wall t'expel the winter's flaw! 216

*Enter King, Queen, Laertes, and the corpse [of
Ophelia, in procession, with Priest, lords, etc.].*

But soft, but soft awhile! Here comes the King, 217

The Queen, the courtiers. Who is this they follow?
And with such maimèd rites? This doth betoken 219
The corpse they follow did with desperate hand
Fordo it own life. 'Twas of some estate. 221
Couch we awhile and mark. 222

[*He and Horatio conceal themselves.
Ophelia's body is taken to the grave.*]

LAERTES   What ceremony else?

HAMLET [*to Horatio*]
That is Laertes, a very noble youth. Mark.

LAERTES   What ceremony else?

PRIEST
Her obsequies have been as far enlarged
As we have warranty. Her death was doubtful, 227
And but that great command o'ersways the order 228
She should in ground unsanctified been lodged 229
Till the last trumpet. For charitable prayers, 230
Shards, flints, and pebbles should be thrown on her. 231
Yet here she is allowed her virgin crants, 232
Her maiden strewments, and the bringing home 233
Of bell and burial. 234

LAERTES
Must there no more be done?

PRIEST   No more be done.
We should profane the service of the dead
To sing a requiem and such rest to her 237
As to peace-parted souls.

LAERTES   Lay her i'th'earth, 238
And from her fair and unpolluted flesh
May violets spring! I tell thee, churlish priest, 240
A ministering angel shall my sister be
When thou liest howling.

HAMLET [*to Horatio*]   What, the fair Ophelia! 242

QUEEN [*scattering flowers*]   Sweets to the sweet! Farewell.
I hoped thou shouldst have been my Hamlet's wife.
I thought thy bride-bed to have decked, sweet maid,
And not t' have strewed thy grave.

LAERTES   Oh, treble woe
Fall ten times treble on that cursèd head
Whose wicked deed thy most ingenious sense 248
Deprived thee of! Hold off the earth awhile,
Till I have caught her once more in mine arms.

[*He leaps into the grave and embraces Ophelia.*]
Now pile your dust upon the quick and dead,
Till of this flat a mountain you have made
T' o'ertop old Pelion or the skyish head 253
Of blue Olympus.

---

171 **sore** keen, veritable.   **whoreson** (An expression of contemptuous familiarity.)   173 **lien you** lain. (See the note at line 166.)   179 **Rhenish** Rhine wine   185 **bore** borne   187 **My gorge rises** i.e., I feel nauseated   189 **gibes** taunts   192 **chopfallen** (1) lacking the lower jaw (2) dejected   193 **favor** aspect, appearance   204 **bunghole** hole for filling or emptying a cask.   205 **curiously** minutely   208 **with . . . lead it** with moderation and plausibility.   211 **loam** a mixture of clay, straw, sand, etc. used to mold bricks, or, in this case, bungs for a beer barrel   213 **Imperious** Imperial   216 **flaw** gust of wind.   217 **soft** i.e., wait, be careful

219 **maimèd** mutilated, incomplete   221 **Fordo it** destroy its.   **estate** rank.   222 **Couch we** Let's hide, lie low   227 **warranty** i.e., ecclesiastical authority.   228 **order** (1) prescribed practice (2) religious order of clerics   229 **She should . . . lodged** she should have been buried in unsanctified ground   230 **For** In place of   231 **Shards** broken bits of pottery   232 **crants** garlands betokening maidenhood   233 **strewments** flowers strewn on a coffin   233–4 **bringing . . . burial** laying the body to rest, to the sound of the bell.   237 **such rest** i.e., to pray for such rest   238 **peace-parted souls** those who have died at peace with God.   240 **violets** (See 4.5.188 and note.)   242 **howling** i.e., in hell.   248 **ingenious sense** a mind that is quick, alert, of fine qualities   253 **Pelion** a mountain in northern Thessaly; compare *Olympus* and *Ossa* in lines 254 and 286. (In their rebellion against the Olympian gods, the giants attempted to heap Ossa on Pelion in order to scale Olympus.)

HAMLET [*coming forward*]   What is he whose grief
 Bears such an emphasis, whose phrase of sorrow   255
 Conjures the wandering stars and makes them stand   256
 Like wonder-wounded hearers? This is I,   257
 Hamlet the Dane.   258
LAERTES [*grappling with him*]   The devil take thy soul!   259
HAMLET   Thou pray'st not well.
 I prithee, take thy fingers from my throat,
 For though I am not splenitive and rash,
 Yet have I in me something dangerous,   262
 Which let thy wisdom fear. Hold off thy hand.
KING   Pluck them asunder.
QUEEN   Hamlet, Hamlet!
ALL   Gentlemen!
HORATIO   Good my lord, be quiet.
 [*Hamlet and Laertes are parted.*]
HAMLET
 Why, I will fight with him upon this theme
 Until my eyelids will no longer wag.   270
QUEEN   Oh, my son, what theme?
HAMLET
 I loved Ophelia. Forty thousand brothers
 Could not with all their quantity of love
 Make up my sum. What wilt thou do for her?
KING   Oh, he is mad, Laertes.
QUEEN   For love of God, forbear him.   276
HAMLET
 'Swounds, show me what thou'lt do.   277
 Woo't weep? Woo't fight? Woo't fast? Woo't tear
   thyself?   278
 Woo't drink up eisel? Eat a crocodile?   279
 I'll do't. Dost come here to whine?
 To outface me with leaping in her grave?
 Be buried quick with her, and so will I.   282
 And if thou prate of mountains, let them throw
 Millions of acres on us, till our ground,
 Singeing his pate against the burning zone,   285
 Make Ossa like a wart! Nay, an thou'lt mouth,   286
 I'll rant as well as thou.
QUEEN   This is mere madness,   287
 And thus awhile the fit will work on him;
 Anon, as patient as the female dove

When that her golden couplets are disclosed,   290
 His silence will sit drooping.
HAMLET   Hear you, sir.
 What is the reason that you use me thus?
 I loved you ever. But it is no matter.
 Let Hercules himself do what he may,   294
 The cat will mew, and dog will have his day.   295
   Exit Hamlet.
KING
 I pray thee, good Horatio, wait upon him.
   [*Exit*] *Horatio.*
 [*To Laertes*] Strengthen your patience in our last
   night's speech;   297
 We'll put the matter to the present push.—   298
 Good Gertrude, set some watch over your son.—
 This grave shall have a living monument.   300
 An hour of quiet shortly shall we see;   301
 Till then, in patience our proceeding be.   *Exeunt.*

❖

[5.2]

Enter Hamlet and Horatio.

HAMLET
 So much for this, sir; now shall you see the other.   1
 You do remember all the circumstance?
HORATIO   Remember it, my lord!
HAMLET
 Sir, in my heart there was a kind of fighting
 That would not let me sleep. Methought I lay
 Worse than the mutines in the bilboes. Rashly,   6
 And praised be rashness for it—let us know   7
 Our indiscretion sometime serves us well   8
 When our deep plots do pall, and that should learn us   9
 There's a divinity that shapes our ends,
 Rough-hew them how we will—
HORATIO   That is most certain.   11
HAMLET   Up from my cabin,
 My sea-gown scarfed about me, in the dark   13
 Groped I to find out them, had my desire,   14
 Fingered their packet, and in fine withdrew   15
 To mine own room again, making so bold,
 My fears forgetting manners, to unseal
 Their grand commission; where I found, Horatio—
 Ah, royal knavery!—an exact command,

---

255 **emphasis** i.e., rhetorical and florid emphasis. (*Phrase* has a similar rhetorical connotation.)   256 **wandering stars** planets   257 **wonder-wounded** struck with amazement   258 **the Dane** (This title normally signifies the King; see 1.1.17 and note.)   259 **s.d. *grappling with him*** The testimony of the First Quarto that *"Hamlet leaps in after Laertes"* and of the ballad "Elegy on Burbage," published in *Gentleman's Magazine* in 1825 ("Oft have I seen him leap into a grave") seem to indicate one way in which this fight was staged; however, the difficulty of fitting two contenders and Ophelia's body into a confined space (probably the trapdoor) suggests to many editors the alternative, that Laertes jumps out of the grave to attack Hamlet.)   262 **splenitive** quick-tempered   270 **wag** move. (A fluttering eyelid is a conventional sign that life has not yet gone.)   276 **forbear him** leave him alone.   277 **'Swounds** By His (Christ's) wounds   278 **Woo't** Wilt thou   279 **Woo't . . . eisel?** Will you drink up a whole draft of vinegar? (An extremely self-punishing task as a way of expressing grief.) **crocodile** (Crocodiles were tough and dangerous, and were supposed to shed crocodile tears.)   282 **quick** alive   285 **his pate** its head, i.e., top.   **burning zone** zone in the celestial sphere containing the sun's orbit, between the tropics of Cancer and Capricorn   286 **Ossa** (See 253n.)   **an thou'lt mouth** if you want to rant   287 **mere** utter

290 **golden couplets** two baby pigeons, covered with yellow down. **disclosed** hatched   294–5 **Let . . . day** i.e., (1) Even Hercules couldn't stop Laertes's theatrical rant (2) I, too, will have my turn; i.e., despite any blustering attempts at interference, every person will sooner or later do what he or she must do.   297 **in** i.e., by recalling   298 **present push** immediate test.   300 **living** lasting. (For Laertes' private understanding, Claudius also hints that Hamlet's death will serve as such a monument.)   301 **hour of quiet** time free of conflict
5.2 Location: The castle.
1 **see the other** hear the other news. (See 4.6.24–6.)   6 **mutines** mutineers.   **bilboes** shackles.   **Rashly** On impulse. (This adverb goes with lines 12 ff.)   7 **know** acknowledge   8 **indiscretion** lack of foresight and judgment (not an indiscreet act)   9 **pall** fail, falter, go stale. **learn** teach   11 **Rough-hew** shape roughly   13 **sea-gown** seaman's coat.   **scarfed** loosely wrapped   14 **them** i.e., Rosencrantz and Guildenstern   15 **Fingered** pilfered, pinched.   **in fine** finally, in conclusion

Larded with many several sorts of reasons 20
Importing Denmark's health and England's too, 21
With, ho! such bugs and goblins in my life, 22
That on the supervise, no leisure bated, 23
No, not to stay the grinding of the ax, 24
My head should be struck off.

HORATIO   Is't possible?

HAMLET [*giving a document*]
Here's the commission. Read it at more leisure.
But wilt thou hear now how I did proceed?

HORATIO   I beseech you.

HAMLET
Being thus benetted round with villainies—
Ere I could make a prologue to my brains, 30
They had begun the play—I sat me down, 31
Devised a new commission, wrote it fair. 32
I once did hold it, as our statists do, 33
A baseness to write fair, and labored much 34
How to forget that learning, but, sir, now
It did me yeoman's service. Wilt thou know
Th'effect of what I wrote?

HORATIO   Ay, good my lord.

HAMLET
An earnest conjuration from the King, 38
As England was his faithful tributary,
As love between them like the palm might flourish, 40
As peace should still her wheaten garland wear 41
And stand a comma 'tween their amities, 42
And many suchlike "as"es of great charge, 43
That on the view and knowing of these contents,
Without debatement further more or less,
He should those bearers put to sudden death,
Not shriving time allowed.

HORATIO   How was this sealed? 47

HAMLET
Why, even in that was heaven ordinant. 48
I had my father's signet in my purse, 49
Which was the model of that Danish seal; 50
Folded the writ up in the form of th'other, 51
Subscribed it, gave't th'impression, placed it safely, 52
The changeling never known. Now, the next day 53
Was our sea fight, and what to this was sequent 54
Thou knowest already.

HORATIO   So Guildenstern and Rosencrantz go to't. 20, 21

HAMLET
Why, man, they did make love to this employment.
They are not near my conscience. Their defeat 58
Does by their own insinuation grow. 59
'Tis dangerous when the baser nature comes 60
Between the pass and fell incensèd points 61
Of mighty opposites.

HORATIO   Why, what a king is this! 62

HAMLET
Does it not, think thee, stand me now upon— 63
He that hath killed my king and whored my mother,
Popped in between th'election and my hopes, 65
Thrown out his angle for my proper life, 66
And with such coz'nage—is't not perfect conscience 67
To quit him with this arm? And is't not to be damned 68
To let this canker of our nature come 69
In further evil? 70

HORATIO
It must be shortly known to him from England
What is the issue of the business there.

HAMLET
It will be short. The interim is mine,
And a man's life's no more than to say "one." 74
But I am very sorry, good Horatio,
That to Laertes I forgot myself,
For by the image of my cause I see
The portraiture of his. I'll court his favors.
But, sure, the bravery of his grief did put me 79
Into a tow'ring passion.

HORATIO   Peace, who comes here?

Enter a Courtier [Osric].

OSRIC   Your Lordship is right welcome back to Denmark.

HAMLET   I humbly thank you, sir. [*To Horatio*] Dost
know this water fly?

HORATIO   No, my good lord.

HAMLET   Thy state is the more gracious, for 'tis a vice to
know him. He hath much land, and fertile. Let a beast 86
be lord of beasts, and his crib shall stand at the King's 87
mess. 'Tis a chuff, but, as I say, spacious in the 88
possession of dirt.

OSRIC   Sweet lord, if Your Lordship were at leisure, I
should impart a thing to you from His Majesty.

HAMLET   I will receive it, sir, with all diligence of spirit.
Put your bonnet to his right use; 'tis for the head. 93

20 **Larded** garnished.   **several** different   21 **Importing** relating to
22 **With . . . life** i.e., with all sorts of warnings of imaginary dangers if
I were allowed to continue living. (*Bugs* are bugbears, hobgoblins.)
23 **That . . . bated** that on the reading of this commission, no delay
being allowed   24 **stay** await   30–1 **Ere . . . play** before I could consciously turn my brain to the matter, it had started working on a plan
32 **fair** in a clear hand.   33 **statists** politicians, men of public affairs
34 **A baseness** beneath my dignity   38 **conjuration** entreaty
40 **palm** (An image of health; see Psalm 92:12.)   41 **still** always.
wheaten garland (Symbolic of fruitful agriculture, of peace and
plenty.)   42 **comma** (Indicating continuity, link.)   43 **"as"es** (1) the
"whereases" of a formal document (2) asses.   **charge** (1) import (2)
burden (appropriate to asses)   47 **shriving time** time for confession
and absolution   48 **ordinant** directing.   49 **signet** small seal
50 **model** replica   51 **writ** writing   52 **Subscribed** signed (with
forged signature).   **impression** i.e., with a wax seal   53 **changeling**
i.e., substituted letter. (Literally, a fairy child substituted for a human
one.)   54 **was sequent** followed

58 **defeat** destruction   59 **insinuation** intrusive intervention, sticking
their noses in my business   60 **baser** of lower social station   61 **pass**
thrust.   **fell** fierce   62 **opposites** antagonists.   63 **stand me now**
upon become incumbent on me now   65 **th'election** (The Danish
monarch was "elected" by a small number of high-ranking electors.)
66 **angle** fishhook.   **proper** very   67 **coz'nage** trickery   68 **quit**
requite, pay back   69 **canker** ulcer   69–70 **come In** grow into
74 **a man's . . . "one"** one's whole life occupies such a short time, only
as long as it takes to count to 1.   79 **bravery** bravado   86–8 **Let . . .**
mess i.e., If a man, no matter how beastlike, is as rich in livestock and
possessions as Osric, he may eat at the King's table.   87 **crib** manger
88 **chuff** boor, churl. (The Second Quarto spelling, "chough," is a
variant spelling that also suggests the meaning here of "chattering
jackdaw.")   93 **bonnet** any kind of cap or hat.   **his** its

OSRIC   I thank Your Lordship, it is very hot.

HAMLET   No, believe me, 'tis very cold. The wind is northerly.

OSRIC   It is indifferent cold, my lord, indeed.   97

HAMLET   But yet methinks it is very sultry and hot for my complexion.   99

OSRIC   Exceedingly, my lord. It is very sultry, as 'twere—I cannot tell how. My lord, His Majesty bade me signify to you that 'a has laid a great wager on your head. Sir, this is the matter—

HAMLET   I beseech you, remember.

[Hamlet moves him to put on his hat.]

OSRIC   Nay, good my lord; for my ease, in good faith.   105
Sir, here is newly come to court Laertes—believe me, an absolute gentleman, full of most excellent differ-   107
ences, of very soft society and great showing. Indeed,   108
to speak feelingly of him, he is the card or calendar of   109
gentry, for you shall find in him the continent of what   110
part a gentleman would see.   111

HAMLET   Sir, his definement suffers no perdition in   112
you, though I know to divide him inventorially would   113
dozy th'arithmetic of memory, and yet but yaw   114
neither in respect of his quick sail. But, in the verity of   115
extolment, I take him to be a soul of great article, and   116
his infusion of such dearth and rareness as, to make   117
true diction of him, his semblable is his mirror and   118
who else would trace him his umbrage, nothing   119
more.   120

OSRIC   Your Lordship speaks most infallibly of him.

HAMLET   The concernancy, sir? Why do we wrap the   122
gentleman in our more rawer breath?   123

OSRIC   Sir?

HORATIO   Is't not possible to understand in another   125
tongue? You will do't, sir, really.   126

HAMLET   What imports the nomination of this gentle-   127
man?

OSRIC   Of Laertes?

HORATIO   *[to Hamlet]*   His purse is empty already; all 's golden words are spent.

HAMLET   Of him, sir.

OSRIC   I know you are not ignorant—

HAMLET   I would you did, sir. Yet in faith if you did,   134
it would not much approve me. Well, sir?   135

OSRIC   You are not ignorant of what excellence Laertes is—

HAMLET   I dare not confess that, lest I should compare   138
with him in excellence. But to know a man well were   139
to know himself.   140

OSRIC   I mean, sir, for his weapon; but in the imputation   141
laid on him by them, in his meed he's unfellowed.   142

HAMLET   What's his weapon?

OSRIC   Rapier and dagger.

HAMLET   That's two of his weapons—but well.   145

OSRIC   The King, sir, hath wagered with him six Barbary horses, against the which he has impawned, as I take   147
it, six French rapiers and poniards, with their assigns,   148
as girdle, hangers, and so. Three of the carriages, in   149
faith, are very dear to fancy, very responsive to the   150
hilts, most delicate carriages, and of very liberal con-   151
ceit.   152

HAMLET   What call you the carriages?   153

HORATIO   *[to Hamlet]*   I knew you must be edified by the margent ere you had done.   155

OSRIC   The carriages, sir, are the hangers.

HAMLET   The phrase would be more germane to the matter if we could carry a cannon by our sides; I would it might be hangers till then. But, on: six Barbary horses against six French swords, their assigns, and three lib-eral-conceited carriages; that's the French bet against the Danish. Why is this impawned, as you call it?

OSRIC   The King, sir, hath laid, sir, that in a dozen   163
passes between yourself and him, he shall not exceed   164
you three hits. He hath laid on twelve for nine, and it would come to immediate trial, if Your Lordship would vouchsafe the answer.   167

HAMLET   How if I answer no?

OSRIC   I mean, my lord, the opposition of your person in trial.

HAMLET   Sir, I will walk here in the hall. If it please His Majesty, it is the breathing time of day with me. Let 172 the foils be brought, the gentleman willing, and the King hold his purpose, I will win for him an I can; if not, I will gain nothing but my shame and the odd hits.

OSRIC   Shall I deliver you so?   177

HAMLET   To this effect, sir—after what flourish your nature will.

OSRIC   I commend my duty to Your Lordship.   180

HAMLET   Yours, yours.   [Exit Osric.]
'A does well to commend it himself; there are no tongues else for 's turn.   183

HORATIO   This lapwing runs away with the shell on his 184 head.

HAMLET   'A did comply with his dug before 'a sucked 186 it. Thus has he—and many more of the same breed 187 that I know the drossy age dotes on—only got the 188 tune of the time, and, out of an habit of encounter, a 189 kind of yeasty collection, which carries them through 190 and through the most fanned and winnowed opin- 191 ions; and do but blow them to their trial, the bubbles 192 are out.   193

Enter a Lord.

LORD   My lord, His Majesty commended him to you by young Osric, who brings back to him that you attend him in the hall. He sends to know if your pleasure hold to play with Laertes, or that you will take longer 197 time.

HAMLET   I am constant to my purposes; they follow the King's pleasure. If his fitness speaks, mine is ready; 200 now or whensoever, provided I be so able as now.

LORD   The King and Queen and all are coming down.

HAMLET   In happy time.   203

LORD   The Queen desires you to use some gentle enter- 204 tainment to Laertes before you fall to play.   205

HAMLET   She well instructs me.   [Exit Lord.]

HORATIO   You will lose, my lord.

HAMLET   I do not think so. Since he went into France, I have been in continual practice; I shall win at the odds.

But thou wouldst not think how ill all's here about my heart; but it is no matter.

HORATIO   Nay, good my lord—

HAMLET   It is but foolery, but it is such a kind of gain- 213 giving as would perhaps trouble a woman.   214

HORATIO   If your mind dislike anything, obey it. I will forestall their repair hither and say you are not fit.   216

HAMLET   Not a whit, we defy augury. There is special 217 providence in the fall of a sparrow. If it be now, 'tis not to come; if it be not to come, it will be now; if it be not now; yet it will come. The readiness is all. Since 220 no man of aught he leaves knows, what is't to leave 221 betimes? Let be.   222

A table prepared. [Enter] trumpets, drums, and officers with cushions; King, Queen, [Osric,] and all the state; foils, daggers, [and wine borne in;] and Laertes.

KING
Come, Hamlet, come and take this hand from me.
          [The King puts Laertes's hand into Hamlet's.]

HAMLET [to Laertes]
Give me your pardon, sir. I have done you wrong,
But pardon't as you are a gentleman.
This presence knows,   226
And you must needs have heard, how I am punished 227
With a sore distraction. What I have done
That might your nature, honor, and exception   229
Roughly awake, I here proclaim was madness.
Was't Hamlet wronged Laertes? Never Hamlet.
If Hamlet from himself be ta'en away,
And when he's not himself does wrong Laertes,
Then Hamlet does it not, Hamlet denies it.
Who does it, then? His madness. If't be so,
Hamlet is of the faction that is wronged;   236
His madness is poor Hamlet's enemy.
Sir, in this audience
Let my disclaiming from a purposed evil
Free me so far in your most generous thoughts
That I have shot my arrow o'er the house
And hurt my brother.

LAERTES   I am satisfied in nature,   242
Whose motive in this case should stir me most   243
To my revenge. But in my terms of honor
I stand aloof, and will no reconcilement
Till by some elder masters of known honor
I have a voice and precedent of peace   247
To keep my name ungored. But till that time   248
I do receive your offered love like love,

172 **breathing time** exercise period.   **Let** i.e., If   **177 deliver you** report what you say   **180 commend** commit to your favor. (A con-ventional salutation, but Hamlet wryly uses a more literal meaning, "recommend," "praise," in line 182.)   **183 for 's turn** for his pur-poses, i.e., to do it for him.   **184 lapwing** (A proverbial type of youthful forwardness. Also, a bird that draws intruders away from its nest and was thought to run about with its head in the shell when newly hatched; a seeming reference to Osric's hat.)   **186 comply . . . dug** observe ceremonious formality toward his nurse's or mother's teat   **187–93 Thus . . . are out** Thus has he—and many like him of the sort our frivolous age dotes on—acquired the trendy manner of speech of the time, and, out of habitual conversation with courtiers of their own kind, have collected together a kind of frothy medley of current phrases, which enables such gallants to hold their own among persons of the most select and well-sifted views; and yet do but test them by merely blowing on them, and their bubbles burst. **197 play** fence.   **that** if   **200 If . . . ready** If he declares his readiness, my convenience waits on his   **203 In happy time** (A phrase of cour-tesy indicating that the time is convenient.)   **204–5 entertainment** greeting

213–14 **gaingiving** misgiving   **216 repair** coming   **217 augury** the attempt to read signs of future events in order to avoid predicted trouble.   **220–2 Since . . . Let be** Since no one has knowledge of what he is leaving behind, what does an early death matter after all? Enough; forbear.   **222.1 trumpets, drums** trumpeters, drummers **222.3 all the state** the entire court   **226 presence** royal assembly **227 punished** afflicted   **229 exception** disapproval   **236 faction** party   **242 in nature** i.e., as to my personal feelings   **243 motive** prompting   **247 voice** authoritative pronouncement.   **of peace** for reconciliation   **248 name ungored** reputation unwounded.

And will not wrong it.

HAMLET   I embrace it freely,
And will this brothers' wager frankly play.—
Give us the foils. Come on.   251

LAERTES   Come, one for me.

HAMLET
I'll be your foil, Laertes. In mine ignorance   253
Your skill shall, like a star i'th' darkest night,
Stick fiery off indeed.

LAERTES   You mock me, sir.   255

HAMLET   No, by this hand.

KING
Give them the foils, young Osric. Cousin Hamlet,
You know the wager?

HAMLET   Very well, my lord.
Your Grace has laid the odds o'th' weaker side.   259

KING
I do not fear it; I have seen you both.
But since he is bettered, we have therefore odds.   261

LAERTES
This is too heavy. Let me see another.
              [*He exchanges his foil for another.*]

HAMLET
This likes me well. These foils have all a length?   263
                        [*They prepare to fence.*]

OSRIC   Ay, my good lord.

KING
Set me the stoups of wine upon that table.
If Hamlet give the first or second hit,
Or quit in answer of the third exchange,   267
Let all the battlements their ordnance fire.
The King shall drink to Hamlet's better breath,   269
And in the cup an union shall he throw   270
Richer than that which four successive kings
In Denmark's crown have worn. Give me the cups,
And let the kettle to the trumpet speak,   273
The trumpet to the cannoneer without,
The cannons to the heavens, the heaven to earth,
"Now the King drinks to Hamlet." Come, begin.
                        Trumpets the while.
And you, the judges, bear a wary eye.

HAMLET   Come on, sir.

LAERTES   Come, my lord. [*They fence. Hamlet scores a hit.*]

HAMLET   One.

LAERTES   No.

HAMLET   Judgment.

OSRIC   A hit, a very palpable hit.   282
                    Drum, trumpets, and shot. Flourish.
                        A piece goes off.

LAERTES   Well, again.

KING
Stay, give me drink. Hamlet, this pearl is thine.
              [*He drinks, and throws a pearl in Hamlet's cup.*]
Here's to thy health. Give him the cup.

HAMLET
I'll play this bout first. Set it by awhile.
Come. [*They fence.*] Another hit; what say you?

LAERTES   A touch, a touch, I do confess't.

KING
Our son shall win.

QUEEN   He's fat and scant of breath.   289
Here, Hamlet, take my napkin, rub thy brows.   290
The Queen carouses to thy fortune, Hamlet.   291

HAMLET   Good madam!

KING   Gertrude, do not drink.

QUEEN
I will, my lord, I pray you pardon me.   [*She drinks.*]

KING [*aside*]
It is the poisoned cup. It is too late.

HAMLET
I dare not drink yet, madam; by and by.

QUEEN   Come, let me wipe thy face.

LAERTES [*aside to the King*]
My lord, I'll hit him now.

KING   I do not think't.

LAERTES [*aside*]
And yet it is almost against my conscience.

HAMLET
Come, for the third, Laertes. You do but dally.
I pray you, pass with your best violence;   301
I am afeard you make a wanton of me.   302

LAERTES   Say you so? Come on.   [*They fence.*]

OSRIC   Nothing neither way.

LAERTES
Have at you now!   305
              [*Laertes wounds Hamlet; then, in scuffling,
              they change rapiers, and Hamlet wounds Laertes.*]

KING   Part them! They are incensed.

HAMLET
Nay, come, again.   [*The Queen falls.*]

OSRIC   Look to the Queen there, ho!

HORATIO
They bleed on both sides. How is it, my lord?

OSRIC   How is't, Laertes?

LAERTES
Why, as a woodcock to mine own springe, Osric;   309
I am justly killed with mine own treachery.

HAMLET
How does the Queen?

KING   She swoons to see them bleed.

---

251 frankly without ill feeling or the burden of rancor   **253 foil** thin metal background which sets a jewel off. (With pun on the blunted rapier for fencing.)   **255 Stick fiery off** stand out brilliantly **259 laid . . . side** backed the weaker side.   **261 is bettered** is the odds-on favorite. (Laertes's handicap is the "three hits" specified in line 165.)   **263 likes** pleases   **267 Or . . . exchange** or draws even with Laertes by winning the third exchange   **269 better breath** improved vigor   **270 union** pearl. (So called, according to Pliny's *Natural History*, 9, because pearls are *unique*, never identical.) **273 kettle** kettledrum   **282.2 *A piece*** A cannon

289 fat not physically fit, out of training   **290 napkin** handkerchief **291 carouses** drinks a toast   **301 pass** thrust   **302 make . . . me** i.e., treat me like a spoiled child, trifle with me.   **305.1–2 *in scuffling, they change rapiers*** (This stage direction occurs in the Folio. According to a widespread stage tradition, Hamlet receives a scratch, realizes that Laertes's sword is unbated, and accordingly forces an exchange.) **309 woodcock** a bird, a type of stupidity or as a decoy.   **springe** trap, snare

QUEEN
No, no, the drink, the drink—Oh, my dear Hamlet—
The drink, the drink! I am poisoned.   [*She dies.*]

HAMLET
Oh, villainy! Ho, let the door be locked!
Treachery! Seek it out.   [*Laertes falls. Exit Osric.*]

LAERTES
It is here, Hamlet. Hamlet, thou art slain.
No med'cine in the world can do thee good;
In thee there is not half an hour's life.
The treacherous instrument is in thy hand,
Unbated and envenomed. The foul practice   320
Hath turned itself on me. Lo, here I lie,
Never to rise again. Thy mother's poisoned.
I can no more. The King, the King's to blame.

HAMLET
The point envenomed too? Then, venom, to thy work.
          [*He stabs the King.*]

ALL   Treason! Treason!

KING
Oh, yet defend me, friends! I am but hurt.

HAMLET [*forcing the King to drink*]
Here, thou incestuous, murderous, damnèd Dane,
Drink off this potion. Is thy union here?   328
Follow my mother.   [*The King dies.*]

LAERTES   He is justly served.
It is a poison tempered by himself.   330
Exchange forgiveness with me, noble Hamlet.
Mine and my father's death come not upon thee,
Nor thine on me!   [*He dies.*]

HAMLET
Heaven make thee free of it! I follow thee.
I am dead, Horatio. Wretched Queen, adieu!
You that look pale and tremble at this chance,   336
That are but mutes or audience to this act,   337
Had I but time—as this fell sergeant, Death,   338
Is strict in his arrest—oh, I could tell you—   339
But let it be. Horatio, I am dead;
Thou livest. Report me and my cause aright
To the unsatisfied.

HORATIO   Never believe it.
I am more an antique Roman than a Dane.   343
Here's yet some liquor left.
          [*He attempts to drink from the poisoned cup.*
          Hamlet prevents him.]

HAMLET   As thou'rt a man,
Give me the cup! Let go! By heaven, I'll ha 't.
Oh, God, Horatio, what a wounded name,
Things standing thus unknown, shall I leave behind
          me!
If thou didst ever hold me in thy heart,
Absent thee from felicity awhile,

And in this harsh world draw thy breath in pain
To tell my story. *A march afar off* [*and a volley within*].
          What warlike noise is this?

          Enter Osric.

OSRIC
Young Fortinbras, with conquest come from Poland,
To th'ambassadors of England gives
This warlike volley.

HAMLET   Oh, I die, Horatio!
The potent poison quite o'ercrows my spirit.   355
I cannot live to hear the news from England,
But I do prophesy th'election lights
On Fortinbras. He has my dying voice.   358
So tell him, with th'occurrents more and less   359
Which have solicited. The rest is silence.   [*He dies.*] 360

HORATIO
Now cracks a noble heart. Good night, sweet prince,
And flights of angels sing thee to thy rest!
          [*March within.*]
Why does the drum come hither?

          Enter Fortinbras, with the [*English*] *Ambassadors*
          [*with drum, colors, and attendants*].

FORTINBRAS
Where is this sight?

HORATIO   What is it you would see?
If aught of woe or wonder, cease your search.

FORTINBRAS
This quarry cries on havoc. O proud Death,   366
What feast is toward in thine eternal cell,   367
That thou so many princes at a shot
So bloodily hast struck?

FIRST AMBASSADOR   The sight is dismal,
And our affairs from England come too late.
The ears are senseless that should give us hearing,
To tell him his commandment is fulfilled,
That Rosencrantz and Guildenstern are dead.
Where should we have our thanks?

HORATIO   Not from his mouth, 374
Had it th'ability of life to thank you.
He never gave commandment for their death.
But since, so jump upon this bloody question,   377
You from the Polack wars and you from England
Are here arrived, give order that these bodies
High on a stage be placèd to the view,   380
And let me speak to th' yet unknowing world
How these things came about. So shall you hear
Of carnal, bloody, and unnatural acts,
Of accidental judgments, casual slaughters,   384

---

320 Unbated not blunted with a button.   **practice** plot   **328 union**
pearl. (See line 270; with grim puns on the word's other meanings:
marriage, shared death.)   **330 tempered** mixed   **336 chance** mischance   **337 mutes** silent observers. (Literally, actors with nonspeaking parts.)   **338 fell sergeant** remorseless arresting officer   **339 strict**
(1) severely just (2) unavoidable.   **arrest** (1) taking into custody (2)
stopping my speech   **343 Roman** (Suicide was an honorable choice
for many Romans as an alternative to a dishonorable life.)

355 o'ercrows triumphs over (like the winner in a cockfight)
358 voice vote.   **359 th'occurrents** the events, incidents
360 solicited moved, urged. (Hamlet doesn't finish saying what the
events have prompted—presumably, his acts of vengeance, or his
reporting of those events to Fortinbras.)   **366 This . . . havoc** This
heap of dead bodies loudly proclaims a general slaughter.   **367 feast**
i.e., Death feasting on those who have fallen.   **toward** in preparation
374 his Claudius's   **377 so jump . . . question** so hard on the heels of
this bloody business   **380 stage** platform   **384 judgments** retribu-
tions.   **casual** occurring by chance

Of deaths put on by cunning and forced cause,   385
And, in this upshot, purposes mistook
Fall'n on th'inventors' heads. All this can I
Truly deliver.

FORTINBRAS   Let us haste to hear it,
And call the noblest to the audience.
For me, with sorrow I embrace my fortune.
I have some rights of memory in this kingdom,   391
Which now to claim my vantage doth invite me.   392

HORATIO
Of that I shall have also cause to speak,
And from his mouth whose voice will draw on more.   394
But let this same be presently performed,   395

385 **put on** instigated. **forced cause** contrivance **391 of memory**
traditional, remembered, unforgotten **392 vantage** favorable opportunity **394 voice . . . more** vote will influence still others.
395 presently immediately

Even while men's minds are wild, lest more
    mischance
On plots and errors happen.

FORTINBRAS   Let four captains   397
Bear Hamlet, like a soldier, to the stage,
For he was likely, had he been put on,   399
To have proved most royal; and for his passage,   400
The soldiers' music and the rite of war
Speak loudly for him.   402
Take up the bodies. Such a sight as this
Becomes the field, but here shows much amiss.   404
Go bid the soldiers shoot.

    Exeunt [*marching, bearing off the dead bodies;
        a peal of ordnance is shot off*].

397 **On** on top of **399 put on** i.e., invested in royal office and so put
to the test **400 for his passage** to mark his passing **402 Speak** (let
them) speak **404 Becomes the field** suits the field of battle

Othello, the Moor of Venice

Othello differs in several respects from the other three major Shakespearean tragedies with which it is usually ranked. Written seemingly about the time of its performance at court by the King's men (Shakespeare's acting company) on November 1, 1604, after *Hamlet* (c. 1599–1601) and before *King Lear* (1605–1606) and *Macbeth* (c. 1606–1607), *Othello* shares with these other plays a fascination with evil in its most virulent and universal aspect. These plays study the devastating effects of ambitious pride, ingratitude, wrath, jealousy, and vengeful hate—the deadly sins of the spirit—with only a passing interest in the political strife to which Shakespeare's Roman or classical tragedies are generally devoted. Of the four, *Othello* is the most concentrated upon one particular evil. The action concerns sexual jealousy, and, although human sinfulness is such that jealousy ceaselessly touches on other forms of depravity, the center of interest always returns in *Othello* to the destruction of a love through jealousy. *Othello* is a tragic portrait of a marriage. The protagonist is not a king or a prince, as in the tragedies already mentioned, but a general recently married. There are no supernatural visitations, as in *Hamlet* and *Macbeth*. Ideas of divine justice, while essential to *Othello*'s portrayal of a battle between good and evil for the allegiance of the protagonist, do not encompass the wide sweep of *King Lear*, nor do we find here the same broad indictment of humanity. Social order is not seriously shaken by Othello's tragedy. The fair-minded Duke of Venice remains firmly in control, and his deputy Lodovico oversees a just conclusion on Cyprus.

By the same token, *Othello* does not offer the remorseless questioning about humanity's relationship to the cosmos that we find in *King Lear, Hamlet,* and *Macbeth.* The battle of good and evil is, of course, cosmic, but in *Othello* that battle is realized through a taut narrative of jealousy and murder. Its poetic images are accordingly focused to a large extent on the natural world. One cluster of images is domestic and animal, having to do with goats, mon-keys, wolves, baboons, guinea hens, wildcats, spiders, flies, asses, dogs, copulating horses and sheep, serpents, and toads; other images, more wide-ranging in scope, include green-eyed monsters, devils, poisons, money purses, tarnished jewels, music untuned, and light extinguished. The story is immediate and direct, retaining the sensational atmosphere of its Italian prose source by Giovanni Baptista Giraldi Cinthio, in his *Hecatommithi* of 1565 (translated into French in 1584). Events move even more swiftly than in Cinthio's work, for Shakespeare has compressed the story into two or three nights and days (albeit with an intervening sea journey and with an elastic use of stage time to allow for the maturing of long-term plans, as when we learn that Iago has begged Emilia "a hundred times" to steal Desdemona's handkerchief, 3.3.308, or that Iago has accused Cassio of making love to Desdemona "A thousand times," 5.2.219). *Othello* does not have a fully developed double plot, as in *King Lear,* or a comparatively large group of characters serving as foils to the protagonist, as in *Hamlet. Othello*'s cast is small, and the plot is concentrated to an unusual degree on Othello, Desdemona, and Iago. What *Othello* may lose in breadth it gains in dramatic intensity.

Daringly, Shakespeare opens this tragedy of love, not with a direct and sympathetic portrayal of the lovers themselves, but with a scene of vicious insinuation about their marriage. The images employed by Iago to describe the coupling of Othello and Desdemona are revoltingly animalistic, sodomistic. "Even now, now, very now, an old black ram / Is tupping your white ewe," he taunts Desdemona's father, Brabantio. (Tupping is a word used specifically for the copulating of sheep.) "You'll have your daughter covered with a Barbary horse; you'll have your nephews neigh to you"; "your daughter and the Moor are now making the beast with two backs"; "the devil will make a grandsire of you" (1.1.90–3, 113–20). This degraded view reduces the marriage to one of utter carnality, with repeated emphasis on the word "gross": Desdemona has yielded "to the gross clasps of a lascivious Moor" and has made "a gross revolt" against her family and society (lines 129, 137). Iago's second theme, one that is habitual with him, is money. "What ho, Brabantio! Thieves, thieves, thieves! / Look to your house, your daughter, and your bags" (lines 81–2). The implication is of a sinister bond between thievery in sex and thievery in gold. Sex and money are both commodities to be protected by watchful fathers against libidinous and opportunistic children.

We as audience make plentiful allowance for Iago's bias in all this, since he has admitted to Roderigo his knavery and resentment of Othello. Even so, the carnal vision of love we confront is calculatedly disturbing, because it seems so equated with a pejorative image of blackness. Othello is unquestionably a black man, referred to disparagingly by his detractors as the "thick-lips," with a "sooty bosom" (1.1.68; 1.2.71); Elizabethan usage applied the term "Moor" without attempting to distinguish between Arabian and African peoples. From the ugly start of the play, Othello and Desdemona have to prove the worth of their love in the face of preset attitudes against miscegenation. Brabantio takes refuge in the thought that Othello must have bewitched Desdemona. His basic assumption—one to be echoed later by Iago and when Othello's confidence is undermined by Othello himself—is that miscegenation is unnatural by definition. In confronting and accusing Othello, he repeatedly appeals "to all things of sense" (that is, to common sense) and asks if it is not "gross in sense" (self-evident) that Othello has practiced magic on her, since nothing else could prompt human nature so to leave its natural path. "For nature so preposterously to err, / Being not deficient, blind, or lame of sense, / Sans witchcraft could not" (1.2.65, 73; 1.3.64–6). We as audience can perceive the racial bias in Brabantio's view and can recognize also in him the type of imperious father who conventionally opposes romantic love. It is sadly ironic that he should now prefer Roderigo as a son-in-law, evidently concluding that any white Venetian would be preferable to the prince of blacks. Still, Brabantio has been hospitable to the Moor and trusting of his daughter. He is a sorrowful rather than ridiculous figure, and the charge he levels at the married pair, however much it is based on a priori assumptions of what is "natural" in human behavior, remains to be answered.

After all, we find ourselves wondering, what did attract Othello and Desdemona to one another? Even though he certainly did not use witchcraft, may Othello not have employed a subtler kind of enchantment in the exotic character of his travels among "the Cannibals that each other eat, / The Anthropophagi, and men whose heads / Do grow beneath their shoulders" (1.3.145–7)? These "passing strange" events fascinate Desdemona as they do everyone, including the Duke of Venice ("I think this tale would win my daughter too"). Othello has not practiced unfairly on her—"This only is the witchcraft I have used" (lines 162, 171–3). Yet may he not represent for Desdemona a radical novelty, being a man at once less devious and more interesting than the dissolute Venetian swaggerers, such as Roderigo and the "wealthy curlèd darlings of our nation" (1.2.69), who follow her about? Was her deceiving of her father by means of the elopement a protest, an escape from conventionality? Why has she been attracted to a man older than herself? For his part, Othello gives the impression of being inexperienced with women, at least of Desdemona's rank and complexion, and is both intrigued and flattered by her attentions. "She loved me for the dangers I had passed, / And I loved her that she did pity them" (1.3.169–70). Desdemona fulfills a place in Othello's view of himself. Does she also represent status for him in Venetian society, where he has been employed as a military commander but treated nonetheless as something of an alien?

These subtle but impertinent ways of doubting the motivations of Othello and Desdemona, adding to the difficulties that are inherent in an attempt to understand the mysteries of attraction in any relationship, are thrust upon us by the play's opening and are later crucial to Iago's strategy of breeding mistrust. Just as importantly, however, these insinuations are refuted by Othello and especially by Desdemona. Whatever others may think, she never gives the slightest indication of regarding her husband as different because he is black and old. In fact, the images of blackness and age are significantly reversed during the play's early scenes. Othello has already embraced the Christian faith, whereas Iago, a white Italian in a Christian culture, emerges as innately evil from the very start of the play. Othello's first appearance onstage, when he confronts a party of torch-bearing men coming to arrest him and bids his followers sheathe their swords (1.2.60), is perhaps reminiscent of Christ's arrest in the Garden of Gethsemane; if so, it suggests a fleeting comparison between Othello and the Christian God whose charity and forbearance he seeks to emulate. Othello's blackness may be used in part as an emblem of fallen humanity, but so are we all fallen. His age similarly strengthens our impression of his wisdom, restraint, and leadership. Any suggestions of comic sexual infidelity in the marriage of an older man and an attractive young bride are confuted by what we see in Desdemona's chaste yet sensual regard for the good man she has chosen.

Desdemona is devoted to Othello, admiring, and faithful. We believe her when she says that she does not even know what it means to be unfaithful; the word *whore* is not in her vocabulary. She is defenseless against the charges brought against her, because she does not even comprehend them and cannot believe that anyone would imagine such things. Her love, both erotic and chaste, is of that transcendent wholesomeness common to several late Shakespearean heroines, such as Cordelia in *King Lear* and Hermione in *The Winter's Tale*. Her "preferring" Othello to her father, like Cordelia's placing her duty to a husband before that to a father, is not ungrateful but natural and proper. And Othello, however much he may regard Desdemona in terms of his own identity (he calls her "my fair warrior"), does cherish Desdemona as she deserves. "I cannot speak enough of this content," he exclaims when he rejoins her on Cyprus. "It stops me here; it is too much of joy" (2.1.181, 196–7). The passionate intensity of his love prepares the way for his tragedy; he speaks more truly than he knows in saying, "when I love thee not, / Chaos is come again" (3.3.99–100). Iago speaks truly also when he observes that Othello "Is of a constant, loving, noble nature" (2.1.290). Othello's tragedy is not that he is easily duped, but that his strong faith can be destroyed at such terrible cost. Othello never forgets how much he is losing. The threat to his love is not an initial lack of his being happily married, but rather the insidious assumption that Desdemona cannot love him because such a love might be unnatural. The fear of being unlovable exists in Othello's mind, but the human instrument of this vicious gospel is Iago.

Iago belongs to a select group of villains in Shakespeare who, while plausibly motivated in human terms, also take delight in evil for its own sake: Aaron the Moor in *Titus Andronicus*, Richard III, Don John in *Much Ado About Nothing*, Iago, Edmund in *King Lear*. They are not, like Macbeth or like Claudius in *Hamlet*, men driven by ambition to commit crimes they clearly recognize to be wrong. Although Edmund does belatedly try to make amends, these villains are essentially conscienceless, sinister, and amused by their own cunning. They are related to one another by a stage metaphor of personified evil derived from the Vice of the morality play, whose typical role is to win the Mankind figure away from virtue and to corrupt him with worldly enticements. Like that engaging tempter, Shakespeare's villains in these plays take the audience into their confidence, boast in soliloquy of their cleverness, exult in the triumph of evil, and improvise plans with daring and resourcefulness. They are all superb actors, deceiving virtually every character onstage until late in the action with their protean and hypocritical display. They take pleasure in this "sport" and amaze us by their virtuosity. The role is paradoxically comic in its use of ingenious and resourceful deception—the grim and ironic comedy of vice. We know that we are to condemn morally even while we applaud the skill.

This theatrical tradition of the Vice may best explain a puzzling feature of Iago, noted long ago and memorably phrased by Samuel Taylor Coleridge as "the motive hunting of a motiveless malignity." To be sure, Iago does offer plausible motives for what he does. Despite his resemblance to the morality Vice, he is no allegorized abstraction but an ensign in the army, a junior field officer who hates being out-ranked by a theoretician or staff officer. As an old-school professional, he also resents that he has not been promoted on the basis of seniority, the "old gradation" (1.1.38). Even his efforts at using influence with Othello have come to naught, and Iago can scarcely be blamed for supposing that Cassio's friendship with Othello has won him special favor. Thus, Iago has reason to plot against Cassio as well as Othello. Nevertheless a further dimension is needed to explain Iago's gloating, his utter lack of moral reflection, his concentration on destroying Desdemona (who has not wronged Iago), his absorption in ingenious methods of plotting, his finesse and style. Hatred precedes any plausible motive in Iago and ultimately does not depend on psychological causality. Probably the tradition of the stage Machiavel (another type of gloating villain based on stereotyped attitudes toward the heretical political ideas of Niccolò Machiavelli), as in Marlowe's *The Jew of Malta*, contributes to the portraiture; this tradition was readily assimilated with that of the Vice.

Iago's machinations yield him both "sport" and "profit" (1.3.387); that is, he enjoys his evildoing, although he is also driven by a motive. This Vice-like behavior in human garb creates a restless sense of a destructive metaphysical reality lying behind his visible exterior. Even his stated motives do not always make sense. When in an outburst of hatred he soliloquizes that "I hate the Moor; / And it is thought abroad that twixt my sheets / He's done my office," Iago goes on to concede the unlikelihood of this charge. "I know not if't be true; / But I, for mere suspicion in that kind, / Will do as if for surety" (lines 387–91). The charge is so absurd, in fact, that we have to look into Iago himself for the origin of this jealous paranoia. The answer may be partly emblematic: as the embodiment and genius of sexual jealousy, Iago suffers with ironic appropriateness from the evil he preaches, and without external cause. Emilia understands that jealousy is not a rational affliction but a self-induced disease of the mind. Jealous persons, she tells Desdemona, "are not ever jealous for the cause, / But jealous for they're jealous. It is a monster / Begot upon itself, born on itself" (3.4.161–3). Iago's own testimonial bears this out, for his jealousy is at once wholly irrational and agonizingly self-destructive. "I do suspect the lusty Moor / Hath leaped into my seat, the thought whereof / Doth, like a poisonous mineral, gnaw my innards" (2.1.296–8). In light of this nightmare, we can see that even his seemingly plausible resentment of Cassio's promotion is jealous envy. The "daily beauty" in Cassio's life makes Iago feel "ugly" by comparison (5.1.19–20), engendering in Iago a profound sense of lack of worth from which he can temporarily find relief only by reducing Othello and others to his own miserable condition. He is adept at provoking self-hatred in others because he suffers from it himself. His declaration to Othello that "I am your own forever"

(3.3.495) is, of course, cynical, but it also signals the extent to which Iago has succeeded in wooing Othello away from Desdemona and Cassio into a murderous union between two women-hating men. The Iago who thus dedicates himself as partner in the fulfillment of Othello's homicidal fantasies is, we learn, capable of fantasizing a bizarre amorous encounter between himself and Cassio (lines 429–41).

Othello comes at last to regard Iago as a "demi-devil" who has tempted Othello to damn himself "beneath all depth in hell"; Lodovico speaks of Iago in the closing lines of the play as a "hellish villain" (5.2.142, 309, 379); and Iago himself boasts that "When devils will the blackest sins put on, / They do suggest at first with heavenly shows, / As I do now" (2.3.345–7). Iago thus bears some affinity to both Vice and the devil, suggesting his relationship both to Othello's inner temptation and to a pre-existent evil force in the universe itself. Conversely, Desdemona is in Emilia's words an "angel," purely chaste; "So come my soul to bliss as I speak true" (5.2.134, 259). When Desdemona lands on Cyprus, she is greeted in words that echo the *Ave Maria:* "Hail to thee, lady! And the grace of heaven . . . Enwheel thee round" (2.1.87–9). These images introduce metaphorically a conflict of good and evil in which Othello, typical of fallen humanity, has chosen evil and destroyed the good at the prompting of a diabolical counselor. Again we see the heritage of the morality play, especially of the later morality play in which the Mankind figure was sometimes damned rather than saved. Even so, to allegorize *Othello* is to obscure and misread its clash of human passion. In fact, we see that the impulse to reduce human complexity to simplistic moral absolutes is a fatal weakness in Othello; by insisting on viewing Desdemona as a type or abstraction, he loses sight of her wonderful humanity. The theological issue of salvation or damnation is not relevant in dramatic terms; the play is not a homily on the dangers of jealousy. The metaphysical dimensions of a homiletic tradition are transmuted into human drama. Acknowledging these limitations, we can notwithstanding see a spiritual analogy in Iago's devil-like method of undoing his victims.

His trick resembles that of the similarly mischief-making Don John in *Much Ado About Nothing:* an optical illusion by which the blameless heroine is impugned as an adulteress. The concealed Othello must watch Cassio boasting of sexual triumphs and believe he is talking about Desdemona. Like the devil, Iago is given power over people's frail senses, especially the eyes. He can create illusions to induce Othello to see what Iago wants him to see, as Don John does with Claudio, but Othello's acceptance of the lie must be his own responsibility, a failure of his corrupted will. Iago practices on Othello with an a priori logic used before on Brabantio and Roderigo, urging the proneness of all mortals to sin and the alleged

unnaturalness of a black-white marriage. All women have appetites; Desdemona is a woman; hence, Desdemona has appetites. "The wine she drinks is made of grapes," he scoffs to Roderigo. "If she had been blessed, she would never have loved the Moor" (2.1.253–5). She is a Venetian, and "In Venice they do let God see the pranks / They dare not show their husbands" (3.3.216–17). Therefore, she, too, is a hypocrite; "She did deceive her father" (line 220). Most of all, it stands to reason that she must long for a man of her own race. Iago succeeds in getting Othello to concur: "And yet, how nature erring from itself—" (line 243). This proposition that Nature teaches all persons, including Desdemona, to seek a harmonious matching of "clime, complexion, and degree" strikes a responsive chord in Othello, since he knows that even though he has authority as a general serving his adopted city he is also black and in some senses a foreigner, an alien. "Haply, for I am black / And have not those soft parts of conversation / That chamberers have." Then, too, he is sensitive that he is older than she, "declined / Into the vale of years" (lines 246, 279–82), "the young affects / In me defunct" (1.3.266–7). And so, if one must conclude from the preceding that Desdemona will seek a lover, the only question is who. "This granted—as it is a most pregnant and unforced position—who stands so eminent in the degree of this fortune as Cassio does?" (2.1.237–9). Once Othello has accepted this syllogistic sequence of proofs, specious not through any lapse in logic but because the axiomatic assumptions about human nature are degraded and do not apply to Desdemona, Othello has arrived at an unshakable conclusion to which all subsequent evidence must be applied. "Villain, be sure thou prove my love a whore," he commissions Iago (3.3.375). Desdemona's innocent pleading for Cassio only makes things look worse. Cassio's reputed muttering while asleep, like the handkerchief seen in his possession or his giddy talk about his mistress Bianca, "speaks against her [Desdemona] with the other proofs" (line 456).

How has Othello fallen so far? His bliss with Desdemona as they are rejoined on Cyprus knows no limit. These two persons represent married love at its very best, erotic and spiritual, she enhancing his manliness, he cherishing her beauty and virtue. His blackness and age are positive images in him, despite earlier insinuations to the contrary. Indeed, we have no reason to suppose that Othello is what we would call "old," despite his worries about being "declined / Into the vale of years" and having lost the "young effects" of sexual desire; he appears to be middle-aged and vigorous, so much so that Desdemona is attracted to him sexually as well as in other ways. He is a man of public worthiness, of command, of self-assurance. Desdemona is the most domestic of Shakespeare's tragic heroines, even while she is also representative of so much that is transcendent. Husband and wife are bound happily in one of Shakespeare's few detailed portraits of serious commitment in marriage. Othello initially has the wisdom to know that Desdemona's feminine attractiveness ought not to be threatening to him: he need not be jealous because she is beautiful, "free of speech," and loves dancing and music, since "Where virtue is, these are more virtuous." Nor does he see any reason at first to fear her "revolt" simply because he is black and older than his wife; "she had eyes, and chose me" (3.3.197–203). Othello's self-assurance through the love he perceives in Desdemona is the strongest sign of his happiness in marriage.

What then gives way? We look at Iago for one important insight, but ultimately the cause must be in Othello himself. Arthur Kirsch has argued persuasively (in *Shakespeare and the Experience of Love*, 1981) that Othello's most grave failing is an insufficient regard for himself. It is in part an inability to counter the effects on him of a culture that regards him as an outsider; he is at last persuaded to see himself with the eyes of Venice, not just of Iago, but of Brabantio (who gladly entertains Othello until he has the presumption to elope with Brabantio's white daughter) and others. The resulting destruction of self-regard is devastating. Othello's jealousy stems from a profound suspicion that others cannot love him because he does not deem himself lovable.

Othello has loved Desdemona as an extention of himself, and, in his moments of greatest contentedness, his marriage is sustained by an idealized vision of himself serving as the object of his exalted romantic passion. When he destroys Desdemona, as he realizes with a terrible clarity, Othello destroys himself; the act is a prelude to his actual suicide. Iago's means of temptation, then, is to persuade Othello to regard himself with the eyes of Venice, to accept the view that Othello is himself alien and that any woman who loves him does so perversely. In Othello's tainted state of mind, Desdemona's very sexuality becomes an unbearable threat to him, her warmth and devotion a "proof" of disloyalty. Othello's most tortured speeches (3.4.57–77, 4.2.49–66) reveal the extent to which he equates the seemingly betraying woman, whom he has so depended on for happiness, with his own mother, who gave Othello's father a handkerchief and threatened him with loss of her love if he should lose it. Othello has briefly learned and then forgotten the precious art of harmonizing erotic passion and spiritual love, and, as these two great aims of love are driven apart in him, he comes to loathe and fear the sexuality that puts him so much in mind of his physical frailty and dependence on woman. The horror and pity of *Othello* rests, above all, in the spectacle of a love that was once so whole and noble made filthy by self-hatred. The tragic flaw thus lies in Othello's maleness, in his fear of betrayal by the innocent woman he loves, and his apparent need to degrade her for the very thing he finds desirable in her—a tendency so common among men that Freud, in the early twentieth century, could declare it to be "the most prevalent form of degradation in erotic life" (in Freud's *Sammlung*, volume 4).

The increasing surrender of Othello's judgment to passion can be measured in three successive trial scenes in the play: the entirely fair trial of Othello himself by the Venetian Senate concerning the elopement, Othello's trial of Cassio for drinking and rioting (when, ominously, Othello's "blood begins my safer guides to rule," 2.3.199), and finally the prejudged sentencing of Desdemona without providing her any opportunity to defend herself. In a corollary decline, Othello falls from the Christian compassion of the opening scenes (he customarily confesses to heaven "the vices of my blood," 1.3.125) to the pagan savagery of his vengeful and ritualistic execution of his wife. "My heart is turned to stone" (4.1.184–5), he vows, and at the play's end he grievingly characterizes himself as a "base Indian" who "threw a pearl away / Richer than all his tribe" (5.2.357–8). Iago knows that he must persuade Othello to sentence and to execute Desdemona himself, for only by active commitment to evil will Othello damn himself. In nothing does Iago so resemble the devil as in his wish to see Othello destroy the innocence and goodness on which his happiness depends.

The fate of some of the lesser characters echoes that of Othello, for Iago's evil intent is to "enmesh them all" (2.3.356). Cassio, in particular, is, like Othello, an attractive man with a single, vulnerable weakness—in his case, a fleshly appetite for wine and women. For him, alternately idolizing and depreciating women as he does, the gap between spiritual and sensual love remains vast, but he is essentially good-natured and trustworthy. His seemingly genial flaws lead to disaster, because they put him at the mercy of a remorseless enemy. Iago is, with fitting irony, the apostle of absolute self-control: "Our bodies are our gardens, to the which our wills are gardeners" (1.3.323–4). Thus, Cassio's tragedy is anything but a straightforward homily on the virtues of temperance. Similarly, Bianca is undone, not through any simple cause-and-effect punishment of her sexual conduct—she is, after all, fond of Cassio and loyal to him, even if he will not marry her—but because Iago is able to turn appearances against her. With his usual appeal to a priori logic, he builds a case that she and Cassio are in cahoots: "I do suspect this trash / To be a party in this injury . . . This is the fruits of whoring" (5.1.86–7, 118). Roderigo is another of Iago's victims, a contemptible one, led by the nose because he, too, has surrendered reason to passion. Emilia cannot escape Iago's evil influence and steals the handkerchief for him, despite knowing its value for Desdemona. Flaws are magnified into disasters by a remorseless evil intelligence. Men and women both must be ceaselessly circumspect; a good reputation is sooner lost than recovered. Emilia is a conventionally decent enough woman—she jests to Desdemona that she would be faithless in marriage only for a very high price—and yet her one small compromise with her conscience contributes to the murder of her mistress. Like Othello, she offers atonement too late, by denouncing her husband in a gesture of defiance toward male authority that says much about the tragic consequences of male mistrust of women. Desdemona is the only person in the play too good to be struck down through some inner flaw, which may explain why Iago is so intent on destroying her along with Othello and Cassio.

As a tragic hero, Othello obtains self-knowledge at a terrible price. He knows finally that what he has destroyed was ineffably good. The discovery is too late for him to make amends, and he dies by his own hand as atonement. The deaths of Othello and Desdemona are, in their separate ways, equally devastating: he is in part the victim of racism, though he nobly refuses to deny his own culpability, and she is the victim of sexism, lapsing sadly into the stereotypical role of passive and silent sufferer that the Venetian world expects of women. Despite the loss, however, Othello's reaffirmation of faith in Desdemona's goodness undoes what the devil-like Iago had most hoped to achieve: the separation of Othello from his loving trust in one who is good. In this important sense, Othello's self-knowledge is cathartic and a compensation for the terrible price he has paid. The very existence of a person as good as Desdemona gives the lie to Iago's creed that everyone has his or her price. She is the sacrificial victim who must die for Othello's loss of faith and, by dying, rekindle that faith. ("My life upon her faith!" Othello prophetically affirms, in response to her father's warning that she may deceive [1.3.297].) She cannot restore him to himself, for self-hatred has done its ugly work, but she is the means by which he understands at last the chimerical and wantonly destructive nature of his jealousy. His greatness appears in his acknowledgment of this truth and in the heroic struggle with which he has confronted an inner darkness we all share.

Onstage and in film and television, *Othello* proves itself to be jarringly relevant to modern concerns about racial conflict and about men's mistreatment of women. Janet Suzman chose to produce the play onstage and subsequently for educational television in Johannesburg,

South Africa, at a time when apartheid was soon to be dismantled, even though that surprising if inevitable event was not yet discernible. A racially mixed audience came to see a racially mixed cast, with John Kani, a well-known South African Black actor, as Othello, and a very fair-haired South African actress as Desdemona. Iago unmistakably represented the mindset of a state police officer obsessed with preserving the purity of the White race and therefore venemous in his racial hatred of Othello for his miscegenated marriage with a White woman. The explosively powerful emotions of that production carry over into a memorable film version. Orson Welles's 1951 film version, recently remastered, featured Othello in blackface as the protagonist; so did Laurence Olivier's film of 1965, based on a National Theatre stage production of 1964 with Frank Finlay as Iago and Maggie Smith as Desdemona. Indeed, most Othellos onstage over the centuries have been White actors (including Edmund Kean, John Philip Kemble, Edwin Booth, Charles Macready, Edwin Forrest, Henry Irving, Tommaso Salvini, and Paul Scofield, many of whom also played Iago), with notable exceptions that include Ira Aldridge, Earle Hyman, and Paul Robeson. Robeson's galvanizing performances at the Savoy Theatre in 1930 with Peggy Ashcroft as Desdemona, and then in Margaret Webster's New York production of 1943–1945 with Uta Hagen as Desdemona and José Ferrer as Iago, helped establish the role of Othello as one that great Black actors could perform. Today racially mixed casting allows for all sorts of permutations, though Kenneth Branagh's recent film chooses the more recognizable pattern with Branagh himself as Iago and Laurence Fishburne as Othello. In another recent development, Emilia has stood out in several productions as the raisonneur and heroic figure in the play, speaking as she does on behalf of maltreated women, urging Desdemona to stand up for her rights. One recent Chicago production went so far as to rewrite the ending: Othello and Iago both survive unpunished for what they have done, while Desdemona and Emilia lie dead as their innocent victims. This deliberate and provocative overstatement might seem extreme to some viewers, but unquestionably did signal the direction of recent performance history of this profoundly disturbing play.

Othello, the Moore of Venice

The Names of the Actors

OTHELLO, *the Moor*
BRABANTIO, [*a senator,*] *father to Desdemona*
CASSIO, *an honorable lieutenant* [*to Othello*]
IAGO, [*Othello's ancient,*] *a villain*
RODERIGO, *a gulled gentleman*
DUKE OF VENICE
SENATORS [*of Venice*]
MONTANO, *Governor of Cyprus*
GENTLEMEN *of Cyprus*
LODOVICO *and* GRATIANO, [*kinsmen to Brabantio,*] *two noble Venetians*
SAILORS
CLOWN

DESDEMONA, [*daughter to Brabantio and*] *wife to Othello*
EMILIA, *wife to Iago*
BIANCA, *a courtesan* [*and mistress to Cassio*]

[A MESSENGER
A HERALD
A MUSICIAN

Servants, Attendants, Officers, Senators, Musicians, Gentlemen

SCENE: *Venice; a seaport in Cyprus*]

1.1

Enter Roderigo and Iago.

RODERIGO
Tush, never tell me! I take it much unkindly   1
That thou, Iago, who hast had my purse
As if the strings were thine, shouldst know of this. 3

IAGO   'Sblood, but you'll not hear me.   4
If ever I did dream of such a matter,
Abhor me.

RODERIGO
Thou toldst me thou didst hold him in thy hate.   6

IAGO   Despise me
If I do not. Three great ones of the city,
In personal suit to make me his lieutenant,
Off-capped to him; and by the faith of man,
I know my price, I am worth no worse a place.
But he, as loving his own pride and purposes,
Evades them with a bombast circumstance   14

Horribly stuffed with epithets of war,   15
And, in conclusion,
Nonsuits my mediators. For, "Certes," says he,   17
"I have already chose my officer."
And what was he?
Forsooth, a great arithmetician,   20
One Michael Cassio, a Florentine,
A fellow almost damned in a fair wife,   22
That never set a squadron in the field
Nor the division of a battle knows   24
More than a spinster—unless the bookish theoric,   25
Wherein the togaed consuls can propose   26
As masterly as he. Mere prattle without practice
Is all his soldiership. But he, sir, had th'election;
And I, of whom his eyes had seen the proof   29
At Rhodes, at Cyprus, and on other grounds

1.1 Location: Venice. A street.
1 never tell me (An expression of incredulity, like "tell me another one.")   **3 this** i.e., Desdemona's elopement.   **4 'Sblood** By His (Christ's) blood   **6 him** Othello   **14 bombast circumstance** wordy evasion. (*Bombast* is cotton padding.)

15 epithets of war military expressions   **17 Nonsuits** rejects the petition of.   **Certes** Certainly   **20 arithmetician** i.e., a man whose military knowledge is merely theoretical, based on books of tactics   **22 A . . . wife** (Cassio does not seem to be married, but his counterpart in Shakespeare's source does have a woman in his house. See also 4.1.131.)   **24 division of a battle** disposition of a military unit   **25 a spinster** i.e., a housewife, one whose regular occupation is spinning.   **theoric** theory   **26 togaed consuls** toga-wearing counselors or senators.   **propose** discuss   **29 his** Othello's

Christened and heathen, must be beleed and calmed   31
By debitor and creditor. This countercaster,   32
He, in good time, must his lieutenant be,   33
And I—God bless the mark!—His Moorship's ancient.   34

RODERIGO
By heaven, I rather would have been his hangman.   35

IAGO
Why, there's no remedy. 'Tis the curse of service;
Preferment goes by letter and affection,   37
And not by old gradation, where each second   38
Stood heir to th' first. Now, sir, be judge yourself
Whether I in any just term am affined   40
To love the Moor.

RODERIGO   I would not follow him then.

IAGO   Oh, sir, content you.
I follow him to serve my turn upon him.   43
We cannot all be masters, nor all masters
Cannot be truly followed. You shall mark   46
Many a duteous and knee-crooking knave
That, doting on his own obsequious bondage,
Wears out his time, much like his master's ass,
For naught but provender, and when he's old,
  cashiered.   50
Whip me such honest knaves. Others there are   51
Who, trimmed in forms and visages of duty,   52
Keep yet their hearts attending on themselves,
And, throwing but shows of service on their lords,
Do well thrive by them, and when they have lined
  their coats,   55
Do themselves homage. These fellows have some
  soul,   56
And such a one do I profess myself. For, sir,
It is as sure as you are Roderigo,
Were I the Moor I would not be Iago.   59
In following him, I follow but myself—
Heaven is my judge, not I for love and duty,
But seeming so for my peculiar end.   62
For when my outward action doth demonstrate
The native act and figure of my heart   64
In compliment extern, 'tis not long after   65

But I will wear my heart upon my sleeve
For daws to peck at. I am not what I am.   67

RODERIGO
What a full fortune does the thick-lips owe   68
If he can carry't thus!

IAGO   Call up her father.   69
Rouse him, make after him, poison his delight,
Proclaim him in the streets; incense her kinsmen,
And, though he in a fertile climate dwell,   72
Plague him with flies. Though that his joy be joy,   73
Yet throw such changes of vexation on't   74
As it may lose some color.   75

RODERIGO
Here is her father's house. I'll call aloud.

IAGO
Do, with like timorous accent and dire yell   77
As when, by night and negligence, the fire   78
Is spied in populous cities.

RODERIGO
What ho, Brabantio! Signor Brabantio, ho!

IAGO
Awake! What ho, Brabantio! Thieves, thieves, thieves!
Look to your house, your daughter, and your bags!
Thieves, thieves!   83

Brabantio [enters] above [at a window].

BRABANTIO
What is the reason of this terrible summons?
What is the matter there?

RODERIGO
Signor, is all your family within?

IAGO
Are your doors locked?

BRABANTIO   Why, wherefore ask you this?

IAGO
Zounds, sir, you're robbed. For shame, put on your
  gown!   88
Your heart is burst; you have lost half your soul.
Even now, now, very now, an old black ram
Is tupping your white ewe. Arise, arise!   91
Awake the snorting citizens with the bell,   92
Or else the devil will make a grandsire of you.   93
Arise, I say!

BRABANTIO   What, have you lost your wits?

RODERIGO
Most reverend signor, do you know my voice?

---

31 beleed and calmed left to leeward without wind, becalmed. (A sailing metaphor.) **32 debitor and creditor** (A name for a system of bookkeeping, here used as a contemptuous nickname for Cassio.) **countercaster** i.e., bookkeeper, one who tallies with *counters*, or "metal disks." (Said contemptuously.) **33 in good time** opportunely, i.e., forsooth **34 God bless the mark** (Perhaps originally a formula to ward off evil; here an expression of impatience.) **ancient** standard-bearer, ensign. **35 his hangman** the executioner of him. **37 Preferment** promotion. **letter and affection** personal influence and favoritism **38 old gradation** step-by-step seniority, the traditional way **40 term** respect. **affined** bound **43 content you** don't you worry about that. **46 truly** faithfully **50 cashiered** dismissed from service. **51 Whip me** Whip, as far as I'm concerned **52 trimmed . . . duty** dressed up in the mere form and show of dutifulness **55 lined their coats** i.e., stuffed their purses **56 Do themselves homage** i.e., attend to self-interest solely. **59 Were . . . Iago** i.e., if I were able to assume command, I certainly would not choose to remain a subordinate, or, I would keep a suspicious eye on a flattering subordinate. **62 peculiar** particular, personal **64 native** innate. **figure** shape, intent **65 compliment extern** outward show (conforming in this case to the inner workings and intention of the heart)

67 daws small crowlike birds, proverbially stupid and avaricious. **I am not what I am** i.e., I am not one who wears his heart on his sleeve. **68 full** swelling. **thick-lips** (Elizabethans often applied the term "Moor" to Negroes.) **owe** own **69 carry't thus** carry this off. **72–3 though . . . flies** though he seems prosperous and happy now, vex him with misery. **73 Though . . . be joy** Although he seems fortunate and happy. (Repeats the idea of line 72.) **74 changes of vexation** vexing changes **75 As . . . color** that may cause it to lose some of its first gloss. **77 timorous** frightening **78 As . . . fire** as when a fire, having gained hold by negligence at night **83.1 at a window** (This stage direction, from the Quarto, probably calls for an appearance on the gallery above and rearstage.) **88 Zounds** By His (Christ's) wounds **91 tupping** covering, copulating with. (Said of sheep.) **92 snorting** snoring **93 the devil** (The devil was conventionally pictured as black.)

BRABANTIO   Not I. What are you?

RODERIGO   My name is Roderigo.

BRABANTIO   The worser welcome.
I have charged thee not to haunt about my doors.
In honest plainness thou hast heard me say
My daughter is not for thee; and now, in madness,
Being full of supper and distemp'ring drafts,   102
Upon malicious bravery dost thou come   103
To start my quiet.   104

RODERIGO
Sir, sir, sir—

BRABANTIO   But thou must needs be sure
My spirits and my place have in their power   106
To make this bitter to thee.

RODERIGO   Patience, good sir.

BRABANTIO
What tell'st thou me of robbing? This is Venice;
My house is not a grange.

RODERIGO   Most grave Brabantio,   109
In simple and pure soul I come to you.   110

IAGO   Zounds, sir, you are one of those that will not
serve God if the devil bid you. Because we come to do
you service and you think we are ruffians, you'll have
your daughter covered with a Barbary horse; you'll   114
have your nephews neigh to you; you'll have coursers   115
for cousins and jennets for germans.   116

BRABANTIO   What profane wretch art thou?

IAGO   I am one, sir, that comes to tell you your daughter
and the Moor are now making the beast with two
backs.

BRABANTIO
Thou art a villain.

IAGO   You are—a senator.   121

BRABANTIO
This thou shalt answer. I know thee, Roderigo.   122

RODERIGO
Sir, I will answer anything. But I beseech you,
If't be your pleasure and most wise consent—   124
As partly I find it is—that your fair daughter,
At this odd-even and dull watch o'th' night,   126
Transported with no worse nor better guard   127
But with a knave of common hire, a gondolier,   128
To the gross clasps of a lascivious Moor—
If this be known to you and your allowance   130
We then have done you bold and saucy wrongs.   131
But if you know not this, my manners tell me
We have your wrong rebuke. Do not believe

That, from the sense of all civility,   134
I thus would play and trifle with your reverence.   135
Your daughter, if you have not given her leave,
I say again, hath made a gross revolt,
Tying her duty, beauty, wit, and fortunes   138
In an extravagant and wheeling stranger   139
Of here and everywhere. Straight satisfy yourself.   140
If she be in her chamber or your house,
Let loose on me the justice of the state
For thus deluding you.

BRABANTIO   [calling]   Strike on the tinder, ho!   144
Give me a taper! Call up all my people!
This accident is not unlike my dream.   146
Belief of it oppresses me already.
Light, I say, light!   *Exit [above]*.

IAGO   Farewell, for I must leave you.
It seems not meet nor wholesome to my place   149
To be produced—as, if I stay, I shall—   150
Against the Moor. For I do know the state,
However this may gall him with some check,   152
Cannot with safety cast him, for he's embarked   153
With such loud reason to the Cyprus wars,   154
Which even now stands in act, that, for their souls,   155
Another of his fathom they have none   156
To lead their business; in which regard,   157
Though I do hate him as I do hell pains,
Yet for necessity of present life   159
I must show out a flag and sign of love,
Which is indeed but sign. That you shall surely find
    him,
Lead to the Sagittary the raisèd search,   162
And there will I be with him. So farewell.   *Exit*. 163

Enter [below] Brabantio [in his nightgown] with
servants and torches.

BRABANTIO
It is too true an evil. Gone she is;
And what's to come of my despisèd time   165
Is naught but bitterness. Now, Roderigo,
Where didst thou see her?—Oh, unhappy girl!—
With the Moor, say'st thou?—Who would be a father!—
How didst thou know 'twas she?—Oh, she deceives
    me
Past thought!—What said she to you?—Get more
    tapers.
Raise all my kindred.—Are they married, think you?

---

102 **distemp'ring** intoxicating   103 **Upon malicious bravery** with hostile intent to defy me   104 **start** startle, disrupt   106 **My . . . power** my temperament and my authority of office have it in their power   109 **grange** isolated country house.   110 **simple** sincere   114 **Barbary** from northern Africa (and hence associated with Othello)   115 **nephews** i.e., grandsons   115–16 **you'll . . . germans** you'll consent to have powerful horses for kinfolks and small Spanish horses for near relatives.   121 **a senator** (Said with mock politeness, as though the word itself were an insult.)   122 **answer** be held accountable for.   124 **wise** well-informed   126 **At . . . night** at this hour that is between day and night, neither the one nor the other   127 **with** by   128 **But with a knave** than by a low fellow, a servant   130 **and your allowance** and has your permission   131 **saucy** insolent

134 **from** contrary to.   **civility** good manners, decency   135 **your reverence** (1) the respect due to you (2) Your Reverence.   138 **wit** intelligence   139–40 **In . . . everywhere** to a wandering and vagabond foreigner of uncertain origins.   140 **Straight** Straightway   144 **tinder** charred linen ignited by a spark from flint and steel, used to light torches or *tapers* (lines 145, 170)   146 **accident** occurrence, event   149 **meet** fitting.   **place** position (as ensign)   150 **produced** produced (as a witness)   152 **gall** rub; oppress.   **check** rebuke   153 **cast** dismiss.   **embarked** engaged   154 **loud** urgent   155 **stands in act** have started.   **for their souls** to save their souls   156 **fathom** i.e., ability, depth of experience   157 **in which regard** out of regard for which   159 **life** livelihood   162 **Sagittary** (An inn or house where Othello and Desdemona are staying, named for its sign of Sagittarius, or Centaur.)   **raisèd search** search party roused out of sleep   163.1 *nightgown* dressing gown. (This costuming is specified in the Quarto text.)   165 **time** i.e., remainder of life

RODERIGO   Truly, I think they are.

BRABANTIO

Oh, heaven! How got she out? Oh, treason of the
    blood!
Fathers, from hence trust not your daughters' minds
By what you see them act. Is there not charms   175
By which the property of youth and maidhood   176
May be abused? Have you not read, Roderigo,   177
Of some such thing?

RODERIGO   Yes, sir, I have indeed.

BRABANTIO

Call up my brother.—Oh, would you had had her!—
Some one way, some another.—Do you know
Where we may apprehend her and the Moor?

RODERIGO

I think I can discover him, if you please   182
To get good guard and go along with me.

BRABANTIO

Pray you, lead on. At every house I'll call;
I may command at most.—Get weapons, ho!   185
And raise some special officers of night.—
On, good Roderigo. I will deserve your pains.   187

Exeunt.

❖

1.2

Enter Othello, Iago, attendants with torches.

IAGO

Though in the trade of war I have slain men,
Yet do I hold it very stuff o'th' conscience
To do no contrived murder. I lack iniquity   2
Sometimes to do me service. Nine or ten times   3
I had thought t'have yerked him here under the ribs. 5

OTHELLO

'Tis better as it is.

IAGO   Nay, but he prated,
And spoke such scurvy and provoking terms
Against your honor
That, with the little godliness I have,
I did full hard forbear him. But, I pray you, sir, 10
Are you fast married? Be assured of this,
That the magnifico is much beloved,   12
And hath in his effect a voice potential   13
As double as the Duke's. He will divorce you,
Or put upon you what restraint or grievance
The law, with all his might to enforce it on,
Will give him cable.

OTHELLO   Let him do his spite.   17
My services which I have done the seigniory   18

Shall out-tongue his complaints. 'Tis yet to know— 19
Which, when I know that boasting is an honor,
I shall promulgate—I fetch my life and being
From men of royal siege, and my demerits   22
May speak unbonneted to as proud a fortune   23
As this that I have reached. For know, Iago,
But that I love the gentle Desdemona,
I would not my unhousèd free condition   26
Put into circumscription and confine   27
For the sea's worth. But look, what lights come yond? 28

Enter Cassio [and officers] with torches.

IAGO

Those are the raisèd father and his friends.
You were best go in.

OTHELLO   Not I. I must be found.
My parts, my title, and my perfect soul   31
Shall manifest me rightly. Is it they?

IAGO   By Janus, I think no.   33

OTHELLO

The servants of the Duke? And my lieutenant?
The goodness of the night upon you, friends!
What is the news?

CASSIO   The Duke does greet you, General,
And he requires your haste-post-haste appearance
Even on the instant.

OTHELLO   What is the matter, think you?

CASSIO

Something from Cyprus, as I may divine.   39
It is a business of some heat. The galleys   40
Have sent a dozen sequent messengers   41
This very night at one another's heels,
And many of the consuls, raised and met,   43
Are at the Duke's already. You have been hotly called
    for;
When, being not at your lodging to be found,
The Senate hath sent about three several quests   46
To search you out.

OTHELLO   'Tis well I am found by you.
I will but spend a word here in the house
And go with you.   [*Exit.*]

CASSIO   Ancient, what makes he here?   49

IAGO

Faith, he tonight hath boarded a land carrack.   50
If it prove lawful prize, he's made forever.   51

---

175 charms spells   **176 property** special quality, nature   **177 abused** deceived.   **182 discover** reveal, uncover   **185 command** demand assistance   **187 deserve** show gratitude for
1.2. Location: Venice. Another street, before Othello's lodgings.
2 very stuff essence, basic material. (Continuing the metaphor of *trade* from line 1.)   **3 contrived** premeditated   **5 yerked** stabbed.   **him** i.e., Roderigo   **10 I . . . him** I restrained myself with great difficulty from assaulting him.   **12 magnifico** Venetian grandee, i.e., Brabantio   **13 in his effect** at his command.   **potential** powerful   **17 cable** i.e., scope.   **18 seigniory** Venetian government

19 yet to know not yet widely known   **22 siege** i.e., rank. (Literally, a seat used by a person of distinction.)   **demerits** deserts   **23 unbonneted** without removing the hat, i.e., on equal terms (? Or "with hat off," "in all due modesty.")   **26 unhousèd** unconfined, undomesticated   **27 circumscription and confine** restriction and confinement   **28 the sea's worth** all the riches at the bottom of the sea.   **28.1 officers** (The Quarto text specifies, "*Enter Cassio with lights, Officers, and torches.*")   **31 My . . . soul** My natural gifts, my position or reputation, and my unflawed conscience   **33 Janus** Roman two-faced god of beginnings   **39 divine** guess.   **40 heat** urgency.   **41 sequent** successive   **43 consuls** senators   **46 about** all over the city.   **several** separate   **49 makes** does   **50 boarded** gone aboard and seized as an act of piracy. (With sexual suggestion.)   **carrack** large merchant ship   **51 prize** booty

CASSIO
I do not understand.

IAGO   He's married.

CASSIO   To who?

[Enter Othello.]

IAGO
Marry, to—Come, Captain, will you go?   53

OTHELLO   Have with you.   54

CASSIO
Here comes another troop to seek for you.   55

Enter Brabantio, Roderigo, with officers and
torches.

IAGO
It is Brabantio. General, be advised.   56
He comes to bad intent.

OTHELLO   Holla! Stand there!

RODERIGO
Signor, it is the Moor.

BRABANTIO   Down with him, thief!
[They draw on both sides.]

IAGO
You, Roderigo! Come, sir, I am for you.

OTHELLO
Keep up your bright swords, for the dew will rust
them.   60
Good signor, you shall more command with years
Than with your weapons.

BRABANTIO
O thou foul thief, where hast thou stowed my
daughter?
Damned as thou art, thou hast enchanted her!
For I'll refer me to all things of sense,   65
If she in chains of magic were not bound
Whether a maid so tender, fair, and happy,
So opposite to marriage that she shunned
The wealthy curlèd darlings of our nation,
Would ever have, t'incur a general mock,
Run from her guardage to the sooty bosom   71
Of such a thing as thou—to fear, not to delight.
Judge me the world if 'tis not gross in sense   73
That thou hast practiced on her with foul charms,
Abused her delicate youth with drugs or minerals   75
That weakens motion. I'll have't disputed on;   76
'Tis probable and palpable to thinking.
I therefore apprehend and do attach thee   78
For an abuser of the world, a practicer   79
Of arts inhibited and out of warrant.—   80
Lay hold upon him! If he do resist,

Subdue him at his peril.

OTHELLO   Hold your hands,
Both you of my inclining and the rest.   83
Were it my cue to fight, I should have known it
Without a prompter.—Whither will you that I go
To answer this your charge?

BRABANTIO   To prison, till fit time
Of law and course of direct session   88
Call thee to answer.

OTHELLO   What if I do obey?
How may the Duke be therewith satisfied,
Whose messengers are here about my side
Upon some present business of the state
To bring me to him?

OFFICER   'Tis true, most worthy signor.
The Duke's in council, and your noble self,
I am sure, is sent for.

BRABANTIO   How? The Duke in council?
In this time of the night? Bring him away.   96
Mine's not an idle cause. The Duke himself,   97
Or any of my brothers of the state,
Cannot but feel this wrong as 'twere their own;
For if such actions may have passage free,   100
Bondslaves and pagans shall our statesmen be.

Exeunt.

❖

1.3

Enter Duke [and] Senators [and sit at a table, with
lights], and Officers. [The Duke and Senators
are reading dispatches.]

DUKE
There is no composition in these news   1
That gives them credit.

FIRST SENATOR   Indeed, they are disproportioned.   3
My letters say a hundred and seven galleys.

DUKE
And mine, a hundred forty.

SECOND SENATOR   And mine, two hundred.
But though they jump not on a just account—   6
As in these cases, where the aim reports   7
'Tis oft with difference—yet do they all confirm
A Turkish fleet, and bearing up to Cyprus.

DUKE
Nay, it is possible enough to judgment.
I do not so secure me in the error   11
But the main article I do approve   12
In fearful sense.

53 Marry (An oath, originally "by the Virgin Mary"; here used
with wordplay on married.)   54 Have with you i.e., Let's go.
55.1–2 officers and torches (The Quarto text calls for "others with lights
and weapons.")   56 be advised be on your guard.   60 Keep up Keep
in the sheath   65 I'll . . . sense I'll submit my case to one and all
71 guardage guardianship   73 gross in sense obvious
75 minerals i.e., poisons   76 weakens motion impair the vital faculties.   disputed on argued in court by professional counsel, debated
by experts   78 attach arrest   79 abuser deceiver   80 arts inhibited
prohibited arts, black magic.   out of warrant illegal.

83 inclining following, party   88 course of direct session regular or
specially convened legal proceedings   96 away right along.   97 idle
trifling   100 may . . . free are allowed to go unchecked
1.3. Location: Venice. A council chamber.
0.1–2 Enter . . . Officers (The Quarto text calls for the Duke and senators to "set at a Table with lights and Attendants.")   1 composition consistency   3 disproportioned inconsistent.   6 jump agree.   just exact
7 the aim conjecture   11–12 I do not . . . approve I do not take such
(false) comfort in the discrepancies that I fail to perceive the main
point, i.e., that the Turkish fleet is threatening

SAILOR (*within*)   What ho, what ho, what ho!

Enter Sailor.

OFFICER   A messenger from the galleys.

DUKE   Now, what's the business?

SAILOR

The Turkish preparation makes for Rhodes.   16
So was I bid report here to the state
By Signor Angelo.

DUKE

How say you by this change?

FIRST SENATOR   This cannot be   19
By no assay of reason. 'Tis a pageant   20
To keep us in false gaze. When we consider   21
Th'importancy of Cyprus to the Turk,
And let ourselves again but understand
That, as it more concerns the Turk than Rhodes,
So may he with more facile question bear it,   25
For that it stands not in such warlike brace,   26
But altogether lacks th'abilities   27
That Rhodes is dressed in—if we make thought of this,   28
We must not think the Turk is so unskillful   29
To leave that latest which concerns him first,   30
Neglecting an attempt of ease and gain
To wake and wage a danger profitless.   32

DUKE

Nay, in all confidence, he's not for Rhodes.

OFFICER   Here is more news.

Enter a Messenger.

MESSENGER

The Ottomites, reverend and gracious,
Steering with due course toward the isle of Rhodes,
Have there injointed them with an after fleet.   37

FIRST SENATOR

Ay, so I thought. How many, as you guess?

MESSENGER

Of thirty sail; and now they do restem   39
Their backward course, bearing with frank
    appearance   40
Their purposes toward Cyprus. Signor Montano,
Your trusty and most valiant servitor,   42
With his free duty recommends you thus,   43
And prays you to believe him.

DUKE   'Tis certain then for Cyprus.
Marcus Luccicos, is not he in town?

FIRST SENATOR   He's now in Florence.

DUKE

Write from us to him, post-post-haste. Dispatch.

FIRST SENATOR

Here comes Brabantio and the valiant Moor.

*Enter Brabantio, Othello, Cassio, Iago,
Roderigo, and officers.*

DUKE

Valiant Othello, we must straight employ you   50
Against the general enemy Ottoman.   51
[*To Brabantio*] I did not see you; welcome, gentle
    signor.   52
We lacked your counsel and your help tonight.

BRABANTIO

So did I yours. Good Your Grace, pardon me;
Neither my place nor aught I heard of business   55
Hath raised me from my bed, nor doth the general
    care
Take hold on me, for my particular grief   57
Is of so floodgate and o'erbearing nature   58
That it engluts and swallows other sorrows   59
And it is still itself.

DUKE   Why, what's the matter?   60

BRABANTIO

My daughter! Oh, my daughter!

DUKE AND SENATORS   Dead?

BRABANTIO   Ay, to me.
She is abused, stol'n from me, and corrupted   62
By spells and medicines bought of mountebanks;
For nature so preposterously to err,
Being not deficient, blind, or lame of sense,   65
Sans witchcraft could not.   66

DUKE

Whoe'er he be that in this foul proceeding
Hath thus beguiled your daughter of herself,
And you of her, the bloody book of law
You shall yourself read in the bitter letter
After your own sense—yea, though our proper son   71
Stood in your action.

BRABANTIO   Humbly I thank Your Grace.   72
Here is the man, this Moor, whom now it seems
Your special mandate for the state affairs
Hath hither brought.

ALL   We are very sorry for't.

DUKE [*to Othello*]

What, in your own part, can you say to this?

BRABANTIO   Nothing, but this is so.

OTHELLO

Most potent, grave, and reverend signors,
My very noble and approved good masters: 79
That I have ta'en away this old man's daughter,
It is most true; true, I have married her.
The very head and front of my offending   82

16 preparation fleet prepared for battle   19 by about   20 assay test.
pageant mere show   21 in false gaze looking the wrong way.   25 So
may . . . it so also he (the Turk) can more easily capture it (Cyprus)
26 For that since.   brace state of defense   27 th'abilities the means
of self-defense   28 dressed in equipped with   29 unskillful deficient in judgment   30 latest last   32 wake and wage stir up and risk
37 injointed them joined themselves.   after second, following
39–40 restem . . . course retrace their original course   40 frank
appearance undisguised intent   42 servitor officer under your command   43 free duty freely given and loyal service.   recommends
commends himself and reports to

50 straight straightway   51 general enemy universal enemy to all
Christendom   52 gentle noble   55 place official position   57 particular personal   58 floodgate i.e., overwhelming (as when floodgates
are opened)   59 engluts engulfs   60 is still itself remains undiminished.   62 abused deceived   65 deficient defective.   lame of sense
deficient in sensory perception   66 Sans without   71 After . . .
sense according to your own interpretation.   our proper my own
72 Stood . . . action were under your accusation.   79 approved
proved, esteemed   82 head and front height and breadth, entire
extent

Hath this extent, no more. Rude am I in my speech,   83
And little blessed with the soft phrase of peace;
For since these arms of mine had seven years' pith,   85
Till now some nine moons wasted, they have used   86
Their dearest action in the tented field;   87
And little of this great world can I speak
More than pertains to feats of broils and battle,
And therefore little shall I grace my cause
In speaking for myself. Yet, by your gracious patience,
I will a round unvarnished tale deliver   92
Of my whole course of love—what drugs, what
    charms,
What conjuration, and what mighty magic,
For such proceeding I am charged withal,   95
I won his daughter.
BRABANTIO   A maiden never bold;
Of spirit so still and quiet that her motion   97
Blushed at herself; and she, in spite of nature,   98
Of years, of country, credit, everything,   99
To fall in love with what she feared to look on!
It is a judgment maimed and most imperfect
That will confess perfection so could err   102
Against all rules of nature, and must be driven
To find out practices of cunning hell   104
Why this should be. I therefore vouch again   105
That with some mixtures powerful o'er the blood,   106
Or with some dram conjured to this effect,   107
He wrought upon her.
DUKE   To vouch this is no proof,
Without more wider and more overt test   109
Than these thin habits and poor likelihoods   110
Of modern seeming do prefer against him.   111
FIRST SENATOR   But Othello, speak.
Did you by indirect and forcèd courses   113
Subdue and poison this young maid's affections?
Or came it by request and such fair question   115
As soul to soul affordeth?
OTHELLO   I do beseech you,
Send for the lady to the Sagittary
And let her speak of me before her father.
If you do find me foul in her report,
The trust, the office I do hold of you
Not only take away, but let your sentence
Even fall upon my life.
DUKE   Fetch Desdemona hither.
OTHELLO [to Iago]
Ancient, conduct them. You best know the place.
                          [Exeunt Iago and attendants.]

And, till she come, as truly as to heaven
I do confess the vices of my blood,   125
So justly to your grave ears I'll present   126
How I did thrive in this fair lady's love,
And she in mine.
DUKE   Say it, Othello.
OTHELLO
Her father loved me, oft invited me,
Still questioned me the story of my life   131
From year to year—the battles, sieges, fortunes
That I have passed.
I ran it through, even from my boyish days
To th' very moment that he bade me tell it,
Wherein I spoke of most disastrous chances,
Of moving accidents by flood and field,   137
Of hairbreadth scapes i'th'imminent deadly breach,   138
Of being taken by the insolent foe
And sold to slavery, of my redemption thence,
And portance in my travels' history,   141
Wherein of antres vast and deserts idle,   142
Rough quarries, rocks, and hills whose heads touch
    heaven,   143
It was my hint to speak—such was my process—   144
And of the Cannibals that each other eat,
The Anthropophagi, and men whose heads   146
Do grow beneath their shoulders. These things to hear
Would Desdemona seriously incline;
But still the house affairs would draw her thence,
Which ever as she could with haste dispatch
She'd come again, and with a greedy ear
Devour up my discourse. Which I, observing,
Took once a pliant hour, and found good means   153
To draw from her a prayer of earnest heart
That I would all my pilgrimage dilate,   155
Whereof by parcels she had something heard,   156
But not intentively. I did consent,   157
And often did beguile her of her tears,
When I did speak of some distressful stroke
That my youth suffered. My story being done,
She gave me for my pains a world of sighs.
She swore, in faith, 'twas strange, 'twas passing
    strange,   162
'Twas pitiful, 'twas wondrous pitiful.
She wished she had not heard it, yet she wished
That heaven had made her such a man. She thanked
    me,   165
And bade me, if I had a friend that loved her,
I should but teach him how to tell my story,
And that would woo her. Upon this hint I spake.   168
She loved me for the dangers I had passed,

---

83 Rude Unpolished **85 since . . . pith** i.e., since I was seven. (*Pith* means "strength, vigor.") **86 Till . . . wasted** until some nine months ago (since when Othello has evidently not been on active duty, but in Venice) **87 dearest** most valuable **92 round** plain **95 withal** with **97–8 her . . . herself** i.e., she blushed easily at herself. (*Motion* can suggest the impulse of the soul or of the emotions, or physical movement.) **99 years** i.e., difference in age. **credit** virtuous reputation **102 confess** concede (that) **104 practices** plots **105 vouch** assert **106 blood** passions **107 dram . . . effect** dose made by magical spells to have this effect **109 more wider** fuller. **test** testimony **110 habits** garments, i.e., appearances. **poor likelihoods** weak inferences **111 modern seeming** commonplace assumption. **prefer** bring forth **113 forcèd courses** means used against her will **115 question** conversation

125 blood passions, human nature **126 justly** truthfully, accurately **131 Still** continually **137 moving accidents** stirring happenings **138 i'th'imminent . . . breach** in death-threatening gaps made in a fortification **141 portance** conduct **142 antres** caverns. **idle** barren, desolate **143 Rough quarries** rugged rock formations **144 hint** occasion, opportunity **146 Anthropophagi** man-eaters. (A term from Pliny's *Natural History*.) **153 pliant** well-suiting **155 dilate** relate in detail **156 by parcels** piecemeal **157 intentively** with full attention, continuously. **162 passing** exceedingly **165 made her** (1) created her to be (2) made for her **168 hint** opportunity. (Othello does not mean that she was dropping hints.)

And I loved her that she did pity them.
This only is the witchcraft I have used.
Here comes the lady. Let her witness it.

Enter Desdemona, Iago, [and] attendants.

DUKE
I think this tale would win my daughter too.
Good Brabantio,
Take up this mangled matter at the best.   175
Men do their broken weapons rather use
Than their bare hands.

BRABANTIO   I pray you, hear her speak.
If she confess that she was half the wooer,
Destruction on my head if my bad blame
Light on the man!—Come hither, gentle mistress.
Do you perceive in all this noble company
Where most you owe obedience?

DESDEMONA   My noble father,
I do perceive here a divided duty.
To you I am bound for life and education;   184
My life and education both do learn me   185
How to respect you. You are the lord of duty;   186
I am hitherto your daughter. But here's my husband,
And so much duty as my mother showed
To you, preferring you before her father,
So much I challenge that I may profess   190
Due to the Moor my lord.

BRABANTIO   God be with you! I have done.
Please it Your Grace, on to the state affairs.
I had rather to adopt a child than get it.   194
Come hither, Moor.   *[He joins the hands of Othello*
                                              and Desdemona.]
I here do give thee that with all my heart   196
Which, but thou hast already, with all my heart   197
I would keep from thee.—For your sake, jewel,   198
I am glad at soul I have no other child,
For thy escape would teach me tyranny,   200
To hang clogs on them.—I have done, my lord.   201

DUKE
Let me speak like yourself, and lay a sentence   202
Which, as a grece or step, may help these lovers   203
Into your favor.
When remedies are past, the griefs are ended   205
By seeing the worst, which late on hopes depended.   206
To mourn a mischief that is past and gone   207
Is the next way to draw new mischief on.   208
What cannot be preserved when fortune takes,   209
Patience her injury a mock'ry makes.   210

The robbed that smiles steals something from the thief;
He robs himself that spends a bootless grief.   212

BRABANTIO
So let the Turk of Cyprus us beguile,
We lose it not, so long as we can smile.
He bears the sentence well that nothing bears   215
But the free comfort which from thence he hears,   216
But he bears both the sentence and the sorrow   217
That, to pay grief, must of poor patience borrow.   218
These sentences, to sugar or to gall,   219
Being strong on both sides, are equivocal.   220
But words are words. I never yet did hear
That the bruised heart was piercèd through the ear.   222
I humbly beseech you, proceed to th'affairs of state.

DUKE   The Turk with a most mighty preparation makes
for Cyprus. Othello, the fortitude of the place is best 225
known to you; and though we have there a substitute   226
of most allowed sufficiency, yet opinion, a sovereign   227
mistress of effects, throws a more safer voice on you. 228
You must therefore be content to slubber the gloss of   229
your new fortunes with this more stubborn and   230
boisterous expedition.   231

OTHELLO
The tyrant custom, most grave senators,
Hath made the flinty and steel couch of war
My thrice-driven bed of down. I do agnize   234
A natural and prompt alacrity
I find in hardness, and do undertake   236
These present wars against the Ottomites.
Most humbly therefore bending to your state,   238
I crave fit disposition for my wife,
Due reference of place and exhibition,   240
With such accommodation and besort   241
As levels with her breeding.   242

DUKE
Why, at her father's.

BRABANTIO   I will not have it so.

OTHELLO
Nor I.

DESDEMONA   Nor I. I would not there reside,
To put my father in impatient thoughts
By being in his eye. Most gracious Duke,
To my unfolding lend your prosperous ear,   247

---

175 **Take . . . best** make the best of a bad bargain.   **184 education** upbringing   **185 learn** teach   **186 of duty** to whom duty is due   **190 challenge** claim   **194 get** beget   **196 with all my heart** wherein my whole affection has been engaged   **197 with all my heart** willingly, gladly   **198 For your sake** Because of you   **200 escape** elopement   **201 clogs** (Literally, blocks of wood fastened to the legs of criminals or animals to inhibit escape.)   **202 like yourself** i.e., as you would, in your proper temper.   **lay a sentence** apply a maxim **203 grece** step   **205–6 When . . . depended** When all hope of remedy is past, our sorrows are ended by realizing that the worst has already happened which lately we hoped would not happen.   **207 mischief** misfortune, injury   **208 next** nearest   **209–10 What . . . makes** When fortune takes away what cannot be saved, patience makes a mockery of fortune's wrongdoing.

212 **spends a bootless grief** indulges in unavailing grief.   **215–18 He bears . . . borrow** A person can easily be comforted by your maxim that enjoys its platitudinous comfort without having to experience the misfortune that occasions sorrow, but anyone whose grief bankrupts his poor patience is left with your saying and his sorrow, too. (*Bears the sentence* also plays on the meaning, "receives judicial sentence.")   **219–20 These . . . equivocal** These fine maxims are equivocal, being equally appropriate to happiness or bitterness. **222 piercèd . . . ear** relieved by mere words reaching it through the ear.   **225 fortitude** strength   **226 substitute** deputy   **227 allowed** acknowledged   **227–8 opinion . . . on you** general opinion, an important determiner of affairs, chooses you as the best man.   **229 slubber** soil, sully   **230–1 stubborn . . . expedition** rough and violent expedition, for which haste is needed.   **234 thrice-driven** thrice sifted, winnowed.   **agnize** know in myself, acknowledge   **236 hardness** hardship   **238 bending . . . state** bowing or kneeling to your authority   **240–2 Due . . . breeding** proper respect for her place (as my wife) and maintenance, with such suitable provision and attendance as befits her upbringing.   **247 my unfolding** what I shall unfold or say.   **prosperous** favorable

And let me find a charter in your voice,   248
T'assist my simpleness.
DUKE   What would you, Desdemona?
DESDEMONA
That I did love the Moor to live with him,
My downright violence and storm of fortunes   252
May trumpet to the world. My heart's subdued
Even to the very quality of my lord.   254
I saw Othello's visage in his mind,
And to his honors and his valiant parts   256
Did I my soul and fortunes consecrate.
So that, dear lords, if I be left behind
A moth of peace, and he go to the war,   259
The rites for why I love him are bereft me,   260
And I a heavy interim shall support   261
By his dear absence. Let me go with him.   262
OTHELLO   Let her have your voice.   263
Vouch with me, heaven, I therefor beg it not
To please the palate of my appetite,
Nor to comply with heat—the young affects   266
In me defunct—and proper satisfaction,   267
But to be free and bounteous to her mind.   268
And heaven defend your good souls that you think   269
I will your serious and great business scant
When she is with me. No, when light-winged toys
Of feathered Cupid seel with wanton dullness   272
My speculative and officed instruments,   273
That my disports corrupt and taint my business,   274
Let huswives make a skillet of my helm,
And all indign and base adversities   276
Make head against my estimation!   277
DUKE
Be it as you shall privately determine,
Either for her stay or going. Th'affair cries haste,
And speed must answer it.
A SENATOR   You must away tonight.
DESDEMONA
Tonight, my lord?
DUKE   This night.
OTHELLO   With all my heart.
DUKE
At nine i'th' morning here we'll meet again.
Othello, leave some officer behind,
And he shall our commission bring to you,
With such things else of quality and respect   285
As doth import you.
OTHELLO   So please Your Grace, my ancient;   286

248 **charter** privilege, authorization   252 **My . . . fortunes** my plain and total breach of social custom   254 **quality** moral and spiritual identity   256 **parts** qualities   259 **moth** i.e., one who consumes merely   260 **rites** rites of love. (With a suggestion, too, of "rights," sharing.)   261 **heavy** burdensome   262 **dear** grievous   263 **voice** consent.   266 **heat** sexual passion.   **young affects** passions of youth, adolescent desires   267 **defunct** done with, at an end.   **proper** personal   268 **free** generous   269 **defend** forbid.   **think** should think   272 **seel** i.e., make blind (as in falconry, by sewing up the eyes of the hawk during training)   273 **My . . . instruments** my eyes, whose function is to see   274 **That . . . business** in such a way that my sexual pastimes interfere with my official duties   276 **indign** unworthy, shameful   277 **Make head** raise an army.   **estimation** reputation.   285 **of quality and respect** of importance and relevance   286 **import** concern

A man he is of honesty and trust.
To his conveyance I assign my wife,
With what else needful Your Good Grace shall think
To be sent after me.
DUKE   Let it be so.
Good night to everyone. [To Brabantio] And, noble
    signor,
If virtue no delighted beauty lack,   292
Your son-in-law is far more fair than black.
FIRST SENATOR
Adieu, brave Moor. Use Desdemona well.
BRABANTIO
Look to her, Moor, if thou hast eyes to see.
She has deceived her father, and may thee.
        Exeunt [Duke, Brabantio, Cassio, Senators, and
                                              officers].
OTHELLO
My life upon her faith!—Honest Iago,
My Desdemona must I leave to thee.
I prithee, let thy wife attend on her,
And bring them after in the best advantage.   300
Come, Desdemona. I have but an hour
Of love, of worldly matters and direction,   302
To spend with thee. We must obey the time.   303
                          Exit [with Desdemona].
RODERIGO   Iago—
IAGO   What say'st thou, noble heart?
RODERIGO   What will I do, think'st thou?
IAGO   Why, go to bed and sleep.
RODERIGO   I will incontinently drown myself.   308
IAGO   If thou dost, I shall never love thee after. Why,
    thou silly gentleman?
RODERIGO   It is silliness to live when to live is torment;
    and then have we a prescription to die when death is 312
    our physician.
IAGO   Oh, villainous! I have looked upon the world for   314
    four times seven years, and, since I could distinguish
    betwixt a benefit and an injury, I never found man
    that knew how to love himself. Ere I would say I
    would drown myself for the love of a guinea hen, I   318
    would change my humanity with a baboon.   319
RODERIGO   What should I do? I confess it is my shame
    to be so fond, but it is not in my virtue to amend it. 321
IAGO   Virtue? A fig! 'Tis in ourselves that we are thus or 322
    thus. Our bodies are our gardens, to the which our
    wills are gardeners; so that if we will plant nettles or
    sow lettuce, set hyssop and weed up thyme, supply it   325
    with one gender of herbs or distract it with many,   326
    either to have it sterile with idleness or manured with 327

292 **delighted** capable of delighting   300 **in . . . advantage** at the most favorable opportunity.   302 **direction** instructions   303 **the time** the urgency of the present crisis.   308 **incontinently** immediately, without self-restraint   312 **prescription** (1) right based on long-established custom (2) doctor's prescription   314 **villainous** i.e., what perfect nonsense.   318 **guinea hen** (A slang term for a prostitute.)   319 **change** exchange   321 **fond** infatuated.   **virtue** strength, nature   322 **fig** (To give a fig is to thrust the thumb between the first and second fingers in a vulgar and insulting gesture.)   325 **hyssop** a herb of the mint family   326 **gender** kind.   **distract it with** divide it among   327 **idleness** want of cultivation

industry—why, the power and corrigible authority of   328
this lies in our wills. If the beam of our lives had not   329
one scale of reason to poise another of sensuality, the   330
blood and baseness of our natures would conduct us   331
to most preposterous conclusions. But we have reason
to cool our raging motions, our carnal stings, our   333
unbitted lusts, whereof I take this that you call love to   334
be a sect or scion.   335

RODERIGO   It cannot be.

IAGO   It is merely a lust of the blood and a permission
of the will. Come, be a man. Drown thyself? Drown
cats and blind puppies. I have professed me thy friend,   339
and I confess me knit to thy deserving with cables of
perdurable toughness. I could never better stead thee   341
than now. Put money in thy purse. Follow thou the
wars; defeat thy favor with an usurped beard. I say,   343
put money in thy purse. It cannot be long that Desdemona should continue her love to the Moor—put
money in thy purse—nor he his to her. It was a violent commencement in her, and thou shalt see an an-   347
swerable sequestration—put but money in thy purse.   348
These Moors are changeable in their wills—fill thy   349
purse with money. The food that to him now is as
luscious as locusts shall be to him shortly as bitter as   351
coloquintida. She must change for youth; when she is   352
sated with his body, she will find the error of her
choice. She must have change, she must. Therefore
put money in thy purse. If thou wilt needs damn thyself, do it a more delicate way than drowning. Make   356
all the money thou canst. If sanctimony and a frail vow   357
betwixt an erring barbarian and a supersubtle Vene-   358
tian be not too hard for my wits and all the tribe of
hell, thou shalt enjoy her. Therefore make money. A
pox of drowning thyself! It is clean out of the way.   361
Seek thou rather to be hanged in compassing thy joy   362
than to be drowned and go without her.

RODERIGO   Wilt thou be fast to my hopes if I depend on   364
the issue?   365

IAGO   Thou art sure of me. Go, make money. I have
told thee often, and I retell thee again and again, I hate
the Moor. My cause is hearted; thine hath no less rea-   368
son. Let us be conjunctive in our revenge against him.   369
If thou canst cuckold him, thou dost thyself a pleasure,
me a sport. There are many events in the womb of
time which will be delivered. Traverse, go, provide thy   372
money. We will have more of this tomorrow. Adieu.

RODERIGO   Where shall we meet i'th' morning?

IAGO   At my lodging.

RODERIGO   I'll be with thee betimes. [*He starts to leave.*]   376

IAGO   Go to, farewell.—Do you hear, Roderigo?   377

RODERIGO   What say you?

IAGO   No more of drowning, do you hear?

RODERIGO   I am changed.

IAGO   Go to, farewell. Put money enough in your
purse.

RODERIGO   I'll sell all my land.   *Exit.*

IAGO
Thus do I ever make my fool my purse;
For I mine own gained knowledge should profane
If I would time expend with such a snipe   386
But for my sport and profit. I hate the Moor;
And it is thought abroad that twixt my sheets   388
He's done my office. I know not if't be true;   389
But I, for mere suspicion in that kind,
Will do as if for surety. He holds me well;   391
The better shall my purpose work on him.
Cassio's a proper man. Let me see now: 393
To get his place and to plume up my will   394
In double knavery—How, how?—Let's see:
After some time, to abuse Othello's ear   396
That he is too familiar with his wife.   397
He hath a person and a smooth dispose   398
To be suspected, framed to make women false.   399
The Moor is of a free and open nature,   400
That thinks men honest that but seem to be so,
And will as tenderly be led by the nose   402
As asses are.
I have't. It is engendered. Hell and night
Must bring this monstrous birth to the world's light.
[*Exit.*]

❖

2.1

Enter Montano and two Gentlemen.

MONTANO
What from the cape can you discern at sea?

FIRST GENTLEMAN
Nothing at all. It is a high-wrought flood.   2
I cannot, twixt the heaven and the main,   3
Descry a sail.

MONTANO
Methinks the wind hath spoke aloud at land;
A fuller blast ne'er shook our battlements.
If it hath ruffianed so upon the sea,   7

328 **corrigible authority** power to correct   329 **beam** balance
330 **poise** counterbalance   331 **blood** natural passions   333 **motions**
appetites   334 **unbitted** unbridled, uncontrolled   335 **sect or scion**
cutting or offshoot.   339 **blind** i.e., newborn and helpless   341 **perdurable** very durable.   **stead** assist   343 **defeat thy favor** disguise
your face.   **usurped** (The suggestion is that Roderigo is not man
enough to have a beard of his own.)   347–8 **an answerable sequestration** a corresponding cutting off or estrangement   349 **wills** carnal
appetites   351 **locusts** fruit of the carob tree (see Matthew 3:4), or
perhaps honeysuckle   352 **coloquintida** colocynth or bitter apple, a
purgative.   356 **Make** Raise, collect   357 **sanctimony** (1) an aura of
goodness (2) love-worship   358 **erring** wandering, vagabond,
unsteady   361 **clean . . . way** entirely unsuitable as a course of action.
362 **compassing** encompassing, embracing   364 **fast** true   365 **issue**
(successful) outcome.   368 **hearted** fixed in the heart, heartfelt
369 **conjunctive** united   372 **Traverse** (A military marching term.)

376 **betimes** early.   377 **Go to** (An expression of impatience or jolly-
ing along others.)   386 **snipe** woodcock, i.e., fool   388 **it is thought
abroad** it is rumored   389 **my office** i.e., my sexual function as husband.   391 **do . . . surety** act as if on certain knowledge.   **holds me
well** regards me favorably   393 **proper** handsome   394 **plume up**
put a feather in the cap of, i.e., glorify, gratify   396 **abuse** deceive
397 **he** Cassio.   **his** Othello's   398 **dispose** disposition   399 **framed**
formed, made   400 **free and open** frank and unsuspecting   402 **tenderly** readily
2.1. Location: A seaport in Cyprus. An open place near the quay.
2 high-wrought flood very agitated sea.   **3 main** ocean. (Also at line
41.)   **7 ruffianed** raged

What ribs of oak, when mountains melt on them, 8
Can hold the mortise? What shall we hear of this? 9

SECOND GENTLEMAN
A segregation of the Turkish fleet. 10
For do but stand upon the foaming shore,
The chidden billow seems to pelt the clouds; 12
The wind-shaked surge, with high and monstrous
mane, 13
Seems to cast water on the burning Bear
And quench the guards of th'ever-fixèd pole. 14
I never did like molestation view 16
On the enchafèd flood. 17

MONTANO If that the Turkish fleet 18
Be not ensheltered and embayed, they are drowned; 19
It is impossible to bear it out. 20

Enter a [Third] Gentleman.

THIRD GENTLEMAN News, lads! Our wars are done.
The desperate tempest hath so banged the Turks
That their designment halts. A noble ship of Venice 23
Hath seen a grievous wreck and sufferance 24
On most part of their fleet.

MONTANO How? Is this true?

THIRD GENTLEMAN The ship is here put in,
A Veronesa; Michael Cassio, 28
Lieutenant to the warlike Moor Othello,
Is come on shore; the Moor himself at sea,
And is in full commission here for Cyprus.

MONTANO
I am glad on't. 'Tis a worthy governor.

THIRD GENTLEMAN
But this same Cassio, though he speak of comfort
Touching the Turkish loss, yet he looks sadly 34
And prays the Moor be safe, for they were parted
With foul and violent tempest.

MONTANO Pray heaven he be,
For I have served him, and the man commands
Like a full soldier. Let's to the seaside, ho! 38
As well to see the vessel that's come in
As to throw out our eyes for brave Othello,
Even till we make the main and th'aerial blue 41
An indistinct regard.

THIRD GENTLEMAN Come, let's do so, 42
For every minute is expectancy 43

---

8 **mountains** i.e., of water   9 **hold the mortise** hold their joints together. (A *mortise* is the socket hollowed out in fitting timbers.) 10 **segregation** dispersal   12 **chidden** i.e., rebuked, repelled (by the shore), and thus shot into the air   13 **monstrous mane** (The surf is like the mane of a wild beast.)   14 **the burning Bear** i.e., the constellation Ursa Minor or the Little Bear, which includes the polestar (and hence regarded as the *guards of th'ever-fixèd pole* in the next line; sometimes the term *guards* is applied to the two "pointers" of the Big Bear or Dipper, which may be intended here.)   16 **like molestation** comparable disturbance   17 **enchafèd** angry   18 **If that** If   19 **embayed** sheltered by a bay   20 **bear it out** survive, weather the storm. 23 **designment halts** enterprise is crippled. (Literally, "is lame.") 24 **wreck** shipwreck.   **sufferance** damage, disaster   28 **Veronesa** from Verona (and perhaps in service with Venice)   34 **sadly** gravely 38 **full** perfect   41 **the main . . . blue** the sea and the sky   42 **An indistinct regard** indistinguishable in our view.   43 **is expectancy** gives expectation

---

Of more arrivance. 44

Enter Cassio.

CASSIO
Thanks, you the valiant of this warlike isle,
That so approve the Moor! Oh, let the heavens 46
Give him defense against the elements,
For I have lost him on a dangerous sea.

MONTANO Is he well shipped?

CASSIO
His bark is stoutly timbered, and his pilot
Of very expert and approved allowance; 51
Therefore my hopes, not surfeited to death, 52
Stand in bold cure.
[*A cry*] *within:* "A sail, a sail, a sail!" 53

CASSIO What noise?

A GENTLEMAN
The town is empty. On the brow o'th' sea 55
Stand ranks of people, and they cry "A sail!"

CASSIO
My hopes do shape him for the governor. 57
[*A shot within.*]

SECOND GENTLEMAN
They do discharge their shot of courtesy; 58
Our friends at least.

CASSIO I pray you, sir, go forth,
And give us truth who 'tis that is arrived.

SECOND GENTLEMAN I shall. *Exit.*

MONTANO
But, good Lieutenant, is your general wived?

CASSIO
Most fortunately. He hath achieved a maid
That paragons description and wild fame, 64
One that excels the quirks of blazoning pens, 65
And in th'essential vesture of creation 66
Does tire the engineer.

Enter [Second] Gentleman.

How now? Who has put in? 67

SECOND GENTLEMAN
'Tis one Iago, ancient to the General.

CASSIO
He's had most favorable and happy speed.
Tempests themselves, high seas, and howling winds,
The guttered rocks and congregated sands— 71
Traitors ensteeped to clog the guiltless keel— 72
As having sense of beauty, do omit 73
Their mortal natures, letting go safely by 74

---

44 **arrivance** arrival.   46 **approve** admire, honor   51 **approved allowance** tested reputation   52–3 **not . . . cure** not worn thin through repeated application or delayed fulfillment, strongly persist. 55 **brow o'th' sea** cliff-edge   57 **My . . . governor** I hope and imagine this ship to be Othello's.   58 **discharge . . . courtesy** fire a salute in token of respect and courtesy   64 **paragons** surpasses.   **wild fame** extravagant report   65 **quirks** witty conceits.   **blazoning** setting forth as though in heraldic language   66–7 **And in . . . engineer** and in her real, God-given, beauty, (she) defeats any attempt to praise her. (An *engineer* is one who devises, here a poet.)   67 **put in** i.e., to harbor.   71 **guttered** jagged, trenched   72 **ensteeped** lying under water   73 **As** as if.   **omit** forbear to exercise   74 **mortal** deadly

The divine Desdemona.

MONTANO   What is she?

CASSIO

She that I spake of, our great captain's captain,
Left in the conduct of the bold Iago,
Whose footing here anticipates our thoughts   78
A sennight's speed. Great Jove, Othello guard,   79
And swell his sail with thine own powerful breath,
That he may bless this bay with his tall ship,   81
Make love's quick pants in Desdemona's arms,
Give renewed fire to our extinced spirits,
And bring all Cyprus comfort!

Enter Desdemona, Iago, Roderigo, and Emilia.

                              Oh, behold,
The riches of the ship is come on shore!
You men of Cyprus, let her have your knees.
        [*The gentlemen make curtsy to Desdemona.*]
Hail to thee, lady! And the grace of heaven
Before, behind thee, and on every hand
Enwheel thee round!

DESDEMONA   I thank you, valiant Cassio.
What tidings can you tell me of my lord?

CASSIO

He is not yet arrived, nor know I aught
But that he's well and will be shortly here.

DESDEMONA

Oh, but I fear—How lost you company?

CASSIO

The great contention of the sea and skies
Parted our fellowship.
                    (*Within*) "A sail, a sail!" [*A shot.*]
                    But hark. A sail!

SECOND GENTLEMAN

They give their greeting to the citadel.
This likewise is a friend.

CASSIO   See for the news.
                    [*Exit Second Gentleman.*]
Good Ancient, you are welcome. [*Kissing Emilia.*]
    Welcome, mistress.
Let it not gall your patience, good Iago,
That I extend my manners; 'tis my breeding   100
That gives me this bold show of courtesy.

IAGO

Sir, would she give you so much of her lips
As of her tongue she oft bestows on me,
You would have enough.

DESDEMONA   Alas, she has no speech!   105

IAGO   In faith, too much.

I find it still, when I have list to sleep.   107
Marry, before Your Ladyship, I grant,
She puts her tongue a little in her heart
And chides with thinking.

EMILIA   You have little cause to say so. 110

IAGO

Come on, come on. You are pictures out of doors,   111
Bells in your parlors, wildcats in your kitchens,   112
Saints in your injuries, devils being offended,   113
Players in your huswifery, and huswives in your beds. 114

DESDEMONA   Oh, fie upon thee, slanderer!

IAGO

Nay, it is true, or else I am a Turk.   116
You rise to play, and go to bed to work.

EMILIA

You shall not write my praise.

IAGO   No, let me not.

DESDEMONA

What wouldst write of me, if thou shouldst praise me?

IAGO

Oh, gentle lady, do not put me to't,
For I am nothing if not critical.   121

DESDEMONA

Come on, essay.—There's one gone to the harbor?   122

IAGO   Ay, madam.

DESDEMONA

I am not merry, but I do beguile
The thing I am by seeming otherwise.   125
Come, how wouldst thou praise me?

IAGO

I am about it, but indeed my invention
Comes from my pate as birdlime does from frieze—   128
It plucks out brains and all. But my Muse labors,   129
And thus she is delivered:
If she be fair and wise, fairness and wit,
The one's for use, the other useth it.   132

DESDEMONA

Well praised! How if she be black and witty?   133

IAGO

If she be black, and thereto have a wit,
She'll find a white that shall her blackness fit.   135

DESDEMONA

Worse and worse.

EMILIA   How if fair and foolish?

IAGO

She never yet was foolish that was fair,
For even her folly helped her to an heir.   138

DESDEMONA   These are old fond paradoxes to make fools 139

laugh i'th'alehouse. What miserable praise hast thou
for her that's foul and foolish?   141

IAGO

There's none so foul and foolish thereunto,   142
But does foul pranks which fair and wise ones do.   143

DESDEMONA   Oh, heavy ignorance! Thou praisest the worst
best. But what praise couldst thou bestow on a deserving woman indeed, one that, in the authority of her merit, did justly put on the vouch of very malice itself?   147

IAGO

She that was ever fair, and never proud,
Had tongue at will, and yet was never loud,   149
Never lacked gold and yet went never gay,   150
Fled from her wish, and yet said, "Now I may,"   151
She that being angered, her revenge being nigh,
Bade her wrong stay and her displeasure fly,   153
She that in wisdom never was so frail
To change the cod's head for the salmon's tail,   155
She that could think and ne'er disclose her mind,
See suitors following and not look behind,
She was a wight, if ever such wight were—

DESDEMONA   To do what?

IAGO

To suckle fools and chronicle small beer.   160

DESDEMONA   Oh, most lame and impotent conclusion! Do
not learn of him, Emilia, though he be thy husband.
How say you, Cassio? Is he not a most profane and   163
liberal counselor?   164

CASSIO   He speaks home, madam. You may relish him   165
more in the soldier than in the scholar.   166

> [*Cassio and Desdemona stand together,
> conversing intimately.*]

IAGO [*aside*]   He takes her by the palm. Ay, well said, 167
whisper. With as little a web as this will I ensnare as
great a fly as Cassio. Ay, smile upon her, do; I will
gyve thee in thine own courtship. You say true; 'tis so, 170
indeed. If such tricks as these strip you out of your
lieutenantry, it had been better you had not kissed
your three fingers so oft, which now again you are
most apt to play the sir in. Very good; well kissed! An 174
excellent courtesy! 'Tis so, indeed. Yet again your fingers to your lips? Would they were clyster pipes for 176
your sake! [*Trumpet within.*] The Moor! I know his
trumpet.

CASSIO   'Tis truly so.

DESDEMONA   Let's meet him and receive him.

CASSIO   Lo, where he comes!

> *Enter Othello and attendants.*

OTHELLO

Oh, my fair warrior!

DESDEMONA   My dear Othello!

OTHELLO

It gives me wonder great as my content
To see you here before me. O my soul's joy,
If after every tempest come such calms,
May the winds blow till they have wakened death,
And let the laboring bark climb hills of seas
Olympus-high, and duck again as low
As hell's from heaven! If it were now to die,
'Twere now to be most happy, for I fear
My soul hath her content so absolute
That not another comfort like to this
Succeeds in unknown fate.

DESDEMONA   The heavens forbid   192
But that our loves and comforts should increase
Even as our days do grow!

OTHELLO   Amen to that, sweet powers!
I cannot speak enough of this content.
It stops me here; it is too much of joy.
And this, and this, the greatest discords be   198
                                        [*They kiss.*]
That e'er our hearts shall make!

IAGO [*aside*]   Oh, you are well tuned now!
But I'll set down the pegs that make this music,   201
As honest as I am.   202

OTHELLO   Come, let us to the castle.
News, friends! Our wars are done, the Turks are
drowned.
How does my old acquaintance of this isle?—
Honey, you shall be well desired in Cyprus;   206
I have found great love amongst them. Oh, my sweet,
I prattle out of fashion, and I dote   208
In mine own comforts.—I prithee, good Iago,
Go to the bay and disembark my coffers.   210
Bring thou the master to the citadel;   211
He is a good one, and his worthiness
Does challenge much respect.—Come, Desdemona.— 213
Once more, well met at Cyprus!

> *Exeunt Othello and Desdemona [and all
> but Iago and Roderigo].*

IAGO [*to a departing attendant*]   Do thou meet me presently at
the harbor. [*To Roderigo*] Come hither. If thou be'st
valiant—as, they say, base men being in love have 217
then a nobility in their natures more than is native to
them—list me. The Lieutenant tonight watches on 219
the court of guard. First, I must tell thee this: 220
Desdemona is directly in love with him.

---

141 **foul** ugly   142 **thereunto** in addition   143 **foul** sluttish   147 **put
. . . vouch** compel the approval   149 **Had . . . will** was never at a loss
for words   150 **gay** extravagantly clothed   151 **Fled . . . may** avoided
temptation where the choice was hers   153 **Bade . . . stay** i.e.,
resolved to put up with her injury and bade her anger to cease
155 **To . . . tail** i.e., to be selfishly demanding and ambitious. (The
fish's lower body, below the rib cage, has fewest bones and is generally the succulent portion. With sexual implication as well: *cod's head*
can be slang for "penis," and *tail* for "pudendum.")   160 **To . . . beer**
i.e., To breastfeed babies and keep petty household accounts.
163–4 **profane and liberal** irreverent and licentious   165 **home** right
to the target. (A term from fencing.)   **relish** appreciate   166 **in** in
the character of   167 **well said** well done   170 **gyve** fetter, shackle.
courtship courtesy, show of courtly manners.   **You say true** i.e.,
That's right, go ahead   174 **the sir** i.e., the fine gentleman
176 **clyster pipes** tubes used for enemas and douches

---

192 **Succeeds . . . fate** i.e., can follow in the unknown future.
198.1 **They kiss** (The direction is from the Quarto.)   201 **set down**
loosen (and hence untune the instrument)   202 **As . . . I am** for all my
supposed honesty.   206 **desired** sought after   208 **out of fashion**
indecorously, incoherently   210 **coffers** chests, baggage.   211 **master**
ship's captain   213 **challenge** lay claim to, deserve   217 **base men**
even ignoble men   219 **list** listen to   220 **court of guard** guardhouse.
(Cassio is in charge of the watch.)

RODERIGO With him? Why, 'tis not possible.

IAGO Lay thy finger thus, and let thy soul be instructed. 223
Mark me with what violence she first loved the Moor,
but for bragging and telling her fantastical lies. To love 225
him still for prating? Let not thy discreet heart think it.
Her eye must be fed; and what delight shall she have
to look on the devil? When the blood is made dull with
the act of sport, there should be, again to inflame it 229
and to give satiety a fresh appetite, loveliness in favor, 230
sympathy in years, manners, and beauties—all which 231
the Moor is defective in. Now, for want of these
required conveniences, her delicate tenderness will 233
find itself abused, begin to heave the gorge, disrelish 234
and abhor the Moor. Very nature will instruct her in it 235
and compel her to some second choice. Now, sir, this
granted—as it is a most pregnant and unforced 237
position—who stands so eminent in the degree of this 238
fortune as Cassio does? A knave very voluble, no 239
further conscionable than in putting on the mere form 240
of civil and humane seeming for the better compass- 241
ing of his salt and most hidden loose affection. Why, 242
none, why, none. A slipper and subtle knave, a finder 243
out of occasions, that has an eye can stamp and 244
counterfeit advantages, though true advantage never 245
present itself; a devilish knave. Besides, the knave is
handsome, young, and hath all those requisites in him
that folly and green minds look after. A pestilent 248
complete knave, and the woman hath found him 249
already.

RODERIGO I cannot believe that in her. She's full of
most blessed condition. 252

IAGO Blessed fig's end! The wine she drinks is made of 253
grapes. If she had been blessed, she would never have
loved the Moor. Blessed pudding! Didst thou not see 255
her paddle with the palm of his hand? Didst not mark
that?

RODERIGO Yes, that I did; but that was but courtesy.

IAGO Lechery, by this hand. An index and obscure pro- 259
logue to the history of lust and foul thoughts. They
met so near with their lips that their breaths embraced
together. Villainous thoughts, Roderigo! When these
mutualities so marshal the way, hard at hand comes 263
the master and main exercise, th'incorporate conclu- 264
sion. Pish! But, sir, be you ruled by me. I have brought

you from Venice. Watch you tonight; for the com- 266
mand, I'll lay't upon you. Cassio knows you not. I'll 267
not be far from you. Do you find some occasion to
anger Cassio, either by speaking too loud, or tainting 269
his discipline, or from what other course you please,
which the time shall more favorably minister. 271

RODERIGO Well.

IAGO Sir, he's rash and very sudden in choler, and haply 273
may strike at you. Provoke him that he may, for
even out of that will I cause these of Cyprus to mutiny, 275
whose qualification shall come into no true taste again 276
but by the displanting of Cassio. So shall you have a
shorter journey to your desires by the means I shall
then have to prefer them, and the impediment most 279
profitably removed, without the which there were no
expectation of our prosperity.

RODERIGO I will do this, if you can bring it to any
opportunity.

IAGO I warrant thee. Meet me by and by at the citadel. 284
I must fetch his necessaries ashore. Farewell.

RODERIGO Adieu.   *Exit.*

IAGO
That Cassio loves her, I do well believe't;
That she loves him, 'tis apt and of great credit. 288
The Moor, howbeit that I endure him not,
Is of a constant, loving, noble nature,
And I dare think he'll prove to Desdemona
A most dear husband. Now, I do love her too,
Not out of absolute lust—though peradventure
I stand accountant for as great a sin— 294
But partly led to diet my revenge 295
For that I do suspect the lusty Moor
Hath leaped into my seat, the thought whereof
Doth, like a poisonous mineral, gnaw my innards;
And nothing can or shall content my soul
Till I am evened with him, wife for wife,
Or failing so, yet that I put the Moor
At least into a jealousy so strong
That judgment cannot cure. Which thing to do,
If this poor trash of Venice, whom I trace 304
For his quick hunting, stand the putting on, 305
I'll have our Michael Cassio on the hip, 306
Abuse him to the Moor in the rank garb— 307
For I fear Cassio with my nightcap too— 308
Make the Moor thank me, love me, and reward me
For making him egregiously an ass
And practicing upon his peace and quiet 311

---

223 thus i.e., on your lips **225 but** only **229 the act of sport** sex
230 favor appearance **231 sympathy** correspondence, similarity
233 required conveniences things conducive to sexual compatibility
234 abused cheated, revolted. **heave the gorge** experience nausea
235 Very nature Her very instincts **237 pregnant** evident, cogent
238 in . . . of as next in line for **239 voluble** facile, glib **240 conscionable** conscientious, conscience-bound **241 humane** polite,
courteous **242 salt** licentious. **affection** passion. **243 slipper** slippery **244 an eye can stamp** an eye that can coin, create **245 advantages** favorable opportunities **248 folly** wantonness. **green**
immature **249 found him** sized him up, perceived his intent
252 condition disposition. **253 fig's end** (See 1.3.322 for the vulgar
gesture of the fig.) **255 pudding** sausage. **259 index** table of contents. **obscure** veiled, hidden **263 mutualities** exchanges, intima-
cies. **hard at hand** closely following **264 th'incorporate** the carnal

266 Watch you Stand watch **266–7 for . . . you** I'll arrange for you to
be appointed, given orders; or, I'll put you in charge. **269 tainting**
disparaging **271 minister** provide. **273 choler** wrath. **haply** perhaps **275 mutiny** riot **276 qualification** pacification. **true taste**
i.e., acceptable state **279 prefer** advance **284 warrant** assure.
by and by immediately **288 apt** probable. **credit** credibility.
294 accountant accountable **295 diet** feed **304 trace** i.e., pursue,
dog; or, keep hungry (?) or perhaps *trash*, a hunting term, meaning to
put weights on a hunting dog in order to slow him down **305 For** to
make more eager for. **stand . . . on** responds properly when I incite
him to quarrel **306 on the hip** at my mercy, where I can throw him.
(A wrestling term.) **307 Abuse** slander. **rank garb** coarse manner,
gross fashion **308 with my nightcap** i.e., as a rival in my bed, as one
who gives me cuckold's horns **311 practicing upon** plotting against

Even to madness. 'Tis here, but yet confused.
Knavery's plain face is never seen till used.   *Exit.*

❧

2.2

Enter Othello's Herald with a proclamation.

HERALD   It is Othello's pleasure, our noble and valiant
general, that, upon certain tidings now arrived, importing the mere perdition of the Turkish fleet, every   3
man put himself into triumph: some to dance, some to   4
make bonfires, each man to what sport and revels his
addiction leads him. For, besides these beneficial   6
news, it is the celebration of his nuptial. So much was
his pleasure should be proclaimed. All offices are open,   8
and there is full liberty of feasting from this present
hour of five till the bell have told eleven. Heaven bless
the isle of Cyprus and our noble general Othello!
                                                      Exit.

❧

[2.3]

*Enter Othello, Desdemona, Cassio, and
attendants.*

OTHELLO
Good Michael, look you to the guard tonight.
Let's teach ourselves that honorable stop   2
Not to outsport discretion.   3
CASSIO
Iago hath direction what to do,
But notwithstanding, with my personal eye
Will I look to't.
OTHELLO   Iago is most honest.
Michael, good night. Tomorrow with your earliest   7
Let me have speech with you. [*To Desdemona*] Come,
    my dear love,
The purchase made, the fruits are to ensue;   9
That profit's yet to come 'tween me and you.—   10
Good night.
          Exit [*Othello, with Desdemona and attendants*].

Enter Iago.

CASSIO   Welcome, Iago. We must to the watch.
IAGO   Not this hour, Lieutenant; 'tis not yet ten o'th'   13
clock. Our general cast us thus early for the love of his   14
Desdemona; who let us not therefore blame. He hath   15
not yet made wanton the night with her, and she is
sport for Jove.
CASSIO   She's a most exquisite lady.
IAGO   And, I'll warrant her, full of game.

CASSIO   Indeed, she's a most fresh and delicate creature.
IAGO   What an eye she has! Methinks it sounds a parley   21
to provocation.
CASSIO   An inviting eye, and yet methinks right modest.
IAGO   And when she speaks, is it not an alarum to love?   24
CASSIO   She is indeed perfection.
IAGO   Well, happiness to their sheets! Come, Lieutenant,
I have a stoup of wine, and here without are a brace of   27
Cyprus gallants that would fain have a measure to the   28
health of black Othello.
CASSIO   Not tonight, good Iago. I have very poor and
unhappy brains for drinking. I could well wish cour-
tesy would invent some other custom of entertain-
ment.
IAGO   Oh, they are our friends. But one cup! I'll drink for   34
you.   35
CASSIO   I have drunk but one cup tonight, and that was
craftily qualified too, and behold what innovation it   37
makes here. I am unfortunate in the infirmity and   38
dare not task my weakness with any more.
IAGO   What, man? 'Tis a night of revels. The gallants
desire it.
CASSIO   Where are they?
IAGO   Here at the door. I pray you, call them in.
CASSIO   I'll do't, but it dislikes me.   *Exit.*   44
IAGO
If I can fasten but one cup upon him,
With that which he hath drunk tonight already,
He'll be as full of quarrel and offense   47
As my young mistress' dog. Now, my sick fool
    Roderigo,
Whom love hath turned almost the wrong side out,
To Desdemona hath tonight caroused   50
Potations pottle-deep; and he's to watch.   51
Three lads of Cyprus—noble swelling spirits,   52
That hold their honors in a wary distance,   53
The very elements of this warlike isle—   54
Have I tonight flustered with flowing cups,
And they watch too. Now, 'mongst this flock of
    drunkards   56
Am I to put our Cassio in some action
That may offend the isle.—But here they come.

Enter Cassio, Montano, and gentlemen; [*servants
following with wine*].

If consequence do but approve my dream,   59
My boat sails freely both with wind and stream.   60
CASSIO   'Fore God, they have given me a rouse already.   61

2.2. Location: Cyprus.
3 mere perdition complete destruction   **4 triumph** public celebration
6 addiction inclination   **8 offices** rooms where food and drink are kept
2.3. Location: Cyprus. The citadel.
2 stop restraint   **3 outsport** celebrate beyond the bounds of   **7 with
your earliest** at your earliest convenience   **9–10 The purchase . . .
you** i.e., though married, we haven't yet consummated our love.
(Possibly, too, Othello is referring to pregnancy. At all events, his
desire for sexual union is manifest.)   **13 Not this hour** Not for an
hour yet   **14 cast** dismissed   **15 who** i.e., Othello

21 sounds a parley calls for a conference, issues an invitation
24 alarum signal calling men to arms. (Continuing the military
metaphor of *parley*, line 21.)   **27 stoup** measure of liquor, two quarts.
without outside.   **brace** pair   **28 fain have a measure** gladly drink a
toast   **34–5 for you** in your place. (Iago will do the steady drinking
to keep the gallants company while Cassio has only one cup.)
37 qualified diluted.   **innovation** disturbance, insurrection   **38 here**
i.e., in my head.   **44 it dislikes me** i.e., I'm reluctant.   **47 offense**
readiness to give or take offense   **50 caroused** drunk off   **51 pottle-
deep** to the bottom of the tankard.   **watch** stand watch.
52 swelling proud   **53 hold . . . distance** i.e., are extremely sensitive
of their honor   **54 elements** lifeblood   **56 watch** are members of the
guard   **59 If . . . dream** If subsequent events will only confirm my
dreams and hopes   **60 stream** current.   **61 rouse** full draft of liquor

MONTANO   Good faith, a little one; not past a pint, as I
am a soldier.

IAGO   Some wine, ho!
[*He sings.*]   "And let me the cannikin clink, clink,   65
And let me the cannikin clink.
A soldier's a man,
Oh, man's life's but a span;   68
Why, then, let a soldier drink."
Some wine, boys!

CASSIO   'Fore God, an excellent song.

IAGO   I learned it in England, where indeed they are
most potent in potting. Your Dane, your German, and   73
your swag-bellied Hollander—drink, ho!—are nothing to your English.

CASSIO   Is your Englishman so exquisite in his drinking?

IAGO   Why, he drinks you, with facility, your Dane   77
dead drunk; he sweats not to overthrow your Almain;   78
he gives your Hollander a vomit ere the next pottle can
be filled.

CASSIO   To the health of our general!

MONTANO   I am for it, Lieutenant, and I'll do you justice.   82

IAGO   O sweet England! [*He sings.*]

"King Stephen was and-a worthy peer,
His breeches cost him but a crown;
He held them sixpence all too dear,
With that he called the tailor lown.   87

He was a wight of high renown,
And thou art but of low degree.
'Tis pride that pulls the country down;   90
Then take thy auld cloak about thee."   91

Some wine, ho!

CASSIO   'Fore God, this is a more exquisite song than
the other.

IAGO   Will you hear't again?

CASSIO   No, for I hold him to be unworthy of his place
that does those things. Well, God's above all; and
there be souls must be saved, and there be souls must
not be saved.

IAGO   It's true, good Lieutenant.

CASSIO   For mine own part—no offense to the General,
nor any man of quality—I hope to be saved.   102

IAGO   And so do I too, Lieutenant.

CASSIO   Ay, but, by your leave, not before me; the lieutenant is to be saved before the ancient. Let's have no
more of this; let's to our affairs.—God forgive us our
sins!—Gentlemen, let's look to our business. Do not
think, gentlemen, I am drunk. This is my ancient; this
is my right hand, and this is my left. I am not drunk
now. I can stand well enough, and speak well enough.

GENTLEMEN   Excellent well.

CASSIO   Why, very well then; you must not think then
that I am drunk.   *Exit.*

MONTANO
To th' platform, masters. Come, let's set the watch.   114
[*Exeunt Gentlemen.*]

IAGO
You see this fellow that is gone before.
He's a soldier fit to stand by Caesar
And give direction; and do but see his vice.
'Tis to his virtue a just equinox,   118
The one as long as th'other. 'Tis pity of him.
I fear the trust Othello puts him in,
On some odd time of his infirmity,
Will shake this island.

MONTANO   But is he often thus?

IAGO
'Tis evermore the prologue to his sleep.
He'll watch the horologe a double set,   124
If drink rock not his cradle.

MONTANO   It were well
The General were put in mind of it.
Perhaps he sees it not, or his good nature
Prizes the virtue that appears in Cassio
And looks not on his evils. Is not this true?

Enter Roderigo.

IAGO   [*aside to him*]   How now, Roderigo?
I pray you, after the Lieutenant; go.   [*Exit Roderigo.*]

MONTANO
And 'tis great pity that the noble Moor
Should hazard such a place as his own second   133
With one of an engraffed infirmity.   134
It were an honest action to say so
To the Moor.

IAGO   Not I, for this fair island.
I do love Cassio well and would do much
To cure him of this evil.   [*Cry within:* "Help! Help!"]
But, hark! What noise?   138

Enter Cassio, pursuing Roderigo.

CASSIO   Zounds, you rogue! You rascal!

MONTANO   What's the matter, Lieutenant?

CASSIO   A knave teach me my duty? I'll beat the knave
into a twiggen bottle.   142

RODERIGO   Beat me?

CASSIO   Dost thou prate, rogue?   [*He strikes Roderigo.*]

MONTANO   Nay, good Lieutenant. [*Restraining him.*] I
pray you, sir, hold your hand.

CASSIO   Let me go, sir, or I'll knock you o'er the
mazard.   148

---

65 cannikin small drinking vessel   **68 span** brief span of time. (Compare Psalm 39:5 as rendered in the Book of Common Prayer: "Thou hast made my days as it were a span long.")   **73 potting** drinking.
77 drinks you drinks.   **your Dane** your typical Dane   **78 sweats not** i.e., need not exert himself.   **Almain** German   **82 I'll . . . justice** i.e., I'll drink as much as you.   **87 lown** lout, rascal.   **90 pride** i.e., extravagance in dress   **91 auld** old   **102 quality** rank

114 set the watch mount the guard.   **118 just equinox** exact counterpart. (*Equinox* is an equal length of days and nights.)   **124 watch . . . set** stay awake twice around the clock or *horologe*   **133–4 hazard . . . With** risk giving such an important position as his second in command to   **134 engraffed** engrafted, inveterate   **138.1 *pursuing*** (The Quarto text reads, "*driuing in.*")   **142 twiggen** wicker-covered. (Cassio vows to assail Roderigo until his skin resembles wickerwork or until he has driven Roderigo through the holes in a wickerwork.)   **148 mazard** i.e., head. (Literally, a drinking vessel.)

MONTANO   Come, come, you're drunk.

CASSIO   Drunk?   [*They fight.*]

IAGO [*aside to Roderigo*]

Away, I say. Go out and cry a mutiny.   151
                                    [*Exit Roderigo.*]
Nay, good Lieutenant—God's will, gentlemen—
Help, ho!—Lieutenant—sir—Montano—sir—
Help, masters!—Here's a goodly watch indeed!   154
                                    [*A bell rings.*]
Who's that which rings the bell?—Diablo, ho!   155
The town will rise. God's will, Lieutenant, hold!1 156
You'll be ashamed forever.

Enter Othello and attendants [with weapons].

OTHELLO

What is the matter here?

MONTANO   Zounds, I bleed still.

I am hurt to th' death. He dies! [*He thrusts at Cassio.*]

OTHELLO   Hold, for your lives!

IAGO

Hold, ho! Lieutenant—sir—Montano—gentlemen—
Have you forgot all sense of place and duty?
Hold! The General speaks to you. Hold, for shame!

OTHELLO

Why, how now, ho! From whence ariseth this?
Are we turned Turks, and to ourselves do that   164
Which heaven hath forbid the Ottomites?   165
For Christian shame, put by this barbarous brawl!
He that stirs next to carve for his own rage   167
Holds his soul light; he dies upon his motion.   168
Silence that dreadful bell. It frights the isle
From her propriety. What is the matter, masters?   170
Honest Iago, that looks dead with grieving,
Speak. Who began this? On thy love, I charge thee.

IAGO

I do not know. Friends all but now, even now,
In quarter and in terms like bride and groom   174
Devesting them for bed; and then, but now—   175
As if some planet had unwitted men—
Swords out, and tilting one at others' breasts
In opposition bloody. I cannot speak   178
Any beginning to this peevish odds;   179
And would in action glorious I had lost
Those legs that brought me to a part of it!

OTHELLO

How comes it, Michael, you are thus forgot?   182

CASSIO

I pray you, pardon me. I cannot speak.

OTHELLO

Worthy Montano, you were wont be civil;   184
The gravity and stillness of your youth   185
The world hath noted, and your name is great
In mouths of wisest censure. What's the matter   187
That you unlace your reputation thus   188
And spend your rich opinion for the name   189
Of a night-brawler? Give me answer to it.

MONTANO

Worthy Othello, I am hurt to danger.
Your officer, Iago, can inform you—
While I spare speech, which something now offends
    me—   193
Of all that I do know; nor know I aught
By me that's said or done amiss this night,
Unless self-charity be sometimes a vice,
And to defend ourselves it be a sin
When violence assails us.

OTHELLO   Now, by heaven,
My blood begins my safer guides to rule,   199
And passion, having my best judgment collied,   200
Essays to lead the way. Zounds, if I stir,   201
Or do but lift this arm, the best of you
Shall sink in my rebuke. Give me to know
How this foul rout began, who set it on;   204
And he that is approved in this offense,   205
Though he had twinned with me, both at a birth,
Shall lose me. What? In a town of war   207
Yet wild, the people's hearts brim full of fear,
To manage private and domestic quarrel?   209
In night, and on the court and guard of safety?   210
'Tis monstrous. Iago, who began't?

MONTANO [*to Iago*]

If partially affined, or leagued in office,   212
Thou dost deliver more or less than truth,
Thou art no soldier.

IAGO   Touch me not so near.
I had rather have this tongue cut from my mouth
Than it should do offense to Michael Cassio;
Yet, I persuade myself, to speak the truth
Shall nothing wrong him. Thus it is, General:
Montano and myself being in speech,
There comes a fellow crying out for help,
And Cassio following him with determined sword
To execute upon him. Sir, this gentleman   222
                            [*indicating Montano*]
Steps in to Cassio and entreats his pause.   223
Myself the crying fellow did pursue,
Lest by his clamor—as it so fell out—
The town might fall in fright. He, swift of foot,

151 mutiny riot.   **154 masters** sirs.   **154.1 *A bell rings*** (This direction is from the Quarto, as are *Exit Roderigo* at line 131, *They fight* at line 150, and *with weapons* at line 157.1.)   **155 Diablo** The devil   **156 rise** grow riotous.   **164–5 to ourselves . . . Ottomites** inflict on ourselves the harm that heaven has prevented the Turks from doing (by destroying their fleet).   **167 carve for** i.e., indulge, satisfy with his sword   **168 Holds . . . light** i.e., places little value on his life.   **upon his motion** if he moves.   **170 propriety** proper state or condition.   **174 In quarter . . . terms** in conduct and speech   **175 Devesting them** undressing themselves   **178 speak** explain   **179 peevish odds** childish quarrel   **182 are thus forgot** have forgotten yourself thus.

184 wont be accustomed to be   **185 stillness** sobriety   **187 censure** judgment.   **188 unlace** undo, lay open (as one might loose the strings of a purse containing reputation)   **189 opinion** reputation   **193 something** somewhat.   **offends** pains   **199 blood** passion (of anger).   **guides** i.e., reason   **200 collied** darkened   **201 Essays** undertakes   **204 rout** riot   **205 approved in** found guilty of   **207 town of** town garrisoned for   **209 manage** undertake   **210 on . . . safety** at the main guardhouse or headquarters and on watch.   **212 If . . . office** If made partial by personal relationship or by your being fellow officers   **222 execute upon him** (1) proceed violently against him (2) execute him.   **223 his pause** him to stop.

Outran my purpose, and I returned, the rather
For that I heard the clink and fall of swords
And Cassio high in oath, which till tonight
I ne'er might say before. When I came back—
For this was brief—I found them close together
At blow and thrust, even as again they were
When you yourself did part them.
More of this matter cannot I report.
But men are men; the best sometimes forget.   235
Though Cassio did some little wrong to him,
As men in rage strike those that wish them best,   237
Yet surely Cassio, I believe, received
From him that fled some strange indignity,
Which patience could not pass.

OTHELLO   I know, Iago,   240
Thy honesty and love doth mince this matter,
Making it light to Cassio. Cassio, I love thee,
But nevermore be officer of mine.

Enter Desdemona, attended.

Look if my gentle love be not raised up.
I'll make thee an example.

DESDEMONA
What is the matter, dear?

OTHELLO   All's well now, sweeting;
Come away to bed. [*To Montano*] Sir, for your hurts,
Myself will be your surgeon.—Lead him off.   248

[*Montano is led off.*]

Iago, look with care about the town
And silence those whom this vile brawl distracted.
Come, Desdemona. 'Tis the soldiers' life
To have their balmy slumbers waked with strife.

Exit [with all but Iago and Cassio].

IAGO What, are you hurt, Lieutenant?

CASSIO Ay, past all surgery.

IAGO Marry, God forbid!

CASSIO Reputation, reputation, reputation! Oh, I have
lost my reputation! I have lost the immortal part of
myself, and what remains is bestial. My reputation,
Iago, my reputation!

IAGO As I am an honest man, I thought you had
received some bodily wound; there is more sense in
that than in reputation. Reputation is an idle and most
false imposition, oft got without merit and lost with-   263
out deserving. You have lost no reputation at all,
unless you repute yourself such a loser. What, man,
there are more ways to recover the General again. You   266
are but now cast in his mood—a punishment more in   267
policy than in malice, even so as one would beat his   268
offenseless dog to affright an imperious lion. Sue to   269
him again and he's yours.

CASSIO I will rather sue to be despised than to deceive   227
so good a commander with so slight, so drunken, and 272
so indiscreet an officer. Drunk? And speak parrot?   273
And squabble? Swagger? Swear? And discourse fustian with one's own shadow? O thou invisible spirit
of wine, if thou hast no name to be known by, let us
call thee devil!

IAGO What was he that you followed with your sword?
What had he done to you?

CASSIO I know not.

IAGO Is't possible?

CASSIO I remember a mass of things, but nothing
distinctly; a quarrel, but nothing wherefore. Oh, God,   283
that men should put an enemy in their mouths to steal
away their brains! That we should, with joy, pleasance, revel, and applause transform ourselves into   286
beasts!

IAGO Why, but you are now well enough. How came
you thus recovered?

CASSIO It hath pleased the devil drunkenness to give
place to the devil wrath. One unperfectness shows me
another, to make me frankly despise myself.

IAGO Come, you are too severe a moraler. As the time,   293
the place, and the condition of this country stands, I
could heartily wish this had not befallen; but since it is
as it is, mend it for your own good.

CASSIO I will ask him for my place again; he shall tell
me I am a drunkard. Had I as many mouths as Hydra,   298
such an answer would stop them all. To be now a
sensible man, by and by a fool, and presently a beast!
Oh, strange! Every inordinate cup is unblessed, and the 301
ingredient is a devil.

IAGO Come, come, good wine is a good familiar
creature, if it be well used. Exclaim no more against it.
And, good Lieutenant, I think you think I love you.

CASSIO I have well approved it, sir. I drunk!   306

IAGO You or any man living may be drunk at a time,   307
man. I'll tell you what you shall do. Our general's wife
is now the general—I may say so in this respect, for   309
that he hath devoted and given up himself to the   310
contemplation, mark, and denotement of her parts   311
and graces. Confess yourself freely to her; importune
her help to put you in your place again. She is of so
free, so kind, so apt, so blessed a disposition, she   314
holds it a vice in her goodness not to do more than she
is requested. This broken joint between you and her
husband entreat her to splinter; and, my fortunes   317
against any lay worth naming, this crack of your love   318
shall grow stronger than it was before.

CASSIO You advise me well.

---

227 **rather** sooner 235 **forget** forget themselves. 237 **those . . . best**
i.e., even those who are well disposed toward them 240 **pass** pass
over, overlook. 248 **be your surgeon** i.e., make sure you receive
medical attention. 263 **false imposition** thing artificially imposed
and of no real value 266 **recover** regain favor with 267 **cast in his
mood** dismissed in a moment of anger 267–8 **in policy** done for
expediency's sake and as a public gesture 268–9 **would . . . lion** i.e.,
would make an example of a minor offender in order to deter more
important and dangerous offenders. 269 **Sue** Petition

272 **slight** worthless 273 **speak parrot** talk nonsense, rant. (*Discourse
fustian*, lines 274–5, has much the same meaning.) 283 **wherefore**
why. 286 **applause** desire for applause 293 **moraler** moralizer.
298 **Hydra** the Lernaean Hydra, a monster with many heads and the
ability to grow two heads when one was cut off, slain by Hercules
as the second of his twelve labors 301 **inordinate** immoderate
306 **approved** proved by experience 307 **at a time** at one time or
another 309–10 **for that** that 311 **mark, and denotement** (Both
words mean "observation.") **parts** qualities 314 **free** generous
317 **splinter** bind with splints 318 **lay** stake, wager

IAGO   I protest, in the sincerity of love and honest 321
kindness.
CASSIO   I think it freely; and betimes in the morning I 323
will beseech the virtuous Desdemona to undertake for
me. I am desperate of my fortunes if they check me 325
here.
IAGO   You are in the right. Good night, Lieutenant. I
must to the watch.
CASSIO   Good night, honest Iago.   *Exit Cassio.*
IAGO
And what's he then that says I play the villain,
When this advice is free I give, and honest,   331
Probal to thinking, and indeed the course   332
To win the Moor again? For 'tis most easy
Th'inclining Desdemona to subdue   334
In any honest suit; she's framed as fruitful   335
As the free elements. And then for her   336
To win the Moor—were't to renounce his baptism,
All seals and symbols of redeemèd sin—   338
His soul is so enfettered to her love
That she may make, unmake, do what she list,
Even as her appetite shall play the god   341
With his weak function. How am I then a villain,   342
To counsel Cassio to this parallel course   343
Directly to his good? Divinity of hell!   344
When devils will the blackest sins put on,   345
They do suggest at first with heavenly shows,   346
As I do now. For whiles this honest fool
Plies Desdemona to repair his fortune,
And she for him pleads strongly to the Moor,
I'll pour this pestilence into his ear,
That she repeals him for her body's lust;   351
And by how much she strives to do him good,
She shall undo her credit with the Moor.
So will I turn her virtue into pitch,   354
And out of her own goodness make the net
That shall enmesh them all.

                  Enter Roderigo.

                       How now, Roderigo?
RODERIGO   I do follow here in the chase, not like a
hound that hunts, but one that fills up the cry. My 358
money is almost spent; I have been tonight exceedingly well cudgeled; and I think the issue will be I shall 360
have so much experience for my pains, and so, 361
with no money at all and a little more wit, return again
to Venice.

IAGO
How poor are they that have not patience!
What wound did ever heal but by degrees?
Thou know'st we work by wit, and not by witchcraft,
And wit depends on dilatory time.
Does't not go well? Cassio hath beaten thee,
And thou, by that small hurt, hast cashiered Cassio. 369
Though other things grow fair against the sun,   370
Yet fruits that blossom first will first be ripe.   371
Content thyself awhile. By the Mass, 'tis morning!
Pleasure and action make the hours seem short.
Retire thee; go where thou art billeted.
Away, I say! Thou shalt know more hereafter.
Nay, get thee gone.   *Exit Roderigo.*
                  Two things are to be done.
My wife must move for Cassio to her mistress;   377
I'll set her on;
Myself the while to draw the Moor apart
And bring him jump when he may Cassio find   380
Soliciting his wife. Ay, that's the way.
Dull not device by coldness and delay.   *Exit.* 382

                         ❧

3.1

Enter Cassio [and] Musicians.

CASSIO
Masters, play here—I will content your pains—   1
Something that's brief, and bid "Good morrow,
General."   [*They play.*]

                  [*Enter*] *Clown.*

CLOWN   Why, masters, have your instruments been in
Naples, that they speak i'th' nose thus?   4
A MUSICIAN   How, sir, how?
CLOWN   Are these, I pray you, wind instruments?
A MUSICIAN   Ay, marry, are they, sir.
CLOWN   Oh, thereby hangs a tail.
A MUSICIAN   Whereby hangs a tale, sir?
CLOWN   Marry, sir, by many a wind instrument that I 10
know. But, masters, here's money for you. [*He gives
money.*] And the General so likes your music that he
desires you, for love's sake, to make no more noise
with it.
A MUSICIAN   Well, sir, we will not.
CLOWN   If you have any music that may not be heard, 16
to't again; but, as they say, to hear music the General
does not greatly care.
A MUSICIAN   We have none such, sir.

---

321 protest insist, declare   **323 freely** unreservedly   **325 check**
repulse   **331 free** (1) free from guile (2) freely given   **332 Probal**
probable, reasonable   **334 Th'inclining** the favorably disposed.
subdue persuade   **335 framed as fruitful** created as generous
336 free·elements i.e., earth, air, fire, and water, unrestrained and
spontaneous.   **338 seals** tokens   **341 her appetite** her desire, or, perhaps, his desire for her   **342 function** exercise of faculties (weakened
by his fondness for her)   **343 parallel** i.e., seemingly in his best interests but at the same time threatening   **344 Divinity of hell!** Inverted
theology of hell (which seduces the soul to its damnation)!   **345 put
on** further, instigate   **346 suggest** tempt   **351 repeals him** attempts
to get him restored   **354 pitch** i.e., (1) foul blackness (2) a snaring
substance   **358 fills up the cry** merely takes part as one of the pack.
360 issue outcome   **361 so much** just so much and no more

369 cashiered dismissed from service   **370–1 Though . . . ripe** i.e.,
Plans that are well prepared and set expeditiously in motion will
soonest ripen into success.   **377 move** plead   **380 jump** precisely
382 device plot.   **coldness** lack of zeal
3.1. Location: Before the chamber of Othello and Desdemona.
1 Masters Good sirs.   **content your pains** reward your efforts
4 speak i'th' nose (1) sound nasal (2) sound like one whose nose has
been attacked by syphilis. (Naples was popularly supposed to have a
high incidence of venereal disease.)   **10 wind instrument** (With a
joke on flatulence. The *tail*, line 8, that hangs nearby the *wind instrument* suggests the penis.)   **16 may not** cannot

CLOWN   Then put up your pipes in your bag, for I'll
away. Go, vanish into air, away!   *Exeunt Musicians.*
CASSIO   Dost thou hear, mine honest friend?
CLOWN   No, I hear not your honest friend; I hear you.
CASSIO   Prithee, keep up thy quillets. There's a poor   24
piece of gold for thee. [*He gives money.*] If the gentlewoman that attends the General's wife be stirring, tell
her there's one Cassio entreats her a little favor of   27
speech. Wilt thou do this?   28
CLOWN   She is stirring, sir. If she will stir hither, I shall   29
seem to notify unto her.   30
CASSIO
Do, good my friend.   *Exit Clown.*

Enter Iago.

In happy time, Iago.   31
IAGO   You have not been abed, then?
CASSIO   Why, no. The day had broke
Before we parted. I have made bold, Iago,
To send in to your wife. My suit to her
Is that she will to virtuous Desdemona
Procure me some access.
IAGO   I'll send her to you presently;
And I'll devise a mean to draw the Moor
Out of the way, that your converse and business
May be more free.
CASSIO
I humbly thank you for't.   *Exit [Iago].*
I never knew
A Florentine more kind and honest.   43

Enter Emilia.

EMILIA
Good morrow, good Lieutenant. I am sorry
For your displeasure; but all will sure be well.   45
The General and his wife are talking of it,
And she speaks for you stoutly. The Moor replies   47
That he you hurt is of great fame in Cyprus   48
And great affinity, and that in wholesome wisdom   49
He might not but refuse you; but he protests he loves
you   50
And needs no other suitor but his likings
To take the safest occasion by the front   52
To bring you in again.
CASSIO   Yet I beseech you,
If you think fit, or that it may be done,
Give me advantage of some brief discourse
With Desdemon alone.
EMILIA   Pray you, come in.
I will bestow you where you shall have time
To speak your bosom freely.   58

CASSIO   I am much bound to you.   [*Exeunt.*]

❖

3.2

Enter Othello, Iago, and Gentlemen.

OTHELLO [*giving letters*]
These letters give, Iago, to the pilot,
And by him do my duties to the Senate.   2
That done, I will be walking on the works;   3
Repair there to me.
IAGO   Well, my good lord, I'll do't.   4
OTHELLO
This fortification, gentlemen, shall we see't?
GENTLEMEN   We'll wait upon Your Lordship.   *Exeunt.*   6

❖

3.3

Enter Desdemona, Cassio, and Emilia.

DESDEMONA
Be thou assured, good Cassio, I will do
All my abilities in thy behalf.
EMILIA
Good madam, do. I warrant it grieves my husband
As if the cause were his.
DESDEMONA
Oh, that's an honest fellow. Do not doubt, Cassio,
But I will have my lord and you again
As friendly as you were.
CASSIO   Bounteous madam,
Whatever shall become of Michael Cassio,
He's never anything but your true servant.
DESDEMONA
I know't. I thank you. You do love my lord;
You have known him long, and be you well assured
He shall in strangeness stand no farther off   12
Than in a politic distance.
CASSIO   Ay, but, lady,   13
That policy may either last so long,
Or feed upon such nice and waterish diet,   15
Or breed itself so out of circumstance,   16
That, I being absent and my place supplied,   17
My general will forget my love and service.
DESDEMONA
Do not doubt that. Before Emilia here   19
I give thee warrant of thy place. Assure thee,   20
If I do vow a friendship I'll perform it
To the last article. My lord shall never rest.
I'll watch him tame and talk him out of patience;   23

---

24 **keep . . . quillets** refrain from quibbling.   **27–8 a little . . . speech**
the favor of a brief talk.   **29 stir** bestir herself. (With a play on
stirring, "rousing herself from rest.")   **30 seem** deem it good, think fit
31 In happy time i.e., Well met   **43 Florentine** i.e., even a fellow Florentine. (Iago is a Venetian; Cassio is a Florentine.)   **45 displeasure**
fall from favor   **47 stoutly** spiritedly.   **48 fame** reputation, importance   **49 affinity** kindred, family connection   **50 protests** insists
52 occasion . . . front opportunity by the forelock   **58 bosom** inmost
thoughts

3.2. Location: The citadel.
2 do my duties convey my respects   **3 works** breastworks, fortifications   **4 Repair** return, come   **6 wait upon** attend
3.3. Location: The garden of the citadel.
12 strangeness aloofness   **13 politic** required by wise policy
15 Or . . . diet or sustain itself at length upon such trivial and meager
technicalities   **16 breed . . . circumstance** continually renew itself so
out of chance events, or yield so few chances for my being pardoned
17 supplied filled by another person   **19 doubt** fear   **20 warrant**
guarantee   **23 watch him tame** tame him by keeping him from sleeping. (A term from falconry.)   **out of patience** past his endurance

His bed shall seem a school, his board a shrift;   24
I'll intermingle everything he does
With Cassio's suit. Therefore be merry, Cassio,
For thy solicitor shall rather die   27
Than give thy cause away.   28

Enter Othello and Iago [at a distance].

EMILIA   Madam, here comes my lord.
CASSIO   Madam, I'll take my leave.
DESDEMONA   Why, stay, and hear me speak.
CASSIO
    Madam, not now. I am very ill at ease,
    Unfit for mine own purposes.
DESDEMONA   Well, do your discretion.   *Exit Cassio.*   34
IAGO   Ha? I like not that.
OTHELLO   What dost thou say?
IAGO
    Nothing, my lord; or if—I know not what.
OTHELLO
    Was not that Cassio parted from my wife?
IAGO
    Cassio, my lord? No, sure, I cannot think it,
    That he would steal away so guiltylike,
    Seeing you coming.
OTHELLO   I do believe 'twas he.
DESDEMONA *[joining them]*   How now, my lord?
    I have been talking with a suitor here,
    A man that languishes in your displeasure.
OTHELLO   Who is't you mean?
DESDEMONA
    Why, your lieutenant, Cassio. Good my lord,
    If I have any grace or power to move you,
    His present reconciliation take;   49
    For if he be not one that truly loves you,
    That errs in ignorance and not in cunning,   51
    I have no judgment in an honest face.
    I prithee, call him back.
OTHELLO   Went he hence now?
DESDEMONA   Yes, faith, so humbled
    That he hath left part of his grief with me
    To suffer with him. Good love, call him back.
OTHELLO
    Not now, sweet Desdemon. Some other time.
DESDEMONA   But shall't be shortly?
OTHELLO   The sooner, sweet, for you.
DESDEMONA   Shall't be tonight at supper?
OTHELLO   No, not tonight.
DESDEMONA   Tomorrow dinner, then?   63
OTHELLO   I shall not dine at home.
    I meet the captains at the citadel.
DESDEMONA
    Why, then, tomorrow night, or Tuesday morn,
    On Tuesday noon, or night, on Wednesday morn.
    I prithee, name the time, but let it not
    Exceed three days. In faith, he's penitent;

And yet his trespass, in our common reason—   70
Save that, they say, the wars must make example   71
Out of her best—is not almost a fault   72
T'incur a private check. When shall he come?   73
Tell me, Othello. I wonder in my soul
What you would ask me that I should deny,
Or stand so mamm'ring on. What? Michael Cassio,   76
That came a-wooing with you, and so many a time,
When I have spoke of you dispraisingly,
Hath ta'en your part—to have so much to do
To bring him in! By'r Lady, I could do much—   80
OTHELLO
    Prithee, no more. Let him come when he will;
    I will deny thee nothing.
DESDEMONA   Why, this is not a boon.
    'Tis as I should entreat you wear your gloves,
    Or feed on nourishing dishes, or keep you warm,
    Or sue to you to do a peculiar profit   86
    To your own person. Nay, when I have a suit
    Wherein I mean to touch your love indeed,   88
    It shall be full of poise and difficult weight,   89
    And fearful to be granted.
OTHELLO   I will deny thee nothing.
    Whereon, I do beseech thee, grant me this,   92
    To leave me but a little to myself.
DESDEMONA
    Shall I deny you? No. Farewell, my lord.
OTHELLO
    Farewell, my Desdemona. I'll come to thee straight.   95
DESDEMONA
    Emilia, come.—Be as your fancies teach you;   96
    Whate'er you be, I am obedient.   *Exit [with Emilia].*
OTHELLO
    Excellent wretch! Perdition catch my soul   98
    But I do love thee! And when I love thee not,   99
    Chaos is come again.   100
IAGO   My noble lord—
OTHELLO   What dost thou say, Iago?
IAGO
    Did Michael Cassio, when you wooed my lady,
    Know of your love?
OTHELLO
    He did, from first to last. Why dost thou ask?
IAGO
    But for a satisfaction of my thought;
    No further harm.
OTHELLO   Why of thy thought, Iago?

---

24 **board** dining table.   **shrift** confessional   27 **solicitor** advocate
28 **away** up.   34 **do your discretion** do as you think fit.   49 **His . . .
take** let him be reconciled to you right away   51 **in cunning** wittingly   63 **dinner** (The noontime meal.)

70 **common reason** everyday judgments   71–2 **Save . . . best** were it
not that, as the saying goes, military discipline requires making an
example of the very best men. (*Her* refers to wars as a singular concept.)   72 **not almost** scarcely   73 **a private check** even a private
reprimand.   76 **mamm'ring on** wavering or muttering about.
80 **bring him in** restore him to favor.   86 **peculiar** particular, personal   88 **touch** test   89 **poise . . . weight** delicacy and weightiness
92 **Whereon** In return for which   95 **straight** straightway.   96 **fancies** inclinations   98 **wretch** (A term of affectionate endearment.)
99–100 **And . . . again** i.e., My love for you will last forever, until the
end of time when chaos will return. (But with an unconscious, ironic
suggestion that, if anything should induce Othello to cease loving
Desdemona, the result would be chaos.)

IAGO

> I did not think he had been acquainted with her.

OTHELLO

> Oh, yes, and went between us very oft.

IAGO   Indeed?

OTHELLO

> Indeed? Ay, indeed. Discern'st thou aught in that?
> Is he not honest?

IAGO   Honest, my lord?

OTHELLO   Honest. Ay, honest.

IAGO   My lord, for aught I know.

OTHELLO   What dost thou think?

IAGO   Think, my lord?

OTHELLO

> "Think, my lord?" By heaven, thou echo'st me,
> As if there were some monster in thy thought
> Too hideous to be shown. Thou dost mean something.
> I heard thee say even now, thou lik'st not that,
> When Cassio left my wife. What didst not like?
> And when I told thee he was of my counsel   123
> In my whole course of wooing, thou criedst "Indeed?"
> And didst contract and purse thy brow together   125
> As if thou then hadst shut up in thy brain
> Some horrible conceit. If thou dost love me,   127
> Show me thy thought.

IAGO   My lord, you know I love you.

OTHELLO   I think thou dost;

> And, for I know thou'rt full of love and honesty,   131
> And weigh'st thy words before thou giv'st them breath,
> Therefore these stops of thine fright me the more;   133
> For such things in a false disloyal knave
> Are tricks of custom, but in a man that's just   135
> They're close dilations, working from the heart   136
> That passion cannot rule.

IAGO   For Michael Cassio,   137

> I dare be sworn I think that he is honest.

OTHELLO

> I think so too.

IAGO   Men should be what they seem;

> Or those that be not, would they might seem none!   140

OTHELLO

> Certain, men should be what they seem.

IAGO

> Why, then, I think Cassio's an honest man.

OTHELLO   Nay, yet there's more in this.

> I prithee, speak to me as to thy thinkings,
> As thou dost ruminate, and give thy worst of thoughts
> The worst of words.

IAGO   Good my lord, pardon me.

> Though I am bound to every act of duty,
> I am not bound to that all slaves are free to.   148
> Utter my thoughts? Why, say they are vile and false,
> As where's that palace whereinto foul things

Sometimes intrude not? Who has that breast so pure
But some uncleanly apprehensions
Keep leets and law days, and in sessions sit   153
With meditations lawful?   154

OTHELLO

> Thou dost conspire against thy friend, Iago,   155
> If thou but think'st him wronged and mak'st his ear
> A stranger to thy thoughts.

IAGO   I do beseech you,

> Though I perchance am vicious in my guess—   158
> As I confess it is my nature's plague
> To spy into abuses, and oft my jealousy   160
> Shapes faults that are not—that your wisdom then,
> From one that so imperfectly conceits,   162
> Would take no notice, nor build yourself a trouble
> Out of his scattering and unsure observance.   164
> It were not for your quiet nor your good,
> Nor for my manhood, honesty, and wisdom,
> To let you know my thoughts.

OTHELLO   What dost thou mean?

IAGO

> Good name in man and woman, dear my lord,
> Is the immediate jewel of their souls.   169
> Who steals my purse steals trash; 'tis something, nothing;
> 'Twas mine, 'tis his, and has been slave to thousands;
> But he that filches from me my good name
> Robs me of that which not enriches him
> And makes me poor indeed.

OTHELLO   By heaven, I'll know thy thoughts.

IAGO

> You cannot, if my heart were in your hand,   176
> Nor shall not, whilst 'tis in my custody.

OTHELLO   Ha?

IAGO   Oh, beware, my lord, of jealousy.

> It is the green-eyed monster, which doth mock   179
> The meat it feeds on. That cuckold lives in bliss   180
> Who, certain of his fate, loves not his wronger;   181
> But oh, what damnèd minutes tells he o'er   182
> Who dotes, yet doubts, suspects, yet fondly loves!

OTHELLO   Oh, misery!

IAGO

> Poor and content is rich, and rich enough,   185
> But riches fineless is as poor as winter   186
> To him that ever fears he shall be poor.

123 of my counsel in my confidence   125 purse knit   127 conceit fancy.   131 for because   133 stops pauses   135 of custom customary   136–7 They're . . . rule they are secret or involuntary expressions of feeling that are too strong to be kept back.   137 For As for   140 seem none not seem at all, not seem to be honest.   148 that that which.   free to free with respect to.

153 Keep leets and law days i.e., hold court, set up their authority in one's heart. (Leets are a kind of manor court; law days are the days courts sit in session, or those sessions.)   153–4 and . . . lawful i.e., and coexist in a kind of spiritual conflict with virtuous thoughts.   155 thy friend i.e., Othello   158 vicious wrong   160 jealousy suspicious nature   162 one i.e., myself, Iago.   conceits judges, conjectures   164 scattering random   169 immediate essential, most precious   176 if even if   179–80 which . . . feeds on (Jealousy mocks both itself and the sufferer of jealousy; it is self-devouring and is its own punishment.)   180–1 That . . . wronger A cuckolded husband who knows his wife to be unfaithful can at least take comfort in knowing the truth, so that he will not continue to love her or to befriend her lover. (Othello echoes this sentiment in lines 204–6, when he vows that he would end uncertainty and cease to love an unfaithful wife.)   182 tells counts   185 Poor . . . enough To be content with what little one has is the greatest wealth of all. (Proverbial.)   186 fineless boundless

Good God, the souls of all my tribe defend
From jealousy!
OTHELLO   Why, why is this?
Think'st thou I'd make a life of jealousy,
To follow still the changes of the moon   192
With fresh suspicions? No! To be once in doubt   193
Is once to be resolved. Exchange me for a goat   194
When I shall turn the business of my soul
To such exsufflicate and blown surmises   196
Matching thy inference. 'Tis not to make me jealous   197
To say my wife is fair, feeds well, loves company,
Is free of speech, sings, plays, and dances well;
Where virtue is, these are more virtuous.
Nor from mine own weak merits will I draw
The smallest fear or doubt of her revolt,   202
For she had eyes, and chose me. No, Iago,
I'll see before I doubt; when I doubt, prove;
And on the proof, there is no more but this—
Away at once with love or jealousy.
IAGO
    I am glad of this, for now I shall have reason
To show the love and duty that I bear you
With franker spirit. Therefore, as I am bound,
Receive it from me. I speak not yet of proof.
Look to your wife; observe her well with Cassio.
Wear your eyes thus, not jealous nor secure.   212
I would not have your free and noble nature,
Out of self-bounty, be abused. Look to't.   214
I know our country disposition well;
In Venice they do let God see the pranks
They dare not show their husbands; their best
    conscience
Is not to leave't undone, but keep't unknown.
OTHELLO   Dost thou say so?
IAGO
    She did deceive her father, marrying you;
And when she seemed to shake and fear your looks,
She loved them most.
OTHELLO   And so she did.
IAGO   Why, go to, then!   222
    She that, so young, could give out such a seeming,   223
To seel her father's eyes up close as oak,   224
He thought 'twas witchcraft! But I am much to blame.
I humbly do beseech you of your pardon
For too much loving you.
OTHELLO   I am bound to thee forever.   228
IAGO
    I see this hath a little dashed your spirits.

OTHELLO
    Not a jot, not a jot.
IAGO   I'faith, I fear it has.
    I hope you will consider what is spoke
Comes from my love. But I do see you're moved.
I am to pray you not to strain my speech
To grosser issues nor to larger reach   234
Than to suspicion.
OTHELLO   I will not.
IAGO   Should you do so, my lord,
    My speech should fall into such vile success   238
Which my thoughts aimed not. Cassio's my worthy
    friend.
My lord, I see you're moved.
OTHELLO   No, not much moved.
    I do not think but Desdemona's honest.   241
IAGO
    Long live she so! And long live you to think so!
OTHELLO
    And yet, how nature erring from itself—
IAGO
    Ay, there's the point! As—to be bold with you—
Not to affect many proposèd matches   245
Of her own clime, complexion, and degree,   246
Whereto we see in all things nature tends—
Foh! One may smell in such a will most rank,   248
Foul disproportion, thoughts unnatural.   249
But pardon me. I do not in position   250
Distinctly speak of her, though I may fear
Her will, recoiling to her better judgment,   252
May fall to match you with her country forms   253
And happily repent.
OTHELLO   Farewell, farewell!   254
    If more thou dost perceive, let me know more.
Set on thy wife to observe. Leave me, Iago.
IAGO [going]   My lord, I take my leave.
OTHELLO
    Why did I marry? This honest creature doubtless
Sees and knows more, much more, than he unfolds.
IAGO [returning]
    My lord, I would I might entreat Your Honor
To scan this thing no farther. Leave it to time.   261
Although 'tis fit that Cassio have his place—
For, sure, he fills it up with great ability—
Yet, if you please to hold him off awhile,
You shall by that perceive him and his means.   265
Note if your lady strain his entertainment   266
With any strong or vehement importunity;
Much will be seen in that. In the meantime,
Let me be thought too busy in my fears—   269

192–3 To follow . . . suspicions? to be constantly imagining new
causes for suspicion, changing incessantly like the moon? 194 once
once and for all.   resolved free of doubt, having settled the matter.
196 exsufflicate and blown inflated and blown up or flyblown,
hence, loathsome, disgusting   197 inference description or allegation.   202 doubt . . . revolt fear of her unfaithfulness   212 not neither.   secure free from uncertainty.   214 self-bounty inherent or
natural goodness and generosity.   abused deceived.   222 go to (An
expression of impatience.)   223 seeming false appearance   224 seel
blind. (A term from falconry.)   oak (A close-grained wood.)
228 bound indebted. (But perhaps with ironic sense of "tied.")

234 issues significances.   reach meaning, scope   238 success effect,
result   241 honest chaste.   245 affect prefer, desire   246 clime . . .
degree country, temperament or skin color, and social position
248 will sensuality, appetite   249 disproportion abnormality   250 in
position in making this argument or proposition   252 recoiling
reverting.   better i.e., more natural and reconsidered   253 fall . . .
forms undertake to compare you with Venetian norms of handsomeness   254 happily repent haply repent her marriage.   261 scan
scrutinize   265 his means the method he uses (to regain his post).
266 strain his entertainment urge his reinstatement   269 busy
officious

As worthy cause I have to fear I am—
And hold her free, I do beseech Your Honor.   271

OTHELLO   Fear not my government.   272

IAGO   I once more take my leave.   *Exit.*

OTHELLO
This fellow's of exceeding honesty,
And knows all qualities, with a learnèd spirit,   275
Of human dealings. If I do prove her haggard,   276
Though that her jesses were my dear heartstrings,   277
I'd whistle her off and let her down the wind   278
To prey at fortune. Haply, for I am black   279
And have not those soft parts of conversation   280
That chamberers have, or for I am declined   281
Into the vale of years—yet that's not much—
She's gone. I am abused, and my relief   283
Must be to loathe her. Oh, curse of marriage,
That we can call these delicate creatures ours
And not their appetites! I had rather be a toad
And live upon the vapor of a dungeon
Than keep a corner in the thing I love
For others' uses. Yet, 'tis the plague of great ones;
Prerogatived are they less than the base.   290
'Tis destiny unshunnable, like death.
Even then this forkèd plague is fated to us   292
When we do quicken. Look where she comes.   293

Enter Desdemona and Emilia.

If she be false, oh, then heaven mocks itself!
I'll not believe't.

DESDEMONA   How now, my dear Othello?
Your dinner, and the generous islanders   296
By you invited do attend your presence.   297

OTHELLO
I am to blame.

DESDEMONA   Why do you speak so faintly?
Are you not well?

OTHELLO
I have a pain upon my forehead here.

DESDEMONA
Faith, that's with watching. 'Twill away again.   301
[She offers her handkerchief.]
Let me but bind it hard, within this hour
It will be well.

OTHELLO   Your napkin is too little.   303
Let it alone. Come, I'll go in with you.   304
[He puts the handkerchief from him, and it drops.]

DESDEMONA
I am very sorry that you are not well.

Exit [with Othello].

EMILIA *[picking up the handkerchief]*
I am glad I have found this napkin.
This was her first remembrance from the Moor.
My wayward husband hath a hundred times   308
Wooed me to steal it, but she so loves the token—
For he conjured her she should ever keep it—
That she reserves it evermore about her
To kiss and talk to. I'll have the work ta'en out,   312
And give't Iago. What he will do with it
Heaven knows, not I;
I nothing but to please his fantasy.   315

Enter Iago.

IAGO
How now? What do you here alone?

EMILIA
Do not you chide. I have a thing for you.

IAGO
You have a thing for me? It is a common thing—   318

EMILIA   Ha?

IAGO   To have a foolish wife.

EMILIA
Oh, is that all? What will you give me now
For that same handkerchief?

IAGO   What handkerchief?

EMILIA   What handkerchief?
Why, that the Moor first gave to Desdemona;
That which so often you did bid me steal.

IAGO   Hast stolen it from her?

EMILIA
No, faith. She let it drop by negligence,
And to th'advantage I, being here, took't up.
Look, here 'tis.   329

IAGO   A good wench! Give it me.

EMILIA
What will you do with't, that you have been so earnest
To have me filch it?

IAGO *[snatching it]*   Why, what is that to you?

EMILIA
If it be not for some purpose of import,
Give't me again. Poor lady, she'll run mad
When she shall lack it.

IAGO   Be not acknown on't.   335
I have use for it. Go, leave me.   *Exit Emilia.*
I will in Cassio's lodging lose this napkin   337
And let him find it. Trifles light as air
Are to the jealous confirmations strong
As proofs of Holy Writ. This may do something.
The Moor already changes with my poison.

271 **hold her free** regard her as innocent   272 **government** self-control, conduct.   275 **qualities** natures, types   276 **haggard** wild (like a wild female hawk)   277 **jesses** straps fastened around the legs of a trained hawk   278 **I'd . . . wind** i.e., I'd let her go forever. (To release a hawk downwind was to turn it loose.)   279 **prey at fortune** fend for herself in the wild.   **Haply, for** Perhaps because   280 **soft . . . conversation** pleasing social graces   281 **chamberers** drawing-room gallants   283 **abused** deceived   290 **Prerogatived** privileged (to have honest wives).   **the base** ordinary citizens. (Socially prominent men are especially prone to the common destiny of being cuckolded and to the public shame that goes with it.)   292 **forkèd** (An allusion to the horns of the cuckold.)   293 **quicken** receive life. (*Quicken* may also mean to swarm with maggots as the body festers, as in 4.2.69, in which case lines 292–3 suggest that *even then*, in death, we are cuckolded by *forkèd* worms.)   296 **generous** noble   297 **attend** await   301 **watching** too little sleep.   303 **napkin** handkerchief   304 **Let it alone** i.e., Never mind.

308 **wayward** capricious   312 **work ta'en out** design of the embroidery copied   315 **fantasy** whim.   318 **common thing** (With bawdy suggestion; *common* suggests coarseness and availability to all comers, and *thing* is a slang term for the pudendum.)   329 **to th'advantage** taking the opportunity   335 **lack** miss.   **Be . . . on't** Do not confess knowledge of it; keep out of this.   337 **lose** (The Folio spelling, "loose," is a normal spelling for "lose," but it may also contain the idea of "let go," "release.")

Dangerous conceits are in their natures poisons,   342
Which at the first are scarce found to distaste,   343
But with a little act upon the blood   344
Burn like the mines of sulfur.

    Enter Othello.

                            I did say so.
Look where he comes! Not poppy nor mandragora   346
Nor all the drowsy syrups of the world
Shall ever medicine thee to that sweet sleep
Which thou owed'st yesterday.

OTHELLO   Ha, ha, false to me?   349

IAGO
  Why, how now, General? No more of that.

OTHELLO
  Avaunt! Begone! Thou hast set me on the rack.
  I swear 'tis better to be much abused
  Than but to know't a little.

IAGO   How now, my lord?

OTHELLO
  What sense had I of her stolen hours of lust?
  I saw't not, thought it not, it harmed not me.
  I slept the next night well, fed well, was free and
    merry;   356
  I found not Cassio's kisses on her lips.
  He that is robbed, not wanting what is stolen,   358
  Let him not know't and he's not robbed at all.

IAGO   I am sorry to hear this.

OTHELLO
  I had been happy if the general camp,
  Pioneers and all, had tasted her sweet body,   362
  So I had nothing known. Oh, now, forever   363
  Farewell the tranquil mind! Farewell content!
  Farewell the plumèd troops and the big wars   365
  That makes ambition virtue! Oh, farewell!
  Farewell the neighing steed and the shrill trump,
  The spirit-stirring drum, th'ear-piercing fife,
  The royal banner, and all quality,   369
  Pride, pomp, and circumstance of glorious war!   370
  And O you mortal engines, whose rude throats   371
  Th'immortal Jove's dread clamors counterfeit,   372
  Farewell! Othello's occupation's gone.

IAGO   Is't possible, my lord?

OTHELLO
  Villain, be sure thou prove my love a whore!
  Be sure of it. Give me the ocular proof,
  Or, by the worth of mine eternal soul,
  Thou hadst been better have been born a dog
  Than answer my waked wrath!

IAGO   Is't come to this?

OTHELLO
  Make me to see't, or at the least so prove it

That the probation bear no hinge nor loop   381
To hang a doubt on, or woe upon thy life!

IAGO   My noble lord—

OTHELLO
  If thou dost slander her and torture me,
  Never pray more; abandon all remorse;   385
  On horror's head horrors accumulate;   386
  Do deeds to make heaven weep, all earth amazed;   387
  For nothing canst thou to damnation add
  Greater than that.

IAGO   O grace! O heaven forgive me!
  Are you a man? Have you a soul or sense?
  God b'wi'you; take mine office. O wretched fool,   391
  That lov'st to make thine honesty a vice!   392
  O monstrous world! Take note, take note, O world,
  To be direct and honest is not safe.
  I thank you for this profit, and from hence   395
  I'll love no friend, sith love breeds such offense. 396

OTHELLO   Nay, stay. Thou shouldst be honest.   397

IAGO
  I should be wise, for honesty's a fool
  And loses that it works for.

OTHELLO   By the world,   399
  I think my wife be honest and think she is not;
  I think that thou art just and think thou art not.
  I'll have some proof. My name, that was as fresh
  As Dian's visage, is now begrimed and black   403
  As mine own face. If there be cords, or knives,
  Poison, or fire, or suffocating streams,
  I'll not endure it. Would I were satisfied!

IAGO
  I see, sir, you are eaten up with passion.
  I do repent me that I put it to you.
  You would be satisfied?

OTHELLO   Would? Nay, and I will.

IAGO
  And may; but how? How satisfied, my lord?
  Would you, the supervisor, grossly gape on?   411
  Behold her topped?

OTHELLO   Death and damnation! Oh!

IAGO
  It were a tedious difficulty, I think,
  To bring them to that prospect. Damn them then,   414
  If ever mortal eyes do see them bolster   415
  More than their own. What then? How then?   416
  What shall I say? Where's satisfaction?
  It is impossible you should see this,
  Were they as prime as goats, as hot as monkeys,   419

---

342 conceits fancies, ideas   **343 distaste** be distasteful   **344 act** action, working   **346 mandragora** an opiate made of the mandrake root   **349 thou owed'st** you did own   **356 free** carefree   **358 wanting** missing   **362 Pioneers** diggers of mines, the lowest grade of soldiers   **363 So** provided   **365 big** mighty   **369 quality** character, essential nature   **370 Pride** rich display.   **circumstance** pageantry **371 mortal engines** i.e., cannon. (*Mortal* means "deadly.")   **372 Jove's dread clamors** i.e., thunder

381 probation proof   **385 remorse** pity, penitent hope for salvation **386 horrors accumulate** add still more horrors   **387 amazed** confounded with horror   **391 O wretched fool** (Iago addresses himself as a fool for having carried honesty too far.)   **392 vice** failing, something overdone.   **395 profit** profitable instruction.   **hence** henceforth   **396 sith** since.   **offense** i.e., harm to the one who offers help and friendship.   **397 Thou shouldst be** It appears that you are. (But Iago replies in the sense of "ought to be.")   **399 that** what   **403 Dian** Diana, goddess of the moon and of chastity   **411 supervisor** onlooker   **414 Damn them then** i.e., They would have to be really incorrigible   **415 bolster** go to bed together, share a bolster **416 More** other.   **own** own eyes.   **419 prime** lustful

As salt as wolves in pride, and fools as gross   420
As ignorance made drunk. But yet I say,
If imputation and strong circumstances   422
Which lead directly to the door of truth
Will give you satisfaction, you might have't.
OTHELLO
Give me a living reason she's disloyal.
IAGO   I do not like the office.
But sith I am entered in this cause so far,   427
Pricked to't by foolish honesty and love,   428
I will go on. I lay with Cassio lately,
And being troubled with a raging tooth
I could not sleep. There are a kind of men
So loose of soul that in their sleeps will mutter
Their affairs. One of this kind is Cassio.
In sleep I heard him say, "Sweet Desdemona,
Let us be wary, let us hide our loves!"
And then, sir, would he grip and wring my hand,
Cry "O sweet creature!", then kiss me hard,
As if he plucked up kisses by the roots
That grew upon my lips; then laid his leg
Over my thigh, and sighed, and kissed, and then
Cried, "Cursèd fate that gave thee to the Moor!"
OTHELLO
Oh, monstrous! Monstrous!
IAGO   Nay, this was but his dream.
OTHELLO
But this denoted a foregone conclusion.   443
'Tis a shrewd doubt, though it be but a dream.   444
IAGO
And this may help to thicken other proofs
That do demonstrate thinly.
OTHELLO   I'll tear her all to pieces.
IAGO
Nay, but be wise. Yet we see nothing done;
She may be honest yet. Tell me but this:
Have you not sometimes seen a handkerchief
Spotted with strawberries in your wife's hand?   450
OTHELLO
I gave her such a one. 'Twas my first gift.
IAGO
I know not that; but such a handkerchief—
I am sure it was your wife's—did I today
See Cassio wipe his beard with.
OTHELLO   If it be that—
IAGO
If it be that, or any that was hers,
It speaks against her with the other proofs.
OTHELLO
Oh, that the slave had forty thousand lives!   457
One is too poor, too weak for my revenge.
Now do I see 'tis true. Look here, Iago,
All my fond love thus do I blow to heaven.   460

'Tis gone.
Arise, black vengeance, from the hollow hell!
Yield up, O love, thy crown and hearted throne   463
To tyrannous hate! Swell, bosom, with thy freight,   464
For 'tis of aspics' tongues!   465
IAGO   Yet be content.   466
OTHELLO   Oh, blood, blood, blood!
IAGO
Patience, I say. Your mind perhaps may change.
OTHELLO
Never, Iago. Like to the Pontic Sea,   469
Whose icy current and compulsive course
Ne'er feels retiring ebb, but keeps due on
To the Propontic and the Hellespont,   472
Even so my bloody thoughts with violent pace
Shall ne'er look back, ne'er ebb to humble love,
Till that a capable and wide revenge   475
Swallow them up. Now, by yond marble heaven,   476
[Kneeling] In the due reverence of a sacred vow
I here engage my words.
IAGO   Do not rise yet.
[He kneels.] Witness, you ever-burning lights above,   479
You elements that clip us round about,   480
Witness that here Iago doth give up
The execution of his wit, hands, heart,   482
To wronged Othello's service. Let him command,
And to obey shall be in me remorse,   484
What bloody business ever.   [They rise.]
OTHELLO   I greet thy love,   485
Not with vain thanks, but with acceptance bounteous,
And will upon the instant put thee to't.   487
Within these three days let me hear thee say
That Cassio's not alive.
IAGO   My friend is dead;
'Tis done at your request. But let her live.
OTHELLO
Damn her, lewd minx! Oh, damn her, damn her!   491
Come, go with me apart. I will withdraw
To furnish me with some swift means of death
For the fair devil. Now art thou my lieutenant.
IAGO   I am your own forever.   Exeunt.

❖

3.4

Enter Desdemona, Emilia, and Clown.

DESDEMONA   Do you know, sirrah, where Lieutenant   1
Cassio lies?   2

---

420 **salt** wanton, sensual.   **pride** heat   422 **imputation . . . circumstances** strong circumstantial evidence   427 **sith** since   428 **Pricked**
spurred   443 **foregone conclusion** previous experience or action.
444 **shrewd doubt** suspicious circumstance   450 **Spotted with strawberries** embroidered with a strawberry pattern   457 **the slave** i.e.,
Cassio   460 **fond** foolish. (But also suggesting "affectionate.")

463 **hearted** fixed in the heart   464 **freight** burden   465 **aspics'**
venomous serpents'   466 **content** calm.   469 **Pontic Sea** Black Sea
472 **Propontic** Sea of Marmora, between the Black Sea and the
Aegean.   **Hellespont** Dardanelles, straits where the Sea of Marmora
joins with the Aegean   475 **capable** ample, comprehensive
476 **marble** i.e., gleaming, polished, and indifferent to human suffering   479 s.d. *He kneels* (In the Quarto text, Iago kneels here after
Othello has knelt at line 477.)   480 **clip** encompass   482 **execution**
exercise, action.   **wit** mind   484 **remorse** pity (for Othello's wrongs)
485 **ever** soever.   487 **to't** to the proof.   491 **minx** wanton.
3.4. Location: Before the citadel.
1 **sirrah** (A form of address to an inferior.)   2 **lies** lodges. (But the
Clown makes the obvious pun.)

CLOWN   I dare not say he lies anywhere.

DESDEMONA   Why, man?

CLOWN   He's a soldier, and for me to say a soldier lies, 'tis stabbing.

DESDEMONA   Go to. Where lodges he?

CLOWN   To tell you where he lodges is to tell you where I lie.

DESDEMONA   Can anything be made of this?

CLOWN   I know not where he lodges, and for me to devise a lodging and say he lies here, or he lies there, were to lie in mine own throat.   13

DESDEMONA   Can you inquire him out, and be edified by report?

CLOWN   I will catechize the world for him; that is, make questions, and by them answer.

DESDEMONA   Seek him, bid him come hither. Tell him I have moved my lord on his behalf and hope all will be   19 well.

CLOWN   To do this is within the compass of man's wit, and therefore I will attempt the doing it.   *Exit Clown.*

DESDEMONA
Where should I lose that handkerchief, Emilia?

EMILIA   I know not, madam.

DESDEMONA
Believe me, I had rather have lost my purse
Full of crusadoes; and but my noble Moor   26
Is true of mind and made of no such baseness
As jealous creatures are, it were enough
To put him to ill thinking.

EMILIA   Is he not jealous?

DESDEMONA
Who, he? I think the sun where he was born
Drew all such humors from him.

EMILIA   Look where he comes.   31

            Enter Othello.

DESDEMONA
I will not leave him now till Cassio
Be called to him.—How is't with you, my lord?

OTHELLO
Well, my good lady. [*Aside*] Oh, hardness to
    dissemble!—
How do you, Desdemona?

DESDEMONA   Well, my good lord.

OTHELLO
Give me your hand. [*She gives her hand.*] This hand is
    moist, my lady.

DESDEMONA
It yet hath felt no age nor known no sorrow.

OTHELLO
This argues fruitfulness and liberal heart.   38
Hot, hot, and moist. This hand of yours requires
A sequester from liberty, fasting and prayer,   40

Much castigation, exercise devout;   41
For here's a young and sweating devil here
That commonly rebels. 'Tis a good hand,
A frank one.

DESDEMONA   You may indeed say so,   44
For 'twas that hand that gave away my heart.

OTHELLO
A liberal hand. The hearts of old gave hands,   46
But our new heraldry is hands, not hearts.   47

DESDEMONA
I cannot speak of this. Come now, your promise.

OTHELLO   What promise, chuck?   49

DESDEMONA
I have sent to bid Cassio come speak with you.

OTHELLO
I have a salt and sorry rheum offends me;   51
Lend me thy handkerchief.

DESDEMONA   Here, my lord.   [*She offers a handkerchief.*]

OTHELLO
That which I gave you.

DESDEMONA   I have it not about me.

OTHELLO   Not?

DESDEMONA   No, faith, my lord.

OTHELLO
That's a fault. That handkerchief
Did an Egyptian to my mother give.
She was a charmer, and could almost read   59
The thoughts of people. She told her, while she kept it
'Twould make her amiable and subdue my father   61
Entirely to her love, but if she lost it
Or made a gift of it, my father's eye
Should hold her loathèd and his spirits should hunt
After new fancies. She, dying, gave it me,   65
And bid me, when my fate would have me wived,
To give it her. I did so; and take heed on't;   67
Make it a darling like your precious eye.
To lose't or give't away were such perdition   69
As nothing else could match.

DESDEMONA   Is't possible?

OTHELLO
'Tis true. There's magic in the web of it.   71
A sibyl, that had numbered in the world
The sun to course two hundred compasses,   73
In her prophetic fury sewed the work;   74
The worms were hallowed that did breed the silk,
And it was dyed in mummy which the skillful   76
Conserved of maidens' hearts.

DESDEMONA   I'faith! Is't true?   77

---

13 **lie . . . throat** lie egregiously and deliberately.   19 **moved my lord** petitioned Othello   26 **crusadoes** Portuguese gold coins   31 **humors** (Refers to the four bodily fluids thought to determine temperament.)   38 **argues** gives evidence of.   **fruitfulness** generosity, amorousness, and fecundity.   **liberal** generous and sexually free   40 **sequester** sequestration

41 **castigation** corrective discipline.   **exercise devout** i.e., prayer, religious meditation, etc.   44 **frank** generous, open. (With sexual suggestion.)   46–7 **The hearts . . . hands** i.e., In former times, people would give their hearts when they gave their hands to something, but in our dedacent present age the joining of hands no longer has that spiritual sense.   49 **chuck** (A term of endearment.)   51 **salt . . . rheum** distressful head cold or watering of the eyes   59 **charmer** sorceress   61 **amiable** desirable   65 **fancies** loves.   67 **her** i.e., to my wife.   69 **perdition** loss   71 **web** fabric, weaving   73 **compasses** annual circlings. (The *sibyl*, or prophetess, was two hundred years old.)   74 **prophetic fury** frenzy of prophetic inspiration.   **work** embroidered pattern   76 **mummy** medicinal or magical preparation drained from mummified bodies   77 **Conserved of** prepared or preserved out of

OTHELLO
  Most veritable. Therefore look to't well.
DESDEMONA
  Then would to God that I had never seen't!
OTHELLO   Ha? Wherefore?
DESDEMONA
  Why do you speak so startingly and rash?   81
OTHELLO
  Is't lost? Is't gone? Speak, is't out o'th' way?   82
DESDEMONA   Heaven bless us!
OTHELLO   Say you?
DESDEMONA
  It is not lost; but what an if it were?   85
OTHELLO   How?
DESDEMONA
  I say it is not lost.
OTHELLO   Fetch't, let me see't.
DESDEMONA
  Why, so I can, sir, but I will not now.
  This is a trick to put me from my suit.
  Pray you, let Cassio be received again.
OTHELLO
  Fetch me the handkerchief! My mind misgives.
DESDEMONA   Come, come,
  You'll never meet a more sufficient man.   93
OTHELLO
  The handkerchief!
DESDEMONA   I pray, talk me of Cassio.   94
OTHELLO
  The handkerchief!
DESDEMONA   A man that all his time   95
  Hath founded his good fortunes on your love,   96
  Shared dangers with you—
OTHELLO   The handkerchief!
DESDEMONA   I'faith, you are to blame.
OTHELLO   Zounds!   Exit Othello.
EMILIA   Is not this man jealous?
DESDEMONA   I ne'er saw this before.
  Sure, there's some wonder in this handkerchief.
  I am most unhappy in the loss of it.   104
EMILIA
  'Tis not a year or two shows us a man.   105
  They are all but stomachs, and we all but food;   106
  They eat us hungerly, and when they are full   107
  They belch us.

        Enter Iago and Cassio.

          Look you, Cassio and my husband.
IAGO [to Cassio]
  There is no other way; 'tis she must do't.
  And, lo, the happiness! Go and importune her.   110

DESDEMONA
  How now, good Cassio? What's the news with you?
CASSIO
  Madam, my former suit. I do beseech you
  That by your virtuous means I may again   113
  Exist and be a member of his love
  Whom I, with all the office of my heart,   115
  Entirely honor. I would not be delayed.
  If my offense be of such mortal kind   117
  That nor my service past, nor present sorrows,   118
  Nor purposed merit in futurity
  Can ransom me into his love again,
  But to know so must be my benefit;   121
  So shall I clothe me in a forced content,
  And shut myself up in some other course,   123
  To fortune's alms.
DESDEMONA   Alas, thrice-gentle Cassio,   124
  My advocation is not now in tune.   125
  My lord is not my lord; nor should I know him,
  Were he in favor as in humor altered.   127
  So help me every spirit sanctified   128
  As I have spoken for you all my best
  And stood within the blank of his displeasure   130
  For my free speech! You must awhile be patient.   131
  What I can do I will, and more I will
  Than for myself I dare. Let that suffice you.
IAGO
  Is my lord angry?
EMILIA   He went hence but now,
  And certainly in strange unquietness.
IAGO
  Can he be angry? I have seen the cannon
  When it hath blown his ranks into the air,
  And like the devil from his very arm
  Puffed his own brother—and is he angry?
  Something of moment then. I will go meet him.   140
  There's matter in't indeed, if he be angry.
DESDEMONA
  I prithee, do so.   Exit [Iago].
                  Something, sure, of state,   142
  Either from Venice, or some unhatched practice   143
  Made demonstrable here in Cyprus to him,
  Hath puddled his clear spirit; and in such cases   145
  Men's natures wrangle with inferior things,
  Though great ones are their object. 'Tis even so;
  For let our finger ache, and it indues   148
  Our other, healthful members even to a sense
  Of pain. Nay, we must think men are not gods,

81 **startingly and rash** disjointedly and impetuously, excitedly.
82 **out o'th' way** lost, misplaced.   85 **an if** if   93 **sufficient** able,
complete   94 **talk** talk to   95–6 **A man . . . love** A man who throughout his career has relied on your favor for his advancement
104 **unhappy** (1) unfortunate (2) sad   105 **'Tis . . . man** A year or two
is not enough time for us women to know what men really are.
106 **but** nothing but   107 **hungerly** hungrily   110 **the happiness** in
happy time, fortunately met.

113 **virtuous** (1) efficacious (2) morally good   115 **office** loyal service
117 **mortal** fatal   118 **nor . . . nor** neither . . . nor   121 **But . . . benefit**
merely to know that my case is hopeless will have to content me (and
will be better than uncertainty)   123 **And shut . . . in** commit myself
to   124 **To fortune's alms** throwing myself on the mercy of fortune.
125 **advocation** advocacy   127 **favor** appearance.   **humor** mood
128 **So . . . sanctified** So help me all the heavenly host   130 **within
the blank** within point-blank range. (The *blank* is the center of the target.)   131 **free** frank   140 **of moment** of immediate importance,
momentous   142 **of state** concerning state affairs   143 **unhatched
practice** as yet unexecuted or undiscovered plot   145 **puddled** muddied   148 **indues** endows, brings to the same condition

Nor of them look for such observancy   151
As fits the bridal. Beshrew me much, Emilia,   152
I was, unhandsome warrior as I am,   153
Arraigning his unkindness with my soul;   154
But now I find I had suborned the witness,   155
And he's indicted falsely.

EMILIA   Pray heaven it be
State matters, as you think, and no conception
Nor no jealous toy concerning you.   158

DESDEMONA
Alas the day! I never gave him cause.

EMILIA
But jealous souls will not be answered so;
They are not ever jealous for the cause,
But jealous for they're jealous. It is a monster   162
Begot upon itself, born on itself.   163

DESDEMONA
Heaven keep that monster from Othello's mind!

EMILIA   Lady, amen.

DESDEMONA
I will go seek him. Cassio, walk hereabout.
If I do find him fit, I'll move your suit
And seek to effect it to my uttermost.

CASSIO
I humbly thank Your Ladyship.
                    Exit [Desdemona with Emilia].

Enter Bianca.

BIANCA
Save you, friend Cassio!

CASSIO   What make you from home?   170
How is't with you, my most fair Bianca?
I' faith, sweet love, I was coming to your house.

BIANCA
And I was going to your lodging, Cassio.
What, keep a week away? Seven days and nights?
Eightscore-eight hours? And lovers' absent hours   175
More tedious than the dial eightscore times?   176
Oh, weary reck'ning!

CASSIO   Pardon me, Bianca.
I have this while with leaden thoughts been pressed;
But I shall, in a more continuate time,   179
Strike off this score of absence. Sweet Bianca,   180
                    [*giving her Desdemona's handkerchief*]
Take me this work out.

BIANCA   Oh, Cassio, whence came this?   181
This is some token from a newer friend.   182
To the felt absence now I feel a cause.
Is't come to this? Well, well.

CASSIO   Go to, woman!
Throw your vile guesses in the devil's teeth,

From whence you have them. You are jealous now
That this is from some mistress, some remembrance.
No, by my faith, Bianca.

BIANCA   Why, whose is it?

CASSIO
I know not, neither. I found it in my chamber.
I like the work well. Ere it be demanded—   190
As like enough it will—I would have it copied   191
Take it and do't, and leave me for this time.

BIANCA   Leave you? Wherefore?

CASSIO
I do attend here on the General,
And think it no addition, nor my wish,   195
To have him see me womaned.

BIANCA   Why, I pray you?

CASSIO   Not that I love you not.

BIANCA   But that you do not love me.
I pray you, bring me on the way a little,   200
And say if I shall see you soon at night.

CASSIO
'Tis but a little way that I can bring you,
For I attend here; but I'll see you soon.

BIANCA
'Tis very good. I must be circumstanced.   204
                    Exeunt omnes.

❖

4.1

Enter Othello and Iago.

IAGO
Will you think so?

OTHELLO   Think so, Iago?

IAGO   What,
To kiss in private?

OTHELLO   An unauthorized kiss!

IAGO
Or to be naked with her friend in bed
An hour or more, not meaning any harm?

OTHELLO
Naked in bed, Iago, and not mean harm?
It is hypocrisy against the devil.
They that mean virtuously and yet do so,
The devil their virtue tempts, and they tempt heaven.

IAGO
If they do nothing, 'tis a venial slip.   9
But if I give my wife a handkerchief—

OTHELLO   What then?

IAGO
Why then, 'tis hers, my lord, and being hers,
She may, I think, bestow't on any man.

OTHELLO
She is protectress of her honor too.
May she give that?

---

151 **observancy** attentiveness   152 **bridal** wedding (when a bridegroom is newly attentive to his bride).   **Beshrew me** (A mild oath.)
153 **unhandsome** insufficient, unskillful   154 **with** before the bar of
155 **suborned the witness** induced the witness to give false testimony
158 **toy** fancy   162 **for** because   163 **Begot upon itself** generated solely from itself   170 **Save** God save.   **make** do   175 **Eightscore-eight** one hundred sixty-eight, the number of hours in a week
176 **the dial** a complete revolution of the clock   179 **continuate** uninterrupted   180 **Strike . . . score** settle this account   181 **Take . . . out** copy this embroidery for me.   182 **friend** mistress.

190 **demanded** inquired for   191 **like** likely   195 **addition** i.e., addition to my reputation   200 **bring** accompany   204 **be circumstanced** be governed by circumstance, yield to your conditions.
4.1. Location: Before the citadel.
9 **venial** pardonable

IAGO
    Her honor is an essence that's not seen;
    They have it very oft that have it not.   17
    But, for the handkerchief—
OTHELLO
    By heaven, I would most gladly have forgot it.
    Thou said'st—Oh, it comes o'er my memory
    As doth the raven o'er the infectious house,   21
    Boding to all—he had my handkerchief.
IAGO
    Ay, what of that?
OTHELLO   That's not so good now.
IAGO   What
    If I had said I had seen him do you wrong?
    Or heard him say—as knaves be such abroad,   25
    Who having, by their own importunate suit,   26
    Or voluntary dotage of some mistress,   27
    Convincèd or supplied them, cannot choose   28
    But they must blab—
OTHELLO   Hath he said anything?   29
IAGO
    He hath, my lord; but, be you well assured,
    No more than he'll unswear.
OTHELLO   What hath he said?
IAGO
    Faith, that he did—I know not what he did.
OTHELLO   What? What?
IAGO
    Lie—
OTHELLO   With her?
IAGO   With her, on her; what you will.
OTHELLO   Lie with her? Lie on her? We say "lie on her"
    when they belie her. Lie with her? Zounds, that's ful-   36
    some.—Handkerchief—confessions—handkerchief!   37
    —To confess and be hanged for his labor—first to be   38
    hanged and then to confess.—I tremble at it. Nature   39
    would not invest herself in such shadowing passion   40
    without some instruction. It is not words that shakes   41
    me thus. Pish! Noses, ears, and lips.—Is't possible?
    —Confess—handkerchief!—O devil!

                             Falls in a trance.

IAGO   Work on,
    My medicine, work! Thus credulous fools are caught,
    And many worthy and chaste dames even thus,
    All guiltless, meet reproach.—What, ho! My lord!
    My lord, I say! Othello!

          Enter Cassio.

             How now, Cassio?

CASSIO   What's the matter?
IAGO
    My lord is fall'n into an epilepsy.
    This is his second fit. He had one yesterday.
CASSIO
    Rub him about the temples.
IAGO   No, forbear.
    The lethargy must have his quiet course.   53
    If not, he foams at mouth, and by and by
    Breaks out to savage madness. Look, he stirs.
    Do you withdraw yourself a little while.
    He will recover straight. When he is gone,
    I would on great occasion speak with you.   58

                             [Exit Cassio.]
    How is it, General? Have you not hurt your head?
OTHELLO
    Dost thou mock me?
IAGO   I mock you not, by heaven.   60
    Would you would bear your fortune like a man!
OTHELLO
    A hornèd man's a monster and a beast.
IAGO
    There's many a beast then in a populous city,
    And many a civil monster.   64
OTHELLO   Did he confess it?
IAGO   Good sir, be a man.
    Think every bearded fellow that's but yoked   67
    May draw with you. There's millions now alive   68
    That nightly lie in those unproper beds   69
    Which they dare swear peculiar. Your case is better.   70
    Oh, 'tis the spite of hell, the fiend's arch-mock,
    To lip a wanton in a secure couch   72
    And to suppose her chaste! No, let me know,
    And knowing what I am, I know what she shall be.   74
OTHELLO   Oh, thou art wise. 'Tis certain.
IAGO   Stand you awhile apart;
    Confine yourself but in a patient list.   77
    Whilst you were here o'erwhelmèd with your grief—
    A passion most unsuiting such a man—
    Cassio came hither. I shifted him away,   80
    And laid good 'scuse upon your ecstasy,   81
    Bade him anon return and here speak with me,
    The which he promised. Do but encave yourself   83
    And mark the fleers, the gibes, and notable scorns   84
    That dwell in every region of his face;
    For I will make him tell the tale anew,
    Where, how, how oft, how long ago, and when
    He hath and is again to cope your wife.   88

---

17 They have it i.e., They enjoy a reputation for it   **21 raven . . . house** (Allusion to the belief that the raven hovered over a house of sickness or infection, such as one visited by the plague.)   **25–9 as . . . blab—** since there are rascals enough who, having seduced a woman either through their own importunity or through the woman's willing infatuation, cannot keep quiet about it—   **36 belie** slander   **36–7 fulsome** foul.   **38–9 first . . . to confess** (Othello reverses the proverbial *confess and be hanged*; Cassio is to be given no time to confess before he dies.)   **39–41 Nature . . . instruction** i.e., Without some foundation in fact, nature would not have dressed herself in such an overwhelming passion that comes over me now and fills my mind with images, or in such a lifelike fantasy as Cassio had in his dream of lying with Desdemona.   **41 words** mere words

53 lethargy coma.   **his** its   **58 on great occasion** on a matter of great importance   **60 mock me** (Othello takes Iago's question about hurting his head to be a mocking reference to the cuckold's horns.)   **64 civil** i.e., dwelling in a city   **67 yoked** (1) married (2) put into the yoke of infamy and cuckoldry   **68 draw with you** pull as you do, like oxen who are yoked, i.e., share your fate as cuckold.   **69 unproper** not exclusively their own   **70 peculiar** private, their own.   **better** i.e., because you know the truth.   **72 lip** kiss.   **secure** free from suspicion   **74 And . . . shall be** and, knowing myself to be a cuckold, I'll know for certain that she's a whore.   **77 in . . . list** within the bounds of patience.   **80–1 I shifted . . . ecstasy** I got him out of the way, using your fit as my excuse for doing so   **83 encave** conceal   **84 fleers** sneers   **88 cope** encounter with, have sex with

I say, but mark his gesture. Marry, patience!
Or I shall say you're all-in-all in spleen,   90
And nothing of a man.
OTHELLO   Dost thou hear, Iago?
I will be found most cunning in my patience;
But—dost thou hear?—most bloody.
IAGO   That's not amiss;
But yet keep time in all. Will you withdraw?   94
    [Othello stands apart.]
Now will I question Cassio of Bianca,
A huswife that by selling her desires   96
Buys herself bread and clothes. It is a creature
That dotes on Cassio—as 'tis the strumpet's plague
To beguile many and be beguiled by one.
He, when he hears of her, cannot restrain   100
From the excess of laughter. Here he comes.

    Enter Cassio.

As he shall smile, Othello shall go mad;
And his unbookish jealousy must conster   103
Poor Cassio's smiles, gestures, and light behaviors
Quite in the wrong.—How do you now, Lieutenant?
CASSIO
The worser that you give me the addition   106
Whose want even kills me.   107
IAGO
Ply Desdemona well and you are sure on't.
[*Speaking lower*] Now, if this suit lay in Bianca's power,
How quickly should you speed!
CASSIO [*laughing*]   Alas, poor caitiff!   111
OTHELLO [*aside*]   Look how he laughs already!
IAGO
I never knew a woman love man so.
CASSIO
Alas, poor rogue! I think, i'faith, she loves me.
OTHELLO [*aside*]
Now he denies it faintly, and laughs it out.
IAGO
Do you hear, Cassio?
OTHELLO [*aside*]   Now he importunes him
To tell it o'er. Go to! Well said, well said.   117
IAGO
She gives it out that you shall marry her.
Do you intend it?
CASSIO   Ha, ha, ha!
OTHELLO [*aside*]
Do you triumph, Roman? Do you triumph?   121
CASSIO   I marry her? What? A customer? Prithee, bear   122
some charity to my wit; do not think it so unwhole-   123
some. Ha, ha, ha!

OTHELLO [*aside*]   So, so, so, so! They laugh that win.   125
IAGO   Faith, the cry goes that you shall marry her.   126
CASSIO   Prithee, say true.
IAGO   I am a very villain else.   128
OTHELLO [*aside*]   Have you scored me? Well.   129
CASSIO   This is the monkey's own giving out. She is
persuaded I will marry her out of her own love and
flattery, not out of my promise.   132
OTHELLO [*aside*]   Iago beckons me. Now he begins the   133
story.
CASSIO   She was here even now; she haunts me in every
place. I was the other day talking on the seabank with   136
certain Venetians, and thither comes the bauble, and,   137
by this hand, she falls me thus about my neck—   138
    [*He embraces Iago.*]
OTHELLO [*aside*]   Crying, "Oh, dear Cassio!" as it were; his
gesture imports it.
CASSIO   So hangs and lolls and weeps upon me, so
shakes and pulls me. Ha, ha, ha!
OTHELLO [*aside*]   Now he tells how she plucked him to my
chamber. Oh, I see that nose of yours, but not that dog   144
I shall throw it to.   145
CASSIO   Well, I must leave her company.
IAGO   Before me, look where she comes.   147

    Enter Bianca [with Othello's handkerchief].

CASSIO   'Tis such another fitchew! Marry, a perfumed   148
one.—What do you mean by this haunting of me?
BIANCA   Let the devil and his dam haunt you! What did   150
you mean by that same handkerchief you gave me
even now? I was a fine fool to take it. I must take out
the work? A likely piece of work, that you should find   153
it in your chamber and know not who left it there!
This is some minx's token, and I must take out the
work? There; give it your hobbyhorse. [*She gives him   156
the handkerchief.*] Wheresoever you had it, I'll take out
no work on't.
CASSIO   How now, my sweet Bianca? How now? How
now?
OTHELLO [*aside*]   By heaven, that should be my hand-   160
kerchief!
BIANCA   If you'll come to supper tonight, you may; if
you will not, come when you are next prepared for.   163
    Exit.
IAGO   After her, after her.
CASSIO   Faith, I must. She'll rail in the streets else.
IAGO   Will you sup there?
CASSIO   Faith, I intend so.
IAGO   Well, I may chance to see you, for I would very
fain speak with you.

90 all-in-all in spleen utterly governed by passionate impulses
94 keep time keep yourself steady (as in music)   **96 huswife** hussy
100 restrain refrain   **103 his unbookish** Othello's uninstructed.
conster construe   **106 addition** title   **107 Whose want** the lack of
which   **111 caitiff** wretch.   **117 Go to** (An expression of remonstrance.)   **Well said** Well done. (Sarcastic.)   **121 Roman** (The
Romans were noted for their *triumphs* or triumphal processions.)
122 A customer? Who, I, the whore's customer? (Or, *customer* could
mean "prostitute.")   **122–3 bear . . . wit** be more charitable to my
judgment

125 They . . . win i.e., They that laugh last laugh best.   **126 cry** rumor
128 I . . . else Call me a complete rogue if I'm not telling the truth.
129 scored me scored off me, beaten me, made up my reckoning,
branded me.   **132 flattery** self-flattery, self-deception   **133 beckons**
signals to   **136 seabank** seashore   **137 bauble** plaything   **138 by
this hand** I make my vow   **144–5 not . . . to** (Othello imagines himself cutting off Cassio's nose and throwing it to a dog.)   **147 Before
me** i.e., On my soul   **148 'Tis . . . fitchew!** What a whore she is! Just
like all the others. (*Fitchew* or "polecat" was a common term of contempt for a courtesan or prostitute.)   **150 dam** mother   **153 A likely
. . . work** A fine story   **156 hobbyhorse** harlot.   **160 should be** must
be   **163 when . . . for** when I'm ready for you (i.e., never).

CASSIO   Prithee, come. Will you?

IAGO   Go to. Say no more.   [Exit Cassio.] 171

OTHELLO [advancing]   How shall I murder him, Iago?

IAGO   Did you perceive how he laughed at his vice?

OTHELLO   Oh, Iago!

IAGO   And did you see the handkerchief?

OTHELLO   Was that mine?

IAGO   Yours, by this hand. And to see how he prizes the foolish woman your wife! She gave it him, and he hath given it his whore.

OTHELLO   I would have him nine years a-killing. A fine woman! A fair woman! A sweet woman!

IAGO   Nay, you must forget that.

OTHELLO   Ay, let her rot and perish, and be damned tonight, for she shall not live. No, my heart is turned to stone; I strike it, and it hurts my hand. Oh, the world hath not a sweeter creature! She might lie by an emperor's side and command him tasks.

IAGO   Nay, that's not your way.   188

OTHELLO   Hang her! I do but say what she is. So delicate with her needle! An admirable musician! Oh, she will sing the savageness out of a bear. Of so high and plenteous wit and invention!   192

IAGO   She's the worse for all this.

OTHELLO   Oh, a thousand, a thousand times! And then, of so gentle a condition!   195

IAGO   Ay, too gentle.   196

OTHELLO   Nay, that's certain. But yet the pity of it, Iago! Oh, Iago, the pity of it, Iago!

IAGO   If you are so fond over her iniquity, give her patent 199 to offend, for if it touch not you it comes near nobody.

OTHELLO   I will chop her into messes. Cuckold me?   201

IAGO   Oh, 'tis foul in her.

OTHELLO   With mine officer?

IAGO   That's fouler.

OTHELLO   Get me some poison, Iago, this night. I'll not expostulate with her, lest her body and beauty unpro- 206 vide my mind again. This night, Iago.   207

IAGO   Do it not with poison. Strangle her in her bed, even the bed she hath contaminated.

OTHELLO   Good, good! The justice of it pleases. Very good.

IAGO   And for Cassio, let me be his undertaker. You 211 shall hear more by midnight.

OTHELLO

Excellent good. [A trumpet within.] What trumpet is that same?

IAGO   I warrant, something from Venice.

Enter Lodovico, Desdemona, and attendants.

'Tis Lodovico. This comes from the Duke.
See, your wife's with him.

LODOVICO

God save you, worthy General!

OTHELLO   With all my heart, sir. 217

LODOVICO [giving him a letter]

The Duke and the senators of Venice greet you.

OTHELLO

I kiss the instrument of their pleasures.

[He opens the letter, and reads.]

DESDEMONA

And what's the news, good cousin Lodovico?

IAGO

I am very glad to see you, signor.
Welcome to Cyprus.

LODOVICO

I thank you. How does Lieutenant Cassio?

IAGO   Lives, sir.

DESDEMONA

Cousin, there's fall'n between him and my lord
An unkind breach; but you shall make all well.   226

OTHELLO   Are you sure of that?

DESDEMONA   My lord?

OTHELLO [reads]   "This fail you not to do, as you will—"

LODOVICO

He did not call; he's busy in the paper.
Is there division twixt my lord and Cassio?

DESDEMONA

A most unhappy one. I would do much
T'atone them, for the love I bear to Cassio.   233

OTHELLO   Fire and brimstone!

DESDEMONA   My lord?

OTHELLO   Are you wise?

DESDEMONA

What, is he angry?

LODOVICO   Maybe the letter moved him;
For, as I think, they do command him home,
Deputing Cassio in his government.   239

DESDEMONA   By my troth, I am glad on't.   240

OTHELLO   Indeed?

DESDEMONA   My lord?

OTHELLO   I am glad to see you mad.   243

DESDEMONA   Why, sweet Othello—

OTHELLO [striking her]   Devil!

DESDEMONA   I have not deserved this.

LODOVICO

My lord, this would not be believed in Venice,
Though I should swear I saw't. 'Tis very much.   248
Make her amends; she weeps.

OTHELLO   Oh, devil, devil!
If that the earth could teem with woman's tears,   250
Each drop she falls would prove a crocodile.   251
Out of my sight!

DESDEMONA   I will not stay to offend you. [Going.]

---

171 Go to (An expression of remonstrance.)   188 your way i.e., the way you should think of her.   192 invention imagination.   195 gentle a condition wellborn and well-bred.   196 gentle generous, yielding (to other men).   199 fond foolish.   patent license   201 messes portions of meat, i.e., bits.   206–7 unprovide weaken, disarm   211 be his undertaker undertake to dispatch him.

217 With all my heart i.e., I thank you most heartily   226 unkind unnatural, contrary to their natures; hurtful   233 T'atone to reconcile   239 government office.   240 on't of it.   243 I am . . . mad i.e., I am glad to see that you are insane enough to rejoice in Cassio's promotion. (? Othello bitterly plays on Desdemona's I am glad.)   248 very much too much, outrageous.   250 teem breed, be impregnated   251 falls lets fall.   crocodile (Crocodiles were supposed to weep hypocritical tears for their victims.)

LODOVICO   Truly, an obedient lady.
I do beseech Your Lordship, call her back.
OTHELLO [*calling*]   Mistress!
DESDEMONA [*returning*]   My lord?
OTHELLO   What would you with her, sir?   257
LODOVICO   Who, I, my lord?
OTHELLO
Ay, you did wish that I would make her turn.
Sir, she can turn, and turn, and yet go on
And turn again; and she can weep, sir, weep;
And she's obedient, as you say, obedient,   262
Very obedient.—Proceed you in your tears.—
Concerning this, sir—Oh, well-painted passion!—   264
I am commanded home.—Get you away;
I'll send for you anon.—Sir, I obey the mandate
And will return to Venice.—Hence, avaunt!
                                        [*Exit Desdemona.*]
Cassio shall have my place. And, sir, tonight
I do entreat that we may sup together.
You are welcome, sir, to Cyprus.—Goats and
        monkeys!   *Exit.* 270
LODOVICO
Is this the noble Moor whom our full Senate
Call all in all sufficient? Is this the nature
Whom passion could not shake? Whose solid virtue
The shot of accident nor dart of chance
Could neither graze nor pierce?
IAGO   He is much changed.
LODOVICO
Are his wits safe? Is he not light of brain?
IAGO
He's that he is. I may not breathe my censure   277
What he might be. If what he might he is not,   278
I would to heaven he were!
LODOVICO   What, strike his wife?   279
IAGO
Faith, that was not so well; yet would I knew
That stroke would prove the worst!
LODOVICO   Is it his use?   281
Or did the letters work upon his blood   282
And new-create his fault?
IAGO   Alas, alas!
It is not honesty in me to speak
What I have seen and known. You shall observe him,
And his own courses will denote him so   286
That I may save my speech. Do but go after,
And mark how he continues.
LODOVICO
I am sorry that I am deceived in him.   *Exeunt.*

❧

257 What . . . sir? (Othello implies that Desdemona is pliant and will do a *turn*, lines 257–9, for any man.)   **262 obedient** (With much the same sexual connotation as *turn* in lines 257–9.)   **264 passion** i.e., grief.   **270 Goats and monkeys** (See 3.3.419.)   **277–9 I may . . . were!** I dare not venture an opinion as to whether he's of unsound mind, as you suggest, but, if he isn't, then it might be better to wish he were in fact insane, since only that could excuse his wild behavior!   **281 use** custom.   **282 blood** passions   **286 courses will denote** actions will reveal

4.2

Enter Othello and Emilia.

OTHELLO   You have seen nothing, then?
EMILIA
Nor ever heard, nor ever did suspect.
OTHELLO
Yes, you have seen Cassio and she together.
EMILIA
But then I saw no harm, and then I heard
Each syllable that breath made up between them.
OTHELLO   What, did they never whisper?
EMILIA   Never, my lord.
OTHELLO   Nor send you out o'th' way?
EMILIA   Never.
OTHELLO
To fetch her fan, her gloves, her mask, nor nothing?
EMILIA   Never, my lord.
OTHELLO   That's strange.
EMILIA
I durst, my lord, to wager she is honest,
Lay down my soul at stake. If you think other,   14
Remove your thought; it doth abuse your bosom.   15
If any wretch have put this in your head,
Let heaven requite it with the serpent's curse!   17
For if she be not honest, chaste, and true,
There's no man happy; the purest of their wives
Is foul as slander.
OTHELLO   Bid her come hither. Go.
                                        Exit Emilia.
She says enough; yet she's a simple bawd   21
That cannot say as much. This is a subtle whore,   22
A closet lock and key of villainous secrets.   23
And yet she'll kneel and pray; I have seen her do't.

Enter Desdemona and Emilia.

DESDEMONA   My lord, what is your will?
OTHELLO   Pray you, chuck, come hither.
DESDEMONA
What is your pleasure?
OTHELLO   Let me see your eyes.
Look in my face.
DESDEMONA   What horrible fancy's this?
OTHELLO [*to Emilia*]   Some of your function, mistress.   29
Leave procreants alone and shut the door;   30
Cough or cry "hem" if anybody come.
Your mystery, your mystery! Nay, dispatch.   32
                                        Exit Emilia.
DESDEMONA [*kneeling*]
Upon my knees, what doth your speech import?

4.2. Location: The citadel.
14 at stake as the wager.   **15 abuse your bosom** deceive your breast, your heart.   **17 the serpent's curse** the curse pronounced by God on the serpent for deceiving Eve, just as some man has done to Othello and Desdemona. (See Genesis 3:14.)   **21–2 she's . . . much** i.e., any procuress or go-between who couldn't make up as plausible a story as Emilia's would have to be pretty stupid.   **22 This** i.e., Desdemona   **23 closet lock and key** i.e., concealer   **29 Some . . . function** i.e., Practice your chosen profession, that of bawd (by guarding the door)   **30 procreants** mating couples   **32 mystery** trade, occupation

I understand a fury in your words,
But not the words.

OTHELLO
Why, what art thou?

DESDEMONA　　　　　　　Your wife, my lord, your true
And loyal wife.

OTHELLO　　　　　　Come, swear it, damn thyself,
Lest, being like one of heaven, the devils themselves　　38
Should fear to seize thee. Therefore be double
　　damned:
Swear thou art honest.

DESDEMONA　　　　　　　Heaven doth truly know it.

OTHELLO
Heaven truly knows that thou art false as hell.

DESDEMONA
To whom, my lord? With whom? How am I false?

OTHELLO [weeping]
Ah, Desdemon! Away, away, away!

DESDEMONA
Alas the heavy day! Why do you weep?
Am I the motive of these tears, my lord?　　45
If haply you my father do suspect
An instrument of this your calling back,
Lay not your blame on me. If you have lost him,
I have lost him too.

OTHELLO　　　　　　Had it pleased heaven
To try me with affliction, had they rained　　50
All kinds of sores and shames on my bare head,
Steeped me in poverty to the very lips,
Given to captivity me and my utmost hopes,
I should have found in some place of my soul
A drop of patience. But, alas, to make me
A fixèd figure for the time of scorn　　56
To point his slow and moving finger at!　　57
Yet could I bear that too, well, very well.
But there where I have garnered up my heart,　　59
Where either I must live or bear no life,
The fountain from the which my current runs　　61
Or else dries up—to be discarded thence!
Or keep it as a cistern for foul toads　　63
To knot and gender in! Turn thy complexion there,　　64
Patience, thou young and rose-lipped cherubin—　　65
Ay, there look grim as hell!　　66

DESDEMONA
I hope my noble lord esteems me honest.　　67

OTHELLO
Oh, ay, as summer flies are in the shambles,　　68
That quicken even with blowing. O thou weed,　　69
Who art so lovely fair and smell'st so sweet
That the sense aches at thee, would thou hadst ne'er
　　been born!

DESDEMONA
Alas, what ignorant sin have I committed?　　72

OTHELLO
Was this fair paper, this most goodly book,
Made to write "whore" upon? What committed?
Committed? Oh, thou public commoner!　　75
I should make very forges of my cheeks,
That would to cinders burn up modesty,
Did I but speak thy deeds. What committed?
Heaven stops the nose at it and the moon winks;　　79
The bawdy wind, that kisses all it meets,　　80
Is hushed within the hollow mine of earth　　81
And will not hear't. What committed?
Impudent strumpet!

DESDEMONA　　　　　　By heaven, you do me wrong.

OTHELLO
Are not you a strumpet?

DESDEMONA　　No, as I am a Christian.
If to preserve this vessel for my lord　　86
From any other foul unlawful touch
Be not to be a strumpet, I am none.

OTHELLO　　What, not a whore?

DESDEMONA　　No, as I shall be saved.

OTHELLO　　Is't possible?

DESDEMONA
Oh, heaven forgive us!

OTHELLO　　　　　　I cry you mercy, then.　　92
I took you for that cunning whore of Venice
That married with Othello. [Calling out] You, mistress,
That have the office opposite to Saint Peter
And keep the gate of hell!

　　　　　Enter Emilia.

　　　　　　　　　You, you, ay, you!
We have done our course. There's money for your
　　pains.　　　　　　　　　　[He gives money.]　　97
I pray you, turn the key and keep our counsel.　　Exit.

EMILIA
Alas, what does this gentleman conceive?　　99
How do you, madam? How do you, my good lady?

DESDEMONA　　Faith, half asleep.　　101

EMILIA
Good madam, what's the matter with my lord?

DESDEMONA　　With who?

EMILIA　　Why, with my lord, madam.

DESDEMONA
Who is thy lord?

EMILIA　　　　　He that is yours, sweet lady.

DESDEMONA
I have none. Do not talk to me, Emilia.
I cannot weep, nor answers have I none
But what should go by water. Prithee, tonight　　108

---

38 being . . . heaven looking like an angel　45 motive cause　50 they
the heavenly powers　56–7 A fixèd . . . finger at a figure of ridicule
to be pointed at scornfully for all of eternity by the slowly moving
finger of Time.　59 garnered stored　61 fountain spring　63 cistern
cesspool　64 To . . . gender in to couple sexually and conceive in.
64–6 Turn . . . hell! Direct your gaze there, Patience, and your youthful and rosy cherubic countenance will turn grim and pale at this
hellish spectacle!　67 honest chaste.　68 shambles slaughterhouse
69 That . . . blowing that come to life with the puffing up of the rotten
meat on which the flies and their maggots are breeding.

72 ignorant sin sin in ignorance　75 commoner prostitute.
79 winks closes her eyes. (The moon symbolizes chastity.)
80 bawdy kissing one and all　81 mine cave (where the winds were
thought to dwell)　86 vessel body　92 cry you mercy beg your pardon. (Sarcastic.)　97 course business. (With an indecent suggestion of
"trick," turn at sex.)　99 conceive suppose, think.　101 half asleep
i.e., dazed.　108 go by water be conveyed by tears.

Lay on my bed my wedding sheets, remember;
And call thy husband hither.
EMILIA   Here's a change indeed!   *Exit.*

DESDEMONA
'Tis meet I should be used so, very meet.   112
How have I been behaved, that he might stick   113
The small'st opinion on my least misuse?   114

              Enter Iago and Emilia.

IAGO
What is your pleasure, madam? How is't with you?
DESDEMONA
I cannot tell. Those that do teach young babes
Do it with gentle means and easy tasks.
He might have chid me so, for, in good faith,
I am a child to chiding.
IAGO   What is the matter, lady?
EMILIA
Alas, Iago, my lord hath so bewhored her,
Thrown such despite and heavy terms upon her,
That true hearts cannot bear it.
DESDEMONA   Am I that name, Iago?
IAGO   What name, fair lady?
DESDEMONA
Such as she said my lord did say I was.
EMILIA
He called her whore. A beggar in his drink
Could not have laid such terms upon his callet.   128
IAGO   Why did he so?
DESDEMONA [*weeping*]
I do not know. I am sure I am none such.
IAGO   Do not weep, do not weep. Alas the day!
EMILIA
Hath she forsook so many noble matches,
Her father and her country and her friends,
To be called whore? Would it not make one weep?
DESDEMONA
It is my wretched fortune.
IAGO   Beshrew him for't!   135
How comes this trick upon him?
DESDEMONA   Nay, heaven doth know.   136
EMILIA
I will be hanged if some eternal villain,   137
Some busy and insinuating rogue,   138
Some cogging, cozening slave, to get some office, 139
Have not devised this slander. I will be hanged else.
IAGO
Fie, there is no such man. It is impossible.
DESDEMONA
If any such there be, heaven pardon him!
EMILIA
A halter pardon him! And hell gnaw his bones!   143

Why should he call her whore? Who keeps her
   company?
What place? What time? What form? What
   likelihood?   145
The Moor's abused by some most villainous knave,
Some base notorious knave, some scurvy fellow.
Oh, heavens, that such companions thou'dst unfold, 148
And put in every honest hand a whip
To lash the rascals naked through the world
Even from the east to th' west!
IAGO   Speak within door.   151
EMILIA
Oh, fie upon them! Some such squire he was   152
That turned your wit the seamy side without   153
And made you to suspect me with the Moor.
IAGO
You are a fool. Go to.
DESDEMONA   O God, Iago,   155
What shall I do to win my lord again?
Good friend, go to him; for, by this light of heaven,
I know not how I lost him. Here I kneel. [*She kneels.*]
If e'er my will did trespass 'gainst his love,
Either in discourse of thought or actual deed,   160
Or that mine eyes, mine ears, or any sense   161
Delighted them in any other form;   162
Or that I do not yet, and ever did,   163
And ever will—though he do shake me off
To beggarly divorcement—love him dearly,
Comfort forswear me! Unkindness may do much,   166
And his unkindness may defeat my life,   167
But never taint my love. I cannot say "whore."
It does abhor me now I speak the word;   169
To do the act that might the addition earn   170
Not the world's mass of vanity could make me.   171
                              [*She rises.*]
IAGO
I pray you, be content. 'Tis but his humor.   172
The business of the state does him offense,
And he does chide with you.
DESDEMONA   If 'twere no other—
IAGO   It is but so, I warrant.   [*Trumpets within.*]
Hark, how these instruments summon you to supper!
The messengers of Venice stays the meat.   178
Go in, and weep not. All things shall be well.
                    Exeunt Desdemona and Emilia.

              Enter Roderigo.

How now, Roderigo?
RODERIGO   I do not find that thou deal'st justly with me.
IAGO   What in the contrary?

---

112 **'Tis . . . very meet** i.e., It must be I somehow have deserved this.
113–14 How . . . misuse? What have I done that prompts Othello to
attach even the slightest censure to whatever little fault I may have
committed?   128 **callet** whore.   135 **Beshrew** May evil befall. (An
oath.)   136 **trick** strange behavior, delusion   137 **eternal** inveterate
138 **insinuating** ingratiating, fawning, wheedling   139 **cogging, cozening** cheating, defrauding   143 **halter** hangman's noose

145 **form** manner, circumstance.   148 **that . . . unfold** would that you
would expose such fellows   151 **within door** i.e., not so loud.
152 **squire** fellow   153 **seamy side without** wrong side out   155 **Go
to** i.e., That's enough.   160 **discourse of thought** process of thinking
161 **that** if. (Also in line 163.)   162 **Delighted them** took delight
163 **yet** still   166 **Comfort forswear** may heavenly comfort forsake
167 **defeat** destroy   169 **abhor** (1) fill me with abhorrence (2) make
me whorelike   170 **addition** title   171 **vanity** showy splendor
172 **humor** mood.   178 **stays the meat** are waiting to dine.

RODERIGO   Every day thou daff'st me with some device, 183
Iago, and rather, as it seems to me now, keep'st
from me all conveniency than suppliest me with the 185
least advantage of hope. I will indeed no longer 186
endure it, nor am I yet persuaded to put up in peace 187
what already I have foolishly suffered.

IAGO   Will you hear me, Roderigo?

RODERIGO   Faith, I have heard too much, for your words
and performances are no kin together.

IAGO   You charge me most unjustly.

RODERIGO   With naught but truth. I have wasted myself
out of my means. The jewels you have had from me to
deliver Desdemona would half have corrupted a vo- 195
tarist. You have told me she hath received them and 196
returned me expectations and comforts of sudden re- 197
spect and acquaintance, but I find none. 198

IAGO   Well, go to, very well.

RODERIGO   "Very well"! "Go to"! I cannot go to, man, 200
nor 'tis not very well. By this hand, I think it is scurvy,
and begin to find myself fopped in it. 202

IAGO   Very well.

RODERIGO   I tell you 'tis not very well. I will make myself 204
known to Desdemona. If she will return me my jewels,
I will give over my suit and repent my unlawful solicitation; if not, assure yourself I will seek satisfaction 207
of you.

IAGO   You have said now? 209

RODERIGO   Ay, and said nothing but what I protest 210
intendment of doing. 211

IAGO   Why, now I see there's mettle in thee, and even
from this instant do build on thee a better opinion
than ever before. Give me thy hand, Roderigo. Thou
hast taken against me a most just exception; but yet I
protest I have dealt most directly in thy affair.

RODERIGO   It hath not appeared.

IAGO   I grant indeed it hath not appeared, and your
suspicion is not without wit and judgment. But,
Roderigo, if thou hast that in thee indeed which I have
greater reason to believe now than ever—I mean
purpose, courage, and valor—this night show it. If
thou the next night following enjoy not Desdemona,
take me from this world with treachery and devise
engines for my life. 225

RODERIGO   Well, what is it? Is it within reason and
compass?

IAGO   Sir, there is especial commission come from
Venice to depute Cassio in Othello's place.

RODERIGO   Is that true? Why, then Othello and Desdemona return again to Venice.

IAGO   Oh, no; he goes into Mauritania and takes away
with him the fair Desdemona, unless his abode be
lingered here by some accident; wherein none can be
so determinate as the removing of Cassio. 235

RODERIGO   How do you mean, removing of him?

IAGO   Why, by making him uncapable of Othello's
place—knocking out his brains.

RODERIGO   And that you would have me to do?

IAGO   Ay, if you dare do yourself a profit and a right.
He sups tonight with a harlotry, and thither will I go to 241
him. He knows not yet of his honorable fortune. If
you will watch his going thence, which I will fashion
to fall out between twelve and one, you may take him 244
at your pleasure. I will be near to second your attempt,
and he shall fall between us. Come, stand not amazed
at it, but go along with me. I will show you such a
necessity in his death that you shall think yourself
bound to put it on him. It is now high suppertime, 249
and the night grows to waste. About it. 250

RODERIGO   I will hear further reason for this.

IAGO   And you shall be satisfied.   *Exeunt.*

❖

4.3

*Enter Othello, Lodovico, Desdemona, Emilia, and
attendants.*

LODOVICO
I do beseech you, sir, trouble yourself no further.

OTHELLO
Oh, pardon me; 'twill do me good to walk.

LODOVICO
Madam, good night. I humbly thank Your Ladyship.

DESDEMONA
Your Honor is most welcome.

OTHELLO   Will you walk, sir?
Oh, Desdemona!

DESDEMONA   My lord?

OTHELLO   Get you to bed on th'instant. I will be returned forthwith. Dismiss your attendant there. Look't
be done.

DESDEMONA   I will, my lord.
                    Exit [Othello, with Lodovico and attendants].

EMILIA   How goes it now? He looks gentler than he did.

DESDEMONA
He says he will return incontinent,   12
And hath commanded me to go to bed,
And bid me to dismiss you.

EMILIA   Dismiss me?

DESDEMONA
It was his bidding. Therefore, good Emilia,
Give me my nightly wearing, and adieu.
We must not now displease him.

EMILIA   I would you had never seen him!

183 **thou daff'st me** you put me off.   **183–4 device** excuse, trick
185 **conveniency** advantage, opportunity   186 **advantage** increase
187 **put up** submit to, tolerate   195 **deliver** deliver to   195–6 **votarist**
nun   197-8 **sudden respect** immediate consideration   200 **I cannot
go to** (Roderigo changes Iago's *go to*, an expression urging patience,
to *I cannot go to*, "I have no opportunity for success in wooing.")
202 **fopped** fooled, duped   204 **not very well** (Roderigo changes
Iago's *very well*, "all right, then," to *not very well*, "not at all good.")
207 **satisfaction** repayment. (The term normally means settling of
accounts in a duel.)   209 **You . . . now?** Have you finished?
210–11 **protest intendment** avow my intention   225 **engines** plots,
snares

235 **determinate** conclusive, instrumental   241 **harlotry** slut
244 **fall out** occur   249 **high** fully   250 **grows to waste** wastes away.
4.3 Location: The citadel.
12 **incontinent** immediately

DESDEMONA
  So would not I. My love doth so approve him
  That even his stubbornness, his checks, his frowns—   21
  Prithee, unpin me—have grace and favor in them.
                   [*Emilia prepares Desdemona for bed.*]
EMILIA   I have laid those sheets you bade me on the
  bed.
DESDEMONA
  All's one. Good faith, how foolish are our minds!   25
  If I do die before thee, prithee shroud me
  In one of these same sheets.
EMILIA   Come, come, you talk.   27
DESDEMONA
  My mother had a maid called Barbary.
  She was in love, and he she loved proved mad   29
  And did forsake her. She had a song of "Willow."
  An old thing 'twas, but it expressed her fortune,
  And she died singing it. That song tonight
  Will not go from my mind; I have much to do   33
  But to go hang my head all at one side   34
  And sing it like poor Barbary. Prithee, dispatch.
EMILIA   Shall I go fetch your nightgown?   36
DESDEMONA   No, unpin me here.
  This Lodovico is a proper man.   38
EMILIA   A very handsome man.
DESDEMONA   He speaks well.
EMILIA   I know a lady in Venice would have walked
  barefoot to Palestine for a touch of his nether lip.
DESDEMONA [*singing*]
    "The poor soul sat sighing by a sycamore tree,
      Sing all a green willow;   44
    Her hand on her bosom, her head on her knee,
      Sing willow, willow, willow.
    The fresh streams ran by her and murmured her
      moans;
      Sing willow, willow, willow;
    Her salt tears fell from her, and softened the
      stones—"
  Lay by these.
  [*Singing*] "Sing willow, willow, willow—"
  Prithee, hie thee. He'll come anon.   52
  [*Singing*] "Sing all a green willow must be my garland.
    Let nobody blame him; his scorn I approve—"
  Nay, that's not next.—Hark! Who is't that knocks?
EMILIA   It's the wind.
DESDEMONA [*singing*]
    "I called my love false love; but what said he
      then?
      Sing willow, willow, willow;
    If I court more women, you'll couch with more
      men."
  So, get thee gone. Good night. Mine eyes do itch;
  Doth that bode weeping?
EMILIA   'Tis neither here nor there.

DESDEMONA
  I have heard it said so. Oh, these men, these men!
  Dost thou in conscience think—tell me, Emilia—
  That there be women do abuse their husbands   64
  In such gross kind?
EMILIA   There be some such, no question.
DESDEMONA
  Wouldst thou do such a deed for all the world?
EMILIA
  Why, would not you?
DESDEMONA   No, by this heavenly light!
EMILIA
  Nor I neither by this heavenly light;
  I might do't as well i'th' dark.
DESDEMONA
  Wouldst thou do such a deed for all the world?
EMILIA
  The world's a huge thing. It is a great price
  For a small vice.
DESDEMONA
  Good troth, I think thou wouldst not.
EMILIA   By my troth, I think I should, and undo't when
  I had done. Marry, I would not do such a thing for a
  joint ring, nor for measures of lawn, nor for gowns,   76
  petticoats, nor caps, nor any petty exhibition. But for   77
  all the whole world! Uds pity, who would not make   78
  her husband a cuckold to make him a monarch? I
  should venture purgatory for't.
DESDEMONA
  Beshrew me if I would do such a wrong
  For the whole world.
EMILIA   Why, the wrong is but a wrong i'th' world, and
  having the world for your labor, 'tis a wrong in your
  own world, and you might quickly make it right.
DESDEMONA
  I do not think there is any such woman.
EMILIA   Yes, a dozen, and as many   87
  To th' vantage as would store the world they played
    for.   88
  But I do think it is their husbands' faults
  If wives do fall. Say that they slack their duties   90
  And pour our treasures into foreign laps,   91
  Or else break out in peevish jealousies,
  Throwing restraint upon us? Or say they strike us,   93
  Or scant our former having in despite?   94
  Why, we have galls, and though we have some grace,   95
  Yet have we some revenge. Let husbands know
  Their wives have sense like them. They see, and smell,   97
  And have their palates both for sweet and sour,
  As husbands have. What is it that they do   99

---

21 stubbornness roughness. **checks** rebukes **25 All's one** All right. It doesn't really matter. **27 talk** i.e., prattle. **29 mad** wild, lunatic **33-4 I . . . hang** I can scarcely keep myself from hanging **36 nightgown** dressing gown. **38 proper** handsome **44 willow** (A conventional emblem of disappointed love.) **52 hie thee** hurry. **anon** right away.

64 abuse deceive **76 joint ring** a ring made in separate halves. **lawn** fine linen **77 exhibition** gift. **78 Uds** God's **87–8 and . . . played for** and enough additionally to stock the world men have gambled and sported sexually for. **90 they** our husbands. **duties** marital duties **91 pour . . . laps** i.e., are unfaithful, give what is rightfully ours (semen) to other women **93 Throwing . . . us** jealously restricting our freedom. **94 Or . . . despite** or spitefully take away from us whatever we enjoyed before. **95 have galls** i.e., are capable of resenting injury and insult. **grace** inclination to be merciful **97 sense** sensory perception and appetite **99 they** husbands

When they change us for others? Is it sport? 100
I think it is. And doth affection breed it? 101
I think it doth. Is't frailty that thus errs?
It is so, too. And have not we affections,
Desires for sport, and frailty, as men have?
Then let them use us well; else let them know,
The ills we do, their ills instruct us so.

DESDEMONA
Good night, good night. God me such uses send 107
Not to pick bad from bad, but by bad mend! 108

Exeunt.

❧

5.1

Enter Iago and Roderigo.

IAGO
Here stand behind this bulk. Straight will he come. 1
Wear thy good rapier bare, and put it home. 2
Quick, quick! Fear nothing. I'll be at thy elbow.
It makes us or it mars us. Think on that,
And fix most firm thy resolution.

RODERIGO
Be near at hand. I may miscarry in't.

IAGO
Here, at thy hand. Be bold, and take thy stand.
[Iago stands aside, Roderigo conceals himself.]

RODERIGO
I have no great devotion to the deed;
And yet he hath given me satisfying reasons.
'Tis but a man gone. Forth, my sword! He dies.
[He draws.]

IAGO
I have rubbed this young quat almost to the sense, 11
And he grows angry. Now, whether he kill Cassio
Or Cassio him, or each do kill the other,
Every way makes my gain. Live Roderigo, 14
He calls me to a restitution large
Of gold and jewels that I bobbed from him 16
As gifts to Desdemona.
It must not be. If Cassio do remain,
He hath a daily beauty in his life
That makes me ugly; and besides, the Moor
May unfold me to him; there stand I in much peril. 21
No, he must die. Be't so. I hear him coming.

Enter Cassio.

RODERIGO *[coming forth]*
I know his gait, 'tis he.—Villain, thou diest!
[He attacks Cassio.]

CASSIO
That thrust had been mine enemy indeed,
But that my coat is better than thou know'st. 25
I will make proof of thine.
[He draws, and wounds Roderigo.]

RODERIGO   Oh, I am slain!   *[He falls.* 26
*Iago, from behind, wounds Cassio
in the leg, and exit.]*

CASSIO
I am maimed forever. Help, ho! Murder! Murder!

Enter Othello.

OTHELLO   The voice of Cassio! Iago keeps his word.
RODERIGO   Oh, villain that I am!
OTHELLO   It is even so.
CASSIO   Oh, help, ho! Light! A surgeon!
OTHELLO
'Tis he. O brave Iago, honest and just,
That hast such noble sense of thy friend's wrong!
Thou teachest me.—Minion, your dear lies dead, 34
And your unblest fate hies. Strumpet, I come. 35
Forth of my heart those charms, thine eyes, are blotted; 36
Thy bed, lust-stained, shall with lust's blood be
   spotted.   *Exit Othello.*

Enter Lodovico and Gratiano.

CASSIO
What ho! No watch? No passage? Murder! Murder! 38
GRATIANO
'Tis some mischance. The voice is very direful.
CASSIO   Oh, help!
LODOVICO   Hark!
RODERIGO   Oh, wretched villain!
LODOVICO
Two or three groan. 'Tis heavy night; 43
These may be counterfeits. Let's think't unsafe
To come in to the cry without more help. 45
[They remain near the entrance.]

RODERIGO
Nobody come? Then shall I bleed to death.

Enter Iago [in his shirtsleeves, with a light].

LODOVICO   Hark!
GRATIANO
Here's one comes in his shirt, with light and weapons.
IAGO
Who's there? Whose noise is this that cries on murder? 49
LODOVICO
We do not know.
IAGO   Did not you hear a cry?
CASSIO
Here, here! For heaven's sake, help me!
IAGO   What's the matter?
[He moves toward Cassio.]

---

100 **change** exchange. **sport** sexual pastime. 101 **affection** passion
107 **uses** habit, practice 108 **Not . . . mend** i.e., not to learn bad conduct from others' badness (as Emilia has suggested women learn
from men), but to mend my ways by perceiving what badness is,
making spiritual benefit out of evil and adversity.
5.1 Location: A street in Cyprus.
1 **bulk** framework projecting from the front of a shop. **2 bare**
unsheathed. **home** all the way into the target. **11 quat** pimple,
pustule. **to the sense** to the quick **14 Live Roderigo** If Roderigo
lives 16 **bobbed** swindled 21 **unfold** expose

25 **coat** (Possibly a garment of mail under the outer clothing, or simply a tougher coat than Roderigo expected.) **26 proof** a test
34 **Minion** Hussy (i.e., Desdemona) 35 **hies** hastens on. 36 **Forth
of** From out 38 **passage** people passing by. 43 **heavy** thick, dark
45 **come in to** approach 49 **cries** cries out

GRATIANO [*to Lodovico*]
      This is Othello's ancient, as I take it.
LODOVICO [*to Gratiano*]
      The same indeed, a very valiant fellow.
IAGO [*to Cassio*]
      What are you here that cry so grievously?   54
CASSIO
      Iago? Oh, I am spoiled, undone by villains!   55
      Give me some help.
IAGO
      Oh, me, Lieutenant! What villains have done this?
CASSIO
      I think that one of them is hereabout,
      And cannot make away.
IAGO   Oh, treacherous villains!   59
      [*To Lodovico and Gratiano*] What are you there? Come
          in, and give some help.   [*They advance.*]
RODERIGO   Oh, help me there!
CASSIO
      That's one of them.
IAGO   Oh, murderous slave! Oh, villain!
                                      [*He stabs Roderigo.*]
RODERIGO
      Oh, damned Iago! Oh, inhuman dog!
IAGO
      Kill men i'th' dark?—Where be these bloody thieves?—
      How silent is this town!—Ho! Murder, murder!—
      [*To Lodovico and Gratiano*] What may you be? Are you
          of good or evil?
LODOVICO   As you shall prove us, praise us.   67
IAGO   Signor Lodovico?
LODOVICO   He, sir.
IAGO
      I cry you mercy. Here's Cassio hurt by villains.   70
GRATIANO   Cassio?
IAGO   How is't, brother?
CASSIO   My leg is cut in two.
IAGO   Marry, heaven forbid!
      Light, gentlemen! I'll bind it with my shirt.
                      [*He hands them the light, and tends to Cassio's
                                                        wound.*]

                      Enter Bianca.

BIANCA
      What is the matter, ho? Who is't that cried?
IAGO   Who is't that cried?
BIANCA   Oh, my dear Cassio!
      My sweet Cassio! Oh, Cassio, Cassio, Cassio!
IAGO
      Oh, notable strumpet! Cassio, may you suspect
      Who they should be that have thus mangled you?
CASSIO   No.
GRATIANO
      I am sorry to find you thus. I have been to seek you.

IAGO
      Lend me a garter. [*He applies a tourniquet.*] So.—Oh, for
          a chair,   83
      To bear him easily hence!
BIANCA
      Alas, he faints! Oh, Cassio, Cassio, Cassio!
IAGO
      Gentlemen all, I do suspect this trash
      To be a party in this injury.—
      Patience awhile, good Cassio.—Come, come;
      Lend me a light. [*He shines the light on Roderigo.*] Know
          we this face or no?
      Alas, my friend and my dear countryman
      Roderigo! No.—Yes, sure.—Oh, heaven! Roderigo!
GRATIANO   What, of Venice?
IAGO   Even he, sir. Did you know him?
GRATIANO   Know him? Ay.
IAGO
      Signor Gratiano? I cry your gentle pardon.   95
      These bloody accidents must excuse my manners   96
      That so neglected you.
GRATIANO   I am glad to see you.
IAGO
      How do you, Cassio?—Oh, a chair, a chair!
GRATIANO   Roderigo!
IAGO
      He, he, 'tis he. [*A litter is brought in.*] Oh, that's well
          said; the chair.   100
      Some good man bear him carefully from hence;
      I'll fetch the General's surgeon. [*To Bianca*] For you,
          mistress,   102
      Save you your labor.—He that lies slain here, Cassio,   103
      Was my dear friend. What malice was between you?   104
CASSIO
      None in the world, nor do I know the man.
IAGO [*to Bianca*]
      What, look you pale?—Oh, bear him out o'th'air.   106
                      [*Cassio and Roderigo are borne off.*]
      Stay you, good gentlemen.—Look you pale,
          mistress?—   107
      Do you perceive the gastness of her eye?—   108
      Nay, if you stare, we shall hear more anon.—   109
      Behold her well; I pray you, look upon her.
      Do you see, gentlemen? Nay, guiltiness
      Will speak, though tongues were out of use.

                      [*Enter Emilia.*]

EMILIA
      'Las, what's the matter? What's the matter, husand?
IAGO
      Cassio hath here been set on in the dark
      By Roderigo and fellows that are scaped.
      He's almost slain, and Roderigo dead.

---

83 chair litter   **95 gentle** noble   **96 accidents** sudden events
100 well said well done   **102 For** As for   **103 Save . . . labor** i.e.,
never you mind tending Cassio.   **104 malice** enmity   **106 bear . . .
air** (Fresh air was thought to be dangerous for a wound.)   **107 Stay
you** (Lodovico and Gratiano are evidently about to leave.)   **108 gast-
ness** terror   **109 stare** (Iago pretends to interpret Bianca's wild looks
as an involuntary confession of guilt.)

---

54 What Who. (Also at lines 60 and 66.)   **55 spoiled** ruined, done for
59 make get   **67 prove us** prove us to be.   **praise** appraise   **70 I cry
you mercy** I beg your pardon.

EMILIA
Alas, good gentleman! Alas, good Cassio!
IAGO
This is the fruits of whoring. Prithee, Emilia,
Go know of Cassio where he supped tonight.   119
[*To Bianca*] What, do you shake at that?
BIANCA
He supped at my house, but I therefore shake not.
IAGO
Oh, did he so? I charge you go with me.
EMILIA   Oh, fie upon thee, strumpet!
BIANCA
I am no strumpet, but of life as honest   124
As you that thus abuse me.
EMILIA   As I? Faugh! Fie upon thee!
IAGO
Kind gentlemen, let's go see poor Cassio dressed.—   127
Come, mistress, you must tell 's another tale.—
Emilia, run you to the citadel
And tell my lord and lady what hath happed.—
Will you go on afore? [*Aside*] This is the night
That either makes me or fordoes me quite.   *Exeunt.* 132

❖

5.2

*Enter Othello [with a light], and Desdemona in
her bed.*

OTHELLO
It is the cause, it is the cause, my soul.   1
Let me not name it to you, you chaste stars!
It is the cause. Yet I'll not shed her blood,
Nor scar that whiter skin of hers than snow,
And smooth as monumental alabaster.   5
Yet she must die, else she'll betray more men.
Put out the light, and then put out the light.   7
If I quench thee, thou flaming minister,   8
I can again thy former light restore,
Should I repent me; but once put out thy light,   10
Thou cunning'st pattern of excelling nature,   11
I know not where is that Promethean heat   12
That can thy light relume. When I have plucked thy
    rose,   13
I cannot give it vital growth again;
It needs must wither. I'll smell thee on the tree.
                                         [*He kisses her.*]
Oh, balmy breath, that dost almost persuade
Justice to break her sword! One more, one more.

Be thus when thou art dead, and I will kill thee,
And love thee after. One more, and that's the last.
                                         [*He kisses her.*]
So sweet was ne'er so fatal. I must weep,
But they are cruel tears. This sorrow's heavenly;   21
It strikes where it doth love. She wakes.   22
DESDEMONA   Who's there? Othello?
OTHELLO   Ay, Desdemona.
DESDEMONA   Will you come to bed, my lord?
OTHELLO   Have you prayed tonight, Desdemon?
DESDEMONA   Ay, my lord.
OTHELLO
If you bethink yourself of any crime   28
Unreconciled as yet to heaven and grace,
Solicit for it straight.   30
DESDEMONA
Alack, my lord, what may you mean by that?
OTHELLO
Well, do it, and be brief. I will walk by.
I would not kill thy unprepar̀ed spirit.
No, heaven forfend! I would not kill thy soul.   34
DESDEMONA
Talk you of killing?
OTHELLO   Ay, I do.
DESDEMONA   Then heaven
Have mercy on me!
OTHELLO   Amen, with all my heart!
DESDEMONA
If you say so, I hope you will not kill me.
OTHELLO   Humh!
DESDEMONA
And yet I fear you; for you're fatal then
When your eyes roll so. Why I should fear I know not,
Since guiltiness I know not; but yet I feel I fear.
OTHELLO
Think on thy sins.
DESDEMONA   They are loves I bear to you.   42
OTHELLO   Ay, and for that thou diest.
DESDEMONA
That death's unnatural that kills for loving.
Alas, why gnaw you so your nether lip?
Some bloody passion shakes your very frame.
These are portents; but yet I hope, I hope,
They do not point on me.
OTHELLO   Peace, and be still!
DESDEMONA   I will so. What's the matter?
OTHELLO
That handkerchief which I so loved and gave thee
Thou gav'st to Cassio.
DESDEMONA   No, by my life and soul!
Send for the man and ask him.
OTHELLO
Sweet soul, take heed, take heed of perjury.
Thou art on thy deathbed.

---

119 know learn   **124 honest** chaste   **127 Cassio dressed** Cassio's
wounds dressed.   **132 fordoes** undoes, ruins
5.2. Location: A bedchamber in the citadel.
0.1–2 *in her bed* (Either the curtains are drawn back to reveal the bed
in a recessed area backstage, or the bed is "thrust out" onstage as the
scene begins.)   **1 cause** i.e., cause of justice, the offense itself, which
must be corrected in the name of justice   **5 monumental** i.e., used in
making tombs and funeral monuments   **7 the light . . . light** the
torch or lamp . . . Desdemona's life.   **8 minister** servant   **10 repent
me** change my mind   **11 Thou . . . pattern** you skillfully wrought
perfect example   **12 Promethean heat** (Alludes to two myths: that of
Prometheus stealing fire from heaven for humanity, and that of his
creating humankind.)   **13 relume** rekindle.

---

21 they are cruel tears these tears betoken a sorrowful cruelty, regrettable but just.   **22 It . . . love** (Compare Hebrews 12:6: "For whom the
Lord loveth he chasteneth.")   **28 crime** sin   **30 Solicit** petition, pray.
straight immediately.   **34 forfend** forbid.   **42 They . . . you** i.e., My
only sins are my idolatry of loving you too much.

DESDEMONA
Ay, but not yet to die.
OTHELLO   Yes, presently.   56
Therefore confess thee freely of thy sin;
For to deny each article with oath
Cannot remove nor choke the strong conception   59
That I do groan withal. Thou art to die.   60
DESDEMONA
Then Lord have mercy on me!
OTHELLO   I say, amen.
DESDEMONA
And have you mercy too! I never did
Offend you in my life; never loved Cassio
But with such general warranty of heaven   64
As I might love. I never gave him token.
OTHELLO
By heaven, I saw my handkerchief in 's hand.
Oh, perjured woman! Thou dost stone my heart,   67
And makes me call what I intend to do
A murder, which I thought a sacrifice.
I saw the handkerchief.
DESDEMONA   He found it, then.
I never gave it him. Send for him hither;
Let him confess a truth.
OTHELLO   He hath confessed.
DESDEMONA   What, my lord?
OTHELLO
That he hath used thee.
DESDEMONA   How? Unlawfully?
OTHELLO   Ay.
DESDEMONA
He will not say so.
OTHELLO   No, his mouth is stopped;
Honest Iago hath ta'en order for 't.   76
DESDEMONA
Oh, my fear interprets. What, is he dead?
OTHELLO
Had all his hairs been lives, my great revenge
Had stomach for them all.
DESDEMONA
Alas, he is betrayed and I undone!   [*She weeps.*]
OTHELLO
Out, strumpet! Weep'st thou for him to my face?
DESDEMONA
Oh, banish me, my lord, but kill me not!
OTHELLO   Down, strumpet!
DESDEMONA
Kill me tomorrow; let me live tonight!
OTHELLO   Nay, if you strive—
DESDEMONA
But half an hour!
OTHELLO   Being done, there is no pause.   86

DESDEMONA
But while I say one prayer!
OTHELLO   It is too late.
                                        Smothers her.
EMILIA (*at the door*)
My lord, my lord! What, ho! My lord, my lord!
OTHELLO
What noise is this? Not dead? Not yet quite dead?
I that am cruel am yet merciful;
I would not have thee linger in thy pain.
                            [*He dispatches her.*]
So, so.
EMILIA (*within*)   What, ho! My lord, my lord!
OTHELLO   Who's there?
EMILIA [*within*]
Oh, good my lord, I would speak a word with you!
OTHELLO
Yes, 'tis Emilia.—By and by.—She's dead.
'Tis like she comes to speak of Cassio's death.—   95
The noise was here. Ha! No more moving?   96
Still as the grave. Shall she come in? Were't good?—
I think she stirs again. No. What's best to do?
If she come in, she'll sure speak to my wife.
My wife! My wife! What wife? I have no wife.
Oh, insupportable! Oh, heavy hour!
Methinks it should be now a huge eclipse
Of sun and moon, and that th'affrighted globe
Should yawn at alteration.
EMILIA [*within*]   I do beseech you   104
That I may speak with you, oh, good my lord!
OTHELLO
I had forgot thee. Oh, come in, Emilia.—
Soft, by and by. Let me the curtains draw.—   107
        [*He closes the bedcurtains and opens the door.*]
Where art thou?

                Enter Emilia.

                        What's the matter with thee now?
EMILIA
Oh, my good lord, yonder's foul murders done!
OTHELLO   What, now?
EMILIA   But now, my lord.
OTHELLO
It is the very error of the moon;   112
She comes more nearer earth than she was wont,   113
And makes men mad.   114
EMILIA
Cassio, my lord, hath killed a young Venetian
Called Roderigo.
OTHELLO   Roderigo killed?

---

56 presently immediately.   **59 conception** (1) belief in your guilt (2) plan in my mind   **60 groan withal** (1) groan at in sorrow (2) as in giving birth.   **64 warranty** sanction   **67 stone** turn to stone, harden **76 ta'en order** taken measures   **86 Being done** i.e., Since justice has begun its relentless course

95 like likely that   **96 here** (The Folio's "high" is possible, suggesting that the commotion of the attack on Cassio was loud.)   **104 Should . . . alteration** should gape wide in an earthquake, as if expressing amazement at an eclipse. (According to Pliny, earthquakes often happen during eclipses. The cataclysmic event here is especially terrifying in that it imagines the impossible concurrence of a solar and lunar eclipse—an apocalyptic scenario befitting the horror of Desdemona's death.)   **107 Soft** Wait a minute   **112 error** aberration, irregularity **113 She** Luna, the moon goddess   **114 mad** i.e., "lunatic."

And Cassio killed?

EMILIA   No, Cassio is not killed.

OTHELLO
Not Cassio killed? Then murder's out of tune,
And sweet revenge grows harsh.

DESDEMONA   Oh, falsely, falsely murdered!

EMILIA   Oh, Lord, what cry is that?

OTHELLO   That? What?

EMILIA
Out and alas, that was my lady's voice.   123
                    [She opens the bedcurtains.]
Help, help, ho, help! O lady, speak again!
Sweet Desdemona! O sweet mistress, speak!

DESDEMONA   A guiltless death I die.

EMILIA   Oh, who hath done this deed?

DESDEMONA   Nobody; I myself. Farewell.
Commend me to my kind lord. Oh, farewell! [She dies.]

OTHELLO
Why, how should she be murdered?

EMILIA   Alas, who knows?

OTHELLO
You heard her say herself it was not I.

EMILIA
She said so. I must needs report the truth.

OTHELLO
She's like a liar gone to burning hell!
'Twas I that killed her.

EMILIA   Oh, the more angel she,
And you the blacker devil!

OTHELLO
She turned to folly, and she was a whore.   136

EMILIA
Thou dost belie her, and thou art a devil.   137

OTHELLO   She was false as water.

EMILIA   Thou art rash as fire to say
That she was false. Oh, she was heavenly true!

OTHELLO
Cassio did top her. Ask thy husband else.   141
Oh, I were damned beneath all depth in hell
But that I did proceed upon just grounds
To this extremity. Thy husband knew it all.

EMILIA   My husband?

OTHELLO   Thy husband.

EMILIA   That she was false to wedlock?

OTHELLO
Ay, with Cassio. Nay, had she been true,
If heaven would make me such another world
Of one entire and perfect chrysolite,   150
I'd not have sold her for it.

EMILIA   My husband?

OTHELLO
Ay, 'twas he that told me on her first.
An honest man he is, and hates the slime
That sticks on filthy deeds.

EMILIA   My husband?

OTHELLO
What needs this iterance, woman? I say thy husband.   157

EMILIA
Oh, mistress, villainy hath made mocks with love!   158
My husband say she was false?

OTHELLO   He, woman;
I say thy husband. Dost understand the word?
My friend, thy husband, honest, honest Iago.

EMILIA
If he say so, may his pernicious soul
Rot half a grain a day! He lies to th' heart.
She was too fond of her most filthy bargain.

OTHELLO   Ha?   [He draws.]

EMILIA   Do thy worst!
This deed of thine is no more worthy heaven
Than thou wast worthy her.

OTHELLO   Peace, you were best.   168

EMILIA
Thou hast not half that power to do me harm
As I have to be hurt. O gull! O dolt!   170
As ignorant as dirt! Thou hast done a deed—
I care not for thy sword; I'll make thee known,
Though I lost twenty lives.—Help! Help, ho, help!
The Moor hath killed my mistress! Murder, murder!

Enter Montano, Gratiano, and Iago.

MONTANO
What is the matter? How now, General?

EMILIA
Oh, are you come, Iago? You have done well,
That men must lay their murders on your neck.   177

GRATIANO   What is the matter?

EMILIA [to Iago]
Disprove this villain, if thou be'st a man.
He says thou told'st him that his wife was false.
I know thou didst not; thou'rt not such a villain.   181
Speak, for my heart is full.

IAGO
I told him what I thought, and told no more
Than what he found himself was apt and true.   184

EMILIA
But did you ever tell him she was false?

IAGO   I did.

EMILIA
You told a lie, an odious, damnèd lie!
Upon my soul, a lie, a wicked lie.
She false with Cassio? Did you say with Cassio?

IAGO
With Cassio, mistress. Go to, charm your tongue.   190

EMILIA
I will not charm my tongue; I am bound to speak.
My mistress here lies murdered in her bed—

ALL   Oh, heavens forfend!

EMILIA
And your reports have set the murder on.

---

123 **Out** (A cry of dismay, intensifying *alas*.)   136 **folly** i.e., wantonness, fleshly sin   137 **belie** slander   141 **else** i.e., if you don't believe me.   150 **chrysolite** precious topaz

157 **iterance** iteration, repetition   158 **made mocks with** made a mockery of   168 **Peace . . . best** You'd better be quiet.   170 **to be hurt** i.e., to endure hurt.   **gull** dupe.   177 **on your neck** to your charge.   181 **such a villain** such a villain as all that.   184 **apt** plausible   190 **charm** control

OTHELLO
Nay, stare not, masters. It is true indeed.
GRATIANO   'Tis a strange truth.
MONTANO
Oh, monstrous act!
EMILIA   Villainy, villainy, villainy!
I think upon't—I think I smell't! O villainy!
I thought so then—I'll kill myself for grief—   199
Oh, villainy, villainy!
IAGO
What, are you mad? I charge you, get you home.
EMILIA
Good gentlemen, let me have leave to speak.
'Tis proper I obey him, but not now.
Perchance, Iago, I will ne'er go home.
OTHELLO
Oh! Oh! Oh!   [Othello falls on the bed.]
EMILIA   Nay, lay thee down and roar,   205
For thou hast killed the sweetest innocent
That e'er did lift up eye.
OTHELLO [rising]   Oh, she was foul!   207
I scarce did know you, uncle. There lies your niece,
Whose breath indeed these hands have newly
     stopped.
I know this act shows horrible and grim.   210
GRATIANO
Poor Desdemon! I am glad thy father's dead.
Thy match was mortal to him, and pure grief
Shore his old thread in twain. Did he live now,   213
This sight would make him do a desperate turn,   214
Yea, curse his better angel from his side,
And fall to reprobance.   216
OTHELLO
'Tis pitiful. But yet Iago knows
That she with Cassio hath the act of shame
A thousand times committed. Cassio confessed it;
And she did gratify his amorous works   220
With that recognizance and pledge of love   221
Which I first gave her. I saw it in his hand;
It was a handkerchief, an antique token
My father gave my mother.
EMILIA   Oh, God! Oh, heavenly God!
IAGO
Zounds, hold your peace.
EMILIA   'Twill out, 'twill out! I peace?
No, I will speak as liberal as the north.   227
Let heaven and men and devils, let them all,
All, all, cry shame against me, yet I'll speak.
IAGO
Be wise, and get you home.
EMILIA   I will not.
                         [Iago threatens Emilia.]
GRATIANO   Fie,

Your sword upon a woman?
EMILIA
Oh, thou dull Moor! That handkerchief thou speak'st of
I found by fortune and did give my husband;
For often, with a solemn earnestness,
More than indeed belonged to such a trifle,   235
He begged of me to steal't.
IAGO   Villainous whore!
EMILIA
She give it Cassio? No, alas! I found it,
And I did give't my husband.
IAGO   Filth, thou liest!
EMILIA
By heaven, I do not, I do not, gentlemen.
Oh, murderous coxcomb! What should such a fool   240
Do with so good a wife?
OTHELLO   Are there no stones in heaven   242
But what serves for the thunder?—Precious villain!   243
     [He runs at Iago; Montano disarms Othello. Iago,
                         from behind, stabs Emilia.]
GRATIANO
The woman falls! Sure he hath killed his wife.
EMILIA
Ay, ay. Oh, lay me by my mistress' side.
                              [Exit Iago.]
GRATIANO   He's gone, but his wife's killed.
MONTANO
'Tis a notorious villain. Take you this weapon,
Which I have here recovered from the Moor.
Come, guard the door without. Let him not pass,
But kill him rather. I'll after that same villain,
For 'tis a damnèd slave.
              Exit [with all but Othello and Emilia,
                  who has been laid by Desdemona's side].
OTHELLO   I am not valiant neither,
But every puny whipster gets my sword.   253
But why should honor outlive honesty?   254
Let it go all.
EMILIA   What did thy song bode, lady?
Hark, canst thou hear me? I will play the swan,
And die in music. [She sings] "Willow, willow, willow."
Moor, she was chaste. She loved thee, cruel Moor.
So come my soul to bliss as I speak true.
So speaking as I think, alas, I die.   [She dies.]
OTHELLO
I have another weapon in this chamber;
It was a sword of Spain, the ice-brook's temper—   262
Oh, here it is. [He finds a sword.] Uncle, I must come
     forth.
GRATIANO [within]
If thou attempt it, it will cost thee dear.

199 then (Perhaps at 3.3.331–2 and 4.2.137–54.)   **205 s.d. Othello . . . bed** (This direction is from the Quarto, as also *He kisses her* at line 19 and *She dies* at line 129.)   **207 lift up eye** i.e., lift her eyes to heaven.   **210 shows** looks   **213 Shore . . . thread** sheared the thread of his old age (as Atropos, one of the three Fates, was thought to do).   **214 turn** deed   **216 reprobance** damnation, i.e., suicide.   **220 gratify** reward   **221 recognizance** token   **227 liberal as the north** freely as the north wind (blows).

235 belonged was appropriate   **240 coxcomb** fool. (Addressed to Othello.)   **242 stones** bolts, such as those used for thunderbolts   **243 Precious** i.e., Arrant, utter.   **243.1–2 He . . . Emilia** (The Quarto text reads, "The Moore runnes at Iago. Iago kils his wife." The Quarto also specifies the exit of Iago at line 245 and the death of Emilia at line 260.)   **253 every . . . sword** every whipper-snapper can get the better of me and my sword.   **254 why . . . honesty?** why should a soldier's reputation for bravery outlive true integrity?   **262 the icebrook's temper** tempered in ice-cold water

Thou hast no weapon, and perforce must suffer.

OTHELLO
Look in upon me then and speak with me,
Or, naked as I am, I will assault thee.　　　　　267

　　　　　[*Enter Gratiano.*]

GRATIANO
What is the matter?

OTHELLO　　　　　Behold, I have a weapon;
A better never did itself sustain
Upon a soldier's thigh. I have seen the day
That, with this little arm and this good sword,
I have made my way through more impediments
Than twenty times your stop. But oh, vain boast!　　273
Who can control his fate? 'Tis not so now.
Be not afraid, though you do see me weaponed;
Here is my journey's end, here is my butt　　　　276
And very seamark of my utmost sail.　　　　　277
　　　　　　　[*Gratiano steps back.*]
Do you go back dismayed? 'Tis a lost fear;　　　278
Man but a rush against Othello's breast　　　　279
And he retires. Where should Othello go?
　　　　　　　[*He turns to Desdemona.*]
Now, how dost thou look now? Oh, ill-starred wench!
Pale as thy smock! When we shall meet at compt,　　282
This look of thine will hurl my soul from heaven,
And fiends will snatch at it. Cold, cold, my girl?
Even like thy chastity. Oh, cursèd, cursèd slave!　　285
Whip me, ye devils,
From the possession of this heavenly sight!
Blow me about in winds! Roast me in sulfur!
Wash me in steep-down gulfs of liquid fire!
Oh, Desdemon! Dead, Desdemon! Dead! Oh! Oh!　　290

Enter Lodovico, Cassio [*carried in a litter*],
Montano, and Iago [*prisoner*], *with officers.*

LODOVICO
Where is this rash and most unfortunate man?

OTHELLO
That's he that was Othello. Here I am.

LODOVICO
Where is that viper? Bring the villain forth.
　　　　　　　[*Iago is led forward.*]

OTHELLO
I look down towards his feet; but that's a fable.　　294
If that thou be'st a devil, I cannot kill thee.
　　　　　　　[*He wounds Iago.*]

LODOVICO
Wrench his sword from him.　　　[*Othello is disarmed.*]

IAGO　　　　　　　　I bleed, sir, but not killed.

OTHELLO
I am not sorry neither. I'd have thee live,

For in my sense 'tis happiness to die.　　　　　298

LODOVICO
O thou Othello, that was once so good,
Fall'n in the practice of a cursèd slave,　　　　300
What shall be said to thee?

OTHELLO　　　　　　　Why, anything.
An honorable murderer, if you will,
For naught I did in hate, but all in honor.

LODOVICO
This wretch hath part confessed his villainy.
Did you and he consent in Cassio's death?　　　305

OTHELLO　Ay.

CASSIO
Dear General, I never gave you cause.

OTHELLO
I do believe it, and I ask your pardon.
Will you, I pray, demand that demi-devil
Why he hath thus ensnared my soul and body?

IAGO
Demand me nothing. What you know, you know.
From this time forth I never will speak word.

LODOVICO　What, not to pray?

GRATIANO　　　Torments will ope your lips.　　314

OTHELLO　Well, thou dost best.　　　　　315

LODOVICO
Sir, you shall understand what hath befall'n,
Which, as I think, you know not. Here is a letter
Found in the pocket of the slain Roderigo;
And here another. [*He produces letters.*] The one of them
　imports
The death of Cassio, to be undertook
By Roderigo.

OTHELLO
Oh, villain!

CASSIO　　　Most heathenish and most gross!　　322

LODOVICO [*showing another paper*]
Now here's another discontented paper　　　　323
Found in his pocket too. And this, it seems,
Roderigo meant t'have sent this damnèd villain;
But that belike Iago in the interim　　　　　326
Came in and satisfied him.　　　　　　　327

OTHELLO [*to Iago*]　Oh, thou pernicious caitiff!—
How came you, Cassio, by that handkerchief
That was my wife's?

CASSIO　　　　　I found it in my chamber;
And he himself confessed but even now
That there he dropped it for a special purpose
Which wrought to his desire.

OTHELLO　　　　　　Oh, fool, fool, fool!　　333

CASSIO
There is besides in Roderigo's letter
How he upbraids Iago, that he made him

---

267 naked unarmed　**273 your stop** the obstruction you present.
276 butt goal, limit. (An archery term.)　**277 seamark** beacon (marking his destination or limit)　**278 lost** groundless　**279 Man . . . rush** wield no more than a reed　**282 compt** account, judgment day
285 slave i.e., Othello himself.　**290.1 in a litter** (The Quarto specifies that Cassio is "*in a Chaire*.")　**294 towards his feet** i.e., to see if they are cloven, as the devil's are fabled to be

298 in my sense to one who feels as I do　**300 in the practice** through the plotting, into the snare.　**slave** villain　**305 consent** agree
314 Torments Torture　**315 thou dost best** you (Iago) do best not to talk.　**322 gross** monstrous.　**323 discontented** full of discontent
326 belike most likely　**327 Came . . . him** interposed and gave him satisfactory explanation.　**333 wrought . . . desire** worked out as he wished, fitted in with his plan.

Brave me upon the watch, whereon it came   336
That I was cast; and even but now he spake,   337
After long seeming dead, Iago hurt him,
Iago set him on.

LODOVICO [*to Othello*]
You must forsake this room and go with us.
Your power and your command is taken off,   341
And Cassio rules in Cyprus. For this slave,
If there be any cunning cruelty
That can torment him much and hold him long,   344
It shall be his. You shall close prisoner rest   345
Till that the nature of your fault be known
To the Venetian state.—Come, bring away.

OTHELLO
Soft you; a word or two before you go.   348
I have done the state some service, and they know't.
No more of that. I pray you, in your letters,
When you shall these unlucky deeds relate,   351
Speak of me as I am; nothing extenuate,
Nor set down aught in malice. Then must you speak
Of one that loved not wisely but too well;
Of one not easily jealous but, being wrought,   355
Perplexed in the extreme; of one whose hand,   356
Like the base Indian, threw a pearl away   357
Richer than all his tribe; of one whose subdued eyes,   358
Albeit unusèd to the melting mood,
Drops tears as fast as the Arabian trees

Their medicinable gum. Set you down this;   361
And say besides that in Aleppo once,
Where a malignant and a turbaned Turk
Beat a Venetian and traduced the state,
I took by th' throat the circumcisèd dog
And smote him, thus.   [*He stabs himself.*] 366

LODOVICO   Oh, bloody period!   367
GRATIANO   All that is spoke is marred.
OTHELLO
I kissed thee ere I killed thee. No way but this,
Killing myself, to die upon a kiss.
       [*He kisses Desdemona and*] *dies.*

CASSIO
This did I fear, but thought he had no weapon;
For he was great of heart.

LODOVICO [*to Iago*]   O Spartan dog,   372
More fell than anguish, hunger, or the sea!   373
Look on the tragic loading of this bed.
This is thy work. The object poisons sight;
Let it be hid. Gratiano, keep the house,   376
       [*The bedcurtains are drawn.*]
And seize upon the fortunes of the Moor,   377
For they succeed on you. [*To Cassio*] To you, Lord
  Governor,   378
Remains the censure of this hellish villain,   379
The time, the place, the torture. Oh, enforce it!
Myself will straight aboard, and to the state
This heavy act with heavy heart relate.   *Exeunt.*

---

336 Brave defy.   **whereon it came** whereof it came about   **337 cast** dismissed   **341 taken off** taken away   **344 hold him long** keep him alive a long time (during his torture)   **345 rest** remain   **348 Soft you** One moment   **351 unlucky** unfortunate   **355 wrought** worked upon, worked into a frenzy   **356 Perplexed** distraught   **357 Indian** (This reading from the Quarto pictures an ignorant savage who cannot recognize the value of a precious jewel. The Folio reading, "Iudean," i.e., infidel or disbeliever, may refer to Herod, who slew Miriamne in a fit of jealousy, or to Judas Iscariot, the betrayer of Christ.)   **358 subdued** i.e., overcome by grief

361 gum i.e., myrrh.   **366 s.d.** *He stabs himself* (This direction is in the Quarto text.)   **367 period** termination, conclusion.   **372 Spartan dog** (Spartan dogs were noted for their savagery and silence.)   **373 fell** cruel   **376 Let it be hid** i.e., draw the bedcurtains. (No stage direction specifies that the dead are to be carried offstage at the end of the play.)   **keep** guard   **377 seize upon** take legal possession of   **378 succeed on** pass as though by inheritance to   **379 censure** sentencing

King Lear

In *King Lear,* Shakespeare pushes to its limit the hypothesis of a malign or at least indifferent universe in which human life is meaningless and brutal. Few plays other than *Hamlet* and *Macbeth* approach *King Lear* in evoking the wretchedness of human existence, and even they cannot match the devastating spectacle of the Earl of Gloucester blinded or Cordelia dead in Lear's arms. The responses of the chief characters are correspondingly searing. "Is man no more than this?" rages Lear. "Unaccommodated man is no more but such a poor, bare, forked animal as thou art" (3.4.101–7). Life he calls a "great stage of fools," an endless torment: "the first time that we smell the air / We wawl and cry" (4.6.179–83). Gloucester's despair takes the form of accusing the gods of gleeful malice toward humanity: "As flies to wanton boys are we to th' gods; / They kill us for their sport" (4.1.36–7). Gloucester's ministering son Edgar can offer him no greater consolation than stoic resolve: "Men must endure / Their going hence, even as their coming hither; / Ripeness is all" (5.2.9–11). These statements need not be read as choric expressions of meaning for the play as a whole, but they do attest to the depth of suffering. In no other Shakespearean play does injustice appear to triumph so ferociously, for so long, and with such impunity. Will the heavens countenance this reign of injustice on earth? Retribution is late in coming and is not certainly the work of the heavens themselves. For, at the last, we must confront the wanton death of the innocent Cordelia—a death no longer willed even by the villain who arranged her execution. "Is this the promised end?" (5.3.268) asks the Earl of Kent, stressing the unparalleled horror of the catastrophe.

Throughout its earlier history, the ancient story of King Lear had always ended happily. In the popular folktale of Cinderella, to which the legend of Lear's daughters bears a significant resemblance, the youngest and virtuous daughter triumphs over her two older wicked sisters and is married to her princely wooer. Geoffrey of Monmouth's *Historia Regum Britanniae* (c. 1136), the ear-liest known version of the Lear story, records that, after Lear is overthrown by his sons-in-law (more than by his daughters), he is restored to his throne by the intervention of the French King and is allowed to enjoy his kingdom and Cordelia's love until his natural death. (Cordelia, as his successor, is later dethroned and murdered by her wicked nephews, but that is another story.) Sixteenth-century Tudor versions of the Lear story with which Shakespeare was familiar—John Higgins's account in *The First Part of the Mirror for Magistrates* (1574), Raphael Holinshed's *Chronicles* (1587), Edmund Spenser's *The Faerie Queene,* 2.10.27–32, and a play called *The True Chronicle History of King Leir* (by 1594, published 1605)—all retain the happy ending. The tragic pattern may have been suggested instead by Shakespeare's probable source for the Gloucester-Edgar-Edmund plot, Sir Philip Sidney's *Arcadia,* 2.10, in which the Paphlagonian King is the victim of filial ingratitude and deceit.

Yet even Shakespeare's authority was not sufficient to put down the craving for a happy resolution. Nahum Tate's adaptation (1681), which banished the Fool as indecorous for a tragedy and united Edgar and Cordelia in marriage, placing Lear once again on his throne, held the English stage for about 150 years. David Garrick restored some of Shakespeare's lines, and Edmund Kean restored the tragic ending, but it was not until 1838 that *King Lear* was again performed more or less as the dramatist wrote it. One of Shakespeare's editors, Dr. Samuel Johnson, evidently spoke for most eighteenth-century audiences when he confessed that he could hardly bring himself to read Shakespeare's text. Cordelia's slaughter violated that age's longing for "poetic justice." Her death implied a wanton universe and so counseled philosophic despair. Today, Shakespeare's relentless honesty and refusal to accept easy answers convince us that he was right to defy the conventions of his source, though no doubt we, too, distort the play to conform with our supposed toughness of vision.

Shakespeare evidently wrote *King Lear* some time before it was performed at court in December of 1606, probably in 1605 and certainly no earlier than 1603–1604; Edgar's speeches as Tom o' Bedlam contain references to Samuel Harsnett's *Declaration of Egregious Popish Impostures,* which was registered for publication in March of 1603. Thus, *King Lear* was probably written between *Othello* (c. 1603–1604) and *Macbeth* (c. 1606–1607), when Shakespeare was at the height of his literary power in the writing of tragedies.

When we look at the play in formal terms, we are apt to be struck first by its complex double plot. Nowhere else in Shakespearean tragedy do we find anything approaching the rich orchestration of the double plotting in *King Lear.* The links and parallels between the two plots are established on a narrative level early in the play and continue to the end. King Lear misjudges his children and disinherits his loving daughter Cordelia in favor of her duplicitous sisters, whereas Gloucester falls prey to Edmund's deceptions and disinherits his loyal son Edgar; Lear is turned out into the storm by his false daughters, while Gloucester is branded as a traitor by Edmund and deprived of his eyesight; Lear in his madness realizes his fault against Cordelia, while the blind Gloucester "sees" at last the truth about Edgar; and both fathers are cared for by their loving children and are belatedly reconciled to them, but then die brokenhearted. As recent criticism has noted, these narrative parallels are not especially significant in themselves; we are moved, not by the mere repetition of events, but by the enlargement of tragic vision that results from the counterpointing of two such actions. When we see juxtaposed to each other two scenes of trial, Lear's mad arraignment of the absent Goneril and Regan and then the cruel imposition of the mere "form of justice" on the pinioned Gloucester (3.6 and 3.7), we begin to measure the extent to which justice and injustice are inverted by cruelty. When at last the two old men come together, during the storm scenes and especially at Dover, the sad comfort they derive from sharing the wreckage of their lives calls forth piercing eloquence against the stench of mortality. The sight is "most pitiful in the meanest wretch, / Past speaking of in a king" (4.6.204–5).

The play's double structure suggests another duality central to *King Lear:* an opposition of parable and realism, in which "divided and distinguished worlds" are bound together for instructive contrast. (These terms are Maynard Mack's, in his *King Lear in Our Time,* 1965.) To a remarkable degree, this play derives its story from folklore and legend, with many of the wondrous and implausible circumstances of popular romance. A prose rendition might almost begin, "Once upon a time there was a king who had three daughters . . . ." Yet Shakespeare arouses romantic expectation only to crush it by aborting the conventional happy ending, setting up a dramatic tension between an idealized world of make-

believe and the actual world of disappointed hopes. We are aware of artifice and convention, and yet are deeply moved by the "truth" of suffering, love, and hatred. The characters pull us two ways at once; we regard them as types with universalized characteristics—a king and father, his cruel daughters, his loving daughter, and the like—and yet we scrutinize them for psychological motivation because they seem so real and individual.

This duality appears in both the central and the secondary characters. The King of France is in part a hero out of romance, who makes selfless choices and rescues the heroine Cordelia from her distress; yet his motive must also be appraised in the context of a bitter struggle for power. Why does he leave the English court "in choler," and why does he return to England with an army? Is it only to aid his wife and her beleaguered father, or is he negotiating for military advantage? Certainly, a French invasion of England on behalf of Lear complicates the issues of loyalty for the well-meaning Duke of Albany (and perhaps as well for an English Renaissance audience, with its habitual mistrust of the French). The dual focus of the play invites conflicting interpretation. Similarly, Edgar is presented to us on the one hand as the traduced victim in a starkly pessimistic story, dominated by his rationalistic brother, Edmund, who scoffs at religion and undertakes to manipulate those around him for personal gain; on the other hand, Edgar's story grows increasingly improbable as he undertakes a series of disguises and emerges finally as an anonymous champion of chivalry, challenging his brother in the lists like a knight-errant out of Arthurian romance. Edgar's motives are hard to follow. Is he the hero of a fabulous story whose disguises and contriving of illusions for his father are simply part of that storytelling tradition, or is he, in more realistic terms, a man whose disguises are a defensive mask and whose elaborate contrivances defeat themselves? Edmund, his brother, is no less complex. Onstage today he is usually interpreted as smooth and plausible, well-motivated by his father's condescending attitude and by the arbitrariness of the law that has excluded him from legitimacy and inheritance. Yet parable elevates Edmund into something monstrous. He becomes an embodiment of gleeful villainy, like Iago in *Othello,* malignantly evil simply because the evil that is in the universe must find a human form through which to express itself. Edmund's belated attempt to do some good adds to our difficulties in appraising his character, but the restless power of the dual conception supplies a vitality not to be found in pure fable or in realistic literature.

What we see then in Edmund and in others is the union of the universal and the particular, making *King Lear* at once parable and compellingly real. The parable or folktale element is prominent at the beginning of the play and focuses attention on the archetypal situations with which the story is concerned: rivalry between siblings, fear of parental rejection, and, at the same time, parental fear of children's callousness. The "unrealistic" contrast between Cordelia and her wicked sisters, or between Edgar and Edmund, is something we accept as a convention of storytelling, because it expresses vividly the psychic truth of rivalry between brothers and sisters. We identify with Cordelia and Edgar as virtuous children whose worth is misjudged, and who are losing to wicked siblings the contest for parental approval. (In folklore, the rejecting parent is usually a stepparent, which signifies our conviction that he or she is not a true parent at all.) Similarly, we accept as a meaningful convention of storytelling the equally "unrealistic" device by which Lear tests the love of his daughters. Like any parent, he wishes to be loved and appreciated in response to the kindnesses he has performed. The tension between fathers and their marriageable daughters is a recurrent pattern in Shakespeare's late plays, as in *Othello* (in which Brabantio accuses Desdemona of deceiving and deserting him), in *Pericles, Cymbeline,* and *The Winter's Tale,* and in *The Tempest,* in which the pattern is best resolved. In *King Lear,* Shakespeare explores the inherently explosive situation of an imperious father who, having provided for his children and having grown old, assumes he has a right to expect that those children will express their love and gratitude by looking after him.

The difficulty is that the parable of Lear and his children presents two contrasting viewpoints—that of the unappreciated child and that of the unwanted aging parent. Tragic misunderstanding is inevitable, and it outweighs the question of assessing blame. From Lear's point of view, Cordelia's silence is a truculent scanting of obedience. What he has devised is, after all, only a prearranged formality, with Cordelia to receive the richest third of England. Cannot such a ceremony be answered with the conventional hyperbole of courtly language, to which the King's ear is attuned? Don't parents have a right to be verbally reassured of their children's love? How can children be so laconic about such a precious matter? For her part, however, Cordelia senses that Lear is demanding love as payment for his parental kindliness, quid pro quo. Genuine love ought rather to be selfless, as the King of France tells the Duke of Burgundy: "Love's not love / When it is mingled with regards that stands / Aloof from th'entire point" (1.1.242–4). Is Cordelia being asked to prefer Lear before her own husband-to-be? Is this the price she must pay for her upbringing? Lear's ego seems fully capable of demanding this sacrifice from his daughters, especially from his favorite, Cordelia; he has given them his whole kingdom, now let them care for him as befits his royal rank and patriarchal role. The "second childishness" of his old age brings with it a self-centered longing to monopolize the lives of his children and to be a child again. Besides, as king, Lear has long grown accustomed to flattery and absolute obedience. Goneril

and Regan are content to flatter and promise obedience, knowing they will turn him out once he has relinquished his authority. Cordelia refuses to lie in this fashion, but she also will not yield to Lear's implicit request for her undivided affection. Part of her must be loyal to her own husband and her children, in the natural cycle of the generations. "When I shall wed, / That lord whose hand must take my plight shall carry / Half my love with him, half my care and duty" (1.1.100–2). Marriage will not prevent her from obeying, loving, and honoring her father as is fit but will establish for her a new priority. To Lear, as to other fathers contemplating a daughter's marriage in late Shakespearean plays, this savors of desertion.

Lear is sadly deficient in self-knowledge. As Regan dryly observes, "he hath ever but slenderly known himself" (1.1.296–7) and has grown ever more changeable and imperious with age. By dividing his kingdom in three, ostensibly so that "future strife / May be prevented now" (lines 44–5), he instead sets in motion a civil war and French invasion. His intention of putting aside his regal authority while still retaining "The name and all th'addition to a king" (line 136) perhaps betrays a lack of comprehension of the realities of power, although Lear may also have plausible political reasons for what he does, in view of the restive ambitions of the Dukes of Cornwall, Albany, and Burgundy. In any case, he welcomes poisoned flattery but interprets well-intended criticism, whether from Cordelia or Kent, as treason. These failures in no sense justify what Lear's ungrateful children do to him; as he later says, just before going mad, "I am a man / More sinned against than sinning" (3.2.59–60). His failures are, however, tokens of his worldly insolence, for which he must fall. The process is a painful one, but, since it brings self-discovery, it is not without its compensations. Indeed, a central paradox of the play is that by no other way could Lear have learned what human suffering and need are all about.

Lear's Fool is instrumental in elucidating this paradox. The Fool offers Lear advice in palatable form as mere foolery or entertainment and thus obtains a hearing when Kent and Cordelia have been angrily dismissed. Beneath his seemingly innocent jibes, however, are plain warnings of the looming disaster Lear blindly refuses to acknowledge. The Fool knows, as indeed any fool could tell, that Goneril and Regan are remorseless and unnatural. The real fool, therefore, is Lear himself, for having placed himself in their power. In a paradox familiar to Renaissance audiences—as in Erasmus's *In Praise of Folly,* Cervantes's *Don Quixote,* and Shakespeare's own earlier *As You Like It* and *Twelfth Night*—folly and wisdom exchange places. By a similar inversion of logic, the Fool offers his coxcomb to the Earl of Kent for siding with Lear in his exile, "for taking one's part that's out of favor" (1.4.97). Worldly wisdom suggests that we serve those whose fortunes are on the rise, as the obsequious and servile Oswald does.

Indeed, the sinister progress of the first half of the play seems to confirm the Fool's contention that kindness and love are a sure way to exile and poverty. "Let go thy hold when a great wheel runs down a hill lest it break thy neck with following; but the great one that goes upward, let him draw thee after" (2.4.70–3). Yet the Fool resolves to ignore his own sardonic advice; "I would have none but knaves follow it, since a fool gives it" (lines 74–5). Beneath his mocking, the Fool expresses the deeper truth that it is better to be a "fool" and suffer than to win on the cynical world's terms. The greatest fools truly are those who prosper through cruelty and become hardened in sin. As the Fool puts it, deriving a seemingly contrary lesson from Lear's rejection of Cordelia: "Why, this fellow has banished two on 's daughters and did the third a blessing against his will" (1.4.99–101).

These inversions find a parallel in Christian teaching, although the play is nominally pagan in setting. (The lack of explicit Christian reference may be in part the result of a parliamentary order in 1606 banning references to "God" onstage as blasphemous.) Christianity does not hold a monopoly on the idea that one must lose the world in order to win a better world, but its expressions of that idea were plentifully available to Shakespeare: "Blessed are the meek, for they shall inherit the earth" (the Sermon on the Mount); "Go and sell that thou hast, and give to the poor, and thou shalt have treasure in heaven" (Matthew 19:21); "He hath put down the mighty from their seats, and exalted them of low degree" (Luke 1:52). Cordelia's vision of genuine love is of this exalted spiritual order. She is, as the King of France extols her, "most rich being poor, / Most choice, forsaken, and most loved, despised" (1.1.254–5). This is the sense in which Lear has bestowed on her an unintended blessing, by exiling her from a worldly prosperity that is inherently pernicious. Now, with poetic fitness, Lear must learn the same lesson himself. He does so, paradoxically, at the very moment he goes mad, parting ways with the conventional truths of the corrupted world. "My wits begin to turn," he says (3.2.67), and then speaks his first kind words to the Fool, who is his companion in the storm. Lear senses companionship with a fellow mortal who is cold and outcast as he is. In his madness, he perceives both the worth of this insight and the need for suffering to attain it: "The art of our necessities is strange, / And can make vile things precious" (lines 70–1). Misery teaches Lear things he never could know as king about other "Poor naked wretches" who "bide the pelting of this pitiless storm." How are such poor persons to be fed and clothed? "Oh, I have ta'en / Too little care of this! Take physic, pomp; / Expose thyself to feel what wretches feel, / That thou mayst shake the superflux to them / And show the heavens more just" (3.4.28–36). This vision of perfect justice is visionary and utopian, utterly mad, in fact, but it is also spiritual wisdom dearly bought.

Gloucester learns a similar truth and expresses it in much the same way. Like Lear, he has driven into exile a virtuous child and has placed himself in the power of the wicked. Enlightenment comes only through suffering. Just as Lear achieves spiritual wisdom when he goes mad, Gloucester achieves spiritual vision when he is physically blinded. His eyes having been ground out by the heel of Cornwall's boot, Gloucester asks for Edmund only to learn that Edmund has betrayed him in return for siding with Lear in the approaching civil war. Gloucester's response, however, is not to accuse Edmund of treachery but to beg forgiveness of the wronged Edgar. No longer does Gloucester need eyes to see this truth: "I stumbled when I saw." Although the discovery is shattering, Gloucester perceives, as does Lear, that adversity is paradoxically of some benefit, since prosperity had previously caused him to be so spiritually blind. "Full oft 'tis seen / Our means secure us, and our mere defects / Prove our commodities" (4.1.19–21). And this realization leads him, as it does Lear, to express a longing for utopian social justice in which arrogant men will be humbled and the poor raised up by redistributed wealth. "Heavens, deal so still! / Let the superfluous and lust-dieted man, / That slaves your ordinance, that will not see / Because he does not feel, feel your pow'r quickly! / So distribution should undo excess / And each man have enough" (lines 65–70).

To say that Lear and Gloucester learn something precious is not, however, to deny that they are also devastated and broken by their savage humiliation. Indeed, Gloucester is driven to a despairing attempt at suicide, and Lear remains obsessed with the rotten stench of his own mortality, "bound / Upon a wheel of fire" (4.7.47–8). Every decent value that we like to associate with civilization is grotesquely inverted during the storm scenes. Justice, for example, is portrayed in two sharply contrasting scenes: the mere "form of justice" by which Cornwall condemns Gloucester for treason (3.7.26) and the earnestly playacted trial by which the mad Lear arraigns Goneril and Regan of filial ingratitude (3.6). The appearance and the reality of justice have exchanged places, as have folly and wisdom or blindness and seeing. The trial of Gloucester is outwardly correct, for Cornwall possesses the legal authority to try his subjects and at least goes through the motions of interrogating his prisoner. The outcome is, however, cruelly predetermined. In the playacting trial concurrently taking place in a wretched hovel, the outward appearance of justice is pathetically absurd. Here, justice on earth is personified by a madman (Lear), Edgar disguised as another madman (Tom o' Bedlam), and a Fool, of whom the latter two are addressed by Lear as "Thou robèd man of justice" and "thou, his yokefellow of equity" (lines 36–7). They are caught up in a pastime of illusion, using a footstool to represent Lear's ungrateful daughters. Yet true justice is here and not inside the manor house.

Similar contrasts invert the values of loyalty, obedience, and family bonds. Edmund becomes, in the language of the villains, the "loyal" son whose loyalty is demonstrated by turning on his own "traitorous" father. Cornwall becomes a new father to Edmund ("thou shalt find a dearer father in my love," 3.5.25–6). Conversely, a servant who tries to restrain Cornwall from blinding Gloucester is, in Regan's eyes, monstrously insubordinate. "A peasant stand up thus?" (3.7.83). Personal and sexual relationships betray signs of the universal malaise. The explicitly sexual ties in the play, notably those of Goneril, Regan, and Edmund, are grossly carnal and lead to jealousy and murder, while in Cordelia's wifely role the sensual is underplayed. The relationships we are invited to cherish—those of Cordelia, Kent, the Fool, and Gloucester to King Lear, and Edgar to Gloucester—are filial or are characterized by loyal service, both of which are pointedly nonsexual. Nowhere do we find an embodiment of love that is both sensual and spiritual, as in Desdemona in *Othello* or Hermione in *The Winter's Tale*. The Fool's and Tom o' Bedlam's (i.e., Edgar's) gibes about codpieces and plackets (3.2.27–40, 3.4.96) anticipate Lear's towering indictment of carnality, in which his fear of woman's insatiable appetite and his revulsion at her body "Down from the waist" ("there is the sulfurous pit, burning, scalding, stench, consumption. Fie, fie, fie! Pah, pah!") combine with a destructive self-hatred (4.6.124–30).

All these inversions and polarizations are subsumed in the inversion of the word "natural." Edmund is the "natural" son of Gloucester, meaning literally that he is illegitimate. Figuratively, he therefore represents a violation of traditional moral order. In appearance he is smooth and plausible, but in reality he is an archdeceiver like the Vice in a morality play, a superb actor who boasts to the audience in soliloquy of his protean villainy. "Nature" is Edmund's goddess, and by this he means something like a naturalistic universe in which the race goes to the swiftest and in which conscience, morality, and religion are empty myths. Whereas Lear invokes Nature as a goddess who will punish ungrateful daughters and defend rejected fathers (1.4.274–88) and whereas Gloucester believes in a cosmic correspondence between eclipses of the moon or sun and mutinous discords among people (1.2.106–17), Edmund scoffs at all such metaphysical speculations. He spurns, in other words, the Boethian conception of a divine harmony uniting the cosmos and humankind, with humankind at the center of the universe. As a rationalist, Edmund echoes Jacobean disruptions of the older world order in politics and religion as well as in science. He is Machiavellian, an atheist, and Epicurean—everything inimical to traditional Elizabethan ideals of order. To him, "natural" means precisely what Lear and Gloucester call "unnatural."

His creed provides the play with its supreme test. Which definition of "natural" is true? Does heaven exist, and will it let Edmund and the other villainous persons get away with their evil? The question is frequently asked, but the answers are ambiguous. "If you do love old men," Lear implores the gods, "if your sweet sway / Allow obedience, if you yourselves are old, / Make it your cause" (2.4.191–3). His exhortations mount into frenzied rant, until finally the heavens do send down a terrible storm— on Lear himself. Witnesses agree that the absence of divine order in the universe would have the gravest consequences. "If that the heavens do not their visible spirits / Send quickly down to tame these vile offenses," says Albany of Lear's ordeal, "It will come, / Humanity must perforce prey on itself, / Like monsters of the deep" (4.2.47–51). And Cornwall's servants (in a passage missing from the Folio text) have perceived earlier the dire implications of their masters' evil deeds. "I'll never care what wickedness I do, / If this man come to good," says one, and his fellow agrees: "If she [Regan] live long, / And in the end meet the old course of death, / Women will all turn monsters" (3.7.102–5). Yet these servants do, in fact, obey their own best instincts, turning on Cornwall and ministering to Gloucester despite danger to themselves. Similarly, Albany abandons his mild attempts to conciliate his domineering wife and instead uses his power for good. Cordelia's ability to forgive and cherish her father, and Edgar's comparable ministering to Gloucester, give the lie to Edmund's "natural" or amoral view of humanity; a few people, at least, are capable of charity, even when it does not serve their own material self-interest. Conversely, the play suggests that villainy will at last destroy itself, and not simply because the gods are just; Albany's hopeful insistence that "This shows you are above, / You justicers" (4.2.79–80) may be a little more than wishful thinking, to be undercut by some fresh disaster, but at least the insatiable ambitions of Edmund, Goneril, Regan, Cornwall, and Oswald do lead to their violent deaths. Edmund's belated attempt to save the life of Cordelia, though unsuccessful, suggests that this intelligent villain has at last begun to understand the great flaw in his naturalistic creed and to see that, like Goneril and Regan, he has been consumed by his own lust.

Even with such reassurances that villainy will eventually undo itself, the devastation at the end of *King Lear* is so appalling that our questions about justice remain finally unanswered. To ask the question "Who must pay for Lear's self-knowledge?" is to remind ourselves that women must often die in Shakespeare's tragedies so that men may learn, and to perceive even further that, in the absurdist world of *Lear,* the Cartesian logic of cause and effect and poetic justice simply will not account for all that we long to understand. As Roland Barthes well expresses the matter in an essay on Racine, "tragedy is only a means of reclaiming human unhappiness, of subsuming it, thus justifying it under the form of necessity, or wisdom, or purification." Tragedy cannot explain away the death of

Cordelia and the heartbreak of her father. The last tableau is a vision of doomsday, with Cordelia strangled, Lear broken and dying, and the "gored state" in such disarray that we cannot be sure what restoration can occur. The very question of political order is dwarfed by the enormity of the personal disaster of Lear and Cordelia. No one wishes longer life for the King: "He hates him / That would upon the rack of this tough world / Stretch him out longer." He is dead; "The wonder is he hath endured so long" (5.3.319–26). Lear's view of life's terrible corruption, pronounced in his madness, seems confirmed in his end. Perhaps the only way in which this tragedy can reclaim so much unhappiness is to suggest that, given the incurable badness of the world, we can at least choose whether to attempt to be like Cordelia and Edgar (knowing what the price may be for such courage) or to settle for being our worst selves, like Edmund, Goneril, and Regan. Overwhelmed as we are by the testimonial before us of humankind's vicious capacity for self-destruction, we are stirred nonetheless by the ability of some men and women to confront their fearful destiny with probity and stoic renunciation, adhering to what they believe to be good and expecting Fortune to give them absolutely nothing. The power of love, though learned too late to avert catastrophe, is at last discovered in its very defeat.

King Lear has become a fable for our times, onstage, in film and television, and in fictional adaptations in novel form. The role of Lear has been a compelling one for so many great Shakespearean actors, including Philip Kemble, Henry Irving, Edwin Forrest, John Gielgud, Donald Wolfit, Donald Sinden, Brian Cox, Michael Gambon, Robert Stephens, and John Wood. Peter Brook's film version of 1970, based on a stage production of 1962, with Paul Scofield as Lear, did much to equate the play's bleak vision with that of our modern existential world. Stimulated by Jan Kott's *Shakespeare Our Contemporary* (translated 1964), a post–World War II apocalyptic interpretation of Shakespeare from the perspective of an ideologically embattled eastern Europe, Brook unfolds a narrative of unrelieved disillusionment. The medium of film enables him to show what it would be like, for example, to have a hundred knights and all their followers descend on Albany's castle at the same time, demanding to be fed and quarreling with the servants of Goneril and Albany; the din and confusion are overwhelming, to such an extent that one can see Goneril's point in wanting to cut back on the King's retinue. A barren, wintry landscape adds visual reinforcement to the savage energies of family and dynastic conflict. Grigori Kozintsev's film of 1971, the work of a great Soviet director, sees the larger movements of the play in Marxist terms as the dialectical imperatives of political and social history; again, the medium of film makes it possible for Kozintsev to do what the stage can-

not do, deploy huge casts of anonymous soldiers and workers as both victims and movers of social change. Laurence Olivier's performance of Lear for Grenada Television (directed by Michael Elliott, 1983, Granada Video, 1984) came at the very end of Olivier's life, as his climactic and final role; his interpretation is deeply enhanced by one's perception that the actor is literally dying of cancer. Olivier, weakened but determined, had to be helped through the rigors of the screening, with the result that his Lear is tender, vulnerable, frail, though capable of the outbursts of rage that often come with advanced age. His *King Lear* is about the approach of death. Akira Kurosawa, in his epic *Ran* (1985), chose a more radical adaptation, that of telling a story of a Japanese warlord and his three sons, one of them (like Cordelia) dear but misunderstood, the others treacherous. One of their wives (the Lady Kaede) turns out to be another Edmund, Goneril, Regan, and Lady Macbeth all combined in one, fiercely and murderously determined that her husband succeed by whatever means possible. Kurosawa's vision of evil in the human heart is meant to be terrifying, and it is. The Royal National Theatre production of *King Lear* won several awards for Best Actor (Ian Holm as Lear) and Best Director (Richard Eyre), and is available on video from the BBC and Mobil Masterpiece Theatre (1998). In fiction, Jane Smiley's *A Thousand Acres* (1991) features a similar transposition, in this case to a midwestern American farm run by an aging farmer who transfers his land to his daughters and then sinks into alcoholism and insanity as two daughters squabble over their inheritance and end up losing everything, including their husbands, while their sister Caroline (Cordelia), unwilling to take part in the dividing of the farm, tries unsuccessfully as a lawyer to have the property restored to her father. Edward Bond's stage play called *Lear* (1971) accentuated *King Lear*'s already formidable bleakness by adding to its cruelty and violence; in it, war became a never-ending cycle of repression and escalating oppression. In these varied reworkings, we see the remarkable malleability of *King Lear* as an endlessly fascinating subject for new historicist, cultural materialist, deconstructive, and feminist readings that open up topics of misogyny and patriarchy, political ideologies, and philosophical pessimism.

King Lear exists in two early texts, the Quarto of 1608 and the considerably changed Folio version of 1623. Similar disparities appear in *Hamlet, Othello, Troilus and Cressida, Henry IV Part II*, and a number of other plays, but the problem is especially acute in *King Lear*. Shakespeare must have had a hand in the revisions that led to the Folio text. It contains new material. At the same time, the Quarto text contains passages not found in the Folio. The revisions may have resulted from a number of circumstances: cutting for performance (the play as it stands in either version is too long to have been produced in its entirety on the Jacobean stage), censorship, errors in transcription, and still more. The Folio version does alter some matters especially having to do with the French invasion; characters like Albany appear in a different light. The very ending is changed as to which characters speak the concluding lines.

Given these factors, many editions today present two or even three texts for the reader, or mark the text with brackets and other indicators of textual variation. This edition does not do so, though the textual notes do indicate the differences that occur. The reasons for choosing to present here the more traditional composite or eclectic text are these: *King Lear*'s textual variations between Quarto and Folio are more extensive than in some other plays, but are not always different in kind, so that it is a distortion to treat this play alone as a multiple-text play.

To choose either Quarto or Folio is to lose important material that is unquestionably Shakespeare's. To print two or even three versions is to add pages to an already weighty collection. And the presentation of multiple texts, or of a single text that is flagged with bracketed markers, also imposes on the reader a task of sorting out a complex and uncertain textual history that, however important ultimately in studying Shakespeare as a writer and as a reviser, is perhaps best left to subsequent investigation in a full-scale critical edition after one has absorbed the greatness of this play as a piece of writing for the theater. The present composite *King Lear*, based on the Folio text but including the 300 or so lines found only in the First Quarto along with some Quarto readings where the Folio version seems less textually reliable, is in a sense a compromise, but it is one that seems well suited to the purposes of this present edition.

King Lear

[*Dramatis Personae*

KING LEAR
GONERIL,
REGAN, } *Lear's daughters*
CORDELIA,
DUKE OF ALBANY, *Goneril's husband*
DUKE OF CORNWALL, *Regan's husband*
KING OF FRANCE, *Cordelia's suitor and husband*
DUKE OF BURGUNDY, *suitor to Cordelia*

EARL OF KENT, *later disguised as Caius*
EARL OF GLOUCESTER
EDGAR, *Gloucester's son and heir, later disguised as poor Tom*
EDMUND, *Gloucester's bastard son*

SCENE: *Britain*]

OSWALD, *Goneril's steward*
A KNIGHT *serving King Lear*
Lear's FOOL
CURAN, *in Gloucester's household*
GENTLEMEN
Three SERVANTS
OLD MAN, *a tenant of Gloucester*
Three MESSENGERS
A GENTLEMAN *attending Cordelia as a Doctor*
Two CAPTAINS
HERALD

Knights, Gentlemen, Attendants, Servants, Officers, Soldiers, Trumpeters

1.1

Enter Kent, Gloucester, and Edmund.

KENT   I thought the King had more affected the Duke of   1
Albany than Cornwall.   2

GLOUCESTER   It did always seem so to us; but now in
the division of the kingdom it appears not which of
the dukes he values most, for equalities are so weighed   5
that curiosity in neither can make choice of either's   6
moiety.   7

KENT   Is not this your son, my lord?

GLOUCESTER   His breeding, sir, hath been at my charge.   9
I have so often blushed to acknowledge him that now
I am brazed to't.   11

KENT   I cannot conceive you.   12

GLOUCESTER   Sir, this young fellow's mother could;
whereupon she grew round-wombed and had indeed,
sir, a son for her cradle ere she had a husband
for her bed. Do you smell a fault?   16

KENT   I cannot wish the fault undone, the issue of it   17
being so proper.   18

GLOUCESTER   But I have a son, sir, by order of law, some   19
year elder than this, who yet is no dearer in my ac-   20
count. Though this knave came something saucily to   21
the world before he was sent for, yet was his mother
fair, there was good sport at his making, and the
whoreson must be acknowledged.—Do you know this   24
noble gentleman, Edmund?

EDMUND   No, my lord.

GLOUCESTER   My lord of Kent. Remember him hereafter
as my honorable friend.

EDMUND   My services to Your Lordship.   29

KENT   I must love you, and sue to know you better.   30

EDMUND   Sir, I shall study deserving.   31

GLOUCESTER   He hath been out nine years, and away   32
he shall again. The King is coming.   33

*Sennet. Enter [one bearing a coronet, then] King
Lear, Cornwall, Albany, Goneril, Regan, Cordelia,
and attendants.*

LEAR
Attend the lords of France and Burgundy, Gloucester.   34

GLOUCESTER   I shall, my liege.   *Exit.*

1.1. Location: King Lear's palace.
1 affected favored   **2 Albany** i.e., Scotland   **5–7 equalities . . .
moiety** the shares balance so equally that close scrutiny cannot find
advantage in either's portion.   **9 breeding** raising, care.   **charge**
expense.   **11 brazed** hardened   **12 conceive** understand. (But
Gloucester puns in the sense of "become pregnant.")   **16 fault** (1) sin
(2) loss of scent by the hounds.   **17 issue** (1) result (2) offspring
18 proper (1) excellent (2) handsome.   **19 by order of law** legitimate
19–20 some year about a year   **20–1 account** estimation.   **21 knave**
young fellow. (Not said disapprovingly, though the word is ironic.)
something somewhat   **24 whoreson** low fellow; suggesting bastardy, but (like *knave* above) used with affectionate condescension
29 services duty   **30 sue** petition, beg   **31 study deserving** strive to
be worthy (of your esteem).   **32 out** i.e., abroad, absent   **33.1 Sennet**
trumpet signal heralding a procession.   *one . . . then* (This direction
is from the Quarto. The *coronet* is perhaps intended for Cordelia or
her betrothed. A coronet signifies nobility below the rank of king.)
34 Attend Wait upon, usher ceremoniously

LEAR
Meantime we shall express our darker purpose.   36
Give me the map there. [*He takes a map.*] Know that we
have divided
In three our kingdom; and 'tis our fast intent   38
To shake all cares and business from our age,
Conferring them on younger strengths while we
Unburdened crawl toward death. Our son of
Cornwall,
And you, our no less loving son of Albany,
We have this hour a constant will to publish   43
Our daughters' several dowers, that future strife   44
May be prevented now. The princes, France and
Burgundy,
Great rivals in our youngest daughter's love,
Long in our court have made their amorous sojourn
And here are to be answered. Tell me, my
daughters—
Since now we will divest us both of rule,
Interest of territory, cares of state—   50
Which of you shall we say doth love us most,
That we our largest bounty may extend
Where nature doth with merit challenge? Goneril,   53
Our eldest born, speak first.

GONERIL
Sir, I love you more than words can wield the matter,
Dearer than eyesight, space, and liberty,   56
Beyond what can be valued, rich or rare,
No less than life, with grace, health, beauty, honor;
As much as child e'er loved, or father found;   59
A love that makes breath poor and speech unable.   60
Beyond all manner of so much I love you.

CORDELIA [*aside*]
What shall Cordelia speak? Love and be silent.

LEAR [*indicating on map*]
Of all these bounds, even from this line to this,
With shadowy forests and with champains riched,   64
With plenteous rivers and wide-skirted meads,   65
We make thee lady. To thine and Albany's issue
Be this perpetual.—What says our second daughter,
Our dearest Regan, wife of Cornwall? Speak.

REGAN
I am made of that self mettle as my sister,   69
And prize me at her worth. In my true heart   70
I find she names my very deed of love;   71
Only she comes too short, that I profess   72
Myself an enemy to all other joys
Which the most precious square of sense possesses,   74

---

36 we, our (The royal plural; also in lines 37–44, etc.)   **darker purpose** undeclared intention.   **38 fast** firm   **43 constant . . . publish**
firm resolve to proclaim   **44 several** individual   **50 Interest of** right
or title to, possession of   **53 Where . . . challenge** where both natural
affection and merit claim our bounty as its due.   **56 space, and liberty** possession of land, and freedom of action   **59 found** i.e., found
himself to be loved   **60 breath . . . unable** utterance impoverished
and speech inadequate.   **64 shadowy** shady.   **champains riched** fertile plains   **65 plenteous . . . meads** abundant rivers bordered with
wide meadows   **69 that self mettle** that same spirited temperament
70 prize . . . worth value myself as her equal (in love for you). (*Prize*
suggests "price.")   **71 names . . . love** describes my love in action
72 that in that   **74 Which . . . possesses** which the most delicately
sensitive part of my nature can enjoy

And find I am alone felicitate   75
In your dear Highness' love.
CORDELIA [aside]   Then poor Cordelia!
And yet not so, since I am sure my love's
More ponderous than my tongue.   78
LEAR
To thee and thine hereditary ever
Remain this ample third of our fair kingdom,
No less in space, validity, and pleasure   81
Than that conferred on Goneril.—Now, our joy,
Although our last and least, to whose young love   83
The vines of France and milk of Burgundy   84
Strive to be interested, what can you say to draw   85
A third more opulent than your sisters'? Speak.
CORDELIA   Nothing, my lord.
LEAR   Nothing?
CORDELIA   Nothing.
LEAR
Nothing will come of nothing. Speak again.
CORDELIA
Unhappy that I am, I cannot heave
My heart into my mouth. I love Your Majesty
According to my bond, no more nor less.   93
LEAR
How, how, Cordelia? Mend your speech a little,
Lest you may mar your fortunes.
CORDELIA   Good my lord,
You have begot me, bred me, loved me. I
Return those duties back as are right fit,   97
Obey you, love you, and most honor you.
Why have my sisters husbands if they say
They love you all? Haply, when I shall wed,   100
That lord whose hand must take my plight shall carry 101
Half my love with him, half my care and duty.
Sure I shall never marry like my sisters,
To love my father all.
LEAR
But goes thy heart with this?
CORDELIA   Ay, my good lord.
LEAR   So young, and so untender?
CORDELIA   So young, my lord, and true.
LEAR
Let it be so! Thy truth then be thy dower!
For, by the sacred radiance of the sun,
The mysteries of Hecate and the night,   110
By all the operation of the orbs   111
From whom we do exist and cease to be,   112
Here I disclaim all my paternal care,
Propinquity, and property of blood,   114
And as a stranger to my heart and me

Hold thee from this forever. The barbarous Scythian,   116
Or he that makes his generation messes   117
To gorge his appetite, shall to my bosom
Be as well neighbored, pitied, and relieved   119
As thou my sometime daughter.
KENT   Good my liege—   120
LEAR   Peace, Kent!
Come not between the dragon and his wrath.
I loved her most, and thought to set my rest   123
On her kind nursery. [To Cordelia] Hence, and avoid
    my sight!—   124
So be my grave my peace, as here I give   125
Her father's heart from her. Call France. Who stirs?   126
Call Burgundy.   [Exit one.]
                Cornwall and Albany,
With my two daughters' dowers digest the third.   128
Let pride, which she calls plainness, marry her.   129
I do invest you jointly with my power,
Preeminence, and all the large effects   131
That troop with majesty. Ourself by monthly course,   132
With reservation of an hundred knights   133
By you to be sustained, shall our abode
Make with you by due turns. Only we shall retain
The name and all th'addition to a king.   136
The sway, revenue, execution of the rest,   137
Belovèd sons, be yours, which to confirm,
This coronet part between you.
KENT   Royal Lear,   139
Whom I have ever honored as my king,
Loved as my father, as my master followed,
As my great patron thought on in my prayers—
LEAR
The bow is bent and drawn. Make from the shaft.   143
KENT
Let it fall rather, though the fork invade   144
The region of my heart. Be Kent unmannerly
When Lear is mad. What wouldst thou do, old man?
Think'st thou that duty shall have dread to speak
When power to flattery bows?
To plainness honor's bound   149
When majesty falls to folly. Reserve thy state,   150
And in thy best consideration check   151
This hideous rashness. Answer my life my judgment,   152

116 this this time forth. **Scythian** (Scythians were famous in antiquity for savagery.) **117 makes . . . messes** makes meals of his children or parents **119 neighbored** helped in a neighborly way
120 sometime former **123 set my rest** rely wholly. (A phrase from a
game of cards, meaning "to stake all.") **124 nursery** nursing, care.
avoid get out of **125 So . . . peace, as** As I hope to rest peacefully in
my grave **126 Who stirs?** i.e., Jump to it; don't just stand there.
128 digest assimilate, incorporate **129 Let . . . her** Let pride, which
she calls plain speaking, be her dowry and get her a husband.
131 effects outward shows **132 troop with** accompany, serve.
Ourself (The royal "we.") **133 With reservation of** reserving to
myself the right to be attended by **136 th'addition** the honors and
prerogatives **137 sway** sovereign authority **139 coronet** (Perhaps
Lear gestures toward this coronet that was to have symbolized
Cordelia's dowry and marriage, hands it to his sons-in-law, or actually attempts to divide it.) **143 Make from** Get out of the way of
144 fall strike. **fork** barbed head of an arrow **149 To . . . bound**
Loyalty demands frankness **150 Reserve thy state** Retain your royal
authority **151 And . . . check** and with wise deliberation restrain
152 Answer . . . judgment I wager my life on my judgment that

75 felicitate made happy **78 ponderous** weighty **81 validity** value.
pleasure pleasing features **83 least** youngest **84 vines** vineyards.
milk pastures (?) **85 be interested** be affiliated, establish a claim, be
admitted as to a privilege. **draw** win **93 bond** filial obligation
97 right fit proper and fitting **100 all** exclusively, and with all of
themselves. **Haply** Perhaps, with luck **101 plight** pledge in marriage **110 mysteries** secret rites. **Hecate** goddess of witchcraft and
the moon **111 operation** influence. **orbs** planets and stars
112 From whom under whose influence **114 Propinquity . . . blood**
close kinship, and rights and duties entailed in blood ties

Thy youngest daughter does not love thee least,
Nor are those emptyhearted whose low sounds
Reverb no hollowness.

LEAR   Kent, on thy life, no more.   155

KENT
My life I never held but as a pawn   156
To wage against thine enemies, nor fear to lose it,   157
Thy safety being motive.

LEAR   Out of my sight!   158

KENT
See better, Lear, and let me still remain
The true blank of thine eye.   160

LEAR   Now, by Apollo—

KENT   Now, by Apollo, King,
Thou swear'st thy gods in vain.

LEAR   Oh, vassal! Miscreant!   164

              [*Laying his hand on his sword.*]

ALBANY, CORNWALL   Dear sir, forbear.

KENT
Kill thy physician, and the fee bestow
Upon the foul disease. Revoke thy gift,
Or whilst I can vent clamor from my throat
I'll tell thee thou dost evil.

LEAR
Hear me, recreant, on thine allegiance hear me!   170
That thou hast sought to make us break our vows,   171
Which we durst never yet, and with strained pride   172
To come betwixt our sentence and our power,   173
Which nor our nature nor our place can bear,   174
Our potency made good, take thy reward.   175
Five days we do allot thee for provision
To shield thee from disasters of the world,
And on the sixth to turn thy hated back
Upon our kingdom. If on the tenth day following
Thy banished trunk be found in our dominions,   180
The moment is thy death. Away! By Jupiter,
This shall not be revoked.

KENT
Fare thee well, King. Sith thus thou wilt appear,   183
Freedom lives hence and banishment is here.
[*To Cordelia*] The gods to their dear shelter take thee,
    maid,
That justly think'st and hast most rightly said!
[*To Regan and Goneril*] And your large speeches may
    your deeds approve,   187
That good effects may spring from words of love.
Thus Kent, O princes, bids you all adieu.

He'll shape his old course in a country new.   *Exit.* 190

*Flourish. Enter Gloucester, with France and
Burgundy; attendants.*

GLOUCESTER
Here's France and Burgundy, my noble lord.

LEAR   My lord of Burgundy,
We first address toward you, who with this king   193
Hath rivaled for our daughter. What in the least   194
Will you require in present dower with her
Or cease your quest of love?

BURGUNDY   Most royal Majesty,
I crave no more than hath Your Highness offered,
Nor will you tender less.

LEAR   Right noble Burgundy,   198
When she was dear to us we did hold her so,   199
But now her price is fallen. Sir, there she stands.
If aught within that little-seeming substance,   201
Or all of it, with our displeasure pieced,   202
And nothing more, may fitly like Your Grace,   203
She's there, and she is yours.

BURGUNDY   I know no answer.

LEAR
Will you, with those infirmities she owes,   205
Unfriended, new-adopted to our hate,
Dowered with our curse and strangered with our
    oath,   207
Take her, or leave her?

BURGUNDY   Pardon me, royal sir.
Election makes not up in such conditions.   209

LEAR
Then leave her, sir, for by the power that made me,
I tell you all her wealth. [*To France*] For you, great King, 211
I would not from your love make such a stray   212
To match you where I hate; therefore beseech you   213
T'avert your liking a more worthier way   214
Than on a wretch whom Nature is ashamed
Almost t'acknowledge hers.

FRANCE   This is most strange,
That she whom even but now was your best object,
The argument of your praise, balm of your age,   218
The best, the dearest, should in this trice of time   219
Commit a thing so monstrous to dismantle   220
So many folds of favor. Sure her offense
Must be of such unnatural degree
That monsters it, or your forevouched affection   223
Fall into taint, which to believe of her

---

155 Reverb no hollowness do not reverberate like a hollow drum,
insincerely.   **156–7 My . . . wage** I never regarded my life other than
as a pledge to hazard in warfare   **158 motive** that which prompts me
to act.   **160 The true . . . eye** i.e., the means to enable you to see better. (*Blank* means "the white center of the target," or, "the true direct
aim," as in "point-blank," traveling in a straight line.)   **164 vassal**
i.e., wretch.   **Miscreant** (Literally, infidel, heretic; hence, villain, rascal.)   **170 recreant** traitor   **171 That** In that, since   **172 strained**
excessive   **173 To . . . power** i.e., to block my power to command and
judge   **174 Which . . . place** which neither my temperament nor my
office as king   **175 Our . . . good** my power enacted, demonstrated
180 trunk body   **183 Sith** Since   **187 your . . . approve** may your
deeds confirm your speeches with their vast claims

190 shape . . . course follow his traditional plainspoken ways.
190.1 *Flourish* trumpet fanfare used for the entrance or exit of important persons   **193 address** address myself   **194 rivaled** competed.
in the least at the lowest   **198 tender** offer   **199 so** i.e., *dear*, beloved
and valued at a high price   **201 little-seeming substance** one who
seems substantial but whose substance is, in fact, little, or, one who
refuses to flatter   **202 pieced** added, joined   **203 like** please
205 owes owns   **207 strangered** disowned   **209 Election . . . conditions** No choice is possible under such conditions.   **211 tell you**
(1) inform you of (2) enumerate for you.   **For** As for   **212 make such
a stray** stray so far   **213 To** as to.   **beseech** I beseech   **214 T'avert**
your liking to turn your affections   **218 argument** theme   **219 trice**
moment   **220 to** as to   **223 monsters it** makes it monstrous
223–4 or . . . taint or else the affection for her you have hitherto
affirmed must fall into suspicion

Must be a faith that reason without miracle
Should never plant in me.

CORDELIA   I yet beseech Your Majesty—
If for I want that glib and oily art   228
To speak and purpose not, since what I well intend   229
I'll do't before I speak—that you make known
It is no vicious blot, murder, or foulness,   231
No unchaste action or dishonored step
That hath deprived me of your grace and favor,
But even for want of that for which I am richer: 234
A still-soliciting eye and such a tongue   235
That I am glad I have not, though not to have it
Hath lost me in your liking.

LEAR   Better thou
Hadst not been born than not t'have pleased me better.

FRANCE
Is it but this? A tardiness in nature
Which often leaves the history unspoke   240
That it intends to do?—My lord of Burgundy,
What say you to the lady? Love's not love
When it is mingled with regards that stands   243
Aloof from th'entire point. Will you have her?   244
She is herself a dowry.

BURGUNDY [to Lear]   Royal King,
Give but that portion which yourself proposed,
And here I take Cordelia by the hand,
Duchess of Burgundy.

LEAR
Nothing. I have sworn. I am firm.

BURGUNDY [to Cordelia]
I am sorry, then, you have so lost a father
That you must lose a husband.

CORDELIA   Peace be with Burgundy!
Since that respects of fortune are his love,   252
I shall not be his wife.

FRANCE
Fairest Cordelia, that art most rich being poor,
Most choice, forsaken, and most loved, despised,
Thee and thy virtues here I seize upon,
Be it lawful I take up what's cast away.   257
                        [He takes her hand.]
Gods, gods! 'Tis strange that from their cold'st neglect   258
My love should kindle to inflamed respect.—   259
Thy dowerless daughter, King, thrown to my chance,   260
Is queen of us, of ours, and our fair France.
Not all the dukes of wat'rish Burgundy   262
Can buy this unprized precious maid of me.—   263
Bid them farewell, Cordelia, though unkind.   264
Thou losest here, a better where to find.   265

LEAR
Thou hast her, France. Let her be thine, for we
Have no such daughter, nor shall ever see
That face of hers again. Therefore begone
Without our grace, our love, our benison.   269
Come, noble Burgundy.
        Flourish. Exeunt [all but France, Goneril, Regan,
                                        and Cordelia].

FRANCE   Bid farewell to your sisters.

CORDELIA
Ye jewels of our father, with washed eyes   272
Cordelia leaves you. I know you what you are,
And like a sister am most loath to call   274
Your faults as they are named. Love well our father.   275
To your professèd bosoms I commit him.   276
But yet, alas, stood I within his grace,
I would prefer him to a better place.   278
So, farewell to you both.

REGAN
Prescribe not us our duty.

GONERIL   Let your study
Be to content your lord, who hath received you
At Fortune's alms. You have obedience scanted,   282
And well are worth the want that you have wanted.   283

CORDELIA
Time shall unfold what plighted cunning hides;   284
Who covers faults, at last shame them derides.   285
Well may you prosper!

FRANCE   Come, my fair Cordelia.
                Exeunt France and Cordelia.

GONERIL   Sister, it is not little I have to say of what most
nearly appertains to us both. I think our father will
hence tonight.

REGAN   That's most certain, and with you; next month
with us.

GONERIL   You see how full of changes his age is; the
observation we have made of it hath not been little.
He always loved our sister most, and with what poor
judgment he hath now cast her off appears too grossly.   295

REGAN   'Tis the infirmity of his age. Yet he hath ever
but slenderly known himself.

GONERIL   The best and soundest of his time hath been   298
but rash. Then must we look from his age to receive   299
not alone the imperfections of long-ingraffed condi-   300
tion, but therewithal the unruly waywardness that in-   301
firm and choleric years bring with them.

REGAN   Such unconstant starts are we like to have from   303
him as this of Kent's banishment.

228 for I want because I lack   229 purpose not not intend to do what
I say   231 foulness immorality   234 for which for lack of which
235 still-soliciting ever begging   240 history tale, narrative
243–4 regards . . . point irrelevant considerations.   252 Since . . . fortune Since concern for wealth and position   257 Be it lawful if it be
lawful that   258 from . . . neglect out of the cold neglect of the gods
259 inflamed respect ardent regard.   260 chance lot   262 wat'rish
(1) well-watered with rivers (2) feeble, watery   263 unprized not
appreciated. (With perhaps a sense also of "priceless.")   264 though
unkind though they have behaved unnaturally.   265 here this place.
where place elsewhere

269 benison blessing.   272 washed tear-washed   274 like a sister i.e.,
because I am your sister   275 as . . . named by their true names.
276 professèd bosoms publicly avowed love   278 prefer advance,
recommend   282 At . . . alms as a pittance or dole from Fortune.
283 And well . . . wanted i.e., and well deserve to be without the
dowry and the parental affection that you have both lacked and
flouted.   284–5 Time . . . derides Time will bring to light what cunning attempts to conceal as if in the folds of a cloak; those who hide
their faults may do so for a while, but in time they will be shamed and
derided.   295 grossly obviously.   298–9 The best . . . rash Even in the
prime of his life, he was stormy and unpredictable.   300–1 long-
ingraffed condition long-implanted habit   301 therewithal added
thereto   303 unconstant starts impulsive outbursts.   like likely

GONERIL   There is further compliment of leave-taking 305
between France and him. Pray you, let us hit together. 306
If our father carry authority with such disposition as 307
he bears, this last surrender of his will but offend us. 308
REGAN   We shall further think of it.
GONERIL   We must do something, and i'th' heat.   310

Exeunt.

❖

1.2

Enter Bastard [Edmund, with a letter].

EDMUND
Thou, Nature, art my goddess; to thy law   1
My services are bound. Wherefore should I
Stand in the plague of custom and permit   3
The curiosity of nations to deprive me,   4
For that I am some twelve or fourteen moonshines   5
Lag of a brother? Why bastard? Wherefore base?   6
When my dimensions are as well compact,   7
My mind as generous, and my shape as true,   8
As honest madam's issue? Why brand they us   9
With base? With baseness? Bastardy? Base, base?
Who in the lusty stealth of nature take   11
More composition and fierce quality   12
Than doth within a dull, stale, tirèd bed
Go to th' creating a whole tribe of fops   14
Got 'tween asleep and wake? Well, then,   15
Legitimate Edgar, I must have your land.
Our father's love is to the bastard Edmund
As to th' legitimate. Fine word, "legitimate"!
Well, my legitimate, if this letter speed   19
And my invention thrive, Edmund the base   20
Shall top th' legitimate. I grow, I prosper.
Now, gods, stand up for bastards!

Enter Gloucester.

GLOUCESTER
Kent banished thus? And France in choler parted?
And the King gone tonight? Prescribed his power,   24
Confined to exhibition? All this done   25
Upon the gad? Edmund, how now? What news?   26
EDMUND   So please Your Lordship, none.
[*Putting up the letter.*]

GLOUCESTER   Why so earnestly seek you to put up that
letter?
EDMUND   I know no news, my lord.
GLOUCESTER   What paper were you reading?
EDMUND   Nothing, my lord.
GLOUCESTER   No? What needed then that terrible dis- 33
patch of it into your pocket? The quality of nothing 34
hath not such need to hide itself. Let's see. Come, if it
be nothing I shall not need spectacles.
EDMUND   I beseech you, sir, pardon me. It is a letter
from my brother, that I have not all o'erread; and for 38
so much as I have perused, I find it not fit for your
o'erlooking.   40
GLOUCESTER   Give me the letter, sir.
EDMUND   I shall offend either to detain or give it. The
contents, as in part I understand them, are to blame. 43
GLOUCESTER   Let's see, let's see.
[*Edmund gives the letter.*]
EDMUND   I hope for my brother's justification he wrote
this but as an essay or taste of my virtue.   46
GLOUCESTER (*reads*)   "This policy and reverence of age 47
makes the world bitter to the best of our times, keeps 48
our fortunes from us till our oldness cannot relish
them. I begin to find an idle and fond bondage in the 50
oppression of aged tyranny, who sways not as it hath 51
power but as it is suffered. Come to me, that of this I 52
may speak more. If our father would sleep till I waked
him, you should enjoy half his revenue forever and live
the beloved of your brother,   Edgar."
Hum! Conspiracy! "Sleep till I waked him, you should
enjoy half his revenue." My son Edgar! Had he
a hand to write this? A heart and brain to breed it
in? When came you to this? Who brought it?   59
EDMUND   It was not brought me, my lord; there's the
cunning of it. I found it thrown in at the casement of 61
my closet.   62
GLOUCESTER   You know the character to be your   63
brother's?
EDMUND   If the matter were good, my lord, I durst   65
swear it were his; but in respect of that I would fain 66
think it were not.
GLOUCESTER   It is his.
EDMUND   It is his hand, my lord, but I hope his heart is
not in the contents.
GLOUCESTER   Has he never before sounded you in this
business?
EDMUND   Never, my lord. But I have heard him oft
maintain it to be fit that, sons at perfect age and fathers 74
declined, the father should be as ward to the son, and 75
the son manage his revenue.

---

305 compliment ceremony   **306 hit** agree   **307–8 If . . . offend us** If
our father continues to boss us around with his accustomed imperi-
ousness, this most recent display of willfulness will do us nothing but
harm.   **310 i'th' heat** i.e., while the iron is hot.
1.2. Location: The Earl of Gloucester's house.
1 Nature i.e., the sanction that governs the material world through
mechanistic amoral forces   **3 Stand . . . custom** submit to the vexatious injustice of convention   **4 The curiosity of nations** arbitrary
social gradations   **5 For that** because.   **moonshines** months
6 Lag of lagging behind   **7 dimensions** proportions.   **compact** knit
together, fitted   **8 generous** noble, refined   **9 honest** chaste
11–12 Who . . . quality Whose begetting in the sexual act both
requires and engenders a fuller mixture and more energetic force
14 fops fools   **15 Got** begotten   **19 speed** succeed, prosper
20 invention thrive scheme prosper   **24 tonight** last night.
Prescribed Limited   **25 exhibition** an allowance, pension.
26 Upon the gad suddenly, as if pricked by a gad or spur.

33–4 terrible dispatch fearful quick disposal   **38 for** as for   **40 o'erlooking** perusal.   **43 to blame** (The Folio reading, "too blame," "too
blameworthy to be shown," may be correct.)   **46 essay or taste** assay,
test   **47 policy and reverence of** policy of reverencing   **48 the best . . .
times** the best years of our lives, i.e., our youth   **50 idle and fond**
useless and foolish   **51 who sways** which rules   **52 suffered** permitted.   **59 to this** upon this (letter).   **61 casement** window   **62 closet**
private room.   **63 character** handwriting   **65 matter** contents   **66 in
. . . that** considering what the contents are.   **fain** gladly   **74 fit** fitting, appropriate.   **perfect age** full maturity   **75 declined** having
become feeble

GLOUCESTER   Oh, villain, villain! His very opinion in the 77
letter! Abhorred villain! Unnatural, detested, brutish 78
villain! Worse than brutish! Go, sirrah, seek him. I'll 79
apprehend him. Abominable villain! Where is he?

EDMUND   I do not well know, my lord. If it shall please
you to suspend your indignation against my brother
till you can derive from him better testimony of his
intent, you should run a certain course; where, if you 84
violently proceed against him, mistaking his purpose,
it would make a great gap in your own honor and
shake in pieces the heart of his obedience. I dare pawn 87
down my life for him that he hath writ this to feel my 88
affection to Your Honor, and to no other pretense of 89
danger. 90

GLOUCESTER   Think you so?

EDMUND   If Your Honor judge it meet, I will place you 92
where you shall hear us confer of this, and by an 93
auricular assurance have your satisfaction, and that 94
without any further delay than this very evening.

GLOUCESTER   He cannot be such a monster—

EDMUND   Nor is not, sure.

GLOUCESTER   To his father, that so tenderly and entirely loves him. Heaven and earth! Edmund, seek
him out; wind me into him, I pray you. Frame the 100
business after your own wisdom. I would unstate 101
myself to be in a due resolution. 102

EDMUND   I will seek him, sir, presently, convey the 103
business as I shall find means, and acquaint you
withal. 105

GLOUCESTER   These late eclipses in the sun and moon 106
portend no good to us. Though the wisdom of nature 107
can reason it thus and thus, yet nature finds itself
scourged by the sequent effects. Love cools, friend- 109
ship falls off, brothers divide; in cities, mutinies; in
countries, discord; in palaces, treason; and the bond
cracked twixt son and father. This villain of mine
comes under the prediction; there's son against father.
The King falls from bias of nature; there's father 114
against child. We have seen the best of our time.
Machinations, hollowness, treachery, and all ruinous
disorders follow us disquietly to our graves. Find out
this villain, Edmund; it shall lose thee nothing. Do it 118
carefully. And the noble and truehearted Kent banished! His offense, honesty! 'Tis strange.   *Exit.*

EDMUND   This is the excellent foppery of the world, that 121
when we are sick in fortune—often the surfeits of our 122
own behavior—we make guilty of our disasters the 123
sun, the moon, and stars, as if we were villains on 124
necessity, fools by heavenly compulsion, knaves,
thieves, and treachers by spherical predominance, 126
drunkards, liars, and adulterers by an enforced obedience of planetary influence, and all that we are evil
in, by a divine thrusting on. An admirable evasion of 129
whoremaster man, to lay his goatish disposition on 130
the charge of a star! My father compounded with my 131
mother under the Dragon's tail and my nativity was 132
under Ursa Major, so that it follows I am rough and 133
lecherous. Fut, I should have been that I am, had the 134
maidenliest star in the firmament twinkled on my
bastardizing. Edgar—

Enter Edgar.

and pat he comes like the catastrophe of the old 137
comedy. My cue is villainous melancholy, with a sigh
like Tom o' Bedlam.—Oh, these eclipses do portend 139
these divisions! Fa, sol, la, mi. 140

EDGAR   How now, brother Edmund, what serious
contemplation are you in?

EDMUND   I am thinking, brother, of a prediction I read
this other day, what should follow these eclipses. 144

EDGAR   Do you busy yourself with that?

EDMUND   I promise you, the effects he writes of succeed 146
unhappily, as of unnaturalness between the child and 147
the parent, death, dearth, dissolutions of ancient amities, divisions in state, menaces and maledictions
against king and nobles, needless diffidences, banish- 150
ment of friends, dissipation of cohorts, nuptial 151
breaches, and I know not what.

EDGAR   How long have you been a sectary astronom- 153
ical? 154

EDMUND   Come, come, when saw you my father last?

EDGAR   The night gone by.

EDMUND   Spake you with him?

EDGAR   Ay, two hours together.

EDMUND   Parted you in good terms? Found you no
displeasure in him by word nor countenance? 160

EDGAR   None at all.

---

77 villain vile wretch, diabolical schemer   **78 Abhorred** Abhorrent.
detested hated and hateful   **79 sirrah** (Form of address used to inferiors or children.)   **84 run a certain course** proceed with safety and
certainty.   **where** whereas   **87–8 pawn down** stake   **88 feel** feel out
89–90 pretense of danger dangerous purpose.   **92 meet** fitting,
proper   **93–4 by an . . . satisfaction** satisfy yourself as to the truth by
what you hear   **100 wind me into him** insinuate yourself into his
confidence. (*Me* is used colloquially.)   **Frame** Arrange   **101 after
your own wisdom** as you think best.   **101–2 I would . . . resolution** I
would give up my wealth and rank to know the truth, have my
doubts resolved.   **103 presently** immediately.   **convey** manage
105 withal therewith.   **106 late** recent   **107 the wisdom of nature**
natural science   **109 sequent effects** i.e., devastating consequences.
114 bias of nature natural inclination   **118 lose thee nothing** i.e.,
earn you a reward.   **121 foppery** foolishness

122–3 surfeits . . . behavior consequences of our own overindulgence
124 on by   **126 treachers** traitors.   **spherical predominance** astrological determinism, because a certain planet was ascendant at the
hour of our birth   **129 divine** supernatural   **130 goatish** lecherous
130–1 on the charge to the responsibility   **131–2 compounded . . .
Dragon's tail** had sex with my mother under the constellation Draco
(not one of the regular signs of the zodiac), or under the descending
point at which the moon's orbit intersects with the ecliptic or apparent orbit of the sun (when an eclipse might occur)   **133 Ursa Major**
the big bear or dipper—not one of the regular signs of the zodiac
134 Fut i.e., 'Sfoot, by Christ's foot.   **that** what   **137 pat** on cue.
catastrophe conclusion, resolution (of a play)   **139 Tom o' Bedlam** a
lunatic patient of Bethlehem Hospital in London turned out to beg for
his bread.   **140 divisions** social and family conflicts. (But with a
musical sense also of florid variations on a theme, thus prompting
Edmund's singing.)   **144 this other day** the other day   **146 promise**
assure   **146–7 succeed unhappily** follow unluckily   **150 needless
diffidences** groundless distrust of others   **151 dissipation of cohorts**
breaking up of military companies, large-scale desertions   **153–4 sectary astronomical** believer in astrology.   **160 countenance** demeanor.

EDMUND   Bethink yourself wherein you may have offended him, and at my entreaty forbear his presence 163
until some little time hath qualified the heat of his 164
displeasure, which at this instant so rageth in him that
with the mischief of your person it would scarcely 166
allay. 167

EDGAR   Some villain hath done me wrong.

EDMUND   That's my fear. I pray you, have a continent 169
forbearance till the speed of his rage goes slower; and, 170
as I say, retire with me to my lodging, from whence I
will fitly bring you to hear my lord speak. Pray ye, go! 172
There's my key. [*He gives a key.*] If you do stir abroad,
go armed.

EDGAR   Armed, brother?

EDMUND   Brother, I advise you to the best. I am no honest man if there be any good meaning toward you. I 177
have told you what I have seen and heard, but faintly, 178
nothing like the image and horror of it. Pray you, 179
away.

EDGAR   Shall I hear from you anon?

EDMUND
I do serve you in this business.   *Exit* [*Edgar*].
A credulous father and a brother noble,
Whose nature is so far from doing harms
That he suspects none; on whose foolish honesty
My practices ride easy. I see the business. 186
Let me, if not by birth, have lands by wit. 187
All with me's meet that I can fashion fit.   *Exit.* 188

❖

1.3

Enter Goneril, and [*Oswald, her*] *steward.*

GONERIL   Did my father strike my gentleman for chiding of his fool?

OSWALD   Ay, madam.

GONERIL   By day and night he wrongs me! Every hour
He flashes into one gross crime or other 5
That sets us all at odds. I'll not endure it.
His knights grow riotous, and himself upbraids us
On every trifle. When he returns from hunting
I will not speak with him. Say I am sick.
If you come slack of former services 10
You shall do well; the fault of it I'll answer. 11
                    [*Horns within.*]

OSWALD   He's coming, madam. I hear him.

GONERIL
Put on what weary negligence you please,
You and your fellows. I'd have it come to question. 14
If he distaste it, let him to my sister, 15

Whose mind and mine, I know, in that are one,
Not to be overruled. Idle old man, 17
That still would manage those authorities 18
That he hath given away! Now, by my life,
Old fools are babes again, and must be used
With checks as flatteries, when they are seen abused. 21
Remember what I have said.

OSWALD   Well, madam.

GONERIL
And let his knights have colder looks among you.
What grows of it, no matter. Advise your fellows so.
I would breed from hence occasions, and I shall, 26
That I may speak. I'll write straight to my sister 27
To hold my very course. Prepare for dinner.   *Exeunt.*

❖

1.4

Enter Kent [*disguised*].

KENT
If but as well I other accents borrow 1
That can my speech diffuse, my good intent 2
May carry through itself to that full issue 3
For which I razed my likeness. Now, banished Kent, 4
If thou canst serve where thou dost stand condemned,
So may it come thy master, whom thou lov'st, 6
Shall find thee full of labors.

Horns within. Enter Lear, [*Knights,*] *and
attendants.*

LEAR   Let me not stay a jot for dinner. Go get it ready. 8
                    [*Exit an Attendant.*]
[*To Kent*] How now, what art thou?

KENT   A man, sir.

LEAR   What dost thou profess? What wouldst thou with 11
us?

KENT   I do profess to be no less than I seem: to serve
him truly that will put me in trust, to love him that is
honest, to converse with him that is wise and says 15
little, to fear judgment, to fight when I cannot choose, 16
and to eat no fish. 17

LEAR   What art thou?

KENT   A very honest-hearted fellow, and as poor as the
King.

17 Idle Foolish   **18 manage those authorities** exercise those prerogatives   **21 With . . . abused** with rebukes in place of flattering attentiveness, when such flattery is seen to be taken advantage of.
26 occasions opportunities for taking offense   **27 speak** speak
bluntly.   **straight** immediately
**1.4. Location: The Duke of Albany's palace still. The sense of time
is virtually continuous.**
1 as well i.e., as well as I have disguised myself by means of costume
2 diffuse render confused or indistinct   **3–4 May . . . likeness** may
achieve the desired result for which I scraped off my beard and
erased my outward appearance.   **6 come** come to pass that   **8 stay**
wait   **8.1 Attendant** (This attendant may be a knight; certainly the
one who speaks at line 50 is a knight.)   **11 What . . . profess?** What is
your special calling? (But Kent puns in his answer on *profess* meaning
to "claim.")   **15 honest** honorable.   **converse** associate   **16 judgment** i.e., God's judgment.   **choose** i.e., choose but to fight   **17 eat
no fish** i.e., eat a manly diet (?), be a good Protestant (?).

163 forbear his presence avoid meeting him   **164 qualified** moderated   **166 with . . . person** with the harmful effect of your presence;
or, even if there were injury done to you   **167 allay** be allayed.
169–70 have . . . forbearance keep a wary distance   **172 fitly** at a fit
time.   **my lord** our father   **177 meaning** intention   **178 but faintly**
only with a faint impression   **179 image and horror** horrid reality
186 practices plots.   **the business** i.e., how my plots should proceed.
187 wit cleverness.   **188 meet** justifiable.   **fit** to my purpose.
1.3. Location: The Duke of Albany's palace.
5 crime offense   **10 come slack** fall short   **11 answer** be answerable
for.   **14 come to question** be made an issue.   **15 distaste** dislike

LEAR   If thou be'st as poor for a subject as he's for a
king, thou'rt poor enough. What wouldst thou?

KENT   Service.

LEAR   Who wouldst thou serve?

KENT   You.

LEAR   Dost thou know me, fellow?

KENT   No, sir, but you have that in your countenance   27
which I would fain call master.

LEAR   What's that?

KENT   Authority.

LEAR   What services canst do?

KENT   I can keep honest counsel, ride, run, mar a curi-   32
ous tale in telling it, and deliver a plain message   33
bluntly. That which ordinary men are fit for I am
qualified in, and the best of me is diligence.

LEAR   How old art thou?

KENT   Not so young, sir, to love a woman for singing,   37
nor so old to dote on her for anything. I have years on
my back forty-eight.

LEAR   Follow me; thou shalt serve me. If I like thee no
worse after dinner, I will not part from thee yet.—
Dinner, ho, dinner! Where's my knave, my fool? Go
you and call my fool hither.   [Exit one.]

Enter steward [Oswald].

You! You, sirrah, where's my daughter?

OSWALD   So please you—   *Exit.*

LEAR   What says the fellow there? Call the clodpoll back.   46
[Exit a knight.]
Where's my fool, ho? I think the world's asleep.

[Enter Knight.]

How now? Where's that mongrel?

KNIGHT   He says, my lord, your daughter is not well.

LEAR   Why came not the slave back to me when I called
him?

KNIGHT   Sir, he answered me in the roundest manner,   53
he would not.

LEAR   He would not?

KNIGHT   My lord, I know not what the matter is, but to
my judgment Your Highness is not entertained with   57
that ceremonious affection as you were wont. There's
a great abatement of kindness appears as well in the
general dependents as in the Duke himself also and   60
your daughter.

LEAR   Ha? Say'st thou so?

KNIGHT   I beseech you, pardon me, my lord, if I be
mistaken, for my duty cannot be silent when I think
Your Highness wronged.

LEAR   Thou but rememberest me of mine own concep-   66
tion. I have perceived a most faint neglect of late,   67
which I have rather blamed as mine own jealous   68

curiosity than as a very pretense and purpose of   69
unkindness. I will look further into't. But where's my
fool? I have not seen him this two days.   71

KNIGHT   Since my young lady's going into France, sir,
the Fool hath much pined away.

LEAR   No more of that. I have noted it well. Go you and
tell my daughter I would speak with her. [Exit one.]
Go you call hither my fool.   [Exit one.]

Enter steward [Oswald].

Oh, you, sir, you, come you hither, sir. Who am I, sir?

OSWALD   My lady's father.

LEAR   "My lady's father"? My lord's knave! You whoreson dog, you slave, you cur!

OSWALD   I am none of these, my lord, I beseech your
pardon.

LEAR   Do you bandy looks with me, you rascal?   83
[He strikes Oswald.]

OSWALD   I'll not be strucken, my lord.   84

KENT   Nor tripped neither, you base football player.   85
[He trips up Oswald's heels.]

LEAR   I thank thee, fellow. Thou serv'st me, and I'll love
thee.

KENT   Come, sir, arise, away! I'll teach you differences.   88
Away, away! If you will measure your lubber's length   89
again, tarry; but away! Go to. Have you wisdom? So.   90
[He pushes Oswald out.]

LEAR   Now, my friendly knave, I thank thee. There's
earnest of thy service.   [He gives Kent money.]   92

Enter Fool.

FOOL   Let me hire him too. Here's my coxcomb.   93
[Offering Kent his cap.]

LEAR   How now, my pretty knave, how dost thou?

FOOL   [to Kent] Sirrah, you were best take my coxcomb.   95

KENT   Why Fool?

FOOL   Why? For taking one's part that's out of favor.
Nay, an thou canst not smile as the wind sits, thou'lt   98
catch cold shortly. There, take my coxcomb. Why, this   99
fellow has banished two on 's daughters and did the   100
third a blessing against his will. If thou follow him, thou   101
must needs wear my coxcomb.—How now, nuncle?   102
Would I had two coxcombs and two daughters.

LEAR   Why, my boy?

69 very pretense true intention   **71 this** these   **83 bandy looks**
exchange glances (in such a way as to imply that Oswald and Lear
are social equals)   **84 strucken** struck   **85 football** (A raucous street
game played by the lower classes.)   **88 differences** distinctions in
rank.   **89–90 If . . . again** i.e., If you want to be laid out flat again, you
clumsy ox   **90 Go to** (An expression of impatience or anger.)   **Have
you wisdom?** i.e., Wise up.   **92 earnest of** a first payment for
93 coxcomb fool's cap, crested with a red comb.   **95 you were best**
you had better   **98–9 an . . . shortly** i.e., if you can't play along with
those in power, you'll find yourself out in the cold.   **100 banished**
(Paradoxically, by giving Goneril and Regan his kingdom, Lear has
lost them, given them power over him.)   **on 's** of his   **101 blessing**
i.e., bestowing Cordelia on France and saving her from the curse of
insolent prosperity   **102 nuncle** (Contraction of "mine uncle," the
Fool's way of addressing Lear.)

27 countenance face and bearing   **32 keep honest counsel** respect
confidences   **32–3 curious** ornate, elaborate   **37 to love** as to love
46 clodpoll blockhead   **53 roundest** bluntest   **57 entertained** treated
60 general dependents servants generally   **66 rememberest** remind
66–7 conception idea, thought.   **67 faint** halfhearted   **68–9 jealous
curiosity** overscrupulous regard for matters of etiquette

FOOL   If I gave them all my living, I'd keep my 105
coxcombs myself. There's mine; beg another of thy 106
daughters. 107

LEAR   Take heed, sirrah—the whip.

FOOL   Truth's a dog must to kennel. He must be
whipped out, when the Lady Brach may stand by th' 110
fire and stink.

LEAR   A pestilent gall to me! 112

FOOL   Sirrah, I'll teach thee a speech.

LEAR   Do.

FOOL   Mark it, nuncle:
Have more than thou showest, 116
Speak less than thou knowest,
Lend less than thou owest, 118
Ride more than thou goest, 119
Learn more than thou trowest, 120
Set less than thou throwest; 121
Leave thy drink and thy whore,
And keep in-a-door, 123
And thou shalt have more 124
Than two tens to a score. 125

KENT   This is nothing, Fool.

FOOL   Then 'tis like the breath of an unfee'd lawyer; you 127
gave me nothing for't. Can you make no use of nothing, nuncle?

LEAR   Why, no, boy. Nothing can be made out of
nothing.

FOOL   [to Kent]   Prithee, tell him; so much the rent of his 132
land comes to. He will not believe a fool. 133

LEAR   A bitter fool! 134

FOOL   Dost know the difference, my boy, between a
bitter fool and a sweet one?

LEAR   No, lad. Teach me.

FOOL
That lord that counseled thee
To give away thy land,
Come place him here by me;
Do thou for him stand. 141
The sweet and bitter fool
Will presently appear: 143
The one in motley here, 144
The other found out there. 145

LEAR   Dost thou call me fool, boy?

FOOL   All thy other titles thou hast given away; that
thou wast born with.

KENT   This is not altogether fool, my lord.

FOOL   No, faith, lords and great men will not let me; if 150
I had a monopoly out, they would have part on't. And 151
ladies too, they will not let me have all the fool to myself; they'll be snatching. Nuncle, give me an egg and 153
I'll give thee two crowns.

LEAR   What two crowns shall they be?

FOOL   Why, after I have cut the egg i'th' middle and eat 156
up the meat, the two crowns of the egg. When thou 157
clovest thy crown i'th' middle and gav'st away both
parts, thou bor'st thine ass on thy back o'er the dirt. 159
Thou hadst little wit in thy bald crown when thou
gav'st thy golden one away. If I speak like myself in 161
this, let him be whipped that first finds it so. 162
[Sings.]   "Fools had ne'er less grace in a year, 163
For wise men are grown foppish 164
And know not how their wits to wear, 165
Their manners are so apish." 166

LEAR   When were you wont to be so full of songs,
sirrah?

FOOL   I have used it, nuncle, e'er since thou mad'st thy 169
daughters thy mothers; for when thou gav'st them the
rod and putt'st down thine own breeches,
[Sings]   "Then they for sudden joy did weep,
And I for sorrow sung,
That such a king should play bo-peep 174
And go the fools among."
Prithee, nuncle, keep a schoolmaster that can teach
thy fool to lie. I would fain learn to lie.

LEAR   An you lie, sirrah, we'll have you whipped. 178

FOOL   I marvel what kin thou and thy daughters are.
They'll have me whipped for speaking true, thou'lt
have me whipped for lying, and sometimes I am
whipped for holding my peace. I had rather be any
kind o' thing than a fool. And yet I would not be thee,
nuncle. Thou hast pared thy wit o' both sides and left
nothing i'th' middle. Here comes one o' th' parings.

Enter Goneril.

LEAR
How now, daughter? What makes that frontlet on? 186
You are too much of late i'th' frown.

---

105 **living** property   105–6 **keep my coxcombs** (as proof of my folly)
106–7 **beg . . . daughters** i.e., beg for the coxcomb that you deserve for
dealing with your daughters as you did.   110 **Brach** bitch hound
(here likened to Goneril and Regan, who have been given favored
places despite their reeking of dishonest flattery)   112 **gall** irritation,
bitterness—literally, a painful swelling, or bile. (Lear is stung by the
Fool's gibe because it is so true.)   116 **Have . . . showest** don't display your wealth ostentatiously   118 **owest** own   119 **goest** i.e., on
foot. (Travel unostentatiously on horseback, not afoot.)   120 **Learn**
i.e., listen to.   **trowest** believe   121 **Set . . . throwest** don't stake
everything on a single throw   123 **in-a-door** indoors, at home
124–5 **And . . . score** and you will do better than break even (since a
score equals two tens, or twenty).   127 **'tis . . . lawyer** i.e., it is free—
and useless—advice. (Lawyers, being proverbially mercenary, would
not give good advice unless paid well.)   132–3 **so . . . to** (Because
Lear has given away his land, he can collect no rent.)   134 **bitter**
satirical   141 **Do . . . stand** take his place.   143 **presently** immediately   144 **motley** the parti-colored dress of the professional fool.
(The Fool identifies himself as the sweet fool, Lear as the bitter fool
who counseled himself to give away his kingdom.)   145 **found out
there** discovered there. (The Fool points at Lear.)

150 **No . . . let me** i.e., Great persons at court will not let me monopolize folly; I am not *altogether fool* in the sense of being "all the fool
there is."   151 **a monopoly out** a corner on the market. (The granting
of monopolies was a common abuse under King James and Queen
Elizabeth.)   **on't** of it.   153 **snatching** seizing their share (including
sexual pleasure).   156–7 **and eat . . . meat** and have eaten the edible
part   159 **bor'st . . . dirt** i.e., bore the ass instead of letting the ass
bear you.   161–2 **If . . . so** If I speak like a fool in saying this, let the
first person to discover the truth of this be whipped (since in this corrupt world those who speak truth are punished for doing so).
163–6 **"Fools . . . apish"** "Fools have never been so out of favor, for
wise men foppishly trade places with the fools and no longer know
how to show off their wit to advantage, they have grown so foolish
in their manners."   169 **used** practiced   174 **bo-peep** (A child's
game.)   178 **An** If   186 **What . . . on?** What is that frown doing on
your forehead?

FOOL Thou wast a pretty fellow when thou hadst no
    need to care for her frowning; now thou art an O with- 189
    out a figure. I am better than thou art now; I am a fool, 190
    thou art nothing. [*To Goneril*] Yes, forsooth, I will
    hold my tongue; so your face bids me, though you say
    nothing.
        Mum, mum,
        He that keeps nor crust nor crumb, 195
        Weary of all, shall want some. 196
    [*Pointing to Lear*] That's a shelled peascod. 197
GONERIL
    Not only, sir, this your all-licensed fool, 198
    But other of your insolent retinue
    Do hourly carp and quarrel, breaking forth 200
    In rank and not-to-be-endurèd riots. Sir, 201
    I had thought by making this well known unto you
    To have found a safe redress, but now grow fearful, 203
    By what yourself too late have spoke and done, 204
    That you protect this course and put it on 205
    By your allowance; which if you should, the fault 206
    Would not scape censure, nor the redresses sleep 207
    Which in the tender of a wholesome weal 208
    Might in their working do you that offense, 209
    Which else were shame, that then necessity 210
    Will call discreet proceeding. 211
FOOL For you know, nuncle,
        "The hedge sparrow fed the cuckoo so long 213
        That it had it head bit off by it young." 214
    So, out went the candle, and we were left darkling. 215
LEAR [*to Goneril*] Are you our daughter?
GONERIL
    I would you would make use of your good wisdom,
    Whereof I know you are fraught, and put away 218
    These dispositions which of late transport you 219
    From what you rightly are.
FOOL May not an ass know when the cart draws the 221
    horse? Whoop, Jug! I love thee. 222
LEAR
    Does any here know me? This is not Lear.
    Does Lear walk thus, speak thus? Where are his eyes?
    Either his notion weakens, or his discernings 225
    Are lethargied—Ha! Waking? 'Tis not so. 226
    Who is it that can tell me who I am?

FOOL Lear's shadow.
LEAR
    I would learn that; for, by the marks of sovereignty, 229
    Knowledge, and reason, I should be false persuaded 230
    I had daughters. 231
FOOL Which they will make an obedient father. 232
LEAR Your name, fair gentlewoman?
GONERIL
    This admiration, sir, is much o'th' savor 234
    Of other your new pranks. I do beseech you 235
    To understand my purposes aright.
    As you are old and reverend, should be wise. 237
    Here do you keep a hundred knights and squires,
    Men so disordered, so debauched and bold 239
    That this our court, infected with their manners,
    Shows like a riotous inn. Epicurism and lust 241
    Makes it more like a tavern or a brothel
    Than a graced palace. The shame itself doth speak 243
    For instant remedy. Be then desired, 244
    By her that else will take the thing she begs,
    A little to disquantity your train, 246
    And the remainders that shall still depend 247
    To be such men as may besort your age, 248
    Which know themselves and you.
LEAR   Darkness and devils! 249
    Saddle my horses! Call my train together! [*Exit one.*] 250
    Degenerate bastard, I'll not trouble thee.
    Yet have I left a daughter.
GONERIL
    You strike my people, and your disordered rabble
    Make servants of their betters.

        Enter Albany.

LEAR
    Woe, that too late repents!—Oh, sir, are you come? 255
    Is it your will? Speak, sir.—Prepare my horses.
                      [*Exit one.*]
    Ingratitude, thou marble-hearted fiend,
    More hideous when thou show'st thee in a child
    Than the sea monster!
ALBANY Pray, sir, be patient.
LEAR [*to Goneril*] Detested kite, thou liest! 261
    My train are men of choice and rarest parts, 262
    That all particulars of duty know
    And in the most exact regard support 264
    The worships of their name. Oh, most small fault, 265

189–90 O without a figure zero, cipher of no value unless preceded by a digit. **195–6 He . . . some** i.e., That person who, having grown weary of his possessions, gives all away, will find himself in need of part of what is gone. **196 want** lack **197 shelled peascod** shelled pea pod, empty of its contents. **198 all-licensed** allowed to speak or act as he pleases **200 carp** find fault **201 rank** gross, excessive **203 safe** certain **204 too late** all too recently **205 put it on** encourage it **206 allowance** approval **207–11 nor . . . proceeding** nor would the punishments lie dormant which, out of care for the common welfare, might prove unpleasant to you—proceedings that the stern necessity of the times will regard as prudent even if under normal circumstances they might seem shameful. **213 cuckoo** a bird that lays its eggs in other birds' nests **214 it its. it young** i.e., the young cuckoo. (A cautionary fable about ungrateful children.) **215 darkling** in the dark. **218 fraught** freighted, provided **219 dispositions** inclinations, moods **221–2 May . . . horse?** i.e., May not even a fool see that matters are backwards when a daughter lectures her father? **222 Jug** i.e., Joan. (The origin of this phrase is uncertain.) **225 notion** intellectual power **225–6 or his . . . lethargied** or his faculties are asleep **226 Waking?** i.e., Am I really awake?

229 that i.e., who I am. **marks of sovereignty** outward and visible evidence of being king **230–1 I should . . . daughters** i.e., all these outward signs of sanity and status would seem to suggest (falsely) that I am the king who had obedient daughters. **232 Which** Whom **234 admiration** (guise of) wonderment **235 other** other of **237 should** i.e., you should **239 Men . . . bold** men so disorderly, so depraved and impudent **241 Shows** appears. **Epicurism** Excess, hedonism **243 graced** dignified **244 desired** requested **246 disquantity your train** diminish the number of your attendants **247 the remainders . . . depend** those who remain to attend you **248 besort** befit **249 Which . . . you** servants who have proper self-knowledge and an awareness of how they should serve you. **250 train** retinue **255 Woe, that** Woe to the person who **261 kite** bird of prey **262 parts** qualities **264 in . . . regard** with close attention to detail **264–5 And . . . name** and with utter scrupulousness may uphold the honor of their reputation.

How ugly didst thou in Cordelia show!
Which, like an engine, wrenched my frame of nature 267
From the fixed place, drew from my heart all love, 268
And added to the gall. Oh, Lear, Lear, Lear! 269
Beat at this gate [*striking his head*] that let thy folly in
And thy dear judgment out!—Go, go, my people. 271
                              [*Exeunt some.*]

ALBANY
My lord, I am guiltless as I am ignorant
Of what hath moved you.
LEAR   It may be so, my lord.—
Hear, Nature, hear! Dear goddess, hear!
Suspend thy purpose if thou didst intend
To make this creature fruitful!
Into her womb convey sterility;
Dry up in her the organs of increase,
And from her derogate body never spring 279
A babe to honor her! If she must teem, 280
Create her child of spleen, that it may live 281
And be a thwart disnatured torment to her! 282
Let it stamp wrinkles in her brow of youth,
With cadent tears fret channels in her cheeks, 284
Turn all her mother's pains and benefits 285
To laughter and contempt, that she may feel
How sharper than a serpent's tooth it is
To have a thankless child! Away, away!
            Exit [*with Kent and the rest of Lear's followers*].
ALBANY
Now, gods that we adore, whereof comes this?
GONERIL
Never afflict yourself to know more of it, 290
But let his disposition have that scope 291
As dotage gives it. 292

            Enter Lear.

LEAR
What, fifty of my followers at a clap?
Within a fortnight?
ALBANY   What's the matter, sir?
LEAR
I'll tell thee. [*To Goneril*] Life and death! I am ashamed
That thou hast power to shake my manhood thus,
That these hot tears, which break from me perforce,
Should make thee worth them. Blasts and fogs upon
    thee! 298
Th'untented woundings of a father's curse 299
Pierce every sense about thee! Old fond eyes, 300
Beweep this cause again, I'll pluck ye out 301
And cast you, with the waters that you loose, 302

To temper clay. Yea, is't come to this? 303
Ha! Let it be so. I have another daughter,
Who, I am sure, is kind and comfortable. 305
When she shall hear this of thee, with her nails
She'll flay thy wolvish visage. Thou shalt find
That I'll resume the shape which thou dost think 308
I have cast off forever.   *Exit.*
GONERIL [*to Albany*] Do you mark that? 309
ALBANY
I cannot be so partial, Goneril,
To the great love I bear you— 311
GONERIL
Pray you, content.—What, Oswald, ho!
[*To the Fool*] You, sir, more knave than fool, after your
    master.
FOOL   Nuncle Lear, nuncle Lear! Tarry, take the Fool 314
    with thee. 315
        A fox, when one has caught her,
        And such a daughter
        Should sure to the slaughter, 318
        If my cap would buy a halter. 319
        So the Fool follows after.   *Exit.*
GONERIL
This man hath had good counsel. A hundred knights? 321
'Tis politic and safe to let him keep 322
At point a hundred knights—yes, that on every
    dream, 323
Each buzz, each fancy, each complaint, dislike, 324
He may enguard his dotage with their powers 325
And hold our lives in mercy.—Oswald, I say! 326
ALBANY   Well, you may fear too far. 327
GONERIL   Safer than trust too far.
Let me still take away the harms I fear, 329
Not fear still to be taken. I know his heart. 330
What he hath uttered I have writ my sister.
If she sustain him and his hundred knights
When I have showed th'unfitness—

            Enter steward [*Oswald*].

                          How now, Oswald?
What, have you writ that letter to my sister?
OSWALD   Ay, madam.
GONERIL
Take you some company and away to horse.
Inform her full of my particular fear,
And thereto add such reasons of your own
As may compact it more. Get you gone, 339

267–8 Which . . . place which, like a powerful mechanical contrivance, wrenched my natural affection away from where it belonged   **269 gall** bitterness.   **271 dear** precious   **279 derogate** debased   **280 teem** produce offspring   **281 spleen** violent ill nature   **282 thwart disnatured** obstinate, perverse, and unnatural, unfilial   **284 cadent** cascading.   **fret** wear away   **285 benefits** pleasures of motherhood   **290 Never . . . know** Don't distress yourself by seeking to know   **291 disposition** humor, mood   **292 As** that   **298 Should . . . them** should seem to suggest that you are worth a king's tears.   **Blasts and fogs** Infectious blights and disease-bearing fogs   **299 untented** too deep to be probed and cleansed   **300 fond** foolish   **301 Beweep** if you weep for   **302 loose** let loose (in tears)

303 To temper clay to mix with earth. (Lear threatens to cast both his eyes and their tears to the ground.)   **305 comfortable** comforting.   **308 the shape** i.e., the kingship   **309 Do . . . that?** i.e., Did you hear his threat to resume royal power?   **311 To** because of   **314–15 take . . . thee** (1) take me with you (2) take the name "fool" with you. (A stock phrase of taunting farewell.)   **318 Should sure** should certainly be sent   **319 halter** (1) rope for leading an animal (2) hangman's noose.   **321 This . . . counsel** (Said sarcastically.)   **322 politic** prudent. (Said ironically.)   **323 At point** armed and ready.   **dream** i.e., imagined wrong   **324 buzz** idle rumor   **325 enguard** protect   **326 in mercy** at his mercy.   **327 fear too far** overestimate the danger.   **329 still take away** always remove   **330 Not . . . taken** rather than dwell continually in the fear of being taken prisoner by such harms.   **339 compact** confirm

And hasten your return.   *[Exit Oswald.]*
                  No, no, my lord,
This milky gentleness and course of yours   341
Though I condemn not, yet, under pardon,   342
You're much more attasked for want of wisdom   343
Than praised for harmful mildness.   344

ALBANY
How far your eyes may pierce I cannot tell.   345
Striving to better, oft we mar what's well.

GONERIL   Nay, then—
ALBANY   Well, well, th'event.   *Exeunt.* 348

❖

1.5

Enter Lear, Kent [disguised as Caius], and Fool.

LEAR *[giving a letter to Kent]*   Go you before to Gloucester   1
with these letters. Acquaint my daughter no further   2
with anything you know than comes from her demand   3
out of the letter. If your diligence be not speedy, I shall   4
be there afore you.
KENT   I will not sleep, my lord, till I have delivered your
letter.   *Exit.*
FOOL   If a man's brains were in 's heels, were't not in   8
danger of kibes?   9
LEAR   Ay, boy.
FOOL   Then, I prithee, be merry. Thy wit shall not go   11
slipshod.   12
LEAR   Ha, ha, ha!
FOOL   Shalt see thy other daughter will use thee kindly,   14
for though she's as like this as a crab's like an apple,   15
yet I can tell what I can tell.
LEAR   What canst tell, boy?
FOOL   She will taste as like this as a crab does to a crab.
Thou canst tell why one's nose stands i'th' middle
on 's face?   20
LEAR   No.
FOOL   Why, to keep one's eyes of either side 's nose,   22
that what a man cannot smell out he may spy into.
LEAR   I did her wrong.   24
FOOL   Canst tell how an oyster makes his shell?
LEAR   No.
FOOL   Nor I neither. But I can tell why a snail has a
house.
LEAR   Why?

FOOL   Why, to put 's head in, not to give it away to his   30
daughters and leave his horns without a case.   31
LEAR   I will forget my nature. So kind a father!—Be my   32
horses ready?
FOOL   Thy asses are gone about 'em. The reason why   34
the seven stars are no more than seven is a pretty   35
reason.
LEAR   Because they are not eight.
FOOL   Yes, indeed. Thou wouldst make a good fool.
LEAR   To take't again perforce! Monster ingratitude!   39
FOOL   If thou wert my fool, nuncle, I'd have thee beaten
for being old before thy time.
LEAR   How's that?
FOOL   Thou shouldst not have been old till thou hadst
been wise.
LEAR
Oh, let me not be mad, not mad, sweet heaven!
Keep me in temper; I would not be mad!   46

[Enter Gentleman.]

How now, are the horses ready?
GENTLEMAN   Ready, my lord.
LEAR   Come, boy.   *[Exeunt Lear and Gentleman.]*
FOOL
She that's a maid now, and laughs at my departure,
Shall not be a maid long, unless things be cut
shorter.   *Exit.* 51

❖

2.1

Enter Bastard [Edmund] and Curan, severally.

EDMUND   Save thee, Curan.   1
CURAN   And you, sir. I have been with your father and
given him notice that the Duke of Cornwall and Regan
his duchess will be here with him this night.
EDMUND   How comes that?
CURAN   Nay, I know not. You have heard of the news
abroad—I mean the whispered ones, for they are yet   7
but ear-kissing arguments?   8
EDMUND   Not I. Pray you, what are they?
CURAN   Have you heard of no likely wars toward twixt   10
the Dukes of Cornwall and Albany?
EDMUND   Not a word.
CURAN   You may do, then, in time. Fare you well, sir.
                              Exit.

---

341 milky . . . course effeminate and gentle way   **342 under pardon** if you'll excuse my saying so   **343 attasked** taken to task for, blamed   **344 harmful mildness** mildness that causes harm.   **345 pierce** i.e., see into matters   **348 th'event** i.e., time will tell.
1.5. Location: Before Albany's palace.
1 Gloucester i.e., the place in Gloucestershire   **2 these letters** this letter.   **3 demand** inquiry   **4 out of** prompted by   **8–9 were't . . . kibes?** wouldn't his brains be in danger of that common affliction of the heel called chilblains?   **11–12 Thy wit . . . slipshod** i.e., Your brains would have no need for slippers to avoid chafing the chilblains, since you have no brains. (Anyone who journeys to Regan in hopes of kind treatment is utterly brainless.)   **14 Shalt** Thou shalt.   **kindly** (1) with filial kindness (2) according to her own nature   **15 crab** crab apple   **20 on 's** of his   **22 of either side 's** on either side of his   **24 her** i.e., Cordelia

30–1 Why, to . . . case i.e., The snail's head and horns are unendangered with its *case* or shell; Lear, conversely, has given away his crown to his daughters, leaving his brows unadorned and vulnerable. (With a suggestion too of the cuckold's horned head, as though Lear's victimization had a sexual dimension.)   **32 nature** natural affection. (Compare line 14 and note.)   **34 Thy . . . 'em** i.e., Your servants (who labor like asses in your service) have gone about readying the horses.   **35 seven stars** Pleiades   **39 To take't . . . perforce!** i.e., To think that Goneril would forcibly take back again the privileges guaranteed to me! (Or perhaps Lear is meditating an armed restoration of his monarchy.)   **46 temper** mental equilibrium
51 things i.e., penises.   **cut shorter** (A bawdy joke addressed to the audience.)
2.1 Location: The Earl of Gloucester's house.
0.1 *severally* separately.   **1 Save** God save   **7 abroad** going the rounds.   **ones** i.e., the news, regarded as plural   **8 ear-kissing arguments** lightly whispered topics.   **10 toward** impending

EDMUND
The Duke be here tonight? The better! Best! 14
This weaves itself perforce into my business.
My father hath set guard to take my brother,
And I have one thing, of a queasy question, 17
Which I must act. Briefness and fortune, work!— 18
Brother, a word. Descend. Brother, I say!

Enter Edgar.

My father watches. Oh, sir, fly this place!
Intelligence is given where you are hid.
You have now the good advantage of the night.
Have you not spoken 'gainst the Duke of Cornwall?
He's coming hither, now, i'th' night, i'th' haste, 24
And Regan with him. Have you nothing said
Upon his party 'gainst the Duke of Albany? 26
Advise yourself.
EDGAR   I am sure on't, not a word. 27
EDMUND
I hear my father coming. Pardon me;
In cunning I must draw my sword upon you.
Draw. Seem to defend yourself. Now, quit you well.—
                                        [*They draw.*] 30
Yield! Come before my father!—Light, ho, here!— 31
Fly, brother.—Torches, torches!—So, farewell. 32
                                        Exit Edgar.
Some blood drawn on me would beget opinion 33
Of my more fierce endeavor. I have seen drunkards 34
Do more than this in sport. [*He wounds himself in the
    arm.*] Father, father!
Stop, stop! No help?

Enter Gloucester, and servants with torches.

GLOUCESTER   Now, Edmund, where's the villain?
EDMUND
Here stood he in the dark, his sharp sword out,
Mumbling of wicked charms, conjuring the moon
To stand 's auspicious mistress.
GLOUCESTER   But where is he? 39
EDMUND
Look, sir, I bleed.
GLOUCESTER   Where is the villain, Edmund?
EDMUND
Fled this way, sir. When by no means he could—
GLOUCESTER   Pursue him, ho! Go after.
                            [*Exeunt some servants.*]
                            By no means what?
EDMUND
Persuade me to the murder of Your Lordship,
But that I told him the revenging gods 44

'Gainst parricides did all the thunder bend, 45
Spoke with how manifold and strong a bond
The child was bound to th' father; sir, in fine, 47
Seeing how loathly opposite I stood 48
To his unnatural purpose, in fell motion 49
With his preparèd sword he charges home 50
My unprovided body, latched mine arm; 51
And when he saw my best alarumed spirits, 52
Bold in the quarrel's right, roused to th'encounter, 53
Or whether ghasted by the noise I made, 54
Full suddenly he fled.
GLOUCESTER   Let him fly far. 55
Not in this land shall he remain uncaught;
And found—dispatch. The noble Duke my master, 57
My worthy arch and patron, comes tonight. 58
By his authority I will proclaim it
That he which finds him shall deserve our thanks,
Bringing the murderous coward to the stake; 61
He that conceals him, death.
EDMUND
When I dissuaded him from his intent
And found him pight to do it, with curst speech 64
I threatened to discover him. He replied, 65
"Thou unpossessing bastard, dost thou think, 66
If I would stand against thee, would the reposal 67
Of any trust, virtue, or worth in thee
Make thy words faithed? No. What I should deny— 69
As this I would, ay, though thou didst produce
My very character—I'd turn it all 71
To thy suggestion, plot, and damnèd practice; 72
And thou must make a dullard of the world 73
If they not thought the profits of my death 74
Were very pregnant and potential spirits 75
To make thee seek it."
GLOUCESTER   Oh, strange and fastened villain! 76
Would he deny his letter, said he?
I never got him.   *Tucket within.* 78
Hark, the Duke's trumpets! I know not why he comes.
All ports I'll bar; the villain shall not scape. 80
The Duke must grant me that. Besides, his picture 81
I will send far and near, that all the kingdom
May have due note of him; and of my land,

---

14 The better! Best! So much the better; in fact, the best that could
happen!   **17 queasy question** matter not for queasy stomachs
18 Briefness and fortune Expeditious dispatch and good luck
24 i'th' haste in great haste   **26 Upon his party** i.e., recklessly on
Cornwall's behalf (? It would be dangerous to speak on either side.)
27 Advise yourself Consider your situation.   **on't** of it   **30 quit you**
defend, acquit yourself   **31–2 Yield . . . farewell** (Edmund speaks
loudly as though trying to arrest Edgar, calls for others to help, and
privately bids Edgar to flee.)   **33–4 beget . . . endeavor** create an
impression of my having fought fiercely.   **39 stand 's** stand his, act as
his   **44 that** when

45 bend aim   **47 in fine** in conclusion   **48 loathly opposite**
loathingly opposed   **49 fell motion** deadly thrust   **50 preparèd**
unsheathed and ready.   **home** to the very heart   **51 unprovided**
unprotected.   **latched** nicked, lanced   **52 best alarumed** thoroughly
aroused to action, as by a trumpet   **53 quarrel's right** justice of the
cause   **54 ghasted** frightened   **55 Let him fly far** i.e., Any fleeing, no
matter how far, will be in vain.   **57 dispatch** i.e., that will be the end
for him.   **58 arch and patron** chief patron   **61 to the stake** i.e., to
reckoning   **64 pight** determined.   **curst** angry   **65 discover** expose
66 unpossessing unable to inherit, beggarly   **67 reposal** placing
69 faithed believed.   **What** That which, whatever   **71 character**
written testimony, handwriting.   **turn** attribute   **72 suggestion** instigation.   **practice** scheming   **73–6 And . . . seek it** and you must
think everyone slow-witted indeed not to suppose that they would
see how the profits to be gained by my death would be fertile and
potent tempters to make you seek my death.   **76 strange and fastened** unnatural and hardened   **78 got** begot.   **s.d.** *Tucket* series of
notes on the trumpet, here indicating Cornwall's arrival   **80 ports**
seaports, or gateways   **81 picture** description

Loyal and natural boy, I'll work the means   84
To make thee capable.   85

Enter Cornwall, Regan, and attendants.

CORNWALL
How now, my noble friend? Since I came hither,
Which I can call but now, I have heard strange news.
REGAN
If it be true, all vengeance comes too short
Which can pursue th'offender. How dost, my lord?
GLOUCESTER
Oh madam, my old heart is cracked, it's cracked!
REGAN
What, did my father's godson seek your life?
He whom my father named? Your Edgar?
GLOUCESTER
Oh, lady, lady, shame would have it hid!
REGAN
Was he not companion with the riotous knights
That tended upon my father?
GLOUCESTER
I know not, madam. 'Tis too bad, too bad.
EDMUND
Yes, madam, he was of that consort.   97
REGAN
No marvel, then, though he were ill affected.   98
'Tis they have put him on the old man's death,   99
To have th'expense and spoil of his revenues.   100
I have this present evening from my sister
Been well informed of them, and with such cautions
That if they come to sojourn at my house
I'll not be there.
CORNWALL   Nor I, assure thee, Regan.
Edmund, I hear that you have shown your father
A childlike office.
EDMUND   It was my duty, sir.   106
GLOUCESTER [*to Cornwall*]
He did bewray his practice, and received   107
This hurt you see striving to apprehend him.   108
CORNWALL   Is he pursued?
GLOUCESTER   Ay, my good lord.
CORNWALL
If he be taken, he shall never more
Be feared of doing harm. Make your own purpose,   112
How in my strength you please. For you, Edmund,   113
Whose virtue and obedience doth this instant
So much commend itself, you shall be ours.
Natures of such deep trust we shall much need;
You we first seize on.
EDMUND   I shall serve you, sir,
Truly, however else.   118
GLOUCESTER   For him I thank Your Grace.

CORNWALL
You know not why we came to visit you—
REGAN
—Thus out of season, threading dark-eyed night:
Occasions, noble Gloucester, of some poise,   122
Wherein we must have use of your advice.
Our father he hath writ, so hath our sister,
Of differences, which I least thought it fit   125
To answer from our home. The several messengers   126
From hence attend dispatch. Our good old friend,   127
Lay comforts to your bosom, and bestow
Your needful counsel to our businesses,
Which craves the instant use.   130
GLOUCESTER   I serve you, madam.
Your Graces are right welcome.   *Flourish. Exeunt.*

❖

2.2

*Enter Kent [disguised as Caius] and steward
[Oswald], severally.*

OSWALD   Good dawning to thee, friend. Art of this   1
house?
KENT   Ay.
OSWALD   Where may we set our horses?
KENT   I'th' mire.
OSWALD   Prithee, if thou lov'st me, tell me.   6
KENT   I love thee not.
OSWALD   Why then, I care not for thee.
KENT   If I had thee in Lipsbury pinfold, I would make   9
thee care for me.   10
OSWALD   Why dost thou use me thus? I know thee not.
KENT   Fellow, I know thee.   12
OSWALD   What dost thou know me for?
KENT   A knave, a rascal, an eater of broken meats;   14
a base, proud, shallow, beggarly, three-suited,   15
hundred-pound, filthy worsted-stocking knave; a   16
lily-livered, action-taking, whoreson, glass-gazing,   17
superserviceable, finical rogue; one-trunk-inheriting   18
slave; one that wouldst be a bawd in way of good ser-   19
vice, and art nothing but the composition of a knave,   20
beggar, coward, pander, and the son and heir of a

---

84 **natural** (1) prompted by natural feelings of loyalty and affection
(2) bastard   85 **capable** legally able to become the inheritor.   97 **consort** crew.   98 **though** if.   **ill affected** ill-disposed, disloyal.   99 **put
him on** incited him to   100 **th'expense and spoil** the squandering
106 **childlike** filial   107 **bewray his practice** expose his (Edgar's)
plot   108 **apprehend** arrest   112–13 **Make . . . please** Go about
achieving your purpose, making free use of my authority and
resources.   113 **For** As for   118 **however else** above all else.

122 **poise** weight   125 **differences** quarrels.   **which** which letters
126 **from our home** while still at our palace in Cornwall.   127 **attend
dispatch** wait to be dispatched.   130 **the instant use** immediate
attention.
2.2 Location: Before Gloucester's house.
0.1 *severally* at separate doors.   **1 dawning** (It is not yet day.)   **6 if
thou lov'st me** i.e., if you bear good will toward me. (But Kent deliberately takes the phrase in its literal, not courtly, sense.)   **9 in Lipsbury pinfold** i.e., within the pinfold of the lips, between my teeth. (A
pinfold is a pound for stray animals.)   **10 care for** i.e., be wary of.
(Playing on *care not for*, "do not like," in line 8.)   **12 I know thee** i.e., I
know you for what you are. (Playing on *know thee not*, "am unacquainted with you," in line 11.)   **14 broken meats** scraps of food
(such as were passed out to the most lowly)   **15–16 three-suited . . .
knave** i.e., a steward of a household, with an allowance of three suits
a year and a comfortable income of one hundred pounds, dressed in
dirty wool stockings appropriate to the servant class   **16–19 a lily-
livered . . . slave** a cowardly, litigious, insufferable, self-infatuated,
officious, foppish rogue, whose personal property all fits into one
trunk   **19–20 bawd . . . service** i.e., pimp or pander as a way of providing whatever is wanted   **20 composition** compound

mongrel bitch; one whom I will beat into clamorous whining if thou deny'st the least syllable of thy addi- 23
tion.   24

OSWALD   Why, what a monstrous fellow art thou thus to rail on one that is neither known of thee nor knows thee!

KENT   What a brazen-faced varlet art thou to deny thou knowest me! Is it two days since I tripped up thy heels and beat thee before the King? Draw, you rogue, for though it be night, yet the moon shines. I'll make a sop o'th' moonshine of you, you whoreson, cullionly 32
barbermonger. Draw!   [He brandishes his sword.] 33

OSWALD   Away! I have nothing to do with thee.

KENT   Draw, you rascal! You come with letters against the King, and take Vanity the puppet's part against 36
the royalty of her father. Draw, you rogue, or I'll so carbonado your shanks—draw, you rascal! Come 38
your ways.   39

OSWALD   Help, ho! Murder! Help!

KENT   Strike, you slave! Stand, rogue, stand, you neat 41
slave, strike!   [He beats him.]

OSWALD   Help, ho! Murder! Murder!

*Enter Bastard [Edmund, with his rapier
drawn], Cornwall, Regan, Gloucester, servants.*

EDMUND   How now, what's the matter? Part!   44

KENT   With you, goodman boy, an you please! Come, 45
I'll flesh ye. Come on, young master.   46

GLOUCESTER   Weapons? Arms? What's the matter here?

CORNWALL   Keep peace, upon your lives! [Kent and Oswald are parted.] He dies that strikes again. What is the matter?

REGAN   The messengers from our sister and the King.

CORNWALL   What's your difference? Speak.   52

OSWALD   I am scarce in breath, my lord.

KENT   No marvel, you have so bestirred your valor. You cowardly rascal, nature disclaims in thee. A tailor 55
made thee.

CORNWALL   Thou art a strange fellow. A tailor make a man?

KENT   A tailor, sir. A stonecutter or a painter could not have made him so ill, though they had been but two years o'th' trade.

CORNWALL   Speak yet, how grew your quarrel?

OSWALD   This ancient ruffian, sir, whose life I have spared at suit of his gray beard—

KENT   Thou whoreson zed! Thou unnecessary letter!— 65
My lord, if you'll give me leave, I will tread this un- 66
bolted villain into mortar and daub the wall of a jakes 67
with him.—Spare my gray beard, you wagtail?   68

CORNWALL   Peace, sirrah!
You beastly knave, know you no reverence?

KENT
Yes, sir, but anger hath a privilege.

CORNWALL   Why art thou angry?

KENT
That such a slave as this should wear a sword,
Who wears no honesty. Such smiling rogues as these,
Like rats, oft bite the holy cords atwain   75
Which are too intrinse t'unloose; smooth every
    passion   76
That in the natures of their lords rebel,   77
Bring oil to fire, snow to their colder moods,   78
Renege, affirm, and turn their halcyon beaks   79
With every gale and vary of their masters,   80
Knowing naught, like dogs, but following.—   81
A plague upon your epileptic visage!   82
Smile you my speeches, as I were a fool?   83
Goose, an I had you upon Sarum plain,   84
I'd drive ye cackling home to Camelot.   85

CORNWALL   What, art thou mad, old fellow?

GLOUCESTER   How fell you out? Say that.

KENT
No contraries hold more antipathy
Than I and such a knave.

CORNWALL
Why dost thou call him knave? What is his fault?

KENT   His countenance likes me not.   91

CORNWALL
No more, perchance, does mine, nor his, nor hers.

KENT
Sir, 'tis my occupation to be plain:
I have seen better faces in my time
Than stands on any shoulder that I see
Before me at this instant.

CORNWALL   This is some fellow
Who, having been praised for bluntness, doth affect 97

---

65 **zed** the letter z (regarded as unnecessary and often not included in dictionaries of the time).   66–7 **unbolted** unsifted; hence, coarse
67 **daub** plaster.   **jakes** privy   68 **wagtail** i.e., bird wagging its tail feathers in pert obsequiousness.   75 **holy cords** sacred bonds of loyalty and order   76 **intrinse** intrinsicate, tightly knotted.   **smooth** flatter, humor   77 **rebel** rebel against reason   78 **Bring . . . moods** flatteringly fuel the flame of their masters' angry passions, while similarly exacerbating their downward mood swings   79 **Renege, affirm** nay-say one moment (when their lords are in a denying mood) and serve as yes-men the next.   **halcyon beaks** (The halcyon or king-fisher, if hung up, would supposedly turn its beak into the wind.)
80 **gale and vary** shifting wind   81 **following** fawning and flattery.
82 **epileptic** i.e., trembling and pale with fright and distorted with a grin   83 **Smile you** Do you smile at.   **as** as if.   84–5 **Goose . . . Camelot** (The reference is obscure, but the general sense is that Kent, if given space and opportunity, would send Oswald packing like a cackling goose. Camelot, the legendary seat of King Arthur and his Knights of the Round Table, was thought to have been in the general vicinity of Salisbury, Sarum, and Gloucester.)   91 **likes** pleases
97 **affect** adopt the style of

23–4 **thy addition** the titles I've given you.   32 **sop o'th' moonshine** something so perforated that it will soak up moonshine as a sop (floating piece of toast) soaks up liquor   32–3 **cullionly barbermonger** base frequenter of barber shops, fop. (*Cullion* originally meant "testicle.")   36 **Vanity . . . part** i.e., the part of Goneril (here personified as a character in a morality play)   38 **carbonado** cut crosswise, like meat for broiling   38–9 **Come your ways** Come on.   41 **neat** (1) foppish (2) calflike. (*Neat* means "horned cattle.")   44 **matter** i.e., trouble. (But Kent takes the meaning "cause for quarrel.")   45 **With you** I'll fight with you; my quarrel is with you.   **goodman boy** (A contemptuous epithet, a title of mock respect, addressed seemingly to Edmund.)   **an** if   46 **flesh** initiate into combat   52 **difference** quarrel.   55 **disclaims in** disowns

A saucy roughness, and constrains the garb   98
Quite from his nature. He cannot flatter, he;   99
An honest mind and plain, he must speak truth!
An they will take 't, so; if not, he's plain.   101
These kind of knaves I know, which in this plainness
Harbor more craft and more corrupter ends
Than twenty silly-ducking observants   104
That stretch their duties nicely.   105

KENT

Sir, in good faith, in sincere verity,   106
Under th'allowance of your great aspect,   107
Whose influence, like the wreath of radiant fire   108
On flickering Phoebus' front—

CORNWALL   What mean'st by this?   109

KENT   To go out of my dialect, which you discommend
so much. I know, sir, I am no flatterer. He that be-   111
guiled you in a plain accent was a plain knave, which   112
for my part I will not be, though I should win your   113
displeasure to entreat me to 't.   114

CORNWALL [to Oswald] What was th'offense you gave him?

OSWALD   I never gave him any.
It pleased the King his master very late   117
To strike at me, upon his misconstruction;   118
When he, compact, and flattering his displeasure,   119
Tripped me behind; being down, insulted, railed,   120
And put upon him such a deal of man   121
That worthied him, got praises of the King   122
For him attempting who was self-subdued;   123
And, in the fleshment of this dread exploit,   124
Drew on me here again.

KENT   None of these rogues and cowards   126
But Ajax is their fool.

CORNWALL   Fetch forth the stocks!   127

You stubborn, ancient knave, you reverend braggart,   128
We'll teach you.

KENT   Sir, I am too old to learn.
Call not your stocks for me. I serve the King,
On whose employment I was sent to you.
You shall do small respect, show too bold malice
Against the grace and person of my master,   133
Stocking his messenger.

CORNWALL
Fetch forth the stocks! As I have life and honor,
There shall he sit till noon.

REGAN
Till noon? Till night, my lord, and all night too.

KENT
Why, madam, if I were your father's dog
You should not use me so.   139

REGAN   Sir, being his knave, I will.   140

CORNWALL
This is a fellow of the selfsame color   141
Our sister speaks of.—Come, bring away the stocks!   142
                              Stocks brought out.

GLOUCESTER
Let me beseech Your Grace not to do so.
His fault is much, and the good King his master
Will check him for't. Your purposed low correction   145
Is such as basest and contemned'st wretches   146
For pilferings and most common trespasses
Are punished with. The King must take it ill
That he, so slightly valued in his messenger,
Should have him thus restrained.

CORNWALL   I'll answer that. 150

REGAN
My sister may receive it much more worse
To have her gentleman abused, assaulted,
For following her affairs. Put in his legs.
                    [Kent is put in the stocks.]
Come, my good lord, away.
                Exeunt [all but Gloucester and Kent].

GLOUCESTER
I am sorry for thee, friend. 'Tis the Duke's pleasure,
Whose disposition, all the world well knows,
Will not be rubbed nor stopped. I'll entreat for thee. 157

KENT
Pray, do not, sir. I have watched and traveled hard.   158
Some time I shall sleep out; the rest I'll whistle.
A good man's fortune may grow out at heels.   160
Give you good morrow!   161

GLOUCESTER
The Duke's to blame in this. 'Twill be ill taken.   Exit.

98–9 constrains . . . nature i.e., distorts plainness quite from its true purpose so that it becomes instead a way of deceiving the listener. **99 He . . . he** He professes to be one who abhors the use of flattering speech. (Said sardonically). **101 An . . . plain** If people will take his rudeness, fine; if not, his excuse is that he speaks plain truth. **104–5 Than . . . nicely** than twenty foolishly bowing, obsequious courtiers who outdo themselves in the punctilious performance of their courtly duties. **106 Sir, in good faith.** (Kent assumes the wordy mannerisms of courtly flattery.) **107 th'allowance** the approval. **aspect** (1) countenance (2) astrological position **108 influence** astrological power **109 Phoebus' front** i.e., the sun's forehead **111–14 He . . . to't** The man who used plain speech to you craftily (see lines 102–5) and thereby taught you to suspect plain speakers of being deceitful was in fact a plain rascal, which part I will not play, much as it would please me to incur your displeasure if speaking thus would have that effect. (Kent would prefer to displease Cornwall, since Cornwell is pleased only by flatterers, and Kent has assumed until now that plain speech was the best way to offend, but he now argues mockingly that he can no longer speak plainly, since his honest utterance would be interpreted as duplicity.) **117 late** recently **118 upon his misconstruction** as a result of the King's misunderstanding (me) **119 When . . . displeasure** whereupon Kent, in cahoots with the King and his party, and wishing to gratify the King's anger at me **120 being down, insulted** when I was down, he exulted over me **121–2 And put . . . him** and acted with a bravado that earned him an accolade **123 For . . . self-subdued** for assailing one (i.e., myself) who chose not to resist **124 And . . . exploit** and, in the excitement of his first success in this fearless deed. (Said ironically.) **126–7 None . . . fool** i.e., You never find any rogues and cowards of this sort who do not outdo the blustering Ajax in their boasting.

128 reverend (because old) **133 grace** sovereignty, royal grace **139 should** would **140 being** since you are **141 color** complexion, character **142 away** along **145 check** rebuke, correct **146 contemned'st** most despised **150 answer** be answerable for **157 rubbed** hindered, obstructed. (A term from bowls.) **158 watched** gone sleepless **160 A . . . heels** i.e., Even good men suffer decline in fortune at times. (To be out at heels is literally to be threadbare, coming through one's stockings.) **161 Give you** i.e., God give you

KENT

Good King, that must approve the common saw,   163
Thou out of heaven's benediction com'st
To the warm sun!   [*He takes out a letter.*]
Approach, thou beacon to this under globe,   166
That by thy comfortable beams I may   167
Peruse this letter. Nothing almost sees miracles   168
But misery. I know 'tis from Cordelia,   169
Who hath most fortunately been informed
Of my obscurèd course, "and shall find time   171
From this enormous state, seeking to give   172
Losses their remedies." All weary and o'erwatched,   173
Take vantage, heavy eyes, not to behold   174
This shameful lodging.   175
Fortune, good night. Smile once more; turn thy wheel!
                                    [*He sleeps.*]   176

❧

[2.3]

Enter Edgar.

EDGAR   I heard myself proclaimed,
And by the happy hollow of a tree   2
Escaped the hunt. No port is free, no place   3
That guard and most unusual vigilance   4
Does not attend my taking. Whiles I may scape   5
I will preserve myself, and am bethought   6
To take the basest and most poorest shape
That ever penury, in contempt of man,   8
Brought near to beast. My face I'll grime with filth,
Blanket my loins, elf all my hairs in knots,   10
And with presented nakedness outface   11
The winds and persecutions of the sky.
The country gives me proof and precedent   13
Of Bedlam beggars who with roaring voices   14
Strike in their numbed and mortifièd arms   15
Pins, wooden pricks, nails, sprigs of rosemary;   16
And with this horrible object, from low farms,   17

Poor pelting villages, sheepcotes, and mills,   18
Sometimes with lunatic bans, sometimes with prayers,   19
Enforce their charity. Poor Turlygod! Poor Tom!   20
That's something yet. Edgar I nothing am.   *Exit.*   21

❧

[2.4]

Enter Lear, Fool, and Gentleman.

LEAR

'Tis strange that they should so depart from home   1
And not send back my messenger.
GENTLEMAN   As I learned,
The night before there was no purpose in them
Of this remove.
KENT   Hail to thee, noble master!   4
LEAR   Ha?
Mak'st thou this shame thy pastime?
KENT   No, my lord.
FOOL   Ha, ha, he wears cruel garters. Horses are tied by   7
the heads, dogs and bears by th' neck, monkeys by
th' loins, and men by th' legs. When a man's over-   9
lusty at legs, then he wears wooden netherstocks.   10
LEAR
What's he that hath so much thy place mistook
To set thee here?
KENT   It is both he and she: 12
Your son and daughter.
LEAR   No.
KENT   Yes.
LEAR   No, I say.
KENT   I say yea.
LEAR   No, no, they would not.
KENT   Yes, they have.
LEAR   By Jupiter, I swear no.
KENT
By Juno, I swear ay.
LEAR   They durst not do't!
They could not, would not do't. 'Tis worse than murder
To do upon respect such violent outrage.   23
Resolve me with all modest haste which way   24
Thou mightst deserve, or they impose, this usage,
Coming from us.

163 approve prove true.   **saw** proverb (i.e., "To run out of God's blessing into the warm sun," meaning "to go from better to worse," from a state of bliss into the pitiless world. Kent sees Lear as heading for trouble.)   **166 beacon . . . globe** i.e., the sun. (Daylight is coming soon.)   **167 comfortable** comforting   **168–9 Nothing . . . misery** Scarcely anything can make one appreciate miracles like being in a state of misery; to the miserable, any relief seems miraculous.   **171 obscurèd** disguised   **171–3 "and shall . . . remedies"** i.e., "and who, in the fullness of time, will bring relief from the monstrous state of affairs under which we suffer, seeking to remedy what has been destroyed." (The passage may be corrupt. Kent may be reading from his letter.)   **173 o'erwatched** exhausted with staying awake   **174 vantage** advantage (of sleep)   **175 lodging** i.e., the stocks.   **176 wheel** (Since Kent is at the bottom of Fortune's wheel, any turning should improve his situation.)
2.3 Location: Scene continues. Kent is dozing in the stocks.
2 happy luckily found   **3 port** (See 2.1.80 and note.)   **4 That** in which   **5 attend my taking** lie in wait to capture me.   **6 bethought** resolved   **8 in . . . man** in order to show how contemptible humankind is   **10 elf** tangle into elflocks   **11 presented** exposed to view, displayed   **13 proof** example   **14 Bedlam** (See the note to 1.2.139.)   **15 Strike** stick.   **mortifièd** deadened   **16 wooden pricks** skewers   **17 object** spectacle.   **low** lowly

18 pelting paltry   **19 bans** curses   **20 Enforce their charity** manage to beg something.   **Poor . . . Tom** (Edgar practices the begging role he is about to adopt. Beggars were known as "poor Toms.")
Turlygod (Meaning unknown.)   **21 That's . . . am** There's some kind of existence for me as poor Tom. I am Edgar no longer.
2.4 Location: Scene continues before Gloucester's house. Kent still dozing in the stocks.
1 they Cornwall and Regan   **4 remove** change of residence.   **7 cruel** (1) unkind (2) crewel (compare the Quarto spelling, "crewell"), a thin yarn of which hose were made   **9–10 overlusty at legs** given to running away, or overly active sexually   **10 netherstocks** stockings.
12 To as to   **23 upon respect** i.e., against my officers (who deserve respect)   **24 Resolve** Enlighten.   **modest** moderate

KENT   My lord, when at their home 26
I did commend Your Highness' letters to them, 27
Ere I was risen from the place that showed 28
My duty kneeling, came there a reeking post, 29
Stewed in his haste, half breathless, panting forth 30
From Goneril his mistress salutations;
Delivered letters, spite of intermission, 32
Which presently they read; on whose contents 33
They summoned up their meiny, straight took horse, 34
Commanded me to follow and attend
The leisure of their answer, gave me cold looks;
And meeting here the other messenger,
Whose welcome, I perceived, had poisoned mine—
Being the very fellow which of late
Displayed so saucily against Your Highness— 40
Having more man than wit about me, drew. 41
He raised the house with loud and coward cries.
Your son and daughter found this trespass worth
The shame which here it suffers.

FOOL Winter's not gone yet if the wild geese fly that 45
way. 46
    Fathers that wear rags
     Do make their children blind, 48
    But fathers that bear bags 49
     Shall see their children kind.
    Fortune, that arrant whore,
     Ne'er turns the key to th' poor. 52
But, for all this, thou shalt have as many dolors for thy 53
daughters as thou canst tell in a year. 54

LEAR
Oh, how this mother swells up toward my heart! 55
Hysterica passio, down, thou climbing sorrow! 56
Thy element's below.—Where is this daughter? 57

KENT With the Earl, sir, here within.

LEAR Follow me not. Stay here.   *Exit.*

GENTLEMAN
Made you no more offense but what you speak of?

KENT None.
How chance the King comes with so small a number? 62

FOOL An thou hadst been set i'th' stocks for that ques- 63
tion, thou'dst well deserved it.

KENT Why, Fool?

FOOL We'll set thee to school to an ant to teach thee 66
there's no laboring i'th' winter. All that follow their 67
noses are led by their eyes but blind men, and there's 68
not a nose among twenty but can smell him that's 69
stinking. Let go thy hold when a great wheel runs 70
down a hill lest it break thy neck with following; but
the great one that goes upward, let him draw thee after. When a wise man gives thee better counsel, give
me mine again. I would have none but knaves follow
it, since a fool gives it.
    That sir which serves and seeks for gain,
     And follows but for form,
    Will pack when it begins to rain   78
     And leave thee in the storm.
    But I will tarry; the fool will stay,
     And let the wise man fly.
    The knave turns fool that runs away; 82
     The fool no knave, pardie. 83

Enter Lear and Gloucester.

KENT Where learned you this, Fool?

FOOL Not i'th' stocks, fool.

LEAR
Deny to speak with me? They are sick? They are
 weary?
They have traveled all the night? Mere fetches, 87
The images of revolt and flying off. 88
Fetch me a better answer.

GLOUCESTER   My dear lord,
You know the fiery quality of the Duke,
How unremovable and fixed he is
In his own course.

LEAR
Vengeance! Plague! Death! Confusion! 93
Fiery? What quality? Why, Gloucester, Gloucester,
I'd speak with the Duke of Cornwall and his wife.

GLOUCESTER
Well, my good lord, I have informed them so.

LEAR
Informed them? Dost thou understand me, man?

GLOUCESTER Ay, my good lord.

LEAR
The King would speak with Cornwall. The dear father
Would with his daughter speak, commands, tends
 service. 100
Are they informed of this? My breath and blood! 101
Fiery? The fiery Duke? Tell the hot Duke that—
No, but not yet. Maybe he is not well.
Infirmity doth still neglect all office 104
Whereto our health is bound; we are not ourselves 105

When nature, being oppressed, commands the mind
To suffer with the body. I'll forbear,
And am fallen out with my more headier will,   108
To take the indisposed and sickly fit   109
For the sound man. [*Looking at Kent*] Death on my
    state! Wherefore   110
Should he sit here? This act persuades me
That this remotion of the Duke and her   112
Is practice only. Give me my servant forth.   113
Go tell the Duke and 's wife I'd speak with them,
Now, presently. Bid them come forth and hear me,   115
Or at their chamber door I'll beat the drum
Till it cry sleep to death.   117

GLOUCESTER   I would have all well betwixt you.   *Exit.*

LEAR
    Oh, me, my heart, my rising heart! But down!

FOOL   Cry to it, nuncle, as the cockney did to the eels   120
when she put 'em i'th' paste alive. She knapped 'em   121
o'th' coxcombs with a stick and cried, "Down, wan-   122
tons, down!" 'Twas her brother that, in pure kindness   123
to his horse, buttered his hay.   124

    Enter Cornwall, Regan, Gloucester, [and]
    servants.

LEAR   Good morrow to you both.
CORNWALL   Hail to Your Grace!
                              Kent here set at liberty.
REGAN   I am glad to see Your Highness.
LEAR
    Regan, I think you are. I know what reason
    I have to think so. If thou shouldst not be glad,
    I would divorce me from thy mother's tomb,   130
    Sepulch'ring an adultress. [*To Kent*] Oh, are you free? 131
    Some other time for that.—Belovèd Regan,
    Thy sister's naught. Oh, Regan, she hath tied   133
    Sharp-toothed unkindness, like a vulture, here.
                    [*He lays his hand on his heart.*]
    I can scarce speak to thee. Thou'lt not believe
    With how depraved a quality—Oh, Regan!   136

REGAN
    I pray you, sir, take patience. I have hope   137
    You less know how to value her desert   138
    Than she to scant her duty.
LEAR   Say? How is that?   139
REGAN
    I cannot think my sister in the least
    Would fail her obligation. If, sir, perchance
    She have restrained the riots of your followers,
    'Tis on such ground and to such wholesome end
    As clears her from all blame.
LEAR   My curses on her!
REGAN   Oh, sir, you are old;
    Nature in you stands on the very verge   147
    Of his confine. You should be ruled and led   148
    By some discretion that discerns your state   149
    Better than you yourself. Therefore, I pray you,
    That to our sister you do make return.
    Say you have wronged her.
LEAR   Ask her forgiveness?
    Do you but mark how this becomes the house: 153
    [*Kneeling*] "Dear daughter, I confess that I am old;
    Age is unnecessary. On my knees I beg
    That you'll vouchsafe me raiment, bed, and food."
REGAN
    Good sir, no more. These are unsightly tricks.
    Return you to my sister.
LEAR [*rising*]   Never, Regan.
    She hath abated me of half my train,   159
    Looked black upon me, struck me with her tongue
    Most serpentlike upon the very heart.
    All the stored vengeances of heaven fall
    On her ingrateful top! Strike her young bones,   163
    You taking airs, with lameness!
CORNWALL   Fie, sir, fie!   164
LEAR
    You nimble lightnings, dart your blinding flames
    Into her scornful eyes! Infect her beauty,
    You fen-sucked fogs drawn by the powerful sun   167
    To fall and blister!   168
REGAN
    O the blest gods! So will you wish on me
    When the rash mood is on.
LEAR
    No, Regan, thou shalt never have my curse.
    Thy tender-hafted nature shall not give   172
    Thee o'er to harshness. Her eyes are fierce, but thine
    Do comfort and not burn. 'Tis not in thee
    To grudge my pleasures, to cut off my train,

108–10 And . . . man and now disapprove of my more impetuous will in having rashly supposed that those who are indisposed and sickly were in sound health.   **110 Death . . . state!** (A common oath, here ironically appropriate to a king whose royal authority is dying.)
112 remotion removal, inaccessibility   **113 practice** deception.
forth out of the stocks.   **115 presently** at once.   **117 cry sleep to death** i.e., puts an end to sleep by the noise.   **120 cockney** i.e., a Londoner, ignorant of ways of cooking eels   **121 paste** pastry pie.
knapped rapped   **122 coxcombs** heads   **122–3 wantons** playful creatures, sexy rogues. (A term of affectionate abuse. The cockney wife is trying to coax and wheedle the eels into laying down their lives for the making of the pastry pie—a plea that is about as ineffectual as Lear's imploring his rising heart to subside.)   **123–4 'Twas . . . hay** (Another city ignorance; the act is well intended, but horses do not like greasy hay. As with Lear, good intentions are not enough. The *brother* is related to the cockney wife in that they are both misguidedly tenderhearted.)   **130–1 I would . . . adultress** i.e., I would cease to honor your dead mother's tomb, since it would surely contain the dead body of an adultress. (Only such a fantasy of illegitimacy could explain to Lear filial ingratitude of the monstrous sort that now confronts him.)   **133 naught** wicked.
136 quality disposition

137–9 I have . . . duty I trust this is more a matter of your undervaluing her merit than of her falling slack in her duty to you.   **139 Say?** Come again?   **147–8 Nature . . . confine** i.e., Your life has almost completed its allotted scope.   **149 By . . . state** by some discreet person who understands your situation and condition   **153 becomes the house** suits domestic decorum and the royal family line. (Said with bitter irony).   **159 abated** deprived   **163 ingrateful top** ungrateful head.   **164 taking** infectious   **167 fen-sucked** (It was supposed that the sun sucked up poisons from fens or marshes.)   **168 To fall and blister** to fall upon her and blister her beauty.   **172 tender-hafted** gentle. (Literally, set in a tender *haft*, i.e., handle or frame.)

To bandy hasty words, to scant my sizes, 176
And, in conclusion, to oppose the bolt 177
Against my coming in. Thou better know'st
The offices of nature, bond of childhood, 179
Effects of courtesy, dues of gratitude. 180
Thy half o'th' kingdom hast thou not forgot,
Wherein I thee endowed.

REGAN   Good sir, to th' purpose. 182

LEAR
Who put my man i'th' stocks?   *Tucket within.*

CORNWALL   What trumpet's that?

REGAN
I know't—my sister's. This approves her letter, 184
That she would soon be here.

        Enter steward [Oswald].

                        Is your lady come?

LEAR
This is a slave, whose easy-borrowed pride 186
Dwells in the fickle grace of her he follows.— 187
Out, varlet, from my sight!

CORNWALL   What means Your Grace? 188

LEAR
Who stocked my servant? Regan, I have good hope
Thou didst not know on't.

        Enter Goneril.

                Who comes here? O heavens,
If you do love old men, if your sweet sway
Allow obedience, if you yourselves are old, 192
Make it your cause; send down, and take my part!
[*To Goneril*] Art not ashamed to look upon this beard?
        [*Goneril and Regan join hands.*] 194
Oh, Regan, will you take her by the hand?

GONERIL
Why not by th' hand, sir? How have I offended?
All's not offense that indiscretion finds 197
And dotage terms so.

LEAR   O sides, you are too tough! 198
Will you yet hold?—How came my man i'th' stocks?

CORNWALL
I set him there, sir; but his own disorders
Deserved much less advancement.

LEAR   You? Did you? 201

REGAN
I pray you, father, being weak, seem so. 202
If till the expiration of your month
You will return and sojourn with my sister,
Dismissing half your train, come then to me.

I am now from home, and out of that provision 206
Which shall be needful for your entertainment. 207

LEAR
Return to her? And fifty men dismissed?
No! Rather I abjure all roofs, and choose
To wage against the enmity o'th'air, 210
To be a comrade with the wolf and owl—
Necessity's sharp pinch. Return with her?
Why, the hot-blooded France, that dowerless took 213
Our youngest born—I could as well be brought
To knee his throne and, squirelike, pension beg 215
To keep base life afoot. Return with her?
Persuade me rather to be slave and sumpter 217
To this detested groom.   [*He points to Oswald.*]

GONERIL   At your choice, sir.

LEAR
I prithee, daughter, do not make me mad.
I will not trouble thee, my child. Farewell.
We'll no more meet, no more see one another.
But yet thou art my flesh, my blood, my daughter—
Or rather a disease that's in my flesh,
Which I must needs call mine. Thou art a boil,
A plague-sore, or embossèd carbuncle 225
In my corrupted blood. But I'll not chide thee;
Let shame come when it will, I do not call it. 227
I do not bid the thunder-bearer shoot, 228
Nor tell tales of thee to high-judging Jove. 229
Mend when thou canst; be better at thy leisure.
I can be patient. I can stay with Regan,
I and my hundred knights.

REGAN   Not altogether so.
I looked not for you yet, nor am provided 234
For your fit welcome. Give ear, sir, to my sister;
For those that mingle reason with your passion 236
Must be content to think you old, and so— 237
But she knows what she does.

LEAR   Is this well spoken?

REGAN
I dare avouch it, sir. What, fifty followers? 239
Is it not well? What should you need of more?
Yea, or so many, sith that both charge and danger 241
Speak 'gainst so great a number? How in one house
Should many people under two commands
Hold amity? 'Tis hard, almost impossible.

GONERIL
Why might not you, my lord, receive attendance
From those that she calls servants, or from mine?

REGAN
Why not, my lord? If then they chanced to slack ye, 247
We could control them. If you will come to me— 248
For now I spy a danger—I entreat you

To bring but five-and-twenty. To no more
Will I give place or notice.   251

LEAR
I gave you all—

REGAN   And in good time you gave it.

LEAR
Made you my guardians, my depositaries,   253
But kept a reservation to be followed   254
With such a number. What, must I come to you
With five-and-twenty? Regan, said you so?

REGAN
And speak't again, my lord. No more with me.

LEAR
Those wicked creatures yet do look well-favored   258
When others are more wicked; not being the worst
Stands in some rank of praise. [*To Goneril*] I'll go with
   thee.   260
Thy fifty yet doth double five-and-twenty,
And thou art twice her love.

GONERIL   Hear me, my lord:
What need you five-and-twenty, ten, or five,
To follow in a house where twice so many   264
Have a command to tend you?

REGAN   What need one?

LEAR
Oh, reason not the need! Our basest beggars   266
Are in the poorest thing superfluous.   267
Allow not nature more than nature needs,   268
Man's life is cheap as beast's. Thou art a lady;
If only to go warm were gorgeous,   270
Why, nature needs not what thou gorgeous wear'st,   271
Which scarcely keeps thee warm. But, for true need—   272
You heavens, give me that patience, patience I need!
You see me here, you gods, a poor old man,
As full of grief as age, wretched in both.
If it be you that stirs these daughters' hearts
Against their father, fool me not so much   277
To bear it tamely; touch me with noble anger,   278
And let not women's weapons, water drops,
Stain my man's cheeks. No, you unnatural hags,
I will have such revenges on you both
That all the world shall—I will do such things—
What they are yet I know not, but they shall be
The terrors of the earth. You think I'll weep;
No, I'll not weep.   *Storm and tempest.*
I have full cause of weeping; but this heart
Shall break into a hundred thousand flaws   287

Or ere I'll weep. Oh, Fool, I shall go mad!   288
           Exeunt [Lear, Gloucester, Kent, Gentleman,
                                                and Fool].

CORNWALL
Let us withdraw. 'Twill be a storm.

REGAN
This house is little. The old man and 's people
Cannot be well bestowed.   291

GONERIL
'Tis his own blame hath put himself from rest,   292
And must needs taste his folly.   293

REGAN
For his particular, I'll receive him gladly,   294
But not one follower.

GONERIL
So am I purposed. Where is my lord of Gloucester?

CORNWALL
Followed the old man forth.

           Enter Gloucester.

                              He is returned.

GLOUCESTER
The King is in high rage.

CORNWALL   Whither is he going?

GLOUCESTER
He calls to horse, but will I know not whither.

CORNWALL
'Tis best to give him way. He leads himself.   300

GONERIL [*to Gloucester*]
My lord, entreat him by no means to stay.   301

GLOUCESTER
Alack, the night comes on, and the bleak winds
Do sorely ruffle. For many miles about   303
There's scarce a bush.

REGAN   Oh, sir, to willful men
The injuries that they themselves procure
Must be their schoolmasters. Shut up your doors.
He is attended with a desperate train,
And what they may incense him to, being apt   308
To have his ear abused, wisdom bids fear.   309

CORNWALL
Shut up your doors, my lord; 'tis a wild night.
My Regan counsels well. Come out o'th' storm.
                                                Exeunt.

                              ♣

3.1

*Storm still. Enter Kent [disguised as Caius]
and a Gentleman, severally.*

KENT   Who's there, besides foul weather?

---

251 place or notice houseroom or recognition.   **253 depositaries**
trustees   **254 kept a reservation** reserved a right   **258 well-favored**
attractive, fair of feature   **260 Stands . . . praise** achieves, by necessity, some relative deserving of praise.   **264 follow** be your attendants   **266 reason not** do not dispassionately analyze.   **266–7 Our . . .
superfluous** Even our most destitute beggars have some wretched
possessions beyond what they absolutely need.   **268 Allow not** If
you do not allow.   **needs** i.e., to survive   **270–2 If . . . warm** If fashions in clothes were determined only by the need for warmth, this
natural standard wouldn't justify the rich robes you wear to be gorgeous—which don't serve well for warmth in any case.   **277–8 fool
. . . To** do not make me so foolish as to   **287 flaws** fragments

288 Or ere before   **291 bestowed** lodged.   **292 blame** fault.   **hath**
that he has, or, that has.   **from rest** i.e., out of the house; also, lacking
peace of mind   **293 taste** experience   **294 For his particular** As for
him individually   **300 give . . . himself** give him his own way. He is
guided only by his own willfulness.   **301 entreat . . . means** by no
means entreat him   **303 ruffle** bluster.   **308–9 being . . . abused** (he)
being inclined to hearken to wild counsel
3.1. Location: An open place in Gloucestershire.
0.2 *severally* at separate doors.

GENTLEMAN
One minded like the weather, most unquietly.
KENT   I know you. Where's the King?
GENTLEMAN
Contending with the fretful elements;
Bids the wind blow the earth into the sea
Or swell the curlèd waters 'bove the main,   6
That things might change or cease; tears his white hair,   7
Which the impetuous blasts with eyeless rage
Catch in their fury and make nothing of;   9
Strives in his little world of man to outstorm   10
The to-and-fro-conflicting wind and rain.
This night, wherein the cub-drawn bear would couch,   12
The lion and the belly-pinchèd wolf
Keep their fur dry, unbonneted he runs
And bids what will take all.
KENT   But who is with him?   15
GENTLEMAN
None but the Fool, who labors to outjest   16
His heart-struck injuries.
KENT   Sir, I do know you,   17
And dare upon the warrant of my note   18
Commend a dear thing to you. There is division,   19
Although as yet the face of it is covered
With mutual cunning, twixt Albany and Cornwall;
Who have—as who have not, that their great stars   22
Throned and set high?—servants, who seem no less,   23
Which are to France the spies and speculations   24
Intelligent of our state. What hath been seen,   25
Either in snuffs and packings of the dukes,   26
Or the hard rein which both of them hath borne   27
Against the old kind King, or something deeper,   28
Whereof perchance these are but furnishings—   29
But true it is, from France there comes a power   30
Into this scattered kingdom, who already,   31
Wise in our negligence, have secret feet   32
In some of our best ports and are at point   33
To show their open banner. Now to you:
If on my credit you dare build so far   35
To make your speed to Dover, you shall find
Some that will thank you, making just report   37
Of how unnatural and bemadding sorrow
The King hath cause to plain.   39
I am a gentleman of blood and breeding,   40

And from some knowledge and assurance offer   41
This office to you.   42
GENTLEMAN
I will talk further with you.
KENT   No, do not.
For confirmation that I am much more
Than my outwall, open this purse and take   45
What it contains. [*He gives a purse and a ring.*] If you
shall see Cordelia—
As fear not but you shall—show her this ring,   47
And she will tell you who that fellow is   48
That yet you do not know. Fie on this storm!
I will go seek the King.
GENTLEMAN
Give me your hand. Have you no more to say?
KENT
Few words, but, to effect, more than all yet: 52
That when we have found the King—in which your
    pain   53
That way, I'll this—he that first lights on him   54
Holla the other.   *Exeunt* [*separately*].

❖

3.2

Storm still. Enter Lear and Fool.

LEAR
Blow, winds, and crack your cheeks! Rage, blow!
You cataracts and hurricanoes, spout   2
Till you have drenched our steeples, drowned the
    cocks!   3
You sulfurous and thought-executing fires,   4
Vaunt-couriers of oak-cleaving thunderbolts,   5
Singe my white head! And thou, all-shaking thunder,
Strike flat the thick rotundity o'th' world!
Crack nature's molds, all germens spill at once   8
That makes ingrateful man!
FOOL   Oh, nuncle, court holy water in a dry house is bet- 10
ter than this rainwater out o'door. Good nuncle, in,
ask thy daughters blessing. Here's a night pities   12
neither wise men nor fools.
LEAR
Rumble thy bellyful! Spit, fire! Spout, rain!
Nor rain, wind, thunder, fire are my daughters.   15
I tax not you, you elements, with unkindness;   16
I never gave you kingdom, called you children.
You owe me no subscription. Then let fall   18

6 **main** mainland   7 **things** all things   9 **make nothing of** blow about contemptuously   10 **little world of man** i.e., microcosm, which is an epitome of the macrocosm or universe   12 **cub-drawn** famished, with udders sucked dry (and hence ravenous).   **couch** lie close in its den   15 **bids . . . all** (A cry of desperate defiance; "take all" is the cry of a gambler in staking his last.)   16 **outjest** exorcise or relieve by jesting   17 **heart-struck injuries** injuries that strike to the very heart.   18–19 **And . . . to you** and dare, on the strength of what I know about you, entrust a precious undertaking to you.   22–3 **as . . . high** as who does not, among those whom a mighty destiny has enthroned on high   23 **no less** i.e., no other than servants   24 **speculations** scouts, spies   25 **Intelligent of** supplying intelligence pertinent to   26 **snuffs and packings** resentments and intrigues   27–8 **Or . . . King** or the harsh reining in they both have inflicted on King Lear   29 **furnishings** outward shows   30 **power** army   31 **scattered** divided   32 **Wise in** taking advantage of.   **feet** footholds   33 **at point** ready   35 **credit** trustworthiness.   **so far** so far as   37 **making just report** for making an accurate report   39 **plain** complain.   40 **blood and breeding** good family and education

41 **assurance** confidence, certainty   42 **office** assignment   45 **outwall** exterior appearance   47 **fear not but** be assured that   48 **fellow** i.e., Kent   52 **to effect** in their consequences   53–4 **in which . . . this** in which task, you search in that direction while I go this way
3.2. Location: An open place, as before.
2 **hurricanoes** waterspouts   3 **drenched** drowned.   **cocks** weathercocks.   4 **thought-executing fires** lightning that acts with the quickness of thought   5 **Vaunt-couriers** forerunners   8 **Crack . . . at once** Crack the molds in which nature makes all life; destroy all seeds at once   10 **court holy water** flattery   12 **ask . . . blessing** (For Lear to do so would be to acknowledge their authority.)   15 **Nor** Neither   16 **tax** accuse.   **with** of   18 **subscription** allegiance.

Your horrible pleasure. Here I stand your slave,
A poor, infirm, weak, and despised old man.
But yet I call you servile ministers,   21
That will with two pernicious daughters join
Your high-engendered battles 'gainst a head   23
So old and white as this. Oho! 'Tis foul.

FOOL   He that has a house to put 's head in has a good
headpiece.   26

    The codpiece that will house   27
        Before the head has any,   28
    The head and he shall louse;   29
        So beggars marry many.   30
    The man that makes his toe   31
        What he his heart should make   32
    Shall of a corn cry woe,   33
        And turn his sleep to wake.   34

For there was never yet fair woman but she made   35
mouths in a glass.   36

LEAR
No, I will be the pattern of all patience;
I will say nothing.

            Enter Kent, [disguised as Caius].

KENT   Who's there?
FOOL   Marry, here's grace and a codpiece; that's a wise   40
man and a fool.

KENT
Alas, sir, are you here? Things that love night
Love not such nights as these. The wrathful skies
Gallow the very wanderers of the dark   44
And make them keep their caves. Since I was man,   45
Such sheets of fire, such bursts of horrid thunder,
Such groans of roaring wind and rain I never
Remember to have heard. Man's nature cannot carry   48
Th'affliction nor the fear.

LEAR   Let the great gods,   49
That keep this dreadful pother o'er our heads,   50
Find out their enemies now. Tremble, thou wretch,
That hast within thee undivulgèd crimes
Unwhipped of justice! Hide thee, thou bloody hand,
Thou perjured, and thou simular of virtue   54
That art incestuous! Caitiff, to pieces shake,   55
That under covert and convenient seeming   56

Has practiced on man's life! Close pent-up guilts,   57
Rive your concealing continents and cry   58
These dreadful summoners grace! I am a man   59
More sinned against than sinning.

FOOL   Alack, bareheaded?
Gracious my lord, hard by here is a hovel;
Some friendship will it lend you 'gainst the tempest.
Repose you there while I to this hard house—
More harder than the stones whereof 'tis raised,
Which even but now, demanding after you,   65
Denied me to come in—return and force
Their scanted courtesy.

LEAR   My wits begin to turn.   67
Come on, my boy. How dost, my boy? Art cold?
I am cold myself.—Where is this straw, my fellow?
The art of our necessities is strange,
And can make vile things precious. Come, your
    hovel.—
Poor fool and knave, I have one part in my heart
That's sorry yet for thee.

FOOL [*sings*]
    "He that has and a little tiny wit,   74
        With heigh-ho, the wind and the rain,
    Must make content with his fortunes fit,
        Though the rain it raineth every day."   77

LEAR
True, boy.—Come, bring us to this hovel.
                            Exit [with Kent].

FOOL   This is a brave night to cool a courtesan. I'll speak   79
a prophecy ere I go:

    When priests are more in word than matter;   81
    When brewers mar their malt with water;   82
    When nobles are their tailors' tutors,   83
    No heretics burned but wenches' suitors,   84
    Then shall the realm of Albion   85
    Come to great confusion.

    When every case in law is right,   87
    No squire in debt, nor no poor knight;
    When slanders do not live in tongues,   89
    Nor cutpurses come not to throngs;

---

21 ministers agents   **23 high-engendered battles** battalions engendered in the heavens   **26 headpiece** (1) helmetlike covering for the head (2) head for common sense.   **27–34 The codpiece . . . wake** i.e., A man who houses his genitals in a sexual embrace before he has a roof over his head can expect the lice-infested penury of a penniless marriage; and anyone who unwisely places his affection on base things will be afflicted with sorrow and sleeplessness. (The *codpiece* is a covering for the genitals worn by men with their close-fitting hose; here representing the genitals themselves. The *corn* is a bunion on the toe.)   **35–6 made . . . glass** practiced making attractive faces in a mirror.   **40 Marry** (An oath, originally "by the Virgin Mary.")   **grace** royal grace.   **codpiece** (Often prominent in the Fool's costume.)
44 Gallow . . . dark frighten the very wild beasts of the night
45 keep occupy, remain inside   **48 carry** endure   **49 Th'affliction** the physical affliction   **50 pother** hubbub, turmoil   **54 simular** pretender   **55 Caitiff** Wretch   **56 convenient seeming** deception fitted to the purpose

57 practiced on plotted against.   **57–9 Close . . . grace!** O you secret and buried consciousnesses of guilt, burst open the hiding places that conceal you, and pray for mercy! (*Summoners* are the officers who cited offenders to appear before ecclesiastical courts.)   **65 Which** i.e., the occupants of which.   **demanding** I inquiring   **67 scanted** stinted
74–7 "He . . . day" (Derived from the popular song that Feste sings in *Twelfth Night,* 5.1.389 ff.)   **79 This . . . courtesan** i.e., This night is stormy enough to cool even the lust of a courtesan. (*Brave* means "fine, excellent.")   **81 When priests . . . matter** i.e., When priests do not practice what they preach. (This and the next three lines satirize the present state of affairs.)   **82 mar** adulterate   **83 are . . . tutors** can instruct their own tailors about fashion   **84 No heretics . . . suitors** i.e., when the prevailing heresy is lechery (a heresy, in other words, against love rather than against true religion), punished by burning not at the stake but by means of venereal infection   **85 realm of Albion** kingdom of England. (The Fool is parodying a pseudo-Chaucerian prophetic verse.)   **87 right** just. (This and the next five lines offer a utopian vision of justice and charity that will never be realized in this corrupted world.)   **89 When slanders . . . tongues** when no tongues speak slanders

When usurers tell their gold i'th' field,   91
And bawds and whores do churches build,
Then comes the time, who lives to see't,   93
That going shall be used with feet.   94

This prophecy Merlin shall make, for I live before his   95
time.   *Exit.*

3.3

Enter Gloucester and Edmund [with lights].

GLOUCESTER   Alack, alack, Edmund, I like not this unnatural dealing. When I desired their leave that I might
pity him, they took from me the use of mine own   3
house, charged me on pain of perpetual displeasure
neither to speak of him, entreat for him, or any way
sustain him.

EDMUND   Most savage and unnatural!

GLOUCESTER   Go to; say you nothing. There is division   8
between the dukes, and a worse matter than that. I
have received a letter this night; 'tis dangerous to be
spoken; I have locked the letter in my closet. These in- 11
juries the King now bears will be revenged home;   12
there is part of a power already footed. We must in-   13
cline to the King. I will look him and privily relieve   14
him. Go you and maintain talk with the Duke, that
my charity be not of him perceived. If he ask for me,   16
I am ill and gone to bed. If I die for't, as no less is
threatened me, the King my old master must be relieved. There is strange things toward, Edmund. Pray   19
you, be careful.   *Exit.*

EDMUND
This courtesy forbid thee shall the Duke   21
Instantly know, and of that letter too.
This seems a fair deserving, and must draw me   23
That which my father loses—no less than all.   24
The younger rises when the old doth fall.   *Exit.*

3.4

Enter Lear, Kent [disguised as Caius], and Fool.

KENT
Here is the place, my lord. Good my lord, enter.

The tyranny of the open night's too rough
For nature to endure.   *Storm still.*
LEAR   Let me alone.   3
KENT
Good my lord, enter here.
LEAR   Wilt break my heart?   4
KENT
I had rather break mine own. Good my lord, enter.
LEAR
Thou think'st 'tis much that this contentious storm
Invades us to the skin. So 'tis to thee,
But where the greater malady is fixed   8
The lesser is scarce felt. Thou'dst shun a bear,
But if thy flight lay toward the roaring sea
Thou'dst meet the bear i'th' mouth. When the mind's
     free,   11
The body's delicate. This tempest in my mind   12
Doth from my senses take all feeling else
Save what beats there. Filial ingratitude!
Is it not as this mouth should tear this hand   15
For lifting food to't? But I will punish home.   16
No, I will weep no more. In such a night
To shut me out? Pour on; I will endure.
In such a night as this? Oh, Regan, Goneril,
Your old kind father, whose frank heart gave all—   20
Oh, that way madness lies; let me shun that!
No more of that.
KENT   Good my lord, enter here.
LEAR
Prithee, go in thyself; seek thine own ease.
This tempest will not give me leave to ponder   24
On things would hurt me more. But I'll go in.   25
[To the Fool] In, boy; go first. You houseless poverty—
Nay, get thee in. I'll pray, and then I'll sleep.
                              Exit [Fool into the hovel].
Poor naked wretches, wheresoe'er you are,
That bide the pelting of this pitiless storm,   29
How shall your houseless heads and unfed sides,   30
Your looped and windowed raggedness, defend you   31
From seasons such as these? Oh, I have ta'en
Too little care of this! Take physic, pomp;   33
Expose thyself to feel what wretches feel,
That thou mayst shake the superflux to them   35
And show the heavens more just.
EDGAR *[within]*   Fathom and half, fathom and half!   37
Poor Tom!

Enter Fool [from the hovel].

---

91 tell count.   **i'th' field** i.e., openly, without fear   **93 who** whoever
94 That . . . feet that walking will be done on foot. (A comical anticlimax: Nothing will have been changed; don't expect these utopian
dreams to have materialized.)   **95 Merlin** (A great wizard of the
court of King Arthur, who came after Lear. The fool's comical inversion ends his song on a note of paradox and impossibility.)
3.3. Location: Gloucester's house.
3 pity be merciful to, relieve   **8 Go to** i.e., No more of that   **11 closet**
private chamber.   **12 home** thoroughly   **13 power** armed force.
footed landed.   **13–14 incline to** side with   **14 look** look for
16 of by   **19 toward** impending   **21 courtesy forbid thee** kindess
(to Lear) which you were forbidden to show   **23–4 This . . . all** i.e.,
This betraying by me of my father is something he has brought on
himself, and will surely confer upon me the earldom of Gloucester
and all his wealth.
3.4. Location: An open place. Before a hovel.

3 nature human nature   **4 Wilt . . . heart?** i.e., Do you want to relieve
my physical wants and thereby force me to remember my daughters'
ingratitude?   **8 fixed** lodged, implanted   **11 i'th' mouth** i.e., head-
on.   **free** free of anxiety   **12 The body's delicate** i.e., the body's
importunate needs can assert themselves.   **15 as** as if   **16 home**
fully.   **20 frank** liberal   **24 will . . . leave** i.e., keeps me too preoccupied   **25 things would** things (such as filial ingratitude) that would
29 bide endure   **30 unfed sides** i.e., lean ribs   **31 looped and windowed** full of openings like windows and loopholes   **33 Take
physic, pomp** Cure yourself, O distempered great ones   **35 superflux** superfluity. (With suggestion of *flux*, "bodily discharge," introduced by *physic*, "purgative," in line 33.)   **37 Fathom and half** (A
sailor's cry while taking soundings, hence appropriate to a deluge.)

FOOL   Come not in here, nuncle; here's a spirit. Help
me, help me!

KENT   Give me thy hand. Who's there?

FOOL   A spirit, a spirit! He says his name's poor Tom.

KENT

What art thou that dost grumble there i'th' straw? 43
Come forth.

Enter Edgar [disguised as a madman].

EDGAR   Away! The foul fiend follows me! Through the 45
sharp hawthorn blows the cold wind. Hum! Go to thy 46
bed and warm thee.

LEAR   Didst thou give all to thy daughters? And art
thou come to this?

EDGAR   Who gives anything to poor Tom? Whom the
foul fiend hath led through fire and through flame,
through ford and whirlpool, o'er bog and quagmire;
that hath laid knives under his pillow and halters in 53
his pew, set ratsbane by his porridge, made him 54
proud of heart to ride on a bay trotting horse over 55
four-inched bridges to course his own shadow for a 56
traitor. Bless thy five wits! Tom's a-cold. Oh, do de, 57
do de, do de. Bless thee from whirlwinds, star-blast- 58
ing, and taking! Do poor Tom some charity, whom the 59
foul fiend vexes. There could I have him now—and 60
there—and there again—and there.   *Storm still.*

LEAR

Has his daughters brought him to this pass?— 62
Couldst thou save nothing? Wouldst thou give 'em
all?

FOOL   Nay, he reserved a blanket, else we had been all 64
shamed.

LEAR

Now, all the plagues that in the pendulous air 66
Hang fated o'er men's faults light on thy daughters! 67

KENT   He hath no daughters, sir.

LEAR

Death, traitor! Nothing could have subdued nature
To such a lowness but his unkind daughters.
Is it the fashion that discarded fathers
Should have thus little mercy on their flesh? 72
Judicious punishment! 'Twas this flesh begot 73
Those pelican daughters. 74

EDGAR   Pillicock sat on Pillicock Hill. Alow, alow, loo, 75
loo!

FOOL   This cold night will turn us all to fools and madmen.

EDGAR   Take heed o'th' foul fiend. Obey thy parents;
keep thy word's justice; swear not; commit not with 80
man's sworn spouse; set not thy sweet heart on proud
array. Tom's a-cold.

LEAR   What hast thou been?

EDGAR   A servingman, proud in heart and mind, that 84
curled my hair, wore gloves in my cap, served the lust 85
of my mistress' heart, and did the act of darkness with
her; swore as many oaths as I spake words, and broke
them in the sweet face of heaven. One that slept in the
contriving of lust and waked to do it. Wine loved I
deeply, dice dearly, and in woman out-paramoured 90
the Turk. False of heart, light of ear, bloody of hand; 91
hog in sloth, fox in stealth, wolf in greediness, dog in
madness, lion in prey. Let not the creaking of shoes 93
nor the rustling of silks betray thy poor heart to 94
woman. Keep thy foot out of brothels, thy hand out of
plackets, thy pen from lenders' books, and defy the 96
foul fiend. Still through the hawthorn blows the cold
wind; says suum, mun, nonny. Dolphin my boy, boy, 98
sessa! Let him trot by.   *Storm still.* 99

LEAR   Thou wert better in a grave than to answer with
thy uncovered body this extremity of the skies. Is man
no more than this? Consider him well. Thou ow'st the 102
worm no silk, the beast no hide, the sheep no wool, 103
the cat no perfume. Ha! Here's three on 's are sophis- 104
ticated; thou art the thing itself. Unaccommodated 105
man is no more but such a poor, bare, forked animal
as thou art. Off, off, you lendings! Come, unbutton
here.   *[Tearing off his clothes.]*

FOOL   Prithee, nuncle, be contented; 'tis a naughty night 109
to swim in. Now a little fire in a wild field were like 110
an old lecher's heart—a small spark, all the rest on 's 111
body cold.

Enter Gloucester, with a torch.

Look, here comes a walking fire.

---

43 **grumble** mutter, mumble   45 **Away!** Keep away!   **45–6 Through . . .
wind** (Possibly a line from a ballad.)   **53–4 that hath . . . porridge** (The
fiend has laid in poor Tom's way tempting means to despairing suicide,
the most damnable of sins: knives under his pillow when he is asleep,
nooses in his church pew when he should be at prayer, and rat poison
set beside his soup when he should eat.)   **54–7 made him . . . traitor**
(The next temptation is a prideful act of great bravado that would be
impossible without the devil's aid: riding a horse over bridges only four
inches wide in pursuit of one's own shadow.)   **57 five wits** (Either the
five physical senses—sight, hearing, etc.—or the five faculties of the
mind: common wit, imagination, fantasy, estimation, and memory.)
58–9 star-blasting being blighted by influence of the stars   **59 taking**
infection, evil influence, enchantment.   **60 There** (Perhaps he slaps at
lice and other vermin as if they were devils.)   **62 pass** miserable plight.
64 reserved a blanket kept a wrap (for his nakedness)   **66 pendulous**
suspended, overhanging   **67 fated** having the power of fate   **72 have . . .
flesh** i.e., punish themselves, as Edgar has done (probably with pins
and thorns stuck in his flesh).   **73 Judicious** Appropriate to the crime
74 pelican greedy. (Young pelicans supposedly smote their parents and
fed on the blood of their mothers' breasts.)

75 **Pillicock** (From an old rhyme, suggested by the sound of *pelican*.
Pillicock in nursery rhyme seems to have been a euphemism for penis;
Pillicock Hill, for the Mount of Venus.)   80 **justice** integrity.   **commit
not** i.e., do not commit adultery. (Edgar's mad homily contains fragments of the Ten Commandments.)   84 **servingman** either a "servant" in the language of courtly love or an ambitious servant in a
household   85 **gloves** i.e., my mistress's favors   **90–1 out-
paramoured the Turk** outdid the Sultan in keeping mistresses.
91 **light of ear** i.e., listening intently for information that can be used
criminally   93 **prey** preying.   **93–4 creaking . . . silks** (Telltale noises
of lovers in a secret assignation.)   96 **plackets** slits in skirts or petticoats.   **thy pen . . . books** i.e., do not sign a contract for a loan
98 **suum . . . nonny** (Imitative of the wind?)   **Dolphin my boy** (A
slang phrase or bit of song?)   99 **sessa** i.e., away, cease (?).
102–4 Thou . . . perfume Stripped of your finery, you are not indebted
to the silkworm for silk, cattle for hide, the sheep for wool, or the civet
cat for the perfume derived from its anal pouch.   **104–5 Here . . .
itself** The three of us here (Kent, the Fool, and Lear) are decked out in
the sophistication of supposedly civilized society; you (Edgar) are the
unadorned, natural essence, the natural man.   105 **Unaccommodated**
Unfurnished with the trappings of civilization, such as clothing
109 **naughty** bad, nasty   110 **wild** barren, uncultivated   111 **on 's**
of his

EDGAR   This is the foul fiend Flibbertigibbet! He begins 114
at curfew and walks till the first cock; he gives the web 115
and the pin, squinnies the eye and makes the harelip, 116
mildews the white wheat, and hurts the poor creature 117
of earth.

> Swithold footed thrice the 'old; 119
> He met the nightmare and her ninefold; 120
>> Bid her alight,
>> And her troth plight,
> And aroint thee, witch, aroint thee! 123

KENT   How fares Your Grace?

LEAR   What's he?

KENT   Who's there? What is't you seek?

GLOUCESTER   What are you there? Your names?

EDGAR   Poor Tom, that eats the swimming frog, the
toad, the tadpole, the wall newt and the water; that in 129
the fury of his heart, when the foul fiend rages, eats
cow dung for salads, swallows the old rat and the
ditch-dog, drinks the green mantle of the standing 132
pool; who is whipped from tithing to tithing and 133
stock-punished and imprisoned; who hath had three 134
suits to his back, six shirts to his body, 135

> Horse to ride, and weapon to wear;
> But mice and rats and such small deer 137
> Have been Tom's food for seven long year.

Beware my follower. Peace, Smulkin! Peace, thou fiend! 139

GLOUCESTER
What, hath Your Grace no better company?

EDGAR   The Prince of Darkness is a gentleman. Modo 141
he's called, and Mahu.

GLOUCESTER [to Lear]
Our flesh and blood, my lord, is grown so vile 143
That it doth hate what gets it. 144

EDGAR   Poor Tom's a-cold.

GLOUCESTER
Go in with me. My duty cannot suffer 146
T'obey in all your daughters' hard commands. 147
Though their injunction be to bar my doors
And let this tyrannous night take hold upon you,

Yet have I ventured to come seek you out
And bring you where both fire and food is ready.

LEAR
First let me talk with this philosopher.
[To Edgar] What is the cause of thunder?

KENT   Good my lord,
Take his offer. Go into th' house.

LEAR
I'll talk a word with this same learnèd Theban. 155
[To Edgar] What is your study? 156

EDGAR   How to prevent the fiend, and to kill vermin. 157

LEAR   Let me ask you one word in private.
                              [Lear and Edgar talk apart.]

KENT [to Gloucester]
Importune him once more to go, my lord.
His wits begin t'unsettle.

GLOUCESTER   Canst thou blame him?
                                        Storm still.
His daughters seek his death. Ah, that good Kent!
He said it would be thus, poor banished man.
Thou sayest the King grows mad; I'll tell thee, friend,
I am almost mad myself. I had a son,
Now outlawed from my blood; he sought my life 165
But lately, very late. I loved him, friend,
No father his son dearer. True to tell thee,
The grief hath crazed my wits. What a night's this!—
I do beseech Your Grace—

LEAR   Oh, cry you mercy, sir. 170
[To Edgar] Noble philosopher, your company.

EDGAR   Tom's a-cold.

GLOUCESTER [to Edgar]
In, fellow, there, in th' hovel. Keep thee warm.

LEAR [starting toward the hovel]
Come, let's in all.

KENT   This way, my lord.

LEAR   With him!
I will keep still with my philosopher.

KENT [to Gloucester]
Good my lord, soothe him. Let him take the fellow. 176

GLOUCESTER [to Kent]   Take you him on. 177

KENT [to Edgar]
Sirrah, come on. Go along with us.

LEAR   Come, good Athenian. 179

GLOUCESTER   No words, no words! Hush.

EDGAR
Child Rowland to the dark tower came; 181
His word was still, "Fie, foh, and fum, 182
I smell the blood of a British man."   Exeunt. 183

114 Flibbertigibbet (A devil from Elizabethan folklore whose name appears in Samuel Harsnett's *Declaration of Egregious Popish Impostures*, 1603, and elsewhere.)   114–15 He . . . cock He walks from nightfall till dawn   115–16 web and the pin cataract of the eye   116 squinnies squints   117 white ripening, ready for harvest   119 Swithold Saint Withold, an Anglo-Saxon exorcist, who here provides defense against the *nightmare,* or demon thought to afflict sleepers, by commanding the nightmare to *alight,* i.e., stop riding over the sleeper, and *plight* her *troth,* i.e., vow true faith, promise to do no harm. (Or, an error for *Swithin.*)   footed . . . 'old thrice traversed the wold (tract of hilly upland)   120 ninefold nine offspring. (With possible pun on *fold, foal.*)   123 aroint thee begone   129 water newt   132 ditch-dog dead dog in a ditch.   mantle scum.   standing stagnant   133 from . . . to tithing from one ward or parish to another   134 stock-punished placed in the stocks   134–5 three suits (Like the menial servant at 2.2.15.)   137 deer animals   139 follower familiar, attendant devil.   Smulkin a devil's name (in Samuel Harsnet's *Declaration,* as are *Modo* and *Mahu* in lines 141–2).   141 The Prince of Darkness The devil   143–4 Our . . . gets it (1) Children have become so hardened in sin that they hate their parents (2) Life is so intolerable that humans cry out at having been born.   146 suffer permit me   147 in all in all matters

155 Theban i.e., one deeply versed in "philosophy" or natural science.   156 study special competence.   157 prevent thwart   165 outlawed . . . blood disowned, disinherited, and legally outlawed   170 cry you mercy I beg your pardon   176 soothe humor   177 Take . . . on i.e., Go on ahead with Edgar.   179 Athenian i.e., philosopher.   181 Child Rowland, etc. (Probably a fragment of a ballad about the hero of the Charlemagne legends. A *child* is a candidate for knighthood.)   182 word watchword   182–3 "Fie . . . man" (This is essentially what the Giant says in "Jack, the Giant Killer.")

3.5

Enter Cornwall and Edmund [with a letter].

CORNWALL   I will have my revenge ere I depart his
house.

EDMUND   How, my lord, I may be censured, that nature 3
thus gives way to loyalty, something fears me to 4
think of.

CORNWALL   I now perceive it was not altogether your
brother's evil disposition made him seek his death, 7
but a provoking merit set awork by a reprovable 8
badness in himself. 9

EDMUND   How malicious is my fortune, that I must 10
repent to be just! This is the letter he spoke of, which 11
approves him an intelligent party to the advantages 12
of France. Oh, heavens! That this treason were not, or 13
not I the detector!

CORNWALL   Go with me to the Duchess.

EDMUND   If the matter of this paper be certain, you have
mighty business in hand.

CORNWALL   True or false, it hath made thee Earl of
Gloucester. Seek out where thy father is, that he may
be ready for our apprehension. 20

EDMUND   [aside]   If I find him comforting the King, it 21
will stuff his suspicion more fully.—I will persevere 22
in my course of loyalty, though the conflict be sore
between that and my blood. 24

CORNWALL   I will lay trust upon thee, and thou shalt
find a dearer father in my love.   *Exeunt.*

3.6

*Enter Kent [disguised as Caius] and
Gloucester.*

GLOUCESTER   Here is better than the open air; take it
thankfully. I will piece out the comfort with what 2
addition I can. I will not be long from you.

KENT   All the power of his wits have given way to his
impatience. The gods reward your kindness! 5

                                 Exit [Gloucester].

Enter Lear, Edgar [as poor Tom], and Fool.

EDGAR   Fraseretto calls me, and tells me Nero is an 6
angler in the lake of darkness. Pray, innocent, and 7
beware the foul fiend.

FOOL   Prithee, nuncle, tell me whether a madman be a
gentleman or a yeoman? 10

LEAR   A king, a king!

FOOL   No, he's a yeoman that has a gentleman to his
son; for he's a mad yeoman that sees his son a
gentleman before him.

LEAR
To have a thousand with red burning spits
Come hizzing in upon 'em— 16

EDGAR   The foul fiend bites my back. 17

FOOL   He's mad that trusts in the tameness of a wolf, a 18
horse's health, a boy's love, or a whore's oath. 19

LEAR
It shall be done; I will arraign them straight. 20
[To Edgar] Come, sit thou here, most learnèd justicer. 21
[To the Fool] Thou, sapient sir, sit here. Now, you she-
foxes! 22

EDGAR   Look where he stands and glares! Want'st thou 23
eyes at trial, madam? 24
[Sings.] "Come o'er the burn, Bessy, to me—" 25

FOOL [sings]
          Her boat hath a leak,
          And she must not speak
    Why she dares not come over to thee.

EDGAR   The foul fiend haunts poor Tom in the voice of a
nightingale. Hoppedance cries in Tom's belly for two 30
white herring. Croak not, black angel; I have no food 31
for thee.

KENT [to Lear]
How do you, sir? Stand you not so amazed. 33
Will you lie down and rest upon the cushions?

LEAR
I'll see their trial first. Bring in their evidence. 35
[To Edgar] Thou robèd man of justice, take thy place; 36
[To the Fool] And thou, his yokefellow of equity, 37

3.5 Location: Gloucester's house.
3 censured judged.   **nature** attachment to family   **4 something
fears** somewhat frightens   **7 his** his father's   **8–9 but . . . himself**
but the promptings of self-worth stimulated by the reprehensible
badness of the Earl of Gloucester.   **10–11 How . . . just!** i.e., How
cruel of fate to oblige me to be upright and loyal by betraying my
own father!   **11–13 which . . . France** which proves him to be a spy
on behalf of the French.   **20 for our apprehension** for our arresting
of him.   **21 If . . . comforting** If I find Gloucester giving aid and comfort to   **22 his suspicion** suspicion of him   **24 blood** family loyalty,
filial instincts.
**3.6. Location: Within a building on Gloucester's estate, near or
adjoining his house, or part of the house itself. See 3.4.146–54.
Cushions are provided, and stools.**
2 piece eke   **5 impatience** rage, inability to endure more.

---

6 Fraseretto (Another of the fiends from Harsnett.)   **6–7 Nero is an
angler** (Chaucer's "Monk's Tale," lines 2474–5, tells how Nero fished
in the Tiber with nets of gold thread; in Rabelais, 2.30, Nero is
described as a hurdy-gurdy player and Trajan an angler for frogs in
the underworld.)   **7 innocent** simpleton, fool (i.e., the Fool)   **10 yeoman** property owner below the rank of gentleman. (The Fool's bitter
jest in lines 12–14 is that such a man might go mad to see his son
advanced over him.)   **16 hizzing** hissing. (Lear imagines his wicked
daughters suffering torments in hell or being attacked by enemies.)
17 bites (i.e., in the shape of a louse.)   **18–19 tameness . . . health**
(Wolves are untamable, and horses are prone to disease.)   **20 arraign
them** (Lear now imagines the trial of his cruel daughters.)   **21 justicer** judge, justice.   **22 sapient** wise   **23 he** (Probably one of Edgar's
devils, or, Lear.)   **23–4 Want'st . . . trial** Do you lack spectators at
your trial? or, Can't you see who's looking at you?   **25 Come . . . me**
(First line of a ballad by William Birche, 1558. A *burn* is a brook. The
Fool makes a ribald reply, in which the *leaky boat* suggests the
woman's easy virtue or perhaps her menstrual period.)   **30 nightingale** (Edgar pretends to take the Fool's singing for that of a fiend disguised as a nightingale.)   **Hoppedance** (Harsnett mentions
"Hoberdidance.")   **31 white** unsmoked (contrasted with *black angel*,
a demon.)   **Croak** (Refers to the rumbling in Edgar's stomach,
denoting hunger.)   **33 amazed** bewildered.   **35 their evidence** the
witnesses against them.   **36 robèd man** i.e., Edgar, with his blanket
37 yokefellow of equity partner in the law

Bench by his side. [*To Kent*] You are o'th' commission; 38
Sit you, too.   [*They sit.*]
EDGAR   Let us deal justly.   [*He sings.*]
        Sleepest or wakest thou, jolly shepherd?
            Thy sheep be in the corn;   42
        And for one blast of thy minikin mouth,   43
            Thy sheep shall take no harm.   44
        Purr the cat is gray.   45
LEAR   Arraign her first; 'tis Goneril, I here take my oath
before this honorable assembly, kicked the poor King 47
her father.
FOOL   Come hither, mistress. Is your name Goneril?
LEAR   She cannot deny it.
FOOL   Cry you mercy, I took you for a joint stool. 51
LEAR
And here's another, whose warped looks proclaim   52
What store her heart is made on. Stop her there!   53
Arms, arms, sword, fire! Corruption in the place!   54
False justicer, why hast thou let her scape?
EDGAR   Bless thy five wits!
KENT
Oh, pity! Sir, where is the patience now
That you so oft have boasted to retain?
EDGAR [*aside*]
My tears begin to take his part so much
They mar my counterfeiting.
LEAR   The little dogs and all,
Tray, Blanch, and Sweetheart, see, they bark at me.
EDGAR   Tom will throw his head at them.—Avaunt, you 63
curs!
        Be thy mouth or black or white,   65
        Tooth that poisons if it bite,
        Mastiff, greyhound, mongrel grim,
        Hound or spaniel, brach or lym,   68
        Bobtail tike or trundle-tail,   69
        Tom will make him weep and wail;
        For, with throwing thus my head,
        Dogs leap the hatch, and all are fled.   72
Do de, de, de. Sessa! Come, march to wakes and fairs 73
and market towns. Poor Tom, thy horn is dry.   74
LEAR   Then let them anatomize Regan; see what breeds 75
about her heart. Is there any cause in nature that makes
these hard hearts? [*To Edgar*] You, sir, I entertain 77

for one of my hundred; only I do not like the fashion of
your garments. You will say they are Persian; but let 79
them be changed.
KENT
Now, good my lord, lie here and rest awhile.
LEAR [*lying on cushions*]   Make no noise, make no
noise. Draw the curtains. So, so. We'll go to supper 83
i'th' morning.   [*He sleeps.*]
FOOL   And I'll go to bed at noon.

        Enter Gloucester.

GLOUCESTER [*to Kent*]
Come hither, friend. Where is the King my master?
KENT
Here, sir, but trouble him not; his wits are gone.
GLOUCESTER
Good friend, I prithee, take him in thy arms.
I have o'erheard a plot of death upon him.   89
There is a litter ready; lay him in't
And drive toward Dover, friend, where thou shalt
    meet
Both welcome and protection. Take up thy master.
If thou shouldst dally half an hour, his life,
With thine and all that offer to defend him,
Stand in assurèd loss. Take up, take up,   95
And follow me, that will to some provision   96
Give thee quick conduct.
KENT   Oppressèd nature sleeps.   97
This rest might yet have balmed thy broken sinews,   98
Which, if convenience will not allow,   99
Stand in hard cure. [*To the Fool*] Come, help to bear thy
    master.   100
Thou must not stay behind.   [*They pick up Lear.*]
GLOUCESTER   Come, come, away!
                        Exeunt [*all but Edgar*].
EDGAR
When we our betters see bearing our woes,   102
We scarcely think our miseries our foes.   103
Who alone suffers suffers most i'th' mind,   104
Leaving free things and happy shows behind;   105
But then the mind much sufferance doth o'erskip   106
When grief hath mates, and bearing fellowship.   107
How light and portable my pain seems now,   108
When that which makes me bend makes the King
    bow—
He childed as I fathered. Tom, away!   110

38 Bench take your place on the bench. **o'th' commission** one commissioned to be a justice   **42 corn** grainfield   **43–4 And . . . harm** i.e., one shout from your dainty (*minikin*) mouth can recall the sheep from the grainfield and thus save them from dangerous overeating. **45 Purr the cat** (A devil or familiar from Harsnett; see the note for 3.4.114. *Purr* may be the sound the familiar makes.)   **47 kicked** who kicked   **51 joint stool** low stool made by a joiner, or maker of furniture with joined parts. (Proverbially, the phrase "I took . . . stool" meant "I beg your pardon for failing to notice you." The reference is also presumably to a real stool onstage.)   **52 another** i.e., Regan **53 store** abundance, material. **on** of.   **54 Corruption in the place!** i.e., There is iniquity or bribery in this court!   **63 throw his head at** i.e., threaten   **65 or black** either black   **68 brach or lym** bitch-hound or bloodhound   **69 Bobtail . . . trundle-tail** mongrel dog with a docked or bobbed tail, or one that is curly-tailed   **72 hatch** lower half of a divided door   **73 Sessa** i.e., Away, cease. **wakes** parish festivals **74 horn** horn-bottle, used by beggars to drink from and to beg for alms   **75 anatomize** dissect   **77 entertain** take into my service

79 Persian (Lear madly asks if Edgar's wretched blanket is a rich Persian fabric.)   **83 curtains** bedcurtains. (They presumably exist only in Lear's mad imagination.)   **89 upon** against   **95 Stand . . . loss** will assuredly be lost.   **96 provision** supplies, or, means of providing for safety   **97 conduct** guidance.   **98 balmed** soothed, healed. **sinews** nerves   **99 convenience** circumstances   **100 Stand . . . cure** will be hard to cure.   **102 our woes** woes like ours   **103 We . . . foes** we almost forget our own miseries (since we see how human suffering afflicts even the great).   **104–7 Who . . . fellowship** Anyone who has no companionship in suffering undergoes the mental anguish of forgetting entirely the carefree ways and happy scenes that were once enjoyed, whereas fellowship in grief enables the mind to rise above such suffering. (I.e., Misery loves company.)   **108 portable** bearable, endurable   **110 He . . . fathered** he suffering cruelty from his children as I from my father.

Mark the high noises, and thyself bewray   111
When false opinion, whose wrong thoughts defile
   thee,   112
In thy just proof repeals and reconciles thee.   113
What will hap more tonight, safe scape the King!   114
Lurk, lurk.   [*Exit.*]   115

♣

3.7

Enter Cornwall, Regan, Goneril, Bastard
[Edmund], and Servants.

CORNWALL [*to Goneril*]   Post speedily to my lord your hus-   1
band; show him this letter. [*He gives a letter.*] The army
of France is landed.—Seek out the traitor Gloucester.
                            [*Exeunt some Servants.*]
REGAN   Hang him instantly.
GONERIL   Pluck out his eyes.
CORNWALL   Leave him to my displeasure. Edmund,
keep you our sister company. The revenges we are   7
bound to take upon your traitorous father are not fit   8
for your beholding. Advise the Duke, where you are   9
going, to a most festinate preparation; we are bound   10
to the like. Our posts shall be swift and intelligent   11
betwixt us. Farewell, dear sister; farewell, my lord of   12
Gloucester.   13

        Enter steward [Oswald].

How now? Where's the King?
OSWALD
My lord of Gloucester hath conveyed him hence.
Some five- or six-and-thirty of his knights,   16
Hot questrists after him, met him at gate,   17
Who, with some other of the lord's dependents,   18
Are gone with him toward Dover, where they boast
To have well-armèd friends.
CORNWALL   Get horses for your mistress. [*Exit Oswald.*]
GONERIL   Farewell, sweet lord, and sister.
CORNWALL
Edmund, farewell.   *Exeunt [Goneril and Edmund].*
          Go seek the traitor Gloucester.
Pinion him like a thief; bring him before us.
                  [*Exeunt Servants.*]
Though well we may not pass upon his life   25
Without the form of justice, yet our power

Shall do a court'sy to our wrath, which men   27
May blame but not control.

    Enter Gloucester, and Servants [leading him].

                Who's there? The traitor?
REGAN   Ingrateful fox! 'Tis he.
CORNWALL   Bind fast his corky arms.   30
GLOUCESTER
What means Your Graces? Good my friends, consider
You are my guests. Do me no foul play, friends.
CORNWALL
Bind him, I say.   [*Servants bind him.*]
REGAN   Hard, hard. Oh, filthy traitor!
GLOUCESTER
Unmerciful lady as you are, I'm none.
CORNWALL
To this chair bind him.—Villain, thou shalt find—
           [*Regan plucks Gloucester's beard.*]
GLOUCESTER
By the kind gods, 'tis most ignobly done
To pluck me by the beard.
REGAN
So white, and such a traitor?
GLOUCESTER   Naughty lady,   38
These hairs which thou dost ravish from my chin
Will quicken and accuse thee. I am your host.   40
With robbers' hands my hospitable favors   41
You should not ruffle thus. What will you do?   42
CORNWALL
Come, sir, what letters had you late from France?   43
REGAN
Be simple-answered, for we know the truth.   44
CORNWALL
And what confederacy have you with the traitors
Late footed in the kingdom?
REGAN   To whose hands   46
You have sent the lunatic King. Speak.
GLOUCESTER
I have a letter guessingly set down,   48
Which came from one that's of a neutral heart,
And not from one opposed.
CORNWALL   Cunning.
REGAN   And false.
CORNWALL   Where hast thou sent the King?
GLOUCESTER   To Dover.
REGAN
Wherefore to Dover? Wast thou not charged at peril—   55
CORNWALL
Wherefore to Dover? Let him answer that.
GLOUCESTER
I am tied to th' stake, and I must stand the course.   57

111–13 Mark . . . thee Observe what is being said about those in high places or about great events, and reveal your identity only when the general opinion that now slanders you, at length establishing your innocence, recalls you from banishment and restores you to favor. **114 What . . . King!** Whatever else happens tonight, may the King escape safely! **115 Lurk** Keep out of sight **3.7. Location: Gloucester's house.** **1 Post speedily** Hurry **7 sister** sister-in-law, Goneril **8 bound** intending; obliged **9 the Duke** Albany **10 festinate** hasty. **are bound** intend, are committed **11 posts** messengers. **intelligent** serviceable in bearing information, knowledgeable **12–13 my . . . Gloucester** i.e., Edmund, the recipient now of his father's forfeited estate and title. (Two lines later, Oswald uses the same title to refer to Edmund's father.) **16 his** Lear's **17 questrists after him** searchers for Lear **18 the lord's** i.e., Gloucester's **25 pass upon his life** pass the death sentence upon him

27 do a court'sy i.e., bow before, yield precedence **30 corky** withered with age **38 white** white-haired, venerable. **Naughty** Wicked **40 quicken** come to life **41–2 With . . . thus** You should not roughly handle my welcoming face with your hands as though you were robbers. **43 late** lately **44 simple-answered** straightforward in your answers **46 Late footed** recently landed **48 guessingly set down** conjecturally written **55 charged at peril** commanded on peril of your life **57 tied to th' stake** i.e., like a bear to be baited with dogs. **the course** the dogs' attack.

REGAN   Wherefore to Dover?

GLOUCESTER
Because I would not see thy cruel nails
Pluck out his poor old eyes, nor thy fierce sister
In his anointed flesh rash boarish fangs.   61
The sea, with such a storm as his bare head
In hell-black night endured, would have buoyed up   63
And quenched the stellèd fires;   64
Yet, poor old heart, he holp the heavens to rain.   65
If wolves had at thy gate howled that dern time,   66
Thou shouldst have said, "Good porter, turn the key."   67
All cruels else subscribe. But I shall see   68
The wingèd Vengeance overtake such children.   69

CORNWALL
See't shalt thou never.—Fellows, hold the chair.
Upon these eyes of thine I'll set my foot.

GLOUCESTER
He that will think to live till he be old,   72
Give me some help!
      [*Servants hold the chair as Cornwall grinds
      out one of Gloucester's eyes with his boot.*]
                     Oh, cruel! O you gods!

REGAN
One side will mock another. Th'other too.

CORNWALL [*to Gloucester*]
If you see Vengeance—

FIRST SERVANT   Hold your hand, my lord!
I have served you ever since I was a child;
But better service have I never done you
Than now to bid you hold.

REGAN   How now, you dog?

FIRST SERVANT [*to Regan*]
If you did wear a beard upon your chin,
I'd shake it on this quarrel.—What do you mean?   80

CORNWALL   My villain?   [*He draws his sword.*] 81

FIRST SERVANT [*drawing*]
Nay, then, come on, and take the chance of anger.   82
                       [*They fight. Cornwall is wounded.*]

REGAN [*to another Servant*]
Give me thy sword. A peasant stand up thus?   83
               [*She takes a sword and runs at him behind.*]

FIRST SERVANT
Oh, I am slain! My lord, you have one eye left
To see some mischief on him. Oh!   [*He dies.*] 85

CORNWALL
Lest it see more, prevent it. Out, vile jelly!
                  [*He puts out Gloucester's other eye.*]

Where is thy luster now?

GLOUCESTER
All dark and comfortless. Where's my son Edmund?
Edmund, enkindle all the sparks of nature   89
To quit this horrid act.

REGAN   Out, treacherous villain!   90
Thou call'st on him that hates thee. It was he
That made the overture of thy treasons to us,   92
Who is too good to pity thee.

GLOUCESTER
Oh, my follies! Then Edgar was abused.   94
Kind gods, forgive me that, and prosper him!

REGAN [*to a Servant*]
Go thrust him out at gates and let him smell
His way to Dover.   *Exit* [*a Servant*] *with Gloucester.*
               How is't, my lord? How look you?   97

CORNWALL
I have received a hurt. Follow me, lady.—
Turn out that eyeless villain. Throw this slave
Upon the dunghill.—Regan, I bleed apace.
Untimely comes this hurt. Give me your arm.
            Exeunt [*Cornwall, supported by Regan*].

SECOND SERVANT
I'll never care what wickedness I do,
If this man come to good.

THIRD SERVANT   If she live long,
And in the end meet the old course of death,   104
Women will all turn monsters.

SECOND SERVANT
Let's follow the old Earl, and get the Bedlam   106
To lead him where he would. His roguish madness 107
Allows itself to anything.   108

THIRD SERVANT
Go thou. I'll fetch some flax and whites of eggs
To apply to his bleeding face. Now, heaven help him! 110
                          Exeunt [*with the body*].

❦

4.1

Enter Edgar [*as poor Tom*].

EDGAR
Yet better thus, and known to be contemned,   1
Than still contemned and flattered. To be worst,   2
The lowest and most dejected thing of fortune,   3
Stands still in esperance, lives not in fear.   4

---

61 anointed consecrated with holy oil.   **rash** slash, stick
63–4 would . . . fires would have swelled high enough, like a wave-lifted buoy, to quench the stars. (*Stellèd* means "starry" or "fixed.")
65 holp helped   **66 dern** dire, dread   **67 turn the key** i.e., let them in.   **68 All . . . subscribe** All other cruel creatures would show forgiveness except you; this cruelty is unparalleled.   **69 The wingèd Vengeance** the swift vengeance of the avenging angel of divine wrath
72 will think hopes   **80 I'd . . . quarrel** i.e., I'd pull your beard in vehement defiance in this cause.   **What do you mean?** i.e., What are you thinking of, what do you think you're doing? (Said perhaps to Cornwall.)   **81 villain** servant, bondman. (Cornwall's question implies, "How dare you do such a thing?")   **82 the chance of anger** the risks of an angry encounter.   **83.1 She . . . behind** (This stage direction appears in the Quarto.)   **85 mischief** injury

89 nature i.e., filial love   **90 quit** requite.   **Out** (An exclamation of anger or impatience.)   **92 overture** disclosure   **94 abused** wronged.
97 How look you? How is it with you?   **104 old** customary, natural
106 Bedlam i.e., lunatic discharged from the insane asylum and licensed to beg   **107–8 His . . . anything** His being a madman and derelict allows him to do anything we ask.   **110.1 Exeunt** (At some point after lines 99–100, the body of the slain First Servant must be removed.)
4.1. Location: An open place.
1–2 Yet . . . flattered It is better to be openly despised as a beggar than continually despised behind one's back and flattered to one's face.
3 dejected cast down   **4 Stands . . . fear** gives one some cause for hope, having nothing to fear (since everything is already lost).

The lamentable change is from the best;   5
The worst returns to laughter. Welcome, then,   6
Thou unsubstantial air that I embrace!
The wretch that thou hast blown unto the worst
Owes nothing to thy blasts.

Enter Gloucester, and an Old Man [leading him].

                             But who comes here?   9
My father, poorly led? World, world, O world!
But that thy strange mutations make us hate thee,   11
Life would not yield to age.   12

OLD MAN
Oh, my good lord, I have been your tenant
And your father's tenant these fourscore years.

GLOUCESTER
Away, get thee away! Good friend, begone.
Thy comforts can do me no good at all;
Thee they may hurt.

OLD MAN   You cannot see your way.

GLOUCESTER
I have no way and therefore want no eyes;
I stumbled when I saw. Full oft 'tis seen
Our means secure us, and our mere defects   20
Prove our commodities. O dear son Edgar,   21
The food of thy abusèd father's wrath!   22
Might I but live to see thee in my touch,   23
I'd say I had eyes again!

OLD MAN   How now? Who's there?

EDGAR [*aside*]
O gods! Who is't can say, "I am at the worst"?
I am worse than e'er I was.

OLD MAN   'Tis poor mad Tom.

EDGAR [*aside*]
And worse I may be yet. The worst is not   27
So long as we can say, "This is the worst."   28

OLD MAN [*to Edgar*]
Fellow, where goest?

GLOUCESTER   Is it a beggar-man?

OLD MAN   Madman and beggar too.

GLOUCESTER
He has some reason, else he could not beg.   31
I'th' last night's storm I such a fellow saw,
Which made me think a man a worm. My son
Came then into my mind, and yet my mind
Was then scarce friends with him. I have heard more
   since.
As flies to wanton boys are we to th' gods;   36

They kill us for their sport.

EDGAR [*aside*]   How should this be?   37
Bad is the trade that must play fool to sorrow,   38
Ang'ring itself and others.—Bless thee, master!   39

GLOUCESTER
Is that the naked fellow?

OLD MAN   Ay, my lord.

GLOUCESTER
Then, prithee, get thee gone. If for my sake
Thou wilt o'ertake us hence a mile or twain   42
I'th' way toward Dover, do it for ancient love,   43
And bring some covering for this naked soul,
Which I'll entreat to lead me.

OLD MAN   Alack, sir, he is mad.

GLOUCESTER
'Tis the time's plague, when madmen lead the blind.   46
Do as I bid thee, or rather do thy pleasure;
Above the rest, begone.   48

OLD MAN
I'll bring him the best 'parel that I have,
Come on't what will.   *Exit.*

GLOUCESTER   Sirrah, naked fellow—   50

EDGAR
Poor Tom's a-cold. [*Aside*] I cannot daub it further.   51

GLOUCESTER   Come hither, fellow.

EDGAR [*aside*]
And yet I must.—Bless thy sweet eyes, they bleed.

GLOUCESTER   Know'st thou the way to Dover?

EDGAR   Both stile and gate, horseway and footpath.
Poor Tom hath been scared out of his good wits. Bless
thee, good man's son, from the foul fiend! Five fiends
have been in poor Tom at once: of lust, as Obidicut;   58
Hobbididance, prince of dumbness; Mahu, of stealing;   59
Modo, of murder; Flibbertigibbet, of mopping   60
and mowing, who since possesses chambermaids and   61
waiting women. So, bless thee, master!

GLOUCESTER [*giving a purse*]
Here, take this purse, thou whom the heavens'
   plagues
Have humbled to all strokes. That I am wretched   64
Makes thee the happier. Heavens, deal so still!
Let the superfluous and lust-dieted man,   66

5–6 The lamentable . . . laughter Any change from the best is griev-ous, just as any change from the worst is bound to be for the better. **9 Owes nothing** can pay no more, is free of obligation **11–12 But . . . age** If it were not for your hateful inconstancy, we would never be reconciled to old age and death. **20–1 Our . . . commodities** Our prosperity makes us proudly overconfident, whereas the sheer afflic-tions we suffer prove beneficial (by teaching us humility). **22 The . . . wrath** on whom thy deceived father's wrath fed, the object of his anger. **23 in** by means of **27–8 The worst . . . worst** So long as we can speak and act and delude ourselves with false hopes, our for-tunes can, in fact, grow worse. **31 reason** sanity **36 wanton** child-ishly cruel

37 How . . . be? i.e., How can he have suffered so much, changed so much? **38–9 Bad . . . others** It's a bad business to have to play the fool to my sorrowing father, vexing myself and others (with this delay in revealing my true identity). **42 o'ertake us** catch up to us (after you have found clothing for Tom o' Bedlam) **43 ancient love** i.e., the mutually trusting relationship of master and tenant that you and I have long enjoyed **46 'Tis the time's plague** It well expresses the spreading sickness of our present state **48 the rest** all **50 Come . . . will** whatever comes of this as regards myself. **51 I . . . further** i.e., I cannot keep up this pretense any longer. (Literally, "I cannot plaster up the wall.") **58–60 Obidicut . . . Flibbertigibbet** (Fiends borrowed, as before in 3.4.114 and 139–42, from Harsnett.) **60–1 mopping and mowing** making grimaces and mouths **61 since** ever since then **64 Have . . . strokes** have brought so low as to bear every blow of Fortune. **66 superfluous and lust-dieted** immoder-ately gluttonous and luxuriously fed

That slaves your ordinance, that will not see   67
Because he does not feel, feel your pow'r quickly!   68
So distribution should undo excess
And each man have enough. Dost thou know Dover?

EDGAR   Ay, master.

GLOUCESTER
There is a cliff, whose high and bending head   72
Looks fearfully in the confinèd deep.   73
Bring me but to the very brim of it
And I'll repair the misery thou dost bear
With something rich about me. From that place   76
I shall no leading need.

EDGAR   Give me thy arm.
Poor Tom shall lead thee.   *Exeunt.*

❧

4.2

Enter Goneril [and] Bastard [Edmund].

GONERIL
Welcome, my lord. I marvel our mild husband   1
Not met us on the way.

        [Enter] steward [Oswald].

                        Now, where's your master?   2

OSWALD
Madam, within, but never man so changed.
I told him of the army that was landed;
He smiled at it. I told him you were coming;
His answer was "The worse." Of Gloucester's
     treachery
And of the loyal service of his son
When I informed him, then he called me sot   8
And told me I had turned the wrong side out.
What most he should dislike seems pleasant to him;
What like, offensive.

GONERIL *[to Edmund]*   Then shall you go no further.
It is the cowish terror of his spirit,   12
That dares not undertake. He'll not feel wrongs   13
Which tie him to an answer. Our wishes on the way 14
May prove effects. Back, Edmund, to my brother;   15
Hasten his musters and conduct his powers.   16
I must change names at home and give the distaff   17

Into my husband's hands. This trusty servant
Shall pass between us. Ere long you are like to hear,   19
If you dare venture in your own behalf,
A mistress's command. Wear this; spare speech.   21
                        [She gives him a favor.]
Decline your head. *[She kisses him.]* This kiss, if it durst
     speak,
Would stretch thy spirits up into the air.
Conceive, and fare thee well.   24

EDMUND
Yours in the ranks of death.   *Exit.*

GONERIL   My most dear Gloucester!
Oh, the difference of man and man!
To thee a woman's services are due;
My fool usurps my body.   28

OSWALD   Madam, here comes my lord.   *[Exit.]*   29

        Enter Albany.

GONERIL
I have been worth the whistling.

ALBANY   Oh, Goneril,   30
You are not worth the dust which the rude wind
Blows in your face. I fear your disposition;   32
That nature which contemns its origin   33
Cannot be bordered certain in itself.   34
She that herself will sliver and disbranch   35
From her material sap perforce must wither   36
And come to deadly use.   37

GONERIL   No more. The text is foolish.   38

ALBANY
Wisdom and goodness to the vile seem vile;
Filths savor but themselves. What have you done? 40
Tigers, not daughters, what have you performed?
A father, and a gracious agèd man,
Whose reverence even the head-lugged bear would
     lick,   43
Most barbarous, most degenerate, have you madded. 44
Could my good brother suffer you to do it?   45
A man, a prince, by him so benefited?
If that the heavens do not their visible spirits   47
Send quickly down to tame these vile offenses,
It will come,
Humanity must perforce prey on itself,
Like monsters of the deep.

GONERIL   Milk-livered man,   51

67 **That . . . ordinance** who enslaves your divine ordinances to his own corrupt will   **67–8 that . . . feel** who is resistant to spiritual insight because, not having suffered himself, he lacks the sympathy of fellow feeling   **72 bending** overhanging   **73 in . . . deep** i.e., into the sea below, which is confined by its shores.   **76 about me** on my person.
4.2. Location: Before the Duke of Albany's palace.
1 Welcome (Goneril, who has just arrived home from Gloucestershire escorted by Edmund, bids him brief welcome before he must return.)
2 Not met has not met   **8 sot** fool   **12 cowish** cowardly   **13 undertake** venture.   **13–14 He'll . . . answer** He will ignore insults that, if he took notice, would oblige him to respond, to fight.   **14–15 Our . . . effects** The hopes we discussed on our journey here (presumably concerning the supplanting of Albany by Edmund) may come to pass.   **15 brother** brother-in-law, Cornwall   **16 musters** assembling of troops.   **powers** armed forces.   **17 change names** i.e., exchange the roles of master and mistress of the household, and exchange the insignia of man and woman: the sword and the *distaff*.   **distaff** spinning staff, symbolizing the wife's role

19 like likely   **21 mistress's** (With sexual double meaning.)   **24 Conceive** Understand, take my meaning. (With sexual double entendre, continuing from *stretch thy spirits* in the previous line and continued in *death*, line 25, and *a woman's services*, line 27.)   **28 My fool . . . body** i.e., my husband claims possession of me but is unfitted to do so.   **29 s.d. Exit** (Oswald could exit later with Goneril, at line 88.)   **30 worth the whistling** i.e., worth the attentions of men. (Alludes to the proverb, "it is a poor dog that is not worth the whistling.")   **32 fear your disposition** mistrust your nature   **33 contemns** spurns   **34 bordered certain** safely restrained, kept within bounds   **35 sliver** tear off   **36 material sap** nourishing substance, the stock from which she grew   **37 to deadly use** to a bad end, to a destructive purpose.   **38 The text** i.e., on which you have been preaching   **40 savor but themselves** hunger only for that which is filthy.   **43 head-lugged** dragged by the head (or by the ring in its nose) and infuriated   **44 madded** driven mad.   **45 brother** brother-in-law (Cornwall)   **47 If that** If.   **visible** manifested   **51 Milk-livered** White-livered, cowardly

That bear'st a cheek for blows, a head for wrongs,
Who hast not in thy brows an eye discerning   53
Thine honor from thy suffering, that not know'st   54
Fools do those villains pity who are punished   55
Ere they have done their mischief. Where's thy drum?   56
France spreads his banners in our noiseless land,   57
With plumèd helm thy state begins to threat,   58
Whilst thou, a moral fool, sits still and cries,   59
"Alack, why does he so?"
ALBANY   See thyself, devil!   60
Proper deformity shows not in the fiend   61
So horrid as in woman.
GONERIL   Oh, vain fool!   62
ALBANY
Thou changèd and self-covered thing, for shame,   63
Bemonster not thy feature. Were't my fitness   64
To let these hands obey my blood,   65
They are apt enough to dislocate and tear   66
Thy flesh and bones. Howe'er thou art a fiend,   67
A woman's shape doth shield thee.   68
GONERIL   Marry, your manhood! Mew!   69

    Enter a Messenger.

ALBANY   What news?
MESSENGER
Oh, my good lord, the Duke of Cornwall's dead,
Slain by his servant, going to put out
The other eye of Gloucester.
ALBANY   Gloucester's eyes!
MESSENGER
A servant that he bred, thrilled with remorse,   74
Opposed against the act, bending his sword   75
To his great master, who, thereat enraged,   76
Flew on him and amongst them felled him dead,   77
But not without that harmful stroke which since
Hath plucked him after.
ALBANY   This shows you are above,   79

You justicers, that these our nether crimes   80
So speedily can venge! But, Oh, poor Gloucester!
Lost he his other eye?
MESSENGER   Both, both, my lord.—
This letter, madam, craves a speedy answer;
'Tis from your sister.   [*He gives her a letter.*]
GONERIL [*aside*]   One way I like this well;   84
But being widow, and my Gloucester with her,   85
May all the building in my fancy pluck   86
Upon my hateful life. Another way   87
The news is not so tart.—I'll read, and answer.   88
                                            [*Exit.*]
ALBANY
Where was his son when they did take his eyes?   89
MESSENGER
Come with my lady hither.
ALBANY   He is not here.
MESSENGER
No, my good lord. I met him back again.   91
ALBANY   Knows he the wickedness?
MESSENGER
Ay, my good lord. 'Twas he informed against him,
And quit the house on purpose that their punishment
Might have the freer course.
ALBANY   Gloucester, I live   95
To thank thee for the love thou show'dst the King
And to revenge thine eyes.—Come hither, friend.
Tell me what more thou know'st.   *Exeunt.*

❖

4.[3]

    Enter Kent [disguised] and a Gentleman.

KENT   Why the King of France is so suddenly gone back
    know you no reason?
GENTLEMAN   Something he left imperfect in the state,   3
    which since his coming forth is thought of, which im- 4
    ports to the kingdom so much fear and danger that his 5
    personal return was most required and necessary.
KENT
Who hath he left behind him general?
GENTLEMAN
The Marshal of France, Monsieur la Far.
KENT   Did your letters pierce the Queen to any demon-
    stration of grief?
GENTLEMAN
Ay, sir. She took them, read them in my presence,
And now and then an ample tear trilled down   12
Her delicate cheek. It seemed she was a queen

53–4 discerning . . . suffering able to tell the difference between an insult to your honor and something you should tolerate   **54–6 that not . . . mischief** you who fail to understand that only fools like yourself are so tenderhearted as to pity villains (like Gloucester, Lear, and Cordelia) who are apprehended and punished before they have committed a crime.   **56 Where's thy drum?** Where is your military preparedness?   **57 noiseless** peaceful, unprepared for war   **58 thy state . . . threat** (France) begins to threaten your kingdom   **59 moral** moralizing   **60 "Alack . . . so?"** (An utterly ineffectual response to invasion.)   **61–2 Proper . . . woman** The deformity that is appropriate in a fiend's features is even uglier in a woman's (since it is so at variance with her nominally feminine appearance).   **63–4 Thou . . . feature** i.e., You creature whose transformation into a fiend now overwhelms your womanliness, do not, however evil you are, take on the outward form of a monster or fiend.   **64 Were't my fitness** If it were suitable for me   **65 blood** passion   **66 apt** ready   **67 Howe'er . . . fiend** However much you may be a fiend in reality   **68 shield** (Since I, as a gentleman, cannot lay violent hands on a lady.)   **69 Mew** (An exclamation of disgust, a derisive catcall: You speak of manhood in shielding me as a woman. Some manhood!)   **74 bred** kept in his household.   **thrilled with remorse** deeply moved with pity   **75 Opposed** opposed himself   **75–6 bending . . . To** directing his sword against   **77 amongst them** together with the others (?) in their midst (?) out of their number (?)   **79 after** along (to death).

80 justicers (heavenly) judges.   **nether** i.e., committed here below, on earth   **84 One way** (i.e., because Edmund is now Duke of Gloucester, and Cornwall, a dangerous rival for the throne, is dead)   **85–7 But . . . life** but she being now a widow, and Edmund in her company, may pull down my imagined happiness (of having the entire kingdom with Edmund), leaving my hopes in ruins.   **88 tart** bitter, sour. (See line 84 and note.)   **89 his son** Edmund.   **his** Gloucester's.   **91 back again** on the way back (from Albany's palace).   **95 Gloucester** The old Earl of Gloucester
4.3. Location: The French camp near Dover.
3 imperfect in the state unsettled in state affairs   **4–5 imports** portends   **12 trilled** trickled

Over her passion, who, most rebel-like,
Sought to be king o'er her.
KENT   Oh, then it moved her?
GENTLEMAN
Not to a rage. Patience and sorrow strove
Who should express her goodliest. You have seen   17
Sunshine and rain at once. Her smiles and tears
Were like a better way; those happy smilets   19
That played on her ripe lip seemed not to know   20
What guests were in her eyes, which parted thence   21
As pearls from diamonds dropped. In brief,
Sorrow would be a rarity most beloved   23
If all could so become it.   24
KENT   Made she no verbal question?   25
GENTLEMAN
Faith, once or twice she heaved the name of "father"   26
Pantingly forth, as if it pressed her heart;
Cried, "Sisters, sisters! Shame of ladies, sisters!
Kent! Father! Sisters! What, i'th' storm, i'th' night?
Let pity not be believed!" There she shook   30
The holy water from her heavenly eyes,
And, clamor-moistened, then away she started   32
To deal with grief alone.
KENT   It is the stars,
The stars above us, govern our conditions,   34
Else one self mate and make could not beget   35
Such different issues. You spoke not with her since?   36
GENTLEMAN   No.
KENT
Was this before the King returned?
GENTLEMAN   No, since.   38
KENT
Well, sir, the poor distressèd Lear's i'th' town,
Who sometime in his better tune remembers   40
What we are come about, and by no means
Will yield to see his daughter.
GENTLEMAN   Why, good sir?   42
KENT
A sovereign shame so elbows him—his own
    unkindness   43
That stripped her from his benediction, turned her   44
To foreign casualties, gave her dear rights   45
To his dog-hearted daughters—these things sting
His mind so venomously that burning shame
Detains him from Cordelia.   48

GENTLEMAN   Alack, poor gentleman!   14
KENT
Of Albany's and Cornwall's powers you heard not?   50
GENTLEMAN   'Tis so. They are afoot.   51
KENT
Well, sir, I'll bring you to our master Lear
And leave you to attend him. Some dear cause   53
Will in concealment wrap me up awhile.
When I am known aright, you shall not grieve   55
Lending me this acquaintance. I pray you, go   56
Along with me.   Exeunt.

✤

4.[4]

*Enter, with drum and colors, Cordelia,
Gentleman, and soldiers.*

CORDELIA
Alack, 'tis he! Why, he was met even now
As mad as the vexed sea, singing aloud,
Crowned with rank fumiter and furrow weeds,   3
With hardocks, hemlock, nettles, cuckooflowers,   4
Darnel, and all the idle weeds that grow   5
In our sustaining corn. A century send forth!   6
Search every acre in the high-grown field
And bring him to our eye.   [*Exit a soldier or soldiers.*]
                              What can man's wisdom   8
In the restoring his bereavèd sense,
He that helps him take all my outward worth.   10
GENTLEMAN   There is means, madam.
Our foster nurse of nature is repose,
The which he lacks. That to provoke in him   13
Are many simples operative, whose power   14
Will close the eye of anguish.
CORDELIA   All blest secrets,
All you unpublished virtues of the earth,   16
Spring with my tears! Be aidant and remediate   17
In the good man's distress! Seek, seek for him,
Lest his ungoverned rage dissolve the life   19
That wants the means to lead it.

Enter Messenger.

MESSENGER   News, madam.   20
The British powers are marching hitherward.   21

---

14 who which   **17 Who . . . goodliest** which of the two could portray
her best.   **19 like a better way** better than that, though similar
20–1 seemed . . . eyes seemed oblivious of her tears   **23 a rarity** i.e., a
precious thing, like a jewel   **24 If . . . it** i.e., if all persons were as
attractive in sorrow as she.   **25 verbal** i.e., as distinguished from her
tears and looks   **26 heaved** breathed out with difficulty   **30 Let . . .
believed!** i.e., Let no show of pity be trusted (since they are proved to
be so false)!   **32 clamor-moistened** i.e., her outcry of grief assuaged
by tears.   **started** i.e., went   **34 conditions** characters   **35 Else . . .
make** otherwise, one couple (husband and wife)   **36 issues** offspring.   **38 before . . . returned** before the King of France returned to
his kingdom.   **40 better tune** more composed state of mind
42 yield consent   **43 sovereign** overruling.   **elbows him** i.e., prods
his memory, jostles him, thrusts him back   **44 turned her** turned her
out   **45 foreign casualties** chances of fortune abroad   **48 Detains
him from** holds him back from seeing

50 powers troops, armies   **51 afoot** on the march.   **53 dear cause**
important purpose   **55–6 grieve . . . acquaintance** regret having
made my acquaintance.
4.4. Location: The French camp.
0.2 Gentleman (The Quarto specifies "Doctor" here and at line 11.)
3 fumiter fumitory, a weed or herb.   **furrow weeds** weeds growing
in plowed furrows   **4 hardocks** probably burdock, a coarse weedy
plant.   **cuckooflowers** flowers of late spring, when the cuckoo is
heard   **5 Darnel** weed of the grass kind.   **idle** worthless   **6 sustaining corn** sustenance-giving grain.   **A century** (Literally, a troop of
one hundred men.)   **8 What . . . wisdom** i.e., What medical knowledge can accomplish   **10 outward** material   **13 That to provoke** To
induce that   **14 Are . . . operative** many herbal remedies are efficacious; or, there are many effective remedies. (*Simples* are prepared
from a single herb.)   **16 unpublished virtues** little-known benign
herbs   **17 Spring** grow.   **aidant and remediate** helpful and remedial
19 rage frenzy   **20 That . . . lead it** that lacks the means to live sanely.
21 powers armies

CORDELIA

    'Tis known before. Our preparation stands
    In expectation of them. O dear father,
    It is thy business that I go about;
    Therefore great France
    My mourning and importuned tears hath pitied.   26
    No blown ambition doth our arms incite,   27
    But love, dear love, and our aged father's right.
    Soon may I hear and see him!   *Exeunt.*

❖

4.[5]

Enter Regan and steward [Oswald].

REGAN   But are my brother's powers set forth?   1
OSWALD   Ay, madam.
REGAN   Himself in person there?
OSWALD   Madam, with much ado.   4
    Your sister is the better soldier.
REGAN
    Lord Edmund spake not with your lord at home?
OSWALD   No, madam.
REGAN
    What might import my sister's letters to him?   8
OSWALD   I know not, lady.
REGAN
    Faith, he is posted hence on serious matter.   10
    It was great ignorance, Gloucester's eyes being out,   11
    To let him live. Where he arrives he moves
    All hearts against us. Edmund, I think, is gone,
    In pity of his misery, to dispatch   14
    His nighted life; moreover to descry   15
    The strength o'th'enemy.
OSWALD
    I must needs after him, madam, with my letter.
REGAN
    Our troops set forth tomorrow. Stay with us;
    The ways are dangerous.
OSWALD   I may not, madam.
    My lady charged my duty in this business.   20
REGAN
    Why should she write to Edmund? Might not you
    Transport her purposes by word? Belike   22
    Something—I know not what. I'll love thee much;
    Let me unseal the letter.
OSWALD   Madam, I had rather—
REGAN
    I know your lady does not love her husband,
    I am sure of that; and at her late being here   26
    She gave strange oeillades and most speaking looks   27
    To noble Edmund. I know you are of her bosom.   28
OSWALD   I, madam?

---

26 importuned importunate   **27 blown** swollen
4.5. Location; Gloucester's house.
1 my brother's powers Albany's forces   **4 with much ado** after much
fuss and persuasion.   **8 import** bear as their purport, express   **10 is
posted** has hurried   **11 ignorance** error, folly   **14 his** Gloucester's
15 nighted benighted, blinded.   **descry** spy out   **20 charged my
duty** laid great stress on my obedience   **22 Belike** It may be   **26 late**
recently   **27 oeillades** amorous glances   **28 of her bosom** in her confidence.

REGAN
    I speak in understanding; y'are, I know't.   30
    Therefore I do advise you, take this note: 31
    My lord is dead; Edmund and I have talked,   32
    And more convenient is he for my hand   33
    Than for your lady's. You may gather more.   34
    If you do find him, pray you, give him this;   35
    And when your mistress hears thus much from you,   36
    I pray, desire her call her wisdom to her.   37
    So, fare you well.
    If you do chance to hear of that blind traitor,
    Preferment falls on him that cuts him off.   40
OSWALD
    Would I could meet him, madam! I should show
    What party I do follow.
REGAN   Fare thee well.
    Exeunt [separately].

❖

4.[6]

*Enter Gloucester, and Edgar [in peasant's clothes,
leading his father].*

GLOUCESTER
    When shall I come to th' top of that same hill?   1
EDGAR
    You do climb up it now. Look how we labor.
GLOUCESTER
    Methinks the ground is even.
EDGAR   Horrible steep.
    Hark, do you hear the sea?
GLOUCESTER   No, truly.
EDGAR
    Why, then, your other senses grow imperfect
    By your eyes' anguish.
GLOUCESTER   So may it be, indeed.
    Methinks thy voice is altered, and thou speak'st
    In better phrase and matter than thou didst.
EDGAR
    You're much deceived. In nothing am I changed
    But in my garments.
GLOUCESTER   Methinks you're better spoken.
EDGAR
    Come on, sir, here's the place. Stand still. How fearful
    And dizzy 'tis to cast one's eyes so low!
    The crows and choughs that wing the midway air   13
    Show scarce so gross as beetles. Halfway down   14
    Hangs one that gathers samphire—dreadful trade!   15
    Methinks he seems no bigger than his head.
    The fishermen that walk upon the beach

---

30 y'are you are   **31 take this note** take note of this   **32 have talked**
have come to an understanding   **33 convenient** fitting   **34 gather
more** infer what I am trying to suggest.   **35 this** i.e., this information,
or a love token, or possibly a letter (though only one letter, Goneril's,
is found on his dead body at 4.6.262)   **36 thus much** what I have told
you   **37 call . . . to her** recall herself to her senses   **40 Preferment**
advancement
4.6. Location: Open place near Dover.
1 that same hill i.e., the cliff we talked about (4.1.72–4).   **13 choughs**
jackdaws.   **midway** halfway down   **14 gross** large   **15 samphire** (A
herb used in pickling.)

Appear like mice, and yond tall anchoring bark 18
Diminished to her cock; her cock, a buoy 19
Almost too small for sight. The murmuring surge,
That on th'unnumbered idle pebble chafes, 21
Cannot be heard so high. I'll look no more,
Lest my brain turn, and the deficient sight 23
Topple down headlong.

GLOUCESTER   Set me where you stand. 24

EDGAR
Give me your hand. You are now within a foot
Of th'extreme verge. For all beneath the moon 26
Would I not leap upright.

GLOUCESTER   Let go my hand. 27
Here, friend, 's another purse; in it a jewel
Well worth a poor man's taking.   [*He gives a purse.*]
    Fairies and gods 29
Prosper it with thee! Go thou further off. 30
Bid me farewell, and let me hear thee going.

EDGAR [*moving away*]
Now fare ye well, good sir.

GLOUCESTER   With all my heart.

EDGAR [*aside*]
Why I do trifle thus with his despair
Is done to cure it.

GLOUCESTER [*kneeling*]   O you mighty gods!
This world I do renounce, and in your sights
Shake patiently my great affliction off.
If I could bear it longer and not fall
To quarrel with your great opposeless wills, 38
My snuff and loathèd part of nature should 39
Burn itself out. If Edgar live, oh, bless him!
Now, fellow, fare thee well.   [*He falls forward.*]

EDGAR   Gone, sir. Farewell.—
And yet I know not how conceit may rob 42
The treasury of life, when life itself
Yields to the theft. Had he been where he thought, 44
By this had thought been past. Alive or dead?— 45
Ho, you, sir! Friend! Hear you, sir! Speak!—
Thus might he pass indeed; yet he revives.— 47
What are you, sir?

GLOUCESTER   Away, and let me die. 48

EDGAR
Hadst thou been aught but gossamer, feathers, air,
So many fathom down precipitating,
Thou'dst shivered like an egg; but thou dost breathe,
Hast heavy substance, bleed'st not, speak'st, art
    sound. 52

Ten masts at each make not the altitude 53
Which thou hast perpendicularly fell.
Thy life's a miracle. Speak yet again.

GLOUCESTER   But have I fall'n or no?

EDGAR
From the dread summit of this chalky bourn. 57
Look up aheight; the shrill-gorged lark so far 58
Cannot be seen or heard. Do but look up.

GLOUCESTER   Alack, I have no eyes.
Is wretchedness deprived that benefit
To end itself by death? 'Twas yet some comfort
When misery could beguile the tyrant's rage 63
And frustrate his proud will.

EDGAR   Give me your arm.
                    [*He lifts him up.*]
Up—so. How is't? Feel you your legs? You stand.

GLOUCESTER
Too well, too well.

EDGAR   This is above all strangeness.
Upon the crown o'th' cliff what thing was that
Which parted from you?

GLOUCESTER   A poor unfortunate beggar.

EDGAR
As I stood here below, methought his eyes
Were two full moons; he had a thousand noses,
Horns whelked and waved like the enridgèd sea. 71
It was some fiend. Therefore, thou happy father, 72
Think that the clearest gods, who make them honors 73
Of men's impossibilities, have preserved thee. 74

GLOUCESTER
I do remember now. Henceforth I'll bear
Affliction till it do cry out itself 76
"Enough, enough," and die. That thing you speak of, 77
I took it for a man; often 'twould say
"The fiend, the fiend." He led me to that place.

EDGAR
Bear free and patient thoughts.

        Enter Lear [*mad, fantastically dressed with wild
        flowers*].

                    But who comes here? 80
The safer sense will ne'er accommodate 81
His master thus. 82

LEAR   No, they cannot touch me for coining. I am the 83
King himself. 84

EDGAR   Oh, thou side-piercing sight! 85

---

18 **bark** small sailing vessel   19 **Diminished . . . cock** reduced to the size of her cockboat, small ship's boat   21 **th'unnumbered idle pebble** innumerable, randomly shifting, pebbles   23–4 **Lest . . . headlong** lest I become dizzy, and my failing sight topple me headlong.   26 **For . . . moon** i.e., For the whole world   27 **upright** i.e., up and down, much less forward.   29–30 **Fairies . . . thee!** May the fairies and gods cause this to multiply in your possession!   38 **To quarrel with** into rebellion against.   **opposeless** irresistible   39 **snuff** i.e., useless residue. (Literally, the smoking wick of a candle.)   **of nature** i.e., of my life   42 **conceit** imagination   44 **Yields** consents   45 **By this** by this time   47 **pass** die   48 **What** Who. (Edgar now speaks in a new voice, differing from that of "poor Tom" and also from the "altered" voice he used at the start of this scene; see lines 7–10.)   52 **heavy substance** the substance of the flesh

53 **at each** end to end   57 **bourn** limit, boundary (i.e., the edge of the sea).   58 **aheight** on high.   **shrill-gorged** shrill-throated   63 **beguile** outwit   71 **whelked** twisted, convoluted.   **enridgèd** furrowed (by the wind)   72 **happy father** lucky old man   73 **clearest** purest, most righteous   73–4 **who . . . impossibilities** who win our awe and reverence by doing things impossible to men   76–7 **till . . . die** i.e., until affliction itself has had enough, or until I die.   80 **free** i.e., free from despair   81–2 **The safer . . . thus** i.e., A person in his right senses would never dress himself in such a fashion. (*His master* is the owner of the *safer sense* or sane mind. *His* means "its.")   83–4 **they . . . himself** they cannot prosecute me for minting coins. As king, I enjoy the exclusive royal prerogative for doing so. (Lear goes on to discuss his need for money to pay his imaginary soldiers.)   85 **side-piercing** heartrending. (With a suggestion of Christ's suffering on the cross.)

LEAR   Nature's above art in that respect. There's your 86
press money. That fellow handles his bow like a crow- 87
keeper. Draw me a clothier's yard. Look, look, a 88
mouse! Peace, peace; this piece of toasted cheese will
do't. There's my gauntlet; I'll prove it on a giant. Bring 90
up the brown bills. Oh, well flown, bird! I'th' clout, 91
i'th' clout—hewgh! Give the word. 92

EDGAR   Sweet marjoram. 93

LEAR   Pass.

GLOUCESTER   I know that voice.

LEAR   Ha! Goneril with a white beard? They flattered
me like a dog and told me I had white hairs in my 97
beard ere the black ones were there. To say ay and 98
no to everything that I said ay and no to was 99
no good divinity. When the rain came to wet me 100
once and the wind to make me chatter, when the 101
thunder would not peace at my bidding, there I found 102
'em, there I smelt 'em out. Go to, they are not men o' 103
their words. They told me I was everything. 'Tis a
lie. I am not ague-proof. 105

GLOUCESTER
The trick of that voice I do well remember. 106
Is't not the King?

LEAR   Ay, every inch a king.
When I do stare, see how the subject quakes.
I pardon that man's life. What was thy cause? 109
Adultery?
Thou shalt not die. Die for adultery? No.
The wren goes to't, and the small gilded fly
Does lecher in my sight.
Let copulation thrive; for Gloucester's bastard son
Was kinder to his father than my daughters
Got 'tween the lawful sheets.
To't, luxury, pell-mell, for I lack soldiers. 117
Behold yond simpering dame,
Whose face between her forks presages snow, 119
That minces virtue and does shake the head 120
To hear of pleasure's name; 121
The fitchew nor the soilèd horse goes to't 122

With a more riotous appetite.
Down from the waist they're centaurs, 124
Though women all above.
But to the girdle do the gods inherit; 126
Beneath is all the fiends'.
There's hell, there's darkness, there is the sulfurous pit,
burning, scalding, stench, consumption. Fie, fie, fie!
Pah, pah! Give me an ounce of civet, good apothecary, 130
sweeten my imagination. There's money for thee.

GLOUCESTER   Oh, let me kiss that hand!

LEAR   Let me wipe it first; it smells of mortality.

GLOUCESTER
Oh, ruined piece of nature! This great world 134
Shall so wear out to naught. Dost thou know me? 135

LEAR   I remember thine eyes well enough. Dost thou
squinny at me? No, do thy worst, blind Cupid; I'll not 137
love. Read thou this challenge. Mark but the penning
of it.

GLOUCESTER
Were all thy letters suns, I could not see.

EDGAR [aside]
I would not take this from report. It is, 141
And my heart breaks at it.

LEAR   Read.

GLOUCESTER   What, with the case of eyes? 144

LEAR   Oho, are you there with me? No eyes in your 145
head, nor no money in your purse? Your eyes are in a
heavy case, your purse in a light, yet you see how this 147
world goes.

GLOUCESTER   I see it feelingly. 149

LEAR   What, art mad? A man may see how this world
goes with no eyes. Look with thine ears. See how
yond justice rails upon yond simple thief. Hark in 152
thine ear: change places and, handy-dandy, which is 153
the justice, which is the thief? Thou hast seen a
farmer's dog bark at a beggar?

GLOUCESTER   Ay, sir.

LEAR   And the creature run from the cur? There thou 157
mightst behold the great image of authority: a dog's 158
obeyed in office. 159
Thou rascal beadle, hold thy bloody hand! 160
Why dost thou lash that whore? Strip thine own back;
Thou hotly lusts to use her in that kind 162
For which thou whipp'st her. The usurer hangs the
cozener. 163

---

86 Nature's . . . respect Real life can offer more heart-piercing examples than art.   **87 press money** enlistment bonus.   **87–8 crowkeeper** laborer hired to scare away the crows.   **88 Draw . . . yard** i.e., Draw your bow to the full length of the arrow, a cloth-yard long.   **90 do't** i.e., capture the mouse, an imagined enemy.   **gauntlet** armored glove thrown down as a challenge.   **prove it on** maintain it against **91 brown bills** soldiers carrying pikes (painted brown), or the pikes themselves.   **well flown, bird** (Lear uses the language of hawking to describe the flight of an arrow.)   **clout** target, bull's-eye   **92 hewgh** (The arrow's noise.)   **word** password.   **93 Sweet marjoram** (A herb used to cure madness.)   **97 like a dog** as a dog fawns   **97–8 told . . . there** i.e., told me I had the white-haired wisdom of old age before I had even attained the manliness of a beard.   **98–100 To . . . divinity** i.e., To agree flatteringly with everything I said was not good theology, since the Bible teaches us to "let your yea be yea and your nay, nay" (James 5:12; see also Matthew 5:37 and 2 Cor. 1:18).   **100–3 When . . . out** i.e., Suffering wet, cold, and storm have taught me about the frailty of the human condition.   **103 Go to** (An expression of impatience.)   **105 ague-proof** immune against illness (literally, fever).   **106 trick** peculiar characteristic   **109 cause** offense.   **117 luxury** lechery   **119 Whose . . . snow** whose frosty countenance seems to suggest frigidity between her legs   **120 minces** affects, mimics   **121 of pleasure's name** the very name of pleasure   **122 The fitchew . . . to't** neither the polecat nor the well-pastured horse indulges in sexual pleasure

124 centaurs fabulous creatures with the head, trunk, and arms of a man joined to the body and legs of a horse   **126 But** Only.   **girdle** waist.   **inherit** have possession   **130 civet** musk perfume **134 piece** (1) fragment (2) masterpiece   **134–5 This . . . naught** Even so will the whole universe come to an apocalyptic end.   **137 squinny** squint   **141 take** believe, credit.   **It is** It is taking place, incredibly enough   **144 case** mere sockets   **145 are . . . me?** is that your meaning, the point you are making?   **147 heavy case** sad plight. (With pun on *case* in line 144.)   **149 feelingly** (1) by touch (2) keenly, painfully. **152 simple** of humble station   **153 handy-dandy** take your choice of hands (as in a well-known child's game)   **157 creature** poor fellow **158–9 a dog's . . . office** i.e., even currish power commands submission.   **160 beadle** parish officer, responsible for giving whippings **162 kind** way   **163 The usurer . . . cozener** The moneylender (who can buy out justice) hangs the con man.

Through tattered clothes small vices do appear;   164
Robes and furred gowns hide all. Plate sin with gold, 165
And the strong lance of justice hurtless breaks;   166
Arm it in rags, a pygmy's straw does pierce it.
None does offend, none, I say, none. I'll able 'em.   168
Take that of me, my friend, who have the power   169
To seal th'accuser's lips. Get thee glass eyes,   170
And like a scurvy politician seem   171
To see the things thou dost not. Now, now, now, now! 172
Pull off my boots. Harder, harder! So.

EDGAR [*aside*]
Oh, matter and impertinency mixed,   174
Reason in madness!

LEAR
If thou wilt weep my fortunes, take my eyes.
I know thee well enough; thy name is Gloucester.
Thou must be patient. We came crying hither.
Thou know'st the first time that we smell the air
We wawl and cry. I will preach to thee. Mark.

GLOUCESTER   Alack, alack the day!

LEAR
When we are born, we cry that we are come
To this great stage of fools.—This' a good block.   183
It were a delicate stratagem to shoe   184
A troop of horse with felt. I'll put 't in proof,   185
And when I have stol'n upon these son-in-laws,
Then, kill, kill, kill, kill, kill, kill!

Enter a Gentleman [with attendants].

GENTLEMAN
Oh, here he is. Lay hand upon him.—Sir,
Your most dear daughter—

LEAR
No rescue? What, a prisoner? I am even
The natural fool of fortune. Use me well;   191
You shall have ransom. Let me have surgeons;
I am cut to th' brains.

GENTLEMAN   You shall have anything.   193

LEAR   No seconds? All myself?   194
Why, this would make a man a man of salt   195
To use his eyes for garden waterpots,
Ay, and laying autumn's dust.
I will die bravely, like a smug bridegroom. What?   198

I will be jovial. Come, come, I am a king,   199
Masters, know you that?   200

GENTLEMAN
You are a royal one, and we obey you.

LEAR   Then there's life in't. Come, an you get it, you 202
shall get it by running. Sa, sa, sa, sa.   203
         Exit [running, followed by attendants].

GENTLEMAN
A sight most pitiful in the meanest wretch,
Past speaking of in a king! Thou hast one daughter
Who redeems nature from the general curse   206
Which twain have brought her to.   207

EDGAR   Hail, gentle sir.   208

GENTLEMAN   Sir, speed you. What's your will?   209

EDGAR
Do you hear aught, sir, of a battle toward?   210

GENTLEMAN
Most sure and vulgar. Everyone hears that   211
Which can distinguish sound.

EDGAR   But, by your favor,   212
How near's the other army?

GENTLEMAN
Near and on speedy foot. The main descry   214
Stands on the hourly thought.   215

EDGAR   I thank you, sir; that's all.

GENTLEMAN
Though that the Queen on special cause is here,   217
Her army is moved on.

EDGAR   I thank you, sir.
                              Exit [Gentleman].

GLOUCESTER
You ever-gentle gods, take my breath from me;
Let not my worser spirit tempt me again   220
To die before you please!

EDGAR   Well pray you, father.   222

GLOUCESTER   Now, good sir, what are you?   223

EDGAR
A most poor man, made tame to fortune's blows,   224
Who, by the art of known and feeling sorrows,   225
Am pregnant to good pity. Give me your hand.   226
I'll lead you to some biding.   [*He offers his arm.*]

GLOUCESTER   Hearty thanks.   227

164–5 Through . . . all i.e., Beggars' small vices are apparent for all to see; rich folk, in expensive clothes, succeed in hiding a great deal. **165 Plate** Arm in plate armor   **166 hurtless breaks** splinters harmlessly   **168 able** empower, give warrant to   **169 Take . . . me** (1) Learn that from me (2) Take that protection from me   **170–2 Get . . . dost not** If Gloucester were to fit himself out with spectacles (or perhaps with glass eyeballs, though they are not mentioned elsewhere until later in the seventeenth century), he would look wise like a hypocritical politician.   **174 matter and impertinency** sense and nonsense   **183 This'** This is.   **block** mold for a felt hat. (Lear may refer to the weeds strewn in his hair, which he removes as though doffing a hat before preaching a sermon.)   **184 delicate** subtle   **185 felt** i.e., padding to deaden the sound of the footfall.   **in proof** to the test   **191 natural fool** born plaything   **193 cut** wounded   **194 seconds** supporters.   **195 of salt** of salt tears   **198 bravely** (1) courageously (2) splendidly attired.   **smug** trimly dressed. (*Bridegroom* continues the punning sexual suggestion of *die bravely*, "have sex successfully.")

199 jovial (1) Jovelike, majestic (2) jolly.   **200 Masters** good sirs   **202 life** i.e., hope still.   **an** if   **203 Sa . . . sa** (A hunting cry.)   **206 general curse** fallen condition of the human race   **207 twain** (1) Goneril and Regan (2) Adam and Eve   **208 gentle** noble   **209 speed you** Godspeed, may God prosper you.   **210 toward** imminent.   **211 vulgar** in everyone's mouth, generally known.   **212 Which** who   **214–15 The main . . . thought** The full view of the main body is expected any hour now.   **217 Though that** Although.   **on special cause** for a special reason, i.e., to minister to Lear   **220 worser spirit** bad angel, or ill thoughts   **222 father** (A term of respect to older men, as also in lines 72, 259, and 290, though with ironic double meaning throughout the scene.)   **223 what** who. (Again, Edgar alters his voice to personate a new stranger assisting Gloucester. See line 48, above, and note.)   **224 tame** submissive   **225 known and feeling** personally experienced and heartfelt   **226 pregnant** prone   **227 biding** abode.

The bounty and the benison of heaven 228
To boot, and boot!

Enter steward [Oswald].

OSWALD   A proclaimed prize! Most happy! 229
                [He draws his sword.]
That eyeless head of thine was first framed flesh 230
To raise my fortunes. Thou old unhappy traitor,
Briefly thyself remember. The sword is out 232
That must destroy thee.
GLOUCESTER   Now let thy friendly hand 233
Put strength enough to't.   *[Edgar intervenes.]*
OSWALD   Wherefore, bold peasant,
Durst thou support a published traitor? Hence, 235
Lest that th'infection of his fortune take 236
Like hold on thee. Let go his arm. 237
EDGAR   'Chill not let go, zir, without vurther 'cagion. 238
OSWALD   Let go, slave, or thou diest!
EDGAR   Good gentleman, go your gait, and let poor volk 240
pass. An 'chud ha' bin zwaggered out of my life, 241
'twould not ha' bin zo long as 'tis by a vortnight. Nay, 242
come not near th' old man; keep out, 'che vor ye, or 243
Ise try whether your costard or my ballow be the 244
harder. 'Chill be plain with you.
OSWALD   Out, dunghill!
EDGAR   'Chill pick your teeth, zir. Come, no matter vor
your foins. *[They fight. Edgar fells him with his cudgel.]* 248
OSWALD
Slave, thou hast slain me. Villain, take my purse. 249
If ever thou wilt thrive, bury my body
And give the letters which thou find'st about me 251
To Edmund, Earl of Gloucester. Seek him out
Upon the English party. Oh, untimely death! 253
Death!   *[He dies.]*
EDGAR
I know thee well: a serviceable villain, 255
As duteous to the vices of thy mistress
As badness would desire.
GLOUCESTER   What, is he dead?
EDGAR   Sit you down, father. Rest you. *[Gloucester sits.]*
Let's see these pockets; the letters that he speaks of
May be my friends. He's dead; I am only sorry
He had no other deathsman. Let us see. 262
               [He finds a letter and opens it.]
Leave, gentle wax, and, manners, blame us not. 263

To know our enemies' minds we rip their hearts;
Their papers is more lawful.   *(Reads the letter.)*
"Let our reciprocal vows be remembered. You have
many opportunities to cut him off; if your will want 267
not, time and place will be fruitfully offered. There is 268
nothing done if he return the conqueror. Then am I 269
the prisoner, and his bed my jail, from the loathed
warmth whereof deliver me and supply the place for 271
your labor. 272
Your—wife, so I would say—affectionate servant,
   and for you her own for venture, Goneril." 274
Oh, indistinguished space of woman's will! 275
A plot upon her virtuous husband's life,
And the exchange my brother! Here in the sands
Thee I'll rake up, the post unsanctified 278
Of murderous lechers; and in the mature time 279
With this ungracious paper strike the sight 280
Of the death-practiced Duke. For him 'tis well 281
That of thy death and business I can tell.
                [Exit with the body.]
GLOUCESTER
The King is mad. How stiff is my vile sense, 283
That I stand up and have ingenious feeling 284
Of my huge sorrows! Better I were distract; 285
So should my thoughts be severed from my griefs,
And woes by wrong imaginations lose 287
The knowledge of themselves.   *Drum afar off.*

[Enter Edgar.]

EDGAR   Give me your hand.
Far off, methinks, I hear the beaten drum.
Come, father, I'll bestow you with a friend. 290
        Exeunt, [Edgar leading his father].

❖

4.7

Enter Cordelia, Kent [dressed still in his disguise
costume], and Gentleman.

CORDELIA
O thou good Kent, how shall I live and work
To match thy goodness? My life will be too short,
And every measure fail me. 3

228–9 The bounty . . . and boot! In addition to my thanks, I wish you the bounty and blessings of heaven. **229 proclaimed prize** one with a price on his head. **happy** fortunate. **230 framed flesh** born **232 thyself remember** i.e., say your prayers. **233 friendly** i.e., welcome, since I desire death **235 published** proclaimed **236 Lest that** lest **237 Like** similar **238 'Chill** I will. (Literally, a contraction of *Ich will.* Edgar adopts Somerset dialect, a stage convention regularly used for peasants.) **vurther 'cagion** further occasion. **240 go your gait** go your own way **241 An 'chud** If I could. **zwaggered** swaggered, bullied **242 'twould . . . vortnight** it (my life) wouldn't have lasted a fortnight. **243 'che vor ye** I warrant you **244 Ise** I shall. **costard** head. (Literally, an apple.) **ballow** cudgel **248 foins** thrusts. **249 Villain** Serf **251 letters** letter. (See 4.5.35 and note.) **about me** upon my person **253 Upon** on. **party** side. **255 serviceable** officious **262 deathsman** executioner. **263 Leave** By your leave. **wax** wax seal on the letter

267 him Albany **267–8 want not** is not lacking **268 fruitfully** plentifully and with results **268–9 There is nothing done** i.e., We will have accomplished nothing **271 supply** fill **271–2 for your labor** (1) as recompense for your efforts (2) as a place for your amorous labors. **274 and for . . . venture** and one ready to venture her own fortunes for your sake **275 indistinguished . . . will** limitless and incalculable expanse of woman's appetite. **278 rake up** cover up. **post unsanctified** unholy messenger **279 in . . . time** when the time is ripe **280 ungracious** wicked. **strike** blast **281 Of . . . well** of Albany, whose death is plotted. It's a good thing for him **283 How . . . sense** How obstinate is my deplorable sanity and power of sensation **284 ingenious** conscious. (Gloucester laments that he remains sane and hence fully conscious of his troubles, unlike Lear.) **285 distract** distracted, crazy **287 wrong imaginations** delusions **290 bestow** lodge. (At the scene's end, Edgar leads off Gloucester; presumably, at line 282 or else here, he must also dispose of Oswald's body in the trapdoor or by lugging it offstage.)
4.7. Location: The French camp.
0.2 Gentleman (*"Doctor"* in Q.) **3 every . . . me** every attempt (to match your goodness) will fall short.

KENT
　　To be acknowledged, madam, is o'erpaid.
　　All my reports go with the modest truth, 　　　　　5
　　Nor more nor clipped, but so.
CORDELIA 　　　　　　　　　Be better suited. 　　　6
　　These weeds are memories of those worser hours; 　　7
　　I prithee, put them off.
KENT 　　　　　　　Pardon, dear madam;
　　Yet to be known shortens my made intent. 　　　　9
　　My boon I make it that you know me not 　　　　10
　　Till time and I think meet. 　　　　　　　　　11
CORDELIA
　　Then be't so, my good lord. [To the Gentleman] How
　　　does the King?
GENTLEMAN 　　Madam, sleeps still.
CORDELIA 　　　O you kind gods,
　　Cure this great breach in his abusèd nature!
　　Th'untuned and jarring senses, oh, wind up 　　　16
　　Of this child-changèd father! 　　　　　　　17
GENTLEMAN 　　So please Your Majesty
　　That we may wake the King? He hath slept long.
CORDELIA
　　Be governed by your knowledge, and proceed
　　I'th' sway of your own will.—Is he arrayed? 　　21

　　　　　Enter Lear in a chair carried by servants.

GENTLEMAN
　　Ay, madam. In the heaviness of sleep
　　We put fresh garments on him.
　　Be by, good madam, when we do awake him.
　　I doubt not of his temperance.
CORDELIA 　　　　　　　Very well. 　　[Music.] 25
GENTLEMAN
　　Please you, draw near.—Louder the music there!
CORDELIA [kissing him]
　　O my dear father! Restoration hang
　　Thy medicine on my lips, and let this kiss
　　Repair those violent harms that my two sisters
　　Have in thy reverence made!
KENT 　　　　　　　Kind and dear princess! 30
CORDELIA
　　Had you not been their father, these white flakes 31
　　Did challenge pity of them. Was this a face 　　32
　　To be opposed against the warring winds?
　　To stand against the deep dread-bolted thunder 34
　　In the most terrible and nimble stroke

Of quick cross lightning? To watch—poor perdu!— 36
With this thin helm? Mine enemy's dog, 　　　　37
Though he had bit me, should have stood that night
Against my fire; and wast thou fain, poor father, 39
To hovel thee with swine and rogues forlorn 　　40
In short and musty straw? Alack, alack! 　　　　41
'Tis wonder that thy life and wits at once
Had not concluded all.—He wakes! Speak to him. 43
GENTLEMAN 　　Madam, do you; 'tis fittest.
CORDELIA
　　How does my royal lord? How fares Your Majesty?
LEAR
　　You do me wrong to take me out o'th' grave.
　　Thou art a soul in bliss; but I am bound
　　Upon a wheel of fire, that mine own tears 　　48
　　Do scald like molten lead.
CORDELIA 　　　　　　Sir, do you know me?
LEAR
　　You are a spirit, I know. Where did you die?
CORDELIA 　　Still, still, far wide! 　　　　　51
GENTLEMAN
　　He's scarce awake. Let him alone awhile.
LEAR
　　Where have I been? Where am I? Fair daylight?
　　I am mightily abused. I should ev'n die with pity 54
　　To see another thus. I know not what to say. 　55
　　I will not swear these are my hands. Let's see;
　　I feel this pinprick. Would I were assured
　　Of my condition!
CORDELIA [kneeling] 　Oh, look upon me, sir,
　　And hold your hands in benediction o'er me.
　　　　　　　　　　　　　[He attempts to kneel.]
　　No, sir, you must not kneel.
LEAR 　　　　　　　Pray, do not mock me.
　　I am a very foolish fond old man, 　　　　　61
　　Fourscore and upward, not an hour more nor less;
　　And, to deal plainly,
　　I fear I am not in my perfect mind.
　　Methinks I should know you, and know this man,
　　Yet I am doubtful; for I am mainly ignorant 　66
　　What place this is, and all the skill I have
　　Remembers not these garments, nor I know not
　　Where I did lodge last night. Do not laugh at me,
　　For, as I am a man, I think this lady
　　To be my child Cordelia.
CORDELIA [weeping] 　And so I am, I am.
LEAR
　　Be your tears wet? Yes, faith. I pray, weep not.
　　If you have poison for me I will drink it.
　　I know you do not love me, for your sisters
　　Have, as I do remember, done me wrong.
　　You have some cause, they have not.

5 **All my reports go** All my reports (of my service as Caius to Lear) conform　6 **Nor ... clipped** i.e., neither more nor less.　**suited** dressed.　7 **weeds** garments.　**memories** remembrances　9 **Yet ... intent** to reveal my true identity now would alter my carefully made plan.　10 **My ... it** The favor I seek is.　**know** acknowledge　11 **meet** appropriate.　16 **wind up** tune (as by tightening the slackened string of an instrument)　17 **child-changèd** changed by children's cruelty　21 **I'th' sway** under the direction　25 **temperance** self-control, calm behavior.　30 **reverence** venerable condition　31 **Had you** Even if you had.　**flakes** locks of hair　32 **Did challenge** would have demanded　34 **deep** bass-voiced.　**dread-bolted** furnished with the dreadful thunderbolt

36 **cross** zigzag.　**watch** stay awake (like a sentry on duty).　**perdu** lost one; a sentinel placed in a position of peculiar danger.　37 **helm** helmet, i.e., scanty hair.　39 **Against** before, in front of.　**fain** constrained　40 **rogues forlorn** abandoned vagabonds　41 **short** broken up and hence uncomfortable　43 **concluded all** come to an end altogether.　48 **wheel of fire** (A hellish torment for the eternally damned.)　**that** so that　51 **wide** wide of the mark, wandering.　54 **abused** confused, deluded.　55 **thus** i.e., thus confused, bewildered.　61 **fond** in my dotage　66 **mainly** entirely

CORDELIA   No cause, no cause.
LEAR   Am I in France?
KENT   In your own kingdom, sir.
LEAR   Do not abuse me.   81
GENTLEMAN
    Be comforted, good madam. The great rage,   82
    You see, is killed in him, and yet it is danger
    To make him even o'er the time he has lost.   84
    Desire him to go in. Trouble him no more
    Till further settling.   86
CORDELIA   Will't please Your Highness walk?   87
LEAR   You must bear with me.
    Pray you now, forget and forgive.
    I am old and foolish.
                    Exeunt [all but Kent and Gentleman].
GENTLEMAN   Holds it true, sir, that the Duke of Corn-   91
    wall was so slain?
KENT   Most certain, sir.
GENTLEMAN   Who is conductor of his people?   94
KENT   As 'tis said, the bastard son of Gloucester.
GENTLEMAN   They say Edgar, his banished son, is with
    the Earl of Kent in Germany.
KENT   Report is changeable. 'Tis time to look about; the   98
    powers of the kingdom approach apace.   99
GENTLEMAN   The arbitrament is like to be bloody. Fare   100
    you well, sir.   *[Exit.]*
KENT
    My point and period will be throughly wrought,   102
    Or well or ill, as this day's battle's fought.   *Exit.* 103

❖

5.1

> *Enter, with drum and colors, Edmund, Regan,*
> *Gentlemen, and soldiers.*

EDMUND   *[to a Gentleman]*
    Know of the Duke if his last purpose hold,   1
    Or whether since he is advised by aught   2
    To change the course. He's full of alteration   3
    And self-reproving. Bring his constant pleasure.   4
                            [Exit Gentleman.]
REGAN
    Our sister's man is certainly miscarried.   5

EDMUND
    'Tis to be doubted, madam.
REGAN   Now, sweet lord,   6
    You know the goodness I intend upon you.   7
    Tell me, but truly—but then speak the truth—
    Do you not love my sister?
EDMUND   In honored love.   9
REGAN
    But have you never found my brother's way
    To the forfended place?   11
EDMUND   That thought abuses you.   12
REGAN
    I am doubtful that you have been conjunct   13
    And bosomed with her, as far as we call hers.   14
EDMUND   No, by mine honor, madam.
REGAN
    I never shall endure her. Dear my lord,
    Be not familiar with her.   17
EDMUND
    Fear me not.—She and the Duke her husband!   18

> *Enter, with drum and colors, Albany, Goneril,*
> *[and] soldiers.*

GONERIL   *[aside]*
    I had rather lose the battle than that sister
    Should loosen him and me.
ALBANY   *[to Regan]*
    Our very loving sister, well bemet.   21
    [To Edmund] Sir, this I heard: the King is come to his
        daughter,
    With others whom the rigor of our state   23
    Forced to cry out. Where I could not be honest,   24
    I never yet was valiant. For this business,   25
    It touches us as France invades our land,   26
    Not bolds the King, with others whom, I fear,   27
    Most just and heavy causes make oppose.   28
EDMUND   Sir, you speak nobly.
REGAN   Why is this reasoned?   30
GONERIL
    Combine together 'gainst the enemy;
    For these domestic and particular broils   32
    Are not the question here.
ALBANY   Let's then determine
    With th'ancient of war on our proceeding.   34
EDMUND
    I shall attend you presently at your tent.
REGAN   Sister, you'll go with us?
GONERIL   No.

---

81 abuse deceive. (Or perhaps Lear feels hurt by the reminder of his having divided the kingdom.)   **82 rage** frenzy   **84 even o'er** fill in, go over in his mind   **86 settling** composing of his mind.   **87 walk** withdraw.   **91 Holds it true** Is it still held to be true   **94 conductor** leader, general   **98 look about** be wary, take stock of the situation   **99 powers of the kingdom** British armies (marching against the French invaders)   **100 arbitrament** decision by arms, decisive encounter   **102 My . . . wrought** i.e., The conclusion of my destiny (literally, the full stop at the end of my life's sentence) will be thoroughly shaped   **103 Or** either.   **as** according as
5.1. Location: The British camp near Dover.
1 Know Inquire.   **last purpose hold** most recent intention (to fight) remains firm   **2 since** since then.   **advised by aught** persuaded by any consideration   **3 alteration** vacillation   **4 constant pleasure** settled decision.   **5 man** i.e., Oswald.   **miscarried** lost, perished.

6 doubted feared   **7 intend** intend to confer   **9 honored** honorable   **11 forfended** forbidden (by the commandment against adultery)   **12 abuses** degrades, wrongs   **13–14 I . . . hers** I fear that you have been sexually intimate with her to the fullest extent possible.   **17 familiar** intimate   **18 Fear me not** Don't worry about me on that score.   **21 bemet** met.   **23 rigor of our state** harshness of our rule   **24 cry out** rebel.   **Where** In a case where.   **honest** honorable   **25 For** As for   **26 touches us as** concerns us insofar as   **27–8 Not . . . oppose** not because the matter emboldens the King and others who, I fear, are driven into opposition by just and weighty grievances.   **30 Why . . . reasoned?** i.e., Why are we arguing about reasons for fighting, instead of fighting?   **32 particular broils** private quarrels   **34 th'ancient of war** the veteran officers

REGAN
 'Tis most convenient. Pray, go with us.   38
GONERIL [aside]
 Oho, I know the riddle.—I will go.   39

  [As they are going out,] enter Edgar [disguised].

EDGAR [to Albany]
 If e'er Your Grace had speech with man so poor,
 Hear me one word.
ALBANY [to the others] I'll overtake you.
         Exeunt both the armies.
          Speak.

EDGAR [giving a letter]
 Before you fight the battle, ope this letter.   42
 If you have victory, let the trumpet sound   43
 For him that brought it. Wretched though I seem,
 I can produce a champion that will prove   45
 What is avouchèd there. If you miscarry,   46
 Your business of the world hath so an end,
 And machination ceases. Fortune love you!   48
ALBANY Stay till I have read the letter.
EDGAR I was forbid it.
 When time shall serve, let but the herald cry
 And I'll appear again.   Exit [Edgar].
ALBANY
 Why, fare thee well. I will o'erlook thy paper.   53

   Enter Edmund.

EDMUND
 The enemy's in view. Draw up your powers.
     [He offers Albany a paper.]
 Here is the guess of their true strength and forces   55
 By diligent discovery; but your haste   56
 Is now urged on you.
ALBANY   We will greet the time.   Exit. 57
EDMUND
 To both these sisters have I sworn my love,
 Each jealous of the other as the stung   59
 Are of the adder. Which of them shall I take?
 Both? One? Or neither? Neither can be enjoyed
 If both remain alive. To take the widow
 Exasperates, makes mad her sister Goneril,
 And hardly shall I carry out my side,   64
 Her husband being alive. Now then, we'll use
 His countenance for the battle, which being done,   66
 Let her who would be rid of him devise
 His speedy taking off. As for the mercy   68
 Which he intends to Lear and to Cordelia,
 The battle done and they within our power,

 Shall never see his pardon, for my state   71
 Stands on me to defend, not to debate.   72
          Exit.

       ❖

5.2

  Alarum within. Enter, with drum and colors, Lear,
  Cordelia, and soldiers, over the stage; and exeunt.

  Enter Edgar and Gloucester.

EDGAR
 Here, father, take the shadow of this tree   1
 For your good host. Pray that the right may thrive.   2
 If ever I return to you again,
 I'll bring you comfort.
GLOUCESTER   Grace go with you, sir!   4
         Exit [Edgar].

  Alarum and retreat within. Enter Edgar.

EDGAR
 Away, old man! Give me thy hand. Away!
 King Lear hath lost, he and his daughter ta'en.
 Give me thy hand. Come on.
GLOUCESTER
 No further, sir. A man may rot even here.
EDGAR
 What, in ill thoughts again? Men must endure
 Their going hence, even as their coming hither;
 Ripeness is all. Come on.
GLOUCESTER   And that's true too.   11
         Exeunt.

       ❖

5.3

  Enter, in conquest, with drum and colors, Edmund;
  Lear and Cordelia, as prisoners; soldiers, Captain.

EDMUND
 Some officers take them away. Good guard   1
 Until their greater pleasures first be known   2
 That are to censure them.
CORDELIA [to Lear] We are not the first   3
 Who with best meaning have incurred the worst.   4
 For thee, oppressèd King, I am cast down;
 Myself could else outfrown false Fortune's frown.
 Shall we not see these daughters and these sisters?   7

---

38 **convenient** proper, fitting. 39 **I know the riddle** i.e., I understand the reason for Regan's enigmatic demand that I accompany her, which is that she wants to keep me away from Edmund. 42 **this letter** i.e., Goneril's letter to Edmund found on Oswald's body. 43 **sound** sound a summons 45 **prove** i.e., in trial by combat 46 **avouchèd** affirmed. **miscarry** lose the battle and die 48 **machination** plotting (against your life) 53 **o'erlook** peruse 55 **guess** estimate 56 **discovery** reconnoitering 57 **We . . . time** We will be ready for whatever happens. 59 **jealous** suspicious 64 **carry . . . side** carry out my end of the bargain in our *reciprocal vows* (4.6.266) 66 **countenance** backing, authority of his name 68 **taking off** killing.

71 **Shall** they shall 71–2 **my state . . . debate** my position depends upon maintenance by forceful action, not by talk.
5.2. Location: The battlefield.
0.1 *Alarum* trumpet call to arms 1 **father** i.e., reverend old man
2 **host** shelterer. 4.2 *retreat* trumpet signal for withdrawal
11 **Ripeness** (Humans shouldn't die before their time, just as fruit doesn't fall until it's ripe.)
5.3. Location: The British camp.
1 **Good guard** Guard them well 2 **their greater pleasures** the wishes of those in command 3 **censure** judge 4 **meaning** intentions
7 **Shall . . . sisters?** i.e., Aren't we even allowed to speak to Goneril and Regan before they order to prison their own father and sister?

LEAR
>   No, no, no, no! Come, let's away to prison.
>   We two alone will sing like birds i'th' cage.
>   When thou dost ask me blessing, I'll kneel down
>   And ask of thee forgiveness. So we'll live,
>   And pray, and sing, and tell old tales, and laugh
>   At gilded butterflies, and hear poor rogues   13
>   Talk of court news; and we'll talk with them too—
>   Who loses and who wins; who's in, who's out—
>   And take upon 's the mystery of things,   16
>   As if we were God's spies; and we'll wear out,   17
>   In a walled prison, packs and sects of great ones,   18
>   That ebb and flow by th' moon.

EDMUND   Take them away.   19

LEAR
>   Upon such sacrifices, my Cordelia,
>   The gods themselves throw incense. Have I caught
>   thee?   21
>   He that parts us shall bring a brand from heaven   22
>   And fire us hence like foxes. Wipe thine eyes;   23
>   The good years shall devour them, flesh and fell,   24
>   Ere they shall make us weep. We'll see 'em starved
>   first.   25
>   Come.   *Exit [with Cordelia, guarded].*

EDMUND   Come hither, Captain. Hark.
>   Take thou this note. [*He gives a paper.*] Go follow them
>   to prison.
>   One step I have advanced thee; if thou dost
>   As this instructs thee, thou dost make thy way
>   To noble fortunes. Know thou this: that men
>   Are as the time is. To be tender-minded   32
>   Does not become a sword. Thy great employment   33
>   Will not bear question; either say thou'lt do't   34
>   Or thrive by other means.

CAPTAIN   I'll do't, my lord.

EDMUND   About it, and write "happy" when th' hast done.   36
>   Mark, I say, instantly, and carry it so   37
>   As I have set it down.

CAPTAIN
>   I cannot draw a cart, nor eat dried oats;
>   If it be man's work, I'll do't.   *Exit Captain.*

>   *Flourish. Enter Albany, Goneril, Regan, [another
>   Captain, and] soldiers.*

ALBANY
>   Sir, you have showed today your valiant strain,
>   And fortune led you well. You have the captives
>   Who were the opposites of this day's strife;   43
>   I do require them of you, so to use them
>   As we shall find their merits and our safety
>   May equally determine.

EDMUND   Sir, I thought it fit
>   To send the old and miserable King
>   To some retention and appointed guard,   49
>   Whose age had charms in it, whose title more,   50
>   To pluck the common bosom on his side   51
>   And turn our impressed lances in our eyes   52
>   Which do command them. With him I sent the Queen,   53
>   My reason all the same; and they are ready
>   Tomorrow, or at further space, t'appear   55
>   Where you shall hold your session. At this time
>   We sweat and bleed; the friend hath lost his friend,
>   And the best quarrels in the heat are cursed   58
>   By those that feel their sharpness.   59
>   The question of Cordelia and her father
>   Requires a fitter place.

ALBANY   Sir, by your patience,   61
>   I hold you but a subject of this war,   62
>   Not as a brother.

REGAN   That's as we list to grace him.   63
>   Methinks our pleasure might have been demanded   64
>   Ere you had spoke so far. He led our powers,
>   Bore the commission of my place and person,
>   The which immediacy may well stand up   67
>   And call itself your brother.

GONERIL   Not so hot!
>   In his own grace he doth exalt himself
>   More than in your addition.

REGAN   In my rights,   70
>   By me invested, he compeers the best.   71

GONERIL
>   That were the most if he should husband you.   72

REGAN
>   Jesters do oft prove prophets.

GONERIL   Holla, holla!   73
>   That eye that told you so looked but asquint.   74

REGAN
>   Lady, I am not well, else I should answer
>   From a full-flowing stomach. [*To Edmund*] General,   76

13 **gilded butterflies** i.e., gaily dressed courtiers and other ephemeral types, or perhaps actual butterflies   16 **take upon 's** assume the burden of, or profess to understand   17 **God's spies** i.e., detached observers surveying the deeds of humanity from an eternal vantage point.   **wear out** outlast   18–19 **packs . . . moon** i.e., followers and cliques attached to persons of high station, whose fortunes change erratically and constantly.   21 **The gods . . . incense** (The gods make offerings to Cordelia instead of receiving them.)   22–3 **He . . . foxes** i.e., Nothing short of a firebrand from heaven will ever part us again. (Firebrands were used to smoke foxes from their lairs; compare also Samson's use of firebrands tied to the tails of foxes in order to punish the Philistines for denying him his wife, in Judges 15:4–5.)   24–5 **The good . . . weep** i.e., the years will be good to us and will utterly foil our enemies' attempts to make us sorrowful as long as we are together (?).   32 **Are . . . is** i.e., must adapt themselves to stern exigencies.   33 **become a sword** i.e., suit a warrior.   34 **bear question** admit of discussion   36 **write "happy"** call yourself fortunate. **th'** thou   37 **carry it** carry it out

43 **opposites** enemies   49 **retention** confinement   50–3 **Whose . . . them** whose advanced age had magic in it, and whose title as king had even more, to win the sympathy of the commoners and turn against us the weapons of those very troops whom we impressed into service. (*In our eyes* may suggest retaliation for the blinding of Gloucester.)   55 **space** interval of time   58–9 **And . . . sharpness** and even the best of causes, at this moment when the passions of battle have not cooled, are viewed with hatred by those who have suffered the painful consequences. (Edmund pretends to worry that Lear and Cordelia would not receive a fair trial.)   61 **by your patience** if you please   62 **subject of** subordinate in   63 **list** please   64 **pleasure** wish.   **demanded** asked about   67 **immediacy** nearness of connection   70 **your addition** the titles you confer.   71 **compeers** is equal with   72 **That . . . most** That investiture would be most complete   73 **prove** turn out to be   74 **asquint** (Jealousy proverbially makes the eye look *asquint*, "furtively, suspiciously.")   76 **full-flowing stomach** full tide of angry rejoinder.

Take thou my soldiers, prisoners, patrimony;   77
Dispose of them, of me; the walls is thine.   78
Witness the world that I create thee here
My lord and master.

GONERIL   Mean you to enjoy him?

ALBANY
The let-alone lies not in your good will.   81

EDMUND
Nor in thine, lord.

ALBANY   Half-blooded fellow, yes.   82

REGAN [to Edmund]
Let the drum strike and prove my title thine.

ALBANY
Stay yet; hear reason. Edmund, I arrest thee
On capital treason; and, in thy attaint   85
This gilded serpent. [Pointing to Goneril] For your
    claim, fair sister,
I bar it in the interest of my wife;
'Tis she is subcontracted to this lord,
And I, her husband, contradict your banns.   89
If you will marry, make your loves to me;   90
My lady is bespoke.

GONERIL   An interlude!   91

ALBANY
Thou art armed, Gloucester. Let the trumpet sound.
If none appear to prove upon thy person
Thy heinous, manifest, and many treasons,
There is my pledge. [He throws down a glove.] I'll make
    it on thy heart,   95
Ere I taste bread, thou art in nothing less   96
Than I have here proclaimed thee.

REGAN   Sick, oh, sick!

GONERIL [aside]   If not, I'll ne'er trust medicine.   99

EDMUND [throwing down a glove]
There's my exchange. What in the world he is   100
That names me traitor, villain-like he lies.
Call by the trumpet. He that dares approach,
On him, on you—who not?—I will maintain
My truth and honor firmly.

ALBANY
A herald, ho!

EDMUND   A herald, ho, a herald!

Enter a Herald.

ALBANY [to Edmund]
Trust to thy single virtue; for thy soldiers,   106
All levied in my name, have in my name
Took their discharge.

REGAN   My sickness grows upon me.

ALBANY [to Soldiers]
She is not well. Convey her to my tent.
    [Exit Regan, supported.]
Come hither, herald. Let the trumpet sound,
And read out this.   [He gives a paper.]

CAPTAIN   Sound, trumpet!   A trumpet sounds.

HERALD (reads)   "If any man of quality or degree within   113
the lists of the army will maintain upon Edmund, sup-   114
posed Earl of Gloucester, that he is a manifold traitor,
let him appear by the third sound of the trumpet. He
is bold in his defense."

EDMUND   Sound!   First trumpet.

HERALD   Again!   Second trumpet.

HERALD   Again!   Third trumpet.
    Trumpet answers within.

*Enter Edgar, armed, [with a trumpeter before
him].*

ALBANY
Ask him his purposes, why he appears
Upon this call o'th' trumpet.

HERALD   What are you?   122
Your name, your quality, and why you answer
This present summons?

EDGAR   Know my name is lost,
By treason's tooth bare-gnawn and canker-bit.   125
Yet am I noble as the adversary
I come to cope.

ALBANY   Which is that adversary?   127

EDGAR
What's he that speaks for Edmund, Earl of
    Gloucester?

EDMUND
Himself. What say'st thou to him?

EDGAR   Draw thy sword,
That, if my speech offend a noble heart,
Thy arm may do thee justice. Here is mine.
    [He draws his sword.]
Behold, it is the privilege of mine honors,   132
My oath, and my profession. I protest,   133
Maugre thy strength, place, youth, and eminence,   134
Despite thy victor sword and fire-new fortune,   135
Thy valor, and thy heart, thou art a traitor—   136
False to thy gods, thy brother, and thy father,
Conspirant 'gainst this high-illustrious prince,
And from th'extremest upward of thy head   139
To the descent and dust below thy foot   140
A most toad-spotted traitor. Say thou no,   141
This sword, this arm, and my best spirits are bent   142
To prove upon thy heart, whereto I speak,
Thou liest.

---

77 patrimony inheritance   **78 the walls is thine** i.e., the citadel of my heart and body surrenders completely to you.   **81 let-alone** preventing, denying   **82 Half-blooded** Only partly of noble blood, bastard **85 in thy attaint** i.e., as partner in your corruption and as one who has (unwittingly) provided the *attaint* or impeachment against you **89 banns** public announcement of a proposed marriage.   **90 make . . . me** i.e., sue to me for permission   **91 An interlude!** A play; i.e., you are being melodramatic, or, what a farce this is!   **95 make** prove **96 in nothing less** in no respect less guilty   **99 medicine** i.e., poison. **100 What** Whoever   **106 single virtue** unaided prowess

113 quality or degree noble birth or rank. (Also in line 123.) **114 lists** roster   **122 What** Who   **125 canker-bit** eaten as by the caterpillar.   **127 cope** encounter.   **132 of mine honors** i.e., of my knighthood   **133 profession** i.e., knighthood.   **134 Maugre** in spite of   **135 victor** victorious.   **fire-new** newly minted   **136 heart** courage   **139 upward** top   **140 descent** lowest extreme   **141 toad-spotted** venomous, or having spots of infamy.   **Say thou** If you say **142 bent** prepared

EDMUND   In wisdom I should ask thy name.   144
But since thy outside looks so fair and warlike,
And that thy tongue some say of breeding breathes,   146
What safe and nicely I might well delay   147
By rule of knighthood, I disdain and spurn.   148
Back do I toss those treasons to thy head,   149
With the hell-hated lie o'erwhelm thy heart,   150
Which—for they yet glance by and scarcely bruise—   151
This sword of mine shall give them instant way,   152
Where they shall rest forever.—Trumpets, speak!   153
               [*He draws.*] *Alarums. Fight.* [*Edmund falls.*]
ALBANY [*to Edgar*]
Save him, save him!
GONERIL   This is practice, Gloucester.   154
By th' law of arms thou wast not bound to answer
An unknown opposite. Thou art not vanquished,
But cozened and beguiled.
ALBANY   Shut your mouth, dame,   157
Or with this paper shall I stopple it.—Hold, sir.   158
Thou worse than any name, read thine own evil.
                         [*He shows the letter.*]
[*To Goneril*] No tearing, lady; I perceive you know it.
GONERIL
Say if I do, the laws are mine, not thine.
Who can arraign me for't?
ALBANY   Most monstrous! Oh!
Know'st thou this paper?
GONERIL   Ask me not what I know.
                                               Exit.
ALBANY
Go after her. She's desperate; govern her.   164
                              [*Exit a soldier.*]
EDMUND
What you have charged me with, that have I done,
And more, much more. The time will bring it out.
'Tis past, and so am I. But what art thou
That hast this fortune on me? If thou'rt noble,   168
I do forgive thee.
EDGAR   Let's exchange charity.   169
I am no less in blood than thou art, Edmund;
If more, the more th' hast wronged me.   171
My name is Edgar, and thy father's son.
The gods are just, and of our pleasant vices   173
Make instruments to plague us.
The dark and vicious place where thee he got   175

Cost him his eyes.
EDMUND   Th' hast spoken right. 'Tis true.
The wheel is come full circle; I am here.   177
ALBANY [*to Edgar*]
Methought thy very gait did prophesy
A royal nobleness. I must embrace thee.
                              [*They embrace.*]
Let sorrow split my heart if ever I
Did hate thee or thy father!
EDGAR   Worthy prince, I know't.
ALBANY   Where have you hid yourself?
How have you known the miseries of your father?
EDGAR
By nursing them, my lord. List a brief tale,   185
And when 'tis told, oh, that my heart would burst!
The bloody proclamation to escape   187
That followed me so near—oh, our lives' sweetness,   188
That we the pain of death would hourly die   189
Rather than die at once!—taught me to shift   190
Into a madman's rags, t'assume a semblance
That very dogs disdained; and in this habit   192
Met I my father with his bleeding rings,   193
Their precious stones new lost; became his guide,   194
Led him, begged for him, saved him from despair;
Never—oh, fault!—revealed myself unto him
Until some half hour past, when I was armed.
Not sure, though hoping, of this good success,   198
I asked his blessing, and from first to last
Told him our pilgrimage. But his flawed heart—   200
Alack, too weak the conflict to support—
Twixt two extremes of passion, joy and grief,
Burst smilingly.
EDMUND   This speech of yours hath moved me,
And shall perchance do good. But speak you on;
You look as you had something more to say.
ALBANY
If there be more, more woeful, hold it in,
For I am almost ready to dissolve,   207
Hearing of this.
EDGAR   This would have seemed a period   208
To such as love not sorrow; but another,   209
To amplify too much, would make much more   210
And top extremity. Whilst I   211
Was big in clamor, came there in a man   212
Who, having seen me in my worst estate,
Shunned my abhorred society; but then, finding
Who 'twas that so endured, with his strong arms
He fastened on my neck and bellowed out

---

144 **wisdom** prudence   146 **say** smack, taste, indication   147 **safe and nicely** prudently and punctiliously   148 **I . . . spurn** i.e., I disdain to insist on my right to refuse combat with one of lower rank.   149 **treasons . . . head** i.e., accusations of treason in your teeth   150 **hell-hated** hated as hell is hated   151 **Which . . . bruise** i.e., which charges of treason—since as yet they merely glance off my armor and do no harm   152 **give . . . way** provide them an immediate pathway (to your heart)   153 **Where . . . forever** i.e., my victory in trial by combat will prove forever that the charges of treason apply to you.   154 **Save** Spare. (Albany wishes to spare Edmund's life so that he may confess and be found guilty.)   **practice** trickery, or (said sardonically) astute management   157 **cozened** tricked   158 **stopple** stop up.   **Hold, sir** (Addressed to Edgar or, more probably, Edmund.)   164 **govern** restrain   168 **fortune on** victory over   169 **charity** forgiveness (for Edmund's wickedness toward Edgar and Edgar's having slain Edmund).   171 **th' hast** thou hast   173 **pleasant** pleasurable   175 **got** begot

177 **The wheel . . . here** (Alludes both to the wheel of fortune and to the idea of a completed circle whereby crime meets its appropriate punishment. Edmund sees that everything has at last come around to where it began.)   185 **List** Listen to   187 **The . . . escape** In order to escape the death-threatening proclamation   188–90 **oh . . . at once!** oh, the perversity of our attachment to our lives' sweetness, that we prefer to suffer continually the fear of death rather than die at once and be done with it!   192 **habit** garb   193 **rings** sockets   194 **stones** i.e., eyeballs   198 **success** outcome   200 **flawed** cracked   207 **dissolve** i.e., in tears   208 **a period** the limit   209–11 **but . . . extremity** i.e., but another sorrowful circumstance, adding to what is already too much, would increase it and exceed the limit.   212 **big in clamor** loud in my lamenting

As he'd burst heaven, threw him on my father,   217
Told the most piteous tale of Lear and him
That ever ear received, which in recounting
His grief grew puissant, and the strings of life   220
Began to crack. Twice then the trumpets sounded,
And there I left him tranced.

ALBANY   But who was this?   222

EDGAR
Kent, sir, the banished Kent, who in disguise
Followed his enemy king and did him service   224
Improper for a slave.

Enter a Gentleman [with a bloody knife].

GENTLEMAN
Help, help, oh, help!

EDGAR   What kind of help?

ALBANY   Speak, man.

EDGAR
What means this bloody knife?

GENTLEMAN   'Tis hot, it smokes.   227
It came even from the heart of—Oh, she's dead!

ALBANY   Who dead? Speak, man.

GENTLEMAN
Your lady, sir, your lady! And her sister
By her is poisoned; she confesses it.

EDMUND
I was contracted to them both. All three
Now marry in an instant.

EDGAR   Here comes Kent.

Enter Kent.

ALBANY
Produce the bodies, be they alive or dead.
                                        [Exit Gentleman.]
This judgment of the heavens, that makes us tremble,
Touches us not with pity.—Oh, is this he?
[*To Kent*] The time will not allow the compliment   237
Which very manners urges.

KENT   I am come   238
To bid my king and master aye good night.   239
Is he not here?

ALBANY   Great thing of us forgot!
Speak, Edmund, where's the King? And where's
     Cordelia?
          Goneril and Regan's bodies [are] brought out.
See'st thou this object, Kent?   242

KENT   Alack, why thus?

EDMUND   Yet Edmund was beloved.
The one the other poisoned for my sake
And after slew herself.

ALBANY   Even so. Cover their faces.

EDMUND
I pant for life. Some good I mean to do,
Despite of mine own nature. Quickly send—
Be brief in it—to th' castle, for my writ
Is on the life of Lear and on Cordelia.
Nay, send in time.

ALBANY   Run, run, oh, run!

EDGAR
To who, my lord? Who has the office? [*To Edmund*]
     Send   253
Thy token of reprieve.

EDMUND   Well thought on. Take my sword. The captain!
Give it the Captain.

EDGAR   Haste thee, for thy life.
                    [Exit one with Edmund's sword.]

EDMUND
He hath commission from thy wife and me
To hang Cordelia in the prison and
To lay the blame upon her own despair,
That she fordid herself.   260

ALBANY
The gods defend her! Bear him hence awhile.
                                        [Edmund is borne off.]

Enter Lear, with Cordelia in his arms; [Captain].

LEAR
Howl, howl, howl! Oh, you are men of stones!
Had I your tongues and eyes, I'd use them so
That heaven's vault should crack. She's gone forever.
I know when one is dead and when one lives;
She's dead as earth. Lend me a looking glass;
If that her breath will mist or stain the stone,   267
Why, then she lives.

KENT   Is this the promised end?   268

EDGAR
Or image of that horror?

ALBANY   Fall and cease!   269

LEAR
This feather stirs; she lives! If it be so,
It is a chance which does redeem all sorrows
That ever I have felt.

KENT [*kneeling*]   O my good master!

LEAR
Prithee, away.

EDGAR   'Tis noble Kent, your friend.

LEAR
A plague upon you, murderers, traitors all!
I might have saved her; now she's gone forever!
Cordelia, Cordelia! Stay a little. Ha?
What is't thou say'st? Her voice was ever soft,
Gentle, and low, an excellent thing in woman.
I killed the slave that was a-hanging thee.

CAPTAIN
'Tis true, my lords, he did.

LEAR   Did I not, fellow?

---

217 As as if.   **threw . . . father** threw himself on my father's body
220 His i.e., Kent's.   **puissant** powerful.   **strings of life** heartstrings
222 tranced entranced, senseless.   **224 his enemy king** i.e., the king
who had rejected and banished him   **227 smokes** steams.   **237 com-**
pliment ceremony   **238 Which . . . urges** which common courtesy
requires.   **239 aye good night** farewell forever. (Kent believes he
himself is near death, his heartstrings having begun to crack.)
242 object sight

253 office commission.   **260 fordid** destroyed   **267 stone** crystal or
polished stone of which the mirror is made   **268 Is . . . end?** (Kent
may mean "Is this what all our hopes have come to?" Edgar replies
by invoking the Last Judgment.)   **269 image** representation.   **Fall**
and cease! i.e., Let all things cease to be!

I have seen the day, with my good biting falchion 281
I would have made them skip. I am old now,
And these same crosses spoil me.—Who are you? 283
Mine eyes are not o'th' best; I'll tell you straight. 284

KENT
If Fortune brag of two she loved and hated, 285
One of them we behold. 286

LEAR
This is a dull sight. Are you not Kent?

KENT   The same, 287
Your servant Kent. Where is your servant Caius? 288

LEAR
He's a good fellow, I can tell you that;
He'll strike, and quickly too. He's dead and rotten.

KENT
No, my good lord, I am the very man—

LEAR   I'll see that straight. 292

KENT
That from your first of difference and decay 293
Have followed your sad steps—

LEAR   You are welcome hither.

KENT
Nor no man else. All's cheerless, dark, and deadly. 295
Your eldest daughters have fordone themselves, 296
And desperately are dead.

LEAR   Ay, so I think. 297

ALBANY
He knows not what he says, and vain is it
That we present us to him.

EDGAR   Very bootless. 299

Enter a Messenger.

MESSENGER   Edmund is dead, my lord.

ALBANY   That's but a trifle here.
You lords and noble friends, know our intent:
What comfort to this great decay may come 303

---

281 **falchion** light sword   283 **crosses spoil me** adversities take away
my strength.   284 **I'll . . . straight** I'll recognize you in a moment.
285–6 **If . . . behold** If Fortune were to brag of two persons whom she
has subjected to the greatest fall from her favor into her hatred, Lear
would have to be one of them.   287 **This . . . sight** i.e., My vision is
clouding, or, this is a dismal spectacle.   288 **Caius** (Kent's disguise
name.)   292 **see that straight** attend to that in a moment.   293 **from
. . . decay** from the beginning of your quarrel (with Cordelia) to your
decline of fortune   295 **Nor . . . else** No, not I nor anyone else, or, I
am the *very man* (line 291), him and no one else.   296 **fordone**
destroyed   297 **desperately** in despair   299 **bootless** in vain.
303 **What . . . come** i.e., whatever means of comforting this ruined
king and state of affairs may present themselves

Shall be applied. For us, we will resign, 304
During the life of this old majesty,
To him our absolute power; [*to Edgar and Kent*] you, to
    your rights,
With boot and such addition as your honors 307
Have more than merited. All friends shall taste
The wages of their virtue, and all foes
The cup of their deservings.—Oh, see, see!

LEAR
And my poor fool is hanged! No, no, no life? 311
Why should a dog, a horse, a rat have life,
And thou no breath at all? Thou'lt come no more,
Never, never, never, never, never!
Pray you, undo this button. Thank you, sir.
Do you see this? Look on her, look, her lips,
Look there, look there!   *He dies.*

EDGAR   He faints.—My lord, my lord!

KENT
Break, heart, I prithee, break!

EDGAR   Look up, my lord.

KENT
Vex not his ghost. Oh, let him pass! He hates him 319
That would upon the rack of this tough world 320
Stretch him out longer.

EDGAR   He is gone indeed.

KENT
The wonder is he hath endured so long.
He but usurped his life.

ALBANY
Bear them from hence. Our present business
Is general woe. [*To Kent and Edgar*] Friends of my soul,
    you twain
Rule in this realm, and the gored state sustain.

KENT
I have a journey, sir, shortly to go. 327
My master calls me; I must not say no.

EDGAR
The weight of this sad time we must obey;
Speak what we feel, not what we ought to say.
The oldest hath borne most; we that are young
Shall never see so much nor live so long. 332

                         Exeunt, with a dead march.

---

304 **For** As for   307 **With . . . honors** with advantage and such further distinctions or titles as your honorable conduct in this war
311 **poor fool** i.e., Cordelia. (*Fool* is here a term of endearment.)
319 **ghost** departing spirit.   320 **rack** torture rack. (With suggestion,
in the Folio and Quarto spelling, "wracke," of shipwreck, disaster.)
327 **journey** i.e., to another world, to death   332.1 *Exeunt* (Presumably the dead bodies are borne out in procession.)

Macbeth

acbeth is seemingly the last of four great Shakespearean tragedies—*Hamlet* (c. 1599–1601), *Othello* (c. 1603–1604), *King Lear* (1605–1606), and *Macbeth* (c. 1606–1607)—that examine the dimensions of spiritual evil, as distinguished from the political strife of Roman tragedies such as *Julius Caesar, Antony* and *Cleopatra*, and *Coriolanus*. Whether or not Shakespeare intended *Macbeth* as a culmination of a series of tragedies on evil, the play does offer a particularly terse and gloomy view of humanity's encounter with the powers of darkness. Macbeth, more consciously than any other of Shakespeare's major tragic protagonists, has to face the temptation of committing what he knows to be a monstrous crime. Like Doctor Faustus in Christopher Marlowe's play, *The Tragedy of Doctor Faustus* (c. 1588–1592), and to a lesser extent like Adam in John Milton's *Paradise Lost* (1667), Macbeth understands the reasons for resisting evil and yet goes ahead with his disastrous plan. His awareness and sensitivity to moral issues, together with his conscious choice of evil, produce an unnerving account of human failure, all the more distressing because Macbeth is so representatively human. He seems to possess freedom of will and accepts personal responsibility for his fate, and yet his tragic doom seems unavoidable. Nor is there eventual salvation to be hoped for, as there is in *Paradise Lost*, since Macbeth's crime is too heinous and his heart too hardened. He is more like Doctor Faustus—damned and in despair.

To an extent not found in the other tragedies, the issue is stated in terms of salvation versus damnation. Macbeth knows before he acts that King Duncan's virtues "Will plead like angels, trumpet-tongued, against / The deep damnation of his taking-off" (1.7.19–20). After the murder, he is equally aware that he has "Put rancors in the vessel of my peace . . . and mine eternal jewel / Given to the common enemy of man" (3.1.68–70). His enemies later describe him as a devil and a "hellhound" (5.8.3). He, like Marlowe's Doctor Faustus before him, has knowingly sold his soul for gain. And, although as a mortal he still has time to repent his crimes, horrible as they are,

Macbeth cannot find the words to be penitent. "Wherefore could not I pronounce 'Amen'?" he implores his wife after they have committed the murder. "I had most need of blessing, and 'Amen' / Stuck in my throat" (2.2.35–7). Macbeth's own answer seems to be that he has committed himself so inexorably to evil that he cannot turn back. Sentence has been pronounced: "Glamis hath murdered sleep, and therefore Cawdor / Shall sleep no more; Macbeth shall sleep no more" (lines 46–7).

Macbeth is not a conventional morality play (even less so than *Doctor Faustus*) and is not concerned primarily with preaching against sinfulness or demonstrating that Macbeth is finally damned for what he does. A tradition of moral and religious drama has been transformed into an intensely human study of the psychological effects of evil on a particular man and, to a lesser extent, on his wife. That moral tradition nevertheless provides as its legacy a perspective on the operation of evil in human affairs. A perverse ambition seemingly inborn in Macbeth himself is abetted by dark forces dwelling in the universe, waiting to catch him off guard. Among Shakespeare's tragedies, indeed, *Macbeth* is remarkable for its focus on evil in the protagonist and on his relationship to the sinister forces tempting him. In no other Shakespearean play is the audience asked to identify to such an extent with the evildoer himself. *Richard III* also focuses on an evil protagonist, but in that play the spectators are distanced by the character's gloating and are not partakers in the introspective soliloquies of a man confronting his own ambition. Macbeth is more representatively human. If he betrays an inclination toward brutality, he also humanely attempts to resist that urge. We witness and struggle to understand his downfall through two phases: the spiritual struggle before he actually commits the crime and the despairing aftermath, with its vain quest for security through continued violence. Evil is thus presented in two aspects: first as an insidious suggestion leading Macbeth on toward an illusory promise of gain and then as a frenzied addiction to the hated thing by which he is possessed.

In the first phase, before the commission of the crime, we wonder to what extent the powers of darkness are a determining factor in what Macbeth does. Can he avoid the fate the witches proclaim? Evidently, he and Lady Macbeth have previously considered murdering Duncan; the witches appear after the thought, not before. Lady Macbeth reminds her wavering husband that he was the first to "break this enterprise" to her, on some previous occasion when "Nor time nor place / Did then adhere, and yet you would make both" (1.7.49–53). Elizabethans would probably understand that evil spirits such as witches appear when summoned, whether by our conscious or unconscious minds. Macbeth is ripe for their insinuations: a mind free of taint would see no sinister invitation in their prophecy of greatness to come. And, in a saner moment, Macbeth knows that his restless desire to interfere with destiny is arrogant and useless. "If chance will have me king, why, chance may crown me / Without my stir" (1.3.145–6). Banquo, his companion, serves as his dramatic opposite by consistently displaying a more stoical attitude toward the witches. "Speak then to me," he addresses them, "who neither beg nor fear / Your favors nor your hate" (lines 60–1). Like Horatio in *Hamlet*, Banquo strongly resists the blandishments of fortune as well as its buffets, though not without an agonizing night of moral struggle. Indeed, promises of success are often more ruinous than setbacks—as in the seemingly paradoxical instance of the farmer, cited by Macbeth's porter, who "hanged himself on th'expectation of plenty" (2.3.4–5). It is by showing Macbeth that he is two-thirds of his way to the throne that the witches tempt him to seize the last third at whatever cost. "Glamis, and Thane of Cawdor! / The greatest is behind" (1.3.116–17).

Banquo comprehends the nature of temptation. "To win us to our harm," he observes, "The instruments of darkness tell us truths, / Win us with honest trifles, to betray 's / In deepest consequence" (1.3.123–6). The devil can speak true, and his strategy is to invite us into a trap we help prepare. Without our active consent in evil (as Othello also learns), we cannot fall. Yet in what sense are the witches trifling with Macbeth or prevaricating? When they address him as one "that shalt be king hereafter" (line 50), they are stating a certainty, for they can "look into the seeds of time / And say which grain will grow and which will not," as Banquo says (lines 58–9). They know that Banquo will be "Lesser than Macbeth, and greater, / Not so happy, yet much happier" (lines 65–6), since Banquo will beget a race of kings and Macbeth will not. How then do they know that Macbeth will be king? If we consider the hypothetical question, what if Macbeth does *not* murder Duncan, we can gain some understanding of the relationship between character and fate; for the only valid answer is that the question remains hypothetical—Macbeth *does* kill Duncan, the witches are right in their prediction. It is idle to speculate that Providence

would have found another way to make Macbeth king, for the witches' prophecy is self-fulfilling in the very way they foresee. Character is fate; they know Macbeth's fatal weakness and know they can "enkindle" him to seize the crown by laying irresistible temptations before him. This does not mean that they determine his choice but, rather, that Macbeth's choice is predictable and therefore unvoidable, even though not preordained. He has free choice, but that choice will, in fact, go only one way—as with Adam and Eve in Milton's *Paradise Lost* and in the medieval tradition from which this poem was derived.

Although the powers of evil cannot determine Macbeth's choice, they can influence the external conditions affecting that choice. By a series of apparently circumstantial events, well timed in their effect, they can repeatedly assail him just when he is about to rally to the call of conscience. The witches, armed with supernatural knowledge, inform Macbeth of his new title shortly before the King's ambassadors confirm that he is to be the Thane of Cawdor. Duncan chooses this night to lodge under Macbeth's roof. And, just when Macbeth resolves to abandon even this unparalleled opportunity, his wife intervenes on the side of the witches. Macbeth commits the murder in part to keep his word to her and to prove he is no coward (like Donwald, the slayer of King Duff in one of Shakespeare's chief sources, Raphael Holinshed's *Chronicles*). Not only the opportunities presented to Macbeth, but also the obstacles put in his way are cannily timed to overwhelm his conscience. When King Duncan announces that his son Malcolm is now Prince of Cumberland and official heir to the throne (1.4.36–42), the unintended threat deflects Macbeth's mood from one of gratitude and acceptance to one of hostility. These are mitigating circumstances that affect our judgment of Macbeth, and, even though they cannot excuse him, they certainly increase our sympathetic identification.

We are moved, too, by the poetic intensity of Macbeth's moral vision. His soliloquies are memorable as poetry, not merely because Shakespeare wrote them, but because Macbeth is sensitive and aware. The horror, indeed, of his crime is that his cultivated self is revolted by what he cannot prevent himself from doing. He understands with a terrible clarity, not only the moral wrong of what he is about to do, but also the inescapably destructive consequences for himself. He is as reluctant as we to see the crime committed, and yet he goes to it with a sad and rational deliberateness rather than in a self-blinding fury. For Macbeth, there is no seeming loss of perspective, and yet there is total alienation of the act from his moral consciousness. The arguments for and against murdering Duncan, as Macbeth pictures them in his acutely visual imagination, when weighed, are overwhelmingly opposed to the deed. Duncan is his king and his guest, deserving Macbeth's duty and hospitality. The King is virtuous and able. He has shown every favor to

Macbeth, thereby removing any sane motive for striving after further promotion. All human history shows that murders of this sort "return / To plague th'inventor" (1.7.9–10), that is, provide only guilt and punishment rather than satisfaction. Finally, judgment in "the life to come" includes the prospect of eternal torment. On the other side of the argument is nothing but Macbeth's "Vaulting ambition, which o'erleaps itself" (line 27)—a perverse refusal to be content with his present good fortune because there is more that beckons. Who could weigh the issues so dispassionately and still choose the wrong? Yet the failure is, in fact, predictable; Macbeth is presented to us as typically human, both in his understanding and in his perverse ambition.

Macbeth's clarity of moral imagination is contrasted with his wife's imperceptiveness. He is always seeing visions or hearing voices—a dagger in the air, the ghost of Banquo, a voice crying "Sleep no more!"—and she is always denying them. "The sleeping and the dead / Are but as pictures," she insists. He knows that "all great Neptune's ocean" cannot wash the blood from his hands; "No, this my hand will rather / The multitudinous seas incarnadine, / Making the green one red." To Lady Macbeth, contrastingly, "A little water clears us of this deed. / How easy is it, then!" (2.2.57–72). Macbeth knows that the murder of Duncan is but the beginning: "We have scorched the snake, not killed it." Lady Macbeth would prefer to believe that "What's done is done" (3.2.14–15). Ironically, it is she, finally, who must endure visions of the most agonizing sort, sleepwalking in her madness and trying to rub away the "damned spot" that before seemed so easy to remove. "All the perfumes of Arabia will not sweeten this little hand," she laments (5.1.34–51). This relationship between Macbeth and Lady Macbeth owes much to traditional contrasts between male and female principles. As in the pairing of Adam and Eve, the man is putatively the more rational of the two but knowingly shares his wife's sin through fondness for her. She has failed to foresee the long-range consequences of sinful ambition and so becomes a temptress to her husband. The fall of man and woman into the bondage of sin takes place in an incongruous atmosphere of domestic intimacy and mutual concern; Lady Macbeth is motivated by ambition for her husband in much the same way that he sins to win her approbation.

The fatal disharmony flawing this domestic accord is conveyed through images of sexual inversion. Lady Macbeth prepares for her ordeal with the incantation, "Come, you spirits / That tend on mortal thoughts, unsex me here . . . Come to my woman's breasts / And take my milk for gall" (1.5.40–8). When she accuses her husband of unmanly cowardice and vows she would dash out the brains of her own infant for such effeminacy as he has displayed, he extols her with "Bring forth men-children only! / For thy undaunted mettle should compose / Nothing but males" (1.7.73–5). She takes the initiative,

devising and then carrying out the plan to drug Duncan's chamber-guards with wine. This assumption of the dominant male role by the woman might well remind Elizabethan spectators of numerous biblical, medieval, and classical parallels deploring the ascendancy of passion over reason: Eve choosing for Adam, Noah's wife taking command of the ark, the Wife of Bath dominating her husbands, Venus emasculating Mars, and others.

In *Macbeth*, sexual inversion also allies Lady Macbeth with the witches or weird sisters, the bearded women. Their unnaturalness betokens disorder in nature, for they can sail in a sieve and "look not like th'inhabitants o'th'earth / And yet are on't" (1.3.41–2). Characteristically, they speak in paradoxes: "When the battle's lost and won," "Fair is foul, and foul is fair" (1.1.4,11). Shakespeare probably drew on numerous sources to depict the witches: Holinshed's *Chronicles* (in which he conflated two accounts, one of Duncan and Macbeth, and the other of King Duff slain by Donwald with the help of his wife), King James's writings on witchcraft, Samuel Harsnett's *Declaration of Egregious Popish Impostures* (used also for *King Lear*), and the accounts of the Scottish witch trials published around 1590. In the last, particularly, Shakespeare could have found mention of witches raising storms and sailing in sieves to endanger vessels at sea, performing threefold rituals blaspheming the Trinity, and brewing witches' broth. Holinshed's *Chronicles* refer to the weird sisters as "goddesses of destiny," associating them with the three fates, Clotho, Lachesis, and Atropos, who hold the spinning distaff, draw off the thread of life, and cut it. In *Macbeth*, the weird sisters' power to control fortune is curtailed, and they are portrayed as witches according to popular contemporary understanding, rather than as goddesses of destiny; nonetheless, witches were thought to be servants of the devil (Banquo wonders if the devil can speak true in their utterances, 1.3.107), and through them Macbeth has made an ominous pact with evil itself. His visit to their seething cauldron in 4.1 brings him to the witches' masters, those unknown powers that know his very thought and who tempt him with those equivocations of which Banquo has warned Macbeth. The popularity of witchlore tempted Shakespeare's acting company to expand the witches' scenes with spectacles of song and dance; even the Folio text we have evidently contains interpolations derived in part from Thomas Middleton's *The Witch* (see especially 3.5 and part of 4.1, containing mention of Middleton's songs "Come away" and "Black spirits"). Nevertheless, Shakespeare's original theme of a disharmony in nature remains clearly visible.

The disharmonies of gender relations in *Macbeth* suggest another disturbing dimension of this tragedy. The play is filled with what Janet Adelman (in *Cannibals, Witches, and Divorce*, edited by Marjorie Garber, 1985) aptly calls fantasies of maternal power. Macbeth, like many males, attempts to cope with his imaginings of a destructive maternal power and his fantasies of escape into a world fashioned and controlled solely by himself. Initially, he submits to his wife's idea of manliness and commits murder in order to win her approval, destroying in the process a fatherly figure whose manhood is nonetheless ambivalently presented to us: Duncan is to be sure a nurturing father-king, but he is also too soft and trusting for his own good. Macbeth chooses to side with his masculinized wife against the gentler side of human nature, lauding her as a woman who should "Bring forth men-children only," since her "undaunted mettle should compose / Nothing but males" (1.7.73–5), but, in the longer term, Macbeth finds himself desiccated by his own vulnerability to this masculinized mother. He turns unsuccessfully to the witches for the power he needs to make him author of himself; in the process of attempting to make himself wholly "masculine," he manages instead to strip away from himself "honor, love, obedience, troops of friends," and all the graces that should "accompany old age" (5.3.24–5). His nemesis is appropriately one who was not, in the normal sense, "of woman born," since Macduff "was from his mother's womb / Untimely ripped" (5.8.13–16). Macduff represents, in other words, the self-creating and invulnerable masculinity that Macbeth cannot fashion for himself. The ending of the play is distressingly absolute in its consolidation of male power—a reestablishment of control that seems necessary in view of the virulence of the maternal power the play has dared to unleash.

Patterns of imagery throughout the play point similarly to disorders in nature and in human relationships. The murder of Duncan, like that of Caesar in *Julius Caesar*, is accompanied by signs of the heavens' anger. Various observers report that chimneys blow down during the unruly night, that owls clamor and attack falcons, that the earth shakes, and that Duncan's horses devour each other. (Some of these portents are from Holinshed.) Banquo's ghost returns from the dead to haunt his murderer, prompting Macbeth to speak in metaphors of charnel houses and graves that send back their dead and of birds of prey that devour the corpses. The drunken porter who opens the gate to Macduff and Lennox after the murder (2.3) invokes images of judgment and everlasting bonfire, through which the scene takes on the semblance of hell gate and the Harrowing of Hell. Owls appear repeatedly in the imagery, along with other creatures associated with nighttime and horror: wolves, serpents, scorpions, bats, toads, beetles, crows, rooks. Darkness itself assumes tangible and menacing shapes of hidden stars or extinguished candles, a thick blanket shrouded "in the dunnest smoke of hell" (1.5.51), an entombment of the earth in place of "living light" (2.4.10), a scarf to hoodwink the eye of "pitiful day" (3.2.50), and a bloody and invisible hand to tear to pieces the lives of the virtuous. Sleep is transformed from "great nature's second course" and a "nourisher" of life that "knits up the raveled sleave

of care" (2.2.41–4) into "death's counterfeit" (2.3.77) and a living hell for Lady Macbeth. Life becomes sterile for Macbeth, a denial of harvest, the lees or dregs of the wine and "the sere, the yellow leaf" (5.3.23). In a theatrical metaphor, life becomes for him unreal, "a walking shadow, a poor player / That struts and frets his hour upon the stage / And then is heard no more" (5.5.24–6). This theme of empty illusion carries over into the recurring image of borrowed or ill-fitting garments that belie the wearer. Macbeth is an actor, a hypocrite, whose "False face must hide what the false heart doth know" (1.7.83) and who must "Look like th'innocent flower, / But be the serpent under't" (1.5.65–6). Even the show of grief is an assumed mask whereby evildoers deceive the virtuous, so much so that Malcolm, Donalbain, and Macduff learn to conceal their true feelings rather than be thought to "show an unfelt sorrow" (2.3.138).

Blood is not only a literal sign of disorder but an emblem of Macbeth's remorseless butchery, a "damned spot" on the conscience, and a promise of divine vengeance: "It will have blood, they say; blood will have blood" (3.4.123). The emphasis on corrupted blood also suggests disease, in which Macbeth's tyranny is a sickness to his country as well as to himself. Scotland bleeds (4.3.32), needing a physician; Macduff and his allies call themselves "the med'cine of the sickly weal" (5.2.27). Lady Macbeth's disease is incurable, something spiritually corrupt wherein "the patient / Must minister to himself" (5.3.47–8). Conversely, the English King Edward is renowned for his divine gift of curing what was called the king's evil, or scrofula. These images are generally paternalistic in their invocation of kings and fathers who heal and unite.

Throughout, the defenders of righteousness are associated with positive images of natural order and with patriarchal control. Duncan rewards his subjects by saying, "I have begun to plant thee, and will labor / To make thee full of growing" (1.4.28–9). His arrival at Inverness Castle is heralded by signs of summer, sweet air, and "the temple-haunting martlet" (1.6.4). He is a fatherly figure, so much so that even Lady Macbeth balks at an act so like patricide. Macduff, too, is a father and husband whose family is butchered. The forest of Birnam marching to confront Macbeth, although rationally explainable as a device of camouflage for Macduff's army, is emblematic of the natural order itself rising up against the monstrosity of Macbeth's crimes. Banquo is, above all, a patriarchal figure, ancestor of the royal line governing Scotland and England at the time the play was written. These harmonies are to an extent restorative. Even the witches' riddling prophecies, "th'equivocation of the fiend" (5.5.43), luring Macbeth into further atrocities with the vain promise of security, anticipate a just retribution.

Nonetheless, the play's vision of evil shakes us deeply. Scotland's peace has been violated, so much so that "to do harm / Is often laudable, to do good sometime /

Accounted dangerous folly" (4.2.76–8). Macduff has been forced to deny his proper manly role of protecting his wife and family; Lady Macduff and her son, along with young Siward, have had to pay with their innocent lives the terrible price of Scotland's tyranny. In his frenzied attempt to prevent the fulfillment of the prophecy about Banquo's lineage inheriting the kingdom, Macbeth has, like King Herod, slaughtered much of the younger generation on whom the future depends. We can only hope that the stability to which Scotland returns after his death will be lasting. Banquo's line is to rule eventually and to produce a line of kings reaching down to the royal occupant to whom Shakespeare will present his play, but, when *Macbeth* ends, it is Malcolm who is king. The killing of a traitor (Macbeth) and the placing of his head on a pole replicate the play's beginning in the treason and beheading of the Thane of Cawdor—a gentleman on whom Duncan built "An absolute trust" (1.4.14). Most troublingly, the humanly representative nature of Macbeth's crime leaves us with little assurance that we could resist his temptation. The most that can be said is that wise and good persons such as Banquo and Macduff have learned to know the evil in themselves and to resist it as nobly as they can.

Along with its timeless interest in murder and the human conscience, *Macbeth* is an intensely political play. It surely was viewed as such when it was first produced in 1606–1607. The drunken porter in 2.3 seemingly refers to the infamous attempt to blow up the houses of Parliament known as the Gunpowder Plot of 1605, and to the subsequent trial of the Jesuit Henry Garnet, the notorious "equivicator," for his part in the conspiracy (2.3.8). Banquo fulfills a historical role as progenitor of the dynastic line that would lead eventually to James VI of Scotland, who had become James I of England in 1603. The pageant of *"eight Kings and Banquo last"* that Macbeth must witness on the occasion of his final visit to the Weird Sisters (4.1.111.1) ends with a *glass* or magic mirror showing many more kings bearing the appurtenances of royal office, including the "twofold balls and treble sceptres" that seemingly refer to James's double coronation in 1603 as King of England and Scotland. James was keenly interested in witchcraft. Scotland was a constant worry on England's northern border, aligning itself with France, marauding across the English border, tearing itself apart through clan violence, and, from an English point of view, manifesting the kind of tyranny that the English especially feared. The Scotland of this play thus helps to define, largely by contrast, what is thought to be truly English. The English King who is described as doing "A most miraculous work" in curing "the evil," or scrofula, by his touch (4.3.147–8) suggests a flattering reference to James, who claimed this power of curing. This unnamed English king lends his support to the military attack against Macbeth through which the tyrant is finally overthrown. The play simultaneously incorporates an uneasy attitude of hostility toward Scotland along with a vision of union between the two countries that is brought about by the subjugation of Scotland to her southern neighbor. A rough kind of harmony is achieved out of disharmony. Macbeth's act of murderous regicide is answered by another regicide in the name of English law. The quandaries of such a resolution may point to the ambivalence that many English people felt about their odd ruler from the north, the man who came to be known as "the wisest fool in Christendom."

Macbeth is a difficult play to present on stage, at least according to stage tradition: ever since the early twentieth century, actors have referred to it superstitiously as "the Scottish play" as a way of avoiding bad luck that otherwise can hover menacingly over the acting company. Presumably this is a theatrical response to the play's dark probing of irrational magic, fatal determinism, and human frailty. Not coincidentally, perhaps, some of the greatest successes in performance have been on film. Akira Kurosawa's *Throne of Blood* (1957) retells the story of Macbeth, in black and white, as a devastating exploration of ambitious strife among Japanese warlords. Although the dialogue and characters' names of Shakespeare's play are altered throughout, this version captures magnificently the mysterious and malign intent of the prophetic figure Macbeth encounters in a forest, tempting him to evil by the ambiguous promises of future greatness. The forest itself is a striking presence in this film, invested as it is with supernatural terror in the midst of a thunderstorm. The Lady Asaji, wife to Washizu (the Macbeth figure), is horrifyingly obsessed with ambition for her husband; her seeming role as an obedient and decorously aristocratic Japanese wife accentuates the contrast between the surfaces of civilized behavior and the dark inner promptings of competitive self-assertion. A film version with Ian McKellen and Judi Dench as Macbeth and his wife, based on a stage version directed by Trevor Nunn (1976–1978) at Stratford-upon-Avon, London, and Newcastle-upon-Tyne, emphasizes the demonic in such a way as to give the Weird Sisters a real power that is both psychologically plausible and frighteningly irrational. Roman Polanski's film version (1971), though faulted for its sponsorship by Playboy Productions and its consequent flaunting of some grotesque nakedness, does successfully portray Macbeth and Lady Macbeth as a vitally young couple for whom sexuality is integral to their ambition. And of course there have been great stage productions, despite the shibboleth of the bad-luck legend, notably Glen Byam Shaw's production at Stratford-upon-Avon in 1955 starring Laurence Olivier and Vivien Leigh that invited admiration for husband and wife as magnificent, courageous, loyal, and of genuinely tragic stature even if fatally flawed by their hearkening to the voice of evil.

Macbeth

[*Dramatis Personae*

DUNCAN, *King of Scotland*
MALCOLM ⎱ *his sons*
DONALBAIN ⎰

MACBETH, *Thane of Glamis, later of Cawdor, later King of*
Scotland
LADY MACBETH

BANQUO, *a thane of Scotland*
FLEANCE, *his son*
MACDUFF, *Thane of Fife*
LADY MACDUFF
SON *of Macduff and Lady Macduff*

LENNOX ⎱
ROSS ⎟
MENTEITH ⎬ *thanes and noblemen of Scotland*
ANGUS ⎟
CAITHNESS ⎰

SIWARD, *Earl of Northumberland*
YOUNG SIWARD, *his son*

SEYTON, *an officer attending Macbeth*
Another LORD
ENGLISH DOCTOR
SCOTTISH DOCTOR
GENTLEWOMAN *attending Lady Macbeth*
CAPTAIN *serving Duncan*
PORTER
OLD MAN
Three MURDERERS *of Banquo*
FIRST MURDERER *at Macduff's castle*
MESSENGER *to Lady Macbeth*
MESSENGER *to Lady Macduff*
SERVANT *to Macbeth*
SERVANT *to Lady Macbeth*
Three WITCHES *or* WEIRD SISTERS
HECATE
Three APPARITIONS

Lords, Gentlemen, Officers, Soldiers, Murderers,
and Attendants

SCENE: *Scotland; England*]

1.1

Thunder and lightning. Enter three Witches.

FIRST WITCH
    When shall we three meet again?
    In thunder, lightning, or in rain?
SECOND WITCH
    When the hurlyburly's done,
    When the battle's lost and won.
THIRD WITCH
    That will be ere the set of sun.   3

FIRST WITCH
    Where the place?
SECOND WITCH   Upon the heath.
THIRD WITCH
    There to meet with Macbeth.
FIRST WITCH   I come, Grimalkin!   8
SECOND WITCH   Paddock calls.   9
THIRD WITCH   Anon.   10

1.1 Location: An open place.
3 hurlyburly tumult

8 Grimalkin i.e., gray cat, name of the witch's familiar—a demon or
evil spirit supposed to answer a witch's call and to allow him or her
to perform black magic.   **9 Paddock** toad; also a familiar   **10 Anon**
At once, right away.

ALL
Fair is foul, and foul is fair.
Hover through the fog and filthy air.   *Exeunt.*

❧

1.2

Alarum within. Enter King [Duncan], Malcolm,
Donalbain, Lennox, with attendants, meeting a
bleeding Captain.

DUNCAN
What bloody man is that? He can report,
As seemeth by his plight, of the revolt
The newest state.
MALCOLM   This is the sergeant   3
Who like a good and hardy soldier fought
'Gainst my captivity.—Hail, brave friend!
Say to the King the knowledge of the broil   6
As thou didst leave it.
CAPTAIN   Doubtful it stood,
As two spent swimmers that do cling together   8
And choke their art. The merciless Macdonwald—   9
Worthy to be a rebel, for to that   10
The multiplying villainies of nature   11
Do swarm upon him—from the Western Isles   12
Of kerns and gallowglasses is supplied;   13
And Fortune, on his damnèd quarrel smiling,   14
Showed like a rebel's whore. But all's too weak; 15
For brave Macbeth—well he deserves that name—   16
Disdaining Fortune, with his brandished steel,
Which smoked with bloody execution,
Like valor's minion carved out his passage   19
Till he faced the slave,   20
Which ne'er shook hands nor bade farewell to him 21
Till he unseamed him from the nave to th' chops, 22
And fixed his head upon our battlements.
DUNCAN
Oh, valiant cousin, worthy gentleman!   24

CAPTAIN
As whence the sun 'gins his reflection   25
Shipwrecking storms and direful thunders break, 26
So from that spring whence comfort seemed to come 27
Discomfort swells. Mark, King of Scotland, mark. 28
No sooner justice had, with valor armed,
Compelled these skipping kerns to trust their heels 30
But the Norweyan lord, surveying vantage,   31
With furbished arms and new supplies of men,
Began a fresh assault.
DUNCAN
Dismayed not this our captains, Macbeth and
     Banquo?
CAPTAIN
Yes, as sparrows eagles, or the hare the lion. 35
If I say sooth, I must report they were   36
As cannons overcharged with double cracks,   37
So they doubly redoubled strokes upon the foe.
Except they meant to bathe in reeking wounds   39
Or memorize another Golgotha,   40
I cannot tell.
But I am faint. My gashes cry for help.
DUNCAN
So well thy words become thee as thy wounds;
They smack of honor both.—Go get him surgeons.
                         [*Exit Captain, attended.*]

Enter Ross and Angus.

Who comes here?
MALCOLM   The worthy Thane of Ross.   45
LENNOX   What a haste looks through his eyes!
So should he look that seems to speak things strange. 47
ROSS   God save the King!
DUNCAN   Whence cam'st thou, worthy thane?
ROSS   From Fife, great King,
Where the Norweyan banners flout the sky   51
And fan our people cold.   52
Norway himself, with terrible numbers,   53
Assisted by that most disloyal traitor,
The Thane of Cawdor, began a dismal conflict,   55
Till that Bellona's bridegroom, lapped in proof, 56
Confronted him with self-comparisons,   57

1.2. Location: A camp near Forres.
0.1 Alarum trumpet call to arms   **3 newest state** latest news.
sergeant i.e., staff officer. (There may be no inconsistency with his
rank of "captain" in the stage direction and speech prefixes in the
Folio.)   **6 broil** battle   **8 spent** tired out   **9 choke their art** render
their skill in swimming useless.   **9–13 The merciless . . . supplied**
The merciless Macdonwald—worthy of the hated name of rebel, for
in the cause of rebellion an ever-increasing number of villainous persons and unnatural qualities swarm about him like vermin—is joined
by light-armed Irish footsoldiers and ax-armed horsemen from the
western islands of Scotland (the Hebrides and perhaps Ireland)
14–15 And Fortune . . . whore i.e., Fortune, proverbially a false
strumpet, smiles at first on Macdonwald's damned rebellion but
deserts him in his hour of need.   **16 well . . . name** well he deserves a
name that is synonymous with "brave"   **19 minion** darling. (Macbeth is Valor's darling, not Fortune's.)   **20 the slave** i.e., Macdonwald   **21 Which . . . to him** i.e., Macbeth paused for no ceremonious
greeting or farewell to Macdonwald.   **22 nave** navel.   **chops** jaws
24 cousin kinsman

25–8 As . . . swells Just as terrible storms at sea arise out of the east,
from the place where the sun first shows itself in the seeming comfort
of the dawn, even thus did a new military threat come on the heels of
the seeming good news of Macdonwald's execution.   **30 skipping**
(1) lightly armed, quick at maneuvering (2) skittish   **31 surveying**
vantage seeing an opportunity   **35 Yes . . . eagles** Yes, about as much
as sparrows terrify eagles. (Said ironically.)   **36 say sooth** tell the
truth   **37 cracks** charges of explosive   **39 Except** Unless   **40 memo-**
rize make memorable or famous.   **Golgotha** "place of a skull,"
where Christ was crucified. (Mark 15:22.)   **45 Thane** Scottish title of
honor, roughly equivalent to "Earl"   **47 seems to** seems about to
51 flout mock, insult   **52 fan . . . cold** fan cold fear into our troops.
53 Norway The King of Norway.   **terrible numbers** terrifying numbers of troops   **55 dismal** ominous   **56 Till . . . proof** i.e., until Macbeth, clad in well-tested armor. (Bellona was the Roman goddess of
war.)   **57 him** i.e., the King of Norway.   **self-comparisons** i.e.,
matching counterthrusts

Point against point, rebellious arm 'gainst arm,
Curbing his lavish spirit; and to conclude,
The victory fell on us.

DUNCAN   Great happiness!

ROSS   That now
Sweno, the Norways' king, craves composition;   62
Nor would we deign him burial of his men
Till he disbursèd at Saint Colme's Inch   64
Ten thousand dollars to our general use.   65

DUNCAN
No more that Thane of Cawdor shall deceive
Our bosom interest. Go pronounce his present death,   67
And with his former title greet Macbeth.

ROSS   I'll see it done.

DUNCAN
What he hath lost noble Macbeth hath won.

                      Exeunt.

❧

1.3

Thunder. Enter the three Witches.

FIRST WITCH   Where hast thou been, sister?
SECOND WITCH   Killing swine.
THIRD WITCH   Sister, where thou?
FIRST WITCH
A sailor's wife had chestnuts in her lap,
And munched, and munched, and munched. "Give
    me," quoth I.
"Aroint thee, witch!" the rump-fed runnion cries.   6
Her husband's to Aleppo gone, master o'th' *Tiger*;   7
But in a sieve I'll thither sail,
And like a rat without a tail   9
I'll do, I'll do, and I'll do.   10
SECOND WITCH
I'll give thee a wind.
FIRST WITCH
Thou'rt kind.
THIRD WITCH
And I another.
FIRST WITCH
I myself have all the other,   14
And the very ports they blow,   15
All the quarters that they know   16
I'th' shipman's card.   17
I'll drain him dry as hay.   18

Sleep shall neither night nor day
Hang upon his penthouse lid.   20
He shall live a man forbid.   21
Weary sev'nnights nine times nine   22
Shall he dwindle, peak, and pine.   23
Though his bark cannot be lost,
Yet it shall be tempest-tossed.
Look what I have.

SECOND WITCH   Show me, show me.

FIRST WITCH
Here I have a pilot's thumb,
Wrecked as homeward he did come.   *Drum within.*

THIRD WITCH
A drum, a drum!
Macbeth doth come.

ALL [*dancing in a circle*]
The Weird Sisters, hand in hand,   32
Posters of the sea and land,   33
Thus do go about, about,
Thrice to thine, and thrice to mine,
And thrice again, to make up nine.
Peace! The charm's wound up.

Enter Macbeth and Banquo.

MACBETH
So foul and fair a day I have not seen.

BANQUO
How far is't called to Forres?—What are these,   39
So withered and so wild in their attire,
That look not like th'inhabitants o'th'earth
And yet are on't?—Live you? Or are you aught
That man may question? You seem to understand me;
By each at once her choppy finger laying   44
Upon her skinny lips. You should be women,
And yet your beards forbid me to interpret
That you are so.

MACBETH   Speak, if you can. What are you?

FIRST WITCH
All hail, Macbeth! Hail to thee, Thane of Glamis!

SECOND WITCH
All hail, Macbeth! Hail to thee, Thane of Cawdor!

THIRD WITCH
All hail, Macbeth, that shalt be king hereafter!

BANQUO
Good sir, why do you start and seem to fear
Things that do sound so fair?—I'th' name of truth,
Are ye fantastical or that indeed   53
Which outwardly ye show? My noble partner   54
You greet with present grace and great prediction   55
Of noble having and of royal hope,
That he seems rapt withal. To me you speak not.   57
If you can look into the seeds of time

And say which grain will grow and which will not,
Speak then to me, who neither beg nor fear   60
Your favors nor your hate.   61

FIRST WITCH   Hail!

SECOND WITCH   Hail!

THIRD WITCH   Hail!

FIRST WITCH
Lesser than Macbeth, and greater.

SECOND WITCH
Not so happy, yet much happier.   66

THIRD WITCH
Thou shalt get kings, though thou be none.   67
So all hail, Macbeth and Banquo!

FIRST WITCH
Banquo and Macbeth, all hail!

MACBETH
Stay, you imperfect speakers, tell me more!   70
By Sinel's death I know I am Thane of Glamis,   71
But how of Cawdor? The Thane of Cawdor lives
A prosperous gentleman; and to be king
Stands not within the prospect of belief,
No more than to be Cawdor. Say from whence   75
You owe this strange intelligence, or why   76
Upon this blasted heath you stop our way   77
With such prophetic greeting? Speak, I charge you.
                                                    Witches vanish.

BANQUO
The earth hath bubbles, as the water has,
And these are of them. Whither are they vanished?

MACBETH
Into the air; and what seemed corporal melted,   81
As breath into the wind. Would they had stayed!

BANQUO
Were such things here as we do speak about?
Or have we eaten on the insane root   84
That takes the reason prisoner?

MACBETH
Your children shall be kings.

BANQUO   You shall be king.

MACBETH
And Thane of Cawdor too. Went it not so?

BANQUO
To th' selfsame tune and words.—Who's here?

                    Enter Ross and Angus.

ROSS
The King hath happily received, Macbeth,
The news of thy success; and when he reads   90
Thy personal venture in the rebels' fight,   91
His wonders and his praises do contend   92
Which should be thine or his. Silenced with that,   93
In viewing o'er the rest o'th' selfsame day

He finds thee in the stout Norweyan ranks,   95
Nothing afeard of what thyself didst make,   96
Strange images of death. As thick as tale   97
Came post with post, and every one did bear   98
Thy praises in his kingdom's great defense,
And poured them down before him.

ANGUS   We are sent
To give thee from our royal master thanks,
Only to herald thee into his sight,
Not pay thee.

ROSS
And, for an earnest of a greater honor,   104
He bade me, from him, call thee Thane of Cawdor;
In which addition, hail, most worthy thane,   106
For it is thine.

BANQUO   What, can the devil speak true?

MACBETH
The Thane of Cawdor lives. Why do you dress me
In borrowed robes?

ANGUS   Who was the thane lives yet,   109
But under heavy judgment bears that life
Which he deserves to lose. Whether he was combined   111
With those of Norway, or did line the rebel   112
With hidden help and vantage, or that with both
He labored in his country's wrack, I know not;   114
But treasons capital, confessed and proved,   115
Have overthrown him.

MACBETH [*aside*]   Glamis, and Thane of Cawdor!
The greatest is behind. [*To Ross and Angus*] Thanks for
    your pains.   117
[*Aside to Banquo*] Do you not hope your children shall
    be kings
When those that gave the Thane of Cawdor to me
Promised no less to them?

BANQUO [*to Macbeth*]   That, trusted home,   120
Might yet enkindle you unto the crown,
Besides the Thane of Cawdor. But 'tis strange;
And oftentimes to win us to our harm
The instruments of darkness tell us truths,
Win us with honest trifles, to betray 's
In deepest consequence.—   126
Cousins, a word, I pray you.   127
        [*He converses apart with Ross and Angus.*]

MACBETH [*aside*]   Two truths are told,
As happy prologues to the swelling act   129
Of the imperial theme.—I thank you, gentlemen.
[*Aside*] This supernatural soliciting   131
Cannot be ill, cannot be good. If ill,
Why hath it given me earnest of success

---

95 stout haughty, determined, valiant   **96 Nothing** not at all
97–8 As . . . with post As fast as could be told, i.e., counted, came
messenger after messenger. (Unless the text should be amended to
"As thick as hail.")   **104 earnest** token payment   **106 addition** title
109 Who He who   **111 combined** confederate   **112 line the rebel**
reinforce Macdonwald   **114 in . . . wrack** to bring about his country's
ruin   **115 capital** deserving death   **117 The greatest is behind** either
(1) Two of the three prophecies (and thus the greatest number of
them) have already been fulfilled, or (2) The greatest one, the kingship, is still to come.   **120 home** all the way   **126 In deepest consequence** in the profoundly important sequel.   **127 Cousins** i.e., Fellow
lords   **129 swelling act** stately drama   **131 soliciting** tempting

---

60–1 beg . . . hate beg your favors nor fear your hate.   **66 happy** fortunate   **67 get** beget   **70 imperfect** cryptic   **71 Sinel's** (Sinel was
Macbeth's father.)   **75–6 Say . . . intelligence** Say from what source
you have this disturbing information   **77 blasted** blighted   **81 corporal** corporeal   **84 on** of.   **insane root** root causing insanity; variously identified   **90–3 and when . . . his** and when he reads of your
extraordinary valor in fighting the rebels, he concludes that your
wondrous deeds outdo any praise he could offer.

Commencing in a truth? I am Thane of Cawdor.
If good, why do I yield to that suggestion
Whose horrid image doth unfix my hair   136
And make my seated heart knock at my ribs,
Against the use of nature? Present fears   138
Are less than horrible imaginings.
My thought, whose murder yet is but fantastical,   140
Shakes so my single state of man   141
That function is smothered in surmise,   142
And nothing is but what is not.   143

BANQUO   Look how our partner's rapt.

MACBETH [*aside*]
If chance will have me king, why, chance may crown
    me
Without my stir.

BANQUO   New honors come upon him,   146
Like our strange garments, cleave not to their mold   147
But with the aid of use.

MACBETH [*aside*]   Come what come may,   148
Time and the hour runs through the roughest day.   149

BANQUO
Worthy Macbeth, we stay upon your leisure.   150

MACBETH
Give me your favor. My dull brain was wrought   151
With things forgotten. Kind gentlemen, your pains
Are registered where every day I turn   153
The leaf to read them. Let us toward the King.
[*Aside to Banquo*]   Think upon what hath chanced,
    and at more time,   155
The interim having weighed it, let us speak   156
Our free hearts each to other.   157

BANQUO [*to Macbeth*]   Very gladly.

MACBETH [*to Banquo*]   Till then, enough.—Come, friends.
                                                          Exeunt.

❖

1.4

*Flourish. Enter King [Duncan], Lennox, Malcolm,
Donalbain, and attendants.*

DUNCAN
Is execution done on Cawdor? Are not
Those in commission yet returned?

MALCOLM   My liege,   2
They are not yet come back. But I have spoke

With one that saw him die, who did report
That very frankly he confessed his treasons,
Implored Your Highness' pardon, and set forth
A deep repentance. Nothing in his life
Became him like the leaving it. He died   8
As one that had been studied in his death   9
To throw away the dearest thing he owed   10
As 'twere a careless trifle.

DUNCAN   There's no art   11
To find the mind's construction in the face.
He was a gentleman on whom I built
An absolute trust.

Enter Macbeth, Banquo, Ross, and Angus.

                    O worthiest cousin!
The sin of my ingratitude even now
Was heavy on me. Thou art so far before   16
That swiftest wing of recompense is slow
To overtake thee. Would thou hadst less deserved,
That the proportion both of thanks and payment   19
Might have been mine! Only I have left to say,   20
More is thy due than more than all can pay.

MACBETH
The service and the loyalty I owe,
In doing it, pays itself. Your Highness' part
Is to receive our duties; and our duties
Are to your throne and state children and servants,   25
Which do but what they should by doing everything
Safe toward your love and honor.

DUNCAN   Welcome hither!   27
I have begun to plant thee, and will labor
To make thee full of growing. Noble Banquo,
That hast no less deserved, nor must be known
No less to have done so, let me infold thee
And hold thee to my heart.

BANQUO   There if I grow,
The harvest is your own.

DUNCAN   My plenteous joys,
Wanton in fullness, seek to hide themselves   34
In drops of sorrow.—Sons, kinsmen, thanes,
And you whose places are the nearest, know
We will establish our estate upon   37
Our eldest, Malcolm, whom we name hereafter
The Prince of Cumberland; which honor must   39
Not unaccompanied invest him only,   40
But signs of nobleness, like stars, shall shine
On all deservers.—From hence to Inverness,   42
And bind us further to you.   43

---

136 unfix my hair make my hair stand on end   **138 use** custom.
fears things feared   **140 whose . . . fantastical** in which the conception of murder is merely imaginary at this point   **141 single . . . man**
weak human condition   **142 function** normal power of action.
surmise speculation, imaginings   **143 And . . . not** and nothing else
has any reality for me.   **146 stir** bestirring (myself).   **come** i.e.,
which have come   **147–8 cleave . . . use** do not take the shape of the
wearer until often worn. (Macbeth is often connected in the text with
clothes that don't really fit him.)   **149 Time . . . day** time moves
relentlessly on, no matter what else happens.   **150 stay** wait
151 favor pardon.   **wrought** shaped, preoccupied   **153 registered**
recorded (in my memory)   **155 at more time** at a time of greater
leisure   **156 weighed it** given opportunity for reflection on its meaning   **157 Our free hearts** our hearts freely
1.4. Location: Forres. The palace.
2 in commission having warrant (to see to the execution of Cawdor)

8 Became graced, befitted   **9 been studied** made it his study
10 owed owned   **11 careless** uncared for   **16 before** ahead (in
deserving)   **19–20 That . . . mine** that I might have thanked and
rewarded you in ample proportion to your worth.   **25 Are . . . servants** are like children and servants in relation to your throne and
dignity, existing only to serve you   **27 Safe** to safeguard
you whom we love and honor.   **34 Wanton** unrestrained   **37 We**
(The royal "we.")   **establish our estate** fix the succession of our state
39 Prince of Cumberland title of the heir apparent to the Scottish
throne   **40 Not . . . only** not be bestowed on Malcolm alone; other
deserving nobles are to share honors   **42 Inverness** the seat or location of Macbeth's castle, Dunsinane   **43 bind . . . you** put me further
in your (Macbeth's) obligation by your hospitality.

MACBETH
  The rest is labor which is not used for you.   44
  I'll be myself the harbinger and make joyful   45
  The hearing of my wife with your approach;
  So humbly take my leave.
DUNCAN   My worthy Cawdor!
MACBETH [aside]
  The Prince of Cumberland! That is a step
  On which I must fall down or else o'erleap,
  For in my way it lies. Stars, hide your fires;
  Let not light see my black and deep desires.   50
  The eye wink at the hand; yet let that be   52
  Which the eye fears, when it is done, to see.   Exit.   53
DUNCAN
  True, worthy Banquo. He is full so valiant,   54
  And in his commendations I am fed;   55
  It is a banquet to me. Let's after him,
  Whose care is gone before to bid us welcome.
  It is a peerless kinsman.   Flourish. Exeunt.

❧

1.5

Enter Macbeth's Wife, alone, with a letter.

LADY MACBETH [reads] "They met me in the day of success; and I have learned by the perfect'st report they   2
have more in them than mortal knowledge. When I
burnt in desire to question them further, they made
themselves air, into which they vanished. Whiles I
stood rapt in the wonder of it came missives from the   6
King, who all-hailed me 'Thane of Cawdor,' by which
title, before, these Weird Sisters saluted me, and referred me to the coming on of time with 'Hail, king
that shalt be!' This have I thought good to deliver thee,   10
my dearest partner of greatness, that thou mightst not
lose the dues of rejoicing by being ignorant of what
greatness is promised thee. Lay it to thy heart, and
farewell."
  Glamis thou art, and Cawdor, and shalt be
  What thou art promised. Yet do I fear thy nature;   16
  It is too full o'th' milk of human kindness
  To catch the nearest way. Thou wouldst be great,
  Art not without ambition, but without
  The illness should attend it. What thou wouldst
    highly,   20
  That wouldst thou holily; wouldst not play false,

  And yet wouldst wrongly win. Thou'dst have, great
    Glamis,
  That which cries "Thus thou must do," if thou have it,   23
  And that which rather thou dost fear to do   24
  Than wishest should be undone. Hie thee hither,   25
  That I may pour my spirits in thine ear
  And chastise with the valor of my tongue
  All that impedes thee from the golden round   28
  Which fate and metaphysical aid doth seem   29
  To have thee crowned withal.

Enter [a servant as] Messenger.

                              What is your tidings?   30
MESSENGER
  The King comes here tonight.
LADY MACBETH   Thou'rt mad to say it!
  Is not thy master with him, who, were't so,
  Would have informed for preparation?   33
MESSENGER
  So please you, it is true. Our thane is coming.
  One of my fellows had the speed of him,   35
  Who, almost dead for breath, had scarcely more
  Than would make up his message.
LADY MACBETH   Give him tending;   37
  He brings great news.   Exit Messenger.
                    The raven himself is hoarse
  That croaks the fatal entrance of Duncan
  Under my battlements. Come, you spirits
  That tend on mortal thoughts, unsex me here   41
  And fill me from the crown to the toe top-full
  Of direst cruelty! Make thick my blood;
  Stop up th'access and passage to remorse,   44
  That no compunctious visitings of nature   45
  Shake my fell purpose, nor keep peace between   46
  Th'effect and it! Come to my woman's breasts   47
  And take my milk for gall, you murd'ring ministers,   48
  Wherever in your sightless substances   49
  You wait on nature's mischief! Come, thick night,   50
  And pall thee in the dunnest smoke of hell,   51
  That my keen knife see not the wound it makes,
  Nor heaven peep through the blanket of the dark
  To cry "Hold, hold!"   54

Enter Macbeth.

                    Great Glamis! Worthy Cawdor!
  Greater than both by the all-hail hereafter!
  Thy letters have transported me beyond   56

---

44 The rest . . . you All activity not devoted to serving you is mere tediousness and hard work.   **45 harbinger** forerunner, messenger **50 in my way it lies** (The monarchy was not hereditary, and Macbeth had a right to believe that he himself might be chosen as Duncan's successor; he here questions whether he will interfere with the course of events.)   **52–3 The eye . . . see** Let the eye shut itself and not see the hand's deed; yet when the deed is done, let it be fearful to behold.   **54 full so valiant** fully as valiant as you say. (Apparently, Duncan and Banquo have been conversing privately on this subject during Macbeth's soliloquy.)   **55 in . . . fed** it nourishes me to hear him praised
1.5. Location: Inverness. Macbeth's castle.
2 perfect'st most accurate   **6 missives** messengers   **10 deliver thee** inform you of   **16 do I fear** I mistrust   **20 illness** evil (that).
highly greatly

23 have are to have, want to have   **24–5 And that . . . undone** i.e., and the thing you ambitiously crave frightens you more in terms of the means needed to achieve it than in the idea of having it; if you could have it without those means, you certainly wouldn't wish it undone.   **25 Hie** Hasten   **28 round** crown   **29 metaphysical** supernatural   **30 withal** with.   **33 informed for preparation** i.e., sent me word so that I might get things ready.   **35 had . . . of** outstripped **37 Give him tending** Tend to his needs   **41 tend . . . thoughts** attend on, act as the instruments of, deadly or murderous thoughts **44 remorse** pity   **45 nature** natural feelings   **46 fell** fierce, cruel **46–7 nor . . . and it** nor intervene between my *fell purpose* and its accomplishment.   **48 for gall** in exchange for gall, or perhaps *as* gall. **ministers** agents   **49 sightless** invisible   **50 You . . . mischief** you aid and abet the wickedness of human nature.   **51 pall** envelop. **dunnest** darkest   **54 Hold** Stop   **56 letters have** i.e., letter has

This ignorant present, and I feel now
The future in the instant.

MACBETH   My dearest love,
Duncan comes here tonight.

LADY MACBETH   And when goes hence?

MACBETH
Tomorrow, as he purposes.

LADY MACBETH   Oh, never
Shall sun that morrow see!
Your face, my thane, is as a book where men
May read strange matters. To beguile the time,   63
Look like the time; bear welcome in your eye,   64
Your hand, your tongue. Look like th'innocent flower,
But be the serpent under't. He that's coming
Must be provided for; and you shall put
This night's great business into my dispatch,   68
Which shall to all our nights and days to come
Give solely sovereign sway and masterdom.

MACBETH
We will speak further.

LADY MACBETH   Only look up clear.   71
To alter favor ever is to fear.   72
Leave all the rest to me.   *Exeut.*

❖

1.6

*Hautboys and torches. Enter King [Duncan],
Malcolm, Donalbain, Banquo, Lennox, Macduff,
Ross, Angus, and attendants.*

DUNCAN
This castle hath a pleasant seat. The air   1
Nimbly and sweetly recommends itself
Unto our gentle senses.

BANQUO   This guest of summer,   3
The temple-haunting martlet, does approve   4
By his loved mansionry that the heaven's breath   5
Smells wooingly here. No jutty, frieze,   6
Buttress, nor coign of vantage but this bird   7
Hath made his pendent bed and procreant cradle.   8
Where they most breed and haunt, I have observed
The air is delicate.

Enter Lady [Macbeth].

DUNCAN   See, see, our honored hostess!
The love that follows us sometime is our trouble,   11
Which still we thank as love. Herein I teach you   12

How you shall bid God 'ild us for your pains,   13
And thank us for your trouble.

LADY MACBETH   All our service
In every point twice done, and then done double,
Were poor and single business to contend   16
Against those honors deep and broad wherewith   17
Your Majesty loads our house. For those of old,   18
And the late dignities heaped up to them,   19
We rest your hermits.

DUNCAN   Where's the Thane of Cawdor?   20
We coursed him at the heels, and had a purpose   21
To be his purveyor; but he rides well,   22
And his great love, sharp as his spur, hath holp him   23
To his home before us. Fair and noble hostess,
We are your guest tonight.

LADY MACBETH   Your servants ever   25
Have theirs, themselves, and what is theirs in compt   26
To make their audit at Your Highness' pleasure,   27
Still to return your own.

DUNCAN   Give me your hand.   28
Conduct me to mine host. We love him highly,
And shall continue our graces towards him.
By your leave, hostess.   *Exeunt.*

❖

1.7

*Hautboys. Torches. Enter a sewer, and divers
servants with dishes and service, [and pass] over
the stage. Then enter Macbeth.*

MACBETH
If it were done when 'tis done, then 'twere well
It were done quickly. If th'assassination   2
Could trammel up the consequence, and catch   3
With his surcease success—that but this blow   4
Might be the be-all and the end-all!—here,   5
But here, upon this bank and shoal of time,
We'd jump the life to come. But in these cases   7

63–4 To beguile . . . time To deceive everyone, look the way people
expect you to look   **68 dispatch** management   **71–2 Only . . . fear**
Whatever else you do, keep a cheerful countenance. To alter one's
countenance is to betray a guilty conscience.
1.6. Location: Before Macbeth's castle.
0.1 *Hautboys* oboelike instruments   **1 seat** site.   **3 gentle** (1) noble
(2) refined (by the delicate air)   **4–5 The . . . mansionry** The house
martin, that loves to nest in churches, proves by his devoted nest
building   **6 jutty** projection of wall or building   **7 coign of vantage**
convenient corner, i.e., for nesting   **8 pendent** hanging, suspended.
procreant for breeding   **11–12 The love . . . love** The love that sometimes forces itself inconveniently upon us we still appreciate, since it
is meant as love. (Duncan is graciously suggesting that his visit is a
bother, but, he hopes, a welcome one.)

13 bid . . . pains ask God to reward me for the trouble I'm giving you.
(This is said in the same gently jocose spirit as lines 11–12.)   **'ild**
yield, repay   **16–17 Were . . . Against** would be poor and small when
compared with   **18–20 For . . . hermits** In gratitude for the dignities
heaped upon us in former days and still others more recently added
to them, we are your thankful worshipers who pray for you like hermits or beadsmen.   **21 coursed** followed (as in a hunt)   **22 purveyor**
an officer sent ahead to provide for entertainment; here, forerunner
23 holp helped   **25 We** (the royal "we," also in lines 13–14 and 29)
25–8 Your . . . own Those who serve you hold their own servants,
themselves, and all their possessions in trust from you, and can render an account whenever you wish, ready always to render back to
you what is yours. (A feudal concept of obligation.)
1.7. Location: Macbeth's castle; an inner courtyard.
0.1 *sewer* chief waiter, butler   **2–4 If . . . success** i.e., If only the assassination of Duncan could proceed without further consequences and
end the matter with the completion of the deed itself. (To *trammel* is to
bind up or entangle in a net; *surcease* means "cessation"; *success*
means "what succeeds or follows.")   **4 that but** so that only   **5 here**
in this world   **7 jump** risk. (But imaging the physical act is characteristic of Macbeth; compare this with line 27.)

We still have judgment here, that we but teach 8
Bloody instructions, which, being taught, return 9
To plague th'inventor. This evenhanded justice 10
Commends th'ingredience of our poisoned chalice 11
To our own lips. He's here in double trust:
First, as I am his kinsman and his subject,
Strong both against the deed; then, as his host,
Who should against his murderer shut the door,
Not bear the knife myself. Besides, this Duncan
Hath borne his faculties so meek, hath been 17
So clear in his great office, that his virtues 18
Will plead like angels, trumpet-tongued, against
The deep damnation of his taking-off; 20
And Pity, like a naked newborn babe
Striding the blast, or heaven's cherubin, horsed 22
Upon the sightless couriers of the air, 23
Shall blow the horrid deed in every eye,
That tears shall drown the wind. I have no spur 25
To prick the sides of my intent, but only
Vaulting ambition, which o'erleaps itself
And falls on th'other— 28

Enter Lady [Macbeth].

How now, what news?
LADY MACBETH
He has almost supped. Why have you left the
      chamber?
MACBETH
Hath he asked for me?
LADY MACBETH   Know you not he has?
MACBETH
We will proceed no further in this business.
He hath honored me of late, and I have bought 33
Golden opinions from all sorts of people,
Which would be worn now in their newest gloss, 35
Not cast aside so soon.
LADY MACBETH   Was the hope drunk
Wherein you dressed yourself? Hath it slept since?
And wakes it now, to look so green and pale 38
At what it did so freely? From this time
Such I account thy love. Art thou afeard
To be the same in thine own act and valor
As thou art in desire? Wouldst thou have that
Which thou esteem'st the ornament of life, 43
And live a coward in thine own esteem,
Letting "I dare not" wait upon "I would," 45

Like the poor cat i'th'adage?
MACBETH   Prithee, peace! 46
I dare do all that may become a man;
Who dares do more is none.
LADY MACBETH   What beast was't, then,
That made you break this enterprise to me? 49
When you durst do it, then you were a man;
And, to be more than what you were, you would
Be so much more the man. Nor time nor place 52
Did then adhere, and yet you would make both. 53
They have made themselves, and that their fitness
      now 54
Does unmake you. I have given suck, and know
How tender 'tis to love the babe that milks me;
I would, while it was smiling in my face,
Have plucked my nipple from his boneless gums
And dashed the brains out, had I so sworn as you
Have done to this.
MACBETH   If we should fail?
LADY MACBETH   We fail?
But screw your courage to the sticking place 61
And we'll not fail. When Duncan is asleep—
Whereto the rather shall his day's hard journey
Soundly invite him—his two chamberlains 64
Will I with wine and wassail so convince 65
That memory, the warder of the brain, 66
Shall be a fume, and the receipt of reason 67
A limbeck only. When in swinish sleep 68
Their drenchèd natures lies as in a death, 69
What cannot you and I perform upon
Th'unguarded Duncan? What not put upon
His spongy officers, who shall bear the guilt 72
Of our great quell?
MACBETH   Bring forth men-children only! 73
For thy undaunted mettle should compose 74
Nothing but males. Will it not be received, 75
When we have marked with blood those sleepy two
Of his own chamber and used their very daggers,
That they have done't?
LADY MACBETH   Who dares receive it other, 78
As we shall make our griefs and clamor roar 79
Upon his death?
MACBETH   I am settled, and bend up 80
Each corporal agent to this terrible feat. 81

8–10 We . . . th'inventor i.e., we still have punishment for crime in this world, whereby our bloody acts establish guilty precedents and thereby invite the just reciprocity of punishing blood with blood. **11 Commends** presents.   **th'ingredience** the contents of a mixture **17 faculties** powers of office   **18 clear** free of taint   **20 taking-off** murder   **22 Striding the blast** bestriding the tempest. (Putti and cherubs are often portrayed this way in Renaissance graphic arts.) **23 sightless couriers** invisible steeds or runners, i.e., the winds **25 tears . . . wind** (Showers of rain were popularly supposed to still the wind.)   **28 th'other** the other side. (The image is of a horseman vaulting into his saddle and ignominiously falling on the opposite side.)   **33 bought** acquired (by bravery in battle)   **35 would** ought to, should   **38 green** sickly   **43 the ornament of life** i.e., the crown **45 wait upon** accompany, always follow

46 adage (i.e., "The cat would eat fish but she will not wet her feet.") **49 break** broach   **52 Nor** Neither   **53 adhere** agree, suit.   **would** wanted to   **54 that their fitness** that very suitability of time and place   **61 But** Only.   **the sticking place** the notch into which is fitted the string of a crossbow cranked taut for shooting   **64 chamberlains** attendants on the bedchamber   **65 wassail** carousal, drink. **convince** overpower   **66–8 warder . . . only** (The brain was thought to be divided into three ventricles: imagination in front, memory at the back, and between them the seat of reason. The fumes of wine, arising from the stomach, would deaden memory and judgment.) **67 receipt** receptacle, ventricle   **68 limbeck** device for distilling liquids   **69 drenchèd** drowned (in wine)   **72 spongy** soaked, drunken **73 quell** murder.   **74 mettle** (the same word as *metal*): substance, temperament   **75 received** i.e., as truth   **78 other** otherwise **79 As** inasmuch as   **80–1 bend up . . . agent** harness and direct every part of me

Away, and mock the time with fairest show.   82
False face must hide what the false heart doth know.
                                                    Exeunt.

❖

2.1

Enter Banquo, and Fleance, with a torch before him.

BANQUO   How goes the night, boy?

FLEANCE
The moon is down. I have not heard the clock.

BANQUO
And she goes down at twelve.

FLEANCE   I take't, 'tis later, sir.

BANQUO
Hold, take my sword. [*He gives him his sword.*] There's
    husbandry in heaven;   4
Their candles are all out. Take thee that too.
                    [*He gives him his belt and dagger.*]
A heavy summons lies like lead upon me,   6
And yet I would not sleep. Merciful powers,   7
Restrain in me the cursèd thoughts that nature
Gives way to in repose!

Enter Macbeth, and a Servant with a torch.

Give me my sword. Who's there? [*He takes his sword.*]

MACBETH   A friend.

BANQUO
What, sir, not yet at rest? The King's abed.
He hath been in unusual pleasure,
And sent forth great largess to your offices.   14
This diamond he greets your wife withal,
By the name of most kind hostess, and shut up   16
In measureless content.   [*He gives a diamond.*]

MACBETH   Being unprepared,   17
Our will became the servant to defect,   18
Which else should free have wrought.   19

BANQUO   All's well.
I dreamt last night of the three Weird Sisters.
To you they have showed some truth.

MACBETH   I think not of them.
Yet, when we can entreat an hour to serve,
We would spend it in some words upon that business,
If you would grant the time.

BANQUO   At your kind'st leisure.

MACBETH
If you shall cleave to my consent when 'tis,   26
It shall make honor for you.

BANQUO   So I lose none   27
In seeking to augment it, but still keep
My bosom franchised and allegiance clear,   29
I shall be counseled.

MACBETH   Good repose the while!   30

BANQUO   Thanks, sir. The like to you.
                        Exit Banquo [*with Fleance*].

MACBETH [*to Servant*]
Go bid thy mistress, when my drink is ready,   32
She strike upon the bell. Get thee to bed.
                                    Exit [*Servant*].
Is this a dagger which I see before me,
The handle toward my hand? Come, let me clutch
    thee.
I have thee not, and yet I see thee still.
Art thou not, fatal vision, sensible   37
To feeling as to sight? Or art thou but
A dagger of the mind, a false creation,
Proceeding from the heat-oppressèd brain?   40
I see thee yet, in form as palpable
As this which now I draw.   [*He draws a dagger.*]
Thou marshall'st me the way that I was going,   43
And such an instrument I was to use.
Mine eyes are made the fools o'th'other senses,
Or else worth all the rest. I see thee still,
And on thy blade and dudgeon gouts of blood,   47
Which was not so before. There's no such thing.
It is the bloody business which informs
Thus to mine eyes. Now o'er the one half world
Nature seems dead, and wicked dreams abuse   51
The curtained sleep. Witchcraft celebrates   52
Pale Hecate's offerings, and withered Murder,   53
Alarumed by his sentinel, the wolf,   54
Whose howl's his watch, thus with his stealthy pace,   55
With Tarquin's ravishing strides, towards his design   56
Moves like a ghost. Thou sure and firm-set earth,
Hear not my steps which way they walk, for fear
Thy very stones prate of my whereabout
And take the present horror from the time   60
Which now suits with it. Whiles I threat, he lives;   61

---

82 **mock** deceive
2.1 Location: Inner courtyard of Macbeth's castle. Time is virtually
continuous from the previous scene.
0.1 torch (This may mean "torchbearer," although it does not at line
9.1.)   **4 husbandry** thrift (careful management of resources in the
domestic economy)   **6 summons** i.e., to sleep   **7 would not** am
reluctant to (owing to my uneasy fears).   **powers** order of angels
deputed by God to resist demons   **14 largess** gifts, gratuities.
offices quarters used for the household work.   **16–17 and shut . . .
content** and went to bed professing himself endlessly pleased.
18–19 Our . . . wrought our good will (to entertain the king) was limited by our meager resources (on such short notice), which otherwise
would have poured forth hospitality without restraint.

26 **cleave . . . 'tis** give me your support, adhere to my view, when the
time comes   **27 So** Provided that   **29 franchised** free (from guilt).
clear unstained   **30 counseled** receptive to suggestion.   **32 drink**
i.e., posset or bedtime drink of hot spiced milk curdled with ale or
wine, as also in 2.2.6   **37 fatal** ominous.   **sensible** perceivable by the
senses   **40 heat-oppressèd** fevered   **43 Thou . . . going** You seem to
guide me toward the destiny I intended, toward Duncan's chambers
47 dudgeon hilt of a dagger.   **gouts** drops   **51 abuse** deceive
52 curtained curtained by night (and by bedcurtains)   **53 Pale**
Hecate's offerings sacrificial offerings to Hecate, the goddess of night
and witchcraft. (She is *pale* because she is identified with the pale
moon.)   **withered** (Murder is pictured as in images of Death,
shrunken and wasted.)   **54 Alarumed** given the signal to action
55 watch watchword or cry   **56 Tarquin's** (Tarquin was a Roman
tyrant who ravished Lucrece.)   **60–1 And take . . . with it** and thus
echo and augment the horror which is so suited to this evil hour, or,
usurp the present horror by breaking the silence.   **61 threat** i.e.,
merely threaten to kill Duncan

Words to the heat of deeds too cold breath gives.   62
                                   A bell rings.
I go, and it is done. The bell invites me.
Hear it not, Duncan, for it is a knell
That summons thee to heaven or to hell.   *Exit.*

❖

2.2

Enter Lady [Macbeth].

LADY MACBETH
That which hath made them drunk hath made me
    bold;
What hath quenched them hath given me fire. Hark!
    Peace!
It was the owl that shrieked, the fatal bellman,   3
Which gives the stern'st good-night. He is about it.   4
The doors are open; and the surfeited grooms   5
Do mock their charge with snores. I have drugged
    their possets,   6
That death and nature do contend about them
Whether they live or die.

MACBETH [*within*]   Who's there? What, ho!

LADY MACBETH
Alack, I am afraid they have awaked,
And 'tis not done. Th'attempt and not the deed
Confounds us. Hark! I laid their daggers ready;   11
He could not miss 'em. Had he not resembled
My father as he slept, I had done't.

Enter Macbeth, [bearing bloody daggers].

My husband!

MACBETH
I have done the deed. Didst thou not hear a noise?

LADY MACBETH
I heard the owl scream and the crickets cry.   16
Did not you speak?

MACBETH   When?

LADY MACBETH   Now.

MACBETH   As I descended?

LADY MACBETH   Ay.

MACBETH   Hark! Who lies i'th' second chamber?

LADY MACBETH   Donalbain.

MACBETH [*looking at his hands*]   This is a sorry sight.

LADY MACBETH
A foolish thought, to say a sorry sight.

MACBETH
There's one did laugh in 's sleep, and one cried
    "Murder!"
That they did wake each other. I stood and heard
    them.

But they did say their prayers, and addressed them   28
Again to sleep.

LADY MACBETH   There are two lodged together.

MACBETH
One cried "God bless us!" and "Amen!" the other,
As they had seen me with these hangman's hands.   31
List'ning their fear, I could not say "Amen"
When they did say "God bless us!"

LADY MACBETH   Consider it not so deeply.

MACBETH
But wherefore could not I pronounce "Amen"?
I had most need of blessing, and "Amen"
Stuck in my throat.

LADY MACBETH   These deeds must not be thought   37
After these ways; so, it will make us mad.   38

MACBETH
Methought I heard a voice cry "Sleep no more!
Macbeth does murder sleep," the innocent sleep,
Sleep that knits up the raveled sleave of care,   41
The death of each day's life, sore labor's bath,   42
Balm of hurt minds, great nature's second course,   43
Chief nourisher in life's feast—

LADY MACBETH   What do you mean?

MACBETH
Still it cried "Sleep no more!" to all the house;
"Glamis hath murdered sleep, and therefore Cawdor
Shall sleep no more; Macbeth shall sleep no more."

LADY MACBETH
Who was it that thus cried? Why, worthy thane,
You do unbend your noble strength to think   49
So brainsickly of things. Go get some water
And wash this filthy witness from your hand.   51
Why did you bring these daggers from the place?
They must lie there. Go, carry them and smear
The sleepy grooms with blood.

MACBETH   I'll go no more.
I am afraid to think what I have done;
Look on't again I dare not.

LADY MACBETH   Infrim of purpose!
Give me the daggers. The sleeping and the dead
Are but as pictures. 'Tis the eye of childhood
That fears a painted devil. If he do bleed,
I'll gild the faces of the grooms withal,   60
For it must seem their guilt.
    [*She takes the daggers, and*] exit. *Knock within.*

MACBETH   Whence is that knocking?
How is't with me, when every noise appalls me?
What hands are here? Ha! They pluck out mine eyes.
Will all great Neptune's ocean wash this blood
Clean from my hand? No, this my hand will rather
The multitudinous seas incarnadine,   66

---

62 Words . . . gives Words give only lifeless expression to live deeds,
are no substitute for deeds.
2.2. Location: Scene continues.
3 bellman one who rings a bell to announce a death or to mark the
hours of the night   **4 Which . . . good-night** i.e., that announces the
last good-night, death.   **5 grooms** servants   **6 mock their charge**
make a mockery of their guard duty.   **possets** hot bedtime drinks (as
in 2.1.32)   **11 Confounds** ruins   **16 owl, crickets** (The sounds of
both could be ominous and prophetic of death.)

28 addressed them settled themselves   **31 As** as if.   **hangman's
hands** bloody hands of the executioner.   **37 thought** thought about
38 so if we do so   **41 raveled sleave** tangled skein   **42 bath** i.e., to
relieve the soreness   **43 second course** (Ordinary feasts had two
courses, of which the second was the *chief nourisher;* here, sleep is
seen as following eating in a restorative process.)   **49 unbend**
slacken (as one would a bow; contrast with "bend up" in 1.7.80)
51 witness evidence   **60 gild** smear, coat, as if with a thin layer of
gold. (Gold was ordinarily spoken of as red.)   **66 multitudinous**
numerous and teeming.   **incarnadine** stain red

Making the green one red.   67

Enter Lady [Macbeth].

LADY MACBETH
My hands are of your color, but I shame
To wear a heart so white. (*Knock.*) I hear a knocking
At the south entry. Retire we to our chamber.
A little water clears us of this deed.
How easy is it, then! Your constancy   72
Hath left you unattended. (*Knock.*) Hark! More   73
    knocking.
Get on your nightgown, lest occasion call us   74
And show us to be watchers. Be not lost   75
So poorly in your thoughts.

MACBETH
To know my deed, 'twere best not know myself.   77
                                                    Knock.
Wake Duncan with thy knocking! I would thou
    couldst!   *Exeunt.*

♣

2.3

Knocking within. Enter a Porter.

PORTER   Here's a knocking indeed! If a man were porter
of hell gate, he should have old turning the key.   2
(*Knock.*) Knock, knock, knock! Who's there, i'th'
name of Beelzebub? Here's a farmer that hanged   4
himself on th'expectation of plenty. Come in time!   5
Have napkins enough about you; here you'll sweat for't.   6
(*Knock.*) Knock, knock! Who's there, in th'other
devil's name? Faith, here's an equivocator, that could   8
swear in both the scales against either scale, who
committed treason enough for God's sake, yet could
not equivocate to heaven. Oh, come in, equivocator.
(*Knock.*) Knock, knock, knock! Who's there? Faith,
here's an English tailor come hither for stealing out of   13
a French hose. Come in, tailor. Here you may roast   14
your goose. (*Knock.*) Knock, knock! Never at quiet!   15

What are you? But this place is too cold for hell. I'll   67
devil-porter it no further. I had thought to have let in
some of all professions that go the primrose way to
th'everlasting bonfire. (*Knock.*) Anon, anon! [*He opens the
gate.*] I pray you, remember the porter.

Enter Macduff and Lennox.

MACDUFF
Was it so late, friend, ere you went to bed,
That you do lie so late?

PORTER   Faith, sir, we were carousing till the second   23
cock; and drink, sir, is a great provoker of three things.   24

MACDUFF   What three things does drink especially
provoke?

PORTER   Marry, sir, nose-painting, sleep, and urine.   27
Lechery, sir, it provokes and unprovokes: it provokes
the desire but it takes away the performance. Therefore much drink may be said to be an equivocator
with lechery: it makes him and it mars him; it sets him
on and it takes him off; it persuades him and disheartens him, makes him stand to and not stand to;   33
in conclusion, equivocates him in a sleep and, giving   34
him the lie, leaves him.   35

MACDUFF   I believe drink gave thee the lie last night.   36

PORTER   That it did, sir, i'the very throat on me. But I   37
requited him for his lie, and, I think, being too strong
for him, though he took up my legs sometimes, yet I   39
made a shift to cast him.   40

MACDUFF   Is thy master stirring?

Enter Macbeth.

Our knocking has awaked him. Here he comes.
                                             [*Exit Porter.*]

LENNOX
Good morrow, noble sir.

MACBETH   Good morrow, both.

MACDUFF
Is the King stirring, worthy thane?

MACBETH   Not yet.

MACDUFF
He did command me to call timely on him.   45
I have almost slipped the hour.

MACBETH   I'll bring you to him.   46

MACDUFF
I know this is a joyful trouble to you,
But yet 'tis one.

---

67 one red one all-pervading red.   **72–3 Your . . . unattended** Your
preoccupation with yourself has left you inattentive to other matters.
74 nightgown dressing gown   **75 to be watchers** to have been awake
and not abed.   **77 To know . . . myself** To come to terms with what I
have done, I would do best to shut out the horror entirely and deny
who I am.
**2.3. Location: Scene continues. The knocking at the door has
already been heard in 2.2. It is not necessary to assume literally,
however, that Macbeth and Lady Macbeth have been talking near
the** *south entry* **(2.2.70) where the knocking is heard.**
2 old plenty of   **4 Beelzebub** a devil.   **4–5 Here's . . . plenty** i.e., Here's
a farmer who has hoarded in anticipation of a scarcity and will be justly
punished by a crop surplus and low prices.   **5 Come in time!** i.e., You
have come in good time!   **6 napkins** handkerchiefs or towels (to mop
up the sweat)   **8 equivocator** (This is regarded by many editors as an
allusion to the trial of the Jesuit Henry Garnet for treason in the spring of
1606 and to the doctrine of equivocation said to have been presented in
his defense; according to this doctrine, a lie was not a lie if the utterer
had in his mind a different meaning in which the utterance was true.)
13–14 for stealing . . . hose (French fashions, much in demand by style-
conscious courtiers, no doubt provided opportunities for tailors to skimp
in the making of garments while charging customers the full amount.)
14–15 roast your goose heat your tailor's smoothing iron—something
easily done in the flames of hell. (With a pun on the sense, "cook your
goose." A *goose* could also be a long-handled iron, or a prostitute.)

23–4 second cock second crowing of the cock before dawn   **27 Marry**
(Originally, an oath, "by the Virgin Mary.")   **nose-painting** i.e., reddening of the nose through drink   **33 makes . . . not stand to** arouses
him sexually but then takes away the ability to perform sexually.
(Repeating the idea of the previous phrases about how it *makes him
and mars him*, etc.)   **34 equivocates . . . sleep** (1) lulls him asleep
(2) gives him an erotic experience in dream only   **34–5 giving him
the lie** (1) deceiving him (2) laying him out flat   **35 leaves him**
(1) dissipates as intoxication (2) is passed off as urine.   **36 gave thee
the lie** (1) called you a liar (2) made you unable to stand and put you
to sleep   **37 i'the . . . me** (1) giving me the deepest insult imaginable
(2) literally, going down my throat. (*On* means "of.")   **39 took . . .
legs** made me unable to stand and threw me to the ground as a
wrestler might do   **40 made a shift** managed.   **cast** (1) throw, as in
wrestling (2) vomit   **45 timely** betimes, early   **46 slipped** let slip

MACBETH
The labor we delight in physics pain.   49
This is the door.
MACDUFF   I'll make so bold to call,
For 'tis my limited service.   *Exit Macduff.*   51
LENNOX   Goes the King hence today?
MACBETH   He does; he did appoint so.
LENNOX
The night has been unruly. Where we lay,
Our chimneys were blown down, and, as they say,
Lamentings heard i'th'air, strange screams of death,
And prophesying with accents terrible   57
Of dire combustion and confused events   58
New hatched to the woeful time. The obscure bird   59
Clamored the livelong night. Some say the earth
Was feverous and did shake.
MACBETH   'Twas a rough night.
LENNOX
My young remembrance cannot parallel
A fellow to it.

    Enter Macduff.

MACDUFF   Oh, horror, horror, horror!
Tongue nor heart cannot conceive nor name thee!
MACBETH AND LENNOX   What's the matter?
MACDUFF
Confusion now hath made his masterpiece!   66
Most sacrilegious murder hath broke ope
The Lord's anointed temple and stole thence
The life o'th' building!
MACBETH   What is't you say? The life?
LENNOX   Mean you His Majesty?
MACDUFF
Approach the chamber and destroy your sight
With a new Gorgon. Do not bid me speak;   73
See, and then speak yourselves.
                    Exeunt Macbeth and Lennox.
                    Awake, awake!
Ring the alarum bell. Murder and treason!
Banquo and Donalbain, Malcolm, awake!
Shake off this downy sleep, death's counterfeit,   77
And look on death itself! Up, up, and see
The great doom's image! Malcolm, Banquo,   79
As from your graves rise up and walk like sprites   80
To countenance this horror! Ring the bell.   *Bell rings.*   81

    Enter Lady [Macbeth].

LADY MACBETH   What's the business,
That such a hideous trumpet calls to parley   83

The sleepers of the house? Speak, speak!
MACDUFF   Oh, gentle lady,
'Tis not for you to hear what I can speak.
The repetition in a woman's ear   87
Would murder as it fell.

    Enter Banquo.

                    Oh, Banquo, Banquo,
Our royal master's murdered!
LADY MACBETH   Woe, alas!
What, in our house?
BANQUO   Too cruel anywhere.
Dear Duff, I prithee, contradict thyself
And say it is not so.

    Enter Macbeth, Lennox, and Ross.

MACBETH
Had I but died an hour before this chance   93
I had lived a blessèd time; for from this instant
There's nothing serious in mortality.   95
All is but toys. Renown and grace is dead;   96
The wine of life is drawn, and the mere lees   97
Is left this vault to brag of.   98

    Enter Malcolm and Donalbain.

DONALBAIN
What is amiss?
MACBETH   You are, and do not know't.
The spring, the head, the fountain of your blood
Is stopped, the very source of it is stopped.
MACDUFF
Your royal father's murdered.
MALCOLM   Oh, by whom?
LENNOX
Those of his chamber, as it seemed, had done't.
Their hands and faces were all badged with blood;   104
So were their daggers, which unwiped we found
Upon their pillows. They stared and were distracted;
No man's life was to be trusted with them.
MACBETH
Oh, yet I do repent me of my fury,
That I did kill them.
MACDUFF   Wherefore did you so?
MACBETH
Who can be wise, amazed, temp'rate and furious,   110
Loyal and neutral, in a moment? No man.
Th'expedition of my violent love   112
Outran the pauser, reason. Here lay Duncan,
His silver skin laced with his golden blood,   114
And his gashed stabs looked like a breach in nature   115
For ruin's wasteful entrance; there the murderers,   116
Steeped in the colors of their trade, their daggers

---

49 physics pain i.e., cures that labor of its troublesome aspect.
51 limited appointed   **57 accents terrible** terrifying utterances
58 combustion tumult   **59 New . . . time** newly born to accompany
the woeful nature of the time.   **obscure bird** owl, the bird of darkness
66 Confusion Destruction   **73 Gorgon** one of three monsters with
hideous faces (Medusa was a Gorgon), whose look turned the beholders to stone   **77 downy** feathery, unsubstantial   **79 great doom's
image** simulacrum of the Last Judgment, of Doomsday.   **80 As . . .
rise up** (At the Last Judgment, the dead will rise from their graves to
be judged.)   **sprites** souls, ghosts   **81 countenance** (1) be in keeping
with (2) witness   **83 trumpet** (Another metaphorical suggestion of
the Last Judgment; the *trumpet* here is the shouting and the bell.)

87 repetition recital, report   **93 chance** occurrence   **95 serious in
mortality** worthwhile in mortal life.   **96 toys** trifles.   **97 lees** dregs
98 vault (1) wine-vault (2) earth, with its vaulted sky   **104 badged**
marked, as with a badge or emblem   **110 amazed** bewildered
112 Th'expedition The haste   **114 golden** (See the note for 2.2.60.)
115 breach in nature gap in the defenses of life. (A metaphor of military siege.)   **116 wasteful** destructive

Unmannerly breeched with gore. Who could refrain 118
That had a heart to love, and in that heart
Courage to make 's love known?

LADY MACBETH [*fainting*]   Help me hence, ho! 120
MACDUFF
    Look to the lady.
MALCOLM [*aside to Donalbain*]
                            Why do we hold our tongues,
That most may claim this argument for ours? 122
DONALBAIN [*aside to Malcolm*]
    What should be spoken here, where our fate,
Hid in an auger hole, may rush and seize us? 124
Let's away. Our tears are not yet brewed. 125
MALCOLM [*aside to Donalbain*]
    Nor our strong sorrow upon the foot of motion. 126
BANQUO   Look to the lady.
                            [*Lady Macbeth is helped out.*]
And when we have our naked frailties hid, 128
That suffer in exposure, let us meet
And question this most bloody piece of work 130
To know it further. Fears and scruples shake us. 131
In the great hand of God I stand, and thence 132
Against the undivulged pretense I fight 133
Of treasonous malice.
MACDUFF   And so do I.
ALL   So all. 134
MACBETH
    Let's briefly put on manly readiness 135
And meet i'th' hall together.
ALL   Well contented.
            Exeunt [all but Malcolm and Donalbain].
MALCOLM
    What will you do? Let's not consort with them. 137
To show an unfelt sorrow is an office
Which the false man does easy. I'll to England. 139
DONALBAIN
    To Ireland, I. Our separated fortune
Shall keep us both the safer. Where we are,
There's daggers in men's smiles; the nea'er in blood, 142
The nearer bloody.
MALCOLM   This murderous shaft that's shot 143
Hath not yet lighted, and our safest way 144
Is to avoid the aim. Therefore to horse,
And let us not be dainty of leave-taking, 146
But shift away. There's warrant in that theft 147

118 breeched with gore covered (as with breeches) to the hilts with
gore.   **120 make 's love known** make manifest his love.   **122 That . . .
ours** to whom this business matters most.   **124 in an auger hole** i.e.,
in some hiding place, in ambush. (An *auger* is a hole-drilling tool.)
125 Our . . . brewed i.e., Our real sorrow has not yet ripened.
126 upon . . . motion yet prepared to express itself fully.   **128 our
naked frailties hid** clothed our poor, shivering bodies (which remind
us of our human frailty)   **130 question** discuss   **131 scruples**
doubts, suspicions   **132–4 thence . . . malice** with God's help, I will
fight against the as-yet-unknown purpose that prompted this treason.
133 pretense design   **134 malice** enmity.   **135 briefly** quickly.
manly readiness men's clothing and resolute purpose   **137 consort**
keep company, associate   **139 easy** easily.   **142–3 the nea'er . . .
bloody** the closer the relationship, the greater the danger to be feared
of bloody intent.   **144 lighted** alighted, descended   **146 dainty of**
tediously ceremonious in   **147 shift away** disappear by stealth.
warrant justification

Which steals itself when there's no mercy left.
                            Exeunt.

❦

2.4

Enter Ross with an Old Man.

OLD MAN
    Threescore and ten I can remember well,
Within the volume of which time I have seen
Hours dreadful and things strange, but this sore night 3
Hath trifled former knowings.
ROSS   Ha, good father, 4
Thou see'st the heavens, as troubled with man's act, 5
Threatens his bloody stage. By th' clock 'tis day, 6
And yet dark night strangles the traveling lamp. 7
Is't night's predominance or the day's shame
That darkness does the face of earth entomb
When living light should kiss it?
OLD MAN   'Tis unnatural,
Even like the deed that's done. On Tuesday last
A falcon, tow'ring in her pride of place, 12
Was by a mousing owl hawked at and killed. 13
ROSS
    And Duncan's horses—a thing most strange and
        certain—
Beauteous and swift, the minions of their race, 15
Turned wild in nature, broke their stalls, flung out, 17
Contending 'gainst obedience, as they would
Make war with mankind.
OLD MAN   'Tis said they eat each other. 18
ROSS
    They did so, to th'amazement of mine eyes
That looked upon't.

Enter Macduff.

                    Here comes the good Macduff.—
How goes the world, sir, now?
MACDUFF   Why, see you not?
ROSS
    Is't known who did this more than bloody deed?
MACDUFF
    Those that Macbeth hath slain.
ROSS   Alas the day,
What good could they pretend?
MACDUFF   They were suborned. 24
Malcolm and Donalbain, the King's two sons,
Are stol'n away and fled, which puts upon them
Suspicion of the deed.
ROSS   'Gainst nature still!

2.4. Location: Outside Macbeth's castle of Inverness.
3 sore dreadful, grievous   **4 trifled former knowings** made trivial all
former experiences.   **father** old man   **5–6 the heavens . . . stage** a
solar eclipse threatens disapprovingly our human scene of murder.
(With a theatrical metaphor in *heavens* [the decorated roof over the
stage], *act*, and *stage*.)   **7 traveling lamp** i.e., sun.   **12 tow'ring** circling higher and higher. (A term in falconry.)   **place** pitch, highest
point in the falcon's flight   **13 mousing** i.e., ordinarily preying on
mice   **15 minions** darlings   **17 as** as if   **18 eat** ate. (Pronounced
"et.")   **24 What . . . pretend?** i.e., what could they hope to gain by it?
suborned bribed, hired.

Thriftless ambition, that will ravin up   28
Thine own life's means! Then 'tis most like   29
The sovereignty will fall upon Macbeth.

MACDUFF
He is already named and gone to Scone   31
To be invested.

ROSS   Where is Duncan's body?

MACDUFF   Carried to Colmekill,   33
The sacred storehouse of his predecessors
And guardian of their bones.

ROSS   Will you to Scone?

MACDUFF
No, cousin, I'll to Fife.

ROSS   Well, I will thither.   36

MACDUFF
Well, may you see things well done there. Adieu,
Lest our old robes sit easier than our new!

ROSS   Farewell, father.

OLD MAN
God's benison go with you, and with those   40
That would make good of bad, and friends of foes!

                                        Exeunt omnes.

❧

3.1

Enter Banquo.

BANQUO
Thou hast it now—King, Cawdor, Glamis, all
As the weird women promised, and I fear
Thou played'st most foully for't. Yet it was said
It should not stand in thy posterity,   4
But that myself should be the root and father
Of many kings. If there come truth from them—
As upon thee, Macbeth, their speeches shine—   7
Why, by the verities on thee made good,
May they not be my oracles as well
And set me up in hope? But hush, no more.   10

        Sennet sounded. Enter Macbeth as King, Lady
        [Macbeth], Lennox, Ross, lords, and attendants.

MACBETH
Here's our chief guest.

LADY MACBETH   If he had been forgotten,
It had been as a gap in our great feast
And all-thing unbecoming.   13

MACBETH
Tonight we hold a solemn supper, sir,   14
And I'll request your presence.

BANQUO   Let Your Highness
Command upon me, to the which my duties   16

Are with a most indissoluble tie
Forever knit.

MACBETH   Ride you this afternoon?

BANQUO   Ay, my good lord.

MACBETH
We should have else desired your good advice,
Which still hath been both grave and prosperous,   22
In this day's council; but we'll take tomorrow.
Is't far you ride?

BANQUO
As far, my lord, as will fill up the time
Twixt this and supper. Go not my horse the better,   26
I must become a borrower of the night
For a dark hour or twain.

MACBETH   Fail not our feast.

BANQUO   My lord, I will not.

MACBETH
We hear our bloody cousins are bestowed   31
In England and in Ireland, not confessing
Their cruel parricide, filling their hearers
With strange invention. But of that tomorrow,   34
When therewithal we shall have cause of state   35
Craving us jointly. Hie you to horse. Adieu,   36
Till you return at night. Goes Fleance with you?

BANQUO
Ay, my good lord. Our time does call upon 's.

MACBETH
I wish your horses swift and sure of foot,
And so I do commend you to their backs.   40
Farewell.   *Exit Banquo.*
Let every man be master of his time
Till seven at night. To make society
The sweeter welcome, we will keep ourself   44
Till suppertime alone. While then, God be with you!   45
        Exeunt Lords [and all but Macbeth and a Servant].
Sirrah, a word with you. Attend those men   46
Our pleasure?

SERVANT
They are, my lord, without the palace gate.

MACBETH
Bring them before us.   *Exit Servant.*
                        To be thus is nothing,   49
But to be safely thus.—Our fears in Banquo   50
Stick deep, and in his royalty of nature   51
Reigns that which would be feared. 'Tis much he
  dares;   52
And to that dauntless temper of his mind   53
He hath a wisdom that doth guide his valor
To act in safety. There is none but he
Whose being I do fear; and under him
My genius is rebuked, as it is said   57

---

28 Thriftless Spendthrift. **ravin up** devour ravenously **29 like** likely **31 named** chosen. (See the note for 1.4.50.) **Scone** ancient royal city of Scotland near Perth **33 Colmekill** Icolmkill, i.e., Cell of St. Columba, the barren islet of Iona in the Western Islands, a sacred spot where the kings were buried; here, called a *storehouse* **36 Fife** (Of which Macduff is Thane.) **40 benison** blessing
3.1. Location: Forres. The palace.
4 stand stay, remain **7 shine** beam favorably **10.1** *Sennet* trumpet call **13 all-thing** in every way **14 solemn** ceremonious **16 Command** lay your command

22 still always. **grave and prosperous** weighty and profitable **26 this** this present moment. **Go . . . better** Unless my horse makes better time than I expect **31 bestowed** lodged **34 invention** falsehood. **35 therewithal** besides that **35–6 cause . . . jointly** questions of state occupying our joint attention. **40 commend** commit, entrust **44 we . . . ourself** I will keep to myself **45 While** Till **46 Sirrah** (A form of address to a social inferior.) **49 thus** i.e., king **50 But** unless. **in** concerning **51 royalty of nature** natural kingly bearing **52 would be** deserves to be **53 to** added to **57 My genius is rebuked** my guardian spirit is daunted or abashed

Mark Antony's was by Caesar. He chid the sisters   58
When first they put the name of king upon me,
And bade them speak to him. Then, prophetlike,
They hailed him father to a line of kings.
Upon my head they placed a fruitless crown
And put a barren scepter in my grip,
Thence to be wrenched with an unlineal hand,   64
No son of mine succeeding. If't be so,
For Banquo's issue have I filed my mind;   66
For them the gracious Duncan have I murdered,
Put rancors in the vessel of my peace   68
Only for them, and mine eternal jewel   69
Given to the common enemy of man   70
To make them kings, the seeds of Banquo kings.
Rather than so, come fate into the list,   72
And champion me to th'utterance!—Who's there?   73

Enter Servant and two Murderers.

Now go to the door, and stay there till we call.
                                         Exit Servant.
Was it not yesterday we spoke together?

MURDERERS
It was, so please Your Highness.

MACBETH   Well then, now
Have you considered of my speeches? Know
That it was he in the times past which held you
So under fortune, which you thought had been   79
Our innocent self. This I made good to you
In our last conference, passed in probation with you   81
How you were borne in hand, how crossed, the
     instruments,   82
Who wrought with them, and all things else that
     might   83
To half a soul and to a notion crazed   84
Say, "Thus did Banquo."

FIRST MURDERER   You made it known to us.

MACBETH
I did so, and went further, which is now
Our point of second meeting. Do you find
Your patience so predominant in your nature
That you can let this go? Are you so gospeled   89
To pray for this good man and for his issue,
Whose heavy hand hath bowed you to the grave
And beggared yours forever?

FIRST MURDERER   We are men, my liege.   92

MACBETH
Ay, in the catalogue ye go for men,   93
As hounds and greyhounds, mongrels, spaniels, curs,

Shoughs, water-rugs, and demi-wolves are clept   95
All by the name of dogs. The valued file   96
Distinguishes the swift, the slow, the subtle,
The housekeeper, the hunter, every one   98
According to the gift which bounteous nature
Hath in him closed, whereby he does receive   100
Particular addition from the bill   101
That writes them all alike; and so of men.   102
Now, if you have a station in the file,   103
Not i'th' worst rank of manhood, say't,   104
And I will put that business in your bosoms
Whose execution takes your enemy off,   106
Grapples you to the heart and love of us,
Who wear our health but sickly in his life,   108
Which in his death were perfect.

SECOND MURDERER   I am one, my liege,
Whom the vile blows and buffets of the world
Hath so incensed that I am reckless what
I do to spite the world.

FIRST MURDERER   And I another,
So weary with disasters, tugged with fortune,   113
That I would set my life on any chance   114
To mend it or be rid on't.

MACBETH   Both of you
Know Banquo was your enemy.

BOTH MURDERERS   True, my lord.

MACBETH
So is he mine, and in such bloody distance   117
That every minute of his being thrusts   118
Against my near'st of life. And though I could   119
With barefaced power sweep him from my sight   120
And bid my will avouch it, yet I must not,   121
For certain friends that are both his and mine,   122
Whose loves I may not drop, but wail his fall   123
Who I myself struck down. And thence it is   124
That I to your assistance do make love,   125
Masking the business from the common eye
For sundry weighty reasons.

SECOND MURDERER   We shall, my lord,
Perform what you command us.

FIRST MURDERER   Though our lives—

MACBETH
Your spirits shine through you. Within this hour at
     most   129
I will advise you where to plant yourselves,

---

58 **Caesar** Octavius Caesar.   64 **with** by.   **unlineal** not of lineal descent from me   66 **filed** defiled   68 **rancors** malignant enemies (here visualized as a poison added to a vessel full of wholesome drink)   69 **eternal jewel** i.e., soul   70 **common . . . man** i.e., devil   72 **list** lists, place of combat   73 **champion me** fight with me in single combat.   **to th'utterance** to the last extremity (French, *à l'outrance*).   79 **under fortune** down in your fortunes   81–3 **passed . . . with them** went over the proof with you how you were deceived by false promises, how you were thwarted, who the agents were, who directed their activities   84 **To . . . crazed** even to a half-wit of unsound mind   89 **gospeled** imbued with the gospel spirit   92 **yours** your family   93 **go for** pass for, are entered for

95 **Shoughs . . . clept** shaggy lap-dogs, long-haired water dogs, and dogs that have been crossbred with wolves are called   96 **valued file** list classified according to value   98 **housekeeper** watchdog   100 **in him closed** enclosed in him   101–2 **Particular . . . alike** particular qualification apart from the catalog that lists them all indiscriminately   103–4 **if . . . manhood** if you occupy not the worst of places in the *rank and file* of men   106 **Whose execution** the doing of which   108 **in his life** while he lives   113 **tugged with** pulled about by (as in wrestling)   114 **set** risk, stake   117 **distance** (1) hostility, enmity (2) interval of distance between fencers   118–19 **thrusts . . . life** stabs me to the heart.   120 **With barefaced power** by open use of my supreme royal authority   121 **And . . . avouch it** and use my mere wish as my justification   122 **For** because of, for the sake of   123–4 **wail . . . Who** I must bewail the death of him who   125 **That . . . love** that I woo your aid   129 **Your . . . you** i.e., Enough; I can see your determination in your faces.

Acquaint you with the perfect spy o'th' time,   131
The moment on't, for't must be done tonight,   132
And something from the palace; always thought   133
That I require a clearness. And with him—   134
To leave no rubs nor botches in the work—   135
Fleance his son, that keeps him company,
Whose absence is no less material to me
Than is his father's, must embrace the fate
Of that dark hour. Resolve yourselves apart;   139
I'll come to you anon.

BOTH MURDERERS   We are resolved, my lord.

MACBETH
I'll call upon you straight. Abide within.

Exeunt [*Murderers*].

It is concluded. Banquo, thy soul's flight,
If it find heaven, must find it out tonight.   [*Exit.*]

❖

3.2

Enter Macbeth's Lady and a Servant.

LADY MACBETH   Is Banquo gone from court?

SERVANT
Ay, madam, but returns again tonight.

LADY MACBETH
Say to the King I would attend his leisure
For a few words.

SERVANT   Madam, I will.   *Exit.*

LADY MACBETH   Naught's had, all's spent,
Where our desire is got without content.   7
'Tis safer to be that which we destroy
Than by destruction dwell in doubtful joy.   9

Enter Macbeth.

How now, my lord? Why do you keep alone,
Of sorriest fancies your companions making,   11
Using those thoughts which should indeed have died   12
With them they think on? Things without all remedy
Should be without regard. What's done is done.   14

MACBETH
We have scorched the snake, not killed it.   15
She'll close and be herself, whilst our poor malice   16
Remains in danger of her former tooth.   17
But let the frame of things disjoint, both the worlds
suffer,   18
Ere we will eat our meal in fear and sleep
In the affliction of these terrible dreams

That shake us nightly. Better be with the dead,
Whom we, to gain our peace, have sent to peace,   22
Than on the torture of the mind to lie   23
In restless ecstasy. Duncan is in his grave;   24
After life's fitful fever he sleeps well.
Treason has done his worst; nor steel, nor poison,   26
Malice domestic, foreign levy, nothing   27
Can touch him further.

LADY MACBETH   Come on,
Gentle my lord, sleek o'er your rugged looks.   30
Be bright and jovial among your guests tonight.

MACBETH
So shall I, love, and so, I pray, be you.
Let your remembrance apply to Banquo;   33
Present him eminence, both with eye and tongue—   34
Unsafe the while, that we   35
Must lave our honors in these flattering streams   36
And make our faces vizards to our hearts,   37
Disguising what they are.

LADY MACBETH   You must leave this.

MACBETH
Oh, full of scorpions is my mind, dear wife!
Thou know'st that Banquo and his Fleance lives.

LADY MACBETH
But in them nature's copy's not eterne.   41

MACBETH
There's comfort yet; they are assailable.
Then be thou jocund. Ere the bat hath flown
His cloistered flight, ere to black Hecate's summons   44
The shard-borne beetle with his drowsy hums   45
Hath rung night's yawning peal, there shall be done   46
A deed of dreadful note.

LADY MACBETH   What's to be done?

MACBETH
Be innocent of the knowledge, dearest chuck,   48
Till thou applaud the deed. Come, seeling night,   49
Scarf up the tender eye of pitiful day,   50
And with thy bloody and invisible hand
Cancel and tear to pieces that great bond   52
Which keeps me pale! Light thickens,   53
And the crow makes wing to th' rooky wood;   54
Good things of day begin to droop and drowse,

131–2 with . . . on't with full and precise instructions as to when it is
to be done. (*Spy* means "espial, observation.")   133 something from
some distance removed from.   thought being borne in mind
134 clearness freedom from suspicion.   135 rubs defects, rough
spots   139 Resolve yourselves apart Make up your minds in private
conference
3.2. Location: The palace.
7 content contentedness.   9 Than . . . joy than by destroying achieve
only an apprehensive joy.   11 sorriest most despicable or wretched
12 Using keeping company with, entertaining   14 without regard
not pondered upon.   15 scorched slashed, cut   16 close heal, close
up again.   poor malice feeble hostility   17 her former tooth her
fang, just as before.   18 let . . . suffer let the universe itself fall apart,
both heaven and earth perish

22 to gain . . . to peace to gain contentedness through satisfied ambition, have sent to eternal rest   23 torture rack   24 ecstasy frenzy.
26 nor steel neither steel   27 Malice domestic civil war.   foreign
levy the levying of troops abroad (against Scotland)   30 Gentle . . .
looks my noble lord, smooth over your rough looks.   33 Let . . .
apply Remember to pay special attention   34 eminence favor
35–6 Unsafe . . . streams we being unsafe at present, we must put on
a show of flattering cordiality to make clean our honor. (To *lave* is to
wash.)   37 vizards masks   41 nature's . . . eterne nature's pattern
will not continue forever.   44 cloistered secluded.   Hecate goddess
of night and witchcraft, as in 2.1.53   45 shard-borne borne on shards,
or horny wing cases, or, *shard-born*, bred in cow-droppings (shards)
46 yawning drowsy   48 chuck (A term of endearment.)   49 seeling
eye-closing. (Night is pictured here as a falconer sewing up the eyes
of day lest it should struggle against the deed that is to be done.)
50 Scarf up blindfold.   pitiful compassionate   52 that . . . bond i.e.,
the bond of natural and moral law (here associated with the full light
of day)   53 pale sickly, pallid (like moonlight, contrasted with the
full light of day); also, pallid from fear.   Light thickens Darkness is
coming on   54 crow rook.   rooky full of rooks

Whiles night's black agents to their preys do rouse.   56
Thou marvel'st at my words, but hold thee still.
Things bad begun make strong themselves by ill.
So, prithee, go with me.   *Exeunt.*

❖

3.3

Enter three Murderers.

FIRST MURDERER [*to the Third Murderer*]
But who did bid thee join with us?

THIRD MURDERER   Macbeth.

SECOND MURDERER [*to the First Murderer*]
He needs not our mistrust, since he delivers   2
Our offices and what we have to do   3
To the direction just.

FIRST MURDERER   Then stand with us.   4
The west yet glimmers with some streaks of day.
Now spurs the lated traveler apace   6
To gain the timely inn, and near approaches   7
The subject of our watch.

THIRD MURDERER   Hark, I hear horses.

BANQUO (*within*)   Give us a light there, ho!

SECOND MURDERER   Then 'tis he. The rest
That are within the note of expectation   12
Already are i'th' court.

FIRST MURDERER   His horses go about.   14

THIRD MURDERER
Almost a mile; but he does usually—
So all men do—from hence to th' palace gate
Make it their walk.

Enter Banquo and Fleance, with a torch.

SECOND MURDERER   A light, a light!

THIRD MURDERER   'Tis he.

FIRST MURDERER   Stand to't.

BANQUO   It will be rain tonight.

FIRST MURDERER   Let it come down!
                    [*They attack Banquo.*]

BANQUO
Oh, treachery! Fly, good Fleance, fly, fly, fly!
Thou mayst revenge.—Oh, slave!
                    [*He dies. Fleance escapes.*]

THIRD MURDERER
Who did strike out the light?

FIRST MURDERER   Was't not the way?   25

THIRD MURDERER
There's but one down; the son is fled.

SECOND MURDERER
We have lost best half of our affair.

FIRST MURDERER
Well, let's away and say how much is done.   28
                    Exeunt.

❖

3.4

*Banquet prepared. Enter Macbeth, Lady
[Macbeth], Ross, Lennox, Lords, and attendants.*

MACBETH
You know your own degrees; sit down. At first   1
And last, the hearty welcome.   [*They sit.*]

LORDS   Thanks to Your Majesty.   2

MACBETH
Ourself will mingle with society   3
And play the humble host.
Our hostess keeps her state, but in best time   5
We will require her welcome.   6

LADY MACBETH
Pronounce it for me, sir, to all our friends,
For my heart speaks they are welcome.

Enter First Murderer [to the door].

MACBETH
See, they encounter thee with their hearts' thanks.   9
Both sides are even. Here I'll sit i'th' midst.   10
Be large in mirth; anon we'll drink a measure   11
The table round. [*He goes to the Murderer.*] There's
    blood upon thy face.

MURDERER   'Tis Banquo's, then.

MACBETH
'Tis better thee without than he within.   14
Is he dispatched?

MURDERER
My lord, his throat is cut. That I did for him.

MACBETH   Thou art the best o'th' cutthroats.
Yet he's good that did the like for Fleance;
If thou didst it, thou art the nonpareil.   19

MURDERER   Most royal sir, Fleance is scaped.

MACBETH
Then comes my fit again. I had else been perfect,
Whole as the marble, founded as the rock,   22
As broad and general as the casing air.   23
But now I am cabined, cribbed, confined, bound in   24
To saucy doubts and fears. But Banquo's safe?   25

---

56 to . . . rouse bestir themselves to hunt their prey.
3.3. Location: A park near the palace.
2–4 He . . . just We need not mistrust this man, since the instructions he brings from Macbeth are so precise.   **6 lated** belated   **7 timely** arrived at in good time   **12 within . . . expectation** in the list of those expected   **14 go about** i.e., can be heard as servants take the horses to the stables (while Banquo and Fleance, provided with a torch, walk from the palace gate to the castle).   **25 way** i.e., thing to do.

28.1 *Exeunt* (Presumably, the murderers drag the body of Banquo offstage as they go.)
3.4. Location: A room of state in the palace.
1 degrees ranks (as a determinant of seating)   **1–2 At . . . last** Once for all   **3 mingle with society** i.e., leave the chair of state and circulate among the guests   **5 keeps her state** remains in her canopied chair of state.   **in best time** when it is most appropriate   **6 require her welcome** call upon her to give the welcome.   **9 encounter** respond to   **10 even** full, with equal numbers on both sides.   **11 large** liberal, free.   **measure** i.e., cup filled to the brim for a toast   **14 'Tis . . . within** It is better for you to have his blood on you than he to have it within him.   **19 the nonpareil** without equal.   **22 founded** firmly established   **23 broad and general** unconfined.   **casing** encasing, enveloping   **24 cribbed** shut in   **25 saucy** sharp, impudent, importunate

MURDERER
Ay, my good lord. Safe in a ditch he bides,
With twenty trenchèd gashes on his head,
The least a death to nature.

MACBETH   Thanks for that.
There the grown serpent lies; the worm that's fled   29
Hath nature that in time will venom breed,
No teeth for th' present. Get thee gone. Tomorrow
We'll hear ourselves again.   *Exit Murderer.*

LADY MACBETH   My royal lord,   32
You do not give the cheer. The feast is sold   33
That is not often vouched, while 'tis a-making,   34
'Tis given with welcome. To feed were best at home;   35
From thence, the sauce to meat is ceremony;   36
Meeting were bare without it.

Enter the Ghost of Banquo, and sits in Macbeth's place.

MACBETH   Sweet remembrancer!   37
Now, good digestion wait on appetite,   38
And health on both!

LENNOX   May't please Your Highness sit?

MACBETH
Here had we now our country's honor roofed   40
Were the graced person of our Banquo present,
Who may I rather challenge for unkindness   42
Than pity for mischance.

ROSS   His absence, sir,
Lays blame upon his promise. Please't Your Highness
To grace us with your royal company?

MACBETH [*seeing his place occupied*]
The table's full.

LENNOX   Here is a place reserved, sir.

MACBETH Where?

LENNOX
Here, my good lord. What is't that moves Your
        Highness?

MACBETH
Which of you have done this?

LORDS   What, my good lord?

MACBETH
Thou canst not say I did it. Never shake
Thy gory locks at me.

ROSS
Gentlemen, rise. His Highness is not well.
                    [*They start to rise.*]

LADY MACBETH
Sit, worthy friends. My lord is often thus,
And hath been from his youth. Pray you, keep seat.
The fit is momentary; upon a thought   55
He will again be well. If much you note him

You shall offend him and extend his passion.   57
Feed, and regard him not.—[*She confers apart with
        Macbeth.*] Are you a man?

MACBETH
Ay, and a bold one, that dare look on that
Which might appall the devil.

LADY MACBETH   Oh, proper stuff!   60
This is the very painting of your fear.
This is the air-drawn dagger which, you said,   62
Led you to Duncan. Oh, these flaws and starts,   63
Impostors to true fear, would well become   64
A woman's story at a winter's fire,
Authorized by her grandam. Shame itself!   66
Why do you make such faces? When all's done,
You look but on a stool.

MACBETH   Prithee, see there!
Behold, look! Lo, how say you?—
Why, what care I? If thou canst nod, speak too.   70
If charnel houses and our graves must send   71
Those that we bury back, our monuments   72
Shall be the maws of kites.   [*Exit Ghost.*] 73

LADY MACBETH What, quite unmanned in folly?

MACBETH
If I stand here, I saw him.

LADY MACBETH   Fie, for shame!

MACBETH
Blood hath been shed ere now, i'th'olden time,
Ere humane statute purged the gentle weal;   77
Ay, and since too, murders have been performed
Too terrible for the ear. The time has been
That, when the brains were out, the man would die,
And there an end; but now they rise again
With twenty mortal murders on their crowns,   82
And push us from our stools. This is more strange
Than such a murder is.

LADY MACBETH   My worthy lord,
Your noble friends do lack you.

MACBETH   I do forget.
Do not muse at me, my most worthy friends;
I have a strange infirmity, which is nothing
To those that know me. Come, love and health to all!
Then I'll sit down. Give me some wine. Fill full.
                    [*He is given wine.*]

Enter Ghost.

I drink to th' general joy o'th' whole table,
And to our dear friend Banquo, whom we miss.
Would he were here! To all, and him, we thirst,   92

---

29 **worm** small serpent   32 **hear ourselves** personally confer
33 **give the cheer** welcome your guests.   33–5 **The feast . . . welcome**
A feast seems grudgingly and mercenarily given unless it is repeatedly graced with assurances of welcome.   35–7 **To feed . . . without it** Plain eating is best done in one's own domestic setting; on more social occasions, the spice to a feast is ceremony; gatherings are too unadorned without it.   38 **wait on** attend   40 **roofed** under one roof
42 **Who . . . unkindness** whom I hope I may reprove for negligence
55 **upon a thought** in a moment

57 **offend him** make him worse   60 **Oh, proper stuff!** Oh, nonsense!
62 **air-drawn** made of thin air, or floating disembodied in space
63 **flaws** gusts, outbursts   64 **to** compared with.   **become** befit
66 **Authorized by** told on the authority of   70 **thou** Banquo
71 **charnel houses** depositories for bones or bodies   72–3 **our . . . kites** i.e., we will have to leave the unburied bodies to scavenging birds of prey.   77 **Ere . . . weal** before the institution of law cleansed the commonwealth of violence and made it civilized. (**Humane,** interchangeable with *human,* means both "appertaining to humankind" and "benevolent, civilizing.")   82 **mortal murders** deadly wounds.
crowns heads   92 **thirst** desire to drink

And all to all.

LORDS   Our duties and the pledge.   93
                                        [*They drink.*]

MACBETH [*seeing the Ghost*]
Avaunt, and quit my sight! Let the earth hide thee!
Thy bones are marrowless, thy blood is cold;
Thou hast no speculation in those eyes   96
Which thou dost glare with!

LADY MACBETH   Think of this, good peers,
But as a thing of custom. 'Tis no other;
Only it spoils the pleasure of the time.

MACBETH   What man dare, I dare.
Approach thou like the rugged Russian bear,
The armed rhinoceros, or th' Hyrcan tiger;   102
Take any shape but that, and my firm nerves   103
Shall never tremble. Or be alive again
And dare me to the desert with thy sword.   105
If trembling I inhabit then, protest me   106
The baby of a girl. Hence, horrible shadow!   107
Unreal mockery, hence!   [*Exit Ghost.*]
                        Why, so; being gone,
I am a man again. Pray you, sit still.

LADY MACBETH
You have displaced the mirth, broke the good meeting
With most admired disorder.

MACBETH   Can such things be,   111
And overcome us like a summer's cloud,   112
Without our special wonder? You make me strange   113
Even to the disposition that I owe,   114
When now I think you can behold such sights
And keep the natural ruby of your cheeks
When mine is blanched with fear.

ROSS   What sights, my lord?

LADY MACBETH
I pray you, speak not. He grows worse and worse;
Question enrages him. At once, good night.   119
Stand not upon the order of your going,   120
But go at once.

LENNOX   Good night, and better health
Attend His Majesty!

LADY MACBETH   A kind good night to all!
                        Exeunt Lords [*and attendants*].

MACBETH
It will have blood, they say; blood will have blood.
Stones have been known to move, and trees to speak;   124
Augurs and understood relations have   125
By maggotpies and choughs and rooks brought forth 126
The secret'st man of blood. What is the night?   127

LADY MACBETH
Almost at odds with morning, which is which.

MACBETH
How say'st thou, that Macduff denies his person   129
At our great bidding?

LADY MACBETH   Did you send to him, sir?

MACBETH
I hear it by the way; but I will send.   131
There's not a one of them but in his house   132
I keep a servant fee'd. I will tomorrow—   133
And betimes I will—to the Weird Sisters.   134
More shall they speak, for now I am bent to know   135
By the worst means the worst. For mine own good
All causes shall give way. I am in blood   137
Stepped in so far that, should I wade no more,   138
Returning were as tedious as go o'er.   139
Strange things I have in head, that will to hand,
Which must be acted ere they may be scanned.   141

LADY MACBETH
You lack the season of all natures, sleep.   142

MACBETH
Come, we'll to sleep. My strange and self-abuse   143
Is the initiate fear that wants hard use.   144
We are yet but young in deed.   *Exeunt.*

❦

3.5

*Thunder. Enter the three Witches, meeting
Hecate.*

FIRST WITCH
Why, how now, Hecate? You look angerly.   1

HECATE
Have I not reason, beldams as you are?   2
Saucy and overbold, how did you dare
To trade and traffic with Macbeth
In riddles and affairs of death,
And I, the mistress of your charms,
The close contriver of all harms,   7
Was never called to bear my part
Or show the glory of our art?
And, which is worse, all you have done
Hath been but for a wayward son,
Spiteful and wrathful, who, as others do,
Loves for his own ends, not for you.
But make amends now. Get you gone,
And at the pit of Acheron   15

93 **all to all** all good wishes to all, or, let all drink to everyone else.
96 **speculation** power of sight   102 **armed** armor-plated.   **Hyrcan** of
Hyrcania, in ancient times a region near the Caspian Sea   103 **nerves**
sinews   105 **the desert** some solitary place   106–7 **If . . . girl** If then I
tremble, proclaim me a baby girl, or a girl's doll.   111 **admired disorder**
wondered-at lack of self-control.   112 **overcome** come over   113–14 **You
make . . . owe** You cause me to feel I do not know my own nature (which
I had presumed to be that of a brave man)   119 **At once** To you all; now
120 **Stand . . . going** Do not take the time to leave in ceremonious order
of rank, as you entered   124 **Stones . . . speak** i.e., Even inanimate
nature speaks in such a way as to reveal the unnatural act of murder
125–7 **Augurs . . . blood** Prophets versed in the interpretation of occult
mysteries have, by reading the signs of magpies and jackdaws, revealed
secret murderers.   127 **the night** i.e., the time of night.

129 **How say'st thou** What do you say to the fact   131 **by the way**
indirectly   132 **them** my Scottish nobles   133 **fee'd** i.e., paid to spy.
134 **betimes** (1) early (2) while there is still time   135 **bent** determined   137 **All causes** all other considerations   138 **should . . . more**
even if I were to wade no farther   139 **were** would be.   **go o'er** to
proceed.   141 **acted . . . scanned** put into performance even before
there is time to scrutinize them.   142 **season** preservative   143–4 **My
. . . use** My strange self-punishing fear is that felt by a novice who
lacks toughening experience.
3.5. Location: A heath. (This scene is probably by another author.)
1 **angerly** angrily, angry.   2 **beldams** hags   7 **close** secret
15 **Acheron** the river of sorrows in Hades; here, hell itself

Meet me i'th' morning. Thither he
Will come to know his destiny.
Your vessels and your spells provide,
Your charms and everything beside.
I am for th'air. This night I'll spend
Unto a dismal and a fatal end.   21
Great business must be wrought ere noon.
Upon the corner of the moon
There hangs a vap'rous drop profound;   24
I'll catch it ere it come to ground,
And that, distilled by magic sleights,
Shall raise such artificial sprites   27
As by the strength of their illusion
Shall draw him on to his confusion.   29
He shall spurn fate, scorn death, and bear
His hopes 'bove wisdom, grace, and fear.
And you all know, security   32
Is mortals' chiefest enemy.   *Music and a song.*
Hark! I am called. My little spirit, see,
Sits in a foggy cloud and stays for me.   [*Exit.*] 35
                    Sing within, "Come away, come away," *etc.*

FIRST WITCH
Come, let's make haste. She'll soon be back again.
                                                  Exeunt.

❖

3.6

Enter Lennox and another Lord.

LENNOX
My former speeches have but hit your thoughts,   1
Which can interpret farther. Only I say   2
Things have been strangely borne. The gracious
    Duncan   3
Was pitied of Macbeth; marry, he was dead.   4
And the right valiant Banquo walked too late,
Whom you may say, if't please you, Fleance killed,
For Fleance fled. Men must not walk too late.
Who cannot want the thought how monstrous   8
It was for Malcolm and for Donalbain
To kill their gracious father? Damnèd fact!   10
How it did grieve Macbeth! Did he not straight   11
In pious rage the two delinquents tear
That were the slaves of drink and thralls of sleep? 13
Was not that nobly done? Ay, and wisely too;
For 'twould have angered any heart alive
To hear the men deny't. So that I say

He has borne all things well; and I do think   17
That had he Duncan's sons under his key—
As, an't please heaven, he shall not—they should find 19
What 'twere to kill a father. So should Fleance.
But peace! For from broad words, and 'cause he failed 21
His presence at the tyrant's feast, I hear   22
Macduff lives in disgrace. Sir, can you tell
Where he bestows himself?

LORD   The son of Duncan,   24
From whom this tyrant holds the due of birth,   25
Lives in the English court, and is received
Of the most pious Edward with such grace   27
That the malevolence of fortune nothing
Takes from his high respect. Thither Macduff   29
Is gone to pray the holy king, upon his aid,   30
To wake Northumberland and warlike Siward,   31
That by the help of these—with Him above
To ratify the work—we may again
Give to our tables meat, sleep to our nights,   34
Free from our feasts and banquets bloody knives,   35
Do faithful homage, and receive free honors—   36
All which we pine for now. And this report
Hath so exasperate the King that he   38
Prepares for some attempt of war.

LENNOX   Sent he to Macduff?

LORD
He did; and with an absolute "Sir, not I,"   41
The cloudy messenger turns me his back   42
And hums, as who should say, "You'll rue the time   43
That clogs me with this answer."

LENNOX   And that well might   44
Advise him to a caution, t' hold what distance   45
His wisdom can provide. Some holy angel   46
Fly to the court of England and unfold
His message ere he come, that a swift blessing   48
May soon return to this our suffering country   49
Under a hand accursed!   50

LORD   I'll send my prayers with him.   *Exeunt.*

❖

17 borne all things well managed everything cleverly   **19 an't if it.
should** would be sure to   **21 from broad words** on account of plain
speech   **22 His presence** i.e., to be present   **24 bestows himself** is
quartered, has taken refuge.   **The son of Duncan** Malcolm
25 holds . . . birth withholds the birthright (i.e., the Scottish crown)
27 Of by.   **Edward** Edward the Confessor, King of England   **29 his
high respect** the high respect paid to him. (Being out of fortune has
not lessened the dignity with which Malcolm is received in England.)
30 upon his aid in aid of Malcolm   **31 wake Northumberland** rouse
the people of Northumberland   **34 meat** food   **35 Free . . . banquets**
free our feasts and banquets from   **36 free** freely bestowed, or, pertaining to freemen   **38 exasperate the King** exasperated Macbeth
41 with . . . I i.e., when Macduff answered the messenger curtly with
a refusal   **42 cloudy** louring, scowling.   **turns me** i.e., turns. (*Me* is
used colloquially for emphasis.)   **43 hums . . . say** says "umph!" as if
to say   **44 clogs** encumbers, loads   **45–6 Advise . . . provide** warn
him (Macduff) to keep what safe distance he can (from Macbeth).
48 His message i.e., the request for aid against Scotland that Macduff
is going to present to King Edward (see lines 29 ff.)   **49–50 suffering
country Under** country suffering under

21 dismal disastrous, ill-omened   **24 profound** i.e., heavily pendent,
ready to drop off   **27 artificial sprites** spirits produced by magical
arts   **29 confusion** ruin.   **32 security** overconfidence   **35.1 "Come
away," etc.** (The song occurs in Thomas Middleton's *The Witch.*)
3.6. Location: Somewhere in Scotland.
1–2 My . . . farther What I've just said has coincided with your own
thought. I needn't say more; you can surmise the rest.   **3 borne** carried on.   **3–4 The gracious . . . dead** (Lennox ironically implies that
Macbeth's show of sorrow was hypocritical and came only after the
murder.)   **8 cannot . . . thought** can help thinking   **10 fact** deed,
crime.   **11 straight** straightway, at once   **13 thralls** slaves

4.1

[A cauldron.] Thunder. Enter the three Witches.

FIRST WITCH
Thrice the brinded cat hath mewed.   1

SECOND WITCH
Thrice, and once the hedgepig whined.   2

THIRD WITCH
Harpier cries. 'Tis time, 'tis time!   3

FIRST WITCH
Round about the cauldron go;
In the poisoned entrails throw.
Toad, that under cold stone
Days and nights has thirty-one   7
Sweltered venom sleeping got,   8
Boil thou first i'th' charmèd pot.

ALL *[as they dance round the cauldron]*
Double, double, toil and trouble;
Fire burn, and cauldron bubble.

SECOND WITCH
Fillet of a fenny snake,   12
In the cauldron boil and bake;
Eye of newt and toe of frog,
Wool of bat and tongue of dog,
Adder's fork and blindworm's sting,   16
Lizard's leg and owlet's wing,
For a charm of powerful trouble,
Like a hell-broth boil and bubble.

ALL
Double, double, toil and trouble;
Fire burn, and cauldron bubble.

THIRD WITCH
Scale of dragon, tooth of wolf,
Witches' mummy, maw and gulf   23
Of the ravined salt-sea shark,   24
Root of hemlock digged i'th' dark,
Liver of blaspheming Jew,
Gall of goat, and slips of yew   27
Slivered in the moon's eclipse,   28
Nose of Turk and Tartar's lips,
Finger of birth-strangled babe
Ditch-delivered by a drab,   31
Make the gruel thick and slab.   32
Add thereto a tiger's chaudron   33
For th'ingredience of our cauldron.   34

ALL
Double, double, toil and trouble;
Fire burn, and cauldron bubble.

SECOND WITCH
Cool it with a baboon's blood,
Then the charm is firm and good.   38

Enter Hecate to the other three Witches.

HECATE
Oh, well done! I commend your pains,   39
And everyone shall share i'th' gains.
And now about the cauldron sing
Like elves and fairies in a ring,
Enchanting all that you put in.   43
Music and a song: "Black spirits," etc.
[Exit Hecate.]

SECOND WITCH
By the pricking of my thumbs,
Something wicked this way comes.
   Open, locks,
   Whoever knocks!

Enter Macbeth.

MACBETH
How now, you secret, black, and midnight hags?   48
What is't you do?

ALL   A deed without a name.

MACBETH
I conjure you, by that which you profess,
Howe'er you come to know it, answer me.
Though you untie the winds and let them fight
Against the churches, though the yeasty waves   53
Confound and swallow navigation up,   54
Though bladed corn be lodged and trees blown down,   55
Though castles topple on their warders' heads,   56
Though palaces and pyramids do slope   57
Their heads to their foundations, though the treasure
Of nature's germens tumble all together   59
Even till destruction sicken, answer me   60
To what I ask you.

FIRST WITCH   Speak.

SECOND WITCH   Demand.

THIRD WITCH   We'll answer.

FIRST WITCH
Say if thou'dst rather hear it from our mouths
Or from our masters?

MACBETH   Call 'em. Let me see 'em.

FIRST WITCH
Pour in sow's blood, that hath eaten
Her nine farrow; grease that's sweaten   65

4.1. Location: A cavern (see 3.5.15). In the middle, a boiling cauldron (provided presumably by means of the trapdoor; see 4.1.106. The trapdoor must also be used in this scene for the apparitions.) 1 brinded marked by streaks (as by fire), brindled **2 hedgepig** hedgehog **3 Harpier** (The name of a familiar spirit; probably derived from *harpy*.) **cries** i.e., gives the signal to begin **7–8 Days . . . got** for thirty-one days and nights has exuded venom formed during sleep **12 Fillet** Slice. **fenny** inhabiting fens or swamps **16 fork** forked tongue. **blindworm** slowworm, a harmless burrowing lizard **23 mummy** mummified flesh made into a magical potion. **maw and gulf** gullet and stomach **24 ravined** ravenous, or glutted with prey (?) **27 Gall** gall bladder. **slips** cuttings for grafting or planting. **yew** (A tree often planted in churchyards and associated with mourning.) **28 Slivered** broken off (as a branch) **31 Ditch . . . drab** born in a ditch of a harlot **32 slab** viscous. **33 chaudron** entrails **34 th'ingredience** the ingredients

38.1 other (Said because Hecate is a witch, too, not because more witches enter.) **39–43 Oh . . . in** (These lines are universally regarded as non-Shakespearean.) **43.1 "Black spirits," etc.** (This song is found in Middleton's *The Witch*.) **48 black** i.e., dealing in black magic **53 yeasty** foamy **54 Confound** destroy **55 Though . . . lodged** though unripe grain be laid flat **56 warders'** guardsmen's **57 slope** bend **59 nature's germens** seed or elements from which all nature operates **60 sicken** be surfeited with its own excess **65 nine farrow** litter of nine. **sweaten** sweated

From the murderer's gibbet throw   66
Into the flame.
ALL   Come high or low,   67
Thyself and office deftly show!   68

Thunder. First Apparition, an armed Head.

MACBETH
Tell me, thou unknown power—
FIRST WITCH   He knows thy thought.
Hear his speech, but say thou naught.
FIRST APPARITION
Macbeth! Macbeth! Macbeth! Beware Macduff,
Beware the Thane of Fife. Dismiss me. Enough.   72
                              He descends.

MACBETH
Whate'er thou art, for thy good caution, thanks;
Thou hast harped my fear aright. But one word
more—   74
FIRST WITCH
He will not be commanded. Here's another,
More potent than the first.   76

Thunder. Second Apparition, a bloody Child.

SECOND APPARITION   Macbeth! Macbeth! Macbeth!
MACBETH   Had I three ears, I'd hear thee.
SECOND APPARITION
Be bloody, bold, and resolute; laugh to scorn
The power of man, for none of woman born
Shall harm Macbeth.   *Descends.*

MACBETH
Then live, Macduff; what need I fear of thee?
But yet I'll make assurance double sure,
And take a bond of fate. Thou shalt not live,   84
That I may tell pale-hearted fear it lies,
And sleep in spite of thunder.   86

*Thunder. Third Apparition, a Child crowned, with
a tree in his hand.*

                    What is this
That rises like the issue of a king   87
And wears upon his baby brow the round   88
And top of sovereignty?
ALL   Listen, but speak not to't.   89
THIRD APPARITION
Be lion-mettled, proud, and take no care
Who chafes, who frets, or where conspirers are.
Macbeth shall never vanquished be until

Great Birnam Wood to high Dunsinane Hill
Shall come against him.   *Descends.*
MACBETH   That will never be.
Who can impress the forest, bid the tree   95
Unfix his earthbound root? Sweet bodements, good!   96
Rebellious dead, rise never till the wood   97
Of Birnam rise, and our high-placed Macbeth   98
Shall live the lease of nature, pay his breath   99
To time and mortal custom. Yet my heart   100
Throbs to know one thing. Tell me, if your art
Can tell so much: shall Banquo's issue ever
Reign in this kingdom?
ALL   Seek to know no more.
MACBETH
I will be satisfied. Deny me this,
And an eternal curse fall on you! Let me know.   105
              [The cauldron descends.] Hautboys.
Why sinks that cauldron? And what noise is this?   106
FIRST WITCH   Show!
SECOND WITCH   Show!
THIRD WITCH   Show!
ALL
Show his eyes, and grieve his heart;
Come like shadows, so depart!   111

*A show of eight Kings and Banquo last; [the eighth
King] with a glass in his hand.*

MACBETH
Thou art too like the spirit of Banquo. Down!
Thy crown does sear mine eyeballs. And thy hair,
Thou other gold-bound brow, is like the first.   114
A third is like the former. Filthy hags,
Why do you show me this? A fourth? Start, eyes!   116
What, will the line stretch out to th' crack of doom?   117
Another yet? A seventh? I'll see no more.
And yet the eighth appears, who bears a glass
Which shows me many more; and some I see
That twofold balls and treble scepters carry.   121
Horrible sight! Now I see 'tis true,
For the blood-boltered Banquo smiles upon me   123
And points at them for his. *[The apparitions vanish.]*
What, is this so?   124

95 **impress** press into service, like soldiers   96 **bodements** prophecies   97–8 **Rebellious . . . rise** i.e., May the souls of those I have murdered (Banquo, Duncan) never rise again, since trees themself cannot rise. (An image of the Day of Judgment, when bodies are prophesied to rise again; see *Henry V*, 4.1.135–8.)   99–100 **Shall . . . custom** will live out his full life span until it is time for him to expire (*pay his breath*) in the way of all mortals.   105.1 *Hautboys* oboelike instruments   106 **noise** music   111.1 *eight Kings* (Banquo was the supposed ancestor of the Stuart dynasty, leading forward to King James VI of Scotland and James I of England, the *eighth King* here.)   111.2 *glass* (magic) mirror (also in line 119)   114 **other** i.e., second   116 **Start** Bulge from their sockets   117 **th' crack of doom** the thunder-peal of Doomsday at the end of time.   121 **twofold balls** (A probable reference to the double coronation of James at Scone and Westminster, as King of England and Scotland.)   **treble scepters** (Probably refers to James' assumed title as King of Great Britain, France, and Ireland.)   123 **blood-boltered** having his hair matted with blood   124 **for his** as his descendants.

66 **gibbet** gallows   67 **high or low** of the upper or lower air, from under the earth or in hell; or, one and all   68 **office** function.   68.1 *armed Head* (Perhaps symbolizes the head of Macbeth cut off by Macduff and presented by him to Malcolm, or else the head of Macduff, armed in rebellion against Macbeth.)   72.1 *He descends* (i.e., by means of the trapdoor).   74 **harped** hit, touched (as in touching a harp to make it sound)   76.1 *bloody Child* (Symbolizes Macduff untimely ripped from his mother's womb; see 5.8.15–16.)   84 **take a bond of** get a guarantee from (i.e., by killing Macduff, to make doubly sure he can do no harm)   86.1-2 *Child . . . hand* (Symbolizes Malcolm, the royal child; the tree anticipates the cutting of boughs in Birnam Wood, 5.4.)   87 **like** in the likeness of   88–9 **round And top** crown

FIRST WITCH

Ay, sir, all this is so. But why   125
Stands Macbeth thus amazedly?   126
Come, sisters, cheer we up his sprites   127
And show the best of our delights.
I'll charm the air to give a sound,
While you perform your antic round,   130
That this great king may kindly say
Our duties did his welcome pay.   132

Music. The Witches dance, and vanish.

MACBETH

Where are they? Gone? Let this pernicious hour
Stand aye accursèd in the calendar!
Come in, without there!

Enter Lennox.

LENNOX   What's Your Grace's will?

MACBETH

Saw you the Weird Sisters?

LENNOX   No, my lord.

MACBETH

Came they not by you?

LENNOX   No, indeed, my lord.

MACBETH

Infected be the air whereon they ride,
And damned all those that trust them! I did hear
The galloping of horse. Who was't came by?   140

LENNOX

'Tis two or three, my lord, that bring you word
Macduff is fled to England.

MACBETH   Fled to England!

LENNOX

Ay, my good lord.

MACBETH [*aside*]

Time, thou anticipat'st my dread exploits.   144
The flighty purpose never is o'ertook   145
Unless the deed go with it. From this moment   146
The very firstlings of my heart shall be   147
The firstlings of my hand. And even now,   148
To crown my thoughts with acts, be it thought and
    done:
The castle of Macduff I will surprise,   150
Seize upon Fife, give to th'edge o'th' sword
His wife, his babes, and all unfortunate souls
That trace him in his line. No boasting like a fool;   153
This deed I'll do before this purpose cool.
But no more sights!—Where are these gentlemen?
Come, bring me where they are.   *Exeunt.*

❧

125–32 **Ay . . . pay** (These lines are assumed to have been written by
someone other than Shakespeare.)   126 **amazedly** stunned
127 **sprites** spirits   130 **antic round** grotesque dance in a circle
132 **pay** repay.   140 **horse** horses.   144 **thou anticipat'st** you forestall
145 **flighty** fleeting   146 **Unless . . . it** unless the execution of the
deed accompanies the conception of it immediately.   147–8 **The
very . . . hand** the firstborn promptings of my heart will become my
first of deeds.   150 **surprise** attack without warning   153 **trace . . .
line** follow him in the line of inheritance.

4.2

Enter Macduff's Wife, her Son, and Ross.

LADY MACDUFF

What had he done to make him fly the land?

ROSS

You must have patience, madam.

LADY MACDUFF   He had none.

His flight was madness. When our actions do not,   3
Our fears do make us traitors.

ROSS   You know not   4

Whether it was his wisdom or his fear.

LADY MACDUFF

Wisdom? To leave his wife, to leave his babes,
His mansion, and his titles in a place   7
From whence himself does fly? He loves us not,
He wants the natural touch; for the poor wren,   9
The most diminutive of birds, will fight,
Her young ones in her nest, against the owl.   11
All is the fear and nothing is the love,
As little is the wisdom, where the flight
So runs against all reason.

ROSS   My dearest coz,   14

I pray you, school yourself. But, for your husband,   15
He is noble, wise, judicious, and best knows
The fits o'th' season. I dare not speak much further,   17
But cruel are the times when we are traitors   18
And do not know ourselves, when we hold rumor   19
From what we fear, yet know not what we fear,   20
But float upon a wild and violent sea
Each way and none. I take my leave of you;   22
Shall not be long but I'll be here again.   23
Things at the worst will cease, or else climb upward
To what they were before.—My pretty cousin,
Blessing upon you!

LADY MACDUFF

Fathered he is, and yet he's fatherless.

ROSS

I am so much a fool, should I stay longer
It would be my disgrace and your discomfort.   29
I take my leave at once.   *Exit Ross.*

LADY MACDUFF   Sirrah, your father's dead;   31
And what will you do now? How will you live?

SON

As birds do, mother.

LADY MACDUFF   What, with worms and flies?

SON

With what I get, I mean; and so do they.

4.2. Location: Fife. Macduff's castle.
3–4 **When . . . traitors** Even when we have committed no treasonous
act, our fearful responses make us look guilty.   7 **titles** possessions to
which he has title   9 **wants . . . touch** lacks the natural instinct to protect his family   11 **Her . . . nest** when her young ones are in the nest
14 **coz** kinswoman   15 **school** control.   **for** as for   17 **fits o'th' season** violent convulsions of the time.   18–19 **are traitors . . . ourselves**
are alienated from one another by a climate of fear and suspected
treason   19–20 **hold . . . From what we fear** believe every fearful
rumor on the basis of what we fear might be   22 **Each . . . none** this
way and that.   23 **Shall** it shall.   **but** before   29 **It . . . discomfort** I
should disgrace my manhood by weeping and cause you distress.
31 **Sirrah** (Here, an affectionate form of address to a child.)

LADY MACDUFF   Poor bird! Thou'dst never fear   35
The net nor lime, the pitfall nor the gin.   36

SON
Why should I, mother? Poor birds they are not set for.   37
My father is not dead, for all your saying.

LADY MACDUFF
Yes, he is dead. How wilt thou do for a father?

SON   Nay, how will you do for a husband?

LADY MACDUFF   Why, I can buy me twenty at any
market.

SON   Then you'll buy 'em to sell again.

LADY MACDUFF
Thou speak'st with all thy wit,
And yet, i'faith, with wit enough for thee.

SON   Was my father a traitor, mother?

LADY MACDUFF   Ay, that he was.

SON   What is a traitor?

LADY MACDUFF   Why, one that swears and lies.

SON   And be all traitors that do so?

LADY MACDUFF
Every one that does so is a traitor,
And must be hanged.

SON
And must they all be hanged that swear and lie?

LADY MACDUFF   Every one.

SON   Who must hang them?

LADY MACDUFF   Why, the honest men.

SON   Then the liars and swearers are fools, for there are
liars and swearers enough to beat the honest men and
hang up them.

LADY MACDUFF   Now, God help thee, poor monkey!
But how wilt thou do for a father?

SON   If he were dead, you'd weep for him; if you would
not, it were a good sign that I should quickly have a
new father.

LADY MACDUFF   Poor prattler, how thou talk'st!

Enter a Messenger.

MESSENGER
Bless you, fair dame! I am not to you known,
Though in your state of honor I am perfect.   67
I doubt some danger does approach you nearly.   68
If you will take a homely man's advice,   69
Be not found here. Hence with your little ones!
To fright you thus, methinks, I am too savage;
To do worse to you were fell cruelty,   72
Which is too nigh your person. Heaven preserve you!   73
I dare abide no longer.   *Exit Messenger.*

LADY MACDUFF   Whither should I fly?
I have done no harm. But I remember now
I am in this earthly world, where to do harm
Is often laudable, to do good sometime
Accounted dangerous folly. Why then, alas,

Do I put up that womanly defense
To say I have done no harm?

Enter Murderers.

What are these faces?

FIRST MURDERER   Where is your husband?

LADY MACDUFF
I hope in no place so unsanctified
Where such as thou mayst find him.

FIRST MURDERER   He's a traitor.

SON
Thou liest, thou shag-haired villain!

FIRST MURDERER   What, you egg?
                                 [*He stabs him.*]
Young fry of treachery!

SON   He has killed me, mother.   85
Run away, I pray you!   [*He dies.*]
      Exit [*Lady Macduff*] *crying* "Murder!"
      [*followed by the Murderers with the Son's body*].

❧

4.3

Enter Malcolm and Macduff.

MALCOLM
Let us seek out some desolate shade, and there
Weep our sad bosoms empty.

MACDUFF   Let us rather
Hold fast the mortal sword, and like good men   3
Bestride our downfall'n birthdom. Each new morn   4
New widows howl, new orphans cry, new sorrows
Strike heaven on the face, that it resounds   6
As if it felt with Scotland and yelled out   7
Like syllable of dolor.

MALCOLM   What I believe, I'll wail;   8
What know, believe; and what I can redress,   9
As I shall find the time to friend, I will.   10
What you have spoke it may be so, perchance.
This tyrant, whose sole name blisters our tongues,   12
Was once thought honest. You have loved him well;
He hath not touched you yet. I am young; but
something   14
You may deserve of him through me, and wisdom   15
To offer up a weak, poor, innocent lamb
T'appease an angry god.

MACDUFF   I am not treacherous.

MALCOLM   But Macbeth is.

---

85 **fry** spawn, progeny
4.3. Location: England. Before King Edward the Confessor's palace.
3 **mortal** deadly   4 **Bestride** stand over in defense.   **birthdom** native
land.   6 **that it resounds** so that it echoes   7–8 **As ... dolor** as if
heaven, feeling itself the blow delivered to Scotland, cried out with a
similar cry of pain.   8–9 **What ... believe** i.e., What I believe to be
amiss in Scotland I will grieve for, and anything I am certain to be
true I will believe. (But one must be cautious in these duplicitous
times.)   10 **to friend** opportune, congenial   12 **sole** mere   14 **He ...
yet** i.e., the fact that Macbeth hasn't hurt you yet makes me suspicious of your loyalties.   **young** i.e., inexperienced   14–15 **something
... me** i.e., you may win favor with Macbeth by delivering me to him
15 **wisdom** i.e., it would be worldly-wise

---

35 **Thou'dst never fear** You are too innocent to be prudently wary of
36 **lime** birdlime (a sticky substance put on branches to snare birds).
gin snare.   37 **Poor ... for** i.e., Traps are not set for *poor* birds, as you
call me.   67 **Though ... perfect** though I am perfectly acquainted
with your honorable state.   68 **doubt** fear   69 **homely** plain
72–3 **To ... person** to do actual harm to you would be savage cruelty,
which cruelty is all too near at hand.

A good and virtuous nature may recoil   20
In an imperial charge. But I shall crave your pardon.   21
That which you are my thoughts cannot transpose;   22
Angels are bright still, though the brightest fell.   23
Though all things foul would wear the brows of grace,   24
Yet grace must still look so.

MACDUFF   I have lost my hopes.   25

MALCOLM
Perchance even there where I did find my doubts.   26
Why in that rawness left you wife and child,   27
Those precious motives, those strong knots of love,
Without leave-taking? I pray you,
Let not my jealousies be your dishonors,   30
But mine own safeties. You may be rightly just,   31
Whatever I shall think.

MACDUFF   Bleed, bleed, poor country!
Great tyranny, lay thou thy basis sure,   33
For goodness dare not check thee; wear thou thy
    wrongs,   34
The title is affeered! Fare thee well, lord.   35
I would not be the villain that thou think'st
For the whole space that's in the tyrant's grasp,
And the rich East to boot.

MALCOLM   Be not offended.   38
I speak not as in absolute fear of you.   39
I think our country sinks beneath the yoke;
It weeps, it bleeds, and each new day a gash
Is added to her wounds. I think withal   42
There would be hands uplifted in my right;   43
And here from gracious England have I offer   44
Of goodly thousands. But, for all this,
When I shall tread upon the tyrant's head,
Or wear it on my sword, yet my poor country
Shall have more vices than it had before,
More suffer, and more sundry ways than ever,   49
By him that shall succeed.

MACDUFF   What should he be?   50

MALCOLM
It is myself I mean, in whom I know

All the particulars of vice so grafted   52
That, when they shall be opened, black Macbeth   53
Will seem as pure as snow, and the poor state
Esteem him as a lamb, being compared
With my confineless harms.

MACDUFF   Not in the legions   56
Of horrid hell can come a devil more damned
In evils to top Macbeth.

MALCOLM   I grant him bloody,   58
Luxurious, avaricious, false, deceitful,   59
Sudden, malicious, smacking of every sin   60
That has a name. But there's no bottom, none,
In my voluptuousness. Your wives, your daughters,
Your matrons, and your maids could not fill up
The cistern of my lust, and my desire
All continent impediments would o'erbear   65
That did oppose my will. Better Macbeth   66
Than such an one to reign.

MACDUFF   Boundless intemperance
In nature is a tyranny; it hath been   68
Th'untimely emptying of the happy throne
And fall of many kings. But fear not yet   70
To take upon you what is yours. You may
Convey your pleasures in a spacious plenty,   72
And yet seem cold; the time you may so hoodwink.   73
We have willing dames enough. There cannot be
That vulture in you to devour so many
As will to greatness dedicate themselves,
Finding it so inclined.

MALCOLM   With this there grows
In my most ill-composed affection such   78
A stanchless avarice that, were I king,   79
I should cut off the nobles for their lands,
Desire his jewels and this other's house,   81
And my more-having would be as a sauce
To make me hunger more, that I should forge   83
Quarrels unjust against the good and loyal,
Destroying them for wealth.

MACDUFF   This avarice
Sticks deeper, grows with more pernicious root
Than summer-seeming lust, and it hath been   87
The sword of our slain kings. Yet do not fear;   88
Scotland hath foisons to fill up your will   89
Of your mere own. All these are portable,   90
With other graces weighed.   91

MALCOLM
But I have none. The king-becoming graces,
As justice, verity, temperance, stableness,

20–1 A good . . . charge i.e., Even as good a virtuous nature as you
have, Macduff, may give way to the insinuations of a royal command
from Macbeth. (With wordplay on the *recoil* of a firearm that is
charged with power and shot.)   **22 That . . . transpose** My suspicious
thoughts cannot change you from what you are, cannot make you
evil   **23 the brightest** i.e., Lucifer   **24–5 Though . . . so** Even though
evil puts on the appearance of good so often as to cast that appearance into deep suspicion, yet goodness must go on looking and acting like itself.   **25 hopes** i.e., hopes of persuading Malcolm to lead
the cause against Macbeth.   **26 Perchance even there** i.e., Perhaps in
that same mistrustful frame of mind.   **doubts** i.e., fears such as that
Macduff may covertly be on Macbeth's side.   **27 rawness** unprotected condition. (Malcolm suggests that Macduff's leaving his family
unprotected could be construed as more evidence of his not having
anything to fear from Macbeth.)   **30–1 Let . . . safeties** may it be true
that my suspicions of your lack of honor are founded only in my own
wariness.   **33 basis** foundation   **34 check** rebuke, call to account.
wear . . . wrongs continue to enjoy your wrongfully gained powers
35 affeered confirmed, certified.   **38 to boot** in addition.
39 absolute fear complete mistrust   **42 withal** in addition   **43 right**
cause   **44 England** the King of England   **49 More . . . ways** suffer
more grievously and in more varied ways   **50 What . . . be?** Whom
could you possibly mean?

52 grafted (1) engrafted, indissolubly mixed (2) grafted like a plant
that will then *open* or unfold   **53 opened** unfolded (like a bud)
56 confineless limitless   **58 top** surpass   **59 Luxurious** lecherous
60 Sudden violent, impetuous   **65 continent** (1) chaste (2) restraining, containing   **66 will** lust. (Also in line 89.)   **68 nature** human
nature   **70 yet** nevertheless   **72 Convey** manage with secrecy
73 cold chaste.   **the time . . . hoodwink** you may thus deceive the
age.   **78 ill-composed affection** evil disposition   **79 stanchless** insatiable   **81 his** one man's.   **this other's** another's   **83 that** so that
87 summer-seeming appropriate to youth (and lessening in later
years)   **88 sword** i.e., cause of overthrow   **89 foisons** resources,
plenty   **90 Of . . . own** out of your own royal estates alone.
portable bearable   **91 weighed** counterbalanced.

Bounty, perseverance, mercy, lowliness,   94
Devotion, patience, courage, fortitude,
I have no relish of them, but abound   96
In the division of each several crime,   97
Acting it many ways. Nay, had I power, I should
Pour the sweet milk of concord into hell,
Uproar the universal peace, confound   100
All unity on earth.
MACDUFF   O Scotland, Scotland!
MALCOLM
If such a one be fit to govern, speak.
I am as I have spoken.
MACDUFF   Fit to govern?
No, not to live. Oh, nation miserable,
With an untitled tyrant bloody-sceptered,   105
When shalt thou see thy wholesome days again,
Since that the truest issue of thy throne
By his own interdiction stands accurst   108
And does blaspheme his breed? Thy royal father   109
Was a most sainted king; the queen that bore thee,
Oft'ner upon her knees than on her feet,
Died every day she lived. Fare thee well.   112
These evils thou repeat'st upon thyself
Hath banished me from Scotland. O my breast,   114
Thy hope ends here!
MALCOLM   Macduff, this noble passion,
Child of integrity, hath from my soul   116
Wiped the black scruples, reconciled my thoughts
To thy good truth and honor. Devilish Macbeth
By many of these trains hath sought to win me   119
Into his power, and modest wisdom plucks me   120
From overcredulous haste. But God above
Deal between thee and me! For even now
I put myself to thy direction and
Unspeak mine own detraction, here abjure   124
The taints and blames I laid upon myself
For strangers to my nature. I am yet   126
Unknown to woman, never was forsworn,   127
Scarcely have coveted what was mine own,
At no time broke my faith, would not betray
The devil to his fellow, and delight
No less in truth than life. My first false speaking
Was this upon myself. What I am truly   132
Is thine and my poor country's to command—
Whither indeed, before thy here-approach,
Old Siward with ten thousand warlike men,
Already at a point, was setting forth.   136

Now we'll together; and the chance of goodness   137
Be like our warranted quarrel!—Why are you silent?   138
MACDUFF
Such welcome and unwelcome things at once
'Tis hard to reconcile.

    Enter a Doctor.

MALCOLM
Well, more anon.—Comes the King forth, I pray you?
DOCTOR
Ay, sir. There are a crew of wretched souls
That stay his cure. Their malady convinces   143
The great essay of art; but at his touch—   144
Such sanctity hath heaven given his hand—
They presently amend.
MALCOLM   I thank you, Doctor.   146

                              Exit [Doctor].

MACDUFF
What's the disease he means?
MALCOLM   'Tis called the evil.   147
A most miraculous work in this good king,
Which often, since my here-remain in England,   149
I have seen him do. How he solicits heaven   150
Himself best knows; but strangely-visited people,   151
All swoll'n and ulcerous, pitiful to the eye,
The mere despair of surgery, he cures,   153
Hanging a golden stamp about their necks   154
Put on with holy prayers; and 'tis spoken,   155
To the succeeding royalty he leaves   156
The healing benediction. With this strange virtue   157
He hath a heavenly gift of prophecy,
And sundry blessings hang about his throne
That speak him full of grace.

    Enter Ross.

MACDUFF   See who comes here.
MALCOLM
My countryman, but yet I know him not.   161
MACDUFF
My ever-gentle cousin, welcome hither.   162
MALCOLM
I know him now. Good God betimes remove   163
The means that makes us strangers!
ROSS   Sir, amen.
MACDUFF
Stands Scotland where it did?
ROSS   Alas, poor country,
Almost afraid to know itself. It cannot

---

94 **lowliness** humility   96 **relish** flavor or trace   97 **division** subdivisions, various possible forms.   **several** separate   100 **Uproar** throw into an uproar   105 **untitled** lacking rightful title, usurping 108 **interdiction** debarring of self   109 **does blaspheme his breed** defames his breeding, i.e., is a disgrace to his royal lineage. 112 **Died . . . lived** lived a life of daily mortification.   114 **breast** heart   116 **Child of integrity** a product of your integrity of spirit; or, you person of perfect integrity   119 **trains** plots, artifices 120 **modest . . . me** wise prudence holds me back   124 **Unspeak . . . detraction** take back all I said in detraction of myself   126 **For** as 127 **Unknown to woman** a virgin   132 **upon** against   136 **at a point** prepared

137–8 **the chance . . . quarrel** may our chance of success be proportionate to the justice of our cause.   143 **stay** wait for.   **convinces** conquers   144 **essay of art** efforts of medical skill   146 **presently** immediately   147 **evil** i.e., scrofula, supposedly cured by the royal touch; James I claimed this power.   149 **here-remain** stay   150 **solicits** prevails by prayer with   151 **strangely-visited** afflicted by strange diseases   153 **mere** utter   154 **stamp** minted coin   155–7 **and 'tis . . . benediction** it is said that he bequeaths this healing blessedness to his royal progeny.   157 **virtue** healing power   161 **My countryman** (So identified by his dress.)   **know** recognize   162 **gentle** noble 163 **betimes** speedily

Be called our mother, but our grave; where nothing   167
But who knows nothing is once seen to smile;   168
Where sighs and groans and shrieks that rend the air
Are made, not marked; where violent sorrow seems   170
A modern ecstasy. The dead man's knell   171
Is there scarce asked for who, and good men's lives
Expire before the flowers in their caps,   173
Dying or ere they sicken.

MACDUFF   Oh, relation   174
Too nice, and yet too true!

MALCOLM   What's the newest grief?   175

ROSS
That of an hour's age doth hiss the speaker;   176
Each minute teems a new one.

MACDUFF   How does my wife?   177

ROSS
Why, well.

MACDUFF   And all my children?

ROSS   Well too.   178

MACDUFF
The tyrant has not battered at their peace?

ROSS
No, they were well at peace when I did leave 'em.

MACDUFF
Be not a niggard of your speech. How goes't?

ROSS
When I came hither to transport the tidings
Which I have heavily borne, there ran a rumor   183
Of many worthy fellows that were out,   184
Which was to my belief witnessed the rather   185
For that I saw the tyrant's power afoot.   186
Now is the time of help. [*To Malcolm*] Your eye in
    Scotland
Would create soldiers, make our women fight,   188
To doff their dire distresses.

MALCOLM   Be't their comfort   189
We are coming thither. Gracious England hath   190
Lent us good Siward and ten thousand men;
An older and a better soldier none   192
That Christendom gives out.

ROSS   Would I could answer   193
This comfort with the like! But I have words
That would be howled out in the desert air,   195
Where hearing should not latch them.

MACDUFF   What concern they?   196

The general cause? Or is it a fee-grief   197
Due to some single breast?

ROSS   No mind that's honest   198
But in it shares some woe, though the main part
Pertains to you alone.

MACDUFF   If it be mine,
Keep it not from me; quickly let me have it.

ROSS
Let not your ears despise my tongue forever,
Which shall possess them with the heaviest sound   203
That ever yet they heard.

MACDUFF   Hum! I guess at it.

ROSS
Your castle is surprised, your wife and babes
Savagely slaughtered. To relate the manner
Were, on the quarry of these murdered deer,   207
To add the death of you.

MALCOLM   Merciful heaven!
What, man, ne'er pull your hat upon your brows;   209
Give sorrow words. The grief that does not speak
Whispers the o'erfraught heart and bids it break.   211

MACDUFF
My children too?

ROSS   Wife, children, servants, all
That could be found.

MACDUFF   And I must be from thence!   213
My wife killed too?

ROSS   I have said.

MALCOLM   Be comforted.
Let's make us med'cines of our great revenge
To cure this deadly grief.

MACDUFF
He has no children. All my pretty ones?   217
Did you say all? O hell-kite! All?   218
What, all my pretty chickens and their dam
At one fell swoop?   220

MALCOLM   Dispute it like a man.   221

MACDUFF   I shall do so;
But I must also feel it as a man.
I cannot but remember such things were,
That were most precious to me. Did heaven look on
And would not take their part? Sinful Macduff,
They were all struck for thee! Naught that I am,   227
Not for their own demerits, but for mine,
Fell slaughter on their souls. Heaven rest them now!

MALCOLM
Be this the whetstone of your sword. Let grief
Convert to anger; blunt not the heart, enrage it.

167–8 nothing But who nobody except a person who   **168 once** ever
170 marked noticed (because they are so common)   **171 modern
ecstasy** commonplace emotion.   **173 flowers** (Often worn in Elizabethan caps.)   **174 or ere they sicken** before they have had time to
fall ill.   **relation** report   **175 nice** minutely accurate, elaborately
phrased   **176 That . . . speaker** The speaker of news that is scarcely
an hour old is hissed at for reporting stale news   **177 teems** teems
with, yields   **178 well** (Ross quibbles, in his reluctance to tell the bad
news. "The dead are well" means they are at rest.)   **183 heavily**
sadly   **184–6 Of . . . afoot** about many worthy Scots who have been
driven into exile and armed rebellion, which rumor was strengthened
all the more when I saw Macbeth's army on the move (in anticipation
of being attacked).   **188 our women** even our women   **189 doff** put
off, get rid of   **190 Gracious England** i.e., Edward the Confessor
192 none there is none   **193 gives out** tells of, proclaims.   **195 would**
should   **196 latch** catch (the sound of)

197 fee-grief a grief with an individual owner, having absolute ownership   **198 Due to** i.e., owned by   **203 possess them with** put them
in possession of   **207 quarry** heap of slaughtered deer at a hunt.
(With a pun on *dear, deer.*)   **209 pull your hat** (A conventional gesture
of grief.)   **211 Whispers** whispers to.   **o'erfraught** overburdened
213 must had to   **217 He has no children** (Referring either to Macbeth, who must not be a father if he can do such a thing, or, to Malcolm, who speaks comfortingly without knowing what such a loss
feels like to a father.)   **218 hell-kite** (The *kite* is a rapacious bird of
prey; a term of disdain and dislike.)   **220 fell** cruel   **221 Dispute**
Strive against, debate   **227 for thee** i.e., as divine punishment for
your sins.   **Naught** Wicked

MACDUFF
> Oh, I could play the woman with mine eyes
> And braggart with my tongue! But, gentle heavens,
> Cut short all intermission. Front to front   234
> Bring thou this fiend of Scotland and myself;
> Within my sword's length set him. If he scape,   236
> Heaven forgive him too!

MALCOLM   This tune goes manly.   237
> Come, go we to the King. Our power is ready;   238
> Our lack is nothing but our leave. Macbeth   239
> Is ripe for shaking, and the powers above
> Put on their instruments. Receive what cheer you may.   241
> The night is long that never finds the day.   *Exeunt.*

❖

5.1

Enter a Doctor of Physic and a Waiting-Gentlewoman.

DOCTOR   I have two nights watched with you, but can perceive no truth in your report. When was it she last walked?

GENTLEWOMAN   Since His Majesty went into the field, I have seen her rise from her bed, throw her nightgown upon her, unlock her closet, take forth paper, fold it, 5 write upon't, read it, afterwards seal it, and again return to bed; yet all this while in a most fast sleep.

DOCTOR   A great perturbation in nature, to receive at once the benefit of sleep and do the effects of 9 watching! In this slumbery agitation, besides her 10 walking and other actual performances, what, at any time, have you heard her say?

GENTLEWOMAN   That, sir, which I will not report after her.

DOCTOR   You may to me, and 'tis most meet you should. 15

GENTLEWOMAN   Neither to you nor anyone, having no witness to confirm my speech.

Enter Lady [Macbeth], with a taper.

Lo you, here she comes! This is her very guise, and, upon my life, fast asleep. Observe her. Stand close.   19
[*They stand aside.*]

DOCTOR   How came she by that light?

GENTLEWOMAN   Why, it stood by her. She has light by her continually. 'Tis her command.

DOCTOR   You see her eyes are open.

GENTLEWOMAN   Ay, but their sense are shut.

DOCTOR   What is it she does now? Look how she rubs her hands.

GENTLEWOMAN   It is an accustomed action with her to seem thus washing her hands. I have known her continue in this a quarter of an hour.

LADY MACBETH   Yet here's a spot.

DOCTOR   Hark, she speaks. I will set down what comes from her, to satisfy my remembrance the more 32 strongly.

LADY MACBETH   Out, damned spot! Out, I say! One—two—why then, 'tis time to do't. Hell is murky.—Fie, my lord, fie, a soldier, and afeard? What need we fear who knows it, when none can call our power to account? Yet who would have thought the old man to have had so much blood in him?

DOCTOR   Do you mark that?

LADY MACBETH   The Thane of Fife had a wife. Where is she now?—What, will these hands ne'er be clean?—No more o'that, my lord, no more o' that; you mar all with this starting.   44

DOCTOR   Go to, go to. You have known what you 45 should not.

GENTLEWOMAN   She has spoke what she should not, I am sure of that. Heaven knows what she has known!

LADY MACBETH   Here's the smell of the blood still. All the perfumes of Arabia will not sweeten this little hand. Oh, oh, oh!

DOCTOR   What a sigh is there! The heart is sorely 52 charged.   53

GENTLEWOMAN   I would not have such a heart in my bosom for the dignity of the whole body.   55

DOCTOR   Well, well, well.

GENTLEWOMAN   Pray God it be, sir.   57

DOCTOR   This disease is beyond my practice. Yet I have known those which have walked in their sleep who have died holily in their beds.

LADY MACBETH   Wash your hands, put on your nightgown; look not so pale! I tell you yet again, Banquo's buried. He cannot come out on 's grave.   63

DOCTOR   Even so?

LADY MACBETH   To bed, to bed! There's knocking at the gate. Come, come, come, come, give me your hand. What's done cannot be undone. To bed, to bed, to bed!   *Exit Lady.*

DOCTOR   Will she go now to bed?

GENTLEWOMAN   Directly.

DOCTOR
> Foul whisperings are abroad. Unnatural deeds
> Do breed unnatural troubles. Infected minds
> To their deaf pillows will discharge their secrets.
> More needs she the divine than the physician.
> God, God forgive us all! Look after her;
> Remove from her the means of all annoyance,   76
> And still keep eyes upon her. So, good night.   77
> My mind she has mated, and amazed my sight.   78
> I think, but dare not speak.

GENTLEWOMAN   Good night, good Doctor.
Exeunt.

---

234 intermission delay, interval.   **Front to front** Face to face
236–7 If . . . too! If I let him escape, may he find forgiveness not only from me but from heaven itself! (This is a condition that Macbeth will not allow to happen.)   **238 power** army   **239 Our . . . leave** we need only to take our leave (of the English King).   **241 Put . . . instruments** set us on as their agents, or, arm themselves.
5.1. Location: Dunsinane. Macbeth's castle.
0.1 *Physic* medicine   **5 closet** chest or cabinet   **9–10 do . . . watching** act as though awake.   **15 meet** suitable   **19 close** concealed.

32 satisfy confirm, support   **44 this starting** these startled movements.
45 Go to (An exclamation of reproof, directed at Lady Macbeth.)
52–3 sorely charged heavily burdened.   **55 dignity** worth, value   **57 Pray . . . sir** Pray God it will turn out well, as you say, sir. (Playing on the Doctor's "*Well, well,*" i.e., "Dear, dear.")   **63 on 's** of his   **76 annoyance** i.e., harming herself   **77 still** constantly   **78 mated** bewildered, stupefied

5.2

Drum and colors. Enter Menteith, Caithness,
Angus, Lennox, [and] soldiers.

MENTEITH
　The English power is near, led on by Malcolm,
　His uncle Siward, and the good Macduff.
　Revenges burn in them, for their dear causes   3
　Would to the bleeding and the grim alarm   4
　Excite the mortified man.
ANGUS   Near Birnam Wood   5
　Shall we well meet them; that way are they coming.   6
CAITHNESS
　Who knows if Donalbain be with his brother?
LENNOX
　For certain, sir, he is not. I have a file   8
　Of all the gentry. There is Siward's son,
　And many unrough youths that even now   10
　Protest their first of manhood.
MENTEITH   What does the tyrant?   11
CAITHNESS
　Great Dunsinane he strongly fortifies.
　Some say he's mad, others that lesser hate him
　Do call it valiant fury; but for certain
　He cannot buckle his distempered cause   15
　Within the belt of rule.
ANGUS   Now does he feel
　His secret murders sticking on his hands;
　Now minutely revolts upbraid his faith-breach.   18
　Those he commands move only in command,   19
　Nothing in love. Now does he feel his title
　Hang loose about him, like a giant's robe
　Upon a dwarfish thief.
MENTEITH   Who then shall blame
　His pestered senses to recoil and start,   23
　When all that is within him does condemn
　Itself for being there?
CAITHNESS   Well, march we on
　To give obedience where 'tis truly owed.
　Meet we the med'cine of the sickly weal,   27
　And with him pour we in our country's purge   28
　Each drop of us.
LENNOX   Or so much as it needs   29
　To dew the sovereign flower and drown the weeds.   30
　Make we our march towards Birnam.

　　　　　　　　　　　　　　　　　　Exeunt, marching.

❧

5.3

Enter Macbeth, Doctor, and attendants.

MACBETH
　Bring me no more reports. Let them fly all!   1
　Till Birnam Wood remove to Dunsinane,
　I cannot taint with fear. What's the boy Malcolm?   3
　Was he not born of woman? The spirits that know
　All mortal consequences have pronounced me thus: 5
　"Fear not, Macbeth. No man that's born of woman
　Shall e'er have power upon thee." Then fly, false
　　　thanes,
　And mingle with the English epicures!   8
　The mind I sway by and the heart I bear   9
　Shall never sag with doubt nor shake with fear.

Enter Servant.

　The devil damn thee black, thou cream-faced loon!   11
　Where got'st thou that goose look?
SERVANT
　There is ten thousand—
MACBETH   Geese, villain?
SERVANT   Soldiers, sir.
MACBETH
　Go prick thy face and over-red thy fear,   14
　Thou lily-livered boy. What soldiers, patch?   15
　Death of thy soul! Those linen cheeks of thine   16
　Are counselors to fear. What soldiers, whey-face?   17
SERVANT   The English force, so please you.
MACBETH   Take thy face hence.   *[Exit Servant.]*
　　　　　　　　[Calling] Seyton!—I am sick at heart
　When I behold—Seyton, I say!—This push   20
　Will cheer me ever, or disseat me now.   21
　I have lived long enough. My way of life   22
　Is fall'n into the sere, the yellow leaf,   23
　And that which should accompany old age,
　As honor, love, obedience, troops of friends,   25
　I must not look to have, but in their stead
　Curses, not loud but deep, mouth-honor, breath
　Which the poor heart would fain deny and dare not.
　Seyton!

Enter Seyton.

SEYTON
　What's your gracious pleasure?
MACBETH   What news more?

5.2. Location: The country near Dunsinane.
3–5 their . . . man their every grievous wrongs would awaken even the
dead to answer the bloody and grim call to battle.　**6 well** conveniently　**8 file** list, roster　**10 unrough** beardless　**11 Protest** assert
publicly　**15 distempered** disease-swollen, dropsical　**18 Now . . .
faith-breach** every minute now, revolts upbraid him for his violation
of all trust and sacred vows.　**19 in command** under orders
23 pestered troubled, tormented　**27 Meet we . . . weal** i.e., Let us
join forces with Malcolm, the physician of our sick land　**28–9 pour
. . . of us** i.e., let us shed all our blood as a bloodletting or *purge* of our
country.　**30 dew** bedew, water.　**sovereign** (1) royal (2) medically
efficacious

5.3. Location: Dunsinane. Macbeth's castle.
1 Let . . . all! Let all the thanes desert!　**3 taint with** become imbued
or infected with, weakened by　**5 All . . . consequences** all that happens in this mortal life　**8 English epicures** luxury-loving Englishmen.　**9 sway** rule myself　**11 loon** stupid fellow.　**14 Go . . . fear**
i.e., Go prick or pinch your pale cheeks to bring some color into them.
(Current medical theory held that fear caused a retreat of the blood to
the abdominal organs, leaving the countenance pale or *lily-livered*,
line 15.)　**15 patch** domestic fool.　**16 Death . . . soul!** May your soul
die an eternal death! (An oath.)　**linen** i.e., pale, white　**17 Are . . .
fear** (The fear is contagious to the rest of the body and to other
observers.)　**20 behold** (Macbeth does not finish this thought.)
push effort, crisis　**21 cheer** (With a suggestion of "chair.")　**disseat**
dethrone　**22 way** course　**23 sere** dry and withered　**25 As** such as

SEYTON

    All is confirmed, my lord, which was reported.

MACBETH

    I'll fight till from my bones my flesh be hacked.

    Give me my armor.

SEYTON   'Tis not needed yet.

MACBETH   I'll put it on.

    Send out more horses. Skirr the country round.   36

    Hang those that talk of fear. Give me mine armor.

    How does your patient, Doctor?

DOCTOR   Not so sick, my lord,

    As she is troubled with thick-coming fancies

    That keep her from her rest.

MACBETH   Cure her of that.

    Canst thou not minister to a mind diseased,

    Pluck from the memory a rooted sorrow,

    Raze out the written troubles of the brain,   44

    And with some sweet oblivious antidote   45

    Cleanse the stuffed bosom of that perilous stuff

    Which weighs upon the heart?

DOCTOR   Therein the patient

    Must minister to himself.

MACBETH

    Throw physic to the dogs! I'll none of it.   49

    Come, put mine armor on. Give me my staff.   50

                    [*Attendants arm him.*]

    Seyton, send out. Doctor, the thanes fly from me.—

    Come, sir, dispatch.—If thou couldst, Doctor, cast   52

    The water of my land, find her disease,   53

    And purge it to a sound and pristine health,

    I would applaud thee to the very echo,

    That should applaud again.—Pull't off, I say.—   56

    What rhubarb, senna, or what purgative drug   57

    Would scour these English hence? Hear'st thou of

        them?   58

DOCTOR

    Ay, my good lord. Your royal preparation

    Makes us hear something.

MACBETH   Bring it after me.—   60

    I will not be afraid of death and bane   61

    Till Birnam Forest come to Dunsinane.

                    Exeunt [*all but the Doctor*].

DOCTOR

    Were I from Dunsinane away and clear,

    Profit again should hardly draw me here.   [*Exit.*]

❖

5.4

Drum and colors. Enter Malcolm, Siward,
Macduff, Siward's Son, Menteith, Caithness,
Angus, [Lennox, Ross,] and soldiers, marching.

MALCOLM

    Cousins, I hope the days are near at hand   1

    That chambers will be safe.

MENTEITH   We doubt it nothing.   2

SIWARD

    What wood is this before us?

MENTEITH   The wood of Birnam.

MALCOLM

    Let every soldier hew him down a bough

    And bear't before him. Thereby shall we shadow

    The numbers of our host and make discovery   6

    Err in report of us.

SOLDIERS   It shall be done.

SIWARD

    We learn no other but the confident tyrant   8

    Keeps still in Dunsinane and will endure   9

    Our setting down before't.

MALCOLM   'Tis his main hope;   10

    For where there is advantage to be given,   11

    Both more and less have given him the revolt,   12

    And none serve with him but constrainèd things

    Whose hearts are absent too.

MACDUFF   Let our just censures   14

    Attend the true event, and put we on   15

    Industrious soldiership.

SIWARD   The time approaches

    That will with due decision make us know

    What we shall say we have and what we owe.   18

    Thoughts speculative their unsure hopes relate,   19

    But certain issue strokes must arbitrate—   20

    Towards which advance the war.   *Exeunt, marching.*   21

❖

5.5

Enter Macbeth, Seyton, and soldiers, with drum
and colors.

MACBETH

    Hang out our banners on the outward walls.

    The cry is still, "They come!" Our castle's strength

    Will laugh a siege to scorn. Here let them lie

    Till famine and the ague eat them up.   4

    Were they not forced with those that should be ours,   5

    We might have met them dareful, beard to beard,   6

---

36 **Skirr** Scour 44 **Raze** scrape; erase. **written troubles of** troubles recorded in 45 **oblivious** causing forgetfulness 49 **physic** medicine 50 **staff** lance or baton of office. 52 **dispatch** hurry. 52–3 **cast The water** diagnose disease by the inspection of urine 56 **Pull't off** (Refers to some part of the armor not properly put on.) 57 **senna** a purgative drug 58 **scour** purge, cleanse, rid 60 **it** i.e., the armor not yet put on 61 **bane** ruin
5.4. Location: Country near Birnam Wood.

1 **Cousins** Kinsmen, peers 2 **chambers . . . safe** i.e., we may sleep safely in our bedchambers. **nothing** not at all. 6 **discovery** scouting reports 8 **no other but** no other news but that 9 **Keeps** remains. **endure** allow, not attempt to prevent 10 **setting down before't** laying siege to it. 11 **advantage** opportunity (i.e., in military operations outside Macbeth's castle in which it is possible for would-be deserters to slip away; in a siege, his forces will be more confined to the castle and under his watchful eye) 12 **more and less** high and low 14–15 **Let . . . event** Let us postpone judgment about these uncertain matters until we've achieved our goal 18 **What . . . owe** what we only claim to have, as distinguished from what we actually have. (*Owe* can mean "own.") 19–20 **Thoughts . . . arbitrate** Speculating can only convey our sense of hope; blows must decide the actual outcome 21 **war** army.
5.5. Location: Dunsinane. Macbeth's castle.
4 **the ague** fever, disease 5 **forced** reinforced 6 **dareful** boldly, in open battle

And beat them backward home.
　　　　　　　　　　A cry within of women.
　　　　　　　　　　What is that noise?

SEYTON
It is the cry of women, my good lord.
　　　　　　　　　　[*He goes to the door.*]

MACBETH
I have almost forgot the taste of fears.
The time has been my senses would have cooled　10
To hear a night-shriek, and my fell of hair　11
Would at a dismal treatise rouse and stir　12
As life were in't. I have supped full with horrors;　13
Direness, familiar to my slaughterous thoughts,
Cannot once start me.

　　　　　　[*Seyton returns.*]

　　　　　　　　　　Wherefore was that cry?　15
SEYTON　　The Queen, my lord, is dead.
MACBETH　　She should have died hereafter;　17
There would have been a time for such a word.
Tomorrow, and tomorrow, and tomorrow　19
Creeps in this petty pace from day to day　20
To the last syllable of recorded time,
And all our yesterdays have lighted fools　22
The way to dusty death. Out, out, brief candle!　23
Life's but a walking shadow, a poor player
That struts and frets his hour upon the stage
And then is heard no more. It is a tale
Told by an idiot, full of sound and fury,
Signifying nothing.　28

　　　　　Enter a Messenger.

Thou com'st to use thy tongue; thy story quickly.
MESSENGER　　Gracious my lord,
I should report that which I say I saw,
But know not how to do't.
MACBETH　　　　　　　Well, say, sir.
MESSENGER
As I did stand my watch upon the hill,
I looked toward Birnam, and anon, methought,
The wood began to move.
MACBETH　　　　　　　Liar and slave!
MESSENGER
Let me endure your wrath if't be not so.
Within this three mile may you see it coming;
I say, a moving grove.
MACBETH　　　　　　If thou speak'st false,
Upon the next tree shall thou hang alive
Till famine cling thee. If thy speech be sooth,　40
I care not if thou dost for me as much.

I pull in resolution, and begin　42
To doubt th'equivocation of the fiend
That lies like truth. "Fear not, till Birnam Wood
Do come to Dunsinane," and now a wood
Comes toward Dunsinane. Arm, arm, and out!
If this which he avouches does appear,
There is nor flying hence nor tarrying here.
I 'gin to be aweary of the sun,
And wish th'estate o'th' world were now undone.　50
Ring the alarum bell! Blow wind, come wrack,　51
At least we'll die with harness on our back.　*Exeunt.*　52

❧

5.6

　　　Drum and colors. Enter Malcolm, Siward,
　　　Macduff, and their army, with boughs.

MALCOLM
Now near enough. Your leafy screens throw down,
And show like those you are. You, worthy uncle,　2
Shall with my cousin, your right noble son,
Lead our first battle. Worthy Macduff and we　4
Shall take upon 's what else remains to do,
According to our order.
SIWARD　　　　　　　Fare you well.　6
Do we but find the tyrant's power tonight,　7
Let us be beaten, if we cannot fight.
MACDUFF
Make all our trumpets speak! Give them all breath,
Those clamorous harbingers of blood and death!　10
　　　　　　　Exeunt. Alarums continued.

❧

5.7

　　　Enter Macbeth.

MACBETH
They have tied me to a stake. I cannot fly,
But bearlike I must fight the course. What's he　2
That was not born of woman? Such a one
Am I to fear, or none.

　　　Enter young Siward.

YOUNG SIWARD　　What is thy name?
MACBETH　　Thou'lt be afraid to hear it.
YOUNG SIWARD
No, though thou call'st thyself a hotter name
Than any is in hell.
MACBETH　　　　　　My name's Macbeth.

---

10 cooled felt the chill of terror　**11 my fell of hair** the hair of my scalp　**12 dismal treatise** sad story　**13 As** as if　**15 start me** make me start.　**17 She . . . hereafter** She would have died someday, or, she should have died at some more appropriate time, freed from the relentless pressures of the moment　**19–28 Tomorrow . . . nothing** (For biblical echoes in this speech, see Psalms 18:28, 22:15, 90:9; Job 8:9, 14:1–2, 18:6.)　**20 in this** in at this　**22 lighted** (The metaphor is of a candle used to light one to bed, just as life is a brief transit for wretched mortals to their deathbeds.)　**23 dusty** (Since life, made out of dust, returns to dust.)　**40 cling** cause to shrivel.　**sooth** truth

42 pull in resolution can no longer give free rein to my self-confident determination　**50 th'estate** the settled order　**51 wrack** ruin　**52 harness** armor
5.6. Location: Dunsinane. Before Macbeth's castle.
2 show appear.　**uncle** i.e., Siward　**4 battle** battalion.　**6 order** plan of battle.　**7 Do we** If we do.　**power** army　**10 harbingers** forerunners
5.7. Location: Before Macbeth's castle; the battle action is continuous here.
2 course bout or round of bearbaiting, in which the bear was tied to a stake and dogs were set upon him.

YOUNG SIWARD
The devil himself could not pronounce a title
More hateful to mine ear.

MACBETH   No, nor more fearful.

YOUNG SIWARD
Thou liest, abhorrèd tyrant! With my sword
I'll prove the lie thou speak'st.

Fight, and young Siward slain.

MACBETH   Thou wast born of woman.   12
But swords I smile at, weapons laugh to scorn,
Brandished by man that's of a woman born.   *Exit.*

Alarums. Enter Macduff.

MACDUFF
That way the noise is. Tyrant, show thy face!
If thou be'st slain, and with no stroke of mine,
My wife and children's ghosts will haunt me still.
I cannot strike at wretched kerns, whose arms   18
Are hired to bear their staves. Either thou, Macbeth,   19
Or else my sword with an unbattered edge
I sheathe again undeeded. There thou shouldst be;   21
By this great clatter one of greatest note
Seems bruited. Let me find him, Fortune,   23
And more I beg not.   *Exit. Alarums.*

Enter Malcolm and Siward.

SIWARD
This way, my lord. The castle's gently rendered: 25
The tyrant's people on both sides do fight,
The noble thanes do bravely in the war,
The day almost itself professes yours,   28
And little is to do.

MALCOLM   We have met with foes
That strike beside us.

SIWARD   Enter, sir, the castle.   30

Exeunt. Alarum.

❖

[5.8]

Enter Macbeth.

MACBETH
Why should I play the Roman fool and die   1
On mine own sword? Whiles I see lives, the gashes   2

Do better upon them.

Enter Macduff.

MACDUFF   Turn, hellhound, turn!

MACBETH
Of all men else I have avoided thee.
But get thee back! My soul is too much charged
With blood of thine already.

MACDUFF   I have no words;
My voice is in my sword, thou bloodier villain
Than terms can give thee out!   *Fight. Alarum.*

MACBETH   Thou losest labor.   8
As easy mayst thou the intrenchant air   9
With thy keen sword impress as make me bleed.   10
Let fall thy blade on vulnerable crests;
I bear a charmèd life, which must not yield
To one of woman born.

MACDUFF   Despair thy charm,   13
And let the angel whom thou still hast served   14
Tell thee, Macduff was from his mother's womb
Untimely ripped.   16

MACBETH
Accursèd be that tongue that tells me so,
For it hath cowed my better part of man!   18
And be these juggling fiends no more believed   19
That palter with us in a double sense,   20
That keep the word of promise to our ear   21
And break it to our hope. I'll not fight with thee.   22

MACDUFF   Then yield thee, coward,
And live to be the show and gaze o'th' time!   24
We'll have thee, as our rarer monsters are,
Painted upon a pole, and underwrit,   26
"Here may you see the tyrant."

MACBETH   I will not yield
To kiss the ground before young Malcolm's feet
And to be baited with the rabble's curse.
Though Birnam Wood be come to Dunsinane,
And thou opposed, being of no woman born,
Yet I will try the last. Before my body   32
I throw my warlike shield. Lay on, Macduff,
And damned be him that first cries, "Hold, enough!"   34

Exeunt, fighting. Alarums.

*Enter fighting, and Macbeth slain. [Exit Macduff
with Macbeth's body.] Retreat, and flourish. Enter,
with drum and colors, Malcolm, Siward, Ross,
thanes, and soldiers.*

---

12 s.d. *young Siward slain* (In some unspecified way, young Siward's body must be removed from the stage; his own father enters at line 24.1 and perceives nothing amiss, and in 5.8.38 young Siward is reported *missing* in action. Perhaps Macbeth drags off the body, or perhaps it is removed by soldiers during the alarums.)   **18 kerns** (Properly, Irish foot soldiers; here, applied contemptuously to the rank and file.)
19 staves spears.   **Either thou** i.e., Either I find you and sheathe my sword in you   **21 undeeded** having seen no action.   **shouldst be** ought to be (judging by the noise)   **23 bruited** announced.   **25 gently rendered** surrendered without fighting   **28 professes** declares itself   **30 strike beside us** fight on our side, or miss us deliberately.
5.8. Location: Before Macbeth's castle, as the battle continues; after line 34, within the castle.
1 Roman fool i.e., suicide, like Brutus, Mark Antony, and others
2 Whiles . . . lives i.e., As long as I see any enemy living

8 give thee out name you, describe you.   **9 intrenchant** that cannot be cut, indivisible   **10 impress** make an impression on   **13 Despair** Despair of   **14 angel** evil angel, Macbeth's genius.   **still** always   **16 Untimely** prematurely, i.e., by Caesarian delivery   **18 better . . . man** i.e., courage.   **19 juggling** deceiving   **20 palter . . . sense** equivocate with us   **21–2 That . . . hope** that make promises we hear (and think we understand) but then break promise with what we hoped and expected.   **24 gaze o'th' time** spectacle or sideshow of the age.   **26 Painted . . . pole** i.e., painted on a board or cloth and suspended on a pole   **32 the last** i.e., my last resort: my own strength and resolution.   **34.3 Retreat** a trumpet call ordering an end to the fighting.   **34.3–4 Enter, with drum and colors, etc.** (The remainder of the play is perhaps imagined as taking place in Macbeth's castle and could be marked as a separate scene. In Shakespeare's theater, however, the shift is so nonrepresentational and without scenic alteration that the action is virtually continuous.)

MALCOLM
I would the friends we miss were safe arrived.

SIWARD
Some must go off; and yet, by these I see   36
So great a day as this is cheaply bought.

MALCOLM
Macduff is missing, and your noble son.

ROSS [to Siward]
Your son, my lord, has paid a soldier's debt.
He only lived but till he was a man,
The which no sooner had his prowess confirmed
In the unshrinking station where he fought,   42
But like a man he died.

SIWARD   Then he is dead?

ROSS
Ay, and brought off the field. Your cause of sorrow
Must not be measured by his worth, for then
It hath no end.

SIWARD   Had he his hurts before?

ROSS
Ay, on the front.

SIWARD   Why then, God's soldier be he!
Had I as many sons as I have hairs
I would not wish them to a fairer death.
And so, his knell is knolled.

MALCOLM   He's worth more sorrow,
And that I'll spend for him.

SIWARD   He's worth no more.
They say he parted well and paid his score,   52
And so, God be with him! Here comes newer comfort.

Enter Macduff, with Macbeth's head.

36 **go off** die.   **by these** to judge by these (assembled)   42 **unshrink-ing station** post from which he did not shrink   52 **parted** departed, died.   **score** reckoning

MACDUFF
Hail, King! For so thou art. Behold where stands   54
Th'usurper's cursèd head. The time is free.   55
I see thee compassed with thy kingdom's pearl,   56
That speak my salutation in their minds,
Whose voices I desire aloud with mine:
Hail, King of Scotland!

ALL   Hail, King of Scotland!   *Flourish.*

MALCOLM
We shall not spend a large expense of time
Before we reckon with your several loves   62
And make us even with you. My thanes and kinsmen,   63
Henceforth be earls, the first that ever Scotland
In such an honor named. What's more to do
Which would be planted newly with the time,   66
As calling home our exiled friends abroad
That fled the snares of watchful tyranny,
Producing forth the cruel ministers   69
Of this dead butcher and his fiendlike queen—
Who, as 'tis thought, by self and violent hands   71
Took off her life—this, and what needful else
That calls upon us, by the grace of Grace
We will perform in measure, time, and place.
So, thanks to all at once and to each one,
Whom we invite to see us crowned at Scone.   76

Flourish. Exeunt omnes.

54 **stands** i.e., on a pole   55 **free** released from tyranny.   56 **com-passed . . . pearl** surrounded by the nobles of your kingdom (literally, the pearls encircling a crown)   62 **reckon** come to a reckoning.   **several** individual   63 **make . . . you** repay your worthi-ness.   66 **would . . . time** should be established at the commence-ment of this new era   69 **Producing forth** bringing forward to trial.   **ministers** agents   71 **self and violent** her own violent   **76.1** *omnes* all.

Timon of Athens

Timon of Athens is Shakespeare's most relentless study in misanthropy. It expresses, with *King Lear*, a moral outrage at human depravity but refuses to soften anger with compassionate tears. The protagonist learns little other than bitterness from his encounters with avarice and ingratitude. In its mordant vision of human folly, *Timon of Athens* resembles a number of other Roman or classical plays. As in *Julius Caesar*, *Coriolanus*, and *Troilus and Cressida*, and to a lesser extent *Titus Andronicus*, the dominant mood is one of futility. Political conflicts end in stalemate or a victory for opportunists; the populace and their leaders are fickle and craven; private virtues of noble men must yield to crass considerations of statecraft. Banishment or self-exile is too often the reward of those who have given their lives to public service. Shakespeare's misanthropic vision in *Timon of Athens* is, then, integral to his portrayal of humanity's political and social nature in the ancient classical world. This is a world to which Shakespeare turned often during his writing career, especially during the period from about 1599 to 1608. As a group, the Roman and classical plays tend to differ from the great tragedies written during this same period (*Hamlet*, *Othello*, *King Lear*, *Macbeth*) in that the classical plays focus on a sardonic and dispiriting view of life's tragic absurdity. Even in *Antony and Cleopatra*, in which Shakespeare offers us an ennobling dream of greatness to offset the worldly failure of his protagonists, the arena of human conflict remains pitiless and disillusioning. *Timon of Athens* offers little compensatory vision; despite the attempts of Flavius and Alcibiades to ameliorate matters, the play remains bleak and dispiriting right to the very end.

Timon of Athens appears to have been written between 1605 and 1608. Evidently Shakespeare collaborated with Thomas Middleton in writing this play. Although the evidence is chiefly internal, and although specific attributions of various parts of the play to one writer or the other remain in dispute, Middleton's style reveals itself in char-acteristic sexual wordplay and Calvinist moralizing. Shakespeare appears to have been the senior partner at all events, the initiator and deviser of the overall scheme, so that, with qualifications, we can study the play as an integral part of the Shakespeare canon. It is often grouped with *King Lear* (c. 1605) on grounds of stylistic and thematic similarity. For its chief source, it uses Thomas North's translation of Plutarch's *Lives of the Noble Grecians and Romans*, a source also for *Julius Caesar*, *Antony and Cleopatra*, *Coriolanus*, and parts of other plays. *Timon of Athens* also makes use, through intermediary versions, of the dialogue called *Timon*, or *The Misanthrope*, by the Greek satirist Lucian. The play may not have been produced; the text, not printed until the 1623 Folio, appears to have been taken from the author's unfinished manuscript, with contradictory uncanceled lines (see Timon's will, 5.4.70–3), unresolved discrepancies as to the amount of money Timon gives or requests, and passages of half-versified prose. Whatever the exact date and circumstance of composition, the play certainly belongs to a period in Shakespeare's artistic career devoted to an unsparing portrayal of human villainy and corruption. The collaboration with Middleton may have given particular impetus to this. Like *Troilus and Cressida*, *Timon of Athens* defies the conventional categories of tragedy, comedy, and history. Generically, the play stands chiefly between tragedy and satire in its preoccupation with dying and sterility. The play portrays a tragic fall from greatness, and presents us with a tragic hero who learns through suffering, but the learning is less about the hero himself than about the failings of humanity. Moreover, Timon's shift from fulsome generosity to embittered misogyny deprives him of the sympathy that is essential to a fully tragic protagonist; as Apemantus says to Timon, "The middle of humanity thou never knewest, but the extremity of both ends" (4.3.305–6). The vision is thus primarily satiric rather than cathartic in its exposure of an unfeeling society. Satire prompts a comic response; we are invited to laugh sardonically at the hypocrisies of Timon's fair-weather friends, and even Timon is himself a problematic figure. The resemblance of his eventual dwelling place *"in the woods"* outside Athens (4.3.0.1) to the forest outside Athens in *A Midsummer Night's Dream* accentuates the difference in genre between romantic comedy and a dark, brooding satire. The play is also a history, drawn from historical sources, as its Folio title, *The Life of Timon of Athens*, suggests. We ought to see or read it with the expectations not simply of tragedy but also of satire and ironic history.

As a genre, in fact, the play most resembles those works that the Painter and the Poet wish to offer Timon himself: a "moral painting" and a "satire against the softness of prosperity" (1.1.95 and 5.1.32–3). Such a deliberately old-fashioned genre recalls the medieval morality plays and the "hybrid" morality plays of the 1570s and 1580s, like Thomas Lupton's *All for Money* (c. 1577) or Thomas Lodge and Robert Greene's *A Looking Glass for London and England* (1587–1591), which inveigh against usury and the neglect of military heroes. John Marston's later quasi-morality, *Histriomastix* (c. 1599), proclaims the decline of civilization through worldly insolence. Ben Jonson's *Volpone* (1605–1606), though "comical" rather than "tragical" in its satire, similarly castigates human greed. The *Parnassus* trilogy (1598–1603), a series of three mordantly satirical plays written to be acted by students at Cambridge, indulges in a massive venting of spleen against a philistine culture. Satire against governmental policies and politicians led to reprisals in the form of prohibitions, imprisonments, and book burning. *Timon of Athens*, though not topically controversial in this sense, follows a tradition of social satire derived from both English and classical models. Like most satire of the 1600s, both dramatic and nondramatic, it is crabbed in style, features a railing protagonist, and denounces through exaggerated caricature an ugly array of types representing a broad social spectrum. The genre of satiric morality play accords well with the play's acerbic view of decadence and "softness."

Human greed, with which *Timon of Athens* is so occupied, lends itself readily to satiric treatment. Avarice does not ordinarily seem terrifying at first, like the spiritual sins of jealousy or prideful ambition as portrayed in *Othello* and *Macbeth;* instead, it is disgusting, ludicrous, and incredibly tenacious. Avarice is, after all, one of the Deadly Sins. Chaucer, in his "Pardoner's Tale," follows a long tradition of medieval commentary in referring to Avarice as the pivotal Sin, the *radix malorum*, or root of all evils. Along with Pride and Envy, it is one of the sins of the spirit. It is insidious and all-embracing. We see its corrupting effects in Timon's friends. Those who sponge off him and then desert him are quick to return when he is rumored to have found gold in his exile. Greed is also self-deceiving and hypocritical. Many are the excuses offered for failing to come to Timon's aid: one friend rates Timon as a bad credit risk, another happens to be short of ready cash at the moment, a third insists that Timon's generosity to him wasn't as great as people suppose, and so on. No wonder Timon feels he must devise for such hypocrites a suitable comeuppance, consisting of a farewell banquet in which their crass expectations are rewarded with a mocking litany of curses and a dinner of water and stones.

Appropriately for this satirical depiction of human greed, the characters are virtually all types or social abstractions. Several represent the crafts and professions and are abstractly labeled as such: the Poet, the Painter, the Jeweler, the Merchant. Others are "flattering lords" or "false friends" or "thieves." Seldom in Shakespeare do we find so many characters without proper names. They are depersonalized, and we are distanced from them. Apemantus is another type, a "churlish philosopher," recognizable in all his appearances by this one feature; we learn little about him other than that he professes to scoff at worldliness with a scabrous wit, derived in part from legends about Diogenes the Cynic philosopher and other devotees of an extravagantly simple mode of life. Abstraction of this sort is close to allegory, especially an allegory of social malaise. Timon himself becomes a type in his conversion to misanthropy, "infected," as Apemantus says, by "A poor unmanly melancholy sprung / From change of fortune" (4.3.204–6). Apemantus's remark appeals to a view of personality as governed by "humors" or dominant traits, such as melancholy or irascibility, which are generated by imbalance in the body of the four "humors": blood, phlegm, bile, and black bile. Images of disease and cannibalism, prominent throughout the play, are often derived from such "humorous" imbalances. The imagery also associates character types, as in Jonson's *Volpone*, with various beasts: the lion, the fox, the ass, the wolf, the bear, and, most of all, the dog.

The nearly total absence of women in the play adds greatly to its bleakness; the tone of the play is distinctly misogynistic as well as misanthropic. Timon addresses the two women named Phrynia and Timandra who appear before him with Alcibiades as "whores" (4.3.84, 142, 170), linking them them imagistically with that "common whore of mankind" called gold (line 43). The women are indeed Alcibiades's mistresses, and are content to put up with Timon's sermonizing as long as he pays them: "More counsel with more money, bounteous Timon" (line 169). Timon's invective against them, as against women generally and all of mankind as well, is rife with images of venereal infection, painful attempts at cures, and the devastating physical consequences of the advanced stages of the disease: a collapsed nose, baldness, boneache, and sterility (see lines 145–66). The ladies who enter as Amazons in the masque at Timon's house in Act 1, scene 2 remain silent other than in a brief expression of thanks for their handsome entertainment; they function as tokens of idle evening pleasure, evoking from Apemantus an outburst against a "sweep of vanity" (1.2.131). The misogyny remains unalleviated by any positive example.

By means of such techniques, Shakespeare portrays those whom Timon comes to despise with a seemingly intentional one-sidedness; the caricatures of avarice are vivid and amusing, with little allowance for subtlety or change. The plot, too, is, by Shakespeare's standard, unusually lacking in complication: Timon discovers the ingratitude and greed of his fellow humans and retires from a world he can no longer tolerate, breathing upon it his dying curse. The dramatic tension of this uneventful story lies instead in Timon's own tortured spiritual saga, in the painful process of realization, in the revulsion, the refusal to compromise, the spuming even of honest friendship, the bitter renunciation and longing for oblivion. Alcibiades, too, is a character who interests us, offering as he does the alternatives of vengeful action against an ungrateful world or of successful conciliation. Then, too, the debate between Apemantus and Timon in which Timon rejects even the companionship of one who wishes, like him, to be the castigator of a corrupt world (4.3.200–402), is an essential part of Timon's working toward total rejection of hope. The true drama of such philosophical debate is increasingly contrasted with a static and superficial society toward which we are asked to feel revulsion.

There are no villains in *Timon of Athens*, though there are plenty of weak and foolish people. What is depressing about greed, in fact, is its insidious normality. Those who desert Timon have many prudent arguments on their side. After all, his original generosity is excessive and reckless. If his friends take advantage of him, they can at least say they have tried to warn him. Even a fool can see what lies in store. Much of Timon's wealth goes into drunken and gluttonous debauchery, into "feasts, pomps, and vainglories" (1.2.247–8). Timon does not know how to use prosperity wisely, and even his loyal servants deplore the "riot" (2.2.3). He is deaf to the friendly counsel of his steward, Flavius. For one who is so open-handed, Timon is surprisingly churlish with his creditors. And is he not presumptuous to assume that his friends will come to his aid when such vast sums are needed? Are they to be blamed for not emulating his prodigal decline into poverty? Clearly, Timon expects too much. We readily though sadly perceive, as do all Timon's friends, that commerce is a god worshiped by all; need he be so shocked at this? As bystanders, we share with Timon's choric servants the certainty that his large requests for help will be refused. And yet, no matter how stupid or blind Timon may be, the desertion of him is still monstrous. Timon suffers, partly at least, from being an idealist, in expecting that people will repay kindness with gratitude. Even Timon's well-intentioned servants know all too well that most people are not like that.

Timon thus tears himself apart in a rage at what we consider the way of the world. We find his misanthropy intemperate, and yet we cannot help being moved by his sweeping indictment of human pettiness and inhumanity. Timon's furor carries him beyond satire. He is, like Lear, all the more clear-sighted for being near to madness. Wisdom and folly exchange places, as Apemantus's friend the Fool has already pointed out (2.2.99–120). In Timon's nearly mad vision, beggars and lords are interchangeable, distinguished only by wealth and position. Love of gold, he sees, inverts everything decent in human life, making "Black white, foul fair, wrong right, / Base noble, old young, coward valiant" (4.3.29–30). Thieves and whores are at least more honest than their counterparts in everyday life, the respectable citizens of Athens and their wives, and so Timon mockingly rewards the thieves and insults the hypocrites. Yet Timon also inveighs furiously against women and all sexuality in a way that suggests feelings of betrayal. Though women occupy virtually no place in Timon's life, he himself has sought to displace women by serving as the generous source of comfort for all his friends—a self-created and narcissistic role that is destined to collapse into self-hatred and dread of all human feeling. His curse embraces the cosmos as well as humanity, inverting all semblance of hierarchical order: obedience must turn to rebellion, fidelity to incontinence, virginity to lasciviousness. "Degrees, observances, customs, and laws" must "Decline to your confounding contraries" (4.1.19–20). Clothing and cosmetics must be stripped away, as in *King Lear*, so that human monstrosity may be revealed for what it truly is.

Three persons, Apemantus, Alcibiades, and Flavius, serve as chief foils to Timon in his estrangement from humanity. Apemantus the Cynic, who first taught Timon to rail at greed, now counsels him to find stoic contentment in renunciation of desire or, conversely, to thrive as a flatterer by preying on those who have undone him (4.3.200–34). Alcibiades, the military commander banished by an ungrateful Athenian Senate for presuming to beg the life of one who had rashly shed blood in a quarrel, offers Timon the example of revenge against his enemies; subsequently, he offers Athens the olive branch with the sword, making "war breed peace" (5.4.83), in an accommodating move that is important for the conclusion of the play and its final mitigating tone. Timon, although resembling both men as railer and as victim of ingratitude, rejects their counsels as too politic, too worldly. His stand is unflinching, absolute, so lacking in compromise that his sole choice can be to curse, die, and hope for oblivion. Only Flavius, his steward, offers brief consolation. Flavius comes to him, like Kent to King Lear, offering love and service in exile. Flavius even speaks in paradoxes reminiscent of *King Lear*, calling Timon "My dearest lord, blest to be most accurst, / Rich only to be wretched" (4.2.43–4). These are precious words, showing that humanity is not utterly irredeemable. Still, this consolation is evidently too late to offset the nightmarish truth that Timon has learned. Timon experiences little of the compassionate love that comes to Lear in his madness, but he at least faces the bleakness of human existence with unbending honesty.

Stage productions in recent years have sought out instructive visual contrasts between the complacent prosperity of the play's first half and the apocalyptic barrenness of Timon's isolated hermitage at the end. The first half works easily in modern dress. Timon in his prosperity has appeared in black-tie evening dress among his money-conscious acquaintances, as in Trevor Nunn's 1971 Young Vic production with David Suchet as Timon. At other times Timon has been represented as a Texas oil tycoon (Jerry Turner's production at Ashland, Oregon, in 1978). Gregory Doran, at Stratford-upon-Avon in 1999, provided a nightclub atmosphere complete with a nightclub pianist, music by Duke Ellington, Apemantus as a master of ceremonies in dark glasses and with a wireless microphone, and a show of Cupid with Amazons in male drag. Conversely, the play's second half has invited desolation: Timon in a loincloth (Michael Pennington in Doran's 1999 production), Timon taking up his abode in a burned-out truck chassis from an automobile graveyard (Larry Yando, directed by Barbara Gaines at the Chicago Shakespeare Theatre in 2000), Timon in the ruins of a dilapidated theater building (Peter Brook's production at Les-Bouffes-du-Nord, Paris, in 1973). Through such contrastive settings, this sometimes neglected play has been shown to have a devastating relevance for a postmodern world of disillusionment.

Timon of Athens

The Actors' Names

TIMON OF ATHENS
LUCIUS *and* } *two flattering lords*
LUCULLUS,
SEMPRONIUS, *another flattering lord*
VENTIDIUS, *one of Timon's false friends*
APEMANTUS, *a churlish philosopher*
ALCIBIADES, *an Athenian captain*
[PHRYNIA, } *mistresses of Alcibiades*
TIMANDRA,
AN OLD ATHENIAN]
Certain SENATORS [*and* LORDS]
[FLAVIUS, *steward to Timon*]
POET, PAINTER, JEWELER, [*and*] MERCHANT
FLAMINIUS, *one of Timon's servants*
[LUCILIUS, *another*]
SERVILIUS, *another*

CAPHIS,
PHILOTUS'S [SERVANT],
TITUS'S [SERVANT],   } *several servants*
HORTENSIUS'S [SERVANT],   *to usurers*
[ISIDORE'S SERVANT,   [*Timon's creditors*]
Two of] VARRO'S [SERVANTS],
[A PAGE
A FOOL
Three STRANGERS
Two MESSENGERS]
Certain THIEVES [*or* BANDITTI]
cupid [*and*] *certain* MASKERS [*as Amazons*]

With divers other Servants and Attendants, [*other Lords,*
Officers, Soldiers]

[SCENE: *Athens, and the neighboring woods*]

1.1

Enter Poet, Painter, Jeweler, and Merchant, at several doors. [The Poet and Painter form one group, the Jeweler and Merchant another.]

POET   Good day, sir.

PAINTER   I am glad you're well.

POET

I have not seen you long. How goes the world?   3

PAINTER

It wears, sir, as it grows.

POET   Ay, that's well known.   4
But what particular rarity? What strange,   5
Which manifold record not matches? See,   6
Magic of bounty, all these spirits thy power   7
Hath conjured to attend! I know the merchant.

PAINTER

I know them both. Th'other's a jeweler.

MERCHANT [*to the Jeweler*]

Oh, 'tis a worthy lord!

JEWELER   Nay, that's most fixed.   10

MERCHANT

A most incomparable man, breathed, as it were,   11
To an untirable and continuate goodness.   12
He passes.   13

JEWELER   I have a jewel here—

MERCHANT

Oh, pray, let's see't. For the Lord Timon, sir?

JEWELER

If he will touch the estimate. But for that—   16

POET [*reciting to himself*]

"When we for recompense have praised the vile,
It stains the glory in that happy verse   18
Which aptly sings the good."

MERCHANT [*looking at the jewel*]   'Tis a good form.   19

JEWELER   And rich. Here is a water, look ye.   20

PAINTER [*to the Poet*]

You are rapt, sir, in some work, some dedication   21
To the great lord.

POET   A thing slipped idly from me.   22
Our poesy is as a gum which oozes   23
From whence 'tis nourished. The fire i'th' flint   24

Shows not till it be struck; our gentle flame
Provokes itself and like the current flies   26
Each bound it chafes. What have you there?   27

PAINTER

A picture, sir. When comes your book forth?

POET

Upon the heels of my presentment, sir.   29
Let's see your piece.   [*He examines the painting.*]

PAINTER   'Tis a good piece.

POET

So 'tis. This comes off well and excellent.

PAINTER

Indifferent.

POET   Admirable! How this grace   33
Speaks his own standing! What a mental power   34
This eye shoots forth! How big imagination   35
Moves in this lip! To th' dumbness of the gesture   36
One might interpret.   37

PAINTER

It is a pretty mocking of the life.   38
Here is a touch; is't good?

POET   I will say of it,
It tutors nature. Artificial strife   40
Lives in these touches, livelier than life.

Enter certain Senators.

PAINTER   How this lord is followed!

POET

The senators of Athens. Happy man!

PAINTER   Look, more!
                         [*The Senators pass over the stage, and exeunt.*]

POET

You see this confluence, this great flood of visitors.
                         [*He shows his poem.*]
I have in this rough work shaped out a man
Whom this beneath world doth embrace and hug   47
With amplest entertainment. My free drift   48
Halts not particularly, but moves itself   49
In a wide sea of tax. No leveled malice   50
Infects one comma in the course I hold,   51
But flies an eagle flight, bold and forth on,   52
Leaving no tract behind.   53

PAINTER   How shall I understand you?   54

POET   I will unbolt to you.   55

1.1. Location: Athens. Timon's house.
0.2 *several* separate   **3 long** for a long time.   **How ... world?** i.e., How are things? (But the Painter quibbles on the literal sense.)
4 wears decays.   **grows** ages.   **5 rarity** unusual occurrence. **strange** strange event   **6 Which ... matches** which all recorded history cannot equal.   **7 Magic of bounty** the remarkable attractive power of generosity.   **spirits** i.e., beings, persons (spoken of as if they were spirits conjured by magic)   **10 worthy lord** i.e., Timon. **fixed** certain.   **11 breathed** conditioned or trained so as not to be wearied (as one "breathes" horses by exercising them)   **12 untirable and continuate** inexhaustible and habitual   **13 passes** surpasses. **16 touch the estimate** offer or meet the price.   **18 happy** felicitous, matching truthful praise to a worthy object   **19 form** shape, appearance. (Refers to the jewel.)   **20 water** luster   **21 dedication** (Such works were regularly dedicated to great nobles.)   **22 idly** casually **23–4 Our ... nourished** The poetry we write oozes from us like gummy sap from the tree that nourishes it.   **24 The fire i'th' flint** (Flint, struck against a stone, yields a spark, and so may seem to have fire latent in it.)

26 Provokes itself is self-generating   **26–7 flies ... chafes** seeks escape from the riverbanks that confine it.   **29 Upon ... presentment** As soon as I have presented it (to Lord Timon, in hopes of obtaining his patronage)   **33 Indifferent** Not bad, so-so.   **this grace** i.e., of the person in the picture   **34 Speaks ... standing** conveys the dignity of its subject.   **35 big** largely   **36–7 To ... interpret** One might easily supply words to express this silent gesture.   **38 mocking** mirroring **40 Artificial strife** The striving of art to surpass nature   **47 beneath** sublunar, beneath the moon   **48 entertainment** welcome.   **drift** design   **49 Halts not particularly** doesn't concern itself with criticizing anyone individually   **50 tax** censure. (The Poet's defense of satire is a familiar one from classical poets like Horace and neoclassicists like Ben Jonson, that the satirist is a moral guardian of society who is entitled to free speech so long as he satirizes types of abuses rather than libeling individuals.)   **leveled** aimed, as a gun is aimed at a particular object   **51 comma** i.e., detail   **52 forth on** straight on **53 tract** track, trace   **54 How ... you?** What do you mean?   **55 unbolt** unlock, interpret

You see how all conditions, how all minds,   56
As well of glib and slippery creatures as
Of grave and austere quality, tender down   58
Their services to Lord Timon. His large fortune,
Upon his good and gracious nature hanging,   60
Subdues and properties to his love and tendance   61
All sorts of hearts; yea, from the glass-faced flatterer   62
To Apemantus, that few things loves better
Than to abhor himself—even he drops down
The knee before him and returns in peace   65
Most rich in Timon's nod.   66
PAINTER   I saw them speak together.
POET
Sir, I have upon a high and pleasant hill
Feigned Fortune to be throned. The base o'th' mount   69
Is ranked with all deserts, all kind of natures,   70
That labor on the bosom of this sphere   71
To propagate their states. Amongst them all   72
Whose eyes are on this sovereign lady fixed,
One do I personate of Lord Timon's frame,   74
Whom Fortune with her ivory hand wafts to her,   75
Whose present grace to present slaves and servants   76
Translates his rivals.
PAINTER   'Tis conceived to scope.   77
This throne, this Fortune, and this hill, methinks,
With one man beckoned from the rest below,
Bowing his head against the steepy mount   80
To climb his happiness, would be well expressed   81
In our condition.
POET   Nay, sir, but hear me on.   82
All those which were his fellows but of late—
Some better than his value—on the moment   84
Follow his strides, his lobbies fill with tendance,   85
Rain sacrificial whisperings in his ear,   86
Make sacred even his stirrup, and through him   87
Drink the free air.
PAINTER   Ay, marry, what of these?   88
POET
When Fortune in her shift and change of mood

Spurns down her late beloved, all his dependents,   90
Which labored after him to the mountain's top
Even on their knees and hands, let him slip down,
Not one accompanying his declining foot.
PAINTER   'Tis common.
A thousand moral paintings I can show   95
That shall demonstrate these quick blows of Fortune's
More pregnantly than words. Yet you do well
To show Lord Timon that mean eyes have seen   98
The foot above the head.   99

*Trumpets sound. Enter Lord Timon, addressing
himself courteously to every suitor; [a Messenger
from Ventidius talking with him; Lucilius and
other servants following].*

TIMON   Imprisoned is he, say you?
MESSENGER
Ay, my good lord. Five talents is his debt,   101
His means most short, his creditors most strait.   102
Your honorable letter he desires   103
To those have shut him up, which failing   104
Periods his comfort.
TIMON   Noble Ventidius! Well,   105
I am not of that feather to shake off   106
My friend when he must need me. I do know him   107
A gentleman that well deserves a help,
Which he shall have. I'll pay the debt and free him.
MESSENGER   Your Lordship ever binds him.   110
TIMON
Commend me to him. I will send his ransom;
And being enfranchised, bid him come to me.   112
'Tis not enough to help the feeble up,
But to support him after. Fare you well.   114
MESSENGER   All happiness to Your Honor!   *Exit.*

Enter an Old Athenian.

OLD ATHENIAN
Lord Timon, hear me speak.
TIMON   Freely, good father.   116
OLD ATHENIAN
Thou hast a servant named Lucilius.
TIMON   I have so. What of him?
OLD ATHENIAN
Most noble Timon, call the man before thee.
TIMON
Attends he here or no? Lucilius!

56 conditions ranks, temperaments   **58 quality** nature.   **tender down** tender, offer   **60 hanging** depending. (The Poet suggests that good nature counts for little without a large fortune to attend it.) **61 properties** appropriates.   **love and tendance** loving and being in attendance on him   **62 glass-faced** reflecting superficially the tastes and whims of his patron   **65 returns** departs   **66 in Timon's nod** for having been acknowledged by Timon.   **69 Feigned** imagined, supposed   **70 ranked … deserts** filled with persons of all degrees of merit standing in ranks   **71 this sphere** i.e., the earth   **72 propagate their states** enlarge their fortunes.   **74 personate** represent.   **frame** mold, shape   **75 ivory** white.   **wafts** beckons, waves   **76–7 Whose … rivals** whose (Fortune's) present gracious favor transforms his (Timon's) rivals immediately into followers and servants.   **77 to scope** to the purpose, in correct proportion.   **80 Bowing his head** i.e., bending forward with the effort.   **steepy** steep   **81 his happiness** to his good fortune   **81–2 would … condition** would find a striking parallel in the human condition.   **82 hear me on** hear me speak further.   **84 better … value** of more worth, and worth more, than he. **on the moment** immediately   **85 his lobbies … tendance** fill the anterooms of his house with their attentive presence   **86 Rain … ear** whisper reverentially to him as if he were a god to be sacrificed to   **87 stirrup** i.e., as they help him to his horse   **87–8 through … air** seem to breathe the free air only through his bounty.   **88 marry** (A mild oath, originally "By the Virgin Mary.")

90 Spurns down kicks or thrusts down   **95 moral paintings** paintings pointing out a moral   **98 mean eyes** even the eyes of persons of low degree   **99 The foot … head** i.e., highest fortune tumbling headlong downward by the turn of Fortune's wheel, or, the foot of Fortune poised over the head of the once-prosperous man.   **101 talents** units of money today worth $2,000 or more. (But Shakespeare was evidently uncertain about the *talent's* value as he wrote this play. *Talents* is also a biblical term; see, for example, Matthew 2:14–29.) **102 short** limited.   **strait** severe, exacting.   **103 Your … letter** A letter from your honor   **104 those** those who   **104–5 which failing Periods** the lack of which puts an end to   **106 feather** i.e., disposition (as in "birds of a feather")   **107 know him** know him to be **110 binds him** i.e., to grateful obligation.   **112 enfranchised** set free **114 But** i.e., but one must continue   **116 Freely** Readily, gladly. **father** (Respectful term of address to an old man.)

LUCILIUS   Here, at Your Lordship's service.

OLD ATHENIAN
This fellow here, Lord Timon, this thy creature,   122
By night frequents my house. I am a man
That from my first have been inclined to thrift,
And my estate deserves an heir more raised   125
Than one which holds a trencher.

TIMON   Well, what further?   126

OLD ATHENIAN
One only daughter have I, no kin else   128
On whom I may confer what I have got.
The maid is fair, o'th' youngest for a bride,   129
And I have bred her at my dearest cost   130
In qualities of the best. This man of thine
Attempts her love. I prithee, noble lord,   132
Join with me to forbid him her resort;   133
Myself have spoke in vain.

TIMON   The man is honest.

OLD ATHENIAN   Therefore he will be, Timon.   136
His honesty rewards him in itself;
It must not bear my daughter.   138

TIMON   Does she love him?

OLD ATHENIAN   She is young and apt.   140
Our own precedent passions do instruct us   141
What levity's in youth.

TIMON [to Lucilius]   Love you the maid?

LUCILIUS
Ay, my good lord, and she accepts of it.   143

OLD ATHENIAN
If in her marriage my consent is missing,
I call the gods to witness, I will choose
Mine heir from forth the beggars of the world
And dispossess her all.   147

TIMON   How shall she be endowed   148
If she be mated with an equal husband?   149

OLD ATHENIAN
Three talents on the present; in future, all.   150

TIMON
This gentleman of mine hath served me long;
To build his fortune I will strain a little,
For 'tis a bond in men. Give him thy daughter.   153
What you bestow, in him I'll counterpoise,   154
And make him weigh with her.

OLD ATHENIAN   Most noble lord,   155
Pawn me to this your honor, she is his.   156

TIMON
My hand to thee; mine honor on my promise.

LUCILIUS
Humbly I thank Your Lordship. Never may
That state or fortune fall into my keeping   159
Which is not owed to you!   160
                    Exeunt [Lucilius and Old Athenian].

POET [presenting his poem]
Vouchsafe my labor, and long live Your Lordship!   161

TIMON
I thank you; you shall hear from me anon.   162
Go not away.—What have you there, my friend?

PAINTER
A piece of painting, which I do beseech   164
Your Lordship to accept.   [He presents his painting.]

TIMON   Painting is welcome.
The painting is almost the natural man;   166
For since dishonor traffics with man's nature,   167
He is but outside; these penciled figures are   168
Even such as they give out. I like your work,   169
And you shall find I like it. Wait attendance   170
Till you hear further from me.

PAINTER   The gods preserve ye!

TIMON
Well fare you, gentleman. Give me your hand;
We must needs dine together.—Sir, your jewel   173
Hath suffered under praise.

JEWELER   What, my lord, dispraise?   174

TIMON
A mere satiety of commendations.   175
If I should pay you for't as 'tis extolled,
It would unclew me quite.

JEWELER   My lord, 'tis rated   177
As those which sell would give; but you well know   178
Things of like value differing in the owners
Are prizèd by their masters. Believe't, dear lord,   180
You mend the jewel by the wearing it.
                            [He presents a jewel.]

TIMON   Well mocked.   182

MERCHANT
No, my good lord, he speaks the common tongue   183
Which all men speak with him.

            Enter Apemantus.

TIMON   Look who comes here. Will you be chid?   185

JEWELER   We'll bear, with Your Lordship.   186

MERCHANT   He'll spare none.

---

122 **creature** dependent, hanger-on   125 **more raised** of higher social position   126 **holds a trencher** i.e., serves at table, handling wooden dishes.   128 **got** acquired.   129 **o'th' . . . bride** just of marriageable age   130 **bred . . . cost** brought her up at great expense   132 **Attempts** tries to win   133 **her resort** access to her   136 **Therefore . . . be** If he really is honest he will continue to be so for honesty's sake   138 **bear my daughter** carry off my daughter into the bargain.   140 **apt** easily wooed, impressionable.   141 **precedent** former (when we were young)   143 **accepts of** accepts   147 **all** wholly.   148 **How . . . endowed** What dowry will she be given   149 **an equal husband** one of equal estate.   150 **on the present** immediately   153 **bond in** obligation among   154 **counterpoise** match, counterbalance   155 **weigh with her** be equal to her in estate.   156 **Pawn . . . honor** If you'll pledge your word of honor to do as you have said

159 **That** i.e., any   160 **owed to you** acknowledged to be from you.   161 **Vouchsafe** Deign to accept   162 **anon** shortly.   164 **piece** example, specimen   166–9 **The painting . . . out** Painting reveals the truth about human nature; for, since deception is inherent in human nature, our outward appearances necessarily conceal much within, whereas paintings are exactly what they show themselves to be.   170 **Wait** Remain in   173 **must needs** must   174 **Hath . . . praise** has been overvalued, to the would-be purchaser's disadvantage. (But the Jeweler misunderstands as "suffered underpraise.")   175 **mere** utter   177 **unclew** unwind, i.e., ruin   178 **As . . . give** at a price which merchants would pay, i.e., at cost   180 **prizèd . . . masters** valued differently by different owners. (Accordingly, the gem will increase in value because Timon will wear it.)   182 **Well mocked** A well-turned bit of flattery, well counterfeited.   183 **common tongue** general opinion   185 **Will you be chid?** Are you prepared to be scolded?   186 **We'll . . Lordship** i.e., We'll put up with it if Your Lordship can.

TIMON
    Good morrow to thee, gentle Apemantus!

APEMANTUS
    Till I be gentle, stay thou for thy good morrow—   189
    When thou art Timon's dog, and these knaves honest. 190

TIMON
    Why dost thou call them knaves? Thou know'st them
    not.

APEMANTUS   Are they not Athenians?

TIMON   Yes.

APEMANTUS   Then I repent not.   194

JEWELER   You know me, Apemantus?

APEMANTUS   Thou know'st I do. I called thee by thy 196
    name.   197

TIMON   Thou art proud, Apemantus.

APEMANTUS   Of nothing so much as that I am not like
    Timon.

TIMON   Whither art going?

APEMANTUS   To knock out an honest Athenian's brains.

TIMON   That's a deed thou'lt die for.

APEMANTUS   Right, if doing nothing be death by th' law. 204

TIMON   How lik'st thou this picture, Apemantus?

APEMANTUS   The best, for the innocence.   206

TIMON   Wrought he not well that painted it?

APEMANTUS   He wrought better that made the painter,
    and yet he's but a filthy piece of work.

PAINTER   You're a dog.   210

APEMANTUS   Thy mother's of my generation. What's 211
    she, if I be a dog?   212

TIMON   Wilt dine with me, Apemantus?

APEMANTUS   No. I eat not lords.   214

TIMON   An thou shouldst, thou'dst anger ladies. 215

APEMANTUS   Oh, they eat lords. So they come by great 216
    bellies.   217

TIMON   That's a lascivious apprehension.   218

APEMANTUS   So thou apprehend'st it. Take it for thy labor. 219

TIMON   How dost thou like this jewel, Apemantus?

APEMANTUS   Not so well as plain dealing, which will
    not cost a man a doit.   222

TIMON   What dost thou think 'tis worth?

APEMANTUS   Not worth my thinking.—How now,
    poet?

POET   How now, philosopher?

APEMANTUS   Thou liest.

POET   Art not one?

APEMANTUS   Yes.

POET   Then I lie not.

APEMANTUS   Art not a poet?

POET   Yes.

APEMANTUS   Then thou liest. Look in thy last work, 233
    where thou hast feigned him a worthy fellow.   234

POET   That's not feigned. He is so.

APEMANTUS   Yes, he is worthy of thee, and to pay thee
    for thy labor. He that loves to be flattered is worthy
    o'th' flatterer. Heavens, that I were a lord!

TIMON   What wouldst do then, Apemantus?

APEMANTUS   E'en as Apemantus does now: hate a lord
    with my heart.

TIMON   What, thyself?

APEMANTUS   Ay.

TIMON   Wherefore?

APEMANTUS   That I had no angry wit to be a lord.—Art 245
    not thou a merchant?

MERCHANT   Ay, Apemantus.

APEMANTUS   Traffic confound thee, if the gods will not! 248

MERCHANT   If traffic do it, the gods do it.   249

APEMANTUS   Traffic's thy god, and thy god confound
    thee!

       Trumpet sounds. Enter a Messenger.

TIMON   What trumpet's that?

MESSENGER
    'Tis Alcibiades and some twenty horse,   253
    All of companionship.   254

TIMON
    Pray, entertain them; give them guide to us. 255
                 [Exeunt some attendants.]
    [To his guests] You must needs dine with me. Go not
    you hence
    Till I have thanked you.—When dinner's done,
    Show me this piece.—I am joyful of your sights. 258

       Enter Alcibiades, with the rest.

    Most welcome, sir!

APEMANTUS   So, so, there! Aches contract 259
    And starve your supple joints! That there should be 260
    Small love amongst these sweet knaves, and all
    This courtesy! The strain of man's bred out 262
    Into baboon and monkey.

ALCIBIADES *[to Timon]*
    Sir, you have saved my longing, and I feed 264

189–90 Till . . . honest i.e., You must wait for my "good morrow" until I have become free of satirical sharpness and until men are free of the faults I criticize, something as likely to happen as Timon changing places with his dog. **194 repent not** don't regret what I said. **196–7 thy name** i.e., "knave." (See line 190.) **204 Right . . . law** i.e., Since Athenians have no brains or honesty, I will be doing nothing that is a capital offense. **206 innocence** innocuous character, inability to do harm. **210 dog** (*Cynic* is derived from the Greek for "dog.") **211 generation** species. **211–12 What's she** i.e., Isn't she a bitch **214 I . . . lords** i.e., I refuse to dine (in sycophantic fashion) at the tables of influential men and consume their wealth. **215 An** If **216 eat** (1) take into their bellies (sexually) (2) consume the substance of. **come by** acquire **216–17 great bellies** (1) pregnant wombs (2) bellies plump from eating. **218 apprehension** interpretation. **219 So . . . labor** That's your interpretation, not mine. You can keep it for your pains. (With a pun on *apprehending* as seizing, and on *labor*, "giving birth.") **222 doit** half a farthing, coin of slight value.

233 Then thou liest (Because poets are supposed to feign.) **234 him** i.e., Timon **245 That . . . lord** (Apemantus quips that since he professes to hate lords, if he were himself a lord he could hate himself with all his angry wit.) **248 Traffic confound** May business or trade ruin **249 If . . . do it** i.e., If I were to suffer financial ruin in merchant shipping (by shipwreck or other disaster), it would be at the behest of the gods. **253 horse** horsemen **254 of companionship** of a company, coming in a body. **255 Pray . . . us** Please receive them hospitably and show them in. **258 of your sights** to see you. **259 So, so, there** Well, well, look at that (i.e., at all the bowing and scraping). **260 starve** destroy **262 strain** race, stock. **bred out** degenerated **264 saved** anticipated and thus prevented

Most hungerly on your sight.

TIMON   Right welcome, sir!   265
Ere we depart, we'll share a bounteous time   266
In different pleasures. Pray you, let us in.   267
                          Exeunt [all except Apemantus].

          Enter two Lords.

FIRST LORD   What time o'day is't, Apemantus?
APEMANTUS   Time to be honest.
FIRST LORD   That time serves still.   270
APEMANTUS   The most accursèd thou, that still omitt'st it.   271
SECOND LORD   Thou art going to Lord Timon's feast?
APEMANTUS   Ay, to see meat fill knaves and wine heat fools.
SECOND LORD   Fare thee well, fare thee well.
APEMANTUS   Thou art a fool to bid me farewell twice.
SECOND LORD   Why, Apemantus?
APEMANTUS   Shouldst have kept one to thyself, for I mean to give thee none.
FIRST LORD   Hang thyself!
APEMANTUS   No, I will do nothing at thy bidding. Make thy requests to thy friend.
SECOND LORD   Away, unpeaceable dog, or I'll spurn   283
thee hence!
APEMANTUS   I will fly, like a dog, the heels o'th' ass.   285
                          [Exit.]
FIRST LORD
He's opposite to humanity. Come, shall we in   286
And taste Lord Timon's bounty? He outgoes   287
The very heart of kindness.   288
SECOND LORD
He pours it out. Plutus, the god of gold,
Is but his steward. No meed but he repays   290
Sevenfold above itself; no gift to him
But breeds the giver a return exceeding
All use of quittance.
FIRST LORD   The noblest mind he carries   293
That ever governed man.
SECOND LORD
Long may he live in fortunes! Shall we in?
FIRST LORD   I'll keep you company.   *Exeunt.*

                    ❖

[1.2]

          Hautboys playing loud music. A great banquet
          served in, [Flavius and others attending]; and
          then enter Lord Timon, the states, the Athenian
          Lords, [Alcibiades, and] Ventidius (which Timon
          redeemed from prison). Then comes, dropping after
          all, Apemantus, discontentedly, like himself.

VENTIDIUS   Most honored Timon,
It hath pleased the gods to remember my father's age
And call him to long peace.   3
He is gone happy and has left me rich.
Then, as in grateful virtue I am bound
To your free heart, I do return those talents,   6
Doubled with thanks and service, from whose help
I derived liberty.   *[He offers money.]*
TIMON   Oh, by no means,
Honest Ventidius. You mistake my love.
I gave it freely ever, and there's none
Can truly say he gives if he receives.   12
If our betters play at that game, we must not dare   13
To imitate them. Faults that are rich are fair.   14
VENTIDIUS   A noble spirit!
          [They all stand ceremoniously looking on Timon.]
TIMON
Nay, my lords, ceremony was but devised at first
To set a gloss on faint deeds, hollow welcomes,   17
Recanting goodness, sorry ere 'tis shown;   18
But where there is true friendship, there needs none.   19
Pray, sit. More welcome are ye my fortunes
Than my fortunes to me.   *[They sit.]*
FIRST LORD
My lord, we always have confessed it.   22
APEMANTUS
Ho, ho, confessed it? Hanged it, have you not?   23
TIMON
Oh, Apemantus, you are welcome.
APEMANTUS   No,
You shall not make me welcome.
I come to have thee thrust me out of doors.   26
TIMON
Fie, thou'rt a churl. You've got a humor there   27
Does not become a man; 'tis much to blame.   28
They say, my lords, *Ira furor brevis est*, but yond   29
man is ever angry. Go, let him have a table by himself,
for he does neither affect company nor is he fit for't,   31
indeed.
APEMANTUS   Let me stay at thine apperil, Timon. I come   33
to observe; I give thee warning on't.
TIMON   I take no heed of thee. Thou'rt an Athenian,
therefore welcome. I myself would have no power;   36
prithee, let my meat make thee silent.   37
APEMANTUS   I scorn thy meat; 'twould choke me, for I   38
should ne'er flatter thee. O you gods, what a number   39

265 **hungerly . . . on your sight** hungrily on the sight of you.
266 **depart** part company   267 **different** various.   **in** enter.
270 **still** always.   271 **The . . . it** The more accursed are you, for continually failing to make good use of time.   283 **unpeaceable** quarrelsome, incessantly barking.   **spurn** kick   285 **fly** flee   286 **opposite to** antagonistic to and out of step with   287 **outgoes** surpasses
288 **heart** essence   290 **meed** merit, or, gift   293 **use of quittance** usual rates of repayment with interest.
1.2. Location: A banqueting room in Timon's house.
0.1 *Hautboys* oboelike instruments.   0.3 *states* i.e., rulers of the state, senators.   0.5 *dropping* entering casually   0.6 *like himself* not in finery.

3 **long peace** eternal rest.   6 **free** generous   12 **gives . . . receives** (Compare with Acts 20:35: "It is more blessed to give than to receive.") 13 **at that game** i.e., at taking in wealth while seeming to be generous 14 **Faults . . . fair** Faults in rich persons are overlooked because they are wealthy.   17 **set a gloss on** give a speciously fair appearance to 18 **Recanting goodness** generosity that takes back what it has offered 19 **there needs none** there is no need for ceremony.   22 **confessed it** acknowledged the truth of what you say.   23 **Hanged it** i.e., Killed it instead. (Apemantus replies with a jesting allusion to the saying, "Confess and be hanged.")   26 **have thee thrust** provoke you into thrusting   27 **churl** surly person.   **humor** disposition   28 **Does** that does   29 *Ira furor brevis est* Wrath is a brief madness (Horace's *Epistles*, 1.2.62)   31 **affect** desire, seek   33 **thine apperil** your peril, risk 36 **would . . . power** do not wish the power (to silence you)   37 **meat** food   38–9 **'twould . . . thee** (Apemantus implies that Timon's food is to reward flatterers; Apemantus, being none, would choke on it.)

of men eats Timon, and he sees 'em not! It grieves me
to see so many dip their meat in one man's blood; and   41
all the madness is, he cheers them up, too.   42
I wonder men dare trust themselves with men.
Methinks they should invite them without knives;   44
Good for their meat, and safer for their lives.   45
There's much example for't. The fellow that sits next
him, now parts bread with him, pledges the breath of   47
him in a divided draft, is the readiest man to kill   48
him. 'T has been proved. If I were a huge man, I   49
should fear to drink at meals,
Lest they should spy my windpipe's dangerous notes.   51
Great men should drink with harness on their throats.   52
TIMON [*toasting a Lord who drinks to him*]
My lord, in heart! And let the health go round.   53
SECOND LORD
Let it flow this way, my good lord.   54
APEMANTUS   Flow this way? A brave fellow! He keeps   55
his tides well. Those healths will make thee and thy   56
state look ill, Timon.   57
Here's that which is too weak to be a sinner: 58
Honest water, which ne'er left man i'th' mire.   59
This and my food are equals; there's no odds.   60
Feasts are too proud to give thanks to the gods.   61

Apemantus' grace.

Immortal gods, I crave no pelf.   62
I pray for no man but myself.
Grant I may never prove so fond   64
To trust man on his oath or bond,   65
Or a harlot for her weeping,
Or a dog that seems a-sleeping,
Or a keeper with my freedom,   68
Or my friends, if I should need 'em.
Amen. So fall to't.   70
Rich men sin, and I eat root. [*He eats and drinks.*]   71
Much good dich thy good heart, Apemantus!   72

TIMON   Captain Alcibiades, your heart's in the field   73
now.
ALCIBIADES   My heart is ever at your service, my lord.
TIMON   You had rather be at a breakfast of enemies   76
than a dinner of friends.   77
ALCIBIADES   So they were bleeding new, my lord,   78
there's no meat like 'em. I could wish my best friend
at such a feast.
APEMANTUS   Would all those flatterers were thine enemies then, that then thou mightst kill 'em—and bid
me to 'em!   83
FIRST LORD   Might we but have that happiness, my lord,
that you would once use our hearts, whereby we   85
might express some part of our zeals, we should think   86
ourselves forever perfect.   87
TIMON   Oh, no doubt, my good friends, but the gods
themselves have provided that I shall have much help
from you. How had you been my friends else? Why
have you that charitable title from thousands, did not   91
you chiefly belong to my heart? I have told more of   92
you to myself than you can with modesty speak in   93
your own behalf; and thus far I confirm you. O you   94
gods, think I, what need we have any friends if we   95
should ne'er have need of 'em? They were the most
needless creatures living should we ne'er have use for   97
'em, and would most resemble sweet instruments   98
hung up in cases, that keeps their sounds to themselves. Why, I have often wished myself poorer, that I
might come nearer to you. We are born to do benefits;   101
and what better or properer can we call our own than   102
the riches of our friends? Oh, what a precious comfort
'tis to have so many, like brothers, commanding one   104
another's fortunes? Oh, joy's e'en made away ere't can   105
be born! Mine eyes cannot hold out water, methinks.
To forget their faults, I drink to you.   107
[*He weeps, and drinks a toast.*]
APEMANTUS   Thou weep'st to make them drink, Timon.   108
SECOND LORD [*to Timon*]
Joy had the like conception in our eyes,
And at that instant like a babe sprung up.   110
APEMANTUS
Ho, ho! I laugh to think that babe a bastard.   111
THIRD LORD [*to Timon*]
I promise you, my lord, you moved me much.   112
APEMANTUS   Much!   *Sound tucket* [*within*].   113

---

41 one man's blood (Possible allusion to the Last Supper; the *fellow* in lines 46–9, who shares food and drink only to betray his host, is like Judas.)   **42 all . . . too** the craziest aspect of his behavior is that he encourages them.   **44 without knives** (Refers to the Renaissance custom of guests bringing their own knives.)   **45 Good . . . lives** Without knives, the guests will consume less food and be less likely to use the knives to commit mayhem.   **47 parts** shares.   **pledges the breath** i.e., drinks to the health   **48 a divided draft** a cup that they share   **49 'T has been proved** There are precedents for it. (Compare with line 143.)   **huge** great in rank and wealth   **51 Lest . . . notes** i.e., lest they should be able to discern where best to slit my throat at the windpipe. (It is the spying that is dangerous, not the *notes* or sounds made by the windpipe.)   **52 harness** armor   **53 in heart** heartily.   **health** toast, and the cup   **54 flow** circulate   **55 brave** fine, foppish. (Said ironically.)   **56 tides** times, seasons. (With quibbling reference to *flow* of tides; Apemantus comments sardonically that the Second Lord is making sure that he will get plenty to drink.)   **57 state** (1) physical condition (2) fortune, estate   **58 a sinner** an incentive to sin   **59 i'th' mire** i.e., in trouble.   **60–1 This . . . gods** There's nothing to choose between this simple water and the honest plain food I eat; feasts, as the products of insolent worldliness, are not a fit offering to the gods.   **62 pelf** property, possessions.   **64 fond** foolish   **65 To** as to   **68 keeper** jailer   **70 fall to't** i.e., begin to eat.   **71 Rich . . root** i.e., The rich sin in gluttony, while I eat sparingly.   **72 dich** may it do. (Originally a contraction of "d' it ye" in the phrase "much good do it you.")

73 field battlefield   **76 a breakfast of enemies** a feast of slaughter on the battlefield   **77 of** among   **78 So** Provided that   **83 to 'em** i.e., to eat them.   **85 use our hearts** make trial of our love   **87 forever perfect** completely happy.   **91 charitable . . . from** beloved name from among   **92 told** (1) recited (2) counted   **92–3 of you** i.e., concerning your deservings   **94 confirm you** endorse your claim (to be my worthy friends).   **95 what** why   **97 needless** useless   **98 instruments** musical instruments   **101 come . . . you** come to you in need.   **102 properer** more fittingly   **104 commanding** having at their disposal   **105 made away** undone, turned to tears   **107 To . . . faults** i.e., To mask my weakness in giving way to tears   **108 Thou . . . drink** i.e., You ought to weep at the way your absurd sentimentalizing is just giving them an excuse to drink up your substance   **110 sprung up** (1) leaped from the womb (2) welled up like a spring of tears.   **111 bastard** i.e., illegitimate, without genuine source. (Refers to the guests' tears.)   **112 promise** assure   **113 Much** (An expression of contemptuous disbelief; playing on *much* in the previous line.)   **s.d. tucket** trumpet call

TIMON

What means that trump?

Enter Servant.

How now?   114

SERVANT   Please you, my lord, there are certain ladies
most desirous of admittance.

TIMON   Ladies? What are their wills?

SERVANT   There comes with them a forerunner, my
lord, which bears that office to signify their pleasures.   119

TIMON   I pray, let them be admitted.   [*Exit Servant.*]

Enter Cupid.

CUPID

Hail to thee, worthy Timon, and to all
That of his bounties taste! The five best senses
Acknowledge thee their patron, and come freely
To gratulate thy plenteous bosom. Th'ear,   124
Taste, touch, and smell, pleased from thy table rise;
They only now come but to feast thine eyes.   126

TIMON

They're welcome all. Let 'em have kind admittance.
Music, make their welcome!

                            [*Cupid summons the maskers.*]

FIRST LORD

You see, my lord, how ample you're beloved.   129

[*Music.*] *Enter a masque of Ladies* [*as*] *Amazons,
with lutes in their hands, dancing and playing.*

APEMANTUS   Hoyday!   130
What a sweep of vanity comes this way!
They dance? They are madwomen.
Like madness is the glory of this life   133
As this pomp shows to a little oil and root.   134
We make ourselves fools to disport ourselves   135
And spend our flatteries to drink those men   136
Upon whose age we void it up again   137
With poisonous spite and envy.   138
Who lives that's not depravèd or depraves?   139
Who dies that bears not one spurn to their graves   140
Of their friends' gift?   141
I should fear those that dance before me now
Would one day stamp upon me. 'T has been done;
Men shut their doors against a setting sun.   144

*The Lords rise from table, with much adoring of
Timon; and to show their loves each singles out an
Amazon, and all dance, men with women, a lofty
strain or two to the hautboys, and cease.*

114 **trump** trumpet blast.   119 **which** who.   **office** function.   **pleasures**
wishes.   124 **To . . . bosom** to greet your generosity of heart.   126 **They**
. . . but the maskers come now only   129 **ample** amply   130 **Hoyday**
(Exclamation denoting surprise; a variety of "heyday.")   133–4 **Like . . .**
root i.e., The insane vaingloriousness of this life is made plain when we
compare the pomp of this lavish entertainment with the bare necessities
needed to maintain life.   135–8 **We . . . envy** We foolishly devise entertainments and lavish our flattering attentions in drinking toasts to men
upon whom, when they are old, we will vomit up what we have drunk
in poisonous spite and malice.   139 **Who . . . depraves?** Who is there
alive that is not either vilified himself or vilifies others?   140–1 **Who . . .**
gift? Who is there that does not go to his grave bearing the injuries of
his dearest friends?   144.1 *adoring of* paying homage to

TIMON

You have done our pleasures much grace, fair ladies,
Set a fair fashion on our entertainment,   146
Which was not half so beautiful and kind.   147
You have added worth unto't and luster,
And entertained me with mine own device.   149
I am to thank you for't.   150

FIRST LADY

My lord, you take us even at the best.   151

APEMANTUS   Faith, for the worst is filthy and would not   152
hold taking, I doubt me.   153

TIMON

Ladies, there is an idle banquet attends you;   154
Please you to dispose yourselves.   155

ALL LADIES   Most thankfully, my lord.
                            Exeunt [*Cupid and Ladies*].

TIMON   Flavius!

FLAVIUS

My lord?

TIMON   The little casket bring me hither.

FLAVIUS   Yes, my lord. [*Aside*] More jewels yet?
There is no crossing him in 's humor;   160
Else I should tell him well, i'faith I should,   161
When all's spent, he'd be crossed then, an he could. 162
'Tis pity bounty had not eyes behind,   163
That man might ne'er be wretched for his mind.   164
                                                                     Exit.

FIRST LORD   Where be our men?

SERVANT   Here, my lord, in readiness.

SECOND LORD

Our horses!

Enter Flavius [*with the casket*].

TIMON   Oh, my friends, I have one word
To say to you. Look you, my good lord,
I must entreat you honor me so much   169
As to advance this jewel; accept it and wear it,   170
Kind my lord.   [*He offers a jewel.*] 171

FIRST LORD

I am so far already in your gifts—   172

ALL   So are we all.

Enter a Servant.

SERVANT

My lord, there are certain nobles of the Senate

146 **Set . . . on** given grace and elegance to   147 **was not** i.e., before
your arrival was not.   **kind** gracious.   149 **And . . . device** (This
could mean that Timon designed the masque himself to surprise his
guests, but more probably he is expressing pleasure at a masque
especially designed for him.)   150 **am to** am under obligation to
151 **take . . . best** i.e., praise us most generously.   152–3 **Faith . . .**
doubt me i.e., Truly, if you were to take your guests at their worst,
take them sexually, you'd find them filthy and rotten with venereal
disease, I fear.   154 **idle** trifling, slight   155 **dispose yourselves** take
your places.   160 **humor** frame of mind   161 **well** plainly
162 **When . . . could** when all the money is gone, he'd be glad enough
to have me try to stop him, if it weren't too late. (Or, he'd be happy to
have someone cross his palm with silver, give him money.)
163–4 **'Tis . . . mind** It's a pity his bounty was not wary, so that he
might not have to suffer privation on account of his bounteous inclination.   169 **you honor** you to honor   170 **advance** raise in value by
accepting   171 **Kind my lord** my kind lord.   172 **in your gifts**
indebted to you for your gifts

Newly alighted and come to visit you.

TIMON
They are fairly welcome.   [*Exit Servant.*]

FLAVIUS   I beseech Your Honor,   176
Vouchsafe me a word; it does concern you near.   177

TIMON
Near? Why then, another time I'll hear thee.
I prithee, let's be provided to show them
entertainment.

FLAVIUS [*aside*]   I scarce know how.

Enter another Servant.

SECOND SERVANT
May it please Your Honor, Lord Lucius,
Out of his free love, hath presented to you
Four milk-white horses trapped in silver.   183

TIMON
I shall accept them fairly. Let the presents   184
Be worthily entertained.   [*Exit Servant.*]

Enter a third Servant.

How now? What news?   185

THIRD SERVANT   Please you, my lord, that honorable
gentleman, Lord Lucullus, entreats your company tomorrow to hunt with him and has sent Your Honor
two brace of greyhounds.   189

TIMON
I'll hunt with him; and let them be received,
Not without fair reward.   [*Exit Servant.*]

FLAVIUS [*aside*]   What will this come to?
He commands us to provide, and give great gifts,
And all out of an empty coffer;
Nor will he know his purse, or yield me this,   194
To show him what a beggar his heart is,
Being of no power to make his wishes good.
His promises fly so beyond his state   197
That what he speaks is all in debt; he owes
For every word. He is so kind that he now
Pays interest for't; his land's put to their books.   200
Well, would I were gently put out of office
Before I were forced out!
Happier is he that has no friend to feed
Than such that do e'en enemies exceed.   204
I bleed inwardly for my lord.   *Exit.*

TIMON [*to the Lords*]   You do yourselves
Much wrong, you bate too much of your own
merits.—   206
Here, my lord, a trifle of our love.   [*He offers a gift.*]

SECOND LORD
With more than common thanks I will receive it.

THIRD LORD   Oh, he's the very soul of bounty!

TIMON   And now I remember, my lord, you gave good   210
words the other day of a bay courser I rode on. 'Tis   211
yours because you liked it.

THIRD LORD
Oh, I beseech you, pardon me, my lord, in that.   213

TIMON
You may take my word, my lord: I know no man
Can justly praise but what he does affect.   215
I weigh my friends' affection with mine own.   216
I'll tell you true, I'll call to you.   217

ALL LORDS   Oh, none so welcome.

TIMON
I take all and your several visitations   219
So kind to heart, 'tis not enough to give.   220
Methinks I could deal kingdoms to my friends
And ne'er be weary. Alcibiades,
Thou art a soldier, therefore seldom rich.
It comes in charity to thee; for all thy living   224
Is 'mongst the dead, and all the lands thou hast
Lie in a pitched field.   226

ALCIBIADES   Ay, defiled land, my lord.   227

FIRST LORD   We are so virtuously bound—

TIMON   And so am I to you.

SECOND LORD   So infinitely endeared—   230

TIMON   All to you. [*To servants*] Lights, more lights!   231

FIRST LORD
The best of happiness, honor, and fortunes
Keep with you, Lord Timon!   233

TIMON   Ready for his friends.   234
Exeunt lords [*and all but Apemantus and Timon*].

APEMANTUS   What a coil's here!   235
Serving of becks and jutting-out of bums!   236
I doubt whether their legs be worth the sums   237
That are given for 'em. Friendship's full of dregs.
Methinks false hearts should never have sound legs.   239
Thus honest fools lay out their wealth on curtsies.   240

TIMON
Now, Apemantus, if thou wert not sullen,
I would be good to thee.

APEMANTUS   No, I'll nothing; for if I should be bribed
too, there would be none left to rail upon thee, and
then thou wouldst sin the faster. Thou giv'st so long,
Timon, I fear me thou wilt give away thyself in paper   246
shortly. What needs these feasts, pomps, and vain-   247
glories?

210–11 gave good words spoke praisingly   **211 bay courser** reddish-brown horse   **213 pardon . . . that** i.e., forgive my mentioning the horse; it was not meant as a hint.   **215 Can . . . affect** who can justly praise a thing unless he likes and desires it.   **216 I . . . own** I judge my friends' desires by my own and give them equal weight.   **217 I'll call to you** I'll call on you when I have need.   **219 all . . . several** your joint and individual   **220 kind** kindly.   **'tis . . . give** there isn't enough wealth in my possession to match my wish to be generous. **224 It . . . thee** i.e., You have need of charity.   **living** (1) existence (2) property, wealth   **226 pitched field** battlefield.   **227 defiled** (1) defiled by dead bodies (2) arrayed with files or rows of soldiers **230 endeared** obligated   **231 All to you** i.e., The obligation is entirely mine, or, all mine is yours.   **233 Keep** dwell, remain   **234 Ready for** Ready to assist   **235 coil** fuss   **236 Serving of becks** Bowing **237 legs** (1) limbs (2) bows, curtsies   **239 sound legs** i.e., healthy legs able to make deceptively flattering bows.   **240 curtsies** (1) bows (2) courtesies.   **246 I fear me** I fear.   **paper** bonds, promises to pay **247 What needs** What necessity is there for

176 fairly sincerely   **177 near** closely.   **183 trapped in silver** in silver-mounted trappings.   **184 fairly** graciously.   **185 entertained** received.   **189 brace** pair   **194 purse** financial situation.   **yield me this** grant me opportunity   **197 state** financial state   **200 put . . . books** mortgaged to those whom he has befriended with gifts. **204 Than . . . exceed** i.e., than he that feeds so-called "friends" who, by consuming his wealth, outdo his enemies in ruining him. **206 bate . . . of** belittle too much

TIMON Nay, an you begin to rail on society once, I am 249
sworn not to give regard to you. Farewell, and come 250
with better music.   *Exit.*

APEMANTUS So.
Thou wilt not hear me now; thou shalt not then.   253
I'll lock thy heaven from thee.   254
Oh, that men's ears should be
To counsel deaf, but not to flattery!   *Exit.*

❖

[2.1]

Enter a Senator [with papers in his hand].

SENATOR
And late, five thousand. To Varro and to Isidore   1
He owes nine thousand, besides my former sum,
Which makes it five-and-twenty. Still in motion   3
Of raging waste? It cannot hold; it will not.   4
If I want gold, steal but a beggar's dog   5
And give it Timon, why, the dog coins gold.
If I would sell my horse and buy twenty more
Better than he, why, give my horse to Timon—
Ask nothing, give it him—it foals me straight,   9
And able horses. No porter at his gate,   10
But rather one that smiles and still invites   11
All that pass by. It cannot hold. No reason   12
Can sound his state in safety.—Caphis, ho!   13
Caphis, I say!

Enter Caphis.

CAPHIS   Here, sir. What is your pleasure?
SENATOR
Get on your cloak and haste you to Lord Timon.
Importune him for my moneys. Be not ceased   16
With slight denial, nor then silenced when   17
"Commend me to your master" and the cap   18
Plays in the right hand, thus, but tell him   19
My uses cry to me; I must serve my turn   20
Out of mine own. His days and times are past,   21
And my reliances on his fracted dates   22
Have smit my credit. I love and honor him,   23
But must not break my back to heal his finger.
Immediate are my needs, and my relief
Must not be tossed and turned to me in words,   26

But find supply immediate. Get you gone.
Put on a most importunate aspect,
A visage of demand, for I do fear
When every feather sticks in his own wing   30
Lord Timon will be left a naked gull,   31
Which flashes now a phoenix. Get you gone.   32
CAPHIS I go, sir.
SENATOR [*giving him bonds*]
Ay, go, sir. Take the bonds along with you
And have the dates in compt.
CAPHIS   I will, sir.
SENATOR   Go.   *Exeunt.* 35

❖

[2.2]

*Enter steward [Flavius] with many bills in his
hand.*

FLAVIUS
No care, no stop! So senseless of expense
That he will neither know how to maintain it   2
Nor cease his flow of riot, takes no account   3
How things go from him nor resumes no care   4
Of what is to continue. Never mind   5
Was to be so unwise to be so kind.   6
What shall be done? He will not hear till feel.   7
I must be round with him, now he comes from
hunting.   8
Fie, fie, fie, fie!

*Enter Caphis [and the Servants of] Isidore and
Varro.*

CAPHIS
Good even, Varro. What, you come for money?   10
VARRO'S SERVANT Is't not your business too?
CAPHIS It is. And yours too, Isidore?
ISIDORE'S SERVANT It is so.
CAPHIS Would we were all discharged!   14
VARRO'S SERVANT I fear it.   15
CAPHIS Here comes the lord.

Enter Timon and his train [with Alcibiades].

TIMON
So soon as dinner's done we'll forth again,   17
My Alcibiades.—With me? What is your will?
CAPHIS [*presenting a bill*]
My lord, here is a note of certain dues.   19
TIMON Dues? Whence are you?

---

249 **an . . . once** if once you begin to criticize 250 **give regard to** take
notice of 253 **thou shalt not then** you won't have the opportunity
later. 254 **thy heaven** i.e., my saving advice
2.1. Location: Athens. A Senator's house.
1 **late** lately 3–4 **Still . . . waste?** Perpetually and ceaselessly squandering? 4 **hold** hold out, last. (Also in line 12.) 5 **steal but** I need
only steal 9 **foals me straight** at once yields me foals, i.e., more
horses (as gifts) 10 **And able horses** i.e., and what's more, they are
full-grown horses, not literally foals. **porter** i.e., one who sternly
denies entrance 11 **still** constantly 12–13 **No . . . safety** No reasonable fathoming of his estate can get to the bottom of Timon's financial
position. 16 **ceased** silenced, put off 17 **slight** negligent, offhand
17–19 **when . . . thus** i.e., when he offers fair greetings and flattering
gestures in lieu of real payment 20 **uses** needs 20–1 **I must . . .
own** I must address my own necessities with my own money.
21 **His . . . times** The deadlines for repayments of his loans
22 **fracted** broken (by failure to meet payments on notes due)
23 **smit** smitten, hurt 26 **tossed and turned** bandied back

30 **When . . . wing** i.e., when everything is in the hands of its rightful
possessor 31 **gull** (1) unfledged bird (2) dupe 32 **Which . . .
phoenix** who now showily looks like a phoenix, a one-of-a-kind
mythical bird, a rare and precious creature that is eventually consumed in flames (according to myth). 35 **in compt** reckoned.
2.2. Location: Athens. Before Timon's house.
2 **know** learn 3 **riot** uncontrolled reveling 4–5 **resumes . . . continue** makes no provision for how it is to continue. 5–6 **Never . . .
kind** Never was there a mind so unwise in being so kind. 7 **till feel**
until he suffers feelingly. 8 **round** plainspoken. **now** now that
10 **Good even** (A greeting used any time after noon.) 14 **discharged**
paid. 15 **fear it** i.e., am apprehensive about our being paid.
17 **forth** go forth 19 **dues** debts.

CAPHIS   Of Athens here, my lord.

TIMON   Go to my steward.

CAPHIS
Please it Your Lordship, he hath put me off
To the succession of new days this month.   24
My master is awaked by great occasion   25
To call upon his own, and humbly prays you   26
That with your other noble parts you'll suit   27
In giving him his right.

TIMON   Mine honest friend,
I prithee but repair to me next morning.   29

CAPHIS
Nay, good my lord—

TIMON   Contain thyself, good friend.

VARRO'S SERVANT
One Varro's servant, my good lord—

ISIDORE'S SERVANT
From Isidore; he humbly prays your speedy payment.

CAPHIS
If you did know, my lord, my master's wants—

VARRO'S SERVANT
'Twas due on forfeiture, my lord, six weeks and past.   34

ISIDORE'S SERVANT
Your steward puts me off, my lord, and I
Am sent expressly to Your Lordship.

TIMON   Give me breath.—   37
I do beseech you, good my lords, keep on;   38
I'll wait upon you instantly.
                          [Exeunt Alcibiades and Lords.]
                          [To Flavius]   Come hither. Pray you,   39
How goes the world, that I am thus encountered
With clamorous demands of broken bonds
And the detention of long-since-due debts   42
Against my honor?

FLAVIUS [to the Servants]   Please you, gentlemen,   43
The time is unagreeable to this business.
Your importunacy cease till after dinner,   45
That I may make His Lordship understand   46
Wherefore you are not paid.

TIMON   Do so, my friends.—   47
See them well entertained.   [Exit.]

FLAVIUS   Pray, draw near.   Exit.   48

Enter Apemantus and Fool.

CAPHIS   Stay, stay, here comes the Fool with Apemantus.
Let's ha' some sport with 'em.

VARRO'S SERVANT   Hang him! He'll abuse us.   51

ISIDORE'S SERVANT   A plague upon him, dog!

VARRO'S SERVANT   How dost, Fool?

APEMANTUS   Dost dialogue with thy shadow?   54

VARRO'S SERVANT   I speak not to thee.

APEMANTUS   No, 'tis to thyself. [To the Fool] Come away.   56

ISIDORE'S SERVANT [to Varro's Servant]   There's the fool   57
hangs on your back already.   58

APEMANTUS   No, thou stand'st single; thou'rt not on   59
him yet.   60

CAPHIS [to Isidore's Servant]   Where's the fool now?   61

APEMANTUS   He last asked the question. Poor rogues   62
and usurers' men, bawds between gold and want!   63

ALL THE SERVANTS   What are we, Apemantus?

APEMANTUS   Asses.

ALL THE SERVANTS   Why?

APEMANTUS   That you ask me what you are, and do not
know yourselves. Speak to 'em, Fool.

FOOL   How do you, gentlemen?

ALL THE SERVANTS   Gramercies, good Fool. How does   70
your mistress?

FOOL   She's e'en setting on water to scald such chickens   72
as you are. Would we could see you at Corinth!   73

APEMANTUS   Good! Gramercy.

Enter Page.

FOOL   Look you, here comes my mistress' page.

PAGE [to the Fool]   Why, how now, captain? What do
you in this wise company?—How dost thou,
Apemantus?

APEMANTUS   Would I had a rod in my mouth, that I   79
might answer thee profitably.   80

PAGE   Prithee, Apemantus, read me the superscription   81
of these letters. I know not which is which.
                          [He shows two letters.]

APEMANTUS   Canst not read?

PAGE   No.

APEMANTUS   There will little learning die then that day
thou art hanged. This is to Lord Timon, this to
Alcibiades. Go, thou wast born a bastard and thou'lt
die a bawd.

PAGE   Thou wast whelped a dog, and thou shalt famish   89
a dog's death. Answer not; I am gone.   Exit.

---

24 To . . . month from one day to another all month.   **25 awaked**
roused, driven   **26 his own** i.e., that which he has lent you   **27 with
. . . parts** in conformity to your other noble qualities   **29 but repair**
only come   **34 on forfeiture** on penalty of forfeiting the security for
it if not paid on the date prescribed   **37 breath** breathing space, time
to breathe.   **38 keep on** go ahead without me   **39 wait . . . instantly**
be with you in a moment.   **42 the detention** the charge of withholding payment   **43 Against my honor** contrary to my honorable reputation.   **45 Your . . . cease** Cease your importunate demands
46 That so that   **47 Wherefore** why   **48 entertained** received,
treated.   **Pray . . . near** Please come this way (to await my return).
51 abuse vilify

54 Dost . . . shadow? i.e., Are you talking with an image of yourself
when you say "Fool"?   **56 No . . . thyself** No, you are speaking to
yourself when you say "fool." (Said to Varro's Servant.)
57–8 There's . . . already i.e., You've just been labeled fool; Apemantus has pinned the label on you.   **59–60 No . . . yet** i.e., No, I didn't
put you, fool that you are, on the back of Varro's Servant; you're still
standing on your own two feet. (Said to Isidore's Servant.)
61 Where's . . . now? i.e., Who is the fool now after what Apemantus
just said to you?   **62 He** He who (i.e., Caphis, who has now been
called a fool like the others)   **63 bawds . . . want** middlemen who,
like panders, bring together usurers and needy men.   **70 Gramercies**
Many thanks   **72 e'en . . . water** just putting water on the fire.   **scald
such chickens** (Allusion to the sweating-tub treatment for venereal
disease, which causes loss of hair, just as a chicken loses its feathers
through scalding. The Fool also implies that they are fools deserving
to be plucked.)   **73 Corinth** a city noted for its brothels; hence, a
brothel or the district for such houses   **79–80 Would . . . profitably**
i.e., I wish that the verbal tongue-lashing I habitually give were an
actual stick to beat you with, that I might teach you a useful lesson.
81 superscription address   **89 whelped** born.   **famish** die

APEMANTUS E'en so thou outrun'st grace. Fool, I will 91
go with you to Lord Timon's.

FOOL Will you leave me there?

APEMANTUS If Timon stay at home.—You three serve 94
three usurers?

ALL THE SERVANTS Ay. Would they served us! 96

APEMANTUS So would I—as good a trick as ever
hangman served thief.

FOOL Are you three usurers' men?

ALL THE SERVANTS Ay, Fool.

FOOL I think no usurer but has a fool to his servant; my 101
mistress is one, and I am her fool. When men come to 102
borrow of your masters, they approach sadly and go
away merry, but they enter my mistress' house
merrily and go away sadly. The reason of this?

VARRO'S SERVANT I could render one. 106

APEMANTUS Do it then, that we may account thee a
whoremaster and a knave; which notwithstanding,
thou shalt be no less esteemed. 109

VARRO'S SERVANT What is a whoremaster, Fool?

FOOL A fool in good clothes, and something like thee.
'Tis a spirit; sometime 't appears like a lord, some- 112
time like a lawyer, sometime like a philosopher,
with two stones more than 's artificial one. He is very 114
often like a knight; and generally, in all shapes that
man goes up and down in from fourscore to thirteen, 116
this spirit walks in.

VARRO'S SERVANT Thou art not altogether a fool.

FOOL Nor thou altogether a wise man. As much
foolery as I have, so much wit thou lack'st.

APEMANTUS That answer might have become Ape- 121
mantus.

ALL THE SERVANTS Aside, aside! Here comes Lord Timon.
[They stand aside.]

Enter Timon and steward [Flavius].

APEMANTUS Come with me, Fool, come.

FOOL I do not always follow lover, elder brother, and 125
woman; sometime the philosopher. 126
[Exeunt Apemantus and Fool.]

FLAVIUS *[to Servants]*
Pray you, walk near. I'll speak with you anon. 127
Exeunt [Servants].

TIMON
You make me marvel wherefore ere this time
Had you not fully laid my state before me, 129
That I might so have rated my expense 130
As I had leave of means.

FLAVIUS   You would not hear me. 131
At many leisures I proposed—

TIMON   Go to! 132
Perchance some single vantages you took, 133
When my indisposition put you back,
And that unaptness made your minister 135
Thus to excuse yourself.

FLAVIUS   O my good lord, 136
At many times I brought in my accounts,
Laid them before you. You would throw them off
And say you found them in mine honesty. 139
When for some trifling present you have bid me
Return so much, I have shook my head and wept; 141
Yea, 'gainst th'authority of manners prayed you 142
To hold your hand more close. I did endure 143
Not seldom nor no slight checks when I have 144
Prompted you in the ebb of your estate 145
And your great flow of debts. My lovèd lord,
Though you hear now too late, yet now's a time; 147
The greatest of your having lacks a half 148
To pay your present debts.

TIMON Let all my land be sold.

FLAVIUS
'Tis all engaged, some forfeited and gone, 151
And what remains will hardly stop the mouth 152
Of present dues. The future comes apace; 153
What shall defend the interim? And at length 154
How goes our reck'ning? 155

TIMON
To Lacedaemon did my land extend. 156

FLAVIUS
Oh, my good lord, the world is but a word.
Were it all yours to give it in a breath,
How quickly were it gone!

TIMON   You tell me true.

91 E'en . . . grace That's just the way you run away from instruction
that might save you. (Said to the departing Page.) 94 If . . . home
i.e., While Timon remains at home, a fool is there. You three Do you
three 96 Would . . . us! Would that they looked after us adequately!
(But Apemantus deliberately misunderstands *serve*, answering, "It
would serve you right to be hanged.") 101–2 my mistress is one (A
bawd is a kind of usurer from whom customers "borrow" pleasure at
great personal expense.) 106 one (Implies that the Fool's mistress's
house is a bawdy house, where men come merrily but leave diseased
and poorer.) 109 no less esteemed i.e., no less esteemed than at present, since these professions are highly regarded in Athens and since
a usurer's servant is universally despised. 112 spirit i.e., one that
can assume various shapes 114 with . . . one i.e., with two testicles
besides the philosopher's *stone*, the quintessence, supposed to change
other metals into gold. 116 from . . . thirteen (The Fool playfully
inverts the normal "from thirteen to eighty," the life span of an adult
male.) 121 become been worthy of, done credit to 125–6 lover . . .
woman (Various sorts of persons proverbially associated with folly;
an *elder brother* is the counterpart of the proverbially wiser younger
brother.)

127 walk near remain nearby. 129 fully . . . state completely
detailed my financial position 130 rated estimated and regulated
131 As . . . means as my means permitted. 132 leisures times when
you were free. Go to (An exclamation of impatience.) 133 single
vantages occasional opportunities 135–6 that . . . yourself i.e., my
disinclination to listen on those occasions served as your excuse
thereafter for remaining silent. (*Made your minister* means "became
your agent or means.") 139 found . . . honesty i.e., found warrant
for believing the books properly kept in knowing me to be honest.
141 Return so much give as in repayment a large gift 142 'gainst . . .
manners contrary to what decorum dictated 143–4 I did . . . checks
I have had to endure rebukes not seldom or slight in nature 145 in
in regard to 147 yet . . . time i.e., late as it is, it is necessary that you
be made acquainted with it 148 The greatest . . . having your total
wealth at a most optimistic reckoning 151 engaged mortgaged
152–3 stop . . . Of satisfy 153 dues debts. apace quickly
154–5 And . . . reckoning? And how are we to provide for the long
term? 156 Lacedaemon Sparta

FLAVIUS
If you suspect my husbandry of falsehood,   160
Call me before th'exactest auditors
And set me on the proof. So the gods bless me,   162
When all our offices have been oppressed   163
With riotous feeders, when our vaults have wept   164
With drunken spilth of wine, when every room   165
Hath blazed with lights and brayed with minstrelsy,
I have retired me to a wasteful cock   167
And set mine eyes at flow.
TIMON   Prithee, no more.
FLAVIUS
Heavens, have I said, the bounty of this lord!
How many prodigal bits have slaves and peasants   170
This night englutted! Who is not Timon's?   171
What heart, head, sword, force, means, but is Lord
        Timon's?   172
Great Timon, noble, worthy, royal Timon!
Ah, when the means are gone that buy this praise,
The breath is gone whereof this praise is made.
Feast-won, fast-lost; one cloud of winter showers,   176
These flies are couched.   [He weeps.]
TIMON   Come, sermon me no further. 177
No villainous bounty yet hath passed my heart;   178
Unwisely, not ignobly, have I given.
Why dost thou weep? Canst thou the conscience lack   180
To think I shall lack friends? Secure thy heart.   181
If I would broach the vessels of my love   182
And try the argument of hearts by borrowing,   183
Men and men's fortunes could I frankly use   184
As I can bid thee speak.
FLAVIUS Assurance bless your thoughts!   186
TIMON
And in some sort these wants of mine are crowned,   187
That I account them blessings; for by these   188
Shall I try friends. You shall perceive how you   189
Mistake my fortunes; I am wealthy in my friends.—
Within there! Flaminius! Servilius!

        *Enter three servants [Flaminius, Servilius, and
        another].*

SERVANTS
My lord? My lord?
TIMON I will dispatch you severally: [*to Servilius*] you 193
to Lord Lucius; [*to Flaminius*] to Lord Lucullus you—
I hunted with His Honor today; [*to the other*] you to

Sempronius. Commend me to their loves, and, I am
proud, say, that my occasions have found time to use   197
'em toward a supply of money. Let the request be fifty 198
talents.
FLAMINIUS   As you have said, my lord.   200
                [*Exeunt Servants.*]
FLAVIUS [*aside*] Lord Lucius and Lucullus? Humh!
TIMON   Go you, sir, to the senators,
Of whom, even to the state's best health, I have   203
Deserved this hearing. Bid 'em send o'th'instant   204
A thousand talents to me.
FLAVIUS   I have been bold—
For that I knew it the most general way—   206
To them to use your signet and your name,   207
But they do shake their heads, and I am here
No richer in return.
TIMON   Is't true? Can 't be?
FLAVIUS
They answer, in a joint and corporate voice,   210
That now they are at fall, want treasure, cannot   211
Do what they would; you are sorry; you are honorable,
But yet they could have wished—they know not—
Something hath been amiss—a noble nature
May catch a wrench—would all were well—'tis pity.   215
And so, intending other serious matters,   216
After distasteful looks and these hard fractions,   217
With certain half-caps and cold-moving nods   218
They froze me into silence.
TIMON   You gods, reward them!
Prithee, man, look cheerly. These old fellows   220
Have their ingratitude in them hereditary.
Their blood is caked, 'tis cold, it seldom flows;   222
'Tis lack of kindly warmth they are not kind;   223
And nature, as it grows again toward earth,   224
Is fashioned for the journey, dull and heavy.
Go to Ventidius. Prithee, be not sad.
Thou art true and honest—ingeniously I speak—   227
No blame belongs to thee. Ventidius lately
Buried his father, by whose death he's stepped
Into a great estate. When he was poor,   230
Imprisoned, and in scarcity of friends,
I cleared him with five talents. Greet him from me.   232
Bid him suppose some good necessity   233
Touches his friend, which craves to be remembered   234
With those five talents. That had, give't these fellows 235

160 **husbandry** management, stewardship   162 **set . . . proof** put me
to the test.   163 **offices** rooms, especially the kitchen and pantries
164 **vaults** wine cellars   165 **spilth** spilling   167 **retired . . . cock**
withdrawn to sit beside the wastefully flowing faucet of a barrel
170 **prodigal bits** wasteful morsels   171 **is not** i.e., does not profess
himself to be   172 **means** financial resources   176 **fast-lost** (1) lost in
time of fast (2) lost quickly and for good   177 **are couched** hide
themselves (to avoid Timon's requests for help).   **sermon** lecture
178 **villainous bounty** generosity that I am ashamed of   180 **conscience** faith, or judgment   181 **Secure** Set at ease   182 **broach** tap,
open.   **my love** the love others have for me   183 **try . . . hearts** test
protestations of love   184 **frankly** as freely   186 **Assurance . . .
thoughts!** May your hopes prove well founded!   187 **sort** manner,
sense.   **crowned** given a special dignity   188 **That** so that   189 **try**
test   193 **severally** separately

197 **occasions** needs.   **time** opportunity   198 **toward** for   200 **As** We
will do as   203 **to . . . health** i.e., for my services in behalf of the state's
welfare. (Compare with 4.3.93–6, where Alcibiades refers to Timon's
sword and fortune offered in the defense of Athens.)   204 **o'th'instant**
at once   206 **For . . . way** because I knew it to be the best overall plan,
trying many at a time   207 **signet** signet ring and seal, token of authority   210 **corporate** united   211 **at fall** at low ebb.   **want** lack
215 **catch a wrench** be twisted from its natural course, run into misfortune   216 **intending** turning their attention to, or pretending   217 **hard
fractions** harsh broken sentences   218 **half-caps** i.e., salutations half-
heartedly given.   **cold-moving** chilling   220 **cheerly** cheerful.
222 **caked** congealed   223 **'Tis . . . kind** it is lack of natural warmth that
makes them not generous. (With pun on *kind*, "natural," "of humankind.")   224 **earth** i.e., the grave   227 **ingeniously** frankly   230–2 **When
. . . talents** (These lines echo Matthew 25:34–7 where Jesus discusses the
Last Judgment.)   233 **good** genuine   234–5 **which . . . talents** which
necessity of mine calls out for the return of those five talents.   235 **That
had** When you have that

To whom 'tis instant due. Ne'er speak or think
That Timon's fortunes 'mong his friends can sink.

FLAVIUS   I would I could not think it.
That thought is bounty's foe;   239
Being free itself, it thinks all others so.   *Exeunt.* 240

❖

[3.1]

[Enter] Flaminius, waiting to speak with a lord,
[Lucullus,] from his master. Enter a Servant to
him.

LUCULLUS'S SERVANT   I have told my lord of you. He is
coming down to you.

FLAMINIUS   I thank you, sir.

Enter Lucullus.

LUCULLUS'S SERVANT   Here's my lord.

LUCULLUS *[aside]*   One of Lord Timon's men? A gift, I
warrant. Why, this hits right; I dreamt of a silver basin   6
and ewer tonight.—Flaminius, honest Flaminius, you   7
are very respectively welcome, sir. *[To Servant]* Fill me 8
some wine.   *[Exit Servant.]*
And how does that honorable, complete, free-hearted   10
gentleman of Athens, thy very bountiful good lord
and master?

FLAMINIUS   His health is well, sir.

LUCULLUS   I am right glad that his health is well, sir.
And what hast thou there under thy cloak, pretty
Flaminius?

FLAMINIUS   Faith, nothing but an empty box, sir,
which, in my lord's behalf, I come to entreat Your
Honor to supply; who, having great and instant   18
occasion to use fifty talents, hath sent to Your Lordship 19
to furnish him, nothing doubting your present assis-   20
tance therein.

LUCULLUS   La, la, la la! "Nothing doubting," says he?
Alas, good lord! A noble gentleman 'tis, if he would   23
not keep so good a house. Many a time and often I ha'   24
dined with him and told him on't, and come again to   25
supper to him of purpose to have him spend less, and   26
yet he would embrace no counsel, take no warning by   27
my coming. Every man has his fault, and honesty is   28
his. I ha' told him on't, but I could ne'er get him
from't.   30

Enter Servant, with wine.

SERVANT   Please Your Lordship, here is the wine.

LUCULLUS   Flaminius, I have noted thee always wise.
Here's to thee.   *[He offers a toast.]*

FLAMINIUS   Your Lordship speaks your pleasure.   34

LUCULLUS   I have observed thee always for a towardly   35
prompt spirit—give thee thy due—and one that   36
knows what belongs to reason; and canst use the time   37
well, if the time use thee well. Good parts in thee! *[To* 38
Servant] Get you gone, sirrah.   *[Exit Servant.]*
Draw nearer, honest Flaminius. Thy lord's a bountiful
gentleman; but thou art wise, and thou know'st well
enough, although thou com'st to me, that this is no
time to lend money, especially upon bare friendship,   43
without security. Here's three solidares for thee. *[He*   44
gives a tip.] Good boy, wink at me, and say thou   45
saw'st me not. Fare thee well.

FLAMINIUS
Is't possible the world should so much differ,   47
And we alive that lived? Fly, damnèd baseness,   48
To him that worships thee! *[He throws the money back.]*

LUCULLUS   Ha? Now I see thou art a fool, and fit for thy
master.   *Exit Lucullus.*

FLAMINIUS
May these add to the number that may scald thee!   52
Let molten coin be thy damnation,
Thou disease of a friend and not himself!   54
Has friendship such a faint and milky heart
It turns in less than two nights? O you gods!   56
I feel my master's passion. This slave   57
Unto his honor has my lord's meat in him.   58
Why should it thrive and turn to nutriment
When he is turned to poison?   60
Oh, may diseases only work upon't!   61
And, when he's sick to death, let not that part of
nature   62
Which my lord paid for be of any power
To expel sickness, but prolong his hour!   *Exit.*

❖

3.2

Enter Lucius, with three Strangers.

LUCIUS   Who, the Lord Timon? He is my very good
friend and an honorable gentleman.

FIRST STRANGER   We know him for no less, though we   3
are but strangers to him. But I can tell you one thing,
my lord, and which I hear from common rumors: now

239 **That . . . foe** i.e., Such naive trusting is the fatal weakness of the
generous mind   240 **free** generous
3.1. Location: Athens. Lucullus's house.
6 **hits right** accords perfectly   7 **ewer** pitcher.   **tonight** last night.
8 **respectively** respectfully   10 **complete** accomplished   18 **supply**
fill   18–19 **instant occasion** urgent need   20 **nothing** not at all.
present immediate   23 **'tis he** is   24 **keep . . . house** be so lavish in
his entertaining.   25 **on't** of it   26 **of** on.   **have him** persuade him to
27 **by** from   28 **honesty** liberality   30 **from't** away from it.   34 **Your**
. . . pleasure It pleases Your Lordship to say so.

35–6 **towardly prompt** alacritous   36–8 **one . . . thee!** one that knows
how to be sensible; and can make the most of an opportunity if it presents itself. These are fine qualities in you!   43 **bare** mere   44 **soli-**
dares small coins. (A term invented by Shakespeare, evidently.)
45 **wink at me** pretend not to see me   47–8 **Is't . . . lived?** Is it possible that so much has changed in a short lifetime?   52 **May . . . thee!**
i.e., May these gold coins be added to the molten gold that will be
poured down your throat in hell!   54 **Thou . . . himself** you who are
no true friend at all but only a diseased resemblance.   56 **It turns**
that it sours like milk. (With quibble on the idea of *turn* as in "turncoat.")   57 **feel . . . passion** i.e., feel angry on my master's behalf,
share his anger and his suffering.   57–8 **slave Unto his honor** person
slavishly devoted to his own dignity. (Said ironically.)   58 **meat** i.e.,
food of a feast   60 **When . . . poison** when his behavior is so poisonous.   61 **may . . . upon't!** i.e., may diseases only thrive on the food
he has eaten at Timon's table!   62 **that . . . nature** i.e., that sustenance
3.2. Location: Athens. A public place.
3 **for no less** to be no less than you say

Lord Timon's happy hours are done and past, and his
estate shrinks from him.

LUCIUS   Fie, no, do not believe it! He cannot want for   8
money.

SECOND STRANGER   But believe you this, my lord, that
not long ago one of his men was with the Lord Lucullus to borrow so many talents, nay, urged extremely   12
for't, and showed what necessity belonged to't, and   13
yet was denied.

LUCIUS   How?   15

SECOND STRANGER   I tell you, denied, my lord.

LUCIUS   What a strange case was that! Now, before the
gods, I am ashamed on't. Denied that honorable
man? There was very little honor showed in't. For my
own part, I must needs confess, I have received some
small kindnesses from him, as money, plate, jewels,
and suchlike trifles, nothing comparing to his; yet had   22
he mistook him and sent to me, I should ne'er have   23
denied his occasion so many talents.   24

Enter Servilius.

SERVILIUS   See, by good hap, yonder's my lord. I have   25
sweat to see his honor. [*To Lucius*] My honored lord—   26

LUCIUS   Servilius? You are kindly met, sir. Fare thee
well. Commend me to thy honorable virtuous lord,
my very exquisite friend.   [*He starts to go.*]   29

SERVILIUS   May it please Your Honor, my lord hath
sent—

LUCIUS   Ha? What has he sent? I am so much endeared   32
to that lord; he's ever sending. How shall I thank him,
think'st thou? And what has he sent now?

SERVILIUS   He's only sent his present occasion now, my
lord, requesting Your Lordship to supply his instant   36
use with so many talents.   37

LUCIUS
I know His Lordship is but merry with me;
He cannot want fifty—five hundred—talents.   39

SERVILIUS
But in the meantime he wants less, my lord.
If his occasion were not virtuous,   41
I should not urge it half so faithfully.

LUCIUS
Dost thou speak seriously, Servilius?

SERVILIUS   Upon my soul, 'tis true, sir.

LUCIUS   What a wicked beast was I to disfurnish myself   45
against such a good time, when I might ha' shown   46

myself honorable! How unluckily it happened that I   47
should purchase the day before for a little part, and   48
undo a great deal of honor! Servilius, now before the   49
gods, I am not able to do—the more beast, I say—I
was sending to use Lord Timon myself, these gentle-   51
men can witness; but I would not for the wealth of   52
Athens I had done't now. Commend me bountifully
to His good Lordship, and I hope His Honor will con-   54
ceive the fairest of me, because I have no power to be   55
kind. And tell him this from me: I count it one of my
greatest afflictions, say, that I cannot pleasure such an   57
honorable gentleman. Good Servilius, will you befriend me so far as to use mine own words to him?

SERVILIUS   Yes, sir, I shall.

LUCIUS   I'll look you out a good turn, Servilius.   61

Exit Servilius.

True, as you said, Timon is shrunk indeed;   62
And he that's once denied will hardly speed.   63

Exit.

FIRST STRANGER   Do you observe this, Hostilius?

SECOND STRANGER   Ay, too well.

FIRST STRANGER   Why, this is the world's soul,   66
And just of the same piece   67
Is every flatterer's sport. Who can call him his friend   68
That dips in the same dish? For, in my knowing,   69
Timon has been this lord's father   70
And kept his credit with his purse,   71
Supported his estate; nay, Timon's money
Has paid his men their wages. He ne'er drinks
But Timon's silver treads upon his lip.   74
And yet—Oh, see the monstrousness of man
When he looks out in an ungrateful shape!—   76
He does deny him, in respect of his,   77
What charitable men afford to beggars.

THIRD STRANGER
Religion groans at it.

FIRST STRANGER   For mine own part,
I never tasted Timon in my life,   80
Nor came any of his bounties over me   81
To mark me for his friend; yet I protest,
For his right noble mind, illustrious virtue,   83
And honorable carriage,   84
Had his necessity made use of me,

---

8 want for lack   **12 urged extremely** begged insistently   **13 what . . . to't** how necessary it was   **15 How?** What's that you say?   **22 his** i.e., Lucullus's receiving of generosity   **23 mistook . . . me** i.e., mistakenly sent to me, who owe him less   **24 occasion** need. (As also in line 35.)   **25 hap** fortune   **25–6 I have sweat** i.e., I have been hurrying   **29 exquisite** sought after, extraordinary   **32 endeared** obliged   **36–7 supply . . . use** provide for his immediate need   **39 He cannot . . . talents** (Probably an indication of Shakespeare's uncertainty over the value of this currency; see also *so many* above in lines 12, 24, and 37.)   **41 were not virtuous** were due to a fault instead of a virtue, i.e., generosity   **45–6 disfurnish . . . time** leave myself unprepared for such an excellent opportunity

47–9 that I . . . honor i.e., that I just yesterday laid out a sum of money in a small investment and thus made it impossible now to acquire a great honor by helping Timon.   **51 use** borrow from   **52 would not** could not bring myself to wish   **54–5 conceive the fairest** think the best   **55 because** i.e., even though   **57 pleasure** satisfy   **61 look you out** seek occasion to do you   **62 shrunk** brought low   **63 speed** prosper.   **66 soul** real essence, vital principle   **67 just . . . piece** exactly the same, cut from the same piece of cloth   **68 sport** plaything, diversion.   **69 dips . . . dish** (Alludes to Judas's betrayal of Christ; see Matthew 26:23.)   **in my knowing** to my knowledge   **70 father** i.e., patron   **71 And . . . purse** and maintained Lucius's credit with Timon's wealth   **74 But . . . lip** without drinking from a silver cup paid for by Timon.   **76 When . . . shape** when he appears in his ungrateful aspect.   **77 He . . . his** Lucius denies Timon an amount that equals, in relation to Lucius's total wealth   **80 tasted Timon** i.e., sampled Timon's liberality   **81 Nor . . . me** nor did any of his generosities light on me   **83 For** because of   **84 carriage** conduct

I would have put my wealth into donation   86
And the best half should have returned to him,
So much I love his heart. But I perceive
Men must learn now with pity to dispense,
For policy sits above conscience.   *Exeunt.*   90

❧

[3.3]

Enter a third Servant [of Timon's] with
Sempronius, another of Timon's friends.

SEMPRONIUS
    Must he needs trouble me in't? Hum! 'Bove all others?
    He might have tried Lord Lucius or Lucullus;
    And now Ventidius is wealthy too,
    Whom he redeemed from prison. All these
    Owe their estates unto him.
SERVANT   My lord,
    They have all been touched and found base metal,   7
    For they have all denied him.
SEMPRONIUS   How? Have they denied him?
    Has Ventidius and Lucullus denied him?
    And does he send to me? Three? Humh!
    It shows but little love or judgment in him.
    Must I be his last refuge? His friends, like physicians,
    Thrive, give him over. Must I take th' cure upon me?   14
    He's much disgraced me in't. I'm angry at him,
    That might have known my place. I see no sense for't   16
    But his occasions might have wooed me first;   17
    For, in my conscience, I was the first man   18
    That e'er receivèd gift from him.
    And does he think so backwardly of me now   20
    That I'll requite it last? No!   21
    So it may prove an argument of laughter   22
    To th' rest, and I 'mongst lords be thought a fool.
    I'd rather than the worth of thrice the sum
    He'd sent to me first, but for my mind's sake;   25
    I'd such a courage to do him good. But now return,   26
    And with their faint reply this answer join:
    Who bates mine honor shall not know my coin.   28
                                            Exit.
SERVANT   Excellent! Your Lordship's a goodly villain.   29
    The devil knew not what he did when he made man
    politic; he crossed himself by't, and I cannot think but   31
    in the end the villainies of man will set him clear.   32

How fairly this lord strives to appear foul! Takes vir-   33
tuous copies to be wicked, like those that under hot   34
ardent zeal would set whole realms on fire!   35
Of such a nature is his politic love.
This was my lord's best hope; now all are fled,
Save only the gods. Now his friends are dead,   38
Doors that were ne'er acquainted with their wards   39
Many a bounteous year must be employed   40
Now to guard sure their master.   41
And this is all a liberal course allows: 42
Who cannot keep his wealth must keep his house.   43
                                            Exit.

❧

[3.4]

Enter [two of] Varro's Men, meeting [Titus's
Servant and] others, all [being servants of] Timon's
creditors, to wait for his coming out. Then enter
Lucius's [Servant] and Hortensius's [Servant].

VARRO'S FIRST SERVANT
    Well met. Good morrow, Titus and Hortensius.
TITUS'S SERVANT
    The like to you, kind Varro.
HORTENSIUS'S SERVANT   Lucius!
    What, do we meet together?
LUCIUS'S SERVANT   Ay, and I think
    One business does command us all;
    For mine is money.
TITUS'S SERVANT   So is theirs and ours.

    Enter Philotus's [Servant].

LUCIUS'S SERVANT
    And Sir Philotus too!
PHILOTUS'S SERVANT   Good day at once.   6
LUCIUS'S SERVANT   Welcome, good brother.
    What do you think the hour?
PHILOTUS'S SERVANT   Laboring for nine.   8
LUCIUS'S SERVANT
    So much?
PHILOTUS'S SERVANT   Is not my lord seen yet?
LUCIUS'S SERVANT   Not yet.   9
PHILOTUS'S SERVANT
    I wonder on't. He was wont to shine at seven.   10
LUCIUS'S SERVANT
    Ay, but the days are waxed shorter with him.   11
    You must consider that a prodigal course

---

86 **I . . . donation** i.e., I would have supposed all my wealth to have
come from him (and thus to be considered his when he needs it back)
90 **policy** self-interest
3.3. Location: Athens. Sempronius's house.
7 **touched** (Metaphor derived from testing metals with a touchstone
to see if they are gold.)   14 **Thrive . . . over** i.e., thrive on his wealth,
but now give him up as beyond help.   16 **That . . . place** who should
have acknowledged my position (among his friends).   **sense** reason
17 **But his occasions** but that he, in his need   18 **in my conscience** to
my knowledge   20 **think . . . me** (1) think I am so backward (2) think
of me last   21 **That . . . last?** that I will repay him when he has
applied last to me among his friends?   22 **argument of** subject for
25 **but . . . sake** if only to satisfy my mind   26 **courage** desire
28 **Who bates** whoever abates, detracts from   29 **goodly** proper.
(Said ironically.)   31 **politic** cunning.   **crossed** foiled (by making
man his rival in treachery)   32 **set him clear** make even the devil
look innocent.

33 **How fairly** With what a plausible appearance of virtue
33–5 **Takes . . . fire!** How this lord appears to model himself on the
virtuous only for wicked purposes, like religious bigots who for zealous purposes would burn down whole kingdoms!   38 **Now** Now
that.   **dead** dead to him, alienated   39–41 **Doors . . . master** doors
that for those many years of Timon's bounty never knew a single bolt
or lock must now be shut tight to shield Timon against arrest for debt
(and also to shield his erstwhile friends from Timon's importunities).
42 **liberal** generous   43 **keep . . . keep** preserve . . . stay inside
3.4. Location: Athens. Timon's house.
6 **at once** to one and all.   8 **Laboring for** Moving toward   9 **much**
i.e., late.   10 **was . . . shine** used to be up   11 **are waxed** have grown

Is like the sun's,
But not, like his, recoverable. I fear   14
'Tis deepest winter in Lord Timon's purse;
That is, one may reach deep enough and yet
Find little.

PHILOTUS'S SERVANT   I am of your fear for that.   17

TITUS'S SERVANT
I'll show you how t'observe a strange event.
Your lord sends now for money?

HORTENSIUS'S SERVANT   Most true, he does.

TITUS'S SERVANT
And he wears jewels now of Timon's gift,
For which I wait for money.   21

HORTENSIUS'S SERVANT   It is against my heart.   22

LUCIUS'S SERVANT   Mark how strange it shows:
Timon in this should pay more than he owes,
And e'en as if your lord should wear rich jewels   25
And send for money for 'em.   26

HORTENSIUS'S SERVANT
I'm weary of this charge, the gods can witness.   27
I know my lord hath spent of Timon's wealth,
And now ingratitude makes it worse than stealth.   29

VARRO'S FIRST SERVANT
Yes, mine's three thousand crowns. What's yours?

LUCIUS'S SERVANT   Five thousand, mine.

VARRO'S FIRST SERVANT
'Tis much deep, and it should seem by th' sum   32
Your master's confidence was above mine,   33
Else surely his had equaled.   34

Enter Flaminius.

TITUS'S SERVANT   One of Lord Timon's men.

LUCIUS'S SERVANT   Flaminius? Sir, a word. Pray, is my
lord ready to come forth?

FLAMINIUS   No, indeed, he is not.

TITUS'S SERVANT   We attend His Lordship. Pray signify   39
so much.

FLAMINIUS   I need not tell him that. He knows you are
too diligent.   [*Exit.*]   41

Enter steward [Flavius] in a cloak, muffled.

LUCIUS'S SERVANT
Ha! Is not that his steward muffled so?
He goes away in a cloud. Call him, call him.   43

TITUS'S SERVANT [*to Flavius*]   Do you hear, sir?

VARRO'S SECOND SERVANT [*to Flavius*]   By your leave, sir.

FLAVIUS
What do ye ask of me, my friend?

TITUS'S SERVANT
We wait for certain money here, sir.

FLAVIUS   Ay,   47
If money were as certain as your waiting,
'Twere sure enough.
Why then preferred you not your sums and bills   50
When your false masters eat of my lord's meat?   51
Then they could smile and fawn upon his debts,
And take down th'interest into their glutt'nous maws.   53
You do yourselves but wrong to stir me up.   54
Let me pass quietly.
Believe't, my lord and I have made an end;   56
I have no more to reckon, he to spend.   57

LUCIUS'S SERVANT   Ay, but this answer will not serve.   58

FLAVIUS
If 'twill not serve, 'tis not so base as you,
For you serve knaves.   [*Exit.*]

VARRO'S FIRST SERVANT   How? What does His cashiered   61
Worship mutter?

VARRO'S SECOND SERVANT   No matter what; he's poor,
and that's revenge enough. Who can speak broader   64
than he that has no house to put his head in? Such   65
may rail against great buildings.   66

Enter Servilius.

TITUS'S SERVANT   Oh, here's Servilius. Now we shall
know some answer.

SERVILIUS   If I might beseech you, gentlemen, to repair   69
some other hour, I should derive much from't. For   70
take't of my soul, my lord leans wondrously to discon-   71
tent. His comfortable temper has forsook him; he's   72
much out of health and keeps his chamber.   73

LUCIUS'S SERVANT
Many do keep their chambers are not sick,   74
And if it be so far beyond his health,   75
Methinks he should the sooner pay his debts
And make a clear way to the gods.

SERVILIUS   Good gods!   77

TITUS'S SERVANT
We cannot take this for an answer, sir.

FLAMINIUS (*within*)   Servilius, help! My lord, my lord!

Enter Timon, in a rage.

---

14 But . . . recoverable i.e., the sun will return from its wintry path,
but Timon cannot recover (since his funds are not *recoverable*).   **17 am
of** share   **21 For . . . money** i.e., while I wait for the money used to
buy those jewels.   **22 It is . . . heart** It goes against my conscience.
25–6 e'en . . . for 'em i.e., it's just as though your master should both
wear the jewels Timon gave him and simultaneously demand the
money that paid for those jewels.   **27 charge** commission   **29 stealth**
theft.   **32 much deep** very great   **33 mine** my master's   **34 his had
equaled** i.e., my master's loan would have equaled in amount your
master's.   **39 attend** are waiting for   **41 diligent** i.e., officious.
43 in a cloud (1) muffled (2) in a state of gloom and ignominy.

47 certain certain sums of. (But Flavius puns bitterly in the next line
on the sense of "reliable," "predictable.")   **50 preferred** presented
51 eat ate. (Pronounced *et.*)   **53 th'interest** i.e., the food and drink
they consumed as though it were interest on a loan.   **maws** stomachs. (A term used of animals.)   **54 do yourselves but** only do yourselves   **56 made an end** severed our relationship   **57 reckon** keep
account of   **58 serve** do. (But Flavius punningly replies in the sense
of "act as servant.")   **61 How?** What's this?   **cashiered** dismissed.
(*His cashiered Worship* is offered sardonically as if it were a title of dignity.)   **64 broader** (1) more freely (2) more in the open, abroad
65–6 Such . . . buildings i.e., A man who is houseless and out of service, like Flavius, has nothing to lose and can inveigh against injustice
and inequality.   **69 repair** return   **70 derive** benefit   **71 take't . . . soul**
i.e., believe I speak sincerely   **72 comfortable temper** cheerful disposition   **73 keeps** stays in   **74 are** who are   **75 if . . . health** if his difficulty is something other than poor physical health   **77 make . . .
gods** i.e., pay all his debts to smooth his way to heaven.   **Good gods!**
(1) The gods are good! (2) Good God!

TIMON

What, are my doors opposed against my passage?
Have I been ever free, and must my house
Be my retentive enemy, my jail?   82
The place which I have feasted, does it now,
Like all mankind, show me an iron heart?

LUCIUS'S SERVANT Put in now, Titus.   85

TITUS'S SERVANT My lord, here is my bill.

LUCIUS'S SERVANT Here's mine.

HORTENSIUS'S SERVANT And mine, my lord.

BOTH VARRO'S SERVANTS And ours, my lord.

PHILOTUS'S SERVANT All our bills.

TIMON

Knock me down with 'em! Cleave me to the girdle!   91

LUCIUS'S SERVANT Alas, my lord—

TIMON Cut my heart in sums!   93

TITUS'S SERVANT Mine, fifty talents.

TIMON Tell out my blood!   95

LUCIUS'S SERVANT Five thousand crowns, my lord.

TIMON

Five thousand drops pays that. What yours? And
    yours?

VARRO'S FIRST SERVANT My lord—

VARRO'S SECOND SERVANT My lord—

TIMON

Tear me, take me, and the gods fall upon you!   100
                                    Exit Timon.

HORTENSIUS'S SERVANT Faith, I perceive our masters
may throw their caps at their money. These debts 102
may well be called desperate ones, for a madman owes 103
'em.   *Exeunt.*

Enter Timon [and Flavius].

TIMON

They have e'en put my breath from me, the slaves.   105
Creditors? Devils!

FLAVIUS My dear lord—

TIMON What if it should be so?   108

FLAVIUS My lord—

TIMON

I'll have it so. My steward!

FLAVIUS   Here, my lord.

TIMON

So fitly? Go, bid all my friends again,   111
Lucius, Lucullus, and Sempronius—all.
I'll once more feast the rascals.

FLAVIUS   Oh, my lord,
You only speak from your distracted soul;
There's not so much left to furnish out   115
A moderate table.

TIMON   Be it not in thy care. Go,   117
I charge thee, invite them all. Let in the tide
Of knaves once more. My cook and I'll provide.
                                    Exeunt.

❖

[3.5]

*Enter three Senators at one door, Alcibiades
meeting them, with attendants.*

FIRST SENATOR   [*to another Senator*]

My lord, you have my voice to't.   1
The fault's bloody;   2
'Tis necessary he should die.
Nothing emboldens sin so much as mercy.

SECOND SENATOR Most true. The law shall bruise 'em.   5

ALCIBIADES

Honor, health, and compassion to the Senate!   6

FIRST SENATOR Now, Captain?

ALCIBIADES

I am an humble suitor to your virtues;
For pity is the virtue of the law,   9
And none but tyrants use it cruelly.
It pleases time and fortune to lie heavy   11
Upon a friend of mine, who in hot blood   12
Hath stepped into the law, which is past depth   13
To those that without heed do plunge into't.   14
He is a man, setting his fate aside,   15
Of comely virtues;
Nor did he soil the fact with cowardice—   17
An honor in him which buys out his fault—   18
But with a noble fury and fair spirit,
Seeing his reputation touched to death,   20
He did oppose his foe;
And with such sober and unnoted passion   22
He did behave his anger, ere 'twas spent,   23
As if he had but proved an argument.   24

FIRST SENATOR

You undergo too strict a paradox,   25
Striving to make an ugly deed look fair.
Your words have took such pains as if they labored
To bring manslaughter into form and set quarreling   28
Upon the head of valor—which indeed   29
Is valor misbegot, and came into the world
When sects and factions were newly born.

82 retentive confining   **85 Put in** i.e., Make payment; let me put in
my bill   **91 Knock, Cleave** (Timon puns on *bills* as weapons.)
girdle belt.   **93 in sums** into sums of money.   **95 Tell out** Count out
by the drop   **100 the gods fall upon you** i.e., may the gods attack
you as with an army.   **102 throw . . . at** i.e., give up hope of recovering   **103 desperate** (1) unlikely to be recovered (2) resulting from
desperate madness   **105 e'en . . . me** left me breathless   **108 What
. . . so?** i.e., What is there to do in that case? (Timon has evidently
thought of the mock banquet he will serve in 3.6.)   **111 fitly** conveniently.   **115 furnish out** supply

117 Be . . . care Don't you worry about it.
3.5. Location: Athens. The Senate House.
1 voice to't vote in favor of it (the death sentence under consideration).   **2 fault's bloody** crime involved bloodshed   **5 'em** i.e., all
such offenders.   **6 compassion to the Senate** i.e., may the Senate
have compassion.   **9 virtue** chief merit, essence   **11–12 lie . . . Upon**
oppress   **13 stepped into** incurred the penalties of   **13–14 past
depth To** over the heads of   **15 setting . . . aside** setting aside his ill-
fated action   **17 fact** deed   **18 buys out** redeems   **20 touched to
death** fatally threatened   **22 unnoted** imperceptible   **23 behave** control   **24 but . . . argument** only been arguing a point.   **25 You . . .
paradox** You split hairs   **28–9 To . . . valor** to make manslaughter
appear legally defensible and dueling the very height of honor

He's truly valiant that can wisely suffer 32
The worst that man can breathe, 33
And make his wrongs his outsides, 34
To wear them like his raiment, carelessly, 35
And ne'er prefer his injuries to his heart, 36
To bring it into danger. 37
If wrongs be evils and enforce us kill, 38
What folly 'tis to hazard life for ill! 39

ALCIBIADES
My lord—

FIRST SENATOR   You cannot make gross sins look clear. 40
To revenge is no valor, but to bear. 41

ALCIBIADES
My lords, then, under favor, pardon me 42
If I speak like a captain.
Why do fond men expose themselves to battle, 44
And not endure all threats? Sleep upon't, 45
And let the foes quietly cut their throats
Without repugnancy? If there be 47
Such valor in the bearing, what make we 48
Abroad? Why then, women are more valiant 49
That stay at home, if bearing carry it, 50
And the ass more captain than the lion, the felon
Loaden with irons wiser than the judge, 52
If wisdom be in suffering. O my lords,
As you are great, be pitifully good. 54
Who cannot condemn rashness in cold blood?
To kill, I grant, is sin's extremest gust, 56
But in defense, by mercy, 'tis most just. 57
To be in anger is impiety,
But who is man that is not angry? 59
Weigh but the crime with this.

SECOND SENATOR   You breathe in vain. 61

ALCIBIADES   In vain? His service done
At Lacedaemon and Byzantium
Were a sufficient briber for his life.

FIRST SENATOR   What's that?

ALCIBIADES
Why, I say, my lords, he's done fair service
And slain in fight many of your enemies.
How full of valor did he bear himself
In the last conflict, and made plenteous wounds!

SECOND SENATOR
He has made too much plenty with 'em. 70

He's a sworn rioter; he has a sin that often 71
Drowns him and takes his valor prisoner.
If there were no foes, that were enough 73
To overcome him. In that beastly fury
He has been known to commit outrages
And cherish factions. 'Tis inferred to us 76
His days are foul and his drink dangerous.

FIRST SENATOR
He dies.

ALCIBIADES   Hard fate! He might have died in war.
My lords, if not for any parts in him— 79
Though his right arm might purchase his own time 80
And be in debt to none—yet, more to move you,
Take my deserts to his and join 'em both; 82
And, for I know your reverend ages love 83
Security, I'll pawn my victories, all 84
My honors, to you, upon his good returns. 85
If by this crime he owes the law his life,
Why, let the war receive't in valiant gore, 87
For law is strict, and war is nothing more.

FIRST SENATOR
We are for law. He dies; urge it no more,
On height of our displeasure. Friend or brother, 90
He forfeits his own blood that spills another. 91

ALCIBIADES
Must it be so? It must not be. My lords,
I do beseech you, know me.

SECOND SENATOR   How?

ALCIBIADES   Call me to your remembrances.

THIRD SENATOR   What?

ALCIBIADES
I cannot think but your age has forgot me. 97
It could not else be I should prove so base 98
To sue and be denied such common grace. 99
My wounds ache at you.

FIRST SENATOR   Do you dare our anger?
'Tis in few words, but spacious in effect: 101
We banish thee forever.

ALCIBIADES   Banish me?
Banish your dotage, banish usury,
That makes the Senate ugly.

FIRST SENATOR
If after two days' shine Athens contain thee,
Attend our weightier judgment. 106
And, not to swell our spirit, 107
He shall be executed presently.   Exeunt [Senators]. 108

32–7 He's . . . danger That person is truly valiant who can endure grave insults with equanimity and treat such injuries as merely external, bearing them lightly and casually as though they were garments, and never take such injuries to heart in such a way as to lead to a dangerous confrontation.   **38 kill** to kill   **39 What . . . ill!** what a folly it is to let this code of honor put life itself at risk in a bad cause!   **40 clear** innocent.   **41 to bear** bearing insults calmly is true valor.   **42 under favor** by your leave   **44 fond** foolish   **45 Sleep upon't** i.e., Why do they not disregard danger   **47 repugnancy** resistance.   **47–9 If . . . Abroad?** If it's valorous to put up with insults, what are we men doing abroad in the world?   **50 bearing** (1) putting up with insults (2) child-bearing (3) bearing the weight of a man in sex.   **carry it** wins the day   **52 Loaden with irons** weighed down with shackles   **54 pitifully good** good by showing mercy.   **56 gust** outburst   **57 defense** self-defense.   **by mercy** by a merciful interpretation of law   **59 not** not sometimes   **61 breathe** speak   **70 He . . . 'em** He has been too free in making wounds, and has rioted too freely after victory.

71 sworn rioter inveterate debauchee.   **a sin** i.e., drunkenness   **73 If . . . enough** Even without enemies, his drinking is enough   **76 cherish factions** encourage dissension and conspiracy.   **inferred** alleged   **79 parts** admirable traits   **80 his . . . time** his ability as a soldier should redeem him   **82 to** in addition to   **83 for** because   **84 Security** (1) safety (2) collateral for a loan (using a financial metaphor found also in *purchase, pawn, good returns,* etc.)   **85 upon . . . returns** as a pledge that he will make a good return on your investment in him, i.e., fight bravely in war.   **87 let . . . gore** i.e., let him pay his debt by bleeding as a soldier   **90 On . . . our** on pain of our highest   **91 another** i.e., another's.   **97 your age has** you, in your advanced age, have   **98 else be** otherwise be (that).   **prove** i.e., be considered   **99 To sue** as to plead for   **101 spacious in effect** of great import. (With quibble on the spacious world to which Alcibiades is banished.)   **106 Attend . . . judgment** expect our more severe sentence.   **107 spirit** anger   **108 presently** immediately.

ALCIBIADES

Now the gods keep you old enough   109
That you may live
Only in bone, that none may look on you!—   111
I'm worse than mad. I have kept back their foes,
While they have told their money and let out   113
Their coin upon large interest, I myself
Rich only in large hurts. All those for this?   115
Is this the balsam that the usuring Senate   116
Pours into captains' wounds? Banishment!
It comes not ill; I hate not to be banished.   118
It is a cause worthy my spleen and fury,   119
That I may strike at Athens. I'll cheer up
My discontented troops and lay for hearts.   121
'Tis honor with most lands to be at odds.   122
Soldiers should brook as little wrongs as gods.   *Exit.* 123

❖

[3.6]

[*Music. Tables and seats set out; servants
attending.*] *Enter divers friends* [*of Timon*] *at
several doors.*

FIRST LORD   The good time of day to you, sir.
SECOND LORD   I also wish it to you. I think this honorable lord did but try us this other day.   3
FIRST LORD   Upon that were my thoughts tiring when   4
we encountered. I hope it is not so low with him as he   5
made it seem in the trial of his several friends.
SECOND LORD   It should not be, by the persuasion of   7
his new feasting.
FIRST LORD   I should think so. He hath sent me an earnest inviting, which many my near occasions did urge   10
me to put off; but he hath conjured me beyond them,   11
and I must needs appear.   12
SECOND LORD   In like manner was I in debt to my im-   13
portunate business, but he would not hear my excuse.
I am sorry, when he sent to borrow of me, that my
provision was out.   16
FIRST LORD   I am sick of that grief too, as I understand 17
how all things go.   18
SECOND LORD   Every man here's so. What would he
have borrowed of you?
FIRST LORD   A thousand pieces.   21

SECOND LORD   A thousand pieces?
FIRST LORD   What of you?
SECOND LORD   He sent to me, sir—Here he comes.

Enter Timon and attendants. [*Music plays.*]

TIMON   With all my heart, gentlemen both! And how
fare you?
FIRST LORD   Ever at the best, hearing well of Your Lordship.
SECOND LORD   The swallow follows not summer more
willing than we Your Lordship.
TIMON [*aside*]   Nor more willingly leaves winter, such
summer birds are men.—Gentlemen, our dinner
will not recompense this long stay. Feast your ears   33
with the music awhile, if they will fare so harshly o'th' 34
trumpet's sound. We shall to't presently.   35
FIRST LORD   I hope it remains not unkindly with Your
Lordship that I returned you an empty messenger.
TIMON   Oh, sir, let it not trouble you.
SECOND LORD   My noble lord—
TIMON   Ah, my good friend, what cheer?
                              The banquet brought in.
SECOND LORD   My most honorable lord, I am e'en sick
of shame that when Your Lordship this other day sent
to me I was so unfortunate a beggar.   43
TIMON   Think not on't, sir.
SECOND LORD   If you had sent but two hours before—
TIMON   Let it not cumber your better remembrance.—   46
Come, bring in all together.
SECOND LORD   All covered dishes!   48
FIRST LORD   Royal cheer, I warrant you.
THIRD LORD   Doubt not that, if money and the season
can yield it.
FIRST LORD   How do you? What's the news?
THIRD LORD   Alcibiades is banished. Hear you of it?
FIRST AND SECOND LORDS   Alcibiades banished?
THIRD LORD   'Tis so, be sure of it.
FIRST LORD   How? How?
SECOND LORD   I pray you, upon what?   57
TIMON   My worthy friends, will you draw near?
THIRD LORD   I'll tell you more anon. Here's a noble
feast toward.   60
SECOND LORD   This is the old man still.   61
THIRD LORD   Will't hold? Will't hold?   62
SECOND LORD   It does; but time will—and so—   63
THIRD LORD   I do conceive.   64
TIMON   Each man to his stool, with that spur as he   65
would to the lip of his mistress. Your diet shall be in   66
all places alike. Make not a city feast of it, to let the 67
meat cool ere we can agree upon the first place; sit, sit. 68
[*They sit.*] The gods require our thanks.

109 keep . . . enough preserve you to such an old age   **111 Only . . .
you** i.e., mere skeletons, forgotten or avoided by everyone.   **113 told**
reckoned.   **let** lent   **115 hurts** injuries.   **116 balsam** balm, medicine
118 It . . . ill It is not such a bad thing after all   **119 worthy** worthy of
121 lay for hearts endeavor to win their affection.   **122 'Tis . . . odds**
It's honorable to be at variance with a country (and its political leaders) in most instances.   **123 brook . . . gods** endure insults as little as
the gods do.
3.6. Location: Athens. A banqueting room in Timon's house.
0.3 *several* separate   **3 did . . . us** was only testing us   **4 tiring** preying, feeding, i.e., busily engaged   **5 I . . . him** I hope his financial situation is not as desperate   **7 persuasion** evidence   **10 inviting**
invitation.   **many . . . occasions** my many urgent necessities or business   **11 conjured . . . them** summoned me so urgently as to overcome my previous commitments   **12 needs** necessarily   **13 in debt**
to obligated to   **16 provision was out** resources were exhausted.
17–18 as . . . go particularly as I now understand the state of affairs.
(Perhaps hinting at Timon's seeming ability to entertain lavishly
again.)   **21 pieces** i.e., gold coins.

33 stay delay.   **34–5 if . . . sound** if your ears will deign to feast on so
harsh a sound as that of the trumpet.   **43 so . . . beggar** so unfortunate as to be out of ready reserves.   **46 cumber . . . remembrance**
trouble your happier thoughts, memories.   **48 covered** lidded.
(Implies particularly elegant fare.)   **57 what** what ground.
60 toward imminent.   **61 old man still** man we once knew.   **62 hold**
last.   **63 will** i.e., will tell   **64 conceive** understand.   **65 that spur**
the same eagerness   **66 diet** food   **66–7 in . . . alike** the same wherever you sit to eat.   **67 city feast** formal occasion, with seating by
rank   **68 first place** place of honor

You great benefactors, sprinkle our society with thankfulness. For your own gifts, make yourselves praised; but reserve still to give, lest your deities be 72 despised. Lend to each man enough, that one need not lend to another; for, were your godheads to borrow of men, men would forsake the gods. Make the meat be beloved more than the man that gives it. Let no assembly of twenty be without a score of villains. If there sit 77 twelve women at the table, let a dozen of them be—as they are. The rest of your fees, O gods—the senators 79 of Athens, together with the common tag of people— 80 what is amiss in them, you gods, make suitable for destruction. For these my present friends, as they are 82 to me nothing, so in nothing bless them, and to nothing are they welcome.

Uncover, dogs, and lap!
[*The dishes are uncovered and seen to contain warm water and stones.*]

SOME SPEAK   What does His Lordship mean?
SOME OTHERS   I know not.
TIMON
May you a better feast never behold,
You knot of mouth-friends! Smoke and lukewarm water   89
Is your perfection. This is Timon's last,   90
Who, stuck and spangled with your flatteries,   91
Washes it off and sprinkles in your faces
Your reeking villainy.
                      [*He throws the water in their faces.*]
                      Live loathed and long,
Most smiling, smooth, detested parasites,
Courteous destroyers, affable wolves, meek bears,
You fools of fortune, trencher-friends, time's flies,   96
Cap-and-knee slaves, vapors, and minute-jacks!   97
Of man and beast the infinite malady   98
Crust you quite o'er! What, dost thou go?
Soft! Take thy physic first! Thou too, and thou!   100
Stay, I will lend thee money, borrow none.
                      [*He assaults them and drives them out.*]
What, all in motion? Henceforth be no feast
Whereat a villain's not a welcome guest.
Burn, house! Sink, Athens! Henceforth hated be
Of Timon, man, and all humanity!   *Exit.* 105

Enter the Senators, with other Lords, [returning].

FIRST LORD   How now, my lords?

SECOND LORD   Know you the quality of Lord Timon's 107 fury?
THIRD LORD   Push! Did you see my cap?   109
FOURTH LORD   I have lost my gown.
FIRST LORD   He's but a mad lord, and naught but hu- 111 mors sways him. He gave me a jewel th'other day, 112 and now he has beat it out of my hat. Did you see my jewel?   [*They search for their belongings.*]
THIRD LORD   Did you see my cap?
SECOND LORD   Here 'tis.
FOURTH LORD   Here lies my gown.
FIRST LORD   Let's make no stay.
SECOND LORD
Lord Timon's mad.
THIRD LORD   I feel't upon my bones.
FOURTH LORD
One day he gives us diamonds, next day stones.
                      Exeunt the Senators [etc.].

❧

4.1

Enter Timon.

TIMON
Let me look back upon thee. O thou wall
That girdles in those wolves, dive in the earth
And fence not Athens! Matrons, turn incontinent!   3
Obedience fail in children! Slaves and fools,   4
Pluck the grave wrinkled Senate from the bench
And minister in their steads! To general filths   6
Convert o'th'instant, green virginity!   7
Do't in your parents' eyes. Bankrupts, hold fast;
Rather than render back, out with your knives
And cut your trusters' throats! Bound servants, steal! 10
Large-handed robbers your grave masters are,   11
And pill by law. Maid, to thy master's bed!   12
Thy mistress is o'th' brothel. Son of sixteen,
Pluck the lined crutch from thy old limping sire;   14
With it beat out his brains! Piety and fear,   15
Religion to the gods, peace, justice, truth,   16
Domestic awe, night rest, and neighborhood,   17
Instruction, manners, mysteries, and trades,   18
Degrees, observances, customs, and laws,   19
Decline to your confounding contraries,   20
And yet confusion live! Plagues, incident to men,   21
Your potent and infectious fevers heap
On Athens, ripe for stroke! Thou cold sciatica,   23

Cripple our senators, that their limbs may halt   24
As lamely as their manners! Lust and liberty   25
Creep in the minds and marrows of our youth,   26
That 'gainst the stream of virtue they may strive   27
And drown themselves in riot! Itches, blains,   28
Sow all th'Athenian bosoms, and their crop   29
Be general leprosy! Breath infect breath,
That their society, as their friendship, may   31
Be merely poison! Nothing I'll bear from thee   32
But nakedness, thou detestable town!

           [He strips off his garments.]

Take thou that too, with multiplying bans!   34
Timon will to the woods, where he shall find
Th'unkindest beast more kinder than mankind.   36
The gods confound—hear me, you good gods all—
Th'Athenians both within and out that wall!
And grant, as Timon grows, his hate may grow
To the whole race of mankind, high and low!
Amen.   *Exit.*

❧

[4.2]

*Enter steward [Flavius], with two or three
Servants.*

FIRST SERVANT
  Hear you, Master Steward, where's our master?
  Are we undone, cast off, nothing remaining?

FLAVIUS
  Alack, my fellows, what should I say to you?
  Let me be recorded by the righteous gods,   4
  I am as poor as you.

FIRST SERVANT   Such a house broke?   5
  So noble a master fall'n? All gone, and not
  One friend to take his fortune by the arm   7
  And go along with him?

SECOND SERVANT   As we do turn our backs
  From our companion thrown into his grave,
  So his familiars to his buried fortunes   11
  Slink all away, leave their false vows with him
  Like empty purses picked; and his poor self,
  A dedicated beggar to the air,   14
  With his disease of all-shunned poverty,
  Walks, like contempt, alone. More of our fellows.   16

Enter other Servants.

FLAVIUS   24
  All broken implements of a ruined house.

THIRD SERVANT
  Yet do our hearts wear Timon's livery;   18
  That see I by our faces. We are fellows still,
  Serving alike in sorrow. Leaked is our bark,   20
  And we, poor mates, stand on the dying deck,   21
  Hearing the surges threat. We must all part   22
  Into this sea of air.

FLAVIUS   Good fellows all,
  The latest of my wealth I'll share amongst you.   24
  Wherever we shall meet, for Timon's sake,
  Let's yet be fellows. Let's shake our heads and say,   26
  As 'twere a knell unto our master's fortunes,   27
  "We have seen better days." Let each take some.

           [He gives them money.]

  Nay, put out all your hands. Not one word more.   29
  Thus part we rich in sorrow, parting poor.   30

    [Servants] embrace, and part several ways.

  Oh, the fierce wretchedness that glory brings us!
  Who would not wish to be from wealth exempt,
  Since riches point to misery and contempt?   33
  Who would be so mocked with glory, or to live
  But in a dream of friendship,
  To have his pomp and all what state compounds   36
  But only painted, like his varnished friends?   37
  Poor honest lord, brought low by his own heart,
  Undone by goodness! Strange, unusual blood,   39
  When man's worst sin is he does too much good!
  Who then dares to be half so kind again?
  For bounty, that makes gods, do still mar men.   42
  My dearest lord, blest to be most accurst,   43
  Rich only to be wretched, thy great fortunes
  Are made thy chief afflictions. Alas, kind lord!
  He's flung in rage from this ingrateful seat   46
  Of monstrous friends,
  Nor has he with him to supply his life,   48
  Or that which can command it.   49
  I'll follow and inquire him out.
  I'll ever serve his mind with my best will;   51
  Whilst I have gold, I'll be his steward still.   *Exit.*

❧

[4.3]

Enter Timon, in the woods [with a spade].

TIMON
  O blessèd breeding sun, draw from the earth

---

24 **halt** limp   25 **liberty** licentiousness   26 **marrows** soft tissues filling the cavities of bone (thought of as the source of vitality and strength)   27 **stream** current   28 **riot** dissoluteness.   **blains** blisters   29 **Sow** fall like seed in   31 **society** associating with one another   32 **merely** entirely   34 **bans** curses.   36 **Th'unkindest** (1) the cruellest (2) the most unnatural, turning against kin and kind. (*Kinder* continues the wordplay.)
4.2. Location: Athens. Timon's house.
4 **Let . . . gods** May the gods note down and confirm what I say
5 **house broke** household disbanded.   7 **his fortune** i.e., Timon in his misfortune. (The dialogue here fulfills the allegorical scene of fallen fortune imagined by the Poet in 1.1.68–93.)   11 **his familiars . . . fortunes** those close to him when he was fortunate, now perceiving his ruin   14 **dedicated . . . air** beggar having nothing and nowhere to go
16 **like contempt** as if he were contemptibility itself

18 **livery** uniform worn by male household servants (here used metaphorically)   20 **bark** sailing vessel   21 **mates** (1) fellows (2) mates of a vessel.   **dying** i.e., sinking   22 **surges** waves
24 **latest** last remnant   26 **yet** still.   **shake our heads** (in sorrow)
27 **knell** tolling of a bell, announcing a death or other misfortune
29 **put out all** all put out   30.1 *several* separate   33 **point to** tend to
36 **what state compounds** that which constitutes dignity and splendor   37 **But only** nothing more than   39 **blood . . . men** i.e., generosity, a godlike attribute, brings mere mortals to ruin.   43 **to be** only to be   46 **flung** rushed off   48 **Nor . . . life** nor has he anything to maintain himself with   49 **that . . . it** i.e., money.
51 **serve his mind** execute his wishes
4.3. Location: Woods and cave, near the seashore; in front of Timon's cave.

Rotten humidity; below thy sister's orb   2
Infect the air! Twinned brothers of one womb,   3
Whose procreation, residence, and birth   4
Scarce is dividant, touch them with several fortunes,   5
The greater scorns the lesser. Not nature,   6
To whom all sores lay siege, can bear great fortune   7
But by contempt of nature.   8
Raise me this beggar, and deny't that lord;   9
The senator shall bear contempt hereditary,   10
The beggar native honor.   11
It is the pasture lards the brother's sides,   12
The want that makes him lean. Who dares, who dares   13
In purity of manhood stand upright
And say "This man's a flatterer"? If one be,
So are they all, for every grece of fortune   16
Is smoothed by that below. The learnèd pate   17
Ducks to the golden fool. All's obliquy;   18
There's nothing level in our cursèd natures   19
But direct villainy. Therefore, be abhorred
All feasts, societies, and throngs of men!
His semblable, yea, himself, Timon disdains.   22
Destruction fang mankind! Earth, yield me roots!   23
                                        [He digs.]
Who seeks for better of thee, sauce his palate   24
With thy most operant poison! [He finds gold.] What
    is here?   25
Gold? Yellow, glittering, precious gold?
No, gods, I am no idle votarist.   27
Roots, you clear heavens! Thus much of this will make   28
Black white, foul fair, wrong right,
Base noble, old young, coward valiant.
Ha, you gods! Why this? What this, you gods? Why,
    this
Will lug your priests and servants from your sides,
Pluck stout men's pillows from below their heads.   33

This yellow slave   34
Will knit and break religions, bless th'accurst,   35
Make the hoar leprosy adored, place thieves   36
And give them title, knee, and approbation   37
With senators on the bench. This is it   38
That makes the wappened widow wed again;   39
She whom the spital house and ulcerous sores   40
Would cast the gorge at, this embalms and spices   41
To th'April day again. Come, damnèd earth,   42
Thou common whore of mankind, that puts odds   43
Among the rout of nations, I will make thee   44
Do thy right nature. (March afar off.) Ha? A drum?
    Thou'rt quick,   45
But yet I'll bury thee. Thou'lt go, strong thief,   46
When gouty keepers of thee cannot stand.   47
                                    [He buries the gold.]
Nay, stay thou out for earnest.   [He keeps some gold.] 48

*Enter Alcibiades, with drum and fife, in warlike
manner, and Phrynia and Timandra.*

ALCIBIADES   What art thou there? Speak.
TIMON
A beast, as thou art. The canker gnaw thy heart   50
For showing me again the eyes of man!
ALCIBIADES
What is thy name? Is man so hateful to thee
That art thyself a man?
TIMON
I am Misanthropos and hate mankind.   54
For thy part, I do wish thou wert a dog,   55
That I might love thee something.
ALCIBIADES   I know thee well,   56
But in thy fortunes am unlearned and strange.   57
TIMON
I know thee too; and more than that I know thee
I not desire to know. Follow thy drum;
With man's blood paint the ground gules, gules.   60
Religious canons, civil laws, are cruel;   61
Then what should war be? This fell whore of thine   62
Hath in her more destruction than thy sword,

2 **Rotten humidity** rot-causing damp.   **thy sister's** i.e., the moon's
3–6 Twinned . . . lesser If, as a test, one were to give unequal fortunes
to identical twins whose lives are otherwise indivisible, the wealthier
twin would end up scorning his poorer twin. (The lust for power and
wealth is greater than the closest of blood ties.)   **6–8 Not . . . nature**
Human nature, subject as it is to such antagonisms and competitive
instincts, cannot experience good fortune without scorning fellow
creatures who are less fortunate.   **9–11 Raise . . . honor** i.e., If Fortune were to raise a beggar to great fortune while simultaneously
impoverishing a lord, the senator would find himself treated with
contempt and the beggar with honor as though this were their
birthright. (*Raise me* means "raise"; the *me* is colloquial.)   **12–13 It is
. . . lean** i.e., It is the inheritance and possessing of pasture that makes
one brother fat, the lack (want) that makes the younger brother lean.
(The Folio reads "leaue" for "lean," which could mean that the
younger brother has to leave in search of riches elsewhere.)   **16 grece**
step   **17 smoothed** assiduously prepared   **17–18 The learnèd . . .
obliquy** The head of the scholar bows obsequiously to the rich fool.
All things deviate from the right path. (*Obliquy* may mean "obliq-
uity," i.e., deviation, or "oblique," or perhaps is a variant of "obloquy," evil-speaking or being spoken against.)   **19 level** direct. (The
contrary to *obliquy*.)   **22 His semblable** i.e., His own kind, his own
image   **23 fang** seize   **24 Who** Whoever.   **sauce** stimulate, tickle
25 operant active, potent   **27 no idle votarist** no trifler in my vows
(of wishing to lead a spare existence).   **28 clear** pure.   **this** i.e., the
gold   **33 Pluck . . . heads** i.e., expedite the death of healthy men by
pulling the pillows from beneath their heads as they sleep (supposedly a way of suffocating them).

34–8 This . . . bench Gold will build up some religious movements
and destroy others, smile with favor on the wicked, cause even lepers
with their white scaly skins to be venerated (if they are rich), and give
to wealthy thieves high office and obsequious attention worthy of a
senator.   **39 makes** enables.   **wappened** worn out   **40–2 She . . .
again** A diseased old woman, whom even hospital inmates with horrible ulcers would vomit to behold, can be so embalmed and spiced
by gold that her greedy wooers will think her as fresh and marriageable as a day in April. (A *spital-house* was usually an unwholesome
institution for foul diseases.)   **42 damnèd earth** i.e., gold   **43–4 puts
. . . nations** causes strife among various peoples   **44–5 I will . . .
nature** i.e., (1) I will make you do according to your true nature as a
whore (2) I will return you to the earth, whence you came and where
you belong.   **45 quick** (1) swift to act (2) alive   **46–7 Thou'lt . . .
stand** i.e., I will put you in the earth where you will dwell unchanged
while those who long to possess you grow gouty and infirm.   **48 for
earnest** for token payments, or as a deposit to secure goods or services.   **48.1 *drum and fife*** i.e., soldiers playing drum and fife
50 The canker May a spreading ulcer   **54 Misanthropos** hater of
mankind   **55 For thy part** As for you   **56 something** somewhat,
a little.   **57 unlearned and strange** uninformed and ignorant.
60 gules (Heraldic name for "red.")   **61 canons** rules, laws
62 fell deadly

For all her cherubin look.

PHRYNIA   Thy lips rot off!

TIMON
I will not kiss thee; then the rot returns   65
To thine own lips again.   66

ALCIBIADES
How came the noble Timon to this change?

TIMON
As the moon does, by wanting light to give.   68
But then renew I could not, like the moon;   69
There were no suns to borrow of.   70

ALCIBIADES   Noble Timon, what friendship may I do thee?

TIMON   None, but to maintain my opinion.

ALCIBIADES   What is it, Timon?

TIMON   Promise me friendship, but perform none. If   74
thou wilt not promise, the gods plague thee, for thou 75
art a man! If thou dost perform, confound thee, for   76
thou art a man!   77

ALCIBIADES
I have heard in some sort of thy miseries.

TIMON
Thou saw'st them when I had prosperity.   79

ALCIBIADES
I see them now. Then was a blessèd time.

TIMON
As thine is now, held with a brace of harlots.   81

TIMANDRA
Is this th'Athenian minion whom the world   82
Voiced so regardfully?

TIMON   Art thou Timandra?

TIMANDRA   Yes.   83

TIMON
Be a whore still. They love thee not that use thee;
Give them diseases, leaving with thee their lust.   85
Make use of thy salt hours. Season the slaves   86
For tubs and baths; bring down rose-cheeked youth   87
To the tub-fast and the diet.

TIMANDRA   Hang thee, monster!

ALCIBIADES
Pardon him, sweet Timandra, for his wits
Are drowned and lost in his calamities.—
I have but little gold of late, brave Timon,
The want whereof doth daily make revolt   92
In my penurious band. I have heard and grieved   93
How cursèd Athens, mindless of thy worth,
Forgetting thy great deeds, when neighbor states,

But for thy sword and fortune, trod upon them—   96

TIMON
I prithee, beat thy drum and get thee gone.

ALCIBIADES
I am thy friend and pity thee, dear Timon.

TIMON
How dost thou pity him whom thou dost trouble?
I had rather be alone.

ALCIBIADES
Why, fare thee well. Here is some gold for thee.
                                    [He offers gold.]

TIMON   Keep it. I cannot eat it.

ALCIBIADES
When I have laid proud Athens on a heap—

TIMON
Warr'st thou 'gainst Athens?

ALCIBIADES   Ay, Timon, and have cause.

TIMON
The gods confound them all in thy conquest,   105
And thee after, when thou hast conquered!

ALCIBIADES   Why me, Timon?

TIMON   That by killing of villains   108
Thou wast born to conquer my country.   109
Put up thy gold. Go on—here's gold—go on.
                                    [He offers gold.]
Be as a planetary plague, when Jove   111
Will o'er some high-viced city hang his poison   112
In the sick air. Let not thy sword skip one.
Pity not honored age for his white beard;
He is an usurer. Strike me the counterfeit matron; 115
It is her habit only that is honest,   116
Herself's a bawd. Let not the virgin's cheek
Make soft thy trenchant sword; for those milk paps, 118
That through the window bars bore at men's eyes,   119
Are not within the leaf of pity writ,   120
But set them down horrible traitors. Spare not the
  babe,   121
Whose dimpled smiles from fools exhaust their mercy; 122
Think it a bastard, whom the oracle
Hath doubtfully pronounced thy throat shall cut,   124
And mince it sans remorse. Swear against objects;   125
Put armor on thine ears and on thine eyes,
Whose proof nor yells of mothers, maids, nor babes, 127
Nor sight of priests in holy vestments bleeding,

---

64 **cherubin** angelic.   **Thy lips** May thy lips   **65–6 I . . . again** Since I will not kiss you (and thereby contract venereal disease), your curse rebounds back on to yourself.   **68 wanting** lacking   **69 renew** become new again. (With a quibble on the idea of renewing a loan.)   **70 suns** (Punning on *sons*, i.e., "men.")   **74–7 If . . . a man!** i.e., May the gods plague you for being a man whether you perform your promises or don't even make promises!   **79 Thou . . . prosperity** i.e., Prosperity itself was my true misery.   **81 brace** pair. (With a quibble on the meaning "clamp," one that holds Alcibiades in its grip.)   **82 th'Athenian minion** the darling of Athens   **83 Voiced so regardfully** spoke of so respectfully.   **85 leaving** since they are leaving   **86 salt** lecherous.   **Season the slaves** i.e., Pickle and spice the villains as if preparing them for the pickling tub; make them ready   **87 tubs and baths** (Allusion to the treatments for venereal diseases, as also in *tub-fast* and *diet* in the next line.)   **92 want** lack.   **make revolt** provoke mutiny   **93 penurious** poverty-stricken

96 **But . . . fortune** (A suggestion of Timon's history as a great military leader, for which Athens ought to be grateful.)   **105 confound** destroy   **108–9 That . . . country** (Timon sees Alcibiades as a scourge, one who is destined to destroy the corrupt city of Athens and then himself be destroyed by the angry gods.)   **111 planetary plague** (Allusion to the belief in the malignant influence of planets.)   **112 high-viced** extremely vicious   **115 Strike me** Strike.   **counterfeit** pretending respectability   **116 habit** costume, outward appearance.   **honest** chaste   **118 trenchant** sharp.   **milk paps** nipples   **119 window bars** i.e., latticework of her bodice, or of her window   **120 Are . . . writ** are not written down on the list of those to whom pity is to be shown   **121 traitors** i.e., betrayers of men.   **122 exhaust** draw forth   **124 doubtfully** ambiguously.   **thy . . . cut** will cut your throat. (However, the phrase can also be ambiguously reversed.)   **125 And . . . remorse** and slash it in small bits without pity.   **Swear . . . objects** Bind yourself by oath to resist any objections or appeals; curse objects of compassion   **127 Whose proof** the tested strength of which armor.   **nor yells** neither the yells

Shall pierce a jot. There's gold to pay thy soldiers.
Make large confusion; and, thy fury spent,   130
Confounded be thyself! Speak not, begone.   131

ALCIBIADES
Hast thou gold yet? I'll take the gold thou givest me,
Not all thy counsel.   [*He takes gold.*]

TIMON
Dost thou or dost thou not, heaven's curse upon thee!   134

PHRYNIA AND TIMANDRA
Give us some gold, good Timon. Hast thou more?

TIMON
Enough to make a whore forswear her trade,   136
And to make whores, a bawd. Hold up, you sluts,   137
Your aprons mountant. [*He throws gold into their
    aprons.*] You are not oathable,   138
Although I know you'll swear—terribly swear—
Into strong shudders and to heavenly agues   140
Th'immortal gods that hear you. Spare your oaths;
I'll trust to your conditions. Be whores still;   142
And he whose pious breath seeks to convert you,
Be strong in whore, allure him, burn him up.   144
Let your close fire predominate his smoke,   145
And be no turncoats. Yet may your pains six months   146
Be quite contrary. And thatch your poor thin roofs   147
With burdens of the dead—some that were hanged,   148
No matter; wear them, betray with them. Whore still;   149
Paint till a horse may mire upon your face.   150
A pox of wrinkles!

PHRYNIA AND TIMANDRA   Well, more gold. What then?   151
Believe't that we'll do anything for gold.

TIMON   Consumptions sow   153
In hollow bones of man; strike their sharp shins,
And mar men's spurring. Crack the lawyer's voice,   155
That he may never more false title plead,
Nor sound his quillets shrilly. Hoar the flamen,   157

That scolds against the quality of flesh   158
And not believes himself. Down with the nose,   159
Down with it flat; take the bridge quite away
Of him that, his particular to foresee,   161
Smells from the general weal. Make curled-pate
    ruffians bald,   162
And let the unscarred braggarts of the war
Derive some pain from you. Plague all,
That your activity may defeat and quell
The source of all erection. There's more gold.   166
                                [*He gives gold.*]
Do you damn others, and let this damn you,
And ditches grave you all!   168

PHRYNIA AND TIMANDRA
More counsel with more money, bounteous Timon.   169

TIMON
More whore, more mischief first. I have given you
    earnest.   170

ALCIBIADES
Strike up the drum towards Athens. Farewell, Timon.
If I thrive well, I'll visit thee again.

TIMON
If I hope well, I'll never see thee more.   173

ALCIBIADES   I never did thee harm.

TIMON
Yes, thou spok'st well of me.

ALCIBIADES   Call'st thou that harm?

TIMON
Men daily find it. Get thee away, and take   176
Thy beagles with thee.

ALCIBIADES   We but offend him. Strike!   177
                [*Drum beats.*] *Exeunt* [*Alcibiades,
                        Phrynia, and Timandra*].

TIMON
That nature, being sick of man's unkindness,   178
Should yet be hungry! [*He digs.*] Common mother,
    thou   179
Whose womb unmeasurable and infinite breast
Teems and feeds all, whose selfsame mettle   181
Whereof thy proud child, arrogant man, is puffed   182
Engenders the black toad and adder blue,
The gilded newt and eyeless venomed worm,   184
With all th'abhorrèd births below crisp heaven   185

130 **large confusion** wholesale destruction   131 **Confounded**
destroyed   134 **Dost . . . not** Whether you do or not   136–7 **Enough . . .
bawd** Enough to let a whore retire from her whoring and turn
madam instead (or, retire from her profession of turning women into
whores).   138 **mountant** (A heraldic coinage, with sexual suggestion
of raising up for erotic purposes; see also *erection* in line 166.)
oathable to be believed on your oath   140 **strong** violent.   **agues**
feverish shivers   142 **your conditions** what you are, your characters.
144 **Be . . . whore** be resolute in whoring.   **burn him up** (1) inflame
him with desire (2) infect him with venereal disease.   145 **Let . . .
smoke** (1) Combat the smoke of the enemy with your close-range
musketry (2) Use your transmitting of venereal infection to overcome
his hypocritical rhetoric, his smokescreen of pious utterances   146 **be
no turncoats** i.e. (continuing the military metaphor), don't betray
your profession of whoring; whore still.   146–7 **Yet . . . contrary**
(Unclear. The *six months* may refer to the time required for syphilitic
infection to take hold, or the time needed to cure a painful venereal
infection, or a prolonged period of menstrual cramping, or the length
of a sentence in a correctional institution.)   147–8 **thatch . . . dead**
cover your balding heads (caused by venereal disease) with wigs
made of the hair of corpses   149 **betray with them** use these wigs to
create false beauty to betray more men.   150 **mire upon** bog down
in. (Timon sardonically urges so thick a cosmetic covering that even a
horse would become mired.)   151 **A pox of wrinkles!** i.e., May you
be plagued with wrinkles!   153 **Consumptions sow** Plant wasting
diseases such as syphilis. (Addressed to Phrynia and Timandra.)
155 **spurring** i.e., riding (here used as a sexual metaphor).   157 **quillets** quibbles.   **Hoar the flamen** Whiten (with venereal disease or
leprosy) the priest. (With a pun on *hoar*, "whore.")

158 **quality of flesh** fleshly desire   159 **And . . . himself** i.e., and
doesn't practice what he preaches.   **Down . . . nose** (An effect of
syphilis.)   161–2 **Of . . . weal** of him that, in furthering his narrow
self-interest, loses the scent of the general welfare, goes down the
wrong path.   162 **curled-pate** curly-headed   166 **erection** (1)
advancement (2) sexual erection.   168 **grave** enclose in the grave.
(With a pun on "ditches" and "damming" continued from line 167.)
169 **More . . . money** i.e., We're glad to listen to your sermon as long
as the money keeps coming   170 **More . . . first** i.e., That's a bargain,
but I insist on more whoring and spreading of disease before I give
more money.   **earnest** earnest money.   173 **If I hope well** If my
hopes are realized   176 **find it** i.e., find it harmful to be spoken well
of.   177 **beagles** i.e., beagle hounds, fawning followers—the prostitutes   178–9 **That . . . hungry!** To think that my human constitution,
sick though it is man's ingratitude and unnaturalness, should still
require food!   179 **Common mother** i.e., The earth   181 **Teems**
abundantly bears offspring.   **mettle** spirit, essence   182 **Whereof**
with which   184 **gilded** iridescent.   **eyeless venomed worm** the
blindworm (wrongly supposed poisonous, as were the toad and the
newt)   185 **crisp** rippled, curled

Whereon Hyperion's quick'ning fire doth shine: 186
Yield him who all thy human sons do hate, 187
From forth thy plenteous bosom, one poor root!
Ensear thy fertile and conceptious womb; 189
Let it no more bring out ingrateful man!
Go great with tigers, dragons, wolves, and bears; 191
Teem with new monsters, whom thy upward face 192
Hath to the marbled mansion all above 193
Never presented! [*He finds a root.*] Oh, a root! Dear
   thanks!—
Dry up thy marrows, vines, and plow-torn leas, 195
Whereof ingrateful man with liquorish drafts 196
And morsels unctuous greases his pure mind, 197
That from it all consideration slips— 198

Enter Apemantus.

More man? Plague, plague!

APEMANTUS
I was directed hither. Men report
Thou dost affect my manners and dost use them. 201
TIMON
'Tis, then, because thou dost not keep a dog, 202
Whom I would imitate. Consumption catch thee! 203
APEMANTUS
This is in thee a nature but infected, 204
A poor unmanly melancholy sprung
From change of fortune. Why this spade? This place? 207
This slavelike habit and these looks of care?
Thy flatterers yet wear silk, drink wine, lie soft,
Hug their diseased perfumes, and have forgot 209
That ever Timon was. Shame not these woods
By putting on the cunning of a carper. 211
Be thou a flatterer now and seek to thrive
By that which has undone thee. Hinge thy knee, 213
And let his very breath whom thou'lt observe 214
Blow off thy cap. Praise his most vicious strain 215
And call it excellent. Thou wast told thus. 216
Thou gav'st thine ears, like tapsters that bade
   welcome, 217
To knaves and all approachers. 'Tis most just 218
That thou turn rascal; hadst thou wealth again,
Rascals should have't. Do not assume my likeness. 220

TIMON
Were I like thee, I'd throw away myself.
APEMANTUS
Thou hast cast away thyself, being like thyself—
A madman so long, now a fool. What, think'st 223
That the bleak air, thy boisterous chamberlain, 224
Will put thy shirt on warm? Will these mossed trees, 225
That have outlived the eagle, page thy heels 226
And skip when thou point'st out? Will the cold brook, 227
Candied with ice, caudle thy morning taste 228
To cure thy o'ernight's surfeit? Call the creatures
Whose naked natures live in all the spite 230
Of wreakful heaven, whose bare unhousèd trunks, 231
To the conflicting elements exposed,
Answer mere nature; bid them flatter thee. 233
Oh, thou shalt find—
TIMON   A fool of thee. Depart. 234
APEMANTUS
I love thee better now than e'er I did.
TIMON
I hate thee worse.
APEMANTUS   Why?
TIMON   Thou flatter'st misery.
APEMANTUS
I flatter not, but say thou art a caitiff. 237
TIMON
Why dost thou seek me out?
APEMANTUS   To vex thee.
TIMON
Always a villain's office or a fool's.
Dost please thyself in't?
APEMANTUS   Ay.
TIMON   What, a knave too? 241
APEMANTUS
If thou didst put this sour cold habit on 242
To castigate thy pride, 'twere well, but thou 243
Dost it enforcedly. Thou'dst courtier be again
Wert thou not beggar. Willing misery 245
Outlives incertain pomp, is crowned before: 246
The one is filling still, never complete, 247
The other at high wish. Best state, contentless, 248
Hath a distracted and most wretched being, 249
Worse than the worst, content. 250
Thou shouldst desire to die, being miserable.

186 Hyperion's i.e., the sun's. **quick'ning** life-giving **187 who . . . hate** who hates all your human offspring **189 Ensear** Dry up. **conceptious** fertile **191 Go great** Be pregnant **192 upward** upturned **193 the marbled . . . above** i.e., the heavens **195 marrows** gourds, squash. (Also, figuratively, the vital strength of the earth.) **plow-torn leas** plowed-up pastureland **196–8 Whereof . . . slips** from ingrateful man, with his delight in alcoholic drink and tasty morsels of meat, greasily indulges his appetites to the point of losing all rationality **201 affect** put on **202 dog** (*Cynic* is derived from the Greek for "dog"; see 1.1.210.) **203 would** would prefer to. **Consumption catch thee!** May a wasting illness lay hold on you! **204 but infected** i.e., not inborn and philosophical but induced by misery and hence shallow **207 habit** garment **209 perfumes** perfumed mistresses **211 putting . . . carper** assuming the manner and profession of a fault-finding cynic. **213–5 Hinge . . . cap** Bow deeply, so low that the breath of the great lord to whom you are so obsequious will virtually blow off your cap. **215 strain** quality **216 Thou . . . thus** This is what you used to be told; you were warned of this. **217–18 Thou . . . approachers** You imprudently gave ear to any rascals that approached you, like a barkeep who welcomes any comer to a tavern. **220 Do . . . likeness** Don't be poor, churlish, and misanthropic, like me.

223–5 think'st . . . warm (Alludes to the practice of having a servant warm one's garment by the fire.) **226 page thy heels** follow at your heels like a page **227 skip . . . out** jump to fulfill your command. **228 Candied** encrusted, as if with sugar. **caudle . . . taste** i.e., provide you with a caudle, a hot spiced drink **230 in** exposed to **231 wreakful** vengeful. **trunks** i.e., bodies **233 Answer . . . nature** contend with nature in its natural state **234 of** in **237 caitiff** wretch. **241 a knave too?** (It is knavish to take pleasure in vexing others rather than doing so with moral intent.) **242 habit** disposition **243 'twere well** it would be a commendable thing **245–6 Willing . . . before** Willingly embraced poverty outlasts the life of insecure ceremony and wealth, and is sooner crowned with spiritual reward **247 The one . . . still** Uncertain pomp is never satisfied **248 at high wish** at the height of contentment. **248–50 Best . . . content** Being at the height of prosperity without contentment means a wretched existence, worse than being at the bottom of prosperity with contentment.

TIMON
Not by his breath that is more miserable. 252
Thou art a slave whom Fortune's tender arm 253
With favor never clasped but bred a dog. 254
Hadst thou, like us from our first swathe, proceeded 255
The sweet degrees that this brief world affords
To such as may the passive drudges of it 257
Freely command, thou wouldst have plunged thyself 258
In general riot, melted down thy youth 259
In different beds of lust, and never learned 260
The icy precepts of respect, but followed
The sugared game before thee. But myself— 262
Who had the world as my confectionary, 263
The mouths, the tongues, the eyes, and hearts of men
At duty, more than I could frame employment, 265
That numberless upon me stuck, as leaves
Do on the oak, have with one winter's brush 267
Fell from their boughs and left me open, bare 268
For every storm that blows—I to bear this, 269
That never knew but better, is some burden. 270
Thy nature did commence in sufferance; time 271
Hath made thee hard in't. Why shouldst thou hate
   men? 272
They never flattered thee. What hast thou given?
If thou wilt curse, thy father, that poor rag, 274
Must be thy subject, who in spite put stuff 275
To some she-beggar and compounded thee 276
Poor rogue hereditary. Hence, begone! 277
If thou hadst not been born the worst of men, 278
Thou hadst been a knave and flatterer.

APEMANTUS
Art thou proud yet?
TIMON   Ay, that I am not thee.
APEMANTUS   I, that I was no prodigal.
TIMON   I, that I am one now. 282
Were all the wealth I have shut up in thee, 283
I'd give thee leave to hang it. Get thee gone. 284
That the whole life of Athens were in this! 285
Thus would I eat it.   [He eats a root.]
APEMANTUS [offering food]   Here, I will mend thy feast.
TIMON
First mend my company: take away thyself.

APEMANTUS
So I shall mend mine own by th' lack of thine.
TIMON
'Tis not well mended so; it is but botched. 289
If not, I would it were. 290
APEMANTUS   What wouldst thou have to Athens? 291
TIMON
Thee thither in a whirlwind. If thou wilt,
Tell them there I have gold. Look, so I have.
                       [He shows his gold.]
APEMANTUS
Here is no use for gold.
TIMON   The best and truest,
For here it sleeps and does no hirèd harm.
APEMANTUS   Where liest anights, Timon? 296
TIMON   Under that's above me. Where feed'st thou 297
adays, Apemantus? 298
APEMANTUS   Where my stomach finds meat; or, rather,
where I eat it.
TIMON   Would poison were obedient and knew my
mind!
APEMANTUS   Where wouldst thou send it?
TIMON   To sauce thy dishes. 304
APEMANTUS   The middle of humanity thou never knew-
est, but the extremity of both ends. When thou wast
in thy gilt and thy perfume, they mocked thee for too 307
much curiosity; in thy rags thou know'st none, but art 308
despised for the contrary. There's a medlar for thee. 309
Eat it.   [He gives a fruit.]
TIMON   On what I hate I feed not.
APEMANTUS   Dost hate a medlar?
TIMON   Ay, though it look like thee. 313
APEMANTUS   An thou'dst hated meddlers sooner, thou 314
shouldst have loved thyself better now. What man
didst thou ever know unthrift that was beloved after 316
his means? 317
TIMON   Who, without those means thou talk'st of, didst
thou ever know beloved?
APEMANTUS   Myself.
TIMON   I understand thee: thou hadst some means to 321
keep a dog. 322
APEMANTUS   What things in the world canst thou
nearest compare to thy flatterers?
TIMON   Women nearest. But men—men are the things

---

252 Not . . . miserable Not when he who speaks (Apemantus) is more wretched than I.   253–4 Thou . . . dog i.e., You are a wretch whom Fortune has never treated any better than a dog. (See note 202 above.) 255 like . . . swathe like us who were born aristocrats. (Swathe means "swaddling clothes.")   proceeded passed through (like a student taking an academic degree)   257–8 To such . . . command i.e., to the status of those who have the world and its sycophants at command 259 riot debauchery   260 different various   262 sugared game sweet-tasting quarry   263 confectionary sweetmeat shop   265 At duty subservient to my wishes.   frame provide with   267 winter's brush gust of wintry wind   268 Fell fallen.   open exposed 269 I . . . this that I should bear this   270 That . . . better who have known only better fortune   271 sufferance suffering, poverty 272 hard in't hardened to it.   274 rag i.e., wretch   275–7 who . . . hereditary who spitefully fornicated with some beggarly woman and begot you as a rogue by right of inheritance.   278 worst lowest in station   282–4 I, that . . . hang it (Timon declares himself now a prodigal in the sense of wishing to give away all his worldly possessions. If that wealth were all contained in Apemantus, Timon would be glad to see Apemantus hanged and thereby have done with the whole lot.)   285 That I wish that

289 botched badly mended (since you remain in your own company). 290 If not If it isn't botched   291 What . . . have What would you have me convey. (But Timon caustically jests in a more literal sense of the phrase.)   296 anights at night   297 that's that which is 298 adays by day   304 sauce flavor   307 gilt fine trappings 308 curiosity fastidiousness, refinement   309 medlar fruit like a small brown-skinned apple, eaten when nearly decayed. (Used here, as often, for the sake of a quibble on meddler, one given to sexual promiscuity.)   313 like thee i.e., in a state of decay, or, as one who meddles.   314 An thou'dst If thou hadst.   meddlers busybodies. (With sexual meaning also.)   316 unthrift to be unthrifty 316–17 after his means (1) after his wealth was gone (2) according to his means.   321–2 thou . . . dog i.e., even in your poverty you were able to keep a dog, and it loved you.

themselves. What wouldst thou do with the world, Apemantus, if it lay in thy power?

APEMANTUS   Give it the beasts, to be rid of the men.

TIMON   Wouldst thou have thyself fall in the confusion 329
of men and remain a beast with the beasts? 330

APEMANTUS   Ay, Timon.

TIMON   A beastly ambition, which the gods grant thee
t'attain to! If thou wert the lion, the fox would beguile
thee. If thou wert the lamb, the fox would eat thee. If
thou wert the fox, the lion would suspect thee when
peradventure thou wert accused by the ass. If thou 336
wert the ass, thy dullness would torment thee, and still 337
thou lived'st but as a breakfast to the wolf. If thou wert 338
the wolf, thy greediness would afflict thee, and oft
thou shouldst hazard thy life for thy dinner. Wert thou
the unicorn, pride and wrath would confound thee 341
and make thine own self the conquest of thy fury. Wert
thou a bear, thou wouldst be killed by the horse. Wert
thou a horse, thou wouldst be seized by the leopard.
Wert thou a leopard, thou wert germane to the lion, 345
and the spots of thy kindred were jurors on thy life; all 346
thy safety were remotion and thy defense absence. 347
What beast couldst thou be, that were not subject to a
beast? And what a beast art thou already, that see'st
not thy loss in transformation! 350

APEMANTUS   If thou couldst please me with speaking to 351
me, thou mightst have hit upon it here. The common- 352
wealth of Athens is become a forest of beasts.

TIMON   How, has the ass broke the wall, that thou art 354
out of the city?

APEMANTUS   Yonder comes a poet and a painter. The 356
plague of company light upon thee! I will fear to catch
it, and give way. When I know not what else to do, I'll 358
see thee again.

TIMON   When there is nothing living but thee, thou
shalt be welcome. I had rather be a beggar's dog than
Apemantus.

APEMANTUS
Thou art the cap of all the fools alive. 363

TIMON
Would thou wert clean enough to spit upon!

APEMANTUS
A plague on thee! Thou art too bad to curse.

TIMON
All villains that do stand by thee are pure. 366

APEMANTUS
There is no leprosy but what thou speak'st.

TIMON   If I name thee.
I'd beat thee, but I should infect my hands.

APEMANTUS
I would my tongue could rot them off!

TIMON
Away, thou issue of a mangy dog! 371
Choler does kill me that thou art alive;
I swoon to see thee.

APEMANTUS
Would thou wouldst burst!

TIMON   Away, thou tedious rogue!
I am sorry I shall lose a stone by thee.
                    [*He throws a stone at Apemantus.*]

APEMANTUS   Beast!

TIMON   Slave!

APEMANTUS   Toad!

TIMON   Rogue, rogue, rogue!
I am sick of this false world, and will love naught
But even the mere necessities upon't. 381
Then, Timon, presently prepare thy grave. 382
Lie where the light foam of the sea may beat
Thy gravestone daily. Make thine epitaph,
That death in me at others' lives may laugh. 385
[*To the gold*] O thou sweet king-killer and dear divorce
Twixt natural son and sire! Thou bright defiler 387
Of Hymen's purest bed! Thou valiant Mars! 388
Thou ever young, fresh, loved, and delicate wooer,
Whose blush doth thaw the consecrated snow 390
That lies on Dian's lap! Thou visible god, 391
That sold'rest close impossibilities 392
And mak'st them kiss; that speak'st with every tongue
To every purpose! O thou touch of hearts! 394
Think thy slave, man, rebels, and by thy virtue 395
Set them into confounding odds, that beasts 396
May have the world in empire!

APEMANTUS   Would 'twere so!
But not till I am dead. I'll say thou'st gold; 398
Thou wilt be thronged to shortly.

TIMON   Thronged to?

APEMANTUS   Ay.

TIMON
Thy back, I prithee.

APEMANTUS   Live, and love thy misery. 400

TIMON
Long live so, and so die! I am quit. 401

                    Enter the Banditti.

329–30 in . . . men i.e., in the destruction of mankind you've just wished for   **336 peradventure** by chance   **337 still** continually   **338 lived'st** wouldst live   **341 unicorn** a legendary creature, supposedly caught by being goaded into charging a tree and embedding its horn in the tree trunk   **345 germane** akin, related   **346 the spots . . . life** i.e., the crimes of those closely related to you would bring down a sentence of death upon you. (With a pun on *spots*, meaning "leopard's spots" and "stains, crimes.")   **346–7 all . . . remotion** your only safety would consist in your constantly going from place to place   **350 in transformation** in being changed into a beast.   **351–2 If . . . here** If it were possible for anything you say to please me, what you've just said (comparing men with beasts) would be pleasing.   **354 How** What is this   **356 Yonder . . . painter** (In fact, they do not appear until 5.1; this line may give evidence of an incompletely revised manuscript.)   **358 give way** (I will) retire.   **363 cap** acme, summit. (With wordplay on "fool's cap.")   **366 that . . . thee** compared to you

371 issue offspring   **381 But even** except   **382 presently** immediately   **385 That** in order that.   **in** through   **387 natural** truly begotten (not illegitimate)   **388 Hymen** god of marriage.   **Mars** i.e., as the adulterous lover of Venus   **390 blush** i.e., reddish glow of gold   **391 Dian** Diana, goddess of the hunt and patroness of chastity   **392 That . . . impossibilities** you who solder tightly together things incapable apparently of being united   **394 touch** touchstone   **395 Think** Consider the fact that.   **virtue** power   **396 Set . . . odds** set men in self-destroying conflict with one another   **398 thou'st** thou hast   **400 Thy back** i.e., Show me your back   **401 quit** rid (of Apemantus).

APEMANTUS
  More things like men! Eat, Timon, and abhor them. 402
                                    Exit Apemantus.
FIRST BANDIT Where should he have this gold? It is 403
  some poor fragment, some slender ort of his remain- 404
  der. The mere want of gold and the falling-from of his 405
  friends drove him into this melancholy.
SECOND BANDIT It is noised he hath a mass of treasure. 407
THIRD BANDIT Let us make the assay upon him. If he 408
  care not for't, he will supply us easily. If he covetously 409
  reserve it, how shall 's get it? 410
SECOND BANDIT True, for he bears it not about him.
  'Tis hid.
FIRST BANDIT Is not this he?
BANDITTI Where?
SECOND BANDIT 'Tis his description.
THIRD BANDIT He. I know him.
BANDITTI [*coming forward*] Save thee, Timon. 417
TIMON Now, thieves?
BANDITTI
  Soldiers, not thieves.
TIMON   Both, too, and women's sons. 419
BANDITTI
  We are not thieves, but men that much do want. 420
TIMON
  Your greatest want is, you want much of meat. 421
  Why should you want? Behold, the earth hath roots;
  Within this mile break forth a hundred springs;
  The oaks bear mast, the briers scarlet hips. 424
  The bounteous huswife Nature on each bush
  Lays her full mess before you. What? Why want? 426
FIRST BANDIT
  We cannot live on grass, on berries, water,
  As beasts and birds and fishes.
TIMON
  Nor on the beasts themselves, the birds and fishes;
  You must eat men. Yet thanks I must you con 430
  That you are thieves professed, that you work not
  In holier shapes; for there is boundless theft
  In limited professions. [*He gives gold.*] Rascal thieves, 433
  Here's gold. Go, suck the subtle blood o'th' grape 434
  Till the high fever seethe your blood to froth, 435
  And so scape hanging. Trust not the physician; 436
  His antidotes are poison, and he slays
  More than you rob. Take wealth and lives together. 438
  Do villainy, do, since you protest to do't, 439

  Like workmen. I'll example you with thievery. 440
  The sun's a thief, and with his great attraction 441
  Robs the vast sea. The moon's an arrant thief, 442
  And her pale fire she snatches from the sun.
  The sea's a thief, whose liquid surge resolves 444
  The moon into salt tears. The earth's a thief,
  That feeds and breeds by a composture stol'n 446
  From gen'ral excrement. Each thing's a thief.
  The laws, your curb and whip, in their rough power 448
  Has unchecked theft. Love not yourselves. Away! 449
  Rob one another. There's more gold. Cut throats.
  All that you meet are thieves. To Athens go,
  Break open shops; nothing can you steal
  But thieves do lose it. Steal less for this I give you, 453
  And gold confound you howsoe'er! Amen. 454
THIRD BANDIT He's almost charmed me from my pro- 455
  fession by persuading me to it.
FIRST BANDIT 'Tis in the malice of mankind that he 457
  thus advises us, not to have us thrive in our mystery. 458
SECOND BANDIT I'll believe him as an enemy, and give 459
  over my trade.
FIRST BANDIT Let us first see peace in Athens. There is 461
  no time so miserable but a man may be true. 462
                                    Exeunt Thieves.

  Enter the steward [Flavius] to Timon.

FLAVIUS O you gods!
  Is yond despised and ruinous man my lord? 464
  Full of decay and failing? O monument 465
  And wonder of good deeds evilly bestowed! 466
  What an alteration of honor has desp'rate want made!
  What viler thing upon the earth than friends,
  Who can bring noblest minds to basest ends! 469
  How rarely does it meet with this time's guise, 470
  When man was wished to love his enemies! 471
  Grant I may ever love, and rather woo 472
  Those that would mischief me than those that do!— 473
  He's caught me in his eye. I will present
  My honest grief unto him, and as my lord
  Still serve him with my life.—My dearest master!

402 them i.e., the bandits. 403 should he have can he have obtained
404 ort fragment 405 mere utter 407 noised rumored 408 assay
trial, test (as one would test gold ore for its content) 409 for't for the
gold 410 shall 's shall we 417 Save God save 419 Both, too You
are both 420 much do want are greatly in need. (But Timon answers
as if they meant "want too much.") 421 Your . . . meat Your main
need arises from the fact that you crave such rich food (as Timon goes
on to explain). 424 mast acorns. hips fruit of the rosebush.
426 mess food, meal 430 thanks . . . con I must offer you thanks
433 limited regulated, legalized. (With a play on *boundless*, line 432,
as the opposite of *limited*.) 434 subtle (1) delicate (2) treacherous in
its influence 435 high fever (Induced by intoxication.) seethe boil
436 scape hanging i.e., avoid execution by dying of excess drinking.
438 Take . . . together i.e., Murder your robbery victims. 439 protest
openly profess

440 example you with give you instances of 441 attraction power to
draw up 442 arrant notorious 444 resolves melts, dissolves.
(Alludes to the belief that the moon draws moisture from the air and
deposits it in the sea, thus creating the effect of tides.) 446 composture compost, manure 448–9 The laws . . . theft The laws, which
restrain and punish men, provide opportunity for unlimited abuse to
those who administer them. 453 But . . . it i.e., without robbing from
persons who are themselves thieves. 453–4 Steal . . . howsoe'er! If
you steal less because of my giving you this gold, may gold destroy
you no matter what happens! 455 charmed dissuaded (as if by
means of enchantment) 457 the malice of i.e., his hating of
458 mystery trade. 459 as as I would. (One can learn even from an
enemy.) 461–2 Let . . . true i.e., Let's not rush into reformation, at
least not until there is peace in Athens; besides, there will always be
time to repent. 464 ruinous brought to ruin 465 failing downfall.
465–6 O . . . bestowed! O admonishing memorial of charitable deeds
sorely misdirected! 469 bring . . . ends reduce even the noblest-
minded (like Timon) to wretchedness. 470–1 How . . . enemies!
How strangely does the commandment to love one's enemies suit
this degenerate age! 472–3 Grant . . . do! May the gods grant that I
continue to love my enemies, but preferring to deal with those who
only intend me harm rather than those who actually do harm!

TIMON
  Away! What art thou?
FLAVIUS   Have you forgot me, sir?
TIMON
  Why dost ask that? I have forgot all men.
  Then, if thou grant'st thou'rt a man, I have forgot thee.
FLAVIUS   An honest poor servant of yours.
TIMON   Then I know thee not.
  I never had honest man about me, I; all
  I kept were knaves, to serve in meat to villains.
FLAVIUS   The gods are witness,
  Ne'er did poor steward wear a truer grief
  For his undone lord than mine eyes for you.
                                        [*He weeps.*]
TIMON
  What, dost thou weep? Come nearer, then, I love thee
  Because thou art a woman and disclaim'st
  Flinty mankind, whose eyes do never give   489
  But thorough lust and laughter. Pity's sleeping. 490
  Strange times, that weep with laughing, not with
    weeping!
FLAVIUS
  I beg of you to know me, good my lord,
  T'accept my grief, and whilst this poor wealth lasts
  To entertain me as your steward still.   494
                            [*He offers money.*]
TIMON   Had I a steward
  So true, so just, and now so comfortable?   496
  It almost turns my dangerous nature mild.   497
  Let me behold thy face. Surely, this man
  Was born of woman.
  Forgive my general and exceptless rashness,   500
  You perpetual-sober gods! I do proclaim   501
  One honest man—mistake me not, but one;   502
  No more, I pray—and he's a steward.
  How fain would I have hated all mankind,   504
  And thou redeem'st thyself! But all, save thee,
  I fell with curses.   506
  Methinks thou art more honest now than wise,
  For by oppressing and betraying me
  Thou mightst have sooner got another service;   509
  For many so arrive at second masters
  Upon their first lord's neck. But tell me true—   511
  For I must ever doubt, though ne'er so sure—   512
  Is not thy kindness subtle, covetous,
  A usuring kindness, and, as rich men deal gifts,
  Expecting in return twenty for one?
FLAVIUS
  No, my most worthy master, in whose breast
  Doubt and suspect, alas, are placed too late.   517
  You should have feared false times when you did
    feast.   518

Suspect still comes where an estate is least.   519
That which I show, heaven knows, is merely love,   520
Duty, and zeal to your unmatchèd mind,
Care of your food and living; and believe it,   522
My most honored lord,
For any benefit that points to me,   524
Either in hope or present, I'd exchange   525
For this one wish: that you had power and wealth
To requite me by making rich yourself.   527
TIMON
  Look thee, 'tis so. Thou singly honest man,   528
  Here, take. [*He offers gold.*] The gods out of my misery
  Has sent thee treasure. Go, live rich and happy,
  But thus conditioned: thou shalt build from men,   531
  Hate all, curse all, show charity to none,
  But let the famished flesh slide from the bone
  Ere thou relieve the beggar. Give to dogs
  What thou deniest to men. Let prisons swallow 'em,
  Debts wither 'em to nothing. Be men like blasted
    woods,   536
  And may diseases lick up their false bloods!
  And so farewell and thrive.
FLAVIUS   Oh, let me stay
  And comfort you, my master.
TIMON   If thou hat'st curses,
  Stay not; fly, whilst thou art blest and free.
  Ne'er see thou man, and let me ne'er see thee.
                Exit [*Flavius; Timon retires to his cave*].

                            ❧

[5.1]

  Enter Poet and Painter. [*Timon enters at some
  point to watch them from his cave.*]

PAINTER   As I took note of the place, it cannot be far
  where he abides.
POET   What's to be thought of him? Does the rumor
  hold for true that he's so full of gold?
PAINTER   Certain. Alcibiades reports it. Phrynia and
  Timandra had gold of him. He likewise enriched poor
  straggling soldiers with great quantity. 'Tis said he
  gave unto his steward a mighty sum.
POET   Then this breaking of his has been but a try for   9
  his friends?
PAINTER   Nothing else. You shall see him a palm in Ath- 11
  ens again, and flourish with the highest. Therefore 'tis
  not amiss we tender our loves to him in this supposed   13
  distress of his. It will show honestly in us and is very

---

519 Suspect . . . least Wariness inevitably arrives (too late) when
one's fortunes are ruined.   **520 merely** purely   **522 Care . . . living**
concern for your having food and maintenance   **524 For** as for.
points to me appears in prospect for me   **525 in hope** in the future
527 requite repay   **528 singly** (1) uniquely (2) earnestly   **531 thus
conditioned** upon this condition.   **from** away from   **536 Be men** Let
men be.   **blasted** withered
5.1. Location: The woods. Before Timon's cave. The scene is virtually continuous; Timon may well remain visible to the audience.
9 breaking bankruptcy.   **try** test   **11 a palm** a dignitary. (Probably
referring to Psalm 92:12: "The righteous man shall flourish like a
palm.")   **13 we tender** that we should offer

489 Flinty hardhearted.   **give** give forth tears   **490 But thorough**
except through   **494 entertain** receive, employ   **496 comfortable**
comforting.   **497 dangerous** savage   **500 exceptless** making no
exception   **501 perpetual-sober** eternally grave and sedate   **502 but**
only   **504 fain** gladly   **506 fell** cut down   **509 service** position
511 Upon . . . neck by stepping on the bowed neck of their former
master.   **512 though . . . sure** however persuasive the evidence
517 suspect suspicion   **518 feast** entertain lavishly.

likely to load our purposes with what they travail for, 15
if it be a just and true report that goes of his having. 16

POET   What have you now to present unto him?

PAINTER   Nothing at this time but my visitation. Only I
will promise him an excellent piece.

POET   I must serve him so too, tell him of an intent 20
that's coming toward him. 21

PAINTER   Good as the best. Promising is the very air o'th' 22
time; it opens the eyes of expectation. Performance
is ever the duller for his act, and but in the plainer 24
and simpler kind of people the deed of saying is quite 25
out of use. To promise is most courtly and fashionable. 26
Performance is a kind of will or testament which 27
argues a great sickness in his judgment that makes it.

Enter Timon from his cave.

TIMON [*aside*]   Excellent workman! Thou canst not
paint a man so bad as is thyself.

POET   I am thinking what I shall say I have provided for 31
him. It must be a personating of himself, a satire 32
against the softness of prosperity, with a discovery of 33
the infinite flatteries that follow youth and opulency.

TIMON [*aside*]   Must thou needs stand for a villain in 35
thine own work? Wilt thou whip thine own faults in 36
other men? Do so, I have gold for thee.

POET   Nay, let's seek him.
Then do we sin against our own estate 39
When we may profit meet and come too late. 40

PAINTER   True.
When the day serves, before black-cornered night, 42
Find what thou want'st by free and offered light. 43
Come.

TIMON [*aside*]
I'll meet you at the turn. What a god's gold, 45
That he is worshiped in a baser temple 46
Than where swine feed!
'Tis thou that rigg'st the bark and plow'st the foam, 48
Settlest admirèd reverence in a slave. 49
To thee be worship, and thy saints for aye 50
Be crowned with plagues, that thee alone obey! 51
Fit I meet them.   [*He comes forward.*] 52

POET   Hail, worthy Timon!

PAINTER   Our late noble master!

TIMON
Have I once lived to see two honest men? 55

POET   Sir,
Having often of your open bounty tasted,
Hearing you were retired, your friends fall'n off, 58
Whose thankless natures—oh, abhorrèd spirits!
Not all the whips of heaven are large enough—
What, to you,
Whose starlike nobleness gave life and influence 62
To their whole being? I am rapt, and cannot cover 63
The monstrous bulk of this ingratitude
With any size of words. 65

TIMON
Let it go naked; men may see't the better.
You that are honest, by being what you are
Make them best seen and known.

PAINTER   He and myself 68
Have traveled in the great show'r of your gifts 69
And sweetly felt it.

TIMON   Ay, you are honest men.

PAINTER
We are hither come to offer you our service.

TIMON
Most honest men! Why, how shall I requite you?
Can you eat roots and drink cold water? No.

BOTH
What we can do we'll do to do you service.

TIMON
You're honest men. You've heard that I have gold;
I am sure you have. Speak truth; you're honest men.

PAINTER
So it is said, my noble lord, but therefor 77
Came not my friend nor I.

TIMON
Good honest men! [*To the Painter*] Thou draw'st a
counterfeit 79
Best in all Athens. Thou'rt indeed the best;
Thou counterfeit'st most lively.

PAINTER   So-so, my lord. 81

TIMON
E'en so, sir, as I say. [*To the Poet*] And for thy fiction, 82
Why, thy verse swells with stuff so fine and smooth 83
That thou art even natural in thine art. 84
But for all this, my honest-natured friends,
I must needs say you have a little fault.
Marry, 'tis not monstrous in you, neither wish I
You take much pains to mend.

BOTH   Beseech Your Honor 88

15 load our purposes i.e., crown our efforts.   travail labor   16 goes
of his having is current about his wealth.   20 intent project
21 coming toward intended for   22 Good as the best i.e., That's perfect.   air style   24 for his act for its being completed.   but in except
among   25 deed of saying actions fulfilling words or promises
26 use fashion.   27 a kind . . . testament i.e., a desperate attempt to
settle accounts, as if one were about to die   31 provided planned
32 personating of himself representation of his case   33 discovery
disclosure   35 needs necessarily.   stand for serve as a model for
36 in in your portrayal of   39 estate worldly well-being   40 may
profit meet have a chance to make a profit   42 black-cornered night
night which darkens as in corners   43 free and offered light the light
of day, freely offered to all.   45 at the turn i.e., trick for trick in a
cheating game.   46 a baser temple i.e., the human body, or, the marketplace   48 rigg'st the bark sets the ship's sail   49 Settlest . . . slave
engenders in the servile worshiper a wondering awe of money.
50–1 thy saints . . . obey! may your saints (i.e., members of your sect)
who obey you only, be eternally crowned with plagues!   52 Fit It is
fit that

55 once actually   58 fall'n off estranged   62–3 Whose . . . being?
whose nobility of character was of such power as to ennoble men.
(An astrological metaphor.)   65 size (1) quantity (2) covering glue
applied by painters   68 them i.e., the ungrateful men you condemn,
or, ungrateful acts   69 traveled walked. (With a suggestion also of
"worked, travailed," as one would labor for a patron.)
77 therefor for that reason   79 counterfeit picture, likeness. (With
quibble on the idea of "fraudulent imitation.")   81 So-so Passably
82 fiction any creative writing; here, poetry. (With connotation of
"lying.")   83 swells . . . smooth (1) is elegantly styled and adorned
(2) is a vainglorious concoction of specious fabrication   84 thou . . .
thine art (1) your art is a triumph of natural verisimilitude and has
become second nature to you (2) you're a born fool and a liar in
your art.   88 mend mend your ways.

To make it known to us.

TIMON   You'll take it ill.

BOTH   Most thankfully, my lord.

TIMON   Will you, indeed?

BOTH   Doubt it not, worthy lord.

TIMON
There's never a one of you but trusts a knave   93
That mightily deceives you.

BOTH   Do we, my lord?

TIMON
Ay, and you hear him cog, see him dissemble,   95
Know his gross patchery, love him, feed him,   96
Keep in your bosom; yet remain assured   97
That he's a made-up villain.   98

PAINTER   I know none such, my lord.

POET   Nor I.

TIMON
Look you, I love you well. I'll give you gold;
Rid me these villains from your companies,   100
Hang them or stab them, drown them in a draft,   101
Confound them by some course, and come to me,   102
I'll give you gold enough.

BOTH   Name them, my lord, let's know them.

TIMON
You that way and you this, but two in company;   105
Each man apart, all single and alone,   106
Yet an archvillain keeps him company.   107
[To one] If where thou art two villains shall not be, 108
Come not near him. [To the other] If thou wouldst not
    reside   109
But where one villain is, then him abandon.—
Hence, pack! There's gold. You came for gold, ye
    slaves.   111
[To one] You have work for me; there's payment.
    Hence!   112
[To the other] You are an alchemist; make gold of that. 113
Out, rascal dogs!

            Exeunt [Poet and Painter, beaten out by Timon,
                    who retires to his cave].

        Enter steward [Flavius] and two Senators.

FLAVIUS
It is in vain that you would speak with Timon;
For he is set so only to himself   116
That nothing but himself which looks like man
Is friendly with him.

FIRST SENATOR   Bring us to his cave.   118
It is our part and promise to th'Athenians   119

To speak with Timon.

SECOND SENATOR   At all times alike
Men are not still the same. 'Twas time and griefs 121
That framed him thus. Time with his fairer hand   122
Offering the fortunes of his former days,
The former man may make him. Bring us to him,   124
And chance it as it may.

FLAVIUS   Here is his cave.—   125
Peace and content be here! Lord Timon! Timon!
Look out, and speak to friends. Th'Athenians,
By two of their most reverend Senate, greet thee.
Speak to them, noble Timon.

            Enter Timon out of his cave.

TIMON
Thou sun that comforts, burn! Speak and be hanged!
For each true word a blister, and each false   131
Be as a cauterizing to the root o'th' tongue,
Consuming it with speaking!

FIRST SENATOR   Worthy Timon—   133

TIMON
Of none but such as you, and you of Timon.   134

FIRST SENATOR
The senators of Athens greet thee, Timon.

TIMON
I thank them, and would send them back the plague,
Could I but catch it for them.

FIRST SENATOR   Oh, forget   137
What we are sorry for ourselves in thee.   138
The senators with one consent of love   139
Entreat thee back to Athens, who have thought
On special dignities which vacant lie
For thy best use and wearing.

SECOND SENATOR   They confess
Toward thee forgetfulness too general gross;   143
Which now the public body, which doth seldom   144
Play the recanter, feeling in itself   145
A lack of Timon's aid, hath sense withal   146
Of its own fail, restraining aid to Timon,   147
And send forth us to make their sorrowed render,   148
Together with a recompense more fruitful
Than their offense can weigh down by the dram—   150
Ay, even such heaps and sums of love and wealth
As shall to thee blot out what wrongs were theirs 152
And write in thee the figures of their love,   153

---

93 There's . . . but i.e., Each of you 95 cog cheat 96 patchery knavery 97 Keep keep him 98 made-up utter, complete 100 Rid me If you'll rid 101 draft privy, cesspool 102 Confound destroy. course means 105–7 You . . . him company (Timon riddlingly suggests that, if the two of them stand apart from each other with no one else around, each has an archvillain—himself—to keep him company.) 108 shall not be are not to be 109 him i.e., the other one. 111 pack be off. 112 there's payment i.e., here's a beating or a thrown stone. 113 alchemist i.e., one who transmutes nature into poetry and art, as the alchemist is supposed to transmute base metals into gold. that i.e., a beating or a thrown stone. 116 set . . . himself so self-absorbed 118 friendly with congenial to 119 our . . . promise the part we have promised to undertake

121 still always 122 framed made, fashioned 124 The former . . . him may turn him into his former self. 125 chance it let it happen 131 each false may each false word 133 Worthy Noble. (But Timon deliberately mistakes the meaning as "deserving.") 134 Of . . . Timon We are worthy of nothing better than each other (each of us being worthless, since we are human). 137 catch (1) snare in such a way that I could send it back (2) contract, as a disease 138 What . . . thee those wrongs that we regret having done you. 139 consent unanimous voice 143 too general gross too all-encompassing and evident 144 public body state 145 Play the recanter i.e., change its mind and apologize 146 Timon's aid aid to Timon. (But suggesting also "aid to be given by Timon to Athens.") withal in addition 147 fail failing. restraining in withholding 148 sorrowed render sorrowful rendering of apologies 150 can . . . dram can outweigh under the most scrupulous measurement 152 theirs of their making 153 figures (1) representations (2) numbers written in a ledger

Ever to read them thine.
TIMON   You witch me in it,   154
Surprise me to the very brink of tears.
Lend me a fool's heart and a woman's eyes,
And I'll beweep these comforts, worthy senators.   157
FIRST SENATOR
Therefore, so please thee to return with us,   158
And of our Athens, thine and ours, to take
The captainship, thou shalt be met with thanks,
Allowed with absolute power, and thy good name   161
Live with authority. So soon we shall drive back   162
Of Alcibiades th'approaches wild,   163
Who, like a boar too savage, doth root up
His country's peace.
SECOND SENATOR   And shakes his threat'ning sword
Against the walls of Athens.
FIRST SENATOR   Therefore, Timon—
TIMON
Well, sir, I will; therefore, I will, sir; thus:
If Alcibiades kill my countrymen,
Let Alcibiades know this of Timon,
That Timon cares not. But if he sack fair Athens
And take our goodly agèd men by th' beards,
Giving our holy virgins to the stain   172
Of contumelious, beastly, mad-brained war,   173
Then let him know, and tell him Timon speaks it
In pity of our agèd and our youth,
I cannot choose but tell him that I care not,
And let him take't at worst—for their knives care not, 177
While you have throats to answer. For myself,   178
There's not a whittle in th'unruly camp   179
But I do prize it at my love before   180
The reverend'st throat in Athens. So I leave you
To the protection of the prosperous gods,   182
As thieves to keepers.
FLAVIUS [to Senators]   Stay not; all's in vain.   183
TIMON
Why, I was writing of my epitaph;
It will be seen tomorrow. My long sickness
Of health and living now begins to mend,
And nothing brings me all things. Go, live still;   187
Be Alcibiades your plague, you his,
And last so long enough!
FIRST SENATOR   We speak in vain.   189
TIMON
But yet I love my country and am not
One that rejoices in the common wrack,   191
As common bruit doth put it.
FIRST SENATOR   That's well spoke.   192

TIMON
Commend me to my loving countrymen—
FIRST SENATOR
These words become your lips as they pass through
them.   194
SECOND SENATOR
And enter in our ears like great triumphers   195
In their applauding gates.
TIMON   Commend me to them,   196
And tell them that, to ease them of their griefs,
Their fears of hostile strokes, their aches, losses,
Their pangs of love, with other incident throes   199
That nature's fragile vessel doth sustain   200
In life's uncertain voyage, I will some kindness do
them:
I'll teach them to prevent wild Alcibiades' wrath.   202
FIRST SENATOR [to the Second Senator]
I like this well. He will return again.
TIMON
I have a tree which grows here in my close,   204
That mine own use invites me to cut down,   205
And shortly must I fell it. Tell my friends,
Tell Athens, in the sequence of degree   207
From high to low throughout, that whoso please
To stop affliction, let him take his haste,
Come hither ere my tree hath felt the ax,
And hang himself. I pray you, do my greeting.
FLAVIUS [to Senators]
Trouble him no further. Thus you still shall find him.
TIMON
Come not to me again. But say to Athens,
Timon hath made his everlasting mansion   214
Upon the beachèd verge of the salt flood,   215
Who once a day with his embossèd froth   216
The turbulent surge shall cover. Thither come,
And let my gravestone be your oracle.   218
Lips, let four words go by and language end!   219
What is amiss, plague and infection mend!
Graves only be men's works and death their gain!
Sun, hide thy beams! Timon hath done his reign.
                              Exit Timon [into his cave].
FIRST SENATOR
His discontents are unremovably
Coupled to nature.   224
SECOND SENATOR
Our hope in him is dead. Let us return
And strain what other means is left unto us

154 Ever . . . thine i.e., to provide a perpetual record of the Athenians' love for you. witch bewitch 157 beweep these comforts weep gratefully at these comforting tidings 158 so if it 161 Allowed vested 162 Live with authority enjoy full authority. 163 Of . . . wild the savage attacks of Alcibiades 172 stain pollution 173 contumelious despiteful 177 take't at worst put the worst possible construction on what I say, or, do the worst destruction possible. their of Alcibiades' troops 178 answer suffer the consequences. 179 whittle small clasp-knife 180 at in. before above 182 prosperous auspicious, favorable 183 As . . . keepers as I would leave thieves to the mercy of their hardhearted jailers. 187 nothing oblivion, death 189 last . . . enough remain in that state as long as possible. 191 wrack destruction 192 bruit rumor

194 become grace, do credit to 195 triumphers those coming in triumph 196 applauding gates i.e., (1) gates crowded with applauding citizens (2) porches of the ears. 199 incident throes naturally occurring agonies 200 nature's . . . vessel i.e., the body 202 prevent frustrate, forestall. (With a quibble on "anticipate.") 204 close enclosure 205 use need 207 in . . . degree in order of social rank 214 everlasting mansion i.e., grave 215 verge . . . flood boundary or margin of the sea. (See 5.4.66.) 216 Who whom or which, i.e., Timon or his grave, his everlasting mansion (line 214), both of which the foaming tide will cover daily. his its. embossèd foaming (like a hunted animal, foaming at the mouth) 218 oracle source of wisdom. 219 four words i.e., few words 224 Coupled to nature integrally part of him.

In our dear peril.

FIRST SENATOR   It requires swift foot.   *Exeunt.* 227

✤

[5.2]

Enter two other Senators, with a Messenger.

THIRD SENATOR
Thou hast painfully discovered. Are his files   1
As full as thy report?

MESSENGER   I have spoke the least.   2
Besides, his expedition promises   3
Present approach.   4

FOURTH SENATOR
We stand much hazard if they bring not Timon.   5

MESSENGER
I met a courier, one mine ancient friend,   6
Whom, though in general part we were opposed,   7
Yet our old love made a particular force   8
And made us speak like friends. This man was riding
From Alcibiades to Timon's cave
With letters of entreaty which imported   11
His fellowship i'th' cause against your city,   12
In part for his sake moved.

Enter the other Senators [from Timon].

THIRD SENATOR   Here come our brothers.   13

FIRST SENATOR
No talk of Timon; nothing of him expect.
The enemies' drum is heard, and fearful scouring   15
Doth choke the air with dust. In, and prepare.   16
Ours is the fall, I fear, our foe's the snare.   *Exeunt.* 17

✤

[5.3]

Enter a Soldier in the woods, seeking Timon.

SOLDIER
By all description this should be the place.
Who's here? Speak, ho! No answer? What is this?
                          [*He finds a rude tomb.*]
"Timon is dead, who hath outstretched his span.   3
Some beast read this; there does not live a man."   4

Dead, sure, and this his grave. What's on this tomb
I cannot read. The character I'll take with wax.   6
                          [*He makes a wax impression.*]
Our captain hath in every figure skill,   7
An aged interpreter, though young in days.   8
Before proud Athens he's set down by this,   9
Whose fall the mark of his ambition is.   *Exit.* 10

✤

[5.4]

*Trumpets sound. Enter Alcibiades with his powers
before Athens.*

ALCIBIADES
Sound to this coward and lascivious town   1
Our terrible approach.   *Sounds a parley.*   2

The Senators appear on the walls.

Till now you have gone on and filled the time
With all licentious measure, making your wills   4
The scope of justice. Till now myself and such   5
As slept within the shadow of your power   6
Have wandered with our traversed arms and
    breathed   7
Our sufferance vainly. Now the time is flush,   8
When crouching marrow in the bearer strong   9
Cries of itself, "No more!" Now breathless wrong   10
Shall sit and pant in your great chairs of ease,
And pursy insolence shall break his wind   12
With fear and horrid flight.

FIRST SENATOR   Noble and young,   13
When thy first griefs were but a mere conceit,   14
Ere thou hadst power or we had cause of fear,
We sent to thee, to give thy rages balm,
To wipe out our ingratitude with loves   17
Above their quantity.

SECOND SENATOR   So did we woo   18
Transformèd Timon to our city's love
By humble message and by promised means.   20

---

227 **dear** costly, dire.   **foot** i.e., action.
5.2. Location: Before the walls of Athens.
1 painfully discovered revealed unsettling news, or, reconnoitered
with painstaking effort.   **files** military ranks   **2 spoke the least**
given the lowest estimate.   **3 expedition** speed   **4 Present** immediate   **5 stand much hazard** are at great risk.   **they** i.e., the senators
who were sent to Timon   **6 one mine ancient friend** a friend of mine
of long standing   **7 Whom** with whom.   **in general part** on many
public issues   **8 made . . . force** exerted a strong personal influence
11–13 which . . . moved which importuned Timon to join Alcibiades
in an attack on Athens, undertaken in part on Timon's behalf.
13 brothers fellow senators.   **15 scouring** hurrying along, aggressive
movement   **16 In** Let us go in   **17 Ours . . . snare** Our part, I fear, is
to fall; our foe's part is to set the trap.
**5.3. Location: The woods. Seemingly near Timon's cave but also at
the edge of the sea; see 5.1.214–17 and 5.4.66. A rude tomb is seen.**
3 outstretched his span stretched out his span of life to its limit.
4 Some . . . man i.e., Whoever reads this will be a beast, since all men
are beasts.

6 I cannot read (Suggests there is another inscription in another language, perhaps Latin, or that this scene shows signs of incomplete
revision and hence apparent inconsistency.)   **The . . . wax** I'll take an
impression of the inscription in wax.   **7 every figure** all kinds of writing   **8 aged** experienced   **9 Before . . . this** By this time he has laid
siege to proud Athens   **10 Whose fall** the fall of which.   **mark** goal
5.4. Location: Before the walls of Athens. Appearances *on the walls*
are presumably located in the gallery, above, to the rear of the stage.
0.1 *powers* armed forces   **1 Sound** Proclaim.   **coward** cowardly
2 terrible terrifying.   **s.d.** *parley* trumpet call to a negotiation.   **4 all
licentious measure** every kind of licentious behavior   **4–5 making
. . . justice** equating justice with your wills.   **6 slept** i.e., dwelled
7 traversed arms weapons not in firing position. (A term in military
drill.)   **7–8 breathed Our sufferance** voiced our sufferings   **8 flush**
at flood, ripe   **9–10 When . . . more!** i.e., when the vital spirit of even
the brave man, crouching in terror, cries out of its own accord, "No
more!" (*Marrow* is literally the fatty substance in the bones.)
10 breathless wrong wrongdoers (i.e., you senators) who are frightened into breathlessness   **12 pursy** short-winded.   **break his wind**
pant for breath. (Perhaps suggesting also to void air from the bowels
in fright.)   **13 horrid** terrified   **14 When . . . conceit** when your
grievances were as yet new and scarcely imagined by us
17–18 loves . . . quantity offers of friendship exceeding the quantity
of your grievances.   **20 means** rewards.

We were not all unkind, nor all deserve
The common stroke of war.

FIRST SENATOR   These walls of ours   22
Were not erected by their hands from whom
You have received your grief; nor are they such
That these great tow'rs, trophies, and schools should
     fall   25
For private faults in them.

SECOND SENATOR   Nor are they living   26
Who were the motives that you first went out.   27
Shame, that they wanted cunning, in excess   28
Hath broke their hearts. March, noble lord,
Into our city with thy banners spread.
By decimation and a tithèd death—   31
If thy revenges hunger for that food
Which nature loathes—take thou the destined tenth,
And by the hazard of the spotted die   34
Let die the spotted.

FIRST SENATOR   All have not offended.   35
For those that were, it is not square to take   36
On those that are, revenge. Crimes, like lands,   37
Are not inherited. Then, dear countryman,   38
Bring in thy ranks, but leave without thy rage.   39
Spare thy Athenian cradle and those kin   40
Which in the bluster of thy wrath must fall
With those that have offended. Like a shepherd
Approach the fold and cull th'infected forth,   43
But kill not all together.

SECOND SENATOR   What thou wilt,
Thou rather shalt enforce it with thy smile
Than hew to't with thy sword.

FIRST SENATOR   Set but thy foot
Against our rampired gates and they shall ope,   47
So thou wilt send thy gentle heart before   48
To say thou'lt enter friendly.

SECOND SENATOR   Throw thy glove,   49
Or any token of thine honor else,   50
That thou wilt use the wars as thy redress
And not as our confusion, all thy powers   52
Shall make their harbor in our town till we   53
Have sealed thy full desire.

ALCIBIADES [throwing a glove]   Then there's my glove.   54
Descend, and open your unchargèd ports.   55

Those enemies of Timon's and mine own
Whom you yourselves shall set out for reproof   57
Fall, and no more; and, to atone your fears   58
With my more noble meaning, not a man   59
Shall pass his quarter or offend the stream   60
Of regular justice in your city's bounds   61
But shall be remedied to your public laws   62
At heaviest answer.

BOTH   'Tis most nobly spoken.   63

ALCIBIADES   Descend, and keep your words.   64
     [The Senators descend, and open the gates.]

     Enter [Soldier as] a messenger [with a wax tablet].

SOLDIER
My noble general, Timon is dead,
Entombed upon the very hem o'th' sea;   66
And on his gravestone this insculpture, which   67
With wax I brought away, whose soft impression
Interprets for my poor ignorance.

ALCIBIADES (reads the epitaph)
"Here lies a wretched corpse, of wretched soul bereft.   70
Seek not my name. A plague consume you wicked
     caitiffs left!   71
Here lie I, Timon, who, alive, all living men did hate.
Pass by and curse thy fill, but pass and stay not here
     thy gait."   73
These well express in thee thy latter spirits.   74
Though thou abhorredst in us our human griefs,
Scorned'st our brains' flow and those our droplets
     which   76
From niggard nature fall, yet rich conceit   77
Taught thee to make vast Neptune weep for aye   78
On thy low grave, on faults forgiven. Dead
Is noble Timon, of whose memory
Hereafter more. Bring me into your city,
And I will use the olive with my sword,   82
Make war breed peace, make peace stint war, make
     each   83
Prescribe to other as each other's leech.   84
Let our drums strike.   [Drums.] Exeunt.

---

22 **common** indiscriminate   25 **trophies** monuments   26 **them** i.e., those from whom you have received your injuries.   27 **motives . . . out** instigators that prompted your banishment.   28 **Shame . . . excess** i.e., An excess of shame for their lack of astuteness in statecraft   31 **decimation . . . tithèd death** selection of every tenth to die. (The two phrases mean the same thing.)   34 **die** singular of *dice.* (With a play on the verb *die.*)   35 **the spotted** the corrupt, wicked. (With a play on the spots on the dice in line 34.)   36 **were** were living then (and were your enemies). **square** just   37 **are** are now alive   37–8 **like . . . inherited** are not inherited, as lands are.   39 **without** outside   40 **thy Athenian cradle** Athens, your birthplace   43 **cull . . . forth** pick out the tainted   47 **rampired** barricaded. **ope** open   48 **So** if only   49 **Throw** If you will throw   50 **token** pledge   52 **confusion** overthrow. **powers** armed forces   53 **make their harbor** find safe lodging   54 **sealed** satisfied, ratified   55 **uncharged ports** unattacked gates.

57 **set out for reproof** pick out for punishment   58 **atone** appease, make "at one"   59–63 **not . . . answer** no soldier of mine will be allowed to leave his assigned duty area or violate the norms set by established law without being remanded to Athenian justice to receive severest punishment.   64.1 **open the gates** (Presumably, the *gates* are a door in the tiring-house facade representing here the *walls* of Athens; the gallery above is *on the walls.*)   66 **hem** i.e., edge, shore   67 **insculpture** inscription   70–3 **"Here . . . gait"** (Of these two inscriptions, both found in Plutarch, Shakespeare would presumably have deleted one, since they contradict one another.)   71 **caitiffs** wretches   73 **gait** journey.   74 **thy latter spirits** your bitter views at the end of your life.   76–7 **Scorned'st . . . fall** scorned our sentiments and our tears, both of which you considered craven and worldly, stemming from our impoverished human spirit   77 **conceit** imagination, fancy   78 **Neptune** the god of the sea in Roman mythology. **aye** ever   82 **olive . . . sword** (Symbols of peace and war.)   83 **Make . . . peace** use war to bring about the security needed for peace (and also, perhaps, to cure the decadent softness of a prolonged peacetime). **stint** stop   84 **leech** physician.

Antony and Cleopatra

Shakespeare probably wrote *Antony and Cleopatra* in 1606 or 1607; it was registered for publication on May 20, 1608, and apparently influenced a revision of Samuel Daniel's *Cleopatra* that was published "newly altered" in 1607. *Antony and Cleopatra* was thus roughly contemporary with *King Lear* and *Macbeth.* Yet the contrast between those two tragedies and *Antony and Cleopatra* is immense. Unlike *Macbeth,* with its taut focus on a murderer and his wife, *Antony and Cleopatra* moves back and forth across the Mediterranean in its epic survey of characters and events, bringing together the fates of Pompey, Octavius Caesar, Octavia, and Lepidus with those of the protagonists. *King Lear* gives proper names to fourteen characters, *Macbeth* to eighteen, *Antony and Cleopatra* to thirty-one. The Roman play requires no less than forty-two separate scenes, of which most occur in what modern editors label Acts 3 and 4, although no play is less suited to the classical rigors of five-act structure, and these divisions are not found in the reliable Folio text of 1623. Indeed, it is as though Shakespeare resolved at the height of his career to show that he could dispense entirely with the classical "rules," which had never taken serious hold of the English popular stage in any case. The flouting of the unities is so extreme that John Dryden, in his *All for Love or The World Well Lost* (1678), undertook not so much to revise Shakespeare as to start afresh on the same subject. Dryden's play is restricted to the last few hours of the protagonists' lives, at Cleopatra's tomb in Alexandria, with a severely limited cast of characters and much of the narrative revealed through recollection. Although a substantial achievement in its own right, *All for Love* surely demonstrates that Shakespeare knew what he was doing, for Dryden has excised a good deal of the panorama, the excitement, and the "infinite variety" (2.2.246).

Shakespeare departs also from the somber tone of his tragedies of evil. He creates, instead, a world that bears affinities to the ambiguous conflicts of the other Roman plays, to the varying humorous perspectives of the come-

dies, and to the imaginative reconstructions of the late romances. As protagonists, Antony and Cleopatra lack tragic stature, or so it first appears: she is a tawny gypsy temptress and he a "strumpet's fool," a once-great general now bound in "strong Egyptian fetters" and lost in "dotage" (1.1.13; 1.2.122–3). Several scenes, especially those set in Egypt, are comic and delightfully bawdy: Charmian learning her fortune from the soothsayer, Cleopatra practicing her charms in vain to keep Antony from leaving Egypt or raunchily daydreaming of being Antony's horse "to bear the weight of Antony" (1.5.22), Cleopatra flying into a magnificent rage at the news of Antony's marriage to Octavia and then consoling herself with catty reflections on Octavia's reported low voice and shortness of stature ("I think so, Charmian. Dull of tongue, and dwarfish," 3.3.17). In its comic texture, the play somewhat resembles *Romeo and Juliet,* an earlier play about a younger pair of lovers, although there the bawdry is used chiefly to characterize the lovers' companions and confidants, whereas in *Antony and Cleopatra* it is central to our vision of Cleopatra especially. In any case, the later play is a tragedy about lovers who, despite their quarrels and uncertainties and betrayals of self, are reconciled in a vision of the greatness of their love. In its depiction of two contrasting worlds, also, *Antony and Cleopatra* recalls the movement of several earlier comedies from the realistic world of political conniving to a dreamworld of the romantic and the unexpected. We can endorse neither world fully in *Antony and Cleopatra,* and, accordingly, the vision of life presented is often ambivalent and ironic as much as it is tragic. The contrast of values separating Egypt and Rome underscores the paradox of humanity's quest for seemingly irreconcilable goals. The ending is neither a triumph nor a defeat for the lovers but something of both. If Antony and Cleopatra seem in one way too small to be tragic protagonists, in another way they seem too large, creating imaginative visions of themselves and their union that escape the realm of

ANTONY AND CLEOPATRA

tragedy altogether. Our attention is focused less on the way in which the protagonists come to understand some meaningful relationship between their character and the fate required of them by a tragic universe than on the almost comic way in which the absurdities of Roman worldly striving and Egyptian dissipation are transfigured in the world of the imagination.

The Roman point of view opens the play and never entirely loses its force. At first, it may seem superior to that of Egypt. Demetrius and Philo, who invite us to view the play's first encounter between Antony and Cleopatra (1.1) from the perspective of the professional Roman soldier, lament the decline of Antony into Circean enslavement. Their tragic concept is of the Fall of Princes, all the more soberly edifying because of the height from which Antony has toppled. "You shall see in him / The triple pillar of the world transformed / Into a strumpet's fool" (1.1.11–13). Egypt is enchanting but clearly enervating—a bizarre assemblage of soothsayers, eunuchs, and waiting-gentlewomen who wish to be "married to three kings in a forenoon and widow them all" (1.2.28–9). Their mirth is all bawdry, tinged with practices, such as transvestitism, that Roman custom views as licentious. The prevailing images are of procreation in various shapes, sleep (mandragora, Lethe), the oriental opulence of Cleopatra's barge (a golden poop, purple sails, silver oars, divers-colored fans), Epicurean feasting, and drinking. As Enobarbus says, "Mine, and most of our fortunes tonight, shall be—drunk to bed" (1.2.47–8).

Antony, for all his reckless defiance of Rome, agrees in his more reflective moments with what Demetrius and Philo have said. "A Roman thought hath struck him," Cleopatra observantly remarks, and Antony has indeed determined that "I must from this enchanting queen break off" (1.2.88, 135). His later return to Cleopatra is at least in part a surrender, a betrayal of his marriage vows to Octavia and his political assurances to Caesar. In the ensuing battles, Antony submits himself dangerously to Cleopatra's governance, and this inversion of dominance in sexual roles, as conventionally understood by the Roman patriarchal world, is emblematic of a deeper disorder within Antony. As Enobarbus concludes bitterly, Antony "would make his will / Lord of his reason" and so has subverted his "judgment" (3.13.3–4, 37) to passion.

From the beginning, Cleopatra has sought dominance over Antony in the war of the sexes. When Antony first came to her on the River Cydnus, we learn, he was so overcome in all his senses that he was "barbered ten times o'er" (2.2.234). Cleopatra boasts that she "angled" for Antony on many occasions, catching him the way fishermen "betray" fish, and that, when she had "drunk him to his bed," she "put my tires and mantles on him, whilst / I wore his sword Philippan" (2.5.10–23). Caesar, affronted by such transvestite debauchery, charges that Antony "is not more manlike / Than Cleopatra, nor the queen of Ptolemy / More womanly than he" (1.4.5–7). During the battle scenes, Antony's followers complain that "Photinus, an eunuch" (probably Mardian), and Cleopatra's maids manage the war: "So our leader's led, / And we are women's men" (3.7.14–15, 70–1). Antony confesses too late that they were right. He becomes a "doting mallard," one whose heart is "tied by th' strings" to Cleopatra's rudder when her ships retreat in the first naval engagement (3.10.20, 3.11.56). In the mythic images used to raise their relationship to heroic proportions, Antony is like Mars to Cleopatra's Venus (1.5.19), both in a positive and a negative sense. The image has positive connotations of the way in which, as Milton puts it, the "two great sexes animate the world," the masterful soldier and his attractive consort complementing one another in a right relationship of martial prowess and beauty, bravery and love, reason and will; however, to the Renaissance, the myth of Mars and Venus could also be read in a destructive sense, as an adulterous relationship in which reason is subverted to appetite. In another mythic comparison, Antony is like Hercules, not in his prime, but with the shirt of Nessus on his back—a poisoned shirt given to Hercules by his wife in a mistaken hope of thereby assuring his love for her (4.12.43). Antony's soldiers understandably believe that the god Hercules has deserted his reputed descendant and onetime champion (4.3.21–2).

Despite Antony's shameful violation of manhood, honor, attention to duty, self-knowledge, and all that Rome stands for, however, the end of his story is anything but a one-sided endorsement for the Roman point of view. The actual Rome, disfigured by political conniving, falls far short of the ideal. Antony has a point when he protests that "Kingdoms are clay" (1.1.37). Alliances are unstable and are governed by mere political expediency. At first, Antony's wife Fulvia and his brother Lucius have fought one another until forced to unite against the greater threat of Octavius Caesar. Similarly, Antony and Caesar come together only because Pompey has become dangerously powerful at sea and has won the favor of the fickle mob, "Our slippery people" (1.2.192). This detente is not meant to last. As Enobarbus bluntly puts it, "if you borrow one another's love for the instant, you may, when you hear no more words of Pompey, return it again" (2.2.109–11). Enobarbus is rebuked for his unstatesmanlike tone, but no one denies the validity of what he says. In this cynical negotiation, Octavia is a pawn between husband and brother, shabbily treated by both. Caesar coldly bargains away the happiness of the one person of whom he protests that "no brother / Did ever love so dearly" (2.2.159–60). Antony, although hating false promises and resolving to be loyal to Octavia, knows within himself that it won't work. To make matters worse for the fair-minded Antony, he has received great favors from Pompey that he must now uncharitably repudiate in the interests of politics. Pompey does not miss the opportunity to remind Antony of his ingratitude, but the prevailing mood is not so much of bitterness as of ironic futility. Old friendships must be sacrificed; no one seems wholly to blame, and no one can stop the game. Pompey is as much in the wrong as anyone and as powerless. Despite his idealistic hope of restoring republican government to Rome, he has had to ally himself with pirates who offer him sinister temptations. He could be "lord of all the world" (2.7.62) if he would only murder on occasion, but Pompey is destined to be trapped between lofty ends and ignoble means. Lepidus is still another dismaying victim of political callousness, used condescendingly by Caesar and permitted to drink himself into oblivion, until he is cashiered on a trumped-up charge and imprisoned for life.

Octavius Caesar embodies most of all the ironic limits of political ambition. He has avoided enslavement to passion at the very real cost of enslaving himself to his public career as general, triumvir, and future emperor. His ideal warrior is one who, driven by military necessity, would "drink / The stale [urine] of horses and the gilded puddle / Which beasts would cough at" (1.4.62–4). As a general, he is Antony's opposite in every way. He attacks only when he has the advantage and places those who have deserted Antony in his own front lines so "That Antony may seem to spend his fury / Upon himself" (4.6.10–11). He controls his supplies cannily, believing it a "waste" to feast his army (4.1.17). He, of course, declines Antony's offers of single combat. Antony meantime recklessly accepts Caesar's challenge to fight at sea, feasts debauchingly in one "gaudy night" after another (3.13.186), and generously refuses to blame or penalize those who leave him. His sending Enobarbus's belongings after him into Caesar's camp convinces that honest soldier he has made a fatal error, for, however imprudent Antony's chivalry may be, it is unquestionably noble and great-hearted. Caesar is a superb general and political genius, but he is also a military automaton, a logistical reckoner, a Machiavellian pragmatist. In his personal life, he is no less austere and puritanical. He deplores loosening his tongue with alcohol. About women, he is deeply cynical, believing that "want will perjure / The ne'er-touched vestal" (3.12.30–1). Between him and Cleopatra, there is a profound antipathy, based in part on his revulsion at her earlier affair with his namesake and adoptive father, Julius Caesar (3.6.6). Cleopatra may entertain briefly the notion of trying to seduce this new Caesar (3.13.46 ff.), for like Charmian she loves long life "better than figs"(1.2.34), but, if so, she soon discovers that she and Caesar are not compatible. All that he represents she must instead grandly repudiate, choosing death and the fantasy of an eternity with Antony as her way to "call great Caesar ass / Unpolicied" (5.2.307–8).

Cleopatra is a "lass unparalleled" (5.2.316), whose greatness is elusive and all the more enthralling because it is so mysterious. She rises above her counterpart in Shakespeare's source, Plutarch's *Lives of the Noble Grecians and Romans,* in which she is an impressive queenly woman but still essentially a temptress causing the lamentable fall of the hero. Shakespeare's Cleopatra is that but is also something indefinable that can be gotten at only through paradox. Her very character is the essence of contradiction: she knows how "to chide, to laugh, / To weep" (1.1.51–2), to be sullen or violent, like a skillful actor keeping Antony continually off guard. Dispassionately examined, she is a woman no longer young who abuses messengers like an oriental despot, who sends Antony a false report of her death out of fear for her own safety, who will not risk leaving her monument even when Antony lies outside mortally wounded, and who lies about her wealth when captured by Caesar (what is she planning to do with that wealth, anyway?). We cannot be sure that she would not have "packed cards with Caesar" (4.14.19) if she had found him susceptible to her charms. Yet we are not invited to see her dispassionately. Her charm is eternal, and so are the myths surrounding that charm. Observers evoking her splendor do not describe her person directly but, rather, her effects and surroundings: Enobarbus says simply that "For her own person, / It beggared all description" and goes on to catalogue her cloth-of-gold pavilion and her mermaidlike attendants. Most of all, she is a paradox: she makes defect perfection, age cannot wither her, and "vilest things / Become themselves in her, that the holy priests / Bless her when she is riggish" (2.2.207–50). She is both a whore and the Lucretian Venus; both sluttish and holy.

Inspired by Cleopatra, Antony shows himself ready to break down conventional barriers between the sexes and to explore new emotional territory by giving up part of his self-protective masculinity. Antony's embracing of an attractive but sexually dangerous woman is all the more remarkable in a play that follows the harrowing depictions of sexual conflict in *Hamlet, Othello,* and *Lear* and the degrading portrait of erotic enslavement in the "Dark Lady" sonnets, for here the relationship of the lovers, though doomed, is also triumphant. Shakespeare takes a look at something like midlife crisis, conceding freely how ridiculous the male appears to himself and to others in his compulsive tendency to polarize women into saints and whores. Yet Shakespeare also explores ways in which the man and the woman attempt to become increasingly like each other, enabling the man to participate in a vision of union with the feminine principle of generative, erotic, fertile, life-giving vitality, and enabling the woman to join her "husband" in the noble resolve of a Roman suicide.

In Cleopatra, "fancy" exceeds "nature"; the fertility of her Egypt overflows the measure, exceeding the sterility of Rome as her own imaginative fertility exceeds reality itself. When she protests that she will not go to Rome to behold herself in a wretched play and thus see "Some squeaking Cleopatra boy my greatness / I'th' posture of a whore" (5.2.220–1), we realize that Shakespeare is calling attention to his own art as well, pointing out how Elizabethan boy actors on a bare stage can transform reality into a dream that we believe. Cleopatra's mystery is like that of poetry itself. The "real" world pales into insignificance of a "little O, the earth," something "No better than a sty," full of illusory shadows that "mock our eyes with air" (5.2.80, 4.15.64, 4.14.7); and Caesar's triumph vanishes with it. In its place, Antony and Cleopatra raise up a vision of themselves as lovers who, through art, have indeed become eternal. Together they will overpicture Venus and Mars, and will be so renowned that "Dido and her Aeneas shall want troops, / And all the haunt be ours" (4.14.53–4). They are virtually husband and wife—"Husband, I come!" exclaims Cleopatra just before she dies (5.2.287)—united at last in a re-creative vision almost appropriate to comedy; and in their marriage they find a kind of redemption for the defeat that history can inflict. Antony is no longer dying Hercules but the god of Cleopatra's dream whose "legs bestrid the ocean; his reared arm / Crested the world; his voice was propertied / As all the tunèd spheres" (lines 81–3). Through Cleopatra's vision, we realize how all the characteristics that made Antony at once so noble and so sure to fall before Caesar—his generosity amounting to imprudence, his spontaneity, his impatience with the ordinary, his staking his all on love when he hears of Cleopatra's supposed death—have not deserted him. His death serves to reaffirm the magnificence of the very qualities that have brought him down. His essential nobility is confirmed, even if it must be defined in non-Roman ways. He and Cleopatra share the "immortal longings" for which she goes willingly to her death, dressed in her "best attires" like a queen (lines 281, 228), for neither lover will accept anything less than greatness.

Antony and Cleopatra is a daunting play to stage, because the main characters take on a mythic character that seems larger than life, larger than art itself. Michael Goldman imagines what it would be like for an actor to try out for the part of Antony only to be instructed by the casting director, "Now, stand there and be a triple pillar of the world." How can an actor convey the charisma of a man whose very name is legendary? The problem in acting Cleopatra is even more acute. The great actresses who have taken on the assignment have all been praised for many things but also faulted for lacking other dimensions of this amazing character. Vivien Leigh, playing opposite Laurence Olivier's Antony at the St. James Theatre, London, in 1951, was applauded by the critics for her coquettish sexiness and magnetism but perhaps deficient in animal heat and duskiness. Peggy Ashcroft, in Glen Byam Shaw's production at Stratford-upon-Avon in 1953, was lauded as impressively intelligent and capable of huge emotional variation, but was seen as physically small and not as sexually glamorous as Leigh. Margaret Whiting, at the Old Vic in 1957, was regarded by most viewers as simply too young for the part. Vanessa Redgrave, at the Bankside Globe Playhouse in 1973, threw cola bottles at her servants in her fits of temper, and somehow lacked dignity for the final scenes. Glenda Jackson, playing Cleopatra in Peter Brook's deromanticized version at Stratford-upon-Avon in 1978, was brilliant for her iciness of tone and angularity in wit combat, but at the expense of tenderness and erotic feeling. The role has attracted the greatest of talent, from Janet Suzman to Helen Mirrin to Judi Dench, with similar praise and qualifications. These limits are a tribute to the play itself but a thorny problem for those who are producing the play. Film versions have tended to succumb to the temptations of visual splendor, in the style of Cecil B. DeMille, thus missing the point of the play's verbal and theatrical invocation of the ineffable. One singularly successful production is that on audiotape with Michael Redgrave as Antony and Peggy Ashcroft as Cleopatra; here the listener can imagine the lovers to be as toweringly great as the play's language suggests, magnificently assisted by the voices of two great actors. This is not to say that *Antony and Cleopatra* is unplayable; to the contrary, it shows Shakespeare at the very height of his powers as a professional writer for the theater. At the same time, few plays have ever posed a greater challenge for an acting ensemble.

Antony and Cleopatra

[*Dramatis Personae*

MARK ANTONY,
OCTAVIUS CAESAR, } *triumvirs*
LEPIDUS,

CLEOPATRA,
CHARMIAN,
IRAS,
ALEXAS,
MARDIAN, *a eunuch,* } *Cleopatra's attendants*
DIOMEDES,
SELEUCUS, *Cleopatra's treasurer,*

OCTAVIA, *sister of Octavius Caesar and wife of Antony*

DEMETRIUS,
PHILO,
DOMITIUS ENOBARBUS,
VENTIDIUS,
SILIUS, } *Antony's friends and followers*
EROS,
CANIDIUS,
SCARUS,
DERCETUS,
A SCHOOLMASTER, *Antony's* AMBASSADOR *to Caesar*

MAECENAS,
AGRIPPA,
TAURUS,
THIDIAS, } *Octavius Caesar's friends and followers*
DOLABELLA,
GALLUS,
PROCULEIUS,

SEXTUS POMPEIUS *or* POMPEY
MENAS,
MENECRATES, } *Pompey's friends*
VARRIUS,

MESSENGERS *to Antony, Octavius, Caesar, and Cleopatra*
A SOOTHSAYER
Two SERVANTS *of Pompey*
SERVANTS *of Antony and Cleopatra*
A BOY
SOLDIERS, SENTRIES, GUARDSMEN *of Antony and Octavius Caesar*
A CAPTAIN *in Antony's army*
An EGYPTIAN
A CLOWN *with figs*

Ladies attending Cleopatra, Eunuchs, Servants, Soldiers, Captains, Officers, silent named characters (Rannius, Lucillius, Lamprius)

SCENE: *In several parts of the Roman Empire*]

1.1

Enter Demetrius and Philo.

PHILO
Nay, but this dotage of our general's   1
O'erflows the measure. Those his goodly eyes,   2

That o'er the files and musters of the war   3
Have glowed like plated Mars, now bend, now turn   4
The office and devotion of their view   5
Upon a tawny front. His captain's heart,   6
Which in the scuffles of great fights hath burst
The buckles on his breast, reneges all temper   8

1.1. Location: Alexandria. Cleopatra's palace.
1 dotage foolish affection, sometimes associated with old age
2 O'erflows the measure exceeds moderation, exceeds the means of measuring it.

3 files and musters orderly formations **4 plated** clothed in armor
5 office function **6 tawny front** dark face. (Literally, forehead.)
8 reneges all temper renounces all moderation

And is become the bellows and the fan
To cool a gypsy's lust.

Flourish. Enter Antony, Cleopatra, her ladies, the
train, with eunuchs fanning her.

        Look, where they come. 10
Take but good note, and you shall see in him
The triple pillar of the world transformed 12
Into a strumpet's fool. Behold and see. 13

CLEOPATRA
If it be love indeed, tell me how much.

ANTONY
There's beggary in the love that can be reckoned. 15

CLEOPATRA
I'll set a bourn how far to be beloved. 16

ANTONY
Then must thou needs find out new heaven, new
  earth. 17

Enter a Messenger.

MESSENGER News, my good lord, from Rome.
ANTONY Grates me! The sum. 19
CLEOPATRA Nay, hear them, Antony. 20
Fulvia perchance is angry, or who knows 21
If the scarce-bearded Caesar have not sent 22
His powerful mandate to you, "Do this, or this;
Take in that kingdom, and enfranchise that; 24
Perform't, or else we damn thee." 25
ANTONY How, my love? 26
CLEOPATRA Perchance? Nay, and most like. 27
You must not stay here longer; your dismission 28
Is come from Caesar. Therefore hear it, Antony.
Where's Fulvia's process? Caesar's, I would say. Both? 30
Call in the messengers. As I am Egypt's queen,
Thou blushest, Antony, and that blood of thine
Is Caesar's homager; else so thy cheek pays shame 33
When shrill-tongued Fulvia scolds. The messengers!
ANTONY
Let Rome in Tiber melt and the wide arch
Of the ranged empire fall! Here is my space. 36
Kingdoms are clay; our dungy earth alike
Feeds beast as man. The nobleness of life

Is to do thus; when such a mutual pair 39
And such a twain can do't, in which I bind, 40
On pain of punishment, the world to weet 41
We stand up peerless.
CLEOPATRA   Excellent falsehood! 42
Why did he marry Fulvia, and not love her? 43
I'll seem the fool I am not. Antony 44
Will be himself.
ANTONY   But stirred by Cleopatra. 45
Now, for the love of Love and her soft hours,
Let's not confound the time with conference harsh. 47
There's not a minute of our lives should stretch 48
Without some pleasure now. What sport tonight?
CLEOPATRA
Hear the ambassadors.
ANTONY   Fie, wrangling queen!
Whom everything becomes—to chide, to laugh,
To weep; whose every passion fully strives
To make itself, in thee, fair and admired!
No messenger but thine; and all alone
Tonight we'll wander through the streets and note
The qualities of people. Come, my queen,
Last night you did desire it.—Speak not to us.
    Exeunt [Antony and Cleopatra] with the train.
DEMETRIUS
Is Caesar with Antonius prized so slight? 58
PHILO
Sir, sometimes when he is not Antony
He comes too short of that great property 60
Which still should go with Antony.
DEMETRIUS   I am full sorry 61
That he approves the common liar, who 62
Thus speaks of him at Rome; but I will hope
Of better deeds tomorrow. Rest you happy! *Exeunt.* 64

❧

[1.2]

Enter Enobarbus, Lamprius, a Soothsayer, Ran-
nius, Lucillius, Charmian, Iras, Mardian the
eunuch, and Alexas.

CHARMIAN Lord Alexas, sweet Alexas, most anything
Alexas, almost most absolute Alexas, where's the 2
soothsayer that you praised so to th' Queen? Oh, that

---

10 gypsy's (Gypsies were widely believed to have come from Egypt, to enjoy magical powers, and to be lustful and cunning.) **s.d.** *Flourish* trumpet fanfare announcing the arrival or departure of important person. *train* retinue **12 triple** one of three. (Alludes to the triumvirate of Antony, Lepidus, and Octavius Caesar; also to tripartite division of the world into Asia, Africa, and Europe.) **13 fool** plaything. **15 There's . . . reckoned** i.e., Love that can be quantified is paltry; ours is infinite. **16 bourn** boundary, limit **17 Then . . . earth** i.e., Only in some new universe could you find a limit to my love. (The language echoes Revelation 21:1 and other biblical passages.) **19 Grates . . . sum** It annoys me! Be brief. **20 them** i.e., the news **21 Fulvia** Antony's wife **22 scarce-bearded Caesar** (Octavius Caesar was twenty-three in 40 B.C., at the time of the play's opening. Antony was forty-three.) **24 Take in** conquer. **enfranchise** set free **25 damn** condemn to death **26 How** i.e., What's that you say? **27 Perchance** (Cleopatra reconsiders what she has said in line 21.) **like** likely. **28 dismission** order to depart **30 process** writ to appear in court. **33 Is . . . shame** is Caesar's vassal, doing homage to him; or else your blushing pays the tribute of shame **36 ranged** well ordered and far-extending

39 thus (May indicate an embrace, or Antony may refer more generally to their way of life.) **40–2 in which . . . peerless** with respect to which I insist that the world, under penalty of punishment if it fails to do so, acknowledge us to be peerless. **43 and not** if he did not **44 I'll . . . not** i.e., I'll pretend to be gullible and believe him, though I know better. **45 be himself** i.e., be the Roman Antony, be the fool and deceiver he always is, etc. **stirred** (1) prompted to noble deeds (2) moved to folly (3) sexually stirred **47 confound** ruin, waste. **conference** conversation **48 should stretch** that should be prolonged **58 prized** valued **60 property** quality, distinction **61 still** always **62 approves** corroborates **64 Of** for **1.2. Location: Alexandria. Cleopatra's palace.** **0.1–2 Lamprius . . . Lucillius** (Lamprius may possibly be the soothsayer, but Rannius and Lucillius have no speaking parts here and do not appear again in the play. Mardian is mute here but does speak in later scenes.) **2 absolute** perfect

I knew this husband, which, you say, must charge his 4
horns with garlands! 5

ALEXAS   Soothsayer!

SOOTHSAYER   Your will?

CHARMIAN
Is this the man?—Is't you, sir, that know things?

SOOTHSAYER
In nature's infinite book of secrecy
A little I can read.

ALEXAS [to Charmian]   Show him your hand.

ENOBARBUS [to servants within]
Bring in the banquet quickly; wine enough 12
Cleopatra's health to drink.

CHARMIAN [giving her hand to the Soothsayer]   Good sir,
give me good fortune.

SOOTHSAYER   I make not, but foresee.

CHARMIAN   Pray, then, foresee me one.

SOOTHSAYER
You shall be yet far fairer than you are.

CHARMIAN   He means in flesh. 19

IRAS   No, you shall paint when you are old. 20

CHARMIAN   Wrinkles forbid!

ALEXAS   Vex not his prescience. Be attentive.

CHARMIAN   Hush!

SOOTHSAYER
You shall be more beloving than beloved.

CHARMIAN   I had rather heat my liver with drinking. 25

ALEXAS   Nay, hear him.

CHARMIAN   Good now, some excellent fortune! Let me 27
be married to three kings in a forenoon and widow
them all. Let me have a child at fifty, to whom Herod 29
of Jewry may do homage. Find me to marry me with 30
Octavius Caesar, and companion me with my mis- 31
tress. 32

SOOTHSAYER
You shall outlive the lady whom you serve.

CHARMIAN   Oh, excellent! I love long life better than figs. 34

SOOTHSAYER
You have seen and proved a fairer former fortune 35
Than that which is to approach.

CHARMIAN   Then belike my children shall have no 37
names. Prithee, how many boys and wenches must I 38
have? 39

SOOTHSAYER
If every of your wishes had a womb,
And fertile every wish, a million.

CHARMIAN   Out, fool! I forgive thee for a witch. 42

ALEXAS   You think none but your sheets are privy to 43
your wishes.

CHARMIAN   Nay, come, tell Iras hers.

ALEXAS   We'll know all our fortunes.

ENOBARBUS   Mine, and most of our fortunes tonight,
shall be—drunk to bed.

IRAS [giving her hand to the Soothsayer]   There's a palm
presages chastity, if nothing else.

CHARMIAN   E'en as the o'erflowing Nilus presageth 51
famine. 52

IRAS   Go, you wild bedfellow, you cannot soothsay. 53

CHARMIAN   Nay, if an oily palm be not a fruitful prog- 54
nostication, I cannot scratch mine ear. Prithee, tell her 55
but a workaday fortune. 56

SOOTHSAYER   Your fortunes are alike.

IRAS   But how, but how? Give me particulars.

SOOTHSAYER   I have said. 59

IRAS   Am I not an inch of fortune better than she?

CHARMIAN   Well, if you were but an inch of fortune better than I, where would you choose it?

IRAS   Not in my husband's nose. 63

CHARMIAN   Our worser thoughts heavens mend! Al- 64
exas—come, his fortune, his fortune! Oh, let him marry
a woman that cannot go, sweet Isis, I beseech thee, 66
and let her die too, and give him a worse, and let
worse follow worse till the worst of all follow him
laughing to his grave, fiftyfold a cuckold! Good Isis,
hear me this prayer, though thou deny me a matter of 70
more weight; good Isis, I beseech thee!

IRAS   Amen, dear goddess, hear that prayer of the people! For, as it is a heart-breaking to see a handsome
man loose-wived, so it is a deadly sorrow to behold a 74
foul knave uncuckolded. Therefore, dear Isis, keep de- 75
corum, and fortune him accordingly! 76

CHARMIAN   Amen.

ALEXAS   Lo now, if it lay in their hands to make me a
cuckold, they would make themselves whores but 79
they'd do't. 80

Enter Cleopatra.

ENOBARBUS
Hush! Here comes Antony.

CHARMIAN   Not he. The Queen.

CLEOPATRA   Saw you my lord?

---

4 this husband (Evidently Alexas has told Charmian that the Sooth-sayer will prophesy a husband for her.) **4–5 must . . . garlands** i.e., must decorate his cuckold's horns with a garland of flowers, like a sacrificial beast. (Cuckolded men were derisively thought of as grow-ing horns, as a badge of their infamy.) **12 banquet** light repast, dessert **19 in flesh** i.e., by putting on weight. **20 paint** i.e., use makeup **25 heat . . . drinking** i.e., heat my liver with wine rather than with unrequited love. (The liver was believed to be the seat of sexual desire.) **27 Good now** Come on, now **29–30 Herod of Jewry** i.e., even the blustering tyrant who massacred the children of Judea **30 Find me** i.e., Find in my palm **31–2 companion . . . mistress** give me equal fortune with Cleopatra; or, perhaps, let Cleopatra become my "companion" or attendant. **34 better than figs** (Probably a proverbial expression; with genital suggestion.) **35 proved** experi-enced **37 belike** probably **37–8 have no names** be illegitimate. **38 wenches** girls **38–9 must I have** am I to have.

42 Out . . . witch (Charmian jokingly says that, since soothsayers, like fools, are allowed to speak freely without penalty, she will forgive him for slander.) **43 privy to** in on the secret of **51–2 E'en . . . famine** (Charmian speaks ironically; the overflowing Nile presages abundance. See 2.7.17–23.) **53 wild** wanton **54 oily palm** sweaty or moist palm (indicating a sensual disposition) **54–5 fruitful prognos-tication** omen of fertility **56 workaday** ordinary **59 I have said** I have no more to say. **63 Not . . . nose** (Iras bawdily hints at some place other than in the nose where she would prefer to see her hus-band well endowed.) **64 Our . . . mend!** (Charmian pretends to be shocked: May heaven improve our dirty minds!) **66 cannot go** (1) is lame (2) cannot make love satisfactorily or cannot bear children. **Isis** Egyptian goddess usually identified with fertility and the moon **70 hear me** hear (on my behalf) **74 loose-wived** with an unfaithful wife **75 foul** ugly **75–6 keep decorum** deal suitably with the case **76 fortune him** grant him fortune **79–80 they . . . do't** i.e., they would stop at nothing, even becoming whores, to cuckold me.

ENOBARBUS   No, lady.
CLEOPATRA   Was he not here?
CHARMIAN   No, madam.
CLEOPATRA
He was disposed to mirth, but on the sudden
A Roman thought hath struck him. Enobarbus!
ENOBARBUS   Madam?
CLEOPATRA
Seek him and bring him hither. Where's Alexas?
ALEXAS
Here at your service.—My lord approaches.

Enter Antony with a Messenger.

CLEOPATRA
We will not look upon him. Go with us.
          Exeunt [all but Antony and the Messenger].
FIRST MESSENGER
Fulvia thy wife first came into the field.   93
ANTONY   Against my brother Lucius?
FIRST MESSENGER   Ay.
But soon that war had end, and the time's state   96
Made friends of them, jointing their force 'gainst
          Caesar,   97
Whose better issue in the war from Italy   98
Upon the first encounter drave them.   99
ANTONY   Well, what worst?
FIRST MESSENGER
The nature of bad news infects the teller.   101
ANTONY
When it concerns the fool or coward. On.
Things that are past are done with me. 'Tis thus:
Who tells me true, though in his tale lie death,
I hear him as he flattered.
FIRST MESSENGER   Labienus—   105
This is stiff news—hath with his Parthian force
Extended Asia; from Euphrates   107
His conquering banner shook, from Syria
To Lydia and to Ionia,
Whilst—
ANTONY   Antony, thou wouldst say.
FIRST MESSENGER   Oh, my lord!
ANTONY
Speak to me home; mince not the general tongue.   111
Name Cleopatra as she is called in Rome;
Rail thou in Fulvia's phrase, and taunt my faults   113
With such full license as both truth and malice
Have power to utter. Oh, then we bring forth weeds
When our quick minds lie still, and our ills told us   116
Is as our earing. Fare thee well awhile.   117

FIRST MESSENGER   At your noble pleasure.
                    Exit [First] Messenger.

Enter another Messenger.

ANTONY
From Sicyon, ho, the news! Speak there.
SECOND MESSENGER
The man from Sicyon—is there such an one?   120
THIRD MESSENGER *[at the door]*
He stays upon your will.
ANTONY   Let him appear.—   121
          [Exeunt Second and Third Messengers.]
These strong Egyptian fetters I must break,
Or lose myself in dotage.

Enter another Messenger, with a letter.

                    What are you?
FOURTH MESSENGER   Fulvia thy wife is dead.
ANTONY   Where died she?
FOURTH MESSENGER   In Sicyon.
Her length of sickness, with what else more serious
Importeth thee to know, this bears.   *[He gives a letter.]*
ANTONY   Forbear me.   128
                    [Exit Fourth Messenger.]
There's a great spirit gone! Thus did I desire it.
What our contempts doth often hurl from us
We wish it ours again. The present pleasure,
By revolution lowering, does become   132
The opposite of itself. She's good, being gone;
The hand could pluck her back that shoved her on.   134
I must from this enchanting queen break off.
Ten thousand harms more than the ills I know
My idleness doth hatch.—How now, Enobarbus!

Enter Enobarbus.

ENOBARBUS   What's your pleasure, sir?
ANTONY   I must with haste from hence.
ENOBARBUS   Why, then, we kill all our women. We see
how mortal an unkindness is to them; if they suffer
our departure, death's the word.
ANTONY   I must be gone.
ENOBARBUS   Under a compelling occasion, let women
die. It were pity to cast them away for nothing, though
between them and a great cause they should be esteemed nothing. Cleopatra, catching but the least noise   147
of this, dies instantly; I have seen her die twenty times   148
upon far poorer moment. I do think there is mettle in   149

---

93 field battlefield.   **96 time's state** circumstances prevailing at the moment   **97 jointing** uniting   **98–9 Whose . . . them** whose better military success drove them from Italy upon the very first encounter.   **101 infects the teller** i.e., makes the teller seem unwelcome.   **105 as** as if.   **Labienus** (Brutus and Cassius [see *Julius Caesar*] had sent Quintus Labienus to Orodes, King of Parthia, to seek aid against Antony and Octavius Caesar; with a force thus obtained, he is now overrunning the Roman provinces in the Middle East.)   **107 Extended** seized upon. (A legal phrase.)   **111 Speak . . . tongue** Speak bluntly; don't minimize the common report.   **113 Rail . . . phrase** Scold me as Fulvia would   **116 quick** alive, inventive   **116–17 our ills . . . earing** hearing our faults told to us improves us, as plowing (*earing*) improves land by rooting out the weeds.

120 The man from Sicyon (The messenger who has just entered, not being from Sicyon, realizes in some confusion that Antony wants to hear the news from Sicyon. This second messenger therefore calls out to ask if the messenger from Sicyon is to be found. Another messenger at the door replies that such a man is indeed waiting, and in a moment that messenger from Sicyon enters with his report. Some editors change the second and third messengers into attendants.) *Sicyon* is an ancient city in Greece, where Antony left Fulvia.   **121 stays upon** awaits   **128 Importeth** concerns.   **Forbear** Leave   **132 By revolution lowering** sinking in our estimation in the course of time and Fortune's turning wheel   **134 could** would be willing to   **147 noise** hint, rumor   **148 die** (Playing on a common second meaning of "achieve sexual orgasm.")   **149 poorer moment** lesser cause. **mettle** i.e., sexual vigor

death, which commits some loving act upon her, she
hath such a celerity in dying.

ANTONY She is cunning past man's thought.

ENOBARBUS Alack, sir, no, her passions are made of
nothing but the finest part of pure love. We cannot call
her winds and waters sighs and tears; they are greater   155
storms and tempests than almanacs can report. This
cannot be cunning in her; if it be, she makes a shower
of rain as well as Jove.

ANTONY Would I had never seen her!

ENOBARBUS Oh, sir, you had then left unseen a wonderful piece of work, which not to have been blessed
withal would have discredited your travel.

ANTONY Fulvia is dead.

ENOBARBUS Sir?

ANTONY Fulvia is dead.

ENOBARBUS Fulvia?

ANTONY Dead.

ENOBARBUS Why, sir, give the gods a thankful sacrifice.
When it pleaseth their deities to take the wife of a man
from him, it shows to man the tailors of the earth;   170
comforting therein, that when old robes are worn out,
there are members to make new. If there were no more   172
women but Fulvia, then had you indeed a cut, and the
case to be lamented. This grief is crowned with consolation; your old smock brings forth a new petticoat,   175
and indeed the tears live in an onion that should water   176
this sorrow.   177

ANTONY
The business she hath broachèd in the state   178
Cannot endure my absence.

ENOBARBUS And the business you have broached here
cannot be without you, especially that of Cleopatra's,
which wholly depends on your abode.   182

ANTONY
No more light answers. Let our officers   183
Have notice what we purpose. I shall break   184
The cause of our expedience to the Queen   185
And get her leave to part. For not alone   186
The death of Fulvia, with more urgent touches,   187
Do strongly speak to us, but the letters too
Of many our contriving friends in Rome   189
Petition us at home. Sextus Pompeius   190
Hath given the dare to Caesar and commands
The empire of the sea. Our slippery people,   192

Whose love is never linked to the deserver
Till his deserts are past, begin to throw   194
Pompey the Great and all his dignities   195
Upon his son, who—high in name and power,
Higher than both in blood and life—stands up   197
For the main soldier; whose quality, going on,   198
The sides o'th' world may danger. Much is breeding,   199
Which, like the courser's hair, hath yet but life,   200
And not a serpent's poison. Say our pleasure,   201
To such whose place is under us, requires   202
Our quick remove from hence.   203

ENOBARBUS I shall do't.   [Exeunt separately.]

❧

[1.3]

Enter Cleopatra, Charmian, Alexas, and Iras.

CLEOPATRA
Where is he?

CHARMIAN I did not see him since.   1

CLEOPATRA [to Alexas]
See where he is, who's with him, what he does.
I did not send you. If you find him sad,   3
Say I am dancing; if in mirth, report
That I am sudden sick. Quick, and return.   5
[Exit Alexas.]

CHARMIAN
Madam, methinks, if you did love him dearly,
You do not hold the method to enforce   7
The like from him.

CLEOPATRA What should I do I do not?   8

CHARMIAN
In each thing give him way. Cross him in nothing.

CLEOPATRA
Thou teachest like a fool: the way to lose him.

CHARMIAN
Tempt him not so too far. I wish, forbear;   11
In time we hate that which we often fear.

Enter Antony.

But here comes Antony.

CLEOPATRA I am sick and sullen.   13

ANTONY
I am sorry to give breathing to my purpose—   14

---

155 **sighs** i.e., mere sighs   170 **tailors** (The gods can fashion a new
wife for a man, much as a tailor can mend or replace a worn-out garment.)   172 **members** (The word has a bawdy suggestion, pursued
in lines 173–4 and 180 in *cut, case, business,* and *broached; cut* and *case*
suggest the female sexual organs; *broached* suggests something that is
stabbed, pricked, opened.)   175 **smock** undergarment. (Also used
defamatorily of women.)   176–7 **the tears ... sorrow** i.e., only an
onion could produce tears on this occasion of Fulvia's death.
178 **broachèd** opened up. (But see the note for line 172.)   182 **abode**
staying.   183 **light** frivolous, indelicate   184 **break** i.e., break the
news of   185 **expedience** haste   186 **leave** consent   187 **urgent
touches** pressing matters   189 **Of ... friends** from many friends
working in our interest   190 **at home** to come home.   **Sextus Pompeius** son of Pompey the Great, who, though outlawed, has been able
to exploit the division between Antony and Octavius and thereby
gain command of Sicily and the sea; he appears in Act 2
192 **slippery** fickle

194 **throw** bestow   195 **Pompey the Great** i.e., the title and honored
status of "Pompey the Great"   197 **blood and life** mettle and vitality
197–8 **stands ... soldier** lays claim to being the greatest soldier
198–9 **whose ... danger** whose aspiring character and situation, if
allowed to continue unchecked, may endanger the frame of the
Roman world.   200 **like ... hair** (Allusion to the popular belief that a
horsehair put into water would turn to a snake.)   200–1 **hath ...
poison** is alive at this point but not yet a poisonous full-grown serpent.   201–3 **Say ... hence** Tell those who serve me that my wish is
to depart quickly.
1.3 Location: Alexandria. Cleopatra's palace.
1 **since** lately.   3 **I did ... you** i.e., Do not let him know I sent you.
sad serious   5 **sudden** suddenly taken   7 **hold the method** follow
the right course   8 **I do not** that I am not doing.   11 **Tempt** Try.
I wish I wish you would   13 **sullen** depressed, melancholy.
14 **breathing** utterance

CLEOPATRA
  Help me away, dear Charmian! I shall fall.
  It cannot be thus long; the sides of nature   16
  Will not sustain it.
ANTONY   Now, my dearest queen—
CLEOPATRA
  Pray you, stand farther from me.
ANTONY   What's the matter?   18
CLEOPATRA
  I know by that same eye there's some good news.
  What, says the married woman you may go?   20
  Would she had never given you leave to come!
  Let her not say 'tis I that keep you here.
  I have no power upon you; hers you are.
ANTONY
  The gods best know—
CLEOPATRA   Oh, never was there queen
  So mightily betrayed! Yet at the first
  I saw the treasons planted.
ANTONY   Cleopatra—
CLEOPATRA
  Why should I think you can be mine, and true—
  Though you in swearing shake the thronèd gods—
  Who have been false to Fulvia? Riotous madness,   29
  To be entangled with those mouth-made vows   30
  Which break themselves in swearing!
ANTONY   Most sweet queen—   31
CLEOPATRA
  Nay, pray you, seek no color for your going,   32
  But bid farewell and go. When you sued staying,   33
  Then was the time for words. No going then.
  Eternity was in our lips and eyes,   35
  Bliss in our brows' bent; none our parts so poor   36
  But was a race of heaven. They are so still,   37
  Or thou, the greatest soldier of the world,
  Art turned the greatest liar.
ANTONY   How now, lady?
CLEOPATRA
  I would I had thy inches. Thou shouldst know   40
  There were a heart in Egypt.
ANTONY   Hear me, Queen: 41
  The strong necessity of time commands
  Our services awhile, but my full heart
  Remains in use with you. Our Italy   44
  Shines o'er with civil swords; Sextus Pompeius   45
  Makes his approaches to the port of Rome;

  Equality of two domestic powers   47
  Breed scrupulous faction; the hated, grown to
    strength,   48
  Are newly grown to love; the condemned Pompey,   49
  Rich in his father's honor, creeps apace   50
  Into the hearts of such as have not thrived
  Upon the present state, whose numbers threaten;   52
  And quietness, grown sick of rest, would purge   53
  By any desperate change. My more particular,   54
  And that which most with you should safe my going,   55
  Is Fulvia's death.
CLEOPATRA
  Though age from folly could not give me freedom,
  It does from childishness. Can Fulvia die?
ANTONY   She's dead, my queen.   [*He offers letters.*]
  Look here, and at thy sovereign leisure read
  The garboils she awaked, at the last, best,   61
  See when and where she died.
CLEOPATRA   Oh, most false love!
  Where be the sacred vials thou shouldst fill   63
  With sorrowful water? Now I see, I see,
  In Fulvia's death how mine received shall be.
ANTONY
  Quarrel no more, but be prepared to know
  The purposes I bear, which are or cease   67
  As you shall give th'advice. By the fire   68
  That quickens Nilus' slime, I go from hence   69
  Thy soldier, servant, making peace or war
  As thou affects.
CLEOPATRA   Cut my lace, Charmian, come!   71
  But let it be; I am quickly ill, and well,
  So Antony loves.
ANTONY   My precious queen, forbear,   73
  And give true evidence to his love which stands   74
  An honorable trial.
CLEOPATRA   So Fulvia told me.   75
  I prithee, turn aside and weep for her;
  Then bid adieu to me, and say the tears
  Belong to Egypt. Good now, play one scene   78

16 It . . . long I can't last long at this rate. **sides of nature** human body, frame   **18 stand farther from me** give me air.   **20 the married woman** Fulvia   **29 Who** you who.   **Riotous madness** What folly on my part   **30 mouth-made** insincerely spoken   **31 in swearing** even while they are being sworn.   **32 color** pretext   **33 sued staying** begged to stay   **35 our** i.e., my. (The royal plural.)   **36 bent** arch, curve.   **none . . . poor** none of my features, however poor   **37 race of heaven** of heavenly origin, or, possibly, of the flavor of heaven.   **40 inches** (1) height (2) manly strength. (With perhaps a bawdy suggestion.)   **41 a heart in Egypt** a mighty courage in the Queen of Egypt.   **44 in use with you** for your use.   **45 Shines . . . swords** glitters everywhere with weapons of civil war

47–8 Equality . . . faction the equal splitting of domestic power between two (Antony and Caesar) breeds petty bickering   **48–9 the hated . . . love** those (like Pompey) who were out of favor, being now strong, have recently come back into popular favor   **49–50 Pompey . . . apace** i.e., Sextus Pompeius, richly inheriting the honor once accorded Pompey the Great, quickly insinuates himself   **52 state** government (of the triumvirate).   **whose** i.e., those supporting Pompey   **53–4 And quietness . . . change** and peace, bored with its own long continuance, longs to purge itself by the violence of war (medically speaking, by vomiting, bowel evacuation, or bloodletting).   **54 particular** personal concern   **55 safe** make safe   **61 garboils** disturbances, commotions.   **best** i.e., best of all   **63 sacred vials** (Alludes to the supposed Roman custom of putting bottles filled with tears in the tombs of the departed.)   **67 which are** which will proceed   **68 fire** i.e., sun   **69 quickens . . . slime** brings to life the mud left by the overflow of the Nile   **71 thou affects** you desire.   **lace** cord or laces fastening the bodice. (Cleopatra pretends she is fainting.)   **73 So** provided that, or, possibly, "in the same way, with changes as sudden as my own"   **74–5 And . . . trial** and bear true witness to the love of one who withstands any honorable test.   **75 So . . . me** i.e., So Fulvia would have said, no doubt. (Said as a taunt.)   **78 Belong to Egypt** are shed for the Queen of Egypt.   **Good now** (An expression of entreaty.)

Of excellent dissembling, and let it look
Like perfect honor.

ANTONY   You'll heat my blood. No more.   80

CLEOPATRA
You can do better yet; but this is meetly.   81

ANTONY
Now, by my sword—

CLEOPATRA   And target. Still he mends.   82
But this is not the best. Look, prithee, Charmian,
How this Herculean Roman does become   84
The carriage of his chafe.   85

ANTONY   I'll leave you, lady.

CLEOPATRA   Courteous lord, one word.
Sir, you and I must part, but that's not it;
Sir, you and I have loved, but there's not it;
That you know well. Something it is I would—   90
Oh, my oblivion is a very Antony,   91
And I am all forgotten.

ANTONY   But that your royalty   92
Holds idleness your subject, I should take you   93
For idleness itself.

CLEOPATRA   'Tis sweating labor   94
To bear such idleness so near the heart   95
As Cleopatra this. But sir, forgive me,   96
Since my becomings kill me when they do not   97
Eye well to you. Your honor calls you hence;   98
Therefore be deaf to my unpitied folly,
And all the gods go with you! Upon your sword
Sit laurel victory, and smooth success   101
Be strewed before your feet!

ANTONY   Let us go. Come;
Our separation so abides and flies   103
That thou, residing here, goes yet with me,
And I, hence fleeting, here remain with thee.
Away!   *Exeunt.*

❖

[1.4]

*Enter Octavius [Caesar], reading a letter, Lepidus,
and their train.*

CAESAR
You may see, Lepidus, and henceforth know,
It is not Caesar's natural vice to hate

Our great competitor. From Alexandria   3
This is the news: he fishes, drinks, and wastes
The lamps of night in revel; is not more manlike
Than Cleopatra, nor the queen of Ptolemy   6
More womanly than he; hardly gave audience, or   7
Vouchsafed to think he had partners. You shall find
there
A man who is the abstract of all faults   9
That all men follow.

LEPIDUS   I must not think there are
Evils enough to darken all his goodness.
His faults in him seem as the spots of heaven,   12
More fiery by night's blackness, hereditary   13
Rather than purchased, what he cannot change   14
Than what he chooses.

CAESAR
You are too indulgent. Let's grant it is not   16
Amiss to tumble on the bed of Ptolemy,
To give a kingdom for a mirth, to sit   18
And keep the turn of tippling with a slave,   19
To reel the streets at noon, and stand the buffet   20
With knaves that smells of sweat. Say this becomes
him—
As his composure must be rare indeed   22
Whom these things cannot blemish—yet must Antony
No way excuse his foils when we do bear   24
So great weight in his lightness. If he filled   25
His vacancy with his voluptuousness,   26
Full surfeits and the dryness of his bones   27
Call on him for't. But to confound such time   28
That drums him from his sport and speaks as loud   29
As his own state and ours, 'tis to be chid   30
As we rate boys who, being mature in knowledge,   31
Pawn their experience to their present pleasure   32
And so rebel to judgment.

Enter a Messenger.

LEPIDUS   Here's more news.   33

FIRST MESSENGER
Thy biddings have been done, and every hour,
Most noble Caesar, shalt thou have report
How 'tis abroad. Pompey is strong at sea,

---

80 heat my blood i.e., anger me.   **81 meetly** i.e., fairly well acted.
(Said mockingly.)   **82 target** shield.   **mends** improves (in his "scene
/ Of excellent dissembling").   **84–5 How . . . chafe** i.e., how Antony,
who claims descent from Hercules, plays the role of his enraged
ancestor well. (Hercules had become a stock figure of the enraged
hero or tyrant.)   **chafe** rage.   **90 would** wished to say   **91 my . . .
Antony** my forgetful memory is like Antony (who is now leaving and
thus forgetting me)   **92 I . . . forgotten** (1) I have forgotten what I
was going to say (2) I am entirely forgotten (by Antony).   **92–4 But . . .
itself** Since you are a queen, your frivolousness must be your subject
(i.e., ruled by you); otherwise, I'd think you were frivolousness itself.
94–6 'Tis . . . this i.e., I am not being frivolous; this is hard for me to
bear. (*Sweating, labor,* and *bear* are all associated with pregnancy.)
97 my becomings (1) those qualities that become me (2) the various
roles that I adopt   **98 Eye** appear   **101 laurel** wreathed with laurel
103 so abides and flies mingles remaining and going in such a paradoxical fashion
1.4 Location: Rome.

3 competitor partner. (With a suggestion also of "rival.")   **6 Ptolemy**
(Cleopatra's royal brother, to whom she had been married according
to Egyptian custom.)   **7 gave audience** i.e., received messengers
9 abstract epitome   **12–13 His . . . blackness** His faults are enhanced
by contrast with his virtues, just as the stars in the sky stand out from
the darkness   **14 purchased** acquired   **16 Let's grant** Even if we
were to grant   **18 mirth** jest, diversion   **19 keep . . . of** take turns
20 stand the buffet exchange blows   **22 As his composure** and a
man's composition or temperament   **24 foils** blemishes   **24–5 when
. . . lightness** when we have to carry the heavy burden imposed by
his levity.   **26 His vacancy** his leisure time   **27–8 Full . . . for't** the
physical disabilities resulting from such voluptuousness (such as
venereal disease) would call him to account and would be adequate
punishment.   **28 confound** waste   **29 drums** summons (as by a military drum).   **sport** amorous pastime   **29–30 speaks . . . ours** summons him urgently in view of his political position and ours as well
30 chid chided, reprimanded   **31 rate** berate.   **mature in knowledge**
old enough to know better   **32 Pawn . . . pleasure** risk for the sake of
immediate gratification what experience tells them will be ultimately
painful   **33 to judgment** against better judgment.

And it appears he is beloved of those 37
That only have feared Caesar. To the ports 38
The discontents repair, and men's reports 39
Give him much wronged. [*Exit.*]
CAESAR I should have known no less. 40
It hath been taught us from the primal state 41
That he which is was wished until he were; 42
And the ebbed man, ne'er loved till ne'er worth love, 43
Comes deared by being lacked. This common body, 44
Like to a vagabond flag upon the stream, 45
Goes to and back, lackeying the varying tide 46
To rot itself with motion.

[*Enter a Second Messenger.*]

SECOND MESSENGER Caesar, I bring thee word
Menecrates and Menas, famous pirates, 49
Makes the sea serve them, which they ear and wound 50
With keels of every kind. Many hot inroads
They make in Italy. The borders maritime 52
Lack blood to think on't, and flush youth revolt. 53
No vessel can peep forth but 'tis as soon
Taken as seen; for Pompey's name strikes more 55
Than could his war resisted. [*Exit.*]
CAESAR Antony, 56
Leave thy lascivious wassails. When thou once 57
Was beaten from Modena, where thou slew'st
Hirtius and Pansa, consuls, at thy heel
Did famine follow, whom thou fought'st against, 60
Though daintily brought up, with patience more
Than savages could suffer. Thou didst drink 62
The stale of horses and the gilded puddle 63
Which beasts would cough at. Thy palate then did
deign 64
The roughest berry on the rudest hedge.
Yea, like the stag, when snow the pasture sheets, 66
The barks of trees thou browsèd. On the Alps 67
It is reported thou didst eat strange flesh,
Which some did die to look on. And all this—
It wounds thine honor that I speak it now—
Was borne so like a soldier that thy cheek
So much as lanked not. 72
LEPIDUS 'Tis pity of him. 73
CAESAR Let his shames quickly
Drive him to Rome. 'Tis time we twain
Did show ourselves i'th' field, and to that end

Assemble we immediate council. Pompey
Thrives in our idleness.
LEPIDUS Tomorrow, Caesar,
I shall be furnished to inform you rightly
Both what by sea and land I can be able 80
To front this present time.
CAESAR Till which encounter 81
It is my business too. Farewell.
LEPIDUS
Farewell, my lord. What you shall know meantime
Of stirs abroad, I shall beseech you, sir, 84
To let me be partaker.
CAESAR
Doubt not, sir, I knew it for my bond. 86
Exeunt [*separately*].

❧

[1.5]

Enter Cleopatra, Charmian, Iras, and Mardian.

CLEOPATRA Charmian!
CHARMIAN Madam?
CLEOPATRA
Ha, ha! Give me to drink mandragora. 3
CHARMIAN Why, madam?
CLEOPATRA
That I might sleep out this great gap of time
My Antony is away.
CHARMIAN You think of him too much.
CLEOPATRA
Oh, 'tis treason!
CHARMIAN Madam, I trust not so.
CLEOPATRA
Thou, eunuch Mardian!
MARDIAN What's Your Highness' pleasure?
CLEOPATRA
Not now to hear thee sing. I take no pleasure
In aught an eunuch has. 'Tis well for thee 11
That, being unseminared, thy freer thoughts 12
May not fly forth of Egypt. Hast thou affections? 13
MARDIAN Yes, gracious madam.
CLEOPATRA Indeed?
MARDIAN
Not in deed, madam, for I can do nothing 16
But what indeed is honest to be done. 17
Yet have I fierce affections, and think
What Venus did with Mars.
CLEOPATRA Oh, Charmian,
Where think'st thou he is now? Stands he or sits he?
Or does he walk? Or is he on his horse?
Oh, happy horse, to bear the weight of Antony!

37 **of** by   38 **That . . . Caesar** that have obeyed Caesar only through fear.   39 **discontents** discontented. (See 1.3.48–52.)   40 **Give him** represent him as   41–4 **It . . . lacked** It is an ironic lesson of history from the earliest times that the man currently in the public eye is avidly sought after only until he becomes ruler, whereas the public figure whose fortunes have decayed, sought after only when he is no longer worthy of love, becomes loved once he is gone.   44 **common body** populace   45 **vagabond flag** shifting and undependable weeds   46 **lackeying** following in servile fashion, like a lackey   49 **famous** notorious   50 **ear** plow   52 **borders maritime** coastal territories   53 **Lack blood** turn pale.   **flush** vigorous; flushed, ruddy (contrasted with those who *Lack blood*)   55–6 **strikes . . . resisted** inflicts more damage than his forces could against our resistance.   57 **wassails** carousals.   60 **whom** i.e., famine   62 **suffer** show in suffering.   63 **stale** urine.   **gilded** covered with iridescent slime   64 **deign** not disdain   66 **sheets** covers   67 **browsèd** fed upon.   72 **lanked not** did not become thin.   73 **of** about

80 **be able** be capable of mustering   81 **front** confront, deal with   84 **stirs** commotions   86 **knew** already knew.   **bond** duty, obligation.   **1.5 Location:** Egypt. Cleopatra's palace.
3 **mandragora** juice of the mandrake (a narcotic).   11 **aught** (With bawdy suggestion.)   12 **unseminared** castrated   13 **of** from.   **affections** passions.   16 **Not in deed** (Mardian punningly takes the *deed* of *Indeed* in line 15 to mean "physical act.")   **do** (With suggestion of sexual intercourse.)   17 **honest** chaste

Do bravely, horse, for wot'st thou whom thou mov'st? 23
The demi-Atlas of this earth, the arm 24
And burgonet of men. He's speaking now, 25
Or murmuring, "Where's my serpent of old Nile?"
For so he calls me. Now I feed myself
With most delicious poison. Think on me, 28
That am with Phoebus' amorous pinches black 29
And wrinkled deep in time. Broad-fronted Caesar, 30
When thou wast here above the ground, I was
A morsel for a monarch. And great Pompey 32
Would stand and make his eyes grow in my brow; 33
There would he anchor his aspect, and die 34
With looking on his life. 35

Enter Alexas.

ALEXAS   Sovereign of Egypt, hail!
CLEOPATRA
How much unlike art thou Mark Antony!
Yet, coming from him, that great med'cine hath 38
With his tinct gilded thee. 39
How goes it with my brave Mark Antony? 40
ALEXAS   Last thing he did, dear Queen,
He kissed—the last of many doubled kisses—
This orient pearl. [*He gives a pearl.*] His speech sticks in
   my heart. 43
CLEOPATRA
Mine ear must pluck it thence.
ALEXAS   "Good friend," quoth he,
"Say the firm Roman to great Egypt sends 45
This treasure of an oyster; at whose foot,
To mend the petty present, I will piece 47
Her opulent throne with kingdoms. All the East,
Say thou, shall call her mistress." So he nodded,
And soberly did mount an arm-gaunt steed, 50
Who neighed so high that what I would have spoke
Was beastly dumbed by him. 52
CLEOPATRA   What, was he sad, or merry?
ALEXAS
Like to the time o'th' year between the extremes
Of hot and cold, he was nor sad nor merry. 55

CLEOPATRA
Oh, well-divided disposition! Note him, 56
Note him, good Charmian, 'tis the man; but note him. 57
He was not sad, for he would shine on those 58
That make their looks by his; he was not merry, 59
Which seemed to tell them his remembrance lay
In Egypt with his joy; but between both.
Oh, heavenly mingle! Be'st thou sad or merry,
The violence of either thee becomes, 63
So does it no man else.—Met'st thou my posts? 64
ALEXAS
Ay, madam, twenty several messengers. 65
Why do you send so thick?
CLEOPATRA   Who's born that day 66
When I forget to send to Antony
Shall die a beggar. Ink and paper, Charmian. 68
Welcome, my good Alexas. Did I, Charmian,
Ever love Caesar so?
CHARMIAN   Oh, that brave Caesar!
CLEOPATRA
Be choked with such another emphasis! 71
Say, "the brave Antony."
CHARMIAN   The valiant Caesar!
CLEOPATRA
By Isis, I will give thee bloody teeth
If thou with Caesar paragon again 74
My man of men.
CHARMIAN   By your most gracious pardon,
I sing but after you.
CLEOPATRA   My salad days,
When I was green in judgment, cold in blood, 77
To say as I said then. But, come, away,
Get me ink and paper.
He shall have every day a several greeting,
Or I'll unpeople Egypt.   *Exeunt.* 81

❖

[2.1]

*Enter Pompey, Menecrates, and Menas, in war-
like manner.*

POMPEY
If the great gods be just, they shall assist
The deeds of justest men.
MENAS   Know, worthy Pompey, 2
That what they do delay they not deny. 3

23 Do (With sexual suggestion, as in line 16.) wot'st thou do you
know   24 demi-Atlas one who (together with Caesar) supports the
weight of the whole world, as Atlas did. (Cleopatra disregards Lepidus as a triumvir.)   arm strong right arm or weapon   25 burgonet
light helmet or steel cap, i.e., protector   28–30 Think . . . time
(Cleopatra reflects on her ability to attract Antony, given the fact that
she is dark-skinned [as from the amorous pinches of her lover, the
sun] and increasingly wrinkled with age.)   29 Phoebus' the sun's
30 Broad-fronted Caesar Broad-foreheaded Julius Caesar   32 great
Pompey Gnaeus Pompey, oldest son of Pompey the Great. (Shakespeare may conflate the two.)   33 make . . . brow i.e., rivet his eyes
on my face   34 aspect look, gaze   die i.e., suffer the extremity of
love. (And with suggestion of orgasm, as at 1.2.148.)   35 his life that
which he lived for.   38 great med'cine the philosopher's stone, the
supposed substance by which alchemists hoped to turn all baser metals into gold   39 his tinct its alchemical potency; also, its color
40 brave splendid   43 orient shining, bright. (The best pearls were
from the East or Orient.)   45 firm constant, true.   Egypt the Queen
of Egypt   47 piece augment   50 arm-gaunt made trim and hard by
warlike service, or hungry for battle   52 dumbed drowned out,
made inaudible   55 nor sad neither sad

56 well-divided disposition well-balanced temperament.   57 the
man i.e., perfectly characteristic of him.   but do but, only   58 would
wished to   59 make . . . his model their demeanor on his look
63 thee becomes is becoming to you   64 posts messengers.   65 several separate, distinct. (Also in line 80.)   66 Who's Anyone who is
68 Shall . . . beggar (since that day, sure never to come, would be ill-
omened)   71 emphasis emphatic expression.   74 paragon match or
compare   77 green immature   81 Or . . . Egypt Or I will send so
many messengers that Egypt will be unpeopled. (Perhaps too with a
darker threat of violence.)
2.1 Location: Pompey's camp, probably at Messina, Sicily.
2 MENAS (The Folio assigns the speeches in this scene to "Mene.";
some could be for Menecrates, but Pompey ignores him entirely at
lines 43–52, and Menecrates never reappears in the play.)   3 not
deny i.e., do not necessarily deny.

POMPEY
Whiles we are suitors to their throne, decays   4
The thing we sue for.
MENAS   We, ignorant of ourselves,   5
Beg often our own harms, which the wise powers
Deny us for our good; so find we profit
By losing of our prayers.
POMPEY   I shall do well.
The people love me, and the sea is mine;
My powers are crescent, and my auguring hope   10
Says it will come to th' full. Mark Antony   11
In Egypt sits at dinner, and will make
No wars without doors. Caesar gets money where   13
He loses hearts. Lepidus flatters both,
Of both is flattered; but he neither loves,   15
Nor either cares for him.
MENAS   Caesar and Lepidus
Are in the field. A mighty strength they carry.   17
POMPEY
Where have you this? 'Tis false.
MENAS   From Silvius, sir.
POMPEY
He dreams. I know they are in Rome together
Looking for Antony. But all the charms of love,   20
Salt Cleopatra, soften thy waned lip!   21
Let witchcraft joined with beauty, lust with both,
Tie up the libertine in a field of feasts,   23
Keep his brain fuming. Epicurean cooks,   24
Sharpen with cloyless sauce his appetite,   25
That sleep and feeding may prorogue his honor   26
Even till a Lethe'd dullness—

Enter Varrius.

                How now, Varrius?   27
VARRIUS
This is most certain that I shall deliver: 28
Mark Antony is every hour in Rome
Expected. Since he went from Egypt 'tis
A space for further travel.   31
POMPEY   I could have given less matter   32
A better ear. Menas, I did not think
This amorous surfeiter would have donned his helm   34
For such a petty war. His soldiership
Is twice the other twain. But let us rear   36
The higher our opinion, that our stirring   37
Can from the lap of Egypt's widow pluck   38

The ne'er-lust-wearied Antony.
MENAS   I cannot hope   39
Caesar and Antony shall well greet together.   40
His wife that's dead did trespasses to Caesar;   41
His brother warred upon him, although, I think,   42
Not moved by Antony.
POMPEY   I know not, Menas,   43
How lesser enmities may give way to greater.
Were't not that we stand up against them all,
'Twere pregnant they should square between
     themselves,   46
For they have entertainèd cause enough   47
To draw their swords. But how the fear of us
May cement their divisions and bind up
The petty difference, we yet not know.
Be't as our gods will have't! It only stands   51
Our lives upon to use our strongest hands.   52
Come, Menas.   *Exeunt.*

❖

[2.2]

Enter Enobarbus and Lepidus.

LEPIDUS
Good Enobarbus, 'tis a worthy deed,
And shall become you well, to entreat your captain
To soft and gentle speech.
ENOBARBUS   I shall entreat him
To answer like himself. If Caesar move him,   4
Let Antony look over Caesar's head   5
And speak as loud as Mars. By Jupiter,
Were I the wearer of Antonio's beard,
I would not shave't today.   8
LEPIDUS
'Tis not a time for private stomaching.
ENOBARBUS   Every time   9
Serves for the matter that is then born in't.
LEPIDUS
But small to greater matters must give way.
ENOBARBUS
Not if the small come first.
LEPIDUS   Your speech is passion;
But pray you stir no embers up. Here comes
The noble Antony.

Enter Antony and Ventidius [in conversation].

ENOBARBUS   And yonder, Caesar.

*Enter Caesar, Maecenas, and Agrippa, [also in
conversation, by another door].*

4–5 Whiles . . . for While we are praying, that for which we pray is being destroyed. **10 My . . . crescent** My armed forces are on the increase. **auguring** prophesying **11 it** i.e., my powers or fortune (seen as a crescent moon, becoming full) **13 without doors** out-doors, i.e., in the battlefield, rather than in the bedroom. **15 Of** by. **neither loves** loves neither **17 A . . . carry** They command a mighty army. **20 Looking for** Awaiting. **charms** spells **21 Salt** lustful. **waned** faded, withered **23 Tie . . . feasts** i.e., tether him like an animal in a rich pasture **24 Epicurean** Let epicurean **25 cloyless** i.e., which will not satiate **26 prorogue** defer the operation of **27 Lethe'd** oblivious. (From the river of the underworld whose waters cause forgetfulness in those who drink.) **28 deliver** report **31 space . . . travel** time enough for an even longer journey and labor (travail). **32 less** less important **34 helm** helmet **36 rear** raise **37 opinion** i.e., of ourselves **38 Egypt's widow** i.e., Cleopatra, widow of the young King Ptolemy

39 hope expect **40 well greet** greet one another kindly **41 did trespasses to** wronged **42 brother** i.e., Lucius Antonius. (See 1.2.94 ff.) **43 moved** provoked, incited **46 pregnant** clear, obvious. **square** quarrel **47 entertainèd** maintained **51–2 It . . . hands** Our very lives depend upon our using our greatest strength.
2.2 Location: Rome. Furniture is put out on which Antony and Caesar are to sit.
4 like himself i.e., in a way befitting his greatness. **move him** i.e., to anger **5 look . . . head** i.e., condescend to Caesar as a smaller man **8 I . . . shave't** i.e., I would continue to wear it and thereby dare Caesar to pluck it (in a symbolic gesture for starting a fight) **9 private stomaching** personal resentment.

ANTONY
    If we compose well here, to Parthia.   15
    Hark, Ventidius.   [*They confer apart.*]
CAESAR
    I do not know, Maecenas, ask Agrippa.
LEPIDUS   Noble friends,
    That which combined us was most great, and let not
    A leaner action rend us. What's amiss,   20
    May it be gently heard. When we debate
    Our trivial difference loud, we do commit
    Murder in healing wounds. Then, noble partners,   23
    The rather for I earnestly beseech,   24
    Touch you the sourest points with sweetest terms,
    Nor curstness grow to th' matter.
ANTONY   'Tis spoken well.   26
    Were we before our armies, and to fight,   27
    I should do thus.   *Flourish.*
CAESAR   Welcome to Rome.
ANTONY   Thank you.
CAESAR   Sit.
ANTONY   Sit, sir.
CAESAR   Nay, then.   [*They sit.*]
ANTONY
    I learn you take things ill which are not so,
    Or being, concern you not.
CAESAR   I must be laughed at   35
    If, or for nothing or a little, I   36
    Should say myself offended, and with you
    Chiefly i'th' world; more laughed at that I should   38
    Once name you derogately, when to sound your name   39
    It not concerned me.   40
ANTONY
    My being in Egypt, Caesar, what was't to you?
CAESAR
    No more than my residing here at Rome
    Might be to you in Egypt. Yet if you there
    Did practice on my state, your being in Egypt   44
    Might be my question.
ANTONY   How intend you "practiced"?   45
CAESAR
    You may be pleased to catch at mine intent   46
    By what did here befall me. Your wife and brother
    Made wars upon me, and their contestation
    Was theme for you. You were the word of war.   49
ANTONY
    You do mistake your business. My brother never
    Did urge me in his act. I did inquire it,   51
    And have my learning from some true reports   52

That drew their swords with you. Did he not rather   53
    Discredit my authority with yours,   54
    And make the wars alike against my stomach,   55
    Having alike your cause? Of this my letters   56
    Before did satisfy you. If you'll patch a quarrel,   57
    As matter whole you have to make it with,   58
    It must not be with this.
CAESAR   You praise yourself   59
    By laying defects of judgment to me, but
    You patched up your excuses.
ANTONY   Not so, not so.
    I know you could not lack—I am certain on't—   62
    Very necessity of this thought, that I,   63
    Your partner in the cause 'gainst which he fought,   64
    Could not with graceful eyes attend those wars   65
    Which fronted mine own peace. As for my wife,   66
    I would you had her spirit in such another.   67
    The third o'th' world is yours, which with a snaffle   68
    You may pace easy, but not such a wife.   69
ENOBARBUS   Would we had all such wives, that the men
    might go to wars with the women!
ANTONY
    So much uncurbable, her garboils, Caesar,   72
    Made out of her impatience—which not wanted   73
    Shrewdness of policy too—I grieving grant   74
    Did you too much disquiet. For that you must   75
    But say I could not help it.
CAESAR   I wrote to you   76
    When rioting in Alexandria; you   77
    Did pocket up my letters and with taunts
    Did gibe my missive out of audience.
ANTONY   Sir,   79
    He fell upon me ere admitted, then.   80
    Three kings I had newly feasted, and did want   81
    Of what I was i'th' morning. But next day   82
    I told him of myself, which was as much   83
    As to have asked him pardon. Let this fellow
    Be nothing of our strife; if we contend,   85
    Out of our question wipe him.
CAESAR   You have broken   86
    The article of your oath, which you shall never   87
    Have tongue to charge me with.
LEPIDUS   Soft, Caesar!   89
ANTONY   No, Lepidus, let him speak.

---

15 **compose** come to an agreement   20 **leaner** lesser, more trivial.
rend divide.   **What's** Whatever is   23 **healing** i.e., attempting to
heal   24 **The rather for** all the more because   26 **Nor . . . grow** nor
let ill humor be added   27 **being** being so, i.e., even
if they are amiss   36 **or . . . or** either . . . or   38 **i'th' world** of all people   39 **Once** under any circumstances.   **derogately** disparagingly
39–40 **when . . . concerned me** i.e., if, as you say, it were none of my
business.   44 **practice on my state** plot against my position
45 **question** business.   **How intend you** What do you mean
46 **catch at** infer   49 **Was . . . war** had you for its theme. They made
war in your name. (*Word* here means "watchword.")   51 **urge . . . act**
claim that he was fighting in my behalf.   **inquire** inquire into
52 **reports** reporters

53 **That . . . you** that fought in your army.   54 **Discredit** injure.   **with**
along with   55 **stomach** desire   56 **Having . . . cause** i.e., I having
just as much reason as you to deplore Lucius's action.   57–9 **If . . .
this** If you insist on manufacturing a quarrel out of shreds and
patches, as if you had substantial material to make it with, you've
chosen a weak matter to use.   62–3 **I know . . . thought** I'm certain
you must have realized   64 **he** i.e., Lucius   65 **with . . . attend** regard
favorably   66 **fronted** confronted, opposed   67 **her . . . another** i.e., a
wife such as she was.   68 **snaffle** bridle bit   69 **pace** put through its
paces, manage   72–5 **So . . . disquiet** I unhappily concede that her
unmanageable commotions, caused by her impatience (at my being
in Egypt) but not lacking in keenness of stratagem, did much to disquiet you, Caesar.   76 **But say** concede that   77 **When** while you
were   79 **Did . . . audience** taunted my messenger out of your presence.   80 **fell** burst in   81–2 **did want . . . morning** was not at my
best as I had been earlier in the day.   83 **of myself** i.e., of my having
had a lot to drink   85 **Be . . . of** have no part in   86 **question** contention   87 **article** terms   89 **Soft** Gently, go easy

The honor is sacred which he talks on now,
Supposing that I lacked it. But, on, Caesar: 92
The article of my oath—

CAESAR
To lend me arms and aid when I required them,   94
The which you both denied.

ANTONY   Neglected, rather;
And then when poisoned hours had bound me up
From mine own knowledge. As nearly as I may   97
I'll play the penitent to you, but mine honesty   98
Shall not make poor my greatness, nor my power   99
Work without it. Truth is that Fulvia,   100
To have me out of Egypt, made wars here,
For which myself, the ignorant motive, do   102
So far ask pardon as befits mine honor
To stoop in such a case.

LEPIDUS   'Tis noble spoken.   104

MAECENAS
If it might please you to enforce no further
The griefs between ye; to forget them quite   106
Were to remember that the present need
Speaks to atone you.

LEPIDUS   Worthily spoken, Maecenas.   108

ENOBARBUS   Or, if you borrow one another's love for the
instant, you may, when you hear no more words of
Pompey, return it again. You shall have time to wrangle in when you have nothing else to do.

ANTONY
Thou art a soldier only. Speak no more.

ENOBARBUS   That truth should be silent I had almost
forgot.

ANTONY
You wrong this presence. Therefore speak no more.   116

ENOBARBUS   Go to, then; your considerate stone.   117

CAESAR
I do not much dislike the matter, but
The manner of his speech; for 't cannot be
We shall remain in friendship, our conditions   120
So diff'ring in their acts. Yet, if I knew
What hoop should hold us staunch, from edge to edge   122
O'th' world I would pursue it.

AGRIPPA   Give me leave, Caesar.

CAESAR   Speak, Agrippa.

AGRIPPA
Thou hast a sister by the mother's side,
Admired Octavia. Great Mark Antony
Is now a widower.

CAESAR   Say not so, Agrippa.
If Cleopatra heard you, your reproof
Were well deserved of rashness.   130

ANTONY
I am not married, Caesar. Let me hear
Agrippa further speak.

AGRIPPA
To hold you in perpetual amity,
To make you brothers, and to knit your hearts
With an unslipping knot, take Antony
Octavia to his wife, whose beauty claims
No worse a husband than the best of men,
Whose virtue and whose general graces speak   138
That which none else can utter. By this marriage   139
All little jealousies, which now seem great,   140
And all great fears, which now import their dangers,   141
Would then be nothing. Truths would be tales,   142
Where now half tales be truths. Her love to both   143
Would each to other and all loves to both
Draw after her. Pardon what I have spoke,
For 'tis a studied, not a present thought,
By duty ruminated.

ANTONY   Will Caesar speak?

CAESAR
Not till he hears how Antony is touched   148
With what is spoke already.   149

ANTONY   What power is in Agrippa
If I would say, "Agrippa, be it so,"
To make this good?

CAESAR   The power of Caesar and
His power unto Octavia.

ANTONY   May I never   153
To this good purpose, that so fairly shows,   154
Dream of impediment! Let me have thy hand
Further this act of grace, and from this hour   156
The heart of brothers govern in our loves
And sway our great designs!

CAESAR   There's my hand.
[They clasp hands.]
A sister I bequeath you whom no brother
Did ever love so dearly. Let her live
To join our kingdoms and our hearts; and never   161
Fly off our loves again!

LEPIDUS   Happily, amen!   162

ANTONY
I did not think to draw my sword 'gainst Pompey,
For he hath laid strange courtesies and great   164
Of late upon me. I must thank him only,   165
Lest my remembrance suffer ill report;   166
At heel of that, defy him.

LEPIDUS   Time calls upon 's.   167
Of us must Pompey presently be sought,   168
Or else he seeks out us.

92 **Supposing** implying   94 **required** requested   97 **From . . . knowledge** from knowing myself.   98–100 **mine . . . it** my honesty (in admitting my overindulgence) will not go so far as to dishonor my greatness, nor, conversely, will my authority be used in a dishonorable way.   102 **motive** moving or inciting cause   104 **noble** nobly 106 **griefs** grievances   108 **atone** reconcile   116 **presence** company. 117 **Go . . . stone** i.e., All right, all right. I'll keep my thoughts to myself.   120 **conditions** temperaments, dispositions   122 **hoop** barrel hoop.   **staunch** firm, watertight   130 **Were . . . rashness** would richly deserve the rebuke it would get for such rashness.

138–9 **Whose . . . utter** whose virtues declare themselves better than any words about them could do.   140 **jealousies** misunderstandings, suspicions   141 **import** imply; carry with them   142–3 **Truths . . . truths** True reports (no matter how distressing) would then be discounted as mere rumors, whereas at present half-true reports are taken for the whole truth.   148–9 **touched With** affected by 153 **unto** over   154 **so fairly shows** looks so promising   156 **Further** in furtherance of   161–2 **never . . . again** may our amity never desert us again.   164 **strange** remarkable   165 **only** at least   166 **Lest . . . report** lest I be accused of ingratitude   167 **At heel of** immediately after   168 **Of** By.   **presently** at once

ANTONY   Where lies he?

CAESAR
About the mount Misena.

ANTONY   What is his strength   171
By land?

CAESAR   Great and increasing; but by sea
He is an absolute master.

ANTONY   So is the fame.   173
Would we had spoke together! Haste we for it.   174
Yet, ere we put ourselves in arms, dispatch we
The business we have talked of.

CAESAR   With most gladness,   176
And do invite you to my sister's view,   177
Whither straight I'll lead you.   178

ANTONY
Let us, Lepidus, not lack your company.

LEPIDUS
Noble Antony, not sickness should detain me.   180
Flourish. Exeunt. Manent Enobarbus, Agrippa,
Maecenas.

MAECENAS   Welcome from Egypt, sir.

ENOBARBUS   Half the heart of Caesar, worthy Maecenas!   182
My honorable friend, Agrippa!

AGRIPPA   Good Enobarbus!

MAECENAS   We have cause to be glad that matters are so
well digested. You stayed well by't in Egypt.   186

ENOBARBUS   Ay, sir, we did sleep day out of counte-   187
nance and made the night light with drinking.   188

MAECENAS   Eight wild boars roasted whole at a breakfast, and but twelve persons there; is this true?

ENOBARBUS   This was but as a fly by an eagle. We had   191
much more monstrous matter of feast, which worthily
deserved noting.

MAECENAS   She's a most triumphant lady, if report be   194
square to her.   195

ENOBARBUS   When she first met Mark Antony, she
pursed up his heart upon the river of Cydnus.   197

AGRIPPA   There she appeared indeed, or my reporter de-   198
vised well for her.   199

ENOBARBUS   I will tell you.
The barge she sat in, like a burnished throne   201
Burnt on the water. The poop was beaten gold;   202
Purple the sails, and so perfumèd that
The winds were lovesick with them. The oars were
    silver,
Which to the tune of flutes kept stroke, and made
The water which they beat to follow faster,

As amorous of their strokes. For her own person,   207
It beggared all description: she did lie
In her pavilion—cloth-of-gold of tissue—   209
O'erpicturing that Venus where we see
The fancy outwork nature. On each side her   211
Stood pretty dimpled boys, like smiling Cupids,
With divers-colored fans, whose wind did seem   213
To glow the delicate cheeks which they did cool,   214
And what they undid did.

AGRIPPA   Oh, rare for Antony!

ENOBARBUS
Her gentlewomen, like the Nereides,   216
So many mermaids, tended her i'th'eyes   217
And made their bends adornings. At the helm   218
A seeming mermaid steers. The silken tackle
Swell with the touches of those flower-soft hands,
That yarely frame the office. From the barge   221
A strange invisible perfume hits the sense
Of the adjacent wharfs. The city cast   223
Her people out upon her; and Antony,
Enthroned i'th' marketplace, did sit alone,
Whistling to th'air, which, but for vacancy,   226
Had gone to gaze on Cleopatra too,
And made a gap in nature.

AGRIPPA   Rare Egyptian!

ENOBARBUS
Upon her landing, Antony sent to her,
Invited her to supper. She replied
It should be better he became her guest,
Which she entreated. Our courteous Antony,
Whom ne'er the word of "No" woman heard speak,
Being barbered ten times o'er, goes to the feast,
And for his ordinary pays his heart   235
For what his eyes eat only.

AGRIPPA   Royal wench!   236
She made great Caesar lay his sword to bed;   237
He plowed her, and she cropped.

ENOBARBUS   I saw her once   238
Hop forty paces through the public street,
And having lost her breath, she spoke and panted,
That she did make defect perfection,   241
And, breathless, power breathe forth.

MAECENAS
Now Antony must leave her utterly.

ENOBARBUS   Never. He will not.
Age cannot wither her, nor custom stale   245
Her infinite variety. Other women cloy
The appetites they feed, but she makes hungry

171 Misena i.e., Misenum, in southern Italy. (Not in Sicily, where 2.1 perhaps takes place.)   **173 So is the fame** So it is reported. **174 Would . . . together!** Would that we had had a chance to parley before battle!   **176 most** the greatest   **177 to my sister's view** to see my sister   **178 straight** straightway   **180.1 *Manent*** They remain onstage   **182 Half . . . Caesar** You who are very close to Caesar, one of his closest advisers   **186 digested** disposed.   **stayed well by't** kept at it   **187–8 we . . . countenance** we insulted day by sleeping right through it   **188 light** (1) brightly lit (2) debauched and giddy **191 This . . . eagle** i.e., This was nothing compared with greater feasting.   **194 triumphant** magnificent   **195 square** just   **197 pursed up** pocketed up, put in her purse   **198–9 devised** invented   **201 burnished** lustrous, shiny   **202 poop** a short deck built over the main deck at the stern of the vessel

207 As As if.   **For** As for   **209 cloth-of-gold of tissue** cloth made of gold thread and silk woven together   **211 fancy** imagination **213 divers-colored** multicolored   **214 glow** cause to glow **216 Nereides** sea nymphs   **217 So . . . i'th'eyes** as if they were so many mermaids, attended to her every glance or nod   **218 made . . . adornings** made their graceful bowings beautiful.   **221 yarely . . . office** nimbly perform their function.   **223 wharfs** banks.   **226 but for vacancy** except that it would have created a vacuum   **235 ordinary** meal, supper (such as one might obtain at a public table in a tavern)   **236 eat** ate. (Pronounced *et*.)   **237 Caesar** i.e., Julius Caesar, by whom Cleopatra had a son named Caesarion   **238 cropped** bore fruit (a son).   **241 That** so that   **245 custom stale** repeated experience make stale

Where most she satisfies; for vilest things
Become themselves in her, that the holy priests 249
Bless her when she is riggish. 250

MAECENAS
If beauty, wisdom, modesty can settle
The heart of Antony, Octavia is
A blessèd lottery to him.

AGRIPPA   Let us go. 253
Good Enobarbus, make yourself my guest
Whilst you abide here.

ENOBARBUS   Humbly, sir, I thank you.
                                        Exeunt.

❧

[2.3]

Enter Antony, Caesar, Octavia between them.

ANTONY
The world and my great office will sometimes
Divide me from your bosom.

OCTAVIA   All which time
Before the gods my knee shall bow my prayers
To them for you.

ANTONY   Good night, sir. My Octavia,
Read not my blemishes in the world's report. 5
I have not kept my square, but that to come 6
Shall all be done by th' rule. Good night, dear lady.
Good night, sir.

CAESAR   Good night.   *Exit [with Octavia].*

Enter Soothsayer.

ANTONY
Now, sirrah: you do wish yourself in Egypt? 10

SOOTHSAYER   Would I had never come from thence,
nor you thither! 12

ANTONY   If you can, your reason?

SOOTHSAYER   I see it in in my motion, have it not in my 14
tongue; but yet hie you to Egypt again. 15

ANTONY
Say to me, whose fortunes shall rise higher,
Caesar's or mine?

SOOTHSAYER   Caesar's.
Therefore, O Antony, stay not by his side.
Thy daemon—that thy spirit which keeps thee—is 20
Noble, courageous, high unmatchable, 21
Where Caesar's is not; but near him thy angel 22
Becomes afeard, as being o'erpowered. Therefore
Make space enough between you.

ANTONY   Speak this no more.

SOOTHSAYER
To none but thee; no more but when to thee. 25
If thou dost play with him at any game,
Thou art sure to lose; and of that natural luck 27
He beats thee 'gainst the odds. Thy luster thickens 28
When he shines by. I say again, thy spirit 29
Is all afraid to govern thee near him;
But, he away, 'tis noble.

ANTONY   Get thee gone.
Say to Ventidius I would speak with him.
                              Exit [Soothsayer].
He shall to Parthia.—Be it art or hap, 33
He hath spoken true. The very dice obey him,
And in our sports my better cunning faints 35
Under his chance. If we draw lots, he speeds; 36
His cocks do win the battle still of mine 37
When it is all to naught, and his quails ever 38
Beat mine, inhooped, at odds. I will to Egypt; 39
And though I make this marriage for my peace,
I'th'East my pleasure lies.

Enter Ventidius.

                              Oh, come, Ventidius.
You must to Parthia. Your commission's ready;
Follow me, and receive't.   *Exeunt.*

❧

[2.4]

Enter Lepidus, Maecenas, and Agrippa.

LEPIDUS
Trouble yourselves no further. Pray you, hasten
Your generals after.

AGRIPPA   Sir, Mark Antony 2
Will e'en but kiss Octavia, and we'll follow. 3

LEPIDUS
Till I shall see you in your soldier's dress, 4
Which will become you both, farewell.

MAECENAS   We shall, 5
As I conceive the journey, be at th' Mount 6
Before you, Lepidus.

LEPIDUS   Your way is shorter;
My purposes do draw me much about. 8
You'll win two days upon me.

MAECENAS, AGRIPPA   Sir, good success!

LEPIDUS   Farewell.   *Exeunt.*

❧

249 **Become themselves** are becoming, attractive.   **that** so that
250 **riggish** lustful.   253 **lottery** prize, gift of fortune
2.3 Location: Rome.
5 **Read** interpret.   **in** according to   6 **kept my square** kept to a
straight course (as guided by a carpenter's square; with pun on *rule,*
"ruler" in next line).   **that** that which is   10 **sirrah** (A form of
address to a social inferior.)   12 **thither** to that place.   14 **in my
motion** intuitively, by inward prompting   15 **hie** hasten   20 **Thy . . .
thee** Your guardian spirit, the spirit that protects you   21 **high
unmatchable** unmatchable in the extreme   22 **Where . . . not** wherever Caesar's spirit is not present (to daunt yours)

25 **no more but when** only when   27 **of** by   28 **thickens** grows dim
29 **by** nearby.   33 **art or hap** skill or luck   35 **cunning** skill
36 **chance** luck.   **speeds** wins   37 **still of** always from   38 **When . . .
naught** when the odds are everything to nothing (in my favor)
39 **inhooped** (The birds were enclosed in hoops to make them fight.)
at odds against the odds.
2.4 Location: Rome.
2 **Your generals after** after your generals.   3 **e'en but** only, just
4 **dress** garb, apparel   5 **become** suit   6 **conceive** understand.
th' Mount i.e., Mount Misenum   8 **about** roundabout.

[2.5]

Enter Cleopatra, Charmian, Iras, and Alexas.

CLEOPATRA
Give me some music; music, moody food
Of us that trade in love.

ALL   The music, ho!

Enter Mardian the eunuch.

CLEOPATRA
Let it alone. Let's to billiards. Come, Charmian.

CHARMIAN
My arm is sore. Best play with Mardian.

CLEOPATRA
As well a woman with an eunuch played
As with a woman. Come, you'll play with me, sir?

MARDIAN   As well as I can, madam.

CLEOPATRA
And when good will is showed, though't come too   8
    short,
The actor may plead pardon. I'll none now.   9
Give me mine angle; we'll to th' river. There,   10
My music playing far off, I will betray
Tawny-finned fishes. My bended hook shall pierce
Their slimy jaws, and as I draw them up
I'll think them every one an Antony,
And say, "Aha! You're caught."

CHARMIAN   'Twas merry when
You wagered on your angling, when your diver
Did hang a salt fish on his hook, which he   17
With fervency drew up.

CLEOPATRA   That time—oh, times!—
I laughed him out of patience; and that night
I laughed him into patience. And next morn,
Ere the ninth hour, I drunk him to his bed,   21
Then put my tires and mantles on him, whilst   22
I wore his sword Philippan.

Enter a Messenger.

                              Oh, from Italy!   23
Ram thou thy fruitful tidings in mine ears,
That long time have been barren.

MESSENGER   Madam, madam—

CLEOPATRA
Antonio's dead! If thou say so, villain,
Thou kill'st thy mistress; but well and free,
If thou so yield him, there is gold, and here   28
My bluest veins to kiss—a hand that kings
Have lipped, and trembled kissing.
                    [*She offers him gold, and her hand to kiss.*]

MESSENGER   First, madam, he is well.

CLEOPATRA
Why, there's more gold. But, sirrah, mark, we use
To say the dead are well. Bring it to that,   33
The gold I give thee will I melt and pour
Down thy ill-uttering throat.

MESSENGER   Good madam, hear me.

CLEOPATRA   Well, go to, I will.   37
But there's no goodness in thy face, if Antony
Be free and healthful—so tart a favor   39
To trumpet such good tidings! If not well,
Thou shouldst come like a Fury crowned with snakes,   41
Not like a formal man.

MESSENGER   Will't please you hear me? 42

CLEOPATRA
I have a mind to strike thee ere thou speak'st.
Yet, if thou say Antony lives, is well,
Or friends with Caesar, or not captive to him,
I'll set thee in a shower of gold and hail
Rich pearls upon thee.

MESSENGER   Madam, he's well.

CLEOPATRA   Well said.

MESSENGER
And friends with Caesar.

CLEOPATRA   Thou'rt an honest man.   48

MESSENGER
Caesar and he are greater friends than ever.

CLEOPATRA
Make thee a fortune from me.

MESSENGER   But yet, madam—

CLEOPATRA
I do not like "But yet"; it does allay   51
The good precedence. Fie upon "But yet"!   52
"But yet" is as a jailer to bring forth
Some monstrous malefactor. Prithee, friend,
Pour out the pack of matter to mine ear,   55
The good and bad together. He's friends with Caesar,
In state of health, thou say'st, and, thou say'st, free.

MESSENGER
Free, madam? No, I made no such report.
He's bound unto Octavia.

CLEOPATRA   For what good turn?   59

MESSENGER
For the best turn i'th' bed.

CLEOPATRA   I am pale, Charmian.

MESSENGER
Madam, he's married to Octavia.

CLEOPATRA
The most infectious pestilence upon thee!
                                        Strikes him down.

MESSENGER
Good madam, patience.

CLEOPATRA   What say you?   *Strikes him.*
                                              Hence,

2.5 Location: Alexandria. Cleopatra's palace.
8 too short (A bawdy joke on Mardian's being castrated; *will* suggests
"sexual desire"; *come* suggests "reach orgasm.")   **9 I'll none now** i.e.,
I won't play billiards after all.   **10 angle** rod and line   **17 salt** dried,
preserved in salt   **21 ninth hour** i.e., 9 A.M.   **drunk** drank   **22 tires**
headdresses, or perhaps attire.   **mantles** garments   **23 Philippan**
(Named for Antony's victory over Brutus and Cassius at Philippi.)
28 yield (1) grant (2) report

33 well i.e., well out of it, in heaven.   **Bring it to that** If that is your
meaning   **37 go to** i.e., all right, then. (Said remonstratingly.)   **39 tart
a favor** sour a face   **41 Fury** avenging goddess of classical mythology
42 like . . . man in ordinary human form.   **48 honest** worthy
51–2 allay . . . precedence annul the good news that preceded it.
55 pack of matter entire contents (as of a peddler's pack)   **59 turn**
favor, purpose. (But the Messenger replies in the sense of "feat, bout,"
with sexual suggestion.)

Horrible villain, or I'll spurn thine eyes   64
Like balls before me! I'll unhair thy head!   65
                    She hales him up and down.
Thou shalt be whipped with wire and stewed in brine,
Smarting in ling'ring pickle!
MESSENGER   Gracious madam,   67
I that do bring the news made not the match.
CLEOPATRA
Say 'tis not so, a province I will give thee
And make thy fortunes proud. The blow thou hadst
Shall make thy peace for moving me to rage,   71
And I will boot thee with what gift beside   72
Thy modesty can beg.
MESSENGER   He's married, madam.   73
CLEOPATRA
Rogue, thou hast lived too long!   *Draw a knife.*
MESSENGER   Nay then, I'll run.
What mean you, madam? I have made no fault.   *Exit.*
CHARMIAN
Good madam, keep yourself within yourself.   76
The man is innocent.
CLEOPATRA
Some innocents scape not the thunderbolt.
Melt Egypt into Nile, and kindly creatures   79
Turn all to serpents! Call the slave again.
Though I am mad, I will not bite him. Call!   81
CHARMIAN
He is afeard to come.
CLEOPATRA   I will not hurt him.
              [The Messenger is sent for.]
These hands do lack nobility, that they strike
A meaner than myself, since I myself   84
Have given myself the cause.

        Enter the Messenger again.

                Come hither, sir.   85
Though it be honest, it is never good
To bring bad news. Give to a gracious message
An host of tongues, but let ill tidings tell   88
Themselves when they be felt.   89
MESSENGER   I have done my duty.
CLEOPATRA   Is he married?
I cannot hate thee worser than I do
If thou again say "Yes."
MESSENGER   He's married, madam.
CLEOPATRA
The gods confound thee! Dost thou hold there still?   94
MESSENGER
Should I lie, madam?
CLEOPATRA   Oh, I would thou didst,

So half my Egypt were submerged and made   96
A cistern for scaled snakes! Go, get thee hence.   97
Hadst thou Narcissus in thy face, to me   98
Thou wouldst appear most ugly. He is married?
MESSENGER
I crave Your Highness' pardon.
CLEOPATRA   He is married?
MESSENGER
Take no offense that I would not offend you.   101
To punish me for what you make me do
Seems much unequal. He's married to Octavia.   103
CLEOPATRA
Oh, that his fault should make a knave of thee,   104
That art not what thou'rt sure of! Get thee hence.   105
The merchandise which thou hast brought from
    Rome
Are all too dear for me. Lie they upon thy hand,   107
And be undone by 'em!   *[Exit Messenger.]*
CHARMIAN   Good Your Highness, patience. 108
CLEOPATRA
In praising Antony, I have dispraised Caesar.
CHARMIAN   Many times, madam.
CLEOPATRA
I am paid for't now. Lead me from hence;
I faint. Oh, Iras, Charmian! 'Tis no matter.
Go to the fellow, good Alexas. Bid him
Report the feature of Octavia: her years,
Her inclination. Let him not leave out   115
The color of her hair. Bring me word quickly.
                [Exit Alexas.]
Let him forever go!—Let him not, Charmian.   117
Though he be painted one way like a Gorgon,   118
The other way's a Mars. *[To Mardian]* Bid you Alexas 119
Bring me word how tall she is.—Pity me, Charmian,
But do not speak to me. Lead me to my chamber.
                   Exeunt.

❖

[2.6]

*Flourish. Enter Pompey [and] Menas at one
door, with drum and trumpet; at another, Caesar, Lepidus, Antony, Enobarbus, Maecenas,
Agrippa, with soldiers marching.*

---

64 spurn kick **65.1** *hales* drags **67 pickle** pickling solution.
71 make thy peace compensate, mollify me **72 boot thee with** give
you into the bargain, or, make amends with. **what** whatever
73 Thy modesty one of your modest expectations **76 keep . . .
yourself** i.e., control yourself. **79 kindly** endowed with innately
good qualities **81 mad** (1) angry (2) insane, and so apt to bite
84 A meaner one of lower social station **84–5 since . . . cause** since I
am the one I ought to blame. **85 the cause** i.e., by loving Antony.
88 host multitude **89 when . . . felt** i.e., by being felt rather than spoken aloud. Let bad tidings announce themselves. **94 confound**
destroy. **hold there still** stick to your story.

96 So even if **97 cistern** tank. **scaled** scaly **98 Narcissus** beautiful
youth of Greek mythology who fell in love with his own reflected
image **101 Take . . . offend you** Don't be offended that I hesitate to
offend you (by telling bad news), or, don't interpret as offense what is
not meant to offend. **103 much unequal** most unjust. **104–5 Oh,
that . . . sure of!** How regrettable that Antony's fault puts you in the
wrong, you who are not yourself hateful even if you have had to
report hateful news as a certain fact! **107 dear** (1) expensive (2) emotionally precious **107–8 Lie . . . by 'em** May they remain in your possession unsold, and may you be bankrupt, financially ruined! (i.e.,
May you never profit from your bad tidings!) **115 inclination** disposition. **117 him** Antony **118–19 Though . . . Mars** (Alludes to a
type of picture known as a perspective, which shows different images
when looked at from different angles of vision. A *Gorgon* is a female
monster with serpents in her hair, capable of turning to stone anything that meets her gaze.)
**2.6. Location: Near Misenum, in southern Italy near modern
Naples. (But 2.1 perhaps took place in Messina, Sicily.)**

POMPEY
Your hostages I have, so have you mine,
And we shall talk before we fight.

CAESAR   Most meet   2
That first we come to words; and therefore have we
Our written purposes before us sent,   4
Which if thou hast considered, let us know
If 'twill tie up thy discontented sword   6
And carry back to Sicily much tall youth   7
That else must perish here.

POMPEY   To you all three,
The senators alone of this great world,   9
Chief factors for the gods: I do not know   10
Wherefore my father should revengers want,   11
Having a son and friends, since Julius Caesar,   12
Who at Philippi the good Brutus ghosted,   13
There saw you laboring for him. What was't   14
That moved pale Cassius to conspire? And what
Made th'all-honored, honest Roman Brutus,   16
With the armed rest, courtiers of beauteous freedom,   17
To drench the Capitol, but that they would   18
Have one man but a man? And that is it   19
Hath made me rig my navy, at whose burden
The angered ocean foams, with which I meant
To scourge th'ingratitude that despiteful Rome
Cast on my noble father.

CAESAR   Take your time.

ANTONY
Thou canst not fear us, Pompey, with thy sails;   24
We'll speak with thee at sea. At land thou know'st   25
How much we do o'ercount thee.

POMPEY   At land indeed   26
Thou dost o'ercount me of my father's house;
But since the cuckoo builds not for himself,   28
Remain in't as thou mayst.

LEPIDUS   Be pleased to tell us—   29
For this is from the present—how you take   30
The offers we have sent you.

CAESAR   There's the point.

ANTONY
Which do not be entreated to, but weigh
What it is worth embraced.   32

CAESAR   And what may follow,   33
To try a larger fortune.

POMPEY   You have made me offer   34
Of Sicily, Sardinia; and I must
Rid all the sea of pirates; then, to send   36
Measures of wheat to Rome. This 'greed upon,
To part with unhacked edges and bear back   38
Our targes undinted.

CAESAR, ANTONY, LEPIDUS   That's our offer.

POMPEY   Know then   39
I came before you here a man prepared
To take this offer, but Mark Antony
Put me to some impatience. Though I lose   42
The praise of it by telling, you must know,   43
When Caesar and your brother were at blows,
Your mother came to Sicily and did find
Her welcome friendly.

ANTONY   I have heard it, Pompey,
And am well studied for a liberal thanks   47
Which I do owe you.

POMPEY   Let me have your hand.
                    [They shake hands.]
I did not think, sir, to have met you here.

ANTONY
The beds i'th'East are soft; and thanks to you,
That called me timelier than my purpose hither,   51
For I have gained by't.

CAESAR   Since I saw you last
There's a change upon you.

POMPEY   Well, I know not
What counts harsh Fortune casts upon my face,   54
But in my bosom shall she never come
To make my heart her vassal.

LEPIDUS   Well met here.

POMPEY
I hope so, Lepidus. Thus we are agreed.
I crave our composition may be written   58
And sealed between us.

CAESAR   That's the next to do.   59

POMPEY
We'll feast each other ere we part, and let's
Draw lots who shall begin.

ANTONY   That will I, Pompey.   61

POMPEY
No, Antony, take the lot. But, first or last,   62

---

2 **meet** fitting 4 **purposes** propositions 6 **tie . . . sword** i.e., satisfy your concerns and allow you to forgo a fight 7 **tall** brave 9 **senators alone** i.e., sole rulers of the state (who have thus supplanted the Senate) 10 **factors** agents 10–14 **I do . . . for him** (Julius Caesar defeated Pompey's father, Pompey the Great, and was subsequently assassinated by Brutus and Cassius, among others. Caesar's ghost appeared to Brutus at Philippi, where the combined forces of Antony, Octavius, and Lepidus defeated Brutus and Cassius. [See *Julius Caesar.*] Since Antony, Octavius, and Lepidus thus defeated the avengers of Pompey the Great's death, Pompey the Great's sons and friends should become his avengers by continuing to war on Antony, Octavius, and Lepidus.) 11 **want** lack 13 **ghosted** haunted 16 **honest** honorable 17 **the armed rest** i.e., the rest of those who were armed. **courtiers . . . freedom** those who serve freedom only 18 **drench** bathe in blood 19 **Have . . . a man** (The republican conspirators acted to keep Julius Caesar from accepting the crown.) 24 **fear** frighten 25 **speak with** confront 26 **o'ercount** outnumber. (But Pompey's use of the word in the next line implies that Antony has cheated him. Plutarch informs us that Antony bought the elder Pompey's house at auction and later refused to pay for it.) 28 **cuckoo** a bird that builds no nest for itself but lays its eggs in other birds' nests. 29 **as thou mayst** as long as you can, or, since you can. 30 **from the present** digressing from the business at hand

32 **do . . . to** i.e., do not accept merely because we ask 33 **embraced** if accepted by you. 34 **To . . . fortune** i.e., if you decide to risk war with the triumvirs, or, if you join with us to share a greater fortune. 36 **to send** I am to send 38 **To part** we are to part company. **edges** swords 39 **targes** shields 42–3 **Though . . . telling** i.e., Though I forfeit praise from others by praising myself 47 **well studied for** well prepared to deliver 51 **timelier** earlier 54 **counts** tally marks. (From the practice of casting accounts or reckonings by means of marks or notches on tallies.) **casts** calculates 58 **composition** agreement 59 **sealed between us** stamped with the official seal of each co-signer. 61 **That will I** I will begin 62 **take the lot** draw lots with the rest of us, accept the results of the lottery. **first or last** whether you win the lottery to go first or last

Your fine Egyptian cookery shall have
The fame. I have heard that Julius Caesar
Grew fat with feasting there.

ANTONY   You have heard much.

POMPEY   I have fair meanings, sir.   67

ANTONY   And fair words to them.   68

POMPEY   Then so much have I heard.   69
And I have heard Apollodorus carried—   70

ENOBARBUS
No more of that. He did so.

POMPEY   What, I pray you?   71

ENOBARBUS
A certain queen to Caesar in a mattress.   72

POMPEY
I know thee now. How far'st thou, soldier?

ENOBARBUS   Well,
And well am like to do, for I perceive   74
Four feasts are toward.

POMPEY   Let me shake thy hand.   75
              [They shake hands.]
I never hated thee. I have seen thee fight
When I have envied thy behavior.

ENOBARBUS   Sir,
I never loved you much, but I ha' praised ye
When you have well deserved ten times as much
As I have said you did.

POMPEY   Enjoy thy plainness;   80
It nothing ill becomes thee.   81
Aboard my galley I invite you all.
Will you lead, lords?

CAESAR, ANTONY, LEPIDUS   Show 's the way, sir.

POMPEY   Come.   83
       Exeunt. Manent Enobarbus and Menas.

MENAS [aside]   Thy father, Pompey, would ne'er have
made this treaty.—You and I have known, sir.   85

ENOBARBUS   At sea, I think.

MENAS   We have, sir.

ENOBARBUS   You have done well by water.

MENAS   And you by land.

ENOBARBUS   I will praise any man that will praise me,
though it cannot be denied what I have done by land.

MENAS   Nor what I have done by water.

ENOBARBUS   Yes, something you can deny for your own
safety: you have been a great thief by sea.

MENAS   And you by land.

ENOBARBUS   There I deny my land service. But give me   96
your hand, Menas. [They shake hands.] If our eyes had
authority, here they might take two thieves kissing.   98

MENAS   All men's faces are true, whatsome'er their hands
are.

ENOBARBUS   But there is never a fair woman has a true   101
face.

MENAS   No slander; they steal hearts.   103

ENOBARBUS   We came hither to fight with you.

MENAS   For my part, I am sorry it is turned to a drinking.   105
Pompey doth this day laugh away his fortune.

ENOBARBUS   If he do, sure he cannot weep't back
again.

MENAS   You've said, sir. We looked not for Mark   109
Antony here. Pray you, is he married to Cleopatra?

ENOBARBUS   Caesar's sister is called Octavia.

MENAS   True, sir. She was the wife of Caius Marcellus.

ENOBARBUS   But she is now the wife of Marcus Antonius.

MENAS   Pray ye, sir?   115

ENOBARBUS   'Tis true.

MENAS   Then is Caesar and he forever knit together.

ENOBARBUS   If I were bound to divine of this unity, I   118
would not prophesy so.

MENAS   I think the policy of that purpose made more in   120
the marriage than the love of the parties.

ENOBARBUS   I think so too. But you shall find the band
that seems to tie their friendship together will be
the very strangler of their amity. Octavia is of a holy, cold,
and still conversation.   125

MENAS   Who would not have his wife so?

ENOBARBUS   Not he that himself is not so, which is
Mark Antony. He will to his Egyptian dish again.
Then shall the sighs of Octavia blow the fire up in
Caesar, and, as I said before, that which is the strength
of their amity shall prove the immediate author of   131
their variance. Antony will use his affection where it   132
is; he married but his occasion here.   133

MENAS   And thus it may be. Come, sir, will you
aboard? I have a health for you.   135

ENOBARBUS   I shall take it, sir. We have used our
throats in Egypt.

MENAS   Come, let's away.   Exeunt.

❖

[2.7]

*Music plays. Enter two or three Servants with a
banquet.*

FIRST SERVANT   Here they'll be, man. Some o' their
plants are ill-rooted already; the least wind i'th' world   2
will blow them down.

---

67 **fair** i.e., friendly   68 **fair** i.e., well-chosen   69 **Then . . . heard** i.e.,
I am not implying more about Antony in Egypt than my words hon-
estly mean.   **70–2 Apollodorus . . . mattress** (Alludes to a tale told by
Plutarch according to which Cleopatra had herself rolled up in a mattress and carried secretly by Apollodorus to meet Julius Caesar.)
74 **like** likely   75 **toward** coming up.   80 **Enjoy thy plainness** Give
free rein to your bluntness   81 **nothing . . . thee** suits you not at all
badly.   **83.1 Manent** They remain onstage   85 **known** known each
other   96 **There** In respect to that   98 **authority** i.e., to make arrests,
like a constable.   **take** arrest.   **two thieves kissing** (1) our two thieving hands shaking (2) two thieves greeting each other.

101 **true** honest (because women use cosmetic art to conceal defects)
103 **No . . . hearts** i.e., You speak true, since women in their own way are
thieves, stealing men's affections.   105 **a drinking** an occasion for drinking.   109 **You've said** You've spoken truly   115 **Pray ye, sir?** Are you in
earnest?   118 **divine of** prophesy about   120 **made more** played more
of a role   125 **conversation** demeanor.   131–2 **author . . . variance** cause
of their falling out.   132–3 **use . . . it is** i.e., satisfy his passion in Egypt
133 **his occasion** what his interests demanded   135 **health** toast
2.7. **Location: On board Pompey's galley, off Misenum in southern
Italy. A table and stools are brought on.**
0.2 *banquet* a course of the feast, probably dessert.   2 **plants**
(1) planted trees (2) soles of the feet

SECOND SERVANT   Lepidus is high-colored.   4
FIRST SERVANT   They have made him drink alms-drink.   5
SECOND SERVANT   As they pinch one another by the   6
disposition, he cries out, "No more," reconciles them   7
to his entreaty, and himself to th' drink.   8
FIRST SERVANT   But it raises the greater war between
him and his discretion.
SECOND SERVANT   Why, this it is to have a name in   11
great men's fellowship. I had as lief have a reed that   12
will do me no service as a partisan I could not heave.   13
FIRST SERVANT   To be called into a huge sphere,   14
and not to be seen to move in't, are the holes where   15
eyes should be, which pitifully disaster the cheeks.   16

A sennet sounded. Enter Caesar, Antony,
Pompey, Lepidus, Agrippa, Maecenas, Enobarbus,
Menas, with other captains [and a Boy].

ANTONY
Thus do they, sir: they take the flow o'th' Nile   17
By certain scales i'th' pyramid. They know   18
By th' height, the lowness, or the mean if dearth   19
Or foison follow. The higher Nilus swells   20
The more it promises; as it ebbs, the seedsman
Upon the slime and ooze scatters his grain,
And shortly comes to harvest.
LEPIDUS   You've strange serpents there.
ANTONY   Ay, Lepidus.
LEPIDUS   Your serpent of Egypt is bred now of your   26
mud by the operation of your sun; so is your crocodile.
ANTONY   They are so.
POMPEY   Sit—and some wine. A health to Lepidus!   29
[They sit and drink.]
LEPIDUS   I am not so well as I should be, but I'll   30
ne'er out.   31
ENOBARBUS   Not till you have slept; I fear me you'll be
in till then.   33
LEPIDUS   Nay, certainly, I have heard the Ptolemies'
pyramises are very goodly things; without contradic-   35
tion I have heard that.

MENAS [aside to Pompey]   Pompey, a word.
POMPEY [to Menas]   Say in mine ear. What is't?
MENAS (whispers in 's ear)
Forsake thy seat, I do beseech thee, captain,
And hear me speak a word.
POMPEY [to Menas]
Forbear me till anon.—This wine for Lepidus!   41
LEPIDUS   What manner o' thing is your crocodile?
ANTONY   It is shaped, sir, like itself, and it is as broad as
it hath breadth. It is just so high as it is, and moves
with it own organs. It lives by that which nourisheth   45
it, and, the elements once out of it, it transmigrates.   46
LEPIDUS   What color is it of?
ANTONY   Of it own color too.
LEPIDUS   'Tis a strange serpent.
ANTONY   'Tis so. And the tears of it are wet.   50
CAESAR   Will this description satisfy him?
ANTONY   With the health that Pompey gives him, else
he is a very epicure.   [Menas whispers again.]   53
POMPEY [aside to Menas]
Go hang, sir, hang! Tell me of that? Away!
Do as I bid you.—Where's this cup I called for?
MENAS [aside to Pompey]
If for the sake of merit thou wilt hear me,   56
Rise from thy stool.
POMPEY [rising]   I think thou'rt mad. The matter?
[They walk aside.]
MENAS
I have ever held my cap off to thy fortunes.   58
POMPEY
Thou hast served me with much faith. What's else to
say?—   59
Be jolly, lords.
ANTONY   These quicksands, Lepidus,
Keep off them, for you sink.
[Menas and Pompey speak aside.]
MENAS
Wilt thou be lord of all the world?
POMPEY   What say'st thou?
MENAS
Wilt thou be lord of the whole world? That's twice.
POMPEY
How should that be?
MENAS   But entertain it,   64
And, though thou think me poor, I am the man
Will give thee all the world.
POMPEY   Hast thou drunk well?
MENAS
No, Pompey, I have kept me from the cup.
Thou art, if thou dar'st be, the earthly Jove.

---

4 **high-colored** flushed.   5 **alms-drink** i.e., drink charitably consumed in the furtherance of reconciliation. (See next speech and note.)   6–8 **As . . . drink** As they chafe one another, prompted by their various temperaments, Lepidus entreats them to stop quarreling, and reconciles himself to the peacemaking business of downing one drink after another in response to their toasts.   11 **a name** a name only   12 **had as lief** would just as soon   13 **partisan** long-bladed spear. (Here, metaphorically, too large a weapon for Lepidus to wield.)   14–16 **To . . . cheeks** To be summoned by fortune to greatness and yet not be able to fulfill the role greatly is like having eye sockets with no eyes in them, a defect that will disfigure (*disaster*) the cheeks. (The underlying image is of a heavenly body that cannot move properly in its sphere, causing *disaster*, meaning both disfigurement and the evil effects of unfavorable aspect of a planet.)
16.1 *sennet* trumpet call signaling the approach of a procession
17 **sir** (Usually thought to refer to Caesar, but the matter is uncertain.)
take measure   18 **scales** graduated markings   19 **mean** middle
20 **foison** plenty   26 **Your serpent** i.e., This serpent that people talk about. (The colloquial indefinite *your*.)   29 **health** toast. (Lepidus is obliged to drink up every time a toast is proposed to him.)   30–1 **I'll ne'er out** i.e., I'll never refuse a toast, never quit.   33 **in** in drink, in your cups. (With a play of antitheses between *in* and *out* in line 31.)
35 **pyramises** (Lepidus's drunken error for *pyramides*, plural of *pyramis* or *pyramid*.)

41 **Forbear . . . anon** Excuse me for a moment.   45 **it own** its own.
(Also in line 48.)   46 **elements** vital elements   50 **tears** (Alludes to the ancient belief that the crocodile wept insincere "crocodile tears" over its victim before devouring it.)   53 **epicure** (1) glutton (2) atheist. (The Epicureans did not believe in an afterlife. Antony's jesting point is that only an atheist or epicure would be skeptical of such a satisfying description as Antony has just given of the crocodile.)
56 **merit** i.e., my merits as a loyal follower, or, the merit of my ideas
58 **held . . . off** i.e., been a respectful and faithful servant   59 **faith** faithfulness.   64 **But entertain it** Only accept the possibility

Whate'er the ocean pales or sky inclips   69
Is thine, if thou wilt ha 't.

POMPEY   Show me which way.

MENAS

These three world-sharers, these competitors,   71
Are in thy vessel. Let me cut the cable,
And, when we are put off, fall to their throats.   73
All there is thine.

POMPEY   Ah, this thou shouldst have done
And not have spoke on't! In me 'tis villainy;   75
In thee 't had been good service. Thou must know,   76
'Tis not my profit that does lead mine honor;
Mine honor, it. Repent that e'er thy tongue   78
Hath so betrayed thine act. Being done unknown,   79
I should have found it afterwards well done,
But must condemn it now. Desist, and drink.
                              [*He returns to the feast.*]

MENAS [*aside*]   For this,
I'll never follow thy palled fortunes more.   83
Who seeks and will not take when once 'tis offered   84
Shall never find it more.

POMPEY   This health to Lepidus!

ANTONY

Bear him ashore. I'll pledge it for him, Pompey.   86

ENOBARBUS

Here's to thee, Menas!   [*They drink.*]

MENAS   Enobarbus, welcome!

POMPEY   Fill till the cup be hid.

ENOBARBUS   There's a strong fellow, Menas.
          [*Pointing to one who carries off Lepidus.*]

MENAS   Why?

ENOBARBUS   'A bears the third part of the world, man;   91
see'st not?

MENAS

The third part, then, is drunk. Would it were all,
That it might go on wheels!   94

ENOBARBUS   Drink thou; increase the reels.   95

MENAS   Come.

POMPEY

This is not yet an Alexandrian feast.

ANTONY

It ripens towards it. Strike the vessels, ho!   98
Here's to Caesar!

CAESAR   I could well forbear 't.
It's monstrous labor when I wash my brain
And it grows fouler.

ANTONY   Be a child o'th' time.

CAESAR   Possess it, I'll make answer.   102
But I had rather fast from all four days   103

Than drink so much in one.   104

ENOBARBUS [*to Antony*]   Ha, my brave emperor!   104
Shall we dance now the Egyptian Bacchanals   105
And celebrate our drink?   106

POMPEY   Let's ha 't, good soldier.

ANTONY   Come, let's all take hands
Till that the conquering wine hath steeped our sense   109
In soft and delicate Lethe.

ENOBARBUS   All take hands.   110
Make battery to our ears with the loud music,   111
The while I'll place you; then the boy shall sing.
The holding every man shall bear as loud   113
As his strong sides can volley.   114
          Music plays. Enobarbus places them hand in hand.

                    The Song.

BOY [*sings*]
Come, thou monarch of the vine,
Plumpy Bacchus with pink eyne!   116
In thy fats our cares be drowned,   117
With thy grapes our hairs be crowned.

ALL   Cup us till the world go round,   119
Cup us till the world go round!

CAESAR
What would you more? Pompey, good night.—Good
     brother,
Let me request you off. Our graver business   122
Frowns at this levity. Gentle lords, let's part;
You see we have burnt our cheeks. Strong Enobarb   124
Is weaker than the wine, and mine own tongue
Splits what it speaks. The wild disguise hath almost   126
Anticked us all. What needs more words? Good night.   127
Good Antony, your hand.

POMPEY   I'll try you on the shore.   128

ANTONY
And shall, sir. Give 's your hand.

POMPEY   Oh, Antony,
You have my father's house. But what? We are
     friends.
Come down into the boat.

ENOBARBUS   Take heed you fall not.   131
          [*Exeunt all but Enobarbus and Menas.*]
Menas, I'll not on shore.

MENAS   No, to my cabin.
These drums, these trumpets, flutes! What!
Let Neptune hear we bid a loud farewell
To these great fellows. Sound and be hanged, sound
     out!   *Sound a flourish, with drums.*

---

69 **pales** impales, fences in. **inclips** embraces **71 competitors** partners. (With secondary sense of "rivals.") **73 are put off** have put to sea **75 on't** of it. **76 Thou must know** I must inform you that **78 Mine honor, it** i.e., my honor comes before my personal profit. **Repent** Regret **79 unknown** i.e., without my knowledge **83 palled** decayed, darkened **84 Who** He who **86 pledge it** i.e., drink the toast (since Lepidus is too far gone to drink) **91 'A** He **94 go on wheels** go fast or easily. (Proverbial.) **95 reels** (1) revels (2) reeling and whirling of drunkenness. **98 Strike the vessels** Broach or tap the casks **102 Possess . . . answer** My answer is, be master of the time; or, possibly, Drink it off, I'll drink in return. **103 all** all nourishment

104 **brave** splendid **105 Bacchanals** drunken dance to Bacchus, god of wine **106 celebrate** consecrate with observances **109 Till that** until **110 Lethe** i.e., forgetfulness. (Literally, the river of oblivion in Hades.) **111 Make battery to** Assault **113 holding** refrain. **bear** carry, sing **114 volley** sing in return, answering the stanza with the refrain. **116 pink eyne** i.e., eyes half-shut, from drinking. **117 fats** vats, vessels **119 Cup** Intoxicate **122 off** to disembark. **124 we . . . cheeks** our complexions are flushed with drinking. **126 disguise** (1) masque (2) transforming drunkenness **127 Anticked us** (1) made dancers of us in a masque (2) made buffoons or fools of us **128 try you** i.e., take you on in a drinking contest **131 boat** small boat for taking the party ashore.

ENOBARBUS   Hoo! says 'a. There's my cap.

[*He flings it in the air.*]

MENAS   Hoo! Noble captain, come.   *Exeunt.*

❧

[3.1]

*Enter Ventidius as it were in triumph [with Silius,
and other Romans, officers, and soldiers], the dead
body of Pacorus borne before him.*

VENTIDIUS

Now, darting Parthia, art thou struck, and now   1
Pleased fortune does of Marcus Crassus' death   2
Make me revenger. Bear the King's son's body
Before our army. Thy Pacorus, Orodes,   4
Pays this for Marcus Crassus.

SILIUS   Noble Ventidius,
Whilst yet with Parthian blood thy sword is warm,
The fugitive Parthians follow. Spur through Media,   7
Mesopotamia, and the shelters whither
The routed fly. So thy grand captain, Antony,
Shall set thee on triumphant chariots and   10
Put garlands on thy head.

VENTIDIUS   Oh, Silius, Silius,
I have done enough. A lower place, note well,   12
May make too great an act. For learn this, Silius:
Better to leave undone than by our deed
Acquire too high a fame when him we serve's away.
Caesar and Antony have ever won
More in their officer than person. Sossius,   17
One of my place in Syria, his lieutenant,   18
For quick accumulation of renown,
Which he achieved by th' minute, lost his favor.   20
Who does i'th' wars more than his captain can   21
Becomes his captain's captain; and ambition,
The soldier's virtue, rather makes choice of loss   23
Than gain which darkens him.   24
I could do more to do Antonius good,
But 'twould offend him, and in his offense   26
Should my performance perish.

SILIUS   Thou hast, Ventidius, that   28
Without the which a soldier and his sword   29
Grants scarce distinction. Thou wilt write to Antony?   30

VENTIDIUS

I'll humbly signify what in his name,

That magical word of war, we have effected: 32
How with his banners and his well-paid ranks
The ne'er-yet-beaten horse of Parthia   34
We have jaded out o'th' field.

SILIUS   Where is he now?   35

VENTIDIUS

He purposeth to Athens, whither, with what haste
The weight we must convey with 's will permit,   37
We shall appear before him.—On, there. Pass along!

Exeunt.

❧

[3.2]

Enter Agrippa at one door, Enobarbus at another.

AGRIPPA   What, are the brothers parted?   1

ENOBARBUS

They have dispatched with Pompey; he is gone.   2
The other three are sealing. Octavia weeps   3
To part from Rome; Caesar is sad; and Lepidus,   4
Since Pompey's feast, as Menas says, is troubled
With the greensickness.

AGRIPPA   'Tis a noble Lepidus.   6

ENOBARBUS

A very fine one. Oh, how he loves Caesar!   7

AGRIPPA

Nay, but how dearly he adores Mark Antony!

ENOBARBUS

Caesar? Why, he's the Jupiter of men.

AGRIPPA

What's Antony? The god of Jupiter.

ENOBARBUS

Spake you of Caesar? How, the nonpareil!

AGRIPPA

O Antony, O thou Arabian bird!   12

ENOBARBUS

Would you praise Caesar, say "Caesar"; go no further.

AGRIPPA

Indeed, he plied them both with excellent praises.

ENOBARBUS

But he loves Caesar best; yet he loves Antony.
Hoo! Hearts, tongues, figures, scribes, bards, poets,
cannot   16
Think, speak, cast, write, sing, number, hoo!   17
His love to Antony. But as for Caesar,
Kneel down, kneel down, and wonder.

AGRIPPA   Both he loves.

3.1. Location: The Middle East.
1 darting (The Parthians were famous for archery and for the Parthian
dart which they discharged as they fled.)   **Parthia** i.e., Orodes, King
of Parthia   **2 Crassus' death** (Crassus, member of the first triumvirate with Pompey the Great and Julius Caesar, was overthrown and
treacherously murdered by Orodes in 53 B.C.)   **4 Pacorus, Orodes**
(Pacorus was the son of Orodes.)   **7 The . . . follow** follow the fleeing
Parthians.   **10 triumphant** triumphal   **12 A lower place** One of
lower rank   **17 More . . . person** more through the actions of their
lieutenants than by their own efforts.   **18 of my place** of the same
rank as I.   **his lieutenant** i.e., the commanding officer acting for
Antony   **20 by th' minute** minute by minute, continually   **21 Who**
He who   **23–4 rather . . . him** prefers to lose rather than gain in such
a way as to darken his reputation.   **26 offense** taking offense
28–30 that . . . distinction i.e., discretion, without the which a soldier
can scarcely be distinguished from the sword he uses.

32 word watchword.   **effected** achieved   **34 horse** cavalry   **35 jaded**
driven exhausted like jades, inferior horses   **37 with 's** with us
3.2. Location: Rome.
1 brothers parted brothers-in-law departed.   **2 dispatched** concluded the business   **3 sealing** affixing seals to their agreements, settling matters.   **4 sad** sober   **6 greensickness** a kind of anemia
supposed to affect young women, especially those afflicted with love-
longing. (Used ironically here to refer to Lepidus's hangover and to
his love for Antony and Caesar.)   **7 fine** (*Lepidus* in Latin means
"fine," "elegant.")   **12 Arabian bird** i.e., the fabled phoenix. (Only
one existed at a time; it re-created itself by arising from its ashes.)
16 figures figures of speech   **17 cast** calculate.   **number** write verses

ENOBARBUS
They are his shards, and he their beetle. [*Trumpets*
within.] So;   20
This is to horse. Adieu, noble Agrippa.   21

AGRIPPA
Good fortune, worthy soldier, and farewell.

Enter Caesar, Antony, Lepidus, and Octavia.

ANTONY   No further, sir.   23

CAESAR
You take from me a great part of myself;
Use me well in't.—Sister, prove such a wife
As my thoughts make thee, and as my farthest bond   26
Shall pass on thy approof.—Most noble Antony,   27
Let not the piece of virtue which is set   28
Betwixt us as the cement of our love
To keep it builded be the ram to batter
The fortress of it; for better might we
Have loved without this mean, if on both parts   32
This be not cherished.

ANTONY   Make me not offended
In your distrust.

CAESAR   I have said.

ANTONY   You shall not find,   34
Though you be therein curious, the least cause   35
For what you seem to fear. So the gods keep you,
And make the hearts of Romans serve your ends!
We will here part.

CAESAR
Farewell, my dearest sister, fare thee well.
The elements be kind to thee, and make   40
Thy spirits all of comfort! Fare thee well.

OCTAVIA [*weeping*]   My noble brother!

ANTONY
The April's in her eyes; it is love's spring,
And these the showers to bring it on.—Be cheerful.

OCTAVIA [*to Caesar*]
Sir, look well to my husband's house; and—   45

CAESAR
What, Octavia?

OCTAVIA   I'll tell you in your ear.
                  [*She whisper to Caesar.*]

ANTONY
Her tongue will not obey her heart, nor can   47
Her heart inform her tongue—the swan's down
feather,   48
That stands upon the swell at full of tide,   49
And neither way inclines.   50

---

20 shards patches of dung, or, perhaps, wings or wing-cases, i.e., protectors, patrons   **21 This is to horse** i.e., The trumpet call gives the
signal to depart.   **23 No further** i.e., You need not go on urging your
point, or, you need accompany me no further   **26–7 as . . . approof**
such that my utmost bond shall be justified in certifying what you
will prove to be.   **28 piece** masterpiece   **32 mean** intermediary, or
means   **34 In by.   I have said** i.e., I stand by what I've said.
35 curious overly inquisitive or touchy   **40 elements** heavens
45 husband's house i.e., Antony's house, as at 2.7.130, though
Octavia is also a widow; see 3.3.29   **47–50 Her . . . inclines** i.e., Her
conflicting emotions make her unable to speak aloud, like a swan's
down feather floating at full tide, moving neither up nor down
stream.

ENOBARBUS [*aside to Agrippa*]   Will Caesar weep?

AGRIPPA [*aside to Enobarbus*]   He has a cloud in 's face.

ENOBARBUS [*aside to Agrippa*]
He were the worse for that, were he a horse;   53
So is he, being a man.

AGRIPPA [*aside to Enobarbus*]   Why, Enobarbus,
When Antony found Julius Caesar dead,
He cried almost to roaring; and he wept
When at Philippi he found Brutus slain.

ENOBARBUS [*aside to Agrippa*]
That year indeed he was troubled with a rheum.   58
What willingly he did confound he wailed,   59
Believe't, till I wept too.

CAESAR   No, sweet Octavia,
You shall hear from me still. The time shall not   61
Outgo my thinking on you.

ANTONY   Come, sir, come,   62
I'll wrestle with you in my strength of love.
Look, here I have you [*embracing him*]; thus I let you
go,
And give you to the gods.

CAESAR   Adieu. Be happy!

LEPIDUS
Let all the number of the stars give light
To thy fair way!

CAESAR   Farewell, farewell!   *Kisses Octavia.*

ANTONY   Farewell!
        Trumpets sound. Exeunt [*in separate groups*].

❖

[3.3]

Enter Cleopatra, Charmian, Iras, and Alexas.

CLEOPATRA
Where is the fellow?

ALEXAS   Half afeard to come.

CLEOPATRA
Go to, go to.

Enter the Messenger as before.

        Come hither, sir.

ALEXAS   Good Majesty,   2
Herod of Jewry dare not look upon you   3
But when you are well pleased.

CLEOPATRA   That Herod's head
I'll have; but how, when Antony is gone,
Through whom I might command it?—Come thou
near.

MESSENGER   Most gracious Majesty!

CLEOPATRA   Didst thou behold Octavia?

---

53 He . . . horse (Alludes to the belief that a horse with a dark spot on
its face was apt to be bad-tempered.)   **58 rheum** i.e., running at the
eyes. (Said of any discharge of secretion from the head.)   **59 What . . .
bewailed** He bewailed what he intentionally destroyed   **61 still** regularly.   **61–2 The time . . . you** Time itself will not outlast my thinking of you.
3.3. Location: Alexandria. Cleopatra's palace.
2 Go to (An expression of impatience.)   **3 Herod of Jewry** i.e., Even
the famous tyrant who slaughtered the children. (See 1.2.29–30.)

MESSENGER
　Ay, dread Queen.

CLEOPATRA　　　　　Where?

MESSENGER　　　　　　Madam, in Rome.
　I looked her in the face, and saw her led
　Between her brother and Mark Antony.

CLEOPATRA
　Is she as tall as me?

MESSENGER　　　　　She is not, madam.

CLEOPATRA
　Didst hear her speak? Is she shrill-tongued or low?

MESSENGER
　Madam, I heard her speak. She is low-voiced.

CLEOPATRA
　That's not so good. He cannot like her long.　　　15

CHARMIAN
　Like her! Oh, Isis, 'tis impossible.

CLEOPATRA
　I think so, Charmian. Dull of tongue, and dwarfish.—
　What majesty is in her gait? Remember,
　If e'er thou looked'st on majesty.

MESSENGER　　　　　She creeps:
　Her motion and her station are as one.　　　　　20
　She shows a body rather than a life,　　　　　　21
　A statue than a breather.

CLEOPATRA　　　　　Is this certain?　　　　　22

MESSENGER
　Or I have no observance.

CHARMIAN　　　　　Three in Egypt　　　　　23
　Cannot make better note.

CLEOPATRA　　　　　He's very knowing,　　　24
　I do perceive't. There's nothing in her yet.
　The fellow has good judgment.

CHARMIAN　　　　　Excellent.

CLEOPATRA　Guess at her years, I prithee.

MESSENGER　Madam,
　She was a widow—

CLEOPATRA　　　　Widow? Charmian, hark.

MESSENGER　And I do think she's thirty.

CLEOPATRA
　Bear'st thou her face in mind? Is't long or round?

MESSENGER　Round, even to faultiness.

CLEOPATRA
　For the most part, too, they are foolish that are so.—
　Her hair, what color?

MESSENGER　Brown, madam; and her forehead
　As low as she would wish it.　　　　　　　　36

CLEOPATRA [giving money]　There's gold for thee.
　Thou must not take my former sharpness ill.
　I will employ thee back again; I find thee　　　39
　Most fit for business. Go make thee ready;

Our letters are prepared.　　　　[Exit Messenger.]

CHARMIAN　　　　　A proper man.　　　　　41

CLEOPATRA
　Indeed, he is so. I repent me much
　That so I harried him. Why, methinks, by him,　　43
　This creature's no such thing.

CHARMIAN　　　　　Nothing, madam.　　　44

CLEOPATRA
　The man hath seen some majesty, and should know.

CHARMIAN
　Hath he seen majesty? Isis else defend,　　　　46
　And serving you so long!　　　　　　　　　47

CLEOPATRA
　I have one thing more to ask him yet, good
　　Charmian—
　But 'tis no matter; thou shalt bring him to me
　Where I will write. All may be well enough

CHARMIAN　I warrant you, madam.　　　Exeunt.　51

❧

[3.4]

Enter Antony and Octavia.

ANTONY
　Nay, nay, Octavia, not only that—
　That were excusable, that and thousands more
　Of semblable import—but he hath waged　　　3
　New wars 'gainst Pompey; made his will, and read it　4
　To public ear;
　Spoke scantly of me; when perforce he could not　　6
　But pay me terms of honor, cold and sickly
　He vented them, most narrow measure lent me;　　8
　When the best hint was given him, he not took't,　　9
　Or did it from his teeth.

OCTAVIA　　　　　Oh, my good lord,　　　10
　Believe not all, or, if you must believe,
　Stomach not all. A more unhappy lady,　　　　12
　If this division chance, ne'er stood between,　　　13
　Praying for both parts.
　The good gods will mock me presently
　When I shall pray, "Oh, bless my lord and husband!"
　Undo that prayer by crying out as loud,　　　　17
　"Oh, bless my brother!" Husband win, win brother,
　Prays and destroys the prayer; no midway
　Twixt these extremes at all.

ANTONY　　　　　Gentle Octavia,
　Let your best love draw to that point which seeks　21
　Best to preserve it. If I lose mine honor,　　　22

---

15 **not so good** i.e., not so good for her.　20 **Her . . . one** i.e., she moves with so little animation that it's all the same whether she's moving or standing.　21 **shows** appears as　22 **breather** living being.　23–4 **Three . . . note** There are not three people in Egypt who are better observers.　36 **As . . . it** i.e., such that she wouldn't wish it to be any lower. (A colloquial way of suggesting she is ugly; high foreheads were thought more beautiful.)　39 **employ . . . again** send you back with a message

41 **proper** good　43 **harried** maltreated.　**by** according to　44 **no such thing** nothing much.　46 **else defend** forbid that it be otherwise. (An interjection.)　47 **serving** i.e., he having served　51 **warrant** assure
3.4. Location: Athens.
3 **semblable** similar　4 **read it** (In order to win the populace by showing them what benefits they might expect from him.)　6 **scantly** slightingly　8 **vented** gave vent to, expressed.　**narrow measure lent me** gave me minimal praise　9 **hint** occasion (to praise Antony)
10 **from his teeth** i.e., between clenched teeth, not from the heart.
12 **Stomach** resent　13 **chance** occur　17 **Undo** i.e., and then undo, or, I shall undo　21–2 **Let . . . it** let your warmest love be given to that one of us who seeks to preserve it (your love) best.

I lose myself; better I were not yours
Than yours so branchless. But, as you requested,   24
Yourself shall go between 's. The meantime, lady,   25
I'll raise the preparation of a war   26
Shall stain your brother. Make your soonest haste;   27
So your desires are yours.

OCTAVIA   Thanks to my lord.   28
The Jove of power make me, most weak, most weak,
Your reconciler! Wars twixt you twain would be
As if the world should cleave, and that slain men   31
Should solder up the rift.   32

ANTONY
When it appears to you where this begins,   33
Turn your displeasure that way, for our faults   34
Can never be so equal that your love   35
Can equally move with them. Provide your going;   36
Choose your own company and command what cost
Your heart has mind to.   *Exeunt.*

❧

[3.5]

Enter Enobarbus and Eros, [meeting].

ENOBARBUS   How now, friend Eros?
EROS   There's strange news come, sir.
ENOBARBUS   What, man?
EROS   Caesar and Lepidus have made wars upon Pompey.
ENOBARBUS   This is old. What is the success?   6
EROS   Caesar, having made use of him in the wars   7
'gainst Pompey, presently denied him rivality, would   8
not let him partake in the glory of the action; and, not
resting here, accuses him of letters he had formerly   10
wrote to Pompey; upon his own appeal seizes him.   11
So the poor third is up, till death enlarge his confine.   12
ENOBARBUS
Then, world, thou hast a pair of chops, no more;   13
And throw between them all the food thou hast,
They'll grind the one the other. Where's Antony?   15
EROS
He's walking in the garden—thus, and spurns   16
The rush that lies before him; cries, "Fool Lepidus!"   17

And threats the throat of that his officer   18
That murdered Pompey.
ENOBARBUS   Our great navy's rigged.   19
EROS
For Italy and Caesar. More, Domitius: 20
My lord desires you presently. My news   21
I might have told hereafter.
ENOBARBUS   'Twill be naught,
But let it be. Bring me to Antony.
EROS   Come, sir.   *Exeunt.*

❧

[3.6]

Enter Agrippa, Maecenas, and Caesar.

CAESAR
Contemning Rome, he has done all this and more   1
In Alexandria. Here's the manner of't:
I'th' marketplace, on a tribunal silvered,   3
Cleopatra and himself in chairs of gold
Were publicly enthroned. At the feet sat
Caesarion, whom they call my father's son,   6
And all the unlawful issue that their lust
Since then hath made between them. Unto her
He gave the stablishment of Egypt, made her   9
Of lower Syria, Cyprus, Lydia,
Absolute queen.
MAECENAS   This in the public eye?
CAESAR
I'th' common showplace, where they exercise.   12
His sons he there proclaimed the kings of kings:
Great Media, Parthia, and Armenia
He gave to Alexander; to Ptolemy he assigned
Syria, Cilicia, and Phoenicia. She
In th' habiliments of the goddess Isis   17
That day appeared, and oft before gave audience,
As 'tis reported, so.
MAECENAS   Let Rome be thus informed.
AGRIPPA   Who, queasy with his insolence already,   21
Will their good thoughts call from him.   22
CAESAR
The people knows it, and have now received
His accusations.
AGRIPPA   Who does he accuse?
CAESAR
Caesar, and that, having in Sicily
Sextus Pompeius spoiled, we had not rated him   26
His part o'th' isle. Then does he say he lent me   27

---

24 branchless pruned (of honor).   **25 The meantime** In the meantime   **26–7 I'll . . . brother** I'll raise an army that will deprive your brother of his luster.   **28 So . . . yours** i.e., thus you have obtained your desire (to go). (Or, *so* may mean "as long as.")   **31 cleave** split **32 Should** would be needed to   **33 where this begins** who started this quarrel   **34 our** i.e., Caesar's and mine   **34–6 our faults . . . them** i.e., you will have to judge between our faults and choose.
36 Provide Make arrangements for
3.5. Location: Athens.
6 success outcome, result.   **7 him** i.e., Lepidus   **8 presently** immediately.   **rivality** rights of a partner. (Caesar and Lepidus have newly gone to war against Pompey and have defeated him.)   **10 resting here** stopping with this insult   **11 his own appeal** Caesar's own accusation   **12 up** shut up (in prison).   **enlarge his confine** set him free.   **13 a pair . . . more** a single pair of jaws, with no third partner **15 They'll . . . other** the jaws will still grind against each other, grind each other down.   **16 thus** (Eros imitates Antony's angry walk.) **spurns** kicks   **17 rush** strewn rushes

18 And . . . officer and threatens the life of the officer of his
19 Pompey (After his defeat by Caesar and Lepidus, Pompey was murdered—perhaps, according to history, on Antony's orders, but here Antony blames his officer.)   **20 More** I have more to say
21 presently immediately.
3.6. Location: Rome.
1 Contemning Disdaining   **3 tribunal** seat of state, dais   **6 my father's** i.e., Julius Caesar's. (Julius Caesar had adopted his grandnephew Octavius as his son.)   **9 stablishment** settled possession **12 exercise** put on entertainments and sports.   **17 habiliments** attire **21 queasy** nauseated, "fed up." (Refers to the Roman people.)
22 call withdraw   **26 spoiled** despoiled, plundered.   **rated him** allotted to Antony   **27 th' isle** i.e., Sicily.

Some shipping, unrestored. Lastly, he frets
That Lepidus of the triumvirate
Should be deposed, and, being, that we detain
All his revenue.

AGRIPPA   Sir, this should be answered.

CAESAR
'Tis done already, and the messenger gone.
I have told him Lepidus was grown too cruel,
That he his high authority abused
And did deserve his change. For what I have
      conquered,
I grant him part; but then in his Armenia,
And other of his conquered kingdoms, I
Demand the like.

MAECENAS   He'll never yield to that.

CAESAR
Nor must not then be yielded to in this.

Enter Octavia with her train.

OCTAVIA
Hail, Caesar, and my lord! Hail, most dear Caesar!

CAESAR
That ever I should call thee castaway!

OCTAVIA
You have not called me so, nor have you cause.

CAESAR
Why have you stol'n upon us thus? You come not
Like Caesar's sister. The wife of Antony
Should have an army for an usher and
The neighs of horse to tell of her approach
Long ere she did appear. The trees by th' way
Should have borne men, and expectation fainted,
Longing for what it had not. Nay, the dust
Should have ascended to the roof of heaven,
Raised by your populous troops. But you are come
A market maid to Rome, and have prevented
The ostentation of our love, which, left unshown,
Is often left unloved. We should have met you
By sea and land, supplying every stage
With an augmented greeting.

OCTAVIA   Good my lord,
To come thus was I not constrained, but did it
On my free will. My lord, Mark Antony,
Hearing that you prepared for war, acquainted
My grievèd ear withal, whereon I begged
His pardon for return.

CAESAR   Which soon he granted,
Being an obstruct 'tween his lust and him.

OCTAVIA
Do not say so, my lord.

CAESAR   I have eyes upon him,
And his affairs come to me on the wind.
Where is he now?

28
29
30

35

46
47

52
53
54
55

61
62

OCTAVIA   My lord, in Athens.

CAESAR
No, my most wrongèd sister. Cleopatra
Hath nodded him to her. He hath given his empire
Up to a whore; who now are levying
The kings o'th'earth for war. He hath assembled
Bocchus, the King of Libya; Archelaus,
Of Cappadocia; Philadelphos, King
Of Paphlagonia; the Thracian king, Adallas;
King Manchus of Arabia; King of Pont;
Herod of Jewry; Mithridates, King
Of Comagene; Polemon and Amyntas,
The Kings of Mede and Lycaonia,
With a more larger list of scepters.

OCTAVIA   Ay me, most wretched,
That have my heart parted betwixt two friends
That does afflict each other!

CAESAR   Welcome hither.
Your letters did withhold our breaking forth
Till we perceived both how you were wrong led
And we in negligent danger. Cheer your heart.
Be you not troubled with the time, which drives
O'er your content these strong necessities,
But let determined things to destiny
Hold unbewailed their way. Welcome to Rome,
Nothing more dear to me. You are abused
Beyond the mark of thought, and the high gods,
To do you justice, makes his ministers
Of us and those that love you. Best of comfort,
And ever welcome to us.

AGRIPPA   Welcome, lady.

MAECENAS   Welcome, dear madam.
Each heart in Rome does love and pity you.
Only th'adulterous Antony, most large
In his abominations, turns you off
And gives his potent regiment to a trull
That noises it against us.

OCTAVIA   Is it so, sir?

CAESAR
Most certain. Sister, welcome. Pray you
Be ever known to patience. My dear'st sister! *Exeunt.*

69

78

82
83
84
85
86
87
88
89
90
91
92

97
98
99

100

102

❖

[3.7]

Enter Cleopatra and Enobarbus.

28 **unrestored** that I did not return to him.   **29 of** from   **30 being** having been deposed   **35 For** As for   **46 horse** horses   **47 by** along   **52 prevented** forestalled (by your unannounced arrival)   **53 ostentation** ceremonial display   **53–4 which . . . unloved** which, if not made manifest through ceremonious display, often remains unappreciated or ceases to exist.   **55 stage** stage of your journey   **61 pardon** permission   **62 Being . . . him** i.e., since your return to Rome removed the obstacle between him and the gratification of his desires.

69 **who** i.e., and they   78 **a more larger** an even longer   82 **withhold . . . forth** restrain my advancing to battle   83 **wrong led** wronged, abused   84 **negligent danger** danger through neglect of taking necessary action.   85 **the time** the present state of affairs   85–6 **which . . . necessities** i.e., which tramples your happiness underfoot like a team of animals pulling a wagon   87–8 **let . . . way** allow inevitable events to go unbewailed to their destined conclusion.   89 **Nothing . . . me** i.e., you who are more dear to me than anything.   90 **mark** reach   90–2 **the high . . . you** i.e., the high gods (here treated as a singular subject of the verb "makes," and referred to as "his" in line 91) make us and those that love you their ministers of justice in your cause.   97 **large** unrestrained   98 **turns you off** rejects you   99 **regiment** government, rule.   **trull** prostitute   100 **noises it** is clamorous   102 **Be . . . patience** be patient.
3.7. Location: Near Actium, on the northwestern coast of Greece. Antony's camp.

CLEOPATRA
I will be even with thee, doubt it not.
ENOBARBUS   But why, why, why?
CLEOPATRA
Thou hast forspoke my being in these wars,
And say'st it is not fit.
ENOBARBUS   Well, is it, is it?   4
CLEOPATRA
If not denounced against us, why should not we   5
Be there in person?
ENOBARBUS [aside]   Well, I could reply.
If we should serve with horse and mares together,   7
The horse were merely lost; the mares would bear   8
A soldier and his horse.
CLEOPATRA   What is't you say?   9
ENOBARBUS
Your presence needs must puzzle Antony,   10
Take from his heart, take from his brain, from's time
What should not then be spared. He is already
Traduced for levity, and 'tis said in Rome   13
That Photinus, an eunuch, and your maids   14
Manage this war.
CLEOPATRA   Sink Rome, and their tongues rot
That speak against us! A charge we bear i'th' war,   16
And as the president of my kingdom will   17
Appear there for a man. Speak not against it.   18
I will not stay behind.

Enter Antony and Canidius.

ENOBARBUS   Nay, I have done.
Here comes the Emperor.
ANTONY   Is it not strange, Canidius,
That from Tarentum and Brundusium
He could so quickly cut the Ionian sea   22
And take in Toryne?—You have heard on't, sweet?   23
CLEOPATRA
Celerity is never more admired   24
Than by the negligent.
ANTONY   A good rebuke,
Which might have well becomed the best of men,   26
To taunt at slackness. Canidius, we
Will fight with him by sea.
CLEOPATRA   By sea, what else?
CANIDIUS   Why will my lord do so?
ANTONY   For that he dares us to't.   30
ENOBARBUS
So hath my lord dared him to single fight.

CANIDIUS
Ay, and to wage this battle at Pharsalia,
Where Caesar fought with Pompey. But these offers,
Which serve not for his vantage, he shakes off,
And so should you.
ENOBARBUS   Your ships are not well manned;
Your mariners are muleteers, reapers, people   36
Engrossed by swift impress. In Caesar's fleet   37
Are those that often have 'gainst Pompey fought;
Their ships are yare, yours heavy. No disgrace   39
Shall fall you for refusing him at sea,   40
Being prepared for land.
ANTONY   By sea, by sea.
ENOBARBUS
Most worthy sir, you therein throw away
The absolute soldiership you have by land,
Distract your army, which doth most consist   44
Of war-marked footmen, leave unexecuted   45
Your own renownèd knowledge, quite forgo
The way which promises assurance, and
Give up yourself merely to chance and hazard   48
From firm security.
ANTONY   I'll fight at sea.
CLEOPATRA
I have sixty sails, Caesar none better.
ANTONY
Our overplus of shipping will we burn,
And with the rest full-manned, from th' head of
      Actium   52
Beat th'approaching Caesar. But if we fail,
We then can do't at land.

Enter a Messenger.

                          Thy business?
MESSENGER
The news is true, my lord; he is descried.   55
Caesar has taken Toryne.
ANTONY
Can he be there in person? 'Tis impossible;
Strange that his power should be. Canidius,   58
Our nineteen legions thou shalt hold by land,
And our twelve thousand horse. We'll to our ship.
Away, my Thetis!

Enter a Soldier.

                          How now, worthy soldier?   61
SOLDIER
O noble Emperor, do not fight by sea;
Trust not to rotten planks. Do you misdoubt
This sword and these my wounds? Let th'Egyptians
And the Phoenicians go a-ducking; we   65

---

3 **forspoke** spoken against   4 **fit** appropriate.   5 **If . . . us** i.e., Even if
the war were not declared against me (which it is)   7 **horse** stallions
8 **merely** utterly   8–9 **bear . . . horse** be mounted by a rider and a
stallion.   10 **puzzle** bewilder   13 **Traduced** criticized, censured
14 **an eunuch** (Probably Mardian. In North's Plutarch, Caesar complains that "Mardian the eunuch, Photinus, and Iras . . . and
Charmian . . . ruled the affairs of Antonius' empire." But Photinus
[or Pothinus] was a eunuch, too.)   16 **charge** responsibility, cost
17 **president** ruler   18 **for** in the capacity of   22 **Ionian** (Often applied
to the Aegean, but here the Adriatic. Tarentum and Brundusium or
Brundisium are in the "heel" of Italy, across the Adriatic from Actium
and Toryne.)   23 **take in** conquer   24 **Celerity** Swiftness.   **admired**
wondered at   26 **becomed** become, suited   30 **For that** Because

36 **muleteers** mule-drivers, peasants   37 **Engrossed** collected wholesale.   **impress** impressment, conscription.   39 **yare** quick, maneu-
verable   40 **fall** befall   44 **Distract** divide, divert.   **most** for the
most part   45 **footmen** foot soldiers.   **unexecuted** unused
48 **merely** entirely   52 **head** promontory   55 **he is descried** he has
been sighted.   58 **his power** i.e., his army, let alone himself
61 **Thetis** sea goddess, the mother of Achilles.   65 **go a-ducking**
(1) get drenched (2) cringe

Have used to conquer standing on the earth   66
And fighting foot to foot.

ANTONY   Well, well, away!

Exeunt Antony, Cleopatra, and Enobarbus.

SOLDIER
By Hercules, I think I am i'th' right.

CANIDIUS
Soldier, thou art; but his whole action grows   69
Not in the power on't. So our leader's led,   70
And we are women's men.

SOLDIER   You keep by land   71
The legions and the horse whole, do you not?   72

CANIDIUS
Marcus Octavius, Marcus Justeius,
Publicola, and Caelius are for sea;
But we keep whole by land. This speed of Caesar's
Carries beyond belief.   76

SOLDIER   While he was yet in Rome
His power went out in such distractions as   78
Beguiled all spies.

CANIDIUS   Who's his lieutenant, hear you?

SOLDIER
They say, one Taurus.

CANIDIUS   Well I know the man.

Enter a Messenger.

MESSENGER   The Emperor calls Canidius.

CANIDIUS
With news the time's in labor, and throws forth   82
Each minute some.   *Exeunt.*   83

❧

[3.8]

*Enter Caesar [and Taurus] with his army,
marching.*

CAESAR   Taurus!

TAURUS   My lord?

CAESAR
Strike not by land; keep whole. Provoke not battle
Till we have done at sea. Do not exceed
The prescript of this scroll. [*He gives a scroll.*] Our
fortune lies   5
Upon this jump.   *Exeunt.*   6

❧

[3.9]

Enter Antony and Enobarbus.

ANTONY
Set we our squadrons on yond side o'th' hill,
In eye of Caesar's battle, from which place
We may the number of the ships behold   2
And so proceed accordingly.   *Exeunt.*

❧

[3.10]

*Canidius marcheth with his land army one way
over the stage, and Taurus, the lieutenant of
Caesar, the other way. After their going in is heard
the noise of a sea fight.*

Alarum. Enter Enobarbus.

ENOBARBUS
Naught, naught, all naught! I can behold no longer.   1
Th'*Antoniad*, the Egyptian admiral,   2
With all their sixty, fly and turn the rudder.
To see't mine eyes are blasted.

Enter Scarus.

SCARUS   Gods and goddesses,
All the whole synod of them!

ENOBARBUS   What's thy passion?   5

SCARUS
The greater cantle of the world is lost   6
With very ignorance; we have kissed away   7
Kingdoms and provinces.

ENOBARBUS   How appears the fight?

SCARUS
On our side like the tokened pestilence,   9
Where death is sure. Yon ribaudred nag of Egypt—   10
Whom leprosy o'ertake!—i'th' midst o'th' fight,
When vantage like a pair of twins appeared   12
Both as the same, or rather ours the elder,   13
The breeze upon her, like a cow in June,   14
Hoists sails and flies.

ENOBARBUS   That I beheld.
Mine eyes did sicken at the sight, and could not
Endure a further view.

SCARUS   She once being loofed,   18
The noble ruin of her magic, Antony,   19
Claps on his sea wing and, like a doting mallard,   20
Leaving the fight in height, flies after her.   21
I never saw an action of such shame.
Experience, manhood, honor, ne'er before

---

66 Have used are accustomed.   **standing on the earth** (1) fighting on
land (2) standing upright, not *ducking*, or "cringing"   **69–70 his . . .
on't** his whole strategy has been developed without regard to where
his power really lies.   **71 men** servingmen.   **72 horse** cavalry.
whole undivided, held in reserve   **76 Carries** surpasses (like an
arrow in archery)   **78 distractions** detachments, divisions
82–3 With . . . some More news is born each minute. (*Throws forth*
means "gives birth.")
3.8. Location: A field near Actium, as before.
5 prescript orders   **6 jump** chance, hazard.
3.9. Location: A field near Actium, as before.

2 eye sight.   **battle** battle line
3.10 Location: A field near Actium, as before.
1 Naught All has come to naught   **2 admiral** flagship   **5 synod**
assembly   **6 cantle** corner; hence, piece or part   **7 With very ignorance** through utter stupidity   **9 tokened pestilence** (Certain red
spots appeared on the bodies of the plague-smitten, called tokens.)
10 ribaudred foul, obscene   **12–13 When . . . same** i.e., when the
advantage was equal on either side   **13 elder** i.e., more advanced,
more likely to inherit   **14 breeze** (1) gadfly (2) light wind   **18 loofed**
luffed, with ship's head brought close to the wind. (With a pun on
aloofed, "becoming distant.")   **19 ruin of** object ruined by   **20 Claps
. . . sea wing** i.e., hoists sail, preparing for flight like a water bird.
mallard drake   **21 in** at its

Did violate so itself.

ENOBARBUS   Alack, alack!

Enter Canidius.

CANIDIUS

Our fortune on the sea is out of breath,
And sinks most lamentably. Had our general
Been what he knew himself, it had gone well.
Oh, he has given example for our flight
Most grossly by his own!

ENOBARBUS

Ay, are you thereabouts? Why then, good night
indeed.   30

CANIDIUS

Toward Peloponnesus are they fled.   31

SCARUS

'Tis easy to't, and there I will attend   32
What further comes.

CANIDIUS   To Caesar will I render   33
My legions and my horse. Six kings already   34
Show me the way of yielding.

ENOBARBUS   I'll yet follow
The wounded chance of Antony, though my reason   36
Sits in the wind against me.   *[Exeunt separately.]*   37

❧

[3.11]

Enter Antony with attendants.

ANTONY

Hark! The land bids me tread no more upon't;
It is ashamed to bear me. Friends, come hither.
I am so lated in the world that I   3
Have lost my way forever. I have a ship
Laden with gold. Take that, divide it; fly,   5
And make your peace with Caesar.

ALL   Fly? Not we.

ANTONY

I have fled myself, and have instructed cowards
To run and show their shoulders. Friends, begone.   8
I have myself resolved upon a course
Which has no need of you. Begone.
My treasure's in the harbor. Take it. Oh,
I followed that I blush to look upon!   12
My very hairs do mutiny, for the white   13
Reprove the brown for rashness, and they them   14

For fear and doting. Friends, begone. You shall
Have letters from me to some friends that will
Sweep your way for you. Pray you, look not sad,   17
Nor make replies of loathness. Take the hint   18
Which my despair proclaims. Let that be left   19
Which leaves itself. To the seaside straightway!   20
I will possess you of that ship and treasure.
Leave me, I pray, a little. Pray you now,
Nay, do so, for indeed I have lost command.   23
Therefore I pray you. I'll see you by and by.   24

[Exeunt attendants. Antony] sits down.

Enter Cleopatra led by Charmian, [Iras,] and Eros.

EROS

Nay, gentle madam, to him, comfort him.

IRAS   Do, most dear Queen.

CHARMIAN   Do; why, what else?

CLEOPATRA   Let me sit down. O Juno!

ANTONY   No, no, no, no, no.

EROS   See you here, sir?

ANTONY   Oh, fie, fie, fie!

CHARMIAN   Madam!

IRAS   Madam, O good Empress!

EROS   Sir, sir!

ANTONY

Yes, my lord, yes. He at Philippi kept   35
His sword e'en like a dancer, while I struck   36
The lean and wrinkled Cassius, and 'twas I
That the mad Brutus ended. He alone   38
Dealt on lieutenantry, and no practice had   39
In the brave squares of war; yet now—no matter.   40

CLEOPATRA

Ah, stand by.

EROS   The Queen, my lord, the Queen.   41

IRAS

Go to him, madam, speak to him.
He's unqualitied with very shame.   43

CLEOPATRA   Well then, sustain me. Oh!

EROS

Most noble sir, arise. The Queen approaches.
Her head's declined, and death will seize her but   46
Your comfort makes the rescue.

ANTONY

I have offended reputation,
A most unnoble swerving.

EROS   Sir, the Queen.   49

---

30 thereabouts i.e., of that mind, thinking of desertion.   **good night
indeed** i.e., it's all over.   **31 Peloponnesus** southern Greece (from
which Antony then crosses the Mediterranean to Egypt)   **32 to't** to
get to it.   **attend** await   **33 render** surrender   **34 horse** cavalry.
36 wounded chance broken fortunes   **37 Sits . . . me** i.e., is on my
downwind side, tracking me and hunting me down.
3.11. Location: Historically, events such as dispatching the Schoolmaster to Caesar took place in Egypt; however, the dramatic
impression of this scene is that it occurs soon after the battle.
3 lated belated, like a traveler still journeying when night falls   **5 fly**
flee   **8 shoulders** i.e., backs.   **12 that** that which   **13 mutiny** contend among themselves   **14 they them** i.e., the brown hairs reprove
the white

17 Sweep your way clear your way (to Caesar)   **18 loathness** unwillingness.   **hint** opportunity   **19 that** i.e., Antony and his cause
20 leaves is untrue to, deserts   **23 lost command** i.e., of myself and
of my authority.   **24 pray** entreat (as opposed to "command")
35 Yes . . . yes (Antony is absorbed in his own bitter thoughts, as also
in lines 29 and 31.)   **He** i.e., Octavius.   **kept** kept in its sheath
36 e'en . . . dancer i.e., as though for ornament only, in a dance
38 ended i.e., defeated. (Not *killed;* Brutus and Cassius committed suicide.)   **He alone** Caesar merely   **39 Dealt on lieutenantry** let his
subordinates do the fighting   **40 brave squares** splendid squadrons,
bodies of troops drawn up in square formation   **41 stand by**
(Cleopatra indicates she is about to faint and needs assistance.)
43 unqualitied dispossessed of his own nature, i.e., not himself
46 but unless   **49 swerving** lapse, transgression.

ANTONY
Oh, whither hast thou led me, Egypt? See 50
How I convey my shame out of thine eyes 51
By looking back what I have left behind 52
'Stroyed in dishonor.

CLEOPATRA　　　　Oh, my lord, my lord, 53
Forgive my fearful sails! I little thought 54
You would have followed.

ANTONY　　　　Egypt, thou knew'st too well
My heart was to thy rudder tied by th' strings, 56
And thou shouldst tow me after. O'er my spirit
Thy full supremacy thou knew'st, and that
Thy beck might from the bidding of the gods 59
Command me.

CLEOPATRA　　Oh, my pardon!

ANTONY　　　　Now I must 60
To the young man send humble treaties, dodge 61
And palter in the shifts of lowness, who 62
With half the bulk o'th' world played as I pleased,
Making and marring fortunes. You did know
How much you were my conqueror, and that
My sword, made weak by my affection, would 66
Obey it on all cause.

CLEOPATRA　　　Pardon, pardon! 67

ANTONY
Fall not a tear, I say; one of them rates 68
All that is won and lost. Give me a kiss.　　*[They kiss.]*
Even this repays me.—We sent our schoolmaster; 70
Is 'a come back?—Love, I am full of lead.—
Some wine, within there, and our viands! Fortune
knows 72
We scorn her most when most she offers blows.
　　　　　　　　　　　　　　　Exeunt.

❦

[3.12]

*Enter Caesar, Agrippa, [Thidias,] and Dolabella,
with others.*

CAESAR
Let him appear that's come from Antony.
Know you him?

DOLABELLA　　Caesar, 'tis his schoolmaster—
An argument that he is plucked, when hither 3
He sends so poor a pinion of his wing, 4
Which had superfluous kings for messengers 5

Not many moons gone by.

Enter Ambassador from Antony.

CAESAR　　　　Approach and speak.

AMBASSADOR
Such as I am, I come from Antony.
I was of late as petty to his ends
As is the morn-dew on the myrtle leaf 8
To his grand sea.

CAESAR　　　Be't so. Declare thine office. 10

AMBASSADOR
Lord of his fortunes he salutes thee, and
Requires to live in Egypt; which not granted, 12
He lessens his requests, and to thee sues 13
To let him breathe between the heavens and earth 14
A private man in Athens. This for him.
Next, Cleopatra does confess thy greatness,
Submits her to thy might, and of thee craves
The circle of the Ptolemies for her heirs, 18
Now hazarded to thy grace.

CAESAR　　　　For Antony, 19
I have no ears to his request. The Queen
Of audience nor desire shall fail, so she 21
From Egypt drive her all-disgracèd friend
Or take his life there. This if she perform
She shall not sue unheard. So to them both.

AMBASSADOR
Fortune pursue thee!

CAESAR　　　Bring him through the bands. 25
　　　　　　[Exit Ambassador, attended.]
[To Thidias] To try thy eloquence now 'tis time.
Dispatch.
From Antony win Cleopatra. Promise,
And in our name, what she requires; add more, 28
From thine invention, offers. Women are not 29
In their best fortunes strong, but want will perjure 30
The ne'er-touched vestal. Try thy cunning, Thidias. 31
Make thine own edict for thy pains, which we 32
Will answer as a law.

THIDIAS　　　　Caesar, I go. 33

CAESAR
Observe how Antony becomes his flaw, 34
And what thou think'st his very action speaks 35
In every power that moves.

THIDIAS　　　Caesar, I shall.　　*Exeunt.* 36

❦

50–3 **See . . . dishonor** i.e., See how ashamed I am to have you see me like this, looking back on what I have left behind dishonorably destroyed. 54 **fearful** timorous 56 **th' strings** (1) the heartstrings (2) towing cable 59–60 **Thy . . . Command me** your mere beckoning would command me away from doing the bidding of the gods themselves. 61 **treaties** entreaties, propositions for settlement. **dodge** shuffle, cringe 62 **palter** use trickery, prevaricate, equivocate. **shifts of lowness** pitiful evasions used by those lacking power 66 **affection** passion 67 **on all cause** whatever the reason. 68 **Fall** Let fall. **rates** equals 70 **Even this** This by itself. **schoolmaster** (Identified in Plutarch as Euphronius, tutor to Antony's children by Cleopatra.) 72 **viands** food.
3.12 Location: Egypt. Caesar's camp.
3 **An argument** an indication 4 **pinion** i.e., pinion-feather, outer feather 5 **Which** who

8 **petty to** insignificant in terms of 10 **To . . . sea** compared to its, the dewdrop's, great source, the sea. **thine office** your official business. 12 **Requires** asks. **which not granted** and if that request is not granted 13 **sues** petitions 14 **breathe** i.e., live 18 **circle** crown 19 **hazarded . . . grace** dependent on your favor. **For** As for 21 **Of audience** neither of hearing. **so** provided that 25 **Bring** Escort. **bands** troops on guard, military lines. 28 **requires** asks 28–9 **add . . . offers** add ideas of your own. 29–31 **Women . . . vestal** Women are not strong even at the height of their good fortune, but need will cause even an untouched vestal virgin to break her vows. 31 **cunning** skill 32 **Make . . . edict** Decree your own reward 33 **answer as a law** confirm as if it were a law. 34 **becomes his flaw** bears his misfortune and disgrace 35–6 **And . . . moves** and what you think his gestures signify in every move he makes.

[3.13]

Enter Cleopatra, Enobarbus, Charmian, and Iras.

CLEOPATRA
What shall we do, Enobarbus?
ENOBARBUS   Think, and die.   1
CLEOPATRA
Is Antony or we in fault for this?   2
ENOBARBUS
Antony only, that would make his will   3
Lord of his reason. What though you fled
From that great face of war, whose several ranges   5
Frighted each other? Why should he follow?
The itch of his affection should not then   7
Have nicked his captainship, at such a point,   8
When half to half the world opposed, he being   9
The mèred question. 'Twas a shame no less   10
Than was his loss, to course your flying flags   11
And leave his navy gazing.
CLEOPATRA   Prithee, peace.

Enter the Ambassador with Antony.

ANTONY   Is that his answer?
AMBASSADOR   Ay, my lord.
ANTONY
The Queen shall then have courtesy, so she   15
Will yield us up.
AMBASSADOR   He says so.
ANTONY   Let her know't.—
To the boy Caesar send this grizzled head,
And he will fill thy wishes to the brim
With principalities.
CLEOPATRA   That head, my lord?
ANTONY [*to the Ambassador*]
To him again. Tell him he wears the rose
Of youth upon him, from which the world should
    note
Something particular. His coin, ships, legions,   22
May be a coward's, whose ministers would prevail   23
Under the service of a child as soon
As i'th' command of Caesar. I dare him therefore
To lay his gay caparisons apart   26
And answer me declined, sword against sword,   27
Ourselves alone. I'll write it. Follow me.
            [*Exeunt Antony and Ambassador.*]
ENOBARBUS [*aside*]
Yes, like enough, high-battled Caesar will   29

Unstate his happiness and be staged to th' show   30
Against a sworder! I see men's judgments are   31
A parcel of their fortunes, and things outward   32
Do draw the inward quality after them   33
To suffer all alike. That he should dream,   34
Knowing all measures, the full Caesar will   35
Answer his emptiness! Caesar, thou hast subdued   36
His judgment too.

Enter a Servant.

SERVANT   A messenger from Caesar.
CLEOPATRA
What, no more ceremony? See, my women,
Against the blown rose may they stop their nose   39
That kneeled unto the buds.—Admit him, sir.
                    [*Exit Servant.*]
ENOBARBUS [*aside*]
Mine honesty and I begin to square.   41
The loyalty well held to fools does make   42
Our faith mere folly; yet he that can endure   43
To follow with allegiance a fall'n lord
Does conquer him that did his master conquer   45
And earns a place i'th' story.

Enter Thidias.

CLEOPATRA   Caesar's will?
THIDIAS
Hear it apart.
CLEOPATRA   None but friends. Say boldly.   47
THIDIAS
So haply are they friends to Antony.   48
ENOBARBUS
He needs as many, sir, as Caesar has,
Or needs not us. If Caesar please, our master   50
Will leap to be his friend. For us, you know   51
Whose he is we are, and that is Caesar's.
THIDIAS   So.   52
Thus then, thou most renowned: Caesar entreats
Not to consider in what case thou stand'st   54
Further than he is Caesar.
CLEOPATRA   Go on: right royal.   55

3.13. Location: Alexandria. Cleopatra's palace.
1 Think, and die Think despondently, and die of melancholy or by
suicide.   **2 we** I   **3 will** desire (especially sexual)   **5 ranges** ranks,
lines (of ships)   **7 affection** sexual passion   **8 nicked** cut short or
maimed, or got the better of.   **point** crisis   **9–10 When . . . question**
when the two halves of the world found themselves in conflict,
Antony being the sole ground of the quarrel.   **11 course** pursue (as in
hunting)   **15 so** provided that   **22 Something particular** some
exceptional exploit.   **23 May be** could as well be.   **ministers** agents,
subordinates   **26 gay caparisons** resplendent trappings   **27 answer
me declined** meet me as I am, lowered in fortune and advanced in
years   **29 like** likely.   **high-battled** provided with a mighty army

30–1 Unstate . . . sworder set aside his advantageous fortune and be
exhibited publicly in a sword-fight contest with a mere gladiator.
31–4 I see . . . alike I see that men's judgments are inextricably linked
to their fortunes, whereby outward circumstances draw after them
inward qualities of character in such a way that both suffer at the
same time.   **35 Knowing all measures** i.e., having experienced every
degree of fortune.   **full** at full fortune   **36 Answer** (1) meet man to
man with (2) correspond with   **39 blown** overblown, starting to
decay   **41 honesty** (With meaning also of "honor.")   **square** quarrel.
42–3 The . . . folly A stubborn loyalty bestowed on fools is folly itself
45 Does . . . conquer i.e., achieves a moral victory over the very fortune or the person that subdued one's own master   **47 apart** in private.   **48 haply** perhaps   **50 Or . . . us** i.e., or else he doesn't need
even us, his case being hopeless.   **51 For** As for   **52 Whose . . .
Caesar's** i.e., we are Antony's friends, and he is Caesar's, so that we,
too, are Caesar's.   **54–5 Not . . . Caesar** i.e., not to worry about your
situation other than to consider that you are dealing with Caesar, the
embodiment of magnanimity.   **55 right royal** i.e., that is very magnanimous.

THIDIAS
He knows that you embrace not Antony
As you did love, but as you feared him.

CLEOPATRA   Oh!

THIDIAS
The scars upon your honor therefore he
Does pity as constrainèd blemishes,
Not as deserved.

CLEOPATRA   He is a god and knows
What is most right. Mine honor was not yielded,   61
But conquered merely.

ENOBARBUS [aside]   To be sure of that,   62
I will ask Antony. Sir, sir, thou art so leaky
That we must leave thee to thy sinking, for
Thy dearest quit thee.   Exit Enobarbus.

THIDIAS   Shall I say to Caesar
What you require of him? For he partly begs   66
To be desired to give. It much would please him
That of his fortunes you should make a staff
To lean upon; but it would warm his spirits
To hear from me you had left Antony
And put yourself under his shroud,
The universal landlord.   71

CLEOPATRA   What's your name?

THIDIAS
My name is Thidias.

CLEOPATRA   Most kind messenger,
Say to great Caesar this in deputation:
I kiss his conquering hand. Tell him I am prompt   74
To lay my crown at 's feet, and there to kneel   75
Till from his all-obeying breath I hear
The doom of Egypt.   77

THIDIAS   'Tis your noblest course.   78
Wisdom and fortune combating together,   79
If that the former dare but what it can,   80
No chance may shake it. Give me grace to lay   81
My duty on your hand.   [He kisses her hand.]

CLEOPATRA   Your Caesar's father oft,   83
When he hath mused of taking kingdoms in,   84
Bestowed his lips on that unworthy place,
As it rained kisses.

Enter Antony and Enobarbus.

ANTONY   Favors? By Jove that thunders!   86
What art thou, fellow?

THIDIAS   One that but performs
The bidding of the fullest man, and worthiest   88
To have command obeyed.

ENOBARBUS [aside]   You will be whipped.

ANTONY [calling for Servants]
Approach, there!—Ah, you kite!—Now, gods and
devils!   90
Authority melts from me of late. When I cried "Ho!",
Like boys unto a muss kings would start forth   92
And cry, "Your will?"—Have you no ears? I am
Antony yet.

Enter a Servant [followed by others].

               Take hence this jack and whip him.   94

ENOBARBUS [aside]
'Tis better playing with a lion's whelp   95
Than with an old one dying.

ANTONY   Moon and stars!
Whip him. Were't twenty of the greatest tributaries   97
That do acknowledge Caesar, should I find them
So saucy with the hand of she here—what's her name
Since she was Cleopatra? Whip him, fellows,
Till like a boy you see him cringe his face   101
And whine aloud for mercy. Take him hence.

THIDIAS
Mark Antony—

ANTONY   Tug him away! Being whipped,
Bring him again. This jack of Caesar's shall
Bear us an errand to him.

Exeunt [Servants] with Thidias.
[To Cleopatra] it You were half blasted ere I knew you.
Ha?   106
Have I my pillow left unpressed in Rome,
Forborne the getting of a lawful race,   108
And by a gem of women, to be abused   109
By one that looks on feeders?   110

CLEOPATRA   Good my lord—

ANTONY   You have been a boggler ever.   112
But when we in our viciousness grow hard—
Oh, misery on't!—the wise gods seel our eyes,   114
In our own filth drop our clear judgments, make us
Adore our errors, laugh at 's while we strut
To our confusion.

CLEOPATRA   Oh, is't come to this?   117

ANTONY
I found you as a morsel cold upon
Dead Caesar's trencher; nay, you were a fragment   119
Of Gnaeus Pompey's, besides what hotter hours,   120
Unregistered in vulgar fame, you have   121
Luxuriously picked out. For I am sure,   122
Though you can guess what temperance should be,

---

61 right true.   62 merely utterly.   66 require ask.   partly i.e., as commensurate with his dignity   71 shroud shelter. (With suggestion too of a burial cloth.)   74 in deputation by you as deputy   75 prompt ready   77 all-obeying obeyed by all   78 The doom of Egypt i.e., my fate.   79–81 Wisdom . . . shake it When wisdom and fortune are at odds, if the wise person will have the resolution to desire only what what fortune will allow, then fortune cannot shake that wisdom.   83 Your Caesar's father i.e., Julius Caesar, actually Octavius' great-uncle. (See note at 3.6.6.)   84 mused . . . in thought about conquering kingdoms   86 As as if   88 fullest most fortunate, best

90 kite a rapacious bird of prey that feeds on ignoble objects, and a slang word for "whore." (Said of Cleopatra.)   92 muss game in which small objects are thrown down to be scrambled for   94 jack fellow. (Contemptuous.)   95 whelp cub   97 tributaries rulers paying tribute   101 cringe contract in pain   106 blasted withered, blighted   108 getting begetting.   lawful legitimate   109 abused deceived, betrayed   110 feeders servants   112 boggler waverer, shifty person. (Often used of shying horses.)   114 seel blind. (A term in falconry for sewing shut the eyes of wild hawks in order to tame them.)   117 confusion destruction.   119 trencher wooden plate.   fragment leftover   120 Gnaeus Pompey's (See 1.5.32 and note.)   121 vulgar fame common gossip   122 Luxuriously lustfully

You know not what it is.

CLEOPATRA   Wherefore is this?   124

ANTONY
To let a fellow that will take rewards
And say "God quit you!" be familiar with   126
My playfellow, your hand, this kingly seal
And plighter of high hearts! Oh, that I were   128
Upon the hill of Basan, to outroar   129
The hornèd herd! For I have savage cause,   130
And to proclaim it civilly were like
A haltered neck which does the hangman thank
For being yare about him.

Enter a Servant with Thidias.

                        Is he whipped?   133

SERVANT   Soundly, my lord.

ANTONY   Cried he? And begged 'a pardon?

SERVANT   He did ask favor.

ANTONY [*to Thidias*]
If that thy father live, let him repent
Thou wast not made his daughter; and be thou sorry
To follow Caesar in his triumph, since
Thou hast been whipped for following him.
    Henceforth
The white hand of a lady fever thee;   141
Shake thou to look on't. Get thee back to Caesar.
Tell him thy entertainment. Look thou say   143
He makes me angry with him; for he seems
Proud and disdainful, harping on what I am,
Not what he knew I was. He makes me angry,
And at this time most easy 'tis to do't,
When my good stars, that were my former guides,
Have empty left their orbs and shot their fires   149
Into th'abysm of hell. If he mislike   150
My speech and what is done, tell him he has
Hipparchus, my enfranchèd bondman, whom   152
He may at pleasure whip, or hang, or torture,
As he shall like, to quit me. Urge it thou.   154
Hence with thy stripes, begone!

        Exit [Servant with] Thidias.
CLEOPATRA   Have you done yet?

ANTONY
Alack, our terrene moon is now eclipsed,   156
And it portends alone the fall of Antony.

CLEOPATRA   I must stay his time.   158

ANTONY
To flatter Caesar, would you mingle eyes

With one that ties his points?

CLEOPATRA   Not know me yet?   160

ANTONY
Coldhearted toward me?

CLEOPATRA   Ah, dear, if I be so,
From my cold heart let heaven engender hail,
And poison it in the source, and the first stone
Drop in my neck; as it determines, so   164
Dissolve my life! The next Caesarion smite,
Till by degrees the memory of my womb,   166
Together with my brave Egyptians all,   167
By the discandying of this pelleted storm   168
Lie graveless till the flies and gnats of Nile
Have buried them for prey!

ANTONY   I am satisfied.   170
Caesar sits down in Alexandria, where   171
I will oppose his fate. Our force by land   172
Hath nobly held; our severed navy too
Have knit again, and fleet, threat'ning most sealike. 174
Where hast thou been, my heart? Dost thou hear,
    lady?   175
If from the field I shall return once more
To kiss these lips, I will appear in blood;   177
I and my sword will earn our chronicle.   178
There's hope in't yet.

CLEOPATRA   That's my brave lord!

ANTONY
I will be treble-sinewed, hearted, breathed,   181
And fight maliciously. For when mine hours   182
Were nice and lucky, men did ransom lives   183
Of me for jests; but now I'll set my teeth   184
And send to darkness all that stop me. Come,   185
Let's have one other gaudy night. Call to me   186
All my sad captains. Fill our bowls once more;
Let's mock the midnight bell.

CLEOPATRA   It is my birthday.
I had thought t'have held it poor; but since my lord   189
Is Antony again, I will be Cleopatra.

ANTONY   We will yet do well.

CLEOPATRA [*to attendants*]
Call all his noble captains to my lord.

ANTONY
Do so. We'll speak to them, and tonight I'll force
The wine peep through their scars. Come on, my
    queen,
There's sap in't yet. The next time I do fight   195

I'll make Death love me, for I will contend   196
Even with his pestilent scythe.   197
                            Exeunt [all but Enobarbus].

ENOBARBUS
Now he'll outstare the lightning. To be furious   198
Is to be frighted out of fear, and in that mood
The dove will peck the estridge; and I see still   200
A diminution in our captain's brain
Restores his heart. When valor preys on reason,   202
It eats the sword it fights with. I will seek   203
Some way to leave him.   *Exit.*

❧

[4.1]

*Enter Caesar, Agrippa, and Maecenas, with his
army, Caesar reading a letter.*

CAESAR
He calls me boy, and chides as he had power   1
To beat me out of Egypt. My messenger
He hath whipped with rods, dares me to personal
    combat,
Caesar to Antony. Let the old ruffian know
I have many other ways to die, meantime
Laugh at his challenge.
MAECENAS   Caesar must think,
When one so great begins to rage, he's hunted   8
Even to falling. Give him no breath, but now   9
Make boot of his distraction. Never anger   10
Made good guard for itself.
CAESAR   Let our best heads   11
Know that tomorrow the last of many battles
We mean to fight. Within our files there are,   13
Of those that served Mark Antony but late,   14
Enough to fetch him in. See it done,   15
And feast the army; we have store to do't,   16
And they have earned the waste. Poor Antony!   17
                                            Exeunt.

❧

[4.2]

*Enter Antony, Cleopatra, Enobarbus,
Charmian, Iras, Alexas, with others.*

ANTONY
He will not fight with me, Domitius?

ENOBARBUS   No.
ANTONY   Why should he not?
ENOBARBUS
He thinks, being twenty times of better fortune,
He is twenty men to one.
ANTONY   Tomorrow, soldier,
By sea and land I'll fight. Or I will live   6
Or bathe my dying honor in the blood
Shall make it live again. Woo't thou fight well?   8
ENOBARBUS
I'll strike, and cry, "Take all."
ANTONY   Well said. Come on!   9
Call forth my household servants. Let's tonight   10

                Enter three or four servitors.

Be bounteous at our meal.—Give me thy hand.
Thou hast been rightly honest—so hast thou—
Thou—and thou—and thou. You have served me   12
    well,
And kings have been your fellows.
CLEOPATRA *[aside to Enobarbus]*   What means this? 14
ENOBARBUS *[aside to Cleopatra]*
'Tis one of those odd tricks which sorrow shoots
Out of the mind.
ANTONY   And thou art honest too.
I wish I could be made so many men,   17
And all of you clapped up together in   18
An Antony, that I might do you service
So good as you have done.
ALL   The gods forbid!
ANTONY
Well, my good fellows, wait on me tonight:
Scant not my cups, and make as much of me   22
As when mine empire was your fellow too,   23
And suffered my command.
CLEOPATRA *[aside to Enobarbus]*   What does he mean?   24
ENOBARBUS *[aside to Cleopatra]*
To make his followers weep.
ANTONY   Tend me tonight;
May be it is the period of your duty.   26
Haply you shall not see me more, or if,   27
A mangled shadow. Perchance tomorrow   28
You'll serve another master. I look on you
As one that takes his leave. Mine honest friends,
I turn you not away, but, like a master
Married to your good service, stay till death.
Tend me tonight two hours, I ask no more,
And the gods yield you for't!
ENOBARBUS   What mean you, sir,   34
To give them this discomfort? Look, they weep,

196–7 **I will . . . scythe** i.e., I will outdo even Death himself and his
scythe of *pestilence* or plague.   **198 outstare** stare down.   **furious**
frenzied   **200 estridge** ostrich, or, a kind of hawk.   **still** constantly
202–3 When . . . with When valor turns to unreasonable fury, it
destroys the very quality of reasonableness that valor depends on in
battle.
4.1 Location: Before Alexandria. Caesar's camp.
1 as as if   **8 rage** rave   **9 breath** breathing space   **10 boot** advantage.
distraction frenzy.   **11 best heads** commanding officers   **13 files** (As
in "rank and file.")   **14 late** lately   **15 fetch him in** surround, capture him.   **16 store** provisions   **17 waste** lavish expenditure.
4.2 Location: Alexandria. Cleopatra's palace.

6 Or Either   **8 Shall** that will.   **Woo't** Wilt   **9 strike . . . Take all**
(1) fight to the finish, crying, "Winner take all" (2) strike sail and surrender.   **10.1 servitors** attendants.   **12 honest** true, loyal   **14 fellows** i.e., fellow servants of me.   **17 made . . . men** divided into as
many men as you are   **18 clapped up** combined   **22 Scant not my
cups** i.e., Provide generously   **23 fellow** i.e., fellow servant   **24 suffered** acknowledged, submitted to   **26 period** end   **27 Haply** Perhaps.   **if** if you do   **28 shadow** ghost.   **34 yield** reward

And I, an ass, am onion-eyed. For shame,
Transform us not to women.
ANTONY   Ho, ho, ho!
Now the witch take me if I meant it thus!   38
Grace grow where those drops fall! My hearty friends,   39
You take me in too dolorous a sense,
For I spake to you for your comfort, did desire you
To burn this night with torches. Know, my hearts,   42
I hope well of tomorrow, and will lead you
Where rather I'll expect victorious life
Than death and honor. Let's to supper, come,
And drown consideration.   *Exeunt.*   46

♣

[4.3]

Enter a company of Soldiers.

FIRST SOLDIER
Brother, good night. Tomorrow is the day.
SECOND SOLDIER
It will determine one way. Fare you well.   2
Heard you of nothing strange about the streets?   3
FIRST SOLDIER   Nothing. What news?
SECOND SOLDIER
Belike 'tis but a rumor. Good night to you.   5
FIRST SOLDIER   Well, sir, good night.

They meet other Soldiers.

SECOND SOLDIER   Soldiers, have careful watch.
THIRD SOLDIER   And you. Good night, good night.
They place themselves in every corner of the stage.
SECOND SOLDIER   Here we. And if tomorrow   9
Our navy thrive, I have an absolute hope
Our landmen will stand up.
FIRST SOLDIER   'Tis a brave army, and full of purpose.   12
Music of the hautboys is under the stage.
SECOND SOLDIER   Peace! What noise?
FIRST SOLDIER   List, list!   14
SECOND SOLDIER   Hark!
FIRST SOLDIER   Music i'th'air.
THIRD SOLDIER   Under the earth.
FOURTH SOLDIER   It signs well, does it not?   18
THIRD SOLDIER   No.
FIRST SOLDIER   Peace, I say! What should this mean?
SECOND SOLDIER
'Tis the god Hercules, whom Antony loved,
Now leaves him.
FIRST SOLDIER   Walk; let's see if other watchmen
Do hear what we do.
[They advance toward their fellow watchmen.]
SECOND SOLDIER   How now, masters?   24

ALL *[speak together]*   How now? How now? Do you
hear this?
FIRST SOLDIER   Ay. Is't not strange?
THIRD SOLDIER   Do you hear, masters? Do you hear?
FIRST SOLDIER
Follow the noise so far as we have quarter;   29
Let's see how it will give off.   30
ALL   Content. 'Tis strange.   *Exeunt.*

♣

[4.4]

*Enter Antony and Cleopatra, with [Charmian and]
others [attending].*

ANTONY
Eros! Mine armor, Eros!
CLEOPATRA   Sleep a little.
ANTONY
No, my chuck.—Eros, come, mine armor, Eros!   2

Enter Eros [with armor].

Come, good fellow, put thine iron on.   3
If fortune be not ours today, it is
Because we brave her. Come.
CLEOPATRA   Nay, I'll help too.   5
What's this for?   *[She helps to arm him.]*
ANTONY   Ah, let be, let be! Thou art
The armorer of my heart. False, false; this, this.   7
CLEOPATRA
Sooth, la, I'll help. Thus it must be.
ANTONY   Well, well,   8
We shall thrive now. See'st thou, my good fellow?
Go, put on thy defenses.
EROS   Briefly, sir.   10
CLEOPATRA
Is not this buckled well?
ANTONY   Rarely, rarely.   11
He that unbuckles this, till we do please   12
To doff't for our repose, shall hear a storm.   13
Thou fumblest, Eros, and my queen's a squire   14
More tight at this than thou. Dispatch. O love,   15
That thou couldst see my wars today, and knew'st   16
The royal occupation! Thou shouldst see   17
A workman in't.

Enter an armed Soldier.

                    Good morrow to thee. Welcome.   18
Thou look'st like him that knows a warlike charge.   19

---

38 the witch take me may I be bewitched   **39 Grace grow** (1) May
rue or herb of grace grow (2) May gracious fortune flourish.   **hearty**
loving   **42 burn . . . torches** i.e., revel through the night.   **46 drown**
consideration drown brooding thought in our winecups.
4.3 Location: Alexandria. Before the palace.
2 determine one way be decided, come to an end one way or the
other.   **3 about** in   **5 Belike** Probably   **9 Here we** Here's our station.   **12 brave** splendid, gallant   **12.1 hautboys** oboelike instruments   **14 List** Listen   **18 signs well** is a good sign   **24 masters**
good sirs. (Also in line 28.)

29 as we have quarter as our watch post extends.   **30 give off** cease.
4.4. Location: Alexandria. The palace.
2 chuck (A term of endearment.)   **3 thine iron** i.e., my armor that
you have there. (Or perhaps he is telling Eros to arm.)   **5 brave** defy
7 False You're putting it on wrong   **8 Sooth** In truth   **10 defenses**
armor.   **Briefly** In a moment   **11 Rarely** Excellently   **12–13 He . . .**
storm i.e., Anyone who attempts to burst my armor in the fight,
before I choose myself to unarm and rest, will be greeted by a storm
of blows.   **14 squire** armor-bearer of a knight   **15 tight** deft, skillful.
Dispatch Finish up.   **16–17 knew'st . . . occupation** (would that) you
could appreciate how excellently I carry out the royal art of warfare.
18 workman craftsman, professional   **19 charge** duty, responsibility.

To business that we love we rise betimes   20
And go to't with delight.
SOLDIER   A thousand, sir,
Early though 't be, have on their riveted trim   22
And at the port expect you.   *Shout. Trumpets flourish.* 23

Enter Captains and soldiers.

CAPTAIN
The morn is fair. Good morrow, General.
ALL
Good morrow, General.
ANTONY   'Tis well blown, lads.   25
This morning, like the spirit of a youth
That means to be of note, begins betimes.
So, so. Come, give me that. This way. Well said.   28
Fare thee well, dame. Whate'er becomes of me,
This is a soldier's kiss. [*He kisses her.*] Rebukable,
And worthy shameful check it were, to stand   31
On more mechanic compliment. I'll leave thee   32
Now like a man of steel.—You that will fight,
Follow me close. I'll bring you to't. Adieu.
        Exeunt [Antony, Eros, Captains, and soldiers].
CHARMIAN
Please you, retire to your chamber?
CLEOPATRA   Lead me.
He goes forth gallantly. That he and Caesar might
Determine this great war in single fight!
Then Antony—but now—Well, on.   *Exeunt.*

❖

[4.5]

*Trumpets sound. Enter Antony and Eros; [a
Soldier meeting them].*

SOLDIER
The gods make this a happy day to Antony!   1
ANTONY
Would thou and those thy scars had once prevailed   2
To make me fight at land!
SOLDIER   Hadst thou done so,
The kings that have revolted, and the soldier   4
That has this morning left thee, would have still
Followed thy heels.
ANTONY   Who's gone this morning?
SOLDIER   Who?
One ever near thee. Call for Enobarbus,
He shall not hear thee, or from Caesar's camp
Say, "I am none of thine."
ANTONY   What sayest thou?
SOLDIER   Sir,
He is with Caesar.
EROS   Sir, his chests and treasure

He has not with him.
ANTONY   Is he gone?
SOLDIER   Most certain.
ANTONY
Go, Eros, send his treasure after. Do it.
Detain no jot, I charge thee. Write to him—
I will subscribe—gentle adieus and greetings.   14
Say that I wish he never find more cause
To change a master. Oh, my fortunes have
Corrupted honest men! Dispatch.—Enobarbus!   17
                                    Exeunt.

❖

[4.6]

*Flourish. Enter Agrippa, Caesar, with Enobarbus,
and Dolabella.*

CAESAR
Go forth, Agrippa, and begin the fight.
Our will is Antony be took alive;
Make it so known.
AGRIPPA   Caesar, I shall.   [*Exit.*]
CAESAR
The time of universal peace is near.   5
Prove this a prosp'rous day, the three-nooked world   6
Shall bear the olive freely.

Enter a Messenger.

MESSENGER   Antony   7
Is come into the field.
CAESAR   Go charge Agrippa   8
Plant those that have revolted in the van,   9
That Antony may seem to spend his fury
Upon himself.   *Exeunt [all but Enobarbus].*
ENOBARBUS
Alexas did revolt and went to Jewry on   12
Affairs of Antony, there did dissuade   13
Great Herod to incline himself to Caesar
And leave his master Antony. For this pains,
Caesar hath hanged him. Canidius and the rest
That fell away have entertainment but   17
No honorable trust. I have done ill,
Of which I do accuse myself so sorely   19
That I will joy no more.

Enter a Soldier of Caesar's.

SOLDIER   Enobarbus, Antony
Hath after thee sent all thy treasure, with
His bounty overplus. The messenger   22

---

20 **betimes** early   22 **riveted trim** i.e., armor riveted into place
23 **port** gate   25 **'Tis well blown** i.e., The morning begins well. (Or,
refers to trumpets in line 23 s.d.)   28 **Well said** Well done.   31 **check**
reproof   31–2 **stand . . . compliment** insist on vulgar and routine ceremonies of leavetaking.
4.5. Location: Before Alexandria. Antony's camp.
1 **happy** fortunate   2 **once** formerly   4 **revolted** deserted

14 **subscribe** sign   17 **Dispatch** Make haste, get on with it.
4.6. Location: Before Alexandria. Caesar's camp.
5 **The . . . near** (The Renaissance identified Octavius Caesar, or the
Emperor Augustus as he was subsequently titled, with this *Pax
Romana*, peace under the Roman Empire.)   6 **Prove this** If this prove
to be.   **three-nooked** three-cornered. (Refers to Asia, Europe, and
Africa.)   7 **bear** (1) bring forth (2) wear as a triumphal garland.
olive symbol of peace   8 **charge Agrippa** order Agrippa to   9 **van**
vanguard, front lines   12 **Jewry** Judaea   13 **dissuade** i.e., from following Antony   17 **entertainment** employment, maintenance
19 **sorely** heavily   22 **overplus** in addition.

Came on my guard, and at thy tent is now   23
Unloading of his mules.

ENOBARBUS   I give it you.

SOLDIER   Mock not, Enobarbus,
I tell you true. Best you safed the bringer   27
Out of the host. I must attend mine office,   28
Or would have done't myself. Your emperor
Continues still a Jove.   *Exit.*

ENOBARBUS
I am alone the villain of the earth,   31
And feel I am so most. O Antony,   32
Thou mine of bounty, how wouldst thou have paid   33
My better service, when my turpitude
Thou dost so crown with gold! This blows my heart.   35
If swift thought break it not, a swifter mean   36
Shall outstrike thought; but thought will do't, I feel. 37
I fight against thee? No, I will go seek
Some ditch wherein to die. The foul'st best fits
My latter part of life.   *Exit.*

❧

[4.7]

*Alarum. Drums and trumpets. Enter Agrippa
[and others].*

AGRIPPA
Retire! We have engaged ourselves too far.
Caesar himself has work, and our oppression   2
Exceeds what we expected.   *Exeunt.*   3

Alarums. Enter Antony, and Scarus wounded.

SCARUS
O my brave Emperor, this is fought indeed!
Had we done so at first, we had droven them home   5
With clouts about their heads.

ANTONY   Thou bleed'st apace.   6

SCARUS
I had a wound here that was like a T,
But now 'tis made an H.   [*Sound retreat*] *far off.*

ANTONY   They do retire.   8

SCARUS
We'll beat 'em into bench holes. I have yet   9
Room for six scotches more.   10

Enter Eros.

EROS
They are beaten, sir, and our advantage serves   11
For a fair victory.

SCARUS   Let us score their backs   12
And snatch 'em up, as we take hares, behind!
'Tis sport to maul a runner.

ANTONY   I will reward thee   14
Once for thy spritely comfort and tenfold
For thy good valor. Come thee on.

SCARUS   I'll halt after.   *Exeunt.*   17

❧

[4.8]

*Alarum. Enter Antony again in a march; Scarus,
with others.*

ANTONY
We have beat him to his camp. Run one before   1
And let the Queen know of our gests. [*Exit a Soldier.*]
Tomorrow,   2
Before the sun shall see 's, we'll spill the blood
That has today escaped. I thank you all,
For doughty-handed are you, and have fought   5
Not as you served the cause, but as't had been   6
Each man's like mine; you have shown all Hectors.   7
Enter the city, clip your wives, your friends,   8
Tell them your feats, whilst they with joyful tears
Wash the congealment from your wounds and kiss
The honored gashes whole.

Enter Cleopatra [attended].

[*To Scarus*] Give me thy hand;
To this great fairy I'll commend thy acts,   12
Make her thanks bless thee. [*To Cleopatra*] O thou day
o'th' world,   13
Chain mine armed neck; leap thou, attire and all,   14
Through proof of harness to my heart, and there   15
Ride on the pants triumphing!   [*They embrace.*]

CLEOPATRA   Lord of lords,   16
O infinite virtue, com'st thou smiling from   17
The world's great snare uncaught?

ANTONY   My nightingale,
We have beat them to their beds. What, girl, though
gray
Do something mingle with our younger brown, yet
ha' we   20
A brain that nourishes our nerves and can   21

---

23 on my guard while I was standing guard   **27 Best you safed** You
would do well to provide safe-conduct for   **28 host** army.   **attend
mine office** see to my duties   **31 alone the** the only, the greatest
32 And . . . most and am the one who feels it most.   **33 mine** abundant
dant store   **35 blows** causes to swell to the bursting point   **36 mean**
i.e., suicide   **37 thought** melancholy.   **do't** i.e., break my heart
4.7. Location: Field of battle between the camps.
2 has work is hard pressed.   **our oppression** the heavy attacks
against us   **3 s.d.** *Exeunt* (The cleared stage technically marks a new
scene, although the alarums provide a sense of continuous action.)
5 droven driven   **6 clouts** (1) bandages (2) blows and knocks
8 H i.e., the bottom of the T has been cut across to make an H lying
on its side. (There is a pun on *ache,* pronounced *aitch.*)   **9 bench
holes** the holes of privies, i.e., any desperate place to hide.
10 scotches cuts

11–12 our . . . victory i.e., we are in such a favorable position that a
complete victory seems in prospect.   **12 score** mark by cuts from a
whip   **14 a runner** one in retreat.   **17 halt** limp
4.8. Location: Before Alexandria. The action is virtually continuous.
1 beat driven.   **Run one** Let someone run   **2 gests** deeds.
5 doughty-handed valiant   **6–7 Not . . . mine** not as if you were
merely serving the general cause, but as if it were your cause personally
ally   **7 shown** shown yourselves   **8 clip** embrace   **12 fairy**
enchantress, dispenser of good fortune   **13 day** light   **14 Chain . . .
neck** hang around my neck in an embrace like a medal on a chain
15 proof of harness proof-armor, tested armor   **16 pants** heartbeats
17 virtue valor   **20 something** somewhat   **21 nerves** sinews, tendons

Get goal for goal of youth. Behold this man;   22
Commend unto his lips thy favoring hand.—   23
Kiss it, my warrior. [*Scarus kisses Cleopatra's hand.*] He
    hath fought today
As if a god, in hate of mankind, had
Destroyed in such a shape.

CLEOPATRA   I'll give thee, friend,
An armor all of gold; it was a king's.

ANTONY
He has deserved it, were it carbuncled   28
Like holy Phoebus' car. Give me thy hand.   29
Through Alexandria make a jolly march;
Bear our hacked targets like the men that owe them.   31
Had our great palace the capacity
To camp this host, we all would sup together   33
And drink carouses to the next day's fate,   34
Which promises royal peril. Trumpeters,   35
With brazen din blast you the city's ear;
Make mingle with our rattling taborins,   37
That heaven and earth may strike their sounds
    together,   38
Applauding our approach. [*Trumpets sound.*] *Exeunt.*

❖

[4.9]

*Enter a Sentry and his company. Enobarbus
follows.*

SENTRY
If we be not relieved within this hour,
We must return to th' court of guard. The night   2
Is shiny, and they say we shall embattle   3
By the second hour i'th' morn.

FIRST WATCH   This last day was a shrewd one to 's.   5

ENOBARBUS   Oh, bear me witness, night—

SECOND WATCH
What man is this?

FIRST WATCH   Stand close, and list him.   8
                            [*They stand aside.*]

ENOBARBUS
Be witness to me, O thou blessèd moon,
When men revolted shall upon record   10
Bear hateful memory: poor Enobarbus did
Before thy face repent.

SENTRY   Enobarbus?

SECOND WATCH   Peace! Hark further.

ENOBARBUS
O sovereign mistress of true melancholy,
The poisonous damp of night disponge upon me,   15
That life, a very rebel to my will,   16
May hang no longer on me. Throw my heart
Against the flint and hardness of my fault,
Which, being dried with grief, will break to powder   20
And finish all foul thoughts. O Antony,
Nobler than my revolt is infamous,
Forgive me in thine own particular,   23
But let the world rank me in register   24
A master-leaver and a fugitive.   25
O Antony! O Antony!   [*He dies.*]

FIRST WATCH   Let's speak to him.

SENTRY
Let's hear him, for the things he speaks
May concern Caesar.

SECOND WATCH   Let's do so. But he sleeps.

SENTRY
Swoons rather, for so bad a prayer as his
Was never yet for sleep.

FIRST WATCH   Go we to him.   31
                    [*They approach Enobarbus.*]

SECOND WATCH   Awake, sir, awake. Speak to us.

FIRST WATCH   Hear you, sir?

SENTRY   The hand of death hath raught him.   34
                            Drums afar off.
Hark, the drums demurely wake the sleepers.   35
Let us bear him to th' court of guard;
He is of note. Our hour is fully out.   37

SECOND WATCH
Come on, then. He may recover yet.

                    Exeunt [*with the body*].

❖

[4.10]

Enter Antony and Scarus, with their army.

ANTONY
Their preparation is today by sea;
We please them not by land.

SCARUS   For both, my lord.

ANTONY
I would they'd fight i'th' fire or i'th'air;   3
We'd fight there too. But this it is: our foot   4
Upon the hills adjoining to the city
Shall stay with us—order for sea is given;   6

22 Get . . . of i.e., stay competitively equal with.   **this man** i.e., Scarus
23 Commend Entrust, commit   **28 carbuncled** set with jewels
29 Phoebus' car the chariot of the sun.   **31 Bear . . . them** bear our
hacked shields, well suited to the warriors who, like their shields,
have sustained blows. (*Owe* means "own.")   **33 camp this host**
accommodate this army   **34 carouses** toasts   **35 royal peril** i.e., war,
the sport of monarchs.   **37 taborins** drums   **38 That . . . together** i.e.,
that the heavens may echo and augment the loud noise of the drums
4.9 Location: Caesar's camp.
2 court of guard guardroom.   **3 shiny** bright, moonlit.   **embattle**
assemble for the combat   **5 shrewd** unlucky   **8 close** concealed.
list listen to   **10 revolted** who have broken their allegiance.   **upon
record** in the record of history

15 mistress . . . melancholy i.e., the moon, so addressed because of
her supposed influence in causing lunacy   **16 disponge** pour down
(as from a squeezed sponge)   **20 Which** i.e., the heart.   **dried with
grief** (Cold and melancholy blood was thought to strangle and dry
up the heart.)   **23 in . . . particular** in your own person   **24 rank me
in register** put me down in its records   **25 master-leaver** (1) one who
deserts his master (2) nonpareil of deserters.   **fugitive** deserter.
31 for a prelude to   **34 raught** reached   **35 demurely** with solemn
sound   **37 of note** of rank.
4.10 Location: The field of battle.
3 fire . . . air (Along with earth and water, where Antony is already
prepared, fire and air make up the traditional four elements of all
matter.)   **4 foot** foot soldiers   **6 for sea** to fight at sea

They have put forth the haven—   7
Where their appointment we may best discover   8
And look on their endeavor.   *Exeunt.*

❧

[4.11]

Enter Caesar and his army.

CAESAR
But being charged, we will be still by land,   1
Which, as I take't, we shall; for his best force   2
Is forth to man his galleys. To the vales,   3
And hold our best advantage.   *Exeunt.*   4

❧

[4.12]

Enter Antony and Scarus.

ANTONY
Yet they are not joined. Where yond pine does stand,
I shall discover all. I'll bring thee word
Straight how 'tis like to go.   *Exit.*
Alarum afar off, as at a sea fight.
SCARUS   Swallows have built   3
In Cleopatra's sails their nests. The augurers   4
Say they know not, they cannot tell, look grimly,
And dare not speak their knowledge. Antony
Is valiant, and dejected, and by starts
His fretted fortunes give him hope and fear   8
Of what he has and has not.

Enter Antony.

ANTONY   All is lost!
This foul Egyptian hath betrayèd me.
My fleet hath yielded to the foe, and yonder
They cast their caps up and carouse together
Like friends long lost. Triple-turned whore! 'Tis thou   13
Hast sold me to this novice, and my heart
Makes only wars on thee. Bid them all fly;
For when I am revenged upon my charm,   16
I have done all. Bid them all fly. Begone!
[Exit Scarus.]
O sun, thy uprise shall I see no more.
Fortune and Antony part here; even here
Do we shake hands. All come to this? The hearts   20
That spanieled me at heels, to whom I gave   21
Their wishes, do discandy, melt their sweets   22

On blossoming Caesar; and this pine is barked   23
That overtopped them all. Betrayed I am.
Oh, this false soul of Egypt! This grave charm,   25
Whose eye becked forth my wars and called them
home,   26
Whose bosom was my crownet, my chief end,   27
Like a right gypsy hath at fast and loose   28
Beguiled me to the very heart of loss.   29
[Calling] What, Eros, Eros!

Enter Cleopatra.

Ah, thou spell! Avaunt!   30
CLEOPATRA
Why is my lord enraged against his love?
ANTONY
Vanish, or I shall give thee thy deserving
And blemish Caesar's triumph. Let him take thee   33
And hoist thee up to the shouting plebeians!
Follow his chariot, like the greatest spot   35
Of all thy sex; most monsterlike be shown   36
For poor'st diminutives, for dolts, and let   37
Patient Octavia plow thy visage up
With her preparèd nails!   *Exit Cleopatra.*
'Tis well thou'rt gone,
If it be well to live; but better 'twere
Thou fell'st into my fury, for one death   41
Might have prevented many.—Eros, ho!—   42
The shirt of Nessus is upon me. Teach me,   43
Alcides, thou mine ancestor, thy rage.   44
Let me lodge Lichas on the horns o'th' moon,   45
And with those hands, that grasped the heaviest club,
Subdue my worthiest self. The witch shall die.
To the young Roman boy she hath sold me, and I fall
Under this plot. She dies for't.—Eros, ho!   *Exit.*

❧

[4.13]

Enter Cleopatra, Charmian, Iras, [and] Mardian.

CLEOPATRA
Help me, my women! Oh, he's more mad

---

7 forth forth from   **8 appointment** disposition of forces, equipment.
discover descry
4.11. Location: The field of battle.
1 But being Unless we are.   **still** inactive   **2 we shall** i.e., we will be
left undistrubed   **3 Is forth** has gone forth.   **vales** valleys   **4 hold . . .**
advantage take the most advantageous position.
4.12 Location: The field of battle at first, though by scene's end the
action appears to be located in Alexandria.
3 Straight immediately.   **like** likely   **4 augurers** augurs, soothsayers
8 fretted worn away, vexed, checkered   **13 Triple-turned** Three times
faithless (to Julius Caesar, Gnaeus Pompey, and now Antony)
16 charm practicer of charms or spells   **20 shake hands** i.e., in parting.   **hearts** good fellows   **21 spanieled** fawned upon like a spaniel
22 Their wishes whatever they wished.   **discandy** melt, dissolve

23 this pine i.e., Antony.   **barked** stripped of its bark and thus killed
25 This grave charm i.e., This sorceress who casts fatal spells
26 becked beckoned   **27 Whose . . . end** whose embraces were the
crown of my achievement and my goal   **28 right** veritable.   **fast and**
loose a cheating game in which the victim bets that he can make fast
a knot in an ingeniously coiled rope, whereupon the knot is pulled
loose   **29 loss** ruin.   **30 spell** enchantment.   **Avaunt!** Begone!
33 blemish Caesar's triumph i.e., mutilate you and thereby frustrate
Caesar's plan to display you in his triumphal procession into Rome.
35 spot blemish, disgrace   **36 shown** exhibited   **37 diminutives**
underlings, i.e., the populace   **41 Thou fell'st into** you had fallen a
victim to   **42 many** i.e., many other deaths resulting from my rage.
43–5 Nessus . . . Lichas (When Hercules or *Alcides* had fatally
wounded the centaur *Nessus* for trying to rape Hercules's wife
Deianira, Nessus vengefully gave his blood-soaked shirt to Deianira
as a supposed love charm for her husband. The poison gave Hercules
such agony that he cast his page *Lichas* into the air.)
4.13 Location: Alexandria. This scene appears to follow scene 12
closely. The sense of location is very fluid, and it is not clear where
the end of scene 12 takes place.

Than Telamon for his shield; the boar of Thessaly   2
Was never so embossed.
CHARMIAN   To th' monument!   3
There lock yourself and send him word you are dead.
The soul and body rive not more in parting   5
Than greatness going off.
CLEOPATRA   To th' monument!   6
Mardian, go tell him I have slain myself.
Say that the last I spoke was "Antony,"
And word it, prithee, piteously. Hence, Mardian,
And bring me how he takes my death. To th'
monument!   *Exeut.*

❧

[4.14]

Enter Antony and Eros.

ANTONY
Eros, thou yet behold'st me?
EROS   Ay, noble lord.
ANTONY
Sometime we see a cloud that's dragonish,   2
A vapor sometime like a bear or lion,
A towered citadel, a pendant rock,
A forkèd mountain, or blue promontory   4
With trees upon't that nod unto the world
And mock our eyes with air. Thou hast seen these
signs;
They are black vesper's pageants.
EROS   Ay, my lord.   8
ANTONY
That which is now a horse, even with a thought
The rack dislimns and makes it indistinct
As water is in water.   10
EROS   It does, my lord.
ANTONY
My good knave Eros, now thy captain is   12
Even such a body. Here I am Antony,
Yet cannot hold this visible shape, my knave.
I made these wars for Egypt, and the Queen,
Whose heart I thought I had, for she had mine—
Which whilst it was mine had annexed unto't
A million more, now lost—she, Eros, has
Packed cards with Caesar and false-played my glory   19
Unto an enemy's triumph.   20

Nay, weep not, gentle Eros. There is left us
Ourselves to end ourselves.

Enter Mardian.

                        Oh, thy vile lady!
She has robbed me of my sword.
MARDIAN   No, Antony,   23
My mistress loved thee, and her fortunes mingled
With thine entirely.
ANTONY   Hence, saucy eunuch, peace!
She hath betrayed me and shall die the death.   26
MARDIAN
Death of one person can be paid but once,   27
And that she has discharged. What thou wouldst do   28
Is done unto thy hand. The last she spake   29
Was, "Antony, most noble Antony!"
Then in the midst a tearing groan did break
The name of Antony; it was divided   32
Between her heart and lips. She rendered life   33
Thy name so buried in her.
ANTONY   Dead, then?
MARDIAN   Dead.   34
ANTONY
Unarm, Eros. The long day's task is done,
And we must sleep. [*To Mardian*] That thou depart'st
hence safe
Does pay thy labor richly; go.   *Exit Mardian.*
                        Off, pluck off! [*Eros unarms him.*]
The sevenfold shield of Ajax cannot keep   38
The battery from my heart. Oh, cleave, my sides!   39
Heart, once be stronger than thy continent;   40
Crack thy frail case! Apace, Eros, apace.   41
No more a soldier. Bruisèd pieces, go;
You have been nobly borne.—From me awhile.   43
                        Exit Eros.
I will o'ertake thee, Cleopatra, and
Weep for my pardon. So it must be, for now
All length is torture; since the torch is out,   46
Lie down, and stray no farther. Now all labor
Mars what it does; yea, very force entangles   48
Itself with strength. Seal then, and all is done.   49
Eros!—I come, my queen.—Eros!—Stay for me.   50
Where souls do couch on flowers, we'll hand in hand,   51
And with our sprightly port make the ghosts gaze.   52

2 Telamon Ajax Telamon, who after the capture of Troy went mad and slew himself when he was not awarded the shield and armor of Achilles.   **the boar of Thessaly** the boar sent by Diana or Artemis to ravage the fields of Calydon, slain by Meleager   **3 embossed** foaming at the mouth from rage and exhaustion.   **monument** tomb presumably built to house Cleopatra's royal remains after her death, like the pyramids.   **5 rive** split, sever   **6 going off** i.e., bidding farewell to its glory.
4.14 Location: Alexandria. (See location of scene 13; again, the sense of time is immediate and the place is fluid.)
2 dragonish shaped like a dragon   **4 pendant** overhanging   **8 black . . . pageants** i.e., the evanescent splendor of a sunset heralding the approach of night.   **10 The rack dislimns** the mass of cloud changes its shape   **12 knave** lad   **19 Packed cards** i.e., stacked the deck.   **false-played** falsely played away   **20 triumph** (1) victory (2) trump card.

23 sword i.e., prowess as a soldier, masculinity.   **26 die the death** be put to death.   **27 of** by   **28 discharged** paid.   **29 unto thy hand** for you, without your having to lift a finger.   **32–3 it . . . lips** i.e., she groaned out half of Antony's name and then died with the unspoken part in her heart only.   **33–4 She . . . in her** She gave back to Nature that part of your name thus buried in her heart.   **38 sevenfold** with seven thicknesses (The shield of Ajax was of brass reinforced with seven thicknesses of oxhide.)   **39 battery** battering   **40 thy continent** that which contains you   **41 Apace** Quickly   **43 From** Go from   **46 length** prolongation of life.   **the torch** i.e., the life of Cleopatra   **48 very force** any resolute action   **49 with strength** i.e., with its own strength.   **Seal** Finish the business (as in sealing a letter)   **50 Eros** (The meaning of Eros's name, erotic love, is especially apt here.)   **51 couch** lie (here, in the Elysian fields)   **52 sprightly** (1) high-spirited (2) spiritlike, ghostly.   **port** bearing

Dido and her Aeneas shall want troops,   53
And all the haunt be ours.—Come, Eros, Eros!   54

Enter Eros.

EROS
What would my lord?
ANTONY   Since Cleopatra died
I have lived in such dishonor that the gods
Detest my baseness. I, that with my sword
Quartered the world, and o'er green Neptune's back   58
With ships made cities, condemn myself to lack   59
The courage of a woman—less noble mind
Than she which by her death our Caesar tells
"I am conqueror of myself." Thou art sworn, Eros,
That when the exigent should come which now   63
Is come indeed, when I should see behind me
Th'inevitable prosecution of   65
Disgrace and horror, that on my command
Thou then wouldst kill me. Do't. The time is come.
Thou strik'st not me, 'tis Caesar thou defeat'st.
Put color in thy cheek.
EROS   The gods withhold me!   69
Shall I do that which all the Parthian darts,
Though enemy, lost aim and could not?
ANTONY   Eros,
Wouldst thou be windowed in great Rome and see   72
Thy master thus with pleached arms, bending down   73
His corrigible neck, his face subdued   74
To penetrative shame, whilst the wheeled seat   75
Of fortunate Caesar, drawn before him, branded   76
His baseness that ensued?
EROS   I would not see't.   77
ANTONY
Come, then, for with a wound I must be cured.
Draw that thy honest sword, which thou hast worn   79
Most useful for thy country.
EROS   Oh, sir, pardon me!   80
ANTONY
When I did make thee free, swor'st thou not then
To do this when I bade thee? Do it at once,
Or thy precedent services are all   83
But accidents unpurposed. Draw, and come.   84
EROS
Turn from me then that noble countenance

Wherein the worship of the whole world lies.   86
ANTONY   Lo thee!   [*He turns away.*]
EROS [*drawing his sword*]
My sword is drawn.
ANTONY   Then let it do at once
That thing why thou hast drawn it.
EROS   My dear master,
My captain, and my emperor, let me say,
Before I strike this bloody stroke, farewell.
ANTONY   'Tis said, man, and farewell.
EROS
Farewell, great chief. Shall I strike now?
ANTONY   Now, Eros.
EROS (*kills himself*)
Why, there then! Thus I do escape the sorrow
Of Antony's death.   [*He dies.*]
ANTONY   Thrice nobler than myself!
Thou teachest me, O valiant Eros, what
I should, and thou couldst not. My queen and Eros   97
Have by their brave instruction got upon me   98
A nobleness in record. But I will be   99
A bridegroom in my death, and run into't
As to a lover's bed. Come, then, and Eros,
Thy master dies thy scholar. To do thus
I learned of thee.   [*He falls on his sword.*]
                  How, not dead? Not dead?
The guard, ho! Oh, dispatch me!   104

Enter [Dercetus and others of] a Guard.

FIRST GUARD   What's the noise?
ANTONY   I have done my work ill, friends.
Oh, make an end of what I have begun!
SECOND GUARD   The star is fallen.
FIRST GUARD   And time is at his period.   109
ALL   Alas, and woe!
ANTONY   Let him that loves me strike me dead.
FIRST GUARD   Not I.
SECOND GUARD   Nor I.
THIRD GUARD   Nor anyone.   *Exeunt [Guard].*
DERCETUS
Thy death and fortunes bid thy followers fly.
This sword but shown to Caesar, with this tidings,
Shall enter me with him. [*He takes up Antony's sword.*]   117

Enter Diomedes.

DIOMEDES   Where's Antony?
DERCETUS   There, Diomed, there.
DIOMEDES
Lives he? Wilt thou not answer, man? [*Exit Dercetus.*]
ANTONY
Art thou there, Diomed? Draw thy sword and give me
Sufficing strokes for death.
DIOMEDES   Most absolute lord,
My mistress Cleopatra sent me to thee.

---

53 **Dido . . . troops** We will be the most distinguished lovers in the Elysian fields, outshining even the Queen of Carthage and her famous lover. (In the *Aeneid*, Aeneas deserts Dido in order to found Rome, putting public good ahead of private passion as Antony does not. Dido scorns Aeneas when they meet in the underworld; Antony here imagines himself and Cleopatra in the Elysian fields.) **want troops** lack followers **54 all . . . ours** i.e., we shall be the objects of everyone's attention. **58–9 Quartered . . . cities** divided and conquered the world, and at sea assembled flotillas as dense and populous as cities **59 to lack** for lacking **63 exigent** exigency, time of compelling need **65 prosecution** consequence **69 The gods withhold me!** i.e., God forbid! **72 windowed** placed as in a window **73 pleached** folded or bound **74 corrigible** submissive to correction **75 penetrative** penetrating. **wheeled seat** chariot **76–7 branded . . . ensued** stigmatized, as by a brand, the shame of him that followed. **79 honest** honorable **80 pardon me!** excuse me from doing this! **83 precedent** former **84 accidents unpurposed** events leading to no purpose.

86 **worship** honor, worth **97 I should . . . not** I should have done for myself and you couldn't do for me. **98–9 got . . . record** won a noble place in history before I have. **104 dispatch** finish **109 his period** its end. **117 enter . . . him** admit me to his service, put me in his good graces.

ANTONY
When did she send thee?
DIOMEDES   Now, my lord.
ANTONY   Where is she?
DIOMEDES
Locked in her monument. She had a prophesying fear
Of what hath come to pass. For when she saw—
Which never shall be found—you did suspect   127
She had disposed with Caesar, and that your rage   128
Would not be purged, she sent you word she was
    dead;
But, fearing since how it might work, hath sent
Me to proclaim the truth, and I am come,
I dread, too late.
ANTONY
Too late, good Diomed. Call my guard, I prithee.
DIOMEDES [calling]
What ho, the Emperor's guard! The guard, what ho!
Come, your lord calls.

        Enter four or five of the Guard of Antony.

ANTONY
Bear me, good friends, where Cleopatra bides.   136
'Tis the last service that I shall command you.
FIRST GUARD
Woe, woe are we, sir, you may not live to wear   138
All your true followers out.
ALL   Most heavy day!   139
ANTONY
Nay, good my fellows, do not please sharp fate
To grace it with your sorrows. Bid that welcome   141
Which comes to punish us, and we punish it,
Seeming to bear it lightly. Take me up.
I have led you oft; carry me now, good friends,
And have my thanks for all.
        Exeunt, bearing Antony [and Eros].

                    ❧

[4.15]

        Enter Cleopatra and her maids aloft, with
        Charmian and Iras.

CLEOPATRA
Oh, Charmian, I will never go from hence.
CHARMIAN
Be comforted, dear madam.
CLEOPATRA   No, I will not.
All strange and terrible events are welcome,
But comforts we despise. Our size of sorrow,
Proportioned to our cause, must be as great
As that which makes it.

        Enter [below] Diomedes.

                    How now? Is he dead?

DIOMEDES
His death's upon him, but not dead.
Look out o'th'other side your monument;
His guard have brought him thither.

        Enter [below] Antony, and the Guard
        [bearing him].

CLEOPATRA   O sun,
Burn the great sphere thou mov'st in; darkling stand 11
The varying shore o'th' world! O Antony,
Antony, Antony! Help, Charmian, help, Iras, help!
Help, friends below! Let's draw him hither.
ANTONY   Peace!
Not Caesar's valor hath o'erthrown Antony,
But Antony's hath triumphed on itself.
CLEOPATRA
So it should be, that none but Antony
Should conquer Antony; but woe 'tis so!
ANTONY
I am dying, Egypt, dying. Only
I here importune death awhile, until   20
Of many thousand kisses the poor last
I lay upon thy lips.
CLEOPATRA   I dare not, dear—   22
Dear my lord, pardon—I dare not,
Lest I be taken. Not th'imperious show   24
Of the full-fortuned Caesar ever shall
Be brooched with me. If knife, drugs, serpents, have 26
Edge, sting, or operation, I am safe.   27
Your wife Octavia, with her modest eyes
And still conclusion, shall acquire no honor   29
Demuring upon me. But come, come, Antony—   30
Help me, my women—we must draw thee up.
Assist, good friends.
ANTONY   Oh, quick, or I am gone.
                        [They begin lifting.]
CLEOPATRA
Here's sport indeed! How heavy weighs my lord!
Our strength is all gone into heaviness,   34
That makes the weight. Had I great Juno's power,
The strong-winged Mercury should fetch thee up
And set thee by Jove's side. Yet come a little;
Wishers were ever fools. Oh, come, come, come!   38
        They heave Antony aloft to Cleopatra.
And welcome, welcome! Die when thou hast lived;   39
Quicken with kissing. Had my lips that power,   40
Thus would I wear them out.   [She kisses him.]
ALL   A heavy sight!   42
ANTONY   I am dying, Egypt, dying.
Give me some wine, and let me speak a little.

---

127 **found** found true   128 **disposed with** come to terms with
136 **bides** abides, dwells.   138–9 **live . . . out** outlive those that serve
you.   141 **To grace** by gracing or honoring
4.15. Location: Alexandria. Cleopatra's monument.
0.1 *aloft* in the gallery above the main stage

11 **sphere** concentric sphere in which, according to Ptolemaic astronomy, the sun moved about the earth as did the planets and stars.
darkling in darkness   20 **importune** i.e., beg a delay of   22 **I dare
not** i.e., I dare not come down   24 **th'imperious show** the imperial
triumphal procession   26 **brooched** adorned (as with a brooch)
27 **operation** power, efficacy   29 **still conclusion** silent judgment
30 **Demuring** looking demurely   34 **heaviness** (1) sadness (2) weight
38 **Wishers . . . fools** Those who wish for things are always fools.
39 **Die . . . lived** i.e., Die after living intensely. (With a pun on *die* suggesting sexual consummation; hence *Quicken* in line 40.)   40 **Quicken**
revive   42 **heavy** doleful

CLEOPATRA
No, let me speak, and let me rail so high
That the false huswife Fortune break her wheel,   46
Provoked by my offense.
ANTONY   One word, sweet Queen: 47
Of Caesar seek your honor, with your safety. Oh!   48
CLEOPATRA
They do not go together.
ANTONY   Gentle, hear me.
None about Caesar trust but Proculeius.
CLEOPATRA
My resolution and my hands I'll trust,
None about Caesar.
ANTONY
The miserable change now at my end
Lament nor sorrow at, but please your thoughts   54
In feeding them with those my former fortunes,
Wherein I lived the greatest prince o'th' world,
The noblest; and do now not basely die,
Not cowardly put off my helmet to
My countryman—a Roman by a Roman
Valiantly vanquished. Now my spirit is going;
I can no more.
CLEOPATRA   Noblest of men, woo't die?   61
Hast thou no care of me? Shall I abide
In this dull world, which in thy absence is
No better than a sty? [*Antony dies.*] Oh, see, my
                women,
The crown o'th'earth doth melt. My lord!
Oh, withered is the garland of the war;
The soldier's pole is fall'n! Young boys and girls   67
Are level now with men. The odds is gone,   68
And there is nothing left remarkable
Beneath the visiting moon.   [*She faints.*]
CHARMIAN   Oh, quietness, lady!
IRAS   She's dead too, our sovereign.
CHARMIAN   Lady!
IRAS   Madam!
CHARMIAN   Oh, madam, madam, madam!
IRAS   Royal Egypt, Empress!   [*Cleopatra stirs.*]
CHARMIAN   Peace, peace, Iras.
CLEOPATRA
No more but e'en a woman, and commanded
By such poor passion as the maid that milks
And does the meanest chares. It were for me   80
To throw my scepter at the injurious gods,
To tell them that this world did equal theirs
Till they had stol'n our jewel. All's but naught;
Patience is sottish, and impatience does   84
Become a dog that's mad. Then is it sin   85
To rush into the secret house of death
Ere death dare come to us? How do you, women?

What, what, good cheer! Why, how now, Charmian?
My noble girls! Ah, women, women! Look,
Our lamp is spent, it's out. Good sirs, take heart.   90
We'll bury him; and then, what's brave, what's noble,   91
Let's do't after the high Roman fashion
And make death proud to take us. Come, away.
This case of that huge spirit now is cold.
Ah, women, women! Come. We have no friend
But resolution, and the briefest end.   96

Exeunt, [those above] bearing off Antony's body.

♣

[5.1]

Enter Caesar, Agrippa, Dolabella, Maecenas,
[Gallus, Proculeius,] with his council of war.

CAESAR
Go to him, Dolabella, bid him yield;
Being so frustrate, tell him, he mocks   2
The pauses that he makes.
DOLABELLA   Caesar, I shall.   [*Exit.*]   3

Enter Dercetus, with the sword of Antony.

CAESAR
Wherefore is that? And what art thou that dar'st
Appear thus to us?
DERCETUS   I am called Dercetus.
Mark Antony I served, who best was worthy
Best to be served. Whilst he stood up and spoke
He was my master, and I wore my life
To spend upon his haters. If thou please   9
To take me to thee, as I was to him
I'll be to Caesar; if thou pleasest not,
I yield thee up my life.
CAESAR   What is't thou say'st?
DERCETUS
I say, O Caesar, Antony is dead.
CAESAR
The breaking of so great a thing should make   14
A greater crack. The round world   15
Should have shook lions into civil streets   16
And citizens to their dens. The death of Antony   17
Is not a single doom; in the name lay   18
A moiety of the world.
DERCETUS   He is dead, Caesar,   19
Not by a public minister of justice,
Nor by a hirèd knife; but that self hand   21
Which writ his honor in the acts it did
Hath, with the courage which the heart did lend it,

---

46 false huswife treacherous hussy   **47 offense** offensive speech.
48 Of from   **54 Lament** i.e., neither lament   **61 woo't** wilt thou
67 pole polestar or battle standard. (Probably with a suggestion of a
sexual potency now withered and fallen through death.)   **68 The
odds is gone** The distinction between great and small has disappeared   **80 chares** chores, drudgery.   **were** would be fitting
84–5 Patience . . . mad i.e., Patience is for fools, and impatience is for
the mad; both are useless here.

90 Good sirs (Addressed to the women.)   **91 brave** fine   **96 briefest**
swiftest
5.1. Location: Alexandria. Caesar's camp.
2 frustrate helpless, baffled   **2–3 mocks . . . makes** makes himself
ridiculous by his delays (in yielding).   **9 spend** expend   **14 breaking** (1) destruction (2) disclosure   **15 crack** (1) cracking apart (2) loud
report.   **16 civil** city   **17 their** i.e., the lions', or else, the citizens
scurry to safety indoors, in their own "dens." (In either case, nature is
inverted in a kind of disorder that earlier accompanied the death of
Julius Caesar.)   **18 Is . . . doom** i.e., signifies the death and destruction of much more than a single man   **19 moiety** half   **21 self** same

Splitted the heart. This is his sword.
[He offers the sword.]
I robbed his wound of it. Behold it stained
With his most noble blood.

CAESAR   Look you sad, friends?
The gods rebuke me, but it is tidings   27
To wash the eyes of kings.

AGRIPPA   And strange it is
That nature must compel us to lament
Our most persisted deeds.

MAECENAS   His taints and honors   30
Waged equal with him.

AGRIPPA   A rarer spirit never   31
Did steer humanity; but you gods will give us   32
Some faults to make us men. Caesar is touched.

MAECENAS
When such a spacious mirror's set before him,
He needs must see himself.

CAESAR   O Antony,
I have followed thee to this; but we do launch   36
Diseases in our bodies. I must perforce   37
Have shown to thee such a declining day,   38
Or look on thine; we could not stall together   39
In the whole world. But yet let me lament
With tears as sovereign as the blood of hearts   41
That thou, my brother, my competitor   42
In top of all design, my mate in empire,   43
Friend and companion in the front of war,   44
The arm of mine own body, and the heart   45
Where mine his thoughts did kindle—that our stars,   46
Unreconciliable, should divide   47
Our equalness to this. Hear me, good friends—   48

Enter an Egyptian.

But I will tell you at some meeter season.   49
The business of this man looks out of him;   50
We'll hear him what he says.—Whence are you?   51

EGYPTIAN
A poor Egyptian yet, the Queen my mistress,   52
Confined in all she has, her monument,
Of thy intents desires instruction,
That she preparedly may frame herself   55
To th' way she's forced to.

CAESAR   Bid her have good heart.
She soon shall know of us, by some of ours,   57

How honorable and how kindly we
Determine for her; for Caesar cannot live
To be ungentle.

EGYPTIAN   So the gods preserve thee!   *Exit.*

CAESAR
Come hither, Proculeius. Go and say
We purpose her no shame. Give her what comforts   62
The quality of her passion shall require,   63
Lest, in her greatness, by some mortal stroke   64
She do defeat us; for her life in Rome   65
Would be eternal in our triumph. Go,   66
And with your speediest bring us what she says   67
And how you find of her.

PROCULEIUS   Caesar, I shall.   68
Exit Proculeius.

CAESAR   Gallus, go you along.   [*Exit Gallus.*]
                        Where's Dolabella,
To second Proculeius?

ALL   Dolabella!

CAESAR
Let him alone, for I remember now   71
How he's employed. He shall in time be ready.
Go with me to my tent, where you shall see
How hardly I was drawn into this war,   74
How calm and gentle I proceeded still   75
In all my writings. Go with me and see   76
What I can show in this.   *Exeunt.*

❧

[5.2]

Enter Cleopatra, Charmian, Iras, and Mardian.

CLEOPATRA
My desolation does begin to make
A better life. 'Tis paltry to be Caesar;   2
Not being Fortune, he's but Fortune's knave,   3
A minister of her will. And it is great
To do that thing that ends all other deeds,   5
Which shackles accidents and bolts up change,   6
Which sleeps and never palates more the dung,   7
The beggar's nurse and Caesar's.   8
Enter [to the gates of the monument] Proculeius.

PROCULEIUS
Caesar sends greeting to the Queen of Egypt,
And bids thee study on what fair demands   10
Thou mean'st to have him grant thee.

CLEOPATRA   What's thy name?

---

27 but it is if it is not   **30 persisted** persistently desired or pursued   **31 Waged equal with** battled equally in   **32 steer humanity** govern any individual.   **will give** insist on giving   **36 followed** pursued   **36–7 but . . . bodies** i.e., I have hurt you to cure myself, as men lance diseases in their own bodies   **37 perforce** necessarily   **38 shown to thee** i.e., suffered myself at your hands   **39 stall** dwell   **41 as sovereign . . . hearts** as precious or efficacious as heart's blood   **42 competitor** associate, partner (and rival)   **43 In . . . design** at the head of every grand enterprise   **44 front** forehead, face   **45–6 the heart . . . kindle** the brave heart where my heart kindled its (*his*) thoughts of courage   **47–8 should . . . this** should divide our equal partnership to this extreme.   **49 meeter season** more suitable time.   **50 looks . . . him** reveals itself in his expression   **51 Whence are you?** Where do you come from?   **52 A . . . yet** i.e., Egyptian Cleopatra, still reduced in circumstance (and awaiting your will), or, I am a poor Egyptian still, though subject to Rome's authority   **55 frame herself** shape her course of action   **57 ours** my people

62 purpose intend   **63 passion** grief   **64 greatness** greatness of spirit   **65 life in Rome** presence in Rome alive   **66 eternal in our triumph** an eternal glory in my triumphal procession.   **67 with your speediest** as quickly as you can   **68 of** concerning   **71 Let him alone** Don't bother about him now   **74 hardly** reluctantly   **75 still** always   **76 writings** i.e., letters to Antony.
5.2. Location: Alexandria. Cleopatra's monument.
2 better i.e., rising above the vicissitudes of fortune   **3 knave** servant   **5–8 To do . . . Caesar's** i.e., to commit suicide, a sleep that arrests accident and change, and in which the sleeper relishes no more the dungy earth that sustains both Caesar and the beggar.   **10 study on** consider carefully

PROCULEIUS
My name is Proculeius.

CLEOPATRA   Antony
Did tell me of you, bade me trust you; but
I do not greatly care to be deceived,   14
That have no use for trusting. If your master   15
Would have a queen his beggar, you must tell him
That majesty, to keep decorum, must
No less beg than a kingdom. If he please
To give me conquered Egypt for my son,
He gives me so much of mine own as I   20
Will kneel to him with thanks.

PROCULEIUS   Be of good cheer;
You're fall'n into a princely hand. Fear nothing.
Make your full reference freely to my lord,   23
Who is so full of grace that it flows over
On all that need. Let me report to him
Your sweet dependency, and you shall find   26
A conqueror that will pray in aid for kindness   27
Where he for grace is kneeled to.

CLEOPATRA   Pray you, tell him
I am his fortune's vassal, and I send him   29
The greatness he has got. I hourly learn   30
A doctrine of obedience, and would gladly
Look him i'th' face.

PROCULEIUS   This I'll report, dear lady.
Have comfort, for I know your plight is pitied
Of him that caused it.   34
          [Roman soldiers enter from
          behind Cleopatra and take her prisoner.]
You see how easily she may be surprised.
[To the soldiers] Guard her till Caesar come.

IRAS   Royal Queen!

CHARMIAN
Oh, Cleopatra! Thou art taken, Queen.

CLEOPATRA [drawing a dagger]
Quick, quick, good hands.

PROCULEIUS   Hold, worthy lady, hold!
                              [He disarms her.]
Do not yourself such wrong, who are in this
Relieved, but not betrayed.

CLEOPATRA   What, of death too,   40
That rids our dogs of languish?

PROCULEIUS   Cleopatra,   41
Do not abuse my master's bounty by
Th'undoing of yourself. Let the world see
His nobleness well acted, which your death   44
Will never let come forth.

CLEOPATRA   Where art thou, Death?   45
Come hither, come! Come, come, and take a queen

Worth many babes and beggars!

PROCULEIUS   Oh, temperance, lady!   47

CLEOPATRA
Sir, I will eat no meat, I'll not drink, sir;
If idle talk will once be necessary,   49
I'll not sleep, neither. This mortal house I'll ruin,
Do Caesar what he can. Know, sir, that I
Will not wait pinioned at your master's court,   52
Nor once be chastised with the sober eye
Of dull Octavia. Shall they hoist me up
And show me to the shouting varletry   55
Of censuring Rome? Rather a ditch in Egypt
Be gentle grave unto me! Rather on Nilus' mud
Lay me stark nak'd and let the waterflies
Blow me into abhorring! Rather make   59
My country's high pyramides my gibbet   60
And hang me up in chains!

PROCULEIUS   You do extend
These thoughts of horror further than you shall
Find cause in Caesar.

          Enter Dolabella.

DOLABELLA   Proculeius,
What thou hast done thy master Caesar knows,
And he hath sent for thee. For the Queen,   65
I'll take her to my guard.

PROCULEIUS   So, Dolabella,
It shall content me best. Be gentle to her.
[To Cleopatra] To Caesar I will speak what you shall
     please,   68
If you'll employ me to him.

CLEOPATRA   Say I would die.
          Exit Proculeius [with soldiers].

DOLABELLA
Most noble Empress, you have heard of me?

CLEOPATRA
I cannot tell.

DOLABELLA   Assuredly you know me.

CLEOPATRA
No matter, sir, what I have heard or known.
You laugh when boys or women tell their dreams;
Is't not your trick?

DOLABELLA   I understand not, madam.   74

CLEOPATRA
I dreamt there was an emperor Antony.
Oh, such another sleep, that I might see
But such another man!

DOLABELLA   If it might please ye—

CLEOPATRA
His face was as the heavens, and therein stuck   78
A sun and moon, which kept their course and lighted

14 do . . . to be am wary of being   15 That since I   20 as that
23 Make . . . reference Refer your case   26 dependency submissiveness   27 pray . . . kindness beg your assistance to ensure that he may
omit no kindness   29–30 I send . . . got i.e., I acknowledge his superiority over all he has won, including myself.   34 Of by.   0.1 Roman
soldiers (Perhaps led by Gallus; see 5.1.69. Possibly some speech for
him has been omitted.)   40 Relieved rescued.   of death too i.e.,
(1) am I relieved or deprived even of death (2) am I betrayed even of the
right to die   41 our dogs of languish even our dogs of lingering disease.   44 acted accomplished   45 let come forth allow to be displayed.

47 babes and beggars i.e., those whom death takes easily and often.
49 If . . . necessary even if on occasion I must resort to idle talk (to
keep myself awake)   52 wait pinioned wait in attendance, like a bird
with clipped wings, unable to fly   55 varletry rabble   59 Blow . . .
abhorring cause me to swell abhorrently with maggots, or, deposit
their eggs on me until I become abhorrent.   60 gibbet gallows
65 For As for   68 what whatever   74 trick manner, way.   78 stuck
were set

The little O, the earth.

DOLABELLA   Most sovereign creature—

CLEOPATRA   His legs bestrid the ocean; his reared arm   81
Crested the world; his voice was propertied   82
As all the tunèd spheres, and that to friends;   83
But when he meant to quail and shake the orb,   84
He was as rattling thunder. For his bounty,   85
There was no winter in't; an autumn 'twas
That grew the more by reaping. His delights   87
Were dolphinlike; they showed his back above   88
The element they lived in. In his livery   89
Walked crowns and crownets; realms and islands
    were   90
As plates dropped from his pocket.

DOLABELLA   Cleopatra—   91

CLEOPATRA
Think you there was or might be such a man
As this I dreamt of?

DOLABELLA   Gentle madam, no.

CLEOPATRA
You lie, up to the hearing of the gods.
But if there be nor ever were one such,   95
It's past the size of dreaming. Nature wants stuff   96
To vie strange forms with fancy; yet t'imagine   97
An Antony were nature's piece 'gainst fancy,   98
Condemning shadows quite.

DOLABELLA   Hear me, good madam: 99
Your loss is as yourself, great; and you bear it
As answering to the weight. Would I might never   101
O'ertake pursued success but I do feel,   102
By the rebound of yours, a grief that smites
My very heart at root.

CLEOPATRA   I thank you, sir.
Know you what Caesar means to do with me?

DOLABELLA
I am loath to tell you what I would you knew.

CLEOPATRA
Nay, pray you, sir.

DOLABELLA   Though he be honorable—

CLEOPATRA   He'll lead me, then, in triumph.

DOLABELLA   Madam, he will, I know't.   *Flourish.*

*Enter Proculeius, Caesar, Gallus, Maecenas,
and others of his train.*

ALL   Make way there! Caesar!

CAESAR   Which is the Queen of Egypt?

DOLABELLA   It is the Emperor, madam.

                              Cleopatra kneels.

CAESAR   Arise, you shall not kneel. I pray you, rise.
Rise, Egypt.

CLEOPATRA [*rising*]   Sir, the gods will have it thus;
My master and my lord I must obey.

CAESAR   Take to you no hard thoughts.   116
The record of what injuries you did us,
Though written in our flesh, we shall remember
As things but done by chance.

CLEOPATRA   Sole sir o'th' world,   119
I cannot project mine own cause so well   120
To make it clear, but do confess I have   121
Been laden with like frailties which before
Have often shamed our sex.

CAESAR   Cleopatra, know
We will extenuate rather than enforce.   124
If you apply yourself to our intents,   125
Which towards you are most gentle, you shall find
A benefit in this change; but if you seek
To lay on me a cruelty by taking   128
Antony's course, you shall bereave yourself   129
Of my good purposes and put your children
To that destruction which I'll guard them from
If thereon you rely. I'll take my leave.

CLEOPATRA
And may, through all the world! 'Tis yours, and we,   133
Your scutcheons and your signs of conquest, shall   134
Hang in what place you please. Here, my good lord.   135
                    [*She gives him a scroll.*]

CAESAR
You shall advise me in all for Cleopatra.   136

CLEOPATRA
This is the brief of money, plate, and jewels   137
I am possessed of. 'Tis exactly valued,
Not petty things admitted. Where's Seleucus?   139

                    [*Enter Seleucus.*]

SELEUCUS   Here, madam.

CLEOPATRA
This is my treasurer. Let him speak, my lord,
Upon his peril, that I have reserved
To myself nothing.—Speak the truth, Seleucus.

SELEUCUS
Madam, I had rather seal my lips
Than to my peril speak that which is not.

CLEOPATRA   What have I kept back?

SELEUCUS
Enough to purchase what you have made known.

81 bestrid straddled (like the Colossus of Rhodes)   **82 Crested** surmounted   **82–3 propertied . . . friends** endowed with qualities
which, when he spoke to friends, recalled the harmony of the heavenly bodies in their spheres   **84 quail** make quail, overawe.   **orb**
world   **85 For** As for   **87–9 His . . . in** i.e., Like the dolphin sport-
fully rising up out of the sea, his pleasures arose out of the element in
which he lived, both glorying in and transcending that element.
89–90 In . . . crownets i.e., Among his retainers (those who would
wear his livery) were kings and princes   **91 plates** coins   **95 nor
ever were** or if there never existed   **96 It's . . . dreaming** no dream
can come up to it, my image of him.   **96–9 Nature . . . quite** Nature
lacks material to equal the remarkable forms produced by fancy or
imagination; yet an Antony such as I have pictured forth would himself be a work of nature, in fact Nature's masterpiece in
competition with the imagination.   **101 As . . . weight** commensurate
with the weightiness of the loss.   **101–2 Would . . . feel** May I never
succeed at what I desire if I do not feel

116 Take . . . thoughts Don't torment yourself with reproaches.
119 sir master   **120 project** set forth   **121 clear** free of blame
124 enforce press home.   **125 If . . . intents** If you comply with my
plans   **128 lay . . . cruelty** force me to be cruel   **129 bereave** rob
133 And may i.e., (1) You may leave when you choose (2) You may
have your will in anything   **134 scutcheons** shields showing armorial bearings; hence, shields hung up as monuments of victory
135 Hang be hung up in display as your trophies. (But with a hidden
suggestion of "be hanged as your captives.")   **136 in all for Cleopatra**
i.e., in all matters pertaining to yourself.   **137 brief** list   **139 Not . . .
admitted** petty things omitted.

CAESAR
Nay, blush not, Cleopatra. I approve
Your wisdom in the deed.
CLEOPATRA   See, Caesar! Oh, behold
How pomp is followed! Mine will now be yours,   150
And, should we shift estates, yours would be mine.   151
The ingratitude of this Seleucus does
Even make me wild.—Oh, slave, of no more trust
Than love that's hired! [*Seleucus retreats from her.*]
What, goest thou back? Thou shalt   154
Go back, I warrant thee! But I'll catch thine eyes,
Though they had wings. Slave, soulless villain, dog!
Oh, rarely base!
CAESAR   Good Queen, let us entreat you. 157
CLEOPATRA
Oh, Caesar, what a wounding shame is this,
That thou vouchsafing here to visit me,   159
Doing the honor of thy lordliness
To one so meek, that mine own servant should
Parcel the sum of my disgraces by   162
Addition of his envy! Say, good Caesar,   163
That I some lady trifles have reserved,   164
Immoment toys, things of such dignity   165
As we greet modern friends withal, and say   166
Some nobler token I have kept apart
For Livia and Octavia, to induce   168
Their mediation; must I be unfolded   169
With one that I have bred? The gods! It smites me   170
Beneath the fall I have. [*To Seleucus*] Prithee, go hence,
Or I shall show the cinders of my spirits   172
Through th'ashes of my chance. Wert thou a man,   173
Thou wouldst have mercy on me.
CAESAR   Forbear, Seleucus.   [*Exit Seleucus.*] 175
CLEOPATRA
Be it known that we, the greatest, are misthought   176
For things that others do; and when we fall
We answer others' merits in our name,   178
Are therefore to be pitied.
CAESAR   Cleopatra,
Not what you have reserved nor what acknowledged
Put we i'th' roll of conquest. Still be't yours;
Bestow it at your pleasure, and believe   182
Caesar's no merchant, to make prize with you   183
Of things that merchants sold. Therefore be cheered.
Make not your thoughts your prisons. No, dear
   Queen,   185
For we intend so to dispose you as   186

Yourself shall give us counsel. Feed and sleep.
Our care and pity is so much upon you
That we remain your friend; and so adieu.
CLEOPATRA
My master, and my lord!
CAESAR   Not so. Adieu.
         Flourish. Exeunt Caesar and his train.
CLEOPATRA
He words me, girls, he words me, that I should not   191
Be noble to myself. But hark thee, Charmian.   192
         [*She whispers to Charmian.*]
IRAS
Finish, good lady. The bright day is done,
And we are for the dark.
CLEOPATRA [*to Charmian*]   Hie thee again.   194
I have spoke already, and it is provided;   195
Go put it to the haste.
CHARMIAN   Madam, I will.

         Enter Dolabella.

DOLABELLA
Where's the Queen?
CHARMIAN   Behold, sir.   [*Exit.*]
CLEOPATRA   Dolabella!
DOLABELLA
Madam, as thereto sworn by your command,
Which my love makes religion to obey,
I tell you this: Caesar through Syria
Intends his journey, and within three days
You with your children will he send before.
Make your best use of this. I have performed
Your pleasure and my promise.
CLEOPATRA   Dolabella,
I shall remain your debtor.
DOLABELLA   I your servant.
Adieu, good Queen. I must attend on Caesar.
CLEOPATRA
Farewell, and thanks.   *Exit [Dolabella].*
                    Now, Iras, what think'st thou?
Thou an Egyptian puppet shall be shown
In Rome as well as I. Mechanic slaves   209
With greasy aprons, rules, and hammers shall   210
Uplift us to the view. In their thick breaths,
Rank of gross diet, shall we be enclouded   212
And forced to drink their vapor.
IRAS   The gods forbid!   213
CLEOPATRA
Nay, 'tis most certain, Iras. Saucy lictors   214
Will catch at us like strumpets, and scald rhymers   215
Ballad us out o' tune. The quick comedians   216
Extemporally will stage us and present   217

---

150 How . . . followed! how greatness is served!   **Mine** All the pomp
and following that attends me   **151 shift estates** reverse fortunes,
exchange places   **154 hired** paid for.   **157 rarely** exceptionally
159 vouchsafing deigning to come   **162 Parcel** particularize
163 envy malice.   **164 lady** ladylike, feminine   **165 Immoment toys**
trifles of no moment or importance   **166 modern** common.   **withal**
with   **168 Livia** Octavius Caesar's wife   **169–70 unfolded . . . bred**
exposed by one of my household.   **172 cinders** smoldering hot coals
173 chance (fallen) fortune.   **175 Forbear** Withdraw   **176 misthought** misjudged   **178 We . . . name** we are accountable for the
deeds of others done in our name   **182 Bestow** Use   **183 make prize**
haggle   **185 Make . . . prisons** i.e., Don't imprison yourself in your
thoughts by misconceiving of your situation.   **186 dispose** dispose of

191–2 he words . . . myself he tries to deceive me with mere words to
keep me from suicide.   **194 Hie thee again** Return quickly.   **195
spoke** given orders (for the means of suicide)   **209 Mechanic slaves**
Common laborers   **210 rules** straight-edged measuring sticks
212 Rank . . . diet reeking of coarse food   **213 drink** drink in, breathe
deeply   **214 lictors** minor officials in attendance on Roman magistrates   **215 scald** scurvy   **216 Ballad us** sing ballads about us.
quick quick-witted   **217 Extemporally** in improvised performance

Our Alexandrian revels; Antony
Shall be brought drunken forth, and I shall see
Some squeaking Cleopatra boy my greatness   220
I'th' posture of a whore.

IRAS   O the good gods!

CLEOPATRA   Nay, that's certain.

IRAS
I'll never see't! For I am sure my nails
Are stronger than mine eyes.

CLEOPATRA   Why, that's the way
To fool their preparation and to conquer
Their most absurd intents.

    Enter Charmian.

                    Now, Charmian!
Show me, my women, like a queen. Go fetch   227
My best attires. I am again for Cydnus,
To meet Mark Antony. Sirrah Iras, go—   229
Now, noble Charmian, we'll dispatch indeed—   230
And when thou hast done this chare I'll give thee
    leave   231
To play till doomsday. Bring our crown and all.   232
                  [Exit Iras.] A noise within.
Wherefore's this noise?

    Enter a Guardsman.

GUARDSMAN   Here is a rural fellow
That will not be denied Your Highness' presence.
He brings you figs.

CLEOPATRA
Let him come in.   *Exit Guardsman.*
               What poor an instrument   236
May do a noble deed! He brings me liberty.
My resolution's placed, and I have nothing   238
Of woman in me. Now from head to foot
I am marble-constant; now the fleeting moon   240
No planet is of mine.

    *Enter Guardsman, and Clown [bringing in a
    basket].*

GUARDSMAN   This is the man.   241

CLEOPATRA   Avoid, and leave him.   *Exit Guardsman.*   242
Hast thou the pretty worm of Nilus there,   243
That kills and pains not?

CLOWN   Truly, I have him, but I would not be the party
that should desire you to touch him, for his biting is
immortal. Those that do die of it do seldom or never   247
recover.

CLEOPATRA   Remember'st thou any that have died on't?

CLOWN   Very many, men and women too. I heard of   250
one of them no longer than yesterday—a very honest
woman, but something given to lie, as a woman   252
should not do but in the way of honesty—how she
died of the biting of it, what pain she felt. Truly, she
makes a very good report o'th' worm. But he that will
believe all that they say shall never be saved by half 256
that they do. But this is most falliable, the worm's an 257
odd worm.

CLEOPATRA   Get thee hence, farewell.

CLOWN   I wish you all joy of the worm.
                [He sets down his basket.]

CLEOPATRA   Farewell.

CLOWN   You must think this, look you, that the worm
will do his kind.   263

CLEOPATRA   Ay, ay; farewell.

CLOWN   Look you, the worm is not to be trusted but in
the keeping of wise people, for indeed there is no
goodness in the worm.

CLEOPATRA   Take thou no care; it shall be heeded.   268

CLOWN   Very good. Give it nothing, I pray you, for it is
not worth the feeding.

CLEOPATRA   Will it eat me?

CLOWN   You must not think I am so simple but I know
the devil himself will not eat a woman. I know that a
woman is a dish for the gods, if the devil dress her   274
not. But truly, these same whoreson devils do the   275
gods great harm in their women, for in every ten that
they make, the devils mar five.

CLEOPATRA   Well, get thee gone. Farewell.

CLOWN   Yes, forsooth. I wish you joy o'th' worm.
                          Exit.

    [Enter Iras with royal attire.]

CLEOPATRA
Give me my robe. Put on my crown. I have
Immortal longings in me. Now no more   281
The juice of Egypt's grape shall moist this lip.
              [The women dress her.]
Yare, yare, good Iras; quick. Methinks I hear   283
Antony call; I see him rouse himself
To praise my noble act. I hear him mock
The luck of Caesar, which the gods give men   286
To excuse their after wrath. Husband, I come!   287
Now to that name my courage prove my title!   288
I am fire and air; my other elements   289

---

220 boy (Allusion to the practice of having women's parts acted by boys on the Elizabethan stage.) **227 Show** Display **229 Sirrah** (Compare *sirs,* addressed to the women, in 4.15.90.) **230 dispatch** (1) finish (2) hasten **231 chare** task, chore **232.1 Exit Iras** (It is possible that Charmian leaves, too.) **236 What** How **238 placed** fixed **240 fleeting** inconstant, changing **241 s.d. Clown** rustic **242 Avoid** Withdraw **243 worm** snake, serpent. (But elsewhere in this scene with the added connotation of "the male sexual organ" and "earthworm.") **247 immortal** (Blunder for "mortal.")

250 heard of heard from **252 to lie** (With sexual second meaning hinted at also in *honest,* i.e., "chaste," *die,* i.e., "reach orgasm," and *worm.*) **256 all . . . half** (The Clown comically reverses the sensible order of these two words.) **257 falliable** (Blunder for "infallible.") **263 his kind** its natural function. **268 Take thou no care** Don't worry **274 dress** prepare, as in cooking. (With a suggestion also of dressing in alluring clothes.) **275 whoreson** i.e., rascally, abominable. (A slang expression.) **281 Immortal longings** longings for immortality **283 Yare** Quickly **286–7 which . . . wrath** the luck that the gods give men when they intend to mock and punish them subsequently for their hubris. **288 to . . . title!** may my courage prove my right to call myself Antony's wife! **289 other elements** i.e., earth and water, the heavier elements

I give to baser life. So, have you done?
Come then, and take the last warmth of my lips.
Farewell, kind Charmian. Iras, long farewell.

> [*She kisses them. Iras falls and dies.*]

Have I the aspic in my lips? Dost fall?   293
If thou and nature can so gently part,
The stroke of death is as a lover's pinch,
Which hurts, and is desired. Dost thou lie still?
If thus thou vanishest, thou tell'st the world
It is not worth leave-taking.   298

CHARMIAN
Dissolve, thick cloud, and rain, that I may say
The gods themselves do weep!

CLEOPATRA   This proves me base.
If she first meet the curlèd Antony,   301
He'll make demand of her, and spend that kiss   302
Which is my heaven to have. [*To an asp*] Come, thou
mortal wretch,   303
With thy sharp teeth this knot intrinsicate   304
Of life at once untie. Poor venomous fool,
Be angry, and dispatch. Oh, couldst thou speak,
That I might hear thee call great Caesar ass
Unpolicied!

CHARMIAN   O eastern star!

CLEOPATRA   Peace, peace!   308
Dost thou not see my baby at my breast,
That sucks the nurse asleep?

CHARMIAN   Oh, break! Oh, break!

CLEOPATRA
As sweet as balm, as soft as air, as gentle—
O Antony!—Nay, I will take thee too.

> [*Applying another asp to her arm.*]

What should I stay—   *Dies.* 313

CHARMIAN
In this wild world? So, fare thee well.   314
Now boast thee, Death, in thy possession lies
A lass unparalleled. Downy windows, close;   316
And golden Phoebus never be beheld
Of eyes again so royal! Your crown's awry;   318
I'll mend it, and then play—   319

> *Enter the Guard, rustling in.*

FIRST GUARD
Where's the Queen?

CHARMIAN   Speak softly. Wake her not.

FIRST GUARD
Caesar hath sent—

CHARMIAN   Too slow a messenger.

> [*She applies an asp to herself.*]

Oh, come apace, dispatch! I partly feel thee.

FIRST GUARD
Approach, ho! All's not well. Caesar's beguiled.   323

SECOND GUARD
There's Dolabella sent from Caesar. Call him.

> [*Exit a guard.*]

FIRST GUARD
What work is here, Charmian? Is this well done?

CHARMIAN
It is well done, and fitting for a princess
Descended of so many royal kings.
Ah, soldier!   *Charmian dies.*

> *Enter Dolabella.*

DOLABELLA
How goes it here?

SECOND GUARD   All dead.

DOLABELLA   Caesar, thy thoughts
Touch their effects in this. Thyself art coming   330
To see performed the dreaded act which thou
So sought'st to hinder.

> *Enter Caesar and all his train, marching.*

ALL   A way there, a way for Caesar!   333

DOLABELLA
Oh, sir, you are too sure an augurer;
That you did fear is done.

CAESAR   Bravest at the last,   335
She leveled at our purposes and, being royal,   336
Took her own way. The manner of their deaths?
I do not see them bleed.

DOLABELLA   Who was last with them?

FIRST GUARD
A simple countryman, that brought her figs.   339
This was his basket.

CAESAR   Poisoned, then.

FIRST GUARD   Oh, Caesar,
This Charmian lived but now; she stood and spake.
I found her trimming up the diadem
On her dead mistress; tremblingly she stood,
And on the sudden dropped.

CAESAR   Oh, noble weakness!
If they had swallowed poison, 'twould appear
By external swelling; but she looks like sleep,   346
As she would catch another Antony   347
In her strong toil of grace.

DOLABELLA   Here on her breast   348
There is a vent of blood and something blown;   349
The like is on her arm.

---

293 aspic asp   **298 is . . . leave-taking** does not deserve a ceremonious farewell.   **301 curlèd** with curled hair   **302 make demand** (1) ask questions (2) ask pleasure.   **spend that kiss** expend his desire on her   **303 mortal** deadly.   **wretch** (An affectionate term of abuse, like *fool* in line 305.)   **304 intrinsicate** intricate   **308 Unpolicied** outwitted.   **eastern star** i.e., Venus, the morning star.   **313 What** Why   **314 wild** savage. (Sometimes emended to *vild*, "vile.")   **316 Downy windows** i.e., Soft eyelids   **318 Of** by   **319 mend** fix, straighten

323 beguiled cheated, tricked.   **330 Touch their effects** meet with realization   **333 A way** Make a path   **335 That** that which   **336 leveled at** aimed at, guessed   **339 simple** humbly born   **346 like sleep** as if asleep   **347 As** as if   **348 toil** net   **349 vent** discharge.   **blown** deposited, or, swollen

FIRST GUARD
　　This is an aspic's trail, and these fig leaves
　　Have slime upon them, such as th'aspic leaves
　　Upon the caves of Nile.
CAESAR　　　　　　　　　　Most probable
　　That so she died; for her physician tells me
　　She hath pursued conclusions infinite　　　　　　　　　355
　　Of easy ways to die. Take up her bed,
　　And bear her women from the monument.
　　She shall be buried by her Antony.
　　No grave upon the earth shall clip in it　　　　　　　359

355 conclusions experiments　　**359 clip** embrace, clasp

　　A pair so famous. High events as these
　　Strike those that make them; and their story is　　361
　　No less in pity than his glory which　　　　　　　362
　　Brought them to be lamented. Our army shall　　363
　　In solemn show attend this funeral,
　　And then to Rome. Come, Dolabella, see
　　High order in this great solemnity.　　　　　　366
　　　　　　Exeunt omnes, [bearing the dead bodies].

361 Strike . . . them touch with sorrow those who brought about these deeds　　**361–3 their story . . . lamented** the story of these famous lovers is no less pitiable than the fame of him who brought them low is glorious.　　**366.1 omnes** all

Coriolanus

oriolanus may be Shakespeare's last tragedy. Even though external evidence is scarce as to its actual date, the style suggests a time around 1608. If so, Shakespeare's final statement on humanity's tragic destiny is disillusioned, wry, almost anticlimactic, in the vein of his Roman and classical tragedies rather than of his tragedies of evil *(Hamlet, Othello, King Lear, Macbeth)*. Shakespeare based *Coriolanus* on Plutarch's *Lives of the Noble Grecians and Romans*, in the translation by Sir Thomas North. As in the presumably earlier Plutarchan plays, *Julius Caesar, Timon of Athens*, and *Antony and Cleopatra*, and in the non-Plutarchan *Titus Andronicus* and *Troilus and Cressida*, Shakespeare's ancient political world is one of constant upheaval. In the clash of ideologies, the plebeian mob turns giddily from one idol to the next, and strong men rise briefly, only to be supplanted by rivals. The result of unceasing change is political stalemate. The great men of the ancient world seem fascinatingly alive to us, but they also seem blind to their own limitations, fatally proud, and hemmed in by circumstance. Their virtues and their defects are inseparable and indeed often identical, for private virtues serve these tragic heroes poorly in the amoral and pitiless arena of politics. Their natures cannot easily be moved from a predilection for catastrophe, and so their downfall proceeds inexorably from what Aristotle, writing of Greek tragedy, termed a tragic flaw, or hamartia, in their characters. The ending, ironic rather than cathartic in its effect, leaves us with an impression of tragic waste.

Coriolanus admirably captures this conflict dividing personal nobility from political reality. The play returns to a political problem that has been studied before in *Julius Caesar:* the rivalry in ancient Rome between republican and absolutist forms of government. *Coriolanus*, although written later than *Julius Caesar*, analyzes an earlier period of Roman history when the tribunes chosen to represent the interests of Rome's common people succeeded in blocking the attempts of the aristocratic party

to install a military leader of their own persuasion (Caius Marcius, given the honorific name of Coriolanus for his triumphal success over Corioles) as consul with an absolute power that could suppress the political and economic demands of the populace. In *Coriolanus*, we thus witness the birth of republicanism in its distinctively Roman form, a blend of aristocratic and democratic elements; in *Julius Caesar*, we see the demise of this delicately balanced regime. Shakespeare views both events with ironic detachment.

Republicanism was potentially a matter of controversy on the Jacobean stage, insofar as spectators might draw analogies between it and parliamentary efforts to curb the power of the English throne. The differences are real, of course, especially in *Julius Caesar*, in which Caesar's claim to absolute rule has no sanction of divine right and Brutus' republicanism is ineffably genteel rather than populist. *Coriolanus*, however, hits closer to home. Here the plebeians are profoundly dissatisfied with aristocratic rule. Popular unrest over famine and high prices leads to rioting and the expression of democratic sentiments such as were heard and feared by the authorities in England. Riots over scarcity of grain occurred in Northamptonshire, Warwickshire, and Leicestershire during the summer of 1607. King James I, who had come to the throne in 1603, adopted a hostile stance toward Puritan efforts to democratize Church government and of corresponding challenges in Parliament on behalf of the common law. From the vantage point of ancient Rome, distant in time and place, *Coriolanus* appraises the conflict in terms that bear no precise relation to Jacobean England but yet have a timeless relevance. Without taking sides, the play dwells on the ambiguity of the struggle and on the indecisive, self-defeating results achieved by both parties.

As in *Julius Caesar*, men on both sides are passionately sincere but driven to shortsighted extremism. The tribunes insist on behalf of the mob that the people's voice is to be the ultimate law of Rome. Coriolanus, in angry response, sees the mob and its elected tribunes as the enemies of hierarchical prerogative, threatening the very existence of the state. Which view is correct? Is the people's voice a brave force of resistance against aristocratic hauteur and class privilege, as exemplified by Coriolanus, or is the tribunes' program a grab for power by demagogues willing to risk anarchy and to weaken Rome's military might? Shakespeare, like Plutarch, explores the weaknesses and strengths of both parties. He uses a dramatic structure, as in *Julius Caesar*, of sustained ambiguity. If any conclusion emerges, it is that violent political struggle leads only to an undoing of those civilized institutions that the few persons of moderation like Menenius, caught in the middle, strive vainly to preserve.

The citizens play a dominant role in *Coriolanus*. The action begins, as in *Julius Caesar*, with a mob scene, setting a tone of ominous instability. The mob is too easily swayed. Lacking any consistent political philosophy of its own, it will follow whatever charismatic orator catches its fancy. It despises Coriolanus one moment and adulates him the next. Its own members agree that the mob is a "many-headed multitude," directionless and irresponsible (2.3.10–17). Other characters besides Coriolanus protest the offensive stench of the crowd, "stinking" breaths, "reechy" necks, "stinking greasy caps," and unclean teeth (2.1.208, 235; 4.6.138). The Roman citizens are a "herd," "apronmen," "garlic eaters," curs, hares, foxes, geese, a "cockle of rebellion, insolence, sedition" (3.1.35, 73; 4.6.101–3). This deliberately repulsive portrayal, part of an excremental motif that runs throughout the play, merely intensifies what is true in the other Roman plays and in the English history plays as well. Nowhere in Shakespeare does mob action lead to anything constructive or even politically acceptable. At the same time, the mob does not bear chief responsibility for disaster either, in *Coriolanus* or elsewhere in Shakespeare. Individually, its members are good-natured, slow to be aroused, quick to forget injury, too credulous indeed for their own good. In *Coriolanus*, they have to be prompted again and again by the tribunes to press forward with their resentment. Many citizens, left to themselves, are wise and patient. They are a neutral force, dangerous only when whipped up to collective frenzy by demagogic persuasion.

Much blame would seem to fall then on the tribunes, and indeed even the more moderate patricians, such as Menenius, are deeply mistrustful of Junius Brutus and Sicinius Velutus. These tribunes are willing to risk mob violence to achieve their ends, especially when they urge the "rabble of plebeians" to "bustle about Coriolanus" (3.1.183–8). Ignoring Menenius's pleas that "This is the way to kindle, not to quench," and that "Confusion's near" (lines 193, 200), the tribunes deliberately goad Coriolanus to anger. Their strategy is to foment clamor, and "with a din confused / Enforce the present execution," shouting down reason with hysteria (3.3.21–2). They care-

fully stage each confrontation with Coriolanus, rehearsing the citizens in what they are to do, cannily timing their provocations. They talk like conspirators. The metadramatic dimension of this emphasis on staging a political campaign suggests that politics can too easily become a theatrical spectacle of manipulating appearances. Shakespeare's audience, accustomed to governmental warnings against mob violence, would probably have understood the menace posed by the tribunes and would have savored the irony that Rome is weakened rather than strengthened by their machinations.

Still, Shakespeare's portrayal of the tribunes is remarkably sympathetic. They honestly fear that Coriolanus seeks "one sole throne, without assistance" (4.6.34), and that as consul he will do everything he can to suppress the people's liberties. This is no idle fear; Coriolanus's own friends merely counsel him to attack the tribunes after he has achieved power, not before. Although the tribunes do arouse the people to actions they would not otherwise take, the tribunes believe they are doing so in the people's best interests, providing leadership for a constituency that has hitherto lacked a voice. They believe in a government "by the consent of all" that can hold aristocratic insolence in check through the "lawful censure" of the common people. "What is the city but the people?" (3.1.202–4; 3.3.50). Moreover, they are not revolutionaries by temperament and do abandon mob tactics once they have made their point. Their achievements mock them when Rome proves defenseless against the return of Coriolanus, but even here they can argue with some reason that Rome would have achieved peace had it not been for Coriolanus's lawless vengeance.

Perhaps, then, Coriolanus must bear the responsibility for provoking democratic extremism through his contempt of the citizenry. From his first appearance, he antagonizes us, as well as the populace, with his curt, insulting manner. He addresses the people as "dissentious rogues," itching with scabby diseases, and dismisses them as "curs" who are "beneath abhorring" (1.1.163–7). His hatred amounts to revulsion, and we fear he is all too ready to employ his sword on "thousands of these quartered slaves" (line 198). He responds to the tribunes' calculated staging of political opposition by demonstrating that he is no actor. Constitutionally unwilling to prostrate himself to the mob by playing the humble role they ask of him in return for their votes ("It is a part / That I shall blush in acting," he tells his friends at 2.2.145–6), Coriolanus prefers to lose on principle rather than to win through catering to popular demand as an actor might do. "You have put me now to such a part which never / I shall discharge to th' life," he insists to his mother (3.2.107–8). The politician's role is one that belies Coriolanus's true nature in the most fundamentally dishonest way. "Away, my disposition, and possess me / Some harlot's spirit!" Reluctantly he consents to "mountebank their loves, / Cog their hearts from them" (3.2.113–35). Small wonder that the commoners are scarcely impressed by any sincerity in his wooing of their votes. When denied the consulship by the tribunes, in fact, he draws his sword in the marketplace, relishing the opportunity for a military solution. His tendency to forget names betrays a coldness and a self-centeredness that is at times nearly babylike in its narcissism. Although he professes not to speak merely in anger, he is too easily baited by the tribunes and too quick to speak his mind. Even those who admire his virtues concede that "to seem to affect the malice and displeasure of the people is as bad as that which he dislikes, to flatter them for their love" (2.2.21–3). Coriolanus is glad to hear of the impending Volscian attack on Rome, for he prefers war to peace and sees conscription as a way of channeling revolutionary energies against an outward foe. He professes love of his country, but, because his attachment is to an exclusively patrician order, he is ready to turn traitor against a Rome that gives a political voice to the plebeians he so abhors.

Nevertheless, the portrayal of Coriolanus, as of the tribunes, is delicately balanced. We admire Coriolanus's hatred of hypocrisy. He is scrupulously honest, refusing all spoils of war except those to which his fellow soldiers are entitled. Despite his pride in family and name, he genuinely dislikes to hear himself praised. Though he disdains to lead cowardly citizen-soldiers and shines most in single deeds of valor rather than in generalship, he is inspiring and even popular among valiant soldiers like himself. He is generous in praising the achievements of his colleagues. Even in matters of state, he shows resoluteness and integrity. He has a consistent political philosophy, bolstered by Menenius's comparison of the state to a body in which the members must harmoniously interact (1.1.94 ff). Jacobean spectators would recognize in this analogy the orthodox appeal to order and degree they heard regularly from pulpit and throne, even though they might also recognize that it is being self-interestedly applied by one who enjoys the perquisites of noble birth. Coriolanus, at any rate, firmly believes that the established prerogatives of the aristocracy are Rome's only safe bulwark against chaos. By granting power to the tribunes, in his view, the Senate has sealed its doom. He sees the people as their own worst enemies, insatiable and irrational in their demands, unable to comprehend the subtleties of government, instinctively envious of their betters. Such base mortals require subjection to their masters, though they cannot be expected to realize this themselves. Coriolanus knows that his views are out of fashion and that the current trend is to appease popular demands with compromise, but he can see no end to the compromises that will be needed once the tribunes have established their prerogatives. He prefers a battle to the death and welcomes the danger to himself. If his courage and consistency are "too absolute," if he is "too noble for the world" (3.2.41; 3.1.261), he would prefer to believe that the fault lies in that world rather than in him.

Between the extremes of democratic and aristocratic rule, the middle position of compromise offers many attractions. Menenius sanely desires to see "On both sides more respect" and pleads with those who would be "truly your country's friend" to "temperately proceed to what you would / Thus violently redress" (3.1.184; 222–4). Although his sympathies are patrician, he acknowledges the tribunes' power as a political reality which must be dealt with. He finds fault with Coriolanus for not having "temporized" (4.6.17). Menenius is a bluff, honest fellow who directs our sympathies, like the equally outspoken Enobarbus in *Antony and Cleopatra*. Yet compromise always has its ridiculous aspect. Menenius increasingly assumes the self-contradictory role of the appeaser, like York of *Richard II*, urging actions that are repugnant to him personally. His seemingly sage advice to the plebeians in his fable of the belly is in part at least a rhetorical strategy calculated to quiet plebeian restiveness without addressing their real demands. At the last, after having denounced the tribunes for betraying Rome, Menenius must go as their ambassador to beg mercy of Coriolanus. When Aufidius's guardsmen scoff at him for having been turned away by Coriolanus, Menenius is beyond caring for their taunts. He does, in fact, hold to a consistent principle—the survival of his beloved city at whatever cost to his pride. He and Rome pragmatically blunder through, though not without loss of dignity.

Coriolanus's mother, Volumnia, is caught in an even more ironic dilemma. She, of course, shares her son's aristocratic pride, having taught him a code of death before dishonor. The bond between mother and son is extraordinarily, even distressingly, close. Emotionally, it takes the place of Coriolanus's bloodless marriage to the chaste and retiring Virgilia. Volumnia, in fact, speaks of Coriolanus metaphorically as her husband and of his warlike prowess as a vicarious substitute for "the embracements of his bed" (1.3.4–5). Throughout, Coriolanus's deeds of war are love offerings to his mother. Every citizen of Rome knows that whatever Coriolanus has done for his country he also did "to please his mother" (1.1.37). Yet, because Volumnia has not been a properly nourishing mother, Coriolanus is poised between two irreconcilable cravings: to please a mother whose demands can never be satisfied and to fashion an identity that is entirely self-made. He needs her approval but also wishes to be beholden to no one, least of all to her. His rigid masculinity in war, we realize, is in part an attempt to escape from his sense of vulnerability to his mother and to the plebeians whom he must beg for votes—indeed, to Rome itself, the city that has banished him like a rejecting mother and that he finally cannot bring himself to destroy. Even Coriolanus's soldiership collapses into an attempt to please his mother.

The conflict reaches its crisis when Volumnia's oppressive demands take the form of insisting that her son achieve fame not only in war but also in politics. Here she must, like Menenius, encourage the compromise and "policy" that they all hate. She and Menenius stage Coriolanus' public appearances with as much care as the tribunes rehearse their plebeians. They "prompt" Coriolanus to "perform a part" for which he has no aptitude (3.2.108–11); as he later says, capitulating to his mother for the last time, "Like a dull actor now, / I have forgot my part, and I am out" (5.3.40–1). This integrity has its admirable side but brings disaster to Volumnia's plans. She is defeated by the very pride she has engendered in him, and he is defeated by her overriding ambition for him. To win her praise, he must put away his true disposition, becoming effeminate and emasculated like a "harlot" or "an eunuch" (3.2.114–16). To satisfy her quest for fame, he must give up his attack on Rome, perjure himself to Aufidius, and die a condemned traitor to the Volscian state. Volumnia's crushing and engulfing love for her son proves ironically fatal to everything they have cherished.

Coriolanus's relationship to Aufidius is one of love as well as hate, and it, too, poses a fatal conflict. Despite their rivalry to the death, these two military heroes are singularly attracted to one another. Coriolanus confesses "I sin in envying his nobility," and considers Aufidius "a lion / That I am proud to hunt" (1.1.231–7). Coriolanus's fate is to love his enemy and hate his birthplace. Aufidius, in turn, greets Coriolanus with more joy "Than when I first my wedded mistress saw / Bestride my threshold" (4.5.122–3). The homoerotic resonances of this metaphor need not be read literally, but they do recall similar images of emotional bonding among men who are enemies in battle such as Hector and Achilles in *Troilus and Cressida*. The animosity of rivalry persists; Aufidius has always resented Coriolanus's superiority in battle and has planned to overcome him by fair means or foul. In their brief military alliance, Coriolanus proves too attractive a rival, overshadowing the achievements of Aufidius. For these reasons, Aufidius secretly exults in Coriolanus's fatal dilemma, since the Volscian general prefers vengeance to victory over Rome. In a final disillusioning scene, he stages one more public outcry against Coriolanus, goading him into a proud rage, and then with his fellow conspirators ingloriously performs an execution "whereat valor will weep" (5.6.139). Aufidius's virtues, like those of Coriolanus, have been betrayed by his worst instincts. Throughout, the Volscians have been cunning enemies, lying in wait for Rome to tear herself apart. The laws governing the relations between states are brutally competitive, characterized by the "slippery turns" (4.4.12) of fortune that ironically bring together former enemies as allies and then turn them against one another. In this world of sudden reversals, Coriolanus's last act is something he could never have foreseen: saving the Roman state and its tribunes from a destruction he himself had wished on it. As Coriolanus wryly observes of his own destiny (5.3.184–5), "The gods look down, and this unnatural scene / They laugh at."

Onstage today, *Coriolanus* works well as a play of disillusionment and psychological diagnosis of charismatic leadership that is easily attuned to our modern-day mistrust of political infighting and machination. Peter Hall's production at Stratford-upon-Avon in 1959, with Lawrence Olivier as Coriolanus, put mordant stress on the cravenness of the mob and presented Coriolanus's hatred of courtly flattery with genuine sympathy while at the same time stressing his emotional and even neurotic dependency on his mother. In death at the play's end, caught by the ankles as he dangled upside down from an upper platform, Olivier reminded viewers of the grisly end of Mussolini. Tyrone Guthrie's 1963 production for the Nottingham Playhouse, in the decor of the French Empire, explored hysterical and homosexual psychological dimensions in the title figure. In John Barton's 1967 production for the Royal Shakespeare Company and that of Terry Hands in 1977, Coriolanus and Aufidius were costumed in identical armor and other matching effects to underscore the narcissism and sibling-rivalry aspects of their competitive love-hate relationship. Politically, the play has lent itself to Marxist readings, as in Prague in 1959 and especially in Bertolt Brecht's adaptation of 1951–1952, for whom the proletarians were heroic and the tribunes honorable. Brecht's collaborators at the Berliner Ensemble in East Berlin continued in this partisan vein in 1964. For Giorgio Strehler in Milan in 1947, the play was about the Marxist dialectic of history, with its emphasis on material causes and the inevitability of historical change. Other directors have seen in Coriolanus a kind of Napoleon. More apolitical presentations have emphasized the ironic and disillusioning aspects of the play, as in Terry Hands's 1977 production, featuring Alan Howard as Coriolanus, a man doomed by his failure to enact his own heroic myths. An especially splendid production is available on long-playing records, in audio only, with Richard Burton as the eponymous hero—surely a role to which Burton's sardonic and intellectually brilliant acting style is singularly well attuned.

Coriolanus

[Dramatis Personae

CAIUS MARCIUS, *afterward* CAIUS MARCIUS
   CORIOLANUS

TITUS LARTIUS,⎫
COMINIUS,   ⎬ *Roman generals*
MENENIUS AGRIPPA, *friend of Coriolanus*
SICINIUS VELUTUS,⎫
JUNIUS BRUTUS, ⎬ *Roman tribunes*
NICANOR, *a Roman traitor*
Two Roman PATRICIANS
Two Roman SENATORS
An AEDILE
Two Roman OFFICERS
A Roman LIEUTENANT
Roman SOLDIERS
A Roman HERALD
Seven Roman CITIZENS
MESSENGERS

VOLUMNIA, *Coriolanus's mother*
VIRGILIA, *Coriolanus's wife*

Young MARCIUS, *son of Coriolanus and Virgilia*
VALERIA, *friend of Virgilia*
A GENTLEWOMAN, *attending Virgilia*

TULLUS AUFIDIUS, *Volscian general*
Two SENATORS *of Corioles*
Three Volscian LORDS
A Volscian LIEUTENANT
A Volscian SOLDIER
Three CONSPIRATORS
ADRIAN, *a Volscian*
A CITIZEN *of Antium*
Two Volscian WATCHMEN
Three SERVINGMEN *of Aufidius*

Roman and Volscian Senators, Patricians, Aediles,
   Lictors, Captains, Soldiers, Citizens, Messengers,
   Servingmen, an Usher attending Valeria, and At-
   tendants

SCENE: *Rome and the neighborhood; Corioles and the neighborhood; Antium*]

1.1

*Enter a company of mutinous Citizens, with
staves, clubs, and other weapons.*

FIRST CITIZEN   Before we proceed any further, hear me
  speak.
ALL   Speak, speak.
FIRST CITIZEN   You are all resolved rather to die than to
  famish?   5
ALL   Resolved, resolved.
FIRST CITIZEN   First, you know Caius Marcius is chief
  enemy to the people.

ALL   We know't, we know't.
FIRST CITIZEN   Let us kill him, and we'll have corn at 10
  our own price. Is't a verdict?   11
ALL   No more talking on't. Let it be done. Away, away! 12
SECOND CITIZEN   One word, good citizens.
FIRST CITIZEN   We are accounted poor citizens, the patricians good. What authority surfeits on would relieve 15
  us. If they would yield us but the superfluity while it 16
  were wholesome, we might guess they relieved us hu- 17
  manely. But they think we are too dear. The leanness 18

---

10 corn grain, such as wheat or barley   **11 Is't a verdict?** Are we
agreed?   **12 on't** of it, about it.   **15 good** i.e., noble, well-to-do.
authority those in authority, the nobility   **16 but the superfluity**
merely the excess   **17 wholesome** good to eat   **18 too dear** costing
more than we are worth (but also, paradoxically, *a gain*; see line 21).

1.1. Location: Rome. A street
5 famish starve.

that afflicts us, the object of our misery, is as an inven- 19
tory to particularize their abundance. Our sufferance is 20
a gain to them. Let us revenge this with our pikes ere 21
we become rakes; for the gods know I speak this in 22
hunger for bread, not in thirst for revenge.

SECOND CITIZEN   Would you proceed especially against
Caius Marcius?

ALL   Against him first. He's a very dog to the common- 26
alty. 27

SECOND CITIZEN   Consider you what services he has
done for his country?

FIRST CITIZEN   Very well, and could be content to give
him good report for't, but that he pays himself with
being proud.

SECOND CITIZEN   Nay, but speak not maliciously.

FIRST CITIZEN   I say unto you, what he hath done fa- 34
mously he did it to that end. Though soft-conscienced 35
men can be content to say it was for his country, he
did it to please his mother and to be partly proud, 37
which he is, even to the altitude of his virtue. 38

SECOND CITIZEN   What he cannot help in his nature you
account a vice in him. You must in no way say he is
covetous.

FIRST CITIZEN   If I must not, I need not be barren of ac- 42
cusations. He hath faults, with surplus, to tire in repe- 43
tition. (Shouts within.) What shouts are these? The 44
other side o'th' city is risen. Why stay we prating 45
here? To th' Capitol! 46

ALL   Come, come.

FIRST CITIZEN   Soft, who comes here? 48

Enter Menenius Agrippa.

SECOND CITIZEN   Worthy Menenius Agrippa, one that
hath always loved the people.

FIRST CITIZEN   He's one honest enough. Would all the
rest were so!

MENENIUS
What work's, my countrymen, in hand? Where go you
With bats and clubs? The matter? Speak, I pray you. 54

FIRST CITIZEN   Our business is not unknown to the
Senate. They have had inkling this fortnight what we
intend to do, which now we'll show 'em in deeds.
They say poor suitors have strong breaths; they shall 58
know we have strong arms too.

MENENIUS
Why, masters, my good friends, mine honest
neighbors,
Will you undo yourselves? 60
61

FIRST CITIZEN
We cannot, sir. We are undone already.

MENENIUS
I tell you, friends, most charitable care
Have the patricians of you. For your wants, 64
Your suffering in this dearth, you may as well 65
Strike at the heaven with your staves as lift them
Against the Roman state, whose course will on 67
The way it takes, cracking ten thousand curbs 68
Of more strong link asunder than can ever
Appear in your impediment. For the dearth, 70
The gods, not the patricians, make it, and
Your knees to them, not arms, must help. Alack, 72
You are transported by calamity 73
Thither where more attends you, and you slander 74
The helms o'th' state, who care for you like fathers, 75
When you curse them as enemies.

FIRST CITIZEN   Care for us? True indeed! They ne'er
cared for us yet: suffer us to famish, and their storehouses crammed with grain; make edicts for usury to 79
support usurers; repeal daily any wholesome act established against the rich; and provide more piercing 81
statutes daily to chain up and restrain the poor. If the
wars eat us not up, they will; and there's all the love
they bear us.

MENENIUS   Either you must
Confess yourselves wondrous malicious,
Or be accused of folly. I shall tell you
A pretty tale. It may be you have heard it,
But, since it serves my purpose, I will venture
To stale't a little more. 90

FIRST CITIZEN   Well, I'll hear it, sir; yet you must not
think to fob off our disgrace with a tale. But, an't 92
please you, deliver. 93

MENENIUS
There was a time when all the body's members
Rebelled against the belly, thus accused it:
That only like a gulf it did remain 96
I'th' midst o'th' body, idle and unactive,
Still cupboarding the viand, never bearing 98
Like labor with the rest, where th'other instruments 99
Did see and hear, devise, instruct, walk, feel, 100
And, mutually participate, did minister 101

19 object spectacle **19–20 is as . . . abundance** serves as a catalogue
or inventory to point out in detail (by means of contrast) how rich
they are. **20 sufferance** suffering **21 pikes** spears, lances; pitch-
forks. (Playing on *rakes*, line 22.) **22 rakes** i.e., as lean as rakes
26 a very dog i.e., inhumanly cruel **26–7 commonalty** common people. **34–5 famously** achieving fame **35 to that end** i.e., in order to
become famous and as an upshot of his pride. **soft-conscienced**
weak-minded, lacking real conviction **37 to be partly proud** partly
out of pride **38 even . . . virtue** i.e., he is as proud as he is brave.
42 If Even if **43–4 to tire in repetition** to tire out the speaker in
reporting them. **45 prating** talking idly **46 Capitol** Temple of
Jupiter on Capitoline Hill; used here to stand for the Senate building.
48 Soft Stay, stop **54 bats** cudgels **58 suitors** petitioners. **strong**
strong-smelling. (With a play in the next line on *strong*, "mighty.")

60 masters i.e., good sirs. (A term appropriate to ordinary citizens.)
61 undo ruin **64 For** As for. (Also in line 70.) **65 dearth** famine
67 on continue on **68 curbs** restraints. (A term from horsemanship;
the curb is attached to the bit.) **70 in your impediment** in any hindrance you may be able to offer. **72 knees** i.e., prayers. (With a play
on *arms* as parts of the body and as weapons.) **73 transported** carried away **74 attends** awaits **75 helms** helmsmen **79 for** permitting **81 piercing** severe **90 stale't** make it stale by repeating it
92 fob . . . disgrace set aside by a trick our feeling of suffering hardship. **an't** if it **93 deliver** tell your tale. **96 gulf** open pit,
whirlpool **98 Still . . . viand** always stowing away the food
99 Like equal. **where** whereas. **instruments** organs **100 devise**
deliberate, think **101 participate** participating, taking part

Unto the appetite and affection common   102
Of the whole body. The belly answered—
FIRST CITIZEN   Well, sir, what answer made the belly?
MENENIUS
Sir, I shall tell you. With a kind of smile,
Which ne'er came from the lungs, but even thus—   106
For, look you, I may make the belly smile
As well as speak—it tauntingly replied
To th' discontented members, the mutinous parts
That envied his receipt; even so most fitly   110
As you malign our senators for that   111
They are not such as you.
FIRST CITIZEN   Your belly's answer—What?
The kingly-crownèd head, the vigilant eye,
The counselor heart, the arm our soldier,
Our steed the leg, the tongue our trumpeter,
With other muniments and petty helps   117
In this our fabric, if that they—
MENENIUS   What then?   118
'Fore me, this fellow speaks! What then? What then?   119
FIRST CITIZEN
Should by the cormorant belly be restrained,   120
Who is the sink o'th' body—
MENENIUS   Well, what then?   121
FIRST CITIZEN
The former agents, if they did complain,   122
What could the belly answer?
MENENIUS   I will tell you.
If you'll bestow a small—of what you have little—   124
Patience awhile, you'st hear the belly's answer.   125
FIRST CITIZEN
You're long about it.
MENENIUS   Note me this, good friend;
Your most grave belly was deliberate,   127
Not rash like his accusers, and thus answered:
"True is it, my incorporate friends," quoth he,   129
"That I receive the general food at first
Which you do live upon; and fit it is,
Because I am the storehouse and the shop
Of the whole body. But, if you do remember,
I send it through the rivers of your blood
Even to the court, the heart, to the seat o'th' brain; 135
And, through the cranks and offices of man,   136
The strongest nerves and small inferior veins   137
From me receive that natural competency   138

Whereby they live. And though that all at once"—
You, my good friends, this says the belly, mark me—
FIRST CITIZEN
Ay, sir, well, well.
MENENIUS   "Though all at once cannot
See what I do deliver out to each,
Yet I can make my audit up, that all   143
From me do back receive the flour of all,   144
And leave me but the bran." What say you to't?   145
FIRST CITIZEN
It was an answer. How apply you this?
MENENIUS
The senators of Rome are this good belly,
And you the mutinous members. For examine
Their counsels and their cares, digest things rightly 149
Touching the weal o'th' common, you shall find   150
No public benefit which you receive
But it proceeds or comes from them to you
And no way from yourselves. What do you think,
You, the great toe of this assembly?
FIRST CITIZEN   I the great toe? Why the great toe?
MENENIUS
For that, being one o'th' lowest, basest, poorest,
Of this most wise rebellion, thou goest foremost.
Thou rascal, that art worst in blood to run,   158
Lead'st first to win some vantage.   159
But make you ready your stiff bats and clubs.   160
Rome and her rats are at the point of battle;
The one side must have bale.

Enter Caius Marcius.

                                   Hail, noble Marcius!   162
MARCIUS
Thanks.—What's the matter, you dissentious rogues,   163
That, rubbing the poor itch of your opinion,
Make yourselves scabs?
FIRST CITIZEN   We have ever your good word.   165
MARCIUS
He that will give good words to thee will flatter   166
Beneath abhorring. What would you have, you curs,   167
That like nor peace nor war? The one affrights you,   168
The other makes you proud. He that trusts to you,   169
Where he should find you lions, finds you hares;

---

102 **affection** inclination   106 **lungs** i.e., supposed organ of laughter
110 **his receipt** what it received.   **fitly** fittingly, justly. (Said ironically.)   111 **for that** because   117 **muniments** furnishings, or
defenses   118 **fabric** body formed by the conjunction of various
parts.   **if that** if   119 **'Fore me** (An oath.)   120 **cormorant** ravenous,
rapacious (like the voracious seabird known by that name)   121 **sink**
cesspool   122 **former** just-named   124 **small** small quantity
125 **you'st** you shall   127 **Your** i.e., this   129 **incorporate** belonging
to one body   135 **to the court . . . brain** i.e., to the heart, which is the
court and vital center, and to the brain, which is the throne
136 **cranks** winding passages.   **offices** service rooms of a household;
kitchen, etc.   137 **nerves** sinews   138 **natural competency** sufficiency for the purposes of nature

143 **audit** balance sheet   144 **the flour** i.e., the nourishing part.
(With a play on *the flower*, "the pick"; spelled "Flowre" in the
Folio.)   145 **bran** chaff.   149 **digest** analyze, interpret. (With a play
on the gastronomic sense.)   150 **weal o'th' common** public welfare
158–9 **Thou . . . vantage** You inferior specimen of mongrel dog, in
the worst of vigor and condition to be leading the pack, are doing
so for some tawdry personal advantage. (*Rascal* can also mean
"lean deer, not worth the hunting.")   160 **stiff bats** sturdy cudgels
162 **The one . . . bale** one side or the other must get the worst of it,
receive injury.   163 **dissentious** rebellious   165 **scabs** (1) scurvy
fellows, rascals (2) sores.   **ever** always   166 **give good words to**
praise   167 **abhorring** contempt.   168 **nor . . . nor** neither . . .
nor.   **The one** War   169 **The other** peace.   **proud** arrogant and
demanding.

Where foxes, geese. You are no surer, no,   171
Than is the coal of fire upon the ice,   172
Or hailstone in the sun. Your virtue is   173
To make him worthy whose offense subdues him,   174
And curse that justice did it. Who deserves greatness 175
Deserves your hate; and your affections are   176
A sick man's appetite, who desires most that
Which would increase his evil. He that depends   178
Upon your favors swims with fins of lead
And hews down oaks with rushes. Hang ye! Trust ye? 180
With every minute you do change a mind
And call him noble that was now your hate,   182
Him vile that was your garland. What's the matter, 183
That in these several places of the city   184
You cry against the noble Senate, who,
Under the gods, keep you in awe, which else   186
Would feed on one another?—What's their seeking? 187

MENENIUS
For corn at their own rates, whereof, they say,   188
The city is well stored.

MARCIUS   Hang 'em! They say?
They'll sit by th' fire and presume to know
What's done i'th' Capitol, who's like to rise,   191
Who thrives and who declines; side factions and
   give out   192
Conjectural marriages, making parties strong   193
And feebling such as stand not in their liking   194
Below their cobbled shoes. They say there's grain
   enough?   195
Would the nobility lay aside their ruth   196
And let me use my sword, I'd make a quarry   197
With thousands of these quartered slaves as high 198
As I could pick my lance.   199

MENENIUS
Nay, these are almost thoroughly persuaded,
For though abundantly they lack discretion,
Yet are they passing cowardly. But I beseech you, 202
What says the other troop?

MARCIUS   They are dissolved. Hang 'em!
They said they were an-hungry; sighed forth
   proverbs,
That hunger broke stone walls, that dogs must eat, 206

That meat was made for mouths, that the gods sent
   not   207
Corn for the rich men only. With these shreds   208
They vented their complainings, which being
   answered   209
And a petition granted them—a strange one,
To break the heart of generosity   211
And make bold power look pale—they threw their
   caps
As they would hang them on the horns o'th' moon, 213
Shouting their emulation.

MENENIUS   What is granted them? 214
MARCIUS
Five tribunes to defend their vulgar wisdoms,   215
Of their own choice. One's Junius Brutus,
Sicinius Velutus, and I know not—'Sdeath!   217
The rabble should have first unroofed the city
Ere so prevailed with me. It will in time
Win upon power and throw forth greater themes 220
For insurrection's arguing.   221
MENENIUS   This is strange.
MARCIUS   Go get you home, you fragments!   223

Enter a Messenger, hastily.

MESSENGER
Where's Caius Marcius?
MARCIUS   Here. What's the matter?
MESSENGER
The news is, sir, the Volsces are in arms.
MARCIUS
I am glad on't. Then we shall ha' means to vent 226
Our musty superfluity.—See, our best elders.   227

*Enter Sicinius Velutus, Junius Brutus,
Cominius, Titus Lartius, with other Senators.*

FIRST SENATOR
Marcius, 'tis true that you have lately told us: 228
The Volsces are in arms.
MARCIUS   They have a leader,
Tullus Aufidius, that will put you to't.   230
I sin in envying his nobility,
And were I anything but what I am
I would wish me only he.
COMINIUS   You have fought together? 233
MARCIUS
Were half to half the world by th' ears and he   234
Upon my party, I'd revolt, to make   235

171–3 You . . . sun You are no more dependable than a pan of burning coals set down on solid ice or hailstones lying in the sun (both short-lived).   173–5 Your . . . it Your distinguishing quality is to glorify the person whose wrongdoing deserves punishment and to curse the justice that punishes him.   175 Who Whoever   176 Deserves incurs. affections desires, propensities   178 evil malady.   180 rushes slender reeds.   182 now just now   183 garland object of highest honor and praise.   184 several different, various   186 which else who otherwise   187 seeking demand.   188 corn grain.   rates prices 191 like likely   192–5 side . . . shoes (they) take sides in factional disputes and gossip about conjectural alliances among the ruling classes, supporting certain factions while working to destroy others whom they regard as contemptible.   196 Would the nobility If only the nobility would.   ruth tenderheartedness   197 quarry heap of slain men (literally, deer)   198 quartered cut into quarters, slaughtered like criminals   199 pick pitch   202 passing exceedingly   205 an-hungry hungry. (The prefix an is an archaic intensifier.)   206 dogs i.e., even dogs

207 meat food   208 shreds bits, scraps (of wisdom)   209 vented discharged, excreted or farted   211 generosity the nobles   213 As as if 214 emulation rivalry of one another in shouting, or, envy of superiors.   215 tribunes official representatives of the people's interests 217 'Sdeath! i.e., By God's death! (An oath.)   220 Win upon gain advantage over   221 For insurrection's arguing to be urged by uprisings.   223 fragments scraps. (A term of contempt.)   226 on't of it.   vent discharge, cast out   227 musty superfluity moldy excess. 228 that what   230 to't i.e., to the test.   233 together against one another.   234 by th' ears at variance (with the other half)   235 Upon my party on my side

Only my wars with him. He is a lion 236
That I am proud to hunt.

FIRST SENATOR   Then, worthy Marcius,
Attend upon Cominius to these wars. 238

COMINIUS
It is your former promise.

MARCIUS   Sir, it is,
And I am constant. Titus Lartius, thou 240
Shalt see me once more strike at Tullus' face.
What, art thou stiff? Stand'st out?

LARTIUS   No, Caius Marcius, 242
I'll lean upon one crutch and fight with t'other
Ere stay behind this business.

MENENIUS   Oh, true bred!

FIRST SENATOR
Your company to th' Capitol, where, I know, 245
Our greatest friends attend us.

LARTIUS [to Cominius]   Lead you on.
[To Marcius] Follow Cominius. We must follow you;
Right worthy you priority.

COMINIUS   Noble Marcius! 248

FIRST SENATOR [to the Citizens]
Hence to your homes, begone!

MARCIUS   Nay, let them follow.
The Volsces have much corn; take these rats thither
To gnaw their garners.—Worshipful mutineers, 251
Your valor puts well forth. Pray follow. 252

         Exeunt. Citizens steal away.
         Manent Sicinius and Brutus.

SICINIUS
Was ever man so proud as is this Marcius?

BRUTUS   He has no equal.

SICINIUS
When we were chosen tribunes for the people—

BRUTUS
Marked you his lip and eyes?

SICINIUS   Nay, but his taunts.

BRUTUS
Being moved, he will not spare to gird the gods. 257

SICINIUS   Bemock the modest moon. 258

BRUTUS
The present wars devour him! He is grown 259
Too proud to be so valiant.

SICINIUS   Such a nature, 260
Tickled with good success, disdains the shadow 261
Which he treads on at noon. But I do wonder

His insolence can brook to be commanded 263
Under Cominius.

BRUTUS   Fame, at the which he aims, 264
In whom already he's well graced, cannot 265
Better be held nor more attained than by
A place below the first; for what miscarries 267
Shall be the general's fault, though he perform
To th'utmost of a man, and giddy censure 269
Will then cry out of Marcius, "Oh, if he
Had borne the business!"

SICINIUS   Besides, if things go well,
Opinion that so sticks on Marcius shall 272
Of his demerits rob Cominius.

BRUTUS   Come. 273
Half all Cominius' honors are to Marcius, 274
Though Marcius earned them not, and all his faults 275
To Marcius shall be honors, though indeed 276
In aught he merit not.

SICINIUS   Let's hence and hear 277
How the dispatch is made, and in what fashion, 278
More than his singularity, he goes 279
Upon this present action.

BRUTUS   Let's along.   *Exeunt.* 280

         ♣

[1.2]

Enter Tullus Aufidius with Senators of Corioles.

FIRST SENATOR
So, your opinion is, Aufidius,
That they of Rome are entered in our counsels 2
And know how we proceed.

AUFIDIUS   Is it not yours?
What ever have been thought on in this state 4
That could be brought to bodily act ere Rome
Had circumvention? 'Tis not four days gone 6
Since I heard thence. These are the words—I think 7
I have the letter here. Yes, here it is. [*Finding a letter.*]
[*He reads*] "They have pressed a power, but it is not
    known 9
Whether for east or west. The dearth is great, 10
The people mutinous; and, it is rumored,
Cominius, Marcius your old enemy,
Who is of Rome worse hated than of you, 13
And Titus Lartius, a most valiant Roman,
These three lead on this preparation

---

236 with against   **238 Attend upon** serve under   **240 constant** true to my promise.   **242 stiff** resistant, reluctant. (But Lartius answers as though the word had meant "stiff with age.")   **Stand'st out?** Do you refuse to engage?   **245 Your company** Let me request your company   **248 Right . . . priority** you well deserve to take precedence.   **251 garners** granaries, storehouses.   **Worshipful mutineers** Worthy mutineers. (Said with mock politeness.)   **252 puts well forth** begins to bud, shows a fair promise. (Said ironically.)   **252.2 *Manent*** They remain onstage   **257 moved** angered.   **spare to gird** refrain from scoffing at   **258 modest** i.e., as representing Diana, goddess of chastity   **259 The present** i.e., May the present   **260 to be** of being. (Or, Brutus may mean that Marcius's excessive pride makes his valor dangerous.)   **261 Tickled with** flattered by, greatly excited by

263–4 can . . . Cominius can endure to be under the command of Cominius.   **265 whom** which   **267 miscarries** goes wrong   **269 giddy censure** thoughtless popular opinion   **272–3 Opinion . . . Cominius** the good reputation that adheres to Marcius will rob Cominius of his deserts.   **274 are to** are given to   **275–7 all his . . . merit not** all Cominius' failings will redound to Marcius' honor, even though Marcius doesn't deserve it.   **278 dispatch** execution of the business   **279 More . . . singularity** i.e., with even more than his usual share of arrogance and idiosyncrasy   **280 along** go, go join.
1.2. Location: Corioles (or Corioli), southeast of Rome.
2 entered in acquainted with   **4 What** What things   **6 circumvention** i.e., warning enabling them to circumvent.   **gone** ago   **7 thence** from there.   **9 pressed a power** raised an army   **10 dearth** famine   **13 of** by

Whither 'tis bent. Most likely 'tis for you.
Consider of it."   16

FIRST SENATOR   Our army's in the field.
We never yet made doubt but Rome was ready
To answer us.

AUFIDIUS   Nor did you think it folly
To keep your great pretenses veiled till when   20
They needs must show themselves, which in the
    hatching,   21
It seemed, appeared to Rome. By the discovery   22
We shall be shortened in our aim, which was   23
To take in many towns ere almost Rome   24
Should know we were afoot.

SECOND SENATOR   Noble Aufidius,
Take your commission; hie you to your bands.   26
Let us alone to guard Corioles.
If they set down before 's, for the remove   28
Bring up your army; but I think you'll find
They've not prepared for us.

AUFIDIUS   Oh, doubt not that;   30
I speak from certainties. Nay, more,
Some parcels of their power are forth already,   32
And only hitherward. I leave Your Honors.   33
If we and Caius Marcius chance to meet,
'Tis sworn between us we shall ever strike   35
Till one can do no more.

ALL   The gods assist you!

AUFIDIUS   And keep your honors safe!

FIRST SENATOR   Farewell.

SECOND SENATOR   Farewell.

ALL   Farewell.   *Exeunt omnes.* 41

❖

[1.3]

*Enter Volumnia and Virgilia, mother and wife to
Marcius. They set them down on two low stools
and sew.*

VOLUMNIA   I pray you, daughter, sing, or express
yourself in a more comfortable sort. If my son were   2
my husband, I should freelier rejoice in that absence   3
wherein he won honor than in the embracements of
his bed where he would show most love. When yet
he was but tender-bodied and the only son of my   6
womb, when youth with comeliness plucked all gaze   7
his way, when for a day of kings' entreaties a mother   8

should not sell him an hour from her beholding, I, con-   9
sidering how honor would become such a person—   10
that it was no better than picturelike to hang by the
wall, if renown made it not stir—was pleased to let   12
him seek danger where he was like to find fame. To a   13
cruel war I sent him, from whence he returned, his
brows bound with oak. I tell thee, daughter, I sprang   15
not more in joy at first hearing he was a man-child than
now in first seeing he had proved himself a man.   17

VIRGILIA   But had he died in the business, madam,
how then?

VOLUMNIA   Then his good report should have been my
son; I therein would have found issue. Hear me pro-   21
fess sincerely: had I a dozen sons, each in my love alike
and none less dear than thine and my good Marcius,
I had rather had eleven die nobly for their country
than one voluptuously surfeit out of action.   25

Enter a Gentlewoman.

GENTLEWOMAN   Madam, the Lady Valeria is come to
visit you.

VIRGILIA
Beseech you, give me leave to retire myself.   28

VOLUMNIA   Indeed, you shall not.
Methinks I hear hither your husband's drum,   30
See him pluck Aufidius down by th' hair;   31
As children from a bear, the Volsces shunning him.   32
Methinks I see him stamp thus, and call thus: 33
"Come on, you cowards! You were got in fear,   34
Though you were born in Rome." His bloody brow
With his mailed hand then wiping, forth he goes   36
Like to a harvestman that's tasked to mow   37
Or all or lose his hire.   38

VIRGILIA
His bloody brow? O Jupiter, no blood!

VOLUMNIA
Away, you fool! It more becomes a man
Than gilt his trophy. The breasts of Hecuba,   41
When she did suckle Hector, looked not lovelier
Than Hector's forehead when it spit forth blood
At Grecian sword, contemning.—Tell Valeria   44
We are fit to bid her welcome.   *Exit Gentlewoman.* 45

VIRGILIA
Heavens bless my lord from fell Aufidius!   46

---

16 Whither 'tis bent wherever it is going. **20 pretenses** intentions
21 needs necessarily **22 appeared** became evident. **discovery** disclosure **23 be shortened in** fall short of **24 take in** capture. **ere**
almost even before **26 hie** hasten. **bands** companies of soldiers.
28 set down before 's lay siege to us. **32 parcels** parts.
30 prepared for us i.e., laid plans to besiege us. **32 parcels** parts.
forth marching forward **33 only hitherward** i.e., marching toward
this place and this alone. **Your Honors** i.e., you. (Plural and honorific.) **35 ever strike** keep on exchanging blows **41 s.d. *omnes*** all.
1.3. Location: Rome. Marcius's house, which may be (as indicated in
Plutarch) his mother's house; see 2.1.194.
2 comfortable sort cheerful manner. **3 freelier** more readily **6 tender-bodied** i.e., young **7 comeliness** beauty. **all gaze** the gaze of
all **8 for** even for

9 should . . . beholding i.e., would not let her son out of her sight
even for an hour at any price **10 such a person** such a fine figure of
a youth **12 if renown . . . stir** if desire for fame did not stir it to
action **13 like** likely **15 bound with oak** i.e., as a badge to signify
that he had saved the life of a Roman citizen. (The *cruel war* was that
against the Latins and Tarquin the Proud; see 2.1.148–9 and note.)
17 now i.e., at that time, when he returned from war **21 issue** offspring. **25 voluptuously surfeit** live extravagantly for pleasure
28 retire myself go in. **30 hither** coming this way **31 See** i.e.,
methinks I see **32 As . . . him** (methinks I see) the Volsces avoiding
him as children flee from a bear. **33 stamp thus** (Volumnia gestures.)
call i.e., exhort his own troops **34 got** begotten **36 mailed** protected by mail, armored **37 tasked** set the task **38 Or** either. **hire**
wages. **41 Than . . . trophy** i.e., than gilding adorns his monument.
Hecuba Queen of Troy, mother of Hector and many other sons
44 contemning scorning the Grecian sword, as if spitting on it.
45 fit ready **46 bless** protect. **fell** cruel

VOLUMNIA
He'll beat Aufidius' head below his knee
And tread upon his neck.   48

Enter Valeria, with an usher and a Gentlewoman.

VALERIA   My ladies both, good day to you.
VOLUMNIA   Sweet madam!
VIRGILIA   I am glad to see Your Ladyship.
VALERIA   How do you both? You are manifest house-   52
keepers. What are you sewing here? A fine spot, in   53
good faith. How does your little son?
VIRGILIA   I thank Your Ladyship; well, good madam.
VOLUMNIA   He had rather see the swords and hear a
drum than look upon his schoolmaster.
VALERIA   O' my word, the father's son. I'll swear 'tis a   58
very pretty boy. O' my troth, I looked upon him
o'Wednesday half an hour together. H'as such a con-   60
firmed countenance! I saw him run after a gilded but-   61
terfly, and when he caught it, he let it go again, and
after it again, and over and over he comes and up   63
again, catched it again. Or whether his fall enraged   64
him, or how 'twas, he did so set his teeth and tear   65
it! Oh, I warrant, how he mammocked it!   66
VOLUMNIA   One on 's father's moods.   67
VALERIA   Indeed, la, 'tis a noble child.
VIRGILIA   A crack, madam.   69
VALERIA   Come, lay aside your stitchery. I must have
you play the idle huswife with me this afternoon.   71
VIRGILIA   No, good madam, I will not out of doors.   72
VALERIA   Not out of doors?
VOLUMNIA   She shall, she shall.
VIRGILIA   Indeed, no, by your patience. I'll not over the   75
threshold till my lord return from the wars.
VALERIA   Fie, you confine yourself most unreasonably.
Come, you must go visit the good lady that lies in.   78
VIRGILIA   I will wish her speedy strength and visit her
with my prayers, but I cannot go thither.
VOLUMNIA   Why, I pray you?
VIRGILIA   'Tis not to save labor, nor that I want love.   82
VALERIA   You would be another Penelope. Yet they   83
say all the yarn she spun in Ulysses' absence did but
fill Ithaca full of moths. Come, I would your cambric   85
were sensible as your finger, that you might leave   86
pricking it for pity. Come, you shall go with us.
VIRGILIA   No, good madam, pardon me; indeed, I will
not forth.

VALERIA   In truth, la, go with me, and I'll tell you
excellent news of your husband.
VIRGILIA   Oh, good madam, there can be none yet.
VALERIA   Verily, I do not jest with you. There came
news from him last night.
VIRGILIA   Indeed, madam?
VALERIA   In earnest, it's true; I heard a senator speak it.
Thus it is: the Volsces have an army forth, against
whom Cominius the general is gone with one part of
our Roman power. Your lord and Titus Lartius are set
down before their city Corioles. They nothing doubt   100
prevailing, and to make it brief wars. This is true, on   101
mine honor, and so, I pray, go with us.
VIRGILIA   Give me excuse, good madam. I will obey
you in everything hereafter.
VOLUMNIA   Let her alone, lady. As she is now, she will
but disease our better mirth.   106
VALERIA   In troth, I think she would. Fare you well,   107
then. Come, good sweet lady. Prithee, Virgilia, turn
thy solemness out o' door and go along with us.
VIRGILIA   No, at a word, madam. Indeed, I must not. I   110
wish you much mirth.
VALERIA   Well, then, farewell.   *Exeunt ladies.*

❖

[1.4]

*Enter Marcius, Titus Lartius, with drum and
colors, with captains and soldiers, as before the city
[of] Corioles. To them a Messenger.*

MARCIUS
Yonder comes news. A wager they have met.
LARTIUS
My horse to yours, no.
MARCIUS   'Tis done.
LARTIUS   Agreed.   2
MARCIUS [*to the Messenger*]
Say, has our general met the enemy?
MESSENGER
They lie in view, but have not spoke as yet.   4
LARTIUS
So, the good horse is mine.
MARCIUS   I'll buy him of you.   5
LARTIUS
No, I'll nor sell nor give him. Lend you him I will   6
For half a hundred years.—Summon the town.   7
MARCIUS   How far off lie these armies?
MESSENGER   Within this mile and half.
MARCIUS
Then shall we hear their 'larum and they ours.   10

48.1 *an usher* a lady's male attendant   **52–3 manifest housekeepers**
out-and-out stay-at-homes.   **53 sewing** embroidering.   **spot** pattern,
figure   **58 O' my** On my   **60 H'as** He has   **60–1 confirmed** resolute
61 gilded brilliantly colored   **63 over and over** head over heels
64 Or whether Whether   **65 set** clench   **66 mammocked** tore into
fragments   **67 on 's** of his   **69 crack** pert little fellow   **71 huswife**
housewife   **72 out** go out.   **75 over** step over   **78 lies in** is expecting
a child.   **82 want** am deficient in   **83 You would be** i.e., One might
take you for.   **Penelope** faithful wife of Ulysses in Homer's *Odyssey*,
who delayed her suitors by insisting she must finish the weaving
which she then unraveled every night.   **85 moths** (1) insects eating
the cloth (2) idle courtiers parasitically consuming her wealth.
85–6 I . . . sensible I wish your fine white linen cambric cloth were as
sensitive   **86 leave** cease

100–1 nothing doubt prevailing have no doubt at all that they will
prevail   **106 disease . . . mirth** trouble our good cheer.   **107 troth**
truth, faith   **110 at a word** once for all
1.4. Location: Before Corioles.
2 My horse . . . no i.e., I'll bet my horse against yours that they,
Cominius's Roman force and the Volscian army under Aufidius, one
and one half miles away, have not met in battle.   **4 in view** i.e., in
view of one another.   **spoke** i.e., encountered   **5 of** (back) from
6 nor sell neither sell   **7 Summon** i.e., Summon by trumpet, to parley   **10 'larum** call to arms

Now, Mars, I prithee, make us quick in work,   11
That we with smoking swords may march from hence   12
To help our fielded friends! Come, blow thy blast.   13

They sound a parley. Enter two Senators, with others, on the walls of Corioles.

Tullus Aufidius, is he within your walls?

FIRST SENATOR
No, nor a man that fears you less than he: 15
That's lesser than a little. (*Drum afar off.*) Hark! Our drums   16
Are bringing forth our youth. We'll break our walls   17
Rather than they shall pound us up. Our gates,   18
Which yet seem shut, we have but pinned with rushes;   19
They'll open of themselves. (*Alarum far off.*) Hark you, far off!
There is Aufidius. List what work he makes   21
Amongst your cloven army.
                    [*Exeunt Volscians from the walls.*]
MARCIUS   Oh, they are at it!   22
LARTIUS
Their noise be our instruction. Ladders, ho!   23

Enter the army of the Volsces [from the city].

MARCIUS
They fear us not, but issue forth their city.   24
Now put your shields before your hearts, and fight
With hearts more proof than shields. Advance, brave Titus!   26
They do disdain us much beyond our thoughts,   27
Which makes me sweat with wrath. Come on, my fellows!
He that retires, I'll take him for a Volsce,
And he shall feel mine edge.   30

*Alarum. The Romans are beat back to their trenches [and thus exeunt].
Enter Marcius, cursing, [with Soldiers].*

MARCIUS
All the contagion of the south light on you,   31
You shames of Rome! You herd of—Boils and plagues
Plaster you o'er, that you may be abhorred   33
Farther than seen, and one infect another   34
Against the wind a mile! You souls of geese,   35
That bear the shapes of men, how have you run

From slaves that apes would beat! Pluto and hell!   37
All hurt behind! Backs red, and faces pale   38
With flight and agued fear! Mend and charge home,   39
Or, by the fires of heaven, I'll leave the foe
And make my wars on you. Look to't. Come on!
If you'll stand fast, we'll beat them to their wives,
As they us to our trenches. Follow 's!

Another alarum; [the Volsces fly back into the city,] and Marcius follows them to [the] gates.

So, now the gates are ope. Now prove good seconds!   44
'Tis for the followers fortune widens them,   45
Not for the fliers. Mark me, and do the like.   46
            Enter the gates and is shut in.
FIRST SOLDIER   Foolhardiness. Not I.
SECOND SOLDIER   Nor I.
FIRST SOLDIER   See, they have shut him in.
ALL   To th' pot, I warrant him.   50
                    Alarum continues.

Enter Titus Lartius.

LARTIUS
What is become of Marcius?
ALL   Slain, sir, doubtless.
FIRST SOLDIER
Following the fliers at the very heels,
With them he enters, who upon the sudden
Clapped to their gates. He is himself alone,   54
To answer all the city.
LARTIUS   Oh, noble fellow!   55
Who sensibly outdares his senseless sword,   56
And, when it bows, stand'st up. Thou art left, Marcius.   57
A carbuncle entire, as big as thou art,   58
Were not so rich a jewel. Thou wast a soldier
Even to Cato's wish, not fierce and terrible   60
Only in strokes, but, with thy grim looks and
The thunderlike percussion of thy sounds,
Thou mad'st thine enemies shake, as if the world
Were feverous and did tremble.

Enter Marcius, bleeding, [from the city], assaulted by the enemy.

FIRST SOLDIER   Look, sir.
LARTIUS   Oh, 'tis Marcius!
Let's fetch him off, or make remain alike.   67
            They fight, and all enter the city.

❧

11 **Mars** Roman god of war   12 **smoking** steaming   13 **fielded** in the field of battle.   13.2 **on the walls** i.e., in the gallery backstage. (Throughout this scene, the tiring-house facade represents the *walls* of Corioles, and a door in that facade represents the *gates*.)   15–16 **nor . . . little** i.e., Aufidius fears you scarcely at all, and others fear even less so, if that were possible.   17 **break** break out of   18 **pound us up** shut us up as in a pound.   19 **rushes** hollow-stemmed reeds   21 **List** Listen to   22 **cloven** split in two, divided, cut to pieces   23 **Their . . . instruction** Let the sound of their battle be an example to us to begin.   24 **issue forth** pour forth from   26 **proof** impenetrable   27 **beyond our thoughts** more than we thought possible   30 **edge** sword edge.   31 **south** south wind (as a supposed source of contagion)   33–4 **abhorred . . . seen** loathed (because of your foul smell) before you are even seen   35 **Against . . . mile** so greatly that it will carry a mile against the wind.

37 **Pluto** Roman god of the underworld   38 **hurt behind** wounded in the back (i.e., in cowardly fashion).   39 **agued** trembling as though with an ague or fever.   **Mend** (1) Do better, reform your battle ranks (2) Recover from this fever of cowardice.   **home** to the heart of the enemy's defenses   44 **seconds** supporters.   45 **followers** pursuers   46 **the fliers** those pursued.   50 **To th' pot** To the cooking pot (i.e., to certain destruction)   54 **Clapped to** shut   55 **answer** confront   56–7 **Who . . . up** Who, though sensitive to pain, dares more than his insensible sword; it might bend to fear, he would not.   57 **left** left alone (in the city); unique   58 **carbuncle entire** flawless brilliant, red gemstone   60 **Cato** Marcus Cato the Censor (234–149 B.C.), celebrated in Plutarch as a staunch soldier and exponent of Roman ethics   67 **fetch him off** rescue him.   **make remain alike** remain to share his fate.

[1.5]

Enter certain Romans, with spoils.

FIRST ROMAN   This will I carry to Rome.
SECOND ROMAN   And I this.
THIRD ROMAN   A murrain on't! I took this for silver.   3
    Exeunt. Alarum continues still afar off.

Enter Marcius and Titus [Lartius] with a trumpet.
    Exeunt [Romans with spoils].

MARCIUS
    See here these movers that do prize their hours   4
    At a cracked drachma! Cushions, leaden spoons,   5
    Irons of a doit, doublets that hangmen would   6
    Bury with those that wore them, these base slaves,   7
    Ere yet the fight be done, pack up. Down with them!
    And hark, what noise the General makes! To him!   9
    There is the man of my soul's hate, Aufidius,
    Piercing our Romans. Then, valiant Titus, take
    Convenient numbers to make good the city,   12
    Whilst I, with those that have the spirit, will haste
    To help Cominius.
LARTIUS   Worthy sir, thou bleed'st.
    Thy exercise hath been too violent
    For a second course of fight.
MARCIUS   Sir, praise me not.   16
    My work hath yet not warmed me. Fare you well.
    The blood I drop is rather physical   18
    Than dangerous to me. To Aufidius thus
    I will appear, and fight.
LARTIUS   Now the fair goddess Fortune
    Fall deep in love with thee, and her great charms   22
    Misguide thy opposers' swords! Bold gentleman,
    Prosperity be thy page!
MARCIUS   Thy friend no less   24
    Than those she placeth highest! So, farewell.   25
LARTIUS   Thou worthiest Marcius!   [*Exit Marcius.*]
    Go sound thy trumpet in the marketplace.
    Call thither all the officers o'th' town,
    Where they shall know our mind. Away!   *Exeunt.*

❖

1.5. Location: The siege of Corioles continues.
0.1 *Enter* i.e., Enter from the city, through the stage door in the facade;
see 1.4.13.2 note. Also at line 3.2.   **3 murrain** plague.   **3.2 trumpet**
trumpeter.   **4–5 See . . . drachma!** i.e., (scornfully) Look at these busy
soldiers that cherish the precious time they should be fighting as
though it were a cracked (and therefore valueless) coin of small
denomination!   **6 Irons of a doit** weapons worth a coin of small
value.   **doublets** tight-fitting coats, usually quilted and decorated
6–7 hangmen . . . them i.e., hangmen, entitled to the clothes of persons they put to death, would not have these   **9 the General** i.e.,
Cominius, fighting Aufidius nearby   **12 Convenient numbers**
appropriate or effective numbers.   **make good** hold, secure
16 course bout, engagement.   **praise me not** (Coriolanus answers
ironically, as though Lartius were praising him for bleeding instead of
cautioning him.)   **18 physical** healthful. (Through bloodletting, a
standard treatment.)   **22 charms** spells   **24 Prosperity be thy page!**
i.e., may success attend on you!   **Thy . . . less** i.e., May prosperity be
no less your friend

[1.6]

Enter Cominius, as it were in retire, with soldiers.

COMINIUS
    Breathe you, my friends. Well fought! We are come off   1
    Like Romans, neither foolish in our stands   2
    Nor cowardly in retire. Believe me, sirs,
    We shall be charged again. Whiles we have struck,   4
    By interims and conveying gusts we have heard   5
    The charges of our friends. The Roman gods   6
    Lead their successes as we wish our own,   7
    That both our powers, with smiling fronts
    encount'ring,   8
    May give you thankful sacrifice!

Enter a Messenger.

    Thy news?
MESSENGER
    The citizens of Corioles have issued   10
    And given to Lartius and to Marcius battle.
    I saw our party to their trenches driven,
    And then I came away.
COMINIUS   Though thou speakest truth,
    Methinks thou speak'st not well. How long is't since?
MESSENGER   Above an hour, my lord.
COMINIUS
    'Tis not a mile; briefly we heard their drums.   16
    How couldst thou in a mile confound an hour   17
    And bring thy news so late?
MESSENGER   Spies of the Volsces   18
    Held me in chase, that I was forced to wheel   19
    Three or four miles about; else had I, sir,   20
    Half an hour since brought my report.   [*Exit.*]

Enter Marcius, [bloody].

COMINIUS   Who's yonder,   21
    That does appear as he were flayed? O gods!   22
    He has the stamp of Marcius, and I have   23
    Before-time seen him thus.
MARCIUS   Come I too late?   24
COMINIUS
    The shepherd knows not thunder from a tabor   25
    More than I know the sound of Marcius' tongue
    From every meaner man.
MARCIUS   Come I too late?   27

**1.6. Location: Near the camp of Cominius. The fighting near Cori-
oles, heard until now at a short distance, is at a lull.**
0.1 *in retire* disengaged from the fighting. (Also in line 3.)   **1 Breathe
you** Catch your breath.   **are come off** have left the field of battle
2 foolish foolhardy   **4 struck** fought, been striking blows   **5 By . . .
gusts** at intervals and borne to us on the wind   **6 friends** i.e., the
besiegers of Corioles.   **The Roman** May the Roman   **7 their successes** the fortunes of our friends (i.e., Lartius and Marcius)   **8 powers** armies.   **fronts** (1) foreheads, brows (2) front lines   **10 issued**
issued forth   **16 briefly** a short time ago (and at short distance)
17 confound consume   **18 Spies** Scouts   **19 that** so that
19–20 wheel . . . about make a detour of three or four miles   **20 else**
otherwise   **21 since** ago   **22 as** as if   **23 stamp** bearing, form
24 Before-time formerly   **25 knows** distinguishes. (Also in line 26.)
tabor small drum   **27 meaner** less noble

COMINIUS
    Ay, if you come not in the blood of others,   28
    But mantled in your own.
MARCIUS   Oh, let me clip ye   29
    In arms as sound as when I wooed, in heart
    As merry as when our nuptial day was done,
    And tapers burnt to bedward!   [*They embrace.*] 32
COMINIUS
    Flower of warriors, how is't with Titus Lartius?
MARCIUS
    As with a man busied about decrees: 34
    Condemning some to death, and some to exile;
    Ransoming him, or pitying, threat'ning th'other;   36
    Holding Corioles in the name of Rome,
    Even like a fawning greyhound in the leash,
    To let him slip at will.
COMINIUS   Where is that slave   39
    Which told me they had beat you to your trenches?
    Where is he? Call him hither.
MARCIUS   Let him alone;
    He did inform the truth. But for our gentlemen,   42
    The common file—a plague! Tribunes for them!—   43
    The mouse ne'er shunned the cat as they did budge 44
    From rascals worse than they.
COMINIUS   But how prevailed you?
MARCIUS
    Will the time serve to tell? I do not think.
    Where is the enemy? Are you lords o'th' field?
    If not, why cease you till you are so?
COMINIUS
    Marcius, we have at disadvantage fought
    And did retire to win our purpose.   50
MARCIUS
    How lies their battle? Know you on which side   51
    They have placed their men of trust?
COMINIUS   As I guess, Marcius,
    Their bands i'th' vaward are the Antiates,   53
    Of their best trust; o'er them Aufidius,   54
    Their very heart of hope.
MARCIUS   I do beseech you,   55
    By all the battles wherein we have fought,
    By th' blood we have shed together, by th' vows we
       have made
    To endure friends, that you directly set me   58
    Against Aufidius and his Antiates,
    And that you not delay the present, but,   60

    Filling the air with swords advanced and darts,   61
    We prove this very hour.
COMINIUS   Though I could wish   62
    You were conducted to a gentle bath
    And balms applied to you, yet dare I never   64
    Deny your asking. Take your choice of those
    That best can aid your action.
MARCIUS   Those are they
    That most are willing. If any such be here—
    As it were sin to doubt—that love this painting   68
    Wherein you see me smeared; if any fear
    Lesser his person than an ill report;   70
    If any think brave death outweighs bad life,
    And that his country's dearer than himself,
    Let him alone, or so many so minded,   73
    Wave thus [*waving his sword*] to express his
       disposition,
    And follow Marcius.
          They all shout and wave their swords,
       take him up in their arms, and cast up their caps.
    Oh, me alone! Make you a sword of me?   76
    If these shows be not outward, which of you   77
    But is four Volsces? None of you but is   78
    Able to bear against the great Aufidius
    A shield as hard as his. A certain number,
    Though thanks to all, must I select from all;
    The rest shall bear the business in some other fight,
    As cause will be obeyed. Please you to march,   83
    And I shall quickly draw out my command,   84
    Which men are best inclined.
COMINIUS   March on, my fellows.
    Make good this ostentation, and you shall   86
    Divide in all with us.   *Exeunt.* 87

❖

[1.7]

Titus Lartius, having set a guard upon Corioles,
going with drum and trumpet toward Cominius
and Caius Marcius, enters [from the city] with a
Lieutenant, other soldiers, and a scout.

LARTIUS
    So, let the ports be guarded. Keep your duties   1
    As I have set them down. If I do send, dispatch
    Those centuries to our aid; the rest will serve   3
    For a short holding. If we lose the field,   4
    We cannot keep the town.
LIEUTENANT   Fear not our care, sir.   5

28–9 Ay . . . own i.e., If you yourself are bleeding all that blood, you are presumably too weak to help, but if it is enemies' blood, you are in time to shed more. **29 clip** embrace **32 tapers . . . bedward** i.e., candles burned low, indicating the approach of bedtime or showing the way to bed. **34 busied about decrees** busy with judicial decisions **36 Ransoming . . . th'other** releasing one man for ransom money, mercifully releasing another without ransom, threatening still another **39 let him slip** unleash him **42 inform** report. **gentlemen** (Said sarcastically of the ordinary soldiers.) **43 common file** ordinary soldiers, plebeians **44 budge** flinch **50 to . . . purpose** i.e., to regroup. **51 battle** army, battle line. **53–4 Their bands . . . trust** the troops in the vanguard are from Antium, their most trustworthy **55 Their . . . hope** the leader on whom their hopes depend. **58 endure** continue. **directly** (1) at once (2) face to face **60 not delay the present** do not delay now

61 advanced raised. **darts** lances **62 prove** try the fortunes of **64 balms** healing ointments **68 painting** i.e., blood **70 Lesser . . . report** less for his safety than for his reputation **73 Let . . . minded** let that individual by himself, or as many as are so minded **76 Oh . . . of me?** Do you make a sword of me alone, choose me as your weapon? (Some editors assign this line to the soldiers.) **77 outward** external, deceptive **78 But is** is not the equal of **83 As . . . obeyed** as necessity shall require. **84 draw . . . command** pick out my chosen troop **86 ostentation** show of zeal **87 Divide** share **1.7. Location: Before the gates of Corioles. The military action near Corioles continues.**
1 ports gates **3 centuries** companies of a hundred **4 short holding** i.e., brief occupation of the city. **5 Fear not** Don't worry about

LARTIUS   Hence, and shut your gates upon 's.   6
[*To the scout*] Our guider, come; to th' Roman camp
   conduct us.
                  Exeunt [*separately, the Lieutenant returning*
                              into the city].

[1.8]

     Alarum as in battle. Enter Marcius and Aufidius
     at several doors.

MARCIUS
   I'll fight with none but thee, for I do hate thee
   Worse than a promise-breaker.
AUFIDIUS   We hate alike.
   Not Afric owns a serpent I abhor   3
   More than thy fame and envy. Fix thy foot.   4
MARCIUS
   Let the first budger die the other's slave,   5
   And the gods doom him after!
AUFIDIUS
   If I fly, Marcius, hollo me like a hare.   7
MARCIUS   Within these three hours, Tullus,
   Alone I fought in your Corioles' walls,
   And made what work I pleased. 'Tis not my blood
   Wherein thou see'st me masked. For thy revenge
   Wrench up thy power to th' highest.
AUFIDIUS   Wert thou the Hector   12
   That was the whip of your bragged progeny,   13
   Thou shouldst not scape me here.   *Here they fight,*
     and certain Volsces come in the aid of Aufidius.
     Marcius fights till they be driven in breathless.
   Officious, and not valiant, you have shamed me
   In your condemnèd seconds.   [*Exeunt.*]   16

[1.9]

     Flourish. Alarum. A retreat is sounded. Enter, at
     one door, Cominius with the Romans; at another
     door Marcius, with his arm in a scarf.

COMINIUS
   If I should tell thee o'er this thy day's work,   1
   Thou't not believe thy deeds. But I'll report it   2
   Where senators shall mingle tears with smiles,

   Where great patricians shall attend and shrug,   4
   I'th'end admire; where ladies shall be frighted   5
   And, gladly quaked, hear more; where the dull
     tribunes,   6
   That with the fusty plebeians hate thine honors,   7
   Shall say against their hearts, "We thank the gods   8
   Our Rome hath such a soldier."
   Yet cam'st thou to a morsel of this feast,   10
   Having fully dined before.
         Enter Titus [*Lartius*] *with his power, from the*
         pursuit.
LARTIUS   Oh, General,   11
   Here is the steed, we the caparison.   12
   Hadst thou beheld—
MARCIUS   Pray now, no more. My mother,
   Who has a charter to extol her blood,   14
   When she does praise me grieves me. I have done
   As you have done—that's what I can;
   Induced as you have been—that's for my country.
   He that has but effected his good will   18
   Hath overta'en mine act.
COMINIUS   You shall not be   19
   The grave of your deserving. Rome must know   20
   The value of her own. 'Twere a concealment
   Worse than a theft, no less than a traducement,   22
   To hide your doings and to silence that
   Which, to the spire and top of praises vouched,   24
   Would seem but modest. Therefore, I beseech you—   25
   In sign of what you are, not to reward   26
   What you have done—before our army hear me.
MARCIUS
   I have some wounds upon me, and they smart
   To hear themselves remembered.
COMINIUS   Should they not,   29
   Well might they fester 'gainst ingratitude   30
   And tent themselves with death. Of all the horses,   31
   Whereof we have ta'en good and good store, of all   32
   The treasure in this field achieved and city,
   We render you the tenth, to be ta'en forth   34
   Before the common distribution
   At your only choice.
MARCIUS   I thank you, General,   36
   But cannot make my heart consent to take

---

6 **Hence** Get a move on
1.8. Location: A field of battle near the Roman camp. The military action near Corioles continues.
0.2 *several* separate   **3 Not . . . serpent** There is no serpent in Africa
4 fame and envy envied reputation.   **Fix thy foot** Stand and fight.
5 budger one who flinches   **7 hollo** cry in pursuit of   **12 Wrench up**
strain, wrest, pull   **13 That . . . progeny** who was foremost among
your boasted Trojan ancestors in scourging the Greeks. (Marcius, as a
Roman, could claim descent from the Trojan prince, Aeneas, legendary founder of Rome.)   **16 condemnèd seconds** futile and
despised efforts at assistance.
1.9. Location: Scene continues. The Roman camp. The military action near Corioles continues.
0.1 *retreat* trumpet signal to call off pursuit   **0.3** *scarf* sling.
1–2 If . . . deeds If I recounted to you this day's work of yours, you'd
not believe it.

4–5 attend . . . admire listen and shrug their shoulders at first but
finally marvel   **6 gladly quaked** thrilling to the *frisson* of danger.
dull sullen   **7 fusty** moldy, ill-smelling   **8 against their hearts**
unwillingly   **10–11 Yet cam'st . . . before** i.e., This battle was just a
small skirmish in comparison with the major battle you had already
fought.   **11 s.d.** *power* army   **12 steed** i.e., Marcius.   **caparison** mere
trappings of a steed.   **14 charter . . . blood** right to praise her child
18 He Anyone.   **effected** manifested in action   **19 overta'en** surpassed   **19–20 You . . . deserving** You shall not conceal your merit (by
your modesty).   **22 traducement** calumny, slander, deceptive hoodwinking   **24 to . . . vouched** proclaimed in the highest possible terms
of praise   **25 modest** moderate, barely sufficient (in relation to all you
did).   **26 sign** token merely   **29 not** i.e., not hear themselves praised.
(A smarting, open wound is less likely to fester.)   **30 'gainst** in the
face of   **31 tent . . . death** i.e., find no remedy short of death. (To *tent* a
wound is to probe and keep it open with a rolled bandage, to prevent
festering.)   **32 good and good store** excellent ones and plenty of them
34 the tenth one tenth   **36 At . . . choice** exactly as you choose.

A bribe to pay my sword. I do refuse it,
And stand upon my common part with those   39
That have beheld the doing.   *A long flourish.* 40
                    They all cry "Marcius! Marcius!",
                    cast up their caps and lances.
                    Cominius and Lartius stand bare.
May these same instruments, which you profane,
Never sound more! When drums and trumpets shall
I'th' field prove flatterers, let courts and cities be
Made all of false-faced soothing! When steel grows   44
Soft as the parasite's silk, let him be made   45
An overture for th' wars. No more, I say!   46
For that I have not washed my nose that bled,   47
Or foiled some debile wretch—which without note   48
Here's many else have done—you shout me forth   49
In acclamations hyperbolical,
As if I loved my little should be dieted   51
In praises sauced with lies.

COMINIUS   Too modest are you,   52
More cruel to your good report than grateful
To us that give you truly. By your patience,   54
If 'gainst yourself you be incensed, we'll put you,
Like one that means his proper harm, in manacles,   56
Then reason safely with you. Therefore be it known,
As to us, to all the world, that Caius Marcius
Wears this war's garland, in token of the which   59
My noble steed, known to the camp, I give him,
With all his trim belonging; and from this time,   61
For what he did before Corioles, call him,
With all th'applause and clamor of the host,
Caius Marcius Coriolanus! Bear
Th'addition nobly ever!   65
                    Flourish. Trumpets sound, and drums.

ALL   Caius Marcius Coriolanus!
CORIOLANUS   I will go wash,
And when my face is fair you shall perceive   68
Whether I blush or no. Howbeit, I thank you.
I mean to stride your steed, and at all times   70
To undercrest your good addition   71
To th' fairness of my power.

COMINIUS   So, to our tent,   72
Where, ere we do repose us, we will write
To Rome of our success. You, Titus Lartius,
Must to Corioles back. Send us to Rome

The best, with whom we may articulate   76
For their own good and ours.
LARTIUS   I shall, my lord.
CORIOLANUS
The gods begin to mock me. I, that now
Refused most princely gifts, am bound to beg   79
Of my lord general.
COMINIUS   Take't, 'tis yours. What is't?
CORIOLANUS
I sometime lay here in Corioles   81
At a poor man's house; he used me kindly.   82
He cried to me; I saw him prisoner;   83
But then Aufidius was within my view,
And wrath o'erwhelmed my pity. I request you
To give my poor host freedom.
COMINIUS   Oh, well begged!
Were he the butcher of my son, he should
Be free as is the wind. Deliver him, Titus.   88
LARTIUS
Marcius, his name?
CORIOLANUS   By Jupiter, forgot!
I am weary; yea, my memory is tired.
Have we no wine here?
COMINIUS   Go we to our tent.
The blood upon your visage dries; 'tis time
It should be looked to. Come.
                    A flourish. Cornets. Exeunt.

❧

[1.10]

*Enter Tullus Aufidius, bloody, with two or three
Soldiers.*

AUFIDIUS   The town is ta'en.
A SOLDIER
'Twill be delivered back on good condition.   2
AUFIDIUS   Condition?
I would I were a Roman, for I cannot,
Being a Volsce, be that I am. Condition?   5
What good condition can a treaty find   6
I'th' part that is at mercy? Five times, Marcius,   7
I have fought with thee; so often hast thou beat me,   8
And wouldst do so, I think, should we encounter
As often as we eat. By th'elements,
If e'er again I meet him beard to beard,
He's mine or I am his. Mine emulation   12
Hath not that honor in't it had; for where   13
I thought to crush him in an equal force,   14
True sword to sword, I'll potch at him some way   15

---

39 **stand . . . part** insist on having only my regular share   **40 beheld the doing** seen the action.   **40.3 bare** bareheaded.   **44 Made . . . soothing** given over utterly to hypocritical flattery.   **44–6 When . . . wars** When steel armor grows as soft as the silk of courtly parasites, let the parasite be made an overture—an excuse or prompting—for us to fight on his behalf. (Cominius implies that Romans would never fight on such conditions, just as cities will never be entirely false, because drums and trumpets, as touchstones of truth, would not permit it.) (A difficult passage to which various emendations have been proposed.)   **47 For that** Because   **48 foiled** have overthrown. **debile** weak.   **note** notice taken   **49 else** others   **51 my little** that the little I have done.   **dieted** fed   **52 In** on, by.   **sauced** seasoned   **54 give** report   **56 means . . . harm** intends to injure himself   **59 garland** (An emblem of victory.)   **61 his trim belonging** the equipment that goes with it   **65 Th'addition** the title   **68 fair** clean   **70 stride** bestride   **71–2 To . . . power** to bear and support the title you have given me to the best of my ability, as if it were a heraldic crest.

76 **best** i.e., best in blood among the Volscians.   **articulate** come to terms (about the return of Corioles to the Volscians)   **79 bound** obliged   **81 sometime lay** once lodged   **82 used** treated   **83 cried** cried out (at the time of the battle just ended)   **88 Deliver** Release   **1.10. Location: Outside of Corioles, after the battle.**
2 **condition** terms.   **5 be . . . am** i.e., be honorable, proud.   **6 good condition** state of well-being. (With a play on "favorable terms," as in line 2.)   **7 I' . . . mercy** for the side that lies at the mercy of the winner.   **8 so** just so   **12 emulation** rivalry   **13 where** whereas   **14 in an equal force** on equal terms   **15 potch** thrust, poke

Or wrath or craft may get him.

A SOLDIER   He's the devil.   16

AUFIDIUS
Bolder, though not so subtle. My valor's poisoned
With only suff'ring stain by him; for him   18
Shall fly out of itself. Nor sleep nor sanctuary,   19
Being naked, sick, nor fane nor Capitol,   20
The prayers of priests nor times of sacrifice,   21
Embarquements all of fury, shall lift up   22
Their rotten privilege and custom 'gainst   23
My hate to Marcius. Where I find him, were it   24
At home, upon my brother's guard, even there,   25
Against the hospitable canon, would I   26
Wash my fierce hand in 's heart. Go you to th' city;
Learn how 'tis held, and what they are that must   28
Be hostages for Rome.

A SOLDIER   Will not you go?   29

AUFIDIUS
I am attended at the cyprus grove. I pray you—   30
'Tis south the city mills—bring me word thither   31
How the world goes, that to the pace of it   32
I may spur on my journey.

A SOLDIER   I shall, sir.

[Exeunt separately.]

❧

2.1

*Enter Menenius with the two tribunes of the
people, Sicinius and Brutus.*

MENENIUS   The augurer tells me we shall have news   1
tonight.

BRUTUS   Good or bad?

MENENIUS   Not according to the prayer of the people,   4
for they love not Marcius.

SICINIUS   Nature teaches beasts to know their friends.   6

MENENIUS   Pray you, who does the wolf love?

SICINIUS   The lamb.

MENENIUS   Ay, to devour him, as the hungry plebeians
would the noble Marcius.

BRUTUS   He's a lamb indeed, that baas like a bear.   11

MENENIUS   He's a bear indeed, that lives like a lamb.   12
You two are old men; tell me one thing that I shall
ask you.

BOTH   Well, sir?

MENENIUS   In what enormity is Marcius poor in, that   16
you two have not in abundance?

BRUTUS   He's poor in no one fault, but stored with all.   18

SICINIUS   Especially in pride.

BRUTUS   And topping all others in boasting.

MENENIUS   This is strange now. Do you two know how
you are censured here in the city, I mean of us o' th'   22
right-hand file? Do you?   23

BOTH   Why, how are we censured?

MENENIUS   Because you talk of pride now—will you
not be angry?

BOTH   Well, well, sir, well?

MENENIUS   Why, 'tis no great matter; for a very little   28
thief of occasion will rob you of a great deal of   29
patience. Give your dispositions the reins and be   30
angry at your pleasures—at the least, if you take it as
a pleasure to you in being so. You blame Marcius for
being proud?

BRUTUS   We do it not alone, sir.

MENENIUS   I know you can do very little alone, for your
helps are many, or else your actions would grow
wondrous single. Your abilities are too infantlike for   37
doing much alone. You talk of pride. Oh, that you
could turn your eyes toward the napes of your necks   39
and make but an interior survey of your good selves!
Oh, that you could!

BOTH   What then, sir?

MENENIUS   Why, then you should discover a brace of   43
unmeriting, proud, violent, testy magistrates, alias   44
fools, as any in Rome.

SICINIUS   Menenius, you are known well enough too.

MENENIUS   I am known to be a humorous patrician, and   47
one that loves a cup of hot wine with not a drop of
allaying Tiber in't; said to be something imperfect in   49
favoring the first complaint, hasty and tinderlike   50
upon too trivial motion; one that converses more with   51
the buttock of the night than with the forehead of the   52
morning. What I think I utter, and spend my malice in   53
my breath. Meeting two such wealsmen as you are—   54

---

16 **Or . . . craft** in which either wrath or craftiness   18 **stain** disgrace,
eclipse   19 **Shall . . . itself** (my valor) shall deviate from its own natural course.   19–24 **Nor . . . Marcius** Neither his being asleep nor
protected by sanctuary (as, for example, in *fane* or temple, or at the
Capitol, guarded by priests when they offer sacrifices to the gods),
nor his being unarmed or ill, nor any restraints (*embarquements*) laid
on my fury, will be able to impose the outmoded sanctions of civilized custom against my hatred for Marcius.   25 **At . . . guard** in my
own house, under my brother's protection   26 **hospitable canon** law
of hospitality   28–9 **what . . . Rome** i.e., who they are that are to be
taken to Rome as hostages during the negotiations about the return
of Corioles to the Volscians. (See 1.9.76.)   30 **attended** waited for
31 **south** south of.   **mills** i.e., grain mills   32 **to the pace of it** in
accordance with the speed of events
2.1. Location: Rome. The ovation prepared for Coriolanus is probably to be imagined as beginning outside the city and moving
toward the Capitol (see line 203).
1 **augurer** auger, Roman religious figure charged with reading signs
to predict the future   4 **Not . . . people** Not what the people would
wish   6 **beasts** i.e., even beasts

11–12 **He's a lamb . . . a lamb** i.e., Some lamb! Have you heard his
growl?—How can you accuse him of being a bear when he acts so
unthreateningly?   16 **enormity** wickedness   18 **stored** well stocked
22 **censured** judged   23 **right-hand file** i.e., party of aristocrats (who
took the honorable right-hand position in battle).   28–30 **a very . . .
patience** any slight pretext will rob you of your patience.   37 **single**
poor, feeble.   39 **turn . . . necks** i.e., turn your gaze in order to see
within   43 **brace** pair   44 **testy** headstrong   47 **humorous** whimsical, governed by humors   49 **allaying Tiber** water used to dilute
49–50 **something . . . complaint** somewhat at fault for deciding in
favor of the complainant before hearing the other side of the case
50 **tinderlike** quick-tempered   51 **motion** cause   51–3 **one . . . morning** one who is better acquainted with the late hours of the night than
with the early hours of the morning.   53 **spend** expend   54 **breath**
words.   **wealsmen** statesmen

I cannot call you Lycurguses—if the drink you give 55
me touch my palate adversely, I make a crooked face 56
at it. I cannot say Your Worships have delivered the 57
matter well, when I find the ass in compound with the 58
major part of your syllables; and though I must be con- 59
tent to bear with those that say you are reverend grave
men, yet they lie deadly that tell you you have good 61
faces. If you see this in the map of my microcosm, 62
follows it that I am known well enough too? What 63
harm can your bisson conspectuities glean out of this 64
character, if I be known well enough too? 65

BRUTUS   Come, sir, come, we know you well enough.

MENENIUS   You know neither me, yourselves, nor anything. You are ambitious for poor knaves' caps and 68
legs. You wear out a good wholesome forenoon in 69
hearing a cause between an orange-wife and a faucet- 70
seller, and then rejourn the controversy of threepence 71
to a second day of audience. When you are hearing a 72
matter between party and party, if you chance to be 73
pinched with the colic, you make faces like mummers, 74
set up the bloody flag against all patience, and, in roar- 75
ing for a chamber pot, dismiss the controversy bleed- 76
ing, the more entangled by your hearing. All the peace 77
you make in their cause is calling both the parties 78
knaves. You are a pair of strange ones. 79

BRUTUS   Come, come, you are well understood to be a 80
perfecter giber for the table than a necessary bencher 81
in the Capitol. 82

MENENIUS   Our very priests must become mockers if
they shall encounter such ridiculous subjects as you 84
are. When you speak best unto the purpose, it is not 85
worth the wagging of your beards, and your beards
deserve not so honorable a grave as to stuff a botcher's 87
cushion or to be entombed in an ass's packsaddle.
Yet you must be saying Marcius is proud; who, in a 89
cheap estimation, is worth all your predecessors since 90
Deucalion, though peradventure some of the best of 91

'em were hereditary hangmen. Good e'en to Your Wor- 92
ships. More of your conversation would infect my 93
brain, being the herdsmen of the beastly plebeians. I 94
will be bold to take my leave of you.

Brutus and Sicinius [stand] aside.

Enter Volumnia, Virgilia, and Valeria.

How now, my as fair as noble ladies—and the moon, 96
were she earthly, no nobler—whither do you follow 97
your eyes so fast? 98

VOLUMNIA   Honorable Menenius, my boy Marcius approaches. For the love of Juno, let's go. 100

MENENIUS   Ha? Marcius coming home?

VOLUMNIA   Ay, worthy Menenius, and with most pros- 102
perous approbation. 103

MENENIUS   Take my cap, Jupiter, and I thank thee. [*He
tosses his cap.*] Hoo! Marcius coming home?

VALERIA, VIRGILIA   Nay, 'tis true.

VOLUMNIA   Look, here's a letter from him. [*Showing a
letter.*] The state hath another, his wife another, and I
think there's one at home for you.

MENENIUS   I will make my very house reel tonight. A
letter for me?

VIRGILIA   Yes, certain, there's a letter for you; I saw't.

MENENIUS   A letter for me! It gives me an estate of seven 113
years' health, in which time I will make a lip at the 114
physician. The most sovereign prescription in Galen 115
is but empiricutic and, to this preservative, of no bet- 116
ter report than a horse drench. Is he not wounded? He 117
was wont to come home wounded. 118

VIRGILIA   Oh, no, no, no.

VOLUMNIA   Oh, he is wounded, I thank the gods for't.

MENENIUS   So do I too, if it be not too much. Brings 'a 121
victory in his pocket, the wounds become him.

VOLUMNIA   On 's brows, Menenius. He comes the 123
third time home with the oaken garland.

MENENIUS   Has he disciplined Aufidius soundly? 125

VOLUMNIA   Titus Lartius writes they fought together,
but Aufidius got off.

MENENIUS   And 'twas time for him too, I'll warrant him
that. An he had stayed by him, I would not have been 129
so fidiused for all the chests in Corioles and the gold 130
that's in them. Is the Senate possessed of this? 131

VOLUMNIA   Good ladies, let's go.—Yes, yes, yes; the
Senate has letters from the General, wherein he gives

---

55 Lycurguses (Said ironically; Lycurgus was the famous Spartan lawgiver.)   **55–7 if the drink . . . at it** i.e., if I don't like the things you say,
I show it in my expression.   **57 delivered** reported   **58–9 I find . . .
syllables** i.e., I find asininity in nearly everything you say. (With a pun
on *ass in compound*, meaning legal phrases ending in *-as,* like *whereas.*)
61 deadly excessively   **62 this** i.e., all that I have freely admitted.
the map of my microcosm my face, or chart of my little world (as
opposed to the macrocosm or great world)   **63 known . . . too** (Menenius mocks their phrase, line 46, and its implication that they "see
through" him.)   **64 bisson conspectuities** blind understandings
65 character character sketch   **68–9 caps and legs** doffing caps and
making obeisances to indicate respect.   **69–72 You . . . audience** You
wear out a morning that might be put to better use in hearing a case
between a woman fruit-seller and one who sells taps for drawing
liquor from barrels, and then adjourn the silly three-penny dispute
until another hearing.   **73 party and party** the two parties in a dispute
74 pinched with the colic afflicted with griping pains in the belly.
mummers masqueraders, performers in dumb shows   **75 set . . . flag**
i.e., declare violent war   **76–7 bleeding** unhealed, unsettled
77–9 All . . . knaves i.e., All you manage to do is to insult both parties.
(Perhaps a reference to the song "Hold thy peace, thou knave"; see
Twelfth Night, 2.3.63–70.)   **80–2 a perfecter . . . Capitol** i.e., better at din-
ner-table jesting than at sitting in the Senate as a counselor.   **84 subjects**
(1) topics (2) citizens   **85 When** i.e., Even when   **87 botcher** one who
patches old clothes or boots   **89–90 in a cheap estimation** even at the
lowest estimation of his worth   **91 Deucalion** the Noah of classical
story, survivor of a great flood.   **peradventure** perhaps

92 hereditary hangmen men serving as executioners (a very ignoble
occupation) generation after generation.   **Good e'en** Good evening
(used for any time after noon)   **93 conversation** society, company
94 being you being   **96 the moon** i.e., Diana, goddess of chastity
97–8 whither . . . fast? where are you going so eagerly in hopes of
some sight?   **100 Juno** wife of Jupiter and Queen of the gods
102–3 prosperous approbation success and acclaim.   **113 It . . . estate
of** It endows me with   **114 make a lip** make a contemptuous face,
mock   **115 sovereign** efficacious.   **Galen** Greek physician and
authority on medicine (born considerably after the time of Coriolanus)
116 empiricutic quacklike.   **to** compared with   **117 report** reputation,
standing.   **horse drench** dose of medicine for horses.   **118 wont**
accustomed   **121 Brings 'a** If he brings   **123 On 's brows** i.e., The
victory is *on his brows* (in the form of a garland) rather than *in his pocket,*
as Menenius suggests. (Said as a pleasantry.)   **125 disciplined** beaten
129 An If   **130 fidiused** (Menenius's coined word, meaning "treated
as Aufidius deserves, beaten.")   **131 possessed** informed

my son the whole name of the war. He hath in this 134
action outdone his former deeds doubly.

VALERIA   In troth, there's wondrous things spoke of
him.

MENENIUS   Wondrous? Ay, I warrant you, and not
without his true purchasing.   139

VIRGILIA   The gods grant them true!

VOLUMNIA   True? Pow waw.   141

MENENIUS   True? I'll be sworn they are true. Where is
he wounded? [*To the tribunes*] God save Your good
Worships! Marcius is coming home. He has more
cause to be proud.—Where is he wounded?

VOLUMNIA   I'th' shoulder and i'th' left arm. There will
be large cicatrices to show the people, when he shall 147
stand for his place. He received in the repulse of 148
Tarquin seven hurts i'th' body.   149

MENENIUS   One i'th' neck and two i'th' thigh—there's
nine that I know.

VOLUMNIA   He had, before this last expedition, twenty-
five wounds upon him.

MENENIUS   Now it's twenty-seven. Every gash was an
enemy's grave. (*A shout and flourish.*) Hark, the trumpets.

VOLUMNIA   These are the ushers of Marcius. Before him
he carries noise, and behind him he leaves tears.
Death, that dark spirit, in 's nervy arm doth lie,   159
Which, being advanced, declines, and then men die.   160

A sennet. Trumpets sound. Enter Cominius the
general, and Titus Lartius; between them,
Coriolanus, crowned with an oaken garland; with
captains and soldiers, and a Herald.

HERALD
Know, Rome, that all alone Marcius did fight
Within Corioles gates, where he hath won,
With fame, a name to Caius Marcius; these   163
In honor follows "Coriolanus."
Welcome to Rome, renownèd Coriolanus!

Sound flourish.

ALL
Welcome to Rome, renownèd Coriolanus!

CORIOLANUS
No more of this. It does offend my heart.
Pray now, no more.

COMINIUS   Look, sir, your mother.

CORIOLANUS   Oh,
You have, I know, petitioned all the gods
For my prosperity!   *Kneels.*

VOLUMNIA   Nay, my good soldier, up,   170
My gentle Marcius, worthy Caius, and
By deed-achieving honor newly named—   172

What is it? Coriolanus must I call thee?—
But, oh, thy wife!

CORIOLANUS [*rising*]   My gracious silence, hail!
Wouldst thou have laughed had I come coffined
home,
That weep'st to see me triumph? Ah, my dear,
Such eyes the widows in Corioles wear,
And mothers that lack sons.

MENENIUS   Now, the gods crown thee!

CORIOLANUS [*to Menenius*]
And live you yet? [*To Valeria*] Oh my sweet lady,
pardon.

VOLUMNIA
I know not where to turn. Oh, welcome home!
[*To Cominius*] And welcome, General! And you're
welcome all.

MENENIUS
A hundred thousand welcomes! I could weep
And I could laugh; I am light and heavy. Welcome.   183
A curse begin at very root on 's heart   184
That is not glad to see thee! You are three
That Rome should dote on; yet, by the faith of men,
We have some old crab trees here at home that will not 187
Be grafted to your relish. Yet welcome, warriors!   188
We call a nettle but a nettle, and   189
The faults of fools but folly.   190

COMINIUS   Ever right.

CORIOLANUS   Menenius ever, ever.   192

HERALD
Give way there, and go on!

CORIOLANUS [*to Volumnia and Virgilia*]
                        Your hand, and yours.
Ere in our own house I do shade my head,   194
The good patricians must be visited,
From whom I have received not only greetings,
But with them change of honors.

VOLUMNIA   I have lived   197
To see inherited my very wishes   198
And the buildings of my fancy. Only   199
There's one thing wanting, which I doubt not but   200
Our Rome will cast upon thee.

CORIOLANUS   Know, good mother,   201
I had rather be their servant in my way
Than sway with them in theirs.

COMINIUS   On, to the Capitol!   203
Flourish. Cornets. Exeunt in state, as before.
Brutus and Sicinius [remain].

BRUTUS
All tongues speak of him, and the blearèd sights   204
Are spectacled to see him. Your prattling nurse   205

---

134 name credit, reputation   **139 his true purchasing** deserving on
his part.   **141 Pow waw** i.e., Pish.   **147 cicatrices** scars   **148 stand**
for his place i.e., seek the consulship.   **148–9 repulse of Tarquin**
(Plutarch reports that Marcius fought his first battle against King Tarquin the Proud in about 496 B.C. on the occasion of Tarquin's last
attempt to regain the kingdom; see 1.3.13–15 and note, and 2.2.88 ff.)
159 in 's nervy in his sinewy   **160 being . . . declines** being raised,
descends   **160.1 A sennet** a trumpet call accompanying an entrance
163 With in addition to.   **to** added to   **170 prosperity** success.
172 deed-achieving achieved by deeds

183 light and heavy merry and sad.   **184 on 's** of his   **187 old crab**
trees old crab apple trees, i.e., sour-natured old men (such as the tribunes)   **188 grafted to your relish** implanted with a liking for you
(something that would sweeten the sourness).   **189–90 We . . . folly**
i.e., Some unpleasant and foolish things cannot be changed and must
be acknowledged for what they are.   **192 Menenius ever** Same old
Menenius   **194 shade** rest   **197 change of honors** promotion, fresh
honors.   **198 inherited** realized, possessed   **199 fancy** imagination.
200 wanting lacking   **201 cast upon** offer   **203 sway with** rule over
204–5 blearèd . . . spectacled people with dimmed vision put on spectacles   **205 Your prattling nurse** The typical chattering nurse

Into a rapture lets her baby cry   206
While she chats him. The kitchen malkin pins   207
Her richest lockram 'bout her reechy neck,   208
Clamb'ring the walls to eye him. Stalls, bulks,
    windows   209
Are smothered up, leads filled and ridges horsed   210
With variable complexions, all agreeing   211
In earnestness to see him. Seld-shown flamens   212
Do press among the popular throngs and puff   213
To win a vulgar station. Our veiled dames   214
Commit the war of white and damask in   215
Their nicely-gauded cheeks to th' wanton spoil   216
Of Phoebus' burning kisses—such a pother   217
As if that whatsoever god who leads him   218
Were slyly crept into his human powers   219
And gave him graceful posture.

SICINIUS   On the sudden   220
I warrant him consul.

BRUTUS   Then our office may,   221
During his power, go sleep.

SICINIUS
He cannot temperately transport his honors   223
From where he should begin and end, but will   224
Lose those he hath won.

BRUTUS   In that there's comfort.

SICINIUS   Doubt not   225
The commoners, for whom we stand, but they   226
Upon their ancient malice will forget   227
With the least cause these his new honors—which   228
That he will give them make I as little question   229
As he is proud to do't.

BRUTUS   I heard him swear,   230
Were he to stand for consul, never would he
Appear i'th' marketplace nor on him put
The napless vesture of humility,   233
Nor, showing, as the manner is, his wounds
To th' people, beg their stinking breaths.

SICINIUS   'Tis right.   235

BRUTUS
It was his word. Oh, he would miss it rather   236
Than carry it but by the suit of the gentry to him   237

And the desire of the nobles.

SICINIUS   I wish no better
Than have him hold that purpose and to put it
In execution.

BRUTUS   'Tis most like he will.   240

SICINIUS
It shall be to him then as our good wills,   241
A sure destruction.

BRUTUS   So it must fall out
To him, or our authority's for an end.   243
We must suggest the people in what hatred   244
He still hath held them; that to 's power he would   245
Have made them mules, silenced their pleaders, and 246
Dispropertied their freedoms, holding them   247
In human action and capacity
Of no more soul nor fitness for the world
Than camels in their war, who have their provand   250
Only for bearing burdens, and sore blows
For sinking under them.

SICINIUS   This—as you say, suggested
At some time when his soaring insolence
Shall touch the people, which time shall not want   254
If he be put upon't, and that's as easy   255
As to set dogs on sheep—will be his fire   256
To kindle their dry stubble; and their blaze   257
Shall darken him forever.

Enter a Messenger.

BRUTUS   What's the matter?   258

MESSENGER
You are sent for to the Capitol. 'Tis thought
That Marcius shall be consul. I have seen
The dumb men throng to see him, and the blind
To hear him speak. Matrons flung gloves,
Ladies and maids their scarves and handkerchiefs,
Upon him as he passed. The nobles bended
As to Jove's statue, and the commons made
A shower and thunder with their caps and shouts.
I never saw the like.

BRUTUS   Let's to the Capitol,
And carry with us ears and eyes for th' time,   268
But hearts for the event.

SICINIUS   Have with you.   *Exeunt.* 269

❖

[2.2]

*Enter two Officers, to lay cushions, as it were in
the Capitol.*

206 **rapture** fit   207 **chats him** gossips about Coriolanus.   **malkin** untidy servantmaid   208 **lockram** coarse linen fabric.   **reechy** dirty, filthy   209 **Stalls** Benches in front of shops displaying wares.   **bulks** structures projecting from the front of a shop   210 **leads** leaded roofs   210–11 **ridges . . . complexions** the roof-ridges bestridden by people of all sorts   211 **agreeing** alike   212 **Seld-shown flamens** Priests (of ancient Rome) who rarely appear in public   213 **popular** plebeian, vulgar.   **puff** pant, exert themselves   214 **vulgar station** place in the crowd.   **215–17 Commit . . . kisses** commit their handsomely made-up complexions, in which white and damask pink contend with each other, to the amorous despoiling of the sun's burning kisses   217 **pother** hubbub   218 **him** Coriolanus   219 **his human powers** Coriolanus's body   220 **graceful posture** godlike bearing.   **220–1 On . . . consul** I predict with confidence that he will quickly be elected consul.   222 **power** term of authority   223 **temperately transport** carry in a temperate and self-controlled way   224 **and end** i.e., to a proper conclusion   225–7 **Doubt not . . . forget** Do not doubt that the commoners, whom we represent, will, because of their long-standing hostility, forget   228 **which** i.e., which provocation   229 **make . . . question** I have as little doubt   230 **As** as that   233 **napless vesture** threadbare garment   235 **breaths** i.e., voices, votes.   236 **miss it** i.e., go without the consulship   237 **carry it but** win it otherwise than

240 **like** likely   241 **as . . . wills** as our interest demands   243 **for an end** doomed.   244 **suggest** insinuate to   245 **still** always.   **to 's power** to the extent of his power   246 **mules** i.e., beasts of burden.   **pleaders** i.e., the tribunes   247 **Dispropertied** dispossessed, deprived (them) of   250 **provand** provender, food   254 **want** be lacking   255 **put upon't** urged, incited to it   256 **his fire** i.e., the spark that kindles his hatred   257 **To kindle . . . stubble** (Coriolanus's fiery wrath will, in turn, kindle the inflammable emotions of the plebeians.)   258 **darken** eclipse, deprive of authority or renown   268 **time** present situation   269 **hearts . . . event** deeper desires and purposes for what is to follow.   **Have with you** I'm with you, let's go.   **2.2. Location:** Rome. The Capitol.

FIRST OFFICER   Come, come, they are almost here. How many stand for consulships?

SECOND OFFICER   Three, they say; but 'tis thought of everyone Coriolanus will carry it.   3

FIRST OFFICER   That's a brave fellow, but he's vengeance proud and loves not the common people.   5

SECOND OFFICER   Faith, there hath been many great men that have flattered the people who ne'er loved them;   8 and there be many that they have loved, they know   9 not wherefore; so that, if they love they know not   10 why, they hate upon no better a ground. Therefore, for Coriolanus neither to care whether they love or hate him manifests the true knowledge he has in their   13 disposition, and out of his noble carelessness lets them   14 plainly see't.

FIRST OFFICER   If he did not care whether he had their love or no, he waved indifferently twixt doing them   17 neither good nor harm; but he seeks their hate with greater devotion than they can render it him, and leaves nothing undone that may fully discover him   20 their opposite. Now, to seem to affect the malice and   21 displeasure of the people is as bad as that which he dislikes, to flatter them for their love.

SECOND OFFICER   He hath deserved worthily of his country, and his ascent is not by such easy degrees as those   25 who, having been supple and courteous to the people, bonneted, without any further deed to have them at   27 all into their estimation and report. But he hath so   28 planted his honors in their eyes and his actions in their hearts that for their tongues to be silent and not confess so much were a kind of ingrateful injury. To report otherwise were a malice that, giving itself the   32 lie, would pluck reproof and rebuke from every ear   33 that heard it.

FIRST OFFICER   No more of him; he's a worthy man. Make way, they are coming.   36

A sennet. Enter the patricians and the tribunes of the people, lictors before them; Coriolanus, Menenius, Cominius the consul. Sicinius and Brutus take their places by themselves. Coriolanus stands.

MENENIUS
Having determined of the Volsces and   37
To send for Titus Lartius, it remains,
As the main point of this our after-meeting,   39
To gratify his noble service that   40
Hath thus stood for his country. Therefore please you,   41

Most reverend and grave elders, to desire
The present consul and last general   43
In our well-found successes to report   44
A little of that worthy work performed
By Caius Marcius Coriolanus, whom
We met here both to thank and to remember
With honors like himself.   [*Coriolanus sits.*]

FIRST SENATOR   Speak, good Cominius.   48
Leave nothing out for length, and make us think
Rather our state's defective for requital   50
Than we to stretch it out. [*To the tribunes*] Masters
o'th' people,   51
We do request your kindest ears and, after,   52
Your loving motion toward the common body   53
To yield what passes here.

SICINIUS   We are convented   54
Upon a pleasing treaty, and have hearts   55
Inclinable to honor and advance
The theme of our assembly.

BRUTUS   Which the rather   57
We shall be blest to do if he remember   58
A kinder value of the people than   59
He hath hereto prized them at.

MENENIUS   That's off, that's off!   60
I would you rather had been silent. Please you
To hear Cominius speak?

BRUTUS   Most willingly;
But yet my caution was more pertinent   63
Than the rebuke you give it.

MENENIUS   He loves your people;
But tie him not to be their bedfellow.   65
Worthy Cominius, speak.
        Coriolanus rises and offers to go away.
                Nay, keep your place.   66

FIRST SENATOR
Sit, Coriolanus. Never shame to hear
What you have nobly done.

CORIOLANUS   Your Honors' pardon.
I had rather have my wounds to heal again
Than hear say how I got them.

BRUTUS   Sir, I hope
My words disbenched you not?

CORIOLANUS   No, sir. Yet oft,   71
When blows have made me stay, I fled from words.
You soothed not, therefore hurt not. But your people,   73
I love them as they weigh—

MENENIUS   Pray now, sit down.   74

---

3 of by   **5 brave** excellent.   **vengeance** terribly   **8 who . . . them** (1) (aristocrats) who never loved the people, or (2) (people) who never loved the aristocrats   **9 they** the people   **10 wherefore** why   **13 in** of   **14 noble carelessness** patrician indifference to public opinion   **17 waved indifferently** would waver impartially   **20–1 discover . . . opposite** reveal him to be their adversary.   **21 affect** seek out, desire   **25 degrees** steps   **27 bonneted** took their hats off.   **have them** gain their way   **28 estimation and report** esteem and good opinion.   **32–3 giving . . . lie** manifesting its own falsehood   **36.2 lictors** officials attendant upon Roman magistrates   **37 determined of** i.e., reached a decision concerning (the terms for returning Corioles, etc.)   **39 after-meeting** follow-up meeting   **40 gratify** reward, requite   **41 stood for** fought for, defended

43 last late, recent   **44 well-found** fortunately met with, found to be good   **48 like himself** i.e., worthy of his greatness.   **50–1 Rather . . . out** that our state lacks means to reward adequately rather than that we are defective in intention to extend what reward we have at our disposal.   **52 after** in addition to that   **53 loving . . . body** friendly intervention with the common people   **54 yield** assent to, grant.   **passes** is voted.   **convented** summoned, convened   **55 Upon** in order to consider.   **treaty** proposal   **57 theme** business.   **rather** sooner   **58 blest** happy   **59 kinder value** more favorable estimation   **60 off** jarring, not pertinent   **63 pertinent** appropriate   **65 tie** oblige   **66 s.d. offers** starts   **71 disbenched you not** did not make you leave your seat.   **73 soothed** flattered   **74 as they weigh** according to their deserts

CORIOLANUS

    I had rather have one scratch my head i'th' sun   75
    When the alarum were struck than idly sit   76
    To hear my nothings monstered.   *Exit Coriolanus.*

MENENIUS   Masters of the people,   77
    Your multiplying spawn how can he flatter—   78
    That's thousand to one good one—when you now see   79
    He had rather venture all his limbs for honor
    Than one on 's ears to hear it?—Proceed, Cominius.   81

COMINIUS

    I shall lack voice. The deeds of Coriolanus
    Should not be uttered feebly. It is held
    That valor is the chiefest virtue and
    Most dignifies the haver; if it be,
    The man I speak of cannot in the world
    Be singly counterpoised. At sixteen years,   87
    When Tarquin made a head for Rome, he fought   88
    Beyond the mark of others. Our then dictator,   89
    Whom with all praise I point at, saw him fight,   90
    When with his Amazonian chin he drove   91
    The bristled lips before him. He bestrid   92
    An o'erpressed Roman, and i'th' Consul's view   93
    Slew three opposers. Tarquin's self he met,
    And struck him on his knee. In that day's feats,   95
    When he might act the woman in the scene,   96
    He proved best man i'th' field, and for his meed   97
    Was brow-bound with the oak. His pupil age   98
    Man-entered thus, he waxèd like a sea,   99
    And in the brunt of seventeen battles since   100
    He lurched all swords of the garland. For this last,   101
    Before and in Corioles, let me say,
    I cannot speak him home. I stopped the fliers,   103
    And by his rare example made the coward   104
    Turn terror into sport. As weeds before
    A vessel under sail, so men obeyed
    And fell below his stem. His sword, death's stamp,   107
    Where it did mark, it took; from face to foot   108
    He was a thing of blood, whose every motion
    Was timed with dying cries. Alone he entered   110

    The mortal gate o'th' city, which he painted   111
    With shunless destiny; aidless came off,   112
    And with a sudden reinforcement struck   113
    Corioles like a planet. Now all's his,   114
    When by and by the din of war 'gan pierce   115
    His ready sense; then straight his doubled spirit   116
    Requickened what in flesh was fatigate,   117
    And to the battle came he, where he did
    Run reeking o'er the lives of men as if   119
    'Twere a perpetual spoil; and till we called   120
    Both field and city ours, he never stood   121
    To ease his breast with panting.

MENENIUS   Worthy man!

FIRST SENATOR

    He cannot but with measure fit the honors   123
    Which we devise him.

COMINIUS   Our spoils he kicked at,   124
    And looked upon things precious as they were   125
    The common muck of the world. He covets less
    Than misery itself would give, rewards   127
    His deeds with doing them, and is content   128
    To spend the time to end it.

MENENIUS   He's right noble.   129
    Let him be called for.

FIRST SENATOR   Call Coriolanus.

OFFICER   He doth appear.

          Enter Coriolanus.

MENENIUS

    The Senate, Coriolanus, are well pleased
    To make thee consul.

CORIOLANUS   I do owe them still   134
    My life and services.

MENENIUS   It then remains
    That you do speak to the people.

CORIOLANUS   I do beseech you,
    Let me o'erleap that custom, for I cannot
    Put on the gown, stand naked, and entreat them   138
    For my wounds' sake to give their suffrage. Please
       you
    That I may pass this doing.

SICINIUS   Sir, the people   140
    Must have their voices; neither will they bate   141
    One jot of ceremony.

MENENIUS [*to Coriolanus*]   Put them not to't.   142
    Pray you, go fit you to the custom and

75–6 have . . . struck i.e., engage in idle pleasure when the battle signal is sounded. **77 monstered** made into unnatural marvels. **78 multiplying spawn** fast-breeding commoners **79 That's . . . one** in which there are a thousand bad ones to one good one, or, a thousand bad ones contrasted to the noble Coriolanus **81 on 's** of his. **it** i.e., praise of his honor. **88 made . . . for** raised a force to attack (and reconquer) **89 mark** ability, reach. **dictator** leader constitutionally given absolute authority to deal with a specific emergency, such as a war **90 point at** i.e., refer to. (The unnamed dictator of those earlier times, probably Aulus Posthumus Regillensis, is not present.) **91 Amazonian** i.e., beardless (like the female warriors, the Amazons) **92 bristled lips** i.e., bearded warriors. **bestrid** stood over in battle, protected **93 o'erpressed** overwhelmed **95 on his knee** to his knees. **96 he . . . scene** i.e., he was young enough not to have been blamed for cowardice. (With an allusion to boys playing women's roles in the theater.) **97 meed** reward **98 brow-bound** i.e., presented with a garland as an emblem of victory **99 Man-entered** initiated into manhood **100 brunt** violence, shock **101 lurched** robbed, cheated. **For** As for **103 speak him home** praise him adequately. **the fliers** those who tried to flee the battle **104 the coward** even the coward **107 stem** main timber of the prow of a ship. **stamp** tool for imprinting a design or pattern **108 took** made an impression, slew **110 Was timed** kept time, was accompanied

111 mortal deadly. **111–12 which . . . destiny** i.e., which city he stained with the blood of those who could not escape his doom **113 reinforcement** fresh assault **114 like a planet** (Refers to the power of striking or blasting, believed in astrology to belong to the planets.) **114–17 Now . . . fatigate** No sooner had he conquered there than at once the noise of battle began to pierce his alert hearing; then at once his renewed or redoubled spirit revivified his fatigued flesh **119 reeking** steaming (with enemies' blood) **120 perpetual spoil** endless slaughter **121 stood** stopped **123 He . . . fit** He can't help but measure up to **124 devise** devise for. **kicked at** spurned **125 as** as if **127 misery** poverty **127–8 rewards . . . doing them** finds reward for his actions in the satisfaction that comes from having acted well **128–9 is content . . . end it** is satisfied to be repaid for his time spent with the pleasure of having spent his time thus. **134 still** ever **138 naked** exposed **140 pass** disregard, omit **141 voices** votes. **bate** abate, do without **142 Put . . . to't** i.e., Do not force the issue.

Take to you, as your predecessors have,
Your honor with your form.

CORIOLANUS   It is a part   145
That I shall blush in acting, and might well
Be taken from the people.

BRUTUS [*to Sicinius*]   Mark you that?

CORIOLANUS
To brag unto them, "Thus I did, and thus!"
Show them th'unaching scars which I should hide,
As if I had received them for the hire   150
Of their breath only!

MENENIUS   Do not stand upon't.—   151
We recommend to you, tribunes of the people,   152
Our purpose to them, and to our noble consul   153
Wish we all joy and honor.

SENATORS
To Coriolanus come all joy and honor!   155

Flourish cornets. Then exeunt. Manent Sicinius
and Brutus.

BRUTUS
You see how he intends to use the people.

SICINIUS
May they perceive 's intent! He will require them   157
As if he did contemn what he requested   158
Should be in them to give.

BRUTUS   Come, we'll inform them   159
Of our proceedings here. On th' marketplace   160
I know they do attend us.   [*Exeunt.*] 161

❧

[2.3]

Enter seven or eight Citizens.

FIRST CITIZEN   Once if he do require our voices, we   1
ought not to deny him.

SECOND CITIZEN   We may, sir, if we will.

THIRD CITIZEN   We have power in ourselves to do it,
but it is a power that we have no power to do; for if he   5
show us his wounds and tell us his deeds, we are to
put our tongues into those wounds and speak for   7
them; so, if he tell us his noble deeds, we must also tell
him our noble acceptance of them. Ingratitude is
monstrous, and for the multitude to be ingrateful were
to make a monster of the multitude; of the which we,
being members, should bring ourselves to be monstrous members.

FIRST CITIZEN   And to make us no better thought of, a   14
little help will serve; for once we stood up about the   15
corn, he himself stuck not to call us the many-headed   16
multitude.

THIRD CITIZEN   We have been called so of many; not that   18
our heads are some brown, some black, some abram,   19
some bald, but that our wits are so diversely colored;
and truly I think if all our wits were to issue out of one
skull, they would fly east, west, north, south, and their
consent of one direct way should be at once to all the   23
points o'th' compass.

SECOND CITIZEN   Think you so? Which way do you
judge my wit would fly?

THIRD CITIZEN   Nay, your wit will not so soon out as   27
another man's will; 'tis strongly wedged up in a blockhead. But if it were at liberty, 'twould, sure, south-   29
ward.   30

SECOND CITIZEN   Why that way?

THIRD CITIZEN   To lose itself in a fog where, being three
parts melted away with rotten dews, the fourth would   33
return for conscience' sake, to help to get thee a wife.

SECOND CITIZEN   You are never without your tricks. You   35
may, you may.   36

THIRD CITIZEN   Are you all resolved to give your
voices? But that's no matter, the greater part carries it. 38
I say, if he would incline to the people, there was   39
never a worthier man.

Enter Coriolanus in a gown of humility, with
Menenius.

Here he comes, and in the gown of humility. Mark his
behavior. We are not to stay all together, but to come
by him where he stands by ones, by twos, and by
threes. He's to make his requests by particulars,   44
wherein every one of us has a single honor in giving him 45
our own voices with our own tongues. Therefore follow me, and I'll direct you how you shall go by him.

ALL   Content, content.   [*Exeunt Citizens.*]

MENENIUS
Oh, sir, you are not right. Have you not known
The worthiest men have done't?

CORIOLANUS   What must I say?
"I pray, sir"—Plague upon't! I cannot bring
My tongue to such a pace. "Look, sir, my wounds!
I got them in my country's service, when
Some certain of your brethren roared and ran
From th' noise of our own drums."

MENENIUS   Oh, me, the gods!
You must not speak of that. You must desire them
To think upon you.

CORIOLANUS   Think upon me? Hang 'em!
I would they would forget me, like the virtues   58
Which our divines lose by 'em.

MENENIUS   You'll mar all.   59
I'll leave you. Pray you speak to 'em, I pray you,

---

145 with your form with the ceremony that custom prescribes to you.
150 hire wages   **151 breath** i.e., votes.   **stand upon't** make a point of
it.   **152 recommend** commit, consign   **153 purpose to them** proposal
to the people   **155.1** *Manent* They remain onstage   **157 require** ask,
solicit   **158 condemn what** scorn that what   **159 in them** theirs
160 On In   **161 attend** wait for
2.3. Location: Rome. The Forum, or marketplace.
1 Once if When once, as soon as   **5 no power to do** i.e., no moral
right to exercise   **7 put . . . wounds** i.e., let the wounds inspire our
tongues   **14–15 And . . . serve** And only a small effort on our part
would be needed to convince the patricians not to think well of us
15 once when   **16 stuck not** did not hesitate

18 of by.   **that** because   **19 abram** auburn   **23 consent of** agreement
upon   **27 out** come out, issue forth   **29–30 southward** (The south
wind was believed to bring pestilence.)   **33 rotten** unwholesome
35–6 You may i.e., Go on, say what you like   **38 greater part** majority
39 incline to sympathize with   **44 by particulars** to individuals, one
by one   **45 single** separate, individual   **58 I would** I wish
58–9 like . . . 'em like the virtuous lessons which our priests vainly
seek to instill in them.

In wholesome manner.   *Exit.*

Enter three of the Citizens.

CORIOLANUS   Bid them wash their faces   61
And keep their teeth clean. So, here comes a brace.—   62
You know the cause, sir, of my standing here.

THIRD CITIZEN
We do, sir. Tell us what hath brought you to't.

CORIOLANUS   Mine own desert.

SECOND CITIZEN   Your own desert?

CORIOLANUS   Ay, but not mine own desire.

THIRD CITIZEN   How, not your own desire?

CORIOLANUS   No, sir, 'twas never my desire yet to
trouble the poor with begging.

THIRD CITIZEN   You must think, if we give you anything, we hope to gain by you.

CORIOLANUS   Well then, I pray, your price o'th' consulship?

FIRST CITIZEN   The price is to ask it kindly.

CORIOLANUS   Kindly, sir, I pray, let me ha 't. I have
wounds to show you, which shall be yours in   77
private.—Your good voice, sir. What say you?

SECOND CITIZEN   You shall ha 't, worthy sir.

CORIOLANUS   A match, sir. There's in all two worthy   80
voices begged. I have your alms. Adieu.

THIRD CITIZEN   But this is something odd.   82

SECOND CITIZEN   An 'twere to give again—but 'tis no   83
matter.   *Exeunt [the three Citizens].*

Enter two other Citizens.

CORIOLANUS   Pray you now, if it may stand with the   85
tune of your voices that I may be consul, I have here
the customary gown.

FOURTH CITIZEN   You have deserved nobly of your
country, and you have not deserved nobly.

CORIOLANUS   Your enigma?   90

FOURTH CITIZEN   You have been a scourge to her   91
enemies; you have been a rod to her friends. You have   92
not indeed loved the common people.

CORIOLANUS   You should account me the more virtuous
that I have not been common in my love. I will, sir,   95
flatter my sworn brother, the people, to earn a dearer   96
estimation of them; 'tis a condition they account gen-   97
tle. And since the wisdom of their choice is rather to   98
have my hat than my heart, I will practice the insin-   99
uating nod and be off to them most counterfeitly. That   100

is, sir, I will counterfeit the bewitchment of some pop-   101
ular man and give it bountiful to the desirers. There-   102
fore, beseech you I may be consul.

FIFTH CITIZEN   We hope to find you our friend, and
therefore give you our voices heartily.

FOURTH CITIZEN   You have received many wounds for
your country.

CORIOLANUS   I will not seal your knowledge with show-   108
ing them. I will make much of your voices and so
trouble you no farther.

BOTH CITIZENS   The gods give you joy, sir, heartily!
                        [Exeunt Citizens.]

CORIOLANUS   Most sweet voices!
Better it is to die, better to starve,
Than crave the hire which first we do deserve.   114
Why in this woolvish toge should I stand here   115
To beg of Hob and Dick that does appear   116
Their needless vouches? Custom calls me to't.   117
What custom wills, in all things should we do't,   118
The dust on antique time would lie unswept   119
And mountainous error be too highly heaped
For truth to o'erpeer. Rather than fool it so,   121
Let the high office and the honor go
To one that would do thus. I am half through;   123
The one part suffered, the other will I do.

Enter three Citizens more.

Here come more voices.—   125
Your voices! For your voices I have fought;
Watched for your voices; for your voices bear   127
Of wounds two dozen odd. Battles thrice six
I have seen and heard of; for your voices have   129
Done many things, some less, some more. Your
voices!
Indeed, I would be consul.

SIXTH CITIZEN   He has done nobly, and cannot go
without any honest man's voice.

SEVENTH CITIZEN   Therefore let him be consul. The gods
give him joy, and make him good friend to the
people!

ALL   Amen, amen. God save thee, noble Consul!
                        [Exeunt Citizens.]

CORIOLANUS   Worthy voices!

Enter Menenius, with Brutus and Sicinius.

MENENIUS
You have stood your limitation, and the tribunes   139

---

61 wholesome calculated to do good. (But Coriolanus answers sarcastically to the sense of "healthful.")   **62 brace** pair. (Used contemptuously here.)   **77 yours** available for your inspection   **80 match**
deal, bargain   **82 something** somewhat   **83 An 'twere** If it were
85 stand with be consistent with   **90 enigma** riddle.   **91 scourge**
instrument of punishment   **92 rod** stick or whip used to inflict punishment   **95 common** vulgar, promiscuous. (Playing on *common* in
line 93.)   **96 sworn brother** one of two friends bound by oath to each
other   **96–7 dearer . . . them** higher esteem on their part   **97–8 'tis . . .
gentle** i.e., they think it genteel to be flattered by an aristocrat and
view flattery as noble.   **99 my hat** i.e., my hat in my hand as a gesture of courtesy   **99–100 insinuating** ingratiating   **100 be off** doff
my hat.   **counterfeitly** hypocritically.

101 bewitchment sorcery, bewitching powers   **101–2 popular man**
demagogue   **102 bountiful** bountifully   **108 seal** confirm
114 crave . . . deserve beg the reward or wages we have already
earned.   **115 woolvish toge** wolf's toga (making me look like a wolf
in sheep's clothing)   **116 Hob and Dick** (Typical names for rustics.)
that does appear who make their appearance   **117 needless vouches**
unnecessary confirmations of approval. (To Coriolanus, only the Senate's appointment is necessary.)   **118 in . . . do't** if we should obey
custom indiscriminately   **119 antique time** old-fashioned traditions
121 o'erpeer overtop, be visible over or be able to see over.   **fool it so**
be so foolhardy (as to challenge ancient custom in its huge accumulation of error)   **123 do thus** i.e., go through with this meaningless ritual.   **125 voices** votes.   **127 Watched** kept watch (in camp)
129 heard of heard, i.e., been present at   **139 limitation** allotted time

Endue you with the people's voice. Remains 140
That, in th'official marks invested, you 141
Anon do meet the Senate.

CORIOLANUS   Is this done? 142

SICINIUS
The custom of request you have discharged. 143
The people do admit you, and are summoned
To meet anon, upon your approbation. 145

CORIOLANUS
Where? At the Senate House?

SICINIUS   There, Coriolanus.

CORIOLANUS
May I change these garments?

SICINIUS   You may, sir.

CORIOLANUS
That I'll straight do and, knowing myself again,
Repair to th' Senate House. 149

MENENIUS
I'll keep you company.—Will you along?

BRUTUS
We stay here for the people.

SICINIUS   Fare you well.
          Exeunt Coriolanus and Menenius.
He has it now, and by his looks methinks
'Tis warm at 's heart.

BRUTUS   With a proud heart he wore
His humble weeds. Will you dismiss the people?

          Enter the Plebeians.

SICINIUS
How now, my masters, have you chose this man? 155

FIRST CITIZEN   He has our voices, sir.

BRUTUS
We pray the gods he may deserve your loves.

SECOND CITIZEN
Amen, sir. To my poor unworthy notice, 158
He mocked us when he begged our voices.

THIRD CITIZEN
Certainly he flouted us downright.

FIRST CITIZEN
No, 'tis his kind of speech. He did not mock us.

SECOND CITIZEN
Not one amongst us, save yourself, but says
He used us scornfully. He should have showed us
His marks of merit, wounds received for 's country.

SICINIUS   Why, so he did, I am sure.

ALL   No, no. No man saw 'em.

THIRD CITIZEN
He said he had wounds, which he could show in
          private,
And with his hat, thus waving it in scorn,
"I would be consul," says he. "Agèd custom,
But by your voices, will not so permit me;
Your voices therefore." When we granted that,
Here was "I thank you for your voices. Thank you.

Your most sweet voices! Now you have left your
          voices,
I have no further with you." Was not this mockery? 174

SICINIUS
Why either were you ignorant to see't, 175
Or, seeing it, of such childish friendliness
To yield your voices?

BRUTUS   Could you not have told him
As you were lessoned? When he had no power, 178
But was a petty servant to the state,
He was your enemy, ever spake against 180
Your liberties and the charters that you bear
I'th' body of the weal; and now, arriving 182
A place of potency and sway o'th' state,
If he should still malignantly remain
Fast foe to th' plebii, your voices might 185
Be curses to yourselves. You should have said
That as his worthy deeds did claim no less
Than what he stood for, so his gracious nature 188
Would think upon you for your voices and 189
Translate his malice towards you into love, 190
Standing your friendly lord.

SICINIUS   Thus to have said, 191
As you were fore-advised, had touched his spirit 192
And tried his inclination; from him plucked
Either his gracious promise, which you might,
As cause had called you up, have held him to; 195
Or else it would have galled his surly nature, 196
Which easily endures not article 197
Tying him to aught. So putting him to rage,
You should have ta'en th'advantage of his choler 199
And passed him unelected.

BRUTUS   Did you perceive
He did solicit you in free contempt 201
When he did need your loves, and do you think
That his contempt shall not be bruising to you
When he hath power to crush? Why, had your bodies
No heart among you? Or had you tongues to cry 205
Against the rectorship of judgment?

SICINIUS   Have you 206
Ere now denied the asker? And now 207
Again, of him that did not ask but mock, 208
Bestow your sued-for tongues?

THIRD CITIZEN   He's not confirmed.
We may deny him yet.

SECOND CITIZEN   And will deny him.
I'll have five hundred voices of that sound.

---

140 **Endue** endow.   **Remains** It remains   141 **in . . . invested** dressed
in the insignia of office   142 **Anon** immediately   143 **The custom . . .
discharged** You have performed the custom of asking the people's voices.
145 **upon your approbation** to confirm your having been elected.
149 **Repair** go   155 **masters** good sirs   158 **notice** observation

174 **further with** further use for   175 **ignorant** too dull
178 **lessoned** instructed.   180 **ever** always   182 **body of the weal**
commonwealth.   **arriving** attaining   185 **plebii** plebeians
188 **what . . . for** the office he was seeking   189 **Would think upon**
should esteem   190 **Translate** transform   191 **Standing . . . lord** acting on your behalf.   192 **had touched** would have tested (as gold
and silver were tested with the touchstone)   195 **As . . . up** if occasion aroused you   196 **galled** irritated, rubbed sore   197 **article** stipulated condition   199 **choler** anger   201 **free** frank   205 **heart** i.e., as
a seat of courage and wisdom.   **to cry** only to rebel   206 **rectorship
of judgment** guidance of common sense.   206–7 **Have . . . asker?**
Haven't you on previous occasions denied one asking for your support?   208 **of** upon

FIRST CITIZEN
I twice five hundred, and their friends to piece 'em.   212
BRUTUS
Get you hence instantly, and tell those friends
They have chose a consul that will from them take
Their liberties, make them of no more voice
Than dogs that are as often beat for barking
As therefor kept to do so.
SICINIUS   Let them assemble,   217
And on a safer judgment all revoke   218
Your ignorant election. Enforce his pride   219
And his old hate unto you. Besides, forget not   220
With what contempt he wore the humble weed,   221
How in his suit he scorned you; but your loves,   222
Thinking upon his services, took from you
Th'apprehension of his present portance,   224
Which most gibingly, ungravely, he did fashion   225
After the inveterate hate he bears you.
BRUTUS   Lay   226
A fault on us, your tribunes, that we labored,   227
No impediment between, but that you must   228
Cast your election on him.
SICINIUS   Say you chose him
More after our commandment than as guided
By your own true affections, and that your minds,
Preoccupied with what you rather must do
Than what you should, made you against the grain   233
To voice him consul. Lay the fault on us.
BRUTUS
Ay, spare us not. Say we read lectures to you,   235
How youngly he began to serve his country,   236
How long continued, and what stock he springs of,
The noble house o'th' Marcians, from whence came
That Ancus Marcius, Numa's daughter's son,   239
Who after great Hostilius here was king;
Of the same house Publius and Quintus were,
That our best water brought by conduits hither;   242
. . . .   243
And nobly namèd so, twice being censor,   244
Was his great ancestor.
SICINIUS   One thus descended,
That hath beside well in his person wrought
To be set high in place, we did commend   246
To your remembrances; but you have found,
Scaling his present bearing with his past,   249

That he's your fixèd enemy, and revoke
Your sudden approbation.
BRUTUS   Say you ne'er had done't—   251
Harp on that still—but by our putting on.   252
And presently, when you have drawn your number,   253
Repair to th' Capitol.
ALL   We will so. Almost all   254
Repent in their election.   Exeunt Plebeians.
BRUTUS   Let them go on.
This mutiny were better put in hazard   256
Than stay, past doubt, for greater.   257
If, as his nature is, he fall in rage
With their refusal, both observe and answer   259
The vantage of his anger.
SICINIUS   To th' Capitol, come.   260
We will be there before the stream o'th' people;
And this shall seem, as partly 'tis, their own,
Which we have goaded onward.   Exeunt.

❖

[3.1]

*Cornets. Enter Coriolanus, Menenius, all the
gentry, Cominius, Titus Lartius, and other
Senators.*

CORIOLANUS
Tullus Aufidius then had made new head?   1
LARTIUS
He had, my lord; and that it was which caused
Our swifter composition.   3
CORIOLANUS
So then the Volsces stand but as at first,
Ready, when time shall prompt them, to make road   5
Upon 's again.
COMINIUS   They are worn, Lord Consul, so,   6
That we shall hardly in our ages see   7
Their banners wave again.
CORIOLANUS [*to Lartius*]   Saw you Aufidius?
LARTIUS
On safeguard he came to me, and did curse   9
Against the Volsces for they had so vilely   10
Yielded the town. He is retired to Antium.   11
CORIOLANUS
Spoke he of me?
LARTIUS   He did, my lord.
CORIOLANUS   How? What?
LARTIUS
How often he had met you, sword to sword;
That of all things upon the earth he hated

212 piece add to, reinforce   **217 therefor** for that purpose   **218 safer** sounder   **219 Enforce** Lay stress upon   **220 forget not** don't forget to mention   **221 weed** garment   **222 suit** petition. (With a pun on "garment.")   **224 Th'apprehension** the perceiving, comprehending. **portance** behavior   **225 gibingly, ungravely** jeeringly, mockingly **226 After** in accord with   **227 A fault** the blame   **228 No impediment between** allowing nothing to stand in the way   **233 against the grain** i.e., against your natural inclination   **235 read lectures to** instructed   **236 youngly** early (in his life)   **239 Numa** legendary successor of Romulus as King of Rome; Tullus Hostilius (line 240) was traditionally the third king; Ancus Martius, the fourth   **242 conduits** aqueducts   **243** (A line is evidently missing here. From Plutarch, editors guess that the line may have read something like "And Censorinus, that was so surnamed.")   **244 censor** Roman magistrate charged also with the supervision of the census   **246 That . . . wrought** who in addition has well deserved by his own actions   **249 Scaling** estimating, weighing

251 sudden hasty   **252 putting on** urging.   **253 presently** immediately.   **drawn your number** assembled your supporters   **254 Repair** go, proceed   **256 put in hazard** risked   **257 Than . . . greater** than wait for the chance of a greater uprising that would certainly occur. **259–60 answer The vantage of** take advantage of
3.1. Location: Rome. A street. The procession is on its way to the marketplace; see line 33.
1 made new head raised another army.   **3 composition** coming to terms (about the return of Corioles to the Volscians).   **5 road** inroad, attack   **6 worn** i.e., militarily weakened   **7 ages** lifetimes   **9 On safeguard** Under safe-conduct   **10 for** because   **11 is retired** has returned

Your person most; that he would pawn his fortunes
To hopeless restitution, so he might　　　　　　　　16
Be called your vanquisher.

CORIOLANUS　At Antium lives he?

LARTIUS　At Antium.

CORIOLANUS
I wish I had a cause to seek him there,
To oppose his hatred fully. Welcome home.

Enter Sicinius and Brutus.

Behold, these are the tribunes of the people,
The tongues o'th' common mouth. I do despise them,
For they do prank them in authority　　　　　　24
Against all noble sufferance.　　　　　　　　　25

SICINIUS [*advancing*]　Pass no further.

CORIOLANUS　Ha? What is that?

BRUTUS
It will be dangerous to go on. No further.

CORIOLANUS　What makes this change?

MENENIUS　The matter?

COMINIUS
Hath he not passed the noble and the common?　31

BRUTUS
Cominius, no.

CORIOLANUS　Have I had children's voices?

FIRST SENATOR
Tribunes, give way. He shall to th' marketplace.

BRUTUS
The people are incensed against him.

SICINIUS　　　　　　　　　　　Stop,
Or all will fall in broil.

CORIOLANUS　　　　　　Are these your herd?　35
Must these have voices, that can yield them now　36
And straight disclaim their tongues? What are your
　offices?　　　　　　　　　　　　　　　　37
You being their mouths, why rule you not their teeth?
Have you not set them on?

MENENIUS　　　　　　　Be calm, be calm.

CORIOLANUS
It is a purposed thing, and grows by plot,　　40
To curb the will of the nobility.
Suffer't, and live with such as cannot rule　　42
Nor ever will be ruled.

BRUTUS　　　　　　　　Call't not a plot.
The people cry you mocked them; and of late,　44
When corn was given them gratis, you repined,　45
Scandaled the suppliants for the people, called them　46
Timepleasers, flatterers, foes to nobleness.

CORIOLANUS
Why, this was known before.

BRUTUS　　　　　　　　　　Not to them all.

CORIOLANUS
Have you informed them sithence?

BRUTUS　　　　　　　　　　How? I inform them?　49

COMINIUS
You are like to do such business.　　　　　　50

BRUTUS
Not unlike, each way, to better yours.　　　　51

CORIOLANUS
Why then should I be consul? By yond clouds,
Let me deserve so ill as you, and make me
Your fellow tribune.

SICINIUS　　　　　　　You show too much of that　54
For which the people stir. If you will pass　　55
To where you are bound, you must inquire your way,　56
Which you are out of, with a gentler spirit,　　57
Or never be so noble as a consul,
Nor yoke with him for tribune.

MENENIUS　　　　　　　　　Let's be calm.　59

COMINIUS
The people are abused, set on. This palt'ring　60
Becomes not Rome, nor has Coriolanus　　61
Deserved this so dishonored rub, laid falsely　62
I'th' plain way of his merit.

CORIOLANUS　　　　　　Tell me of corn?　63
This was my speech, and I will speak't again.

MENENIUS　Not now, not now.

FIRST SENATOR　Not in this heat, sir, now.

CORIOLANUS　Now, as I live, I will.
My nobler friends, I crave their pardons. For　68
The mutable, rank-scented meiny, let them　69
Regard me as I do not flatter, and　　　　　70
Therein behold themselves. I say again,　　71
In soothing them, we nourish 'gainst our Senate
The cockle of rebellion, insolence, sedition,　73
Which we ourselves have plowed for, sowed, and
　scattered
By mingling them with us, the honored number,　75
Who lack not virtue, no, nor power, but that
Which they have given to beggars.

MENENIUS　　　　　　　　　Well, no more.

FIRST SENATOR
No more words, we beseech you.

CORIOLANUS　　　　　　　　How? No more?
As for my country I have shed my blood,
Not fearing outward force, so shall my lungs

---

16 To . . . restitution beyond hope of recovery.　so provided that
24 prank them dress themselves up　25 Against . . . sufferance
beyond the power of nobility to tolerate.　31 passed . . . common
been approved by the nobility and the common people.　35 broil
tumult.　36 yield grant, bestow.　now one instant　37 straight
immediately afterward.　offices duties.　40 purposed premeditated
42 live i.e., you will have to live　44 of late lately　45 repined
demurred　46 Scandaled defamed

49 sithence since.　50 like likely　51 Not . . . yours Not unlikely to
prove, in any case, a better way (of providing for the welfare of the
state) than yours.　54 that that quality　55 stir are aroused, angry.
55–6 If . . . bound i.e., If you wish to get to the marketplace and attain
the consulship　57 are out of have strayed from　59 yoke be joined.
(Sicinius insults Coriolanus by treating his sarcastic offer to be a tribune, lines 52–4, as though it were serious.)　60–1 The people . . .
Rome The commoners are being misled and incited by their tribunes.
Rome does not deserve this equivocating trickery　62–3 this . . .
merit this dishonoring obstacle treacherously placed (as in the game
of bowls) in the clear path of his deserving.　68–71 For . . . themselves As for the changeable, foul-smelling multitude, let them see
themselves in the unflattering truth I show to them.　73 cockle weed
75 honored honorable

Coin words till their decay against those measles   81
Which we disdain should tetter us, yet sought   82
The very way to catch them.
BRUTUS   You speak o'th' people   83
As if you were a god to punish, not
A man of their infirmity.
SICINIUS   'Twere well   85
We let the people know't.
MENENIUS   What, what? His choler?
CORIOLANUS   Choler?
Were I as patient as the midnight sleep,
By Jove, 'twould be my mind.
SICINIUS   It is a mind   89
That shall remain a poison where it is,
Not poison any further.
CORIOLANUS   "Shall remain"?
Hear you this Triton of the minnows? Mark you   92
His absolute "shall"?
COMINIUS   'Twas from the canon.
CORIOLANUS   "Shall"?   93
O good but most unwise patricians! Why,
You grave but reckless senators, have you thus
Given Hydra here to choose an officer,   96
That with his peremptory "shall," being but   97
The horn and noise o'th' monster's, wants not spirit   98
To say he'll turn your current in a ditch   99
And make your channel his? If he have power,   100
Then vail your ignorance; if none, awake   101
Your dangerous lenity. If you are learned,   102
Be not as common fools; if you are not,
Let them have cushions by you. You are plebeians   104
If they be senators; and they are no less   105
When, both your voices blended, the great'st taste   106
Most palates theirs. They choose their magistrate,   107
And such a one as he, who puts his "shall,"
His popular "shall," against a graver bench   109
Than ever frowned in Greece. By Jove himself,   110
It makes the consuls base! And my soul aches
To know, when two authorities are up,   112
Neither supreme, how soon confusion   113

May enter twixt the gap of both and take   114
The one by th'other.
COMINIUS   Well, on to th' marketplace.   115
CORIOLANUS
Whoever gave that counsel to give forth
The corn o'th' storehouse gratis, as 'twas used   117
Sometime in Greece—
MENENIUS   Well, well, no more of that.   118
CORIOLANUS
Though there the people had more absolute power,
I say they nourished disobedience, fed
The ruin of the state.
BRUTUS   Why shall the people give
One that speaks thus their voice?
CORIOLANUS   I'll give my reasons,
More worthier than their voices. They know the corn
Was not our recompense, resting well assured   124
They ne'er did service for't. Being pressed to the war,   125
Even when the navel of the state was touched,   126
They would not thread the gates. This kind of service   127
Did not deserve corn gratis. Being i'th' war,
Their mutinies and revolts, wherein they showed
Most valor, spoke not for them. Th'accusation   130
Which they have often made against the Senate,
All cause unborn, could never be the native   132
Of our so frank donation. Well, what then?   133
How shall this bosom multiplied digest   134
The Senate's courtesy? Let deeds express
What's like to be their words: "We did request it;   136
We are the greater poll, and in true fear   137
They gave us our demands." Thus we debase
The nature of our seats and make the rabble
Call our cares fears, which will in time   140
Break ope the locks o'th' Senate and bring in
The crows to peck the eagles.
MENENIUS   Come, enough.
BRUTUS
Enough, with overmeasure.
CORIOLANUS   No, take more!
What may be sworn by, both divine and human,   144
Seal what I end withal! This double worship—   145
Where one part does disdain with cause, the other
Insult without all reason, where gentry, title, wisdom   147
Cannot conclude but by the yea and no   148
Of general ignorance—it must omit   149
Real necessities, and give way the while   150

81–3 till . . . them till my lungs can utter no more against those loathsome diseases (i.e., the common people), which, though we disdain to be infected by them, we have nonetheless left ourselves open to infection by discoursing with them. **85 of their infirmity** sharing their human imperfections. **89 mind** opinion. **92 Triton of the minnows** i.e., god of the little fish. (Triton was Neptune's son and trumpeter.) **93 from the canon** i.e., out of order, exceeding the authority granted the tribunes. **96 Given** permitted. **Hydra** many-headed monster slain by Hercules; here, the mob **97 his peremptory "shall"** his use of the command form of the verb (*shall*) **98 horn and noise** noisy horn. (See allusion to Triton above.) **wants** lacks **99–100 he'll . . . his** he'll divert the current of your power into a ditch and preempt for himself your channel of authority. **101 vail your ignorance** bow down to him in your ignorant yielding **101–2 awake . . . lenity** arouse yourselves from your dangerous mildness. **102 learned** wise **104 cushions** i.e., seats in the Senate **105–7 and . . . theirs** and they are to all intents and purposes senators if, when their voices are mingled with yours, the resulting action savors of them more than of you. **109 popular** on behalf of the populace. **graver bench** more august deliberative body **110 frowned** looked austere in judgment. **Greece** (Famous for its law-giving institutions.) **112 up** established, in action **113 confusion** chaos

114 gap of both space between the two. **take** destroy **115 by** by means of **117 used** practiced, customary **118 Sometime** formerly **124 our recompense** reward from us **125 pressed** conscripted, enlisted **126 navel** vital center. **touched** threatened **127 thread** pass through **130 spoke not** did not speak well **132 All cause unborn** unjustifiably. **native** natural source or origin **133 frank** freely granted and generous **134 bosom multiplied** multiple stomach. **digest** i.e., consider, regard. (With also the literal sense of eating the grain.) **136 like** likely **137 greater poll** majority, greater number of heads **140 cares** concern (for them and for the state). **which** i.e., which insubordination **144 What** May whatever **145 Seal** confirm. **withal** with. **double worship** divided authority **147 Insult without** behave insolently beyond. **gentry** noble birth **148 conclude** come to a final decision **149 general** popular, common. **omit** neglect **150 the while** in the meanwhile

To unstable slightness. Purpose so barred, it follows   151
Nothing is done to purpose. Therefore, beseech you—   152
You that will be less fearful than discreet,   153
That love the fundamental part of state   154
More than you doubt the change on't, that prefer   155
A noble life before a long, and wish
To jump a body with a dangerous physic   157
That's sure of death without it—at once pluck out
The multitudinous tongue; let them not lick   159
The sweet which is their poison. Your dishonor   160
Mangles true judgment and bereaves the state   161
Of that integrity which should become't,   162
Not having the power to do the good it would
For th'ill which doth control't.

BRUTUS   He's said enough.   164
SICINIUS
He's spoken like a traitor and shall answer   165
As traitors do.

CORIOLANUS   Thou wretch, despite o'erwhelm thee!   166
What should the people do with these bald tribunes,   167
On whom depending, their obedience fails
To th' greater bench? In a rebellion,   169
When what's not meet, but what must be, was law,   170
Then were they chosen. In a better hour,
Let what is meet be said it must be meet,   172
And throw their power i'th' dust.

BRUTUS   Manifest treason!

SICINIUS   This a consul? No!

BRUTUS
The aediles, ho!

Enter an Aedile.

Let him be apprehended.   176

SICINIUS   Go, call the people,   [*Exit an Aedile.*]
in whose name myself
Attach thee as a traitorous innovator,   178
A foe to th' public weal. Obey, I charge thee,   179
And follow to thine answer.

CORIOLANUS   Hence, old goat!   180

ALL PATRICIANS
We'll surety him.

COMINIUS [*to Sicinius*]   Aged sir, hands off.   181

CORIOLANUS [*to Sicinius*]
Hence, rotten thing! Or I shall shake thy bones
Out of thy garments.

SICINIUS   Help, ye citizens!

Enter a rabble of plebeians, with the aediles.

MENENIUS   On both sides more respect.   184
SICINIUS
Here's he that would take from you all your power.
BRUTUS   Seize him, aediles!
ALL PLEBEIANS   Down with him! Down with him!
SECOND SENATOR   Weapons, weapons, weapons!
                              They all bustle about Coriolanus.
ALL
Tribunes!—Patricians!—Citizens!—What, ho!—
Sicinius!—Brutus!—Coriolanus!—Citizens!—
Peace, peace, peace!—Stay, hold, peace!
MENENIUS
What is about to be? I am out of breath.
Confusion's near; I cannot speak. You, tribunes
To th' people! Coriolanus, patience!
Speak, good Sicinius.
SICINIUS   Hear me, people. Peace!
ALL PLEBEIANS
Let's hear our tribune. Peace! Speak, speak, speak.
SICINIUS
You are at point to lose your liberties.   197
Marcius would have all from you—Marcius,   198
Whom late you have named for consul.
MENENIUS   Fie, fie, fie!   199
This is the way to kindle, not to quench.
FIRST SENATOR
To unbuild the city and to lay all flat.
SICINIUS
What is the city but the people?
ALL PLEBEIANS   True,
The people are the city.
BRUTUS
By the consent of all, we were established
The people's magistrates.
ALL PLEBEIANS   You so remain.
MENENIUS   And so are like to do.   207
COMINIUS
That is the way to lay the city flat,
To bring the roof to the foundation,
And bury all which yet distinctly ranges   210
In heaps and piles of ruin.
SICINIUS   This deserves death.   211
BRUTUS
Or let us stand to our authority   212
Or let us lose it. We do here pronounce,
Upon the part o'th' people, in whose power
We were elected theirs, Marcius is worthy
Of present death.
SICINIUS   Therefore lay hold of him!   216

---

151 **slightness** vacillation, trifling.   **Purpose so barred** Sound policy and planning being thus obstructed   152 **purpose** any effect.   153 **less . . . discreet** actuated less by fear than by foresight   154–5 **That . . . on't** i.e., you that love the essentials of our government more than you fear changes in it (such as getting rid of the tribunes)   157 **jump** risk (treating).   **physic** cure   159 **The multitudinous tongue** the voice of the multitude, i.e., the tribunes   160 **sweet . . . poison** i.e., power which in their hands will undo them as well as Rome.   **dishonor** present dishonorable state   161 **bereaves** deprives   162 **become't** adorn it   164 **For . . . control't** because of the dangerous tribunal power that overmasters it.   165 **answer** answer for it   166 **despite** scorn   167 **bald** petty, barren (literally and figuratively)   169 **greater bench** i.e., senators collectively.   170 **When . . . was law** when "might makes right" prevailed   172 **Let . . . be meet** i.e., let us openly say that what is right is what should be done   176 **aediles** officers attached to the tribunes   178 **Attach** arrest.   **innovator** revolutionary   179 **weal** welfare.   180 **answer** defense, answer to a charge.   181 **surety** go bail for

184 **more** let there be more   197 **at point to lose** on the verge of losing   198 **Marcius** (Sicinius pointedly omits the title "Coriolanus.")   199 **late** recently   207 **like** likely   210 **distinctly ranges** stretches out in proper order   211 **This** i.e., Coriolanus's defiance of the tribunes   212 **Or** Either.   **stand to** maintain   216 **present** immediate

Bear him to th' rock Tarpeian, and from thence   217
Into destruction cast him.

BRUTUS   Aediles, seize him!

ALL PLEBEIANS
Yield, Marcius, yield!

MENENIUS   Hear me one word.
Beseech you, tribunes, hear me but a word.

AEDILES   Peace, peace!

MENENIUS [to the tribunes]
Be that you seem, truly your country's friend,   222
And temperately proceed to what you would
Thus violently redress.

BRUTUS   Sir, those cold ways,
That seem like prudent helps, are very poisonous
Where the disease is violent.—Lay hands upon him
And bear him to the rock.

                          Coriolanus draws his sword.

CORIOLANUS   No, I'll die here.
There's some among you have beheld me fighting.
Come, try upon yourselves what you have seen me.

MENENIUS
Down with that sword! Tribunes, withdraw awhile.

BRUTUS
Lay hands upon him.

MENENIUS   Help Marcius, help!
You that be noble, help him, young and old!

ALL PLEBEIANS   Down with him, down with him!   233
            In this mutiny, the tribunes, the aediles,
                    and the people are beat in.

MENENIUS [to Coriolanus]
Go, get you to your house. Begone, away!
All will be naught else.

SECOND SENATOR   Get you gone.

CORIOLANUS   Stand fast!   235
We have as many friends as enemies.

MENENIUS
Shall it be put to that?

FIRST SENATOR   The gods forbid!
I prithee, noble friend, home to thy house;
Leave us to cure this cause.   239

MENENIUS   For 'tis a sore upon us
You cannot tent yourself. Begone, beseech you.   241

COMINIUS   Come, sir, along with us.

CORIOLANUS
I would they were barbarians, as they are,
Though in Rome littered; not Romans, as they are not,
Though calved i'th' porch o'th' Capitol.

MENENIUS   Begone!
Put not your worthy rage into your tongue.
One time will owe another.

CORIOLANUS   On fair ground   247
I could beat forty of them.

MENENIUS   I could myself

Take up a brace o'th' best of them; yea, the two
tribunes.   249

COMINIUS
But now 'tis odds beyond arithmetic,   250
And manhood is called foolery when it stands   251
Against a falling fabric. Will you hence   252
Before the tag return, whose rage doth rend   253
Like interrupted waters and o'erbear   254
What they are used to bear?

MENENIUS   Pray you, begone.   255
I'll try whether my old wit be in request   256
With those that have but little. This must be patched 257
With cloth of any color.   258

COMINIUS   Nay, come away.

            Exeunt Coriolanus and Cominius [with others].

A PATRICIAN   This man has marred his fortune.

MENENIUS
His nature is too noble for the world.
He would not flatter Neptune for his trident   262
Or Jove for 's power to thunder. His heart's his mouth. 263
What his breast forges, that his tongue must vent, 264
And, being angry, does forget that ever
He heard the name of death.   A noise within.
                          Here's goodly work!

A PATRICIAN   I would they were abed!

MENENIUS
I would they were in Tiber! What the vengeance!   268
Could he not speak 'em fair?

            Enter Brutus and Sicinius, with the rabble again.

SICINIUS   Where is this viper   269
That would depopulate the city and
Be every man himself?

MENENIUS   You worthy tribunes—

SICINIUS
He shall be thrown down the Tarpeian rock
With rigorous hands. He hath resisted law,   273
And therefore law shall scorn him further trial   274
Than the severity of the public power
Which he so sets at naught.

FIRST CITIZEN   He shall well know   276
The noble tribunes are the people's mouths,
And we their hands.

ALL PLEBEIANS   He shall, sure on't.   279

MENENIUS   Sir, sir—

SICINIUS   Peace!

---

217 rock Tarpeian famous precipice on the Capitoline Hill in ancient Rome from which persons condemned for offenses against the state were thrown down   **222 that** what   **233.2 beat in** i.e., driven offstage. **235 naught else** ruined otherwise.   **239 cause** disease.   **241 tent** treat (by probing a wound), cure   **247 One . . . another** Another time will compensate for this setback.

249 Take . . . brace take on a pair   **250 'tis . . . arithmetic** i.e., we are thoroughly outnumbered   **251 manhood** manliness.   **foolery** folly **252 fabric** building.   **hence** leave   **253 tag** rabble   **253–5 doth rend . . . bear** breaks and overflows, like dammed-up waters, the banks that normally contain them.   **256 request** demand **257–8 patched . . . color** i.e., mended in any way possible. **262 trident** three-pronged spear, the symbol of Neptune, Roman god of the sea   **263 His . . . mouth** i.e., What he feels is exactly what he speaks.   **264 vent** express   **268 What the vengeance!** (An oath.) **269 speak 'em fair** speak to them courteously.   **273 rigorous** severe **274 scorn** refuse.   **further** any further   **276 sets at naught** views as worthless.   **279 sure on't** be sure of it.

MENENIUS
Do not cry havoc, where you should but hunt   282
With modest warrant.

SICINIUS   Sir, how comes 't that you   283
Have holp to make this rescue?

MENENIUS   Hear me speak.   284
As I do know the Consul's worthiness,
So can I name his faults.

SICINIUS   Consul? What consul?

MENENIUS   The Consul Coriolanus.

BRUTUS   He consul?

ALL PLEBEIANS   No, no, no, no, no.

MENENIUS
If, by the tribunes' leave and yours, good people,   291
I may be heard, I would crave a word or two,
The which shall turn you to no further harm
Than so much loss of time.

SICINIUS   Speak briefly then,
For we are peremptory to dispatch   295
This viperous traitor. To eject him hence   296
Were but one danger, and to keep him here
Our certain death; therefore it is decreed
He dies tonight.

MENENIUS   Now the good gods forbid
That our renownèd Rome, whose gratitude
Towards her deservèd children is enrolled   301
In Jove's own book, like an unnatural dam   302
Should now eat up her own!

SICINIUS
He's a disease that must be cut away.

MENENIUS
Oh, he's a limb that has but a disease—
Mortal to cut it off; to cure it easy.   306
What has he done to Rome that's worthy death?
Killing our enemies, the blood he hath lost—
Which I dare vouch is more than that he hath
By many an ounce—he dropped it for his country;
And what is left, to lose it by his country   311
Were to us all that do't and suffer it
A brand to th'end o'th' world.

SICINIUS   This is clean kam.   313

BRUTUS
Merely awry. When he did love his country,   314
It honored him.

SICINIUS   The service of the foot,
Being once gangrened, is not then respected
For what before it was.

BRUTUS   We'll hear no more.
Pursue him to his house and pluck him thence,
Lest his infection, being of catching nature,
Spread further.

MENENIUS   One word more, one word.
This tiger-footed rage, when it shall find

The harm of unscanned swiftness, will too late   323
Tie leaden pounds to 's heels. Proceed by process,   324
Lest parties—as he is beloved—break out   325
And sack great Rome with Romans.

BRUTUS   If it were so—   326

SICINIUS   What do ye talk?   327
Have we not had a taste of his obedience?
Our aediles smote? Ourselves resisted? Come.

MENENIUS
Consider this: he has been bred i'th' wars
Since 'a could draw a sword, and is ill schooled   331
In bolted language; meal and bran together   332
He throws without distinction. Give me leave,   333
I'll go to him and undertake to bring him
Where he shall answer, by a lawful form,   335
In peace, to his utmost peril.

FIRST SENATOR   Noble tribunes,   336
It is the humane way. The other course
Will prove too bloody, and the end of it
Unknown to the beginning.

SICINIUS   Noble Menenius,
Be you then as the people's officer.—
Masters, lay down your weapons.

BRUTUS   Go not home.

SICINIUS
Meet on the marketplace.—We'll attend you there,   342
Where, if you bring not Marcius, we'll proceed
In our first way.

MENENIUS   I'll bring him to you.
[*To the Senators*] Let me desire your company. He must
  come,
Or what is worst will follow.

FIRST SENATOR   Pray you, let's to him.   347
                                    Exeunt omnes.

❧

[3.2]

Enter Coriolanus, with Nobles.

CORIOLANUS
Let them pull all about mine ears, present me   1
Death on the wheel or at wild horses' heels,   2
Or pile ten hills on the Tarpeian rock,
That the precipitation might down stretch   4
Below the beam of sight, yet will I still   5
Be thus to them.

A PATRICIAN   You do the nobler.

CORIOLANUS   I muse my mother   8
Does not approve me further, who was wont   9

---

282 **cry havoc** give the order for general slaughter (as in *Julius Caesar*, 3.1.275)   283 **modest warrant** limited license.   284 **holp . . . rescue** helped to remove this prisoner from custody by force.   291 **leave** permission   295 **peremptory** determined   296 **eject him hence** exile him   301 **deservèd** deserving   302 **dam** mother   306 **Mortal** fatal   311 **by** at the hands of   313 **brand** i.e., brand of infamy, stigma.   **clean kam** quite beside the point.   314 **Merely** Completely

323 **unscanned** unconsidered   324 **Tie . . . heels** tie leaden weights to his heels.   **process** legal method   325 **parties** factions   326 **with** by means of; along with   327 **'a** he   331 **bolted** sifted, refined   332–3 **meal . . . throws** he throws flour and husks together   333 **Give** If you give   335–6 **answer . . . peril** stand trial peacefully even though his life is at stake.   342 **attend** await   347.1 *omnes* all.   3.2. Location: Rome. Coriolanus's house.
1 **pull . . . ears** pull everything down on top of me, crush me.   **present me** i.e., sentence me to   2 **wheel** instrument of torture and death by which the victim's limbs were broken   4 **precipitation** precipitousness   5 **Below . . . sight** further than the eye can see   8 **muse** wonder that   9 **further** to a greater degree.   **was wont** used

To call them woolen vassals, things created   10
To buy and sell with groats, to show bare heads   11
In congregations, to yawn, be still, and wonder   12
When one but of my ordinance stood up   13
To speak of peace or war.

Enter Volumnia.

                    I talk of you.
Why did you wish me milder? Would you have me
False to my nature? Rather say I play
The man I am.

VOLUMNIA   Oh, sir, sir, sir,
I would have had you put your power well on   18
Before you had worn it out.

CORIOLANUS   Let go.   20

VOLUMNIA
You might have been enough the man you are
With striving less to be so. Lesser had been
The thwartings of your dispositions if
You had not showed them how ye were disposed
Ere they lacked power to cross you.

CORIOLANUS   Let them hang!   25

VOLUMNIA   Ay, and burn too.

Enter Menenius with the Senators.

MENENIUS
Come, come, you have been too rough, something too
    rough;   27
You must return and mend it.

FIRST SENATOR   There's no remedy,
Unless, by not so doing, our good city
Cleave in the midst and perish.

VOLUMNIA   Pray be counseled.
I have a heart as little apt as yours,   31
But yet a brain that leads my use of anger
To better vantage.

MENENIUS   Well said, noble woman!
Before he should thus stoop to th' herd, but that   34
The violent fit o'th' time craves it as physic   35
For the whole state, I would put mine armor on,
Which I can scarcely bear.

CORIOLANUS   What must I do?   37

MENENIUS
Return to th' tribunes.

CORIOLANUS   Well, what then? What then?

MENENIUS   Repent what you have spoke.

CORIOLANUS
For them? I cannot do it to the gods.
Must I then do't to them?

VOLUMNIA   You are too absolute,   41

Though therein you can never be too noble,   42
But when extremities speak. I have heard you say   43
Honor and policy, like unsevered friends,   44
I'th' war do grow together. Grant that, and tell me
In peace what each of them by th'other lose
That they combine not there.

CORIOLANUS   Tush, tush!

MENENIUS   A good demand.   47

VOLUMNIA
If it be honor in your wars to seem
The same you are not, which for your best ends
You adopt your policy, how is it less or worse   50
That it shall hold companionship in peace
With honor as in war, since that to both
It stands in like request?

CORIOLANUS   Why force you this?   53

VOLUMNIA
Because that now it lies you on to speak   54
To th' people, not by your own instruction,   55
Nor by th' matter which your heart prompts you,
But with such words that are but roted in   57
Your tongue, though but bastards and syllables
Of no allowance to your bosom's truth.   59
Now, this no more dishonors you at all
Than to take in a town with gentle words,   61
Which else would put you to your fortune and   62
The hazard of much blood.
I would dissemble with my nature where   64
My fortunes and my friends at stake required
I should do so in honor. I am in this   66
Your wife, your son, these senators, the nobles;   67
And you will rather show our general louts   68
How you can frown than spend a fawn upon 'em   69
For the inheritance of their loves and safeguard   70
Of what that want might ruin.

MENENIUS   Noble lady!—   71
Come, go with us; speak fair. You may salve so,   72
Not what is dangerous present, but the loss   73
Of what is past.

VOLUMNIA   I prithee now, my son,   74
Go to them, with this bonnet in thy hand,   75
And thus far having stretched it—here be with them—   76
Thy knee bussing the stones—for in such business   77
Action is eloquence, and the eyes of th'ignorant

---

10 **woolen** coarsely clad   11 **To . . . groats** i.e., to be nothing more than petty traders. (*Groats* are fourpenny pieces.)   12 **congregations** assemblies.   **yawn** i.e., gape with amazement   13 **ordinance** rank
18 **I would . . . well on** I would have preferred that you had learned to achieve and use your authority well   20 **Let go** Enough.   25 **Ere . . . you** before they lost the power to thwart your attempt to become consul.   27 **something** somewhat   31 **apt** compliant   34–5 **but that . . . physic** were it not that the feverish convulsions of the time need it as medicine   37 **Which . . . bear** i.e., which I am nearly too old for.
41 **absolute** uncompromising

42–3 **therein . . . speak** i.e., being uncompromising in your nobility is a fine thing, except when the situation is critically extreme.   44 **policy** the proper consideration of stratagem and craft.   **unsevered** inseparable   47 **demand** question.   50 **adopt** adopt as   53 **It . . . request** it is equally needed.   **force** urge   54 **lies you on** is your duty   55 **instruction** i.e., conviction, inner prompting   57 **are but roted in** have been learned merely by rote in   59 **Of . . . to** unacknowledged by   61 **take in** capture   62 **else . . . fortune** otherwise would force you to take your chance (in battle)   64 **dissemble . . . nature** pretend to be other than I was   66 **in honor** in compliance with the requirements of honor.   66–7 **I am . . . wife** In this I represent your wife   68 **And . . . louts** and yet you'd rather show our vulgar commoners   69 **fawn** flattering appeal   70 **inheritance** obtaining   71 **that want** i.e., the lack of their loves   72 **salve** remedy   73–4 **Not . . . past** not only the present danger but what has been lost already.   75 **bonnet** cap   76 **And . . . them** and go to them holding your hat out thus—do this to please them. (She gestures.)
77 **bussing** kissing

More learnèd than the ears—waving thy head,   79
With often thus correcting thy stout heart,   80
Now humble as the ripest mulberry   81
That will not hold the handling. Or say to them   82
Thou art their soldier, and being bred in broils   83
Hast not the soft way which, thou dost confess,
Were fit for thee to use as they to claim,   85
In asking their good loves; but thou wilt frame   86
Thyself, forsooth, hereafter theirs, so far   87
As thou hast power and person.

MENENIUS   This but done   88
Even as she speaks, why, their hearts were yours;   89
For they have pardons, being asked, as free   90
As words to little purpose.

VOLUMNIA   Prithee now,
Go, and be ruled; although I know thou hadst rather
Follow thine enemy in a fiery gulf   93
Than flatter him in a bower.

                    Enter Cominius.

                                    Here is Cominius.   94

COMINIUS
I have been i'th' marketplace; and, sir, 'tis fit   95
You make strong party, or defend yourself   96
By calmness or by absence. All's in anger.

MENENIUS
Only fair speech.

COMINIUS   I think 'twill serve, if he
Can thereto frame his spirit.

VOLUMNIA   He must, and will.
Prithee, now, say you will, and go about it.

CORIOLANUS
Must I go show them my unbarbed sconce? Must I   101
With my base tongue give to my noble heart
A lie that it must bear? Well, I will do't.
Yet, were there but this single plot to lose,   104
This mold of Marcius, they to dust should grind it   105
And throw't against the wind. To th' marketplace!
You have put me now to such a part which never
I shall discharge to th' life.

COMINIUS   Come, come, we'll prompt you.   108

VOLUMNIA
I prithee now, sweet son, as thou hast said
My praises made thee first a soldier, so,
To have my praise for this, perform a part
Thou hast not done before.

CORIOLANUS   Well, I must do't.

Away, my disposition, and possess me
Some harlot's spirit! My throat of war be turned,   114
Which choirèd with my drum, into a pipe   115
Small as an eunuch or the virgin voice   116
That babies lulls asleep! The smiles of knaves   117
Tent in my cheeks, and schoolboys' tears take up   118
The glasses of my sight! A beggar's tongue   119
Make motion through my lips, and my armed knees,
Who bowed but in my stirrup, bend like his
That hath received an alms! I will not do't,   122
Lest I surcease to honor mine own truth   123
And by my body's action teach my mind
A most inherent baseness.

VOLUMNIA   At thy choice, then.   125
To beg of thee, it is my more dishonor
Than thou of them. Come all to ruin. Let   127
Thy mother rather feel thy pride than fear   128
Thy dangerous stoutness, for I mock at death   129
With as big heart as thou. Do as thou list.   130
Thy valiantness was mine, thou suck'st it from me,
But owe thy pride thyself.

CORIOLANUS   Pray, be content.   132
Mother, I am going to the marketplace.
Chide me no more. I'll mountebank their loves,   134
Cog their hearts from them, and come home beloved 135
Of all the trades in Rome. Look, I am going.
Commend me to my wife. I'll return consul,
Or never trust to what my tongue can do
I'th' way of flattery further.

VOLUMNIA   Do your will.
                                        Exit Volumnia.

COMINIUS
Away! The tribunes do attend you. Arm yourself   140
To answer mildly; for they are prepared
With accusations, as I hear, more strong
Than are upon you yet.

CORIOLANUS
The word is "mildly." Pray you, let us go.   144
Let them accuse me by invention; I   145
Will answer in mine honor.

MENENIUS   Ay, but mildly.   146

CORIOLANUS
Well, mildly be it then. Mildly!   *Exeunt.*

                              ❧

[3.3]

                    Enter Sicinius and Brutus.

---

79 learnèd i.e., receptive.   **waving** bowing up and down   **80 stout** proud   **81 Now . . . mulberry** now as soft and malleable as overripe fruit. (Or *humble* may mean "abase, let droop.")   **82 hold** bear, tolerate   **83 broils** battles   **85 fit** as fit.   **as they** as for them   **86 In asking** in your asking for.   **frame** conform   **87 forsooth** truly, indeed. **theirs** to suit their wish   **87–8 so far . . . person** to the full extent of your ability and authority.   **89 were** would be, will be   **90 as free** i.e., which they will grant as freely   **93 in** into   **94 bower** (1) arbor (2) lady's private chamber.   **95 fit** appropriate   **96 make strong party** support your side strongly, or gather a strong faction around you   **101 unbarbed sconce** unhelmeted head.   **104 this single plot** this piece of earth only (i.e., my own person)   **105 mold** (1) bodily form (2) earth   **108 discharge to th' life** perform convincingly.

114 harlot's (1) rascal's (2) whore's.   **throat of war** i.e., soldier's voice   **115 choirèd** harmonized, sang in tune   **116 Small** high-pitched   **117 babies lulls** lulls babies   **118 Tent** lodge, set up camp **118–19 take up . . . sight** occupy my eyeballs.   **122 an alms** a gift of charity.   **123 surcease** cease   **125 inherent** irremovable, fixed **127–9 Let . . . stoutness** Let me rather suffer the worst your pride can do for us than fear to confront your dangerous obstinacy   **130 big heart** noble courage.   **list** please.   **132 owe** own   **134 mountebank** win over as with the tricks of a quack medicine salesman   **135 Cog** cheat, beguile   **140 attend** await.   **Arm** Prepare   **144 word** watchword   **145 accuse . . . invention** invent charges against me all they like   **146 in** in accordance with
3.3. Location: Rome. The Forum or marketplace.

BRUTUS

In this point charge him home, that he affects   1
Tyrannical power. If he evade us there,
Enforce him with his envy to the people,   3
And that the spoil got on the Antiates   4
Was ne'er distributed.

Enter an Aedile.

                              What, will he come?   5

AEDILE   He's coming.

BRUTUS   How accompanied?

AEDILE

With old Menenius, and those senators
That always favored him.

SICINIUS   Have you a catalogue
Of all the voices that we have procured
Set down by th' poll?

AEDILE   I have; 'tis ready.   11

SICINIUS

Have you collected them by tribes?

AEDILE   I have.   12

SICINIUS

Assemble presently the people hither;   13
And when they hear me say "It shall be so
I'th' right and strength o'th' commons," be it either
For death, for fine, or banishment, then let them,
If I say "Fine," cry "Fine!", if "Death," cry "Death!",
Insisting on the old prerogative   18
And power i'th' truth o'th' cause.

AEDILE   I shall inform them.   19

BRUTUS

And when such time they have begun to cry,   20
Let them not cease, but with a din confused
Enforce the present execution   22
Of what we chance to sentence.

AEDILE   Very well.

SICINIUS

Make them be strong, and ready for this hint
When we shall hap to give't them.

BRUTUS   Go about it.   25

                              [*Exit Aedile.*]

Put him to choler straight. He hath been used   26
Ever to conquer and to have his worth   27
Of contradiction. Being once chafed, he cannot   28
Be reined again to temperance; then he speaks
What's in his heart, and that is there which looks   30
With us to break his neck.   31

*Enter Coriolanus, Menenius, and Cominius, with
others [Senators and patricians].*

---

1 charge him home press home your charges.   **affects** aspires to,
desires   **3 Enforce . . . to** confront him with his inveterate malice
toward   **4 spoil got on** property taken from   **5 s.d. Aedile** (See note
at 3.1.176.)   **11 by th' poll** by individual names, by head count
12 tribes divisions of the Roman populace.   **13 presently** immediately   **18 old prerogative** traditional privilege or position   **19 truth**
justice.   **cause** case.   **20 cry** cry out, shout   **22 Enforce . . . execution**
insist on immediate carrying out   **25 hap** happen   **26 Put . . .**
straight Incense him to anger straightway.   **used** accustomed
27–8 his worth . . . contradiction plenty of opportunity to answer
back, giving as good as he gets.   **30–1 looks With us** promises, with
our help

SICINIUS   Well, here he comes.

MENENIUS   Calmly, I do beseech you.

CORIOLANUS

Ay, as an hostler, that for th' poorest piece   34
Will bear the knave by th' volume.—Th' honored gods   35
Keep Rome in safety and the chairs of justice
Supplied with worthy men! Plant love among 's!
Throng our large temples with the shows of peace,   38
And not our streets with war!

FIRST SENATOR   Amen, amen.

MENENIUS   A noble wish.

Enter the Aedile, with the plebeians.

SICINIUS   Draw near, ye people.

AEDILE

List to your tribunes. Audience! Peace, I say!   43

CORIOLANUS   First, hear me speak.

BOTH TRIBUNES   Well, say.—Peace, ho!

CORIOLANUS

Shall I be charged no further than this present?   46
Must all determine here?

SICINIUS   I do demand   47
If you submit you to the people's voices,   48
Allow their officers, and are content   49
To suffer lawful censure for such faults   50
As shall be proved upon you?

CORIOLANUS   I am content.

MENENIUS

Lo, citizens, he says he is content.
The warlike service he has done, consider. Think
Upon the wounds his body bears, which show
Like graves i'th' holy churchyard.

CORIOLANUS   Scratches with briers,
Scars to move laughter only.

MENENIUS   Consider further,
That when he speaks not like a citizen,
You find him like a soldier. Do not take
His rougher accents for malicious sounds,
But, as I say, such as become a soldier
Rather than envy you.

COMINIUS   Well, well, no more.   61

CORIOLANUS   What is the matter
That, being passed for consul with full voice,
I am so dishonored that the very hour
You take it off again?

SICINIUS   Answer to us.   66

CORIOLANUS   Say, then. 'Tis true, I ought so.   67

SICINIUS

We charge you that you have contrived to take
From Rome all seasoned office and to wind   69
Yourself into a power tyrannical,

34–5 an hostler . . . volume a horse-groom, who for a measly coin will
put up with being called knave any number of times.   **35 Th' hon-**
ored May the honored   **38 shows** ceremonies   **43 List** Listen.
Audience! Listen, give heed!   **46 this present** this present occasion,
the matter in hand.   **47 determine** come to an end, be concluded.
demand ask   **48 If** whether   **49 Allow** acknowledge the authority of
50 censure judgment   **61 Rather . . . you** rather than such as show
malice toward you.   **66 Answer to us** i.e., We'll do the asking, not
you.   **67 so** to do so.   **69 seasoned** established.   **wind** insinuate

For which you are a traitor to the people.

CORIOLANUS
How? Traitor?

MENENIUS   Nay, temperately! Your promise.

CORIOLANUS
The fires i'th' lowest hell fold in the people!   73
Call me their traitor? Thou injurious tribune!   74
Within thine eyes sat twenty thousand deaths,   75
In thy hands clutched as many millions, in   76
Thy lying tongue both numbers, I would say   77
"Thou liest" unto thee with a voice as free
As I do pray the gods.

SICINIUS   Mark you this, people?

ALL PLEBEIANS   To th' rock, to th' rock with him!

SICINIUS   Peace!
We need not put new matter to his charge.   83
What you have seen him do and heard him speak,
Beating your officers, cursing yourselves,
Opposing laws with strokes, and here defying   86
Those whose great power must try him—even this,
So criminal and in such capital kind,   88
Deserves th'extremest death.

BRUTUS   But since he hath
Served well for Rome—

CORIOLANUS   What do you prate of service?   90

BRUTUS   I talk of that that know it.

CORIOLANUS   You?

MENENIUS
Is this the promise that you made your mother?

COMINIUS   Know, I pray you—

CORIOLANUS   I'll know no further.
Let them pronounce the steep Tarpeian death,
Vagabond exile, flaying, pent to linger   97
But with a grain a day, I would not buy   98
Their mercy at the price of one fair word,
Nor check my courage for what they can give,   100
To have't with saying "Good morrow."   101

SICINIUS   For that he has,   101
As much as in him lies, from time to time   102
Envied against the people, seeking means   103
To pluck away their power, as now at last   104
Given hostile strokes, and that not in the presence   105
Of dreaded justice, but on the ministers
That doth distribute it: in the name o'th' people
And in the power of us the tribunes, we,
Ev'n from this instant, banish him our city,
In peril of precipitation   110
From off the rock Tarpeian, never more
To enter our Rome gates. I'th' people's name,
I say it shall be so.

ALL PLEBEIANS
It shall be so, it shall be so! Let him away!

He's banished, and it shall be so!

COMINIUS
Hear me, my masters, and my common friends—

SICINIUS
He's sentenced. No more hearing.

COMINIUS   Let me speak.
I have been consul, and can show for Rome
Her enemies' marks upon me. I do love
My country's good with a respect more tender,   120
More holy and profound, than mine own life,
My dear wife's estimate, her womb's increase,   122
And treasure of my loins. Then if I would
Speak that—

SICINIUS   We know your drift. Speak what?

BRUTUS
There's no more to be said, but he is banished   126
As enemy to the people and his country.
It shall be so.

ALL PLEBEIANS   It shall be so, it shall be so!

CORIOLANUS
You common cry of curs, whose breath I hate   130
As reek o'th' rotten fens, whose loves I prize   131
As the dead carcasses of unburied men
That do corrupt my air, I banish you!
And here remain with your uncertainty!   134
Let every feeble rumor shake your hearts!
Your enemies, with nodding of their plumes,   136
Fan you into despair! Have the power still   137
To banish your defenders, till at length
Your ignorance—which finds not till it feels,   139
Making but reservation of yourselves,   140
Still your own foes—deliver you   141
As most abated captives to some nation   142
That won you without blows! Despising
For you the city, thus I turn my back.   144
There is a world elsewhere.

        Exeunt Coriolanus, Cominius,
        [Menenius, Senators, and patricians].

AEDILE   The people's enemy is gone, is gone!

ALL PLEBEIANS
Our enemy is banished! He is gone! Hoo! Hoo!
        They all shout and throw up their caps.

SICINIUS
Go see him out at gates, and follow him,
As he hath followed you, with all despite;   149
Give him deserved vexation. Let a guard   150
Attend us through the city.

ALL PLEBEIANS
Come, come, let's see him out at gates! Come.
The gods preserve our noble tribunes! Come.
                                        Exeunt.

73 **fold in** enfold, envelop   74 **their traitor** a traitor to them.   **injurious** insulting   75–7 **Within . . . numbers** (Understand "although" before each of the three clauses.)   83 **put new matter** add new particulars   86 **strokes** blows   88 **capital** death-deserving   90 **prate** talk idly   97–8 **pent . . . day** imprisoned to starve with but a small particle of food a day   100 **check** restrain   101 **To have't with saying** if I might have it merely by saying.   **For that** Because   102 **in him lies** he could   103 **Envied against** showed malice toward   104 **as** i.e., and inasmuch as (he has)   105 **not** not merely   110 **precipitation** being thrown

120 **respect** regard, feeling   122 **estimate** reputation   126 **but** but that   130 **cry** pack   131 **reek** vapor   134 **remain** may you remain.   **uncertainty** inconstancy, fickleness; also, insecurity (as explained in the following lines).   136 **Your** May your.   **with** merely with   137 **Have** May you have   139–41 **which . . . foes** which learns only through experience, seeking only to preserve yourselves (or, leaving no one unbanished except yourselves), you being always your own worst enemies   142 **abated** humbled   144 **For** because of   149 **despite** disdain, contempt   150 **vexation** torment.

4.1

Enter Coriolanus, Volumnia, Virgilia, Menenius,
Cominius, with the young nobility of Rome.

CORIOLANUS
Come, leave your tears. A brief farewell. The beast   1
With many heads butts me away. Nay, mother,
Where is your ancient courage? You were used   3
To say extremities was the trier of spirits;   4
That common chances common men could bear;
That when the sea was calm all boats alike
Showed mastership in floating; fortune's blows   7
When most struck home, being gentle wounded
  craves   8
A noble cunning. You were used to load me   9
With precepts that would make invincible
The heart that conned them.   11

VIRGILIA
O heavens! O heavens!

CORIOLANUS   Nay, I prithee, woman—

VOLUMNIA
Now the red pestilence strike all trades in Rome,   13
And occupations perish!

CORIOLANUS   What, what, what!   14
I shall be loved when I am lacked. Nay, mother,   15
Resume that spirit when you were wont to say,   16
If you had been the wife of Hercules,
Six of his labors you'd have done and saved   18
Your husband so much sweat. Cominius,
Droop not. Adieu. Farewell, my wife, my mother.
I'll do well yet. Thou old and true Menenius,
Thy tears are salter than a younger man's,
And venomous to thine eyes.—My sometime general,   23
I have seen thee stern, and thou hast oft beheld
Heart-hard'ning spectacles; tell these sad women
'Tis fond to wail inevitable strokes   26
As 'tis to laugh at 'em. My mother, you wot well   27
My hazards still have been your solace, and—   28
Believe't not lightly—though I go alone,
Like to a lonely dragon that his fen   30
Makes feared and talked of more than seen, your son
Will or exceed the common or be caught   32
With cautelous baits and practice.

VOLUMNIA   My first son,   33
Whither wilt thou go? Take good Cominius
With thee awhile. Determine on some course
More than a wild exposture to each chance   36

That starts i'th' way before thee.

VIRGILIA   O the gods!   37

COMINIUS
I'll follow thee a month, devise with thee   38
Where thou shalt rest, that thou mayst hear of us
And we of thee; so if the time thrust forth
A cause for thy repeal, we shall not send   41
O'er the vast world to seek a single man,
And lose advantage, which doth ever cool   43
I'th'absence of the needer.

CORIOLANUS   Fare ye well.   44
Thou hast years upon thee, and thou art too full
Of the wars' surfeits to go rove with one   46
That's yet unbruised. Bring me but out at gate.   47
Come, my sweet wife, my dearest mother, and
My friends of noble touch; when I am forth,   49
Bid me farewell, and smile. I pray you, come.
While I remain above the ground, you shall
Hear from me still, and never of me aught
But what is like me formerly.

MENENIUS   That's worthily
As any ear can hear. Come, let's not weep.
If I could shake off but one seven years
From these old arms and legs, by the good gods,
I'd with thee every foot.

CORIOLANUS   Give me thy hand.
Come.   *Exeunt.*

❖

[4.2]

Enter the two tribunes, Sicinius and Brutus, with
the Aedile.

SICINIUS [*to the Aedile*]
Bid them all home. He's gone, and we'll no further.   1
The nobility are vexed, whom we see have sided
In his behalf.

BRUTUS   Now we have shown our power,
Let us seem humbler after it is done
Than when it was a-doing.

SICINIUS   Bid them home.
Say their great enemy is gone, and they
Stand in their ancient strength.

BRUTUS   Dismiss them home.   7
                              [*Exit Aedile.*]
Here comes his mother.

Enter Volumnia, Virgilia, and Menenius.

SICINIUS Let's not meet her.
BRUTUS Why?
SICINIUS They say she's mad.

4.1. Location: Rome, near the gates of the city (see line 47).
1 leave cease, leave off   **3 ancient** former.   **used** accustomed
4 extremities crisis   **7–9 fortune's . . . cunning** i.e., when fortune
strikes her hardest blows, to bear one's afflictions like true gentlefolk
requires great nobility and understanding.   **11 conned** studied,
memorized   **13 red pestilence** (Red spots presaged death to those
stricken with the plague.)   **14 occupations** trades, handicrafts
15 lacked missed.   **16 wont** accustomed   **18 Six of his labors** i.e.,
half of the twelve labors of Hercules   **23 sometime** former. (Said to
Cominius.)   **26 fond** foolish   **27 wot** know   **28 still** always   **30 fen**
lurking place, marsh   **32 or . . . common** either exceed the ordinary
deeds of men   **33 cautelous** crafty, deceitful.   **practice** treacherous
methods.   **36 exposture** exposure (of yourself)

37 starts breaks from cover, darts across your path   **38 follow** go
with   **41 repeal** recall from banishment   **43 advantage** the opportune moment   **44 the needer** the person who needs to seize the
moment.   **46 wars' surfeits** wearing effects of military service
47 Bring Conduct   **49 noble touch** approved nobility. (From the use
of the touchstone with precious metal.)
4.2. Location: Rome. A street.
1 home go home.   **7 ancient** former

BRUTUS
They have ta'en note of us. Keep on your way.
[*They start to leave.*]

VOLUMNIA
Oh, you're well met. Th' hoarded plague o'th' gods   13
Requite your love!

MENENIUS   Peace, peace! Be not so loud.   14

VOLUMNIA
If that I could for weeping, you should hear—   15
Nay, and you shall hear some. Will you be gone?

VIRGILIA
You shall stay too. I would I had the power   17
To say so to my husband.

SICINIUS   Are you mankind?   18

VOLUMNIA
Ay, fool, is that a shame?—Note but this fool.—   19
Was not a man my father? Hadst thou foxship   20
To banish him that struck more blows for Rome
Than thou hast spoken words?

SICINIUS   O blessèd heavens!

VOLUMNIA
More noble blows than ever thou wise words,
And for Rome's good. I'll tell thee what—yet go.
Nay, but thou shalt stay too. I would my son   25
Were in Arabia, and thy tribe before him,   26
His good sword in his hand.

SICINIUS   What then?

VIRGILIA   What then?
He'd make an end of thy posterity.   28

VOLUMNIA Bastards and all.
Good man, the wounds that he does bear for Rome!

MENENIUS Come, come, peace.

SICINIUS
I would he had continued to his country
As he began, and not unknit himself   33
The noble knot he made.

BRUTUS   I would he had.   34

VOLUMNIA
"I would he had"? 'Twas you incensed the rabble—
Cats, that can judge as fitly of his worth   36
As I can of those mysteries which heaven
Will not have earth to know!

BRUTUS
Pray, let's go.

VOLUMNIA   Now, pray, sir, get you gone.
You have done a brave deed. Ere you go, hear this:
As far as doth the Capitol exceed
The meanest house in Rome, so far my son—   42
This lady's husband here, this, do you see?—
Whom you have banished, does exceed you all.

BRUTUS
Well, well, we'll leave you.

SICINIUS   Why stay we to be baited   45
With one that wants her wits?   *Exeunt tribunes.*

VOLUMNIA   Take my prayers with you.   46
I would the gods had nothing else to do
But to confirm my curses! Could I meet 'em   48
But once a day, it would unclog my heart   49
Of what lies heavy to't.

MENENIUS   You have told them home,   50
And, by my troth, you have cause. You'll sup with me?   51

VOLUMNIA
Anger's my meat. I sup upon myself,
And so shall starve with feeding. [*To Virgilia*] Come,
let's go.
Leave this faint puling and lament as I do,   54
In anger, Juno-like. Come, come, come.   55

MENENIUS Fie, fie, fie!   *Exeunt.*

❖

4.3

*Enter [Nicanor,] a Roman, and [Adrian,] a
Volsce.*

ROMAN I know you well, sir, and you know me. Your
name, I think, is Adrian.

VOLSCE It is so, sir. Truly, I have forgot you.

ROMAN I am a Roman; and my services are, as you are,
against 'em. Know you me yet?   5

VOLSCE Nicanor, no?

ROMAN The same, sir.

VOLSCE You had more beard when I last saw you, but
your favor is well approved by your tongue. What's the   9
news in Rome? I have a note from the Volscian state   10
to find you out there. You have well saved me a day's
journey.

ROMAN There hath been in Rome strange insurrections:
the people against the senators, patricians, and nobles.

VOLSCE Hath been? Is it ended, then? Our state thinks
not so. They are in a most warlike preparation, and
hope to come upon them in the heat of their division.

ROMAN The main blaze of it is past, but a small thing
would make it flame again; for the nobles receive so to
heart the banishment of that worthy Coriolanus that
they are in a ripe aptness to take all power from the
people and to pluck from them their tribunes forever.
This lies glowing, I can tell you, and is almost mature   23
for the violent breaking out.

VOLSCE Coriolanus banished?

ROMAN Banished, sir.

VOLSCE You will be welcome with this intelligence,
Nicanor.

---

13 hoarded stored up   **14 Requite** repay   **15 If that** If   **17 You shall
stay too** (Sometimes read as if addressed to the second of the two tribunes, but it may mean "you shall too stay," i.e., whether you want to
or not. See line 25.)   **18 mankind** masculine (i.e., railing like a man),
or, infuriated. (Volumnia responds as though it meant "of the human
race.")   **19 Note but this fool** (The line could read, "Note but this,
fool," addressed to Sicinius.)   **20 foxship** craftiness   **25 would** wish
26 Arabia i.e., a deserted spot, with no place to hide.   **tribe** family,
clan, set   **28 posterity** descendants.   **33–4 unknit . . . made** i.e.,
untied the knot of service and gratitude binding him and Rome
together.   **36 Cats** (A term of contempt.)   **42 meanest** poorest

45–6 baited With harassed by   **48 'em** i.e., the tribunes   **49 unclog**
unburden   **50 to't** upon it.   **told them home** berated them thoroughly   **51 sup** dine   **54 puling** whimpering   **55 Juno-like** resembling Juno, chief goddess of the Romans (whose unforgiving anger is
mentioned by Virgil in *Aeneid* 1.4).
4.3. Location: A road between Rome and Antium.
5 against 'em i.e., on behalf of the Volsces against Rome.   **9 your . . .
tongue** your face and appearance are well confirmed by your voice.
10 note instruction   **23 glowing** smoldering

ROMAN   The day serves well for them now. I have heard   29
it said the fittest time to corrupt a man's wife is when
she's fall'n out with her husband. Your noble Tullus
Aufidius will appear well in these wars, his great
opposer Coriolanus being now in no request of his   33
country.

VOLSCE   He cannot choose. I am most fortunate thus   35
accidentally to encounter you. You have ended my
business, and I will merrily accompany you home.

ROMAN   I shall, between this and supper, tell you most   38
strange things from Rome, all tending to the good of
their adversaries. Have you an army ready, say you?

VOLSCE   A most royal one: the centurions and their   41
charges, distinctly billeted, already in th'entertain-   42
ment, and to be on foot at an hour's warning.   43

ROMAN   I am joyful to hear of their readiness, and am
the man, I think, that shall set them in present action.   45
So, sir, heartily well met, and most glad of your
company.

VOLSCE   You take my part from me, sir; I have the most   48
cause to be glad of yours.

ROMAN   Well, let us go together.   *Exeunt.*

❖

[4.4]

*Enter Coriolanus in mean apparel, disguised
and muffled.*

CORIOLANUS
A goodly city is this Antium. City,
'Tis I that made thy widows. Many an heir
Of these fair edifices 'fore my wars   3
Have I heard groan and drop. Then know me not,
Lest that thy wives with spits and boys with stones
In puny battle slay me.

Enter a Citizen.

Save you, sir.   6

CITIZEN
And you.

CORIOLANUS   Direct me, if it be your will,
Where great Aufidius lies. Is he in Antium?   8

CITIZEN
He is, and feasts the nobles of the state
At his house this night.

CORIOLANUS   Which is his house, beseech you?

CITIZEN
This here before you.

CORIOLANUS   Thank you, sir. Farewell.
Exit Citizen.

O world, thy slippery turns! Friends now fast sworn,   12
Whose double bosoms seems to wear one heart,
Whose hours, whose bed, whose meal and exercise
Are still together, who twin, as 'twere, in love   15
Unseparable, shall within this hour,   16
On a dissension of a doit, break out   17
To bitterest enmity; so fellest foes,   18
Whose passions and whose plots have broke their
sleep   19
To take the one the other, by some chance,   20
Some trick not worth an egg, shall grow dear friends   21
And interjoin their issues. So with me: 22
My birthplace hate I, and my love's upon
This enemy town. I'll enter. If he slay me,
He does fair justice; if he give me way,   25
I'll do his country service.   *Exit.*

❖

[4.5]

Music plays. Enter a Servingman.

FIRST SERVINGMAN   Wine, wine, wine! What service is
here? I think our fellows are asleep.   *[Exit.]*   2

Enter another Servingman.

SECOND SERVINGMAN   Where's Cotus? My master calls
for him. Cotus!   *Exit.*

Enter Coriolanus.

CORIOLANUS
A goodly house. The feast smells well, but I
Appear not like a guest.

Enter the First Servingman.

FIRST SERVINGMAN   What would you have, friend?
Whence are you? Here's no place for you. Pray go to   8
the door.   *Exit.*   9

CORIOLANUS
I have deserved no better entertainment   10
In being Coriolanus.

Enter Second Servingman.

SECOND SERVINGMAN   Whence are you, sir? Has the
porter his eyes in his head, that he gives entrance
to such companions? Pray, get you out.   14

CORIOLANUS   Away!

SECOND SERVINGMAN   Away? Get you away.

---

29 them i.e., the Volsces   **33 of** by   **35 choose** do otherwise (than
appear well).   **38 this** this present time   **41 centurions** officers each
in command of a hundred men or "century"   **41–2 their charges** the
men under their command   **42 distinctly billeted** separately enrolled
42–3 in th'entertainment mobilized, on the payroll   **45 present**
immediate   **48 my part** i.e., the words I should say
4.4. Location: Antium. Before Aufidius's house.
3 'fore my wars in the face of my onslaught   **6 puny** petty.   **Save**
God save   **8 lies** dwells.

12 slippery turns fickle shifts of fortune.   **fast** firmly   **15 still** ever
16 this hour an hour   **17 dissension of a doit** i.e., paltry dispute. (A
doit is a small coin.)   **18 so fellest** similarly fiercest   **19–20 Whose . . .
other** whose passionate plotting to undo each other have kept them
awake at night   **21 trick** trifle   **22 interjoin . . . issues** (1) bind
together their fortunes and affairs (2) link themselves by marriage of
their children.   **25 give me way** let me have my will and do what I
want, accede to my request
4.5. Location: Antium. The house of Aufidius. The sense of time
here is virtually continuous; the stage is imaginatively transformed
from the outside to the inside of Aufidius's house.
2 fellows fellow servants   **8–9 go to the door** get out.   **10 entertainment** reception.   **14 companions** rascals, base persons.

CORIOLANUS   Now thou'rt troublesome.

SECOND SERVINGMAN   Are you so brave? I'll have you 18
talked with anon. 19

Enter Third Servingman. The First, [entering,]
meets him.

THIRD SERVINGMAN   What fellow's this?

FIRST SERVINGMAN   A strange one as ever I looked on.
I cannot get him out o'th' house. Prithee, call my
master to him.

THIRD SERVINGMAN   What have you to do here, fellow?
Pray you, avoid the house. 25

CORIOLANUS   Let me but stand. I will not hurt your
hearth.

THIRD SERVINGMAN   What are you?

CORIOLANUS   A gentleman.

THIRD SERVINGMAN   A marvelous poor one.

CORIOLANUS   True, so I am.

THIRD SERVINGMAN   Pray you, poor gentleman, take
up some other station; here's no place for you. Pray 33
you, avoid. Come.

CORIOLANUS   Follow your function, go, and batten on 35
cold bits.   *Pushes him away from him.*

THIRD SERVINGMAN   What, you will not?—Prithee, tell
my master what a strange guest he has here.

SECOND SERVINGMAN   And I shall.
Exit Second Servingman.

THIRD SERVINGMAN   Where dwell'st thou?

CORIOLANUS   Under the canopy. 41

THIRD SERVINGMAN   Under the canopy?

CORIOLANUS   Ay.

THIRD SERVINGMAN   Where's that?

CORIOLANUS   I'th' city of kites and crows. 45

THIRD SERVINGMAN   I'th' city of kites and crows?
What an ass it is! Then thou dwell'st with daws too? 47

CORIOLANUS   No, I serve not thy master.

THIRD SERVINGMAN   How, sir? Do you meddle with 49
my master?

CORIOLANUS   Ay, 'tis an honester service than to meddle
with thy mistress. Thou prat'st and prat'st. Serve
with thy trencher. Hence! 53
Beats him away. [Exit Third Servingman.]

Enter Aufidius with the [Second] Servingman.

AUFIDIUS   Where is this fellow?

SECOND SERVINGMAN   Here, sir. I'd have beaten him
like a dog, but for disturbing the lords within. 56
[He and First Servingman stand aside.]

AUFIDIUS *[to Coriolanus]*
Whence com'st thou? What wouldst thou? Thy name?
Why speak'st not? Speak, man. What's thy name?

CORIOLANUS *[unmuffling]*   If, Tullus,
Not yet thou know'st me, and, seeing me, dost not
Think me for the man I am, necessity
Commands me name myself.

AUFIDIUS   What is thy name?

CORIOLANUS
A name unmusical to the Volscians' ears,
And harsh in sound to thine.

AUFIDIUS   Say, what's thy name?
Thou hast a grim appearance, and thy face
Bears a command in't; though thy tackle's torn, 66
Thou show'st a noble vessel. What's thy name? 67

CORIOLANUS
Prepare thy brow to frown. Know'st thou me yet?

AUFIDIUS   I know thee not. Thy name?

CORIOLANUS
My name is Caius Marcius, who hath done
To thee particularly and to all the Volsces 71
Great hurt and mischief; thereto witness may 72
My surname, Coriolanus. The painful service, 73
The extreme dangers, and the drops of blood
Shed for my thankless country are requited
But with that surname—a good memory, 76
And witness of the malice and displeasure
Which thou shouldst bear me. Only that name
remains.
The cruelty and envy of the people,
Permitted by our dastard nobles, who
Have all forsook me, hath devoured the rest,
And suffered me by th' voice of slaves to be
Whooped out of Rome. Now this extremity 83
Hath brought me to thy hearth; not out of hope—
Mistake me not—to save my life, for if
I had feared death, of all the men i'th' world
I would have 'voided thee, but in mere spite, 87
To be full quit of those my banishers, 88
Stand I before thee here. Then if thou hast
A heart of wreak in thee, that wilt revenge 90
Thine own particular wrongs and stop those maims 91
Of shame seen through thy country, speed thee
straight 92
And make my misery serve thy turn. So use it
That my revengeful services may prove
As benefits to thee, for I will fight
Against my cankered country with the spleen 96
Of all the under fiends. But if so be 97
Thou dar'st not this, and that to prove more fortunes 98
Thou'rt tired, then, in a word, I also am
Longer to live most weary, and present
My throat to thee and to thy ancient malice; 101
Which not to cut would show thee but a fool,

---

18 brave insolent. **19 anon** immediately. **25 avoid** leave **33 station** place to stand. (With a play on the idea of a gentleman's "station" or rank.) **35 Follow your function** Go back to your ordinary business. **batten** grow fat **41 canopy** i.e., of heaven. (With ironic suggestion of a canopied royal throne.) **45 kites and crows** i.e., scavengers and birds of prey. **47 daws** jackdaws. (Conventional emblems of foolishness.) **49 meddle** concern yourself with. (But Coriolanus answers in the sense of "have sexual intercourse with.") **53 trencher** wooden plate. **56 but for** were it not for (fear of)

66 a command authority. **tackle** rigging of a ship (i.e., Coriolanus's clothing) **67 show'st** appear to be. **vessel** (1) ship (2) body containing the soul. **71 particularly** personally **72 mischief** injury **73 painful** arduous **76 memory** reminder **83 Whooped** driven with hoots **87 mere** utter **88 full quit of** fully even with **90 wreak** vengeance **91–2 maims Of shame** dishonoring injuries **92 through** throughout **96 cankered** ulcerated, corrupted **97 under fiends** fiends of the underworld. **98 prove more fortunes** try your fortunes further **101 ancient** long-standing

Since I have ever followed thee with hate,
Drawn tuns of blood out of thy country's breast, 104
And cannot live but to thy shame, unless
It be to do thee service.

AUFIDIUS   Oh, Marcius, Marcius!
Each word thou hast spoke hath weeded from my
  heart
A root of ancient envy. If Jupiter
Should from yond cloud speak divine things
And say "'Tis true," I'd not believe them more
Than thee, all-noble Marcius. Let me twine
Mine arms about that body, whereagainst
My grainèd ash an hundred times hath broke 113
And scarred the moon with splinters. [*They embrace.*]
    Here I clip 114
The anvil of my sword, and do contest 115
As hotly and as nobly with thy love
As ever in ambitious strength I did
Contend against thy valor. Know thou first,
I loved the maid I married; never man
Sighed truer breath. But that I see thee here,
Thou noble thing, more dances my rapt heart 121
Than when I first my wedded mistress saw
Bestride my threshold. Why, thou Mars, I tell thee 123
We have a power on foot, and I had purpose 124
Once more to hew thy target from thy brawn, 125
Or lose mine arm for't. Thou hast beat me out 126
Twelve several times, and I have nightly since 127
Dreamt of encounters twixt thyself and me—
We have been down together in my sleep, 129
Unbuckling helms, fisting each other's throat— 130
And waked half dead with nothing. Worthy Marcius, 131
Had we no other quarrel else to Rome but that
Thou art thence banished, we would muster all 133
From twelve to seventy and, pouring war 134
Into the bowels of ungrateful Rome,
Like a bold flood o'erbear't. Oh, come, go in, 136
And take our friendly senators by th' hands,
Who now are here, taking their leaves of me,
Who am prepared against your territories, 139
Though not for Rome itself.

CORIOLANUS   You bless me, gods!
AUFIDIUS
Therefore, most absolute sir, if thou wilt have 141
The leading of thine own revenges, take
Th'one half of my commission; and set down— 143
As best thou art experienced, since thou know'st

Thy country's strength and weakness—thine own
  ways,
Whether to knock against the gates of Rome
Or rudely visit them in parts remote
To fright them ere destroy. But come in.
Let me commend thee first to those that shall 149
Say yea to thy desires. A thousand welcomes!
And more a friend than e'er an enemy;
Yet, Marcius, that was much. Your hand. Most
  welcome!   *Exeunt* [*Coriolanus and Aufidius*].
                       Two of the Servingmen [*come forward*].

FIRST SERVINGMAN   Here's a strange alteration!
SECOND SERVINGMAN   By my hand, I had thought to
  have strucken him with a cudgel; and yet my mind
  gave me his clothes made a false report of him. 156
FIRST SERVINGMAN   What an arm he has! He turned me
  about with his finger and his thumb as one would
  set up a top. 159
SECOND SERVINGMAN   Nay, I knew by his face that there
  was something in him. He had, sir, a kind of face,
  methought—I cannot tell how to term it.
FIRST SERVINGMAN   He had so, looking as it were—
  Would I were hanged but I thought there was more 164
  in him than I could think.
SECOND SERVINGMAN   So did I, I'll be sworn. He is
  simply the rarest man i'th' world. 167
FIRST SERVINGMAN   I think he is. But a greater soldier
  than he you wot on. 169
SECOND SERVINGMAN   Who, my master?
FIRST SERVINGMAN   Nay, it's no matter for that. 171
SECOND SERVINGMAN   Worth six on him. 172
FIRST SERVINGMAN   Nay, not so neither. But I take him 173
  to be the greater soldier.
SECOND SERVINGMAN   Faith, look you, one cannot tell
  how to say that. For the defense of a town our general
  is excellent.
FIRST SERVINGMAN   Ay, and for an assault too.

             Enter the Third Servingman.

THIRD SERVINGMAN   Oh, slaves, I can tell you news—
  news, you rascals!
FIRST AND SECOND SERVINGMEN   What, what, what?
  Let's partake.
THIRD SERVINGMAN   I would not be a Roman, of all
  nations; I had as lief be a condemned man. 184
FIRST AND SECOND SEVINGMAN   Wherefore? Wherefore? 185
THIRD SERVINGMAN   Why, here's he that was wont to 186
  thwack our general, Caius Marcius.
FIRST SERVINGMAN   Why do you say "thwack our general"?
THIRD SERVINGMAN   I do not say "thwack our general,"
  but he was always good enough for him.

---

104 tuns large barrels   **113 grainèd ash** spear with long-grained ashen shaft   **114 clip** embrace   **115 anvil** i.e., Coriolanus, in fighting against whom Aufidius has formed and shaped his martial prowess   **121 dances** makes to dance.   **rapt** enraptured   **123 Bestride** step across   **124 power on foot** force in the field   **125 hew . . . brawn** cut your shield from your muscular arm   **126 out** thoroughly   **127 several** distinct, separate   **129 down together** fighting on the ground.   **sleep** i.e., dreams   **130 helms** helmets.   **fisting** clutching   **131 And . . . nothing** and I have awakened exhausted from sleeplessness for no reason, spent but alone.   **133 muster all** enlist everyone   **134 twelve** i.e., aged twelve   **136 o'erbear't** overflow, surge over, beat down Rome.   **139 am prepared** i.e., have forces ready to move   **141 absolute** perfect   **143 commission** command.   **set down** determine upon

149 commend present   **156 gave** told   **159 set up** set going   **164 but I thought** if I didn't think   **167 rarest** most remarkable   **169 you wot on** you know of, know who I mean—i.e., Aufidius.   **171 Nay . . . that** i.e., Never mind about names.   **172 on** of   **173 him** i.e., Aufidius. (Some commentators argue that *him* is Coriolanus; the servingmen tend to contradict themselves in their newfound admiration for Coriolanus and their loyalty toward their own general.)   **184 as lief** as soon   **185 Wherefore?** Why?   **186 was wont** used

SECOND SERVINGMAN   Come, we are fellows and
friends. He was ever too hard for him; I have heard
him say so himself.

FIRST SERVINGMAN   He was too hard for him, directly
to say the truth on't, before Corioles; he scotched him   195
and notched him like a carbonado.   196

SECOND SERVINGMAN   An he had been cannibally   197
given, he might have boiled and eaten him too.

FIRST SERVINGMAN   But, more of thy news.

THIRD SERVINGMAN   Why, he is so made on here within   200
as if he were son and heir to Mars; set at upper end o'th'   201
table; no question asked him by any of the senators
but they stand bald before him. Our general himself   203
makes a mistress of him, sanctifies himself   204
with 's hand, and turns up the white o'th' eye to his   205
discourse. But the bottom of the news is, our general is   206
cut i'th' middle and but one half of what he was
yesterday, for the other has half by the entreaty and
grant of the whole table. He'll go, he says, and sowl   209
the porter of Rome gates by th'ears. He will mow all
down before him, and leave his passage polled.   211

SECOND SERVINGMAN   And he's as like to do't as any
man I can imagine.

THIRD SERVINGMAN   Do't? He will do't! For look you, sir,
he has as many friends as enemies; which friends, sir,
as it were, durst not, look you, sir, show themselves,
as we term it, his friends whilst he's in directitude.   217

FIRST SERVINGMAN   Directitude? What's that?

THIRD SERVINGMAN   But when they shall see, sir, his crest
up again, and the man in blood, they will out of their   220
burrows like coneys after rain, and revel all with him.   221

FIRST SERVINGMAN   But when goes this forward?

THIRD SERVINGMAN   Tomorrow, today, presently. You   223
shall have the drum struck up this afternoon. 'Tis,
as it were, a parcel of their feast, and to be executed   225
ere they wipe their lips.

SECOND SERVINGMAN   Why, then we shall have a stirring   227
world again. This peace is nothing but to rust iron,
increase tailors, and breed ballad makers.

FIRST SERVINGMAN   Let me have war, say I. It exceeds
peace as far as day does night. It's spritely walking,   231
audible, and full of vent. Peace is a very apoplexy,   232
lethargy; mulled, deaf, sleepy, insensible; a getter of   233
more bastard children than war's a destroyer of men.

SECOND SERVINGMAN   'Tis so. And as wars in some
sort may be said to be a ravisher, so it cannot be
denied but peace is a great maker of cuckolds.

FIRST SERVINGMAN   Ay, and it makes men hate one
another.

THIRD SERVINGMAN   Reason: because they then less need
one another. The wars for my money! I hope to see
Romans as cheap as Volscians.—They are rising,   242
they are rising.

FIRST AND SECOND SERVINGMEN   In, in, in, in!

Exeunt.

❖

[4.6]

Enter the two tribunes, Sicinius and Brutus.

SICINIUS
We hear not of him, neither need we fear him.
His remedies are tame: the present peace   2
And quietness of the people, which before
Were in wild hurry. Here do we make his friends   4
Blush that the world goes well, who rather had,
Though they themselves did suffer by't, behold
Dissentious numbers pest'ring streets than see   7
Our tradesmen singing in their shops and going
About their functions friendly.

BRUTUS
We stood to't in good time.

Enter Menenius.

                              Is this Menenius?   10

SICINIUS
'Tis he, 'tis he. Oh, he is grown most kind
Of late.—Hail, sir!

MENENIUS   Hail to you both!

SICINIUS
Your Coriolanus is not much missed
But with his friends. The commonwealth doth stand,   14
And so would do were he more angry at it.   15

MENENIUS
All's well, and might have been much better if
He could have temporized.   17

SICINIUS   Where is he, hear you?

MENENIUS   Nay, I hear nothing.
His mother and his wife hear nothing from him.

Enter three or four Citizens.

ALL CITIZENS
The gods preserve you both!

SICINIUS   Good e'en, our neighbors.

BRUTUS
Good e'en to you all, good e'en to you all.

FIRST CITIZEN
Ourselves, our wives, and children, on our knees

195 on't of it.   scotched scored, gashed   196 carbonado meat scored
across for broiling.   197 An If   200 made on made much of   201 at
upper end i.e., at the place of honor   203 but unless.   bald bareheaded   204–5 sanctifies . . . hand touches his (Coriolanus's) hand
as though it were a holy relic or that of his mistress   206 bottom last
item, gist   209 sowl drag   211 polled stripped (as one would strip
branches or foliage).   217 directitude (A blunder for something like
discretitude or *discredit*.)   220 in blood in full vigor. (Usually said of
hounds.)   will out will come out   221 coneys rabbits   223 presently
immediately.   225 parcel part   227 stirring active   231–2 It's . . .
vent (War is like a hunting hound: lively, audible in full cry, and
quick to pick up the scent.)   232 apoplexy paralysis   233 mulled
insipid, drowsy.   getter begetter

242 rising i.e., rising from table
4.6. Location: Rome. A public place.
2 His . . . tame (Sicinius argues that the quietness of the populace
affords no opportunity for those who hope to foment further trouble
and thereby bring about Coriolanus's return.)   4 hurry commotion.
7 pest'ring crowding, blocking   10 stood to't i.e., stood up against
Coriolanus   14 But with except among   15 were even were
17 temporized compromised.

Are bound to pray for you both.

SICINIUS   Live and thrive!

BRUTUS
Farewell, kind neighbors. We wished Coriolanus
Had loved you as we did.

ALL CITIZENS   Now the gods keep you!

BOTH TRIBUNES   Farewell, farewell.   *Exeunt Citizens.*

SICINIUS
This is a happier and more comely time   28
Than when these fellows ran about the streets
Crying confusion.

BRUTUS   Caius Marcius was
A worthy officer i'th' war, but insolent,
O'ercome with pride, ambitious, past all thinking
Self-loving.

SICINIUS
And affecting one sole throne, without assistance.   34

MENENIUS   I think not so.

SICINIUS
We should by this, to all our lamentation,   36
If he had gone forth consul, found it so.   37

BRUTUS
The gods have well prevented it, and Rome
Sits safe and still without him.

Enter an Aedile.

AEDILE   Worthy tribunes,
There is a slave, whom we have put in prison,
Reports the Volsces with two several powers   41
Are entered in the Roman territories,
And with the deepest malice of the war
Destroy what lies before 'em.

MENENIUS   'Tis Aufidius,
Who, hearing of our Marcius' banishment,
Thrusts forth his horns again into the world,   46
Which were inshelled when Marcius stood for Rome,   47
And durst not once peep out.

SICINIUS   Come, what talk you of Marcius?   49

BRUTUS
Go see this rumorer whipped. It cannot be
The Volsces dare break with us.

MENENIUS   Cannot be?   51
We have record that very well it can,
And three examples of the like hath been
Within my age. But reason with the fellow   54
Before you punish him, where he heard this,
Lest you shall chance to whip your information   56
And beat the messenger who bids beware
Of what is to be dreaded.

SICINIUS   Tell not me.
I know this cannot be.

BRUTUS   Not possible.

Enter a Messenger.

MESSENGER
The nobles in great earnestness are going
All to the Senate House. Some news is come
That turns their countenances.

SICINIUS   'Tis this slave—   62
Go whip him 'fore the people's eyes—his raising,   63
Nothing but his report.

MESSENGER   Yes, worthy sir,
The slave's report is seconded, and more,   65
More fearful, is delivered.

SICINIUS   What more fearful?   66

MESSENGER
It is spoke freely out of many mouths—
How probable I do not know—that Marcius,
Joined with Aufidius, leads a power 'gainst Rome,
And vows revenge as spacious as between   70
The young'st and oldest thing.

SICINIUS   This is most likely!   71

BRUTUS
Raised only that the weaker sort may wish   72
Good Marcius home again.

SICINIUS   The very trick on't.   74

MENENIUS   This is unlikely.
He and Aufidius can no more atone   76
Than violent'st contrariety.   77

Enter [a Second] Messenger.

SECOND MESSENGER
You are sent for to the Senate.
A fearful army, led by Caius Marcius   79
Associated with Aufidius, rages
Upon our territories, and have already
O'erborne their way, consumed with fire, and took   82
What lay before them.

Enter Cominius.

COMINIUS   Oh, you have made good work!

MENENIUS   What news? What news?

COMINIUS
You have holp to ravish your own daughters and   86
To melt the city leads upon your pates,   87
To see your wives dishonored to your noses—   88

MENENIUS   What's the news? What's the news?

COMINIUS
Your temples burnèd in their cement, and   90
Your franchises, whereon you stood, confined   91
Into an auger's bore.

MENENIUS   Pray now, your news?—   92
You have made fair work, I fear me.—Pray, your
news?

---

62 turns changes   **62–3 'Tis . . . raising** It is this slave's rumor-raising, for which let him be publicly whipped   **65 seconded** confirmed   **66 delivered** reported.   **70–1 as spacious . . . thing** comprehensive enough to embrace every living person.   **72 Raised** Invented, stirred up. (See *raising*, line 63 above.)   **74 trick on't** stratagem of it.   **76 atone** come to a reconciliation   **77 violent'st contrariety** most extreme opposites.   **79 fearful** frightening   **82 O'erborne their way** carried all before them   **86 holp** helped   **87 leads** roofs of lead.   **pates** heads   **88 to** before   **90 in their cement** i.e., to their foundations   **91 franchises** political rights.   **stood** insisted   **92 auger's bore** hole drilled by an auger, i.e., narrow space.

---

28 comely gracious   **34 affecting . . . assistance** desiring to rule alone, without any help or partnership in rule.   **36 this** this time   **37 found** have found   **41 several powers** separate armed forces   **46 Thrusts . . . again** (i.e., like a snail)   **47 inshelled** i.e., drawn in the shell like a snail's horns.   **stood** fought   **49 what** why   **51 break** break their treaty   **54 age** lifetime.   **56 information** source of information

If Marcius should be joined wi'th' Volscians—

COMINIUS   If?
He is their god. He leads them like a thing
Made by some other deity than Nature,
That shapes man better; and they follow him
Against us brats with no less confidence   98
Than boys pursuing summer butterflies
Or butchers killing flies.

MENENIUS   You have made good work,
You and your apron-men, you that stood so much   101
Upon the voice of occupation and   102
The breath of garlic eaters!

COMINIUS   He'll shake your Rome about your ears.

MENENIUS
As Hercules did shake down mellow fruit.   105
You have made fair work!

BRUTUS   But is this true, sir?

COMINIUS   Ay, and you'll look pale
Before you find it other. All the regions   109
Do smilingly revolt, and who resists   110
Are mocked for valiant ignorance   111
And perish constant fools. Who is't can blame him? 112
Your enemies and his find something in him.   113

MENENIUS   We are all undone, unless
The noble man have mercy.

COMINIUS   Who shall ask it?
The tribunes cannot do't for shame; the people
Deserve such pity of him as the wolf
Does of the shepherds. For his best friends, if they 118
Should say "Be good to Rome," they charged him
even   119
As those should do that had deserved his hate   120
And therein showed like enemies.

MENENIUS   'Tis true.   121
If he were putting to my house the brand   122
That should consume it, I have not the face
To say "Beseech you, cease." You have made fair
hands,   124
You and your crafts! You have crafted fair!

COMINIUS   You have brought   125
A trembling upon Rome, such as was never
S' incapable of help.

BOTH TRIBUNES   Say not we brought it.

MENENIUS
How? Was't we? We loved him, but, like beasts
And cowardly nobles, gave way unto your clusters, 129

Who did hoot him out o'th' city.

COMINIUS   But I fear
They'll roar him in again. Tullus Aufidius,   131
The second name of men, obeys his points   132
As if he were his officer. Desperation
Is all the policy, strength, and defense
That Rome can make against them.

Enter a troop of Citizens.

MENENIUS   Here come the clusters.—
And is Audifius with him? You are they
That made the air unwholesome when you cast
Your stinking greasy caps in hooting at
Coriolanus' exile. Now he's coming,
And not a hair upon a soldier's head
Which will not prove a whip. As many coxcombs   141
As you threw caps up will he tumble down,
And pay you for your voices. 'Tis no matter;
If he could burn us all into one coal,   144
We have deserved it.

ALL CITIZENS   Faith, we hear fearful news.

FIRST CITIZEN   For mine own part,
When I said, banish him, I said, 'twas pity.

SECOND CITIZEN   And so did I.

THIRD CITIZEN   And so did I; and, to say the truth, so
did very many of us. That we did, we did for the best; 151
and though we willingly consented to his banishment,
yet it was against our will.

COMINIUS   You're goodly things, you voices!

MENENIUS   You have made good work,
You and your cry!—Shall 's to the Capitol?   156

COMINIUS   Oh, ay, what else?
                    Exeunt both [Cominius and Menenius].

SICINIUS
Go, masters, get you home, be not dismayed.
These are a side that would be glad to have   159
This true which they so seem to fear. Go home,
And show no sign of fear.

FIRST CITIZEN   The gods be good to us! Come, masters,
let 's home. I ever said we were i'th' wrong when we
banished him.

SECOND CITIZEN   So did we all. But, come, let 's home.
                                        Exeunt Citizens.

BRUTUS   I do not like this news.

SICINIUS   Nor I.

BRUTUS
Let 's to the Capitol. Would half my wealth   168
Would buy this for a lie!

SICINIUS   Pray, let 's go.   169
                                        Exeunt tribunes.

❖

---

98 **brats** mere children   101 **apron-men** artisans (who wore aprons)
102 **voice of occupation** votes of the laboring men   105 **Hercules . . .
fruit** (Hercules's eleventh labor was to carry off the golden apples of
the Hesperides.)   109 **other** otherwise.   110 **smilingly** gladly.
who whoever   111 **valiant ignorance** foolish valor   112 **constant**
loyal   113 **Your . . . him** i.e., Both your enemies, the patricians, and
his enemies, the Volscians, find cause to ally themselves with him, or,
all find him irresistible.   118 **For** As for   119–21 **they charged . . .
enemies** they would be urging him with the same language that
those who deserved his hate (the tribunes and plebeians) would use
and in that respect would be behaving as his enemies would behave.
122 **brand** torch   124 **made fair hands** done fine work. (Said ironically.)   125 **crafted fair** (1) cleverly advanced the interests of the
crafts or occupations (2) shown your expert craft or cunning.
129 **clusters** mobs

131 **roar . . . again** i.e., roar with pain when he returns.   132 **second . . .
men** second greatest name among men.   **his points** Coriolanus's
instructions   141 **coxcombs** i.e., fools' heads   144 **into one coal** into
one cindery mass   151 **That** What   156 **cry** pack.   **Shall 's** Shall we
go   159 **side** party, faction   168–9 **Would . . . lie!** I would give half of
my fortune if this could be proven a lie!

[4.7]

Enter Aufidius with his Lieutenant.

AUFIDIUS   Do they still fly to th' Roman?

LIEUTENANT
  I do not know what witchcraft's in him, but
  Your soldiers use him as the grace 'fore meat,
  Their talk at table, and their thanks at end;
  And you are darkened in this action, sir,   5
  Even by your own.

AUFIDIUS   I cannot help it now,   6
  Unless by using means I lame the foot   7
  Of our design. He bears himself more proudlier,   8
  Even to my person, than I thought he would
  When first I did embrace him. Yet his nature
  In that's no changeling, and I must excuse   11
  What cannot be amended.

LIEUTENANT   Yet I wish, sir—
  I mean for your particular—you had not   13
  Joined in commission with him, but either
  Have borne the action of yourself or else   15
  To him had left it solely.

AUFIDIUS
  I understand thee well, and be thou sure,
  When he shall come to his account, he knows not   18
  What I can urge against him. Although it seems—   19
  And so he thinks, and is no less apparent
  To th' vulgar eye—that he bears all things fairly   21
  And shows good husbandry for the Volscian state,   22
  Fights dragonlike, and does achieve as soon   23
  As draw his sword, yet he hath left undone   24
  That which shall break his neck or hazard mine
  Whene'er we come to our account.

LIEUTENANT
  Sir, I beseech you, think you he'll carry Rome?   27

AUFIDIUS
  All places yields to him ere he sits down,   28
  And the nobility of Rome are his;
  The senators and patricians love him too.
  The tribunes are no soldiers, and their people
  Will be as rash in the repeal as hasty   32
  To expel him thence. I think he'll be to Rome
  As is the osprey to the fish, who takes it   34
  By sovereignty of nature. First he was
  A noble servant to them, but he could not
  Carry his honors even. Whether 'twas pride,   37

  Which out of daily fortune ever taints   38
  The happy man; whether defect of judgment,   39
  To fail in the disposing of those chances   40
  Which he was lord of; or whether nature,   41
  Not to be other than one thing, not moving   42
  From th' casque to th' cushion, but commanding
    peace   43
  Even with the same austerity and garb   44
  As he controlled the war; but one of these—
  As he hath spices of them all—not all,   46
  For I dare so far free him—made him feared,   47
  So hated, and so banished. But he has a merit   48
  To choke it in the utt'rance. So our virtues   49
  Lie in th'interpretation of the time;   50
  And power, unto itself most commendable,   51
  Hath not a tomb so evident as a chair   52
  T'extol what it hath done.   53
  One fire drives out one fire; one nail, one nail;
  Rights by rights falter, strengths by strengths do fail.   55
  Come, let 's away. When, Caius, Rome is thine,
  Thou art poor'st of all; then shortly art thou mine.

                        Exeunt.

❖

[5.1]

Enter Menenius, Cominius; Sicinius, Brutus,
the two tribunes; with others.

MENENIUS
  No, I'll not go. You hear what he hath said   1
  Which was sometime his general, who loved him   2
  In a most dear particular. He called me father;   3
  But what o' that? Go you that banished him;
  A mile before his tent fall down and knee   5
  The way into his mercy. Nay, if he coyed   6
  To hear Cominius speak, I'll keep at home.

COMINIUS
  He would not seem to know me.

MENENIUS   Do you hear?   8

COMINIUS
  Yet one time he did call me by my name.
  I urged our old acquaintance, and the drops

4.7. Location: A camp, at a small distance from Rome.
5 you . . . action your glory is dimmed in this undertaking **6 your own** i.e., your followers, or, your own action (in making Coriolanus your fellow general). **7–8 means . . . design** i.e., such means as would cripple our assault on Rome. **11 changeling** i.e., fickle thing **13 for your particular** regarding your self-interest **15 Have . . . yourself** had led the campaign yourself **18 account** day of reckoning **19 urge against him** accuse him of. **21 vulgar** common. **bears** carries out **22 husbandry for** management on behalf of **23 achieve** accomplish his goals **24 As draw** as he does draw **27 carry** capture **28 sits down** besieges **32 repeal** recall from exile **34 osprey** fish hawk, said to have had the power to fascinate fishes so by its kingly *sovereignty* (line 35) that they would turn belly up and allow themselves to be taken without a struggle **37 Carry . . . even** bear his honors temperately.

38–9 out of . . . man as a result of continuous success always corrupts the fortunate man **40 disposing** clever using **41 whether nature** whether it was his nature **42 Not . . . thing** i.e., always rigidly the same, in peace as in war **43 casque** helmet (as symbolic of the warrior). **cushion** i.e., seat for a senator **44 austerity and garb** austere behavior **46 spices** tastes, traces. **not all** not all in full measure **47 free** free from blame **48 So . . . banished** because he was feared he was hated, and because he was hated he was banished. **48–9 he . . . utt'rance** i.e., his merit is of the perverse sort that undoes itself; it *chokes* itself by its very *utt'rance*. (Also interpreted as meaning, "He has so many counterbalancing good points that the words stick in my throat.") **50 the time** contemporary opinion **51–3 power . . . done** i.e., power, however worthy in itself, is quickly forgotten even while it is being commemorated from the public rostrum. **55 Rights . . . fail** i.e., great deeds, eclipsed by the subsequent deeds of others, are soon forgotten.

5.1. Location: Rome. A public place.
1 he i.e., Cominius **2 Which** who. **sometime** formerly **3 In . . . particular** with warmest personal affection. **He** i.e., Coriolanus **5 knee** crawl on your knees **6 coyed** showed reluctance, disdained **8 would not seem** pretended not

That we have bled together. "Coriolanus"
He would not answer to; forbade all names.
He was a kind of nothing, titleless,
Till he had forged himself a name o'th' fire
Of burning Rome.
MENENIUS   Why, so; you have made good work!
A pair of tribunes that have wracked for Rome   16
To make coals cheap! A noble memory!   17
COMINIUS
I minded him how royal 'twas to pardon   18
When it was less expected. He replied,
It was a bare petition of a state   20
To one whom they had punished.
MENENIUS   Very well.
Could he say less?
COMINIUS
I offered to awaken his regard   23
For 's private friends. His answer to me was,
He could not stay to pick them in a pile   25
Of noisome musty chaff. He said 'twas folly,   26
For one poor grain or two, to leave unburnt
And still to nose th'offense.   28
MENENIUS   For one poor grain or two!
I am one of those! His mother, wife, his child,
And this brave fellow too, we are the grains;
You are the musty chaff, and you are smelt
Above the moon. We must be burnt for you.
SICINIUS
Nay, pray, be patient. If you refuse your aid
In this so-never-needed help, yet do not
Upbraid 's with our distress. But sure, if you
Would be your country's pleader, your good tongue,
More than the instant army we can make,   38
Might stop our countryman.
MENENIUS   No, I'll not meddle.
SICINIUS
Pray you, go to him.
MENENIUS   What should I do?
BRUTUS
Only make trial what your love can do
For Rome, towards Marcius.
MENENIUS
Well, and say that Marcius return me,
As Cominius is returned, unheard—what then?
But as a discontented friend, grief-shot   45
With his unkindness? Say't be so?
SICINIUS   Yet your good will
Must have that thanks from Rome after the measure 48
As you intended well.
MENENIUS   I'll undertake't.   49
I think he'll hear me. Yet, to bite his lip   50

And hum at good Cominius much unhearts me.   51
He was not taken well; he had not dined.   52
The veins unfilled, our blood is cold, and then
We pout upon the morning, are unapt   54
To give or to forgive; but when we have stuffed
These pipes and these conveyances of our blood   56
With wine and feeding, we have suppler souls
Than in our priestlike fasts. Therefore I'll watch him
Till he be dieted to my request,   59
And then I'll set upon him.
BRUTUS
You know the very road into his kindness,
And cannot lose your way.
MENENIUS   Good faith, I'll prove him,   62
Speed how it will. I shall ere long have knowledge   63
Of my success.   Exit.
COMINIUS   He'll never hear him.
SICINIUS   Not?   64
COMINIUS
I tell you, he does sit in gold, his eye   65
Red as 'twould burn Rome; and his injury   66
The jailer to his pity. I kneeled before him;
'Twas very faintly he said "Rise"; dismissed me 68
Thus, with his speechless hand. What he would do
He sent in writing after me; what he would not, 70
Bound with an oath to yield to his conditions;   71
So that all hope is vain
Unless his noble mother and his wife,   73
Who, as I hear, mean to solicit him
For mercy to his country. Therefore, let 's hence
And with our fair entreaties haste them on.   Exeunt.

[5.2]

Enter Menenius to the Watch, or Guard.

FIRST WATCH   Stay! Whence are you?
SECOND WATCH   Stand, and go back.   2
MENENIUS
You guard like men; 'tis well. But, by your leave,
I am an officer of state, and come
To speak with Coriolanus.
FIRST WATCH   From whence?
MENENIUS   From Rome.
FIRST WATCH
You may not pass; you must return. Our general
Will no more hear from thence.

---

16 **wracked for** brought ruin to. (With a play on "striven for.")
17 **coals** charcoal (which will be cheap because Rome will be burnt to cinders; see 4.6.144).   **memory** memorial.   18 **minded** reminded
20 **bare** barefaced, paltry   23 **offered** attempted   25 **stay . . . them** take time to pick them out   26 **noisome** evil-smelling   28 **nose th' offense** smell the offensive stuff.   38 **instant army** army we can raise at this instant   45 **But as** i.e., What if he send me back only as.
grief-shot grief-stricken   48–9 **after . . . As** in proportion that
50 **to bite his lip** (An expression of anger, like humming in line 51; see below, 5.4.21.)

51 **unhearts** disheartens, discourages   52 **taken well** approached at the right time   54 **pout upon** are out of temper with   56 **conveyances** channels   59 **dieted to** fed properly so as to be in a mood for   62 **prove** attempt   63 **Speed** turn out, succeed   64 **success** outcome.   65 **in gold** in a golden chair   66 **Red** i.e., with anger; also the color normally used to describe gold.   **his injury** his sense of having been wronged   68 **faintly** coldly, indifferently   70–1 **what . . . conditions** i.e., what terrible actions he would not take against Rome if we bound ourselves under oath to agree to his terms. (See 5.3.14.) Or Cominius may mean that Coriolanus is bound by his own oath not to relent.   73 **Unless** if it were not for, except for
5.2. Location: The Volscian camp before Rome.
2 Stand Stop

SECOND WATCH
You'll see your Rome embraced with fire before
You'll speak with Coriolanus.

MENENIUS   Good my friends,
If you have heard your general talk of Rome
And of his friends there, it is lots to blanks   13
My name hath touched your ears. It is Menenius.

FIRST WATCH
Be it so; go back. The virtue of your name
Is not here passable.   15

MENENIUS   I tell thee, fellow,   16
Thy general is my lover. I have been   17
The book of his good acts, whence men have read
His fame unparalleled happily amplified;   19
For I have ever verified my friends—   20
Of whom he's chief—with all the size that verity   21
Would without lapsing suffer. Nay, sometimes,   22
Like to a bowl upon a subtle ground,   23
I have tumbled past the throw, and in his praise   24
Have almost stamped the leasing. Therefore, fellow,   25
I must have leave to pass.

FIRST WATCH   Faith, sir, if you had told as many lies in   27
his behalf as you have uttered words in your own, you
should not pass here; no, though it were as virtuous
to lie as to live chastely. Therefore go back.   30

MENENIUS   Prithee, fellow, remember my name is
Menenius, always factionary on the party of your   32
general.

SECOND WATCH   Howsoever you have been his liar, as
you say you have, I am one that, telling true under   35
him, must say you cannot pass. Therefore go back.   36

MENENIUS   Has he dined, canst thou tell? For I would
not speak with him till after dinner.

FIRST WATCH   You are a Roman, are you?

MENENIUS   I am, as thy general is.

FIRST WATCH   Then you should hate Rome, as he does.
Can you, when you have pushed out your gates the   42
very defender of them, and, in a violent popular ig-   43
norance, given your enemy your shield, think to front   44
his revenges with the easy groans of old women, the   45
virginal palms of your daughters, or with the palsied   46
intercession of such a decayed dotant as you seem to   47
be? Can you think to blow out the intended fire your
city is ready to flame in with such weak breath as
this? No, you are deceived; therefore, back to Rome

and prepare for your execution. You are condemned;
our general has sworn you out of reprieve and pardon.   52

MENENIUS   Sirrah, if thy captain knew I were here, he   53
would use me with estimation.   54

FIRST WATCH   Come, my captain knows you not.

MENENIUS   I mean thy general.

FIRST WATCH   My general cares not for you. Back, I say,
go, lest I let forth your half-pint of blood. Back! That's
the utmost of your having. Back!   59

MENENIUS   Nay, but, fellow, fellow—

Enter Coriolanus with Aufidius.

CORIOLANUS   What's the matter?

MENENIUS   Now, you companion, I'll say an errand for   62
you. You shall know now that I am in estimation; you   63
shall perceive that a Jack guardant cannot office me   64
from my son Coriolanus. Guess but by my entertain-   65
ment with him if thou stand'st not i'th' state of hang-   66
ing or of some death more long in spectatorship and   67
crueller in suffering; behold now presently, and   68
swoon for what's to come upon thee. [*To Coriolanus*]
The glorious gods sit in hourly synod about thy partic-   70
ular prosperity and love thee no worse than thy old
father Menenius does! O my son, my son! Thou art
preparing fire for us; look there, here's water to quench   73
it. I was hardly moved to come to thee; but being as-   74
sured none but myself could move thee, I have been
blown out of our gates with sighs, and conjure thee
to pardon Rome and thy petitionary countrymen. The   77
good gods assuage thy wrath, and turn the dregs of it
upon this varlet here—this, who, like a block, hath   79
denied my access to thee.

CORIOLANUS   Away!

MENENIUS   How? Away?

CORIOLANUS
Wife, mother, child, I know not. My affairs
Are servanted to others. Though I owe   84
My revenge properly, my remission lies   85
In Volscian breasts. That we have been familiar,   86
Ingrate forgetfulness shall poison rather   87
Than pity note how much. Therefore, begone.   88
Mine ears against your suits are stronger than
Your gates against my force. Yet, for I loved thee,   90
Take this along; I writ it for thy sake,   [*giving a letter*]
And would have sent it. Another word, Menenius,
I will not hear thee speak.—This man, Aufidius,
Was my beloved in Rome; yet thou behold'st!

---

13 **lots to blanks** i.e., a thousand to one. (Literally, prize-winning tick-
ets compared with valueless ones.) 15 **virtue** strength 16 **passable**
current (like a coin), and able to provide passage. 17 **lover** friend.
19 **happily** aptly, felicitously 20–2 **For . . . suffer** for I have always
expatiated on the good name of my friends—of whom he is chief—to
the fullest extent possible without distorting the facts. 23 **bowl** ball
used in bowls. **subtle** deceptively irregular 24 **tumbled . . . throw**
overshot the mark 25 **stamped the leasing** given the stamp of truth
to lying (i.e., overstated praise of him). 27 **if** even if 30 **chastely**
honestly. (But with a sexual quibble, taking *lie* in a sexual sense.)
32 **factionary** active as a partisan 35–6 **telling . . . him** telling the
truth in his service 42 **out** out at; out of 43–4 **violent popular ignorance** folly of mob violence 44 **shield** defender, i.e., Coriolanus.
front confront, oppose 45 **easy groans** i.e., groans that are easily
provoked 46 **virginal . . . daughters** uplifted hands of your virgin
daughters 47 **dotant** dotard, old fool

52 **out of** beyond the reach of 53 **Sirrah** (Term of address to inferiors.) 54 **use** treat. **estimation** esteem. 59 **the utmost of your having** all you are going to get. 62 **companion** fellow. **say an errand**
deliver a message 63 **in estimation** well regarded 64 **Jack
guardant** knave on guard duty. **office** officiously keep 65–6 **entertainment with** reception by 66 **stand'st . . . state** are not at risk
67 **spectatorship** watching 68 **presently** immediately 70 **synod**
council, assembly 73 **water** i.e., tears 74 **hardly moved** with difficulty persuaded 77 **petitionary** suppliant, petitioning 79 **block**
(1) impediment (2) blockhead 84 **servanted** subjected. **owe** own,
possess 85 **properly** as my own. **remission** power to forgive
86–8 **That . . . much** i.e., Close as we have been, I will allow ungrateful forgetfulness (prompted by Rome's ingratitude) to poison the
memory of our friendship rather than allow my pity to recall how
much we meant to each other. 90 **for** because

AUFIDIUS   You keep a constant temper.   95

Exeunt. Manent the Guard and Menenius.

FIRST WATCH   Now, sir, is your name Menenius?

SECOND WATCH   'Tis a spell, you see, of much power. You know the way home again.

FIRST WATCH   Do you hear how we are shent for keeping your greatness back?   99

SECOND WATCH   What cause, do you think, I have to swoon?

MENENIUS   I neither care for the world nor your general. For such things as you, I can scarce think there's any, 104 you're so slight. He that hath a will to die by himself 105 fears it not from another. Let your general do his worst. For you, be that you are, long; and your misery 107 increase with your age! I say to you, as I was said to, Away!   *Exit.*

FIRST WATCH   A noble fellow, I warrant him.

SECOND WATCH   The worthy fellow is our general. He's the rock, the oak not to be wind-shaken.   *Exit Watch.*

❖

[5.3]

Enter Coriolanus and Aufidius [with Volscian soldiers. Coriolanus and Aufidius sit.]

CORIOLANUS
We will before the walls of Rome tomorrow
Set down our host. My partner in this action,   2
You must report to th' Volscian lords how plainly   3
I have borne this business.

AUFIDIUS   Only their ends   4
You have respected, stopped your ears against
The general suit of Rome, never admitted
A private whisper, no, not with such friends
That thought them sure of you.

CORIOLANUS   This last old man,
Whom with a cracked heart I have sent to Rome,
Loved me above the measure of a father,
Nay, godded me indeed. Their latest refuge   11
Was to send him, for whose old love I have—
Though I showed sourly to him—once more offered   13
The first conditions, which they did refuse
And cannot now accept. To grace him only   15
That thought he could do more, a very little   16
I have yielded to. Fresh embassies and suits,   17
Nor from the state nor private friends, hereafter   18
Will I lend ear to. (*Shout within.*) Ha? What shout is this?

Shall I be tempted to infringe my vow
In the same time 'tis made? I will not.

Enter Virgilia, Volumnia, Valeria, young Marcius, with attendants.

My wife comes foremost; then the honored mold   22
Wherein this trunk was framed, and in her hand   23
The grandchild to her blood. But, out, affection!
All bond and privilege of nature, break!   25
Let it be virtuous to be obstinate.   [*The women bow.*]   26
What is that curtsy worth? Or those doves' eyes,   27
Which can make gods forsworn? I melt, and am not
Of stronger earth than others. My mother bows,
As if Olympus to a molehill should
In supplication nod, and my young boy
Hath an aspect of intercession which   32
Great Nature cries "Deny not." Let the Volsces   33
Plow Rome and harrow Italy, I'll never
Be such a gosling to obey instinct, but stand   35
As if a man were author of himself
And knew no other kin.

VIRGILIA   My lord and husband!

CORIOLANUS
These eyes are not the same I wore in Rome.   38

VIRGILIA
The sorrow that delivers us thus changed   39
Makes you think so.

CORIOLANUS   Like a dull actor now,   40
I have forgot my part, and I am out,   41
Even to a full disgrace. Best of my flesh,
Forgive my tyranny, but do not say   43
For that, "Forgive our Romans." Oh, a kiss
Long as my exile, sweet as my revenge!   [*They kiss.*]
Now, by the jealous queen of heaven, that kiss   46
I carried from thee, dear, and my true lip
Hath virgined it e'er since. You gods! I prate,   48
And the most noble mother of the world
Leave unsaluted. Sink, my knee, i'th' earth.   *Kneels.*
Of thy deep duty more impression show   51
Than that of common sons.

VOLUMNIA   Oh, stand up blest!
[*He rises.*]

Whilst with no softer cushion than the flint
I kneel before thee, and unproperly   54
Show duty, as mistaken all this while
Between the child and parent.   [*She kneels.*]

CORIOLANUS   What's this?

---

95 **constant temper** firm mind.   95.1 *Manent* They remain onstage   99 **shent** rebuked   104 **For** As for. (Also in line 107.)   105 **slight** insignificant.   **by himself** by his own hand   107 **that** what.   **long** through a long (and tedious) lifetime   5.3. **Location:** The Volscian camp, as in scene 2. The tent of Coriolanus.   2 **Set down our host** lay siege with our army.   3 **plainly** openly, straightforwardly   4 **their ends** i.e., the Volscians' purposes   11 **godded** deified.   **latest refuge** last resource   13 **showed** acted   15 **grace** gratify   16–17 **a very . . . yielded to** I have conceded a little, but almost nothing.   18 **Nor** neither

22 **mold** form, body (of my mother)   23 **this trunk** my body   25 **bond . . . nature** natural ties and claims of love   26 **obstinate** hard-hearted.   27 **curtsy** (1) bow (2) courtesy.   **doves' eyes** i.e., beautiful and seductive eyes. (See Song of Solomon 1:15.)   32 **aspect of intercession** pleading look   33 **Let** Even should   35 **gosling** baby goose (i.e., foolish, inexperienced person).   **to** as to   38–40 **These . . . so** (Coriolanus says, "I see differently now that I am not in Rome." Virgilia replies, taking his words literally, "Our sorrow has so changed us that you cannot recognize us." *Delivers* means "presents.")   41 **I am out** I have forgotten my lines, I am at a loss for words   43 **tyranny** cruelty   46 **jealous . . . heaven** i.e., Juno, patroness of marriage   48 **virgined it** remained untouched.   **prate** talk idly   51 **more impression** (1) a deeper mark (in the earth) (2) a clearer sign (of filial obedience)   54 **unproperly** unfittingly, violating due propriety

Your knees to me? To your corrected son?   57
                              [*He raises her.*]
Then let the pebbles on the hungry beach   58
Fillip the stars! Then let the mutinous winds   59
Strike the proud cedars 'gainst the fiery sun,   60
Murd'ring impossibility, to make   61
What cannot be slight work.

VOLUMNIA   Thou art my warrior;   62
I holp to frame thee. Do you know this lady?   63

CORIOLANUS
The noble sister of Publicola,
The moon of Rome, chaste as the icicle   65
That's curded by the frost from purest snow   66
And hangs on Dian's temple—dear Valeria!

VOLUMNIA [*indicating young Marcius*]
This is a poor epitome of yours,   68
Which by th'interpretation of full time   69
May show like all yourself.

CORIOLANUS [*to his son*]   The god of soldiers,   70
With the consent of supreme Jove, inform   71
Thy thoughts with nobleness, that thou mayst prove
To shame unvulnerable, and stick i'th' wars   73
Like a great seamark, standing every flaw   74
And saving those that eye thee!

VOLUMNIA [*to young Marcius*]   Your knee, sirrah.   75
                              [*Young Marcius kneels.*]

CORIOLANUS   That's my brave boy!

VOLUMNIA
Even he, your wife, this lady, and myself
Are suitors to you.

CORIOLANUS   I beseech you, peace.
Or, if you'd ask, remember this before:
The thing I have forsworn to grant may never   80
Be held by you denials. Do not bid me   81
Dismiss my soldiers or capitulate   82
Again with Rome's mechanics. Tell me not   83
Wherein I seem unnatural; desire not
T'allay my rages and revenges with
Your colder reasons.

VOLUMNIA   Oh, no more, no more!
You have said you will not grant us anything;
For we have nothing else to ask but that
Which you deny already. Yet we will ask,
That, if you fail in our request, the blame   90
May hang upon your hardness. Therefore hear us.

CORIOLANUS
Aufidius, and you Volsces, mark; for we'll
Hear naught from Rome in private. [*He sits.*] Your
    request?

VOLUMNIA
Should we be silent and not speak, our raiment   94
And state of bodies would bewray what life   95
We have led since thy exile. Think with thyself   96
How more unfortunate than all living women
Are we come hither; since that thy sight, which
    should   98
Make our eyes flow with joy, hearts dance with
    comforts,
Constrains them weep and shake with fear and
    sorrow,
Making the mother, wife, and child to see
The son, the husband, and the father tearing
His country's bowels out. And to poor we
Thine enmity's most capital. Thou barr'st us   104
Our prayers to the gods, which is a comfort
That all but we enjoy; for how can we,
Alas, how can we for our country pray,
Whereto we are bound, together with thy victory,
Whereto we are bound? Alack, or we must lose   109
The country, our dear nurse, or else thy person,
Our comfort in the country. We must find
An evident calamity, though we had   112
Our wish, which side should win; for either thou   113
Must as a foreign recreant be led   114
With manacles through our streets, or else
Triumphantly tread on thy country's ruin,
And bear the palm for having bravely shed   117
Thy wife and children's blood. For myself, son,
I purpose not to wait on fortune till   119
These wars determine. If I cannot persuade thee   120
Rather to show a noble grace to both parts   121
Than seek the end of one, thou shalt no sooner
March to assault thy country than to tread—
Trust to't, thou shalt not—on thy mother's womb   124
That brought thee to this world.

VIRGILIA   Ay, and mine,
That brought you forth this boy to keep your name
Living to time.

YOUNG MARCIUS   'A shall not tread on me;   127
I'll run away till I am bigger, but then I'll fight.

CORIOLANUS
Not of a woman's tenderness to be   129
Requires nor child nor woman's face to see.   130
I have sat too long.   [*He rises.*]

VOLUMNIA   Nay, go not from us thus.   131
If it were so that our request did tend

---

57 **corrected** chastised 58 **hungry** unfertile, barren 59 **Fillip** strike 60 **Strike . . . sun** uproot huge cedar trees and throw them against the sun 61 **Murd'ring** negating the very concept of 62 **What . . . slight work** an easy task of what cannot be, is impossible. 63 **holp** helped 65 **moon of Rome** (Allusion to Diana, goddess of chastity and associated with the moon.) 66 **curded** congealed 68 **epitome** abridgement 69 **by . . . time** when time shall have revealed and fulfilled all. (Time will expand the *epitome*, giving *interpretation* to its full meaning.) 70 **show** look. **The god of soldiers** i.e., Mars 71 **inform** inspire 73 **To . . . unvulnerable** (1) incapable of shameful deeds (2) proof against being shamed. **stick** stand out 74 **seamark** reference object used by mariners in navigating. **standing . . . flaw** withstanding every gust 75 **eye thee** i.e., guide themselves by you, use you as a *seamark*. 80–1 **The thing . . . denials** i.e., it would be unjust to regard me as refusing to grant what I have sworn not to grant and hence no longer have the power of granting. 82 **capitulate** come to terms 83 **mechanics** tradesmen. 90 **fail in** do not grant

94 **Should we** Even if we should. **raiment** clothes 95 **bewray** reveal 96 **Think with thyself** Reflect 98 **thy sight** the sight of you 104 **capital** fatal. 109 **or** either 112 **evident** certain 113 **which** whichever 114 **recreant** traitor 117 **palm** i.e., emblem of victory 119 **purpose** propose 120 **determine** come to an end, settle matters. 121 **grace** favor, mercy. **parts** sides 124 **Trust . . . not** (Read this parenthetical phrase after *sooner* in line 122.) 127 **'A** He 129–30 **Not . . . see** If a man is not to yield to a womanly tenderness, he must not look upon any child's or woman's face. 131 **sat** i.e., stayed here listening

To save the Romans, thereby to destroy
The Volsces whom you serve, you might condemn us
As poisonous of your honor. No, our suit
Is that you reconcile them, while the Volsces   136
May say, "This mercy we have showed," the Romans,
"This we received," and each in either side   138
Give the all-hail to thee and cry, "Be blest   139
For making up this peace!" Thou know'st, great son,
The end of war's uncertain, but this certain,
That, if thou conquer Rome, the benefit
Which thou shalt thereby reap is such a name
Whose repetition will be dogged with curses,
Whose chronicle thus writ: "The man was noble,
But with his last attempt he wiped it out,   146
Destroyed his country, and his name remains
To th'ensuing age abhorred." Speak to me, son.
Thou hast affected the fine strains of honor,   149
To imitate the graces of the gods,
To tear with thunder the wide cheeks o'th' air,   151
And yet to charge thy sulfur with a bolt   152
That should but rive an oak. Why dost not speak?   153
Think'st thou it honorable for a nobleman
Still to remember wrongs? Daughter, speak you;   155
He cares not for your weeping. Speak thou, boy;   156
Perhaps thy childishness will move him more
Than can our reasons. There's no man in the world
More bound to 's mother, yet here he lets me prate   159
Like one i'th' stocks.—Thou hast never in thy life   160
Showed thy dear mother any courtesy,
When she, poor hen, fond of no second brood,   162
Has clucked thee to the wars and safely home,   163
Loaden with honor. Say my request's unjust,
And spurn me back; but if it be not so,
Thou art not honest, and the gods will plague thee   166
That thou restrain'st from me the duty which   167
To a mother's part belongs.—He turns away.
Down, ladies! Let us shame him with our knees.
To his surname Coriolanus 'longs more pride   170
Than pity to our prayers. Down! [*They kneel.*] An end;
This is the last. So we will home to Rome,
And die among our neighbors.—Nay, behold 's!
This boy, that cannot tell what he would have,   174
But kneels and holds up hands for fellowship,   175
Does reason our petition with more strength   176
Than thou hast to deny't.—Come, let us go.

                                                    [*They rise.*]

136 **while** so that   at the same time   138 **each** everyone.   **in** on
139 **all-hail** general acclaim   146 **attempt** undertaking.   **it** i.e., his
nobility   149 **affected** sought, cherished   151 **cheeks** (On Renaissance maps, the winds were often portrayed as issuing from the
cheeks of Aeolus, Greek god of the winds.)   152–3 **And . . . oak** and
yet to load your lightning with a thunderbolt that should only split
an oak. (Volumnia cautions against the unwise use of such power.)
155 **Still** always   156 **cares not for** is unmoved by   159–60 **prate . . .
stocks** i.e., talk uselessly like a prisoner who has been publicly humiliated.   162 **When** whereas.   **fond** desirous   163 **clucked** marshaled
as a hen her brood   166 **honest** honorable, just   167 **thou restrain'st**
you withhold   170 **'longs** belongs   174 **This . . . have** This boy, Coriolanus's son, who does not understand what he is asking for   175 **for
fellowship** merely to keep us company   176 **reason** argue for

This fellow had a Volscian to his mother;   178
His wife is in Corioles, and his child   179
Like him by chance.—Yet give us our dispatch.   180
I am hushed until our city be afire,
And then I'll speak a little.

                    [*He*] *holds her by the hand, silent.*
CORIOLANUS   Oh, mother, mother!
What have you done? Behold, the heavens do ope,
The gods look down, and this unnatural scene
They laugh at. Oh, my mother, mother! Oh!
You have won a happy victory to Rome;
But for your son—believe it, oh, believe it!—
Most dangerously you have with him prevailed,
If not most mortal to him. But let it come.—   189
Aufidius, though I cannot make true wars,   190
I'll frame convenient peace. Now, good Aufidius,   191
Were you in my stead, would you have heard
A mother less? Or granted less, Aufidius?
AUFIDIUS
I was moved withal.
CORIOLANUS   I dare be sworn you were.   194
And, sir, it is no little thing to make
Mine eyes to sweat compassion. But, good sir,   196
What peace you'll make, advise me. For my part,
I'll not to Rome. I'll back with you; and pray you,   198
Stand to me in this cause.—Oh, mother! Wife!   199
AUFIDIUS [*aside*]
I am glad thou hast set thy mercy and thy honor
At difference in thee. Out of that I'll work
Myself a former fortune.
                    [*The ladies make signs to Coriolanus.*]
CORIOLANUS [*to the ladies*]   Ay, by and by;   202
But we will drink together; and you shall bear
A better witness back than words, which we,   204
On like conditions, will have countersealed.   205
Come, enter with us. Ladies, you deserve
To have a temple built you. All the swords
In Italy, and her confederate arms,   208
Could not have made this peace.   *Exeunt.*

                              ❖

[5.4]

                Enter Menenius and Sicinius.

MENENIUS   See you yond coign o'th' Capitol, yond cor-   1
nerstone?
SICINIUS   Why, what of that?

178 **to** for   179 **his child** this boy, supposed his son   180 **dispatch**
dismissal, leave to go. (With implication also of "demise.")   189 **mortal** fatally   190 **true** i.e., as I vowed to do   191 **convenient** fitting,
proper   194 **withal** by it.   196 **sweat compassion** i.e., weep with
pity.   198 **back** go back   199 **Stand to** stand by   202 **former fortune**
fortune great as formerly.   204 **better witness** i.e., formal document
of peace   205 **On . . . countersealed** having agreed to the same conditions, will both have sealed and guaranteed.   208 **her confederate
arms** the weapons of her allies
5.4. Location: Rome. A public place.
1 **coign** corner

MENENIUS   If it be possible for you to displace it with your little finger, there is some hope the ladies of Rome, especially his mother, may prevail with him. But I say there is no hope in't; our throats are sentenced, and stay upon execution.   8

SICINIUS   Is't possible that so short a time can alter the condition of a man?   10

MENENIUS   There is differency between a grub and a butterfly, yet your butterfly was a grub. This Marcius is grown from man to dragon. He has wings; he's more than a creeping thing.

SICINIUS   He loved his mother dearly.

MENENIUS   So did he me; and he no more remembers his mother now than an eight-year-old horse. The tartness of his face sours ripe grapes. When he walks, he moves like an engine, and the ground shrinks before his treading. He is able to pierce a corslet with his eye, 20 talks like a knell, and his hum is a battery. He sits in 21 his state as a thing made for Alexander. What he bids 22 be done is finished with his bidding. He wants noth- 23 ing of a god but eternity and a heaven to throne in. 24

SICINIUS   Yes, mercy, if you report him truly. 25

MENENIUS   I paint him in the character. Mark what 26 mercy his mother shall bring from him. There is no more mercy in him than there is milk in a male tiger; that shall our poor city find. And all this is long of you. 29

SICINIUS   The gods be good unto us!

MENENIUS   No, in such a case the gods will not be good unto us. When we banished him, we respected not them; and, he returning to break our necks, they respect not us.

Enter a Messenger.

MESSENGER [*to Sicinius*]
Sir, if you'd save your life, fly to your house!
The plebeians have got your fellow tribune
And hale him up and down, all swearing, if 37
The Roman ladies bring not comfort home,
They'll give him death by inches.

Enter another Messenger.

SICINIUS   What's the news? 39

SECOND MESSENGER
Good news, good news! The ladies have prevailed,
The Volscians are dislodged, and Marcius gone. 41
A merrier day did never yet greet Rome,
No, not th'expulsion of the Tarquins. 43

SICINIUS
Friend, art thou certain this is true?
Is't most certain?

SECOND MESSENGER
As certain as I know the sun is fire.
Where have you lurked, that you make doubt of it?
Ne'er through an arch so hurried the blown tide 48
As the recomforted through th' gates. Why, hark you! 49
    Trumpets, hautboys, drums beat, all together.
The trumpets, sackbuts, psalteries, and fifes, 50
Tabors and cymbals, and the shouting Romans, 51
Make the sun dance. Hark you!   *A shout within.*

MENENIUS   This is good news.
I will go meet the ladies. This Volumnia
Is worth of consuls, senators, patricians,
A city full; of tribunes, such as you,
A sea and land full. You have prayed well today.
This morning for ten thousand of your throats
I'd not have given a doit. Hark, how they joy! 58
    Sound still, with the shouts.

SICINIUS
First, the gods bless you for your tidings!
Next, accept my thankfulness.

SECOND MESSENGER
Sir, we have all great cause to give great thanks.

SICINIUS   They are near the city?

SECOND MESSENGER   Almost at point to enter. 63

SICINIUS   We'll meet them, and help the joy. *Exeunt.*

[5.5]

Enter two Senators with ladies [Volumnia, Virgilia, Valeria] passing over the stage, with other lords.

FIRST SENATOR
Behold our patroness, the life of Rome!
Call all your tribes together, praise the gods,
And make triumphant fires! Strew flowers before them!
Unshout the noise that banished Marcius; 4
Repeal him with the welcome of his mother. 5
Cry, "Welcome, ladies, welcome!"

ALL   Welcome, ladies, welcome!
    A flourish with drums and trumpets. [Exeunt.]

---

8 stay upon await **10 condition** nature **19 engine** heavy instrument of war, such as a battering ram **20 corslet** body armor **21 a knell** the tolling of a bell announcing a death. **hum** (An expression of anger.) **battery** artillery assault. **22 state** chair of state. **as . . . Alexander** as though he were a statue of Alexander the Great (who lived after Coriolanus). **23 finished . . . bidding** i.e., as good as done once he orders it. **23–4 wants nothing** lacks no attribute **24 throne** be enthroned **25 mercy** i.e., he lacks mercy **26 in the character** to the life. **29 long of** owing to **37 hale** drag **39 death by inches** slow and lingering death. **41 dislodged** gone from their camp **43 th'expulsion of the Tarquins** i.e., the expulsion of Rome's last kings and beginning of the Republic.

48 arch i.e., arch of a bridge, such as London Bridge. **blown** swollen, driven by the wind **49.1 hautboys** oboelike instruments **50 sackbuts** early trombones. **psalteries** stringed instruments played by plucking the strings **51 Tabors** small drums **58 doit** very small coin. **63 at point** ready **5.5. Location:** Rome. A street near the gate, seemingly continuous from the previous scene; the time is virtually continuous. **4 Unshout** Recall, or, cancel by more shouting **5 Repeal** recall

[5.6]

Enter Tullus Aufidius, with attendants.

AUFIDIUS
Go tell the lords o'th' city I am here.
Deliver them this paper. [*He gives a paper.*] Having read
   it,
Bid them repair to th' marketplace, where I,   3
Even in theirs and in the commons' ears,
Will vouch the truth of it. Him I accuse   5
The city ports by this hath entered and   6
Intends t'appear before the people, hoping
To purge himself with words. Dispatch.
                              [*Exeunt attendants.*]

*Enter three or four Conspirators of Aufidius's
faction.*

                              Most welcome!

FIRST CONSPIRATOR
How is it with our general?
AUFIDIUS   Even so
As with a man by his own alms empoisoned
And with his charity slain.
SECOND CONSPIRATOR   Most noble sir,   11
If you do hold the same intent wherein
You wished us parties, we'll deliver you   13
Of your great danger.
AUFIDIUS   Sir, I cannot tell.   14
We must proceed as we do find the people.
THIRD CONSPIRATOR
The people will remain uncertain whilst
Twixt you there's difference, but the fall of either 17
Makes the survivor heir of all.
AUFIDIUS   I know it,
And my pretext to strike at him admits   19
A good construction. I raised him, and I pawned   20
Mine honor for his truth; who, being so heightened, 21
He watered his new plants with dews of flattery,   22
Seducing so my friends; and to this end
He bowed his nature, never known before
But to be rough, unswayable, and free.   25
THIRD CONSPIRATOR   Sir, his stoutness   26
When he did stand for consul, which he lost
By lack of stooping—
AUFIDIUS   That I would have spoke of.   28
Being banished for't, he came unto my hearth,
Presented to my knife his throat. I took him,

Made him joint servant with me, gave him way   31
In all his own desires; nay, let him choose
Out of my files, his projects to accomplish,   33
My best and freshest men; served his designments   34
In mine own person; holp to reap the fame
Which he did end all his; and took some pride   36
To do myself this wrong—till at the last
I seemed his follower, not partner, and
He waged me with his countenance, as if   39
I had been mercenary.
FIRST CONSPIRATOR   So he did, my lord.   40
The army marveled at it, and, in the last,   41
When he had carried Rome and that we looked   42
For no less spoil than glory—
AUFIDIUS   There was it   43
For which my sinews shall be stretched upon him.   44
At a few drops of women's rheum, which are   45
As cheap as lies, he sold the blood and labor
Of our great action. Therefore shall he die,
And I'll renew me in his fall. But hark!   48
                *Drums and trumpets sounds,
                with great shouts of the people.*

FIRST CONSPIRATOR
Your native town you entered like a post,   49
And had no welcomes home; but he returns,
Splitting the air with noise.
SECOND CONSPIRATOR   And patient fools,
Whose children he hath slain, their base throats tear
With giving him glory.
THIRD CONSPIRATOR   Therefore, at your vantage,   53
Ere he express himself or move the people
With what he would say, let him feel your sword,
Which we will second. When he lies along,   56
After your way his tale pronounced shall bury   57
His reasons with his body.
AUFIDIUS   Say no more.   58
Here come the lords.

Enter the Lords of the city.

ALL LORDS
You are most welcome home.
AUFIDIUS   I have not deserved it.
But, worthy lords, have you with heed perused   61
What I have written to you?
ALL LORDS   We have.
FIRST LORD   And grieve to hear't.
What faults he made before the last, I think   65

5.6. **Location:** Corioles. A Volscian city. (Plutarch sets this action in Antium, Aufidius's "native town" [in line 49], but in line 94 and following, the place is Corioles.)
3 repair go   **5 vouch** affirm.   **Him** He whom   **6 ports** gates.   **by this** by this time   **11 with his** by his own   **13 parties** as allies, partners   **14 Of** from   **17 difference** disagreement   **19 pretext** intention, motive   **20 construction** interpretation.   **pawned** pledged   **21 truth** loyalty.   **heightened** raised to power   **22 He . . . flattery** i.e., he bestowed flattering honors on those who now depended on him for patronage   **25 free** plainspoken.   **26 stoutness** obstinacy   **28 That . . . of** I was about to mention that.

31 joint servant partner   **33 files** ranks, troops   **34 designments** designs, enterprises   **36 end all his** gather in as all his own   **39 waged** remunerated.   **countenance** patronage, favor   **40 mercenary** a hired soldier.   **41 last** end   **42 had carried** had virtually overcome, or, might have overcome   **43 There was it** That was the thing   **44 my . . . upon** I shall exert all my strength against   **45 rheum** i.e., tears   **48 renew me** restore my reputation   **49 post** messenger   **53 at your vantage** seizing your opportune moment   **56 along** prostrate   **57 After . . . pronounced** telling your own version of the story   **58 reasons** justifications   **61 with heed** carefully   **65 made** committed

Might have found easy fines; but there to end
Where he was to begin, and give away
The benefit of our levies, answering us
With our own charge, making a treaty where
There was a yielding—this admits no excuse.   70

AUFIDIUS He approaches. You shall hear him.

Enter Coriolanus, marching with drum and colors;
the commoners being with him.

CORIOLANUS
Hail, lords! I am returned your soldier,
No more infected with my country's love   73
Than when I parted hence, but still subsisting   74
Under your great command. You are to know
That prosperously I have attempted, and   76
With bloody passage led your wars even to
The gates of Rome. Our spoils we have brought home
Doth more than counterpoise a full third part   79
The charges of the action. We have made peace   80
With no less honor to the Antiates
Than shame to th' Romans; and we here deliver,
Subscribed by th' consuls and patricians,   83
Together with the seal o'th' Senate, what
We have compounded on.   [*He offers a document.*]   85
AUFIDIUS Read it not, noble lords,
But tell the traitor, in the highest degree
He hath abused your powers.
CORIOLANUS "Traitor"? How now?
AUFIDIUS Ay, traitor, Marcius.
CORIOLANUS "Marcius"?
AUFIDIUS
Ay, Marcius, Caius Marcius. Dost thou think
I'll grace thee with that robbery, thy stol'n name
Coriolanus, in Corioles?
You lords and heads o'th' state, perfidiously
He has betrayed your business and given up,
For certain drops of salt, your city Rome—   97
I say your city—to his wife and mother,
Breaking his oath and resolution like
A twist of rotten silk, never admitting   100
Counsel o'th' war, but at his nurse's tears   101
He whined and roared away your victory,
That pages blushed at him and men of heart   103
Looked wond'ring each at other.
CORIOLANUS   Hear'st thou, Mars?
AUFIDIUS Name not the god, thou boy of tears!

CORIOLANUS Ha?   66
AUFIDIUS No more.   67   107
CORIOLANUS   68
Measureless liar, thou hast made my heart
Too great for what contains it. "Boy"? O slave!   109
Pardon me, lords, 'tis the first time that ever
I was forced to scold. Your judgments, my grave lords,
Must give this cur the lie; and his own notion—   112
Who wears my stripes impressed upon him, that
Must bear my beating to his grave—shall join
To thrust the lie unto him.
FIRST LORD Peace, both, and hear me speak.
CORIOLANUS
Cut me to pieces, Volsces. Men and lads,
Stain all your edges on me. "Boy"? False hound!   118
If you have writ your annals true, 'tis there   119
That, like an eagle in a dovecote, I   120
Fluttered your Volscians in Corioles.
Alone I did it. "Boy"!
AUFIDIUS   Why, noble lords,
Will you be put in mind of his blind fortune,   123
Which was your shame, by this unholy braggart,
'Fore your own eyes and ears?
ALL CONSPIRATORS   Let him die for't.
ALL PEOPLE Tear him to pieces!—Do it presently!—   126
He killed my son!—My daughter!—He killed my
cousin Marcus!—He killed my father!
SECOND LORD Peace, ho! No outrage! Peace!
The man is noble, and his fame folds in   130
This orb o'th' earth. His last offenses to us
Shall have judicious hearing. Stand, Aufidius,   132
And trouble not the peace.
CORIOLANUS   Oh, that I had him,
With six Aufidiuses, or more, his tribe,
To use my lawful sword!
AUFIDIUS   Insolent villain!
ALL CONSPIRATORS Kill, kill, kill, kill, kill him!
Draw the Conspirators, and kill Marcius,
who falls. Aufidius stands on him.
LORDS Hold, hold, hold, hold!
AUFIDIUS
My noble masters, hear me speak.
FIRST LORD   Oh, Tullus!
SECOND LORD
Thou hast done a deed whereat valor will weep.   139
THIRD LORD
Tread not upon him, masters. All be quiet;
Put up your swords.
AUFIDIUS
My lords, when you shall know—as in this rage,
Provoked by him, you cannot—the great danger

---

66 easy fines light penalties   **66–7 there . . . begin** to give up right at
the threshold of his potentially greatest victory   **68 levies** expenses
incurred in raising an army   **68–9 answering . . . charge** rewarding
us with our own expenses, or, answering our protests with the claim
that he acted with the authority we had given him in charge
70 yielding surrender   **73 infected with** influenced by. (But with the
suggestion of contamination.)   **74 hence** i.e., from Antium.
subsisting continuing   **76 prosperously . . . attempted** my warlike
enterprise has been prosperous   **79 Doth . . . part** outweigh by a full
third   **80 charges** costs   **83 Subscribed** signed   **85 compounded**
agreed   **97 certain . . . salt** some particular tears (i.e., those of Volumnia and Virgilia)   **100 twist** twisted thread   **100–1 never . . . war**
never taking counsel from other officers   **103 heart** courage

107 No more i.e., (1) No more than a boy (2) Do not dare to ally yourself with Mars.   **109 Too . . . it** swollen with rage so that my breast
cannot contain it.   **112 notion** understanding, sense of the truth
118 edges swords   **119 there** recorded there   **120 dovecote** pigeon
house   **123 blind fortune** gift of Fortune, the blind goddess; mere
good luck   **126 presently** immediately.   **130 folds in** overspreads,
enwraps   **132 judicious** judicial.   **Stand** Stop   **139 whereat** at
which

Which this man's life did owe you, you'll rejoice   144
That he is thus cut off. Please it Your Honors
To call me to your Senate, I'll deliver   146
Myself your loyal servant, or endure
Your heaviest censure.

FIRST LORD   Bear from hence his body,
And mourn you for him. Let him be regarded
As the most noble corpse that ever herald
Did follow to his urn.

SECOND LORD   His own impatience   151
Takes from Aufidius a great part of blame.

Let's make the best of it.

AUFIDIUS   My rage is gone,
And I am struck with sorrow. Take him up.
Help, three o'th' chiefest soldiers; I'll be one.   155
Beat thou the drum that it speak mournfully;
Trail your steel pikes. Though in this city he   157
Hath widowed and unchilded many a one,
Which to this hour bewail the injury,
Yet he shall have a noble memory.   160
Assist.   *Exeunt, bearing the body of Marcius.*
                                   A dead march sounded.

---

144 did owe you had for you, held in store for you   **146 deliver**
show, demonstrate   **151 impatience** rage

155 be one i.e., be the fourth.   **157 Trail . . . pikes** Carry your lances
reversed with the point trailing along the ground (as a sign of mourning).   **160 memory** memorial.

The Romances

Pericles

Pericles is a deceptively simple play. Although it was popular in its own time and in recent years has proved to be successful and deeply moving onstage, the play may seem naive and trivial on the printed page. Its apparent lack of "depth" seems especially striking when we compare it with its contemporaries, *King Lear, Macbeth, Timon of Athens*, and *Antony and Cleopatra*. It purports to be the work of a medieval poet, John Gower, who, as presenter, or chorus, apologizes to his sophisticated Jacobean audience ("born in these latter times/When wit's more ripe") for the "lame feet of my rhyme" and the quaintness of his ditty (1.0.11–12; 4.0.48). The narrative offers a series of sea voyages, separations, hairbreadth escapes, and reunions. Thrilling circumstances abound: Pericles fleeing the wrath of Antiochus; his wife, Thaisa, giving birth to their daughter, Marina, on board ship in the midst of a gigantic storm; and Marina later being rescued by pirates from a would-be murderer only to be sold by her new captors to a house of prostitution. Time leaps forward from Pericles's own youth to that of his daughter. The action takes place in remote lands, shifting constantly back and forth among six eastern Mediterranean localities: Antioch, Tyre, Tarsus, Pentapolis, Ephesus, and Mytilene. Conventional devices of plot include the expounding of riddles, the discovery of incest at court, the exposure of infants to the hostile elements, the miraculous restoration of life after seeming death, the appearance of the gods in a vision, and recognition of long-lost loved ones by means of signs or tokens.

These are the attributes of popular romance, a distinctly old-fashioned genre in 1606–1608 when *Pericles* was apparently written. Robert Greene had composed prose romances of this sort in the 1580s and early 1590s, including *Pandosto*, Shakespeare's source for *The Winter's Tale*. Sir Philip Sidney's *Arcadia* had endowed romance with noble eloquence and literary fashionableness, but that, too, was in the late 1580s. (The name Pericles may

well owe something to the *Arcadia's* Pyrocles, though Shakespeare may also have been attracted to the Pericles of fifth-century Athens and to the mellifluous quality of the name.) One source for *Pericles* itself, a prose history of Apollonius of Tyre by Laurence Twine, was registered for publication in 1576, although no edition exists before that of 1594 or 1595. Earlier accounts of Apollonius (as the hero was originally named), going back to Greek romance, include a ninth-century *Historia Apollonii Regis Tyri*, Godfrey of Viterbo's *Pantheon* (c. 1186), John Gower's *Confessio Amantis* (c. 1383–1393), and the *Gesta Romanorum*. Why did Shakespeare's company refurbish such an outmoded romantic story in 1606–1608?

The puzzle is aggravated by questions of authorship and textual reliability. The editors of the First Folio did not include *Pericles* in the canon of Shakespeare's plays. Perhaps they experienced copyright difficulties or could not lay their hands on the playbook, but it is also possible they either suspected or knew that Shakespeare was not the sole author. Printed editions were available to them: the First Quarto of 1609 and the subsequent quartos of 1609, 1611, and 1619, each based on the preceding edition. The First Quarto was, however, a bad text with occasional glaring contradictions. In 1.2, for example, Pericles's lords wish him a safe journey when no one has yet spoken of his departure, and Helicanus rebukes these same lords for flattery even though they have not said anything remotely sycophantic. Other scenes present similar difficulties, especially in the first two acts. The characters do not always seem consistent: Cleon is condemned in Act 5 for having tried to murder Marina, even though our earlier impression of him is of a man who is genuinely horrified at his wife's villainy. He weakly bends to the will of Dionyza but is no murderer. Such inconsistencies and errors, and the naiveté of the whole, have generally led to three hypotheses: that Shakespeare worked with a collaborator such as Thomas Heywood or George Wilkins, that he revised an older play and left the first two acts pretty much as they were, or that he wrote the entire play, which was then "pirated" by two unemployed actors whose portions differed markedly in accuracy.

To complicate matters still further, a prose version of the story called *The Painful Adventures of Pericles* by George Wilkins appeared in 1608, purporting to be "the true History of the Play of Pericles," that is, to be a prose account of a dramatic performance. This redaction is indeed close at times to the play we have, but at other times it departs widely. The departures of the later work are sometimes explained with the hypothesis that Wilkins based his account on an older play, to which Wilkins might have contributed himself; another and more current opinion favors the notion that Wilkins took what he needed from the play we have, borrowing also from Twine's prose version or from his own imagination. Apparently, then, *Pericles* was such a popular stage success that it inspired Wilkins's *Painful Adventures* in 1608, a new reprint in 1607 of Twine's *Pattern of Painful Adventures* on which the play itself had been partly based, and a botched surreptitious quarto edition of the play in 1609. Shakespeare's sole authorship must remain in doubt, although the incongruities, especially in the first two acts, are sometimes explained as the result of faulty memorial reporting and compositorial error. Onstage, to be sure, even the first two acts make fine dramatic sense, establishing motifs and situations that are essential to the rest of the play, so that the overall impression in the theater is of cohesion.

The naiveté of *Pericles* is probably deliberate. Its romantic motifs continue on into that group of plays known generally as the late romances: *Cymbeline* (c. 1608–1610), *The Winter's Tale* (c. 1609–1611), and *The Tempest* (c. 1610–1611). Nor are these motifs entirely new in *Pericles*: the "problem" comedies *All's Well That Ends Well* and *Measure for Measure* use a tragicomic structure in which miraculous cures or providential interventions triumph over the semblance of death. *Pericles* occupies an integral place, then, in the development of Shakespearean comedy during the period of his great tragedies. To that development, it offers a new emphasis on the simplicity of folk legend. Of the four late romances, *Pericles*, the earliest, is also the nearest in tone to the romances of the 1580s. The play seems to have constituted a revival of that old genre and was so immensely popular that it did much to establish the vogue of tragicomedy exploited by Beaumont and Fletcher.

The Chorus, old Gower, gives to the episodic materials of the play a unified point of view. He speaks with the authority of one who has told the story before, even though his *Confessio Amantis* (c. 1383–1393) was probably not Shakespeare's immediate source. Gower adopts a kind of Chaucerian persona, appealing to "what mine authors say" (1.0.20) and apologizing for his rude simplicity. Like the Chorus of *Henry V*, he repeatedly urges his auditors to transcend the limitations of his naive art, using the power of imagination to bridge gaps in time and to suppose the stage a storm-tossed ship or the city of Antioch. His appearances divide the action into seven episodic segments, surely a more authentic structure than the five "acts" conventionally employed by later editions. He offers moral appraisals of his various characters, often before we have had a chance to see them, contrasting the good with the bad. Most important, he presides as a sort of benign deity over the changing fortunes of his characters, assuring us that as narrator he will not allow the virtuous to come to grief or the wicked to escape punishment. He thus paces our expectations and provides a comic reassurance appropriate to romance. He promises to "show you those in trouble's reign, / Losing a mite, a mountain gain." To the virtuous, he will ultimately give his "benison." Under his direction, the vacillations of fortune take on a predictable rhythm, whereby the rewards of virtuous conduct may be delayed but cannot eventually fail. Pericles, he tells us, will suffer adversity "Till fortune, tired with doing bad, / Threw him ashore, to give him glad" (2.0.7–38). This pattern is repeated several times.

The characters often remind us of characters from a fairy story, outwardly stereotyped and one-dimensional, divided for the most part into contrasting types of villainy and virtue, and yet suggesting beneath their conventional surfaces the conflicts in family relationships that are essential to the fairy story. Incest is a recurrent motif, from its most blunt and evil manifestation in the court of Antiochus to more subtle inversions and variations in the relationships of Simonides and his daughter Thaisa, and, most centrally, of Pericles and his daughter Marina. The interest in fathers and daughters, and in the difficulties fathers have in coming to terms with their daughters' marrying other younger men, continues to fascinate Shakespeare from *Othello* and *King Lear* into all of his late romances. The mystery of incest is posed in terms of a riddle at the start of *Pericles*, and the moving dramatic conclusion in which the hero is reunited at last with his daughter seems to represent at some level a resolution of conflict between father and daughter. Pericles and Marina have "found" each other and themselves, literally in the narrative sense and also in some deeper psychic and spiritual way.

The characters expressing this and other conflicts are repeatedly paired opposite to one another as contrasting foils, illustrating a type of human depravity and its ideal opposite. One such contrast is that of tyranny and true monarchy. For example, both Antiochus and Simonides seem to welcome the various suitors who flock to their courts, seeking the hand in marriage of the two kings' daughters. Antiochus does so deceitfully, however, since he is his daughter's incestuous lover. Pericles learns in Antioch the danger of perceiving too much about the private affairs of a suspicious and vengeful tyrant. Simonides is, on the other hand, a true prince, beloved by even the simplest of his subjects, generous, lacking in envy, courteous to strangers, and more impressed with inner substance than with outward show. He approves of Pericles as a son-in-law, though (like Prospero in *The Tempest*) he imposes artificial restraints on the lovers to make their eventual triumph of love seem all the more sweet. Antiochus and his daughter are eventually shriveled up by a fire from heaven, whereas Simonides and Thaisa earn the just rewards of gracious hospitality. Another opposing pair of characters, Thaliard and Helicanus, are conventionally typed as false and true courtiers. Thaliard, ordered by Antiochus to murder Pericles, is evasive and self-serving; Helicanus, when offered the opportunity to supplant Pericles as ruler of Tyre, loyally awaits his master's return.

Pericles is apparently conceived in these same conventional terms as a prince of chivalry, young, brave, admirable both as a romantic wooer and as a resolute adventurer. His visit to the city of Tarsus, which has recently been toppled from wealth to poverty, shows him practicing the generosity that befits his lofty rank and innately noble qualities. Even when fortune strips him of his finery, his princely bearing is evident to discerning observers like King Simonides and Thaisa. Pericles thus differs outwardly from the flawed tragicomic protagonists more often found in the late romances, such as Posthumus in *Cymbeline* and Leontes in *The Winter's Tale*, who bring grief upon themselves and must suffer agonizing contrition before gaining an unexpected second chance. Pericles seems to be virtually without fault, a hero of romance rather than of tragedy. His soliloquies and eloquent speeches are not darkly introspective and psychological, like Leontes's. Although he grieves in sackcloth and ashes, he does so for undeserved misfortune rather than for his own follies. The play accordingly has little to say about humanity's perverse instinct for self-destruction. Yet critics have been unable to agree as to whether Pericles is simply a good man buffeted by misfortune or a man somehow perplexed by inner conflict. Are there unresolved wishes in his relationships to Thaisa and Marina that link him to the manifestly flawed protagonists of *Cymbeline* and *The Winter's Tale*, and, more explicitly, to Antiochus and his daughter in this play? What is it that causes his excessive despair in his grief and his withdrawal into absolute silence? On the surface, his story is one of undeserved misfortune, leading at last to happy reunion and an end of his trials. He learns a more affirmative and patient response from his courageous daughter Marina, whereupon his trials have run their necessary course. Even his learning such a lesson is of less importance than the sublime sense of mystery and joy that accompanies his reunion with Marina.

In several ways, Marina is a typical heroine of Shakespeare's late romances. Her name, like that of Perdita in *The Winter's Tale*, signifies loss and recovery. Marina is the gift of the sea, that mysterious power of fortune in *Pericles* that takes with one hand even while it gives with the other. Just as the sea tosses Pericles on the coast of Pentapolis and then returns to him the suit of armor in which he will joust for the love of fair Thaisa, so in another storm at sea Thaisa apparently dies giving birth to Marina. The child is a "fresh new seafarer" on the troubled voyage of life (3.1.41). The sea parts her from her mother and father and leads to the misunderstandings whereby Marina is supposed dead, but the sea also eventually deposits Pericles on the coast of Mytilene, where he finds his long-lost daughter. Like Perdita, Marina is associated with flowers and with Tellus, a divinity of the earth. The inscription on her monument, when she is thought dead, speaks of elemental strife between the sea and the shore caused by her death, in which the angry sea gods "Make raging battery upon shores of flint" (4.4.39–43). She is a princess from folk legend, like Snow White or like Imogen in *Cymbeline*, who must flee the envious wrath of a witchlike stepmother and queen. Her true mother, Thaisa, another princess in a folktale, is washed ashore in a treasure-filled chest, smelling sweetly and betokening some miraculous change of fortune.

Most important, Marina is one who can preach conversion to the sinful and cure distempered souls. She recovers her husband-to-be, Lysimachus, from the brothels of Mytilene, and even converts pimps and prostitutes by her innocent faith. As one with a strange power to bring new life to dead hope, she resembles a number of mysterious artist-figures and magicians in the late romances (or, earlier, in *All's Well That Ends Well*). One such is Cerimon, who restores life to Thaisa. Like him, or like Paulina in *The Winter's Tale*, whose devices are "lawful" though seemingly magical, Marina offers cures that can be rationally explained and yet appear to be miraculous. To Pericles, her ministrations seem "the rarest dream that e'er dull sleep / Did mock sad fools withal" (5.1.166–7). Yet what she has taught him, by her own example, is simple patience; she has suffered even more than he but nevertheless knows how to endure, how to "look / Like Patience gazing on kings' graves and smiling / Extremity out of act" (lines 140–2). Marina has the power to renew her father and restore him to life, perhaps because she represents the way in which the sexuality of women can be legitimated: she dwells for a time in a house of prostitution and is eminently desirable to men, and yet at the same time is so pure that she can teach men the way to control their own libidinousness. She is thus whore and saint in one person, able to refute the low premise about the carnality of the human condition that Pericles elsewhere finds so threatening. In his recovery of Marina and in his glad disposing of her as the bride of Lysimachus, Pericles at last comes to terms with the incestuous bond between father and daughter that had posed itself so menacingly for him in the court of King Antiochus.

Through Marina's ministrations, Pericles is reunited with his wife as well. Here, too, the narrative suggests a successful resolution of guilt after long years of inner conflict. Pericles is obliged to throw his wife's body overboard in a storm after she has died in childbirth. The fault is not his, since the sailors insist that the storm cannot be abated until the ship is cleared of the dead (3.1.47–9), but the emotional burden of loss is incalculable. Thaisa's miraculous recovery makes possible an eventual reunion that coincides with the rediscovery of the daughter. Viewed in these terms, the tale is one in which a husband finds it possible to love again a wife he lost and in a sense abandoned long ago. As in *The Winter's Tale*, where King Leontes causes the death of his queen at the time of her childbearing and then regains her after years of penance, the husband learns again, late in life, to cherish a long-lost wife who has aged and whom he is now able to love in spite of that aging. In *Pericles*, the husband's guilt is not manifest, nor is his wife's sexuality an open threat to him in her youthful childbearing vitality, and yet the narrative itself of separation and reunion resembles a slow and difficult coming to terms with the emotional demands of marriage. Perhaps it is significant in some way that Shakespeare lived apart from his family most of his working life and that when he wrote his late romances he was about to retire from London to Stratford.

Whatever the psychological dimension of the story of Pericles, his daughter, and his wife, old Gower as Chorus searches for meaning in simpler, pious terms. Gower wishes us to understand finally why Providence has allowed so much misfortune to afflict the virtuous: only by such testing can humanity learn to conquer time and death. Time will always remain "the king of men;/He's both their parent and he is their grave, / And gives them

what he will, not what they crave" (2.3.47–9). Nevertheless, Providence can turn the accidents of time and fortune to good purpose for those who are Joblike in their patient faith. Even pirates unknowingly take part in a divine plan, rescuing Marina from the clutches of the evil Dionyza. As Gower puts it, those who are "assailed with fortune fierce and keen" are also "Led on by heaven, and crowned with joy at last" (5.3.90–2). To Pericles, such a delayed reward is ample compensation for his sorrows, almost indeed an unbearable joy. "No more, you gods!" he movingly pleads. "Your present kindness / Makes my past miseries sports" (lines 41–2).

After centuries of neglect, other than in an occasional much-transmuted alteration, *Pericles* has come into its own in recent decades on stage. The tendency of late is to emphasize the play's fairy-tale-like and paradoxical elements in such a way as to call attention to the contrivances of theatrical illusion. Terry Hands, at Stratford-upon-Avon in 1969, employed a bare stage to emphasize the fluidity of movement and need for the audience's complicity in the creation of theatrical illusion; Gower (Emrys James) was a Welsh bard, and the parts of Thaisa and Marina were doubled by Susan Fleetwood—not without some contrivance at the end, when the two are onstage together. Toby Robertson chose a Brechtian modern-dress decor in order to emphasize the corruption of the brothel scenes (1973, the Roundhouse Theatre, London). Gower has taken on a number of modern guises, including that of a calypso singer (Edric Connor) in Tony Richardson's 1958 production at Stratford-upon-Avon, a blues gospel singer (Renee Rogers) in Richard Ouzounian's fine production at Stratford, Canada, in 1986, and a singing bus driver in Barbara Gaines's production for the Chicago Shakespeare Theatre in 1998. The play lends itself to oriental opulence and romance-like variety of setting. Its continued success in the theater is an effective antidote to the problems of textual uncertainty that afflict the play on the printed page.

Pericles

[Dramatis Personae

GOWER, *as Presenter or Chorus*

ANTIOCHUS, *King of Antioch*
DAUGHTER *of Antiochus*
THALIARD, *a lord of Antioch*
MESSENGER *to Antiochus*

PERICLES, *Prince of Tyre*
THAISA, *his wife, daughter of Simonides*
MARINA, *their daughter*
HELICANUS,
ESCANES, } *two lords of Tyre*
Three other LORDS *of Tyre*

CLEON, *Governor of Tarsus*
DIONYZA, *his wife*
LEONINE, *a murderer*
A LORD *of Tarsus*

SIMONIDES, *King of Pentapolis*
Three FISHERMEN *of Pentapolis*
Five KNIGHTS *who compete for Thaisa's hand*
Three LORDS *of Pentapolis*
A MARSHAL

LYCHORIDA, *Marina's nurse*

MASTER *of a ship*
A SAILOR *of the ship*

CERIMON, *a lord of Ephesus*
PHILEMON, *his servant*
Two GENTLEMEN *of Ephesus*
Two SERVANTS *of Ephesus*

Three PIRATES

LYSIMACHUS, *Governor of Mytilene*
PANDER,
BAWD, *his wife,* } *three bawds, or dealers*
BOLT, *their man,* } *in prostitution*
Two GENTLEMEN *of Mytilene*

SAILOR *of Tyre*
SAILOR *of Mytilene*
GENTLEMAN *of Tyre*
LORD *of Mytilene*

DIANA, *goddess of chastity*

Lords, Ladies, Gentlemen, Attendants, Servants,
Messengers, young Ladies accompanying Marina,
Vestal Virgins, inhabitants of Ephesus

SCENE: *In various eastern Mediterranean countries*]

1. Chorus

Enter Gower [before the palace of Antioch, on the
walls of which can be seen a row of impaled heads].

GOWER
    To sing a song that old was sung,   1
    From ashes ancient Gower is come,   2
    Assuming man's infirmities   3
    To glad your ear and please your eyes.
    It hath been sung at festivals,
    On ember eves and holy-ales;   6
    And lords and ladies in their lives
    Have read it for restoratives.   8
    The purchase is to make men glorious,   9

1.0. (Gower is seen to be standing before the palace of Antioch,
where scene 1 will take place.)
1 old of old   **2 ancient Gower** the fourteenth-century poet John
Gower, who related the adventures of Apollonius of Tyre (of which
Pericles is a version) in his *Confessio Amantis*

3 Assuming man's infirmities taking on a mortal body   **6 ember**
eves evenings before the ember days—the periodic fast days which
coincide with the four changes of the seasons.   **holy-ales** i.e., church
ales or festivals   **8 for restoratives** for its nourishing or healing properties.   **9 purchase** gain, benefit.   **glorious** renowned

Et bonum quo antiquius, eo melius.
If you, born in these latter times   10
When wit's more ripe, accept my rhymes,   12
And that to hear an old man sing   13
May to your wishes pleasure bring,
I life would wish, and that I might
Waste it for you, like taper light.   16
This Antioch, then. Antiochus the Great   17
Built up this city for his chiefest seat,
The fairest in all Syria—
I tell you what mine authors say.   20
This king unto him took a peer,   21
Who died and left a female heir,
So buxom, blithe, and full of face   23
As heaven had lent her all his grace;   24
With whom the father liking took   25
And her to incest did provoke.
Bad child, worse father, to entice his own
To evil should be done by none!   28
But custom what they did begin   29
Was with long use account'd no sin.
The beauty of this sinful dame
Made many princes thither frame   32
To seek her as a bedfellow,
In marriage pleasures playfellow;
Which to prevent he made a law,
To keep her still, and men in awe,   36
That whoso asked her for his wife,
His riddle told not, lost his life.   38
So for her many a wight did die,   39
As yon grim looks do testify.

> [*He points to the heads of the unsuccessful
> suitors, displayed on the walls.*]

What now ensues, to the judgment of your eye
I give my cause, who best can justify.   *Exit.* 42

❧

[1.1]

Enter Antiochus, Prince Pericles, and followers.

ANTIOCHUS
Young Prince of Tyre, you have at large received   1
The danger of the task you undertake.
PERICLES
I have, Antiochus, and with a soul
Emboldened with the glory of her praise
Think death no hazard in this enterprise.

ANTIOCHUS   Music!   10
Bring in our daughter, clothèd like a bride
For th'embracements even of Jove himself,
At whose conception, till Lucina reigned,   9
Nature this dowry gave: to glad her presence,   10
The senate house of planets all did sit   11
To knit in her their best perfections.   12

[*Music.*] *Enter Antiochus's Daughter.*

PERICLES
See where she comes, appareled like the spring,
Graces her subjects, and her thoughts the king   14
Of every virtue gives renown to men!   15
Her face the book of praises, where is read   16
Nothing but curious pleasures, as from thence   17
Sorrow were ever razed, and testy wrath   18
Could never be her mild companion.   19
You gods that made me man, and sway in love,   20
That have inflamed desire in my breast
To taste the fruit of yon celestial tree
Or die in the adventure, be my helps,
As I am son and servant to your will,
To compass such a boundless happiness!   25
ANTIOCHUS   Prince Pericles—
PERICLES
That would be son to great Antiochus.
ANTIOCHUS
Before thee stands this fair Hesperides,   28
With golden fruit, but dangerous to be touched,
For deathlike dragons here affright thee hard.   30
Her face, like heaven, enticeth thee to view
Her countless glory, which desert must gain;   32
And which, without desert, because thine eye   33
Presumes to reach, all the whole heap must die.   34
Yon sometimes famous princes, like thyself,   35

> [*pointing to the heads on the walls*]

Drawn by report, advent'rous by desire,
Tell thee with speechless tongues and semblance pale   37
That without covering, save yon field of stars,
Here they stand martyrs slain in Cupid's wars,
And with dead cheeks advise thee to desist
For going on death's net, whom none resist.   41

PERICLES

> Antiochus, I thank thee, who hath taught
> My frail mortality to know itself,
> And by those fearful objects to prepare
> This body, like to them, to what I must;   45
> For death remembered should be like a mirror,   46
> Who tells us life's but breath, to trust it error.
> I'll make my will then, and, as sick men do,
> Who know the world, see heaven, but, feeling woe,   49
> Grip not at earthly joys as erst they did,   50
> So I bequeath a happy peace to you
> And all good men, as every prince should do;
> My riches to the earth from whence they came,
> [To the Princess] But my unspotted fire of love to you.
> Thus ready for the way of life or death,
> I wait the sharpest blow, Antiochus.

ANTIOCHUS

> Scorning advice, read the conclusion, then;   57
> Which read and not expounded, 'tis decreed,
> As these before thee, thou thyself shalt bleed.

DAUGHTER

> Of all 'sayed yet, mayst thou prove prosperous!   60
> Of all 'sayed yet, I wish thee happiness!   61

PERICLES

> Like a bold champion, I assume the lists,   62
> Nor ask advice of any other thought
> But faithfulness and courage.   [He reads] the riddle.
>> I am no viper, yet I feed   65
>> On mother's flesh which did me breed.   66
>> I sought a husband, in which labor
>> I found that kindness in a father.   68
>> He's father, son, and husband mild;
>> I mother, wife, and yet his child.
>> How they may be, and yet in two,   71
>> As you will live, resolve it you.
> [Aside] Sharp physic is the last! But, O you powers   73
> That gives heaven countless eyes to view men's acts,   74
> Why cloud they not their sights perpetually   75
> If this be true which makes me pale to read it?
> Fair glass of light, I loved you, and could still,   77
> Were not this glorious casket stored with ill.
> But I must tell you now my thoughts revolt,
> For he's no man on whom perfections wait   80
> That, knowing sin within, will touch the gate.   81
> You are a fair viol, and your sense the strings   82
> Who, fingered to make man his lawful music,

> Would draw heaven down and all the gods to
>   hearken,
> But, being played upon before your time,   85
> Hell only danceth at so harsh a chime.   86
> Good sooth, I care not for you.   87

ANTIOCHUS

> Prince Pericles, touch not, upon thy life,   88
> For that's an article within our law
> As dangerous as the rest. Your time's expired.
> Either expound now, or receive your sentence.

PERICLES   Great King,

> Few love to hear the sins they love to act;
> 'Twould braid yourself too near for me to tell it.   94
> Who has a book of all that monarchs do,   95
> He's more secure to keep it shut than shown.
> For vice repeated is like the wand'ring wind,   97
> Blows dust in others' eyes to spread itself;   98
> And yet the end of all is bought thus dear,   99
> The breath is gone, and the sore eyes see clear   100
> To stop the air would hurt them. The blind mole
>   casts   101
> Copped hills towards heaven to tell the earth is
>   thronged   102
> By man's oppression, and the poor worm doth die
>   for 't.   103
> Kings are earth's gods; in vice their law's their will;
> And if Jove stray, who dares say Jove doth ill?
> It is enough you know; and it is fit,   106
> What being more known grows worse, to smother it. 107
> All love the womb that their first being bred;
> Then give my tongue like leave to love my head.   109

ANTIOCHUS [aside]

> Heaven, that I had thy head! He has found the
>   meaning.
> But I will gloze with him.—Young Prince of Tyre,   111
> Though by the tenor of our strict edict,
> Your exposition misinterpreting,   113
> We might proceed to cancel of your days,   114
> Yet hope, succeeding from so fair a tree   115
> As your fair self, doth tune us otherwise.   116
> Forty days longer we do respite you,

---

45 **must** must someday be   46 **remembered** called to mind   49 **Who . . . woe** i.e., who, weary of this world's miseries and seeing the imminence of heavenly bliss   50 **Grip** clutch.   **erst** formerly   57 **conclusion** problem, riddle   60 **'sayed** who have assayed, attempted. (Also in line 61.)   62 **assume the lists** i.e., undertake the combat, enter the tournament ground   65–6 **I am . . . breed** (Vipers at birth were thought to gnaw their way through their mother's sides, thus killing the mother.)   68 **kindness** (1) affection (2) kinship   71 **two** i.e., two people   73 **Sharp . . . last!** i.e., This last condition—to stake my life on solving this riddle—is bitter medicine!   **powers** celestial beings who control destiny   74 **eyes** i.e., the stars   75 **Why . . . perpetually** i.e., why do the gods not forever turn their gaze aside in dismay   77 **glass of light** beautiful (but deceptive) glass vessel   80–1 **For . . . gate** i.e., the man who will meddle with incest is not one on whom virtues attend.   82 **sense** senses

85 **before your time** i.e., before marriage   86 **only** alone   87 **Good sooth** In truth   88 **touch not** (Antiochus evidently believes Pericles is about to touch the Princess's hand or some such forbidden thing.)   94 **braid . . . near** upbraid you too directly   95 **Who** He who   97 **repeated** proclaimed   98–101 **Blows . . . hurt them** which, in seeking to disseminate its report of vice, manages only to blow dust in people's eyes, the result being costly to the one attempting to tell the truth; his breath is spent in vain, whereas the offenders can see clearly enough, despite the irritation, how to prevent the talk from hurting them.   101–3 **The blind . . . for 't** (Pericles's example is of a lowly creature like the worm who dares to sound a warning against incest and tyranny only to suffer for the attempt, while spiritually blind figures of authority, like the mole, insolently build up peaked [copped] monuments, thereby demonstrating how the earth is beset [thronged] with such oppressive uses of power.)   106 **you know** i.e., that you know that I know your riddle   107 **What . . . it** to cover up a deed that is only worsened by revelation.   109 **like leave** similar permission   111 **gloze** talk smoothly and speciously   113 **Your . . . misinterpreting** since your exposition interprets wrongly   114 **to cancel . . . days** to end your life   115 **Yet . . . tree** yet hope (or fear) of your answering correctly, issuing from so fair a royal stock   116 **doth . . . otherwise** alters my intention. (Us is the royal "we.")

If by which time our secret be undone,   118
This mercy shows we'll joy in such a son.
And until then your entertain shall be   120
As doth befit our honor and your worth.   121
                    [*Exeunt.*] *Manet Pericles solus.*

PERICLES
How courtesy would seem to cover sin,   122
When what is done is like an hypocrite,
The which is good in nothing but in sight!   124
If it be true that I interpret false,   125
Then were it certain you were not so bad
As with foul incest to abuse your soul,
Where now you're both a father and a son   128
By your untimely claspings with your child,
Which pleasures fits a husband, not a father,
And she an eater of her mother's flesh
By the defiling of her parents' bed;
And both like serpents are, who, though they feed
On sweetest flowers, yet they poison breed.
Antioch, farewell, for wisdom sees those men   135
Blush not in actions blacker than the night
Will 'schew no course to keep them from the light.   137
One sin, I know, another doth provoke;
Murder's as near to lust as flame to smoke.   139
Poison and treason are the hands of sin,
Ay, and the targets, to put off the shame.   141
Then, lest my life be cropped to keep you clear,   142
By flight I'll shun the danger which I fear.   *Exit.*

            Enter Antiochus.

ANTIOCHUS   He hath found the meaning,
For which we mean to have his head.
He must not live to trumpet forth my infamy,
Nor tell the world Antiochus doth sin
In such a loathèd manner;
And therefore instantly this prince must die,
For by his fall my honor must keep high.
[*Calling*] Who attends us there?

            Enter Thaliard.

THALIARD   Doth Your Highness call?
ANTIOCHUS
Thaliard, you are of our chamber, Thaliard,   153
And our mind partakes her private actions   154
To your secrecy; and for your faithfulness
We will advance you, Thaliard. Behold.
                    [*He gives poison and money.*]
Here's poison and here's gold. We hate the Prince
Of Tyre, and thou must kill him. It fits thee not
To ask the reason why: because we bid it.

Say, is it done?
THALIARD   My lord, 'tis done.
ANTIOCHUS   Enough.

            Enter a Messenger.

Let your breath cool yourself, telling your haste.   161
MESSENGER   My lord, Prince Pericles is fled.   [*Exit.*]
ANTIOCHUS [*to Thaliard*]   As thou wilt live, fly after,
and like an arrow shot from a well-experienced archer
hits the mark his eye doth level at, so thou never re-   165
turn unless thou say Prince Pericles is dead.
THALIARD   My lord, if I can get him within my pistol's
length, I'll make him sure enough. So farewell to Your   168
Highness.
ANTIOCHUS   Thaliard, adieu!   [*Exit Thaliard.*]
                    Till Pericles be dead,
My heart can lend no succor to my head.   [*Exit.*]   171

❖

[1.2]

            Enter Pericles with his Lords.

PERICLES
Let none disturb us.   [*The Lords stay at the door.*]
                    Why should this change of thoughts,   1
The sad companion, dull-eyed melancholy,
Be my so used a guest as not an hour   3
In the day's glorious walk or peaceful night,   4
The tomb where grief should sleep, can breed me
            quiet?
Here pleasures court mine eyes, and mine eyes shun
            them,
And danger, which I feared, is at Antioch,
Whose arm seems far too short to hit me here.
Yet neither pleasure's art can joy my spirits,
Nor yet the other's distance comfort me.
Then it is thus: the passions of the mind,   11
That have their first conception by misdread,   12
Have after-nourishment and life by care;   13
And what was first but fear what might be done   14
Grows elder now, and cares it be not done.   15
And so with me: the great Antiochus,
'Gainst whom I am too little to contend,
Since he's so great can make his will his act,   18
Will think me speaking, though I swear to silence;
Nor boots it me to say I honor him,   20
If he suspect I may dishonor him.
And what may make him blush in being known,   22
He'll stop the course by which it might be known.

118 undone unraveled, solved   **120 entertain** entertainment, reception   **121.1 *Manet*** He remains onstage.   ***solus*** alone.   **122 would
seem** speciously endeavors   **124 sight** appearance.   **125 If . . . false**
If I were mistaken (which I am not)   **128 Where** whereas   **135 sees
those men** sees that those men who   **137 'schew** eschew. (Or "shew,"
the Quarto reading, could mean "show, reveal.")   **keep . . . light** i.e.,
keep their guilty actions hidden.   **139 Murder's . . . lust** (A sententious truism of the time.)   **141 targets** shields.   **put off** deflect
142 cropped harvested, cut down.   **clear** free from accusation
153 of our chamber my chamberlain
154 partakes imparts

161 Let . . . haste Cool your hot haste by breathing or panting out
your report.   **165 level** aim   **168 length** range.   **sure** harmless (i.e.,
dead)   **171 My . . . head** i.e., my anxieties cannot calm my fears.
1.2. Location: Tyre. The palace.
1 us i.e., me.   **change of thoughts** altered disposition of mind   **3 Be . . .
guest as** be so familiar a guest with me that   **4 walk** i.e., traversing of
the sun   **11–15 the passions . . . not done** passions such as fear, that
originate in apprehension of some evil, are kept alive by anxiety; and
what at first was simple apprehension gives way in time to an anxious care to prevent from happening what at first had seemed only a
worrisome possibility.   **18 so great can** so powerful that he can
20 boots avails   **22 known** publicly revealed

With hostile forces he'll o'erspread the land,
And with th'ostent of war will look so huge   25
Amazement shall drive courage from the state,   26
Our men be vanquished ere they do resist,
And subjects punished that ne'er thought offense;
Which care of them, not pity of myself—
Who am no more but as the tops of trees
Which fence the roots they grow by, and defend
   them—   31
Makes both my body pine and soul to languish,
And punish that before that he would punish.   33

Enter [Helicanus and] all the Lords to Pericles.

FIRST LORD
Joy and all comfort in your sacred breast!
SECOND LORD
And keep your mind, till you return to us,   35
Peaceful and comfortable!
HELICANUS
Peace, peace, and give experience tongue.   37
They do abuse the King that flatter him.
For flattery is the bellows blows up sin;   39
The thing the which is flattered, but a spark   40
To which that blast gives heat and stronger glowing;   41
Whereas reproof, obedient and in order,
Fits kings as they are men, for they may err.
When Signor Sooth here does proclaim peace,   44
He flatters you, makes war upon your life.
Prince, pardon me, or strike me, if you please;
I cannot be much lower than my knees.   *[He kneels.]*
PERICLES
All leave us else; but let your cares o'erlook   48
What shipping and what lading's in our haven,   49
And then return to us.   *[Exeunt Lords.]*
     Helicanus,
Thou hast moved us. What see'st thou in our looks?   51
HELICANUS   An angry brow, dread lord.
PERICLES
If there be such a dart in princes' frowns,
How durst thy tongue move anger to our face?
HELICANUS
How dares the plants look up to heaven,
From whence they have their nourishment?

25 **th'ostent** the display   26 **Amazement** fear, terror   31 **fence** shield, shelter. (As a virtuous prince, Pericles sees his exalted role at the top of the hierarchy, like a treetop, as one of defending the common people, who are lowly and earthbound like the tree's roots but are also its center of life and source of sustenance.)   33 **And . . . would punish** and punishes me beforehand (through fear) whom he (Antiochus) wishes to punish.   35 **till you return to us** (Here, the lords of Tyre appear to know of Pericles's departure. In the next scene, we find that he left *unlicensed of their loves,* i.e., without their knowledge. The prose narratives that recount the same story state that his departure was accomplished secretly. This is one of the several inconsistencies of this rather garbled text.)   37 **give . . . tongue** listen to the voice of experience. 39 **blows up** that inflames, heats   40 **the which** which   41 **blast** i.e., flattering speech. (In Wilkins's *Painful Adventures,* this scene is more clearly presented: Helicanus upbraids Pericles for his bad humor and then justifies such plain talk as preferable to flattery.)   44 **When Signor Sooth** When Sir Flattery. (Though, puzzlingly, no one in this scene has, in fact, flattered Pericles; see the note for line 41.)   48 **else** i.e., except Helicanus.   **cares o'erlook** watchfulness supervise 49 **lading's** cargo is   51 **moved** angered

PERICLES
Thou knowest I have power to take thy life from thee.
HELICANUS   I have ground the ax myself;
Do you but strike the blow.
PERICLES
Rise, prithee, rise. *[He rises.]* Sit down. Thou art no
   flatterer,
I thank thee for't, and heaven forbid
That kings should let their ears hear their faults hid!   62
Fit counselor and servant for a prince,
Who by thy wisdom makes a prince thy servant,
What wouldst thou have me do?
HELICANUS   To bear with patience such griefs
As you yourself do lay upon yourself.
PERICLES
Thou speak'st like a physician, Helicanus,
That ministers a potion unto me
That thou wouldst tremble to receive thyself.
Attend me, then: I went to Antioch,   71
Where, as thou know'st, against the face of death
I sought the purchase of a glorious beauty   73
From whence an issue I might propagate,   74
Are arms to princes and bring joys to subjects.   75
Her face was to mine eye beyond all wonder;
The rest—hark in thine ear—as black as incest,
Which by my knowledge found, the sinful father
Seemed not to strike, but smooth. But thou know'st
   this,   79
'Tis time to fear when tyrants seem to kiss.
Which fear so grew in me, I hither fled
Under the covering of a careful night,   82
Who seemed my good protector, and, being here,
Bethought me what was past, what might succeed.   84
I knew him tyrannous, and tyrants' fears
Decrease not, but grow faster than the years;
And should he doubt—as doubt no doubt he doth—   87
That I should open to the list'ning air   88
How many worthy princes' bloods were shed
To keep his bed of blackness unlaid ope,   90
To lop that doubt he'll fill this land with arms   91
And make pretense of wrong that I have done him;
When all for mine—if I may call't—offense   93
Must feel war's blow, who spares not innocence;   94
Which love to all, of which thyself art one,   95
Who now reprov'st me for't—   96
HELICANUS   Alas, sir!
PERICLES
Drew sleep out of mine eyes, blood from my cheeks,
Musings into my mind, with thousand doubts
How I might stop this tempest ere it came;

62 **hear . . . hid** listen to flattery that glosses over their faults. 71 **Attend** Listen to   73 **purchase** acquisition   74–5 **From . . . princes** upon whose body I might beget an heir, such as are the props and supports of princes   79 **Seemed** pretended.   **smooth** gloss over, conciliate.   82 **careful** protecting   84 **succeed** follow.   87 **And should . . . doth** and should he fear—as no doubt he does fear— 88 **open** reveal   90 **unlaid ope** unrevealed   91 **lop that doubt** cut off that fear   93–4 **When . . . innocence** in which event, all my subjects will, because of my offense (if I may call it that), be subjected to the blows of war that spare not the innocent   95 **Which . . . one** which love for all my subjects, of whom you are one   96 **now** just now

And finding little comfort to relieve them,
I thought it princely charity to grieve for them.

HELICANUS
Well, my lord, since you have given me leave to speak,
Freely will I speak. Antiochus you fear,
And justly too, I think, you fear the tyrant,
Who either by public war or private treason
Will take away your life.
Therefore, my lord, go travel for a while,
Till that his rage and anger be forgot,
Or till the Destinies do cut his thread of life.
Your rule direct to any; if to me,   111
Day serves not light more faithful than I'll be.

PERICLES I do not doubt thy faith;
But should he wrong my liberties in my absence?   114

HELICANUS
We'll mingle our bloods together in the earth,   115
From whence we had our being and our birth.

PERICLES
Tyre, I now look from thee, then, and to Tarsus
Intend my travel, where I'll hear from thee,   118
And by whose letters I'll dispose myself.
The care I had and have of subjects' good
On thee I lay, whose wisdom's strength can bear it.
I'll take thy word for faith, not ask thine oath.
Who shuns not to break one will sure crack both.   123
But in our orbs we'll live so round and safe   124
That time of both this truth shall ne'er convince: 125
Thou showed'st a subject's shine, I a true prince'.   126

Exeunt.

❖

[1.3]

Enter Thaliard solus.

THALIARD So, this is Tyre, and this the court. Here
must I kill King Pericles; and if I do it not, I am sure to
be hanged at home. 'Tis dangerous. Well, I perceive he   3
was a wise fellow and had good discretion that, being
bid to ask what he would of the King, desired he might
know none of his secrets. Now do I see he had some   6
reason for't; for if a king bid a man be a villain, he's
bound by the indenture of his oath to be one. Husht!   8
Here comes the lords of Tyre.

*Enter Helicanus [and] Escanes, with other
Lords [of Tyre. Thaliard stands aside.]*

HELICANUS
You shall not need, my fellow peers of Tyre,
Further to question me of your king's departure.
His sealed commission left in trust with me
Does speak sufficiently he's gone to travel.   12

THALIARD [aside] How? The King gone?

HELICANUS
If further yet you will be satisfied
Why, as it were, unlicensed of your loves   16
He would depart, I'll give some light unto you.
Being at Antioch—

THALIARD [aside]   What from Antioch?

HELICANUS
Royal Antiochus—on what cause I know not—
Took some displeasure at him, at least he judged so;
And doubting lest he had erred or sinned,   21
To show his sorrow, he'd correct himself;   22
So puts himself unto the shipman's toil,   23
With whom each minute threatens life or death.

THALIARD [aside] Well, I perceive
I shall not be hanged now, although I would;   26
But since he's gone, the King's ears it must please
He scaped the land, to perish at the seas.
I'll present myself.—Peace to the lords of Tyre!

HELICANUS
Lord Thaliard from Antiochus is welcome.

THALIARD From him I come
With message unto princely Pericles;
But since my landing I have understood
Your lord has betaken himself to unknown travels;
Now message must return from whence it came.   35

HELICANUS
We have no reason to desire it,   36
Commended to our master, not to us.   37
Yet ere you shall depart, this we desire,
As friends to Antioch, we may feast in Tyre.

Exeunt.

❖

[1.4]

*Enter Cleon, the Governor of Tarsus, with
[Dionyza] his wife, and others.*

CLEON
My Dionyza, shall we rest us here
And, by relating tales of others' griefs,
See if 'twill teach us to forget our own?

DIONYZA
That were to blow at fire in hope to quench it,
For who digs hills because they do aspire   5

---

111 direct delegate **114 should he** what if he (Antiochus) should.
liberties royal rights and prerogatives, and those of my subjects
115 mingle . . . earth i.e., die fighting him **118 Intend** direct, purpose **123 Who** He who **124 orbs** orbits, spheres. **round** with probity. (But punning on the idea of circularity in *round*. A line appears
to be lost here, rhyming with *safe*.) **125 time . . . convince** time will
never confute this truth regarding us two **126 shine** brightness,
honor (as of true gold). **prince'** prince's.
1.3. Location: Tyre. The palace.
3–6 he . . . secrets (So the poet Philippides asked of Lysimachus; mentioned by Plutarch and Barnabe Riche.) **8 indenture** terms by which
a servant is bound to his master

12 sealed bearing the royal seal **16 unlicensed . . . loves** without your
loving assent. (Compare with the note for 1.2.35.) **21 doubting lest**
fearing that **22 he'd correct himself** he wished to impose a penalty
on himself **23 toil** travail, hence dangers **26 although I would**
even if I wished to be **35 message** my message **36 desire it** i.e., wish
to know the message's contents **37 Commended** directed as it is
1.4. Location: Tarsus. The Governor's house.
5 who digs whoever digs up, removes. **aspire** mount up

Throws down one mountain to cast up a higher.
Oh, my distressed lord, even such our griefs are;
Here they are but felt, and seen with mischief's eyes,   8
But like to groves, being topped, they higher rise.   9
CLEON   Oh, Dionyza,
Who wanteth food and will not say he wants it,   11
Or can conceal his hunger till he famish?   12
Our tongues and sorrows do sound deep our woes   13
Into the air; our eyes do weep till lungs
Fetch breath that may proclaim them louder, that,   15
If heaven slumber while their creatures want,   16
They may awake their helps to comfort them.   17
I'll then discourse our woes, felt several years,
And, wanting breath to speak, help me with tears.   19
DIONYZA   I'll do my best, sir.
CLEON
This Tarsus, o'er which I have the government,   21
A city on whom Plenty held full hand,   22
For Riches strewed herself even in her streets;   23
Whose towers bore heads so high they kissed the
    clouds,
And strangers ne'er beheld but wondered at;
Whose men and dames so jetted and adorned,   26
Like one another's glass to trim them by;   27
Their tables were stored full, to glad the sight,
And not so much to feed on as delight;
All poverty was scorned, and pride so great,
The name of help grew odious to repeat.   31
DIONYZA   Oh, 'tis too true.
CLEON
But see what heaven can do by this our change: 33
These mouths who but of late earth, sea, and air
Were all too little to content and please,
Although they gave their creatures in abundance,
As houses are defiled for want of use,   37
They are now starved for want of exercise.
Those palates who, not yet two summers younger,
Must have inventions to delight the taste,   40
Would now be glad of bread and beg for it.
Those mothers who, to nuzzle up their babes,   42
Thought naught too curious, are ready now   43
To eat those little darlings whom they loved.
So sharp are hunger's teeth that man and wife

Draw lots who first shall die to lengthen life.   46
Here stands a lord and there a lady weeping;
Here many sink, yet those which see them fall
Have scarce strength left to give them burial.
Is not this true?
DIONYZA
Our cheeks and hollow eyes do witness it.
CLEON
Oh, let those cities that of Plenty's cup
And her prosperities so largely taste,
With their superfluous riots, hear these tears!   54
The misery of Tarsus may be theirs.

    Enter a Lord.

LORD   Where's the Lord Governor?
CLEON   Here.
Speak out thy sorrows which thou bring'st in haste,
For comfort is too far for us to expect.
LORD
We have descried, upon our neighboring shore,
A portly sail of ships make hitherward.   61
CLEON   I thought as much.
One sorrow never comes but brings an heir
That may succeed as his inheritor,
And so in ours. Some neighboring nation,
Taking advantage of our misery,
Hath stuffed these hollow vessels with their power   67
To beat us down, the which are down already,
And make a conquest of unhappy men,
Whereas no glory's got to overcome.   70
LORD
That's the least fear, for by the semblance   71
Of their white flags displayed they bring us peace,
And come to us as favorers, not as foes.
CLEON
Thou speak'st like him 's untutored to repeat: 74
Who makes the fairest show means most deceit.   75
But bring they what they will and what they can,
What need we fear?
Our ground's the lowest, and we are halfway there.   78
Go tell their general we attend him here,
To know for what he comes and whence he comes
And what he craves.
LORD   I go, my lord.   [*Exit.*]
CLEON
Welcome is peace, if he on peace consist;   83
If wars, we are unable to resist.

    Enter Pericles with attendants.

PERICLES
Lord Governor, for so we hear you are,

8–9 Here . . . rise our misfortunes seem bad enough when we mutely behold them with the eyes of calamity, but will only grow worse if we talk about them, like trees that, being cut off at the top, merely sprout new growth.   **11 wanteth** lacks   **12 famish** starve to death.
13 sound deep sound forth solemnly. (With suggestion of plumbing unfathomable depths.)   **15 them** our woes   **16–17 while . . . them** while living beings are in need, our tears and prayers may awaken the help of the heavens to provide comfort.   **19 wanting** i.e., when I lack.   **help me** i.e., you help me   **21 This Tarsus** This is Tarsus
22 on whom . . . hand over which Plenty poured her gifts generously
23 Riches (A singular concept, probably derived from the French *richesse*, equivalent to "plenty"; the image is that of the cornucopia being held aloft over the city.)   **her** i.e., the city's   **26 jetted and adorned** strutted and adorned themselves   **27 glass . . . by** mirror by which to adorn themselves, or, to mirror each other's finery   **31 The name . . . repeat** i.e., that it became odious even to mention the very possibility of asking for help.   **33 see . . . change** see by our change in fortune what heaven can do   **37 for want** through lack   **40 Must have inventions** insisted on novelties   **42 nuzzle up** nurture
43 naught too curious nothing too choice (for their babes)

46 lengthen life i.e., provide food for the other to cannibalize.
54 superfluous riots prodigal living.   **tears** i.e., sounds of weeping.
61 A portly . . . hitherward a stately fleet of ships sails toward us.
67 power force of armed men   **70 Whereas . . . overcome** whereby no glory is gained by the conqueror.   **71 the least fear** i.e., something not to be feared in the least   **74 him 's . . . repeat** one who has never been taught to recite (the following maxim) and is therefore unaware of its truth   **75 Who** He who   **78 Our . . . lowest** i.e., One who's already down on the ground can fall no lower. (Proverbial.)   **83 on peace consist** is resolved on peace.

Let not our ships and number of our men
Be like a beacon fired t'amaze your eyes.
We have heard your miseries as far as Tyre   87
And seen the desolation of your streets;
Nor come we to add sorrow to your tears,
But to relieve them of their heavy load;
And these our ships, you happily may think   92
Are like the Trojan horse was stuffed within   93
With bloody veins expecting overthrow,   94
Are stored with corn to make your needy bread   95
And give them life whom hunger starved half dead.

ALL [*kneeling*]   The gods of Greece protect you!
And we'll pray for you.

PERICLES   Arise, I pray you, rise.
We do not look for reverence but for love,
And harborage for ourself, our ships, and men.

CLEON [*rising*]
The which when any shall not gratify,   102
Or pay you with unthankfulness in thought,
Be it our wives, our children, or ourselves,
The curse of heaven and men succeed their evils!   105
Till when—the which I hope shall ne'er be seen—
Your Grace is welcome to our town and us.

PERICLES
Which welcome we'll accept, feast here awhile,
Until our stars that frown lend us a smile.   *Exeunt.*

❖

[2. Chorus]

Enter Gower.

GOWER
Here have you seen a mighty king
His child, iwis, to incest bring;
A better prince and benign lord,   2
That will prove awful both in deed and word.   3
Be quiet then, as men should be,   4
Till he hath passed necessity.
I'll show you those in trouble's reign,   6
Losing a mite, a mountain gain.   7
The good in conversation,
To whom I give my benison,   9
Is still at Tarsus, where each man   10
Thinks all is writ he spoken can;
And, to remember what he does,   12
Build his statue to make him glorious.   13

But tidings to the contrary   15
Are brought your eyes. What need speak I?

Dumb Show.

*Enter at one door Pericles talking with Cleon, all
the train with them. Enter at another door a
Gentleman, with a letter to Pericles; Pericles shows
the letter to Cleon; Pericles gives the Messenger a
reward, and knights him. Exit Pericles at one door,
and Cleon at another.*

Good Helicane, that stayed at home—
Not to eat honey like a drone   18
From others' labors, for though he strive   19
To killen bad, keep good alive,   20
And to fulfill his prince' desire—   21
Sends word of all that haps in Tyre:
How Thaliard came full bent with sin   23
And hid intent to murder him,   24
And that in Tarsus was not best
Longer for him to make his rest.
He, doing so, put forth to seas,   27
Where when men been there's seldom ease;   28
For now the wind begins to blow;
Thunder above and deeps below
Makes such unquiet that the ship
Should house him safe is wrecked and split,   32
And he, good prince, having all lost,
By waves from coast to coast is tossed.
All perishen of man, of pelf,   35
Ne aught escapend but himself;   36
Till fortune, tired with doing bad,
Threw him ashore, to give him glad.   38
And here he comes. What shall be next,
Pardon old Gower—this 'longs the text.   [*Exit.*] 40

❖

[2.1]

Enter Pericles, wet.

PERICLES
Yet cease your ire, you angry stars of heaven!
Wind, rain, and thunder, remember earthly man   2
Is but a substance that must yield to you,
And I, as fits my nature, do obey you.
Alas, the seas hath cast me on the rocks,
Washed me from shore to shore, and left me breath
Nothing to think on but ensuing death.
Let it suffice the greatness of your powers
To have bereft a prince of all his fortunes,
And, having thrown him from your wat'ry grave,

87 t'amaze to terrify   **92 you happily** which you perchance   **93 was**
which was   **94 bloody veins** i.e., bloodthirsty Greek warriors.
expecting overthrow i.e., in anticipation of the overthrow of Troy. (Or
the phrase perhaps modifies *you* in line 92.)   **95 corn** grain.   **your
needy bread** desperately needed bread, or, bread for your needy people   **102 gratify** show gratitude for or toward   **105 succeed** follow
as a consequence of
2.0.
2 iwis certainly   **3 A better prince** i.e., and you have also seen a better prince, Pericles   **4 awful** deserving of awe, respect   **6 necessity**
those hardships imposed by fate.   **7 those** i.e., those who   **9 The
good in conversation** The good man (Pericles) in matters of conduct
10 benison blessing   **12 writ** holy writ.   **he speken can** that he (Pericles) speaks. (A deliberately medieval expression, as also in *killen,
been, perishen,* and *Ne aught escapend,* lines 20, 28, 35, and 36.)
13 remember commemorate

15 to the contrary adverse   **18–21 Not . . . desire** (Helicanus strives
to punish evildoers and reward the virtuous, much as a good bee
refuses to be a drone, choosing instead to labor in the interests of the
hive's ruler.)   **23 bent with** intent upon   **24 hid** hidden   **27 so** i.e.,
as advised   **28 been** are   **32 Should** that should   **35 pelf** goods,
property   **36 Ne aught escapend** nothing escaping   **38 glad** gladness.
40 'longs the text belongs to the text of the play proper. (Or Gower
may be saying that his speech is already long enough or too long.)
2.1. Location: Pentapolis. The seaside.
2 remember remember that

Here to have death in peace is all he'll crave.

Enter three Fishermen.

FIRST FISHERMAN   What, ho, Pilch!   12

SECOND FISHERMAN   Ha, come and bring away the nets!   13

FIRST FISHERMAN   What, Patchbreech, I say!   14

THIRD FISHERMAN   What say you, master?

FIRST FISHERMAN   Look how thou stirr'st now! Come   16
away, or I'll fetch th' with a wanion.   17

THIRD FISHERMAN   Faith, master, I am thinking of the
poor men that were cast away before us even now.   19

FIRST FISHERMAN   Alas, poor souls, it grieved my heart
to hear what pitiful cries they made to us to help them,
when, welladay, we could scarce help ourselves.   22

THIRD FISHERMAN   Nay, master, said not I as much
when I saw the porpoise how he bounced and tum-   24
bled? They say they're half fish, half flesh. A plague
on them, they ne'er come but I look to be washed.   26
Master, I marvel how the fishes live in the sea.

FIRST FISHERMAN   Why, as men do aland: the great   28
ones eat up the little ones. I can compare our rich misers to nothing so fitly as to a whale: 'a plays and tum-   30
bles, driving the poor fry before him, and at last devours them all at a mouthful. Such whales have I heard   32
on o'th' land, who never leave gaping till they swal-   33
lowed the whole parish, church, steeple, bells, and all.

PERICLES [*aside*]   A pretty moral.

THIRD FISHERMAN   But, master, if I had been the sexton,
I would have been that day in the belfry.

SECOND FISHERMAN   Why, man?

THIRD FISHERMAN   Because he should have swallowed
me too, and when I had been in his belly I would
have kept such a jangling of the bells that he should
never have left till he cast bells, steeple, church, and   42
parish up again. But if the good King Simonides were
of my mind—

PERICLES [*aside*]   Simonides?

THIRD FISHERMAN   We would purge the land of these
drones that rob the bee of her honey.

PERICLES [*aside*]
How from the finny subject of the sea   48
These fishers tell the infirmities of men,
And from their wat'ry empire recollect   50
All that may men approve or men detect!—   51
Peace be at your labor, honest fishermen.   52

SECOND FISHERMAN   "Honest," good fellow? What's that?   53
If it be a day fits you, search out of the calendar, and   54
nobody look after it.   55

PERICLES
May see the sea hath cast upon your coast—   56

SECOND FISHERMAN   What a drunken knave was the
sea to cast thee in our way!   58

PERICLES
A man whom both the waters and the wind,
In that vast tennis court, hath made the ball
For them to play upon, entreats you pity him.
He asks of you that never used to beg.   62

FIRST FISHERMAN   No, friend, cannot you beg? Here's
them in our country of Greece gets more with begging
than we can do with working.

SECOND FISHERMAN   Canst thou catch any fishes, then?

PERICLES   I never practiced it.

SECOND FISHERMAN   Nay, then, thou wilt starve, sure,
for here's nothing to be got nowadays unless thou
canst fish for't.   70

PERICLES
What I have been I have forgot to know,
But what I am, want teaches me to think on:
A man thronged up with cold. My veins are chill,   73
And have no more of life than may suffice
To give my tongue that heat to ask your help—
Which if you shall refuse, when I am dead,
For that I am a man, pray you see me buried.   77

FIRST FISHERMAN   Die, quotha? Now gods forbid't, an I   78
have a gown here! Come, put it on, keep thee warm.
[*He gives a garment; Pericles puts it on.*] Now, afore me, a   80
handsome fellow! Come, thou shalt go home, and
we'll have flesh for holidays, fish for fasting days, and
moreo'er puddings and flapjacks, and thou shalt be   83
welcome.

PERICLES   I thank you, sir.

SECOND FISHERMAN   Hark you, my friend. You said
you could not beg?

PERICLES   I did but crave.   88

SECOND FISHERMAN   But crave? Then I'll turn craver
too, and so I shall scape whipping.   90

PERICLES   Why, are your beggars whipped, then?

SECOND FISHERMAN   Oh, not all, my friend, not all; for if
all your beggars were whipped, I would wish no better
office than to be beadle. But, master, I'll go draw up   94
the net.   [*Exit with Third Fisherman.*]

PERICLES [*aside*]
How well this honest mirth becomes their labor!   96

FIRST FISHERMAN   Hark you, sir, do you know where
ye are?

PERICLES   Not well.

FIRST FISHERMAN   Why, I'll tell you. This is called
Pentapolis, and our king the good Simonides.

---

12 Pilch (A name derived from what he wears, a leather garment.)
13 bring away bring along   **14 Patchbreech** (Comically named for his
patched breeches.)   **16 Look . . . now!** i.e., Get a move on!   **17 I'll . . .
wanion** I'll deal you a blow, a vengeance take you!   **19 before us** before
our eyes   **22 welladay** alas   **24 porpoise** (Porpoises were popularly
supposed to be prognosticators of storms.)   **26 washed** wetted by a
storm.   **28 aland** on the land   **30 'a** he   **32–3 heard on** heard of
42 cast vomited   **48 subject** i.e., residents, citizens   **50 recollect** gather
up   **51 may . . . detect** may commend men or expose them.   **52–5 Peace
. . . after it** (Most commentators think something has been lost here, perhaps a line in which Pericles bids the fishermen good day; if so, the Second Fisherman's reply could mean, "if the day fits your wretched
condition, scratch it out of the calendar and let no one miss it.")

56 May You may   **58 cast** (Punning on *vomit*, as suggested by
drunken; see line 42.)   **62 used** made it a practice   **70 fish for't** i.e.,
angle for it, look out for one's own interests.   **73 thronged up** overwhelmed   **77 For that** because   **78 quotha** says he.   **an** if, so long as
80 afore me (A mild oath.)   **83 puddings** sausages   **88 crave**
request.   **90 scape whipping** i.e., escape the punishment for begging
(as required by Elizabethan law. The Second Fisherman jokes that
crave is only a polite term for *beg.*)   **94 beadle** parish official responsible for administering corporal punishment (who would be busy and
well paid if all those who beg under the pretext of seeking favor at
court were to be whipped as beggars)   **96 becomes** suits

PERICLES   "The good Simonides" do you call him?

FIRST FISHERMAN   Ay, sir, and he deserves so to be called for his peaceable reign and good government.

PERICLES   He is a happy king, since he gains from his subjects the name of "good" by his government. How far is his court distant from this shore?

FIRST FISHERMAN   Marry, sir, half a day's journey. And 108 I'll tell you, he hath a fair daughter, and tomorrow is her birthday; and there are princes and knights come from all parts of the world to joust and tourney for her 111 love.

PERICLES   Were my fortunes equal to my desires, I could wish to make one there. 114

FIRST FISHERMAN   Oh, sir, things must be as they may; and what a man cannot get, he may lawfully deal for 116 his wife's soul. 117

Enter the two [other] Fishermen, drawing up a net.

SECOND FISHERMAN   Help, master, help! Here's a fish hangs in the net like a poor man's right in the law; 'twill hardly come out. Ha! Bots on't, 'tis come at last, 120 and 'tis turned to a rusty armor.

[He hauls in Pericles's armor.]

PERICLES
An armor, friends? I pray you, let me see it.
Thanks, Fortune, yet that after all thy crosses 123
Thou givest me somewhat to repair myself;
And though it was mine own, part of my heritage
Which my dead father did bequeath to me
With this strict charge, even as he left his life:
"Keep it, my Pericles; it hath been a shield
Twixt me and death," and pointed to this brace; 129
"For that it saved me, keep it. In like necessity— 130
The which the gods protect thee from!—may't defend thee."
It kept where I kept, I so dearly loved it, 132
Till the rough seas, that spares not any man,
Took it in rage, though calmed have given't again.
I thank thee for't. My shipwreck now's no ill,
Since I have here my father gave in his will. 136

FIRST FISHERMAN   What mean you, sir?

PERICLES
To beg of you, kind friends, this coat of worth, 138
For it was sometime target to a king; 139
I know it by this mark. He loved me dearly,
And for his sake I wish the having of it,
And that you'd guide me to your sovereign's court,
Where with it I may appear a gentleman.
And if that ever my low fortune's better,

I'll pay your bounties; till then rest your debtor. 145

FIRST FISHERMAN   Why, wilt thou tourney for the lady?

PERICLES
I'll show the virtue I have borne in arms. 147

FIRST FISHERMAN   Why, d' ye take it, and the gods give thee good on't!   *[Pericles puts it on.]* 149

SECOND FISHERMAN   Ay, but hark you, my friend, 'twas we that made up this garment through the rough seams of the waters. There are certain condolements, 152 certain vails. I hope, sir, if you thrive, you'll remember 153 from whence you had them. 154

PERICLES   Believe't, I will.
By your furtherance I am clothed in steel,
And spite of all the rapture of the sea 157
This jewel holds his building on my arm. 158
Unto thy value I will mount myself 159
Upon a courser, whose delightful steps 160
Shall make the gazer joy to see him tread.
Only, my friend, I yet am unprovided
Of a pair of bases. 163

SECOND FISHERMAN   We'll sure provide. Thou shalt have my best gown to make thee a pair; and I'll bring thee to the court myself.

PERICLES
Then honor be but equal to my will,
This day I'll rise, or else add ill to ill.   *[Exeunt.]*

❖

[2.2]

Enter [King] Simonides, with attendance, and Thaisa, [and take their places].

SIMONIDES
Are the knights ready to begin the triumph? 1

FIRST LORD   They are, my liege,
And stay your coming to present themselves. 3

SIMONIDES
Return them we are ready; and our daughter, 4
In honor of whose birth these triumphs are,
Sits here like Beauty's child, whom Nature gat 6
For men to see and, seeing, wonder at.   *[Exit one.]*

THAISA
It pleaseth you, my royal father, to express
My commendations great, whose merit's less.

145 **pay your bounties** repay your generosity.   **rest** I will remain
147 **virtue** bravery, knightly qualities   149 **on't** of it, from it.
152 **seams** (The metaphor is from tailoring, as if the waves of the sea were seams.)   **condolements** (Probably confused with "dole," portion or share, or with "emoluments." The Fisherman hopes for a gratuity.)
153 **vails** (1) perquisites, tips (2) tailors' remnants of cloth.   154 **them** the pieces of armor.   157 **rapture** plundering   158 **This . . . arm** i.e., this armor is my strength and my defense.   159 **Unto thy value** In keeping with the worthiness of you, my armor   160 **courser** spirited horse   163 **bases** pleated skirts attached to the doublet and reaching from the waist to the knee, worn under the armor by a mounted knight.
2.2. Location: Pentapolis. A public way leading to the lists. A pavilion by the side of it for the reception of the King, Princess, Lords, etc.
1 **triumph** tournament, festive spectacle.   3 **stay** await   4 **Return** Reply to   6 **gat** begot

108 **Marry** (A mild oath, originally "by the Virgin Mary.")   111 **tourney** take part in a tournament   114 **make one** be among those
116–17 **what . . . soul** (A difficult line. Perhaps the Fisherman jokes that if a man cannot prosper any other way, he could prostitute his wife, at the expense of her—and his—soul.)   120 **'twill . . . out** it will hardly ever be disentangled, set to rights.   **Bots on't** i.e., Plague take it. (*Bots* is a disease of horses.)   123 **crosses** thwartings, misfortunes
129 **brace** mailed arm protector   130 **For that** because.   **like** similar
132 **kept** lodged   136 **my father** what my father   138 **coat** i.e., armor, coat of mail   139 **target** shield, i.e., protector

SIMONIDES
It's fit it should be so, for princes are   10
A model which heaven makes like to itself.
As jewels lose their glory if neglected,
So princes their renowns if not respected.
'Tis now your honor, daughter, to entertain   14
The labor of each knight in his device.   15

THAISA
Which, to preserve mine honor, I'll perform.

*The First Knight passes by [and his Squire presents
his shield to the Princess].*

SIMONIDES
Who is the first that doth prefer himself?   17

THAISA
A knight of Sparta, my renownèd father,
And the device he bears upon his shield
Is a black Ethiop reaching at the sun;
The word, *Lux tua vita mihi.*   21

SIMONIDES
He loves you well that holds his life of you.
                                        The Second Knight [passes by].
Who is the second that presents himself?

THAISA
A prince of Macedon, my royal father,
And the device he bears upon his shield
Is an armed knight that's conquered by a lady;
The motto thus, in Spanish, *Piùe per dolcezza che per
forza.*   *Third Knight [passes by].*   27

SIMONIDES
And what's the third?

THAISA   The third of Antioch,
And his device, a wreath of chivalry;   29
The word, *Me pompae provexit apex.*   30
                                        Fourth Knight [passes by].

SIMONIDES   What is the fourth?

THAISA
A burning torch that's turnèd upside down;
The word, *Quod me alit, me extinguit.*   33

SIMONIDES
Which shows that beauty hath his power and will,   34
Which can as well inflame as it can kill.
                                        Fifth Knight [passes by].

THAISA
The fifth, an hand environèd with clouds,
Holding out gold that's by the touchstone tried;   37
The motto thus, *Sic spectanda fides.*   38
                                        *Sixth Knight, [Pericles, passes by;
he himself presents his device to Thaisa].*

SIMONIDES   And what's

The sixth and last, the which the knight himself
With such a graceful courtesy delivered?

THAISA
He seems to be a stranger; but his present is   42
A withered branch, that's only green at top;
The motto, *In hac spe vivo.*   44

SIMONIDES   A pretty moral;
From the dejected state wherein he is,
He hopes by you his fortunes yet may flourish.

FIRST LORD
He had need mean better than his outward show   48
Can any way speak in his just commend,   49
For by his rusty outside he appears
To have practiced more the whipstock than the lance.   51

SECOND LORD
He well may be a stranger, for he comes
To an honored triumph strangely furnished.   53

THIRD LORD
And on set purpose let his armor rust
Until this day, to scour it in the dust.   55

SIMONIDES
Opinion's but a fool, that makes us scan   56
The outward habit by the inward man.   57
But stay, the knights are coming.
We will withdraw into the gallery.   [*Exeunt.*]   59
                                        *Great shouts [within], and all cry
"The mean knight!"*

❧

[2.3]

*[A banquet prepared.] Enter the King [Simonides,
Thaisa, Marshal, Ladies, Lords, attendants], and
Knights from tilting, [in armor].*

SIMONIDES   Knights,
To say you're welcome were superfluous.
To place upon the volume of your deeds,
As in a title page, your worth in arms
Were more than you expect or more than's fit,
Since every worth in show commends itself.   6
Prepare for mirth, for mirth becomes a feast.   7
You are princes and my guests.

THAISA [*to Pericles*]   But you my knight and guest,   9
To whom this wreath of victory I give,
And crown you king of this day's happiness.
                                        [She crowns Pericles with a wreath.]

---

10 **princes** royalty of either sex   14 **honor** i.e., honorable duty.
entertain receive, review   15 **device** emblem with motto on the
knights' shields.   17 **prefer** present   21 **word** motto. *Lux . . . mihi*
Your light is my life. (Latin; also at lines 30, 33, 38, 44.)   27 *Piùe . . .
forza* More by gentleness than by force. (Italian, not Spanish.)
29 **wreath of chivalry** twisted band joining the crest to the knight's
helmet   30 *Me . . . apex* The highest summit of honor has led me on.
33 *Quod . . . extinguit* The person who feeds my flame puts out my
light.   34 **his** its   37 **touchstone** black quartz, used to test gold for
purity   38 *Sic spectanda fides* Thus is faith to be tried.

42 **present** presented device   44 *In . . . vivo* In this hope I live.
48–9 **He . . . commend** He'd certainly better have some nobler meaning, more than his present wretched outward appearance can in any
way speak to commend him.   51 **whipstock** handle of a whip (which
he would use to drive workhorses)   53 **strangely** (The witticism
plays on *strangely*, "oddly," and *stranger*, "a visitor from a foreign
land.")   55 **scour** (The joke is that he will polish his rusty armor by
falling off his horse in the dust.)   56 **Opinion** Judgment of a person's
worth in terms of mere reputation   56–7 **Opinion's . . . man** i.e., Only
a fool belives that one can judge a person's inner qualities by outward
appearance.   59.2 **mean** humble, undistinguished in appearance
2.3. Location: Pentapolis. The palace.
6 **in show** by being revealed through deeds   7 **becomes** suits   9 **you**
you are

PERICLES
'Tis more by fortune, lady, than by merit.

SIMONIDES
Call it by what you will, the day is yours,
And here, I hope, is none that envies it.
In framing an artist, art hath thus decreed: 15
To make some good but others to exceed;
And you are her labored scholar.—Come, queen o'th'
feast—   17
For, daughter, so you are—here take your place.
[To the Marshal] Marshal, the rest, as they deserve their
grace.   19

KNIGHTS
We are honored much by good Simonides.
[They take their places.]

SIMONIDES
Your presence glads our days. Honor we love,
For who hates honor hates the gods above.   22

MARSHAL [to Pericles]   Sir, yonder is your place.

PERICLES   Some other is more fit.

FIRST KNIGHT
Contend not, sir, for we are gentlemen   25
Have neither in our hearts nor outward eyes   26
Envies the great, nor shall the low despise.   27

PERICLES   You are right courteous knights.

SIMONIDES   Sit, sir, sit.   [They sit.]
[Aside] By Jove, I wonder, that is king of thoughts,   30
These cates resist me, he not thought upon.   31

THAISA [aside]
By Juno, that is queen of marriage,
All viands that I eat do seem unsavory,
Wishing him my meat. [To Simonides] Sure he's a
gallant gentleman.

SIMONIDES [to Thaisa]
He's but a country gentleman.
He's done no more than other knights have done;
He's broken a staff or so. So let it pass.   37

THAISA [aside]
To me he seems like diamond to glass.   38

PERICLES [aside]
Yon king's to me like to my father's picture,
Which tells me in that glory once he was—   40
Had princes sit like stars about his throne,
And he the sun for them to reverence.
None that beheld him but, like lesser lights,
Did vail their crowns to his supremacy;   44
Where now his son's like a glowworm in the night,   45
The which hath fire in darkness, none in light.   46

Whereby I see that Time's the king of men;
He's both their parent and he is their grave,
And gives them what he will, not what they crave.

SIMONIDES   What, are you merry, knights?

KNIGHTS
Who can be other in this royal presence?

SIMONIDES
Here, with a cup that's stored unto the brim—
As you do love, fill to your mistress' lips—   53
We drink this health to you.   [He drinks a toast.]

KNIGHTS   We thank Your Grace.

SIMONIDES   Yet pause awhile.
Yon knight doth sit too melancholy,
As if the entertainment in our court
Had not a show might countervail his worth.   58
Note it not you, Thaisa?

THAISA   What is't to me, my father?

SIMONIDES
Oh, attend, my daughter. Princes in this
Should live like gods above, who freely give
To everyone that come to honor them;
And princes not doing so are like to gnats,
Which make a sound but, killed, are wondered at.   65
Therefore to make his entrance more sweet,
Here, say we drink this standing-bowl of wine to him.   67
[He drinks a toast.]

THAISA
Alas, my father, it befits not me
Unto a stranger knight to be so bold.
He may my proffer take for an offense,
Since men take women's gifts for impudence.

SIMONIDES   How?
Do as I bid you, or you'll move me else.   73

THAISA [aside]
Now, by the gods, he could not please me better.

SIMONIDES
And furthermore tell him we desire to know of him
Of whence he is, his name and parentage.

THAISA [going to Pericles]
The King my father, sir, has drunk to you—

PERICLES   I thank him.

THAISA
Wishing it so much blood unto your life.   79

PERICLES
I thank both him and you, and pledge him freely.   80

THAISA
And further, he desires to know of you
Of whence you are, your name and parentage.

PERICLES
A gentleman of Tyre, my name Pericles,
My education been in arts and arms;   84
Who, looking for adventures in the world,
Was by the rough seas reft of ships and men,   86

15 **framing** making   17 **her labored scholar** the one on whom art has bestowed the most pains.   19 **the rest** i.e., place the rest of the company.   **grace** favor.   22 **who** one who   25–7 **for . . . despite** for we are gentlemen who have nothing in our hearts or outward-seeing eyes that envies the great or shall despise those of low birth.   30–1 **By Jove . . . upon** By Jove, who rules over human thoughts, I marvel that these delicacies do not seem appealing to me, since I would rather be thinking about him (Pericles).   37 **broken a staff** (Shattering the lance became the aim in sixteenth-century tilting matches.)   38 **to** compared with   40 **Which . . . was** a picture that recalls to me my father's former glory   44 **vail** lower, remove submissively   45–6 **Where . . . light** i.e., whereas I, my kingly father's son, am a pale light by comparison, one best seen at night like a glowworm.

53 **fill . . . lips** i.e., drink a full cup to your mistress   58 **might countervail** that could equal   65 **are wondered at** i.e., cause amazement at the loud noise such small insects could make while living.   67 **standing-bowl** drinking vessel that stands on feet or on stem and base   73 **move me else** anger me otherwise.   79 **Wishing . . . life** (Wine was thought to replenish the blood.)   80 **pledge him** drink his health (in a return toast)   84 **been . . . arms** has been in humane learning and the arts of warfare   86 **reft** bereft

And after shipwreck driven upon this shore.
THAISA [*returning to the King*]
    He thanks Your Grace; names himself Pericles,
    A gentleman of Tyre,
    Who only by misfortune of the seas,
    Bereft of ships and men, cast on this shore.   91
SIMONIDES
    Now, by the gods, I pity his misfortune
    And will awake him from his melancholy.—
    Come, gentlemen, we sit too long on trifles
    And waste the time which looks for other revels.
    Even in your armors, as you are addressed,   96
    Will well become a soldier's dance.   97
    I will not have excuse with saying this: 98
    Loud music is too harsh for ladies' heads,   99
    Since they love men in arms as well as beds.   100
                                            They dance.
    So this was well asked, 'twas so well performed.   101
    Come, sir,   [*presenting Thaisa to Pericles*]
    Here's a lady that wants breathing too.   103
    And I have heard you knights of Tyre
    Are excellent in making ladies trip,   105
    And that their measures are as excellent.   106
PERICLES
    In those that practice them they are, my lord.
SIMONIDES
    Oh, that's as much as you would be denied   108
    Of your fair courtesy.   *They dance.*
                    Unclasp, unclasp!   109
    Thanks, gentlemen, to all; all have done well,
        [*To Pericles*] But you the best.—Pages and lights, to
        conduct
    These knights unto their several lodgings!
        [*To Pericles*] Yours, sir,   112
    We have given order to be next our own.
PERICLES   I am at Your Grace's pleasure.
SIMONIDES
    Princes, it is too late to talk of love,
    And that's the mark I know you level at.   116
    Therefore each one betake him to his rest.
    Tomorrow all for speeding do their best.   [*Exeunt.*]   118

                    ❧

91 cast was cast   **96 addressed** accoutered   **97 Will** you will
98–100 I will . . . beds I won't allow any of you to beg off by saying
that the clanging of armor on the dance floor is too loud for the
ladies, since they love men as soldiers no less than as bed-partners.
(With a pun on "men in armor" and "men in ladies' arms.")
100.1 They dance (Dancing in armor gave courtly dancers opportunity to display strength and swordsmanship.)   **101 So . . . performed**
As I did well to suggest that you dance, so you have done it well.
103 breathing exercise   **105 trip** dance lightly. (With a suggestion of
"go astray.")   **106 measures** stately, formal dances. (With suggestion
of "stratagems in wooing.")   **108–9 that's . . . courtesy** i.e., that's as
much as to say you wish to claim inexperience in courtly ways as
your reason for asking not to dance with Thaisa (but I won't let you
get away with your denial).   **Unclasp** either (1) Time for you to stop
dancing, or (2) Remove your armor so that you can dance in more
courtly fashion.   **112 several** various   **116 level** aim   **118 speeding**
succeeding (as wooers)

[2.4]

Enter Helicanus and Escanes.

HELICANUS   No, Escanes, know this of me,
    Antiochus from incest lived not free;
    For which, the most high gods not minding longer   3
    To withhold the vengeance that they had in store
    Due to this heinous capital offense,
    Even in the height and pride of all his glory,
    When he was seated in a chariot of
    An inestimable value, and his daughter with him,
    A fire from heaven came and shriveled up
    Those bodies even to loathing; for they so stunk
    That all those eyes adored them ere their fall   11
    Scorn now their hand should give them burial.
ESCANES
    'Twas very strange.
HELICANUS   And yet but justice, for though
    This king were great, his greatness was no guard
    To bar heaven's shaft, but sin had his reward.   15
ESCANES   'Tis very true.

        Enter two or three Lords.

FIRST LORD
    See, not a man in private conference
    Or council has respect with him but he.   18
SECOND LORD
    It shall no longer grieve without reproof.   19
THIRD LORD
    And curst be he that will not second it.
FIRST LORD
    Follow me, then.—Lord Helicane, a word.
HELICANUS
    With me? And welcome. Happy day, my lords.
FIRST LORD
    Know that our griefs are risen to the top,   23
    And now at length they overflow their banks.
HELICANUS
    Your griefs? For what? Wrong not your prince you
        love.
FIRST LORD
    Wrong not yourself, then, noble Helicane;
    But if the Prince do live, let us salute him,
    Or know what ground's made happy by his breath.   28
    If in the world he live, we'll seek him out;
    If in his grave he rest, we'll find him there,
    And be resolved he lives to govern us,   31
    Or dead, give 's cause to mourn his funeral
    And leave us to our free election.
SECOND LORD
    Whose death's indeed the strongest in our censure;   34
    And knowing this kingdom is without a head—
    Like goodly buildings left without a roof   36

2.4. Location: Tyre. The Governor's house.
3 minding intending   **11 adored** that adored   **15 shaft** bolt, arrow.
his its   **18 respect** influence.   **he** i.e., Escanes.   **19 grieve without
reproof** cause grievance without (our) protest.   **23 griefs** grievances.
(Also in line 25.)   **28 ground** i.e., country.   **breath** i.e., presence.
31 resolved satisfied, assured   **34 Whose . . . censure** And indeed his
death is the likeliest probability in our judgment   **36 Like** as

Soon fall to ruin—your noble self,
That best know how to rule and how to reign,
We thus submit unto, our sovereign.
ALL   Live, noble Helicane!
HELICANUS
Try honor's cause; forbear your suffrages.   41
If that you love Prince Pericles, forbear.   42
Take I your wish, I leap into the seas,   43
Where's hourly trouble for a minute's ease.
A twelvemonth longer let me entreat you
To forbear the absence of your king,   46
If in which time expired he not return,
I shall with agèd patience bear your yoke.
But if I cannot win you to this love,   49
Go search like nobles, like noble subjects,
And in your search spend your adventurous worth;   51
Whom if you find, and win unto return,   52
You shall like diamonds sit about his crown.
FIRST LORD
To wisdom he's a fool that will not yield;
And since Lord Helicane enjoineth us,
We with our travels will endeavor.   56
HELICANUS
Then you love us, we you, and we'll clasp hands.
When peers thus knit, a kingdom ever stands.
                                        [*Exeunt.*]

❧

[2.5]

*Enter the King [Simonides] reading of a letter, at
one door; the Knights meet him.*

FIRST KNIGHT
Good morrow to the good Simonides.
SIMONIDES
Knights, from my daughter this I let you know,
That for this twelvemonth she'll not undertake
A married life.
Her reason to herself is only known,
Which from her by no means can I get.
SECOND KNIGHT
May we not get access to her, my lord?
SIMONIDES
Faith, by no means. She hath so strictly tied
Her to her chamber that 'tis impossible.
One twelve moons more she'll wear Diana's livery.   10
This by the eye of Cynthia hath she vowed,   11
And on her virgin honor will not break it.

THIRD KNIGHT
Loath to bid farewell, we take our leaves.
                                  [*Exeunt Knights.*]
SIMONIDES   So,
They are well dispatched. Now to my daughter's
    letter.
She tells me here she'll wed the stranger knight,
Or never more to view nor day nor light.   17
'Tis well, mistress. Your choice agrees with mine;
I like that well. Nay, how absolute she's in 't,   19
Not minding whether I dislike or no!
Well, I do commend her choice
And will no longer have it be delayed.
Soft, here he comes. I must dissemble it.

                    Enter Pericles.

PERICLES
All fortune to the good Simonides!
SIMONIDES
To you as much! Sir, I am beholding to you   25
For your sweet music this last night. I do
Protest my ears were never better fed
With such delightful pleasing harmony.
PERICLES
It is Your Grace's pleasure to commend,
Not my desert.
SIMONIDES   Sir, you are music's master.
PERICLES
The worst of all her scholars, my good lord.
SIMONIDES   Let me ask you one thing:
What do you think of my daughter, sir?
PERICLES   A most virtuous princess.
SIMONIDES   And she is fair too, is she not?
PERICLES
As a fair day in summer, wondrous fair.
SIMONIDES
Sir, my daughter thinks very well of you,
Ay, so well that you must be her master,
And she will be your scholar. Therefore look to it.
PERICLES
I am unworthy for her schoolmaster.
SIMONIDES
She thinks not so. Peruse this writing else.   41
                            [*He gives a letter.*]
PERICLES [*aside*]   What's here?
A letter, that she loves the knight of Tyre!
'Tis the King's subtlety to have my life.—   44
Oh, seek not to entrap me, gracious lord,
A stranger and distressèd gentleman,
That never aimed so high to love your daughter,   47
But bent all offices to honor her.   48
SIMONIDES
Thou hast bewitched my daughter, and thou art
A villain.
PERICLES   By the gods, I have not!

---

41 **Try . . . suffrages** i.e., Follow the honorable course; refrain from
choosing me in your *free election* (line 33).   42 **If that** If   43 **Take . . .
wish** If I should act on your wish   46 **forbear** put up with   49 **love**
act of loyal devotion   51 **spend . . . worth** use up your noble adventurous spirits   52 **Whom . . . return** i.e., and if you find Pericles during this year of probation and persuade him to return   56 **endeavor**
i.e., try to find him.
2.5. Location: Pentapolis. The palace.
10 **wear Diana's livery** continue to serve Diana, goddess of chastity.
11 **Cynthia** the moon goddess, equated with Diana

17 **nor day nor** either day or. (A double negative.)   19 **absolute**
unconditional, positive   25 **beholding** beholden   41 **else** i.e., if you
don't believe me.   44 **subtlety** trick   47 **to** as to   48 **bent all offices**
devoted all my service

Never did thought of mine levy offense,   52
Nor never did my actions yet commence
A deed might gain her love or your displeasure.   54

SIMONIDES
Traitor, thou liest!

PERICLES   Traitor?

SIMONIDES   Ay, traitor.

PERICLES
Even in his throat—unless it be the King—   56
That calls me traitor, I return the lie.   57

SIMONIDES [aside]
Now, by the gods, I do applaud his courage.

PERICLES
My actions are as noble as my thoughts,
That never relished of a base descent.   60
I came unto your court for honor's cause,
And not to be a rebel to her state;   62
And he that otherwise accounts of me,
This sword shall prove he's honor's enemy.

SIMONIDES   No?
Here comes my daughter. She can witness it.

Enter Thaisa.

PERICLES [to Thaisa]
Then, as you are as virtuous as fair,
Resolve your angry father if my tongue   68
Did e'er solicit, or my hand subscribe
To any syllable that made love to you.

THAISA
Why, sir, say if you had, who takes offense
At that would make me glad?   72

SIMONIDES
Yea, mistress, are you so peremptory?   73
(*Aside*) I am glad on't with all my heart.—
[*To her*] I'll tame you; I'll bring you in subjection!
Will you, not having my consent,
Bestow your love and your affections
Upon a stranger? (*Aside*) Who, for aught I know,
May be, nor can I think the contrary,
As great in blood as I myself.—
Therefore hear you, mistress: either frame   81
Your will to mine—and you, sir, hear you—
Either be ruled by me, or I'll make you—
Man and wife.
Nay, come, your hands and lips must seal it too.
And being joined, I'll thus your hopes destroy;
And for further grief—God give you joy!
What, are you both pleased?

THAISA   Yes, if you love me, sir.

PERICLES
Even as my life my blood that fosters it.   90

SIMONIDES   What, are you both agreed?

BOTH   Yes, if't please Your Majesty.

SIMONIDES
It pleaseth me so well that I will see you wed,
And then, with what haste you can, get you to bed.
                                Exeunt.

❖

[3. Chorus]

Enter Gower.

GOWER
Now sleep yslakèd hath the rout;   1
No din but snores the house about,
Made louder by the o'erfed breast
Of this most pompous marriage feast.   4
The cat, with eyne of burning coal,   5
Now couches 'fore the mouse's hole,
And crickets sing at the oven's mouth,
Are the blither for their drouth.   8
Hymen hath brought the bride to bed,   9
Where, by the loss of maidenhead,
A babe is molded. Be attent,   11
And time that is so briefly spent   12
With your fine fancies quaintly eche.   13
What's dumb in show I'll plain with speech.   14

[*Dumb Show.*]

*Enter Pericles and Simonides, at one door, with
attendants. A Messenger meets them, kneels, and
gives Pericles a letter. Pericles shows it Simonides;
the Lords kneel to him [Pericles]. Then enter
Thaisa with child, with Lychorida, a nurse. The
King shows her [Thaisa] the letter; she rejoices. She
and Pericles take leave of her father, and depart [with
Lychorida and their attendants. Then exeunt
Simonides and the rest.]*

By many a dern and painful perch   15
Of Pericles the careful search,
By the four opposing coigns   17
Which the world together joins,
Is made with all due diligence
That horse and sail and high expense
Can stead the quest. At last from Tyre,   21
Fame answering the most strange inquire,   22
To th' court of King Simonides
Are letters brought, the tenor these:
Antiochus and his daughter dead,
The men of Tyrus on the head
Of Helicanus would set on
The crown of Tyre, but he will none.
The mutiny he there hastes t'appease;

---

52 **levy** i.e., level, aim at; or undertake   54 **might** that might
56–7 **Even . . . lie** i.e., to any man except you as king I would give the
lie in the throat, the deepest kind of insult and challenge to a duel.
60 **relished of** showed any trace of   62 **her** i.e., honor's   68 **Resolve**
satisfy, explain to   72 **that** that which   73 **peremptory** willfully
determined.   81 **frame** accommodate, shape   90 **my life** i.e., my
life loves

3.0.
1 **yslakèd . . . rout** has laid to rest the whole assembly   4 **pompous**
ceremonial, splendid   5 **eyne** eyes   8 **Are . . . drouth** (and) are the
happier for their dryness.   9 **Hymen** god of marriage   11 **attent**
attentive   12–13 **And time . . . eche** and use your fine imaginations to
eke or stretch out the time that I can describe here only briefly.
14 **plain** make plain   15 **By many . . . perch** By many a dreary and
laborious measure of distance, many a weary mile   17 **opposing
coigns** opposite corners, compass points   21 **stead** assist   22 **Fame . . .
inquire** rumor answering inquiry into the most remote areas

Says to 'em, if King Pericles
Come not home in twice six moons,
He, obedient to their dooms,
Will take the crown. The sum of this, 32
Brought hither to Pentapolis,
Y-ravishèd the regions round, 35
And everyone with claps can sound, 36
"Our heir apparent is a king!
Who dreamt, who thought of such a thing?"
Brief, he must hence depart to Tyre. 39
His queen, with child, makes her desire—
Which who shall cross?—along to go. 41
Omit we all their dole and woe. 42
Lychorida, her nurse, she takes,
And so to sea. Their vessel shakes
On Neptune's billow; half the flood 45
Hath their keel cut. But Fortune's mood 46
Varies again; the grizzled North 47
Disgorges such a tempest forth
That, as a duck for life that dives,
So up and down the poor ship drives.
The lady shrieks, and well-a-near 51
Does fall in travail with her fear; 52
And what ensues in this fell storm 53
Shall for itself perform;
I nill relate; action may 55
Conveniently the rest convey,
Which might not what by me is told. 57
In your imagination hold 58
This stage the ship, upon whose deck
The sea-tossed Pericles appears to speak. [Exit.] 60

❧

[3.1]

Enter Pericles, a-shipboard.

PERICLES
Thou god of this great vast, rebuke these surges, 1
Which wash both heaven and hell! And thou that hast 2
Upon the winds command, bind them in brass,
Having called them from the deep! Oh, still
Thy deaf'ning, dreadful thunders; gently quench 5
Thy nimble, sulfurous flashes! [*Calling*] Oh, how,
  Lychorida,
How does my queen?—Thou stormest venomously;
Wilt thou spit all thyself? The seaman's whistle 8

Is as a whisper in the ears of death, 9
Unheard. [*Calling*] Lychorida!—Lucina, O 10
Divinest patroness and midwife gentle
To those that cry by night, convey thy deity
Aboard our dancing boat; make swift the pangs
Of my queen's travails!

Enter Lychorida [with an infant].

Now, Lychorida!
LYCHORIDA
Here is a thing too young for such a place,
Who, if it had conceit, would die, as I 16
Am like to do. Take in your arms this piece 17
Of your dead queen.
PERICLES   How? How, Lychorida?
LYCHORIDA
Patience, good sir. Do not assist the storm. 19
Here's all that is left living of your queen,
A little daughter. For the sake of it,
Be manly and take comfort. [*She gives him the child.*]
PERICLES   O you gods!
Why do you make us love your goodly gifts
And snatch them straight away? We here below
Recall not what we give, and therein may 25
Use honor with you.
LYCHORIDA   Patience, good sir, 26
Even for this charge.
PERICLES [*to the babe*]   Now, mild may be thy life! 27
For a more blustrous birth had never babe.
Quiet and gentle thy conditions! For 29
Thou art the rudeliest welcome to this world 30
That ever was prince's child. Happy what follows! 31
Thou hast as chiding a nativity 32
As fire, air, water, earth, and heaven can make
To herald thee from the womb. Poor inch of nature! 34
Even at the first thy loss is more than can 35
Thy portage quit, with all thou canst find here. 36
Now the good gods throw their best eyes upon't! 37

Enter two Sailors, [one the ship's Master].

MASTER   What courage, sir? God save you!
PERICLES
Courage enough. I do not fear the flaw; 39
It hath done to me the worst. Yet for the love
Of this poor infant, this fresh new seafarer,
I would it would be quiet.

9–10 Is . . . Unheard is no more audible than a whisper in the ears of a dead person.   10 Lucina goddess of childbirth (as in 1.1.9)   16 conceit understanding (of its precarious position)   17 like likely   19 assist i.e., with your sighs and tears   25 Recall take back. therein in that respect   26 Use . . . you i.e., challenge our right to be treated by you in like honorable fashion.   27 for this charge for the sake of this infant, this responsibility.   29 Quiet . . . conditions! May the conditions of your life be quiet and gentle!   30 the rudeliest welcome the most rudely welcomed   31 Happy what follows! May what is to come be happy for you!   32 chiding clamorous   34 Poor . . . nature! i.e., Poor tiny babe! (This half-line is from Wilkins's *Painful Adventures*.)   35–6 Even . . . here Your loss at birth (of your mother) exceeds anything that your life can offer by way of compensation. (*Portage* is the cargo that one has aboard at the start of a voyage, i.e., one's natural endowments; *quit* means "requite.")   37 best eyes most auspicious looks   39 flaw gust, squall

32 dooms judgments   35 Y-ravishèd delighted   36 can sound began to proclaim   39 Brief In short   41 cross thwart, deny   42 dole sorrow (of leave-taking)   45 On Neptune's billow on the foaming ocean   45–6 half . . . cut i.e., their vessel has completed half the voyage.   47 grizzled gray, grizzly.   North north wind   51 well-a-near alas   52 travail labor   53 fell fierce   55 nill will not   57 Which . . . told which action could not dramatize easily the story I've just told. 58 hold suppose   60 appears to speak appears and speaks.
3.1. Location: A ship at sea.
1 Thou god i.e., Neptune.   vast expanse (of sea)   2 thou i.e., Aeolus, god of the winds   5 Thy i.e., Jupiter, god of thunder's   8 Wilt . . . thyself? Are you going to spit all of yourself at us? (Said to the storm.)

MASTER [*calling*]   Slack the bowlines there!—Thou wilt not, 43
wilt thou? Blow, and split thyself. 44
SAILOR   But sea room, an the brine and cloudy billow 45
kiss the moon, I care not.
MASTER   Sir, your queen must overboard. The sea
works high, the wind is loud, and will not lie till the 48
ship be cleared of the dead.
PERICLES   That's your superstition.
MASTER   Pardon us, sir. With us at sea it hath been still 51
observed, and we are strong in custom. Therefore
briefly yield 'er, for she must overboard straight. 53
PERICLES   As you think meet. Most wretched queen!
LYCHORIDA   Here she lies, sir. 55
PERICLES
A terrible childbed hast thou had, my dear;
No light, no fire. Th'unfriendly elements
Forgot thee utterly, nor have I time
To give thee hallowed to thy grave, but straight
Must cast thee, scarcely coffined, in the ooze; 60
Where, for a monument upon thy bones, 61
And aye-remaining lamps, the belching whale 62
And humming water must o'erwhelm thy corpse,
Lying with simple shells. Oh, Lychorida,
Bid Nestor bring me spices, ink and paper, 65
My casket and my jewels; and bid Nicander
Bring me the satin coffin. Lay the babe 67
Upon the pillow. Hie thee, whiles I say 68
A priestly farewell to her. Suddenly, woman. 69
[*Exit Lychorida.*]
SAILOR   Sir, we have a chest beneath the hatches,
caulked and bitumed ready. 71
PERICLES
I thank thee. Mariner, say what coast is this?
MASTER   We are near Tarsus.
PERICLES   Thither, gentle mariner,
Alter thy course for Tyre. When canst thou reach it? 75
MASTER   By break of day, if the wind cease.
PERICLES   Oh, make for Tarsus!
There will I visit Cleon, for the babe
Cannot hold out to Tyrus. There I'll leave it
At careful nursing. Go thy ways, good mariner. 80
I'll bring the body presently.   *Exeunt.* 81

❖

43–4 Thou wilt . . . thyself (Addressed to the storm.)   **45 But sea room**
So long as we have room enough to maneuver without being driven on
the rocks.   **an** even if.   **cloudy billow** waves breaking into misty
spray, high as the clouds   **48 lie** subside   **51 still** always   **53 briefly**
quickly.   **straight** straightway. (Also in line 59.)   **55 Here she lies**
(Perhaps Lychorida reveals Thaisa's body by drawing the curtains of a
"discovery space" rearstage, or possibly the sailors have brought the
Queen's body onstage, but it may be that Pericles apostrophizes her in
her absence in lines 56–64. Line 55 could mean, "Here is what is left of
the Queen; here is her daughter.")   **60 ooze** muddy ocean bed   **61 for**
in place of   **62 aye-remaining** ever burning.   **belching** blowing,
spouting   **65 Nestor** (A servant who remains silent. So too with
Nicander in line 66.)   **67 coffin** coffer.   **68 Hie thee** Hasten   **69 Suddenly** Quickly   **69.1 *Exit Lychorida*** (Probably she takes the babe with
her.)   **71 bitumed** caulked with pitch   **75 Alter . . . Tyre** change your
course, which has been for Tyre.   **80 Go thy ways** i.e., About it
81 presently immediately.   **s.d. *Exeunt*** (If Thaisa's body was brought
onstage before line 55, it must presumably be carried off now.)

[3.2]

*Enter Lord Cerimon, with a Servant [and one or
more other persons who have suffered from the
storm].*

CERIMON   Philemon, ho!

Enter Philemon.

PHILEMON   Doth my lord call?
CERIMON
Get fire and meat for these poor men. 3
[*Exit Philemon.*]
'T has been a turbulent and stormy night.
SERVANT
I have been in many, but such a night as this
Till now I ne'er endured.
CERIMON [*to a Servant*]
Your master will be dead ere you return; 7
There's nothing can be ministered to nature 8
That can recover him. [*To another*] Give this to the
pothecary, 9
And tell me how it works.   [*Exeunt all but Cerimon.*]

Enter two Gentlemen.

FIRST GENTLEMAN   Good morrow.
SECOND GENTLEMAN   Good morrow to Your Lordship.
CERIMON
Gentlemen, why do you stir so early?
FIRST GENTLEMAN   Sir,
Our lodgings , standing bleak upon the sea, 15
Shook as the earth did quake; 16
The very principals did seem to rend 17
And all to topple. Pure surprise and fear 18
Made me to quit the house.
SECOND GENTLEMAN
That is the cause we trouble you so early;
'Tis not our husbandry. 21
CERIMON   Oh, you say well.
FIRST GENTLEMAN
But I much marvel that Your Lordship, having
Rich tire about you, should at these early hours 24
Shake off the golden slumber of repose.
'Tis most strange
Nature should be so conversant with pain, 27
Being thereto not compelled.
CERIMON   I hold it ever 28
Virtue and cunning were endowments greater 29
Than nobleness and riches. Careless heirs
May the two latter darken and expend, 31

3.2. Location: Ephesus. Cerimon's house.
3 meat food   **7 Your master** i.e., One of those who have suffered in
the storm and have been brought to Cerimon for help   **8 can . . .**
nature that can be administered in aid of nature   **9 recover** restore.
pothecary druggist   **15 bleak upon** exposed to   **16 as** as if   **17 prin-**
cipals main timbers of houses.   **rend** come apart   **18 all to topple**
(or "**to-topple**") topple completely.   **Pure** Sheer   **21 husbandry**
industrious habits, zeal for rising early.   **24 tire** accoutrement, furnishings   **27 pain** toil   **28 hold it ever** have always believed that
29 cunning knowledge, skill   **31 May . . . expend** may sully the gloss
of nobility and squander riches

But immortality attends the former,
Making a man a god. 'Tis known I ever
Have studied physic, through which secret art,   34
By turning o'er authorities, I have,   35
Together with my practice, made familiar
To me and to my aid the blest infusions   37
That dwells in vegetives, in metals, stones;   38
And can speak of the disturbances
That nature works, and of her cures; which doth give
me
A more content in course of true delight   41
Than to be thirsty after tottering honor,   42
Or tie my pleasure up in silken bags   43
To please the fool and death.   44

SECOND GENTLEMAN
Your Honor has through Ephesus poured forth   45
Your charity, and hundreds call themselves
Your creatures, who by you have been restored;   47
And not your knowledge, your personal pain, but
even   48
Your purse, still open, hath built Lord Cerimon   49
Such strong renown as time shall never—   50

Enter two or three [Servants] with a chest.

FIRST SERVANT
So, lift there.

CERIMON   What's that?

FIRST SERVANT   Sir, even now
Did the sea toss up upon our shore this chest.
'Tis of some wreck.

CERIMON   Set 't down. Let's look upon't.

SECOND GENTLEMAN
'Tis like a coffin, sir.

CERIMON   Whate'er it be,
'Tis wondrous heavy. Wrench it open straight.
If the sea's stomach be o'ercharged with gold,
'Tis a good constraint of fortune it belches upon us.   57

SECOND GENTLEMAN
'Tis so, my lord.

CERIMON   How close 'tis caulked and bitumed!   58
Did the sea cast it up?

FIRST SERVANT
I never saw so huge a billow, sir,
As tossed it upon shore.

CERIMON   Wrench it open.
Soft! It smells most sweetly in my sense.   62

SECOND GENTLEMAN   A delicate odor.

CERIMON
As ever hit my nostril. So, up with it.
                         [They open the chest.]
O you most potent gods! What's here? A corpse?

SECOND GENTLEMAN   Most strange!

CERIMON
Shrouded in cloth of state, balmed and entreasured   67
With full bags of spices! A passport too!   68
Apollo, perfect me in the characters!   69
                         [He reads from a scroll.]
"Here I give to understand,
If e'er this coffin drives aland,
I, King Pericles, have lost
This queen, worth all our mundane cost.   73
Who finds her, give her burying;   74
She was the daughter of a king.
Besides this treasure for a fee,
The gods requite his charity!"   77
If thou livest, Pericles, thou hast a heart
That even cracks for woe! This chanced tonight.   79

SECOND GENTLEMAN
Most likely, sir.

CERIMON   Nay, certainly tonight,
For look how fresh she looks. They were too rough   81
That threw her in the sea. Make a fire within.
Fetch hither all my boxes in my closet.
                         [Exit a Servant.]
Death may usurp on nature many hours,
And yet the fire of life kindle again
The o'erpressed spirits. I heard of an Egyptian
That had nine hours lain dead,
Who was by good appliance recovered.

Enter one with [boxes,] napkins, and fire.

Well said, well said! The fire and cloths.   89
The rough and woeful music that we have,   90
Cause it to sound, beseech you.
The vial once more. How thou stirr'st, thou block!   92
The music there! *[Music.]* I pray you, give her air.
Gentlemen, this queen will live. Nature awakes;
A warmth breathes out of her. She hath not been
Entranced above five hours. See how she 'gins   96
To blow into life's flower again!

FIRST GENTLEMAN   The heavens,   97
Through you, increase our wonder and sets up
Your fame forever.

CERIMON   She is alive! Behold,
Her eyelids, cases to those heavenly jewels
Which Pericles hath lost, begin to part

---

34 physic medicine **35–7 By . . . infusions** by turning the pages of learned texts, together with practical experiments, I have familiarized myself with and made available to my art the sacred medicinal properties **38 vegetives** herbs, plants **41 more** greater. **course** pursuit **42 tottering honor** wavering, unstable reputation **43 tie . . . bags** confine my pleasures to the hoarding of silken moneybags **44 the fool** anyone who is fool enough to trust in wealth. **death** (since all wealth ends in death). **45 through** throughout **47 Your creatures** i.e., people dependent for their very lives on your restoratives **48 not** not only. **pain** labor **49 still** always **50.1 two or three** (One of these may well be Philemon or at least the same actor; also at line 88.1). **57 'Tis . . . us** it's a lucky thing that it disgorges this chest upon our shore. **58 close** tightly. **bitumed** (See 3.1.71.) **62 Soft!** Gently, wait a minute!

67 cloth of state fabric fit for royalty; literally, a canopy for a chair of state. **balmed** anointed. **entreasured** laid up like valuables in a treasury **68 passport** document identifying the bearer **69 Apollo** god of eloquence and of medicine. **perfect . . . characters** enable me to read the writing. **73 mundane cost** worldly wealth. **74 Who** Whoever **77 his** the finder's **79 chanced tonight** happened last night. **81 rough** i.e., hasty **89 Well said** Well done **90 rough and woeful** i.e., discordant in such a way as to stimulate and awaken **92 vial** (The Quarto text reads "Violl," appropriate perhaps to the music just ordered, but it could mean a *vial* of medicine.) **How thou stirr'st** i.e., How slow you are. **block** blockhead. **96 Entranced** unconscious **97 blow** bloom

Their fringes of bright gold. The diamonds
Of a most praisèd water doth appear,   103
To make the world twice rich.—Live, and make
Us weep to hear your fate, fair creature,
Rare as you seem to be.   *She moves.*
THAISA   O dear Diana,   106
Where am I? Where's my lord? What world is this?
SECOND GENTLEMAN   Is not this strange?
FIRST GENTLEMAN   Most rare.
CERIMON   Hush, my gentle neighbors!
Lend me your hands. To the next chamber bear her.
Get linen. Now this matter must be looked to,   112
For her relapse is mortal. Come, come!   113
And Aesculapius guide us!   114
                    They carry her away. Exeunt omnes.

❖

[3.3]

*Enter Pericles at Tarsus, with Cleon and Dionyza
[and Lychorida with Marina in her arms].*

PERICLES
Most honored Cleon, I must needs be gone.
My twelve months are expired, and Tyrus stands   2
In a litigious peace. You and your lady   3
Take from my heart all thankfulness! The gods   4
Make up the rest upon you!   5
CLEON
Your shakes of fortune, though they haunt you
    mortally,   6
Yet glance full wonderingly on us.   7
DIONYZA
Oh, your sweet queen! That the strict fates had pleased
You had brought her hither, to have blessed mine eyes
    with her!
PERICLES
We cannot but obey the powers above us.
Could I rage and roar as doth the sea
She lies in, yet the end must be as 'tis.
My gentle babe Marina,
Whom, for she was born at sea, I have named so,   14
Here I charge your charity withal,   15
Leaving her the infant of your care,
Beseeching you to give her princely training,
That she may be mannered as she is born.   18
CLEON   Fear not, my lord, but think
Your Grace, that fed my country with your corn,
For which the people's prayers still fall upon you,

Must in your child be thought on. If neglection   22
Should therein make me vile, the common body,   23
By you relieved, would force me to my duty.
But if to that my nature need a spur,   25
The gods revenge it upon me and mine
To the end of generation!
PERICLES   I believe you.   27
Your honor and your goodness teach me to't   28
Without your vows. Till she be married, madam,
By bright Diana, whom we honor, all
Unscissored shall this hair of mine remain,
Though I show ill in't. So I take my leave.   32
Good madam, make me blessèd in your care   33
In bringing up my child.
DIONYZA   I have one myself,
Who shall not be more dear to my respect   35
Than yours, my lord.
PERICLES   Madam, my thanks and prayers.
CLEON
We'll bring Your Grace e'en to the edge o'th' shore,
Then give you up to the masked Neptune and   38
The gentlest winds of heaven.
PERICLES
I will embrace your offer.—Come, dearest madam.—
Oh, no tears, Lychorida, no tears.
Look to your little mistress, on whose grace   42
You may depend hereafter.—Come, my lord.
                                    [Exeunt.]

❖

[3.4]

Enter Cerimon and Thaisa.

CERIMON
Madam, this letter and some certain jewels
Lay with you in your coffer, which are
At your command. Know you the character?   3
                    [He shows her the letter.]
THAISA
It is my lord's. That I was shipped at sea
I well remember, even on my eaning time;   5
But whether there delivered, by the holy gods,   6
I cannot rightly say. But since King Pericles,
My wedded lord, I ne'er shall see again,
A vestal livery will I take me to,   9
And never more have joy.
CERIMON
Madam, if this you purpose as ye speak,

---

103 water luster and clearness. (Used about precious stones.)
106 Rare of rare beauty and excellence   **112 Now** Right now   **113 is
mortal** would be fatal.   **114 Aesculapius** god of healing
3.3. Location: Tarsus. Cleon's (the Governor's) house.
2 twelve months (Pericles was given a year to return to Tyre; see
3.0.30–3.)   **3 litigious** disturbed by disputes (especially legal)   **4 Take**
receive   **4–5 The gods . . . you!** May the gods requite your goodness
as fully as it deserves (of which my gratitude can supply only part)!
6–7 Your . . . on us Your violent shocks of fortune, though they prey
upon you with deadly intent, fill us, too, with amazement and sor-
row.   **14 for** since   **15 charge** burden.   **withal** with   **18 mannered . . .
born** taught manners and graces to accord with her high birth.

22 Must . . . on must be recompensed by our kind treatment of
Marina.   **neglection** neglect   **23 common body** common people
25 But . . . spur But if my own nature needed to be prodded to do
what the commoners will insist on in any case   **27 of generation** of
my line of descent or of the human race.   **28 to't** to do so   **32 show
ill** look unattractive. (The Quarto's "shew will" could mean "display
willfulness.")   **33 blessèd in your care** fortunate in having the care
you provide   **35 to my respect** in my regard   **38 masked** i.e., deceivingly calm   **42 grace** favor
3.4. Location: Ephesus. Cerimon's house.
3 character handwriting.   **5 eaning** time of delivery
6 whether there delivered whether I gave birth there   **9 A vestal livery** garments of chastity, nun's habit

Diana's temple is not distant far,
Where you may abide till your date expire. 13
Moreover, if you please, a niece of mine
Shall there attend you.

THAISA
My recompense is thanks, that's all;
Yet my good will is great, though the gift small.

Exeunt.

❧

[4. Chorus]

Enter Gower.

GOWER
Imagine Pericles arrived at Tyre,
Welcomed and settled to his own desire. 2
His woeful queen we leave at Ephesus,
Unto Diana there 's a votaress. 4
Now to Marina bend your mind,
Whom our fast-growing scene must find
At Tarsus, and by Cleon trained
In music, letters, who hath gained
Of education all the grace,
Which makes high both the art and place 10
Of general wonder. But, alack, 11
That monster Envy, oft the wrack 12
Of earnèd praise, Marina's life
Seeks to take off by treason's knife. 14
And in this kind hath our Cleon 15
One daughter, and a wench full grown,
Even ripe for marriage rite. This maid
Hight Philoten, and it is said 18
For certain in our story, she
Would ever with Marina be.
Be't when she weaved the sleided silk 21
With fingers long, small, white as milk; 22
Or when she would with sharp needle wound
The cambric, which she made more sound 24
By hurting it; or when to th' lute
She sung, and made the night bird mute, 26
That still records with moan; or when 27
She would with rich and constant pen 28
Vail to her mistress Dian; still 29
This Philoten contends in skill
With absolute Marina. So 31
With the dove of Paphos might the crow
Vie feathers white. Marina gets 33

All praises, which are paid as debts, 34
And not as given. This so darks 35
In Philoten all graceful marks
That Cleon's wife, with envy rare, 37
A present murder does prepare 38
For good Marina, that her daughter
Might stand peerless by this slaughter. 40
The sooner her vile thoughts to stead, 41
Lychorida, our nurse, is dead;
And cursèd Dionyza hath
The pregnant instrument of wrath 44
Prest for this blow. The unborn event 45
I do commend to your content; 46
Only I carry wingèd Time
Post on the lame feet of my rhyme, 48
Which never could I so convey
Unless your thoughts went on my way.
Dionyza does appear,
With Leonine, a murderer. *Exit.*

❧

[4.1]

Enter Dionyza with Leonine.

DIONYZA
Thy oath remember. Thou hast sworn to do't.
'Tis but a blow, which never shall be known.
Thou canst not do a thing in the world so soon
To yield thee so much profit. Let not conscience, 4
Which is but cold, inflaming love i'thy bosom, 5
Inflame too nicely; nor let pity, which 6
Even women have cast off, melt thee, but be 7
A soldier to thy purpose.

LEONINE   I will do't;
But yet she is a goodly creature.

DIONYZA
The fitter, then, the gods should have her.
Here she comes, weeping for her only nurse's death. 11
Thou art resolved?

LEONINE   I am resolved.

Enter Marina, with a basket of flowers.

MARINA
No, I will rob Tellus of her weed 14
To strew thy green with flowers. The yellows, blues, 15
The purple violets, and marigolds
Shall as a carpet hang upon thy grave
While summer days doth last. Ay me, poor maid,
Born in a tempest when my mother died,

13 **date** term of life
4.0.
2 to in accordance with   **4 there 's** there as, or there (she) is
10–11 Which . . . wonder which raises to an exalted level both her art
(in music and literature) and the general wonderment it occasions.
12 wrack ruin, destruction   **14 treason's** treachery's   **15 kind** manner   **18 Hight** was called   **21 sleided** divided into filaments for
embroidery   **22 small** slender   **24 cambric** a fine white linen.   **more
sound** more whole, with its embroidery   **26 night bird** nightingale
with its sad song (*moan,* line 27)   **27 still records with moan** incessantly tells her story in plaintive song   **28 constant** fixedly loyal.
pen (Used in writing hymns of praise.)   **29 Vail** do homage
31 absolute free from any imperfection   **31–3 So . . . white** With
equal ill success might the crow attempt to outdo the white plumage
of Venus's doves. (*Paphos* is a city in Cyprus sacred to Venus.)

34 as debts as owed to her   **35 given** i.e., gratuitous gifts, compliments.   **darks** darkens, obscures   **37 rare** keen   **38 present** immediate   **40 by** by means of   **41 stead** assist   **44 pregnant** willing,
45 Prest prepared.   **event** outcome   **46 content** pleasure (in watching)   **48 Post** swiftly
4.1. Location: Tarsus. An open place near the seashore.
4–6 Let . . . nicely Do not let conscience, thus far unawakened,
inflame your heart with love of goodness and scruples. (*Too nicely*
means "overscrupulously.")   **6–7 which . . . off** i.e., which even some
women, such as I, have cast off   **11 only nurse's** i.e., Lychorida's.
(*Only* means "one and only.")   **14 Tellus** goddess of the earth.
weed garment (here, flowers)   **15 green** i.e., grass-covered grave

This world to me is a lasting storm
Whirring me from my friends.   21
DIONYZA
How now, Marina? Why do you keep alone?   22
How chance my daughter is not with you?   23
Do not consume your blood with sorrowing;   24
Have you a nurse of me. Lord, how your favor's   25
Changed with this unprofitable woe!
Come, give me your flowers. On the sea margent   27
Walk with Leonine; the air is quick there,   28
And it pierces and sharpens the stomach.   29
Come, Leonine, take her by the arm, walk with her.
MARINA   No, I pray you,
I'll not bereave you of your servant.
DIONYZA   Come, come,
I love the King your father and yourself
With more than foreign heart. We every day   35
Expect him here. When he shall come and find
Our paragon to all reports thus blasted,   37
He will repent the breadth of his great voyage,
Blame both my lord and me that we have taken
No care to your best courses. Go, I pray you,   40
Walk, and be cheerful once again. Reserve   41
That excellent complexion which did steal
The eyes of young and old. Care not for me;   43
I can go home alone.
MARINA   Well, I will go,
But yet I have no desire to it.
DIONYZA
Come, come, I know 'tis good for you.—
Walk half an hour, Leonine, at the least.
Remember what I have said.
LEONINE   I warrant you, madam.   48
DIONYZA
I'll leave you, my sweet lady, for a while.
Pray walk softly; do not heat your blood.   50
What, I must have a care of you.
MARINA   My thanks, sweet madam.   [Exit Dionyza.]
Is this wind westerly that blows?
LEONINE   Southwest.
MARINA
When I was born, the wind was north.
LEONINE   Was't so?
MARINA
My father, as Nurse says, did never fear,
But cried "Good seamen!" to the sailors,
Galling his kingly hands, haling ropes,   57
And, clasping to the mast, endured a sea
That almost burst the deck.
LEONINE   When was this?

MARINA   When I was born.
Never was waves nor wind more violent;
And from the ladder-tackle washes off   63
A canvas-climber. "Ha!" says one, "wolt out?"   64
And with a dropping industry they skip   65
From stem to stern. The boatswain whistles, and
The master calls and trebles their confusion.
LEONINE   Come, say your prayers.
MARINA   What mean you?
LEONINE
If you require a little space for prayer,
I grant it. Pray, but be not tedious, for   71
The gods are quick of ear, and I am sworn
To do my work with haste.
MARINA   Why will you kill me?
LEONINE   To satisfy my lady.
MARINA   Why would she have me killed?
Now, as I can remember, by my troth,   77
I never did her hurt in all my life.
I never spake bad word nor did ill turn
To any living creature. Believe me, la,
I never killed a mouse nor hurt a fly.
I trod upon a worm against my will,
But I wept for 't. How have I offended,
Wherein my death might yield her any profit,
Or my life imply her any danger?
LEONINE   My commission
Is not to reason of the deed, but do't.
MARINA
You will not do't for all the world, I hope.
You are well favored, and your looks foreshow   89
You have a gentle heart. I saw you lately,
When you caught hurt in parting two that fought;   91
Good sooth, it showed well in you. Do so now.   92
Your lady seeks my life; come you between
And save poor me, the weaker.
LEONINE   I am sworn,
And will dispatch.   [He seizes her.]

                    Enter Pirates.

FIRST PIRATE   Hold, villain!   [Leonine runs away.]
SECOND PIRATE   A prize, a prize!
THIRD PIRATE   Half-part, mates, half-part. Come, let's   98
have her aboard suddenly.   99
                    Exeunt [Pirates with Marina].

                    Enter Leonine.

LEONINE
These roguing thieves serve the great pirate Valdes,   100
And they have seized Marina. Let her go.
There's no hope she will return. I'll swear she's dead
And thrown into the sea. But I'll see further;

---

21 Whirring whirling, blowing   22 keep remain   23 How chance
How does it happen that   24 with sorrowing i.e., with sighs, thought
to cost the heart its blood   25 Have . . . me i.e., Take me as your
nurse.   favor's face is, appearance is   27 margent margin, shore
28 quick fresh, invigorating   29 stomach appetite.   35 more . . .
heart i.e., as though we were related by blood.   37 Our . . . blasted
the person whom all regard as a paragon of beauty thus withered
40 courses interests.   41 Reserve Preserve, maintain   43 Care not
for me Don't concern yourself about me   48 warrant promise
50 softly gently, slowly   57 Galling chafing, blistering.   haling
hauling on

63 ladder-tackle rope ladder in the ship's rigging   64 "wolt out?" so
you want to get out? (Addressed perhaps as a cruel jest to the canvas-
climber or sailor in the rigging who is washed overboard.)   65 with
. . . industry dripping wet as they labor   71 tedious long-winded
77 as as far as   89 well favored pleasant-looking.   foreshow proclaim   91 caught hurt received an injury   92 Good sooth (A mild
oath.)   98 Half-part Let's share   99 suddenly immediately.
100 roguing roving about like rogues

Perhaps they will but please themselves upon her,   104
Not carry her aboard. If she remain,
Whom they have ravished must by me be slain. *Exit.*

❖

[4.2]

Enter the three bawds [Pander, Bawd, and Bolt].

PANDER   Bolt!

BOLT   Sir?

PANDER   Search the market narrowly. Mytilene is full of   3
gallants. We lost too much money this mart by being   4
too wenchless.

BAWD   We were never so much out of creatures. We   6
have but poor three, and they can do no more than
they can do; and they with continual action are even
as good as rotten.   9

PANDER   Therefore let's have fresh ones, whate'er we
pay for them. If there be not a conscience to be used in   11
every trade, we shall never prosper.

BAWD   Thou say'st true. 'Tis not our bringing up of poor   13
bastards—as, I think, I have brought up some   14
eleven—

BOLT   Ay, to eleven, and brought them down again.   16
But shall I search the market?

BAWD   What else, man? The stuff we have, a strong   18
wind will blow it to pieces, they are so pitifully
sodden.   20

PANDER   Thou sayest true. There's two unwholesome,   21
o' conscience. The poor Transylvanian is dead that lay   22
with the little baggage.   23

BOLT   Ay, she quickly pooped him. She made him   24
roast meat for worms. But I'll go search the market.   25

Exit.

PANDER   Three or four thousand chequins were as   26
pretty a proportion to live quietly, and so give over.   27

BAWD   Why to give over, I pray you? Is it a shame to get   28
when we are old?

PANDER   Oh, our credit comes not in like the commodity,   30
nor the commodity wages not with the danger. There-   31
fore, if in our youths we could pick up some pretty

estate, 'twere not amiss to keep our door hatched. Be-   33
sides, the sore terms we stand upon with the gods will
be strong with us for giving o'er.   35

BAWD   Come, other sorts offend as well as we.   36

PANDER   As well as we? Ay, and better too; we offend   37
worse. Neither is our profession any trade; it's no   38
calling. But here comes Bolt.   39

Enter Bolt with the Pirates and Marina.

BOLT   Come your ways, my masters. You say she's a   40
virgin?

FIRST PIRATE   Oh, sir, we doubt it not.

BOLT   Master, I have gone through for this piece you   43
see. If you like her, so; if not, I have lost my earnest.   44

BAWD   Bolt, has she any qualities?

BOLT   She has a good face, speaks well, and has excellent good clothes. There's no farther necessity of qualities can make her be refused.   48

BAWD   What's her price, Bolt?

BOLT   I cannot be bated one doit of a thousand pieces.   50

PANDER   Well, follow me, my masters; you shall have
your money presently. Wife, take her in. Instruct her   52
what she has to do, that she may not be raw in her   53
entertainment.   *[Exeunt Pander and Pirates.]*   54

BAWD   Bolt, take you the marks of her, the color of her
hair, complexion, height, her age, with warrant of her
virginity, and cry, "He that will give most shall have
her first." Such a maidenhead were no cheap thing, if
men were as they have been. Get this done as I
command you.

BOLT   Performance shall follow.   *Exit.*

MARINA
Alack that Leonine was so slack, so slow!
He should have struck, not spoke; or that these pirates,
Not enough barbarous, had not o'erboard thrown me
For to seek my mother!

BAWD   Why lament you, pretty one?

MARINA   That I am pretty.

BAWD   Come, the gods have done their part in you.

MARINA   I accuse them not.

BAWD   You are light into my hands, where you are like   70
to live.   71

---

104 **please . . . her** take their sexual pleasure with her
4.2. Location: Mytilene, on the island of Lesbos. A brothel.
0.1 *bawds* (Used for either sex to mean dealers in prostitution.)   *Bolt*
(The name phallically suggests a shaft, projectile, or arrow.)   3 **narrowly** carefully.   4 **this mart** at the last market time   6 **creatures** i.e.,
prostitutes.   9 **rotten** i.e., with venereal disease.   11 **If . . . used** i.e., If
one does not conscientiously offer good quality   13–14 'Tis . . . bastards** i.e., Raising bastard children doesn't bring us enough wealth.
(As Bolt points out, the children are raised only to be introduced into
prostitution.)   16 **to eleven** to the age of eleven.   **brought . . . again**
i.e., lowered them into debauchery. (With a pun on going to bed with
customers.)   18 **stuff** goods   20 **sodden** boiled (by being treated in
the sweating tub for venereal disease).   21 **unwholesome** who are
diseased   22 **o 'conscience** i.e., I must admit.   **Transylvanian** a customer from Transylvania (in modern Romania and Hungary)
23 **baggage** whore.   24 **pooped him** i.e., did for him, by infecting
him with venereal disease   24–5 **She . . . worms** She made a corpse
of him, a feast for worms.   26 **chequins** gold coins   26–7 **were . . .
over** would be a fine portion to live on quietly in retirement.   28 **get**
earn money   30–1 **our . . . danger** i.e., our reputation does not keep
pace with our profit, and such profits as we make aren't worth the
risk (of dealing in whores, disease, etc.).

33 **estate** savings for a rainy day.   **'twere . . . hatched** it wouldn't be a
bad idea to close our door to business. (*Hatched* doors, common in
brothels, were divided at the middle so that business could be conducted through the upper door.)   35 **strong** strong inducement
36 **sorts** kinds of people.   **as well as we** in addition to ourselves.
37–8 **Ay . . . worse** (The Pander plays with the meanings of *better* and
worse: we bawds and panders may offend *worse* in the sense of profiting from degrading sexual activity, whereas the better-born, no less
sinful, may be said to offend *better* because of their higher social
standing.)   38–9 **it's no calling** i.e., it is not a recognized and ostensibly legitimate vocation (even if it is, as the saying goes, the oldest of
the professions).   40 **Come . . . masters** Come along, my good fellows.   43 **I . . . piece** I have made the best deal I could for this piece
of flesh   44 **so** well and good.   **earnest** earnest money, deposit.
48 **can** i.e., the lack of which can   50 **I . . . pieces** i.e., They won't settle for anything less than a thousand gold coins (each worth about a
pound).   52 **presently** immediately.   53 **raw** inexperienced
54 **entertainment** servicing of customers.   70 **are light** have chanced
to light. (With a pun on becoming a *light* or immoral woman.)   **like**
likely   71 **live** remain.

MARINA   The more my fault,   72
    To scape his hands where I was like to die.
BAWD   Ay, and you shall live in pleasure.
MARINA   No.
BAWD   Yes, indeed shall you, and taste gentlemen of all
    fashions. You shall fare well; you shall have the dif- 77
    ference of all complexions. What do you stop your ears? 78
MARINA   Are you a woman?
BAWD   What would you have me be, an I be not a 80
    woman?
MARINA   An honest woman, or not a woman. 82
BAWD   Marry, whip the gosling! I think I shall have 83
    something to do with you. Come, you're a young fool- 84
    ish sapling and must be bowed as I would have you.
MARINA   The gods defend me!
BAWD   If it please the gods to defend you by men, then 87
    men must comfort you, men must feed you, men must
    stir you up. Bolt's returned.

[Enter Bolt.]

    Now, sir, hast thou cried her through the market? 90
BOLT   I have cried her almost to the number of her 91
    hairs; I have drawn her picture with my voice. 92
BAWD   And, I prithee, tell me how dost thou find the
    inclination of the people, especially of the younger
    sort?
BOLT   Faith, they listened to me as they would have
    hearkened to their father's testament. There was a 97
    Spaniard's mouth watered an he went to bed to her 98
    very description.
BAWD   We shall have him here tomorrow with his best
    ruff on. 101
BOLT   Tonight, tonight. But, mistress, do you know
    the French knight that cowers i'th' hams? 103
BAWD   Who, Monsieur Verolles? 104
BOLT   Ay, he. He offered to cut a caper at the procla- 105
    mation, but he made a groan at it, and swore he
    would see her tomorrow.
BAWD   Well, well, as for him, he brought his disease 108
    hither; here he does but repair it. I know he will come 109
    in our shadow, to scatter his crowns in the sun. 110
BOLT   Well, if we had of every nation a traveler, we
    should lodge them with this sign. 112

BAWD   *[to Marina]* Pray you, come hither awhile. You
    have fortunes coming upon you. Mark me: you must
    seem to do that fearfully which you commit willingly,
    despise profit where you have most gain. To weep 116
    that you live as ye do makes pity in your lovers; sel-
    dom but that pity begets you a good opinion, and that
    opinion a mere profit. 119
MARINA   I understand you not.
BOLT   Oh, take her home, mistress, take her home! 121
    These blushes of hers must be quenched with some
    present practice.
BAWD   Thou sayest true, i'faith, so they must, for your 124
    bride goes to that with shame which is her way to go 125
    with warrant. 126
BOLT   Faith, some do and some do not. But, mistress,
    if I have bargained for the joint— 128
BAWD   Thou mayst cut a morsel off the spit. 129
BOLT   I may so.
BAWD   Who should deny it?—Come, young one, I like
    the manner of your garments well.
BOLT   Ay, by my faith, they shall not be changed 133
    yet. 134
BAWD   Bolt, spend thou that in the town. *[She gives
    money.]* Report what a sojourner we have; you'll lose
    nothing by custom. When nature framed this piece, 137
    she meant thee a good turn; therefore say what a para- 138
    gon she is, and thou hast the harvest out of thine own
    report.
BOLT   I warrant you, mistress, thunder shall not so
    awake the beds of eels as my giving out her beauty 142
    stirs up the lewdly inclined. I'll bring home some
    tonight.   *[Exit.]*
BAWD   Come your ways. Follow me. 145
MARINA
    If fires be hot, knives sharp, or waters deep,
    Untied I still my virgin knot will keep.
    Diana aid my purpose! 148
BAWD   What have we to do with Diana? Pray you, will
    you go with us?   *Exeunt.*

❧

[4.3]

Enter Cleon and Dionyza.

DIONYZA
    Why, are you foolish? Can it be undone?

---

72 fault misfortune   **77–8 difference . . . complexions** variety of men of all races and temperaments.   **78 What** Why   **80 an** if   **82 honest** chaste   **83 whip the gosling!** i.e., the devil take this goose of a young whore!   **84 something to do** i.e., my hands full   **87 by men** by way of men   **90 cried** proclaimed, advertised   **91–2 almost . . . hairs** almost to the point of numbering the hairs of her head   **97 testament** will.   **98 an** as if   **101 ruff** (The large starched collars worn by Spanish gentlemen were a matter of jest to the English.)   **103 cowers i'th' hams** i.e., crouches, showing a weakness typical of venereal disease. **104 Verolles** (From the French *vérole*, "pox," "syphilis.")   **105 offered** tried, made as if.   **cut a caper** leap up and click his heels together   **108–9 brought . . . hither** was already diseased when he came. (Syphilis was popularly known in England as "the French disease.")   **109 repair** (1) return with (2) mend, renew   **110 in our shadow** i.e., under our roof.   **crowns in the sun** i.e., gold coins, known as "crowns of the sun," with perhaps the suggestion of squandering gold on bright beauty. (A French crown also plays on the idea of a bald head resulting from venereal disease.)   **112 lodge . . . sign** i.e., attract them to lodge here by means of Marina's picture, metaphorically hung out as though it were a shop sign.

116 despise and must seem to despise   **119 mere** utter, absolute **121 take her home** talk plainly, i.e., be direct with her, or, take her inside **124–5 your bride** even your ordinary bride   **125 that** i.e., first sex **126 with warrant** with lawful sanction.   **128 joint** roast of meat **129 off the spit** while it is still roasting on the spit, before it is served up to customers. (Bolt is bargaining for the right to take Marina's chastity.) **133–4 they shall . . . yet** (Marina's clothes proclaim her to be a wellborn virgin; she does not wear a prostitute's distinctive dress.)   **137 by custom** by increasing our trade (since you'll get a commission).   **piece** (1) masterpiece (2) piece of woman's flesh, as in line 43   **138 a good turn** (1) a favor (2) an occasion for sex, a *piece* in the sexual sense   **142 beds of eels** (Seager, *Natural History,* p. 98, quotes *Hortus Sanitatus*: the eel "is disturbed by the sound of thunder." Used here with possible bawdy connotation; eels are often associated with the penis.)   **145 Come your ways** Come along.   **148 Diana** goddess of chastity, as in 2.5.10 **4.3. Location: Tarsus. Cleon's (the Governor's) house.**

CLEON

    Oh, Dionyza, such a piece of slaughter
    The sun and moon ne'er looked upon!

DIONYZA

    I think you'll turn a child again.

CLEON

    Were I chief lord of all this spacious world,
    I'd give it to undo the deed. A lady   6
    Much less in blood than virtue, yet a princess   7
    To equal any single crown o'th'earth
    I'th' justice of compare! O villain Leonine!   9
    Whom thou hast poisoned too.
    If thou hadst drunk to him, 't had been a kindness   11
    Becoming well thy fact. What canst thou say   12
    When noble Pericles shall demand his child?

DIONYZA

    That she is dead. Nurses are not the Fates;
    To foster is not ever to preserve.   15
    She died at night; I'll say so. Who can cross it,   16
    Unless you play the impious innocent   17
    And, for an honest attribute, cry out,   18
    "She died by foul play"?

CLEON   Oh, go to. Well, well,   19
    Of all the faults beneath the heavens, the gods
    Do like this worst.

DIONYZA   Be one of those that thinks
    The petty wrens of Tarsus will fly hence
    And open this to Pericles. I do shame   23
    To think of what a noble strain you are,
    And of how coward a spirit.

CLEON   To such proceeding   25
    Whoever but his approbation added,   26
    Though not his prime consent, he did not flow   27
    From honorable courses.

DIONYZA   Be it so, then.   28
    Yet none does know but you how she came dead,
    Nor none can know, Leonine being gone.
    She did distain my child and stood between   31
    Her and her fortunes. None would look on her,
    But cast their gazes on Marina's face,
    Whilst ours was blurted at and held a malkin   34
    Not worth the time of day. It pierced me through;
    And though you call my course unnatural,   36
    You not your child well loving, yet I find   37
    It greets me as an enterprise of kindness   38

    Performed to your sole daughter.

CLEON   Heavens forgive it!

DIONYZA   And as for Pericles,
    What should he say? We wept after her hearse,
    And yet we mourn. Her monument   43
    Is almost finished, and her epitaphs
    In glitt'ring golden characters express
    A general praise to her and care in us
    At whose expense 'tis done.

CLEON   Thou art like the harpy,   47
    Which, to betray, dost, with thine angel's face,
    Seize with thine eagle's talons.

DIONYZA

    You're like one that superstitiously   50
    Do swear to th' gods that winter kills the flies.   51
    But yet I know you'll do as I advise.   [*Exeunt.*]

❧

[4.4]

[*Enter Gower, before the monument of Marina at Tarsus.*]

GOWER

    Thus time we waste and long leagues make short,   1
    Sail seas in cockles, have and wish but for't,   2
    Making to take your imagination   3
    From bourn to bourn, region to region.   4
    By you being pardoned, we commit no crime
    To use one language in each several clime   6
    Where our scenes seem to live. I do beseech you
    To learn of me, who stand i'th' gaps to teach you,   8
    The stages of our story. Pericles
    Is now again thwarting the wayward seas,   10
    Attended on by many a lord and knight,
    To see his daughter, all his life's delight.
    Old Helicanus goes along. Behind
    Is left to govern, if you bear in mind,
    Old Escanes, whom Helicanus late   15
    Advanced in time to great and high estate.
    Well-sailing ships and bounteous winds have brought
    This King to Tarsus—think his pilot thought;   18
    So with his steerage shall your thoughts grow on—   19
    To fetch his daughter home, who first is gone.   20

6 lady i.e., Marina   **7 Much . . . virtue** i.e., noble in birth but even more so in virtue   **9 I'th' . . . compare** if justly compared.   **11 drunk to him** i.e., drunk poison yourself while giving him poison   **12 Becoming . . . fact** well suited to the horror of your crime.   **15 To . . . preserve** i.e., one can foster life, but one cannot preserve it forever; that is in the hands of the Fates.   **16 cross** contradict   **17 play . . . innocent** impiously play the innocent. (*Impious* suggests "undutiful to me, your wife.")   **18 for** to gain   **attribute** reputation   **19 go to** (A term of reproach or anger.)   **23 open** reveal. (In ancient times, birds were thought to reveal murders.)   **25–8 To . . . courses** Anyone who would merely assent to such a proceeding, let alone conspiring in the first place, would betray his dishonorable origins.   **31 distain** tarnish by comparison   **34 blurted at** scorned (by means of a derisive noise made with the lips).   **malkin** slut   **36–8 And though . . . kindness** and though you, who do not know how to love your daughter properly, call my course unnatural, my deed strikes me as an enterprise of natural affection

43 yet still   **47 harpy** monstrous bird with the face and torso of a woman   **50–1 You're . . . flies** i.e., You are one of those bleeding hearts who protest against the harsh necessity of death; you'd appeal to the gods to take pity on flies that die in the wintertime.
4.4. Location: Tarsus.
0.1 the monument of Marina (Perhaps Gower reveals this monument by drawing a curtain hung before the "discovery space" here, or perhaps Cleon draws back the curtain at line 22.1)   **1 waste** i.e., pass quickly over   **2 cockles** scallop shells, or, small boats. (Supernatural creatures sometimes sail in this fashion. Gower is alluding to the imaginary crossing of the seas between scenes of the play.)   **have . . . for't** have something if we but wish it   **3 Making** proceeding   **4 bourn** frontier   **6 several clime** different region   **8 stand i'th' gaps** bridge the gaps (of time and space between scenes)   **10 thwarting** crossing.   **wayward** unruly, hostile   **15 late** recently   **18 think . . . thought** imagine that he is being piloted by our swift thoughts as we accompany him   **19 with his steerage** with Thought as pilot steering our thoughts.   **grow on** proceed   **20 first** already

Like motes and shadows see them move awhile; 21
Your ears unto your eyes I'll reconcile. 22

[*Dumb Show.*]

*Enter Pericles at one door with all his train, Cleon
and Dionyza at the other. Cleon shows Pericles the
tomb, whereat Pericles makes lamentation, puts on
sackcloth, and in a mighty passion departs.* [*Then
exeunt Cleon and Dionyza.*]

See how belief may suffer by foul show! 23
This borrowed passion stands for true-owed woe; 24
And Pericles, in sorrow all devoured,
With sighs shot through and biggest tears o'er-
showered,
Leaves Tarsus and again embarks. He swears
Never to wash his face nor cut his hairs;
He puts on sackcloth, and to sea. He bears 29
A tempest, which his mortal vessel tears, 30
And yet he rides it out. Now please you wit 31
The epitaph is for Marina writ 32
By wicked Dionyza.

[*He reads the inscription on Marina's monument.*]

"The fairest, sweetest, and best lies here,
Who withered in her spring of year.
She was of Tyrus the King's daughter,
On whom foul death hath made this slaughter.
Marina was she called, and at her birth,
Thetis, being proud, swallowed some part o'th'earth. 39
Therefore the earth, fearing to be o'erflowed,
Hath Thetis' birth-child on the heavens bestowed;
Wherefore she does, and swears she'll never stint, 42
Make raging battery upon shores of flint." 43
No visor does become black villainy
So well as soft and tender flattery.
Let Pericles believe his daughter's dead
And bear his courses to be orderèd 47
By Lady Fortune, while our scene must play 48
His daughter's woe and heavy welladay 49
In her unholy service. Patience, then, 50
And think you now are all in Mytilene. *Exit.*

[4.5]

Enter [*from the brothel*] *two Gentlemen.*

FIRST GENTLEMAN Did you ever hear the like?
SECOND GENTLEMAN No, nor never shall do in such a
place as this, she being once gone.
FIRST GENTLEMAN But to have divinity preached there!
Did you ever dream of such a thing?
SECOND GENTLEMAN No, no. Come, I am for no more
bawdy houses. Shall 's go hear the vestals sing? 7
FIRST GENTLEMAN I'll do anything now that is virtuous,
but I am out of the road of rutting forever. *Exeunt.* 9

❧

[4.6]

Enter three bawds [*Pander, Bawd, and Bolt*].

PANDER Well, I had rather than twice the worth of her
she had ne'er come here.
BAWD Fie, fie upon her! She's able to freeze the god
Priapus and undo a whole generation. We must ei- 4
ther get her ravished or be rid of her. When she
should do for clients her fitment and do me the kind- 6
ness of our profession, she has me her quirks, her reasons, her master reasons, her prayers, her knees, that
she would make a puritan of the devil if he should
cheapen a kiss of her. 10
BOLT Faith, I must ravish her, or she'll disfurnish us 11
of all our cavalleria and make our swearers priests. 12
PANDER Now, the pox upon her greensickness for me! 13
BAWD Faith, there's no way to be rid on't but by the 14
way to the pox. Here comes the Lord Lysimachus dis- 15
guised.
BOLT We should have both lord and loon, if the pee- 17
vish baggage would but give way to customers. 18

Enter Lysimachus.

LYSIMACHUS How now? How a dozen of virginities? 19
BAWD Now, the gods to-bless Your Honor! 20
BOLT I am glad to see Your Honor in good health.
LYSIMACHUS You may so; 'tis the better for you that
your resorters stand upon sound legs. How now? 23
Wholesome iniquity have you, that a man may deal 24
withal and defy the surgeon? 25

---

21 **motes** specks in a beam of light. **shadows** (With a suggestion of
the ever-changing images created by actors.) 22.5 *passion* grief
23 **suffer by foul show** be abused by dissembling. 24 **This . . . woe**
This feigned lamentation (of Cleon and Dionyza) usurps the place
that should be occupied by genuine woe 29 **He bears** i.e., He bears
within him 30 **his mortal vessel tears** afflicts with anguish his
human body, racks his frame 31 **wit** know 32 **is that** is 39 **Thetis**
a sea nymph, often confused (as here) with Tethys, a Titaness and
consort of Oceanus. **swallowed . . . earth** (The fanciful image is that
of the oceans rejoicing over Marina's birth at sea with such destructive flood tides that the earth resolves to be rid of Marina by sending
her to heaven; it is in angry reprisal that the sea continues to beat
against the shore.) 42 **she** i.e., Thetis. **stint** cease 43 **Make . . .
flint** continuously beat upon rocky shores. 47–8 **bear . . . Fortune**
direct his passage as Fortune orders 49 **welladay** grief, lamentation
50 **In her unholy service** i.e., in the brothel.

4.5. Location: Mytilene. The brothel.
7 Shall 's Shall we. **vestals** virgins consecrated to tend the sacred
altar **9 rutting** sexual indulgence
4.6. Location: The brothel, as before.
4 Priapus god of fertility and lechery. **undo . . . generation** (1) prevent the engendering of the next generation (2) prevent the pleasures
of the present generation. **6 fitment** sexual duty. **do me** do. (*Me* is
an emphatic marker; see also *has me* in the next line.) **10 cheapen**
bargain for **11 disfurnish** deprive **12 cavalleria** cavaliers.
swearers profane swaggerers **13 the pox . . . me!** i.e., a curse upon
her moody obstinacy and squeamishness (literally, an anemia suffered by young women), as far as I'm concerned! **14 on't** of it, of this
difficulty **15 pox** syphilis. (Playing on *pox* as a familiar curse in line
13.) **17 loon** low fellow, person of low birth **17–18 peevish baggage** stubborn hussy **19 How a** What price for **20 to-bless** bless
completely **23 your resorters** those who resort to your place, customers **24 Wholesome iniquity** Healthy prostitutes **25 withal**
with. **surgeon** barber-surgeon (to treat syphilis).

BAWD We have here one, sir, if she would—but there never came her like in Mytilene.

LYSIMACHUS If she'd do the deeds of darkness, thou wouldst say.

BAWD Your Honor knows what 'tis to say well enough. 30

LYSIMACHUS Well, call forth, call forth. [*Exit Pander.*]

BOLT For flesh and blood, sir, white and red, you shall see a rose; and she were a rose indeed, if she had but— 34

LYSIMACHUS What, prithee?

BOLT Oh, sir, I can be modest.

LYSIMACHUS That dignifies the renown of a bawd no 37
less than it gives a good report to a number to be 38
chaste. 39

[Enter Pander with Marina.]

BAWD Here comes that which grows to the stalk; never plucked yet, I can assure you. Is she not a fair creature?

LYSIMACHUS Faith, she would serve after a long voyage 43
at sea. Well, there's for you. [*He gives money.*] Leave us. 44

BAWD I beseech Your Honor, give me leave a word, and 45
I'll have done presently. 46

LYSIMACHUS I beseech you, do.

BAWD [*aside to Marina*] First, I would have you note this is an honorable man.

MARINA I desire to find him so, that I may worthily 50
note him. 51

BAWD Next, he's the Governor of this country, and a man whom I am bound to. 53

MARINA If he govern the country, you are bound to 54
him indeed, but how honorable he is in that, I know not.

BAWD Pray you, without any more virginal fencing, will you use him kindly? He will line your apron with gold.

MARINA What he will do graciously, I will thankfully receive.

LYSIMACHUS Ha' you done?

BAWD My lord, she's not paced yet. You must take 63
some pains to work her to your manage.—Come, we 64
will leave His Honor and her together. Go thy ways.
[Exeunt Bawd, Pander, and Bolt.]

LYSIMACHUS Now, pretty one, how long have you been at this trade?

MARINA What trade, sir?

LYSIMACHUS Why, I cannot name 't but I shall offend. 69

MARINA I cannot be offended with my trade. Please you to name it.

LYSIMACHUS How long have you been of this profession?

MARINA E'er since I can remember.

LYSIMACHUS Did you go to't so young? Were you a 75
gamester at five, or at seven? 76

MARINA Earlier too, sir, if now I be one.

LYSIMACHUS Why, the house you dwell in proclaims you to be a creature of sale.

MARINA Do you know this house to be a place of such 80
resort, and will come into't? I hear say you're of hon- 81
orable parts and are the governor of this place. 82

LYSIMACHUS Why, hath your principal made known unto you who I am?

MARINA Who is my principal?

LYSIMACHUS Why, your herbwoman, she that sets seeds and roots of shame and iniquity. Oh, you have heard something of my power, and so stand aloof for more serious wooing. But I protest to thee, pretty one, my authority shall not see thee, or else look friendly 90
upon thee. Come, bring me to some private place. Come, come.

MARINA
If you were born to honor, show it now;
If put upon you, make the judgment good 94
That thought you worthy of it.

LYSIMACHUS
How's this? How's this? Some more. Be sage.

MARINA   For me,
That am a maid, though most ungentle fortune
Have placed me in this sty, where, since I came,
Diseases have been sold dearer than physic— 99
That the gods
Would set me free from this unhallowed place,
Though they did change me to the meanest bird 102
That flies i'th' purer air!

LYSIMACHUS   I did not think
Thou couldst have spoke so well, ne'er dreamt thou
couldst.
Had I brought hither a corrupted mind,
Thy speech had altered it. Hold, here's gold for thee. 106
Persevere in that clear way thou goest, 107
And the gods strengthen thee!   [*He gives gold.*]

MARINA The good gods preserve you!

LYSIMACHUS For me, be you thoughten 110
That I came with no ill intent, for to me
The very doors and windows savor vilely.
Fare thee well. Thou art a piece of virtue, and
I doubt not but thy training hath been noble.
Hold, here's more gold for thee.   [*He gives gold.*]
A curse upon him, die he like a thief,

---

30 what 'tis to say what I'm trying to say   **34 but** (To catch the sexual innuendo of this remark, compare the completed phrase, "No roses without prickles.")   **37–9 That . . . chaste** i.e., Modesty in speech gives good reputation to a bawd, as well as attesting to the chastity of many women who deserve no such reputation.   **43–4 she . . . sea** i.e., She is just the thing for a man who is sexually ravenous.   **45 a word** i.e., to say a few words in private to her   **46 have done presently** be done in a moment.   **50–1 I . . . him** I hope to find him truly honorable (not merely *honorable* in the sense used in line 49, "of high rank").   **53, 54 bound** (1) obligated (2) subject   **63 paced** broken in. (A term from horse training.)   **64 manage** handling. (Again from horse training.)   **69 but . . . offend** without offending.

75 go to't i.e., practice sexual acts   **76 gamester** wanton woman   **80–1 of such resort** to be visited for such a purpose   **82 parts** qualities   **90 my authority . . . thee** i.e., I'll wink at your offenses, not enforce the laws against prostitutes   **94 If put upon you** i.e., if your high position was conferred after birth, not through inheritance   **99 Diseases . . . physic** venereal diseases have been transmitted for higher prices than their curative remedies would cost   **102 meanest** lowest   **106 had** would have   **107 clear** virtuous   **110 be you thoughten** assure yourself

That robs thee of thy goodness! If thou dost
Hear from me, it shall be for thy good.

[Enter Bolt.]

BOLT   I beseech Your Honor, one piece for me.

LYSIMACHUS   Avaunt, thou damnèd doorkeeper!
Your house, but for this virgin that doth prop it,
Would sink and overwhelm you. Away!   *[Exit.]*

BOLT   How's this? We must take another course with
you. If your peevish chastity, which is not worth a
breakfast in the cheapest country under the cope, shall 125
undo a whole household, let me be gelded like a spaniel. Come your ways.

MARINA   Whither would you have me?

BOLT   I must have your maidenhead taken off, or the 129
common hangman shall execute it. Come your ways. 130
We'll have no more gentlemen driven away. Come
your ways, I say.

Enter bawds [Bawd and Pander].

BAWD   How now, what's the matter?

BOLT   Worse and worse, mistress. She has here spoken
holy words to the Lord Lysimachus.

BAWD   Oh, abominable!

BOLT   She makes our profession as it were to stink afore
the face of the gods.

BAWD   Marry, hang her up forever!

BOLT   The nobleman would have dealt with her like a 140
nobleman, and she sent him away as cold as a snow- 141
ball, saying his prayers too.

BAWD   Bolt, take her away. Use her at thy pleasure.
Crack the glass of her virginity and make the rest
malleable.

BOLT   An if she were a thornier piece of ground than 146
she is, she shall be plowed.

MARINA   Hark, hark, you gods!

BAWD   She conjures. Away with her! Would she had
never come within my doors!—Marry, hang you!—
She's born to undo us.—Will you not go the way of
womenkind? Marry, come up, my dish of chastity 152
with rosemary and bays!   *[Exeunt Bawd and Pander.]* 153

BOLT   Come, mistress, come your ways with me.

MARINA   Whither wilt thou have me?

BOLT   To take from you the jewel you hold so dear.

MARINA   Prithee, tell me one thing first.

BOLT   Come now, your one thing.   158

MARINA
What canst thou wish thine enemy to be?   159

BOLT   Why, I could wish him to be my master, or
rather, my mistress.

MARINA
Neither of these are so bad as thou art,
Since they do better thee in their command.   163
Thou hold'st a place for which the pained'st fiend   164
Of hell would not in reputation change.
Thou art the damnèd doorkeeper to every
Coistrel that comes inquiring for his Tib.   167
To the choleric fisting of every rogue   168
Thy ear is liable; thy food is such
As hath been belched on by infected lungs.

BOLT   What would you have me do? Go to the wars,
would you, where a man may serve seven years for 172
the loss of a leg and have not money enough in the
end to buy him a wooden one?

MARINA
Do anything but this thou doest. Empty
Old receptacles, or common shores, of filth;   176
Serve by indenture to the common hangman.   177
Any of these ways are yet better than this;
For what thou professest, a baboon, could he speak, 179
Would own a name too dear. That the gods   180
Would safely deliver me from this place!
Here, here's gold for thee.   *[She gives gold.]*
If that thy master would gain by me,   183
Proclaim that I can sing, weave, sew, and dance,
With other virtues, which I'll keep from boast,   185
And will undertake all these to teach.
I doubt not but this populous city will
Yield many scholars.   188

BOLT   But can you teach all this you speak of?

MARINA
Prove that I cannot, take me home again   190
And prostitute me to the basest groom   191
That doth frequent your house.

BOLT   Well, I will see what I can do for thee. If I can
place thee, I will.

MARINA   But amongst honest women.

BOLT   Faith, my acquaintance lies little amongst them.
But since my master and mistress hath bought you,
there's no going but by their consent. Therefore I will
make them acquainted with your purpose, and I
doubt not but I shall find them tractable enough.
Come, I'll do for thee what I can. Come your ways.

Exeunt.

[5. Chorus]

Enter Gower.

---

125 **cope** firmament   129–30 **or . . . execute it** (As if taking the maidenhead were a kind of beheading.)   140–1 **like a nobleman** i.e., as a
nobleman would have done, using her and rewarding her   146 **An if**
Even if   152 **Marry, come up** i.e., Hoity-toity   153 **rosemary and
bays** (Customary garnishes for certain foods; the Bawd sees Marina
as a fancy dish.)   158 **thing** (Bolt plays on Marina's *one thing* [line
157] in a lewd sense, referring to her sexual anatomy.)   159 **What . . .
to be?** i.e., Who is your worst enemy imaginable? (Marina means the
devil. Bolt, in reply, can think only in terms of his master and mistress, who presumably make his life miserable.)

163 **Since . . . command** i.e., since they give the orders but you do the
actual dirty work.   164 **pained'st** most tormented   167 **Coistrel**
knave.   **Tib** common woman.   168 **choleric fisting** angry blows
172 **would you** would you have me.   **for** i.e., to end up with
176 **shores** sewers, or, garbage dumps at the water's edge   177 **by
indenture** i.e., as an apprentice   179 **what thou professest** your profession   180 **Would . . . dear** would consider himself and his reputation too good for that.   **That** Would that   183 **If that** If   185 **virtues**
accomplishments   188 **scholars** pupils.   190 **Prove** If you find
191 **groom** menial
5.0.

GOWER

Marina thus the brothel scapes and chances
　Into an honest house, our story says.
She sings like one immortal, and she dances
　As goddesslike to her admirèd lays.   4
Deep clerks she dumbs, and with her neele
　composes   5
　Nature's own shape, of bud, bird, branch, or
　　berry,
That even her art sisters the natural roses;   7
　Her inkle, silk, twin with the rubied cherry,   8
That pupils lacks she none of noble race,   9
　Who pour their bounty on her, and her gain
She gives the cursèd bawd. Here we her place,
　And to her father turn our thoughts again,
Where we left him, on the sea. We there him lost,
　Where, driven before the winds, he is arrived
Here where his daughter dwells; and on this coast
　Suppose him now at anchor. The city strived
God Neptune's annual feast to keep, from whence
　Lysimachus our Tyrian ship espies,
His banners sable, trimmed with rich expense,
　And to him in his barge with fervor hies.
In your supposing once more put your sight;   21
　Of heavy Pericles think this his bark,   22
Where what is done in action—more, if might—   23
　Shall be discovered. Please you, sit and hark.   24
　　　　　　　　　　　　　　　　　　　　Exit.

❧

[5.1]

*Enter Helicanus. To him two Sailors, [one
belonging to the Tyrian vessel, the other to a barge
of Mytilene that is evidently alongside, out of
view].*

TYRIAN SAILOR [*to the Sailor of Mytilene*]
Where is Lord Helicanus? He can resolve you.   1
Oh, here he is.—
Sir, there is a barge put off from Mytilene,
And in it is Lysimachus the Governor,
Who craves to come aboard. What is your will?
HELICANUS
That he have his. Call up some gentlemen.
TYRIAN SAILOR Ho, gentlemen! My lord calls.

Enter two or three Gentlemen.

FIRST GENTLEMAN Doth Your Lordship call?

HELICANUS Gentlemen,
There is some of worth would come aboard.   10
I pray, greet him fairly.   11
　　　　　　[*The Gentlemen and the two Sailors
　　　　　　　　　　go to greet Lysimachus.*]

Enter [as from the barge] Lysimachus, [escorted].

TYRIAN SAILOR [*to Lysimachus*] Sir,
This is the man that can, in aught you would,   13
Resolve you.
LYSIMACHUS
Hail, reverend sir! The gods preserve you!
HELICANUS And you, to outlive the age I am,
And die as I would do.
LYSIMACHUS 　　　　　　You wish me well.   17
Being on shore, honoring of Neptune's triumphs,   18
Seeing this goodly vessel ride before us,
I made to it, to know of whence you are.
HELICANUS First, what is your place?   21
LYSIMACHUS
I am the governor of this place you lie before.   22
HELICANUS Sir,
Our vessel is of Tyre, in it the King,
A man who for this three months hath not spoken
To anyone, nor taken sustenance
But to prorogue his grief.   27
LYSIMACHUS
Upon what ground is his distemperature?   28
HELICANUS
'Twould be too tedious to repeat,
But the main grief springs from the loss
Of a belovèd daughter and a wife.
LYSIMACHUS May we not see him?
HELICANUS You may,
But bootless is your sight. He will not speak   34
To any.
LYSIMACHUS Yet let me obtain my wish.
HELICANUS
Behold him. [*Pericles is discovered to view, in rough
　clothing and with long hair and beard.*]
This was a goodly person,
Till the disaster that, one mortal night,
Drove him to this.   38
LYSIMACHUS [*to Pericles*]
Sir King, all hail! The gods preserve you!
Hail, royal sir!
HELICANUS
It is in vain. He will not speak to you.
A LORD Sir,
We have a maid in Mytilene, I durst wager,
Would win some words of him.
LYSIMACHUS 　　　　　　'Tis well bethought.
She questionless, with her sweet harmony

---

4 lays songs.   **5 Deep . . . dumbs** She silences profound scholars.
neele needle   **7 That . . . roses** in such a way that her embroidery is
just as natural as real roses are   **8 inkle** linen thread or yarn.   **twin
with** resemble closely   **9 race** class, family   **21 In . . . sight** Visualize
the scene again in your imagination   **22 heavy** sorrowful   **23 if
might** if we could   **24 discovered** revealed, shown.
5.1. Location: On board Pericles's ship, off Mytilene. A pavilion for
Pericles is provided onstage, with a curtain before it, perhaps by
means of a "discovery space"; Pericles, reclining within, is "discovered" at line 37 by the drawing back of the curtain.
1 resolve answer, satisfy

10 some of worth some nobleman (who)   **11 fairly** courteously.
13 in aught you would in whatever you wish to know   **17 as I
would do** i.e., at the end of a long and honorable life.   **18 honoring
. . . triumphs** celebrating a festival in honor of Neptune   **21 place**
office.   **22 lie** lie at anchor   **27 prorogue** prolong   **28 Upon . . . distemperature?** What is the cause of his disturbance of mind?
34 bootless fruitless   **38 mortal** fatal

And other chosen attractions, would allure,   47
And make a batt'ry through his deafened ports,   48
Which now are midway stopped.   49
She is all happy as the fairest of all   50
And, with her fellow maids, is now upon
The leafy shelter that abuts against
The island's side.   [*He signals to the Lord, who goes
                                 off to bring Marina.*]

HELICANUS
Sure, all effectless; yet nothing we'll omit   54
That bears recovery's name. But since your kindness   55
We have stretched thus far, let us beseech you
That for our gold we may provision have,
Wherein we are not destitute for want,
But weary for the staleness.

LYSIMACHUS   Oh, sir, a courtesy   59
Which if we should deny, the most just gods
For every graft would send a caterpillar,   61
And so inflict our province. Yet once more   62
Let me entreat to know at large the cause   63
Of your king's sorrow.

HELICANUS
Sit, sir, I will recount it to you.—
But, see, I am prevented.   66

          [*Enter, as though from the barge, the Lord, with
          Marina, and a young lady.*]

LYSIMACHUS
Oh, here's the lady that I sent for.—
Welcome, fair one!—Is't not a goodly presence?   68

HELICANUS   She's a gallant lady.   69

LYSIMACHUS
She's such a one that, were I well assured
Came of a gentle kind and noble stock,   71
I'd wish no better choice, and think me rarely wed.—   72
Fair one, all goodness that consists in bounty   73
Expect even here, where is a kingly patient;
If that thy prosperous and artificial feat   75
Can draw him but to answer thee in aught,
Thy sacred physic shall receive such pay   77
As thy desires can wish.

MARINA   Sir, I will use
My utmost skill in his recovery, provided
That none but I and my companion maid
Be suffered to come near him.

LYSIMACHUS   Come, let us leave her;   81
And the gods make her prosperous!   82
          [*They stand aside.*] *The song* [*by Marina*].

LYSIMACHUS [*advancing*]
Marked he your music?

MARINA   No, nor looked on us.

LYSIMACHUS [*to Helicanus*] See, she will speak to him.

MARINA [*to Pericles*]   Hail, sir! My lord, lend ear.

PERICLES   Hum, ha!   [*He pushes her away.*]

MARINA
I am a maid, my lord, that ne'er before
Invited eyes, but have been gazèd on   88
Like a comet. She speaks,   89
My lord, that maybe hath endured a grief
Might equal yours, if both were justly weighed.
Though wayward fortune did malign my state,   92
My derivation was from ancestors
Who stood equivalent with mighty kings;
But time hath rooted out my parentage,
And to the world and awkward casualties   96
Bound me in servitude. [*Aside*] I will desist;
But there is something glows upon my cheek,
And whispers in mine ear, "Go not till he speak."

PERICLES
My fortunes—parentage—good parentage—
To equal mine!—Was it not thus? What say you?

MARINA
I said, my lord, if you did know my parentage,
You would not do me violence.

PERICLES
I do think so. Pray you, turn your eyes upon me.   104
You're like something that—What countrywoman?
Here of these shores?

MARINA   No, nor of any shores.
Yet I was mortally brought forth, and am   107
No other than I appear.

PERICLES
I am great with woe and shall deliver weeping.   109
My dearest wife was like this maid, and such a one
My daughter might have been. My queen's square
    brows;
Her stature to an inch; as wandlike straight;
As silver-voiced; her eyes as jewel-like
And cased as richly; in pace another Juno;   114
Who starves the ears she feeds, and makes them
    hungry
The more she gives them speech.—Where do you
    live?

MARINA
Where I am but a stranger. From the deck
You may discern the place.

PERICLES
Where were you bred? And how achieved you these
Endowments which you make more rich to owe?   120

MARINA
If I should tell my history, it would seem

---

47 chosen choice   **48 make . . . ports** i.e., force an entrance through
his deafened sense of hearing   **49 midway stopped** shut so that com-
munications get only halfway through.   **50 all happy** completely fortunate (in having such beauty)   **54 effectless** useless   **55 bears
recovery's name** deserves the name of cure.   **59 for** because of
61 graft scion, shoot, grafted plant   **62 inflict** afflict   **63 at large** in
detail   **66 prevented** forestalled.   **68 Is't . . . presence?** Isn't her
demeanor fine?   **69 gallant** splendid   **71 gentle kind** noble kindred
72 rarely excellently   **73 all . . . bounty** (In the Quarto, which reads
"beautie" for "bounty," this phrase could mean: You, Marina, possessed of all good that beauty can contain.)   **75 prosperous** producing favorable results.   **artificial** skillful   **77 physic** medicine
81 suffered permitted   **82.1 The song** (Not given in the Quarto.)

88 Invited eyes asked to be looked at   **88–9 gazèd . . . comet** i.e.,
stared at in astonishment.   **92 wayward** contrary.   **did . . . state** has
dealt malignantly with my condition   **96 awkward casualties**
adverse misfortunes   **104 I do think so** I agree.   **107 mortally**
humanly   **109 great** (1) pregnant (2) heavy.   **deliver** (1) give birth
(2) speak   **114 cased** enclosed, framed.   **pace** gait, carriage   **120 to
owe** by possessing.

Like lies disdained in the reporting.
PERICLES   Prithee, speak.   122
Falseness cannot come from thee, for thou lookest
Modest as Justice, and thou seemest a palace
For the crownèd Truth to dwell in. I will believe thee
And make my senses credit thy relation   126
To points that seem impossible, for thou lookest
Like one I loved indeed. What were thy friends?   128
Didst thou not say, when I did push thee back—
Which was when I perceived thee—that thou cam'st
From good descending?
MARINA   So indeed I did.   131
PERICLES
  Report thy parentage. I think thou said'st
Thou hadst been tossed from wrong to injury,
And that thou thought'st thy griefs might equal mine,
If both were opened.
MARINA   Some such thing   135
  I said, and said no more but what my thoughts
Did warrant me was likely.
PERICLES   Tell thy story.
If thine, considered, prove the thousand part   138
Of my endurance, thou art a man, and I   139
Have suffered like a girl. Yet thou dost look
Like Patience gazing on kings' graves and smiling   141
Extremity out of act. What were thy friends?   142
How lost thou them? Thy name, my most kind virgin?
Recount, I do beseech thee. Come, sit by me.
MARINA [sitting]   My name is Marina.
PERICLES   Oh, I am mocked,
And thou by some incensèd god sent hither   147
To make the world to laugh at me.
MARINA   Patience, good sir, or here I'll cease.
PERICLES
  Nay, I'll be patient. Thou little know'st how thou
Dost startle me to call thyself Marina.
MARINA   The name
Was given me by one that had some power:
My father, and a king.
PERICLES   How, a king's daughter?
And called Marina?
MARINA   You said you would believe me;
But, not to be a troubler of your peace,
I will end here.
PERICLES   But are you flesh and blood?
Have you a working pulse, and are no fairy?   158
Motion? Well, speak on. Where were you born?   159
And wherefore called Marina?
MARINA   Called Marina
For I was born at sea.
PERICLES
  At sea! What mother?   161

MARINA
  My mother was the daughter of a king,
Who died the minute I was born,
As my good nurse Lychorida hath oft
Delivered weeping.
PERICLES   Oh, stop there a little!   165
This is the rarest dream that e'er dull sleep
Did mock sad fools withal. This cannot be   167
My daughter—buried!—Well, where were you bred?
I'll hear you more, to th' bottom of your story,
And never interrupt you.
MARINA
  You scorn. Believe me, 'twere best I did give o'er.   171
PERICLES
  I will believe you by the syllable   172
Of what you shall deliver. Yet give me leave:
How came you in these parts? Where were you bred?
MARINA
  The King my father did in Tarsus leave me,
Till cruel Cleon, with his wicked wife,
Did seek to murder me; and having wooed
A villain to attempt it, who having drawn to do't,   178
A crew of pirates came and rescued me,
Brought me to Mytilene. But, good sir,
Whither will you have me? Why do you weep? It may
  be   181
You think me an impostor. No, good faith,
I am the daughter to King Pericles,
If good King Pericles be.   184
PERICLES [calling]   Ho, Helicanus!
HELICANUS   Calls my lord?
PERICLES
  Thou art a grave and noble counselor,
Most wise in general. Tell me, if thou canst,
What this maid is, or what is like to be,   189
That thus hath made me weep?
HELICANUS   I know not,
But here's the regent, sir, of Mytilene
Speaks nobly of her.
LYSIMACHUS   She never would tell   192
Her parentage; being demanded that,
She would sit still and weep.
PERICLES
  Oh, Helicanus, strike me, honored sir,
Give me a gash, put me to present pain,
Lest this great sea of joys rushing upon me
O'erbear the shores of my mortality,   198
And drown me with their sweetness.—Oh, come
  hither,
Thou that beget'st him that did thee beget,   200
Thou that wast born at sea, buried at Tarsus,
And found at sea again!—Oh, Helicanus,

Down on thy knees! Thank the holy gods as loud   203
As thunder threatens us. This is Marina.—   204
What was thy mother's name? Tell me but that,
For truth can never be confirmed enough,
Though doubts did ever sleep.   207

MARINA
First, sir, I pray, what is your title?

PERICLES
I am Pericles of Tyre. But tell me now
My drowned queen's name, as in the rest you said
Thou hast been godlike perfect, the heir of kingdoms, 211
And another life to Pericles thy father.   212

MARINA
Is it no more to be your daughter than   213
To say my mother's name was Thaisa?
Thaisa was my mother, who did end
The minute I began.

PERICLES
Now, blessing on thee! Rise, thou'rt my child.—
Give me fresh garments.—Mine own Helicanus,   218
She is not dead at Tarsus, as she should have been, 219
By savage Cleon. She shall tell thee all,   220
When thou shalt kneel, and justify in knowledge   221
She is thy very princess.—Who is this?

HELICANUS
Sir, 'tis the Governor of Mytilene,
Who, hearing of your melancholy state,
Did come to see you.

PERICLES [to Lysimachus]   I embrace you.
Give me my robes. I am wild in my beholding.   227
                        [He is freshly attired.]
O heavens bless my girl! But, hark, what music?
Tell Helicanus, my Marina, tell him
O'er, point by point, for yet he seems to doubt,   230
How sure you are my daughter. But, what music?   231

HELICANUS   My lord, I hear none.

PERICLES   None?
The music of the spheres! List, my Marina.   233

LYSIMACHUS
It is not good to cross him. Give him way.

PERICLES   Rarest sounds! Do ye not hear?

LYSIMACHUS
Music, my lord? I hear.

PERICLES   Most heavenly music!   236

It nips me unto list'ning, and thick slumber   237
Hangs upon mine eyes. Let me rest.   [He sleeps.]

LYSIMACHUS
A pillow for his head. So, leave him all.
Well, my companion friends,
If this but answer to my just belief,   241
I'll well remember you.   [Exeunt all but Pericles.] 242

    Diana [appears to Pericles as in a vision].

DIANA
My temple stands in Ephesus. Hie thee thither
And do upon mine altar sacrifice.
There, when my maiden priests are met together
Before the people all,
Reveal how thou at sea didst lose thy wife.
To mourn thy crosses, with thy daughter's, call   248
And give them repetition to the life.   249
Or perform my bidding, or thou livest in woe;   250
Do't, and happy, by my silver bow!
Awake, and tell thy dream.   [She disappears.]

PERICLES
Celestial Dian, goddess argentine,   253
I will obey thee.—Helicanus!

    [Enter Helicanus, Lysimachus, and Marina.]

HELICANUS   Sir?
PERICLES
My purpose was for Tarsus, there to strike
The inhospitable Cleon, but I am
For other service first. Toward Ephesus
Turn our blown sails; eftsoons I'll tell thee why. 258
[To Lysimachus] Shall we refresh us, sir, upon your
    shore
And give you gold for such provision
As our intents will need?

LYSIMACHUS   Sir,
With all my heart; and, when you come ashore,
I have another suit.

PERICLES   You shall prevail,
Were it to woo my daughter, for it seems
You have been noble towards her.

LYSIMACHUS   Sir, lend me your arm.
PERICLES   Come, my Marina.   Exeunt.

                     ❖

[5.2]

[Enter Gower, before the temple of Diana of
Ephesus; Thaisa standing near the altar, as high
priestess; a number of virgins on each side;
Cerimon and other inhabitants of Ephesus
attending.]

203–4 as loud . . . us i.e., with hosannas as loud as the thunder with
which the gods threaten us.   207 Though . . . sleep i.e., even though
all doubts were laid to rest forever.   211 godlike perfect all-knowing
like a god.   the heir i.e., if you can do this, you will show yourself to
be the heir   212 another life i.e., the bringer of a new life   213 Is it
no more Is nothing more required   218 Mine own Helicanus (Perhaps this should read "Mine own, Helicanus!"—i.e., she is my own
daughter.)   219 should have been was thought to be, or, was
intended to have been   220 By at the hands of   221 justify in
knowledge acknowledge   227 wild . . . beholding elated and deliri-
ous in everything I see, or, possibly, unkempt, savage in appearance.
230 doubt (Or perhaps dote, be in a daze; the Quarto reads "doat.")
231 sure certainly   233 music of the spheres celestial harmony, supposedly produced by the ordered movements of the heavenly bodies.
(Whether the music is to be heard in the theater is not clear.)
236 I hear (Lysimachus may hear music or may say this to humor
Pericles and give him way [line 234]. Editors sometimes regard the
word music in line 236 as a stage direction or assign I hear to Pericles.)

237 nips overpowers and compels   241 but . . . belief turns out as I
expect it to   242 remember reward.   242.1 Diana (Perhaps she
descends from the heavens and reascends at line 252.)   248 crosses
misfortunes.   call lift your voice   249 give . . . life repeat them point
for point.   250 Or Either   253 argentine silvery in appearance (as
appropriate to the moon goddess)   258 blown inflated by the wind.
eftsoons shortly, later on
5.2. Location: The temple of Diana at Ephesus.
0.1 before the temple (Perhaps Gower reveals this scene, by means of
a curtain, at line 17.)

GOWER

Now our sands are almost run;
More a little, and then dumb.
This my last boon give me,
For such kindness must relieve me:
That you aptly will suppose   5
What pageantry, what feats, what shows,
What minstrelsy, and pretty din
The regent made in Mytilin
To greet the King. So he thrived   9
That he is promised to be wived
To fair Marina, but in no wise
Till he had done his sacrifice   12
As Dian bade; whereto being bound,   13
The interim, pray you, all confound.   14
In feathered briefness sails are filled,   15
And wishes fall out as they're willed.
At Ephesus the temple see,
Our King and all his company.
That he can hither come so soon
Is by your fancies' thankful doom.   [Exit.] 20

❀

[5.3]

[Enter Pericles, with his train; Lysimachus,
Helicanus, Marina, and a lady.]

PERICLES

Hail, Dian! To perform thy just command,
I here confess myself the King of Tyre,
Who, frighted from my country, did wed
At Pentapolis the fair Thaisa.
At sea in childbed died she, but brought forth
A maid child called Marina, who, O goddess,   6
Wears yet thy silver livery. She at Tarsus   7
Was nursed with Cleon, who at fourteen years   8
He sought to murder; but her better stars
Brought her to Mytilene, 'gainst whose shore
Riding, her fortunes brought the maid aboard us,   11
Where, by her own most clear remembrance, she
Made known herself my daughter.

THAISA   Voice and favor!   13
You are, you are—O royal Pericles!   [She faints.]

PERICLES

What means the nun? She dies! Help, gentlemen!

CERIMON   Noble sir,
If you have told Diana's altar true,
This is your wife.

PERICLES   Reverend appearer, no;   18
I threw her overboard with these very arms.

CERIMON

Upon this coast, I warrant you.
PERICLES   'Tis most certain.   2
CERIMON

Look to the lady; Oh, she's but overjoyed.
Early one blustering morn this lady was
Thrown upon this shore. I oped the coffin,
Found there rich jewels, recovered her, and placed her 24
Here in Diana's temple.
PERICLES   May we see them?
CERIMON

Great sir, they shall be brought you to my house,
Whither I invite you. Look, Thaisa is
Recovered.

THAISA [rising]   Oh, let me look!
If he be none of mine, my sanctity   30
Will to my sense bend no licentious ear,   31
But curb it, spite of seeing.—O my lord,   32
Are you not Pericles? Like him you spake,
Like him you are. Did you not name a tempest,
A birth, and death?

PERICLES   The voice of dead Thaisa!
THAISA

That Thaisa am I, supposèd dead
And drowned.

PERICLES

Immortal Dian!
THAISA   Now I know you better.
When we with tears parted Pentapolis,   39
The King my father gave you such a ring.   40
                          [She points to his ring.]

PERICLES

This, this! No more, you gods! Your present kindness
Makes my past miseries sports. You shall do well   42
That on the touching of her lips I may   43
Melt and no more be seen.—Oh, come, be buried   44
A second time within these arms!   [They embrace.]

MARINA [kneeling]   My heart
Leaps to be gone into my mother's bosom.

PERICLES

Look who kneels here! Flesh of thy flesh, Thaisa,
Thy burden at the sea, and called Marina
For she was yielded there.

THAISA   Blest, and mine own!   49
                               [They embrace.]

HELICANUS

Hail, madam, and my queen!
THAISA   I know you not.
PERICLES

You have heard me say, when I did fly from Tyre

2 More . . . dumb A little more of the story, and then I shall be silent.
5 aptly readily   9 So he thrived He (Lysimachus) fared so well
12 he i.e., Pericles   13 bade commanded   14 confound do away
with, omit.   15 feathered winged   20 Is . . . doom is thanks to the
consent (and willing participation) of your imaginations.
5.3. Location: Scene continues; the temple, as before.
6 maid child baby girl   7 Wears . . . livery i.e., is still a virgin.
8 with Cleon under Cleon's care   11 Riding (we) riding at anchor
13 favor face, appearance.   18 Reverend appearer You who appear
reverend

24 recovered revived   30–2 If . . . seeing If he is not my husband, my
holy way of life will lend no credence to my physical sense of sight
and my sensual inclination but will curb my longings (for marriage,
my lost life of domestic pleasure), despite what I see before me.
39 parted departed from   40.1 She points to his ring (Possibly Pericles included this ring among the jewels he laid in Thaisa's casket, or,
more probably, she may recognize it on his finger now.)   42 sports
mere amusements.   42–4 You . . . seen You gods would give me a
good death if, when I touch her lips with mine, I should die of happiness.   49 For because.   yielded brought forth, born

I left behind an ancient substitute.
Can you remember what I called the man?
I have named him oft.
THAISA 'Twas Helicanus then.
PERICLES   Still confirmation!
Embrace him, dear Thaisa, this is he.   [*They embrace.*]
Now do I long to hear how you were found,
How possibly preserved, and who to thank,   59
Besides the gods, for this great miracle.
THAISA
Lord Cerimon, my lord; this man,
Through whom the gods have shown their power,
    that can
From first to last resolve you.
PERICLES [*to Cerimon*]   Reverend sir,   63
The gods can have no mortal officer   64
More like a god than you. Will you deliver   65
How this dead queen re-lives?
CERIMON   I will, my lord.
Beseech you, first go with me to my house,
Where shall be shown you all was found with her,   68
How she came placed here in the temple,
No needful thing omitted.
PERICLES
Pure Dian, I bless thee for thy vision, and   71
Will offer night oblations to thee. Thaisa,   72
This prince, the fair betrothèd of your daughter,   73
Shall marry her at Pentapolis. And now
This ornament   75
Makes me look dismal will I clip to form;   76
And what this fourteen years no razor touched,
To grace thy marriage day, I'll beautify.

---

59 possibly by what possible means   **63 resolve you** satisfy your
curiosity.   **64 mortal officer** human agent   **65 deliver** recount
68 all was all that was   **71 thy vision** appearing to me in a vision
72 night oblations nightly sacrifices, evening prayers   **73 This prince**
Lysimachus   **75 ornament** i.e., hair and beard   **76 Makes** which
makes.   **to form** to proper shape

THAISA
Lord Cerimon hath letters of good credit, sir,   79
My father's dead.
PERICLES
Heavens make a star of him! Yet there, my queen,   81
We'll celebrate their nuptials, and ourselves
Will in that kingdom spend our following days.
Our son and daughter shall in Tyrus reign.
Lord Cerimon, we do our longing stay   85
To hear the rest untold. Sir, lead 's the way.   86
                                          [*Exeunt.*]

[*Enter Gower.*]

GOWER
In Antiochus and his daughter you have heard
Of monstrous lust the due and just reward.
In Pericles, his queen, and daughter seen,
Although assailed with fortune fierce and keen,
Virtue preserved from fell destruction's blast,   91
Led on by heaven, and crowned with joy at last.
In Helicanus may you well descry
A figure of truth, of faith, of loyalty.
In reverend Cerimon there well appears
The worth that learnèd charity aye wears.
For wicked Cleon and his wife, when fame   97
Had spread his cursèd deed to the honored name   98
Of Pericles, to rage the city turn,   99
That him and his they in his palace burn;   100
The gods for murder seemèd so content
To punish—although not done, but meant.   102
So, on your patience evermore attending,
New joy wait on you! Here our play has ending.
                                          [*Exit.*]

---

79 of good credit trustworthy   **81 there** i.e., in Pentapolis   **85 do . . .
stay** merely postpone the completion of our desires   **86 untold** that
is not yet told.   **91 fell** cruel   **97 fame** report; common talk   **98 his . . .
deed to** i.e., the deed done by him and his family, especially Dionyza,
against   **99 turn** did turn   **100 That** so that.   **and his** and his family,
notably Dionyza   **102 although . . . meant** i.e., even though the crime
was only intended and not actually carried out.

Cymbeline

Cymbeline's remarkable blending of romantic narrative and quasi-history urges us to think about the play as a genealogical fantasy about British origins. By choosing a setting in ancient Britain, the play searches for a national identity through a rediscovered national history. To be truly British, Britain must have a history, a story about its origins. Chroniclers since Geoffrey of Monmouth (c. 1136) had undertaken to provide Britain with a mythical past, from the supposed settlement of the British Isles by a great-grandson of Aeneas down through the days of Roman occupation around the beginning of the Christian Era. The accounts were by and large fabulous, and were under increasing pressure of skepticism in Shakespeare's day. Perhaps for those very reasons, they offered rich material for poetic and dramatic exploration. How do these myths of origin enter into the dramatic world of *Cymbeline*?

One possible line of inquiry is to ask how the play dramatizes anxieties about national identity in relation to gender identities. As Coppélia Kahn, Janet Adelman, and others have argued, Imogen's sufferings of virtual rape and subsequent slander by a scheming Italian (Iachimo) may suggest the island nation's fear of invasion and mistrust of Catholic Italy. Conversely, the saga of Posthumus Leonatus, as he loses faith in his wife, attempts to arrange her murder, and eventually repents what he has done, suggests a testing and definition of British manhood through which the final emergence of Posthumus as Britain's martial champion is emblematic of the emergence of Britain as a specifically masculine nation. (Imogen's prospects of inheriting the kingdom from her father, Cymbeline, are set aside by the rediscovery of her two lost brothers.) The vexed relationship of Britain to Rome points to an ambivalent feeling about the period of Roman occupation, and, more generally, to Britain's indebtedness to the cultural legacy of ancient Rome as opposed to its own nascent literary nationalism. The Roman presence may also have prompted Shakespeare's

audience to think of their own monarch, James I, and his aspirations to a kind of neo-Augustan empire in the shape of a united Britain and a pan-European peace. In a period of difficult transition, we see glimmerings at least of an emerging Britain that is able to appropriate the virtues of Rome for its own national identity.

The genre of *Cymbeline* can be suggested by such critical terms as romance, tragicomedy, and the comedy of forgiveness. As in *Pericles, The Winter's Tale*, and other late plays, Shakespeare turns to the improbable fictions of romance: a stepmother-queen skilled in the use of poisons and envious of her fair and virtuous stepdaughter (as in *Snow White*), lost sons recognized by the inevitable birthmark, the reunion of many persons long separated by exile and wandering, the intervention of the gods by means of a riddling and inane prophecy. These are the distinguishing features of English romance in the 1580s, a titillating vogue exploited by Robert Greene and other professional writers of the period. From two romantic plays of the 1580s—*Sir Clyomon and Sir Clamydes* and *The Rare Triumphs of Love and Fortune*—Shakespeare may, in fact, have drawn source material. Why did he turn to such old-fashioned models in 1608–1610? The choice has puzzled many critics and has prompted them to speak condescendingly of Shakespeare's dotage or to assign parts of the play (notably the descent of Jupiter) to some other dramatist.

Shakespeare nevertheless courted the improbabilities, even the deliberate absurdities, of romance with a serious artistic purpose. In part, he was responding to a new literary fashion, evident especially in the private theaters, for a tragicomedy of refined sensibility—a literary fashion that produced Francis Beaumont and John Fletcher's *Philaster*. This play of about 1609 features, like *Cymbeline*, a rapidly moving and ingeniously woven plot of separation and reunion, a king's daughter betrothed by her father to a churl and then wrongly accused of infidelity, a young maiden in male disguise, and other comparable details. Whether *Cymbeline* preceded or followed *Philaster* is a matter that is difficult to determine, since *Cymbeline* can be dated only approximately as from 1608–1610 on grounds of style; in any case, Shakespeare's fascination with romance goes back at least to *All's Well That Ends Well* (c. 1601–1604) and *Pericles* (c. 1606–1608). His experiments in the genre must be viewed as innovative and unique. Despite the affinities to Fletcherian tragicomedy, Shakespeare never indulges in the cloying sensationalism, the exaggerated heightening of exotic emotion, and (except in *The Winter's Tale*) the trickery of concealing essential information from the audience, such as we find in works of Beaumont and Fletcher. Shakespeare's interest in romantic improbability is related to the serious motif of redemption, of an unexpected and undeserved second chance for erring humanity.

The tragic possibilities are manifold. Cymbeline, like Lear (another king from British legendary history in Raphael Holinshed's *Chronicles*, 1578), tyrannically repulses a virtuous daughter and rewards the vicious members of his family, with predictably unhappy consequences. Posthumus Leonatus, like Othello, commands the death of his beloved mistress because he believes a groundless but cunningly presented accusation of her infidelity; finally, concluding that he has destroyed the only person capable of giving order to his life, he despairingly longs for death. Whereas in a similar situation Lear and Othello suffer the tragic consequences of their choice, Cymbeline and Posthumus are spared. Some benign force, integral to the world of this play, prevents fallible mortals from pursuing their misguided intentions to the point of irreversible injury. Posthumus relies for his vengeance on the virtuous Pisanio, who cannot bring himself to slay Imogen. The Queen's box of "poison," given ultimately to Imogen by the well-meaning but duped Pisanio, is only a sleeping potion concocted by that kindly manipulator behind the scenes, Doctor Cornelius. These fortunate avoidances of disaster recall other such narrow escapes in *Much Ado About Nothing*, *All's Well That Ends Well*, and *Measure for Measure*. They also anticipate similar events in *The Winter's Tale*.

Because *Cymbeline* begins with dilemmas like those of *King Lear* and *Othello*, the prevailing tone is at first serious. (The editors of the 1623 First Folio printed the play among the tragedies.) The King's behavior toward Imogen and her virtuous but nonaristocratic husband, Posthumus, is tyrannical. Disinterested observers condemn the wicked Queen's dominance over Cymbeline and laugh privately at the Queen's cowardly and ridiculous son Cloten. A good man like Belarius suffers lifelong banishment from the envious court and spends his exile dwelling in caves. Many conventional features of romantic narrative—wandering and return, loss and rediscovery, apparent death and rebirth—are set in motion by the need to escape from a court dominated by the wicked Queen. One by one, honest persons of the play—Posthumus, Imogen, Pisanio—leave society in disfavor to be reunited in the wild landscape of Belarius and his foster sons. Italy is no better a place than the English court. Its evil genius is Iachimo, apostle of animal appetite, duplicity, and cynical indifference to human values.

Despite the prevailing tragic mood at first, there are promises of brighter prospects. Posthumus's birth is attended by wondrous circumstances that would appear to single him out for an extraordinary career. In the first scene, moreover, we learn that the King's only two sons were stolen from their nursery in their infancy—an obvious hint that they will turn up sooner or later. Cloten, too, strikes us as a ludicrous suitor for Imogen, the type of buffoonish rival appropriate to a love comedy. Because he is witless, superficial, and preoccupied with clothes, he deserves to be exposed and ridiculed. Even his death is grotesquely comic. He acts as a foil or caricature to Posthumus, in whose clothes he is erroneously taken by Imogen to be her dead husband; the outward resemblance of the two men suggests to us that Posthumus has not been unlike Cloten when he has suspected Imogen of betraying him and has vowed revenge. Cloten's death signals an end to Posthumus's disposition to be fooled by appearances.

The initial somber mood, with its threat of tragic outcome, is further lightened by the juxtaposition of sorrow and hope. When Arviragus and Guiderius mourn the "death" of Imogen with an exquisite song on the vanity of human striving, we respond to the appropriateness of the sentiment and yet qualify our sorrow with our consoling knowledge that she has really taken a sleeping potion. Similarly, when Posthumus jests eloquently about death with his jailer and prepares to find his only freedom in surcease, we cannot ignore Jupiter's assurance of eventual redress. As in *Measure for Measure*, suffering and regret are framed in the benign context of a providential design that the audience alone can fully appreciate.

Tragicomedy threatens and consoles at the same time. The chief source of anxiety is Posthumus's renunciation of Imogen. The sensationalism of the plot derives in part from the use of the "wager" motif found in several Italianate *novelle*, such as the ninth tale of the second day in Giovanni Boccaccio's *Decameron*. The psychological portrait of Posthumus's wavering and fall, like that of Othello or Leontes, is intense and ugly, fraught with grotesque images of sexual coupling. As with Othello and Leontes, Posthumus is threatened by his wife's sexuality and is unable to respond securely to her offered love that is appropriately sensual and spiritual. He is comfortable only when he thinks of her as sexually restrained even in her marriage bed, praying forbearance of her husband with "A pudency so rosy the sweet view on't / Might well have warmed old Saturn" (2.5.11–12). He is aroused by virginal unresponsiveness but repelled by too great a responsiveness. Such unbalanced expectations leave him prone to insinuations that women practice deception. Once Imogen has been made to appear carnal to him, she becomes monstrous and insatiable in his imagination. He conjures up the imagined sexual triumph of Iachimo in animalistic terms: "Perchance he spoke not, but, / Like a full-acorned boar, a German one, / Cried 'Oh!' and mounted" (lines 15–17). Like Othello, he insists on being proved a cuckold; once he has experienced jealousy, he can expect only one conclusion. He longs "to tear her limbmeal," and like Lear he would violently destroy "The woman's part in me" (2.4.150; 2.5.20).

Posthumus suffers from dark fantasies about women such as we find elsewhere in Shakespeare. Because he regards women as male property, he is all too ready to engage in a contest with other males "in praise of our country mistresses" and to boast that Imogen is (in the terms of the contest) "more fair, virtuous, wise, chaste, constant, qualified, and less attemptable" than any other lady alive (1.4.57–61). The results are predictably disastrous, as they were earlier in Shakespeare's *The Rape of Lucrece*. By engaging in the objectification of women, Posthumus betrays his emotional kinship to Iachimo, who takes advantage of his concealment in Imogen's bedchamber to catalogue in clinical detail her physical charms along with the furniture of the room itself (2.2). Posthumus's misogynistic outburst against women as "half-workers" in the act of generation (2.5.1 ff.) reveals his fear of betrayal by all women (including his own mother) and hence his own helpless vulnerability to what he supposes to be women's lying, flattering, deceiving, "Lust and rank thoughts," revenges, "Nice longing, slanders, mutability, / All faults that have a name, nay, that hell knows" (lines 22–7). This male phobia is deeply sculpted in the male world of *Cymbeline*, for we see it also in Cloten's warped desire to possess Imogen and in Cymbeline's troubled patriarchal relations with his daughter and his domineering wife. In Posthumus, this typically male perversity threatens disaster and demands either a tragic ending or the contrived happy ending of tragicomedy. His failure places a special burden on Imogen to endure his frailty and to redeem it; only through her can Posthumus receive a second chance. Meantime, his failure has raised a familiarly Shakespearean question about his responsibility for his fall. How could he have avoided accusing Imogen falsely?

Powerful forces militate against Posthumus. Iachimo is a plausible villain, in the vein of Don John (*Much Ado About Nothing*), Iago (*Othello*), and Edmund (*King Lear*). Like them, he plots to arouse envy and dissension in others, by means of appearances falsely presented to the senses. We can readily understand him in human terms as a quarrelsome and lecherous man, and yet his sinster delight in mischief also suggests a more all-encompassing and diabolical evil. His contention is that every woman has her price (and every man, too). When he discovers in Imogen a wholesomeness that will not yield to his insinuations, he seeks to destroy her as a dangerous refutation of his low premise about human nature. He states the confrontation between them in cosmic terms: "Though this a heavenly angel, hell is here" (2.2.50). He does not, to be sure, boast gleefully to the audience or dominate the play as Iago does; moreover, he himself experiences the beneficent change brought about by the play's happy ending and speaks in praise of Imogen's virtue. As befits a tragicomedy, he is more sinister than potent, almost at times a travesty of a tragic villain. Nevertheless, in his scenes of villainy, his function is that of a diabolical tempter working through humanity's frail senses. His use of the ring as evidence recalls the handkerchief in *Othello*. Iachimo creates a minutely circumstantial inference of Imogen's transgression and lets Posthumus's inclination to believe the worst do the rest.

Like Othello, then, Posthumus must bear the blame for his loss of faith. The tempter can prevail upon his senses, but humanity's own wavering heart chooses evil. Trustworthy observers perceive Posthumus's fallacy and indicate the correct response; as Philario says, "This is not strong enough to be believed / Of one persuaded well of" (2.4.134–5). True faith urges that, being what she is, Imogen could not do the thing alleged. She is, like Helena and Desdemona before her, a virtuous woman who responds to her undeserved tribulations with forbearance (though even her patience has a limit, and she, too, is capable of overreacting and misjudging). She overbalances male faithlessness with her forgiveness. Her perseverance in virtue confounds Iachimo's thesis and rescues Posthumus from his worst self. Iachimo and she are spiritual contestants for the allegiance of Posthumus's faith. She triumphs, not through Posthumus's choice (which is for evil), but through her own unassailable goodness. Belatedly, too, Posthumus makes the amends that are necessary if we are to accept him as the restored hero. He forgives Imogen even before he knows of her innocence, seeks death as an atonement, and moves by degrees through sin to regret, confession of guilt, and penance. His peasant costume in Act 5 signals the resignation of worldly desire he must achieve to be worthy of an almost miraculous second chance. As fallen man, he can never truly deserve that mercy, but he can strive at least to atone for what he has done.

The story of King Cymbeline's long-lost sons is similarly tragicomic and is even more explicitly indebted to the conventions of romance with its motifs of banishment, wandering, and eventual recognition and reunion. The sylvan setting of this romantic narrative lends to the second half of the play a primal vigor and mystery (as also in *The Winter's Tale*). Arviragus and Guiderius remind us of medieval legends about Parzival; that is, like Parzival, they are young princes raised in a wilderness, lacking courtly training and yet possessing an "invisible instinct" (4.2.179) that prompts them to assert their royal blood. Ignoring their stepfather's warnings about the ingratitude and decadence of the courtly society he has abandoned, the princes long to prove themselves in deeds of chivalry. They are a rejuvenating force in this play, bringing together the ideals of medieval knighthood and the unsullied strength of their sylvan world. Cloten, that effete semblance of a courtier and their foil in every respect, is appropriately killed by these agents of "divine Nature" (line 172). They cherish Imogen as one of their own and grieve for her seeming death with the vivid immediacy of those who have lived with nature. Her seeming death and reawakening is for them something like the restorative cycle of the seasons, bringing a renewal of natural vigor that nicely complements the spiritual grace she embodies for Posthumus. Her name to them is appropriately "Fidele." Old Belarius's reconciliation with Cymbeline signals an end to political injustice, still another consequence of humanity's fallen condition for which grace must be provided.

The story of the war between Britain and Rome, derived in part from Holinshed's *Chronicles*, contributes also to the process of spiritual rebirth. The war sets in motion a series of apparently unrelated events, including the return to Britain of Posthumus and Iachimo, without which the play's happy conclusion would be impossible. Although the war itself is destructive and is supported chiefly by Cloten and the Queen (whose patriotic speeches show us just how hollow a thing patriotism can be), the war does lead ultimately to new life for Britain, as well as for the romantic lovers. Sudden turns in the battle, especially when an old man and two boys defend a narrow lane against an army, are seen as marvels directed by some higher power. In the benign aftermath of peace, the King, no longer misled by evil counselors, finds reconciliation with his daughter and her husband, as well as with Rome. The final scene, in which the seeming accidents of fortune are unraveled, is a structural tour de force of comic discovery.

The three main plots of *Cymbeline*—of Posthumus and Imogen, of the King's lost sons, and of the war between Britain and Rome—may seem outwardly unconnected with one another. Certainly, the play ranges over a wide geographical space and introduces a host of characters, many of whom never meet until the final scene. Yet the three plots are unified by being structurally like one another. In each, we perceive a pattern of fall from innocence, followed by conflict and eventual redemption. Posthumus is tempted into a loss of faith and attempted murder, from which he recovers through penance. The saga of the King's sons provides a secular equivalent in its story of estrangement, mistaken identity, and eventual recovery of loss. Politically, Britain is alienated from Rome through the machinations of the Queen only to rediscover

after many years a new harmony. The plots impinge on one another in ways that seem contrived (as, for example, when the accidents of war finally bring together Imogen, Posthumus, and Iachimo in the presence of Cymbeline), and yet we understand at last that the contrivance is providential and benign, intended to test humanity and then reward those who have persevered or at least have found true contrition.

Despite the symmetries of structure among the various plots of *Cymbeline*, the play manages to keep us constantly off balance. Its tragicomic pattern of innocence, conflict, and eventual redemption is repeatedly disturbed by the odd juxtapositions of imperial Rome, Renaissance Rome, and prehistoric Britain contrived from chronicle, romance, and pastoral. The play yields weird moments, such as Imogen's awakening near Milford Haven to find herself next to Cloten's headless body and to mistake it for Posthumus's body (4.2.294–335), or Jupiter's descent to earth on the back of an eagle (5.4.92 ff.). The play's denouement relies on the unraveling of an absurdly infantile riddle. The final accommodation of Britain into the Roman empire may add topical complexity by casting oblique glances in the direction of King James I of England and his dream of assuming a central role in the forging of a pacified Europe. Generically, the play is a deliberate mingling of history and romance, however successfully it may attempt to harmonize these genres; formally, it opts for instability through the intrusion of the comic into the serious. An implicit relationship between the psychosexual in the private realm and the political in the public realm is everywhere apparent and yet elusive.

Through such boldly experimental means, Shakespeare creates his dramatic world of accident and design, of odd juxtapositions and symmetry. The dramatist chooses by experimental and outrageous means to bring together disparate elements and to flaunt the lack of a perfectly smooth resolution, even while suggesting an overall sense of purpose and harmony that human witnesses can only imperfectly comprehend. Jupiter becomes the spokesman for a providential view in his role as *deus ex machina*—literally illustrating that term, since he "descends" from the stage roof by means of some mechanical device. The scene of this divine intervention (5.4) is so blatantly unrealistic that, as we have seen, many critics have wished to exonerate Shakespeare of having written it, but this very unreality is the key to the play's ending. Jupiter places the human suffering of the play in a larger perspective: "Whom best I love I cross, to make my gift, / The more delayed, delighted. Be content" (5.4.101–2). In the tragicomic view, suffering is the manifestation of a design engineered and supervised by a loving deity to test and strengthen humankind. Understood as such, the test affirms Imogen's strength, shows Posthumus a reason to cherish what he would otherwise destroy, and even reclaims the evil agent by whom the test had been put in operation. As Caius Lucius insists to the long-suffering Fidele, "Some falls are means the happier to arise" (4.2.406).

In the theater, *Cymbeline* calls for sensational effects. The nineteenth century often went for opulent splendor, as in Henry Irving's expensively realistic renditions of Celtic Britain and ancient Rome in his 1896 production at the Lyceum Theater, London. More recent interpretations have preferred theatrical wizardry of a more updated sort. Robin Phillips, at Stratford, Canada, in 1986, set the battle scenes in World War I garb, with Jupiter as a flying ace in goggles, appearing from above in a burst of light.

Wales was the primitive land of Tarzan. Directors have to choose whether to play Jupiter's epiphany as straight romance, emphasizing the wonder of it, or send the scene up as campy impossibility; if audiences laugh, the actors will go for parody and exaggeration. Since the play itself daringly courts improbability, styles of performance are likely to succeed best when the production is consciously aware of its own contrivances. Romance becomes metatheater; the theatrical space becomes one of magical virtuosity, inspiring in audiences an assent to the "truth" of the story as one of theatrical artifice at its best and as its own best excuse.

Cymbeline

[*Dramatis Personae*

CYMBELINE, *King of Britain*
QUEEN, *wife of Cymbeline*
CLOTEN, *her son by a former husband*
IMOGEN, *daughter of Cymbeline by a former queen*
POSTHUMUS LEONATUS, *a gentleman, Imogen's husband*
BELARIUS, *a banished lord, disguised as Morgan*
GUIDERIUS, } *sons of Cymbeline, disguised as Polydore*
ARVIRAGUS, } *and Cadwal, supposed sons of Morgan*

PISANIO, *servant of Posthumus*
CORNELIUS, *a physician*
Two LORDS *attending Cloten*
Two GENTLEMEN *of Cymbeline's court*
HELEN, *a lady attending Imogen*
Another LADY *attending Imogen, or possibly the same*
A LADY *attending the Queen*
A British LORD
Two British CAPTAINS
Two JAILERS
Two MESSENGERS

PHILARIO, *friend of Posthumus,* } *Italians*
IACHIMO, *friend of Philario,* }
A FRENCHMAN, *friend of Philario*

CAIUS LUCIUS, *general of the Roman forces*
Two Roman SENATORS
A TRIBUNE
A Roman CAPTAIN
Philharmonus, *a* SOOTHSAYER

JUPITER
The Ghost of SICILIUS *Leonatus, father of Posthumus*
The Ghost of Leonatus's MOTHER
The Ghosts of Leonatus's two BROTHERS

Lords, Ladies, Attendants, Musicians attending Cloten, a Dutchman, a Spaniard, Senators, Tribunes, Captains, and Soldiers

SCENE: *Britain; Italy*]

1.1

Enter two Gentlemen.

FIRST GENTLEMAN
You do not meet a man but frowns. Our bloods   1
No more obey the heavens than our courtiers'
Still seem as does the King's.

SECOND GENTLEMAN   But what's the matter?   3

FIRST GENTLEMAN
His daughter, and the heir of 's kingdom, whom
He purposed to his wife's sole son—a widow   5
That late he married—hath referred herself   6
Unto a poor but worthy gentleman. She's wedded,
Her husband banished, she imprisoned. All
Is outward sorrow, though I think the King   9
Be touched at very heart.

SECOND GENTLEMAN   None but the King?

FIRST GENTLEMAN
He that hath lost her, too. So is the Queen,   11
That most desired the match. But not a courtier,
Although they wear their faces to the bent   13
Of the King's looks, hath a heart that is not
Glad at the thing they scowl at.

SECOND GENTLEMAN   And why so?

FIRST GENTLEMAN
He that hath missed the Princess is a thing
Too bad for bad report, and he that hath her—
I mean, that married her, alack, good man!
And therefore banished—is a creature such
As, to seek through the regions of the earth
For one his like, there would be something failing   21
In him that should compare. I do not think   22
So fair an outward and such stuff within   23
Endows a man but he.

SECOND GENTLEMAN   You speak him far.   24

FIRST GENTLEMAN
I do extend him, sir, within himself,   25
Crush him together rather than unfold   26
His measure duly.

SECOND GENTLEMAN   What's his name and birth?   27

FIRST GENTLEMAN
I cannot delve him to the root. His father   28
Was called Sicilius, who did join his honor   29
Against the Romans with Cassibelan,   30

But had his titles by Tenantius, whom   31
He served with glory and admired success,
So gained the sur-addition Leonatus;   33
And had, besides this gentleman in question,
Two other sons, who in the wars o'th' time
Died with their swords in hand; for which their father,
Then old and fond of issue, took such sorrow   37
That he quit being, and his gentle lady,   38
Big of this gentleman our theme, deceased   39
As he was born. The King he takes the babe   40
To his protection, calls him Posthumus Leonatus,
Breeds him and makes him of his bedchamber,   42
Puts to him all the learnings that his time   43
Could make him the receiver of, which he took,
As we do air, fast as 'twas ministered,
And in 's spring became a harvest, lived in court—   46
Which rare it is to do—most praised, most loved,
A sample to the youngest, to th' more mature   48
A glass that feated them, and to the graver   49
A child that guided dotards. To his mistress,   50
For whom he now is banished, her own price   51
Proclaims how she esteemed him; and his virtue
By her election may be truly read   53
What kind of man he is.

SECOND GENTLEMAN   I honor him
Even out of your report. But pray you, tell me,   55
Is she sole child to th' King?

FIRST GENTLEMAN   His only child.
He had two sons; if this be worth your hearing,
Mark it: The eldest of them at three years old,
I'th' swaddling-clothes the other, from their nursery
Were stol'n, and to this hour no guess in knowledge   60
Which way they went.

SECOND GENTLEMAN   How long is this ago?

FIRST GENTLEMAN   Some twenty years.

SECOND GENTLEMAN
That a king's children should be so conveyed,
So slackly guarded, and the search so slow
That could not trace them!

FIRST GENTLEMAN   Howso'er 'tis strange,
Or that the negligence may well be laughed at,
Yet is it true, sir.

SECOND GENTLEMAN   I do well believe you.

FIRST GENTLEMAN
We must forbear. Here comes the gentleman,   69
The Queen, and Princess.   *Exeunt.*

Enter the Queen, Posthumus, and Imogen.

1.1. Location: Britain. At the court of King Cymbeline.
1–3 Our . . . King's The constitutions and dispositions of us mortals are no more obedient to the influence of the heavenly bodies than our courtiers' demeanors and looks follow those of the King.   5 purposed to intended for   6 late lately.   referred given (in marriage)   9 outward mere pretense of (as explained in lines 12–22)   11 He . . . her i.e., Cloten, the Queen's son, Imogen's unsuccessful wooer. (Also in line 16.)   13 bent inclination   21 his like like him   22 him . . . compare anyone chosen for comparison.   23 stuff (1) substance (2) fabric (as the imagery of lines 26–7 further suggests)   24 speak him far go far in praising him.   25 I . . . himself I expand his virtues within the limits of what he actually is   26–7 unfold . . . duly disclose his dimensions to the degree that he merits.   28 delve . . . root i.e., account fully for his lineage.   29 join his honor give his honorable assistance in arms   30 Cassibelan Cymbeline's uncle; see 3.1.5. (According to Holinshed, Cassibelan was Cymbeline's great-uncle, being younger brother and successor to King Lud.)

31 Tenantius Cymbeline's father, son of King Lud. (In Holinshed, Tenantius is Cassibelan's nephew.)   33 sur-addition additional title, surname.   Leonatus lion-born   37 fond of issue devoted to his children   38 quit being died.   gentle noble   39 Big . . . theme pregnant with this Posthumus we are talking about   40 King he i.e., King   42 Breeds raises, educates.   of his bedchamber one of his intimate retinue   43 Puts to sets before.   time time of life, age   46 in 's . . . harvest i.e., in his youth became ripe in learning   48 sample example   49 A glass . . . them a mirror that furnished them an image of virtue   49–50 to . . . dotards i.e., to older courtiers he offered wise example as if a child were to instruct doddering old men.   50 To As for; or, In the eyes of   51 her own price the price she willingly paid (of her father's hostility)   53 election choice (of him)   55 out of judging by   60 guess in knowledge credible conjecture   69 forbear stop talking and withdraw.

QUEEN
    No, be assured you shall not find me, daughter,
    After the slander of most stepmothers,   72
    Evil-eyed unto you. You're my prisoner, but
    Your jailer shall deliver you the keys
    That lock up your restraint. For you, Posthumus, 75
    So soon as I can win th'offended King
    I will be known your advocate. Marry, yet 77
    The fire of rage is in him, and 'twere good
    You leaned unto his sentence with what patience 79
    Your wisdom may inform you.
POSTHUMUS   Please Your Highness, 80
    I will from hence today.
QUEEN   You know the peril.
    I'll fetch a turn about the garden, pitying
    The pangs of barred affections, though the King
    Hath charged you should not speak together.   *Exit.*
IMOGEN   Oh,
    Dissembling courtesy! How fine this tyrant
    Can tickle where she wounds! My dearest husband,
    I something fear my father's wrath, but nothing— 87
    Always reserved my holy duty—what 88
    His rage can do on me. You must be gone,
    And I shall here abide the hourly shot
    Of angry eyes, not comforted to live 91
    But that there is this jewel in the world
    That I may see again.
POSTHUMUS   My queen, my mistress!
    Oh, lady, weep no more, lest I give cause 94
    To be suspected of more tenderness 95
    Than doth become a man. I will remain 96
    The loyal'st husband that did e'er plight troth;
    My residence in Rome at one Philario's,
    Who to my father was a friend, to me
    Known but by letter; thither write, my queen,
    And with mine eyes I'll drink the words you send,
    Though ink be made of gall.

       Enter Queen.

QUEEN   Be brief, I pray you.
    If the King come, I shall incur I know not
    How much of his displeasure. [*Aside*] Yet I'll move him
    To walk this way. I never do him wrong 105
    But he does buy my injuries, to be friends, 106
    Pays dear for my offenses.   [*Exit.*] 107
POSTHUMUS [*to Imogen*] Should we be taking leave
    As long a term as yet we have to live,
    The loathness to depart would grow. Adieu!
IMOGEN   Nay, stay a little!
    Were you but riding forth to air yourself, 112

    Such parting were too petty. Look here, love:
    This diamond was my mother's. Take it, heart,
    But keep it till you woo another wife
    When Imogen is dead.
      [*She gives a ring, or puts it on his finger.*]
POSTHUMUS   How, how? Another?
    You gentle gods, give me but this I have,
    And cere up my embracements from a next 118
    With bonds of death! Remain, remain thou here 119
    While sense can keep it on. And, sweetest, fairest, 120
    As I my poor self did exchange for you 121
    To your so infinite loss, so in our trifles 122
    I still win of you. For my sake wear this. 123
    It is a manacle of love; I'll place it
    Upon this fairest prisoner.
      [*He puts a bracelet upon her arm.*]
IMOGEN   O the gods!
    When shall we see again?

      Enter Cymbeline and lords.

POSTHUMUS   Alack, the King! 126
CYMBELINE [*to Posthumus*]
    Thou basest thing, avoid hence, from my sight! 127
    If after this command thou freight the court 128
    With thy unworthiness, thou diest. Away!
    Thou'rt poison to my blood.
POSTHUMUS   The gods protect you,
    And bless the good remainders of the court! 131
    I am gone.   *Exit.*
IMOGEN There cannot be a pinch in death 132
    More sharp than this is.
CYMBELINE   O disloyal thing,
    That shouldst repair my youth, thou heap'st 134
    A year's age on me.
IMOGEN   I beseech you, sir, 135
    Harm not yourself with your vexation.
    I am senseless of your wrath; a touch more rare 137
    Subdues all pangs, all fears.
CYMBELINE   Past grace? Obedience?
IMOGEN
    Past hope and in despair; that way past grace. 139
CYMBELINE
    That mightst have had the sole son of my queen!
IMOGEN
    O blessèd, that I might not! I chose an eagle 141

72 After the slander according to what is slanderously told **75 For** As for **77 Marry** i.e., Indeed. (Originally, "by the Virgin Mary.") **79 leaned unto** deferred to **80 inform** instill in **87 something** somewhat. **nothing** not in the least **88 Always . . . duty** although never forgetting my sacred duty to him. (Though dutiful and even fearful, Imogen will not let her father's rage alter her determination.) **91 not . . . live** finding no comfort in living **94–6 lest . . . man** i.e., lest I, too, shed tears, which would be unmanly in me. **105–7 I . . . offenses** Whenever I wrong him, he interprets those injuries as kindnesses and submits to them in order to remain on good terms. **112 air yourself** take some fresh air

118 cere up wrap in cerecloth or waxed cloth used for wrapping a dead body; perhaps with a play on sealing a document with wax. (See *bonds* in the next line.) **a next** another wife **119 Remain** (The ring will remind him of Imogen always.) **120 sense** sensory feeling. **it** (Said of the ring.) **121 exchange** (In their wedding vows, they have given themselves to each other.) **122 trifles** i.e., love tokens **123 I . . . you** I still am enriched in the exchange, receive better than I give. **126 see** see each other **127 avoid hence** begone **128 freight** burden **131 remainders of** those who remain at **132 pinch** pang **134 repair** restore **134–5 thou . . . on me** you've added a year to my age. **137 senseless of** insensible to. **a touch** a feeling (of love for Posthumus and pain at his banishment). **139 despair . . . grace** (Imogen puns bitterly on grace, by which the King meant "gracious dutifulness"; in her religious metaphor, to despair is to be beyond God's grace.) **141 blessèd** (Imogen continues the religious paradox: she is *blessèd* in her love, though *past grace*, or damned, in terms of the King's favor.)

And did avoid a puttock. 142

CYMBELINE
Thou took'st a beggar, wouldst have made my throne
A seat for baseness.

IMOGEN   No, I rather added
A luster to it.

CYMBELINE   O thou vile one!

IMOGEN   Sir,
It is your fault that I have loved Posthumus.
You bred him as my playfellow, and he is
A man worth any woman, overbuys me 148
Almost the sum he pays.

CYMBELINE   What, art thou mad? 149

IMOGEN
Almost, sir. Heaven restore me! Would I were
A neatherd's daughter, and my Leonatus 151
Our neighbor shepherd's son!

Enter Queen.

CYMBELINE   Thou foolish thing!—
[*To the Queen*] They were again together. You have done
Not after our command. Away with her 154
And pen her up.

QUEEN   Beseech your patience.—Peace, 155
Dear lady daughter, peace!—Sweet sovereign,
Leave us to ourselves, and make yourself some comfort
Out of your best advice.

CYMBELINE   Nay, let her languish 158
A drop of blood a day, and, being aged, 159
Die of this folly!   *Exit* [*with lords*].

QUEEN   Fie, you must give way. 160

Enter Pisanio.

Here is your servant.—How now, sir? What news?

PISANIO
My lord your son drew on my master.

QUEEN   Ha? 162
No harm, I trust, is done?

PISANIO   There might have been,
But that my master rather played than fought
And had no help of anger. They were parted 165
By gentlemen at hand.

QUEEN   I am very glad on't. 166

IMOGEN
Your son's my father's friend; he takes his part 167
To draw upon an exile. Oh, brave sir! 168

I would they were in Afric both together, 169
Myself by with a needle, that I might prick 170
The goer-back.—Why came you from your master?

PISANIO
On his command. He would not suffer me 172
To bring him to the haven, left these notes
Of what commands I should be subject to
When't pleased you to employ me.

QUEEN [*to Imogen*]   This hath been
Your faithful servant. I dare lay mine honor 176
He will remain so.

PISANIO   I humbly thank Your Highness.

QUEEN [*to Imogen*]   Pray, walk awhile. 179

IMOGEN [*to Pisanio*]   About some half hour hence,
Pray you, speak with me. You shall at least
Go see my lord aboard. For this time leave me.

Exeunt.

♣

1.[2]

Enter Cloten and two Lords.

FIRST LORD   Sir, I would advise you to shift a shirt. The 1
violence of action hath made you reek as a sacrifice.
Where air comes out, air comes in; there's none
abroad so wholesome as that you vent. 4

CLOTEN   If my shirt were bloody, then to shift it. Have 5
I hurt him?

SECOND LORD [*aside*]   No, faith, not so much as his 7
patience. 8

FIRST LORD   Hurt him? His body's a passable carcass if 9
he be not hurt. It is a thoroughfare for steel if it be not 10
hurt.

SECOND LORD [*aside*]   His steel was in debt; it went o'th' 12
backside the town. 13

CLOTEN   The villain would not stand me. 14

SECOND LORD [*aside*]   No, but he fled forward still, 15
toward your face. 16

FIRST LORD   Stand you? You have land enough of your
own, but he added to your having, gave you some 18
ground. 19

SECOND LORD [*aside*]   As many inches as you have 20
oceans. Puppies! 21

---

142 puttock kite, bird of prey.   **148–9 overbuys . . . pays** pays more for me than I am worth by almost as much as the price he pays (which is his banishment).   **149 mad** insane. (But Imogen uses the word to mean "mad with grief"; compare with her pun on *grace* in line 139.)   **151 neatherd's** cowherd's   **154 after** according to **155 Beseech** I beseech   **158 best advice** most mature reflection. **languish** pine away   **159 drop of blood** (Each sigh was supposed to deprive the heart of a drop of blood.)   **160 Fie . . . way** (Said to the departing King as a way of pretending, for Imogen's benefit, the Queen's concern for her.)   **162 My . . . master** i.e., Cloten drew his sword on Posthumus.   **165 had . . . anger** was not whetted on by anger.   **166 on't** of it.   **167 takes his part** sides with the King, or, plays the role one would expect of him   **168 To draw** in drawing

169 in Afric i.e., in some deserted spot   **170 prick** urge forward **172 suffer** allow   **176 lay** wager   **179 walk awhile** i.e., walk with me awhile.
1.2. Location: Britain. At the court of Cymbeline, as before. The time is virtually continuous; Cloten still sweats from his duel (1.1.162). 1 shift change   **4 abroad** outside you. (The First Lord flatteringly suggests that the outside air is not as wholesome as that of Cloten's own sweet body, as though the outside air were the cause of the odor of perspiration, but the effect of *reek* and *vent* is to inform us at any rate that the odor is his.)   **5 then to shift it** in that case, I would change it.   **7–8 his patience** (Posthumus's patience has been sorely tried by this encounter, but little else.)   **9 passable** (1) penetrable (2) tolerably good   **9–10 if . . . hurt** i.e., I don't know what you mean by "hurt" otherwise.   **12–13 His . . . town** ie., Cloten's rapier avoided the fight in a cowardly fashion, as a debtor hides in back streets. (With an antithetical play on *backside / thoroughfare*.)   **14 stand me** stand up to me. **15–16 No . . . face** i.e., What you call fleeing looked instead like his charging relentlessly toward you. (Said sardonically.)   **18–19 gave . . . ground** fell back before your advance. (With pun on literal meaning.) **20–1 As . . . oceans** i.e., None.   **21 Puppies!** Arrogant, vain cubs!

CLOTEN   I would they had not come between us.

SECOND LORD [*aside*]   So would I, till you had measured how long a fool you were upon the ground.

CLOTEN   And that she should love this fellow and
refuse me!

SECOND LORD [*aside*]   If it be a sin to make a true
election, she is damned.   28

FIRST LORD   Sir, as I told you always, her beauty and
her brain go not together. She's a good sign, but I have   30
seen small reflection of her wit.   31

SECOND LORD [*aside*]   She shines not upon fools, lest
the reflection should hurt her.   33

CLOTEN   Come, I'll to my chamber. Would there had
been some hurt done!

SECOND LORD [*aside*]   I wish not so, unless it had been
the fall of an ass, which is no great hurt.

CLOTEN   You'll go with us?   38

FIRST LORD   I'll attend Your Lordship.

CLOTEN   Nay, come, let's go together.

SECOND LORD   Well, my lord.   *Exeunt.*

❧

1.[3]

Enter Imogen and Pisanio.

IMOGEN
I would thou grew'st unto the shores o'th' haven
And questioned'st every sail. If he should write
And I not have it, 'twere a paper lost   3
As offered mercy is. What was the last   4
That he spake to thee?

PISANIO   It was his queen, his queen!

IMOGEN
Then waved his handkerchief?

PISANIO   And kissed it, madam.

IMOGEN
Senseless linen, happier therein than I!
And that was all?   7

PISANIO   No, madam; for so long
As he could make me with this eye or ear
Distinguish him from others, he did keep
The deck, with glove, or hat, or handkerchief
Still waving, as the fits and stirs of 's mind
Could best express how slow his soul sailed on,
How swift his ship.

IMOGEN   Thou shouldst have made him
As little as a crow, or less, ere left   15
To after-eye him.

PISANIO   Madam, so I did.   16

IMOGEN
I would have broke mine eyestrings, cracked them,
but
To look upon him till the diminution   17
Of space had pointed him sharp as my needle—   18
Nay, followed him till he had melted from   19
The smallness of a gnat to air, and then
Have turned mine eye and wept. But, good Pisanio,
When shall we hear from him?

PISANIO   Be assured, madam,
With his next vantage.   24

IMOGEN
I did not take my leave of him, but had
Most pretty things to say. Ere I could tell him
How I would think on him at certain hours
Such thoughts and such; or I could make him swear
The shes of Italy should not betray   29
Mine interest and his honor; or have charged him   30
At the sixth hour of morn, at noon, at midnight
T'encounter me with orisons, for then   32
I am in heaven for him; or ere I could   33
Give him that parting kiss which I had set
Betwixt two charming words, comes in my father,   35
And like the tyrannous breathing of the north   36
Shakes all our buds from growing.

Enter a Lady.

LADY   The Queen, madam,
Desires Your Highness' company.

IMOGEN
Those things I bid you do, get them dispatched.   39
I will attend the Queen.

PISANIO   Madam, I shall.   *Exeunt.*

❧

1.[4]

*Enter Philario, Iachimo, a Frenchman, a
Dutchman, and a Spaniard.*

IACHIMO   Believe it, sir, I have seen him in Britain. He
was then of a crescent note, expected to prove so   2
worthy as since he hath been allowed the name of. But   3
I could then have looked on him without the help of
admiration, though the catalogue of his endowments   5
had been tabled by his side and I to peruse him by   6
items.

---

28 election choice. (With a pun on the theological meaning.)   **30 go
not together** do not match.   **sign** semblance, appearance   **31 wit**
intelligence.   **33 reflection** (The Second Lord plays on *reflection,*
"shining," in line 31, suggesting here that, if Imogen were to show
favor to fools, it would *reflect on,* or bring reproach on, her character.)
38 You'll . . . us? (Addressed to the Second Lord or to both.)
1.3. Location: Britain. At the court of Cymbeline.
3–4 'twere . . . is i.e., the loss of such a letter would be as unfortunate
as a pardon offered but failing to arrive before the execution, or as
God's mercy similarly having no effect.   **7 Senseless** Unfeeling
15–16 ere . . . him before you left off following him with your gaze.

17 eyestrings the muscles, nerves, or tendons of the eye, thought to
break or crack at loss of sight.   **but merely   18–19 till . . . needle**
until the increase of distance had made him appear as small as my
needle's point   **24 next vantage** first opportunity.   **29 shes** women
30 Mine interest my legitimate claim to his loyalty   **32 T'encounter**
to join.   **orisons** prayers   **33 in heaven** i.e., praying   **35 charming**
having magical potency (to protect Posthumus from evil)   **36 north**
north wind   **39 bid** bade, ordered
1.4. Location: Rome. Philario's house. Perhaps a feast is in progress;
see 5.5.157.
2 crescent note growing reputation   **3 allowed the name of** granted
to have the reputation for.   **5 admiration** wonder. (Iachimo insists he
was not dazzled by Posthumus.)   **6 tabled** set down in a list

PHILARIO   You speak of him when he was less furnished than now he is with that which makes him both with- 9
out and within. 10

FRENCHMAN   I have seen him in France. We had very many there could behold the sun with as firm eyes 12
as he.

IACHIMO   This matter of marrying his king's daughter, wherein he must be weighed rather by her value than his own, words him, I doubt not, a great deal from the 16
matter. 17

FRENCHMAN   And then his banishment.

IACHIMO   Ay, and the approbation of those that weep 19
this lamentable divorce under her colors are wonder- 20
fully to extend him, be it but to fortify her judgment, 21
which else an easy battery might lay flat for taking a 22
beggar without less quality. But how comes it he is to 23
sojourn with you? How creeps acquaintance? 24

PHILARIO   His father and I were soldiers together, to whom I have been often bound for no less than my life.

Enter Posthumus.

Here comes the Briton. Let him be so entertained amongst you as suits, with gentlemen of your know- 29
ing, to a stranger of his quality.—I beseech you all, be 30
better known to this gentleman, whom I commend to you as a noble friend of mine. How worthy he is I will leave to appear hereafter rather than story him in his 33
own hearing.

FRENCHMAN   Sir, we have known together in Orleans. 35

POSTHUMUS   Since when I have been debtor to you for courtesies which I will be ever to pay and yet pay still. 37

FRENCHMAN   Sir, you o'errate my poor kindness. I was glad I did atone my countryman and you. It had been 39
pity you should have been put together with so mortal 40
a purpose as then each bore, upon importance of so 41
slight and trivial a nature.

POSTHUMUS   By your pardon, sir, I was then a young traveler; rather shunned to go even with what I heard 44
than in my every action to be guided by others' experiences. But upon my mended judgment—if I 46
offend not to say it is mended—my quarrel was not altogether slight.

FRENCHMAN   Faith, yes, to be put to the arbitrament of 49
swords, and by such two that would by all likelihood 50
have confounded one the other or have fallen both. 51

IACHIMO   Can we, with manners, ask what was the difference? 53

FRENCHMAN   Safely, I think; 'twas a contention in public, which may without contradiction suffer the 55
report. It was much like an argument that fell out last 56
night, where each of us fell in praise of our country 57
mistresses, this gentleman at that time vouching—and 58
upon warrant of bloody affirmation—his to be more 59
fair, virtuous, wise, chaste, constant, qualified, and less 60
attemptable than any the rarest of our ladies in France. 61

IACHIMO   That lady is not now living, or this gentleman's opinion by this worn out. 63

POSTHUMUS   She holds her virtue still, and I my mind. 64

IACHIMO   You must not so far prefer her 'fore ours of 65
Italy.

POSTHUMUS   Being so far provoked as I was in France, I would abate her nothing, though I profess myself 68
her adorer, not her friend. 69

IACHIMO   As fair and as good—a kind of hand-in-hand 70
comparison—had been something too fair and too 71
good for any lady in Britain. If she went before others 72
I have seen, as that diamond of yours outlusters many 73
I have beheld, I could not but believe she excelled many. But I have not seen the most precious diamond that is, nor you the lady.

POSTHUMUS   I praised her as I rated her. So do I my stone.

IACHIMO   What do you esteem it at?

POSTHUMUS   More than the world enjoys. 80

IACHIMO   Either your unparagoned mistress is dead, or 81
she's outprized by a trifle. 82

POSTHUMUS   You are mistaken. The one may be sold or given, or if there were wealth enough for the purchase 84
or merit for the gift. The other is not a thing for sale, and only the gift of the gods. 86

IACHIMO   Which the gods have given you?

POSTHUMUS   Which, by their graces, I will keep.

IACHIMO   You may wear her in title yours; but you 89
know strange fowl light upon neighboring ponds. 90

9–10 makes . . . within establishes him as regards both his fortune and his character.   12 behold the sun i.e., like an eagle, a royal bird supposedly able to stare at the sun unblinkingly   16–17 words . . . matter causes him to be described in accounts that go beyond the truth.   19–23 Ay . . . quality Yes, and those who weep for this lamentable forced separation, taking Imogen's side in the matter (literally, carrying her banner), approvingly seek every means possible to praise Posthumus beyond his merit, if only to justify her choice of him, which otherwise would be vulnerable to attack for having chosen a beggar of no rank or merit.   24 How creeps acquaintance? How has he crept into your favor?   29–30 knowing knowledge of affairs, *savoir faire*   30 stranger foreigner.   quality rank.   33 story give an account of   35 known together been acquainted   37 which . . . still which I will always be indebted to you for, even if I go on paying forever.   39 atone reconcile   40 put together set opposite one another in a duel.   mortal deadly   41 importance matter, occasion   44 shunned . . . even declined to agree   46 upon even upon. mended improved

49–50 arbitrament of swords settlement by a duel   51 confounded destroyed   53 difference quarrel.   55–6 without . . . report without objection be reported or told.   57–8 our country mistresses the lady each of us loves in his native land   59 bloody affirmation affirming the truth in a duel   60 qualified having fine qualities   61 attempt-able open to attempts on her virtue.   any the rarest any of the finest   63 by this by now   64 mind opinion.   65 prefer her advance her claims   68 would abate her nothing would not lower my estimate of her in the slightest   68–9 though . . . friend even though I should (as at that time, in France) profess myself to be her adorer or worshiper in the "courtly" sense, not her accepted lover.   70–1 hand-in-hand comparison comparison claiming equality only, not superiority   71 had would have   72 went before excelled   73 diamond i.e., the ring Imogen gave Posthumus   80 the world enjoys anything in the world.   81–2 Either . . . trifle (In that case, jests Iachimo, you must love your jewel more than her, for if she is alive she is "in the world.")   84 or if if either   86 only . . . gods the gift of the gods alone.   89 wear . . . yours possess her in name, claim title to her 90 strange . . . ponds i.e., claiming possession doesn't prevent strangers from infiltrating one's private domain.

Your ring may be stolen too. So your brace of unpriz- 91
able estimations, the one is but frail and the other ca- 92
sual. A cunning thief or a that-way-accomplished cour- 93
tier would hazard the winning both of first and last.

POSTHUMUS   Your Italy contains none so accomplished a
courtier to convince the honor of my mistress if, in 96
the holding or loss of that, you term her frail. I do
nothing doubt you have store of thieves; notwith- 98
standing, I fear not my ring. 99

PHILARIO   Let us leave here, gentlemen. 100

POSTHUMUS   Sir, with all my heart. This worthy signor,
I thank him, makes no stranger of me; we are familiar 102
at first. 103

IACHIMO   With five times so much conversation I
should get ground of your fair mistress, make her go 105
back even to the yielding, had I admittance and 106
opportunity to friend. 107

POSTHUMUS   No, no.

IACHIMO   I dare thereupon pawn the moiety of my estate 109
to your ring, which in my opinion o'ervalues it some- 110
thing. But I make my wager rather against your confi- 111
dence than her reputation, and, to bar your offense 112
herein too, I durst attempt it against any lady in the
world.

POSTHUMUS   You are a great deal abused in too bold a 115
persuasion, and I doubt not you sustain what you're 116
worthy of by your attempt.

IACHIMO   What's that?

POSTHUMUS   A repulse—though your attempt, as you
call it, deserve more: a punishment too.

PHILARIO   Gentlemen, enough of this. It came in too
suddenly; let it die as it was born, and, I pray you, be
better acquainted.

IACHIMO   Would I had put my estate and my neighbor's 124
on th'approbation of what I have spoke! 125

POSTHUMUS   What lady would you choose to assail?

IACHIMO   Yours, whom in constancy you think stands
so safe. I will lay you ten thousand ducats to your ring 128
that, commend me to the court where your lady is, 129
with no more advantage than the opportunity of a
second conference, and I will bring from thence that
honor of hers which you imagine so reserved. 132

POSTHUMUS   I will wage against your gold, gold to it. 133
My ring I hold dear as my finger; 'tis part of it.

IACHIMO   You are a friend, and therein the wiser. If you 135
buy ladies' flesh at a million a dram, you cannot 136
preserve it from tainting. But I see you have some
religion in you, that you fear. 138

POSTHUMUS   This is but a custom in your tongue. You
bear a graver purpose, I hope.

IACHIMO   I am the master of my speeches and would
undergo what's spoken, I swear. 142

POSTHUMUS   Will you? I shall but lend my diamond till
your return. Let there be covenants drawn between 's.
My mistress exceeds in goodness the hugeness of your
unworthy thinking. I dare you to this match; here's
my ring.   [He wagers his ring.] 147

PHILARIO   I will have it no lay. 148

IACHIMO   By the gods, it is one. If I bring you no
sufficient testimony that I have enjoyed the dearest
bodily part of your mistress, my ten thousand ducats
are yours; so is your diamond too. If I come off and
leave her in such honor as you have trust in, she your
jewel, this your jewel, and my gold are yours—
provided I have your commendation for my more free 155
entertainment. 156

POSTHUMUS   I embrace these conditions. Let us have
articles betwixt us. Only, thus far you shall answer: if
you make your voyage upon her and give me directly 159
to understand you have prevailed, I am no further your
enemy; she is not worth our debate. If she remain un-
seduced, you not making it appear otherwise, for your
ill opinion and th'assault you have made to her chastity you shall answer me with your sword.

IACHIMO   Your hand; a covenant. [They shake hands.]
We will have these things set down by lawful counsel,
and straight away for Britain, lest the bargain should
catch cold and starve. I will fetch my gold and have 168
our two wagers recorded.

POSTHUMUS   Agreed.   [Exeunt Posthumus and Iachimo.]

FRENCHMAN   Will this hold, think you?

PHILARIO   Signor Iachimo will not from it. Pray let us 172
follow 'em.   Exeunt.

✤

1.[5]

Enter Queen, Ladies, and Cornelius.

QUEEN
Whiles yet the dew's on ground, gather those flowers.
Make haste. Who has the note of them?

A LADY   I, madam. 2

91 ring (Often, as here, symbolic of a chastity that can be lost.)
91–2 your . . . estimations of the pair of objects (lady and ring) that
you esteem beyond value   92–3 casual susceptible to accident (such
as theft).   93 that-way-accomplished i.e., accomplished in seducing
women   96 to convince as to overcome   98 nothing not at all.
store plenty   99 fear not fear not for   100 leave leave off, cease
102–3 familiar at first on familiar terms right from the start.   105 get
ground gain the advantage   105–6 go back succumb, give way. (The
metaphor is from fencing, with sexual suggestion.)   107 to friend to
assist me.   109 moiety half   110–11 something somewhat.   112 bar
your offense avoid offending you individually   115–16 abused . . .
persuasion deceived in your excessively bold belief   116 sustain
will sustain, receive   124 put wagered   125 th'approbation the
attestation, confirmation   128 lay wager   129 commend me provide
me a letter of introduction   132 reserved kept safe.   133 to it in
equal amount.

135 You . . . wiser i.e., You know her too well, being her lover, to bet
your ring on her.   136 at . . . dram i.e., at an inordinately high price
for a very small amount   138 that since.   fear (1) experience "the
fear of the Lord" that is the beginning of true wisdom (2) are fearful.
142 undergo undertake   147 s.d. wagers his ring (Possibly Posthumus hands the ring to Iachimo or to Philario as official of the wager,
or perhaps he still keeps it himself; see 2.4.108.)   148 I . . . lay I will
not let it be a wager.   155 commendation introduction (to Imogen)
155–6 free entertainment ready welcome.   159 directly straightforwardly, unequivocally   168 starve die (through second thoughts and
cooling of resolve).   172 from it depart from it.
1.5. Location: Britain. At the court of Cymbeline.
2 note list

QUEEN   Dispatch.   *Exeunt Ladies.*
Now, Master Doctor, have you brought those drugs?

CORNELIUS
Pleaseth Your Highness, ay. Here they are, madam.   5
   [*He presents a small box.*]
But I beseech Your Grace, without offense—
My conscience bids me ask—wherefore you have   7
Commanded of me these most poisonous
   compounds,
Which are the movers of a languishing death,
But though slow, deadly.

QUEEN   I wonder, Doctor,
Thou ask'st me such a question. Have I not been
Thy pupil long? Hast thou not learned me how   12
To make perfumes? Distill? Preserve? Yea, so
That our great king himself doth woo me oft
For my confections? Having thus far proceeded—   15
Unless thou think'st me devilish—is't not meet   16
That I did amplify my judgment in   17
Other conclusions? I will try the forces   18
Of these thy compounds on such creatures as
We count not worth the hanging—but none human—
To try the vigor of them and apply   21
Allayments to their act, and by them gather   22
Their several virtues and effects.

CORNELIUS   Your Highness   23
Shall from this practice but make hard your heart.   24
Besides, the seeing these effects will be
Both noisome and infectious.

QUEEN   Oh, content thee.   26

Enter Pisanio.

[*Aside*] Here comes a flattering rascal; upon him
Will I first work. He's for his master,   28
And enemy to my son.—How now, Pisanio?—
Doctor, your service for this time is ended;
Take your own way.

CORNELIUS [*aside*]   I do suspect you, madam,   31
But you shall do no harm.

QUEEN [*to Pisanio*]   Hark thee, a word.

CORNELIUS [*aside*]
I do not like her. She doth think she has
Strange ling'ring poisons. I do know her spirit
And will not trust one of her malice with
A drug of such damned nature. Those she has
Will stupefy and dull the sense awhile,
Which first, perchance, she'll prove on cats and dogs, 38
Then afterward up higher; but there is
No danger in what show of death it makes
More than the locking-up the spirits a time,

To be more fresh, reviving. She is fooled
With a most false effect, and I the truer   43
So to be false with her.

QUEEN   No further service, Doctor,
Until I send for thee.

CORNELIUS   I humbly take my leave.   *Exit.*

QUEEN [*to Pisanio*]
Weeps she still, say'st thou? Dost thou think in time
She will not quench, and let instructions enter   49
Where folly now possesses? Do thou work.
When thou shalt bring me word she loves my son,
I'll tell thee on the instant thou art then
As great as is thy master; greater, for
His fortunes all lie speechless, and his name   54
Is at last gasp. Return he cannot, nor
Continue where he is. To shift his being   56
Is to exchange one misery with another,
And every day that comes comes to decay   58
A day's work in him. What shalt thou expect   59
To be depender on a thing that leans,   60
Who cannot be new built, nor has no friends,
So much as but to prop him? [*The Queen drops the box:*
   Pisanio takes it up.] Thou tak'st up
Thou know'st not what; but take it for thy labor.
It is a thing I made, which hath the King
Five times redeemed from death. I do not know
What is more cordial. Nay, I prithee, take it;   66
It is an earnest of a farther good   67
That I mean to thee. Tell thy mistress how
The case stands with her; do't as from thyself.   69
Think what a chance thou changest on, but think   70
Thou hast thy mistress still—to boot, my son,   71
Who shall take notice of thee. I'll move the King   72
To any shape of thy preferment such   73
As thou'lt desire; and then myself, I chiefly,
That set thee on to this desert, am bound   75
To load thy merit richly. Call my women.
Think on my words.   *Exit Pisanio.*
                A sly and constant knave,
Not to be shaked; the agent for his master,   78
And the remembrancer of her to hold   79
The handfast to her lord. I have given him that   80
Which, if he take, shall quite unpeople her   81
Of liegers for her sweet, and which she after,   82

---

5 Pleaseth If it please   **5.1** *He presents . . . box* (Perhaps Cornelius hesitates before actually giving it to her; she may snatch it from him.)   **7 wherefore** why   **12 learned** taught   **15 confections** compounds (of drugs)   **16 meet** fitting   **17 did** should   **18 conclusions** experiments.   **try** test   **21–3 To try . . . effects** to test their efficacy and apply antidotes to their action, and by these experiments determine their various operative powers and effects.   **24 but** only   **26 noisome** noxious, foul-smelling.   **content thee** do not trouble yourself.   **28 He's for** i.e., He's an agent for   **31 Take your own way** Be off, go about your business.   **38 prove** test

43 truer more honest   **49 quench** become cool.   **instructions** good counsel   **54 name** reputation   **56 shift his being** change his abode   **58–9 And . . . him** i.e., and every new day that arrives means the undoing of a day's fruitful endeavor as far as he's concerned.   **59 What . . . expect** What can you expect for yourself   **60 To . . . leans** to be a dependent of a creature (Posthumus) who is about to fall   **66 cordial** restorative (literally, to the heart).   **67 earnest** first payment   **69 as from thyself** as if from your own advice.   **70 Think . . . on** Think what an improvement in your fortunes you come upon in this change of service   **71 Thou . . . still** i.e., you will have Imogen as your patroness still, as the wife of Cloten, your new lord.   **to boot** and besides her (you will have)   **72 take notice of thee** look out for you, offer advancement to you.   **73 preferment** advancement   **75 That . . . desert** who urged you to take this action for which you will be rewarded   **78 shaked** shaken (in his loyalty)   **79 remembrancer of her** one who reminds her   **80 handfast** marriage contract   **81–2 shall . . . sweet** will thoroughly deprive her of the services of any ambassadors to her sweet Posthumus

Except she bend her humor, shall be assured   83
To taste of too.

Enter Pisanio, and Ladies [with flowers].

         So, so. Well done, well done.
The violets, cowslips, and the primroses
Bear to my closet. Fare thee well, Pisanio;   86
Think on my words.   *Exeunt Queen and Ladies.*

PISANIO And shall do.
But when to my good lord I prove untrue,
I'll choke myself. There's all I'll do for you.   *Exit.*

          ❦

1.[6]

Enter Imogen alone.

IMOGEN
A father cruel and a stepdame false,
A foolish suitor to a wedded lady
That hath her husband banished. Oh, that husband!   3
My supreme crown of grief, and those repeated   4
Vexations of it! Had I been thief-stol'n,
As my two brothers, happy! But most miserable   6
Is the desire that's glorious. Blest be those,   7
How mean soe'er, that have their honest wills,   8
Which seasons comfort.—Who may this be? Fie!   9

Enter Pisanio and Iachimo.

PISANIO
Madam, a noble gentleman of Rome,
Comes from my lord with letters.
IACHIMO   Change you, madam?   11
The worthy Leonatus is in safety
And greets Your Highness dearly.
                  [He presents a letter.]
IMOGEN   Thanks, good sir.
You're kindly welcome.   *[She reads.]*
IACHIMO *[aside]*
All of her that is out of door most rich!   15
If she be furnished with a mind so rare,
She is alone th'Arabian bird, and I   17
Have lost the wager. Boldness be my friend!
Arm me, audacity, from head to foot!
Or, like the Parthian, I shall flying fight—   20
Rather, directly fly.
IMOGEN *(reads)* "He is one of the noblest note, to   22
whose kindnesses I am most infinitely tied. Reflect   23

upon him accordingly, as you value your trust—
                        Leonatus."
So far I read aloud.
But even the very middle of my heart
Is warmed by th' rest and takes it thankfully.
You are as welcome, worthy sir, as I
Have words to bid you, and shall find it so
In all that I can do.
IACHIMO   Thanks, fairest lady.
What, are men mad? Hath nature given them eyes
To see this vaulted arch and the rich crop   33
Of sea and land, which can distinguish twixt
The fiery orbs above and the twinned stones   35
Upon th'unnumbered beach, and can we not   36
Partition make with spectacles so precious   37
Twixt fair and foul?
IMOGEN   What makes your admiration?   38
IACHIMO
It cannot be i'th'eye, for apes and monkeys
Twixt two such shes would chatter this way and   40
Contemn with mows the other; nor i'th' judgment,   41
For idiots in this case of favor would   42
Be wisely definite; nor i'th'appetite: 43
Sluttery, to such neat excellence opposed,   44
Should make desire vomit emptiness,   45
Not so allured to feed.   46
IMOGEN
What is the matter, trow?
IACHIMO   The cloyèd will—   47
That satiate yet unsatisfied desire, that tub   48
Both filled and running—ravening first the lamb,   49
Longs after for the garbage.
IMOGEN   What, dear sir,
Thus raps you? Are you well?   51
IACHIMO
Thanks, madam, well. *[To Pisanio]* Beseech you, sir,
Desire my man's abode where I did leave him.   53
He's strange and peevish.
PISANIO   I was going, sir,   54
To give him welcome.   *Exit.*
IMOGEN
Continues well my lord? His health, beseech you?
IACHIMO Well, madam.
IMOGEN
Is he disposed to mirth? I hope he is.
IACHIMO
Exceeding pleasant; none a stranger there   59

---

83 Except . . . humor unless she changes her mind (about not accepting Cloten) **86 closet** private chamber.
1.6. Location: Britain. At the court.
3 That . . . banished whose husband is banished. **4 repeated** already enumerated **6 happy!** how happy and fortunate would I be! **7 the desire . . . glorious** i.e., the ungratified yearnings of those of us who are born to high social station—in this case my yearning for Posthumus. **8 mean** lowly. **honest wills** simple desires **9 seasons** adds relish to **11 Comes** who comes. **letters** i.e., (probably) a letter. **Change you, Madam?** Does your expression change at news of letters from Rome? **15 out of door** external **17 th'Arabian bird** i.e., the phoenix, therefore unique **20 Parthian** (The Parthians were proverbial in ancient times for discharging a flight of arrows as they fled.) **22 note** reputation **23 Reflect** Bestow favor

33 vaulted arch sky. **crop** harvest, produce **35 fiery orbs** stars. **twinned** exactly alike **36 th'unnumbered** the numberless **37 Partition** distinction. **with . . . precious** i.e., with organs of vision so acutely sensitive **38 admiration** wonder. **40 chatter this way** i.e., indicate approval of Imogen **41 Contemn** scorn. **mows** grimaces, wry faces **42 in . . . favor** in question concerning a face of such grace and beauty **43 Be wisely definite** choose wisely **44–6 Sluttery . . . feed** sluttishness itself, confronted with such pure excellence, would void its own empty desire, not being tempted to feed its lust.
47 trow do you think. **will** lustful appetite **48 satiate** glutted, *cloyèd,* as in line 47. (The perverted sexual appetite is at once glutted and insatiable.) **49 running** emptying itself. **ravening** devouring greedily **51 raps** transports, makes rapt **53 Desire . . . abode** bid my servant remain **54 strange and peevish** a foreigner and easily upset. **59 none a stranger** no other foreigner

So merry and so gamesome. He is called   60
The Briton reveler.

IMOGEN   When he was here
He did incline to sadness, and ofttimes   62
Not knowing why.

IACHIMO   I never saw him sad.
There is a Frenchman his companion, one
An eminent monsieur that, it seems, much loves
A Gallian girl at home. He furnaces   66
The thick sighs from him, whiles the jolly Briton—   67
Your lord, I mean—laughs from 's free lungs, cries
"Oh,   68
Can my sides hold, to think that man, who knows
By history, report, or his own proof   70
What woman is, yea, what she cannot choose
But must be, will 's free hours languish   72
For assurèd bondage?"

IMOGEN   Will my lord say so?   73

IACHIMO
Ay, madam, with his eyes in flood with laughter.
It is a recreation to be by
And hear him mock the Frenchman. But heavens
    know
Some men are much to blame.

IMOGEN   Not he, I hope.

IACHIMO
Not he; but yet heaven's bounty towards him might   78
Be used more thankfully. In himself, 'tis much;   79
In you, which I account his, beyond all talents.   80
Whilst I am bound to wonder, I am bound   81
To pity too.

IMOGEN   What do you pity, sir?   82

IACHIMO
Two creatures heartily.

IMOGEN   Am I one, sir?   83
You look on me. What wrack discern you in me   84
Deserves your pity?

IACHIMO   Lamentable! What,   85
To hide me from the radiant sun, and solace   86
I'th' dungeon by a snuff?

IMOGEN   I pray you, sir,   87
Deliver with more openness your answers
To my demands. Why do you pity me?   89

IACHIMO   That others do—
I was about to say—enjoy your—But

It is an office of the gods to venge it,   92
Not mine to speak on't.

IMOGEN   You do seem to know   93
Something of me, or what concerns me. Pray you—
Since doubting things go ill often hurts more   95
Than to be sure they do; for certainties
Either are past remedies, or, timely knowing,   97
The remedy then born—discover to me   98
What both you spur and stop.

IACHIMO   Had I this cheek   99
To bathe my lips upon; this hand, whose touch,
Whose every touch, would force the feeler's soul
To th'oath of loyalty; this object, which
Takes prisoner the wild motion of mine eye,
Fixing it only here; should I, damned then,
Slaver with lips as common as the stairs
That mount the Capitol; join grips with hands   106
Made hard with hourly falsehood—falsehood as   107
With labor; then by-peeping in an eye   108
Base and illustrous as the smoky light   109
That's fed with stinking tallow—it were fit
That all the plagues of hell should at one time
Encounter such revolt.

IMOGEN   My lord, I fear,   112
Has forgot Britain.

IACHIMO   And himself. Not I,   113
Inclined to this intelligence, pronounce   114
The beggary of his change, but 'tis your graces   115
That from my mutest conscience to my tongue   116
Charms this report out.

IMOGEN   Let me hear no more.

IACHIMO
O dearest soul, your cause doth strike my heart
With pity that doth make me sick. A lady
So fair, and fastened to an empery   120
Would make the great'st king double—to be partnered 121
With tomboys hired with that self exhibition   122
Which your own coffers yield; with diseased ventures 123
That play with all infirmities for gold   124
Which rottenness can lend nature; such boiled stuff 125
As well might poison poison! Be revenged,
Or she that bore you was no queen, and you
Recoil from your great stock.   128

---

60 gamesome sportive. (With a sexual suggestion, as also, in the following lines, in *reveler, jolly, free,* etc.)   **62 sadness** seriousness
66 Gallian Gallic, French.   **furnaces** gives forth like a furnace
67 thick coming thick and fast   **68 from 's free lungs** i.e., without restraint, heartily   **70 proof** experience   **72 will 's . . . languish** will give up his free time and licentious opportunities   **73 assurèd** (1) certain (2) betrothed   **78–82 heaven's . . . pity too** i.e., the graces that heaven has lent him might be more thankfully acknowledged and employed. His own graces are considerable; but his having you as his wife (or so I understand) bestows on him a gift of such rarity that I am bound to wonder at and at the same time to pity.   **83 two creatures** (Iachimo implies that he pities Imogen for having a faithless husband and, in a different sense, pities Posthumus for abusing such a rich gift.)   **84 wrack** ruin   **85 Deserves** that deserves   **86 hide me** i.e., hide.   **solace** take delight   **87 snuff** smoking candlewick.
89 demands inquiries.

92 office function   **93 on't** of it.   **95 doubting** fearing (that)
97 timely knowing if one knows in time   **98 then born** i.e., is then born.   **discover** reveal   **99 What . . . stop** i.e., what you simultaneously urge toward disclosure and then conceal, as if spurring and then reining in a horse.   **106 grips** claspings   **107–8 as With labor** as much as if they had been made hard by actual labor   **108 by-peeping** giving sidelong glances   **109 illustrous** not lustrous   **112 Encounter . . . revolt** confront and punish such infidelity.   **113–15 Not . . . change** It is not through any inclination to disclose this information that I report his contemptible alteration   **116 mutest conscience** most silent inner being   **120–1 fastened . . . double** endowed with an empire (of graces and inheritance) that would make any king's wealth twice what it was before   **121–3 to be . . . yield** to be made to share him as sexual partner with wantons paid for with that very allowance of money that he received from your own treasure chests
123–5 with diseased . . . nature with diseased prostitutes who, for gold, play around with all the infirmities that rottenness (venereal disease) can lend to human nature.   **125 boiled stuff** i.e., women treated by "sweating" for venereal disease   **128 Recoil** fall away, degenerate

IMOGEN   Revenged?
How should I be revenged? If this be true—
As I have such a heart that both mine ears   131
Must not in haste abuse—if it be true,   132
How should I be revenged?
IACHIMO   Should he make me
Live like Diana's priest betwixt cold sheets   134
Whiles he is vaulting variable ramps,   135
In your despite, upon your purse? Revenge it.   136
I dedicate myself to your sweet pleasure,
More noble than that runagate to your bed,   138
And will continue fast to your affection,   139
Still close as sure.
IMOGEN [calling]   What, ho, Pisanio!   140
IACHIMO
Let me my service tender on your lips.
IMOGEN
Away! I do condemn mine ears that have
So long attended thee. If thou wert honorable,   143
Thou wouldst have told this tale for virtue, not
For such an end thou seek'st—as base as strange.
Thou wrong'st a gentleman who is as far
From thy report as thou from honor, and
Solicits here a lady that disdains
Thee and the devil alike.—What ho, Pisanio!—
The King my father shall be made acquainted
Of thy assault. If he shall think it fit
A saucy stranger in his court to mart   152
As in a Romish stew and to expound   153
His beastly mind to us, he hath a court
He little cares for and a daughter who
He not respects at all.—What, ho, Pisanio!
IACHIMO
O happy Leonatus! I may say
The credit that thy lady hath of thee   158
Deserves thy trust, and thy most perfect goodness
Her assured credit.—Blessèd live you long,   160
A lady to the worthiest sir that ever
Country called his, and you his mistress, only   162
For the most worthiest fit! Give me your pardon.
I have spoke this to know if your affiance   164
Were deeply rooted, and shall make your lord   165
That which he is new o'er; and he is one   166
The truest mannered, such a holy witch   167
That he enchants societies into him.   168
Half all men's hearts are his.
IMOGEN   You make amends. 169

IACHIMO
He sits 'mongst men like a descended god.
He hath a kind of honor sets him off   171
More than a mortal seeming. Be not angry,   172
Most mighty Princess, that I have adventured
To try your taking of a false report, which hath
Honored with confirmation your great judgment
In the election of a sir so rare,   176
Which you know cannot err. The love I bear him   177
Made me to fan you thus, but the gods made you,   178
Unlike all others, chaffless. Pray, your pardon. 179
IMOGEN
All's well, sir. Take my power i'th' court for yours.
IACHIMO
My humble thanks. I had almost forgot
T'entreat Your Grace but in a small request,
And yet of moment too, for it concerns   183
Your lord, myself, and other noble friends
Are partners in the business.
IMOGEN   Pray, what is't?   185
IACHIMO
Some dozen Romans of us and your lord—
The best feather of our wing—have mingled sums   187
To buy a present for the Emperor;
Which I, the factor for the rest, have done   189
In France. 'Tis plate of rare device, and jewels 190
Of rich and exquisite form, their values great,
And I am something curious, being strange,   192
To have them in safe stowage. May it please you
To take them in protection?
IMOGEN   Willingly;
And pawn mine honor for their safety. Since
My lord hath interest in them, I will keep them   196
In my bedchamber.
IACHIMO   They are in a trunk,
Attended by my men. I will make bold
To send them to you, only for this night;
I must aboard tomorrow.
IMOGEN   Oh, no, no.
IACHIMO
Yes, I beseech, or I shall short my word   201
By length'ning my return. From Gallia   202
I crossed the seas on purpose and on promise
To see Your Grace.
IMOGEN   I thank you for your pains.
But not away tomorrow!
IACHIMO   Oh, I must, madam.
Therefore I shall beseech you, if you please
To greet your lord with writing, do't tonight.
I have outstood my time, which is material   208

131 As i.e., I say "if," since   132 Must . . . abuse must not overhastily
wrong (by being too credulous)   134 Diana's priest i.e., priestess
devoted to the goddess of chastity   135 vaulting . . . ramps mounting various prostitutes   136 In . . . purse treating you contemptuously, while spending your money.   138 runagate renegade
139 fast firm   140 Still . . . sure always as secret as I am true.
143 attended listened to   152 to mart should bargain   153 Romish
stew Roman house of prostitution   158 credit faith.   of in   160 Her
assured credit deserves her faith in you, Leonatus.   162 called his
called its own   164 affiance fidelity   165–6 and shall . . . o'er and
my report will confirm anew in Leonatus an assurance that he is
indeed your lord   166–7 one . . . mannered uniquely, above all others
honorably disposed   167–8 such . . . him such a virtuous yet charming man that he draws all sorts of people to him as if by magic.
169 Half . . . his All persons give him half their hearts.

171–2 sets . . . seeming that sets him apart as if he were a god.
176 election choice   177 Which who   178 fan test. (A metaphor
from winnowing of grain.)   179 chaffless without chaff, i.e., perfect.
183 moment importance   185 Are who are   187 The best . . . wing
i.e., the choicest spirit of our company   189 factor agent   190 plate
ware plated with precious metal.   192 something curious somewhat
anxious.   strange a foreigner   196 interest a stake   201 short fall
short of   202 Gallia Gaul, France   208 outstood overstayed

To th' tender of our present.

IMOGEN   I will write. 209
Send your trunk to me; it shall safe be kept
And truly yielded you. You're very welcome. *Exeunt.* 211

✤

2.1

Enter Cloten and the two Lords.

CLOTEN Was there ever man had such luck? When I
kissed the jack upon an upcast, to be hit away! I had 2
a hundred pound on't. And then a whoreson jacka- 3
napes must take me up for swearing, as if I borrowed 4
mine oaths of him and might not spend them at my
pleasure.

FIRST LORD What got he by that? You have broke his 7
pate with your bowl. 8

SECOND LORD [*aside*] If his wit had been like him that
broke it, it would have run all out.

CLOTEN When a gentleman is disposed to swear, it is
not for any standers-by to curtail his oaths, ha? 12

SECOND LORD No, my lord; [*aside*] nor crop the ears of
them.

CLOTEN Whoreson dog! I gave him satisfaction? Would 15
he had been one of my rank! 16

SECOND LORD [*aside*] To have smelled like a fool.

CLOTEN I am not vexed more at anything in the earth. A 18
pox on't! I had rather not be so noble as I am. They 19
dare not fight with me because of the Queen my
mother. Every jack-slave hath his bellyful of fighting, 21
and I must go up and down like a cock that nobody 22
can match. 23

SECOND LORD [*aside*] You are cock and capon too, and 24
you crow, cock, with your comb on. 25

CLOTEN Sayest thou? 26

SECOND LORD It is not fit Your Lordship should under- 27
take every companion that you give offense to. 28

CLOTEN No, I know that, but it is fit I should commit 29
offense to my inferiors. 30

SECOND LORD Ay, it is fit for Your Lordship only.

CLOTEN Why, so I say.

FIRST LORD Did you hear of a stranger that's come to
court tonight? 34

CLOTEN A stranger, and I not know on't?

SECOND LORD [*aside*] He's a strange fellow himself,
and knows it not.

FIRST LORD There's an Italian come, and, 'tis thought,
one of Leonatus' friends.

CLOTEN Leonatus? A banished rascal; and he's another,
whatsoever he be. Who told you of this stranger?

FIRST LORD One of Your Lordship's pages.

CLOTEN Is it fit I went to look upon him? Is there no
derogation in't? 44

SECOND LORD You cannot derogate, my lord. 45

CLOTEN Not easily, I think.

SECOND LORD [*aside*] You are a fool granted; therefore 47
your issues, being foolish, do not derogate. 48

CLOTEN Come, I'll go see this Italian. What I have lost
today at bowls I'll win tonight of him. Come, go.

SECOND LORD I'll attend Your Lordship.

                                 Exeunt [Cloten and First Lord].
That such a crafty devil as is his mother
Should yield the world this ass! A woman that
Bears all down with her brain, and this her son 54
Cannot take two from twenty, for his heart, 55
And leave eighteen. Alas, poor Princess,
Thou divine Imogen, what thou endur'st,
Betwixt a father by thy stepdame governed,
A mother hourly coining plots, a wooer
More hateful than the foul expulsion is
Of thy dear husband, than that horrid act 61
Of the divorce he'd make! The heavens hold firm 62
The walls of thy dear honor, keep unshaked
That temple, thy fair mind, that thou mayst stand
T'enjoy thy banished lord and this great land! *Exit.*

✤

2.2

Enter Imogen in her bed, and a lady [Helen, attending. A trunk is brought on.]

IMOGEN
Who's there? My woman Helen?

HELEN   Please you, madam.

---

209 tender of our present offering of our gift.   **211 truly yielded you** duly returned to you.
2.1. Location: Britain. At the court.
2 kissed the jack touched and lay near the small bowl used as target in the game of bowls.   **upcast** i.e., crucial throw in the game of bowls **3–4 whoreson jackanapes** wretched coxcomb   **4 take me up** take me to task   **7–8 broke his pate** i.e., given him a blow to the head. (But the Second Lord jokes as though a *broken* head would allow brains to run out.)   **12 curtail** shorten, as one might bob the tail (and sometimes the ears) of a curtal dog; hence, *crop the ears* (of the *oaths*) in the next speech   **15 gave** was to give. (To *give satisfaction* is to accept a challenge to a duel from one who feels himself insulted—something that Cloten professes himself unwilling to do because the opponent is of lower social rank, though Cloten's real motive appears to have been cowardice.)   **16 rank** social class. (But the Second Lord takes it in the sense of "rankness of smell.")   **18–19 A pox on't!** i.e., A plague on it!   **21 jack-slave** lowborn fellow   **22–3 like a cock . . . match** (Like the champion cock in cockfighting, complains Cloten, I am unchallenged because all are socially unequal to me.)   **24 capon** castrated rooster. (Used quibblingly for *cap-on*, i.e., with fool's cap or coxcomb.)   **25 with your comb on** (There is a play here on "coxcomb" and "cock's comb.")   **26 Sayest thou?** What do you say? **27–8 undertake** engage with, give satisfaction to   **28 companion** fellow.   **give offense to** attack or insult in the code of dueling. (But the speaker also suggests that Cloten gives offense to virtually everyone by being who he is. The insinuation is present in line 31 as well: no one but Your Lordship is so adept at giving offense.)

29–30 commit offense to attack, initiate action against. (With unintended sense of "defecate upon.")   **34 tonight** last night.   **44 derogation** loss of dignity   **45 cannot derogate** (1) cannot do anything undignified (2) have no dignity to lose.   **47 a fool granted** an acknowledged fool   **48 issues** offspring, i.e., deeds, actions **54 Bears all down** carries all before her, triumphs over everyone **55 for his heart** for the life of him   **61–2 than . . . make** more hateful than his horrid undertaking to separate Imogen from Posthumus. **2.2 Location: Britain. Imogen's bedchamber in Cymbeline's palace. 0.1. in her bed** (On the Elizabethan stage, a curtain presumably would be withdrawn from a recessed area backstage, revealing a bed and trunk within. Alternatively, a bed could be "thrust out" at this point and the trunk carried on containing Iachimo, unless he uses the trapdoor or other such device. Imogen has a book; a lighted candle is provided.)

IMOGEN
What hour is it?

HELEN   Almost midnight, madam.

IMOGEN
I have read three hours then. Mine eyes are weak.
                              [*She gives her the book.*]
Fold down the leaf where I have left. To bed.
Take not away the taper; leave it burning.
And if thou canst awake by four o'th' clock,
I prithee, call me. Sleep hath seized me wholly.
                    [*Exit Helen, leaving the book beside the bed.*]
To your protection I commend me, gods.
From fairies and the tempters of the night   9
Guard me, beseech ye!
                    Sleeps. Iachimo [comes] from the trunk.

IACHIMO
The crickets sing, and man's o'erlabored sense
Repairs itself by rest. Our Tarquin thus   12
Did softly press the rushes ere he wakened   13
The chastity he wounded. Cytherea,   14
How bravely thou becom'st thy bed, fresh lily,   15
And whiter than the sheets! That I might touch!
But kiss, one kiss! Rubies unparagoned,   17
How dearly they do't! 'Tis her breathing that   18
Perfumes the chamber thus. The flame o'th' taper
Bows toward her and would underpeep her lids
To see th'enclosèd lights, now canopied
Under these windows, white and azure-laced   22
With blue of heaven's own tinct. But my design—   23
To note the chamber. I will write all down.
                                      [*He writes.*]
Such and such pictures; there the window; such
Th'adornment of her bed; the arras, figures,   26
Why, such and such; and the contents o'th' story. 27
Ah, but some natural notes about her body   28
Above ten thousand meaner movables   29
Would testify t'enrich mine inventory.
O sleep, thou ape of death, lie dull upon her,   31
And be her sense but as a monument   32
Thus in a chapel lying! Come off, come off;
                              [*taking off her bracelet*]
As slippery as the Gordian knot was hard!   34
'Tis mine; and this will witness outwardly,
As strongly as the conscience does within,   36
To th' madding of her lord. On her left breast   37
A mole cinque-spotted, like the crimson drops   38
I'th' bottom of a cowslip. Here's a voucher

Stronger than ever law could make. This secret
Will force him think I have picked the lock and ta'en
The treasure of her honor. No more. To what end?
Why should I write this down that's riveted,
Screwed to my memory? She hath been reading late
The tale of Tereus; here the leaf's turned down   45
Where Philomel gave up. I have enough.
To th' trunk again, and shut the spring of it.
Swift, swift, you dragons of the night, that dawning
May bare the raven's eye! I lodge in fear;   49
Though this a heavenly angel, hell is here.
                                    Clock strikes.
One, two, three. Time, time!   51
                    [*He goes into the trunk.*] *Exeunt.*

♣

2.3

Enter Cloten and Lords.

FIRST LORD   Your Lordship is the most patient man in
    loss, the most coldest that ever turned up ace.   2

CLOTEN   It would make any man cold to lose.   3

FIRST LORD   But not every man patient after the noble
    temper of Your Lordship. You are most hot and furious
    when you win.

CLOTEN   Winning will put any man into courage. If I
    could get this foolish Imogen, I should have gold
    enough. It's almost morning, is't not?

FIRST LORD   Day, my lord.

CLOTEN   I would this music would come. I am advised
    to give her music o' mornings; they say it will pene-   12
    trate.   13

Enter Musicians.

Come on, tune. If you can penetrate her with your
fingering, so; we'll try with tongue too. If none will   15
do, let her remain, but I'll never give o'er. First, a very
excellent good-conceited thing; after, a wonderful   17
sweet air, with admirable rich words to it—and then   18
let her consider.   [*Music plays.*]

MUSICIAN [*sings*]

            Song.

    Hark, hark, the lark at heaven's gate sings,
        And Phoebus 'gins arise,   21

---

9 fairies i.e., evil spirits   **12 Our Tarquin** the Roman Sextus Tarquinius, who raped Lucrece   **13 rushes** (Elizabethan floors were strewn with rushes or reeds.)   **14 Cytherea** Venus   **15 bravely** handsomely   **17 Rubies** Red lips   **18 do't** i.e., kiss each other.   **22 windows** i.e., eyelids   **23 tinct** color, hue.   **26 arras** tapestry.   **figures** carvings   **27 contents . . . story** narrative represented in the tapestry (?).   **28 notes** marks   **29 meaner movables** less important furnishings   **31 ape** i.e., imitator.   **dull** heavy   **32 be . . . monument** let her be as insensible as a horizontal effigy on a tomb   **34 slippery** easy to slip off.   **Gordian knot** (According to prophecy, whoever untied the knot binding the yoke to the pole of the chariot of Gordius, peasant King of Phrygia, should be king of all Asia. Alexander severed the knot with his sword.)   **36 conscience** consciousness, internal conviction   **37 madding** maddening   **38 cinque-spotted** with five spots

45 Tereus mythical king of Thrace, who raped Philomela, sister of his wife, Procne. (He had Philomela's tongue cut out so that she could not tell the story, but she wove it into a tapestry.)   **49 raven's eye** (The raven was supposed to wake at early dawn.)   **51.1 Exeunt** (Presumably the bed, and trunk with Iachimo inside, are carried offstage, unless Iachimo exits by a trapdoor or other means as a way of reentering the "trunk.")
2.3. Location: Britain. Adjoining Imogen's apartments. The sense of time is nearly continuous, since it is early morn.
2 the most . . . ace the least impatient person that ever threw the lowest throw of one at dice. (With a pun on *ass*.)   **3 cold** gloomy, dispirited   **12–13 penetrate** affect the feelings. (With suggestion of penetrating her sexually; continued in *fingering* and *tongue*, line 15. See also lines 72, 77, and notes.)   **15 so it** is well   **17 good-conceited** imaginatively invented   **18 air** accompanied song for single voice   **21 Phoebus** i.e., the sun-god with his chariot and horses

His steeds to water at those springs
  On chaliced flowers that lies;   23
And winking marybuds begin   24
  To ope their golden eyes.
With everything that pretty is,
  My lady sweet, arise,
    Arise, arise!

CLOTEN   So, get you gone. If this penetrate, I will con-   29
sider your music the better; if it do not, it is a vice in   30
her ears, which horsehairs and calves' guts, nor the   31
voice of unpaved eunuch to boot, can never amend.   32
                           [*Exeunt Musicians.*]

     Enter Cymbeline and Queen.

SECOND LORD   Here comes the King.
CLOTEN   I am glad I was up so late, for that's the reason
I was up so early. He cannot choose but take this ser-
vice I have done fatherly.—Good morrow to Your   36
Majesty, and to my gracious mother.
CYMBELINE
Attend you here the door of our stern daughter?
Will she not forth?
CLOTEN   I have assailed her with musics, but she vouch-
safes no notice.
CYMBELINE
The exile of her minion is too new;   42
She hath not yet forgot him. Some more time   43
Must wear the print of his remembrance on't,   44
And then she's yours.
QUEEN   You are most bound to th' King,
Who lets go by no vantages that may   46
Prefer you to his daughter. Frame yourself   47
To orderly solicits, and be friended   48
With aptness of the season; make denials   49
Increase your services; so seem as if
You were inspired to do those duties which
You tender to her; that you in all obey her,
Save when command to your dismission tends,   53
And therein you are senseless.   54
CLOTEN   Senseless? Not so.

    [*Enter a Messenger.*]

MESSENGER
So like you, sir, ambassadors from Rome;   56
The one is Caius Lucius.
CYMBELINE   A worthy fellow,   57
Albeit he comes on angry purpose now;
But that's no fault of his. We must receive him

According to the honor of his sender;
And towards himself, his goodness forespent on us,   61
We must extend our notice. Our dear son,   62
When you have given good morning to your mistress,
Attend the Queen and us. We shall have need
T'employ you towards this Roman.—Come, our
  queen.   *Exeunt [all but Cloten].*
CLOTEN
If she be up, I'll speak with her; if not,
Let her lie still and dream.—By your leave, ho!—
I know her women are about her. What
If I do line one of their hands? 'Tis gold   69
Which buys admittance—oft it doth—yea, and makes   70
Diana's rangers false themselves, yield up   71
Their deer to th' stand o' th' stealer; and 'tis gold   72
Which makes the true man killed and saves the thief,   73
Nay, sometimes hangs both thief and true man. What   74
Can it not do and undo? I will make
One of her women lawyer to me, for   76
I yet not understand the case myself.—   77
By your leave.   *Knocks.*

    Enter a Lady.

LADY
Who's there that knocks?
CLOTEN   A gentleman.
LADY   No more?
CLOTEN
Yes, and a gentlewoman's son.
LADY [*aside*]   That's more
Than some, whose tailors are as dear as yours,   81
Can justly boast of.—What's Your Lordship's
  pleasure?
CLOTEN
Your lady's person. Is she ready?
LADY   Ay,   83
[*Aside*] To keep her chamber.
CLOTEN   There is gold for you;
Sell me your good report.   [*He offers money.*]   85
LADY
How? My good name? Or to report of you
What I shall think is good?—The Princess!   87
                         [*Exit Lady.*]

    Enter Imogen.

---

23 **chaliced** with cuplike blossoms   24 **winking marybuds** closed buds of marigolds, as though with closed eyes   29–30 **consider** reward, value   31 **horsehairs and calves' guts** i.e., bow hair and fiddle strings   32 **unpaved** unstoned, castrated   36 **fatherly** as a father would receive it, graciously and thankfully.   42 **minion** darling   43–4 **more . . . on't** more time must elapse, erasing the image of him on the memory   46 **vantages** favorable occasions   47 **Prefer** recommend.   **Frame** Prepare   48 **To** with.   **solicits** soliciting, importunings   48–9 **be . . . season** make timely use of your best opportunity   49 **denials** i.e., Imogen's refusals   53–4 **Save . . . senseless** except when she orders you to leave—a command you profess not to understand. (Cloten, however, understands *senseless* as meaning "stupid.")   56 **So like you** If you please   57 **The one** the chief one

61 **his . . . us** in light of the honorable conduct he has shown on past occasions   62 **extend our notice** show special attentiveness.   69 **line** i.e., with gold   70–2 **makes . . . stealer** prompts the nymphs who serve as Diana's chaste gamekeepers to falsify their oaths by betraying the deer to the marauding huntsman—i.e., they admit a would-be seducing male in return for a bribe. (*Deer* puns on "dear"; *stand*, meaning the station for the huntsman waiting to shoot the game, has erotic connotations of male erection.)   73–5 **Which . . . true man** (Gold can corrupt justice, sometimes with wantonly arbitrary consequences.)   76 **her** Imogen's.   **lawyer to** advocate for   77 **understand the case** know how to conduct my suit. (With bawdy pun on *stand* again, line 72, and on *case*, meaning "vagina," as well as a legal *case* requiring a *lawyer*.)   81 **dear** costly. (The Lady jests that expensive clothes are no guarantee of gentility.)   83 **person** (1) presence (2) body.   **ready** dressed. (But the Lady quibbles in another sense of "prepared, inclined.")   85 **Sell . . . report** i.e., Let me offer this money in return for your speaking favorably on my behalf to Imogen. (But the Lady quibbles on *report* in the sense of "reputation, good name.")   87 **What . . . good** what seems good to me to report (favorable or unfavorable).

CLOTEN

   Good morrow, fairest. Sister, your sweet hand.

IMOGEN

   Good morrow, sir. You lay out too much pains
   For purchasing but trouble. The thanks I give
   Is telling you that I am poor of thanks
   And scarce can spare them.

CLOTEN   Still, I swear I love you.

IMOGEN

   If you but said so, 'twere as deep with me.   93
   If you swear still, your recompense is still   94
   That I regard it not.

CLOTEN   This is no answer.

IMOGEN

   But that you shall not say I yield being silent,   96
   I would not speak. I pray you, spare me. Faith,
   I shall unfold equal discourtesy   98
   To your best kindness. One of your great knowing   99
   Should learn, being taught, forbearance.

CLOTEN

   To leave you in your madness, 'twere my sin.
   I will not.

IMOGEN

   Fools are not mad folks.

CLOTEN   Do you call me fool?   103

IMOGEN   As I am mad, I do.   104

   If you'll be patient, I'll no more be mad;
   That cures us both. I am much sorry, sir,
   You put me to forget a lady's manners
   By being so verbal; and learn now for all   108
   That I, which know my heart, do here pronounce,   109
   By th' very truth of it, I care not for you,
   And am so near the lack of charity   111
   To accuse myself I hate you—which I had rather   112
   You felt than make 't my boast.

CLOTEN   You sin against   113

   Obedience, which you owe your father. For   114
   The contract you pretend with that base wretch,   115
   One bred of alms and fostered with cold dishes,
   With scraps o'th' court, it is no contract, none.
   And though it be allowed in meaner parties—   118
   Yet who than he more mean?—to knit their souls,

On whom there is no more dependency   120
But brats and beggary, in self-figured knot,   121
Yet you are curbed from that enlargement by   122
The consequence o'th' crown, and must not foil   123
The precious note of it with a base slave,   124
A hilding for a livery, a squire's cloth,   125
A pantler—not so eminent.

IMOGEN   Profane fellow!   126

   Wert thou the son of Jupiter and no more
   But what thou art besides, thou wert too base
   To be his groom. Thou wert dignified enough,   129
   Even to the point of envy, if 'twere made   130
   Comparative for your virtues, to be styled   131
   The underhangman of his kingdom, and hated
   For being preferred so well.

CLOTEN   The south fog rot him!   133

IMOGEN

   He never can meet more mischance than come
   To be but named of thee. His mean'st garment   135
   That ever hath but clipped his body is dearer   136
   In my respect than all the hairs above thee,   137
   Were they all made such men.—How now, Pisanio!   138

       Enter Pisanio.

CLOTEN   "His garment!" Now the devil—

IMOGEN

   To Dorothy my woman hie thee presently.   140

CLOTEN

   "His garment!"

IMOGEN   I am sprited with a fool,   141

   Frighted, and angered worse. Go bid my woman
   Search for a jewel that too casually
   Hath left mine arm. It was thy master's. 'Shrew me   144
   If I would lose it for a revenue
   Of any king's in Europe. I do think
   I saw't this morning; confident I am
   Last night 'twas on mine arm; I kissed it.
   I hope it be not gone to tell my lord
   That I kiss aught but he.

PISANIO   'Twill not be lost.

IMOGEN

   I hope so. Go and search.   [*Exit Pisanio.*]

CLOTEN   You have abused me.
   "His meanest garment!"

IMOGEN   Ay, I said so, sir.

---

93 **deep** binding, efficacious. (Imogen's point is that Cloten's oath adds nothing to his unwelcome protestation of love.)   94 **still** constantly. (Imogen puns on Cloten's *Still*, "nonetheless," in line 92.) 96 **But ... silent** If it were not for the fact that you might interpret my silence as giving consent   98 **unfold equal discourtesy** display discourtesy equal   99 **knowing** knowledge, discernment. (Said with tactful irony.)   103 **Fools ... folks** i.e., I may seem a fool to refuse you or to waste time talking with you, but that doesn't make me mad (?), or, if I'm mad, as you say, at least I'm not a fool like you (?) 104 **As I am mad** Insofar as I am mad (and you, after all, were the one who said I was mad)   108 **By ... verbal** (If the phrase refers to Cloten, the meaning of *verbal* is "verbose"; if it refers to Imogen, "plainspoken.") **for all** once and for all   109 **which** who 111–13 **And ... boast** and am so nearly lacking in Christian charity as to be obliged to accuse myself of hating you—which I would rather you perceived without my having to say it.   114 **For** As for 115 **pretend** allege   118 **meaner parties** persons of lower social rank, who, says Cloten, are allowed to choose in marriage because the only consequence is their own child-burdened poverty

120–1 **On ... knot** from whose marriage there are no consequences other than many children and poverty, in a self-contracted union 122 **enlargement** liberty, freedom of action   123 **consequence** succession, all that follows as a result of your being heir to the throne. **foil** defile, foul   124 **note** reputation   125 **hilding for a livery** good-for-nothing fellow fit only for wearing a servant's uniform. **cloth** uniform, livery   126 **pantler** pantry-servant. **not** not even   129 **his** Posthumus's   129–33 **Thou wert ... so well** If you and Posthumus were to be compared in virtue, you would be given high enough status, even to the point of being envied and hated for your promotion, if you were given the title of assistant hangman of his kingdom.   133 **south fog** (The south wind was supposed to be laden with poisonous vapors and diseases.)   135 **of** by   136 **clipped** embraced   137 **respect** regard. **above thee** on your head   138 **such men** such men as you are. 140 **hie thee presently** go at once.   141 **sprited with** haunted by 144 **'Shrew me** Beshrew me. (A mild oath.)

If you will make 't an action, call witness to't. 153

CLOTEN
I will inform your father.

IMOGEN   Your mother too.
She's my good lady and will conceive, I hope, 155
But the worst of me. So, I leave you, sir,
To th' worst of discontent.   *Exit.*

CLOTEN   I'll be revenged.
"His mean'st garment!" Well.   *Exit.*

             ❧

2.4

Enter Posthumus and Philario.

POSTHUMUS
Fear it not, sir. I would I were so sure
To win the King as I am bold her honor 2
Will remain hers.

PHILARIO   What means do you make to him? 3

POSTHUMUS
Not any, but abide the change of time,
Quake in the present winter's state, and wish
That warmer days would come. In these feared hopes 6
I barely gratify your love; they failing, 7
I must die much your debtor.

PHILARIO
Your very goodness and your company
O'erpays all I can do. By this, your king 10
Hath heard of great Augustus; Caius Lucius 11
Will do 's commission throughly. And I think 12
He'll grant the tribute, send th'arrearages, 13
Or look upon our Romans, whose remembrance 14
Is yet fresh in their grief.

POSTHUMUS   I do believe, 15
Statist though I am none, nor like to be, 16
That this will prove a war; and you shall hear
The legions now in Gallia sooner landed
In our not-fearing Britain than have tidings
Of any penny tribute paid. Our countrymen
Are men more ordered than when Julius Caesar 21
Smiled at their lack of skill but found their courage
Worthy his frowning at. Their discipline, 23
Now mingled with their courages, will make known

To their approvers they are people such 25
That mend upon the world.

        Enter Iachimo.

PHILARIO   See! Iachimo! 26

POSTHUMUS
The swiftest harts have posted you by land, 27
And winds of all the corners kissed your sails, 28
To make your vessel nimble.

PHILARIO   Welcome, sir.

POSTHUMUS
I hope the briefness of your answer made 30
The speediness of your return.

IACHIMO   Your lady
Is one of the fairest that I have looked upon.

POSTHUMUS
And therewithal the best, or let her beauty
Look through a casement to allure false hearts 34
And be false with them.

IACHIMO   Here are letters for you.
         [He gives a letter or letters.]

POSTHUMUS
Their tenor good, I trust.

IACHIMO   'Tis very like. 36

PHILARIO
Was Caius Lucius in the Briton court
When you were there?

IACHIMO   He was expected then,
But not approached. 39

POSTHUMUS   All is well yet. 40
Sparkles this stone as it was wont, or is 't not
Too dull for your good wearing? *[Indicating the ring.]*

IACHIMO   If I have lost it, 42
I should have lost the worth of it in gold.
I'll make a journey twice as far t'enjoy
A second night of such sweet shortness which
Was mine in Britain, for the ring is won.

POSTHUMUS
The stone's too hard to come by.

IACHIMO   Not a whit,
Your lady being so easy.

POSTHUMUS   Make not, sir,
Your loss your sport. I hope you know that we
Must not continue friends.

IACHIMO   Good sir, we must,
If you keep covenant. Had I not brought
The knowledge of your mistress home, I grant 52

---

153 **action** action at law   155 **good lady** i.e., patroness. (Said ironically.)   **conceive** believe, think.   **hope** (Continues the irony, though it can also mean "expect.")
2.4. Location: Rome. Philario's house.
2 bold confident   **3 means** overtures.   **him** i.e., the King.   **6 feared** mixed with fear   **7 gratify** repay   **10 this** this time   **11 of** from **12 do 's** do his.   **throughly** thoroughly.   **13 He'll** i.e., Cymbeline will. **13–15 send . . . grief** (and) send the part of the tribute still in arrears, sooner than face the Romans, the remembrance of whom is yet fresh in the Britons' grief. (*Or* can mean "ere," "sooner than," or possibly "or else"; *grief* could refer to the grief inflicted by the Romans.)
16 Statist statesman.   **like** likely   **21 more ordered** better disciplined and governed.   **Julius Caesar** (As proconsul in Gaul in 58–49 B.C., Caesar extended Roman dominion into Britain.)   **23 frowning** i.e., in stern military resolve and concern, not disapproval

25 **their approvers** those who test their courage   **25–6 such . . . world** such as are able to improve their standing in the world's estimation. **27 The swiftest . . . land** i.e., You have made speed as if conveyed on land by the swiftest of deer   **28 of all the corners** from every corner **30 hope** expect.   **your answer** the answer you were given   **34 Look through a casement** (As a whore might show herself to attract customers. The *casement* here is her body or perhaps her laced bodice.) **36 like** likely.   **39 not** had not   **40 All is well yet** (Posthumus is evidently reassured by what he has read of the letter.)   **42 s.d.** *Indicating the ring* (The ring possibly is in the custody of Philario as official of the wager; although Posthumus appears to have it himself at line 108, he may then take it from Philario and give it to Iachimo.)
52 knowledge i.e., carnal knowledge

We were to question farther; but I now
Profess myself the winner of her honor,
Together with your ring, and not the wronger
Of her or you, having proceeded but
By both your wills.

POSTHUMUS   If you can make 't apparent
That you have tasted her in bed, my hand
And ring is yours; if not, the foul opinion
You had of her pure honor gains or loses
Your sword or mine, or masterless leaves both
To who shall find them.

IACHIMO   Sir, my circumstances,
Being so near the truth as I will make them,
Must first induce you to believe; whose strength
I will confirm with oath, which I doubt not
You'll give me leave to spare when you shall find
You need it not.

POSTHUMUS   Proceed.

IACHIMO   First, her bedchamber—
Where, I confess, I slept not, but profess
Had that was well worth watching—it was hanged
With tapestry of silk and silver; the story
Proud Cleopatra when she met her Roman,
And Cydnus swelled above the banks, or for
The press of boats or pride. A piece of work
So bravely done, so rich, that it did strive
In workmanship and value, which I wondered
Could be so rarely and exactly wrought,
Since the true life on 't was—

POSTHUMUS   This is true;
And this you might have heard of here, by me
Or by some other.

IACHIMO   More particulars
Must justify my knowledge.

POSTHUMUS   So they must,
Or do your honor injury.

IACHIMO   The chimney
Is south the chamber, and the chimneypiece
Chaste Dian bathing. Never saw I figures
So likely to report themselves. The cutter
Was as another nature, dumb; outwent her,
Motion and breath left out.

POSTHUMUS   This is a thing
Which you might from relation likewise reap,
Being, as it is, much spoke of.

IACHIMO   The roof o'th' chamber
With golden cherubins is fretted. Her andirons—

53
60
61
62
66
69
72
74
75
77
80
81
82
83
84
85
86
87
89

I had forgot them—were two winking Cupids
Of silver, each on one foot standing, nicely
Depending on their brands.

POSTHUMUS   This is her honor!
Let it be granted you have seen all this—and praise
Be given to your remembrance—the description
Of what is in her chamber nothing saves
The wager you have laid.

IACHIMO   Then, if you can
Be pale, I beg but leave to air this jewel. See!

[He shows the bracelet.]

And now 'tis up again. It must be married
To that your diamond; I'll keep them.

POSTHUMUS   Jove!
Once more let me behold it. Is it that
Which I left with her?

IACHIMO   Sir—I thank her—that.
She stripped it from her arm; I see her yet;
Her pretty action did outsell her gift,
And yet enriched it too. She gave it me
And said she prized it once.

POSTHUMUS   Maybe she plucked it off
To send it me.

IACHIMO   She writes so to you, doth she?

POSTHUMUS
Oh, no, no, no! 'Tis true. Here, take this too.

[He gives the ring.]

It is a basilisk unto mine eye,
Kills me to look on't. Let there be no honor
Where there is beauty, truth where semblance, love
Where there's another man. The vows of women
Of no more bondage be to where they are made
Than they are to their virtues, which is nothing.
Oh, above measure false!

PHILARIO   Have patience, sir,
And take your ring again; 'tis not yet won.
It may be probable she lost it; or
Who knows if one her women, being corrupted,
Hath stolen it from her?

POSTHUMUS   Very true,
And so, I hope, he came by't. Back my ring!

[He takes back the ring.]

Render to me some corporal sign about her
More evident than this; for this was stolen.

IACHIMO
By Jupiter, I had it from her arm.

POSTHUMUS
Hark you, he swears; by Jupiter he swears.
'Tis true—nay, keep the ring—'tis true. I am sure
She would not lose it. Her attendants are
All sworn and honorable. They induced to steal it?

90
91
92
94
95
96
97
98
103
109
111
114
118
123
128

---

53 question dispute, i.e., settle matters by a duel   **60–1 gains . . . mine** i.e., means that we must fight a duel   **62 who** whoever.   **circumstances** detailed observations   **66 spare** leave out   **69 that** that which.   **watching** remaining awake (for)   **72 Cydnus** a river in Cilicia, or modern-day southern Turkey, the scene of the meeting of Antony and Cleopatra. (See *Antony and Cleopatra,* 2.2.196–236.)   **or for** either because of   **74 bravely** handsomely   **74–5 it did . . . value** it was a question whether the workmanship or the monetary value was the greater   **77 on't** of it   **80 justify** confirm   **81 chimney** fireplace   **82 chimneypiece** sculptured mantelpiece   **83 Dian** Diana, goddess of chastity   **84 So . . . themselves** so like what they purported to represent, speaking likenesses.   **84–6 The cutter . . . out** The sculptor rivaled nature in creative power, albeit mute; indeed, he outwent nature, except that his creation lacked motion and the ability to breathe.   **87 relation** hearsay, report   **89 fretted** carved.

90 winking i.e., blind   **91–2 nicely . . . brands** ingeniously leaning on their torches.   **92 This . . . honor!** i.e., Is this what you can allege to impugn her honor? (Said sarcastically.)   **94 remembrance** ability to remember   **95 nothing** not at all   **96–7 if . . . pale** if you are prepared to look aghast   **98 up** put up, pocketed   **103 outsell** exceed in value   **109 basilisk** fabulous serpent or dragon whose look was fatal   **111 semblance** mere seeming   **114 Than . . . virtues** than women are bound to their virtuousness   **118 one** one of   **123 evident** conclusive   **128 sworn** bound by oath

And by a stranger? No, he hath enjoyed her.
The cognizance of her incontinency   130
Is this. She hath bought the name of whore thus
  dearly.
There, take thy hire, and all the fiends of hell   132
Divide themselves between you!

                       [*He gives the ring again.*]

PHILARIO   Sir, be patient.   133
This is not strong enough to be believed
Of one persuaded well of.

POSTHUMUS   Never talk on't.   135
She hath been colted by him.

IACHIMO   If you seek   136
For further satisfying, under her breast—
Worthy the pressing—lies a mole, right proud
Of that most delicate lodging. By my life,
I kissed it, and it gave me present hunger
To feed again, though full. You do remember
This stain upon her?

POSTHUMUS   Ay, and it doth confirm
Another stain, as big as hell can hold,
Were there no more but it.

IACHIMO   Will you hear more?

POSTHUMUS
Spare your arithmetic! Never count the turns.   145
Once, and a million!

IACHIMO   I'll be sworn—

POSTHUMUS   No swearing.   146
If you will swear you have not done't, you lie,
And I will kill thee if thou dost deny
Thou'st made me cuckold.

IACHIMO   I'll deny nothing.

POSTHUMUS
Oh, that I had her here, to tear her limbmeal!   150
I will go there and do't, i'th' court, before
Her father. I'll do something—   *Exit.*

PHILARIO   Quite besides   152
The government of patience! You have won.
Let's follow him and pervert the present wrath   154
He hath against himself.

IACHIMO   With all my heart.   *Exeunt.*

❖

[2.5]

Enter Posthumus.

POSTHUMUS
Is there no way for men to be, but women   1
Must be half-workers? We are all bastards,   2
And that most venerable man which I
Did call my father was I know not where

When I was stamped. Some coiner with his tools   5
Made me a counterfeit; yet my mother seemed
The Dian of that time. So doth my wife   7
The nonpareil of this. Oh, vengeance, vengeance!   8
Me of my lawful pleasure she restrained
And prayed me oft forbearance; did it with
A pudency so rosy the sweet view on't   11
Might well have warmed old Saturn, that I thought
  her   12
As chaste as unsunned snow. Oh, all the devils!
This yellow Iachimo, in an hour, was't not?   14
Or less? At first? Perchance he spoke not, but,   15
Like a full-acorned boar, a German one,   16
Cried "Oh!" and mounted; found no opposition
But what he looked for should oppose and she   18
Should from encounter guard. Could I find out
The woman's part in me! For there's no motion   20
That tends to vice in man but I affirm
It is the woman's part. Be it lying, note it,
The woman's; flattering, hers; deceiving, hers;
Lust and rank thoughts, hers, hers; revenges, hers;
Ambitions, covetings, change of prides, disdain,   25
Nice longing, slanders, mutability,   26
All faults that have a name, nay, that hell knows,
Why, hers, in part or all, but rather all.
For even to vice
They are not constant, but are changing still   30
One vice but of a minute old for one
Not half so old as that. I'll write against them,   32
Detest them, curse them. Yet 'tis greater skill   33
In a true hate to pray they have their will;   34
The very devils cannot plague them better.   *Exit.*

❖

3.1

*Enter in state, Cymbeline, Queen, Cloten, and
lords at one door, and at another, Caius Lucius
and attendants.*

CYMBELINE
Now say, what would Augustus Caesar with us?

LUCIUS
When Julius Caesar, whose remembrance yet   2

---

130 **cognizance** token   132–3 **all . . . you!** i.e., may you and Imogen suffer equal torments in hell!   135 **persuaded well of** well thought of.   **on't** of it.   136 **colted** enjoyed sexually   145 **turns** (With a bitter suggestion of "tricks," sexual encounters with a customer.)   146 **Once, and a million** i.e., What does it matter if once or a million times; it's all the same.   150 **limbmeal** limb from limb.   152 **besides** beyond   154 **pervert** divert
2.5. Location: Philario's house, as before. The scene may be virtually continuous.
1 **be** exist   2 **half-workers** partners, collaborators.

5 **stamped** (The image of procreation as an act of coinage by the father occurs often in Shakespeare.)   **tools** (With bitter suggestion of the male sexual organ.)   7 **Dian** Diana, goddess of chastity   8 **nonpareil** one who has no equal.   **this** this time.   11 **pudency** modesty. **rosy** blushing (that).   **on't** of it   12 **Saturn** father of Jupiter, associated with old age   14 **yellow** sallow   15 **At first?** Right at first?   16 **full-acorned** full of acorns, favorite food of boars. (In German, *eichel,* "acorn," also means "penis" because of its glanslike shape.)   18 **But . . . oppose** i.e., except for the pleasant physical friction or barrier (the hymen) he expected in entering. (Imogen is no longer a virgin, being married, but the hymen still symbolizes what she should *guard* from *encounter,* line 19.)   20 **part** (With bitter sexual suggestion.)   **motion** impulse   25 **change of prides** varying vanities (in dress, etc.)   26 **Nice** fastidious, wanton.   **mutability** inconstancy **30 still** continuously   32 **write against** denounce   33–4 **Yet . . . will** Yet the best way to damn women in a spirit of true hatred is simply to pray that they be encouraged to have their desire (since they will proceed then to damn themselves).
3.1. Location: Britain. At the court of Cymbeline.
2 **whose remembrance** the remembrance of whom

Lives in men's eyes, and will to ears and tongues
Be theme and hearing ever, was in this Britain
And conquered it, Cassibelan, thine uncle—
Famous in Caesar's praises no whit less
Than in his feats deserving it—for him
And his succession granted Rome a tribute,   8
Yearly three thousand pounds, which by thee lately
Is left untendered.

QUEEN   And, to kill the marvel,   10
Shall be so ever.

CLOTEN   There be many Caesars
Ere such another Julius. Britain's a world
By itself, and we will nothing pay
For wearing our own noses.

QUEEN   That opportunity   14
Which then they had to take from 's, to resume   15
We have again. Remember, sir, my liege,   16
The kings your ancestors, together with
The natural bravery of your isle, which stands
As Neptune's park, ribbed and paled in   19
With rocks unscalable and roaring waters,
With sands that will not bear your enemies' boats,
But suck them up to th' topmast. A kind of conquest
Caesar made here, but made not here his brag
Of "Came and saw and overcame." With shame—
The first that ever touched him—he was carried
From off our coast, twice beaten; and his shipping,
Poor ignorant baubles, on our terrible seas   27
Like eggshells moved upon their surges, cracked   28
As easily 'gainst our rocks. For joy whereof
The famed Cassibelan, who was once at point—   30
O giglot fortune!—to master Caesar's sword,   31
Made Lud's Town with rejoicing fires bright   32
And Britons strut with courage.

CLOTEN   Come, there's no more tribute to be paid. Our
kingdom is stronger than it was at that time; and, as I
said, there is no more such Caesars. Other of them may
have crooked noses, but to owe such straight arms,   37
none.

CYMBELINE   Son, let your mother end.   39

CLOTEN   We have yet many among us can grip as hard   40
as Cassibelan. I do not say I am one; but I have a hand.
Why tribute? Why should we pay tribute? If Caesar
can hide the sun from us with a blanket, or put the
moon in his pocket, we will pay him tribute for light;
else, sir, no more tribute, pray you now.

CYMBELINE [to Lucius]   You must know,
Till the injurious Romans did extort   47
This tribute from us, we were free. Caesar's ambition,

Which swelled so much that it did almost stretch
The sides o'th' world, against all color here   50
Did put the yoke upon 's, which to shake off
Becomes a warlike people, whom we reckon
Ourselves to be. We do say then to Caesar,
Our ancestor was that Mulmutius which   54
Ordained our laws, whose use the sword of Caesar   55
Hath too much mangled, whose repair and franchise   56
Shall, by the power we hold, be our good deed,
Though Rome be therefore angry. Mulmutius made
    our laws,
Who was the first of Britain which did put
His brows within a golden crown and called
Himself a king.

LUCIUS   I am sorry, Cymbeline,
That I am to pronounce Augustus Caesar—
Caesar, that hath more kings his servants than
Thyself domestic officers—thine enemy.
Receive it from me, then: war and confusion   65
In Caesar's name pronounce I 'gainst thee. Look
For fury not to be resisted. Thus defied,   67
I thank thee for myself.

CYMBELINE   Thou art welcome, Caius.   68
Thy Caesar knighted me; my youth I spent
Much under him. Of him I gathered honor,
Which he to seek of me again perforce   71
Behooves me keep at utterance. I am perfect   72
That the Pannonians and Dalmatians for   73
Their liberties are now in arms, a precedent   74
Which not to read would show the Britons cold.   75
So Caesar shall not find them.

LUCIUS   Let proof speak.   76

CLOTEN   His Majesty bids you welcome. Make pastime
with us a day or two, or longer. If you seek us afterwards in other terms, you shall find us in our saltwater   79
girdle. If you beat us out of it, it is yours; if you fall in   80
the adventure, our crows shall fare the better for you,   81
and there's an end.

LUCIUS   So, sir.

CYMBELINE
I know your master's pleasure and he mine.
All the remain is "Welcome!"   Exeunt.   85

❦

50 against all color in defiance of all rightful claim. (*Color*, "arguable
ground or claim," may also pun on *yoke*, "collar," in the next line.)
54 Mulmutius (according to legend, the first King of Britain)
55 whose use the exercise of which laws   **56 whose . . . franchise** the
repair and free exercise of which laws   **65 confusion** destruction
67 Thus defied You having been thus defied   **68 thank . . . myself**
thank you personally for this welcome.   **71–2 Which . . . utterance**
which honor, since he seeks to take it away from me, I must defend to
the last extremity of death. (From the French *à l'outrance*.)   **72 perfect**
well aware   **73–4 That . . . liberties** that the inhabitants of Hungary
and Dalmatia (along the Adriatic coast), in order to defend their liberties   **74–5 a precedent . . . cold** (Cymbeline implies that Britons should
be quick to see the military advantage to them of Rome's facing an
insurrection in the Balkans, draining off military resources and thus
providing Britons a *precedent* in refusing to pay tribute. *Cold* means
"lacking spirit.")   **76 proof** the outcome. (The proof of the pudding is
in the eating.)   **79–80 our saltwater girdle** our ocean-surrounded
island.   **81 crows** i.e., scavenger birds, like vultures   **85 All the
remain** All that remains (to be said)

8 succession heirs   **10 untendered** unpaid.   **to kill . . . marvel** to
end the suspense   **14 our own noses** i.e., British, not Roman, noses.
(See Cloten's gibe at the Romans' *crooked noses* in line 37.)   **15–16 to
resume . . . again** we now have the opportunity to take back.
19 ribbed and palèd in enclosed and fenced in   **27 ignorant baubles**
silly trifles   **28 their surges** the waves of the sea   **30 Cassibelan**
(The incident referred to is recorded of Nennius, brother of Cassibelan, in Holinshed.)   **30 at point** ready   **31 giglot** lewd, wanton
32 Lud's Town London (supposedly named after King Lud, Cymbeline's grandfather)   **37 owe** own.   **straight** i.e., strong   **39 end** finish speaking.   **40 can grip** who can grasp (a sword)   **47 injurious**
insolent

3.2

Enter Pisanio, reading of a letter.

PISANIO
How? Of adultery? Wherefore write you not
What monster's her accuser? Leonatus,
Oh, master, what a strange infection
Is fall'n into thy ear! What false Italian,
As poisonous-tongued as handed, hath prevailed   5
On thy too ready hearing? Disloyal? No.   6
She's punished for her truth, and undergoes,   7
More goddesslike than wifelike, such assaults
As would take in some virtue. O my master,   9
Thy mind to her is now as low as were   10
Thy fortunes. How? That I should murder her,
Upon the love and truth and vows which I
Have made to thy command? I, her? Her blood?
If it be so to do good service, never
Let me be counted serviceable. How look I,
That I should seem to lack humanity
So much as this fact comes to? [*He reads.*] "Do't. The
    letter   17
That I have sent her, by her own command
Shall give thee opportunity." O damned paper,
Black as the ink that's on thee! Senseless bauble,   20
Art thou a fedarie for this act, and look'st   21
So virginlike without? Lo, here she comes.

    Enter Imogen.

I am ignorant in what I am commanded.   23
IMOGEN How now, Pisanio?
PISANIO
Madam, here is a letter from my lord.
IMOGEN [*taking the letter*]
Who, thy lord that is my lord, Leonatus?
Oh, learned indeed were that astronomer   27
That knew the stars as I his characters;   28
He'd lay the future open. You good gods,
Let what is here contained relish of love,   30
Of my lord's health, of his content—yet not   31
That we two are asunder; let that grieve him.
Some griefs are med'cinable; that is one of them,   33
For it doth physic love—of his content   34
All but in that! Good wax, thy leave. [*She breaks the
    seal.*] Blest be
You bees that make these locks of counsel! Lovers   36

And men in dangerous bonds pray not alike;   37
Though forfeiters you cast in prison, yet   38
You clasp young Cupid's tables. Good news, gods!   39
    [*She reads.*] "Justice and your father's wrath, should
he take me in his dominion, could not be so cruel to me 41
as you, O the dearest of creatures, would even renew   42
me with your eyes. Take notice that I am in Cambria,   43
at Milford Haven. What your own love will out of this
advise you, follow. So he wishes you all happiness
that remains loyal to his vow, and your increasing in   46
love.   Leonatus Posthumus." 47
Oh, for a horse with wings! Hear'st thou, Pisanio?
He is at Milford Haven. Read, and tell me
How far 'tis thither. If one of mean affairs   50
May plod it in a week, why may not I
Glide thither in a day? Then, true Pisanio,
Who long'st like me to see thy lord, who long'st—
Oh, let me bate—but not like me, yet long'st,   54
But in a fainter kind—oh, not like me,
For mine's beyond beyond; say, and speak thick—   56
Love's counselor should fill the bores of hearing,   57
To th' smothering of the sense—how far it is   58
To this same blessèd Milford. And by th' way   59
Tell me how Wales was made so happy as
T'inherit such a haven. But first of all,   61
How we may steal from hence, and for the gap
That we shall make in time from our hence-going
And our return, to excuse. But first, how get hence?
Why should excuse be born or ere begot?   65
We'll talk of that hereafter. Prithee, speak,
How many score of miles may we well ride
Twixt hour and hour?
PISANIO   One score twixt sun and sun,   68
Madam, 's enough for you—and too much too.   69
IMOGEN
Why, one that rode to 's execution, man,
Could never go so slow. I have heard of riding wagers   71
Where horses have been nimbler than the sands
That run i'th' clock's behalf. But this is fool'ry.   73

3.2. Location: Britain. At the court of Cymbeline.
0.1 *reading of* reading **5 As . . . handed** as skilled in slander as in the art of secret poisoning (for which the Italians were notorious) **6 ready** credulous **7 truth** fidelity **9 take in** cause to yield **10 to her** compared to hers **17 fact** deed **20 Senseless bauble** Trifle incapable of feeling **21 fedarie** accomplice **23 am ignorant in** will pretend not to know **27 astronomer** astrologer **28 characters** handwriting. (With a suggestion, too, of astrological symbols.) **30 relish** taste **31 not** i.e., not content **33 med'cinable** curative, health-giving **34 physic** make healthy, strong **36 locks of counsel** waxen seals enclosing confidential matters.

36–9 Lovers . . . tables People in love don't address the same prayers to you wax-making bees as do men at risk of penalties for contracts they've signed; your beeswax, used to seal documents, puts forfeiters of contracts in prison, whereas you bees seal with wax the writing tablets or love letters used in the affairs of Cupid. **41 take** apprehend **42 as** but that. (The letter, however, is studiously ambiguous and suggests also that no one can be so cruel as she.) **43 Cambria** Wales **46 that remains loyal** more ambiguity: (1) to you who remain loyal (2) on condition that you remain loyal **46–7 your increasing in love** (he wishes) your advancement and prosperity in love. (Suggesting, too, he wishes your love for your husband were greater.) **50 mean affairs** ordinary business **54 bate** moderate my speech **56 beyond beyond** i.e., even greater than something already great. **thick** many words quickly **57 the bores of hearing** the ears **58 To . . . sense** to the point of overwhelming the sense of hearing **59 by th' way** as we go **61 T'inherit** to come to possess **65 Why . . . begot?** i.e., Why worry about how to excuse our absence before we've figured how to get away? **68 Twixt hour and hour** in an hour. **One . . . and sun** twenty miles a day **69 too much too** i.e., even that would exhaust you. (But suggesting also that she will arrive too soon at her fatal destiny. Her answer unconsciously picks up the irony.) **71 riding** racing **73 That . . . behalf** that run in the hourglass, doing the service of a clock.

Go bid my woman feign a sickness, say
She'll home to her father; and provide me presently   75
A riding suit no costlier than would fit
A franklin's huswife.

PISANIO   Madam, you're best consider.   77

IMOGEN
I see before me, man. Nor here, nor here,   78
Nor what ensues, but have a fog in them   79
That I cannot look through. Away, I prithee!
Do as I bid thee. There's no more to say.
Accessible is none but Milford way.

                                        Exeunt [*separately*].

❖

3.3

Enter [*from the cave*] *Belarius; Guiderius, and
Arviragus* [*following*].

BELARIUS
A goodly day not to keep house with such   1
Whose roof's as low as ours. Stoop, boys; this gate
Instructs you how t'adore the heavens and bows you   3
To a morning's holy office. The gates of monarchs   4
Are arched so high that giants may jet through   5
And keep their impious turbans on, without
Good morrow to the sun.—Hail, thou fair heaven!
We house i'th' rock, yet use thee not so hardly   8
As prouder livers do.

GUIDERIUS   Hail, heaven!
ARVIRAGUS   Hail, heaven!   9
BELARIUS
Now for our mountain sport. Up to yond hill;
Your legs are young. I'll tread these flats. Consider,
When you above perceive me like a crow,   12
That it is place which lessens and sets off,   13
And you may then revolve what tales I have told you   14
Of courts, of princes, of the tricks in war.
This service is not service, so being done,   16
But being so allowed. To apprehend thus   17
Draws us a profit from all things we see;
And often, to our comfort, shall we find

The sharded beetle in a safer hold   20
Than is the full-winged eagle. Oh, this life
Is nobler than attending for a check,   22
Richer than doing nothing for a bauble,   23
Prouder than rustling in unpaid-for silk;   24
Such gain the cap of him that makes him fine,   25
Yet keeps his book uncrossed. No life to ours.   26

GUIDERIUS
Out of your proof you speak. We poor unfledged   27
Have never winged from view o'th' nest, nor know
not
What air's from home. Haply this life is best,   29
If quiet life be best, sweeter to you
That have a sharper known, well corresponding
With your stiff age; but unto us it is
A cell of ignorance, traveling abed,   33
A prison for a debtor that not dares
To stride a limit.

ARVIRAGUS   What should we speak of   35
When we are old as you? When we shall hear
The rain and wind beat dark December, how,   37
In this our pinching cave, shall we discourse   38
The freezing hours away? We have seen nothing.
We are beastly: subtle as the fox for prey,
Like warlike as the wolf for what we eat.   41
Our valor is to chase what flies. Our cage   42
We make a choir, as doth the prisoned bird,
And sing our bondage freely.

BELARIUS   How you speak!   44
Did you but know the city's usuries
And felt them knowingly; the art o'th' court,
As hard to leave as keep, whose top to climb   47
Is certain falling, or so slipp'ry that
The fear's as bad as falling; the toil o'th' war,   49
A pain that only seems to seek out danger   50
I'th' name of fame and honor, which dies i'th' search
And hath as oft a slanderous epitaph
As record of fair act; nay, many times
Doth ill deserve by doing well; what's worse,   54
Must curtsy at the censure. Oh, boys, this story
The world may read in me. My body's marked
With Roman swords, and my report was once   57
First with the best of note. Cymbeline loved me,   58

75 **She'll . . . father** (The waiting woman's pretended emergency will
justify her asking for a riding habit that Imogen can then use.)
77 **franklin's** yeoman's. (A franklin was a farmer who owned his
own land but was not of noble birth.) **you're best** you had better
78 **before me** immediately in front of me. **Nor . . . here** (She gestures: not to this side, not to that.) 79 **ensues** happens later. (Imogen
can only look directly ahead to Milford Haven, nowhere else and
not beyond.)
3.3. Location: Wales. Before the cave of Belarius.
1 **keep house** stay at home 3 **bows you** makes you bow 4 **holy
office** i.e., a morning prayer. 5 **jet** strut 8 **use . . . hardly** treat you
not so badly, do not offend heaven as much. (With a play on the idea
of *rock* and *hard*.) 9 **prouder livers** those who live more proudly and
magnificently 12 **like a crow** appearing through distance as small as
a crow 13 **place** position. **sets off** enhances 14 **revolve** ponder
16–17 **This . . . allowed** i.e., Any act of service is valued not for itself,
but is valued as proof of the greatness of the person for whom the
service is performed.

20 **sharded** living in dung, or, covered with the sheaths of insects'
wings. **hold** stronghold 22 **attending . . . check** doing service (at
court) only to be rewarded with a rebuke 23 **bauble** trifle
24 **unpaid-for** for which the wearer is in debt to his tailor
25–6 **Such . . . uncrossed** such finery wins the respectful greeting of
his tailor, but does nothing to cancel his record of debts. 26 **to compared** with 27 **proof** experience. **unfledged** not yet feathered
29 **What . . . home** what things are like away from home. **Haply**
Perhaps 33 **abed** i.e., in imagination only, in dreams 35 **stride a
limit** overpass a bound (where the debtor will be liable for arrest).
37 **beat dark December** beat down, as befitting dark December
38 **pinching** nippingly cold, or, confining 41 **Like** as 42 **flies** flees.
44 **freely** (Said ironically: the only freedom is to sing of one's
bondage.) 47 **keep** dwell in 49 **the toil o'th' war** i.e., did you but
know the toil of war 50 **pain** labor 54 **Doth . . . deserve** earns
ungrateful treatment 57 **report** reputation 58 **the best of note** persons of the highest distinction.

And when a soldier was the theme, my name
Was not far off. Then was I as a tree
Whose boughs did bend with fruit. But in one night,   61
A storm, or robbery, call it what you will,
Shook down my mellow hangings, nay, my leaves,   63
And left me bare to weather.

GUIDERIUS   Uncertain favor!   64

BELARIUS
My fault being nothing—as I have told you oft—
But that two villains, whose false oaths prevailed
Before my perfect honor, swore to Cymbeline
I was confederate with the Romans. So
Followed my banishment, and this twenty years
This rock and these demesnes have been my world,   70
Where I have lived at honest freedom, paid   71
More pious debts to heaven than in all
The fore-end of my time. But up to th' mountains!   73
This is not hunters' language. He that strikes
The venison first shall be the lord o'th' feast;
To him the other two shall minister,
And we will fear no poison, which attends   77
In place of greater state. I'll meet you in the valleys.
                      Exeunt [Guiderius and Arviragus].
How hard it is to hide the sparks of nature!
These boys know little they are sons to th' King,
Nor Cymbeline dreams that they are alive.
They think they are mine; and though trained up thus
    meanly
I'th' cave wherein they bow, their thoughts do hit
The roofs of palaces, and nature prompts them
In simple and low things to prince it much   85
Beyond the trick of others. This Polydore,   86
The heir of Cymbeline and Britain, who
The King his father called Guiderius—Jove!
When on my three-foot stool I sit and tell
The warlike feats I have done, his spirits fly out
Into my story; say, "Thus mine enemy fell,
And thus I set my foot on 's neck," even then
The princely blood flows in his cheek, he sweats,
Strains his young nerves, and puts himself in posture   94
That acts my words. The younger brother, Cadwal,
Once Arviragus, in as like a figure   96
Strikes life into my speech and shows much more   97
His own conceiving. [*Sounds of hunting are heard.*]
      Hark, the game is roused!—   98
O Cymbeline, heaven and my conscience knows
Thou didst unjustly banish me; whereon,
At three and two years old, I stole these babes,
Thinking to bar thee of succession as
Thou refts me of my lands. Euriphile,   103
Thou wast their nurse; they took thee for their mother,

And every day do honor to her grave.   105
Myself, Belarius, that am Morgan called,
They take for natural father.—The game is up.   107
                                                    Exit.

❖

3.4

Enter Pisanio and Imogen.

IMOGEN
Thou toldst me, when we came from horse, the place   1
Was near at hand. Ne'er longed my mother so
To see me first as I have now. Pisanio, man,   3
Where is Posthumus? What is in thy mind
That makes thee stare thus? Wherefore breaks that
    sigh
From th'inward of thee? One but painted thus
Would be interpreted a thing perplexed   7
Beyond self-explication. Put thyself   8
Into a havior of less fear, ere wildness   9
Vanquish my staider senses. What's the matter?   10
            [*He offers her a letter.*]
Why tender'st thou that paper to me with   11
A look untender? If't be summer news,
Smile to't before; if winterly, thou need'st
But keep that countenance still. My husband's hand?
That drug-damned Italy hath outcraftied him,   15
And he's at some hard point. Speak, man. Thy tongue   16
May take off some extremity, which to read   17
Would be even mortal to me.

PISANIO   Please you, read,   18
And you shall find me, wretched man, a thing
The most disdained of fortune.

IMOGEN (*reads*) "Thy mistress, Pisanio, hath played the
    strumpet in my bed, the testimonies whereof lies
    bleeding in me. I speak not out of weak surmises but
    from proof as strong as my grief and as certain as I
    expect my revenge. That part thou, Pisanio, must act
    for me, if thy faith be not tainted with the breach of
    hers. Let thine own hands take away her life. I shall
    give thee opportunity at Milford Haven—she hath
    my letter for the purpose—where, if thou fear to strike
    and to make me certain it is done, thou art the pander
    to her dishonor and equally to me disloyal."

PISANIO
What shall I need to draw my sword? The paper
Hath cut her throat already. No, 'tis slander,
Whose edge is sharper than the sword, whose tongue
Outvenoms all the worms of Nile, whose breath   35

---

105 her (Belarius shifts easily from apostrophizing the dead Euriphile
to speaking about her.)   **107 up** roused. (Belarius hears a hunting cry.)
3.4. Location: Wales. Country near Milford Haven.
1 came from horse dismounted   **3 have** i.e., have longing to see
Posthumus   **7–8 perplexed . . . self-explication** bewildered beyond
the ability to express his condition.   **9 havior of less fear** less fearsome behavior   **9–10 ere . . . senses** before frenzy and panic overcome my calm.   **11 tender'st** offerest. (With a play on *untender* in the
next line.)   **15 That . . . him** That country notorious for its poisons
has overcome him by craft   **16 hard point** dangerous crisis.   **17 take
. . . extremity** reduce somewhat the shock   **18 mortal** fatal
35 worms serpents

---

61 Whose . . . fruit laden with rewards, the harvest of my efforts.
63 hangings hanging fruit   **64 Uncertain favor!** How unreliable is
the favor bestowed on one by great men!   **70 demesnes** domains,
regions   **71 at honest freedom** (Compare the phrases "at peace," "at
liberty.")   **73 fore-end** earlier part   **77 attends** is present, renders
service   **85 prince it** play the prince   **86 trick** manner   **94 nerves**
sinews   **96 in . . . figure** acting his part equally well   **97–8 shows . . .
conceiving** i.e., adds to my story his own conception.   **103 Thou
refts** you have bereft, deprived

Rides on the posting winds and doth belie   36
All corners of the world. Kings, queens, and states,   37
Maids, matrons, nay, the secrets of the grave
This viperous slander enters.—What cheer, madam?

IMOGEN
False to his bed? What is it to be false?
To lie in watch there and to think on him?   41
To weep twixt clock and clock? If sleep charge nature,   42
To break it with a fearful dream of him   43
And cry myself awake? That's false to's bed, is it?

PISANIO   Alas, good lady!

IMOGEN
I false? Thy conscience witness, Iachimo,   46
Thou didst accuse him of incontinency.
Thou then looked'st like a villain; now methinks
Thy favor's good enough. Some jay of Italy,   49
Whose mother was her painting, hath betrayed him.   50
Poor I am stale, a garment out of fashion,   51
And, for I am richer than to hang by th' walls,   52
I must be ripped. To pieces with me! Oh,   53
Men's vows are women's traitors! All good seeming,
By thy revolt, O husband, shall be thought   55
Put on for villainy; not born where't grows,   56
But worn a bait for ladies.

PISANIO   Good madam, hear me.

IMOGEN
True honest men being heard like false Aeneas   58
Were in his time thought false, and Sinon's weeping   59
Did scandal many a holy tear, took pity   60
From most true wretchedness. So thou, Posthumus,   61
Wilt lay the leaven on all proper men;   62
Goodly and gallant shall be false and perjured   63
From thy great fail.—Come, fellow, be thou honest;   64
Do thou thy master's bidding. When thou see'st him,
A little witness my obedience. Look,   66

   [drawing her sword and offering it to him]

36 posting hastening.   **belie** spread lies throughout   **37 states**
statesmen   **41 in watch** awake   **42 twixt . . . clock** from hour to
hour.   **charge nature** i.e., overcome wakefulness   **43 fearful dream
of him** fearful dream about his safety   **46 Thy conscience witness**
Let your conscience bear me witness. (She apostrophizes the absent
Iachimo; see next note.)   **49 Thy . . . enough** your appearance is good
enough (since what you said about Posthumus must sadly be true
after all.) (Imogen thinks that some whore of Italy, not Iachimo, is to
blame for this.)   **jay** i.e., flashy or light woman   **50 Whose . . . painting** i.e., who owed her beauty to cosmetics   **51 stale** no longer fresh.
(But with bitter suggestion of "harlot.")   **52 And . . . walls** and,
because I am too expensive to hang up idly like discarded clothing
53 ripped torn apart (1) in murder (2) like rich garments unsewn to
recover the cloth.   **55 revolt** inconstancy   **56 born** i.e., innate
58 being heard like when they were heard to speak like.   **Aeneas**
(Thought of as the pattern of faithless love because of his desertion of
Dido.)   **59 Were . . . false** i.e., were mistrusted because of Aeneas's
deceptive speech, which was indeed false; his smooth falsehood cast
doubt even on perfectly honest professions of love.   **Sinon** Greek
who by his guile persuaded the Trojans to introduce within the walls
of Troy the wooden horse filled with armed men   **60 scandal** bring
scandal to, discredit   **60–1 took pity From** prevented the bestowing
of well-deserved pity upon   **62 lay . . . men** take credit away from all
well-deserving and honorable men (just as sour *leaven* or fermenting
dough causes more dough to ferment and spoil)   **63 be** be thought
64 fail fault, offense.   **honest** loyal to your vow of obedience. (Said
with bitter irony.)   **66 A little witness** testify somewhat to

I draw the sword myself. Take it, and hit
The innocent mansion of my love, my heart.
Fear not; 'tis empty of all things but grief.
Thy master is not there, who was indeed
The riches of it. Do his bidding; strike.
Thou mayst be valiant in a better cause,   72
But now thou seem'st a coward.

PISANIO [rejecting the sword]   Hence, vile instrument!
Thou shalt not damn my hand.

IMOGEN   Why, I must die;
And if I do not by thy hand, thou art
No servant of thy master's. Against self-slaughter
There is a prohibition so divine
That cravens my weak hand. Come, here's my heart.   78
Something's afore't. Soft, soft! We'll no defense;   79
Obedient as the scabbard. What is here?   80
           [She takes letters from her bodice.]
The scriptures of the loyal Leonatus,   81
All turned to heresy? Away, away,
Corrupters of my faith! [She throws away the letters.]
     You shall no more
Be stomachers to my heart. Thus may poor fools   84
Believe false teachers. Though those that are betrayed
Do feel the treason sharply, yet the traitor
Stands in worse case of woe. And thou, Posthumus,   87
That didst set up   88
My disobedience 'gainst the King my father
And make me put into contempt the suits
Of princely fellows, shalt hereafter find   91
It is no act of common passage, but   92
A strain of rareness; and I grieve myself   93
To think, when thou shalt be disedged by her   94
That now thou tirest on, how thy memory   95
Will then be panged by me.—Prithee, dispatch.   96
The lamb entreats the butcher. Where's thy knife?
Thou art too slow to do thy master's bidding
When I desire it too.

PISANIO   Oh, gracious lady,
Since I received command to do this business
I have not slept one wink.

IMOGEN   Do't, and to bed then.

PISANIO
I'll wake mine eyeballs blind first.

IMOGEN   Wherefore then   102
Didst undertake it? Why hast thou abused
So many miles with a pretense? This place?
Mine action and thine own? Our horses' labor?
The time inviting thee? The perturbed court,

72 Thou mayst be Maybe you are   **78 cravens** makes cowardly
79 Something's i.e., Posthumus's letter is.   **Soft** i.e., Wait a minute
80 Obedient i.e., as willing to receive the sword   **81 scriptures** writings, letters. (With a play on "Holy Scriptures.")   **84 stomachers**
ornamental coverings for the breast worn by women under their
bodices   **87 Stands . . . woe** i.e., risks the penalty of damnation.
88 set up incite, encourage   **91 princely fellows** those of equal social
rank with me   **92–3 It . . . rareness** that my choice (of you) was no act
of a common sort but a rare trait   **94 disedged** surfeited, having the
edge of appetite taken off   **95 thou tirest on** you tear or devour ravenously (as a bird of prey)   **96 panged** pierced by thought of
102 wake . . . blind remain awake until I can no longer see

For my being absent, whereunto I never
Purpose return? Why hast thou gone so far,
To be unbent when thou hast ta'en thy stand,   109
Th'elected deer before thee?

PISANIO   But to win time   110
To lose so bad employment, in the which   111
I have considered of a course. Good lady,
Hear me with a patience.

IMOGEN   Talk thy tongue weary. Speak.
I have heard I am a strumpet, and mine ear,
Therein false struck, can take no greater wound,   115
Nor tent to bottom that. But speak.

PISANIO   Then, madam,   116
I thought you would not back again.

IMOGEN   Most like,   117
Bringing me here to kill me.

PISANIO   Not so, neither.
But if I were as wise as honest, then   119
My purpose would prove well. It cannot be   120
But that my master is abused. Some villain,   121
Ay, and singular in his art, hath done   122
You both this cursèd injury.

IMOGEN
Some Roman courtesan.

PISANIO   No, on my life.
I'll give but notice you are dead, and send him
Some bloody sign of it, for 'tis commanded
I should do so. You shall be missed at court,
And that will well confirm it.

IMOGEN   Why, good fellow,
What shall I do the while? Where bide? How live?
Or in my life what comfort, when I am
Dead to my husband?

PISANIO   If you'll back to th' court—

IMOGEN
No court, no father, nor no more ado
With that harsh, noble, simple nothing,
That Cloten, whose love suit hath been to me
As fearful as a siege.

PISANIO   If not at court,
Then not in Britain must you bide.

IMOGEN   Where, then?
Hath Britain all the sun that shines? Day, night,
Are they not but in Britain? I'th' world's volume   138
Our Britain seems as of it but not in't,   139
In a great pool a swan's nest. Prithee, think
There's livers out of Britain.

PISANIO   I am most glad   141
You think of other place. Th'ambassador,
Lucius the Roman, comes to Milford Haven

Tomorrow. Now, if you could wear a mind   144
Dark as your fortune is, and but disguise   145
That which, t'appear itself, must not yet be   146
But by self-danger, you should tread a course   147
Pretty and full of view; yea, haply near   148
The residence of Posthumus, so nigh at least
That, though his actions were not visible, yet
Report should render him hourly to your ear
As truly as he moves.

IMOGEN   Oh, for such means!
Though peril to my modesty, not death on't,   153
I would adventure.

PISANIO   Well, then, here's the point.
You must forget to be a woman, change
Command into obedience; fear and niceness—   156
The handmaids of all women, or, more truly,
Woman its pretty self—into a waggish courage;   158
Ready in gibes, quick-answered, saucy, and
As quarrelous as the weasel. Nay, you must   160
Forget that rarest treasure of your cheek,
Exposing it—but oh, the harder heart!   162
Alack, no remedy—to the greedy touch
Of common-kissing Titan, and forget   164
Your laborsome and dainty trims, wherein   165
You made great Juno angry.

IMOGEN   Nay, be brief.   166
I see into thy end and am almost
A man already.

PISANIO   First, make yourself but like one.
Forethinking this, I have already fit—   169
'Tis in my cloak bag—doublet, hat, hose, all
That answer to them. Would you in their serving,   171
And with what imitation you can borrow
From youth of such a season, 'fore noble Lucius   173
Present yourself, desire his service, tell him   174
Wherein you're happy—which will make him know,   175
If that his head have ear in music—doubtless   176
With joy he will embrace you, for he's honorable,   177
And, doubling that, most holy. Your means abroad,   178

144–7 if . . . self-danger if you could adapt your spirit to the obscurity of your fortune and simply disguise your womanhood, which, if it were to reveal itself for what it truly is, remains full of self-danger for the present   **148 Pretty . . . view** advantageous and promising, affording a fair prospect. **haply** perhaps. (With a suggestion also of "happily" [the Folio spelling], "fortunately.")   **153 Though . . . on't** As long as the risk to my modesty would not be fatal to it   **156 Command** i.e., as befitting one of royal birth. (Imogen will be disguising her royal birth and assuming the guise of one who must obey orders.) **niceness** daintiness   **158 waggish** roguish, masculine   **160 quarrelous** quarrelsome   **162 harder** too hard. (Pisanio is either reproaching the cruel necessity of his speaking so, or blaming Posthumus, or suggesting that Imogen must harden her heart.)   **164 common-kissing Titan** the sun god who kisses (i.e., shines on) everybody and everything   **165 laborsome . . . trims** elaborate and dainty apparel **166 angry** i.e., jealous.   **169 Forethinking** Anticipating.   **fit** ready **171 answer to** go along with. **Would . . . serving** If you would, assisted by them   **173 of . . . season** of such an age as you will represent   **174 his service** employment in his service   **175 happy** gifted, skillful.   **make him know** convince him   **176 If . . . music** i.e., if he has an ear for music, since he then cannot fail to appreciate your voice   **177 embrace you** take you in (to his service)   **178 doubling that** twice as important.   **Your means abroad** As for your financial means while you are abroad

109 To be unbent to unbend your bow again (and thus refuse to shoot).   **stand** place from which to shoot game   **110 Th'elected** the chosen.   **But** Only   **111 which** which time   **115 take** receive **116 tent . . . that** probe that wound to the bottom.   **117 back** go back (to court).   **like** likely   **119–20 But . . . well** (Pisanio hopes the plan he is going to propose will be as clever as he is honest in intent.) **121 abused** deceived.   **122 singular** unexcelled   **138 but** except **139 as . . . in't** i.e., as part of it but a small and relatively insignificant part, on the periphery, like a page torn out of a volume   **141 livers** persons living

You have me, rich, and I will never fail   179
Beginning nor supplyment. [*He gives her a cloak bag.*]
IMOGEN   Thou art all the comfort   180
The gods will diet me with. Prithee, away.   181
There's more to be considered, but we'll even   182
All that good time will give us. This attempt
I am soldier to, and will abide it with   184
A prince's courage. Away, I prithee.
PISANIO
Well, madam, we must take a short farewell,
Lest, being missed, I be suspected of
Your carriage from the court. My noble mistress,   188
Here is a box; I had it from the Queen.
                              [*He gives a box.*]
What's in't is precious. If you are sick at sea
Or stomach-qualmed at land, a dram of this
Will drive away distemper. To some shade,   192
And fit you to your manhood. May the gods
Direct you to the best!
IMOGEN   Amen. I thank thee.
                    Exeunt [*separately*].

❧

3.5

Enter Cymbeline, Queen, Cloten, Lucius,
[*Attendants,*] *and Lords.*

CYMBELINE
Thus far, and so farewell.
LUCIUS   Thanks, royal sir.   1
My emperor hath wrote I must from hence;   2
And am right sorry that I must report ye
My master's enemy.
CYMBELINE   Our subjects, sir,
Will not endure his yoke, and for ourself
To show less sovereignty than they must needs
Appear unkinglike.
LUCIUS   So, sir. I desire of you   7
A conduct overland to Milford Haven.   8
Madam, all joy befall Your Grace, and you!   9
CYMBELINE
My lords, you are appointed for that office;   10
The due of honor in no point omit.
So farewell, noble Lucius.
LUCIUS [*to Cloten*]   Your hand, my lord.
CLOTEN
Receive it friendly; but from this time forth

I wear it as your enemy.
LUCIUS   Sir, the event   14
Is yet to name the winner. Fare you well.
CYMBELINE
Leave not the worthy Lucius, good my lords,
Till he have crossed the Severn. Happiness!   17
                         Exeunt Lucius etc.
QUEEN
He goes hence frowning, but it honors us
That we have given him cause.
CLOTEN   'Tis all the better;
Your valiant Britons have their wishes in it.
CYMBELINE
Lucius hath wrote already to the Emperor
How it goes here. It fits us therefore ripely   22
Our chariots and our horsemen be in readiness.
The powers that he already hath in Gallia   24
Will soon be drawn to head, from whence he moves   25
His war for Britain.
QUEEN   'Tis not sleepy business,
But must be looked to speedily and strongly.
CYMBELINE
Our expectation that it would be thus
Hath made us forward. But, my gentle queen,   29
Where is our daughter? She hath not appeared
Before the Roman, nor to us hath tendered
The duty of the day. She looks us like   32
A thing more made of malice than of duty.
We have noted it.—Call her before us, for
We have been too slight in sufferance.
                         [*Exit an Attendant.*]
QUEEN   Royal sir,   35
Since the exile of Posthumus, most retired
Hath her life been; the cure whereof, my lord,
'Tis time must do. Beseech Your Majesty,
Forbear sharp speeches to her. She's a lady
So tender of rebukes that words are strokes
And strokes death to her.

Enter [*Attendant as*] *a messenger.*

CYMBELINE   Where is she, sir? How
Can her contempt be answered?
ATTENDANT   Please you, sir,   42
Her chambers are all locked, and there's no answer
That will be given to th' loud'st of noise we make.
QUEEN
My lord, when last I went to visit her,
She prayed me to excuse her keeping close,   46
Whereto constrained by her infirmity
She should that duty leave unpaid to you   48
Which daily she was bound to proffer. This
She wished me to make known, but our great court   50

---

179 rich adequately supplied with funds   **180 Beginning nor supplyment** from first to last in supplying your needs.   **181 diet** feed   **182 even** keep pace with, profit by   **184 soldier to** enlisted in, courageously prepared for.   **abide it** sustain it, stick with it   **188 Your carriage** having removed you   **192 distemper** illness.   **shade** secluded and protected spot
3.5. Location: At the court of Cymbeline.
1 Thus far Thus far we can escort you   **2 wrote** written. (Also in line 21.)   **7 So** i.e., Very good. (A polite way of closing the discussion.)
8 conduct safe-conduct, escort   **9 and you** (Possibly addressed to Cloten, or, more probably, to the King. Lucius bids farewell to Cloten in line 12.)   **10 office** duty (as escorts of Lucius)

14 event outcome   **17 Severn** river between England and Wales.
22 fits befits.   **ripely** speedily   **24 powers** armed forces   **25 drawn to head** brought together, assembled   **29 forward** well prepared.
32 looks us seems to me   **35 slight in sufferance** permissive.
42 answered accounted for.   **46 close** in private   **48 She . . . leave** she found herself obliged to leave that duty   **50 great court** important courtly business

Made me to blame in memory.
CYMBELINE   Her doors locked?
Not seen of late? Grant, heavens, that which I fear
Prove false!   *Exit.*
QUEEN   Son, I say, follow the King.
CLOTEN
That man of hers, Pisanio, her old servant,
I have not seen these two days.
QUEEN   Go, look after.
                                          Exit [Cloten].
Pisanio, thou that stand'st so for Posthumus!   56
He hath a drug of mine; I pray his absence
Proceed by swallowing that, for he believes   58
It is a thing most precious. But for her,
Where is she gone? Haply despair hath seized her,
Or, winged with fervor of her love, she's flown
To her desired Posthumus. Gone she is
To death or to dishonor, and my end   63
Can make good use of either. She being down,
I have the placing of the British crown.

          Enter Cloten.

How now, my son?
CLOTEN   'Tis certain she is fled.
Go in and cheer the King. He rages; none
Dare come about him.
QUEEN   All the better. May
This night forestall him of the coming day!   69
                                        Exit Queen.
CLOTEN
I love and hate her. For she's fair and royal,   70
And that she hath all courtly parts more exquisite 71
Than lady, ladies, woman—from every one   72
The best she hath, and she, of all compounded,   73
Outsells them all—I love her therefore. But   74
Disdaining me and throwing favors on   75
The low Posthumus slanders so her judgment   76
That what's else rare is choked; and in that point 77
I will conclude to hate her, nay, indeed,
To be revenged upon her. For when fools
Shall—

          Enter Pisanio. [He attempts to avoid Cloten.]

                    Who is here? What, are you packing, sirrah?   80
Come hither. Ah, you precious pander! Villain,
Where is thy lady? In a word, or else
Thou art straightway with the fiends.
                    [He threatens him with his sword.]
PISANIO   Oh, good my lord!
CLOTEN
Where is thy lady? Or, by Jupiter,
I will not ask again. Close villain,   85

I'll have this secret from thy heart or rip
Thy heart to find it. Is she with Posthumus,
From whose so many weights of baseness cannot   88
A dram of worth be drawn?
PISANIO   Alas, my lord,   89
How can she be with him? When was she missed?
He is in Rome.
CLOTEN   Where is she, sir? Come nearer.   91
No farther halting. Satisfy me home   92
What is become of her.
PISANIO
Oh, my all-worthy lord!
CLOTEN   All-worthy villain!
Discover where thy mistress is at once,   95
At the next word. No more of "worthy lord"!
Speak, or thy silence on the instant is
Thy condemnation and thy death.
PISANIO   Then, sir,
This paper is the history of my knowledge
Touching her flight.   *[He presents a letter.]*
CLOTEN   Let's see't. I will pursue her
Even to Augustus' throne.
PISANIO *[aside]*   Or this or perish.   101
She's far enough, and what he learns by this
May prove his travel, not her danger.
CLOTEN *[reading]*   Hum!
PISANIO *[aside]*
I'll write to my lord she's dead. O Imogen,
Safe mayst thou wander, safe return again!
CLOTEN   Sirrah, is this letter true?
PISANIO   Sir, as I think.
CLOTEN   It is Posthumus' hand, I know't. Sirrah, if thou
wouldst not be a villain, but do me true service, un-   109
dergo those employments wherein I should have   110
cause to use thee with a serious industry—that is,
what villainy soe'er I bid thee do, to perform it directly
and truly—I would think thee an honest man. Thou
shouldst neither want my means for thy relief nor my
voice for thy preferment.   115
PISANIO   Well, my good lord.
CLOTEN   Wilt thou serve me? For since patiently and
constantly thou hast stuck to the bare fortune of that
beggar Posthumus, thou canst not, in the course of
gratitude, but be a diligent follower of mine. Wilt thou
serve me?
PISANIO   Sir, I will.
CLOTEN   Give me thy hand; here's my purse. *[He gives* 123
money.] Hast any of thy late master's garments in thy   124
possession?
PISANIO   I have, my lord, at my lodging the same suit
he wore when he took leave of my lady and mistress.
CLOTEN   The first service thou dost me, fetch that suit
hither. Let it be thy first service. Go.

---

56 thou that stand'st so you who stand up for, look out for the
interests of   **58 Proceed by** results from   **63 end** intent   **69 forestall**
deprive (i.e., bring about his death)   **70 For** Because   **71 that** because.
parts endowments, graces   **72 Than lady, ladies, woman** than any
lady, or all ladies, or indeed womankind   **72–3 from . . . she hath** she
has the best qualities of each   **74 Outsells** outvalues, excels   **75 Disdaining** her disdaining   **76 slanders** discredits   **77 rare** excellent
80 packing plotting and sneaking away.   **sirrah** (Form of address to
a social inferior; also in lines 106 and 108.)   **85 Close** Secretive

88–9 From . . . drawn from whom not even a tiny amount of worthiness can be extracted, so heavy is the preponderance of baseness.
91 Come nearer Answer more to the point.   **92 home** completely
95 Discover Disclose   **101 Or** Either   **109–10 undergo** undertake
115 preferment advancement.   **123 purse** (Cloten is not giving
Pisanio salary but making him his purse bearer.)   **124 late** recent.
(Not "dead.")

PISANIO   I shall, my lord.   *Exit.*

CLOTEN   Meet thee at Milford Haven!—I forgot to ask him one thing; I'll remember't anon.—Even there, thou villain Posthumus, will I kill thee. I would these garments were come. She said upon a time—the bitterness of it I now belch from my heart—that she held the very garment of Posthumus in more respect than **136** my noble and natural person, together with the adornment of my qualities. With that suit upon my back will I ravish her; first kill him, and in her eyes. There shall she see my valor, which will then be a torment to her contempt. He on the ground, my speech of insult- **141** ment ended on his dead body, and when my lust hath **142** dined—which, as I say, to vex her I will execute in the clothes that she so praised—to the court I'll knock her back, foot her home again. She hath despised me re- **145** joicingly, and I'll be merry in my revenge.

Enter Pisanio [with the clothes].

Be those the garments?

PISANIO   Ay, my noble lord.

CLOTEN   How long is't since she went to Milford Haven?

PISANIO   She can scarce be there yet.

CLOTEN   Bring this apparel to my chamber; that is the second thing that I have commanded thee. The third is that thou wilt be a voluntary mute to my design. Be but duteous, and true preferment shall tender itself to thee. My revenge is now at Milford. Would I had wings to follow it! Come, and be true.   *Exit.*

PISANIO
Thou bidd'st me to my loss; for true to thee
Were to prove false, which I will never be,
To him that is most true. To Milford go,
And find not her whom thou pursuest. Flow, flow,
You heavenly blessings, on her! This fool's speed   **162**
Be crossed with slowness; labor be his meed!   *Exit.* **163**

❧

3.6

Enter Imogen alone [in boy's clothes].

IMOGEN
I see a man's life is a tedious one.
I have tired myself, and for two nights together   **2**
Have made the ground my bed. I should be sick
But that my resolution helps me. Milford,
When from the mountain top Pisanio showed thee,
Thou wast within a ken. O Jove, I think   **6**
Foundations fly the wretched—such, I mean,   **7**
Where they should be relieved. Two beggars told me
I could not miss my way. Will poor folks lie,
That have afflictions on them, knowing 'tis

A punishment or trial? Yes; no wonder,   **11**
When rich ones scarce tell true. To lapse in fullness   **12**
Is sorer than to lie for need, and falsehood   **13**
Is worse in kings than beggars. My dear lord!
Thou art one o'th' false ones. Now I think on thee,
My hunger's gone; but even before I was   **16**
At point to sink for food. [*She sees the cave.*] But what is this?   **17**
Here is a path to't. 'Tis some savage hold.   **18**
I were best not call; I dare not call. Yet famine,
Ere clean it o'erthrow nature, makes it valiant.   **20**
Plenty and peace breeds cowards; hardness ever   **21**
Of hardiness is mother.—Ho! Who's here?   **22**
If anything that's civil, speak; if savage,   **23**
Take or lend. Ho!—No answer? Then I'll enter.   **24**
Best draw my sword; an if mine enemy   **25**
But fear the sword like me, he'll scarcely look on't.
Such a foe, good heavens!   **27**

[*She draws her sword, and*]
exit [into the cave].

Enter Belarius, Guiderius, and Arviragus.

BELARIUS
You, Polydore, have proved best woodman and   **28**
Are master of the feast. Cadwal and I
Will play the cook and servant; 'tis our match.   **30**
The sweat of industry would dry and die   **31**
But for the end it works to. Come, our stomachs   **32**
Will make what's homely savory; weariness   **33**
Can snore upon the flint, when resty sloth   **34**
Finds the down pillow hard. Now peace be here,
Poor house, that keep'st thyself!

GUIDERIUS   I am throughly weary.   **36**

ARVIRAGUS
I am weak with toil, yet strong in appetite.

GUIDERIUS
There is cold meat i'th' cave. We'll browse on that   **38**
Whilst what we have killed be cooked.

BELARIUS [*looking into the cave*]   Stay, come not in.
But that it eats our victuals, I should think
Here were a fairy.

GUIDERIUS   What's the matter, sir?

BELARIUS
By Jupiter, an angel! Or, if not,
An earthly paragon! Behold divineness
No elder than a boy!

Enter Imogen.

---

136 more respect higher regard   **141–2 insultment** contemptuous triumph   **145 foot** kick   **162 This fool's** May this fool's   **163 crossed** thwarted.   **meed** reward.
3.6. Location: Wales. Before the cave of Belarius.
2 tired (1) exhausted (2) attired   **6 within a ken** within sight.
7 Foundations (1) certainties, fixed places (2) charitable institutions.
fly the wretched i.e., are never there when most needed

11 trial test of virtue. (Poverty may be a Job-like affliction visited on those God wishes to test, in which case lying is dangerously sinful.)
12 lapse in fullness lie and commit other sins in a state of prosperity
13 sorer worse, more wicked   **16 but even before** just now   **17 for** for lack of   **18 hold** stronghold, fastness.   **20 clean** altogether
21 hardness hardship   **22 Of hardiness is mother** breeds courage.
23 civil civilized   **24 Take or lend** rob me (or something worse), or give me food.   **25 Best** It were best to.   **an if** if   **27 Such ... heavens!** May the heavens grant me a foe as timid as myself!   **28 woodman** woodsman, huntsman   **30 match** agreement, bargain.
31–2 The sweat ... works to Human labor would dry up and cease if it were not for the desired end.   **33 homely** plain   **34 resty** sluggish, indolent   **36 keep'st thyself** i.e., is untended, empty.   **throughly** thoroughly   **38 browse** nibble

IMOGEN Good masters, harm me not.
Before I entered here, I called, and thought
To have begged or bought what I have took. Good
truth,
I have stol'n naught, nor would not, though I had
found
Gold strewed i'th' floor. Here's money for my meat.
[*She offers money.*]
I would have left it on the board so soon
As I had made my meal, and parted
With prayers for the provider.
GUIDERIUS   Money, youth?
ARVIRAGUS
All gold and silver rather turn to dirt,
As 'tis no better reckoned but of those
Who worship dirty gods.
IMOGEN   I see you're angry.
Know, if you kill me for my fault, I should
Have died had I not made it.
BELARIUS   Whither bound?
IMOGEN To Milford Haven.
BELARIUS What's your name?
IMOGEN
Fidele, sir. I have a kinsman who
Is bound for Italy. He embarked at Milford,
To whom being going, almost spent with hunger,
I am fall'n in this offense.
BELARIUS   Prithee, fair youth,
Think us no churls, nor measure our good minds
By this rude place we live in. Well encountered!
'Tis almost night. You shall have better cheer
Ere you depart, and thanks to stay and eat it.
Boys, bid him welcome.
GUIDERIUS   Were you a woman, youth,
I should woo hard but be your groom in honesty,
Ay, bid for you as I do buy.
ARVIRAGUS [*to Guiderius*] I'll make't my comfort
He is a man; I'll love him as my brother.
[*To Imogen*] And such a welcome as I'd give to him
After long absence, such is yours. Most welcome!
Be sprightly, for you fall 'mongst friends.
IMOGEN   'Mongst friends,
If brothers. [*Aside*] Would it had been so that they
Had been my father's sons! Then had my prize
Been less, and so more equal ballasting
To thee, Posthumus.
BELARIUS   He wrings at some distress.

45
47

53
54

57

61

63

69
70

73

75
76
77
78

79

GUIDERIUS
Would I could free't!
ARVIRAGUS   Or I; whate'er it be,
What pain it cost, what danger! Gods!
BELARIUS   Hark, boys.
[*He whispers to them.*]
IMOGEN [*to herself*] Great men
That had a court no bigger than this cave,
That did attend themselves and had the virtue
Which their own conscience sealed them, laying by
That nothing-gift of differing multitudes,
Could not outpeer these twain. Pardon me, gods!
I'd change my sex to be companion with them,
Since Leonatus's false.
BELARIUS   It shall be so.
Boys, we'll go dress our hunt. Fair youth, come in.
Discourse is heavy, fasting; when we have supped,
We'll mannerly demand thee of thy story,
So far as thou wilt speak it.
GUIDERIUS   Pray draw near.
ARVIRAGUS
The night to th'owl and morn to th' lark less welcome.
IMOGEN Thanks, sir.
ARVIRAGUS I pray, draw near.   *Exeunt.*

45
47

81

84
85
86
87

89
90
91

❧

3.[7]

Enter two Roman Senators and Tribunes.

FIRST SENATOR
This is the tenor of the Emperor's writ:
That since the common men are now in action
'Gainst the Pannonians and Dalmatians,
And that the legions now in Gallia are
Full weak to undertake our wars against
The fall'n-off Britons, that we do incite
The gentry to this business. He creates
Lucius proconsul, and to you the tribunes,
For this immediate levy, he commends
His absolute commission. Long live Caesar!
A TRIBUNE
Is Lucius general of the forces?
SECOND SENATOR   Ay.
A TRIBUNE
Remaining now in Gallia?
FIRST SENATOR   With those legions
Which I have spoke of, whereunto your levy

6

8
9
10

45 masters i.e., sirs. (A form of address to ordinary folk.) **47 Good truth** In truth **53 All gold** Let all gold **54 but of** except by **57 made** committed **61 embarked** was to have embarked **63 in** into **69–70 I . . . buy** I would woo earnestly rather than fail to be your swain in all honesty, yes, and propose marriage to you as if offering to buy something precious. **73 him** i.e., such a brother **75–6 'Mongst . . . brothers** i.e., Certainly I am among friends, if the three of us are to be like brothers. **77–9 Then . . . Posthumus** Then my value would be less (since my brothers would take my place as heirs to the throne) and thus more equal in social station and wealth to that of you, Posthumus. (*Prize* also suggests a captured vessel at sea, in the nautical metaphor continued with *ballasting*, which gives a ship stability). **79 wrings** writhes

81 What whatever **84–6 That . . . multitudes** who had no one to attend them but themselves and no moral excellence to boast of other than what their own self-knowledge could swear to, disregarding the valueless gift of adulation from the fickle populace **87 outpeer** excel **89 It shall be so** (Belarius finishes his conversation apart with Arviragus and Guiderius.) **90 hunt** game taken in the hunt. **91 Discourse . . . fasting** Conversation is difficult when one has not eaten.
3.7. Location: Rome. A public place, perhaps the Senate House.
6 fall'n-off revolted **8 proconsul** provincial governor **9 commends** entrusts **10 absolute commission** unlimited authority.

Must be supplyant. The words of your commission 14
Will tie you to the numbers and the time 15
Of their dispatch.

A TRIBUNE   We will discharge our duty.

Exeunt.

❧

4.1

Enter Cloten alone, [dressed in Posthumus's garments].

CLOTEN   I am near to th' place where they should meet,
if Pisanio have mapped it truly. How fit his garments 2
serve me! Why should his mistress, who was made
by Him that made the tailor, not be fit too? The 4
rather—saving reverence of the word—for 'tis said a 5
woman's fitness comes by fits. Therein I must play the 6
workman. I dare speak it to myself, for it is not vainglory for a man and his glass to confer in his own 8
chamber—I mean, the lines of my body are as well
drawn as his; no less young, more strong, not beneath
him in fortunes, beyond him in the advantage of the 11
time, above him in birth, alike conversant in general 12
services, and more remarkable in single oppositions. 13
Yet this imperceiverant thing loves him in my despite. 14
What mortality is! Posthumus, thy head, which now is 15
growing upon thy shoulders, shall within this hour be
off, thy mistress enforced, thy garments cut to pieces
before her face; and all this done, spurn her home to her
father, who may haply be a little angry for my so rough 19
usage; but my mother, having power of his testiness, 20
shall turn all into my commendations. My horse is tied
up safe. Out, sword, and to a sore purpose! [*He draws.*] 22
Fortune put them into my hand! This is the very description of their meeting place, and the fellow dares
not deceive me.   *Exit.*

❧

4.2

Enter Belarius, Guiderius, Arviragus, and Imogen from the cave.

BELARIUS [*to Imogen*]
You are not well. Remain here in the cave;
We'll come to you after hunting.

ARVIRAGUS [*to Imogen*]   Brother, stay here.

Are we not brothers?

IMOGEN   So man and man should be, 3
But clay and clay differs in dignity, 4
Whose dust is both alike. I am very sick. 5

GUIDERIUS [*to Arviragus and Belarius*]
Go you to hunting. I'll abide with him.

IMOGEN
So sick I am not, yet I am not well; 7
But not so citizen a wanton as 8
To seem to die ere sick. So please you, leave me; 9
Stick to your journal course. The breach of custom 10
Is breach of all. I am ill, but your being by me
Cannot amend me; society is no comfort
To one not sociable. I am not very sick,
Since I can reason of it. Pray you, trust me here— 14
I'll rob none but myself—and let me die, 15
Stealing so poorly.

GUIDERIUS   I love thee—I have spoke it— 16
How much the quantity, the weight as much, 17
As I do love my father.

BELARIUS   What? How? How?

ARVIRAGUS
If it be sin to say so, sir, I yoke me 19
In my good brother's fault. I know not why
I love this youth; and I have heard you say
Love's reason's without reason. The bier at door,
And a demand who is't shall die, I'd say
"My father, not this youth."

BELARIUS [*aside*]   Oh, noble strain! 24
Oh, worthiness of nature! Breed of greatness!
Cowards father cowards and base things sire base;
Nature hath meal and bran, contempt and grace. 27
I'm not their father; yet who this should be 28
Doth miracle itself, loved before me. 29
[*Aloud*] 'Tis the ninth hour o'th' morn.

ARVIRAGUS [*to Imogen*]   Brother, farewell.

IMOGEN
I wish ye sport.

ARVIRAGUS   You health. [*To Belarius*] So please you, sir. 31

IMOGEN [*aside*]
These are kind creatures. Gods, what lies I have heard!
Our courtiers say all's savage but at court.
Experience, oh, thou disprov'st report!
Th'imperious seas breeds monsters; for the dish, 35
Poor tributary rivers as sweet fish. 36

3–5 So . . . alike i.e., We are brothers, as all humans should be, being made out of the same dust, though social distinctions impose their artificial differences.   7 So sick I am not I am not that sick   8–9 But . . . sick but I am not so city-bred a weakling as to fear I am dying when I am not even really sick yet.   10 journal daily   14 reason of it talk coherently about it.   15–16 I'll . . . poorly (Imogen's witticism is that, since she will only be robbing herself of their company, not taking their food as in 3.6, only she should pay the penalty of loneliness for such a petty "crime.")   17 How . . . as much just as much in quantity and weight   19 yoke me join company   24 strain inherited disposition.   27 Nature . . . grace in human nature we find both flour and husks, the worthy and the contemptible.   28–9 who . . . before me it is miraculous that this youth, whoever he is, should be loved in preference to me.   31 You i.e., I wish you.   So please you At your service   35 Th'imperious The imperial, as contrasted with *tributary*   35–6 for . . . fish when it comes to providing delicious fish to eat, small tributaries do at least as well as the sea. (By analogy, humble surroundings breed at least as great virtue as can be found at court.)

14 supplyant reinforcing, auxiliary.   15 tie you to specify for you
4.1. Location: Wales. Near the cave of Belarius.
2 his Posthumus's   4 Him i.e., God   5 saving reverence asking pardon (i.e., for the indecent punning on *fitness* and *fit.*)   for because
6 fitness sexual inclination.   fits fits and starts.   8 glass mirror
11–12 the advantage of the time superiority in social opportunity
12–13 alike . . . services equally versed in military matters   13 single oppositions single combat.   14 imperceiverant dull of perception.
in my despite to spite me.   15 What mortality is! What a thing life is!   19 haply perchance   20 power of control over   22 sore grievous
4.2. Location: Before the cave of Belarius. The scene may be virtually continuous.

I am sick still, heartsick. Pisanio,
I'll now taste of thy drug.
                    [*She swallows some. The men speak apart.*]
GUIDERIUS   I could not stir him.   38
He said he was gentle, but unfortunate;   39
Dishonestly afflicted, but yet honest.   40

ARVIRAGUS
Thus did he answer me, yet said hereafter
I might know more.

BELARIUS   To th' field, to th' field!—
We'll leave you for this time. Go in and rest.

ARVIRAGUS
We'll not be long away.

BELARIUS   Pray be not sick,
For you must be our huswife.

IMOGEN   Well or ill,
I am bound to you.   *Exit [to the cave]*.

BELARIUS   And shalt be ever.   47
This youth, howe'er distressed, appears he hath had   48
Good ancestors.

ARVIRAGUS   How angel-like he sings!

GUIDERIUS
But his neat cookery! He cut our roots in characters   50
And sauced our broths as Juno had been sick   51
And he her dieter.

ARVIRAGUS   Nobly he yokes   52
A smiling with a sigh, as if the sigh
Was that it was for not being such a smile;   54
The smile mocking the sigh, that it would fly
From so divine a temple to commix   56
With winds that sailors rail at.

GUIDERIUS   I do note   57
That grief and patience, rooted in him both,
Mingle their spurs together.

ARVIRAGUS   Grow, patience,   59
And let the stinking elder, grief, untwine   60
His perishing root with the increasing vine!   61

BELARIUS
It is great morning. Come, away!—Who's there?   62

Enter Cloten, [not seeing them at first].

CLOTEN
I cannot find those runagates. That villain   63
Hath mocked me. I am faint.

BELARIUS   "Those runagates"?
Means he not us? I partly know him. 'Tis
Cloten, the son o' th' Queen. I fear some ambush.
I saw him not these many years, and yet
I know 'tis he. We are held as outlaws. Hence!

GUIDERIUS
He is but one. You and my brother search
What companies are near. Pray you, away.   70
Let me alone with him.

                    [*Exeunt Belarius and Arviragus.*]

CLOTEN   Soft, what are you   71
That fly me thus? Some villain mountaineers?
I have heard of such. What slave art thou?

GUIDERIUS   A thing
More slavish did I ne'er than answering
A slave without a knock.

CLOTEN   Thou art a robber,   75
A lawbreaker, a villain. Yield thee, thief.

GUIDERIUS
To who? To thee? What art thou? Have not I
An arm as big as thine? A heart as big?
Thy words, I grant, are bigger, for I wear not
My dagger in my mouth. Say what thou art,
Why I should yield to thee.

CLOTEN   Thou villain base,
Know'st me not by my clothes?   82

GUIDERIUS   No, nor thy tailor, rascal,   83
Who is thy grandfather. He made those clothes,   84
Which, as it seems, make thee.

CLOTEN   Thou precious varlet,   85
My tailor made them not.

GUIDERIUS   Hence, then, and thank
The man that gave them thee. Thou art some fool;
I am loath to beat thee.

CLOTEN   Thou injurious thief,   88
Hear but my name, and tremble.

GUIDERIUS   What's thy name?

CLOTEN   Cloten, thou villain.

GUIDERIUS
Cloten, thou double villain, be thy name,
I cannot tremble at it. Were it toad, or adder, spider,
'Twould move me sooner.

CLOTEN   To thy further fear,
Nay, to thy mere confusion, thou shalt know   94
I am son to th' Queen.

GUIDERIUS   I am sorry for't; not seeming
So worthy as thy birth.

CLOTEN   Art not afeard?

GUIDERIUS
Those that I reverence, those I fear—the wise.   97
At fools I laugh, not fear them.

CLOTEN   Die the death!   98
When I have slain thee with my proper hand,   99
I'll follow those that even now fled hence
And on the gates of Lud's Town set your heads.
Yield, rustic mountaineer!   *Fight, and exeunt.*

Enter Belarius and Arviragus.

---

38 stir him persuade him to tell about himself.   **39 gentle** wellborn
40 Dishonestly afflicted afflicted by adverse and ignominious fortune   **47 bound** obligated. (But Belarius answers in the sense of
"bound by affection.")   **48 he hath had** i.e., to have had   **50 characters** letters, designs   **51 as** as if   **52 dieter** cook.   **54 that** what
56 commix join   **57 winds . . . at** i.e., the rude wind, so infinitely
rougher than the sigh.   **59 spurs** roots   **60–1 And let . . . vine!** and
let the strong-smelling elder tree (on which Judas is supposed to have
hanged himself after betraying Jesus) cease to twine its deadly root
around that of the bounteous vine! i.e., may grief cease to afflict
Fidele's well-being!   **62 great morning** broad day.   **63 runagates**
renegades, runaways.   **That villain** Pisanio

70 companies companions   **71 Let . . . him** Leave me alone to deal
with him.   **Soft** i.e., Wait a minute   **75 without a knock** without giving him a blow.   **82 Know'st . . . clothes?** (Cloten is dressed as one
from the court.)   **83–5 No . . . thee** (A jest on the proverbial idea that
"The tailor makes the man.")   **85 precious varlet** arrant rascal
88 injurious insulting, malicious   **94 mere confusion** utter ruin
97 fear regard with awe   **98 Die the death!** (A solemn pronouncement of the sentence of death.)   **99 proper** own

BELARIUS   No company's abroad?

ARVIRAGUS

None in the world. You did mistake him, sure.

BELARIUS

I cannot tell. Long is it since I saw him,
But time hath nothing blurred those lines of favor   106
Which then he wore. The snatches in his voice   107
And burst of speaking were as his. I am absolute   108
'Twas very Cloten.

ARVIRAGUS   In this place we left them.   109
I wish my brother make good time with him,   110
You say he is so fell.

BELARIUS   Being scarce made up,   111
I mean to man, he had not apprehension   112
Of roaring terrors; for defect of judgment   113
Is oft the cause of fear.

Enter Guiderius [with Cloten's head].

                But see, thy brother.   114

GUIDERIUS

This Cloten was a fool, an empty purse;
There was no money in't. Not Hercules
Could have knocked out his brains, for he had none.
Yet I not doing this, the fool had borne   118
My head as I do his.

BELARIUS   What hast thou done?

GUIDERIUS

I am perfect what: cut off one Cloten's head,   120
Son to the Queen, after his own report,   121
Who called me traitor, mountaineer, and swore
With his own single hand he'd take us in,   123
Displace our heads where—thanks, ye gods!—they
    grow,   124
And set them on Lud's Town.

BELARIUS   We are all undone.

GUIDERIUS

Why, worthy father, what have we to lose
But that he swore to take, our lives? The law   127
Protects not us. Then why should we be tender   128
To let an arrogant piece of flesh threat us,   129
Play judge and executioner all himself,
For we do fear the law? What company   131
Discover you abroad?

BELARIUS   No single soul
Can we set eye on; but in all safe reason
He must have some attendants. Though his humor   134
Was nothing but mutation—ay, and that   135
From one bad thing to worse—not frenzy,

Not absolute madness could so far have raved
To bring him here alone. Although perhaps
It may be heard at court that such as we
Cave here, hunt here, are outlaws, and in time
May make some stronger head, the which he
    hearing—   141
As it is like him—might break out and swear   142
He'd fetch us in, yet is't not probable   143
To come alone, either he so undertaking   144
Or they so suffering. Then on good ground we fear,   145
If we do fear this body hath a tail
More perilous than the head.

ARVIRAGUS   Let ord'nance   147
Come as the gods foresay it. Howsoe'er,   148
My brother hath done well.

BELARIUS   I had no mind   149
To hunt this day. The boy Fidele's sickness
Did make my way long forth.

GUIDERIUS   With his own sword,   151
Which he did wave against my throat, I have ta'en
His head from him. I'll throw't into the creek
Behind our rock, and let it to the sea
And tell the fishes he's the Queen's son, Cloten.
That's all I reck.   *Exit.*

BELARIUS   I fear 'twill be revenged.   156
Would, Polydore, thou hadst not done't, though valor
Becomes thee well enough.

ARVIRAGUS   Would I had done't,
So the revenge alone pursued me! Polydore,   159
I love thee brotherly, but envy much
Thou hast robbed me of this deed. I would revenges   161
That possible strength might meet would seek us
    through   162
And put us to our answer.

BELARIUS   Well, 'tis done.   163
We'll hunt no more today, nor seek for danger
Where there's no profit. I prithee, to our rock.
You and Fidele play the cooks. I'll stay
Till hasty Polydore return, and bring him   167
To dinner presently.

ARVIRAGUS   Poor sick Fidele!
I'll willingly to him. To gain his color   169
I'd let a parish of such Clotens blood,   170
And praise myself for charity.   *Exit [into the cave].*

BELARIUS   O thou goddess,
Thou divine Nature, how thyself thou blazon'st   172
In these two princely boys! They are as gentle
As zephyrs blowing below the violet,

---

106 **nothing** not at all. **lines of favor** facial features 107 **snatches** hesitations 108 **absolute** positive 109 **very Cloten** Cloten himself. 110 **make good time** acquit himself well 111 **fell** fierce. 111–14 **Being . . . fear** Even when he was barely full-grown, Cloten had no clear apprehension of danger, for a defective judgment like his often produces a recklessness that is to be feared (as evidenced in Cloten's behavior as reported in lines 120–43 below). 118 **Yet . . . this** Yet if I had not done this. **had** would have 120 **perfect** well aware 121 **after** according to 123 **take us in** capture us 124 **where** from where 127 **that** that which 128–9 **be . . . let** be so meek as to allow 131 **For** simply because 134 **humor** disposition 135 **mutation** changeability

141 **make** assemble. **head** armed force 142 **break out** burst out (in speech) 143 **fetch us in** capture us 144 **To come** that he would come 145 **suffering** permitting. 147 **ord'nance** what is ordained 148 **foresay** predetermine 149 **mind** inclination 151 **Did . . . forth** made my wanderings (from the cave) seem long. **his** i.e., Cloten's 156 **reck** care. 159 **alone . . . me** would have pursued me only. 161 **Thou** that thou 161–3 **I would . . . answer** I wish that revenges equal to all the human strength that we could muster would seek us out and put us to the test. 167 **hasty** rash 169 **gain his color** restore the color (to his cheeks) 170 **I'd . . . blood** I'd drain the blood from a parish full of such Clotens 172 **how . . . blazon'st** how you proudly display yourself

Not wagging his sweet head; and yet as rough,
Their royal blood enchafed, as the rud'st wind   176
That by the top doth take the mountain pine
And make him stoop to th' vale. 'Tis wonder
That an invisible instinct should frame them   179
To royalty unlearned, honor untaught,
Civility not seen from other, valor   181
That wildly grows in them but yields a crop   182
As if it had been sowed. Yet still it's strange
What Cloten's being here to us portends,
Or what his death will bring us.

Enter Guiderius.

GUIDERIUS   Where's my brother?
I have sent Cloten's clodpoll down the stream   186
In embassy to his mother. His body's hostage   187
For his return.   *Solemn music.*
BELARIUS   My ingenious instrument!   188
Hark, Polydore, it sounds. But what occasion
Hath Cadwal now to give it motion? Hark!
GUIDERIUS
Is he at home?
BELARIUS   He went hence even now.
GUIDERIUS
What does he mean? Since death of my dear'st mother
It did not speak before. All solemn things   193
Should answer solemn accidents. The matter?   194
Triumphs for nothing and lamenting toys   195
Is jollity for apes and grief for boys.   196
Is Cadwal mad?

Enter Arviragus, with Imogen, [as] dead, bearing
her in his arms.

BELARIUS   Look, here he comes,
And brings the dire occasion in his arms
Of what we blame him for.
ARVIRAGUS   The bird is dead
That we have made so much on. I had rather   200
Have skipped from sixteen years of age to sixty,
To have turned my leaping-time into a crutch,   202
Than have seen this.
GUIDERIUS   O sweetest, fairest lily!
My brother wears thee not the one half so well   204
As when thou grew'st thyself.
BELARIUS   O Melancholy,   205

Who ever yet could sound thy bottom, find   206
The ooze to show what coast thy sluggish crare   207
Might eas'liest harbor in?—Thou blessèd thing,   208
Jove knows what man thou mightst have made; but I, 209
Thou diedst, a most rare boy, of melancholy.—
How found you him?
ARVIRAGUS   Stark, as you see,   211
Thus smiling, as some fly had tickled slumber,   212
Not as death's dart being laughed at; his right cheek   213
Reposing on a cushion.
GUIDERIUS   Where?
ARVIRAGUS   O'th' floor,
His arms thus leagued. I thought he slept, and put   215
My clouted brogues from off my feet, whose rudeness   216
Answered my steps too loud.
GUIDERIUS   Why, he but sleeps.
If he be gone, he'll make his grave a bed;
With female fairies will his tomb be haunted,
And worms will not come to thee.
ARVIRAGUS   With fairest flowers   220
Whilst summer lasts and I live here, Fidele,
I'll sweeten thy sad grave. Thou shalt not lack
The flower that's like thy face, pale primrose, nor
The azured harebell, like thy veins, no, nor   224
The leaf of eglantine, whom, not to slander,   225
Outsweetened not thy breath. The ruddock would   226
With charitable bill—O bill sore shaming
Those rich-left heirs that let their fathers lie
Without a monument!—bring thee all this,
Yea, and furred moss besides, when flowers are none,
To winter-ground thy corpse.
GUIDERIUS   Prithee, have done,   231
And do not play in wenchlike words with that   232
Which is so serious. Let us bury him
And not protract with admiration what   234
Is now due debt. To th' grave!
ARVIRAGUS   Say, where shall 's lay him?   235
GUIDERIUS
By good Euriphile, our mother.
ARVIRAGUS   Be't so.
And let us, Polydore, though now our voices
Have got the mannish crack, sing him to th' ground,
As once to our mother; use like note and words,   239

176 **enchafed** being heated (with anger).   **rud'st** roughest
179 **frame** shape, direct   181 **not seen from other** not learned by
observing it in some other persons   182 **wildly grows** grows wild
186 **clodpoll** blockhead, head. (With a play on Cloten's name.)
187–8 **His . . . return** Cloten's body will be held as hostage to ensure
the safe return of his head, which is being sent as though it were the
ambassador to a parley. (That return will of course never occur;
Guiderius speaks sardonically.)   188 **ingenious** skillfully made
193 **did not speak** has not sounded   194 **answer** correspond to.
accidents events.   195–6 **Triumphs . . . boys** Holding ceremonies
about nothing and grieving over trivialities are foolish and jejune.
200 **on** of.   202 **leaping-time** time of energetic youth   204–5 **My . . .
thyself** i.e., It is not even half so beautiful a sight to see you carried
by my brother, as though he were wearing a lily, as when you lived
and grew.

206–8 **find . . . harbor in?** dredge up muddy bottoms to show where
your sluggish skiff might best seek quiet harbor? (Who can ever
know where Melancholy will lodge, says Belarius, when she afflicts
even so fair a youth as this? They all conclude that "Fidele" died of
melancholy.)   208 **thing** i.e., Fidele   209 **but I** i.e., but I know that
211 **Stark** Stiff   212 **as** as if   213 **Not as . . . laughed at** not as though
laughing at death's dart (which Arviragus believes Fidele to be
doing)   215 **leagued** folded.   216 **clouted brogues** hobnailed boots
220 **to thee** (Addressed to Imogen.)   224 **The azured . . . veins** the
blue hyacinth, as blue as the blood in your veins   225 **eglantine** i.e.,
the sweetbrier rose or honeysuckle   225–6 **whom . . . breath** it is no
slander to the eglantine to say that its fragrance was not sweeter than
your breath.   226–31 **The ruddock . . . corpse** (According to fable the
ruddock or robin redbreast would cover graves with flowers and
moss, thus showing more tenderness and reverence than forgetful
humans. To *winter-ground* is to cover protectively against frost.)
231 **have done** stop   232 **wenchlike** womanish   234 **admiration**
wonder   235 **due debt** i.e., a ceremonial obligation (of burial) that
must be paid now.   **shall 's** shall we   239 **like note** a similar tune

Save that "Euriphile" must be "Fidele."
GUIDERIUS   Cadwal,
I cannot sing. I'll weep, and word it with thee;   242
For notes of sorrow out of tune are worse
Than priests and fanes that lie.
ARVIRAGUS   We'll speak it, then.   244
BELARIUS
Great griefs, I see, med'cine the less, for Cloten   245
Is quite forgot. He was a queen's son, boys,
And, though he came our enemy, remember
He was paid for that. Though mean and mighty,
        rotting   248
Together, have one dust, yet reverence,   249
That angel of the world, doth make distinction   250
Of place 'tween high and low. Our foe was princely,
And though you took his life as being our foe,
Yet bury him as a prince.
GUIDERIUS   Pray you, fetch him hither.
Thersites' body is as good as Ajax'   255
When neither are alive.
ARVIRAGUS   If you'll go fetch him,
We'll say our song the whilst. Brother, begin.
                        [Exit Belarius.]
GUIDERIUS
Nay, Cadwal, we must lay his head to th'east.   258
My father hath a reason for't.
ARVIRAGUS   'Tis true.
GUIDERIUS
Come on, then, and remove him.
            [They lay out Imogen with her head to the east.]
ARVIRAGUS   So. Begin.

                    Song.
GUIDERIUS
    Fear no more the heat o'th' sun,
        Nor the furious winter's rages;
    Thou thy worldly task hast done,
        Home art gone, and ta'en thy wages.
    Golden lads and girls all must,
        As chimney sweepers, come to dust.
ARVIRAGUS
    Fear no more the frown o'th' great;
        Thou art past the tyrant's stroke.
    Care no more to clothe and eat;
        To thee the reed is as the oak.   270
    The scepter, learning, physic, must   271
        All follow this and come to dust.
GUIDERIUS
    Fear no more the lightning flash,
ARVIRAGUS
    Nor th'all-dreaded thunderstone.   274

GUIDERIUS
Fear not slander, censure rash;
ARVIRAGUS
Thou hast finished joy and moan.
BOTH
    All lovers young, all lovers must
        Consign to thee and come to dust.   278
GUIDERIUS
    No exorciser harm thee!   279
ARVIRAGUS
    Nor no witchcraft charm thee!
GUIDERIUS
    Ghost unlaid forbear thee!   281
ARVIRAGUS
    Nothing ill come near thee!
BOTH
    Quiet consummation have,   283
    And renownèd be thy grave!

        Enter Belarius, with the [headless] body of Cloten.

GUIDERIUS
We have done our obsequies. Come, lay him down.
                    [Cloten is laid next to Imogen.]
BELARIUS
Here's a few flowers, but 'bout midnight, more.
                        [They strew flowers.]
The herbs that have on them cold dew o'th' night
Are strewings fitt'st for graves. Upon their faces.   288
You were as flowers, now withered; even so
These herblets shall, which we upon you strew.   290
Come on, away; apart upon our knees.   291
The ground that gave them first has them again.
Their pleasures here are past, so is their pain.
        Exeunt [Belarius, Guiderius, and Arviragus].
IMOGEN (awakes)
Yes, sir, to Milford Haven. Which is the way?
I thank you. By yond bush? Pray, how far thither?
Ods pittikins! Can it be six mile yet?   296
I have gone all night. Faith, I'll lie down and sleep.   297
But soft, no bedfellow? [She sees or touches Cloten's
        body.] O gods and goddesses!
These flowers are like the pleasures of the world,
This bloody man the care on't. I hope I dream,   300
For so I thought I was a cave keeper   301
And cook to honest creatures. But 'tis not so.
'Twas but a bolt of nothing, shot of nothing,   303
Which the brain makes of fumes. Our very eyes   304
Are sometimes like our judgments, blind. Good faith,
I tremble still with fear; but if there be

242 **word** speak   244 **fanes** temples   245 **med'cine** cure   248 **mean** those lowly born   249–50 **reverence . . . world** i.e., the great principle of reverence, through which the hierarchy of order and degree in human affairs mirrors that of the angels   255 **Thersites' . . . Ajax'** (Thersites was the base scoffer in the *Iliad*; Ajax, a Greek hero.)
258 **lay . . . east** (Opposite to the Christian custom and hence suggestive here of Celtic pre-Christian worship.)   270 **reed, oak** (Contrasting symbols of a fragility that survives by being flexible and a mightiness often overthrown. Fidele is past caring for the lesson contained in this contrast.)   271 **physic** medical learning   274 **thunderstone** (The supposed solid body accompanying a stroke of lightning.)

278 **Consign to** co-sign with, share a similar fate with, submit to the same terms with   279 **exorciser** conjurer   281 **unlaid** not laid to rest   283 **consummation** end, death   288 **Upon their faces** i.e., Strew flowers on the dead persons' faces or perhaps on the front of their bodies, since Cloten is headless. (The line may be corrupt.)   290 **shall** shall wither   291 **apart** let us depart   296 **Ods pittikins!** (A diminutive oath.)   297 **gone** walked   300 **the care on't** i.e., is like the troubles of this world.   301 **For so** for then.   **cave keeper** dweller in a cave   303 **bolt** arrow.   **shot of nothing** shot from nowhere
304 **fumes** vapors engendered of humors which, according to current theory, rose up into the brain and, by affecting imagination in the forechamber of the brain, caused dreams.

Yet left in heaven as small a drop of pity
As a wren's eye, feared gods, a part of it!   308
The dream's here still. Even when I wake, it is
Without me, as within me; not imagined, felt.   310
A headless man? The garments of Posthumus?
I know the shape of 's leg; this is his hand,
His foot Mercurial, his Martial thigh,   313
The brawns of Hercules; but his Jovial face—   314
Murder in heaven? How? 'Tis gone. Pisanio,
All curses madded Hecuba gave the Greeks,   316
And mine to boot, be darted on thee! Thou,
Conspired with that irregulous devil, Cloten,   318
Hath here cut off my lord. To write and read   319
Be henceforth treacherous! Damned Pisanio
Hath with his forgèd letters—damned Pisanio—
From this most bravest vessel of the world
Struck the maintop! O Posthumus! Alas,   323
Where is thy head? Where's that? Ay me, where's
    that?
Pisanio might have killed thee at the heart
And left this head on. How should this be? Pisanio?
'Tis he and Cloten. Malice and lucre in them   327
Have laid this woe here. Oh, 'tis pregnant, pregnant!   328
The drug he gave me, which he said was precious
And cordial to me, have I not found it   330
Murd'rous to th' senses? That confirms it home.   331
This is Pisanio's deed, and Cloten.—Oh,   332
Give color to my pale cheek with thy blood,   333
That we the horrider may seem to those
Which chance to find us. Oh, my lord, my lord!
                            [*She falls on the body.*]

            Enter Lucius, Captains, and a Soothsayer.

CAPTAIN
To them the legions garrisoned in Gallia,   336
After your will, have crossed the sea, attending   337
You here at Milford Haven with your ships.
They are in readiness.
LUCIUS   But what from Rome?
CAPTAIN
The Senate hath stirred up the confiners   340
And gentlemen of Italy, most willing spirits,
That promise noble service, and they come
Under the conduct of bold Iachimo,
Siena's brother.
LUCIUS   When expect you them?   344

CAPTAIN
With the next benefit o'th' wind.
LUCIUS   This forwardness
Makes our hopes fair. Command our present numbers
Be mustered; bid the captains look to't.—Now, sir,
What have you dreamed of late of this war's purpose?   348
SOOTHSAYER
Last night the very gods showed me a vision—
I fast and prayed for their intelligence—thus: 350
I saw Jove's bird, the Roman eagle, winged
From the spongy south to this part of the west,   352
There vanished in the sunbeams, which portends—
Unless my sins abuse my divination—   354
Success to th' Roman host.
LUCIUS   Dream often so,
And never false. [*He sees Cloten and Imogen.*] Soft, ho,
    what trunk is here
Without his top? The ruin speaks that sometime
It was a worthy building. How? A page?
Or dead or sleeping on him? But dead rather;   359
For nature doth abhor to make his bed
With the defunct, or sleep upon the dead.
Let's see the boy's face.
CAPTAIN   He's alive, my lord.
LUCIUS
He'll then instruct us of this body.—Young one,
Inform us of thy fortunes, for it seems
They crave to be demanded. Who is this   365
Thou mak'st thy bloody pillow? Or who was he
That, otherwise than noble nature did,   367
Hath altered that good picture? What's thy interest
In this sad wrack? How came't? Who is't?   369
What art thou?
IMOGEN   I am nothing; or if not,   370
Nothing to be were better. This was my master,   371
A very valiant Briton and a good,
That here by mountaineers lies slain. Alas,
There is no more such masters. I may wander
From east to occident, cry out for service,
Try many, all good, serve truly, never
Find such another master.
LUCIUS   'Lack, good youth!
Thou mov'st no less with thy complaining than   378
Thy master in bleeding. Say his name, good friend.
IMOGEN
Richard du Champ. [*Aside*] If I do lie and do
No harm by it, though the gods hear, I hope
They'll pardon it.—Say you, sir?
LUCIUS   Thy name?
IMOGEN   Fidele, sir.
LUCIUS
Thou dost approve thyself the very same;   383
Thy name well fits thy faith, thy faith thy name.
Wilt take thy chance with me? I will not say

---

308 wren's eye i.e., a very small eye, rendering a small teardrop.
a part i.e., give me a part   **310 Without me** outside of me, externally
real and not just imagined (within)   **313 Mercurial** nimble and swift
like the foot of Mercury.   **Martial** powerful for war like that of Mars
314 brawns muscles   **316 madded Hecuba** the
widow of King Priam of Troy, driven insane by her longing for
revenge on the Greeks who had killed her husband and sacked Troy
318 Conspired conspiring.   **irregulous** lawless   **319 Hath** hast   **323**
maintop top of mainmast, i.e., head.   **327 lucre** greed   **328 pregnant**
evident   **330 cordial** restorative to the heart   **331 home** utterly.   **332**
Cloten i.e., Cloten's.   **333 Give . . . blood** (Imogen may daub her
cheeks with what she supposes to be Posthumus's blood, or she may
simply fall on the body.)   **336 To them** i.e., In addition to the forces
we've already mentioned   **337 After** according to   **340 confiners**
inhabitants   **344 Siena's** the Duke of Siena's

348 purpose effect, outcome.   **350 fast** fasted   **352 spongy** damp
354 abuse falsify   **359 Or** Either   **365 demanded** asked about.
367 That . . . did who, in a manner different from the way that noble
nature fashioned him   **369 wrack** ruin.   **370–1 or . . . better** or if I am
not nothing, it would be better to be nothing.   **378 mov'st** i.e., to pity
383 approve prove.   **the very same** (*Fidele* means "faithful.")

Thou shalt be so well mastered, but be sure
No less beloved. The Roman Emperor's letters
Sent by a consul to me should not sooner
Than thine own worth prefer thee. Go with me.   389

IMOGEN
I'll follow, sir. But first, an't please the gods,   390
I'll hide my master from the flies as deep
As these poor pickaxes can dig; and when   392
With wild-wood leaves and weeds I ha' strewed his
    grave
And on it said a century of prayers,   394
Such as I can, twice o'er I'll weep and sigh,
And leaving so his service, follow you,
So please you entertain me.

LUCIUS   Ay, good youth,   397
And rather father thee than master thee.—
My friends,
The boy hath taught us manly duties. Let us
Find out the prettiest daisied plot we can
And make him with our pikes and partisans   402
A grave. Come, arm him. Boy, he's preferred   403
By thee to us, and he shall be interred
As soldiers can. Be cheerful; wipe thine eyes.
Some falls are means the happier to arise.
                              Exeunt, [bearing Cloten's body].

❧

4.3

*Enter Cymbeline, Lords, [Attendants,] and
Pisanio.*

CYMBELINE
Again, and bring me word how 'tis with her.
                              [*Exit an Attendant.*]
A fever with the absence of her son,   2
A madness, of which her life's in danger. Heavens,
How deeply you at once do touch me! Imogen,   4
The great part of my comfort, gone; my queen
Upon a desperate bed, and in a time
When fearful wars point at me; her son gone,
So needful for this present! It strikes me past
The hope of comfort. [*To Pisanio*] But for thee, fellow,
Who needs must know of her departure and
Dost seem so ignorant, we'll enforce it from thee   11
By a sharp torture.

PISANIO   Sir, my life is yours;
I humbly set it at your will. But for my mistress,
I nothing know where she remains, why gone,
Nor when she purposes return. Beseech Your
    Highness,
Hold me your loyal servant.

A LORD   Good my liege,   16

The day that she was missing he was here.
I dare be bound he's true and shall perform
All parts of his subjection loyally. For Cloten,   19
There wants no diligence in seeking him,   20
And will no doubt be found.

CYMBELINE   The time is troublesome. 21
[*To Pisanio*] We'll slip you for a season, but our jealousy 22
Does yet depend.

A LORD   So please Your Majesty,   23
The Roman legions, all from Gallia drawn,
Are landed on your coast with a supply
Of Roman gentlemen by the Senate sent.

CYMBELINE
Now for the counsel of my son and queen!   27
I am amazed with matter.

A LORD   Good my liege,   28
Your preparation can affront no less   29
Than what you hear of. Come more, for more you're
    ready.   30
The want is but to put those powers in motion   31
That long to move.

CYMBELINE   I thank you. Let's withdraw,
And meet the time as it seeks us. We fear not
What can from Italy annoy us, but   34
We grieve at chances here. Away!   35
                              Exeunt [all but Pisanio].

PISANIO
I heard no letter from my master since
I wrote him Imogen was slain. 'Tis strange.
Nor hear I from my mistress, who did promise
To yield me often tidings. Neither know I
What is betid to Cloten, but remain   40
Perplexed in all. The heavens still must work.
Wherein I am false I am honest; not true, to be true.
These present wars shall find I love my country,
Even to the note o'th' King, or I'll fall in them.   44
All other doubts, by time let them be cleared;   45
Fortune brings in some boats that are not steered.
                                              Exit.

❧

4.4

Enter Belarius, Guiderius, and Arviragus.

GUIDERIUS
The noise is round about us.

BELARIUS   Let us from it.

---

389 prefer recommend   **390 an't** if it   **392 pickaxes** i.e., fingers
394 century of hundred   **397 entertain** employ   **402 partisans** long-
handled weapons, halberds   **403 arm him** lift him up.   **preferred**
recommended
4.3. Location: Britain. At the court of Cymbeline.
2 with brought on by   **4 touch** wound, afflict   **11 seem** pretend to be
13 for as for. (Also in line 19.)   **16 Hold me** regard me as

19 subjection duty as a subject   **20 wants** is lacking   **21 will** he will.
troublesome filled with deep troubles.   **22 slip you** let you go.
22–3 but . . . depend but our suspicions still hold.   **27 Now for** If
only I now had   **28 amazed with matter** confused and overwhelmed
by the pressure of affairs.   **29–30 Your . . . . hear of** your military
force already mustered can confront as large an army as you hear
reported.   **30 Come more** If more (enemy) come   **31 want is but**
sole thing needed is.   **powers** armed forces   **34 annoy** injure
35 chances accidents (the Queen's illness, etc.)   **40 is betid** has happened   **44 Even . . . King** to the extent of attracting the favorable
notice of the King (for my bravery)   **45 let them** i.e., let us pray
that they
4.4. Location: Wales. Before the cave of Belarius.

ARVIRAGUS
    What pleasure, sir, find we in life, to lock it
    From action and adventure?
GUIDERIUS   Nay, what hope
    Have we in hiding us? This way the Romans   4
    Must or for Britons slay us or receive us   5
    For barbarous and unnatural revolts   6
    During their use, and slay us after.
BELARIUS   Sons,   7
    We'll higher to the mountains, there secure us.
    To the King's party there's no going. Newness
    Of Cloten's death—we being not known, not
        mustered
    Among the bands—may drive us to a render   11
    Where we have lived, and so extort from 's that
    Which we have done, whose answer would be death   13
    Drawn on with torture.
GUIDERIUS   This is, sir, a doubt   14
    In such a time nothing becoming you   15
    Nor satisfying us.
ARVIRAGUS   It is not likely
    That when they hear the Roman horses neigh,
    Behold their quartered fires, have both their eyes   18
    And ears so cloyed importantly as now,   19
    That they will waste their time upon our note,   20
    To know from whence we are.
BELARIUS   Oh, I am known
    Of many in the army. Many years,
    Though Cloten then but young, you see, not wore him   23
    From my remembrance. And besides, the King
    Hath not deserved my service nor your loves,
    Who find in my exile the want of breeding,   26
    The certainty of this hard life, aye hopeless   27
    To have the courtesy your cradle promised,   28
    But to be still hot summer's tanlings and   29
    The shrinking slaves of winter.
GUIDERIUS   Than be so,   30
    Better to cease to be. Pray, sir, to th'army.
    I and my brother are not known; yourself   32
    So out of thought, and thereto so o'ergrown,   33
    Cannot be questioned.
ARVIRAGUS   By this sun that shines,   34
    I'll thither. What thing is't that I never   35
    Did see man die, scarce ever looked on blood
    But that of coward hares, hot goats, and venison!   37

4 This way i.e., If we take such a course of conduct   **5 Must or** must either   **6 revolts** deserters, rebels   **7 During their use** as long as they find us useful   **11 bands** troops.   **render** rendering of an account   **13 answer** consequence   **14 Drawn on with** brought about and lengthened by   **15 nothing** not at all   **18 quartered fires** campfires   **19 cloyed importantly** filled with urgent business   **20 upon our note** in observing us   **23 then** was then.   **not wore him** did not erase him   **26–8 Who . . . promised** you who find in exile with me a lack of proper education and hardship from which there is no escape, without hope of ever achieving the cultivated existence promised you by your gentle birth (as sons of a onetime courtier and soldier)   **29 But** i.e., but destined instead.   **tanlings** those tanned by the sun   **30 shrinking** i.e., shrinking from the cold and cowering in servitude   **32–3 yourself . . . o'ergrown** yourself so forgotten by now, and besides that overgrown with hair and beard as well as years   **34 questioned** looked at with suspicion.   **35 What thing** What a disgraceful thing   **37 hot** lecherous

    Never bestrid a horse, save one that had
    A rider like myself, who ne'er wore rowel   39
    Nor iron on his heel! I am ashamed
    To look upon the holy sun, to have
    The benefit of his blest beams, remaining
    So long a poor unknown.
GUIDERIUS   By heavens, I'll go.
    If you will bless me, sir, and give me leave,
    I'll take the better care, but if you will not,   45
    The hazard therefore due fall on me by   46
    The hands of Romans!
ARVIRAGUS   So say I. Amen.
BELARIUS
    No reason I, since of your lives you set
    So slight a valuation, should reserve
    My cracked one to more care. Have with you, boys!   50
    If in your country wars you chance to die,   51
    That is my bed too, lads, and there I'll lie.
    Lead, lead. [*Aside*] The time seems long; their blood
        thinks scorn   53
    Till it fly out and show them princes born.   *Exeunt.*

❖

5.1

Enter Posthumus alone [in Italian dress, with a bloody handkerchief].

POSTHUMUS
    Yea, bloody cloth, I'll keep thee, for I wished
    Thou shouldst be colored thus. You married ones,
    If each of you should take this course, how many
    Must murder wives much better than themselves
    For wrying but a little! O Pisanio!   5
    Every good servant does not all commands;
    No bond but to do just ones. Gods, if you   7
    Should have ta'en vengeance on my faults, I never   8
    Had lived to put on this; so had you saved   9
    The noble Imogen to repent, and struck
    Me, wretch, more worth your vengeance. But alack,
    You snatch some hence for little faults; that's love,   12
    To have them fall no more; you some permit   13
    To second ills with ills, each elder worse,   14
    And make them dread it, to the doers' thrift.   15
    But Imogen is your own. Do your best wills,
    And make me blest to obey! I am brought hither
    Among th'Italian gentry, and to fight
    Against my lady's kingdom. 'Tis enough

39 rowel wheel of a spur   **45 take . . . care** be more careful, proceed with better prospects of success   **46 The hazard therefore due** may the danger resulting from disobedience and lack of parental blessing   **50 cracked** i.e., weakened with age.   **Have with you** Come on, then   **51 country** country's   **53 The time . . . scorn** i.e., They are eager to go. Their blood disdains itself   **5.1. Location: Britain. An open place.**   **5 wrying** swerving from the right course   **7 bond but** obligation except   **8 Should have** had, as you should have   **9 put on this** undertake this deed   **12–13 that's . . . more** that is a loving act, since it makes them sin no more   **14 second** follow up.   **elder** subsequent (sin)   **15 and make . . . thrift** and make those evildoers repent their deeds, to their ultimate spiritual profit.

That, Britain, I have killed thy mistress; peace,   20
I'll give no wound to thee. Therefore, good heavens,
Hear patiently my purpose: I'll disrobe me
Of these Italian weeds and suit myself   23
As does a Briton peasant; so I'll fight
Against the part I come with; so I'll die   25
For thee, O Imogen, even for whom my life
Is every breath a death; and thus, unknown,   27
Pitied nor hated, to the face of peril   28
Myself I'll dedicate. Let me make men know
More valor in me than my habits show.   30
Gods, put the strength o'th' Leonati in me!
To shame the guise o'th' world, I will begin   32
The fashion: less without and more within.   *Exit.*   33

❖

5.2

> *Enter Lucius, Iachimo, and the Roman army at
> one door, and the Briton army at another,
> Leonatus Posthumus following like a poor soldier.
> They march over and go out. Then enter again, in
> skirmish, Iachimo and Posthumus; he vanquisheth
> and disarmeth Iachimo, and then leaves him.*

IACHIMO
The heaviness and guilt within my bosom
Takes off my manhood. I have belied a lady,
The princess of this country, and the air on't   3
Revengingly enfeebles me; or could this carl,   4
A very drudge of nature's, have subdued me   5
In my profession? Knighthoods and honors borne
As I wear mine are titles but of scorn.
If that thy gentry, Britain, go before   8
This lout as he exceeds our lords, the odds
Is that we scarce are men and you are gods.   *Exit.*

> *The battle continues; the Britons fly; Cymbeline is
> taken. Then enter, to his rescue, Belarius,
> Guiderius, and Arviragus.*

BELARIUS
Stand, stand! We have th'advantage of the ground;
The lane is guarded. Nothing routs us but
The villainy of our fears.
GUIDERIUS, ARVIRAGUS   Stand, stand, and fight!

> *Enter Posthumus, and seconds the Britons. They
> rescue Cymbeline, and exeunt. Then enter Lucius,
> Iachimo, and Imogen.*

LUCIUS
Away, boy, from the troops, and save thyself!
For friends kill friends, and the disorder's such

As war were hoodwinked.
IACHIMO   'Tis their fresh supplies.   16
LUCIUS
It is a day turned strangely. Or betimes   17
Let's reinforce, or fly.   *Exeunt.*

❖

5.3

> *Enter Posthumus [dressed as a British peasant
> still], and a Briton Lord.*

LORD
Cam'st thou from where they made the stand?
POSTHUMUS   I did,
Though you, it seems, come from the fliers?
LORD   I did.
POSTHUMUS
No blame be to you, sir, for all was lost,
But that the heavens fought. The King himself   4
Of his wings destitute, the army broken,   5
And but the backs of Britons seen, all flying
Through a strait lane; the enemy fullhearted,   7
Lolling the tongue with slaught'ring, having work   8
More plentiful than tools to do't, struck down
Some mortally, some slightly touched, some falling   10
Merely through fear, that the strait pass was dammed
With dead men hurt behind, and cowards living   12
To die with lengthened shame.
LORD   Where was this lane?   13
POSTHUMUS
Close by the battle, ditched, and walled with turf;
Which gave advantage to an ancient soldier,
An honest one, I warrant, who deserved   16
So long a breeding as his white beard came to,   17
In doing this for's country. Athwart the lane,
He, with two striplings—lads more like to run   19
The country base than to commit such slaughter,   20
With faces fit for masks, or rather fairer   21
Than those for preservation cased or shame—   22
Made good the passage, cried to those that fled,   23
"Our Britain's harts die flying, not our men.
To darkness fleet souls that fly backwards. Stand!   25
Or we are Romans and will give you that   26

16 As as if.   **hoodwinked** blindfolded. (War swings his weapons
blindly, without looking to see who is struck.)   **17 Or betimes** Either
swiftly
5.3. Location: The field of battle, as before.
4 But that if it had not been for the fact that   **5 wings** flanks of the
army   **7 strait** narrow.   **fullhearted** full of courage and confidence
8 Lolling letting hang out   **10 touched** wounded   **12 behind** from
the rear (while running away)   **13 lengthened** lingering (for the rest
of their lives)   **16 honest** worthy   **16–17 who . . . to** whose white
beard betokened the length of years that he deserves to live still in
honor   **19 like** likely   **20 base** prisoner's base, a game in which
rapid running is the means to victory   **21 fit for masks** refined
enough to deserve sheltering from the elements   **22 Than . . . shame**
than ladies' faces masked (*cased*) either for protection against the elements or for modesty   **23 Made good** secured   **25 darkness** i.e.,
ignominy, hell.   **fleet** hasten   **26 we are Romans** i.e., we three will
act like Romans.   **that** i.e., death blows

20 peace i.e., calm yourself, be reassured   **23 suit** clothe   **25 part**
party, side   **27 Is . . . death** i.e., is like dying again and again, every
instant, from painful remorse   **28 Pitied** neither pitied   **30 habits**
clothes   **32 guise** custom   **33 The fashion: less without** the fashion
of relying less on outward show
5.2. Location: Britain. Field of battle. The scene is probably continuous with the previous.
0.3 *poor* of low rank and poorly outfitted   **3 on't** of it   **4 or** otherwise.   **carl** churl, peasant   **5 drudge** slave   **8 go before** excel

Like beasts which you shun beastly, and may save 27
But to look back in frown. Stand, stand!" These three, 28
Three thousand confident, in act as many— 29
For three performers are the file when all 30
The rest do nothing—with this word "Stand, stand,"
Accommodated by the place, more charming 32
With their own nobleness, which could have turned 33
A distaff to a lance, gilded pale looks, 34
Part shame, part spirit renewed, that some, turned
  coward 35
But by example—oh, a sin in war, 36
Damned in the first beginners!—'gan to look 37
The way that they did and to grin like lions 38
Upon the pikes o'th' hunters. Then began 39
A stop i'th' chaser, a retire, anon 40
A rout, confusion thick. Forthwith they fly 41
Chickens, the way which they stooped eagles; slaves, 42
The strides they victors made. And now our cowards, 43
Like fragments in hard voyages, became 44
The life o'th' need. Having found the back door open 45
Of the unguarded hearts, heavens, how they wound!
Some slain before, some dying, some their friends 47
O'erborne i'th' former wave, ten chased by one, 48
Are now each one the slaughterman of twenty.
Those that would die or ere resist are grown 50
The mortal bugs o'th' field.

LORD   This was strange chance: 51
A narrow lane, an old man, and two boys!

POSTHUMUS
Nay, do not wonder at it. You are made
Rather to wonder at the things you hear
Than to work any. Will you rhyme upon't 55
And vent it for a mockery? Here is one: 56
"Two boys, an old man twice a boy, a lane, 57
Preserved the Britons, was the Romans' bane."

LORD
Nay, be not angry, sir.
POSTHUMUS   'Lack, to what end? 59
Who dares not stand his foe, I'll be his friend; 60
For if he'll do as he is made to do, 61
I know he'll quickly fly my friendship too. 62
You have put me into rhyme.
LORD   Farewell. You're angry.
                                           Exit.
POSTHUMUS
Still going? This is a lord! Oh, noble misery, 64
To be i'th' field, and ask "What news?" of me!
Today how many would have given their honors
To have saved their carcasses! Took heel to do't,
And yet died too! I, in mine own woe charmed, 68
Could not find Death where I did hear him groan,
Nor feel him where he struck. Being an ugly monster,
'Tis strange he hides him in fresh cups, soft beds, 71
Sweet words, or hath more ministers than we 72
That draw his knives i'th' war. Well, I will find him; 73
For being now a favorer to the Briton, 74
                    [*removing his British garb*]
No more a Briton, I have resumed again 75
The part I came in. Fight I will no more, 76
But yield me to the veriest hind that shall 77
Once touch my shoulder. Great the slaughter is 78
Here made by th' Roman; great the answer be 79
Britons must take. For me, my ransom's death.
On either side I come to spend my breath, 81
Which neither here I'll keep nor bear again,
But end it by some means for Imogen.

        Enter two [British] Captains and soldiers.

FIRST CAPTAIN
Great Jupiter be praised! Lucius is taken.
'Tis thought the old man and his sons were angels.
SECOND CAPTAIN
There was a fourth man, in a silly habit, 86
That gave th'affront with them.
FIRST CAPTAIN   So 'tis reported, 87
But none of 'em can be found.—Stand! Who's there?
POSTHUMUS   A Roman,
Who had not now been drooping here if seconds 90
Had answered him.
SECOND CAPTAIN   Lay hands on him; a dog! 91

27 **Like beasts** i.e., like savage lions. **beastly** like cowards   **27–8 and may . . . frown** and which you may prevent only by turning and facing us in defiance.   **29 Three . . . many** as confident as if they were three thousand men, doing the deeds of that many   **30 file** i.e., entire force (as in "rank and file")   **32–9 Accommodated . . . hunters** assisted by the place, casting a spell on their fellow soldiers by exemplary action so noble that it could have inspired even a housewife to become a soldier, imparted a flush of color to the cheeks of palefaced men, partly through shame and partly through a renewing of courage, so that some soldiers who had turned coward only by others' display of cowardice—oh, a terrible sin in war, damnable in those who first cower in time of danger!—now began to model themselves on the looks and actions of the three brave warriors and to bare their teeth like lions at the weapons of those who had hunted them down.   **40 stop i'th' chaser** stopping of those who had been the pursuers, i.e., the Romans.   **retire** retreat   **41–3 Forthwith . . . made** Immediately the Romans fled like chickens along the narrow passage down which they had just swooped down like eagles, retracing, like slaves, the steps thay had taken as victors.   **44 fragments** scraps, fragments of food, something to fall back on as a last resort   **45 The life o'th' need** vital support in time of necessity.   **back door** i.e., vulnerable soft spot of the Romans   **47–8 Some . . . by one** i.e., some who were given up for dead or dying, and some comrades overwhelmed in the previous Roman assault who had yielded by the tens to each Roman soldier   **50 would . . . ere** previously were ready to die rather than   **51 mortal bugs** deadly bugbears, terrors   **55 work any** perform any such wonders yourself. (Said reproachfully.)   **55–6 Will . . . one** i.e., Would you like to compose rhymes on this event in ballad fashion and thus make a mockery of it with your cheap exploitation? Here is a sample. (*Vent* means "air, circulate.")   **57 twice a boy** in his second childhood

59 **'Lack . . . end?** Alack, why should I be angry?   **60–2 Who . . . too** i.e., I can put up with the friendship of any coward (like yourself), for, if he is true to his colors, he'll run away and rid me of his company. (*Who* means "whoever," *stand* "stand against," *made* "inclined.")   64 **Still . . . misery** Still running away? This is a fine lord! What a miserable specimen of the nobility   68 **too** anyway.   **charmed** made invulnerable as if by a spell   71 **cups** cups of wine   72–3 **Sweet . . . war** sweet whisperings of lovers, and yet has more agents to carry out his (Death's) work than we soldiers have weapons.   74 **For . . . Briton** for since Death now favors the British side   75 **No . . . Briton** I remaining no longer a Briton   76 **The part . . . in** i.e., my Roman guise (in which my capture and execution seem assured).   77 **hind** peasant   78 **touch my shoulder** i.e., place me under arrest.   79 **answer be** retaliation is that   81 **spend my breath** give up my life   86 **silly** simple, rustic   87 **th'affront** the attack   90 **drooping** languishing.   **seconds** supporters   91 **answered him** followed his lead, or answered his call for help.

A leg of Rome shall not return to tell   92
What crows have pecked them here. He brags his
    service
As if he were of note. Bring him to th' King.

Enter Cymbeline, Belarius, Guiderius, Arvira-
gus, Pisanio, [soldiers, attendants,] and Roman
captives. The Captains present Posthumus to
Cymbeline, who delivers him over to a Jailer.

                          [Then exeunt.]

❖

5.4

Enter Posthumus [in chains] and [two] Jailer[s].

FIRST JAILER
You shall not now be stol'n; you have locks upon you.
So graze as you find pasture.
SECOND JAILER   Ay, or a stomach.   2
                     [Exeunt Jailers.]
POSTHUMUS
Most welcome, bondage! For thou art a way,
I think, to liberty. Yet am I better
Than one that's sick o'th' gout, since he had rather
Groan so in perpetuity than be cured
By th' sure physician, Death, who is the key
T'unbar these locks. My conscience, thou art fettered
More than my shanks and wrists. You good gods,
    give me
The penitent instrument to pick that bolt,   10
Then, free forever! Is't enough I am sorry?
So children temporal fathers do appease;
Gods are more full of mercy. Must I repent,   13
I cannot do it better than in gyves,   14
Desired more than constrained. To satisfy,   15
If of my freedom 'tis the main part, take   16
No stricter render of me than my all.   17
I know you are more clement than vile men,
Who of their broken debtors take a third,   19
A sixth, a tenth, letting them thrive again
On their abatement. That's not my desire.   21
For Imogen's dear life take mine; and though
'Tis not so dear, yet 'tis a life; you coined it.   23

'Tween man and man they weigh not every stamp;   24
Though light, take pieces for the figure's sake;   25
You rather mine, being yours. And so, great powers, 26
If you will take this audit, take this life   27
And cancel these cold bonds. O Imogen!   28
I'll speak to thee in silence.   *[He sleeps.]*

Solemn music. Enter, as in an apparition, Sicilius
Leonatus, father to Posthumus, an old man, attired
like a warrior; leading in his hand an ancient
matron, his wife, and mother to Posthumus, with
music before them. Then, after other music, follows
the two young Leonati, brothers to Posthumus,
with wounds as they died in the wars. They circle
Posthumus round, as he lies sleeping.

SICILIUS
No more, thou Thunder-master, show   30
    Thy spite on mortal flies.   31
With Mars fall out, with Juno chide,
    That thy adulteries   33
    Rates and revenges.   34
Hath my poor boy done aught but well,
    Whose face I never saw?
I died whilst in the womb he stayed
    Attending nature's law;   38
Whose father then—as men report   39
    Thou orphans' father art—   40
Thou shouldst have been, and shielded him
    From this earth-vexing smart.   42
MOTHER
Lucina lent not me her aid,   43
    But took me in my throes,
That from me was Posthumus ripped,
    Came crying 'mongst his foes,
        A thing of pity!
SICILIUS
Great nature, like his ancestry,   48
    Molded the stuff so fair   49
That he deserved the praise o'th' world
    As great Sicilius' heir.
FIRST BROTHER
When once he was mature for man,   52
    In Britain where was he   53
That could stand up his parallel,
    Or fruitful object be
In eye of Imogen, that best
    Could deem his dignity?   57

---

92 leg i.e., one of the lower extremities, one who does the walking
(and the running away)
5.4. Location: A British prison or stockade. Possibly the scene is
continuous; see the next note.
0.1 Enter (The scene may be continuous, with Posthumus and the jailers remaining onstage, though the Folio does mark an entrance for
Posthumus and one jailer, and the scene does appear to call for manacles [lines 9, 191]. On the unlocalized Elizabethan stage, the change
of scene is achieved chiefly by the actors and their dialogue.) **2 graze**
. . . pasture i.e., like a horse, fettered by one leg.   **10 The penitent . . .**
bolt the penitence to unlock the fetters encumbering my conscience
and to find the death I seek   **13 Must I** If I must   **14 gyves** fetters
15 constrained forced (upon me).   **satisfy** make atonement   **16 If . . .**
part i.e., if such atonement is essential to freeing my conscience
17 stricter render sterner repayment   **19 broken** bankrupt   **21 abate-**
ment diminished principal.   **23 so dear** as valuable as hers

24–6 'Tween . . . yours In commercial transactions, men do not weigh
each coin exactly; even if some coins may be under the exact weight,
men accept them for the sake of the image stamped thereon of the
King; you gods should all the more readily take my coin (i.e., me),
even though I am a light (worthless) coin, since I am stamped in your
image.   **27 take this audit** accept this accounting   **28 bonds** (1) fetters, both literal and figurative (2) legal contracts.   **30 Thunder-mas-**
ter i.e., Jupiter   **31 mortal flies** i.e., petty creatures, mere humans.
33 That who (i.e., Juno)   **34 Rates** scolds   **38 Attending nature's law**
i.e., awaiting the completion of his term in the womb   **39–40 Whose**
father . . . art (Psalm 68:5 praises God as "A father of the fatherless.")
42 earth-vexing smart suffering to which all life is prone.   **43 Lucina**
goddess of childbirth   **48 like** acting in concert with, or, taking the
part of   **49 stuff** substance   **52 mature for man** grown to manhood
53 he any man   **57 deem his dignity** judge his worth.

MOTHER
   With marriage wherefore was he mocked,
     To be exiled and thrown
   From Leonati seat, and cast
     From her his dearest one,
     Sweet Imogen?

SICILIUS
   Why did you suffer Iachimo,
     Slight thing of Italy,   64
   To taint his nobler heart and brain
     With needless jealousy,
   And to become the geck and scorn   67
     O'th'other's villainy?

SECOND BROTHER
   For this from stiller seats we came,   69
     Our parents and us twain,
   That striking in our country's cause   71
     Fell bravely and were slain,
   Our fealty and Tenantius' right   73
     With honor to maintain.

FIRST BROTHER
   Like hardiment Posthumus hath   75
     To Cymbeline performed.
   Then, Jupiter, thou king of gods,
     Why hast thou thus adjourned   78
   The graces for his merits due,
     Being all to dolors turned?

SICILIUS
   Thy crystal window ope; look out.
     No longer exercise
   Upon a valiant race thy harsh
     And potent injuries.

MOTHER
   Since, Jupiter, our son is good,
     Take off his miseries.

SICILIUS
   Peep through thy marble mansion. Help,
     Or we poor ghosts will cry
   To th' shining synod of the rest   89
     Against thy deity.

BROTHERS
   Help, Jupiter, or we appeal,
     And from thy justice fly.

Jupiter descends in thunder and lightning, sitting
upon an eagle. He throws a thunderbolt. The
ghosts fall on their knees.

JUPITER
  No more, you petty spirits of region low,
    Offend our hearing. Hush! How dare you ghosts
  Accuse the Thunderer, whose bolt, you know,
    Sky-planted, batters all rebelling coasts?   96
  Poor shadows of Elysium, hence, and rest
    Upon your never-withering banks of flowers.
  Be not with mortal accidents oppressed.   99

  No care of yours it is; you know 'tis ours.
  Whom best I love I cross, to make my gift,   101
    The more delayed, delighted. Be content.   102
  Your low-laid son our godhead will uplift.   103
    His comforts thrive, his trials well are spent.   104
  Our Jovial star reigned at his birth, and in   105
    Our temple was he married. Rise, and fade.   106
  He shall be lord of Lady Imogen,
    And happier much by his affliction made.
  This tablet lay upon his breast, wherein   109
    Our pleasure his full fortune doth confine.   110
            [He delivers a tablet.]
  And so away! No farther with your din
    Express impatience, lest you stir up mine.
    Mount, eagle, to my palace crystalline.   *Ascends.*

SICILIUS
  He came in thunder; his celestial breath
    Was sulfurous to smell. The holy eagle
  Stooped, as to foot us. His ascension is   116
  More sweet than our blest fields. His royal bird   117
  Prunes the immortal wing and cloys his beak,   118
  As when his god is pleased.

ALL   Thanks, Jupiter!

SICILIUS
  The marble pavement closes; he is entered   120
    His radiant roof. Away! And, to be blest,
    Let us with care perform his great behest.
          [The ghosts place the tablet on
           Posthumus's breast, and] vanish.

POSTHUMUS *[waking]*
  Sleep, thou hast been a grandsire and begot
  A father to me; and thou hast created
  A mother and two brothers. But, oh scorn,   125
  Gone! They went hence so soon as they were born.
  And so I am awake. Poor wretches that depend
  On greatness' favor dream as I have done,
  Wake and find nothing. But, alas, I swerve!   129
               [He sees the tablet.]
  Many dream not to find, neither deserve,   130
  And yet are steeped in favors; so am I,
  That have this golden chance and know not why.
  What fairies haunt this ground? A book? Oh, rare one! 133
  Be not, as is our fangled world, a garment   134
  Nobler than that it covers. Let thy effects
  So follow, to be most unlike our courtiers,   136
  As good as promise.

---

64 Slight worthless   **67 geck** dupe   **69 stiller seats** quieter abodes (i.e., the Elysian Fields)   **71 That** who   **73 Tenantius'** Cymbeline's father's   **75 Like hardiment** Similar bold exploits   **78 adjourned** deferred   **89 synod of the rest** assembly of the gods   **96 Sky-planted** growing out of the sky   **99 accidents** events

101 cross thwart   **102 delighted** (the more) delighted in.   **103 Your... uplift** I, in my godhead, will raise up your humbled son.   **104 spent** ended.   **105 Jovial star** the planet Jupiter   **106 fade** vanish. **109–10 wherein . . . confine** wherein I am pleased to set forth precisely his happy fortune to come.   **116 Stooped . . . us** swooped down, as if to seize us in his talons.   **116–17 His . . . fields** His ascent gives a favorable aspect and a sweet odor surpassing that of the Elysian Fields.   **118 Prunes** preens.   **cloys** claws, strokes with the claw   **120 The marble pavement** i.e., the aperture giving access to the hut over the stage in which machinery for ascents and descents was housed. The floor of this hut, serving as a roof over the stage, was decorated with celestial emblems to represent the heavens. (Compare with *marble mansion* in line 87.)   **125 scorn** mockery **129 swerve** mistake, go astray.   **130 to find** of finding   **133 book** i.e., the tablet or scroll.   **rare** excellent   **134 fangled** characterized by fripperies or gaudiness   **136 to** so as to

(*Reads.*) "Whenas a lion's whelp shall, to himself 138
unknown, without seeking find and be embraced by
a piece of tender air; and when from a stately cedar
shall be lopped branches which, being dead many
years, shall after revive, be jointed to the old stock, and
freshly grow; then shall Posthumus end his miseries,
Britain be fortunate and flourish in peace and plenty."
'Tis still a dream, or else such stuff as madmen   145
Tongue and brain not; either both or nothing,   146
Or senseless speaking or a speaking such   147
As sense cannot untie. Be what it is,   148
The action of my life is like it, which
I'll keep, if but for sympathy.   150

Enter [First] Jailer.

FIRST JAILER   Come, sir, are you ready for death?
POSTHUMUS   Overroasted rather; ready long ago.
FIRST JAILER   Hanging is the word, sir. If you be ready 153
for that, you are well cooked.
POSTHUMUS   So, if I prove a good repast to the spectators, the dish pays the shot.   156
FIRST JAILER   A heavy reckoning for you, sir. But the
comfort is, you shall be called to no more payments,
fear no more tavern bills, which are often the sadness 159
of parting as the procuring of mirth. You come in faint
for want of meat, depart reeling with too much drink;
sorry that you have paid too much, and sorry that you
are paid too much; purse and brain both empty; the 163
brain the heavier for being too light, the purse too 164
light, being drawn of heaviness. Of this contradiction 165
you shall now be quit. Oh, the charity of a penny cord! 166
It sums up thousands in a trice. You have no true 167
debitor and creditor but it; of what's past, is, and to 168
come, the discharge. Your neck, sir, is pen, book, and 169
counters; so the acquittance follows.   170
POSTHUMUS   I am merrier to die than thou art to live.
FIRST JAILER   Indeed, sir, he that sleeps feels not the
toothache. But a man that were to sleep your sleep, 173
and a hangman to help him to bed, I think he would
change places with his officer; for, look you, sir, you 175
know not which way you shall go.   176
POSTHUMUS   Yes, indeed do I, fellow.

FIRST JAILER   Your death has eyes in 's head then; I
have not seen him so pictured. You must either be 179
directed by some that take upon them to know, or to 180
take upon yourself that which I am sure you do not
know, or jump the after-inquiry on your own peril. 182
And how you shall speed in your journey's end, I 183
think you'll never return to tell one.
POSTHUMUS   I tell thee, fellow, there are none want eyes 185
to direct them the way I am going but such as wink 186
and will not use them.
FIRST JAILER   What an infinite mock is this, that a man
should have the best use of eyes to see the way of 189
blindness! I am sure hanging's the way of winking.   190

Enter a Messenger.

MESSENGER   Knock off his manacles. Bring your prisoner to the King.
POSTHUMUS   Thou bring'st good news. I am called to
be made free.   [*He is freed from his irons.*] 194
FIRST JAILER   I'll be hanged then.   195
POSTHUMUS   Thou shalt be then freer than a jailer; no
bolts for the dead.   *Exeunt [all but the First Jailer].*
FIRST JAILER   Unless a man would marry a gallows and
beget young gibbets, I never saw one so prone. Yet, 199
on my conscience, there are verier knaves desire to 200
live, for all he be a Roman; and there be some of them 201
too that die against their wills. So should I, if I were 202
one. I would we were all of one mind, and one mind 203
good. Oh, there were desolation of jailers and gal- 204
lowses! I speak against my present profit, but my wish 205
hath a preferment in't.   [*Exit.*] 206

5.5

*Enter Cymbeline, Belarius, Guiderius, Arviragus,
Pisanio, [officers, attendants,] and lords.*

CYMBELINE
Stand by my side, you whom the gods have made
Preservers of my throne. Woe is my heart
That the poor soldier that so richly fought,
Whose rags shamed gilded arms, whose naked breast 4
Stepped before targes of proof, cannot be found.   5

---

138 **Whenas** When   145–8 **'Tis . . . untie** It is a dream or else the sort
of thing that madmen speak without understanding; either it is the
senseless babbling of a madman or a language that reason cannot
unravel; it may be both of these things, or neither.   150 **sympathy**
i.e., resemblance (between my life and this mystery).   153 **Hanging**
(1) Hanging up like cooking meat (2) Being hanged as a criminal
156 **the dish . . . shot** (1) the food is worth the tavern reckoning
(2) my death settles my account.   159 **often** as often   163 **are paid**
are subdued (by excessive drink)   164 **light** foolish   165 **being . . .
heaviness** being emptied of the money that weighed it down.
166 **charity** benevolent action, one that settles all debts   167 **sums up**
(1) totals up a reckoning (2) collects, summarizes.   **trice** (1) instant
(2) tricing up, hauling up by a rope.   168 **debitor and creditor**
account book   169 **discharge** (1) payment of debt (2) disburdening,
release, as in death.   170 **counters** metal disks used for calculating.
acquittance (1) discharge of an account (2) deliverance   173 **a man
that were to** if there were a man who was sentenced to   175 **officer**
i.e., the hangman   176 **which . . . go** i.e., to heaven or hell; but
Posthumus answers in the sense of knowing that death will release
all sorrows.

179 **so pictured** (The traditional death's-head is an eyeless skull.)
180 **take upon them** undertake, profess   182 **jump** finesse   183 **speed**
succeed   185 **want** lacking   186 **wink** close the eyes   189–90 **the
way of blindness** i.e., the way to death.   190 **hanging's . . . winking**
hanging will close up the eyes.   194 **made free** i.e., executed and
thereby freed from existence.   195 **I'll be hanged then** (The jailer is
using a conventional expression, like "I'll be damned if that's so," but
Posthumus replies that he means *free* in a spiritual sense.)   199 **prone**
ready, eager.   200–3 **there . . . were one** i.e., he's not such a bad fellow, even if he is a Roman; worse men than he desire to live when
they're to be executed, as I would in such a plight. (Romans were
supposed to be stoical in the face of death.)   204–5 **there . . . gal-
lowses!** i.e., if all men were good, there would be no work left for jailers and gallows!   206 **a preferment** i.e., a preference for us all to live
in a better world (with a hope that this pious wish may stand me in
good stead at my day of reckoning and thus "prefer" me to bliss). Possibly, the jailer thinks of more worldly promotion to a better office.
5.5. Location: Britain. The camp of King Cymbeline.
4 **gilded arms** glittering armor   5 **targes of proof** shields hardened to
withstand tests

He shall be happy that can find him, if
Our grace can make him so.
BELARIUS   I never saw   7
Such noble fury in so poor a thing,
Such precious deeds in one that promised naught
But beggary and poor looks.
CYMBELINE   No tidings of him?
PISANIO
He hath been searched among the dead and living,
But no trace of him.
CYMBELINE   To my grief, I am
The heir of his reward, [*to Belarius, Guiderius, and
    Arviragus*] which I will add
To you, the liver, heart, and brain of Britain,   14
By whom I grant she lives. 'Tis now the time
To ask of whence you are. Report it.
BELARIUS   Sir,
In Cambria are we born, and gentlemen.
Further to boast were neither true nor modest,
Unless I add we are honest.
CYMBELINE   Bow your knees.
                              [*They kneel.*]
Arise my knights o'th' battle. I create you   20
Companions to our person and will fit you
With dignities becoming your estates.   [*They rise.*]   22

Enter Cornelius and Ladies.

There's business in these faces. Why so sadly
Greet you our victory? You look like Romans,
And not o'th' court of Britain.
CORNELIUS   Hail, great King!
To sour your happiness, I must report
The Queen is dead.
CYMBELINE   Who worse than a physician   27
Would this report become? But I consider   28
By med'cine life may be prolonged, yet death
Will seize the doctor too. How ended she?
CORNELIUS
With horror, madly dying, like her life,
Which, being cruel to the world, concluded
Most cruel to herself. What she confessed
I will report, so please you. These her women
Can trip me, if I err, who with wet cheeks   35
Were present when she finished.
CYMBELINE   Prithee, say.
CORNELIUS
First, she confessed she never loved you, only
Affected greatness got by you, not you;   38
Married your royalty, was wife to your place,
Abhorred your person.
CYMBELINE   She alone knew this;
And, but she spoke it dying, I would not   41
Believe her lips in opening it. Proceed.   42

CORNELIUS
Your daughter, whom she bore in hand to love   43
With such integrity, she did confess
Was as a scorpion to her sight, whose life,
But that her flight prevented it, she had   46
Ta'en off by poison.
CYMBELINE   Oh, most delicate fiend!   47
Who is't can read a woman? Is there more?
CORNELIUS
More, sir, and worse. She did confess she had
For you a mortal mineral which, being took,   50
Should by the minute feed on life and, ling'ring,   51
By inches waste you. In which time she purposed,
By watching, weeping, tendance, kissing, to   53
O'ercome you with her show and, in fine,   54
When she had fitted you with her craft, to work   55
Her son into th'adoption of the crown;   56
But, failing of her end by his strange absence,
Grew shameless desperate; opened, in despite   58
Of heaven and men, her purposes; repented   59
The evils she hatched were not effected; so
Despairing died.
CYMBELINE   Heard you all this, her women?
LADIES   We did, so please Your Highness.
CYMBELINE   Mine eyes
Were not in fault, for she was beautiful;
Mine ears, that heard her flattery; nor my heart,
That thought her like her seeming. It had been vicious   66
To have mistrusted her. Yet, O my daughter,
That it was folly in me thou mayst say,
And prove it in thy feeling. Heaven mend all!   69

*Enter Lucius, Iachimo, [the Soothsayer,] and other
Roman prisoners, [guarded; Posthumus] Leonatus
behind, and Imogen [disguised as Fidele].*

Thou com'st not, Caius, now for tribute. That
The Britons have rased out, though with the loss   71
Of many a bold one, whose kinsmen have made suit
That their good souls may be appeased with slaughter
Of you their captives, which ourself have granted.
So think of your estate.   75
LUCIUS
Consider, sir, the chance of war. The day
Was yours by accident. Had it gone with us,
We should not, when the blood was cool, have
    threatened
Our prisoners with the sword. But since the gods
Will have it thus, that nothing but our lives
May be called ransom, let it come. Sufficeth

---

7 **grace** favor   14 **liver, heart, and brain** i.e., heart and soul
20 **knights o'th' battle** knights created on the battlefield.   22 **estates**
i.e., new status.   27–8 **Who . . . become?** i.e., A report of death does
not speak well for the doctor, of all people.   35 **trip** refute, contradict
38 **Affected** desired   41 **but** were it not that   42 **opening** revealing

43 **bore in hand** pretended   46 **had** would have   47 **Ta'en off**
ended.   **delicate** subtle   50 **mortal mineral** deadly poison   51 **by
the minute** minute by minute   53 **watching** staying awake (as
nurse).   **tendance** attentiveness   54 **in fine** in conclusion   55 **fitted
you** shaped you to her wish   56 **th'adoption** the right of an adopted
heir   58 **opened** revealed   59 **repented** regretted   66 **That . . .
vicious** that thought her to be what she appeared to be. It would have
been wrong   69 **in thy feeling** by feeling it, by what you have suffered. (Cymbeline apostrophizes the absent Imogen, who then ironically enters in disguise.)   71 **rased out** erased   75 **estate** spiritual
estate (in preparation for your death).

A Roman with a Roman's heart can suffer.
Augustus lives to think on't; and so much   83
For my peculiar care. This one thing only   84
I will entreat: my boy, a Briton born,
Let him be ransomed. Never master had
A page so kind, so duteous, diligent,
So tender over his occasions, true,   88
So feat, so nurselike. Let his virtue join   89
With my request, which I'll make bold Your Highness   90
Cannot deny. He hath done no Briton harm,
Though he have served a Roman. Save him, sir,
And spare no blood beside.

CYMBELINE   I have surely seen him;   93
His favor is familiar to me.—Boy,   94
Thou hast looked thyself into my grace   95
And art mine own. I know not why, wherefore,
To say "Live, boy." Ne'er thank thy master. Live,   97
And ask of Cymbeline what boon thou wilt,   98
Fitting my bounty and thy state, I'll give it,
Yea, though thou do demand a prisoner,
The noblest ta'en.

IMOGEN   I humbly thank Your Highness.

LUCIUS
I do not bid thee beg my life, good lad,
And yet I know thou wilt.

IMOGEN   No, no, alack,
There's other work in hand. I see a thing   104
Bitter to me as death. Your life, good master,
Must shuffle for itself.

LUCIUS   The boy disdains me,
He leaves me, scorns me. Briefly die their joys   107
That place them on the truth of girls and boys.   108
Why stands he so perplexed?   [She studies Iachimo.]

CYMBELINE   What wouldst thou, boy?
I love thee more and more. Think more and more
What's best to ask. Know'st him thou look'st on?
  Speak,
Wilt have him live? Is he thy kin? Thy friend?

IMOGEN
He is a Roman, no more kin to me
Than I to Your Highness; who, being born your vassal,   114
Am something nearer.

CYMBELINE   Wherefore ey'st him so?   115

IMOGEN
I'll tell you, sir, in private, if you please
To give me hearing.

CYMBELINE   Ay, with all my heart,
And lend my best attention. What's thy name?

IMOGEN
Fidele, sir.

CYMBELINE   Thou'rt my good youth, my page;

I'll be thy master. Walk with me; speak freely.
        [Cymbeline and Imogen converse apart.]

BELARIUS [to Arviragus and Guiderius]
Is not this boy revived from death?

ARVIRAGUS   One sand another   122
Not more resembles that sweet rosy lad   123
Who died, and was Fidele. What think you?   124

GUIDERIUS   The same dead thing alive.

BELARIUS
Peace, peace! See further. He eyes us not; forbear.
Creatures may be alike. Were't he, I am sure
He would have spoke to us.

GUIDERIUS   But we saw him dead.

BELARIUS
Be silent; let's see further.

PISANIO [aside]   It is my mistress.
Since she is living, let the time run on   130
To good or bad. [Cymbeline and Imogen come forward.]

CYMBELINE [to Imogen]   Come, stand thou by our side.   131
Make thy demand aloud. [To Iachimo] Sir, step you
  forth;
Give answer to this boy, and do it freely,
Or, by our greatness and the grace of it,   134
Which is our honor, bitter torture shall
Winnow the truth from falsehood.—On, speak to him.

IMOGEN
My boon is that this gentleman may render   137
Of whom he had this ring.
        [She points to the ring Iachimo wears.]

POSTHUMUS [aside]   What's that to him?

CYMBELINE [to Iachimo]
That diamond upon your finger, say
How came it yours?

IACHIMO
Thou'lt torture me to leave unspoken that   141
Which, to be spoke, would torture thee.

CYMBELINE   How? Me?

IACHIMO
I am glad to be constrained to utter that
Which torments me to conceal. By villainy
I got this ring. 'Twas Leonatus' jewel,
Whom thou didst banish; and—which more may
  grieve thee,
As it doth me—a nobler sir ne'er lived
Twixt sky and ground. Wilt thou hear more, my lord?

CYMBELINE
All that belongs to this.

IACHIMO   That paragon, thy daughter,
For whom my heart drops blood and my false spirits   150
Quail to remember—Give me leave; I faint.

CYMBELINE
My daughter? What of her? Renew thy strength.
I had rather thou shouldst live while nature will   153

83 think on't i.e., consider what revenge to take   84 my peculiar care my concern for myself.   88 tender . . . occasions solicitous of his master's needs   89 feat graceful   90 make bold venture   93 And even if (you)   94 favor face   95 looked . . . grace won my favor by your appearance   97 Ne'er thank thy master i.e., Don't attribute your being saved to Lucius's request.   98 ask if you ask   104 thing i.e., the ring on Iachimo's finger   107–8 Briefly . . . That Swiftly die the joys of those who   108 truth fidelity   114 who i.e., I, Fidele   115 something somewhat

122–4 One . . . died One grain of sand does not resemble another more than this youth resembles the sweet rose-cheeked lad who died   130–1 let . . . bad i.e., let come what must come.   134 the grace of it that which adorns it   137 render give account   141 to leave for leaving, if I leave.   150 and and whom   153 live . . . will continue to live as long as nature permits (with your death sentence forgiven)

Than die ere I hear more. Strive, man, and speak.
IACHIMO
Upon a time—unhappy was the clock
That struck the hour!—it was in Rome—accurst
The mansion where!—'twas at a feast—Oh, would
Our viands had been poisoned, or at least
Those which I heaved to head!—the good
    Posthumus—   159
What should I say? He was too good to be
Where ill men were, and was the best of all
Amongst the rar'st of good ones—sitting sadly,
Hearing us praise our loves of Italy   163
For beauty that made barren the swelled boast   164
Of him that best could speak; for feature, laming   165
The shrine of Venus or straight-pight Minerva,   166
Postures beyond brief nature; for condition,   167
A shop of all the qualities that man   168
Loves woman for, besides that hook of wiving,   169
Fairness which strikes the eye—
CYMBELINE   I stand on fire.   170
Come to the matter.
IACHIMO   All too soon I shall,
Unless thou wouldst grieve quickly. This Posthumus,
Most like a noble lord in love and one
That had a royal lover, took his hint,   174
And not dispraising whom we praised—therein
He was as calm as virtue—he began
His mistress' picture; which by his tongue being
    made,
And then a mind put in't, either our brags   178
Were cracked of kitchen trulls, or his description   179
Proved us unspeaking sots.
CYMBELINE   Nay, nay, to th' purpose.   180
IACHIMO
Your daughter's chastity—there it begins.
He spake of her as Dian had hot dreams   182
And she alone were cold; whereat I, wretch,
Made scruple of his praise and wagered with him   184
Pieces of gold 'gainst this which then he wore
Upon his honored finger, to attain
In suit the place of 's bed and win this ring   187
By hers and mine adultery. He, true knight,
No lesser of her honor confident
Than I did truly find her, stakes this ring;
And would so, had it been a carbuncle   191
Of Phoebus' wheel, and might so safely, had it   192
Been all the worth of 's car. Away to Britain   193
Post I in this design. Well may you, sir,   194

Remember me at court, where I was taught
Of your chaste daughter the wide difference   196
Twixt amorous and villainous. Being thus quenched
Of hope, not longing, mine Italian brain   198
'Gan in your duller Britain operate   199
Most vilely; for my vantage, excellent.   200
And, to be brief, my practice so prevailed   201
That I returned with simular proof enough   202
To make the noble Leonatus mad
By wounding his belief in her renown   204
With tokens thus and thus; averring notes   205
Of chamber hanging, pictures, this her bracelet—   206
                         [*showing the bracelet*]
Oh, cunning, how I got it!—nay, some marks
Of secret on her person, that he could not
But think her bond of chastity quite cracked,
I having ta'en the forfeit. Whereupon—   210
Methinks, I see him now—
POSTHUMUS [*advancing*]   Ay, so thou dost,
Italian fiend! Ay me, most credulous fool,
Egregious murderer, thief, anything
That's due to all the villains past, in being,
To come! Oh, give me cord, or knife, or poison,
Some upright justicer! Thou, King, send out   216
For torturers ingenious! It is I
That all th'abhorred things o'th'earth amend   218
By being worse than they. I am Posthumus,
That killed thy daughter—villain-like, I lie—
That caused a lesser villain than myself,
A sacrilegious thief, to do't. The temple
Of virtue was she, yea, and she herself.   223
Spit, and throw stones, cast mire upon me, set
The dogs o'th' street to bay me! Every villain
Be called Posthumus Leonatus, and
Be "villainy" less than 'twas! O Imogen!   227
My queen, my life, my wife! O Imogen,
Imogen, Imogen!
IMOGEN   Peace, my lord. Hear, hear—
POSTHUMUS
Shall 's have a play of this? Thou scornful page,   230
There lie thy part.   [*He strikes her; she falls.*]
PISANIO   Oh, gentlemen, help!   231
                    [*He goes to her assistance.*]
Mine and your mistress! Oh, my lord Posthumus,
You ne'er killed Imogen till now. Help, help!
Mine honored lady!
CYMBELINE   Does the world go round?   234

---

159 **heaved to head** raised to my lips 163–70 **Hearing ... eye** hearing us praise our Italian mistresses for beauty that surpassed even the exaggerated boast of the most eloquent speaker, attributing to them graces surpassing those of ordinary mortals and able indeed to make the enshrined Venus and stately, straight-backed Minerva seem lame by comparison, praising these women for qualities that are the sum of all that men love women for, and in addition the physical attractiveness that serves as a bait to inveigle men into marriage 174 **hint** occasion 178 **put in't** inserted into the picture 179 **cracked of kitchen trulls** boastfully offered in praise of kitchen maids 180 **unspeaking sots** inarticulate blockheads. 182 **as** as if 184 **Made scruple of** expressed doubts as to 187 **In suit** by urging my suit 191 **would so** would have done so 192 **Phoebus' wheel** i.e., the wheel of the sun-god's chariot 193 **'s car** his chariot. 194 **Post** hasten

196 **Of** by 198 **not longing** though not of my desire 199 **duller** i.e., slower-minded (supposedly caused by the northern climate) 200 **vantage** profit 201 **practice** scheming 202 **simular** simulated, or, pretended, plausible 204 **renown** good name 205 **averring** avouching, citing 206 **hanging** hangings 210 **the forfeit** i.e., what was forfeited by the breaking of her bond of chaste loyalty. 216 **justicer** judge. 218 **That ... amend** who make all loathsome things seem better in comparison 223 **she herself** she was Virtue herself. 227 **Be ... 'twas!** let the name "villainy" signify something less heinous than it used to! 230 **Shall 's** Shall we 231 **There lie thy part** Your part is to lie there on the ground. 234 **Does ... round?** i.e., Is the ground turning under my feet? (An expression of dizziness.)

POSTHUMUS
How comes these staggers on me?

PISANIO   Wake, my mistress! 235

CYMBELINE
If this be so, the gods do mean to strike me
To death with mortal joy.

PISANIO   How fares my mistress?

IMOGEN   Oh, get thee from my sight!
Thou gav'st me poison. Dangerous fellow, hence!
Breathe not where princes are.

CYMBELINE   The tune of Imogen!   241

PISANIO   Lady,
The gods throw stones of sulfur on me if   243
That box I gave you was not thought by me
A precious thing. I had it from the Queen.

CYMBELINE
New matter still?

IMOGEN   It poisoned me.

CORNELIUS   O gods!
I left out one thing which the Queen confessed,
[To Pisanio] Which must approve thee honest. "If
  Pisanio   248
Have," said she, "given his mistress that confection   249
Which I gave him for cordial, she is served
As I would serve a rat."

CYMBELINE   What's this, Cornelius?

CORNELIUS
The Queen, sir, very oft importuned me
To temper poisons for her, still pretending   253
The satisfaction of her knowledge only
In killing creatures vile, as cats and dogs,
Of no esteem. I, dreading that her purpose
Was of more danger, did compound for her
A certain stuff which, being ta'en, would cease   258
The present power of life, but in short time
All offices of nature should again
Do their due functions.—Have you ta'en of it?

IMOGEN
Most like I did, for I was dead.

BELARIUS [to Guiderius and Arviragus]   My boys,   262
There was our error.

GUIDERIUS   This is, sure, Fidele.

IMOGEN [to Posthumus]
Why did you throw your wedded lady from you?
                                   [She embraces him.]
Think that you are upon a rock, and now   265
Throw me again.   [They embrace.]

POSTHUMUS   Hang there like fruit, my soul,
Till the tree die!

CYMBELINE   How now, my flesh, my child?
What, mak'st thou me a dullard in this act?   268
Wilt thou not speak to me?

IMOGEN [kneeling]   Your blessing, sir.

BELARIUS [to Guiderius and Arviragus]
Though you did love this youth, I blame ye not;

You had a motive for't.

CYMBELINE   My tears that fall
Prove holy water on thee! Imogen,
Thy mother's dead.

IMOGEN [rising]   I am sorry for't, my lord.

CYMBELINE
Oh, she was naught; and long of her it was   274
That we meet here so strangely. But her son
Is gone, we know not how nor where.

PISANIO   My lord,
Now fear is from me, I'll speak truth. Lord Cloten,
Upon my lady's missing, came to me
With his sword drawn, foamed at the mouth, and
  swore
If I discovered not which way she was gone   280
It was my instant death. By accident
I had a feignèd letter of my master's   282
Then in my pocket, which directed him
To seek her on the mountains near to Milford;
Where, in a frenzy, in my master's garments,
Which he enforced from me, away he posts
With unchaste purpose and with oath to violate
My lady's honor. What became of him
I further know not.

GUIDERIUS   Let me end the story:
I slew him there.

CYMBELINE   Marry, the gods forfend!   290
I would not thy good deeds should from my lips   291
Pluck a hard sentence. Prithee, valiant youth,
Deny't again.   293

GUIDERIUS   I have spoke it, and I did it.

CYMBELINE   He was a prince.

GUIDERIUS
A most incivil one. The wrongs he did me
Were nothing princelike, for he did provoke me
With language that would make me spurn the sea
If it could so roar to me. I cut off 's head,
And am right glad he is not standing here
To tell this tale of mine.

CYMBELINE   I am sorrow for thee.   301
By thine own tongue thou art condemned and must
Endure our law. Thou'rt dead.

IMOGEN   That headless man
I thought had been my lord.

CYMBELINE   Bind the offender,
And take him from our presence.
                    [Guards start to bind Guiderius.]

BELARIUS   Stay, sir King.
This man is better than the man he slew,
As well descended as thyself, and hath
More of thee merited than a band of Clotens
Had ever scar for. [To the Guard] Let his arms alone;   309

---

235 staggers dizziness, bewilderment   241 tune accent, voice
243 stones of sulfur thunderbolts   248 approve prove   249 confection composition of drugs   253 temper mix   258 cease cause to
cease   262 like likely   265 a rock i.e., solid ground (?) (Some editors
conjecture lock, "a wrestling embrace.")   268 dullard sluggish performer

274 naught wicked.   long of on account of   280 discovered disclosed   282 feignèd (Pisanio would not have wished to show Cloten
the real letter, since it ordered Pisanio to kill Imogen.)   290 forfend
forbid.   291 thy good deeds i.e., that you, who fought so valiantly
against the Romans   293 Deny't again take back what you just said.
301 tell . . . mine i.e., tell of cutting off my head.   sorrow sorry
309 Had ever scar for ever merited by their battle scars.

They were not born for bondage.
CYMBELINE   Why, old soldier,
Wilt thou undo the worth thou art unpaid for
By tasting of our wrath? How of descent
As good as we?
ARVIRAGUS   In that he spake too far.
CYMBELINE [*to Belarius*]
And thou shalt die for't.
BELARIUS   We will die all three
But I will prove that two on 's are as good   315
As I have given out him. My sons, I must   316
For mine own part unfold a dangerous speech,   317
Though, haply, well for you.
ARVIRAGUS   Your danger's ours.
GUIDERIUS
And our good his.
BELARIUS   Have at it then, by leave.   319
Thou hadst, great King, a subject who
Was called Belarius.
CYMBELINE   What of him? He is
A banished traitor.
BELARIUS   He it is that hath
Assumed this age; indeed a banished man,   323
I know not how a traitor.
CYMBELINE   Take him hence!
The whole world shall not save him.
BELARIUS   Not too hot.
First pay me for the nursing of thy sons,
And let it be confiscate all so soon
As I have received it.
CYMBELINE   Nursing of my sons?
BELARIUS
I am too blunt and saucy. Here's my knee. [*He kneels.*]
Ere I arise, I will prefer my sons;   330
Then spare not the old father. Mighty sir,
These two young gentlemen, that call me father
And think they are my sons, are none of mine;
They are the issue of your loins, my liege,
And blood of your begetting.
CYMBELINE   How? My issue?
BELARIUS
So sure as you your father's. I, old Morgan,
Am that Belarius whom you sometime banished.
Your pleasure was my mere offense, my punishment   338
Itself, and all my treason; that I suffered   339
Was all the harm I did. These gentle princes—   340
For such and so they are—these twenty years   341
Have I trained up; those arts they have as I
Could put into them. My breeding was, sir, as
Your Highness knows. Their nurse, Euriphile,
Whom for the theft I wedded, stole these children

Upon my banishment. I moved her to't,   346
Having received the punishment before
For that which I did then. Beaten for loyalty   348
Excited me to treason. Their dear loss,
The more of you 'twas felt, the more it shaped   350
Unto my end of stealing them. But, gracious sir,   351
Here are your sons again, and I must lose
Two of the sweet'st companions in the world.
The benediction of these covering heavens
Fall on their heads like dew! For they are worthy
To inlay heaven with stars.
CYMBELINE   Thou weep'st and speak'st.   356
The service that you three have done is more   357
Unlike than this thou tell'st. I lost my children;   358
If these be they, I know not how to wish
A pair of worthier sons.
BELARIUS [*rising*]   Be pleased awhile.   360
This gentleman, whom I call Polydore,
Most worthy prince, as yours, is true Guiderius;
This gentleman, my Cadwal, Arviragus,
Your younger princely son. He, sir, was lapped   364
In a most curious mantle, wrought by th' hand   365
Of his queen mother, which for more probation   366
I can with ease produce.
CYMBELINE   Guiderius had
Upon his neck a mole, a sanguine star;   368
It was a mark of wonder.
BELARIUS   This is he,   369
Who hath upon him still that natural stamp.
It was wise nature's end in the donation   371
To be his evidence now.
CYMBELINE   Oh, what, am I   372
A mother to the birth of three? Ne'er mother   373
Rejoiced deliverance more. Blest pray you be,   374
That, after this strange starting from your orbs,   375
You may reign in them now! O Imogen,   376
Thou hast lost by this a kingdom.
IMOGEN   No, my lord,
I have got two worlds by't. O my gentle brothers,
Have we thus met? Oh, never say hereafter
But I am truest speaker. You called me brother,
When I was but your sister; I you brothers,
When ye were so indeed.
CYMBELINE   Did you e'er meet?
ARVIRAGUS
Ay, my good lord.
GUIDERIUS   And at first meeting loved;
Continued so until we thought he died.

---

315 **But I will** if I do not.   **on 's** of us   316 **given out** reported
317 **For . . . speech** unfold a speech that is dangerous for me   319 **And
our good his** i.e., and whatever fortune comes to us we share with
him, Belarius.   **Have . . . leave** Here goes, with your permission.
323 **Assumed** reached, attained   330 **prefer** promote   338–40 **Your . . .
did** Your displeasure toward me was all the offense I committed; so,
too, my punishment and my supposed treason were the creation of
your royal whim; what I suffered was the extent of my wrongdoing.
340 **gentle** nobly born   341 **such and so** i.e., both princes and gentle

346 **moved** persuaded   348 **Beaten** Being beaten   350 **of** by
350–1 **shaped . . . of** fitted my purpose in   356 **To . . . stars** to be
inlaid in heaven, like stars.   356–8 **Thou . . . tell'st** i.e., Your weeping
seems a testimony of the truth of what you speak, and your story is,
in any event, more credible—strange though it seems—than the
brave service you three did in battle.   360 **Be pleased awhile** i.e., Be
so kind as to listen a while longer.   364 **lapped** enfolded   365 **curious** exquisitely made   366 **probation** proof   368 **sanguine** blood-red
369 **of wonder** to be wondered at.   371 **end in the donation** aim in
giving it to him   372 **his evidence** evidence of his identity
373–4 **Ne'er . . . more** Never did deliverance (in childbed) more
rejoice a mother.   375 **starting . . . orbs** shooting from your orbits,
i.e., leaving your places at court   376 **reign** i.e., both as royal persons
and as planets with influence

CORNELIUS
By the Queen's dram she swallowed.

CYMBELINE   Oh, rare instinct!
When shall I hear all through? This fierce abridgement   386
Hath to it circumstantial branches, which   387
Distinction should be rich in. Where, how lived you?   388
And when came you to serve our Roman captive?
How parted with your brothers? How first met them?
Why fled you from the court? And whither? These,
And your three motives to the battle, with   392
I know not how much more, should be demanded,   393
And all the other by-dependencies   394
From chance to chance; but nor the time nor place   395
Will serve our long interrogatories. See,
Posthumus anchors upon Imogen,
And she, like harmless lightning, throws her eye
On him, her brothers, me, her master, hitting   399
Each object with a joy; the counterchange   400
Is severally in all. Let's quit this ground   401
And smoke the temple with our sacrifices.   402
[To Belarius] Thou art my brother; so we'll hold thee
    ever.

IMOGEN [to Belarius]
You are my father too, and did relieve me   404
To see this gracious season.

CYMBELINE   All o'erjoyed,
Save these in bonds. Let them be joyful too,
For they shall taste our comfort.

IMOGEN [to Lucius]   My good master,
I will yet do you service.

LUCIUS   Happy be you!

CYMBELINE
The forlorn soldier, that so nobly fought,   409
He would have well becomed this place and graced   410
The thankings of a king.

POSTHUMUS   I am, sir,
The soldier that did company these three
In poor beseeming; 'twas a fitment for   413
The purpose I then followed. That I was he,
Speak, Iachimo. I had you down and might
Have made you finish.

IACHIMO [kneeling]   I am down again;   416
But now my heavy conscience sinks my knee,   417
As then your force did. Take that life, beseech you,
Which I so often owe; but your ring first;   419
And here the bracelet of the truest princess
That ever swore her faith.   [He gives ring and bracelet.]

POSTHUMUS   Kneel not to me.
The power that I have on you is to spare you;

The malice towards you to forgive you. Live,
And deal with others better.   [Iachimo rises.]

CYMBELINE   Nobly doomed!   424
We'll learn our freeness of a son-in-law;   425
Pardon's the word to all.

ARVIRAGUS [to Posthumus] You holp us, sir,   426
As you did mean indeed to be our brother;   427
Joyed are we that you are.

POSTHUMUS
Your servant, princes. [To Lucius] Good my lord of
    Rome,
Call forth your soothsayer. As I slept, methought
Great Jupiter, upon his eagle backed,
Appeared to me, with other spritely shows   432
Of mine own kindred. When I waked, I found
This label on my bosom [showing tablet], whose
    containing   434
Is so from sense in hardness that I can   435
Make no collection of it. Let him show   436
His skill in the construction.

LUCIUS   Philharmonus!   437

SOOTHSAYER
Here, my good lord.

LUCIUS   Read, and declare the meaning.

SOOTHSAYER (reads) "Whenas a lion's whelp shall, to
himself unknown, without seeking find and be embraced by a piece of tender air; and when from a stately
cedar shall be lopped branches which, being dead
many years, shall after revive, be jointed to the old
stock and freshly grow; then shall Posthumus end his
miseries, Britain be fortunate and flourish in peace
and plenty."
Thou, Leonatus, art the lion's whelp;
The fit and apt construction of thy name,
Being Leo-natus, doth import so much.   449
[To Cymbeline] The piece of tender air, thy virtuous
    daughter,
Which we call "mollis aer," and "mollis aer"   451
We term it "mulier"; which "mulier" I divine
Is this most constant wife; who, even now,   453
Answering the letter of the oracle,   [to Posthumus]   454
Unknown to you, unsought, were clipped about   455
With this most tender air.

CYMBELINE   This hath some seeming.   456

SOOTHSAYER
The lofty cedar, royal Cymbeline,
Personates thee, and thy lopped branches point
Thy two sons forth; who, by Belarius stol'n,
For many years thought dead, are now revived,

---

386 **fierce abridgment** drastically compressed account   387–8 **cir-cumstantial . . . in** details and ramifications to be distinguished in all their abundance.   392 **your three motives** the motives of you three   393 **demanded** inquired into   394 **by-dependencies** attendant circumstances   395 **chance to chance** event to event.   **nor the** neither the   399 **her master** i.e., Lucius   400–1 **the counterchange . . . all** the exchange (of happy glances) involves each of us to everyone else.   402 **smoke** fill with incense   404 **relieve** save   409 **forlorn** missing, or, poorly dressed   410 **graced** adorned   413 **beseeming** appearance.   **fitment** makeshift disguise   416 **made you finish** put an end to you.   417 **sinks** causes to sink   419 **often** many times over

424 **doomed** decreed, judged.   425 **freeness** liberality, generosity   426 **holp** helped   427 **As** as if   432 **spritely shows** ghostly appearances   434 **label** tablet, paper   434–5 **whose . . . hardness** whose meaning is so remote from sense in its difficulty   436 **collection** interpretation   437 **construction** construing of it.   449 **Leo-natus** one born of the lion   451 **mollis aer** tender air. (A fanciful derivation of Latin *mulier*, "woman.")   453 **who** (Perhaps referring to Posthumus, but the grammar is loose and the point of reference may shift after line 454.)   454 **Answering . . . of** fulfilling the exact terms of   455 **were clipped about** i.e., you were embraced   456 **seeming** plausibility.

To the majestic cedar joined, whose issue
Promises Britain peace and plenty.

CYMBELINE   Well,
My peace we will begin. And, Caius Lucius,
Although the victor, we submit to Caesar
And to the Roman empire, promising
To pay our wonted tribute, from the which
We were dissuaded by our wicked queen,
Whom heavens in justice both on her and hers   468
Have laid most heavy hand.

SOOTHSAYER
The fingers of the powers above do tune
The harmony of this peace. The vision
Which I made known to Lucius ere the stroke
Of this yet scarce-cold battle at this instant
Is full accomplished; for the Roman eagle,
From south to west on wing soaring aloft,

Lessened herself, and in the beams o'th' sun   476
So vanished; which foreshowed our princely eagle, 477
Th'imperial Caesar, should again unite
His favor with the radiant Cymbeline,
Which shines here in the west.

CYMBELINE   Laud we the gods,   480
And let our crooked smokes climb to their nostrils 481
From our blest altars. Publish we this peace
To all our subjects. Set we forward. Let
A Roman and a British ensign wave
Friendly together. So through Lud's Town march,
And in the temple of great Jupiter
Our peace we'll ratify, seal it with feasts.
Set on there! Never was a war did cease,   488
Ere bloody hands were washed, with such a peace. 489
                                        Exeunt.

468 **Whom** on whom.   **hers** i.e., Cloten

476 **Lessened herself** i.e., grew smaller to sight   477 **foreshowed**
foreshowed that   480 **Laud** Praise   481 **crooked** curling, twining
488 **Set on there** Forward march.   **was a war** was there a war that
489 **Ere . . . washed** before hands were washed in blood or free of
blood

The Winter's Tale

*T*he Winter's Tale (c. 1609–1611), with its almost symmetrical division into two halves of bleak tragedy and comic romance, illustrates perhaps more clearly than any other Shakespearean play the genre of tragicomedy. To be sure, all the late romances feature journeys of separation, apparent deaths, and tearful reconciliations. Marina and Thaisa in *Pericles*, Imogen in *Cymbeline*, and Ferdinand in *The Tempest*, all supposed irrecoverably lost, are brought back to life by apparently miraculous devices. Of the four late romances, however, *The Winter's Tale* uses the most formal structure to evoke the antithesis of tragedy and romance. It is sharply divided into contrasting halves by a gap of sixteen years. The tragic first half takes place almost entirely in Sicilia, whereas the action of the second half is limited for the most part to Bohemia. At the court of Sicilia, we see tyrannical jealousy producing a spiritual climate of "winter / In storm perpetual"; in Bohemia, we witness a pastoral landscape and a sheepshearing evoking "the sweet o'th' year," "When daffodils begin to peer" (3.2.212–13; 4.3.1–3). Paradoxically, the contrast between the two halves is intensified by parallels between the two: both begin with Camillo onstage and proceed to scenes of confrontation and jealousy in which, ironically, the innocent cause of jealousy in the first half, Polixenes, becomes the jealous tyrant of the second half. The mirroring reminds us of the cyclical nature of time and the hope it brings of renewal as we move from tragedy to romantic comedy.

Although this motif of a renewing journey from jaded court to idealized countryside reminds us of *As You Like It* and other early comedies, we sense in the late romances and especially in *The Winter's Tale* a new preoccupation with humanity's tragic folly. The vision of human depravity is world-weary and pessimistic, as though infected by the gloomy spirit of the great tragedies. And because humanity is so bent on destroying itself, the restoration is at once more urgently needed and more miraculous than in the

"festive" world of early comedy. Renewal is mythically associated with the seasonal cycle from winter to summer.

King Leontes's tragedy seems at first irreversible and terrifying, like that of Shakespeare's greatest tragic protagonists. He suffers from irrational jealousy, as does Othello, and attempts to destroy the person on whom all his happiness depends. As with Othello, his jealousy stems from a characteristically male fear of inadequacy and rejection. Unlike Othello, however, Leontes needs no diabolical tempter such as Iago to poison his mind against Queen Hermione. Leontes is undone by his own fantasies. No differences in race or age can explain Leontes's fears of estrangement from Hermione. She is not imprudent in her conduct, like her counterpart in Robert Greene's *Pandosto* (1588), the prose romance from which Shakespeare drew his narrative. Although Hermione is graciously fond of Leontes's dear friend Polixenes and urges him to stay longer in Sicilia, she does so only with a hospitable warmth demanded by the occasion and encouraged by her husband. In every way, then, Shakespeare strips away from Leontes the motive and the occasion for plausible doubting of his wife. All observers in the Sicilian court are incredulous and shocked at the King's accusations. Even so, Leontes is neither an unsympathetic nor an unbelievable character. Like Othello, Leontes cherishes his wife and perceives with a horrifying intensity what a fearful cost they both must pay for his suspicions. Not only his marriage, but also his lifelong friendship with Polixenes, his sense of pride in his children, and his enjoyment of his subjects' warm regard, all must be sacrificed to a single overwhelming compulsion.

Whatever may be the psychological cause of this obsession, it manifests itself as a revulsion against all sexual behavior. Like mad Lear, Leontes imagines lechery to be the unavoidable fact of the cosmos and of the human condition, the lowest common denominator to which all persons (including Hermione) must stoop. He is persuaded that "It is a bawdy planet," in which cuck-olded man has "his pond fished by his next neighbor, by / Sir Smile, his neighbor" (1.2.195–201). Leontes's tortured soliloquies are laden with sexual images, of unattended "gates" letting in and out the enemy "With bag and baggage," and of a "dagger" that must be "muzzled / Lest it should bite its master" (lines 197, 206, 156–7). As in *King Lear*, order is inverted to disorder, sanity to madness, legitimacy to illegitimacy. Sexual misconduct is emblematic of a universal malaise: "Why, then the world and all that's in 't is nothing, / The covering sky is nothing, Bohemia nothing, / My wife is nothing" (lines 292–4). Other characters, too, see the trial of Hermione as a testing of humanity's worth: if Hermione proves false, Antigonus promises, he will treat his own wife as a stable horse and will "geld" his three daughters (2.1.148). Prevailing images are of spiders, venom, infection, sterility, and the "dungy earth" (line 158).

Cosmic order is never really challenged, however, even though the human suffering is very real and the injustice to women especially apparent. Leontes's fantasies of universal disorder are chimerical. His wife is, in fact, chaste, Polixenes true, and the King's courtiers loyal. Camillo refuses to carry out Leontes's order to murder Polixenes, not only because he knows murder to be wrong, but also because history offers not one example of a man "that had struck anointed kings / And flourished after" (1.2.357–8). The cosmos of this play is one in which crimes are invariably and swiftly punished. The Delphic oracle vindicates Hermione and gives Leontes stern warning. When Leontes persists in his madness, his son Mamillius's death follows as an immediate consequence. As Leontes at once perceives, "Apollo's angry, and the heavens themselves / Do strike at my injustice" (3.2.146–7). Leontes paradoxically welcomes the lengthy contrition he must undergo, for it confirms a pattern in the universe of just cause and effect. Although as tragic protagonist he has discovered the truth about Hermione moments too late and so must pay richly for his error, Leontes has at least recovered faith in Hermione's transcendent goodness. His nightmare now over, he accepts and embraces suffering as a necessary atonement.

The transition to romance is therefore anticipated to an extent by the play's first half, even though the tone of the last two acts is strikingly different. The old Shepherd signals a momentous change when he speaks to his son of a cataclysmic storm and a ravenous bear set in opposition to the miraculous discovery of a child: "Now bless thyself. Thou mett'st with things dying, I with things newborn" (3.3.110–11). Time comes onstage as Chorus, like Gower in *Pericles*, to remind us of the conscious artifice of the dramatist. He can "o'erthrow law" and carry us over sixteen years as if we had merely dreamed out the interim (4.1). Shakespeare flaunts the improbability

of his story by giving Bohemia a seacoast (much to the distress of Ben Jonson) and by bringing onstage either a live bear or an actor costumed as one (*"Exit, pursued by a bear"*; 3.3.57 s.d.). The narrative uses many typical devices of romance: a babe abandoned to the elements, a princess brought up by shepherds, a prince disguised as a swain, a sea voyage, and a recognition scene. Love is threatened, not by the internal psychic obstacle of jealousy, but by the external obstacles of parental opposition and a seeming disparity of social rank between the lovers. Comedy easily finds solutions for such difficulties by the unraveling of illusion. This comic world also properly includes clownish shepherds, coy shepherdesses, and Autolycus, the roguish peddler, whose machinations contribute in an unforeseen manner to the working out of the love plot. Autolycus is in many ways the presiding genius of the play's second half, as dominant a character as Leontes in the first half and one whose delightful function is to do good "against my will" (5.2.125). In this paradox of knavery converted surprisingly to benign ends, we see how the comic providence of Shakespeare's tragicomic world makes use of the most implausible and outrageous happenings in pursuit of its own inscrutable design.

The conventional romantic ending is infused, however, with a sadness and a mystery that take the play well beyond what is usual in comedy. Mamillius and Antigonus are really dead, and that irredeemable fact is not forgotten in the play's final happy moments. Hermione, although vindicated by the gods, has suffered public shame, the death of one child, separation from her other child, and prolonged isolation from her husband; like Imogen in *Cymbeline*, she has had to endure the consequences of male frailty and thereby redeem her husband through her suffering. Her husband, having thrown her aside, must, like Pericles, rediscover and learn to cherish the woman he once chose who now has aged; he must reconfirm his marriage to her, even as he learns to accept the marriage of his daughter to a younger man. All of these crucial turnings hinge upon Shakespeare's most notable departure from his source, Greene's *Pandosto*: Hermione is brought back to life. All observers regard this event, and the rediscovery of Perdita, as grossly implausible, "so like an old tale that the verity of it is in strong suspicion" (5.2.29–30). The play's very title, *The Winter's Tale*, reinforces this sense of naive improbability. Why does Shakespeare stress this riddling paradox of an unbelievable reality, and why does he deliberately mislead his audience into believing that Hermione has, in fact, died (3.3.15–45), using a kind of theatrical trickery found in no other Shakespearean play? The answer may well be that, in Paulina's words, we must awake our faith, accepting a narrative of death and return to life that cannot ultimately be comprehended by reason. On the rational level, we are told that Hermione has been kept in hiding for sixteen years, in order to fulfill the condition of the oracle that Leontes is to live without an heir (and hence without a wife) until Perdita is found. Such an explanation seems psychologically incomprehensible, however, for it demands that Hermione live in extended isolation and that Paulina serve as the King's conscience for such a long period of time without any way for the participants to know when their suffering will end. Instead, we are drawn toward an emblematic interpretation, bearing in mind that it is more an evocative hint than a complete truth. Throughout the play, Hermione has been repeatedly associated with "Grace" and with the goddess Proserpina, whose return from the underworld, after "Three crabbèd months had soured themselves to death" (1.2.102), signals the coming of spring. Perdita, also associated with Proserpina (4.4.116), is welcomed by her father "As is the spring to th' earth" (5.1.152). The emphasis on the bond of father and daughter, so characteristic of Shakespeare's late plays and especially his romances, goes importantly beyond the patriarchalism of Shakespeare's earlier history plays in its exploration of family relationships. Paulina has a similarly emblematic role, that of Conscience, patiently guiding the King to a divinely appointed renewal of his joy. Paulina speaks of herself as an artist figure, like Prospero in *The Tempest*, performing wonders of illusion, though she rejects the assistance of wicked powers. These emblematic hints do not rob the story of its human drama, but they do lend a transcendent significance to Leontes's bittersweet story of sinful error, affliction, and an unexpected second happiness.

On stage in recent decades, the play has shown its remarkable dramaturgic effectiveness, especially in the restoration of Hermione to her husband as a living and breathing statue. Peter Brook, at the Phoenix Theatre in London, 1951, chose a permanent set to underscore the play's malleable swift action and its need for the audience to participate imaginatively in the fashioning of theatrical illusion. Trevor Nunn's set at Stratford-upon-Avon in 1969 was a three-sided white box in which nothing was realistically represented. Nunn and John Barton, at Stratford-upon-Avon in 1976, visualized bears everywhere: in motifs of wall hangings and carpets, in a bearskin draped on a couch. The violent irrationality of Ian McKellan's Leontes seemed plausible in such a symbolic and mythic landscape. In Terry Hands's 1986 production also at Stratford-upon-Avon, a huge bear rug on the cool marble floor of Leontes's Regency palace during the play's first half became, in Bohemia, the live bear that tore into the shoulder of Antigonus. Above all, the apparent bringing back to life of Hermione's statue in the final scene has proven again and again to be a masterful *coup de théâtre*. What we see in the theater is of course an illusion, but at what level? Are we to understand that a statue comes to life? Much depends on the actress's skill in appearing motionless and then warm to her husband's touch. The moment is indeed one calculated to awaken our faith in the miracle of renewal and in the power of art to confound illusion and reality. We are led to ponder deeply the mysteries of our own uncertain existence.

The Winter's Tale

The Names of the Actors

LEONTES, *King of Sicilia*
MAMILLIUS, *young prince of Sicilia*
CAMILLO,
ANTIGONUS,
CLEOMENES,   } *four Lords of Sicilia*
DION,

HERMIONE, *Queen to Leontes*
PERDITA, *daughter to Leontes and Hermione*
PAULINA, *wife to Antigonus*
EMILIA, *a lady [attending on Hermione]*

POLIXENES, *King of Bohemia*
FLORIZEL, *Prince of Bohemia*
ARCHIDAMUS, *a lord of Bohemia*
Old SHEPHERD, *reputed father of Perdita*
CLOWN, *his son*
AUTOLYCUS, *a rogue*

[SCENE: *Sicilia, and Bohemia.*]

[MOPSA,
[DORCAS,   } *Shepherdesses.*]

[A MARINER
A JAILER
Two LADIES *attending Hermione*
Two SERVANTS *attending Leontes*
One or more LORDS *attending Leontes*
An OFFICER *of the court*
A GENTLEMAN *attending Leontes*
Three GENTLEMEN *of the court of Sicilia*
A SERVANT *of the Old Shepherd*

TIME, *as Chorus*]

Other Lords and Gentlemen, [Ladies, Officers,] and
Servants; Shepherds and Shepherdesses; [Twelve
Countrymen disguised as Satyrs]

1.1

Enter Camillo and Archidamus.

ARCHIDAMUS   If you shall chance, Camillo, to visit Bohemia on the like occasion whereon my services are ²
now on foot, you shall see, as I have said, great ³
difference betwixt our Bohemia and your Sicilia.
CAMILLO   I think this coming summer the King of Sicilia
means to pay Bohemia the visitation which he justly ⁶
owes him.
ARCHIDAMUS   Wherein our entertainment shall shame ⁸
us, we will be justified in our loves; for indeed— ⁹
CAMILLO   Beseech you—

ARCHIDAMUS   Verily, I speak it in the freedom of my ¹¹
knowledge. We cannot with such magnificence—in ¹²
so rare—I know not what to say. We will give you
sleepy drinks, that your senses, unintelligent of our ¹⁴
insufficience, may, though they cannot praise us, as
little accuse us.
CAMILLO   You pay a great deal too dear for what's
given freely.
ARCHIDAMUS   Believe me, I speak as my understanding
instructs me and as mine honesty puts it to utterance.
CAMILLO   Sicilia cannot show himself overkind to Bo- ²¹
hemia. They were trained together in their childhoods,
and there rooted betwixt them then such an affection
which cannot choose but branch now. Since their ²⁴
more mature dignities and royal necessities made
separation of their society, their encounters, though ²⁶

<hr/>

1.1 Location: Sicilia. The court of Leontes.
2–3 on the . . . foot on an occasion like this one that I am engaged in
(attending on King Polixenes)   **6 Bohemia** the King of Bohemia.
(Also at lines 21–2.)   **8–9 Wherein . . . loves** In whatever way our
attempts to entertain you will shame us by falling short, we will
make up for by our affection

11–12 in . . . knowledge as my knowledge entitles me to speak.
14 sleepy sleep-inducing.   **unintelligent** unaware   **21 Sicilia** The
King of Sicilia   **24 branch** put forth new growth, flourish. (Also perhaps with opposite and unconscious suggestion of "divide.")
26 their society their being together

1530

not personal, hath been royally attorneyed with   27
interchange of gifts, letters, loving embassies, that
they have seemed to be together though absent,
shook hands as over a vast, and embraced as it were   30
from the ends of opposed winds. The heavens con-   31
tinue their loves!

ARCHIDAMUS   I think there is not in the world either
malice or matter to alter it. You have an unspeakable
comfort of your young prince Mamillius. It is a   35
gentleman of the greatest promise that ever came into
my note.   37

CAMILLO   I very well agree with you in the hopes of
him. It is a gallant child, one that indeed physics the   39
subject, makes old hearts fresh. They that went on   40
crutches ere he was born desire yet their life to see him   41
a man.

ARCHIDAMUS   Would they else be content to die?

CAMILLO   Yes, if there were no other excuse why they
should desire to live.

ARCHIDAMUS   If the King had no son, they would desire   46
to live on crutches till he had one.   *Exeunt.*   47

1.2

Enter Leontes, Hermione, Mamillius, Polixenes,
Camillo.

POLIXENES
Nine changes of the wat'ry star hath been   1
The shepherd's note since we have left our throne   2
Without a burden. Time as long again   3
Would be filled up, my brother, with our thanks,
And yet we should for perpetuity   5
Go hence in debt. And therefore, like a cipher,   6
Yet standing in rich place, I multiply   7
With one "We thank you" many thousands more
That go before it.

LEONTES   Stay your thanks awhile
And pay them when you part.

POLIXENES   Sir, that's tomorrow.
I am questioned by my fears of what may chance   11
Or breed upon our absence, that may blow   12
No sneaping winds at home to make us say,   13
"This is put forth too truly." Besides, I have stayed   14

To tire your royalty.

LEONTES   We are tougher, brother,
Than you can put us to't.

POLIXENES   No longer stay.   16

LEONTES
One sev'nnight longer.

POLIXENES   Very sooth, tomorrow.   17

LEONTES
We'll part the time between 's, then, and in that   18
I'll no gainsaying.

POLIXENES   Press me not, beseech you, so.   19
There is no tongue that moves, none, none i' th' world
So soon as yours could win me. So it should now,
Were there necessity in your request, although
'Twere needful I denied it. My affairs
Do even drag me homeward, which to hinder
Were in your love a whip to me, my stay   25
To you a charge and trouble. To save both,   26
Farewell, our brother.

LEONTES   Tongue-tied, our Queen? Speak you.

HERMIONE
I had thought, sir, to have held my peace until   28
You had drawn oaths from him not to stay. You, sir,   29
Charge him too coldly. Tell him you are sure
All in Bohemia's well; this satisfaction   31
The bygone day proclaimed. Say this to him,   32
He's beat from his best ward.

LEONTES   Well said, Hermione.   33

HERMIONE
To tell he longs to see his son were strong.   34
But let him say so then, and let him go.
But let him swear so and he shall not stay;   36
We'll thwack him hence with distaffs.   37
[*To Polixenes*] Yet of your royal presence I'll adventure   38
The borrow of a week. When at Bohemia   39
You take my lord, I'll give him my commission
To let him there a month behind the gest   41
Prefixed for 's parting.—Yet, good deed, Leontes,   42
I love thee not a jar o' th' clock behind   43
What lady she her lord.—You'll stay?

POLIXENES   No, madam.   44

HERMIONE
Nay, but you will?

POLIXENES   I may not, verily.

HERMIONE   Verily?

---

27 **personal** in person.   **attorneyed** carried out by deputy   30 **vast** boundless space   31 **ends . . . winds** i.e., opposite ends of the earth. **The heavens** May the heavens   35 **of** in the person of   37 **note** observation.   39–40 **physics the subject** brings health to the subjects of this kingdom   41 **their life** to continue living   46–7 **If . . . one** Even if there were no living heir to the throne, these old people would still wish to go on living in hopes of one.
1.2. Location: The same.   1 wat'ry star moon   **2 note** observation. **we** I. (The royal "we.")   **3 burden** occupant.   **5 for perpetuity** forever   **6–7 like . . . place** like a zero at the end of a number, increasing its value by powers of ten, though of itself without value   **11–14 I am . . . truly** I am anxious about what may happen in my absence, especially a stirring up of envy and backbiting that would cause me to say my fears were all too plausible.

16 **Than . . . to't** than anything you can do to try me.   17 **sev'nnight** week.   **Very sooth** Truly   18 **part the time** split the difference, i.e., divide a week in two   19 **I'll no gainsaying** I won't take "no" for an answer.   25 **Were . . . whip** would be a punishment to me, though done through love   26 **charge** expense, burden   28–9 **I . . . to stay** i.e., I almost thought that you were going to get him to swear he *won't* stay, before I got a chance to say anything.   31–2 **this . . . proclaimed** yesterday brought news to satisfy on that score.   32 **Say** If you say   33 **ward** defensive posture. (A fencing term.)   34 **tell** tell us that. **strong** a strong argument.   36 **he shall not stay** i.e., we wouldn't let him stay even if he wanted to.   37 **distaffs** sticks used in spinning, here employed as a domestic kind of weapon.   38 **adventure** risk   39 **borrow** borrowing   41–2 **To . . . parting** to let him stay there a month longer than the originally agreed-upon time for his departure.   42 **good deed** indeed   43–4 **I love . . . lord** I love you not even a tiny bit (literally, a tick of the clock) less than any noble lady loves her husband.

You put me off with limber vows; but I,
Though you would seek t'unsphere the stars with
   oaths,
Should yet say, "Sir, no going." Verily,
You shall not go. A lady's "verily" is
As potent as a lord's. Will you go yet?
Force me to keep you as a prisoner,
Not like a guest: so you shall pay your fees   53
When you depart, and save your thanks. How say
   you?
My prisoner or my guest? By your dread "verily,"
One of them you shall be.

POLIXENES   Your guest, then, madam.
To be your prisoner should import offending,   57
Which is for me less easy to commit
Than you to punish.

HERMIONE   Not your jailer, then,
But your kind hostess. Come, I'll question you
Of my lord's tricks and yours when you were boys.
You were pretty lordings then?

POLIXENES   We were, fair Queen,
Two lads that thought there was no more behind   63
But such a day tomorrow as today,
And to be boy eternal.

HERMIONE   Was not my lord
The verier wag o'th' two?   66

POLIXENES
We were as twinned lambs that did frisk i'th' sun
And bleat the one at th'other. What we changed   68
Was innocence for innocence; we knew not
The doctrine of ill-doing, nor dreamed
That any did. Had we pursued that life,
And our weak spirits ne'er been higher reared
With stronger blood, we should have answered
   heaven   73
Boldly "Not guilty," the imposition cleared   74
Hereditary ours.

HERMIONE   By this we gather   75
You have tripped since.

POLIXENES   Oh, my most sacred lady,
Temptations have since then been born to 's, for
In those unfledged days was my wife a girl;   78
Your precious self had then not crossed the eyes
Of my young playfellow.

HERMIONE   Grace to boot!   80
Of this make no conclusion, lest you say   81
Your queen and I are devils. Yet go on.
Th'offenses we have made you do we'll answer,
If you first sinned with us, and that with us
You did continue fault, and that you slipped not

With any but with us.   47

LEONTES   Is he won yet?   86
HERMIONE
He'll stay, my lord.
LEONTES   At my request he would not.
Hermione, my dearest, thou never spok'st
To better purpose.
HERMIONE   Never?
LEONTES   Never but once.
HERMIONE
What? Have I twice said well? When was 't before?
I prithee, tell me. Cram 's with praise and make 's
As fat as tame things. One good deed dying
   tongueless   92
Slaughters a thousand waiting upon that.   93
Our praises are our wages. You may ride 's
With one soft kiss a thousand furlongs ere
With spur we heat an acre. But to th' goal: 96
My last good deed was to entreat his stay.
What was my first? It has an elder sister,
Or I mistake you. Oh, would her name were Grace!
But once before I spoke to the purpose. When?
Nay, let me have't; I long.
LEONTES   Why, that was when
Three crabbèd months had soured themselves to
   death
Ere I could make thee open thy white hand
And clap thyself my love. Then didst thou utter, 104
"I am yours forever."
HERMIONE   'Tis grace indeed.
Why, lo you now, I have spoke to th' purpose twice:
The one forever earned a royal husband,
Th'other for some while a friend.
        [She gives her hand to Polixenes.]
LEONTES [aside]   Too hot, too hot!
To mingle friendship far is mingling bloods.   109
I have *tremor cordis* on me. My heart dances,   110
But not for joy, not joy. This entertainment   111
May a free face put on, derive a liberty   112
From heartiness, from bounty, fertile bosom,   113
And well become the agent. 'T may, I grant.   114
But to be paddling palms and pinching fingers,
As now they are, and making practiced smiles
As in a looking glass, and then to sigh, as 'twere
The mort o'th' deer; oh, that is entertainment   118
My bosom likes not, nor my brows.—Mamillius,   119
Art thou my boy?
MAMILLIUS   Ay, my good lord.
LEONTES   I'fecks,   120

---

47 **limber** limp 53 **fees** payments demanded by jailers of prisoners at the time of their release 57 **import offending** imply my having offended 63 **behind** still to come 66 **The verier wag** truly the more mischievous 68 **changed** exchanged 73 **stronger blood** mature sexual passions 74–5 **the imposition . . . ours** i.e., being freed from original sin itself (if we had continued in that state); or, excepting of course the original sin that is the common condition of all mortals. 78 **unfledged** not yet feathered, i.e., immature 80 **Grace to boot!** Heaven help me! 81 **Of . . . conclusion** Don't follow your implied line of reasoning to its logical conclusion

86 **Is he won yet**? (Leontes has been out of hearing for much of their conversation.) 92 **tongueless** unpraised, unsung 93 **Slaughters . . . that** i.e., will inhibit many other good deeds that would have been inspired by that praise. 96 **heat** traverse as in a race. **to th' goal** to come to the point 104 **clap** clasp hands, pledge 109 **mingling bloods** (Sexual intercourse was thought to produce a mingling of bloods.) 110 *tremor cordis* fluttering of the heart 111 **entertainment** i.e., of Polixenes by Hermione 112 **free face** innocent appearance 113 **fertile bosom** i.e., generous affection 114 **well . . . agent** do credit to the doer. 118 **mort** note sounded on a horn at the death of the hunted deer 119 **brows** (Alludes to cuckolds' horns, the supposed badge of men whose wives are unfaithful.) 120 **I'fecks** in faith

Why, that's my bawcock. What, hast smutched thy
   nose?   121
They say it is a copy out of mine. Come, captain,
We must be neat; not neat, but cleanly, captain.   123
And yet the steer, the heifer, and the calf
Are all called neat.—Still virginaling   125
Upon his palm?—How now, you wanton calf?   126
Art thou my calf?
MAMILLIUS   Yes, if you will, my lord.
LEONTES
Thou want'st a rough pash and the shoots that I have 128
To be full like me. Yet they say we are   129
Almost as like as eggs. Women say so,
That will say anything. But were they false
As o'erdyed blacks, as wind, as waters, false   132
As dice are to be wished by one that fixes   133
No bourn twixt his and mine, yet were it true   134
To say this boy were like me. Come, sir page,
Look on me with your welkin eye. Sweet villain!   136
Most dear'st! My collop! Can thy dam?—may't be?—   137
Affection, thy intention stabs the center.   138
Thou dost make possible things not so held,   139
Communicat'st with dreams—how can this be?—   140
With what's unreal thou coactive art,   141
And fellow'st nothing. Then 'tis very credent   142
Thou mayst cojoin with something; and thou dost,   143
And that beyond commission, and I find it,   144
And that to the infection of my brains
And hard'ning of my brows.
POLIXENES   What means Sicilia?   146
HERMIONE
He something seems unsettled.
POLIXENES   How, my lord?   147
What cheer? How is't with you, best brother?
HERMIONE   You look
As if you held a brow of much distraction.
Are you moved, my lord?
LEONTES   No, in good earnest.   150
How sometimes nature will betray its folly,   151
Its tenderness, and make itself a pastime   152
To harder bosoms! Looking on the lines   153

Of my boy's face, methoughts I did recoil   154
Twenty-three years, and saw myself unbreeched,   155
In my green velvet coat, my dagger muzzled   156
Lest it should bite its master and so prove,
As ornaments oft do, too dangerous.
How like, methought, I then was to this kernel,
This squash, this gentleman.—Mine honest friend,   160
Will you take eggs for money?   161
MAMILLIUS   No, my lord, I'll fight.
LEONTES
You will? Why, happy man be 's dole!—My brother,   163
Are you so fond of your young prince as we
Do seem to be of ours?
POLIXENES   If at home, sir,
He's all my exercise, my mirth, my matter,   166
Now my sworn friend and then mine enemy,
My parasite, my soldier, statesman, all.
He makes a July's day short as December,
And with his varying childness cures in me   170
Thoughts that would thick my blood.
LEONTES   So stands this squire 171
Officed with me. We two will walk, my lord,   172
And leave you to your graver steps. Hermione,
How thou lov'st us, show in our brother's welcome.   174
Let what is dear in Sicily be cheap.   175
Next to thyself and my young rover, he's
Apparent to my heart.
HERMIONE   If you would seek us,   177
We are yours i'th' garden. Shall 's attend you there? 178
LEONTES
To your own bents dispose you. You'll be found,   179
Be you beneath the sky. [*Aside*] I am angling now,
Though you perceive me not how I give line.   181
Go to, go to!   182
How she holds up the neb, the bill to him,   183
And arms her with the boldness of a wife   184
To her allowing husband!
                 [*Exeunt Polixenes and Hermione.*]
              Gone already!   185
Inch thick, knee-deep, o'er head and ears a forked
   one!—   186
Go play, boy, play. Thy mother plays, and I   187
Play too, but so disgraced a part, whose issue   188

---

121 bawcock i.e., fine fellow. (French *beau coq*.) **123 not . . . cleanly**
(Leontes changes the word because *neat* also means "cattle" and hence
reminds him of cuckolds' horns.) **125 virginaling** touching hands, as
in playing on the virginals, a keyboard instrument **126 wanton** frisky
128 Thou . . . have You lack a shaggy head and the horns that I have.
(Again alluding to cuckolds' horns.) **129 full** fully **132 o'erdyed
blacks** black garments that have been weakened by too much dye or
that have been dyed over another color (thereby betraying a falseness
in the mourner) **132–4 false . . . mine** as false as dice are wished false
by one who intends to cheat me, and who respects no boundary
between what is his and mine **136 welkin** sky-blue **137 collop** small
piece of meat; i.e., of my own flesh. **dam** mother **138–43 Affection
. . . something** Strong passion, your intense power pierces to the very
center, the soul. You make possible things normally considered fantastic, partaking as you do of the nature of dreams. How can this be?
You collaborate with unreality and imagined fantasies. It's all the
likelier, then, that such imaginings may also fasten on a real object
144 commission what is lawful **146 What means Sicilia?** Why is the
King of Sicilia looking so distracted? **147 something** somewhat
150 moved angry **151 nature** i.e., affectionate feeling between parent and child **152 pastime** occasion for amusement **153 To harder
bosoms** for persons who are less tender-hearted.

154 methoughts it seemed to me. **recoil** i.e., go back in memory
155 unbreeched not yet wearing breeches **156 muzzled** i.e., sheathed.
(With phallic suggestion.) **160 squash** unripe peascod or pea pod.
honest worthy **161 take eggs for money** i.e., be imposed upon, taken
advantage of, cheated. (Proverbial.) **163 happy . . . dole** may good
fortune be his lot. (Proverbial.) **166 matter** concern **170 childness**
childlike ways **171 thick my blood** (Melancholy thoughts were supposed to thicken the blood.) **172 Officed** placed in particular function
174–5 How . . . cheap (A hidden second meaning in these lines may be
intentional: show just how much you love me by the way you encourage Polixenes's attentions and thereby cheapen the most precious thing
in Sicily.) **177 Apparent** heir apparent (perhaps with a suggestion too
of "evident, revealed") **178 Shall 's** Shall we **179 To . . . dispose you**
Act according to your inclinations. (With more bitter double meaning,
continued in *You'll be found*, i.e., found out.) **181 give line** pay out line
(to let the fish hook itself well). **182 Go to** (An expression of remonstrance.) **183 neb** beak, i.e., nose, mouth **184 arms her with** assumes
185 allowing approving **186 forked** horned **187 play** play games.
plays i.e., in a sexual liaison **188 Play** play a role. **issue** outcome.
(With a pun on the sense of "offspring" and "theatrical exit.")

Will hiss me to my grave. Contempt and clamor
Will be my knell. Go play, boy, play. There have been,
Or I am much deceived, cuckolds ere now;
And many a man there is, even at this present,
Now while I speak this, holds his wife by th' arm,
That little thinks she has been sluiced in 's absence   194
And his pond fished by his next neighbor, by
Sir Smile, his neighbor. Nay, there's comfort in 't
Whiles other men have gates and those gates opened,   197
As mine, against their will. Should all despair
That have revolted wives, the tenth of mankind   199
Would hang themselves. Physic for 't there's none.   200
It is a bawdy planet, that will strike   201
Where 'tis predominant; and 'tis powerful, think it,   202
From east, west, north, and south. Be it concluded,
No barricado for a belly. Know 't,   204
It will let in and out the enemy
With bag and baggage. Many thousand on 's   206
Have the disease and feel 't not.—How now, boy?

MAMILLIUS
I am like you, they say.

LEONTES   Why, that's some comfort.
What, Camillo there?

CAMILLO [coming forward]   Ay, my good lord.

LEONTES
Go play, Mamillius; thou'rt an honest man.
                              [Exit Mamillius.]
Camillo, this great sir will yet stay longer.

CAMILLO
You had much ado to make his anchor hold.
When you cast out, it still came home.

LEONTES   Didst note it?   213

CAMILLO
He would not stay at your petitions, made
His business more material.

LEONTES   Didst perceive it?   215
[Aside] They're here with me already, whisp'ring,
     rounding,   216
"Sicilia is a so-forth." 'Tis far gone   217
When I shall gust it last.—How came 't, Camillo,   218
That he did stay?

CAMILLO   At the good Queen's entreaty.

LEONTES
"At the Queen's" be 't. "Good" should be pertinent,   220
But so it is, it is not. Was this taken   221
By any understanding pate but thine?

For thy conceit is soaking, will draw in   223
More than the common blocks. Not noted, is 't,   224
But of the finer natures? By some severals   225
Of headpiece extraordinary? Lower messes   226
Perchance are to this business purblind? Say.   227

CAMILLO
Business, my lord? I think most understand
Bohemia stays here longer.

LEONTES
Ha?

CAMILLO   Stays here longer.

LEONTES   Ay, but why?

CAMILLO
To satisfy Your Highness and the entreaties
Of our most gracious mistress.

LEONTES   Satisfy?   232
Th'entreaties of your mistress? Satisfy?
Let that suffice. I have trusted thee, Camillo,
With all the nearest things to my heart, as well   235
My chamber councils, wherein, priestlike, thou   236
Hast cleansed my bosom. I from thee departed
Thy penitent reformed. But we have been
Deceived in thy integrity, deceived
In that which seems so.

CAMILLO   Be it forbid, my lord!   240

LEONTES
To bide upon 't, thou art not honest; or,   241
If thou inclin'st that way, thou art a coward,   242
Which hoxes honesty behind, restraining   243
From course required; or else thou must be counted   244
A servant grafted in my serious trust   245
And therein negligent; or else a fool
That see'st a game played home, the rich stake drawn,   247
And tak'st it all for jest.

CAMILLO   My gracious lord,
I may be negligent, foolish, and fearful;
In every one of these no man is free
But that his negligence, his folly, fear,
Among the infinite doings of the world
Sometime puts forth. In your affairs, my lord,   253
If ever I were willful-negligent,
It was my folly; if industriously   255
I played the fool, it was my negligence,
Not weighing well the end; if ever fearful
To do a thing where I the issue doubted,   258

---

194 **sluiced** drawn off, as by a sluice. (The water in his pond, so to speak, has been drawn off by a cheating neighbor.)   197 **gates** sluice gates, suggestive of the wife's chastity that has been opened and robbed   199 **revolted** unfaithful   200 **Physic** Medicine   201 **It . . . planet** i.e., This unchastity is like the planet Venus.   **strike** blast, destroy by a malign influence   202 **predominant** in the ascendant. (Said of a planet.)   **think it** be assured of this   204 **barricado** barricade.   **Know 't** Be certain of this   206 **bag and baggage** (With sexual suggestion, as earlier in *dagger* [line 156], *sluiced, gates, let in and out,* etc.)   **on 's** of us   213 **still came home** always came back to the ship, failed to hold.   215 **material** important.   216 **They're . . . already** People are already onto my situation.   **rounding** whispering, gossiping   217 **a so-forth** a so-and-so, a you-know-what.   218 **gust** taste, i.e., hear of   220 **pertinent** i.e., appropriately applied   221 **so it is** as things stand.   **taken** perceived

223 **conceit is soaking** understanding is receptive   224 **blocks** blockheads.   225 **But . . . natures** except by those of rarefied intellect.   **severals** individuals   226 **Lower messes** Those who sit lower at table, i.e., inferior persons   227 **purblind** totally blind.   232 **Satisfy?** (Leontes takes the word in a sexual sense.)   235–6 **as well . . . councils** as well as with my private affairs   240 **Be it forbid** i.e., God forbid I should do such a thing   241–4 **To bide . . . required** If you hold back from saying what you think, you are not being honest; or, if you would like to speak but remain silent, you are a coward, allowing frankness to be hamstrung or shackled from carrying out the duty it should perform   245 **grafted . . . trust** taken into my complete confidence. (*Grafted* means "deeply embedded," like a graft.)   247 **home** i.e., for keeps, in earnest. (With perhaps a sexual double meaning, continued in *rich stake drawn*.)   **drawn** won   253 **Sometime puts forth** sometimes shows itself.   255 **industriously** deliberately   258 **the issue doubted** feared the outcome

Whereof the execution did cry out   259
Against the nonperformance, 'twas a fear   260
Which oft infects the wisest. These, my lord,
Are such allowed infirmities that honesty   262
Is never free of. But, beseech Your Grace,
Be plainer with me. Let me know my trespass
By its own visage. If I then deny it,   265
'Tis none of mine.

LEONTES   Ha' not you seen, Camillo—
But that's past doubt; you have, or your eyeglass   267
Is thicker than a cuckold's horn—or heard—   268
For to a vision so apparent, rumor   269
Cannot be mute—or thought—for cogitation
Resides not in that man that does not think—   271
My wife is slippery? If thou wilt confess,
Or else be impudently negative   273
To have nor eyes nor ears nor thought, then say   274
My wife's a hobbyhorse, deserves a name   275
As rank as any flax-wench that puts to   276
Before her trothplight. Say't and justify't.   277

CAMILLO
I would not be a stander-by to hear
My sovereign mistress clouded so without
My present vengeance taken. 'Shrew my heart,   280
You never spoke what did become you less
Than this, which to reiterate were sin   282
As deep as that, though true.

LEONTES   Is whispering nothing?   283
Is leaning cheek to cheek? Is meeting noses?
Kissing with inside lip? Stopping the career   285
Of laughter with a sigh—a note infallible
Of breaking honesty? Horsing foot on foot?   287
Skulking in corners? Wishing clocks more swift,
Hours minutes, noon midnight? And all eyes   289
Blind with the pin and web but theirs, theirs only,   290
That would unseen be wicked? Is this nothing?
Why, then the world and all that's in't is nothing,
The covering sky is nothing, Bohemia nothing,
My wife is nothing, nor nothing have these nothings,
If this be nothing.

CAMILLO   Good my lord, be cured
Of this diseased opinion, and betimes,   296
For 'tis most dangerous.

LEONTES   Say it be, 'tis true.   297

CAMILLO
No, no, my lord.

LEONTES   It is. You lie, you lie!
I say thou liest, Camillo, and I hate thee,
Pronounce thee a gross lout, a mindless slave,
Or else a hovering temporizer, that   301
Canst with thine eyes at once see good and evil,
Inclining to them both. Were my wife's liver   303
Infected as her life, she would not live   304
The running of one glass.

CAMILLO   Who does infect her?   305

LEONTES
Why, he that wears her like her medal, hanging   306
About his neck, Bohemia—who, if I
Had servants true about me, that bare eyes   308
To see alike mine honor as their profits,
Their own particular thrifts, they would do that   310
Which should undo more doing. Ay, and thou,   311
His cupbearer—whom I from meaner form   312
Have benched and reared to worship, who mayst see 313
Plainly as heaven sees earth and earth sees heaven
How I am galled—mightst bespice a cup   315
To give mine enemy a lasting wink,   316
Which draft to me were cordial.

CAMILLO   Sir, my lord,   317
I could do this, and that with no rash potion,   318
But with a ling'ring dram that should not work
Maliciously like poison. But I cannot   320
Believe this crack to be in my dread mistress,   321
So sovereignly being honorable.   322
I have loved thee—

LEONTES   Make that thy question, and go rot! 323
Dost think I am so muddy, so unsettled,   324
To appoint myself in this vexation, sully   325
The purity and whiteness of my sheets—
Which to preserve is sleep, which being spotted
Is goads, thorns, nettles, tails of wasps—
Give scandal to the blood o' th' prince my son,
Who I do think is mine and love as mine,
Without ripe moving to't? Would I do this?   331
Could man so blench?

CAMILLO   I must believe you, sir.   332
I do, and will fetch off Bohemia for't;   333
Provided that, when he's removed, Your Highness
Will take again your queen as yours at first,

259–60 Whereof . . . nonperformance in which the completion of the task showed how wrong I was in being reluctant to undertake it **262 allowed** acknowledged.   **that** as   **265 visage** face, i.e., plain appearance.   **267 eyeglass** lens of the eye   **268 cuckold's horn** (A thin sheet of horn can be seen through like a lens, though a cuckold's horn is another matter.)   **269 to a vision so apparent** about something so plainly visible   **271 think** i.e., think so   **273–4 Or . . . eyes** or, as the only possible alternative, insist impudently that you have neither eyes   **275 hobbyhorse** wanton woman   **276 flax-wench** common slut.   **puts to** engages in sex   **277 justify't** affirm it. **280 present** immediate.   **'Shrew** Beshrew, curse   **282–3 which . . . true** i.e., to repeat which accusation would be to sin as deeply as her supposed adultery, even if it were true (which it isn't).   **285 career** full gallop   **287 honesty** chastity.   **Horsing foot on foot** Placing one's foot on that of another person and then moving the feet up and down together.   **289 Hours minutes** wishing hours were minutes **290 pin and web** cataract of the eye. (The lovers wish to think themselves unobserved.)   **296 betimes** quickly   **297 Say it be** Even if it is dangerous

301 hovering wavering   **303 Inclining . . . both** being tolerant of evil along with the good.   **304 Infected as her life** as full of disease as is her moral conduct   **305 glass** hourglass.   **306 like her medal** like a miniature portrait of her, worn in a locket   **308 bare** bore, had **310 thrifts** gains   **311 undo** prevent   **312 meaner form** humbler station   **313 benched** placed on the bench of authority.   **worship** dignity, honor   **315 galled** rubbed, chafed   **316 lasting wink** everlasting closing of the eyes (in death)   **317 were cordial** would be restorative.   **318 rash** quick-acting (and therefore easily detected) **320 Maliciously** virulently   **321 crack** flaw.   **dread** worthy of awe **322 sovereignly** supremely   **323 Make . . . rot!** i.e., If you're going to question my accusations, may you rot in hell!   **324 muddy** muddle-headed   **325 To . . . vexation** to give myself this vexation   **331 ripe** ample, urgent   **332 blench** swerve (from sensible conduct). **333 fetch off** do away with; or, with deliberate ambiguity, rescue. (As also in *removed* in the next line.)

Even for your son's sake, and thereby for sealing   336
The injury of tongues in courts and kingdoms
Known and allied to yours.

LEONTES   Thou dost advise me
Even so as I mine own course have set down.
I'll give no blemish to her honor, none.

CAMILLO   My lord,
Go then, and with a countenance as clear
As friendship wears at feasts, keep with Bohemia   343
And with your queen. I am his cupbearer.
If from me he have wholesome beverage,
Account me not your servant.

LEONTES   This is all.
Do't and thou hast the one half of my heart;
Do't not, thou splitt'st thine own.

CAMILLO   I'll do't, my lord.

LEONTES
I will seem friendly, as thou hast advised me.   *Exit.*

CAMILLO
Oh, miserable lady! But, for me,
What case stand I in? I must be the poisoner
Of good Polixenes, and my ground to do't
Is the obedience to a master, one
Who in rebellion with himself will have
All that are his so too. To do this deed,   355
Promotion follows. If I could find example   356
Of thousands that had struck anointed kings
And flourished after, I'd not do't; but since   358
Nor brass, nor stone, nor parchment bears not one,   359
Let villainy itself forswear't. I must
Forsake the court. To do't or no is certain   361
To me a breakneck. Happy star reign now!   362
Here comes Bohemia.

        Enter Polixenes.

POLIXENES [*to himself*]   This is strange. Methinks
My favor here begins to warp. Not speak?—   364
Good day, Camillo.

CAMILLO   Hail, most royal sir!

POLIXENES
What is the news i'th' court?

CAMILLO   None rare, my lord.   366

POLIXENES
The King hath on him such a countenance
As he had lost some province and a region   368
Loved as he loves himself. Even now I met him
With customary compliment, when he,
Wafting his eyes to th' contrary and falling   371
A lip of much contempt, speeds from me, and

So leaves me to consider what is breeding   373
That changeth thus his manners.

CAMILLO   I dare not know, my lord.

POLIXENES
How, dare not? Do not? Do you know, and dare not?   376
Be intelligent to me. 'Tis thereabouts,   377
For to yourself what you do know you must,   378
And cannot say you dare not. Good Camillo,   379
Your changed complexions are to me a mirror
Which shows me mine changed too; for I must be   381
A party in this alteration, finding   382
Myself thus altered with't.

CAMILLO   There is a sickness
Which puts some of us in distemper, but
I cannot name the disease; and it is caught
Of you that yet are well.

POLIXENES   How? Caught of me?   386
Make me not sighted like the basilisk.   387
I have looked on thousands who have sped the better   388
By my regard, but killed none so. Camillo,   389
As you are certainly a gentleman, thereto   390
Clerklike experienced, which no less adorns   391
Our gentry than our parents' noble names,   392
In whose success we are gentle, I beseech you,   393
If you know aught which does behoove my
        knowledge
Thereof to be informed, imprison't not
In ignorant concealment.

CAMILLO   I may not answer.   396

POLIXENES
A sickness caught of me, and yet I well?
I must be answered. Dost thou hear, Camillo?
I conjure thee, by all the parts of man   399
Which honor does acknowledge, whereof the least   400
Is not this suit of mine, that thou declare   401
What incidency thou dost guess of harm   402
Is creeping toward me; how far off, how near;
Which way to be prevented, if to be;   404
If not, how best to bear it.

CAMILLO   Sir, I will tell you,
Since I am charged in honor and by him   406
That I think honorable. Therefore mark my counsel,
Which must be even as swiftly followed as
I mean to utter it, or both yourself and me

---

336 **for sealing** for the sake of silencing. (Some editors prefer *forsealing*, sealing up tight.)   343 **keep** remain in company   355 **All . . . too** i.e., all his followers like him in rebelling against the best in themselves and in obeying his worst self.   **To do** If I do   356 **If** Even if   358–9 **but . . . one** but since recorded history shows no instances of persons who have killed a king and prospered afterwards   361 **To do 't or no** i.e., Either to kill Polixenes or not to kill him   362 **breakneck** destruction, ruin.   **Happy** Propitious, favorable   364 **warp** change, shrivel, grow askew (as wood warps).   **Not speak?** (Leontes has just passed by Polixenes without speaking.)   366 **rare** noteworthy   368 **As** as if   371 **Wafting . . . contrary** averting his eyes. **falling** letting fall

373 **breeding** hatching   376 **Do not?** i.e., Or do you mean you don't know?   377 **intelligent** intelligible.   **'Tis thereabouts** It must be something of this sort, i.e., that you know and dare not tell   378–9 **For . . . dare not** i.e., for in your heart, whatever it is you know, you must in fact know, and can't claim it's a matter of not daring to know.   381–2 **for . . . alteration** i.e., for my looks must have changed, too, reflecting this change in my position   386 **Of** from   387 **sighted** provided with a gaze.   **basilisk** a fabled serpent whose gaze was fatal.   388 **sped** prospered   389 **regard** look   390–3 **thereto . . . gentle** in addition to which you are a cultivated and educated person— something that graces our gentlemanlike condition no less than the worthy name of our ancestors, by succession from whom we are made noble   396 **ignorant concealment** concealment that would keep me ignorant or that would proceed from pretended ignorance on your part.   399 **parts** obligations   400–1 **whereof . . . not** not the least of which is (to answer)   402 **incidency** likely incident   404 **if to be** if it can be (prevented)   406 **by him** i.e., by you yourself

Cry lost, and so good night!

POLIXENES   On, good Camillo.   410

CAMILLO

I am appointed him to murder you.   411

POLIXENES

By whom, Camillo?

CAMILLO   By the King.

POLIXENES   For what?

CAMILLO

He thinks, nay, with all confidence he swears,
As he had seen't or been an instrument
To vice you to't, that you have touched his queen   415
Forbiddenly.

POLIXENES   Oh, then my best blood turn
To an infected jelly, and my name
Be yoked with his that did betray the Best!   418
Turn then my freshest reputation to
A savor that may strike the dullest nostril   420
Where I arrive, and my approach be shunned,
Nay, hated too, worse than the great'st infection
That e'er was heard or read!

CAMILLO   Swear his thought over   423
By each particular star in heaven and
By all their influences, you may as well
Forbid the sea for to obey the moon   426
As or by oath remove or counsel shake   427
The fabric of his folly, whose foundation   428
Is piled upon his faith and will continue   429
The standing of his body.

POLIXENES   How should this grow?   430

CAMILLO

I know not. But I am sure 'tis safer to
Avoid what's grown than question how 'tis born.
If therefore you dare trust my honesty,
That lies enclosèd in this trunk which you   434
Shall bear along impawned, away tonight!   435
Your followers I will whisper to the business,   436
And will by twos and threes at several posterns   437
Clear them o'th' city. For myself, I'll put
My fortunes to your service, which are here
By this discovery lost. Be not uncertain,   440
For, by the honor of my parents, I
Have uttered truth, which if you seek to prove,   442
I dare not stand by; nor shall you be safer   443
Than one condemned by the King's own mouth,
     thereon
His execution sworn.

POLIXENES   I do believe thee;

I saw his heart in 's face. Give me thy hand.
Be pilot to me, and thy places shall   447
Still neighbor mine. My ships are ready, and   448
My people did expect my hence departure
Two days ago. This jealousy
Is for a precious creature. As she's rare,
Must it be great; and as his person's mighty,
Must it be violent; and as he does conceive
He is dishonored by a man which ever
Professed to him, why, his revenges must   455
In that be made more bitter. Fear o'ershades me.
Good expedition be my friend, and comfort   457
The gracious Queen, part of his theme, but nothing   458
Of his ill-ta'en suspicion! Come, Camillo,   459
I will respect thee as a father if
Thou bear'st my life off. Hence! Let us avoid.   461

CAMILLO

It is in mine authority to command
The keys of all the posterns. Please Your Highness
To take the urgent hour. Come, sir, away.   *Exeunt.*

❧

2.1

Enter Hermione, Mamillius, [and] Ladies.

HERMIONE

Take the boy to you. He so troubles me,
'Tis past enduring.

FIRST LADY [*taking Mamillius from the Queen*]
                          Come, my gracious lord,
Shall I be your playfellow?

MAMILLIUS

No, I'll none of you.

FIRST LADY   Why, my sweet lord?   4

MAMILLIUS

You'll kiss me hard and speak to me as if
I were a baby still.—I love you better.

SECOND LADY

And why so, my lord?

MAMILLIUS   Not for because   7
Your brows are blacker; yet black brows, they say,
Become some women best, so that there be not   9
Too much hair there, but in a semicircle,
Or a half-moon made with a pen.

SECOND LADY   Who taught' this?   11

MAMILLIUS

I learned it out of women's faces. Pray now,
What color are your eyebrows?

FIRST LADY   Blue, my lord.

MAMILLIUS

Nay, that's a mock. I have seen a lady's nose

---

410 good night i.e., this is the end.   **411 him** by him (Leontes), or, the one   **415 vice** force, as with a carpenter's tool, or, impel, tempt. (The *Vice* was a tempter in the morality play.)   **418 his . . . Best** the name of him (Judas) who betrayed Christ.   **420 savor** stench   **423 Swear . . . over** i.e., Even if you should deny his suspicion with oaths   **426 for to** to   **427 or . . . or** either . . . or   **428 fabric** edifice   **428–30 whose . . . body** the foundation of which is built upon an unshaken conviction and which will last as long as his body exists.   **430 How . . . grow?** How could this suspicion have arisen?   **434 trunk** body. (With a suggestion too of a traveling trunk.)   **435 impawned** i.e., as a pledge of good faith   **436 whisper to** secretly inform of and urge   **437 posterns** rear gates   **440 discovery** revelation, disclosure   **442 prove** test   **443 stand by** affirm publicly; stay

447–8 thy . . . mine your official position will always be near to me.   **455 Professed** openly professed friendship   **457–9 Good . . . suspicion!** May good speed befriend me, and may my quick departure ease the predicament of the gracious Queen, who is the object of the King's suspicions but who is guiltless of them!   **461 bear'st my life off** can get me out of this alive.   **avoid** depart.
2.1. Location: Sicilia. The royal court.
4 none of you have nothing to do with you.   **7 for because** because   **9 so** provided   **11 taught'** taught you

That has been blue, but not her eyebrows.
FIRST LADY   Hark ye,
The Queen your mother rounds apace. We shall
Present our services to a fine new prince
One of these days, and then you'd wanton with us,   18
If we would have you.
SECOND LADY   She is spread of late
Into a goodly bulk. Good time encounter her!   20
HERMIONE [*calling to her women*]
What wisdom stirs amongst you?—Come, sir, now
I am for you again. Pray you, sit by us   22
And tell 's a tale.
MAMILLIUS   Merry or sad shall 't be?
HERMIONE   As merry as you will.
MAMILLIUS
A sad tale's best for winter. I have one
Of sprites and goblins.
HERMIONE   Let's have that, good sir.
Come on, sit down. Come on, and do your best
To fright me with your sprites. You're powerful at it.
MAMILLIUS
There was a man—
HERMIONE   Nay, come sit down, then on.
                              [*Mamillius sits.*]
MAMILLIUS
Dwelt by a churchyard. I will tell it softly;
Yond crickets shall not hear it.   31
HERMIONE
Come on, then, and give't me in mine ear.
                    [*They converse privately.*]

    [*Enter*] Leontes, Antigonus, Lords, [*and others*].

LEONTES
Was he met there? His train? Camillo with him?
A LORD
Behind the tuft of pines I met them. Never
Saw I men scour so on their way. I eyed them   35
Even to their ships.
LEONTES   How blest am I
In my just censure, in my true opinion!   37
Alack, for lesser knowledge! How accurst   38
In being so blest! There may be in the cup   39
A spider steeped, and one may drink, depart,   40
And yet partake no venom, for his knowledge
Is not infected; but if one present
Th'abhorred ingredient to his eye, make known
How he hath drunk, he cracks his gorge, his sides,   44
With violent hefts. I have drunk, and seen the spider. 45
Camillo was his help in this, his pander.
There is a plot against my life, my crown.
All's true that is mistrusted. That false villain   48

Whom I employed was pre-employed by him.
He has discovered my design, and I   50
Remain a pinched thing, yea, a very trick   51
For them to play at will. How came the posterns   52
So easily open?
A LORD   By his great authority,
Which often hath no less prevailed than so
On your command.
LEONTES   I know't too well.
[*To Hermione*] Give me the boy. I am glad you did not
    nurse him.
Though he does bear some signs of me, yet you
Have too much blood in him.
HERMIONE   What is this? Sport?   59
LEONTES [*to a Lord*]
Bear the boy hence; he shall not come about her.
Away with him! And let her sport herself
With that she's big with, [*to Hermione*] for 'tis Polixenes
Has made thee swell thus.   [*Mamillius is led out.*]
HERMIONE   But I'd say he had not,   63
And I'll be sworn you would believe my saying,
Howe'er you lean to th' nayward.
LEONTES   You, my lords,   65
Look on her, mark her well. Be but about
To say "She is a goodly lady," and   67
The justice of your hearts will thereto add
"'Tis pity she's not honest, honorable."   69
Praise her but for this her without-door form,   70
Which on my faith deserves high speech, and straight 71
The shrug, the hum or ha, these petty brands   72
That calumny doth use—oh, I am out,   73
That mercy does, for calumny will sear   74
Virtue itself—these shrugs, these hums and ha's,
When you have said she's goodly, come between   76
Ere you can say she's honest. But be't known,
From him that has most cause to grieve it should be,
She's an adulteress.
HERMIONE   Should a villain say so,
The most replenished villain in the world,   80
He were as much more villain. You, my lord,   81
Do but mistake.
LEONTES   You have mistook, my lady,   82
Polixenes for Leontes. Oh, thou thing!
Which I'll not call a creature of thy place,   84
Lest barbarism, making me the precedent,
Should a like language use to all degrees   86
And mannerly distinguishment leave out   87

---

18 **wanton** sport, play   20 **Good . . . her!** May she have a happy issue!   22 **for you** ready for you   31 **crickets** i.e., the court ladies, tittering and laughing   35 **scour** scurry   37 **censure** judgment   38 **Alack . . . knowledge!** Would that there were less for me to know!   39 **blest** i.e., with knowledge (that causes unhappiness).   40 **A spider** (The superstition referred to here is that the drinker is not poisoned by the spider in the cup unless the spider is known to be there.)   44 **gorge** throat   45 **hefts** heavings, retchings.   48 **mistrusted** suspected.

50 **discovered** disclosed   51 **pinched** tortured, ridiculous.   **trick** plaything   52 **play** play with   59 **Sport?** A joke?   63 **I'd** I need only   65 **th' nayward** the contrary.   67 **goodly** attractive   69 **honest** chaste   70 **without-door** outward, external   71 **straight** straightaway, at once   72 **brands** i.e., signs, stigmas   73 **out** wrong, in error   74 **does** uses. (Leontes's point is that no one commits calumny by suggesting with a shrug that Hermione is unchaste; calumny attacks *virtue itself*, whereas Hermione has only the false appearance of virtue.)   76 **come between** interrupt   80 **replenished** complete   81 **He . . . villain** his saying so would double his villainy.   82 **mistook** taken wrongfully. (Playing bitterly on *mistake*, "misapprehend.")   84 **Which . . . place** whose exalted rank I will not desecrate by calling you what you really are   86 **like** similar.   **degrees** social ranks   87 **And . . . out** and leave out proper distinctions

Betwixt the prince and beggar. I have said
She's an adult'ress; I have said with whom.
More, she's a traitor, and Camillo is
A fedarie with her, and one that knows 91
What she should shame to know herself 92
But with her most vile principal, that she's 93
A bed-swerver, even as bad as those 94
That vulgars give bold'st titles, ay, and privy 95
To this their late escape.

HERMIONE   No, by my life, 96
Privy to none of this. How will this grieve you,
When you shall come to clearer knowledge, that
You thus have published me! Gentle my lord, 99
You scarce can right me throughly then to say 100
You did mistake.

LEONTES   No. If I mistake
In those foundations which I build upon,
The center is not big enough to bear 103
A schoolboy's top.—Away with her to prison!
He who shall speak for her is afar off guilty 105
But that he speaks.

HERMIONE   There's some ill planet reigns. 106
I must be patient till the heavens look
With an aspect more favorable. Good my lords,
I am not prone to weeping, as our sex
Commonly are, the want of which vain dew 110
Perchance shall dry your pities; but I have
That honorable grief lodged here which burns
Worse than tears drown. Beseech you all, my lords,
With thoughts so qualified as your charities 114
Shall best instruct you, measure me; and so 115
The King's will be performed!

LEONTES   Shall I be heard? 116

HERMIONE
Who is't that goes with me? Beseech Your Highness
My women may be with me, for you see
My plight requires it.—Do not weep, good fools; 119
There is no cause. When you shall know your mistress
Has deserved prison, then abound in tears
As I come out. This action I now go on 122
Is for my better grace.—Adieu, my lord. 123
I never wished to see you sorry; now
I trust I shall. My women, come, you have leave. 125

LEONTES   Go, do our bidding. Hence!
                    [Exit Queen, guarded, with Ladies.]

A LORD
Beseech Your Highness, call the Queen again.

ANTIGONUS
Be certain what you do, sir, lest your justice

Prove violence, in the which three great ones suffer:
Yourself, your queen, your son.

A LORD   For her, my lord,
I dare my life lay down and will do't, sir,
Please you t'accept it, that the Queen is spotless
I'th'eyes of heaven and to you—I mean
In this which you accuse her.

ANTIGONUS   If it prove
She's otherwise, I'll keep my stables where 135
I lodge my wife. I'll go in couples with her; 136
Than when I feel and see her no farther trust her. 137
For every inch of woman in the world,
Ay, every dram of woman's flesh is false,
If she be.

LEONTES   Hold your peaces.

A LORD   Good my lord— 140

ANTIGONUS
It is for you we speak, not for ourselves.
You are abused, and by some putter-on 142
That will be damned for't. Would I knew the villain;
I would land-damn him. Be she honor-flawed, 144
I have three daughters—the eldest is eleven,
The second and the third, nine and some five— 146
If this prove true, they'll pay for't. By mine honor,
I'll geld 'em all! Fourteen they shall not see 148
To bring false generations. They are co-heirs, 149
And I had rather glib myself than they 150
Should not produce fair issue.

LEONTES   Cease, no more! 151
You smell this business with a sense as cold
As is a dead man's nose; but I do see't and feel't
As you feel doing thus, and see withal 154
The instruments that feel.

ANTIGONUS   If it be so, 155
We need no grave to bury honesty;
There's not a grain of it the face to sweeten
Of the whole dungy earth.

LEONTES   What? Lack I credit? 158

A LORD
I had rather you did lack than I, my lord,
Upon this ground; and more it would content me 160
To have her honor true than your suspicion,
Be blamed for't how you might.

LEONTES   Why, what need we 162
Commune with you of this, but rather follow

---

91 fedarie confederate   **92–3 to know . . . principal** to acknowledge privately even with her contemptible partner   **94 bed-swerver** adulteress   **95 That . . . titles** that common people call by the rudest names.   **privy** in on the secret   **96 late** recent   **99 published** proclaimed.   **Gentle my** My noble   **100 You . . . say** you scarcely can do me full justice then merely by saying   **103 center** earth   **105 afar off** indirectly   **106 But . . . speaks** merely by speaking.   **110 want** lack **114 qualified** tempered   **115 measure** judge   **116 heard** i.e., obeyed. **119 fools** (Here, a term of endearment.)   **122 come out** am released from prison.   **122–3 The action . . . grace** What I now must undergo will ultimately make me seem more gracious in others' eyes and ennoble me by suffering.   **125 leave** permission (to attend me).

135–6 I'll . . . wife (If Hermione is an adulteress, says Antigonus, then all women are no better than animals, to be penned up and guarded suspiciously.)   **136 in couples** i.e., like two hounds leashed together and hence inseparable   **137 Than . . . her** trust her no further than I can feel her next to me and actually see her.   **140 she** i.e., Hermione   **142 abused** deceived.   **putter-on** instigator   **144 land-damn** lambaste (? Meaning uncertain.)   **146 some** about   **148 geld** sterilize, de-sex   **149 bring false generations** have illegitimate children.   **They are co-heirs** i.e., They will share my inheritance (since I have no son to inherit all)   **150 glib** castrate, geld   **151 fair issue** legitimate offspring.   **154 thus** (Leontes presumably grasps Antigonus by the arm or pinches him or tweaks his nose.)   **154–5 and see . . . feel** i.e., just as you and I see these fingers that pinch, I see in my mind's eye the amorous touching of Hermione and Polixenes. (*Withal* means "in addition.")   **158 credit** credibility.   **160 Upon this ground** in this matter   **162 we** I. (The royal "we.")

Our forceful instigation? Our prerogative   164
Calls not your counsels, but our natural goodness   165
Imparts this; which if you—or stupefied   166
Or seeming so in skill—cannot or will not   167
Relish a truth like us, inform yourselves   168
We need no more of your advice. The matter,
The loss, the gain, the ordering on't, is all   170
Properly ours.
ANTIGONUS   And I wish, my liege,
You had only in your silent judgment tried it,
Without more overture.
LEONTES   How could that be?   173
Either thou art most ignorant by age,   174
Or thou wert born a fool. Camillo's flight,
Added to their familiarity—
Which was as gross as ever touched conjecture,   177
That lacked sight only, naught for approbation   178
But only seeing, all other circumstances
Made up to th' deed—doth push on this proceeding.   180
Yet, for a greater confirmation—
For in an act of this importance 'twere
Most piteous to be wild—I have dispatched in post   183
To sacred Delphos, to Apollo's temple,   184
Cleomenes and Dion, whom you know
Of stuffed sufficiency. Now from the oracle   186
They will bring all, whose spiritual counsel had   187
Shall stop or spur me. Have I done well?
A LORD   Well done, my lord.
LEONTES
Though I am satisfied, and need no more
Than what I know, yet shall the oracle
Give rest to th' minds of others, such as he   192
Whose ignorant credulity will not
Come up to th' truth. So have we thought it good   194
From our free person she should be confined,   195
Lest that the treachery of the two fled hence
Be left her to perform. Come, follow us.
We are to speak in public, for this business
Will raise us all.
ANTIGONUS [aside]   To laughter, as I take it,   199
If the good truth were known.   Exeunt.

♣

2.2

Enter Paulina, a Gentleman, [and attendants].

PAULINA
The keeper of the prison, call to him.
Let him have knowledge who I am.
                    [The Gentleman goes to the door.]
                                        Good lady,   2
No court in Europe is too good for thee;
What dost thou then in prison?

        [Enter] Jailer.

                                    Now, good sir,
You know me, do you not?
JAILER   For a worthy lady
And one who much I honor.
PAULINA   Pray you then,
Conduct me to the Queen.
JAILER   I may not, madam.
To the contrary I have express commandment.
PAULINA
Here's ado, to lock up honesty and honor from
Th'access of gentle visitors! Is't lawful, pray you,
To see her women? Any of them? Emilia?
JAILER   So please you, madam,
To put apart these your attendants, I   13
Shall bring Emilia forth.
PAULINA   I pray now, call her.—
Withdraw yourselves.
                [Gentleman and attendants withdraw.]
JAILER   And, madam,
I must be present at your conference.
PAULINA   Well, be't so, prithee.   [Exit Jailer.]
Here's such ado, to make no stain a stain   19
As passes coloring.

        [Enter Jailer, with] Emilia.

                        Dear gentlewoman,   20
How fares our gracious lady?
EMILIA
As well as one so great and so forlorn
May hold together. On her frights and griefs—   23
Which never tender lady hath borne greater—   24
She is something before her time delivered.   25
PAULINA
A boy?
EMILIA   A daughter, and a goodly babe,
Lusty and like to live. The Queen receives   27
Much comfort in't, says, "My poor prisoner,
I am innocent as you."
PAULINA   I dare be sworn.
These dangerous unsafe lunes i'th' King, beshrew
them!   30
He must be told on't, and he shall. The office   31
Becomes a woman best; I'll take't upon me.   32

164 **Our . . . instigation** my own strong inclination.   **164–6 Our prerogative . . . this** My royal prerogative is under no obligation to consult you, but rather out of natural generosity I inform you of the
matter   **166 or** either   **167 Or . . . skill** or pretending to be stupefied
out of cunning   **168 Relish** savor, appreciate   **170 on't** of it
173 overture public disclosure.   **174 by age** through the folly of old
age   **177 as gross . . . conjecture** as palpably evident as any conjecture ever touched upon and verified   **178 approbation** proof
180 Made up added up.   **push on** urge onward   **183 wild** rash.
post haste   **184 Delphos** (See note at 3.1.2.)   **186 Of stuffed sufficiency** abundantly qualified and trustworthy.   **187 all** the whole
truth.   **had** having been obtained   **192 he** any person (such as
Antigonus)   **194 Come up to** face   **195 From** away from.   **free**
accessible   **199 raise** rouse
2.2 Location: Sicilia. A prison.

2 **Good lady** (Addressed to the absent Hermione.)   **13 put apart** dismiss   **19–20 to make . . . coloring** to make out of no stain at all a
besmirching of honor that surpasses any justification. (Expressed in a
metaphor of dyeing and painting.)   **23 On** In consequence of
24 Which than which   **25 something** somewhat. (Also in line 55.)
27 Lusty vigorous.   **like** likely   **30 lunes** fits of lunacy   **31 on't** of it
32 Becomes suits

If I prove honeymouthed, let my tongue blister   33
And never to my red-looked anger be   34
The trumpet any more. Pray you, Emilia,
Commend my best obedience to the Queen.   36
If she dares trust me with her little babe,
I'll show't the King and undertake to be
Her advocate to th' loud'st. We do not know   39
How he may soften at the sight o'th' child.
The silence often of pure innocence
Persuades when speaking fails.

EMILIA   Most worthy madam,
Your honor and your goodness is so evident
That your free undertaking cannot miss   44
A thriving issue. There is no lady living   45
So meet for this great errand. Please Your Ladyship   46
To visit the next room, I'll presently   47
Acquaint the Queen of your most noble offer,
Who but today hammered of this design,   49
But durst not tempt a minister of honor   50
Lest she should be denied.

PAULINA   Tell her, Emilia,
I'll use that tongue I have. If wit flow from't   52
As boldness from my bosom, let 't not be doubted
I shall do good.

EMILIA   Now be you blest for it!
I'll to the Queen.—Please you, come something nearer.   55

JAILER
Madam, if't please the Queen to send the babe,
I know not what I shall incur to pass it,   57
Having no warrant.

PAULINA   You need not fear it, sir.
This child was prisoner to the womb and is
By law and process of great Nature thence
Freed and enfranchised, not a party to
The anger of the King nor guilty of—
If any be—the trespass of the Queen.

JAILER   I do believe it.

PAULINA
Do not you fear. Upon mine honor, I
Will stand betwixt you and danger.   *Exeunt.*

❧

2.3

Enter Leontes.

LEONTES
Nor night nor day, no rest! It is but weakness
To bear the matter thus, mere weakness. If
The cause were not in being—part o'th' cause,   3
She th'adulteress, for the harlot King   4

Is quite beyond mine arm, out of the blank   5
And level of my brain, plot-proof, but she   6
I can hook to me—say that she were gone,   7
Given to the fire, a moiety of my rest   8
Might come to me again.—Who's there?

[Enter a] Servant.

SERVANT   My lord?
LEONTES   How does the boy?
SERVANT
He took good rest tonight; 'tis hoped   11
His sickness is discharged.

LEONTES   To see his nobleness!
Conceiving the dishonor of his mother,   13
He straight declined, drooped, took it deeply,   14
Fastened and fixed the shame on't in himself,   15
Threw off his spirit, his appetite, his sleep,
And downright languished.—Leave me solely. Go,   17
See how he fares.   *[Exit Servant.]*
                      Fie, fie! No thought of him.   18
The very thought of my revenges that way
Recoil upon me—in himself too mighty,
And in his parties, his alliance. Let him be,   21
Until a time may serve. For present vengeance,
Take it on her. Camillo and Polixenes
Laugh at me, make their pastime at my sorrow.
They should not laugh if I could reach them, nor
Shall she, within my power.

*Enter Paulina [with a baby]; Antigonus and Lords
[trying to hold her back].*

A LORD   You must not enter.
PAULINA
Nay, rather, good my lords, be second to me.   27
Fear you his tryannous passion more, alas,
Than the Queen's life? A gracious innocent soul,
More free than he is jealous.

ANTIGONUS   That's enough.   30
SERVANT
Madam, he hath not slept tonight, commanded
None should come at him.

PAULINA   Not so hot, good sir.
I come to bring him sleep. 'Tis such as you,
That creep like shadows by him and do sigh
At each his needless heavings, such as you   35
Nourish the cause of his awaking. I   36
Do come with words as medicinal as true,
Honest as either, to purge him of that humor   38
That presses him from sleep.

LEONTES   What noise there, ho?

33 blister (It was popularly supposed that lying blistered the tongue.)
34 red-looked red-faced   **36 Commend** deliver   **39 to th' loud'st** as
loudly as I can.   **44 free** generous   **45 thriving issue** successful outcome.   **46 meet** suited.   **Please** If it please   **47 presently** at once
49 hammered of mused upon   **50 tempt** solicit (to serve as ambassador in such a case)   **52 wit** wisdom   **55 come . . . nearer** i.e., come
into the next room (as in lines 46–7).   **57 to pass it** if I let it pass
2.3. Location: Sicilia. The royal court.
3 not in being dead   **4 harlot** lewd. (Originally applied to either sex.)

5–6 out . . . level beyond the range. (Archery terms: *blank* is the center
of the target or the close range needed for a direct shot at it, as in
"point-blank"; *level* is the action of aiming.)   **7 hook** (As with grappling hooks.)   **8 Given to the fire** burned at the stake (as a traitor
conspiring against the King).   **moiety** portion   **11 tonight** last night
13 Conceiving Grasping the enormity of   **14 straight** immediately
15 on't of it   17 solely alone.   **18 him** i.e., Polixenes.   **21 his parties
. . . alliance** his supporters and allies.   **27 be second to** aid, second
30 free innocent   **35 heavings** sighs or groans   **36 awaking** inability
to sleep.   **38 humor** distemper

PAULINA
  No noise, my lord, but needful conference
  About some gossips for Your Highness.
LEONTES   How?   41
  Away with that audacious lady! Antigonus,
  I charged thee that she should not come about me.
  I knew she would.
ANTIGONUS   I told her so, my lord,
  On your displeasure's peril and on mine,
  She should not visit you.
LEONTES   What, canst not rule her?
PAULINA
  From all dishonesty he can. In this,
  Unless he take the course that you have done—
  Commit me for committing honor—trust it,   49
  He shall not rule me.
ANTIGONUS   La you now, you hear!   50
  When she will take the rein I let her run,
  But she'll not stumble.
PAULINA   Good my liege, I come—
  And, I beseech you hear me, who professes
  Myself your loyal servant, your physician,
  Your most obedient counselor, yet that dares
  Less appear so in comforting your evils   56
  Than such as most seem yours—I say, I come   57
  From your good queen.
LEONTES Good queen?
PAULINA
  Good queen, my lord, good queen, I say good queen,
  And would by combat make her good, so were I   61
  A man, the worst about you.
LEONTES [to Lords]   Force her hence.   62
PAULINA
  Let him that makes but trifles of his eyes
  First hand me. On mine own accord I'll off,
  But first I'll do my errand. The good Queen,
  For she is good, hath brought you forth a daughter—
  Here 'tis—commends it to your blessing.
                    [She lays down the baby.]
LEONTES   Out!
  A mankind witch! Hence with her, out o' door!   68
  A most intelligencing bawd!
PAULINA   Not so.   69
  I am as ignorant in that as you
  In so entitling me, and no less honest
  Than you are mad; which is enough, I'll warrant,
  As this world goes, to pass for honest.
LEONTES [to Lords]   Traitors!
  Will you not push her out? [To Antigonus] Give her the
    bastard.
  Thou dotard, thou art woman-tired, unroosted   75

By thy Dame Partlet here. Take up the bastard!   76
Take't up, I say. Give't to thy crone.
PAULINA [to Antigonus]   Forever
  Unvenerable be thy hands if thou
  Tak'st up the Princess by that forcèd baseness   79
  Which he has put upon't!
LEONTES   He dreads his wife.
PAULINA
  So I would you did. Then 'twere past all doubt
  You'd call your children yours.
LEONTES   A nest of traitors!
ANTIGONUS
  I am none, by this good light.
PAULINA   Nor I, nor any   83
  But one that's here, and that's himself; for he
  The sacred honor of himself, his queen's,
  His hopeful son's, his babe's, betrays to slander,
  Whose sting is sharper than the sword's; and will
    not—
  For, as the case now stands, it is a curse   88
  He cannot be compelled to't—once remove   89
  The root of his opinion, which is rotten   90
  As ever oak or stone was sound.
LEONTES   A callet   91
  Of boundless tongue, who late hath beat her husband   92
  And now baits me! This brat is none of mine;   93
  It is the issue of Polixenes.
  Hence with it, and together with the dam
  Commit them to the fire!
PAULINA   It is yours;
  And, might we lay th'old proverb to your charge,
  So like you, 'tis the worse. Behold, my lords,   98
  Although the print be little, the whole matter
  And copy of the father—eye, nose, lip,
  The trick of 's frown, his forehead, nay, the valley,   101
  The pretty dimples of his chin and cheek, his smiles,
  The very mold and frame of hand, nail, finger.
  And thou, good goddess Nature, which hast made it
  So like to him that got it, if thou hast   105
  The ordering of the mind too, 'mongst all colors
  No yellow in't, lest she suspect, as he does,   107
  Her children not her husband's!
LEONTES   A gross hag!
  And, lozel, thou art worthy to be hanged,   109
  That wilt not stay her tongue.
ANTIGONUS   Hang all the husbands   110
  That cannot do that feat, you'll leave yourself

---

41 gossips godparents for the baby at its baptism **49 Commit** i.e., to prison **50 La . . . hear!** i.e., There now, you hear how she will go on talking! **56–7 in comforting . . . yours** when it comes to encouraging your evil courses than those flatterers who seem to be your most loyal servants **61 by combat** by trial by combat. **make** prove **62 worst** least manly, or, lowest in rank **68 mankind** masculine, behaving like a man **69 intelligencing bawd** acting as go-between and spy (for the Queen and Polixenes). **75 woman-tired** henpecked. (From *tire* in falconry, meaning "tear with the beak.") **unroosted** driven from perch

76 Partlet or Pertilote, a common name for a hen (as in *Reynard the Fox* and in Chaucer's "Nun's Priest's Tale") **79 by that forcèd baseness** under that wrongfully imposed name of bastard **83 by this good light** by the light of day. (A common oath.) **88–90 as . . . opinion** i.e., since he is King, he regrettably can't be compelled to change his deeply rooted opinion **91 callet** scold **92 late** recently **93 baits** (With a pun on *beat* in the previous line, pronounced "bate.") **98 So . . . worse** he's so like you that he fares the worse for it. **101 trick** characteristic expression. **valley** cleft above the upper lip **105 got** begot **107 No yellow** let there be no yellow, i.e., the color of jealousy. (A chaste woman could hardly expect that her own children are illegitimate, but Paulina may be hyperbolically ridiculing Leontes's suspicions.) **109 lozel** worthless person, scoundrel. (Addressed to Antigonus.) **110 stay** restrain

Hardly one subject.
LEONTES   Once more, take her hence.
PAULINA
A most unworthy and unnatural lord
Can do no more.
LEONTES   I'll ha' thee burnt.
PAULINA   I care not.
It is an heretic that makes the fire,   115
Not she which burns in't. I'll not call you tyrant;   116
But this most cruel usage of your queen,
Not able to produce more accusation   118
Than your own weak-hinged fancy, something savors
Of tyranny and will ignoble make you,
Yea, scandalous to the world.
LEONTES [*to Antigonus*]   On your allegiance,
Out of the chamber with her! Were I a tyrant,
Where were her life? She durst not call me so   123
If she did know me one. Away with her!
PAULINA
I pray you, do not push me; I'll be gone.
Look to your babe, my lord; 'tis yours. Jove send her
A better guiding spirit!—What needs these hands?   127
You that are thus so tender o'er his follies
Will never do him good, not one of you.
So, so. Farewell, we are gone.   *Exit.*
LEONTES [*to Antigonus*]
Thou, traitor, hast set on thy wife to this.
My child? Away with't! Even thou, that hast
A heart so tender o'er it, take it hence
And see it instantly consumed with fire;
Even thou and none but thou. Take it up straight.
Within this hour bring me word 'tis done,
And by good testimony, or I'll seize thy life,
With what thou else call'st thine. If thou refuse
And wilt encounter with my wrath, say so;
The bastard brains with these my proper hands   140
Shall I dash out. Go, take it to the fire,
For thou set'st on thy wife.
ANTIGONUS   I did not, sir.
These lords, my noble fellows, if they please,
Can clear me in't.
LORDS   We can. My royal liege,
He is not guilty of her coming hither.
LEONTES You're liars all.
A LORD
Beseech Your Highness, give us better credit.   147
We have always truly served you, and beseech'   148
So to esteem of us; and on our knees we beg,
As recompense of our dear services   150
Past and to come, that you do change this purpose,
Which being so horrible, so bloody, must
Lead on to some foul issue. We all kneel.

LEONTES
I am a feather for each wind that blows.
Shall I live on to see this bastard kneel
And call me father? Better burn it now
Than curse it then. But be it; let it live.
It shall not neither. [*To Antigonus*] You, sir, come you
     hither,
You that have been so tenderly officious
With Lady Margery, your midwife there,   160
To save this bastard's life—for 'tis a bastard,
So sure as this beard's gray. What will you adventure 162
To save this brat's life?
ANTIGONUS   Anything, my lord,
That my ability may undergo
And nobleness impose. At least thus much:
I'll pawn the little blood which I have left
To save the innocent—anything possible.
LEONTES [*holding his sword*]
It shall be possible. Swear by this sword
Thou wilt perform my bidding.
ANTIGONUS [*his hand on the hilt*]   I will, my lord.
LEONTES
Mark and perform it, see'st thou; for the fail   170
Of any point in't shall not only be
Death to thyself but to thy lewd-tongued wife,
Whom for this time we pardon. We enjoin thee,
As thou art liegeman to us, that thou carry   174
This female bastard hence, and that thou bear it
To some remote and desert place quite out
Of our dominions, and that there thou leave it,
Without more mercy, to it own protection   178
And favor of the climate. As by strange fortune
It came to us, I do in justice charge thee,
On thy soul's peril and thy body's torture,
That thou commend it strangely to some place   182
Where chance may nurse or end it. Take it up.
ANTIGONUS [*taking up the baby*]
I swear to do this, though a present death
Had been more merciful.—Come on, poor babe.
Some powerful spirit instruct the kites and ravens
To be thy nurses! Wolves and bears, they say,
Casting their savageness aside, have done
Like offices of pity.—Sir, be prosperous
In more than this deed does require!—And blessing   190
Against this cruelty fight on thy side,
Poor thing, condemned to loss!   *Exit* [*with the baby*].
LEONTES   No, I'll not rear   192
Another's issue.

            Enter a Servant.

SERVANT   Please Your Highness, posts   193
From those you sent to th'oracle are come
An hour since. Cleomenes and Dion,

115–16 It is . . . in 't i.e., In burning me, you who would be making or
building the fire are the heretic, not me (since loss of faith in innocence is a kind of heresy), or, you can burn a woman if you like, but
it's a heretic's fire only if she is, in fact, a heretic. **118 Not able** you
not being able **123 Where . . . life?** how could she escape execution
at my command? **127 What . . . hands?** What need is there to push
me? **140 proper** own **147 credit** belief. **148 beseech'** beseech you
150 dear loyal, heartfelt

160 Margery (A derisive term, evidently equivalent to *Partlet* in line
76.) **162 this beard's** (Probably Antigonus's.) **170 see'st thou** i.e.,
do you hear. **fail** failure **174 liegeman** loyal subject **178 it** its
182 commend . . . place commit it to some foreign place **190 more**
i.e., more ways, more extent. **require** deserve. **192 loss** destruction. **193 posts** messengers

Being well arrived from Delphos, are both landed,
Hasting to th' court.
A LORD   So please you, sir, their speed
Hath been beyond account.
LEONTES   Twenty-three days   198
They have been absent. 'Tis good speed, foretells
The great Apollo suddenly will have   200
The truth of this appear. Prepare you, lords.
Summon a session, that we may arraign   202
Our most disloyal lady; for, as she hath
Been publicly accused, so shall she have
A just and open trial. While she lives
My heart will be a burden to me. Leave me,
And think upon my bidding.   *Exeunt [separately].*

❖

3.1

Enter Cleomenes and Dion.

CLEOMENES
The climate's delicate, the air most sweet,
Fertile the isle, the temple much surpassing   2
The common praise it bears.
DION   I shall report,
For most it caught me, the celestial habits—   4
Methinks I so should term them—and the reverence
Of the grave wearers. Oh, the sacrifice!
How ceremonious, solemn, and unearthly
It was i'th'offering!
CLEOMENES   But of all, the burst
And the ear-deaf'ning voice o'th'oracle,
Kin to Jove's thunder, so surprised my sense   10
That I was nothing.
DION   If th'event o'th' journey   11
Prove as successful to the Queen—O, be't so!—
As it hath been to us rare, pleasant, speedy,
The time is worth the use on't.
CLEOMENES   Great Apollo   14
Turn all to th' best! These proclamations,
So forcing faults upon Hermione,
I little like.
DION   The violent carriage of it   17
Will clear or end the business. When the oracle,
Thus by Apollo's great divine sealed up,   19
Shall the contents discover, something rare   20
Even then will rush to knowledge. Go. Fresh horses!
And gracious be the issue!   *Exeunt.*

198 **beyond account** unprecedented, or, beyond explanation.
200 **suddenly** at once   202 **session** trial
3.1. Location: Sicilia. On the way to Leontes's court.
2 **isle** (Shakespeare follows Greene's *Pandosto* in fictitiously placing Delphi on an island. Delphi, sometimes known as Delphos [see 2.1.184, 2.3.196, and 3.2.126], was often confused with Delos, the island birthplace of Apollo and location also of an oracle.)   4 **habits** vestments   10 **surprised** overwhelmed   11 **th'event** the outcome
14 **is worth . . . on't** has been well employed.   17 **carriage** execution, management   19 **great divine** chief priest   20 **discover** reveal

3.2

Enter Leontes, Lords, [and] Officers.

LEONTES
This sessions, to our great grief we pronounce,
Even pushes 'gainst our heart: the party tried
The daughter of a king, our wife, and one
Of us too much beloved. Let us be cleared   4
Of being tyrannous, since we so openly
Proceed in justice, which shall have due course
Even to the guilt or the purgation.   7
Produce the prisoner.
OFFICER
It is His Highness' pleasure that the Queen
Appear in person here in court. Silence!

*[Enter] Hermione, as to her trial, [Paulina, and]
Ladies.*

LEONTES   Read the indictment.
OFFICER *[reads]* "Hermione, Queen to the worthy
Leontes, King of Sicilia, thou art here accused and ar-
raigned of high treason, in committing adultery with
Polixenes, King of Bohemia, and conspiring with
Camillo to take away the life of our sovereign lord the
King, thy royal husband; the pretense whereof being   17
by circumstances partly laid open, thou, Hermione,
contrary to the faith and allegiance of a true subject,
didst counsel and aid them, for their better safety, to
fly away by night."
HERMIONE
Since what I am to say must be but that
Which contradicts my accusation, and
The testimony on my part no other
But what comes from myself, it shall scarce boot me   25
To say "not guilty." Mine integrity,
Being counted falsehood, shall, as I express it,
Be so received. But thus: if powers divine
Behold our human actions, as they do,
I doubt not then but innocence shall make
False accusation blush and tyranny
Tremble at patience. You, my lord, best know,
Who least will seem to do so, my past life
Hath been as continent, as chaste, as true
As I am now unhappy; which is more
Than history can pattern, though devised   36
And played to take spectators. For behold me—   37
A fellow of the royal bed, which owe   38
A moiety of the throne, a great king's daughter,   39
The mother to a hopeful prince—here standing
To prate and talk for life and honor 'fore

3.2. Location: Sicilia. A place of justice, probably at court.
4 **Of us** by me   7 **purgation** acquittal.   17 **pretense** purpose, design
25 **boot** avail   36 **history** story, drama.   **pattern** show a similar example for   37 **take** please, charm   38 **which owe** who owns
39 **moiety** share

Who please to come and hear. For life, I prize it 42
As I weigh grief, which I would spare. For honor, 43
'Tis a derivative from me to mine, 44
And only that I stand for. I appeal 45
To your own conscience, sir, before Polixenes 46
Came to your court, how I was in your grace,
How merited to be so; since he came,
With what encounter so uncurrent I 49
Have strained t'appear thus; if one jot beyond 50
The bound of honor, or in act or will
That way inclining, hardened be the hearts 52
Of all that hear me, and my near'st of kin
Cry "Fie" upon my grave!

LEONTES   I ne'er heard yet
That any of these bolder vices wanted 55
Less impudence to gainsay what they did 56
Than to perform it first.

HERMIONE   That's true enough,
Though 'tis a saying, sir, not due to me. 58

LEONTES
You will not own it.

HERMIONE   More than mistress of 59
Which comes to me in name of fault, I must not 60
At all acknowledge. For Polixenes, 61
With whom I am accused, I do confess
I loved him as in honor he required; 63
With such a kind of love as might become
A lady like me; with a love even such,
So, and no other, as yourself commanded;
Which not to have done I think had been in me
Both disobedience and ingratitude
To you and toward your friend, whose love had
    spoke, 69
Even since it could speak, from an infant, freely 70
That it was yours. Now, for conspiracy, 71
I know not how it tastes, though it be dished 72
For me to try how. All I know of it
Is that Camillo was an honest man;
And why he left your court, the gods themselves,
Wotting no more than I, are ignorant. 76

LEONTES
You knew of his departure, as you know
What you have underta'en to do in 's absence.

HERMIONE Sir,
You speak a language that I understand not.
My life stands in the level of your dreams, 81

Which I'll lay down.

LEONTES   Your actions are my dreams. 82
You had a bastard by Polixenes,
And I but dreamed it. As you were past all shame—
Those of your fact are so—so past all truth, 85
Which to deny concerns more than avails; for as 86
Thy brat hath been cast out, like to itself, 87
No father owning it—which is indeed
More criminal in thee than it—so thou
Shalt feel our justice, in whose easiest passage 90
Look for no less than death.

HERMIONE   Sir, spare your threats. 91
The bug which you would fright me with I seek. 92
To me can life be no commodity. 93
The crown and comfort of my life, your favor,
I do give lost, for I do feel it gone, 95
But know not how it went. My second joy
And firstfruits of my body, from his presence
I am barred, like one infectious. My third comfort,
Starred most unluckily, is from my breast, 99
The innocent milk in it most innocent mouth, 100
Haled out to murder; myself on every post 101
Proclaimed a strumpet; with immodest hatred 102
The childbed privilege denied, which longs 103
To women of all fashion; lastly, hurried 104
Here to this place, i'th'open air, before
I have got strength of limit. Now, my liege, 106
Tell me what blessings I have here alive
That I should fear to die? Therefore proceed.
But yet hear this; mistake me not. No life, 109
I prize it not a straw. But for mine honor,
Which I would free, if I shall be condemned 111
Upon surmises, all proofs sleeping else
But what your jealousies awake, I tell you
'Tis rigor and not law. Your Honors all, 114
I do refer me to the oracle.
Apollo be my judge!

A LORD   This your request
Is altogether just. Therefore bring forth,
And in Apollo's name, his oracle.

                        [*Exeunt certain Officers.*]

HERMIONE
The Emperor of Russia was my father.
Oh, that he were alive and here beholding
His daughter's trial! That he did but see

---

42 Who please whoever chooses   **42–5 For . . . stand for** As for life, I value it as I value grief, and would as willingly do without; as for honor, it is transmitted from me to my descendants, and that only I make a stand for.   **46 conscience** consideration, inward knowledge   **49–50 With . . . thus** (I ask) by what behavior so unacceptable I have transgressed so that I appear thus (in disgrace and on trial)   **52 hardened** hardened against me   **55–6 wanted Less** were more lacking in   **58 due** applicable   **59–61 More . . . acknowledge** I must not acknowledge more faults than I actually have.   **61 For** As for   **63 required** deserved   **69–71 your friend . . . yours** i.e., Polixenes, who professed love for you from earliest childhood (as you for him).   **71 for** as for   **72 though . . . dished** even if it were to be served up   **76 Wotting** supposing they know   **81 level** aim, range

82 Which i.e., my life.   **Your . . . dreams** i.e., You have performed what I have fantasized, and what you have done preys on my mind. **85 Those of your fact** All those who do what you did   **86 Which . . . avails** your denial of which is understandable, but it won't do you any good   **87 like to itself** as an outcast, fatherless brat ought to be **90–1 in whose . . . death** i.e., which will impose the death sentence at least, perhaps torture also.   **92 bug** bugbear, bogey, imaginary object of terror   **93 commodity** asset   **95 give** reckon as, or give up for **99 Starred most unluckily** born under a most unlucky star   **100 it** its **101 post** posting place for public notices   **102 immodest** immoderate **103 The childbed . . . longs** denied the privilege of bedrest after giving birth, something that is the right   **104 all fashion** every rank   **106 got . . . limit** regained my strength after having borne a child.   **109 No life** i.e., I do not ask for life   **111 free** vindicate   **114 rigor** tyranny

The flatness of my misery, yet with eyes   122
Of pity, not revenge!

[*Enter Officers, with*] Cleomenes [*and*] Dion.

OFFICER [*holding a sword*]
You here shall swear upon this sword of justice
That you, Cleomenes and Dion, have
Been both at Delphos, and from thence have brought
This sealed up oracle, by the hand delivered
Of great Apollo's priest, and that since then
You have not dared to break the holy seal
Nor read the secrets in't.
CLEOMENES, DION   All this we swear.
LEONTES
Break up the seals and read.   131
OFFICER [*reads*]   "Hermione is chaste, Polixenes blame-
less, Camillo a true subject, Leontes a jealous tyrant,
his innocent babe truly begotten, and the King shall
live without an heir if that which is lost be not
found."
LORDS
Now blessèd be the great Apollo!
HERMIONE   Praised!
LEONTES
Hast thou read truth?
OFFICER   Ay, my lord, even so
As it is here set down.
LEONTES
There is no truth at all i'th'oracle.
The sessions shall proceed. This is mere falsehood.

[*Enter a Servant.*]

SERVANT
My lord the King, the King!
LEONTES   What is the business?
SERVANT
Oh, sir, I shall be hated to report it!   143
The Prince your son, with mere conceit and fear   144
Of the Queen's speed, is gone.
LEONTES   How? Gone?
SERVANT   Is dead.   145
LEONTES
Apollo's angry, and the heavens themselves
Do strike at my injustice. [*Hermione swoons.*] How now
there?
PAULINA
This news is mortal to the Queen. Look down
And see what death is doing.
LEONTES   Take her hence.
Her heart is but o'ercharged; she will recover.
I have too much believed mine own suspicion.
Beseech you, tenderly apply to her
Some remedies for life.
     [*Exeunt Paulina and Ladies, with Hermione.*]
                    Apollo, pardon
My great profaneness 'gainst thine oracle!
I'll reconcile me to Polixenes,

New woo my queen, recall the good Camillo,
Whom I proclaim a man of truth, of mercy;
For, being transported by my jealousies
To bloody thoughts and to revenge, I chose
Camillo for the minister to poison
My friend Polixenes; which had been done,
But that the good mind of Camillo tardied   162
My swift command, though I with death and with
Reward did threaten and encourage him,
Not doing it and being done. He, most humane   165
And filled with honor, to my kingly guest
Unclasped my practice, quit his fortunes here,   167
Which you knew great, and to the hazard
Of all incertainties himself commended,   169
No richer than his honor. How he glisters   170
Through my rust! And how his piety   171
Does my deeds make the blacker!

[*Enter Paulina.*]

PAULINA   Woe the while!
Oh, cut my lace, lest my heart, cracking it,   173
Break too!
A LORD   What fit is this, good lady?
PAULINA
What studied torments, tyrant, hast for me?   175
What wheels, racks, fires? What flaying, boiling   176
In leads or oils? What old or newer torture
Must I receive, whose every word deserves   178
To taste of thy most worst? Thy tyranny,   179
Together working with thy jealousies—
Fancies too weak for boys, too green and idle   181
For girls of nine—oh, think what they have done,
And then run mad indeed, stark mad! For all
Thy bygone fooleries were but spices of it.   184
That thou betrayed'st Polixenes, 'twas nothing;
That did but show thee, of a fool, inconstant   186
And damnable ingrateful. Nor was 't much
Thou wouldst have poisoned good Camillo's honor,
To have him kill a king—poor trespasses,   189
More monstrous standing by; whereof I reckon   190
The casting forth to crows thy baby daughter   191
To be or none or little, though a devil   192
Would have shed water out of fire ere done't.   193
Nor is't directly laid to thee, the death
Of the young Prince, whose honorable thoughts,
Thoughts high for one so tender, cleft the heart   196
That could conceive a gross and foolish sire   197

---

162 **tardied** delayed   165 **Not . . . done** i.e., death if he did not do it
and reward if he did.   167 **Unclasped my practice** disclosed my plot
169 **himself commended** entrusted himself   170 **No richer than** with
no riches except   170–1 **How . . . rust!** How he shines in contrast with
my fault!   173 **my lace** the lace of my stays   175 **studied** ingeniously
devised   176 **wheels . . . flaying** (Various methods of torture: being
stretched on a wheel or rack until the bones are broken or pulled
apart at the joints, being burned or skinned alive.)   178–9 **whose . . .
worst?** I, whose every word seems to invite your severest punishment?   181 **idle** foolish   184 **spices** foretastes, samples   186 **of** for
189 **To have** by having.   **poor** slight   190 **More . . . by** when more
monstrous sins are at hand for comparison   191 **crows** carrion birds
192 **or none** either none   193 **shed . . . fire** wept from his fiery eyes or
while surrounded by hellfire   196 **tender** young   197 **conceive**
apprehend that

---

122 **flatness** boundlessness   131 **up** open   143 **to report** for reporting
144 **conceit and fear** i.e., anxious concern   145 **speed** fate, fortune

Blemished his gracious dam. This is not, no,   198
Laid to thy answer. But the last—Oh, lords,   199
When I have said, cry woe! The Queen, the Queen,   200
The sweet'st, dear'st creature's dead, and vengeance
   for't
Not dropped down yet.

A LORD   The higher powers forbid!

PAULINA
I say she's dead. I'll swear't. If word nor oath
Prevail not, go and see. If you can bring
Tincture or luster in her lip, her eye,   205
Heat outwardly or breath within, I'll serve you
As I would do the gods. But, O thou tyrant!
Do not repent these things, for they are heavier
Than all thy woes can stir. Therefore betake thee   209
To nothing but despair. A thousand knees
Ten thousand years together, naked, fasting,
Upon a barren mountain, and still winter   212
In storm perpetual, could not move the gods
To look that way thou wert.

LEONTES   Go on, go on.   214
Thou canst not speak too much. I have deserved
All tongues to talk their bitt'rest.

A LORD [to Paulina]   Say no more.
Howe'er the business goes, you have made fault
I'th' boldness of your speech.

PAULINA   I am sorry for't.
All faults I make, when I shall come to know them,   219
I do repent. Alas, I have showed too much
The rashness of a woman! He is touched
To th' noble heart. What's gone and what's past help
Should be past grief.—Do not receive affliction   223
At my petition. I beseech you, rather   224
Let me be punished, that have minded you   225
Of what you should forget. Now, good my liege,
Sir, royal sir, forgive a foolish woman.
The love I bore your queen—lo, fool again!
I'll speak of her no more, nor of your children;
I'll not remember you of my own lord,   230
Who is lost too. Take your patience to you,   231
And I'll say nothing.

LEONTES   Thou didst speak but well
When most the truth, which I receive much better
Than to be pitied of thee. Prithee, bring me
To the dead bodies of my queen and son.
One grave shall be for both. Upon them shall
The causes of their death appear, unto
Our shame perpetual. Once a day I'll visit
The chapel where they lie, and tears shed there
Shall be my recreation. So long as nature   240
Will bear up with this exercise, so long

I daily vow to use it. Come and lead me
To these sorrows.   *Exeunt.*

❧

3.3

Enter Antigonus [and] a Mariner, [with a] babe.

ANTIGONUS
Thou art perfect then, our ship hath touched upon   1
The deserts of Bohemia?

MARINER   Ay, my lord, and fear   2
We have landed in ill time. The skies look grimly
And threaten present blusters. In my conscience,   4
The heavens with that we have in hand are angry
And frown upon 's.

ANTIGONUS   Their sacred wills be done! Go, get aboard;
Look to thy bark. I'll not be long before   8
I call upon thee.

MARINER   Make your best haste, and go not
Too far i'th' land. 'Tis like to be loud weather.   10
Besides, this place is famous for the creatures
Of prey that keep upon't.

ANTIGONUS   Go thou away.   12
I'll follow instantly.

MARINER   I am glad at heart
To be so rid o'th' business.   *Exit.*

ANTIGONUS   Come, poor babe.
I have heard, but not believed, the spirits o'th' dead
May walk again. If such thing be, thy mother
Appeared to me last night, for ne'er was dream
So like a waking. To me comes a creature,
Sometimes her head on one side, some another;   19
I never saw a vessel of like sorrow,
So filled and so becoming. In pure white robes,   21
Like very sanctity, she did approach
My cabin where I lay, thrice bowed before me,
And, gasping to begin some speech, her eyes
Became two spouts. The fury spent, anon
Did this break from her: "Good Antigonus,
Since fate, against thy better disposition,
Hath made thy person for the thrower-out
Of my poor babe, according to thine oath,
Places remote enough are in Bohemia;
There weep and leave it crying. And, for the babe   31
Is counted lost forever, Perdita,   32
I prithee, call't. For this ungentle business   33
Put on thee by my lord, thou ne'er shalt see
Thy wife Paulina more." And so, with shrieks,
She melted into air. Affrighted much,
I did in time collect myself and thought
This was so and no slumber. Dreams are toys;   38

---

198 dam mother.   **199 Laid . . . answer** presented as a charge that
you must answer.   **200 said** finished speaking   **205 Tincture** color
209 woes can stir penance can remove.   **212 still** always   **214 To look
. . . wert** to regard you.   **219 I make** that I make   **223–4 Do . . . petition** Do not afflict yourself with remorse at my urging.   **225 minded
you** put you in mind   **230 remember** remind   **231 Take . . . you** Arm
yourself with patience   **240 my recreation** (1) my sole diversion (2) my
spiritual regeneration.   **nature** my physical being

3.3 Location: Bohemia. The seacoast.
1 perfect certain   **2 deserts of Bohemia** i.e., deserted region on the
coast. (Shakespeare follows Greene's *Pandosto* in giving Bohemia a
seacoast.)   **4 present** immediate.   **conscience** opinion   **8 bark** ship.
10 like likely.   **loud** stormy   **12 keep upon't** inhabit it.   **19 some
another** sometimes the other   **21 So . . . becoming** i.e., so filled with
sorrow and able to bear it so gracefully.   **31 for** because   **32 Perdita**
i.e., the lost one   **33 ungentle** ignoble   **38 toys** trifles

Yet for this once, yea, superstitiously,
I will be squared by this. I do believe   40
Hermione hath suffered death, and that
Apollo would, this being indeed the issue
Of King Polixenes, it should here be laid,
Either for life or death, upon the earth
Of its right father. Blossom, speed thee well!
                                    [*He lays down the baby.*]
There lie, and there thy character; there these,   46
           [*He places a box and a fardel beside the baby.*]
Which may, if fortune please, both breed thee, pretty,   47
And still rest thine. [*Thunder.*] The storm begins. Poor
       wretch,   48
That for thy mother's fault art thus exposed
To loss and what may follow! Weep I cannot,   50
But my heart bleeds; and most accurst am I
To be by oath enjoined to this. Farewell!
The day frowns more and more. Thou'rt like to have
A lullaby too rough. I never saw
The heavens so dim by day. A savage clamor!
Well may I get aboard! This is the chase.
I am gone forever!   *Exit, pursued by a bear.*

              [*Enter a*] Shepherd.

SHEPHERD   I would there were no age between ten and
three-and-twenty, or that youth would sleep out the
rest, for there is nothing in the between but getting
wenches with child, wronging the ancientry, stealing,   61
fighting—Hark you now, would any but these boiled   62
brains of nineteen and two-and-twenty hunt this   63
weather? They have scared away two of my best sheep,
which I fear the wolf will sooner find than the master.
If anywhere I have them, 'tis by the seaside, browsing
of ivy. Good luck, an't be thy will! [*Seeing the child.*]   67
What have we here? Mercy on 's, a bairn, a very pretty   68
bairn! A boy or a child, I wonder? A pretty one, a very   69
pretty one. Sure some scape. Though I am not bookish,   70
yet I can read waiting-gentlewoman in the scape.
This has been some stair-work, some trunk-work,   72
some behind-door-work. They were warmer that got   73
this than the poor thing is here. I'll take it up for pity.
Yet I'll tarry till my son come; he hallooed but even
now.—Whoa, ho, hoa!   76

              Enter Clown.

CLOWN   Hilloa, loa!

SHEPHERD   What, art so near? If thou'lt see a thing to
talk on when thou art dead and rotten, come hither.
What ail'st thou, man?
CLOWN   I have seen two such sights, by sea and by
land! But I am not to say it is a sea, for it is now the sky;
betwixt the firmament and it you cannot thrust a
bodkin's point.   84
SHEPHERD   Why, boy, how is it?
CLOWN   I would you did but see how it chafes, how it
rages, how it takes up the shore! But that's not to the   87
point. Oh, the most piteous cry of the poor souls! Sometimes to see 'em, and not to see 'em; now the ship
boring the moon with her mainmast, and anon swal-
lowed with yeast and froth, as you'd thrust a cork into   91
a hogshead. And then for the land service, to see how   92
the bear tore out his shoulder bone; how he cried to
me for help and said his name was Antigonus, a nobleman. But to make an end of the ship: to see how
the sea flapdragoned it! But first, how the poor souls   96
roared and the sea mocked them, and how the poor
gentleman roared and the bear mocked him, both
roaring louder than the sea or weather.
SHEPHERD   Name of mercy, when was this, boy?
CLOWN   Now, now. I have not winked since I saw these   101
sights. The men are not yet cold under water, nor the
bear half dined on the gentleman. He's at it now.
SHEPHERD   Would I had been by, to have helped the
old man!
CLOWN   I would you had been by the ship side, to have
helped her. There your charity would have lacked
footing.   108
SHEPHERD   Heavy matters, heavy matters! But look thee
here, boy. Now bless thyself. Thou met'st with things
dying, I with things newborn. Here's a sight for thee;
look thee, a bearing cloth for a squire's child! Look   112
thee here; take up, take up, boy. Open't. So, let's see.
It was told me I should be rich by the fairies. This is
some changeling. Open't. What's within, boy?   115
                        [*The Clown opens the box.*]
CLOWN   You're a made old man. If the sins of your
youth are forgiven you, you're well to live. Gold, all   117
gold!
SHEPHERD   This is fairy gold, boy, and 'twill prove so.
Up with't, keep it close. Home, home, the next way.   120
We are lucky, boy, and to be so still requires nothing   121
but secrecy. Let my sheep go. Come, good boy, the   122
next way home.

---

40 **squared** directed in my course   46 **thy character** the written
account of you (i.e., the one that subsequently will serve to identify
Perdita).   **these** i.e., the gold and jewels found by the Shepherd, also
later used to identify her.   46.1 *box, fardel* (The box, containing gold
and jewels, is later produced by the old Shepherd and the Clown; see
4.4.758–9. They also have a *fardel*, or "bundle," consisting evidently of
the bearing cloth [3.3.112] and/or mantle [5.2.34] in which the babe
was found.)   47 **breed thee** keep you, pay for your support.   **pretty**
pretty one   48 **And still rest thine** i.e., and still provide a heritage with
what is unspent.   50 **Weep I cannot** i.e., I cannot weep as the Queen
instructed me (line 31)   61 **ancientry** old people   62–3 **boiled brains**
addlepated youths   67 **Good . . . will!** i.e., May God grant me good
luck in finding my sheep!   68 **bairn** child   69 **child** i.e., female infant
70 **scape** sexual escapade.   72–3 **stair-work . . . behind-door-work** i.e.,
sexual liaisons under or behind the stairs or using a room or a trunk for
concealment.   73 **got** begot   76.1 *Clown* country fellow, rustic.

84 **bodkin's** needle's. (A *bodkin* can also be a dagger, awl, etc.)   87 **takes
up** (1) contends with, rebukes (2) swallows   91 **yeast** foam   92 **hogshead**
large barrel. (The image is of a cork swimming in a turbulent expanse
of frothing liquid.)   **land service** (1) dish of food served on land
(2) military service on land (as distinguished from naval service);
here, the doings on land   96 **flapdragoned** swallowed as one would
a flapdragon, i.e., a raisin or the like swallowed out of burning brandy
in the game of snapdragon   101 **winked** blinked an eye   108 **footing** (1) foothold (2) establishment of a charitable foundation, one that
would provide *charity* (line 107).   112 **bearing cloth** rich cloth or
mantle in which a child was carried to its baptism   115 **changeling**
child left or taken by fairies.   117 **well to live** well-to-do.   120 **close**
secret.   **next** nearest   121–2 **to be . . . secrecy** (To talk about fairy
gifts would be to insure bad luck.)   121 **still** on a continuing basis

CLOWN   Go you the next way with your findings. I'll go
see if the bear be gone from the gentleman, and how
much he hath eaten. They are never curst but when   126
they are hungry. If there be any of him left, I'll bury it.
SHEPHERD   That's a good deed. If thou mayest discern
by that which is left of him what he is, fetch me to th'   129
sight of him.
CLOWN   Marry, will I; and you shall help to put him i'th'   131
ground.
SHEPHERD   'Tis a lucky day, boy, and we'll do good
deeds on't.   *Exeunt.*

❖

4.1

Enter Time, the Chorus.

TIME
I, that please some, try all, both joy and terror   1
Of good and bad, that makes and unfolds error,   2
Now take upon me, in the name of Time,
To use my wings. Impute it not a crime
To me or my swift passage that I slide
O'er sixteen years and leave the growth untried   6
Of that wide gap, since it is in my power
To o'erthrow law and in one self-born hour   8
To plant and o'erwhelm custom. Let me pass   9
The same I am ere ancient'st order was   10
Or what is now received. I witness to   11
The times that brought them in; so shall I do   12
To th' freshest things now reigning, and make stale
The glistering of this present as my tale   14
Now seems to it. Your patience this allowing,   15
I turn my glass and give my scene such growing   16
As you had slept between. Leontes leaving   17
Th'effects of his fond jealousies, so grieving   18
That he shuts up himself, imagine me,
Gentle spectators, that I now may be
In fair Bohemia. And remember well
I mentioned a son o'th' King's, which Florizel
I now name to you; and with speed so pace   23
To speak of Perdita, now grown in grace   24
Equal with wond'ring. What of her ensues   25
I list not prophesy; but let Time's news   26
Be known when 'tis brought forth. A shepherd's
daughter,

And what to her adheres, which follows after,   28
Is th'argument of Time. Of this allow,   29
If ever you have spent time worse ere now;
If never, yet that Time himself doth say   31
He wishes earnestly you never may.   *Exit.*

❖

4.2

Enter Polixenes and Camillo.

POLIXENES   I pray thee, good Camillo, be no more
importunate. 'Tis a sickness denying thee anything, a
death to grant this.
CAMILLO   It is fifteen years since I saw my country.   4
Though I have for the most part been aired abroad, I   5
desire to lay my bones there. Besides, the penitent
King, my master, hath sent for me, to whose feeling   7
sorrows I might be some allay—or I o'erween to think   8
so—which is another spur to my departure.
POLIXENES   As thou lov'st me, Camillo, wipe not out the
rest of thy services by leaving me now. The need I
have of thee thine own goodness hath made. Better
not to have had thee than thus to want thee. Thou,   13
having made me businesses which none without thee
can sufficiently manage, must either stay to execute
them thyself or take away with thee the very services
thou hast done; which if I have not enough
considered—as too much I cannot—to be more thank-   18
ful to thee shall be my study, and my profit therein the
heaping friendships. Of that fatal country, Sicilia,   20
prithee, speak no more, whose very naming punishes
me with the remembrance of that penitent, as thou
call'st him, and reconciled King, my brother, whose
loss of his most precious queen and children are even
now to be afresh lamented. Say to me, when saw'st
thou the Prince Florizel, my son? Kings are no less
unhappy, their issue not being gracious, than they are   27
in losing them when they have approved their virtues.   28
CAMILLO   Sir, it is three days since I saw the Prince.
What his happier affairs may be are to me unknown;
but I have missingly noted he is of late much retired   31
from court and is less frequent to his princely exercises 32
than formerly he hath appeared.
POLIXENES   I have considered so much, Camillo, and   34
with some care, so far that I have eyes under my ser-   35
vice which look upon his removedness; from whom I   36
have this intelligence, that he is seldom from the   37
house of a most homely shepherd—a man, they say,   38

---

126 curst mean, fierce   **129 what he is** what is his identity or rank
131 Marry i.e., Indeed. (Originally an oath, "by the Virgin Mary.")
4.1.
1 try test   **2 that . . . error** i.e., I who make error, thus bringing joy to
the bad and terror to the good, and then at last unfold or disclose error,
thus bringing joy to the good and terror to the bad   **6 growth untried**
developments unexplored   **8 law** any established order (including the
rule of the unity of time in a dramatic performance, conventionally
limiting the action to twenty-four hours).   **self-born** selfsame, or born
of myself (since hours are the creations of Time)   **9–11 Let . . . received**
Let me continue as I have been from before the beginning of time to the
present.   **12 them** i.e., law and custom   **14 glistering** glittering shine
15 seems to it seems (stale) when compared with the present.
16 glass hourglass   **17 As** as if   **18 fond** foolish   **23 pace** proceed
24–5 now . . . wondering now grown so gracious (and graceful) as to
inspire wonderment.   **26 list not** do not care to

28 to her adheres concerns her   **29 th'argument** the subject matter
31 yet that i.e., yet allow that
4.2. Location: Bohemia. The court of Polixenes.
4 fifteen (Compare "sixteen" at 4.1.6.)   **5 been aired abroad** lived
abroad   **7 feeling** heartfelt   **8 allay** means of abatement.   **o'erween**
am presumptuous enough   **13 want** lack   **18 considered** rewarded
20 heaping friendships accumulation of your kind services and our
mutual affection.   **27 their . . . gracious** if their children behave ungra-
ciously   **28 approved** proved   **31 missingly** being aware that he is
missing   **32 frequent to** devoted to   **34 so much** as much   **35–6 eyes
. . . removedness** spies who keep an eye on him in his absence
37 intelligence news.   **from** away from   **38 homely** simple

that from very nothing, and beyond the imagination
of his neighbors, is grown into an unspeakable estate.   40

CAMILLO   I have heard, sir, of such a man, who hath a
daughter of most rare note. The report of her is   42
extended more than can be thought to begin from
such a cottage.

POLIXENES   That's likewise part of my intelligence; but,
I fear, the angle that plucks our son thither. Thou shalt   46
accompany us to the place, where we will, not appearing what we are, have some question with the shep-   48
herd; from whose simplicity I think it not uneasy to   49
get the cause of my son's resort thither. Prithee, be my
present partner in this business, and lay aside the
thoughts of Sicilia.

CAMILLO   I willingly obey your command.

POLIXENES   My best Camillo! We must disguise ourselves.   *Exit [with Camillo].*

❖

4.3

Enter Autolycus, singing.

AUTOLYCUS

When daffodils begin to peer,   1
   With heigh, the doxy over the dale!   2
Why, then comes in the sweet o'the year,
   For the red blood reigns in the winter's pale.   4

The white sheet bleaching on the hedge,
   With heigh, the sweet birds, oh, how they
      sing!
Doth set my pugging tooth on edge,   7
   For a quart of ale is a dish for a king.   8

The lark, that tirralirra chants,
   With heigh, with heigh, the thrush and the jay!
Are summer songs for me and my aunts,   11
   While we lie tumbling in the hay.

I have served Prince Florizel and in my time wore
three-pile, but now I am out of service.   14

But shall I go mourn for that, my dear?   15
   The pale moon shines by night,
And when I wander here and there,   17
   I then do most go right.   18

If tinkers may have leave to live,   19
   And bear the sow-skin budget,   20

Then my account I well may give,   21
   And in the stocks avouch it.   22

My traffic is sheets; when the kite builds, look to lesser   23
linen. My father named me Autolycus, who, being, as   24
I am, littered under Mercury, was likewise a snap-   25
per-up of unconsidered trifles. With die and drab I   26
purchased this caparison, and my revenue is the silly   27
cheat. Gallows and knock are too powerful on the   28
highway; beating and hanging are terrors to me. For   29
the life to come, I sleep out the thought of it. A prize,   30
a prize!

Enter Clown.

CLOWN   Let me see: every 'leven wether tods; every tod   32
yields pound and odd shilling; fifteen hundred shorn,
what comes the wool to?

AUTOLYCUS [*aside*]   If the springe hold, the cock's mine.   35

CLOWN   I cannot do't without counters. Let me see;   36
what am I to buy for our sheepshearing feast? Three
pound of sugar, five pound of currants, rice—what
will this sister of mine do with rice? But my father hath
made her mistress of the feast, and she lays it on. She
hath made me four-and-twenty nosegays for the shear-   41
ers—three-man-song men all, and very good ones;   42
but they are most of them means and basses, but one   43
Puritan amongst them, and he sings psalms to horn-   44
pipes. I must have saffron to color the warden pies;   45
mace; dates?—none, that's out of my note; nutmegs,   46
seven; a race or two of ginger, but that I may beg; four   47
pound of prunes, and as many of raisins o'th' sun.   48

AUTOLYCUS   Oh, that ever I was born! [*He grovels on the
ground.*]

CLOWN   I'th' name of me!   50

AUTOLYCUS   Oh, help me, help me! Pluck but off these
rags, and then death, death!

21 my account an account of myself   **22 in . . . avouch it** i.e., affirm
that I am a tinker if I find myself sitting in the stocks, where vagabonds
often end up. (Autolycus passes himself off as a tinker to mask his real
calling of thief.)   **23–4 when . . . linen** (The kite, a bird of prey, was
thought to carry off small pieces of linen with which to construct its
nest, whereas Autolycus makes off with larger linen or sheets hung out
to dry.)   **24 Autolycus** (Like his namesake, Ulysses's grandfather, the
son of Mercury, this Autolycus is an expert thief.)   **who** (Refers
ambiguously to Autolycus and "My father"; see next note.)   **25 littered under Mercury** (1) sired by Mercury, the god of thieves (2) born
when the planet Mercury was in the ascendant   **26 unconsidered** left
unattended, not worth thinking about   **26–8 With . . . cheat** Gambling
and whoring have brought me to the wearing of these tattered rags,
and my source of income is petty trickery used to cheat simpletons.
28–9 Gallows . . . to me i.e., Hanging and being beaten, the ordinary
hazards of being a highwayman, are too much for me; I'll stick to being
a petty thief.   **29 For** As for   **30 sleep . . . it** i.e., don't give a thought to
punishment in the next world.   **prize** booty   **32 every . . . tods** every
eleven sheep yield a *tod*, i.e., a bulk of wool weighing twenty-eight
pounds   **35 springe** snare.   **cock** woodcock. (A proverbially stupid
bird.)   **36 counters** metal disks used in reckoning.   **41 made me**
made. (*Me* is used colloquially.)   **nosegays** bouquets   **42 three-man-
song men** singers of songs for three male voices: bass, tenor, and treble
43 means tenors   **43–5 but . . . hornpipes** (Puritans were often laughed
at for their pious singing; this Puritan is imagined as singing hymns
even to the sounds of raucous merriment at a fair.)   **45 warden** made
of the warden pear   **46 out of my note** not on my list   **47 race** root
48 o'th' sun dried in the sun.   **50 I'th' name of me!** (An unusual and
perhaps comic oath.)

40 unspeakable beyond description   **42 note** distinction.   **46 angle**
baited fishhook.   **our** (The royal plural; also in *us*, line 47.)   **48 question** talk   **49 uneasy** difficult
4.3. Location: Bohemia. A road near the Shepherd's cottage.
1 peer peep out, appear   **2 doxy** beggar's wench   **4 pale** (1) paleness
(2) domain, region of authority. (The image is of red blood restoring
vitality to a pale complexion.)   **7 set . . . on edge** i.e., whets the
appetite of my thieving tooth, my taste for thieving. (To *pug* is to
"pull, tug.")   **8 quart of ale** (To be paid for perhaps with profits from
theft of sheets.)   **11 aunts** i.e., whores   **14 three-pile** velvet having
very rich pile or nap   **15 for that** i.e., for being out of service
17 wander (i.e., as a thief)   **18 most go right** i.e., live the life that is
meant for me.   **19 leave to live** permission to practice their trade
20 budget tool bag

CLOWN Alack, poor soul! Thou hast need of more rags to lay on thee, rather than have these off.

AUTOLYCUS Oh, sir, the loathsomeness of them offend me more than the stripes I have received, which are mighty ones and millions.

CLOWN Alas, poor man! A million of beating may come to a great matter.

AUTOLYCUS I am robbed, sir, and beaten; my money and apparel ta'en from me, and these detestable things put upon me.

CLOWN What, by a horseman or a footman?   63

AUTOLYCUS A footman, sweet sir, a footman.

CLOWN Indeed, he should be a footman by the garments he has left with thee. If this be a horseman's coat, it hath seen very hot service. Lend me thy hand; I'll help thee. Come, lend me thy hand. [*He helps him up.*]

AUTOLYCUS Oh, good sir, tenderly. Oh!

CLOWN Alas, poor soul!

AUTOLYCUS Oh, good sir, softly, good sir! I fear, sir, my shoulder blade is out.

CLOWN How now? Canst stand?

AUTOLYCUS [*picking his pocket*] Softly, dear sir; good sir, softly. You ha' done me a charitable office.

CLOWN [*reaching for his purse*] Dost lack any money? I   76
have a little money for thee.   77

AUTOLYCUS No, good sweet sir; no, I beseech you, sir. I have a kinsman not past three quarters of a mile hence, unto whom I was going; I shall there have money or anything I want. Offer me no money, I pray you. That kills my heart.

CLOWN What manner of fellow was he that robbed you?

AUTOLYCUS A fellow, sir, that I have known to go about with troll-my-dames. I knew him once a servant of the   85
Prince. I cannot tell, good sir, for which of his virtues it was, but he was certainly whipped out of the court.

CLOWN His vices, you would say. There's no virtue whipped out of the court. They cherish it to make it stay there; and yet it will no more but abide.   90

AUTOLYCUS Vices, I would say, sir. I know this man well. He hath been since an ape bearer, then a process   92
server, a bailiff. Then he compassed a motion of   93
the Prodigal Son and married a tinker's wife within a mile where my land and living lies, and, having flown   95
over many knavish professions, he settled only in rogue. Some call him Autolycus.

CLOWN Out upon him! Prig, for my life, prig! He   98
haunts wakes, fairs, and bearbaitings.   99

AUTOLYCUS Very true, sir. He, sir, he. That's the rogue that put me into this apparel.

CLOWN Not a more cowardly rogue in all Bohemia. If you had but looked big and spit at him, he'd have run.

AUTOLYCUS I must confess to you, sir, I am no fighter. I am false of heart that way, and that he knew, I   106
warrant him.

CLOWN How do you now?

AUTOLYCUS Sweet sir, much better than I was. I can stand and walk. I will even take my leave of you and pace softly towards my kinsman's.   111

CLOWN Shall I bring thee on the way?   112

AUTOLYCUS No, good-faced sir, no, sweet sir.

CLOWN Then fare thee well. I must go buy spices for our sheepshearing.   *Exit.*

AUTOLYCUS Prosper you, sweet sir! Your purse is not   116
hot enough to purchase your spice. I'll be with you at   117
your sheep shearing too. If I make not this cheat bring   118
out another, and the shearers prove sheep, let me be   119
unrolled and my name put in the book of virtue!   120

> *Song.*
>
> Jog on, jog on, the footpath way,
>   And merrily hent the stile-a;   122
> A merry heart goes all the day,
>   Your sad tires in a mile-a.   *Exit.*

❖

4.4

Enter Florizel [in shepherd's garb, and] Perdita [in holiday attire].

FLORIZEL
These your unusual weeds to each part of you   1
Does give a life; no shepherdess, but Flora   2
Peering in April's front. This your sheepshearing   3
Is as a meeting of the petty gods,   4
And you the queen on't.

PERDITA   Sir, my gracious lord,
To chide at your extremes it not becomes me.   6
Oh, pardon that I name them! Your high self,
The gracious mark o'th' land, you have obscured   8
With a swain's wearing, and me, poor lowly maid,   9

---

63 **horseman** highwayman.   **footman** footpad. (As the Clown observes in line 65, a common robber on foot would have poorer clothes than a mounted highwayman.)   **76–7 I have . . . thee** (The Clown reaches for his money and might have discovered the robbery if Autolycus had not quickly begged him not to bother.)   **85 troll-my-dames** or troll-madams (from the French *trou-madame*), a game in which the object was to *troll* balls through arches set on a board. (Autolycus uses the word to suggest women who *troll* or saunter about.)   **90 no more but abide** make only a temporary or unwilling stay.   **92 ape bearer** one who carries a trained monkey about for exhibition   **92–3 process server** sheriff's officer who serves processes or summonses   **93 compassed a motion** devised a puppet show   **95 living** property

98 **Prig** Thief   99 **wakes** village festivals   106 **false** cowardly   111 **softly** slowly   112 **bring . . . way** go part of the way with you.   116 **Prosper . . . sir!** (Said to the departing Clown.)   116–17 **Your . . . spice** i.e., You'll find but a cold purse to pay for your hot spices; an empty purse is a cold one. (Said after the Clown's departure.)   118–19 **cheat bring out** swindle lead to   120 **unrolled** taken off the roll (of rogues and vagabonds)   122 **hent** take hold of (as a means of leaping over)
4.4. Location: Bohemia. The Shepherd's cottage. (See lines 181–2, 187, etc.)
1 **unusual weeds** special, holiday attire   2 **Flora** goddess of flowers   3 **Peering . . . front** peeping forth in early April, or, in April's countenance or garb.   4 **petty** minor   6 **extremes** extravagant statements   8 **mark o'th' land** one who is noted and used as a model by everyone   9 **wearing** garb

Most goddesslike pranked up. But that our feasts 10
In every mess have folly, and the feeders 11
Digest it with a custom, I should blush 12
To see you so attired, swoon, I think,
To show myself a glass.

FLORIZEL   I bless the time 14
When my good falcon made her flight across
Thy father's ground.

PERDITA   Now Jove afford you cause! 16
To me the difference forges dread; your greatness 17
Hath not been used to fear. Even now I tremble
To think your father by some accident
Should pass this way as you did. Oh, the Fates!
How would he look to see his work, so noble, 21
Vilely bound up? What would he say? Or how 22
Should I, in these my borrowed flaunts, behold 23
The sternness of his presence?

FLORIZEL   Apprehend
Nothing but jollity. The gods themselves,
Humbling their deities to love, have taken
The shapes of beasts upon them. Jupiter 27
Became a bull, and bellowed; the green Neptune 28
A ram, and bleated; and the fire-robed god, 29
Golden Apollo, a poor humble swain, 30
As I seem now. Their transformations
Were never for a piece of beauty rarer,
Nor in a way so chaste, since my desires 33
Run not before mine honor, nor my lusts
Burn hotter than my faith.

PERDITA   Oh, but sir,
Your resolution cannot hold when 'tis
Opposed, as it must be, by th' power of the King.
One of these two must be necessities,
Which then will speak: that you must change this
    purpose
Or I my life.

FLORIZEL   Thou dearest Perdita, 40
With these forced thoughts, I prithee, darken not 41
The mirth o'th' feast. Or I'll be thine, my fair, 42
Or not my father's. For I cannot be
Mine own, nor anything to any, if
I be not thine. To this I am most constant,
Though destiny say no. Be merry, gentle! 46
Strangle such thoughts as these with anything 47
That you behold the while. Your guests are coming. 48

Lift up your countenance as it were the day 49
Of celebration of that nuptial which
We two have sworn shall come.

PERDITA   O Lady Fortune,
Stand you auspicious!

FLORIZEL   See, your guests approach.
Address yourself to entertain them sprightly, 53
And let's be red with mirth.

[Enter] Shepherd, Clown; Polixenes, Camillo
[disguised]; Mopsa, Dorcas; servants.

SHEPHERD
Fie, daughter! When my old wife lived, upon
This day she was both pantler, butler, cook, 56
Both dame and servant; welcomed all, served all; 57
Would sing her song and dance her turn; now here,
At upper end o'th' table, now i'th' middle;
On his shoulder, and his; her face afire 60
With labor, and the thing she took to quench it 61
She would to each one sip. You are retired, 62
As if you were a feasted one and not
The hostess of the meeting. Pray you, bid
These unknown friends to 's welcome, for it is 65
A way to make us better friends, more known. 66
Come, quench your blushes and present yourself
That which you are, mistress o'th' feast. Come on,
And bid us welcome to your sheepshearing,
As your good flock shall prosper.

PERDITA [to Polixenes]   Sir, welcome.
It is my father's will I should take on me
The hostess-ship o'th' day. [To Camillo] You're
    welcome, sir.—
Give me those flowers there, Dorcas.—Reverend sirs,
For you there's rosemary and rue; these keep
Seeming and savor all the winter long. 75
Grace and remembrance be to you both, 76
And welcome to our shearing! [Giving them flowers.]

POLIXENES   Shepherdess—
A fair one are you—well you fit our ages
With flowers of winter.

PERDITA   Sir, the year growing ancient, 79
Not yet on summer's death nor on the birth
Of trembling winter, the fairest flow'rs o'th' season
Are our carnations and streaked gillyvors, 82
Which some call nature's bastards. Of that kind 83
Our rustic garden's barren, and I care not
To get slips of them.

POLIXENES   Wherefore, gentle maiden, 85
Do you neglect them?

PERDITA   For I have heard it said 86

---

10 **pranked up** bedecked.   10–12 **But . . . custom** Were it not that whenever folks gather for merry feasting one encounters some folly, which
the guests take in their stride as to be expected   14 **To show . . . glass** if
I were to see myself in a mirror.   16 **Jove . . . cause!** May Jove grant that
you have good reason to be thankful!   17 **To me . . . dread** To me, the
difference in our social rank is a source of dread   21–2 **How . . . bound
up?** What would he think to see the nobly-born son he created so vilely
outfitted? (The *work*, Florizel, is metaphorically a piece of writing,
and his garments are the binding of the book.)   23 **flaunts** finery
27–30 **Jupiter . . . swain** (Jupiter in the guise of a bull wooed Europa,
Neptune disguised as a ram deceived Bisaltes or Theophane [Ovid,
Metamorphoses, 6.117], and Apollo took the guise of a humble shepherd
to enable Admetus to woo Alcestis.)   33 **in a way** i.e., pursuing a purpose   40 **Or I my life** i.e., or I will be threatened with loss of life (as
Polixenes indeed threatens at lines 436–43).   41 **forced** farfetched,
unnatural   42 **Or** Either   46 **gentle** i.e., my gentle love.   47–8 **Strangle
. . . while** i.e., Put down such thoughts by attending to matters at hand.

49 **as** as if   53 **Address** Prepare   56 **pantler** pantry servant
57 **dame** mistress of the household   60 **On his . . . his** at one person's
. . . another's   61–2 **and . . . sip** and she would toast each one with
the drink she took to quench the fire of her labor.   65 **to 's** each to his
66 **more known** better acquainted.   75 **Seeming** outward appearance, color   76 **Grace and remembrance** Divine grace and remembrance after death. (Equated respectively with rue and rosemary.)
79 **the year . . . ancient** i.e., when autumn arrives   82 **gillyvors**
gillyflowers, a kind of carnation   83 **nature's bastards** i.e., the
result of artificial breeding. (See lines 86–8.)   85 **slips** cuttings
86 **For** Because

There is an art which in their piedness shares   87
With great creating nature.

POLIXENES   Say there be;
Yet nature is made better by no mean   89
But nature makes that mean. So, over that art   90
Which you say adds to nature is an art
That nature makes. You see, sweet maid, we marry
A gentler scion to the wildest stock,   93
And make conceive a bark of baser kind
By bud of nobler race. This is an art
Which does mend nature—change it, rather—but
The art itself is nature.

PERDITA   So it is.

POLIXENES
Then make your garden rich in gillyvors,
And do not call them bastards.

PERDITA   I'll not put
The dibble in earth to set one slip of them,   100
No more than, were I painted, I would wish   101
This youth should say 'twere well, and only therefore
Desire to breed by me. Here's flowers for you:
                    [giving them flowers]
Hot lavender, mints, savory, marjoram,   104
The marigold, that goes to bed wi'th' sun
And with him rises weeping. These are flowers
Of middle summer, and I think they are given   107
To men of middle age. You're very welcome.

CAMILLO
I should leave grazing, were I of your flock,
And only live by gazing.

PERDITA   Out, alas!   110
You'd be so lean that blasts of January
Would blow you through and through. [To Florizel]
        Now, my fair'st friend,
I would I had some flow'rs o'th' spring that might
Become your time of day; [to the Shepherdesses] and
        yours, and yours,
That wear upon your virgin branches yet
Your maidenheads growing. O Proserpina,   116
For the flow'rs now that, frighted, thou let'st fall
From Dis's wagon! Daffodils,
That come before the swallow dares, and take   119
The winds of March with beauty; violets dim,   120
But sweeter than the lids of Juno's eyes
Or Cytherea's breath; pale primroses,   122
That die unmarried ere they can behold

Bright Phoebus in his strength—a malady   124
Most incident to maids; bold oxlips and   125
The crown imperial; lilies of all kinds,   126
The flower-de-luce being one. Oh, these I lack   127
To make you garlands of, and my sweet friend,   128
To strew him o'er and o'er!

FLORIZEL   What, like a corpse?

PERDITA
No, like a bank for Love to lie and play on,   130
Not like a corpse; or if, not to be buried,   131
But quick and in mine arms. Come, take your flowers.
                    [Giving flowers.]   132
Methinks I play as I have seen them do
In Whitsun pastorals. Sure this robe of mine   134
Does change my disposition.

FLORIZEL   What you do
Still betters what is done. When you speak, sweet,   136
I'd have you do it ever. When you sing,
I'd have you buy and sell so, so give alms,
Pray so; and, for the ord'ring your affairs,
To sing them too. When you do dance, I wish you
A wave o'th' sea, that you might ever do
Nothing but that—move still, still so,
And own no other function. Each your doing,   143
So singular in each particular,   144
Crowns what you are doing in the present deeds,   145
That all your acts are queens.

PERDITA   Oh, Doricles,   146
Your praises are too large. But that your youth,   147
And the true blood which peeps fairly through't
Do plainly give you out an unstained shepherd,   149
With wisdom I might fear, my Doricles,
You wooed me the false way.

FLORIZEL   I think you have
As little skill to fear as I have purpose   152
To put you to't. But come, our dance, I pray.   153
Your hand, my Perdita. So turtles pair,   154
That never mean to part.

PERDITA   I'll swear for 'em.   155
                    [They speak apart.]

POLIXENES [to Camillo]
This is the prettiest lowborn lass that ever

---

87 **art** i.e., of crossbreeding.   **piedness** particolored appearance.
(Perdita disclaims the art of crossbreeding, since it infringes on what
nature itself does so well.)   **89 mean** means   **90 But** unless. (Polixenes's point is that the art of improving on nature is itself natural.)
93 gentler nobler, more cultivated   **100 dibble** trowel   **101 painted**
made artificially beautiful by cosmetics   **104 Hot** eager, ardent, aromatic (?) (Spices were classified as hot or cold.)   **107 middle summer**
(Having no autumn flowers in any case [lines 79–82], since it is too
early in the season, Perdita flatters her older guests by giving them
flowers appropriate to *middle age*.)   **110 Out** (An exclamation of dismay.)   **116 Proserpina** daughter of Ceres, stolen away by Pluto
(*Dis*) and taken to Hades when, according to Ovid, she was gathering
flowers   **119 take** charm   **120 dim** with hanging heads
122 Cytherea's Venus's

124 **Phoebus** the sun-god   **124–5 a malady . . . maids** (Young maids,
suffering from greensickness, a kind of anemia, are pale like the primrose.)   **126 crown imperial** flower from the Levant, cultivated in
English gardens   **127 flower-de-luce** fleur-de-lis.   **I lack** (Because
the season is too late for them.)   **128 To . . . friend** to make garlands
of them for you (Polixenes and Camillo) and for my sweet friend
(Florizel)   **130 like . . . play on** as if one were strewing a bank where
Cupid himself might lie in amorous play   **131 or if** or like a corpse,
that is, a living body   **132 quick** alive   **134 Whitsun pastorals** plays
(including Robin Hood plays) and English morris dances often performed at Whitsuntide, seven Sundays after Easter. (The part of
Maid Marian strikes Perdita as immodest for her usual behavior.)
136 Still . . . done gets better and better.   **143 Each your doing** Each
thing you do and how you do it   **144 singular** unique and peerless
145 Crowns . . . deeds makes whatever you are doing at the moment
seem supremely wonderful   **146 Doricles** (Florizel's disguise name.)
147 large lavish.   **But that** Were it not that   **149 give you out** proclaim you to be   **152 skill** reason   **153 To . . . to't** i.e., to woo you
"the false way," with intent to seduce you.   **154 turtles** turtledoves,
as symbols of faithful love   **155 I'll swear for 'em** i.e., I'll be sworn
they do.

Ran on the greensward. Nothing she does or seems 157
But smacks of something greater than herself,
Too noble for this place.

CAMILLO   He tells her something
That makes her blood look out. Good sooth, she is 160
The queen of curds and cream.

CLOWN   Come on, strike up!

DORCAS
Mopsa must be your mistress. Marry, garlic, 162
To mend her kissing with!

MOPSA   Now, in good time! 163

CLOWN
Not a word, a word. We stand upon our manners. 164
Come, strike up! 165
                    [*Music.*] *Here a dance of shepherds and*
                                        shepherdesses.

POLIXENES
Pray, good shepherd, what fair swain is this
Which dances with your daughter?

SHEPHERD
They call him Doricles, and boasts himself 168
To have a worthy feeding; but I have it 169
Upon his own report and I believe it.
He looks like sooth. He says he loves my daughter. 171
I think so too, for never gazed the moon
Upon the water as he'll stand and read,
As 'twere, my daughter's eyes; and, to be plain,
I think there is not half a kiss to choose
Who loves another best.

POLIXENES   She dances featly. 176

SHEPHERD
So she does anything—though I report it
That should be silent. If young Doricles
Do light upon her, she shall bring him that 179
Which he not dreams of.

                    Enter Servant.

SERVANT   Oh, master, if you did but hear the peddler at
the door, you would never dance again after a tabor 182
and pipe; no, the bagpipe could not move you. He
sings several tunes faster than you'll tell money. He 184
utters them as he had eaten ballads and all men's ears 185
grew to his tunes.

CLOWN   He could never come better. He shall come in. 187
I love a ballad but even too well, if it be doleful matter 188
merrily set down, or a very pleasant thing indeed and 189
sung lamentably. 190

SERVANT   He hath songs for man or woman, of all sizes. 191
No milliner can so fit his customers with gloves. He 192

has the prettiest love songs for maids, so without
bawdry, which is strange, with such delicate burdens 194
of dildos and fadings, "Jump her and thump her"; and 195
where some stretchmouthed rascal would, as it were, 196
mean mischief and break a foul gap into the matter, 197
he makes the maid to answer, "Whoop, do me no
harm, good man"; puts him off, slights him, with
"Whoop, do me no harm, good man."

POLIXENES   This is a brave fellow. 201

CLOWN   Believe me, thou talkest of an admirable con- 202
ceited fellow. Has he any unbraided wares? 203

SERVANT   He hath ribbons of all the colors i'th'
rainbow; points more than all the lawyers in Bohemia 205
can learnedly handle, though they come to him by th'
gross; inkles, caddisses, cambrics, lawns. Why, he 207
sings 'em over as they were gods or goddesses; you
would think a smock were a she-angel, he so chants to 209
the sleevehand and the work about the square on't. 210

CLOWN   Prithee, bring him in, and let him approach
singing.

PERDITA   Forewarn him that he use no scurrilous words
in 's tunes.   [*The Servant goes to the door.*]

CLOWN   You have of these peddlers that have more in 215
them than you'd think, sister.

PERDITA   Ay, good brother, or go about to think. 217

                Enter Autolycus, singing.

AUTOLYCUS
Lawn as white as driven snow,
Cyprus black as e'er was crow, 219
Gloves as sweet as damask roses, 220
Masks for faces and for noses,
Bugle bracelet, necklace amber, 222
Perfume for a lady's chamber,
Golden coifs and stomachers, 224
For my lads to give their dears,
Pins and poking-sticks of steel, 226
What maids lack from head to heel,
Come buy of me, come. Come buy, come buy.
Buy, lads, or else your lasses cry.
Come buy.

CLOWN   If I were not in love with Mopsa, thou shouldst

---

157 **greensward** grassy turf.   160 **makes . . . out** makes her blush.
162 **mistress** i.e., partner in the dance.   163 **kissing** i.e., bad breath.
(Dorcas jests that even garlic would improve Mopsa's breath.)   **in
good time** (An expression of indignation.)   164 **stand upon** set store
by   165.1 *dance* (Probably a morris dance.)   168 **and** i.e., and they
say he   169 **feeding** pasturage, lands   171 **He . . . sooth** He appears
to be honest.   176 **another** the other.   **featly** gracefully.   179 **light
upon** choose   182 **tabor** small drum   184 **several** various.   **tell**
count   185 **as** as if. (Also in line 208.)   187 **better** at a better time.
188 **but even too well** all too well   189 **pleasant** merry   190 **lamentably** mournfully.   191 **sizes** sorts.   192 **milliner** vendor of fancy
ware and apparel, including gloves, ribbons, and bonnets

194 **burdens** refrains   195 **dildos and fadings** words used as part of
the refrains of ballads. (But with bawdy double meaning unperceived
by the servant, as also in *jump her, thump her, do me no harm*, etc.)
196 **stretchmouthed** widemouthed, foulmouthed   197 **break . . .
matter** insert some gross obscenity into the song, or, act in a suggestive way   201 **brave** excellent   202–3 **admirable conceited** wonderfully witty and clever   203 **unbraided** not shopworn, new
205 **points** (1) laces for fastening clothes (2) headings in an argument
207 **inkles . . . lawns** linen tapes, worsted tape used for garters, fine
heavy linen fabrics, fine sheer linens.   209 **smock** petticoat
210 **sleevehand** wristband.   **square on't** embroidered bosom or yoke
of the garment.   215 **You . . . peddlers** You'll find peddlers   217 **go
about** intend, wish.   217.1 *Enter Autolycus* (Apparently he is wearing a false beard; later in this scene, he removes it to impersonate a
courtier to the Clown and Shepherd.)   219 **Cyprus** crepe   220 **sweet**
i.e., perfumed. (Also in line 249.)   222 **Bugle bracelet** bracelet of
black glossy beads   224 **coifs** close-fitting caps.   **stomachers**
embroidered fronts for ladies' dresses   226 **poking-sticks** rods used
for ironing and stiffening the plaits of ruffs. (With bawdy suggestion.)

take no money of me, but being enthralled as I am, it 232
will also be the bondage of certain ribbons and gloves. 233

MOPSA   I was promised them against the feast, but they 234
come not too late now.

DORCAS   He hath promised you more than that, or 236
there be liars. 237

MOPSA   He hath paid you all he promised you. Maybe
he has paid you more, which will shame you to give 239
him again. 240

CLOWN   Is there no manners left among maids? Will 241
they wear their plackets where they should bear their 242
faces? Is there not milking time, when you are going to 243
bed, or kilnhole, to whistle of these secrets, but you 244
must be tittle-tattling before all our guests? 'Tis well
they are whisp'ring. Clamor your tongues, and not a 246
word more.

MOPSA   I have done. Come, you promised me a tawdry 248
lace and a pair of sweet gloves. 249

CLOWN   Have I not told thee how I was cozened by the 250
way and lost all my money?

AUTOLYCUS   And indeed, sir, there are cozeners abroad;
therefore it behooves men to be wary.

CLOWN   Fear not thou, man, thou shalt lose nothing
here.

AUTOLYCUS   I hope so, sir, for I have about me many
parcels of charge. 257

CLOWN   What hast here? Ballads?

MOPSA   Pray now, buy some. I love a ballad in print
alife, for then we are sure they are true. 260

AUTOLYCUS   Here's one to a very doleful tune, how a
usurer's wife was brought to bed of twenty moneybags at a burden, and how she longed to eat adders' 263
heads and toads carbonadoed. 264

MOPSA   Is it true, think you?

AUTOLYCUS   Very true, and but a month old.

DORCAS   Bless me from marrying a usurer! 267

AUTOLYCUS   Here's the midwife's name to't, one
Mistress Taleporter, and five or six honest wives that 269
were present. Why should I carry lies abroad?

MOPSA   Pray you now, buy it.

CLOWN   Come on, lay it by, and let's first see more
ballads. We'll buy the other things anon.

AUTOLYCUS   Here's another ballad, of a fish that appeared upon the coast on Wednesday the fourscore of 275
April, forty thousand fathom above water, and sung 276
this ballad against the hard hearts of maids. It was

thought she was a woman and was turned into a cold
fish for she would not exchange flesh with one that 279
loved her. The ballad is very pitiful and as true.

DORCAS   Is it true too, think you?

AUTOLYCUS   Five justices' hands at it, and witnesses 282
more than my pack will hold.

CLOWN   Lay it by too. Another.

AUTOLYCUS   This is a merry ballad, but a very pretty
one.

MOPSA   Let's have some merry ones.

AUTOLYCUS   Why, this is a passing merry one and goes 288
to the tune of "Two Maids Wooing a Man." There's
scarce a maid westward but she sings it. 'Tis in 290
request, I can tell you.

MOPSA   We can both sing it. If thou'lt bear a part, thou
shalt hear; 'tis in three parts.

DORCAS   We had the tune on't a month ago. 294

AUTOLYCUS   I can bear my part; you must know 'tis my
occupation. Have at it with you. 296

Song.

AUTOLYCUS
      Get you hence, for I must go
      Where it fits not you to know.
DORCAS
            Whither?
MOPSA   Oh, whither?
DORCAS   Whither?
MOPSA
      It becomes thy oath full well,
      Thou to me thy secrets tell.
DORCAS
            Me too. Let me go thither.
MOPSA
      Or thou goest to th' grange or mill. 303
DORCAS
      If to either, thou dost ill.
AUTOLYCUS
            Neither.
DORCAS   What, neither?
AUTOLYCUS   Neither.
DORCAS
      Thou hast sworn my love to be.
MOPSA
      Thou hast sworn it more to me.
            Then whither goest? Say, whither?

CLOWN   We'll have this song out anon by ourselves. 309
My father and the gentlemen are in sad talk, and we'll 310
not trouble them. Come, bring away thy pack after
me. Wenches, I'll buy for you both. Peddler, let's have
the first choice. Follow me, girls.
                    [*Exit with Dorcas and Mopsa.*]

AUTOLYCUS   And you shall pay well for 'em.
                    [*He follows singing.*]

232–3 it will . . . bondage it will mean the taking into custody (by
means of purchase and tying up into a parcel)   234 against in anticipation of, in time for   236–7 He . . . liars i.e., He promised to marry
you, too, or else rumor is a liar.   239 paid you more i.e., made you
pregnant   239–40 which . . . again i.e., which will shame you by giving birth to his child.   241–3 Will . . . faces? i.e., Will they always be
talking and revealing personal secrets?   plackets slits in petticoats.
(With bawdy suggestion of the pudendum, as in line 613.)   244 kilnhole fire hole of a baking oven (where maids might gossip).   whistle
whisper   246 Clamor i.e., Silence   248–9 tawdry lace cheap and
showy lace, or, neckerchief. (So called from St. Audrey's Fair.)
250 cozened cheated   257 parcels of charge valuable items.
260 alife on my life   263 at a burden in one childbirth   264 carbonadoed scored across and grilled.   267 Bless God protect, keep
269 Taleporter i.e., talebearer, gossip   275 fourscore eightieth (!)
276 forty thousand fathom 240,000 feet

279 exchange flesh have sex   282 hands at it signatures on it
288 passing surpassingly   290 westward in the West Country
294 on't of it   296 Have at it Here goes   303 Or Either.   grange
farm   309 have this song out finish this song   310 sad serious

Song.

> Will you buy any tape,
> Or lace for your cape,
> My dainty duck, my dear-a?
> Any silk, any thread,
> And toys for your head,   319
> Of the new'st and fin'st, fin'st wear-a?
> Come to the peddler;
> Money's a meddler,   322
> That doth utter all men's ware-a.   *Exit.* 323

[*Enter a Servant.*]

SERVANT   Master, there is three carters, three shep- 324
herds, three neatherds, three swineherds, that have 325
made themselves all men of hair. They call themselves 326
saultiers, and they have a dance which the wenches say 327
is a gallimaufry of gambols, because they are not in't; 328
but they themselves are o'th' mind, if it be not too
rough for some that know little but bowling, it will 330
please plentifully.

SHEPHERD   Away! We'll none on't. Here has been too
much homely foolery already.—I know, sir, we 333
weary you.

POLIXENES   You weary those that refresh us. Pray, let's
see these four threes of herdsmen.

SERVANT   One three of them, by their own report, sir, 337
hath danced before the King, and not the worst of the
three but jumps twelve foot and a half by the square. 339

SHEPHERD   Leave your prating. Since these good men 340
are pleased, let them come in; but quickly now.

SERVANT   Why, they stay at door, sir.

[*He goes to the door.*]

Here a dance of twelve Satyrs.

POLIXENES [*to the Shepherd*]
Oh, father, you'll know more of that hereafter.   343
[*To Camillo*] Is it not too far gone? 'Tis time to part
them.
He's simple and tells much. [*To Florizel*] How now, fair
shepherd?   345
Your heart is full of something that does take
Your mind from feasting. Sooth, when I was young
And handed love as you do, I was wont   348
To load my she with knacks. I would have ransacked
The peddler's silken treasury and have poured it
To her acceptance; you have let him go,   351
And nothing marted with him. If your lass   352

Interpretation should abuse and call this   353
Your lack of love or bounty, you were straited   354
For a reply, at least if you make a care
Of happy holding her.
FLORIZEL   Old sir, I know   356
She prizes not such trifles as these are.
The gifts she looks from me are packed and locked 358
Up in my heart, which I have given already,
But not delivered. [*To Perdita*] Oh, hear me breathe my
life   360
Before this ancient sir, who, it should seem,   361
Hath sometime loved! I take thy hand, this hand,
As soft as dove's down and as white as it,
Or Ethiopian's tooth, or the fanned snow that's bolted 364
By th' northern blasts twice o'er.   [*He takes her hand.*]
POLIXENES   What follows this?
How prettily the young swain seems to wash
The hand was fair before! I have put you out.   367
But to your protestation; let me hear   368
What you profess.
FLORIZEL   Do, and be witness to't.
POLIXENES
And this my neighbor too?
FLORIZEL   And he, and more
Than he, and men—the earth, the heavens, and all:
That, were I crowned the most imperial monarch,
Thereof most worthy, were I the fairest youth   373
That ever made eye swerve, had force and knowledge 374
More than was ever man's, I would not prize them
Without her love; for her employ them all,
Commend them and condemn them to her service   377
Or to their own perdition.
POLIXENES   Fairly offered.   378
CAMILLO
This shows a sound affection.
SHEPHERD   But, my daughter,
Say you the like to him?
PERDITA   I cannot speak
So well, nothing so well; no, nor mean better.
By th' pattern of mine own thoughts I cut out   382
The purity of his.
SHEPHERD   Take hands, a bargain!   383
And, friends unknown, you shall bear witness to't:
I give my daughter to him and will make
Her portion equal his.
FLORIZEL   Oh, that must be
I'th' virtue of your daughter. One being dead,   387

---

319 **toys** trifles   322 **meddler** i.e., go-between in commercial transactions   323 **utter** put on the market   324 **carters** cart drivers
325 **neatherds** cowherds   326 **of hair** dressed in skins   327 **saultiers**
leapers or vaulters. (With perhaps a play on *Saltiers* as a blunder for
"satyrs.")   328 **gallimaufry** jumble   330 **bowling** (A more gentle
sport than the vigorous satyr dancing.)   333 **homely** unpolished
337 **three** threesome   339 **by the square** precisely.   340 **Leave** Leave
off   343 **Oh, . . . hereafter** (Polixenes completes the conversation he
has been having with the old Shepherd during the dance. *Father* is a
respectful term of address for older men.)   345 **He's simple** The old
Shepherd is guileless   348 **handed** handled, dealt in   351 **To her
acceptance** for her to choose   352 **nothing marted with** have done
no business with

353 **Interpretation should abuse** should interpret wrongly   354 **were
straited** would be hard-pressed   356 **happy holding her** keeping her
happy.   358 **looks** looks for   360 **But not delivered** i.e., but I have
not confirmed it by a solemn vow before witnesses, making binding
the contract.   **breathe my life** i.e., pronounce eternal vows   361 **this
ancient sir** Polixenes   364 **fanned** blown.   **bolted** sifted   367 **was**
that was.   **put you out** interrupted what you were saying.   368 **to
your protestation** on with your public affirmation   373 **Thereof
most worthy** the most worthy of monarchs   374 **swerve** turn in my
direction (out of awe and respect)   377–8 **Commend . . . perdition**
either commend them to her service, or, failing that, condemn them
to deserved destruction.   382–3 **By . . . of his** By the purity of my
own thoughts I can define the purity of his. (A metaphor of clothes-
making; Perdita has formed her own thoughts on the model of his.)
387 **One being dead** When a certain person dies

I shall have more than you can dream of yet;
Enough then for your wonder. But come on: 389
Contract us 'fore these witnesses.

SHEPHERD   Come, your hand;
And, daughter, yours.

POLIXENES   Soft, swain, awhile, beseech you. 391
Have you a father?

FLORIZEL   I have, but what of him?

POLIXENES   Knows he of this?

FLORIZEL   He neither does nor shall.

POLIXENES   Methinks a father
Is at the nuptial of his son a guest
That best becomes the table. Pray you, once more,
Is not your father grown incapable
Of reasonable affairs? Is he not stupid   400
With age and altering rheums? Can he speak? Hear?   401
Know man from man? Dispute his own estate?   402
Lies he not bedrid, and again does nothing
But what he did being childish?

FLORIZEL   No, good sir,   404
He has his health and ampler strength indeed
Than most have of his age.

POLIXENES   By my white beard,
You offer him, if this be so, a wrong
Something unfilial. Reason my son   408
Should choose himself a wife, but as good reason
The father, all whose joy is nothing else
But fair posterity, should hold some counsel   411
In such a business.

FLORIZEL   I yield all this;   412
But for some other reasons, my grave sir,
Which 'tis not fit you know, I not acquaint
My father of this business.

POLIXENES   Let him know't.

FLORIZEL
He shall not.

POLIXENES   Prithee, let him.

FLORIZEL   No, he must not.

SHEPHERD
Let him, my son. He shall not need to grieve
At knowing of thy choice.

FLORIZEL   Come, come, he must not.
Mark our contract.

POLIXENES [*discovering himself*]   Mark your divorce,
          young sir,
Whom son I dare not call. Thou art too base
To be acknowledged. Thou a scepter's heir,
That thus affects a sheephook?—Thou old traitor,   422
I am sorry that by hanging thee I can
But shorten thy life one week.—And thou, fresh piece

Of excellent witchcraft, who of force must know   425
The royal fool thou cop'st with—

SHEPHERD   Oh, my heart!   426

POLIXENES
I'll have thy beauty scratched with briers and made
More homely than thy state.—For thee, fond boy,   428
If I may ever know thou dost but sigh
That thou no more shalt see this knack—as never   430
I mean thou shalt—we'll bar thee from succession,
Not hold thee of our blood, no, not our kin,
Farre than Deucalion off. Mark thou my words.   433
Follow us to the court.—Thou churl, for this time,   434
Though full of our displeasure, yet we free thee
From the dead blow of it.—And you, enchantment,   436
Worthy enough a herdsman—yea, him too,   437
That makes himself, but for our honor therein,   438
Unworthy thee—if ever henceforth thou   439
These rural latches to his entrance open,
Or hoop his body more with thy embraces,
I will devise a death as cruel for thee
As thou art tender to't.   *Exit.*

PERDITA   Even here undone!
I was not much afeard; for once or twice
I was about to speak and tell him plainly
The selfsame sun that shines upon his court
Hides not his visage from our cottage, but
Looks on alike. Will't please you, sir, begone?   448
I told you what would come of this. Beseech you,
Of your own state take care. This dream of mine—
Being now awake, I'll queen it no inch farther,
But milk my ewes and weep.

CAMILLO   Why, how now, father?
Speak ere thou diest.

SHEPHERD   I cannot speak, nor think,   453
Nor dare to know that which I know. [*To Florizel*] Oh,
          sir,
You have undone a man of fourscore three,
That thought to fill his grave in quiet, yea,
To die upon the bed my father died,   457
To lie close by his honest bones; but now
Some hangman must put on my shroud and lay me
Where no priest shovels in dust. [*To Perdita*] Oh,
          cursed wretch,
That knew'st this was the Prince, and wouldst adven-
          ture
To mingle faith with him! Undone, undone!   462
If I might die within this hour, I have lived
To die when I desire.   *Exit.*

FLORIZEL [*to Perdita*]   Why look you so upon me?

---

389 **Enough . . . wonder** there will be enough then for you to wonder
at.   391 **Soft** Wait a minute   400 **reasonable affairs** matters requiring the use of reason.   401 **altering rheums** weakening catarrhs or
other diseases.   402 **Dispute** Discuss.   **estate** affairs, condition.
404 **being childish** when he was a child.   408 **Something** somewhat.
Reason my son It is reasonable that my son. (The disguised Polixenes
seems to be speaking hypothetically, using himself as an example, but
of course the application to Florizel is direct.)   411 **hold some counsel** be consulted   412 **yield** concede   422 **affects** desires, shows
inclination for

425 **of force** of necessity   426 **thou cop'st** you deal   428 **homely**
(1) unattractive (2) humble.   **fond** foolish   430 **knack** trifle, schemer
433 **Farre . . . off** farther in kinship than Deucalion (the Noah of classical legend and hence the primal, distant ancestor of the whole human
race).   434 **churl** i.e., the Shepherd   436 **dead** deadly.   **enchantment**
i.e., Perdita   437–9 **him too . . . thee** worthy indeed of him (Florizel)
whose behavior renders him unworthy even of you, if we were to set
aside for the moment the question of the dignity of our royal house
448 **alike** both alike.   453 **ere thou diest** before you die of grief (?).
(Although Polixenes has relented of his threat to hang the Shepherd,
the Shepherd is gloomily sure it will come to a hanging, lines 459–60.)
457 **died** died on   462 **mingle faith** exchange pledges

I am but sorry, not afeard; delayed,
But nothing altered. What I was, I am,
More straining on for plucking back, not following   468
My leash unwillingly.
CAMILLO   Gracious my lord,
You know your father's temper. At this time
He will allow no speech, which I do guess
You do not purpose to him; and as hardly
Will he endure your sight as yet, I fear.
Then, till the fury of His Highness settle,
Come not before him.
FLORIZEL   I not purpose it.
I think Camillo?
CAMILLO   Even he, my lord.
PERDITA
How often have I told you 'twould be thus?
How often said my dignity would last   478
But till 'twere known?
FLORIZEL   It cannot fail but by
The violation of my faith; and then   480
Let nature crush the sides o'th'earth together
And mar the seeds within! Lift up thy looks.   482
From my succession wipe me, father; I   483
Am heir to my affection.
CAMILLO   Be advised.   484
FLORIZEL
I am, and by my fancy. If my reason   485
Will thereto be obedient, I have reason;   486
If not, my senses, better pleased with madness,
Do bid it welcome.
CAMILLO   This is desperate, sir.
FLORIZEL
So call it, but it does fulfill my vow;
I needs must think it honesty. Camillo,
Not for Bohemia nor the pomp that may
Be thereat gleaned, for all the sun sees or
The close earth wombs or the profound seas hides   493
In unknown fathoms, will I break my oath
To this my fair beloved. Therefore, I pray you,
As you have ever been my father's honored friend,
When he shall miss me—as, in faith, I mean not
To see him any more—cast your good counsels
Upon his passion. Let myself and fortune   499
Tug for the time to come. This you may know   500
And so deliver: I am put to sea   501
With her who here I cannot hold on shore;   502
And most opportune to our need I have
A vessel rides fast by, but not prepared   504

For this design. What course I mean to hold
Shall nothing benefit your knowledge nor   506
Concern me the reporting.
CAMILLO   Oh, my lord,   507
I would your spirit were easier for advice,   508
Or stronger for your need.
FLORIZEL   Hark, Perdita.
[To Camillo] I'll hear you by and by.
[He draws Perdita aside.]
CAMILLO [aside]   He's irremovable,   510
Resolved for flight. Now were I happy if
His going I could frame to serve my turn,   512
Save him from danger, do him love and honor,
Purchase the sight again of dear Sicilia
And that unhappy king, my master, whom
I so much thirst to see.
FLORIZEL   Now, good Camillo,
I am so fraught with curious business that   517
I leave out ceremony.
CAMILLO   Sir, I think   518
You have heard of my poor services i'th' love
That I have borne your father?
FLORIZEL   Very nobly
Have you deserved. It is my father's music
To speak your deeds, not little of his care
To have them recompensed as thought on.
CAMILLO   Well, my lord,   523
If you may please to think I love the King
And through him what's nearest to him, which is
Your gracious self, embrace but my direction,   526
If your more ponderous and settled project   527
May suffer alteration. On mine honor,   528
I'll point you where you shall have such receiving
As shall become Your Highness, where you may   530
Enjoy your mistress—from the whom I see
There's no disjunction to be made but by,
As heavens forfend, your ruin—marry her,   533
And, with my best endeavors in your absence   534
Your discontenting father strive to qualify   535
And bring him up to liking.
FLORIZEL   How, Camillo,   536
May this, almost a miracle, be done,
That I may call thee something more than man,
And after that trust to thee?
CAMILLO   Have you thought on   539
A place whereto you'll go?
FLORIZEL   Not any yet.
But as th'unthought-on accident is guilty   541
To what we wildly do, so we profess   542

Ourselves to be the slaves of chance and flies   543
Of every wind that blows.

CAMILLO   Then list to me.
This follows, if you will not change your purpose
But undergo this flight: make for Sicilia,
And there present yourself and your fair princess—
For so I see she must be—'fore Leontes.
She shall be habited as it becomes   549
The partner of your bed. Methinks I see
Leontes opening his free arms and weeping   551
His welcomes forth; asks thee there "Son,
    forgiveness!"
As 'twere i'th' father's person; kisses the hands
Of your fresh princess; o'er and o'er divides him   554
Twixt his unkindness and his kindness. Th'one   555
He chides to hell, and bids the other grow
Faster than thought or time.

FLORIZEL   Worthy Camillo,   557
What color for my visitation shall I   558
Hold up before him?

CAMILLO   Sent by the King your father   559
To greet him and to give him comforts. Sir,
The manner of your bearing towards him, with
What you, as from your father, shall deliver—   562
Things known betwixt us three—I'll write you down,
The which shall point you forth at every sitting   564
What you must say, that he shall not perceive
But that you have your father's bosom there   566
And speak his very heart.

FLORIZEL   I am bound to you.
There is some sap in this.

CAMILLO   A course more promising
Than a wild dedication of yourselves
To unpathed waters, undreamed shores, most certain
To miseries enough; no hope to help you,
But as you shake off one to take another;   572
Nothing so certain as your anchors, who   573
Do their best office if they can but stay you   574
Where you'll be loath to be. Besides, you know   575
Prosperity's the very bond of love,   576
Whose fresh complexion and whose heart together   577
Affliction alters.

PERDITA   One of these is true: 578
I think affliction may subdue the cheek,   579
But not take in the mind.

CAMILLO   Yea, say you so?   580

There shall not at your father's house these seven
    years   581
Be born another such.

FLORIZEL   My good Camillo,
She's as forward of her breeding as she is   583
I'th' rear 'our birth.   584

CAMILLO   I cannot say 'tis pity
She lacks instructions, for she seems a mistress   585
To most that teach.

PERDITA   Your pardon, sir; for this
I'll blush you thanks.

FLORIZEL   My prettiest Perdita!
But oh, the thorns we stand upon! Camillo,
Preserver of my father, now of me,
The medicine of our house, how shall we do?
We are not furnished like Bohemia's son,
Nor shall appear so in Sicilia.

CAMILLO My lord,
Fear none of this. I think you know my fortunes
Do all lie there. It shall be so my care
To have you royally appointed as if   595
The scene you play were mine. For instance, sir,
That you may know you shall not want, one word.

                                        [*They talk aside.*]

    Enter Autolycus.

AUTOLYCUS Ha, ha, what a fool Honesty is! And Trust,
his sworn brother, a very simple gentleman! I have
sold all my trumpery; not a counterfeit stone, not a
ribbon, glass, pomander, brooch, table book, ballad,   601
knife, tape, glove, shoe tie, bracelet, horn ring, to
keep my pack from fasting. They throng who should   603
buy first, as if my trinkets had been hallowed and   604
brought a benediction to the buyer; by which means
I saw whose purse was best in picture, and what I   606
saw, to my good use I remembered. My clown, who
wants but something to be a reasonable man, grew so   608
in love with the wenches' song that he would not stir
his pettitoes till he had both tune and words, which   610
so drew the rest of the herd to me that all their other
senses stuck in ears. You might have pinched a   612
placket, it was senseless. 'Twas nothing to geld a cod- 613
piece of a purse. I could have filed keys off that hung 614
in chains. No hearing, no feeling, but my sir's song,   615
and admiring the nothing of it. So that in this time of 616
lethargy I picked and cut most of their festival purses;
and had not the old man come in with hubbub

---

543 **flies** i.e., insignificant insects, blown about by the winds of chance
549 **habited** (richly) dressed   551 **free** generous, noble   554 **fresh**
young and beautiful   554–5 **divides . . . kindness** divides his speech
between his former unkindness (which he condemns) and his present
intention of kindness.   557 **Faster** firmer; also, more swiftly
558 **color** excuse, pretext   559 **Hold up before** present to.   **Sent** i.e.,
Say you are sent   562 **deliver** say   564 **point you forth** indicate to
you.   **sitting** conference   566 **bosom** inmost thoughts   572 **one** one
misery, one misfortune.   **take** encounter   573 **Nothing** not at all.
573–5 **who . . . to be** which are doing as well as can be hoped if they
simply hold you in some undesirable place (rather than allowing you
to proceed on toward even greater disaster).   576–8 **Prosperity's . . .
alters** i.e., young love flourishes while things are going well but loses
its fresh complexion and strength of feeling under the test of adversity.   579 **subdue the cheek** make the complexion look pale and
wasted   580 **take in** overcome

581 **your father's** (Said either to Florizel or Perdita.)   **these seven
years** i.e., for a long time to come. (Camillo's point is that she is a
nonpareil.)   583 **forward . . . breeding** far in advance of her lowly
upbringing   584 **I'th' rear 'our** below me in   585 **instructions** formal
schooling.   **a mistress** a teacher   595 **appointed** equipped, outfitted
601 **pomander** scent-ball.   **table book** notebook   603 **from fasting**
i.e., from being empty.   604 **hallowed** made sacred, like a relic
606 **best in picture** i.e., best to look at, most promising   608 **wants
but something** lacks one thing only (i.e., intelligence)   610 **pettitoes**
pig's toes; here, toes   612 **stuck in ears** were occupied with hearing.
613 **placket** (Literally, slit in a petticoat; with bawdy suggestion.)
senseless insensible.   613–14 **geld . . . purse** cut a purse loose from
the pouch worn at the front of a man's breeches   615 **my sir's** i.e., the
Clown's   616 **nothing** (1) vacuity (2) noting, tune. (*Nothing* and
noting were sounded alike in Elizabethan English.)

against his daughter and the King's son and scared my
choughs from the chaff, I had not left a purse alive in   620
the whole army.

[*Camillo, Florizel, and Perdita come forward.*]

CAMILLO
Nay, but my letters, by this means being there
So soon as you arrive, shall clear that doubt.
FLORIZEL
And those that you'll procure from King Leontes—
CAMILLO
Shall satisfy your father.
PERDITA   Happy be you!
All that you speak shows fair.
CAMILLO [*seeing Autolycus*]   Who have we here?
We'll make an instrument of this, omit
Nothing may give us aid.   628
AUTOLYCUS [*aside*]   If they have overheard me now,
why, hanging.
CAMILLO   How now, good fellow? Why shak'st thou so?
Fear not, man, here's no harm intended to thee.
AUTOLYCUS   I am a poor fellow, sir.
CAMILLO   Why, be so still. Here's nobody will steal that
from thee. Yet for the outside of thy poverty we must   635
make an exchange. Therefore disce thee instantly—   636
thou must think there's a necessity in't—and change   637
garments with this gentleman. Though the penny-   638
worth on his side be the worst, yet hold thee, there's   639
some boot.   [*He gives money.*]   640
AUTOLYCUS   I am a poor fellow, sir. [*Aside*] I know ye
well enough.
CAMILLO   Nay, prithee, dispatch. The gentleman is half   643
flayed already.   644
AUTOLYCUS   Are you in earnest, sir? [*Aside*] I smell the
trick on't.
FLORIZEL   Dispatch, I prithee.
AUTOLYCUS   Indeed, I have had earnest, but I cannot   648
with conscience take it.
CAMILLO   Unbuckle, unbuckle.

[*Florizel and Autolycus exchange garments.*]

Fortunate mistress—let my prophecy   651
Come home to ye!—you must retire yourself   652
Into some covert. Take your sweetheart's hat   653
And pluck it o'er your brows, muffle your face,
Dismantle you, and, as you can, disliken   655
The truth of your own seeming, that you may—   656
For I do fear eyes—over to shipboard   657
Get undescried.
PERDITA   I see the play so lies
That I must bear a part.
CAMILLO   No remedy.—

Have you done there?
FLORIZEL   Should I now meet my father,
He would not call me son.
CAMILLO   Nay, you shall have no hat.
                          [*He gives it to Perdita.*]
Come, lady, come. Farewell, my friend.
AUTOLYCUS   Adieu, sir.
FLORIZEL
Oh, Perdita, what have we twain forgot?
Pray you, a word.   [*They speak aside.*]
CAMILLO [*aside*]
What I do next shall be to tell the King
Of this escape and whither they are bound;
Wherein my hope is I shall so prevail
To force him after, in whose company
I shall re-view Sicilia, for whose sight   670
I have a woman's longing.
FLORIZEL   Fortune speed us!
Thus we set on, Camillo, to th' seaside.
CAMILLO   The swifter speed the better.
                    Exit [*with Florizel and Perdita*].
AUTOLYCUS   I understand the business; I hear it. To
have an open ear, a quick eye, and a nimble hand is
necessary for a cutpurse; a good nose is requisite also,
to smell out work for th'other senses. I see this is the
time that the unjust man doth thrive. What an
exchange had this been without boot! What a boot is   679
here with this exchange! Sure the gods do this year
connive at us, and we may do anything extempore.   681
The Prince himself is about a piece of iniquity, stealing   682
away from his father with his clog at his heels. If I   683
thought it were a piece of honesty to acquaint the King
withal, I would not do't. I hold it the more knavery to   685
conceal it; and therein am I constant to my profession.

Enter Clown and Shepherd [*carrying a bundle and
a box*].

Aside, aside! Here is more matter for a hot brain.
Every lane's end, every shop, church, session, hang-   688
ing, yields a careful man work.   [*He stands aside.*]
CLOWN   See, see, what a man you are now! There is no
other way but to tell the King she's a changeling and   691
none of your flesh and blood.
SHEPHERD   Nay, but hear me.
CLOWN   Nay, but hear me.
SHEPHERD   Go to, then.   695
CLOWN   She being none of your flesh and blood, your
flesh and blood has not offended the King, and so
your flesh and blood is not to be punished by him.
Show those things you found about her, those secret
things, all but what she has with her. This being done,
let the law go whistle, I warrant you.
SHEPHERD   I will tell the King all, every word, yea, and
his son's pranks too; who, I may say, is no honest

620 **choughs** jackdaws   628 **Nothing** nothing that   635 **the outside . . .
poverty** i.e., your ragged clothing   636 **disce** undress   637 **think**
understand   638–9 **pennyworth** i.e., value of the bargain   640 **some
boot** something in addition.   643 **dispatch** hurry. (Also in line 647.)
644 **flayed** skinned, i.e., undressed   648 **earnest** advance payment.
(Playing on *in earnest* in line 645.)   651–2 **let . . . to ye!** i.e., let my
prophecy that you, Perdita, will be fortunate be fulfilled for you!
653 **covert** hidden place.   655–6 **as you . . . seeming** as much as you
can, disguise your outward appearance   657 **eyes** spying eyes

670 **re-view** see again   679 **without boot** i.e., even without added
payment.   **What a boot** What a profit   681 **connive at** look indul-
gently at   682 **about** engaged in   683 **clog** encumbrance (i.e.,
Perdita)   685 **withal** with it   688 **session** court session   691
changeling child left by the fairies   695 **Go to** Go ahead. (Or, an
expression of impatience.)

man, neither to his father nor to me, to go about to 704
make me the King's brother-in-law.

CLOWN   Indeed, brother-in-law was the farthest off you
could have been to him, and then your blood had
been the dearer by I know not how much an ounce.

AUTOLYCUS [aside]   Very wisely, puppies!

SHEPHERD   Well, let us to the King. There is that in this
fardel will make him scratch his beard.   711

AUTOLYCUS [aside]   I know not what impediment this
complaint may be to the flight of my master.   713

CLOWN   Pray heartily he be at' palace.   714

AUTOLYCUS [aside]   Though I am not naturally honest,
I am so sometimes by chance. Let me pocket up my
peddler's excrement. [He takes off his false beard.] How 717
now, rustics, whither are you bound?

SHEPHERD   To the palace, an it like Your Worship.   719

AUTOLYCUS   Your affairs there, what, with whom, the
condition of that fardel, the place of your dwelling, 721
your names, your ages, of what having, breeding, and 722
anything that is fitting to be known, discover.   723

CLOWN   We are but plain fellows, sir.   724

AUTOLYCUS   A lie; you are rough and hairy. Let me have
no lying. It becomes none but tradesmen, and they
often give us soldiers the lie, but we pay them for it 727
with stamped coin, not stabbing steel; therefore they
do not give us the lie.   729

CLOWN   Your Worship had like to have given us one, if 730
you had not taken yourself with the manner.   731

SHEPHERD   Are you a courtier, an't like you, sir?

AUTOLYCUS   Whether it like me or no, I am a courtier.
See'st thou not the air of the court in these enfoldings? 734
Hath not my gait in it the measure of the court? Re- 735
ceives not thy nose court odor from me? Reflect I not
on thy baseness court contempt? Think'st thou, for 737
that I insinuate to toze from thee thy business, I am 738
therefore no courtier? I am courtier cap-à-pie, and one 739
that will either push on or pluck back thy business
there. Whereupon I command thee to open thy affair. 741

SHEPHERD   My business, sir, is to the King.

AUTOLYCUS   What advocate hast thou to him?

SHEPHERD   I know not, an't like you.

CLOWN [aside to Shepherd]   "Advocate" 's the court
word for a pheasant. Say you have none.   746

SHEPHERD   None, sir. I have no pheasant, cock nor hen.

AUTOLYCUS [aside]
How blessed are we that are not simple men!
Yet nature might have made me as these are;
Therefore I will not disdain.

CLOWN [to Shepherd]   This cannot be but a great courtier.

SHEPHERD   His garments are rich, but he wears them
not handsomely.

CLOWN   He seems to be the more noble in being fantas- 755
tical. A great man, I'll warrant. I know by the picking 756
on's teeth.   757

AUTOLYCUS   The fardel there? What's i'th' fardel?
Wherefore that box?

SHEPHERD   Sir, there lies such secrets in this fardel and
box which none must know but the King, and which
he shall know within this hour if I may come to the
speech of him.

AUTOLYCUS   Age, thou hast lost thy labor.   764

SHEPHERD   Why, sir?

AUTOLYCUS   The King is not at the palace. He is gone
aboard a new ship to purge melancholy and air
himself; for, if thou be'st capable of things serious, 768
thou must know the King is full of grief.

SHEPHERD   So 'tis said, sir; about his son, that should
have married a shepherd's daughter.

AUTOLYCUS   If that shepherd be not in handfast, let him 772
fly. The curses he shall have, the tortures he shall feel,
will break the back of man, the heart of monster.

CLOWN   Think you so, sir?

AUTOLYCUS   Not he alone shall suffer what wit can make 776
heavy and vengeance bitter, but those that are ger- 777
mane to him, though removed fifty times, shall all 778
come under the hangman—which, though it be great
pity, yet it is necessary. An old sheep-whistling rogue, 780
a ram tender, to offer to have his daughter come into 781
grace? Some say he shall be stoned; but that death is 782
too soft for him, say I. Draw our throne into a sheep- 783
cote? All deaths are too few, the sharpest too easy. 784

CLOWN   Has the old man e'er a son, sir, do you hear,
an't like you, sir?

AUTOLYCUS   He has a son, who shall be flayed alive; then,
'nointed over with honey, set on the head of a wasp's
nest; then stand till he be three-quarters and a dram 789
dead; then recovered again with aqua vitae or some 790
other hot infusion; then, raw as he is, and in the hottest day prognostication proclaims, shall he be set 792
against a brick wall, the sun looking with a southward
eye upon him, where he is to behold him with flies 794
blown to death. But what talk we of these traitorly ras- 795
cals, whose miseries are to be smiled at, their offenses

704 go about make it his object   **711 fardel** bundle   **713 my master**
i.e., Florizel. (See 4.3.13.)   **714 at'** at the   **717 excrement** outgrowth of
hair, beard.   **719 an it like** if it please   **721 condition** nature
722 having property   **723 discover** reveal.   **724 plain** simple. (But
Autolycus plays on the meaning "smooth.")   **727 give . . . lie** i.e.,
cheat us. (But *giving the lie* also means to accuse a person to his face of
lying, an affront which a soldier would repay with *stabbing steel*.)
729 give (Autolycus punningly observes that, since soldiers pay
tradesmen for their wares, the tradesmen cannot be said to have *given*
the lie, and so a duel is avoided.)   **730 had like** was about   **731 taken
. . . manner** i.e., caught yourself in the act, stopped short. (The Clown
observes that Autolycus has once again avoided the "giving of the lie"
and its consequences in a duel by his clever equivocation. Compare
with Touchstone in *As You Like It*, 5.4)   **734 enfoldings** clothes.   **735
measure** stately tread   **737–8 for that . . . business** because I undertake to pry out of you what your business may be   **739 cap-à-pie**
from head to foot   **741 open** reveal   **746 pheasant** (The rustics suppose that Autolycus has asked them what gift they propose to present
as a bribe, as one might do to a judge in a court of law.)

755–6 fantastical eccentric.   **756–7 picking on's teeth** (A stylish
affectation in Shakespeare's time.)   **764 Age** Old man   **768 be'st
capable of** know anything about   **772 handfast** custody. (With a play
on "betrothal.")   **776 wit** ingenuity (in devising tortures)   **777–8 germane** related   **780 sheep-whistling** tending sheep by whistling after
them   **781 offer** dare   **782 grace** favor.   **783–4 sheepcote** pen for
sheep   **789 a dram** i.e., a small amount, a fraction   **790 aqua vitae**
brandy   **792 prognostication** forecasting (in the almanac)   **794 he**
i.e., the sun   **795 blown** swollen.   **what** i.e., why

being so capital? Tell me, for you seem to be honest
plain men, what you have to the King. Being some- 798
thing gently considered, I'll bring you where he is 799
aboard, tender your persons to his presence, whisper 800
him in your behalfs; and if it be in man besides the
King to effect your suits, here is man shall do it.

CLOWN [*to Shepherd*]   He seems to be of great authority.
Close with him, give him gold; and though authority 804
be a stubborn bear, yet he is oft led by the nose
with gold. Show the inside of your purse to the outside of his hand, and no more ado. Remember—
"stoned," and "flayed alive."

SHEPHERD   An't please you, sir, to undertake the
business for us, here is that gold I have. [*He offers
money.*] I'll make it as much more and leave this young
man in pawn till I bring it you.   812

AUTOLYCUS   After I have done what I promised?

SHEPHERD   Ay, sir.

AUTOLYCUS [*taking the money*]   Well, give me the moiety. 815
[*To the Clown*] Are you a party in this business?

CLOWN   In some sort, sir. But, though my case be a piti- 817
ful one, I hope I shall not be flayed out of it.

AUTOLYCUS   Oh, that's the case of the shepherd's son.
Hang him, he'll be made an example.

CLOWN [*to Shepherd*]   Comfort, good comfort! We must
to the King and show our strange sights. He must
know 'tis none of your daughter nor my sister; we are
gone else.—Sir, I will give you as much as this old 824
man does when the business is performed, and
remain, as he says, your pawn till it be brought you.

AUTOLYCUS   I will trust you. Walk before toward the
seaside; go on the right hand. I will but look upon the 828
hedge and follow you.   829

CLOWN [*to Shepherd*]   We are blessed in this man, as I
may say, even blessed.

SHEPHERD   Let's before, as he bids us. He was provided
to do us good.   *Exeunt [Shepherd and Clown].*

AUTOLYCUS   If I had a mind to be honest, I see Fortune
would not suffer me; she drops booties in my mouth.
I am courted now with a double occasion: gold, and a 836
means to do the Prince my master good, which who
knows how that may turn back to my advancement? I 838
will bring these two moles, these blind ones, aboard 839
him. If he think it fit to shore them again and that the 840
complaint they have to the King concerns him noth- 841
ing, let him call me rogue for being so far officious, for 842
I am proof against that title and what shame else 843
belongs to't. To him will I present them. There may be
matter in it.   [*Exit.*]

❖

798 **what you have to** what business you have with   **798–9 Being . . .
considered** i.e., (1) Being a gentleman of some influence (2) If I receive
a gentlemanly consideration, a bribe   **800 tender your persons** introduce you   **804 Close with him** Accept his offer   **812 in pawn** as
security   **815 moiety** half.   **817 case** (1) cause (2) skin   **824 gone
else** undone otherwise.   **828–9 look . . . hedge** i.e., relieve myself
836 occasion opportunity   **838 turn back** redound   **839–40 aboard
him** i.e., to him (Prince Florizel) aboard his ship.   **840 shore** put
ashore   **841–2 nothing** not at all   **843 proof against** invulnerable to

5.1

*Enter Leontes, Cleomenes, Dion, Paulina, [and]
servants.*

CLEOMENES
Sir, you have done enough, and have performed
A saintlike sorrow. No fault could you make
Which you have not redeemed—indeed, paid down
More penitence than done trespass. At the last,
Do as the heavens have done: forget your evil.
With them, forgive yourself.

LEONTES   Whilst I remember
Her and her virtues, I cannot forget
My blemishes in them, and so still think of   8
The wrong I did myself, which was so much
That heirless it hath made my kingdom and
Destroyed the sweet'st companion that e'er man
Bred his hopes out of. True?

PAULINA   Too true, my lord.
If one by one you wedded all the world,
Or from the all that are took something good   14
To make a perfect woman, she you killed
Would be unparalleled.

LEONTES   I think so. Killed?
She I killed? I did so, but thou strik'st me
Sorely to say I did. It is as bitter
Upon thy tongue as in my thought. Now, good now,   19
Say so but seldom.

CLEOMENES   Not at all, good lady.
You might have spoken a thousand things that would
Have done the time more benefit and graced
Your kindness better.

PAULINA   You are one of those
Would have him wed again.

DION   If you would not so,
You pity not the state nor the remembrance   25
Of his most sovereign name, consider little   26
What dangers by His Highness' fail of issue   27
May drop upon his kingdom and devour
Incertain lookers-on. What were more holy   29
Than to rejoice the former queen is well?   30
What holier than, for royalty's repair,
For present comfort and for future good,
To bless the bed of majesty again
With a sweet fellow to't?

PAULINA   There is none worthy,
Respecting her that's gone. Besides, the gods   35
Will have fulfilled their secret purposes;   36
For has not the divine Apollo said,
Is't not the tenor of his oracle,
That King Leontes shall not have an heir

5.1. Location: Sicilia. The royal court.
8 in them in comparison with them   **14 the all that are** all the women
that there are   **19 good now** i.e., if you please   **25 nor the remembrance** i.e., nor give consideration to the perpetuation (through bearing a child and heir)   **26 consider** you consider   **27 fail of issue**
failure to produce an heir   **29 Incertain** not knowing what to think or
do (about the royal succession)   **30 well** happy, at rest (in heaven).
35 Respecting in comparison with   **36 Will . . . purposes** are determined to have their secret purposes fulfilled

Till his lost child be found? Which that it shall
Is all as monstrous to our human reason
As my Antigonus to break his grave   42
And come again to me, who, on my life,
Did perish with the infant. 'Tis your counsel   44
My lord should to the heavens be contrary,
Oppose against their wills. [*To Leontes*] Care not for
   issue.   46
The crown will find an heir. Great Alexander
Left his to th' worthiest; so his successor   48
Was like to be the best.

LEONTES   Good Paulina,
Who hast the memory of Hermione,
I know, in honor, oh, that ever I
Had squared me to thy counsel! Then even now   52
I might have looked upon my queen's full eyes,
Have taken treasure from her lips—

PAULINA   And left them
More rich for what they yielded.

LEONTES   Thou speak'st truth.
No more such wives, therefore no wife. One worse,   56
And better used, would make her sainted spirit   57
Again possess her corpse, and on this stage,   58
Where we're offenders now, appear soul-vexed,
And begin, "Why to me?"

PAULINA   Had she such power,   60
She had just cause.

LEONTES   She had, and would incense me   61
To murder her I married.

PAULINA   I should so.   62
Were I the ghost that walked, I'd bid you mark
Her eye and tell me for what dull part in't
You chose her. Then I'd shriek, that even your ears
Should rift to hear me, and the words that followed   66
Should be, "Remember mine."

LEONTES   Stars, stars,   67
And all eyes else dead coals! Fear thou no wife;   68
I'll have no wife, Paulina.

PAULINA   Will you swear
Never to marry but by my free leave?

LEONTES
Never, Paulina, so be blest my spirit!

PAULINA
Then, good my lords, bear witness to his oath.

CLEOMENES
You tempt him overmuch.

PAULINA   Unless another,   73
As like Hermione as is her picture,

Affront his eye.

CLEOMENES   Good madam—

PAULINA   I have done.   75
Yet if my lord will marry—if you will, sir,
No remedy, but you will—give me the office
To choose you a queen. She shall not be so young
As was your former, but she shall be such
As, walked your first queen's ghost, it should take joy   80
To see her in your arms.

LEONTES   My true Paulina,
We shall not marry till thou bidd'st us.

PAULINA   That
Shall be when your first queen's again in breath;
Never till then.   84

         Enter a Gentleman.

GENTLEMAN
One that gives out himself Prince Florizel,   85
Son of Polixenes, with his princess—she
The fairest I have yet beheld—desires access
To your high presence.

LEONTES   What with him? He comes not   88
Like to his father's greatness. His approach,   89
So out of circumstance and sudden, tells us   90
'Tis not a visitation framed, but forced   91
By need and accident. What train?

GENTLEMAN   But few,   92
And those but mean.

LEONTES   His princess, say you, with him?   93

GENTLEMAN
Ay, the most peerless piece of earth, I think,
That e'er the sun shone bright on.

PAULINA   Oh, Hermione,
As every present time doth boast itself   96
Above a better gone, so must thy grave   97
Give way to what's seen now! [*To the Gentleman*] Sir,
   you yourself   98
Have said and writ so, but your writing now
Is colder than that theme. She had not been   100
Nor was not to be equaled—thus your verse   101
Flowed with her beauty once. 'Tis shrewdly ebbed   102
To say you have seen a better.

GENTLEMAN   Pardon, madam.
The one I have almost forgot—your pardon!
The other, when she has obtained your eye,
Will have your tongue too. This is a creature,   106
Would she begin a sect, might quench the zeal

42 As as for   **44 'Tis your counsel** It's your advice that   **46 Oppose** oppose himself.   **Care not for** Do not be anxious about   **48 Left . . . worthiest** (When Alexander the Great died in 323 B.C., his son Alexander was yet unborn, necessitating the choice of an heir.)
52 squared me adjusted or regulated myself   **56–7 One . . . used** i.e., If I took a new, less excellent wife and treated her better   **57 her** Hermione's   **58 possess her corpse** i.e., return to earth (*this stage*) in Hermione's human shape   **60 Why to me?** Why this offense to me?   **61 had** would have.   **incense** stir up, incite   **62 should so** would similarly incite you.   **66 rift** rive, split   **67 mine** my eyes.   **Stars** i.e., Her eyes were stars   **68 all eyes else** all other eyes   **73 tempt** bear down on

75 Affront confront   **80 walked . . . ghost** if your first queen's ghost were to walk.   **take joy** be overjoyed   **84.1 *Enter a Gentleman*** (He is called a "Servant" in the Folio text, but his writing poetry in lines 100–4 is more consistent with his being a courtier. Any such person at court is a servant of the king.)   **85 gives out himself** reports himself to be   **88 What** What retinue   **89 Like to** in a manner consistent with   **90 out of circumstance** without ceremony   **91 framed** planned   **92 train** retinue.   **93 mean** lowly.   **96–8 As . . . now!** As every present age boasts its superiority to past times that were in point of fact better, so you, long dead, must give way to present fashion!   **100 that theme** i.e., Hermione, the subject of your verses.   **100–1 She . . . equaled** (Presumably, the poet wrote "She has not been nor is not to be equaled.")   **102 'Tis shrewdly ebbed** i.e., You've egregiously gone back on your word   **106 tongue** i.e., approval

Of all professors else, make proselytes 108
Of who she but bid follow.

PAULINA   How? Not women! 109

GENTLEMAN
Women will love her that she is a woman
More worth than any man; men, that she is
The rarest of all women.

LEONTES   Go, Cleomenes.
Yourself, assisted with your honored friends,
Bring them to our embracement.
          Exit [Cleomenes with others].
          Still, 'tis strange
He thus should steal upon us.

PAULINA   Had our prince,
Jewel of children, seen this hour, he had paired
Well with this lord. There was not full a month
Between their births.

LEONTES   Prithee, no more, cease. Thou know'st
He dies to me again when talked of. Sure,
When I shall see this gentleman, thy speeches
Will bring me to consider that which may
Unfurnish me of reason. They are come. 123
    Enter Florizel, Perdita, Cleomenes, and others.
Your mother was most true to wedlock, Prince,
For she did print your royal father off,
Conceiving you. Were I but twenty-one,
Your father's image is so hit in you, 127
His very air, that I should call you brother,
As I did him, and speak of something wildly
By us performed before. Most dearly welcome!
And your fair princess—goddess! Oh! Alas,
I lost a couple that twixt heaven and earth
Might thus have stood begetting wonder as
You, gracious couple, do. And then I lost—
All mine own folly—the society,
Amity too, of your brave father, whom, 136
Though bearing misery, I desire my life 137
Once more to look on him.

FLORIZEL   By his command 138
Have I here touched Sicilia, and from him
Give you all greetings that a king, at friend, 140
Can send his brother; and but infirmity, 141
Which waits upon worn times, hath something seized 142
His wished ability, he had himself 143
The lands and waters twixt your throne and his
Measured to look upon you, whom he loves— 145
He bade me say so—more than all the scepters
And those that bear them living.

LEONTES   O my brother! 147
Good gentleman, the wrongs I have done thee stir

Afresh within me, and these thy offices, 149
So rarely kind, are as interpreters 150
Of my behindhand slackness. Welcome hither, 151
As is the spring to th'earth. And hath he too
Exposed this paragon to th' fearful usage—
At least ungentle—of the dreadful Neptune, 154
To greet a man not worth her pains, much less
Th'adventure of her person?

FLORIZEL   Good my lord, 156
She came from Libya.

LEONTES   Where the warlike Smalus,
That noble honored lord, is feared and loved?

FLORIZEL
Most royal sir, from thence, from him, whose daughter 159
His tears proclaimed his, parting with her. Thence, 160
A prosperous south wind friendly, we have crossed,
To execute the charge my father gave me
For visiting Your Highness. My best train
I have from your Sicilian shores dismissed,
Who for Bohemia bend, to signify 165
Not only my success in Libya, sir,
But my arrival and my wife's in safety
Here where we are.

LEONTES   The blessèd gods
Purge all infection from our air whilst you
Do climate here! You have a holy father, 170
A graceful gentleman, against whose person, 171
So sacred as it is, I have done sin,
For which the heavens, taking angry note,
Have left me issueless; and your father's blest,
As he from heaven merits it, with you,
Worthy his goodness. What might I have been,
Might I a son and daughter now have looked on,
Such goodly things as you?

          Enter a Lord.

LORD   Most noble sir,
That which I shall report will bear no credit
Were not the proof so nigh. Please you, great sir,
Bohemia greets you from himself by me;
Desires you to attach his son, who has— 182
His dignity and duty both cast off— 183
Fled from his father, from his hopes, and with
A shepherd's daughter.

LEONTES   Where's Bohemia? Speak.

LORD
Here in your city. I now came from him.
I speak amazedly, and it becomes 187
My marvel and my message. To your court 188
Whiles he was hast'ning—in the chase, it seems,
Of this fair couple—meets he on the way

---

108 professors else believers in other sects or deities   **109 Of . . . follow** of all those whom she merely told to follow her.   **How? Not women!** What do you mean? Surely women wouldn't become converts!   **123 Unfurnish** deprive, divest   **127 hit** exactly reproduced   **136 brave** noble   **137 my life** i.e., to live long enough   **138 him** (Redundant in modern syntax.)   **140 at friend** in friendship   **141 but** were it not that   **142 waits . . . times** attends old age   **142–3 something . . . ability** to some extent taken away his ability (to travel) as he wishes   **145 Measured** traversed   **147 those . . . living** those living kings who bear scepters.

149 offices messages of good will, courteous attentions   **150 rarely** exceptionally   **150–1 are . . . slackness** are like commentators on my slowness in greeting you.   **154 Neptune** god of the sea   **156 Th'adventure** the hazard   **159–60 whose . . . her** whose tears, as he parted with her, proclaimed her to be his daughter.   **165 bend** direct their course   **170 climate** dwell, reside (in this clime)   **171 graceful** full of grace, gracious   **182 attach** arrest   **183 dignity and duty** princely dignity and filial duty   **187–8 I . . . message** i.e., I speak perplexedly as befits my perplexity and my astonishing news.

The father of this seeming lady and
Her brother, having both their country quitted
With this young prince.

FLORIZEL   Camillo has betrayed me,
Whose honor and whose honesty till now
Endured all weathers.

LORD   Lay't so to his charge.   195
He's with the King your father.

LEONTES   Who? Camillo?

LORD
Camillo, sir. I spake with him, who now
Has these poor men in question. Never saw I   198
Wretches so quake. They kneel, they kiss the earth,
Forswear themselves as often as they speak.
Bohemia stops his ears and threatens them
With divers deaths in death.

PERDITA   Oh, my poor father!   202
The heaven sets spies upon us, will not have
Our contract celebrated.

LEONTES   You are married?

FLORIZEL
We are not, sir, nor are we like to be.   205
The stars, I see, will kiss the valleys first;
The odds for high and low's alike.

LEONTES   My lord,   207
Is this the daughter of a king?

FLORIZEL   She is,
When once she is my wife.

LEONTES
That "once," I see, by your good father's speed
Will come on very slowly. I am sorry,
Most sorry, you have broken from his liking
Where you were tied in duty, and as sorry
Your choice is not so rich in worth as beauty,   214
That you might well enjoy her.

FLORIZEL [to Perdita]   Dear, look up.
Though Fortune, visible an enemy,   216
Should chase us with my father, power no jot   217
Hath she to change our loves.—Beseech you, sir,
Remember since you owed no more to time   219
Than I do now. With thought of such affections,   220
Step forth mine advocate. At your request
My father will grant precious things as trifles.

LEONTES
Would he do so, I'd beg your precious mistress,
Which he counts but a trifle.

PAULINA   Sir, my liege,
Your eye hath too much youth in't. Not a month
'Fore your queen died, she was more worth such
    gazes
Than what you look on now.

LEONTES   I thought of her

Even in these looks I made. [To Florizel] But your
    petition
Is yet unanswered. I will to your father.
Your honor not o'erthrown by your desires,   230
I am friend to them and you. Upon which errand
I now go toward him. Therefore follow me,
And mark what way I make. Come, good my lord.   233
                               Exeunt.

❖

5.2

Enter Autolycus and a Gentleman.

AUTOLYCUS   Beseech you, sir, were you present at this
relation?   2

FIRST GENTLEMAN   I was by at the opening of the fardel,
heard the old shepherd deliver the manner how he   4
found it; whereupon, after a little amazedness, we
were all commanded out of the chamber. Only this,
methought, I heard the shepherd say: he found the
child.

AUTOLYCUS   I would most gladly know the issue of it.   9

FIRST GENTLEMAN   I make a broken delivery of the busi-   10
ness, but the changes I perceived in the King and Camillo were very notes of admiration. They seemed al-   12
most, with staring on one another, to tear the cases of   13
their eyes. There was speech in their dumbness, lan-   14
guage in their very gesture. They looked as they had   15
heard of a world ransomed, or one destroyed. A notable
passion of wonder appeared in them, but the wisest
beholder, that knew no more but seeing, could not say   18
if th'importance were joy or sorrow; but in the ex-   19
tremity of the one it must needs be.   20

Enter another Gentleman.

Here comes a gentleman that haply knows more.—   21
The news, Rogero?

SECOND GENTLEMAN   Nothing but bonfires. The oracle
is fulfilled; the King's daughter is found. Such a deal of   24
wonder is broken out within this hour that ballad
makers cannot be able to express it.

Enter another Gentleman.

Here comes the Lady Paulina's steward. He can deliver
you more.—How goes it now, sir? This news which is
called true is so like an old tale that the verity of it is in
strong suspicion. Has the King found his heir?

THIRD GENTLEMAN   Most true, if ever truth were preg-   31
nant by circumstance. That which you hear you'll   32

---

195 **Lay't . . . charge** Confront him with it directly.   **198 in question**
under interrogation.   **202 deaths** i.e., tortures   **205 like** likely   **207
The odds . . . alike** Fortune treats high and low alike.   **214 worth**
rank   **216–17 Though . . . father** Though the goddess Fortune herself
were to manifest herself as our enemy and join my father in chasing
us   **219–20 since . . . now** when you were no older than I am now.
220 With . . . affections Recalling what it was to be in love at that age

230 **Your . . . desires** If your chaste honor has not been overcome by
sexual desire, or, if what you want in this match is compatible with
your royal honor   **233 way** progress
5.2. Location: Sicilia. At court.
2 relation narrative, account.   **4 deliver** report   **9 issue** outcome
10 broken disjointed, fragmented   **12 very notes of admiration** veritable marks of wonderment.   **13–14 cases of their eyes** eyelids.   **15 as**
as if   **18 no . . . seeing** nothing except what he could see   **19 th'importance** the import, meaning   **20 of the one** of one or the other
21 haply perhaps   **24 deal** huge quantity   **31–2 pregnant by circumstance** made apparent by circumstantial evidence.

swear you see, there is such unity in the proofs. The mantle of Queen Hermione's, her jewel about the neck of it, the letters of Antigonus found with it which they know to be his character, the majesty of the creature in 36 resemblance of the mother, the affection of nobleness 37 which nature shows above her breeding, and many 38 other evidences proclaim her with all certainty to be the King's daughter. Did you see the meeting of the two kings?

SECOND GENTLEMAN   No.

THIRD GENTLEMAN   Then have you lost a sight which was to be seen, cannot be spoken of. There might you have beheld one joy crown another, so and in such manner that it seemed Sorrow wept to take leave of them, for their joy waded in tears. There was casting up of eyes, holding up of hands, with countenance of 48 such distraction that they were to be known by garment, not by favor. Our king, being ready to leap 50 out of himself for joy of his found daughter, as if that joy were now become a loss, cries, "Oh, thy mother, thy mother!" then asks Bohemia forgiveness; then embraces his son-in-law; then again worries he his 54 daughter with clipping her; now he thanks the old 55 shepherd, which stands by like a weather-bitten con- 56 duit of many kings' reigns. I never heard of such 57 another encounter, which lames report to follow it and 58 undoes description to do it. 59

SECOND GENTLEMAN   What, pray you, became of Antigonus, that carried hence the child?

THIRD GENTLEMAN   Like an old tale still, which will have matter to rehearse though credit be asleep and not an 63 ear open. He was torn to pieces with a bear. This 64 avouches the shepherd's son, who has not only his 65 innocence, which seems much, to justify him, but a 66 handkerchief and rings of his that Paulina knows. 67

FIRST GENTLEMAN   What became of his bark and his followers?

THIRD GENTLEMAN   Wrecked the same instant of their master's death and in the view of the shepherd; so that all the instruments which aided to expose the child were even then lost when it was found. But oh, the noble combat that twixt joy and sorrow was fought in Paulina! She had one eye declined for the loss of her 75 husband, another elevated that the oracle was fulfilled. 76 She lifted the Princess from the earth, and so locks her in embracing as if she would pin her to her heart, that she might no more be in danger of losing. 79

FIRST GENTLEMAN   The dignity of this act was worth the audience of kings and princes, for by such was it acted.

THIRD GENTLEMAN   One of the prettiest touches of all, and that which angled for mine eyes—caught the water, though not the fish—was when, at the relation of the Queen's death, with the manner how she came to't bravely confessed and lamented by the King, how attentiveness wounded his daughter; till, from 88 one sign of dolor to another, she did, with an "Alas!" I 89 would fain say, bleed tears, for I am sure my heart wept blood. Who was most marble there changed 91 color; some swooned, all sorrowed. If all the world could have seen't, the woe had been universal.

FIRST GENTLEMAN   Are they returned to the court?

THIRD GENTLEMAN   No. The Princess hearing of her mother's statue, which is in the keeping of Paulina—a piece many years in doing and now newly performed 97 by that rare Italian master, Julio Romano, who, had he 98 himself eternity and could put breath into his work, would beguile Nature of her custom, so perfectly he is 100 her ape; he so near to Hermione hath done Hermione 101 that they say one would speak to her and stand in hope of answer—thither with all greediness of affec- 103 tion are they gone, and there they intend to sup. 104

SECOND GENTLEMAN   I thought she had some great matter there in hand, for she hath privately twice or thrice a day, ever since the death of Hermione, visited that removed house. Shall we thither and with our com- 108 pany piece the rejoicing? 109

FIRST GENTLEMAN   Who would be thence that has the benefit of access? Every wink of an eye some new grace will be born. Our absence makes us unthrifty to 112 our knowledge. Let's along.   Exeunt [Gentlemen].

AUTOLYCUS   Now, had I not the dash of my former life 114 in me, would preferment drop on my head. I brought 115 the old man and his son aboard the Prince, told him I 116 heard them talk of a fardel and I know not what. But he at that time overfond of the shepherd's daughter—so he then took her to be—who began to be much seasick, and himself little better, extremity of weather continuing, this mystery remained undiscov- ered. But 'tis all one to me, for had I been the finder 122 out of this secret, it would not have relished among 123 my other discredits.

Enter Shepherd and Clown, [dressed in finery].

Here come those I have done good to against my will, and already appearing in the blossoms of their fortune.

SHEPHERD   Come, boy. I am past more children, but thy sons and daughters will be all gentlemen born.

36 **character** handwriting   37 **affection of** natural disposition to 38 **breeding** rearing   48 **countenance** bearing, demeanor   50 **favor** features.   54 **worries he** he pesters   55 **clipping** embracing 56–7 **which . . . reigns** who stands by weeping like a weather-beaten fountain that has stood there over the course of many kings' reigns. 58–9 **which . . . do it** which makes any account of it seem inadequate and beggars the powers of description in an attempt to do justice to it.   63 **rehearse** relate.   **credit** belief   64 **with** by   65 **avouches** confirms, corroborates   66 **innocence** simplemindedness (such that he would seem unable to invent such a story)   67 **his** Antigonus's 75–6 **She . . . fulfilled** i.e., She wept and laughed at the same time. 79 **losing** being lost.

88 **attentiveness** listening to it   89 **dolor** grief   91 **Who . . . marble** Even the most hardhearted   97 **performed** completed   98 **Julio Romano** Italian painter and sculptor of the sixteenth century, better known as a painter (and an anachronism in this play)   100 **beguile** deprive, cheat.   **custom** trade   101 **ape** imitator   103–4 **greediness of affection** eagerness born of love   104 **sup** i.e., feed their hungry eyes (?) or, perhaps, have a commemorative banquet (?). 108 **removed** sequestered   109 **piece** add to, augment   112 **unthrifty to** passing up an opportunity to increase   114–15 **had I . . . head** if it weren't for the lingering reputation of petty thievery that hangs about me, royal favor would be sure to fall to my lot.   116 **the Prince** the Prince's ship   122 **'tis all one** it's all the same   123 **relished** tasted well, suited

CLOWN [*to Autolycus*] You are well met, sir. You denied to fight
with me this other day because I was no gentleman   131
born. See you these clothes? Say you see them not and
think me still no gentleman born. You were best say
these robes are not gentlemen born. Give me the lie,   134
do, and try whether I am not now a gentleman born.

AUTOLYCUS   I know you are now, sir, a gentleman born.

CLOWN   Ay, and have been so any time these four
hours.

SHEPHERD   And so have I, boy.

CLOWN   So you have. But I was a gentleman born before
my father; for the King's son took me by the hand
and called me brother; and then the two kings called
my father brother; and then the Prince my brother and
the Princess my sister called my father father; and so
we wept, and there was the first gentlemanlike tears
that ever we shed.

SHEPHERD   We may live, son, to shed many more.

CLOWN   Ay, or else 'twere hard luck, being in so pre-   148
posterous estate as we are.   149

AUTOLYCUS   I humbly beseech you, sir, to pardon me
all the faults I have committed to Your Worship, and to
give me your good report to the Prince my master.   152

SHEPHERD   Prithee, son, do; for we must be gentle, now   153
we are gentlemen.

CLOWN [*to Autolycus*]   Thou wilt amend thy life?

AUTOLYCUS   Ay, an it like Your good Worship.   156

CLOWN   Give me thy hand. I will swear to the Prince
thou art as honest a true fellow as any is in Bohemia.   158

SHEPHERD   You may say it, but not swear it.

CLOWN   Not swear it, now I am a gentleman? Let boors   160
and franklins say it; I'll swear it.   161

SHEPHERD   How if it be false, son?

CLOWN   If it be ne'er so false, a true gentleman may
swear it in the behalf of his friend.—And I'll swear to
the Prince thou art a tall fellow of thy hands and that   165
thou wilt not be drunk; but I know thou art no tall
fellow of thy hands and that thou wilt be drunk. But
I'll swear it, and I would thou wouldst be a tall fellow
of thy hands.

AUTOLYCUS   I will prove so, sir, to my power.   170

CLOWN   Ay, by any means prove a tall fellow. If I do not
wonder how thou dar'st venture to be drunk, not
being a tall fellow, trust me not. Hark, the kings and
the princes, our kindred, are going to see the Queen's
picture. Come, follow us. We'll be thy good masters.   175

Exeunt.

❧

5.3

Enter Leontes, Polixenes, Florizel, Perdita,
Camillo, Paulina, lords, etc.

LEONTES
O grave and good Paulina, the great comfort
That I have had of thee!

PAULINA   What, sovereign sir,   2
I did not well, I meant well. All my services
You have paid home. But that you have vouchsafed,   4
With your crowned brother and these your contracted
Heirs of your kingdoms, my poor house to visit,
It is a surplus of your grace which never   7
My life may last to answer.

LEONTES   O Paulina,   8
We honor you with trouble. But we came   9
To see the statue of our queen. Your gallery
Have we passed through, not without much content
In many singularities; but we saw not   12
That which my daughter came to look upon,
The statue of her mother.

PAULINA   As she lived peerless,
So her dead likeness, I do well believe,
Excels whatever yet you looked upon
Or hand of man hath done. Therefore I keep it
Lonely, apart. But here it is. Prepare   18
To see the life as lively mocked as ever   19
Still sleep mocked death. Behold, and say 'tis well.   20
[*Paulina draws a curtain, and discovers*]
Hermione [*standing*] *like a statue.*
I like your silence; it the more shows off
Your wonder. But yet speak; first, you, my liege.
Comes it not something near?

LEONTES   Her natural posture!   23
Chide me, dear stone, that I may say indeed
Thou art Hermione; or rather, thou art she
In thy not chiding, for she was as tender
As infancy and grace. But yet, Paulina,
Hermione was not as much wrinkled, nothing   28
So agèd as this seems.

POLIXENES   Oh, not by much.

PAULINA
So much the more our carver's excellence,
Which lets go by some sixteen years and makes her
As she lived now.

LEONTES   As now she might have done,   32
So much to my good comfort as it is
Now piercing to my soul. Oh, thus she stood,
Even with such life of majesty—warm life,
As now it coldly stands—when first I wooed her!
I am ashamed. Does not the stone rebuke me
For being more stone than it? O royal piece!   38

131 **this other** the other   134 **Give me the lie** Accuse me to my face
of lying (an insult that requires a challenge to a duel)   148–9 **prepos-**
terous (Blunder for "prosperous.")   152 **me** on my behalf   153 **gen-**
tle nobly generous   156 **an it like** if it please   158 **honest a true**
worthy an honest   160 **boors** peasants   161 **franklins** farmers owning their own small farms   165 **tall . . . hands** brave fellow   170 **my**
power the best of my ability. (Autolycus slyly promises to use his hands
well—in picking pockets.)   175 **picture** i.e., likeness, painted statue.

5.3. Location: Sicilia. Paulina's house.
2 **What** Whatever   4 **home** fully.   7–8 **which . . . answer** which I can
never live long enough to be able to repay.   9 **We . . . trouble** i.e., we
trouble you with the demands of hospitality, though you are kind
enough to call it an honor.   12 **singularities** rarities, curiosities
18 **Lonely** isolated   19 **as lively mocked** as realistically counterfeited
20 **Still** motionless   23 **something** somewhat   28 **nothing** not at all
32 **As she** as if she   38 **piece** work of art.

There's magic in thy majesty, which has
My evils conjured to remembrance and
From thy admiring daughter took the spirits,   41
Standing like stone with thee.

PERDITA   And give me leave,
And do not say 'tis superstition, that
I kneel and then implore her blessing. Lady,
                                    [kneeling]
Dear Queen, that ended when I but began,
Give me that hand of yours to kiss.

PAULINA   Oh, patience!
The statue is but newly fixed; the color's   47
Not dry.

CAMILLO
My lord, your sorrow was too sore laid on,   49
Which sixteen winters cannot blow away,
So many summers dry. Scarce any joy   51
Did ever so long live; no sorrow
But killed itself much sooner.

POLIXENES   Dear my brother,
Let him that was the cause of this have power   54
To take off so much grief from you as he
Will piece up in himself.

PAULINA   Indeed, my lord,   56
If I had thought the sight of my poor image
Would thus have wrought you—for the stone is
      mine—   58
I'd not have showed it.

LEONTES   Do not draw the curtain.

PAULINA
No longer shall you gaze on't, lest your fancy
May think anon it moves.

LEONTES   Let be, let be.
Would I were dead but that methinks already—
What was he that did make it? See, my lord,
Would you not deem it breathed? And that those veins
Did verily bear blood?

POLIXENES   Masterly done.
The very life seems warm upon her lip.

LEONTES
The fixture of her eye has motion in't,   67
As we are mocked with art.

PAULINA   I'll draw the curtain.   68
My lord's almost so far transported that
He'll think anon it lives.

LEONTES   Oh, sweet Paulina,
Make me to think so twenty years together!
No settled senses of the world can match   72
The pleasure of that madness. Let't alone.

PAULINA
I am sorry, sir, I have thus far stirred you; but

I could afflict you farther.

LEONTES   Do, Paulina;
For this affliction has a taste as sweet
As any cordial comfort. Still methinks   77
There is an air comes from her. What fine chisel
Could ever yet cut breath? Let no man mock me,
For I will kiss her.

PAULINA   Good my lord, forbear.
The ruddiness upon her lip is wet;
You'll mar it if you kiss it, stain your own
With oily painting. Shall I draw the curtain?   83

LEONTES
No, not these twenty years.

PERDITA   So long could I
Stand by, a looker on.

PAULINA   Either forbear,
Quit presently the chapel, or resolve you   86
For more amazement. If you can behold it,
I'll make the statue move indeed, descend
And take you by the hand. But then you'll think—
Which I protest against—I am assisted
By wicked powers.

LEONTES   What you can make her do
I am content to look on, what to speak
I am content to hear; for 'tis as easy
To make her speak as move.

PAULINA   It is required
You do awake your faith. Then all stand still.
On; those that think it is unlawful business   96
I am about, let them depart.

LEONTES   Proceed.
No foot shall stir.

PAULINA   Music, awake her; strike!   [Music.]   98
'Tis time. Descend. Be stone no more. Approach.
Strike all that look upon with marvel. Come,   100
I'll fill your grave up. Stir, nay, come away,
Bequeath to death your numbness, for from him   102
Dear life redeems you.—You perceive she stirs.
                        [Hermione comes down.]
Start not. Her actions shall be holy as
You hear my spell is lawful. Do not shun her   105
Until you see her die again, for then   106
You kill her double. Nay, present your hand.   107
When she was young you wooed her. Now in age
Is she become the suitor?   [Leontes touches her.]

LEONTES   Oh, she's warm!
If this be magic, let it be an art
Lawful as eating.

POLIXENES   She embraces him.

CAMILLO   She hangs about his neck.
If she pertain to life, let her speak too.   114

POLIXENES
Ay, and make it manifest where she has lived,
Or how stol'n from the dead.

PAULINA   That she is living,

---

41 admiring filled with wonder.   **spirits** vital spirits   **47 fixed** made fast in its color   **49 sore** heavily   **51 So . . . dry** i.e., and sixteen summers cannot dry up. (Camillo tells the King that he has imposed too heavy a sorrow on himself if even sixteen years' time cannot end it.) **54 him** i.e., myself (as an innocent cause, but still a cause)   **56 piece up in himself** add to his own burden.   **58 wrought** affected   **67 The fixture . . . in't** i.e., Her eye, though motionless, gives the appearance of motion   **68 As . . . art** in such a way that we are fooled by artistic illusion.   **72 No settled . . . world** No calm mind in the world

77 cordial restorative, heartwarming   **83 painting** paint.
86 presently immediately   **96 On; those** (Often emended to *Or those.*)   **98 strike** strike up.   **100 upon** on   **102 him** i.e., death   **105–7 Do . . . double** i.e., If you ever shun her during the rest of her life, you will kill her again.   **114 pertain to life** be truly alive

Were it but told you, should be hooted at
Like an old tale; but it appears she lives,
Though yet she speak not. Mark a little while.
[*To Perdita*] Please you to interpose, fair madam. Kneel,   120
And pray your mother's blessing.—Turn, good lady;
Our Perdita is found.

HERMIONE   You gods, look down
And from your sacred vials pour your graces
Upon my daughter's head!—Tell me, mine own,
Where hast thou been preserved? Where lived? How
     found
Thy father's court? For thou shalt hear that I,
Knowing by Paulina that the oracle
Gave hope thou wast in being, have preserved
Myself to see the issue.   129

PAULINA   There's time enough for that,
Lest they desire upon this push to trouble   131
Your joys with like relation. Go together,   132
You precious winners all; your exultation
Partake to everyone. I, an old turtle,   134
Will wing me to some withered bough and there

My mate, that's never to be found again,   136
Lament till I am lost.

LEONTES   Oh, peace, Paulina!   137
Thou shouldst a husband take by my consent,
As I by thine a wife. This is a match,
And made between 's by vows. Thou hast found
     mine,
But how is to be questioned, for I saw her,
As I thought, dead, and have in vain said many
A prayer upon her grave. I'll not seek far—
For him, I partly know his mind—to find thee   144
An honorable husband. Come, Camillo,
And take her by the hand, whose worth and honesty   146
Is richly noted and here justified   147
By us, a pair of kings. Let's from this place.
[*To Hermione*] What? Look upon my brother. Both your
     pardons,
That e'er I put between your holy looks
My ill suspicion. This' your son-in-law   151
And son unto the King, whom, heavens directing,
Is trothplight to your daughter. Good Paulina,   153
Lead us from hence, where we may leisurely
Each one demand and answer to his part
Performed in this wide gap of time since first
We were dissevered. Hastily lead away.   *Exeunt.*

---

120 madam (Addressed to Perdita as Princess and affianced to be married.)   **129 the issue** (1) the outcome (2) my child.   **131–2 Lest . . . relation** lest they (bystanders) insist, at this critical juncture, on interrupting this moment of joy with your relating of your story or with their telling what has happened to them.   **134 Partake to** share with, communicate.   **turtle** turtledove

136–7 My mate . . . lost grieve for my lost mate until I die.   **144 For** as for   **146 whose** i.e., Camillo's   **147 richly noted** abundantly acknowledged.   **justified** avouched   **151 This'** This is   **153 trothplight** betrothed

The Tempest

Shakespeare creates in *The Tempest* a world of the imagination, a place of conflict and ultimately of magical rejuvenation, like the forests of *A Midsummer Night's Dream* and *As You Like It*. The journey to Shakespeare's island is to a realm of art where everything is controlled by the artist-figure. Yet the journey is no escape from reality, for the island shows people what they are, as well as what they ought to be. Even its location juxtaposes the "real" world with an idealized landscape: like Plato's New Atlantis or Thomas More's Utopia, Shakespeare's island is to be found both somewhere and nowhere. On the narrative level, it is located in the Mediterranean Sea. Yet there are overtones of the New World, the Western Hemisphere, where Thomas More had situated his island of Utopia. Ariel fetches dew at Prospero's command from the "Bermudas" (1.2.230). Caliban when prostrate reminds Trinculo of a "dead Indian" (2.2.33) who might be displayed before gullible crowds eager to see such a prodigious creature from across the seas, and Caliban's god, Setebos, was, according to Richard Eden's account of Magellan's circumnavigation of the globe (in *History of Travel*, 1577), worshiped by South American natives. An inspiration for Shakespeare's story (for which no direct literary source is known) may well have been various accounts of the shipwreck in the Bermudas in 1609 of the *Sea Venture,* which was carrying settlers to the new Virginian colony. Shakespeare borrowed details from Sylvester Jourdain's *A Discovery of the Bermudas, Otherwise Called the Isle of Devils,* published in 1610, and from William Strachey's *A True Reportory of the Wreck and Redemption . . . from the Islands of the Bermudas,* which Shakespeare must have seen in manuscript since it was not published until after his death. He wrote the play shortly after reading these works, for *The Tempest* was acted at court in 1611. He may also have known or heard of various accounts of Magellan's circumnavigation of the world in 1519–1522 (including Richard Eden's shortened English version, as part of his *History of Travel,*

of an Italian narrative by Antonio Pigafetta), Francis Fletcher's journal of Sir Francis Drake's circumnavigation in 1577–1580, Richard Rich's *News from Virginia* (1610), and still other potential sources of information. Shakespeare's fascination with the Western Hemisphere gave him, not the actual location of his story, which remains Mediterranean, but a state of mind associated with newness and the unfamiliar. From this strange and unknown place, we gain a radical perspective on the old world of European culture. Miranda sees on the island a "new world" in which humankind appears "brave" (5.1.185), and, although her wonder must be tempered by Prospero's rejoinder that "'Tis new to thee" (line 186) and by Aldous Huxley's still more ironic use of her phrase in the title of his satirical novel *Brave New World*, the island endures as a restorative vision. Even though we experience it fleetingly, as in a dream, this nonexistent realm assumes a permanence enjoyed by all great works of art.

Prospero rules autocratically as artist-king and patriarch over this imaginary world, conjuring up trials and visions to test people's intentions and awaken their consciences. To the island come an assortment of persons who, because they require varied ordeals, are separated by Prospero and Ariel into three groups: King Alonso and those accompanying him; Alonso's son, Ferdinand; and Stephano and Trinculo. Prospero's authority over them, though strong, has limits. As Duke of Milan, he was bookishly inattentive to political matters and thus vulnerable to the Machiavellian conniving of his younger brother, Antonio. Only in this world apart, the artist's world, do his powers derived from learning find their proper sphere. Because he cannot control the world beyond his isle, he must wait for "strange, bountiful Fortune, / Now my dear lady" (1.2.179–80) to bring his enemies near his shore. He eschews, moreover, the black arts of diabolism. His is a white magic, devoted ultimately to what he considers moral ends: rescuing Ariel from the spell of the witch Sycorax, curbing the appetite of Caliban, spying on Antonio and Sebastian in the role of Conscience. He thus comes to see Fortune's gift of delivering his enemies into his hands as an opportunity for him to forgive and restore them, not be revenged.

Such an assumption of godlike power is close to arrogance, even blasphemy, for Prospero is no god. His chief power, learned from books and exercised through Ariel, is to control the elements so as to create illusion—of separation, of death, of the gods' blessing. Yet, since he is human, even this power is an immense burden and temptation. Prospero has much to learn, like those whom he controls. He must subdue his anger, his self-pity, his readiness to blame others, his domineering over Miranda. He must overcome the vengeful impulse he experiences toward those who have wronged him, and he must conquer the longing many a father feels to hold on to his daughter when she is desired by another man. He struggles with these problems through his art, devising games and shows in which his angry self-pity and jealousy are transmuted into playacting scenes of divine warning and forgiveness toward his enemies and watchful parental austerity toward Miranda and Ferdinand. Prospero's responsibilities cause him to behave magisterially and to be resented by the spirits of the isle. His authority is problematic to us because he seems so patriarchal, colonialist, even sexist and racist in his arrogating to himself the right and responsibility to control others in the name of values they may not share. Ariel longs to be free of this authority. Perhaps our sympathy for Prospero is greatest when we perceive that he, too, with mixed feelings of genuine relief and melancholy, is ready to lay aside his demanding and self-important role as creative moral intelligence.

Alonso and his court party variously illustrate the unregenerate world left behind in Naples and Milan. We first see them on shipboard, panicky and desperate, their titles and finery mocked by roaring waves. Futile ambition seems destined for a watery demise. Yet death by water in this play is a transfiguration rather than an end, a mystical rebirth, as in the regenerative cycle of the seasons from winter to summer. Ariel suggests as much in his song about a drowned father: "Those are pearls that were his eyes. / Nothing of him that doth fade / But doth suffer a sea change / Into something rich and strange" (1.2.402–5). Still, this miracle is not apparent at first to those who are caught in the illusion of death. As in T. S. Eliot's *The Waste Land*, which repeatedly alludes to *The Tempest,* self-blinded human beings fear a disaster that is ironically the prelude to reawakening.

The illusions created on the island serve to test these imperfect men and to make them reveal their true selves. Only Gonzalo, who long ago aided Prospero and Miranda when they were banished from Milan, responds affirmatively to illusion. In his eyes, their having been saved from drowning is a miracle: they breathe fresh air, the grass is green on the island, and their very garments appear not to have been stained by the salt water. His ideal commonwealth (2.1.150–71), which Shakespeare drew in part from an essay by Montaigne, postulates a natural goodness in humanity and makes no allowance for the darker propensities of human behavior, but at least Gonzalo's cheerfulness is in refreshing contrast to the jaded sneers of some of his companions. Sebastian and Antonio react to the magic isle, as to Gonzalo's commonwealth, by cynically refusing to believe in miracles. They scoff at Gonzalo for insistently looking on the bright side; if he were to examine his supposedly unstained clothes more carefully, they jest, he would discover that his pockets are filled with mud. Confident that they are unobserved, they seize the opportunity afforded by Alonso's being asleep to plot a murder and political coup. This attempt is not only despicable but also madly ludicrous, for they are all shipwrecked and no longer have kingdoms over which to quarrel. Even more ironically, Sebastian and Antonio, despite their insolent belief in their self-sufficiency, are being observed. The villains must be taught that an unseen power keeps track of their misdeeds. However presumptuous Prospero may be to assume through Ariel's means the role of godlike observer, he does awaken conscience and prevent murder. The villains may revert to type when returned to their usual habitat, but even they are at least briefly moved to an awareness of the unseen (3.3.21–7). Alonso, more worthy than they, though burdened, too, with sin, responds to his situation with guilt and despair, for he assumes that his son Ferdinand's death is the just punishment of the gods for Alonso's part in the earlier overthrow of Prospero. Alonso must be led, by means of curative illusions, through the purgative experience of contrition to the reward he thinks impossible and undeserved: reunion with his lost son.

Alonso is thus, like Posthumus in *Cymbeline* or Leontes in *The Winter's Tale*, a tragicomic figure—sinful, contrite, forgiven. Alonso's son Ferdinand must also undergo ordeals and visions devised by Prospero to test his worth, but more on the level of romantic comedy. Ferdinand is young, innocent, and hopeful, well-matched to Miranda. From the start, Prospero obviously approves of his prospective son-in-law. Yet even Prospero, needing to prepare himself for a life in which Miranda will no longer be solely his, is not ready to lay aside at least the comic fiction of parental opposition. He invents difficulties, imposes tasks of logbearing (like those assigned Caliban), and issues stern warnings against premarital lust. In the comic mode, parents are expected to cross their children in matters of the heart. Prospero is so convincing in his role of overbearing parent, insisting on absolute unthinking obedience from his daughter, that we remain unsure whether he is truly like that or whether we are meant to sense in his performance a grappling with his own deepest feelings of possessiveness and autocratic authority, tempered finally by his awareness of the arbitrariness of such a role and his readiness to let Miranda decide for herself. As a teacher of youth, moreover, Prospero is convinced by long experience that prizes too easily won are too lightly esteemed. Manifold are the temptations urging Ferdinand to surrender to the natural rhythms of the isle as Caliban would. In place of ceremonies conducted in civilized societies by the church, Prospero must create the illusion of ceremony by his art. The betrothal of Ferdinand and Miranda accordingly unites the best of both worlds: the natural innocence of the island, which teaches them to avoid the corruptions of civilization at its worst, and the higher law of nature achieved through moral wisdom at its best. To this marriage, the goddesses Iris, Ceres, and Juno bring promises of bounteous harvest, "refreshing showers," celestial harmony, and a springtime brought back to the earth by Proserpina's return from Hades (4.1.76–117). In Ferdinand and Miranda, "nurture" is wedded to "nature." This bond unites spirit and flesh, legitimizing erotic pleasure by incorporating it within Prospero's vision of a cosmic moral order.

At the lowest level of this traditional cosmic and moral framework, in Prospero's view, are Stephano and Trinculo. Their comic scenes juxtapose them with Caliban, for he represents untutored Nature, whereas they represent the unnatural depths to which human beings brought up in civilized society can fall. In this they resemble Sebastian and Antonio, who have learned in supposedly civilized Italy arts of intrigue and political murder. The antics of Stephano and Trinculo burlesque the conduct of their presumed betters, thereby exposing to ridicule the self-deceptions of ambitious men. The clowns desire to exploit the natural wonders of the isle by taking Caliban back to civilization to be shown in carnivals or by plying him with strong drink and whetting his resentment against authority. These plottings are in vain, however, for, like Sebastian and Antonio, the clowns are being watched. The clowns teach Caliban to cry out for "freedom" (2.2.184), by which they mean license to do as one pleases, but are foiled by Ariel as comic nemesis. Because they are degenerate buffoons, Prospero as satirist devises for them an exposure that is appropriately humiliating and satirical.

In contrast with them, Caliban is in many ways a sympathetic character. His sensitivity to natural beauty, as in his descriptions of the "nimble marmoset" or the dreaming music he so often hears (2.2.168; 3.2.137–45), is entirely appropriate to this child of nature. He is, to be sure, the child of a witch and is called many harsh names by Miranda and Prospero, such as "Abhorrèd slave" and "a born devil, on whose nature / Nurture can never stick" (1.2.354; 4.1.188–9). Yet he protests with some justification that the island was his in the first place and that Prospero and Miranda are interlopers. His very existence calls radically into question the value of civilization, which has shown itself capable of limitless depravity. What profit has

Caliban derived from learning Prospero's language other than, as he puts it, to "know how to curse" (1.2.367)? With instinctive cunning, he senses that books are his chief enemy and plots to destroy them first in his attempt at rebellion. The unspoiled natural world does indeed offer civilization a unique perspective on itself. In this it resembles Gonzalo's ideal commonwealth, which, no matter how laughably implausible from the cynic's point of view, does at least question some assumptions—economic, political, and social—common in western societies.

Radical perspectives of this kind invite consideration of many unsettling questions about exploration, colonialist empire building, and sexual imperialism. The fleeting comparison of Caliban to an indigenous native (2.2.33), although ignored in stage productions of the play until the late nineteenth century, suggests a discourse on colonialism in *The Tempest* that anticipates to a remarkable degree a doleful history of exploitation, of providing rum and guns to the natives, and of taking away land through violent expropriation in the name of bringing civilization and God to the New World. Stephano and Trinculo, pouring wine down Caliban's throat and thus reducing him to a worshiping slave, show exploitation at its worst, but surely the play allows us to wonder also if Prospero's enslavement of Caliban, however high-minded in its claims of preventing disorder and rape, is not tainted by the same imperatives of possession and control. The issue is wonderfully complex. Caliban is a projection of both the naturally depraved savage described in many explorers' accounts and the nobly innocent savage described by Montaigne. By dramatizing the conflict without taking sides, Shakespeare leaves open a debate about the worth of Prospero's endeavor to contain Caliban's otherness and produces an ambivalent result in which the apparent victory of colonialism and censorship does not entirely conceal the contradictory struggle through which those values are imposed. The play's many open-ended questions apply not only to the New World but also, nearer at hand, to Ireland—an island on the margins of Britain that was regarded as both savage and threatening.

The play's discourse also raises issues of class and political justice. The battle between Prospero and Caliban is one of "master" and "man" (2.2.183); even if Caliban's cry of "freedom" leads him only into further enslavement by Stephano and Trinculo (who are themselves masterless men), the play does not resolve the conflict by simply reimposing social hierarchy. Caliban, Stephano, and Trinculo are all taught a lesson and are satirically punished for their rebellious behavior, but Caliban at least is pardoned and is left behind on the island at the play's end where presumably he will no longer be a slave. In political terms, Prospero resolves the long-standing hostilities between Milan and Naples by his astute arranging of the betrothal of Miranda to Ferdinand. However much it is idealized as a romantic match presided over harmoniously by the gods, it is also a political union aimed at bringing together the ruling families of those two city states. Prospero's masque, his ultimate vision of the triumph of civilization, transforms the myth of the rape of a daughter (Proserpina) in such a way as to preserve the daughter's chaste honor in a union that will repair the political and social damage done by the ouster of Prospero from his dukedom of Milan. For these reasons, the betrothal of Ferdinand and Miranda must have seemed politically relevant to Shakespeare's audience when *The Tempest* was performed before King James at Whitehall in November of 1611 and then again at court in 1613 in celebration of the marriage of James's daughter Elizabeth to Frederick, the Elector Palatine.

The play's ending is far from perfectly stable. Antonio never repents, and we cannot be sure what the island will be like once Prospero has disappeared from the scene. Since Prospero's occupation of the island replicates in a sense the process by which he himself was overthrown, we cannot know when the cycle of revolution will ever cease. We cannot even be sure of the extent to which Shakespeare is master of his own colonial debate in *The Tempest* or, conversely, the extent to which today we should feel ourselves free to relativize, ironize, or in other ways criticize this play for apparent or probable prejudices. Not even a great author like Shakespeare can escape the limits of his own time, any more than we can escape the limits of our own. Perhaps we can nonetheless project ourselves, as spectators and readers, into Shakespeare's attempt to celebrate humanity's highest achievement in the union of the island with the civilized world. Miranda and Ferdinand have bright hopes for the future, even if those hopes must be qualified by Prospero's melancholic observation that the "brave new world" with "such people in't" is only "new to thee," to those who are young and not yet experienced in the world's vexations. Even Caliban may be at last reconciled to Prospero's insistent idea of a harmony between will and reason, no matter how perilously and delicately achieved. Prospero speaks of Caliban as a "thing of darkness I / Acknowledge mine," and Caliban vows to "be wise hereafter / And seek for grace" (5.1.278–9, 298–9). Prospero's view is that the natural human within is more contented, better understood, and more truly free when harmonized with reason.

Caliban is a part of humanity; Ariel is not. Ariel can comprehend what compassion and forgiveness would be like, "were I human" (5.1.20), and can take good-natured part in Prospero's designs to castigate or reform his fellow mortals, but Ariel longs to be free in quite another sense from that meant by Caliban. Ariel takes no part in the final integration of human society. This spirit belongs to a magic world of song, music, and illusion that the artist borrows for his use but that exists eternally outside of him. Like the elements of air, earth, fire, and water in which it mysteriously dwells, this spirit is morally neutral but incredibly vital. From it the artist achieves powers of imagination, enabling him to bedim the noontide sun or call forth the dead from their graves. These visions are illusory in the profound sense that all life is illusory, an "insubstantial pageant" melted into thin air (4.1.150–5). Prospero the artist cherishes his own humanity, as a promise of surcease from his labors. Yet the artifact created by the artist endures, existing apart from time and place, as does Ariel: "Then to the elements / Be free, and fare thou well!" (5.1.321–2). No doubt it is a romantic fiction to associate the dramatist Shakespeare with Prospero's farewell to his art, but it is an almost irresistible idea, because we are so moved by the sense of completion and yet humility, the exultation and yet the calm contained in this leave-taking.

As though to demonstrate the summation of his artistry as magician-poet in what he may indeed have designed as his farewell to the stage, Shakespeare puts on a dazzling display of the verbal artistry for which he had already become famous. His command of blank verse is, by this time, more flexible and protean than ever before, with a marked increase in run-on lines, caesuras in mid line, the sharing of blank verse lines between two or more speakers, feminine endings, and other features of the late Shakespearean style. (See General Introduction, pp. lxxx–lxxxi). The play is notable for its bravura passages, such as those that begin "Our revels now are ended" (4.1.148–58) and "Ye elves of hills" (5.1.33–57). With its opening storm scene and its solemn shows and masques—the *"several strange shapes"* bringing in a banquet and the appearance of Ariel *"like a harpy"* in 3.3, the masque of Iris, Ceres, and Juno in 4.1, and Prospero's confining the Neapolitans to a charmed circle in 5.1—*The Tempest* presents itself as a tour de force of spectacle and grandeur in which all of these dazzling events are also astutely interrupted by the resurgence of human appetite and by satiric correction. At every turn the drama manifests a deft compression of time and event. The tone is masterfully assured, in prose as in verse. Images of a dreamlike world come together in a remarkable amalgam whereby the characters participate in a fluid world that moves through them even as they move through it, becoming one with the tempest of time.

In performance, *The Tempest* reveals an extraordinary range of interpretive possibilities. Caliban, in nineteenth-century stage versions, was apt to be a grotesque specimen of Darwinian evolution, outfitted with gills, fishy scales, and long fingernails for prying shellfish out of rocks (the long fingernails are in fact mentioned, at 2.2.166). Herbert Beerbohm Tree, in 1904, saw Caliban as hairy from head to foot, with unkempt beard, pointed ears, sinister eyes, and long fingernails. To Frank Benson, at Stratford-upon-Avon in 1891, Caliban (played by Benson himself) was the missing link in an evolutionary chain of monkeys, baboons, and other presumably human ancestors; the Caliban of this production climbed a tree on stage, hung upside down, and gibbered. More recently, in accord with critical interest in the play as a potential critique of colonialism, Caliban has often been seen as a Caribbean native, physically imposing and even handsome, restive under his slavery, a man of immense human dignity. An example is that of David Suchet in Clifford Williams's 1987 production for the Royal Shakespeare Company; Suchet's Caliban, a sympathetic victim of imperialism, evoked unmistable echoes of third-world exploited populations from the West Indies and sub-Saharan Africa. Prospero has undergone no less of a sea change, from the benign authorial stand-in of traditional nineteenth-century productions to a man who can be tyrannical, arbitrary, menacing, close to violence, deeply angry, as in Derek Jarman's 1980 film. Interpretations of Ariel have varied from saccharine sweetness to the punk-haired and drug-inebriated, as in Mark Rylance's Ariel in

Ron Daniels's 1982 RSC production. Underlying sexual tensions are evident on all sides in recent productions. Some of the most remarkable versions of the play have abandoned Shakespeare's script to varying degrees, as in Peter Brook's Round House production of 1968 featuring an enormous Sycorax giving birth to Caliban, a takeover of the island and capture of Prospero by Caliban, and a wild orgy. Derek Jarman's film version of 1980 saw the play as dominantly gay, with Caliban as an aging "queen." Giorgio Strehler's *La Tempesta*, Milan, 1977, pictured Ariel as a commedia dell'arte Pierrot attached to a wire, soaring through the air and landing as though on Prospero's raised finger. Peter Greenaway's 1991 film called *Prospero's Books* presented the entire play through Prospero's eyes; John Gielgud, as Prospero, spoke virtually all the lines. The extraordinary range of theatrical innovations that has been brought to this play testifies to the script's own remarkable theatrical self-consciousness and its delight in magic and illusion.

The Tempest

Names of the Actors

ALONSO, *King of Naples*
SEBASTIAN, *his brother*
PROSPERO, *the right Duke of Milan*
ANTONIO, *his brother, the usurping Duke of Milan*
FERDINAND, *son to the King of Naples*
GONZALO, *an honest old counselor*
ADRIAN *and* ⎫
FRANCISCO, ⎬ *lords*
CALIBAN, *a savage and deformed slave*
TRINCULO, *a jester*
STEPHANO, *a drunken butler*
MASTER *of a ship*

BOATSWAIN
MARINERS

MIRANDA, *daughter to Prospero*

ARIEL, *an airy spirit*
IRIS ⎫
CERES, ⎪
JUNO, ⎬ *[presented by] spirits*
NYMPHS ⎪
REAPERS, ⎭

[Other Spirits attending on Prospero]

THE SCENE: *An island*

1.1

*A tempestuous noise of thunder and lightning
heard. Enter a Shipmaster and a Boatswain.*

MASTER Boatswain!

BOATSWAIN Here, Master. What cheer?

MASTER Good, speak to th' mariners. Fall to't yarely,   3
or we run ourselves aground. Bestir, bestir!   *Exit.*

Enter Mariners.

BOATSWAIN Heigh, my hearts! Cheerly, cheerly, my
hearts! Yare, yare! Take in the topsail. Tend to th' Mas-   6
ter's whistle.—Blow till thou burst thy wind, if room   7
enough!   8

*Enter Alonso, Sebastian, Antonio, Ferdinand,
Gonzalo, and others.*

ALONSO Good Boatswain, have care. Where's the Master? Play the men.   10

BOATSWAIN I pray now, keep below.

ANTONIO Where is the Master, Boatswain?

BOATSWAIN Do you not hear him? You mar our labor.
Keep your cabins! You do assist the storm.   14

GONZALO Nay, good, be patient.   15

BOATSWAIN When the sea is. Hence! What cares these
roarers for the name of king? To cabin! Silence! Trou-   17
ble us not.

GONZALO Good, yet remember whom thou hast
aboard.

BOATSWAIN None that I more love than myself. You are
a councillor; if you can command these elements to
silence and work the peace of the present, we will not   23
hand a rope more. Use your authority. If you cannot,   24
give thanks you have lived so long and make yourself
ready in your cabin for the mischance of the hour, if it
so hap.—Cheerly, good hearts!—Out of our way,   27
I say.   *Exit.*

GONZALO I have great comfort from this fellow. Methinks he hath no drowning mark upon him; his com-   30
plexion is perfect gallows. Stand fast, good Fate, to his   31
hanging! Make the rope of his destiny our cable, for
our own doth little advantage. If he be not born to be   33

hanged, our case is miserable.   *Exeunt [courtiers].*   34

Enter Boatswain.

BOATSWAIN Down with the topmast! Yare! Lower,
lower! Bring her to try wi'th' main course. (*A cry*   36
within.) A plague upon this howling! They are louder
than the weather or our office.   38

Enter Sebastian, Antonio, and Gonzalo.

Yet again? What do you here? Shall we give o'er and   39
drown? Have you a mind to sink?

SEBASTIAN A pox o'your throat, you bawling, blasphemous, incharitable dog!

BOATSWAIN Work you, then.

ANTONIO Hang, cur! Hang, you whoreson, insolent
noisemaker! We are less afraid to be drowned than
thou art.

GONZALO I'll warrant him for drowning, though the   47
ship were no stronger than a nutshell and as
leaky as an unstanched wench.   49

BOATSWAIN Lay her ahold, ahold! Set her two courses.   50
Off to sea again! Lay her off!

Enter Mariners, wet.

MARINERS All lost! To prayers, to prayers! All lost!
[*The Mariners run about in confusion, exiting at
random.*]

BOATSWAIN What, must our mouths be cold?   53

GONZALO
The King and Prince at prayers! Let's assist them,
For our case is as theirs.

SEBASTIAN   I am out of patience.

ANTONIO
We are merely cheated of our lives by drunkards.   56
This wide-chapped rascal! Would thou mightst lie
drowning   57
The washing of ten tides!

GONZALO   He'll be hanged yet,   58
Though every drop of water swear against it
And gape at wid'st to glut him.
(*A confused noise within:*)   "Mercy on us!"—   60
"We split, we split!"—"Farewell my wife and
children!"—   61
"Farewell, brother!"—"We split, we split, we split!"
[*Exit Boatswain.*]

ANTONIO Let's all sink wi'th' King.

SEBASTIAN Let's take leave of him.

Exit [with Antonio].

GONZALO Now would I give a thousand furlongs of sea

Names of the Actors This list appears at the end of the play in the
First Folio, in this order, with Miranda's name below that of the men,
as was conventional in lists of the period. **PROSPERO, *the right***
the rightful **CALIBAN . . . *slave*** The Folio reads "*saluage*," a common alternative spelling of *savage* but perhaps also with a resonance
of being salvaged from shipwreck. *Slave* has a range of meanings:
wretch, rascal, servile creature, one who is owned by another person,
one who is divested of freedom and personal rights.
1.1 Location: On board ship, off the island's coast.
3 Good i.e., It's good you've come, or, my good fellow. **yarely** nimbly **6 Tend** Attend **7 Blow** (Addressed to the wind.) **7–8 if room
enough** as long as we have sea room enough. **10 Play the men** Act
like men, with spirit. **14 Keep** Remain in **15 good** good fellow
17 roarers waves or winds, or both; spoken to as though they were
"bullies" or "blusterers" **23 work . . . present** bring calm to our present circumstances **24 hand** handle **27 hap** happen. **30–1 complexion . . . gallows** appearance shows he was born to be hanged
(and therefore, according to the proverb, in no danger of drowning)
33 our . . . advantage our own cable is of little benefit.

34 case is miserable circumstances are desperate. **36 Bring . . .
course** Sail her close to the wind by means of the mainsail. **38 our
office** i.e., the noise we make at our work. **39 give o'er** give up
47 warrant him for drowning guarantee that he will never be
drowned **49 unstanched** insatiable, loose, unrestrained. (Suggesting
also "incontinent" and "menstrual.") **50 ahold** ahull, close to the
wind. **courses** sails, i.e., foresail as well as mainsail, set in an
attempt to get the ship back out into open water. **53 must . . . cold?**
i.e., must we drown in the cold sea? **56 merely** utterly **57 wide-
chapped** big-mouthed **57–8 Would . . . tides!** (Pirates were hanged
on the shore and left until three tides had come in.) **60 at wid'st**
wide open. **glut** swallow **61 split** break apart.

for an acre of barren ground: long heath, brown furze, 66
anything. The wills above be done! But I would fain 67
die a dry death. *Exit.*

❖

1.2

Enter Prospero [in his magic cloak] and Miranda.

MIRANDA
If by your art, my dearest father, you have 1
Put the wild waters in this roar, allay them. 2
The sky, it seems, would pour down stinking pitch,
But that the sea, mounting to th' welkin's cheek, 4
Dashes the fire out. Oh, I have suffered
With those that I saw suffer! A brave vessel, 6
Who had, no doubt, some noble creature in her,
Dashed all to pieces. Oh, the cry did knock
Against my very heart! Poor souls, they perished.
Had I been any god of power, I would
Have sunk the sea within the earth or ere 11
It should the good ship so have swallowed and
The freighting souls within her.
PROSPERO   Be collected. 13
No more amazement. Tell your piteous heart 14
There's no harm done.
MIRANDA   Oh, woe the day!
PROSPERO   No harm.
I have done nothing but in care of thee, 16
Of thee, my dear one, thee, my daughter, who
Art ignorant of what thou art, naught knowing
Of whence I am, nor that I am more better 19
Than Prospero, master of a full poor cell, 20
And thy no greater father.
MIRANDA   More to know
Did never meddle with my thoughts.
PROSPERO   'Tis time 22
I should inform thee farther. Lend thy hand
And pluck my magic garment from me. So,
          [laying down his magic cloak and staff]
Lie there, my art.—Wipe thou thine eyes. Have
    comfort.
The direful spectacle of the wreck, which touched 26
The very virtue of compassion in thee, 27
I have with such provision in mine art
So safely ordered that there is no soul—
No, not so much perdition as an hair 30
Betid to any creature in the vessel 31
Which thou heard'st cry, which thou saw'st sink. Sit
    down, 32

For thou must now know farther.
MIRANDA *[sitting]*   You have often
Begun to tell me what I am, but stopped
And left me to a bootless inquisition, 35
Concluding, "Stay, not yet."
PROSPERO   The hour's now come;
The very minute bids thee ope thine ear.
Obey, and be attentive. Canst thou remember
A time before we came unto this cell?
I do not think thou canst, for then thou wast not
Out three years old.
MIRANDA   Certainly, sir, I can. 41
PROSPERO
By what? By any other house or person?
Of anything the image, tell me, that
Hath kept with thy remembrance.
MIRANDA   'Tis far off,
And rather like a dream than an assurance 45
That my remembrance warrants. Had I not 46
Four or five women once that tended me?
PROSPERO
Thou hadst, and more, Miranda. But how is it
That this lives in thy mind? What see'st thou else
In the dark backward and abysm of time? 50
If thou rememb'rest aught ere thou cam'st here, 51
How thou cam'st here thou mayst.
MIRANDA   But that I do not.
PROSPERO
Twelve year since, Miranda, twelve year since,
Thy father was the Duke of Milan and
A prince of power.
MIRANDA   Sir, are not you my father?
PROSPERO
Thy mother was a piece of virtue, and 56
She said thou wast my daughter; and thy father
Was Duke of Milan, and his only heir
And princess no worse issued.
MIRANDA   Oh, the heavens! 59
What foul play had we, that we came from thence?
Or blessèd was't we did?
PROSPERO   Both, both, my girl.
By foul play, as thou say'st, were we heaved thence,
But blessedly holp hither.
MIRANDA   O, my heart bleeds 63
To think o'th' teen that I have turned you to, 64
Which is from my remembrance! Please you, farther. 65
PROSPERO
My brother and thy uncle, called Antonio—
I pray thee mark me—that a brother should
Be so perfidious!—he whom next thyself 68
Of all the world I loved, and to him put
The manage of my state, as at that time 70
Through all the seigniories it was the first, 71

---

66 **heath** heather.   **furze** gorse, a weed growing on wasteland
67 **fain** rather
1.2 Location: The island, near Prospero's cell. On the Elizabethan
stage, this cell is implicitly at hand throughout the play, although
in some scenes the convention of flexible distance allows us to
imagine characters in other parts of the island.
1 **art** magic   2 **allay** pacify   4 **welkin's cheek** sky's face   6 **brave**
gallant, splendid   11 **or ere** before   13 **freighting souls** cargo of
souls.   **collected** calm, composed.   14 **amazement** consternation.
piteous pitying   16 **but** except   19 **more better** of higher rank
20 **full** very   22 **meddle** mingle   26 **wreck** shipwreck   27 **virtue**
essence   30 **perdition** loss   31 **Betid** happened   32 **Which** whom

35 **bootless inquisition** profitless inquiry   41 **Out** fully   45–6 **assurance . . . warrants** certainty that my memory guarantees.   50 **backward**
. . . time abyss of the past.   51 **aught** anything   56 **piece** masterpiece,
exemplar   59 **no worse issued** no less nobly born, descended.   63 **holp**
helped   64 **teen . . . to** trouble I've caused you to remember or put you
to   65 **from** out of   68 **next** next to   70 **manage** management, administration   71 **seigniories** i.e., city-states of northern Italy

And Prospero the prime duke, being so reputed　72
In dignity, and for the liberal arts
Without a parallel; those being all my study,
The government I cast upon my brother
And to my state grew stranger, being transported　76
And rapt in secret studies. Thy false uncle—
Dost thou attend me?
MIRANDA　　　　　　　　Sir, most heedfully.
PROSPERO
Being once perfected how to grant suits,　79
How to deny them, who t'advance and who
To trash for overtopping, new created　81
The creatures that were mine, I say, or changed 'em,　82
Or else new formed 'em; having both the key　83
Of officer and office, set all hearts i'th' state　84
To what tune pleased his ear, that now he was　85
The ivy which had hid my princely trunk
And sucked my verdure out on't. Thou attend'st not.　87
MIRANDA
Oh, good sir, I do.
PROSPERO　　　　　I pray thee, mark me.
I, thus neglecting worldly ends, all dedicated
To closeness and the bettering of my mind　90
With that which, but by being so retired,　91
O'erprized all popular rate, in my false brother　92
Awaked an evil nature; and my trust,
Like a good parent, did beget of him　94
A falsehood in its contrary as great
As my trust was, which had indeed no limit,
A confidence sans bound. He being thus lorded　97
Not only with what my revenue yielded
But what my power might else exact, like one　99
Who, having into truth by telling of it,　100
Made such a sinner of his memory　101
To credit his own lie, he did believe　102
He was indeed the Duke, out o'th' substitution　103
And executing th'outward face of royalty　104
With all prerogative. Hence his ambition growing—　105
Dost thou hear?
MIRANDA　　　　　Your tale, sir, would cure deafness.

PROSPERO
To have no screen between this part he played　107
And him he played it for, he needs will be　108
Absolute Milan. Me, poor man, my library　109
Was dukedom large enough. Of temporal royalties　110
He thinks me now incapable; confederates—　111
So dry he was for sway—wi'th' King of Naples　112
To give him annual tribute, do him homage,　113
Subject his coronet to his crown, and bend　114
The dukedom yet unbowed—alas, poor Milan!—　115
To most ignoble stooping.
MIRANDA　　　　　　　　O the heavens!
PROSPERO
Mark his condition and th'event, then tell me　117
If this might be a brother.
MIRANDA　　　　　　　　I should sin
To think but nobly of my grandmother.　119
Good wombs have borne bad sons.
PROSPERO　　　　　　　　　　　　Now the condition.
This King of Naples, being an enemy
To me inveterate, hearkens my brother's suit,　122
Which was that he, in lieu o'th' premises　123
Of homage and I know not how much tribute,
Should presently extirpate me and mine　125
Out of the dukedom and confer fair Milan,
With all the honors, on my brother. Whereon,
A treacherous army levied, one midnight
Fated to th' purpose did Antonio open
The gates of Milan, and, i'th' dead of darkness,
The ministers for th' purpose hurried thence　131
Me and thy crying self.
MIRANDA　　　　　　　　Alack, for pity!
I, not remembering how I cried out then,
Will cry it o'er again. It is a hint　134
That wrings mine eyes to 't.
PROSPERO　　　　　　　　Hear a little further,　135
And then I'll bring thee to the present business
Which now's upon 's, without the which this story
Were most impertinent.
MIRANDA　　　　　　　　Wherefore did they not　138
That hour destroy us?
PROSPERO　　　　　　　Well demanded, wench.　139
My tale provokes that question. Dear, they durst not,
So dear the love my people bore me, nor set　141
A mark so bloody on the business, but　142

---

72 **prime** first in rank and importance　76 **to . . . stranger** i.e., withdrew from my responsibilities as duke.　**transported** carried away　79 **perfected** grown skillful　81 **trash** check a hound by tying a cord or weight to its neck.　**overtopping** running too far ahead of the pack; surmounting, exceeding one's authority　81–3 **new . . . formed 'em** won the loyalty of my officers by appointing them to new posts, or replaced them with others who would be loyal to Antonio, or else redefined the positions and their occupants　83–5 **having . . . ear** having now under his control both the officers and the positions, he set a tone for his rule according to his own inclination. (*Key* is also a metaphor for tuning stringed instruments.)　87 **verdure** vitality.　**on't** of it.　90 **closeness** retirement, seclusion　91–2 **but . . . rate** i.e., were it not that its private nature caused me to neglect my public responsibilities, had a value far beyond what public opinion could appreciate, or, simply because it was done in such seclusion, had a value not appreciated by popular opinion　94 **good parent** (Alludes to the proverb that good parents often bear bad children; see also line 120.)　**of** in　97 **sans** without.　**lorded** raised to lordship, with power and wealth　99 **else** otherwise, additionally　100–2 **Who . . . lie** i.e., who, by repeatedly telling the lie (that he was indeed Duke of Milan), made his memory such a confirmed sinner against truth that he began to believe his own lie.　103–5 **out . . . prerogative** as a result of his making himself my substitute and carrying out all the visible functions of royalty with all its rights and privileges.

107–9 **To have . . . Milan** In order to eliminate all separation between his role and himself, he insisted on becoming the Duke of Milan in name as well as in fact.　110 **temporal royalties** practical prerogatives and responsibilities of a sovereign　111 **confederates** conspires, allies himself　112 **dry** thirsty.　**sway** power　113 **him** i.e., the King of Naples　114 **his . . . his** Antonio's . . . the King of Naples'.　**bend** make bow down　115 **yet** hitherto　117 **condition** pact.　**th'event** the outcome　119 **but** other than　122 **hearkens** listens to　123 **he** the King of Naples.　**in . . . premises** in return for the stipulation　125 **presently extirpate** at once remove　131 **ministers . . . purpose** agents employed to do this.　**thence** from there　134 **hint** prompting　135 **wrings** (1) constrains (2) wrings tears from　138 **impertinent** irrelevant.　**Wherefore** Why　139 **demanded** asked.　**wench** (Here a term of endearment.)　141–2 **set . . . bloody** i.e., make obvious their murderous intent. (From the practice of marking with the blood of the prey those who have participated in a successful hunt.)

With colors fairer painted their foul ends.   143
In few, they hurried us aboard a bark,   144
Bore us some leagues to sea, where they prepared
A rotten carcass of a butt, not rigged,   146
Nor tackle, sail, nor mast; the very rats   147
Instinctively have quit it. There they hoist us,   148
To cry to th' sea that roared to us, to sigh
To th' winds whose pity, sighing back again,
Did us but loving wrong.

MIRANDA   Alack, what trouble   151
Was I then to you!

PROSPERO   Oh, a cherubin
Thou wast that did preserve me. Thou didst smile,
Infusèd with a fortitude from heaven,   154
When I have decked the sea with drops full salt,   155
Under my burden groaned, which raised in me   156
An undergoing stomach, to bear up   157
Against what should ensue.

MIRANDA   How came we ashore?

PROSPERO   By Providence divine.
Some food we had, and some fresh water, that
A noble Neapolitan, Gonzalo,
Out of his charity, who being then appointed
Master of this design, did give us, with
Rich garments, linens, stuffs, and necessaries,   165
Which since have steaded much. So, of his
   gentleness,   166
Knowing I loved my books, he furnished me
From mine own library with volumes that
I prize above my dukedom.

MIRANDA   Would I might   169
But ever see that man!

PROSPERO   Now I arise.   170
                    [He puts on his magic cloak.]
Sit still, and hear the last of our sea sorrow.   171
Here in this island we arrived; and here
Have I, thy schoolmaster, made thee more profit   173
Than other princes can, that have more time   174
For vainer hours and tutors not so careful.   175

MIRANDA
Heavens thank you for't! And now, I pray you, sir—
For still 'tis beating in my mind—your reason
For raising this sea storm?

PROSPERO   Know thus far forth:
By accident most strange, bountiful Fortune,
Now my dear lady, hath mine enemies   180
Brought to this shore; and by my prescience
I find my zenith doth depend upon   182

A most auspicious star, whose influence   183
If now I court not, but omit, my fortunes   184
Will ever after droop. Here cease more questions.
Thou art inclined to sleep. 'Tis a good dullness,   186
And give it way. I know thou canst not choose.   187
                              [Miranda sleeps.]
Come away, servant, come! I am ready now.   188
Approach, my Ariel, come.

        Enter Ariel.

ARIEL
All hail, great master, grave sir, hail! I come
To answer thy best pleasure; be't to fly,
To swim, to dive into the fire, to ride
On the curled clouds, to thy strong bidding task   193
Ariel and all his quality.

PROSPERO   Hast thou, spirit,   194
Performed to point the tempest that I bade thee?   195

ARIEL   To every article.
I boarded the King's ship. Now on the beak,   197
Now in the waist, the deck, in every cabin,   198
I flamed amazement. Sometime I'd divide   199
And burn in many places; on the topmast,
The yards, and bowsprit would I flame distinctly,   201
Then meet and join. Jove's lightning, the precursors
O'th' dreadful thunderclaps, more momentary
And sight-outrunning were not. The fire and cracks   204
Of sulfurous roaring the most mighty Neptune   205
Seem to besiege and make his bold waves tremble,
Yea, his dread trident shake.

PROSPERO   My brave spirit!   207
Who was so firm, so constant, that this coil   208
Would not infect his reason?

ARIEL   Not a soul
But felt a fever of the mad and played   210
Some tricks of desperation. All but mariners
Plunged in the foaming brine and quit the vessel,
Then all afire with me. The King's son, Ferdinand,
With hair up-staring—then like reeds, not hair—   214
Was the first man that leapt; cried, "Hell is empty,
And all the devils are here!"

PROSPERO   Why, that's my spirit!
But was not this nigh shore?

ARIEL   Close by, my master.

PROSPERO
But are they, Ariel, safe?

ARIEL   Not a hair perished.
On their sustaining garments not a blemish,   219
But fresher than before; and, as thou bad'st me,   220

---

143 **fairer** apparently more attractive   144 **few** few words.   **bark** ship   146 **butt** cask, tub   147 **Nor tackle** neither rigging   148 **quit** abandoned   151 **Did . . . wrong** i.e., pitied us even as they drove us on.   154 **Infusèd** filled, suffused   155 **decked** covered (with salt tears); adorned   156 **which** i.e., the smile   157 **undergoing stomach** courage to go on   165 **stuffs** supplies   166 **steaded much** been of much use.   **So, of** Similarly, out of   169 **Would** I wish   170 **But ever** i.e., someday   171 **sea sorrow** sorrowful adventure at sea.
173–4 **made . . . can** provided a more valuable education than other royal children (of either sex) can enjoy   175 **vainer** more foolishly spent   180 **my dear lady** (Refers to Fortune, not Miranda.)
182 **zenith** height of fortune. (Astrological term.)

183 **influence** astrological power   184 **but omit** but ignore instead   186 **dullness** drowsiness   187 **give it way** let it happen (i.e., don't fight it).   188 **Come away** Come   193 **task** make demands upon   194 **quality** (1) fellow spirits (2) abilities.   195 **to point** to the smallest detail   197 **beak** prow   198 **waist** midships.   **deck** poop deck at the stern   199 **flamed amazement** struck terror in the guise of fire, i.e., Saint Elmo's fire.   201 **distinctly** in different places   204 **sight-out-running** swifter than sight.   **were not** could not have been.
205 **Neptune** Roman god of the sea   207 **trident** three-pronged weapon   208 **coil** tumult   210 **of the mad** such as madmen feel   214 **up-staring** standing on end   219 **sustaining** protecting
220 **bad'st** ordered

In troops I have dispersed them 'bout the isle.   221
The King's son have I landed by himself,
Whom I left cooling of the air with sighs   223
In an odd angle of the isle, and sitting,   224
His arms in this sad knot.   [*He folds his arms.*]

PROSPERO   Of the King's ship,   225
The mariners, say how thou hast disposed,
And all the rest o'th' fleet.

ARIEL   Safely in harbor
Is the King's ship; in the deep nook, where once   228
Thou called'st me up at midnight to fetch dew   229
From the still-vexed Bermudas, there she's hid;   230
The mariners all under hatches stowed,
Who, with a charm joined to their suffered labor,   232
I have left asleep. And for the rest o'th' fleet,
Which I dispersed, they all have met again
And are upon the Mediterranean float   235
Bound sadly home for Naples,
Supposing that they saw the King's ship wrecked
And his great person perish.

PROSPERO   Ariel, thy charge
Exactly is performed. But there's more work.
What is the time o'th' day?

ARIEL   Past the mid season.   240

PROSPERO
At least two glasses. The time twixt six and now   241
Must by us both be spent most preciously.

ARIEL
Is there more toil? Since thou dost give me pains,   243
Let me remember thee what thou hast promised,   244
Which is not yet performed me.

PROSPERO   How now? Moody?
What is't thou canst demand?

ARIEL   My liberty.

PROSPERO
Before the time be out? No more!

ARIEL   I prithee,
Remember I have done thee worthy service,
Told thee no lies, made thee no mistakings, served
Without or grudge or grumblings. Thou did promise
To bate me a full year.

PROSPERO   Dost thou forget   251
From what a torment I did free thee?

ARIEL   No.

PROSPERO
Thou dost, and think'st it much to tread the ooze
Of the salt deep,
To run upon the sharp wind of the north,
To do me business in the veins o'th' earth   256

When it is baked with frost.

ARIEL   I do not, sir.   257

PROSPERO
Thou liest, malignant thing! Hast thou forgot
The foul witch Sycorax, who with age and envy   259
Was grown into a hoop? Hast thou forgot her?   260

ARIEL   No, sir.

PROSPERO
Thou hast. Where was she born? Speak. Tell me.

ARIEL
Sir, in Argier.

PROSPERO   Oh, was she so? I must   263
Once in a month recount what thou hast been,
Which thou forget'st. This damned witch Sycorax,
For mischiefs manifold and sorceries terrible
To enter human hearing, from Argier,
Thou know'st, was banished. For one thing she did   268
They would not take her life. Is not this true?

ARIEL   Ay, sir.

PROSPERO
This blue-eyed hag was hither brought with child   271
And here was left by th' sailors. Thou, my slave,
As thou report'st thyself, was then her servant;
And, for thou wast a spirit too delicate   274
To act her earthy and abhorred commands,
Refusing her grand hests, she did confine thee,   276
By help of her more potent ministers
And in her most unmitigable rage,
Into a cloven pine, within which rift
Imprisoned thou didst painfully remain
A dozen years; within which space she died
And left thee there, where thou didst vent thy
    groans
As fast as mill wheels strike. Then was this island—   283
Save for the son that she did litter here,   284
A freckled whelp, hag-born—not honored with   285
A human shape.

ARIEL   Yes, Caliban her son.   286

PROSPERO
Dull thing, I say so: he, that Caliban   287
Whom now I keep in service. Thou best know'st
What torment I did find thee in. Thy groans
Did make wolves howl, and penetrate the breasts
Of ever-angry bears. It was a torment
To lay upon the damned, which Sycorax
Could not again undo. It was mine art,
When I arrived and heard thee, that made gape   294
The pine and let thee out.

ARIEL   I thank thee, master.

---

221 **troops** groups   223 **cooling of** cooling   224 **angle** corner
225 **sad knot** (Folded arms are indicative of melancholy.)   228 **nook**
bay   229 **dew** (Collected at midnight for magical purposes; compare
with line 324.)   230 **still-vexed Bermudas** ever stormy Bermudas.
(Perhaps refers to the then recent Bermuda shipwreck; see play Introduction. The Folio text reads "*Bermoothes*.")   232 **with . . . labor** by
means of a spell added to all the labor they have undergone
235 **float** sea   240 **mid season** noon.   241 **glasses** hourglasses.
243 **pains** labors   244 **remember** remind   251 **bate** remit, deduct
256 **do me** do for me.   **veins** veins of minerals, or, underground
streams, thought to be analogous to the veins of the human body

257 **baked** hardened   259 **envy** malice   260 **grown into a hoop** i.e.,
so bent over with age as to resemble a hoop.   263 **Argier** Algiers
268 **one . . . did** (Perhaps a reference to her pregnancy, for which her
life would be spared.)   271 **blue-eyed** with dark circles under the
eyes or with blue eyelids, implying pregnancy.   **with child** pregnant
274 **for** because   276 **hests** commands   283 **as mill wheels strike** as
the blades of a mill wheel strike the water.   284 **Save** except.   **litter**
give birth to   285 **whelp** offspring. (Used of animals.)   **hag-born**
born of a female demon   286 **Yes . . . son** (Ariel is probably concurring with Prospero's comment about a "freckled whelp," not contradicting the point about "A human shape.")   287 **Dull . . . so** i.e.,
Exactly, that's what I said, you dullard.   294 **gape** open wide

PROSPERO
If thou more murmur'st, I will rend an oak
And peg thee in his knotty entrails till   297
Thou hast howled away twelve winters.
ARIEL   Pardon, master.
I will be correspondent to command   299
And do my spriting gently.   300
PROSPERO   Do so, and after two days
I will discharge thee.
ARIEL   That's my noble master!
What shall I do? Say what? What shall I do?
PROSPERO
Go make thyself like a nymph o'th' sea. Be subject
To no sight but thine and mine, invisible
To every eyeball else. Go take this shape
And hither come in't. Go, hence with diligence!
                                    Exit [Ariel].
[To Miranda] Awake, dear heart, awake! Thou hast
    slept well.
Awake!
MIRANDA   The strangeness of your story put
Heaviness in me.
PROSPERO   Shake it off. Come on,   310
We'll visit Caliban, my slave, who never
Yields us kind answer.
MIRANDA   'Tis a villain, sir,
I do not love to look on.
PROSPERO   But, as 'tis,
We cannot miss him. He does make our fire,   314
Fetch in our wood, and serves in offices   315
That profit us.—What ho! Slave! Caliban!
Thou earth, thou! Speak.
CALIBAN (within)   There's wood enough within.
PROSPERO
Come forth, I say! There's other business for thee.
Come, thou tortoise! When?   319

        Enter Ariel like a water nymph.

Fine apparition! My quaint Ariel,   320
Hark in thine ear.   [He whispers.]
ARIEL   My lord, it shall be done.   Exit.
PROSPERO
Thou poisonous slave, got by the devil himself   322
Upon thy wicked dam, come forth!   323

            Enter Caliban.

CALIBAN
As wicked dew as e'er my mother brushed   324
With raven's feather from unwholesome fen   325
Drop on you both! A southwest blow on ye   326
And blister you all o'er!
PROSPERO
For this, be sure, tonight thou shalt have cramps,

Side-stitches that shall pen thy breath up. Urchins   329
Shall forth at vast of night that they may work   330
All exercise on thee. Thou shalt be pinched
As thick as honeycomb, each pinch more stinging   332
Than bees that made 'em.
CALIBAN   I must eat my dinner.   333
This island's mine, by Sycorax my mother,
Which thou tak'st from me. When thou cam'st first,
Thou strok'st me and made much of me, wouldst give
    me
Water with berries in't, and teach me how
To name the bigger light, and how the less,   338
That burn by day and night. And then I loved thee
And showed thee all the qualities o'th'isle,
The fresh springs, brine pits, barren place and fertile.
Cursed be I that did so! All the charms   342
Of Sycorax, toads, beetles, bats, light on you!
For I am all the subjects that you have,
Which first was mine own king; and here you sty me 345
In this hard rock, whiles you do keep from me
The rest o'th'island.
PROSPERO   Thou most lying slave,
Whom stripes may move, not kindness! I have used
    thee,   348
Filth as thou art, with humane care, and lodged thee 349
In mine own cell, till thou didst seek to violate
The honor of my child.
CALIBAN
Oho, Oho! Would't had been done!
Thou didst prevent me; I had peopled else   353
This isle with Calibans.
MIRANDA   Abhorrèd slave,   354
Which any print of goodness wilt not take,   355
Being capable of all ill! I pitied thee,
Took pains to make thee speak, taught thee each hour
One thing or other. When thou didst not, savage,
Know thine own meaning, but wouldst gabble like
A thing most brutish, I endowed thy purposes   360
With words that made them known. But thy vile race, 361
Though thou didst learn, had that in't which good
    natures
Could not abide to be with; therefore wast thou
Deservedly confined into this rock,
Who hadst deserved more than a prison.   365
CALIBAN
You taught me language, and my profit on't
Is I know how to curse. The red plague rid you   367

---

297 his its   299 correspondent responsive, submissive   300 spriting
gently duties as a spirit willingly.   310 Heaviness drowsiness
314 miss do without   315 offices functions, duties   319 When (An
exclamation of impatience.)   320 quaint ingenious   322 got begotten, sired   323 dam mother. (Used of animals.)   324 wicked mischievous, harmful   325 fen marsh, bog   326 southwest i.e., wind
thought to bring disease

329 Urchins Hedgehogs; here, suggesting goblins in the guise of
hedgehogs   330 vast lengthy, desolate time. (Malignant spirits were
thought to be restricted to the hours of darkness.)   332 as honeycomb i.e., as a honeycomb full of bees   333 'em i.e., the honeycomb
338 the bigger . . . less i.e., the sun and the moon. (See Genesis 1:16:
"God then made two great lights: the greater light to rule the day, and
the less light to rule the night.")   342 charms spells   345 sty confine
as in a sty   348 stripes lashes   349 humane (Not distinguished as a
word from human.)   353 peopled else otherwise populated   354–65
Abhorrèd . . . prison (Sometimes assigned by editors to Prospero.)
355 print imprint, impression   360 purposes meanings, desires
361 race natural disposition; species, nature   367 red plague plague
characterized by red sores and evacuation of blood.   rid destroy

For learning me your language!

PROSPERO   Hagseed, hence!   368
Fetch us in fuel, and be quick, thou'rt best,   369
To answer other business. Shrugg'st thou, malice?   370
If thou neglect'st or dost unwillingly
What I command, I'll rack thee with old cramps,   372
Fill all thy bones with aches, make thee roar   373
That beasts shall tremble at thy din.

CALIBAN   No, pray thee.
[Aside] I must obey. His art is of such power
It would control my dam's god, Setebos,   376
And make a vassal of him.

PROSPERO   So, slave, hence!   377

Exit Caliban.

*Enter Ferdinand; and Ariel, invisible, playing and
singing. [Ferdinand does not see Prospero and
Miranda.]*

Ariel's Song.

ARIEL

Come unto these yellow sands,
      And then take hands;
Curtsied when you have, and kissed   380
      The wild waves whist;   381
Foot it featly here and there,   382
      And, sweet sprites, bear   383
The burden. Hark, hark!   384
      Burden, dispersedly [*within*].Bow-wow.   385
The watchdogs bark.
      [*Burden, dispersedly within.*] Bow-wow.
Hark, hark! I hear
The strain of strutting chanticleer
Cry Cock-a-diddle-dow.

FERDINAND

Where should this music be? I'th'air or th'earth?
It sounds no more; and sure it waits upon   392
Some god o'th'island. Sitting on a bank,   393
Weeping again the King my father's wreck,
This music crept by me upon the waters,
Allaying both their fury and my passion   396
With its sweet air. Thence I have followed it,   397
Or it hath drawn me rather. But 'tis gone.
No, it begins again.

Ariel's Song.

ARIEL

Full fathom five thy father lies.
Of his bones are coral made.

Those are pearls that were his eyes.
      Nothing of him that doth fade
But doth suffer a sea change
Into something rich and strange.
Sea nymphs hourly ring his knell.   406
      Burden [*within*]. Ding dong.
Hark, now I hear them, ding dong bell.

FERDINAND

The ditty does remember my drowned father.   409
This is no mortal business, nor no sound
That the earth owes. I hear it now above me.   411

PROSPERO [*to Miranda*]
The fringèd curtains of thine eye advance   412
And say what thou see'st yond.

MIRANDA   What is't? A spirit?
Lord, how it looks about! Believe me, sir,
It carries a brave form. But 'tis a spirit.   415

PROSPERO
No, wench, it eats and sleeps and hath such senses
As we have, such. This gallant which thou see'st
Was in the wreck; and, but he's something stained   418
With grief, that's beauty's canker, thou mightst
      call him   419
A goodly person. He hath lost his fellows
And strays about to find 'em.

MIRANDA   I might call him
A thing divine, for nothing natural
I ever saw so noble.

PROSPERO [*aside*]   It goes on, I see,
As my soul prompts it.—Spirit, fine spirit, I'll free thee
Within two days for this.

FERDINAND [*seeing Miranda*]   Most sure, the goddess
On whom these airs attend!—Vouchsafe my prayer   426
May know if you remain upon this island,   427
And that you will some good instruction give
How I may bear me here. My prime request,   429
Which I do last pronounce, is—O you wonder!—   430
If you be maid or no?

MIRANDA   No wonder, sir,   431
But certainly a maid.

FERDINAND   My language? Heavens!
I am the best of them that speak this speech,   433
Were I but where 'tis spoken.

PROSPERO [*coming forward*]   How? The best?
What wert thou if the King of Naples heard thee?

FERDINAND
A single thing, as I am now, that wonders   436
To hear thee speak of Naples. He does hear me,   437

---

368 learning teaching. **Hagseed** Offspring of a female demon
369 thou'rt best you'd be well advised   **370 answer other business**
perform other tasks.   **372 old** such as old people suffer, or, plenty of
373 aches (Pronounced "aitches.")   **376 Setebos** (A god of the Patago-
nians, named in Richard Eden's *History of Travel*, 1577.)   **377.2 Ariel,
invisible** (Ariel wears a garment that by convention indicates he is invisible to the other characters.)   **380 Curtsied . . . have** when you have curtsied   **380–1 kissed . . . whist** kissed the waves into silence, or, kissed
while the waves are being hushed   **382 Foot it featly** dance nimbly
383 sprites spirits   **384 burden** refrain, undersong.   **385 s.d. *dispersedly*** i.e., from all directions, not in unison   **392 waits upon** serves,
attends   **393 bank** sandbank   **396 passion** grief   **397 Thence** i.e.,
From the bank on which I sat

406 knell announcement of a death by the tolling of a bell.
409 remember commemorate   **411 owes** owns   **412 advance** raise
415 brave excellent   **418 but . . . stained** were it not that his luster is
somewhat darkened   **419 canker** cankerworm (feeding on buds and
leaves)   **426 airs** songs.   **Vouchsafe** Grant   **427 remain** dwell
429 bear me conduct myself.   **prime** chief   **430 wonder** (Miranda's
name means "to be wondered at.")   **431 maid** (1) a human maiden as
opposed to a goddess (2) unmarried (3) a virgin   **433 best** i.e., in
birth   **436 A single . . . now** (1) A single figure who combines into
one person both self and King of Naples (since Ferdinand believes he
has inherited the kingship) (2) A lonely shipwrecked figure
437 Naples the King of Naples.   **He . . . me** I who hear my own
words am the King of Naples

And that he does I weep. Myself am Naples, 438
Who with mine eyes, never since at ebb, beheld 439
The King my father wrecked.
MIRANDA   Alack, for mercy!
FERDINAND
Yes, faith, and all his lords, the Duke of Milan
And his brave son being twain.
PROSPERO [aside]   The Duke of Milan 442
And his more braver daughter could control thee, 443
If now 'twere fit to do't. At the first sight
They have changed eyes.—Delicate Ariel, 445
I'll set thee free for this. [To Ferdinand] A word, good
    sir.
I fear you have done yourself some wrong. A word! 447
MIRANDA [aside]
Why speaks my father so ungently? This
Is the third man that e'er I saw, the first
That e'er I sighed for. Pity move my father
To be inclined my way!
FERDINAND [to Miranda]   Oh, if a virgin,
And your affection not gone forth, I'll make you
The Queen of Naples.
PROSPERO   Soft, sir! One word more.
    [Aside] They are both in either's powers; but this swift
    business 454
I must uneasy make, lest too light winning 455
Make the prize light. [To Ferdinand] One word more: I
    charge thee 456
That thou attend me. Thou dost here usurp 457
The name thou ow'st not, and hast put thyself 458
Upon this island as a spy, to win it
From me, the lord on't.
FERDINAND   No, as I am a man. 460
MIRANDA
There's nothing ill can dwell in such a temple.
If the ill spirit have so fair a house,
Good things will strive to dwell with't.
PROSPERO   Follow me.— 463
Speak not you for him; he's a traitor.—Come,
I'll manacle thy neck and feet together.
Seawater shalt thou drink; thy food shall be
The fresh-brook mussels, withered roots, and husks
Wherein the acorn cradled. Follow.
FERDINAND   No!
I will resist such entertainment till 469
Mine enemy has more pow'r. 470
            He draws, and is charmed from moving.
MIRANDA   O dear father,
Make not too rash a trial of him, for 471

He's gentle, and not fearful.
PROSPERO   What, I say, 472
My foot my tutor?—Put thy sword up, traitor, 473
Who mak'st a show but dar'st not strike, thy
    conscience
Is so possessed with guilt. Come, from thy ward, 475
For I can here disarm thee with this stick
And make thy weapon drop. [He brandishes his staff.]
MIRANDA [trying to hinder him]   Beseech you, father!
PROSPERO
Hence! Hang not on my garments.
MIRANDA   Sir, have pity!
I'll be his surety.
PROSPERO   Silence! One word more 479
Shall make me chide thee, if not hate thee. What,
An advocate for an impostor? Hush!
Thou think'st there is no more such shapes as he,
Having seen but him and Caliban. Foolish wench,
To th' most of men this is a Caliban, 484
And they to him are angels.
MIRANDA   My affections
Are then most humble; I have no ambition
To see a goodlier man.
PROSPERO [to Ferdinand]   Come on, obey.
Thy nerves are in their infancy again 488
And have no vigor in them.
FERDINAND   So they are.
My spirits, as in a dream, are all bound up. 490
My father's loss, the weakness which I feel,
The wreck of all my friends, nor this man's threats
To whom I am subdued, are but light to me, 493
Might I but through my prison once a day
Behold this maid. All corners else o'th'earth 495
Let liberty make use of; space enough
Have I in such a prison.
PROSPERO [aside]   It works. [To Ferdinand] Come on.—
Thou hast done well, fine Ariel! [To Ferdinand] Follow
me.
[To Ariel] Hark what thou else shalt do me.
MIRANDA [to Ferdinand]   Be of comfort. 499
My father's of a better nature, sir,
Than he appears by speech. This is unwonted 501
Which now came from him.
PROSPERO [to Ariel]   Thou shalt be as free
As mountain winds; but then exactly do 503
All points of my command.
ARIEL   To th' syllable.
PROSPERO [to Ferdinand]
Come, follow. [To Miranda] Speak not for him.
                                        Exeunt.

❧

438 And . . . weep i.e., and I weep at this reminder that my father is
seemingly dead, leaving me heir.   439 never . . . ebb never dry, continually weeping   442 son (The only reference in the play to a son of
Antonio.)   443 more braver more splendid.   control refute
445 changed eyes exchanged amorous glances.   447 done . . . wrong
i.e., spoken falsely.   454 both in either's each in the other's
455 uneasy difficult   456 light cheap. (Playing on light, "easy," in
455.)   457 attend follow, obey   458 ow'st ownest   460 on't of it.
463 strive . . . with't i.e., expel the evil and occupy the temple, the
body.   469 entertainment treatment   470 s.d. charmed magically
prevented   471 rash harsh

472 gentle (1) wellborn (2) easily managed.   fearful frightening,
dangerous.   473 My . . . tutor? i.e., Do you, as my daughter and thus
bound to me by obedience, dare presume to teach me what to do?
475 ward defensive posture (in fencing)   479 surety guarantee.
484 To compared with   488 nerves sinews   490 spirits vital powers
493 light unimportant   495 corners else other corners, regions
499 me for me.   501 unwonted unusual   503 then if so, then

2.1

Enter Alonso, Sebastian, Antonio, Gonzalo,
Adrian, Francisco, and others.

GONZALO [*to Alonso*]
  Beseech you, sir, be merry. You have cause,
  So have we all, of joy, for our escape
  Is much beyond our loss. Our hint of woe   3
  Is common; every day some sailor's wife,
  The masters of some merchant, and the merchant,   5
  Have just our theme of woe. But for the miracle,   6
  I mean our preservation, few in millions
  Can speak like us. Then wisely, good sir, weigh   8
  Our sorrow with our comfort.
ALONSO   Prithee, peace.   9
SEBASTIAN [*aside to Antonio*] He receives comfort like
  cold porridge.   11
ANTONIO [*aside to Sebastian*] The visitor will not give   12
  him o'er so.   13
SEBASTIAN Look, he's winding up the watch of his wit;
  by and by it will strike.
GONZALO [*to Alonso*] Sir—
SEBASTIAN [*aside to Antonio*] One. Tell.   17
GONZALO When every grief is entertained   18
  That's offered, comes to th'entertainer—   19
SEBASTIAN A dollar.   20
GONZALO Dolor comes to him, indeed. You have spo-
  ken truer than you purposed.
SEBASTIAN You have taken it wiselier than I meant you
  should.
GONZALO [*to Alonso*] Therefore, my lord—
ANTONIO Fie, what a spendthrift is he of his tongue!
ALONSO [*to Gonzalo*] I prithee, spare.   27
GONZALO Well, I have done. But yet—
SEBASTIAN [*aside to Antonio*] He will be talking.
ANTONIO [*aside to Sebastian*] Which, of he or Adrian,   30
  for a good wager, first begins to crow?   31
SEBASTIAN The old cock.   32
ANTONIO The cockerel.   33
SEBASTIAN Done. The wager?
ANTONIO A laughter.   35

SEBASTIAN A match!   36
ADRIAN Though this island seem to be desert—   37
ANTONIO Ha, ha, ha!
SEBASTIAN So, you're paid.   39
ADRIAN Uninhabitable and almost inaccessible—
SEBASTIAN Yet—
ADRIAN Yet—
ANTONIO He could not miss't.   43
ADRIAN It must needs be of subtle, tender, and delicate   44
  temperance.   45
ANTONIO Temperance was a delicate wench.   46
SEBASTIAN Ay, and a subtle, as he most learnedly   47
  delivered.   48
ADRIAN The air breathes upon us here most sweetly.
SEBASTIAN As if it had lungs, and rotten ones.
ANTONIO Or as 'twere perfumed by a fen.   51
GONZALO Here is everything advantageous to life.
ANTONIO True, save means to live.   53
SEBASTIAN Of that there's none, or little.
GONZALO How lush and lusty the grass looks! How   55
  green!
ANTONIO The ground indeed is tawny.   57
SEBASTIAN With an eye of green in't.   58
ANTONIO He misses not much.
SEBASTIAN No. He doth but mistake the truth totally.   60
GONZALO But the rarity of it is—which is indeed
  almost beyond credit—
SEBASTIAN As many vouched rarities are.   63
GONZALO That our garments, being, as they were,
  drenched in the sea, hold notwithstanding their fresh-
  ness and glosses, being rather new-dyed than stained
  with salt water.
ANTONIO If but one of his pockets could speak, would   68
  it not say he lies?   69
SEBASTIAN Ay, or very falsely pocket up his report.   70
GONZALO Methinks our garments are now as fresh as
  when we put them on first in Afric, at the marriage of
  the King's fair daughter Claribel to the King of Tunis.
SEBASTIAN 'Twas a sweet marriage, and we prosper
  well in our return.
ADRIAN Tunis was never graced before with such a
  paragon to their queen.   77

2.1. Location: Another part of the island.
3 hint occasion   **5 The masters . . . the merchant** the officers or owners of some merchant vessel and the merchant who owns the cargo
6 for as for   **8–9 weigh . . . comfort** balance our sorrow against our
comfort.   **11 porridge** (Punningly suggested by *peace*, i.e., "peas" or
"pease," a common ingredient of porridge.)   **12 visitor** one bringing
nourishment and comfort to the sick, as Gonzalo is doing   **12–13 give
him o'er** abandon him   **17 Tell** Keep count.   **18–19 When . . . entertainer** When every sorrow that presents itself is accepted without
resistance, there comes to the recipient   **20 dollar** widely circulated
coin, the German thaler and the Spanish piece of eight. (Sebastian
puns on *entertainer* in the sense of paid performer or innkeeper; to
Gonzalo, *dollar* suggests "dolor," grief.)   **27 spare** forbear, cease.
30–1 Which . . . crow? Which of the two, Gonzalo or Adrian, do you
bet will speak (crow) first?   **32 The old cock** Gonzalo.   **33 The cockerel** Adrian.   **35 laughter** (1) burst of laughter (2) sitting of eggs.
(When Adrian, the *cockerel*, begins to speak two lines later, Sebastian
loses the bet. The Folio speech prefixes in lines 38–9 are here reversed
so that Antonio enjoys his laugh as the prize for winning, as in the
proverb "He who laughs last laughs best" or "He laughs that wins."
The Folio assignment can work in the theater, however, if Sebastian
pays for losing with a sardonic laugh of concession.)

36 A match! A bargain; agreed!.   **37 desert** uninhabited   **39 you're
paid** i.e., you've had your laugh.   **43 miss't** (1) avoid saying "Yet"
(2) miss the island.   **44 must needs be** has to be   **45 temperance**
mildness of climate.   **46 Temperance** a girl's name.   **delicate** (Here
it means "given to pleasure, voluptuous"; in line 44, "pleasant."
Antonio is evidently suggesting that *tender, and delicate temperance*
sounds like a Puritan phrase, which Antonio then mocks by applying
the words to a woman rather than an island. He began this bawdy
comparison with a double entendre on *inaccessible,* line 40.)   **47 subtle** (Here it means "tricky, sexually crafty"; in line 44, "delicate.")
48 delivered uttered. (Sebastian joins Antonio in baiting the Puritans
with his use of the pious cant phrase *learnedly delivered.*)   **51 fen** evil-
smelling marshland.   **53 save** except   **55 lusty** healthy   **57 tawny**
dull brown, yellowish.   **58 eye** tinge, or spot. (Sebastian is mocking
Gonzalo's optimism by saying there's precious little green to see anywhere. Antonio echoes him in line 59 with similar sarcasm.)   **60 He
. . . totally** i.e., He's only a tiny 100% wrong. (Sarcastic.)   **63 As . . . are**
(More sarcasm: Just as many alleged strange sights are doubtful,
including this one.)   **68–70 If . . . report** (More wisecracking: Gonzalo's mud-filled pockets would surely give the lie to his talk of clean
fresh garments, thereby *pocketing up* or tabling the *report.*)   **77 to** for

GONZALO   Not since widow Dido's time.   78

ANTONIO   [*aside to Sebastian*]   Widow? A pox o' that!
How came that "widow" in? Widow Dido!

SEBASTIAN   What if he had said "widower Aeneas"
too? Good Lord, how you take it!   82

ADRIAN   [*to Gonzalo*]   "Widow Dido" said you? You make
me study of that. She was of Carthage, not of Tunis.   84

GONZALO   This Tunis, sir, was Carthage.

ADRIAN   Carthage?

GONZALO   I assure you, Carthage.

ANTONIO   His word is more than the miraculous harp.   88

SEBASTIAN   He hath raised the wall, and houses too.

ANTONIO   What impossible matter will he make easy
next?

SEBASTIAN   I think he will carry this island home in his
pocket and give it his son for an apple.

ANTONIO   And, sowing the kernels of it in the sea,   94
bring forth more islands.

GONZALO   Ay.   96

ANTONIO   Why, in good time.   97

GONZALO   [*to Alonso*]   Sir, we were talking that our
garments seem now as fresh as when we were at
Tunis at the marriage of your daughter, who is now
queen.

ANTONIO   And the rarest that e'er came there.   101

SEBASTIAN   Bate, I beseech you, widow Dido.   102

ANTONIO   Oh, widow Dido? Ay, widow Dido.

GONZALO   Is not, sir, my doublet as fresh as the first   104
day I wore it? I mean, in a sort.   105

ANTONIO   That "sort" was well fished for.   106

GONZALO   When I wore it at your daughter's marriage.

ALONSO
You cram these words into mine ears against
The stomach of my sense. Would I had never   109
Married my daughter there! For, coming thence,   110
My son is lost and, in my rate, she too,   111
Who is so far from Italy removed
I ne'er again shall see her. O thou mine heir
Of Naples and of Milan, what strange fish
Hath made his meal on thee?

FRANCISCO   Sir, he may live.
I saw him beat the surges under him   116
And ride upon their backs. He trod the water,

Whose enmity he flung aside, and breasted
The surge most swoll'n that met him. His bold head
'Bove the contentious waves he kept, and oared   120
Himself with his good arms in lusty stroke   121
To th' shore, that o'er his wave-worn basis bowed,   122
As stooping to relieve him. I not doubt   123
He came alive to land.

ALONSO   No, no, he's gone.

SEBASTIAN   [*to Alonso*]
Sir, you may thank yourself for this great loss,
That would not bless our Europe with your daughter,   126
But rather loose her to an African,   127
Where she at least is banished from your eye,   128
Who hath cause to wet the grief on't.

ALONSO   Prithee, peace.   129

SEBASTIAN
You were kneeled to and importuned otherwise   130
By all of us, and the fair soul herself   131
Weighed between loathness and obedience at   132
Which end o'th' beam should bow. We have lost your
son,   133
I fear, forever. Milan and Naples have
More widows in them of this business' making   135
Than we bring men to comfort them.
The fault's your own.

ALONSO   So is the dear'st o'th' loss.   138

GONZALO   My lord Sebastian,
The truth you speak doth lack some gentleness
And time to speak it in. You rub the sore   141
When you should bring the plaster.

SEBASTIAN   Very well.   142

ANTONIO   And most chirurgeonly.   143

GONZALO   [*to Alonso*]
It is foul weather in us all, good sir,
When you are cloudy.

SEBASTIAN   [*to Antonio*]   Fowl weather?

ANTONIO   [*to Sebastian*]   Very foul.   145

GONZALO
Had I plantation of this isle, my lord—   146

ANTONIO   [*to Sebastian*]
He'd sow't with nettle seed.

SEBASTIAN   Or docks, or mallows.   147

GONZALO
And were the king on't, what would I do?

---

78 widow Dido Queen of Carthage, deserted by Aeneas. (She was, in fact, a widow when Aeneas, a widower, met her, but Antonio may be amused at Gonzalo's prudish use of the term "widow" to describe a woman deserted by her lover.)   **82 take** understand, respond to, interpret   **84 study of** think about   **88 miraculous harp** (Alludes to Amphion's harp, with which he raised the walls of Thebes; Gonzalo has exceeded that deed by recreating ancient Carthage—*wall and houses*—mistakenly on the site of modern-day Tunis. Some Renaissance commentators believed, like Gonzalo, that the two sites were near each other.)   **94 kernels** seeds   **96 Ay** (Gonzalo may be reasserting his point about Carthage, or he may be responding ironically to Antonio, who, in turn, answers sarcastically.)   **97 in good time** (An expression of ironical acquiescence or amazement, i.e., "sure, right away.")   **101 rarest** most remarkable, beautiful   **102 Bate** Abate, except, leave out. (Sebastian says sardonically, surely you should allow widow Dido to be an exception.)   **104 doublet** close-fitting jacket   **105 in a sort** in a way.   **106 sort** (Antonio plays on the idea of drawing lots and on "fishing" for something to say.)   **109 The stomach . . . sense** my appetite for hearing them.   **110 Married** given in marriage   **111 rate** estimation, opinion   **116 surges** waves

120 oared propelled as by an oar   **121 lusty** vigorous   **122 that . . . bowed** that projected out over its (*his*) surf-eroded base, bending down toward the sea   **123 As** as if   **126 That** you who   **127 But . . . her** but would rather turn her loose (or, "lose her")   **128–9 Where . . . on't** where at least she is not a constant reproach in your eye, which has good reason to weep sorrowfully for this unhappy development.   **130 importuned** urged, implored   **131–3 the fair . . . bow** Claribel herself was poised uncertainly, as in a balancing scale, between being unwilling to marry and yet wishing to obey her father.   **135 of . . . making** on account of this marriage and subsequent shipwreck   **138 dear'st** heaviest, most costly   **141 time** appropriate time   **142 plaster** (A medical application.)   **143 chirurgeonly** like a skilled surgeon. (Antonio mocks Gonzalo's medical analogy of a *plaster* applied curatively to a wound.)   **145 Fowl** (With a pun on *foul*, returning to the imagery of lines 30–5.)   **146 plantation** colonial settlement. (With subsequent wordplay on the literal meaning, "planting.")   **147 docks . . . mallows** (Weeds; the first was used as an antidote for nettle stings.)

SEBASTIAN   Scape being drunk for want of wine.   149

GONZALO

I'th' commonwealth I would by contraries   150
Execute all things; for no kind of traffic   151
Would I admit; no name of magistrate;
Letters should not be known; riches, poverty,   153
And use of service, none; contract, succession,   154
Bourn, bound of land, tilth, vineyard, none;   155
No use of metal, corn, or wine, or oil;   156
No occupation; all men idle, all,
And women too, but innocent and pure;
No sovereignty—

SEBASTIAN   Yet he would be king on't.

ANTONIO   The latter end of his commonwealth forgets
the beginning.

GONZALO

All things in common nature should produce
Without sweat or endeavor. Treason, felony,
Sword, pike, knife, gun, or need of any engine   164
Would I not have; but nature should bring forth,
Of it own kind, all foison, all abundance,   166
To feed my innocent people.

SEBASTIAN   No marrying 'mong his subjects?

ANTONIO   None, man, all idle—whores and knaves.

GONZALO

I would with such perfection govern, sir,
T'excel the Golden Age.

SEBASTIAN   'Save His Majesty!   171

ANTONIO

Long live Gonzalo!

GONZALO   And—do you mark me, sir?

ALONSO

Prithee, no more. Thou dost talk nothing to me.

GONZALO   I do well believe Your Highness, and did it
to minister occasion to these gentlemen, who are of   175
such sensible and nimble lungs that they always use   176
to laugh at nothing.

ANTONIO   'Twas you we laughed at.

GONZALO   Who in this kind of merry fooling am nothing
to you; so you may continue, and laugh at nothing
still.

ANTONIO   What a blow was there given!

SEBASTIAN   An it had not fallen flat-long.   182

GONZALO   You are gentlemen of brave mettle; you   183
would lift the moon out of her sphere if she would   184

continue in it five weeks without changing.

Enter Ariel [invisible] playing solemn music.

SEBASTIAN   We would so, and then go a-batfowling.   186

ANTONIO   Nay, good my lord, be not angry.

GONZALO   No, I warrant you, I will not adventure my   188
discretion so weakly. Will you laugh me asleep? For I   189
am very heavy.   190

ANTONIO   Go sleep, and hear us.   191

[*All sleep except Alonso, Sebastian, and Antonio.*]

ALONSO

What, all so soon asleep? I wish mine eyes
Would, with themselves, shut up my thoughts. I find   193
They are inclined to do so.

SEBASTIAN   Please you, sir,
Do not omit the heavy offer of it.   195
It seldom visits sorrow; when it doth,
It is a comforter.

ANTONIO   We two, my lord,
Will guard your person while you take your rest,
And watch your safety.

ALONSO   Thank you. Wondrous heavy.

[*Alonso sleeps. Exit Ariel.*]

SEBASTIAN

What a strange drowsiness possesses them!

ANTONIO

It is the quality o'th' climate.

SEBASTIAN   Why
Doth it not then our eyelids sink? I find not
Myself disposed to sleep.

ANTONIO   Nor I. My spirits are nimble.
They fell together all, as by consent;   204
They dropped, as by a thunderstroke. What might,
Worthy Sebastian, oh, what might—? No more.
And yet methinks I see it in thy face
What thou shouldst be. Th'occasion speaks thee, and   208
My strong imagination sees a crown
Dropping upon thy head.

SEBASTIAN   What, art thou waking?

ANTONIO

Do you not hear me speak?

SEBASTIAN   I do, and surely
It is a sleepy language, and thou speak'st   212
Out of thy sleep. What is it thou didst say?
This is a strange repose, to be asleep
With eyes wide open—standing, speaking, moving—
And yet so fast asleep.

ANTONIO   Noble Sebastian,
Thou let'st thy fortune sleep—die, rather; wink'st   217

---

149 Scape Escape.   **want** lack. (Sebastian jokes sarcastically that this
hypothetical ruler would be saved from dissipation only by the barrenness of the island.)   **150 by contraries** by what is directly opposite to usual custom   **151 traffic** trade   **153 Letters** learning   **154
use of service** custom of employing servants.   **succession** holding
of property by right of inheritance   **155 Bourn . . . tilth** boundaries,
property limits, tillage of soil   **156 corn** grain   **164 pike** lance.
engine instrument of warfare   **166 it** its.   **foison** plenty   **171 the
Golden Age** an age of prelapsarian abundance and peace; the first of
four "ages" of human history, followed by silver, bronze, and lead.
'Save God save   **175 minister occasion** furnish opportunity (for
laughter)   **176 sensible** sensitive.   **use** are accustomed   **182 An** If.
flat-long with the flat of the sword, i.e., ineffectually.   **183 mettle**
temperament, courage. (The sense of *metal*, indistinguishable as a
form from *mettle*, continues the metaphor of the sword. F reads
"mettall.")   **184 sphere** orbit. (Literally, one of the concentric zones
occupied by planets in Ptolemaic astronomy.)

186 a-batfowling hunting birds at night with lantern and *bat*, or
"stick"; also, gulling a simpleton. (Gonzalo is the simpleton, or fowl,
and Sebastian will use the moon as his lantern.)   **188–9 adventure . . .
weakly** risk my reputation for discretion for so trivial a cause (by getting angry).   **190 heavy** sleepy.   **191 Go . . . us** i.e., Get ready for
sleep, and we'll do our part by laughing.   **193 Would . . . thoughts**
would shut off my melancholy brooding when they (my eyes) close
themselves in sleep.   **195 Do . . . it** do not decline the invitation to
drowsiness.   **204 They . . . consent** The others all fell asleep simultaneously, as if by common agreement   **208 Th' occasion . . . thee** The
opportunity of the moment calls upon you   **212 sleepy** dreamlike,
fantastic   **217 wink'st** (you) shut your eyes

Whiles thou art waking.

SEBASTIAN   Thou dost snore distinctly;   218
There's meaning in thy snores.

ANTONIO
I am more serious than my custom. You
Must be so too if heed me, which to do   221
Trebles thee o'er.

SEBASTIAN   Well, I am standing water.   222

ANTONIO
I'll teach you how to flow.

SEBASTIAN   Do so. To ebb   223
Hereditary sloth instructs me.

ANTONIO   Oh,   224
If you but knew how you the purpose cherish   225
Whiles thus you mock it! How, in stripping it,   226
You more invest it! Ebbing men, indeed,   227
Most often do so near the bottom run   228
By their own fear or sloth.

SEBASTIAN   Prithee, say on.
The setting of thine eye and cheek proclaim   230
A matter from thee, and a birth indeed   231
Which throes thee much to yield.

ANTONIO   Thus, sir: 232
Although this lord of weak remembrance, this   233
Who shall be of as little memory   234
When he is earthed, hath here almost persuaded—   236
For he's a spirit of persuasion, only   236
Professes to persuade—the King his son's alive,   237
'Tis as impossible that he's undrowned
As he that sleeps here swims.

SEBASTIAN   I have no hope
That he's undrowned.

ANTONIO   Oh, out of that "no hope"
What great hope have you! No hope that way is   241
Another way so high a hope that even   242
Ambition cannot pierce a wink beyond,   243
But doubt discovery there. Will you grant with me   244
That Ferdinand is drowned?

SEBASTIAN   He's gone.

ANTONIO   Then tell me,
Who's the next heir of Naples?

SEBASTIAN   Claribel.

ANTONIO
She that is Queen of Tunis; she that dwells
Ten leagues beyond man's life; she that from Naples   248
Can have no note, unless the sun were post—   249
The Man i'th' Moon's too slow—till newborn chins
Be rough and razorable; she that from whom   251
We all were sea-swallowed, though some cast again,   252
And by that destiny to perform an act
Whereof what's past is prologue, what to come
In yours and my discharge.   255

SEBASTIAN   What stuff is this? How say you?
'Tis true my brother's daughter's Queen of Tunis,
So is she heir of Naples, twixt which regions
There is some space.

ANTONIO   A space whose ev'ry cubit   259
Seems to cry out, "How shall that Claribel
Measure us back to Naples? Keep in Tunis,   261
And let Sebastian wake." Say this were death   262
That now hath seized them, why, they were no worse
Than now they are. There be that can rule Naples   264
As well as he that sleeps, lords that can prate   265
As amply and unnecessarily
As this Gonzalo. I myself could make   267
A chough of as deep chat. Oh, that you bore   268
The mind that I do! What a sleep were this
For your advancement! Do you understand me?

SEBASTIAN
Methinks I do.

ANTONIO   And how does your content   271
Tender your own good fortune?

SEBASTIAN   I remember   272
You did supplant your brother Prospero.

ANTONIO   True.
And look how well my garments sit upon me,
Much feater than before. My brother's servants   275
Were then my fellows. Now they are my men.

SEBASTIAN   But, for your conscience?   277

ANTONIO
Ay, sir, where lies that? If 'twere a kibe,   278
'Twould put me to my slipper; but I feel not   279
This deity in my bosom. Twenty consciences   280
That stand twixt me and Milan, candied be they   281
And melt ere they molest! Here lies your brother,   282
No better than the earth he lies upon,
If he were that which now he's like—that's dead,
Whom I, with this obedient steel, three inches of it,

---

218 distinctly articulately   **221 if heed** if you heed   **222 Trebles thee o'er** makes you three times as great and rich.   **standing water** water that neither ebbs nor flows, at a standstill.   **223 ebb** recede, decline **224 Hereditary sloth** i.e., natural laziness and the position of younger brother, one who cannot inherit   **225–6 If . . . mock it!** If you only knew how much you secretly cherish ambition even while your words mock it!   **226–7 How . . . invest it!** How the more you speak flippantly of ambition, the more you, in effect, affirm it, clothing what you have stripped!   **228 the bottom** i.e., on which unadventurous men may go aground and miss the tide of fortune   **230 setting** set expression (of earnestness)   **231 matter** matter of importance   **232 throes** causes pain, as in giving birth.   **yield** give forth, speak about.   **233–7 Although . . . alive** Although this owner of weak memory, he who will be only weakly remembered when he is dead, has nearly persuaded— since he's a mind or soul devoted solely to persuade—King Alonso that Ferdinand lives   **241 that way** i.e., in regard to Ferdinand's being saved   **242–4 that . . . there** that even ambition for high status cannot see anything higher, and even there it doubts the reality of what it sees (because the place is so supremely high). (What then follows is Antonio's analysis of why they can proceed without fear.)

248 Ten . . . life i.e., further than the journey of a lifetime   **249 note** news, intimation.   **post** messenger   **251 razorable** ready for shaving.   **from** on our voyage from   **252 cast** were disgorged. (With a pun on *casting* of parts for a play.)   **255 discharge** part to play.   **259 cubit** ancient measure of length of about twenty inches   **261 Measure us** retrace our journey.   **Keep** You, Claribel, stay   **262 wake** i.e., to his good fortune.   **264 There be** There are those   **265 prate** speak foolishly   **267–8 I . . . chat** I could teach a jackdaw to talk as wisely, or, be such a garrulous talker myself.   **271–2 And . . . fortune?** And how does your contentment with what I've just said further your good fortune?   **275 feater** more becomingly, fittingly   **277 for** as for **278 kibe** chilblain, here a sore on the heel   **279 put me to** oblige me to wear   **280–2 Twenty . . . molest!** Even if there were twenty consciences between me and the dukedom of Milan, may they be lumped together or crystallized like candy and then melted down before I'd let them interfere!

Can lay to bed forever; whiles you, doing thus,   286
To the perpetual wink for aye might put   287
This ancient morsel, this Sir Prudence, who
Should not upbraid our course. For all the rest,   289
They'll take suggestion as a cat laps milk;   290
They'll tell the clock to any business that   291
We say befits the hour.

SEBASTIAN   Thy case, dear friend,
Shall be my precedent. As thou got'st Milan,
I'll come by Naples. Draw thy sword. One stroke
Shall free thee from the tribute which thou payest,   295
And I the king shall love thee.

ANTONIO   Draw together;
And when I rear my hand, do you the like
To fall it on Gonzalo.   [*They draw.*]

SEBASTIAN   Oh, but one word.   298
                                                            [*They talk apart.*]

Enter Ariel [invisible], with music and song.

ARIEL [*to Gonzalo*]
My master through his art foresees the danger
That you, his friend, are in, and sends me forth—
For else his project dies—to keep them living.
                                              Sings in Gonzalo's ear.
    While you here do snoring lie,
    Open-eyed conspiracy
       His time doth take.   304
    If of life you keep a care,
    Shake off slumber, and beware.
       Awake, awake!

ANTONIO   Then let us both be sudden.

GONZALO [*waking*]   Now, good angels preserve the King!
                                              [*The others wake.*]

ALONSO
Why, how now, ho, awake? Why are you drawn?
Wherefore this ghastly looking?

GONZALO   What's the matter?

SEBASTIAN
Whiles we stood here securing your repose,   312
Even now, we heard a hollow burst of bellowing
Like bulls, or rather lions. Did 't not wake you?
It struck mine ear most terribly.

ALONSO   I heard nothing.

ANTONIO
Oh, 'twas a din to fright a monster's ear,
To make an earthquake! Sure it was the roar
Of a whole herd of lions.

ALONSO   Heard you this, Gonzalo?

GONZALO
Upon mine honor, sir, I heard a humming,
And that a strange one too, which did awake me.
I shaked you, sir, and cried. As mine eyes opened,   322
I saw their weapons drawn. There was a noise,

That's verily. 'Tis best we stand upon our guard,   324
Or that we quit this place. Let's draw our weapons.

ALONSO
Lead off this ground, and let's make further search
For my poor son.

GONZALO   Heavens keep him from these beasts!
For he is, sure, i'th'island.

ALONSO   Lead away.

ARIEL [*aside*]
Prospero my lord shall know what I have done.
So, King, go safely on to seek thy son.
                                              Exeunt [separately].

                                    ✤

2.2

*Enter Caliban with a burden of wood. A noise
of thunder heard.*

CALIBAN
All the infections that the sun sucks up
From bogs, fens, flats, on Prosper fall, and make him   2
By inchmeal a disease! His spirits hear me,   3
And yet I needs must curse. But they'll nor pinch,   4
Fright me with urchin shows, pitch me i'th' mire,   5
Nor lead me, like a firebrand, in the dark   6
Out of my way, unless he bid 'em. But
For every trifle are they set upon me,
Sometimes like apes, that mow and chatter at me   9
And after bite me; then like hedgehogs, which
Lie tumbling in my barefoot way and mount
Their pricks at my footfall. Sometime am I
All wound with adders, who with cloven tongues   13
Do hiss me into madness.

Enter Trinculo.

                          Lo, now, lo!
Here comes a spirit of his, and to torment me
For bringing wood in slowly. I'll fall flat.
Perchance he will not mind me.   [*He lies down.*]   17

TRINCULO   Here's neither bush nor shrub to bear off   18
any weather at all. And another storm brewing; I hear
it sing i'th' wind. Yond same black cloud, yond huge
one, looks like a foul bombard that would shed his   21
liquor. If it should thunder as it did before, I know not
where to hide my head. Yond same cloud cannot
choose but fall by pailfuls. [*Seeing Caliban*] What have
we here, a man or a fish? Dead or alive? A fish, he
smells like a fish; a very ancient and fishlike smell; a
kind of not-of-the-newest Poor John. A strange fish!   27
Were I in England now, as once I was, and had but
this fish painted, not a holiday fool there but would   29

286 thus similarly. (The actor makes a stabbing gesture.)   **287 wink** sleep, closing of eyes.   **aye** ever   **289 Should not** must not be allowed to   **290 take suggestion** respond to prompting   **291 tell the clock** i.e., agree, answer appropriately, chime   **295 tribute** (See 1.2.113–24.)   **298 fall it** let it fall   **304 time** opportunity   **312 securing** standing guard over   **322 cried** called out.

324 verily true.
2.2. Location: Another part of the island.
2 flats swamps   **3 By inchmeal** inch by inch   **4 needs must** have to.
nor neither   **5 urchin shows** elvish apparitions shaped like hedgehogs   **6 like a firebrand** they in the guise of a will-o'-the-wisp   **9 mow** make faces   **13 wound with** entwined by   **17 mind** notice   **18 bear off** keep off   **21 foul bombard** dirty leather jug.   **his** its   **27 Poor John** salted fish, type of poor fare   **29 painted** i.e., painted on a sign set up outside a booth or tent at a fair

give a piece of silver. There would this monster make 30
a man. Any strange beast there makes a man. When 31
they will not give a doit to relieve a lame beggar, they 32
will lay out ten to see a dead Indian. Legged like a
man, and his fins like arms! Warm, o' my troth! I do 34
now let loose my opinion, hold it no longer: this is no 35
fish, but an islander, that hath lately suffered by a
thunderbolt. [*Thunder.*] Alas, the storm is come again!
My best way is to creep under his gaberdine. There is 38
no other shelter hereabout. Misery acquaints a man
with strange bedfellows. I will here shroud till the 40
dregs of the storm be past. 41

[*He creeps under Caliban's garment.*]

Enter Stephano, singing, [a bottle in his hand].

STEPHANO
"I shall no more to sea, to sea,
      Here shall I die ashore—"
This is a very scurvy tune to sing at a man's funeral.
Well, here's my comfort.   *Drinks.*
(*Sings.*)
      "The master, the swabber, the boatswain, and I, 46
            The gunner and his mate,
      Loved Mall, Meg, and Marian, and Margery,
            But none of us cared for Kate.
      For she had a tongue with a tang, 50
      Would cry to a sailor, 'Go hang!'
      She loved not the savor of tar nor of pitch,
      Yet a tailor might scratch her where'er she did itch. 53
            Then to sea, boys, and let her go hang!"
This is a scurvy tune too. But here's my comfort.
                                                  Drinks.
CALIBAN   Do not torment me! Oh! 56
STEPHANO   What's the matter? Have we devils here? Do 57
you put tricks upon 's with savages and men of Ind, 58
ha? I have not scaped drowning to be afeard now of
your four legs. For it hath been said, "As proper a man 60
as ever went on four legs cannot make him give 61
ground"; and it shall be said so again while Stephano
breathes at' nostrils. 63
CALIBAN   This spirit torments me! Oh!
STEPHANO   This is some monster of the isle with four
legs, who hath got, as I take it, an ague. Where the 66
devil should he learn our language? I will give him 67
some relief, if it be but for that. If I can recover him 68
and keep him tame and get to Naples with him, he's

a present for any emperor that ever trod on neat's 70
leather. 71
CALIBAN   Do not torment me, prithee. I'll bring my
wood home faster.
STEPHANO   He's in his fit now and does not talk after 74
the wisest. He shall taste of my bottle. If he have never 75
drunk wine afore, it will go near to remove his fit. If I 76
can recover him and keep him tame, I will not take too 77
much for him. He shall pay for him that hath him, and 78
that soundly.
CALIBAN   Thou dost me yet but little hurt; thou wilt
anon, I know it by thy trembling. Now Prosper works
upon thee.
STEPHANO   Come on your ways. Open your mouth. Here
is that which will give language to you, cat. Open your 84
mouth. This will shake your shaking, I can tell you, 85
and that soundly. [*Giving Caliban a drink.*] You cannot 86
tell who's your friend. Open your chaps again. 87
TRINCULO   I should know that voice. It should be—but
he is drowned, and these are devils. Oh, defend me!
STEPHANO   Four legs and two voices—a most delicate 90
monster! His forward voice now is to speak well of his
friend; his backward voice is to utter foul speeches and 92
to detract. If all the wine in my bottle will recover him, 93
I will help his ague. Come. [*Giving a drink.*] Amen! I
will pour some in thy other mouth.
TRINCULO   Stephano!
STEPHANO   Doth thy other mouth call me? Mercy,
mercy! This is a devil, and no monster. I will leave
him. I have no long spoon. 99
TRINCULO   Stephano! If thou be'st Stephano, touch me
and speak to me, for I am Trinculo—be not afeard—
thy good friend Trinculo.
STEPHANO   If thou be'st Trinculo, come forth. I'll pull
thee by the lesser legs. If any be Trinculo's legs, these
are they. [*Pulling him out.*] Thou art very Trinculo
indeed! How cam'st thou to be the siege of this 106
mooncalf? Can he vent Trinculos? 107
TRINCULO   I took him to be killed with a thunderstroke.
But art thou not drowned, Stephano? I hope now thou
art not drowned. Is the storm overblown? I hid me 110
under the dead mooncalf's gaberdine for fear of the
storm. And art thou living, Stephano? Oh, Stephano,
two Neapolitans scaped!   [*He capers with Stephano.*]

30–1 make a man (1) make a man's fortune (2) pass for a human
being.   **32 doit** small coin   **34 o' my troth** by my faith.   **35 hold it**
hold it in   **38 gaberdine** cloak, loose upper garment.   **40 shroud**
take shelter   **41 dregs** i.e., last remains (as in a *bombard* or jug, line 21)
46 swabber crew member whose job is to wash the decks   **50 tang**
sting   **53 tailor . . . itch** (A dig at tailors for their supposed effeminacy and a bawdy suggestion of satisfying a sexual craving.)   **56 Do
. . . me!** (Caliban assumes that one of Prospero's spirits has come to
punish him.)   **57 What's the matter?** What's going on here?   **58 put
tricks upon 's** trick us with conjuring shows.   **Ind** India   **60 proper**
handsome   **61 four legs** (The conventional phrase would supply *two
legs*, but the creature Stephano thinks he sees has four.)   **63 at'** at the
66 ague fever. (Probably both Caliban and Trinculo are quaking; see
lines 56 and 81.)   **67 should he learn** could he have learned   **68 for
that** i.e., for knowing our language.   **recover** revive. (Also in line 77.)

70–1 neat's leather cowhide.   **74–5 after the wisest** in the wisest
fashion.   **76 afore** before.   **go near to** be in a fair way to   **77 recover**
restore   **77–8 I will . . . much** i.e., no sum can be too much   **78 He
shall . . . hath him** Anyone who wants him will have to pay dearly
for him   **84–5 cat . . . mouth** (Allusion to the proverb "Good liquor
will make a cat speak.")   **85 shake** shake off   **86–7 You . . . friend**
i.e., You can't tell who's your friend until someone like me provides
you with a drink.   **87 chaps** jaws   **90 delicate** ingenious   **92 backward voice** (Trinculo and Caliban are facing in opposite directions.
Stephano supposes the monster to have a rear end that can emit *foul
speeches* or foul-smelling wind at the monster's *other mouth*, line 95.)
93 If . . . him Even if it takes all the wine in my bottle to cure him
99 long spoon (Allusion to the proverb "He that sups with the devil
has need of a long spoon.")   **106 siege** excrement   **107 mooncalf**
monstrous or misshapen creature (whose deformity is caused by the
malignant influence of the moon).   **vent** excrete, defecate
110 overblown blown over.

STEPHANO   Prithee, do not turn me about. My stomach
is not constant.   115

CALIBAN

These be fine things, an if they be not spirits.   116
That's a brave god, and bears celestial liquor.   117
I will kneel to him.

STEPHANO   How didst thou scape? How cam'st thou
hither? Swear by this bottle how thou cam'st hither. I
escaped upon a butt of sack which the sailors heaved   121
o'erboard—by this bottle, which I made of the bark of   122
a tree with mine own hands since I was cast ashore.

CALIBAN [*kneeling*]   I'll swear upon that bottle to be
thy true subject, for the liquor is not earthly.

STEPHANO   Here. Swear then how thou escaped'st.

TRINCULO   Swum ashore, man, like a duck. I can swim
like a duck, I'll be sworn.

STEPHANO   Here, kiss the book. Though thou canst   129
swim like a duck, thou art made like a goose.
            [*Giving him a drink.*]

TRINCULO   Oh, Stephano, hast any more of this?

STEPHANO   The whole butt, man. My cellar is in a rock
by th' seaside, where my wine is hid.—How now,
mooncalf? How does thine ague?

CALIBAN   Hast thou not dropped from heaven?

STEPHANO   Out o'th' moon, I do assure thee. I was the
man i'th' moon when time was.   137

CALIBAN

I have seen thee in her, and I do adore thee.
My mistress showed me thee, and thy dog, and thy
bush.   139

STEPHANO   Come, swear to that. Kiss the book. I will
furnish it anon with new contents. Swear.
            [*Giving him a drink.*]

TRINCULO   By this good light, this is a very shallow   142
monster! I afeard of him? A very weak monster! The
man i'th' moon? A most poor credulous monster!
Well drawn, monster, in good sooth!   145

CALIBAN [*to Stephano*]

I'll show thee every fertile inch o'th'island,
And I will kiss thy foot. I prithee, be my god.

TRINCULO   By this light, a most perfidious and drunken
monster! When 's god's asleep, he'll rob his bottle.   149

CALIBAN

I'll kiss thy foot. I'll swear myself thy subject.

STEPHANO   Come on then. Down, and swear.
            [*Caliban kneels.*]

TRINCULO   I shall laugh myself to death at this puppy-
headed monster. A most scurvy monster! I could find
in my heart to beat him—

STEPHANO   Come, kiss.

TRINCULO   But that the poor monster's in drink. An   156
abominable monster!

CALIBAN

I'll show thee the best springs. I'll pluck thee berries.
I'll fish for thee and get thee wood enough.
A plague upon the tyrant that I serve!
I'll bear him no more sticks, but follow thee,
Thou wondrous man.

TRINCULO   A most ridiculous monster, to make a
wonder of a poor drunkard!

CALIBAN

I prithee, let me bring thee where crabs grow,   165
And I with my long nails will dig thee pignuts,   166
Show thee a jay's nest, and instruct thee how
To snare the nimble marmoset. I'll bring thee   168
To clust'ring filberts, and sometimes I'll get thee
Young scamels from the rock. Wilt thou go with me?   170

STEPHANO   I prithee now, lead the way without any
more talking.—Trinculo, the King and all our com-   172
pany else being drowned, we will inherit here.—   173
Here, bear my bottle.—Fellow Trinculo, we'll fill him
by and by again.

CALIBAN (*sings drunkenly*)
Farewell, master, farewell, farewell!

TRINCULO   A howling monster; a drunken monster!

CALIBAN

No more dams I'll make for fish,
   Nor fetch in firing   179
   At requiring,
Nor scrape trenchering, nor wash dish.   181
   'Ban, 'Ban, Ca–Caliban
   Has a new master. Get a new man!   183
Freedom, high-day! High-day, freedom! Freedom,   184
high-day, freedom!

STEPHANO   O brave monster! Lead the way.   *Exeunt.*

❧

3.1

Enter Ferdinand, bearing a log.

FERDINAND

There be some sports are painful, and their labor   1
Delight in them sets off. Some kinds of baseness   2
Are nobly undergone, and most poor matters   3
Point to rich ends. This my mean task   4
Would be as heavy to me as odious, but   5

---

115 **constant** steady.   116 **an if** if   117 **brave** fine, magnificent
121 **butt of sack** barrel of Canary wine   122 **by this bottle** i.e., I swear
by this bottle   129 **book** i.e., bottle. (But with ironic reference to the
practice of kissing the Bible in swearing an oath; see *I'll be sworn* in line
128.)   137 **when time was** once upon a time.   139 **dog . . . bush** (The
man in the moon was popularly imagined to have with him a dog and
a bush of thorn.)   142 **By . . . light** By God's light, by this good light
from heaven   145 **Well . . . sooth!** Well pulled on the bottle, truly!
149 **When . . . bottle** i.e., Caliban wouldn't even stop at robbing his
god (i.e., Stephano) of his bottle if he could catch him asleep.

156 **But that** were it not that.   **in drink** drunk.   165 **crabs** crab apples,
or crabs   166 **pignuts** earthnuts, edible tuberous roots   168 **marmoset** small monkey.   170 **scamels** (Possibly *seamews*, mentioned in
Strachey's letter, or shellfish, or perhaps from *squamelle*, "furnished
with little scales." Contemporary French and Italian travel accounts
report that the natives of Patagonia in South America ate small fish
described as *fort scameux* and *squame*.)   172–3 **all . . . else** all the rest
of our shipboard companions   173 **inherit** take possession   179 **firing** firewood   181 **trenchering** trenchers, wooden plates   183 **Get a
new man** (Addressed to Prospero.)   184 **high-day** holiday.
3.1. Location: Before Prospero's cell.
1–2 **There . . . sets off** Some pastimes are laborious, but the pleasure
we get from them compensates for the effort. (Pleasure is *set off* by
labor as a jewel is set off by its foil.)   2 **baseness** menial activity
3 **undergone** undertaken.   **most poor** poorest   4 **mean** lowly   5 **but**
were it not that

The mistress which I serve quickens what's dead 6
And makes my labors pleasures. Oh, she is
Ten times more gentle than her father's crabbed,
And he's composed of harshness. I must remove
Some thousands of these logs and pile them up,
Upon a sore injunction. My sweet mistress 11
Weeps when she sees me work and says such baseness
Had never like executor. I forget; 13
But these sweet thoughts do even refresh my labors,
Most busy lest when I do it.

Enter Miranda; and Prospero [at a distance, unseen].

MIRANDA   Alas now, pray you, 15
Work not so hard. I would the lightning had
Burnt up those logs that you are enjoined to pile! 17
Pray, set it down and rest you. When this burns, 18
'Twill weep for having wearied you. My father 19
Is hard at study. Pray now, rest yourself.
He's safe for these three hours.

FERDINAND   O most dear mistress, 21
The sun will set before I shall discharge 22
What I must strive to do.

MIRANDA   If you'll sit down,
I'll bear your logs the while. Pray, give me that.
I'll carry it to the pile.

FERDINAND   No, precious creature,
I had rather crack my sinews, break my back,
Than you should such dishonor undergo
While I sit lazy by.

MIRANDA   It would become me
As well as it does you; and I should do it
With much more ease, for my good will is to it,
And yours it is against.

PROSPERO *[aside]*   Poor worm, thou art infected!
This visitation shows it.

MIRANDA   You look wearily. 32

FERDINAND
No, noble mistress, 'tis fresh morning with me
When you are by at night. I do beseech you— 34
Chiefly that I might set it in my prayers—
What is your name?

MIRANDA   Miranda.—O my father,
I have broke your hest to say so.

FERDINAND   Admired Miranda! 37
Indeed the top of admiration, worth
What's dearest to the world! Full many a lady 39
I have eyed with best regard, and many a time 40
The harmony of their tongues hath into bondage

Brought my too diligent ear. For several virtues 42
Have I liked several women, never any
With so full soul but some defect in her
Did quarrel with the noblest grace she owed 45
And put it to the foil. But you, oh, you, 46
So perfect and so peerless, are created
Of every creature's best!

MIRANDA   I do not know 48
One of my sex; no woman's face remember,
Save, from my glass, mine own. Nor have I seen
More that I may call men than you, good friend,
And my dear father. How features are abroad 52
I am skilless of; but, by my modesty, 53
The jewel in my dower, I would not wish
Any companion in the world but you;
Nor can imagination form a shape,
Besides yourself, to like of. But I prattle 57
Something too wildly, and my father's precepts 58
I therein do forget.

FERDINAND   I am in my condition 59
A prince, Miranda; I do think, a king—
I would, not so!—and would no more endure 61
This wooden slavery than to suffer 62
The flesh-fly blow my mouth. Hear my soul speak: 63
The very instant that I saw you did
My heart fly to your service, there resides
To make me slave to it, and for your sake
Am I this patient log-man.

MIRANDA   Do you love me?

FERDINAND
O heaven, O earth, bear witness to this sound,
And crown what I profess with kind event 69
If I speak true! If hollowly, invert 70
What best is boded me to mischief! I 71
Beyond all limit of what else i'th' world 72
Do love, prize, honor you.

MIRANDA *[weeping]*   I am a fool
To weep at what I am glad of.

PROSPERO *[aside]*   Fair encounter
Of two most rare affections! Heavens rain grace
On that which breeds between 'em!

FERDINAND   Wherefore weep you?

MIRANDA
At mine unworthiness, that dare not offer
What I desire to give, and much less take
What I shall die to want. But this is trifling, 79
And all the more it seeks to hide itself
The bigger bulk it shows. Hence, bashful cunning, 81

---

6 **quickens** gives life to   11 **sore injunction** severe command.
13 **Had . . . executor** was never before undertaken by so noble a
being.   **I forget** i.e., I forget that I'm supposed to be working
15 **Most . . . do it** (Ferdinand seems to say that the busier he is, the
less likely he is to forget the sweet thoughts that make his labors
pleasant. The line may be in need of emendation.)   17 **enjoined** commanded   18 **this** i.e., the log   19 **weep** i.e., exude resin   21 **these** the
next   22 **discharge** complete   32 **visitation** (1) Miranda's visit to
Ferdinand (2) visitation of the plague, i.e., infection of love   34 **by**
nearby   37 **hest** command.   **Admired Miranda** (Her name means
"to be admired or wondered at.")   39 **dearest** most treasured
40 **best regard** thoughtful and approving attention

42 **diligent** attentive.   **several** various. (Also in line 43.)   45 **owed**
owned   46 **put . . . foil** (1) overthrew it (as in fencing or wrestling)
(2) served as a *foil*, or "contrast," to set it off.   48 **Of** out of   52 **How . . .
abroad** What people look like in other places   53 **skilless** ignorant.
modesty virginity   57 **like of** be pleased with, be fond of.   58 **Something** somewhat   59 **condition** rank   61 **I would** I wish it were
62 **wooden slavery** being compelled to carry wood   62–3 **than . . .
mouth** than I would allow flying insects to deposit their eggs in my
mouth as if in decaying flesh.   69 **kind event** favorable outcome
70 **hollowly** insincerely, falsely.   **invert** turn   71 **boded** in store for.
mischief harm.   72 **what** whatever   79 **die** (Probably with an
unconscious sexual meaning that underlies all of lines 77–81.)   **to
want** through lacking.   81 **bashful cunning** coyness

And prompt me, plain and holy innocence!
I am your wife, if you will marry me;
If not, I'll die your maid. To be your fellow   84
You may deny me, but I'll be your servant
Whether you will or no.

FERDINAND   My mistress, dearest,   86
And I thus humble ever.

MIRANDA   My husband, then?

FERDINAND   Ay, with a heart as willing   89
As bondage e'er of freedom. Here's my hand.

MIRANDA [*clasping his hand*]
And mine, with my heart in't. And now farewell
Till half an hour hence.

FERDINAND   A thousand thousand!   92

Exeunt [Ferdinand and Miranda, separately].

PROSPERO
So glad of this as they I cannot be,
Who are surprised with all; but my rejoicing   94
At nothing can be more. I'll to my book,
For yet ere suppertime must I perform
Much business appertaining.   *Exit.*   97

❖

3.2

Enter Caliban, Stephano, and Trinculo.

STEPHANO   Tell not me. When the butt is out, we will   1
drink water, not a drop before. Therefore bear up and   2
board 'em. Servant monster, drink to me.   3

TRINCULO   Servant monster? The folly of this island!   4
They say there's but five upon this isle. We are three
of them; if th'other two be brained like us, the state   6
totters.

STEPHANO   Drink, servant monster, when I bid thee.
Thy eyes are almost set in thy head.   [*Giving a drink.*]   9

TRINCULO   Where should they be set else? He were a   10
brave monster indeed if they were set in his tail.   11

STEPHANO   My man-monster hath drowned his tongue
in sack. For my part, the sea cannot drown me. I
swam, ere I could recover the shore, five and thirty   14
leagues off and on. By this light, thou shalt be my   15
lieutenant, monster, or my standard.   16

TRINCULO   Your lieutenant, if you list; he's no standard.   17

STEPHANO   We'll not run, Monsieur Monster.   18

TRINCULO   Nor go neither, but you'll lie like dogs and   19
yet say nothing neither.

STEPHANO   Mooncalf, speak once in thy life, if thou
be'st a good mooncalf.

CALIBAN
How does Thy Honor? Let me lick thy shoe.
I'll not serve him. He is not valiant.

TRINCULO   Thou liest, most ignorant monster, I am in   25
case to jostle a constable. Why, thou deboshed fish,   26
thou, was there ever man a coward that hath drunk so   27
much sack as I today? Wilt thou tell a monstrous lie,   28
being but half a fish and half a monster?

CALIBAN
Lo, how he mocks me! Wilt thou let him, my lord?

TRINCULO   "Lord," quoth he? That a monster should be
such a natural!   32

CALIBAN
Lo, lo, again! Bite him to death, I prithee.

STEPHANO   Trinculo, keep a good tongue in your head.
If you prove a mutineer—the next tree! The poor mon-   35
ster's my subject, and he shall not suffer indignity.

CALIBAN
I thank my noble lord. Wilt thou be pleased
To hearken once again to the suit I made to thee?

STEPHANO   Marry, will I. Kneel and repeat it. I will   39
stand, and so shall Trinculo.   [*Caliban kneels.*]   40

Enter Ariel, invisible.

CALIBAN
As I told thee before, I am subject to a tyrant,
A sorcerer, that by his cunning hath
Cheated me of the island.

ARIEL [*mimicking Trinculo*]
Thou liest.

CALIBAN   Thou liest, thou jesting monkey, thou!
I would my valiant master would destroy thee.
I do not lie.

STEPHANO   Trinculo, if you trouble him any more in 's
tale, by this hand, I will supplant some of your teeth.   48

TRINCULO   Why, I said nothing.

STEPHANO   Mum, then, and no more.—Proceed.

CALIBAN
I say by sorcery he got this isle;
From me he got it. If Thy Greatness will
Revenge it on him—for I know thou dar'st,
But this thing dare not—   54

STEPHANO   That's most certain.

CALIBAN
Thou shalt be lord of it, and I'll serve thee.

---

84 maid handmaiden, servant.   **fellow** mate   **86 will** desire it.   **My mistress** i.e., The woman I adore and serve (not an illicit sexual partner)   **89 willing** desirous   **92 A thousand thousand!** A thousand thousand farewells!   **94 with all** by everything that has happened, or, *withal*, "by it"   **97 appertaining** related to this.
3.2 Location: Another part of the island.
1 out empty   **2–3 bear . . . 'em** (Stephano uses the terminology of maneuvering at sea and boarding a vessel under attack as a way of urging an assault on the liquor supply.)   **4 folly of** i.e., stupidity found on   **6 be brained** are endowed with intelligence   **9 set . . . head** fixed in a drunken stare. (But Trinculo answers in a literal sense.)   **10 set** placed   **11 brave** fine, splendid   **14 recover** gain, reach   **14–15 five . . . on** i.e., a little over a hundred miles, give or take, or, off and on, intermittently. (A drunken hyperbole.)   **15 By this light** (An oath: By the light of the sun.)   **16 standard** standard-bearer, ensign. (But Trinculo answers in the literal sense: Caliban is *no standard*, not able to stand up because he's so drunk.)   **17 list** prefer

18 run run away, retreat (as a standard-bearer should not do)
19 Nor . . . dogs i.e., You won't even walk, much less run; you'll lie down in the field like the proverbial cowardly dog. (With a play on *lie*, tell falsehoods.)   **25–6 in case** ready, valiant enough
26 deboshed debauched, drunken   **27 ever . . . coward** ever a coward. (Trinculo appeals to his gargantuan drinking as refutation of the charge that he is *not valiant*, line 24.)   **28 sack** Spanish white wine   **32 natural** fool, idiot.   **35 the next tree** i.e., you'll hang.   **39 Marry** i.e., Indeed. (Originally an oath, "by the Virgin Mary.")
40.1 invisible i.e., wearing a garment to connote invisibility, as at 1.2.377.2.   **48 supplant** uproot, displace   **54 this thing** i.e., Trinculo

STEPHANO   How now shall this be compassed? Canst   57
thou bring me to the party?

CALIBAN
Yea, yea, my lord. I'll yield him thee asleep,
Where thou mayst knock a nail into his head.

ARIEL   [*mimicking Trinculo*]   Thou liest; thou canst not.

CALIBAN
What a pied ninny's this! Thou scurvy patch!—   62
I do beseech Thy Greatness, give him blows
And take his bottle from him. When that's gone
He shall drink naught but brine, for I'll not show
him
Where the quick freshes are.   66

STEPHANO   Trinculo, run into no further danger. Interrupt the monster one word further and, by this hand,
I'll turn my mercy out o' doors and make a stockfish of   69
thee.

TRINCULO   Why, what did I? I did nothing. I'll go farther
off.

STEPHANO   Didst thou not say he lied?

ARIEL   [*mimicking Trinculo*]   Thou liest.

STEPHANO   Do I so? Take thou that.   [*He beats Trinculo.*]
As you like this, give me the lie another time.   76

TRINCULO   I did not give the lie. Out o' your wits and
hearing too? A pox o' your bottle! This can sack and   78
drinking do. A murrain on your monster, and the   79
devil take your fingers!

CALIBAN   Ha, ha, ha!

STEPHANO   Now, forward with your tale. [*To Trinculo*]
Prithee, stand further off.

CALIBAN
Beat him enough. After a little time
I'll beat him too.

STEPHANO   Stand farther.—Come, proceed.

CALIBAN
Why, as I told thee, 'tis a custom with him
I'th'afternoon to sleep. There thou mayst brain him,
Having first seized his books; or with a log
Batter his skull, or paunch him with a stake,   90
Or cut his weasand with thy knife. Remember   91
First to possess his books, for without them
He's but a sot, as I am, nor hath not   93
One spirit to command. They all do hate him
As rootedly as I. Burn but his books.
He has brave utensils—for so he calls them—   96
Which, when he has a house, he'll deck withal.   97
And that most deeply to consider is
The beauty of his daughter. He himself
Calls her a nonpareil. I never saw a woman
But only Sycorax my dam and she;
But she as far surpasseth Sycorax
As great'st does least.

STEPHANO   Is it so brave a lass?   104

CALIBAN
Ay, lord. She will become thy bed, I warrant,   105
And bring thee forth brave brood.

STEPHANO   Monster, I will kill this man. His daughter
and I will be king and queen—save Our Graces!—and
Trinculo and thyself shall be viceroys. Dost thou like
the plot, Trinculo?

TRINCULO   Excellent.

STEPHANO   Give me thy hand. I am sorry I beat thee;
but, while thou liv'st, keep a good tongue in thy head.

CALIBAN
Within this half hour will he be asleep.
Wilt thou destroy him then?

STEPHANO   Ay, on mine honor.

ARIEL   [*aside*]   This will I tell my master.

CALIBAN
Thou mak'st me merry; I am full of pleasure.
Let us be jocund. Will you troll the catch   119
You taught me but whilere?   120

STEPHANO   At thy request, monster, I will do reason,   121
any reason.—Come on, Trinculo, let us sing.   *Sings.*   122
"Flout 'em and scout 'em   123
And scout 'em and flout 'em!
Thought is free."

CALIBAN   That's not the tune.   126
Ariel plays the tune on a tabor and pipe.

STEPHANO   What is this same?

TRINCULO   This is the tune of our catch, played by the
picture of Nobody.   129

STEPHANO   If thou be'st a man, show thyself in thy
likeness. If thou be'st a devil, take't as thou list.   131

TRINCULO   Oh, forgive me my sins!

STEPHANO   He that dies pays all debts. I defy thee.   133
Mercy upon us!

CALIBAN   Art thou afeard?

STEPHANO   No, monster, not I.

CALIBAN
Be not afeard. The isle is full of noises,
Sounds, and sweet airs, that give delight and hurt not.
Sometimes a thousand twangling instruments
Will hum about mine ears, and sometimes voices
That, if I then had waked after long sleep,
Will make me sleep again; and then, in dreaming,
The clouds methought would open and show riches
Ready to drop upon me, that when I waked
I cried to dream again.   145

STEPHANO   This will prove a brave kingdom to me,
where I shall have my music for nothing.

CALIBAN   When Prospero is destroyed.

---

57 **compassed** achieved.   62 **pied ninny** fool in motley.   **patch** fool.
66 **quick freshes** running springs   69 **turn . . . o' doors** banish all
merciful feelings.   **stockfish** dried cod beaten before cooking
76 **give me the lie** call me a liar to my face   78 **A pox** i.e., A plague.
(A curse.)   79 **murrain** plague. (Literally, a cattle disease.)   90 **paunch**
stab in the belly   91 **weasand** windpipe   93 **sot** fool   96 **brave utensils** fine furnishings   97 **deck withal** furnish it with.

104 **brave** splendid, attractive   105 **become** suit (sexually)   119 **jocund**
jovial, merry.   **troll the catch** sing the round   120 **but whilere** only a
short time ago.   121–2 **reason, any reason** anything reasonable.
123 **Flout** Scoff at.   **scout** deride   126.1 *tabor* small drum   129 **picture of Nobody** (Refers to a familiar figure with head, arms, and legs
but no trunk.)   131 **take't . . . list** (A proverbial formula of bravado
and defiance, as in *Romeo and Juliet*, 1.1.40–1.)   133 **He . . . debts**
(Another proverbial swagger: Death settles all scores, I'm not afraid
to fight.)   145 **to dream** desirous of dreaming

STEPHANO   That shall be by and by. I remember the 149
story.

TRINCULO   The sound is going away. Let's follow it,
and after do our work.

STEPHANO   Lead, monster; we'll follow. I would I could
see this taborer! He lays it on.   154

TRINCULO   Wilt come? I'll follow, Stephano.
                    Exeunt [following Ariel's music].

❖

3.3

*Enter Alonso, Sebastian, Antonio, Gonzalo,
Adrian, Francisco, etc.*

GONZALO
By'r lakin, I can go no further, sir.   1
My old bones aches. Here's a maze trod indeed
Through forthrights and meanders! By your patience,   3
I needs must rest me.

ALONSO   Old lord, I cannot blame thee,
Who am myself attached with weariness,   5
To th' dulling of my spirits. Sit down and rest.   6
Even here I will put off my hope, and keep it
No longer for my flatterer. He is drowned
Whom thus we stray to find, and the sea mocks
Our frustrate search on land. Well, let him go.   10
                    [Alonso and Gonzalo sit.]

ANTONIO *[aside to Sebastian]*
I am right glad that he's so out of hope.
Do not, for one repulse, forgo the purpose   12
That you resolved t'effect.

SEBASTIAN *[to Antonio]*   The next advantage
Will we take throughly.

ANTONIO *[to Sebastian]*   Let it be tonight,   14
For, now they are oppressed with travel, they   15
Will not, nor cannot, use such vigilance   16
As when they are fresh.

SEBASTIAN *[to Antonio]*   I say tonight. No more.   17

*Solemn and strange music; and Prospero on
the top, invisible.*

ALONSO
What harmony is this? My good friends, hark!

GONZALO   Marvelous sweet music!

*Enter several strange shapes, bringing in a ban-
quet, and dance about it with gentle actions of
salutations; and, inviting the King, etc., to eat,
they depart.*

ALONSO
Give us kind keepers, heavens! What were these?   20

SEBASTIAN
A living drollery. Now I will believe   21
That there are unicorns; that in Arabia
There is one tree, the phoenix' throne, one phoenix   23
At this hour reigning there.

ANTONIO   I'll believe both;
And what does else want credit, come to me   25
And I'll be sworn 'tis true. Travelers ne'er did lie,
Though fools at home condemn 'em.

GONZALO   If in Naples
I should report this now, would they believe me
If I should say I saw such islanders?
For, certes, these are people of the island,   30
Who, though they are of monstrous shape, yet note,
Their manners are more gentle, kind, than of
Our human generation you shall find
Many, nay, almost any.

PROSPERO *[aside]*   Honest lord,
Thou hast said well, for some of you there present
Are worse than devils.

ALONSO   I cannot too much muse   36
Such shapes, such gesture, and such sound,
expressing—
Although they want the use of tongue—a kind   38
Of excellent dumb discourse.

PROSPERO *[aside]*   Praise in departing.   39

FRANCISCO
They vanished strangely.

SEBASTIAN   No matter, since
They have left their viands behind, for we have
stomachs.   41
Will 't please you taste of what is here?

ALONSO   Not I.

GONZALO
Faith, sir, you need not fear. When we were boys,
Who would believe that there were mountaineers   44
Dewlapped like bulls, whose throats had hanging at
'em   45
Wallets of flesh? Or that there were such men   46
Whose heads stood in their breasts? Which now we
find   47
Each putter-out of five for one will bring us   48
Good warrant of.

ALONSO   I will stand to and feed,   49

---

149 **by and by** very soon.   154 **lays it on** i.e., plays the drum vigorously.
3.3. Location: Another part of the island.
1 **By'r lakin** By our Ladykin, by our Lady   3 **forthrights and meanders** paths straight and crooked.   5 **attached with** seized by   6 **To . . .
spirits** to the point of being dull-spirited.   10 **frustrate** frustrated
12 **for** because of   14 **throughly** thoroughly.   15 **now** now that.
travel (Spelled "trauaile" in the Folio and carrying the sense of labor
as well as traveling.)   16 **use such vigilance** be as vigilant   17.1–2 *on
the top* at some high point of the tiring-house or the theater, on a
third level above the gallery

20 **kind keepers** guardian angels   21 **living drollery** comic entertainment, caricature, or puppet show put on by live actors.   23 **phoenix**
mythical bird consumed to ashes every five hundred to six hundred
years, only to be renewed into another cycle   25 **want credit** lack
credibility   30 **certes** certainly   36 **muse** wonder at   38 **want** lack
39 **Praise in departing** i.e., Save your praise until the end of the performance. (Proverbial.)   41 **viands** provisions.   **stomachs** appetites.
44 **mountaineers** mountain dwellers   45 **Dewlapped** having a
dewlap, or fold of skin hanging from the neck, like cattle   46 **Wallets**
pendent folds of skin, wattles   47 **in their breasts** (I.e., like the
Anthropophagi described in *Othello*, 1.3.146.)   48 **putter-out . . . one**
one who invests money or gambles on the risks of travel on the condition that the traveler who returns safely is to receive five times the
amount deposited; hence, any traveler   49 **Good warrant** assurance.
stand to come forward, fall to. (Also in line 52.)

Although my last—no matter, since I feel 50
The best is past. Brother, my lord the Duke, 51
Stand to, and do as we.   [*They approach the table.*] 52

Thunder and lightning. Enter Ariel, like a harpy,
claps his wings upon the table, and with a quaint
device the banquet vanishes.

ARIEL
You are three men of sin, whom Destiny— 53
That hath to instrument this lower world 54
And what is in't—the never-surfeited sea 55
Hath caused to belch up you, and on this island 56
Where man doth not inhabit, you 'mongst men
Being most unfit to live. I have made you mad;
And even with suchlike valor men hang and drown 59
Their proper selves.   [*Alonso, Sebastian, and Antonio*
draw their swords.]
                    You fools! I and my fellows 60
Are ministers of Fate. The elements
Of whom your swords are tempered may as well 62
Wound the loud winds, or with bemocked-at stabs 63
Kill the still-closing waters, as diminish 64
One dowl that's in my plume. My fellow ministers 65
Are like invulnerable. If you could hurt, 66
Your swords are now too massy for your strengths 67
And will not be uplifted. But remember—
For that's my business to you—that you three
From Milan did supplant good Prospero;
Exposed unto the sea, which hath requit it, 71
Him and his innocent child; for which foul deed
The powers, delaying, not forgetting, have
Incensed the seas and shores, yea, all the creatures,
Against your peace. Thee of thy son, Alonso,
They have bereft; and do pronounce by me
Ling'ring perdition, worse than any death 77
Can be at once, shall step by step attend
You and your ways; whose wraths to guard you
    from— 79
Which here, in this most desolate isle, else falls 80
Upon your heads—is nothing but heart's sorrow 81
And a clear life ensuing. 82

He vanishes in thunder; then, to soft music,
enter the shapes again, and dance, with mocks
and mows, and carrying out the table.

PROSPERO
Bravely the figure of this harpy hast thou 83
Performed, my Ariel; a grace it had devouring. 84
Of my instruction hast thou nothing bated 85
In what thou hadst to say. So, with good life 86
And observation strange, my meaner ministers 87
Their several kinds have done. My high charms work, 88
And these mine enemies are all knit up
In their distractions. They now are in my power; 90
And in these fits I leave them, while I visit
Young Ferdinand, whom they suppose is drowned,
And his and mine loved darling.   [*Exit above.*]
GONZALO
I'th' name of something holy, sir, why stand you 94
In this strange stare?
ALONSO   Oh, it is monstrous, monstrous! 95
Methought the billows spoke and told me of it; 96
The winds did sing it to me, and the thunder,
That deep and dreadful organ pipe, pronounced
The name of Prosper; it did bass my trespass. 99
Therefor my son i'th'ooze is bedded; and
I'll seek him deeper than e'er plummet sounded, 101
And with him there lie mudded.   *Exit.*
SEBASTIAN   But one fiend at a time, 103
I'll fight their legions o'er.
ANTONIO   I'll be thy second. 104
                    Exeunt [*Sebastian and Antonio*].
GONZALO
All three of them are desperate. Their great guilt, 105
Like poison given to work a great time after, 106
Now 'gins to bite the spirits. I do beseech you, 107
That are of suppler joints, follow them swiftly 108
And hinder them from what this ecstasy 109
May now provoke them to.
ADRIAN   Follow, I pray you.
                    Exeunt omnes.

❖

4.1

Enter Prospero, Ferdinand, and Miranda.

PROSPERO
If I have too austerely punished you,
Your compensation makes amends, for I

---

50 Although my last even if this were to be my last meal   **51 best** best part of life   **52.1 harpy** a fabulous monster with a woman's face and breasts and a vulture's body, supposed to be a minister of divine vengeance.   **52.2–3 with . . . vanishes** by means of some ingenious stage contrivance, the food vanishes. (The table remains until line 82.)   **53–6 whom . . . up** you whom Destiny, acting through this sublunary world as its instrument, has caused the ever-hungry sea to belch up   **59 suchlike valor** i.e., the reckless valor derived from madness   **60 proper** own   **62 whom** which.   **tempered** made hard   **63 bemocked-at** scorned   **64 still-closing** always closing again when parted   **65 dowl** soft, fine feather   **66 like** likewise, similarly.   **If** Even if   **67 massy** heavy   **71 requit** requited, avenged   **77 perdition** ruin, destruction   **79 whose . . . from** to guard you from which heavenly wrath   **80 else** otherwise   **81 is nothing** there is no way   **82 clear** unspotted, innocent   **82.2–3 mocks and mows** mocking gestures and grimaces

83 Bravely Finely, dashingly   **84 a grace . . . devouring** your impersonation displayed a ravishing grace. (With a punning suggestion of having caused the banquet to disappear as if by consuming it.)   **85 bated** abated, omitted   **86–8 So . . . done** Similarly, my lesser spirits assisting you have done their various tasks with observant care and attention to detail.   **90 distractions** trancelike state.   **94–5 why . . . stare?** (Gonzalo was not addressed in Ariel's speech to the *three men of sin*, line 53, and is not, as they are, in a maddened state; see lines 105–7.)   **95 it** i.e., my sin. (Also in line 96.)   **96 billows** waves   **99 bass my trespass** proclaim my trespass like a bass note on the music.   **101 than . . . sounded** than ever a lead weight attached to a line tested the depth   **103–4 But . . . o'er** If the demons come at me one at a time, I'll fight them all.   **105 desperate** despairing and reckless.   **106 Like . . . after** like poison, starting to work long after it has been administered   **107 bite the spirits** sap their vital powers through anguish   **107–8 you . . . joints** Adrian, Francisco, and others not under Ariel's numbing spell   **109 ecstasy** mad frenzy
4.1. Location: Before Prospero's cell.

Have given you here a third of mine own life, 3
Or that for which I live; who once again
I tender to thy hand. All thy vexations 5
Were but my trials of thy love, and thou
Hast strangely stood the test. Here, afore heaven, 7
I ratify this my rich gift. O Ferdinand,
Do not smile at me that I boast her off, 9
For thou shalt find she will outstrip all praise
And make it halt behind her.

FERDINAND   I do believe it 11
Against an oracle. 12

PROSPERO
Then, as my gift and thine own acquisition
Worthily purchased, take my daughter. But
If thou dost break her virgin-knot before
All sanctimonious ceremonies may 16
With full and holy rite be ministered,
No sweet aspersion shall the heavens let fall 18
To make this contract grow; but barren hate,
Sour-eyed disdain, and discord shall bestrew
The union of your bed with weeds so loathly 21
That you shall hate it both. Therefore take heed,
As Hymen's lamps shall light you.

FERDINAND   As I hope 23
For quiet days, fair issue, and long life, 24
With such love as 'tis now, the murkiest den,
The most opportune place, the strong'st suggestion 26
Our worser genius can, shall never melt 27
Mine honor into lust, to take away 28
The edge of that day's celebration 29
When I shall think or Phoebus' steeds are foundered 30
Or Night kept chained below.

PROSPERO   Fairly spoke.
Sit then and talk with her. She is thine own.
    [Ferdinand and Miranda sit and talk together.]
What, Ariel! My industrious servant, Ariel! 33

    Enter Ariel.

ARIEL
What would my potent master? Here I am.

PROSPERO
Thou and thy meaner fellows your last service 35
Did worthily perform, and I must use you
In such another trick. Go bring the rabble, 37

O'er whom I give thee power, here to this place.
Incite them to quick motion, for I must
Bestow upon the eyes of this young couple
Some vanity of mine art. It is my promise, 41
And they expect it from me.

ARIEL   Presently? 42
PROSPERO   Ay, with a twink. 43

ARIEL
Before you can say "Come" and "Go,"
And breathe twice, and cry "So, so,"
Each one, tripping on his toe,
Will be here with mop and mow. 47
Do you love me, master? No?

PROSPERO
Dearly, my delicate Ariel. Do not approach
Till thou dost hear me call.

ARIEL   Well; I conceive.   Exit. 50
PROSPERO
Look thou be true; do not give dalliance 51
Too much the rein. The strongest oaths are straw
To th' fire i'th' blood. Be more abstemious,
Or else good night your vow!

FERDINAND   I warrant you, sir, 54
The white cold virgin snow upon my heart 55
Abates the ardor of my liver.

PROSPERO   Well. 56
Now come, my Ariel! Bring a corollary, 57
Rather than want a spirit. Appear, and pertly!— 58
No tongue! All eyes! Be silent.   Soft music. 59

    Enter Iris.

IRIS
Ceres, most bounteous lady, thy rich leas 60
Of wheat, rye, barley, vetches, oats, and peas; 61
Thy turfy mountains, where live nibbling sheep,
And flat meads thatched with stover, them to keep; 63
Thy banks with pionèd and twillèd brims, 64
Which spongy April at thy hest betrims 65
To make cold nymphs chaste crowns; and thy
    broom groves, 66
Whose shadow the dismissèd bachelor loves, 67
Being lass-lorn; thy poll-clipped vineyard; 68
And thy sea marge, sterile and rocky hard, 69
Where thou thyself dost air: the queen o'th' sky, 70

3 a third i.e., Miranda, into whose education I have put a third of my life, or (less precisely) who represents a large part of what I have cared about, along with my dukedom and my magical art   5 tender offer   7 strangely exceptionally   9 boast her off i.e., praise her so, or, perhaps an error for "boast of her"; the Folio reads "boast her of"   11 halt limp   12 Against an oracle even if an oracle should declare otherwise.   16 sanctimonious sacred   18 aspersion dew, shower   21 weeds (In place of the flowers customarily strewn on the marriage bed.)   23 As . . . you i.e., as you long for happiness and concord in your marriage. (Hymen was the Greek and Roman god of marriage; his symbolic torches, the wedding torches, were supposed to burn brightly for a happy marriage and smokily for a troubled one.)   24 issue offspring   26–7 the strong'st . . . can the strongest temptation that the evil spirit within us can propose   28 to so as to   29 edge keen enjoyment, sexual ardor   30 or . . . foundered either that the horses of the sun's chariot have gone lame (thus delaying the night for which I will be so eager)   33 What Now then   35 meaner fellows subordinates   37 trick device.   rabble band, i.e., the *meaner fellows* of line 35

41 vanity (1) illusion (2) trifle (3) desire for admiration, conceit   42 Presently? Immediately?   43 with a twink in the twinkling of an eye.   47 mop and mow grimaces.   50 conceive understand.   51 true true to your promise   54 good night i.e., say good-bye to.   warrant guarantee   55 The white . . . heart i.e., the chaste ideal to which my heart is devoted   56 liver (The presumed seat of the passions.)   57 corollary surplus, extra supply   58 want lack.   pertly briskly.   59 No tongue! Quiet, everyone!   59.1 Iris goddess of the rainbow and Juno's messenger.   60 Ceres goddess of the generative power of nature.   leas meadows   61 vetches plants for forage, fodder   63 meads meadows.   stover winter fodder for cattle   64 pionèd and twillèd undercut by the swift current and protected by roots and branches that tangle to form a barricade   65 spongy wet.   hest command   66 broom groves clumps of broom, gorse, yellow-flowered shrub   67 dismissèd bachelor rejected male lover   68 poll-clipped pruned, lopped at the top, or pole-clipped, "hedged in with poles"   69 sea marge shore   70 thou . . . air you take the air, go for walks.   queen o'th' sky i.e., Juno

Whose wat'ry arch and messenger am I,   71
Bids thee leave these, and with her sovereign grace,   72

> *Juno descends [slowly in her car].*

Here on this grass plot, in this very place,
To come and sport. Her peacocks fly amain.   74
Approach, rich Ceres, her to entertain.   75

> *Enter Ceres.*

CERES
Hail, many-colored messenger, that ne'er
Dost disobey the wife of Jupiter,
Who with thy saffron wings upon my flowers   78
Diffusest honeydrops, refreshing showers,
And with each end of thy blue bow dost crown   80
My bosky acres and my unshrubbed down,   81
Rich scarf to my proud earth. Why hath thy queen   82
Summoned me hither to this short-grassed green?

IRIS
A contract of true love to celebrate,
And some donation freely to estate   85
On the blest lovers.

CERES   Tell me, heavenly bow,
If Venus or her son, as thou dost know,   87
Do now attend the Queen? Since they did plot   88
The means that dusky Dis my daughter got,   89
Her and her blind boy's scandaled company   90
I have forsworn.

IRIS   Of her society   91
Be not afraid. I met Her Deity   92
Cutting the clouds towards Paphos, and her son   93
Dove-drawn with her. Here thought they to have
done   94
Some wanton charm upon this man and maid,   95
Whose vows are that no bed-right shall be paid   96
Till Hymen's torch be lighted; but in vain.
Mars's hot minion is returned again;   98
Her waspish-headed son has broke his arrows,   99
Swears he will shoot no more, but play with
sparrows   100
And be a boy right out.

> *[Juno alights.]*

CERES   Highest Queen of state,   101
Great Juno, comes; I know her by her gait.   102

JUNO
How does my bounteous sister? Go with me   103
To bless this twain, that they may prosperous be,
And honored in their issue.   *They sing:*   105

JUNO
Honor, riches, marriage blessing,
Long continuance, and increasing,
Hourly joys be still upon you!   108
Juno sings her blessings on you.

CERES
Earth's increase, foison plenty,   110
Barns and garners never empty,   111
Vines with clust'ring bunches growing,
Plants with goodly burden bowing;

Spring come to you at the farthest
In the very end of harvest!   115
Scarcity and want shall shun you;
Ceres' blessing so is on you.

FERDINAND
This is a most majestic vision, and
Harmonious charmingly. May I be bold   119
To think these spirits?

PROSPERO   Spirits, which by mine art
I have from their confines called to enact
My present fancies.

FERDINAND   Let me live here ever!
So rare a wondered father and a wife   123
Makes this place Paradise.

> *Juno and Ceres whisper, and send*
> *Iris on employment.*

PROSPERO   Sweet now, silence!
Juno and Ceres whisper seriously;
There's something else to do. Hush and be mute,
Or else our spell is marred.

IRIS *[calling offstage]*
You nymphs, called naiads, of the windring brooks,   128
With your sedged crowns and ever-harmless looks,   129
Leave your crisp channels, and on this green land   130
Answer your summons; Juno does command.
Come, temperate nymphs, and help to celebrate   132
A contract of true love. Be not too late.

> *Enter certain nymphs.*

You sunburned sicklemen, of August weary,   134
Come hither from the furrow and be merry.   135

---

71 wat'ry arch rainbow   **72.1 *Juno descends*** i.e., starts her descent
from the "heavens" above the stage   **74 peacocks** birds sacred to
Juno and used to pull her chariot.   **amain** with full speed.   **75 enter-**
tain receive.   **78 saffron** yellow   **80 bow** rainbow   **81 bosky**
wooded.   **unshrubbed down** open upland   **82 scarf** (The rainbow is
like a colored silk band adorning the earth.)   **85 estate** bestow   **87**
son i.e., Cupid.   **as** as far as   **88–91 Since . . . forsworn** Since Venus
and her blind son Cupid plotted the means by which Dis (Pluto) carried off my daughter Proserpina to be his bride in Hades, I have forsworn their scandalous company.   **92 Her Deity** i.e., Her Highness
93 Paphos place on the island of Cyprus, sacred to Venus   **94 Dove-**
drawn (Venus's chariot was drawn by doves.)   **94–5 done . . . charm**
inflicted some lustful spell   **96 that . . . paid** that their union will not
be sexually consummated   **98 Mars's hot minion** i.e., Venus, the
beloved of Mars.   **returned** i.e., returned to Paphos   **99 waspish-**
headed hotheaded, peevish   **100 sparrows** (Supposed lustful, and
sacred to Venus.)   **101 right out** outright.   **Highest . . . state** Most
majestic Queen   **102 gait** i.e., majestic bearing.

103 sister i.e., fellow goddess.   **105 issue** offspring.   **108 still** always
110 foison plenty plentiful harvest   **111 garners** granaries   **115 In . . .**
harvest i.e., with no winter in between.   **119 charmingly** enchantingly.   **123 wondered** wonder-performing, wondrous.   **wise** (The
Folio appears to read "wise" here, but with a tall "s" that resembles an
"f," leading to much dispute over this reading. In some copies of the
Folio the "s" looks like an "f," perhaps damaged, but evidently as the
result of an inkblot, so that the true reading is "s." Even so, an error in
transmission would be easy, so that the author's intention is uncertain.
The matter bears importantly on whether or not Ferdinand includes
Miranda in his vision of paradise.)   **128 naiads** nymphs of springs,
rivers, or lakes.   **windring** wandering, winding (?)   **129 sedged**
made of reeds.   **ever-harmless** ever innocent   **130 crisp** curled, rippled   **132 temperate** chaste   **134 sicklemen** harvesters, field workers who cut down grain and grass.   **of August weary** i.e., weary of
the hard work of the harvest   **135 furrow** i.e., plowed fields

Make holiday; your rye-straw hats put on,
And these fresh nymphs encounter every one   137
In country footing.   138

> *Enter certain reapers, properly habited. They join
> with the nymphs in a graceful dance, towards the
> end whereof Prospero starts suddenly, and speaks;
> after which, to a strange, hollow, and confused
> noise, they heavily vanish.*

PROSPERO [*aside*]
I had forgot that foul conspiracy
Of the beast Caliban and his confederates
Against my life. The minute of their plot
Is almost come. [*To the Spirits*] Well done! Avoid; no
    more!   142
FERDINAND [*to Miranda*]
This is strange. Your father's in some passion
That works him strongly.
MIRANDA   Never till this day 144
Saw I him touched with anger so distempered.
PROSPERO
You do look, my son, in a moved sort,   146
As if you were dismayed. Be cheerful, sir.
Our revels now are ended. These our actors,   148
As I foretold you, were all spirits and
Are melted into air, into thin air;
And, like the baseless fabric of this vision,   151
The cloud-capped towers, the gorgeous palaces,
The solemn temples, the great globe itself,   153
Yea, all which it inherit, shall dissolve,   154
And, like this insubstantial pageant faded,
Leave not a rack behind. We are such stuff   156
As dreams are made on, and our little life   157
Is rounded with a sleep. Sir, I am vexed.   158
Bear with my weakness. My old brain is troubled.
Be not disturbed with my infirmity.   160
If you be pleased, retire into my cell   161
And there repose. A turn or two I'll walk
To still my beating mind.
FERDINAND, MIRANDA   We wish your peace.   163
                    Exeunt [*Ferdinand and Miranda*].
PROSPERO
Come with a thought! I thank thee, Ariel. Come.   164

> *Enter Ariel.*

ARIEL
Thy thoughts I cleave to. What's thy pleasure?   165
PROSPERO   Spirit,
We must prepare to meet with Caliban.

ARIEL
Ay, my commander. When I presented Ceres,   167
I thought to have told thee of it, but I feared
Lest I might anger thee.
PROSPERO
Say again, where didst thou leave these varlets?
ARIEL
I told you, sir, they were red-hot with drinking;
So full of valor that they smote the air
For breathing in their faces, beat the ground
For kissing of their feet; yet always bending   174
Towards their project. Then I beat my tabor,
At which, like unbacked colts, they pricked their ears, 176
Advanced their eyelids, lifted up their noses   177
As they smelt music. So I charmed their ears   178
That calflike they my lowing followed through   179
Toothed briers, sharp furzes, pricking gorse, and
    thorns,   180
Which entered their frail shins. At last I left them
I'th' filthy-mantled pool beyond your cell,   182
There dancing up to th' chins, that the foul lake
O'erstunk their feet.
PROSPERO   This was well done, my bird.   184
Thy shape invisible retain thou still.
The trumpery in my house, go bring it hither,   186
For stale to catch these thieves.
ARIEL   I go, I go.   *Exit.* 187
PROSPERO
A devil, a born devil, on whose nature
Nurture can never stick; on whom my pains,
Humanely taken, all, all lost, quite lost!
And as with age his body uglier grows,
So his mind cankers. I will plague them all,   192
Even to roaring.

> *Enter Ariel, loaden with glistering apparel, etc.*

                Come, hang them on this line.   193

> [*Ariel hangs up the showy finery; Prospero and
> Ariel remain, invisible.*] *Enter Caliban, Stephano,
> and Trinculo, all wet.*

CALIBAN
Pray you, tread softly, that the blind mole may
Not hear a foot fall. We now are near his cell.
STEPHANO Monster, your fairy, which you say is a
harmless fairy, has done little better than played the
jack with us.   198

---

137 encounter join **138 country footing** country dancing.
138.1 *properly* suitably. **138.5** *heavily* slowly, dejectedly **142 Avoid**
Withdraw **144 works** affects, agitates **146 moved sort** troubled
state, condition **148 revels** entertainment, pageant **151 baseless
fabric** unsubstantial theatrical edifice or contrivance **153 great
globe** (With a glance at the Globe Theatre.) **154 which it inherit**
who subsequently occupy it **156 rack** wisp of cloud **157 on** of
158 rounded surrounded (before birth and after death), or crowned,
rounded off **160 with** by **161 retire** withdraw, go **163 beating**
agitated **164 with a thought** i.e., on the instant, or, summoned by
my thought, no sooner thought of than here. **165 cleave** cling,
adhere

167 presented acted the part of, or, introduced **174 bending** aiming
176 unbacked unbroken, unridden **177 Advanced** lifted up **178 As**
as if **179 lowing** mooing **180 furzes . . . gorse** prickly shrubs
182 filthy-mantled covered with a slimy coating **184 O'erstunk**
smelled worse than, or, caused to stink terribly **186 trumpery** cheap
goods, the *glistering apparel* mentioned in the following stage direction **187 stale** (1) decoy (2) out-of-fashion garments. (With possible
further suggestions of "horse piss," as in line 199, and "steal," pronounced like *stale. For stale* could also mean "fit for a prostitute.")
192 cankers festers, grows malignant. **193 line** lime tree or linden.
193.1–2 *Prospero and Ariel remain* (The staging is uncertain. They
may instead exit here and return with the spirits at line 256.)
198 jack (1) knave (2) will-o'-the-wisp

TRINCULO   Monster, I do smell all horse piss, at which
my nose is in great indignation.

STEPHANO   So is mine. Do you hear, monster? If I
should take a displeasure against you, look you—

TRINCULO   Thou wert but a lost monster.

CALIBAN
Good my lord, give me thy favor still.
Be patient, for the prize I'll bring thee to
Shall hoodwink this mischance. Therefore speak
softly.   206
All's hushed as midnight yet.

TRINCULO   Ay, but to lose our bottles in the pool—

STEPHANO   There is not only disgrace and dishonor in
that, monster, but an infinite loss.

TRINCULO   That's more to me than my wetting. Yet this
is your harmless fairy, monster!

STEPHANO   I will fetch off my bottle, though I be o'er 213
ears for my labor.   214

CALIBAN
Prithee, my king, be quiet. See'st thou here,
This is the mouth o'th' cell. No noise, and enter.
Do that good mischief which may make this island
Thine own forever, and I thy Caliban
For aye thy footlicker.

STEPHANO   Give me thy hand. I do begin to have bloody
thoughts.

TRINCULO   [seeing the finery] O King Stephano! O peer! 222
O worthy Stephano! Look what a wardrobe here is
for thee!

CALIBAN
Let it alone, thou fool, it is but trash.

TRINCULO   Oho, monster! We know what belongs to a
frippery. O King Stephano!   [He puts on a gown.] 227

STEPHANO   Put off that gown, Trinculo. By this hand,
I'll have that gown.

TRINCULO   Thy Grace shall have it.

CALIBAN
The dropsy drown this fool! What do you mean   231
To dote thus on such luggage? Let't alone   232
And do the murder first. If he awake,
From toe to crown he'll fill our skins with pinches, 234
Make us strange stuff.

STEPHANO   Be you quiet, monster.—Mistress line, is 236
not this my jerkin? [He takes it down.] Now is the jerkin 237
under the line. Now, jerkin, you are like to lose your 238
hair and prove a bald jerkin.   239

TRINCULO   Do, do! We steal by line and level, an't like 240
Your Grace.

STEPHANO   I thank thee for that jest. Here's a garment
for't. [He gives a garment.] Wit shall not go unrewarded
while I am king of this country. "Steal by line and
level" is an excellent pass of pate. There's another 245
garment for't.

TRINCULO   Monster, come, put some lime upon your 247
fingers, and away with the rest.

CALIBAN
I will have none on't. We shall lose our time,
And all be turned to barnacles, or to apes   250
With foreheads villainous low.   251

STEPHANO   Monster, lay to your fingers. Help to bear 252
this away where my hogshead of wine is, or I'll turn 253
you out of my kingdom. Go to, carry this.   254

TRINCULO   And this.

STEPHANO   Ay, and this.
[They load Caliban with more and more garments.]

A noise of hunters heard. Enter divers spirits, in
shape of dogs and hounds, hunting them about,
Prospero and Ariel setting them on.

PROSPERO   Hey, Mountain, hey!

ARIEL   Silver! There it goes, Silver!

PROSPERO   Fury, Fury! There, Tyrant, there! Hark! Hark!
[Caliban, Stephano, and Trinculo are driven out.]
Go, charge my goblins that they grind their joints
With dry convulsions, shorten up their sinews   261
With agèd cramps, and more pinch-spotted make
them   262
Than pard or cat o' mountain.

ARIEL   Hark, they roar!   263

PROSPERO
Let them be hunted soundly. At this hour   264
Lies at my mercy all mine enemies.
Shortly shall all my labors end, and thou
Shalt have the air at freedom. For a little   267
Follow, and do me service.   Exeunt.

❖

5.1

Enter Prospero in his magic robes, [with his
staff,] and Ariel.

---

206 hoodwink this mischance cover up (literally, blindfold) this mistake.   213–14 o'er ears over my ears in the filthy horse pond (line
182)   222 King . . . peer (Alludes to the old ballad beginning, "King
Stephen was a worthy peer.")   227 frippery second-hand-clothing
shop. (Trinculo knows that what they have just found is much finer.)
231 The dropsy drown (An oath. Dropsy is a disease characterized by
the accumulation of fluid in the connective tissue of the body.)
232 luggage cumbersome trash.   234 crown head   236 Mistress line
(Addressed to the linden or lime tree upon which, at line 193, Ariel
hung the glistering apparel.)   237 jerkin jacket made of leather
238 under the line under the lime tree. (With punning sense of being
south of the equinoctial line or equator; sailors on long voyages to the
southern regions were popularly supposed to lose their hair from
scurvy or other diseases. Stephano also quibbles bawdily on losing
hair through syphilis, and puns in Mistress and jerkin.)   like likely
239 bald (1) hairless, napless (2) meager

240 Do, do! i.e., Bravo! (Said in response to the jesting or to the taking
of the jerkin, or both.)   steal . . . level i.e., steal by means of plumb
line and carpenter's level, methodically. (With pun on line, "lime
tree," line 238, and steal, pronounced like stale, i.e., prostitute, continuing Stephano's bawdy quibble.)   an't like if it please   245 pass of
pate sally of wit. (The metaphor is from fencing.)   247 lime birdlime,
sticky substance (to give Caliban sticky fingers)   250 barnacles bar-
nacle geese, formerly supposed to be hatched from barnacles
attached to trees or to rotting timber; here, evidently used, like apes,
as types of simpletons   251 villainous vilely   252 lay to start using
253 this i.e., the glistering apparel.   hogshead large cask   254 Go to
(An expression of exhortation or remonstrance.)   261 dry convulsions racking cramps   262 agèd characteristic of old age   263 pard
panther or leopard.   cat o' mountain wildcat.   264 soundly
severely.   267 little little while longer
5.1. Location: Before Prospero's cell.

PROSPERO

Now does my project gather to a head.
My charms crack not, my spirits obey, and Time   2
Goes upright with his carriage. How's the day?   3

ARIEL

On the sixth hour, at which time, my lord,   4
You said our work should cease.

PROSPERO   I did say so,
When first I raised the tempest. Say, my spirit,
How fares the King and 's followers?

ARIEL   Confined together
In the same fashion as you gave in charge,
Just as you left them; all prisoners, sir,
In the line grove which weather-fends your cell.   10
They cannot budge till your release. The King,   11
His brother, and yours abide all three distracted,   12
And the remainder mourning over them,
Brim full of sorrow and dismay; but chiefly
Him that you termed, sir, the good old lord,
    Gonzalo.
His tears runs down his beard like winter's drops
From eaves of reeds. Your charm so strongly works
    'em   17
That if you now beheld them your affections   18
Would become tender.

PROSPERO   Dost thou think so, spirit?

ARIEL

Mine would, sir, were I human.

PROSPERO   And mine shall.
Hast thou, which art but air, a touch, a feeling   21
Of their afflictions, and shall not myself,
One of their kind, that relish all as sharply   23
Passion as they, be kindlier moved than thou art?   24
Though with their high wrongs I am struck to th'
    quick,
Yet with my nobler reason 'gainst my fury
Do I take part. The rarer action is   27
In virtue than in vengeance. They being penitent,
The sole drift of my purpose doth extend
Not a frown further. Go release them, Ariel.
My charms I'll break, their senses I'll restore,
And they shall be themselves.

ARIEL   I'll fetch them, sir.

                                             Exit.
    [Prospero traces a charmed circle with his staff.]

PROSPERO

Ye elves of hills, brooks, standing lakes, and groves,   33
And ye that on the sands with printless foot
Do chase the ebbing Neptune, and do fly him

When he comes back; you demi-puppets that   36
By moonshine do the green sour ringlets make,   37
Whereof the ewe not bites; and you whose pastime
Is to make midnight mushrooms, that rejoice   39
To hear the solemn curfew; by whose aid,   40
Weak masters though ye be, I have bedimmed   41
The noontide sun, called forth the mutinous winds,
And twixt the green sea and the azured vault   43
Set roaring war; to the dread rattling thunder   44
Have I given fire, and rifted Jove's stout oak   45
With his own bolt; the strong-based promontory   46
Have I made shake, and by the spurs plucked up   47
The pine and cedar; graves at my command
Have waked their sleepers, oped, and let 'em forth
By my so potent art. But this rough magic   50
I here abjure, and when I have required   51
Some heavenly music—which even now I do—
To work mine end upon their senses that   53
This airy charm is for, I'll break my staff,
Bury it certain fathoms in the earth,
And deeper than did ever plummet sound
I'll drown my book.   Solemn music.

    *Here enters Ariel before; then Alonso, with a
    frantic gesture, attended by Gonzalo; Sebastian and
    Antonio in like manner, attended by Adrian and
    Francisco. They all enter the circle which Prospero
    had made, and there stand charmed; which
    Prospero observing, speaks:*

[*To Alonso*] A solemn air, and the best comforter   58
To an unsettled fancy, cure thy brains,   59
Now useless, boiled within thy skull! [*To Sebastian
    and Antonio*] There stand,   60
For you are spell-stopped.—
Holy Gonzalo, honorable man,
Mine eyes, e'en sociable to the show of thine,   63
Fall fellowly drops. [*Aside*] The charm dissolves
    apace,   64
And as the morning steals upon the night,
Melting the darkness, so their rising senses
Begin to chase the ignorant fumes that mantle   67
Their clearer reason.—O good Gonzalo,   68
My true preserver, and a loyal sir
To him thou follow'st! I will pay thy graces   70
Home both in word and deed.—Most cruelly   71
Didst thou, Alonso, use me and my daughter.
Thy brother was a furtherer in the act.—   73

2 **crack** collapse, fail. (The metaphor is probably alchemical, as in *project* and *gather to a head*, line 1.) 3 **his carriage** its burden. (Time is no longer heavily burdened and so can go *upright*, "standing straight and unimpeded.") 4 **On** Approaching 10 **line grove** grove of lime trees. **weather-fends** protects from the weather 11 **your release** you release them. 12 **distracted** out of their wits 17 **eaves of reeds** thatched roofs. 18 **affections** disposition, feelings 21 **touch** sense, apprehension 23–4 **that . . . they** I who experience human passions as acutely as they 24 **kindlier** (1) more sympathetically (2) more naturally, humanly 27 **rarer** nobler 33 **Ye . . . groves** This passage, down through line 50, is an embellished paraphrase of Golding's translation of Ovid's *Metamorphoses*, 7.197–219.)

36 **demi-puppets** puppets of half size, i.e., elves and fairies 37 **green sour ringlets** fairy rings, circles in grass (actually produced by mushrooms) 39 **midnight mushrooms** mushrooms appearing overnight 40 **curfew** evening bell, usually rung at nine o'clock, ushering in the time when spirits are abroad 41 **Weak masters** i.e., subordinate spirits, as in 4.1.35 43 **the azured vault** i.e., the sky 44–5 **to . . . fire** I have discharged the dread rattling thunderbolt 45 **rifted** riven, split. **oak** a tree that was sacred to Jove 46 **bolt** thunderbolt 47 **spurs** roots 50 **rough** violent 51 **required** demanded 53 **their senses that** the senses of those whom 58 **air** song. **and** i.e., which is 59 **fancy** imagination 60 **boiled** i.e., extremely agitated 63 **sociable** sympathetic. **show** appearance 64 **Fall** let fall 67 **ignorant fumes** fumes that render them incapable of comprehension. **mantle** envelop 68 **clearer** growing clearer 70 **pay thy graces** requite your favors and virtues 71 **Home** fully 73 **furtherer** accomplice

Thou art pinched for't now, Sebastian. [*To Antonio*]
    Flesh and blood,   74
You, brother mine, that entertained ambition,
Expelled remorse and nature, whom, with Sebastian,   76
Whose inward pinches therefore are most strong,
Would here have killed your king, I do forgive thee,
Unnatural though thou art.—Their understanding
Begins to swell, and the approaching tide
Will shortly fill the reasonable shore   81
That now lies foul and muddy. Not one of them
That yet looks on me, or would know me.—Ariel,
Fetch me the hat and rapier in my cell.
            [*Ariel goes to the cell and returns immediately.*]
I will discase me and myself present   85
As I was sometime Milan. Quickly, spirit!   86
Thou shalt ere long be free.
                    Ariel sings and helps to attire him.

ARIEL
        Where the bee sucks, there suck I.
        In a cowslip's bell I lie;
        There I couch when owls do cry.   90
        On the bat's back I do fly
        After summer merrily.   92
    Merrily, merrily shall I live now
    Under the blossom that hangs on the bough.

PROSPERO
    Why, that's my dainty Ariel! I shall miss thee,
    But yet thou shalt have freedom. So, so, so.   96
    To the King's ship, invisible as thou art!
    There shalt thou find the mariners asleep
    Under the hatches. The Master and the Boatswain
    Being awake, enforce them to this place,
    And presently, I prithee.   101

ARIEL
    I drink the air before me, and return
    Or ere your pulse twice beat.   *Exit.* 103

GONZALO
    All torment, trouble, wonder, and amazement
    Inhabits here. Some heavenly power guide us
    Out of this fearful country!

PROSPERO   Behold, sir King,   106
    The wrongèd Duke of Milan, Prospero.
    For more assurance that a living prince
    Does now speak to thee, I embrace thy body;
    And to thee and thy company I bid
    A hearty welcome.   [*Embracing him.*]

ALONSO   Whe'er thou be'st he or no,
    Or some enchanted trifle to abuse me,   112
    As late I have been, I not know. Thy pulse   113
    Beats as of flesh and blood; and, since I saw thee,
    Th' affliction of my mind amends, with which

I fear a madness held me. This must crave—   116
An if this be at all—a most strange story.   117
Thy dukedom I resign, and do entreat   118
Thou pardon me my wrongs. But how should
    Prospero   119
Be living, and be here?
PROSPERO [*to Gonzalo*]   First, noble friend,
    Let me embrace thine age, whose honor cannot   121
    Be measured or confined.   [*Embracing him.*]
GONZALO   Whether this be
    Or be not, I'll not swear.
PROSPERO   You do yet taste
    Some subtleties o'th'isle, that will not let you   124
    Believe things certain. Welcome, my friends all!
    [*Aside to Sebastian and Antonio*] But you, my brace of
        lords, were I so minded,   126
    I here could pluck His Highness' frown upon you
    And justify you traitors. At this time   128
    I will tell no tales.
SEBASTIAN   The devil speaks in him.
PROSPERO   No.
    [*To Antonio*] For you, most wicked sir, whom to call
        brother
    Would even infect my mouth, I do forgive
    Thy rankest fault—all of them; and require
    My dukedom of thee, which perforce I know
    Thou must restore.
ALONSO   If thou be'st Prospero,
    Give us particulars of thy preservation,
    How thou hast met us here, whom three hours since   136
    Were wrecked upon this shore; where I have lost—
    How sharp the point of this remembrance is!—
    My dear son Ferdinand.
PROSPERO   I am woe for't, sir.   139
ALONSO
    Irreparable is the loss, and Patience
    Says it is past her cure.
PROSPERO   I rather think
    You have not sought her help, of whose soft grace
    For the like loss I have her sovereign aid   143
    And rest myself content.
ALONSO   You the like loss?
PROSPERO
    As great to me as late, and supportable   145
    To make the dear loss, have I means much weaker   146
    Than you may call to comfort you; for I   147
    Have lost my daughter.
ALONSO   A daughter?
    O heavens, that they were living both in Naples,

---

74 pinched punished, afflicted   **76 remorse and nature** pity and natural feeling.   **whom** you who   **81 reasonable shore** shores of reason, i.e., minds. (Their reason returns, like the incoming tide.)
85 discase disrobe   **86 As . . . Milan** in my former appearance as Duke of Milan.   **90 couch** lie   **92 After summer** following summer as it moves to various parts of the world   **96 So, so, so** (Expresses approval of Ariel's help as valet.)   **101 presently** immediately
103 Or ere before   **106 fearful** frightening   **112 trifle** trick of magic. **abuse** deceive   **113 late** lately

116 crave require   **117 An . . . all** if this is actually happening.   **story** i.e., explanation.   **118 Thy . . . resign** (Alonso made arrangement with Antonio at the time of Prospero's banishment for Milan to pay tribute to Naples; see 1.2.113–27.)   **119 wrongs** wrongdoings.
121 thine age your venerable self   **124 subtleties** illusions, magical powers. (Playing on the idea of "pastries, concoctions.")   **126 brace** pair   **128 justify you** prove you to be   **136 whom** we who   **139 woe** sorry   **143 sovereign** efficacious   **145 late** recent   **145–7 and supportable . . . you** and I have much weaker means to make my loss supportable than you can call upon to comfort you

The king and queen there! That they were, I wish   151
Myself were mudded in that oozy bed   152
Where my son lies. When did you lose your daughter?   153
PROSPERO
    In this last tempest. I perceive these lords
    At this encounter do so much admire   155
    That they devour their reason and scarce think   156
    Their eyes do offices of truth, their words   157
    Are natural breath. But, howsoever you have   158
    Been jostled from your senses, know for certain
    That I am Prospero and that very duke
    Which was thrust forth of Milan, who most strangely   161
    Upon this shore, where you were wrecked, was
         landed
    To be the lord on't. No more yet of this,
    For 'tis a chronicle of day by day,   164
    Not a relation for a breakfast nor
    Befitting this first meeting. Welcome, sir.
    This cell's my court. Here have I few attendants,
    And subjects none abroad. Pray you, look in.   168
    My dukedom since you have given me again,
    I will requite you with as good a thing,   170
    At least bring forth a wonder to content ye
    As much as me my dukedom.   172

    Here Prospero discovers Ferdinand and Miranda,
    playing at chess.

MIRANDA   Sweet lord, you play me false.   173
FERDINAND   No, my dearest love,
    I would not for the world.
MIRANDA
    Yes, for a score of kingdoms you should wrangle,   176
    And I would call it fair play.
ALONSO   If this prove   177
    A vision of the island, one dear son   178
    Shall I twice lose.
SEBASTIAN   A most high miracle!
FERDINAND *[approaching his father]*
    Though the seas threaten, they are merciful;
    I have cursed them without cause.   *[He kneels.]*
ALONSO   Now all the blessings
    Of a glad father compass thee about!   182
    Arise, and say how thou cam'st here.
                              [Ferdinand rises.]
MIRANDA   Oh, wonder!
    How many goodly creatures are there here!
    How beauteous mankind is! Oh, brave new world   185

That has such people in't!
PROSPERO   'Tis new to thee.
ALONSO
    What is this maid with whom thou wast at play?
    Your eld'st acquaintance cannot be three hours.   188
    Is she the goddess that hath severed us,
    And brought us thus together?
FERDINAND   Sir, she is mortal;
    But by immortal Providence she's mine.
    I chose her when I could not ask my father
    For his advice, nor thought I had one. She
    Is daughter to this famous Duke of Milan,
    Of whom so often I have heard renown,
    But never saw before; of whom I have
    Received a second life; and second father
    This lady makes him to me.
ALONSO   I am hers.
    But oh, how oddly will it sound that I
    Must ask my child forgiveness!
PROSPERO   There, sir, stop.
    Let us not burden our remembrances with
    A heaviness that's gone.
GONZALO   I have inly wept,   202
    Or should have spoke ere this. Look down, you gods,
    And on this couple drop a blessèd crown!
    For it is you that have chalked forth the way   205
    Which brought us hither.
ALONSO   I say amen, Gonzalo!
GONZALO
    Was Milan thrust from Milan, that his issue   207
    Should become kings of Naples? Oh, rejoice
    Beyond a common joy, and set it down
    With gold on lasting pillars: In one voyage
    Did Claribel her husband find at Tunis,
    And Ferdinand, her brother, found a wife
    Where he himself was lost; Prospero his dukedom
    In a poor isle; and all of us ourselves   214
    When no man was his own.
ALONSO *[to Ferdinand and Miranda]*   Give me your hands. 215
    Let grief and sorrow still embrace his heart   216
    That doth not wish you joy!
GONZALO   Be it so! Amen!

    Enter Ariel, with the Master and Boatswain
    amazedly following.

    Oh, look, sir, look, sir! Here is more of us.
    I prophesied, if a gallows were on land,
    This fellow could not drown.—Now, blasphemy,   220
    That swear'st grace o'erboard, not an oath on shore? 221
    Hast thou no mouth by land? What is the news?
BOATSWAIN
    The best news is that we have safely found

151–3 That . . . lies I would wish myself buried in that muddy bed
where my son's body lies drowned if that would somehow make
them alive and reigning in Naples.   **155 admire** wonder   **156 devour
their reason** i.e., are openmouthed, dumbfounded   **156–8 and scarce
. . . breath** and scarcely can believe their eyes or their own words.
161 of from   **164 of day by day** requiring days to tell, or covering a
long span of time   **168 abroad** anywhere else.   **170 requite** repay
172.1 *discovers* i.e., by opening a curtain, presumably rearstage
173 play me false cheat.   **176–7 Yes . . . play** i.e., Yes, even if we were
playing for twenty kingdoms, something less than the whole world,
you would still press your advantage against me, and I would lovingly let you do it as though it were fair play.   **178 vision** illusion
182 compass encompass, embrace   **185 brave** splendid, gorgeously
appareled, handsome

---

188 eld'st longest   **202 heaviness** sadness.   **inly** inwardly
205 chalked . . . way marked as with a piece of chalk the pathway
207 Was Milan Was the Duke of Milan.   **issue** child   **214–15 all . . .
own** all of us have found ourselves and our sanity when we all had
lost our senses.   **216 still** always.   **his** that person's   **220 blasphemy** i.e., blasphemer   **221 That swear'st grace o'erboard** i.e., you
who expel heavenly grace from the ship by your blasphemies.   **not
an oath** aren't you going to swear an oath

Our King and company; the next, our ship—
Which, but three glasses since, we gave out split— 225
Is tight and yare and bravely rigged as when 226
We first put out to sea.
ARIEL [*aside to Prospero*]   Sir, all this service
Have I done since I went.
PROSPERO [*aside to Ariel*]   My tricksy spirit! 228
ALONSO
These are not natural events; they strengthen 229
From strange to stranger. Say, how came you hither?
BOATSWAIN
If I did think, sir, I were well awake,
I'd strive to tell you. We were dead of sleep,   232
And—how we know not—all clapped under hatches,
Where but even now, with strange and several noises 234
Of roaring, shrieking, howling, jingling chains,
And more diversity of sounds, all horrible,
We were awaked; straightway at liberty;
Where we, in all her trim, freshly beheld
Our royal, good, and gallant ship, our Master
Cap'ring to eye her. On a trice, so please you,   240
Even in a dream, were we divided from them   241
And were brought moping hither.
ARIEL [*aside to Prospero*]   Was't well done? 242
PROSPERO [*aside to Ariel*]
Bravely, my diligence. Thou shalt be free.
ALONSO
This is as strange a maze as e'er men trod,
And there is in this business more than nature
Was ever conduct of. Some oracle   246
Must rectify our knowledge.
PROSPERO   Sir, my liege,
Do not infest your mind with beating on   248
The strangeness of this business. At picked leisure, 249
Which shall be shortly, single I'll resolve you,   250
Which to you shall seem probable, of every   251
These happened accidents; till when, be cheerful   252
And think of each thing well. [*Aside to Ariel*] Come
    hither, spirit.   253
Set Caliban and his companions free.
Untie the spell.   [*Exit Ariel.*]
    [*To Alonso*]   How fares my gracious sir?
There are yet missing of your company
Some few odd lads that you remember not.   257

    Enter Ariel, driving in Caliban, Stephano, and
    Trinculo, in their stolen apparel.

STEPHANO   Every man shift for all the rest, and let no 258
man take care for himself; for all is but fortune. *Corag-* 259

gio, bully monster, *coraggio!*   260
TRINCULO   If these be true spies which I wear in my 261
head, here's a goodly sight.
CALIBAN
O Setebos, these be brave spirits indeed!   263
How fine my master is! I am afraid   264
He will chastise me.
SEBASTIAN   Ha, ha!
What things are these, my lord Antonio?
Will money buy 'em?
ANTONIO   Very like. One of them
Is a plain fish, and no doubt marketable.
PROSPERO
Mark but the badges of these men, my lords,   270
Then say if they be true. This misshapen knave,   271
His mother was a witch, and one so strong
That could control the moon, make flows and ebbs,
And deal in her command without her power.   274
These three have robbed me, and this demidevil—
For he's a bastard one—had plotted with them   276
To take my life. Two of these fellows you
Must know and own. This thing of darkness I   278
Acknowledge mine.
CALIBAN   I shall be pinched to death.
ALONSO
Is not this Stephano, my drunken butler?
SEBASTIAN   He is drunk now. Where had he wine?
ALONSO
And Trinculo is reeling ripe. Where should they   282
Find this grand liquor that hath gilded 'em?   283
[*To Trinculo*] How cam'st thou in this pickle?   284
TRINCULO   I have been in such a pickle since I saw you
last that, I fear me, will never out of my bones. I shall
not fear flyblowing.   287
SEBASTIAN   Why, how now, Stephano?
STEPHANO   Oh, touch me not! I am not Stephano, but a
cramp.
PROSPERO   You'd be king o'the isle, sirrah?   291
STEPHANO   I should have been a sore one, then.   292
ALONSO [*pointing to Caliban*]
This is a strange thing as e'er I looked on.
PROSPERO
He is as disproportioned in his manners
As in his shape.—Go, sirrah, to my cell.
Take with you your companions. As you look
To have my pardon, trim it handsomely.   297

---

225 **glasses** hourglasses.   **gave out split** reported shipwrecked, gave
up for lost   226 **yare** ready.   **bravely** splendidly   228 **tricksy** ingenious, sportive   229 **strengthen** increase   232 **dead of sleep** deep in
sleep   234 **several** diverse   240 **Cap'ring to eye** dancing for joy to
see.   **On a trice** In an instant   241 **them** i.e., the other crew members
242 **moping** in a daze   246 **conduct** director   248 **infest** harass, disturb.   **beating on** worrying about   249 **picked** chosen, convenient
250 **single** privately.   **resolve** satisfy, explain to   251 **probable** plausible   251–2 **of every These** about every one of these   252 **accidents**
occurrences   253 **well** favorably.   257 **odd** unaccounted for
258–9 **Every . . . himself** (Stephano drunkenly inverts the saying
"Every man for himself.")

259–60 **Coraggio . . . monster** Have courage, gallant monster   261 **true
spies** accurate observers (i.e., sharp eyes)   263 **brave** handsome
264 **fine** splendidly attired   270 **badges** emblems worn by servants
to indicate whom they serve   271 **say . . . true** say if they are worthy
and loyal servants.   274 **And . . . power** and usurp the moon's command (over tides) without her authority. (Sycorax could control the
moon and hence the tides.)   276 **bastard** counterfeit   278 **own**
acknowledge.   282 **reeling ripe** staggeringly drunk.   283 **gilded 'em**
flushed their complexion (from the drink), giving them a ruddy or
gilded appearance.   284 **pickle** (1) fix, predicament (2) pickling brine
(in this case, horse urine).   287 **flyblowing** i.e., being fouled by fly
eggs (from which he is saved by being pickled).   291 **sirrah** (Standard form of address to an inferior, here expressing reprimand.)
292 **sore** (1) tyrannical (2) sorry, inept (3) wracked by pain   297 **trim**
prepare, decorate

CALIBAN
    Ay, that I will; and I'll be wise hereafter
    And seek for grace. What a thrice-double ass   299
    Was I to take this drunkard for a god
    And worship this dull fool!
PROSPERO   Go to. Away!
ALONSO
    Hence, and bestow your luggage where you found it.
SEBASTIAN   Or stole it, rather.
                [*Exeunt Caliban, Stephano, and Trinculo.*]
PROSPERO
    Sir, I invite Your Highness and your train
    To my poor cell, where you shall take your rest
    For this one night; which, part of it, I'll waste   306
    With such discourse as, I not doubt, shall make it
    Go quick away: the story of my life,
    And the particular accidents gone by   309
    Since I came to this isle. And in the morn
    I'll bring you to your ship, and so to Naples,
    Where I have hope to see the nuptial
    Of these our dear-belovèd solemnized;
    And thence retire me to my Milan, where
    Every third thought shall be my grave.
ALONSO   I long
    To hear the story of your life, which must
    Take the ear strangely.
PROSPERO   I'll deliver all;   317
    And promise you calm seas, auspicious gales,
    And sail so expeditious that shall catch   319
    Your royal fleet far off. [*Aside to Ariel*] My Ariel, chick,   320

299 **grace** pardon, favor.   306 **waste** spend   309 **accidents** occurrences   317 **Take** take effect upon, enchant.   **deliver** declare, relate   319–20 **catch . . . far off** enable you to catch up with the main part of your royal fleet, now afar off en route to Naples. (See 1.2.235–6.)

That is thy charge. Then to the elements
Be free, and fare thou well!
                [*To the others*] Please you, draw near.   322
                Exeunt omnes [except Prospero].

Epilogue   *Spoken by* PROSPERO.

Now my charms are all o'erthrown,
And what strength I have 's mine own,
Which is most faint. Now, 'tis true,
I must be here confined by you
Or sent to Naples. Let me not,
Since I have my dukedom got
And pardoned the deceiver, dwell
In this bare island by your spell,
But release me from my bands   9
With the help of your good hands.   10
Gentle breath of yours my sails   11
Must fill, or else my project fails,
Which was to please. Now I want   13
Spirits to enforce, art to enchant,
And my ending is despair,
Unless I be relieved by prayer,   16
Which pierces so that it assaults   17
Mercy itself, and frees all faults.   18
As you from crimes would pardoned be,   19
Let your indulgence set me free.   *Exit.* 20

322 draw near i.e., enter my cell.
Epilogue.
9 bands bonds   **10 hands** i.e., applause (the noise of which could break a charm).   **11 Gentle breath** Favorable breeze (produced by hands clapping or favorable comment)   **13 want** lack   **16 prayer** i.e., Prospero's petition to the audience   **17 assaults** penetrates the heart of   **18 frees** obtains forgiveness for   **19 crimes** sins   **20 indulgence** (1) humoring, lenient approval (2) remission of punishment for sin

The Two Noble Kinsmen

The Two Noble Kinsmen, seemingly the very last play in which Shakespeare had a hand, returns to a theme he had pursued in *The Two Gentlemen of Verona*, one of his early plays and possibly even the first. As in that early comedy, two friends vie for the affection of a lady in such a way as to put their warm friendship to a severe test. In the late play, as Bruce Smith, Jeffrey Masten, and others have observed, the famous friendship of Palamon and Arcite is rich in a sexual innuendo of which they seem innocently unaware until they both fall in love with Emilia. "We are one another's wife, ever begetting / New births of love," declares Arcite to his cousin as they find themselves imprisoned together in Athens. "We are father, friends, acquaintance; / We are in one another, families; / I am your heir, and you are mine" (2.2.80–3). The sentiment is close to that of Aufidius in *Coriolanus*, when he says of his former enemy, Coriolanus: "that I see thee here, / Thou noble thing, more dances my rapt heart / Than when I first wedded mistress saw / Bestride my threshold" (4.5.120–3). This is not to argue that Palamon and Arcite become lovers in their imprisonment. Nonetheless, at its most exalted, same-sex friendship fulfills the emotional role expected of matrimony and is indeed put in conflict with matrimonial intent.

The Two Noble Kinsmen was probably first performed in 1613 or 1614, and was revived for performance at court in 1619 and again seemingly in 1625–1626. Rights were subsequently assigned to the publisher of the so-called Beaumont and Fletcher Folio, 1646. The play actually appeared in print in a second edition, entitled *Fifty Comedies and Tragedies, Written by Francis Beaumont, and John Fletcher, Gentlemen*, 1679—of which, in fact, a good number were by Beaumont or by Fletcher alone, with many others by Fletcher in collaboration with other dramatists. The play did not appear in the First Folio of Shakespeare's plays in 1623 or in subsequent editions of that work. Perhaps for these reasons, *The Two Noble Kinsmen* was for

centuries excluded from the Shakespeare canon and is still only occasionally studied or performed. Shakespeare was so famous that his name was often attached to plays in which he had no part; was *The Two Noble Kinsmen* one of these? Why would Shakespeare want to collaborate when his name was so well known?

Whatever his personal reasons, however, Shakespeare does seem to have done just that. Perhaps his own retirement, seemingly announced in *The Tempest*, turned out to be a semi-retirement. John Fletcher was his younger colleague and, in effect, successor as playwright for the King's Men. The two seemingly collaborated in writing *Henry VIII* at about the same time, although there the evidence is less certain and Shakespeare's role in any case more dominant. He appears to have collaborated with Thomas Middleton in the writing of *Timon of Athens*. Earlier, in the 1590s, Shakespeare had agreed to help revise a controversial play by writing a new scene for *The Book of Sir Thomas More*, originally perhaps by Anthony Munday and others. Shakespeare's name was linked with that of Fletcher in the authorship of the seemingly lost play *Cardenio*, c. 1612–1613. Shakespeare was loyal to his acting company and may have helped them out with collaborations on other occasions. And, as Jeffrey Masten has suggested, the dominant theme of male friendship in *The Two Noble Kinsmen* is one that offers itself as an apt subject for authors working in collaboration.

On the basis of style, metrics, distinctive rhythms, vocabulary, linguistic preferences for forms like *ye* and *'em* (both of these characteristic of Fletcher), tone, characterization, and a kind of theatrical abruptness that Fletcher seems to have cultivated, many editors and critics come to a general consensus, not shared by all, that Shakespeare seems to have written all of Act 1, the first scene of Act 2, the first two scenes of Act 3, scene 3 of Act 4, and most of the final act except scene 2. This division would give to Shakespeare the scenes that dramatize Duke Theseus's resolve to defend the cause of three slain kings against Creon of Thebes, Palamon and Arcite's dilemma in serving the tyrant Creon and their brave defeat in battle by Theseus's Athenian army, Emilia's defense of friendship between women, Arcite and Palamon's quarrel in the forest after one has been released from captivity by Theseus and the other freed from prison by the Jailer's enamored daughter, the Jailer's Daughter's forlorn lament at Palamon's neglect of her, a touching scene in which the Jailer and a Doctor overhear manifestations of the Jailer's Daughter's mad affliction, and the long concluding action in which Palamon and Arcite's rival claims to Emilia are sorted out by divine will.

Fletcher is then left with the bulk of the play's middle action, including the startling scene (2.2) in which the imprisoned Palamon and Arcite declare their love for each other but then fall instantly into bitter enmity once they have both seen Emilia, Arcite's encounter (after he has been released from prison) with some country rustics who tell him of public games in which Arcite resolves to compete, his success there in winning the right to be Emilia's "servant," several scenes of the Jailer's Daughter's increasing madness, some broadly comic subplot business in which a pedantic schoolmaster and his rustic companions prepare a Morris dance to be performed in Theseus's presence, Palamon and Arcite's determination to fight each other even at the certain cost of their being captured and sentenced to death by Theseus, Emilia's inability to choose between Palamon and Arcite even when it appears that her choice would save one of them from death, and still more.

Even a quick outline suggests how Fletcher seems to have preferred the scenes of unexpected reversals of the action in which plausibility of motivation yields precedence to self-conscious theatrical artifice. Some of the scenes assigned to Fletcher exploit sexuality in novel situations, as when the Doctor advises the Wooer of the Jailer's Daughter to disguise himself as Palamon, for whose love the Daughter has lost her wits. The Doctor insists that her whim is to be indulged in every detail, even if the Wooer must climb into bed with her. When the father protests that marriage should come before sexual fulfillment, the Doctor is curt with such a prudish idea: "Nev'r cast away your child for honesty [chastity]," he admonishes (5.2.22). This droll exploitation of a tittilating situation is characteristic of Fletcher. The Prologue and Epilogue are almost certainly by him.

Whatever their mode of collaboration in writing *The Two Noble Kinsmen*, Shakespeare and Fletcher chose to dramatize a tale from Chaucer's *Canterbury Tales*, the Knight's tale, which is about noble friendship. Palamon and Arcite are cousins and devoted friends, "dearer in

love than blood" (1.2.1). When we first see them, they are considering what guidance their friendship can provide them in the corrupted world of Thebes. Under the rule of their uncle Creon, "a most unbounded tyrant" (line 63), Thebes is a place of carnal temptation and political favoritism. Their virtuous behavior makes them aliens and the subjects of mockery. "Not to be ev'n jump / As they are here were to be strangers" (lines 40–1), Arcite insists, and yet the alternative of swimming along in "The common stream" would be enough to turn them both into "mere monsters" (lines 10, 42). They resolve not to ape the mannerisms and dress of their contemporaries, and long for war as a means of purging the enervating softness of peace. Yet war, when it comes, provides only another dilemma, for military action in support of a tyrant undermines the very purpose for which they wish to fight. Ultimately the calling of military duty prevails, and they are captured by Theseus's Athenian army after having surpassed all others in the battle.

The mutual fondness of these cousins is not the only study in this play of friendship under duress. Duke Theseus of Athens and his general, Pirithous, are friends in the tradition of Alexander and Hephaestion, Damon and Pythias, and other figures from classical legend and history. Pirithous is reputed to have descended into Hades with Theseus to help carry off Persephone. "How his longing / Follows his friend!" exclaims Theseus's sister-in-law Emilia as she sees Pirithous eagerly depart to join Theseus in the military campaign against Thebes (1.3.26–7). Delayed for a time by Theseus's command that he see to the ceremonies that the war has interrupted, Pirithous cannot devote his full energies to matters of peace; his heart is with Theseus on the field of battle. Theseus's bride, Hippolyta, quite agrees with her sister Emilia: Theseus and Pirithous have shared so many dangers, she says, that "Their knot of love, / Tied, weaved, entangled . . . May be outworn, never undone" (lines 41–4). As is always the case in such conventional debates about friendship and love, or love and honor, rival claims test friendship to prove its durability. Pirithous's loyalty to Theseus overcomes all other considerations.

Emilia and Hippolyta, as sisters, discuss friendship between women, comparing it to friendship between men. "Theirs has more ground," concedes Emilia, "is more maturely seasoned, / More buckled with strong judgment." Yet Emilia's own love for the now-dead Flavina, whom she once enjoyed as a playfellow, had qualities of innocence, of mutual devotion to chastity, and of intermingling of souls that men seemingly cannot match. "Like the elements / That know not what nor why, yet do effect / Rare issues by their operance, our souls / Did so to one another," Emilia longingly recalls. Their tastes were instinctively identical; their mannerisms and garments were so alike that neither could discern who had begun the fashion. Emilia's conclusion is that "true love 'tween maid and maid may be / More than in sex divid-ual"—that is, between persons of the opposite sex (1.3.55–82). At first, then, both men and women in this play find bonding to a person of the same sex more per-fect and fulfilling than heterosexual love. The situation recalls that of *A Midsummer Night's Dream*, where that play's Duke Theseus also marries Hippolyta, Queen of the Amazons. The very image of the Amazonian maiden is of a woman armed to defend herself against men.

These familiar topics of love versus honor and the battle of the sexes, eloquently set up by Shakespeare in the first act, inevitably lead to complications and testings in the second and third acts. Even in the first act, choices must be faced in terms of a code of chivalric honor. The-seus, about to marry Hippolyta but petitioned by three widows to avenge the dishonor done to their royal hus-bands by Creon, postpones his marital happiness to march against Thebes. Pirithous must reconcile the claims of duty and of his longing to be with Theseus on the field of battle. Palamon and Arcite seek ways to jus-tify their military service in support of a tyrant and a cor-rupt state. Emilia announces her resolution to live and die a virgin, while her sister Hippolyta determines to go ahead with her marriage to Theseus, in a sisterly debate that reminds us of Luciana and her married sister Adri-ana in *The Comedy of Errors*.

Fletcher's theatrical strategy in the middle acts of the play is to subject these conventional polarities of love and honor to surprising and disarmingly improbable turns of events. In the prison where Palamon and Arcite lie lan-guishing after their capture by Theseus's army, the Jailer's Daughter falls immediately and disastrously in love with Palamon, even though she readily concedes that Arcite is as handsome (2.4.16) and that "To marry him [Palamon] is hopeless, / To be his whore is witless" (lines 4–5). For their part, the two young men, resolving in the best stoical fashion to embrace their imprisonment as a way to repu-diate a bad world and rely instead on their own sustain-ing friendship, fall instantly to quarreling when Emilia appears in the courtyard below their window (2.2.1–284). Palamon claims precedence because he has seen Emilia first. Whereas they previously regarded women as "The poison of pure spirits" and worse than a distraction (1ine 75), they now devote their loyalties to love alone and look upon each other as villains worthy only of sudden death. Neither has yet spoken a word with the lady in question.

The pattern of flamboyant theatrical artifice continues to unfold. Once Arcite is released from prison for some unexplained reason and banished from Athens (lines 251–2), his only wish is to return in some disguise so that he may be near Emilia; once Palamon in turn is freed by the lovesick Jailer's Daughter at considerable risk to her-self and her poor father, Palamon's sole hope is to see Emilia again. When the two cousins encounter one another by chance in the forest near Athens (another rec-ollection of *A Midsummer Night's Dream*), their fierce determination to undo each other is almost comically mediated by the solicitude of each warrior that the other be properly armed. The hyperbolic vaunting, the unex-pected coincidences, the lack of plausible motivation are highly theatrical and self-conscious in a way that is char-acteristic not only of Fletcher's other plays but of Jacobean drama in the 1610s and indeed of some of Shakespeare's own final work.

Throughout, the major characters operate in response to a code of aristocratic behavior that is eminently suited to a play about heroic chivalry. Arcite, in disguise as one who is competing in the "pastimes" devised to entertain Theseus and his court (2.3.78), amply displays his "noble qualities" to all who see him, even though they suppose him a stranger. "His body / And fiery mind illustrate a brave father," says Hippolyta; that is, he is nobly descended (2.5.21–2). He speaks well: "All his words are worthy" (line 29). With a modesty and *sprezzatura* aptly suited to his noble station, he allows that he knows well the aristocratic pursuits of hawking and hunting, and most of all horsemanship. "I dare not praise / My feat in horsemanship," he says, "yet they that know me / Would say it was my best piece" (lines 11–14). Elsewhere, as often is the case in Shakespeare, horsemanship is a sure sign of aristocratic bearing, as when Pirithous describes Arcite as able to hold his saddle "bravely" even on a vicious horse that eventually topples over backward on its rider and crushes him (5.4.48–84). Arcite is "as brave a knight as e'er / Did spur a noble steed" (5.3.115–16). Palamon and Arcite's insistence on duelling even at the risk of the law's judgment is another mark of their inherent nobleness, even if the play also dramatizes the conflict between that aristocratic code of duelling and Theseus's insistence (reflecting Elizabethan and Jacobean official policy) that quarrels must be submitted to the authority of the state (3.6.132 ff.). Palamon and Arcite's followers in the climactic trial by combat in Act 5 are elaborately described as worthy of their greatness, with "all the ornament of honor" in their outward appearance and behavior; they "are all the sons of honor" (4.2.75–141). Theseus too is governed by the code of aris-tocratic honor, and his final resolution to allow Palamon and Arcite to settle their differences in a state-sponsored public arena through trial by combat is presented as a suitable solution for chivalric strife.

Even the comedy of this play, chiefly by Fletcher, is well suited to the aristocratic presuppositions of the main plot. The countrymen who tell Arcite about the upcom-ing pastimes in which he can compete to win the favor of Theseus and Emilia are country rustics whose rude man-nerisms are contrasted at every turn with those of Arcite.

Their conversation is often about sexuality, about jealous wives who must be "boarded" and "stowed" in suitable fashion, about the "wenches" with whom they will dance before the Duke, and so on (2.3.25–66). Like the shipwrecked hero of *Pericles*, who similarly obtains from poor country folk a means of competing in courtly games as a stranger, Arcite is beholden to these good-natured bumpkins and immeasurably far above them in noble graces. "'Tis a pretty fellow," one of them allows (line 79). The pedantic Schoolmaster Gerald, who, with his tedious Latinisms, presents a Morris dance before the Duke, reminds us of the schoolmaster Holofernes in *Love's Labor's Lost* and Peter Quince in *A Midsummer Night's Dream*; indeed, the business of devising a play within the play, witnessed by an amused critical audience onstage, is a medley of motifs out of Shakespeare. The plot line of the distraught Jailer's Daughter, sometimes comic, sometimes touching, borrows elements of mad talk from Ophelia in *Hamlet* and of medical eavesdropping from Lady Macbeth's sleepwalking in *Macbeth*. The Jailer's Daughter's song of "Willow, willow, willow" (4.1.80) would appear to be an explicit allusion to Desdemona's song in *Othello*. At every point, the play's subplot material seems intended to reflect through parody and comic exaggeration the heroic themes of love versus honor and the display of chivalric nobility. At the same time, the play's depiction of madness and erotic desire is serious and even clinical, in much the way that madness and desire come together in *Hamlet*'s depiction of the deranged Ophelia.

Staging is appropriately ceremonial and elaborate. The play opens with a procession headed by Hymen, god of marriage, and including a courtly entourage of Theseus, his bride-to-be, and others, all elaborately robed in costumes and garlands symbolic of their ceremonial roles. A boy sings a hymn to love and marriage. The interruption of this grand entrance by the three widowed petitioners signals the sorts of conflicts that will continue to challenge the courtly ideals of perfect love, friendship, and honor. The battle between Thebes and Athens and later athletic contests are decorously conducted offstage (1.4.0.1–5, 2.5.0.1–3), but the entrances of Theseus and other dignitaries continue to be heralded by the blaze of cornets and other flourishes. Repeated kneelings underscore the hierarchical structure of the Athenian court and the obedience that Theseus expects to his authority. Music accompanies the ceremonials of interment devised for the three dead kings (1.5.0.1–3). The theater building is used to its fullest extent, as when Palamon and Arcite appear in prison *"above"* (2.0.51.1) and look down upon Emilia on the main stage gathering flowers as though in a garden adjacent to the prison. The sounds of cornets and halooing are heard from various directions to signify the celebration of May Day (3.1.0.1–2).

Doors are used to suggest locations: Palamon enters, presumably in the forest, *"as out of a bush"* (3.1.30.1), and Palamon and Arcite enter to their final trial at opposite doors (5.1.7.1–2). A Morris dance provides opportunity for numerous quaint characters in costume, including a baboon, the Lord and Lady of May (i.e., Robin Hood and Maid Marian), the Chambermaid, the Servingman, mine Host and his fat Spouse, the rustic countryman called the Clown, and the Fool (3.5.128–35). The dance itself is an elaborate if lower-class entertainment that is hard to recapture through reading the play text, and it certainly required music, including a taborer or player on pipe and drum. Palamon and Arcite fight a duel in full armor; the dialogue makes much of the stage business of their dressing each other for the encounter (3.6.16–131).

The play's last act is especially ceremonial, as though calling upon ceremony as a visual language of closure. Palamon and Arcite are brought onstage from opposite doors at the beginning of Act 5 to "tender their holy prayers" before the gods, asking for divine judgment in their strife. First Arcite and then Palamon approach the altars of their respective immortal patrons, Mars and Venus. The staging is uncertain. Conceivably, one altar is to stand in turn for the altar of Mars and Venus, and then for Diana when Emilia in her turn implores the gods' assistance; the elaborate stage business requires a trapdoor, of which the theater where the play was performed might have provided only one. Still, it is quite possible that three altars were provided onstage at once, giving the balanced, antithetical, and symbolic sense of location that the last act visually demands. Mars's altar answers Arcite's entreaties with *"clanging of armor, with a short thunder"* (5.1.61.2) in an auspicious sign that Mars will grant Arcite the desired ascendancy. Palamon and his followers hear *"music"* at Venus's altar and see doves (line 129.1) as a "fair token" of truth in love. Emilia's ceremonial at Diana's altar is the most elaborate, requiring as it does *"still music,"* garlands and flowers, and a *"silver hind, in which is conveyed incense and sweet odors."* The oblation being set afire on the altar, *"the hind vanishes under the altar, and in the place ascends a rose tree, having one rose upon it."* This rose subsequently falls from a tree to the accompaniment of *"a sudden twang of instruments"* (lines 136.1–8, 168.1–2). These symbolic actions, signifying that virginity will yield chastely to love's erotic fulfillment, demand the services of a trapdoor, but the first two ceremonies do not. Perhaps then Diana's altar is centrally placed and is flanked by the representations of war and love. Such a configuration would give visual confirmation to the last act's movement toward a reconciliation in which the seemingly competing demands of military prowess, eros, and chaste denial are finally given their respective places in the crowning ceremonial of marriage. Staging thus embodies the antitheses of this chivalric play by visually juxtaposing male and female, friendship and love, love and honor, and by seeking a way to bring these opposites together.

Whatever Shakespeare's exact share may have been, *The Two Noble Kinsmen* displays many of the characteristics of the late Shakespeare, not only in the freedom of the verse, with its run-on lines and hypermetric effects, but also in the play's fascination with romantic plotting. The play that Shakespeare and Fletcher fashioned out of an old Chaucerian tale is one that portrays chivalric ideals through the medium of theatrical artifice. Like *Pericles*, whose narrator is Chaucer's contemporary John Gower, *The Two Noble Kinsmen* goes back to a quaint and improbable fiction of medieval times where fancy and imagination can do their work of theatrical transformation. Staging is elaborate, especially at the close, as in *Cymbeline*. The gods intervene directly in the play's denouement, as in all the late romances (though the gods in *The Tempest* are of Prospero's devising).

As in the romances as a group, the audience is asked to approach, in a spirit of wonder combined perhaps with ironic detachment, a work that is self-consciously theatrical in its depiction of supernatural effects. The gods have their way in *The Two Noble Kinsmen*. The human protagonists stand in awe at their final deliverance from their own worst selves. Palamon and Arcite, in their perverse but noble attempts to destroy each other for love, fulfill the will of destiny that is revealed to them at the altars of Mars, Venus, and Diana: the brave Arcite is to die on horseback, the lover Palamon is to win the lady Emilia, and she is to find marital happiness even while preserving her ideal of chaste marriage. The ending is contrived to a striking degree, in that it depends on a physical accident; and yet it is no more arbitrary than the ending of *Cymbeline*. What seems accident to mere mortals is seen finally by the play's protagonists as part of a deeper heavenly design. "O you heavenly charmers," Theseus apostrophizes the gods in a choric close, "What things you make of us! For what we lack / We laugh, for what we have are sorry, still / Are children in some kind." Theseus's conclusion from this is one of pious acceptance: "Let us be thankful / For that which is" (5.4.131–5). The audience, even while it is openly encouraged to see the play's romantic structure as theatrical artifice, is also invited to ponder what deeper ideologies may be embodied in Shakespeare's and Fletcher's depiction of dramatic art as pattern, order, ornament, contrivance, and vision.

The Two Noble Kinsmen has been seen on stage only occasionally, more so in recent decades than in the preceding centuries. Productions have tended to focus on the play's fairy-tale-like qualities, its fascination with sexual ambiguities, and its penchant for the theatrically surprising. A French version, *Deux Nobles Cousins,* for the Centre Dramatique de Courneuve in 1979, directed by Pierre Constant, saw the play as an extended debate about heterosexual versus homosexual love. Barry Kyle, directing the play in 1986 for the Royal Shakespeare Theatre, chose a large Japanese decor to emphasize a culture of chivalric warriors locked into an antique code of honor. Theseus has sometimes been seen as a problematic and tyrannical figure of authority, browbeating Emilia into making her difficult choice between Palamon and Arcite. The Jailer's Daughter has come into her own as perhaps the most believable character in the play, with her forthright sexuality and her Ophelia-like pathos.

The Two Noble Kinsmen

[*Dramatis Personae*

PROLOGUE

THESEUS, *Duke of Athens*
HIPPOLYTA, *Queen of the Amazons, later married to Theseus*
EMILIA, *her sister*
PIRITHOUS, *friend of Theseus*

PALAMON ⎫ *the two noble kinsmen, cousins, nephews*
ARCITE ⎭ *of Creon, the King of Thebes*

HYMEN, *god of marriage*
A BOY
ARTESIUS, *an Athenian soldier*
Three QUEENS, *widows of three kings killed at the siege of Thebes*
VALERIUS, *a Theban*
A HERALD
A WOMAN *attending Emilia*
An Athenian GENTLEMAN
MESSENGERS

Six KNIGHTS, *three following Palamon and three Arcite*
A SERVANT
THE JAILER *in charge of Theseus's prison*
THE JAILER'S DAUGHTER
THE JAILER'S BROTHER
THE WOOER *of the Jailer's Daughter*
Two FRIENDS *of the Jailer*
A DOCTOR
Six COUNTRYMEN, *one dressed as a babion, or baboon*
A SCHOOLMASTER *named Gerald*
NELL, *a country wench*
Four other country wenches: Friz, Maudline, Luce, and Barbery
A TABORER *named Timothy*
Nymphs, attendants, maids, executioner, guard

EPILOGUE

SCENE: *Athens and Thebes.*]

Prologue

Flourish. [*Enter Prologue.*]

PROLOGUE
New plays and maidenheads are near akin:
Much followed both, for both much money gi'en, 2
If they stand sound and well. And a good play, 3
Whose modest scenes blush on his marriage day 4
And shake to lose his honor, is like her 5
That after holy tie and first night's stir 6
Yet still is modesty, and still retains 7
More of the maid to sight than husband's pains. 8
We pray our play may be so; for I am sure
It has a noble breeder and a pure, 10
A learnèd, and a poet never went 11
More famous yet 'twixt Po and silver Trent. 12
Chaucer, of all admired, the story gives; 13
There, constant to eternity, it lives. 14

0.1 *Flourish* fanfare to announce the arrival or departure of a notable person **2 Much followed** eagerly sought after **3 stand sound** seem healthy **4 his marriage day** i.e., its first day of performance **5 shake . . . honor** (1) tremble at the thought of loss of virginity (2) fear disgrace at the hands of the audience **6 holy . . . stir** marriage and sexual consummation that night

7 is modesty (1) remains chaste (2) is modest about the play's success **7–8 still retains . . . pains** still appears more like a virgin than like a woman transformed into a wife by her husband's exertions. (The moral edge that is given to virginity over married chastity is characteristic of the play as a whole.) **10 breeder** (1) sire (2) author **11–12 a poet . . . Trent** there never was a more famous poet anywhere in Europe (literally, between the river Po in northern Italy and the Trent in England). **13 of** by **14 There** i.e., in "The Knight's Tale" of *The Canterbury Tales*

If we let fall the nobleness of this,   15
And the first sound this child hear be a hiss,   16
How will it shake the bones of that good man,
And make him cry from under ground, "Oh, fan
From me the witless chaff of such a writer
That blasts my bays and my famed works makes
   lighter   20
Than Robin Hood!" This is the fear we bring;   21
For, to say truth, it were an endless thing,
And too ambitious, to aspire to him,   23
Weak as we are, and almost breathless swim
In this deep water. Do but you hold out
Your helping hands, and we shall tack about   26
And something do to save us. You shall hear
Scenes, though below his art, may yet appear   28
Worth two hours' travail. To his bones sweet sleep;   29
Content to you. If this play do not keep   30
A little dull time from us, we perceive   31
Our losses fall so thick we must needs leave.

Flourish. [Exit.]

❖

1.1

*[Music.] Enter Hymen with a torch burning; a boy
in a white robe before, singing and strewing
flowers; after Hymen a nymph, encompassed in her
tresses, bearing a wheaten garland; then Theseus
between two other nymphs with wheaten chaplets
on their heads; then Hippolyta, the bride, led by
Pirithous, and another holding a garland over her
head, her tresses likewise hanging; after her,
Emilia, holding up her train; [Artesius and
attendants].*

BOY [*singing as they enter*]
   Roses, their sharp spines being gone,
   Not royal in their smells alone,
      But in their hue;
   Maiden pinks, of odor faint,
   Daisies smell-less, yet most quaint,   5
      And sweet thyme true;

   Primrose, firstborn child of Ver,   7
   Merry springtime's harbinger,
      With her bells dim;   9
   Oxlips, in their cradles growing,   10

Marigolds, on deathbeds blowing,   11
   Lark's-heels trim;   12

(*Strew flowers*) All dear Nature's children sweet
Lie 'fore bride and bridegroom's feet,
   Blessing their sense.   15
Not an angel of the air,
Bird melodious or bird fair,
   Is absent hence.

The crow, the sland'rous cuckoo, nor   19
The boding raven, nor chough hoar   20
   Nor chatt'ring pie,   21
May on our bridehouse perch or sing,
Or with them any discord bring,
   But from it fly.   24

*Enter three Queens in black, with veils stained,
with imperial crowns. The first Queen falls down
at the foot of Theseus; the second falls down at the
foot of Hippolyta; the third before Emilia.*

FIRST QUEEN [*to Theseus*]
   For pity's sake and true gentility's,   25
   Hear and respect me.
SECOND QUEEN [*to Hippolyta*]   For your mother's sake,   26
   And as you wish your womb may thrive with fair
      ones,
   Hear and respect me.
THIRD QUEEN [*to Emilia*]
   Now for the love of him whom Jove hath marked   29
   The honor of your bed, and for the sake   30
   Of clear virginity, be advocate   31
   For us and our distresses. This good deed
   Shall raze you out o'th' book of trespasses   33
   All you are set down there.   34
THESEUS [*to First Queen*]
   Sad lady, rise.
HYPPOLYTA [*to Second Queen*]   Stand up.
EMILIA [*to Third Queen*]   No knees to me.
   What woman I may stead that is distressed   36
   Does bind me to her.   37
                     [*The Second and Third Queens rise.*]
THESEUS [*to First Queen*]
   What's your request? Deliver you for all.   38
FIRST QUEEN [*kneeling still*]
   We are three queens whose sovereigns fell before
   The wrath of cruel Creon; who endured   40
   The beaks of ravens, talons of the kites,

15 let fall allow to collapse   **16 child** i.e., play   **20 blasts my bays** withers my poetic reputation   **21 Than Robin Hood** i.e., than popular ballad material.   **23 him** Chaucer   **26 tack about** turn about in the water, as though sailing, in response to the wind generated by the audience's applause   **28 his** Chaucer's.   **may** which may   **29 travail** (Spelled *"travell"* in the original Quarto, suggesting [1] the actors' exertions [2] the audience's journey of imagination.)   **30–1 If . . . from us** i.e., If we don't manage to be entertaining and thereby able to fend off boredom
1.1 Location: Athens. Enroute to the temple where the marriage is to take place.
0.1 Hymen god of marriage.   **0.3–4 a nymph . . . tresses** a young woman with her hair unbound, as a token of virginity   **0.4 wheaten garland** symbol of fecundity   **0.5 chaplets** garlands   **5 quaint** beautiful, trim   **7 Ver** spring personified   **9 bells dim** pale bell-shaped flowers   **10 Oxlips . . . growing** cowslip-like flowers with the bud cradled by surrounding petals and leaves

11 on deathbeds blowing flowering on graves   **12 Lark's-heels** larkspur   **15 Blessing their sense** pleasing all their senses.   **19 sland'rous cuckoo** (The cuckoo was despised for seeming to mock married men as potential cuckolds and for laying its eggs in other birds' nests.)   **20 boding** prophesying bad fortune.   **chough hoar** gray-feathered jackdaw   **21 pie** magpie   **24.1 stained** dyed black to betoken mourning   **25 gentility's** nobility's   **26 respect** pay considerate attention to   **29–30 marked . . . bed** destined to be your honorable husband   **31 clear** pure   **33–4 raze . . . there** erase from the book of heaven's judgment all your sins set down there.   **36–7 What . . . to her** Whatsoever woman in distress that I can assist will by her very situation obligate me to her (without further kneeling on her part).   **37.1 rise** (The stage directions to rise and kneel again are conjectural in their placement.)   **38 Deliver** Speak   **40 who** i.e., our three husbands

And pecks of crows in the foul fields of Thebes.   42
He will not suffer us to burn their bones,
To urn their ashes, nor to take th'offense
Of mortal loathsomeness from the blest eye   45
Of holy Phoebus, but infects the winds   46
With stench of our slain lords. Oh, pity, Duke!
Thou purger of the earth, draw thy feared sword   48
That does good turns to th' world; give us the bones
Of our dead kings, that we may chapel them;   50
And of thy boundless goodness take some note   51
That for our crownèd heads we have no roof
Save this, which is the lion's and the bear's,   53
And vault to everything.

THESEUS   Pray you, kneel not;   54
I was transported with your speech and suffered
Your knees to wrong themselves. I have heard the
    fortunes
Of your dead lords, which gives me such lamenting
As wakes my vengeance and revenge for 'em.
[*To the First Queen*] King Capaneus was your lord; the
    day
That he should marry you, at such a season   60
As now it is with me, I met your groom   61
By Mars's altar. You were that time fair—
Not Juno's mantle fairer than your tresses,
Nor in more bounty spread her. Your wheaten wreath   64
Was then nor threshed nor blasted; Fortune at you   65
Dimpled her cheek with smiles. Hercules, our
    kinsman—
Then weaker than your eyes—laid by his club;   67
He tumbled down upon his Nemean hide   68
And swore his sinews thawed. O Grief and Time,   69
Fearful consumers, you will all devour!   70

FIRST QUEEN   Oh, I hope some god,
Some god hath put his mercy in your manhood,
Whereto he'll infuse power and press you forth   73
Our undertaker.

THESEUS   Oh, no knees, none, widow;   74
Unto the helmeted Bellona use them   75
And pray for me, your soldier.
                        [*The First Queen rises.*]
Troubled I am.   [*He*] *turns away.*

SECOND QUEEN [*kneeling*]   Honored Hippolyta,
Most dreaded Amazonian, that hast slain   78
The scythe-tusked boar; that with thy arm, as strong   79

As it is white, wast near to make the male   80
To thy sex captive, but that this thy lord,
Born to uphold creation in that honor   82
First nature styled it in, shrunk thee into   83
The bound thou wast o'erflowing, at once subduing   84
Thy force and thy affection; soldieress
That equally canst poise sternness with pity,   86
Whom now I know hast much more power on him   87
Then ever he had on thee, who ow'st his strength   88
And his love too, who is a servant for   89
The tenor of thy speech: dear glass of ladies,   90
Bid him that we, whom flaming war doth scorch,
Under the shadow of his sword may cool us!
Require him he advance it o'er our heads.   93
Speak 't in a woman's key, like such a woman   94
As any of us three; weep ere you fail.   95
Lend us a knee;
But touch the ground for us no longer time   97
Than a dove's motion when the head's plucked off.   98
Tell him if he i'th' blood-sized field lay swoll'n,   99
Showing the sun his teeth, grinning at the moon,   100
What you would do.

HIPPOLYTA   Poor lady, say no more.
I had as lief trace this good action with you   102
As that whereto I am going, and never yet   103
Went I so willing way. My lord is taken   104
Heart-deep with your distress. Let him consider.
I'll speak anon.   [*The Second Queen rises.*]

THIRD QUEEN [*kneel to Emilia*]   Oh, my petition was   106
Set down in ice, which by hot grief uncandied   107
Melts into drops; so sorrow, wanting form,   108
Is pressed with deeper matter.

EMILIA   Pray stand up;   109
Your grief is written in your cheek.

THIRD QUEEN   Oh, woe!
You cannot read it there; there through my tears,   111
Like wrinkled pebbles in a glassy stream,   112
You may behold 'em. Lady, lady, alack!   113
He that will all the treasure know o'th'earth

---

80 wast near to make was on the verge of making   **82–3 Born . . . it in** i.e., destined to restore and maintain the natural hierarchy of the sexes, as ordained since the beginning of time   **84 The bound . . . o'erflowing** the circumscribed limits that you were attempting to exceed, like a river overflowing its banks   **86 poise** counterpoise, balance   **87 on** over   **88 who ow'st** you who now own or control   **89–90 who . . . ladies** i.e., Theseus, who is obedient in love to your every command: you who are a mirror or model for all ladies   **93 Require . . . it** Request of him that he hold it aloft   **94 key** tone, style   **95 weep . . . fail** weep rather than give up.   **97–8 But . . . off** i.e., we ask that you touch your knee to the ground for us only for a moment or two, in the time it would take a beheaded dove to cease moving.   **99 blood-sized field** blood-soaked battlefield. (*Size* is a gelatinous glue-like coating that soaks into a wall, paper, leather, etc. as a way of filling pores.)   **100 Showing . . . moon** grinning as a skull does   **102–4 I had . . . way** I would just as gladly speak on your behalf as go ahead with my impending marriage, which I look forward to more willingly than anything I've ever done.   **104 taken** struck, afflicted   **106–9 my petition . . . matter** i.e., my petition, coldly formal when expressed in mere words, is melted by my hot grief into teardrops; thus my sorrow, lacking shape or power of expression, is pressed out in tears by the deep cause of my grief.   **111–13 You . . . 'em** i.e., You cannot read my grief truly on my cheek, in the external sign; look through my tears into my eyes, as you would look at pebbles distorted in their shape through the rippling water of a clear stream.

---

42 fields battlefields   **45–6 from . . . Phoebus** out of the sun (which hastens the process of putrefaction)   **48 Thou . . . earth** You who are renowned for defending the innocent against monsters and evil-doers   **50 chapel** inter in a chapel   **51 of** out of   **53 this** the sky   **54 vault** roof   **60 should** was about to   **61 groom** bridegroom   **64 Nor . . . her** nor enveloped her in more luxuriant tresses.   **64–5 Your . . . blasted** Your garland woven of wheat (a token of fecundity, as at 1.1.0.4) was neither threshed (punning on "thrashed," beaten) nor withered   **67 weaker than your eyes** subdued by your gaze   **68 Nemean hide** (One of Hercules's twelve labors was to kill and skin the Nemean lion.)   **69 thawed** i.e., rendered powerless (by love).   **70 all devour** devour all things.   **73–4 press . . . undertaker** press you into service as our champion.   **75 Bellona** goddess of war   **78–9 that . . . boar** (Atalanta, a huntress like Hippolyta, helped kill the fearful wild boar of Calydon; see Chaucer's "The Knight's Tale" and Ovid, *Metamorphoses*, Book 8.)

Must know the center too; he that will fish 115
For my least minnow, let him lead his line 116
To catch one at my heart. Oh, pardon me!
Extremity, that sharpens sundry wits, 118
Makes me a fool.

[The Third Queen rises.]

EMILIA   Pray you say nothing, pray you. 119
Who cannot feel nor see the rain, being in't, 120
Knows neither wet nor dry. If that you were 121
The ground-piece of some painter, I would buy you 122
T'instruct me 'gainst a capital grief, indeed 123
Such heart-pierced demonstration; but alas, 124
Being a natural sister of our sex, 125
Your sorrow beats so ardently upon me 126
That it shall make a counter-reflect 'gainst 127
My brother's heart and warm it to some pity, 128
Though it were made of stone. Pray have good
    comfort.

THESEUS
Forward to th' temple. Leave not out a jot
O'th' sacred ceremony.

FIRST QUEEN   Oh, this celebration 131
Will longer last and be more costly than 132
Your suppliants' war. Remember that your fame 133
Knolls in the ear o'th' world; what you do quickly 134
Is not done rashly; your first thought is more
Than others' labored meditance, your premeditating 136
More than their actions. But, O Jove, your actions,
Soon as they move, as ospreys do the fish, 138
Subdue before they touch. Think, dear Duke, think 139
What beds our slain kings have.

SECOND QUEEN   What griefs our beds, 140
That our dear lords have none.

THIRD QUEEN   None fit for th' dead. 141
Those that with cords, knives, drams, precipitance, 142
Weary of this world's light, have to themselves
Been death's most horrid agents, human grace
Affords them dust and shadow.

FIRST QUEEN   But our lords 145

Lie blist'ring 'fore the visiting sun, 146
And were good kings when living. 147

THESEUS
It is true, and I will give you comfort
To give your dead lords graves; 149
The which to do must make some work with Creon. 150

FIRST QUEEN
And that work presents itself to th' doing. 151
Now 'twill take form; the heats are gone tomorrow. 152
Then, bootless toil must recompense itself 153
With its own sweat. Now he's secure, 154
Not dreams we stand before your puissance, 155
Rinsing our holy begging in our eyes
To make petition clear.

SECOND QUEEN   Now you may take him, 157
Drunk with his victory.

THIRD QUEEN   And his army full
Of bread and sloth.

THESEUS *[to Artesius]*   Artesius, that best knowest
How to draw out, fit to this enterprise, 160
The prim'st for this proceeding, and the number 161
To carry such a business: forth and levy 162
Our worthiest instruments, whilst we dispatch 163
This grand act of our life, this daring deed 164
Of fate in wedlock.

FIRST QUEEN *[to the other Queens]* Dowagers, take hands. 165
Let us be widows to our woes; delay 166
Commends us to a famishing hope.

ALL [THE QUEENS]   Farewell. 167

SECOND QUEEN
We come unseasonably; but when could grief
Cull forth, as unpanged judgment can, fitt'st time 169
For best solicitation?

THESEUS   Why, good ladies,
This is a service, whereto I am going,
Greater than any was; it more imports me 172
Than all the actions that I have foregone, 173
Or futurely can cope.

FIRST QUEEN   The more proclaiming 174
Our suit shall be neglected, when her arms, 175
Able to lock Jove from a synod, shall 176
By warranting moonlight corslet thee. Oh, when 177

---

115 Must . . . too must mine deeply   **116 lead** attach a lead weight to (so that the fishing gear may sink deeply)   **118–19 Extremity . . . fool** Extremity of grief, which sharpens some people's minds, prompts me to speak distractedly.   **120–1 Who . . . dry** i.e., Anyone who would not be moved by your eloquence simply has no feeling.   **121–4 If that . . . demonstration** If you were merely depicted by some painter as an image intended to provide moral example, I would buy the painting to help me anticipate and thus ward off a deadly grief, indeed just such a heart-piercing instance as your sad case represents   **125 Being . . . sex** i.e., since you are a living woman, not a painting   **126 ardently** burningly, sunlike in intensity   **127 make a counter-reflect** reflect back from me as from a mirror   **128 My brother's** my prospective brother-in-law's, Theseus'   **131–3 Oh, this . . . war** (The First Queen urges Theseus to consider that the wedding ceremony will consume precious time, during which the queens' supplications and their struggle with Creon will languish.)   **134 Knolls** tolls   **136 labored meditance** laborious thought   **138–9 as ospreys . . . touch** (Osprey hawks, which dive spectacularly on fish in the water, were thought to subdue their prey with a powerful emanating influence even before they struck.)   **140 What griefs our beds** i.e., Think in what beds of grief we lie, so to speak   **141 None . . . dead** i.e., the cold ground on which they lie is no fit bed for a dead warrior.   **142 drams** poisons. **precipitance** suicidal leaps. (The Third Queen's point is that even suicides are allowed some kind of burial.)   **145 dust and shadow** i.e., to lie in quiet darkness in the earth.

146 visitating surveying, overseeing   **147 And** i.e., and yet, unlike suicides   **149 To give** by giving   **150 must . . . work** necessitates dealing   **151–4 presents . . . sweat** calls for action immediately. It can be shaped, like heated metal, now, but will soon cool. Tomorrow, all effort will be fruitless and will have to be content with the effort itself.   **154 he's** i.e., Creon is   **155 your puissance** your mighty self   **157 To . . . clear** to purify our supplication and stress our point.   **160 draw out** choose   **161 prim'st** best   **162 carry** carry out.   **forth** go forth   **163 instruments** agents, i.e., soldiers   **164–5 This . . . wedlock** (Theseus's view here of his marriage as a heroic deed, a counter-adventure, is quite different from the view that the queens are presenting [e.g., lines 174 ff.].)   **166–7 delay . . . hope** the delay (occasioned by this marriage) commits us to a dying hope.   **169 Cull forth** choose, select.   **unpanged** unafflicted by the pangs of sorrow   **172 more imports me** is more important to me   **173 foregone** previously achieved   **174 futurely can cope** can achieve in the future.   **The more proclaiming** Making it all the more clear that   **175–7 when . . . thee** when the arms of her (Hippolyta) whose charms would keep Jupiter himself from an assembly of the gods will, by the light of the love-authorizing moon, encircle you like close-fitting armor.

Her twinning cherries shall their sweetness fall 178
Upon thy tasteful lips, what wilt thou think 179
Of rotten kings or blubbered queens? What care 180
For what thou feel'st not, what thou feel'st being able 181
To make Mars spurn his drum? Oh, if thou couch 182
But one night with her, every hour in't will
Take hostage of thee for a hundred, and 184
Thou shalt remember nothing more than what
That banquet bids thee to.
HIPPOLYTA [*to Theseus*]   Though much unlike 186
You should be so transported, as much sorry 187
I should be such a suitor, yet I think, 188
Did I not, by th'abstaining of my joy— 189
Which breeds a deeper longing—cure their surfeit 190
That craves a present med'cine, I should pluck 191
All ladies' scandal on me. [*She kneels.*] Therefore, sir, 192
As I shall here make trial of my prayers,
Either presuming them to have some force,
Or sentencing for aye their vigor dumb, 195
Prorogue this business we are going about, and hang 196
Your shield afore your heart, about that neck
Which is my fee, and which I freely lend 198
To do these poor queens service.
ALL [THE] QUEENS [*to Emilia*]   Oh, help now!
Our cause cries for your knee.
EMILIA [*to Theseus, kneeling*]   If you grant not
My sister her petition in that force, 201
With that celerity and nature which 202
She makes it in, from henceforth I'll not dare 203
To ask you anything, nor be so hardy
Ever to take a husband.
THESEUS   Pray stand up.
[*Hippolyta and Emilia rise.*]
I am entreating of myself to do
That which you kneel to have me.—Pirithous, 207
Lead on the bride; get you and pray the gods 208
For success and return; omit not anything 209
In the pretended celebration.—Queens, 210
Follow your soldier. [*To Artesius*] As before, hence you, 211
And at the banks of Aulis meet us with
The forces you can raise, where we shall find

The moiety of a number for a business 214
More bigger looked.   [*Exit Artesius.*]
[*To Hippolyta*]   Since that our theme is haste, 215
I stamp this kiss upon thy current lip; 216
Sweet, keep it as my token.—Set you forward, 217
For I will see you gone.
[*The marriage procession moves*] *towards the temple.*
[*To Emilia*] Farewell, my beauteous sister.—Pirithous, 219
Keep the feast full; bate not an hour on't.
PIRITHOUS   Sir, 220
I'll follow you at heels. The feast's solemnity 221
Shall want till your return.
THESEUS   Cousin, I charge you, 222
Budge not from Athens. We shall be returning
Ere you can end this feast, of which I pray you
Make no abatement.—Once more, farewell all.
Exeunt [*in procession, all but Theseus*
and the Queens].
FIRST QUEEN
Thus dost thou still make good the tongue o'th' world. 226
SECOND QUEEN
And earn'st a deity equal with Mars.
THIRD QUEEN   If not above him, for
Thou, being but mortal, makest affections bend 229
To godlike honors; they themselves, some say, 230
Groan under such a mast'ry. 231
THESEUS   As we are men,
Thus should we do; being sensually subdued, 232
We lose our human title. Good cheer, ladies! 233
Now turn we towards your comforts.
Flourish. Exeunt.

♣

1.2

Enter Palamon and Arcite.

ARCITE
Dear Palamon, dearer in love than blood, 1
And our prime cousin, yet unhardened in 2
The crimes of nature, let us leave the city 3
Thebes, and the temptings in't, before we further 4
Sully our gloss of youth. 5

---

178 twinning cherries cherry lips.   **fall** let fall   **179 tasteful** capable of tasting   **180 rotten** with decaying flesh.   **blubbered** tear-stained
180–2 What . . . drum? Why should you care for something that does not touch you personally, at a time when your sexual desire is enough to make you set aside military duty?   **182 couch** lie
184 Take . . . hundred i.e., commit you to a hundred more such hours
186–8 Though . . . suitor Even though it would be much unlike you to be lifted into transports thus, and as much as I regret being the one to request (that you postpone the wedding)   **189 of** from   **190 Which . . . longing** Hippolyta's point is that by abstaining virtuously from the joys of marriage, she (and Theseus, too) can engender a deeper longing by making more precious and well-earned the reward.
surfeit excess (of grief)   **191 present** immediate   **191–2 I should . . . on me** I should invite the scorn of all ladies for my scandalous behavior.   **195 Or . . . dumb** or condemning them forever as ineffectual (if they fail), as if they had never been spoken   **196 Prorogue** postpone
198 my fee due to me (in marriage)   **201–3 in that force . . . it in** with the same intensity, speed, and natural feeling she uses in making her petition   **207 have me** have me do.   **208 get you** get you hence, depart   **209 return** our victorious return   **210 pretended** intended
211 your soldier i.e., Theseus himself.

214–15 The moiety . . . looked a part of an armed force raised to deal with a larger enterprise. (An army, raised for some other campaign, is now to be turned against Thebes.)   **215 Since that our theme** Since our business   **216 current** (1) legal and genuine, like a coin stamped with the royal image (2) currant-red. (The Quarto spelling, "currant," allows for both meanings.)   **217 token** (1) keepsake (2) stamped coin   **219 sister** sister-in-law-to-be.   **220 full** fully.   **bate . . . on't** don't abate one hour of it.   **221 solemnity** ceremonial dignity
222 want be lacking.   **Cousin** (A term used by royal figures to address their courtiers.)   **226 the tongue o'th' world** your reputation among all peoples.   **229–31 makest . . . mast'ry** subdue your passions to your godlike sense of honor; the gods themselves, some people say, suffer under passions that master them.   **232 being sensually subdued** if we allow ourselves to be subdued by our sensual natures   **233 human title** claim to be called human.
1.2 Location: Thebes.
1 blood kinship   **2 prime cousin** nearest kin   **3 The crimes of nature** those vices to which the human race is prone   **4 temptings** temptations   **5 Sully . . . youth** stain the luster of our youth.

And here to keep in abstinence we shame 6
As in incontinence; for not to swim 7
I'th'aid o'th' current were almost to sink, 8
At least to frustrate striving; and to follow 9
The common stream, 'twould bring us to an eddy 10
Where we should turn or drown; if labor through, 11
Our gain but life and weakness. 12

PALAMON   Your advice
Is cried up with example. What strange ruins, 13
Since first we went to school, may we perceive
Walking in Thebes? Scars and bare weeds 15
The gain o'th' martialist, who did propound 16
To his bold ends honor and golden ingots, 17
Which though he won, he had not, and now flirted 18
By peace for whom he fought. Who then shall offer 19
To Mars's so scorned altar? I do bleed 20
When such I meet, and wish great Juno would 21
Resume her ancient fit of jealousy 22
To get the soldier work, that peace might purge 23
For her repletion, and retain anew 24
Her charitable heart, now hard and harsher 25
Than strife or war could be.

ARCITE   Are you not out? 26
Meet you no ruin but the soldier in
The cranks and turns of Thebes? You did begin 28
As if you met decays of many kinds.
Perceive you none that do arouse your pity
But th'unconsidered soldier?

PALAMON   Yes, I pity 31
Decays where'er I find them, but such most
That, sweating in an honorable toil,
Are paid with ice to cool 'em.

ARCITE   'Tis not this 34
I did begin to speak of; this is virtue 35
Of no respect in Thebes. I spake of Thebes, 36
How dangerous, if we will keep our honors, 37
It is for our residing, where every evil
Hath a good color; where ev'ry seeming good's 39

A certain evil; where not to be ev'n jump 40
As they are here were to be strangers, and 41
Such things to be, mere monsters.

PALAMON   'Tis in our power 42
(Unless we fear that apes can tutor's) to 43
Be masters of our manners. What need I
Affect another's gait, which is not catching 45
Where there is faith? Or to be fond upon 46
Another's way of speech, when by mine own
I may be reasonably conceived—saved, too— 48
Speaking it truly? Why am I bound 49
By any generous bond to follow him 50
Follows his tailor, haply so long until 51
The followed make pursuit? Or let me know 52
Why mine own barber is unblessed, with him 53
My poor chin too, for 'tis not scissored just 54
To such a favorite's glass? What canon is there 55
That does command my rapier from my hip 56
To dangle't in my hand, or to go tip-toe 57
Before the street be foul? Either I am 58
The fore-horse in the team, or I am none
That draw i'th' sequent trace. These poor slight sores 60
Need not a plantain. That which rips my bosom 61
Almost to th' heart's—

ARCITE   Our uncle Creon.

PALAMON   He,
A most unbounded tyrant, whose successes
Makes heaven unfeared and villainy assured 64
Beyond its power there's nothing; almost puts 65
Faith in a fever, and deifies alone 66
Voluble chance; who only attributes 67
The faculties of other instruments 68
To his own nerves and act; commands men service, 69
And what they win in't, boot and glory; one 70

6–12 And . . . weakness And we shame ourselves as much by practicing abstinence here in this corrupt city as we would by indulging in licentious conduct; the first is to resist the current at the risk of drowning or frustration at the very least, whereas the second is to go with the flow and thereby either fall into deadly sin or eddy about aimlessly, or, at best, be weakened by sinfulness.   **13 cried up with example** proclaimed by many instances.   **ruins** persons ruined by extravagance   **15–20 Scars . . . altar?** Scars and threadbare garments are the reward of the soldier, who had proposed instead as a reward for his martial deeds honor and wealth, which, though he had indeed earned in battle, he had not received, and instead was jeered at by the very peace-loving (and craven) citizens for whom he fought. Who now would wish to be a soldier?   **20 I do bleed** i.e., my heart bleeds   **21–6 wish . . . could be** (Palamon wishes that war might break out again, renewing the conflict that came about when Juno vented her hatred on Thebes in retaliation for her husband Jupiter's affair with Alcmena in that city. War would put honorable soldiers to work. Peace, purging herself through war of her own excesses of decadent indolence, would paradoxically be more charitable than the harsh present reality of unchaste behavior.)   **26 out** mistaken (in pitying only the soldier).   **28 cranks** winding streets   **31 th'unconsidered** the neglected   **34 Are . . . 'em** i.e., are treated coldly.   **35–6 this . . . respect** i.e., no one cares for military honor   **37 will** wish to   **39 Hath a good color** assumes a pleasant appearance

40–2 where . . . monsters where not to go along exactly with Theban customs will brand us as strangers; yet to be as the Thebans are would make us utter monsters.   **43 Unless . . . tutor's** unless we are so insecure as to copy the behavior of those who are themselves mere imitators of others   **45–6 Affect . . . faith** model myself on another person's bearing, which should have no attraction for me when I practice self-reliance.   **46 fond upon** infatuated with   **48 conceived** understood   **48–9 saved . . . truly** i.e., I can reasonably hope to be saved from eternal damnation by my own speech, if I speak the truth.   **50 generous bond** honorable and gentlemanly obligation   **50–2 to follow . . . pursuit** to follow one who puts himself in obligation to his tailor, perchance until the tailor ends up pursuing that gentleman in order to recover what that gentleman owes.   **53 unblessed** not in favor   **54 for** because   **54–5 just . . . glass** precisely according to the latest fashion as reflected in the mirror of one who is much in favor.   **55 canon** law   **56–8 That . . . foul** (Carrying one's rapier in one's hand and tiptoeing even when the streets are not dirty are here seen as affectations of the dandy.)   **60 That . . . trace** that pull in the traces among a team of horses following behind the leader. (Palamon insists on being the leader or else no part of the team.)   **60–1 These . . . plantain** i.e., These social inanities are not what really needs curing. (*Plantain* is a plant used in healing wounds.)   **64–5 Makes . . . nothing** seem to suggest that villains need not fear heaven's justice and that no superior divine authority exists beyond human power   **65–7 puts . . . chance** undermines religious faith and makes mutable Chance the only goddess   **67–9 who . . . act** who attributes the capabilities and achievements of those who serve him to his own sinews (*nerves*) and deeds alone   **69–70 commands . . . glory** forces men to follow him and then arrogates to himself both the glory and the spoils they have won in battle

That fears not to do harm; good, dares not. Let 71
The blood of mine that's sib to him be sucked 72
From me with leeches! Let them break and fall 73
Off me with that corruption.

ARCITE   Clear-spirited cousin, 74
Let's leave his court, that we may nothing share
Of his loud infamy; for our milk 76
Will relish of the pasture, and we must 77
Be vile or disobedient, not his kinsmen 78
In blood unless in quality.

PALAMON   Nothing truer. 79
I think the echoes of his shames have deafed 80
The ears of heav'nly justice: widows' cries
Descend again into their throats, and have not
Due audience of the gods.

Enter Valerius.

Valerius! 83

VALERIUS
The King calls for you; yet be leaden-footed 84
Till his great rage be off him. Phoebus, when 85
He broke his whipstock and exclaimed against 86
The horses of the sun, but whispered to 87
The loudness of his fury.

PALAMON   Small winds shake him. 88
But what's the matter?

VALERIUS
Theseus, who where he threats appalls, hath sent 90
Deadly defiance to him and pronounces
Ruin to Thebes, who is at hand to seal 92
The promise of his wrath.

ARCITE   Let him approach.
But that we fear the gods in him, he brings not 94
A jot of terror to us. Yet what man 95
Thirds his own worth—the case is each of ours— 96
When that his action's dregged with mind assured 97
'Tis bad he goes about.

PALAMON   Leave that unreasoned. 98
Our services stand now for Thebes, not Creon.
Yet to be neutral to him were dishonor, 100
Rebellious to oppose; therefore we must 101

With him stand to the mercy of our fate, 102
Who hath bounded our last minute.

ARCITE   So we must. 103
Is't said this war's afoot, or it shall be 104
On fail of some condition?

VALERIUS   'Tis in motion; 105
The intelligence of state came in the instant 106
With the defier.

PALAMON   Let's to the King, who, were he 107
A quarter carrier of that honor which 108
His enemy come in, the blood we venture 109
Should be as for our health, which were not spent, 110
Rather laid out for purchase. But alas, 111
Our hands advanced before our hearts, what will 112
The fall o'th' stroke do damage?

ARCITE   Let th'event, 113
That never-erring arbitrator, tell us
When we know all ourselves, and let us follow
The becking of our chance.   *Exeunt.* 116

❧

1.3

Enter Pirithous, Hippolyta, Emilia.

PIRITHOUS
No further.

HIPPOLYTA   Sir, farewell. Repeat my wishes 1
To our great lord, of whose success I dare not
Make any timorous question; yet I wish him
Excess and overflow of power, an't might be, 4
To dure ill-dealing fortune. Speed to him! 5
Store never hurts good governors.

PIRITHOUS   Though I know 6
His ocean needs not my poor drops, yet they 7
Must yield their tribute there. [*To Emilia*] My precious
        maid,
Those best affections that the heaven infuse 9
In their best-tempered pieces keep enthroned 10
In your dear heart!

EMILIA   Thanks, sir. Remember me
To our all-royal brother, for whose speed 12

---

71 good, dares not dares not do any good (lest it leave him vulnerable to those he might trust).   **72 sib** akin   **73 leeches . . . break** (These bloodsucking worms, used by physicians to purge the blood, were allowed to fill to bursting and then fall off.)   **74 Clear-spirited** Noble-minded   **76 loud** notorious   **76–9 our . . . quality** our milk (like that of cows) will acquire the flavor of what we have eaten, so that we must either be vile like him or resist his corrupt authority; to be his kinsman in blood is to risk becoming like him in quality.   **80 deafed** deafened   **83 Due audience of** proper attention from   **84 be leaden-footed** answer the summons slowly   **85–8 Phoebus . . . fury** The sun god, when he vented his fury on the horses that drew his chariot (after his son Phaethon had had to be destroyed for misgoverning his father's chariot), merely whispered compared to the loudness of Creon's present anger. (See Ovid, *Metamorphoses*, 2.398 ff.)   **88 Small . . . him** The most trivial things put him in a rage.   **90 appalls** makes pale, terrifies   **92 who** i.e., Theseus.   **seal** ratify, carry out   **94 But** Were it not that   **95–8 Yet . . . about** Yet any man whatever cuts down by one third his own worth as a soldier—as we all do—when what he is about to do seems to him unworthy.   **98 Leave that unreasoned** Consider it not so deeply.   **100 Yet to be** To continue to be.   **were** would be   **101 Rebellious** treasonous

102–3 stand . . . minute submit to our fate, which has determined when we will die.   **104–5 or . . . condition?** or is war contingent on Thebes's accepting or refusing certain conditions?   **106–7 The intelligence . . . defier** the tidings of Creon's decision to fight were virtually synchronous with the arrival of Theseus's challenge.   **108–9 A quarter . . . come in** possessed of a mere fourth of the honor that his enemy (Theseus) brings to the battle   **110–11 Should . . . purchase** would be therapeutic, like a medical bloodletting, the blood being not wasted but put to profitable use (in defending an honorable cause).   **112–13 Our . . . damage?** if we lift our hands in battle before our hearts are engaged, what can our half-hearted blows be expected to accomplish?   **113 th'event** the outcome   **116 The becking . . . chance** the beckoning of our destiny (which will reveal all to us in the fullness of time).

1.3 Location: Athens, at the edge of the city, toward Thebes.
1 No further (Hippolyta and Emilia have escorted Pirithous to the city gates for his departure; here they must stay behind.)   **4 an't . . . be** if it (such an overflow of power) were possible   **5 dure** endure   **5–6 Speed . . . governors** May he prosper! Abundance (the "overflow of power" in line 4) never hurts those who manage things well.   **7 drops** i.e., drops of blood   **9 affections** good dispositions   **10 their best-tempered pieces** those persons whom the heavens have made of best temper or quality   **12 speed** success

The great Bellona I'll solicit; and 13
Since in our terrene state petitions are not 14
Without gifts understood, I'll offer to her
What I shall be advised she likes. Our hearts
Are in his army, in his tent.

HIPPOLYTA   In 's bosom.
We have been soldiers, and we cannot weep
When our friends don their helms, or put to sea,
Or tell of babes broached on the lance, or women 20
That have sod their infants in—and after ate them— 21
The brine they wept at killing 'em; then if
You stay to see of us such spinsters, we 23
Should hold you here forever.

PIRITHOUS   Peace be to you
As I pursue this war, which shall be then 25
Beyond further requiring.   *Exit Pirithous.*

EMILIA   How his longing 26
Follows his friend! Since his depart, his sports, 27
Though craving seriousness and skill, passed slightly 28
His careless execution, where nor gain 29
Made him regard, or loss consider, but
Playing one business in his hand, another
Directing in his head, his mind nurse equal 32
To these so diff'ring twins. Have you observed him 33
Since our great lord departed?

HIPPOLYTA   With much labor;
And I did love him for't. They two have cabined 35
In many as dangerous as poor a corner, 36
Peril and want contending; they have skiffed 37
Torrents whose roaring tyranny and power 38
I'th' least of these was dreadful, and they have 39
Fought out together where Death's self was lodged; 40
Yet fate hath brought them off. Their knot of love, 41
Tied, weaved, entangled, with so true, so long,
And with a finger of so deep a cunning, 43
May be outworn, never undone. I think 44
Theseus cannot be umpire to himself,
Cleaving his conscience into twain and doing
Each side like justice, which he loves best.

EMILIA   Doubtless 47
There is a best, and reason has no manners 48

To say it is not you. I was acquainted
Once with a time when I enjoyed a playfellow;
You were at wars when she the grave enriched,
Who made too proud the bed; took leave o'th' moon— 52
Which then looked pale at parting—when our count 53
Was each eleven.

HIPPOLYTA   'Twas Flavina.
EMILIA   Yes.
You talk of Pirithous' and Theseus' love.
Theirs has more ground, is more maturely seasoned, 56
More buckled with strong judgment, and their needs 57
The one of th'other may be said to water
Their intertangled roots of love. But I,
And she I sigh and spoke of, were things innocent; 60
Loved for we did, and, like the elements 61
That know not what nor why, yet do effect 62
Rare issues by their operance, our souls 63
Did so to one another. What she liked 64
Was then of me approved, what not, condemned—
No more arraignment. The flower that I would pluck 66
And put between my breasts—Oh, then but beginning
To swell about the blossom—she would long 68
Till she had such another, and commit it
To the like innocent cradle, where, phoenix-like, 70
They died in perfume. On my head no toy 71
But was her pattern; her affections—pretty, 72
Though happily her careless wear—I followed 73
For my most serious decking. Had mine ear 74
Stol'n some new air, or at adventure hummed one 75
From musical coinage, why, it was a note 76
Whereon her spirits would sojourn—rather dwell
    on—
And sing it in her slumbers. This rehearsal— 78
Which seely innocence wots well, comes in 79
Like old importment's bastard—has this end: 80
That the true love 'tween maid and maid may be 81
More than in sex dividual.

HIPPOLYTA   You're out of breath, 82
And this high-speeded pace is but to say

---

13 Bellona goddess of war   **14 terrene** earthly   **20 broached** spitted, impaled   **21 sod** boiled   **23 spinsters** women involved solely in domestic chores   **25 As** while, as long as   **25–6 which . . . requiring** which war, when I have triumphed, will no longer require your prayers.   **27 his depart** Theseus's departure.   **his sports** Pirithous's amusements, diversions   **28–9 passed . . . execution** received only Pirithous's cursory attention   **29 nor** neither   **32–3 nurse . . . twins** i.e., evenly divided between his caring for his sports (such as hunting and martial practice) and his longing to be with Theseus.   **35–7 have . . . contending** have shared soldiers' quarters in many a place that was as dangerous as poorly furnished, the danger and the paucity of comfort contending as to which was more oppressive   **37–8 skiffed Torrents** braved turbulent waters in light skiffs   **39 I'th' least of these** at their least threatening   **40 Fought . . . lodged** battled it out with Death itself in Death's own dominion. (According to legend; Theseus descended with Pirithous, King of the Lapithae, to Hades to help him carry off Persephone, for which crime he suffered imprisonment in Hades until rescued by Hercules.)   **41 brought them off** rescued them.   **43 cunning** skill   **44 outworn** worn out (by death)   **47 like** equal.   **which** i.e., Hippolyta or Pirithous   **48 There is a best** (Emilia responds to Hippolyta's modest disclaimer by insisting that of course Theseus loves his bride best.)

52 Who . . . moon who was too fine to grace the bed of death; who departed from this mortal sublunary sphere and from the service of the goddess of chastity   **53 count** age   **56 ground** firm foundation   **57 buckled with** joined together, held in by   **60 things innocent** innocent young beings   **61** for simply because.   **61–4 like . . . another** like the four elements of earth, water, air, and fire, out of which the universe is composed, which, acting instinctively in obedience to some higher law of nature, bring about amazing results by their interaction, our souls responded to each other.   **66 No more arraignment** without needing any further inquiry or trial.   **68 To swell . . . blossom** (The image applies to the flower and to Emilia's breasts.)   **70–1 phoenix-like . . . perfume** (The phoenix was said to build a nest of "sweet-smelling sticks" that was then set on fire by the sun, consuming the mythical bird to ashes from which arose a new and unique phoenix. An emblem of immortality.)   **71–2 no toy . . . pattern** no bit of finery that was not emulated by her   **72–3 her affections . . . wear** what she chose to wear—pretty even when perchance casual   **74 serious decking** carefully thought out attire.   **75–6 Stol'n . . . coinage** caught some new tune, or randomly hummed an improvised one of my own   **78–82 This . . . dividual** This narrative of mine, which blissful innocence recognizes as the imperfect representation (as if it were an illegitimate child) of some meaningful old tale, is meant to show that true love between two young women can be greater than the love between persons of the opposite sex.

That you shall never—like the maid Flavina—
Love any that's called man.
EMILIA   I am sure I shall not.
HIPPOLYTA   Now alack, weak sister,
I must no more believe thee in this point—
Though in't I know thou dost believe thyself—
Than I will trust a sickly appetite,
That loathes even as it longs. But sure, my sister,
If I were ripe for your persuasion, you   92
Have said enough to shake me from the arm
Of the all-noble Theseus, for whose fortunes
I will now in and kneel, with great assurance
That we, more than his Pirithous, possess
The high throne in his heart.
EMILIA   I am not
Against your faith, yet I continue mine.   *Exeunt.*

❖

1.4

Cornets. A battle struck within; then a retreat.
Flourish. Then enter [from one door] Theseus,
victor. [A Herald follows with attendants bearing
Palamon and Arcite. From another door] the three
Queens meet him and fall on their faces before him.

FIRST QUEEN
To thee no star be dark!
SECOND QUEEN   Both heaven and earth   1
Friend thee forever!
THIRD QUEEN   All the good that may
Be wished upon thy head, I cry amen to't!
THESEUS
Th'impartial gods, who, from the mounted heavens,   4
View us their mortal herd, behold who err
And in their time chastise. Go and find out
The bones of your dead lords, and honor them
With treble ceremony; rather than a gap
Should be in their dear rites, we would supply't.
But those we will depute, which shall invest   10
You in your dignities, and even each thing   11
Our haste does leave imperfect. So adieu,
And heaven's good eyes look on you.
                              Exeunt Queens.
                    [Theseus points to Palamon and Arcite.]
                              What are those?
HERALD
Men of great quality, as may be judged   14
By their appointment. Some of Thebes have told 's   15

They are sisters' children, nephews to the King.
THESEUS
By th' helm of Mars, I saw them in the war,
Like to a pair of lions, smeared with prey,
Make lanes in troops aghast. I fixed my note   19
Constantly on them, for they were a mark   20
Worth a god's view. What prisoner was't that told me
When I inquired their names?
HERALD   Wi' leave, they're called 22
Arcite and Palamon.
THESEUS   'Tis right; those, those.
They are not dead?
HERALD
Nor in a state of life. Had they been taken
When their last hurts were given, 'twas possible
They might have been recovered. Yet they breathe
And have the name of men.
THESEUS   Then like men use 'em.   28
The very lees of such, millions of rates,   29
Exceed the wine of others. All our surgeons   30
Convent in their behoof; our richest balms,   31
Rather than niggard, waste; their lives concern us   32
Much more than Thebes is worth. Rather than have
    'em   33
Freed of this plight, and in their morning state,   34
Sound and at liberty, I would 'em dead;   35
But forty-thousandfold we had rather have 'em
Prisoners to us than death. Bear 'em speedily
From our kind air, to them unkind, and minister   38
What man to man may do—for our sake more,
Since I have known frights, fury, friends' behests,   40
Love's provocations, zeal, a mistress' task,   41
Desire of liberty, a fever, madness,   42
Hath set a mark which nature could not reach to   43
Without some imposition, sickness in will   44
O'er-wrestling strength in reason. For our love   45
And great Apollo's mercy, all our best   46
Their best skill tender.—Lead into the city,
Where, having bound things scattered, we will post   48
To Athens 'fore our army.   *Flourish. Exeunt.*

❖

19 **Make . . . aghast** hew their way through troops that were aghast.
note attention   20 **mark** object of attention   22 **Wi' leave** By your
leave, if you'll allow me to say so   28 **have . . . men** are nominally
still alive.   29 **The very . . . rates** The mere dregs or last physical remnants of such men, by millions of times   30–1 **All . . . behoof** Call
together all our surgeons on their behalf   32 **Rather . . . waste** rather
than be niggardly with, expend lavishly   33–5 **Rather . . . dead** i.e., If
it were the previous morning, before the battle began, I would have
wished them dead rather than healthy and free, ready to fight on the
enemy side   38 **kind . . . unkind** (The air that Theseus cherishes is
dangerous to his enemies, especially since air was thought to be
infectious to open wounds.)   40–5 **Since . . . reason** Theseus has
known men like Palamon and Arcite to strive for something nearly
impossible and quite unreasonable, when their natural common
sense is overwhelmed by some compelling desire to please friends,
lovers, or country, or in response to some equally impulsive emotion.
46 **Apollo** here invoked as god of healing.   **all our best** let all our
best surgeons   48 **post** hasten

92 **ripe . . . persuasion** disposed to be won over by your argument
1.4 Location: At the siege of Thebes.
0.1 *Cornets* trumpet calls signifying battle.   *within* offstage, behind
the stage façade.   *retreat* withdrawal after combat, not necessarily in
flight.   **1 no star be dark** may no planet or heavenly body be obscure
and unfavorable.   **4 mounted** high   **10–11 But . . . dignities** But I
will deputize others to perform these ceremonies which will clothe
you in the dignities that you and your dead husbands have deserved.
(Having performed his vow to guarantee the burial of the dead kings,
Theseus is eager to return to his marriage.)   **11 even** make even,
complete   **14 quality** rank   **15 appointment** accoutrement, armor.

1.5

Music. Enter the Queens with [attendants bearing] the hearses of their knights in a funeral solemnity, etc.

[*Song*]

Urns and odors bring away;   1
Vapors, sighs darken the day;
    Our dole more deadly looks than dying;   3
Balms and gums and heavy cheers,   4
Sacred vials filled with tears,
    And clamors through the wild air flying.

Come all sad and solemn shows
That are quick-eyed Pleasure's foes;
We convent naught else but woes,   9
We convent naught else but woes.

THIRD QUEEN
    This funeral path brings to your household's grave;   11
    Joy seize on you again; peace sleep with him!
SECOND QUEEN
    And this to yours.
FIRST QUEEN   Yours this way. Heavens lend   13
    A thousand differing ways to one sure end.
THIRD QUEEN
    This world's a city full of straying streets,
    And death's the market-place where each one meets.   16
                                        Exeunt severally.

❖

2.1

Enter Jailer and Wooer.

JAILER   I may depart with little while I live; something I   1
may cast to you, not much. Alas, the prison I keep,   2
though it be for great ones, yet they seldom come;
before one salmon you shall take a number of min-
nows. I am given out to be better lined than it can   5
appear to me report is a true speaker. I would I were   6
really that I am delivered to be. Marry, what I   7

have—be it what it will—I will assure upon my   8
daughter at the day of my death.
WOOER   Sir, I demand no more than your own offer,
and I will estate your daughter in what I have   11
promised.
JAILER   Well, we will talk more of this when the   13
solemnity is past. But have you a full promise of her?   14
When that shall be seen, I tender my consent.   15
WOOER   I have, sir.

Enter [Jailer's] Daughter [with rushes].

Here she comes.
JAILER [*to Daughter*]   Your friend and I have chanced
to name you here, upon the old business; but no
more of that now. So soon as the court hurry is over
we will have an end of it. I'th' meantime look   21
tenderly to the two prisoners. I can tell you they are   22
princes.
JAILER'S DAUGHTER   These strewings are for their cham-   24
ber. 'Tis pity they are in prison, and 'twere pity they   25
should be out. I do think they have patience to make   26
any adversity ashamed. The prison itself is proud   27
of 'em, and they have all the world in their chamber.   28
JAILER   They are famed to be a pair of absolute men.   29
JAILER'S DAUGHTER   By my troth, I think fame but stam-   30
mers 'em; they stand a grece above the reach of report.   31
JAILER   I heard them reported in the battle to be the   32
only doers.   33
JAILER'S DAUGHTER   Nay, most likely, for they are
noble suff'rers. I marvel how they would have looked
had they been victors, that with such a constant
nobility enforce a freedom out of bondage, making   37
misery their mirth and affliction a toy to jest at.   38
JAILER   Do they so?
JAILER'S DAUGHTER   It seems to me they have no more
sense of their captivity than I of ruling Athens. They
eat well, look merrily, discourse of many things, but
nothing of their own restraint and disasters. Yet some-
time a divided sigh, martyred as 'twere i'th' deliver-   44
ance, will break from one of them, when the other
presently gives it so sweet a rebuke that I could   46
wish myself a sigh to be so chid, or at least a sigher to
be comforted.
WOOER   I never saw 'em.
JAILER   The Duke himself came privately in the night,   50

1.5. Location: Outside Thebes. A marginal note in the Quarto specifies at line 26 in the previous scene that the "hearses" are to be made
"ready" for this present scene.
0.2 *their knights* their husband kings.   **0.3** *etc.* This notation invites
the use of extras, conventional props, and blocking through which
the acting company is to stage a solemn procession suitable to the
weight of the occasion.   **0.4** *Song* The song may be sung by the three
queens, but possibly by attendant singers.   **1** *odors* incense.   **away**
along   **3** *Our . . . dying* our mourning has a more grim appearance
than death itself   **4** *gums* resins burned to produce incense.   **heavy**
cheers sad countenances   **9** *convent* (1) assemble (2) suit   **11** *brings*
leads.   **household's grave** family monument and burial plot
13 *And this* And this path   **16.1** *severally* separately. (The funeral
procession divides into three, each queen going through a stage door
accompanied by the hearse of her dead husband.)
2.1. Location: Athens. A prison garden, on the main stage, with the
prison cell above in the theater gallery.
1 *depart with* part with, give away   **2** *cast to* confer upon (in the
way of dowry)   **5–6** *I . . . speaker* I am reputed to have more wealth
than I can see any reason for the rumor of it to be believed.   **7** *that*
that which.   **delivered** rumored, said.   **Marry** an oath, originally
"by the Virgin Mary"

8 *assure* guarantee to settle   **11** *estate* settle an estate upon   **13–14** *the*
solemnity i.e., the royal wedding of Theseus and Hippolyta; the "court
hurry" of line 20   **14** *of* from   **15** *seen* understood to have occurred.
tender offer   **21–2** *look tenderly to* tend carefully   **24** *strewings*
rushes or reeds strewn on the floor and changed from time to time
25 *pity . . . pity* (The Jailer's Daughter takes pity on them as prisoners,
but would hate to see them set free.)   **26–7** *to make . . . ashamed* to
put to shame any adversity by their noble resolution.   **28** *they have . . .*
chamber i.e., their friendship is a world unto itself.   **29** *absolute men*
complete gentlemen.   **30–1** *stammers* describes only haltingly
31 *grece* step. (They stand above anything reputation can say of them.)
32–3 *the only doers* the ones whose brave feats immeasurably outdid
those of any others.   **37** *enforce . . . bondage* manage to make themselves free in spirit even in their captivity   **38** *toy* trifle   **44** *divided*
broken, incomplete   **46** *presently* instantly   **50** *privately* secretly. (The
Duke returned home with his prisoners at night; unobserved.)

and so did they; what the reason of it is, I know not.   51

Enter Palamon and Arcite above [in shackles].

Look, yonder they are. That's Arcite looks out.   52

JAILER'S DAUGHTER   No, sir, no, that's Palamon. Arcite
is the lower of the twain; you may perceive a part of   54
him.

JAILER   Go to, leave your pointing. They would not   56
make us their object. Out of their sight!   57

JAILER'S DAUGHTER   It is a holiday to look on them.
Lord, the diff'rence of men!   59

Exeunt [Jailer, Wooer, and Daughter].

❖

2.2

PALAMON
How do you, noble cousin?

ARCITE   How do you, sir?

PALAMON
Why, strong enough to laugh at misery
And bear the chance of war; yet we are prisoners
I fear forever, cousin.

ARCITE   I believe it,
And to that destiny have patiently
Laid up my hour to come.

PALAMON   Oh, cousin Arcite,   6
Where is Thebes now? Where is our noble country?
Where are our friends and kindreds? Never more
Must we behold those comforts, never see
The hardy youths strive for the games of honor,
Hung with the painted favors of their ladies,   11
Like tall ships under sail; then start amongst 'em
And, as an east wind, leave 'em all behind us,
Like lazy clouds, whilst Palamon and Arcite,
Even in the wagging of a wanton leg,   15
Outstripped the people's praises, won the garlands
Ere they have time to wish 'em ours. Oh, never
Shall we two exercise, like twins of honor,
Our arms again, and feel our fiery horses   19
Like proud seas under us. Our good swords, now—
Better the red-eyed god of war nev'r wore—   21
Ravished our sides, like age must run to rust   22
And deck the temples of those gods that hate us;
These hands shall never draw 'em out like lightning
To blast whole armies more.

ARCITE   No, Palamon,   25
Those hopes are prisoners with us. Here we are,

And here the graces of our youths must wither
Like a too-timely spring. Here age must find us,   28
And—which is heaviest, Palamon—unmarried.   29
The sweet embraces of a loving wife,
Loaden with kisses, armed with thousand Cupids,   31
Shall never clasp our necks; no issue know us;   32
No figures of ourselves shall we ev'r see   33
To glad our age, and, like young eagles, teach 'em   34
Boldly to gaze against bright arms, and say   35
"Remember what your fathers were, and conquer!"
The fair-eyed maids shall weep our banishments
And in their songs curse ever-blinded Fortune,
Till she for shame see what a wrong she has done
To youth and nature. This is all our world;
We shall know nothing here but one another;
Hear nothing but the clock that tells our woes.   42
The vine shall grow, but we shall never see it;
Summer shall come, and with her all delights,
But dead-cold winter must inhabit here still.

PALAMON
'Tis too true, Arcite. To our Theban hounds
That shook the agèd forest with their echoes
No more now must we hollo; no more shake   48
Our pointed javelins, whilst the angry swine   49
Flies like a Parthian quiver from our rages,   50
Struck with our well-steeled darts. All valiant uses—   51
The food and nourishment of noble minds—
In us two here shall perish; we shall die—
Which is the curse of honor—lastly,   54
Children of grief and ignorance.

ARCITE   Yet, cousin,   55
Even from the bottom of these miseries,
From all that fortune can inflict upon us,
I see two comforts rising, two mere blessings,   58
If the gods please: to hold here a brave patience,
And the enjoying of our griefs together.
Whilst Palamon is with me, let me perish
If I think this our prison.

PALAMON   Certainly
'Tis a main goodness, cousin, that our fortunes   63
Were twinned together. 'Tis most true, two souls   64
Put in two noble bodies, let 'em suffer   65
The gall of hazard, so they grow together,   66
Will never sink; they must not, say they could.   67
A willing man dies sleeping and all's done.   68

ARCITE
Shall we make worthy uses of this place

51.1 *above* in the gallery over the stage.   52 **looks out** who looks out.
54 **lower** less tall   56 **Go to** i.e., Come, come, enough of that
56–7 **They . . . object** They wouldn't be so rude as to point to us; they
have no wish to see us.   59 **the diff'rence of men!** how much finer
some men are than others!
2.2. Palamon and Arcite probably remain onstage in a continuation
of scene 1, but since the Quarto explicitly has them "*Exeunt*" and
then "*Enter . . . in prison*," the Q scene division is retained.
6 **Laid up . . . come** devoted the rest of my life.   11 **painted favors**
brightly colored tokens of favor in love, such as a scarf or glove
15 **Even . . . leg** i.e., with seemingly effortless motion, sportively
19 **arms** armor, weapons   21 **red-eyed god of war** Mars, red-eyed with
fury   22 **Ravished** seized violently from   25 **blast** blight, destroy

28 **too-timely** prematurely blooming   29 **heaviest** most burdensome
31 **Loaden** loaded   32 **issue** offspring   33 **figures** likenesses
34 **glad** gladden   34–5 **like . . . arms** we will never be able to teach
our children to look fearlessly at the arms of opponents, much as
eagles are reputed to be able to gaze directly at the sun   42 **tells**
counts   48 **hollo** cry encouragement   49 **swine** wild boar
50 **Parthian** (The Parthians, fierce warriors, were famed for their ability to shoot while in real or feigned retreat.)   51 **uses** pursuits (such
as hunting)   54 **lastly** finally   55 **Children . . . ignorance** i.e., sadly
and forgotten.   58 **mere** unmixed   63 **main goodness** major blessing, piece of good luck   64 **twinned** (The Quarto spelling,"twyn'd,"
suggests [1] paired inseparably [2] entwined.)   65–6 **let . . . hazard**
even if they should suffer the rubs of misfortune   66 **so** provided
that   67 **say** even if   68 **A willing . . . sleeping** One who is stoically
prepared for death dies as though going gently to sleep

That all men hate so much?
PALAMON   How, gentle cousin?   70
ARCITE
    Let's think this prison holy sanctuary,
    To keep us from corruption of worse men.
    We are young and yet desire the ways of honor
    That liberty and common conversation,   74
    The poison of pure spirits, might, like women,   75
    Woo us to wander from. What worthy blessing   76
    Can be but our imaginations   77
    May make it ours? And here being thus together,   78
    We are an endless mine to one another.   79
    We are one another's wife, ever begetting
    New births of love; we are father, friends,
        acquaintance;
    We are in one another, families;
    I am your heir, and you are mine. This place
    Is our inheritance; no hard oppressor
    Dare take this from us. Here, with a little patience,
    We shall live long and loving. No surfeits seek us;
    The hand of war hurts none here, nor the seas
    Swallow their youth. Were we at liberty,
    A wife might part us lawfully, or business;
    Quarrels consume us; envy of ill men   90
    Crave our acquaintance. I might sicken, cousin,   91
    Where you should never know it, and so perish
    Without your noble hand to close mine eyes,
    Or prayers to the gods. A thousand chances,
    Were we from hence, would sever us.
PALAMON   You have made me—
    I thank you, cousin Arcite—almost wanton   96
    With my captivity. What a misery
    It is to live abroad, and everywhere!   98
    'Tis like a beast, methinks. I find the court here,   99
    I am sure, a more content; and all those pleasures   100
    That woo the wills of men to vanity
    I see through now, and am sufficient
    To tell the world 'tis but a gaudy shadow
    That old Time, as he passes by, takes with him.
    What had we been, old in the court of Creon,   105
    Where sin is justice, lust and ignorance
    The virtues of the great ones? Cousin Arcite,
    Had not the loving gods found this place for us,
    We had died as they do, ill old men, unwept,   109
    And had their epitaphs, the people's curses.   110
    Shall I say more?
ARCITE   I would hear you still.
PALAMON   Ye shall.

Is there record of any two that loved
Better than we do, Arcite?
ARCITE   Sure there cannot.
PALAMON
    I do not think it possible our friendship
    Should ever leave us.
ARCITE   Till our deaths it cannot.

        Enter Emilia and her Woman [below].

    And after death our spirits shall be led
    To those that love eternally.
            [*Palamon sees Emilia and is speechless.*]
                              Speak on, sir.   117
EMILIA [*as she and her Woman gather flowers*]
    This garden has a world of pleasures in't.
    What flower is this?
WOMAN   'Tis called narcissus, madam.   119
EMILIA
    That was a fair boy, certain, but a fool   120
    To love himself. Were there not maids enough?   121
ARCITE [*to Palamon*]
    Pray, forward.
PALAMON   Yes.
EMILIA [*to her Woman*]   Or were they all hard-hearted?   122
WOMAN
    They could not be to one so fair.
EMILIA   Thou wouldst not.
WOMAN
    I think I should not, madam.
EMILIA   That's a good wench;
    But take heed to your kindness, though.
WOMAN   Why, madam?
EMILIA
    Men are mad things.
ARCITE [*to Palamon*]   Will ye go forward, cousin?   126
EMILIA [*to her Woman*]
    Canst not thou work such flowers in silk, wench?
WOMAN   Yes.   127
EMILIA
    I'll have a gown full of 'em, and of these.
    This is a pretty color; will't not do
    Rarely upon a skirt, wench?
WOMAN   Dainty, madam.   130
ARCITE [*to Palamon*]
    Cousin, cousin, how do you, sir? Why, Palamon!
PALAMON
    Never till now was I in prison, Arcite.
ARCITE
    Why, what's the matter, man?
PALAMON [*indicating Emilia*]   Behold and wonder!

---

70 **gentle** well-born, gracious   74 **common conversation** indiscriminate dealings with people   75 **like women** as if they were women. (Liberty and common conversation are personified as temptresses wooing the young men away from honor.)   76–8 **What . . . ours?** What worthy blessing can there be that in our imaginations we cannot make ours?   79 **mine** resource   90–1 **Quarrels . . . acquaintance** becoming involved in the quarrels might destroy our friendship; we might succumb to the vice of envying or imitating bad men   96 **wanton** sportive   98 **abroad** at liberty   99 **the court** i.e., the court that we create for ourselves, as distinguished from the courts of Creon or Theseus   100 **more** greater   105 **What . . . old** What would we have been like, if we had grown old   109 **they** i.e., the "great ones" of line 107.   **ill** evil   110 **their epitaphs** i.e., the same remembrance they got

117 **To . . . eternally** to those lovers whose spirits dwell in the Elysian Fields.   119–21 **narcissus . . . himself** (As punishment for his refusal to return the love of the nymph Echo, Narcissus fell fruitlessly in love with his own image in a fountain; eventually he was transformed into the flower that bears his name. Ovid, *Metamorphoses*, 3.)   122 **forward** continue with what you were saying. (Also in line 126.)   126 **Men are mad things** (Emilia warns her Woman that a kindly disposition toward handsome young men, however indicative of goodness of heart, may get a young woman into trouble.)   127 **work** embroider   130 **Rarely** excellently

By heaven, she is a goddess.

ARCITE [*seeing Emilia*]   Ha!

PALAMON   Do reverence;
She is a goddess, Arcite.

EMILIA [*to her Woman*]   Of all flowers
Methinks a rose is best.

WOMAN   Why, gentle madam?

EMILIA
It is the very emblem of a maid;
For when the west wind courts her gently,
How modestly she blows, and paints the sun   139
With her chaste blushes! When the north comes near
  her,   140
Rude and impatient, then, like chastity,
She locks her beauties in her bud again,
And leaves him to base briers.

WOMAN   Yet, good madam,   143
Sometimes her modesty will blow so far   144
She falls for't; a maid,   145
If she have any honor, would be loath
To take example by her.

EMILIA   Thou art wanton.   147

ARCITE [*to Palamon*]
She is wondrous fair.

PALAMON   She is all the beauty extant.

EMILIA [*to her Woman*]
The sun grows high; let's walk in. Keep these flowers;
We'll see how near art can come near their colors. 150
I am wondrous merry-hearted; I could laugh now.   151

WOMAN
I could lie down, I am sure.

EMILIA   And take one with you?   152

WOMAN
That's as we bargain, madam.

EMILIA   Well, agree then.
                  Exeunt Emilia and [her] Woman.

PALAMON
What think you of this beauty?

ARCITE   'Tis a rare one.

PALAMON
Is't but a rare one?

ARCITE   Yes, a matchless beauty.

PALAMON
Might not a man well lose himself and love her?

ARCITE
I cannot tell what you have done; I have,
Beshrew mine eyes for't! Now I feel my shackles.   158

PALAMON   You love her, then?

ARCITE   Who would not?

PALAMON   And desire her?

ARCITE   Before my liberty.

PALAMON   I saw her first.

ARCITE   That's nothing.

PALAMON   But it shall be.

ARCITE   I saw her too.

PALAMON   Yes, but you must not love her.

ARCITE
I will not, as you do, to worship her
As she is heavenly and a blessèd goddess.
I love her as a woman, to enjoy her;
So both may love.

PALAMON   You shall not love at all.

ARCITE   Not love at all? Who shall deny me?

PALAMON
I, that first saw her; I, that took possession
First with mine eye of all those beauties
In her revealed to mankind. If thou lov'st her,
Or entertain'st a hope to blast my wishes,   177
Thou art a traitor, Arcite, and a fellow
False as thy title to her. Friendship, blood,
And all the ties between us I disclaim
If thou once think upon her.

ARCITE   Yes, I love her,
And if the lives of all my name lay on it,   182
I must do so. I love her with my soul;
If that will lose ye, farewell, Palamon.
I say again I love, and, in loving her, maintain
I am as worthy and as free a lover,   186
And have as just a title to her beauty,
As any Palamon or any living
That is a man's son.

PALAMON   Have I called thee friend?

ARCITE
Yes, and have found me so. Why are you moved thus? 190
Let me deal coldly with you. Am not I   191
Part of your blood, part of your soul? You have told
  me
That I was Palamon, and you were Arcite.

PALAMON   Yes.

ARCITE
Am not I liable to those affections,   194
Those joys, griefs, angers, fears, my friend shall suffer?

PALAMON
Ye may be.

ARCITE   Why then would you deal so cunningly,
So strangely, so unlike a noble kinsman,
To love alone? Speak truly, do you think me
Unworthy of her sight?

PALAMON   No, but unjust
If thou pursue that sight.

ARCITE   Because another
First sees the enemy, shall I stand still
And let mine honor down, and never charge?

PALAMON
Yes, if he be but one.

ARCITE   But say that one   203

---

139 she blows . . . sun the rose blooms, and adds color to the sun's rays **140 north** north wind   **143 And . . . briers** and leaves the north wind with nothing but her briers.   **144–45 Sometimes . . . for't** (The Woman observes that the rose eventually blooms so openly, in despite of modesty, that it goes past its prime and decays. *Blow* can suggest being puffed up with vanity. A woman following such an example might well fall into temptation.)   **147 Thou art wanton** You're being witty. **150 art** i.e., embroidery. (See line 127.)   **151–2 laugh . . . lie down** The Woman continues the sexual joking with her reference to a proverb and a card game called "Laugh and lay (or lie) down."   **152 one** someone, a man   **158 Beshrew** i.e., May the devil take. (A mild curse.)

177 blast blight, destroy   **182 name** family.   **lay** depended   **186 free** noble   **190 moved** angered   **191 coldly** calmly   **194 affections** feelings   **203 but one** (The code of chivalry would forbid Arcite to join Palamon in engaging with a single opponent, two against one.)

Had rather combat me?

PALAMON   Let that one say so,   204
And use thy freedom; else, if thou pursuest her,   205
Be as that cursèd man that hates his country,
A branded villain.

ARCITE   You are mad.

PALAMON   I must be.
Till thou art worthy, Arcite, it concerns me;   208
And in this madness if I hazard thee   209
And take thy life, I deal but truly.

ARCITE   Fie, sir!
You play the child extremely. I will love her,
I must, I ought to do so, and I dare,
And all this justly.

PALAMON   Oh, that now, that now   213
Thy false self and thy friend had but this fortune   214
To be one hour at liberty, and grasp   215
Our good swords in our hands! I would quickly teach
    thee
What 'twere to filch affection from another.
Thou art baser in it than a cutpurse.
Put but thy head out of this window more,
And, as I have a soul, I'll nail thy life to't.   220

ARCITE
Thou dar'st not, fool, thou canst not, thou art feeble.
Put my head out? I'll throw my body out
And leap the garden, when I see her next,   223

        Enter Jailer [above].

And pitch between her arms to anger thee.   224

PALAMON
No more; the keeper's coming. I shall live
To knock thy brains out with my shackles.

ARCITE   Do.

JAILER
By your leave, gentlemen.

PALAMON   Now, honest keeper?   227

JAILER
Lord Arcite, you must presently to th' Duke.
The cause I know not yet.

ARCITE   I am ready, keeper.

JAILER
Prince Palamon, I must awhile bereave you
Of your fair cousin's company.

        Exeunt Arcite and Jailer.

PALAMON   And me too,
Even when you please, of life. Why is he sent for?
It may be he shall marry her; he's goodly,   233
And like enough the Duke hath taken notice   234

Both of his blood and body. But his falsehood!   235
Why should a friend be treacherous? If that
Get him a wife so noble and so fair,
Let honest men ne'er love again. Once more
I would but see this fair one. Blessèd garden,
And fruit and flowers more blessèd, that still blossom
As her bright eyes shine on ye! Would I were,
For all the fortune of my life hereafter,
Yon little tree, yon blooming apricot.
How I would spread and fling my wanton arms
In at her window! I would bring her fruit
Fit for the gods to feed on; youth and pleasure
Still as she tasted should be doubled on her,   247
And, if she be not heavenly, I would make her   248
So near the gods in nature they should fear her;

        Enter Jailer [above].

And then I am sure she would love me.—How now,
    keeper?
Where's Arcite?

JAILER   Banished. Prince Pirithous
Obtained his liberty; but never more,
Upon his oath and life, must he set foot
Upon this kingdom.

PALAMON   He's a blessèd man.
He shall see Thebes again, and call to arms
The bold young men that, when he bids 'em charge,
Fall on like fire. Arcite shall have a fortune,   257
If he dare make himself a worthy lover,
Yet in the field to strike a battle for her;   259
And if he lose her then, he's a cold coward.
How bravely may he bear himself to win her
If he be noble Arcite—thousand ways!
Were I at liberty, I would do things
Of such a virtuous greatness that this lady,
This blushing virgin, should take manhood to her   265
And seek to ravish me.

JAILER   My lord, for you
I have this charge too.

PALAMON   To discharge my life.   267

JAILER
No, but from this place to remove Your Lordship;
The windows are too open.

PALAMON   Devils take 'em
That are so envious to me! Prithee kill me.

JAILER
And hang for't afterward.

PALAMON   By this good light,
Had I a sword I would kill thee.

JAILER   Why, my lord?

PALAMON
Thou bring'st such pelting scurvy news continually,   273
Thou art not worthy life. I will not go.

204–5 Let . . . freedom If that opponent were to indicate a preference for engaging with you, not me, you could go ahead and exercise your free choice by engaging with that person. (The "opponent" in this argument has become Emilia, not a hypothetical warrior.) **208 Till . . . me** i.e., Until you behave worthily to me once again, by forgoing your claim to Emilia, the issue engages my honor   **209 hazard thee** put your life at hazard   **213–15 Oh . . . liberty** Would that you and I had but one hour of freedom from this prison   **220 to't** i.e., to the window frame. (Palamon will not allow Arcite to gaze any more at Emilia in the garden below their window.)   **223 leap** leap down into   **224 pitch** thrust myself   **227 honest** worthy   **233 goodly** handsome   **234 like** likely

235 blood breeding, lineage   **247 Still as** whenever   **248 be not** is not already   **257 Fall on** begin the battle.   **fortune** chance   **259 strike a battle** fight a battle, engage the enemy force   **265 take manhood to her** go on the offensive, like a male. (Palamon pictures himself here as the raped object of desire.)   **267 discharge my life** release me from life. (Playing sardonically on the Jailer's *charge*, "order," and on the idea of discharging a firearm.)   **273 pelting** paltry, contemptible

JAILER
Indeed you must, my lord.

PALAMON   May I see the garden?

JAILER
No.

PALAMON   Then I am resolved, I will not go.

JAILER
I must constrain you then; and, for you are dangerous, 277
I'll clap more irons on you.

PALAMON   Do, good keeper.
I'll shake 'em so, ye shall not sleep;
I'll make ye a new morris. Must I go?   280

JAILER
There is no remedy.

PALAMON   Farewell, kind window;
May rude wind never hurt thee.—Oh, my lady,
If ever thou hast felt what sorrow was,
Dream how I suffer!—Come, now bury me.   284

Exeunt Palamon and Jailer.

♣

2.3

Enter Arcite.

ARCITE
Banished the kingdom? 'Tis a benefit,
A mercy I must thank 'em for; but banished
The free enjoying of that face I die for,   3
Oh, 'twas a studied punishment, a death   4
Beyond imagination—such a vengeance
That, were I old and wicked, all my sins
Could never pluck upon me. Palamon,
Thou hast the start now; thou shalt stay and see
Her bright eyes break each morning 'gainst thy
    window
And let in life into thee; thou shalt feed
Upon the sweetness of a noble beauty
That nature nev'r exceeded, nor nev'r shall.
Good gods, what happiness has Palamon!
Twenty to one he'll come to speak to her,   14
And if she be as gentle as she's fair,
I know she's his; he has a tongue will tame
Tempests and make the wild rocks wanton.
Come what can come,
The worst is death. I will not leave the kingdom.
I know mine own is but a heap of ruins,   20
And no redress there; if I go, he has her.
I am resolved another shape shall make me   22
Or end my fortunes. Either way I am happy;
I'll see her, and be near her or no more.   24

*Enter four Country people and one with a garland
before them. [Arcite stands apart.]*

FIRST COUNTRYMAN   My masters, I'll be there, that's 25
certain.

SECOND COUNTRYMAN   And I'll be there.

THIRD COUNTRYMAN   And I.

FOURTH COUNTRYMAN   Why then, have with ye, boys! 29
'Tis but a chiding. Let the plough play today; I'll 30
tickle't out of the jades' tails tomorrow.   31

FIRST COUNTRYMAN   I am sure to have my wife as
jealous as a turkey; but that's all one. I'll go through; 33
let her mumble.

SECOND COUNTRYMAN   Clap her aboard tomorrow 35
night, and stow her, and all's made up again.

THIRD COUNTRYMAN   Ay, do but put a fescue in her 37
fist, and you shall see her take a new lesson out and be 38
a good wench. Do we all hold against the maying?   39

FOURTH COUNTRYMAN   Hold? What should ail us?   40

THIRD COUNTRYMAN   Arcas will be there.

SECOND COUNTRYMAN   And Sennois and Rycas, and
three better lads nev'r danced under green tree; and
ye know what wenches, ha! But will the dainty   44
dominie, the schoolmaster, keep touch, do you think? 45
For he does all, ye know.   46

THIRD COUNTRYMAN   He'll eat a hornbook e'er he fail. 47
Go to, the matter's too far driven between him and the 48
tanner's daughter to let slip now; and she must see the 49
Duke, and she must dance too.   50

FOURTH COUNTRYMAN   Shall we be lusty?   51

SECOND COUNTRYMAN   All the boys in Athens blow 52
wind i'th' breech on 's! And here I'll be and there   53
I'll be, for our town, and here again and there again. 54
Ha, boys, hey for the weavers!   55

FIRST COUNTRYMAN   This must be done i'th' woods.

FOURTH COUNTRYMAN   Oh, pardon me.   57

SECOND COUNTRYMAN   By any means, our thing of   58
learning says so; where he himself will edify the Duke 59
most parlously in our behalfs. He's excellent i'th' 60

---

25 **masters** sirs. (Used often among workmen and citizens.)
29–30 have . . . chiding I'll join you, boys; the worst thing that can
happen to me is a scolding (for not ploughing).   **30–1 I'll . . . tomorrow** i.e., I'll make up for lost time tomorrow by whipping the old
horses into working faster.   **33 that's all one** no matter.   **35 Clap her
aboard** Board her. The sexual wordplay continues in *stow her*, "place
your cargo belowdecks in her," and in *all's made up*: (1) all's supplied
for a journey (2) the quarrel is patched up (3) the hole is stopped up.
37 a fescue a pointer used in pointing out letters for children learning
to read   **38 take . . . out** learn a new lesson   **39 hold against the
maying** hold to our intention with respect to the May Day celebration.   **40 ail us** prevent us from taking part.   **44–5 dainty dominie**
fastidious schoolmaster   **45 keep touch** keep faith, keep his promise
46 he does all all depends on him   **47 hornbook** an alphabet, etc.
protected by a layer of cowhorn or similar animal horn cut thin
enough to be virtually transparent, used in classrooms   **48 Go to** (An
expression of impatience.)   **the matter's . . . driven** things have gone
too far   **49–50 she must see . . . too** she insists on seeing the Duke
and dancing too.   **51 lusty** jolly, lively.   **52–3 All . . . on 's!** i.e., May
all the lads of Athens have to pant and puff to keep up with us!
53–4 And . . . town And I'll be here, there, and everywhere in the
morris dance, for honor of our town   **55 hey . . . weavers!** hooray for
the weavers! (the guild to which the First Countryman evidently
belongs)   **57 Oh, pardon me** i.e., I beg to differ.   **58–9 By . . . so** In
the woods, certainly; our schoolmaster says so. (The morris dance
will be more fitting as part of the hunt in the woods; it is too rustic for
performance at court.)   **60 parlously** cleverly, amazingly

---

277 **for** since   280 **morris** a morris dance, in which the dancers wore
bells around their legs; the sound might be thought to resemble the
clanking of chains.   284 **bury me** i.e., remove me where I cannot see
Emilia, which will be tantamount to death.
2.3. Location: Outside Athens.
3 **die** would die   4 **studied** premeditated   14 **come** find occasion
20 **mine own** my own kingdom (Thebes)   22 **another shape** i.e., a
disguise   24 **no more** be no more, perish.

woods; bring him to th' plains, his learning makes no 61
cry. 62

THIRD COUNTRYMAN   We'll see the sports, then every
man to 's tackle. And, sweet companions, let's re- 64
hearse, by any means, before the ladies see us, and do
sweetly, and God knows what may come on't. 66

FOURTH COUNTRYMAN   Content. The sports once
ended, we'll perform. Away, boys, and hold! 68
[They start to go.]

ARCITE *[coming forward]*   By your leaves, honest 69
friends; pray you, whither go you?

FOURTH COUNTRYMAN   Whither? Why, what a question's that?

ARCITE   Yes, 'tis a question to me that know not.

THIRD COUNTRYMAN   To the games, my friend.

SECOND COUNTRYMAN *[to Arcite]*
Where were you bred, you know it not?

ARCITE   Not far, sir.
Are there such games today?

FIRST COUNTRYMAN   Yes, marry, are there,
And such as you never saw. The Duke himself
Will be in person there.

ARCITE   What pastimes are they?

SECOND COUNTRYMAN
Wrestling and running. *[To his companions]* 'Tis a
pretty fellow.

THIRD COUNTRYMAN *[to Arcite]*
Thou wilt not go along?

ARCITE   Not yet, sir.

FOURTH COUNTRYMAN   Well, sir,
Take your own time.—Come, boys.

FIRST COUNTRYMAN   My mind misgives me, 81
This fellow has a vengeance trick o'th' hip; 82
Mark how his body's made for't.

SECOND COUNTRYMAN   I'll be hanged, though,
If he dare venture. Hang him, plum porridge! 84
He wrestle? He roast eggs! Come, let's be gone, lads. 85
Exeunt four. [Arcite remains.]

ARCITE
This is an offered opportunity
I durst not wish for. Well I could have wrestled— 87
The best men called it excellent—and run
Swifter than wind upon a field of corn, 89
Curling the wealthy ears, never flew. I'll venture, 90
And in some poor disguise be there. Who knows
Whether my brows may not be girt with garlands,
And happiness prefer me to a place 93
Where I may ever dwell in sight of her?
Exit Arcite.

❖

2.4

Enter Jailer's Daughter, alone.

JAILER'S DAUGHTER
Why should I love this gentleman? 'Tis odds 1
He never will affect me. I am base, 2
My father the mean keeper of his prison, 3
And he a prince. To many him is hopeless,
To be his whore is witless. Out upon't, 5
What pushes are we wenches driven to 6
When fifteen once has found us! First I saw him; 7
I, seeing, thought he was a goodly man;
He has as much to please a woman in him—
If he please to bestow it so—as ever
These eyes yet looked on. Next I pitied him,
And so would any young wench, o' my conscience, 12
That ever dreamed, or vowed her maidenhead 13
To a young handsome man. Then I loved him,
Extremely loved him, infinitely loved him,
And yet he had a cousin, fair as he too.
But in my heart was Palamon, and there,
Lord, what a coil he keeps! To hear him 18
Sing in an evening, what a heaven it is!
And yet his songs are sad ones. Fairer spoken
Was never gentleman. When I come in
To bring him water in a morning, first
He bows his noble body, then salutes me thus: 23
"Fair, gentle maid, good morrow; may thy goodness
Get thee a happy husband." Once he kissed me;
I loved my lips the better ten days after.
Would he would do so ev'ry day! He grieves much,
And me as much to see his misery.
What should I do to make him know I love him?
For I would fain enjoy him. Say I ventured 30
To set him free? What says the law then? *[She snaps her
fingers]* Thus much
For law or kindred! I will do it,
And this night; ere tomorrow he shall love me.
Exit.

❖

2.5

*[A] short flourish of cornets, and shouts within.
Enter Theseus, Hippolyta, Pirithous, Emilia,
Arcite [disguised] with a garland, etc.*

THESEUS *[to Arcite]*
You have done worthily. I have not seen,
Since Hercules, a man of tougher sinews.
Whate'er you are, you run the best and wrestle 3
That these times can allow.

ARCITE   I am proud to please you. 4

61–2 bring . . . cry if we were to bring this morris dance and the
schoolmaster's presentation of it to court, his learning would look out
of place, like confused hunting dogs no longer yelping after their
prey.   **64 tackle** i.e., bells and other gear for the morris dance.
66 on't of it.   **68 hold** hold to your promise.   **69 honest** worthy
81–2 My mind . . . hip I suspect that this fellow may have a fearsome
ability to catch his opponent on the hip in wrestling   **84 plum porridge** i.e., weakling, milksop. (Literally, stewed fruit.)   **85 He roast
eggs!** i.e., He might as soon turn cook as wrestler.   **87 Well . . . wrestled** I used to know how to wrestle well   **89–90 Swifter . . . flew**
swifter than the wind ever flew through a grainfield, curling back the
fruitful ears of the grain.   **93 happiness prefer** good fortune advance
2.4. Location: Somewhere near the prison.
1 'Tis odds The likelihood is that   **2 affect** love.   **base** of low social
station   **3 mean** lowly   **5 Out upon't** (An expression of dismay.)
6 pushes exertions, extremes   **7 fifteen** the age of fifteen   **12 o' my
conscience** on my word of honor   **13 vowed** dedicated   **18 coil he
keeps** tumult he stirs up.   **23 salutes** greets   **30 fain** willingly
2.5. Location: The arena for wrestling, running, etc., near Athens.
3 run . . . wrestle are the best runner and wrestler   **4 allow** boast of.

THESEUS
   What country bred you?
ARCITE   This; but far off, prince.
THESEUS
   Are you a gentleman?
ARCITE   My father said so,
   And to those gentle uses gave me life.   7
THESEUS
   Are you his heir?
ARCITE   His youngest, sir.
THESEUS   Your father
   Sure is a happy sire, then. What proves you?   9
ARCITE
   A little of all noble qualities.   10
   I could have kept a hawk and well have hallooed   11
   To a deep cry of dogs; I dare not praise   12
   My feat in horsemanship, yet they that knew me   12
   Would say it was my best piece; last, and greatest,   14
   I would be thought a soldier.
THESEUS   You are perfect.   15
PIRITHOUS
   Upon my soul, a proper man.
EMILIA   He is so.   16
PIRITHOUS [to Hippolyta]
   How do you like him, lady?
HIPPOLYTA   I admire him.   17
   I have not seen so young a man, so noble—
   If he say true—of his sort.
EMILIA   Believe,   19
   His mother was a wondrous handsome woman;
   His face, methinks, goes that way.
HIPPOLYTA   But his body
   And fiery mind illustrate a brave father.
PIRITHOUS
   Mark how his virtue, like a hidden sun,   23
   Breaks through his baser garments.
HIPPOLYTA   He's well got, sure.   24
THESEUS [to Arcite]
   What made you seek this place, sir?
ARCITE   Noble Theseus,
   To purchase name, and do my ablest service   26
   To such a well-found wonder as thy worth;   27
   For only in thy court, of all the world,
   Dwells fair-eyed honor.
PIRITHOUS   All his words are worthy.
THESEUS [to Arcite]
   Sir, we are much indebted to your travel,   30
   Nor shall you lose your wish.—Pirithous,

Dispose of this fair gentleman.
PIRITHOUS   Thanks, Theseus.   32
   [To Arcite] Whate'er you are, you're mine, and I shall
      give you
   To a most noble service, to this lady,
   This bright young virgin; pray observe her goodness.   35
   You have honored her fair birthday with your virtues,
   And as your due you're hers. Kiss her fair hand, sir.
ARCITE
   Sir, you're a noble giver. [To Emilia] Dearest beauty,
   Thus let me seal my vowed faith.
                          [He kisses her hand.]
                                When your servant,
   Your most unworthy creature, but offends you,   40
   Command him die, he shall.
EMILIA   That were too cruel.
   If you deserve well, sir, I shall soon see't.
   You're mine, and somewhat better than your rank
   I'll use you.
PIRITHOUS [to Arcite]
   I'll see you furnished, and because you say
   You are a horseman, I must needs entreat you
   This afternoon to ride—but 'tis a rough one.   47
ARCITE
   I like him better, prince; I shall not then
   Freeze in my saddle.
THESEUS [to Hippolyta]   Sweet, you must be ready—
   And you, Emilia, and you, friend, and all—
   Tomorrow by the sun, to do observance   51
   To flow'ry May in Dian's wood.—Wait well, sir,
   Upon your mistress.—Emily, I hope
   He shall not go afoot.
EMILIA   That were a shame, sir,
   While I have horses. [To Arcite] Take your choice; and
      what
   You want at any time, let me but know it.   56
   If you serve faithfully, I dare assure you
   You'll find a loving mistress.
ARCITE   If I do not,
   Let me find that my father ever hated: 59
   Disgrace and blows.
THESEUS   Go lead the way; you have won it.   60
   It shall be so: you shall receive all dues
   Fit for the honor you have won; 'twere wrong else.—
   Sister, beshrew my heart, you have a servant   63
   That, if I were a woman, would be master;
   But you are wise.
EMILIA   I hope too wise for that, sir.
                                Flourish. Exeunt omnes.

❧

7 to . . . life my father bred me to the accomplishments of a gentleman.   **9 What proves you?** What accomplishments do you have to demonstrate your gentlemanly breeding?   **10 qualities** accomplishments.   **11 could have kept** was trained to keep   **12 deep cry** deepmouthed yelping (of hounds in pursuit of game)   **13 feat** skill   **14 piece** example, accomplishment   **15 would be thought** profess myself to be   **16 proper** excellent, handsome   **17 admire** marvel at   **19 sort** class, rank.   **Believe** You may rest assured that   **23 virtue** moral and personal excellence, strength   **24 got** begotten, born   **26 purchase name** gain reputation   **27 well-found** well-deserved   **30 travel** (1) coming to this court (2) endeavoring so nobly (in the contests)

32 Dispose of make provision for, find a place for   **35 observe** show respect for, honor   **40 but offends you** offends you in the smallest way   **47 a rough one** i.e., a temperamental horse.   **51 by the sun** at dawn   **56 want** lack   **59 that** that which   **60 it** i.e., the honor of leading the return to court.   **63 Sister** Sister-in-law.   **servant** (Arcite has formally become Emilia's "servant" in the sense of being her courtly admirer, devoted to the service of his "mistress," line 58, not her lover in an explicitly sexual sense.)

2.6

Enter Jailer's Daughter, alone.

JAILER'S DAUGHTER
Let all the dukes and all the devils roar!
He is at liberty. I have ventured for him,   2
And out I have brought him. To a little wood
A mile hence I have sent him, where a cedar,
Higher than all the rest, spreads like a plane,   5
Fast by a brook, and there he shall keep close   6
Till I provide him files and food, for yet
His iron bracelets are not off. O Love,   8
What a stout-hearted child thou art! My father
Durst better have endured cold iron than done it.   10
I love him beyond love and beyond reason,   11
Or wit, or safety. I have made him know it;   12
I care not, I am desperate. If the law
Find me and then condemn me for't, some wenches,
Some honest-hearted maids, will sing my dirge,
And tell to memory my death was noble,
Dying almost a martyr. That way he takes   17
I purpose is my way too. Sure, he cannot
Be so unmanly as to leave me here.
If he do, maids will not so easily
Trust men again. And yet he has not thanked me
For what I have done; no, not so much as kissed me,
And that, methinks, is not so well; nor scarcely
Could I persuade him to become a free man,
He made such scruples of the wrong he did
To me and to my father. Yet I hope,
When he considers more, this love of mine
Will take more root within him. Let him do
What he will with me, so he use me kindly;   29
For use me so he shall, or I'll proclaim him,
And to his face, no man. I'll presently   31
Provide him necessaries and pack my clothes up,
And where there is a path of ground I'll venture,   33
So he be with me. By him, like a shadow   34
I'll ever dwell. Within this hour the hubbub
Will be all o'er the prison; I am then
Kissing the man they look for. Farewell, father!
Get many more such prisoners, and such daughters,   38
And shortly you may keep yourself. Now to him.   39

[Exit.]

3.1

*Cornets in sundry places. Noise and hallooing as
people a-maying. Enter Arcite, alone.*

ARCITE
The Duke has lost Hippolyta; each took   1
A several laund. This is a solemn rite   2
They owe bloomed May, and the Athenians pay it   3
To th' heart of ceremony. O Queen Emilia,   4
Fresher than May, sweeter
Than her gold buttons on the boughs, or all   6
Th'enameled knacks o'th' mead or garden—yea,   7
We challenge too the bank of any nymph   8
That makes the stream seem flowers; thou, O jewel   9
O'th' wood, o'th' world, hast likewise blessed a pace   10
With thy sole presence; in thy rumination   11
That I, poor man, might eftsoons come between   12
And chop on some cold thought! Thrice blessèd
chance   13
To drop on such a mistress, expectation   14
Most guiltless on't! Tell me, O Lady Fortune,   15
Next after Emily my sovereign, how far   16
I may be proud. She takes strong note of me,   17
Hath made me near her, and this beauteous morn,
The prim'st of all the year, presents me with   19
A brace of horses; two such steeds might well
Be by a pair of kings backed, in a field   21
That their crowns' titles tried. Alas, alas,   22
Poor cousin Palamon, poor prisoner, thou
So little dream'st upon my fortune that
Thou think'st thyself the happier thing, to be
So near Emilia! Me thou deem'st at Thebes,
And therein wretched, although free; but if
Thou knew'st my mistress breathed on me, and that
I eared her language, lived in her eye, O coz,   29
What passion would enclose thee!

*Enter Palamon as out of a bush, with his shackles;
[he] bends his fist at Arcite.*

PALAMON   Traitor kinsman,   30

2.6. Location: Athens. Somewhere near the prison.
2 He Palamon.   **ventured** risked dangers   **5 plane** plane tree,
sycamore   **6 Fast by** near by.   **close** concealed   **8 Love** Cupid
10 Durst . . . it would rather have encountered armed assailants than
to have done this deed.   **11 him** Palamon   **12 wit** human understanding   **17 way** direction, path   **29 so** provided.   **kindly**
(1) benevolently (2) as my sexual nature requires   **31 no man** (1) no
gentleman (2) impotent.   **33 a path of ground** a path to be found
anywhere (in the forest)   **34 So** provided that   **38 Get** (1) Acquire
(2) Beget   **39 And . . . yourself** i.e., and soon you can have the jail to
yourself, with neither prisoners nor daughter.   **him** Palamon.

3.1. Location: A forest near Athens.
0.1 in sundry places i.e., from various locations offstage.   **1–2 took . . .
laund** headed for a different glade.   **3 bloomed** in full blossom   **4 To
. . . ceremony** with full ceremony.   **6 buttons** buds   **7 Th'enameled
knacks** the ornamental delicacies (i.e., flowers).   **mead** meadow
8–9 We . . . flowers i.e., I dare compare my mistress's beauty with any
bank of a stream belonging to a guardian spirit (or nymph) and reflecting its flowered beauty in the water   **10 pace** narrow passage (through
the woods)   **11–15 in thy . . . on't!** O, would that I, poor man, meditating on you, might enter into your thoughts from time to time and, by
interrupting them, bring about an exchange of some cold thought for
thoughts of love! What a thrice blessed fortune, to happen upon such a
mistress, when least expecting to do so!   **16–17 how . . . proud** i.e., how
far may I bask in good fortune like this without growing worrisomely
overconfident.   **17 She . . . me** Emilia pays a lot of attention to me
19 prim'st finest   **21 backed** mounted   **21–2 field . . . tried** battlefield
on which their titles to their crowns were being contested.   **29 eared . . .
eye** took in her speech at my ear and lived under her gaze.   **coz** cousin
30 passion anger.   **enclose thee** enfold you in its grasp.   **s.d. as out of
a bush** i.e., either through a door understood to represent a hiding place
in the forest, or possibly out of a stage structure provided for this act.
bends shakes, aims

Thou shouldst perceive my passion if these signs
Of prisonment were off me, and this hand
But owner of a sword. By all oaths in one,
I and the justice of my love would make thee
A confessed traitor, O thou most perfidious
That ever gently looked, the void'st of honor   36
That ev'r bore gentle token, falsest cousin   37
That ever blood made kin! Call'st thou her thine?
I'll prove it in my shackles, with these hands,   39
Void of appointment, that thou liest, and art   40
A very thief in love, a chaffy lord,   41
Not worth the name of villain. Had I a sword,
And these house-clogs away—

ARCITE   Dear cousin Palamon—   43
PALAMON
Cozener Arcite, give me language such   44
As thou hast showed me feat.
ARCITE   Not finding in   45
The circuit of my breast any gross stuff   46
To form me like your blazon holds me to   47
This gentleness of answer: 'tis your passion   48
That thus mistakes, the which, to you being enemy,   49
Cannot to me be kind. Honor and honesty   50
I cherish and depend on, howsoev'r
You skip them in me, and with them, fair coz,   52
I'll maintain my proceedings. Pray be pleased   53
To show in generous terms your griefs, since that   54
Your question's with your equal, who professes   55
To clear his own way with the mind and sword   56
Of a true gentleman.
PALAMON   That thou durst, Arcite!   57
ARCITE
My coz, my coz, you have been well advertised   58
How much I dare; you've seen me use my sword
Against th'advice of fear. Sure of another   60
You would not hear me doubted, but your silence   61
Should break out, though i'th' sanctuary.
PALAMON   Sir,   62
I have seen you move in such a place which well   63
Might justify your manhood; you were called

A good knight and a bold. But the whole week's not
fair   65
If any day it rain; their valiant temper   66
Men lose when they incline to treachery,
And then they fight like compelled bears—would fly   68
Were they not tied.
ARCITE   Kinsman, you might as well
Speak this and act it in your glass as to   70
His ear which now disdains you.
PALAMON   Come up to me;
Quit me of these cold gyves, give me a sword,   72
Though it be rusty, and the charity
Of one meal lend me. Come before me then,
A good sword in thy hand, and do but say
That Emily is thine, I will forgive
The trespass thou hast done me—yea, my life,   77
If then thou carry't; and brave souls in shades   78
That have died manly, which will seek of me
Some news from earth, they shall get none but this:
That thou art brave and noble.
ARCITE   Be content;
Again betake you to your hawthorn house.   82
With counsel of the night I will be here   83
With wholesome viands. These impediments   84
Will I file off. You shall have garments and
Perfumes to kill the smell o'th' prison. After,
When you shall stretch yourself and say but "Arcite, 87
I am in plight," there shall be at your choice   88
Both sword and armor.
PALAMON   O you heavens, dares any   89
So noble bear a guilty business? None   90
But only Arcite; therefore none but Arcite
In this kind is so bold.
ARCITE   Sweet Palamon—
PALAMON
I do embrace you and your offer; for   93
Your offer do't I only; sir, your person   94
Without hypocrisy I may not wish   95
More than my sword's edge on't.

Wind horns off. Cornets [sounded].

ARCITE   You hear the horns. 96
Enter your muset, lest this match between 's   97

---

36 **gently looked** had the appearance of a gentleman 37 **bore gentle token** wore signs of gentility 39 **in my shackles** even with these shackles on 40 **Void of appointment** lacking accouterments of arms 41 **chaffy** worthless as chaff 43 **house-clogs** shackles confining the prisoner to his cell 44 **Cozener** Deceiver. (With a familiar pun on *cousin* in line 43.) 44–5 **give . . . feat** match your words to your (perfidious) deeds. (*Feat* means "apt, apropos.") 45–8 **Not . . . answer** Not finding anything base in my conduct that corresponds to your accusation, I answer gently. (A *blazon* is a description or catalogue, as on a shield in heraldry.) 48 **passion** anger 49–50 **the which . . . kind** which show of anger, wherein you are your own worst enemy, makes you also unfair to me. 52 **skip** fail to see 53–6 **Pray . . . way** Please use courteous speech in setting forth your grievances, since your dispute is with one who is your equal, and who affirms his intention of vindicating his own behavior 57 **That thou durst** If only you would dare to do that 58 **advertised** informed, put on notice 60–2 **Against . . . sanctuary** when prudence would advise caution. Surely you would not permit my honor to be doubted by some other person; you would break silence to defend me even if you were in hiding. 63 **place** i.e., field of battle or lists for a tournament

65–6 **But . . . rain** i.e., Unless you are perfectly consistent all the time in honorable behavior, the evidence of your bravery at other times proves nothing about the present instance 66 **temper** temperament 68 **compelled bears** (In bear-baiting, bears were tied to a stake and attacked by dogs.) **would** who would 70 **in your glass** to yourself, in your mirror 72 **Quit me of** release me from. **gyves** shackles 77 **trespass** insult, wrong 78 **carry't** win the fight between us. **shades** the dark world of Hades, the abode of the dead 82 **betake . . . house** i.e., go to your place of hiding in the woods. 83 **With . . . night** Under cover of darkness, witnessed only by the night 84 **viands** food. 87 **stretch** rouse 88 **in plight** in readiness 89–90 **dares . . . business?** dare anyone venture so nobly in a cause so guilty? 93–6 **for . . . on't** (Palamon accepts Arcite's offer, but without acknowledging any personal thanks to one whom he frankly wishes only to kill.) 96 s.d. **Wind horns off** Sound horns offstage (indicative of a hunt). 97 **muset** meuse or opening in a hedge used by hunted game for concealment

Be crossed ere met. Give me your hand; farewell. 98
I'll bring you every needful thing; I pray you,
Take comfort and be strong.

PALAMON   Pray hold your promise,
And do the deed with a bent brow. Most certain 101
You love me not; be rough with me, and pour
This oil out of your language. By this air, 103
I could for each word give a cuff, my stomach 104
Not reconciled by reason.

ARCITE   Plainly spoken.
Yet pardon me hard language. When I spur 106
My horse, I chide him not; content and anger
In me have but one face.

Wind horns.

                         Hark, sir, they call 108
The scattered to the banquet. You must guess 109
I have an office there.

PALAMON   Sir, your attendance 110
Cannot please heaven, and I know your office
Unjustly is achieved.

ARCITE   'Tis a good title. 112
I am persuaded this question, sick between's, 113
By bleeding must be cured. I am a suitor 114
That to your sword you will bequeath this plea, 115
And talk of it no more.

PALAMON   But this one word:
You are going now to gaze upon my mistress—
For note you, mine she is—

ARCITE   Nay then—

PALAMON   Nay, pray you—
You talk of feeding me to breed me strength;
You are going now to look upon a sun
That strengthens what it looks on. There you have
A vantage o'er me, but enjoy't till
I may enforce my remedy. Farewell.

Exeunt [separately, Palamon as into his hawthorn house].

❖

3.2

Enter Jailer's Daughter alone [with a file].

JAILER'S DAUGHTER
He has mistook the brake I meant, is gone 1
After his fancy. 'Tis now well-nigh morning. 2
No matter; would it were perpetual night,
And darkness lord o'th' world. Hark, 'tis a wolf!

In me hath grief slain fear, and but for one thing,
I care for nothing, and that's Palamon.
I reck not if the wolves would jaw me, so 7
He had this file. What if I hallooed for him?
I cannot halloo. If I whooped, what then?
If he not answered, I should call a wolf,
And do him but that service. I have heard 11
Strange howls this livelong night; why may't not be
They have made prey of him? He has no weapons;
He cannot run; the jingling of his gyves
Might call fell things to listen, who have in them 15
A sense to know a man unarmed, and can
Smell where resistance is. I'll set it down 17
He's torn to pieces; they howled many together,
And then they fed on him. So much for that.
Be bold to ring the bell. How stand I then? 20
All's chared when he is gone. No, no, I lie; 21
My father's to be hanged for his escape, 22
Myself to beg, if I prized life so much 23
As to deny my act, but that I would not, 24
Should I try death by dozens. I am moped; 25
Food took I none these two days,
Sipped some water. I have not closed mine eyes
Save when my lids scoured off their brine. Alas, 28
Dissolve, my life! Let not my sense unsettle, 29
Lest I should drown, or stab, or hang myself.
O state of nature, fail together in me, 31
Since thy best props are warped! So which way now? 32
The best way is the next way to a grave; 33
Each errant step beside is torment. Lo, 34
The moon is down, the crickets chirp, the screech owl
Calls in the dawn. All offices are done 36
Save what I fail in; but the point is this—
An end, and that is all. 38

                                        Exit.

❖

3.3

Enter Arcite with meat, wine, and files.

ARCITE
I should be near the place.—Ho! Cousin Palamon!
PALAMON [*from the bush*]
Arcite?
ARCITE   The same. I have brought you food and files.

---

98 **crossed ere met** thwarted before it takes place.   101 **bent** frowning   103 **oil** i.e., calming and reconciling words   104 **stomach** anger   106 **pardon . . . language** pardon me if I refrain from using harsh speech.   108 **have but one face** look outwardly alike.   109 **The scattered** the hunters, who have separated during the hunt   110 **office** function (of waiting on Emilia)   112 **'Tis . . . title** It is a title I have justly earned.   113–15 **I am . . . plea** I am convinced that the contention that afflicts us both can be cured only by our swords, drawing blood as a doctor bleeds patients to effect a cure. I beg of you to refer this lawsuit to your sword
3.2. Location: The forest.
1 **brake** thicket   2 **After his fancy** as his wishes prompt him.

7 **reck** care.   **jaw** gnaw.   **so** provided   11 **And . . . service** i.e., and accomplish nothing more than to bring a wolf who would then threaten Palamon's life as well as mine.   15 **fell things** savage beasts   17 **set it down** record it as for a fact that   20 **the bell** i.e., the bell rung by the bellman to announce a person's death.   **How stand I** What plight am I in   21 **chared** done for. (To *chare* is to accomplish a turn of work, a chore.)   22 **his** Palamon's   23 **Myself to beg** I would be forced to beg for my living (as the daughter of an executed man)   24 **deny my act** deny allowing Palamon to escape   25 **Should . . . dozens** even if I had to suffer death many times or in many forms.   **moped** stupefied, dazed   28 **scoured . . . brine** skimmed off the briny tears from my eyes.   29 **sense** sanity   31 **state of nature** existence.   **together** altogether   32 **props** supports   33 **next** nearest   34 **Each . . . beside** each step that deviates from the quickest way to the grave   36 **offices** duties   38 **An end** i.e., death
3.3. Location: The forest, as before.

Come forth and fear not. Here's no Theseus.

Enter Palamon [as out of a bush].

PALAMON
Nor none so honest, Arcite.

ARCITE   That's no matter;
We'll argue that hereafter. Come, take courage;
You shall not die thus beastly. Here, sir, drink;
I know you are faint. Then I'll talk further with you.

PALAMON
Arcite, thou mightst now poison me.

ARCITE   I might;
But I must fear you first. Sit down and, good now,   9
No more of these vain parleys. Let us not,
Having our ancient reputation with us,   11
Make talk for fools and cowards. To your health, sir!
                                        [He drinks.]

PALAMON
Do.

ARCITE   Pray sit down, then, and let me entreat you,
By all the honesty and honor in you,
No mention of this woman; 'twill disturb us.
We shall have time enough.

PALAMON   Well, sir, I'll pledge you.   16
                                        [He drinks.]

ARCITE
Drink a good hearty draught; it breeds good blood,
  man.   17
Do not you feel it thaw you?

PALAMON
Stay, I'll tell you after a draught or two more.

ARCITE
Spare it not; the Duke has more, coz. Eat now.

PALAMON
Yes.   *[He eats.]*

ARCITE   I am glad you have so good a stomach.   21

PALAMON
I am gladder I have so good meat to't.

ARCITE
Is't not mad lodging here in the wild woods, cousin?

PALAMON
Yes, for them that have wild consciences.

ARCITE   How tastes your victuals?
Your hunger needs no sauce, I see.

PALAMON   Not much.
But if it did, yours is too tart, sweet cousin.   27
What is this?

ARCITE   Venison.

PALAMON   'Tis a lusty meat.   28
Give me more wine. Here, Arcite, to the wenches
We have known in our days!   *[He drinks.]*
                The Lord Steward's daughter—
Do you remember her?

ARCITE   After you, coz.   31

9 **must** should have to.   **good now** i.e., please, for goodness' sake
11 **ancient** long-established   16 **pledge** drink a toast to   17 **breeds
good blood** (Wine was thought to resupply the blood.)   21 **stomach**
appetite.   27 **yours . . . tart** (1) your sauce is too sharp (2) your insolence is too keen   28 **lusty** agreeable, fortifying; lust-provoking
31 **After you** i.e., Go ahead with your toast, and I'll reciprocate

PALAMON
She loved a black-haired man.

ARCITE   She did so. Well, sir?

PALAMON
And I have heard some call him Arcite, and—

ARCITE
Out with't, faith.

PALAMON   She met him in an arbor.
What did she there, coz? Play o'th' virginals?   35

ARCITE
Something she did, sir.

PALAMON   Made her groan a month for't—   36
Or two, or three, or ten.

ARCITE   The marshal's sister   37
Had her share, too, as I remember, cousin,
Else there be tales abroad. You'll pledge her?

PALAMON   Yes.   39
                                        [They drink.]

ARCITE
A pretty brown wench 'tis. There was a time   40
When young men went a-hunting—and a wood,
And a broad beech—and thereby hangs a tale.
Heigh ho!

PALAMON   For Emily, upon my life! Fool,
Away with this strained mirth. I say again,
That sigh was breathed for Emily. Base cousin,
Dar'st thou break first?

ARCITE   You are wide.

PALAMON   By heaven and earth, 46
There's nothing in thee honest.

ARCITE   Then I'll leave you;
You are a beast now.

PALAMON   As thou mak'st me, traitor.

ARCITE
There's all things needful: files, and shirts, and
  perfumes.
I'll come again some two hours hence and bring
That that shall quiet all.

PALAMON   A sword and armor.   51

ARCITE
Fear me not. You are now too foul. Farewell.   52
Get off your trinkets; you shall want naught.

PALAMON   Sirrah—   53

ARCITE
I'll hear no more.   *Exit.*

PALAMON   If he keep touch, he dies for't.   54
                        Exit, [as into the bush].

❧

35 **virginals** a spinet-like keyboard instrument. (With sexual suggestion here.)   36–7 **groan . . . ten** i.e., suffer a pregnancy. (*Ten* is an
approximation for nine).   39 **tales** false rumors   40 **brown** dark-
complexioned, brunette   46 **break** i.e., break our convenant not to
speak of Emilia.   **wide** wide of the mark.   51 **quiet** put an end to
52 **Fear me not** i.e., Don't worry about my not doing all I promised.
(Palamon has just reiterated his demands.)   **foul** beastly.   53 **trinkets** i.e., the shackles, still to be filed off.   **want naught** lack nothing.
54 **keep touch** keeps his promise

3.4

Enter Jailer's Daughter.

JAILER'S DAUGHTER
I am very cold, and all the stars are out too,
The little stars and all, that look like aglets.   2
The sun has seen my folly.—Palamon!—
Alas, no; he's in heaven. Where am I now?
Yonder's the sea, and there's a ship. How't tumbles!
And there's a rock lies watching under water.
Now, now, it beats upon it; now, now, now,
There's a leak sprung, a sound one. How they cry!   8
Open her before the wind, you'll lose all else.   9
Up with a course or two, and tack about, boys.   10
Good night, good night, you're gone. I am very
    hungry;
Would I could find a fine frog! He would tell me
News from all parts o'th' world. Then would I make
A carrack of a cockleshell, and sail   14
By east and north-east to the king of pygmies,
For he tells fortunes rarely. Now my father,   16
Twenty to one, is trussed up in a trice   17
Tomorrow morning. I'll say never a word.
(Sing)
        For I'll cut my green coat a foot above my knee,
        And I'll clip my yellow locks an inch below
            mine e'e;
        Hey, nonny, nonny, nonny.
            He s' buy me a white cut, forth for to ride,   22
            And I'll go seek him through the world that is
                so wide;
        Hey, nonny, nonny, nonny.
Oh, for a prick now, like a nightingale,   25
To put my breast against! I shall sleep like a top else.
                                                            Exit.

❖

3.[5]

*Enter a schoolmaster [Gerald], six Countrymen,
[one of whom is dressed as a] babion, five
Wenches, with a taborer [Timothy].*

SCHOOLMASTER   Fie, Fie,
What tediosity and disinsanity   2
Is here among ye? Have my rudiments   3

Been labored so long with ye, milked unto ye,
And, by a figure, even the very plum broth   5
And marrow of my understanding laid upon ye?   6
And do you still cry "Where?" and "How?" and
    "Wherefore?"
You most coarse frieze capacities, ye jean judgments,   8
Have I said, "Thus let be," and "There let be,"
And "Then let be," and no man understand me?
Proh deum, medius fidius, ye are all dunces!   11
Forwhy, here stand I. Here the Duke comes. There are
    you,   12
Close in the thicket. The Duke appears. I meet him,   13
And unto him I utter learnèd things
And many figures. He hears, and nods, and hums,   15
And then cries, "Rare!", and I go forward. At length   16
I fling my cap up; mark there! Then do you,
As once did Meleager and the boar,   18
Break comely out before him. Like true lovers,
Cast yourselves in a body decently,
And sweetly, by a figure, trace and turn, boys.   21
FIRST COUNTRYMAN
And sweetly we will do it, Master Gerald.
SECOND COUNTRYMAN
Draw up the company. Where's the taborer?
THIRD COUNTRYMAN *[calling]*
Why, Timothy!
TABORER   Here, my mad boys. Have at ye!   24
SCHOOLMASTER
But I say, where's their women?
FOURTH COUNTRYMAN   Here's Friz and Maudline.
SECOND COUNTRYMAN
And little Luce with the white legs, and bouncing
    Barbery.   26
FIRST COUNTRYMAN
And freckled Nell, that never failed her master.
SCHOOLMASTER
Where be your ribbons, maids? Swim with your
    bodies,   28
And carry it sweetly and deliverly,   29
And now and then a favor and a frisk.   30
NELL
Let us alone, sir.
SCHOOLMASTER   Where's the rest o'th' music?   31

3.4. Location: The forest, as before.
2 aglets spangles, ornamental studs peeping through eyelet-holes.
8 sound robust   **9 Open her** Unfurl her sails. (The talk of storms and sailing vessels is indicative of the Daughter's madness and is filled with sexual double meanings, as in the leaky vessel of line 8.)
10 course sails furled on the lower yard until they are hauled up and unfurled   **14 carrack** large merchant ship or fighting vessel
16 rarely excellently.   **17 is . . . trice** will be hanged quickly
22 s' buy shall buy.   **cut** common laboring horse (with cut tail or a gelding). Also a slang word suggesting the female sexual anatomy.
25 prick thorn, against which the nightingale was thought to lean in order to stay awake. (With bawdy suggestion.)
3.5. Location: The forest still.
0.2 babion baboon   **0.3 taborer** player on the tabor or small drum (and probably on the pipe as well)   **2 tediosity and disinsanity** pedantic Latinisms for *tediousness and complete folly*   **3 rudiments** basic teachings

5 by a figure to use a figure of speech   **5–6 plum . . . marrow** i.e., essence   **8 frieze capacities** persons with homespun mental capacities.   **jean** made of twilled cotton (named originally for Genoa)
11 Proh . . . fidius So help me the God of faith   **12 Forwhy** Wherefore, because   **13 Close** hidden   **15 figures** figures of speech.
16 Rare! Remarkable, excellent!   **18 Meleager and the boar** Evidently the Schoolmaster instructs the rustics to present themselves before Duke Theseus as though acting out the story of the Greek warrior's slaying of the Calydonian boar; Hippolyta, at 1.1.78–9, is seemingly associated with the story. They are to come forward gracefully (*break comely out*), arrange themselves in order (*cast . . . decently*), and dance (*by a figure, trace and turn*). To trace is to step, "tread a measure," dance.   **21 trace** step, "tread a measure," dance   **24 Have at ye!** i.e., Here we go, have a go at it.   **26 bouncing** strapping, plump   **28 Swim** Move gracefully   **29 carry it** execute the dance movement.   **deliverly** nimbly   **30 favor** gesture of friendly regard, such as bowing or blowing a kiss.   **frisk** caper, jig.   **31 Let us alone** Leave it to us.   **music** musicians.

THIRD COUNTRYMAN
Dispersed, as you commanded.

SCHOOLMASTER   Couple then,   32
And see what's wanting. Where's the babion?—   33
My friend, carry your tail without offense
Or scandal to the ladies; and be sure
You tumble with audacity and manhood,
And when you bark, do it with judgment.

BABION   Yes, sir.

SCHOOLMASTER
Quousque tandem? Here is a woman wanting.   38

FOURTH COUNTRYMAN
We may go whistle; all the fat's i'th' fire.   39

SCHOOLMASTER   We have,
As learnèd authors utter, washed a tile;   40
We have been *fatuus* and labored vainly.   41

SECOND COUNTRYMAN
This is that scornful piece, that scurvy hilding   42
That gave her promise faithfully she would be here—
Cicely, the seamster's daughter.   44
The next gloves that I give her shall be dogskin.   45
Nay, an she fail me once—you can tell, Arcas,
She swore by wine and bread she would not break.   47

SCHOOLMASTER   An eel and woman,
A learnèd poet says, unless by th' tail
And with thy teeth thou hold, will either fail.   50
In manners this was false position.   51

FIRST COUNTRYMAN
A fire ill take her! Does she flinch now?

THIRD COUNTRYMAN   What   52
Shall we determine, sir?

SCHOOLMASTER   Nothing;   53
Our business is become a nullity,
Yea, and a woeful and a piteous nullity.

FOURTH COUNTRYMAN
Now, when the credit of our town lay on it,
Now to be frampold, now to piss o'th' nettle!   57
Go thy ways, I'll remember thee, I'll fit thee!   58

Enter Jailer's Daughter.

JAILER'S DAUGHTER [*sings*]
The *George Alow* came from the south,   59
From the coast of Barbary-a;
And there he met with brave gallants of war,   61
By one, by two, by three-a.

"Well hailed, well hailed, you jolly gallants,
And whither now are you bound-a?
Oh, let me have your company
Till I come to the sound-a."

There was three fools fell out about an owlet—

[*She sings*]
The one he said it was an owl,   68
The other he said nay,
The third he said it was a hawk,
And her bells were cut away.   71

THIRD COUNTRYMAN
There's a dainty madwoman, master,
Comes i'th' nick, as mad as March hare.   73
It we can get her dance, we are made again.   74
I warrant her, she'll do the rarest gambols.   75

FIRST COUNTRYMAN
A madwoman? We are made, boys.

SCHOOLMASTER [*to the Jailer's Daughter*]
And are you mad, good woman?

JAILER'S DAUGHTER
I would be sorry else. Give me your hand.

SCHOOLMASTER   Why?

JAILER'S DAUGHTER   I can tell your fortune.
You are a fool. Tell ten; I have posed him. Buzz!   81
Friend, you must eat no white bread; if you do,
Your teeth will bleed extremely. Shall we dance, ho?
I know you, you're a tinker. Sirrah tinker,   84
Stop no more holes but what you should.

SCHOOLMASTER   *Dii boni!*   85
A tinker, damsel?

JAILER'S DAUGHTER   Or a conjurer.
Raise me a devil now, and let him play   87
Qui passa o'th' bells and bones.

SCHOOLMASTER   Go take her,   88
And fluently persuade her to a peace.   89
Et opus exegi, quod nec Iovis ira, nec ignis.
Strike up, and lead her in.

SECOND COUNTRYMAN   Come, lass, let's trip it.   91

JAILER'S DAUGHTER   I'll lead.

THIRD COUNTRYMAN   Do, do.

SCHOOLMASTER
Persuasively and cunningly.

Wind horns.

Away, boys!   94
I hear the horns. Give me some meditation,   95

---

32 Couple Arrange yourself in pairs   **33 wanting** lacking.
38 *Quousque tandem?* How long, then? (From the beginning of Cicero's Latin oration *Contra Catiline:* "How long, then, Catiline, will you abuse our patience?")   **39 We . . . fire** i.e., We are out of luck, all's come to nothing.   **40 washed a tile** i.e., striven in vain
41 *fatuus* foolish   **42 This . . . hilding** That's a scornful wench, that wretched jade   **44 seamster's** tailor's   **45 dogskin** cheap leather.
47 by wine and bread by the Mass.   **break** break her promise.
50 either fail both prove too slippery. (Proverbial.)   **51 In . . . position** i.e., Cicely's failed promise was a false assertion in logic.
52 A fire . . . her! (1) May a fire consume her! (2) May venereal disease infect her!   **53 determine** decide to do   **57 be frampold . . . piss o'th' nettle** be ill-tempered . . . recalcitrant.   **58 Go . . . fit thee** Go right ahead, I'll be even with you. (Said to the absent Cicely.)   **59 The *George Alow*** (This ship was featured in a popular ballad, of which the Jailer's Daughter sings a fragment.)   **61 gallants of war** warships

68–71 The one . . . away (A nursery rhyme.)   **71 bells** (In falconry, the birds flew with bells hung from their legs.)   **73 th' nick** the nick of time   **74 dance** to dance.   **we are made again** our fortunes are restored.   **75 rarest gambols** most elegant leaps in dancing.   **81 Tell . . . Buzz!** Count to ten; he can't, I've stumped him. Pshaw!   **84 tinker** itinerant peddlers who mended kitchenware and the like were thought of as rogues and vagabonds. (The reference to stopping holes [line 85] is given a sexual double meaning.)   **85 *Dii boni!*** Good gods!   **87–8 let . . . bones** let him play a popular dance tune, *Qui (Chi) passa per questa strada* ("Who passes through this street"), using bells and bones as musical and percussion instruments.   **89–91 fluently . . . Strike up** with graceful speech, persuade her to dance peacefully with us. "And I have completed a work which neither the anger of love nor fire [shall undo]." Start the music. (The Latin quotation is from Ovid's *Metamorphoses*.)   **94 s.d. *Wind*** Sound   **95 meditation** time to think

And mark your cue.

> *Exeunt all but [the] Schoolmaster.*
> Pallas, inspire me!   96

> *Enter Theseus, Pirithous, Hippolyta, Emilia,*
> *Arcite, and train.*

THESEUS   This way the stag took.

SCHOOLMASTER   Stay and edify.   98

THESEUS   What have we here?

PIRITHOUS   Some country sport, upon my life, sir.

THESEUS *[to the Schoolmaster]*
Well, sir, go forward; we will edify.

> *[Seats are brought for Theseus and the ladies.]*
Ladies, sit down; we'll stay it.   *[They sit.]*   102

SCHOOLMASTER
Thou doughty Duke, all hail! All hail, sweet ladies!   103

THESEUS *[to Pirithous and the ladies]*
This is a cold beginning.   104

SCHOOLMASTER
If you but favor, our country pastime made is.   105
We are a few of those collected here
That ruder tongues distinguish "villager";   107
And to say verity, and not to fable,
We are a merry rout, or else a rabble,   109
Or company, or, by a figure, chorus,   110
That 'fore thy dignity will dance a morris.   111
And I that am the rectifier of all,   112
By title *pedagogus*, that let fall   113
The birch upon the breeches of the small ones,
And humble with a ferula the tall ones,   115
Do here present this machine, or this frame;   116
And, dainty Duke, whose doughty dismal fame   117
From Dis to Daedalus, from post to pillar,   118
Is blown abroad, help me, thy poor well-willer,
And with thy twinkling eyes, look right and straight
Upon this mighty "Morr" of mickle weight.   121
"Is" now comes in, which, being glued together,   122
Makes "Morris," and the cause that we came hither.   123
The body of our sport, of no small study,   124
I first appear, though rude, and raw, and muddy,
To speak before thy noble grace this tenner,   126

At whose great feet I offer up my penner.   127
The next, the Lord of May and Lady bright;   128
The Chambermaid and Servingman, by night
That seek out silent hanging; then mine Host   130
And his fat Spouse, that welcomes to their cost   131
The gallèd traveller, and with a beck'ning   132
Informs the tapster to inflame the reck'ning;   133
Then the beest-eating Clown; and next the Fool;   134
The Babion with long tail and eke long tool,   135
Cum multis aliis that make a dance;   136
Say "ay," and all shall presently advance.   137

THESEUS
Ay, ay, by any means, dear dominie.

PIRITHOUS   Produce!   138

SCHOOLMASTER *(knock for [the] school)*
Intrate, filii; come forth and foot it.   139

> *Music.*

> *Enter the [Countrymen, the Taborer, the Wenches,*
> *and the Jailer's Daughter. They] dance [a morris].*

Ladies, if we have been merry,
And have pleased ye with a derry,   141
And a derry and a down,
Say the schoolmaster's no clown.
Duke, if we have pleased thee too,
And have done as good boys should do,
Give us but a tree or twain
For a maypole, and again,
Ere another year run out,
We'll make thee laugh, and all this rout.

THESEUS
Take twenty, dominie. *[To Hippolyta]* How does my
sweetheart?

HIPPOLYTA
Never so pleased, sir.

EMILIA   'Twas an excellent dance,
And for a preface, I never heard a better.   152

THESEUS
Schoolmaster, I thank you.—One see 'em all
rewarded.   153

PIRITHOUS
And here's something to paint your pole withal.
> *[He gives them money.]*

THESEUS   Now to our sports again.   155

SCHOOLMASTER
May the stag thou hunt'st stand long,   156
And thy dogs be swift and strong;

---

96 Pallas Pallas Athene   **98 edify** be instructed.   **102 stay it** stay to attend the presentation.   **103 doughty** valiant, worthy   **104 cold** (Theseus puns on the meteorological meaning of "hail.")   **105 favor** grant the favor of your attention   **107 ruder** county-bred.   **distinguish** classify or characterize as   **109 rout** assembly   **110 figure** figure of speech   **111 'fore thy dignity** in your royal presence   **112 rectifier** one who corrects, the director, but also the one who corrects and spanks students (in lines 113–15)   **113 pedagogus** schoolmaster   **115 ferula** cane used to punish older students   **116 this machine . . . frame** this device, this construction (the entertainment)   **117 dainty** gracious.   **dismal** unpropitious (to your enemies). (The words are chosen partly for their alliteration.)   **118 From Dis to Daedalus** from the underworld to the labyrinth of Daedalus. (Again with alliterative effect.)   **121–3 "Morr" . . . "Is" . . . "Morris"** To achieve this pedantry, the Schoolmaster has evidently outfitted two of his dancers to depict "Morr" (perhaps signifying "Moor") and "Is" (perhaps "ice"); when they stand together, the result is "Morris."   **121 mickle** much   **124 The body . . . study** (1) The substance of our entertainment, mastered with no small amount of effort (2) I, as the structural centerpiece of our entertainment, a person of considerable learning   **126 tenner** i.e., ten-syllable line. (Punning also on *tenor*, purport.)

127 penner leather sheath for pens.   **128 Lady** i.e., Queen of May, Maid Marian   **130 silent hanging** wall or bed curtains behind which to seek concealment   **131–2 to their . . . traveller** chafed and weary travelers, who find their welcome a costly one   **133 inflame the reck'ning** inflate the bill   **134 beest-eating** eating the first milk to be drawn from a cow after it gives birth. (Such a diet characterizes the Clown as a country bumpkin.)   **135 tool** penis.   **136 Cum multis aliis** with many others   **137 presently** immediately   **138 dominie** schoolmaster.   **Produce!** Bring them forth!   **139 s.d. knock for [the] school** The schoolmaster signals for those under his tutelage to enter.   **139 Intrate, filii** Come in, my boys.   **foot it** dance.   **141 derry** ballad, refrain. ("Derry down derry" is a common nonsense refrain.)   **152 for** as for   **153 One** Someone   **155 sports** hunting   **156 stand long** hold out a long time (thus providing good sport)

May they kill him without lets,   158
And the ladies eat his dowsets.   159
    Wind horns [within. Exeunt Theseus and train.]
Come, we are all made. *Dii deaeque omnes!*   160
Ye have danced rarely, wenches.   *Exeunt.*

❧

3.[6]

Enter Palamon from the bush.

PALAMON
About this hour my cousin gave his faith
To visit me again, and with him bring
Two swords and two good armors. If he fail,   3
He's neither man nor soldier. When he left me,
I did not think a week could have restored
My lost strength to me, I was grown so low
And crest-fall'n with my wants. I thank thee, Arcite,
Thou art yet a fair foe; and I feel myself,
With this refreshing, able once again
To outdure danger. To delay it longer   10
Would make the world think, when it comes to
   hearing,   11
That I lay fatting like a swine to fight,   12
And not a soldier. Therefore this blest morning
Shall be the last; and that sword he refuses,   14
If it but hold, I kill him with; 'tis justice.   15
So, love and fortune for me!

Enter Arcite with [suits of] armor and swords.

              Oh, good morrow.

ARCITE
Good morrow, noble kinsman.
PALAMON   I have put you
To too much pains, sir.
ARCITE   That too much, fair cousin,
Is but a debt to honor and my duty.
PALAMON
Would you were so in all, sir. I could wish ye   20
As kind a kinsman as you force me find   21
A beneficial foe, that my embraces   22
Might thank ye, not my blows.
ARCITE   I shall think either,
Well done, a noble recompense.
PALAMON   Then I shall quit you.   24
ARCITE
Defy me in these fair terms, and you show   25

---

158 lets hindrances   **159 dowsets** testicles—considered a delicacy.
160 *Dii deaeque omnes!* All gods and goddesses!
3.6. Location: The forest still. Palamon's entrance "from the bush"
suggests some sort of visual indication at a stage door or structure.
3 armors suits of armor.   **10 outdure** endure, outlast
11 when . . . hearing when the matter is generally known   **12 fatting
. . . fight** lazing about in my preparations for fighting like a swine
being fattened for the kill   **14–15 that sword . . . hold** the sword he
brings for me to use (having chosen the other one for himself), so
long as it remains whole. (At line 45 Palamon offers Arcite his choice
of weapons.)   **20–2 Would . . . foe** I wish you were as honorable in all
things as you are in providing these weapons and armor. I could wish
you were as kind a kinsman as what you oblige me to find you are
instead: an enemy who does me this benefit (of providing armor and
food.)   **24 quit** repay   **25 show** show yourself to be

More than a mistress to me. No more anger,
As you love anything that's honorable!
We were not bred to talk, man; when we are armed,
And both upon our guards, then let our fury,
Like meeting of two tides, fly strongly from us,
And then to whom the birthright of this beauty   31
Truly pertains—without upbraidings, scorns,   32
Despisings of our persons, and such poutings,
Fitter for girls and schoolboys—will be seen,
And quickly, yours or mine. Will't please you arm, sir?
Or if you feel yourself not fitting yet   36
And furnished with your old strength, I'll stay, cousin,
And ev'ry day discourse you into health,
As I am spared. Your person I am friends with,   39
And I could wish I had not said I loved her,
Though I had died; but loving such a lady,   41
And justifying my love, I must not fly from't.
PALAMON
Arcite, thou art so brave an enemy
That no man but thy cousin's fit to kill thee.
I am well and lusty; choose your arms.
ARCITE   Choose you, sir.   45
PALAMON
Wilt thou exceed in all, or dost thou do it   46
To make me spare thee?
ARCITE   If you think so, cousin,
You are deceivèd, for, as I am a soldier,
I will not spare you.
PALAMON   That's well said.
ARCITE   You'll find it.   49
PALAMON
Then, as I am an honest man, and love
With all the justice of affection,
I'll pay thee soundly.   *[He chooses one suit of armor.]*
        This I'll take.
ARCITE *[indicating the other suit]*   That's mine, then.   52
I'll arm you first.
PALAMON   Do. Pray thee tell me, cousin,
Where got'st thou this good armor?
ARCITE *[arming Palamon]*   'Tis the Duke's,
And to say true, I stole it. Do I pinch you?
PALAMON
No.
ARCITE   Is't not to heavy?
PALAMON   I have worn a lighter,
But I shall make it serve.
ARCITE   I'll buckle't close.
PALAMON
By any means.
ARCITE   You care not for a grand guard?   58
PALAMON
No, no, we'll use no horses. I perceive

31–2 to whom . . . pertains the one who can claim the beautiful
Emilia by right of birth   **36 fitting** prepared   **39 As I am spared** as
far as I have time.   **41 Though I had died** even if my remaining
silent had killed me   **45 lusty** healthy, strong   **46 exceed in all** go
beyond me in everything that is chivalrous   **49 You'll find it** i.e., I
mean to do what I've said I'll do.   **52 pay** reward, punish   **58 grand
guard** armor plate covering the breast and left shoulder, used in tournaments and hence appropriate for tilting on horseback (as Palamon
implies in line 59).

You would fain be at that fight.

ARCITE   I am indifferent.   60

PALAMON

Faith, so am I. Good cousin, thrust the buckle
Through far enough.

ARCITE   I warrant you.

PALAMON   My casque now.   62

ARCITE

Will you fight bare-armed?

PALAMON   We shall be the nimbler.

ARCITE

But use your gauntlets, though. Those are o'th' least.   64
Prithee take mine, good cousin

PALAMON   Thank you, Arcite.

How do I look? Am I fall'n much away?   66

ARCITE

Faith, very little; love has used you kindly.

PALAMON

I'll warrant thee, I'll strike home.

ARCITE   Do, and spare not.   68

I'll give you cause, sweet cousin.

PALAMON   Now to you, sir.

[Arming Arcite] Methinks this armor's very like that,
    Arcite,

Thou wor'st that day the three kings fell, but lighter.

ARCITE

That was a very good one, and that day,
I well remember, you outdid me, cousin;
I never saw such valor. When you charged
Upon the left wing of the enemy,
I spurred hard to come up, and under me   76
I had a right good horse.

PALAMON   You had indeed;

A bright bay, I remember.

ARCITE   Yes, but all   78

Was vainly labored in me; you outwent me,
Nor could my wishes reach you. Yet a little
I did by imitation.

PALAMON   More by virtue.   81

You are modest, cousin.

ARCITE   When I saw you charge first,

Methought I heard a dreadful clap of thunder
Break from the troop.

PALAMON   But still before that flew

The lightning of your valor. Stay a little;
Is not this piece too strait?

ARCITE   No, no, 'tis well.   86

PALAMON

I would have nothing hurt thee but my sword;
A bruise would be dishonor.

ARCITE   Now I am perfect.   88

PALAMON

Stand off, then.

ARCITE   Take my sword; I hold it better.   89

PALAMON

I thank ye. No, keep it; your life lies on it.   90
Here's one; if it but hold, I ask no more
For all my hopes. My cause and honor guard me!

ARCITE

And me my love!

                They bow several ways, then advance and stand.

                          Is there aught else to say?   93

PALAMON

This only, and no more: thou art mine aunt's son,
And that blood we desire to shed is mutual—
In me, thine, and in thee, mine. My sword
Is in my hand, and if thou kill'st me,
The gods and I forgive thee! If there be
A place prepared for those that sleep in honor,
I wish his weary soul that falls may win it.
Fight bravely, cousin. Give me thy noble hand.

ARCITE [as they clasp hands]

Here, Palamon. This hand shall never more
Come near thee with such friendship.

PALAMON   I commend thee.   103

ARCITE

If I fall, curse me, and say I was a coward,
For none but such dare die in these just trials.   105
Once more farewell, my cousin.

PALAMON   Farewell, Arcite.

                [They] fight. Horns within. They stand.

ARCITE

Lo, cousin, lo, our folly has undone us.

PALAMON   Why?

ARCITE

This is the Duke, a-hunting, as I told you.
If we be found, we are wretched. Oh, retire
For honor's sake, and safely, presently,
Into your bush again. Sir, we shall find
Too many hours to die in. Gentle cousin,
If you be seen, you perish instantly
For breaking prison, and I, if you reveal me,
For my contempt. Then all the world will scorn us,   115
And say we had a noble difference,   116
But base disposers of it.

PALAMON   No, no, cousin,   117

I will no more be hidden, nor put off
This great adventure to a second trial.   119
I know your cunning, and I know your cause;
He that faints now, shame take him! Put thyself   121
Upon thy present guard.

ARCITE   You are not mad?   122

PALAMON

Or I will make th'advantage of this hour

---

60 would . . . fight would prefer to fight that way, mounted.   **62 warrant** promise.   **casque** helmet   **64 gauntlets** plated gloves.   **o'th' least** too small.   **66 fall'n much away** much thinner.   **68 home** to the heart.   **76 come up** come up from the rear   **78 bay** reddish brown   **81 virtue** manliness.   **86 strait** tight-fitting.   **88 perfect** i.e., correctly armed in every detail.   **89 hold it better** regard it as the better one.

90 lies depends   **93 s.d. several ways** in various directions, as though to those witnessing a tournament   **103 commend thee** commend you to the gods.   **105 For none . . . trials** i.e., only the unworthy are sure to lose in trial by combat, since the gods will give victory to the just.   **115 contempt** i.e., disobedience of the decree of banishment.   **116–17 we had . . . of it** we had a noble quarrel but were guilty of conducting it in defiance of royal command.   **119 adventure** venture   **121 faints** proves fainthearted   **122 Upon . . . guard** on guard at once.

Mine own, and what to come shall threaten me   124
I fear less than my fortune. Know, weak cousin,   125
I love Emilia, and in that I'll bury
Thee and all crosses else.

ARCITE   Then come what can come,   127
Thou shalt know, Palamon, I dare as well
Die as discourse or sleep. Only this fears me: 129
The law will have the honor of our ends.   130
Have at thy life!

PALAMON   Look to thine own well, Arcite!

[They] fight again.

Horns. Enter Theseus, Hippolyta, Emilia,
Pirithous, and train. [Palamon and Arcite are
separated.]

THESEUS
What ignorant and mad malicious traitors
Are you, that 'gainst the tenor of my laws
Are making battle, thus like knights appointed,   134
Without my leave and officers of arms?   135
By Castor, both shall die.

PALAMON   Hold thy word, Theseus.   136
We are certainly both traitors, both despisers
Of thee and of thy goodness. I am Palamon,
That cannot love thee, he that broke thy prison;
Think well what that deserves. And this is Arcite;
A bolder traitor never trod thy ground,
A falser nev'r seemed friend. This is the man
Was begged and banished, this is he contemns thee   143
And what thou dar'st do, and in this disguise,
Against thine own edict, follows thy sister,
That fortunate bright star, the fair Emilia,
Whose servant—if there be a right in seeing,   147
And first bequeathing of the soul to—justly
I am; and, which is more, dares think her his.
This treachery, like a most trusty lover,
I called him now to answer. If thou be'st
As thou art spoken, great and virtuous,
The true decider of all injuries,   153
Say "Fight again," and thou shalt see me, Theseus,
Do such a justice thou thyself wilt envy.
Then take my life; I'll woo thee to't.

PIRITHOUS   O heaven,   156
What more than man is this!

THESEUS   I have sworn.

ARCITE   We seek not
Thy breath of mercy, Theseus. 'Tis to me   158
A thing as soon to die as thee to say it,
And no more moved. Where this man calls me traitor,   160

Let me say thus much: if in love be treason,
In service of so excellent a beauty,
As I love most, and in that faith will perish,
As I have brought my life here to confirm it,
As I have served her truest, worthiest,
As I dare kill this cousin that denies it,
So let me be most traitor, and ye please me.   167
For scorning thy edict, Duke, ask that lady   168
Why she is fair, and why her eyes command me
Stay here to love her; and if she say "traitor,"
I am a villain fit to lie unburied.

PALAMON
Thou shalt have pity of us both, O Theseus,
If unto neither thou show mercy. Stop,
As thou art just, thy noble ear against us;
As thou art valiant, for thy cousin's soul,   175
Whose twelve strong labors crown his memory,
Let's die together at one instant, Duke.   177
Only a little let him fall before me,
That I may tell my soul he shall not have her.

THESEUS
I grant your wish, for to say true, your cousin
Has ten times more offended, for I gave him
More mercy than you found, sir, your offenses   182
Being no more than his.—None here speak for 'em,
For ere the sun set both shall sleep for ever.

HIPPOLYTA *[to Emilia]*
Alas, the pity! Now or never, sister,
Speak not to be denied. That face of yours
Will bear the curses else of after ages
For these lost cousins.

EMILIA   In my face, dear sister,
I find no anger to 'em, nor no ruin;
The misadventure of their own eyes kill 'em.   190
Yet that I will be woman and have pity, *[kneeling]*
My knees shall grow to th' ground but I'll get mercy.   192
Help me, dear sister; in a deed so virtuous,
The powers of all women will be with us.—
Most royal brother—

HIPPOLYTA *[kneeling]*   Sir, by our tie of marriage—

EMILIA
By your own spotless honor—

HIPPOLYTA   By that faith,
That fair hand, and that honest heart you gave me—

EMILIA
By that you would have pity in another,   198
By your own virtues infinite—

HIPPOLYTA   By valor,
By all the chaste nights I have ever pleased you—   200

THESEUS
These are strange conjurings.

PIRITHOUS *[kneeling]*   Nay then, I'll in too.

124–5 **what . . . fortune** I fear whatever the future may threaten me with less than the outcome of this present fight.   127 **crosses else** other thwartings or afflictions.   129 **fears** frightens   130 **The law . . . ends** The law will execute us rather than allowing us to settle this matter honorably.   134 **appointed** accoutered in arms   135 **officers of arms** referees of chivalric combat.   136 **Castor** one of Jupiter's sons, twin brother of Pollux.   **Hold** Keep   143 **Was begged** whose life was begged of you. (See 2.2.251–4.)   **contemns** scorns   147 **servant** knight devoted to the service of the lady he loves. (Palamon claims a prior right to be Emilia's "servant" by virtue of having seen her first and having given his soul to her, lines 147–8.)   153 **injuries** wrongful acts   156 **Then** After that   158–60 **'Tis . . . moved** My death would mean no more to me than it would to you in uttering the judgment.

167 **So . . . me** if that is what "traitor" means, you will gratify me by calling me such.   168 **For** As for   175 **thy cousin's** Hercules's, who was famous for his twelve labors (line 176)   177 **Let's** let the two of us   182 **More . . . found** (Theseus released Arcite from prison, though banishing him, while Palamon remained in prison.)   190 **The misadventure . . . 'em** i.e., they are sentenced to die not by my anger but by their own rash quarreling over me.   192 **but** unless and until   198 **that** your hope that.   **in** from   200 **chaste nights** nights spent in monogamous wedded happiness

By all our friendship, sir, by all our dangers,
By all you love most, wars and this sweet lady—
EMILIA
By that you would have trembled to deny   204
A blushing maid—
HIPPOLYTA   By your own eyes, by strength,   205
In which you swore I went beyond all women,   206
Almost all men, and yet I yielded, Theseus—
PIRITHOUS
To crown all this, by your most noble soul,
Which cannot want due mercy, I beg first—   209
HIPPOLYTA
Next hear my prayers—
EMILIA   Last let me entreat, sir—
PIRITHOUS
For mercy.
HIPPOLYTA   Mercy.
EMILIA   Mercy on these princes.
THESEUS
Ye make my faith reel. [*To Emilia*] Say I felt   212
Compassion to 'em both, how would you place it?
                                          [*They rise.*]
EMILIA
Upon their lives—but with their banishments.
THESEUS
You are a right woman, sister; you have pity,   215
But want the understanding where to use it.
If you desire their lives, invent a way
Safer than banishment. Can these two live,
And have the agony of love about 'em,
And not kill one another? Every day
They'd fight about you, hourly bring your honor   221
In public question with their swords. Be wise, then,   222
And here forget 'em; it concerns your credit
And my oath equally. I have said they die;
Better they fall by th' law than one another.
Bow not my honor.
EMILIA   O my noble brother,   226
That oath was rashly made, and in your anger;
Your reason will not hold it. If such vows   228
Stand for express will, all the world must perish.   229
Beside, I have another oath 'gainst yours,
Of more authority, I am sure more love,
Not made in passion neither, but good heed.   232
THESEUS
What is it, sister?
PIRITHOUS   Urge it home, brave lady.   233
EMILIA
That you would nev'r deny me anything
Fit for my modest suit and your free granting.
I tie you to your word now; if ye fail in't,

Think how you maim your honor—
For now I am set a-begging, sir, I am deaf
To all but your compassion—how their lives   239
Might breed the ruin of my name, opinion.   240
Shall anything that loves me perish for me?
That were a cruel wisdom. Do men prune
The straight young boughs that blush with thousand
    blossoms
Because they may be rotten? O Duke Theseus,   244
The goodly mothers that have groaned for these,   245
And all the longing maids that ever loved,
If your vow stand, shall curse me and my beauty,
And in their funeral songs for these two cousins
Despise my cruelty, and cry woe worth me,   249
Till I am nothing but the scorn of women.
For heaven's sake, save their lives and banish 'em.
THESEUS
On what conditions?
EMILIA   Swear 'em never more   252
To make me their contention, or to know me,   253
To tread upon thy dukedom, and to be,
Wherever they shall travel, ever strangers
To one another.
PALAMON   I'll be cut a-pieces
Before I take this oath. Forget I love her?
O all ye gods, despise me then. Thy banishment   258
I not mislike, so we may fairly carry   259
Our swords and cause along; else never trifle,
But take our lives, Duke. I must love and will,
And for that love must and dare kill this cousin
On any piece the earth has.
THESEUS   Will you, Arcite,   263
Take these conditions?
PALAMON   He's a villain, then.
PIRITHOUS   These are men!
ARCITE
No, never, Duke. 'Tis worse to me than begging
To take my life so basely. Though I think
I never shall enjoy her, yet I'll preserve
The honor of affection, and die for her,   268
Make death a devil.   269
THESEUS
What may be done? For now I feel compassion.
PIRITHOUS
Let it not fall again, sir.
THESEUS   Say, Emilia,   271
If one of them were dead, as one must, are you
Content to take th'other to your husband?   273
They cannot both enjoy you. They are princes
As goodly as your own eyes, and as noble
As ever fame yet spoke of. Look upon 'em,

And, if you can love, end this difference.
I give consent.—Are you content too, princes?

PALAMON AND ARCITE
With all our souls.

THESEUS   He that she refuses
Must die, then.

PALAMON AND ARCITE   Any death thou canst invent, Duke.

PALAMON
If I fall from that mouth, I fall with favor,   281
And lovers yet unborn shall bless my ashes.

ARCITE
If she refuse me, yet my grave will wed me,
And soldiers sing my epitaph.

THESEUS [to Emilia]   Make choice, then.

EMILIA
I cannot, sir; they are both too excellent.
For me, a hair shall never fall of these men.   286

HIPPOLYTA
What will become of 'em?

THESEUS   Thus I ordain it,
And by mine honor, once again, it stands,
Or both shall die. [To Palamon and Arcite] You shall
    both to your country,
And each, within this month, accompanied
With three fair knights, appear again in this place,
In which I'll plant a pyramid; and whether,   292
Before us that are here, can force his cousin
By fair and knightly strength to touch the pillar,
He shall enjoy her; the other lose his head,
And all his friends; nor shall he grudge to fall,   296
Nor think he dies with interest in this lady.   297
Will this content ye?

PALAMON   Yes. Here, cousin Arcite,
I am friends again till that hour.

ARCITE   I embrace ye.
                    [They embrace.]

THESEUS
Are you content, sister?

EMILIA   Yes, I must, sir,
Else both miscarry.

THESEUS [to Palamon and Arcite]
                    Come, shake hands again, then,
And take heed, as you are gentlemen, this quarrel
Sleep till the hour prefixed, and hold your course.

PALAMON
We dare not fail thee, Theseus.

THESEUS   Come, I'll give ye
Now usage like to princes and to friends.
When ye return, who wins I'll settle here;   306
Who loses yet I'll weep upon his bier.

                    Exeunt.

281 **from that mouth** as a result of the decision she pronounces
286 **For me** On my account   292 **plant a pyramid** erect an obelisk or
pillar.   **whether** whichever of you two   296–7 **And . . . lady** and all
his followers shall die also; nor shall he protest that the sentence is
unjust, or that he continues to have a claim upon Emilia.   306 **who . . .
here** whoever wins I'll make a member of my court here in Athens

4.1

Enter Jailer and his Friend.

JAILER
Hear you no more? Was nothing said of me
Concerning the escape of Palamon?
Good sir, remember.

FIRST FRIEND   Nothing that I heard,
For I came home before the business
Was fully ended. Yet I might perceive,
Ere I departed, a great likelihood
Of both their pardons; for Hippolyta
And fair-eyed Emily, upon their knees,
Begged with such handsome pity that the Duke,
Methought, stood staggering whether he should
    follow
His rash oath or the sweet compassion
Of those two ladies; and to second them
That truly noble prince, Pirithous—
Half his own heart—set in too, that I hope   14
All shall be well; neither heard I one question
Of your name or his scape.

Enter Second Friend.

JAILER   Pray heaven it hold so.

SECOND FRIEND
Be of good comfort, man! I bring you news,
Good news.

JAILER   They are welcome.

SECOND FRIEND   Palamon has cleared you,   18
And got your pardon, and discovered how   19
And by whose means he escaped, which was your
    daughter's,
Whose pardon is procured too, and the prisoner,
Not to be held ungrateful to her goodness,
Has given a sum of money to her marriage—
A large one, I'll assure you.

JAILER   Ye are a good man
And ever bring good news.

FIRST FRIEND   How was it ended?

SECOND FRIEND
Why, as it should be: they that nev'r begged
But they prevailed had their suits fairly granted;
The prisoners have their lives.

FIRST FRIEND   I knew 'twould be so.

SECOND FRIEND
But there be new conditions, which you'll hear of
At better time.

JAILER   I hope they are good.

SECOND FRIEND   They are honorable;
How good they'll prove I know not.

Enter Wooer.

FIRST FRIEND   'Twill be known.

WOOER
Alas, sir, where's your daughter?

JAILER   Why do you ask?

4.1. Location: The prison.
14 that so that   **18 They** The news   **19 discovered** revealed

WOOER
Oh, sir, when did you see her?

SECOND FRIEND [*aside*]   How he looks!

JAILER
This morning.

WOOER   Was she well? Was she in health?
Sir, when did she sleep?

FIRST FRIEND   These are strange questions.

JAILER
I do not think she was very well, for now
You make me mind her, but this very day   37
I asked her questions, and she answered me
So far from what she was, so childishly,   39
So sillily, as if she were a fool,
An innocent, and I was very angry.   41
But what of her, sir?

WOOER   Nothing but my pity;
But you must know it, and as good by me
As by another that less loves her.

JAILER
Well, sir?

FIRST FRIEND   Not right?

SECOND FRIEND   Not well?

WOOER   No, sir, not well.   45
'Tis too true, she is mad.

FIRST FRIEND   It cannot be.

WOOER
Believe you'll find it so.

JAILER   I half suspected
What you told me. The gods comfort her!
Either this was her love to Palamon,
Or fear of my miscarrying on his scape,   50
Or both.

WOOER   'Tis likely.

JAILER   But why all this haste, sir?

WOOER
I'll tell you quickly. As I late was angling   52
In the great lake that lies behind the palace,
From the far shore, thick set with reeds and sedges,
As patiently I was attending sport,   55
I heard a voice—a shrill one; and attentive,
I gave my ear, when I might well perceive
'Twas one that sung, and by the smallness of it   58
A boy or woman. I then left my angle   59
To his own skill, came near, but yet perceived not   60
Who made the sound, the rushes and the reeds
Had so encompassed it. I laid me down
And listened to the words she sung, for then,
Through a small glade cut by the fishermen,   64
I saw it was your daughter.

JAILER   Pray go on, sir.

WOOER
She sung much, but no sense, only I heard her
Repeat this often: "Palamon is gone,

Is gone to th' wood to gather mulberries;
I'll find him out tomorrow."

FIRST FRIEND   Pretty soul!

WOOER
"His shackles will betray him; he'll be taken,
And what shall I do then? I'll bring a bevy,
A hundred black-eyed maids that love as I do,
With chaplets on their heads of daffadillies,   73
With cherry lips and cheeks of damask roses,   74
And all we'll dance an antic 'fore the Duke,   75
And beg his pardon." Then she talked of you, sir—   76
That you must lose your head tomorrow morning,
And she must gather flowers to bury you,
And see the house made handsome. Then she sung
Nothing but "Willow, willow, willow," and between
Ever was "Palamon, fair Palamon,"
And "Palamon was a tall young man." The place   82
Was knee-deep where she sat. Her careless tresses   83
A wreath of bulrush rounded; about her stuck   84
Thousand freshwater flowers of several colors,
That methought she appeared like the fair nymph
That feeds the lake with waters, or as Iris,   87
Newly dropped down from heaven. Rings she made
Of rushes that grew by, and to 'em spoke
The prettiest posies: "Thus our true love's tied,"   90
"This you may lose, not me," and many a one;
And then she wept, and sung again, and sighed,
And with the same breath smiled and kissed her hand.

SECOND FRIEND
Alas, what pity it is!

WOOER   I made in to her.   94
She saw me, and straight sought the flood. I saved her   95
And set her safe to land, when presently
She slipped away, and to the city made
With such a cry and swiftness that, believe me,
She left me far behind her. Three or four
I saw from far off cross her—one of 'em   100
I knew to be your brother—where she stayed   101
And fell, scarce to be got away. I left them with her   102

*Enter [Jailer's] Brother, [Jailer's] Daughter, and
others.*

And hither came to tell you. Here they are.

JAILER'S DAUGHTER [*sings*]
May you never more enjoy the light . . . (etc.)
Is not this a fine song?

JAILER'S BROTHER   Oh, a very fine one.

JAILER'S DAUGHTER
I can sing twenty more.

JAILER'S BROTHER   I think you can.

JAILER'S DAUGHTER
Yes, truly can I; I can sing "The Broom,"

---

37 **mind** think of. **but** only   39 **So far . . . was** so differently from
her usual way   41 **innocent** simpleton   45 **right** in her right mind.
50 **miscarrying on** suffering misfortune on account of   52 **late**
recently. **angling** fishing   55 **attending sport** i.e., waiting for a bite
58 **smallness** high pitch   59 **angle** fishing tackle.   60 **To his own
skill** to manage itself   64 **glade** clearing

73 **chaplets** garlands of flowers   74 **of damask roses** rose-colored
75 **antic** quaint or grotesque pageant   76 **beg his pardon** beg the life
of Palamon.   82 **tall** handsome, valiant   83–4 **Her . . . rounded** A
garland of bulrushes encircled her disheveled tresses   87 **Iris** goddess of the rainbow and messenger of Hera   90 **posies** short mottoes,
often inscribed within rings   94 **made in to** advanced toward
95 **straight . . . flood** immediately got in the water   100 **cross** intercept   101 **stayed** halted   102 **scarce . . . away** almost unremovable.

And "Bonny Robin." Are not you a tailor?

JAILER'S BROTHER
  Yes.

JAILER'S DAUGHTER
  Where's my wedding gown?

JAILER'S BROTHER   I'll bring it tomorrow.

JAILER'S DAUGHTER
  Do, very rarely; I must be abroad else   110
  To call the maids and pay the minstrels,
  For I must lose my maidenhead by cocklight;   112
  'Twill never thrive else.
    (*Sings*) O fair, O sweet . . . (etc.)

JAILER'S BROTHER [*to the Jailer*]
  You must ev'n take it patiently.

JAILER   'Tis true.

JAILER'S DAUGHTER
  Good ev'n, good men. Pray, did you ever hear
  Of one young Palamon?

JAILER   Yes, wench, we know him.

JAILER'S DAUGHTER
  Is't not a fine young gentleman?

JAILER   'Tis, love.

JAILER'S BROTHER [*to the others*]
  By no mean cross her; she is then distempered   119
  Far worse than now she shows.

FIRST FRIEND [*to the Jailer's Daughter*]
                     Yes, he's a fine man.

JAILER'S DAUGHTER
  Oh, is he so? You have a sister.

FIRST FRIEND   Yes.

JAILER'S DAUGHTER
  But she shall never have him, tell her so,
  For a trick that I know. You'd best look to her,   123
  For if she see him once, she's gone—she's done
  And undone in an hour. All the young maids
  Of our town are in love with him, but I laugh at 'em
  And let 'em all alone. Is't not a wise course?

FIRST FRIEND   Yes. 127

JAILER'S DAUGHTER
  There is at least two hundred now with child by him—
  There must be four; yet I keep close for all this,   129
  Close as a cockle; and all these must be boys—   130
  He has the trick on't—and at ten years old   131
  They must be all gelt for musicians,   132
  And sing the wars of Theseus.

SECOND FRIEND [*to the others*]   This is strange.

JAILER'S BROTHER [*to the Second Friend*]
  As ever you heard; but say nothing.

FIRST FRIEND   No.

JAILER'S DAUGHTER
  They come from all parts of the dukedom to him.

I'll warrant ye, he had not so few last night   136
As twenty to dispatch. He'll tickle't up   137
In two hours, if his hand be in.

JAILER [*to the others*]   She's lost 138
  Past all cure.

JAILER'S BROTHER   Heaven forbid, man!

JAILER'S DAUGHTER [*to the Jailer*]
  Come hither; you are a wise man.

FIRST FRIEND [*to the Second Friend*]   Does she know him?

SECOND FRIEND [*to the First Friend*]
  No; would she did.

JAILER'S DAUGHTER   You are master of a ship?

JAILER   Yes.

JAILER'S DAUGHTER   Where's your compass?

JAILER   Here.

JAILER'S DAUGHTER   Set it to th' north; 145
  And now direct your course to th' wood, where Palamon
  Lies longing for me. For the tackling, 147
  Let me alone. Come, weigh, my hearts, cheerly all. 148
  Owgh, owgh, owgh! 'Tis up. 149
  The wind's fair. Top the bowline. 150
  Out with the mainsail! Where's your whistle, master?

JAILER'S BROTHER   Let's get her in.

JAILER   Up to the top, boy!

JAILER'S BROTHER   Where's the pilot?

FIRST FRIEND   Here.

JAILER'S DAUGHTER   What kenn'st thou? 156

SECOND FRIEND   A fair wood.

JAILER'S DAUGHTER   Bear for it, master. Tack about. 158
  (*Sings*)
    When Cynthia with her borrowed light . . . (etc.)
                         Exeunt.

❖

4.2

Enter Emilia alone with two pictures.

EMILIA
  Yet I may bind those wounds up, that must open
  And bleed to death for my sake else; I'll choose,
  And end their strife. Two such young handsome men
  Shall never fall for me; their weeping mothers,
  Following the dead cold ashes of their sons,
  Shall never curse my cruelty. Good heaven,
  What a sweet face has Arcite! If wise Nature,
  With all her best endowments, all those beauties
  She sows into the births of noble bodies,
  Were here a mortal woman, and had in her 10
  The coy denials of young maids, yet doubtless 11

136–7 **not so few . . . As** no fewer than 137 **tickle't up** finish up. (With sexual suggestion.) 138 **if . . . in** if he's in good form. (With sexual suggestion.) 145 **Set** Orient 147–8 **For . . . alone** As for the rigging, leave it to me. 148 **weigh** weigh anchor 149 **Owgh** a grunting sound of exertion 150 **Top the bowline** Haul in on the line used to hold steady the edge of a square sail in sailing close to the wind. 156 **kenn'st thou** do you discern. 158 **Bear** Head
4.2 Location: Theseus's palace, Athens.
10–11 **and had . . . maids** and possessed the modest inclination of virtuous young maids to resist male blandishments

110 **rarely** early; excellently. **abroad else** away from home otherwise 112 **cocklight** dawn 119 **mean** means. **cross** contradict. **distempered** mentally disordered 123 **For** because of 127 **let . . . alone** pay no attention to them. 129 **keep close** keep to myself, keep still 130 **cockle** clam-like mollusk 131 **on't** i.e., of begetting sons 132 **gelt for musicians** castrated before puberty to preserve the soprano or contralto voice

She would run mad for this man. What an eye,
Of what a fiery sparkle and quick sweetness,   13
Has this young prince! Here Love himself sits smiling;   14
Just such another wanton Ganymede   15
Set Jove afire with, and enforced the god
Snatch up the goodly boy and set him by him,
A shining constellation. What a brow,   18
Of what a spacious majesty, he carries,
Arched like the great-eyed Juno's, but far sweeter,
Smoother than Pelops' shoulder! Fame and Honor,   21
Methinks, from hence, as from a promontory   22
Pointed in heaven, should clap their wings and sing   23
To all the under world the loves and fights   24
Of gods and such men near 'em. Palamon   25
Is but his foil, to him a mere dull shadow;
He's swart and meager, of an eye as heavy   27
As if he had lost his mother, a still temper,   28
No stirring in him, no alacrity,
Of all this sprightly sharpness not a smile.   30
Yet these that we count errors may become him;
Narcissus was a sad boy but a heavenly.   32
Oh, who can find the bent of woman's fancy?   33
I am a fool; my reason is lost in me;
I have no choice, and I have lied so lewdly   35
That women ought to beat me. On my knees
I ask thy pardon! Palamon, thou art alone
And only beautiful, and these the eyes,
These the bright lamps of beauty, that command
And threaten love, and what young maid dare cross
  'em?   40
What a bold gravity, and yet inviting,   42
Has this brown manly face! O Love, this only
From this hour is complexion. Lie there, Arcite;   43
Thou art a changeling to him, a mere gypsy,   44
And this the noble body. I am sotted,   45
Utterly lost; my virgin's faith has fled me.
For if my brother but even now had asked me
Whether I loved, I had run mad for Arcite;   48
Now if my sister, more for Palamon.
Stand both together. Now come ask me, brother;

Alas, I know not! Ask me now, sweet sister;
I may go look. What a mere child is Fancy,   52
That, having two fair gauds of equal sweetness,   53
Cannot distinguish, but must cry for both!

Enter a Gentleman.

How now, sir?
GENTLEMAN   From the noble Duke, your brother,
Madam, I bring you news: the knights are come.
EMILIA
To end the quarrel?
GENTLEMAN   Yes.
EMILIA   Would I might end first!
What sins have I committed, chaste Diana,   58
That my unspotted youth must now be soiled
With blood of princes, and my chastity
Be made the altar where the lives of lovers—
Two greater and two better never yet
Made mothers joy—must be the sacrifice   63
To my unhappy beauty?

*Enter Theseus, Hippolyta, Pirithous, and
attendants.*

THESEUS   Bring 'em in   64
Quickly, by any means; I long to see 'em.
                              [*Exit one or more.*]
[*To Emilia*] Your two contending lovers are returned,
And with them their fair knights. Now, my fair sister,
You must love one of them.
EMILIA   I had rather both,
So neither for my sake should fall untimely.
THESEUS
Who saw 'em?
PIRITHOUS   I awhile.
GENTLEMAN   And I.   70

Enter a Messenger.

THESEUS
From whence come you, sir?
MESSENGER   From the knights.
THESEUS   Pray speak,
You that have seen them, what they are.
MESSENGER   I will, sir,
And truly what I think. Six braver spirits
Than these they have brought, if we judge by the
  outside,
I never saw nor read of. He that stands
In the first place with Arcite, by his seeming   76
Should be a stout man, by his face a prince;   77
His very looks so say him, his complexion   78
Nearer a brown than black—stern and yet noble—
Which shows him hardy, fearless, proud of dangers.
The circles of his eyes show fire within him,
And as a heated lion, so he looks.   82

---

13 **quick** lively   14 **Love himself** Cupid. (Emilia is comparing the two portraits; see also lines 43 and 50.)   15 **Ganymede** the young man whom Jove, infatuated, took to be his cupbearer   18 **constellation** (The zodiacal sign Aquarius was often thought to have been Ganymede transported to the sky.)   21 **Pelops' shoulder** (Pelops's father, Tantalus, served the child to the gods in a banquet to see if they could tell the flesh from that of some animal. He managed to fool Demeter into eating part of the shoulder. The gods restored Pelops to life with the missing shoulder replaced by ivory.)   22 **hence** Arcite's brow   23 **Pointed** coming to a point   24 **the under world** the earth as seen from the heavens   25 **near 'em** close to the gods in achievement. 27 **He's . . . meager** Palamon is swarthy and of deficient build.   **heavy** sad   28 **still temper** lethargic temperament   30 **Of . . . smile** with not even a smile to match Arcite's sprightly keenness.   32 **Narcissus . . . heavenly** i.e., Narcissus too had a sad look about him (owing to his being punished for repulsing the love of Echo by becoming enamored of his own image in a fountain), and yet he was immortalized. 33 **bent** inclination   35 **choice** ability to choose.   **lewdly** basely, ignorantly   40 **cross** encounter, oppose   42–3 **this only . . . complexion** from this day forth, Palamon's dark complexion is the only one for me.   44 **a changeling** a child (usually stupid or ugly) thought to have been left by fairies in exchange for one stolen   45 **sotted** besotted 48 **Whether** which of the two.   **had** would have

52 **I . . . look** i.e., for all my looking, I find no answer.   **Fancy** love 53 **gauds** toys, baubles   58 **Diana** goddess associated with the moon and with chastity   63 **joy** rejoice   64 **unhappy** causing misfortune 70 **awhile** recently.   76 **seeming** appearance   77 **stout** valiant 78 **say** proclaim   82 **heated** angry

His hair hangs long behind him, black and shining
Like ravens' wings; his shoulders broad and strong,
Armed long and round; and on his thigh a sword   85
Hung by a curious baldric, when he frowns,   86
To seal his will with. Better, o' my conscience,   87
Was never soldier's friend.

THESEUS
Thou hast well described him.

PIRITHOUS   Yet a great deal short,
Methinks, of him that's first with Palamon.

THESEUS
Pray speak him, friend.

PIRITHOUS   I guess he is a prince too,   91
And, if it may be, greater, for his show   92
Has all the ornament of honor in't.
He's somewhat bigger than the knight he spoke of,   94
But of a face far sweeter; his complexion
Is, as a ripe grape, ruddy. He has felt
Without doubt what he fights for, and so apter   97
To make this cause his own. In 's face appears
All the fair hopes of what he undertakes,
And when he's angry, then a settled valor,
Not tainted with extremes, runs through his body,
And guides his arm to brave things. Fear he cannot;
He shows no such soft temper. His head's yellow,
Hard-haired and curled, thick-twined like ivy-tods,   104
Not to undo with thunder. In his face   105
The livery of the warlike maid appears,   106
Pure red and white, for yet no beard has blessed him;
And in his rolling eyes sits Victory,
As if she ever meant to court his valor.   109
His nose stands high, a character of honor;   110
His red lips, after fights, are fit for ladies.

EMILIA
Must these men die too?

PIRITHOUS   When he speaks, his tongue
Sounds like a trumpet. All his lineaments
Are as a man would wish 'em—strong and clean.
He wears a well-steeled ax, the staff of gold;
His age some five-and-twenty.

MESSENGER   There's another—
A little man, but of a tough soul, seeming
As great as any. Fairer promises
In such a body yet I never looked on.

PIRITHOUS
Oh, he that's freckle-faced?

MESSENGER   The same, my lord.
Are they not sweet ones?

PIRITHOUS   Yes, they are well.

MESSENGER   Methinks,   121
Being so few, and well disposed, they show   122

Great and fine art in nature. He's white-haired—   123
Not wanton white, but such a manly color   124
Next to an auburn; tough and nimble-set,   125
Which shows an active soul. His arms are brawny,
Lined with strong sinews. To the shoulder-piece   127
Gently they swell, like women new-conceived,   128
Which speaks him prone to labor, never fainting   129
Under the weight of arms; stout-hearted still,   130
But when he stirs, a tiger. He's grey-eyed,   131
Which yields compassion where he conquers; sharp   132
To spy advantages, and where he finds 'em,
He's swift to make 'em his. He does no wrongs,
Nor takes none. He's round-faced, and when he
    smiles   135
He shows a lover, when he frowns, a soldier.   136
About his head he wears the winner's oak,   137
And in it stuck the favor of his lady;   138
His age some six-and-thirty. In his hand
He bears a charging-staff embossed with silver.   140

THESEUS
Are they all thus?

PIRITHOUS   They are all the sons of honor.

THESEUS
Now, as I have a soul, I long to see 'em.
[To Hippolyta] Lady, you shall see men fight, now.

HIPPOLYTA   I wish it,
But not the cause, my lord. They would show   144
Bravely about the titles of two kingdoms;   145
'Tis pity love should be so tyrannous.

                    [Emilia weeps.]
Oh, my soft-hearted sister, what think you?
Weep not till they weep blood. Wench, it must be.

THESEUS [to Emilia]
You have steeled 'em with your beauty. [To Pirithous]
    Honored friend,   149
To you I give the field; pray order it   150
Fitting the persons that must use it.

PIRITHOUS   Yes, sir.

THESEUS
Come, I'll go visit 'em; I cannot stay,   152
Their fame has fired me so. Till they appear,
Good friend, be royal.

PIRITHOUS   There shall want no bravery.   154

EMILIA [to herself]
Poor wench, go weep, for whosoever wins
Loses a noble cousin for thy sins.

                                    Exeunt.

❧

85 Armed ... round with long, well-shaped arms   **86–7 Hung ...
with** hung from an intricately designed sword belt (worn across one
shoulder), which he uses to execute his furious will.   **91 speak**
describe   **92 show** appearance   **94 he** the messenger   **97 what ...
for** i.e., love   **104 Hard-haired and curled** tightly curled.   **ivy-tods**
ivy bushes   **105 undo** be undone or destroyed   **106 the warlike maid**
Athene, warlike goddess, protector of Athens   **109 As ... valor** as if
Victory were constantly drawn to woo him for his valor.   **110 His ...
honor** (The prominent Roman nose was thought to indicate honorableness.)   **121 they** the freckles   **122 disposed** placed, situated

123 white-haired blond   **124 wanton** effeminate   **125 nimble-set**
nimble of build   **127 Lined** fortified   **128 new-conceived** newly pregnant   **129 speaks ... labor** bespeaks one willing to strive hard. (With a
pun on the "labor" of pregnancy.)   **130 still** (1) always, under any conditions (2) at rest   **131 grey-eyed** blue-eyed   **132 Which ... conquers**
which indicates his inclination to be compassionate to those he conquers   **135 Nor takes none** and does not tolerate anyone injuring him.
136 shows looks like   **137 oak** garland of oak leaves   **138 favor** glove,
scarf or other token   **140 charging-staff** tilting lance   **144–5 They ...
kingdoms** Their splendor would be well suited to a contention
between two kingdoms   **149 steeled** hardened   **150 the field** the
management of the contest   **152 stay** wait   **154 be royal** arrange matters with royal generosity.   **want no bravery** lack no splendor.

4.3

Enter Jailer, Wooer, Doctor.

DOCTOR   Her distraction is more at some time of the
    moon than at other some, is it not?   2

JAILER   She is continually in a harmless distemper,   3
    sleeps little; altogether without appetite, save often
    drinking; dreaming of another world, and a better;
    and what broken piece of matter soe'er she's about,
    the name "Palamon" lards it, that she farces ev'ry   7
    business withal, fits it to every question.

Enter [Jailer's] Daughter.

Look where she comes. You shall perceive her behav-
    ior.   [*They stand apart.*]

JAILER'S DAUGHTER   I have forgot it quite; the burden   11
    on't was "Down-a, down-a," and penned by no   12
    worse man than Geraldo, Emilia's schoolmaster. He's
    as fantastical, too, as ever he may go upon 's legs; for   14
    in the next world will Dido see Palamon, and then will   15
    she be out of love with Aeneas.

DOCTOR   What stuff's here! Poor soul!

JAILER   Ev'n thus all day long.

JAILER'S DAUGHTER   Now for this charm that I told you
    of, you must bring a piece of silver on the tip of your
    tongue, or no ferry; then if it be your chance to come   21
    where the blessed spirits are—there's a sight now!
    We maids that have our livers perished, cracked to   23
    pieces with love, we shall come there, and do nothing
    all day long but pick flowers with Proserpine. Then   25
    will I make Palamon a nosegay, then let him mark me,   26
    then—

DOCTOR   How prettily she's amiss! Note her a little
    further.

JAILER'S DAUGHTER   Faith, I'll tell you: sometime we go
    to barley-break, we of the blessèd. Alas, 'tis a sore   31
    life they have i'th'other place. Such burning, frying,   32
    boiling, hissing, howling, chatt'ring, cursing—Oh,
    they have shrewd measure, take heed! If one be mad,   34
    or hang or drown themselves, thither they go, Jupiter
    bless us, and there shall we be put in a cauldron of
    lead and usurers' grease, amongst a whole million of   37
    cutpurses, and there boil like a gammon of bacon that   38
    will never be enough.   39

DOCTOR   How her brain coins!   40

4.3. Location: The prison.
2 at other some at other times   **3 distemper** state of mental disorder
7 lards is inserted into.   **farces** stuffs. (Cooking terms.)   **11–12 bur-**
den on't refrain of it   **14 fantastical** filled with lively imagination.
ever . . . legs anyone who can walk, any person   **15 Dido** Queen of
Carthage, deserted by Aeneas in Virgil's *Aeneid*   **21 or no ferry** (A
coin was placed on the tongue of a deceased person as fare for being
ferried across the Styx to the underworld by Charon.)   **23 livers** supposed seat of the passions   **25 Proserpine** (As this beautiful goddess
was picking flowers in Sicily, she was carried off by Hades to be his
queen in the lower world.)   **26 nosegay** bouquet of flowers.   **mark**
me pay attention to me   **31 barley-break** a game played by various
couples, one couple in the center (called "hell") trying to catch the
others   **32 i'th'other place** i.e., in hell.   **34 shrewd measure** dire
punishment   **37 grease** i.e., sweat   **38 gammon** ham   **38–9 that . . .**
enough i.e., the torment will never cease.   **40 coins** fabricates.

JAILER'S DAUGHTER   Lords and courtiers that have got
    maids with child, they are in this place; they shall
    stand in fire up to the navel and in ice up to th' heart,
    and there th'offending part burns and the deceiv-
    ing part freezes—in truth a very grievous punishment,
    as one would think, for such a trifle. Believe me,
    one would marry a leprous witch to be rid on't, I'll
    assure you.

DOCTOR   How she continues this fancy! 'Tis not an en-   49
    grafted madness, but a most thick and profound   50
    melancholy.   51

JAILER'S DAUGHTER   To hear there a proud lady and a
    proud city wife howl together! I were a beast an I'd call   53
    it good sport. One cries, "Oh, this smoke!," th'other,
    "This fire!"; one cries, "Oh, that ever I did it behind
    the arras!", and then howls; th'other curses a   56
    suing fellow and her garden house.   57

(*Sings*)
    I will be true, my stars, my fate . . . (etc.)

Exit [Jailer's] Daughter.

JAILER   What think you of her, sir?

DOCTOR   I think she has a perturbed mind, which I
    cannot minister to.

JAILER   Alas, what then?

DOCTOR   Understand you she ever affected any man   63
    ere she beheld Palamon?

JAILER   I was once, sir, in great hope she had fixed her
    liking on this gentleman, my friend.

WOOER   I did think so too, and would account I had a   67
    great penn'orth on 't to give half my state that both she   68
    and I, at this present, stood unfeignedly on the same
    terms.

DOCTOR   That intemp'rate surfeit of her eye hath dis-
    tempered the other senses. They may return and
    settle again to execute their preordained faculties, but
    they are now in a most extravagant vagary. This you   74
    must do: confine her to a place where the light may
    rather seem to steal in than be permitted. Take upon
    you, young sir, her friend, the name of Palamon; say
    you come to eat with her, and to commune of love.
    This will catch her attention, for this her mind beats
    upon; other objects that are inserted 'tween her mind
    and eye become the pranks and friskins of her   81
    madness. Sing to her such green songs of love as she   82
    says Palamon hath sung in prison; come to her stuck   83
    in as sweet flowers as the season is mistress of, and
    thereto make an addition of some other compounded
    odors which are grateful to the sense. All this shall
    become Palamon, for Palamon can sing, and Palamon   87
    is sweet and ev'ry good thing. Desire to eat with her,
    carve her, drink to her, and still among intermingle   89

49–51 'Tis . . . melancholy It's not insanity in the psychotic sense, but
a profound lovesickness.   **53 I . . . an** I would be a beast if   **56 arras**
hanging screen placed in front of walls, allowing space behind for
concealment and assignations   **57 suing fellow** suitor.   **garden**
house (A suitable place for a seduction.)   **63 affected** felt passion for
67–8 would . . . on 't would consider it a great bargain   **68 state**
estate   **74 in . . . vagary** wandering out of bounds.   **81 friskins** playful encounters   **82 green** youthful   **83 stuck** decked out   **87 become**
suit your role as   **89 carve** carve meat for.   **still among** mingled
with these activities

your petition of grace and acceptance into her favor.
Learn what maids have been her companions and
playferes, and let them repair to her with "Palamon"   92
in their mouths, and appear with tokens, as if they   93
suggested for him. It is a falsehood she is in, which is   94
with falsehoods to be combatted. This may bring her
to eat, to sleep, and reduce what's now out of square   96
in her into their former law and regiment. I have seen   97
it approved, how many times I know not; but, to   98
make the number more, I have great hope in this. I
will between the passages of this project come in   100
with my appliance. Let us put it in execution, and   101
hasten the success, which doubt not will bring forth   102
comfort.

                                                    Exeunt.

❖

5.1

*Flourish. Enter Theseus, Pirithous, Hippolyta,
attendants. [Three altars are visible.]*

THESEUS
Now let 'em enter, and before the gods
Tender their holy prayers. Let the temples
Burn bright with sacred fires, and the altars
In hallowed clouds commend their swelling incense
To those above us. Let no due be wanting;
They have a noble work in hand, will honor   6
The very powers that love 'em.

*Flourish of cornets. Enter Palamon and Arcite
and their knights [at opposite doors].*

PIRITHOUS
THESEUS   Sir, they enter.
You valiant and strong-hearted enemies,
You royal german foes, that this day come   9
To blow that nearness out that flames between ye,   10
Lay by your anger for an hour, and, dove-like,
Before the holy altars of your helpers,
The all-feared gods, bow down your stubborn bodies.
Your ire is more than mortal; so your help be,   14
And as the gods regard ye, fight with justice.   15
I'll leave you to your prayers, and betwixt ye
I part my wishes.
PIRITHOUS   Honor crown the worthiest!
*Exeunt Theseus and his train, [including Pirithous
                                      and Hippolyta].*

PALAMON *[to Arcite]*
The glass is running now that cannot finish   18
Till one of us expire. Think you but thus,

That were there aught in me which strove to show   20
Mine enemy in this business, were't one eye
Against another, arm oppressed by arm,
I would destroy th'offender, coz—I would,
Though parcel of myself. Then from this gather   24
How I should tender you.
ARCITE   I am in labor   25
To push your name, your ancient love, our kindred,   26
Out of my memory, and i'th' selfsame place
To seat something I would confound. So hoist we   28
The sails that must these vessels port even where   29
The heavenly limiter pleases.
PALAMON   You speak well.   30
Before I turn, let me embrace thee, cousin.   31
                                    [They embrace.]
This I shall never do again.
ARCITE   One farewell.
PALAMON
Why, let it be so; farewell, coz.
ARCITE   Farewell, sir.
                        Exeunt Palamon and his knights.
Knights, kinsmen, lovers, yea, my sacrifices,
True worshipers of Mars, whose spirit in you
Expels the seeds of fear and th'apprehension   36
Which still is father of it: go with me   37
Before the god of our profession. There   38
Require of him the hearts of lions and   39
The breath of tigers, yea, the fierceness too,   40
Yea, the speed also—to go on, I mean;
Else wish we to be snails. You know my prize
Must be dragged out of blood; force and great feat
Must put my garland on, where she sticks,   44
The queen of flowers. Our intercession, then,   45
Must be to him that makes the camp a cistern   46
Brimmed with the blood of men. Give me your aid,   47
And bend your spirits towards him.

*They [advance to Mars's altar, fall prostrate, and]
kneel.*

Thou mighty one, that with thy power hast turned
Green Neptune into purple; whose havoc in vast field comets prewarn,
Whose havoc in vast field comets prewarn,   50
Unearthèd skulls proclaim; whose breath blows down   51
The teeming Ceres' foison; who dost pluck   53
With hand armipotent from forth blue clouds   54
The masoned turrets, that both mak'st and break'st   55
The stony girths of cities: me thy pupil,   56

92 **playferes** playfellows. **repair** come 93 **tokens** love tokens
94 **suggested** pleaded. **falsehood** delusion 96 **reduce** lead back
97 **regiment** order. 98 **it approved** this course of treatment confirmed in practice 100 **passages** transactions 101 **appliance** application, administering 102 **success** outcome
5.1. Location: The forest, where Palamon and Arcite fought (in 3.6)
and where the tournament is now to be held. Visible onstage are
temples to Mars, Venus, and Diana, each with an altar.
6 **will** that will 9 **german** cousin 10 **blow that nearness out** blow
out or extinguish the friendship and nearness of blood 14 **be** must
be 15 **regard** watch over 18 **glass** hourglass

20 **show** appear as 24 **parcel** part 25 **tender** behave toward, treat
26 **kindred** kinship 28 **confound** destroy. 29 **port** transport, convey to port 30 **The heavenly limiter** the god who controls all life
31 **turn** turn away 36–7 **th'apprehension . . . of it** the anticipation or
perception of danger which is ever the cause of fear 38 **of our profession** to whom we offer our services and who is patron of our military calling. 39 **Require** request 40 **breath** endurance, "wind"
44–5 **Must . . . flowers** must win for me the victory laurel wreath, of
which Emilia, who already reigns in my heart, is the chiefest flower.
46 **him** Mars 47 **Brimmed** filled to the brim 50 **Green Neptune** i.e.,
the sea 51 **field** battlefield 53 **The . . . foison** the teeming crops
ready for harvesting, the gift of Ceres, goddess of agriculture
53–5 **pluck . . . turrets** pull down with your mighty arm, from out of
the sky, the stone-built fortifications
56 **girths** walls

Youngest follower of thy drum, instruct this day
With military skill, that to thy laud   58
I may advance my streamer, and by thee   59
Be styled the lord o'th' day. Give me, great Mars,   60
Some token of thy pleasure.   61

> *Here they fall on their faces as formerly, and there*
> *is heard clanging of armor, with a short thunder,*
> *as the burst of a battle, whereupon they all rise and*
> *bow to the altar.*

O great corrector of enormous times,   62
Shaker of o'er-rank states, thou grand decider   63
Of dusty and old titles, that heal'st with blood   64
The earth when it is sick, and cur'st the world
O'th' plurisy of people, I do take   66
Thy signs auspiciously, and in thy name
To my design march boldly. [*To his knights*] Let us go.
                                                                          Exeunt.   68

> *Enter Palamon and his knights, with the former*
> *observance.*

PALAMON
Our stars must glister with new fire, or be   69
Today extinct. Our argument is love,
Which, if the goddess of it grant, she gives
Victory too. Then blend your spirits with mine,
You whose free nobleness do make my cause
Your personal hazard. To the goddess Venus
Commend we our proceeding, and implore
Her power unto our party.

> *Here they [advance to Venus's altar, prostrate*
> *themselves, and] kneel as formerly.*

Hail, sovereign queen of secrets, who hast power
To call the fiercest tyrant from his rage
And weep unto a girl; that hast the might   79
Even with an eye-glance to choke Mars's drum
And turn th'alarm to whispers; that canst make   81
A cripple flourish with his crutch, and cure him   82
Before Apollo; that mayst force the king   83
To be his subject's vassal, and induce
Stale gravity to dance! The polled bachelor—   85
Whose youth, like wanton boys through bonfires,
Have skipped thy flame—at seventy thou canst catch,
And make him, to the scorn of his hoarse throat,
Abuse young lays of love. What godlike power   89
Hast thou not power upon? To Phoebus thou
Add'st flames hotter than his; the heavenly fires

Did scorch his mortal son, thine him. The huntress,   92
All moist and cold, some say, began to throw
Her bow away and sigh. Take to thy grace
Me, thy vowed soldier, who do bear thy yoke
As 'twere a wreath of roses, yet is heavier   96
Than lead itself, stings more than nettles.
I have never been foul-mouthed against thy law;
Nev'r revealed secret, for I knew none; would not,
Had I kenned all that were. I never practiced   100
Upon man's wife, nor would the libels read   101
Of liberal wits. I never at great feasts   102
Sought to betray a beauty, but have blushed   103
At simp'ring sirs that did. I have been harsh
To large confessors, and have hotly asked them   105
If they had mothers; I had one, a woman,
And women 'twere they wronged. I knew a man
Of eighty winters—this I told them—who
A lass of fourteen brided; 'twas thy power   109
To put life into dust. The agèd cramp
Had screwed his square foot round;   111
The gout had knit his fingers into knots;
Torturing convulsions from his globy eyes   113
Had almost drawn their spheres, that what was life   114
In him seemed torture. This anatomy   115
Had by his young fair fere a boy, and I   116
Believed it was his, for she swore it was,
And who would not believe her? Brief, I am   118
To those that prate and have done, no companion;   119
To those that boast and have not, a defier;
To those that would and cannot, a rejoicer.
Yea, him I do not love that tells close offices   122
The foulest way, nor names concealments in
The boldest language. Such a one I am,   124
And vow that lover never yet made sigh
Truer than I. Oh, then, most soft sweet goddess,
Give me the victory of this question, which   127
Is true love's merit, and bless me with a sign   128
Of thy great pleasure.

> *Here music is heard. Doves are seen to flutter.*
> *They fall again upon their faces, then on their*
> *knees.*

O thou that from eleven to ninety reign'st
In mortal bosoms, whose chase is this world   131
And we in herds thy game, I give thee thanks   132
For this fair token, which, being laid unto

---

58 to thy laud in praise of thee   **59 streamer** banner   **60 styled** titled
61.3 burst eruption   **62 enormous** abnormal, monstrous   **63 o'er-
rank** overripe, decadent   **64 with blood** through bloodletting (a
common medical treatment for sickness)   **66 plurisy** diseased superabundance. (Pleurisy, an inflammation of the lung sacks or pleura,
was wrongly thought to be derived from the Latin *plus, plur-,*
"more.")   **68.1–2 the former observance.** Palamon and his knights
fulfill ceremonies at Venus's altar like those performed by Arcite and
his knights at Mars's altar.   **69 stars** fortunes   **79 weep unto** make
him weep before, imploring the favor of   **81 th'alarm** the alarum,
call to arms   **82 flourish with** wave about vigorously   **83 Before
Apollo** even sooner than Apollo, the god of medicine   **85 polled**
bald   **89 Abuse** butcher (with his hoarse singing)

92 his mortal son Phaethon, who drove the sun god Phoebus's chariot too near the sun.   **The huntress** Diana or Artemis, goddess of
chastity and of the moon, who fell in love with a shepherd
(Endymion)   **96 is** it is   **100 kenned** known   **100–1 practiced Upon**
attempted to seduce   **102 liberal** licentious   **103 betray** (1) tattle
about (2) seduce   **105 large confessors** men who boast unre-
strainedly of their sexual prowess with many women   **109 brided**
took as his bride   **111 Had . . . round** had twisted his well-
proportioned foot into a gouty misshapen mass   **113 globy** protrud-
ing   **114 drawn their spheres** popped out the eyeballs.   **that** so that
115 anatomy mere skeleton   **116 fere** partner (in marriage)
118 Brief In brief   **119 and have done** and did what they boast about
122 close offices secret affairs   **124 Such a one** i.e., One who condemns male boastfulness   **127 question** contention   **128 Is . . . merit**
is the reward of the true lover   **131 chase** hunting-ground
132 game quarry

Mine innocent true heart, arms in assurance
My body to this business. [*To his knights*] Let us rise
And bow before the goddess.   *They* [*rise and*] *bow.*
                    Time comes on.   *Exeunt.* 136

> *Still music of record*[*er*]*s. Enter Emilia in white,*
> *her hair about her shoulders,* [*wearing*] *a wheaten*
> *wreath; one in white holding up her train, her hair*
> *stuck with flowers; one before her carrying a silver*
> *hind, in which is conveyed incense and sweet*
> *odors; which being set upon the altar* [*of Diana*]*,*
> *her maids standing aloof, she sets fire to it. Then*
> *they curtsy and kneel.*

EMILIA
O sacred, shadowy, cold, and constant queen,   137
Abandoner of revels, mute contemplative,
Sweet, solitary, white as chaste, and pure
As wind-fanned snow, who to thy female knights
Allow'st no more blood than will make a blush,
Which is their order's robe: I here, thy priest,   142
Am humbled 'fore thine altar. Oh, vouchsafe
With that thy rare green eye, which never yet   144
Beheld thing maculate, look on thy virgin!   145
And, sacred silver mistress, lend thine ear—
Which nev'r heard scurril term, into whose port   147
Ne'er entered wanton sound—to my petition,
Seasoned with holy fear. This is my last
Of vestal office; I am bride-habited,   150
But maiden-hearted. A husband I have 'pointed,   151
But do not know him. Out of two I should
Choose one, and pray for his success, but I
Am guiltless of election. Of mine eyes   154
Were I to lose one—they are equal precious—
I could doom neither; that which perished should   156
Go to't unsentenced. Therefore, most modest queen,   157
He of the two pretenders that best loves me   158
And has the truest title in't, let him
Take off my wheaten garland, or else grant   160
The file and quality I hold I may   161
Continue in thy band.   162

> *Here the hind vanishes under the altar, and in the*
> *place ascends a rose tree, having one rose upon it.*

See what our general of ebbs and flows   163
Out from the bowels of her holy altar
With sacred act advances—but one rose!   165
If well inspired, this battle shall confound   166

Both these brave knights, and I, a virgin flower,
Must grow alone, unplucked.

> *Here is heard a sudden twang of instruments, and*
> *the rose falls from the tree.*   [*The tree descends.*]

The flower is fall'n, the tree descends. Oh, mistress,
Thou here dischargest me. I shall be gathered;   170
I think so, but I know not thine own will.
Unclasp thy mystery!—I hope she's pleased;
Her signs were gracious.
                    They curtsy and exeunt.

5.2

> *Enter Doctor, Jailer, and Wooer in* [*the*] *habit of*
> *Palamon.*

DOCTOR   Has this advice I told you done any good
upon her?
WOOER   Oh, very much. The maids that kept her com-
pany have half persuaded her that I am Palamon.
Within this half-hour she came smiling to me, and
asked me what I would eat, and when I would kiss
her. I told her presently, and kissed her twice.
DOCTOR
'Twas well done. Twenty times had been far better,
For there the cure lies mainly.
WOOER   Then she told me
She would watch with me tonight, for well she knew   10
What hour my fit would take me.
DOCTOR   Let her do so.   11
And when your fit comes, fit her home,   12
And presently.
WOOER   She would have me sing.
DOCTOR
You did so?
WOOER   No.
DOCTOR   'Twas very ill done, then;
You should observe her ev'ry way.
WOOER   Alas,   15
I have no voice, sir, to confirm her that way.   16
DOCTOR
That's all one, if ye make a noise.   17
If she entreat again, do anything;
Lie with her if she ask you.
JAILER   Whoa there, doctor!
DOCTOR
Yes, in the way of cure.
JAILER   But first, by your leave,
I'th' way of honesty.
DOCTOR   That's but a niceness.   21
Nev'r cast your child away for honesty.   22

136.1 *Still* Quiet   **136.2** *her hair . . . shoulders* (Betokening a virginal
and yet-unmarried woman.)   **136.2–3** *wheaten wreath* symbol of
fecundity and of marriage, as at 1.1.0.4   **136.5** *hind* doe. (Also at 162.1.)
136.7 *aloof* apart   **137 shadowy** associated with the night.   **cold** chaste
142 Which . . . robe which blush is the visible garb of those who worship you   **144 rare** excellent   **145 maculate** spotted, defiled   **147 scurril** scurrilous.   **port** portal (of the ear)   **150 bride-habited** dressed as a
bride   **151 I have 'pointed** has been appointed for me   **154 election**
having made a choice.   **156 doom** condemn   **157 Go to't** go to execution   **158 pretenders** suitors   **160 Take . . . garland** take my virginity.
(See 136.2–3.)   **161–2 The file . . . band** that the position and status I
hold (as a virgin) may continue, with me as a valued and ranking member of your entourage   **163 our general . . . flows** our goddess of the
moon and of tides   **165 advances** lifts up   **166 If well inspired** If this
omen and my prophetic reading of it are true.   **confound** destroy

170 Thou . . . me you release me from your service.   **gathered** harvested, i.e., married and thus be a virgin no longer
5.2. Location: The prison.
0.1 *habit* garb   **10 watch** stay awake   **11 fit** sudden inclination
12 fit her home humor her in every way   **15 observe** humor   **16 confirm** fortify, encourage   **17 That's all one** It's all the same   **21 honesty**
chaste marriage.   **niceness** fastidiousness.   **22 Nev'r . . . honesty** Don't
abandon her to her affliction merely out of regard for her chastity.

Cure her first this way; then if she will be honest,   23
She has the path before her.

JAILER
Thank ye, doctor.

DOCTOR   Pray bring her in,
And let's see how she is.

JAILER   I will, and tell her
Her Palamon stays for her. But, doctor,   27
Methinks you are i'th' wrong still.   *Exit Jailer.*

DOCTOR   Go, go;
You fathers are fine fools! Her honesty?
An we should give her physic till we find that—   30

WOOER
Why, do you think she is not honest, sir?

DOCTOR
How old is she?

WOOER   She's eighteen.

DOCTOR   She may be,
But that's all one; 'tis nothing to our purpose.
Whate'er her father says, if you perceive
Her mood inclining that way that I spoke of,
Videlicet, the way of flesh—you have me?   36

WOOER
Yes, very well, sir.

DOCTOR   Please her appetite,
And do it home; it cures her, *ipso facto*,   38
The melancholy humor that infects her.

WOOER
I am of your mind, doctor.

Enter Jailer [and his] Daughter, [mad].

DOCTOR
You'll find it so. She comes; pray humor her.
                                         [Doctor and Wooer stand aside.]

JAILER
Come, your love Palamon stays for you, child,
And has done this long hour, to visit you.

JAILER'S DAUGHTER
I thank him for his gentle patience.
He's a kind gentleman, and I am much bound to him.
Did you nev'r see the horse he gave me?

JAILER   Yes.

JAILER'S DAUGHTER
How do you like him?

JAILER   He's a very fair one.   47

JAILER'S DAUGHTER
You never saw him dance?

JAILER   No.

JAILER'S DAUGHTER   I have, often.
He dances very finely, very comely,
And for a jig, come cut and long tail to him,   50
He turns ye like a top.

JAILER   That's fine indeed.   51

JAILER'S DAUGHTER
He'll dance the morris twenty mile an hour,
And that will founder the best hobby-horse,   53
If I have any skill, in all the parish;   54
And gallops to the tune of "Light o' love."   55
What think you of this horse?

JAILER   Having these virtues,
I think he might be brought to play at tennis.

JAILER'S DAUGHTER
Alas, that's nothing.

JAILER   Can he write and read too?   58

JAILER'S DAUGHTER
A very fair hand, and casts himself th'accounts   59
Of all his hay and provender. That hostler   60
Must rise betime that cozens him. You know   61
The chestnut mare the Duke has?

JAILER   Very well.

JAILER'S DAUGHTER
She is horribly in love with him, poor beast,   63
But he is like his master, coy and scornful.   64

JAILER
What dowry has she?

JAILER'S DAUGHTER   Some two hundred bottles,   65
And twenty strike of oats, but he'll ne'er have her.   66
He lisps in 's neighing able to entice   67
A miller's mare. He'll be the death of her.   68

DOCTOR   What stuff she utters!
                                         [The Wooer approaches her.]

JAILER
Make curtsy; here your love comes.

WOOER   Pretty soul,
How do ye? *[She curtsies]* That's a fine maid; there's a
   curtsy!

JAILER'S DAUGHTER
Yours to command i'th' way of honesty.
How far is't now to th' end o'th' world, my masters?   73

DOCTOR
Why, a day's journey, wench.

JAILER'S DAUGHTER *[to the Wooer]*
                                         Will you go with me?

WOOER
What shall we do there, wench?

JAILER'S DAUGHTER   Why, play at stool-ball.   75
What is there else to do?

WOOER   I am content,
If we shall keep our wedding there.

JAILER'S DAUGHTER   'Tis true,   77

---

23 will wishes to be **27 stays** waits **30 An . . . that** If we were to give her medical treatment until we were assured of her chastity **36 *Videlicet*** namely. **have** understand **38 home** thoroughly. **cures her** cures her of. *ipso facto* by that very act **47 fair** good-looking **50 come . . . to him** i.e., no matter what other kinds of horse (with docked or long tails) there are to compete with him. (With sexual double entendres, as throughout this scene.) **51 ye** for you

53 founder lame, disable, cause to collapse. **hobby-horse** a morris dancer with a figure of a horse fastened around his waist, or a toy horse **54 skill** judgment **55 "Light o' love"** a ballad on the subject of inconstancy in love **58 that's nothing** that's easy, he can do that already. **59 A very . . . accounts** He writes with beautiful penmanship and keeps track of his own expenses **60–1 That hostler . . . him** Any caretaker of horses who wants to cheat this horse will have to get up early to do so. **63 She . . . him** The mare is horribly in love with the talented stallion **64 his master** i.e., Palamon, who is imagined to have given the Jailer's Daughter this horse. **coy** disdainful **65 bottles** bundles **66 strike** bundles, usually bushel or half-bushel **67–8 He lisps . . . mare** This stallion has an ingratiating manner of speech able to seduce even the most plodding and stolid of mares. **73 my masters** my good sirs. **75 stool-ball** a cricket-like game with a stool-like wicket. **77 keep** celebrate

For there, I will assure you, we shall find
Some blind priest for the purpose, that will venture
To marry us; for here they are nice, and foolish.   80
Besides, my father must be hanged tomorrow,
And that would be a blot i'th' business.
Are not you Palamon?
WOOER   Do not you know me?
JAILER'S DAUGHTER
Yes, but you care not for me. I have nothing
But this poor petticoat and two coarse smocks.   85
WOOER
That's all one; I will have you.
JAILER'S DAUGHTER   Will you surely?   86
WOOER
Yes, by this fair hand, will I.
JAILER'S DAUGHTER   We'll to bed then.
WOOER   Ev'n when you will.   [He kisses her.]
JAILER'S DAUGHTER [wiping her mouth]
                Oh, sir, you would fain be nibbling.
WOOER
Why do you rub my kiss off?
JAILER'S DAUGHTER   'Tis a sweet one,
And will perfume me finely against the wedding.   90
[Pointing to the Doctor] Is not this your cousin Arcite?
DOCTOR   Yes, sweetheart,
And I am glad my cousin Palamon
Has made so fair a choice.
JAILER'S DAUGHTER   Do you think he'll have me?
DOCTOR
Yes, without doubt.
JAILER'S DAUGHTER [to the Jailer]   Do you think so too?
JAILER   Yes.
JAILER'S DAUGHTER
We shall have many children. [To the Doctor] Lord,
    how you're grown!
My Palamon, I hope, will grow too, finely,
Now he's at liberty. Alas, poor chicken,
He was kept down with hard meat and ill lodging,   98
But I'll kiss him up again.

        Enter a Messenger.

MESSENGER
What do you here? You'll lose the noblest sight
That ev'r was seen.
JAILER   Are they i'th' field?
MESSENGER   They are.
You bear a charge there too.
JAILER   I'll away straight.   102
[To the others] I must ev'n leave you here.
DOCTOR   Nay, we'll go with you.
I will not lose the fight.
JAILER   How did you like her?   104
DOCTOR
I'll warrant you, within these three or four days

I'll make her right again. [To the Wooer] You must not
    from her,
But still preserve her in this way.
WOOER   I will.
DOCTOR
Let's get her in.
WOOER [to the Jailer's Daughter]
                Come, sweet, we'll go to dinner,
And then we'll play at cards.
JAILER'S DAUGHTER   And shall we kiss too?
WOOER
A hundred times.
JAILER'S DAUGHTER   And twenty.
WOOER   Ay, and twenty.
JAILER'S DAUGHTER
And then we'll sleep together.
DOCTOR [to the Wooer]   Take her offer.
WOOER [to the Jailer's Daughter]
Yes, marry, will we.
JAILER'S DAUGHTER   But you shall not hurt me.
WOOER
I will not, sweet.
JAILER'S DAUGHTER   If you do, love, I'll cry.   *Exeunt.*

                ❖

5.3

        *Flourish. Enter Theseus, Hippolyta, Emilia,
        Pirithous, and some attendants.*

EMILIA [to Pirithous]
I'll no step further.
PIRITHOUS   Will you lose this sight?
EMILIA
I had rather see a wren hawk at a fly   2
Than this decision. Ev'ry blow that falls   3
Threats a brave life; each stroke laments
The place whereon it falls, and sounds more like
A bell than blade. I will stay here.   6
It is enough my hearing shall be punished
With what shall happen, 'gainst the which there is
No deafing, but to hear; not taint mine eye   9
With dread sights it may shun.
PIRITHOUS [to Theseus]   Sir, my good lord,
Your sister will no further.
THESEUS   Oh, she must.
She shall see deeds of honor in their kind,   12
Which sometime show well, pencilled. Nature now   13
Shall make and act the story, the belief   14
Both sealed with eye and ear. [To Emilia] You must be
    present;   15
You are the victor's meed—the prize and garland   16
To crown the question's title.
EMILIA   Pardon me;

---

80 **nice** fastidious   85 **smocks** petticoats, undergarments.   86 **That's
all one** It doesn't matter   90 **against** in preparation for   98 **kept . . .
meat** kept from growing by harsh fare. (And with sexual meaning in
kept down, kiss him up [line 99], and throughout this passage.)
102 **bear a charge** have official responsibilities   104 **lose the fight**
lose the chance to see this armed encounter.   **like** find (medically)

5.3. Location: Near the tournament field, as in 5.1.
2 **hawk** fly on the attack   3 **decision** contest through which the
rivalry will be decided.   6 **bell** bell toll announcing a death   9 **No . . .
hear** no way of preventing one's hearing.   **not** I will not   12–15 **deeds
. . . ear** those honorable deeds in real life which are often so well represented in art. Nature now will both create and enact the story, so
that belief in it will be confirmed by eye and ear.   16 **meed** prize

If I were there, I'd wink.

THESEUS   You must be there;   18
This trial is as 'twere i'th' night, and you
The only star to shine.

EMILIA   I am extinct.   20
There is but envy in that light which shows   21
The one the other. Darkness, which ever was   22
The dam of Horror, who does stand accurst   23
Of many mortal millions, may even now,   24
By casting her black mantle over both,
That neither could find other, get herself   26
Some part of a good name, and many a murder   27
Set off whereto she's guilty.

HIPPOLYTA   You must go.   28
EMILIA
In faith, I will not.

THESEUS   Why, the knights must kindle
Their valor at your eye. Know, of this war
You are the treasure, and must needs be by
To give the service pay.

EMILIA   Sir, pardon me;   32
The title of a kingdom may be tried   33
Out of itself.

THESEUS   Well, well, then; at your pleasure.   34
Those that remain with you could wish their office   35
To any of their enemies.

HIPPOLYTA [to Emilia]   Farewell, sister.   36
I am like to know your husband 'fore yourself   37
By some small start of time. He whom the gods
Do of the two know best, I pray them he   39
Be made your lot.
        Exeunt Theseus, Hippolyta, Pirithous, etc. [Emilia
        remains, attended, comparing two pictures of Palamon
                                          and Arcite.]

EMILIA
Arcite is gently visaged, yet his eye
Is like an engine bent, or a sharp weapon   42
In a soft sheath; mercy and manly courage
Are bedfellows in his visage. Palamon   44
Has a most menacing aspect; his brow
Is graved, and seems to bury what it frowns on;   46
Yet sometime 'tis not so, but alters to   47
The quality of his thoughts. Long time his eye   48
Will dwell upon his object. Melancholy   49
Becomes him nobly; so does Arcite's mirth;   50
But Palamon's sadness is a kind of mirth,

So mingled as if mirth did make him sad
And sadness merry. Those darker humors that   53
Stick misbecomingly on others, on him   54
Live in fair dwelling.   55

        Cornets. Trumpets sound as to a charge.

Hark how yon spurs to spirit do incite   56
The princes to their proof! Arcite may win me,   57
And yet may Palamon wound Arcite to   58
The spoiling of his figure. Oh, what pity   59
Enough for such a chance? If I were by,   60
I might do hurt, for they would glance their eyes
Toward my seat, and in that motion might
Omit a ward or forfeit an offense   63
Which craved that very time. It is much better   64
I am not there. Oh, better never born
Than minister to such harm!

        Cornets. A great cry and noise within,
                          crying "A Palamon!"

        Enter Servant.

                          What is the chance?   66
SERVANT   The cry's "A Palamon!"
EMILIA
Then he has won. 'Twas ever likely;
He looked all grace and success, and he is
Doubtless the prim'st of men. I prithee run   70
And tell me how it goes.

        Shout and cornets, crying "A Palamon!"

SERVANT   Still "Palamon."
EMILIA
Run and inquire.   [Exit Servant.]
                          [To the picture in her right hand]
                          Poor servant, thou hast lost.
Upon my right side still I wore thy picture,   73
Palamon's on the left—why so, I know not;
I had no end in't else; chance would have it so.   75
On the sinister side the heart lies; Palamon   76
Had the best-boding chance.

        Another cry and shout within, and cornets.

                          This burst of clamor   77
Is sure th'end o'th' combat.

        Enter Servant.

SERVANT
They said that Palamon had Arcite's body
Within an inch o'th' pyramid, that the cry

---

18 wink close my eyes.   20 extinct extinguished.   21 envy malice
22 The one the other Palamon and Arcite to each other.   23 dam
mother   24 Of by   26 That so that   27 name reputation   27–8 and
. . . whereto and thus make compensation for many a murder of which
32 give . . . pay reward the service of the knight who triumphs.
33–4 The title . . . itself i.e., I need not be present at a contest over
myself, just as a contest over a kingdom can be conducted in some
other land.   35–6 Those . . . enemies i.e., Any persons staying in
your company are the envy of even their worst enemies.   37 like
likely   39 Do . . . best do know to be the better for you.   them to the
gods   42 an engine bent i.e., a bow bent and ready to be discharged
44 Are bedfellows keep company, are seen together   46 graved
engraved, furrowed   47 to in accordance with   48 quality nature
49 his its   50 so . . . mirth Arcite's mirth becomes Arcite

53–5 Those . . . dwelling Those darker moods that seem out of place
in others seem well suited to him.   56 spirit bravery   57 proof trial.
58–9 to . . . figure sufficiently to disfigure him.   59–60 what . . .
chance? what pity would suffice for such a misfortune?   63 ward
defensive posture.   offense attack   64 craved . . . time needed to
seize that very moment.   66 s.d. "A Palamon!" A cry of support
from Palamon's supporters. The "A"-prefix is customary in such a
shout.   70 prim'st of first among, finest of   73 still unceasingly   75 end in't else purpose
in it otherwise   76 sinister left   77 best-boding best-portending

Was general "A Palamon!" But anon
Th'assistants made a brave redemption, and   82
The two bold titlers at this instant are
Hand to hand at it.

EMILIA   Were they metamorphosed   84
Both into one!—Oh, why? There were no woman   85
Worth so composed a man; their single share,   86
Their nobleness peculiar to them, gives   87
The prejudice of disparity, value's shortness   88
To any lady breathing.   89

Cornets. Cry within, "Arcite, Arcite!"

                    More exulting?
"Palamon" still?

SERVANT   Nay, now the sound is "Arcite."

EMILIA
I prithee lay attention to the cry;   91
Set both thine ears to th' business.

Cornets. A great shout and cry, "Arcite! Victory!"

SERVANT   The cry is
"Arcite" and "Victory!" Hark, "Arcite, victory!"
The combat's consummation is proclaimed   94
By the wind instruments.

EMILIA   Half-sights saw   95
That Arcite was no babe. God's lid, his richness   96
And costliness of spirit looked through him; it could 97
No more be hid in him that fire in flax,
Than humble banks can go to law with waters   99
That drift-winds force to raging. I did think   100
Good Palamon would miscarry, yet I knew not
Why I did think so. Our reasons are not prophets
When oft our fancies are. They are coming off.   103
Alas, poor Palamon!

*Cornets. Enter Theseus, Hippolyta, Pirithous,
Arcite as victor, and attendants, etc.*

THESEUS
Lo, where our sister is in expectation,
Yet quaking and unsettled! Fairest Emily,
The gods by their divine arbitrament   107
Have given you this knight; he is a good one
As ever struck at head. [*To Emilia and Arcite*] Give me
    your hands.
[*To Arcite*] Receive you her, [*to Emilia*] you him; be
    plighted with
A love that grows as you decay.

ARCITE   Emily,

To buy you I have lost what's dearest to me   112
Save what is bought, and yet I purchase cheaply,   113
As I do rate your value.

THESEUS   O loved sister,   114
He speaks now of as brave a knight as e'er
Did spur a noble steed. Surely the gods
Would have him die a bachelor, lest his race   117
Should show i'th' world too godlike. His behavior
So charmed me that methought Alcides was   119
To him a sow of lead. If I could praise   120
Each part of him to th'all I have spoke, your Arcite   121
Did not lose by't; for he that was thus good   122
Encountered yet his better. I have heard
Two emulous Philomels beat the ear o'th' night   124
With their contentious throats, now one the higher,
Anon the other, then again the first,
And by and by out-breasted, that the sense   127
Could not be judge between 'em. So it fared
Good space between these kinsmen, till heavens did   129
Make hardly one the winner. [*To Arcite*] Wear the
    garland   130
With joy that you have won.—For the subdued,   131
Give them our present justice, since I know   132
Their lives but pinch 'em. Let it here be done.   133
The scene's not for our seeing; go we hence
Right joyful, with some sorrow. [*To Arcite*] Arm your
    prize;   135
I know you will not lose her.

[Arcite takes Emilia's arm in his.]
                              Hippolyta,   136
I see one eye of yours conceives a tear,
The which it will deliver.

EMILIA   Is this winning?
O all you heavenly powers, where is your mercy?
But that your wills have said it must be so,
And charge me live to comfort this unfriended,   141
This miserable prince, that cuts away
A life more worthy from him than all women,
I should and would die too.

HIPPOLYTA   Infinite pity
That four such eyes should be so fixed on one
That two must needs be blind for't.

THESEUS   So it is.
                    Flourish. Exeunt.

❧

82 **Th'assistants** the knights seconding Arcite.   **redemption** rescue
84 **Were they** Would that they   85 **were** would be, could be   86 **so composed a man** a man thus made of both their best qualities
86-9 **their . . . breathing** the worthiness of either and the nobleness unique to each puts any woman at a disadvantage by comparison.
91 **lay** apply   94 **consummation** completion   95 **Half-sights** Even a quick glance   96 **God's lid** By God's eyelid. (An oath.)   97 **looked through** shone out of   99 **humble** low.   **go to law** i.e., contend
100 **drift-winds** driving winds   103 **off** off the field.   107 **arbitrament** decision, deciding of a dispute

112-14 **To buy . . . value** to win you I have lost Palamon, dearest of all persons excepting only yourself, and yet the cost is comparatively little since I value you so highly.   117 **his race** his descendants
119-20 **that . . . lead** that I thought Hercules himself a mere ingot of lead (i.e., dull and heavy) compared with Palamon.   121 **to . . . spoke** to the extent that I have praised all of him   122 **Did** would
124 **emulous Philomels** contending nightingales   127 **out-breasted** outsung.   **sense** sense of hearing   129 **Good space** for some length of time   130 **hardly** by a close judgment call; or, after hard fighting
131 **For** As for   132 **our present justice** immediate execution
133 **but pinch** only torment   135 **Arm** Give your arm to   136 **lose** (1) lose possession of (2) forget (3) release (spelled "loose" in the Quarto)   141 **this unfriended** Arcite, who has lost his best friend

5.4

*Enter, [guarded,] Palamon and his knights pin-
ioned; Jailer, Executioner, etc.*

PALAMON
There's many a man alive that hath outlived
The love o'th' people; yea, i'th' selfsame state
Stands many a father with his child. Some comfort
We have by so considering. We expire,
And not without men's pity; to live still,
Have their good wishes. We prevent　　　　　　　6
The loathsome misery of age, beguile
The gout and rheum that in lag hours attend　　　8
For grey approachers. We come towards the gods
Young and unwappered, not halting under crimes　10
Many and stale. That sure shall please the gods　11
Sooner than such, to give us nectar with 'em,　12
For we are more clear spirits. My dear kinsmen,　13
Whose lives for this poor comfort are laid down,
You have sold 'em too too cheap.

FIRST KNIGHT　　　　　　　What ending could be
Of more content? O'er us the victors have
Fortune, whose title is as momentary
As to us death is certain. A grain of honor
They not o'erweigh us.

SECOND KNIGHT　　　　　　Let us bid farewell,
And with our patience anger tott'ring Fortune,
Who at her certain'st reels.

THIRD KNIGHT　　　　　　Come, who begins?　　21

PALAMON
Ev'n he that led you to this banquet shall
Taste to you all. *[To the Jailer]* Aha, my friend, my
　　friend,　　　　　　　　　　　　　　　　　23
Your gentle daughter gave me freedom once;
You'll see't done now forever. Pray, how does she?　25
I heard she was not well; her kind of ill　　　26
Gave me some sorrow.

JAILER　　　　　　　Sir, she's well restored,
And to be married shortly.

PALAMON　　　　　　　By my short life,
I am most glad on't; 'tis the latest thing　　　29
I shall be glad of. Prithee tell her so.
Commend me to her, and to piece her portion　31

Tender her this.　　　　*[He gives the Jailer his purse.]*
FIRST KNIGHT　　Nay, let's be offerers all.
SECOND KNIGHT
Is it a maid?
PALAMON　　　　　　Verily, I think so—
A right good creature, more to me deserving
Than I can quit or speak of.
ALL THE KNIGHTS　　　　　Commend us to her.　35
　　　　　　　　　　　　　They give their purses.
JAILER
The gods requite you all, and make her thankful!
PALAMON
Adieu, and let my life be now as short
As my leave-taking!
　　*[He mounts the scaffold and] lays [his head] on
　　　　　　　　　　　　　　　　　the block.*
FIRST KNIGHT　　　　　Lead, courageous cousin.
SECOND *AND* THIRD KNIGHTS
We'll follow cheerfully.

　　*A great noise within, crying "Run!" "Save!"
　　"Hold!" Enter in haste a Messenger.*

MESSENGER
Hold, hold! Oh, hold, hold, hold!

　　　Enter Pirithous in haste.

PIRITHOUS
Hold, ho! It is a cursèd haste you made　　　41
If you have done so quickly. Noble Palamon,　42
The gods will show their glory in a life
That thou art yet to lead.
PALAMON　　　　　　　Can that be,
When Venus, I have said, is false? How do things fare?
PIRITHOUS
Arise, great sir, and give the tidings ear
That are most rarely sweet and bitter.
PALAMON *[rising and descending from the scaffold]*　What
Hath waked us from our dream?
PIRITHOUS　　　　　　List, then. Your cousin,
Mounted upon a steed that Emily
Did first bestow on him, a black one, owing　　50
Not a hair-worth of white—which some will say　51
Weakens his price, and many will not buy
His goodness with this note, which superstition　53
Here finds allowance—on this horse is Arcite　54
Trotting the stones of Athens, which the calkins　55
Did rather tell than trample, for the horse　　56
Would make his length a mile, if't pleased his rider　57
To put pride in him. As he thus went counting　58

5.4. Location: Near the tournament field, as in 3.6, 5.1, and 5.3. A
scaffold is visible onstage.
6 prevent forestall　**8 rheum . . . approachers** catarrh and rheumatic
pains that in the lag end of life await grey-haired old persons
approaching their sickly end.　**10 unwappered** unwearied.　**halting**
limping　**11 stale** out of date.　**11–13 That . . . spirits** Such youthful
service offered to the gods will surely please them sooner than the
service of those who are old and sin-ridden, prompting the gods to
invite us to feed on nectar with them, since we are more unsullied
spirits.　**21 Who . . . reels** who is unstable even when she seems most
favoring.　**23 Taste . . . all** i.e., go first, like the official taster whose
assignment it was to taste food before distinguished persons ate to
see if the food was poisoned.　**25 You'll . . . forever** you will now
give me freedom forever, in death.　**26 her kind of ill** her distressing
madness　**29 latest** last　**31 piece her portion** piece out her dowry

---

35 quit requite, repay　**41 made** would have made　**42 have done** had
completed the execution　**50 owing** owning, having　**51–3 which . . .
note** (A uniformly dark color was widely regarded as a sign of
viciousness in horses.)　**53 note** distinguishing feature, stigma
54 allowance approbation, confirmation　**55 calkins** turned-down
edges of a horseshoe that raise the horse's foot and heel from the
ground and help prevent skidding　**56 tell** count, i.e., enumerate as
markers in the horse's swift and feathery touch　**57 make . . . mile**
make each stride a mile in length　**58 put pride in him** i.e., give him
his head, let him show his stuff.

The flinty pavement, dancing, as 'twere, to th' music
His own hooves made—for, as they say, from iron 60
Came music's origin—what envious flint, 61
Cold as old Saturn, and like him possessed 62
With fire malevolent, darted a spark, 63
Or what fierce sulfur else, to this end made, 64
I comment not—the hot horse, hot as fire, 65
Took toy at this and fell to what disorder 66
His power could give his will; bounds, comes on end, 67
Forgets school-doing, being therein trained 68
And of kind manège. Pig-like he whines
At the sharp rowel, which he frets at rather 70
Than any jot obeys; seeks all foul means 71
Of boist'rous and rough jadery to disseat 72
His lord, that kept it bravely. When naught served, 73
When neither curb would crack, girth break, nor
    diff'ring plunges 74
Disroot his rider whence he grew, but that
He kept him 'tween his legs, on his hind hooves
On end he stands,
That Arcite's legs, being higher than his head,
Seemed with strange art to hang. His victor's wreath
Even then fell off his head; and presently
Backward the jade comes o'er, and his full poise 81
Becomes the rider's load. Yet is he living, 82
But such a vessel 'tis that floats but for 83
The surge that next approaches. He much desires 84
To have some speech with you. Lo, he appears.

*Enter Theseus, Hippolyta, Emilia, [with] Arcite in
a chair [carried by attendants. Palamon approaches
Arcite.]*

PALAMON

Oh, miserable end of our alliance!
The gods are mighty, Arcite. If thy heart,
Thy worthy, manly heart, be yet unbroken,
Give me thy last words. I am Palamon,

One that yet loves thee dying.
ARCITE   Take Emilia,
And with her all the world's joy. Reach thy hand; 91
Farewell. I have told my last hour. I was false, 92
Yet never treacherous. Forgive me, cousin.
One kiss from fair Emilia. [*Kisses her.*] 'Tis done.
Take her; I die.   [*He dies.*]
PALAMON   Thy brave soul seek Elysium!
EMILIA
I'll close thine eyes, prince. Blessèd souls be with thee!
Thou art a right good man, and while I live,
This day I give to tears.
PALAMON   And I to honor. 98
THESEUS [*to Palamon*]
In this place first you fought; ev'n very here
I sundered you. Acknowledge to the gods 100
Our thanks that you are living.
His part is played, and, though it were too short,
He did it well. Your day is lengthened, and
The blissful dew of heaven does arrose you. 104
The powerful Venus well hath graced her altar,
And given you your love. Our master, Mars,
Hath vouched his oracle, and to Arcite gave 107
The grace of the contention. So the deities 108
Have showed due justice. [*To the attendants*] Bear this
    hence.   [*Exeunt attendants with Arcite's body.*]
PALAMON   Oh, cousin,
That we should things desire which do cost us
The loss of our desire! That naught could buy
Dear love but loss of dear love!
THESEUS   Never Fortune
Did play a subtler game: the conquered triumphs,
The victor has the loss. Yet in the passage 114
The gods have been most equal. Palamon, 115
Your kinsman hath confessed the right o'th' lady
Did lie in you, for you first saw her and
Even then proclaimed your fancy. He restored her
As your stol'n jewel, and desired your spirit
To send him hence forgiven. The gods my justice
Take from my hand, and they themselves become
The executioners. Lead your lady off,
And call your lovers from the stage of death, 123
Whom I adopt my friends.
        [*The knights approach from the scaffold.*]
                    A day or two
Let us look sadly, and give grace unto
The funeral of Arcite, in whose end 126
The visages of bridegrooms we'll put on
And smile with Palamon, for whom an hour,
But one hour since, I was as dearly sorry
As glad of Arcite, and am now as glad

60–1 from iron . . . origin (Pythagoras supposedly came upon the idea of harmonic relationships in music by observing how hammers of differing sizes produced pure intervals of fourths, fifths, and octaves when struck upon an anvil. Tubalcain, the first "artificer in brass and iron" [Genesis 4:22], was popularly credited with earlier discoveries of this sort.) **61–5 what . . . not** whatever malicious flint it was, or else some other violent sulfurous device make for this purpose, cold as the gloomy saturnine god associated with the cold and moist "humour" in the body called phlegm and yet filled with burning malevolence (like Saturn in Chaucer's "The Knight's Tale," who sends a fury to goad Arcite's horse into wild action) that sent out a hot spark, I do not care to speculate **66 Took toy at** took a capricious dislike to. **fell to what** started acting out whatever **67 comes on end** rears straight up **68 school-doing** the *kind manège* or trained movements he has been schooled in (lines 68–9) **70 rowel** sharp-pointed disk on a spur **71 jot** slightest bit **72 jadery** tricks characteristic of a vicious horse **73 that . . . bravely** who nonetheless kept in his saddle superbly. **74 curb** strap attached to the bit to control the horse. **girth** belt under the horse's belly to hold the saddle in place. **diff'ring** different kinds of **81–2 his full . . . load** the full weight of the horse now becomes the rider's load to be carried, as though the rider were the horse. **82 Yet** (1) Still (2) Nonetheless **83–4 But . . . approaches** but Arcite is like a ship that needs only one more big wave to founder.

91 Reach Extend **92 told** counted out **98 to honor** i.e., to honor the memory of Arcite. **100 Acknowledge** Let us acknowledge **104 arrose** bedew, sprinkle **107 vouched** affirmed, guaranteed the truth of **108 grace** honor **114 passage** (1) occurrence (2) exchange of blows **115 equal** impartial, fair and balanced. **123 lovers** devoted followers **126 in whose end** after which

As for him sorry. O you heavenly charmers,   131
What things you make of us! For what we lack
We laugh, for what we have are sorry, still
Are children in some kind. Let us be thankful
For that which is, and with you leave dispute   135
That are above our question. Let's go off,   136
And bear us like the time.   *Flourish. Exeunt.*   137

❦

Epilogue

[*Enter Epilogue.*]

EPILOGUE
I would now ask ye how ye like the play,
But, as it is with schoolboys, cannot say;   2

---

131 charmers i.e., gods, with their magical powers capable of
enchanting us   **135–6 and . . . question** and leave off disputing with
you, whose high will we must not question.   **137 bear . . . time** bear
ourselves in a matter suitable to the sad and yet joyful occasion.
Epilogue
2 schoolboys (Probably it is a juvenile actor who speaks.)   **say** speak

I am cruel fearful. Pray yet stay awhile,   3
And let me look upon ye. No man smile?
Then it goes hard, I see. He that has
Loved a young handsome wench, then, show his
    face—
'Tis strange if none be here—and if he will,
Against his conscience, let him hiss, and kill   8
Our market. 'Tis in vain, I see, to stay ye.   9
Have at the worst can come, then! Now, what say ye?   10
And yet mistake me not; I am not bold:
We have no such cause. If the tale we have told—
For 'tis no other—any way content ye,
For to that honest purpose it was meant ye,
We have our end; and ye shall have ere long,   15
I dare say, many a better to prolong
Your old loves to us. We and all our might
Rest at your service. Gentlemen, good night.
                                    Flourish. [*Exit.*]

---

3 cruel extremely   **8–9 kill Our market** spoil the demand for this
play.   **9 stay** restrain   **10 Have . . . then!** Go ahead, then, do your
damnedst!   **15 end** intent, wish

The Poems

Venus and Adonis

Like most of his contemporaries, Shakespeare apparently did not regard the writing of plays as an elegant literary pursuit. He must have known that he was good at it, and he certainly became famous in his day as a playwright, but he took no pains over the publication of his plays. We have no literary prefaces for them, no indication that Shakespeare saw them through the press. Writing for the theater was rather like writing for the movies today: a profitable and even glamorous venture but subliterary. When Ben Jonson brought out his collected *Works* (mostly plays) during his lifetime, he was jeered at for his pretensions.

The writing of sonnets and other "serious" poetry, on the other hand, was conventionally a bid for true literary fame. Shakespeare's prefatory epistle to his *Venus and Adonis* betrays an eagerness for recognition. Deferentially, he seeks the sponsorship of the Earl of Southampton, in hopes of literary prestige as well as financial support. He speaks of *Venus and Adonis* as "the first heir of my invention," as though he had written no plays earlier, and promises Southampton a "graver labor" to appear shortly. *Venus and Adonis* in 1593 and *The Rape of Lucrece* in 1594 were, in fact, Shakespeare's first publications. Both were carefully and correctly printed. They were probably composed between June of 1592 and May of 1594, a period when the theaters were closed because of the plague. Shakespeare's belief in their importance to his literary career is confirmed by the reports of his contemporaries. Richard Barnfield singled them out as the works most likely to assure a place for Shakespeare in "fame's immortal book." Francis Meres, in his *Palladis Tamia: Wit's Treasury*, exclaimed in 1598 that "the sweet witty soul of Ovid lives in mellifluous and honey-tongued Shakespeare: witness his *Venus and Adonis*, his *Lucrece*, his sugared sonnets among his private friends, etc." Gabriel Harvey, although preferring *Lucrece* and *Hamlet* as more pleasing to "the wiser sort," conceded that "the younger sort takes much delight in Shakespeare's *Venus and Ado-*nis." John Weever and still others add further testimonials to the extraordinary reputation of Shakespeare's nondramatic poems.

As Gabriel Harvey's puritanical comment on *Venus and Adonis* suggests, this poem was regarded as amatory and even risqué. It mirrored a current vogue for Ovidian erotic poetry, as exemplified by Thomas Lodge's *Scilla's Metamorphosis*, 1589 (in which an amorous nymph courts a reluctant young man), and by Christopher Marlowe's *Hero and Leander*. This latter poem, left unfinished at Marlowe's death in 1593 and published in 1598 with a continuation by George Chapman, was evidently circulated in manuscript, as were so many poems of this sophisticated sort, including Shakespeare's sonnets. Shakespeare may well have been influenced by Marlowe's tone of wryly comic detachment and sensuous grace. He may also have read Michael Drayton's *Endymion and Phoebe* (published in 1595 but written earlier), in which the erotic tradition is somewhat idealized into moral allegory. Most important, however, Shakespeare knew his Ovid, both firsthand and in Golding's English translation (1567). He appears to have combined three mythical tales from the *Metamorphoses*. The narrative outline is to be found in Venus's pursuit of Adonis (Book 10), but the bashful reluctance of the young man is more reminiscent of Hermaphroditus (Book 4) and Narcissus (Book 3). Hermaphroditus pleads youth as his reason for wishing to escape the clutches of the water nymph Salmacis and so is transformed with her into a single body containing both sexes; Narcissus evades the nymph Echo out of self-infatuation. Shakespeare has thus drawn a composite portrait of male coyness, a subject he was to explore further in the sonnets. Such a theme was suited to a nobleman of Southampton's youth and prospects. In tone it was also well suited to the aristocratic and intellectual set who read such poetry. Shakespeare here aimed at a more refined audience than that for which he wrote plays, though his theatrical audience must also have been generally intelligent. The ornate qualities of

Venus and Adonis should be judged in the fashionable context of a sophisticated audience.

The poem is, among other things, a tour de force of stylized poetic techniques. The story itself is relatively uneventful, and the characters are static. For two-thirds of the poem, very little happens other than a series of amorous claspings, from which Adonis feebly attempts to extricate himself. Even his subsequent fight with the boar and his violent death are occasions for rhetorical pathos rather than for vivid narrative description. The story is essentially a frame. Similarly, we must not expect psychological insight or meaningful self-discovery. The conventions of amatory verse do not encourage a serious interest in character. Venus and Adonis are mouthpieces for contrasting attitudes toward love. They debate a favorite courtly topic in the style of John Lyly. Both appeal to conventional wisdom and speak in *sententiae*, or aphoristic pronouncements. Venus, for example, warning Adonis of the need for caution in pursuing the boar, opines that "Danger deviseth shifts; wit waits on fear" (line 690). Adonis, pleading his unreadiness for love, cites commonplace analogies: "No fisher but the ungrown fry forbears. / The mellow plum doth fall, the green sticks fast" (lines 526–7). In substance, their arguments are equally conventional. Venus urges a carpe diem philosophy of seizing the moment of pleasure. "Make use of time, let not advantage slip; / Beauty within itself should not be wasted" (lines 129–30). She bolsters her claim with an appeal to the "law of nature," according to which all living things are obliged to reproduce themselves; only by begetting can humans conquer time and death. Yet, however close this position may be to a major theme of the sonnets, it does not go unchallenged. Adonis charges vigorously that Venus is only rationalizing her lust: "O strange excuse, / When reason is the bawd to lust's abuse!" (lines 791–2). His plea for more time in which to mature and prove his manliness is understandable, however much we may smile at his inability to be aroused by Venus's blandishments. Thus, neither contestant wins the argument. Venus is proved right in her fear that Adonis will be killed by the boar he hunts, but Adonis's rejection of idle lust for manly activity affirms a conventional idea of masculinity that requires the fleshing of one's killing sword as ritual prerequisite to the fleshing of one's phallic sword. The debate is, in a sense, an ingeniously elaborate literary exercise, yet it also allows for reflection on contrasting views of love as sensual and spiritual, absurd and magnificent, funny and serious.

The narrator's persona is central to the ambivalence in the debate. He, too, speaks in *sententiae*, and his aphorisms appear to sympathize with both contestants. At times, he affirms the irresistible force of love: "What though the rose have prickles, yet 'tis plucked" (line 574). At other times, he laughs at Venus for her vacillation of mood: "Thy weal and woe are both of them extremes. /

Despair and hope makes thee ridiculous" (lines 987–8). Like Ovid's usual persona, the speaker here is both intrigued and amused by love, compelled to heed its power and yet aware of the absurdities. The result is a characteristic Ovidian blend of irony and pathos. The irony is especially evident in the delightful comic touches that undermine the potential seriousness of the action: Venus like an Amazon pulling Adonis off his mount and tucking him under one arm, pouting and blushing; Adonis's horse chasing away after a mare in heat, leaving Adonis to fend for himself; Venus fainting at the thought of the boar and pulling Adonis right on top of her, "in the very lists of love, / Her champion mounted for the hot encounter" (lines 595–6). These devices distance us from the action and create an atmosphere of elegant if prurient entertainment. Yet the poem is also suffused with the rich pathos of sensuous emotion. Venus's sorrow over the death of Adonis is quite genuine. The sensuousness would cloy without the ironic humor, whereas the humor would seem frivolous without the pathos.

The poem hints at moral allegory, in the manner of Ovidian mythologizing. Venus represents herself as the goddess, not only of erotic passion, but also of eternal love conquering time and death. Because Adonis perversely spurns this ideal, Venus concludes that human beauty must perish and that human happiness must be subject to mischance. Yet this reading is only one part of the argument and is contradicted by an opposing suggestion that Adonis is the rational principle attempting unsuccessfully to govern human lust (the boar and Adonis's unbridled horse). These contradictions, which derive from the structure of the poem as a debate and also from Renaissance Neoplatonism, confirm our impression that the allegory is not the true "meaning" of the poem but is part of an ambiguous view of love as both exalted and earthly, a mystery that we will never comprehend in single terms. The allegory elevates the seriousness, adding poetic dignity to what might otherwise appear to be an unabashedly erotic poem. We should not minimize the sexual teasing or fail to acknowledge our own erotic pleasure in it. Venus's repeated encounters with Adonis take the form of ingeniously varied positions, ending in coital embrace, although without consummation. Adonis's passive role invites the male reader to fantasize himself in Adonis's place, being seduced by the goddess of beauty. The famous passage comparing Venus's body to a deer park with "pleasant fountains," "sweet bottom grass," and "round rising hillocks" (lines 229–40) is graphic through the use of double entendre without being pornographic. The poem is equally explicit in its "banquet" of the five senses (lines 433–50). This is the "naughty" Ovid of the *Ars Amatoria*.

Shakespeare's poem is an embroidery of poetic flourishes, of "conceits" or ingeniously wrought similes, of artfully constructed digressions, such as the narrative of

Adonis's horse, and of color symbolism. Images usually are drawn from nature (eagles, birds caught in nets, wolves, berries) or connote burning, blazing, and shining (torches, jewels). The dominant colors are red and white, usually paired antithetically: the red of the rising sun or Adonis's blushing face or Mars's ensign, the white of an alabaster hand or fresh bed linen or "ashy-pale" anger. Ironically, too, the boar's frothy-white mouth is stained with red, and Adonis's red blood blemishes his "wonted lily white." Adonis's flower, the anemone, is reddish-purple and white. A similarly balanced antithesis per-

vades the poem's rhetorical figures, as in the symmetrical repetition of words in grammatically parallel phrases (*parison*), or in phrases of equal length (*isocolon*), or in inverted order (*antimetabole*), or at the beginning and ending of a line (*epanalepsis*), and so on. These pyrotechnics may at first seem mechanical, but they, too, have a place in a work of art that celebrates both the erotic and the spiritual in love. Decoration has its function and is not mere embellishment for its own sake. At all events Shakespeare has created a powerful poetic variation on an ancient myth that is at the same time a rhetorical tour de force.

Venus and Adonis

"*Vilia miretur vulgus; mihi flavus Apollo*
Pocula Castalia plena ministret aqua."

To the RIGHT HONORABLE HENRY WRIOTHESLEY,
Earl of Southampton, and Baron of Titchfield.

RIGHT HONORABLE,

I know not how I shall offend in dedicating my unpolished lines to Your Lordship, nor how the world will censure me for choosing so strong a prop to support so weak a burden; only if Your Honor seem but pleased, I account

myself highly praised, and vow to take advantage of all idle hours, till I have honored you with some graver labor. But if the first heir of my invention prove deformed,   7
I shall be sorry it had so noble a godfather, and never after ear so barren a land, for fear it yield me still so bad a har-   9
vest. I leave it to your honorable survey, and Your Honor to your heart's content, which I wish may always answer your own wish and the world's hopeful expectation.

Your Honor's in all duty,

William Shakespeare.

Motto: *Vilia miretur,* etc. Let the base vulgar admire trash; may golden-haired Apollo serve me goblets filled from the Castalian spring. (Ovid, *Amores,* 1.15.35–6.)
Dedication: Henry Wriothesley, Earl of Southampton (A popular and brilliant young gentleman of nineteen years, already prominent at court. Subsequent dedications by Shakespeare and others indicate that he was a genuinely devoted patron of literature throughout his life.)

7 the first . . . invention (This phrase has been variously interpreted to mean Shakespeare's first written work, his first printed work, his first "invented" work in the sense that the plots of his plays were usually not original with him, his first work independent of collaborators, or his first "literary" work, since plays were unliterary in the Elizabethan sense. The second and last are the most probable.)   **9 ear** sow, cultivate

Even as the sun with purple-colored face
Had ta'en his last leave of the weeping morn,
Rose-cheeked Adonis hied him to the chase.
Hunting he loved, but love he laughed to scorn.
　　Sick-thoughted Venus makes amain unto him,
　　And like a boldfaced suitor 'gins to woo him.

"Thrice-fairer than myself," thus she began,
"The field's chief flower, sweet above compare,
Stain to all nymphs, more lovely than a man,
More white and red than doves or roses are:
　　Nature that made thee, with herself at strife,
　　Saith that the world hath ending with thy life.

"Vouchsafe, thou wonder, to alight thy steed,
And rein his proud head to the saddlebow.
If thou wilt deign this favor, for thy meed
A thousand honey secrets shalt thou know.
　　Here come and sit, where never serpent hisses,
　　And being set, I'll smother thee with kisses;

"And yet not cloy thy lips with loathed satiety,
But rather famish them amid their plenty,
Making them red and pale with fresh variety—
Ten kisses short as one, one long as twenty.
　　A summer's day will seem an hour but short,
　　Being wasted in such time-beguiling sport."

With this she seizeth on his sweating palm,
The precedent of pith and livelihood,
And, trembling in her passion, calls it balm,
Earth's sovereign salve, to do a goddess good.
　　Being so enraged, desire doth lend her force
　　Courageously to pluck him from his horse.

Over one arm the lusty courser's rein,
Under her other was the tender boy,
Who blushed and pouted in a dull disdain,
With leaden appetite, unapt to toy;
　　She red and hot as coals of glowing fire,
　　He red for shame, but frosty in desire.

The studded bridle on a ragged bough
Nimbly she fastens. Oh, how quick is love!

The steed is stallèd up, and even now
To tie the rider she begins to prove.
　　Backward she pushed him, as she would be thrust,
　　And governed him in strength, though not in lust.

So soon was she along as he was down,
Each leaning on their elbows and their hips.
Now doth she stroke his cheek, now doth he frown,
And 'gins to chide, but soon she stops his lips
　　And kissing speaks, with lustful language broken,
　　"If thou wilt chide, thy lips shall never open."

He burns with bashful shame; she with her tears
Doth quench the maiden burning of his cheeks.
Then with her windy sighs and golden hairs
To fan and blow them dry again she seeks.
　　He saith she is immodest, blames her miss;
　　What follows more, she murders with a kiss.

Even as an empty eagle, sharp by fast,
Tires with her beak on feathers, flesh, and bone,
Shaking her wings, devouring all in haste,
Till either gorge be stuffed or prey be gone,
　　Even so she kissed his brow, his cheek, his chin,
　　And where she ends she doth anew begin.

Forced to content, but never to obey,
Panting he lies and breatheth in her face.
She feedeth on the steam as on a prey,
And calls it heavenly moisture, air of grace,
　　Wishing her cheeks were gardens full of flowers,
　　So they were dewed with such distilling showers.

Look how a bird lies tangled in a net,
So fastened in her arms Adonis lies;
Pure shame and awed resistance made him fret,
Which bred more beauty in his angry eyes.
　　Rain added to a river that is rank
　　Perforce will force it overflow the bank.

Still she entreats, and prettily entreats,
For to a pretty ear she tunes her tale.
Still is he sullen, still he lours and frets,
Twixt crimson shame and anger ashy-pale.
　　Being red, she loves him best; and being white,
　　Her best is bettered with a more delight.

Look how he can, she cannot choose but love;
And by her fair immortal hand she swears
From his soft bosom never to remove,
Till he take truce with her contending tears,

1 **purple-colored** red, blushing　2 **the weeping morn** the goddess of the dawn, Aurora, weeping tears (i.e., the dew of morning) at being left by the sun-god. (In the Greek myth, she weeps for the death of her lover, Tithonus.)　3 **hied him** betook himself, hastened　5 **Sick-thoughted** lovesick.　**makes amain** hastens　9 **Stain . . . nymphs** eclipsing in beauty all young beautiful women　11–12 **Nature . . . life** Nature, having striven to surpass herself in making you her masterpiece, says that if you die the world will cease. (The story of Adonis's death, and of the anemone that springs from his blood, is a vegetation myth.)　13 **Vouchsafe** Deign.　**alight** alight from　14 **the saddlebow** the arch in, or the pieces forming, the front of the saddle. (The image is of reining the horse's head sharply back.)　15 **meed** reward　16 **honey** sweet　24 **wasted** spent　25 **sweating** i.e., indicative of youth; not dried with age　26 **The precedent . . . livelihood** the sign of sexual strength and vitality　28 **sovereign** efficacious　29 **enraged** ardent　30 **Courageously** lustfully and boldly　31 **lusty courser's** vigorous horse's　33 **dull** moody, listless　34 **unapt to toy** undisposed to dally amorously

39 **stallèd** fastened, secured (as in a stall)　40 **prove** try.　43 **along** lying at his side　47 **broken** interrupted　53 **miss** offense, misconduct　55 **sharp by fast** hungry for lack of food　56 **Tires** tears, feeds ravenously　58 **gorge** bird's crop　61 **content** acquiesce.　**obey** i.e., answer her lust　66 **So** provided that.　**distilling** gently falling, in fine droplets　67 **Look how** Just as　69 **awed** daunted, overborne　71 **rank** full to overflowing　77 **Being** i.e., He being　78 **more** greater　81 **remove** move, remove herself　82 **take truce** come to terms

Which long have rained, making her cheeks all wet;
And one sweet kiss shall pay this countless debt.   84

Upon this promise did he raise his chin,
Like a divedapper peering through a wave,   86
Who, being looked on, ducks as quickly in.
So offers he to give what she did crave;
    But when her lips were ready for his pay,   89
    He winks and turns his lips another way.   90

Never did passenger in summer's heat   91
More thirst for drink than she for this good turn.
Her help she sees, but help she cannot get;
She bathes in water, yet her fire must burn.   94
    "Oh, pity," 'gan she cry, "flint-hearted boy!
    'Tis but a kiss I beg. Why art thou coy?

"I have been wooed, as I entreat thee now,
Even by the stern and direful god of war,   98
Whose sinewy neck in battle ne'er did bow,
Who conquers where he comes in every jar;   100
    Yet hath he been my captive and my slave,
    And begged for that which thou unasked shalt have.

"Over my altars hath he hung his lance,
His battered shield, his uncontrollèd crest,   104
And for my sake hath learned to sport and dance,
To toy, to wanton, dally, smile, and jest,   106
    Scorning his churlish drum and ensign red,
    Making my arms his field, his tent my bed.   108

"Thus he that overruled I overswayed,
Leading him prisoner in a red-rose chain.
Strong-tempered steel his stronger strength obeyed,
Yet was he servile to my coy disdain.   112
    Oh, be not proud, nor brag not of thy might,
    For mastering her that foiled the god of fight!   114

"Touch but my lips with those fair lips of thine—   115
Though mine be not so fair, yet are they red—
The kiss shall be thine own as well as mine.   117
What see'st thou in the ground? Hold up thy head.
    Look in mine eyeballs, there thy beauty lies;   119
    Then why not lips on lips, since eyes in eyes?

"Art thou ashamed to kiss? Then wink again,   121
And I will wink; so shall the day seem night.
Love keeps his revels where there are but twain;
Be bold to play, our sport is not in sight.   124

These blue-veined violets whereon we lean
Never can blab, nor know not what we mean.   126

"The tender spring upon thy tempting lip   127
Shows thee unripe, yet mayst thou well be tasted.
Make use of time, let not advantage slip;   129
Beauty within itself should not be wasted.   130
    Fair flowers that are not gathered in their prime
    Rot and consume themselves in little time.

"Were I hard-favored, foul, or wrinkled old,   133
Ill-nurtured, crooked, churlish, harsh in voice,
O'erworn, despisèd, rheumatic, and cold,   135
Thick-sighted, barren, lean, and lacking juice,   136
    Then mightst thou pause, for then I were not for thee;
    But having no defects, why dost abhor me?

"Thou canst not see one wrinkle in my brow;
Mine eyes are gray and bright and quick in turning;   140
My beauty as the spring doth yearly grow,   141
My flesh is soft and plump, my marrow burning;   142
    My smooth moist hand, were it with thy hand felt,   143
    Would in thy palm dissolve, or seem to melt.

"Bid me discourse, I will enchant thine ear,
Or like a fairy, trip upon the green,   146
Or like a nymph, with long disheveled hair,
Dance on the sands, and yet no footing seen.   148
    Love is a spirit all compact of fire,   149
    Not gross to sink, but light, and will aspire.   150

"Witness this primrose bank whereon I lie;
These forceless flowers like sturdy trees support me.   152
Two strengthless doves will draw me through the sky,   153
From morn till night, even where I list to sport me.   154
    Is love so light, sweet boy, and may it be   155
    That thou shouldst think it heavy unto thee?   156

"Is thine own heart to thine own face affected?   157
Can thy right hand seize love upon thy left?   158
Then woo thyself, be of thyself rejected;   159
Steal thine own freedom and complain on theft.   160

---

84 **countless** beyond reckoning   86 **divedapper** dabchick, a common
English waterbird   89 **for his pay** to be paid by him (with a kiss)
90 **winks** shuts his eyes (and winces)   91 **passenger** wayfarer
94 **water** i.e., her tears.   **fire** (of passion)   98 **direful** inspiring dread.
god of war Mars   100 **where** wherever.   **jar** fight   104 **uncontrollèd**
unconquered, unbowed.   **crest** i.e., of helmet   106 **toy, wanton,
dally** sport amorously   108 **arms** (With a pun on "weapons.")
112 **coy** aloof, teasing   114 **foiled** vanquished   115 **Touch** If you
touch   117 **thine . . . mine** i.e., mutual, shared.   119 **there . . . lies** i.e.,
(1) see your beauty reflected there (2) your beauty lies in my beholding   121 **wink** close the eyes   124 **not in sight** observed by no one.

126 **mean** intend.   127 **spring** growth (i.e., downy hair)   129 **advantage** opportunity   130 **Beauty . . . wasted** beauty should not be
wasted by being kept to itself.   133 **hard-favored** ugly.   **foul** ugly
135 **O'erworn** worn by time   136 **Thick-sighted** dim-eyed   140 **gray**
i.e., blue.   **quick in turning** animated   141 **as . . . grow** is perennially renewed, like spring   142 **marrow** vital animal spirit.   **burning**
sexually ardent   143 **moist** (Indicative of youth and passion, as with
sweating in line 25.)   146 **trip** dance   148 **footing** footprint
149 **compact** composed   150 **gross** heavy. (The heavy elements, earth
and water, sink; fire and air rise.)   **aspire** rise.   152 **forceless** frail
153 **doves** (Venus's chariot was depicted as being drawn by doves.)
154 **list** desire   155 **light** (1) rising, weightless (2) wanton
156 **heavy** (1) weighty (2) troublous   157 **affected** drawn by affection.   158–60 **Can . . . theft** i.e., Do you think you can you find love
by having one hand woo the other, as if love were wholly contained
within oneself? Then go ahead, play all the roles of love yourself: woo
yourself, find yourself rejected by yourself, make captive your own
heart to yourself and complain of yourself as the thief of love.
159 **of** by

Narcissus so himself himself forsook, 161
And died to kiss his shadow in the brook. 162

"Torches are made to light, jewels to wear,
Dainties to taste, fresh beauty for the use,
Herbs for their smell, and sappy plants to bear. 165
Things growing to themselves are growth's abuse. 166
    Seeds spring from seeds, and beauty breedeth beauty.
    Thou wast begot; to get it is thy duty. 168

"Upon the earth's increase why shouldst thou feed,
Unless the earth with thy increase be fed?
By law of nature thou art bound to breed,
That thine may live when thou thyself art dead; 172
    And so, in spite of death, thou dost survive,
    In that thy likeness still is left alive."

By this the lovesick queen began to sweat, 175
For where they lay the shadow had forsook them,
And Titan, tirèd in the midday heat, 177
With burning eye did hotly overlook them, 178
    Wishing Adonis had his team to guide, 179
    So he were like him, and by Venus' side. 180

And now Adonis, with a lazy sprite, 181
And with a heavy, dark, disliking eye,
His louring brows o'erwhelming his fair sight, 183
Like misty vapors when they blot the sky,
    Souring his cheeks, cries, "Fie, no more of love! 185
    The sun doth burn my face; I must remove." 186

"Ay me," quoth Venus, "young, and so unkind? 187
What bare excuses mak'st thou to be gone!
I'll sigh celestial breath, whose gentle wind
Shall cool the heat of this descending sun.
    I'll make a shadow for thee of my hairs;
    If they burn too, I'll quench them with my tears.

"The sun that shines from heaven shines but warm, 193
And, lo, I lie between that sun and thee.
The heat I have from thence doth little harm;
Thine eye darts forth the fire that burneth me,
    And were I not immortal, life were done 197
    Between this heavenly and earthly sun.

"Art thou obdurate, flinty, hard as steel?
Nay, more than flint, for stone at rain relenteth. 200
Art thou a woman's son, and canst not feel
What 'tis to love, how want of love tormenteth? 202
    Oh, had thy mother borne so hard a mind,
    She had not brought forth thee, but died unkind. 204

"What am I, that thou shouldst contemn me this? 205
Or what great danger dwells upon my suit? 206
What were thy lips the worse for one poor kiss? 207
Speak, fair, but speak fair words, or else be mute. 208
    Give me one kiss, I'll give it thee again, 209
    And one for interest, if thou wilt have twain.

"Fie, lifeless picture, cold and senseless stone, 211
Well-painted idol, image dull and dead,
Statue contenting but the eye alone,
Thing like a man, but of no woman bred!
    Thou art no man, though of a man's complexion, 215
    For men will kiss even by their own direction." 216

This said, impatience chokes her pleading tongue,
And swelling passion doth provoke a pause.
Red cheeks and fiery eyes blaze forth her wrong; 219
Being judge in love, she cannot right her cause. 220
    And now she weeps, and now she fain would speak, 221
    And now her sobs do her intendments break. 222

Sometime she shakes her head and then his hand, 223
Now gazeth she on him, now on the ground;
Sometime her arms enfold him like a band. 225
She would, he will not in her arms be bound;
    And when from thence he struggles to be gone,
    She locks her lily fingers one in one.

"Fondling," she saith, "since I have hemmed thee here 229
Within the circuit of this ivory pale, 230
I'll be a park, and thou shalt be my deer. 231
Feed where thou wilt, on mountain or in dale;
    Graze on my lips; and if those hills be dry,
    Stray lower, where the pleasant fountains lie. 234

"Within this limit is relief enough, 235
Sweet bottom grass and high delightful plain, 236

---

161 Narcissus a beautiful youth in classical mythology who, leaning over a pool to drink, fell in love with his reflection and stayed there until he died. He was afterward changed into a flower. (Ovid, *Metamorphoses*, 3.339–510.) **himself himself forsook** i.e., abandoned himself to a hopeless passion for himself **162 to kiss his shadow** seeking fruitlessly to kiss his own reflection **165 sappy plants** sapbearing fruit trees **166 Things . . . abuse** Things that grow solely for their own use abuse the very purpose of growth. **168 get** beget, procreate **172 thine** your progeny **175 By this** By this time **177 Titan** the sun-god. **tirèd** (1) attired (2) weary **178 overlook** look upon **179 his team** i.e., Titan's team of horses **180 So . . . side** i.e., so that he, Titan, might be in Adonis's place. **181 lazy sprite** dull spirit **183 o'erwhelming** overhanging so as to cover. **sight** eyes **185 Souring his cheeks** scowling **186 remove** move. **187 unkind** unrelenting; unnatural. **193 shines but warm** merely makes me warm (whereas you burn me up) **197 were done** would be done for, finished

200 relenteth wears slowly away. **202 want of love** being denied reciprocal love **204 unkind** unnaturally unrelenting, not fulfilling her natural function. **205 contemn me this** scornfully refuse me this request, or, scorn me thus. **206 dwells upon** attends **207 What** In what way **208 Speak, fair** Speak, handsome youth. **fair words** kind words **209 Give** If you give **211 senseless** insensible **215 complexion** outward appearance **216 direction** inclination. **219 blaze forth** proclaim. (With a metaphorical sense of "seem to burn," "show by their flaming.") **220 Being . . . cause** although goddess and hence arbiter of love, Venus cannot prevail in her own case. **221 fain** gladly **222 do . . . break** interrupt what she intends to say. **223 his hand** (i.e., not in a handshake but in a gesture of frustration) **225 like a band** as in a bond or fetter. **229 Fondling** Foolish one **230 pale** fence (i.e., the sexual topography is continued in *fountains, bottom grass, hillocks, brakes,* etc.) **231 park** deer preserve. **deer** (With a pun on *dear*.) **234 fountains** (1) springs (2) breasts **235 limit** boundary. **relief** (1) pasture (2) sexual pleasure (3) variety of landscape **236 bottom grass** valley grass. (With an allusion to pubic hair.) **plain** i.e., mons veneris or the stomach (?)

Round rising hillocks, brakes obscure and rough, 237
To shelter thee from tempest and from rain.
　　Then be my deer, since I am such a park;
　　No dog shall rouse thee, though a thousand bark." 240

At this Adonis smiles as in disdain,
That in each cheek appears a pretty dimple. 242
Love made those hollows, if himself were slain, 243
He might be buried in a tomb so simple, 244
　　Foreknowing well, if there he came to lie,
　　Why, there Love lived; and there he could not die. 246

These lovely caves, these round enchanting pits,
Opened their mouths to swallow Venus' liking. 248
Being mad before, how doth she now for wits? 249
Struck dead at first, what needs a second striking?
　　Poor queen of love, in thine own law forlorn, 251
　　To love a cheek that smiles at thee in scorn!

Now which way shall she turn? What shall she say?
Her words are done, her woes the more increasing;
The time is spent; her object will away,
And from her twining arms doth urge releasing.
　　"Pity," she cries, "some favor, some remorse!" 257
　　Away he springs and hasteth to his horse.

But, lo, from forth a copse that neighbors by, 259
A breeding jennet, lusty, young, and proud, 260
Adonis' trampling courser doth espy,
And forth she rushes, snorts, and neighs aloud.
　　The strong-necked steed, being tied unto a tree,
　　Breaketh his rein, and to her straight goes he. 264

Imperiously he leaps, he neighs, he bounds,
And now his woven girths he breaks asunder. 266
The bearing earth with his hard hoof he wounds, 267
Whose hollow womb resounds like heaven's thunder.
　　The iron bit he crusheth 'tween his teeth,
　　Controlling what he was controllèd with.

His ears up-pricked, his braided hanging mane
Upon his compassed crest now stand on end; 272
His nostrils drink the air, and forth again,
As from a furnace, vapors doth he send.
　　His eye, which scornfully glisters like fire,
　　Shows his hot courage and his high desire. 276

Sometime he trots, as if he told the steps, 277
With gentle majesty and modest pride;
Anon he rears upright, curvets, and leaps, 279
As who should say, "Lo, thus my strength is tried, 280
　　And this I do to captivate the eye
　　Of the fair breeder that is standing by."

What recketh he his rider's angry stir, 283
His flattering "Holla," or his "Stand, I say"? 284
What cares he now for curb or pricking spur?
For rich caparisons or trappings gay? 286
　　He sees his love, and nothing else he sees,
　　For nothing else with his proud sight agrees.

Look when a painter would surpass the life, 289
In limning out a well-proportioned steed, 290
His art with nature's workmanship at strife,
As if the dead the living should exceed, 292
　　So did this horse excel a common one
　　In shape, in courage, color, pace, and bone. 294

Round-hoofed, short-jointed, fetlocks shag and long, 295
Broad breast, full eye, small head, and nostril wide,
High crest, short ears, straight legs and passing strong, 297
Thin mane, thick tail, broad buttock, tender hide: 298
　　Look what a horse should have he did not lack, 299
　　Save a proud rider on so proud a back.

Sometime he scuds far off, and there he stares;
Anon he starts at stirring of a feather;
To bid the wind a base he now prepares, 303
And whe'er he run or fly they know not whether; 304
　　For through his mane and tail the high wind sings,
　　Fanning the hairs, who wave like feathered wings.

He looks upon his love and neighs unto her;
She answers him as if she knew his mind.
Being proud, as females are, to see him woo her,
She puts on outward strangeness, seems unkind, 310
　　Spurns at his love and scorns the heat he feels, 311
　　Beating his kind embracements with her heels. 312

Then, like a melancholy malcontent,
He vails his tail that, like a falling plume, 314

---

237 **hillocks** buttocks (?)　**brakes** patches of dense fern and bracken. (Again with sexual suggestion.)　**obscure** dark.　**rough** shaggy, dense　240 **rouse** cause to start from cover　242 **That** so that 243 **Love** Cupid.　**if** so that if　244 **simple** unadorned　246 **Love** (1) the essence of love, loveliness (2) Cupid himself　248 **Opened . . . liking** i.e., looked so winsome in their dimpling that Venus was engulfed, swallowed up, by love.　**liking** desire.　249 **how . . . wits?** how may she keep her sanity now?　251 **in . . . forlorn** condemned to suffer under your own rule of love　257 **remorse** compassion. 259 **copse . . . by** neighboring thicket　260 **breeding jennet** small Spanish mare in heat.　**lusty** spirited　264 **straight** straightway 266 **girths** cloth belts securing the saddle　267 **bearing** receiving 272 **compassed crest** arched ridge of the neck.　**stand on end** (The hairs of the mane stand on end.)　276 **courage** passion

277 **told** numbered　279 **curvets** raises his forelegs and then springs with his hind legs before the forelegs reach the ground　280 **As who should** as one might.　**tried** tested　283 **What recketh he** What does he care about or pay attention to.　**stir** bustle, agitation　284 **flattering** cajoling.　**Holla** Stop　286 **caparisons** gaily ornamental cloth coverings for the saddle and harness　289 **Look when** Just as when 290 **limning out** portraying, drawing　292 **dead** inanimate　294 **bone** frame.　295 **short-jointed** with short pasterns, the part of the horse's foot between the hoof and the fetlock.　**fetlocks** lower part of horses' legs where the tuft of hair grows behind, just above the hoof.　**shag** shaggy　297 **crest** ridge of the neck.　**passing** surpassingly　298 **tender hide** i.e., delicate of hide, not coarse　299 **Look what** whatever 303 **bid the wind a base** challenge the wind to a contest. (From the children's game of prisoner's base.)　304 **whe'er** whether.　**whether** which of the two　310 **outward strangeness** seeming indifference. **unkind** unattracted sexually, not responding to natural feeling 311 **Spurns at** (1) kicks at (2) repels　312 **kind** (1) affectionate, passionate (2) prompted by nature　314 **vails** lowers

Cool shadow to his melting buttock lent;
He stamps and bites the poor flies in his fume.   316
 His love, perceiving how he was enraged,
 Grew kinder, and his fury was assuaged.

His testy master goeth about to take him,   319
When, lo, the unbacked breeder, full of fear,   320
Jealous of catching, swiftly doth forsake him,   321
With her the horse, and left Adonis there.   322
 As they were mad, unto the wood they hie them,   323
 Outstripping crows that strive to overfly them.   324

All swoll'n with chafing, down Adonis sits,   325
Banning his boisterous and unruly beast;   326
And now the happy season once more fits   327
That lovesick Love by pleading may be blest;   328
 For lovers say the heart hath treble wrong
 When it is barred the aidance of the tongue.   330

An oven that is stopped, or river stayed,   331
Burneth more hotly, swelleth with more rage;
So of concealèd sorrow may be said.   333
Free vent of words love's fire doth assuage;   334
 But when the heart's attorney once is mute,   335
 The client breaks, as desperate in his suit.   336

He sees her coming and begins to glow,
Even as a dying coal revives with wind,
And with his bonnet hides his angry brow,
Looks on the dull earth with disturbèd mind,   339
 Taking no notice that she is so nigh,   341
 For all askance he holds her in his eye.   342

Oh, what a sight it was, wistly to view   343
How she came stealing to the wayward boy!
To note the fighting conflict of her hue,
How white and red each other did destroy!
 But now her cheek was pale, and by and by   347
 It flashed forth fire, as lightning from the sky.

Now was she just before him as he sat,
And like a lowly lover down she kneels;
With one fair hand she heaveth up his hat,
Her other tender hand his fair cheek feels.
 His tenderer cheek receives her soft hand's print,   353
 As apt as new-fall'n snow takes any dint.   354

Oh, what a war of looks was then between them!
Her eyes petitioners to his eyes suing,
His eyes saw her eyes as they had not seen them;   357
Her eyes wooed still, his eyes disdained the wooing;
 And all this dumb play had his acts made plain   359
 With tears which, choruslike, her eyes did rain.   360

Full gently now she takes him by the hand,
A lily prisoned in a jail of snow,
Or ivory in an alabaster band;
So white a friend engirts so white a foe.   364
 This beauteous combat, willful and unwilling,
 Showed like two silver doves that sit a-billing.   366

Once more the engine of her thoughts began: 367
"O fairest mover on this mortal round,   368
Would thou wert as I am, and I a man,
My heart all whole as thine, thy heart my wound!   370
 For one sweet look thy help I would assure thee,   371
 Though nothing but my body's bane would cure thee."   372

"Give me my hand," saith he. "Why dost thou feel it?"   373
"Give me my heart," saith she, "and thou shalt have it.   374
Oh, give it me, lest thy hard heart do steel it,   375
And being steeled, soft sighs can never grave it.   376
 Then love's deep groans I never shall regard,
 Because Adonis' heart hath made mine hard."

"For shame," he cries, "let go, and let me go!
My day's delight is past, my horse is gone,
And 'tis your fault I am bereft him so.   381
I pray you hence, and leave me here alone;   382
 For all my mind, my thought, my busy care,
 Is how to get my palfrey from the mare."   384

Thus she replies: "Thy palfrey, as he should,
Welcomes the warm approach of sweet desire.
Affection is a coal that must be cooled,   387
Else, suffered, it will set the heart on fire.   388
 The sea hath bounds, but deep desire hath none;
 Therefore no marvel though thy horse be gone.

"How like a jade he stood, tied to the tree,   391
Servilely mastered with a leathern rein!
But when he saw his love, his youth's fair fee,   393

---

316 **fume** anger.   319 **testy** irritated.   **goeth about** makes an effort
320 **unbacked breeder** unbroken and riderless mare in heat
321 **Jealous of catching** wary of being caught   322 **horse** i.e., stallion
323 **As** As if.   **hie them** hasten   324 **overfly them** fly faster than
they can run, or, keep pace above them in flight.   325 **swoll'n with
chafing** puffed with anger   326 **Banning** cursing   327 **fits** is fitting,
is suited   328 **Love** i.e., Venus, the goddess of love (not Cupid, as in
lines 243–6)   330 **aidance** help   331 **stopped** stopped up.   **stayed**
dammed   333 **may** it may   334 **love's . . . assuage** assuages love's fire
335 **the heart's attorney** i.e., the tongue   336 **breaks** (1) goes bankrupt
(2) breaks asunder, as the heart is said to break in rejected love
339 **And . . . brow** and pulls his hat down over his frowning brows
341 **Taking** i.e., pretending to take   342 **all . . . eye** he watches her out
of the corner of his eye.   343 **wistly** earnestly, attentively   347 **But
now** A short time ago   353 **tenderer** i.e., even more tender than her
hand   354 **dint** impression.

357 **as** as if   359–60 **And . . . rain** and all this silent action, as if in a
dumbshow preceding a play, was interpreted by her choruslike tears.
(In line 359, *his* means "its.")   364 **engirts** surrounds   366 **Showed**
looked   367 **the engine of her thoughts** her tongue   368 **mover** one
who moves or walks; also, one who imparts motion to the universe
itself.   **mortal round** earth   370 **thy heart my wound** would that
your heart suffered my wound.   371 **For** In return for.   **thy help . . .
thee** I would promise to help you   372 **bane** ruin, death. (With a suggestion of sexual surrender.)   373 **Give me** Let go   374 **it** your hand.
375 **give . . . it** give me back my heart, lest your hardness of heart turn
it to steel. (With a suggestion of *steal*: don't steal my heart from me.)
376 **grave** engrave, make an impression on   381 **bereft** deprived of
382 **hence** go away   384 **palfrey** saddle horse   387 **Affection . . .
cooled** Passion is an ember that must be quenched through satisfaction of desire   388 **suffered** permitted to continue   391 **jade** spiritless, worn-out nag   393 **fair fee** due reward

He held such petty bondage in disdain,
    Throwing the base thong from his bending crest,   395
    Enfranchising his mouth, his back, his breast.   396

"Who sees his true love in her naked bed,   397
Teaching the sheets a whiter hue than white,
But when his glutton eye so full hath fed,   399
His other agents aim at like delight?   400
    Who is so faint that dares not be so bold
    To touch the fire, the weather being cold?

"Let me excuse thy courser, gentle boy;
And learn of him, I heartily beseech thee,
To take advantage on presented joy.   405
Though I were dumb, yet his proceedings teach thee.   406
    Oh, learn to love; the lesson is but plain,
    And once made perfect, never lost again."   408

"I know not love," quoth he, "nor will not know it,
Unless it be a boar, and then I chase it;
'Tis much to borrow, and I will not owe it;   411
My love to love is love but to disgrace it;   412
    For I have heard it is a life in death,
    That laughs and weeps, and all but with a breath.   414

"Who wears a garment shapeless and unfinished?
Who plucks the bud before one leaf put forth?
If springing things be any jot diminished,   417
They wither in their prime, prove nothing worth.
    The colt that's backed and burdened being young   419
    Loseth his pride and never waxeth strong.

"You hurt my hand with wringing. Let us part
And leave this idle theme, this bootless chat.   422
Remove your siege from my unyielding heart;
To love's alarms it will not ope the gate.   424
    Dismiss your vows, your feignèd tears, your flatt'ry;
    For where a heart is hard they make no batt'ry."   426

"What, canst thou talk?" quoth she. "Hast thou a
    tongue?
Oh, would thou hadst not, or I had no hearing!
Thy mermaid's voice hath done me double wrong;   429
I had my load before, now pressed with bearing: 430
    Melodious discord, heavenly tune harsh sounding,
    Ear's deep sweet music, and heart's deep sore
        wounding.

"Had I no eyes but ears, my ears would love
That inward beauty and invisible;   434
Or were I deaf, thy outward parts would move   435
Each part in me that were but sensible.   436
    Though neither eyes nor ears, to hear nor see,
    Yet should I be in love by touching thee.

"Say that the sense of feeling were bereft me,
And that I could not see, nor hear, nor touch,
And nothing but the very smell were left me,
Yet would my love to thee be still as much;
    For from the stillitory of thy face excelling   443
    Comes breath perfumed that breedeth love by smelling.

"But oh, what banquet wert thou to the taste,
Being nurse and feeder of the other four!
Would they not wish the feast might ever last,
And bid Suspicion double-lock the door,   448
    Lest Jealousy, that sour unwelcome guest,
    Should, by his stealing in, disturb the feast?"

Once more the ruby-colored portal opened,   451
Which to his speech did honey passage yield,   452
Like a red morn, that ever yet betokened
Wreck to the seaman, tempest to the field,   454
    Sorrow to shepherds, woe unto the birds,
    Gusts and foul flaws to herdmen and to herds.   456

This ill presage advisedly she marketh.   457
Even as the wind is hushed before it raineth,
Or as the wolf doth grin before he barketh,   459
Or as the berry breaks before it staineth,
    Or like the deadly bullet of a gun,
    His meaning struck her ere his words begun.

And at his look she flatly falleth down,
For looks kill love, and love by looks reviveth;
A smile recures the wounding of a frown.   465
But blessèd bankrupt, that by love so thriveth!   466
    The silly boy, believing she is dead,   467
    Claps her pale cheek, till clapping makes it red;

And all amazed brake off his late intent,   469
For sharply he did think to reprehend her,
Which cunning Love did wittily prevent.
Fair fall the wit that can so well defend her!   472
    For on the grass she lies as she were slain,   473
    Till his breath breatheth life in her again.

---

395 base worthless, paltry. **bending crest** arching ridge of the neck **396 Enfranchising** freeing **397 in . . . bed** naked in her bed **399 But when** but that when **400 agents** organs, senses **405 on presented joy** of joy that presents itself. **406 dumb** unable to speak **408 made perfect** learned completely **411 borrow** assume as an obligation. **owe** obligate myself to repay **412 My . . . disgrace it** my only inclination toward love is a desire to render it contemptible, discredit it **414 all . . . breath** all in the same breath. **417 springing** sprouting, immature **419 backed** broken in **422 idle** useless. **bootless** profitless **424 alarms** signals of attack **426 batt'ry** breach in a fortified wall. **429 mermaid's** siren's **430 I . . . bearing** I was already burdened with desire; now I am oppressed by the weight of it, hearing your voice

434 That . . . invisible i.e., the unseen beauty of your voice **435 deaf** i.e., deaf as well as blind. **outward parts** i.e., tangible body **436 sensible** susceptible to sensual impressions. **443 For . . . excelling** for from the distillery of your unmatchable face **448 Suspicion** watchfulness against danger **451 portal** i.e., mouth **452 honey** sweet **454 Wreck** shipwreck. (A red sun at sunrise proverbially betokens a storm.) **tempest to the field** a heavy storm that beats down the grain **456 flaws** gusts of wind **457 ill presage** prediction of storm. **advisedly** attentively **459 grin** bare its teeth **465 recures** cures **466 blessèd bankrupt** (In becoming like a bankrupt, she paradoxically regains a fortune, i.e., Adonis's attention.) **467 silly** naive **469 amazed** perplexed, distraught. **brake** broke **472 Fair fall** Good luck befall. (With a pun on the idea of her falling down without hurting herself.) **473 as** as if

He wrings her nose, he strikes her on the cheeks,   475
He bends her fingers, holds her pulses hard,   476
He chafes her lips; a thousand ways he seeks
To mend the hurt that his unkindness marred.   478
    He kisses her, and she, by her good will,   479
    Will never rise, so he will kiss her still.   480

The night of sorrow now is turned to day.
Her two blue windows faintly she upheaveth,
Like the fair sun, when in his fresh array
He cheers the morn and all the earth relieveth;
    And as the bright sun glorifies the sky,
    So is her face illumined with her eye,

Whose beams upon his hairless face are fixed,
As if from thence they borrowed all their shine.
Were never four such lamps together mixed,   489
Had not his clouded with his brow's repine;   490
    But hers, which through the crystal tears gave light,
    Shone like the moon in water seen by night.

"Oh, where am I?" quoth she, "in earth or heaven,
Or in the ocean drenched, or in the fire?   494
What hour is this? Or morn or weary even?   495
Do I delight to die, or life desire?
    But now I lived, and life was death's annoy;   497
    But now I died, and death was lively joy.   498

"Oh, thou didst kill me; kill me once again!
Thy eyes' shrewd tutor, that hard heart of thine,   500
Hath taught them scornful tricks and such disdain
That they have murdered this poor heart of mine;
    And these mine eyes, true leaders to their queen, 503
    But for thy piteous lips no more had seen.   504

"Long may they kiss each other, for this cure!   505
Oh, never let their crimson liveries wear!   506
And as they last, their verdure still endure,   507
To drive infection from the dangerous year,
    That the stargazers, having writ on death,   509
    May say the plague is banished by thy breath!

"Pure lips, sweet seals in my soft lips imprinted,   511
What bargains may I make, still to be sealing?   512
To sell myself I can be well contented,

So thou wilt buy and pay and use good dealing,   514
    Which purchase if thou make, for fear of slips   515
    Set thy seal manual on my wax-red lips.   516

"A thousand kisses buys my heart from me;
And pay them at thy leisure, one by one.
What is ten hundred touches unto thee?   519
Are they not quickly told and quickly gone?   520
    Say for nonpayment that the debt should double,
    Is twenty hundred kisses such a trouble?"

"Fair queen," quoth he, "if any love you owe me,   523
Measure my strangeness with my unripe years.   524
Before I know myself, seek not to know me.   525
No fisher but the ungrown fry forbears.   526
    The mellow plum doth fall; the green sticks fast,
    Or being early plucked is sour to taste.

"Look the world's comforter, with weary gait,   529
His day's hot task hath ended in the west;
The owl, night's herald, shrieks; 'tis very late;
The sheep are gone to fold, birds to their nest,
    And coal-black clouds that shadow heaven's light
    Do summon us to part and bid good night.

"Now let me say 'Good night,' and so say you;
If you will say so, you shall have a kiss."
"Good night," quoth she, and, ere he says "Adieu,"
The honey fee of parting tendered is.   538
    Her arms do lend his neck a sweet embrace;
    Incorporate then they seem; face grows to face; 540

Till, breathless, he disjoined, and backward drew
The heavenly moisture, that sweet coral mouth,
Whose precious taste her thirsty lips well knew,
Whereon they surfeit, yet complain on drouth.   544
    He with her plenty pressed, she faint with dearth, 545
    Their lips together glued, fall to the earth.

Now quick desire hath caught the yielding prey,
And gluttonlike she feeds, yet never filleth;
Her lips are conquerors, his lips obey,
Paying what ransom the insulter willeth,   550
    Whose vulture thought doth pitch the price so high 551
    That she will draw his lips' rich treasure dry.

And having felt the sweetness of the spoil,   553
With blindfold fury she begins to forage;

---

475 He . . . nose (A standard first-aid remedy; briefly stopping the air supply can induce the patient to resume breathing.)   **476 bends her fingers** (as a stimulus or test of consciousness).   **holds . . . hard** takes her pulse   **478 marred** caused to her detriment.   **479 good will** consent   **480 so** so that, or, provided.   **still** continually.   **489 Were never** Never before were   **490 repine** vexation   **494 drenched** drowned   **495 Or** Either   **497 death's annoy** i.e., as wretched as death   **498 lively joy** i.e., as joyous as life.   **500 shrewd** sharp, harsh   **503 leaders** guides.   **queen** i.e., the heart   **504 But for** were it not for.   **seen** had the power of sight.   **505 they** i.e., your lips.   **for** in payment for, as a means of effecting   **506 crimson liveries** uniforms or costumes of crimson.   **wear** wear out.   **507 their verdure** may their fresh fragrance. (Alludes to belief in the efficacy of certain herbs to ward off contagion.)   **509 writ on death** predicted (by means of astrology) an epidemic of deadly plague   **511 seals . . . imprinted** stamps that have left their impression on my soft lips   **512 still to be sealing** (1) to continue kissing always (2) to seal a bargain.

514 So provided that   **515 slips** errors or fraudulent payment (which Venus suggests they avoid by means of a *seal manual* or seal placed on the contract of their love)   **516 wax-red** (since wax would be used in sealing)   **519 touches** i.e., kisses   **520 told** counted   **523 owe** bear   **524 Measure . . . with** i.e., explain my reserve by   **525 to know me** (With erotic suggestion of carnal knowledge.)   **526 No . . . forbears** There is no fisherman who does not throw back immature fish.   **529 Look . . . comforter** See how the sun   **538 honey** sweet.   **tendered is** is given.   **540 Incorporate** united into one body   **544 on drouth** of drought, of not having enough.   **545 with . . . pressed** oppressed with the plenty she has bestowed on him   **550 insulter** boasting conqueror   **551 Whose . . . high** whose ravenous desire demands so high a price (in kisses)   **553 spoil** plunder, conquest

Her face doth reek and smoke, her blood doth boil,   555
And careless lust stirs up a desperate courage,   556
    Planting oblivion, beating reason back,   557
    Forgetting shame's pure blush and honor's wrack.   558

Hot, faint, and weary with her hard embracing,
Like a wild bird being tamed with too much handling,
Or as the fleet-foot roe that's tired with chasing,   561
Or like the froward infant stilled with dandling,   562
    He now obeys, and now no more resisteth,
    While she takes all she can, not all she listeth.   564

What wax so frozen but dissolves with temp'ring   565
And yields at last to every light impression?
Things out of hope are compassed oft with vent'ring,   567
Chiefly in love, whose leave exceeds commission.   568
    Affection faints not like a pale-faced coward,   569
    But then woos best when most his choice is froward.   570

When he did frown, oh, had she then gave over,   571
Such nectar from his lips she had not sucked.
Foul words and frowns must not repel a lover.   573
What though the rose have prickles, yet 'tis plucked.
    Were beauty under twenty locks kept fast,
    Yet love breaks through and picks them all at last.   576

For pity now she can no more detain him;   577
The poor fool prays her that he may depart.   578
She is resolved no longer to restrain him,
Bids him farewell, and look well to her heart,   580
    The which, by Cupid's bow she doth protest,   581
    He carries thence encagèd in his breast.

"Sweet boy," she says, "this night I'll waste in sorrow,   583
For my sick heart commands mine eyes to watch.   584
Tell me, Love's master, shall we meet tomorrow?
Say, shall we, shall we? Wilt thou make the match?"
    He tells her no, tomorrow he intends
    To hunt the boar with certain of his friends.

"The boar!" quoth she, whereat a sudden pale,   589
Like lawn being spread upon the blushing rose,   590
Usurps her cheek. She trembles at his tale,
And on his neck her yoking arms she throws.
    She sinketh down, still hanging by his neck;
    He on her belly falls, she on her back.

Now is she in the very lists of love,   595
Her champion mounted for the hot encounter.
All is imaginary she doth prove.   597
He will not manage her, although he mount her,   598
    That worse than Tantalus' is her annoy,   599
    To clip Elysium and to lack her joy.   600

Even so poor birds, deceived with painted grapes,   601
Do surfeit by the eye and pine the maw;   602
Even so she languisheth in her mishaps,
As those poor birds that helpless berries saw.   604
    The warm effects which she in him finds missing   605
    She seeks to kindle with continual kissing.

But all in vain; good queen, it will not be.
She hath assayed as much as may be proved.   608
Her pleading hath deserved a greater fee;   609
She's Love, she loves, and yet she is not loved.
    "Fie, fie," he says, "you crush me, let me go!
    You have no reason to withhold me so."

"Thou had'st been gone," quoth she, "sweet boy, ere this,
But that thou told'st me thou wouldst hunt the boar.
Oh, be advised! Thou know'st not what it is   615
With javelin's point a churlish swine to gore,
    Whose tushes, never sheathed, he whetteth still,   617
    Like to a mortal butcher bent to kill.   618

"On his bow-back he hath a battle set   619
Of bristly pikes, that ever threat his foes;   620
His eyes like glowworms shine when he doth fret;   621
His snout digs sepulchers where'er he goes;
    Being moved, he strikes whate'er is in his way,   623
    And whom he strikes his crooked tushes slay.

"His brawny sides, with hairy bristles armed,
Are better proof than thy spear's point can enter;   626
His short thick neck cannot be easily harmed;
Being ireful, on the lion he will venter.   628
    The thorny brambles and embracing bushes,
    As fearful of him, part, through whom he rushes.   630

"Alas, he naught esteems that face of thine,
To which Love's eyes pays tributary gazes,

---

595 lists tournament field (here a site of sexual encounter)   597 All . . .
prove She finds out, however, that the hot encounter is merely in her
imagination.   598 manage control, ride (as one manages a horse)
599 Tantalus a son of Zeus who was punished by perpetual hunger
and thirst with food and drink always in sight yet untouchable.
annoy vexation, torment   600 To clip Elysium and to embrace the
joys of afterlife of classical mythology and yet   601 birds . . . grapes
(Allusion to Zeuxis, a Greek painter of the fifth century B.C., so skillful an artist that birds were said to peck at his picture of a bunch of
grapes.)   602 Do . . . maw gorge themselves visually but starve the
stomach   604 As like.   helpless affording no sustenance   605 warm
effects sexual response   608 assayed tried.   proved experienced,
tried.   609 Her pleading . . . fee (A legal metaphor; she is pleading
her own case.)   615 advised warned.   617 tushes tusks.   still continually   618 Like . . . kill like a deadly butcher intent on killing.
619 bow-back arched back, but suggestive also of a bowman's quiver.
battle i.e., martial array   620 ever threat continually threaten
621 fret i.e., gnash his teeth   623 moved angered   626 proof armor
628 ireful wrathful.   venter venture.   630 As as if

555 reek i.e., steam   556 careless heedless   557 Planting oblivion
implanting or causing forgetfulness of all that she ought to remember
558 wrack ruin.   561 with chasing with being chased   562 froward
fretful   564 listeth desires.   565 temp'ring heating and working
with the fingers   567 out of beyond.   compassed encompassed,
accomplished   568 whose . . . commission which intemperately goes
beyond its instructions.   569 Affection . . . not Passion does not
relent   570 when . . . froward when the object of its choice is unwilling.   571 gave given   573 Foul Hostile, disagreeable   576 picks
them all (Picking a lock often has sexual meaning in Shakespeare.)
577 For pity Appealing to his sense of pity   578 fool (An affectionate
term.)   580 and look well to i.e., and bids him take good care of
581 protest vow, affirm   583 waste spend   584 watch stay awake.
589 pale pallor   590 lawn fine linen

Nor thy soft hands, sweet lips, and crystal eyne, 633
Whose full perfection all the world amazes;
   But having thee at vantage—wondrous dread!— 635
   Would root these beauties as he roots the mead. 636

"Oh, let him keep his loathsome cabin still! 637
Beauty hath naught to do with such foul fiends.
Come not within his danger by thy will; 639
They that thrive well take counsel of their friends.
   When thou didst name the boar, not to dissemble, 641
   I feared thy fortune, and my joints did tremble. 642

"Didst thou not mark my face? Was it not white?
Sawest thou not signs of fear lurk in mine eye?
Grew I not faint, and fell I not downright? 645
Within my bosom, whereon thou dost lie,
   My boding heart pants, beats, and takes no rest,
   But, like an earthquake, shakes thee on my breast.

"For where Love reigns, disturbing Jealousy 649
Doth call himself Affection's sentinel,
Gives false alarms, suggesteth mutiny, 651
And in a peaceful hour doth cry 'Kill, kill!', 652
   Distemp'ring gentle Love in his desire, 653
   As air and water do abate the fire. 654

"This sour informer, this bate-breeding spy, 655
This canker that eats up Love's tender spring, 656
This carry-tale, dissentious Jealousy, 657
That sometime true news, sometime false doth bring,
   Knocks at my heart and whispers in mine ear
   That if I love thee, I thy death should fear;

"And more than so, presenteth to mine eye 661
The picture of an angry chafing boar,
Under whose sharp fangs on his back doth lie
An image like thyself, all stained with gore,
   Whose blood upon the fresh flowers being shed
   Doth make them droop with grief and hang the head.

"What should I do, seeing thee so indeed, 667
That tremble at th'imagination? 668
The thought of it doth make my faint heart bleed,
And fear doth teach it divination. 670
   I prophesy thy death, my living sorrow,
   If thou encounter with the boar tomorrow.

"But if thou needs wilt hunt, be ruled by me; 673
Uncouple at the timorous flying hare, 674
Or at the fox which lives by subtlety,
Or at the roe which no encounter dare.
   Pursue these fearful creatures o'er the downs, 677
   And on thy well-breathed horse keep with thy hounds. 678

"And when thou hast on foot the purblind hare, 679
Mark the poor wretch, to overshoot his troubles 680
How he outruns the wind, and with what care
He cranks and crosses with a thousand doubles. 682
   The many musets through the which he goes 683
   Are like a labyrinth to amaze his foes. 684

"Sometime he runs among a flock of sheep,
To make the cunning hounds mistake their smell,
And sometime where earth-delving coneys keep, 687
To stop the loud pursuers in their yell, 688
   And sometime sorteth with a herd of deer. 689
   Danger deviseth shifts; wit waits on fear. 690

"For there his smell with others being mingled,
The hot scent-snuffing hounds are driven to doubt,
Ceasing their clamorous cry till they have singled
With much ado the cold fault cleanly out. 694
   Then do they spend their mouths; echo replies, 695
   As if another chase were in the skies.

"By this, poor Wat, far off upon a hill, 697
Stands on his hinder legs with list'ning ear,
To hearken if his foes pursue him still.
Anon their loud alarums he doth hear,
   And now his grief may be comparèd well
   To one sore sick that hears the passing bell. 702

"Then shalt thou see the dew-bedabbled wretch
Turn, and return, indenting with the way; 704
Each envious brier his weary legs do scratch, 705
Each shadow makes him stop, each murmur stay;
   For misery is trodden on by many,
   And, being low, never relieved by any.

"Lie quietly, and hear a little more.
Nay, do not struggle, for thou shalt not rise.
To make thee hate the hunting of the boar,
Unlike myself thou hear'st me moralize, 712
   Applying this to that, and so to so;
   For love can comment upon every woe.

"Where did I leave?" "No matter where," quoth he, 715
"Leave me, and then the story aptly ends;
The night is spent." "Why, what of that?" quoth she.
"I am," quoth he, "expected of my friends, 718
  And now 'tis dark, and going I shall fall."
  "In night," quoth she, "desire sees best of all.

"But if thou fall, oh, then imagine this,
The earth, in love with thee, thy footing trips,
And all is but to rob thee of a kiss.
Rich preys make true men thieves; so do thy lips 724
  Make modest Dian cloudy and forlorn, 725
  Lest she should steal a kiss and die forsworn. 726

"Now of this dark night I perceive the reason: 727
Cynthia for shame obscures her silver shine 728
Till forging Nature be condemned of treason 729
For stealing molds from heaven that were divine,
  Wherein she framed thee, in high heaven's despite, 731
  To shame the sun by day and her by night. 732

"And therefore hath she bribed the Destinies
To cross the curious workmanship of Nature, 734
To mingle beauty with infirmities,
And pure perfection with impure defeature, 736
  Making it subject to the tyranny
  Of mad mischances and much misery;

"As burning fevers, agues pale and faint, 739
Life-poisoning pestilence and frenzies wood, 740
The marrow-eating sickness, whose attaint 741
Disorder breeds by heating of the blood;
  Surfeits, impostumes, grief, and damned despair 743
  Swear Nature's death for framing thee so fair. 744

"And not the least of all these maladies
But in one minute's fight brings beauty under. 746
Both favor, savor, hue, and qualities, 747
Whereat th'impartial gazer late did wonder, 748
  Are on the sudden wasted, thawed, and done, 749
  As mountain snow melts with the midday sun.

"Therefore, despite of fruitless chastity, 751
Love-lacking vestals and self-loving nuns,

715 **leave** leave off. (But Adonis answers with another sense, "go away from.") **718 of** by **724 Rich . . . thieves** The chance of rich spoils (*preys*) will make thieves even of honest (*true*) men **725 Dian** Diana, goddess of the moon, chastity, and the hunt. (Even Diana would fall in love with Adonis.) **cloudy** obscured with clouds; sorrowful **726 forsworn** having broken her vow as the goddess of chastity. **727 of** for **728 Cynthia** Diana, the moon **729 forging** counterfeiting **731 she** Nature. **in . . . despite** in defiance of high heaven **732 her** the moon **734 cross** thwart. **curious** ingenious **736 defeature** disfigurement **739 As** such as **740 frenzies wood** mad seizures **741 The marrow-eating sickness** (Probably venereal disease; love is said to burn or melt the marrow, as in line 142; hence the *heating of the blood* in line 742.) **attaint** infection **743 impostumes** abscesses **744 Swear . . . fair** (all these diseases) swear to undo Nature because she formed you so beautiful. **746 brings beauty under** subdues beauty. **747 Both . . . qualities** Beauty of feature, sweetness of smell, color and shape, and other qualities **748 late** lately **749 wasted** wasted away. **done** destroyed **751 despite of fruitless** in defiance of barren

That on the earth would breed a scarcity
And barren dearth of daughters and of sons,
  Be prodigal. The lamp that burns by night
  Dries up his oil to lend the world his light. 756

"What is thy body but a swallowing grave,
Seeming to bury that posterity
Which by the rights of time thou needs must have,
If thou destroy them not in dark obscurity?
  If so, the world will hold thee in disdain,
  Sith in thy pride so fair a hope is slain. 762

"So in thyself thyself art made away, 763
A mischief worse than civil homebred strife, 764
Or theirs whose desperate hands themselves do slay,
Or butcher sire that reaves his son of life. 766
  Foul cank'ring rust the hidden treasure frets, 767
  But gold that's put to use more gold begets."

"Nay, then," quoth Adon, "you will fall again
Into your idle overhandled theme. 770
The kiss I gave you is bestowed in vain,
And all in vain you strive against the stream; 772
  For, by this black-faced night, desire's foul nurse, 773
  Your treatise makes me like you worse and worse. 774

"If love have lent you twenty thousand tongues,
And every tongue more moving than your own,
Bewitching like the wanton mermaids' songs, 777
Yet from mine ear the tempting tune is blown;
  For know, my heart stands armèd in mine ear
  And will not let a false sound enter there,

"Lest the deceiving harmony should run
Into the quiet closure of my breast; 782
And then my little heart were quite undone,
In his bedchamber to be barred of rest.
  No, lady, no. My heart longs not to groan,
  But soundly sleeps, while now it sleeps alone.

"What have you urged that I cannot reprove? 787
The path is smooth that leadeth on to danger.
I hate not love, but your device in love, 789
That lends embracements unto every stranger.
  You do it for increase. Oh, strange excuse,
  When reason is the bawd to lust's abuse! 792

"Call it not love, for Love to heaven is fled
Since sweating Lust on earth usurped his name,
Under whose simple semblance he hath fed 795
Upon fresh beauty, blotting it with blame; 796

756 **Dries up** expends. **his** its **762 Sith** since **763 thyself art made away** i.e., your futurity is destroyed **764 mischief** evil **766 reaves** bereaves **767 cank'ring** consuming (like the cankerworm). **frets** eats away **770 idle** profitless **772 stream** current **773 night . . . nurse** i.e., night, the foul nourisher of evil desire **774 treatise** discourse **777 mermaids'** i.e., sirens' **782 closure** enclosure **787 urged** argued for. **reprove** refute. **789 device** cunning, deceitful conduct **792 bawd** procuress **795 Under . . . fed** and under the guileless appearance of Love, Lust has fed **796 blotting** soiling

Which the hot tyrant stains and soon bereaves, 797
As caterpillars do the tender leaves.

"Love comforteth like sunshine after rain,
But Lust's effect is tempest after sun.
Love's gentle spring doth always fresh remain;
Lust's winter comes ere summer half be done.
    Love surfeits not, Lust like a glutton dies;
    Love is all truth, Lust full of forgèd lies.

"More I could tell, but more I dare not say;
The text is old, the orator too green. 806
Therefore, in sadness, now I will away. 807
My face is full of shame, my heart of teen; 808
    Mine ears, that to your wanton talk attended
    Do burn themselves for having so offended." 810

With this, he breaketh from the sweet embrace
Of those fair arms which bound him to her breast
And homeward through the dark laund runs apace, 813
Leaves Love upon her back deeply distressed.
    Look how a bright star shooteth from the sky,
    So glides he in the night from Venus' eye;

Which after him she darts, as one on shore
Gazing upon a late-embarkèd friend, 818
Till the wild waves will have him seen no more, 819
Whose ridges with the meeting clouds contend.
    So did the merciless and pitchy night
    Fold in the object that did feed her sight. 822

Whereat amazed, as one that unaware 823
Hath dropped a precious jewel in the flood, 824
Or stonished as night wand'rers often are, 825
Their light blown out in some mistrustful wood, 826
    Even so confounded in the dark she lay, 827
    Having lost the fair discovery of her way. 828

And now she beats her heart, whereat it groans,
That all the neighbor caves, as seeming troubled,
Make verbal repetition of her moans.
Passion on passion deeply is redoubled: 832
    "Ay me!" she cries, and twenty times "Woe, woe!"
    And twenty echoes twenty times cry so.

She marking them begins a wailing note
And sings extemporally a woeful ditty
How love makes young men thrall and old men dote, 837
How love is wise in folly, foolish witty.

Her heavy anthem still concludes in woe, 839
And still the choir of echoes answer so.

Her song was tedious and outwore the night,
For lovers' hours are long, though seeming short.
If pleased themselves, others, they think, delight
In suchlike circumstance, with suchlike sport.
    Their copious stories, oftentimes begun,
    End without audience and are never done.

For who hath she to spend the night withal 847
But idle sounds resembling parasits, 848
Like shrill-tongued tapsters answering every call, 849
Soothing the humor of fantastic wits? 850
    She says " 'Tis so," they answer all " 'Tis so,"
    And would say after her, if she said "No."

Lo here the gentle lark, weary of rest,
From his moist cabinet mounts up on high, 854
And wakes the morning, from whose silver breast 855
The sun ariseth in his majesty,
    Who doth the world so gloriously behold 857
    That cedar tops and hills seem burnished gold.

Venus salutes him with this fair good morrow:
"O thou clear god, and patron of all light, 860
From whom each lamp and shining star doth borrow
The beauteous influence that makes him bright, 862
    There lives a son that sucked an earthly mother 863
    May lend thee light, as thou dost lend to other." 864

This said, she hasteth to a myrtle grove,
Musing the morning is so much o'erworn, 866
And yet she hears no tidings of her love.
She hearkens for his hounds and for his horn.
    Anon she hears them chant it lustily, 869
    And all in haste she coasteth to the cry. 870

And as she runs, the bushes in the way
Some catch her by the neck, some kiss her face,
Some twine about her thigh to make her stay.
She wildly breaketh from their strict embrace, 874
    Like a milch doe, whose swelling dugs do ache, 875
    Hasting to feed her fawn hid in some brake. 876

By this, she hears the hounds are at a bay, 877
Whereat she starts, like one that spies an adder

Wreathed up in fatal folds just in his way, 879
The fear whereof doth make him shake and shudder;
 Even so the timorous yelping of the hounds
 Appalls her senses and her spirit confounds.

For now she knows it is no gentle chase,
But the blunt boar, rough bear, or lion proud,
Because the cry remaineth in one place,
Where fearfully the dogs exclaim aloud.
 Finding their enemy to be so curst, 887
 They all strain court'sy who shall cope him first. 888

This dismal cry rings sadly in her ear, 889
Through which it enters to surprise her heart, 890
Who, overcome by doubt and bloodless fear, 891
With cold-pale weakness numbs each feeling part. 892
 Like soldiers, when their captain once doth yield, 893
 They basely fly and dare not stay the field. 894

Thus stands she in a trembling ecstasy, 895
Till, cheering up her senses all dismayed,
She tells them 'tis a causeless fantasy 897
And childish error that they are afraid;
 Bids them leave quaking, bids them fear no more—
 And with that word she spied the hunted boar,

Whose frothy mouth, bepainted all with red,
Like milk and blood being mingled both together,
A second fear through all her sinews spread,
Which madly hurries her she knows not whither.
 This way she runs, and now she will no further,
 But back retires to rate the boar for murther. 906

A thousand spleens bear her a thousand ways; 907
She treads the path that she untreads again; 908
Her more than haste is mated with delays, 909
Like the proceedings of a drunken brain,
 Full of respects, yet naught at all respecting, 911
 In hand with all things, naught at all effecting. 912

Here kenneled in a brake she finds a hound, 913
And asks the weary caitiff for his master, 914
And there another licking of his wound,
'Gainst venomed sores the only sovereign plaster; 916
 And here she meets another sadly scowling,
 To whom she speaks, and he replies with howling.

When he hath ceased his ill-resounding noise,
Another flapmouthed mourner, black and grim, 920
Against the welkin volleys out his voice; 921
Another and another answer him,
 Clapping their proud tails to the ground below,
 Shaking their scratched ears, bleeding as they go.

Look how the world's poor people are amazed 925
At apparitions, signs, and prodigies,
Whereon with fearful eyes they long have gazed,
Infusing them with dreadful prophecies; 928
 So she at these sad signs draws up her breath
 And, sighing it again, exclaims on Death. 930

"Hard-favored tyrant, ugly, meager, lean, 931
Hateful divorce of love!"—thus chides she Death— 932
"Grim-grinning ghost, earth's worm, what dost thou mean 933
To stifle beauty and to steal his breath,
 Who, when he lived, his breath and beauty set
 Gloss on the rose, smell to the violet?

"If he be dead—Oh, no, it cannot be,
Seeing his beauty, thou shouldst strike at it!
Oh, yes, it may; thou hast no eyes to see, 939
But hatefully at random dost thou hit.
 Thy mark is feeble age, but thy false dart 941
 Mistakes that aim and cleaves an infant's heart.

"Hadst thou but bid beware, then he had spoke, 943
And, hearing him, thy power had lost his power. 944
The Destinies will curse thee for this stroke;
They bid thee crop a weed, thou pluck'st a flower.
 Love's golden arrow at him should have fled,
 And not Death's ebon dart, to strike him dead. 948

"Dost thou drink tears, that thou provok'st such weeping?
What may a heavy groan advantage thee?
Why hast thou cast into eternal sleeping
Those eyes that taught all other eyes to see?
 Now Nature cares not for thy mortal vigor, 953
 Since her best work is ruined with thy rigor." 954

Here overcome, as one full of despair,
She vailed her eyelids, who, like sluices, stopped 956
The crystal tide that from her two cheeks fair
In the sweet channel of her bosom dropped; 958
 But through the floodgates breaks the silver rain,
 And with his strong course opens them again. 960

---

879 **folds** coils   887 **curst** savage   888 **strain court'sy** are punctiliously polite, stand upon ceremony; i.e., they hold back.   **cope** cope with   889 **dismal** foreboding ill   890 **surprise** assail suddenly 891 **bloodless fear** i.e., fear that causes the blood to draw to the heart and desert the features, leaving one *cold, pale,* and *weak* (line 892) 892 **feeling part** bodily part and organ of sense.   893 **when . . . yield** once their commanding officer has yielded   894 **stay the field** remain in the battlefield.   895 **ecstasy** agitated state   897 **them** i.e., her senses   906 **rate** berate   907 **spleens** impulses   908 **untreads** retraces   909 **mated** confounded, checked   911–12 **Full . . . effecting** full of considerations yet not considering anything at all, preoccupied with everything yet attending to nothing.   913 **kenneled** hiding as if in its kennel   914 **caitiff** wretch   916 **only sovereign plaster** best all-curing application

920 **flapmouthed** having broad, hanging lips or jowls   921 **welkin** sky   925 **Look how** Just as   928 **Infusing** imbuing.   **prophecies** prophetic qualities   930 **exclaims on** denounces   931 **Hard-favored** Ugly-faced   932 **divorce** terminator   933 **Grim-grinning** i.e., grinning like a skull.   **worm** i.e., cankerworm, consumer of flowers. (With the suggestion also of worms that devour corpses.)   939 **no eyes** (The eye sockets of the skull of Death are empty.)   941 **mark** target   943 **bid beware** i.e., issued a warning of your approach.   **he** Adonis   944 **his** its   948 **ebon** ebony, black   953 **cares . . . vigor** does not fear your deadly power   954 **with** by   956 **vailed** lowered. **who . . . stopped** which, like floodgates, stopped up   958 **channel** i.e., cleavage   960 **his** its

Oh, how her eyes and tears did lend and borrow!   961
Her eye seen in the tears, tears in her eye,
Both crystals, where they viewed each other's sorrow,   963
Sorrow that friendly sighs sought still to dry;   964
    But like a stormy day, now wind, now rain,
    Sighs dry her cheeks, tears make them wet again.

Variable passions throng her constant woe,
As striving who should best become her grief.   968
All entertained, each passion labors so   969
That every present sorrow seemeth chief,
    But none is best; then join they all together,   971
    Like many clouds consulting for foul weather.   972

By this, far off she hears some huntsman hallow;   973
A nurse's song ne'er pleased her babe so well.
The dire imagination she did follow   975
This sound of hope doth labor to expel;
    For now reviving joy bids her rejoice
    And flatters her it is Adonis' voice.

Whereat her tears began to turn their tide,   979
Being prisoned in her eye like pearls in glass;
Yet sometimes falls an orient drop beside,   981
Which her cheek melts, as scorning it should pass,   982
    To wash the foul face of the sluttish ground,   983
    Who is but drunken when she seemeth drowned.   984

O hard-believing love, how strange it seems   985
Not to believe, and yet too credulous!   986
Thy weal and woe are both of them extremes.
Despair and hope makes thee ridiculous: 988
    The one doth flatter thee in thoughts unlikely;   989
    In likely thoughts the other kills thee quickly.

Now she unweaves the web that she hath wrought;
Adonis lives, and Death is not to blame;
It was not she that called him all to naught.   993
Now she adds honors to his hateful name;
    She clepes him king of graves and grave for kings,   995
    Imperious supreme of all mortal things.   996

"No, no," quoth she, "sweet Death, I did but jest.
Yet pardon me, I felt a kind of fear
Whenas I met the boar, that bloody beast,   999
Which knows no pity, but is still severe.   1000

Then, gentle shadow—truth I must confess—   1001
    I railed on thee, fearing my love's decesse.   1002

" 'Tis not my fault; the boar provoked my tongue.
Be wreaked on him, invisible commander.   1004
'Tis he, foul creature, that hath done thee wrong;
I did but act, he's author of thy slander.   1006
    Grief hath two tongues, and never woman yet   1007
    Could rule them both without ten women's wit."

Thus hoping that Adonis is alive,
Her rash suspect she doth extenuate;   1010
And that his beauty may the better thrive,   1011
With Death she humbly doth insinuate;   1012
    Tells him of trophies, statues, tombs, and stories   1013
    His victories, his triumphs, and his glories.

"O Jove," quoth she, "how much a fool was I
To be of such a weak and silly mind
To wail his death who lives and must not die
Till mutual overthrow of mortal kind!   1018
    For, he being dead, with him is beauty slain,
    And, beauty dead, black chaos comes again.

"Fie, fie, fond love, thou art as full of fear   1021
As one with treasure laden, hemmed with thieves;   1022
Trifles, unwitnessèd with eye or ear,   1023
Thy coward heart with false bethinking grieves."   1024
    Even at this word she hears a merry horn,
    Whereat she leaps that was but late forlorn.   1026

As falcon to the lure, away she flies—
The grass stoops not, she treads on it so light—
And in her haste unfortunately spies
The foul boar's conquest on her fair delight;
    Which seen, her eyes, as murdered with the view,   1031
    Like stars ashamed of day, themselves withdrew;   1032

Or, as the snail, whose tender horns being hit,
Shrinks backward in his shelly cave with pain,
And there, all smothered up, in shade doth sit,
Long after fearing to creep forth again;
    So, at his bloody view, her eyes are fled
    Into the deep dark cabins of her head,

Where they resign their office and their light
To the disposing of her troubled brain,   1040

---

961 lend and borrow i.e., reflect each other.   **963 crystals** i.e., mirrors or magic crystals   **964 friendly** i.e., consoling   **968 As** as if.   **who** which (passion).   **become** suit   **969 entertained** having been admitted   **971 best** supreme   **972 consulting for** gathering and conspiring to produce   **973 By this** By this time.   **hallow** halloo   **975 dire imagination** tragic train of thought.   **follow** pursue in her thoughts   **979 turn their tide** ebb   **981 orient** shining.   **beside** to one side   **982 melts** i.e., dries.   **as** as if   **983 foul** dirty   **984 Who . . . drowned** i.e., the earth greedily drinks up her tears while she seems drowned in grief.   **985–6 O . . . credulous!** O suspicious love, how strange it appears that you don't believe, even though you are too credulous!   **988 Despair and hope** i.e., The rapid oscillation between despair and hope   **989 The one** i.e., hope   **993 called . . . naught** called Death wholly evil.   **995 clepes** names, calls   **996 Imperious supreme** imperial ruler   **999 Whenas** when   **1000 still severe** incessantly ruthless.

1001 shadow specter   **1002 railed on** reviled.   **decesse** decease.   **1004 wreaked** revenged.   **invisible commander** i.e., Death, a specter that orders our final destiny.   **1006 act** i.e., act as agent   **1007 two tongues** i.e., a double tongue, twice as loud and hard to control as a usual tongue. (Women are conventionally unable to rule their tongues in any case.)   **1010 rash suspect** too hasty suspicion (of Death).   **extenuate** excuse   **1011 his** Adonis's   **1012 insinuate** ingratiate herself   **1013 trophies** memorial monuments.   **stories** narrates   **1018 mutual** i.e., universal   **1021 fond** foolish   **1022 hemmed with** hemmed about by   **1023–4 Trifles . . . grieves** mere trifles, not actually seen by eye or heard by ear, grieve your cowardly heart with false imaginings.   **1026 leaps** i.e., leaps for joy.   **late** lately   **1031 as** as if   **1032 ashamed of day** ashamed to be seen by daylight.   **themselves withdrew** shut themselves up   **withdrew** i.e., closed   **1040 disposing** direction, ordering

Who bids them still consort with ugly night   1041
And never wound the heart with looks again—   1042
　　Who, like a king perplexèd in his throne,   1043
　　By their suggestion gives a deadly groan.   1044

Whereat each tributary subject quakes,   1045
As when the wind, imprisoned in the ground,   1046
Struggling for passage, earth's foundation shakes,
Which with cold terror doth men's minds confound.
　　This mutiny each part doth so surprise   1049
　　That from their dark beds once more leap her eyes;

And, being opened, threw unwilling light
Upon the wide wound that the boar had trenched
In his soft flank, whose wonted lily white   1053
With purple tears, that his wound wept, was drenched.
　　No flower was nigh, no grass, herb, leaf, or weed,
　　But stole his blood and seemed with him to bleed.   1056

This solemn sympathy poor Venus noteth.
Over one shoulder doth she hang her head.
Dumbly she passions, franticly she doteth;   1059
She thinks he could not die, he is not dead.
　　Her voice is stopped, her joints forget to bow;   1061
　　Her eyes are mad that they have wept till now.   1062

Upon his hurt she looks so steadfastly
That her sight, dazzling, makes the wound seem three;   1064
And then she reprehends her mangling eye,
That makes more gashes where no breach should be.
　　His face seems twain, each several limb is doubled;
　　For oft the eye mistakes, the brain being troubled.

"My tongue cannot express my grief for one,
And yet," quoth she, "behold two Adons dead!
My sighs are blown away, my salt tears gone;
Mine eyes are turned to fire, my heart to lead.
　　Heavy heart's lead, melt at mine eyes' red fire!   1073
　　So shall I die by drops of hot desire.   1074

"Alas, poor world, what treasure hast thou lost!
What face remains alive that's worth the viewing?
Whose tongue is music now? What canst thou boast
Of things long since, or anything ensuing?   1078
　　The flowers are sweet, their colors fresh and trim,
　　But true sweet beauty lived and died with him.

"Bonnet nor veil henceforth no creature wear!   1081
Nor sun nor wind will ever strive to kiss you.
Having no fair to lose, you need not fear;   1083
The sun doth scorn you, and the wind doth hiss you.
　　But when Adonis lived, sun and sharp air
　　Lurked like two thieves, to rob him of his fair.

"And therefore would he put his bonnet on,
Under whose brim the gaudy sun would peep;
The wind would blow it off and, being gone,   1089
Play with his locks. Then would Adonis weep;
　　And straight, in pity of his tender years,   1091
　　They both would strive who first should dry his tears.

"To see his face the lion walked along
Behind some hedge, because he would not fear him;   1094
To recreate himself when he hath song,   1095
The tiger would be tame and gently hear him;
　　If he had spoke, the wolf would leave his prey
　　And never fright the silly lamb that day.   1098

"When he beheld his shadow in the brook,   1099
The fishes spread on it their golden gills;
When he was by, the birds such pleasure took
That some would sing, some other in their bills   1102
　　Would bring him mulberries and ripe-red cherries;
　　He fed them with his sight, they him with berries.

"But this foul, grim, and urchin-snouted boar,   1105
Whose downward eye still looketh for a grave,   1106
Ne'er saw the beauteous livery that he wore—   1107
Witness the entertainment that he gave.   1108
　　If he did see his face, why then I know
　　He thought to kiss him, and hath killed him so.

" 'Tis true, 'tis true! Thus was Adonis slain:
He ran upon the boar with his sharp spear,
Who did not whet his teeth at him again,   1113
But by a kiss thought to persuade him there;   1114
　　And, nuzzling in his flank, the loving swine
　　Sheathed unaware the tusk in his soft groin.

"Had I been toothed like him, I must confess,   1117
With kissing him I should have killed him first;
But he is dead, and never did he bless

1041 **still consort** always remain   1042 **with looks** by looking
1043 **Who** which, i.e., the heart   1044 **By their suggestion** incited by
the eyes   1045 **tributary subject** i.e., subordinate part of the body
1046 **wind . . . ground** (The common Elizabethan explanation of
earthquakes; compare with *1 Henry IV*, 3.1.30.)   1049 **surprise** attack
suddenly   1053 **wonted** customary   1056 **But stole** that did not steal
1059 **passions** shows grief   1061 **forget to bow** cannot bend
1062 **till now** before now (in a lesser cause).   1064 **dazzling** being
dazzled   1073–4 **Heavy . . . desire** i.e., May my leaden heart be
melted by my hot tears! In that way I will die, as my desire melts me.
1078 **long . . . ensuing** past or to come.

1081 **Bonnet nor veil** Neither hat nor veil (worn to guard a fair complexion, regarded as particularly beautiful, against the sun)
1083 **fair** beauty. (Also in line 1086.)   1089 **being gone** it (the hat)
being gone   1091 **straight** at once   1094 **would not fear** did not wish
to frighten   1095 **To recreate . . . song** whenever he sang for his own
recreation   1098 **silly** innocent   1099 **shadow** reflected image
1102 **other** others   1105 **urchin-snouted** having a snout like a hedgehog   1106 **still** continually.   **for a grave** i.e., as if for a grave in which
to bury victims. (Compare with line 622, where the boar's snout *digs
sepulchers* as it roots in the earth.)   1107 **livery** i.e., outside appearance.   **he** Adonis   1108 **entertainment** treatment, reception
1113 **again** in return   1114 **persuade** win over, or, persuade to stay
1117 **toothed** tusked

My youth with his—the more am I accurst."
    With this, she falleth in the place she stood,   1121
    And stains her face with his congealèd blood.

She looks upon his lips, and they are pale;
She takes him by the hand, and that is cold;
She whispers in his ears a heavy tale,   1125
As if they heard the woeful words she told;
    She lifts the coffer-lids that close his eyes,   1127
    Where, lo, two lamps, burnt out, in darkness lies;

Two glasses, where herself herself beheld   1129
A thousand times, and now no more reflect,
Their virtue lost, wherein they late excelled,   1131
And every beauty robbed of his effect.   1132
    "Wonder of time," quoth she, "this is my spite,   1133
    That, thou being dead, the day should yet be light.

"Since thou art dead, lo, here I prophesy:
Sorrow on love hereafter shall attend.
It shall be waited on with jealousy,   1137
Find sweet beginning but unsavory end,
    Ne'er settled equally, but high or low,   1139
    That all love's pleasure shall not match his woe.   1140

"It shall be fickle, false, and full of fraud,
Bud and be blasted in a breathing while;   1142
The bottom poison, and the top o'erstrawed   1143
With sweets that shall the truest sight beguile.
    The strongest body shall it make most weak,
    Strike the wise dumb and teach the fool to speak.

"It shall be sparing and too full of riot,   1147
Teaching decrepit age to tread the measures;   1148
The staring ruffian shall it keep in quiet,   1149
Pluck down the rich, enrich the poor with treasures;
    It shall be raging mad and silly mild,   1151
    Make the young old, the old become a child.

"It shall suspect where is no cause of fear;   1153
It shall not fear where it should most mistrust;
It shall be merciful and too severe,

And most deceiving when it seems most just;   1156
    Perverse it shall be where it shows most toward,   1157
    Put fear to valor, courage to the coward.

"It shall be cause of war and dire events
And set dissension twixt the son and sire,
Subject and servile to all discontents,   1161
As dry combustious matter is to fire.
    Sith in his prime Death doth my love destroy,   1163
    They that love best their loves shall not enjoy."

By this, the boy that by her side lay killed   1165
Was melted like a vapor from her sight,
And in his blood that on the ground lay spilled
A purple flow'r sprung up, checkered with white,   1168
    Resembling well his pale cheeks and the blood
    Which in round drops upon their whiteness stood.

She bows her head, the new-sprung flower to smell,
Comparing it to her Adonis' breath,
And says within her bosom it shall dwell,
Since he himself is reft from her by death.   1174
    She crops the stalk, and in the breach appears
    Green dropping sap, which she compares to tears.

"Poor flower," quoth she, "this was thy father's guise—   1177
Sweet issue of a more sweet-smelling sire—   1178
For every little grief to wet his eyes;   1179
To grow unto himself was his desire,   1180
    And so 'tis thine; but know, it is as good
    To wither in my breast as in his blood.

"Here was thy father's bed, here in my breast;
Thou art the next of blood, and 'tis thy right.
Lo, in this hollow cradle take thy rest;
My throbbing heart shall rock thee day and night.
    There shall not be one minute in an hour
    Wherein I will not kiss my sweet love's flower."

Thus, weary of the world, away she hies
And yokes her silver doves, by whose swift aid
Their mistress mounted through the empty skies   1191
In her light chariot quickly is conveyed,   1192
    Holding their course to Paphos, where their queen   1193
    Means to immure herself and not be seen.

1121 **place** place where   1125 **heavy** sad   1127 **coffer-lids** lids covering chests of treasure, i.e., eyelids   1129 **glasses** mirrors   1131 **virtue** power (to see and to reflect)   1132 **his** its   1133 **time** i.e., the ages, human existence.   **spite** torment, vexation   1137 **It** Love.   **with** by 1139 **Ne'er . . . low** i.e., (love will be) never equal between the two lovers; they will be from high and low social stations, or of different intensities   1140 **his** its   1142 **blasted** blighted.   **breathing while** moment   1143 **The bottom . . . o'erstrawed** the inner substance poison, and the surface strewn over   1147 **sparing . . . riot** i.e., both niggardly and excessive   1148 **tread the measures** dance. (An inappropriate action for the old.)   1149 **staring** looking savage, glaring 1151 **silly** innocently, feebly, humbly, weak-mindedly   1153 **is** there is

1156 **just** trustworthy   1157 **Perverse** stubborn, contrary.   **shows** looks.   **toward** tractable   1161 **Subject . . . discontents** (love will be) both the cause and the unwilling slave of every kind of dissension 1163 **Sith** Since   1165 **By this** By this time   1168 **flow'r** anemone 1174 **reft** torn   1177 **guise** manner, way   1178 **Sweet issue** i.e., you, the anemone, who are the sweet offspring   1179 **For . . . eyes** to weep compassionately at every little sorrow   1180 **To grow unto himself** to mature self-made and independent   1191–2 **mounted . . . conveyed** is quickly conveyed, mounted in her light chariot, through the empty skies   1193 **Paphos** Venus's dwelling in Cyprus

The Rape of Lucrece

The Rape of Lucrece is closely related to *Venus and Adonis*. The two were published about a year apart, in 1594 and 1593, respectively, and both were printed by Richard Field. Both are dedicated to the young Earl of Southampton, Henry Wriothesley, whose confidence and friendship Shakespeare appears to have gained during the interim between the two poems; the dedicatory preface to *The Rape of Lucrece* expresses assurance that the poem will be accepted. Stylistically, the two poems are of a piece: both are reliant on Petrarchan ornament and rhetorical showmanship and are steeped in Ovidian pathos. Yet they are complementary rather than similar in attitude and subject. *The Rape of Lucrece* appears to be the "graver labor" promised to Southampton in the dedication of the earlier poem, a planned sequel in which love would be subjected to a darker treatment. *Venus and Adonis* is chiefly about sensual pleasure, whereas *The Rape of Lucrece* is about heroic chastity. The first poem is amatory, erotic, and amusing, despite its sad end; the second is moral, declamatory, and lugubrious. As Gabriel Harvey observed (c. 1598–1601), "The younger sort takes much delight in Shakespeare's *Venus and Adonis*, but his *Lucrece* and his *Tragedy of Hamlet, Prince of Denmark*, have it in them to please the wiser sort."

Harvey's pairing of this poem with *Hamlet* suggests that, to Harvey at least, Shakespeare aspires to sublime effects in *Lucrece*. For his verse pattern, Shakespeare chooses the seven-line rhyme royal stanza, traditionally used for tragic expression, as in Geoffrey Chaucer's *Troilus and Criseyde* and several of the more formal *Canterbury Tales*, in John Lydgate's *The Fall of Princes* (1430–1438) and its continuation in *A Mirror for Magistrates* (1559), in Samuel Daniel's *The Complaint of Rosamond*, and others. Although Shakespeare turns to Ovid once again as his chief source, he chooses a tale of ravishment, suicide, and vengeance rather than one of titillating amatory pursuit. The story of Lucrece had gained wide currency in the ancient and medieval worlds as an exemplum of chaste conduct in women. Shakespeare seems to have known Livy's *History of Rome* (Book 1, chaps. 57–59), though he relied primarily on Ovid's *Fasti* (2.721–852). Among later versions, he may have known Chaucer's *The Legend of Good Women* and a translation of Livy in William Painter's *The Palace of Pleasure* (1566, 1575). He encountered other "complaints" in *A Mirror for Magistrates* and in Daniel's *The Complaint of Rosamond*, and it is to this well-established genre that *Lucrece* belongs. The poem had the desired effect of enhancing Shakespeare's reputation for elegant poetry; it was reprinted five times during his lifetime and was frequently admired by his contemporaries. *Venus and Adonis* was, to be sure, more popular still (it was reprinted nine times during Shakespeare's lifetime), but no one in Shakespeare's day seems to have regarded *Lucrece* as anything other than a noble work.

To understand the poem in terms of its own generic sense of form, we must recognize its conventions and not expect it to be other than what it professes to be. As in *Venus and Adonis*, plot and character are secondary. Although the story outlined in "The Argument" is potentially sensational and swift-moving, Shakespeare deliberately cuts away most of the action. We do not see Lucius Tarquinius's murder of his father-in-law and tyrannical seizure of Rome, or Collatinus's rash boasting of his wife Lucrece's virtue in the presence of the King's lustful son Sextus Tarquinius, nor, at the conclusion of the story, do we learn much about the avenging of Lucrece's rape. Shakespeare's focus is on the attitudes of the two protagonists immediately before and after the ravishment. Even here, despite opportunities for psychological probing, Shakespeare's real interest is not in the characters themselves so much as in the social ramifications of their actions. As Coppélia Kahn has shown (in *Shakespeare Studies 9*), the rape serves as a means of examining the nature of marriage in a patriarchal society in which competition for ownership and struggles for power characterize men's attitudes toward politics and sex. Using Rome as a familiar mirror for English customs, Shakespeare presents Lucrece as a heroine acting to uphold the institution of marriage. However innocently, she is the one who acquires the stain through being violated and must pay the cost of wifely duty in marriage. Her husband accepts the decorousness of her suicide as necessary for the preservation of his honor, however much he may grieve over her wrong. Like a number of Shakespeare's later heroines, such as Imogen in *Cymbeline*, Lucrece is portrayed as beautiful but not alluring, restrained even in her marriage bed. She arranges her death so as to make the most of its social implications.

Along with his interest in patriarchy and violence, Shakespeare frames the story of *The Rape of Lucrece* in terms of the political events that lead to the founding of the Roman republic. The corruption of the Tarquin dynasty raises issues about Roman values generally, and the poem ends with a strong repudiation of the old order. The villain of the poem is at once rapist and tyrant; the resolution is both a vindication of women as victims and a movement toward republicanism. To be sure, the patriarchy that has dictated the conditions of Lucrece's life and honor will remain intact in the republic; the wife is still her husband's possession, and her greatest obligation to state and family must be to ensure that the husband's honor remains unbesmirched. Nonetheless, the assumptions of Roman hierarchy have been held up to scrutiny.

Shakespeare casts his narrative in the form of a series of rhetorical disputations, each a set piece presented as a debate or as a formal declamation. The debates are built around familiar antitheses: honor versus lust, rude will versus conscience, "affection" versus reason, nobility versus baseness, and so on. Many of the images are similarly arranged in contrasting pairs: dove and owl, daylight and darkness, clear and cloudy weather, white and red. Tarquin debates with himself the reasons for and against rape; Lucrece tries to persuade him of the depravity of his course; Lucrece ponders suicide. These debates generate, in turn, a number of rhetorical apostrophes to marital fidelity (lines 22–8), to the ideal of kingship as a moral example to others (lines 610–37), to Night (lines 764–812), to Opportunity (lines 876–924), and to Time (lines 925–1022). Another rhetorical formula, perhaps the most successful in the poem, is the use of structural digression. The most notable describes a painting or tapestry of Troy with obvious relevance to Lucrece's sad fate: Troy is a city destroyed by a rape, Paris achieves his selfish pleasure at the expense of the public good, and Sinon wins his sinister victory through deceitful appearance (lines 1366–1568).

Throughout, the poem's ornament strives after heightened and elaborate effects. The comparisons, or "conceits," as the Elizabethans called them, are intentionally contrived and reliant on ingenious wordplay. Shakespeare puns on the word *will*, for example, as he does in his sonnets, where he takes advantage of his own first name being Will (see sonnet 135), and in *Venus and Adonis* (see line 365). In *The Rape of Lucrece*, the word is central to Shakespeare's depiction of Tarquin, as we see the ravisher holding a disputation between "frozen conscience and hot-burning will" (line 247), forcing the locks "between her chamber and his will" (line 302), feeding ravenously "in his will his willful eye" (line 417), and the like. These and other passages often frame the word in a polarity of "will" and "heart," and range over numerous meanings that include inclination, desire, appetite, sexual lust, request or command, volition, pleasure, permission, good will, and spontaneity. The fact that the word rhymes with "kill" and "ill" adds to its usefulness. Another kind of "conceit" found throughout *The Rape of Lucrece*—one that arises integrally from the poem's deepest concerns—is the extended military metaphor of a city under siege. Tarquin's heart beats an alarum, Lucrece's breasts are "round turrets" made pale by the assault (lines 432–41), and, in her subsequent death, she is likened to a "late-sacked island" surrounded by rivers of her own blood (line 1740). Elsewhere she is a house that has been pillaged, "Her mansion battered by the enemy" (lines 1170–1). Classical allusions are, of course, common, notably to the story of the rape of Philomel or Philomela (lines 1079, 1128, etc.). Rhetorical devices of antithesis are displayed with the same ornate versatility as in *Venus and Adonis*. In a poem on a serious subject, these devices may seem overly contrived to us. We should nevertheless recognize them as conventional in the genre to which *The Rape of Lucrece* belongs. We find a similar blending of the sensuous and the moral in the sometimes grotesque conceits of the Catholic poet Robert Southwell (d. 1595) and in the later baroque paradoxes of Richard Crashaw (d. 1649). Among Shakespeare's dramatic works, *Titus Andronicus* seems closest to *The Rape of Lucrece* in its pathos, refined sensationalism, and use of classical allusion, and specifically in the character of Lavinia, whose misfortunes and chaste dignity so much resemble those of Lucrece.

Throughout *The Rape of Lucrece*, we find a consciousness of the poem's own artistry. In Lucrece's tragic plight, Shakespeare explores art's ability to communicate through its various means of expression. Especially in the long passage on the painting of the fall of Troy (lines 1366–1568), Lucrece shows an understandable anxiety about art's ability to deceive. The painting is in some ways more realistic than life itself; the figures in the painting seem to move and are so cunningly rendered that they "mock the mind" (line 1414). The imaginary work is "conceit deceitful" (line 1423), able through synecdoche (using the part to represent the whole) to suggest a series of general truths lying behind the particulars that are shown. This power of art to deceive is most troublesome in the case of Sinon, the betrayer of Troy—"In him the painter labored with his skill / To hide deceit" (lines 1506–7)—and has succeeded with such devastating effect that the viewer cannot tell from Sinon's mild appearance that he is, in fact, capable of lim-

itless evil. In his capacity for deception, Sinon is like Tarquin, the seemingly attractive prince who has ravaged Lucrece. Art is thus capable of misrepresentation for purposes of evil; its persuasive power, its imaginative vision, can be perverted to wrong ends. Seen through such art, Rome, too, is at once a great source of civilization and a nation whose values are cast seriously in doubt. *The Rape of Lucrece* thus grapples with issues of serious consequences—ones that also concerned Shakespeare in his early plays (such as *Titus Andronicus*) and indeed throughout his career as a dramatist.

The Rape of Lucrece

To the RIGHT HONORABLE HENRY WRIOTHESLEY, *Earl of Southampton, and Baron of Titchfield.*

The love I dedicate to Your Lordship is without end; whereof this pamphlet without beginning is but a super- 2
fluous moiety. The warrant I have of your honorable dis- 3
position, not the worth of my untutored lines, makes it assured of acceptance. What I have done is yours; what I have to do is yours; being part in all I have, devoted yours. 6
Were my worth greater, my duty would show greater; meantime, as it is, it is bound to Your Lordship, to whom I wish long life still lengthened with all happiness. 9

Your Lordship's in all duty,

William Shakespeare.

The Argument

Lucius Tarquinius, for his excessive pride surnamed Superbus, after he had caused his own 2
father-in-law Servius Tullius to be cruelly murdered and, contrary to the Roman laws and customs, not requiring or staying for the peo- 5
ple's suffrages, had possessed himself of the 6
kingdom, went, accompanied with his sons and other noblemen of Rome, to besiege Ardea. During which siege, the principal men of the army meeting one evening at the tent of Sextus Tarquinius, the King's son, in their discourses after supper everyone commended the virtues of his own wife; among whom Collatinus extolled the incomparable chastity of his wife Lucretia. In that pleasant humor they all posted to Rome; 15
and intending, by their secret and sudden arrival, to make trial of that which everyone had before avouched, only Collatinus finds his wife, 18

Dedication.
2 without beginning i.e., beginning *in medias res,* in the middle of the action **3 moiety** part. **warrant** assurance **6 being . . . have** since you are part of everything I have done and have to do **9 still** continually

The Argument.
2 Superbus "the Proud" **5 requiring** requesting **6 suffrages** consent **15 pleasant** merry. **posted** hastened **18 avouched** affirmed

though it were late in the night, spinning amongst her maids; the other ladies were all found dancing and reveling, or in several dis- 21 ports. Whereupon the noblemen yielded Collat- 22 inus the victory and his wife the fame. At that time Sextus Tarquinius, being inflamed with Lucrece' beauty, yet smothering his passions for the present, departed with the rest back to the camp; from whence he shortly after privily 27 withdrew himself and was, according to his estate, royally entertained and lodged by Lu- 29 crece at Collatium. The same night he treacherously stealeth into her chamber, violently ravished her, and early in the morning speedeth away. Lucrece, in this lamentable plight, hastily dispatcheth messengers, one to Rome for her father, another to the camp for Collatine. They came, the one accompanied with Junius Brutus, the other with Publius Valerius; and finding Lucrece attired in mourning habit, demanded 38 the cause of her sorrow. She, first taking an oath of them for her revenge, revealed the actor and 40 whole manner of his dealing, and withal suddenly stabbed herself. Which done, with one consent they all vowed to root out the whole hated family of the Tarquins; and, bearing the dead body to Rome, Brutus acquainted the people with the doer and manner of the vile deed, with a bitter invective against the tyranny of the King, wherewith the people were so moved that with one consent and a general acclamation the Tarquins were all exiled and the state government changed from kings to consuls.

From the besieged Ardea all in post,   1
Borne by the trustless wings of false desire,   2
Lust-breathèd Tarquin leaves the Roman host   3
And to Collatium bears the lightless fire   4
Which, in pale embers hid, lurks to aspire   5
    And girdle with embracing flames the waist
    Of Collatine's fair love, Lucrece the chaste.

Haply that name of "chaste" unhapp'ly set   8
This bateless edge on his keen appetite,   9
When Collatine unwisely did not let   10
To praise the clear unmatchèd red and white
Which triumphed in that sky of his delight,   12
    Where mortal stars, as bright as heaven's beauties, 13
    With pure aspects did him peculiar duties.   14

For he the night before, in Tarquin's tent,
Unlocked the treasure of his happy state,   16
What priceless wealth the heavens had him lent
In the possession of his beauteous mate,
Reck'ning his fortune at such high-proud rate
    That kings might be espousèd to more fame,   20
    But king nor peer to such a peerless dame.   21

Oh, happiness enjoyed but of a few!
And, if possessed, as soon decayed and done   23
As is the morning's silver melting dew
Against the golden splendor of the sun!
An expired date, canceled ere well begun.   26
    Honor and beauty in the owner's arms
    Are weakly fortressed from a world of harms. 28

Beauty itself doth of itself persuade   29
The eyes of men without an orator;
What needeth then apology be made
To set forth that which is so singular?
Or why is Collatine the publisher   33
    Of that rich jewel he should keep unknown
    From thievish ears, because it is his own?

Perchance his boast of Lucrece' sovereignty   36
Suggested this proud issue of a king,   37
For by our ears our hearts oft tainted be.
Perchance that envy of so rich a thing,   39
Braving compare, disdainfully did sting   40
    His high-pitched thoughts, that meaner men should
      vaunt   41
    That golden hap which their superiors want. 42

But some untimely thought did instigate
His all too timeless speed, if none of those.   44
His honor, his affairs, his friends, his state,   45
Neglected all, with swift intent he goes
To quench the coal which in his liver glows.   47
    O rash false heat, wrapped in repentant cold,
    Thy hasty spring still blasts and ne'er grows old! 49

When at Collatium this false lord arrived,
Well was he welcomed by the Roman dame,
Within whose face beauty and virtue strived
Which of them both should underprop her fame.
When virtue bragged, beauty would blush for shame;
    When beauty boasted blushes, in despite   55
    Virtue would stain that o'er with silver white. 56

21–2 **several disports** various pastimes.   **27 privily** secretly   **29 estate** rank   **38 habit** attire   **40 actor** doer
1 Ardea a city twenty-four miles south of Rome.   **post** haste   **2 trustless** treacherous   **3 Lust-breathèd** excited by lust   **4 Collatium** a city about ten miles east of Rome.   **lightless** i.e., smoldering invisibly   **5 aspire** rise, i.e., break into flames   **8 Haply** Perchance.   **unhapp'ly** (1) unhappily (2) by mischance   **9 bateless** not to be blunted   **10 let** forbear   **12 sky** i.e., Lucrece's face   **13 mortal stars** i.e., Lucrece's eyes   **14 aspects** (1) looks (2) astrologically favorable position.   **peculiar** exclusively for him

16 Unlocked the treasure i.e., opened and revealed (in conversation) the riches   **20 espousèd** i.e., joined, linked   **21 But king** but neither king   **23 done** done with   **26 date** period of time   **28 fortressed from** defended against   **29 of itself** by its own nature   **33 publisher** publicizer   **36 sovereignty** supremacy   **37 Suggested** tempted. **issue** offspring, son (i.e., Tarquin)   **39 Perchance that** Perhaps it was that   **40 Braving compare** defying comparison   **41 meaner** less nobly born   **42 hap** fortune.   **want** lack.   **44 timeless** unseemly, unseasonable   **45 state** position   **47 liver** (Regarded as the seat of the passions.)   **49 blasts** is nipped by frost   **55 When . . . despite** when beauty boasted of its rosy blushing countenance, in defiance of that beauty   **56 o'er** (Perhaps with a pun on *or*, "gold.")

But beauty, in that white entitulèd 57
From Venus' doves, doth challenge that fair field. 58
Then virtue claims from beauty beauty's red, 59
Which virtue gave the golden age to gild 60
Their silver cheeks, and called it then their shield,
    Teaching them thus to use it in the fight:
    When shame assailed, the red should fence the white. 63

This heraldry in Lucrece' face was seen,
Argued by beauty's red and virtue's white. 65
Of either's color was the other queen,
Proving from world's minority their right. 67
Yet their ambition makes them still to fight, 68
    The sovereignty of either being so great
    That oft they interchange each other's seat. 70

This silent war of lilies and of roses,
Which Tarquin viewed in her fair face's field,
In their pure ranks his traitor eye encloses, 73
Where, lest between them both it should be killed,
The coward captive vanquishèd doth yield 75
    To those two armies, that would let him go
    Rather than triumph in so false a foe. 77

Now thinks he that her husband's shallow tongue,
The niggard prodigal that praised her so, 79
In that high task hath done her beauty wrong,
Which far exceeds his barren skill to show. 81
Therefore that praise which Collatine doth owe 82
    Enchanted Tarquin answers with surmise, 83
    In silent wonder of still-gazing eyes.

This earthly saint, adorèd by this devil,
Little suspecteth the false worshiper,
For unstained thoughts do seldom dream on evil;
Birds never limed no secret bushes fear. 88
So, guiltless, she securely gives good cheer 89
    And reverend welcome to her princely guest, 90
    Whose inward ill no outward harm expressed.

For that he colored with his high estate, 92
Hiding base sin in pleats of majesty, 93

That nothing in him seemed inordinate 94
Save sometimes too much wonder of his eye,
Which, having all, all could not satisfy;
    But, poorly rich, so wanteth in his store 97
    That, cloyed with much, he pineth still for more.

But she, that never coped with stranger eyes, 99
Could pick no meaning from their parling looks, 100
Nor read the subtle shining secrecies
Writ in the glassy margins of such books. 102
She touched no unknown baits, nor feared no hooks,
    Nor could she moralize his wanton sight 104
    More than his eyes were opened to the light. 105

He stories to her ears her husband's fame, 106
Won in the fields of fruitful Italy,
And decks with praises Collatine's high name,
Made glorious by his manly chivalry
With bruisèd arms and wreaths of victory. 110
    Her joy with heaved-up hand she doth express
    And, wordless, so greets heaven for his success.

Far from the purpose of his coming thither
He makes excuses for his being there.
No cloudy show of stormy blust'ring weather
Doth yet in his fair welkin once appear, 116
Till sable Night, mother of dread and fear, 117
    Upon the world dim darkness doth display
    And in her vaulty prison stows the day.

For then is Tarquin brought unto his bed,
Intending weariness with heavy sprite; 121
For, after supper, long he questionèd 122
With modest Lucrece, and wore out the night.
Now leaden slumber with life's strength doth fight,
    And everyone to rest himself betakes,
    Save thieves and cares and troubled minds that wakes.

As one of which doth Tarquin lie revolving 127
The sundry dangers of his will's obtaining; 128
Yet ever to obtain his will resolving,
Though weak-built hopes persuade him to abstaining. 130
Despair to gain doth traffic oft for gaining; 131
    And when great treasure is the meed proposed, 132
    Though death be adjunct, there's no death supposed. 133

57–8 But . . . field But beauty, asserting title to that white from the whiteness of Venus's turtledoves that draw her chariot, lays claim to Lucrece's face, which is both a battlefield for the contest of beauty and virtue and a heraldic shield where armorial devices are displayed in red and white.   **59 Then . . . red** Then modesty claims that the color red really belongs to it, not to beauty (since modesty blushes)   **60 gave the golden age** i.e., bestowed on those who live innocently and purely, as in ancient times before the world grew corrupt.   **gild** i.e., cover with a blush of modesty. (Gold and red were often considered interchangeable as colors.)   **63 fence** defend   **65 Argued** disputed and demonstrated   **67 from world's minority** from the beginning of time   **68 still** always   **70 seat** throne.   **73 In . . . encloses** virtue and beauty, arrayed in battle formation, close in on Tarquin's eye, that is treacherously willing to come to terms with either side   **75 coward captive** Tarquin's eye   **77 in** over   **79 niggard prodigal** unwisely lavish yet coming too short in praise   **81 show** describe.   **82 doth owe** must still render, having fallen short on previous occasions   **83 answers with surmise** makes up for with wondering admiration   **88 limed** snared with birdlime, a sticky substance placed on branches   **89 she . . . cheer** she unsuspectingly provides hospitable entertainment   **90 reverend** respectful   **92 that he colored** i.e., he disguised his harmful intent   **93 pleats** cunning folds, concealments

94 That so that   **97 so . . . store** feels such a craving despite the abundance   **99 stranger eyes** eyes of a stranger   **100 parling** speaking   **102 glassy . . . books** (Refers to the custom of printing explanatory comments in book margins; compare *Romeo and Juliet*, 1.3.87.)   **104 moralize** interpret.   **sight** looking   **105 More . . . light** i.e., other than to see that his eyes are open and seemingly without concealing a hidden motive.   **106 stories** relates   **110 bruisèd arms** armor battered in combat   **116 welkin** sky, i.e., appearance, face   **117 sable** black   **121 Intending** pretending.   **sprite** spirit   **122 questionèd** conversed   **127 revolving** considering   **128 his will's obtaining** obtaining his will   **130 weak-built hopes** the fact that his hopes are built on a weak foundation   **131 Despair . . . gaining** i.e., Even a despairing hope often perversely undertakes to venture for gain; or, though frail hopes of wooing her urge him to hold back, despair of gaining her unviolently often urges him (bargains with him) to gain her violently.   **132 meed** reward   **133 adjunct** adjoined, resultant.   **supposed** thought of.

Those that much covet are with gain so fond 134
That what they have not, that which they possess 135
They scatter and unloose it from their bond, 136
And so, by hoping more, they have but less;
Or, gaining more, the profit of excess 138
    Is but to surfeit, and such griefs sustain 139
    That they prove bankrupt in this poor-rich gain.

The aim of all is but to nurse the life 141
With honor, wealth, and ease in waning age;
And in this aim there is such thwarting strife 143
That one for all or all for one we gage: 144
As life for honor in fell battle's rage, 145
    Honor for wealth; and oft that wealth doth cost
    The death of all, and all together lost.

So that in vent'ring ill we leave to be 148
The things we are for that which we expect; 149
And this ambitious foul infirmity, 150
In having much, torments us with defect 151
Of that we have. So then we do neglect
    The thing we have, and, all for want of wit, 153
    Make something nothing by augmenting it.

Such hazard now must doting Tarquin make,
Pawning his honor to obtain his lust,
And for himself himself he must forsake. 157
Then where is truth, if there be no self-trust?
When shall he think to find a stranger just,
    When he himself himself confounds, betrays
    To sland'rous tongues and wretched hateful days?

Now stole upon the time the dead of night,
When heavy sleep had closed up mortal eyes.
No comfortable star did lend his light; 164
No noise but owls' and wolves' death-boding cries
Now serves the season, that they may surprise
    The silly lambs. Pure thoughts are dead and still, 167
    While lust and murder wakes to stain and kill.

And now this lustful lord leapt from his bed,
Throwing his mantle rudely o'er his arm;
Is madly tossed between desire and dread;
Th'one sweetly flatters, th'other feareth harm; 172
But honest fear, bewitched with lust's foul charm,
    Doth too too oft betake him to retire, 174
    Beaten away by brainsick rude desire.

His falchion on a flint he softly smiteth, 176
That from the cold stone sparks of fire do fly,
Whereat a waxen torch forthwith he lighteth,
Which must be lodestar to his lustful eye; 179
And to the flame thus speaks advisedly: 180
    "As from this cold flint I enforced this fire,
    So Lucrece must I force to my desire."

Here pale with fear he doth premeditate
The dangers of his loathsome enterprise,
And in his inward mind he doth debate
What following sorrow may on this arise.
Then, looking scornfully, he doth despise
    His naked armor of still-slaughtered lust, 188
    And justly thus controls his thoughts unjust: 189

"Fair torch, burn out thy light, and lend it not
To darken her whose light excelleth thine;
And die, unhallowed thoughts, before you blot
With your uncleanness that which is divine.
Offer pure incense to so pure a shrine.
    Let fair humanity abhor the deed
    That spots and stains love's modest snow-white weed. 196

"Oh, shame to knighthood and to shining arms!
Oh, foul dishonor to my household's grave! 198
Oh, impious act, including all foul harms! 199
A martial man to be soft fancy's slave! 200
True valor still a true respect should have; 201
    Then my digression is so vile, so base, 202
    That it will live engraven in my face.

"Yea, though I die, the scandal will survive
And be an eyesore in my golden coat; 205
Some loathsome dash the herald will contrive 206
To cipher me how fondly I did dote; 207
That my posterity, shamed with the note, 208
    Shall curse my bones, and hold it for no sin
    To wish that I their father had not been.

"What win I, if I gain the thing I seek?
A dream, a breath, a froth of fleeting joy.
Who buys a minute's mirth to wail a week?
Or sells eternity to get a toy? 214
For one sweet grape who will the vine destroy?
    Or what fond beggar, but to touch the crown,
    Would with the scepter straight be strucken down? 217

134 **fond** infatuated   135 **what** for what   136 **bond** possession
138 **profit of excess** only advantage of having more than enough
139 **such griefs sustain** i.e., to sustain such griefs as accompany surfeit   141 **The aim . . . life** The ultimate aim of the good life should be to sustain that life   143 **And yet**   144 **gage** stake, risk   145 **As** such as.   **fell** fierce   148 **leave to be** cease being   149 **expect** i.e., hope to be   150 **infirmity** i.e., covetousness   151 **In having much** though we have much.   **defect** the imagined deficiency   153 **want of wit** lack of common sense   157 **for . . . forsake** i.e., he must forsake his honorable self to satisfy his lustful self.   164 **comfortable** cheering, benevolent.   **his** its   167 **silly** helpless, defenseless   172 **Th'one . . . flatters** i.e., desire deceives him into thinking he can go ahead safely
174 **retire** withdraw, retreat

176 **falchion** curved sword   179 **lodestar** the guiding polestar
180 **advisedly** deliberately   188 **His . . . lust** the armor supplied by lust that effectively leaves him naked and unprotected, the lust that continually undoes itself   189 **controls** rebukes   196 **weed** garment (i.e., chastity).   198 **my household's grave** memorial tomb of my forebears.   199 **including** encompassing   200 **fancy's** love's, infatuation's   201 **true respect** proper consideration for virtue
202 **digression** transgression   205 **coat** coat of arms   206 **dash** bar, stroke (devised by the heralds to indicate something dishonorable in the pedigree)   207 **cipher** express in characters, indicate.   **fondly** foolishly   208 **note** stigma, the heraldic bar (line 206)   214 **toy** trifle.
217 **straight** at once

"If Collatinus dream of my intent,
Will he not wake and in a desp'rate rage
Post hither, this vile purpose to prevent?—   220
This siege that hath engirt his marriage,   221
This blur to youth, this sorrow to the sage,   222
    This dying virtue, this surviving shame,
    Whose crime will bear an ever-during blame.   224

"Oh, what excuse can my invention make
When thou shalt charge me with so black a deed?   226
Will not my tongue be mute, my frail joints shake,
Mine eyes forgo their light, my false heart bleed?   228
The guilt being great, the fear doth still exceed;
    And extreme fear can neither fight nor fly,
    But cowardlike with trembling terror die.

"Had Collatinus killed my son or sire,
Or lain in ambush to betray my life,
Or were he not my dear friend, this desire
Might have excuse to work upon his wife,
As in revenge or quittal of such strife;   236
    But as he is my kinsman, my dear friend,
    The shame and fault finds no excuse nor end.

"Shameful it is; ay, if the fact be known,   239
Hateful it is. There is no hate in loving.
I'll beg her love. But she is not her own.   241
The worst is but denial and reproving.
My will is strong, past reason's weak removing.
    Who fears a sentence or an old man's saw   244
    Shall by a painted cloth be kept in awe."   245

Thus, graceless, holds he disputation
'Tween frozen conscience and hot-burning will,
And with good thoughts makes dispensation,
Urging the worser sense for vantage still,   248
Which in a moment doth confound and kill
    All pure effects, and doth so far proceed   251
    That what is vile shows like a virtuous deed.

Quoth he, "She took me kindly by the hand
And gazed for tidings in my eager eyes,
Fearing some hard news from the warlike band
Where her belovèd Collatinus lies.
Oh, how her fear did make her color rise!
    First red as roses that on lawn we lay,   258
    Then white as lawn, the roses took away.

"And how her hand, in my hand being locked,
Forced it to tremble with her loyal fear!

Which struck her sad, and then it faster rocked,
Until her husband's welfare she did hear;
Whereat she smilèd with so sweet a cheer   264
    That had Narcissus seen her as she stood   265
    Self-love had never drowned him in the flood.

"Why hunt I then for color or excuses?   267
All orators are dumb when beauty pleadeth;
Poor wretches have remorse in poor abuses;   269
Love thrives not in the heart that shadows dreadeth.   270
Affection is my captain, and he leadeth;   271
    And when his gaudy banner is displayed,
    The coward fights and will not be dismayed.   273

"Then, childish fear, avaunt! Debating, die!   274
Respect and reason, wait on wrinkled age!   275
My heart shall never countermand mine eye.   276
Sad pause and deep regard beseems the sage;   277
My part is youth, and beats these from the stage.   278
    Desire my pilot is, beauty my prize;
    Then who fears sinking where such treasure lies?"

As corn o'ergrown by weeds, so heedful fear   281
Is almost choked by unresisted lust.
Away he steals with open list'ning ear,
Full of foul hope and full of fond mistrust,   284
Both which, as servitors to the unjust,
    So cross him with their opposite persuasion   286
    That now he vows a league, and now invasion.   287

Within his thought her heavenly image sits,
And in the selfsame seat sits Collatine.
That eye which looks on her confounds his wits;   290
That eye which him beholds, as more divine,   291
Unto a view so false will not incline,
    But with a pure appeal seeks to the heart,   293
    Which once corrupted takes the worser part;

And therein heartens up his servile powers,   295
Who, flattered by their leader's jocund show,   296
Stuff up his lust, as minutes fill up hours;
And as their captain, so their pride doth grow,

---

264 a cheer an expression **265 Narcissus** youth who fell in love with his own reflection in the water (but who would have fallen in love with Lucrece if he had seen her) **267 color** pretext **269 Poor . . . abuses** lowborn, cowardly men feel remorse for their paltry misdeeds **270 shadows** i.e., the chimeras of conscience **271 Affection** Passion **273 The coward** i.e., even the coward **274 avaunt** begone. **275 Respect** Circumspection. **wait on** attend, accompany **276 heart** (Here, "moral sense"; compare with lines 293 ff., where the heart is corrupted.) **277 Sad** Serious, reflective **278 My . . . stage** (Tarquin visualizes himself as taking the role of hotheaded Youth in a morality play, driving away [offstage] his wise older counselors.) **281 corn** grain **284 fond** foolish **286 cross** thwart **287 league** treaty (of peace) **290 eye** eye of lust. **confounds his wits** over-whelms his reason with lust. **291 That eye . . . divine** The eye of divine reason, reflecting on Collatine **293 seeks to** looks to (for moral support) **295 his servile powers** i.e., the heart's servants, i.e., appetites. (The image is the common one of the faculties as an army: the heart as captain of the sensible soul commands all the affections to serve him. Compare with lines 433 ff., below.) **296 jocund** sprightly

220 Post hasten **221 engirt** engirdled, as in a siege **222 blur** blot, disgrace **224 ever-during** everlasting **226 thou** i.e., Collatinus **228 forgo their light** lose their power of vision **236 quittal** requital **239 fact** deed **241 she . . . own** i.e., she is not entirely independent, since she has duties to her husband. **244 Who** Whoever. **sentence** moral sentiment. **saw** saying, proverb **245 painted cloth** wall hanging in which moral tales and maxims were sometimes depicted. (Compare with lines 1366–1456, where such a painted cloth is described.) **248 makes dispensation** dispenses, sets aside **251 effects** intents and consequences **258 lawn** fine white linen

Paying more slavish tribute than they owe.   299
  By reprobate desire thus madly led,
  The Roman lord marcheth to Lucrece' bed.

The locks between her chamber and his will,
Each one by him enforced, retires his ward;   303
But, as they open, they all rate his ill,   304
Which drives the creeping thief to some regard.   305
The threshold grates the door to have him heard;
  Night-wand'ring weasels shriek to see him there;   307
  They fright him, yet he still pursues his fear.   308

As each unwilling portal yields him way,
Through little vents and crannies of the place
The wind wars with his torch to make him stay,
And blows the smoke of it into his face,
Extinguishing his conduct in this case;   313
  But his hot heart, which fond desire doth scorch,
  Puffs forth another wind that fires the torch.

And being lighted, by the light he spies
Lucretia's glove, wherein her needle sticks.
He takes it from the rushes where it lies,   318
And gripping it, the needle his finger pricks,
As who should say, "This glove to wanton tricks   320
  Is not inured. Return again in haste;   321
  Thou see'st our mistress' ornaments are chaste."

But all these poor forbiddings could not stay him;   323
He in the worst sense consters their denial.   324
The doors, the wind, the glove that did delay him
He takes for accidental things of trial,   326
Or as those bars which stop the hourly dial,   327
  Who with a ling'ring stay his course doth let   328
  Till every minute pays the hour his debt.

"So, so," quoth he, "these lets attend the time,   330
Like little frosts that sometime threat the spring,
To add a more rejoicing to the prime,   332
And give the sneapèd birds more cause to sing.   333
Pain pays the income of each precious thing;   334
  Huge rocks, high winds, strong pirates, shelves, and
    sands   335
  The merchant fears, ere rich at home he lands."

Now is he come unto the chamber door
That shuts him from the heaven of his thought,
Which with a yielding latch, and with no more,
Hath barred him from the blessèd thing he sought.
So from himself impiety hath wrought   341
  That for his prey to pray he doth begin,
  As if the heavens should countenance his sin.

But in the midst of his unfruitful prayer,
Having solicited th'eternal power
That his foul thoughts might compass his fair fair,   346
And they would stand auspicious to the hour,   347
Even there he starts. Quoth he, "I must deflower.   348
  The powers to whom I pray abhor this fact;   349
  How can they then assist me in the act?

"Then Love and Fortune be my gods, my guide!
My will is backed with resolution.
Thoughts are but dreams till their effects be tried;
The blackest sin is cleared with absolution;
Against love's fire fear's frost hath dissolution.
  The eye of heaven is out, and misty night   356
  Covers the shame that follows sweet delight."

This said, his guilty hand plucked up the latch,
And with his knee the door he opens wide.
The dove sleeps fast that this night owl will catch.
Thus treason works ere traitors be espied.
Who sees the lurking serpent steps aside;   362
  But she, sound sleeping, fearing no such thing,
  Lies at the mercy of his mortal sting.   364

Into the chamber wickedly he stalks,   365
And gazeth on her yet unstainèd bed.
The curtains being close, about he walks,   367
Rolling his greedy eyeballs in his head.
By their high treason is his heart misled,
  Which gives the watchword to his hand full soon
  To draw the cloud that hides the silver moon.   371

Look as the fair and fiery-pointed sun,   372
Rushing from forth a cloud, bereaves our sight,
Even so, the curtain drawn, his eyes begun
To wink, being blinded with a greater light.   375
Whether it is that she reflects so bright   376
  That dazzleth them, or else some shame supposed;
  But blind they are, and keep themselves enclosed.

Oh, had they in that darksome prison died,
Then had they seen the period of their ill!   380
Then Collatine again by Lucrece' side

---

299 Paying . . . owe i.e., paying tribute to the heart as its vassals, and doing so in an overdone and corrupting way.   **303 retires his ward** draws back its guard, i.e., the locking mechanism   **304 rate his ill** chide his evil (by creaking)   **305 regard** caution.   **307 weasels** (Weasels were sometimes kept in houses as rat catchers.)   **308 his fear** i.e., the cause of his fear.   **313 conduct** conductor, i.e., his torch. (With a play on "behavior.")   **318 rushes** reeds used as floor covering   **320 who should** one might   **320–1 to wanton . . . inured** has not become habituated to lascivious stratagems.   **323 stay** restrain   **324 consters** construes   **326 accidental . . . trial** i.e., accidents that test his resolve, not portents   **327 bars . . . dial** minute marks on a clock face at which the minute hand seems to pause slightly   **328 Who** which.   **his** its.   **let** hinder   **330 these . . . time** i.e., these hindrances (like the minute marks) are part of the passage of time   **332 more** greater.   **prime** spring   **333 sneapèd** nipped or pinched with cold   **334 pays . . . of** is the price of obtaining, or, pays court to, as though attending the arrival of   **335 shelves** sandbars

341 So . . . wrought Impiety has so wrested him away from his better nature   **346 compass** encompass, possess.   **fair fair** virtuous fair one   **347 they** i.e., that they, the eternal powers of heaven   **348 starts** i.e., startled, taken aback.   **349 fact** deed   **356 The eye . . . out** i.e., The sun is set   **362 Who** Whoever   **364 mortal** deadly.   **sting** bite. (Suggesting also "lust" and "penis.")   **365 stalks** steals   **367 close** (around a four-poster bed)   **371 draw the cloud** i.e., draw back the bedcurtains   **372 Look as** See how, just as   **375 wink** shut   **376 reflects** shines   **380 period** end.   **ill** wrongdoing.

In his clear bed might have reposèd still.   382
But they must ope, this blessèd league to kill,   383
   And holy-thoughted Lucrece to their sight   384
   Must sell her joy, her life, her world's delight.

Her lily hand her rosy cheek lies under,
Cozening the pillow of a lawful kiss,   387
Who, therefore angry, seems to part in sunder,
Swelling on either side to want his bliss;   389
Between whose hills her head entombèd is;
   Where, like a virtuous monument, she lies,   391
   To be admired of lewd unhallowed eyes.

Without the bed her other fair hand was,   393
On the green coverlet, whose perfect white
Showed like an April daisy on the grass,
With pearly sweat resembling dew of night.
Her eyes, like marigolds, had sheathed their light,
   And canopied in darkness sweetly lay,
   Till they might open to adorn the day.

Her hair, like golden threads, played with her breath—
Oh, modest wantons, wanton modesty!—
Showing life's triumph in the map of death   402
And death's dim look in life's mortality.   403
Each in her sleep themselves so beautify   404
   As if between them twain there were no strife,
   But that life lived in death and death in life.

Her breasts like ivory globes circled with blue,
A pair of maiden worlds unconquerèd,
Save of their lord no bearing yoke they knew,
And him by oath they truly honorèd.
These worlds in Tarquin new ambition bred,
   Who, like a foul usurper, went about
   From this fair throne to heave the owner out.

What could he see but mightily he noted?
What did he note but strongly he desired?
What he beheld, on that he firmly doted,
And in his will his willful eye he tired.   417
With more than admiration he admired
   Her azure veins, her alabaster skin,
   Her coral lips, her snow-white dimpled chin.

As the grim lion fawneth o'er his prey,   421
Sharp hunger by the conquest satisfied,
So o'er this sleeping soul doth Tarquin stay,
His rage of lust by gazing qualified—   424
Slacked, not suppressed, for, standing by her side,   425

His eye, which late this mutiny restrains,   426
Unto a greater uproar tempts his veins.

And they, like straggling slaves for pillage fighting,   428
Obdurate vassals fell exploits effecting,   429
In bloody death and ravishment delighting,
Nor children's tears nor mothers' groans respecting,   431
Swell in their pride, the onset still expecting.   432
   Anon his beating heart, alarum striking,
   Gives the hot charge and bids them do their liking.

His drumming heart cheers up his burning eye,
His eye commends the leading to his hand;   436
His hand, as proud of such a dignity,
Smoking with pride, marched on to make his stand
On her bare breast, the heart of all her land;
   Whose ranks of blue veins, as his hand did scale,   440
   Left their round turrets destitute and pale.

They, must'ring to the quiet cabinet   442
Where their dear governess and lady lies,
Do tell her she is dreadfully beset,
And fright her with confusion of their cries.
She, much amazed, breaks ope her locked-up eyes,
   Who, peeping forth this tumult to behold,
   Are by his flaming torch dimmed and controlled.   448

Imagine her as one in dead of night
From forth dull sleep by dreadful fancy waking,
That thinks she hath beheld some ghastly sprite,
Whose grim aspect sets every joint a-shaking.
What terror 'tis! But she, in worser taking,   453
   From sleep disturbèd, heedfully doth view
   The sight which makes supposèd terror true.

Wrapped and confounded in a thousand fears,
Like to a new-killed bird she trembling lies.
She dares not look; yet, winking, there appears   458
Quick-shifting antics, ugly in her eyes.   459
Such shadows are the weak brain's forgeries,
   Who, angry that the eyes fly from their lights,   461
   In darkness daunts them with more dreadful sights.

His hand, that yet remains upon her breast—
Rude ram, to batter such an ivory wall!—   464
May feel her heart—poor citizen!—distressed,
Wounding itself to death, rise up and fall,
Beating her bulk, that his hand shakes withal.   467
   This moves in him more rage and lesser pity
   To make the breach and enter this sweet city.

---

382 clear pure, innocent **383 league** i.e., marriage **384 to their sight** for the sake of what they (his eyes) will see **387 Cozening** cheating **389 to want his** i.e., protesting the lack of its **391 monument** effigy on a tomb **393 Without the bed** Outside the bedclothes **402 the map of death** i.e., sleep. (*Map* means "image, picture.") **403 life's mortality** life's least-living aspect, i.e., sleep. **404 Each** i.e., Life and death **417 will** lust. **tired** (1) exhausted (2) glutted, fed ravenously. (A term from falconry.) **421 fawneth** shows delight **424 qualified** softened, abated **425 Slacked** moderated. (The Quarto reading, "Slakt," could be modernized as "Slaked," with the same meaning.)

426 late lately, a moment ago **428 slaves** i.e., base-born soldiers **429 fell** fierce. **effecting** carrying out **431 Nor** neither **432 pride** lust. **still** continually **436 commends** entrusts, commissions **440 scale** ascend (as in military attack) **442 mustering** gathering. **cabinet** i.e., heart **448 controlled** overpowered. **453 taking** plight **458 winking** closing the eyes **459 antics** phantoms, fantastic appearances, shapes **461 angry . . . lights** i.e., angry that the eyes abandon their stations as guardians of light **464 ram** battering ram **467 bulk** i.e., chest, breast. **that** so that

First, like a trumpet, doth his tongue begin
To sound a parley to his heartless foe,   471
Who o'er the white sheet peers her whiter chin,   472
The reason of this rash alarm to know,
Which he by dumb demeanor seeks to show;   474
    But she with vehement prayers urgeth still   475
    Under what color he commits this ill.   476

Thus he replies: "The color in thy face,   477
That even for anger makes the lily pale,   478
And the red rose blush at her own disgrace,
Shall plead for me and tell my loving tale.
Under that color am I come to scale   481
    Thy never-conquered fort; the fault is thine,
    For those thine eyes betray thee unto mine.

"Thus I forestall thee, if thou mean to chide:
Thy beauty hath ensnared thee to this night,   485
Where thou with patience must my will abide—
My will that marks thee for my earth's delight,
Which I to conquer sought with all my might.
    But as reproof and reason beat it dead,   489
    By thy bright beauty was it newly bred.

"I see what crosses my attempt will bring;   491
I know what thorns the growing rose defends;
I think the honey guarded with a sting;   493
All this beforehand counsel comprehends.   494
But will is deaf and hears no heedful friends;
    Only he hath an eye to gaze on beauty
    And dotes on what he looks, 'gainst law or duty.   497

"I have debated even in my soul
What wrong, what shame, what sorrow I shall breed,
But nothing can affection's course control   500
Or stop the headlong fury of his speed.
I know repentant tears ensue the deed,   502
    Reproach, disdain, and deadly enmity;
    Yet strive I to embrace mine infamy."

This said, he shakes aloft his Roman blade,
Which, like a falcon towering in the skies,
Coucheth the fowl below with his wings' shade,   507
Whose crooked beak threats if he mount he dies.   508
So under his insulting falchion lies   509
    Harmless Lucretia, marking what he tells
    With trembling fear, as fowl hear falcon's bells.   511

"Lucrece," quoth he, "this night I must enjoy thee.
If thou deny, then force must work my way,
For in thy bed I purpose to destroy thee.
That done, some worthless slave of thine I'll slay,
To kill thine honor with thy life's decay;   516
    And in thy dead arms do I mean to place him,
    Swearing I slew him, seeing thee embrace him.

"So thy surviving husband shall remain
The scornful mark of every open eye,   520
Thy kinsmen hang their heads at this disdain,
Thy issue blurred with nameless bastardy;   522
And thou, the author of their obloquy,
    Shalt have thy trespass cited up in rhymes   524
    And sung by children in succeeding times.

"But if thou yield, I rest thy secret friend.   526
The fault unknown is as a thought unacted;
A little harm done to a great good end
For lawful policy remains enacted.   529
The poisonous simple sometime is compacted   530
    In a pure compound; being so applied,   531
    His venom in effect is purified.

"Then, for thy husband and thy children's sake,
Tender my suit. Bequeath not to their lot   534
The shame that from them no device can take,   535
The blemish that will never be forgot,
Worse than a slavish wipe or birth hour's blot.   537
    For marks descried in men's nativity
    Are nature's faults, not their own infamy."

Here with a cockatrice' dead-killing eye   540
He rouseth up himself and makes a pause,
While she, the picture of pure piety,
Like a white hind under the gripe's sharp claws,   543
Pleads, in a wilderness where are no laws,   544
    To the rough beast that knows no gentle right,   545
    Nor aught obeys but his foul appetite.

But when a black-faced cloud the world doth threat,
In his dim mist th'aspiring mountains hiding,   548
From earth's dark womb some gentle gust doth get,   549
Which blows these pitchy vapors from their biding,   550
Hind'ring their present fall by this dividing;   551

471 **a parley** a summoning of the defenders to a negotiation.   **heartless**
terrified   472 **peers** causes to peep out (as a defender would peer out
over the fortifications)   474 **dumb demeanor** mute gesture
475 **urgeth** cries out to know   476 **color** pretext   477 **color** hue. (Punning on the previous line.)   478 **That . . . pale** that makes even the lily
turn pale in anger (at being surpassed in paleness)   485 **ensnared thee to** led you into the
trap of   489 **as** as soon as.   **it** my will or passion   491 **crosses** vexations   493 **think the honey** know the honey to be   494 **counsel** wisdom, reason   497 **looks** sees   500 **affection's** passion's   502 **ensue**
follow upon   507 **Coucheth** causes to couch, i.e., remain concealed.
his i.e., the falcon's (whose shadow frightens the fowl)   508 **Whose . . .
dies** (The crooked beak of the falcon threatens that if the fowl dare
emerge from hiding, it dies.)   509 **insulting falchion** triumphantly
exulting sword   511 **bells** (Falcons had bells attached to their feet.)

516 **To kill . . . decay** i.e., to destroy your honor even while also taking your life   520 **open eye** i.e., observer   522 **Thy . . . bastardy** your
children sullied with the suspicion of being bastards of some
unknown father   524 **in rhymes** i.e., in ballads   526 **rest** remain.
friend lover.   529 **For . . . enacted** is accepted as a lawful expedient.
530 **simple** ingredient, drug.   **compacted** mixed   531 **pure** i.e.,
benign, medically efficacious   534 **Tender my suit** regard my plea.
535 **device** (1) contrivance (2) heraldic motto   537 **slavish wipe**
brand with which slaves were marked.   **birth hour's blot** unsightly
birthmark.   540 **cockatrice** the basilisk, said to be hatched by a serpent from a cock's egg and to kill by its breath and the rays it emitted
from its eyes   **gripe's** vulture's, or griffin's
544 **Pleads** (With play on legal meaning.)   545 **gentle right** law of
gentility   548 **th'aspiring** the high-rising   549 **doth get** comes into
being   550 **pitchy** black.   **their biding** where they hang   551 **their
present fall** i.e., the imminent onset of the storm

So his unhallowed haste her words delays,   552
And moody Pluto winks while Orpheus plays.   553

Yet, foul night-waking cat, he doth but dally,
While in his hold-fast foot the weak mouse panteth.
Her sad behavior feeds his vulture folly,   556
A swallowing gulf that even in plenty wanteth. 557
His ear her prayers admits, but his heart granteth
    No penetrable entrance to her plaining;   559
    Tears harden lust, though marble wear with raining.

Her pity-pleading eyes are sadly fixed
In the remorseless wrinkles of his face;   562
Her modest eloquence with sighs is mixed,
Which to her oratory adds more grace.
She puts the period often from his place,   565
    And midst the sentence so her accent breaks 566
    That twice she doth begin ere once she speaks.

She conjures him by high almighty Jove,
By knighthood, gentry, and sweet friendship's oath, 569
By her untimely tears, her husband's love,   570
By holy human law and common troth,   571
By heaven and earth, and all the power of both,
    That to his borrowed bed he make retire   573
    And stoop to honor, not to foul desire.   574

Quoth she, "Reward not hospitality
With such black payment as thou hast pretended. 576
Mud not the fountain that gave drink to thee;   577
Mar not the thing that cannot be amended.   578
End thy ill aim before thy shoot be ended;   579
    He is no woodman that doth bend his bow   580
    To strike a poor unseasonable doe.   581

"My husband is thy friend; for his sake spare me.
Thyself art mighty; for thine own sake leave me.
Myself a weakling; do not then ensnare me.
Thou look'st not like deceit; do not deceive me.
My sighs, like whirlwinds, labor hence to heave thee.
    If ever man were moved with woman's moans,
    Be movèd with my tears, my sighs, my groans;

"All which together, like a troubled ocean,
Beat at thy rocky and wreck-threat'ning heart,
To soften it with their continual motion;

For stones dissolved to water do convert.   592
Oh, if no harder than a stone thou art,
    Melt at my tears, and be compassionate!
    Soft pity enters at an iron gate.

"In Tarquin's likeness I did entertain thee.
Hast thou put on his shape to do him shame?
To all the host of heaven I complain me.
Thou wrong'st his honor, wound'st his princely name.
Thou art not what thou seem'st; and if the same, 600
    Thou seem'st not what thou art, a god, a king;
    For kings like gods should govern everything.

"How will thy shame be seeded in thine age,   603
When thus thy vices bud before thy spring?
If in thy hope thou dar'st do such outrage,   605
What dar'st thou not when once thou art a king?
Oh, be remembered, no outrageous thing   607
    From vassal actors can be wiped away;   608
    Then kings' misdeeds cannot be hid in clay. 609

"This deed will make thee only loved for fear, 610
But happy monarchs still are feared for love.   611
With foul offenders thou perforce must bear,   612
When they in thee the like offenses prove.
If but for fear of this, thy will remove;   614
    For princes are the glass, the school, the book, 615
    Where subjects' eyes do learn, do read, do look.

"And wilt thou be the school where Lust shall learn?
Must he in thee read lectures of such shame?
Wilt thou be glass wherein it shall discern
Authority for sin, warrant for blame,
To privilege dishonor in thy name?   621
    Thou back'st reproach against long-living laud 622
    And mak'st fair reputation but a bawd.

"Hast thou command? By Him that gave it thee,   624
From a pure heart command thy rebel will.
Draw not thy sword to guard iniquity,
For it was lent thee all that brood to kill.   627
Thy princely office how canst thou fulfill,
    When, patterned by thy fault, foul Sin may say 629
    He learned to sin, and thou didst teach the way?

"Think but how vile a spectacle it were
To view thy present trespass in another.
Men's faults do seldom to themselves appear;

---

552 **So . . . delays** thus her words delay his unhallowed haste
553 **winks** closes his eyes.   **Orpheus** husband of Eurydice, who went
to the underworld for her and charmed Pluto, ruler of the underworld,
with his playing the lyre   556 **vulture folly** ravenous lewdness and
madness   557 **gulf** maw, belly.   **wanteth** craves insatiably.
559 **plaining** lamentation   562 **wrinkles** i.e., frowns   565 **his place** its
place (in the sentence; i.e., she speaks in broken phrases)   566 **accent**
speech   569 **gentry** nobleness of birth and breeding   570 **untimely
tears** i.e., tears occasioned by an inopportune and unwelcome happening   571 **troth** good faith   573 **borrowed** lent him for the night
574 **stoop to** (1) subject himself to (2) pursue (3) swoop down to (as to
the lure or prey, like a falcon)   576 **pretended** proposed.   577 **Mud**
Muddy   578 **amended** returned to its former purity.   579 **shoot** shooting, hunting   580 **woodman** huntsman   581 **unseasonable** in foal or
not yet bearing, out of the hunting season

592 **stones . . . convert** stones are worn away in time by water.
convert change.   600 **if the same** i.e., if you are actually Tarquin
603 **be seeded** ripen   605 **in thy hope** i.e., while you are yet only heir
to the kingdom   607 **be remembered** bear in mind   608 **vassal
actors** vassals or ordinary subjects who commit crimes   609 **in clay**
i.e., even in death.   610 **loved for fear** obeyed out of fear   611 **still . . .
love** always are regarded with reverential awe stemming from love.
612 **With . . . bear** You will have to put up with others' foul offenses
614 **but** only.   **thy will remove** dissuade your lust   615 **glass** mirror
and paradigm   621 **privilege** license   622 **Thou back'st** You support.   **laud** praise   624 **Him** i.e., God   627 **that brood** i.e., the progeny of evil   629 **patterned** shown a precedent

Their own transgressions partially they smother.
This guilt would seem death-worthy in thy brother.   634
　　Oh, how are they wrapped in with infamies
　　That from their own misdeeds askance their eyes!   637

"To thee, to thee, my heaved-up hands appeal,   638
Not to seducing lust, thy rash relier.   639
I sue for exiled majesty's repeal;   640
Let him return, and flatt'ring thoughts retire.   641
His true respect will prison false desire   642
　　And wipe the dim mist from thy doting eyne,   643
　　That thou shalt see thy state and pity mine."

"Have done," quoth he. "My uncontrollèd tide   645
Turns not, but swells the higher by this let.   646
Small lights are soon blown out; huge fires abide,
And with the wind in greater fury fret.
The petty streams that pay a daily debt
　　To their salt sovereign, with their fresh falls' haste   650
　　Add to his flow but alter not his taste."

"Thou art," quoth she, "a sea, a sovereign king;
And lo, there falls into thy boundless flood
Black lust, dishonor, shame, misgoverning,
Who seek to stain the ocean of thy blood.   655
If all these petty ills shall change thy good,
　　Thy sea within a puddle's womb is hearsed,   657
　　And not the puddle in thy sea dispersed.   658

"So shall these slaves be king, and thou their slave;   659
Thou nobly base, they basely dignified;
Thou their fair life, and they thy fouler grave;
Thou loathèd in their shame, they in thy pride.
The lesser thing should not the greater hide;
　　The cedar stoops not to the base shrub's foot,
　　But low shrubs wither at the cedar's root.

"So let thy thoughts, low vassals to thy state—"
"No more," quoth he, "by heaven, I will not hear thee.
Yield to my love; if not, enforcèd hate,
Instead of love's coy touch, shall rudely tear thee.   668
That done, despitefully I mean to bear thee   669
　　Unto the base bed of some rascal groom,
　　To be thy partner in this shameful doom."   671

This said, he sets his foot upon the light,
For light and lust are deadly enemies;
Shame folded up in blind concealing night,
When most unseen, then most doth tyrannize.
The wolf hath seized his prey, the poor lamb cries;

Till with her own white fleece her voice controlled   678
Entombs her outcry in her lips' sweet fold.   679

For with the nightly linen that she wears
He pens her piteous clamors in her head,
Cooling his hot face in the chastest tears
That ever modest eyes with sorrow shed.
Oh, that prone lust should stain so pure a bed!   684
　　The spots whereof could weeping purify,   685
　　Her tears should drop on them perpetually.

But she hath lost a dearer thing than life,
And he hath won what he would lose again.   688
This forcèd league doth force a further strife;
This momentary joy breeds months of pain;
This hot desire converts to cold disdain.   691
　　Pure Chastity is rifled of her store,   692
　　And Lust, the thief, far poorer than before.

Look as the full-fed hound or gorgèd hawk,   694
Unapt for tender smell or speedy flight,   695
Make slow pursuit, or altogether balk   696
The prey wherein by nature they delight,
So surfeit-taking Tarquin fares this night.
　　His taste delicious, in digestion souring,
　　Devours his will, that lived by foul devouring.

Oh, deeper sin than bottomless conceit   701
Can comprehend in still imagination!   702
Drunken Desire must vomit his receipt   703
Ere he can see his own abomination.
While Lust is in his pride, no exclamation   705
　　Can curb his heat or rein his rash desire,
　　Till like a jade Self-will himself doth tire.   707

And then with lank and lean discolored cheek,
With heavy eye, knit brow, and strengthless pace,
Feeble Desire, all recreant, poor, and meek,   710
Like to a bankrupt beggar wails his case.   711
The flesh being proud, Desire doth fight with Grace,   712
　　For there it revels, and when that decays,   713
　　The guilty rebel for remission prays.   714

So fares it with this faultful lord of Rome,
Who this accomplishment so hotly chased;
For now against himself he sounds this doom,   717

---

634 **partially . . . smother** they hide from themselves.   637 **askance** avert   638 **heaved-up** raised   639 **thy rash relier** on which you rashly rely.   640 **repeal** recall from exile   641 **and flatt'ring thoughts retire** and let those thoughts that flatter and egg on lust go away.   642 **His . . . respect** His true authority and concern for truth.   **prison** imprison   643 **eyne** eyes   645 **Have done** Cease talking   646 **let** hindrance.   650 **salt sovereign** i.e., the sea   655 **blood** heritage; character.   657–8 **Thy . . . dispersed** in that case your royal sea is now buried in a foul puddle, rather than the puddle being dispersed in your royal sea.   659 **these slaves** i.e., lust, dishonor, etc.; see line 654   668 **enforcèd hate** force impelled by hatred   669 **coy** gentle   671 **groom** servant

678–9 **Till . . . fold** until, overmastering her voice with her own night-wear or bedlinen, he buries her outcry as though in the fold of her sweet lips. (*Fold* refers to her folded or compressed lips and to a sheep-fold; hence *pens* in line 681.)   684 **prone** eager, headlong   685 **could weeping** if weeping could   688 **what . . . again** what he soon wished he could undo.   691 **converts** changes   692 **Pure . . . store** i.e., Pure chastity loses all that it has, loses all itself   694 **Look as** Just as   695 **tender smell** delicate scent   696 **balk** turn away from, let slip   701 **bottomless conceit** limitless imagination   702 **in still imagina-tion** in imagination alone.   703 **his receipt** what it has swallowed   705 **exclamation** protest   707 **jade** recalcitrant horse   710 **recreant** craven, cowed   711 **Like to** like   712 **proud** stubborn, willful   713 **there** i.e., in the flesh.   **when that decays** when the reveling in pleasure subsides   714 **The guilty . . . prays** the flesh prays for for-giveness.   717 **sounds this doom** pronounces this judgment

That through the length of times he stands disgraced.
Besides, his soul's fair temple is defaced,
　　To whose weak ruins muster troops of cares
　　To ask the spotted princess how she fares.　　721

She says her subjects with foul insurrection　　722
Have battered down her consecrated wall,
And by their mortal fault brought in subjection　　724
Her immortality, and made her thrall
To living death and pain perpetual,
　　Which in her prescience she controllèd still,　　727
　　But her foresight could not forestall their will.　　728

Ev'n in this thought through the dark night he stealeth,
A captive victor that hath lost in gain,　　730
Bearing away the wound that nothing healeth,
The scar that will, despite of cure, remain,
Leaving his spoil perplexed in greater pain.　　733
　　She bears the load of lust he left behind,
　　And he the burden of a guilty mind.

He like a thievish dog creeps sadly thence;
She like a wearied lamb lies panting there.
He scowls and hates himself for his offense;
She, desperate, with her nails her flesh doth tear.
He faintly flies, sweating with guilty fear;　　740
　　She stays, exclaiming on the direful night;　　741
　　He runs, and chides his vanished, loathed delight.

He thence departs a heavy convertite;　　743
She there remains a hopeless castaway.
He in his speed looks for the morning light;
She prays she never may behold the day.
"For day," quoth she, "night's scapes doth open lay,　　747
　　And my true eyes have never practiced how
　　To cloak offenses with a cunning brow.

"They think not but that every eye can see
The same disgrace which they themselves behold;
And therefore would they still in darkness be,
To have their unseen sin remain untold.
For they their guilt with weeping will unfold,　　754
　　And grave, like water that doth eat in steel,　　755
　　Upon my cheeks what helpless shame I feel."

Here she exclaims against repose and rest　　757
And bids her eyes hereafter still be blind.　　758
She wakes her heart by beating on her breast,
And bids it leap from thence, where it may find

Some purer chest to close so pure a mind.　　761
　　Frantic with grief thus breathes she forth her spite　　762
　　Against the unseen secrecy of night:

"O comfort-killing Night, image of hell,
Dim register and notary of shame,　　765
Black stage for tragedies and murders fell,　　766
Vast sin-concealing chaos, nurse of blame!　　767
Blind muffled bawd, dark harbor for defame,　　768
　　Grim cave of death, whisp'ring conspirator
　　With close-tongued treason and the ravisher!　　770

"O hateful, vaporous, and foggy Night,
Since thou art guilty of my cureless crime,
Muster thy mists to meet the eastern light,
Make war against proportioned course of time;　　774
Or if thou wilt permit the sun to climb
　　His wonted height, yet ere he go to bed
　　Knit poisonous clouds about his golden head.

"With rotten damps ravish the morning air;
Let their exhaled unwholesome breaths make sick
The life of purity, the supreme fair,　　780
Ere he arrive his weary noontide prick;　　781
And let thy musty vapors march so thick
　　That in their smoky ranks his smothered light
　　May set at noon and make perpetual night.

"Were Tarquin Night, as he is but Night's child,
The silver-shining queen he would distain;　　786
Her twinkling handmaids too, by him defiled,　　787
Through Night's black bosom should not peep again.
So should I have copartners in my pain;
　　And fellowship in woe doth woe assuage,
　　As palmers' chat makes short their pilgrimage.　　791

"Where now I have no one to blush with me,　　792
To cross their arms and hang their heads with mine,　　793
To mask their brows and hide their infamy;　　794
But I alone alone must sit and pine,　　795
Seasoning the earth with showers of silver brine,
　　Mingling my talk with tears, my grief with groans,
　　Poor wasting monuments of lasting moans.　　798

"O Night, thou furnace of foul reeking smoke!
Let not the jealous Day behold that face
Which underneath thy black all-hiding cloak
Immodestly lies martyred with disgrace!　　802
Keep still possession of thy gloomy place,

---

721 **spotted princess** i.e., his contaminated soul, of whom the *temple*, line 719, is the body.　　722 **subjects** i.e., the senses or passions 724 **mortal** deadly　　727–8 **Which . . . will** i.e., which senses or passions she theoretically governed in anticipation of any act but could not, despite her foresight, restrain in their state of sexual arousal. 730 **A captive . . . gain** one who has gained the prize at the cost of perpetual durance in sin　　733 **spoil** prey, i.e., Lucrece　　740 **faintly** cowardly　　741 **exclaiming on** denouncing　　743 **heavy convertite** sad penitent　　747 **night's . . . lay** exposes night's transgressions to view　　754 **unfold** reveal　　755 **grave** engrave.　**water** i.e., aqua fortis, nitric acid　　757 **exclaims against** reproaches　　758 **still** forever

761 **close** enclose　　762 **spite** vexation　　765 **register** registrar.　**notary** recorder　　766 **Black stage** (Referring seemingly to a practice of hanging the stage with black for the performance of a tragedy.)　**fell** savage　　767 **blame** evil.　　768 **defame** infamy　　770 **close-tongued** closemouthed, secretive of speech　　774 **proportioned** i.e., orderly in the regulated interchange of day and night　　780 **supreme fair** i.e., the sun　　781 **arrive** arrive at.　**prick** mark (as on a dial)　　786 **queen** i.e., moon.　**distain** stain, soil　　787 **handmaids** i.e., stars　　791 **palmers' pilgrims'**　　792 **Where** Whereas　　793–4 **To cross . . . infamy** (Folding the arms and pulling the hat over the brows were conventional gestures of grief.)　　795 **I alone alone** only I alone　　798 **monuments** tokens, mementos　　802 **martyred** i.e., disfigured

That all the faults which in thy reign are made
May likewise be sepulch'red in thy shade.

"Make me not object to the telltale Day.   806
The light will show charactered in my brow   807
The story of sweet chastity's decay,   808
The impious breach of holy wedlock vow.
Yea, the illiterate, that know not how
    To cipher what is writ in learnèd books,   811
    Will quote my loathsome trespass in my looks.   812

"The nurse, to still her child, will tell my story,
And fright her crying babe with Tarquin's name;
The orator, to deck his oratory,   815
Will couple my reproach to Tarquin's shame;
Feast-finding minstrels, tuning my defame,   817
    Will tie the hearers to attend each line,
    How Tarquin wrongèd me, I Collatine.

"Let my good name, that senseless reputation,   820
For Collatine's dear love be kept unspotted.
If that be made a theme for disputation,   822
The branches of another root are rotted,   823
And undeserved reproach to him allotted
    That is as clear from this attaint of mine   825
    As I, ere this, was pure to Collatine.

"O unseen shame, invisible disgrace!
O unfelt sore, crest-wounding, private scar!   828
Reproach is stamped in Collatinus' face,
And Tarquin's eye may read the mot afar,   830
How he in peace is wounded, not in war.
    Alas, how many bear such shameful blows,
    Which not themselves but he that gives them knows!

"If, Collatine, thine honor lay in me,
From me by strong assault it is bereft;
My honey lost, and I, a dronelike bee,
Have no perfection of my summer left,   837
But robbed and ransacked by injurious theft.
    In thy weak hive a wand'ring wasp hath crept
    And sucked the honey which thy chaste bee kept.

"Yet am I guilty of thy honor's wrack;
Yet for thy honor did I entertain him.
Coming from thee, I could not put him back,
For it had been dishonor to disdain him.
Besides, of weariness he did complain him,
    And talked of virtue. Oh, unlooked-for evil,
    When virtue is profaned in such a devil!

"Why should the worm intrude the maiden bud?
Or hateful cuckoos hatch in sparrows' nests?
Or toads infect fair founts with venom mud?
Or tyrant folly lurk in gentle breasts?   851
Or kings be breakers of their own behests?   852
    But no perfection is so absolute
    That some impurity doth not pollute.

"The agèd man that coffers up his gold
Is plagued with cramps and gouts and painful fits,
And scarce hath eyes his treasure to behold,
But like still-pining Tantalus he sits,   858
And useless barns the harvest of his wits,   859
    Having no other pleasure of his gain
    But torment that it cannot cure his pain.

"So then he hath it when he cannot use it,
And leaves it to be mastered by his young,   863
Who in their pride do presently abuse it.   864
Their father was too weak, and they too strong,   865
To hold their cursèd-blessèd fortune long.
    The sweets we wish for turn to loathèd sours
    Even in the moment that we call them ours.

"Unruly blasts wait on the tender spring;
Unwholesome weeds take root with precious flowers;
The adder hisses where the sweet birds sing;
What virtue breeds, iniquity devours.
We have no good that we can say is ours
    But ill-annexèd Opportunity   874
    Or kills his life or else his quality.   875

"O Opportunity, thy guilt is great!
'Tis thou that execut'st the traitor's treason;   877
Thou sets the wolf where he the lamb may get;
Whoever plots the sin, thou 'point'st the season.   879
'Tis thou that spurn'st at right, at law, at reason;
    And in thy shady cell, where none may spy him,
    Sits Sin, to seize the souls that wander by him.

"Thou makest the vestal violate her oath;   883
Thou blowest the fire when temperance is thawed;
Thou smother'st honesty, thou murderest troth.   885
Thou foul abettor, thou notorious bawd,
Thou plantest scandal and displacest laud.   887
    Thou ravisher, thou traitor, thou false thief,
    Thy honey turns to gall, thy joy to grief!

---

806 object a thing exposed to sight, object of gossip **807 charactered** inscribed **808 decay** ruin **811 cipher** decipher, read **812 quote** note, observe **815 deck** adorn **817 Feast-finding** searching out feasts at which to sing **820 senseless** impalpable **822–3 If . . . rotted** i.e., If my reputation comes in question, then Collatine's will also be attacked **825 attaint** stain, imputation of dishonor **828 crest-wounding** disgraceful to the crest or device above the shield in one's coat of arms **830 mot** motto **837 Have . . . left** have nothing left of the honey I perfected in the summer

851 folly sensuality. **gentle** noble (in rank and temperament) **852 behests** biddings, injunctions. **858 still-pining** continually starving. **Tantalus** a son of Zeus who was punished by perpetual hunger and thirst with unreachable food and drink always in sight. (Renaissance commentators on Ovid glossed Tantalus as a usurer; hence the image of lines 859 ff.) **859 barns** stores, as in a barn **863 mastered** possessed. **young** heirs **864 presently** immediately **865 strong** headstrong **874–5 But . . . quality** but circumstance, joining itself to evil purpose at the critical moment, either kills the good entirely or at least destroys its nature. **877 'Tis . . . treason** It is you that fulfills the traitor's treasonous plan by providing the opportunity **879 thou . . . season** you appoint the time. **883 vestal** vestal virgin, priestess of Vesta, the Roman goddess of hearth and home **885 honesty** chastity. **troth** honesty. **887 laud** praise.

"Thy secret pleasure turns to open shame,
Thy private feasting to a public fast,
Thy smoothing titles to a ragged name, 892
Thy sugared tongue to bitter wormwood taste.
Thy violent vanities can never last.
    How comes it then, vile Opportunity,
    Being so bad, such numbers seek for thee?

"When wilt thou be the humble suppliant's friend,
And bring him where his suit may be obtained?
When wilt thou sort an hour great strifes to end? 899
Or free that soul which wretchedness hath chained?
Give physic to the sick, ease to the pained? 901
    The poor, lame, blind, halt, creep, cry out for thee,
    But they ne'er meet with Opportunity.

"The patient dies while the physician sleeps;
The orphan pines while the oppressor feeds; 905
Justice is feasting while the widow weeps; 906
Advice is sporting while infection breeds. 907
Thou grant'st no time for charitable deeds.
    Wrath, envy, treason, rape, and murder's rages, 909
    Thy heinous hours wait on them as their pages. 910

"When Truth and Virtue have to do with thee,
A thousand crosses keep them from thy aid. 912
They buy thy help; but Sin ne'er gives a fee; 913
He gratis comes; and thou art well apaid 914
As well to hear as grant what he hath said. 915
    My Collatine would else have come to me
    When Tarquin did, but he was stayed by thee.

"Guilty thou art of murder and of theft,
Guilty of perjury and subornation,
Guilty of treason, forgery, and shift, 920
Guilty of incest, that abomination—
An accessory by thine inclination 922
    To all sins past and all that are to come,
    From the creation to the general doom. 924

"Misshapen Time, copesmate of ugly Night, 925
Swift subtle post, carrier of grisly care, 926
Eater of youth, false slave to false delight,
Base watch of woes, sin's packhorse, virtue's snare! 928
Thou nursest all, and murd'rest all that are.
    Oh, hear me then, injurious, shifting Time! 930
    Be guilty of my death, since of my crime. 931

"Why hath thy servant Opportunity
Betrayed the hours thou gav'st me to repose,
Canceled my fortunes, and enchainèd me
To endless date of never-ending woes? 935
Time's office is to fine the hate of foes, 936
    To eat up errors by opinion bred, 937
    Not spend the dowry of a lawful bed.

"Time's glory is to calm contending kings,
To unmask falsehood and bring truth to light,
To stamp the seal of time in agèd things,
To wake the morn and sentinel the night, 942
To wrong the wronger till he render right,
    To ruinate proud buildings with thy hours,
    And smear with dust their glitt'ring golden towers;

"To fill with wormholes stately monuments,
To feed oblivion with decay of things,
To blot old books and alter their contents, 948
To pluck the quills from ancient ravens' wings, 949
To dry the old oak's sap and cherish springs, 950
    To spoil antiquities of hammered steel,
    And turn the giddy round of Fortune's wheel;

"To show the beldam daughters of her daughter, 953
To make the child a man, the man a child, 954
To slay the tiger that doth live by slaughter,
To tame the unicorn and lion wild,
To mock the subtle in themselves beguiled, 957
    To cheer the plowman with increaseful crops, 958
    And waste huge stones with little waterdrops. 959

"Why work'st thou mischief in thy pilgrimage,
Unless thou couldst return to make amends?
One poor retiring minute in an age 962
Would purchase thee a thousand thousand friends,
Lending him wit that to bad debtors lends. 964
    O, this dread night, wouldst thou one hour come back,
    I could prevent this storm and shun thy wrack! 966

"Thou ceaseless lackey to Eternity, 967
With some mischance cross Tarquin in his flight! 968
Devise extremes beyond extremity
To make him curse this cursèd crimeful night.
Let ghastly shadows his lewd eyes affright,
    And the dire thought of his committed evil
    Shape every bush a hideous shapeless devil.

892 smoothing flattering. **ragged** faulty, irregular **899 sort** choose, appoint **901 physic** medicine **905 pines** starves **906 Justice** i.e., wealthy, complacent Justices of the Peace **907 Advice** i.e., doctors who enjoy the idle pleasures of wealth gained from the medical advice they give **909–10 Wrath . . . pages** The heinous hours that you, Opportunity, give over to crime are like page boys serving wrath, envy, treason, rape, and murder. **912 crosses** hindrances **913–15 They . . . said** Truth and Virtue have to pay for any opportunity they get, whereas Sin never has to pay; Opportunity comes free to Sin. You, contrastingly, have to be satisfied to listen to and obey whatever conditions Opportunity lays down for you. **920 shift** fraud **922 inclination** natural disposition **924 general doom** Doomsday, Day of Judgment. **925 copesmate** companion, accomplice **926 post** messenger **928 watch** crier, one who announces woes **930 shifting** ever changing and treacherous **931 since of** since you are guilty of

935 date duration **936 Time's . . . foes** Time's function should be to end or punish hatred **937 opinion** popular rumor **942 sentinel** stand guard over **948 blot** erase, obliterate **949 To pluck . . . wings** i.e., to end even the existence of long-lived ravens **950 springs** new growth, shoots **953 To . . . daughter** to show to the aging women her granddaughters **954 a child** i.e., in the second childishness of old age **957 subtle . . . beguiled** crafty who are foiled by their own cleverness **958 increaseful** fruitful **959 waste** wear away **962 retiring** returning (thereby allowing sinners an opportunity to undo their evil) **964 Lending . . . lends** giving the would-be lender the foresight and second chance to avoid the mistake he has made. **966 prevent** anticipate, forestall **967 ceaseless lackey** untiring and relentless servant **968 cross** thwart

"Disturb his hours of rest with restless trances; 974
Afflict him in his bed with bedrid groans; 975
Let there bechance him pitiful mischances
To make him moan, but pity not his moans.
Stone him with hardened hearts harder than stones,
    And let mild women to him lose their mildness, 979
    Wilder to him than tigers in their wildness.

"Let him have time to tear his curlèd hair,
Let him have time against himself to rave,
Let him have time of Time's help to despair,
Let him have time to live a loathèd slave,
Let him have time a beggar's orts to crave, 985
    And time to see one that by alms doth live 986
    Disdain to him disdainèd scraps to give. 987

"Let him have time to see his friends his foes,
And merry fools to mock at him resort; 989
Let him have time to mark how slow time goes
In time of sorrow, and how swift and short
His time of folly and his time of sport;
    And ever let his unrecalling crime 933
    Have time to wail th'abusing of his time.

"O Time, thou tutor both to good and bad,
Teach me to curse him that thou taught'st this ill! 996
At his own shadow let the thief run mad,
Himself himself seek every hour to kill!
Such wretched hands such wretched blood should spill;
    For who so base would such an office have
    As sland'rous deathsman to so base a slave? 1001

"The baser is he, coming from a king,
To shame his hope with deeds degenerate. 1003
The mightier man, the mightier is the thing
That makes him honored or begets him hate;
For greatest scandal waits on greatest state. 1006
    The moon being clouded presently is missed, 1007
    But little stars may hide them when they list.

"The crow may bathe his coal-black wings in mire,
And unperceived fly with the filth away,
But if the like the snow-white swan desire,
The stain upon his silver down will stay.
Poor grooms are sightless night, kings glorious day. 1013
    Gnats are unnoted wheresoe'er they fly,
    But eagles gazed upon with every eye.

"Out, idle words, servants to shallow fools, 1016
Unprofitable sounds, weak arbitrators!

Busy yourselves in skill-contending schools; 1018
Debate where leisure serves with dull debaters;
To trembling clients be you mediators.
    For me, I force not argument a straw, 1021
    Since that my case is past the help of law. 1022

"In vain I rail at Opportunity,
At Time, at Tarquin, and uncheerful Night;
In vain I cavil with mine infamy, 1025
In vain I spurn at my confirmed despite. 1026
This helpless smoke of words doth me no right. 1027
    The remedy indeed to do me good
    Is to let forth my foul-defilèd blood. 1029

"Poor hand, why quiver'st thou at this decree?
Honor thyself to rid me of this shame!
For if I die, my honor lives in thee,
But if I live, thou liv'st in my defame.
Since thou couldst not defend thy loyal dame,
    And wast afeard to scratch her wicked foe,
    Kill both thyself and her for yielding so."

This said, from her betumbled couch she starteth,
To find some desp'rate instrument of death;
But this, no slaughterhouse, no tool imparteth 1039
To make more vent for passage of her breath,
Which, thronging through her lips, so vanisheth
    As smoke from Etna, that in air consumes, 1042
    Or that which from dischargèd cannon fumes.

"In vain," quoth she, "I live, and seek in vain
Some happy means to end a hapless life. 1045
I feared by Tarquin's falchion to be slain, 1046
Yet for the selfsame purpose seek a knife;
But when I feared, I was a loyal wife.
    So am I now.—Oh, no, that cannot be!
    Of that true type hath Tarquin rifled me. 1050

"Oh, that is gone for which I sought to live,
And therefore now I need not fear to die.
To clear this spot by death, at least I give 1053
A badge of fame to slander's livery, 1054
A dying life to living infamy.
    Poor helpless help, the treasure stol'n away,
    To burn the guiltless casket where it lay!

974 **trances** visions, fits 975 **bedrid** bedridden 979 **to** confronted with 985 **orts** refuse, fragments of food 986–7 **And . . . give** and may he live long enough to see the most miserable charity-supported beggar disdain to give him the leftover scraps from that beggar's meal. 989 **And . . . resort** and merry fools gather (*resort*) to mock him 993 **unrecalling crime** crime that cannot be undone 996 **that** to whom 1001 **sland'rous deathsman** despised executioner 1003 **his hope** the hope people had of him as heir to the crown 1006 **waits . . . state** potentially attends those of most exalted rank. 1007 **presently** at once 1013 **Poor . . . night** Poor lowly commoners are like pitch-dark night, unnoticed 1016 **Out** (An exclamation of disapproval.)

1018 **in . . . schools** i.e., among scholars who perennially debate with words 1021 **For . . . straw** As for me, I do not value argument as worth so much as a straw 1022 **Since that** since 1025 **cavil with** raise objections to 1026 **spurn at** (Literally, kick against.) **confirmed despite** unrecoverable injury. 1027 **helpless . . . words** unavailing rhetoric 1029 **let . . . blood** bleed (1) as a *remedy* (line 1028) for illness, a standard form of medical treatment (2) as a means of death. 1039 **no slaughterhouse** being no slaughterhouse. **imparteth** provides 1042 **Etna** famous volcano in northeast Sicily. **consumes** vanishes 1045 **happy** fit. (With a play of antithesis on *hapless*.) 1046 **falchion** curved sword 1050 **type** pattern (of virtue) 1053 **To clear** i.e., in clearing. **spot** stain 1054 **fame** good reputation. **livery** clothing or uniform worn by those in service, bearing a heraldic *badge* on the sleeve to indicate in whose service the livery is worn. (Lucrece says that the livery of shame will be partially redeemed by the badge of an honorable death.)

"Well, well, dear Collatine, thou shalt not know
The stainèd taste of violated troth;
I will not wrong thy true affection so
To flatter thee with an infringèd oath;   1061
This bastard graft shall never come to growth.   1062
      He shall not boast who did thy stock pollute
      That thou art doting father of his fruit.

"Nor shall he smile at thee in secret thought,
Nor laugh with his companions at thy state,
But thou shalt know thy int'rest was not bought   1067
Basely with gold, but stol'n from forth thy gate.
For me, I am the mistress of my fate,   1069
      And with my trespass never will dispense   1070
      Till life to death acquit my forced offense.   1071

"I will not poison thee with my attaint,   1072
Nor fold my fault in cleanly coined excuses;   1073
My sable ground of sin I will not paint,   1074
To hide the truth of this false night's abuses.
My tongue shall utter all; mine eyes, like sluices,
      As from a mountain spring that feeds a dale,
      Shall gush pure streams to purge my impure tale."

By this, lamenting Philomel had ended   1079
The well-tuned warble of her nightly sorrow,
And solemn night with slow sad gait descended
To ugly hell, when, lo, the blushing morrow
Lends light to all fair eyes that light will borrow.   1083
      But cloudy Lucrece shames herself to see,   1084
      And therefore still in night would cloistered be.

Revealing day through every cranny spies
And seems to point her out where she sits weeping,
To whom she sobbing speaks: "O eye of eyes,
Why pry'st thou through my window? Leave thy peeping.
Mock with thy tickling beams eyes that are sleeping.
      Brand not my forehead with thy piercing light,
      For day hath naught to do what's done by night."   1092

Thus cavils she with everything she sees.
True grief is fond and testy as a child   1094
Who, wayward once, his mood with naught agrees.   1095
Old woes, not infant sorrows, bear them mild: 1096
Continuance tames the one; the other, wild,
      Like an unpracticed swimmer plunging still,
      With too much labor drowns for want of skill.

So she, deep-drenchèd in a sea of care,
Holds disputation with each thing she views,
And to herself all sorrow doth compare;
No object but her passion's strength renews,   1103
And as one shifts, another straight ensues.   1104
      Sometimes her grief is dumb and hath no words,
      Sometimes 'tis mad and too much talk affords.

The little birds that tune their morning's joy
Make her moans mad with their sweet melody,
For mirth doth search the bottom of annoy;   1109
Sad souls are slain in merry company.
Grief best is pleased with grief's society.
      True sorrow then is feelingly suffced   1112
      When with like semblance it is sympathized.   1113

'Tis double death to drown in ken of shore;   1114
He ten times pines that pines beholding food;   1115
To see the salve doth make the wound ache more;
Great grief grieves most at that would do it good;   1117
Deep woes roll forward like a gentle flood,
      Who, being stopped, the bounding banks o'erflows;   1119
      Grief dallied with nor law nor limit knows.   1120

"You mocking birds," quoth she, "your tunes entomb
Within your hollow-swelling feathered breasts,
And in my hearing be you mute and dumb.
My restless discord loves no stops nor rests;   1124
A woeful hostess brooks not merry guests.   1125
      Relish your nimble notes to pleasing ears;   1126
      Distress likes dumps, when time is kept with tears.   1127

"Come, Philomel, that sing'st of ravishment,
Make thy sad grove in my disheveled hair.
As the dank earth weeps at thy languishment,
So I at each sad strain will strain a tear   1131
And with deep groans the diapason bear;   1132
      For burden-wise I'll hum on Tarquin still,   1133
      While thou on Tereus descants better skill.   1134

"And whiles against a thorn thou bear'st thy part   1135
To keep thy sharp woes waking, wretched I,
To imitate thee well, against my heart
Will fix a sharp knife to affright mine eye,

1061 To flatter . . . oath i.e., to deceive you by presenting you with a bastard child, born through an enforced violation of my vow of chastity, as though the child were your own   1062 graft scion   1067 int'rest claim, property   1069 For As for   1070 with . . . dispense never will pardon my offense. (To *dispense* is to grant dispensation.)   1071 acquit atone for   1072 attaint infection   1073 fold wrap up, conceal.   cleanly coined cleverly counterfeited   1074 sable ground dark surface on a heraldic device   1079 Philomel i.e., the nightingale. (Philomela was raped by her brother-in-law, Tereus, who cut out her tongue so that she could not disclose his villainy; she was changed into a nightingale.)   1083 that . . . borrow that wish to behold the light of dawn and reflect the light in their eyes.   1084 cloudy sorrowful.   shames is ashamed   1092 to do to do with   1094 fond foolish   1095 wayward once once in a peevish mood   1096 bear . . . mild behave themselves mildly

1103 No . . . renews everything she considers renews the strength of her sorrows   1104 shifts moves, yields place.   straight at once   1109 search probe.   annoy grief, injury   1112 suffced contented   1113 sympathized matched.   1114 ken sight   1115 He Anyone. pines hungers   1117 would which would   1119 Who . . . o'erflows which, being dammed up, overflows the banks that should contain it   1120 dallied trifled.   nor . . . nor neither . . . nor   1124 restless agitated. (With a pun on the musical sense of having no *stops* or *rests*, i.e., being ceaseless, without pause.)   1125 brooks enjoys   1126 Relish (1) Warble, make attractive (2) Elaborate with musical ornamentation.   pleasing capable of being pleased   1127 dumps mournful songs   1131 strain . . . strain melody . . . force, squeeze   1132 diapason bass accompaniment below the melody   1133 burden-wise in the manner of an undersong or bass. (With a play on *burden*, meaning "sorrow.")   1134 While . . . skill while, singing of Philomel's ravisher (see note 1079), you warble your musical elaboration in the upper register with better skill (than my bass accompaniment).   1135 against a thorn (According to popular belief, the nightingale perched deliberately with a thorn against her breast to keep herself awake.)

Who, if it wink, shall thereon fall and die. 1139
    These means, as frets upon an instrument, 1140
    Shall tune our heartstrings to true languishment.

"And for, poor bird, thou sing'st not in the day, 1142
As shaming any eye should thee behold, 1143
Some dark deep desert seated from the way, 1144
That knows not parching heat nor freezing cold,
Will we find out; and there we will unfold
    To creatures stern sad tunes, to change their kinds. 1147
    Since men prove beasts, let beasts bear gentle minds."

As the poor frighted deer, that stands at gaze, 1149
Wildly determining which way to fly,
Or one encompassed with a winding maze,
That cannot tread the way out readily,
So with herself is she in mutiny,
    To live or die which of the twain were better
    When life is shamed and death reproach's debtor. 1155

"To kill myself," quoth she, "alack, what were it
But with my body my poor soul's pollution? 1157
They that lose half with greater patience bear it
Than they whose whole is swallowed in confusion. 1159
That mother tries a merciless conclusion 1160
    Who, having two sweet babes, when death takes one,
    Will slay the other and be nurse to none.

"My body or my soul, which was the dearer,
When the one pure, the other made divine?
Whose love of either to myself was nearer, 1165
When both were kept for heaven and Collatine?
Ay me! The bark pilled from the lofty pine, 1167
    His leaves will wither and his sap decay;
    So must my soul, her bark being pilled away.

"Her house is sacked, her quiet interrupted,
Her mansion battered by the enemy,
Her sacred temple spotted, spoiled, corrupted,
Grossly engirt with daring infamy. 1173
Then let it not be called impiety
    If in this blemished fort I make some hole 1175
    Through which I may convey this troubled soul. 1176

"Yet die I will not till my Collatine
Have heard the cause of my untimely death,

That he may vow, in that sad hour of mine,
Revenge on him that made me stop my breath.
My stainèd blood to Tarquin I'll bequeath,
    Which, by him tainted, shall for him be spent,
    And as his due writ in my testament. 1183

"My honor I'll bequeath unto the knife
That wounds my body so dishonorèd.
'Tis honor to deprive dishonored life; 1186
The one will live, the other being dead. 1187
So of shame's ashes shall my fame be bred, 1188
    For in my death I murder shameful scorn;
    My shame so dead, mine honor is new born.

"Dear lord of that dear jewel I have lost, 1191
What legacy shall I bequeath to thee?
My resolution, love, shall be thy boast,
By whose example thou revenged mayst be.
How Tarquin must be used, read it in me:
    Myself, thy friend, will kill myself, thy foe,
    And for my sake serve thou false Tarquin so.

"This brief abridgment of my will I make:
My soul and body to the skies and ground;
My resolution, husband, do thou take;
Mine honor be the knife's that makes my wound;
My shame be his that did my fame confound;
    And all my fame that lives disbursèd be 1203
    To those that live and think no shame of me.

"Thou, Collatine, shalt oversee this will.
How was I overseen that thou shalt see it! 1206
My blood shall wash the slander of mine ill;
My life's foul deed my life's fair end shall free it. 1208
Faint not, faint heart, but stoutly say 'So be it.'
    Yield to my hand; my hand shall conquer thee.
    Thou dead, both die, and both shall victors be."

This plot of death when sadly she had laid,
And wiped the brinish pearl from her bright eyes,
With untuned tongue she hoarsely calls her maid, 1214
Whose swift obedience to her mistress hies; 1215
For fleet-winged duty with thought's feathers flies.
    Poor Lucrece' cheeks unto her maid seem so
    As winter meads when sun doth melt their snow.

Her mistress she doth give demure good morrow 1219
With soft slow tongue, true mark of modesty,
And sorts a sad look to her lady's sorrow, 1221
Forwhy her face wore sorrow's livery; 1222

1139 **Who** which, i.e., my heart. **if it wink** i.e., if my eye should close in sleep 1140 **frets** bars placed on the fingerboards of stringed instruments to regulate the fingering. (With a pun on *frets,* meaning "vexations.") 1142 **for** because. **sing'st not in the day** (One of the common errors of the poem; nightingales sing both day and night.) 1143 **As shaming** as though being ashamed that, or, since you are ashamed that 1144 **desert** deserted place. **seated from** situated away from 1147 **kinds** natures. 1149 **at gaze** transfixed, bewildered 1155 **death reproach's debtor** i.e., death by suicide would incur reproach. 1157 **But . . . pollution** but to add my poor soul's pollution (through suicide) to that of my body (through the rape). 1159 **confusion** ruin. 1160 **conclusion** experiment 1165 **Whose . . . either** Love of which of the two 1167 **pilled** peeled, stripped off, rifled 1173 **daring** audacious 1175 **fort** i.e., body 1176 **convey** spirit away

1183 **writ** written. **testament** last will and testament. 1186 **deprive** take away 1187 **the one** honor. **the other** life 1188 **So . . . bred** Thus will my fame be born out of the ashes of my shame, like the mythical Phoenix bird 1191 **that dear jewel** i.e., my chastity (which) 1203 **disbursèd** i.e., paid out as legacies 1206 **overseen** deluded, taken advantage of. (With quibble on *oversee,* line 1205, i.e., attend to as an executor of an estate.) 1208 **My . . . free it** my life's virtuous end will free my reputation of my life's foul deed. 1214 **untuned** discordant 1215 **Whose . . . hies** who in swift obedience hastens to her mistress 1219 **Her** To her 1221 **sorts** suits 1222 **Forwhy** because

But durst not ask of her audaciously
    Why her two suns were cloud-eclipsèd so,
    Nor why her fair cheeks over-washed with woe.

But as the earth doth weep, the sun being set,
Each flower moist'ned like a melting eye,
Even so the maid with swelling drops 'gan wet
Her circled eyne, enforced by sympathy   1229
Of those fair suns set in her mistress' sky,
    Who in a salt-waved ocean quench their light,
    Which makes the maid weep like the dewy night.

A pretty while these pretty creatures stand,   1233
Like ivory conduits coral cisterns filling.   1234
One justly weeps; the other takes in hand   1235
No cause but company of her drops' spilling.   1236
Their gentle sex to weep are often willing,
    Grieving themselves to guess at others' smarts,   1238
    And then they drown their eyes or break their hearts.

For men have marble, women waxen, minds,   1240
And therefore are they formed as marble will.   1241
The weak oppressed, th'impression of strange kinds   1242
Is formed in them by force, by fraud, or skill.   1243
Then call them not the authors of their ill,
    No more than wax shall be accounted evil
    Wherein is stamped the semblance of a devil.

Their smoothness, like a goodly champaign plain,   1247
Lays open all the little worms that creep;   1248
In men, as in a rough-grown grove, remain
Cave-keeping evils that obscurely sleep.   1250
Through crystal walls each little mote will peep.   1251
    Though men can cover crimes with bold stern looks,
    Poor women's faces are their own faults' books.

No man inveigh against the withered flower,   1254
But chide rough winter that the flower hath killed.
Not that devoured, but that which doth devour,
Is worthy blame. Oh, let it not be hild   1257
Poor women's faults that they are so fulfilled   1258
    With men's abuses. Those proud lords, to blame,   1259
    Make weak-made women tenants to their shame.   1260

The precedent whereof in Lucrece view,   1261
Assailed by night with circumstances strong   1262
Of present death, and shame that might ensue   1263

By that her death, to do her husband wrong.   1264
Such danger to resistance did belong   1265
    That dying fear through all her body spread;   1266
    And who cannot abuse a body dead?

By this, mild patience bid fair Lucrece speak   1268
To the poor counterfeit of her complaining: 1269
"My girl," quoth she, "on what occasion break
Those tears from thee, that down thy cheeks are raining?
If thou dost weep for grief of my sustaining,   1272
    Know, gentle wench, it small avails my mood.   1273
    If tears could help, mine own would do me good.

"But tell me, girl, when went"—and there she stayed
Till after a deep groan—"Tarquin from hence?"
"Madam, ere I was up," replied the maid,
"The more to blame my sluggard negligence.   1278
Yet with the fault I thus far can dispense: 1279
    Myself was stirring ere the break of day,
    And, ere I rose, was Tarquin gone away.

"But, lady, if your maid may be so bold,
She would request to know your heaviness."   1283
"Oh, peace!" quoth Lucrece. "If it should be told,
The repetition cannot make it less;   1285
For more it is than I can well express,
    And that deep torture may be called a hell
    When more is felt than one hath power to tell.

"Go, get me hither paper, ink, and pen.
Yet save that labor, for I have them here.
What should I say? One of my husband's men
Bid thou be ready by and by to bear
A letter to my lord, my love, my dear.
    Bid him with speed prepare to carry it;
    The cause craves haste, and it will soon be writ."

Her maid is gone, and she prepares to write,
First hovering o'er the paper with her quill.
Conceit and grief an eager combat fight;   1298
What wit sets down is blotted straight with will;   1299
This is too curious-good, this blunt and ill.   1300
    Much like a press of people at a door
    Throng her inventions, which shall go before.   1302

At last she thus begins: "Thou worthy lord
Of that unworthy wife that greeteth thee,
Health to thy person! Next vouchsafe t'afford—
If ever, love, thy Lucrece thou wilt see—

1229 circled eyne rounded eyes, or, circled with red. **enforced** compelled **1233 pretty while** considerable while **1234 conduits** (Alludes to conduit spouts and fountains shaped in the form of human figures; the women's eyes run like conduits.) **1235–6 takes ... spilling** acknowledges no cause for the shedding of teardrops other than to keep her mistress company. **1238 to guess at** merely when they conjecture **1240 waxen** i.e., soft, impressionable **1241 will** wills, wishes. **1242 The weak** When the weak are. **strange kinds** alien natures **1243 skill** cunning. **1247 champaign** level, open **1248 Lays open** reveals **1250 Cave-keeping** concealed **1251 mote** speck **1254 No man** Let no one **1257 worthy** deserving of. **hild** held **1258 fulfilled** filled to the brim **1259 to blame** who are to blame **1260 tenants ... shame** i.e., occupying and sharing a shame that is properly men's. **1261 precedent** proof, example **1262–3 circumstances ... death** a situation strongly threatening immediate death

1264 By that her death by her very death **1265 danger** i.e., the danger of being defamed by Tarquin **1266 dying** i.e., paralyzing **1268 By this** By this time **1269 counterfeit of her complaining** i.e., the maid, weeping like her **1272 of my sustaining** borne by me **1273 small avails** little helps **1278 to blame** at fault **1279 dispense** give dispensation, find excuse **1283 know your heaviness** know the reason for your sadness. **1285 repetition** recital **1298 Conceit** Thought (of what she will write). **eager** fierce **1299–1300 What ... ill** i.e., whatever thought wishes to say is immediately ruled out as inadequate to express what she feels; one phrase is too fastidiously elaborate, another too blunt and ugly. **1302 which ... before** contending as to who is to enter first.

Some present speed to come and visit me.   1307
　　So, I commend me from our house in grief.   1308
　　My woes are tedious, though my words are brief."   1309

Here folds she up the tenor of her woe,   1310
Her certain sorrow writ uncertainly.   1311
By this short schedule Collatine may know   1312
Her grief, but not her grief's true quality.
She dares not thereof make discovery,   1314
　　Lest he should hold it her own gross abuse,   1315
　　Ere she with blood had stained her stained excuse.   1316

Besides, the life and feeling of her passion
She hoards, to spend when he is by to hear her,
When sighs and groans and tears may grace the fashion   1319
Of her disgrace, the better so to clear her
From that suspicion which the world might bear her.
　　To shun this blot, she would not blot the letter   1322
　　With words, till action might become them better.

To see sad sights moves more than hear them told,
For then the eye interprets to the ear
The heavy motion that it doth behold,   1326
When every part a part of woe doth bear.   1327
'Tis but a part of sorrow that we hear.
　　Deep sounds make lesser noise than shallow fords,   1329
　　And sorrow ebbs, being blown with wind of words.

Her letter now is sealed, and on it writ,
"At Ardea to my lord with more than haste."
The post attends, and she delivers it,   1333
Charging the sour-faced groom to hie as fast
As lagging fowls before the northern blast.   1335
　　Speed more than speed but dull and slow she deems;   1336
　　Extremity still urgeth such extremes.   1337

The homely villain curtsies to her low;   1338
And, blushing on her, with a steadfast eye
Receives the scroll without or yea or no,   1340
And forth with bashful innocence doth hie.
But they whose guilt within their bosoms lie
　　Imagine every eye beholds their blame;
　　For Lucrece thought he blushed to see her shame,

When, silly groom, God wot, it was defect   1345
Of spirit, life, and bold audacity.

Such harmless creatures have a true respect   1347
To talk in deeds, while others saucily   1348
Promise more speed, but do it leisurely.
　　Even so this pattern of the worn-out age   1350
　　Pawned honest looks but laid no words to gage.   1351

His kindled duty kindled her mistrust,   1352
That two red fires in both their faces blazed.
She thought he blushed as knowing Tarquin's lust,
And, blushing with him, wistly on him gazed.   1355
Her earnest eye did make him more amazed.   1356
　　The more she saw the blood his cheeks replenish,
　　The more she thought he spied in her some blemish.

But long she thinks till he return again,   1359
And yet the duteous vassal scarce is gone.
The weary time she cannot entertain,   1361
For now 'tis stale to sigh, to weep, and groan.
So woe hath wearied woe, moan tirèd moan,
　　That she her plaints a little while doth stay,   1364
　　Pausing for means to mourn some newer way.

At last she calls to mind where hangs a piece   1366
Of skillful painting, made for Priam's Troy,   1367
Before the which is drawn the power of Greece,   1368
For Helen's rape the city to destroy,
Threat'ning cloud-kissing Ilion with annoy,   1370
　　Which the conceited painter drew so proud   1371
　　As heaven, it seemed, to kiss the turrets bowed.

A thousand lamentable objects there,
In scorn of nature, art gave lifeless life.   1374
Many a dry drop seemed a weeping tear,   1375
Shed for the slaughtered husband by the wife.
The red blood reeked, to show the painter's strife,   1377
　　And dying eyes gleamed forth their ashy lights
　　Like dying coals burnt out in tedious nights.

There might you see the laboring pioneer   1380
Begrimed with sweat and smearèd all with dust;
And from the towers of Troy there would appear
The very eyes of men through loopholes thrust,
Gazing upon the Greeks with little lust.   1384
　　Such sweet observance in this work was had   1385
　　That one might see those far-off eyes look sad.

1307 present immediate   **1308 commend me** ask to be remembered
1309 tedious prolonged, painful   **1310 tenor** gist, summary
1311 uncertainly not in precise detail; in great uncertainty of feeling.
1312 schedule document, summary   **1314 thereof make discovery**
reveal its true extent and nature   **1315 abuse** wrongdoing   **1316 Ere
. . . excuse** before she had had a chance to put a better appearance on
her unsatisfactory excuse by shedding her own blood.   **1319 fashion**
fashioning   **1322 blot . . . blot** stain . . . mark   **1326 heavy motion**
sad action   **1327 every part** i.e., of the body   **1329 Deep sounds**
Deep waters. (With pun on *sounds*, i.e., inlets of the sea, and "noise.")
1333 post messenger   **1335 lagging** falling behind in migratory flight
1336 Speed . . . deems She considers even extraordinary speed too
tedious and slow   **1337 still** ever   **1338 The homely . . . curtsies** The
plain-mannered servant bows   **1340 or . . . or** either . . . or   **1345 silly
groom** simple menial.   **wot** knows

1347–8 have . . . deeds eagerly express their duty in their acts of service (rather than flowery speech)   **1350–1 Even . . . gage** In just this
fashion, this perfect model of old-fashioned loyalty pledged his service in wordless, honest looks.   **1352 kindled duty** i.e., blushing obeisance.   **mistrust** i.e., fear of her shame being known   **1355 wistly**
intently   **1356 amazed** embarrassed.   **1359 long she thinks** she thinks
it long   **1361 entertain** occupy   **1364 stay** halt   **1366 piece** picture
(evidently in a tapestry)   **1367 made for** depicting   **1368 drawn**
drawn up, arrayed.   **power** army   **1370 cloud-kissing Ilion** i.e.,
lofty-towered Troy.   **annoy** harm   **1371 conceited** ingenious
1374 In scorn of i.e., defiantly rivaling.   **lifeless** inanimate
1375 dry drop i.e., drop of paint depicting a tear   **1377 strife** rivalry,
i.e., with Nature; also the strife depicted in the painting   **1380 pioneer** digger of trenches and mines   **1384 lust** pleasure, delight.
1385 sweet observance i.e., verisimilitude created with loving attention to detail

In great commanders grace and majesty
You might behold, triumphing in their faces;
In youth, quick bearing and dexterity;   1389
And here and there the painter interlaces
Pale cowards marching on with trembling paces,
    Which heartless peasants did so well resemble   1392
    That one would swear he saw them quake and tremble.

In Ajax and Ulysses, oh, what art
Of physiognomy might one behold!
The face of either ciphered either's heart;   1396
Their face their manners most expressly told.
In Ajax' eyes blunt rage and rigor rolled,
    But the mild glance that sly Ulysses lent
    Showed deep regard and smiling government.   1400

There pleading might you see grave Nestor stand,   1401
As 'twere encouraging the Greeks to fight,
Making such sober action with his hand
That it beguiled attention, charmed the sight.
In speech, it seemed, his beard, all silver white,
    Wagged up and down, and from his lips did fly
    Thin winding breath, which purled up to the sky.   1407

About him were a press of gaping faces,
Which seemed to swallow up his sound advice,
All jointly list'ning, but with several graces,   1410
As if some mermaid did their ears entice;
Some high, some low, the painter was so nice.   1412
    The scalps of many, almost hid behind,   1413
    To jump up higher seemed, to mock the mind.   1414

Here one man's hand leaned on another's head,
His nose being shadowed by his neighbor's ear;
Here one being thronged bears back, all boll'n and red;   1417
Another, smothered, seems to pelt and swear;   1418
And in their rage such signs of rage they bear
    As, but for loss of Nestor's golden words,   1420
    It seemed they would debate with angry swords.

For much imaginary work was there,   1422
Conceit deceitful, so compact, so kind,   1423
That for Achilles' image stood his spear
Gripped in an armèd hand; himself, behind,
Was left unseen, save to the eye of mind.
    A hand, a foot, a face, a leg, a head,
    Stood for the whole to be imaginèd.

And from the walls of strong-besiegèd Troy,
When their brave hope, bold Hector, marched to field,
Stood many Trojan mothers, sharing joy
To see their youthful sons bright weapons wield;
And to their hope they such odd action yield   1433
    That through their light joy seemèd to appear,
    Like bright things stained, a kind of heavy fear.

And from the strand of Dardan where they fought   1436
To Simois' reedy banks the red blood ran,   1437
Whose waves to imitate the battle sought
With swelling ridges; and their ranks began
To break upon the gallèd shore and then   1440
    Retire again, till, meeting greater ranks,
    They join and shoot their foam at Simois' banks.

To this well-painted piece is Lucrece come,
To find a face where all distress is stelled.   1444
Many she sees where cares have carvèd some,
But none where all distress and dolor dwelled,
Till she despairing Hecuba beheld,   1447
    Staring on Priam's wounds with her old eyes,
    Which bleeding under Pyrrhus' proud foot lies.

In her the painter had anatomized   1450
Time's ruin, beauty's wrack, and grim care's reign.
Her cheeks with chaps and wrinkles were disguised;   1452
Of what she was no semblance did remain.
Her blue blood, changed to black in every vein,
    Wanting the spring that those shrunk pipes had fed,   1455
    Showed life imprisoned in a body dead.

On this sad shadow Lucrece spends her eyes,   1457
And shapes her sorrow to the beldam's woes,   1458
Who nothing wants to answer her but cries   1459
And bitter words to ban her cruel foes.   1460
The painter was no god to lend her those;
    And therefore Lucrece swears he did her wrong,
    To give her so much grief and not a tongue.

"Poor instrument," quoth she, "without a sound,
I'll tune thy woes with my lamenting tongue,   1465
And drop sweet balm in Priam's painted wound,
And rail on Pyrrhus that hath done him wrong,
And with my tears quench Troy that burns so long,
    And with my knife scratch out the angry eyes
    Of all the Greeks that are thine enemies.

"Show me the strumpet that began this stir,
That with my nails her beauty I may tear.
Thy heat of lust, fond Paris, did incur   1473

1389 **quick** lively   1392 **heartless** cowardly   1396 **ciphered** showed, expressed   1400 **deep . . . government** profound wisdom and calm self-control.   1401 **pleading** making a persuasive oration   1407 **purled** curled   1410 **with several graces** i.e., in differing attitudes   1412 **nice** accurate, particular.   1413 **scalps** heads of hair   1414 **To . . . mind** (The artistic illusion deceives the mind of the viewer into thinking he sees the movement of those in the back of the crowd who are jumping higher to catch Nestor's oration.)   1417 **thronged** crowded.   **bears** pushes.   **boll'n** swollen up   1418 **pelt** scold   1420 **but . . . words** were it not that they would thereby miss Nestor's speech   1422 **imaginary work** work of the imagination   1423 **Conceit . . . kind** a contrived artifice, so efficiently composed, so seemingly natural

1433 **they . . . yield** they add such actions and emotions at odds with the joy   1436 **strand** shore   1437 **Simois** river near Troy   1440 **gallèd** eroded   1444 **stelled** portrayed, engraved.   1447 **Hecuba** Queen of Troy, wife of King Priam   1450 **anatomized** laid open, dissected   1452 **chaps** cracks and lines in the skin.   **disguised** disfigured   1455 **spring** i.e., source of blood and life.   **pipes** i.e., veins   1457 **shadow** image, likeness   1458 **beldam's** old woman's   1459 **wants to answer her** lacks in order to be perfectly like Lucrece in her sorrow   1460 **ban** curse   1465 **tune** sing   1473 **fond** doting

This load of wrath that burning Troy doth bear.
Thine eye kindled the fire that burneth here,
    And here in Troy, for trespass of thine eye,
    The sire, the son, the dame, and daughter die.

"Why should the private pleasure of some one
Become the public plague of many moe?   1479
Let sin, alone committed, light alone   1480
Upon his head that hath transgressèd so;
Let guiltless souls be freed from guilty woe.
    For one's offense why should so many fall,
    To plague a private sin in general?   1484

"Lo, here weeps Hecuba, here Priam dies,
Here manly Hector faints, here Troilus swounds,   1486
Here friend by friend in bloody channel lies,   1487
And friend to friend gives unadvisèd wounds,   1488
And one man's lust these many lives confounds.
    Had doting Priam checked his son's desire,
    Troy had been bright with fame and not with fire."

Here feelingly she weeps Troy's painted woes,
For sorrow, like a heavy-hanging bell
Once set on ringing, with his own weight goes;   1494
Then little strength rings out the doleful knell.
So Lucrece, set a-work, sad tales doth tell
    To penciled pensiveness and colored sorrow;   1497
    She lends them words, and she their looks doth borrow.

She throws her eyes about the painting round,
And who she finds forlorn she doth lament.   1500
At last she sees a wretched image bound,   1501
That piteous looks to Phrygian shepherds lent.   1502
His face, though full of cares, yet showed content;
    Onward to Troy with the blunt swains he goes,   1504
    So mild that patience seemed to scorn his woes.   1505

In him the painter labored with his skill
To hide deceit and give the harmless show   1507
An humble gait, calm looks, eyes wailing still,   1508
A brow unbent that seemed to welcome woe;
Cheeks neither red nor pale, but mingled so
    That blushing red no guilty instance gave,   1511
    Nor ashy pale the fear that false hearts have.

But, like a constant and confirmèd devil,
He entertained a show so seeming just,   1514
And therein so ensconced his secret evil,   1515

That jealousy itself could not mistrust   1516
False-creeping craft and perjury should thrust
    Into so bright a day such black-faced storms,
    Or blot with hell-born sin such saintlike forms.

The well-skilled workman this mild image drew
For perjured Sinon, whose enchanting story   1521
The credulous old Priam after slew;   1522
Whose words like wildfire burnt the shining glory   1523
Of rich-built Ilion, that the skies were sorry,
    And little stars shot from their fixèd places
    When their glass fell wherein they viewed their faces.   1526

This picture she advisedly perused,   1527
And chid the painter for his wondrous skill,
Saying, some shape in Sinon's was abused;   1529
So fair a form lodged not a mind so ill.
And still on him she gazed, and gazing still,
    Such signs of truth in his plain face she spied   1532
    That she concludes the picture was belied.   1533

"It cannot be," quoth she, "that so much guile—"
She would have said "can lurk in such a look";
But Tarquin's shape came in her mind the while,
And from her tongue "can lurk" from "cannot" took.
"It cannot be" she in that sense forsook,
    And turned it thus: "It cannot be, I find,
    But such a face should bear a wicked mind.

"For even as subtle Sinon here is painted,
So sober-sad, so weary, and so mild,
As if with grief or travail he had fainted,   1543
To me came Tarquin armèd, too beguiled   1544
With outward honesty, but yet defiled
    With inward vice. As Priam him did cherish,
    So did I Tarquin; so my Troy did perish.

"Look, look, how list'ning Priam wets his eyes,
To see those borrowed tears that Sinon sheeds!   1549
Priam, why art thou old and yet not wise?
For every tear he falls, a Trojan bleeds.   1551
His eye drops fire, no water thence proceeds;
    Those round clear pearls of his, that move thy pity,
    Are balls of quenchless fire to burn thy city.

"Such devils steal effects from lightless hell,   1555
For Sinon in his fire doth quake with cold,

1479 moe more.   1480 alone committed committed by one person alone.   light alight   1484 in general collectively, publicly. 1486 swounds swoons   1487 channel gutter   1488 unadvised wounds wounds they never intended for each other   1494 his its   1497 penciled painted.   colored painted   1500 who whoever   1501 image i.e., of Sinon, betrayer of Troy.   bound onward bound   1502 piteous . . . lent i.e., drew pitying looks from Phrygian shepherds. (Sinon deceived humble Trojans into pitying him as a deserter from the Greeks, thereby persuading them to admit the wooden horse.)   1504 blunt swains rustic peasants   1505 patience his patience.   scorn make light of 1507 harmless show outwardly harmless appearance   1508 still continually   1511 guilty instance symptom of guilt   1514 entertained a show kept up an appearance   1515 ensconced hid

1516 jealousy suspicion.   mistrust suspect (that)   1521 For to represent.   enchanting bewitching   1522 The . . . slew subsequently brought about the slaughter of credulous old Priam   1523 wildfire a highly inflammable mixture of tar, sulfur, grease, etc., used in war 1526 glass mirror (i.e., rich-built Troy)   1527 advisedly studiously 1529 some shape i.e., the figure of some other person.   abused slanderously portrayed   1532 plain honest   1533 belied falsified. 1543 travail (The Quarto's "trauaile" also contains the idea of "travel.")   1544 armèd equipped, accoutered.   too beguiled too concealed or disguised by guile; or, "to beguile"   1549 borrowed counterfeited.   sheeds sheds.   1551 he falls that Sinon lets fall Such devils (The ability to weep without real tears—effects—was attributed to devils.)   effects illusions. (Devils were supposedly able to weep without real tears.)

And in that cold hot-burning fire doth dwell.
These contraries such unity do hold 1558
Only to flatter fools and make them bold. 1559
    So Priam's trust false Sinon's tears doth flatter 1560
    That he finds means to burn his Troy with water."

Here, all enraged, such passion her assails
That patience is quite beaten from her breast.
She tears the senseless Sinon with her nails, 1564
Comparing him to that unhappy guest 1565
Whose deed hath made herself herself detest.
    At last she smilingly with this gives o'er: 1567
    "Fool, fool!" quoth she, "his wounds will not be sore." 1568

Thus ebbs and flows the current of her sorrow,
And time doth weary time with her complaining. 1570
She looks for night, and then she longs for morrow,
And both she thinks too long with her remaining.
Short time seems long in sorrow's sharp sustaining; 1573
    Though woe be heavy, yet it seldom sleeps, 1574
    And they that watch see time how slow it creeps. 1575

Which all this time hath overslipped her thought
That she with painted images hath spent,
Being from the feeling of her own grief brought
By deep surmise of others' detriment, 1579
Losing her woes in shows of discontent. 1580
    It easeth some, though none it ever cured,
    To think their dolor others have endured.

But now the mindful messenger, come back, 1583
Brings home his lord and other company,
Who finds his Lucrece clad in mourning black,
And round about her tear-distainèd eye 1586
Blue circles streamed, like rainbows in the sky.
    These water galls in her dim element 1588
    Foretell new storms to those already spent. 1589

Which when her sad-beholding husband saw,
Amazedly in her sad face he stares.
Her eyes, though sod in tears, looked red and raw, 1592
Her lively color killed with deadly cares.
He hath no power to ask her how she fares;
    Both stood like old acquaintance in a trance,
    Met far from home, wond'ring each other's chance. 1596

At last he takes her by the bloodless hand
And thus begins: "What uncouth ill event 1598
Hath thee befall'n, that thou dost trembling stand?
Sweet love, what spite hath thy fair color spent? 1600
Why art thou thus attired in discontent? 1601
    Unmask, dear dear, this moody heaviness, 1602
    And tell thy grief, that we may give redress."

Three times with sighs she gives her sorrow fire 1604
Ere once she can discharge one word of woe. 1605
At length addressed to answer his desire, 1606
She modestly prepares to let them know
Her honor is ta'en prisoner by the foe,
    While Collatine and his consorted lords 1609
    With sad attention long to hear her words. 1610

And now this pale swan in her wat'ry nest 1611
Begins the sad dirge of her certain ending:
"Few words," quoth she, "shall fit the trespass best,
Where no excuse can give the fault amending.
In me more woes than words are now depending, 1615
    And my laments would be drawn out too long,
    To tell them all with one poor tirèd tongue.

"Then be this all the task it hath to say:
Dear husband, in the interest of thy bed 1619
A stranger came, and on that pillow lay
Where thou wast wont to rest thy weary head;
And what wrong else may be imaginèd
    By foul enforcement might be done to me,
    From that, alas, thy Lucrece is not free.

"For in the dreadful dead of dark midnight,
With shining falchion in my chamber came
A creeping creature with a flaming light,
And softly cried, 'Awake, thou Roman dame,
And entertain my love! Else lasting shame 1629
    On thee and thine this night I will inflict,
    If thou my love's desire do contradict.

" 'For some hard-favored groom of thine,' quoth he, 1632
'Unless thou yoke thy liking to my will,
I'll murder straight, and then I'll slaughter thee 1634
And swear I found you where you did fulfill
The loathsome act of lust, and so did kill
    The lechers in their deed. This act will be
    My fame and thy perpetual infamy.'

"With this, I did begin to start and cry;
And then against my heart he set his sword,

1558–9 These . . . bold This illusory corresponding of opposites serves to encourage and embolden such slaves to passion as Tarquin and Sinon.   **1560 flatter** encourage   **1564 senseless** inanimate; unfeeling   **1565 unhappy** causing unhappiness and misfortune **1567 gives o'er** ceases   **1568 his . . . sore** i.e., I am not hurting Tarquin in the least by this fruitless scratching at Sinon's picture with my fingernails.   **1570 time . . . time** time seems to exhaust itself **1573 sharp sustaining** painful enduring   **1574 heavy** exhausting; sorrowful   **1575 watch** stay awake   **1579 surmise** contemplation. **detriment** suffering   **1580 shows of discontent** representations of sorrow, i.e., the painted scene of Troy's woe.   **1583 mindful** diligent **1586 tear-distainèd** tear-stained   **1588 water galls** fragments of rainbow, secondary rainbows (foretelling stormy weather).   **dim** cloudy. **element** sky, i.e., face or eye   **1589 to** besides   **1592 sod** sodden, steeped   **1596 wond'ring . . . chance** wondering at or about each other's fortune.

1598 uncouth unknown, strange   **1600 spite** injury. **spent** expended, taken away.   **1601 attired in discontent** (1) wrapped up in melancholy (2) dressed in mourning black (line 1585).   **1602 Unmask** Reveal   **1604–5 Three . . . woe** (The metaphor is that of discharging firearms by means of a match.)   **1606 addressed** prepared **1609 consorted** companion   **1610 sad** serious   **1611 swan** (Alludes to the belief that the swan, ordinarily without a song, sings beautifully at its own death.)   **1615 depending** belonging, impending. (With Latin sense of "weighing heavier.")   **1619 in the interest** claiming possession   **1629 entertain** receive   **1632 hard-favored** ugly **1634 straight** at once

Swearing, unless I took all patiently,
I should not live to speak another word;
So should my shame still rest upon record,
     And never be forgot in mighty Rome
     Th'adulterate death of Lucrece and her groom.   1645

"Mine enemy was strong, my poor self weak,
And far the weaker with so strong a fear.
My bloody judge forbade my tongue to speak;
No rightful plea might plead for justice there.
His scarlet lust came evidence to swear   1650
     That my poor beauty had purloined his eyes;
     And when the judge is robbed the prisoner dies.

"Oh, teach me how to make mine own excuse!
Or at the least this refuge let me find:
Though my gross blood be stained with this abuse,
Immaculate and spotless is my mind.
That was not forced, that never was inclined
     To accessory yieldings, but still pure   1658
     Doth in her poisoned closet yet endure."   1659

Lo, here the hopeless merchant of this loss,   1660
With head declined and voice dammed up with woe,   1661
With sad set eyes and wreathèd arms across,   1662
From lips new waxen pale begins to blow   1663
The grief away that stops his answer so.
     But, wretched as he is, he strives in vain;
     What he breathes out his breath drinks up again.

As through an arch the violent roaring tide   1667
Outruns the eye that doth behold his haste,
Yet in the eddy boundeth in his pride
Back to the strait that forced him on so fast,
In rage sent out, recalled in rage, being past;
     Even so his sighs, his sorrows, make a saw,   1672
     To push grief on and back the same grief draw.   1673

Which speechless woe of his poor she attendeth,   1674
And his untimely frenzy thus awaketh: 1675
"Dear lord, thy sorrow to my sorrow lendeth
Another power; no flood by raining slaketh.   1677
My woe too sensible thy passion maketh   1678
     More feeling-painful. Let it then suffice   1679
     To drown one woe, one pair of weeping eyes.

"And for my sake, when I might charm thee so,   1681
For she that was thy Lucrece, now attend me:
Be suddenly revengèd on my foe,   1683
Thine, mine, his own. Suppose thou dost defend me   1684
From what is past. The help that thou shalt lend me
     Comes all too late, yet let the traitor die;
     For sparing justice feeds iniquity.   1687

"But ere I name him, you fair lords," quoth she,
Speaking to those that came with Collatine,
"Shall plight your honorable faiths to me,   1690
With swift pursuit to venge this wrong of mine;
For 'tis a meritorious fair design
     To chase injustice with revengeful arms.
     Knights, by their oaths, should right poor ladies'
          harms."

At this request, with noble disposition
Each present lord began to promise aid,
As bound in knighthood to her imposition,   1697
Longing to hear the hateful foe bewrayed.   1698
But she, that yet her sad task hath not said,   1699
     The protestation stops. "Oh, speak," quoth she,   1700
     "How may this forcèd stain be wiped from me?

"What is the quality of my offense,   1702
Being constrained with dreadful circumstance?   1703
May my pure mind with the foul act dispense,   1704
My low-declinèd honor to advance?   1705
May any terms acquit me from this chance?   1706
     The poisoned fountain clears itself again,
     And why not I from this compellèd stain?"

With this they all at once began to say
Her body's stain her mind untainted clears,
While with a joyless smile she turns away
The face, that map which deep impression bears   1712
Of hard misfortune, carved in it with tears.
     "No, no," quoth she, "no dame hereafter living
     By my excuse shall claim excuse's giving."   1715

Here with a sigh, as if her heart would break,
She throws forth Tarquin's name: "He, he," she says,
But more than "he" her poor tongue could not speak;
Till after many accents and delays,   1719
Untimely breathings, sick and short assays,
     She utters this: "He, he, fair lords, 'tis he,
     That guides this hand to give this wound to me."

1645 Th'adulterate the adulterous 1650 came evidence supplied
evidence 1658 To accessory yieldings to a yielding that would
make me an accessory to crime 1659 poisoned closet i.e., violated
body 1660 merchant of this loss i.e., owner who has sustained this
loss, Collatine 1661 declined bent down 1662 wreathèd arms (See
line 793–4 and note.) 1663 new waxen newly turned 1667 arch i.e.,
of a bridge, such as London Bridge or Clopton Bridge 1672 saw i.e.,
sawlike back-and-forth motion 1673 and . . . draw and draw the
same grief back. (Collatine breathes and sighs, in and out.)
1674 Which . . . attendeth To which speechless woe of Collatine poor
Lucrece pays heed 1675 And . . . awaketh and awakens him from
his ill-timed distraction 1677 Another power added strength.
no . . . slaketh no flood is lessened by more rain. 1678–9 My . . .
painful Your passionate grief makes my woe, already too keenly felt,
even more painfully perceived.

1681 so i.e., in the person of my former self, still unravished
1683 suddenly quickly 1684 his own i.e., his own worst enemy.
Suppose Imagine, think that 1687 sparing too lenient. feeds iniquity encourages wrongdoing. 1690 plight pledge 1697 imposition
injunction 1698 bewrayed revealed, named. 1699 her . . . said had
not yet finished her sad task of speaking 1700 The protestation
their vows (to revenge her) 1702 quality nature 1703 with dreadful circumstance in a situation filled with dread. 1704 with . . .
dispense receive pardon for the foul deed 1705 advance raise up.
1706 terms mitigating grounds 1712 map i.e., image 1715 By . . .
giving will be able to claim the right to offer (give) an excuse using
my excuse as her precedent. 1719 accents sounds expressive of
emotion

Even here she sheathèd in her harmless breast
A harmful knife, that thence her soul unsheathed.
That blow did bail it from the deep unrest   1725
Of that polluted prison where it breathed.
Her contrite sighs unto the clouds bequeathed
 Her wingèd sprite, and through her wounds doth fly
 Life's lasting date from canceled destiny.   1729

Stone-still, astonished with this deadly deed,
Stood Collatine and all his lordly crew,
Till Lucrece' father, that beholds her bleed,
Himself on her self-slaughtered body threw,
And from the purple fountain Brutus drew   1734
 The murd'rous knife, and, as it left the place,
 Her blood, in poor revenge, held it in chase;

And bubbling from her breast, it doth divide
In two slow rivers, that the crimson blood
Circles her body in on every side,
Who, like a late-sacked island, vastly stood   1740
Bare and unpeopled in this fearful flood.
 Some of her blood still pure and red remained,
 And some looked black, and that false Tarquin stained. 1743

About the mourning and congealèd face
Of that black blood a wat'ry rigol goes,   1745
Which seems to weep upon the tainted place;
And ever since, as pitying Lucrece' woes,
Corrupted blood some watery token shows,
 And blood untainted still doth red abide,
 Blushing at that which is so putrified.

"Daughter, dear daughter," old Lucretius cries,
"That life was mine which thou hast here deprived.   1752
If in the child the father's image lies,
Where shall I live now Lucrece is unlived?   1754
Thou wast not to this end from me derived.
 If children predecease progenitors,
 We are their offspring, and they none of ours.

"Poor broken glass, I often did behold   1758
In thy sweet semblance my old age new born;
But now that fair fresh mirror dim and old
Shows me a bare-boned death by time outworn.   1761
Oh, from thy checks my image thou hast torn,
 And shivered all the beauty of my glass,
 That I no more can see what once I was!

"O Time, cease thou thy course and last no longer,
If they surcease to be that should survive!   1766

Shall rotten Death make conquest of the stronger
And leave the faltering feeble souls alive?
The old bees die, the young possess their hive.
 Then live, sweet Lucrece, live again and see
 Thy father die, and not thy father thee!"

By this, starts Collatine as from a dream,
And bids Lucretius give his sorrow place;   1773
And then in key-cold Lucrece' bleeding stream   1774
He falls, and bathes the pale fear in his face,   1775
And counterfeits to die with her a space,   1776
 Till manly shame bids him possess his breath
 And live to be revengèd on her death.

The deep vexation of his inward soul
Hath served a dumb arrest upon his tongue,   1780
Who, mad that sorrow should his use control
Or keep him from heart-easing words so long,
Begins to talk; but through his lips do throng
 Weak words, so thick come in his poor heart's aid   1784
 That no man could distinguish what he said.

Yet sometime "Tarquin" was pronouncèd plain,
But through his teeth, as if the name he tore.
This windy tempest, till it blow up rain,
Held back his sorrow's tide, to make it more.
At last it rains, and busy winds give o'er;
 Then son and father weep with equal strife
 Who should weep most, for daughter or for wife.

The one doth call her his, the other his,
Yet neither may possess the claim they lay.   1794
The father says, "She's mine." "Oh, mine she is,"
Replies her husband. "Do not take away
My sorrow's interest. Let no mourner say   1797
 He weeps for her, for she was only mine,
 And only must be wailed by Collatine."

"Oh," quoth Lucretius, "I did give that life
Which she too early and too late hath spilled."   1801
"Woe, woe," quoth Collatine, "She was my wife;
I owed her, and 'tis mine that she hath killed."   1803
"My daughter" and "my wife" with clamors filled
 The dispersed air, who, holding Lucrece' life,
 Answered their cries, "my daughter" and "my wife." 1806

Brutus, who plucked the knife from Lucrece' side,
Seeing such emulation in their woe,
Began to clothe his wit in state and pride,   1809
Burying in Lucrece' wound his folly's show.   1810

1725 **bail it** pay for its release   1729 **Life's . . . destiny** i.e., the life
that now has a perpetual existence, its subjugation to corporeal existence having been canceled.   1734 **Brutus** Lucius Junius Brutus,
whose brother had been put to death by the father of the Tarquin in
this poem   1740 **Who** which.   **late-sacked** recently pillaged.
vastly in desolation   1743 **and that . . . stained** and false Tarquin had
stained that blood.   1745 **rigol** rim of pale serum that forms around
congealing blood   1752 **deprived** taken away.   1754 **unlived** bereft
of life.   1758 **glass** mirror (i.e., Lucrece, the image of her father)
1761 **death** death's-head, skull   1766 **surcease** cease

1773 **give . . . place** yield him precedence in sorrowing   1774 **key-
cold** cold as steel   1775 **pale fear** fearful pallor   1776 **counterfeits to
die** gives the appearance of dying.   **a space** for a period of time
1780 **dumb arrest** injunction to be silent   1784 **so . . . aid** coming too
thick and fast to aid his heart   1794 **possess . . . lay** take possession
of what they claim (since she is dead).   1797 **interest** claim to possession.   1801 **late** recently   1803 **owed** owned   1806 **Answered**
echoed   1809 **state** dignity   1810 **folly's show** pretense of folly.
(Lucius Junius Brutus had feigned madness to escape the fate of his
brother; see the note for line 1734.)

He with the Romans was esteemèd so
    As silly jeering idiots are with kings, 1812
      For sportive words and uttering foolish things.

But now he throws that shallow habit by 1814
Wherein deep policy did him disguise, 1815
And armed his long-hid wits advisedly 1816
To check the tears in Collatinus' eyes.
"Thou wrongèd lord of Rome," quoth he, "arise!
    Let my unsounded self, supposed a fool, 1819
      Now set thy long-experienced wit to school.

"Why, Collatine, is woe the cure for woe?
Do wounds help wounds, or grief help grievous deeds?
Is it revenge to give thyself a blow
For his foul act by whom thy fair wife bleeds?
Such childish humor from weak minds proceeds. 1825
    Thy wretched wife mistook the matter so
      To slay herself, that should have slain her foe.

"Courageous Roman, do not steep thy heart
In such relenting dew of lamentations,
But kneel with me and help to bear thy part
To rouse our Roman gods with invocations
That they will suffer these abominations— 1832

Since Rome herself in them doth stand disgraced—
    By our strong arms from forth her fair streets chased. 1834

"Now, by the Capitol that we adore,
And by this chaste blood so unjustly stained,
By heaven's fair sun that breeds the fat earth's store, 1837
By all our country rights in Rome maintained, 1838
And by chaste Lucrece' soul that late complained
    Her wrongs to us, and by this bloody knife,
      We will revenge the death of this true wife."

This said, he struck his hand upon his breast,
And kissed the fatal knife, to end his vow;
And to his protestation urged the rest, 1844
Who, wond'ring at him, did his words allow. 1845
Then jointly to the ground their knees they bow,
    And that deep vow which Brutus made before
      He doth again repeat, and that they swore.

When they had sworn to this advisèd doom, 1849
They did conclude to bear dead Lucrece thence,
To show her bleeding body thorough Rome, 1851
And so to publish Tarquin's foul offense; 1852
Which being done with speedy diligence,
    The Romans plausibly did give consent 1854
      To Tarquin's everlasting banishment.

1812 **silly jeering idiots** i.e., innocent court jesters   1814 **habit** cloak and disposition   1815 **policy** cunning   1816 **advisedly** with deliberation   1819 **unsounded** unplumbed, unexplored   1825 **humor** disposition   1832 **suffer** permit

1834 **chased** i.e., to be chased away.   1837 **fat** fertile.   **store** abundance   1838 **country rights** rights we have as a people   1844 **to his protestation** to join in his vow   1845 **wond'ring** marveling.   **allow** approve.   1849 **advisèd doom** considered judgment   1851 **thorough** throughout   1852 **publish** make public   1854 **plausibly** with applause

The Phoenix and Turtle

"The Phoenix and Turtle" first appeared in a collection of poems called *Love's Martyr: Or, Rosalins Complaint* by Robert Chester (1601). This quarto volume offered various poetic exercises about the phoenix and the turtle "by the best and chiefest of our modern writers." The poem assigned to Shakespeare has been universally accepted as his and is one of his most remarkable productions. With a deceptively simple diction, in gracefully pure tetrameter quatrains and triplets, the poem effortlessly evokes the transcendental ideal of a love existing eternally beyond death. The occasion is an assembly of birds to observe the funeral rites of the phoenix (always found alone) and the turtledove (always found in pairs). The phoenix, legendary bird of resurrection from its own ashes, once more finds life through death in the company of the turtledove, emblem of pure constancy in affection. Their spiritual union becomes a mystical oneness in whose presence Reason stands virtually speechless. Baffled human discourse must resort to paradox in order to explain how two beings become one essence, "Hearts remote yet not asunder." Mathematics and logic are "confounded" by this joining of two spirits into a "concordant one." This paradox of oneness echoes scholastic theology and its expounding of the doctrine of the Trinity, in terms of persons, substance, accident, triunity, and the like, although, somewhat in the manner of John Donne's poetry, this allusion is more a part of the poem's serious wit than its symbolic meaning. The poignant brevity of this vision and its medieval bird-mass setting is rendered all the more mysterious by our not knowing what, if any, human tragedy may have prompted this metaphysical affirmation.

The Phoenix and Turtle

Let the bird of loudest lay	1
On the sole Arabian tree	2
Herald sad and trumpet be,	3
To whose sound chaste wings obey.	4

But thou shrieking harbinger,	5
Foul precurrer of the fiend,	6
Augur of the fever's end,	7
To this troop come thou not near.

From this session interdict
Every fowl of tyrant wing,	10
Save the eagle, feathered king;
Keep the obsequy so strict.

Let the priest in surplice white,
That defunctive music can,	14
Be the death-divining swan,	15
Lest the requiem lack his right.	16

And thou treble-dated crow,	17
That thy sable gender mak'st	18
With the breath thou giv'st and tak'st,	19
'Mongst our mourners shalt thou go.

Here the anthem doth commence.
Love and constancy is dead;

Phoenix and the turtle fled
In a mutual flame from hence.

So they loved, as love in twain	25
Had the essence but in one,
Two distincts, division none;	27
Number there in love was slain.	28

Hearts remote yet not asunder,
Distance and no space was seen
Twixt this turtle and his queen;
But in them it were a wonder.	32

So between them love did shine,	33
That the turtle saw his right	34
Flaming in the phoenix' sight;	35
Either was the other's mine.	36

Property was thus appalled	37
That the self was not the same;	38
Single nature's double name	39
Neither two nor one was called.	40

Reason, in itself confounded,	41
Saw division grow together,	42
To themselves yet either neither,	43
Simple were so well compounded,	44

Title: Phoenix mythical bird that was thought to be consumed in flame and reborn in its own ashes, symbol of immortality; here regarded as female, though traditionally of both sexes. **Turtle** turtledove, symbol of constancy in love; here regarded as male (line 31) **1 the bird . . . lay** the bird (possibly the nightingale) of loudest song **2 sole Arabian tree** (The phoenix was thought to build its nest in a unique tree in Arabia.) **3 sad** solemn. **trumpet** trumpeter **4 chaste wings** i.e., the wings of the good birds that are being summoned. **obey** are obedient. **5 shrieking harbinger** i.e., screech owl **6 precurrer** forerunner **7 Augur . . . end** i.e., prognosticator of death **10 fowl . . . wing** bird of prey **14 That . . . can** that is skilled in funereal music **15 death-divining swan** (Alludes to the belief that the swan foresees its own death and sings when it is about to die.) **16 his right** its proper ceremony, or, its proper due. (Referring either to the *requiem* or to the *swan*.) **17 treble-dated** i.e., living thrice the normal span **18–19 That . . . tak'st** (Compare with *Hortus Sanitatis*, Bk. 3, sec. 34, in Seager's *Natural History in Shakespeare's Time*: "They [ravens] are said to conceive and to lay eggs at the bill. The young become black on the seventh day.") **sable gender** black offspring

25 So . . . as They so loved that **27 distincts** separate or individual persons or things **28 Number . . . slain** i.e., their love, being of one essence, paradoxically renders the very concept of number meaningless; "one [in the numerological tradition] is no number." **32 But . . . wonder** this phenomenon, had it been seen anywhere but in them, would have seemed amazing. **33 So** In such a way **34 his right** his true nature, what pertained uniquely and rightly to him, or, what was due to him **35 sight** eyes **36 mine** i.e., very own. (The phoenix and turtle are so merged in one another's identity that each contains the other's being. *Mine* also suggests "source of each other's treasure.") **37–8 Property . . . same** i.e., The very idea of a peculiar or essential quality was thus confounded by the paradoxical revelation here that each lover's identity was merged into the other's and was no longer itself **39–40 Single . . . called** i.e., their nature was at once so single and double that it could not properly be called either one or two. **40–4 Reason . . . compounded** i.e., Reason, which proceeds by making discriminations between separate entities, is confounded when it beholds a paradoxical union of such entities, each at once discrete and fused into a single being, at once a simple (i.e., made of one substance) and a compound

That it cried, "How true a twain
Seemeth this concordant one!
Love hath reason, Reason none, 47
If what parts can so remain." 48

Whereupon it made this threne 49
To the phoenix and the dove,
Co-supremes and stars of love, 51
As chorus to their tragic scene.

THRENOS

Beauty, truth, and rarity, 53
Grace in all simplicity,
Here enclosed, in cinders lie. 55

Death is now the phoenix' nest, 45
And the turtle's loyal breast
To eternity doth rest, 58

Leaving no posterity;
'Twas not their infirmity, 60
It was married chastity. 61

Truth may seem, but cannot be; 62
Beauty brag, but 'tis not she; 63
Truth and beauty buried be. 64

To this urn let those repair
That are either true or fair;
For these dead birds sigh a prayer.

---

45 it i.e., Reason   **47–8 Love . . . remain** i.e., Love represents a higher reason than reason itself owing to its embodiment of the paradoxical unity of two in one.   **49 threne** lamentation, funeral song. (From Greek *threnos*.)   **51 Co-supremes** joint rulers   **53 truth** constancy in love. (Also in line 62.)   **55 enclosed** i.e., enclosed in *this urn* (line 65)

58 To eternity for all eternity   **60–1 'Twas . . . chastity** i.e., it was not a defect in them to leave no posterity but an emblem of their mystical eternal trothplight.   **62–4 Truth . . . be** Anything calling itself fidelity or beauty is only a shadow or approximation of the metaphysical reality hinted at in those words.

A Lover's Complaint

Thomas Thorpe published "A Lover's Complaint" in his 1609 Quarto of Shakespeare's *Sonnets*, ascribing the poem to "William Shakespeare" in its title heading (sig. K^v). The ascription must not be given too much weight, for Thorpe evidently did not have Shakespeare's authorization to publish the sonnets and may possibly have added the last two sonnets from some other source. Yet the attribution of "A Lover's Complaint" to Shakespeare is entirely plausible and is refuted by no other claim. The poem was never assigned to any other author during Shakespeare's lifetime, and no convincing alternative candidate has come forward since then. Although some critics used to wonder if the poem were worthy of Shakespeare's genius, its density of metaphor and energy of wordplay are stylistically and intellectually very much like that of Shakespeare's mature work around or before the date of publication.

The poem takes as its point of departure the conventions of a familiar Elizabethan poetic genre: the "complaint." Often choosing as their setting a stylized pastoral landscape inhabited by rustic shepherds and shepherdesses, poems in this genre generally depicted the plaintive laments of deserted or unrequited lovers. Typically, the poet might catalogue the fickle lover's features and bewail in moralistic terms the dangerous consequences of blind passion. Elizabethans often expected this sort of didacticism in the genre and might, indeed, have been tempted to read Shakespeare's poem as a useful and moving object lesson to young women about the honeyed tongues of young wooers.

Yet the value of Shakespeare's poem goes far beyond the conventional demands of the genre, as did the contributions of other exceptional writers. Much as *As You Like It* shows us a complex, ironic vision of the pastoral, this poem explores the genre of the pastoral "complaint" with subtlety and range. Its multiple point of view is noteworthy. Beginning with the sympathetic voice of the poet-narrator, "A Lover's Complaint" introduces us to the forlorn maiden and then the old shepherd who becomes an audience for her tale of woe. He is a good listener, partly because he has sowed his own wild oats in his day (11. 58–60). The story he hears incorporates also the voice of the young man who has seduced the maiden; the passage in which the young man speaks directly to her, as reported to the old man and thus to us as readers, takes up much of the poem (11. 177–280).

Framed successively and concentrically by the points of view of the sad maiden, the old man, the poet, and ourselves, the male wooer is given free rein of expression in pleading for sympathy. The old man provides his own sympathy of regret and male acknowledgment of a kind of complicity, while the poet hovers in the background not simply as narrator but also as one who understands. The moralism is evident and yet is less important for us than the multiplicity of voices expressing in rich metaphorical language the tense and ultimately bitter struggle over sexuality that is so much a key to the "Dark Lady" sonnets as well. Thorpe's inclusion of the poem in his volume of the *Sonnets* suggests an integrity in that publishing venture.

A Lover's Complaint

From off a hill whose concave womb reworded   1
A plaintful story from a sist'ring vale,   2
My spirits t'attend this double voice accorded,   3
And down I laid to list the sad-tuned tale;   4
Ere long espied a fickle maid full pale,   5
Tearing of papers, breaking rings a-twain,   6
Storming her world with sorrow's wind and rain.

Upon her head a platted hive of straw,   8
Which fortified her visage from the sun,   9
Whereon the thought might think sometimes it saw   10
The carcass of a beauty spent and done.   11
Time had not scythèd all that youth begun,   12
Nor youth all quit, but spite of heaven's fell rage   13
Some beauty peeped through lattice of seared age.   14

Oft did she heave her napkin to her eyne,   15
Which on it had conceited characters,   16
Laund'ring the silken figures in the brine
That seasoned woe had pelleted in tears,   18
And often reading what contents it bears;
As often shrieking undistinguished woe,   20
In clamors of all size, both high and low.

Sometimes her leveled eyes their carriage ride,   22
As they did batt'ry to the spheres intend;   23
Sometimes diverted, their poor balls are tied   24
To th'orbèd earth; sometimes they do extend   25

Their view right on; anon their gazes lend   26
To every place at once, and, nowhere fixed,   27
The mind and sight distractedly commixed.   28

Her hair, nor loose nor tied in formal plat,   29
Proclaimed in her a careless hand of pride;   30
For some, untucked, descended her sheaved hat,   31
Hanging her pale and pinèd cheek beside;   32
Some in her threaden fillet still did bide,   33
And, true to bondage, would not break from thence,
Though slackly braided in loose negligence.

A thousand favors from a maund she drew   36
Of amber, crystal, and of beaded jet,   37
Which one by one she in a river threw,
Upon whose weeping margent she was set,   39
Like usury applying wet to wet,   40
Or monarch's hands that lets not bounty fall   41
Where want cries some, but where excess begs all.   42

Of folded schedules had she many a one,   43
Which she perused, sighed, tore, and gave the flood;   44
Cracked many a ring of posied gold and bone,   45
Bidding them find their sepulchers in mud;
Found yet more letters sadly penned in blood,
With sleided silk feat and affectedly   48
Enswathed and sealed to curious secrecy.   49

---

1 **concave womb** hollow-shaped hillside. **reworded** echoed
2 **plaintful story** i.e., mournful sound (which turns out to be the grieving of a maiden). **sist'ring** neighboring 3 **t'attend** to listen to. **double** (because echoed). **accorded** inclined, consented 4 **list** listen to. **sad-tuned** i.e., sung in a minor key 5 **fickle** i.e., perturbed, moody 6 **papers** i.e., love letters 8 **platted hive** i.e., woven hat 9 **fortified** protected 10 **the thought** the mind, the imagination 11 **carcass** decaying, lifeless remnant. **spent** consumed 12–13 **all ... quit** all the beauty of her youth, nor had youth abandoned her entirely 13 **fell** deadly, cruel 14 **seared** dried up 15 **heave** lift. **napkin** handkerchief. **eyne** eyes 16 **conceited characters** fanciful or emblematic devices 18 **seasoned** (1) matured (2) salted. **pelleted** formed into small globules 20 **undistinguished woe** incoherent cries of grief 22 **her ... ride** i.e., her eyes, directed and aimed like a cannon, swiveled about as on a gun carriage 23 **As ... intend** as if they did intend to direct their fire against the heavens 24 **balls** eyeballs 24–5 **are ... earth** seem fixed to the orb-shaped earth, to the ground

26 **right on** straight in front of her 26–7 **lend ... once** i.e., roll distractedly everywhere 28 **The mind ... commixed** her mind and sight wildly confused or mingled. 29 **nor ... nor** neither ... nor. **in formal plat** neatly braided 30 **careless ... pride** hand careless of appearances 31 **descended** hung from. **sheaved** straw 32 **Hanging ... beside** hanging beside her pale cheek wasted with pining 33 **threaden fillet** i.e., ribbon binding her hair 36 **favors** love tokens. **maund** woven basket with handles 37 **beaded jet** jet beads 39 **weeping margent** moist bank. (Though *weeping* also applies to her.) 40 **usury** i.e., adding money to money; she adds tears to the river's water 41–2 **Or ... all** or like the monarch who distributes his bounty not among those whose need cries out for some aid, but among the excessively wealthy who beg for absolutely everything. 43 **schedules** papers containing writing, i.e., letters 44 **gave the flood** threw in the stream 45 **posied** inscribed with a motto 48 **sleided** separated into threads. **feat** featly, adroitly. **affectedly** lovingly 49 **Enswathed ... secrecy** wrapped about (with the silk) and sealed (with wax) into careful secrecy.

These often bathed she in her fluxive eyes, 50
And often kissed, and often 'gan to tear;
Cried, "O false blood, thou register of lies, 52
What unapprovèd witness dost thou bear! 53
Ink would have seemed more black and damnèd here!"
This said, in top of rage the lines she rents, 55
Big discontent so breaking their contents. 56

A reverend man that grazed his cattle nigh— 57
Sometime a blusterer, that the ruffle knew 58
Of court, of city, and had let go by
The swiftest hours, observèd as they flew— 60
Towards this afflicted fancy fastly drew, 61
And, privileged by age, desires to know
In brief the grounds and motives of her woe.

So slides he down upon his grainèd bat, 64
And comely-distant sits he by her side, 65
When he again desires her, being sat, 66
Her grievance with his hearing to divide. 67
If that from him there may be aught applied 68
Which may her suffering ecstasy assuage, 69
'Tis promised in the charity of age. 70

"Father," she says, "though in me you behold 71
The injury of many a blasting hour, 72
Let it not tell your judgment I am old;
Not age, but sorrow, over me hath power.
I might as yet have been a spreading flower, 75
Fresh to myself, if I had self-applied 76
Love to myself and to no love beside.

"But, woe is me! Too early I attended 78
A youthful suit—it was to gain my grace— 79
Oh, one by nature's outwards so commended 80
That maidens' eyes stuck over all his face. 81
Love lacked a dwelling and made him her place; 82
And when in his fair parts she did abide,
She was new lodged and newly deified. 84

"His browny locks did hang in crooked curls,
And every light occasion of the wind 86

Upon his lips their silken parcels hurls. 87
What's sweet to do, to do will aptly find; 88
Each eye that saw him did enchant the mind,
For on his visage was in little drawn 90
What largeness thinks in Paradise was sawn. 91

"Small show of man was yet upon his chin;
His phoenix down began but to appear 93
Like unshorn velvet on that termless skin 94
Whose bare outbragged the web it seemed to wear. 95
Yet showed his visage by that cost more dear; 96
And nice affections wavering stood in doubt 97
If best were as it was, or best without. 98

"His qualities were beauteous as his form, 99
For maiden-tongued he was, and thereof free; 100
Yet, if men moved him, was he such a storm 101
As oft twixt May and April is to see, 102
When winds breathe sweet, unruly though they be.
His rudeness so with his authorized youth 104
Did livery falseness in a pride of truth. 105

"Well could he ride, and often men would say,
'That horse his mettle from his rider takes. 107
Proud of subjection, noble by the sway, 108
What rounds, what bounds, what course, what stop he
    makes!' 109
And controversy hence a question takes, 110
Whether the horse by him became his deed, 111
Or he his manage by th' well-doing steed. 112

"But quickly on this side the verdict went:
His real habitude gave life and grace 114
To appertainings and to ornament, 115
Accomplished in himself, not in his case. 116
All aids, themselves made fairer by their place, 117

---

50 **fluxive** flowing   52 **blood** i.e., the blood in which the letters were written (line 47), but with a sense also of the *blood* or passion that has played her false.   **register** record   53 **unapprovèd** unconfirmed, false   55 **in top of** in the height of.   **rents** rends, tears   56 **discontent . . . contents** (With a play of antithesis.)   57 **reverend** aged   58 **Sometime** at one time.   **blusterer** swaggerer.   **ruffle** commotion, bustle   60 **swiftest hours** i.e., time of youth.   **observèd as they flew** (This man has let his youth go by and disappear, but not without observing and learning from the years as they flew.)   61 **fancy** i.e., amorous passion and the person expressing it.   **fastly** (1) quickly (2) in close proximity   64 **So . . . bat** And so he lowers himself by means of his club or staff that is worn and showing the grain   65 **comely-distant** at a decorous distance   66 **being** he being   67 **divide** share.   68 **If that** If   69 **ecstasy** frenzy (of grief)   70 **in the charity of age** in the loving-kindness that old people can offer.   71 **Father** i.e., Old man   72 **blasting** blighting, withering   75 **spreading** unfolding   76 **Fresh to myself** i.e., like a flower that lives and dies unseen and unplucked   78 **attended** heeded   79 **grace** favor   80 **nature's outwards** the physical appearance given him by nature   81 **stuck over** i.e., were glued to   82 **Love** Venus   84 **She . . . deified** Love, already a goddess, was made doubly so when she dwelt with him.   86 **occasion** chance breath

87 **Upon . . . hurls** (the wind) tosses the *silken parcels*, the curls, against his lips.   88 **to do will aptly find** i.e., will find a doer or an occasion   90 **in little** in miniature   91 **What . . . sawn** what one supposes was seen in full scale in Paradise.   93 **phoenix** i.e., suggesting his unique perfection (since only one phoenix, a mythical bird, exists at one time)   94 **Like . . . skin** like velvet with its nap not yet trimmed or shaved, on that skin which words are inadequate to describe   95 **Whose . . . wear** the unadorned surface of which could outboast in handsomeness the downy covering it seemed to wear.   96 **Yet . . . dear** Yet his face seemed all the lovelier for its rich covering   97 **nice affections** carefully discriminating tastes   98 **without** i.e., lacking the downy beard.   99 **qualities were** manner was as   100 **maiden-tongued** modest of speech, soft-spoken.   **free** eloquent, well-spoken   101 **moved** i.e., to anger   102 **to see** to be seen   104–5 **His . . . truth** His roughness, privileged by his youth, thereby did dress falseness in a magnificent garment or concealment of truth.   107 **mettle** vigor and strength of spirit   108 **noble by the sway** made noble by the way he's controlled   109 **stop** sudden check in a horse's "career" or trial gallop at full speed. (All the terms here are terms of *manage*, line 112, the schooling or handling of a horse.)   110 **takes** takes up, considers   111–12 **Whether . . . steed** whether it was owing to his horsemanship that his horse acted so becomingly or whether he seemed such a good rider because he had so good a horse.   114 **habitude** constitution, temperament   115 **appertainings** external attributes   116 **case** appearance and circumstances, e.g., the possession of so good a horse.   117 **place** i.e., place near to him or on his person

Came for additions, yet their purposed trim 118
Pieced not his grace, but were all graced by him. 119

"So on the tip of his subduing tongue
All kind of arguments and question deep,
All replication prompt and reason strong, 122
For his advantage still did wake and sleep. 123
To make the weeper laugh, the laugher weep,
He had the dialect and different skill, 125
Catching all passions in his craft of will, 126

"That he did in the general bosom reign 127
Of young, of old, and sexes both enchanted,
To dwell with him in thoughts, or to remain
In personal duty, following where he haunted. 130
Consents bewitched, ere he desire, have granted, 131
And dialogued for him what he would say, 132
Asked their own wills, and made their wills obey. 133

"Many there were that did his picture get
To serve their eyes, and in it put their mind, 135
Like fools that in th'imagination set 136
The goodly objects which abroad they find 137
Of lands and mansions, theirs in thought assigned, 138
And laboring in more pleasures to bestow them 139
Than the true gouty landlord which doth owe them; 140

"So many have, that never touched his hand, 141
Sweetly supposed them mistress of his heart. 142
My woeful self, that did in freedom stand,
And was my own fee simple, not in part, 144
What with his art in youth, and youth in art,
Threw my affections in his charmèd power, 146
Reserved the stalk and gave him all my flower.

"Yet did I not, as some my equals did, 148
Demand of him, nor being desirèd yielded; 149
Finding myself in honor so forbid, 150

With safest distance I mine honor shielded. 151
Experience for me many bulwarks builded 152
Of proofs new-bleeding, which remained the foil 153
Of this false jewel and his amorous spoil. 154

"But, ah, who ever shunned by precedent
The destined ill she must herself assay? 156
Or forced examples, 'gainst her own content 157
To put the by-past perils in her way? 158
Counsel may stop awhile what will not stay; 159
For when we rage, advice is often seen 160
By blunting us to make our wits more keen. 161

"Nor gives it satisfaction to our blood 162
That we must curb it upon others' proof, 163
To be forbade the sweets that seems so good 164
For fear of harms that preach in our behoof. 165
O appetite, from judgment stand aloof! 166
The one a palate hath that needs will taste, 167
Though Reason weep and cry, 'It is thy last.'

"For further I could say 'This man's untrue,' 169
And knew the patterns of his foul beguiling; 170
Heard where his plants in others' orchards grew, 171
Saw how deceits were gilded in his smiling; 172
Knew vows were ever brokers to defiling; 173
Thought characters and words merely but art, 174
And bastards of his foul adulterate heart.

"And long upon these terms I held my city, 176
Till thus he 'gan besiege me: 'Gentle maid,
Have of my suffering youth some feeling pity,
And be not of my holy vows afraid.
That's to ye sworn to none was ever said; 180
For feasts of love I have been called unto, 181
Till now did ne'er invite, nor never woo. 182

" 'All my offenses that abroad you see 183
Are errors of the blood, none of the mind.

118–19 Came . . . him added to his attractiveness, yet their intended function as ornament did not so much augment his grace as take grace from him. **122–3 All . . . sleep** all prompt riposte and persuasive argument served him at all hours, like servants always ready whenever called. **125 dialect** manner of expression. **different** varied, readily adaptable **126 passions** (1) passions of his hearers (2) passions incorporated into his moving speech. **craft of will** skill in persuasion **127 That** so that. **general bosom** hearts of all **130 In personal duty** i.e., like a personal servant. **haunted** frequented. **131–3 Consents . . . obey** i.e., Women have consented to his will before he even asked them, have made up his love speeches to them for him, and have made themselves obey as if obeying their own desires. **135 in it . . . mind** let their minds become engrossed with it **136–40 Like . . . owe them** like fools who imagine certain goodly lands and mansions they have happened on in their travels to be their own, and try harder to make them habitable and pleasurable than does the gout-afflicted landlord who owns them **141 So many** Thus many women **142 them** themselves **144 was . . . part** i.e., had total control of my own destiny, as of land held in perpetuity, not partial control **146 charmèd power** power to charm or cast a spell **148 my equals** i.e., of those equal to me in age and station **149 Demand . . . yielded** i.e., ask him to take me, or, yield myself to him the moment he desired me to **150 in honor so forbid** forbidden by (maidenly) honor to do so (i.e., to yield at once)

151 With safest distance by staying at a safe distance **152–3 Experience . . . new-bleeding** i.e., The experience of those recently undone in love by him provided me with many defenses **153 foil** dark background used to show off the brilliance of a jewel **154 this false jewel** i.e., the young man. **spoil** plunder; that which is spoiled. **156 assay** learn by experience. **157–8 Or . . . way?** Or, in order to deter her own present inclination, urged the dangers experienced by others in the past? **159 stay** stop forever **160 rage** i.e., in passion **161 By . . . keen** in attempting to stop us, merely making us all the more ingenious and eager. **162 blood** passion **163 proof** experience **164 seems** seem **165 preach in our behoof** offer us good advice aimed at benefiting us. **166 O appetite . . . aloof!** O desire, you will always remain distant from judgment! **167 The one** i.e., Passion, *appetite*. **needs will taste** insists upon gratification **169 say . . . untrue** tell of this man's faithlessness **170 knew . . . beguiling** had examples of his treachery before me **171 plants** i.e., children illegitimately begotten. **orchards** i.e., wombs **172 gilded** given a gilded (false) surface **173 brokers** panders **174 characters and words** i.e., the written and spoken word. **art** artifice **176 city** citadel (of chastity) **180 That's** That which is **181–2 For . . . woo** I have been invited to other feasts of love before now, but never until now did I do the inviting and the wooing. **183 abroad** in the world around us

Love made them not. With acture they may be,   185
Where neither party is nor true nor kind.   186
They sought their shame that so their shame did find;
And so much less of shame in me remains   188
By how much of me their reproach contains.   189

" 'Among the many that mine eyes have seen,
Not one whose flame my heart so much as warmed,   191
Or my affection put to th' smallest teen,   192
Or any of my leisures ever charmed.   193
Harm have I done to them, but ne'er was harmed;
Kept hearts in liveries, but mine own was free,   195
And reigned, commanding in his monarchy.

" 'Look here what tributes wounded fancies sent me,   197
Of pallid pearls and rubies red as blood,
Figuring that they their passions likewise lent me   199
Of grief and blushes, aptly understood
In bloodless white and the encrimsoned mood—   201
Effects of terror and dear modesty,   202
Encamped in hearts but fighting outwardly.   203

" 'And, lo, behold these talents of their hair,   204
With twisted metal amorously impleached,   205
I have received from many a several fair,   206
Their kind acceptance weepingly beseeched,
With th'annexions of fair gems enriched,   208
And deep-brained sonnets that did amplify   209
Each stone's dear nature, worth, and quality.

" 'The diamond? Why, 'twas beautiful and hard,
Whereto his invised properties did tend;   212
The deep-green emerald, in whose fresh regard   213
Weak sights their sickly radiance do amend;   214
The heaven-hued sapphire and the opal blend   215
With objects manifold—each several stone,   216
With wit well blazoned, smiled or made some moan.   217

" 'Lo, all these trophies of affections hot,   218
Of pensived and subdued desires the tender,   219
Nature hath charged me that I hoard them not,
But yield them up where I myself must render,
That is, to you, my origin and ender;   222
For these, of force, must your oblations be,   223
Since, I their altar, you enpatron me.   224

" 'Oh, then, advance of yours that phraseless hand,   225
Whose white weighs down the airy scale of praise!   226
Take all these similes to your own command,   227
Hallowed with sighs that burning lungs did raise;   228
What me, your minister for you, obeys,   229
Works under you; and to your audit comes   230
Their distract parcels in combinèd sums.   231

" 'Lo, this device was sent me from a nun,
Or sister sanctified of holiest note,   233
Which late her noble suit in court did shun,   234
Whose rarest havings made the blossoms dote;   235
For she was sought by spirits of richest coat,   236
But kept cold distance, and did thence remove   237
To spend her living in eternal love.   238

" 'But oh, my sweet, what labor is't to leave   239
The thing we have not, mast'ring what not strives,   240
Paling the place which did no form receive,   241
Playing patient sports in unconstrainèd gyves?   242
She that her fame so to herself contrives   243
The scars of battle scapeth by the flight,
And makes her absence valiant, not her might.   245

" 'Oh, pardon me, in that my boast is true!   246
The accident which brought me to her eye
Upon the moment did her force subdue,   248

185–6 With . . . kind They may be physically performed where nei-ther partner is faithful or truly in love. 188–9 And . . . contains and I am all the less to blame by how little their reproaches really accuse me (rather than themselves). 191 Not one . . . warmed i.e., there is not one whose flame of passion so much as warmed my heart 192 Or . . . teen or gave my affection the least sorrow (teen) 193 Or . . . charmed or put a spell on any of my times of leisure. 195 in liveries in the uniform of a person in service, i.e., almost enslaved 197 wounded fancies i.e., doting young women 199 Figuring signifying 201 mood mode, form, emotional state (i.e., blushing) 202 Effects the signs or results. dear precious; deeply felt 203 Encamped . . . outwardly (White and red contend visually in the alternation of pallor and blushing cheeks, while fear and maidenly shame occupy the hearts of the women who have been seduced.) 204 talents i.e., treasures, riches 205 impleached intertwined 206 a several fair different beautiful young women 208 th'annexions the additions 209 deep-brained intricate. amplify enlarge upon, go into detail about 212 Whereto . . . tend toward which its invisible properties incline. (Invised, used nowhere else, may be an error for incised, "engraved.") The young man, too, is beautiful and hard. 213 regard aspect, sight 214 radiance power of vision. (The emerald helps repair weak vision in those who look at it, just as the young man refreshes the eyes by his beauty.) 215–16 blend . . . manifold blended of many colors (?), or, blended with (or that blends with) many objects presented to the sight (?) 216 several partic-ular 217 blazoned proclaimed, cataloged (in the accompanying son-nets). smiled . . . moan symbolized joy or grief in love.

218 affections passions 219 pensived saddened. tender offering 222 ender end, conclusion. (You are the source of my life and that without which I cannot live.) 223 of force perforce. your oblations offerings made at the altar of love for you 224 Since . . . me since I am the altar (on which these gifts are offered) and you are my patron saint (to whom the altar is dedicated). 225 phraseless indescribable 226 weighs . . . praise outweighs in the scales any praise that can be offered to it in airy words. 227 similes i.e., symbolic love tokens or gems accompanied by symbolic explanation in the sonnets 228 Hal-lowed consecrated. burning i.e., hot with passion 229–30 What . . . you whatever is at the command of me, your minister or agent acting on your authority, is thus yours also 230 audit account 231 dis-tract parcels component parts 233 note reputation 234 Which . . . shun who recently (before she became nun) shunned those who sued for her attention at court 235 Whose . . . dote whose rare gift of beauty made the young courtiers (in the blossom of their life) dote on her 236 spirits spirited young men. coat coat of arms, i.e., descent 237 remove depart 238 living lifetime. eternal love love of the eternal God (i.e., she became a nun). 239–42 what . . . gyves? how can it be called a difficult thing to give up something we haven't tried yet, mastering an emotion that offers no resistance, paling or fencing in the heart upon which no lover yet has made any impression, patiently pretending to endure restraints that, in fact, impose no restraint and that one is not obliged to endure? 243 her fame . . . contrives devises for herself a reputation (for renouncing love) 245 makes . . . might i.e., shows valor only in avoiding temptation, not in con-fronting it directly. 246 my boast i.e., that she could resist me only by fleeing, not when she saw me 248 Upon the moment at once

And now she would the cagèd cloister fly.   249
Religious love put out religion's eye.   250
Not to be tempted, would she be immured,   251
And now to tempt all liberty procured.   252

" 'How mighty then you are, oh, hear me tell!
The broken bosoms that to me belong   254
Have emptied all their fountains in my well,   255
And mine I pour your ocean all among.   256
I strong o'er them, and you o'er me being strong,   257
Must for your victory us all congest,   258
As compound love to physic your cold breast.   259

" 'My parts had power to charm a sacred nun,   260
Who, disciplined, ay, dieted in grace,   261
Believed her eyes when they t'assail begun,   262
All vows and consecrations giving place.
O most potential love! Vow, bond, nor space,   264
In thee hath neither sting, knot, nor confine,   265
For thou art all, and all things else are thine.

" 'When thou impressest, what are precepts worth   267
Of stale example? When thou wilt inflame,   268
How coldly those impediments stand forth
Of wealth, of filial fear, law, kindred, fame!
Love's arms are peace, 'gainst rule, 'gainst sense, 'gainst
    shame,   271
And sweetens, in the suff'ring pangs it bears,   272
The aloes of all forces, shocks, and fears.   273

" 'Now all these hearts that do on mine depend,
Feeling it break, with bleeding groans they pine,   275
And supplicant their sighs to you extend   276
To leave the batt'ry that you make 'gainst mine,   277

Lending soft audience to my sweet design,   278
And credent soul to that strong-bonded oath   279
That shall prefer and undertake my troth.'   280

"This said, his wat'ry eyes he did dismount,   281
Whose sights till then were leveled on my face;   282
Each cheek a river running from a fount
With brinish current downward flowed apace.
Oh, how the channel to the stream gave grace!   285
Who glazed with crystal gate the glowing roses   286
That flame through water which their hue encloses.   287

"Oh, father, what a hell of witchcraft lies   288
In the small orb of one particular tear!   289
But with the inundation of the eyes
What rocky heart to water will not wear?
What breast so cold that is not warmèd here?
Oh, cleft effect! Cold modesty, hot wrath,   293
Both fire from hence and chill extincture hath.   294

"For, lo, his passion, but an art of craft,   295
Even there resolved my reason into tears;   296
There my white stole of chastity I daffed,   297
Shook off my sober guards and civil fears;   298
Appear to him as he to me appears,   299
All melting, though our drops this difference bore: 300
His poisoned me, and mine did him restore.

"In him a plenitude of subtle matter,   302
Applied to cautels, all strange forms receives,   303
Of burning blushes, or of weeping water,
Or swooning paleness; and he takes and leaves,   305
In either's aptness, as it best deceives,   306
To blush at speeches rank, to weep at woes,   307
Or to turn white and swoon at tragic shows;

"That not a heart which in his level came   309
Could scape the hail of his all-hurting aim,   310
Showing fair nature is both kind and tame;   311

249 she would . . . fly she wished to flee the locked convent.
250 Religious . . . eye i.e., Love of me put out love of the divine.
251–2 Not . . . procured Before she wished to be shut up from temptation, but now she sought liberty to venture everything. (The Quarto
reads "enur'd" for "immured" and perhaps should be "inured,"
habituated.) 254 bosoms hearts 255–6 Have . . . among have emptied all their affections into me as into a spring, and I in turn, like a
river, pour all these fountains of affection into your ocean.
257 strong victorious 258–9 Must . . . breast must as a consequence
of your victory gather together all of us (my admirers and myself) as
a compound of various ingredients applied as a medicine to cure and
thaw your resisting heart. 260 parts qualities 261 dieted in sustained by 262 they t'assail begun they (my qualities or parts) began
to assail her heart 264 potential powerful 264–5 Vow . . . confine
Against you vows have no strength (sting), bonds have no binding
force (knot), and space is no barrier or impediment (confine)
267 thou impressest you make an impression on a heart or conscript
it into your service 267–8 what . . . example? of what worth are
moralistic warnings based on stale old instances? 271 Love's . . .
shame Love's might enforces its own peace in the teeth of reason,
good sense, and decorum 272 pangs it bears pangs that it (love)
brings, the pangs that lovers must suffer 273 aloes bitter drugs,
medicines 275 break i.e., break in disappointment at the threat of
your rejecting me. bleeding groans (Each groan was thought to cost
the heart a drop of blood.) 276 supplicant as supplicants 277 leave
leave off. mine my heart

278–80 Lending . . . troth lending their support to my suit to you and
credibility to the inviolable oath that thereby guarantees the truth of
what I say. 281 dismount lower (as in dismounting an artillery
piece) 282 leveled on aimed at 285 channel . . . stream cheek to
the flow of tears 286–7 Who . . . encloses i.e., which river of tears
glazed over the cheeks (the roses) with a kind of crystal covering, in
such a way that the cheeks' rosy color shines through the water.
288 father i.e., the old man to whom she is talking 289 particular
single 293 cleft twofold. 293–4 Cold . . . hath Cold modesty
receives warmth and hot desire is cooled by such tears. 295 passion
passionate wooing. but an art merely an artifice 296 resolved dissolved 297 stole vestment. daffed doffed, put off 298 guards
defenses. civil decorous, grave 299 Appear I did appear
300 drops teardrops 302 subtle matter malleable material and cunning 303 cautels crafty devices 305 takes and leaves uses one and
avoids the other 306 In either's aptness whichever is more appropriate 307 rank gross 309 That So that. level range and aim.
(Continues the metaphor of siege.) 310 hail i.e., of artillery
311 Showing . . . tame i.e., his aim being to represent his true nature
as loving and docile

And, veiled in them, did win whom he would maim.   312
Against the thing he sought he would exclaim;   313
When he most burnt in heart-wished luxury,   314
He preached pure maid and praised cold chastity.   315

"Thus merely with the garment of a grace   316
The naked and concealèd fiend he covered,   317
That th'unexperient gave the tempter place,   318
Which like a cherubin above them hovered.   319

Who, young and simple, would not be so lovered?   320
Ay me! I fell, and yet do question make   321
What I should do again for such a sake.   322

"Oh, that infected moisture of his eye,   323
Oh, that false fire which in his cheek so glowed,   324
Oh, that forced thunder from his heart did fly,   325
Oh, that sad breath his spongy lungs bestowed,   326
Oh, all that borrowed motion seeming owed,   327
Would yet again betray the fore-betrayed,   328
And new pervert a reconcilèd maid!"   329

312 **And . . . maim** and, disguised thus in kindness and docility, or in *blushes, weeping*, and *paleness* (lines 304–5), won the heart of the woman he intended to harm.   314 **heart-wished luxury** deeply desired lechery   315 **pure maid** as if he were an untouched virgin   316 **with . . . grace** with a charming outward show or appearance. (Perhaps suggesting also one of the three Graces.)   317 **The naked . . . covered** he covered his fiendish inner self   318 **th'unexperient** the inexperienced.   **place** entry   319 **Which . . . hovered** who, resembling a cherub, hovered over his victims as though offering them protection.

320 **simple** naive.   **be so lovered** surrender to a lover like him.   321 **question make** i.e., ask myself   322 **for such a sake** for someone like him, or, for the sake of falling into such pleasure, however brief.   323 **infected** infectious   325 **forced** feigned.   **from** that from   326 **spongy lungs** lungs that are spongelike (as all lungs are; perhaps with the suggestion of "blown up with flattery and pretended grief")   327 **all . . . owed** all that passion he seemed to possess himself but had, in fact, borrowed   329 **reconcilèd** penitent

Sonnets

Shakespeare seems to have cared more about his reputation as a lyric poet than as a dramatist. He contributed to the major nondramatic genres of his day: to amatory Ovidian narrative in *Venus and Adonis,* to the Complaint in *The Rape of Lucrece,* to philosophical poetry in "The Phoenix and Turtle." He cooperated in the publication of his first two important poems, dedicating them to the young Earl of Southampton with a plea to him for sponsorship. To write poetry in this vein was more fashionable than to write plays, which one did mainly for money.

A poet with ambitions of this sort simply had to write a sonnet sequence. Sonneteering was the rage in England in the early and mid 1590s. Based on the sonneteering tradition of Francesco Petrarch, Sir Thomas Wyatt, and others, and gaining new momentum in 1591 with the publication of Sir Philip Sidney's *Astrophel and Stella,* the vogue ended almost as suddenly as it began, in 1596 or 1597. The sonnet sequences of this brief period bear the names of most well-known and minor poets of the day: *Amoretti* by Edmund Spenser (1595), *Delia* by Samuel Daniel (1591 and 1592), *Caelica* by Fulke Greville (not published until 1633), *Idea's Mirror* by Michael Drayton (1594), *Diana* by Henry Constable (1592), *Phyllis* by Thomas Lodge (1593), and the more imitative sequences of Barnabe Barnes, Giles Fletcher, William Percy, Bartholomew Griffin, William Smith, and Robert Tofte.

Shakespeare wrote sonnets during the heyday of the genre, for in 1598 Francis Meres, in his *Palladis Tamia: Wit's Treasury,* praised Shakespeare's "sugared sonnets among his private friends." Even though they were not printed at the time, we know from Meres's remark that they were circulated in manuscript among the cognoscenti and commanded respect. Shakespeare may actually have preferred to delay the publication of his sonnets, not through indifference to their literary worth, but through a desire not to seem too professional. The "courtly makers" of the English Renaissance, those gentlemen whose chivalric accomplishments were supposed to include versifying, looked on the writing of poetry as an avocation designed to amuse one's peers or to court a lady. Publication was not quite genteel, and many such authors affected dismay when their verses were pirated into print. The young wits about London of the 1590s, whether aristocratic or not, sometimes imitated this fashion. Like young John Donne, they sought the favorable verdict of their fellow wits at the Inns of Court (where young men studied law) and professed not to care about wider recognition. Whether Shakespeare was motivated in this way we do not know, but, in any event, his much-sought-after sonnet sequence was not published until 1609, long after the vogue had passed. The publisher, Thomas Thorpe, seems not to have obtained Shakespeare's authorization. Two sonnets, numbers 138 and 144, had been pirated ten years earlier by William Jaggard in *The Passionate Pilgrim,* 1599, a little anthology with some poems by Shakespeare and some wrongly attributed to him. The sonnets were not reprinted until 1640, either because the sonnet vogue had passed or because Thorpe's edition had been suppressed.

The unexplained circumstances of publication have given rise to a host of vexing and apparently unanswerable questions. Probably no puzzle in all English literature has provoked so much speculation and produced so little agreement. To whom are the sonnets addressed? Do they tell a consistent story, and, if so, do they tell us anything about Shakespeare's life? The basic difficulty is that we cannot be sure that the order in which Thorpe published the sonnets represents Shakespeare's intention, nor can we assume that Thorpe spoke for Shakespeare when he dedicated the sonnets to "Mr. W. H." As they stand, most of the first 126 sonnets appear to be addressed in warm friendship to a handsome young aristocrat, whereas sonnets 127–52 mostly speak of the poet's dark-haired mistress. Yet the last two sonnets, 153–4, seem unrelated to anything previous and cast some doubt on the reliability of the ordering. Within each large grouping of the sonnets, moreover, we find evident inconsistencies: jealousies disappear and suddenly reappear, the poet bewails his absolute rejection by the friend and then speaks a few sonnets later of harmonious affection as though nothing had happened, and so on. Some sonnets are closely linked to their predecessors; some are apparently disconnected (although even here we must allow for the real possibility that Shakespeare intends juxtaposition and contrast). We cannot be sure if the friend of sonnets 1–126 is really one person or several. We can only speculate that the unhappy love triangle described in sonnets 40–2, in which the friend has usurped the poet's mistress, can be identified with the love triangle of the "Dark Lady" sonnets, 127–52. Most readers sense a narrative continuity of the whole yet find blocks of sonnets stubbornly out of place. The temptation to rearrange the order has proved irresistible, but no alternative order has ever won acceptance. The consensus is that Thorpe's order is at times suspect but may have more rationale than at first appears. It is, in any case, the only authoritative order we have.

No less frustrating is Thorpe's dedication "To the Only Begetter of These Ensuing Sonnets, Mr. W. H." Given the late and unauthorized publication, we cannot assume that Thorpe speaks for Shakespeare. Quite possibly he is only thanking the person who obtained the sonnets for him, making publication possible. Mundanely enough, Mr. W. H. could be William Hall, an associate of Thorpe's in the publishing business. Yet Elizabethan usage affords few instances of "begetter" in this sense of "obtainer." Donald Foster has offered new and persuasive arguments for the idea that "Mr. W. H." is only a typographical error of a common sort and that Thorpe meant to say "Mr. W. S.," Master William Shakespeare. In this case, "begetter" would mean simply "creator." This solution has a wonderful neatness about it, but other readers have wondered if it answers the seeming contradiction when Thorpe speaks of "Mr. W. H." and "our ever-living poet" in the dedication as though they are two people. Thorpe offers to Mr. W. H. "that eternity promised by our ever-living poet," as though Mr. W. H. were the very subject of those sonnets whom Shakespeare vows to immortalize.

This interpretation of "begetter" as "inspirer" has prompted many enthusiasts to search for a Mr. W. H. in Shakespeare's life, a nobleman who befriended him. The chief candidates are two. First is the young Earl of Southampton, to whom Shakespeare had dedicated *Venus and Adonis* and *The Rape of Lucrece*. The dedication to the second of these poems bespeaks a warmth and gratitude that had been less evident in the first. The Earl's name, Henry Wriothesley, yields initials that are the reverse of W. H. If this correspondence seems unconvincing, W. H. could stand for Sir William Harvey, third husband of Mary, Lady Southampton, the young Earl's

mother. Some researchers would have us believe that Shakespeare wrote the sonnets for Lady Southampton, especially those urging a young man (her son) to marry and procreate. This entire case is speculative, however, and we have no evidence that Shakespeare had any dealings with Southampton after *The Rape of Lucrece*. The plain ascription "Mr. W. H." seems an oddly uncivil way for Thorpe to have addressed an earl. If meant for Southampton, the sonnets must have been written fairly early in the 1590s, for they give no hint of Southampton's later career: his courtship of Elizabeth Vernon, her pregnancy and their secret marriage in 1598, and his later involvement in Essex's Irish campaign and abortive uprising against Queen Elizabeth. Those literary sleuths who stress similarities to the Southampton relationship are too willing to overlook dissimilarities.

The next chief candidate for Mr. W. H. is William Herbert, third Earl of Pembroke, to whom, along with his brother, Shakespeare's colleagues dedicated the First Folio of 1623. In 1595, Pembroke's parents were attempting to arrange his marriage with Lady Elizabeth Carey, granddaughter of the first Lord Hunsdon, who was Lord Chamberlain and patron of Shakespeare's company. In 1597, another alliance was attempted with Bridget Vere, granddaughter of Lord Burghley. In both negotiations, young Pembroke objected to the girl in question. This hypothesis requires, however, an uncomfortably late date for the sonnets and postulates a gap in age between Shakespeare and Pembroke that would have afforded little opportunity for genuine friendship. Pembroke was only fifteen in 1595; Shakespeare was thirty-one. Besides, no evidence supports the claim other than historical coincidence. The common initials W. H. can be made to produce other candidates as well, such as the Lincolnshire lawyer named William Hatcliffe proposed (to no one's satisfaction) by Leslie Hotson. Hotson wants to date most of the sonnets before 1589, since Hatcliffe came to London in 1587–1588. When such speculations are constructed on the single enigmatic testimonial of the dedication by Thomas Thorpe, who may well have had no connection with Shakespeare, we are left with a case that would not be worth describing had it not captured the imagination of so many researchers.

Biographical identifications have also been proposed for the various personages in the sonnet sequence, predictably with no better success. The rival poet, with "the proud full sail of his great verse" (sonnet 86), has been linked to Christopher Marlowe (who died in 1593), George Chapman, and others. The sequence gives us little to go on, other than that the rival poet possesses a considerable enough talent to intimidate the author of the sonnets and to ingratiate himself with the author's aristocratic friend. No biographical circumstances resembling this rivalry have come to light. Various candidates have also been found for the "Dark Lady." One is Mary

Fitton, a lady-in-waiting at court who bore a child by Pembroke in 1601. Again, we have no evidence that Shakespeare knew her, nor is he likely to have carried on an affair with one of such high rank. A. L. Rowse has proposed Emilia Lanier, wife of Alfonso Lanier and daughter of a court musician named Bassano, a woman of suitably dark complexion perhaps but whose presumed connection with Shakespeare rests only on the reported rumor that she was a mistress of Lord Hunsdon. We are left finally without knowing who any of these people were, or whether indeed Shakespeare was attempting to be biographical at all.

The same irresolution afflicts the dating of the sonnets. Do they give hints of a personal chronicle extending over some years, following Thorpe's arrangement of the sonnets or some alternative order? Sonnet 104 speaks of three years having elapsed since the poet met his friend. Are there other signposts that relate to contemporary events? A line in sonnet 107 ("The mortal moon hath her eclipse endured") is usually linked to the death of Queen Elizabeth (known as Diana or Cynthia) in 1603, though Leslie Hotson prefers to see in it an allusion to the Spanish Armada, shaped for sea battle in a moonlike crescent when it met defeat in 1588. The newly built pyramids in sonnet 123 remind Hotson of the obelisks built by Pope Sixtus V in Rome, 1586–1589; other researchers have discovered pyramids erected on London's streets in 1603 to celebrate the coronation of James I. As these illustrations suggest, speculative dating can be used to support a hypothesis of early or late composition. The wary consensus of most scholars is that the sonnets were written over a number of years; a large number, certainly, before 1598, but some perhaps later and even up to the date of publication in 1609.

However fruitless this quest for nonexistent certainties, it does at least direct us to a meaningful critical question: should we expect sonnets of this "personal" nature to be at least partly autobiographical? Shakespeare's sonnets have struck many readers as cries from the heart, voicing at times fears of rejection, self-hatred, and humiliation, and at other times a serene gratitude for reciprocated affection. This power of expression may, however, be a tribute to Shakespeare's dramatic gift rather than evidence of personal involvement. Earlier sonnet sequences, both Elizabethan and pre-Elizabethan, had established a variety of artistic conventions that tended to displace biography. Petrarch's famous *Rime*, or sonnets, later collected in his *Canzoniere*, though addressed to Laura in two sequences (during her life and after her death), idealized her into the unapproachable lady worshiped by the self-abasing and miserable lover. Petrarch's imitators—Serafino Aquilano, Pietro Bembo, Ludovico Ariosto, and Torquato Tasso among the Italians, Clement Marot, Joachim du Bellay, Pierre de Ronsard, and Philippe Desportes among the French Pléiade—reworked these conventions in countless variations. In England, the fashion was taken up by Sir Thomas Wyatt, the Earl of Surrey, George Gascoigne, Thomas Watson, and others. Spenser's *Amoretti* and Sidney's *Astrophel and Stella,* though inspired at least in part by real women in the poets' lives, are also deeply concerned with theories of writing poetry. Rejection of the stereotyped attitudes and relationships that had come to dominate the typical Petrarchan sonnet sequence is evidence not of biographical literalism in art but of a new insistence on lifelike emotion in art; as Sidney's muse urges him, "look in thy heart and write." Thus, both the Petrarchan and the anti-Petrarchan schools avoid biographical writing for its own sake. This is essentially true of all Elizabethan sonneteering, from Drayton's serious pursuit of platonic abstraction in his *Idea's Mirror* to the facile chorusing of lesser sonnet writers about Diana, Phyllis, Zepheria, or Fidessa.

The "story" connecting the individual poems of an Elizabethan sonnet sequence is never very important or consistent, even when we can be sure of the order in which the sonnets were written. Dante had used prose links in his *La Vita Nuova* (c. 1282) to stress narrative continuity, and so had Petrarch, but this sturdy framework had been abandoned by the late sixteenth century. Rather than telling a chronological story, the typical Elizabethan sonnet sequence offers a thematically connected series of lyrical meditations, chiefly on love but also on poetic theory, the adversities of fortune, death, or what have you. The narrative events mentioned from time to time are not the substance of the sequence but the occasion for meditative reflection. Attitudes need not be consistent throughout, and the characters need not be consistently motivated like dramatis personae in a play.

Shakespeare's sonnet sequence retains these conventions of Elizabethan sonneteering and employs many archetypal situations and themes that had been explored by his predecessors and contemporaries. His emphasis on friendship seems new, for no other sequence addressed a majority of its sonnets to a friend rather than to a mistress, but even here the anti-Petrarchan quest for spontaneity and candor is in the best Elizabethan tradition of Sidney and Spenser. Besides, the exaltation of friendship over love was itself a widespread Neoplatonic commonplace recently popularized in the writings of John Lyly. Shakespeare's sequence makes use of the structural design found in contemporary models. Even though we cannot reconstruct a rigorously consistent chronological narrative from the sonnets, we can discern overall patterns out of which the poet's emotional crises arise and upon which he constructs his meditative lyrics. Certain groupings, such as the sonnets addressed to the "Dark Lady," 127–52, in which individually they comment on one another through reinforcement or antithetical design and are thus enhanced by their context, achieve a plausible cohesion; a case can be made, in other words, for the order of the poems as Thorpe printed them. Even the last two sonnets, 153 and 154, have their defenders (see Michael J. B. Allen's essay in *Shakespeare Survey*, 1978). Juxtaposition is a favorite technique in Shakespeare's plays, and we must remember that he alone among the major Elizabethan sonneteers wrote for the stage.

Taking note of such considerations, we can account for most of the situations portrayed in Shakespeare's sonnets by postulating four figures: the poet-speaker himself, his friend, his mistress, and a rival poet. The order of events in this tangled relationship is not what the poet wishes to describe; instead, he touches upon this situation from time to time as he explores his own reaction to love in its various aspects.

The poet's relationship to his friend is a vulnerable one. This friend to whom he writes is aristocratic, handsome, and younger than he is. The poet is beholden to this friend as a sponsor and must consider himself as subservient, no matter how deep their mutual affection. Even at its happiest, their relationship is hierarchical. The poet abases himself in order to extol his friend's beauty and virtues (sonnets 52–4, 105–6). He confesses that his love would be idolatry, except that the friend's goodness excels all poetic hyperbole. As the older of the two, the poet sententiously urges his young friend to marry and eternize his beauty through the engendering of children (sonnets 1–17). Such a course, he argues, is the surest way to conquer devouring Time, the enemy of all earthly beauty and love. Yet elsewhere the poet exalts his own art as the surest defense against Time (sonnets 55, 60, 63–5, etc.). These conclusions are nominally contradictory, offering procreation in one instance and poetry in another as the best hope for immortality, but thematically the two are obviously related. In even the happiest of the sonnets, such as those giving thanks for "the marriage of true minds" (116, 123), the consciousness of devouring Time is inescapable. If love and celebratory poetry can sometimes triumph over Time, the victory is all the more precious because it is achieved in the face of such odds.

Love and perfect friendship are a refuge for the poet faced with hostile fortune and an indifferent world. He is too often "in disgrace with fortune and men's eyes" (sonnet 29), oppressed by his own failings, saddened by the facile success of opportunists (sonnets 66–8), ashamed of having sold himself cheap in his own profession (sonnets 110–11). If taken biographically, this could mean that Shakespeare was not happy about his career as actor and playwright, but the motif makes complete sense in the sonnet sequence without resort to biography. A biographical reading also raises the question of homosexual attraction, as urged by Joseph Pequigney in his *Such Is My Love* (University of Chicago Press, 1985). The bawdy reference in sonnet 20.12 to the friend's possession of "one thing to my purpose nothing" would seem to militate against the idea of a consummated homosexual relationship, while conversely many sonnets (such as 138) do point to the poet's consummation with his mistress. Still, the bond between poet and friend is extraordinarily strong, and certainly there is a danger that traditional scholarship has minimized the erotic bond between the poet and his friend out of a distaste for the idea. Occasional absences torture the poet with the physical separation, even though he realizes that pure love of the spirit ought not to be hampered by distance or time (sonnets 43–51). The absence is especially painful when the poet must confess his own disloyalty (sonnets 117–18). The chronology of these absences cannot be worked out satisfactorily, but the haunting theme of separation is incessant and overwhelming. By extension, it includes the fear of separation through death (sonnets 71–3, 126). The concern with absence is closely related to the poet's obsession with devouring Time.

All the poet's misfortunes would be bearable if love were constant, but his dependency on the aristocratic friend leaves him at the mercy of that friend's changeable moods. The poet must not complain when his wellborn friend entertains a rival poet (sonnets 78–86) or forms other emotional attachments, even with the poet's own mistress (sonnets 40–2). These disloyalties evoke outbursts of jealousy. The poet vacillates between forgiveness and recrimination. Sometimes even his forgiveness is self-loathing, in which the poet confesses he would take back the friend on any terms (sonnets 93–5). At times the poet grovels, conceding that he deserves no better treatment (sonnets 57–8), but at other times his stored-up resentment bursts forth (sonnets 93–5). The poet's fears, though presented in no clear chronological order, run the gamut from a fatalistic sense that rejection will come one day (sonnet 49) to an abject and bitter final farewell (sonnet 87). Sometimes he is tormented by jealousy (sonnet 61) and sometimes by self-hate (sonnets 88–9).

The sonnets addressed to the poet's mistress, the "Dark Lady," similarly convey fear, self-abasement, and a panicky awareness of loss of self-control. In rare moments of happiness, the poet praises her dark features as proof of her being a real woman, not a Petrarchan goddess (sonnet 130). Too often, however, her lack of ideal beauty reminds the poet of his irrational enchantment (sonnets 148–50). She is tyrannous, disdainful, spiteful, disloyal, a "female evil" (sonnet 144) who has tempted away from the poet his better self, his friend. The poet is distressed not so much by her perfidy as by his own self-betrayal; he sees bitterly that he offends his nobler reason by his attachment to the rebellious flesh. He worships what others abhor and perjures himself by swearing to what he knows to be false (sonnets 150–2). His only hope for escape is to punish his flesh and renounce the vanity of all worldly striving (sonnet 146), but this solution evades him as he plunges helplessly back into the perverse enslavement of a sickened appetite.

This sketch of only some themes of the sequence may suggest the range and yet the interconnection of Shakespeare's meditations on love, friendship, and poetry. Patterns are visible, even if the exact chronology (never important in the Elizabethan sonnet sequence) cannot be determined. The pattern suggests a pivotal role for the sonnets in Shakespeare's development, as Richard Wheeler has urged in his *Shakespeare's Development* (University of California Press, 1981): the early sonnets about love and marriage pursue relationships central to the comedies, whereas subsequent sonnets move with increasing intensity toward the portrayal of promiscuity and degradation in erotic love and toward new assaults upon the binding power of friendship in such a way as to anticipate the darker vision of the tragedies. The playful and unthreatening heroine of the comedies gives way to a dark lady who inspires in the poet a compulsive and humiliating self-hatred; mutuality in friendship finds itself threatened by a one-sided relationship in which the abasement of the poet is answered by the indifference and infidelity of the friend. It as though in the sonnets Shakespeare opened the Pandora's box of hazardous erotic entanglements he was to dramatize in his late plays.

Shakespeare's concern with patterning is equally evident in matters of versification and imagery. The sonnets are written throughout in the "Shakespearean" or English form, *abab cdcd efef gg*. (Sonnet 126, written entirely in couplets, is an exception, perhaps because it was intended as the envoi to the series addressed to the poet's friend.) This familiar sonnet form, introduced by Wyatt and developed by Sidney, differs markedly from the octave-sestet division of the Petrarchan, or Italian, sonnet. The English form of three quatrains and a concluding couplet lends itself to a step-by-step development of idea and image, culminating in an epigrammatic two-line conclusion that may summarize the thought of the preceding twelve lines or give a sentMAtious interpretation of the images developed up to this point. Sonnet 7 pursues the image of the sun at morning, noon, and evening through three quatrains, one for each phase of the day, and then in the couplet "applies" the image to the friend's unwillingness to beget children. Sonnet 29 moves from resentment of misfortune to a rejoicing in the friend's love and rhetorically mirrors this sudden elevation of mood in the image of the lark "at break of day arising / From sullen earth." Shakespeare's rhetorical and imagistic devices exploit the sonnet structure he inherited and perfected, and remind us again of the strong element of convention and artifice in these supremely "personal" sonnets. The recurring images—the canker on the rose, the pleading of a case at law, the seasonal rhythms of summer and winter, the alternations of day and night, the harmonies and dissonances of music—also testify to the artistic unity of the whole and to the artist's extraordinary discipline in evoking a sense of helpless loss of self-control.

Sonnets

To the Only Begetter of These Ensuing Sonnets

Mr. W. H.

All Happiness and That Eternity Promised
    by Our Ever-living Poet
Wisheth the Well-wishing Adventurer in
    Setting Forth

                                                    T. T.

1

From fairest creatures we desire increase,
That thereby beauty's rose might never die,
But as the riper should by time decease,
His tender heir might bear his memory;
But thou, contracted to thine own bright eyes,   4
Feed'st thy light's flame with self-substantial fuel,
Making a famine where abundance lies,
Thyself thy foe, to thy sweet self too cruel.
Thou that art now the world's fresh ornament   8
And only herald to the gaudy spring,
Within thine own bud buriest thy content,
And, tender churl, mak'st waste in niggarding.
    Pity the world, or else this glutton be: 12
    To eat the world's due, by the grave and thee.

2

When forty winters shall besiege thy brow
And dig deep trenches in thy beauty's field,

Thy youth's proud livery, so gazed on now,
Will be a tattered weed, of small worth held.   4
Then being asked where all thy beauty lies,
Where all the treasure of thy lusty days,
To say within thine own deep-sunken eyes
Were an all-eating shame and thriftless praise.   8
How much more praise deserved thy beauty's use
If thou couldst answer, "This fair child of mine
Shall sum my count and make my old excuse,"
Proving his beauty by succession thine.   12
    This were to be new made when thou art old,
    And see thy blood warm when thou feel'st it cold.

3

Look in thy glass, and tell the face thou viewest
Now is the time that face should form another,
Whose fresh repair if now thou not renewest
Thou dost beguile the world, unless some mother.   4
For where is she so fair whose uneared womb
Disdains the tillage of thy husbandry?
Or who is he so fond will be the tomb
Of his self-love, to stop posterity?   8
Thou art thy mother's glass, and she in thee
Calls back the lovely April of her prime;
So thou through windows of thine age shalt see,
Despite of wrinkles, this thy golden time.   12
    But if thou live remembered not to be,
    Die single, and thine image dies with thee.

3 proud livery handsome garments   **4 weed** garment. (With a play on a *weed* growing in *beauty's field*, line 2.)   **6 lusty** (1) vigorous (2) lustful   **8 Were . . . praise** would be a shameful admission of gluttony and praise of idle extravagance.   **9 deserved . . . use** would be the proper investment and employment of your beauty deserve   **11 Shall . . . excuse** will balance my account and make amends in my old age   **12 thine** derived from you.   **13 were** would be
3.1 glass mirror   **3 fresh repair** youthful condition   **4 beguile** cheat. **unless some mother** withhold the happiness of childbearing from some woman.   **5 uneared** untilled, uncultivated   **6 husbandry** cultivation. (With obvious suggestion of "playing the husband.")   **7 fond** foolish, (self-)loving.   **will be** i.e., that he is willing to be   **9 thy mother's glass** the image of your mother   **11–12 So . . . time** in just the same way, you, looking through eyes dimmed by advancing years, and despite your own wrinkles of age, will see in your child an image of your own happy youth.   **13 remembered not to be** in such a way as not to be remembered, without children

---

1.1 increase procreation   **3 as** just as, while   **4 His** its, the ripening creation (including the young man).   **bear his memory** i.e., immortalize it by bearing its features   **5 contracted** (1) engaged, espoused (2) shrunk   **6 self-substantial** of your own substance   **10 only herald** to principal or unique messenger of   **11 thy content** (1) that which is contained in you; potential fatherhood (2) your contentment   **12 mak'st . . . niggarding** squander your substance by being miserly. (An oxymoron, like *tender churl*, "youthful old miser.")   **14 the world's due** i.e., the offspring you owe to posterity.   **by . . . thee** (consumed) by death and by your willfully remaining childless.
2.2 trenches i.e., wrinkles.   **field** (1) meadow (2) battlefield (3) heraldic background

4

Unthrifty loveliness, why dost thou spend
Upon thyself thy beauty's legacy?
Nature's bequest gives nothing, but doth lend,
And being frank she lends to those are free.   4
Then, beauteous niggard, why dost thou abuse
The bounteous largess given thee to give?
Profitless usurer, why dost thou use
So great a sum of sums, yet canst not live?   8
For having traffic with thyself alone,
Thou of thyself thy sweet self dost deceive.
Then how, when Nature calls thee to be gone,
What acceptable audit canst thou leave?   12
      Thy unused beauty must be tombed with thee,
      Which, usèd, lives th'executor to be.

5

Those hours, that with gentle work did frame
The lovely gaze where every eye doth dwell,
Will play the tyrants to the very same
And that unfair which fairly doth excel;   4
For never-resting Time leads summer on
To hideous winter and confounds him there,
Sap checked with frost and lusty leaves quite gone,
Beauty o'ersnowed and bareness everywhere.   8
Then, were not summer's distillation left
A liquid prisoner pent in walls of glass,
Beauty's effect with beauty were bereft,
Nor it nor no remembrance what it was.   12
      But flowers distilled, though they with winter meet,
      Leese but their show; their substance still lives sweet.

6

Then let not winter's ragged hand deface
In thee thy summer ere thou be distilled.
Make sweet some vial; treasure thou some place
With beauty's treasure ere it be self-killed.   4
That use is not forbidden usury
Which happies those that pay the willing loan;
That's for thyself to breed another thee,

Or ten times happier, be it ten for one.   8
Ten times thyself were happier than thou art,
If ten of thine ten times refigured thee;
Then what could death do, if thou shouldst depart,
Leaving thee living in posterity?   12
      Be not self-willed, for thou art much too fair
      To be death's conquest and make worms thine heir.

7

Lo, in the orient when the gracious light
Lifts up his burning head, each under eye
Doth homage to his new-appearing sight,
Serving with looks his sacred majesty;   4
And having climbed the steep-up heavenly hill,
Resembling strong youth in his middle age,
Yet mortal looks adore his beauty still,
Attending on his golden pilgrimage;   8
But when from highmost pitch, with weary car,
Like feeble age, he reeleth from the day,
The eyes, 'fore duteous, now converted are
From his low tract and look another way.   12
      So thou, thyself outgoing in thy noon,
      Unlooked on diest, unless thou get a son.

8

Music to hear, why hear'st thou music sadly?
Sweets with sweets war not, joy delights in joy.
Why lov'st thou that which thou receiv'st not gladly,
Or else receiv'st with pleasure thine annoy?   4
If the true concord of well-tunèd sounds,
By unions married, do offend thine ear,
They do but sweetly chide thee, who confounds
In singleness the parts that thou shouldst bear.   8
Mark how one string, sweet husband to another,
Strikes each in each by mutual ordering,
Resembling sire and child and happy mother
Who, all in one, one pleasing note do sing;   12
      Whose speechless song, being many, seeming one,
      Sings this to thee: "Thou single wilt prove none."

4.1 Unthrifty (1) Prodigal (2) Unavailing   **2 thy beauty's legacy** the
beauty you inherited (and should pass on to your children).   **4 frank**
liberal, bounteous.   **are free** who are generous.   **7 use** (1) use up
(2) fail to invest for profit. (See sonnet 6.5 and note.)   **8 live** (1) have a
livelihood (2) live in your posterity.   **9 traffic** commerce. (The commercial and financial metaphor hints at sexual self-fascination.)
10 deceive cheat.   **13 unused** (1) unemployed (2) not invested for
profit   **14 lives** would live (in your son)
5.1 frame make   **2 gaze** object of gazes   **3 play . . . to** oppress
4 unfair make unlovely.   **fairly** (1) in beauty (2) truly, honestly
5 leads summer on (1) guides the steps of summer (2) lures summer
6 confounds destroys   **7 lusty** vigorous   **9 summer's distillation**
distilled perfume of flowers   **10 walls of glass** glass containers
11 with . . . bereft would be lost along with beauty itself   **12 Nor it
nor no** (leaving behind) neither it (beauty) nor any   **14 Leese** lose.
still (1) notwithstanding (2) always
6.1 ragged rough   **3 vial** (With suggestion of a womb.)   **treasure** enrich
5 use lending money at interest   **6 happies** makes happy.   **pay . . .
loan** willingly borrow on these terms and repay the loan   **7 That's . . .
thee** i.e., such would be the case if you were to sire a child like you

8 Or . . . one i.e., or indeed the happy mother (of line 6) would be ten
times happier were she to bear you ten children instead of one. (*Ten
for one* alludes to the highest legal rate of interest, one for ten.)
9 Ten . . . art i.e., Ten children of yours would be a tenfold blessing
and would make you happier   **10 refigured** duplicated, copied (producing one hundred grandchildren)   **13 self-willed** (1) obstinate
(2) bequeathed to self
7.1 orient east.   **light** i.e., sun   **2 under** earthly   **9 pitch** highest
point (as of a falcon's flight before it attacks).   **car** chariot (of the sun-
god)   **11 converted** turned away   **12 tract** course   **14 get** beget
8.1 Music to hear i.e., You whom it is music to hear.   **2 Sweets** Sweet
things   **3–4 Why . . . annoy?** Why do you not gladly love the sweet
things you hear, or find irksome that which is pleasurable?   **6 By
unions married** perfectly blended in harmonious chords   **7–8 who . . .
bear** you who destroy, by playing a single part only, the harmony
(i.e., marriage) that you should sustain.   **9 sweet husband** i.e.,
paired, as on the double strings of the lute, one string vibrating sympathetically to the other   **10 each in each** i.e., with double resonance,
sounding mutually   **13 Whose** i.e., the strings'.   **being . . . one** i.e.,
making harmony out of several voices   **14 Thou . . . none** (Alludes to
the proverb, "One is no number." The single person who dies without
posterity leaves nothing of himself behind.)

9

Is it for fear to wet a widow's eye
That thou consum'st thyself in single life?
Ah, if thou issueless shalt hap to die,
The world will wail thee like a makeless wife.   4
The world will be thy widow and still weep
That thou no form of thee hast left behind,
When every private widow well may keep,
By children's eyes, her husband's shape in mind.   8
Look what an unthrift in the world doth spend
Shifts but his place, for still the world enjoys it;
But beauty's waste hath in the world an end,
And, kept unused, the user so destroys it.   12
　　No love toward others in that bosom sits
　　That on himself such murd'rous shame commits.

10

For shame, deny that thou bear'st love to any,
Who for thyself art so unprovident!
Grant, if thou wilt, thou art beloved of many,
But that thou none lov'st is most evident;   4
For thou art so possessed with murd'rous hate
That 'gainst thyself thou stick'st not to conspire,
Seeking that beauteous roof to ruinate
Which to repair should be thy chief desire.   8
Oh, change thy thought, that I may change my mind!
Shall hate be fairer lodged than gentle love?
Be, as thy presence is, gracious and kind,
Or to thyself at least kindhearted prove: 12
　　Make thee another self, for love of me,
　　That beauty still may live in thine or thee.

11

As fast as thou shalt wane, so fast thou grow'st
In one of thine from that which thou departest;
And that fresh blood which youngly thou bestow'st
Thou mayst call thine when thou from youth convertest.   4
Herein lives wisdom, beauty, and increase;
Without this, folly, age, and cold decay.
If all were minded so, the times should cease
And threescore year would make the world away.   8
Let those whom Nature hath not made for store,
Harsh, featureless, and rude, barrenly perish;

Look whom she best endowed she gave the more,
Which bounteous gift thou shouldst in bounty cherish.   12
　　She carved thee for her seal, and meant thereby
　　Thou shouldst print more, not let that copy die.

12

When I do count the clock that tells the time,
And see the brave day sunk in hideous night;
When I behold the violet past prime,
And sable curls all silvered o'er with white;   4
When lofty trees I see barren of leaves
Which erst from heat did canopy the herd,
And summer's green, all girded up in sheaves,
Borne on the bier with white and bristly beard,   8
Then of thy beauty do I question make
That thou among the wastes of time must go,
Since sweets and beauties do themselves forsake
And die as fast as they see others grow;   12
　　And nothing 'gainst Time's scythe can make defense
　　Save breed, to brave him when he takes thee hence.

13

Oh, that you were yourself! But, love, you are
No longer yours than you yourself here live.
Against this coming end you should prepare,
And your sweet semblance to some other give.   4
So should that beauty which you hold in lease
Find no determination; then you were
Yourself again after yourself's decease,
When your sweet issue your sweet form should bear.   8
Who lets so fair a house fall to decay,
Which husbandry in honor might uphold
Against the stormy gusts of winter's day
And barren rage of death's eternal cold?   12
　　Oh, none but unthrifts! Dear my love, you know
　　You had a father; let your son say so.

14

Not from the stars do I my judgment pluck,
And yet methinks I have astronomy—
But not to tell of good or evil luck,
Of plagues, of dearths, or seasons' quality;   4
Nor can I fortune to brief minutes tell,
'Pointing to each his thunder, rain, and wind,

Or say with princes if it shall go well
By oft predict that I in heaven find.
But from thine eyes my knowledge I derive,
And, constant stars, in them I read such art
As truth and beauty shall together thrive
If from thyself to store thou wouldst convert.
      Or else of thee this I prognosticate:
      Thy end is truth's and beauty's doom and date.

15

When I consider every thing that grows
Holds in perfection but a little moment,
That this huge stage presenteth naught but shows
Whereon the stars in secret influence comment;
When I perceive that men as plants increase,
Cheerèd and checked even by the selfsame sky,
Vaunt in their youthful sap, at height decrease,
And wear their brave state out of memory;
Then the conceit of this inconstant stay
Sets you most rich in youth before my sight,
Where wasteful Time debateth with Decay
To change your day of youth to sullied night;
      And, all in war with Time for love of you,
      As he takes from you I engraft you new.

16

But wherefore do not you a mightier way
Make war upon this bloody tyrant, Time,
And fortify yourself in your decay
With means more blessèd than my barren rhyme?
Now stand you on the top of happy hours,
And many maiden gardens yet unset
With virtuous wish would bear your living flowers,
Much liker than your painted counterfeit.
So should the lines of life that life repair
Which this time's pencil, or my pupil pen,
Neither in inward worth nor outward fair
Can make you live yourself in eyes of men.
      To give away yourself keeps yourself still,
      And you must live, drawn by your own sweet skill.

17

Who will believe my verse in time to come
If it were filled with your most high deserts?
Though yet, heaven knows, it is but as a tomb
Which hides your life and shows not half your parts.
If I could write the beauty of your eyes
And in fresh numbers number all your graces,
The age to come would say, "This poet lies;
Such heavenly touches ne'er touched earthly faces."
So should my papers, yellowed with their age,
Be scorned like old men of less truth than tongue,
And your true rights be termed a poet's rage
And stretchèd meter of an antique song.
      But were some child of yours alive that time,
      You should live twice, in it and in my rhyme.

18

Shall I compare thee to a summer's day?
Thou art more lovely and more temperate.
Rough winds do shake the darling buds of May,
And summer's lease hath all too short a date.
Sometime too hot the eye of heaven shines,
And often is his gold complexion dimmed;
And every fair from fair sometimes declines,
By chance or nature's changing course untrimmed.
But thy eternal summer shall not fade
Nor lose possession of that fair thou ow'st;
Nor shall Death brag thou wand'r'st in his shade,
When in eternal lines to time thou grow'st.
      So long as men can breathe or eyes can see,
      So long lives this, and this gives life to thee.

19

Devouring Time, blunt thou the lion's paws,
And make the earth devour her own sweet brood;
Pluck the keen teeth from the fierce tiger's jaws,
And burn the long-lived phoenix in her blood;
Make glad and sorry seasons as thou fleet'st,
And do whate'er thou wilt, swift-footed Time,
To the wide world and all her fading sweets.
But I forbid thee one most heinous crime:
Oh, carve not with thy hours my love's fair brow,
Nor draw no lines there with thine antique pen;
Him in thy course untainted do allow
For beauty's pattern to succeeding men.

---

7 **Or . . . well** or say if things will go well for certain rulers   8 **oft predict** frequent predictions   10–11 **read . . . As** gather such learning as, in effect, that   12 **store** replenishment (through the begetting of children). **convert** turn.   14 **doom and date** limit of duration, destruction.
15.2 **Holds in perfection** maintains its prime   3 **stage** i.e., the world   5 **as** like   6 **Cheerèd and checked** (1) urged on, nourished, and held back, starved (2) applauded and hissed   7 **Vaunt** boast, exult.   **sap** vigor.   **at height decrease** i.e., no sooner reach full maturity but they (humans) start to decline   8 **brave** splendid.   **out of memory** until forgotten   9 **conceit** notion.   **inconstant stay** mutable brief time (on earth)   11 **debateth** competes   13 **all in war** I, fighting with might and main   14 **engraft you new** renew you by grafting, infusing new life into you (by means of my verse).
16.4 **barren** (1) unable to produce offspring (2) poetically sterile   6 **unset** (1) unplanted (2) unimpregnated   7 **virtuous wish** desire that is still chaste   8 **liker** more resembling you.   **painted** rendered by art (including poetry), artificial.   **counterfeit** portrait.   9 **lines of life** lineage, i.e., children (whose lineaments are more lifelike than lines of verse or of a portrait)   10 **this time's pencil** a portraiture done in this present age.   **pupil** apprenticed, inexpert   11 **fair** beauty   12 **live** survive as   13 **give away yourself** i.e., marry and beget children.   **keeps** preserves   14 **skill** i.e., artistry in reproducing yourself, mightier than the poet's pen.

17.3 **yet** as yet   4 **parts** qualities.   6 **numbers** verses   10 **of . . . tongue** more garrulous than truthful   11 **rage** exaggerated inspiration   12 **stretchèd meter** overstrained poetry, poetic license
18.4 **lease** allotted time.   **date** duration.   5 **eye** i.e., sun   7 **fair from fair** beautiful thing from beauty   8 **untrimmed** stripped of ornament and beauty.   10 **fair thou ow'st** beauty you own   12 **lines** i.e., of poetry.   **to . . . grow'st** you become incorporated into time, engrafted upon it.   14 **this** i.e., this sonnet
19.4 **phoenix** legendary bird reputed to live for hundreds of years and then to be consumed alive (*in her blood*) in its own ashes, from which it is then reborn   5 **sorry** i.e., miserable, uncomfortable.   **thou fleet'st** you fleet, hurry   10 **antique** (1) old (2) antic, capricious, fantastic   11 **untainted** unsullied; uninjured

Yet, do thy worst, old Time. Despite thy wrong,
My love shall in my verse ever live young.

20

A woman's face with Nature's own hand painted
Hast thou, the master-mistress of my passion;
A woman's gentle heart, but not acquainted
With shifting change, as is false women's fashion;   4
An eye more bright than theirs, less false in rolling,
Gilding the object whereupon it gazeth;
A man in hue, all hues in his controlling,
Which steals men's eyes and women's souls amazeth.   8
And for a woman wert thou first created,
Till Nature, as she wrought thee, fell a-doting,
And by addition me of thee defeated,
By adding one thing to my purpose nothing.   12
   But since she pricked thee out for women's pleasure,
   Mine be thy love and thy love's use their treasure.

21

So is it not with me as with that muse,
Stirred by a painted beauty to his verse,
Who heaven itself for ornament doth use
And every fair with his fair doth rehearse,   4
Making a couplement of proud compare
With sun and moon, with earth and sea's rich gems,
With April's firstborn flowers, and all things rare
That heaven's air in this huge rondure hems.   8
Oh, let me, true in love, but truly write,
And then, believe me, my love is as fair
As any mother's child, though not so bright
As those gold candles fixed in heaven's air.   12
   Let them say more that like of hearsay well;
   I will not praise that purpose not to sell.

22

My glass shall not persuade me I am old
So long as youth and thou are of one date;
But when in thee Time's furrows I behold,
Then look I death my days should expiate.   4
For all that beauty that doth cover thee
Is but the seemly raiment of my heart,
Which in thy breast doth live, as thine in me.
How can I then be elder than thou art?   8
Oh, therefore, love, be of thyself so wary
As I, not for myself, but for thee will,
Bearing thy heart, which I will keep so chary
As tender nurse her babe from faring ill.   12
   Presume not on thy heart when mine is slain;
   Thou gav'st me thine, not to give back again.

23

As an unperfect actor on the stage
Who with his fear is put beside his part,
Or some fierce thing replete with too much rage,
Whose strength's abundance weakens his own heart,   4
So I, for fear of trust, forget to say
The perfect ceremony of love's rite,
And in mine own love's strength seem to decay,
O'ercharged with burden of mine own love's might.   8
Oh, let my books be then the eloquence
And dumb presagers of my speaking breast,
Who plead for love and look for recompense
More than that tongue that more hath more expressed.   12
   Oh, learn to read what silent love hath writ.
   To hear with eyes belongs to love's fine wit.

24

Mine eye hath played the painter and hath stelled
Thy beauty's form in table of my heart;
My body is the frame wherein 'tis held,
And perspective it is best painter's art.   4
For through the painter must you see his skill

---

14 My love (1) my beloved (2) my affection for him
20.1 with . . . hand i.e., naturally beautiful   **2 master-mistress** i.e.,
both master and mistress, male and female.   **passion** love   **4 as . . .
fashion** as is the way with women, who are false by nature
5 rolling i.e., roving   **6 Gilding** causing to shine brightly   **7 A man
. . . controlling** one who has a manly appearance surpassing all other
forms. (Suggesting, too, that he captivates all beholders and that his
hue is womanly as well as manly.)   **10 fell a-doting** fell infatuated
in love with you and so went mildly crazy   **11 defeated** defrauded,
deprived   **12 to my purpose nothing** out of line with my wishes
13 pricked designated. (With bawdy suggestion; the *thing* in line 12
is a phallus.)   **for women's pleasure** to give (sexual) pleasure to
women   **14 Mine . . . treasure** I will have your love in the truest
sense, while women will enjoy you sexually and bear you children.
(Expressed as a metaphor of financial capital or principal, which
belongs to the poet, versus the *use* or interest, which belongs to
women.)
21.1 muse i.e., poet   **2 Stirred** inspired.   **painted** artificial, created
by cosmetics   **3 Who . . . use** who does not scruple to invoke heaven
itself as an ornament of praise for his mistress   **4 every . . . rehearse**
compares his lady fair with every lovely thing   **5 Making . . . compare** joining (her) in proud comparison   **8 rondure** sphere.   **hems**
encloses, encircles.   **12 gold candles** i.e., stars. (The trite and exaggerated metaphor is of the sort the poet hopes to eschew.)   **13 like . . .
well** like to deal in secondhand or trite expressions   **14 I will . . . sell**
I, who do not intend to sell as a merchant might, will accordingly not
indulge in extravagant and empty praise.

22.1 glass mirror   **2 of one date** of an age, i.e., young   **4 look I** I
foresee that.   **expiate** end.   **5–7 For . . . me** Since my heart dwells in
your breast (and yours in mine), your beauty is in effect a becoming
cover for my heart.   **10 will** i.e., will take wary care of myself for
your sake   **11 Bearing** since I bear.   **chary** carefully   **13 Presume . . .
slain** Do not expect to receive back your heart when mine is slain (as
would happen if you were to stop loving me)
23.1 unperfect one who has not learned his lines sufficiently   **2 is . . .
part** forgets his lines   **3 Or . . . rage** i.e., or some wild creature overfilled with ungovernable rage   **4 Whose . . . heart** whose excess of
emotion collapses on itself   **5 for . . . trust** mistrusting myself and
fearful of not being trusted.   **forget** forget how   **9 books** (Possibly
refers to the sonnets or to *Venus and Adonis* and *The Rape of Lucrece* or,
more generally, the works of the persona poet.)   **10 dumb presagers**
silent messengers or presenters   **12 that tongue** the tongue of some
rival speaker.   **more hath more expressed** has more often or more
fully said more.   **14 fine wit** sharp intelligence.
24.1 played acted the part of.   **stelled** fixed, installed; or perhaps steeled,
i.e., engraved. (The Quarto reads "steeld.")   **2 table** tablet, wooden panel
used for painting   **3 frame** (1) picture frame (2) bodily frame   **4 perspective** an artist's method of producing a distorted picture that looks
right only from an oblique point of view; or, a painter's technique used
to produce the illusion of reality; or, the science of optics   **5 For . . .
skill** i.e., You must look through the eyes of me, the skillful painter

To find where your true image pictured lies,
Which in my bosom's shop is hanging still,
That hath his windows glazèd with thine eyes.   8
Now see what good turns eyes for eyes have done:
Mine eyes have drawn thy shape, and thine for me
Are windows to my breast, wherethrough the sun
Delights to peep, to gaze therein on thee.   12
    Yet eyes this cunning want to grace their art:
    They draw but what they see, know not the heart.

25

Let those who are in favor with their stars
Of public honor and proud titles boast,
Whilst I, whom fortune of such triumph bars,
Unlooked for joy in that I honor most.   4
Great princes' favorites their fair leaves spread
But as the marigold at the sun's eye,
And in themselves their pride lies burièd,
For at a frown they in their glory die.   8
The painful warrior famousèd for fight,
After a thousand victories once foiled,
Is from the book of honor rasèd quite,
And all the rest forgot for which he toiled.   12
    Then happy I, that love and am beloved
    Where I may not remove nor be removed.

26

Lord of my love, to whom in vassalage
Thy merit hath my duty strongly knit,
To thee I send this written embassage
To witness duty, not to show my wit—   4
Duty so great, which wit so poor as mine
May make seem bare, in wanting words to show it,
But that I hope some good conceit of thine
In thy soul's thought, all naked, will bestow it;   8
Till whatsoever star that guides my moving
Points on me graciously with fair aspect,
And puts apparel on my tattered loving
To show me worthy of thy sweet respect.   12
    Then may I dare to boast how I do love thee;
    Till then not show my head where thou mayst prove
    me.

27

Weary with toil, I haste me to my bed,
The dear repose for limbs with travel tirèd;
But then begins a journey in my head,
To work my mind when body's work's expirèd.   4
For then my thoughts, from far where I abide,
Intend a zealous pilgrimage to thee,
And keep my drooping eyelids open wide,
Looking on darkness which the blind do see;   8
Save that my soul's imaginary sight
Presents thy shadow to my sightless view,
Which, like a jewel hung in ghastly night,
Makes black night beauteous and her old face new.   12
    Lo, thus by day my limbs, by night my mind,
    For thee and for myself no quiet find.

28

How can I then return in happy plight
That am debarred the benefit of rest?
When day's oppression is not eased by night,
But day by night, and night by day, oppressed?   4
And each, though enemies to either's reign,
Do in consent shake hands to torture me,
The one by toil, the other to complain
How far I toil, still farther off from thee.   8
I tell the day, to please him, thou art bright
And dost him grace when clouds do blot the heaven;
So flatter I the swart-complexioned night,
When sparkling stars twire not, thou gild'st th' even.   12
    But day doth daily draw my sorrows longer,
    And night doth nightly make grief's strength seem
    stronger.

29

When, in disgrace with fortune and men's eyes,
I all alone beweep my outcast state,
And trouble deaf heaven with my bootless cries,
And look upon myself and curse my fate,   4
Wishing me like to one more rich in hope,
Featured like him, like him with friends possessed,
Desiring this man's art and that man's scope,

---

7 bosom's shop i.e., heart **8 his** its. **glazèd** fitted with glass, paned.
(The friend, looking into the poet's eyes where his own eyes are
reflected, sees into the poet's heart.) **13 this cunning want** lack this
skill. **grace** enhance **14 know not** do not perceive the thoughts of
25.3 of from **4 Unlooked for** (1) unexpectedly (2) out of the public
eye. **that** that which **5 their ... spread** i.e., flourish, blossom, prosper **6 But** only **7 lies burièd** i.e., will die with the ending of their
brief glory **8 a frown** (1) a prince's frown (2) a cloud obscuring the
sun **9 painful** enduring much, striving. **famousèd** renowned.
fight (Reads "worth" in the 1609 Quarto; some editors retain and
emend "quite" in line 11 to "forth." Other editors prefer "might.")
11 rasèd erased (or **razèd**, scraped out) **12 the rest** i.e., his *thousand
victories* **14 remove** i.e., be unfaithful. **removed** i.e., removed from
favor.
26.1 vassalage allegiance **4 witness** bear witness to. **wit** skill, literary ingenuity **5 wit** intelligence and skill **6 wanting** lacking
7 good conceit good conception, favorable opinion **8 all naked** i.e.,
poor verse though it is. **bestow** give lodging to **9 moving** life and
deeds **10 Points on** directs its rays at. **aspect** influence (as of a
star) **14 prove** test

27.2 travel (With connotation also of *travail*; spelled "trauaill" in the
Quarto.) **5 from far** i.e., far away from you **6 Intend** (1) set out
upon (2) have purposefully in mind **8 Looking ... see** while my
thoughts try to peer (toward you) through the darkness, like the
blind, who see only darkness **9 Save** except **10 thy shadow** the
image of you **14 For** on account of
28.4 But ... oppressed i.e., but experiencing sleeplessness at night
and fatigue during the day. **6 in ... hands** i.e., come to a mutual
agreement **7 the other to complain** i.e., the night by causing me to
complain **10 And ... heaven** i.e., and that you shine in place of the
sun when the sun is overclouded **11 So flatter I** similarly I gratify.
swart dark **12 When ... even** i.e., by saying that, when sparkling
stars do not twinkle or peep out, you make bright the evening.
29.3 bootless useless **4 look upon myself** consider my predicament **5 more rich in hope** with better prospects of success
6 Featured formed, i.e., having good looks. **like him, like him** like
a second man, like a third **7 art** literary skill, learning. **scope**
range of powers

With what I most enjoy contented least;   8
Yet in these thoughts myself almost despising,
Haply I think on thee, and then my state,
Like to the lark at break of day arising
From sullen earth, sings hymns at heaven's gate;   12
> For thy sweet love remembered such wealth brings
> That then I scorn to change my state with kings.

30

When to the sessions of sweet silent thought
I summon up remembrance of things past,
I sigh the lack of many a thing I sought,
And with old woes new wail my dear time's waste.   4
Then can I drown an eye, unused to flow,
For precious friends hid in death's dateless night,
And weep afresh love's long-since-canceled woe,
And moan th'expense of many a vanished sight.   8
Then can I grieve at grievances foregone,
And heavily from woe to woe tell o'er
The sad account of fore-bemoanèd moan,
Which I new pay as if not paid before.   12
> But if the while I think on thee, dear friend,
> All losses are restored and sorrows end.

31

Thy bosom is endearèd with all hearts
Which I by lacking have supposèd dead,
And there reigns love and all love's loving parts,
And all those friends which I thought burièd.   4
How many a holy and obsequious tear
Hath dear religious love stol'n from mine eye
As interest of the dead, which now appear
But things removed that hidden in thee lie!   8
Thou art the grave where buried love doth live,
Hung with the trophies of my lovers gone,
Who all their parts of me to thee did give;
That due of many now is thine alone.   12
> Their images I loved I view in thee,
> And thou, all they, hast all the all of me.

32

If thou survive my well-contented day
When that churl Death my bones with dust shall cover,
And shalt by fortune once more re-survey
These poor rude lines of thy deceasèd lover,   4
Compare them with the bett'ring of the time,
And though they be outstripped by every pen,
Reserve them for my love, not for their rhyme,
Exceeded by the height of happier men.   8
Oh, then vouchsafe me but this loving thought:
"Had my friend's Muse grown with this growing age,
A dearer birth than this his love had brought
To march in ranks of better equipage;   12
> But since he died and poets better prove,
> Theirs for their style I'll read, his for his love."

33

Full many a glorious morning have I seen
Flatter the mountaintops with sovereign eye,
Kissing with golden face the meadows green,
Gilding pale streams with heavenly alchemy;   4
Anon permit the basest clouds to ride
With ugly rack on his celestial face,
And from the forlorn world his visage hide,
Stealing unseen to west with this disgrace.   8
Even so my sun one early morn did shine
With all-triumphant splendor on my brow.
But out, alack! He was but one hour mine;
The region cloud hath masked him from me now.   12
> Yet him for this my love no whit disdaineth;
> Suns of the world may stain when heaven's sun
>   staineth.

34

Why didst thou promise such a beauteous day
And make me travel forth without my cloak,
To let base clouds o'ertake me in my way,
Hiding thy brav'ry in their rotten smoke?   4
'Tis not enough that through the cloud thou break,
To dry the rain on my storm-beaten face,
For no man well of such a salve can speak
That heals the wound and cures not the disgrace.   8

8 **most enjoy** possess most securely and take greatest pleasure in
10 **Haply** perchance; happily.   **state** state of mind. (Suggesting also
"fortunes.")   14 **change** exchange
30.1 **sessions** (The metaphor is that of a court of law, continued in
summon up, line 2.)   3 **sigh** sigh for   4 **new . . . waste** lament anew
the wasting of precious time or time's erosion of those things held
precious.   5 **unused to flow** not prone to weep   6 **dateless** endless
7 **canceled** paid in full (by grieving)   8 **th'expense** the loss, expenditure   9 **grievances foregone** sorrows past   10 **heavily** sadly.   **tell**
count   11 **account** (1) narrative (2) financial reckoning.   **fore-
bemoanèd moan** previously uttered laments
31.1 **endearèd with all hearts** (1) beloved by all (2) made dear to me
by representing and including those I have loved   2 **lacking** not having   3 **parts** attributes   5 **obsequious** suitable to mourning   6 **religious** dutiful, reverent   7 **interest of** that which is rightfully due to.
which who   8 **But . . . lie** i.e., no more than absent persons (now
dead), whose best qualities are to be found buried in you.
10 **Hung . . . gone** festooned with symbolic memorials of my past triumphs in being loved by many   11 **parts** shares   12 **That due of
many** that which was both owed by, and paid to, many   13 **I loved**
which I loved   14 **all they** (you) who comprise all of them

32.1 **my . . . day** i.e., the day of my death, which will content me well
3 **And . . . fortune** and if by chance you happen   4 **rude** unpolished.
lover friend   5 **bett'ring** i.e., improved writing, greater cultural
sophistication   7 **Reserve** preserve.   **for my love** (1) out of love for
me (2) for the sake of my love for you.   **rhyme** i.e., poetic skill
8 **height** superiority, highest achievement.   **happier** more gifted or
fortunate   9 **vouchsafe me but** deign to bestow on me just   11 **dearer
birth** i.e., better poem, better artistic creation   12 **better equipage** i.e.,
more finely wrought verse   13 **better prove** turn out to be superior
33.1 **Full** Very   2 **sovereign eye** i.e., morning sunlight   5 **Anon** soon
afterward.   **basest** darkest   6 **rack** mass of cloud scudding before
the wind   11 **out, alack!** (An expression of dismay.)   12 **region** of the
upper air   14 **Suns** i.e., great men. (With a pun on *sons of the world*,
"mortal men.")   **stain** grow dim, be obscured, soiled.   **staineth** is
clouded over.
34.3 **To** only to   4 **brav'ry** finery.   **rotten smoke** foul vapors.   8 **disgrace** i.e., the scar, the disfigurement caused by his friend's neglect or
harsh treatment; the *loss* main mentioned in line 10.

Nor can thy shame give physic to my grief;
Though thou repent, yet I have still the loss.
Th'offender's sorrow lends but weak relief
To him that bears the strong offense's cross.   12
    Ah, but those tears are pearl which thy love sheds,
    And they are rich, and ransom all ill deeds.

35

No more be grieved at that which thou hast done.
Roses have thorns, and silver fountains mud,
Clouds and eclipses stain both moon and sun,
And loathsome canker lives in sweetest bud.   4
All men make faults, and even I in this,
Authorizing thy trespass with compare,
Myself corrupting, salving thy amiss,
Excusing thy sins more than thy sins are.   8
For to thy sensual fault I bring in sense—
Thy adverse party is thy advocate—
And 'gainst myself a lawful plea commence.
Such civil war is in my love and hate   12
    That I an accessary needs must be
    To that sweet thief which sourly robs from me.

36

Let me confess that we two must be twain,
Although our undivided loves are one;
So shall those blots that do with me remain,
Without thy help, by me be borne alone.   4
In our two loves there is but one respect,
Though in our lives a separable spite,
Which, though it alter not love's sole effect,
Yet doth it steal sweet hours from love's delight.   8
I may not evermore acknowledge thee,
Lest my bewailèd guilt should do thee shame,
Nor thou with public kindness honor me
Unless thou take that honor from thy name.   12
    But do not so; I love thee in such sort
    As, thou being mine, mine is thy good report.

37

As a decrepit father takes delight
To see his active child do deeds of youth,

So I, made lame by Fortune's dearest spite,
Take all my comfort of thy worth and truth.   4
For whether beauty, birth, or wealth, or wit,
Or any of these all, or all, or more,
Entitled in thy parts do crownèd sit,
I make my love engrafted to this store.   8
So then I am not lame, poor, nor despised,
Whilst that this shadow doth such substance give
That I in thy abundance am sufficed
And by a part of all thy glory live.   12
    Look what is best, that best I wish in thee.
    This wish I have; then ten times happy me!

38

How can my Muse want subject to invent
While thou dost breathe, that pour'st into my verse
Thine own sweet argument, too excellent
For every vulgar paper to rehearse?   4
Oh, give thyself the thanks, if aught in me
Worthy perusal stand against thy sight,
For who's so dumb that cannot write to thee,
When thou thyself dost give invention light?   8
Be thou the tenth Muse, ten times more in worth
Than those old nine which rhymers invoke;
And he that calls on thee, let him bring forth
Eternal numbers to outlive long date.   12
    If my slight Muse do please these curious days,
    The pain be mine, but thine shall be the praise.

39

Oh, how thy worth with manners may I sing,
When thou art all the better part of me?
What can mine own praise to mine own self bring?
And what is't but mine own when I praise thee?   4
Even for this let us divided live,
And our dear love lose name of single one,
That by this separation I may give
That due to thee which thou deserv'st alone.   8
O absence, what a torment wouldst thou prove,
Were it not thy sour leisure gave sweet leave
To entertain the time with thoughts of love,
Which time and thoughts so sweetly doth deceive,   12

---

9 **shame** repentance for the wrong done. **physic** remedy **12 cross**
affliction. **14 ransom** atone for
35.3 stain dim, obscure **4 canker** cankerworm **6 Authorizing** sanctioning, justifying. **compare** comparisons (as in this sonnet)
7 Myself . . . amiss excusing your misdeed, thereby bringing blame
on myself **8 Excusing . . . are** going further to excuse your sins than
they warrant, or, excusing you for even worse sins than you have
actually committed. **9 For . . . sense** I reason away your fleshly
offenses **10 Thy . . . advocate** I who profess to be your accuser find
myself, instead, pleading your case **13 That . . . be** that I am compelled (by my love) to be a guilty accomplice
36.1 twain parted **3 blots** defects, stains of dishonor **5 but one
respect** a mutual regard, singleness of attitude **6 separable spite**
vexing separation **7 sole effect** unique effect (of making the two of
us into one) **9 not evermore acknowledge** nevermore admit my
acquaintance with **12 Unless . . . from** without consequent loss of
honor to **13 in such sort** in such a way **14 As . . . report** that since
you are mine, your good reputation sustains me also.

37.3 made lame handicapped in life. **dearest** most bitter **4 of** in,
from **5 wit** intelligence **7 Entitled . . . sit** sit enthroned among your
qualities **8 I make . . . store** I add my love to this abundance (and
thereby flourish by drawing on their strength). **10 shadow** idea (in
the platonic sense). **substance** actuality **13 Look what** Whatever
38.1 want . . . invent lack something to write about **2 that** you who
3 Thine . . . argument yourself as subject **4 vulgar paper** common
piece of writing. **rehearse** recite, repeat. **5–6 if . . . sight** if any of
my writing strikes you as worthy of perusal **7 dumb** silent, lacking
in subject **8 When . . . light** when you bring such a light of invention
to yourself as poetic subject. **12 numbers** verses. **long date** even a
very distant limit in time. **13 curious** finicky **14 pain** labor
39.1 with manners decently, becomingly **3–4 What . . . thee?** i.e.,
Since my better self is entirely yours, what can I gain from praising
you but a kind of vainglorious self-praise? **5 Even for** Precisely
because of **10 not** not that **11 entertain** pass, occupy **12 Which . . .
deceive** (thoughts of love), which sweetly beguile away time and
(sad) thoughts

And that thou teachest how to make one twain
By praising him here who doth hence remain!

40

Take all my loves, my love, yea, take them all;
What hast thou then more than thou hadst before?
No love, my love, that thou mayst true love call;
All mine was thine before thou hadst this more.   4
Then if for my love thou my love receivest,
I cannot blame thee for my love thou usest;
But yet be blamed if thou this self deceivest
By willful taste of what thyself refusest.   8
I do forgive thy robb'ry, gentle thief,
Although thou steal thee all my poverty;
And yet love knows it is a greater grief
To bear love's wrong than hate's known injury.   12
  Lascivious grace, in whom all ill well shows,
  Kill me with spites; yet we must not be foes.

41

Those pretty wrongs that liberty commits
When I am sometime absent from thy heart,
Thy beauty and thy years full well befits,
For still temptation follows where thou art.   4
Gentle thou art, and therefore to be won,
Beauteous thou art, therefore to be assailed;
And when a woman woos, what woman's son
Will sourly leave her till he have prevailed?   8
Ay me, but yet thou mightst my seat forbear,
And chide thy beauty and thy straying youth,
Who lead thee in their riot even there
Where thou art forced to break a twofold truth: 12
  Hers, by thy beauty tempting her to thee,
  Thine, by thy beauty being false to me.

42

That thou hast her, it is not all my grief,
And yet it may be said I loved her dearly;
That she hath thee is of my wailing chief,
A loss in love that touches me more nearly.   4
Loving offenders, thus I will excuse ye:

Thou dost love her because thou know'st I love her,
And for my sake even so doth she abuse me,
Suff'ring my friend for my sake to approve her.   8
If I lose thee, my loss is my love's gain,
And, losing her, my friend hath found that loss;
Both find each other, and I lose both twain,
And both for my sake lay on me this cross.   12
  But here's the joy: my friend and I are one.
  Sweet flattery! Then she loves but me alone.

43

When most I wink, then do mine eyes best see,
For all the day they view things unrespected;
But when I sleep, in dreams they look on thee,
And, darkly bright, are bright in dark directed.   4
Then thou, whose shadow shadows doth make bright,
How would thy shadow's form form happy show
To the clear day with thy much clearer light,
When to unseeing eyes thy shade shines so!   8
How would, I say, mine eyes be blessèd made
By looking on thee in the living day,
When in dead night thy fair imperfect shade
Through heavy sleep on sightless eyes doth stay!   12
  All days are nights to see till I see thee,
  And nights bright days when dreams do show thee
  me.

44

If the dull substance of my flesh were thought,
Injurious distance should not stop my way;
For then despite of space I would be brought,
From limits far remote, where thou dost stay.   4
No matter then although my foot did stand
Upon the farthest earth removed from thee;
For nimble thought can jump both sea and land
As soon as think the place where he would be.   8
But, ah, thought kills me that I am not thought,
To leap large lengths of miles when thou art gone,
But that, so much of earth and water wrought,
I must attend time's leisure with my moan,   12

---

14 **here** (1) here where I am (2) here in this poem
40.1 all my loves (1) all those whom I love (2) all the love I have. (The young man addressed has taken away the poet's mistress.)   **3 No . . . call** i.e., Any love more than you had already—my complete affection—cannot be called true love   **5 my love . . . my love** love of me . . . her whom I love   **6 for** because.   **thou usest** you enjoy (sexually)   **7 this self** i.e., me, your other self. (Often emended to "thyself.")   **8 By . . . refusest** i.e., by tasting sexual pleasures that your best self would refuse.   **10 steal . . . poverty** take for your own the poor little that I have   **12 To . . . injury** to endure injuries arising out of a loving relationship than those stemming from calculated hatred.   **13 Lascivious grace** i.e., You who are gracious even in your lasciviousness
41.1 pretty graciously committed, sportive.   **liberty** licentiousness   **3 befits** (The subject is *wrongs*, line 1.)   **4 still** constantly   **7–8 And . . . prevailed** i.e., When a woman woos, what man can resist until he has scored? (*He* is sometimes emended to "she.")   **9 seat** place, that which belongs to me (i.e., my mistress)   **11 Who** which.   **riot** debauchery   **12 twofold truth** i.e., her plighted love to me and your plighted friendship to me
42.3 is . . . chief is chief cause of my lamentation

7 abuse betray, wrong   **8 Suff'ring** allowing.   **approve** try, test (in a sexual sense)   **9 my love's** hers whom I love, my mistress's   **10 losing her** i.e., I losing her   **12 for my sake** as though out of love for me.   **cross** torment.   **14 flattery** gratifying deception.
43.1 wink close my eyes in sleep   **2 unrespected** unnoticed, unregarded; not deserving notice   **4 And . . . directed** and, able to see in the darkness (though still shut), are directed toward your brightness in the dark.   **5 whose . . . bright** whose image makes darkness bright   **6 thy shadow's . . . show** the substance of the shadow, i.e., your presence, make a gladdening sight   **8 unseeing eyes** i.e., closed eyes of the dreamer   **11 imperfect** unsubstantial, indistinct as in a dream   **12 stay** linger, dwell.   **13 All . . . to see** All days are gloomy to behold   **14 thee** me you to me. (But also suggesting "me to you.")
44.1 dull heavy   **4 limits** regions, bounds.   **where** to the place where   **6 farthest earth removed** that part of the earth farthest removed   **8 he** thought   **9 ah, thought** ah, the thought   **11 so . . . wrought** i.e., I, compounded to such an extent of the heavier elements, earth and water. (The lighter elements are fire and air.)
12 attend time's leisure i.e., wait until time has leisure to reunite us

Receiving naught by elements so slow
But heavy tears, badges of either's woe.

45

The other two, slight air and purging fire,
Are both with thee, wherever I abide;
The first my thought, the other my desire,
These present-absent with swift motion slide. 4
For when these quicker elements are gone
In tender embassy of love to thee,
My life, being made of four, with two alone
Sinks down to death, oppressed with melancholy; 8
Until life's composition be recured
By those swift messengers returned from thee,
Who even but now come back again, assured
Of thy fair health, recounting it to me. 12
 This told, I joy; but then no longer glad,
 I send them back again and straight grow sad.

46

Mine eye and heart are at a mortal war
How to divide the conquest of thy sight;
Mine eye my heart thy picture's sight would bar,
My heart mine eye the freedom of that right. 4
My heart doth plead that thou in him dost lie—
A closet never pierced with crystal eyes—
But the defendant doth that plea deny
And says in him thy fair appearance lies. 8
To 'cide this title is impanelèd
A quest of thoughts, all tenants to the heart,
And by their verdict is determinèd
The clear eye's moiety and the dear heart's part, 12
 As thus: mine eye's due is thy outward part,
 And my heart's right thy inward love of heart.

47

Betwixt mine eye and heart a league is took,
And each doth good turns now unto the other.
When that mine eye is famished for a look,
Or heart in love with sighs himself doth smother, 4

With my love's picture then my eye doth feast
And to the painted banquet bids my heart;
Another time mine eye is my heart's guest
And in his thoughts of love doth share a part. 8
So, either by thy picture or my love,
Thyself, away, are present still with me;
For thou no farther than my thoughts canst move,
And I am still with them and they with thee; 12
 Or, if they sleep, thy picture in my sight
 Awakes my heart to heart's and eye's delight.

48

How careful was I, when I took my way,
Each trifle under truest bars to thrust,
That to my use it might unusèd stay
From hands of falsehood, in sure wards of trust! 4
But thou, to whom my jewels trifles are,
Most worthy comfort, now my greatest grief,
Thou best of dearest and mine only care,
Art left the prey of every vulgar thief. 8
Thee have I not locked up in any chest,
Save where thou art not—though I feel thou art—
Within the gentle closure of my breast,
From whence at pleasure thou mayst come and part; 12
 And even thence thou wilt be stol'n, I fear,
 For truth proves thievish for a prize so dear.

49

Against that time, if ever that time come,
When I shall see thee frown on my defects,
Whenas thy love hath cast his utmost sum,
Called to that audit by advised respects; 4
Against that time when thou shalt strangely pass
And scarcely greet me with that sun, thine eye,
When love, converted from the thing it was,
Shall reasons find of settled gravity— 8
Against that time do I ensconce me here
Within the knowledge of mine own desart,
And this my hand against myself uprear,
To guard the lawful reasons on thy part. 12
 To leave poor me thou hast the strength of laws,
 Since why to love I can allege no cause.

13 by from   14 badges signs, tokens.   either's (1) both earth's and water's, because the earth is heavy and the sea is salt and wet like tears (2) both your and my
45.1 other two (i.e., of the four elements discussed in sonnet 44). slight insubstantial.   purging purifying   4 present-absent (1) now here and immediately gone (2) simultaneously both present and absent   7 two alone i.e., earth and water   8 melancholy a humor thought to be induced by an excess of earth and water   9 composition proper balance among the four elements.   recured restored
10 swift messengers i.e., fire and air, thought and desire   14 straight straightway
46.1 mortal deadly   2 How . . . sight how to divide the spoils of war, namely, the sight of you   3–4 Mine . . . right my eye wishes to bar my heart from seeing your image (perhaps a painting), and conversely my heart would like to deny my eye the free enjoyment of that right.   6 closet (1) small private room (2) cabinet   7 the defendant the eye   9 'cide decide   10 quest inquest, jury   12 moiety portion   13 mine . . . part i.e., the eye gets the outward appearance of you. (The jury, composed entirely of those who are loyal to the heart, being its tenants, awards true love to the heart.)
47.1 a league is took an agreement is reached   3 When that When
4 Or heart or when my heart.   himself itself

5 With i.e., on   6 painted banquet i.e., visual feast, perhaps an actual picture of the friend   12 still constantly
48.1 took my way set out on my journey   2 truest most trusty   3 to my use for my own use and profit   3–4 stay . . . falsehood remain out of the hands of thieves   5 to compared to   6 worthy valuable. grief anxiety, cause of sorrow (i.e., because of your absence and likeliness of being stolen)   8 vulgar common   12 part depart   14 truth i.e., even honesty itself
49.1 Against In anticipation of   3 Whenas when.   cast . . . sum added up the sum total. (The metaphor is from closing accounts on a dissolution of partnership.)   4 advised respects careful consideration
5 strangely as a stranger   8 of settled gravity (1) for a dignified reserve or continued coldness (2) of sufficient weight   9 ensconce fortify, shelter   10 desart i.e., deserving, such as it is. (This Quarto spelling of desert, "desart," indicates the rhyme with part.)   11 this . . . uprear I raise my own hand (as a witness) against my own interest
12 To . . . part i.e., to testify in behalf of the lawful reasons on your side of the case.   14 Since . . . cause since I can urge no lawful cause why you should love me.

50

How heavy do I journey on the way,
When what I seek, my weary travel's end,
Doth teach that ease and that repose to say,
"Thus far the miles are measured from thy friend!"   4
The beast that bears me, tirèd with my woe,
Plods dully on, to bear that weight in me,
As if by some instinct the wretch did know
His rider loved not speed being made from thee.   8
The bloody spur cannot provoke him on
That sometimes anger thrusts into his hide,
Which heavily he answers with a groan,
More sharp to me than spurring to his side;   12
 For that same groan doth put this in my mind:
 My grief lies onward and my joy behind.

51

Thus can my love excuse the slow offense
Of my dull bearer when from thee I speed:
From where thou art why should I haste me thence?
Till I return, of posting is no need.   4
Oh, what excuse will my poor beast then find
When swift extremity can seem but slow?
Then should I spur, though mounted on the wind;
In wingèd speed no motion shall I know.   8
Then can no horse with my desire keep pace;
Therefore desire, of perfect'st love being made,
Shall neigh—no dull flesh—in his fiery race.
But love, for love, thus shall excuse my jade: 12
 Since from thee going he went willful slow,
 Towards thee I'll run, and give him leave to go.

52

So am I as the rich whose blessèd key
Can bring him to his sweet up-lockèd treasure,
The which he will not ev'ry hour survey,
For blunting the fine point of seldom pleasure.   4
Therefore are feasts so solemn and so rare,
Since, seldom coming, in the long year set,
Like stones of worth they thinly placèd are,
Or captain jewels in the carcanet.   8
So is the time that keeps you as my chest,
Or as the wardrobe which the robe doth hide,
To make some special instant special blest

By new unfolding his imprisoned pride.   12
 Blessèd are you whose worthiness gives scope,
 Being had, to triumph; being lacked, to hope.

53

What is your substance, whereof are you made,
That millions of strange shadows on you tend?
Since everyone hath, every one, one shade,
And you, but one, can every shadow lend.   4
Describe Adonis, and the counterfeit
Is poorly imitated after you;
On Helen's cheek all art of beauty set,
And you in Grecian tires are painted new.   8
Speak of the spring and foison of the year;
The one doth shadow of your beauty show,
The other as your bounty doth appear,
And you in every blessèd shape we know.   12
 In all external grace you have some part,
 But you like none, none you, for constant heart.

54

Oh, how much more doth beauty beauteous seem
By that sweet ornament which truth doth give!
The rose looks fair, but fairer we it deem
For that sweet odor which doth in it live.   4
The canker blooms have full as deep a dye
As the perfumèd tincture of the roses,
Hang on such thorns, and play as wantonly
When summer's breath their maskèd buds discloses;   8
But, for their virtue only is their show,
They live unwooed and unrespected fade,
Die to themselves. Sweet roses do not so;
Of their sweet deaths are sweetest odors made.   12
 And so of you, beauteous and lovely youth,
 When that shall vade, by verse distills your truth.

55

Not marble nor the gilded monuments
Of princes shall outlive this powerful rhyme,

50.1 **heavy** sadly and slowly   **2–4 When . . . friend** when the ease and repose I seek at journey's end will merely remind me that I have gone so many miles from my friend.
51.1 **slow offense** offense consisting in slowness   **2 my dull bearer** i.e., the horse   **4 posting** riding swiftly   **6 swift extremity** extreme swiftness (in returning to you)   **8 In . . . know** even at the speed of flight I won't perceive the motion at all, won't feel as though I'm moving.   **11 Shall . . . race** i.e., shall neigh proudly in its fire-swift race, since it, composed like fire of a lighter element, is not held back by the heavy flesh. (See sonnet 45.)   **12 for love** for love's sake. **jade** nag   **14 go** travel on at his own pace.
52.1 **as the rich** like the rich man   **4 For . . . pleasure** lest he blunt the delicacy of pleasure sparingly enjoyed.   **5 feasts** feast days. **solemn** ceremonious, festive.   **rare** excellent; uncommon   **8 captain** principal.   **carcanet** necklace of jewels.   **9 keeps you** (1) watches over you (2) keeps you from me.   **as** like

12 his its.   **pride** splendor, proud treasure.   **13–14 gives . . . hope** gives me opportunity, when you are with me, to rejoice, and when you are away from me, to hope for reunion.
53.2 **strange** (1) exotic (2) not belonging to you.   **tend** attend.
3 shade shadow (as cast by the sun)   **4 And . . . lend** and yet you, being only one person, can cast all sorts of shadowy images or reflections (such as Adonis, Helen, etc.).   **5 Adonis** beautiful youth beloved of Venus.   **counterfeit** likeness, portrait   **7–8 On . . . new** set forth the entire art use to beautify the cheek of Helen of Troy, and the result will be a portrait of you in Grecian attire or headdress.
9 foison abundance, i.e., autumn   **12 you . . . know** we recognize you in every beautiful image.   **14 But . . . heart** but in the matter of constancy you resemble no one and no one can resemble you.
54.2 **By** by means of.   **truth** (1) constancy (2) substance, integrity
5 canker blooms dog roses (outwardly attractive but not as sweetly scented as the damask rose).   **dye** tincture   **7 wantonly** sportively
8 discloses causes to open   **9 for** because.   **their show** in their appearance   **10 unrespected** unregarded   **11 to themselves** i.e., without profit to others.   **12 Of . . . made** i.e., perfumes are made from the crushed petals of these roses.   **13 of you** (1) distilled from you (2) with regard to you.   **lovely** (1) lovable (2) handsome   **14 When . . . truth** when your physical beauty fades, your true substance will be distilled and preserved by (my) verse. (See sonnet 5.)   **vade** (1) fade (2) go away

But you shall shine more bright in these contents
Than unswept stone besmeared with sluttish time.   4
When wasteful war shall statues overturn,
And broils root out the work of masonry,
Nor Mars his sword nor war's quick fire shall burn
The living record of your memory.   8
'Gainst death and all-oblivious enmity
Shall you pace forth; your praise shall still find room
Even in the eyes of all posterity
That wear this world out to the ending doom.   12
 So, till the judgment that yourself arise,
 You live in this, and dwell in lovers' eyes.

56

Sweet love, renew thy force! Be it not said
Thy edge should blunter be than appetite,
Which but today by feeding is allayed,
Tomorrow sharpened in his former might.   4
So, love, be thou; although today thou fill
Thy hungry eyes even till they wink with fullness,
Tomorrow see again, and do not kill
The spirit of love with a perpetual dullness.   8
Let this sad interim like the ocean be
Which parts the shore where two contracted new
Come daily to the banks, that, when they see
Return of love, more blest may be the view;   12
 As call it winter, which being full of care
 Makes summer's welcome thrice more wished, more
  rare.

57

Being your slave, what should I do but tend
Upon the hours and times of your desire?
I have no precious time at all to spend,
Nor services to do, till you require.   4
Nor dare I chide the world-without-end hour
Whilst I, my sovereign, watch the clock for you,
Nor think the bitterness of absence sour
When you have bid your servant once adieu.   8
Nor dare I question with my jealous thought
Where you may be, or your affairs suppose,

But, like a sad slave, stay and think of naught
Save where you are how happy you make those.   12
 So true a fool is love that in your will,
 Though you do anything, he thinks no ill.

58

That god forbid, that made me first your slave,
I should in thought control your times of pleasure,
Or at your hand th'account of hours to crave,
Being your vassal, bound to stay your leisure!   4
Oh, let me suffer, being at your beck,
Th'imprisoned absence of your liberty,
And, patience-tame to sufferance, bide each check,
Without accusing you of injury.   8
Be where you list, your charter is so strong
That you yourself may privilege your time
To what you will; to you it doth belong
Yourself to pardon of self-doing crime.   12
 I am to wait, though waiting so be hell,
 Not blame your pleasure, be it ill or well.

59

If there be nothing new, but that which is
Hath been before, how are our brains beguiled,
Which, laboring for invention, bear amiss
The second burden of a former child!   4
Oh, that record could with a backward look,
Even of five hundred courses of the sun,
Show me your image in some antique book,
Since mind at first in character was done!   8
That I might see what the old world could say
To this composèd wonder of your frame;
Whether we are mended, or whe'er better they,
Or whether revolution be the same.   12
 Oh, sure I am the wits of former days
 To subjects worse have given admiring praise.

60

Like as the waves make towards the pebbled shore,
So do our minutes hasten to their end,
Each changing place with that which goes before,

55.3 these contents i.e., the contents of my poems written in praise of you **4 Than unswept stone** than in a memorial stone that has been left unswept, unattended. **sluttish** neglectful, slovenly, whorish **5 wasteful** laying waste **6 broils** uprisings, battles **7 Nor Mars his sword** Neither Mars's sword (shall destroy) **9 all-oblivious enmity** oblivion, at enmity with everything **12 That . . . doom** that will last from now till doomsday. (*That* may refer to *eyes, praise,* or *posterity*.) **13 till . . . arise** until the Judgment Day, when you will arise from the dead
56.1 love i.e., the spirit of love. (The friend is not directly mentioned in this sonnet.) **1–2 Be . . . appetite** Let no one attempt to argue that true love should be any less sharp-edged in desire than sexual appetite **3 but** only for **4 his** its **6 wink** shut **9 sad interim** a period of love's abatement or absence **10 parts the shore** separates the shores. **contracted new** newly betrothed **11 banks** shores **12 love** the loved one **13 As** just as appropriately
57.1 tend attend **5 world-without-end** interminable **6 Whilst . . . you** while I count the minutes, my sovereign, waiting for your command **7 Nor think** nor dare I think **9 question with** (1) debate with (2) seek to know by means of **10 suppose** make conjectures about

13 true (1) constant (2) utter. **in your will** with regard to your desire (with perhaps an allusion to "Will Shakespeare"; "will" is capitalized in the 1609 Quarto, as in sonnet 135)
58.3 th'account . . . crave should crave an accounting of how you spend your time **4 stay** await **6 Th'imprisoned . . . liberty** the lack of freedom I suffer in being absent from you, arising from (*of*) your freedom and licentious behavior **7 And . . . check** and, trained to endure any suffering, let me put up with each rebuke **9 list** please. **charter** privilege **10 privilege** authorize **12 self-doing** committed by yourself **13 am to** must
59.1 that everything **3–4 laboring . . . child** striving to give birth to a new creation, merely miscarry with the repetition of something created before. **5 record** memory, especially memory preserved in writing **6 courses . . . sun** years **8 Since . . . done** since thought was first expressed in writing. **10 composèd wonder** wonderful composition **11 mended** improved. **whe'er** whether **12 revolution . . . same** the revolving of the ages brings only repetition. **13 wits** discerning persons; poets
60.1 Like . . . shore Just as waves move up the shingle beach **3 changing place with** replacing

In sequent toil all forwards do contend.   4
Nativity, once in the main of light,
Crawls to maturity, wherewith being crowned,
Crookèd eclipses 'gainst his glory fight,
And Time that gave doth now his gift confound.   8
Time doth transfix the flourish set on youth
And delves the parallels in beauty's brow,
Feeds on the rarities of nature's truth,
And nothing stands but for his scythe to mow.   12
    And yet to times in hope my verse shall stand,
    Praising thy worth despite his cruel hand.

61

Is it thy will thy image should keep open
My heavy eyelids to the weary night?
Dost thou desire my slumbers should be broken
While shadows like to thee do mock my sight?   4
Is it thy spirit that thou send'st from thee
So far from home into my deeds to pry,
To find out shames and idle hours in me,
The scope and tenor of thy jealousy?   8
Oh, no, thy love, though much, is not so great;
It is my love that keeps mine eye awake,
Mine own true love that doth my rest defeat,
To play the watchman ever for thy sake.   12
    For thee watch I whilst thou dost wake elsewhere,
    From me far off, with others all too near.

62

Sin of self-love possesseth all mine eye,
And all my soul, and all my every part;
And for this sin there is no remedy,
It is so grounded inward in my heart.   4
Methinks no face so gracious is as mine,
No shape so true, no truth of such account,
And for myself mine own worth do define
As I all other in all worths surmount.   8
But when my glass shows me myself indeed,
Beated and chapped with tanned antiquity,
Mine own self-love quite contrary I read;
Self so self-loving were iniquity.   12
    'Tis thee, my self, that for myself I praise,
    Painting my age with beauty of thy days.

63

Against my love shall be, as I am now,
With Time's injurious hand crushed and o'erworn;
When hours have drained his blood and filled his brow
With lines and wrinkles; when his youthful morn   4
Hath traveled on to age's steepy night,
And all those beauties whereof now he's king
Are vanishing or vanished out of sight,
Stealing away the treasure of his spring;   8
For such a time do I now fortify
Against confounding age's cruel knife,
That he shall never cut from memory
My sweet love's beauty, though my lover's life.   12
    His beauty shall in these black lines be seen,
    And they shall live, and he in them still green.

64

When I have seen by Time's fell hand defaced
The rich proud cost of outworn buried age;
When sometime lofty towers I see down-razed
And brass eternal slave to mortal rage;   4
When I have seen the hungry ocean gain
Advantage on the kingdom of the shore,
And the firm soil win of the wat'ry main,
Increasing store with loss and loss with store;   8
When I have seen such interchange of state,
Or state itself confounded to decay,
Ruin hath taught me thus to ruminate
That Time will come and take my love away.   12
    This thought is as a death, which cannot choose
    But weep to have that which it fears to lose.

65

Since brass, nor stone, nor earth, nor boundless sea,
But sad mortality o'ersways their power,
How with this rage shall beauty hold a plea,
Whose action is no stronger than a flower?   4
Oh, how shall summer's honey breath hold out
Against the wrackful siege of batt'ring days,

---

4 In . . . contend one after another, all struggle onward.   5 Nativity . . . light The newborn infant, no sooner born into the broad expanse of this world and the light of day   7 Crookèd perverse, malignant   8 doth . . . confound now destroys what it gave.   9 doth . . . flourish pierces through and destroys the ornament, i.e., the physical beauty   10 delves the parallels digs the wrinkles, furrows   11 Feeds . . . truth consumes the most precious things created by the fidelity of nature   12 but . . . mow that can escape the mowing of Time's scythe.   13 times in hope times to come
61.4 shadows images. (But also suggesting spirits.)   8 The scope . . . jealousy the aim and purport of your suspicion. (Probably in apposition to shames and idle hours.)   13 watch stay awake.   wake revel
62.5 Methinks It seems to me   7 for myself (1) by my own reckoning (2) for my own pleasure   8 As as if.   other others   9 glass mirror.   indeed as I actually am   10 Beated battered, weather-beaten.   tanned antiquity i.e., leathery old age   12 Self . . . iniquity it would be wicked for the self to love such an aged and unattractive self.   13 thee, my self you, with whom I identify myself.   for as   14 days i.e., youth.

63.1 Against Anticipating the time when.   love beloved   2 crushed and o'erworn creased and worn threadbare (like a long-used garment)   5 traveled (1) journeyed (2) labored.   steepy precipitous, i.e., descending swiftly toward death   9 For such a time (Parallel in construction with Against in line 1.)   fortify raise works of defense   10 confounding destroying   11 That so that   12 though i.e., though he cut   13 black (1) inscribed in ink (2) the opposite of fair or beautiful   14 still (1) even in death (2) forever.   green i.e., as in springtime and youth.
64.1 fell cruel   2 The rich . . . age i.e., those monuments that were the product of proud wealth and magnificent outlay in times now past and forgotten   3 sometime formerly   4 brass . . . rage i.e., seemingly indestructible brass subdued by the destructive power of decay   7 of . . . main at the expense of the ocean   8 Increasing . . . store one gaining as the other loses, and losing as the other gains   9 state condition   10 state pomp, greatness; condition in the abstract.   confounded to decay destroyed to the point of being in ruins   12 love beloved   13 which cannot choose (Modifies thought.)   14 to have at having
65.1 Since i.e., Since there is neither   3 How . . . plea how against this destructive force can beauty hope to make its case   4 action (1) efficacy (2) case (in law)   6 wrackful destructive

When rocks impregnable are not so stout,
Nor gates of steel so strong, but Time decays?
Oh, fearful meditation! Where, alack,
Shall Time's best jewel from Time's chest lie hid?
Or what strong hand can hold his swift foot back?
Or who his spoil of beauty can forbid? 12
    Oh, none, unless this miracle have might,
    That in black ink my love may still shine bright.

66

Tired with all these, for restful death I cry:
As, to behold desert a beggar born,
And needy nothing trimmed in jollity,
And purest faith unhappily forsworn, 4
And gilded honor shamefully misplaced,
And maiden virtue rudely strumpeted,
And right perfection wrongfully disgraced,
And strength by limping sway disablèd, 8
And art made tongue-tied by authority,
And folly doctorlike controlling skill,
And simple truth miscalled simplicity,
And captive good attending captain ill. 12
    Tired with all these, from these would I be gone,
    Save that, to die, I leave my love alone.

67

Ah, wherefore with infection should he live,
And with his presence grace impiety,
That sin by him advantage should achieve
And lace itself with his society? 4
Why should false painting imitate his cheek
And steal dead seeming of his living hue?
Why should poor beauty indirectly seek
Roses of shadow, since his rose is true? 8

Why should he live, now Nature bankrupt is,
Beggared of blood to blush through lively veins,
For she hath no exchequer now but his,
And, proud of many, lives upon his gains? 12
    Oh, him she stores, to show what wealth she had
    In days long since, before these last so bad.

68

Thus is his cheek the map of days outworn,
When beauty lived and died as flowers do now,
Before these bastard signs of fair were born,
Or durst inhabit on a living brow; 4
Before the golden tresses of the dead,
The right of sepulchers, were shorn away
To live a second life on second head;
Ere beauty's dead fleece made another gay. 8
In him those holy antique hours are seen
Without all ornament, itself and true,
Making no summer of another's green,
Robbing no old to dress his beauty new; 12
    And him as for a map doth Nature store,
    To show false art what beauty was of yore.

69

Those parts of thee that the world's eye doth view
Want nothing that the thought of hearts can mend;
All tongues, the voice of souls, give thee that due,
Utt'ring bare truth, even so as foes commend. 4
Thy outward thus with outward praise is crowned,
But those same tongues that give thee so thine own
In other accents do this praise confound
By seeing farther than the eye hath shown. 8
They look into the beauty of thy mind,
And that, in guess, they measure by thy deeds;
Then, churls, their thoughts, although their eyes were
      kind,
To thy fair flower add the rank smell of weeds. 12

---

7 stout sturdy, impregnable **8 decays** brings about their decay.
9–10 Where . . . hid? Where, alas, shall the youth and beauty of my
friend (*Time's best jewel*) be hidden away from being deposited by
Time in its repository of forgetfulness? **12 spoil** despoliation, rav-
aging **14 my love** (1) my beloved (2) the love I feel for him
66.1 all these i.e., the following **2 As** for instance, namely. **desert**
one who is deserving **3 And needy . . . jollity** and empty worthless-
ness adorned in finery **4 unhappily forsworn** wretchedly and evilly
betrayed **5 gilded** golden, splendid. (Not here suggesting mere
appearance of splendor.) **6 strumpeted** accused of profligacy, or violated **7 right** true. **disgraced** banished from favor **8 limping
sway** halting leadership **9 And art . . . authority** and literature and
learning stifled by censorship **10 doctorlike** assuming a learned
bearing. **controlling** dominating, curbing **11 miscalled simplicity**
slandered as foolishness, naivetè **12 attending** waiting on, subordinated to **14 to die** in dying
67.1 wherefore why. **with infection** i.e., with the world's ills, as
enumerated in the preceding sonnet. **he** i.e., the poet's friend
3 That . . . achieve with the result that sin should flourish by being
associated with him **4 lace . . . society** (1) adorn itself with his company (2) weave its way into his company. **6 dead seeming of** lifeless
appearance from **7 poor** inferior. **indirectly** imitatively, or, falsely
8 Roses of shadow i.e., painted roses, cosmetically applied. **since**
(1) just because (2) since after all

9–12 Why . . . gains? Why should he continue to live in this bad
world, seeing that Nature has now squandered all her resources of
beauty on him, with no genuine way left to produce a natural blush
on the cheek, since she has no treasury of natural beauty other than
what is vested in him, and, though (falsely) taking pride in her abundance (of offspring), lives solely on the wealth (of beauty) that he provides? **13 stores** preserves, keeps in store **14 last** i.e., recent days,
the present
68.1 map embodiment, image **3 bastard . . . fair** i.e., cosmetics.
born (Suggesting also *borne*, "worn.") **4 inhabit** dwell **5–7 Before
. . . head** i.e., before the deplorable current fad of making wigs out of
dead persons' hair **8 gay** lovely, gaudy. **9 holy antique hours**
blessed ancient times **10 all** any **13 store** stock (with beauty) and
preserve
69.2 Want lack. **mend** improve upon **3–4 the voice . . . commend**
i.e., uttering heartfelt conviction, allow that as your due, thus saying
what even your enemies would concede to be the bare truth. **5 outward praise** the kind of praise suited to mere outward qualities
6 thine own your due **7 In other accents** in other terms and with
another emphasis. **confound** confute, destroy **10 in guess** at a
guess **12 To . . . weeds** i.e., to the flower of your outward beauty,
they contrastingly suggest something putrid within.

But why thy odor matcheth not thy show,
The soil is this, that thou dost common grow.

70

That thou art blamed shall not be thy defect,
For slander's mark was ever yet the fair;
The ornament of beauty is suspect,
A crow that flies in heaven's sweetest air.   4
So thou be good, slander doth but approve
Thy worth the greater, being wooed of time,
For canker vice the sweetest buds doth love,
And thou present'st a pure unstainèd prime.   8
Thou hast passed by the ambush of young days,
Either not assailed, or victor being charged;
Yet this thy praise cannot be so thy praise
To tie up envy, evermore enlarged.   12
    If some suspect of ill masked not thy show,
    Then thou alone kingdoms of hearts shouldst owe.

71

No longer mourn for me when I am dead
Than you shall hear the surly sullen bell
Give warning to the world that I am fled
From this vile world, with vilest worms to dwell.   4
Nay, if you read this line, remember not
The hand that writ it, for I love you so
That I in your sweet thoughts would be forgot
If thinking on me then should make you woe.   8
Oh, if, I say, you look upon this verse
When I perhaps compounded am with clay,
Do not so much as my poor name rehearse,
But let your love even with my life decay,   12
    Lest the wise world should look into your moan
    And mock you with me after I am gone.

72

Oh, lest the world should task you to recite
What merit lived in me that you should love,

After my death, dear love, forget me quite;
For you in me can nothing worthy prove—
Unless you would devise some virtuous lie   4
To do more for me than mine own desert,
And hang more praise upon deceasèd I
Than niggard truth would willingly impart.   8
Oh, lest your true love may seem false in this,
That you for love speak well of me untrue,
My name be buried where my body is,
And live no more to shame nor me nor you.   12
    For I am shamed by that which I bring forth,
    And so should you, to love things nothing worth.

73

That time of year thou mayst in me behold
When yellow leaves, or none, or few, do hang
Upon those boughs which shake against the cold,
Bare ruined choirs where late the sweet birds sang.   4
In me thou see'st the twilight of such day
As after sunset fadeth in the west,
Which by and by black night doth take away,
Death's second self, that seals up all in rest.   8
In me thou see'st the glowing of such fire
That on the ashes of his youth doth lie
As the deathbed whereon it must expire,
Consumed with that which it was nourished by.   12
    This thou perceiv'st, which makes thy love more
        strong,
    To love that well which thou must leave ere long.

74

But be contented when that fell arrest
Without all bail shall carry me away;
My life hath in this line some interest,
Which for memorial still with thee shall stay.   4
When thou reviewest this, thou dost review
The very part was consecrate to thee.
The earth can have but earth, which is his due;
My spirit is thine, the better part of me.   8

---

13 odor i.e., reputation   **14 soil** (1) blemish, fault (2) origin, source, ground.   **common** cheapened by being too familiar and available to all, inferior (like a weed)
70.1 defect fault   **2 mark** target   **3 The . . . suspect** i.e., Beauty is always attended by suspicion (*suspect*), as though suspicion were a necessary ornament to beauty   **5 So** Provided that.   **approve** prove   **6 being . . . time** i.e., since it shows you are courted by the world   **7 canker vice** i.e., slander, that is like the cankerworm   **8 unstainèd prime** unspotted youth (like the pure, unspoiled flower that attracts the cankerworm).   **9 ambush . . . days** temptations of youth   **10 being charged** when you were assailed   **11–12 Yet . . . enlarged** yet the praise you receive cannot be enough to silence malice, which is always at liberty to do its worst.   **13 If . . . show** If some suspicion (*suspect*) of ill doing did not partly obscure your outward attractiveness   **14 owe** own.
71.2 bell a passing bell for one who has died, rung once for each year of that person's life   **8 on** of, about.   **make you woe** cause you woe or make you woeful.   **10 compounded** mingled   **11 rehearse** repeat   **12 even with** at the same time as   **13 look . . . moan** investigate the cause of your sorrow   **14 with** because of; for loving; along with
72.1 recite tell

7 hang (as in hanging trophies on a funeral monument)   **10 of me untrue** (1) about me untruly (2) about me, flawed and inconstant as I am   **11 My name be** let my name be   **12 nor . . . nor** neither . . . nor   **13 that . . . forth** (Perhaps a deprecatory reference to the author's acting and writing of plays, but more probably his verse or his written work generally.)   **14 should you** i.e., you ought to be ashamed
73.4 Bare . . . sang (In their arched shape, the bare trees resemble the church choir where the service is sung; with a hint of *quires*, gatherings of *leaves* [see line 2] in a book or manuscript, and evoking memories of church buildings left in ruins by the dissolution of the monasteries in the English Reformation. *Late* means "lately.")   **8 seals** closes   **10 his** its   **12 with** (1) by (2) along with   **14 that** (1) me, your beloved (2) youth and life itself.   **leave** i.e., lose by the speaker's death
74.1 be contented . . . arrest do not be distressed when that cruel arrest (carried out by Death)   **3 line** verse.   **interest** legal concern, right, or title   **4 still** (1) always (2) despite death   **5 reviewest this** see this again (and view it with a critical eye)   **6 part was consecrate** part (of me) that was dedicated solemnly (as in a religious service)   **7 his** its

So then thou hast but lost the dregs of life,
The prey of worms, my body being dead,
The coward conquest of a wretch's knife,
Too base of thee to be rememberèd.   12
    The worth of that is that which it contains,
    And that is this, and this with thee remains.

75

So are you to my thoughts as food to life,
Or as sweet-seasoned showers are to the ground.
And for the peace of you I hold such strife
As twixt a miser and his wealth is found: 4
Now proud as an enjoyer, and anon
Doubting the filching age will steal his treasure;
Now counting best to be with you alone,
Then bettered that the world may see my pleasure;   8
Sometime all full with feasting on your sight,
And by and by clean starvèd for a look;
Possessing or pursuing no delight
Save what is had or must from you be took.   12
    Thus do I pine and surfeit day by day,
    Or gluttoning on all, or all away.

76

Why is my verse so barren of new pride?
So far from variation or quick change?
Why with the time do I not glance aside
To newfound methods and to compounds strange?   4
Why write I still all one, ever the same,
And keep invention in a noted weed,
That every word doth almost tell my name,
Showing their birth and where they did proceed?   8
Oh, know, sweet love, I always write of you,
And you and love are still my argument;
So all my best is dressing old words new,
Spending again what is already spent.   12
    For as the sun is daily new and old,
    So is my love still telling what is told.

77

Thy glass will show thee how thy beauties wear,
Thy dial how thy precious minutes waste;
The vacant leaves thy mind's imprint will bear,
And of this book this learning mayst thou taste: 4
The wrinkles which thy glass will truly show
Of mouthèd graves will give thee memory;
Thou by thy dial's shady stealth mayst know
Time's thievish progress to eternity.   8
Look what thy memory cannot contain
Commit to these waste blanks, and thou shalt find
Those children nursed, delivered from thy brain,
To take a new acquaintance of thy mind.   12
    These offices, so oft as thou wilt look,
    Shall profit thee and much enrich thy book.

78

So oft have I invoked thee for my Muse
And found such fair assistance in my verse
As every alien pen hath got my use
And under thee their poesy disperse.   4
Thine eyes, that taught the dumb on high to sing
And heavy ignorance aloft to fly,
Have added feathers to the learnèd's wing
And given grace a double majesty.   8
Yet be most proud of that which I compile,
Whose influence is thine and born of thee.
In others' works thou dost but mend the style,
And arts with thy sweet graces gracèd be;   12
    But thou art all my art, and dost advance
    As high as learning my rude ignorance.

79

Whilst I alone did call upon thy aid,
My verse alone had all thy gentle grace,
But now my gracious numbers are decayed,
And my sick Muse doth give another place.   4

---

11 **The coward . . . knife** i.e., the cowardly conquest that even such a poor wretch as Mortality, or Death, can make with his scythe   **12 of . . . rememberèd** to be remembered by you.   **13–14 The worth . . . remains** The only worth of my body is the spirit it contains, i.e., this verse, which will remain with you and endure through you.
75.1 as food to life what food is to life   **2 sweet-seasoned** of the sweet season, i.e., spring   **3 of you** to be found in loving you   **6 Doubting** suspecting, fearing that.   **filching** thieving   **7 counting** (1) thinking it (2) reckoning, like a miser   **8 bettered** made happier, better pleased. **see my pleasure** i.e., see me with you, enjoying your company **10 clean** completely, absolutely.   **a look** (1) a glimpse of you (2) an exchange of glances   **12 Save . . . took** except what is had or must be received from you alone.   **13 pine and surfeit** starve and overeat **14 Or . . . or** either . . . or.   **all away** i.e., all food being taken away. **76.1 pride** ornament.   **2 quick change** fashionable innovation. **3 time** way of the world, fashion   **4 compounds** strange literary inventions, or perhaps, compound words, neologisms.   **5 still all one** continually one way   **6 invention** literary creation.   **noted weed** familiar garment   **8 where** whence   **10 still** always. **argument** subject, theme   **14 telling** (1) retelling (2) counting over. (Continuing the financial wordplay of *Spending* and *spent* in line 12, and in 75.7.)

77.1 glass mirror.   **wear** wear away   **2 dial** sundial   **3 vacant leaves** blank pages. (Apparently these lines accompanied the gift of a book of blank pages, a memorandum book.)   **thy mind's imprint** i.e., your reflections and ideas, to be set down in the memorandum book **4 this learning** i.e., mental profit derived from reflecting and keeping a journal, as explained in lines 9 ff.   **6 mouthèd** all-devouring, gaping.   **memory** reminder   **7 shady stealth** stealthy shadow   **9 Look what** Whatever   **10 waste blanks** blank pages   **10–12 thou . . . mind** you will see those thoughts, the children of your brain, nursed to maturity and ready to be newly reencountered by your mind. **13 offices** duties (of meditation and reflection)   **14 thy book** i.e., the memorandum book, where these reflections are to be set down. **78.2 fair** favorable   **3 As** that.   **alien** belonging to others.   **got my use** adopted my practice   **4 under thee** i.e., with you as their muse or patron; under your influence.   **disperse** circulate.   **5 on high** aloud. (Also anticipating *aloft*.)   **7 added . . . wing** i.e., enabled learned poets to fly higher still. (A falconry metaphor; birds could be given extra wing feathers.)   **8 And . . . majesty** and have added to the majesty of poets already capable of it.   **9 compile** compose, write **10 influence** inspiration. (With suggestion of astrological meaning.) **11 mend the style** correct or improve the style. (Also with a suggestion of repairing the point of a writing quill or stylus, continuing the metaphor of *pen* and *feathers*.)   **12 arts** learning, literary culture **13 advance** lift up
79.3 numbers verse   **4 doth . . . place** yields place to another.

I grant, sweet love, thy lovely argument
Deserves the travail of a worthier pen,
Yet what of thee thy poet doth invent
He robs thee of and pays it thee again.   8
He lends thee virtue, and he stole that word
From thy behavior; beauty doth he give,
And found it in thy cheek; he can afford
No praise to thee but what in thee doth live.   12
     Then thank him not for that which he doth say,
     Since what he owes thee thou thyself dost pay.

80

Oh, how I faint when I of you do write,
Knowing a better spirit doth use your name,
And in the praise thereof spends all his might
To make me tongue-tied, speaking of your fame!   4
But since your worth, wide as the ocean is,
The humble as the proudest sail doth bear,
My saucy bark, inferior far to his,
On your broad main doth willfully appear.   8
Your shallowest help will hold me up afloat,
Whilst he upon your soundless deep doth ride;
Or, being wrecked, I am a worthless boat,
He of tall building and of goodly pride.   12
     Then if he thrive and I be cast away,
     The worst was this: my love was my decay.

81

Or I shall live your epitaph to make,
Or you survive when I in earth am rotten,
From hence your memory death cannot take,
Although in me each part will be forgotten.   4
Your name from hence immortal life shall have,
Though I, once gone, to all the world must die;
The earth can yield me but a common grave,
When you entombèd in men's eyes shall lie.   8
Your momument shall be my gentle verse,
Which eyes not yet created shall o'erread,
And tongues to be your being shall rehearse
When all the breathers of this world are dead.   12
     You still shall live—such virtue hath my pen—
     Where breath most breathes, even in the mouths of
        men.

82

I grant thou wert not married to my Muse,
And therefore mayst without attaint o'erlook
The dedicated words which writers use
Of their fair subject, blessing every book.   4
Thou art as fair in knowledge as in hue,
Finding thy worth a limit past my praise,
And therefore art enforced to seek anew
Some fresher stamp of these time-bettering days.   8
And do so, love; yet when they have devised
What strainèd touches rhetoric can lend,
Thou, truly fair, wert truly sympathized
In true plain words by thy true-telling friend;   12
     And their gross painting might be better used
     Where cheeks need blood; in thee it is abused.

83

I never saw that you did painting need,
And therefore to your fair no painting set;
I found, or thought I found, you did exceed
The barren tender of a poet's debt;   4
And therefore have I slept in your report,
That you yourself, being extant, well might show
How far a modern quill doth come too short,
Speaking of worth, what worth in you doth grow.   8
This silence for my sin you did impute,
Which shall be most my glory, being dumb;
For I impair not beauty, being mute,
When others would give life and bring a tomb.   12
     There lives more life in one of your fair eyes
     Than both your poets can in praise devise.

84

Who is it that says most which can say more
Than this rich praise: that you alone are you,
In whose confine immurèd is the store
Which should example where your equal grew?   4

5 **thy lovely argument** the theme of your lovable qualities   **6 travail** labor   **7–8 Yet . . . again** yet whatever a poet under your patronage discovers as a literary subject concerning you he merely robs from you and gives you back your own again.   **11 afford** furnish, extend   **80.1 faint** grow weak, falter   **2 better spirit** i.e., rival poet, whom the speaker admires   **5 wide . . . is** as wide as is the ocean   **6 as** as well as   **8 main** ocean.   **willfully** perversely, audaciously   **9 Your . . . afloat** i.e., My genius is so slight that I derive only minimal benefit from the greatness of you as my subject   **10 soundless** unfathomable   **11 wrecked** shipwrecked   **12 tall building** i.e., sturdy construction.   **pride** splendor.   **13 cast away** (1) shipwrecked (2) abandoned   **14 my love** (1) my love for you, which led me to be so reckless in my inferior boat (2) you, my beloved.   **decay** ruin.
81.1 Or Whether   **3 hence** (1) this poetry (2) the world   **4 in . . . part** every quality of mine (as distinguished from the poetry)   **5 from hence** (1) from this poetry (2) henceforth   **11 to be** i.e., of persons yet unborn.   **rehearse** recite   **12 breathers** living people.   **this world** this present time   **13 virtue** power   **14 even in the** in the very

82.2 attaint blame, discredit.   **o'erlook** look at, peruse   **3 dedicated** devoted. (With suggestion of "dedicatory.")   **writers** i.e., other writers   **4 blessing every book** i.e., you bestowing favor thus on the writings presented to you, or, writers commending their own work.   **5 hue** complexion, appearance   **6 a limit . . . praise** an area extending beyond the capacities of my praise   **8 Some . . . days** some more recently issued imprint, i.e., more up-to-date literary product of this culturally sophisticated age.   **11 wert truly sympathized** would be faithfully matched and described   **13 gross painting** flattery that is heavily laid on, like a cosmetic   **14 abused** misused, misapplied.
83.1 painting i.e., artificial enhancement of beauty   **2 fair** beauty.   **set** applied   **4 The barren . . . debt** the worthless homage that a poet can offer you   **5 slept . . . report** been neglectful in writing praisingly of you   **6 That** because, so that.   **extant** still alive and much in the public eye   **7 modern** (1) commonplace (2) up-to-date   **7–8 doth come . . . grow** comes too short, in describing your worth, of the actual worth that flourishes in you.   **9–10 This . . . dumb** You imputed my silence to willful failure when, in fact, it will prove most to my credit   **11 being mute** (Modifies I.)   **12 bring a tomb** i.e., instead, they bring an inadequate monument that conceals lifelessly rather than enhances.   **14 both your poets** i.e., (probably,) I and the rival poet
84.1–2 Who . . . praise What extravagant writer of praise can say more than this in way of praise   **3–4 In . . . grew** in whose person are contained all those rich qualities that would be needed as a model to produce again your equal in beauty.

Lean penury within that pen doth dwell
That to his subject lends not some small glory;
But he that writes of you, if he can tell
That you are you, so dignifies his story.   8
Let him but copy what in you is writ,
Not making worse what nature made so clear,
And such a counterpart shall fame his wit,
Making his style admirèd everywhere.   12
    You to your beauteous blessings add a curse,
      Being fond on praise, which makes your praises
        worse.

85

My tongue-tied Muse in manners holds her still,
While comments of your praise, richly compiled,
Reserve thy character with golden quill
And precious phrase by all the Muses filed.   4
I think good thoughts whilst other write good words,
And like unlettered clerk still cry "Amen"
To every hymn that able spirit affords
In polished form of well-refinèd pen.   8
Hearing you praised, I say "'Tis so, 'tis true,"
And to the most of praise add something more;
But that is in my thought, whose love to you,
Though words come hindmost, holds his rank before.   12
    Then others for the breath of words respect,
    Me for my dumb thoughts, speaking in effect.

86

Was it the proud full sail of his great verse,
Bound for the prize of all-too-precious you,
That did my ripe thoughts in my brain inhearse,
Making their tomb the womb wherein they grew?   4
Was it his spirit, by spirits taught to write
Above a mortal pitch, that struck me dead?
No, neither he, nor his compeers by night
Giving him aid, my verse astonishèd.   8
He, nor that affable familiar ghost

Which nightly gulls him with intelligence,
As victors of my silence cannot boast;
I was not sick of any fear from thence.   12
    But when your countenance filled up his line,
    Then lacked I matter; that enfeebled mine.

87

Farewell! Thou art too dear for my possessing,
And like enough thou know'st thy estimate.
The charter of thy worth gives thee releasing;
My bonds in thee are all determinate.   4
For how do I hold thee but by thy granting,
And for that riches where is my deserving?
The cause of this fair gift in me is wanting,
And so my patent back again is swerving.   8
Thyself thou gav'st, thy own worth then not knowing,
Or me, to whom thou gav'st it, else mistaking;
So thy great gift, upon misprision growing,
Comes home again, on better judgment making.   12
    Thus have I had thee as a dream doth flatter,
    In sleep a king, but waking no such matter.

88

When thou shalt be disposed to set me light
And place my merit in the eye of scorn,
Upon thy side against myself I'll fight
And prove thee virtuous, though thou art forsworn.   4
With mine own weakness being best acquainted,
Upon thy part I can set down a story
Of faults concealed, wherein I am attainted,
That thou in losing me shall win much glory.   8
And I by this will be a gainer too;
For, bending all my loving thoughts on thee,
The injuries that to myself I do,
Doing thee vantage, double-vantage me.   12
    Such is my love, to thee I so belong,
    That for thy right myself will bear all wrong.

89

Say that thou didst forsake me for some fault,
And I will comment upon that offense;
Speak of my lameness, and I straight will halt,

5–6 Lean . . . glory It is a poor piece of writing indeed that does not confer at least some glory on its subject **8 so** sufficiently, thus **10 clear** glorious, shining **11 counterpart** copy, likeness. **fame** endow with fame **13 curse** (1) defect in character (2) burden for those seeking to praise you **14 Being fond** doting. **which . . . worse** (1) which encourages false flattery (2) which makes all praise seem inadequate in comparison to you.
85.1 in . . . still politely remains silent **2 comments . . . compiled** eulogies of you composed in fine language **3 Reserve thy character** store up praise of you in their writings. **golden** aureate, affected **4 precious** affected. **filed** polished. **5 other** others **6–7 like . . . affords** like an illiterate assistant to a priest continually give my approval to every praising verse that the rival poet (and others like him) provides **10 most** highmost **11 that . . . thought** that which I add is added silently **12 holds . . . before** is second to none in love. **13 Then . . . respect** Then take notice of others for what they say **14 speaking in effect** conveying what speech would say.
86.1 his i.e., an unidentified rival poet's **2 prize** capture, booty (as in a seized cargo vessel) **3 inhearse** coffin up **5 spirits** i.e., literary ancestors or contemporaries. (With a suggestion also of *daemons*, attendant spirits.) **6 pitch** height. (A term from falconry.) **dead** i.e., dumb, silent. **7 compeers by night** spirits (see line 5) visiting and aiding the poet in his dreams or nighttime reading **8 astonishèd** struck dumb. **9 ghost** spirit (as in lines 5 and 7)

10 gulls misleads. **intelligence** information, ideas **12 of** with **13 countenance filled up** (1) approval repaired any defect in (2) beauty served as subject for **14 lacked I matter** I had nothing left to write about
87.1 dear precious **2 like** likely, probably. **estimate** value. **3 charter of** privilege derived from. **releasing** i.e., release from obligations of love **4 determinate** ended, expired. (A legal term, as throughout this sonnet.) **8 my . . . swerving** my rights of possession revert to you. **10 mistaking** i.e., overvaluing **11 upon misprision growing** arising out of error **12 on . . . making** on your forming a more accurate judgment.
88.1 set me light make light of me, value me slightingly **3 Upon thy side** supporting your case. (Also *Upon thy part* in line 6.) **7 concealed** not publicly known. **attainted** dishonored **8 That** so that. **losing** i.e., separating from. (With a suggestion of "loosing," "setting free," the Quarto spelling.) **12 vantage** advantage
89.1 Say Assert, claim **2 comment** enlarge **3 Speak . . . halt** i.e., If you ascribe to me any kind of handicap, I immediately will limp to show that you are right. (*Halt* also has the suggestion of ceasing to object, remaining silent.)

Against thy reasons making no defense.
Thou canst not, love, disgrace me half so ill,
To set a form upon desirèd change,
As I'll myself disgrace, knowing thy will.
I will acquaintance strangle and look strange,   8
Be absent from thy walks, and in my tongue
Thy sweet belovèd name no more shall dwell,
Lest I, too much profane, should do it wrong
And haply of our old acquaintance tell.   12
    For thee against myself I'll vow debate,
    For I must ne'er love him whom thou dost hate.

90

Then hate me when thou wilt; if ever, now;
Now, while the world is bent my deeds to cross,
Join with the spite of fortune, make me bow,
And do not drop in for an after-loss.   4
Ah, do not, when my heart hath scaped this sorrow,
Come in the rearward of a conquered woe;
Give not a windy night a rainy morrow,
To linger out a purposed overthrow.   8
If thou wilt leave me, do not leave me last,
When other petty griefs have done their spite,
But in the onset come; so shall I taste
At first the very worst of fortune's might,   12
    And other strains of woe, which now seem woe,
    Compared with loss of thee will not seem so.

91

Some glory in their birth, some in their skill,
Some in their wealth, some in their body's force,
Some in their garments, though newfangled ill,
Some in their hawks and hounds, some in their horse;   4
And every humor hath his adjunct pleasure,
Wherein it finds a joy above the rest.
But these particulars are not my measure;
All these I better in one general best.   8
Thy love is better than high birth to me,
Richer than wealth, prouder than garments' cost,
Of more delight than hawks or horses be;
And having thee, of all men's pride I boast—   12
    Wretched in this alone, that thou mayst take
    All this away and me most wretched make.

92

But do thy worst to steal thyself away,
For term of life thou art assurèd mine,
And life no longer than thy love will stay,
For it depends upon that love of thine.   4
Then need I not to fear the worst of wrongs,
When in the least of them my life hath end;
I see a better state to me belongs
Than that which on thy humor doth depend.   8
Thou canst not vex me with inconstant mind,
Since that my life on thy revolt doth lie.
Oh, what a happy title do I find,
Happy to have thy love, happy to die!   12
    But what's so blessèd-fair that fears no blot?
    Thou mayst be false, and yet I know it not.

93

So shall I live, supposing thou art true,
Like a deceivèd husband; so love's face
May still seem love to me, though altered new,
Thy looks with me, thy heart in other place.   4
For there can live no hatred in thine eye,
Therefore in that I cannot know thy change.
In many's looks the false heart's history
Is writ in moods and frowns and wrinkles strange,   8
But heaven in thy creation did decree
That in thy face sweet love should ever dwell;
Whate'er thy thoughts or thy heart's workings be,
Thy looks should nothing thence but sweetness tell.   12
    How like Eve's apple doth thy beauty grow,
    If thy sweet virtue answer not thy show!

94

They that have power to hurt and will do none,
That do not do the thing they most do show,
Who, moving others, are themselves as stone,
Unmovèd, cold, and to temptation slow,   4
They rightly do inherit heaven's graces
And husband nature's riches from expense;

4 **reasons** charges, arguments 5 **disgrace** discredit 6 **To . . . change** to provide a pretext for (in the interest of justifying) your change of affection and to set it in proper order 7 **As . . . disgrace** as I will disfigure and depreciate myself 8 **acquaintance strangle** put an end to familiarity (with you). **strange** like a stranger 9 **walks** haunts 12 **haply** perchance 13 **vow debate** declare hostility, quarrel **90.2 bent** determined. **cross** thwart 4 **drop . . . after-loss** crushingly add to my sorrow. 5–6 **do not . . . woe** do not, when I have just recovered from my present grief, attack me from the rear 7 **windy, rainy** (Suggestive of sighs and tears.) 8 **linger out** protract. **purposed** intended, inevitable 11 **in the onset** at the outset 13 **strains** (1) kinds (2) stresses **91.3 newfangled ill** fashionably unattractive 4 **horse** horses 5 **humor** disposition, temperament. **his adjunct** its corresponding 7 **measure** standard (of happiness); lot in life 8 **better** surpass, improve upon 10 **prouder** more splendid 12 **of . . . boast** I boast of having the equivalent of all that is a source of pride in other men

92.1 But do i.e., But even if you do **2 term of life** i.e., my lifetime **5–6 Then . . . end** I need not fear what most people would call the worst of misfortunes, since the seemingly lesser misfortune—loss of your friendship—would prove fatal to me **7–8 I see . . . depend** i.e., I see that I am happier than most people whose happiness ends when they are cast from favor, since my very existence will cease when I am cast from favor and thus will end my misery. **humor** whim, fancy **10 Since . . . lie** since if you desert me it will cost me my life. **11 happy title** right to be thought happy; fortunate legal right of ownership **13 that fears** as to fear **14 Thou . . . not** i.e., My worst fate would be to lose your affection without knowing it and thereby live on in an unloved state, unreleased by the death that certainty of your desertion would bring. **93.1 So** (Continues the thought of sonnet 92.) **supposing** I supposing (incorrectly) **2 face** appearance **3 new** to something new **5 For** Since **6 in . . . change** I won't be able to detect your changed affection from your eyes. **8 moods** moody looks. **strange** unfriendly **14 answer . . . show** does not conform with your outward appearance. **94.1 and . . . none** and do not willfully try to do hurt **2 show** i.e., show themselves capable of, or, seem to do **4 cold** dispassionate **5 inherit** (1) receive through inheritance (2) enjoy, make use of **6 husband** carefully manage, preserve. **expense** waste, expenditure.

They are the lords and owners of their faces,
Others but stewards of their excellence.
The summer's flower is to the summer sweet,
Though to itself it only live and die,
But if that flower with base infection meet,
The basest weed outbraves his dignity.   12
    For sweetest things turn sourest by their deeds;
    Lilies that fester smell far worse than weeds.

95

How sweet and lovely dost thou make the shame
Which, like a canker in the fragrant rose,
Doth spot the beauty of thy budding name!
Oh, in what sweets dost thou thy sins enclose!   4
That tongue that tells the story of thy days,
Making lascivious comments on thy sport,
Cannot dispraise, but, in a kind of praise,
Naming thy name, blesses an ill report.   8
Oh, what a mansion have those vices got
Which for their habitation chose out thee,
Where beauty's veil doth cover every blot,
And all things turns to fair that eyes can see!   12
    Take heed, dear heart, of this large privilege;
    The hardest knife ill used doth lose his edge.

96

Some say thy fault is youth, some wantonness;
Some say thy grace is youth and gentle sport;
Both grace and faults are loved of more and less;
Thou mak'st faults graces that to thee resort.   4
As on the finger of a thronèd queen
The basest jewel will be well esteemed,
So are those errors that in thee are seen
To truths translated and for true things deemed.   8
How many lambs might the stern wolf betray,
If like a lamb he could his looks translate!
How many gazers mightst thou lead away,
If thou wouldst use the strength of all thy state!   12
    But do not so; I love thee in such sort
    As, thou being mine, mine is thy good report.

97

How like a winter hath my absence been
From thee, the pleasure of the fleeting year!
What freezings have I felt, what dark days seen!
What old December's bareness everywhere!   4
And yet this time removed was summer's time,
The teeming autumn, big with rich increase,
Bearing the wanton burden of the prime,
Like widowed wombs after their lords' decease.   8
Yet this abundant issue seemed to me
But hope of orphans and unfathered fruit,
For summer and his pleasures wait on thee,
And, thou away, the very birds are mute;   12
    Or, if they sing, 'tis with so dull a cheer
    That leaves look pale, dreading the winter's near.

98

From you have I been absent in the spring,
When proud-pied April, dressed in all his trim,
Hath put a spirit of youth in everything,
That heavy Saturn laughed and leapt with him.   4
Yet nor the lays of birds nor the sweet smell
Of different flowers in odor and in hue
Could make me any summer's story tell,
Or from their proud lap pluck them where they grew.   8
Nor did I wonder at the lily's white,
Nor praise the deep vermilion in the rose;
They were but sweet, but figures of delight
Drawn after you, you pattern of all those.   12
    Yet seemed it winter still, and, you away,
    As with your shadow I with these did play.

99

The forward violet thus did I chide:
"Sweet thief, whence didst thou steal thy sweet that
    smells,
If not from my love's breath? The purple pride
Which on thy soft cheek for complexion dwells   4
In my love's veins thou hast too grossly dyed."
The lily I condemnèd for thy hand,
And buds of marjoram had stol'n thy hair;
The roses fearfully on thorns did stand,   8

---

7 They . . . faces they are completely masters of themselves and of the qualities that appear in them   **8 but stewards** are merely custodians or dispensers   **9–10 The . . . die** i.e., Such self-contained persons may seem like flowers that live and die unto themselves, but, in fact, they have much sweetness and beauty to bestow   **12 outbraves his dignity** surpasses in show its worth.   **14 Lilies . . . weeds** (This line appears in the anonymous play *Edward III*, usually dated before 1595 and attributed in part by some editors to Shakespeare.)
95.2 canker cankerworm that destroys buds and leaves   **3 name** reputation.   **6 sport** amours   **8 blesses** graces   **12 all . . . fair** makes everything deceptively beautiful   **13 large** unlimited, licentious   **14 his** its
96.1 wantonness (1) exuberance (2) lechery   **2 gentle sport** gentlemanlike amorousness   **3 of more and less** by high and low   **4 Thou . . . resort** you convert into graces the faults that attend you.   **8 translated** transformed   **9 stern** cruel   **10 like** i.e., unto those of   **11 away** astray   **12 the strength . . . state** the full power at your command, i.e., your wealth, charm, and social rank.   **13–14 But . . . report** (The same couplet ends sonnet 36.)   **report** reputation.

97.5 time removed time of separation   **6 big** pregnant   **7 the wanton . . . prime** the fruit or offspring of wanton spring, i.e., the crops planted in springtime   **9 issue** offspring   **10 hope of orphans** orphaned hope   **11 his** its.   **wait on thee** attend on you, are at your disposal   **13 with . . . cheer** in so melancholy a fashion
98.2 proud-pied gorgeously multicolored.   **trim** finery   **4 That** so that.   **Saturn** (A planet associated with melancholy, *heavy*.)   **5 nor the lays** neither the songs   **6 different flowers** flowers differing   **7 any summer's story** i.e., any pleasant story   **8 proud lap** i.e., the earth   **11 but sweet . . . delight** mere sweetness, mere delightful forms or emblems   **12 after** resembling   **14 shadow** image, portrait.   **these** i.e., the flowers
99.1 forward early and presumptuous. (This sonnet has fifteen lines, the first being introductory.)   **2 thy sweet** your scent   **3 pride** splendor   **5 grossly** obviously and heavily   **6 for thy hand** i.e., because it has stolen its whiteness from your hand   **7 And . . . hair** i.e., and I condemned the buds of marjoram for having stolen your hair.   **buds of marjoram** (These are dark purple-red or auburn, and it may be that the reference is to color, although marjoram is noted for its sweet scent.)   **8 on thorns did stand** grew on thorny stems. (With a suggestion of being apprehensive.)

One blushing shame, another white despair;
A third, nor red nor white, had stol'n of both
And to his robbery had annexed thy breath,
But, for his theft, in pride of all his growth   12
A vengeful canker ate him up to death.
        More flowers I noted, yet I none could see
        But sweet or color it had stol'n from thee.

100

Where art thou, Muse, that thou forget'st so long
To speak of that which gives thee all thy might?
Spend'st thou thy fury on some worthless song,
Dark'ning thy pow'r to lend base subjects light?   4
Return, forgetful Muse, and straight redeem
In gentle numbers time so idly spent;
Sing to the ear that doth thy lays esteem
And gives thy pen both skill and argument.   8
Rise, resty Muse, my love's sweet face survey
If Time have any wrinkle graven there;
If any, be a satire to decay,
And make Time's spoils despisèd everywhere.   12
        Give my love fame faster than Time wastes life;
        So thou prevent'st his scythe and crooked knife.

101

O truant Muse, what shall be thy amends
For thy neglect of truth in beauty dyed?
Both truth and beauty on my love depends;
So dost thou too, and therein dignified.   4
Make answer, Muse. Wilt thou not haply say,
"Truth needs no color with his color fixed,
Beauty no pencil, beauty's truth to lay,
But best is best, if never intermixed"?   8
Because he needs no praise, wilt thou be dumb?
Excuse not silence so, for 't lies in thee
To make him much outlive a gilded tomb
And to be praised of ages yet to be.   12
        Then do thy office, Muse; I teach thee how
        To make him seem, long hence, as he shows now.

102

My love is strengthened, though more weak in seeming;
I love not less, though less the show appear.
That love is merchandized whose rich esteeming
The owner's tongue doth publish everywhere.   4
Our love was new and then but in the spring
When I was wont to greet it with my lays,
As Philomel in summer's front doth sing
And stops her pipe in growth of riper days—   8
Not that the summer is less pleasant now
Than when her mournful hymns did hush the night,
But that wild music burdens every bough
And sweets grown common lose their dear delight.   12
        Therefore like her I sometime hold my tongue,
        Because I would not dull you with my song.

103

Alack, what poverty my Muse brings forth,
That, having such a scope to show her pride,
The argument all bare is of more worth
Than when it hath my added praise beside.   4
Oh, blame me not if I no more can write!
Look in your glass, and there appears a face
That overgoes my blunt invention quite,
Dulling my lines and doing me disgrace.   8
Were it not sinful then, striving to mend,
To mar the subject that before was well?
For to no other pass my verses tend
Than of your graces and your gifts to tell;   12
        And more, much more, than in my verse can sit
        Your own glass shows you when you look in it.

104

To me, fair friend, you never can be old,
For, as you were when first your eye I eyed,
Such seems your beauty still. Three winters cold
Have from the forests shook three summers' pride,   4
Three beauteous springs to yellow autumn turned
In process of the seasons have I seen,
Three April perfumes in three hot Junes burned
Since first I saw you fresh, which yet are green.   8

9 **shame** i.e., red for shame   10 **nor red** neither (purely) red   11 **to . . . annexed** to this robbery had added the robbery of   12 **But, for** although, in punishment for.   **in pride . . . growth** in his prime   13 **canker** cankerworm   15 **But** except.   **sweet** scent (as in line 2)
100.3 **fury** poetic inspiration   4 **Dark'ning** debasing   5 **straight** straightway   6 **gentle numbers** noble verses.   **idly** foolishly   7 **lays** songs   8 **argument** subject.   9 **resty** inactive, lazy   10 **If** to see if   11 **If any** if there are any.   **satire** to satirist of, here one composing a satire on Time as a despoiler   12 **spoils** acts of destruction, ravages   13 **faster** (1) more quickly (2) more firmly   14 **thou prevent'st** you forestall, thwart.   **crooked knife** curved blade.
101.1 **what . . . amends** what reparation will you make   2 **truth . . . dyed** truth made integrally a part of the beauty which it inhabits.   3–4 **Both . . . dignified** i.e., Both faith and beauty depend on my love for their proper appreciation and recognition, and you, my Muse, depend for your very office and dignity on that same function.   5 **haply** perhaps   6 **no . . . fixed** no artificial color (with suggestion of *pretense*) added to its natural and permanent color or hue   7 **pencil** paintbrush.   **lay** apply color to, as with a brush   8 **intermixed** adulterated.   9 **dumb** silent.   12 **of** by   13 **office** function   14 **long hence** long in the future.   **shows** appears

102.1 **seeming** outward appearance   3 **merchandized** degraded by being treated as a thing of sale.   **esteeming** valuation   4 **publish** announce, advertise   5 **in the spring** only just beginning   6 **wont . . . lays** accustomed to salute it (our love) with my song
7 **Philomel** the nightingale.   **front** forehead, beginning   8 **stops her pipe** stops singing.   **riper** i.e., those of late summer and autumn   11 **But . . . music** i.e., but because a profusion of wild birds' singing. (Refers to other poets.)   **burdens** weighs down. (But with a musical sense as well; a *burden* is a chorus.)   14 **dull** surfeit
103.1 **poverty** poor stuff   2 **pride** splendor   3 **argument all bare** subject alone, unadorned   5 **no more can write** i.e., (1) am silent (2) cannot go beyond what you yourself are, cannot excel my own poverty of invention.   6 **glass** mirror   7 **overgoes** surpasses; overwhelms.   **blunt invention** unpolished style, writing   8 **Dulling** i.e., making dull by comparison   11 **pass** purpose, issue   13 **sit** reside
104.4 **pride** splendor   6 **process** the progression   8 **which yet** who still

Ah, yet doth beauty, like a dial hand,
Steal from his figure and no pace perceived.
So your sweet hue, which methinks still doth stand,
Hath motion, and mine eye may be deceived,   12
    For fear of which, hear this, thou age unbred:
    Ere you were born was beauty's summer dead.

105

Let not my love be called idolatry,
Nor my belovèd as an idol show,
Since all alike my songs and praises be
To one, of one, still such, and ever so.   4
Kind is my love today, tomorrow kind,
Still constant in a wondrous excellence;
Therefore my verse, to constancy confined,
One thing expressing, leaves out difference.   8
"Fair, kind, and true" is all my argument,
"Fair, kind, and true" varying to other words;
And in this change is my invention spent,
Three themes in one, which wondrous scope affords.   12
    Fair, kind, and true have often lived alone,
    Which three till now never kept seat in one.

106

When in the chronicle of wasted time
I see descriptions of the fairest wights,
And beauty making beautiful old rhyme
In praise of ladies dead and lovely knights,   4
Then, in the blazon of sweet beauty's best,
Of hand, of foot, of lip, of eye, of brow,
I see their antique pen would have expressed
Even such a beauty as you master now.   8
So all their praises are but prophecies
Of this our time, all you prefiguring;
And, for they looked but with divining eyes,
They had not skill enough your worth to sing.   12
    For we, which now behold these present days,
    Have eyes to wonder, but lack tongues to praise.

107

Not mine own fears nor the prophetic soul
Of the wide world dreaming on things to come
Can yet the lease of my true love control,
Supposed as forfeit to a confined doom.   4
The mortal moon hath her eclipse endured,
And the sad augurs mock their own presage;
Incertainties now crown themselves assured,
And peace proclaims olives of endless age.   8
Now with the drops of this most balmy time
My love looks fresh, and Death to me subscribes,
Since, spite of him, I'll live in this poor rhyme,
While he insults o'er dull and speechless tribes;   12
    And thou in this shalt find thy monument,
    When tyrants' crests and tombs of brass are spent.

108

What's in the brain that ink may character
Which hath not figured to thee my true spirit?
What's new to speak, what now to register,
That may express my love or thy dear merit?   4
Nothing, sweet boy; but yet, like prayers divine,
I must each day say o'er the very same,
Counting no old thing old—thou mine, I thine—
Even as when first I hallowed thy fair name.   8
So that eternal love in love's fresh case
Weighs not the dust and injury of age,
Nor gives to necessary wrinkles place,
But makes antiquity for aye his page,   12
    Finding the first conceit of love there bred
    Where time and outward form would show it dead.

109

Oh, never say that I was false of heart,
Though absence seemed my flame to qualify.

9–10 yet . . . perceived yet beauty slips almost imperceptibly away, from you, like the dial hand of a watch making its stealthy progress away from number to number on the dial face.   **11 hue** appearance, complexion.   **still doth stand** remains seemingly unaltered   **13 unbred** not yet born
105.2 show appear   **4 To . . . so** (The poet loves his friend in phrases that recall the paradoxical and mysterious duality of two in one, as in "The Phoenix and Turtle." Such sacred love, by analogy, cannot be idolatry.)   **8 difference** diversity of theme and the seeming diversity of two persons (the poet and his friend) who are essentially one; also the seeming diversity of "Fair, kind, and true" which is also a variation on a single theme.   **11 this change** variations on this theme.   **invention** inventiveness.   **spent** expended
13 alone separately (in different people)   **14 kept seat** resided; sat enthroned
106.1 wasted past, used up   **2 wights** persons   **3 beauty** (1) beauty of style and language (2) beauty of the persons described   **5 blazon** i.e., glorification, cataloguing of qualities. (A heraldic metaphor.)
8 master possess, control   **11 for** because.   **divining** guessing or predicting as to the future   **13 For we** For even we   **14 praise** i.e., praise you worthily, sufficiently.

107.1–2 soul . . . world collective consciousness of humanity   **3–4 Can . . . doom** can set a limit to the time allotted to me to love you, though imagined to be destined to expire after a limited term.   **5 mortal moon** (Probably a reference to Queen Elizabeth, ill or deceased, most probably to her death in 1603; she was known as Diana, Cynthia, etc.)
6 And . . . presage and the solemn prophets of disaster now mock their earlier predictions   **7 Incertainties . . . assured** uncertainties have triumphantly given way to certainties. (Probably a reference to the accession and coronation of King James VI of Scotland and I of England.)   **8 olives** (Conventionally associated with peace and probably pointing here to King James I's resolutions of war with Spain and strife in Ireland.)   **of endless age** without foreseen end.   **9 with the drops** i.e., healed as though by a balmy dew. (Balm was employed in the coronation ceremony for James in 1603, as in all such coronations.)
10 subscribes yields   **12 insults . . . tribes** triumphs scornfully over endless generations of dead who have no poet to celebrate them   **14 crests** trophies adorning a tomb.   **spent** expended, wasted away.
108.1 character write   **2 figured** revealed, represented.   **true** constant   **3 register** record   **7 Counting . . . thine** dismissing no old truth as out of date or shopworn, such as the truth that you are mine and I yours   **8 hallowed** (As in "hallowed be thy name" from the Lord's Prayer.)   **9 fresh case** new exterior and circumstance
10 Weighs not is unconcerned about   **11 place** consideration, primacy   **12–14 But . . . dead** Love makes age serve its grand purposes, finding in age and antiquity the first stirrings of love, in a place where conventionally one would suppose it to be dead.
109.2 flame passion.   **qualify** temper, moderate.

As easy might I from myself depart
As from my soul, which in thy breast doth lie.   4
That is my home of love; if I have ranged,
Like him that travels I return again,
Just to the time, not with the time exchanged,
So that myself bring water for my stain.   8
Never believe, though in my nature reigned
All frailties that besiege all kinds of blood,
That it could so preposterously be stained
To leave for nothing all thy sum of good;   12
    For nothing this wide universe I call
    Save thou, my rose; in it thou art my all.

110

Alas, 'tis true, I have gone here and there
And made myself a motley to the view,
Gored mine own thoughts, sold cheap what is most dear,
Made old offenses of affections new;   4
Most true it is that I have looked on truth
Askance and strangely. But, by all above,
These blenches gave my heart another youth,
And worse essays proved thee my best of love.   8
Now all is done, have what shall have no end.
Mine appetite I never more will grind
On newer proof, to try an older friend,
A god in love, to whom I am confined.   12
    Then give me welcome, next my heaven the best,
    Even to thy pure and most most loving breast.

111

Oh, for my sake do you with Fortune chide,
The guilty goddess of my harmful deeds,
That did not better for my life provide
Than public means which public manners breeds.   4
Thence comes it that my name receives a brand,
And almost thence my nature is subdued
To what it works in, like the dyer's hand.
Pity me then, and wish I were renewed,   8
Whilst, like a willing patient, I will drink

Potions of eisel 'gainst my strong infection;
No bitterness that I will bitter think,
Nor double penance, to correct correction.   12
    Pity me then, dear friend, and I assure ye
    Even that your pity is enough to cure me.

112

Your love and pity doth th'impression fill
Which vulgar scandal stamped upon my brow;
For what care I who calls me well or ill,
So you o'ergreen my bad, my good allow?   4
You are my all the world, and I must strive
To know my shames and praises from your tongue;
None else to me, nor I to none alive,
That my steeled sense or changes, right or wrong.   8
In so profound abysm I throw all care
Of others' voices that my adder's sense
To critic and to flatterer stoppèd are.
Mark how with my neglect I do dispense: 12
    You are so strongly in my purpose bred
    That all the world besides, methinks, are dead.

113

Since I left you, mine eye is in my mind,
And that which governs me to go about
Doth part his function and is partly blind,
Seems seeing, but effectually is out;   4
For it no form delivers to the heart
Of bird, of flower, or shape, which it doth latch;
Of his quick objects hath the mind no part,
Nor his own vision holds what it doth catch;   8
For if it see the rud'st or gentlest sight,
The most sweet-favor or deformd'st creature,
The mountain or the sea, the day or night,
The crow or dove, it shapes them to your feature.   12

5 **ranged** traveled, wandered   7 **Just . . . exchanged** punctual to the minute, not changed by the period of separation   8 **water for my stain** i.e., repentant tears, to wash away the stain of my offense. 10 **blood** temperament, sensual nature   12 **for** in exchange for 110.2 **motley** jester, fool.   **to the view** in the eyes of the world 3 **Gored** wounded   4 **Made . . . new** i.e., repeated old offenses or made offense against old friendship in forming new attachments 5 **truth** constancy   6 **Askance and strangely** disdainfully, obliquely and at a distance.   **by all above** by heaven   7 **blenches** swervings. **another youth** i.e., a renewal of true friendship   8 **essays** experiments (in friendship)   9 **Now all** Now that all that.   **have what . . . end** take what is eternal (my friendship).   10 **grind** whet, sharpen 11 **newer proof** further experiment, experience.   **try** test   13 **next my heaven** you, who are to me second only to heaven itself 111.1 **do you** (A command: "Do")   2 **guilty goddess of** goddess responsible for   3 **life** livelihood   4 **Than . . . breeds** than providing me a means of livelihood that depends on catering to the public. (A probable reference to Shakespeare's career as an actor.)   5 **receives a brand** is disgraced (through prejudice against my occupation) 7 **like the dyer's hand** (The dyer's hand is stained by the dye it handles, just as the dramatist's or actor's nature is almost overpowered by the medium in which he works—the theater.)   8 **renewed** restored to what I was by nature, cleansed

10 **eisel** vinegar, used as an antiseptic against the plague and also as an agent for removing stains   11 **No bitterness** there is no bitterness 12 **Nor . . . correction** nor will I think it bitter to undertake a twofold penance in order to correct what must be doubly corrected.   14 **Even that your pity** that very pity of yours
112.1 **doth th'impression fill** effaces the scar   2 **vulgar scandal** notoriety (for being an actor?)   4 **So you o'ergreen** provided that you cover as with green growth.   **allow** approve.   5 **my all the world** everything to me   7–8 **None . . . wrong** no one else but you affects my fixed and hardened sensibilities, whether for better or for worse. 9–11 **In . . . are** Into so deep an abyss do I throw all concern as to what others may think that, adderlike, my ears are deaf to critic and flatterer alike. (Adders were popularly supposed to have no sense of hearing.)   12 **Mark . . . dispense** See how I justify my disregard of the opinion of others   13 **You . . . bred** you are so nurtured in my thoughts and are such a powerful influence over my intentions 113.1 **mine . . . mind** i.e., I'm guided by my mind's eye   2 **that . . . about** i.e., my physical sight   3 **part** (1) divide (2) abandon.   **his** its, i.e., the physical eye's. (Also in lines 7 and 8.)   4 **Seems . . . out** seems to be seeing, but in reality is blind   5 **heart** (Here portrayed as capable of receiving sense impressions and of consciousness, as in sonnet 47.)   6 **latch** catch or receive the sight of   7 **Of . . . part** i.e., the mind, attuned to its inner eye, takes no part in the fleeting and lively (*quick*) things seen by the physical sight   8 **Nor . . . holds** nor does the eye itself retain.   **catch** see glimpsingly   9 **For . . . sight** for whether it see the most uncouth or most gracious sight   10 **sweet-favor** sweet-featured   12 **shapes . . . feature** makes them resemble you.

Incapable of more, replete with you,
My most true mind thus maketh mine eye untrue.

114

Or whether doth my mind, being crowned with you,
Drink up the monarch's plague, this flattery?
Or whether shall I say mine eye saith true,
And that your love taught it this alchemy, 4
To make of monsters and things indigest
Such cherubins as your sweet self resemble,
Creating every bad a perfect best
As fast as objects to his beams assemble? 8
Oh, 'tis the first, 'tis flatt'ry in my seeing,
And my great mind most kingly drinks it up;
Mine eye well knows what with his gust is greeing,
And to his palate doth prepare the cup. 12
      If it be poisoned, 'tis the lesser sin
      That mine eye loves it and doth first begin.

115

Those lines that I before have writ do lie,
Even those that said I could not love you dearer;
Yet then my judgment knew no reason why
My most full flame should afterwards burn clearer. 4
But reckoning Time, whose millioned accidents
Creep in twixt vows and change decrees of kings,
Tan sacred beauty, blunt the sharp'st intents,
Divert strong minds to th' course of alt'ring things— 8
Alas, why, fearing of Time's tyranny,
Might I not then say, "Now I love you best,"
When I was certain o'er incertainty,
Crowning the present, doubting of the rest? 12
      Love is a babe; then might I not say so,
      To give full growth to that which still doth grow.

116

Let me not to the marriage of true minds
Admit impediments. Love is not love

Which alters when it alteration finds,
Or bends with the remover to remove. 4
Oh, no, it is an ever-fixèd mark
That looks on tempests and is never shaken;
It is the star to every wand'ring bark,
Whose worth's unknown, although his height be taken. 8
Love's not Time's fool, though rosy lips and cheeks
Within his bending sickle's compass come;
Love alters not with his brief hours and weeks,
But bears it out even to the edge of doom. 12
      If this be error and upon me proved,
      I never writ, nor no man ever loved.

117

Accuse me thus: that I have scanted all
Wherein I should your great deserts repay,
Forgot upon your dearest love to call,
Whereto all bonds do tie me day by day; 4
That I have frequent been with unknown minds,
And given to time your own dear-purchased right;
That I have hoisted sail to all the winds
Which should transport me farthest from your sight. 8
Book both my willfulness and errors down,
And on just proof surmise accumulate;
Bring me within the level of your frown,
But shoot not at me in your wakened hate, 12
      Since my appeal says I did strive to prove
      The constancy and virtue of your love.

118

Like as to make our appetites more keen
With eager compounds we our palate urge;
As to prevent our maladies unseen
We sicken to shun sickness when we purge: 4
Even so, being full of your ne'er-cloying sweetness,
To bitter sauces did I frame my feeding
And, sick of welfare, found a kind of meetness

114.1, 3 Or whether (Indicates alternative possibilities.) 1 crowned with you elevated by possession of you 2 the monarch's . . . flattery this pleasing delusion to which all monarchs are prone. 4 your love my love of you. alchemy science of transmuting base metals 5 indigest chaotic, formless 6 cherubins angelic forms (suggesting the youth and beauty of the friend) 7 Creating creating out of 8 his beams its (the eye's) gaze 9 'tis flatt'ry . . . seeing my eye is flattering my mind (see lines 1–2) 11 what . . . greeing what agrees with the mind's taste 12 to to suit 13–14 'tis . . . begin it extenuates the eye's sinful deed (of misleading the mind) that it tastes of the poison first, like an official taster sampling food before it is given to the king. 115.5 reckoning Time (1) Time, which we reckon up (2) Time, which demands a reckoning and settles all accounts. millioned accidents multitudinous unforeseen occurrences 6 twixt vows i.e., between the making of vows and their fulfillment 7 Tan darken, i.e., coarsen 8 Divert . . . things divert the most resolute of intentions into the current of changing circumstances 9 fearing of fearing 10 Might . . . say i.e., wasn't it understandable for me to say then, when I wrote *Those lines* (line 1) 11 certain o'er incertainty i.e., certain of my love's perfection then, as contrasted with the uncertainty of the future 12 Crowning exalting. doubting of fearing 13 then might . . . so i.e., therefore it was wrong of me to say then, "Now I love you best" (line 10) 14 To give thereby giving
116.2 Admit concede that there might be, allow consideration of. (An echo of the marriage service.)

3 alteration i.e., in age, beauty, affection, health, circumstance 4 Or . . . remove or changes simply because there is change (by ill health, mental deterioration, death, absence, or inconstancy) in the person loved. 5 mark seamark, conspicuous object distinguishable at sea as an aid to navigation 7 wand'ring bark lost ship 8 Whose . . . taken whose value is beyond estimation, although its altitude above the horizon can be determined (for purposes of navigation). 9 fool plaything, laughingstock 10 his i.e., Time's. (Also in line 11.) bending curved. compass range 12 bears . . . doom endures or holds out to the very Day of Judgment.
117.1 scanted come short in 3 Forgot . . . call forgot to invoke or call upon your most precious love 5 frequent familiar. unknown minds strangers of no consequence 6 And . . . right and wasted time that should have been devoted to you, to which you had every right 8 should were likely to 9 Book . . . down Record both my willful faults and errors 10 on . . . accumulate to sure proof add surmise, suspicion 11 level point-blank range, aim 13 appeal legal appealing of the case. I . . . prove my intention was to test
118.1 Like as Just as 2 eager compounds pungent, bitter concoctions. urge stimulate 3 As just as. prevent anticipate, forestall 4 We . . . purge we induce a kind of sickness through purging (i.e., evacuation of stomach or bowel), in order to ward off greater sickness 5 Even so in just the same way 6 bitter sauces i.e., other loves, undesirable in comparison with you. frame adapt, direct 7 sick of welfare surfeited by health and happiness (in love). meetness suitability

To be diseased ere that there was true needing.
Thus policy in love, t'anticipate
The ills that were not, grew to faults assured,
And brought to medicine a healthful state
Which, rank of goodness, would by ill be cured.   12
    But thence I learn, and find the lesson true:
    Drugs poison him that so fell sick of you.

119

What potions have I drunk of siren tears,
Distilled from limbecks foul as hell within,
Applying fears to hopes and hopes to fears,
Still losing when I saw myself to win!   4
What wretched errors hath my heart committed,
Whilst it hath thought itself so blessèd never!
How have mine eyes out of their spheres been fitted
In the distraction of this madding fever!   8
Oh, benefit of ill! Now I find true
That better is by evil still made better;
And ruined love, when it is built anew,
Grows fairer than at first, more strong, far greater.   12
    So I return rebuked to my content,
    And gain by ills thrice more than I have spent.

120

That you were once unkind befriends me now,
And for that sorrow which I then did feel
Needs must I under my transgression bow,
Unless my nerves were brass or hammered steel.   4
For if you were by my unkindness shaken
As I by yours, you've passed a hell of time,
And I, a tyrant, have no leisure taken
To weigh how once I suffered in your crime.   8
Oh, that our night of woe might have remembered
My deepest sense how hard true sorrow hits,
And soon to you, as you to me then, tendered

The humble salve which wounded bosoms fits!   12
    But that your trespass now becomes a fee;
    Mine ransoms yours, and yours must ransom me.

121

'Tis better to be vile than vile esteemed
When not to be receives reproach of being,
And the just pleasure lost which is so deemed
Not by our feeling but by others' seeing.   4
For why should others' false adulterate eyes
Give salutation to my sportive blood?
Or on my frailties why are frailer spies,
Which in their wills count bad what I think good?   8
No, I am that I am, and they that level
At my abuses reckon up their own.
I may be straight though they themselves be bevel.
By their rank thoughts my deeds must not be shown,   12
    Unless this general evil they maintain:
    All men are bad, and in their badness reign.

122

Thy gift, thy tables, are within my brain
Full charactered with lasting memory,
Which shall above that idle rank remain
Beyond all date, even to eternity—   4
Or at the least, so long as brain and heart
Have faculty by nature to subsist;
Till each to razed oblivion yield his part
Of thee, thy record never can be missed.   8
That poor retention could not so much hold,
Nor need I tallies thy dear love to score;
Therefore to give them from me was I bold,

---

8 ere . . . needing before there was any real necessity for it.   **9 policy** shortsighted calculation. **t'anticipate** to forestall   **10 assured** actual   **11 to medicine** into a state of needing medical care   **12 rank of goodness** gorged and sickened by good health   **14 Drugs . . . you** a rash and unnecessary course of treatment inflicted true sickness on one (myself) who had thought himself weary of your company.
119.1 siren i.e., deceitful. (The poet seems to speak of an affair.) **2 limbecks** vessels used in distillation.   **foul as hell within** i.e., possessing an inner ugliness contrasted with a beautiful and seductive appearance   **3 Applying . . . fears** trying vainly to control my wild hopes with a sense of fear and to assuage my fears with hope   **4 Still** always.   **saw myself** vainly expected   **6 so blessèd never** never before so fortunate.   **7 How . . . fitted** How my eyes have popped out in convulsive fit   **8 distraction** frenzy.   **madding fever** fever that drives me mad.
120.1 befriends benefits (by giving me perspective on what I now need to do)   **2–3 for . . . bow** i.e., realizing the sorrow I felt from your unkindness, I must now acknowledge my own guilt in being unkind to you   **4 nerves** sinews   **6 hell of** hellish   **7 have . . . taken** have not taken the opportunity   **8 weigh** consider.   **in your crime** i.e., from your unkindness; or, from erring as you did. (If I suffered so, I should realize you've suffered, too, from my unkindness.)   **9 that our night of woe** would that the dark and woeful time of our earlier estrangement.   **remembered** reminded   **10 sense** consciousness, apprehension   **11 And . . . tendered** i.e., and would that I had quickly offered to you, as you did to me

12 humble salve i.e., apology and remorse.   **which . . . fits** which is just what wounded hearts need.   **13 that your trespass** that unkindness of yours.   **fee** payment, compensation   **14 ransoms** redeems, excuses
121.1 vile esteemed (to be) considered vile   **2 When . . . being** when not to be vile receives the reproach of vileness. (It's even worse to be unjustly accused of wickedness than to be reproved when one's conduct is truly vile.)   **3–4 And . . . seeing** and to lose justifiable pleasure because its justification has to depend not on our feelings but on the censorious attitudes of others.   **5 false adulterate eyes** i.e., the eyes of those whose own wickedness prompts them to misconstrue my innocent love   **6 Give . . . blood** i.e., greet me, in my lusty merriment, with familiarity and with a knowing wink of the eye.   **7 Or . . . spies** Or why should there be persons more faulty than I spying on my fleshly indulgences   **8 Which in their wills** who by the measure of their prurient, licentious minds   **9 am that** am what.   **level** (1) aim (2) guess   **10 abuses** misdoings.   **reckon up their own** i.e., merely enumerate their own misdeeds.   **11 bevel** out of square, crooked.   **12 rank** ugly, foul.   **shown** viewed, interpreted   **14 reign** i.e., prosper. (Only a cynic would interpret my success in love as a paradoxical proof of my sharing in general human depravity.)
122.1 tables writing tablet, memorandum book   **2 charactered with** written by   **3 that idle rank** i.e., the relative unimportance of that memorandum book (as compared with the memory itself)   **6 faculty . . . subsist** natural power to survive   **7–8 Till . . . missed** until both heart and brain have given up their memory of you to the ravages of time, what you have written never can be lost. (Hence the memorandum book itself, which the poet has given away, is not essential.)
9 retention i.e., the book, an instrument for retaining memoranda. **so much** i.e., as much as is in my memory   **10 tallies** sticks notched to serve for reckoning. (The notebook is such a mere *tally*.)   **score** reckon   **11 to . . . me** i.e., to give away the writing tablet.   **bold** i.e., bold in taking the liberty

To trust those tables that receive thee more.   12
    To keep an adjunct to remember thee
    Were to import forgetfulness in me.

123

No, Time, thou shalt not boast that I do change.
Thy pyramids built up with newer might
To me are nothing novel, nothing strange;
They are but dressings of a former sight.   4
Our dates are brief, and therefore we admire
What thou dost foist upon us that is old,
And rather make them born to our desire
Than think that we before have heard them told.   8
Thy registers and thee I both defy,
Not wond'ring at the present nor the past,
For thy records and what we see doth lie,
Made more or less by thy continual haste.   12
    This I do vow and this shall ever be:
    I will be true, despite thy scythe and thee.

124

If my dear love were but the child of state,
It might for Fortune's bastard be unfathered,
As subject to Time's love or to Time's hate,
Weeds among weeds, or flowers with flowers gathered.   4
No, it was builded far from accident;
It suffers not in smiling pomp, nor falls
Under the blow of thrallèd discontent,
Whereto th'inviting time our fashion calls.   8
It fears not Policy, that heretic,
Which works on leases of short-numbered hours,
But all alone stands hugely politic,
That it nor grows with heat nor drowns with showers.   12
    To this I witness call the fools of Time,
    Which die for goodness, who have lived for crime.

125

Were't aught to me I bore the canopy,
With my extern the outward honoring,
Or laid great bases for eternity
Which proves more short than waste or ruining?   4
Have I not seen dwellers on form and favor
Lose all, and more, by paying too much rent,
For compound sweet forgoing simple savor,
Pitiful thrivers, in their gazing spent?   8
No, let me be obsequious in thy heart,
And take thou my oblation, poor but free,
Which is not mixed with seconds, knows no art
But mutual render, only me for thee.   12
    Hence, thou suborned informer! A true soul
    When most impeached stands least in thy control.

126

O thou, my lovely boy, who in thy power
Dost hold Time's fickle glass, his sickle hour;
Who hast by waning grown, and therein show'st
Thy lovers withering as thy sweet self grow'st;   4
If Nature, sovereign mistress over wrack,
As thou goest onwards, still will pluck thee back,
She keeps thee to this purpose, that her skill
May Time disgrace and wretched minutes kill.   8
Yet fear her, O thou minion of her pleasure!
She may detain, but not still keep, her treasure.
Her audit, though delayed, answered must be,
And her quietus is to render thee.   12

---

12 those tables i.e., those of memory.   **receive thee more** retain more of you.   **13 adjunct** aid   **14 Were** would be.   **import** imply, impute   **123.2 pyramids** (May refer to obelisks or other structures erected in Rome in 1586 or in London in 1603.)   **3 nothing** not at all   **4 dressings . . . sight** reconstructions in new form of things from the past.   **5 dates** life spans   **7 make . . . desire** consider them newly created to our liking and reinvented by us   **8 told** reckoned, told about.   **9 registers** visual records, monuments   **10 wond'ring** marveling   **11 doth lie** deceives us   **12 Made . . . haste** i.e., raised one minute and ruined the next (by Time), and alternately overvalued and undervalued by us.
124.1–2 If . . . unfathered If my love for you were merely the product of circumstances and your high position, we might disavow it as nothing but the bastard child of Fortune   **4 Weeds . . . gathered** either despised as worthless like a weed or cherished like a flower as Fortune dictates.   **5 accident** chance, fortune   **6–8 It . . . calls** it does not grow acquiescent to the dictates of pomp and finery, nor does it weaken under the blows of slavish adversity, both of which the insidious mores of our present age tempt us to regard as fashionable.
9 Policy, that heretic cunning expediency, false to the spirit of love   **10 Which . . . hours** which thinks only shortsightedly of short-term gain and makes only short-term commitments   **11 hugely politic** prudent in a long-term sense   **12 That . . . showers** so that it neither pins its hopes unrealistically on rising fortunes nor grows desperate in times of adversity.   **13–14 To . . . crime** I call as witnesses those creatures of Time who succumb to the moral weaknesses described in this sonnet, and who repent their evil ways only after having lived corruptly.

125.1–4 Were't . . . ruining? Would it mean anything to me if I did public homage to great persons by carrying over their heads a cloth of state as they go in procession, thereby honoring what is external by means of a purely external action, or if I laid foundations for supposedly eternal monuments which then prove to last no longer than the forces of decay and ruin allow?   **5 dwellers . . . favor** those who depend on court etiquette and influence peddling; also, in figure and face   **6 by paying . . . rent** i.e., by overdoing flattery and depending too much on hopes of obtaining favor   **7 For . . . savor** i.e., foregoing wholesome sincerity for the sake of obsequious flattery   **8 Pitiful . . . spent** pitiful in their unsuccessful attempts, their means consumed in their ineffectual fawning on greatness.   **9 obsequious** (1) courtly (2) devoted   **10 oblation** offering.   **free** freely offered   **11 seconds** inferior matter, adulterants.   **art** artifice   **12 render** exchange   **13 suborned informer** perjured witness, the envious one who has charged the poet with self-interested flattery.   **14 impeached** accused
126.1 (This sonnet is made up of six couplets.)   **2 Time's . . . hour** Time's treacherous and inexorable hourglass, his reaping time   **3 Who . . . grown** you who have grown more youthfully beautiful as you have aged.   **show'st** show by way of contrast with yourself   **4 Thy lovers** (including the poet)   **5 wrack** ruin. (Nature is mistress over decay in that she decays and renews.)   **6 onwards** i.e., in life's journey   **7 to** for   **8 May . . . kill** may put Time to shame and render powerless the passing of the minutes.   **9 Yet . . . pleasure!** Yet fear Nature too, you who as her darling are subject to her will!   **10 She . . . treasure** i.e., Nature may keep and restore you for a time, but Time will ultimately triumph.   **11 Her audit** i.e., The proverbial paying of one's debt to Nature through death; also, Nature's account to Time.   **answered** paid   **12 quietus** discharge, quittance.   **render** surrender

127

In the old age black was not counted fair,
Or if it were, it bore not beauty's name;
But now is black beauty's successive heir,
And beauty slandered with a bastard shame.   4
For since each hand hath put on nature's power,
Fairing the foul with art's false borrowed face,
Sweet beauty hath no name, no holy bower,
But is profaned, if not lives in disgrace.   8
Therefore my mistress' eyes are raven black,
Her brows so suited, and they mourners seem
At such who, not born fair, no beauty lack,
Sland'ring creation with a false esteem.   12
   Yet so they mourn, becoming of their woe,
   That every tongue says beauty should look so.

128

How oft, when thou, my music, music play'st
Upon that blessèd wood whose motion sounds
With thy sweet fingers when thou gently sway'st
The wiry concord that mine ear confounds,   4
Do I envy those jacks that nimble leap
To kiss the tender inward of thy hand,
Whilst my poor lips, which should that harvest reap,
At the wood's boldness by thee blushing stand!   8
To be so tickled, they would change their state
And situation with those dancing chips
O'er whom thy fingers walk with gentle gait,
Making dead wood more blest than living lips.   12
   Since saucy jacks so happy are in this,
   Give them thy fingers, me thy lips to kiss.

129

Th'expense of spirit in a waste of shame
Is lust in action; and, till action, lust

Is perjured, murd'rous, bloody, full of blame,
Savage, extreme, rude, cruel, not to trust,   4
Enjoyed no sooner but despisèd straight,
Past reason hunted, and no sooner had
Past reason hated, as a swallowed bait
On purpose laid to make the taker mad;   8
Mad in pursuit, and in possession so;
Had, having, and in quest to have, extreme;
A bliss in proof, and proved, a very woe;
Before, a joy proposed; behind, a dream.   12
   All this the world well knows; yet none knows well
   To shun the heaven that leads men to this hell.

130

My mistress' eyes are nothing like the sun;
Coral is far more red than her lips' red;
If snow be white, why then her breasts are dun;
If hairs be wires, black wires grow on her head.   4
I have seen roses damasked, red and white,
But no such roses see I in her cheeks;
And in some perfumes is there more delight
Than in the breath that from my mistress reeks.   8
I love to hear her speak, yet well I know
That music hath a far more pleasing sound.
I grant I never saw a goddess go;
My mistress, when she walks, treads on the ground.   12
   And yet, by heaven, I think my love as rare
   As any she belied with false compare.

131

Thou art as tyrannous, so as thou art,
As those whose beauties proudly make them cruel;
For well thou know'st to my dear doting heart
Thou art the fairest and most precious jewel.   4
Yet, in good faith, some say that thee behold
Thy face hath not the power to make love groan;
To say they err I dare not be so bold,
Although I swear it to myself alone.   8
And, to be sure that is not false I swear,
A thousand groans, but thinking on thy face,
One on another's neck, do witness bear
Thy black is fairest in my judgment's place.   12
   In nothing art thou black save in thy deeds,
   And thence this slander, as I think, proceeds.

127.1 old age olden times.   **black** darkness of hair and eyes.   **fair** (1) beautiful (2) light-complexioned   **2 it bore . . . name** i.e., it was not called so   **3 now . . . heir** nowadays black has been named lawful successor to the title of beauty   **4 beauty . . . shame** i.e., blonde beauty is declared illegitimate, created artificially by cosmetics.   **5 put on** assumed   **6 Fairing the foul** making the ugly beautiful.   **borrowed face** i.e., cosmetics   **7 no name . . . bower** no reputation or pride of family, and no sacred abode   **8 if not** or even   **10 so suited** decked out in the same color and for the same reason   **11 At** for.   **no beauty lack** i.e., nonetheless make themselves attractive   **12 Sland'ring . . . esteem** i.e., dishonoring nature by blurring the distinction between real and false beauty.   **13 they** i.e., my mistress' eyes.   **becoming of** gracing or being graced by   **128.2 wood** keys of the spinet or virginal.   **motion** mechanism   **3 thou gently sway'st** you gently control   **4 wiry concord** harmony produced by strings.   **confounds** i.e., pleasurably overwhelms   **5 jacks** (Literally, upright pieces of wood fixed to the key lever and fitted with a quill that plucks the strings of the virginal; here used of the keys and with a pun on *jacks* in the sense of "common fellows," as in line 13.)   **8 by** beside, or, with. (The poet stands beside the lady as she plays, blushing to his very lips; he blushes in vexation at the *jacks'* boldness with her hand.)   **9 they** i.e., my lips   **13 jacks** (With a pun on "knaves, fellows" as in line 5.)   **129.1–2 Th'expense . . . action** Lust being consummated is the expenditure or dissipation of vital energy in an orgy of shameful extravagance and guilt. (*Spirit* also suggests "sperm.")   **2 till action** until it achieves consummation

3 blame (1) guilt (2) recrimination   **4 rude** brutal.   **to trust** to be trusted   **5 straight** immediately   **6 Past reason** madly, intemperately   **11 in proof** while experienced.   **proved** i.e., afterward   **12 Before** in prospect   **14 the heaven** the seeming bliss of sexual consumation.   **hell** (Often equated imagistically with the vagina.)   **130.1 nothing** not at all   **3 dun** dull grayish brown, mouse-colored   **5 damasked** mingled red and white   **8 reeks** emanates.   **11 go** walk   **13 rare** extraordinary and unique   **14 As . . . compare** as any woman misrepresented with false comparison.   **131.1 tyrannous** pitiless and domineering.   **so as thou art** just as you are (dark, not considered handsome)   **3 dear** fond   **9 to be sure** as proof.   **false I false that I**   **10 but thinking on** when I do no more than think of   **11 One . . . neck** one rapidly after another   **12 black** dark complexion.   **my judgment's place** my opinion.   **14 this slander** (See lines 5–6.)   **proceeds** originates.

132

Thine eyes I love, and they, as pitying me,
Knowing thy heart torment me with disdain,
Have put on black, and loving mourners be,
Looking with pretty ruth upon my pain.
And truly not the morning sun of heaven
Better becomes the gray cheeks of the east,
Nor that full star that ushers in the even
Doth half that glory to the sober west
As those two mourning eyes become thy face.
Oh, let it then as well beseem thy heart
To mourn for me, since mourning doth thee grace,
And suit thy pity like in every part.
      Then will I swear beauty herself is black,
      And all they foul that thy complexion lack.

133

Beshrew that heart that makes my heart to groan
For that deep wound it gives my friend and me!
Is't not enough to torture me alone,
But slave to slavery my sweet'st friend must be?
Me from myself thy cruel eye hath taken,
And my next self thou harder hast engrossed.
Of him, myself, and thee I am forsaken—
A torment thrice threefold thus to be crossed.
Prison my heart in thy steel bosom's ward,
But then my friend's heart let my poor heart bail;
Whoe'er keeps me, let my heart be his guard;
Thou canst not then use rigor in my jail.
      And yet thou wilt; for I, being pent in thee,
      Perforce am thine, and all that is in me.

134

So, now I have confessed that he is thine,
And I myself am mortgaged to thy will,
Myself I'll forfeit, so that other mine
Thou wilt restore to be my comfort still.
But thou wilt not, nor he will not be free,
For thou art covetous and he is kind;

He learned but surety-like to write for me
Under that bond that him as fast doth bind.
The statute of thy beauty thou wilt take,
Thou usurer, that put'st forth all to use,
And sue a friend came debtor for my sake;
So him I lose through my unkind abuse.
      Him have I lost; thou hast both him and me;
      He pays the whole, and yet am I not free.

135

Whoever hath her wish, thou hast thy Will,
And Will to boot, and Will in overplus;
More than enough am I that vex thee still,
To thy sweet will making addition thus.
Wilt thou, whose will is large and spacious,
Not once vouchsafe to hide my will in thine?
Shall will in others seem right gracious,
And in my will no fair acceptance shine?
The sea, all water, yet receives rain still
And in abundance addeth to his store;
So thou, being rich in Will, add to thy Will
One will of mine, to make thy large Will more.
      Let no unkind no fair beseechers kill;
      Think all but one, and me in that one Will.

136

If thy soul check thee that I come so near,
Swear to thy blind soul that I was thy Will,
And will, thy soul knows, is admitted there;
Thus far for love my love suit, sweet, fulfill.
Will will fulfill the treasure of thy love,
Ay, fill it full with wills, and my will one.
In things of great receipt with ease we prove
Among a number one is reckoned none.
Then in the number let me pass untold,

132.1 as as if   **2 Knowing . . . torment** knowing that your heart torments   **4 ruth** pity   **6 becomes** adorns.   **cheeks** i.e., clouds   **7 that full star** the evening star, Hesperus, i.e., Venus.   **even** evening   **8 Doth** i.e., lends.   **sober** somber, subdued in color   **9 mourning** black. (Spelled "morning" in the Quarto, suggesting a pun on line 5.)   **10 beseem** suit   **11 since . . . grace** since you look very attractive in mourning black   **12 And suit . . . part** and dress your pity similarly, in your heart and eyes.   **14 And . . . that** and that all those are ugly who
133.1 Beshrew i.e., A plague upon   **4 slave to slavery** utterly enslaved   **6 And . . . engrossed** i.e., and you have put my dearest friend, my other self, under even greater restraint.   **engrossed** (1) driven into obsession (2) bought up wholesale.   **8 crossed** thwarted, afflicted.   **9 Prison** Imprison.   **thy . . . ward** the prison cell of your hard heart   **10 bail** set free by taking its place   **11 keeps** has custody of.   **his guard** my friend's guardhouse   **12 rigor** harshness.   **my jail** i.e., my heart, where my friend is kept (and where I can protect him from your harsh authority).   **13 pent** shut up   **14 and all** along with everything (including my friend's heart)
134.1 now now that   **2 will** (1) wishes (2) fleshly desire   **3 so . . . mine** provided that my other self, my friend   **5 will not** does not wish to, won't

7 surety-like as security, as guarantor.   **write** sign the bond, endorse (suggesting that the friend has taken the poet's place with the mistress)   **8 Under . . . bind** under that mortgage or bond (of sexual enslavement) that now binds him as securely as it does me.   **9 statute** a usurer's security or amount of money secured under his bond.   **take** call in, invoke. (The lady will exact the full forfeiture specified in the mortgage as the amount to which her beauty entitles her.)   **10 use** (1) usury (2) sexual pleasure   **11 sue** (With suggestion also of "woo.")   **came** i.e., who became   **12 my unkind abuse** your ill usage and unkind deceiving (of me).   **14 pays** (With sexual suggestion.)
135.1 Will (This and the following sonnet and sonnet 143 ring changes on the word *will*—sexual desire, temper, passion, and the poet's name; possibly also the friend's name. The word can also suggest the sexual organs, male and female.)   **3 vex** (by unwelcome wooing).   **still** continually   **6 hide . . . thine** (With sexual suggestion.)   **7 will in others** others' wills   **10 his** its   **13 Let . . . kill** Let no unkind word kill any who seek your favors, or, *Let "no" unkind*, etc., do not kill your wooers with the word *no*   **14 Think . . . Will** i.e., think all your wooers and their wills to be but one, all comprised in me.
136.1 check rebuke.   **come so near** i.e., come so near the truth about you (in my previous sonnet); with suggestion of physical nearness also   **2 blind** unperceptive; shut up in the body without sensory organs   **4 fulfill** grant.   **5 fulfill the treasure** fill full the treasury. (With suggestion of sexual entry.)   **6 my will** (Suggesting "my penis.")   **one** one of them.   **7 receipt** capacity. (Suggesting profligacy.)   **8 one . . . none** (A variant of the common saying "one is no number.")   **9 untold** uncounted

Though in thy store's account I one must be;
For nothing hold me, so it please thee hold
That nothing me, a something, sweet, to thee.   12
    Make but my name thy love, and love that still,
    And then thou lovest me for my name is Will.

137

Thou blind fool, Love, what dost thou to mine eyes
That they behold and see not what they see?
They know what beauty is, see where it lies,
Yet what the best is take the worst to be.   4
If eyes corrupt by overpartial looks
Be anchored in the bay where all men ride,
Why of eyes' falsehood hast thou forgèd hooks,
Whereto the judgment of my heart is tied?   8
Why should my heart think that a several plot
Which my heart knows the wide world's common place?
Or mine eyes seeing this, say this is not,
To put fair truth upon so foul a face?   12
    In things right true my heart and eyes have erred,
    And to this false plague are they now transferred.

138

When my love swears that she is made of truth
I do believe her, though I know she lies,
That she might think me some untutored youth,
Unlearnèd in the world's false subtleties.   4
Thus vainly thinking that she thinks me young,
Although she knows my days are past the best,
Simply I credit her false-speaking tongue;
On both sides thus is simple truth suppressed.   8
But wherefore says she not she is unjust?
And wherefore say not I that I am old?
Oh, love's best habit is in seeming trust,
And age in love loves not to have years told.   12

Therefore I lie with her, and she with me,
And in our faults by lies we flattered be.

139

Oh, call not me to justify the wrong
That thy unkindness lays upon my heart;
Wound me not with thine eye but with thy tongue;
Use power with power, and slay me not by art.   4
Tell me thou lov'st elsewhere, but in my sight,
Dear heart, forbear to glance thine eye aside;
What need'st thou wound with cunning when thy might
Is more than my o'erpressed defense can bide?   8
Let me excuse thee: "Ah, my love well knows
Her pretty looks have been mine enemies,
And therefore from my face she turns my foes,
That they elsewhere might dart their injuries."   12
    Yet do not so; but since I am near slain,
    Kill me outright with looks and rid my pain.

140

Be wise as thou art cruel; do not press
My tongue-tied patience with too much disdain,
Lest sorrow lend me words, and words express
The manner of my pity-wanting pain.   4
If I might teach thee wit, better it were,
Though not to love, yet, love, to tell me so,
As testy sick men, when their deaths be near,
No news but health from their physicians know.   8
For if I should despair, I should grow mad,
And in my madness might speak ill of thee.
Now this ill-wresting world is grown so bad,
Mad slanderers by mad ears believèd be.   12
    That I may not be so, nor thou belied,
    Bear thine eyes straight, though thy proud heart go
    wide.

141

In faith, I do not love thee with mine eyes,
For they in thee a thousand errors note;
But 'tis my heart that loves what they despise,
Who in despite of view is pleased to dote.   4
Nor are mine ears with thy tongue's tune delighted,

---

10 **in . . . account** in your (huge) inventory (of lovers)   **11–12 For . . .
thee** i.e., consider me too insignificant to think of, provided that you
deign to hold insignificant me to you, my sweet, thereby making me
something of worth. (*Something* is sexually suggestive of "some
thing.")   **13 my name** i.e., "will," that is, desire.   **still** continually
14 for because
137.1 Love Cupid, portrayed as blind   **2 see not** do not comprehend
3 lies resides (and deceives through false appearance)   **4 Yet . . . be**
yet take the worst for the best.   **5 corrupt by overpartial looks** corrupted by doting and frankly prejudiced gazing   **6 Be . . . ride** seek
harbor where all men do so, i.e., *ride* in the arms of promiscuous
women   **7 Why . . . hooks** why have you, Love, fashioned snares out
of my eyes' delusion   **9 think . . . plot** think that to be a private field,
i.e., that woman to be the exclusive property of one man   **10 knows**
knows to be.   **common place** (1) a commons, a common pasture
(2) a woman's body that is open, promiscuous.   **11 Or** Or why
should.   **not** not so   **14 false plague** (1) plague of judging falsely
(2) false woman
138.1 (A version of this sonnet appears in *The Passionate Pilgrim*.)
truth fidelity, constancy   **2 believe** i.e., pretend to believe   **5 vainly
thinking** acting as though I thought   **7 Simply** (1) pretending to be
foolish (2) unconditionally.   **credit** give credence to   **9 unjust**
unfaithful, deceitful.   **11 habit** demeanor. (With, however, a suggestion of *garb*, i.e., "something put on.")   **seeming trust** apparent
fidelity   **12 age in love** an aging person in love, or, in matters of love.
told (1) counted (2) divulged.

---

13 lie with (1) deceive (2) have sex with   **14 And . . . be** and so by
lies we flatteringly deceive ourselves about our moral lapses.
139.1 call ask.   **justify the wrong** i.e., condone something actually
taking place under my eyes   **2 unkindness** i.e., flagrant infidelity
3 with thine eye i.e., with a roving eye. (See lines 5–6.)   **4 with
power** i.e., candidly, directly.   **art** artifice, cunning.   **7 What** why
8 bide abide, withstand.   **11 foes** i.e., the *pretty looks*, the beauty and
wanton glances of line 10   **13 near** nearly   **14 rid** end. (*Rid my pain*
also suggests "satiate my craving.")
140.4 pity-wanting (1) unpitied by you (2) pity-craving   **5 wit** wisdom, prudence   **5–6 better . . . so** (I would teach you that) even
though you don't love me, yet, dear friend, it would be better to tell
me that you do   **8 know** i.e., hear.   **11 ill-wresting** misinterpreting
in an evil sense.   **bad** bad (that)   **13 so** i.e., a *mad slanderer* who is
believèd.   **belied** slandered   **14 Bear . . . straight** keep your eyes on
me.   **wide** astray.
141.2 errors flaws in beauty   **4 Who . . . view** which (i.e., the heart),
in spite of what the eyes see

Nor tender feeling to base touches prone,
Nor taste, nor smell, desire to be invited
To any sensual feast with thee alone. 8
But my five wits nor my five senses can
Dissuade one foolish heart from serving thee,
Who leaves unswayed the likeness of a man,
Thy proud heart's slave and vassal wretch to be. 12
    Only my plague thus far I count my gain,
    That she that makes me sin awards me pain.

142

Love is my sin, and thy dear virtue hate,
Hate of my sin, grounded on sinful loving.
Oh, but with mine compare thou thine own state,
And thou shalt find it merits not reproving; 4
Or, if it do, not from those lips of thine
That have profaned their scarlet ornaments
And sealed false bonds of love as oft as mine,
Robbed others' beds' revenues of their rents. 8
Be it lawful I love thee as thou lov'st those
Whom thine eyes woo as mine importune thee.
Root pity in thy heart, that when it grows
Thy pity may deserve to pitied be. 12
    If thou dost seek to have what thou dost hide,
    By self-example mayst thou be denied.

143

Lo, as a careful huswife runs to catch
One of her feathered creatures broke away,
Sets down her babe and makes all swift dispatch
In pursuit of the thing she would have stay, 4
Whilst her neglected child holds her in chase,
Cries to catch her whose busy care is bent
To follow that which flies before her face,

Not prizing her poor infant's discontent: 8
So run'st thou after that which flies from thee,
Whilst I, thy babe, chase thee afar behind;
But if thou catch thy hope, turn back to me,
And play the mother's part: kiss me, be kind. 12
    So will I pray that thou mayst have thy Will,
    If thou turn back and my loud crying still.

144

Two loves I have, of comfort and despair,
Which like two spirits do suggest me still:
The better angel is a man right fair,
The worser spirit a woman colored ill. 4
To win me soon to hell, my female evil
Tempteth my better angel from my side,
And would corrupt my saint to be a devil,
Wooing his purity with her foul pride. 8
And whether that my angel be turned fiend
Suspect I may, yet not directly tell;
But being both from me, both to each friend,
I guess one angel in another's hell. 12
    Yet this shall I ne'er know, but live in doubt
    Till my bad angel fire my good one out.

145

Those lips that Love's own hand did make
Breathed forth the sound that said "I hate"
To me that languished for her sake;
But when she saw my woeful state, 4
Straight in her heart did mercy come,
Chiding that tongue that ever sweet
Was used in giving gentle doom,
And taught it thus anew to greet: 8
"I hate" she altered with an end,
That followed it as gentle day
Doth follow night, who like a fiend
From heaven to hell is flown away. 12
    "I hate" from hate away she threw,
    And saved my life, saying "not you."

---

6 Nor . . . prone nor (is) my delicate sense of touch inclined toward carnal contact (with you)   9 my five wits (neither) my five intellectual senses, i.e., the common sense, imagination, fancy, estimation (judgment), and memory   11 Who . . . man i.e., which heart abandons the proper government of my person, leaving me the mere likeness of a man   13 thus far to the following extent   14 That . . . pain i.e., that the sin brings with it its own punishment and contrition, thus presumably shortening my torment after death. (With a suggestion in pain of "sexual pleasure"; see sonnet 139.)
142.1–2 Love . . . loving My sin is to love you, and your best virtue is to hate—hate that sin in me, but also because of your uncontrolled sexual longing for other men. (The bitter paradox here is that hatred of sin must be virtue, and yet the lady is herself deeply implicated in this sin; her hatred is more a disdainful rejection of the poet's love than a noble virtue.)   4 it i.e., my state   6–7 That . . . mine i.e., that have forsworn themselves in love as often as my lips have. (The scarlet ornaments are lips and also red wax used to seal documents; they seal with a kiss.)   8 Robbed . . . rents i.e., and committed adultery with other women's husbands. (The metaphor is of income-yielding estates, revenues, whose rents or payments made by tenants are not properly paid; the husband does not pay what is owed to the wife in terms of marital affection and the producing of children.)
9–10 Be . . . thee i.e., I am as justified in loving you and imploring you with my eyes as you are in pursuing other men. (Be it lawful is a legal phrase meaning "Let it be considered lawful that.")   12 deserve make you deserving   13 what . . . hide what you withhold, i.e., pity   143.1 careful distressed, full of cares, busy.   huswife housewife   2 feathered . . . away domestic fowl which has broken away from the flock   5 holds her in chase chases after her   7 flies flees

8 Not prizing disregarding   13 Will (See sonnets 135, 136.)   14 still hush, make quiet.
144.1 (This sonnet appears, somewhat altered, in The Passionate Pilgrim.)   2 suggest urge, offer counsel, tempt.   still continually   3 right fair very handsome and blond   4 ill i.e., dark of complexion.   11 from me away from me. (The poet suspects they are together.)   both . . . friend friends to each other   12 I . . . hell I suspect that she (the evil angel) has him in her power (i.e., her sexual embracement; hell is slang for the pudenda).   14 fire . . . out drive out my good angel, stop seeing him. (With the suggestion of driving him out of the lady's sexual body as one would use fire and smoke to drive an animal out of its burrow, and with the further suggestion that the fire is venereal disease. Bad angel also hints at bad coinage driving out good money.)
145.1 (This sonnet is in eight-syllable meter.)   5 Straight at once   7 used . . . doom accustomed to passing a mild sentence   13 "I hate" . . . threw i.e., She separated the phrase "I hate" from the hatred I feared it expressed, from hateful meaning   13–14 hate away . . . And (Punning perhaps on the name of Shakespeare's wife, Anne Hathaway.)

146

Poor soul, the center of my sinful earth,
Thrall to these rebel powers that thee array,
Why dost thou pine within and suffer dearth,
Painting thy outward walls so costly gay?   4
Why so large cost, having so short a lease,
Dost thou upon thy fading mansion spend?
Shall worms, inheritors of this excess,
Eat up thy charge? Is this thy body's end?   8
Then, soul, live thou upon thy servant's loss,
And let that pine to aggravate thy store;
Buy terms divine in selling hours of dross;
Within be fed, without be rich no more.   12
    So shalt thou feed on Death, that feeds on men,
    And Death once dead, there's no more dying then.

147

My love is as a fever, longing still
For that which longer nurseth the disease,
Feeding on that which doth preserve the ill,
Th'uncertain sickly appetite to please.   4
My reason, the physician to my love,
Angry that his prescriptions are not kept,
Hath left me, and I desperate now approve
Desire is death, which physic did except.   8
Past cure I am, now reason is past care,
And frantic-mad with evermore unrest;
My thoughts and my discourse as madmen's are,
At random from the truth vainly expressed;   12
    For I have sworn thee fair and thought thee bright,
    Who art as black as hell, as dark as night.

148

Oh, me, what eyes hath love put in my head,
Which have no correspondence with true sight!
Or, if they have, where is my judgment fled,
That censures falsely what they see aright?   4
If that be fair whereon my false eyes dote,
What means the world to say it is not so?

If it be not, then love doth well denote
Love's eye is not so true as all men's "no."   8
How can it? Oh, how can love's eye be true,
That is so vexed with watching and with tears?
No marvel then though I mistake my view;
The sun itself sees not till heaven clears.   12
    O cunning love, with tears thou keep'st me blind,
    Lest eyes well-seeing thy foul faults should find.

149

Canst thou, O cruel, say I love thee not,
When I against myself with thee partake?
Do I not think on thee when I forgot
Am of myself, all tyrant for thy sake?   4
Who hateth thee that I do call my friend?
On whom frown'st thou that I do fawn upon?
Nay, if thou lour'st on me, do I not spend
Revenge upon myself with present moan?   8
What merit do I in myself respect
That is so proud thy service to despise,
When all my best doth worship thy defect,
Commanded by the motion of thine eyes?   12
    But, love, hate on, for now I know thy mind:
    Those that can see thou lov'st, and I am blind.

150

Oh, from what power hast thou this powerful might
With insufficiency my heart to sway?
To make me give the lie to my true sight
And swear that brightness doth not grace the day?   4
Whence hast thou this becoming of things ill,
That in the very refuse of thy deeds
There is such strength and warrantise of skill
That, in my mind, thy worst all best exceeds?   8
Who taught thee how to make me love thee more,
The more I hear and see just cause of hate?
Oh, though I love what others do abhor,
With others thou shouldst not abhor my state.   12
    If thy unworthiness raised love in me,
    More worthy I to be beloved of thee.

146.1 **sinful earth** body   2 **Thrall ... array** made captive by the rebellious flesh that decks you in finery and lines you up in battle array. ("Thrall to" is one of several conjectures; the Quarto repeats "My sinfull earth" from line 1.)   4 **outward walls** i.e., the body, decked out in finery, cosmetics, etc.   5 **having ... lease** having so brief a period of residence in this world   6 **mansion** dwelling, i.e., the body   8 **charge** expense, outlay.   **Is ... end?** Is this what your body was intended to be used for?   9 **thy servant's** i.e., the body's   10 **let that ... store** let the body starve to increase your stock of spiritual riches   11 **Buy ... dross** i.e., purchase eternal life in return for giving up (selling) mere hours of wasteful pleasure; secure *terms* that only God can provide
147.1 **still** always   2 **nurseth** nourishes   3 **preserve the ill** sustain the illness   4 **Th'uncertain** the finicky   7–8 **and I ... except** and I now, desperately sick and in desperation, discover by experience that desire, which rejected medicine (or, which medical advice warned against), is fatal.   9 **care** medical care. (The line is an inversion of the proverb, "things past cure are past care," i.e., don't worry about what can't be helped. Reason, the physician, has ceased to care for his patient.)   10 **evermore** constant and increasing   12 **vainly** to no sensible purpose
148.4 **censures** judges

7 **love** i.e., the self-deceiving nature of my love.   **denote** indicate, demonstrate (that)   8 **eye** (With a pun on "ay," yes.)   10 **vexed** troubled.   **watching** remaining awake   11 **I** (Punning on "eye.")   **mistake my view** err in what I see
149.2 **partake** take part (against myself).   3–4 **Do ... sake?** Do I not put consideration of you foremost when I am tyrannously neglectful of, or oblivious of, myself and my best interests on your behalf?
7 **spend** vent   8 **present moan** immediate suffering and lamentation.   9 **respect** value   10 **thy ... despise** as to think it demeaning to serve you   11 **all my best** all that is best in me.   **defect** flaws   14 **Those ... blind** i.e., you scorn one who loves you in a blind passion, in defiance of reason, and are drawn instead to those who know you for what you are.
150.2 **With insufficiency** by means of all your shortcomings.   **sway** rule.   3 **give the lie to** accuse flatly of lying   4 **And ... day** i.e., and swear that what is so is not so, that what is fair and beautiful is not fair and beautiful, since you are dark.   5 **becoming ... ill** i.e., ability to show ill things in a becoming light   6 **in ... deeds** in the most debased of your actions   7 **warrantise of skill** warrant or assurance of expertise   12 **state** i.e., condition of being helplessly in love.

151

Love is too young to know what conscience is;
Yet who knows not conscience is born of love?
Then, gentle cheater, urge not my amiss,
Lest guilty of my faults thy sweet self prove.   4
For, thou betraying me, I do betray
My nobler part to my gross body's treason.
My soul doth tell my body that he may
Triumph in love; flesh stays no farther reason,   8
But, rising at thy name, doth point out thee
As his triumphant prize. Proud of this pride,
He is contented thy poor drudge to be,
To stand in thy affairs, fall by thy side.   12
        No want of conscience hold it that I call
        Her "love" for whose dear love I rise and fall.

152

In loving thee thou know'st I am forsworn,
But thou art twice forsworn, to me love swearing:
In act thy bed-vow broke, and new faith torn
In vowing new hate after new love bearing.   4
But why of two oaths' breach do I accuse thee,
When I break twenty? I am perjured most,
For all my vows are oaths but to misuse thee,
And all my honest faith in thee is lost.   8
For I have sworn deep oaths of thy deep kindness,
Oaths of thy love, thy truth, thy constancy,
And, to enlighten thee, gave eyes to blindness,
Or made them swear against the thing they see;   12

For I have sworn thee fair. More perjured eye,
To swear against the truth so foul a lie!

153

Cupid laid by his brand and fell asleep.
A maid of Dian's this advantage found,
And his love-kindling fire did quickly steep
In a cold valley-fountain of that ground,   4
Which borrowed from this holy fire of Love
A dateless lively heat, still to endure,
And grew a seething bath, which yet men prove
Against strange maladies a sovereign cure.   8
But at my mistress' eye Love's brand new-fired,
The boy for trial needs would touch my breast;
I, sick withal, the help of bath desired,
And thither hied, a sad distempered guest,   12
        But found no cure. The bath for my help lies
        Where Cupid got new fire—my mistress' eyes.

154

The little love god lying once asleep
Laid by his side his heart-inflaming brand,
Whilst many nymphs that vowed chaste life to keep
Came tripping by; but in her maiden hand   4
The fairest votary took up that fire
Which many legions of true hearts had warmed,
And so the general of hot desire
Was, sleeping, by a virgin hand disarmed.   8
This brand she quenchèd in a cool well by,
Which from Love's fire took heat perpetual,
Growing a bath and healthful remedy
For men diseased; but I, my mistress' thrall,   12
        Came there for cure, and this by that I prove:
        Love's fire heats water, water cools not love.

151.1 **too young** (Love is personified as the young Cupid.) **2 conscience** guilty knowing, carnal knowledge. (Playing on *conscience*,
"moral sense," in line 1.) **3 urge** stress, invoke. **amiss** sin **5 betraying** (1) cheating on (2) leading into temptation **6 nobler part** i.e., soul
7–8 that . . . in love that he, the soul, may triumph in virtuous love. (But
ambiguously misinterpretable as urging the flesh to triumph carnally.)
8 flesh . . . reason my flesh waits no longer to hear reason's lecture
9 rising (With bawdy suggestion of erection, continued in *point, Proud,
stand, fall.* Metaphors of conjuration and of the compass needle's point
are also invoked.) **10 triumphant prize** spoils to be enjoyed in victory.
Proud of Swelling with. **pride** splendor; erection **12 stand** (1) serve,
undertake business (2) be erect. **fall** (as in battle; with sexual suggestion of detumescence) **13 want** lack
152.1 **forsworn** i.e., faithless to my vows of love (perhaps marriage
vows) **3 act** sexual act. **bed-vow** marriage vows to your husband
3–4 new . . . bearing i.e., a new contract of fidelity is torn up by your
swearing hatred toward me, to whom you have only recently professed love. (Or the *new faith* that is torn up may be that which the
lady has sworn to the friend.) **7 but to misuse** merely to deceive
8 And . . . lost i.e., all my professions of honesty are belied when I
perjure myself by praising you for loving constancy. **11 And . . .
blindness** i.e., and, to invest you with brightness, I made my eyes testify to things they did not see

13 eye (With a pun on "I.")
153 (This sonnet and the following seemingly have no direct connection with those preceding. They are derived ultimately, through
Renaissance adaptations, from an epigram by the fifth-century Byzan-
tine poet Marianus Scholasticus in the Greek Anthology.) **1 brand**
torch. (With phallic suggestion.) **2 maid** attendant virgin, votaress.
Dian Diana, goddess of chastity **4 of that ground** i.e., nearby. (*Valley-
fountain* suggests the female sexual anatomy; compare with 154.9.)
6 dateless endless, eternal. **still** always **7–8 And grew . . . cure** and
became a spring of hot medicinal waters, which even today men discover to be an efficacious cure against strange maladies. (Syphilis was
conventionally treated with hot medicinal baths.) **9 new-fired** having
been reignited **10 for trial** by way of test **11 withal** from it **12 hied**
hastened. **distempered** sick. (The bath is suggestive again of the
sweating cure for venereal disease.)
154.7 **general** inspirer and commander, i.e., Cupid **9 by** nearby
11 Growing becoming **12 thrall** slave, bondman **13 cure** (With suggestion of treatment for venereal disease, as in 153.7–14.) **this** i.e., the
following proposition. **that** i.e., my coming, which failed to cure me

❧

Canon, Dates, and Early Texts

By "canon" we mean a listing of plays that can be ascribed to Shakespeare on the basis of reliable evidence. Such evidence is either "internal," derived from matters of style or poetics in the plays themselves (see General Introduction), or "external," derived from outside the play. The latter includes any reference by Shakespeare's contemporaries to his plays, any allusions in the plays themselves to contemporary events, the entering of Shakespeare's plays for publication in the Stationers' Register (S. R.), actual publication of the plays, and records of early performances. These matters of external evidence are also essential in attempting to date the plays.

The greatest single source of information is the First Folio text of Shakespeare's plays, sponsored by Shakespeare's fellow actors John Heminges and Henry Condell and published in 1623. It contains all the plays included in this present edition of Shakespeare except *Pericles* and *The Two Noble Kinsmen* and offers strong presumptive evidence of being a complete and accurate compilation of Shakespeare's work by men who knew him and cherished his memory. It provides the only texts we have for these eighteen plays: *The Comedy of Errors, The Two Gentlemen of Verona, The Taming of the Shrew, I Henry VI, King John, As You Like It, Twelfth Night, Julius Caesar, All's Well That Ends Well, Measure for Measure, Timon of Athens, Macbeth, Antony and Cleopatra, Coriolanus, Cymbeline, The Winter's Tale, The Tempest,* and *Henry VIII.* This includes nearly half the known canon of Shakespeare's plays. Our debt to the First Folio is incalculable and confirms our impression of its reliability.

The information of the First Folio is further confirmed by contemporary references. In 1598, a cleric and minor writer of the period named Francis Meres wrote in his *Palladis Tamia, Wit's Treasury*:

As the soul of Euphorbus was thought to live in Pythagoras, so the sweet, witty soul of Ovid lives in mellifluous and honey-tongued Shakespeare: witness his *Venus and Adonis*, his *Lucrece*, his sugared sonnets among his private friends, etc.

As Plautus and Seneca are accounted the best for comedy and tragedy among the Latins, so Shakespeare among the English is the most excellent in both kinds for the stage; for comedy, witness his *Gentlemen of Verona*, his *Errors*, his *Love's Labor's Lost*, his *Love's Labor's Won*, his *Midsummer's Night Dream*, and his *Merchant of Venice*; for tragedy his *Richard the II, Richard the III, Henry the IV, King John, Titus Andronicus* and his *Romeo and Juliet*.

Though this list was meant to offer praise, not to be an exhaustive catalogue, it is remarkably full. If the tantalizing *Love's Labor's Won* refers to *The Taming of the Shrew*, Meres's list of comedies is substantially complete down almost to 1598. It does not include the comedies that Shakespeare appears to have written around that date or soon afterward: *Much Ado About Nothing, The Merry Wives of Windsor, As You Like It,* and *Twelfth Night*. Meres correctly names all of Shakespeare's history plays except the *Henry VI* trilogy and of course the later histories, *Henry V* (1599) and *Henry VIII* (1613). He names both of Shakespeare's early tragedies that are not based on English history: *Titus Andronicus* and *Romeo and Juliet*. He tells us about the important nondramatic poems, which did not appear in the First Folio, since that volume is devoted exclusively to plays. Not much can be made of the order in which Meres names the plays, however, for we learn from other sources that *Richard III* clearly precedes *Richard II* in date of composition and that *King John* precedes the *Henry IV* plays.

Other writers of the 1590s add further confirming evidence. John Weever, in an epigram *Ad Gulielmum Shakespeare*," published in 1599, refers to "Rose-cheeked Adonis" and "Fair fire-hot Venus," to "Chaste Lucretia" and "Proud lust-stung Tarquin," and to "*Romeo, Richard*—more whose names I know not." Richard Barnfield, in

Poems in Divers Humors (1598), praises Shakespeare for *"Venus"* and *"Lucrece."* Both Thomas Nashe and Robert Greene seemingly refer to the *Henry VI* plays, missing from Meres's list. Nashe, in his *Pierce Penniless* (1592), speculates how it would "have joyed brave Talbot (the terror of the French) to think that after he had lain two hundred years in his tomb, he should triumph again on the stage." Talbot is the hero of *1 Henry VI*, and we know of no other play on the subject. Greene, in his *Greene's Groats-worth of Wit* (1592), lashes out at an "upstart crow, beautified with our feathers, that with his *'Tiger's heart wrapped in a player's hide'* supposes he is as well able to bombast out a blank verse as the best of you, and, being an absolute *Johannes Factotum*, is in his own conceit the only Shake-scene in a country." The line about "Tiger's heart" is deliberately misquoted from *3 Henry VI*, 1.4.137. (It is possible that this famous attack on Shakespeare was actually written not by Greene himself but by Henry Chettle, his literary executor.)

The Comedy of Errors (c. 1589–1594)

The earliest known edition of *The Comedy of Errors* is in the First Folio of 1623. Its first-mentioned production, however, was on Innocents Day, December 28, 1594, when a "Comedy of Errors (like to *Plautus* his *Menechmus*)" was performed by professional actors as part of the Christmas Revels at Gray's Inn (one of the Inns of Court, where young men studied law) in London. The evening's festivities are set down in *Gesta Grayorum*, a contemporary account of the revels, though not published until 1688. According to this record, the evening was marred by such tumult and disorder that the invited guests from the Inner Temple (another of the Inns of Court) refused to stay; thereafter, the night became known as "The Night of Errors." References to sorcery and enchantment in the play leave little doubt that it was Shakespeare's.

Some scholars argue that the play was not newly written for this occasion. To them, the play seems early: slight in characterization, and full of punning wit reminiscent of *Love's Labor's Lost* and *The Two Gentlemen of Verona*. Topical clues are suggestive but not conclusive. Chief of these is the joke about France being "armed and reverted, making war against her heir" (3.2.123–4). Unquestionably, this refers to France's civil wars between Henry of Navarre and his Catholic opposition. Since Henry became a Catholic and the King of France in 1593, most scholars prefer a date before 1593. Peter Alexander (*Shakespeare's Life and Art*, 1961) has even argued for a date prior to 1589, since Henry III died in that year, leaving Henry of Navarre as nominal king rather than heir. The sad truth is that we probably cannot attach too much weight to either conclusion. Allusions to the French civil wars during the early 1590s were common but also imprecise; the

joke would have seemed relevant at almost any time up to 1595. The same is probably true of the allusion to Spain's sending "whole armadas of carracks" (3.2.135–6). This is often taken to refer to the Spanish Armada, 1588, but may refer instead to the Portuguese *Madre de Dios*, captured and brought to England in 1592, or to a similar venture. In short, it is virtually impossible to prove that *The Comedy of Errors* precedes *Love's Labor's Lost, The Two Gentlemen of Verona*, or *The Taming of the Shrew*. Those scholars who think it unlikely that the young gentlemen of Gray's Inn would have bestowed their attention on a play already five years old prefer a date of 1594.

A lost play called *The History of Error* was acted before the Queen by the Children of Paul's (a company of boy actors from St. Paul's School) at Hampton Court on New Year's night, 1577. About this play we know nothing other than its suggestive title, and speculation that Shakespeare may have adapted it has been generally abandoned.

The Folio text, based probably on Shakespeare's own manuscript, is generally a good text, although, as is common in authorial manuscripts, the form of the characters' names frequently varies in the stage directions and speech prefixes. Perhaps a few performance-oriented annotations have been added to the authorial manuscript.

Love's Labor's Lost (c. 1588–1597)

Love's Labor's Lost first appeared in a Quarto dated 1598, without entry in the Stationers' Register, the official record book of the London Company of Stationers (booksellers and printers). Its title page reads:

A PLEASANT Conceited Comedie CALLED Loues labors lost. As it vvas presented before her Highnes this last Christmas. Newly corrected and augmented *By W. Shakespere.* Imprinted at London by W. W. [William White] for *Cutbert Burby.* 1598.

Because the phrase "newly corrected and augmented" also appears on the title page of the second Quarto of *Romeo and Juliet*, issued in 1599 to correct an unauthorized Quarto of 1597, many scholars suspect that *Love's Labor's Lost* may similarly have appeared in an unauthorized Quarto that is now lost. Such a circumstance would explain why the existing Quarto of *Love's Labor's Lost* was not registered: if the play had already been published, even in an unauthorized version, relicensing would have been unnecessary. (The *Romeo and Juliet* second Quarto was not registered for this reason.) But it is also entirely possible that the 1598 Quarto is simply reprinting an earlier lost good Quarto and that Burby is exaggerating his claims of correcting and augmenting.

The text shows clear signs of revision. Two long passages (see textual notes at 4.3.291 and 5.2.812) give duplicate readings of the same speeches, suggesting the printer mistakenly copied both the canceled version in his copy and the revision. Speech headings are unusually confused, sometimes referring to characters by their personal names (Navarre, Armado, Holofernes) and at other times by their generic titles (King, Braggart, Pedant). Some of these errors, notably the long uncanceled passages, suggest that the printer of the 1598 Quarto or of an earlier lost Quarto, perhaps new and relatively inexperienced, was copying from Shakespeare's working draft. Whether Shakespeare wrote this draft on one occasion or whether he revised an earlier version is, however, a matter on which scholars disagree. The First Folio text was set from the Quarto and thus gives us little additional information as to when or in what stages the play was written, though it may also have had occasional reference to a playhouse manuscript.

Francis Meres refers to the play in October 1598 in his *Palladis Tamia*. The performance before Queen Elizabeth "last Christmas" was probably in late 1597. Robert Tofte tells us in his *Alba* (1598) that *"Love's Labour Lost*, I once did see a play / ycleped so." His phrasing suggests a performance seen sometime in the past, although he could mean that he saw it only once. Apart from these allusions, dating of the play must rely on its presumed internal allusions to contemporary events. The play has attracted a lot of highly speculative topical hypotheses. One such describes a "School of Night" to which Sir Walter Ralegh, Matthew Roydon, George Chapman, and others are supposed to have belonged. No objective evidence exists to prove the existence of such a school. Ralegh was tried for atheism but was acquitted. Other topical hypotheses are discussed briefly in the Introduction to the play. Some allusions to the historical King of Navarre and to his supporters, the Duc de Biron and the Duc de Longueville, are undeniable. These allusions tend to argue either for an early date (c. 1588–1589), when these persons had not yet become the chief figures in a bloody religious civil war in France and hence inappropriate subjects for light comedy, or for a date after 1594, when a satire of Navarre's perjury might seem relevant to the historical Navarre's renunciation of Protestantism in 1593. The influence of John Lyly and the children's drama also argues for an early date. If, on the other hand, the Muscovite masque in 5.2 contains a reference to the Gray's Inn (one of the Inns of Court, where young men studied law) revels of 1594, as several scholars have urged, some portions of the play may be from after that date. The hypothesis that Shakespeare revived an old play of his shortly before publication in 1598, although not universally accepted, offers at least a plausible explanation of the phrase "newly corrected and augmented" on the title page.

The Two Gentlemen of Verona (c. 1590–1594)

The Two Gentlemen of Verona was not published until the First Folio of 1623. Other than Francis Meres's listing of it

in 1598 in his *Palladis Tamia* (a slender volume on contemporary literature and art, valuable because it lists most of the plays of Shakespeare that existed at that time), evidence as to dating is scarce. No convincing allusions to contemporary events have been found. From the internal evidence of style, such as the relative density and sophistication of the dialogue, most scholars prefer an early date. The influence of John Lyly's romantic comedies, such as *Campaspe* (1584) and *Endymion* (1588), is still perceptible in the play's overly ingenious wit-combat.

A notable feature of the text, its grouping of characters' names at the beginning of each scene and the absence of any other stage directions except exits, seems to indicate that the manuscript was copied at some point by the scrivener Ralph Crane, probably from an authorial manuscript still containing a number of inconsistencies. The speech prefixes are sufficiently regular, on the other hand, that the text may have been prepared for the theater or else tidied up by Crane.

The Taming of the Shrew (c. 1590–1593)

The Taming of the Shrew was not printed until the First Folio of 1623. Francis Meres does not mention the play in 1598 in his *Palladis Tamia*, unless it is the mysterious *"Loue labours wonne"* on his list. (Meres is not totally accurate, for he omits *Henry VI* from the history plays.) The play must have existed prior to 1598, however, for its style is comparable with that of *The Two Gentlemen of Verona* and other early comedies. Moreover, a play called *The Taming of a Shrew* appeared in print in 1594 (Stationers' Register, 1594). Four theories can be adduced to explain the problematic relationship of *A Shrew* to Shakespeare's play. The two least plausible theories are that Shakespeare, for some reason, reworked someone else's play shortly after its first performance or else wrote *A Shrew* himself as an early version. The third theory is that *A Shrew* represents an imitation of Shakespeare's play by some rival dramatist, who relied chiefly on his memory and who changed characters' names and the location to make the play seem his. Fourth and most plausibly, *A Shrew* may be a somewhat uncharacteristic kind of reported or memorially reconstructed Quarto, "improved" upon by a writer who also borrowed admiringly from Christopher Marlowe and other Elizabethan dramatists. In either of the latter two scenarios, Shakespeare's play would have to be dated earlier than May 1594.

The title page of *A Shrew* proclaims that "it was sundry times acted by the *Right honorable the Earle of* Pembrook his seruants." Quite possibly this derivative version was merely trying to capitalize on the original's stage success and was, in fact, describing performances of Shakespeare's play. Theater owner and manager Philip Henslowe's record of a performance of *"the Tamynge of A Shrowe"* in 1594 at Newington Butts, a mile south of London Bridge, may also refer to Shakespeare's play; certainly, the minute distinction between "A Shrew" and "The Shrew" is one that the official records of the time would overlook. The Admiral's men and the Lord Chamberlain's men, acting companies, were playing at Newington Butts at the time, either jointly or alternatingly. Since Shakespeare's company, the Lord Chamberlain's, later owned *The Shrew*, they may well have owned and acted it on this occasion in 1594, having obtained it from the Earl of Pembroke's men when that company disbanded in 1593. Many of Pembroke's leading players joined the Lord Chamberlain's, Shakespeare being quite possibly among them. (The possibility that he came to the Lord Chamberlain's from Lord Strange's men seems less certain today than it once did.) Several echoes of Shakespeare's play in other plays of the early 1590s tend to confirm a date in or before 1593. It is entirely possible, then, that *The Shrew* was acted by Pembroke's men in 1592–1593 and subsequently passed along to the Lord Chamberlain's.

The Folio text of this play is now generally thought to have been printed from Shakespeare's working manuscript or possibly from a transcript of his papers, with perhaps some theatrical annotations as well. Some signs of revision are discernible.

A Midsummer Night's Dream (c. 1595)

A Midsummer Night's Dream was entered on the Stationers' Register, the official record book of the London Company of Stationers (booksellers and printers), by Thomas Fisher on October 8, 1600, and printed by him that same year in Quarto:

A Midsommer nights dreame. As it hath beene sundry times pub*lickely acted, by the Right honoura*ble, the Lord Chamberlaine his *seruants. Written by William Shakespeare.* Imprinted at London, for *Thomas Fisher,* and are to be soulde at his shoppe, at the Signe of the White Hart, in *Fleetestreete.* 1600.

This text appears to have been set from Shakespeare's working manuscript. Its inconsistencies in time scheme and other irregularities may reflect some revision, although the inconsistencies are not noticeable in performance. A Second Quarto appeared in 1619, though falsely dated 1600; it was a reprint of the First Quarto, with some minor corrections and many new errors. A copy of this Second Quarto, evidently with some added stage directions and other minor changes from a theatrical manuscript in the company's possession, served as the basis for the First Folio text of 1623. Changes of speech assignment in the Folio text, especially in Act 5, may reflect a late revival over which Shakespeare had no

control. Essentially, the First Quarto remains the authoritative text.

Other than Francis Meres's listing of the play in 1598 in his *Palladis Tamia,* external clues as to date are elusive. Possibly the worry that a lion in a play might frighten the ladies (3.1.24–31) echoes published accounts of a baptismal feast at court in August 1594, when a blackamoor was chosen to draw in a chariot in place of a lion for fear of alarming nearby spectators. The description of unruly weather (2.1.88–114) has been related to the bad summer of 1594, but complaints about the weather are perennial. On the assumption that the play celebrates some noble wedding of the period, scholars have come up with a number of suitable marriages. Chief are those of Sir Thomas Heneage to Mary, Countess of Southampton, in 1594; of William Stanley, Earl of Derby, to Elizabeth Vere, daughter of the Earl of Oxford, in 1595; and of Thomas, son of Lord Berkeley, to Elizabeth, daughter of Lord Carey, in 1596. The Countess of Southampton was the widowed mother of the young Earl of Southampton, to whom Shakespeare had dedicated his *Venus and Adonis* and *The Rape of Lucrece.* No one has ever proved convincingly, however, that the play was written for any occasion other than commercial public performance. The play makes sense for a general audience and does not need to depend on references to a private marriage. Shakespeare was, after all, in the business of writing plays for his fellow actors, who earned their livelihood chiefly by public acting before large paying audiences. In any event, the search for a court marriage is a circular argument in terms of dating; suitable court marriages can be found for any year of the decade. In the last analysis, the play has to be dated on the basis of its stylistic affinity to plays like *Romeo and Juliet* and *Richard II,* works of the "lyric" mid-1590s. The "Pyramus and Thisbe" performance in *A Midsummer Night's Dream* would seem to bear an obvious relation to *Romeo and Juliet,* although no one can say for sure which came first.

The Merchant of Venice (c. 1596–1597)

The Stationers' Register, the official record book of the London Company of Stationers (booksellers and printers), for July 22, 1598, contains an entry on behalf of the printer James Roberts for "a booke of the Marchaunt of Venyce, or otherwise called the Iewe of Venyce, Prouided, that yt bee not prynted by the said James Robertes or anye other whatsoeuer without lycence first had from the Right honorable the lord Chamberlen." Roberts evidently enjoyed a close connection with the Chamberlain's men (Shakespeare's acting company) and seemingly was granted the special favor of registering the play at this time, even though the company did not wish to see the play published until later (or until they were paid). In 1600, at any rate, Roberts transferred his rights as publisher to Thomas Heyes and printed the volume for him with the following title:

The most excellent Historie of the *Merchant of Venice*. VVith the extreme crueltie of *Shylocke* the Iewe towards the sayd Merchant, in cutting a iust pound of his flesh: and the obtayning of *Portia* by the choyse of three chests. *As it hath beene diuers times acted by the Lord Chamberlaine his Seruants.* Written by William Shakespeare. AT LONDON, Printed by *I. R.* [James Roberts] for Thomas Heyes, and are to be sold in Paules Church-yard, at the signe of the Greene Dragon. 1600.

The text of this 1600 Quarto is generally a good one, based seemingly on an accurate copy of Shakespeare's papers by the dramatist himself or some reliable transcriber. It served as copy for the Second Quarto of 1619 (printed by William Jaggard for Thomas Pavier and fraudulently dated 1600) and for the First Folio of 1623. Although some theatrical manuscript seems also to have been consulted in preparation for the Folio text, the Folio variations appear to have little authority.

Francis Meres mentions the play in 1598 in his *Palladis Tamia*. Establishing an earlier limit for dating has proven not so easy. Many scholars have urged a connection with the Roderigo Lopez affair of 1594 (see the Introduction to the play). The supposed allusion to Lopez in the lines about "a wolf, who, hanged for human slaughter" (4.1.134) may simply indicate, however, that wolves were actually hanged for attacking men in Shakespeare's day (as dogs were for killing sheep). Besides, the Lopez case remained so notorious throughout the 1590s that even a proven allusion to it in *The Merchant* would not limit the play to 1594 or 1595. Christopher Marlowe's play, *The Jew of Malta*, was revived in 1594 to exploit anti-Lopez sentiment but was also revived in 1596. There may be, moreover, an allusion in 1.1.27 to the *St. Andrew*, a Spanish ship captured at Cadiz in 1596, and Shylock's allusion to Jacob and Laban (1.3.69–88) may well echo Miles Mosse's *The Arraignment and Conviction of Usury*, 1595. If so, the likeliest date is 1596–1597.

Much Ado About Nothing (1598–1599)

"The Commedie of muche A doo about nothing a booke" was entered in the Stationers' Register, the official record book of the London Company of Stationers (booksellers and printers), on August 4, 1600, along with *As You Like It*, *Henry V*, and Ben Jonson's *Every Man in His Humor*, all marked as plays of "My lord chamberlens men" (Shakespeare's acting company) and all "to be staied"—that is, not published without further permission. Earlier in the same memorandum, written on a spare page in the Register, occurs the name of the printer James Roberts, whose

registration of *The Merchant of Venice* in 1598 was similarly stayed, pending further permission to publish. Evidently, the Chamberlain's men were attempting to ensure that they were paid for any plays printed or else to prevent unauthorized publication of these very popular plays. If the latter was their motive, they were too late to forestall the appearance of a bad Quarto of *Henry V* in August 1600, but they did manage to control release of the others. *Much Ado About Nothing* appeared later that same year in a seemingly authorized version:

Much adoe about Nothing. *As it hath been sundrie times publikely acted by the right honourable, the Lord Chamberlaine his seruants. Written by William Shakespeare.* LONDON Printed by V. S. [Valentine Sims] for Andrew Wise, and William Aspley. 1600.

Once thought to have been set up from a theatrical playbook and then used itself in the theater as a playbook before serving as copy for the First Folio of 1623, this 1600 Quarto text is now generally regarded as having been set from Shakespeare's own manuscript. The names of the actors Will Kempe and Richard Cowley appear among the speech prefixes in 4.2, indicating that Shakespeare had them in mind as he wrote; other irregularities in speech prefixes and scene headings (including "ghost" characters, such as Leonato's wife Innogen) read more like a manuscript in the last stages of revision than a playbook for a finished production. The Folio text was based on this 1600 Quarto, lightly annotated with reference to the playbook but providing little in the way of new readings other than the correction of obvious error.

Francis Meres does not mention the play in September 1598 in his *Palladis Tamia*, unless (and this seems unlikely) it is his "*Loue labours wonne.*" Will Kempe, who played Dogberry, left the Chamberlain's men early in 1599. The likeliest date, then, is the winter of 1598–1599, though publication was not until 1600.

The Merry Wives of Windsor (1597–1601)

The Stationers' Register, the official record book of the London Company of Stationers (booksellers and printers), for January 18, 1602, carries an entry for "A booke called an excellent and pleasant conceited commedie of Sir John Faulstof and the merry wyves of Windesor," by assignment from John Busby to Arthur Johnson. Later that year, Thomas Creed printed the following Quarto:

A Most pleasaunt and excellent conceited Comedie, of Syr *Iohn Falstaffe*, and the merrie Wiues of *Windsor*. Entermixed with sundrie variable and pleasing humors, of Syr *Hugh* the Welch Knight, Iustice *Shallow*, and his wise Cousin M. *Slender*. With the swaggering vaine of Auncient *Pistoll*, and Corporall *Nym*. By *William Shakespeare*. As it hath bene diuers times Acted by the right Honorable my Lord Chamberlaines seruants. Both before her Maiestie, and else-where. LONDON Printed by T. C. [Thomas Creed] for Arthur Iohnson, and are to be sold at his shop in Powles Church-yard, at the signe of the Flower de Leuse and the Crowne. 1602.

This text is now generally regarded as a memorially reconstructed Quarto, perhaps assembled by the actors who played the Host and Falstaff. A Second Quarto in 1619, printed by William Jaggard for Thomas Pavier, was based on it. The First Folio text of 1623, however, was taken from a manuscript evidently transcribed by Ralph Crane (hence, the "massed entries" of characters' names at the beginnings of scenes) and based perhaps on a theatrical playbook. It is the most authoritative text. Several interesting variant readings occur in the memorially reconstructed Quarto, despite its unreliability, and seem to indicate original readings that were altered in the Folio version for reasons of prudence. We find "garmombles" in place of the Folio "germans" at 4.5.74, and "Brook" in place of the Folio "Broome" throughout as the disguise name for the jealous Ford. "Garmombles" is often interpreted as an unflattering allusion to Frederick, Count Mömpelgard (see the Introduction to the play). "Brook" is a seeming dig at the family name of the powerful Henry Brooke (a descendant of Sir John Oldcastle), eighth Lord Cobham, whose intervention probably led to the similar changing of "Oldcastle" to "Falstaff" in *Henry IV*. The First Quarto can also be used sparingly to correct errors and omissions in the Folio text when, as seems likely in a small number of instances, the omission looks like eyeskip in the Folio text, rather than actors' or reporters' interpolations in the Quarto.

On dating, two irreconcilable choices are still possible: 1597, when the Lord Chamberlain was elected to the Order of the Garter, and 1600–1601, after *Henry V* (1599), in which Nym had been introduced. (There is more on the Order of the Garter in the Introduction.) The Stationers' Register entry in January 1602 provides a forward limit in time. Recent scholarly work tends to argue for the earlier date of 1597, though Francis Meres does not mention it in 1598 in his *Palladis Tamia*.

As You Like It (1598–1600)

"As you like yt, a booke" was entered in the Stationers' Register, the official record book of the London Company of Stationers (booksellers and printers), on August 4, 1600, along with *Much Ado About Nothing, Henry V*, and Ben Jonson's *Every Man in His Humor*, all labeled as "My lord chamberlens mens plaies" and all ordered "to be staied" from publication until further notice. Evidently, the Chamberlain's men (Shakespeare's acting company) were anxious to ensure payment or otherwise protect their rights to these very popular plays. Despite their

efforts, *Henry V* appeared in an unauthorized Quarto that same month. *As You Like It* did not appear in print, however, until the First Folio of 1623. The Folio text is a good one, based seemingly on the theatrical playbook that still retained certain authorial features (conceivably, because an autograph fair copy served as the basis for it) or on a literary transcript either of the playbook or of an authorial manuscript.

Francis Meres does not mention the play in September 1598 in his *Palladis Tamia*. However, the play contains an unusually clear allusion to Christopher Marlowe's *Hero and Leander* ("Who ever loved that loved not at first sight?" 3.5.82), of which the first extant edition appeared in 1598, although Shakespeare may well have known it earlier in manuscript or in some lost edition. Even so, other possible allusions, to the burning of satirical books in June 1599 (see 1.2.85–6) and to the new Globe Theater ("All the world's a stage," 2.7.138), point to a date between late 1598 and the summer of 1600, probably after *Much Ado About Nothing*.

Twelfth Night (1600–1602)

Twelfth Night was registered with the London Company of Stationers (booksellers and printers) in 1623 and was first published in the First Folio of that year in a good text set up from what may have been a scribal transcript of Shakespeare's draft manuscript or possibly the playbook (assuming that the scribe might omit theatrical notations). There was a brief delay in printing *Twelfth Night* in the First Folio, possibly because a transcript was being prepared. The play was first mentioned, however, in the *Diary* of a Middle Temple law student or barrister named John Manningham, who describes the festivities for Candlemas Day, February 2, 1602, as follows:

At our feast wee had a play called "Twelue Night, or What you Will," much like the Commedy of Errores, or Menechmi in Plautus, but most like and neere to that in Italian called *Inganni*. A good practise in it to make the Steward beleeve his Lady widdowe was in love with him, by couterfeyting a letter as from his Lady in generall termes, telling him what shee liked best in him, and prescribing his gesture in smiling, his apparaile, & c., and then when he came to practise making him beleeue they tooke him to be mad.

This entry was once suspected to be a forgery perpetrated by John Payne Collier, who published the *Diary* in 1831, but its authenticity is now generally accepted. The date accords with several possible allusions in the play itself. When Fabian jokes about "a pension of thousands to be paid from the Sophy" (2.5.176–7), he seems to be recalling Sir Anthony Shirley's reception by the Shah of Persia (the Sophy) between the summer of 1598 and late 1601. An account of this visit was entered in the Stationers' Register in November 1601. Viola's description of Feste as "wise enough to play the fool" (3.1.60) may recall a poem beginning "True it is, he plays the fool indeed," published in 1600–1601 by Robert Armin (who had played the role of Feste). Maria's comparison of Malvolio's smiling face to "the new map with the augmentation of the Indies" (3.2.77–8) refers to new maps published in 1599 in which America (the Indies) was increased in size. Fabian's reference to sailing north and to the icicle on a Dutchman's beard (3.2.25–6) sounds like an allusion to William Barentz's Arctic expedition, first described in English in an account entered in the Stationers' Register on June 13, 1598, though no edition survives before 1609. Leslie Hotson (*The First Night of Twelfth Night*, 1954) has argued for a first performance at court on Twelfth Night in January 1601, when Queen Elizabeth entertained Don Virginio Orsino, Duke of Bracciano, but this hypothesis has not gained general acceptance, partly because the role of Orsino in the play would scarcely flatter such a noble visitor and partly because there is no proof that any of Shakespeare's plays were originally commissioned for private performance. Nevertheless, the episode may have suggested to Shakespeare the name Orsino. All in all, a date between 1600 and early 1602 seems most likely. Francis Meres does not mention the play in 1598 in his *Palladis Tamia*.

All's Well That Ends Well (c. 1601–1605)

All's Well That Ends Well was first registered in the Stationers' Register, the official record book of the London Company of Stationers (booksellers and printers), in November 1623 and was published in the First Folio of that same year. The text contains numerous inconsistencies in speech headings, "ghost" characters, anomalies of punctuation, and vague or literary stage directions, indicating it was set from the author's working papers, but these errors are not as extensive as once thought and the text is basically sound. Shakespeare's manuscript may have been sporadically annotated by the bookkeeper. Its printing in the First Folio is unusually laden with errors.

Information on the date of the play is sparse. Francis Meres does not mention it in 1598 in his *Palladis Tamia*, unless it is the intriguing "*Loue labours wonne*" on his list. Its themes and style are more suggestive of the period of *Hamlet* and *Troilus and Cressida*. The common assumption today is that the play was written sometime around 1601–1605. It may be later than *Measure for Measure*; the two plays are closely related, but the order of composition is hard to determine. The role of Lavatch is clearly designed for the actor Robert Armin, who did not join Shakespeare's acting company until 1599 or 1600. Scholars once argued that *All's Well* is an early play later revised, but this means of explaining the inconsistencies in the text no longer seems necessary.

Measure for Measure (1603–1604)

Measure for Measure first appeared in the First Folio of 1623. The text was evidently set from scrivener Ralph Crane's copy, possibly of Shakespeare's own draft; the usual inconsistencies of composition have not yet been smoothed away by use in the theater. On the other hand, spellings tend to suggest that Crane was copying a transcript. A recent and controversial hypothesis is that Crane based his copy on a playbook in use after Shakespeare's death, which incorporated some theatrical adaptation by Thomas Middleton and some other reviser, including a song (4.1.1–6) that could have originated in *Rollo, Duke of Normandy* (c. 1617) by John Fletcher and others.

The first recorded performance (according to a Revels account document) was on December 26, 1604, St. Stephen's Night, when "a play Caled Mesur for Mesur" by "Shaxberd" was acted in the banqueting hall at Whitehall "by his Maiesties plaiers." Shakespeare's acting company, previously the Lord Chamberlain's men, had become the King's men after the accession to the throne of James I in 1603. Several allusions in the play seem to point to the summer of 1604, when the theaters, having been closed for a year because of the plague, were reopened. A reference to the King of Hungary (1.2.1–5) may reflect anxieties in England over James's negotiations for a settlement with Spain; censorship would forbid a direct mentioning of Spain. Mistress Overdone's complaint about the war, the "sweat" (plague), the "gallows" (public executions), and poverty (1.2.81–3) are all suggestive of events in 1603–1604, when war with Spain and the plague were still very much in evidence. Duke Vincentio's reticent habits have been seen as a flattering reference to James's well-known dislike of crowds. Stylistically, the play is clearly later than *Twelfth Night* (1600–1602), so that a date close to the first recorded performance in 1604 is a necessity, even if we cannot be positive about all the supposed allusions to King James.

Troilus and Cressida (c. 1601)

The textual history of *Troilus and Cressida* is complicated. On February 7, 1603, James Roberts entered in the Stationers' Register, the official record book of the London Company of Stationers (booksellers and printers), "when he hath gotten sufficient aucthority for yt, The booke of Troilus and Cresseda as yt is acted by my lord Chamberlens Men." On January 28, 1609, however, a new entry appeared in the Register, as though the first had never been made: "Richard Bonion Henry Walleys. Entred for their Copy vnder thandes of Master Segar deputy to Sir George Bucke and master warden Lownes a booke called the history of Troylus and Cressida." Later that year appeared the First Quarto with the following title:

THE Historie of Troylus and Cresseida. *As it was acted by the Kings Maiesties seruants at the Globe. Written by* William Shakespeare. LONDON Imprinted by *G. Eld* for *R Bonian* and *H. Walley*, and are to be sold at the spred Eagle in Paules Church-yeard, ouer against the great North doore. 1609.

Before the first printing had sold out, still in 1609, the original title leaf was replaced by two new leaves containing a new title and an epistle. The title reads:

THE Famous Historie of Troylus *and* Cresseid. *Excellently expressing the beginning* of their loues, with the conceited wooing of *Pandarus* Prince of *Licia. Written by* William Shakespeare.

The epistle is addressed "A neuer writer, to an euer reader. Newes," and begins, "Eternall reader, you haue heere a new play, neuer stal'd with the Stage, neuer clapperclawd with the palmes of the vulger, and yet passing full of the palme comicall."

The First Folio editors originally intended *Troilus and Cressida* to follow *Romeo and Juliet.* After three pages and a title page had been set up in this position, however, the play was removed (perhaps owing to copyright difficulties) and *Timon of Athens* was inserted instead. Later, *Troilus* was placed between the Histories and the Tragedies, almost entirely without pagination. See the Introduction for some possible explanations of the unusual publishing history.

The Quarto text was evidently set from a transcript of Shakespeare's working draft, made either by Shakespeare or by a scribe, or more probably from the working draft itself. The first three pages of the Folio text, those originally intended to follow *Romeo and Juliet,* were set from this First Quarto. The remaining pages of the First Folio, however, seem to have been based on a copy of the Quarto that had been collated with a manuscript, either Shakespeare's draft or more probably the playbook, which could itself have been a transcript of Shakespeare's fair copy of his original papers. As a result, both the Quarto and Folio texts have independent textual authority. Recent editorial study has paid increasing attention to the Folio text on the theory that its readings, when not manifestly corrupt, may represent either Shakespeare's second throughts as he fair copied or at least what the Folio collator found in Shakespeare's draft or the playbook. Hence, this edition, though using the First Quarto as its control text, introduces more Folio readings than are usually found in some previous editions; the Folio readings have been rejected only when there is some textual evidence against them.

The possibility that the play may not have been publicly performed and the failure of Shakespeare's company to provide the sequel promised at the end of *Troilus*

suggest that the play was written not long before the first Stationers' Register entry of February 1603. Certainly the play was not an old favorite in the company's repertoire. Failure as a stage play might have led to an attempt at quick publication, aimed at sophisticated readers. The current fad for satire would also have provided a motive for prompt publication. Stylistically, *Troilus* belongs to the period of *Hamlet* (c. 1599–1601). A seeming allusion in the Prologue of *Troilus* to the "armed" Prologue of Ben Jonson's *Poetaster* (1601) helps set a probable early limit for date of composition; although the Prologue first appears in the First Folio of 1623 and may be an addition to the original play, it probably is not much later in date of composition. George Chapman's *The Seauen Bookes of Homers Iliads,* a source of information about the Trojan war, had appeared in 1598. The play is not mentioned by Francis Meres in 1598.

The Henry VI Plays (c. 1589–1592)

The date and textual situation for *1 Henry VI* needs to be discussed in the context of all three *Henry VI* plays. *1 Henry VI* was not the first to be published. Shortened versions of *2* and *3 Henry VI* appeared in 1594 and 1595. One was titled as follows:

The First part of the Contention betwixt the two famous Houses of Yorke and Lancaster, with the death of the good Duke Humphrey: And the banishment and death of the Duke of *Suffolke,* and the Tragicall end of the proud Cardinall of VVinchester, vvith the notable Rebellion of *Iacke Cade: And the Duke of Yorkes first claime vnto the Crowne.* LONDON Printed by Thomas Creed, for Thomas Millington, and are to be sold at his shop vnder Saint Peters Church in Cornwall. 1594.

Its sequel was titled as follows:

The true Tragedie of Richard *Duke of Yorke, and the death of* good King Henrie the Sixt, *with the whole contention betweene* the two Houses Lancaster and Yorke, as it was sundrie times acted by the Right Honourable the Earle of Pembrooke his seruants. Printed at London by P. S. [Peter Short] for Thomas Milling*ton, and are to be sold at his shoppe vnder Saint Peters Church in Cornwal.* 1595.

Once thought to be source plays for Shakespeare's 2 and 3 *Henry VI,* these texts, the first a Quarto and the second an Octavo, may represent early authorial drafts, or they may have had their origins in memorially reconstructed transcripts of performance versions of the plays made by actors. As such, their textual authority is questionable but may be of significance in those occasional passages where the Folio compositors seem to have had recourse to later reprints (the Third Quartos) of these texts. In 1619 they were combined in a reprint by the printer William Jaggard called *The Whole Contention betweene the two Famous Houses, Lancaster and Yorke.* These texts are considerably shorter than the First Folio versions of 1623, which appeared there under the titles "The second Part of Henry the Sixt, with the death of the Good Duke HVMFREY," and "The third Part of Henry the Sixt, with the death of the Duke of YORKE." Since, as memorially reconstructed texts, they are ultimately derived from the playbook, these texts may contain some materials that were revised as the plays were put into performance, but the likelihood of contamination through reporting, actors' interpolations, and transmission are so great that the textual authority here must be regarded with great caution. The Folio texts seem to have been based on authorial manuscripts, although there is evidence, too, that both plays or portions thereof were printed from pages of the Third Quartos of each play or at least with some consultation of the respective Third Quartos by the Folio compositors. The Third Quarto of 2 *Henry VI* may embody some independent authority (perhaps a theatrical manuscript), although not necessarily the author's; Q3 of 3 *Henry VI* seems to have no such independent authority.

The text of 1 *Henry VI*, based seemingly on an authorial manuscript that may have been annotated in the theater and possibly recopied, was first published in the First Folio of 1623. It alone of the three parts was registered for publication at this time. The Stationers' Register entry refers to this play as "The thirde parte of Henry the sixt." These circumstances have prompted many scholars to suspect that 1 *Henry VI* was written after the other two plays, especially since those two plays do not often recall events of 1 *Henry VI*—for example, they make no mention of its hero, Lord Talbot. The seeming fact that the 1594 and 1595 Quartos were pirated editions would, however, explain their publication before 1 *Henry VI* and the necessity of registering Part One later. In other ways, 1 *Henry VI* has shown itself to be no hasty afterthought, but a play with thematic unity throughout and a sense of direction anticipating the remainder of the series. Hence, some scholars now support Dr. Johnson's commonsense hunch that these three plays in Shakespeare's first historical tetralogy were written in order, though the issue remains in doubt.

Although scholars have long questioned Shakespeare's authorship, especially in parts of 1 *Henry VI*, the series as a whole is best regarded as his own work or at the very least dominated by his artistic conception throughout. The once prevailing and recently reasserted hypotheses of multiple authorship rest on questionable internal evidence, such as vocabulary or versification. What sounds like Thomas Nashe, Robert Greene, or George Peele in these very early plays may simply be the result of those men's undoubted influence on Shakespeare during his apprenticeship. Greene's famous diatribe at Shakespeare (see below) suggests that he was keenly aware of Shakespeare's facility for learning quickly from his contemporaries. The inconsistencies in these early plays, especially in Part One—mislineation, defective verse, inaccuracy in speech prefixes, confusion about time, discrepancy in facts—may be the result not of multiple authorship but of reliance on various sources, hasty composition, and problems of transcription. Again, however, the issue has not been finally resolved.

Several contemporary allusions to the *Henry VI* plays help considerably with dating the series. Thomas Nashe wrote in his *Pierce Penniless* (registered August 1592) that it would "have joyed brave Talbot (the terror of the French) to think that after he had lain two hundred years in his tomb, he should triumph again on the stage." Probably he was referring to Shakespeare's play. The reference in Henslowe's diary to a "ne" (new?) performance of *Harey the vi* in March 1592 may or may not refer to Shakespeare's work, however, for this performance was by Lord Strange's men, whereas Shakespeare's *Henry VI* series is associated elsewhere with Pembroke's men. In any event, 3 *Henry VI* must have been completed by the time of Robert Greene's death in September 1592, when Greene (or his literary executor, Chettle) alludes plainly to it (1.4.137) in his angry remark about "an upstart crow, beautified with our feathers, that with his '*Tiger's heart wrapped in a player's hide*' supposes he is as well able to bombast out a blank verse as the best of you." These contemporary references are confirmed by allusions in the texts themselves, for all the *Henry VI* plays seem to contain echoes of Books 1–3 of Edmund Spenser's *Faerie Queene* (printed 1590), whereas 3 *Henry VI* seems to have influenced parts of *The Troublesome Reign of King John* (printed 1591). An inclusive date of 1589–1591 or 1592 ought to account for the entire series.

Richard III (c. 1592–1594)

A Quarto edition of *Richard III*, registered by Andrew Wise on October 20, 1597, appeared later that same year with the following title:

THE TRAGEDY of King Richard the third. Containing, His treacherous Plots against his brother Clarence: the pittiefull murther of his iunocent nephewes: his tyrannicall vsurpation: with the whole course of his detested life, and most deserued death. As it hath beene lately Acted by the Right honourable the Lord Chamberlaine his seruants. AT LONDON Printed by Valentine Sims, for Andrew Wise, dwelling in Paules Chu[r]ch-yard, at the Signe of the Angell. 1597.

This text, one of the most perplexing in all Shakespeare, is sometimes regarded as one that was created when the acting company banded together to reconstruct a play of which the copy was missing. The reconstructed version may have been cut, perhaps for provincial performance. This defective text was the basis of the 1597 Quarto, which was reprinted in 1598, 1602, 1605, 1612, 1622, 1629, and 1634, each of which was successively more error-laden than the previous one. The First Folio text of 1623 seems to have been set mainly from copies of the Third and Sixth Quartos (1602 and 1622), which had been sporadically but heavily corrected against an independent manuscript—possibly Shakespeare's own working manuscript or a copy of it. This manuscript source, some of which may have been interleaved into the printers' copy, represents a generally superior authority to that of the First Quarto. Parts of the Folio text, however, were set from an uncorrected copy of the Third Quarto (1602), and for those passages (3.1.1–158 and 5.3.48 to end of play) the First Quarto, from which the Third Quarto was derived, must serve as copy text. Otherwise, the Folio text is the most authoritative, though it must be approached with caution.

The situation is indeed fraught with unusual uncertainty, since there are many opportunities for the Folio to have perpetuated errors of the earlier Quartos; moreover, its "improvements" over the readings of those Quartos could in some instances be editorial sophistications. The First Quarto offers some readings that demand serious attention. Especially when the Folio's reading differs from those of the First Quarto and is instead derived from Quartos Two through Six, the First Quarto should be preferred unless it is manifestly wrong. At the same time, however, since the First Quarto may reflect adaptation of the original acting text, its changes may not represent Shakespeare's artistic intention either. For these reasons, one must be wary of the First Quarto's assignment of speeches when they vary from the Folio's assignments and also of the First Quarto's cuts, some of which are substantial.

The play is mentioned by Francis Meres in 1598 in his *Palladis Tamia*. John Weever names a *"Richard"* in his *Epigrams*, published in 1599. Most scholars date *Richard III* as 1592–1594, on the basis of its style and its close affinity to the *Henry VI* series (completed probably in 1591–1592). The play may have been influenced by the anonymous *The True Tragedy of Richard III*, registered in June 1594 but probably written in 1590–1592 or even earlier. Shakespeare's play may also have been influenced by Thomas Kyd's *The Spanish Tragedy* (c. 1587) and by Christopher Marlowe's dramas (he died in 1593).

King John (c. 1594–1596)

The Life and Death of King John, as it is called in the original text, first appeared in the First Folio of 1623. That text appears to have been set up from Shakespeare's working manuscript as copied by two scribes with a view to future theatrical use, although the manuscript does not show signs of having been actually employed as a playbook. Apart from Francis Meres's listing of the play (in his

Palladis Tamia, 1598), dating clues are scarce. Editors have suggested dates ranging from 1590 to 1598 and have proposed topical allusions to bolster their various arguments. The consensus today is that *King John* was probably written shortly before or after *Richard II* in about 1594–1595, or 1596, and that it was based primarily on an anonymous two-part play, *The Troublesome Reign of King John*, published in 1591. Many editors assume that Shakespeare would have preferred to write this historically independent play in the interim between his two four-play series (*Henry VI* through *Richard III* and *Richard II* through *Henry V*), rather than interrupt the flow of composition on either of those series. This suggestion is scarcely provable, however. In any case, the link between *Richard II* and *1 Henry IV* is not so close as to preclude interruption.

A major critic of the consensus view is E. A. J. Honigmann, editor of the Arden *King John* (1954), who argues for a date in 1590 preceding the publication in 1591 of *The Troublesome Reign of King John* (which he regards as an unauthorized Quarto). Honigmann is joined by William Matchett in his Signet edition of *King John* (1966) and, earlier, by Peter Alexander in 1939. Otherwise, this argument has aroused controversy but has received little acceptance.

Richard II (c. 1595–1596)

On August 29, 1597, "The Tragedye of Richard the Second" was entered in the Stationers' Register, the official record book of the London Company of Stationers (booksellers and printers), by Andrew Wise, and was published by him later that same year:

THE Tragedie of King Richard the second. *As it hath beene publikely acted by the right Honourable the Lorde Chamberlaine his Seruants.* LONDON Printed by Valentine Simmes for Androw Wise, and are to be sold at his shop in Paules church yard at the signe of the Angel. 1597.

This is a good text, printed evidently from the author's papers or a nontheatrical transcript of them. Wise issued two more quartos of this popular play in 1598, each set from the previous quarto, and then in 1603 transferred his rights to the play to Matthew Law. This publisher issued in 1608 a Fourth Quarto "With new additions of the Parliament Sceane, and the deposing of King Richard" (according to the title page in some copies). The deposition scene has indeed been omitted from the earlier quartos, probably through censorship. A Fifth Quarto appeared in 1615, based on the Fourth Quarto. All the quartos after the first attribute the play to Shakespeare. The added deposition scene in Quartos 4 and 5 seems to have been memorially reconstructed. The First Folio text of 1623 gives a better version of the deposition scene, seemingly because the printers of the Folio had access to the manuscript playbook for this portion of the text. (Some scholars maintain that the Folio text was derived from an earlier quarto or quartos that had been marked up and used as a playbook, but that case has been weakened by recent research.) Most of the Folio text was probably set from an annotated copy of the Third Quarto, and perhaps a leaf in Act 5 from the Fifth Quarto. The annotation was evidently quite uneven, and so the most authoritative text for all but the deposition scene remains the First Quarto; nevertheless, at certain points (especially the first 900 lines, part of 3.2, and much of Act 5), the annotation with reference to the playbook seems to have been more thorough. At such points, the Folio readings deserve serious attention, and the stage directions are often illuminating.

Francis Meres mentions the play in 1598 in his *Palladis Tamia*. Clearly it had been written and performed prior to the Stationers' Register entry in August 1597. Its earliest probable date is 1595, since the play seemingly is indebted to Samuel Daniel's poem, *The First Four Books of the Civil Wars*, published in that year. Shakespeare follows Daniel, for example, in increasing the Queen's age from eleven (according to the chronicles) to maturity, and in other significant details. On December 7, 1595, Sir Edward Hoby invited Sir Robert Cecil to his house in Cannon Row, "where as late as it shall please you a gate for your supper shall be open, and King Richard present himself to your view." Although it is by no means certain that this passage refers to a private performance of Shakespeare's play, stylistic considerations favor a date around 1595 rather than 1597. If, as some scholars contend, Daniel's *Civil Wars* was written after Shakespeare's play rather than before it, the date of *Richard II* might be as early as 1594.

Henry IV, Part I (1596–1597)

On February 25, 1598, "The historye of Henry the IIIJth with his battaile of Shrewsburye against Henry Hottspurre of the Northe with the conceipted mirthe of Sir John Ffalstoff" was entered in the Stationers' Register, the official record book of the London Company of Stationers (booksellers and printers), by Andrew Wise. Later that year appeared the following Quarto:

THE HISTORY OF HENRIE THE FOVRTH; With the battell at Shrewsburie, *betweene the King and Lord* Henry Percy, surnamed Henrie Hotspur of the North. *With the humorous conceits of Sir* Iohn Falstalffe. AT LONDON, Printed by P. S. [Peter Short] for *Andrew Wise*, dwelling in Paules Churchyard, at the signe of the Angell. 1598.

Actually this was not the first quarto, for an earlier fragment of eight pages has survived, part of a text that served as copy for the first complete extant Quarto. Together, these quartos make up an excellent authoritative text,

based seemingly on the author's papers or, more probably, a scribal transcript of them. Four more quartos appeared before the First Folio of 1623, each based on the previous quarto. The Folio itself was based on the last of these, perhaps with reference also to some kind of manuscript, although the number of authoritative readings that can be claimed for the Folio is small.

1 Henry IV shows signs of revision in the use of characters' names, most notably that of Falstaff. Plainly, the original version of the play called him Sir John Oldcastle, after one of the prince's companions in the anonymous *Famous Victories of Henry the Fifth* (c. 1588). The name "Oldcastle" was originally intended for *2 Henry IV* as well. The speech prefix "Old." is left standing at 1.2.119 in the Quarto of *2 Henry IV*, one or two lines of verse in *1 Henry IV* are one syllable short, evidently because "Oldcastle" has been altered to "Falstaff," and Falstaff is jokingly referred to as "my old lad of the castle" (*1 Henry IV*, 1.2.41). Moreover, there are several contemporary allusions to a play about a fat knight named Oldcastle. Apparently, Henry Brooke, Lord Cobham, a living descendant of the Lollard martyr Oldcastle of Henry V's reign, took umbrage at the profane use Shakespeare had made of this revered name, whereupon Shakespeare's acting company shifted to another less controversial name from the chronicles, Sir John Fastolfe or Falstaff (called "Falstaffe" in the Folio text of Shakespeare's *1 Henry VI* and assigned a cowardly role in the French wars of that play). The revision also changed the names of Oldcastle's cronies from Harvey and Russell to Peto and Bardolph. This edition retains the name "Falstaff," since Shakespeare clearly accepted it as the new name of the character in all his "Falstaff" plays.

Cobham was Lord Chamberlain from July 1596 until his death in March 1597, during which interval Shakespeare's company bore the name of Lord Hunsdon's men. Quite possibly, the difficulty over the name "Oldcastle" erupted during that period, for *1 Henry IV* seems to have been written and performed in late 1596 and early 1597, not long after Shakespeare had finished *Richard II* (c. 1595–1596).

Francis Meres, in his *Palladis Tamia*, 1598, refers to "*Henry the IV*" without specifying one or two parts. Publication of *1 Henry IV* in 1598 confirmed to the Elizabethan public that the changes in names to Falstaff, Peto, and Bardolph had taken place.

Henry IV, Part II (1597–1598)

"The second parte of the history of Kinge Henry the IIIJth with the humours of Sir John Fallstaff: Wrytten by master Shakespere" was entered in the Stationers' Register, the official record book of the London Company of Stationers (booksellers and printers), by Andrew Wise and William

Aspley on August 23, 1600. (This is the first time Shakespeare's name appeared in the Stationers' Register.) The Quarto was published later that year as

THE Second part of Henrie the fourth, continuing to his death, *and coronation of Henrie* the fift. With the humours of sir Iohn Fal*staffe, and swaggering* Pistoll. *As it hath been sundrie times publikely* acted by the right honourable, the Lord Chamberlaine his seruants. *Written by William Shakespeare.* LONDON Printed by V. S. [Valentine Sims] for Andrew Wise, and William Aspley. 1600.

One scene, 3.1, was omitted from Sims's first printing [Qa] of this Quarto, whereupon Sims reset two leaves as four new leaves [Qb] including not only the omitted 3.1, but also 2.4.340–390 and 3.2.1–104. Qb is therefore the best copy text for 3.1 and Qa for those portions that were reset. In addition, still other passages were omitted from both versions of the 1600 Quarto; they were later restored in, or added to, the First Folio. No further quartos appeared prior to the First Folio of 1623—an odd fact in view of *1 Henry IV*'s continued popularity but perhaps the result of a large printing of *2 Henry IV* in anticipation of heavy sales. At any rate, this Quarto text seems to have been based on Shakespeare's papers and was a reliable one except for some substantial omissions and for some misreadings, owing to the compositors' difficulty in reading an authorial manuscript that may have been unfinished. Speech prefixes are at times quite irregular, indicative of author's papers before they have received the attentions of the prompter. Of the omitted passages, some may have been the result of shortening for performance, but some suggest political censorship. Others suggest authorial revision. The Folio text restores or adds the omitted readings.

The relationship of Folio to Quarto text is extraordinarily difficult to determine. Perhaps the Folio compositors were using a manuscript that had been transcribed either from an extensively annotated copy of the Quarto or from a Quarto and a manuscript source jointly compared. Another hypothesis is that the copy for the Folio was made up from actors' parts. The Folio copy was, in any case, a strange transcript, showing perhaps some stage influence and possibly used as a playbook but less adequately provided with stage directions than most playbooks; perhaps the scribe imposed certain literary features. It seems to have been a special case. George Walton Williams (*Shakespeare Studies* 9:173) speculates that it was an edited transcript of a playbook prepared for Lord Cobham. Whatever its identity, it embodied tendencies toward sophistication and regularization that frequently render the Folio readings less authoritative than those of the Quarto. The Folio text does restore the passages excised from the Quarto, however, and on other occasions as well it provides what appear to be authentic corrections of, and authorial additions to, the Quarto. The Quarto text is generally the most authoritative when it is not manifestly in error or lacking material found in the Folio, but the Folio corrections and additions have to be regarded with close attention.

Like *Part One* of *Henry IV*, *Part Two* shows signs of revision in the use of characters' names, most notably that of Falstaff. Plainly, the original version of both plays called him Sir John Oldcastle, after one of the prince's companions in the anonymous *Famous Victories of Henry the Fifth* (c. 1588). The speech prefix "Old." is left standing at 1.2.119 in the Quarto of *2 Henry IV*, and in *1 Henry IV* Falstaff is jokingly referred to as "my old lad of the castle" (1.2.41). Moreover, there are several contemporary allusions to a play about a fat knight named Oldcastle. See above, *Henry IV, Part I,* for an account of how Shakespeare's company appears to have changed to the less controversial name of Falstaff (along with Peto and Bardolph in place of Harvey and Russell) in order to avoid offending the family of Henry Brooke, Lord Cobham, a living descendant of the Lollard martyr Oldcastle of Henry V's reign.

Cobham was Lord Chamberlain from July 1596 until his death in March 1597, during which interval Shakespeare's company bore the name of Lord Hunsdon's men. Quite possibly, the difficulty over the name Oldcastle erupted during that period, for *1 Henry IV* seems to have been written and performed in late 1596 and early 1597, not long after Shakespeare had finished *Richard II* (c. 1595–1596). *2 Henry IV* must have been written before the end of 1598, so that Shakespeare could then begin *Henry V* in early 1599. Since *2 Henry IV* was begun using the names Oldcastle, Harvey, and Russell, however, there is reason to date it somewhat earlier, in 1597, before the squabble over the names broke out. Scholars who prefer a date in 1597 for *The Merry Wives* also date *2 Henry IV* early in 1597, since it appears to have introduced Shallow and Pistol before they appeared in *The Merry Wives*. Francis Meres refers in 1598 to "Henry the 4" without specifying one or two parts. Publication of *1 Henry IV* in 1598 assured the Elizabethan public that the changes in names to Falstaff, Peto, and Bardolph had taken place; a revised epilogue to the 1600 Quarto of *2 Henry IV* protests that "Oldcastle died a martyr, and this [Falstaff] is not the man," as though by way of apology or disclaimer. A play defending the reputation of the Lollard Oldcastle and attacking Falstaff, called *The History of the Life of Sir John Oldcastle, Lord Cobham, with his Martyrdom*, had been performed by the rival Admiral's men in 1599.

Henry V (1599)

An entry in the Stationers' Register, the official record book of the London Company of Stationers (booksellers and printers), for August 4, 1600, provides that "Henry the ffift" and three other plays belonging to the Lord Chamberlain's men (Shakespeare's acting company) are "to be staied" from publication until further permission is granted. Evidently, the Chamberlain's men were anxious to ensure they were paid or to prevent unauthorized publication. They did not succeed, in any event, in preventing the appearance of an unauthorized text of *Henry V*. An entry in the Stationers' Register for August 14 assigns to Thomas Pavier an already published work entitled "The historye of Henry the Vth with the battell of Agencourt." The Quarto volume to which this entry refers is the following:

THE CHRONICLE History of Henry the fift, With his battell fought at *Agin Court* in France. Togither with *Auntient Pistoll. As it hath bene sundry times playd by the Right honorable the Lord Chamberlaine his seruants.* LONDON Printed by *Thomas Creede,* for Tho. Millington, and Iohn Busby. And are to be sold at his house in Carter Lane, next the Powle head. 1600.

The text of this play is manifestly corrupt. It is considerably shorter than the First Folio version and completely omits the choruses and three entire scenes (1.1, 3.1, and 4.2). The remainder seems to have been put together by memorial reconstruction. This unauthorized Quarto served as the basis for a Second Quarto printed by Thomas Creed for Thomas Pavier in 1602 and a third printed by William Jaggard for Thomas Pavier in 1619 but fraudulently dated 1608. The Folio text was printed seemingly from an authorial manuscript, perhaps with occasional reference to the Third Quarto (which contains some potentially troublesome contamination). The Folio text is thus the most reliable version, though the First Quarto is also an interesting witness, especially for visual effects recorded in its stage directions, for a few readings in the text, and for verse lineation of Pistol's speeches.

Francis Meres does not mention the play in 1598 in his *Palladis Tamia,* though he does mention *"Henry the IV."* The epilogue to *2 Henry IV* (written probably in 1597) promises that "our humble author will continue the story, with Sir John in it, and make you merry with fair Katharine of France"; since the prediction is not really accurate regarding Falstaff, we can be reasonably certain that Shakespeare had not yet begun *Henry V* in 1597. An allusion in the Chorus of Act 5 to "the General of our gracious Empress," who may in good time come home from Ireland with "rebellion broachèd on his sword," has been taken by virtually all editors to refer to the Earl of Essex, who left in March 1599 to quell the Irish rebellion headed by Tyrone. Although Essex returned on September 28 of that same year, having failed utterly in his assignment, the departure of such a charismatic figure could have inspired Shakespeare's praising remark. A minority view holds that the choruses (which do not appear in the unauthorized Quarto of 1600) could have been written later in 1601 for Essex's far more victorious successor, Lord Mountjoy (see Warren D. Smith on *Henry V* in *JEGP*, 1954). Still, Essex

was more center stage during those exciting years, more likely to have been the subject of adulation. In any case, the play itself must have been written before August 1600, most probably in 1599. The reference to "this wooden O" in the Chorus of Act 1 is often thought to be Shakespeare's compliment to the company's new theater, the Globe, which was ready for their use probably in 1599; but the play may have been produced at the Curtain instead.

King Henry VIII (1613)

The Famous History of the Life of King Henry the Eighth was first printed in the First Folio of 1623. The text is a good one, set from a careful transcript of an authorial manuscript. The stage directions are unusually elaborate. The first recorded performance was on June 29, 1613. A letter of July 2 in that year from Sir Henry Wotton to Sir Edmund Bacon tells of a performance of "a new play, called *All Is True,* representing some principal pieces of the reign of Henry VIII." During this performance, as King Henry was arriving as a masker at the house of Cardinal Wolsey (1.4), "certain chambers [cannons] being shot off at his entry, some of the paper, or other stuff, wherewith one of them was stopped, did light on the thatch, where being thought at first but an idle smoke, and their eyes more attentive to the show, it kindled inwardly, and ran round like a train, consuming within less than an hour the whole house to the very grounds." The identification of this *All Is True* with Shakespeare's play is certain. Other accounts include a letter from Thomas Lorkin to Sir Thomas Puckering, June 1613, asserting the fire to have started "while Burbage his company were acting at the Globe the play of Henry 8," a letter of 4 July from Henry Bluett to Richard Weeks, another of 8 July from John Chamberlain to Sir Ralph Winwood, and an account in John Stow's *Annals* as continued by Edmund Howe (1618).

Wotton calls it a new play, and stylistic considerations confirm this characterization. The play may also have helped provide entertainment for the betrothal and marriage of James I's daughter Elizabeth to the Elector Palatine earlier in 1613, though *Henry VIII* is not listed among the many plays acted on this occasion.

On the question of Shakespeare's collaboration with John Fletcher in the authorship of *Henry VIII,* see the play's Introduction.

Titus Andronicus (c. 1589–1592)

On February 6, 1594, "a Noble Roman Historye of Tytus Andronicus" was entered in the Stationers' Register, the official record book of the London Company of Stationers (booksellers and printers), to John Danter, along with "the ballad thereof." The entry probably, though not certainly, refers to Shakespeare's play. Later in that same year, at any rate, Danter published a Quarto volume with the following title:

THE MOST LAmentable Romaine Tragedie of Titus Andronicus: As it was Plaide by the Right Honourable the Earle of *Darbie*, Earle of *Pembrooke*, and Earle of *Sussex* their Seruants. LONDON, Printed by Iohn Danter, and are to be sold by *Edward White* & *Thomas Millington*, at the little North doore of Paules at the signe of the Gunne. 1594.

This text seems to have been set from Shakespeare's manuscript in an unpolished state. A Second Quarto appeared in 1600, adding the name of the Lord Chamberlain's company to those who had acted the play. It was set up from a slightly damaged copy of the First Quarto. Although the Second Quarto made some improvements, these were probably by the compositor and not the author, or may have been made in a press-corrected Q1 no longer extant (since we have only one copy today). A Third Quarto (1611), set up from the second, contributed new errors. The First Folio text of 1623 was derived from the Third Quarto, but with an authentic added scene (3.2) from a manuscript source and with additional stage directions that suggest a playhouse playbook. One theory is that the copy used by the Folio printers, the Third Quarto, had been corrected from an annotated copy of the Second Quarto that had been used as a playbook, or perhaps directly from the playbook. Despite these improvements, the First Quarto clearly remains the authoritative text except for 3.2.

The date of *Titus* must be prior to 1594. Philip Henslowe's *Diary* records a performance of a "Titus & Ondronicus" by the Earl of Sussex's men on January 24, 1594, and indicates it was "ne" or new. This could certainly mean a new play, but it could also mean it was newly revised or newly acquired. Since the players on this occasion, Sussex's men, were listed third on the 1594 title page after Derby's and Pembroke's men, they may just have acquired *Titus*. Two allusions may point to an earlier date: *A Knack to Know a Knave* (performed in 1592) and *The Troublesome Reign of King John* (published 1591) may contain echoes of *Titus*, though the text of the former is memorially reconstructed and could therefore contain a remembered reference up to the date of publication in 1594. Stylistic considerations favor a date around 1589–1592 or even earlier.

The authorship of *Titus* would appear at first glance to belong entirely to Shakespeare. Although the 1594 Quarto does not mention Shakespeare's name (a common omission in such early texts, especially since the author was as yet relatively unknown), Francis Meres in his *Palladis Tamia*, 1598, assigns the play to Shakespeare, and the Folio editors include it in the 1623 edition. Doubts began to arise, however, when Edward Ravenscroft observed in 1687 that he had been "told by some ancient-

ly conversant with the stage that it was not originally his, but brought by a private author to be acted, and he only gave some master touches to one or two of the principal parts or characters." This remark touched off a controversy that continues today; for example, J. Dover Wilson in his New Cambridge Shakespeare (1948), J. C. Maxwell in his Arden edition (1953), and Jonathan Bate in his Arden 3 edition (1995). Plausible arguments have been brought forward that George Peele may have contributed scenes 1 through 3 of Act 1, scenes 1 and 2 of Act 2, and scene 1 of Act 4. Ravenscroft's testimonial is suspect, to be sure, both because it came one hundred years after the fact and because Ravenscroft himself was embarked on an adaptation of *Titus* and so might have wished to denigrate the original. The efforts at assigning portions of the play to Shakespeare's contemporaries have sometimes been motivated by a wish to rescue Shakespeare's reputation from the violent and garish effects of this play. Most recent criticism prefers to regard the play as an interesting experiment in revenge tragedy by a young artist, with many shrewdly characteristic Shakespearean touches. Even so, joint authorship remains a lively possibility. See the Introduction to the play in this volume.

Henslowe's *Diary* records the performance of a "Tittus & Vespacia" on April 11, 1592, a "ne" play by Strange's men. Despite the similarity of the title, this play was probably on an independent subject.

Romeo and Juliet (1594–1596)

A corrupt and unregistered Quarto of *Romeo and Juliet* appeared in 1597 with the following title:

AN excellent conceited Tragedie OF Romeo and Iuliet, As it hath been often (with great applause) plaid publiquely, by the right Honourable the L. of *Hunsdon* his Seruants. LONDON, Printed by Iohn Danter. 1597.

This edition, intended no doubt to capitalize on the play's great popularity, seems to have been memorially reconstructed by two or more actors (probably those playing Romeo and Paris), and possibly thereafter to have been used as a playbook. Its appearance seems to have caused the issuance two years later of a clearly authoritative version:

THE MOST EXcellent and lamentable Tragedie, of Romeo and Iuliet. *Newly corrected, augmented, and amended*: As it hath bene sundry times publiquely acted, by the right Honourable the Lord Chamberlaine his Seruants. LONDON Printed by Thomas Creede, for Cuthbert Burby, and are to be sold at his shop neare the Exchange. 1599.

This text is some 800 lines longer than the first and corrects errors in that earlier version. It seems at one point, however, to have been contaminated by the First Quarto, as though the manuscript source for the Second Quarto (probably the author's rough draft) was defective at some point. A passage from 1.2.53 to 1.3.34 was apparently set directly from the First Quarto. (On this matter, see George W. Williams's old-spelling edition of the play, Duke Univ. Press, 1964.) Q1 may also have influenced Q2 in some other isolated instances. Despite this contamination, however, the Second Quarto is the authoritative text, except for the passage of direct indebtedness to Q1. Q2 served as the basis for the Third Quarto (1609), which in turn served as copy for the Fourth Quarto (undated, but placed in 1622) and the First Folio of 1623. A Fifth Quarto appeared in 1637. The Folio text may embody a few authoritative readings of its own, perhaps by way of reference to a theatrical manuscript.

Francis Meres, in his *Palladis Tamia*, 1598, assigns the play to Shakespeare. So does John Weever in his *Epigrams* of 1599. Internal evidence on dating is not reliable. The Nurse observes that "'Tis since the earthquake now eleven years" (1.3.24); however, it has been discovered that suitable earthquakes occurred in 1580, 1583, 1584, and 1585, giving us a wide choice of dates even if we accept the dubious proposition that the Nurse is speaking accurately. Astronomical reckoning of the position of the moon at the time the play purportedly takes place ("A fortnight and odd days" before Lammastide, August 1, 1.3.16) indicates the year 1596; again, however, we have no reason to assume Shakespeare cared about this sort of internal accuracy. More suggestive perhaps is the argument that Danter's unauthorized publication in 1597 was seeking to exploit a popular new play—one the acting company certainly did not yet wish to see published, since it was a moneymaker. Danter assigns the play to Lord Hunsdon's servants, a name that Shakespeare's company could have used only from July 22, 1596 (when the old Lord Chamberlain, Henry Carey, first Lord Hunsdon, died) to March 17, 1597 (when George Carey, second Lord Hunsdon, was appointed to his father's erstwhile position as Lord Chamberlain). Danter could simply have been using the name of the company at the time he obtained the play, but he may also have indicated performance in late 1596. Danter printed only the first four sheets, but he must have done so by February–March 1597, when his presses were seized. Stylistically, the play is clearly of the "lyric" period of *A Midsummer Night's Dream* and *Richard II*. There are also stylistic affinities to the sonnets and to the narrative poems of 1593–1594. A date between 1594 and 1596 is likely, especially toward the latter end of this period. Whether the play comes before or after *A Midsummer Night's Dream* is, however, a matter of conjecture.

Julius Caesar (1599)

Julius Caesar was first published in the First Folio of 1623. The text is an excellent one, based evidently on a theater playbook or a transcript of it; some theatrical features, such as a provision for the doubling of Cassius and Caius Ligarius, appear to represent a staging configuration that Shakespeare had not anticipated. On the other hand, some stage directions sound authorial, as though Shakespeare's own words had survived into the playbook. Some confusions have survived as well, notably in the handling of Lucilius, Lucius, Titinius, and Pindarus in 4.2. In the Folio, the play is included among the tragedies and entitled *The Tragedy of Julius Caesar*, although the table of contents lists it as *The Life and death of Julius Caesar*.

The play's first performance must have occurred in 1599 or slightly earlier. On September 21, 1599, a Swiss visitor named Thomas Platter crossed the River Thames after lunch with a company of spectators to see "the tragedy of the first Emperor Julius Caesar" performed in a thatched-roofed building. The description fits the Globe, the Rose, and the Swan theaters, but the last of these was not in regular use. The Admiral's men at the Rose are not known to have had a Caesar play, whereas the Chamberlain's men certainly had Shakespeare's play about this time. They had only recently moved from their Theatre in the northeast suburbs of London to the Globe south of the river, and *Julius Caesar* was probably a new play for the occasion.

John Weever, in *The Mirror of Martyrs* (1601), is surely referring to Shakespeare's play when he describes "the many-headed multitude" listening first to "Brutus' speech, that Caesar was ambitious" and then to "eloquent Mark Antony." (The dedication to Weever's book claims he wrote it "some two years ago," in 1599; however, since this book has been shown to be heavily indebted to a work that first appeared in 1600, Weever's allusion is not as helpful in limiting the date as was once thought.) Ben Jonson's *Every Man in His Humor*, acted in 1599, may also contain allusions to Shakespeare's play. Francis Meres does not mention it in 1598 in his *Palladis Tamia*.

Hamlet (c. 1599–1601)

Like everything else about *Hamlet*, the textual problem is complicated. On July 26, 1602, James Roberts entered in the Stationers' Register, the official record book of the London Company of Stationers (booksellers and printers), "A booke called the Revenge of Hamlett Prince Denmarke as yt was latelie Acted by the Lord Chamberleyne his servantes." For some reason, however, Roberts did not print his copy of *Hamlet* until 1604, by which time the following unauthorized edition had appeared:

THE Tragicall Historie of HAMLET *Prince of Denmarke*. By William Shake-speare. As it hath beene diuerse times acted by his

Highnesse seruants in the Cittie of London: as also in the two Vniuersities of Cambridge and Oxford, and else-where. At London printed for N. L. [Nicholas Ling] and Iohn Trundell. 1603.

This edition, the First Quarto of *Hamlet*, seems to have been memorially reconstructed by actors who toured the provinces (note the references to Cambridge, Oxford, and so on), with some recollection of an earlier *Hamlet* play (the *Ur-Hamlet*) written before 1589 and acted during the 1590s. The actors seemingly had no recourse to an authoritative manuscript. One of these actors may have played Marcellus and possibly Lucianus and Voltimand. Their version appears to have been based on an adaptation of the company's original playbook, which itself stood once removed from Shakespeare's working papers by way of an intermediate manuscript. The resulting text is very corrupt, and yet it seems to have affected the more authentic text, because the compositors of the Second Quarto made use of it, especially when they typeset the first act.

The authorized Quarto of *Hamlet* appeared in 1604. Roberts, the printer, seems to have reached some agreement with Ling, one of the publishers of the First Quarto, for their initials are now paired on the title page:

THE Tragicall Historie of HAMLET, *Prince of Denmarke.* By William Shakespeare. Newly imprinted and enlarged to almost as much againe as it was, according to the true and perfect Coppie. AT LONDON, Printed by I. R. [James Roberts] for N. L. [Nicholas Ling] and are to be sold at his shoppe vnder Saint Dunstons Church in Fleetstreet. 1604.

Some copies of this edition are dated 1605. This text was based seemingly on Shakespeare's own papers, with the bookkeeper's annotations, but is marred by printing errors and is at times contaminated by the First Quarto—presumably, when the printers found Shakespeare's manuscript unreadable. This Second Quarto served as copy for a Third Quarto in 1611, Ling having meanwhile transferred his rights in the play to John Smethwick. A Fourth Quarto, undated but before 1623, was based on the Third.

The First Folio text of 1623 omits more than two hundred lines found in the Second Quarto, yet it supplies some clearly authentic passages. It seems to derive from a transcript of Shakespeare's draft, in which cuts made by the author were observed—cuts made by Shakespeare quite possibly because he knew the draft to be too long for performance and which had either not been marked in the Second Quarto copy or had been ignored there by the compositors. The Folio also incorporates other alterations seemingly made for clarity or in anticipation of performance. To this theatrically motivated transcript, Shakespeare apparently contributed some revisions. Subsequently, this version evidently was copied again by a careless scribe who took many liberties with the text. Typesetting from this inferior manuscript, the Folio compositors occasionally consulted the Fourth Quarto, but not

often enough. Thus, even though the Folio supplies some genuine readings, as does the First Quarto when both the Folio and the Second Quarto are wrong, the Second Quarto remains the most authentic version of the text.

Since the text of the Second Quarto is too long to be accommodated in the two hours' traffic of the stage and since it becomes even longer when the words found only in the Folio are added, Shakespeare must have known it would have to be cut for performance and probably marked at least some omissions himself. Since he may have consented to such cuts primarily because of the constraints of time, however, this present edition holds to the view that the passages in question should not be excised from the text we read. The *Hamlet* presented here is doubtless longer than any version ever acted in Shakespeare's day and thus does not represent a script for any actual performance, but it may well represent the play as Shakespeare wrote it and then expanded it somewhat while also including passages that he may reluctantly have consented to cut for performance. It is also possible that some cuts were artistically intended, but, in the face of real uncertainty in this matter, an editorial policy of inclusion gives to the reader those passages that would otherwise have to be excised or put in an appendix on questionable grounds of authorial "intent."

Hamlet must have been produced before the Stationers' Register entry of July 26, 1602. Francis Meres does not mention the play in 1598 in his *Palladis Tamia.* Gabriel Harvey attributes the "tragedy of Hamlet, Prince of Denmark" to Shakespeare in a marginal note in Harvey's copy of Speght's Chaucer; Harvey acquired the book in 1598, but he could have written the note any time between then and 1601, or even 1603. More helpful in dating is *Hamlet*'s clear reference to the so-called War of the Theaters, the rivalry between the adult actors and the boy actors whose companies had newly revived in 1598–1599 after nearly a decade of inactivity (see 2.2.337–62). The Children of the Chapel Royal began acting at Blackfriars in 1598 and provided such keen competition in 1599–1601 that the adult actors were at times forced to tour the provinces (see *Hamlet*, 2.2.332–62). *Hamlet*'s reference to the rivalry appears, however, only in the Folio text and could represent a late addition. The reference to an "inhibition" imposed on acting companies "by the means of the late innovation" (2.2.332–3), printed in the 1604 Quarto, may possibly refer to the abortive uprising of the Earl of Essex on February 8, 1601, or to a decree issued by the Privy Council on June 22, 1600, restricting London companies to two performances a week in each of two playhouses. Revenge tragedy was also in fashion during these years: John Marston's *Antonio's Revenge*, for example, dates from 1599–1601, and *The Malcontent* is from about the same time or slightly later, though it is hard to tell who influenced whom. *Hamlet*'s apparent indebtedness to John Florio's translation of Montaigne suggests that

Shakespeare had access to that work in manuscript before its publication in 1603; the Florio had been registered for publication in 1595 and 1600.

Othello (c. 1603–1604)

On October 6, 1621, Thomas Walkley entered in the Stationers' Register, the official record book of the London Company of Stationers (booksellers and printers), "The Tragedie of Othello, the moore of Venice," and published the play in the following year:

THE Tragoedy of Othello, The Moore of Venice. *As it hath beene diuerse times acted at the* Globe, and at the Black-Friers, by *his Maiesties Seruants. Written by* VVilliam Shakespeare. LONDON, Printed by N. O. [Nicholas Okes] for *Thomas Walkley,* and are to be sold at his shop, at the Eagle and Child, in Brittans Bursse. 1622.

This text of this Quarto is a good one, based probably on a scribal transcript of Shakespeare's working manuscript, although it is some one hundred and sixty lines shorter than the Folio text of 1623, mostly in scattered small omissions. The Folio text may have been derived (via an intermediate transcript) from a revision of the original authorial manuscript, in which Shakespeare himself copied over his work and made a large number of synonymous or nearly synonymous changes as he did so. These papers, edited by someone else to remove profanity as required by law and introducing other stylistic changes in the process, seemingly became the basis of the playbook and also of the Folio text. E. A. J. Honigmann (*The Texts of "Othello" and Shakespearian Revision,* 1996) proposes that Ralph Crane prepared a transcript to serve as copy for the Folio text, though not all scholars have agreed.

The textual situation is thus complex. The Folio text appears to contain a significant number of authorial changes, but it was also worked on by one or more sophisticating scribes and by compositors whose changes are sometimes hard to distinguish from those of Shakespeare. The Quarto text was printed by a printing establishment that was not known for careful work but does stand close in some ways to a Shakespearean original. Editorially, then, the Folio is the copy text, and its readings are to be preferred when the Quarto is not clearly correct and especially when the Folio gives us genuinely new words, but the Quarto's readings demand careful consideration when the Folio text may be suspected of mechanical error (e.g., the shortening of words in full lines) or compositorial substitution of alternative forms, normalizations, and easy adjustments of meter. There are times when the Folio's compositor may have been misled by nearby words or letters in his copy. And, because the Folio's stage directions are probably scribal, attention should be paid to those in the Quarto.

According to a Revels account that was suspected of being a forgery soon after its publication in 1842 but is now generally accepted, the earliest mention of the play is on "Hallamas Day, being the first of Nouembar," 1604, when "the Kings Maiesties plaiers" performed "A Play in the Banketinge house att Whit Hall Called The Moor of Venis." Possible echoes of *Othello* in *The Honest Whore, Part I,* by Thomas Dekker and Thomas Middleton (1604) and in Richard Knolles's *History of the Turks* (1603) help fix a forward date of composition. Francis Meres does not list the play in 1598. On stylistic grounds, the play is usually dated in 1603 or 1604, although arguments are sometimes presented for a date as early as 1601 or 1602.

King Lear (c. 1605–1606)

On November 26, 1607, Nathaniel Butter and John Busby entered in the Stationers' Register, the official record book of the London Company of Stationers (booksellers and printers), "A booke called. Master William Shakespeare his historye of Kinge Lear, as yt was played before the Kinges maiestie at Whitehall vppon Sainct Stephens night at Christmas Last, by his maiesties servantes playinge vsually at the Globe on the Banksyde." Next year appeared the following Quarto:

M. William Shak-speare: HIS True Chronicle Historie of the life and death of King LEAR and his three Daughters. *With the vnfortunate life* of Edgar, *sonne* and heire to the Earle of Gloster, and his sullen and assumed humor of Tom of Bedlam: *As it was played before the Kings Maiestie at Whitehall vpon S.* Stephans *night in Christmas Hollidayes.* By his Maiesties seruants playing vsually at the Gloabe on the Bancke-side. LONDON, Printed for *Nathaniel Butter,* and are to be sold at his shop in *Pauls* Church-yard at the signe of the Pide Bull neere St. *Austins* Gate. 1608.

This Quarto is often called the "Pied Bull" Quarto in reference to its place of sale. Twelve copies exist today, in ten different "states," because proofreading was being carried on while the sheets were being run off in the press; the copies variously combine corrected and uncorrected sheets. A Second Quarto, printed in 1619 by William Jaggard for Thomas Pavier with the fraudulent date of 1608, was based on a copy of the First Quarto, combining corrected and uncorrected sheets.

The First Folio text of 1623 may have been typeset from a playbook cut for performance or from a transcript of such a manuscript, and the playbook in its turn appears to have been based on Shakespeare's fair copy (with revisions) of his first draft. The Folio compositors also almost certainly consulted a copy of the Second Quarto from time to time or may have typeset directly from this Quarto as annotated with reference to Shakespeare's fair copy. In writing the fair copy, Shakespeare may have marked some three hundred lines for deletion, but it is possible that he did so chiefly to shorten the time of performance. He also seems to have added some one hundred lines, an apparent contradiction in view of the need for cutting, but possibly dictated by Shakespeare's developing sense of his play. It is also possible that the cuts were carried out by someone else in the preparation of the playbook.

The First Quarto, on the other hand, appears to have been printed from Shakespeare's unrevised and evidently untidy working papers. It is often corrupt, owing in part to type shortages, compositorial uncertainties with the manuscript, and other difficulties in Nicholas Okes's shop. Still, in some matters—especially variants indifferent in meaning (such as *an/if* or *thine/thy*)— the First Quarto may be closer to Shakespeare's preferences than the Folio, behind which are several stages of transmission.

This edition agrees with most recent students of the *Lear* text that the Folio represents a theatrical revision, in which the cuts were devised for performance by Shakespeare's company and quite possibly by Shakespeare himself as a member of that company. The case for artistic preference in the making of those cuts, on the other hand, is less certain and may have been overstated. Many of the cuts have the effect of shortening scenes, especially in the latter half of the play. Some scenes, like 3.6, show open gaps as a result of the cutting: Lear's "Then let them anatomize Regan" (line 75) implies the trial of Goneril as it is dramatized in the First Quarto but cut from the Folio. Other omissions also read like expedients, although they can also be explained by a hypothesis of literary and theatrical rewriting; if Shakespeare himself undertook the cutting, he would presumably do so as expertly as possible. The fact that the Folio text gives almost no rewritten speeches may suggest that the large cuts were motivated by the need for shortening. This edition holds to the principle that it is unwise to omit the material cut from the Folio text, since we cannot be sure that Shakespeare would have shortened the text had there been no external constraints. At the same time, the added material in the Folio is clearly his and belongs in his conception of the play. The resulting text is a conflation, but one that avoids cutting material that Shakespeare may well have regretted having to excise.

The Stationers' Register entry for November 26, 1607, describes a performance at court on the previous St. Stephen's night, December 26, 1606. The title page of the First Quarto confirms this performance on St. Stephen's night. Such a performance at court was not likely to have been the first, however. Shakespeare's repeated use of Samuel Harsnett's *Declaration of Egregious Popish Impostures*, registered on March 16, 1603, sets an early limit for composition of the play. Other circumstances point to composition of the Quarto text in 1605 or 1606. In May 1605, an old play called *The True Chronicle History of King Leir* was entered in the Stationers' Register as a "Tragecall historie," a phrase possibly suggesting the influence of Shakespeare's play, since the old *King Leir* does not end tragically. Moreover, the title page of the old *King Leir*, issued in 1605, proclaims the text to be "as it hath bene diuers and sundry times lately acted." In view of the unlikelihood that such an old play (written before 1594) would be revived in 1605, scholars have suggested that the title page was the publisher's way of trying to capitalize on the recent popularity of Shakespeare's play. In this case, the likeliest date for the composition of Shakespeare's *King Lear* would be in the winter of 1604–1605. Shakespeare certainly used the old *King Leir* as a chief source, but he need not have waited for its publication in 1605 if, as seems perfectly plausible, his company owned the playbook. This hypothesis of the publication of the old *King Leir* after performances of Shakespeare's play must do battle, however, with indications that Shakespeare did not write *King Lear* until late 1605 or 1606. Gloucester's mentioning of "These late eclipses in the sun and moon" (1.2.106) seems to refer to an eclipse of the moon in September and of the sun in October 1605.

There may be echoes in the First Quarto of *King Lear* of *Eastward Ho!* by George Chapman, Ben Jonson, and John Marston, written in early 1605, and *Miseries of Enforced Marriage*, written by mid-1605. *King Lear* may allude to concerns at court about the King's frequent absences for hunting, about monopolies, the giving away of knighthoods, the King's need of money, and the like, all of which would have seemed pertinent in 1605–1606. The Folio revisions may date from some time around 1610, according to the editors of the Oxford Shakespeare.

Macbeth (c. 1606–1607)

Macbeth was first printed in the First Folio of 1623. It was set up from a playbook or a transcript of one. The text is unusually short and seems to have been cut for reasons of censorship or for some special performance. Moreover, all of 3.5 and parts of 4.1 (39–43, 125–32) appear to be interpolations, containing songs from Thomas Middleton's *The Witch* (c.1609–1616). Middleton may have been responsible for other alterations and additions.

Simon Forman, in his manuscript *The Book of Plays and Notes thereof per Formans for Common Policy*, records the first known performance of *Macbeth* on April 20, 1611, at the Globe Theatre. The play must have been in existence by 1607, however, for allusions to it seemingly occur in *Lingua* and *The Puritan* (both published in 1607) and in *The Knight of the Burning Pestle* (probably acted in 1607). On the other hand, the play itself seemingly alludes to James I's royal succession in 1603, to his touching for "the king's evil" (see 4.3.147), and to the trial of the notorious Gunpowder Plot conspirators in March 1606. The interpolations from Middleton's *The Witch* are probably from a later date, perhaps after 1613.

Timon of Athens (c. 1605–1608)

Timon of Athens first appeared in the First Folio of 1623. The text seems to have been based on an unusually early draft of the author's papers, with manifest inconsistencies still present that would have been straightened out in a final draft. If Thomas Middleton was coauthor of the play with Shakespeare, as seems very likely (see play Introduction), the collaboration might have contributed to the discrepancies about the value of money and the like. The play seems to have been a last-minute substitution in the Folio, to replace *Troilus and Cressida* when, for some reason (probably copyright difficulties), that play had to be removed from its original position following *Romeo and Juliet*. The Folio editors possibly had not intended to use *Timon* at all. The manuscript used by the printers seems to have been copied over in places by a second hand, as though the manuscript was too illegible for the printer to use. H. J. Oliver's suggestion (in his Arden edition of 1959, reprinted 1977) that Ralph Crane acted as transcriber has not found general acceptance.

Dating of the play is unusually difficult. No records of performances exist from the early seventeenth century; nor is there any trace of the play until it was registered for publication on November 8, 1623. Stylistically, it seems close to the late tragedies. Its pessimism reminds us of *King Lear,* and its use of Plutarch suggests *Antony and Cleopatra.*

Antony and Cleopatra (1606–1607)

On May 20, 1608, Edward Blount entered in the Stationers' Register, the official record book of the London Company of Stationers (booksellers and printers), "A booke Called. Anthony. and Cleopatra," along with "A booke called. The booke of Pericles prynce of Tyre." Blount was friendly with Shakespeare's company, and his entry may have been a "staying entry" designed to forestall unauthorized publication of these texts. If so, the tactic did not succeed with *Pericles*, issued in 1609 by another publisher, but it did succeed with *Antony and Cleopatra.* The play was first printed in the First Folio of 1623. It is a good text, set evidently from Shakespeare's own draft in a more finished state than most of his working papers, or possibly from a transcript of those papers, though not yet prepared to be a playbook.

The year 1608 is thus the latest possible date for *Antony and Cleopatra.* Evidently, it was written in 1606–1607, however, for a "newly altered" edition in 1607 of Samuel Daniel's play *Cleopatra* seems to have been influenced by Shakespeare's play. Shakespeare himself had probably consulted the original edition of *Cleopatra*, published in 1594, or the slightly revised edition of 1599, but Daniel's more thorough revision in 1607

shows signs of his having seen Shakespeare's play in the interim. Also, a play by Barnabe Barnes called *The Devil's Charter* (1607) may contain a parody of Cleopatra's death by asps. Although the printed text of this play advertises corrections and augmentations that could postdate a court performance in February 1607, recent scholarship favors the likelihood that Barnes saw *Antony and Cleopatra* before that—perhaps in late 1606.

Coriolanus (c. 1608)

Coriolanus was first printed in the First Folio of 1623. Its text was perhaps set from a transcript of the playbook that clarified Shakespeare's stage directions while also preserving some authorial flavor in them and some Shakespearean spellings. Although printing errors are numerous, they are, for the most part, easy to correct. Dating of the play is uncertain. No early performance is on record. The late style and some possible allusions point to sometime around 1608. Menenius's fable of the belly (1.1.94 ff.) is probably indebted to William Camden's *Remains*, published 1605. The demonstrations of the plebeians about distribution of grain may allude to the Midland riots of 1607–1608. Echoes of the play may appear in Robert Armin's *The Italian Taylor and His Boy* and in Ben Jonson's *Epicene*, both from 1609. Thus, a date in 1608 is plausible but only approximate.

Pericles (c. 1606–1608)

On May 20, 1608, Edward Blount entered in the Stationers' Register, the official record book of the London Company of Stationers (booksellers and printers), "A booke called. The booke of Pericles prynce of Tyre." He also entered *Antony and Cleopatra* at this time, possibly hoping to forestall unauthorized publishing of these two texts. If so, the plan succeeded with *Antony* but not with *Pericles*. A corrupt Quarto of this play was printed in 1609 by William White:

THE LATE, And much admired Play, Called Pericles, Prince of Tyre. With the true Relation of the whole Historie, aduentures, and fortunes of the said Prince: As also, The no lesse strange, and worthy accidents, in the Birth and Life, of his Daughter MARIANA. As it hath been diuers and sundry times acted by his Maiesties Seruants, at the Globe on the Banck-side. By William Shakespeare. Imprinted at London for *Henry Gosson*, and are to be sold at the signe of the Sunne in Pater-noster row, &c. 1609.

Blount was a friend of the players, and the text he registered is likely to have been the playbook. (This would explain why it is referred to as "A booke called the booke of Pericles" in the Stationers' Register, since playbooks were known technically as "books.") White's text, on the other hand, appears to be a memorially constructed text and at times it is unintelligible. Two reporters may have been at work, and the printing was done by at least three compositors. See the play's Introduction for some examples of inconsistency in the text. Unfortunately, this bad text is the best we have, though George Wilkins's *The Painful Adventures of Pericles* (see below) may have been influenced directly by the play and may well afford some clues as to the wording of the text; a recent and controversial hypothesis argues that *The Painful Adventures* is as much a "report" of the play as is the corrupt Quarto. Subsequent quartos appeared in 1609, 1611, 1619, and 1630, but each was set up from the previous edition, and all attempts in them at improvement are editorial rather than authorial. *Pericles* did not appear at all in the First Folio of 1623, perhaps because the editors suspected it to be partly non-Shakespearean or because they did not possess a reliable text. Arguments for multiple authorship, though based essentially on internal evidence of the play's manifest inconsistencies, are still taken seriously by scholars. George Wilkins especially has been proposed as collaborator in the first two acts. The defects of the first two acts are generally more extensive than those found even in such unauthorized Quartos as *Hamlet* or *Romeo and Juliet*. Philip Edwards has argued, on the other hand (*Shakespeare Survey 5*, 1952), that the differences between the first two acts and the last three can be accounted for by memorial reporting and compositorial error. This matter is still in dispute.

Pericles (though probably differing textually from the play we have today) must have been in existence by the date of the Stationers' Register entry in May 1608. A play of *Pericles* was seen by the Venetian ambassador to England, Zorzi Giustinian, sometime during his official stay from January 5, 1606, to November 23, 1608. George Wilkins's *The Painful Adventures of Pericles, Prince of Tyre*, published in 1608, was certainly derived in part from a play about Pericles: its title page offers the work "as it was lately presented by the worthy and ancient poet John Gower," and the final sentence of the Argument urges the reader "to receive this history in the same manner as it was under the habit of ancient Gower, the famous English poet, by the Kings Majesty's players excellently presented." The play to which Wilkins refers may have been Shakespeare's or perhaps some earlier version—just how early, no one can say. As it stands, however, the play appears to represent the beginning of Shakespeare's fascination with the genre of romance. As such, its date is usually set between 1606 and 1608.

Cymbeline (c. 1608–1610)

Cymbeline was first printed in the First Folio of 1623, where it was included among the tragedies. The text, a

good one, was evidently set from a careful transcript (perhaps by the scrivener Ralph Crane) of an earlier manuscript, one in which two copyists may have been involved, basing their work either on Shakespeare's own papers or on a theatrical playbook that had incorporated many authorial stage directions. The first recorded performance was in 1611. Dr. Simon Forman jotted down a description of *Cymbeline* in his commonplace book for that year; although he did not record the actual date he saw the play, he must have done so sometime between April and his sudden death on September 8 of that year. Stylistically, the play appears to follow *Pericles* (c. 1606–1608) and to precede *The Winter's Tale* (c. 1609–1611). *Cymbeline* may also follow and imitate Beaumont and Fletcher's *Philaster*, produced with great success in 1609, although the relative order of these similar plays remains doubtful. If *Cymbeline* is the later of the two, it may have been written as late as 1610.

The Winter's Tale (c. 1609–1611)

The Winter's Tale was first printed in the First Folio of 1623. Its text is a good one, taken evidently from Ralph Crane's transcript of Shakespeare's own well-finished draft or possibly the playbook. As in most other Crane transcriptions, the stage directions are sparse, and the characters' names are grouped at the beginning of each scene. The first recorded performance was on May 15, 1611, when Simon Forman saw the play at the Globe Theater and recorded a summary of it in his commonplace book. Another performance that year at court, on November 5, is recorded in the *Revels Account* and still another, during the winter of 1612–1613. Quite possibly, the play was new at the time Forman saw it. It apparently contains an allusion to the dance of ten or twelve satyrs in Ben Jonson's *Masque of Oberon*, performed at court on January 1, 1611. A 1623 entry in the *Office book* of Sir Henry Herbert, Master of the Revels, refers to *The Winter's Tale* as "an old play . . . formerly allowed of by Sir George Bucke." Bucke (or Buc) was first appointed Master of the Revels in 1610 but had occasionally licensed plays before that date during his predecessor's illness, so that the backward limit of 1610 cannot be considered absolute. Still, matters of style confirm the likelihood that Forman was seeing a new play in 1611.

The Tempest (c. 1611)

The Tempest was first printed in the First Folio of 1623. It occupies first place in the volume and is a scrupulously prepared text from a transcript by Ralph Crane of a theater playbook or of Shakespeare's draft after it had been annotated for production; or, Crane may have provided some of the elaboration of stage directions. Shakespeare's colleagues may have placed *The Tempest* first in the Folio because they considered it his most recent complete play. The first recorded performance was at court on November 1, 1611: "Hallomas nyght was presented att Whithall before ye kinges Maiestie a play Called the Tempest." The actors were "the Kings players" (*Revels Account*). The play was again presented at court during the winter of 1612–1613, this time "before the Princes Highnes the Lady Elizabeth and the Prince Pallatyne Elector." The festivities for this important betrothal and wedding were sumptuous and included at least thirteen other plays. Various arguments have been put forward that Shakespeare composed parts of *The Tempest*, especially the masque, for this occasion, but there is absolutely no evidence that the play was singled out for special prominence among the many plays presented, and the masque is integral to the play as it stands. Probably the 1611 production was of a fairly new play. Simon Forman, who saw *Cymbeline* and *The Winter's Tale* in 1611, does not mention *The Tempest*. He died in September 1611. According to every stylistic test, such as run-on and hypermetric lines, the play is very late. Shakespeare probably knew Sylvester Jourdain's *A Discovery of the Bermudas*, published in 1610, and William Strachey's *A True Reportory of the Wreck and Redemption*, dated July 1610, although not published until 1625.

The Two Noble Kinsmen (1613–1614)

The Two Noble Kinsmen did not appear in the Shakespeare First Folio of 1623. Publishing rights were first assigned in the Stationers' Register to John Waterson on April 8, 1634, as "a TragiComedy called the two noble kinsmen by Jo: ffletcher & Wm. Shakespeare." It was first published in 1634 in quarto by John Waterson as:

THE TWO NOBLE KINSMEN: Presented at the Blackfriers by the Kings Maiesties servants, with great applause: Written by the memorable Worthies of their time; Mr. *John Fletcher*, and Mr. *William Shakspeare*, Gent. Printed at *London* by *Tho. Cotes*, for *Iohn Waterson*: and are to be sold at the signe of the *Crowne* in *Pauls* Church-yard. 1634.

Waterson transferred his rights in the play on October 31, 1646, to Humphrey Moseley, along with two other plays, as by "Mr fflesher." Moseley's first collection of plays by Beaumont and Fletcher in 1647 did not in fact include *The Two Noble Kinsmen*. It did appear finally in Moseley's 1679 edition of *Fifty Comedies and Tragedies, Written by Francis Beaumont, and John Fletcher, Gentlemen*. Despite the attribution to Fletcher and Shakespeare in 1634, the omission of the play from the Beaumont and Fletcher collected works led to its being excluded from the Shakespeare canon until well into the nineteenth century. Today nearly all editors view the play as a collaboration between Shakespeare, who was entering on his retirement, and the dramatist who succeeded him at the King's men.

The 1634 Quarto text is a good one, perhaps based on a scribal transcript and containing theatrical annotations by the "bookkeeper" or prompter in the form of marginal notes warning the acting company to get properties ready and naming minor actors.

The likely date of first performance is in 1613 or 1614. An expanded version of the morris dance in 3.5 had served as the antimasque (a kind of grotesque comic subplot) for Beaumont's *Masque of the Inner Temple and Gray's Inn* on February 20, 1613, presented at court during the marriage festivities for James I's daughter Elizabeth to Frederick, the Elector Palatine. It seems likely that this highly celebratory court occasion would have taken precedence over commercial performance. Ben Jonson's *Bartholomew Fair*, first performed on October 31, 1614, alludes to a play called "Palamon." Shakespeare died in 1616 and may have been in failing health toward the very end; 1613 and 1614 seem to have been his last years of writing.

Venus and Adonis (1592–1593)

On April 18, 1593, "a booke intituled, Venus and Adonis" was entered by Richard Field in the Stationers' Register, the official record book of the London Company of Stationers (booksellers and printers), and was published by him the same year. The Quarto contains a dedication written by Shakespeare to the Earl of Southampton. The text seems to have been carefully supervised through the press and to have been based on the author's manuscript. The poem was very popular and was reprinted nine times before Shakespeare's death. The First Folio of 1623, being limited to plays, did not include it or any other nondramatic poems. Contemporary references are numerous: Francis Meres and Richard Barnfield in 1598, Gabriel Harvey in 1598–1601, and John Weever in 1599, among others. Shakespeare probably wrote this poem shortly before its publication, since his intention was to present it to Southampton. The theaters closed from June 1592 to May 1594, giving Shakespeare a period of enforced leisure in which to write poetry.

The Rape of Lucrece (1593–1594)

Shakespeare promised a "graver labour" to Southampton in his dedication of *Venus and Adonis*, 1593, and *The Rape of Lucrece* is almost surely that promised sequel. It was registered in the Stationers' Register, the official record book of the London Company of Stationers (booksellers and printers), by John Harrison on May 9, 1594, and issued that same year as "printed by Richard Field, for Iohn Harrison." The printed text was probably based on Shakespeare's manuscript. Although not quite as popular as *Venus and Adonis*, the poem was reprinted five times during Shakespeare's lifetime. Contemporaries of Shakespeare who allude favorably to the poem include W. Har and Michael Drayton in 1594, William Covell in 1595, Francis Meres in 1598, Gabriel Harvey in 1598–1601, John Weever in 1599, and others. The date of composition of the poem is well fixed between the publication of *Venus and Adonis* in 1593 and that of *The Rape of Lucrece* itself in 1594.

The Phoenix and Turtle (by 1601)

"The Phoenix and Turtle" first appeared in a volume with the following title:

LOVES MARTYR: OR, ROSALINS COMPLAINT. *Allegorically shadowing the truth of Loue*, in the constant Fate of the Phoenix and Turtle....by ROBERT CHESTER....*To these are added some new compositions, of seuerall moderne Writers whose names are subscribed to their seuerall workes, vpon the first subiect: viz. the* Phoenix and Turtle.

The date 1601 appears on a separate title page. One poem is signed "William Shake-speare"; others are assigned to John Marston, George Chapman, and Ben Jonson.

A Lover's Complaint (c. 1601–1605)

A Lover's Complaint first appeared in Thomas Thorpe's 1609 edition of the sonnets. It may have been printed from the same transcript as that used to print the sonnets. The poem is not mentioned on the title page of the volume but has its own head-title on sig. K^v: "A Louers complaint. BY William Shake-speare." For the reliability of this attribution, see the Introduction to *A Lover's Complaint*. Stylistic tests suggest a date around the time of *Hamlet* and *All's Well That Ends Well*, though any such suggestion is approximate.

The Sonnets (c. 1593–1603)

On May 20, 1609, "Thomas Thorpe Entred for his copie vnder thandes of master Wilson and master Lownes Warden a Booke called Shakespeares sonnettes." In the same year appeared the following volume:

SHAKE-SPEARES SONNETS. Neuer before Imprinted. AT LONDON By *G. Eld* for *T. T.* [Thomas Thorpe] and are to be solde by *Iohn Wright*, dwelling at Christ Church gate. 1609.

Some copies of this same edition are marked to be sold by William Aspley rather than John Wright; evidently, Thorpe had set up two sellers to distribute the volume. The sonnets were not reprinted until John Benson's rearranged edition of 1640, possibly because the first edition had been suppressed or because sonnets were no longer in vogue. The 1609 edition may rest on a transcript of Shakespeare's sonnets by someone other than the author, and the edition itself is marred by misprints, though Thorpe was a reputable printer. Clearly, the collection was not supervised through the press as were *Venus and Adonis* and *The Rape of Lucrece*. All the evidence suggests that it was obtained without Shakespeare's permission from a manuscript that had been in private circulation (as we know from Francis Meres's 1598 allusion, in his *Palladis Tamia*, to Shakespeare's "sugared sonnets among his private friends"). Two sonnets, 138 and 144, had appeared in 1599 in *The Passionate Pilgrim*. On questions of dating and order of the sonnets, see the Introduction to *The Sonnets* in this volume.

Appendix 2

Sources

The Comedy of Errors

The Comedy of Errors is based chiefly on the *Menaechmi* of Plautus (c. 254–184 B.C.). Shakespeare appears to have used the Latin, which was available to him in numerous Renaissance texts. He may also have known in manuscript the translation into English by "W.W." (? William Warner), published in 1595.

A comparison of the *Menaechmi* with Shakespeare's play suggests how much he has retained and what he has changed. As in Plautus, the story concerns two separated twins, one of whom (Menaechmus the Traveler of Syracuse) has come by chance, accompanied by his servant, Messenio, to the city of Epidamnum, where his long-lost brother, Menaechmus the Citizen, lives. Menaechmus the Citizen, in the company of the parasite Peniculus, quarrels with his wife and arranges lunch with the courtesan Erotium. The confusion begins when Menaechmus the Traveler is mistaken for his twin by Erotium's cook, Cylindrus, and then by Erotium herself, who invites him to lunch and to her bed. She bids him take a cloak (which Menaechmus the Citizen had given her that morning) to the dyer's for alteration. A short time later, Peniculus, too, mistakes Menaechmus the Traveler for the Epidamnian twin, upbraids him for having dined while the parasite was absent, and threatens to tell Menaechmus's wife of his carryings-on. Erotium's maid brings Menaechmus the Traveler a chain or bracelet to be mended at the goldsmith's. Menaechmus the Citizen now returns home from a busy day to a furious wife and a vindictive Peniculus. Among other matters, the wife demands the return of her cloak, which, as she suspects, her husband stole from her and gave to Erotium. The husband, locked out of his own house by his angry wife, must now confront Erotium, who insists

that she gave her chain and the cloak to him. The Citizen goes to seek the help of his friends. Menaechmus the Traveler shows up at this point and is angrily abused by the wife and by her father, both of whom consider the supposed husband to be mad. They send for a doctor, who arrives after Menaechmus the Traveler has fled; they detain Menaechmus the Citizen instead as a madman. Messenio the servant now returns to his supposed master and fights manfully with his master's captors. Finally, the two twins confront one another and unravel the mystery.

Shakespeare creates the two Dromios in place of Messenio, plays down the role of the courtesan, dignifies the part of the wife, invents the sympathetic role of Luciana her sister, eliminates the parasite and the wife's father, and replaces the courtesan's maid and cook with comic servants such as Luce, or Nell, the kitchen-wench in the household of Antipholus of Ephesus. The conventional doctor, Medicus, becomes the zany Dr. Pinch. The setting is Ephesus rather than Epidamnum. Plautus's detached ironic tone and his matter-of-fact depiction of courtesans and parasites are replaced by a thematic emphasis on patience and loyalty in marriage. The name "Dromio" may have come from John Lyly's *Mother Bombie*.

The dual identity of the servants and the superb confusion in Act 3 when Antipholus of Ephesus is locked out of his own house are derived in good part from Plautus's *Amphitruo*. In the relevant portion of that play, Amphitryon's wife Alcmena is courted by Jupiter, disguised as her husband, while Mercury guards the door in the guise of Amphitryon's slave Sosia. The real Sosia approaches but is so bewildered by Mercury's inventive wit that he begins to doubt his own identity. Later, at Jupiter's behest, Mercury again poses as Sosia to dupe

Amphitryon and to deny him entrance to his own house. Ultimately, after Alcmena has given birth to twins, one by Jupiter (Hercules) and one by Amphitryon (Iphiclus), Jupiter tells Amphitryon the truth.

The "framing" action of *The Comedy of Errors*, concerning old Egeon's painful separation from his wife and their eventual reunion, is derived not from Plautus but from the story of Apollonius of Tyre. Shakespeare later used this story for *Pericles*, and for that play his sources were chiefly two: the *Confessio Amantis* by John Gower, Book 8, and Laurence Twine's *The Pattern of Painful Adventures*, translated from a French version based in turn on a popular story in the *Gesta Romanorum*. Perhaps Shakespeare was acquainted with these same versions when he wrote *The Comedy of Errors*; in 1576, Twine's account was entered in the Stationers' Register, the official record book of the London Company of Stationers (booksellers and printers), although the earliest extant edition dates from around 1594–1595. Gower's account had been printed by William Caxton (England's first printer) in 1493 and reprinted in 1532 and 1554.

In Gower's *Confessio*, Apollonius's wife Lucina gives birth to a daughter on board ship and, having apparently died in childbirth, is put into a chest and committed to the sea. Washing ashore at Ephesus, she is restored by the physician Cerimon. She becomes a priestess in the Temple of Diana. Years later, Apollonius comes to Ephesus, is first reunited with his daughter Thaisa, and then is told in a vision to go to the Temple. There he discovers the "Abbess" to be his long-lost wife. Shakespeare has added the threatened hanging from which Egeon is finally rescued.

Love's Labor's Lost

No main source exists for *Love's Labor's Lost*. For his conception of an "academy" of aristocratic scholars, Shakespeare may have drawn on Pierre de la Primaudaye's *L'Académie française* (1577), translated into English in 1586, in which the ideals of scholarly withdrawal are discussed. The notion was, however, commonplace. Certain historical facts about Henry of Navarre may well have provided Shakespeare with a model for the play's action, especially the visit of Catherine de Medici with her daughter and the famous *l'escadron volant* (flying squadron) to Henry's court in 1578, and a similar visit in 1586 (see the Introduction to the play). Published accounts of these visits were not available when Shakespeare wrote his play, but he may well have heard the gossip. John Lyly's plays provided Shakespeare with a literary model for the saucy boyish wit of Mote, Boyet, and others, and Armado and Mote are often thought to resemble Sir Tophas and the page Epiton in Lyly's *Endymion*. Traditions of the *commedia dell' arte* provided Shakespeare with stock comic models, especially those of the *dottore* or pedant (Holofernes), his parasite (Nathaniel, the curate), the *capitano* or braggart soldier (Armado), and the rustic servant (Costard). All of these types are individualized and rendered in English terms, however. Many literary quarrels in England in the 1590s have been adduced as possible sources for Shakespeare's play, especially the controversy between Thomas Nashe and Gabriel Harvey, but the evidence remains inconclusive.

The Two Gentlemen of Verona

Shakespeare appears to have combined two kinds of stories in *The Two Gentlemen of Verona:* one of romantic love triumphing over inconstancy and one of perfect friendship triumphing over perfidy. For the story of the deserted heroine and her inconstant lover, Shakespeare's main source was evidently *Diana Enamorada*, a Spanish pastoral by Jorge de Montemayor (published c. 1559). This work was translated into French in 1578 and 1587, and was published in English in 1598 by Bartholomew Yonge. Yonge states that he began his translation some nineteen years earlier. Possibly, then, Shakespeare saw it in manuscript, or he may have relied on the Spanish original or the French translation. A play, now lost, was performed at court in 1585 called *The History of Felix & Philiomena* (i.e., Felismena). It must surely have been based on Montemayor's prose pastoral and may have provided Shakespeare with a dramatic model.

The story of Felix and Felismena is only one of the many narratives in *Diana Enamorada* that are set in contrast to the central story of Diana the shepherdess. It is told by Felismena as her own narrative, beginning in Book 2. The story contains no character corresponding to Valentine, but Proteus and Julia find their equivalents in Felix and Felismena. The latter is attended by a maid, Rosina, like Julia's Lucetta, who is hypocritically scolded by her mistress for delivering a letter from Felix that Felismena, in fact, longs to have. Like Proteus in Shakespeare's play, Don Felix is sent off to court (in this case, the court of Princess Augusta Caesarina) to prevent his marriage to the orphaned Felismena. She follows after, appareled as a young man named Valerius (as Julia travels under the name of Sebastian). Stopping at an inn, she is invited by the host of the inn to hear some music, whereupon she happens to overhear the faithless Felix courting a lady named Celia (Shakespeare's Silvia). Disguised as Valerius, Felismena ingratiates herself with Felix's servant Fabius and takes service with Don Felix. She is sent on embassages to Celia, with whom she converses about Felix's first love. Celia falls in love with "Valerius," like Olivia in *Twelfth Night*, and subsequently dies of unrequited passion. Hereupon the distraught Felix disappears. Later, in Book 7, we hear how Felismena, disguised as an Amazonian shepherdess, rescues Felix from his attackers and is reconciled with him. Felix acknowledges her beauty to be superior to that of Celia. Shakespeare has changed some important matters, notably Celia's falling in love with "Valerius" and her dying of unrequited love; Silvia's remaining faithful to Valentine and following him into banishment are essential parts of her character in Shakespeare's account. Shakespeare also adds several new characters: the Duke of Milan (Silvia's father), Thurio, Eglamour, Lance, Speed, and the outlaws. Still, the debt to *Diana Enamorada* is considerable.

In Sir Philip Sidney's *Arcadia* (1590), Zelmane follows Felismena's example by disguising herself as a page (Daiphantus) in the service of her beloved Pyrocles. When she falls ill and is on the verge of death, Zelmane's identity is revealed to Pyrocles. *Arcadia* also offers a noble example of perfect friendship in the relation between Pyrocles and Musidorus. Shakespeare used the *Arcadia* as a source elsewhere, especially in the Gloucester plot of *King Lear*.

The story of perfect friendship has many antecedents, including the fourteenth-century *Amis and Amiloun* and Richard Edwards's play about *Damon and Pythias* (1565). The falling-out of sworn friends over a woman is the central theme of Geoffrey Chaucer's "The Knight's Tale" and of John Lyly's *Euphues* (1578). Perhaps the most suggestive example of perfect friendship is the story of Titus and Gisippus as it appears in Book 2, Chapter 12, of Sir Thomas Elyot's *The Governor* (1531). Elyot derived his account from Day 10, Novel 8, of Giovanni Boccaccio's *Decameron*. Titus and Gisippus were proverbially famous friends, like Damon and Pythias, and other Renaissance versions of the story were available (including a Latin school play of 1546[?] and a children's play at court in 1577, both now lost). Perhaps Shakespeare knew the story as a commonplace rather than having to depend on one particular literary source.

Elyot's version tells of two look-alike friends dwelling in Athens, of whom one, Gisippus, is persuaded by his kindred and acquaintances to marry. Despite a preference for the study of philosophy, he finds his fiancée most attractive. When, however, his Roman-born friend Titus falls desperately in love with the same lady and confesses as much to Gisippus, the husband-to-be generously proposes that Titus take his place on the wedding night. Because the binding element of the marriage contract is the bestowing of the ring in bed and the undoing of the girdle of virginity, the lady is now Titus's legal wife and returns with him to Rome. Gisippus, accused by the Athenians of having mismanaged the affair, follows his friend to Rome and is there wrongly accused of a murder. Titus's turn has now arrived to be magnanimous, and he insists that he be punished for the murder. Eventually, the real culprit, touched by this selflessness, confesses the crime, allowing Titus to return with Gisippus to Athens and forcibly to restore him to his rightful possessions.

Valentine's sojourn in the forest and his leadership of a band of outlaws would seem to be indebted to the tradition of Robin Hood, although no single source has been found. An analogue to the outlaw episode does appear in Henry Wotton's *A Courtly Controversy of Cupid's Cautels* (1578), where it is linked to a story of perfidy in friendship. Valentine's unwelcome rival Thurio may owe something to the braggart soldier, Captain Spavento, of the *commedia dell' arte* tradition. Silvia's father, the Duke, is a similarly conventional comic stage type.

One final analogue worthy of note is a German play, *Julio und Hyppolita*, from a collection called *Englische Comedien und Tragedien* (1620). It may have been derived from performances by English players around 1600. Although some of its lines are suggestively close to those of Shakespeare's play, we cannot determine which version is prior to the other.

The Taming of the Shrew

Scholars do not agree on the relationship of *The Taming of the Shrew* to the play called *The Taming of a Shrew*, published in 1594. *A Shrew* has been argued to be an earlier version of Shakespeare's play, or a memorial reconstruction of it, or derived from a common original. Some recent critics argue that the two versions should be treated as distinct texts. An often-held view is that *A Shrew* is derived from a now-lost earlier version of Shakespeare's play, to which the compiler added original material and borrowed or even plagiarized from other literary sources as well. If so, *A Shrew* would not appear to be a source for Shakespeare's play, as Geoffrey Bullough has argued in his *Narrative and Dramatic Sources of Shakespeare*. Apart from this question, all critics agree that Shakespeare's play consists of three elements, each with its own source: the romantic love plot of Lucentio and Bianca, the wife-taming plot of Petruchio and Kate, and the framing plot, or induction, of Christopher Sly.

The romantic love plot is derived from George Gascoigne's *Supposes*, a neoclassical comedy performed at Gray's Inn (one of the Inns of Court, where young men studied law in London) in 1566. Gascoigne's play was a rather close translation of Ludovico Ariosto's *I Suppositi* (1509), which in turn was based on two classical plays, Terence's *Eunuchus* and Plautus's *Captivi*. The heroine of Gascoigne's version (as of Ariosto's) is Polynesta, the resourceful daughter of Damon, a widower of Ferrara. Two suitors vie for Polynesta's hand: Dr. Cleander, an aged and miserly lawyer, and Erostrato, a Sicilian gentleman who has purportedly come to Ferrara to study. In fact, however, this "Erostrato" is the servant Dulippo in disguise, having changed places with his master. (These disguisings are the "supposes" of the title.) As a servant in Damon's household, "Dulippo" has secretly become the lover of Polynesta and has made her pregnant. Balia, the nurse or duenna, is their go-between. Meanwhile, "Erostrato" takes great delight in outwitting Dr. Cleander and his unattractive parasite, Pasiphilo. The counterfeit Erostrato's ruse is to produce a rich father who will guarantee a handsome dowry and thereby outbid Cleander in the contest for Polynesta's hand. The "father" he produces, however, is actually an old Sienese stranger, who is persuaded that he is in danger in Ferrara unless he cloaks his identity. Complications arise when Damon learns of his daughter's affair and throws the lover, "Dulippo," into a dungeon. The crafty Pasiphilo overhears this compromising information and resolves to cause mischief for all the principals. Moreover, when Erostrato's real father, Philogano, arrives in Ferrara, he is barred from his son's house by the counterfeit Philogano and resolves to get help. His clever servant, Litio, suggests employing the famous lawyer, Cleander. All is happily resolved when the real Dulippo proves to be the son of Dr. Cleander and the real Erostrato is revealed to be rich and socially eligible for Polynesta's hand in marriage. Cleander is even reconciled to his parasite, Pasiphilo.

Shakespeare, in his play, has almost entirely eliminated the satire of the law that is in his source. Gremio is aged and wealthy, but no shyster. The lover is not imprisoned in a dungeon. The parasite is gone, as also in *The Comedy of Errors*. Bianca does not consummate her affair with Lucentio, as does Polynesta, and hence has no need for a go-between like Balia. Shakespeare adapts a sophisticated neoclassical comedy, racy and cosmopolitan, to the moral standards of his public theater. The witless Hortensio, the tutoring in Latin, and the music lesson are Shakespeare's inventions.

The wife-taming plot of Petruchio and Kate reflects an ancient comic misogynistic tradition, still extant today in the Scottish folksong "The Cooper of Fife" or "The Wife Wrapped in Wether's Skin" (Francis James Child, *The English and Scottish Popular Ballads* [1888–1898], 5:104). Richard Hosley has argued (in *Huntington Library Quarterly, 27*, 1964) that Shakespeare's likeliest source was *A Merry Jest of a Shrewd and Curst Wife Lapped in Morel's Skin, for her Good Behavior* (printed c. 1550). In this version, the husband beats his shrewish wife with birch rods until she bleeds and faints, whereupon he wraps her in the raw salted skin of an old plow-horse named Morel. Like Kate, this shrewish wife has a gentle younger sister who is their father's favorite. This father warns the man who proposes to marry his older daughter that she is shrewish, but the suitor goes ahead and subsequently tames his wife with Morel's skin. Thereafter, at a celebratory dinner, everyone is impressed by the thoroughness of the taming.

Shakespeare avoids the misogynistic extremes of this story, despite the similarity of the narrative. Instead, he seems to have had in mind the more humanistic spirit of Erasmus's *A Merry Dialogue Declaring the Properties of Shrewd Shrews and Honest Wives* (translated 1557) and Juan Luis Vives's *The Office and Duty of an Husband* (translated 1555). Specific elements of the wife-taming plot have been traced to other possible sources. The scolding of a tailor occurs in Gerard Legh's *Accidence of Armory* (1562); a wife agrees with her husband's assertion of a patent falsehood in Don Juan Manuel's *El Conde Lucanor* (1335); and three husbands wager on the obedience of their wives in *The Book of the Knight of La Tour-Landry* (printed 1484).

The induction story, of the beggar duped into believing himself a rich lord, is an old tale occurring in the *Arabian Nights*. An interesting analogue occurs in P. Heuterus's *De Rebus Burgundicis* (1584), translated into the French of S. Goulart (1606?) and thence into the English of Edward Crimeston (1607). According to Heuterus, in 1440, Philip the Good of Burgundy actually entertained a drunken beggar in his palace "to make trial of the vanity of our life," plying him with fine clothes, bed, a feast, and the performance of "a pleasant comedy."

A Midsummer Night's Dream

No single source has been discovered that unites the various elements that we find in *A Midsummer Night's Dream*, but the four main strands of action can be individually discussed in terms of sources. The four strands are: (1) the marriage of Theseus (Duke of Athens) and Queen Hippolyta, (2) the romantic tribulations and triumphs of the four young lovers, (3) the quarrel of King Oberon and Queen Titania, together with the fairies' manipulations of human affairs, and (4) the "rude mechanicals" and their play of "Pyramus and Thisbe."

For his conception of Theseus, Shakespeare went chiefly to Geoffrey Chaucer's "The Knight's Tale" and to Thomas North's 1579 translation of "The Life of Theseus" in Plutarch's *Lives of the Noble Grecians and Romans*. Chaucer's Theseus is a duke of "wisdom" and "chivalrye," renowned for his conquest of the Amazons and his marriage to Hippolyta. Plutarch provides information concerning Theseus's other conquests (to which Oberon alludes in 2.1.77 ff.), including that of Antiopa. Shakespeare could have learned more about Theseus from Chaucer's *The Legend of Good Women* and from Ovid's *Metamorphoses*. He seems to have blended all or some of these impressions together with his own notion of a noble yet popular Renaissance ruler.

The romantic narrative of the four lovers appears to be original with Shakespeare, although one can find many analogous situations of misunderstanding and rivalry in love. Chaucer's "The Knight's Tale" tells of two friends battling over one woman. Shakespeare's own *The Two Gentlemen of Verona* gives us four lovers, properly matched at first until one of the men shifts his attentions to his friend's ladylove; eventually, all is righted when the false lover recovers his senses. Parallel situations arise in Sir Philip Sidney's *Arcadia* (1590) and in Jorge de Montemayor's *Diana Enamorada* (c. 1559), a source for *The Two Gentlemen*. What Shakespeare adds in *A Midsummer* is the intervention of the fairies in human love affairs.

Shakespeare's knowledge of fairy lore must have been extensive and is hard to trace exactly. Doubtless, much of it was from oral traditions about leprechauns, gremlins, and elves, who were thought to cause such mischief as spoiling fermentation or preventing milk from churning into butter; Puck's tricks mentioned in 2.1.34 ff. are derived from such lore. Some of the oral tales circulating about Robin Goodfellow later reached print, probably somewhat modified, in the prose pamphlet *Robin Good Fellow, His Mad Pranks and Merry Jests* (London, 1628) and a ballad, "The Mad Merry Pranks of Robbin Good-fellow" (c. 1600) in Roxburghe Ballads, vol. 2, ed. William Chappell (Hertford: Stephen Austin for the Ballad Society, 1872), p. 83. Shakespeare seems to have consulted literary sources as well. In Chaucer's "The Merchant's Tale," Pluto and Proserpina as King and Queen of the fairies intervene in the affairs of old January, his young wife May, and her lover Damyan. Fairies appear on stage in John Lyly's *Endymion* (1588), protecting true lovers and tormenting those who are morally tainted. Shakespeare later reflects this tradition in *The Merry Wives of Windsor* (1597–1601). The name Oberon probably comes from the French romance *Huon of Bordeaux* (translated by Lord Berners by about 1540), where Oberon is a dwarfish fairy King from the mysterious East who practices enchantment in a haunted wood. In Edmund Spenser's *The Faerie Queene*, Oberon is the Elfin father of Queen Gloriana (2.10. 75–76). Robert Greene's *James IV* (c. 1591) also features Oberon as the fairy King, and a lost play called *Huon of Bordeaux* was performed by Sussex's men, an acting company, at about this same time. The name "Titania" comes from Ovid's *Metamorphoses*, where it is used as a synonym for both the enchantress Circe and the chaste goddess Diana. The name "Titania" does not appear in Arthur Golding's translation (1567), suggesting that Shakespeare found it in the original. Puck, or Robin Goodfellow, is essentially the product of oral tradition, although Reginald Scot's *The Discovery of Witchcraft* (1584) discusses Robin in pejorative terms as an incubus or hobgoblin in whom intelligent people no longer believe.

Scot also reports the story of a man who finds an ass's head placed on his shoulders by enchantment. Similar legends of transformation occur in Apuleius's *The Golden Ass* (translated by William Adlington, 1566) and in the well-known story of the ass's ears bestowed by Phoebus Apollo on King Midas for his presumption. Perhaps the most suggestive possible source for Shakespeare's clownish actors, however, is Anthony Munday's play *John a Kent and John a Cumber* (c. 1587–1590). In it a group of rude artisans, led by the intrepid Turnop, stage a ludicrous interlude written by their churchwarden in praise of his millhorse. Turnop's prologue is a medley of lofty comparisons. The entertainment is presented before noble spectators, who are graciously amused. *John a Kent* also features a lot of magic trickery, a boy named Shrimp whose role is comparable to that of Puck, and a multiple love plot.

"Pyramus and Thisbe" itself is based on the *Metamorphoses* (4.55 ff.). Other versions that Shakespeare may have known include Chaucer's *The Legend of Good Women*, a poem by William Griffith in 1562, George Pettie's *A Petite Palace of Pettie His Pleasure* (1576), *A Gorgeous Gallery of Gallant Inventions* (1578), and "A New Sonnet of Pyramus and Thisbe" from Clement Robinson's *A Handful of Pleasant Delights* (1584). Several of these, especially the last three, are bad enough to have given Shakespeare materials to lampoon, though the sweep of his parody goes beyond the particular story of Pyramus and Thisbe. The occasionally stilted phraseology of Golding's translation of the *Metamorphoses* contributed to the fun. According to Kenneth Muir (*Shakespeare's Sources*, 1957), Shakespeare must also have known Thomas Mouffet's *Of the Silkworms and Their Flies* (published 1599, but possibly circulated earlier in manuscript), which contains perhaps the most ridiculous of all versions of the Pyramus and Thisbe story. Shakespeare also appears to have been spoofing the inept dramatic style and lame verse of English dramas of the 1560s, 1570s, and 1580s, especially in their treatment of tragic sentiment and high emotion; *Cambises, Damon and Pythias*, and *Appius and Virginia* are examples.

The Merchant of Venice

Shakespeare's probable chief source for *The Merchant of Venice* was the first story of the fourth day of *Il Pecorone* (*The Dunce*), by Ser Giovanni Fiorentino. This collection of tales dates from the late fourteenth century but was first published in 1558 at Milan and was not published in English translation in Shakespeare's time. If Shakespeare was unable to read it in Italian, he may conceivably have consulted a translation in some now-lost manuscript; such translations did sometimes circulate. Behind Ser Giovanni's story lies an old tradition of a bond given for human flesh, as found in Persia, India, and the Twelve Tables of Roman Law. This legend first appears in English in the thirteenth-century *Cursor Mundi*, with a Jew as the creditor. A thirteenth-century version of the *Gesta Romanorum* (a popular collection of stories in Latin) adds a romantic love plot; the evil moneylender in this story is not Jewish. The hero pawns his own flesh to a merchant in order to win a lady. He succeeds on his third attempt, having learned to avoid a magic spell that had previously put him to sleep and cost him a large number of florins. When he goes to pay his forfeit, the lady follows him disguised as a knight, and foils the evil merchant by pointing out a quibbling distinction between flesh and blood.

Il Pecorone provided Shakespeare with a number of essential elements, although not all that he has included. Ser Giovanni's story tells of Giannetto, the adventurous youngest son of a Florentine merchant, who goes to live with his father's dearest friend, Ansaldo, in Venice. This worthy merchant gives him money to seek his fortune at sea. Unbeknownst to Ansaldo, Giannetto twice risks everything to woo the lady of Belmont: if he can succeed in sleeping with her, he will win her and her country, but, if he fails, he loses all his wealth. Twice Giannetto is given a sleeping medicine and has to forfeit everything. Returning destitute to Venice twice, he is reunited each time with Ansaldo and given the means to seek his fortune again. For the third such voyage, however, Ansaldo is driven to borrow ten thousand florins from a Jew, using the forfeiture of a pound of flesh as a guarantee. This time, one of the lady's maids warns Giannetto not to drink his wine, and he finally possesses the lady as his wife. Sometime later, remembering that the day of Ansaldo's forfeiture has arrived, Giannetto explains the predicament to his wife and is sent by her to Venice with a hundred thousand florins, but he arrives after the forfeiture has fallen due. The lady, however, following after him in the disguise of a doctor of laws, decrees that the Jew may have no blood and must take no more or no less than one pound of flesh. The Jew is jeered at and receives no money. The "doctor of laws" refuses any payment other than the ring Giannetto was given by his lady. Giving it up unwillingly, he returns to Belmont, where his lady vexes him about the ring but finally relents and tells him all. Shakespeare could thus have found in one source the wooing, the borrowing from a Jewish moneylender, the pound of flesh, the trial, and the business of the rings. The story provides no casket episode, courtship of Nerissa by Gratiano, elopement of Jessica, or clowning of Lancelot Gobbo. The Jew's motive is not prompted by the way he has been treated.

Shakespeare may also have known "The Ballad of Gernutus," a popular English work that seems to be older than the play. It has no love plot but dwells on the unnatural cruelty of a Jewish Venetian usurer who takes a bond of flesh for "a merry jest." Anthony Munday's prose *Zelauto* (1580), though its villain is a Christian rather than a Jewish moneylender, also features a bond of this sort, taken purportedly as a mere sport but with

hidden malice. Truculento, the villain, takes the bond of two young men, Rodolfo and his friend Strabino, as surety for a loan. If they forfeit the loan, the young men are to lose their lands and their right eyes as well. The villain has a daughter, Brisana, whom he permits to marry Rodolfo, since Truculento expects to marry Rodolfo's sister Cornelia himself. When Cornelia instead marries Strabino, Truculento angrily takes the young men to court to demand his bond. The two brides disguise themselves as scholars and go to court, where they appeal for mercy and then foil Truculento by means of the legal quibble about blood.

Another possible source for the courtroom scene is *The Orator*, translated into English in 1596 from the French of Alexandre Sylvain. An oration, entitled "Of a Jew, who would for his debt have a pound of the flesh of a Christian," uses many specious arguments also employed by Shylock, and is forthrightly confuted in "The Christian's Answer."

Shylock's relationship to his daughter finds obvious earlier parallels in *Zelauto* and in Christopher Marlowe's play, *The Jew of Malta* (c. 1589), in which Barabas's daughter Abigail loves a Christian and ultimately renounces her faith. The actual elopement, however, is closer to the fourteenth story in Masuccio of Salerno's fifteenth-century *Il Novellino* (not published in English translation in Shakespeare's day).

The casket-choosing episode, not found in *Il Pecorone*, was a widespread legend, occurring, for example, in the story of *Barlaam and Josophat* (ninth-century Greek, translated into Latin by the thirteenth century), in Vincent of Beauvais's *Speculum Historiale*, in the *Legenda Aurea*, in Giovanni Boccaccio's *Decameron* (Day 10, Story 1), in John Gower's *Confessio Amantis*, and—closest to Shakespeare—in the *Gesta Romanorum* (translated into English in 1577 by Richard Robinson and "bettered" by him in 1595). In this last account, the choice is between a gold, silver, and lead casket, each with its own inscription. The first two inscriptions are like Shakespeare's; the third reads, "Thei that chese me, shulle fynde [in] me that God hathe disposid." The chooser, however, is a maiden, and she is not preceded by other contestants.

An old play called *The Jew* is referred to by Stephen Gosson in 1579 as containing "the greediness of worldly choosers, and bloody minds of usurers." Scholars have speculated that this was a source play for Shakespeare, but actually we have too little to go on to make a reliable judgment. Gosson was surely not referring to Robert Wilson's *The Three Ladies of London* (c. 1581) in any case, even though it is sometimes suggested as an analogue to *The Merchant of Venice*, for its Jewish figure, named Gerontus (compare Gernutus in the ballad), is an exemplary person. Besides, the probable date of this play is later than Gosson's remark.

Much Ado About Nothing

Shakespeare's probable chief source for the Hero-Claudio plot of *Much Ado* was the twenty-second story from the *Novelle* of Matteo Bandello (Lucca, 1554). A French translation by François de Belleforest, in his *Histoires Tragiques* (1569 edition), was available to Shakespeare, as was the Italian original. The story of the maiden falsely accused was, however, much older than the story by Bandello. Perhaps the earliest version that has been found is the Greek romance *Chaereas and Callirrhoe*, fourth or fifth century A.D., in which the hero Chaereas, warned by envious rivals of his wife's purported infidelity, watches at dusk while an elegantly attired stranger is admitted by the maid to the house where Callirrhoe lives. Chaereas rushes in and strikes mistakenly at his wife in the dark but is acquitted of murder when the maid confesses her part in a conspiracy to delude Chaereas. Callirrhoe is buried in a deathlike trance but awakens in time to be carried off by pirates. The story reappears in a fifteenth-century Spanish romance, *Tirante el Blanco*, in which the princess Blanche is courted seemingly by a repulsive black man. This Spanish version probably inspired the account in Canto 5 of Ludovico Ariosto's *Orlando Furioso* (1516), to which all subsequent Renaissance versions are ultimately indebted.

In Ariosto's account, as translated into English by Sir John Harington (1591), the narrator is Dalinda, maid to the virtuous Scottish princess Genevra. Dalinda tells how she has fallen guiltily in love with Polynesso, Duke of Albany, an evil man who often makes love to Dalinda in her mistress's rooms but who longs in fact to marry Genevra. Consequently, Polynesso arranges for Genevra's noble Italian suitor, Ariodante, and Ariodante's brother Lurcanio, to witness the Duke's ascent to Genevra's window by a rope ladder. The woman who admits the Duke is, of course, not Genevra but Dalinda disguised as her mistress, having been duped into believing that the Duke merely wishes to satisfy his craving for Genevra by making love to her image. Lurcanio publicly accuses the innocent Genevra and offers to fight anyone who defends her cause (compare Claudio's quarrel with Leonato). The evil Duke tries to get rid of Dalinda, but all is finally put to rights by Rinaldo (the hero of *Orlando Furioso*) and Ariodante. This account gives an unusually vivid motivation for the maid and the villain—a clearer motivation than in Shakespeare's play. A lost dramatic version, *Ariodante and Genevora*, was performed at the English court in 1583.

Shakespeare probably consulted not only Ariosto but also Edmund Spenser's *The Faerie Queene* (2.4), based on Ariosto. Spenser's emphasis is on the blind rage of Phedon, a young squire in love with Claribell. Phedon is tricked by his erstwhile friend Philemon and by Claribell's maid Pryene into believing Claribell false. Pryene's motive in dressing up as Claribell is to prove she is as beautiful as her mistress. When, after having slain Claribell for her supposed perfidy, Phedon learns the truth, he poisons Philemon and furiously pursues Pryene until he is utterly possessed by a mad frenzy.

Shakespeare's greatest debt is, however, to Bandello's story. In a number of details, the story is closer to Shakespeare's play than are those already discussed. Several names are substantially the same as in Shakespeare: the location is Messina, the father of the slandered bride is Lionato di' Lionati (compare Shakespeare's Leonato), and her lover is in the service of King Piero of Aragon (compare Don Pedro of Aragon). As in Shakespeare, a young knight (named Sir Timbreo) seeks the hand in marriage of his beloved (Fenicia) through the matchmaking offices of a noble emissary. The complication of this wooing is somewhat different in that Timbreo's friend Girondo also falls in love with Fenicia, but Girondo then plots with a mischief-loving courtier (resembling Shakespeare's Don John) to poison Timbreo's mind against Fenicia, and Girondo thereupon escorts Timbreo to a garden, where they see Girondo's servant, elegantly dressed, enter Fenicia's window. No maid takes part in the ruse, however, nor indeed is any woman seen at the window. When Fenicia is wrongly accused, she falls into a deathlike trance and is pronounced dead by a doctor, but she is revived. Her father, believing in her innocence, sends her off to a country retreat and circulates the report that she is, in fact, dead. Soon both Timbreo and Girondo are stricken with remorse, Timbreo magnanimously spares his friend's life, and both confess the truth to Fenicia's family. A year later, Timbreo marries a wife chosen for him by Lionato who turns out, of course, to be Fenicia. Girondo marries her sister Belfiore. This account does not provide any equivalent for Beatrice and Benedick. Shakespeare enhances the Friar's role and provides a brother for Leonato. Claudio and Leonato are of comparable social station in Shakespeare, whereas Bandello makes a point of Timbreo's superior social rank.

A lost play, *Panecia* (1574–1575), may have been based on Bandello's work. One other version Shakespeare may have known is George Whetstone's *The Rock of Regard* (1576), based on Ariosto and Bandello. It contains a suggestive parallel to Claudio's rejection of Hero in church. Various Italian plays in the tradition of Luigi Pasqualigo's *Il Fedele* (1579), and also a version perhaps by Anthony Munday, *Fedele and Fortunio* (published 1585), are analogous in situation, though Shakespeare need not have known any of them.

For the Beatrice-Benedick plot, no source has been discovered, apart from Shakespeare's own earlier fascination with wit-combat and candid wooing in *Love's Labor's Lost* and *The Taming of the Shrew*. Nor has a plausible source been found for Dogberry and the watch.

The Merry Wives of Windsor

The Merry Wives of Windsor is indebted to no single source that combines the various elements found in the play: the courtship of Anne Page, the hoodwinking of Falstaff by the merry wives, the horse-stealing business, and the various "humors" portraits. Nor does any one element derive from a single source. The entire play is brilliantly improvised.

Many analogues exist to the courtship of Anne Page, for it is essentially a plot in which parents and unwelcome wooers are outwitted by resourceful young people. The Bianca-Lucentio plot of Shakespeare's own *The Taming of the Shrew* is a good enough instance. Similarly, analogues have been found to the discomfiture of Falstaff. In Ser Giovanni Fiorentino's *Il Pecorone* (Day 1, Novella 2), for example, a student twice cuckolds the very professor who is instructing him in the art of love. Comically, the student reports back to the professor at every turn and is coached in his next move. He doesn't know that the lady is the professor's wife, but the professor begins to suspect and so follows after. On the first occasion, the student escapes detection by hiding under a pile of newly washed linen. The second time, he slips out the door, whereupon the neighbors arrive and, finding no intruder, berate the professor for his mad suspicions. The wife's brothers even search the linen pile at the professor's suggestion but find nothing. They thrash the professor and chain him up as a madman. Next day, intending once again to report to the professor what has happened, the student discovers the truth. This version differs markedly from Shakespeare's in that the husband is the chief comic butt. Nevertheless, Shakespeare may have known it. Although *Il Pecorone* (1558) is not known to have been translated into English in the sixteenth century, Shakespeare had already used it (or some now-lost manuscript translation) as his chief source for *The Merchant of Venice*.

Certainly available to Shakespeare was a similar story, "Two Lovers of Pisa," from *Tarlton's News Out of Purgatory* (1590). In this story, the husband is again the one who is duped. An old doctor, wedded to a beautiful young wife, becomes by chance the confidential adviser of a young man who has fallen in love with the wife. The young man reports to the husband his plans and successes in detail. The lover thrice escapes detection (when warned by the lady's maid of the husband's approach) by hiding in a vat of feathers, in a false ceiling, and in an old chest full of legal documents. When on the third occasion the jealous husband sets fire to his own house, the lover is saved by the husband's order to carry out the chest of documents. At last, the lover reveals his knowledge of the husband's identity, and everyone laughs at the old fool. Elsewhere, Tarlton's book has suggestive references to Robin Goodfellow and other prankish spirits that may have influenced the concluding scene of *The Merry Wives of Windsor*.

The story "Of Two Brethren and Their Wives" in *Riche His Farewell to Military Profession* (1581) features two wives: one of "light disposition" and much given to adultery, and the other a tedious scold. The first wife desires to rid herself of her two erstwhile lovers, a doctor and a lawyer, in order to enjoy a new liaison with a soldier, Accordingly, she pretends to encourage the lawyer's advances, but when the lawyer comes to her she feigns the approach of her husband and enjoins the lawyer to hide in a large mailbag. Meanwhile, the merry wife has arranged for the doctor to come and pick up the mailbag, on the assumption that she will be hiding in it. The doctor thus carries off the lawyer, nearly suffocating from his close confinement, into the country, where the doctor expects to enjoy his rendezvous. Instead, the soldier accosts them, cudgeling first the body in the bag and then the one who has done the laborious carrying. The lawyer is no less astonished to discover where he has arrived than is the doctor to discover what he has been carrying.

For the background of Shakespeare's horse-stealing episodes and "humors" portraits, see the Introduction to the play. The explicit comparison between Falstaff's ludicrous fate in Windsor Forest and the legend of Actaeon is ultimately indebted to Ovid's *Metamorphoses* (3, 150–304 in Arthur Golding's translation, 1567). In this account, Actaeon, grandson of Cadmus and a mighty hunter, happens to disturb Diana and her nymphs while they are bathing naked. Transformed by the vengeful Diana into a horned stag, he is hunted to death by his own hounds.

As You Like It

Shakespeare's chief source for *As You Like It* was Thomas Lodge's graceful pastoral romance, *Rosalynde: Euphues' Golden Legacy* (1590). Lodge was indebted in turn to *The Tale of Gamelyn*, a fourteenth-century poem wrongly included by some medieval scribes as "The Cook's Tale" in Chaucer's *Canterbury Tales*. *Gamelyn* was not printed until 1721, but Lodge clearly had access to a manuscript of it. Although Shakespeare may not have known *Gamelyn* directly, his play still retains the hearty spirit of this Robin Hood legend. (In later Robin Hood ballads, Gamelyn or Gandelyn is identified with Will Scarlet, a member of Robin Hood's band.)

Even a brief account of *Gamelyn* suggests how greatly the original tale is inspired by Robin Hood legends of outlaws valiantly defying the corrupt social order presided over by the Sheriff and his henchmen. Gamelyn, the youngest of three brothers, is denied his inheritance by his churlish eldest brother John. When Gamelyn demands his rights, John orders his men to beat Gamelyn, but the young man arms himself with a pestle and proves to be a formidable fighter. After defeating the champion wrestler in a local wrestling match (a lower-class sport befitting the social milieu of this story), Gamelyn returns home to find himself locked out by his brother. He kills the porter, flings the man's body down a well, and feasts his companions day and night for a week. John feigns a reconciliation and slyly asks if he can bind Gamelyn hand and foot merely to satisfy an oath he has sworn over the death of the porter. Gamelyn trustingly agrees and is made prisoner. After his bonds have been secretly loosed by Adam the Spencer (the steward), Gamelyn pretends to remain bound until the propitious moment for revenge and escape. The moment arrives during a feast of monks who churlishly refuse to help Gamelyn. With Adam's help, he fells many of them, ties up his brother, and escapes to the woods, where he and Adam are rescued from hunger by a band of merry outlaws. As their chief, Gamelyn becomes a champion of the poor and an enemy of rich churchmen. His brother, now sheriff, brands Gamelyn an outlaw and manages to imprison him, but Gamelyn's second brother, Sir Ote, stands bail for him. On the day of the trial, Gamelyn frees Sir Ote and hangs the sheriff and the jury. Gamelyn finally obtains his inheritance and becomes chief officer of the King's royal forests. This story is uninfluenced by the pastoral tradition and contains no love plot. Its Robin Hood traditions are very much present, nonetheless, in Shakespeare's contrasting portrayal of a tyrannical court and of a just society in banishment.

Lodge retains the primitive vigor of *Gamelyn* but adds generous infusions of pastoral sentiment in the manner of Sir Philip Sidney's *Arcadia* (1590) and sententious moralizing in the manner of John Lyly's *Euphues* (1578). The pastoralism is presented in conventional terms, with none of the genial self-reflexive satire we find in Shakespeare. Psychological motive is intricate, often more so than in Shakespeare's play. The style is also heavily influenced by Lyly's exquisitely balanced, antithetical, and ornamented prose. For his pastoralism, Lodge was indebted not only to Sidney but also to the ancient pastoral tradition that included the Greek Theocritus and the Roman Virgil, the Italian Sannazaro (*Arcadia*), and the Portuguese Jorge de Montemayor (*Diana*). Pastoralism by Lodge's time had become thoroughly imbued with artificial conventions: abject lovers writing sonnets to their disdainful mistresses, princes and princesses in shepherds' disguise, idealized landscapes, stylized debate as to the relative merits of love and friendship, youth and age, city life and country life, and so on. Some of these conventions were derived also from the vogue of sonneteering pioneered by Francesco Petrarch and can thus be described as the stereotypes of "Petrarchism." Lodge accepts these conventions and gives us typical pastoral lovers even in his hero and heroine, although the elements he derived from *Gamelyn* certainly add a contrasting note of violence and danger.

Lodge's account begins much like that of *Gamelyn*. Saladyne, the envious eldest brother, bribes the champion wrestler to do away with Rosader (Orlando) in the wrestling match. Rosader succeeds instead in killing the wrestler and in winning the heart of Rosalynde, daughter of the banished King Gerismond. When she sends him a jewel, Rosader is not at all at a loss for words; indeed, he composes a Petrarchan sonnet on the spot. The usurping King Torismond (no relation to Gerismond), despite his evil nature, is impressed by Rosader's grace and martial prowess. Rosader returns home with friends, breaks open the door, and feasts his company. The wily Saladyne overwhelms Rosader in his sleep and binds him to a post, but Rosader is untied by Adam and makes havoc among the eldest brother's guests, as in *Gamelyn*. In this case, however, the guests are Saladyne's kindred and allies, all of whom have refused to help Rosader. The sheriff tries to arrest Rosader and Adam, but they make good their escape to the Forest of Arden in France. They are saved from starvation by the kindly King Gerismond and his exiled followers. Rosalynde and King Torismond's daughter Alinda meanwhile have been banished from court and have taken abode in the forest under the names of Ganymede and Aliena. They befriend old Corydon (Corin) and young Montanus (Silvius), who is hopelessly in love with the haughty Phoebe. "Ganymede" poses as a woman to test Rosader in his wooing, and they are joined in a mock marriage. Saladyne, now repenting of his evil deeds, comes to the forest, is saved by his brother from a lion, and falls in love with Alinda (whom he helps to rescue from ruffians). The denouement is as in Shakespeare, although the triumphant return to society is more complete: King Torismond is slain, Gerismond is restored to his throne, Rosader is named heir-apparent, and all the friends are appropriately rewarded.

Despite Shakespeare's extensive indebtedness to this charming romance, there is a crucial difference: Lodge's pastoral world is never subjected to a wry or satirical exploration. Lodge offers no equivalent for Touchstone, the fool who sees the absurdity of both country and city; Jaques, the malcontent traveler; William and Audrey, the clownishly simple peasants; or Sir Oliver Martext, the ridiculous hedge-priest. Nor does Lodge tell of Le Beau, the court butterfly. Hymen is a Shakespearean addition, and the conversion of Duke Frederick by a hermit instead of his being overthrown and killed is a characteristically Shakespearean softening touch. Shakespeare's added characters are virtually all foils to the conventional pastoral vision he found in his source.

Twelfth Night

John Manningham's description of a performance of *Twelfth Night* on February 2, 1602, at the Middle Temple (one of the Inns of Court, where young men studied law in London), compares the play to Plautus's *Menaechmi* and to an Italian play called *Inganni*. The comment offers a helpful hint on sources. The *Menaechmi* had been the chief source for Shakespeare's earlier play, *The Comedy of Errors*, and that farce of mistaken identity clearly resembles *Twelfth Night* in the hilarious mix-ups resulting from the confusion of two look-alike twins. Shakespeare certainly profited from his earlier experimenting with this sort of comedy. *Twelfth Night* is not necessarily directly indebted to the *Menaechmi*, however, for Renaissance Italian comedy offered many imitations of Plautus from which Shakespeare could have taken his *Twelfth Night* plot. These include *Gl'Inganni* (1562) by Nicolò Secchi, another *Gl'Inganni* (1592) by Curzio Gonzaga, and, most important, an anonymous *Gl'Ingannati* (published 1537). This last play was translated into French by Charles Estienne as *Les Abusés* (1543) and adapted into Spanish by Lope de Rueda in *Los Engaños* (1567). A Latin version, *Laelia*, based on the French, was performed at Cambridge in the 1590s but never printed. Obviously, *Gl'Ingannati* was widely known, and Manningham was probably referring to it in his diary. To trace Shakespeare's own reading in this matter is difficult, owing to the large number of versions available to him, but we can note the suggestive points of comparison in each.

Both *Inganni* plays feature a brother and a sister mistaken for one another. In the later play (by Gonzaga), the sister uses the disguise name of "Cesare." In Secchi's *Inganni*, the disguised sister is in love with her master, who is told that a woman the exact age of his supposed page is secretly in love with him. Another play by Secchi, *L'Interesse* (1581), has a comic duel involving a disguised heroine. Of the Italian plays considered here, however, *Gl'Ingannati* is closest to Shakespeare's play. A short prefatory entertainment included with it in most editions features the name Malevolti. In the play itself, the heroine, Lelia, disguises herself as a page in the service of Flaminio, whom she secretly loves, and is sent on embassies to Flaminio's disdainful mistress Isabella. This lady falls in love with "Fabio," as Lelia calls herself. Lelia's father, Virginio, learning of her disguise and resolving to marry her to old Gherardo (Isabella's father), seeks out Lelia but instead mistakenly arrests her long-lost twin brother, Fabrizio, who has just arrived in Modena. Fabrizio is locked up as a madman in Isabella's room, whereupon Isabella takes the opportunity to betroth herself to the person she mistakes for "Fabio." A recognition scene clears up everything and leads to the marriages of Fabrizio to Isabella and Flaminio to Lelia. This story lacks the subplot of Malvolio, Sir Toby, *et al.* Nor is there a shipwreck.

Matteo Bandello based one of the stories in his *Novelle* (1554) on *Gl'Ingannati*, and this prose version was then translated into French by François de Belleforest in his *Histoires Tragiques* (1579 edition). Shakespeare may well have read both, for he consulted these collections of stories in writing *Much Ado About Nothing*. His most direct source, however, seems to have been the story of "Apollonius and Silla" by Barnabe Riche (an English soldier and fiction writer), in *Riche His Farewell to Military Profession* (1581), which was derived from Belleforest. Riche involves his characters in more serious moral predicaments than Shakespeare allows in his festive comedy. The plot situation is much the same: Silla (the equivalent of Shakespeare's Viola) is washed ashore near Constantinople, where, disguised as "Silvio," she takes service with a duke, Apollonius (Shakespeare's Orsino), and goes on embassies to the wealthy widow Julina (Shakespeare's Olivia), who proceeds at once to fall in love with "Silvio." When Silla's twin brother, the real Silvio, arrives, he is mistaken by Julina for his twin and is invited to a rendezvous, like Shakespeare's Sebastian. The differences at this point are marked, however, for Silvio becomes Julina's lover and leaves her pregnant when he departs the next day on his quest for Silla. Apollonius is understandably furious to learn of "Silvio's" apparent success with Julina and throws his page into prison. Julina is no less distressed when she learns that the supposed father of her child is in actuality a woman. Only Silvio's eventual return to marry Julina resolves these complications. Shakespeare eschews the pregnancy, the desertion, the imprisonment, and all of Riche's stern moralizing about the bestiality of lust that accompanies this lurid tale. Moreover, he adds the plot of Malvolio, for which Riche provides little suggestion. Shakespeare changes the location to Illyria, with its hint of delirium and illusion, and provides an English flavor in the comic scenes that intensifies the festive character of the play.

Shakespeare's reading may also have included the anonymous play *Sir Clyomon and Sir Clamydes* (c. 1570–1583), Sir Philip Sidney's *Arcadia* (1590), and Emmanuel Forde's prose romance *Parismus* (1598), in which one "Violetta" borrows the disguise of a page. Scholars have suggested that the Malvolio plot may reflect an incident at Queen Elizabeth's court in which the Comptroller of the Household, Sir William Knollys, interrupted a noisy late-night party dressed in only his nightshirt and a pair of spectacles, with a copy of the Italian pornographic writer Aretino's work in his hand. A similar confrontation between revelry and sobriety occurred in 1598: Ambrose Willoughby quieted a disturbance after the Queen had gone to bed and was afterward thanked by her for doing his duty. Such incidents were no doubt common, however, and there is no compelling reason to suppose Shakespeare was sketching from current court gossip.

All's Well That Ends Well

Shakespeare's only known source for *All's Well That Ends Well* is the tale of Giglietta of Nerbone from Boccaccio's *Decameron* (c. 1348–1358), as translated into English by

William Painter in *The Palace of Pleasure* (1566, 1575). Painter may have based his translation on a French intermediary by Antoine le Maçon, and Shakespeare possibly knew the Italian and French versions, although the English was the most available to him. All three are essentially the same, except for the forms of the proper names. The Helena story is also widely dispersed in folktales.

In Painter's account, Giletta is the daughter of Gerardo of Narbona, physician to the ailing Count of Rossiglione. Giletta falls in love with the Count's son, Beltramo. When the Count dies, Beltramo is "left under the royal custody of the King" and is sent to Paris. Giletta's father dies soon after, and she, refusing many favorable offers of marriage, journeys to Paris and cures the King of a fistula. The King has promised her any husband as her reward but is loath to give her Beltramo. The young man, no less reluctant, goes through with the marriage ceremony but then escapes into Italy before the marriage is consummated. In Italy he joins the Florentines in a military campaign against the Senois (Sienese). His deserted wife, now countess, returns home and governs the domain of Rossiglione with great skill. When she writes to Beltramo, offering to depart if her presence displeases him, Beltramo sets for her the "impossible" demand of obtaining his ring and begetting a son by him. Hereupon she calls together the leaders of her domain and announces her intention of going on a pilgrimage of renunciation. Despite her people's great lamentation, she departs for Florence where she inquires after Beltramo and discovers that he is paying court to a poor gentlewoman (unnamed) who dwells with her mother. Giletta offers to obtain a dowry for this daughter if she will demand the ring from Beltramo and arrange an assignation so that Giletta may secretly take her place in Beltramo's bed. Beltramo reluctantly agrees to give up the cherished ring, and Giletta becomes his lover on not one but numerous occasions. When she is pregnant, she rewards the daughter with a dowry and then remains living in Florence until she is delivered of two sons. Beltramo has meanwhile been called home by his people. Giletta arrives home in time for a great feast, at which she prostrates herself before Beltramo and proves that she has performed the terms of his "impossible" task. Beltramo is persuaded by her constancy and wit to be true to his promise and reclaim her as his wife.

Except for Helena, many of the characters' names in Shakespeare's play are derived from Painter's version. Helena is Giletta in Painter, but her father is Gerardo of Narbona (compare Shakespeare's Gerard de Narbon or Narbonne), and the young man she vainly loves is Beltramo, Count of Rossiglione (i.e., Bertram, Count of Rossillion), who is left after his father's death as a ward in the custody of the King of France. Giletta is no ward and helpless dependent, however, as in Shakespeare; she is well-to-do, is cared for by her kinsfolk after her father's death, and refuses many favorable offers of marriage before journeying to Paris to cure the King of a fistula and claim her reward. Shakespeare's Helena, on the other hand, is not rich and so can serve as an example of innate virtue or "gentleness," in contrast with Bertram's hereditary nobility. Shakespeare enhances the roles of the Countess and Lafew, and makes the King more sympathetic than in Painter to Helena's (or Giletta's) cause: in Painter, the King is reluctant to give Giletta to Beltramo, whereas in Shakespeare the King becomes a spokesman for faith in the miraculous. Other courtiers in Shakespeare's play join the King in approving of Helena, so that, however much Bertram's resistance to an enforced marriage might seem understandable in most circumstances, his refusal of Helena is made to appear willful. Lavatch, the Countess's fool, quizzically expounds questions of moral consequence that are absent in Painter. Conversely, the added character Parolles highlights the callowness and insensitivity of Bertram, and serves as a scapegoat when Bertram belatedly gains a better understanding of himself. At the same time, Shakespeare eschews Painter's easy romantic ending for one that is highly problematic: he does not offer Bertram much opportunity to show a real change of heart toward Helena, as Painter does, and thus places a greater strain on credibility in this comedy of forgiveness. Helena, because she is so far below Bertram in wealth and position, is obliged to be more aggressive than her counterpart in Painter, which raises troublesome issues of female assertiveness. She does not enjoy Giletta's prerogative of governing Rossiglione in her husband's absence and winning such love from her advisers and subjects that they all lament her public resolution to go on a pilgrimage; Helena is thrown more on her own resources and so is at once more self-reliant and self-asserting.

Another possible though minor source is the epic romance *Girart de Roussillon* set in the ninth-century Burgundian court, featuring a scene of forced marriage and an atmosphere of chivalric glory. Shakespeare may also have been thinking of the *Chanson de Roland*. Parolles's interchange with Helena in 1.1 on virginity closely resembles Donne's Paradox, "That Virginity Is a Virtue," written in the 1590s.

Shakespeare gives his play a unity of construction and an economy of time not found in the sources. Characters such as the King and Diana are not discarded once their primary role has been discharged but are brought importantly into the denouement. As in his use of other Italianate fictional sources, Shakespeare compresses time: for example, Helena vows to cure the King in two days rather than eight (as in Painter), and Helena sleeps with Bertram once rather than often. No convincing source has been found for the comic exposure of Parolles.

Measure for Measure

Stories about corrupt magistrates are ancient and universal, but Shakespeare's particular story in *Measure for Measure* seems to go back to an actual incident in the sixteenth-century Italian court of Don Ferdinando de Gonzaga. A Hungarian student named Joseph Macarius, writing from Vienna, tells about an Italian citizen accused of murder whose wife submitted to the embraces of the magistrate in hopes of saving her husband. When the magistrate executed her husband despite her having fulfilled her bargain, she appealed to the Duke, who ordered the magistrate to give her a dowry and marry her. Thereafter, the Duke ordered the magistrate to be executed. This incident seems to have inspired a Senecan drama by Claude Rouillet called *Philanira* (1556), a French translation of this play (1563), a novella in the *Hecatommithi* of G. B. Giraldi Cinthio (1565), and a play by Cinthio called *Epitia* (posthumously published in 1583). Shakespeare may have known both the prose and the dramatic versions by Cinthio.

In Cinthio's story, the wise Emperor Maximian appoints his friend Juriste to govern Innsbruck, warning him to rule justly or expect no mercy from the Emperor. Juriste rules long and well, to the satisfaction of his master and the people of Innsbruck. When a young man named Vico is brought before him for ravishing a virgin, Juriste assigns the mandatory sentence of death. Vico's sister, Epitia, an extraordinarily beautiful virgin of eighteen, pleads for Vico's life, urging that his deed was one of passion and that he stands ready to marry the girl he forced. The judge, secretly inflamed with lust for Epitia, promises to consider the matter carefully. She reports this seemingly encouraging news to Vico, who urges her to persevere. When, however, the judge proposes to take her chastity in return for her brother's life, Epitia is mortified and refuses unless Juriste will marry her. During another interim in these negotiations, Vico begs his sister to save his life at any cost. She then submits to Juriste on the condition that he will both marry her and spare Vico. Next morning, however, the jailer brings her the body of her decapitated brother. She lays her complaint before the Emperor, who confronts Juriste with his guilt. Conscience-stricken, Juriste confesses and begs for mercy. At first, Epitia demands strict justice, but when the Emperor compels Juriste to marry her and then be beheaded, she reveals "her natural kindness" and begs successfully for the life of her wronger. There are several important differences between this account and Shakespeare's play: Vico is actually killed, unlike Claudio, and Epitia sleeps with Juriste and then is married to him. No equivalent to Mariana appears, or to Lucio, Pompey, Mistress Overdone, Elbow, and other characters in the comic scenes of Shakespeare's play. No duke oversees the career of Juriste and ensures that no fatal wrong will occur.

Shakespeare may also have consulted Cinthio's play *Epitia*, but his chief source was George Whetstone's two-part play *Promos and Cassandra* (1578) and a novella on the same subject. In the English play, the corrupt judge is Promos, administrator of the city of Julio under the King of Hungary. The law forbidding adultery has lain in abeyance for some years when a young gentleman named Andrugio is arrested and condemned for "incontinency." His sister Cassandra, like Epitia in Cinthio's play, lays down her precious chastity to Promos in response to her brother's piteous entreaties. Promos gives his assurance that he will marry her and save Andrugio's life. When Promos instead treacherously orders the execution of Andrugio, the jailer secretly substitutes the head of a felon, newly executed and so mutilated as to be unrecognizable even by Cassandra. (This rescue is seen as an intervention "by the providence of God.") The King sentences Promos, just as the Emperor sentences Juriste in Cinthio's play, but in Whetstone's play the King refuses Cassandra's pleas for the life of her new husband until Andrugio reveals himself to be still alive and offers to die for Promos. The King forgives Andrugio on condition that he marry Polina, whom he has wronged. The play also features a courtesan named Lamia and her man, Rosko, who ingratiate themselves with the corrupt officer (Phallax) in charge of investigating their case. Phallax is ultimately caught and dismissed from office while Lamia is publicly humiliated.

Whetstone wrote a prose novella of this same story in the *Heptameron of Civil Discourses* (1582). Shakespeare appears to have consulted it as well as the play, for the prose version mentions the names of Isabella (as the narrator of the story) and Crassus (compare *Measure for Measure*, 4.5.8), and the King's awarding of measure for measure in his sentencing of Promos—"You shall be measured with the grace you bestowed on Andrugio"—may have given Shakespeare an idea for the title of his play. Shakespeare was also indebted for a few details to a version in Thomas Lupton's *Too Good to Be True* (1581).

Even though Shakespeare's play is closely related to Whetstone's play and novella, Shakespeare has changed much. He adds the motif of the Duke's mysterious disguise. (A not very compelling analogue to this motif occurs in Sir Thomas Elyot's *The Image of Governance*, 1541.) Shakespeare introduces the use of the bed trick, found also in his presumably earlier play *All's Well That Ends Well*. Most important, Shakespeare stresses the moral and legal complexity of his story. Isabella is about to renounce the world by entering a convent. By contrast, Lucio, a Shakespearean addition, is an engaging cynic, hedonist, and slanderer. Claudio, although guilty of fornication, is only technically in violation of the laws against sexual license. Isabella does not surrender her chastity. Her breakdown in the scene with Claudio intensifies her emotional crisis and renders all the more triumphant her final ability to forgive Angelo. Angelo himself is made puritanical in temperament and is spared the actual consequences of his worst intentions so that he can be worthy of being forgiven. Isabella need not marry Angelo, since he has not actually seduced her; she is thus free to marry the Duke. No felon need be executed in Claudio's stead, for Providence provides a natural death in the prison. In the subplot, going well beyond the merest hints in Whetstone, Pompey is a brilliantly original innovation, Elbow a characteristically Shakespearean clown modeled on the earlier Dogberry of *Much Ado About Nothing*, and Escalus a significant spokesman for a moderate and practical course of equity in the law.

Troilus and Cressida

Shakespeare had access to Homer for information about the Trojan War, since George Chapman's translation of *Seven Books of the Iliads of Homer* had appeared in 1598, and earlier English translations of parts of the *Iliad* were also available. Shakespeare ends his play with the death of Hector, as do Homer and some post-Homeric historians of the war, and portrays Achilles as a figure in tragic conflict with his sense of pride, as did Homer. Thersites and Nestor are based ultimately on the *Iliad*. Ajax's ludicrous boastfulness may owe something to Homer's Ajax Telamon, as well as to Ovid's account of the quarrel between Ulysses and Ajax over Achilles's armor (*Metamorphoses*, 12–13). Yet, for Shakespeare, and for most Englishmen of his time, the chief sources of information about the Trojan War were medieval romances. These were all pro-Trojan in their bias, since Englishmen traced their own mythic history to the lineage of Aeneas and tended to look on Homer as suspiciously pro-Greek. Medieval European culture generally was far more oriented to Roman than to Greek civilization; Greek texts went almost unread. In these circumstances, a pro-Trojan account of the war emerged and grew to considerable proportions, in which non-Homeric material became increasingly important.

The central work dealing with this expanded account of the war was Benoît de Sainte-Maure's *Roman de Troie* (c. 1160), a romance freely based on earlier accounts of two supposed eyewitnesses named Dictys the Cretan and Dares the Phrygian. Benoît not only narrates the war from Troy's point of view but introduces the love story of Troilus, "Breseida," and Diomedes. Benoît found a hint for this story in the *Iliad*, in which two Trojan maidens named Chryseis and Briseis are captured and given to Agamemnon and Achilles, respectively. When Chryseis's father calls down a plague on the Greeks for refusing to return Chryseis, Agamemnon reluctantly gives her up but then seizes Briseis from Achilles, thereby precipitat-

ing Achilles's angry retirement to his tent and all that disastrously follows. Benoît freely transforms this situation into the rivalry of Troilus and Diomed, who appear in Homer but in entirely different roles.

Benoît's *Roman de Troie* became the inspiration for subsequent medieval accounts of the Trojan War. Guido delle Colonne translated Benoît in his *Historia Troiana* (completed 1287). Giovanni Boccaccio based his *Il Filostrato* (c. 1338) on Guido and Benoît but made significant alterations: the love story became the focus of attention, and Pandarus assumed the important role of go-between. (In Homer, Pandarus is a fierce warrior.) Geoffrey Chaucer based his *Troilus and Criseyde* (c. 1385–1386) on Boccaccio, giving still greater attention to the states of mind of the two lovers and endowing Pandarus with a humorous disposition. Shakespeare certainly knew Chaucer's masterpiece. He also consulted, however, at least two other medieval accounts of the war: John Lydgate's *The History, Siege, and Destruction of Troy* (first printed 1513), based on Guido and Chaucer and known also as the *Troy Book*, and William Caxton's *The Recuyell of the Histories of Troy* (printed 1474, the first book printed in English), a translation from the French of Raoul Lefevre, who had followed Guido rather closely. In Caxton, for example, Shakespeare found materials for the Trojan debate in 2.2 and for Hector's visit to the Greek camp (4.5). In addition, Shakespeare was certainly familiar with the degeneration of Cressida's character since the time of Chaucer, as reflected for example in Robert Henryson's *The Testament of Cresseid* (published 1532), in which Cressida is punished for her faithlessness by leprosy and poverty.

Shakespeare pays a good deal more attention to the war than does Chaucer and portrays the lovers as caught in a conflict beyond their control. Shakespeare's Cressida is more sardonic and experienced in the ways of the world than is Chaucer's heroine, even though Chaucer's Criseyde is a widow and Shakespeare's Cressida is unmarried. The subtle and elaborate code of courtly love evoked by Chaucer has almost completely disappeared in Shakespeare's work, leaving in its wake a more dispiriting and cynical impression. Shakespeare's Troilus is still a faithful and earnest lover, as in Chaucer, but betrayed by his own chauvinistic ideals about honor and patriotism in a way that Chaucer's Troilus is not. Pandarus is more leering, giddy, vapid, and coarse than his Chaucerian counterpart. Diomedes is also changed for the worse, being more hard and cynical.

Among the non-Chaucerian characters, Achilles is made to appear more guilty and brutal than in Shakespeare's sources: Achilles orders his Myrmidons (i.e., his soldiers) to murder the unarmed Hector, even though Hector had previously spared Achilles in battle. Lydgate and Caxton report that Achilles's Myrmidons kill Troilus, not Hector (in Caxton, Achilles cuts off Troilus's head and then drags Troilus's body behind his horse), whereas in Homer Achilles kills Hector in battle and only then do his Myrmidons desecrate the body. Shakespeare refuses to glamorize the war, just as he refuses to glamorize the love story. He also compresses time, as he did with so many of his sources. The play begins only a short time before Cressida surrenders to Troilus; she is transferred to the Greeks immediately after she and Troilus become lovers; her surrender to Diomedes follows quickly after her transfer. This telescoping provides not only dramatic unity but also a sense of sudden and violent change.

Other plays on Troilus and Cressida are known to have existed in Shakespeare's time, such as a "new" play acted by the Admiral's men, an acting company, in 1596 and another by Thomas Dekker and Henry Chettle in 1599. Shakespeare may have known and even written in response to such productions by rival theatrical companies, but today nothing is known about these lost plays.

The Henry VI Plays

The chief source for Shakespeare's conception of the entire *Henry VI* trilogy is Edward Hall's *The Union of the Two Noble and Illustre Families of Lancaster and York* (1542), a work written to glorify the Tudor monarchs by demonstrating how their lineage reconciled the fatally warring factions of Lancaster and York. Shakespeare may actually have done much of his reading for historical particulars in the second edition of Raphael Holinshed's *The Chronicles of England, Scotland, and Ireland* (1587), which included much of Hall's material. He may also have used John Foxe's *Acts and Monuments of Martyrs* (1583 edition), and still other sources. Richard Grafton's *Chronicle* (1568) plagiarized so heavily from Hall that one cannot always be sure which of the two Shakespeare may have consulted. In any event, Hall's interpretation provided an overview, although Shakespeare carefully distances himself from the Tudor apologetics and providential view of history we find in Hall.

To intensify Hall's theme of the horrors of civil dissension, Shakespeare takes considerable liberties with the chronicles. He frequently disregards chronology, telescopes events of many years into a single sequence, invents scenes and characters, and transfers details from one historical scene to another. The artistic unity of each play is his overriding consideration, not historical accuracy.

In *1 Henry VI*, for example, Shakespeare shows the English losing Orleans to the French and then retaking the city (1.5–2.1). In fact, Orleans was never retaken once it had fallen. Shakespeare has transferred events from the recapture of Le Mans to his partly invented account of Orleans. Talbot's visit to the Countess of Auvergne (2.3) is fictitious. The scene in the Temple Garden when the leaders of Lancaster and York pluck red and white roses (2.4) is fictitious in a different sense: antagonisms between the two factions certainly did exist, but not in the allegorically schematized fashion here pictured. In 3.2 Shakespeare shows us Rouen lost and recaptured in a day, whereas, in fact, the city was (like Orleans) never recovered. Shakespeare's intention is to suggest that France is lost through England's political divisions at home, not through any failure on the part of Lord Talbot. Shakespeare exalts Talbot's might and chivalry (hence the scene with the Countess of Auvergne), and contrastingly overstates the cowardice of Falstaff (called Falstolfe in Holinshed and Fastolfe in some other historical sources). Joan la Pucelle is another exaggeratedly evil foil to Talbot; Shakespeare combines her worst traits from Hall and Holinshed. The play covers the events of about three decades. When Henry V died in 1422, his son was less than one year old; by the time of Talbot's fall in 1453, the King was over thirty.

In *2 Henry VI*, Shakespeare accentuates the threat of popular unrest in a number of ways. He conflates reports of the Jack Cade rebellion in 1450 with those of the Peasants' Revolt in 1381, using the most unattractive features of each. Shakespeare ridicules the peasants' utopian aims and omits a list of sympathetic demands. Similarly, the dispute between the Armorer and his apprentice (1.3) is put into a context of courtly politics that we do not find in the chronicles. Simpcox's name and his lameness (2.1) are added to stress the farcical nature of this "miracle." (Shakespeare could have found this account in Thomas More's *Dialogue...of the Veneration and Worship of Images*, 1529, or in Foxe's *Acts and Monuments*.) Although the indictment of Suffolk (3.2) was historically an act of the House of Commons, Shakespeare portrays it as a near riot in which the people hammer at the King's very door with their strident demands. In every way, *2 Henry VI* stresses the fickleness, inhumanity, and ignorance of men caught up in a mob. Despite all this, however, the play alters its sources less than does *1 Henry VI*. And, for all its disapproval of mob unrest, Shakespeare's play is considerably less hostile toward the populace than an anonymous contemporary play, *The Life and Death of Jack Straw* (1590–1593).

3 Henry VI similarly alters its sources less than does *1 Henry VI*. The alterations are chiefly those of telescoping and highlighting for emphasis. The ritual killings, which form an integral part of the spectacle in *3 Henry VI*, are cleverly adapted or rearranged from chronicle accounts. Concerning the death of the Duke of York (1.4), for example, Hall reports merely that York died fighting manfully, whereas Holinshed tells us that the remorseless Clifford caused the dead York's head to be struck off "and set on it a crown of paper, fixed it on a pole, and presented it to the Queen." Shakespeare's version goes still further:

Queen Margaret mocks York while he is still alive by putting a paper crown on his head. The ritual killing of the Lancastrian Prince Edward (5.5) is similarly enhanced. Throughout, Shakespeare's purpose is to intensify the scourgelike role of the Yorkist Edward IV and his brethren. Among the three, Richard of Gloucester is the most ominous. Shakespeare introduces crookbacked Richard into the fighting (2.1) when historically this man was abroad.

According to Andrew Cairncross's Arden edition, *3 Henry VI* contains occasional allusions to Edmund Spenser's *The Faerie Queene* (see 2.1.9 ff. and *The Faerie Queene*, 1.5.2), to *A Mirror for Magistrates* (especially in the sections "Richard, Duke of York" and "King Henry the Sixth"), and to Arthur Brooke's *The Tragical History of Romeus and Juliet* (see 5.4.1–33 and *Romeus* 2.1359–1377). David Riggs argues (*Shakespeare's Heroical Histories: "Henry VI" and Its Literary Tradition*, 1971) that Christopher Marlowe's *Tamburlaine* (1587–1588) was an important source for Shakespeare's *Henry VI* plays and that behind *Tamburlaine* lay a classical rhetorical tradition of praise for heroism. Shakespeare would have thoroughly absorbed this tradition through the Tudor grammar-school curriculum.

Richard III

Richard III, like the *Henry VI* series, is based on Edward Hall's *The Union of the Two Noble and Illustre Families of Lancaster and York* (1542) and on the 1587 edition of Raphael Holinshed's *The Chronicles of England, Scotland, and Ireland*. Both of these historical compilations were deeply indebted for their hostile view of Richard III to Polydore Vergil and Thomas More. Vergil, a papal tax collector who came to England in 1501, spent many years under the patronage of Henry VII writing in Latin his *Anglica Historia* (first published in Basel, 1534). This work portrayed Richard negatively in order to glorify the claim of the Tudor monarch who had deposed Richard in 1485. Vergil argued that England's suffering was a divinely sent scourge, intended to cleanse England of rebelliousness and to prepare the English people for the providential reward of Tudor rule.

Thomas More's *The History of King Richard III*, left unfinished in 1513, was published in two slightly different versions: one in English (1557) and one in Latin (1566). Thomas More obtained much information and possibly an early draft of his narrative from Cardinal Morton, in whose household More lived as a youth. Morton had figured in the struggles of Richard III's reign—he was the Bishop of Ely from whom Richard requested the strawberries (3.4.32–3)—and had become a bitter enemy of the Yorkist king. Thomas More's own purpose in writing the life of Richard III was surely not to glorify Henry VII,

with whom More had a strained relationship, but to characterize the evil of political opportunism. His portrait of Richard becomes that of the generic tyrant, behaving as such tyrants behaved in the various literary models from Renaissance Italy with which More was doubtless familiar. The result was, in any case, one-sided. The historical Richard seems to have been no worse than many another late medieval ruler and had indeed some admirable ideas on efficiency in government. More's blackened portrait, because it served the purposes of the Tudor state, became part of the legend and was available to Shakespeare in many versions. Holinshed incorporated verbatim a good deal of More's account.

Apart from Hall's and Holinshed's chronicles, those of Robert Fabyan (first published in 1516) and the *Annals* of John Stow (1580, 1592) may have provided Shakespeare with further details. Another possible source is *A Mirror for Magistrates* (first published in 1559), in which, for example, in "The Complaint of George, Duke of Clarence," we find the riddling prophecy about the letter G (see 1.1.39). A second edition of the *Mirror* (1563) contains the Complaints of Edward IV, Anthony Woodville (Lord Rivers), Hastings, Buckingham, Shore's wife, and others. Shakespeare's particular indebtedness to the *Mirror* is not great, though he certainly was familiar with it. The same is probably true of the Latin tragedy *Richardus Tertius* by Thomas Legge (1579) at Cambridge, which contains an interesting scene of Richard's wooing of the Lady Anne not reported in the chronicles. The anonymous *The True Tragedy of Richard III* (published 1594, written c. 1590–1592) may have been useful in its fusing of Senecan revenge motifs with English history and in its focus on the single figure of Richard. The Richard of this anonymous play is an overreacher, a worshiper of Fortune who meets his nemesis in the devoutly Christian Earl of Richmond. Opinion is divided as to whether Shakespeare actually used the play, chiefly because by 1590 he could have found the legend of Richard III set forth in so many works.

King John

To understand Shakespeare's use of sources in *King John*, we must first understand the play's relationship to the anonymous play *The Troublesome Reign of King John*, published in 1591. According to E. A. J. Honigmann (in his Arden edition of *King John*, 1954), *Troublesome Reign* is an unauthorized Quarto plagiarized from Shakespeare's text rather than a source for it. *Troublesome Reign* does indeed show features of an unauthorized Quarto. Moreover, a 1611 reprint of this play is attributed to "W. Sh." and another in 1622 to "W. Shakespeare." The Folio editors did not register *King John* for publication in 1623, as though assuming it had already been published in some form. Nevertheless, most scholars still hold to the view that *Troublesome Reign* is a source. (See "Canon, Dates, and Early Texts.") Its early date, by 1591, would mean a still earlier date for a play on which it was based. Honigmann's argument for dating *King John* in 1590 has not won general acceptance.

If, on the other hand, we accept the argument that Shakespeare was substantially rewriting an earlier play on King John, the pattern of his indebtedness becomes clear on two points: (1) *Troublesome Reign* was his main, though not his only, source, and (2) Shakespeare consciously toned down the earlier play's anti-Catholic excesses and scurrilous humor. His characters are more thoughtful and complex; the paradoxes of kingship, more disturbing. Shakespeare's alteration of a crude and chauvinistic source play into a subtle exploration of political rule anticipates his similar transformation of the irrepressible *Famous Victories of Henry V* (c. 1586–1587) into the *Henry IV* plays and *Henry V*.

Briefly, some differences between *Troublesome Reign* and *King John* are as follows. In *Troublesome Reign*, John is a hero and a martyr for his defiance of Rome. His claim to the English throne is unquestioned. The barons who rise against him are loyal to Rome. Vice is rampant in monasteries and other ecclesiastical institutions. An abbot is discovered to be hiding a nun in his treasure chest. John is poisoned by a monk who is in league with the abbot and who receives absolution for his deed. The Bastard, John's loyal supporter, is an invincible foe of ecclesiastical corruption and treason against the state. In Shakespeare, on the other hand, John's claim to the throne is dynastically questionable, and his treatment of his nephew Arthur is reprehensible. The barons' opposition to him is prompted by a genuine moral revulsion. Although they learn belatedly that rebellion is more destructive than the evil it seeks to correct, since rebellion provides a fatal opportunity for foreign opportunists such as the French Dauphin, the barons are not simply tools of the papacy. The Bastard struggles, too, with his conscience over John's treatment of Arthur. The Church is often guilty of political duplicity, as are virtually all the kings and political leaders in the play, but the Church shows no signs of moral decadence. John is poisoned by a monk, but without evidence of conspiracy.

These contrasting estimates of King John reflect the two views of him held concurrently in Tudor England. One, the older and more critical, is that of medieval historians generally and Polydore Vergil in particular. The other, a more favorable estimate, is essentially a Protestant defense of John, a rewriting of history in order to view him (despite his failures) as a martyr of Catholic oppression and hence a forerunner of the Reformation. William Tyndale began this revisionist view of John in his *The Obedience of a Christian Man* (1528). The case was vividly expounded by John Bale in his *King Johan*, a play begun before 1536 and rewritten in 1538 and 1561. Whether the author of *Troublesome Reign*, or Shakespeare, consulted Bale is uncertain, but the author of *Troublesome Reign* was certainly heir to the Protestant tradition. A major repository of the Protestant view, in any event, was John Foxe's *Acts and Monuments* (1583 edition), known as the *Book of Martyrs;* more copies of this work were to be found in English households than of any other book except the Bible, and Shakespeare must have known it, even if the influence on *King John* is largely negative; the interpretation in Shakespeare's play is notably at variance with the nearly hagiographical account found in Foxe. Richard Grafton and Raphael Holinshed took the Protestant line in their chronicles and thus passed on the tradition to *Troublesome Reign*.

Shakespeare's play, though based primarily for its materials on *Troublesome Reign*, allows the expression of the more critical attitude toward John of the older non-Protestant line. Honigmann argues that Shakespeare also consulted the *Historia Maior* of Matthew Paris (published 1571) and perhaps the Latin manuscript *Wakefield Chronicle*, but scholarly opinion on this point is divided.

Richard II

Shakespeare's primary source for *Richard II* was the 1587 edition of Raphael Holinshed's *Chronicles* covering the years 1398 to 1400. As in his earlier *Henry VI* plays and *Richard III*, Shakespeare departs from historical accuracy in the interests of artistic design. Queen Isabel's part is almost wholly invented, for historically she was a child of eleven at the time the events in this play occurred. Her "Garden Scene" (3.4) is a fine piece of invention, bringing together images of order and disorder that are found in the rest of the play. The Duchess of York's role is entirely original; Holinshed reports the scene in which York's son Aumerle (the Earl of Rutland) rides to the new king and begs for mercy while his father simultaneously denounces him as a traitor, but the Duchess is never mentioned. Shakespeare has added the poignant conflict between husband and wife. Northumberland's role as conspirator against Richard and as hatchet man for Bolingbroke is greatly enlarged; for example, Holinshed never names the persons who engage in the original plotting against Richard. Shakespeare's Bolingbroke returns to England on his own initiative, whereas in Holinshed he does so at the barons' invitation, a change that accentuates the puzzle of Bolingbroke's motive. Another invention is the meeting between John of Gaunt and the Duchess of Gloucester (1.2). In fact, most of Gaunt's character and behavior has no basis in Holinshed at all. Shakespeare creates him to fill the role of thoughtfully conservative statesman, agonized by his son's banishment but doggedly obedient to his monarch. Finally, and most important, Shakespeare has greatly enlarged the role and the poetic nature of King Richard, especially in the final two acts.

Many of these alterations are Shakespeare's own; others derive from his reading in other sources. Samuel Daniel's *The First Four Books of the Civil Wars* (1595) may have had an important influence. Although we cannot discount the possibility that Shakespeare's play may have been written first, the consensus today is that he knew Daniel's poem. It gave him the idea of the Queen's maturity and grief (although not the Garden Scene), and the final meeting of King and Queen. Daniel's Hotspur is unhistorically a young man, as in 2.3 of Shakespeare's play. Like Shakespeare, Daniel sees York as a man of "a mild temperateness." Daniel's Richard and Bolingbroke ride together into London, not separately as in Holinshed. In Daniel's poem, Bolingbroke's indirect manner of insinuating his desire for Richard's death ("And wished that some would so his life esteem/As rid him of these fears wherein he stood") is verbally close to Shakespeare's depiction of this scene. Richard's final soliloquies in these two works show an unmistakable similarity to one another.

Richard II's reign was a controversial subject in the 1590s and produced other plays of varying political coloration that Shakespeare must have known. *The Life and Death of Jack Straw* (anonymous, 1590–1593) distorts history in its friendly portrayal of Richard's role in the Peasants' Revolt of 1381 and whitewashes government policy. In contrast, the anonymous play *Thomas of Woodstock*, sometimes known as *1 Richard II* (1591–1595), is almost a call for open rebellion against tyranny. Many verbal similarities link this latter play with Shakespeare's *Richard II*, and, although scholars have difficulty in determining which was written first, the wary consensus is that Shakespeare borrowed from *Woodstock*. Such a hypothesis would explain some of the mysterious references to Woodstock's death in the first act of *Richard II*, since the anonymous play deals with historical events preceding those of Shakespeare's play. Shakespeare's debt to *Jack Straw*, on the other hand, is slight, even though he probably knew the play. Christopher Marlowe's *Edward II* (c. 1592), although dealing with another reign, probably taught Shakespeare much about constructing a play in which a weak king gains sympathy in his suffering, while his successor becomes morally tainted by the act of deposition.

Other sources have been proposed—so many, in fact, that Shakespeare's task of writing the play has been compared to that of a historical researcher. More probably he assimilated his wide and varied reading without any formal program of study. He had certainly read Edward Hall's *Union of the Two Noble and Illustre Families of Lancaster and York* (1542), a chief source for his earlier history plays, but in *Richard II* he seems to have recalled little more than its overall thematic pattern. Shakespeare must have known the Complaints of Mowbray and Richard in *A Mirror for Magistrates*, but the verbal echoes are slight in this case. The same is essentially true of *The Chronicles of England* by Jean Froissart, translated by Lord Berners (1525), and two French eyewitness accounts available to Shakespeare only in manuscript: the anonymous *Chronique de la Traïson et Mort de Richard Deux Roi d'Angleterre* and Jean Créton's *Histoire du Roi d'Angleterre Richard*. The Froissart *Chronicles* perhaps gave some hints for Gaunt's refusal to avenge Gloucester's death, for Richard's insensitivity at Gaunt's death, and for Northumberland's role as conspirator. The *Traïson* is notably sympathetic to Richard in his decline, although Shakespeare might also have found this sympathy in Daniel's *Civil Wars*.

Shakespeare's second series of English history plays (*Richard II*, *1 and 2 Henry IV*, *Henry V*) is even freer of the Tudor providential view of history than his first. The second series does not lead forward by any direct link to the reign of the Tudors, as does the first. Henry A. Kelly has shown (*Divine Providence in the England of Shakespeare's Histories*, 1970) that Shakespeare does not follow a single "Tudor myth" but allows spokesmen for both Richard II and his opponents to repeat arguments found in the various chronicles. This practice is especially evident in *Richard II*, in which some spokesmen eloquently warn of the disasters that will follow Bolingbroke's assumption of the throne, while other spokesmen are sympathetic to Bolingbroke's takeover as a political necessity.

Henry IV, Part I

Shakespeare's chief historical source for *1 Henry IV* was the 1587 edition of Raphael Holinshed's *Chronicles*, but he also took some important ideas from Samuel Daniel's *The First Four Books of the Civil Wars* (1595). Following Daniel, Shakespeare readjusts the age of Hotspur (who was historically older than Henry IV) to match that of Prince Hal. Daniel's Hotspur is, like Shakespeare's, dauntless and stubborn, a turbulent yet noble spirit. The theme of a nemesis of rebellion afflicting Henry IV for his usurpation, only touched upon in Shakespeare's play, owes something to Daniel's presentation, although the idea of nemesis is to be found also in Holinshed. Both Holinshed and Daniel err in confusing the Edmund Mortimer whom Glendower captured with his nephew Edmund Mortimer, claimant to the throne; Shakespeare perpetuates this error. Hal's killing of Hotspur is unhistorical, since both Holinshed and Daniel report only that Hal bravely helped rescue his father from attack and that Hotspur was killed in the melee.

Daniel does give prominence to Prince Henry in the battle, however, and implies that he and Hotspur will meet face-to-face. Shakespeare invents the scenes in which we see Mortimer as a devoted husband and Hotspur as a fond combatant in wit with his wife Kate; Holinshed merely informs us that these two men were married. Shakespeare greatly expands Glendower's fascination with magic and poetry, changing him from a ruthless barbarian (in Holinshed) into a cranky but charismatic Welshman. Hotspur, despite hints from Daniel and Holinshed, is chiefly Shakespeare's creation.

The most impressive transformations are those of Hal and Falstaff. Shakespeare knew many legends of Hal's wild youth: some from John Stow's *The Chronicles of England* (1580) and *The Annals of England* (1592); others from oral tradition. Many of these stories were also available in Holinshed. Shakespeare's readiest source, however, was a rowdy and chauvinistic play called *The Famous Victories of Henry the Fifth*, registered 1594 but usually ascribed to Richard Tarlton or Samuel Rowley around 1587 or 1588. This play covers all the events of the *Henry IV* plays and *Henry V* in one chaotic sequence. Prince Hal has three companions, Sir John Oldcastle, Tom, and Ned (cf. Ned Poins), in whose company he robs the King's receivers of 1,000 pounds, visits the old tavern in Eastcheap, vexes his father, and strikes the Lord Chief Justice. A crucial difference is that this Hal is truly unregenerate. He not only chases after women and robs, but encourages his companions to look forward to unrestricted license when he is king. Hal seems consciously to desire his father's death. Yet he does reform and banishes his companions beyond a ten-mile limit with a promise to assist them if they amend their conduct. Although Hal's reform is crude and sudden, his popularity aids him when he goes to war against the French. He is followed by a comic crew of London artisans and thieves, who prove invincible against the effete enemy.

Shakespeare owes much to this unsophisticated, vibrant account of Hal's riotous youth, but he has transformed it to his own use. He limits himself in *1 Henry IV* to the action leading up to the Battle of Shrewsbury in order to focus on the coming of age of Prince Henry and the pairing and contrasting of Hotspur, Falstaff, and King Henry IV as alternative models for Hal's behavior. He invents unforgettable comic characters, such as Mistress Quickly, Francis, and Bardolph. Most of all, Shakespeare's portrayal of Falstaff is essentially his own. Sir John Oldcastle of the anonymous play is a minor character, not Hal's closest companion. Falstaff owes something to the tradition of the guileful and inventive Vice of the Tudor morality play (especially when Falstaff is called jestingly "that reverend Vice, that gray Iniquity," 2.4.448), but the influence of the morality play is general rather than specific. To label Falstaff a "Vice" is to reduce him to comic

tempter and villain. Falstaff is in part an allowed fool, a parasite, and a *miles gloriosus* or braggart soldier, but he transcends all these conventionalized types with his own unique vitality.

1 Henry IV suggests some acquaintance with the anonymous play *Thomas of Woodstock* (c. 1591–1595), which Shakespeare may also have used for *Richard II*, and with the Complaints of Owen Glendower and Northumberland in *A Mirror for Magistrates* (1559). In neither case is the debt extensive. More suggestive as possible sources are events and social conditions in Shakespeare's England: the Northern Rebellion of 1569 against Queen Elizabeth's government, abuses of military authority by unscrupulous officers, the dangerous state of the highways, the raucous vitality of tavern life in Eastcheap, and the like.

Henry IV, Part II

As in the case of *1 Henry IV*, Shakespeare's chief historical source for *2 Henry IV* is the 1587 edition of Raphael Holinshed's *Chronicles*. Samuel Daniel's *Civil Wars* provides less pertinent material here than for *1 Henry IV*, so that Shakespeare is particularly indebted to Holinshed for historical information about the rebels' grievances, negotiations with the rebel leaders, King Henry IV's illness and death, and the Prince's succession to the throne. Changes are nonetheless prominent and telling. Shakespeare condenses time, giving an impression of failing health on the part of King Henry IV almost immediately after Shrewsbury, whereas historically the King reigned vigorously for ten years after that battle. The Earl of Northumberland is presented as more "crafty-sick" than in Holinshed, and Prince John, too, is shown in a disagreeable light by his cold-blooded handling of negotiations that in Holinshed are the responsibility of the Earl of Westmorland; Shakespeare thus tarnishes the integrity of both sides, accentuating (as he does also in the Induction spoken by Rumor) a mood of cynicism and world-weariness. The theme of nemesis for Henry IV's usurpation is touched upon in *2 Henry IV*, as in Daniel, and Henry is accordingly plagued by sleeplessness and mournful reflection.

Like Shakespeare's first play about Prince Hal, *2 Henry IV* makes extensive use of legends of Hal's wild youth. Some are from John Stow's *Chronicles of England* (1588) and *Annals of England* (1592). Sir Thomas Elyot's *The Governor* (1531) is the ultimate source of an account of Hal's boxing the ear of the Lord Chief Justice. Shakespeare evidently knew *The Governor* firsthand, though he could also have found the story reproduced almost verbatim in Stow; by the 1590s, it was widely circulated. Shakespeare certainly used the anonymous play (usually attributed to Richard Tarlton or Samuel Rowley) called *The Famous Vic-*

tories of Henry the Fifth, usually dated around 1587–1588. He had already used parts of this play for 1 Henry IV. In Famous Victories, Shakespeare found a dramatization of the famous blow to the Lord Chief Justice's ear, interpreted there as a blow for freedom and against authority. He found also a vivid account of Hal's entry into his father's death chamber and the final reconciliation of father and son, followed by the coronation and the young King's rejection of his disreputable companions, Sir John Oldcastle, Tom, and Ned; they are banished beyond a ten-mile limit, though the new king will assist them if they behave. The anonymous play then goes on to recount King Henry's successful campaign against the French, as dramatized in Henry V.

Shakespeare's changes are as significant as his extensive borrowings. He mutes the parricidal suggestions of Hal's interview with his dying father; in the anonymous play, Hal can hardly wait to see his father in the grave. Shakespeare greatly expands the tavern scenes, with an added emphasis on Falstaff's age and dissipation; new characters, such as Pistol and Doll Tearsheet, with their rowdiness and colorful vituperation, surround Falstaff with signs of his increasing isolation from Hal. The venal country justices, Shallow and Silence, have no counterparts in Famous Victories, though that play does show a scene of farcical recruitment. Most of all, Shakespeare has immeasurably added to the humor and pathos of his chief comic character. Sir John Oldcastle of the anonymous play is a minor figure whose banishment at King Henry V's coronation is simply an appropriate gesture of the new King's reform. The characterization of Falstaff owes something to many traditional stage types, including the Vice of the morality play and the cowardly braggart soldier of classical comedy, but the richness and complexity are Shakespeare's own.

Henry V

Shakespeare's principal historical source for Henry V, as for Richard II and the Henry IV plays, was the 1587 edition of Raphael Holinshed's Chronicles. Holinshed's account of Henry V, however, depended so heavily on Edward Hall's The Union of the Two Noble and Illustre Families of Lancaster and York (1542) that we sometimes have difficulty knowing whether Shakespeare consulted Holinshed or Hall. He was certainly familiar with both. Shakespeare's sources all acclaim Henry V a hero-king. Samuel Daniel's The First Four Books of the Civil Wars (1595), which Shakespeare may have used for his account of the treasonous plot against Henry (2.2), also praises the King in encomiastic terms.

Shakespeare follows the order of events laid down in Holinshed and Hall: the personal rivalry between Henry and the French Dauphin, Henry's request for reassurance from the clergy as to the legitimacy of the war, the maneuvering of the clergy to forestall a bill in Parliament threatening to seize Church land, the foiling of a plot against Henry's life, the siege of Harfleur, and the glorious victory at Agincourt. Both Holinshed and Hall offer Shakespeare many particulars about the English claim to France: in both accounts, the Archbishop quotes the law—In terram Salicam mulieres ne succedant—and goes on at length about King Pharamond, the rivers Elbe and Saale, King Pepin, Hugh Capet, the Book of Numbers, and the rest. On the other hand, Shakespeare omits a three-year campaign that historically intervened between Agincourt and the peace treaty of Troyes. He passes over the Lollard controversy in England, with the execution of Sir John Oldcastle. And, of course, he adds unforgettable characters whom we do not find in the chronicles—Welshmen, Irishmen, Scots, common soldiers, thieves—who show the unity of the British nation under King Henry's charismatic leadership.

For many of his additions to the chronicles, Shakespeare was indebted to the anonymous The Famous Victories of Henry the Fifth (c. 1588), a work to which he had turned earlier in writing 1 and 2 Henry IV. This old play, not registered until 1594 and not printed until 1598, exists today only in a corrupt text; quite possibly Shakespeare knew a fuller and more authentic version that would have given him still more material. Other plays may have existed on the subject, for the Admiral's men (a rival acting company) acted a "harey the v" in 1595 and 1596 that may or may not have been The Famous Victories. In any event, the relationship between Henry V and Famous Victories is at times close. Famous Victories omits Henry's long campaign between Agincourt and the final peace treaty, as does Shakespeare's play. The Archbishop of Famous Victories discusses the French claim just before the arrival of the French Ambassador with the tennis balls. (In Holinshed, the tennis-ball incident occurs first, at Kenilworth, whereas the Archbishop's lecture occurs sometime later at a meeting of Parliament in Leicester.) Henry assures the French ambassador that he has "free liberty and license to speak." To the Dauphin's insolent gift, taunting Henry about his wild youth, the King suavely replies that "My lord prince Dauphin is very pleasant with me" and promises to repay the insult with balls of brass and iron. (Holinshed mentions this apparently nonhistorical legend only briefly.) When the French noblemen assembled at the French court hear of Henry's arrival on their shores, they tremble with fear, even though the Dauphin recklessly scoffs at so young and prodigal a king. Henry is accompanied to France by a ludicrous assortment of London artisans and thieves, such as John Cobbler, who bids farewell to his wife in a comic scene similar to Pistol's parting from the Hostess, and Derick, who turns the tables on a French soldier much as Pistol deals with Monsieur le Fer. When King Henry woos Katharine of France, he protests to her that he cannot speak flatteringly because he is a plain soldier. She asks in return: "How should I love him, that hath dealt so hardly / With my father?" Despite these resemblances, however, Shakespeare's *Henry V* is incomparably superior to the old play and contains many original scenes and characters, such as King Henry's touring of his camp incognito, the quarrel between Henry and Williams, and above all the scenes involving Fluellen and his fellow captains.

Other possible sources include the *Henrici Quinti Angliae Regis Gesta*, written by a chaplain in Henry V's army; the *Vita et Gesta Henrici Quinti*, erroneously ascribed to Thomas Elmham; the *Vita Henrici Quinti* by "Titus Livius," translated in 1513 (in which the French brag about their horses and armor); a ballad called "The Battle of Agincourt" (c. 1530); and *The Annals of Cornelius Tacitus*, translated in 1598 (in which Germanicus walks disguised through his camp at night "to sound the soldiers' mind," and hears his leadership praised).

King Henry VIII

Shakespeare's chief source for the first four acts of *Henry VIII*, as for many of his earlier history plays, was Raphael Holinshed's *Chronicles* (1587 edition). Holinshed presented him with conflicting views of Cardinal Wolsey, however, and traces of the conflict remain in Shakespeare's play. Much of Holinshed's work is actually a compilation of the writings of earlier historiographers. In this case, some of Holinshed's material is from the bitterly anti-Wolseyan *Anglica Historia* (1534) of Polydore Vergil. Accordingly, Holinshed gives decidedly unfavorable interpretations of Wolsey's animosity toward the Duke of Buckingham and his unscrupulous meddling in the question of the King's marriage. Vergil was particularly distressed by the way in which Katharine had been shabbily treated; he (and Holinshed) report her speeches in her own behalf with manifest approval. Shakespeare preserves this alignment of sympathies in which Katharine is the wrongly accused wife and Wolsey the scheming Machiavellian.

Other portions of Holinshed, on the other hand, derive from George Cavendish's *The Life and Death of Thomas Wolsey*, written some time around 1557 and extensively used by the chroniclers, though not separately printed until 1641. Cavendish was a gentleman usher in the household of Cardinal Wolsey from 1526 to 1530. Although he moralizes about the lesson to be learned from Wolsey's ambitious rise and sudden fall, Cavendish speaks admiringly of the Cardinal as an extraordinarily great man. He captures in minutely observed detail the magnificence of Wolsey's prosperous estate. He gives a

moving portrait of Wolsey after his fall, on his sickbed and near the end, saying to a companion: "If I had served God as diligently as I have done the King, he would not have given me over in my gray hairs." This passage, borrowed verbatim by Holinshed from Cavendish, produces in turn the famous lines from Shakespeare: "Had I but served my God with half the zeal / I served my King, he would not in mine age / Have left me naked to mine enemies" (3.2.456–8).

For his fifth act, Shakespeare turned to John Foxe's *Acts and Monuments of Martyrs* (1583 edition). Here he encountered a particularly rabid Protestant point of view, which has left its impression not only on the fifth act but on portrayals of Wolsey (whom Foxe naturally deplored) in earlier scenes. Foxe's hero, Thomas Cranmer, emerges as the victor of Shakespeare's play. Although the triumphantly Protestant ending contrasts oddly with Shakespeare's earlier manifest sympathy for Queen Katharine, the duality of attitudes is somehow plausible and perhaps even typically Elizabethan: Katharine suffered lamentably, and Henry and Wolsey treated her shabbily, but these great events did, after all, lead to the English Reformation and the rule of Queen Elizabeth. The ambiguity so often noted in *Henry VIII*, then, is an essential part of Shakespeare's sources, not merely because he used conflicting accounts, but because many Elizabethan Englishmen necessarily felt mixed emotions toward this chapter of their past.

Shakespeare may also have made use of Edward Hall's *The Union of the Two Noble and Illustre Families of Lancaster and York* (1542) and John Speed's *History of Great Britain* (1611). In addition, he probably knew a dramatic version of the reign of Henry VIII that had appeared about eight years before, *When You See Me You Know Me*, by Samuel Rowley (1603–1605).

Titus Andronicus

We do not possess today any work that Shakespeare and (probably) his collaborator could have used for their immediate source in writing *Titus Andronicus*. An eighteenth-century chapbook called *The History of Titus Andronicus*, once thought to provide a reliable account of a prose original to which the dramatists had access, has now been shown to be an expansion of the story based on a ballad of 1594 which in turn was modeled on the extant play. Some scholars once argued that the Stationers' Register entry in 1594 by the printer John Danter for his publication of "a Noble Roman Historye of Tytus Andronicus" with "the ballad thereof" refers to a lost prose account. This hypothesis seems no longer tenable. Danter did, after all, publish Shakespeare's play in that same year, and the ballad appears to owe some of its details to the play. The existence of a prose *History of*

Titus when the play was written remains nothing more than a tantalizing possibility. (A ballad of "Titus Andronicus's Complaint," published in 1620 in Richard Johnson's *The Golden Garland of Princely Pleasures*, attests to the continued currency of the story in the early seventeenth century.)

The prose *History* is a fictitious medley of revenge stories inspired by Seneca and Ovid. It is set in the last days of the Roman Empire but contains no recognizable historical characters or events. Titus Andronicus is a Roman senator who defends Rome against the Goths in a protracted ten-year struggle, losing twenty-two of his own sons in the conflict. He slays the Gothic King Tottilius in battle and captures the Queen, Attava. When Tottilius's two sons Alaricus and Abonus continue the assault on Rome, the Roman Emperor wearies of the conflict and resolves to marry Attava against the advice of his general, Andronicus. The Queen, naturally regarding Titus as an enemy, proceeds to obtain powerful positions for her own kinsmen. She succeeds in having Titus banished, but he is recalled by popular insistence. Attava has an affair with her nameless Moorish servant and has a black child by him. Discovery of the child leads to the Moor's banishment, but he, too, is later recalled. Attava opposes the marriage of Titus's daughter Lavinia to the Emperor's only son (by a former marriage), since she desires the possession of the empire for her own sons. The remainder of the story proceeds much as in the play, except that we do not learn what happens to Rome after Titus's death. Shakespeare's chief additions include Titus's candidacy for, and rejection of, the throne, the struggle between Saturninus and Bassianus, the sacrifice of Tamora's son Alarbus, and a greatly magnified role for Aaron the Moor.

Although the prose version itself made use of Ovid and Seneca, Shakespeare evidently consulted these authors directly as well. The play contains many explicit references to classical authors, most notably when Lavinia turns the pages of Ovid's *Metamorphoses* to the story of Philomela's rape (4.1). In Ovid's famous account (Book 6, 526 ff.), King Tereus of Thrace rapes Philomela, cuts out her tongue (but not her hands) to prevent her from revealing the crime, and keeps her prisoner. She nevertheless manages to weave her story into a tapestry and send it to her sister, Procne, who liberates Philomela and plots with her to serve Tereus's and Procne's son Itys to him at a banquet.

A similar grisly feast takes place in Seneca's *Thyestes*, from which Shakespeare may well have drawn some particulars. Atreus, the wronged avenger, murders the two sons of Thyestes and serves them to him. As in Shakespeare's play, there are two sons rather than one. Of these two sons, one is guilty of ambition, whereas Ovid's Itys is an innocent victim. The slayer is a male avenger, not (as in Ovid's account) the mother of the slain victim. Senecan conventions of underworld spirits of revenge and the like are also present in the play, though they may have reached Shakespeare by way of Thomas Kyd's *The Spanish Tragedy* and other plays of the late 1580s. The works of both Ovid and Seneca were commonly taught in Elizabethan grammar schools, though they were also available in English translation: Ovid by Arthur Golding (1567) and Seneca by Jasper Heywood (1560). Christopher Marlowe's *Tamburlaine* and *The Jew of Malta* certainly had an influence, especially on Shakespeare's conception of Aaron the Moor.

Two continental plays about Titus, the German *Tragaedia von Tito Andronico* (1620) and the Dutch *Aran en Titus* by Jan Vos (1641), were once thought to have been derived from an English play before 1594, which might then have served as a source for Shakespeare. In the German play, the name of Titus's son Lucius is Vespasian, and this fact has caused scholars to wonder if the "Tittus & Vespasia" acted in April 1592 by the acting company known as Lord Strange's men (as mentioned in Philip Henslowe's *Diary*) was about Titus Andronicus. Lucius's part is small for such prominence in a title, however, and the prevailing opinion today is that Henslowe's play was on an independent subject.

Romeo and Juliet

Shakespeare's chief source for *Romeo and Juliet* was a long narrative poem by Arthur Brooke called *The Tragical History of Romeus and Juliet, written first in Italian by Bandell and now in English by Ar. Br.* (1562). Other English versions of this popular legend were available to Shakespeare, in particular William Painter's *The Palace of Pleasure* (1566), but Shakespeare shows only a passing indebtedness to it. Brooke mentions having seen (prior to 1562) a play about the two lovers, but such an old play is not likely to have been of much service to Shakespeare. Nor does he appear to have extensively consulted the various continental versions that lay behind Brooke's poem. Still, these versions help explain the genesis of the story.

The use of a sleeping potion to escape an unwelcome marriage goes back at least to the *Ephesiaca* of Xenophon of Ephesus (by the fifth century A.D.). Masuccio of Salemo, in his *Il Novellino* (1476), seems to have been the first to combine this sleeping potion story with an ironic aftermath of misunderstanding and suicide (as found in the Pyramus and Thisbe story of Ovid's *Metamorphoses*). In Masuccio's account, the lovers Mariotto and Giannozza of Siena are secretly married by a friar. When Mariotto kills a prominent citizen of Siena in a quarrel, he is banished to Alexandria. Giannozza, to avoid marriage with a suitor of her father's choosing, takes a sleeping potion given her by the friar and is buried as though dead. She is thereupon taken from the tomb by the friar and sent on her way to Alexandria. Mariotto, however, having failed to hear from her because the messenger is intercepted by pirates, returns in disguise to her tomb where he is discovered and executed. Giannozza, hearing this sad news, retires to a Sienese convent and dies of a broken heart.

In Luigi da Porto's *Historia novellamente ritrovata di due Nobili Amanti* (published c. 1530), based on Masuccio's account, the scene shifts to Verona. Despite the feuding of their two families, the Montecchi and the Cappelletti, Romeo and Guilietta meet and fall in love at a carnival ball. Romeo at once forgets his unrequited passion for a scornful lady. Friar Lorenzo, an experimenter in magic, secretly marries the lovers. Romeo tries to avoid brawling with the Cappelletti, but when some of his own kinsmen suffer defeat, he kills Theobaldo Cappelletti. After Romeo's departure for Mantua, Guilietta's family arranges a match for her with the Count of Lodrone. Friar Lorenzo gives Guilietta a sleeping potion and sends a letter to Romeo by a fellow friar, but this messenger is unable to find Romeo in Mantua. Romeo, hearing of Guilietta's supposed death from her servant Peter, returns to Verona with a poison he already possesses. Guilietta awakens in time to converse with Romeo before he dies. Then, refusing the Friar's advice to retire to a convent, she dies by stopping her own breath. This story provides no equivalents for Mercutio and the Nurse, although a young man named Marcuccio appears briefly at the Cappellettis's ball.

Da Porto's version inspired that of Matteo Bandello in his *Novelle* of 1554. Some details are added: Romeo goes to the ball in a vizard (mask), he has a servant named Pietro, a rope ladder is given to the Nurse enabling Romeo to visit Julietta's chamber before their marriage, Romeo obtains a poison from one Spolentino, and so on. The young man at the ball, Marcuccio, is now named Mercutio but is still a minor figure. This Bandello version was translated into French by Pierre Boaistuau in his *Histoires Tragiques* (1559); Boaistuau adds the Apothecary (who is racked and hanged for his part in the tragedy) and has Romeo die before Juliet awakens and slays herself with Romeo's dagger.

Despite Arthur Brooke's implication on the title page that his version is based on Bandello, the narrative poem *Romeus and Juliet* is taken from Boaistuau. Brooke's poem is a severely pious work written in "Poulter's Measure," couplets with alternating lines of six and seven feet. Brooke openly disapproves of the lovers' carnality and haste, although fortunately the story itself remains sympathetic to Romeus and Juliet. Brooke stresses starcrossed fortune and the antithesis of love and hate. He reduces Juliet's age from eighteen (as in Bandello) to sixteen. (Shakespeare further reduces her age to less than fourteen.) Brooke's narrative is generally close to Shakespeare's, though with important exceptions. Shakespeare compresses time from some nine months to a few days. In Brooke, for example, some two weeks elapse between the masked ball and Romeus's encounter with Juliet in her garden, and about two months elapse between the marriage and Tybalt's death. Shakespeare also unifies his play by such devices as introducing Tybalt and Paris early in the story; in Brooke's poem, Tybalt appears only at the time he is slain, and Juliet's proposed marriage to Count Paris emerges as a threat only after Romeus's banishment. Shakespeare's greatest transformation is of the characters. Brooke's Juliet is scheming. His Mercutio remains a shadowy figure, as in Bandello *et al.* Brooke's Nurse is unattractive, although she does occasionally hint at comic greatness: for example, she garrulously confides to Romeus the details of Juliet's infancy and then keeps Juliet on tenterhooks while she prates about Romeus's fine qualities (lines 631–714). Even if Shakespeare's play is incomparably superior to Brooke's drably versified poem, the indebtedness is extensive.

Julius Caesar

Julius Caesar represents Shakespeare's first extensive use of the work of the first-century Greek biographer Plutarch, in Thomas North's translation (based on the French of Jacques Amyot) of *The Lives of the Noble Grecians and Romans* (1579 and 1595). Plutarch was to become Shakespeare's most often used source in the 1600s; prior to 1599 he had consulted it briefly on a number of other occasions. In *Julius Caesar*, he borrows details from three lives: Caesar, Brutus, and Antonius. He uses particular traits of character, such as Caesar's belief that it is "better to die once than always to be afraid of death," Brutus's determination to "frame his manners of life by the rules of virtue and study of philosophy," Cassius's choleric disposition and his "hating Caesar privately more than he did the tyranny openly," and Antonius's inclination to "rioting and banqueting."

The events of the play are substantially present in Plutarch, especially in "The Life of Julius Caesar." Antonius runs the course on the Feast of Lupercal to cure barrenness and offers the diadem to Caesar. Flavius and Marullus despoil the images of Caesar. Caesar observes that he mistrusts pale and lean men such as Brutus and Cassius. Papers are thrown by the conspirators where Brutus can find them, proclaiming "Thou sleepest, Brutus, and art not Brutus indeed." Caesar's death is preceded by prodigies: a slave's hand burns but is unconsumed, a sacrificial beast is found to contain no heart. When Caesar encounters the soothsayer who previously had warned him of his fate and boasts that "the ides of March be come," the soothsayer has the last word: "So they be, but yet are they not past." Brutus's wife Portia complains to him of being treated "like a harlot," not like a partner. Brutus commits what Plutarch calls two serious errors when he forbids his fellow conspirators to kill Antonius and when he permits Antonius to speak at Caesar's funeral. Cinna the Poet is slain by an angry crowd mistaking him for Cinna the conspirator. A ghost appears to Brutus shortly before the last battle saying, "I am thy ill angel, Brutus, and thou shalt see me by the city of Phillippes," to which Brutus replies, "Well, I shall see thee then." Antonius says of the vanquished conspirators that "there was none but Brutus only that was moved to do it, as thinking the act commendable of itself: but that all the other conspirators did conspire his death for some private malice or envy." Shakespeare's debt to Plutarch is greater than these few examples can indicate.

Of course, Shakespeare reshapes and selects, as in his history plays. He compresses into one day Caesar's triumphant procession, the disrobing of the images, and the offer of the crown to Caesar on the Lupercal, when, in fact, these events were chronologically separate. Casca is by and large an invented character, and Octavius's role is considerably enlarged. Brutus's servant Lucius is a minor but effective addition, illustrating Brutus's capacity for warmth and humanity. Brutus's two speeches after the assassination (as mentioned by Plutarch) become one, and Antonius's speech is made to follow immediately after. (In Plutarch, Antonius speaks the following day, after the reading of the will.) Shakespeare accentuates the irrationality and vacillation of the mob, for in Plutarch the people are never much swayed by Brutus's rhetoric, even though they respectfully allow him to speak. The unforgettable speeches of both Brutus and Antonius are not set down at all in Plutarch. More compression of time occurs after the assassination: in Plutarch, Octavius does not arrive in Rome until some six weeks afterward and does not agree to the formation of the Triumvirate until more than a year of quarreling has taken place. The inexorable buildup of tension in Shakespeare's play is the result of careful selection from a vast amount of material. Shakespeare's borrowing from "The Life of Marcus Brutus" is no less extensive and is at the same time reshaped and given new emphasis.

Although Shakespeare depended heavily on Plutarch, he was also aware of later and conflicting traditions about Caesar. On the one hand, Dante's *Divine Comedy* (c. 1310–1321) consigns Brutus and Cassius to the lowest circle of hell, along with Judas Iscariot and other betrayers of their masters. Geoffrey Chaucer's "The Monk's Tale," from the *Canterbury Tales*, similarly portrays Caesar as the manly and uncorruptible victim of envious attackers. On the other hand, Montainge stresses the hubris of Caesar in aspiring to divinity. (Shakespeare could have read Montaigne in the French original or, if he had access to a manuscript, in John Florio's English translation, pub-

lished in 1603.) A pro-Brutus view could also be found in the Latin *Julius Caesar* of Marc-Antoine Muret (1553) and the French *César* of Jacques Grévin (1561). That Shakespeare knew these works is unlikely, but they kept alive a tradition with which he was certainly familiar. Possibly he knew such Roman works as Lucan's account of Caesar in the *Pharsalia* and Cicero's letters and orations, which were republican in tenor. Other possible sources include the *Chronicle of the Romans' Wars* by Appian of Alexandria (translated 1578), the anonymous play *Caesar's Revenge* (published 1606–1607, performed in the early 1590s at Oxford), and Thomas Kyd's *Cornelia* (translated from the French Senecan tragedy by Garnier). *Il Cesare* by Orlando Pescetti (1594) is now almost universally rejected as a possible source. The result of Shakespeare's acquaintance with both pro- and anti-Caesar traditions is that he subordinates his own political vision to a balanced presentation of history, showing the significant strengths and disabling weaknesses in both Caesar and the conspirators.

Hamlet

The ultimate source of the *Hamlet* story is Saxo Grammaticus's *Historia Danica* (1180–1208), the saga of one Amlothi or (as Saxo calls him) Amlethus. The outline of the story is essentially that of Shakespeare's play, even though the emphasis of the Danish saga is overwhelmingly on cunning, brutality, and bloody revenge. Amlethus's father is Horwendil, a Governor of Jutland, who bravely kills the King of Norway in single combat and thereby wins the hand in marriage of Gerutha, daughter of the King of Denmark. This good fortune goads the envious Feng into slaying his brother Horwendil and marrying Gerutha, "capping unnatural murder with incest." Though the deed is known to everyone, Feng invents excuses and soon wins the approbation of the fawning courtiers. Young Amlethus vows revenge but, perceiving his uncle's cunning, feigns madness. His mingled words of craft and candor awaken suspicions that he may be playing a game of deception.

Two attempts are made to lure Amlethus into revealing that he is actually sane. The first plan is to tempt him into lechery, on the theory that one who lusts for women cannot be truly insane. Feng causes an attractive woman to be placed in a forest where Amlethus will meet her as though by chance; but Amlethus, secretly warned of the trap by a kindly foster brother, spirits the young lady off to a hideaway where they can make love unobserved by Feng's agents. She confesses the plot to Amlethus. In a second stratagem, a courtier who is reported to be "gifted with more assurance than judgment" hides himself under some straw in the Queen's chamber in order to overhear her private conversations with Amlethus. The hero, suspecting just such a trap, feigns madness and begins crowing like a noisy rooster, bouncing up and down on the straw until he finds the eavesdropper. Amlethus stabs the man to death, drags him forth, cuts the body into morsels, boils them, and flings the bits "through the mouth of an open sewer for the swine to eat." Thereupon he returns to his mother to accuse her of being an infamous harlot. He wins her over to repentant virtue and even cooperation. When Feng, returning from a journey, looks around for his counselor, Amlethus jestingly (but in part truly) suggests that the man went to the sewer and fell in.

Feng now sends Amlethus to the King of Britain with secret orders for his execution. However, Amlethus finds the letter to the British King in the coffers of the two unnamed retainers accompanying him on the journey and substitutes a new letter ordering their execution instead. The new letter, purportedly written and signed by Feng, goes on to urge that the King of Britain marry his daughter to a young Dane being sent from the Danish court. By this means, Amlethus gains an English wife and rids himself of the escorts. A year later Amlethus returns to Jutland, gets the entire court drunk, flings a tapestry (knitted for him by his mother) over the prostrate courtiers, secures the tapestry with stakes, and then sets fire to the palace. Feng escapes this holocaust, but Amlethus cuts him down with the King's own sword. (Amlethus exchanges swords because his own has been nailed fast into its scabbard by his enemies.) Subsequently, Amlethus convinces the people of the justice of his cause and is chosen King of Jutland. After ruling for several years, he returns to Britain, bigamously marries a Scottish Queen, fights a battle with his first father-in-law, is betrayed by his second wife, and is finally killed in battle.

In Saxo's account, we thus find the prototypes of Hamlet, Claudius, Gertrude, Polonius, Ophelia, Rosencrantz, and Guildenstern. Several episodes are close in narrative detail to Shakespeare's play: the original murder and incestuous marriage, the feigned madness, the woman used as a decoy, the eavesdropping counselor, and especially the trip to England. A translation of Saxo into French by François de Belleforest, in *Histoires Tragiques* (1576 edition), adds a few details, such as Gertrude's adultery before the murder and Hamlet's melancholy. Belleforest's version is longer than Saxo's, with more psychological and moral observation and more dialogue. Shakespeare probably consulted it.

Shakespeare need not have depended extensively on these older versions of his story, however. His main source was almost certainly an old play of *Hamlet*. Much evidence testifies to the existence of such a play. The *Diary* of Philip Henslowe, a theater owner and manager, records a performance, not marked as "new," of a *Hamlet*

at Newington Butts on June 11, 1594, by "my Lord Admiral's men" or "my Lord Chamberlain's men," probably the latter. Thomas Lodge's pamphlet, *Wit's Misery, and the World's Madness* (1596), refers to "the visard of the ghost which cried so miserably at the theater, like an oyster wife, 'Hamlet, revenge!'" And Thomas Nashe, in his *Epistle* prefixed to Robert Greene's romance *Menaphon* (1589), offers the following observation:

It is a common practice nowadays amongst a sort of shifting companions, that run through every art and thrive by none, to leave the trade of noverint, whereto they were born, and busy themselves with the endeavors of art, that could scarcely Latinize their neck verse if they should have need; yet English Seneca read by candlelight yields many good sentences, as "Blood is a beggar," and so forth; and if you entreat him fair in a frosty morning, he will afford you whole *Hamlets*, I should say handfuls, of tragical speeches. But O grief! *Tempus edax rerum*, what's that will last always? The sea exhaled by drops will in continuance be dry, and Seneca, let blood line by line and page by page, at length must needs die to our stage; which makes his farnished followers to imitate the Kid in Aesop, who, enamored with the Fox's newfangles, forsook all hopes of life to leap into a new occupation; and these men, renouncing all possibilities of credit or estimation, to intermeddle with Italian translations . . .

Nashe's testimonial describes a *Hamlet* play, written in the Senecan style by some person born to the trade of "noverint," or scrivener, who has turned to hack writing and translation. The description has often been fitted to Thomas Kyd, though this identification is not certain. (Nashe could be punning on Kyd's name when he refers to "the Kid in Aesop.") Certainly Thomas Kyd's *The Spanish Tragedy* (c. 1587) shows many affinities with Shakespeare's play and provides many Senecan ingredients missing from Saxo and Belleforest: the ghost, the difficulty in ascertaining whether the ghost's words are believable, the resulting need for delay and a feigning of madness, the moral perplexities afflicting a sensitive man called upon to revenge, the play within the play, the clever reversals and ironically caused deaths in the catastrophe, the rhetoric of tragic passion. Whether or not Kyd, in fact, wrote the *Ur-Hamlet*, his extant play enables us to see more clearly what that lost play must have contained. The unauthorized First Quarto of *Hamlet* (1603) also offers a few seemingly authentic details that are not found in the authoritative Second Quarto but are found in the earlier sources and may have been a part of the *Ur-Hamlet*. For example, after Hamlet has killed Corambis (corresponding to Polonius), the Queen vows to assist Hamlet in his strategies against the King; later, when Hamlet has returned to England, the Queen sends him a message by Horatio warning him to be careful.

One last document sheds light on the *Ur-Hamlet*. A German play, *Der bestrafte Brudermord (Fratricide Punished)*, from a now-lost manuscript dated 1710, seems to have been based on a text used by English actors traveling in Germany in 1586 and afterward. Though changed by translation and manuscript transmission, and too entirely different from Shakespeare's play to have been based on it, this German version may well have been based on Shakespeare's source-play. Polonius's name in this text, Corambus, is the Corambis of the First Quarto of 1603. (The name may mean "cabbage cooked twice," from *coramblebis*, a proverbially dull dish.)

Der bestrafte Brudermord begins with a prologue in the Senecan manner, followed by the appearance of the ghost to Francisco, Horatio, and sentinels of the watch. Within the palace, meanwhile, the King carouses. Hamlet joins the watch, confiding to Horatio that he is "sick at heart" over his father's death and his mother's hasty remarriage. The ghost appears to Hamlet, tells him how the juice of hebona was poured into his ear, and urges revenge. When Hamlet swears Horatio and Francisco to silence, the ghost (now invisible) says several times "We swear," his voice following the men as they move from place to place. Hamlet reveals to Horatio the entire circumstance of the murder. Later, in a formal session of the court, the new King speaks hypocritically of his brother's death and explains the reasons for his marriage to the Queen. Hamlet is forbidden to return to Wittenberg, though Corambus's son Leonhardus has already set out for France.

Some time afterward, Corambus reports the news of Hamlet's madness to the King and Queen, and presumes on the basis of his own youthful passions to diagnose Hamlet's malady as lovesickness. Concealed, he and the King overhear Hamlet tell Ophelia to "go to a nunnery." When players arrive from Germany, Hamlet instructs them in the natural style of acting and then requests them to perform a play before the King about the murder of King Pyrrus by his brother. (Death is again inflicted by hebona poured in the ear.) After the King's guilty reaction to the play, Hamlet finds him alone at prayers but postpones the killing lest the King's soul be sent to heaven. Hamlet kills Corambus behind the tapestry in the Queen's chamber and is visited again by the ghost (who says nothing, however). Ophelia, her mind deranged, thinks herself in love with a court butterfly named Phantasmo. (This creature is also involved in a comic action to help the clown Jens with a tax problem.)

The King sends Hamlet to England with two unnamed courtiers who are instructed to kill Hamlet after their arrival. A contrary wind takes them instead to an island near Dover, where Hamlet foils his two enemies by kneeling between them and asking them to shoot him on signal; at the proper moment, he ducks and they shoot one another. He finishes them off with their own swords and discovers letter on their persons ordering Hamlet's execution by the English King if the original plot should fail. When Hamlet returns to Denmark, the King arranges a duel between him and Corambus's son Leonhardus. If Leonhardus's poisoned dagger misses its mark, a beaker of wine containing finely ground oriental diamond dust is to do the rest. Hamlet is informed of the impending duel by Phantasmo (compare Osric), whom Hamlet taunts condescendingly and calls "Signora Phantasmo." Shortly before the duel takes place, Ophelia is reported to have thrown herself off a hill to her death. The other deaths occur much as in Shakespeare's play. The dying Hamlet bids that the crown be conveyed to his cousin, Duke Fortempras of Norway, of whom we have not heard earlier.

From the extensive similarities between *Hamlet* and this German play, we can see that Shakespeare inherited his narrative material almost intact, though in a jumble and so pitifully mangled that the modern reader can only laugh at the contrast. No source study in Shakespeare reveals so clearly the extent of Shakespeare's wholesale borrowing of plot and the incredible transformation he achieved in reordering his materials.

Othello

Shakespeare's main source for *Othello* was the seventh story from the third decade of G. B. Giraldi Cinthio's *Hecatommithi* (1565). Cinthio was available in French but not in English translation during Shakespeare's lifetime. The verbal echoes in Shakespeare's play are usually closer to the Italian original than to Gabriel Chappuys's French version of 1584. Cinthio's account may have been based on an actual incident occurring in Venice around 1508.

Shakespeare is considerably indebted to Cinthio's story for the essentials of the narrative: the marriage of a Moorish captain to a Venetian lady, Disdemona, whose relatives wish her to marry someone else, the mutual attraction to noble qualities of mind in both husband and wife, their happiness together at first, the dispatching of the Moor to Cyprus to take charge of the garrison there, Disdemona's insistence on accompanying her husband through whatever dangers may occur (though the sea voyage, as it turns out, is a very calm one), the ensign's treachery and resolve to destroy the Moor's happiness with Disdemona, her begging her husband to reinstate the squadron leader whom the Moor has demoted for fighting on guard duty (although no mention is made of drunkenness or of the ensign's role in starting the trouble), the ensign's insinuations to the Moor that his wife is cuckolding him because she is becoming weary of her marriage with a black man, the ensign's difficulty in providing ocular proof, his planting of Disdemona's handkerchief in the squadron leader's quarters and his showing the Moor that the handkerchief is now in the squadron leader's possession, his arranging for the Moor to witness at a distance a conversation between the ensign and squadron leader that is, in fact, not about Disdemona, Disdemona's confusion when she is asked to produce the handkerchief, the attack on the squadron leader in the dark, the murder of Disdemona in her bed, the Moor's deep regret at the loss of his wife, the eventual punishment of both the Moor and and the ensign, and the telling of the story publicly by the ensign's wife, who has heretofore kept silent because of her fear of her husband.

Although these correspondences in the story are many, Shakespeare has changed a great deal. He provides Desdemona with a caring and saddened father, Brabantio, out of Cinthio's brief suggestion of family opposition to her marriage, and adds the entire opening scene in which Iago arouses the prejudices of Brabantio. Roderigo is a brilliantly invented character used to reveal Iago's skill in manipulation. Cinthio's ensign, though thoroughly wicked, never expresses a resentment for the squadron leader's promotion and favored treatment by the Moor; instead, the ensign lusts for Disdemona and turns against her and the Moor only when his passion is unrequited. In his complex portrayal of a consuming and irrational jealousy in Iago, Shakespeare goes far beyond his source, making use as well of the inventive villainy of the Vice in the English late medieval morality play. In Cinthio's account, the ensign filches the handkerchief from Disdemona while she is hugging the ensign's three-year-old daughter; the ensign's wife is uninvolved in this mischief, though she does unwillingly learn of her husband's villainy (since he has an idea of using her in his plot) and later feels constrained to hold her tongue when Disdemona asks her if she knows why the Moor is behaving so strangely. (As is usual in prose narrative, the passage of time is much more extended than in Shakespeare's play.)

In the later portions of the story, the changes are more marked. Cinthio relates an episode in which the squadron leader, finding the handkerchief in his room, takes it back to Disdemona while the Moor is out but is interrupted by the Moor's unexpected return home; Shakespeare instead has Cassio approach Desdemona (earlier in the story) to beg her assistance in persuading Othello to reinstate him. Cinthio tells of a woman in the squadron leader's household who copies the embroidery of the handkerchief before it is returned and is seen with it at a window by the Moor; here, Shakespeare finds a suggestion for Bianca, but her role is considerably augmented, partly with the help of a passing remark in Cinthio's account that the squadron leader is attacked and wounded as he leaves the house of a courtesan with whom he occasionally takes his pleasure. In the absence of any character corresponding to Roderigo, the Cinthio narrative assigns to the ensign himself the role of wounding the squadron leader. The manner in which Disdemona is murdered is strik-

ingly different. Cinthio has nothing equivalent to the tender scene between Desdemona and Emilia as Desdemona prepares to go to bed. Cinthio's Moor hides the ensign in a dressing room next to his bedroom and commissions the ensign to bludgeon her to death with a sand-filled stocking, after which the two murderers cause the ceiling of the room to collapse on her and create the impression that a rafter has smashed her skull.

Cinthio also treats the aftermath of the murder in a very different way. The Moor, distracted with grief, turns on the ensign and demotes him, whereupon the ensign persuades the squadron commander to take vengeance on the Moor as his attacker (according to the lying ensign) and killer of Disdemona. When the squadron commander accuses the Moor before the Seigniory, the Moor keeps silent but is banished and eventually killed by Disdemona's relatives. The ensign, returning to his own country, gets in trouble by making a false accusation and dies as the result of torture. Cinthio sees this as God's retribution. The ensign's wife lives to tell her story, unlike Shakespeare's Emilia.

The changed ending is essential to Shakespeare's play. Emilia becomes a more complex figure than the ensign's wife: Shakespeare implicates her in the stealing of the handkerchief but also accentuates her love for Desdemona and her brave denunciation of her husband when at last she knows the full truth. Othello's ritual slaying of Desdemona avoids the appalling butchery of the source story. Shakespeare's ending is more unified, and brings both Othello and Iago to account for the deeds they have committed in this play. Most important, Shakespeare transforms a sensational murder story into a moving tragedy of love.

King Lear

The story of Lear goes back into ancient legend. The motif of two wicked sisters and a virtuous youngest sister reminds us of Cinderella. Lear himself appears to come from Celtic mythology. Geoffrey of Monmouth, a Welshman in close contact with Celtic legend, included a Lear or Leir as one of the pseudo-historical Kings in his *Historia Regum Britanniae* (c. 1136). This fanciful mixture of history and legend traces a supposed line of descent from Brut, great-grandson of Aeneas of Troy, through Locrine, Bladud, Leir, Gorboduc, Ferrex and Porrex, Lud, Cymbeline, Bonduca, Vortigern, Arthur, and so forth, to the historical Kings of England. The Tudor monarchs made much of their purported claim to such an ancient dynasty, and in Shakespeare's day this mythology had a quasi-official status demanding a certain reverential suspension of disbelief.

King Leir, according to Geoffrey, is the father of three daughters, Gonorilla, Regan, and Cordeilla, among whom he intends to divide his kingdom. To determine who deserves most, he asks them who loves him most. The two eldest sisters protest undying devotion, but Cordeilla, perceiving how the others flatter and deceive him, renounces hyperbole and promises only to love him as a daughter should love a father. Furious, the King denies Cordeilla her third of the kingdom but permits her to marry Aganippus, King of the Franks, without dowry. Thereafter, Leir bestows his two eldest daughters on the Dukes of Albania and Cornubia (Albany and Cornwall), together with half the island during his lifetime and the possession of the remainder after his death. In due course, his two sons-in-law rebel against Leir and seize his power. Thereafter Maglaunus, Duke of Albania, agrees to maintain Leir with sixty retainers, but, after two years of chafing at this arrangement, Gonorilla insists that the number be reduced to thirty. Angrily, the King goes to Henvin, Duke of Cornubia, where all goes well for a time; within a year, however, Regan demands that Leir reduce his retinue to five knights. When Gonorilla refuses to take him back with more than one retainer, Leir crosses into France and is generously received by Cordeilla and Aganippus. An invasion restores Leir to his throne. Three years later, he and Aganippus die, after which Cordeilla rules successfully for five years until overthrown by the sons of Maglaunus and Henvin. In prison she commits suicide.

This story, as part of England's mythic genealogy, was repeated in various Tudor versions, such as *The First Part of the Mirror for Magistrates* (1574), William Warner's *Albion's England* (1586), and Raphael Holinshed's *Chronicles* (second edition, 1587). Warner refers to the King's sons-in-law as "the Prince of Albany" and "the Cornish prince"; Holinshed refers to them as "the Duke of Albania" and "the Duke of Cornwall" but reports that it is Cornwall who marries the eldest daughter Gonorilla. *The Mirror*, closer to Shakespeare in these details, speaks of "Gonerell" as married to "Albany" and of "Cordila" as married to "the King of France." Edmund Spenser's *The Faerie Queene* (2.10.27–32) reports that "Cordeill" or "Cordelia" ends her life by hanging herself. Other retellings appear in Gerard Legh's *Accidence of Armory* and William Camden's *Remains*. All of these accounts leave the story virtually unchanged.

Shakespeare's immediate source for *King Lear* was an old play called *The True Chronicle History of King Leir*. It was published in 1605 but plainly is much earlier in style. The Stationers' Register, the official record of the London Company of Stationers (booksellers and printers), for May 14, 1594, lists "A booke called the Tragecall historie of Kinge Leir and his Three Daughters &c.," and a short time earlier Philip Henslowe's *Diary* records the performance of a "Kinge Leare" at the Rose Theatre on April 6 and 8, 1594. The actors were either the Queen's or the Earl of Sussex's men (two acting companies), though probably the Queen's. The play may have been written as early as 1588. George Peele, Robert Greene, Thomas Lodge, and Thomas Kyd have all been suggested as possible authors. Shakespeare probably knew the play before its publication in 1605.

This play of *Leir* ends happily, with the restoration of Leir to his throne. Essentially, the play is a legendary history with a strong element of romance. The two wicked sisters are warned of the King's plans for dividing his Kingdom by an obsequious courtier named Skalliger (compare Oswald). It is Skalliger, in fact, who proposes the idea of apportioning the Kingdom in accord with the lovingness of the daughters' responses. Cordella receives the ineffectual support of an honest courtier, Perillus (compare Kent) but is disinherited by her angry father. Trusting herself to God's mercy and setting forth alone to live by her own labor, Cordella is found by the Gallian King and his bluff companion Mumford, who have come to England disguised as palmers to see if the English King's daughters are as beautiful as reported. The King hears Cordella's sad story, falls in love with her, and woos her (still wearing his disguise) in the name of the Gallian King. When she virtuously suggests the palmer woo for himself, he throws off his disguise and marries her forthwith.

Meanwhile the other sons-in-law, Cornwall and Combria (compare Albany), draw lots for their shares of the kingdom. Leir announces that he will sojourn with Cornwall and Gonorill first. Cornwall treats the King with genuine solicitude, but Gonorill, abetted by Skalliger, tauntingly drives her father away. The King acknowledges to his loyal companion Perillus that he has wronged Cordella. Regan, who rules her mild husband as she pleases, receives the King with seeming tenderness but secretly hires an assassin to end his life. (Gonorill is partner in this plot.) The suborned agent, frightened into remorse by a providentially sent thunderstorm, shows his intended victim the letter ordering the assassination.

The Gallian King and Cordella, who have previously sent ambassadors to Leir urging him to come to France, now decide to journey with Mumford into Britain disguised as countryfolk. Before they can do so, however, Leir and Perillus arrive in France, in mariners' garb, where they encounter Cordella and her party dressed as country folk. Cordella recognizes Leir's voice, and father and daughter are tearfully reunited. The Gallian King invades England and restores Leir to his throne.

Shakespeare has changed much in the narrative of his source. He discards not only the happy ending but also the attempted assassination and the numerous romance-like uses of disguise (although Tom o' Bedlam, in an added plot, repeatedly uses disguise). Shakespeare eliminates the humorous Mumford and replaces Perillus with both Kent and the Fool. He turns Cornwall into a villain and Albany into a belated champion of justice. He creates the storm scene out of a mere suggestion of such an event, serving a very different purpose, in his source.

Most of all, he adds the parallel plot of Gloucester, Edgar, and Edmund. Here Shakespeare derived some of his material from Sir Philip Sidney's *Arcadia* (1590). In Book 2, chapter 10 of this greatest of Elizabethan prose romances, the two heroes, Pyrocles and Musidorus, encounter a son leading his blind old father. The old man tells his pitiful tale. He is the deposed King of Paphlagonia, father of a bastard son named Plexirtus who, he now bitterly realizes, turned the King against his true son Leonatus—the very son who is now his guide and guardian. The true son, having managed to escape his father's order of execution, has been forced to live poorly as a soldier, while the bastard son has proceeded to usurp his father's throne. In his wretchedness, the King has been succored by his forgiving true son and has been prevented from casting himself off the top of a hill. At the conclusion of this narrative, the villain Plexirtus arrives and attacks Leonatus; reinforcements arrive on both sides, but eventually Plexirtus is driven off, enabling the King to return to his court and bestow the crown on Leonatus. The old King thereupon dies, his heart having been stretched beyond the limits of endurance.

Other parts of the *Arcadia* may have given Shakespeare further suggestions; for example, the disguises adopted by Kent and Edgar are like those of Zelmane and Pyrocles in Sidney's prose work, and Albany's speeches about anarchy and the monstrosity that results from assaults on the rule of law recall one of Sidney's deepest concerns. Edmund is decidedly indebted to the allegorical Vice figure of the late medieval morality play tradition. For Tom o' Bedlam's mad language, Shakespeare consulted Samuel Harsnett's *Declaration of Egregious Popish Impostures*, 1603. (See Kenneth Muir's Arden edition of *King Lear*, pp. 253–6, for an extensive comparison.)

Macbeth

Shakespeare's chief source for *Macbeth* was Raphael Holinshed's *Chronicles* (1587 edition). Holinshed had gone for most of his material to Hector Boece, *Scotorum Historiae* (1526–1527), who in turn was indebted to a fourteenth-century priest named John of Fordun and to a fifteenth-century chronicler, Andrew of Wyntoun. By the time Holinshed found it, the story of Macbeth had become more fiction than fact. The historical Macbeth, who ruled from 1040 to 1057, did take the throne by killing Duncan, but in a civil conflict between two clans contending for the kingship. Contemporary observers credit him with having been a good ruler. Although he

was defeated by the Earl of Northumbria (the Siward of Shakespeare's play) at Birnam Wood in 1054, the Earl was forced by his own losses to retire, and Macbeth ruled three years longer before being slain by Duncan's son Malcolm. Banquo and Fleance are fictional characters apparently invented by Boece.

In Holinshed's telling of the story, Duncan is a King with a soft and gentle nature, negligent in punishing his enemies and thereby an unwitting encourager of sedition. It falls to his cousin, Macbeth, a critic of this soft line, and to Banquo, the Thane of Lochaber, to defend Scotland against her enemies: first against Macdowald (Macdonwald in Shakespeare), with his Irish kerns and gallowglasses, and then against Sueno, King of Norway. (Shakespeare fuses these battles into one.) Shortly thereafter, Macbeth and Banquo encounter "three women in strange and wild apparel, resembling creatures of elder world," who predict their futures as in the play. Although Macbeth and Banquo jest about the matter, common opinion later maintains that "these women were either the Weird Sisters, that is (as ye would say), the goddesses of destiny, or else some nymphs or fairies, endued with knowledge of prophecy." Certainly Macbeth soon becomes the Thane of Cawdor, whereupon, jestingly reminded of the three sisters' promise by Banquo, he resolves to seek the throne. His way is blocked, however, by Duncan's naming of his eldest but still underage son Malcolm to be Prince of Cumberland and heir to the throne. Macbeth's resentment at this is understandable, since Scottish law provides that, until the King's son is of age, the "next of blood unto him"—that is, Macbeth himself, as Duncan's cousin—should reign. Accordingly, Macbeth begins to plot with his associates how to usurp the kingdom by force. His "very ambitious" wife urges him on because of her "unquenchable desire" to be Queen. Banquo is one among many trusted friends with whose support Macbeth slays the King at Inverness or at Bothgowanan. (No mention is made of a visit to Macbeth's castle.) Malcolm and Donald Bane, the dead King's sons, fly for their safety to Cumberland, where Malcolm is well received by Edward the Confessor of England; Donald Bane proceeds on to Ireland.

Holinshed's Macbeth is at first no brutal tyrant, as in Shakespeare. For some ten years he rules well, using great liberality and correcting the laxity of his predecessor's reign. (Holinshed does suggest, to be sure, that his justice is only contrived to court popularity among his subjects.) Inevitably, however, the Weird Sisters' promise of a posterity to Banquo goads Macbeth into ordering the murder of his onetime companion. Fleance escapes Macbeth's henchmen in the dark and afterward founds the lineage of the Stuart Kings. (This genealogy is fictitious.) Macbeth's vain quest for absolute power further causes him to build Dunsinane fortress. When Macduff refuses to help, the King turns against him and would kill him except that "a certain witch, whom he had in great trust," tells the King he need never fear a man born of woman nor any vanquishment till Birnam Wood come to Dunsinane. Macduff flees for his safety into England and joins Malcolm, whereupon Macbeth's agents slaughter Macduff's wife and children at Fife. Malcolm, fearing that Macduff may be an agent of Macbeth, dissemblingly professes to be a voluptuary, miser, and tyrant, but, when Macduff responds as he should in righteous sorrow at Scotland's evil condition, Malcolm reveals his steadfast commitment to the cause of right. These leaders return to Scotland and defeat Macbeth at Birnam Wood, with their soldiers carrying branches before them. Macduff, proclaiming that he is a man born of no woman since he was "ripped out" of his mother's womb, slays Macbeth.

Despite extensive similarities, Shakespeare has made some significant changes. Duncan is no longer an ineffectual king. Macbeth can no longer justify his claim to the throne. Most important, Banquo is no longer partner in a broadly based though secret conspiracy against Duncan. Banquo is, after all, ancestor of James I (at least according to this legendary history), and so his hands must be kept scrupulously clean; King James disapproved of all tyrannicides, whatever the circumstances. Macbeth is no longer a just lawgiver. The return of Banquo's ghost to Macbeth's banqueting table is an added scene. Macbeth hears the prophecy about Birnam Wood and Macduff from the Weird Sisters, not, as in Holinshed, from some witch. Lady Macbeth's role is considerably enhanced, and her sleepwalking scene is original. Shakespeare compresses time, as he usually does.

In making some of these alterations, Shakespeare turned to another story in Holinshed's chronicle of Scotland: the murder of King Duff by Donwald. King Duff, never suspecting any treachery in Donwald, often spends time at the castle of Forres, where Donwald is captain of the castle. On one occasion, Donwald's wife, bearing great malice toward the King, shows Donwald (who already bears a grudge against Duff) "the means whereby he might soonest accomplish" the murder. The husband and wife ply Duff's few chamberlains with much to eat and drink. Donwald abhors the act "greatly in heart" but perseveres "through instigation of his wife." Four of Donwald's servants actually commit the murder under his instruction. Next morning, Donwald breaks into the King's chamber and slays the chamberlains, as though believing them guilty. Donwald is so overzealous in his investigation of the murder that many lords begin to suspect him of having done it. For six months afterward, the sun refuses to appear by day and the moon by night.

The chronicle accounts in Holinshed of Malcolm and Edward the Confessor supplied Shakespeare with further details. A more important supplementary source may have been George Buchanan's *Rerum Scoticarum Historia* (1582), a Latin history not translated in Shakespeare's lifetime, presenting a more complex psychological portrait of the protagonist than in Holinshed. Finally, Shakespeare may have used King James I's *Daemonology* (1597), John Studley's early seventeenth-century version of Seneca's *Medea*, Samuel Harsnett's *Declaration of Egregious Popish Impostures* (1603), and accounts of the Scottish witch trials published around 1590.

Timon of Athens

Shakespeare certainly made use of a brief passage from "The Life of Marcus Antonius" in Thomas North's English translation (from the French of Jacques Amyot) of the first-century Greek biographer Plutarch's *Lives of the Noble Grecians and Romans* (1579). This passage is a digression used to illustrate Antonius's embittered withdrawal to an Egyptian island after his defeat at Actium, in which he compares himself to the famous misanthrope of Athens, Timon. As Plutarch reports Timon's story, citing Plato and Aristophanes as his sources, Timon is a hater of mankind because he has been victimized by deception and ingratitude. Timon shuns all company but that of young Alcibiades and occasionally that of Apemantus. When asked by Apemantus why he favors Alcibiades, Timon replies that he knows Alcibiades will some day do great mischief to the Athenians. On another occasion, Timon mounts a public rostrum and invites his Athenian listeners to come hang themselves on a fig tree growing in his yard before he cuts it down (see 5.1.204–11). When Timon dies, he is buried upon the seashore (5.1.213–17). Plutarch transcribes two epitaphs—one by the poet Callimachus and one by Timon himself—both of which appear virtually word for word in Shakespeare's play (5.4.70–3). (Shakespeare probably meant to cancel one, for dramatically they are inconsistent with each other.) Plutarch thus provides Shakespeare not only with several incidents in the life of Timon but also with the link connecting Timon, Alcibiades, and Apemantus. The twenty-eighth novel in William Painter's *The Palace of Pleasure* (1566) retells the events narrated by Plutarch but without adding any new information.

Oddly, Shakespeare seems to have absorbed little from Plutarch's "Life of Alcibiades," though that account does tell how the general leaves Athens in disgrace and sides with Athens's enemies but ultimately relents when he sees that the Athenians are sorry for the injury they have done him. Alcibiades is a handsome young man and is fond of women; his concubine Timandra buries him. Despite these scattered hints, however, Plutarch's "Life of Alcibiades" provides no basis for Shakespeare's plot.

The comedy of Timon by Aristophanes, to which Plutarch alludes, has not survived. Nor has Plato's description. Apparently, these accounts were based on a historical figure of fifth-century Athens, Timon the son of Echecratides. Allusions to him in classical literature are common enough to suggest that his name had become synonymous with misanthropy. The fullest surviving classical record of this tradition is a dialogue by Lucian of Samosata (c. A.D. 125–180) called *Timon, or The Misanthrope*. No English translation was available in Shakespeare's lifetime, but he could have read Lucian in Italian, Latin, or French translation.

The dialogue begins as Timon, impoverished and abandoned by his fair-weather friends, calls upon Zeus to punish such injustice. Zeus hears this diatribe and learns from Hermes the sad tale of Timon's victimization by his ungrateful fellow mortals. Aware that he has been neglectful of this case, Zeus orders Hermes to descend with Plutus (Riches) and restore Timon to prosperity. Although Plutus fears he will be treated improvidently as before, Zeus is insistent. Plutus (personifying Riches) confesses to Hermes, as they descend, how he (i.e., wealth) deceives people. Hermes and Plutus find Timon digging, accompanied by Poverty, Toil, Endurance, and other such allegorical companions. Poverty and his fellows are reluctant to leave Timon, for they know he has been happier with them than in his former days; Timon, too, protests that he wants nothing to do with prosperity. Still, the will of the gods must be obeyed, and Timon discovers treasure where he is digging.

Just as he mordantly predicts, opportunists now seek him out. One is Gnathonides the flatterer, a former recipient of Timon's hospitality who only recently has repaid that kindness by offering Timon a noose. Another, Philiades, once received from Timon a farm as a dowry for his daughters but has spurned Timon in his poverty; now he makes a pretense of offering money, knowing Timon not to be in need. A third petitioner is the orator Demea, whose debt Timon once paid to obtain his release from jail; now, having insulted Timon in his poverty, Demea comes with a fulsome and patently fictitious decree that he has composed in Timon's honor. Fourth is Thrasicles, a hypocritical philosopher who preaches self-denial but drinks to excess and who professes to come now, not for his own benefit, but for those to whom he will gladly distribute Timon's new wealth. Timon drives them off one by one and then resorts to throwing stones at the ever increasing crowd of flatterers. (This parade of villains, and their satirical discomfiture, bear an interesting resemblance to Aristophanes's *The Birds*.)

Many details here are suggestive of Shakespeare's play and are not in Plutarch: Timon's generosity to friends (including the payment of a debt and the providing of a marriage dowry), his friends' ungrateful response when he is in need, the finding of gold in the ground followed by the reappearance of his former friends, the insincere offer of money, the flattering composition in praise of Timon. The personified abstractions are parablelike, as in Shakespeare's play. Yet verbal parallels between Shakespeare and Lucian are tenuous at best. Probably, Shakespeare knew some later version based on Lucian. Renaissance works inspired by Lucian are not hard to find, but none seems to be the direct source for Shakespeare. He is not likely to have known an Italian play called *Timone* by Matteo Maria Boiardo (c. 1487).

More suggestive of Shakespeare's play is an English academic play written at Cambridge (c. 1581–1600, or perhaps c. 1609–1610?) and preserved in the Dyce manuscript. (The editor Alexander Dyce first published this Elizabethan manuscript in 1842.) In this version, Timon's servant Laches warns against the effects of prodigality. When one friend, Eutrapelus, experiences financial trouble, Timon gives him five talents. Laches is driven out by Timon but returns disguised as a soldier to serve his master. At a final banquet, Timon mocks his guests with stones painted to resemble artichokes. When he finds gold, Timon's false mistress shows her readiness to take it. Even a farcical comic subplot reminds us that Shakespeare's *Timon* contains an unrelated and perhaps vestigial Fool scene. Yet this academic play may have been written after Shakespeare's play, though surely not based on it (since *Timon* was not published until 1623 and apparently was never acted), and the likeliest explanation for the similarities is a common source. Perhaps Shakespeare knew and used a play that is now lost.

Apemantus does not have a prominent role in any of the versions here discussed, though he is mentioned in Plutarch. Apemantus bears a resemblance to many satirical railers and crabbed philosophers in Renaissance literature, such as Diogenes in John Lyly's play of *Campaspe* (1584) and Jaques in Shakespeare's *As You Like It*.

Antony and Cleopatra

In writing *Antony* and *Cleopatra*, Shakespeare relied to an unusual extent on his chief source, "The Life of Marcus Antonius" in the first-century Greek biographer Plutarch's *The Lives of the Noble Grecians and Romans* (in an English version by Sir Thomas North, 1579). Perhaps the best-known example in all Shakespeare of his skillful use of source material is in 2.2.201–36, when Enobarbus describes the first meeting of Antony and Cleopatra on the river Cydnus. Putarch reports the event as follows:

She disdained to set forward otherwise but to take her barge in the river of Cydnus, the poop whereof was of gold, the sails of purple, and the oars of silver, which kept stroke in rowing after the sound of the music of flutes, hautboys, citterns, viols, and such other instruments as they played upon in the barge. And now for the person of herself: she was laid under a pavilion of cloth of gold of tissue, appareled and attired like the goddess

Venus, commonly drawn in picture; and hard by her, on either hand of her, pretty fair boys appareled as painters do set forth god Cupid, with little fans in their hands with the which they fanned wind upon her. Her ladies and gentlewomen also, the fairest of them, were appareled like the nymphs Nereides (which are the mermaids of the waters) and like the Graces, some steering the helm, others tending the tackle and ropes of the barge, out of the which there came a wonderful passing sweet savor of perfumes that perfumed the wharf's side, pestered with innumerable multitudes of people. Some of them followed the barge all alongst the river's side; others also ran out of the city to see her coming in. So that in the end, there ran such multitudes of people one after another to see her that Antonius was left post alone in the marketplace, in his imperial seat, to give audience.

Shakespeare retains virtually every detail describing Cleopatra's barge: the poop of gold, the sails of purple, the oars of silver, the flutes, the boys with fans, the gentlewomen like the Nereides, and so on. He borrows phrases and images virtually intact from North, as in the account of Cleopatra's own person. Yet Shakespeare also transforms this scene by putting the description in the mouth of Enobarbus, a largely invented character. Enobarbus's sardonic view derived from military experience, his wry but genuine admiration for Cleopatra, and the prurient curiosity of his Roman listeners—all combine to produce the paradox of cloying appetite and insatiable hunger that helps to define the unforgettable greatness of Cleopatra as a character.

Shakespeare turns to Plutarch for other fabulous stories as well: eight wild boars roasted whole for only twelve guests (2.2.189–90), Cleopatra teasing Antony by causing an old dried salt fish to be placed on his fishing line (2.5.15–18), Menas the pirate suggesting to Pompey that they cut the anchor cable with all their noble guests still aboard (2.7.62–85), Cleopatra's sudden changes from weeping to laughing, and her willingness to be flattered by those who tell her Antony has married Octavia solely out of necessity (3.3), Octavius's tenderness for his sister, the ill-omened nesting of swallows in Cleopatra's sails (4.12.3–4), Antony's disregarding the advice of a valiant captain not to fight at sea (3.7.62–71), Cleopatra's study of swift means of death (5.2.353–6), Antony's jealous reaction to the embassy of the young Thyreus, or Thidias (3.13.86–170), the suicide of Antony's servant Eros (4.14.85–97), Cleopatra's difficulty in lifting Antony up to her tomb or monument (4.15.30–8), his warning that she should trust none but Proculeius (4.15.50), Cleopatra's deception of Caesar through persuading him that she desires to live (5.2.110–90), the countryman with the basket of figs (5.2.233–5), Cleopatra's death "attired and arrayed in her royal robes" attended by Charmian and Iras, and much more.

Despite these extensive and detailed borrowings, Shakespeare is highly innovative in his use of his sources.

He compresses time in order to give a sense of dramatic momentum to the events of many years. He creates vibrant characters like Enobarbus, Charmian, Iras, Mardian, the Soothsayer, Menas, Thidias, Dollabella, and many others for whom the historical sources provide only a sketchy impression or no information at all. In his characterization of the main figures as well, Shakespeare is not content to rely on Plutarch's estimate. To Plutarch, Antony is the tragic victim of infatuation. For all Cleopatra's cultivation and fascination—she knows several languages and rules her country with royal bearing—she is the source of Antony's downfall. Plutarch's attitude is, like Enobarbus's, admiring but ironic. "In the end," he writes, "the horse of the mind, as Plato termeth it, that is so hard of rein (I mean the unreined lust of concupiscence) did put out of Antonius's head all honest and commendable thoughts." This "Roman" view is present in *Antony and Cleopatra*, to be sure, but is counterbalanced by the "Egyptian" view that finds greatness in Antony and Cleopatra's capacity for love. Shakespeare's play sets up a debate among conflicting traditions, as found in various medieval and Renaissance treatments of this famous story. The moralistic perspective condemning vice was popular in medieval texts, such as *De Casibus Virorum Illustrium* and its continuation, John Lydgate's *The Fall of Princes*. The interpretation of Cleopatra as love's martyr was to be found in Geoffrey Chaucer's *The Legend of Good Women*. And, finally, the view of Antony and Cleopatra as heroic protagonists rising above their guilt found expression in several neo-Senecan dramas of the later sixteenth century. Most important for Shakespeare were *The Tragedy of Antony*, translated from Robert Garnier's *Marc Antoine* by Mary Herbert, Countess of Pembroke, in about 1590 (published 1592 and 1595), and *The Tragedy of Cleopatra* by Samuel Daniel (1594), a companion play dealing mainly with the end of Cleopatra's life. Garnier's play had been based on Étienne Jodelle's *Cléopâtre Captive* (1552), the first regular French tragedy. Shakespeare certainly gained from such works as these a sense of tragic greatness in his protagonists. He seems also to have been aware of favorable and unfavorable historical appraisals of Octavius Caesar as both a great ruler and a ruthless and even treacherous politician. One influential work on the more critical side may have been the *Chronicle of the Romans' Wars* by Appian of Alexandria (translated 1578). Virgil's *Aeneid* gave Shakespeare a model for a drama of passion set in the context of Roman history.

Coriolanus

Coriolanus probably represents Shakespeare's last use of the first-century Greek biographer Plutarch's *The Lives of the Noble Grecians and Romans*, as translated by Sir Thomas North (1579) from a French version by Jacques Amyot.

"The Life of Caius Marcius Coriolanus" provided most of the material for Shakespeare's play, just as "The Life of Marcus Antonius" had provided most of the material for *Antony and Cleopatra*. Plutarch's Coriolanus is a man of exceeding nobility but also of excessive impatience and churlish incivility. In war he practices *virtus*, or "valiantness" as North translates it. He wins his title of Coriolanus by storming the city of Corioles (Corioli) almost single-handed. He is the son of a widow whose good opinion he cherishes; as Plutarch reports, "he thought nothing made him so happy and honorable as that his mother might hear everybody praise and commend him, that she might always see him return with a crown upon his head, and that she might still embrace him with tears running down her cheeks for joy." Coriolanus vehemently disapproves of leniency toward the populace, believing it to be an invitation to anarchy. He is, naturally, an enemy of the people's first tribunes, Junius Brutus and Sicinius Velutus, who, in Plutarch's estimation, "had only been the causers and procurers of this sedition."

Plutarch informs us that, when Coriolanus stands for consul and follows the custom of appearing in the marketplace clad only in a poor gown, the people remember his martial prowess; on the day of the election itself, however, they recall their old hate of him and refuse his candidacy. Coriolanus, in his typically choleric and intemperate fashion, makes no attempt to conceal his outrage at this insult. (Plutarch comments editorially on his behavior as "the fruits of self-will and obstinacy.") When he is banished, Coriolanus goes in disguise to Antium, to the house of Tullus Aufidius, his great rival, knowing perfectly well that "Tullus did more malice and envy him than he did all the Romans besides." Coriolanus and Tullus have long been admiring rivals: "they were ever at the encounter one against another, like lusty courageous youths striving in all emulation of honor, and had encountered many times together." Returning vengefully to Rome, Coriolanus is "determined at the first to persist in his obstinate and inflexible rancor," but finally relents through "natural affection," and receives his wife and mother. Volumnia's oration to him, reported in full by Plutarch, causes Coriolanus to cry out: "you have won a happy victory for your country, but mortal and unhappy for your son."

Shakespeare's changes simultaneously enhance the haughtiness of Coriolanus and the volatility of the commoners, thereby increasing the distance between the two sides. Shakespeare's Coriolanus is revolted by the custom of wearing a robe and showing his wounds to the people, and shows his contempt more snarlingly than in Plutarch's *Lives*. He is, unlike Plutarch's protagonist, reluctant to seek office and has to be persuaded to it by his mother and friends. Shakespeare minimizes the legitimate griefs of the Roman people—Plutarch makes it plain that the Senate does favor the rich and that the people are oppressed by usurers—and accentuates their political instability. Shakespeare shows them as being manipulated against Coriolanus by the scheming tribunes, whereas in Plutarch the people make up their own minds to oppose Coriolanus for the consulship. Shakespeare also magnifies the roles of Volumnia and of Menenius. Volumnia, though she is mentioned by Plutarch, takes no active part in the story until Coriolanus attacks Rome; Menenius's chief function in Plutarch is to relate the fable of the belly. Shakespeare compresses and rearranges events as he usually does: for example, in Plutarch the people actually leave Rome to demonstrate their grievances and agree to return only when granted the election of tribunes to represent their interests, whereas in Shakespeare the tribunes have already been elected when the play begins. In Shakespeare, Coriolanus is banished as the result of a dispute over his consulship, not (as in Plutarch) as the result of an insurrection over scarcity of grain.

Shakespeare probably also knew the story of Coriolanus in another classical source, Livy's *Roman History*, Book 2, as translated by Philemon Holland (1600). Other versions of the story were available to him, including an outline of Roman history by L. Annaeus Florus (also called Publius Annius Florus), written in the second century A.D., based chiefly on Livy. Plutarch, however, seems to have provided Shakespeare with virtually everything he needed. Even Shakespeare's alterations of Plutarch tend to enhance rather than revise Plutarch's overall thesis and appraisal of the characters in his history.

Pericles

This play, at least partly by Shakespeare, is based on the ancient Greek romance of Apollonius of Tyre. Shakespeare had used the story once before, in *The Comedy of Errors*. Medieval versions of this enduringly popular legend include the ninth-century Latin *Historia Apollonii Regis Tyri*, Godfrey of Viterbo's *Pantheon* (c. 1186), the *Gesta Romanorum* (a collection of ancient tales in Latin), John Gower's *Confessio Amantis* (c. 1383–1393), and an English chronicle of *Appolyn of Thyre* translated for the printer Wynkyn de Worde by Robert Copland from a French source (1510). Shakespeare, and perhaps a collaborator or the author of a lost earlier dramatic version, were chiefly indebted to Gower's *Confessio* and to Laurence Twine's *The Pattern of Painful Adventures*, a prose version registered in 1576 but existing today only in two editions from about 1594–1595 and 1607.

The order of events in Twine is much the same as in the play: the hero Apollonius's difficulty with the incestuous King Antiochus, his relieving of the city of Tharsus, his shipwreck at Pentapolis and his falling in love with the King's daughter Lucina (Thaisa in the play), her child-bearing and apparent death at sea, the discovery of her floating casket at Ephesus, her revival by the physician Cerimon and her retirement to the Temple of Diana in Ephesus, her daughter Tharsia's (i.e., Marina's) capture by pirates and enslavement in a brothel, her conversion of Athanagoras (Lysimachus), the Governor of Machilenta (Mytilene), and Apollonius's eventual reunion with his daughter and wife. Gower's account, too, is much the same, with slightly different forms of the proper names: Appolinus's (Apollonius's) wife is referred to as the King's daughter, Appolinus's daughter is Thaise, the man she marries is Atenagoras (or Athenagoras) of Mytilene, and so on.

Other than changing some proper names, including that of the hero, Shakespeare did not introduce many significant alterations. To be sure, Shakespeare has given a more sordid impression of the brothel in which Marina must dwell, and has dignified the character of Lysimachus so as to render him worthy of marrying Marina. In Twine's prose account, Athanagoras actually tries to buy Tharsia from the pirates at an auction; when he is outbid by a bawd, he resolves to be the first to visit Tharsia in her new residence. Shakespeare has provided a more decorous action for Lysimachus, although traces of the older and more licentious character occasionally show through and create the impression of inconsistency. For the most part, however, Shakespeare's play stays unusually close to the episodic narrative structure of his sources.

The relationship of George Wilkins's *The Painful Adventures of Pericles, Prince of Tyre* (1608) to Shakespeare's play is complex and uncertain. Beyond doubt, Wilkins's prose account is based in part on a *Pericles* play; Wilkins acknowledges in his Argument that this same story has been recently presented "by the King's Majesty's Players." The play he used may, however, not have been the *Pericles* we know from the corrupt 1609 Quarto. Parts of Wilkins's narrative are very close to the earlier *Pattern of Painful Adventures* by Twine. Kenneth Muir suggests (*Shakespeare's Sources*, 1957) that because Wilkins's novel is closer to the first two acts of Shakespeare's play than to the last three acts, Wilkins may have been using an older play that Shakespeare then revised, substantially rewriting the last three acts but changing little in the first two. Whether the presumed *Ur-Pericles* might have been Wilkins's own play is a matter of conjecture. The very existence of an *Ur-Pericles* is by no means universally accepted but cannot be ruled out as a possibility.

Cymbeline

Cymbeline mingles legendary history with elements of romance. Traces of historical events lie dimly behind the narrative, but only insofar as they are incorporated in a much larger legendary purpose. A Cunobelinus, or Cymbeline, was leader of the Celtic chieftains in southeast England during the period of Roman hegemony there, following Julius Caesar's invasion of the island in 54 B.C. Cunobelinus ruled from about 5 to 40 A.D., with his capital at Camulodunum (Colchester). He was a friend and ally of Augustus Caesar and enjoyed a peaceful reign. When the Kingdom had passed to his sons (one of whom apparently was Caractacus), the Romans under Claudius pursued once again their conquest of England and subdued much of the southeast, though Caractacus escaped to Wales and became a leader of the resistance.

Beginning with Geoffrey of Monmouth's *Historia Regum Britanniae* (c. 1136), King Kymbelinus becomes a quasi-legendary figure. Geoffrey adds him to the genealogy of Kings (along with Leir, Locrine, etc.) descended from Aeneas's great-grandson Brut, the mythical founder of Britain. Kymbelinus's reign was peaceful, according to Geoffrey, since the King, having been raised in Augustus Caesar's household, willingly paid tribute to Rome without being asked. When Kymbelinus's elder son Guiderius succeeded to the throne, however, said Geoffrey, he defied the Emperor Claudius over the tribute. Guiderius fell in battle and was succeeded by his brother Arviragus, who more than held his own against Claudius, eventually settling matters by negotiation.

By the time of Raphael Holinshed's *Chronicles* (1587 edition), history is scarcely distinguishable from legend. Holinshed admits he cannot be sure whether Kymbeline or some other British leader fought against Augustus Caesar, or whether Kymbeline paid tribute; he does report that Guiderius fought Augustus Caesar (rather than Claudius) but is uncertain as to whether the Romans lost or won. Edmund Spenser's *The Faerie Queene* (2.10.50–1) affirms that Kimbeline fought the Romans over tribute and was slain in battle, whereupon his brother Arviragus took his place and compelled the Roman Claudius to a peace. (In other words, Spenser has conflated Cymbeline and Guiderius.) Shakespeare, like Spenser, imagines the great struggle with Rome and subsequent peace settlement to have taken place during Cymbeline's reign; following Holinshed, he assumes that Rome was then governed by Augustus Caesar. Shakespeare also seems to have consulted a vivid account of the battle in Thomas Blenerhasset's contribution to *The Second Part of the Mirror for Magistrates* (1578) and another account of Cymbeline's reign by John Higgins in the 1587 *Mirror for Magistrates*. Finally, Shakespeare turned for his background material to quite a different story in Holinshed, concerning a Scottish farmer named Hay who with his two sons helped defend Scotland against the Danes in 976. Shakespeare presumably found this story when reading for *Macbeth*, since it stands between the two accounts—Donwald's murder of Duff and Macbeth's murder of Duncan—that Shakespeare used in writing *Macbeth*. The exploits of Hay and his two sons resemble those of Belarius and the two princes in the final battle of *Cymbeline*.

The quasi-historical setting accounts for only a small part of *Cymbeline*, and Shakespeare had no special reason to regard the story of Cymbeline as historically "true." Most of his material is, after all, romantic. The central plot of a wager over a wife's virtue may have come from Giovanni Boccaccio's *Decameron*, Day 2, Story 9, although as a type this ancient story was widespread and presumably available to Shakespeare in many forms. Earlier versions include the thirteenth-century French *Roi Flore et la belle Jeanne*, the *Roman de la Violette* by Gerbert de Montreuil, a miracle play by Gautier de Coincy, and others. Boccaccio was available to Shakespeare in French translation but not in English.

A summary of Boccaccio's story suggests a number of particulars to which Shakespeare was indebted. Boccaccio tells of an Italian merchant, Bernabò of Genoa, who, at a gathering in Paris of fellow merchants discussing the wantonness of their wives, dares to affirm the absolute chastity of his own wife, Zinevra. A young merchant, Ambrogiuolo, makes a wager that he can seduce Zinevra and return with proof in three months. Going at once to Genoa, Ambrogiuolo discovers that Zinevra is indeed incorruptible. He therefore bribes an elderly lady, whom Zinevra has befriended, to convey him hidden in a chest to the lady's bedroom. When the lady is asleep, he steals forth from hiding, memorizes details of her room, notes particularly a mole upon her left breast, and takes with him a purse, gown, ring, and sash. Returning to Paris, he convinces his fellow merchants and Bernabò that he has succeeded. Bernabò hereupon travels to within a few miles of Genoa, summons his wife, and secretly orders his servant to kill her on the way. The servant is reluctant to do so, however, and gladly takes only her cloak as evidence of having finished the job. Zinevra now makes her way disguised as a man to Alexandria and enters the service of the Sultan. One day she happens to recognize her own purse and girdle in a Venetian clothes shop in Palestine, inquires as to their owner, meets Ambrogiuolo in this way (who has journeyed to Palestine selling merchandise), and hears from Ambrogiuolo's own boastful lips the story of his treachery. She cannily manages to bring Ambrogiuolo and Bernabò before the Sultan, throws off her male disguise, and reveals the whole story. She pardons Bernabò and is reunited with him, but Ambrogiuolo is sentenced by the Sultan to be tied to a stake, smeared with honey, and left to be devoured by insects.

Shakespeare has altered the setting and has surrounded the story with other matters, such as King Cymbeline's lost sons, his quarrel with Rome, his difficulties with his Queen and her son, Cloten, and the like. Shakespeare's ending is much more forgiving toward Iachimo than in the narrative source. The circumstances of the denouement are changed. Still, the plot of Posthumus, Imogen, and Iachimo is extensively indebted to Boccaccio.

Shakespeare seems also to have known an English version, *Frederyke of Jennen* (Antwerp, 1518; London, 1520 and 1560), translated from the Dutch. In some details, it is closer to Shakespeare's play than is Boccaccio's story. For example, the merchants who witness the wager include a Spaniard, a Frenchman, a Florentine, and a Genoese (compare 1.4). Three of these merchants are not present when the villain returns to prove his victory, just as in 2.4 of Shakespeare's play. Also, the husband repents even before learning of his wife's innocence, as does Posthumus. Shakespeare greatly accentuates this motif of penance and forgiveness. Another source is a romantic play called *The Rare Triumphs of Love and Fortune*, acted before Queen Elizabeth in 1582, in which the princess Fidelia is banished by her father for falling in love, is betrayed and pursued by her boorish brother Armenio (compare Cloten), and is hospitably received by a banished courtier named Bomelio who lives hermitlike in a cave. "Fidele" is the name used by Shakespeare's Imogen to disguise her identity. Folk motifs are apparent throughout *Cymbeline*; the cruel Queen inevitably reminds us of Snow White's stepmother. Although Shakespeare may not have been acquainted with that particular story, he clearly was interested in folk legend when he wrote *Cymbeline*. One other anonymous romantic play, *Sir Clyomon and Sir Clamydes* (c. 1570–1583), may have given Shakespeare some suggestions for his Welsh scenes.

Francis Beaumont and John Fletcher's *Philaster* was written about the same time as *Cymbeline* and seems to bear a significant resemblance to Shakespeare's play. Philaster is, like Posthumus, in love with a princess whose father intends her for another suitor. Many of the similarities can be attributed to the conventions of the romance genre just then coming into vogue, and no one can be sure whether Shakespeare's play came after or before *Philaster*. If *Cymbeline* is the later of the two, however, *Philaster* must be considered as a source.

The Winter's Tale

Shakespeare based *The Winter's Tale* on Robert Greene's romantic novella called *Pandosto: The Triumph of Time* (1588), or *The History of Dorastus and Fawnia* in its running title. Shakespeare changes the names, reverses the two Kingdoms of Sicilia and Bohemia, and alters the unhappy ending that afflicts King Pandosto and Queen Bellaria of Bohemia (Leontes and Hermione of Sicilia). Otherwise, the narrative outline remains intact. The story begins with the state visit of King Egistus of Sicilia (Polixenes of Bohemia) to his boyhood companion, King Pandosto of Bohemia. Queen Bellaria entertains their guest with such warmth, "oftentimes coming herself into his bedchamber to see that nothing should be amiss to mislike him," that Pandosto grows jealous. He commands his cupbearer Franion (Camillo) to murder Egistus, and the latter seems to agree but instead warns his victim to flee with him. Their hasty departure appears to confirm Pandosto's worst suspicions. He sends the guard to arrest Bellaria as she plays with her young son Garinter (Mamillius). When the Queen gives birth to a daughter in prison, the King orders the child destroyed, but he relents upon the insistence of his courtiers and causes the infant to be set adrift in a small boat. The Queen nobly defends herself at her trial (in language that Shakespeare has copied in some detail). She herself requests that the oracle at Delphos be consulted. The oracle replies in words that Shakespeare has altered only slightly: "Bellaria is chaste, Egistus blameless, Franion a true subject, Pandosto treacherous, his babe an innocent; and the King shall live without an heir if that which is lost be not found." Pandosto is immediately stricken with remorse, and, when Queen Bellaria collapses at the news of her son Garinter's death, she is truly and irrecoverably dead.

A similarly close parallel in the narrative, along with telling changes in a number of details, characterizes the story's second half. The babe is conveyed by a tempest to the coast of Sicilia and is discovered by an impoverished shepherd named Porrus. He and his wife Mopsa adopt the child, naming her Fawnia. By the age of sixteen, Fawnia's natural beauty rivals that of the goddess Flora. At a meeting of the farmers' daughters of Sicilia, where she is chosen mistress of the feast, Fawnia is seen by the King's son Dorastus on his way home from hawking. She counters his importunate suit with the argument that she is too lowly a match for him, but he replies that the gods themselves sometimes take earthly lovers. Her foster father, distressed by the Prince's repeated visits (though he comes in shepherd's costume), resolves to carry the jewels he found with Fawnia to the King and reveal her story, thereby escaping blame for the goings-on. Dorastus escapes with Fawnia to a ship, aided by his servant Capnio (compare Camillo). Capnio also fulfills a role given by Shakespeare to Autolycus, for he manages to trick the shepherd Porrus into thinking he can see the King if he comes aboard Dorastus's ship. A storm drives these voyagers to Bohemia where, because of the ancient enmity between Egistus and Pandosto, they disguise themselves. Pandosto, happening to hear of Fawnia's beauty, orders her and the others to be arrested as spies and summoned to court, whereupon he falls incestuously in love with the disguised Fawnia. He promises to free the young man (who has taken the name of Meleagrus to conceal his identity) only if he will relinquish his claim to Fawnia. King Egistus meanwhile has discovered his son's whereabouts and sends ambassadors to Bohemia demanding the return of Dorastus and the execution of Fawnia, Capnio, and Porrus. Pandosto, his love for Fawnia having turned to hate, is about to comply when Porrus reveals the circumstances of Fawnia's infancy. Overjoyed to rediscover his daughter, Pandosto permits her to marry Dorastus but then falls into a melancholy fit and commits suicide.

Shakespeare has almost entirely created some characters, such as Paulina, Antigonus, the clownish shepherd's son, and Autolycus, though Capnio does perform one of Autolycus's functions by inveigling the old shepherd aboard ship. Antigonus's journey to the seacoast of Bohemia with the infant Perdita and his fatal exit *"pursued by a bear"* are Shakespearean additions. The character of Time is also added, and the shift in tone from tragedy to tragicomedy averts the catastrophe in Greene's novella (in which Pandosto commits suicide). The shepherdesses at the sheepshearing are Shakespearean. The old shepherd has a more substantial and comic role; Camillo is a stronger person than Capnio. Greene's Mopsa, the shrewish wife of old Porrus, disappears from the play. Shakespeare omits the incestuous love of Pandosto for his daughter and brings Hermione back to life. (For this motif of a statue made to breathe, he may well have recalled Ovid's account of Pygmalion in Ovid's *Metamorphoses*, Book 10.) Shakespeare's Leontes is more irrationally jealous than in Greene's account. Leontes's purgative sorrow is more intense and also more restorative than in the source; he is a truly noble and tragicomic figure, the center of a play about forgiveness and renewal.

Shakespeare may also have known Francis Sabie's *The Fisherman's Tale* (1595) and its continuation, *Flora's Fortune* (1595). From Greene's pamphlets, describing in vividly colloquial detail the life of London's underworld, Shakespeare probably derived many of Autolycus's tricks.

The Tempest

No direct literary source for the whole of *The Tempest* has been found. Shakespeare does seem to have drawn material from various accounts of the shipwreck of the *Sea Venture* in the Bermudas, in 1609, although the importance of these materials should not be overstated. Several of the survivors wrote narratives of the shipwreck itself and of their life on the islands for some nine months. Sylvester Jourdain, in *A Discovery of the Bermudas*, published 1610, speaks of miraculous preservation despite the island's reputation for being "a most prodigious and enchanted place." William Strachey's letter, written in July of 1610 and published much later (1625) as *A True Reportory of the*

Wreck and Redemption . . . from the Islands of the Bermudas, describes the panic among the passengers and crew, the much feared reputation of the island as the habitation of devils and wicked spirits, the actual beauty and fertility of the place with its abundance of wild life (compare Caliban's descriptions), and the treachery of the Indians they later encounter in Virginia. Shakespeare seems to have read Strachey's letter in manuscript and may have been acquainted with him. The storm scene in Chapter 4 of Laurence Twine's *The Pattern of Painful Adventures*, a major source for *Pericles*, may also have given Shakespeare material for the first scene of *The Tempest*. Shakespeare also kept up with travel accounts of Sir Walter Ralegh and Thomas Harriot, and knew various classical evocations of a New World. The name "Setebos" came from Richard Eden's *History of Travel* (1577), translated from Peter Martyr's *De Novo Orbe* and from other travel accounts of the period. (See the Introduction to *The Tempest* for the potential relevance of various journals of the circumnavigation of the globe.) All these hints are indeed suggestive, but they are scattered and relate more to the setting and general circumstance of Shakespeare's play than to the plot.

Shakespeare certainly consulted Michel de Montaigne's essay "Of the Cannibals," as translated by John Florio in 1603. Gonzalo's reverie on an ideal commonwealth (2.1.150–71) contains many verbal echoes of the essay. Montaigne's point is that supposedly civilized men who condemn as barbarous any society not conforming with their own are simply refusing to examine their own shortcomings. A supposedly primitive society may well embody perfect religion, justice, and harmony; civilized art can never rival the achievements of nature. The ideal commonwealth has no need of magistrates, riches, poverty, and contracts, all of which breed dissimulation and covetousness. The significance of these ideas for *The Tempest* extends well beyond the particular passage in which they are found. And Caliban himself, whose name is an anagram of "cannibal," illustrates (even though he is not an eater of human flesh) the truth of Montaigne's observation apropos of the intense and wanton cruelty he finds so widespread in so-called Western civilization: "I think there is more barbarism in eating men alive than to feed upon them being dead."

Prospero's famous valedictory speech to "Ye elves of hills, brooks, standing lakes, and groves" (5.1.33–57) owes its origin to Medea's similar invocation in Ovid's *Metamorphoses* (Book 7), which Shakespeare knew both in the Latin original and in Golding's translation: "Ye airs and winds, ye elves of hills, of brooks, of woods alone, / Of standing lakes . . . " Medea also anticipates Shakespeare's Sycorax. Medea thus provides material for the representation of both black and white magic in *The Tempest*, so carefully differentiated by Shakespeare. Ariel is part English fairy, like Puck, and part daemon. The pastoral situation in *The Tempest* is perhaps derived from Edmund Spenser's *The Faerie Queene*, Book 6 (with its distinctions between savage lust and true courtesy, between nature and art). Italian pastoral drama as practiced by Guarini and (in England) by John Fletcher may also have been an influence. The masque element in *The Tempest*, prominent as in much late Shakespeare, bears the imprint of the courtly masque tradition of Ben Jonson, Francis Beaumont, and John Fletcher. Virgil's *Aeneid* may have provided Shakespeare with a more indirect source, with its story of wandering in the Mediterranean and storm at sea, love in Carthage, the intervention of the gods, and the fulfillment of destiny in Italy. Donna Hamilton (*Virgil and "The Tempest,"* 1990) contends that Shakespeare "imitated" Virgil so as to argue for a politics of retrenchment.

A German play, *Die Schöne Sidea* by Jacob Ayrer, written before 1605, was once thought to have been based on an earlier version of *The Tempest* as performed by English players traveling in Germany. Today, the similarities between the two plays are generally attributed to conventions found everywhere in romance.

The Two Noble Kinsmen

For their chief source, John Fletcher and William Shakespeare turned to "The Knight's Tale" in Chaucer's *Canterbury Tales*. "Chaucer, of all admired, the story gives," the Prologue tells us (line 13). In general, the dramatists follow their source for their main plot, especially in the middle acts.

"The Knight's Tale" relates how Duke Theseus, "lord and governour" of Athens, conquers the reign of "Femenye" and leads home Queen Ipolita to be his wife in "greet solempnitee," bringing with them Ipolita's younger sister Emelye. Their approach to Athens is interrupted by the petitions of widowed Queens whose royal husbands have been slain at Thebes by the tyrant Creon. Complaining that their husbands' bodies have been desecrated, they implore Theseus to avenge the outrage. The Duke, filled with pity and anger, marches to battle forthwith and slays Creon, restoring to the widows the bones of their dead husbands.

On the field of battle are discovered two wounded cousins, Palamon and Arcite, nephews of the dead Creon. Taken back to Athens as prisoners for whom Theseus will accept no ransom, they languish in prison for some years, until it happens one May morning that they see Emelye from their prison tower as she gathers flowers. Palamon sees her first and is immediately stricken with love; Arcite, inquiring into his cousin's distress, soon follows his example. Despite their being sworn friends, they quarrel over her.

Arcite, it turns out, is a long-time acquaintance of The-seus's dearest friend, Perotheus, who many years ago made a dangerous journey to hell with Theseus. At Perotheus's behest, Arcite is freed but is also banished from Athens on pain of death. This condition of being separated from Emelye is a torment to him. The still-imprisoned Palamon is no less inconsolable, fearing that Arcite will assemble an army to attack Athens and thus gain his advantage with Emelye. The narrator asks: Which lover is in a worse plight?

After a year or two of this misery, Arcite, in Thebes, is visited by the god Mercury in a dream, bidding him return to Athens. He does so in disguise, and manages to obtain the office of chamberlain in Emelye's dwelling, where he remains "A yeer or two" as "Page of the chambre of Emelye the brighte." Theseus appoints the admirable young man as squire of his chamber as well. Three more years pass in this happy circumstance. Palamon meantime has been in his dark and horrible prison for seven years. At length, with the help of "a freend," he manages to break prison and flee Athens, hiding in a grove of trees until he can make his way to Thebes and obtain armed assistance in winning Emelye as his wife.

One May morning, out hunting with Theseus, Arcite happens upon Palamon's grove and encounters his furi-ous cousin. Arcite agrees to bring arms and armor so that they can fight it out over Emelye. Their subsequent match is interrupted by Theseus, who objects that they may not fight thus "With-outen juge or other officere." Revealing their identities, the two cousins confess that they have incurred Theseus's just wrath. When the Duke condemns both to death, however, Ipolyta and Emelye intervene for mercy's sake until he relents. Theseus decrees that the cousins are to contend for Emelye, each with a hundred knights, in the lists, some fifty weeks hence. The cousins each repair to Thebes to prepare for the event.

The lists are set up in grand fashion, with three altars: for Venus, goddess of love, to the east; for Mars, god of war, to the west; and for Diana, goddess of chastity, to the north. Each altar is elaborately decorated with sym-bolic paintings, statuary, and the like. The contenders arrive with their supporting kings, who are presented to the reader in elaborate detail. The fateful day com-mences with prayers offered by the protagonists to their respective patron-gods: Palamon to Venus, Emelye to Diana, and Arcite to Mars. Each petitioner is answered with enigmatic but seemingly hopeful signs: Palamon is to have his love, Emelye is to have (though not the life of virginal purity she most wishes) the suitor who loves her most, and Arcite is to have the victory. Saturn will oversee the way in which these seemingly conflicting demands among mortals and gods alike can be amica-bly resolved.

All is fulfilled as destined. When Palamon falls in the lists, Theseus awards Emelye to Arcite—much to the dis-tress of Venus, who complains to Saturn, only to be told to await the final end. Sure enough, an infernal fury, sent by Pluto at the behest of Saturn, causes Arcite's steed to shy and buck, throwing Arcite head-first to the ground. Dying, Arcite bestows Emelye on his dear cousin. The-seus orders an elaborate funeral for Arcite. After a deco-rous interval of some years, the Duke decrees an end to mourning so that the marriage of Palamon and Emelye can take place. They live happily ever afterward, with never a word of jealousy or other vexation.

The playwrights' alterations of this tale are revealing, especially in Shakespeare's contributions in the first and fifth act. Theseus's friend Pirithous plays a larger role at first than in Chaucer, giving Shakespeare opportunity to develop the motif of friendship in various guises. Emil-ia's loving remembrance of her dearest childhood friend is newly provided, for much the same thematic purpose. The extensive philosophical debate between Palamon and Arcite about the corruptions of Theban civic life and their need for stoical withdrawal is not even hinted at in Chaucer. In the play's last act, Shakespeare substitutes for Chaucer's rich description of the tournament a report of off-stage combat, so that the focus is on Emilia and her emotional response to the news of changing fortunes in the battle. Saturn's role is eliminated in the play; the one mention of his name (5.4.62) is an indirect reminder that he no longer controls the action. The fury that Saturn sends via Pluto to goad Arcite's horse becomes, in Shake-speare's account, a "fire malevolent" or "fierce sulfur," of hellish origin only in a metaphorical sense. Venus's direct intervention on behalf of Palamon forms no part of Shakespeare's dramatized account. The gods are still invoked as presiding deities over a destiny that humans cannot predict, but with a far less immediate role for the Olympians.

Time passes in Chaucer in narrative fashion over a succession of years. The playwrights are understandably more interested in a dramatic compression of events. Arcite's release from prison at Perotheus's (Pirithous's) behest is more carefully explained in Chaucer as the result of an old friendship. The appearance to Arcite of Mercury in a dream, urging him to return to Athens, has no counterpart in the play; throughout, actions of this sort are apt to be motivated more by human feeling than by divine ordinance. Palamon's escape from prison is accomplished with the help of a friend; it is at this point that the playwrights, especially Fletcher, devise a subplot of the infatuated Jailer's Daughter to assist in the escape.

Chaucer's interest is in chivalric pageantry and in the soliloquies of his protagonists, as they ponder the seem-ing cruelties of their fates. Chaucer focuses a good deal on Duke Theseus, as we might expect from a tale told by a knight in defense of knightly ideals. Theseus is a mighty warrior, a defender of the innocent, and an equitable judge. Chaucer seemingly does not hold it against Theseus that he condemns Arcite and Palamon to death for their crimes of disobedience, and in any case he listens mercifully to his petitioners. Theseus presides over a courtly world in which the god of love is mighty and that those who fall under love's spell, gods and humans alike, are likely to act with noble foolishness. The play's serious thematic treatment of friendship seems a conscious choice on the part of the dramatists, especially Shakespeare.

Occasional verbal echoes attest to the playwrights' direct acquaintance with "The Knight's Tale," perhaps in Thomas Speght's edition first published in 1598 and enlarged in 1602. They may also have known Chaucer's source, the *Teseida* of Boccaccio, in which that author undertook to acclimatize the Roman epic (especially Virgil's *Aeneid* and Statius's *Thebiad*) to Renaissance themes. Shakespeare made use of Sir Thomas North's translation of Plutarch's "Life of Theseus" for the friendship of Theseus and Pirithous. Shakespeare's own earlier *A Midsummer Night's Dream* afforded the playwrights a portrait of Duke Theseus as he sets about to marry Hippolyta and to adjudicate amorous conflicts among the courtiers.

The plot of the Jailer's Daughter is apparently an invention, albeit with generous infusions from earlier models in the depiction of the Daughter's madness, especially from the mad songs of Ophelia in *Hamlet*. The treatment of the Daughter's mental and emotional illness by a doctor in 4.3 (see especially lines 59–61) has some affinities to Lady Macbeth's plight; see *Macbeth*, 5.1 and 5.3.47–8. The Daughter's pathetic situation also recalls some earlier work of Fletcher, as for example *The Coxcomb* (c. 1609); the story is similar, too, to that of Mopsa in Book 4 of Philip Sidney's *Arcadia* (first printed in 1593).

Other elements of comic subplot material in *The Two Noble Kinsmen* borrow freely from Shakespeare's earlier plays and other materials. When Palamon returns to Athens and is helped by some countrymen to learn about the games in which he can compete (2.3 and 2.5), the story is close to that of Pericles's being assisted by some fishermen when he is washed ashore at Pentapolis (2.1). Fletcher's pedantic schoolmaster in 3.5 reminds us of Holofernes in *Love's Labor's Lost*, who, like Fletcher's Gerald, helps put on a ridiculous entertainment for royalty. *A Midsummer Night's Dream* presents a similar pageant devised by clownish countrymen, with a burgomask dance not unlike the antimasque of twelve dancers in *The Two Noble Kinsmen*. Shakespeare and Fletcher took this antimasque, featuring a clown, a baboon, etc., and pedant as usher, from an antimasque devised for Francis Beaumont's *Masque of the Inner Temple*. Philip Sidney's entertainment, "The Lady of May," provides still another model for this buffoonish entertainment.

Two earlier plays on the subject of Palamon and Arcite have not survived. The first (in two parts) was written and staged in 1566 by Richard Edwards, whose surviving play about friendship, *Damon and Pythias* (c. 1560–1565), gives us some indication of the importance of friendship in Renaissance discourse. Castiglione's *The Courtier* and Sidney's *Arcadia* are but two of many models here. A second lost play about Palamon and Arcite was staged by the Admiral's men in 1594, and a lost play about Damon and Pythias by Henry Chettle was acted by the same company in 1600.

Venus and Adonis

Venus and Adonis was Shakespeare's contribution to the vogue of Ovidian and erotic poetry in the 1580s and 1590s that included Thomas Lodge's *Scilla's Metamorphosis* (1589), Michael Drayton's *Endimion and Phoebe* (published 1595), Christopher Marlowe's *Hero and Leander* (registered 1593), and John Marston's *Metamorphosis of Pygmalion's Image* (1598). On Shakespeare's combining of three passages from Ovid's *Metamorphoses*, see the Introduction to *Venus and Adonis*. A disdainful Adonis had evidently become a commonplace in the 1590s, for it appears in *Hero and Leander*, lines 12–14, Edmund Spenser's *Faerie Queene*, 3.1.35, and elsewhere.

The Rape of Lucrece

Shakespeare's chief source for *The Rape of Lucrece* was Ovid's *Fasti* (2, 721–852), which had not yet been translated into English. He also seems to have known Livy's *History of Rome* (1, 57–9), which had been translated by William Painter in his *The Palace of Pleasure* (1566), and Chaucer's *The Legend of Good Women* (which is, like Shakespeare's poem, indebted to Ovid and Livy). Shakespeare's version is considerably longer than any of these sources. Ovid, Livy, and Chaucer give narrative, swift-moving accounts; Shakespeare follows, instead, the literary tradition of the "Complaint," as in *A Mirror for Magistrates* and in Samuel Daniel's *The Complaint of Rosamond*.

The Phoenix and Turtle

"The Phoenix and Turtle" is sometimes related to Chaucer's *The Parlement of Fowles*, an allegorical treatment of an assembly of birds. No indebtedness can be proved, however. Instead, as F. T. Price has shown in his Arden edition of *The Poems*, Shakespeare's chief "source" was the very anthology to which he contributed this remarkable piece. Called *Love's Martyr*, assembled by one Robert Chester, it contains some execrable verse but was built around a single vivid and intriguing emblem: the union in death of two mythic birds expressing a love beyond human reason. The idea was sufficiently compelling to attract not only Shakespeare but Jonson, Chapman, and Marston. The cooperation of these highly sophisticated writers may have been prompted by some kind of private *jeu d'esprit*, but Shakespeare's venture into fantasy produced extraordinary results.

A Lover's Complaint

This poem resembles other complaints of forsaken women, as in Ovid's *Amores* and Chaucer's *Legend of Good Women*, but no specific source is known.

The Sonnets

See the Introduction to *The Sonnets* for a discussion of the sonnet vogue in England of the 1590s, and the previous history of the sonnet in England and on the Continent.

Appendix 3

Shakespeare in Performance

Lois Potter, University of Delaware

Although we know a good deal about the conditions of performance at the time Shakespeare's plays were first produced, much of this information (summarized in the Introduction, pp. xliv–xlvii) raises as many questions as it answers. We know, for example, that Shakespeare wrote most of his plays for the Lord Chamberlain's men, first formed in 1594 after a period of plague and theater closures, and that the company (officially servants of the courtier whose duties included supervising court entertainments) was honored with the title of the King's men at the accession of James I. Elizabethan acting companies were all male, with boys or young men playing women's roles, but we know almost nothing about how they acted, or who played which parts. We know that the stages of the public, partially roofed playhouses jutted into the yard where the audience stood on three sides, looking up at the actors; the rest of the spectators sat in covered galleries looking down on them. But we are not sure whether the gallery above the stage, pictured in the contemporary illustration of the Swan Theatre interior shown on page xlvi, was meant for musicians, spectators, or both. (And of course we do not know how much the Globe's interior resembled the Swan's.) If, as appears from the illustrations of theater interiors on pages xlvi and lxiv, some spectators normally watched the action from behind the stage, the actors would have had to move a great deal during a scene, as in modern theater-in-the-round productions, to make sure that they were visible and audible to all parts of their audience.

However much information we have, we still cannot know if aspects of the theater that were common then but unusual in our eyes were taken for granted by the spectators who watched the plays in the reigns of Elizabeth and James I. Did they think of the boy actresses as boys or believe in them as women? Those who had traveled to France and Italy would have known that women played women's parts in those countries and were often as famous as the male actors. What was the acting style for love scenes between a man and a cross-dressed boy, and what was the range of responses to it? The players in the open theaters performed by day (normally beginning at 2 P.M.), but used torches and candles to indicate when the action was supposed to be taking place at night. Did audiences find it difficult to accept a convention by which actors, fully visible to the audience, declare that they are unable to see anything? There is probably no single answer. It is likely that then, as always, audience members differed in the extent to which they preferred to believe in the performance or feel superior to it.

To the audiences of Shakespeare's time, the theaters were sumptuous and impressive buildings. Their wooden interiors were painted to look like marble, and the ceiling of the Globe was apparently decorated with the signs of the zodiac (perhaps, when Hamlet and Othello addressed the heavens, they looked at both a real and an artificial sky). Visitors from abroad were taken to see plays; actors traveled with them as far as Prague; versions of them were being translated into German as early as 1618. All this indicates how much English plays and players were respected. By about 1597, the company for which Shakespeare wrote was the one most frequently invited to perform at court, evidence that it was considered the best in London.

The theater in fact offered a great deal of visual and musical pleasure even for those who could not understand the language. Vast sums of money were spent on costumes. The most valuable surviving evidence, an account book of Philip Henslowe, manager of the Rose playhouse, shows that their bright or striking colors (often red and black, with silver and gold) allowed them to stand out on a stage that depended on daylight for most of its illumination. These were not "costumes" but clothes, sometimes bought in secondhand shops and sometimes donated or sold by gentlemen patrons. Characters normally wore contemporary dress, but with some indications of historical costume, like togas for classical characters (see the contemporary drawing, usually taken to be an illustration of *Titus Andronicus*, on p. lxi). Costumes and wigs, as well as false beards, were obviously important for a theater in which twelve to fourteen actors frequently doubled in as many as thirty roles. Music was frequently used in productions and a number of writers, including Shakespeare, incorporated popular contemporary songs into their plays. Robert Johnson, who is credited with the songs to a number of Jacobean plays, may have been the company's in-house composer. Some plays may have had as much music as a modern musical comedy, though very little of it has been identified.

Shakespeare's plays were designed to show off the actors' talents: singing, playing an instrument, dancing, and fencing. Most of his most popular plays end with either a dance or a fight, and nearly all of his tragic heroes (with the interesting exceptions of Othello and Antony) have at least one heroic fight scene. Since memorization and oratory were part of every grammar school education, audiences could recognize the superior memories of the actors who learned the long and complicated speeches that Shakespeare wrote for them. The combination of great actors and a dramatist who wrote great roles for them was attractive to other playwrights, and helped to ensure the company's continuing preeminence.

Shakespeare's practice of writing plays dominated by one very large starring role probably followed Richard Burbage's rise to stardom. Many contemporary references identify him with Richard III (see the anecdote on pp. lxx–lxxi), and he is also known to have played Romeo, Hamlet, Othello, and Lear. John Lowin, who joined the company in 1602–1603, seems to have partnered Burbage in plays with two substantial roles. Shakespeare was unusual in that he wrote equally well for tragic and comic actors, and for the company clown, a type of performer traditionally famous for his ad-libs. Will Kemp, the most famous comedian of his day, certainly created the role of Dogberry—his name accidentally replaces the character's in one quarto of the play. It is not absolutely certain that he played Falstaff, but his departure from the Lord Chamberlain's men in 1599 is often linked with Shakespeare's writing the character out of *Henry V* after having apparently promised (at the end of *2 Henry IV*) to include him in the sequel. Those who think that Shakespeare was in agreement with Hamlet's advice to the players ("Let those that play your clowns speak no more than is set down for them") wonder whether Kemp's inability to refrain from "speaking" led to friction with his leading playwright.

Kemp's successor was Robert Armin, and it is often said that the more literary quality of Shakespeare's later fools resulted from their being tailored for the new actor.

Little is known about the other chief sharers in the company, though attempts have been made to identify them with, for example, references to exceptionally thin or exceptionally fat actors. It is not known whether any particular young actor inspired Shakespeare to write his best female roles, but many boys seem to have been good enough to have a personal following. A spectator who saw *Othello* in Oxford in 1610 mentions how moved the spectators were at the sight of Desdemona after her death.

It has often been suggested that Hamlet's insistence on naturalness, and the First Player's modest claim to have "reformed" the practice of overacting at least to some extent, reflect a perceived difference between the actors for whom Shakespeare wrote and the more melodramatic ones in the company led by Philip Henslowe and its leading actor Edward Alleyn. Yet Alleyn, who created the major Marlowe roles, was no less intelligent and talented than Burbage. It was Alleyn who retired early to live the life of a gentleman (in 1597, when he was only 31), with one brief comeback in 1601–1604. Burbage, on the other hand, went on acting up to his death at the age of 46, a fact that suggests a more theatrical personality than Alleyn's. If there was a movement toward greater naturalism in the 1590s, it probably resulted from greater professionalization and better training of actors, along with greater sophistication of the audiences themselves.

As the Lord Chamberlain's men grew more successful, they looked for a more select location. In 1597 James Burbage, Richard's father, purchased part of the disused monastic site of Blackfriars in the City of London. Protests from the local residents forced him to rent out the building to boys' companies (which performed less frequently) until, early in the reign of James I, times became more favorable. Finally moving into the new premises some time after 1607, the company was able to restrict its public to those who could afford the higher admission prices. In the indoor theaters, all the spectators were seated. Comfortable spectators cause less trouble than uncomfortable ones. The smaller size may have allowed for a more "realistic" style of playing. At the same time, the company continued to use the Globe throughout the period, as well as acting at court and elsewhere, so the actors must have been able to adapt their style to circumstances. In many ways, Shakespeare's last plays are his least "realistic," since they often involve magic, but the technology available in the Blackfriars playhouse may have made the magic convincing.

Besides, if realistic acting means acting that makes one forget that one is watching a play, it is unlikely that the drama was ever truly realistic. Other dramatists' allusions to Shakespeare are obviously meant to break the dramatic illusion: "What, Hamlet, are you mad?" asks a character in *Eastward Ho!* (1605), speaking to a servant who is named Hamlet only so that someone can ask him that question. Shakespeare himself also refers to his own plays. It is likely that the lovers' suicides in "Pyramus and Thisbe," performed at the end of *A Midsummer Night's Dream*, are meant as an absurd version of the end of *Romeo and Juliet*; Malvolio's madness, in *Twelfth Night*, probably parodies Hamlet's. Perhaps a comedy can make jokes about a tragedy without destroying the atmosphere, but *Hamlet* does the same thing. When Polonius tells Hamlet about playing Julius Caesar "at the university," and being killed by Brutus, many of their audience would remember that, not long before, the two actors speaking these lines had played Caesar and Brutus, respectively, in *Julius Caesar*.

The deaths of Shakespeare in 1616 and of Burbage in 1619 may have temporarily affected Shakespeare's theatrical popularity. Burbage was so much identified with the major roles that, according to one elegy, these characters seemed to have died with him. The Earl of Pembroke may have been typical when, in a letter, he expresses reluctance to go to the theater again. John Taylor, who replaced Burbage in 1619, inherited a number of his roles. He and Lowin led the company for the next twenty years, with first John Fletcher and then Philip Massinger as their leading dramatist. The company had been called the King's men since 1603, but the name was even more appropriate under Charles I than under his father, since the actors were much closer to the court. Taylor even served as acting coach to Queen Henrietta Maria and her ladies when they put on a pastoral tragicomedy in 1633.

Though not all Puritans or parliamentarians were hostile to the theater, and not all of Charles I's courtiers approved of it, the English civil war created a further association between theater and crown. Parliament closed the theaters at the start of the war in 1642, refusing to reopen them even when hostilities had ended. Performances continued nevertheless: professionals acted illegally in the theater buildings that were still usable, or, like amateurs, legally in private houses and inns. Some also went abroad and acted for English royalists in exile. Since the prohibition applied only to plays, scenes involving popular characters (Hamlet and the gravediggers, Falstaff, Bottom) were adapted and disguised as "drolls"—comic sketches—that could be performed in a mixed program of music, dance, and drama. The 1662 frontispiece to a collection of these drolls (p. lxiv) shows how Falstaff and Mrs. Quickly were probably costumed in this period.

The Restoration and the Eighteenth Century (1660–1776)

At the Restoration of 1660, one of Charles II's first acts was to establish two licensed acting companies, one patronized by him, the other by his brother the Duke of York. Each company was assigned a selection of plays from the prewar period. Shakespeare's were among the first to be revived; indeed, actors were already playing them in London before the new theaters had opened. Although one of the speakers in Dryden's dialogue on drama (*An Essay of Dramatic Poesy*, 1665) says that Beaumont and Fletcher's plays were more popular than Shakespeare's or Jonson's, the evidence indicates that Shakespeare went on being a frequently acted dramatist throughout this period. Since the King's company seems to have received preferential treatment, it is likely that the plays awarded to them—*1 Henry IV*, *The Merry Wives of Windsor*, and Othello—were the most popular of Shakespeare's works in 1660.

It was natural that Shakespeare's works would need updating; nearly fifty years after their author's death, their language, grammar, and jokes were already becoming obsolete. Audiences saw themselves as too refined for plays with clowns and devils. Both theater managers (Thomas Killigrew and William Davenant) had been playwrights before the war, and both produced the prewar drama with extensive alterations. *The Taming of the Shrew*, as produced in 1667 by the King's company under Killigrew, was called, improbably, *Sauny the Scot*, after the new comic servant who replaced Grumio; the actor John Lacy wrote the title role for himself, exploiting the anti-Scots feeling that had been exacerbated by the Civil War. "Scenes," or scenery, the norm in the theaters of France and Italy, had already been used in prewar masques, and in the 1630s Davenant had already been planning to open a theater equipped to use it for plays. As manager of the Duke's company, he set about revising old plays to create more possibilities for spectacle. His *The Law Against Lovers* (1662) conflated *Measure for Measure* and *Much Ado About Nothing*, neither of which was well known at the period. The result was an emphasis on the romantic part of both plays, as opposed to their low comedy. He added more music and scenery in his adaptations of *Macbeth* (1664) and *The Tempest* (1667); in later revivals, these two works became almost operatic. The new theaters were rather small, and actors still played at the front of the stage, with the wings and backdrop of the new scenery stretching away behind them. Scene changes could be made quickly by rolling away one sliding backdrop to reveal another one behind it, sometimes with a new set of characters already in place. The same painted wings and backdrop were expected to serve for a number of plays, acting as a kind of shorthand to distinguish indoor from outdoor settings. The idea that each play belonged to its own particular visual world did not gain currency until well into the nineteenth century.

Charles II had insisted, in his patent for the new theaters, that the custom of boy actors—unique to England—must end. Most of the women who became actresses during the early years of the Restoration were, inevitably, untrained. The famous Nell Gwyn, mistress of Charles II, was a star of the King's company. She was considered delightful in contemporary comedies, some of which were written especially for her; however, Pepys always insisted that she was disastrous in serious roles, and there is no record of her playing Shakespeare. The new actresses could exploit their natural gifts, their beauty, and their novelty, but no one wanted to see them in character parts, especially those of elderly women. As a result, roles like the witches in *Macbeth* were taken by men, often the company's low comedians, a practice that continued for centuries. The small number of parts for attractive young women in Shakespeare now became a problem. Davenant was skillful at multiplying them. He expanded the part of Lady Macduff; Miranda, no longer the only woman in *The Tempest*, acquired a naïve younger sister, while Caliban and Ariel were likewise paired off with a female monster and spirit respectively.

Some of these changes also had a moral purpose. Davenant balanced the wickedness of Macbeth and his Lady by developing the virtuous Macduffs as foils to them. He also gave Macbeth a death speech (only one line long) to show that the dying man recognized the vanity of his ambition. Later adaptations were still more concerned with "poetic justice." This term meant simply that art ought to reward virtue and punish vice, not because this is what happens in the real world, but because art's duty is to offer virtuous models whenever possible. John Dryden, who had worked with Davenant on *The Tempest*, later wrote free adaptations of both *Antony and Cleopatra* and *Troilus and Cressida*, in which the lovers, far from being unfaithful, are only sympathetic victims of misunderstanding. His version of *Antony and Cleopatra*, called *All for Love, or, the World Well Lost* (1675–1677), largely replaced its model for much of the next century, and was often played under Shakespeare's title. Though Dryden claimed that he had made Antony's wife Octavia a virtuous foil to Cleopatra, the play's success was due less to its superior morality (indeed, its most popular scene was one in which the two women insult each other) than to its simplification of the structure, which subordinated political history to the love story. Shadwell's *Timon of Athens* (1678) provided a faithful woman as well as a faithful steward, to contrast with the mercenary friends and mistress who desert the hero. Thomas Otway's *Caius Marius* (1679) made the suicides of Romeo and Juliet more acceptable by locating them in a classical world. One of Otway's other innovations—letting the heroine revive in time to converse with the hero before they die—was to outlast the adaptation itself. Nahum Tate's *King Lear* (1681) made the virtuous Cordelia a large and dramatic role, worthy of a star actress. He also added a love interest between her and Edgar, and provided a happy ending in which Lear is restored to his throne. The adaptation remained in the repertory for 150 years, and Samuel Johnson defended it in 1765 on the grounds that,

although the unjust tragic ending might be more true to life, "all reasonable beings naturally love justice." Tate's omission of the Fool, a character associated with old-fashioned theater, was not even noticed.

After 1679, the Popish Plot and uncertainty over the royal succession led to Shakespearean adaptations designed to score political points. In 1680, John Crowne wrote *The Misery of Civil War* (1680), the first of two adaptations based on the *Henry VI* plays, while Tate's *The Sicilian Usurper*, adapted from *Richard II*, fell foul of the censor, even though its deposed ruler was more sympathetic than Shakespeare's. In the following year, Tate reversed the order of scenes in *King Lear*, beginning with Edmund's first soliloquy: a bastard son claiming his right to inherit was bound to be topical in the reign of a king who had no legitimate children and whose next heir was a Roman Catholic brother. The turbulent political climate kept audiences away, and the two companies amalgamated in 1682. Very few plays of any kind survive from the last years of Charles II's reign and the three years of James II's leading to the revolution of 1688. In the reign of William and Mary (James's daughter), *King Lear* was once again so topical that it could not be staged. Mary and her sister Anne looked all too much like Lear's daughters, especially since Tate's version ends with the king's abdication in favor of his daughter and son-in-law.

Colley Cibber's *Richard III* (1699), the most successful of all adaptations, benefited from the fact that a number of Shakespeare's history plays had dropped out of the repertory by the end of the century, thus providing a quarry from which the adapter could borrow. Feeling that he had a free hand, Cibber removed Queen Margaret and, since he intended to play Richard himself, gave him some good lines from other histories, including (from *2 Henry IV*) the death speech that Shakespeare had neglected to write for his hero. This Richard, literally an actor's dream, was more theatrically popular than Shakespeare's had been, a fact that kept the version alive well into the twentieth century (the Olivier film, which also cut Margaret's role, used two recognizable Cibber lines). Cibber had some difficulties with the licenser just before the first performance because it was feared that his opening scene, showing the deposed Henry VI in the Tower, would remind its audiences of the deposed James II. He made sure to show his loyalty in his next adaptation— *King John*, under the title *Papal Tyranny*, coincided with the threatened invasion, in 1715, of James II's exiled Catholic son. As one of the managers of Drury Lane, and as poet laureate (from 1730), Cibber became a popular target for satire, and he is best remembered for Pope's attacks on him in *The Dunciad* (1743). But his entertaining autobiography, *An Apology for the Life of Colley Cibber, Comedian* (1740), is still the best source of information on the early eighteenth-century theater.

Indeed, without Cibber's book, it would be difficult to say much about Shakespearean acting at the turn of the eighteenth century. Though Thomas Betterton was recognized as the greatest actor of his age from the first years of the Restoration, those, like Samuel Pepys, who saw him at this time, praised him highly but in vague terms. Because of the division of the theatrical repertory, Betterton acquired some major Shakespearean roles, like Othello, only after the unification of the two companies in 1682, when senior actors of the King's company took the opportunity to retire. After this, he had virtually a monopoly, and went on playing a much-acclaimed Hamlet until he was seventy, as well as taking the role of Falstaff in what seems to have been his own adaptation of the *Henry IV* plays. Cibber's description of Betterton's Hamlet reacting to the first sight of his father's ghost became a point of comparison for later Hamlets well into the nineteenth century. It is clear that his effects had to do with "presence" rather than with movement—though, of course, Cibber was describing him in his last years, when he was presumably less active.

The early female performers are still more shadowy figures. Women had appeared on stage as singers, or singing actresses, in "operas" performed in the 1650s, and one of these, perhaps Margaret Hughes, may have been the first to play a Shakespearean role (probably Desdemona). Mary Sanderson, who became Mrs. Betterton, was the first Lady Macbeth. Her successor, Elizabeth Barry, was primarily a tragic actress. She is said to have owed her initial success to careful instruction by her lover, the Earl of Rochester, who recognized the importance of constant repetition and, like a modern director, insisted that she should rehearse in the dress that she was going to wear in performance. The best-loved comic actress of Cibber's youth, Anne Bracegirdle, played several Shakespearean comedy heroines alongside the Congreve roles for which she was famous. The popularity of *The Merry Wives of Windsor* may have been due not only to Betterton's playing of Falstaff but also to its two excellent roles for actresses past their first youth, probably the only women in the company experienced enough to do justice to Shakespearean comedy.

Though the history of Shakespeare editing begins in the early eighteenth century, the plays still belonged essentially to the theater; hence, the publication of acting editions, which allowed audiences to read what they were actually going to see in the theater, usually heavily cut and partially modernized. Even so, the first half of the century saw a steady return to original versions, as one role after another was suddenly revealed to be a superb vehicle for a particular actor. Shylock, for instance, had been a not-very-interesting comic miser in a not-very-interesting romantic comedy, often replaced by George Granville's adaptation, *The Jew of Venice* (1701). When Shakespeare's original was revived in 1741, Charles Macklin astonished his fellow-actors as much as the audience by emphasizing Shylock's terrifying malevolence.

Although later actors would play the character more sympathetically, Macklin made him what he has been ever since: a disturbing character who cannot be assimilated into a comic structure. Something of a theorist on acting, Macklin, in teaching other actors, insisted on clear and intelligent diction. Perhaps for that reason, his Iago was the most convincing of the period.

Richard III, in Cibber's version, was the role in which David Garrick made his London debut in 1741. The actor became famous almost instantly and went on to manage the Drury Lane Theatre from 1747 to 1776. Garrick was a self-proclaimed idolater of Shakespeare whose "Jubilee" at Stratford-upon-Avon in 1769 not only inaugurated the practice of celebrations and festivals but also led contemporaries to regard him as almost equal in importance with his author. Despite his reputation for restoring Shakespeare, Garrick was as much of an adapter as his famous predecessors, turning *The Taming of the Shrew* and the last part of *The Winter's Tale* into short three-act plays and making operas out of *A Midsummer Night's Dream* and *The Tempest*. His *Macbeth* had a death speech, much more dramatic and pathetic than the one-line moral that Davenant had given him. His *Romeo and Juliet* had a pathetic farewell scene based on the one in Otway's *Caius Marius*. In response to French criticisms, he even directed a *Hamlet* in 1771 with the low comedy of the gravediggers omitted. Yet he also revived many plays not seen in their Shakespearean form since the Restoration, showing by his acting what superb roles they contained. He was equally gifted at comedy and tragedy. Two of his most popular roles were Benedick and (Tate's) King Lear. *Julius Caesar* and *Othello,* plays in which Betterton had been particularly successful, were better acted by Garrick's chief rival, Spranger Barry, a tall and handsome actor with a beautiful voice. Garrick, shorter and less romantic in appearance, was famous for his mobile and expressive features that allowed him to delineate the transitions between the "passions." It was this grasp of human psychology that he praised in Shakespeare and that others praised in him. His most significant leading lady, Hannah Pritchard, must have been equally versatile, since she was famous both as Rosalind and as Lady Macbeth. It was, however, characteristic of Garrick that he was able to form an excellent company around himself, including a number of fine actresses and low comedians. Without these conditions, it would have been impossible to revive so many of the comedies.

The Romantic Period (1776–1850)

Between Garrick's retirement in 1776 and the end of the century, the theaters changed to the point where a rapid, subtle style like Garrick's was becoming almost impossible. The Licensing Act of 1737 had limited spoken drama to Drury Lane and Covent Garden, the descendents of the two London theaters licensed in 1660 by Charles II. The late eighteenth century saw the rapid growth of a London population in search of entertainment. The two theaters responded by increasing their audience capacity until, at the end of the century, Covent Garden held over 3,000 spectators, and Drury Lane 3,600. When much of the audience was too far from the stage to see facial expressions or hear the softer tones of an actor's voice, the most successful performers were those who could establish themselves through their volume or through visual effects. Two tall and statuesque actors, John Philip Kemble and his more gifted sister, Sarah Siddons, dominated the theater of this period. Siddons's Lady Macbeth was probably the finest performance of the age: when she said that she could smell blood, at least one contemporary spectator declared that he could smell it too. Her other finest Shakespearean roles were Isabella in *Measure for Measure* and Hermione in *The Winter's Tale*, both of them strong women whose sublime moral grandeur dwarfed everyone else. Kemble's attempt to impose greater discipline and unity on theatrical productions, with more historically "correct" sets and costumes, resulted in what must have been the most genuinely classical theater yet seen in Britain. *Coriolanus*, with Kemble in the title role and Siddons as a heroically obsessed Volumnia, was the triumph of their approach. It was ironic that it should have come in an age dominated by the spirit of revolution and of the complex attitudes that are summed up as Romanticism.

It was to this spirit that Edmund Kean appealed. Those who saw him make his famous London debut as Shylock in 1814, wearing a black wig instead of the traditional red one, would have realized at once that he was going to play, not a tragic villain, but a tragic victim. He had been a singer, dancer, and Harlequin before taking London by storm, and his acting benefited from these other skills. Unlike Kemble, who expressed authority and aristocratic dignity, he excelled as Shakespeare's outsiders and outlaws: the hunchbacked Richard III (still in Cibber's softened version), the Moor Othello, and the melancholy Hamlet. Knowing his gift for pathos, he starred in an adaptation of *3 Henry VI* (where York sobs over his murdered son) and attempted to bring back the original ending of *King Lear* (where Lear grieves over the dead Cordelia), but audiences were not yet ready for either. Those who saw him at his best never forgot his haunting delivery of Richard III's forebodings before Bosworth and Othello's farewell to arms, which provided the kind of appreciative, poetic commentary on Shakespeare that characterized the best contemporary criticism.

Kean's career was short, wrecked by drink and scandal. In 1833, just as he had reached his miserable end, another actor, using the stage name of Keane, made his Covent Garden debut in the role of Othello. Ira Aldridge, a black American, may have hoped to announce himself as Kean's successor, but racial prejudice in England prevented him from being accepted as a leading tragedian. He would, however, play Othello all over Europe, and especially in Russia, in bilingual productions with local casts. Like Kean, he sought out the roles of victims and social outcasts: Aaron in his own adaptation of *Titus Andronicus*, as well as (in white make-up) Macbeth, Shylock, and King Lear; like Kean, he was also capable of singing songs in dialect or even a Russian folksong. The excitement that German and Russian spectators felt at the sight of a black actor playing a black character would become an important part of theatrical experience a century later; at this point, it was a novelty. In the 1860s Aldridge finally acted in major London theaters and might have returned to the United States after the Civil War if he had not died unexpectedly while on tour in Poland.

Meanwhile, both of the unruly London theaters were managed, in turn, by William Macready, who, as his diary makes clear, took seriously his responsibility to a dramatist he worshipped. Still more than Kemble, he behaved like a modern director, with a vision of the production as a whole. His revivals of the history plays showed the possibilities of historical reconstruction. He is best known for restoring the Fool to *King Lear* in 1838, though he gave the role to a young woman to ensure that it would be played for pathos rather than low comic effects that might distract from his own scenes. A number of fine actresses played opposite him: Helen Faucit, young, fragile, refined, who would later write a perceptive if sentimental account of her approach to acting some of Shakespeare's female characters; Fanny Kemble, a member of the famous Kemble family, whose memoirs indicate the struggle involved for women in a star-dominated theater; Charlotte Cushman, a powerful visitor from America who sometimes played male roles. The plays were still heavily cut and showed the influence of earlier adaptations, but by the end of his career, Macready could fairly claim to have restored a good deal of Shakespeare's text and to have made the theater more respectable. The repeal of the Licensing Act in 1843, which allowed smaller theaters to cater to different publics, also encouraged gentrification. Samuel Phelps, who managed the working-class Sadler's Wells Theatre from 1844 to 1869, did even more than Macready had, performing thirty-four of Shakespeare's plays; he even restored the original *Richard III*, though other actors continued to prefer the Cibber version. Charles Kean (son of Edmund), at the Princess's Theatre from 1850 to 1859, carried the historicizing process still further; his "archaeological" productions were likely to be accompanied by notes explaining the reason for the choice of period, costumes, and props.

Still, it was only rarely that anyone had the opportunity to impose a concept of Shakespearean production on an acting company in his own theater. Star actors tended to spend much of their time on tour, both in England and America, performing their favorite roles after perhaps one rehearsal with the resident company. Far from seeking new ways to interpret a play, these actors had to rely on standardized stage business (when Mr. Wopsle plays Hamlet in Dickens's *Great Expectations*, an unsympathetic audience comments loudly on each theatrical cliché as it occurs). They naturally tended to conceive of their characters in isolation and to favor tragedy over comedy, which requires ensemble playing. (Similarly, nineteenth-century critics usually focus on the analysis of individual characters.) A common practice was the pitting of one actor against another in a famous role, arguing over which one was the "true" Hamlet or Lear. In one case, the rivalry developed a nationalistic dimension. Macready's visit to America, in 1849, is notorious for the riot at Astor Place in New York, when soldiers fired on and killed some of the crowd outside the theater. The rioters had been trying to drown out Macready's performance of *Macbeth* out of a mistaken loyalty to the American tragedian, Edwin Forrest. On a visit to Britain, Forrest had hissed Macready for some foppish business with a handkerchief that the actor, as Hamlet, had used to illustrate the phrase "I must be idle." Now his personal hostility became a quarrel about effete English acting versus the manly American tradition. In fact, the distinction was largely meaningless: many well-known American actors had begun their careers in England or Ireland. While some American Shakespeareans might have seen themselves as part of the Forrest tradition, and some (like the touring performers depicted by Mark Twain in *Huckleberry Finn*) were of no tradition at all, most American actors continued to look to Europe for models.

The Victorian Era and the Early Twentieth Century (1850–1912)

The greatest American actor of the next generation, Edwin Booth, was a refined and melancholy figure whose readings of the great Shakespearean roles were psychological and poetic. Booth was the son of Junius Brutus Booth, who had acted in London opposite Edmund Kean, and the brother of John Wilkes Booth, the assassin of Abraham Lincoln. (Ironically, all three members of this acting family had once performed together in the great assassination play, *Julius Caesar*.) Though Booth briefly attempted theater management, he spent much of his time in the exhausting business of touring. He clearly thought deeply about his own roles, and about the moments when other characters interacted with him. His correspondence with the New Variorum Shakespeare

editor, H.H. Furness, is quoted in many notes of that edition—an early example of successful communication between the theater and the scholarly world. Yet when Booth was alternating the two leading roles of *Othello* with Henry Irving in 1881, he sent his servant to take notes at rehearsal for him. Nothing in his experience had prepared him for a theater in which the actor-manager expected everyone to fit into a total artistic conception.

It was Irving, the first actor to be knighted, who dominated English Shakespearean acting in the late Victorian era. His pictorial sense was even stronger than that of the actor-managers who preceded him, and the technical means at his disposal in the Lyceum Theatre, which he began to manage in 1878, were much better. The old system of sliding screens in grooves, flanked by a series of wings, had been replaced by the "box set," which was built like a piece of architecture, creating a complete environment. Electric lighting, introduced in the 1880s, provided new, subtle visual effects. The elaborate and beautiful sets often required interminable scene changes and, sometimes, rearrangement of the plays to accommodate them. Irving's own performances were usually controversial. His Malvolio, like his Shylock, was a tragic figure, while his Iago was so witty and likeable that, playing opposite Booth's Othello, he stole all the sympathy from the hero. His theater offered a beautiful dream for the spectator to share: if it also disturbed the spectator, it was through its revelation of the psychological depths of character, never through its comments on social and political issues. Irving's leading lady, Ellen Terry, was both beautiful and brilliant; in most productions she was allowed to be only the former. Bernard Shaw, longing for her to appear in plays about "grownup" topics, by himself or Henrik Ibsen, resented her imprisonment in Irving's world. For Shaw and other modern thinkers, Shakespeare was becoming synonymous with nostalgia and with the moralistic and idealistic thinking that the new drama regarded as a vice. The early twentieth-century theater was finally affected by these critical attempts to reform it, but two kinds of production coexisted for some time. At His Majesty's Theatre, Herbert Beerbohm Tree, like Irving, offered psychologically based character acting in a beautiful scenic environment, recreating Cleopatra's Egypt and Henry VIII's England; having seen his lavish production of *Macbeth*, one critic commented that "Nature put up a pretty feeble imitation of what several barrels of stones and a few sheets of tin could do in His Majesty's." At the Savoy, on the other hand, Harley Granville Barker, a disciple of Bernard Shaw, developed a decorative visual style that was not tied to a specific historical period.

Meanwhile, a more experimental approach to acting was being developed in Germany. The country's unusual political structure, with small dukedoms and cities sponsoring their own theaters, made it possible for the

Duke of Saxe-Meiningen to sponsor his own company of players, sixty-six in all. His leading actors were unremarkable but, when he took them on tour in the 1880s, audiences were impressed by his handling of large groups. The Duke insisted that those who played major roles in one production should be walk-ons in another, so that crowds could be properly rehearsed instead of being assembled from those gathered around the stage door and drilled by the stage manager immediately before each performance.

Frank Benson, a young Oxford graduate, saw the Saxe-Meiningen company at Drury Lane in 1881, and was inspired to develop his own touring company—though, unlike the Duke, he acted in his own productions and consequently shaped them from a star's point of view. From 1886 on, the Bensonians became regular visitors at Stratford-upon-Avon. Shakespeare's birthplace had been briefly famous in 1769, the year of Garrick's Jubilee, but it was only in 1879, when the first Memorial Theatre was built, that tourists had any reason to visit for more than a few hours. Benson essentially created the first Stratford company, though it used the theater only during a short "Festival" season. Having a regular venue and a devoted audience enabled him to revive unusual works, if often drastically cut. In 1901 he inaugurated the new century with a "Grand Cycle" of Shakespeare's histories—the first English production of the plays as a group.

The desire to return to fuller texts and something like the original conditions of Shakespearean performance was initially associated with Germany and then with outsiders like William Poel, who founded the English Stage Society in 1894. Previously, Poel had given an experimental matinee of the First Quarto *Hamlet* at St. George's Hall in 1881. More surprisingly (though his friendship with Bernard Shaw in part explains it), the popular London actor Johnston Forbes-Robertson played an unusually full text of *Hamlet* in 1897, with characters like Reynaldo and Fortinbras appearing for the first time in centuries. Then Benson's company played an uncut *Hamlet* in 1899 and 1900. Poel, who often worked with amateurs, using all-purpose curtains rather than scenery on what was meant to be an Elizabethan stage, revived works previously considered unperformable, by Shakespeare's contemporaries as well as by Shakespeare. For example, he gave the first important *Troilus and Cressida* to be seen in London since 1734, dressing it in Elizabethan rather than classical costume. It was 1912. He had discovered the play's antiwar potential.

The Twentieth Century

World War I drastically curtailed many Shakespearean projects, including those for a gigantic celebration of the anniversary of his death in 1916, which at one point was intended to include the opening of a National Theatre. Although this theater did not come into existence until nearly 100 years after Irving had first suggested it, other developments were creating the conditions that would make Shakespeare plays, with their large casts, commercially viable.

One was the rise of repertory theaters, which could support a large company and a varied range of plays. The most famous of these was London's Royal Victoria, or "Old Vic," founded in 1914. Under a number of gifted directors (notably Robert Atkins, who had directed all the plays in the 1623 Folio by 1923, Harcourt Williams, and Tyrone Guthrie), it was the home to many legendary productions, including John Gielgud's first *Hamlet* (1929) and Olivier's first *Hamlet* (1937). At the Birmingham Repertory Theatre, Barry Jackson had already directed a modern-dress *Hamlet* in 1925. Modern dress had been common practice until the nineteenth century; it now seemed eccentric, but would by the end of the century become almost the norm. The Memorial Theatre at Stratford, after struggling to find its identity, saw some brilliant productions by Peter Brook in the 1940s and 1950s, including three plays traditionally considered minor: *Love's Labor's Lost* (1946), *Measure for Measure* (1948), and a *Titus Andronicus* (1955), starring Olivier, at which audience members regularly fainted at what was then unusual stage violence: the amputation of the hero's hand and the cutting of the villains' throats. Stratford and the Old Vic were becoming rival Shakespeare companies and in the 1960s each achieved a new status. The Memorial Theatre was renamed the Royal Shakespeare Theatre in 1960, with Peter Hall as director, whereas the Old Vic was designated the National Theatre in 1963. Olivier directed its opening production of *Hamlet*, with Peter O'Toole in the title role, and played a famous Othello in 1964. The National Theatre eventually moved into new premises in an arts complex, with three stages, on the South Bank of the Thames.

In the United States, the most exciting Shakespeare productions also occurred during a period of government subsidy: it was depression-era financing that enabled Orson Welles to direct Shakespeare on radio, and, for the Mercury Theatre, his "voodoo" *Macbeth* (1938) with an all-black cast, his anti-Fascist *Julius Caesar* (1937), and his condensation of the major history plays, *Five Kings*, which, although unsuccessful, later influenced his Falstaff film, *Chimes at Midnight* (1966). The other significant development in North America was the growth of summer Shakespeare festivals at outdoor Elizabethan-style theaters, beginning with the Elizabethan Stage at Ashland, Oregon (founded 1935), and the Guthrie-designed Festival Theatre at Stratford, Ontario (1953). Festival seasons allowed juxtapositions of related plays and the yearly performance of successive plays in a history cycle.

It was the English Stratford-upon-Avon, however, that fully seized on the history plays, performing the *Richard II–Henry V* group in 1951, during the Festival of Britain that celebrated the country's emergence from wartime and postwar rationing. For the rest of the century, the "cycle" of history plays would be recognized as a national epic, to be performed for special occasions. For the new Royal Shakespeare Company, Peter Hall and John Barton produced the *Henry VI–Richard III* group of plays— rewritten, reduced to three plays, and called *The Wars of the Roses*. They revived these, along with the other *Henry* plays, for the Shakespeare quatercentenary in 1964. The histories were produced again in 1975 by Terry Hands, with Alan Howard playing all the kings except Henry IV; in 1982 the *Henry IV* plays opened the company's new London theater at the Barbican under Trevor Nunn; and the company, now under Adrian Noble, marked the arrival of the millennium with a freshly conceived production of the *Richard II–Richard III* sequence. Just as the 1951 production showed the influence of Tillyard's essays on the histories as a unified cycle, the plays of the year 2000, deliberately disparate in style and even venue, were the product of a critical movement that emphasized discontinuity and diversity.

Contemporary Critical Approaches

By now, productions might require as much interpretation as plays. In the last half of the twentieth century, the spread of school and university education had created a substantial population that had studied at least one Shakespeare play and a smaller population, including some theater practitioners, that had read not only the plays but also the criticism. Stratford's John Barton, a former Cambridge don, directed *Twelfth Night* (1969) as if it were by Chekhov, encouraging the audience to imagine the unspoken feelings of the characters—not only Viola (Judi Dench), smiling through heartbreak, but Maria, in her apparently hopeless love for Sir Toby, and Sir Andrew in his even more hopeless love for Olivia. This attention to character, often created out of masses of tiny realistic details, informed some of the theater's most highly praised productions. Barton's *Richard II* (1973) worked very differently, externalizing the play's images in ways that were clearly independent of the characters' awareness: for instance, a glimpse of a melting snowman echoed Richard's wish that he were "a mockery king of snow" and linked the fall and rise of kings to a natural cycle of dissolution and renewal.

Other major critical approaches, easier to categorize, quickly found their way onto the stage. Political readings, often influenced by a Brechtian production style, dominated the 1960s and 1970s. These were usually Marxist and anti-authority: lines in which characters expressed high moral sentiments might be juxtaposed (legitimately) with those in which they showed themselves less noble, or (illegitimately) by setting them in a context that undermined them, as when, in Peter Zadek's *Held Henry* (Hero Henry), Henry V delivers the St. Crispin's Day speech to his bored mistress. Even before its first English publication in 1964, *Shakespeare Our Contemporary*, by the Polish critic Jan Kott, had powerfully influenced theater with his comparison of *Hamlet* and the histories to life under a totalitarian regime, *King Lear* to Theater of the Absurd, and the comedies to a Freudian nightmare. Both Brecht and Kott could be recognized behind Peter Brook's *King Lear* (1962), which, in place of the traditional sympathy with the king (a frighteningly harsh Paul Scofield), emphasized his and his followers' brutality toward Goneril's servants, and ruthlessly cut anything that might be cathartic; the Dover cliff meeting between Lear and Gloucester frankly drew on the stage imagery of Samuel Beckett's *Waiting for Godot*. Brook's *A Midsummer Night's Dream* (1970), which based its erotic treatment of Titania and Bottom on Kott's work, found a purely theatrical language for the critical commonplaces about the play's metatheatricality. Without makeup, under bright light, in a white-walled gymnasium that replaced the traditional moonlit forest, Oberon and Puck sat on trapezes and passed the aphrodisiac "flower," a metal plate, from one spinning metallic wand to another. The fact that this operation could, and occasionally did, go wrong was the point: it reminded the audience that the real magic lay in its own willingness to trust the actors. Even the "Pyramus and Thisbe" actors in the final scene were treated as serious artists, representatives of working-class culture who deserved respect. For many of his later productions, Peter Brook went abroad in search of a multilingual, multiethnic cast, searching for ways of escaping the "easy" assumptions about Shakespeare.

It was in fact race and gender rather than class that dominated Shakespeare production in the last quarter of the century. The concern with race began with the great American theatrical event of the 1940s, Margaret Webster's production of *Othello* with the charismatic Paul Robeson in the title role. After the longest run of any Shakespeare play on Broadway, it was taken on tour all over America in 1945, playing only in desegregated theaters. Although Robeson had already played Othello in London (1930), and would do so again at Stratford-upon-Avon, England, in 1959, his long period of disgrace in the politically polarized United States of the 1950s delayed the movement toward race-based casting as a norm. After initial embarrassment about racist language in Shakespeare, the theater began deliberately to explore its implications, as race became a subject for academic study. The range of *Othello* videos available by the 1990s indicates the play's performance history: besides Orson

Welles's film from 1952, these include the National Theatre production of 1964 starring Laurence Olivier and the BBC one with Antony Hopkins (1981), both with white actors in the title role; Trevor Nunn's Chekhovian version originally staged in 1989; the historic South African production by Janet Suzman, a political act at a time when apartheid still existed; and Oliver Parker's 1994 version, with Laurence Fishburne (opposite Kenneth Branagh's convincingly ordinary Iago), consciously conveying the concentrated power and sensuality associated with blackness. Confusion between "color-blind casting" (when the audience is supposed to ignore the race of both actor and character) and "race-based casting" (when the audience is being told something about race through the casting) was deliberately cultivated in Jude Kelly's *Othello* (Washington, D.C., 1997). This production enabled Patrick Stewart to achieve his otherwise unrealizable ambition of playing the title role by surrounding a white Othello with African American and Hispanic actors, yet with the play's racial references unaltered.

Just as some critics of racism felt that *Othello* and *The Merchant of Venice* had become theatrically unacceptable, some feminist responses to Shakespeare argued the same about *The Taming of the Shrew*, in which a female character is made to acquiesce in her humiliation by a husband who uses patriarchal arguments to justify his behavior. The play had usually been directed to soften its final moral, either by making it clear that the protagonists have fallen in love at first sight or by emphasizing its nature as a play within a play, safely distant from real life. A famous production by Michael Bogdanov (Royal Shakespeare Theatre, 1978) doubled the drunken tinker Sly with Petruchio and showed Kate being brutalized into a dazed submission that horrified even her husband. Obviously, the play in this version was no longer a comedy. A less obvious effect of feminism has been the increasing attention paid to Shakespeare's female characters. They tend now to be on stage more than the text directs, as when Ophelia stands appalled while her father reads Hamlet's love letters to the court or Gertrude enters in time to hear Claudius and Laertes plan to poison Hamlet, so that her decision to drink from the cup is recognized as a heroic device to save her son's life. The young Elizabeth of York, who does not appear in the text of *Richard III* although she is important to its plot, has frequently been seen and even heard in stage versions, as in the 1995 film by Richard Loncraine. The fact that women are often denied speech at crucial moments can be turned to an advantage, as when John Barton and a number of subsequent directors of *Measure for Measure* in the 1980s made Isabella silently refuse the Duke's proposal, which earlier actors and directors had assumed she would eagerly accept.

Still more important, in a theater in which women are far more likely than men to be underemployed, were devices that increased the number of Shakespearean roles for women. Cross-dressed performances, parallel to the productions focused on race, hovered between gender based and gender blind. Deborah Warner's *Richard II* in 1995, with Fiona Shaw as the title character (National Theatre, London), suggested a troubled and potentially erotic relationship between Richard and Bolingbroke without defining it further. In the all-male Cheek-by-Jowl production of *As You Like It* (1995), the audience was never certain whether it was meant to be thinking of Rosalind (Adrian Lester) as male or female. A similar confusion was exploited when Michael Kahn's *King Lear* (Washington, D.C., 1999) cast Cordelia as a deaf-mute, signing her lines, which were then interpreted by the Fool. This decision, which would have been meaningless if the audience had not known that the actress (Monique Holt) really was a deaf-mute, might be seen either as a return to the self-conscious theatricality of the Renaissance stage or as an example of identity politics.

Shakespeare on Film

Of course, the sense of identity between actor and role is strongest in the cinema, where physical appearance matters more and where audiences are particularly likely to bring with them recollections of an actor's previous roles. Films of Shakespeare plays are as old as film itself. Their transfer to videotape and then laserdisc and DVD, a process that began in the 1970s, has given them a much wider circulation and canonized some performances: Olivier's Richard III, for instance, now has much the same iconic status that Cibber gave to Betterton's Hamlet. Orson Welles's film versions of *Macbeth* (1947) and *Othello* (1952), visually remarkable as they were, have benefited from remastering to make their soundtracks more intelligible. The BBC made-for-TV versions of Shakespeare, 1979–1985, often disappointed both film and Shakespeare enthusiasts, though for different reasons, but have been widely used in schools. Kenneth Branagh's films, including a remarkable four-hour uncut *Hamlet* (1996), have been surprisingly successful in making the plays accessible to a popular audience. His *Henry V* (1989) was unfairly praised for being more "real" than Olivier's; both films were star-centered, with Olivier playing a more controlled king, Branagh a more vulnerable one. Whereas Olivier began his film with a view of an idealized Elizabethan London, then of a playhouse viewed from a superior perspective as old-fashioned and in some ways comic, Branagh introduced his Chorus (Derek Jacobi) in a room full of movie cameras, though he later allowed him to move among the actors in the film. As often in films, the moments most remembered were visual: Henry's (Branagh's) grief when, in order to enforce proper discipline, he is obliged to order the hanging of Bardolph, or the long shot, after the Battle of Agincourt, that shows Henry carrying the dead boy in a procession of English soldiers singing *Non nobis Domine*.

Branagh's youth was an asset in bringing Shakespeare to a young audience. Later filmmakers have aimed at a still younger group. *William Shakespeare's Romeo and Juliet* (directed by Baz Luhrmann, 1996), filled as it was with icons of contemporary youth culture, is perhaps the first of these, though it retains Shakespeare's language, juxtaposing it with contradictory images, so that it can be understood either as a complex visual-verbal experience or as a rather simple visual one. The *Hamlet* directed by Michael Almereyda (2000) represents its young characters as college students obsessed with modern technology: Hamlet (Ethan Hawke) is an amateur filmmaker and Ophelia is a photographer; "To be or not to be" is spoken in a video store against a background of videos labeled "Action." For students of the new field of Shakespeare in Popular Culture, Teenage Shakespeare, with the stories rewritten in contemporary language and settings, is becoming a genre in its own right. *Ten Things I Hate About You* (directed by Gil Junger, 1999) and *O* (directed by Tim Blake Nelson, 2001) retell *The Taming of the Shrew* and *Othello* in American high school settings. *The Children's Midsummer Night's Dream* (directed by Christine Edzard, 2001) has a cast of primary school children.

International Contexts and Contemporary Adaptations

Not only have the plays been adapted for every age group, they have turned out to speak an international language. This had not always been true, though English and French actors had visited each other's countries since the seventeenth century: in 1629 French actresses were booed by English audiences, still accustomed to an all-male stage; one group of English actors was booed in the Paris of 1818, but another visiting company in 1827 inspired French writers and actors to try to understand Shakespeare. English and American audiences saw *Othello* with new eyes when the Italian actor Tommaso Salvini, followed by several other famous Italians, performed on tour in the late nineteenth century. Along with the visit of the Berliner Ensemble to London in 1956, the most important influences in the late twentieth century came from Asian, especially Japanese, theater and from central and eastern Europe. Kurosawa's films, *Throne of Blood* (*Macbeth*, 1957) and *Ran* (*King Lear*, 1986), transpose Shakespearean plots into Japanese culture and images. Successful Russian films have ranged from the visually stunning colors of Yan Fried's *Twelfth Night* and Sergei Yutkevitch's *Othello* (both 1955) to Grigori Kozintsev's black-and-white *Hamlet* (1964) and *King Lear* (1971).

The opening up of contacts with central and eastern Europe after 1989 has resulted in visits from theater companies of the former eastern bloc countries. When London audiences in 1990 saw *Hamlet* by the Bulandra Theatre of Romania (directed by Alexander Tocilescu), they discovered that plays often regarded in Britain and America as "conservative" tools of the "establishment" had elsewhere been a powerful vehicle for the expression of political dissent. When first produced in 1985, Tocilescu's *Hamlet* was clearly understood to be equating the rottenness of Elsinore with the world created by Nicolae Ceaucescu, the dictator executed in 1989; Ion Caramitru, the actor who played Hamlet, had been one of the leaders of the revolution. In Czech productions of Shakespeare, similarly, actors and audience had gathered in a deliberate act of misreading directed at the occupying Russians: in *Love's Labor's Lost*, of all plays, the princess's suggestion that the courtiers disguised as Muscovites should "be gone" was the high point of the evening.

Western directors have sometimes attempted to deal with a difficult text by interpreting it as "Other," particularly as Japanese: the samurai warrior culture was the background to Barry Kyle's *The Two Noble Kinsmen* (Swan Theatre, Stratford, 1986) and to David Farr's *Coriolanus* (Royal Shakespeare Theatre, 2002), whereas Ron Daniels's *Timon of Athens* (The Other Place, Stratford, 1980) drew on the concept of a society based on gift-giving. Conversely, Yukio Ninagawa's Japanese Shakespeare productions have combined Japanese costumes with a soundtrack of European music (*Macbeth*) and interpreted *The Tempest* through the story of the famous Japanese exile, Shunkan. Such cross-cultural borrowings have sometimes been denigrated as "cultural tourism," by which critics seem to mean that it is illegitimate to appropriate the merely visual aspects of a culture to which one does not belong.

Similarly, the reconstructed "Shakespeare's Globe" in London, which opened in 1997, was accused of attempting to appropriate the emotions of another historical period. Perhaps because the opening production was *Henry V*, the "groundlings" who stood in the yard for only £5 apiece seemed to be modeling themselves on their counterparts in the Globe sequence of Olivier's film, who boo when they hear that Falstaff has been banished. Their willingness to boo the French (and, in the next season, Shylock) at first shocked the critics, and it was suggested that this theater might be suited only to comedies and histories demanding a presentational style, but productions of *Hamlet* (2000) and *King Lear* (2001) showed that it was possible to control audience response to the tragedies. Mark Rylance's *Hamlet* skillfully played his line about groundlings "capable of nothing but inexplicable dumbshow," so that he could respond to their laughter by adding "*and* noise." Whether or not the theater can really tell anyone anything about Elizabethan stage conventions and audience response, it has given considerable pleasure. Other Globes, more and less historically based, now can be found in several countries (the United States, Japan, Poland, and the Czech Republic, among others), while the open stage of Stratford, Canada, remains one of the most successful modifications of the Elizabethan model. In a reversal of the search for authenticity, the Shakespeare Theatre in Washington, D.C., has abandoned its home in the reconstructed Fortune Theatre at the Folger Shakespeare Library for a purpose-built modern auditorium. In fact, the two kinds of theater can coexist. The well-established Shakespeare festivals of Stratford, Ontario; Ashland, Oregon; and Santa Cruz, California, have added well-equipped indoor theaters to their outdoor acting spaces, and an indoor auditorium is projected as an addition to Shakespeare's Globe in London. A reconstruction of the Blackfriars Playhouse opened in Staunton, Virginia, in 2001.

Although it has been impossible to discuss the theatrical fortunes of every Shakespeare play, it may be interesting to end by reflecting how greatly these have fluctuated. If some plays, like *Hamlet* and *Macbeth*, have always been popular, the history of others is more checkered. Some of the comedies most popular today, such as *As You Like It* and *Twelfth Night*, were regarded as insipid in the eighteenth century, redeemed only by their scenes of low comedy and occasional sententious speeches. *The Merry Wives of Windsor* was the most popular comedy during the Restoration; *King John* and *Henry VIII* were more popular in the nineteenth century than *Richard II* or *2 Henry IV*. *Othello* was acted without the "willow scene" (4.3) for most of the eighteenth and nineteenth centuries, and *Troilus and Cressida* and *Titus Andronicus* were performed, if at all, only in heavily adapted versions. It is arguable that the attitude to Shakespeare that Bernard Shaw ridiculed as "Bardolatry" reached its height, not in the Victorian age, but at the end of the twentieth century, a time when any Shakespeare play, however minor, was likely to find a director and an audience. One reason might be that the subsidized theaters had been giving fewer controversial productions since 1980, emphasizing instead what the plays have in common with musical comedies and films. An important American contribution to Shakespeare in performance has taken the form of musicals like *The Boys from Syracuse* (1938), *Kiss Me Kate* (1948), and *West Side Story* (1957), based respectively on *The Comedy of Errors*, *The Taming of the Shrew*, and *Romeo and Juliet*; now, many productions of the comedies followed the Restoration practice of filling them with popular music. What was new was not the practice of adaptation but the attitude toward it. In the mid century, the plays were taken to be fixed quantities: the job of the theater director, as of the critic, was to uncover the "real" work, whether through more authentic staging, a more accurate text, or a better understanding of its meaning. By the end of the millennium, when some theorists were insisting that the text itself was unknowable, it is not surprising to find a much greater tolerance for re-creations and explorations of the plays in other forms.

THE ROYAL GENEALOGY OF ENGLAND, 1154–1625

THE PLANTAGENET KINGS

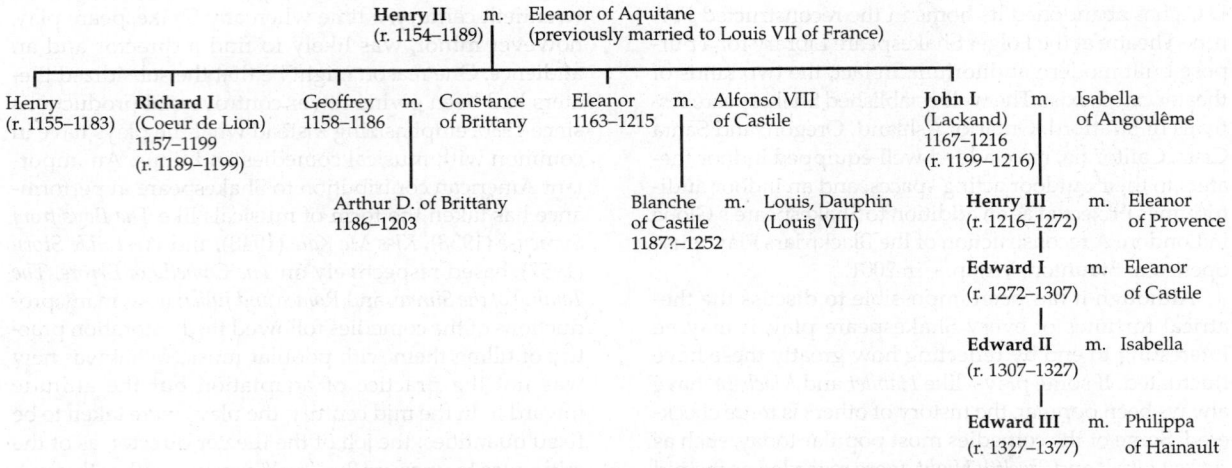

THE LANCASTRIAN KINGS

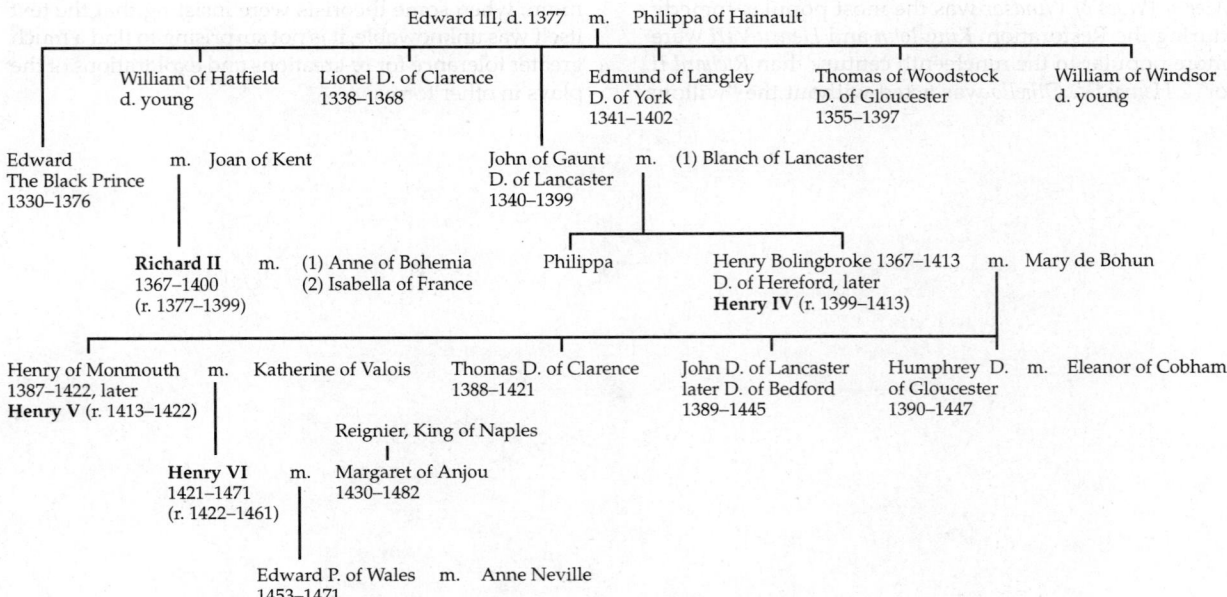

In these diagrams, reigning dates are given in parentheses; other dates indicate life span. Abbreviations: P., Prince, D., Duke, E., Earl; b., born, d., died, m., married, r., reigned. English monarchs are printed in boldface type. The spatial arrangement of names in a family indicates order of birth.

In 1 Henry IV, Shakespeare confuses the Edmund Mortimer who married Glendower's daughter and died in 1409 with his nephew Edmund, fifth Earl of March, who asserted a claim to the English throne (see "The Yorkist Kings"). Shakespeare also refers to Henry Percy's (Hotspur's) wife as "Kate," though historically she was named Elizabeth.

Catherine Swynford, third wife of John of Gaunt (see "The Tudor Kings"), bore him children before their eventual marriage. These Beauforts, although later legitimized, were specifically barred from any claim to the English throne.

THE YORKIST KINGS

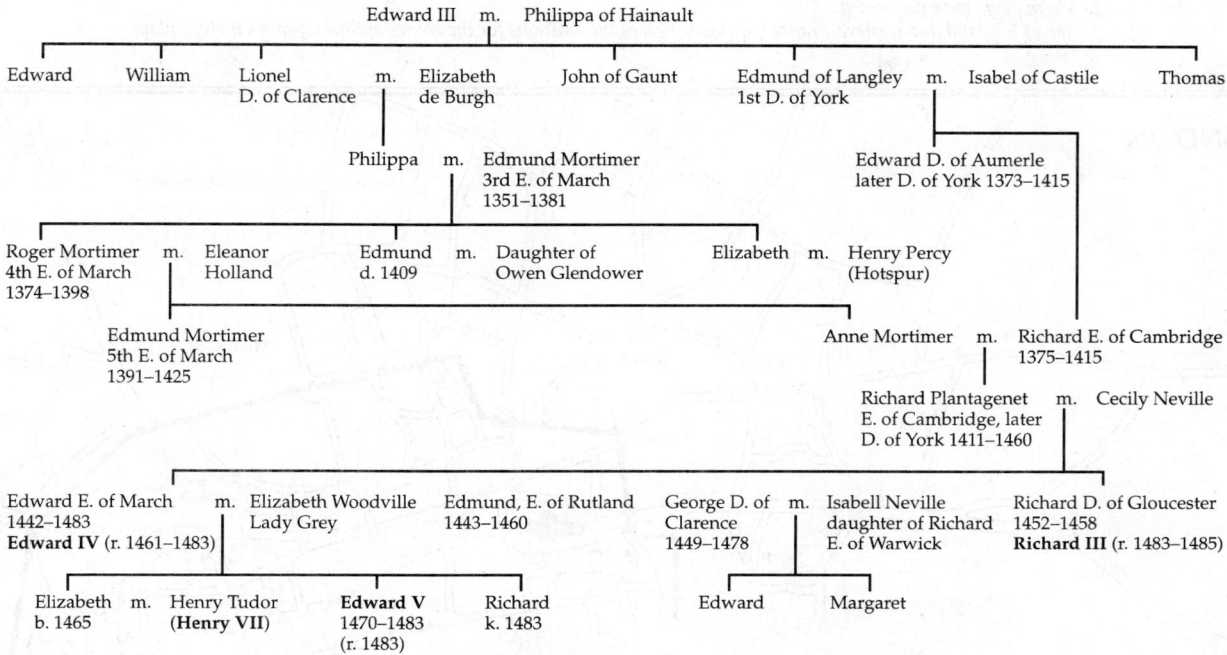

THE TUDOR KINGS

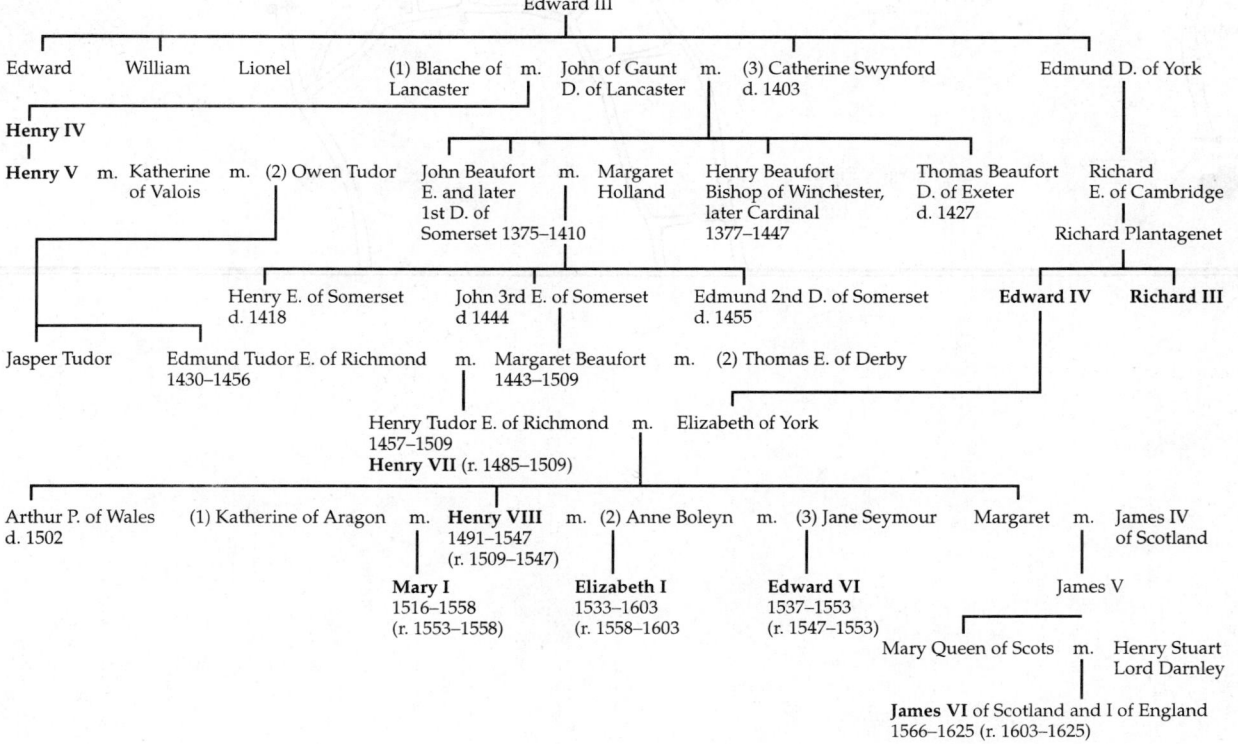

Maps.

A map of London (below) of Shakespeare's time shows the prominent landmarks, as well as the theaters and other places where plays were performed.
A map of England and western France (opposite) gives the locations for the scenes of Shakespeare's history plays.

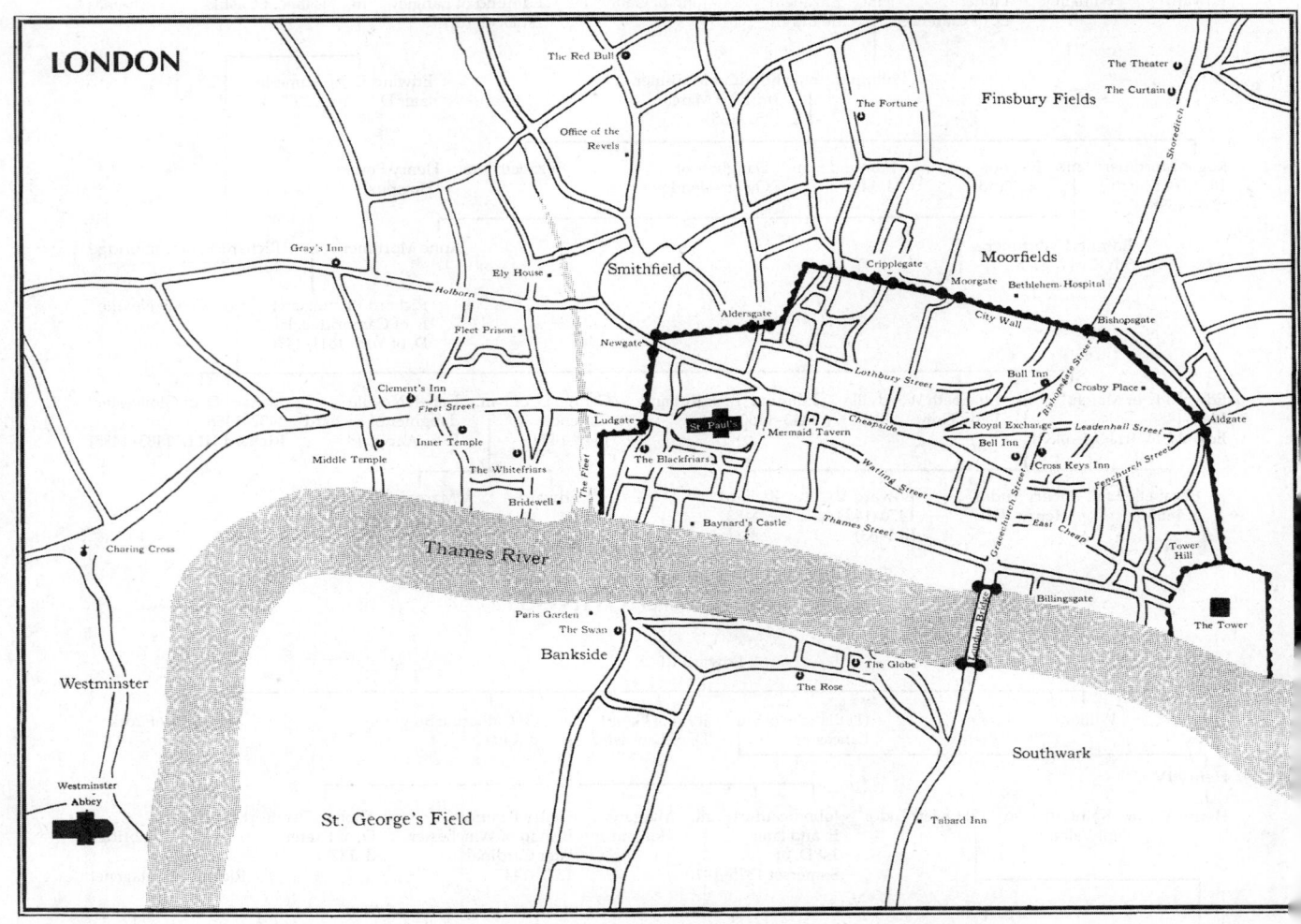

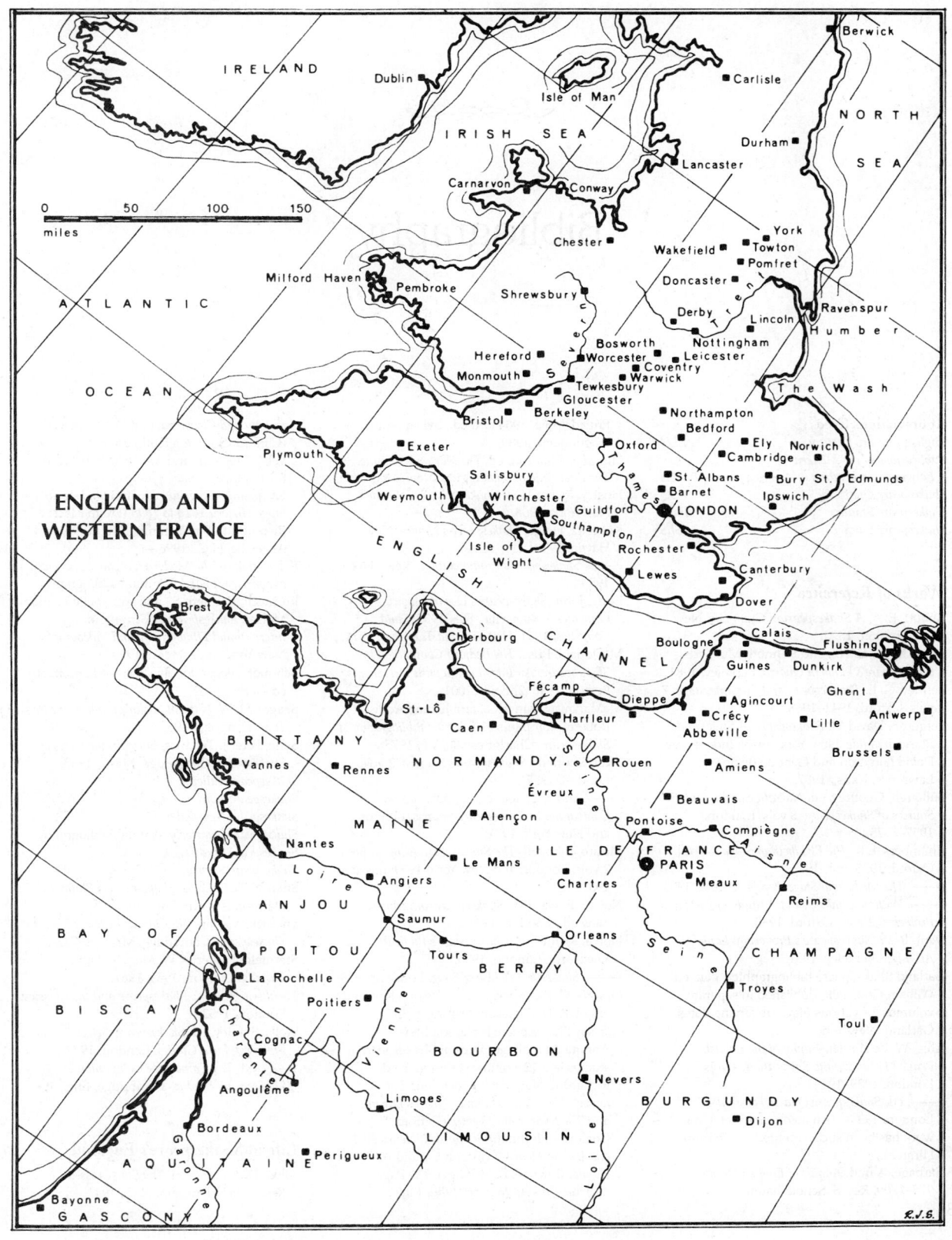

ENGLAND AND
WESTERN FRANCE

Bibliography

Abbreviations Used

English Literary History	*ELH*
Publications of the Modern Language Association of America	*PMLA*
Shakespeare Quarterly	*SQ*
Shakespeare Studies	*ShakS*
Shakespeare Survey	*ShS*

Works of Reference

Abbott, E. A. *A Shakespearian Grammar*. New ed., London, 1870.

Allen, Michael J. B., and Kenneth Muir, eds. *Shakespeare's Plays in Quarto*. Berkeley, 1981.

Bentley, G. E. *The Jacobean and Caroline Stage*. 7 vols. Oxford, 1941–1968.

Bergeron, David M. *Shakespeare: A Study and Research Guide*. New York, 1975; 2nd ed., rev. David Bergeron and Geraldo de Sousa. Lawrence, Kans., 1987.

Bullough, Geoffrey, ed. *Narrative and Dramatic Sources of Shakespeare*. 8 vols. London, 1957–1975.

Chambers, E.K. *The Elizabethan Stage*. 4 vols. Oxford, 1923; rev., 1945.

——. *The Mediaeval Stage*. 2 vols. Oxford, 1903.

——. *William Shakespeare: A Study of Facts and Problems*. 2 vols. Oxford, 1930.

Dent, R. W. *Shakespeare's Proverbial Language: An Index*. Berkeley, 1981.

Garland Shakespeare Bibliographies, gen. ed. William Godshalk. Published in separate volumes, at varying dates. Garland: New York.

Greg, W. W. *A Bibliography of the English Printed Drama to the Restoration*. 4 vols. London, 1939–1959.

——, ed. *Shakespeare Quarto Facsimiles*. London, 1939–. (An incomplete set; Greg's work has been supplemented by Charlton Hinman.)

Harbage, Alfred. *Annals of English Drama, 975–1700*. Rev. S. Schoenbaum.

Philadelphia, 1964; 3rd ed., Sylvia Stoler Wagonheim, 1989.

Hinman, Charlton, ed. *The Norton Facsimile: The First Folio of Shakespeare*. New York, 1968.

Hosley, Richard, ed. *Shakespeare's Holinshed*. New York, 1968.

Kökeritz, Helge. *Shakespeare's Names*. New Haven, 1959.

——. *Shakespeare's Pronunciation*. New Haven, 1953.

Long, John. *Shakespeare's Use of Music: Comedies*. Gainesville, Fla., 1955. *Final Comedies*, 1961; *Histories and Tragedies*, 1971.

McDonald, Russ. *The Bedford Companion to Shakespeare: An Introduction with Documents*. Boston, 1996; 2nd ed., 2001.

McManaway, James G., and Jeanne Addison Roberts, compilers. *A Selective Bibliography of Shakespeare*. Charlottesville, Va., 1975.

Muir, Kenneth. *Shakespeare's Sources*. 2 vols. London, 1957.

——, and S. Schoenbaum, eds. *A New Companion to Shakespeare Studies*. London and New York, 1971.

Munro, John, ed. *The Shakespeare Allusion Book*. 2 vols. London and New York, 1909; reissued 1932.

Naylor, Edward W. *Shakespeare and Music*. New ed., London, 1931.

Noble, Richmond. *Shakespeare's Biblical Knowledge*. London, 1935.

——. *Shakespeare's Use of Song*. London, 1923.

Onions, C. T. *A Shakespeare Glossary*. Rev. and enlgd. R. D. Eagleson. Oxford, 1986.

Pegasus Shakespeare Bibliographies. Annotated bibliographies of Shakespeare studies in a 12-volume series, gen. ed. Richard L. Nochimson, including *Love's Labor's Lost, A Midsummer Night's Dream*, and *The Merchant of Venice* (Clifford Chalmers Huffman), *Richard II, Henry IV, I and II*, and *Henry V* (Joseph Candido), *Hamlet* (Michael E. Mooney), *The Rape of Lucrece, Titus Andronicus, Julius Caesar,*

Antony and Cleopatra, and *Coriolanus* (Clifford Chalmers Huffman and John W. Velz), *King Lear* and *Macbeth* (Rebecca W. Bushnell), and *Shakespeare and the Renaissance Stage to 1616* and *Shakespearean Stage History 1616 to 1998* (Hugh Macrae Richmond). Binghamton, N.Y. (1995) and Asheville, N.C., 1996—.

Publications of the Modern Language Association of America (PMLA). Annual Bibliography.

Rothwell, Kenneth S., and Annabelle Henkin Melzer. *Shakespeare on Screen: An International Filmography and Videography*. New York and London, 1990.

Schmidt, Alexander. *Shakespeare-Lexicon*. 5th ed. Berlin, 1962.

Seager, H. W. *Natural History in Shakespeare's Time*. London, 1896.

Seng, Peter J. *The Vocal Songs in the Plays of Shakespeare*. Cambridge, Mass., 1967.

Shakespeare Bulletin.

Shakespeare-Jahrbuch.

Shakespeare Newsletter.

Shakespeare Quarterly. Annual Bibliography.

Shakespeare Studies.

Shakespeare Survey.

Spencer, T. J. B., ed. *Shakespeare's Plutarch*. Harmondsworth, Eng., 1964.

Spevack, Marvin. *The Harvard Concordance to Shakespeare*. Cambridge, Mass., 1973.

Sternfeld, Frederick W. *Music in Shakespearean Tragedy*. London, 1963, 1967.

Thomson, J. A. K. *Shakespeare and the Classics*. London, 1952.

Wells, Stanley, ed. *Shakespeare: Select Bibliographical Guides*. London, 1973.

——, ed. *The Cambridge Companion to Shakespeare Studies*. Cambridge, Eng., 1986.

Life in Shakespeare's England

Allen, Don Cameron. *The Star-Crossed Renaissance*. Durham, N.C., 1941.

Baker, Herschel. *The Image of Man: A Study of the Idea of Human Dignity in Classical Antiquity, the Middle Ages, and the Renaissance*. Cambridge, Mass., 1961. (First published in 1947 as *The Dignity of Man*.)

———. *The Wars of Truth: Studies in the Decay of Christian Humanism in the Earlier Seventeenth Century*. Cambridge, Mass., 1952.

Bakhtin, Mikhail M. *Rabelais and His World*, trans. H. Iswolsky. Cambridge, Mass., 1968.

Barkan, Leonard, *Nature's Work of Art: The Human Body as Image of the World*. New Haven, 1975.

———. *The Gods Made Flesh: Metamorphosis and the Pursuit of Paganism*. New Haven, 1986.

Barroll, J. Leeds. *Politics, Plague, and Shakespeare's Theater: The Stuart Years*. Ithaca, N.Y., 1991.

Bindoff, S. T., et al., eds. *Elizabethan Government and Society*. Essays presented to Sir John Neale. London, 1961.

Bush, Douglas. *The Renaissance and English Humanism*. Toronto, 1939.

Buxton, John. *Elizabethan Taste*. London, 1963.

Byrne, Muriel St. Clare. *Elizabethan Life in Town and Country*. 8th ed. London, 1970.

Camden, Carroll. *The Elizabethan Woman*. Houston, 1952.

Caspari, Fritz. *Humanism and the Social Order in Tudor England*. Chicago, 1954.

Cassirer, Ernst. *The Platonic Renaissance in England*, trans. J. E. Pettegrove. Austin, Tex., 1953.

De Grazia, Margreta, Maureen Quilligan, and Peter Stallybrass, eds. *Subject and Object in Renaissance Culture*. Cambridge, Eng., 1996.

Einstein, Lewis. *Tudor Ideals*. New York, 1921.

Elizabeth I. *Collected Works*, eds. Leah S. Marcus, Janel Mueller, and Mary Beth Rose. Chicago, 2000.

Elton, G. R. *The Tudor Revolution in Government*. Cambridge, Eng., 1959.

Fumerton, Patricia, and Simon Hunt, eds. *Renaissance Culture and the Everyday*. Philadelphia, 1999.

Gallagher, Lowell. *Medusa's Gaze: Casuistry and Conscience in the Renaissance*. Stanford, 1991.

Harrison, G. B. *An Elizabethan Journal*. London, 1928; supplements.

———. *A Jacobean Journal . . . 1603–1606*. London, 1941.

———. *A Second Jacobean Journal . . . 1607 to 1610*. Ann Arbor, Mich., 1958.

Haydn, Hiram. *The Counter-Renaissance*. New York, 1950.

Helgerson, Richard. *Forms of Nationhood: The Elizbethan Writing of England*. Chicago, 1992.

Heninger, S. K., Jr. *A Handbook of Renaissance Meteorology*. Durham, N.C., 1960.

Hirst, Derek. *Authority and Conflict: England, 1603–1658*. Cambridge, Mass., 1986.

Huizinga, Johan. *The Waning of the Middle Ages*. London, 1924; Baltimore, 1955.

Hurstfield, Joel, *Elizabeth I and the Unity of England*. London, 1960.

Jones, Ann Rosalind, and Peter Stallybrass. *Renaissance Clothing and the Materials of Memory*. Cambridge, Eng., 2000.

Jordan, Constance. *Renaissance Feminism: Literary Texts and Political Models*. Ithaca, N.Y., 1990.

Judges, A. V., ed. *The Elizabethan Underworld*. London and New York, 1930. Rpt., London, 1965.

Kewes, Paulina, ed. *Plagiarism in Early Modern England*. Basingstoke, Hampshire, Eng., 2003.

Knights, L. C. *Drama and Society in the Age of Jonson*. London, 1937.

Kocher, Paul. *Science and Religion in Elizabethan England*. San Marino, Calif., 1953.

Lee, Morris. *Great Britain's Solomon: James VI and I in His Three Kingdoms*. Urbana, Ill., 1990.

Lovejoy, A. O. *The Great Chain of Being*. Cambridge, Mass., 1936.

MacCaffrey, Wallace T. *The Shaping of the Elizabethan Regime*. Princeton, 1968.

Marotti, Arthur F., ed. *Catholicism and Anti-Catholicism in Early Modern English Texts*. Basingstoke, Hampshire, Eng., 1999.

Matar, Nabil. *Turks, Moors, and Englishmen in the Age of Discovery*. New York, 1999.

Mattingly, Garrett. *The Armada*. Boston, 1959.

McEachern, Claire, and Debora Shuger, eds. *Religion and Culture in Renaissance England*. Cambridge, Eng., 1997.

McElwee, W. *The Wisest Fool in Christendom*. [About James VI and I.] New York, 1958.

McPeek, James A. S. *The Black Book of Knaves and Unthrifts in Shakespeare and Other Renaissance Authors*. Storrs, Conn., 1969.

Neale, John E. *Elizabeth I and Her Parliaments*. 2 vols. London and New York, 1953–1958.

———. *The Elizabethan House of Commons*. London, 1949.

———. *Queen Elizabeth I*. London, 1934; New York, 1957.

Nichols, John, ed. *The Progresses and Public Processions of Queen Elizabeth*. 3 vols. London, 1823.

Patterson, Annabel M. *Reading Holinshed's Chronicles*. Chicago, 1994.

Peck, Linda Levy. *Court Patronage and Corruption in Early Stuart England*. Boston, 1990.

Penrose, Boies. *Travel and Discovery in the Renaissance, 1420–1620*. Cambridge, Mass., 1955.

Quinones, Ricardo J. *The Renaissance Discovery of Time*. Cambridge, Mass., 1972.

Rowse, A. L. *The England of Elizabeth: The Structure of Society*. London, 1951.

Stallybrass, Peter, and Allon White. *The Politics and Poetics of Transgression*. Ithaca, N.Y., and London, 1986.

Stone, Lawrence. *The Crisis of the Aristocracy, 1558–1641*. Oxford, 1965.

———. *The Family, Sex and Marriage in England, 1500–1800*. London, 1977.

Stow, John. *Survey of London*, ed. C. L. Kingsford. Oxford, 1971.

Targoff, Ramie. *Common Prayer: The Language of Public Devotion in Early Modern England*. Chicago, 2001.

Tawney, R. H. *Religion and the Rise of Capitalism*. New York, 1926, 1962.

Tillyard, E. M. W. *The Elizabethan World Picture*. London, 1943, 1967.

Underdown, David. *Revel, Riot, and Rebellion: Popular Politics and Culture in England, 1603–1660*. Oxford, 1985.

Whigham, Frank. *Ambition and Privilege: The Social Tropes of Elizabethan Courtesy Theory*. Berkeley, 1984.

Willson, David Harris. *King James VI & I*. New York, 1956.

Wilson, F. P. *Elizabethan and Jacobean*. Oxford, 1945.

Wilson, J. Dover, ed. *Life in Shakespeare's England*. Cambridge, Eng., 1911; 2nd ed., 1926.

Woodbridge, Linda. *Women and the English Renaissance*. Urbana, Ill., 1984.

Wright, Louis B. *Middle-Class Culture in Elizabethan England*. Chapel Hill, N.C., 1935.

Wrightson, Keith. *English Society, 1580–1680*. New Brunswick, N.J., 1982.

Zeeveld, W. Gordon. *Foundations of Tudor Policy*. Cambridge, Mass., 1948.

Shakespeare's Predecessors and Contemporaries

See also, under *Works of Reference*, Bentley, Chambers, Greg, and Harbage; under *London Theaters and Dramatic Companies*, McMillin and MacLean; under *Shakespeare Criticism Since 1980*, Dollimore, Garber (*Cannibals*), Goldberg, Greenblatt, Jardine, Loomba, Mullaney, Newman, and Skura; under *The Histories*, Ribner; and under *The Tragedies*, Bushnell.

Altman, Joel B. *The Tudor Play of Mind: Rhetorical Inquiry and the Development of Elizabethan Drama*. Berkeley, 1978.

Bamford, Karen. *Sexual Violence on the Jacobean Stage*. New York, 2000.

Barber, C. L. *Creating Elizabethan Tragedy: The Theater of Kyd and Marlowe*. Chicago, 1988.

Bartels, Emily C. *Spectacles of Strangeness: Imperialism, Alienation, and Marlowe*. Philadelphia, 1993.

Bednarz, James P. *Shakespeare and the Poets' War*. New York, 2001.

Belsey, Catherine. *The Subject of Tragedy: Identity and Difference in Renaissance Drama*. London, 1985.

Berry, Philippa. *Of Chastity and Power: Elizabethan Literature and the Unmarried Queen*. London and New York, 1989.

Bevington, David. *From "Mankind" to Marlowe: Growth of Structure in the Popular Drama of Tudor England*. Cambridge, Mass., 1962.

———. *Tudor Drama and Politics*. Cambridge, Mass., 1968.

———, and Peter Holbrook, eds. *The Politics of the Stuart Court Masque*. Cambridge, Eng., 1991.

Bowers, Fredson T. *Elizabethan Revenge Tragedy, 1587–1642*. Princeton, 1940.

Braden, Gordon. *Renaissance Tragedy and the Senecan Tradition*. New Haven, 1985.

Braunmuller, A. R., and Michael Hattaway, eds. *The Cambridge Companion to English Renaissance Drama*. Cambridge, Eng., 1990.

Bristol, Michael D. *Carnival and Theater: Plebeian Culture and the Structure of Authority in Renaissance England.* London, 1985.

Brooke, C. F. Tucker, ed. *The Shakespeare Apocrypha.* Oxford, 1908.

Brooks, Douglas A. *From Playhouse to Printing House: Drama and Authorship in Early Modern England.* Cambridge, Eng., 2000.

Bruster, Douglas. *Drama and the Market in the Age of Shakespeare.* Cambridge, Eng., 1992.

Burt, Richard. *Licensed by Authority: Ben Jonson and the Discourses of Censorship.* Ithaca, N.Y., 1993.

Bushnell, Rebecca W. *Tragedies of Tyrants: Political Thought and Theater in the English Renaissance.* Ithaca, N.Y., 1990.

Butterworth, Philip. *Theatre of Fire: Special Effects in Early English and Scottish Theatre.* London, 1998.

Caputi, Anthony. *John Marston, Satirist.* Ithaca, N.Y., 1961.

Cohen, Walter. *Drama of a Nation: Public Theater in Renaissance England and Spain.* Ithaca, N.Y., 1985.

Comensoli, Viviana, and Anna Russell, eds. *Enacting Gender on the English Renaissance Stage.* Urbana, Ill., 1999.

Cox, John D., and David Scott Kastan, eds. *A New History of Early English Drama.* New York, 1997.

Craik, T. W. *The Tudor Interlude.* Leicester, 1958, 1962.

Dawson, Anthony B., and Paul Yachnin. *The Culture of Playgoing in Shakespeare's England: A Collaborative Debate.* Cambridge, Eng., 2001.

Deats, Sara Munson. *Sex, Gender, and Desire in the Plays of Christopher Marlowe.* Newark, Del., 1997.

Dessen, Alan C. *Elizabethan Drama and the Viewer's Eye.* Chapel Hill, N.C., 1977.

Diehl, Huston. *Staging Reform, Reforming the Stage: Protestantism and Popular Theater in Early Modern England.* Ithaca, N.Y., 1997.

Dillon, Janette. *Theatre, Court and City, 1595–1610: Drama and Social Space in London.* Cambridge, Eng., 2000.

DiGangi, Mario. *The Homoerotics of Early Modern Drama.* Cambridge, Eng., 1997.

Dolan, Frances E. *Dangerous Familiars: Representations of Domestic Crime in England, 1550–1700.* Ithaca, N.Y., 1994.

Doran, Madeleine. *Endeavors of Art: A Study of Form in Elizabethan Drama.* Madison, Wis., 1954, 1972.

Farley-Hills, David. *Shakespeare and the Rival Playwrights, 1600–1606.* London, 1990.

Findlay, Alison. *A Feminist Perspective on Renaissance Drama.* Oxford, 1999.

———. *Illegitimate Power: Bastards in Renaissance Drama.* Manchester, Eng., 1994.

Finkelpearl, Philip. *John Marston of the Middle Temple.* Cambridge, Mass., 1969.

Freer, Coburn. *The Poetics of Jacobean Drama.* Baltimore, 1981.

Gardiner, H. C. *Mysteries' End.* New Haven, 1946.

Gibbons, Brian. *Jacobean City Comedy.* London, 1968.

Hall, Kim F. *Things of Darkness: Economies of Race and Gender in Early Modern England.* Ithaca, N.Y., 1995.

Hardison, O. B., Jr. *Christian Rite and Christian Drama in the Middle Ages.* Baltimore, 1965.

Hassel, R. Chris. *Renaissance Drama and the English Church Year.* Lincoln, Neb., 1979.

Hattaway, Michael. *Elizabethan Popular Theatre: Plays in Performance.* London, 1982.

Hawkins, Harriett. *Likenesses of Truth in Elizabethan and Restoration Drama.* Oxford, 1972.

Helgerson, Richard. *Adulterous Alliances: Home, State, and History in Early Modern European Drama and Painting.* Chicago, 2000.

Hendricks, Margo, and Patricia Parker, eds. *Women, "Race," and Writing in the Early Modern Period.* London and New York, 1994.

Holbrook, Peter. *Literature and Degree in Renaissance England: Nashe, Bourgeois Tragedy, Shakespeare.* Newark, Del., 1994.

Howard, Jean. *The Stage and Social Struggle in Early Modern England.* London and New York, 1994.

Hunter, G. K. *John Lyly: The Humanist as Courtier.* Cambridge, Mass., 1962.

Kastan, David Scott, and Peter Stallybrass, eds. *Staging the Renaissance: Reinterpretations of Elizabethan and Jacobean Drama.* New York and London, 1991.

Kernan, Alvin. *The Cankered Muse: Satire of the English Renaissance.* New Haven, 1959.

Kiefer, Frederick. *Writing on the Renaissance Stage: Written Words, Printed Pages, Metaphoric Books.* Newark, Del., 1996.

Kirsch, Arthur C. *Jacobean Dramatic Perspectives.* Charlottesville, Va., 1972.

Kolve, V. A. *The Play Called Corpus Christi.* Palo Alto and London, 1966.

Leggatt, Alexander. *Citizen Comedy in the Age of Shakespeare.* Toronto, 1973.

———. *Jacobean Public Theatre.* London, 1992.

Leishman, J. B., ed. *The Three Parnassus Plays (1598–1601).* London, 1949.

Levin, Harry. *The Overreacher: A Study of Christopher Marlowe.* Cambridge, Mass., 1952, 1964.

Levin, Richard. *The Multiple Plot in English Renaissance Drama.* Chicago, 1971.

Margeson, J. M. R. *The Origins of English Tragedy.* Oxford, 1967.

Marrapodi, Michele, ed., with A. J. Hoenselaars. *The Italian World of English Renaissance Drama: Cultural Exchange and Intertextuality.* Newark, Del., 1998.

Maus, Katharine Eisaman. *Inwardness and Theater in the English Renaissance Drama.* Chicago, 1995.

McAlindon, T. *English Renaissance Tragedy.* London, 1986.

McLuskie, Kathleen. *Renaissance Dramatists.* (Feminist Readings.) Atlantic Highlands, N.J., 1989.

Orgel, Stephen. *The Illusion of Power: Political Theater in the English Renaissance.* Berkeley, 1975.

———. *Impersonations: The Performance of Gender in Shakespeare's England.* Cambridge, Eng., 1996.

Orgel, Stephen, and Roy Strong. *Inigo Jones: The Theatre of the Stuart Court.* 2 vols. London and Berkeley, 1973.

Ornstein, Robert. *The Moral Vision of Jacobean Tragedy.* Madison, Wis., 1960.

Rabkin, Norman, ed: *Reinterpretations of Elizabethan Drama.* New York, 1969.

Rasmussen, Mark David, ed. *Renaissance Literature and Its Formal Engagements.* Basingstoke, Hampshire, 2002.

Rose, Mary Beth. *The Expense of Spirit: Love and Sexuality in English Renaissance Drama.* Ithaca, N.Y., 1988.

———. *Gender and Heroism in Early Modern English Literature.* Chicago, 2002.

———. ed. *Renaissance Drama as Cultural History.* Evanston, Ill., 1990.

Sanders, Wilbur. *The Dramatist and the Received Idea: Studies in the Plays of Marlowe and Shakespeare.* Cambridge, Eng., 1968.

Shannon, Laurie. *Sovereign Amity: Figures of Friendship in Shakespearean Contexts.* Chicago, 2002.

Shapiro, James. *Rival Playwrights: Marlowe, Jonson, Shakespeare.* New York, 1991.

Smith, Bruce R. *The Acoustic World of Early Modern England.* Chicago, 1999.

Smith, David L., Richard Strier, and David Bevington, eds. *The Theatrical City: Culture, Theatre and Politics in London, 1567–1649.* Cambridge, Eng., 1995.

Southern, Richard. *The Medieval Theatre in the Round.* London, 1957.

Spivack, Bernard. *Shakespeare and the Allegory of Evil.* New York, 1958.

Traub, Valerie, M. Lindsay Kaplan, and Dympna C. Callaghan, eds. *Feminist Readings of Early Modern Culture: Emerging Subjects.* Cambridge, Eng., 1996.

Vickers, Brian. *"Counterfeiting" Shakespeare: Evidence, Authorship, and John Ford's "Funeral Elegye."* Cambridge, Eng., 2002.

Waith, Eugene M. *The Herculean Hero in Marlowe, Chapman, Shakespeare, and Dryden.* New York, 1962.

Whigham, Frank. *Seizures of the Will in Early Modern English Drama.* Cambridge, Eng., 1996.

White, Paul Whitfield. *Marlowe, History, and Sexuality: New Critical Essays on Christopher Marlowe.* New York, 1998.

———. *Theatre and Reformation: Protestantism, Patronage and Playing in Tudor England.* Cambridge, Eng., 1993.

Wickham, Glynne. *Early English Stages, 1300 to 1660.* 3 vols. London, 1959–1972.

Wilson, F. P. *Marlowe and the Early Shakespeare.* Oxford, 1953.

Woodbridge, Linda. *Women and the English Renaissance: Literature and the Nature of Womankind, 1540–1620.* Urbana, Ill., 1984.

Woolf, Rosemary. *The English Mystery Plays.* Berkeley and Los Angeles, 1972.

Yachnin, Paul. *Stage-Wrights: Shakespeare, Jonson, Middleton, and the Making of Theatrical Value.* Philadelphia, 1997.

Zimmerman, Susan, ed. *Erotic Politics: Desire on the Renaissance Stage.* London and New York, 1992.

London Theaters and Dramatic Companies

See also, under *Works of Reference*, Bentley, and Chambers (*Elizabethan Stage*).

Astington, John H., ed. *The Development of Shakespeare's Theater.* New York, 1992.

Beckerman, Bernard. *Shakespeare at the Globe, 1599–1609.* New York, 1962, 1967.

Bentley, Gerald Eades. *The Profession of Dramatist in Shakespeare's Time, 1590–1642.* Princeton, 1971.

———. *The Profession of Player in Shakespeare's Time, 1590–1642.* Princeton, 1984.

Berry, Herbert. *Shakespeare's Playhouses.* New York, 1987.

Bradley, David. *From Text to Performance in the Elizabethan Theatre: Preparing the Play for the Stage.* Cambridge, Eng., 1992.

Clare, Janet. *"Art Made Tongue-Tied by Authority": Elizabethan and Jacobean Dramatic Censorship.* Manchester, Eng., 1990.

Cook, Ann Jennalie. *The Privileged Playgoers of Shakespeare's London, 1576–1642.* Princeton, 1981.

Dutton, Richard. *Mastering the Revels: The Regulation and Censorship of English Renaissance Drama.* Iowa City, 1991.

Feuillerat, Albert, ed. *Documents Relating to the Office of the Revels in the Time of Queen Elizabeth.* Louvain (Louven), Belgium, 1908.

Foakes, R. A., ed. *The Henslowe Papers: The Diary, Theatre Papers, and Bear Garden Papers.* In full and in facsimile. 3 vols. in 2. London, 1976.

Foakes, R. A., and R. T. Rickert, eds. *Henslowe's Diary.* London, 1961.

Gair, W. Reavley. *The Children of Paul's.* Cambridge, Eng., 1982.

Greg, W. W., ed. *Dramatic Documents from the Elizabethan Playhouses: Stage Plots; Actors' Parts; Prompt Books.* 2 vols. Oxford, 1931.

Gurr, Andrew. *Playgoing in Shakespeare's London.* Cambridge, Eng., 1987; 2nd ed., 1996.

———. *The Shakespearian Playing Companies.* Oxford, 1996.

——— *The Shakespearean Stage, 1574–1642.* Cambridge, Eng., 1970; 2nd ed., 1980.

Gurr, Andrew, and John Orrell. *Rebuilding Shakespeare's Globe.* London and New York, 1989.

Harbage, Alfred. *Shakespeare's Audience.* New York, 1941.

Hodges, C. Walter. *The Globe Restored.* London, 1953; 2nd ed., New York, 1968.

Hosley, Richard. "Was There a Music-room in Shakespeare's Globe?" *ShS* 13 (1960), 113–23.

Ingram, William. *The Business of Playing: The Beginnings of the Adult Professional Theater in Elizabethan London.* Ithaca, N.Y., 1992.

King, T. J. *Casting Shakespeare's Plays: London Actors and Their Roles, 1590–1642.* Cambridge, Eng., 1992.

———. *Shakespearean Staging, 1599–1642.* Cambridge, Mass., 1971.

Knutson, Roslyn Lander. *The Repertory of Shakespeare's Company, 1594–1613.* Fayetteville, Ark., 1991.

———. *Playing Companies and Commerce in Shakespeare's Time.* Cambridge, Eng., 2001.

Linthicum, Marie C. *Costume in the Drama of Shakespeare and His Contemporaries.* Oxford, 1936.

Mann, David. *The Elizabethan Player: Contemporary Stage Representation.* London, 1991.

McMillin, Scott. *The Elizabethan Theatre and "The Book of Sir Thomas More."* Ithaca, N.Y., 1987.

McMillin, Scott, and Sally-Beth MacLean. *The Queen's Men and Their Plays.* Cambridge, Eng., 1998.

Nelson, Alan H. *Early Cambridge Theatres: College, University, and Town Stages, 1464–1720.* Cambridge, Eng., 1994.

Nungezer, Edwin. *A Dictionary of Actors.* London and New Haven, 1929.

Shapiro, Michael. *Children of the Revels: The Boys' Companies of Shakespeare's Time and Their Plays.* New York, 1977.

Wickham, Glynne. *Early English Stages, 1300 to 1660.* 3 vols. London, 1959–1972.

Shakespeare's Life and Work

Alexander, Peter. *Shakespeare's Life and Art.* New ed., New York, 1961.

Baldwin, T. W. *William Shakspere's Small Latine and Lesse Greeke.* 2 vols. Urbana, Ill., 1944.

Chambers, E. K. *William Shakespeare: A Study of Facts and Problems.* 2 vols. Oxford, 1930.

Eccles, Mark. *Shakespeare in Warwickshire.* Madison, Wis., 1961.

Honan, Park. *Shakespeare: A Life.* Oxford, 1998.

Matus, Irvin Leigh, *Shakespeare, In Fact.* New York, 1994.

Schoenbaum, S. *Shakespeare's Lives.* Oxford and New York, 1970.

———. *William Shakespeare: A Documentary Life.* Oxford, 1975. Also published with fewer illustrations and a slightly revised text as *A Compact Documentary Life.* 1977.

———. *William Shakespeare: Records and Images.* Oxford, 1981.

Wells, Stanley. *Shakespeare: A Life in Drama.* New York and London, 1995.

Wheeler, Richard P. "Deaths in the Family: The Loss of a Son and the Rise of Shakespearean Comedy," *SQ* 51 (2000), 127–53.

Shakespeare's Language: His Development as Poet and Dramatist

See also, under *Works of Reference*, Abbott, Onions, and Schmidt; and under *The Comedies*, Elam.

Barton, Anne. "Shakespeare and the Limits of Language," *ShS* 24 (1971), 19–30.

Byrne, Muriel St. Clare. "The Foundations of Elizabethan Language," *ShS* 17 (1964), 223–39.

Charney, Maurice. *Shakespeare's Roman Plays: The Function of Imagery in the Drama.* Cambridge, Mass., 1961.

———. *Style in Hamlet.* Princeton, 1969.

Clemen, Wolfgang H. *The Development of Shakespeare's Imagery.* Cambridge, Mass., 1951.

Cruttwell, Patrick. *The Shakespearean Moment and Its Place in the Poetry of the Seventeenth Century.* London, 1954.

Desmet, Christy. *Reading Shakespeare's Characters: Rhetoric, Ethics, and Identity.* Amherst, Mass., 1992.

Dobson, E. J. *English Pronunciation, 1500–1700.* 2 vols. 2nd ed. Oxford, 1968.

Donawerth, Jane. *Shakespeare and the Sixteenth-Century Study of Language.* Urbana, Ill., 1984.

Doran, Madeleine. *Shakespeare's Dramatic Language.* Madison, Wis., 1976.

Empson, William. *The Structure of Complex Words.* London, 1951; 3rd ed., 1977.

Hulme, Hilda M. *Explorations in Shakespeare's Language.* London, 1962.

Kermode, Frank. *Shakespeare's Language.* New York, 2000.

Kökeritz, Helge. *Shakespeare's Names.* New Haven, 1959.

———. *Shakespeare's Pronunciation.* New Haven, 1953.

Lanham, Richard A. *The Motives of Eloquence: Literary Rhetoric in the Renaissance.* New Haven, 1976.

Magnussen, Lynne. *Shakespeare and Social Dialogue: Dramatic Language and Elizabethan Letters.* Cambridge, Eng., 1999.

Mahood, M. M. *Shakespeare's Wordplay.* London, 1957.

Miriam Joseph, Sister. *Shakespeare's Use of the Arts of Language.* New York, 1947. Rpt. in part as *Rhetoric in Shakespeare's Time.* 1962.

Nares, Robert. *A Glossary . . . of Shakespeare and His Contemporaries.* New ed. J. O. Halliwell and Thomas Wright. 2 vols. London, 1859, 1905, Rpt. Detroit, 1966.

Partridge, Eric. *Shakespeare's Bawdy.* London, 1947, 1955.

Spurgeon, Caroline. *Shakespeare's Imagery and What it Tells Us.* Cambridge, Eng., 1935.

Thompson, Ann and John O. *Shakespeare: Meaning and Metaphor.* Iowa City, 1987.

Thorne, Alison. *Vision and Rhetoric in Shakespeare: Looking Through Language.* Basingstoke and New York, 2000.

Vickers, Brian. *The Artistry of Shakespeare's Prose.* London, 1968.

Willbern, David. *Poetic Will: Shakespeare and the Play of Language*. Philadelphia, 1997.

Willcock, Gladys D. "Shakespeare and Elizabethan English," *ShS* 7 (1954), 12–24.

Wright, George T. *Shakespeare's Metrical Art*. Berkeley, 1988.

Textual Criticism and Bibliography

See also under *King Lear*, Urkowitz.

Alexander, Peter. *Shakespeare's "Henry VI" and "Richard III."* Cambridge, Eng., 1929.

Blayney, Peter W. M. *The First Folio of Shakespeare*. Washington D.C., 1991.

———. *The Texts of "King Lear" and Their Origins*. Vol. 1. Cambridge, Eng., 1982.

Bowers, Fredson. *Bibliography and Textual Criticism*. Oxford, 1964.

———. *On Editing Shakespeare*. Charlottesville, Va., 1966.

———. *Principles of Bibliographical Description*. Princeton, 1949.

———. *Textual and Literary Criticism*. Cambridge, Eng., 1959.

Chambers, E. K. *William Shakespeare: A Study of Facts and Problems*. 2 vols. Oxford, 1930.

De Grazia, Margreta. *Shakespeare Verbatim: The Reproduction of Authenticity and the 1790 Apparatus*. Oxford, 1991.

Doran, Madeleine. *"Henry VI," Parts II and III: Their Relation to "The Contention" and "The True Tragedy."* Iowa City, 1928.

Duthie, G. I. *Elizabethan Shorthand and the First Quarto of "King Lear."* Oxford, 1949.

Gaskell, Philip. *A New Introduction to Bibliography*. New York and Oxford, 1972.

Greg, W. W. *The Editorial Problem in Shakespeare*. 3rd ed. Oxford, 1954.

———. *Principles of Emendation in Shakespeare*. London, 1928.

———. *The Shakespeare First Folio: Its Bibliographical and Textual History*. Oxford, 1955.

Hart, Alfred. *Stolne and Surreptitious Copies: A Comparative Study of Shakespeare's Bad Quartos*. Melbourne and London, 1942.

Hinman, Charlton. *The Printing and Proof-Reading of the First Folio of Shakespeare*. 2 vols. Oxford, 1963.

Honigmann, E. A. J. *The Stability of Shakespeare's Text*. London and Lincoln, Neb., 1965.

Long, William B. " 'A bed for woodstock': A Warning for the Unwary," *Medieval and Renaissance Drama in England* 2 (1985), 91–118.

Maguire, Laurie E., and Thomas L. Berger, eds. *Textual Formations and Reformations*. Newark, Del., 1998.

Masten, Jeffrey. *Textual Intercourse: Collaboration, Authorship, and Sexualities in Renaissance Drama*. Cambridge, Eng., 1997.

McKerrow, Ronald B. *An Introduction to Bibliography for Literary Students*. Oxford, 1927.

———. *Prolegomena for the Oxford Shakespeare*. Oxford, 1939.

McLeod, Randall, ed. *Crisis in Editing: Texts of the English Renaissance*. New York, 1994.

Mowat, Barbara, and Paul Werstine, eds. *The New Folger Library Shakespeare*. New York, 1992–.

Nosworthy, J. M. *Shakespeare's Occasional Plays: Their Origin and Transmission*. London and New York, 1965.

Pechter, Edward, ed. *Textual and Theatrical Shakespeare: Questions of Evidence*. Iowa City, Iowa, 1996.

Pollard, Alfred W. *Shakespeare Folios and Quartos: A Study in the Bibliography of Shakespeare's Plays, 1594–1685*. London, 1909.

———. *Shakespeare's Fight with the Pirates and the Problems of the Transmission of His Text*. Rev. ed. Cambridge, Eng., 1937.

Sisson, C. J. *New Readings in Shakespeare*. 2 vols. Cambridge, Eng., 1956.

Taylor, Gary, and Michael Warren, eds. *The Division of the Kingdoms: Shakespeare's Two Versions of "King Lear."* Oxford, 1983.

Walker, Alice. *Textual Problems of the First Folio*. Cambridge, Eng., 1953.

Wells, Stanley. *Re-editing Shakespeare for the Modern Reader*. Oxford, 1984.

Wells, Stanley, and Gary Taylor. *Modernizing Shakespeare's Spelling*. Oxford, 1979.

Werstine, Paul. "'Foul Papers' and 'Prompt-books': Printer's Copy for Shakespeare's *Comedy of Errors*," *Studies in Bibliography* 41 (1988), 232–46.

Shakespeare Criticism to the 1930s

Badawi, M. M. *Coleridge: Critic of Shakespeare*. Cambridge, Eng., 1973.

Bradby, Anne, ed. *Shakespeare Criticism, 1919–35*. London, 1936.

Coleridge, S. T. *Coleridge on Shakespeare: The Text of the Lectures of 1811–12*, ed. R. A. Foakes. Charlottesville, Va., 1971.

———. *Coleridge's Writings on Shakespeare*, ed. Terence Hawkes. New York, 1959.

Evans, G. Blakemore, ed. *Shakespeare: Aspects of Influence*. Cambridge, Mass., 1976.

Hazlitt, William. *Characters of Shakespear's Plays*. London, 1817.

Johnson, Samuel. *Johnson on Shakespeare*, ed. Arthur Sherbo. Vol. 7 of *The Yale Edition of the Works of Samuel Johnson*. New Haven, 1968.

Kermode, Frank, ed. *Four Centuries of Shakespearean Criticism*. New York, 1965.

Knight, G. Wilson. *The Shakespearian Tempest*. London, 1932, 1953.

Muir, Kenneth. "Fifty Years of Shakespearian Criticism: 1900–1950," *ShS* 4 (1951), 1–25.

Rabkin, Norman, ed. *Approaches to Shakespeare*. New York, 1964.

Ralli, Augustus. *A History of Shakespearian Criticism*. 2 vols. London, 1932.

Raysor, T. M., ed. *Samuel Taylor Coleridge: Shakespearean Criticism*. 2 vols. 2nd ed. London, 1960.

Schlegel, August Wilhelm. *Lectures on Dramatic Art and Literature*, trans. John Black, 1846. Rpt., New York, 1965.

Schücking, Levin L. *Character Problems in Shakespeare's Plays*. London, 1917; trans., 1922.

Shaw, G. B. *Shaw on Shakespeare*, ed. Edwin Wilson. New York, 1961.

Sherbo, Arthur. *Samuel Johnson, Editor of Shakespeare*. Urbana, Ill., 1956.

Smith, David Nichol, ed. *Shakespeare Criticism: A Selection*. World's Classics, Oxford, 1916.

———, ed. *Eighteenth Century Essays on Shakespeare*. 2nd ed. Oxford, 1963.

Stoll, E. E. *Art and Artifice in Shakespeare*. Cambridge, Eng., 1933, 1962.

Vickers, Brian, ed. *Shakespeare: The Critical Heritage*. Several volumes. London and Boston, 1974—.

Welsford, Enid. *The Fool: His Social and Literary History*. London, 1935; rpt. 1966.

Westfall, A. V. *American Shakespearean Criticism, 1607–1865*. New York, 1939.

Shakespeare Criticism from the 1940s to the 1970s

Armstrong, Edward A. *Shakespeare's Imagination: A Study of the Psychology of Association and Inspiration*. London, 1946.

Bethell, S. L. *Shakespeare and the Popular Dramatic Tradition*. London and Durham, N.C., 1944.

Bevington, David, and Jay L. Halio, eds. *Shakespeare: Pattern of Excelling Nature*. Newark, Del., 1978.

Bloom, Allan, with Harry V. Jaffa. *Shakespeare's Politics*. New York and London, 1964.

Brown, John Russell. *Shakespeare's Plays in Performance*. London, 1966.

Bryant, J. A., Jr. *Hippolyta's View: Some Christian Aspects of Shakespeare's Plays*. Lexington, Ky., 1961.

Burckhardt, Sigurd. *Shakespearean Meanings*. Princeton, 1968.

Burke, Kenneth. *Language as Symbolic Action*. Berkeley, 1966.

Calderwood, James L. *Shakespearean Metadrama*. Minneapolis, 1971.

Coghill, Neville. *Shakespeare's Professional Skills*. Cambridge, Eng., 1964.

Colie, Rosalie L. *Shakespeare's Living Art*. Princeton, 1974.

Council, Norman. *When Honour's at the Stake: Ideas of Honour in Shakespeare's Plays*. London, 1973.

Danby, John F. *Poets on Fortune's Hill: Studies in Sidney, Shakespeare, and Beaumont and Fletcher*. London, 1952.

Dean, Leonard F., ed. *Shakespeare: Modern Essays in Criticism*. New York, 1967.

Driver, Tom F. *The Sense of History in Greek and Shakespearean Drama*. New York, 1960.

Dusinberre, Juliet. *Shakespeare and the Nature of Women*. New York, 1975. 2nd ed., 1996.

Eagleton, Terence. *Shakespeare and Society*. New York and London, 1967.

Edwards, Philip. *Shakespeare and the Confines of Art*. London and New York, 1968.

Empson, William. *The Structure of Complex Words*. London, 1951.

Fiedler, Leslie A. *The Stranger in Shakespeare*. New York, 1972.

Fly, Richard. *Shakespeare's Mediated World*. Amherst, Mass., 1976.

Frye, Roland M. *Shakespeare and Christian Doctrine*. Princeton, 1963.

Garber, Marjorie B. *Dream in Shakespeare: From Metaphor to Metamorphosis.* New Haven and London, 1974.

Goddard, Harold C. *The Meaning of Shakespeare.* Chicago, 1951.

Goldman, Michael. *Shakespeare and the Energies of Drama.* Princeton, 1972.

Granville-Barker, Harley. *Prefaces to Shakespeare.* 2 vols. Princeton, 1946–1947.

Harbage, Alfred. *As They Liked it.* New York, 1947.

———. *Shakespeare and the Rival Traditions.* New York, 1952.

Hawkes, Terence. *Shakespeare's Talking Animals: Language and Drama in Society.* London, 1973.

Hawkins, Harriett. *Poetic Freedom and Poetic Truth: Chaucer, Shakespeare, Marlowe, Milton.* Oxford, 1976.

Holland, Norman. *Psychoanalysis and Shakespeare.* New York, 1966.

———. *The Shakespearean Imagination.* New York, 1964.

Jones, Emrys. *The Origins of Shakespeare.* Oxford, 1977.

Jorgensen, Paul A. *Shakespeare's Military World.* Berkeley and Los Angeles, 1956.

Kernan, Alvin B. *The Playwright as Magician: Shakespeare's Image of the Poet in the English Public Theater.* New Haven, 1979.

———, ed. *Modern Shakespearean Criticism.* New York, 1970.

Kettle, Arnold, ed. *Shakespeare in a Changing World.* London and New York, 1964.

Knights, L. C. *Some Shakespearean Themes.* London, 1959.

Kott, Jan. *Shakespeare Our Contemporary.* New York, 1964.

Leavis, F. R. *The Common Pursuit.* London, 1952.

Levin, Richard. *New Readings vs. Old Plays: Recent Trends in the Reinterpretation of English Renaissance Drama.* Chicago, 1979.

McAlindon, T. *Shakespeare and Decorum.* London and New York, 1973.

Rabkin, Norman. *Shakespeare and the Common Understanding.* New York, 1967.

Righter, Anne. *Shakespeare and the Idea of the Play.* London, 1962.

Rossiter, A. P. *Angel with Horns.* London, 1961.

Sanders, Wilbur. *The Dramatist and the Received Idea: Studies in the Plays of Marlowe and Shakespeare.* Cambridge, Eng., 1968.

Sewell, Arthur. *Character and Society in Shakespeare.* London, 1951.

Soellner, Rolf. *Shakespeare's Patterns of Self-Knowledge.* Columbus, Ohio, 1972.

Spencer, Theodore. *Shakespeare and the Nature of Man.* New York, 1942.

Spivack, Bernard. *Shakespeare and the Allegory of Evil.* New York, 1958.

Stewart, J. I. M. *Character and Motive in Shakespeare.* London, 1949.

Stirling, Brents. *The Populace in Shakespeare.* New York, 1949.

Traversi, Derek. *An Approach to Shakespeare.* 2 vols. Rev. ed. London, 1968.

Van Laan, Thomas F. *Role-Playing in Shakespeare.* Toronto, 1978.

Watson, Curtis Brown. *Shakespeare and the Renaissance Concept of Honor.* Princeton, 1960.

Weimann, Robert. *Shakespeare and the Popular Tradition in the Theater,* ed. Robert Schwartz. Baltimore, 1978.

Whitaker, Virgil K. *Shakespeare's Use of Learning.* San Marino, Calif., 1953.

Zeeveld, W. Gordon. *The Temper of Shakespeare's Thought.* New Haven and London, 1974.

Shakespeare Criticism Since 1980, including New Historicism, Gender Studies, and Poststructuralism

See also, under *Shakespeare's Predecessors and Contemporaries,* Bednarz, Belsey, Braden, Bristol, Bruster, Cohen, Dolan, Farley-Hills, Findlay (two items), Freer, McLuskie, Orgel, Rasmussen, Rose, Shannon, and Vickers; and under *Shakespeare Criticism from the 1940s to the 1970s,* Weimann.

Adelman, Janet. *Suffocating Mothers: Fantasies of Maternal Origin in Shakespeare's Plays, "Hamlet" to "The Tempest."* Chicago, 1992.

Alexander, Catherine M. S., and Stanley Wells, eds. *Shakespeare and Race.* Cambridge, Eng., 2000.

Auden, W. H. *Lectures on Shakespeare,* ed. Arthur Kirsch. Princeton, 2000.

Bamber, Linda. *Comic Women, Tragic Men: A Study of Gender and Genre in Shakespeare.* Stanford, 1982.

Barber, C. L. *The Whole Journey: Shakespeare's Power of Development.* Berkeley, 1986.

Bate, Jonathan. *The Genius of Shakespeare.* Oxford, 1997.

Belsey, Catherine. *Shakespeare and the Loss of Eden: The Construction of Family Values in Early Modern Culture.* New Brunswick, N.J., 1999.

Berger, Harry, Jr. *Making Trifles of Terrors: Redistributing Complicities in Shakespeare.* ed. Peter Erickson. Stanford, 1997.

Bergeron, David, ed. *Pageantry in the Shakespearean Theater.* Athens, Ga., 1985.

Bevington, David. *Shakespeare.* Oxford, 2002.

Boose, Lynda E. "The Father and the Bride in Shakespeare," *PMLA* 97 (1982), 325–47.

Bristol, Michael. *Shakespeare's America, America's Shakespeare.* London and New York, 1990.

Bulman, James C., ed. *Shakespeare, Theory, and Performance.* London and New York, 1996.

Calderwood, James. *Shakespeare and the Denial of Death.* Amherst, Mass., 1987.

Callaghan, Dympna C. *Shakespeare Without Women: Representing Gender and Race on the Renaissance Stage.* London and New York, 2000.

———, ed. *A Feminist Companion to Shakespeare.* Oxford, 2000.

Callaghan, Dympna, Lorraine Helms, and Jyotsna Singh. *The Weyward Sisters: Shakespeare and Feminist Politics.* Cambridge, Eng., 1994.

Carey, John, ed. *English Renaissance Studies.* Oxford, 1980.

Cartelli, Thomas. *Repositioning Shakespeare: National Formations, Postcolonial Appropriations.* London and New York, 1999.

Cavell, Stanley. *Disowning Knowledge in Six Plays of Shakespeare.* Cambridge, Eng., 1987.

Charnes, Linda. *Notorious Identity: Materializing the Subject in Shakespeare.* Cambridge, Mass., 1993.

Cook, Ann Jennalie. *Making a Match: Courtship in Shakespeare and His Society.* Princeton, 1991.

Cox, John D. *Shakespeare and the Dramaturgy of Power.* Princeton, 1989.

Daileder, Celia R. *Eroticism on the Renaissance Stage: Transcendence, Desire, and the Limits of the Visible.* Cambridge, Eng., 1998.

Danson, Lawrence. *Shakespeare's Dramatic Genres.* Oxford, 2000.

Dawson, Anthony B. *Indirections: Shakespeare and the Art of Illusion.* Toronto, 1984.

De Grazia, Margreta, Maureen Quilligan, and Peter Stallybrass, eds. *Subject and Object in Renaissance Culture.* Cambridge, Eng., 1996.

Desmet, Christy. *Reading Shakespeare's Characters: Rhetoric, Ethics, and Identity.* Amherst, Mass., 1992.

Desmet, Christy, and Robert Sawyer, eds. *Shakespeare and Appropriation.* London and New York, 1999.

Dobson, Michael. *The Making of the National Poet: Shakespeare, Adaptation, and Authorship, 1660–1769.* Oxford, 1992.

Dolan, Frances E. *Dangerous Familiars: Representations of Domestic Crime in England, 1550–1700.* Ithaca, N.Y., 1994.

Dollimore, Jonathan. *Radical Tragedy: Religion, Ideology and Power in the Drama of Shakespeare and His Contemporaries.* Chicago, 1984; New York, 1989.

Dollimore, Jonathan, and Alan Sinfield. *Political Shakespeare: New Essays in Cultural Materialism.* Manchester, Eng., 1985.

Drakakis, John, ed. *Alternative Shakespeares.* London, 1985.

Dubrow, Heather, and Richard Strier, eds. *The Historical Renaissance: New Essays on Tudor and Stuart Literature and Culture.* Chicago, 1988.

Eagleton, Terence. *William Shakespeare.* Oxford, 1986.

Edwards, Philip, et al., eds. *Shakespeare's Styles.* Cambridge, Eng., 1980.

Engle, Lars. *Shakespearean Pragmatism: Market of His Time.* Chicago, 1993.

Erickson, Peter. *Patriarchal Structures in Shakespeare's Drama.* Berkeley, 1985.

Erickson, Peter, and Coppélia Kahn, eds. *Shakespeare's Rough Magic: Essays in Honor of C. L. Barber.* Newark, Del., 1985.

French, Marilyn. *Shakespeare's Division of Experience.* New York, 1981.

Frye, Northrop. *Northrop Frye on Shakespeare,* ed. Robert Sandler. New Haven, 1986.

Fumerton, Patricia, and Simon Hunt, eds. *Renaissance Culture and the Everyday.* Philadelphia, 1999.

Garber, Marjorie. *Coming of Age in Shakespeare.* London, 1981.

———. *Shakespeare's Ghost Writers: Literature as Uncanny Causality.* London and New York, 1987.

———, ed. *Cannibals, Witches, and Divorce: Estranging the Renaissance.* Baltimore, 1987.

Gibbons, Brian. *Shakespeare and Multiplicity.* Cambridge, Eng., 1993.

Gillies, John. *Shakespeare and the Geography of Difference*. Cambridge, Eng., 1994.

Goldberg, Jonathan. *James I and the Politics of Literature: Jonson, Shakespeare, Donne, and Their Contemporaries*. Baltimore, 1983.

——. *Sodometries: Renaissance Texts, Modern Sexualities*. Stanford, 1992.

Grady, Hugh, ed. *Shakespeare and Modernity: Early Modern to Millennium*. London and New York, 2000.

Greenblatt, Stephen. *Learning to Curse: Essays in Early Modern Culture*. London and New York, 1990.

——. *Marvelous Possessions: The Wonder of the New World*. Chicago, 1991.

——. *Renaissance Self-Fashioning: From More to Shakespeare*. Chicago, 1980.

——. *Shakespearean Negotiations: The Circulation of Social Energy in Renaissance England*. Berkeley, 1988.

Habib, Imtiaz. *Shakespeare and Race: Postcolonial Praxis in the Early Modern Period*. Lanham and Oxford, 2000.

Hall, Kim F. *Things of Darkness: Economies of Race and Gender in Early Modern England*. Ithaca, N.Y., 1994.

Hamilton, Donna B. *Shakespeare and the Politics of Protestant England*. Lexington, Ky., 1992.

Hamlin, William M. *The Image of America in Montaigne, Spenser, and Shakespeare: Renaissance Ethnography and Literary Tradition*. New York, 1995.

Hawkes, Terence. *Meaning by Shakespeare*. London and New York, 1992.

——, ed. *Alternative Shakespeares*. Vol. 2. London and New York, 1996.

Holland, Norman, et al., eds. *Shakespeare's Personality*. Berkeley, 1989.

Howard, Jean E. *Shakespeare's Art of Orchestration: Stage Technique and Audience Response*. Urbana, Ill., 1984.

——. *The Stage and Social Struggle in Early Modern England*. London, 1994.

——, and Marion F. O'Connor, eds. *Shakespeare Reproduced: The Text in History and Ideology*. London and New York, 1987.

——, and Scott Cutler Shershow, eds. *Marxist Shakespeares*. London and New York, 2000.

James, Heather. *Shakespeare's Troy: Drama, Politics, and the Translation of Empire*. Cambridge, Eng., 1997.

Jardine, Lisa. *Reading Shakespeare Historically*. London and New York, 1996.

——. *Still Harping on Daughters: Women and Drama in the Age of Shakespeare*. Sussex and Totowa, N.J., 1983; New York, 1989.

Kahn, Coppélia. *Man's Estate: Masculine Identity in Shakespeare*. Berkeley, 1981.

——. *Roman Shakespeare: Warriors, Wounds, and Women*. London and New York, 1997.

Kamps, Ivo, ed. *Materialist Shakespeare: A History*. London, 1995.

——, ed. *Shakespeare Left and Right*. New York and London, 1991.

Kastan, David Scott. *Shakespeare After Theory*. London, 1999.

——. *Shakespeare and the Book*. Cambridge, Eng., 2001.

——. *Shakespeare and the Shapes of Time*. Hanover, N.H., 1982.

——, ed. *A Companion to Shakespeare*. Oxford, 1999.

Kernan, Alvin. *Shakespeare, the King's Playwright: Theater in the Stuart Court, 1603–1613*. New Haven, 1995.

Kerrigan, William. *Shakespeare's Promises*. Baltimore, 1999.

Kirsch, Arthur. *Shakespeare and the Experience of Love*. Cambridge, Eng., 1981.

Knapp, Robert S. *Shakespeare—The Theater and the Book*. Princeton, 1989.

Knowles, Richard, ed. *Shakespeare and Carnival: After Bakhtin*. London and New York, 1998.

Lenz, Carolyn, et al., eds. *The Woman's Part: Feminist Criticism of Shakespeare*. Urbana, Ill., 1980.

Little, Arthur L., Jr. *Shakespeare Jungle Fever: National-Imperial Re-Visions of Race, Rape, and Sacrifice*. Stanford, 2000.

Loomba, Ania. *Gender, Race, Renaissance Drama*. Manchester, Eng., 1989.

Loomba, Ania, and Martin Orkin, eds. *Post-colonial Shakespeares*. London and New York, 1998.

Mahon, John W., and Thomas A. Pendleton, eds. *"Fanned and Winnowed Opinion": Shakespearean Essays Presented to Harold Jenkins*. London, 1987.

Mallin, Eric. *Inscribing the Time: Shakespeare and the End of Elizabethan England*. Berkeley, 1995.

Marcus, Leah. *Puzzling Shakespeare: Local Reading and its Discontents*. Berkeley, 1988.

Mazzio, Carla, and Douglas Trevor, eds. *Historicism, Psychoanalysis, and Early Modern Culture*. London and New York, 2000.

McDonald, Russ, ed. *Shakespeare Reread: The Texts in New Contexts*. Ithaca, N.Y., 1994.

McMullan, Gordon, and Jonathan Hope, eds. *The Politics of Tragicomedy: Shakespeare and After*. London and New York, 1992.

Melchiori, Giorgio. *Shakespeare's Garter Plays: "Edward III" to "Merry Wives of Windsor."* Newark, Del., 1994.

Miola, Robert S. *Shakespeare's Reading*. Oxford and New York, 2000.

——. *Shakespeare's Rome*. Cambridge, Eng., 1983.

Montrose, Louis. *The Purpose of Playing: Shakespeare and Cultural Politics of the Elizabethan Theatre*. Chicago, 1996.

Mullaney, Steven. *The Place of the Stage: License, Play, and Power in Renaissance England*. Chicago, 1988.

Neely, Carol Thomas. *Broken Nuptials in Shakespeare's Plays*. New Haven, 1985.

Newman, Karen. *Fashioning Femininity and the English Renaissance Drama*. Chicago, 1991.

Novy, Marianne. *Love's Argument: Gender Relations in Shakespeare*. Chapel Hill, N.C., 1984.

——, ed. *Women's Re-Visions of Shakespeare*. Urbana, Ill., 1990.

Nuttall, A. D. *A New Mimesis: Shakespeare and the Representation of Reality*. London, 1983.

Orgel, Stephen. *The Authentic Shakespeare and Other Problems of the Early Modern Stage*. London and New York, 2002.

Orgel, Stephen, and Sean Keilen, eds. *Shakespeare and History; Post-modern Shakespeare; Shakespeare and the Interpretive Tradition; Shakespeare and the Literary Tradition; Shakespeare and Gender; Political Shakespeare*. In separate volumes, New York, 1999.

Parker, Patricia. *Shakespeare from the Margins: Language, Culture, Context*. Chicago, 1996.

——, and Geoffrey Hartman, eds. *Shakespeare and the Question of Theory*. London, 1985.

Paster, Gail Kern. *The Body Embarrassed: Drama and the Disciplines of Shame in Early Modern England*. Ithaca, N.Y., 1993.

Patterson, Annabel. *Shakespeare and the Popular Voice*. Oxford, 1989.

Rabkin, Norman. *Shakespeare and the Problem of Meaning*. Chicago, 1981.

Salingar, Leo. *Dramatic Form in Shakespeare and the Jacobeans*. Cambridge, Eng., 1986.

Schwartz, Murray, and Coppélia Kahn, eds. *Representing Shakespeare: New Psychoanalytic Essays*. Baltimore, 1980.

Siemon, James R. *Shakespearean Iconoclasm*. Berkeley, 1985.

Sinfield, Alan. *Faultlines: Cultural Materialism and the Politics of Dissident Reading*. Berkeley, 1992.

Skura, Meredith Anne. *The Literary Use of the Psychoanalytic Process*. New Haven, 1981.

——. *Shakespeare the Actor and the Purposes of Playing*. Chicago, 1993.

Smith, Bruce R. *Homosexual Desire in Shakespeare's England*. Chicago, 1991.

——. *Shakespeare and Masculinity*. Oxford, 2000.

Stockholder, Kay. *Dream Works: Lovers and Families in Shakespeare's Plays*. Toronto, 1987.

Taylor, Gary. *Reinventing Shakespeare: A Cultural History from the Restoration to the Present*. New York, 1989.

Traub, Valerie. *Desire and Anxiety: Circulations of Sexuality in Shakespearean Drama*. London, 1992.

Vickers, Brian. *Appropriating Shakespeare: Contemporary Critical Quarrels*. New Haven, 1993.

Watson, Robert N. *The Rest is Silence: Death as Annihilation in the English Renaissance*. Berkeley, 1994.

——. *Shakespeare and the Hazards of Ambition*. Cambridge, Mass., 1984.

Wayne, Valerie, ed. *The Matter of Difference: Materialist Feminist Criticism of Shakespeare*. Ithaca, N.Y., 1991.

Weimann, Robert. *Author's Pen and Actor's Voice: Playing and Writing in Shakespeare's Theatre*. Cambridge, Eng., 2000.

Wells, Robin Headlam. *Shakespeare on Masculinity*. Cambridge, Eng., 2000.

——. *Shakespeare, Politics, and the State*. London, 1986.

Wheeler, Richard P. *Shakespeare's Development and the Problem Comedies: Turn and Counter-Turn*. Berkeley, 1981.

White, Paul Whitfield, and Suzanne R. Westfall, eds. *Shakespeare and Theatrical Patronage in Early Modern England*. Cambridge, Eng., 2002.

Williams, Gordon. *Shakespeare, Sex, and the Print Revolution*. London and Atlantic Highlands, N.J., 1996.

Woodbridge, Linda. *The Scythe of Saturn: Shakespeare's Magical Thinking*. Urbana, Ill., 1994.

Woodbridge, Linda, and Edward Berry, eds. *True Rites and Maimed Rites: Ritual and Anti-Ritual in Shakespeare and His Age*. Urbana, Ill., 1992.

Ziegler, Georgianna, ed. *Shakespeare's Unruly Women*. Washington, D.C., 1997.

Shakespeare in Performance; Dramaturgy

See also, under *Shakespeare Criticism from the 1940s to the 1970s*, Goldman and Granville-Barker.

Bartholomeusz, Dennis. *Macbeth and the Players*. Cambridge, Eng., 1969.

Barton, John. *Playing Shakespeare*. London, 1984.

Bevington, David. *Action is Eloquence: Shakespeare's Language of Gesture*. Cambridge, Mass., 1984.

Brockbank, Philip, ed. *Players of Shakespeare*. Cambridge, Eng., 1985.

Brown, Ivor. *Shakespeare and the Actors*. London, 1970.

Brown, John Russell. *Shakespeare's Plays in Performance*. London, 1966.

——. *Shakespeare's Dramatic Style*. London, 1970.

Bulman, J. C., and H. R. Coursen, eds. *Shakespeare on Television*. Hanover, N.H., 1988.

Carlisle, Carol Jones. *Shakespeare from the Greenroom: Actors' Criticisms of Four Major Tragedies*. Chapel Hill, N.C., 1969.

Cohn, Ruby. *Modern Shakespeare Offshoots*. Princeton, 1976.

Cook, Judith. *Shakespeare's Players*. London, 1983.

Davies, Anthony, and Stanley Wells, eds. *Shakespeare and the Moving Image: The Plays on Film and Television*. Cambridge, Eng., 1994.

Dessen, Alan C. *Recovering Shakespeare's Theatrical Vocabulary*. Cambridge, Eng., 1995.

——. *Rescripting Shakespeare: The Text, the Director, and Modern Productions*. Cambridge, Eng., 2002.

——, and Leslie Thomson. *A Dictionary of Stage Directions in English Drama, 1580–1642*. Cambridge, Eng., 1999.

Donohue, Joseph W., Jr. *Dramatic Character in the English Romantic Age*. Princeton, 1970.

Downer, Alan S. *The Eminent Tragedian, William Charles Macready*. Cambridge, Mass., 1966.

Edelman, Charles. *Brawl Ridiculous: Swordfighting in Shakespeare's Plays*. Manchester, Eng., 1992.

Hodgdon, Barbara. *The Shakespeare Trade: Performances and Appropriations*. Philadelphia, 1998.

Hogan, Charles B. *Shakespeare in the Theatre, 1701–1800*. 2 vols. Oxford, 1952–1957.

Jackson, Russell, and Robert Smallwood, eds. *Players of Shakespeare 2*. Cambridge, Eng., 1988. Followed by Vols. 3 (1993); and 4, ed. Smallwood (1998).

Jones, Emrys. *Scenic Form in Shakespeare*. Oxford, 1971.

Jorgens, Jack L. *Shakespeare on Film*. Bloomington, Ind., 1977.

Manvell, Roger. *Shakespeare and the Film*. London and New York, 1971.

McGuire, Philip C. *Speechless Dialect: Shakespeare's Open Silences*. Berkeley, 1985.

McGuire, Philip C., and David A. Samuelson. *Shakespeare: The Theatrical Dimension*. New York, 1979.

Odell, George C. D. *Shakespeare from Betterton to Irving*. 2 vols. New York, 1920, 1966.

Poel, William. *Shakespeare in the Theatre*. London, 1913, 1968.

Price, Joseph G., ed. *The Triple Bond: Plays, Mainly Shakespearean, in Performance*. University Park, Pa., 1975.

Rutter, Carol Chillington, ed. *Documents of the Rose Playhouse*. Manchester, Eng., 1999.

Rutter, Carol, et al. *Clamorous Voices: Shakespeare's Women Today*. New York, 1989.

Shapiro, Michael. *Gender in Play on the Shakespearean Stage: Boy Heroines and Female Pages*. Ann Arbor, Mich., 1994.

Shattuck, Charles H. *The Shakespeare Promptbooks: A Descriptive Catalogue*. Urbana, Ill., 1965.

——. *Shakespeare on the American Stage from the Hallams to Edwin Booth*. Washington, D.C., 1976; *from Booth and Barrett to Sothern and Marlowe*, Washington, D.C., 1987.

Slater, Ann Pasternak. *Shakespeare the Director*. Brighton, Sussex, and Totowa, N.J., 1982.

Speaight, Robert. *William Poel and the Elizabethan Revival*. London, 1954.

Sprague, Arthur Colby. *Shakespeare and the Actors*. Cambridge, Mass., 1944.

——. *Shakespearian Players and Performances*. Cambridge, Mass., 1953.

Styan, J. L. *Shakespeare's Stagecraft*. Cambridge, Eng., 1967.

Wells, Stanley. *Royal Shakespeare: Four Major Productions at Stratford-upon-Avon*. Manchester, Eng., 1977.

The Comedies

See also, under *Shakespeare Criticism Since 1980*, Drakakis (essay by Belsey), Erickson and Kahn (essay by Adelman), and Paster (Chapter 7).

Anderson, Linda. *A Kind of Wild Justice: Revenge in Shakespeare's Comedies*. Newark, Del., 1987.

Barber, C. L. *Shakespeare's Festive Comedy*. Princeton, 1959.

Barton, Anne. *The Names of Comedy*. Toronto, 1990.

Berry, Edward. *Shakespeare's Comic Rites*. Cambridge, Eng., 1984.

Berry, Ralph. *Shakespeare's Comedies: Explorations in Form*. Princeton, 1972.

——. *The Shakespearean Metaphor: Studies in Language and Form*. Totowa, N.J., 1978.

Bloom, Harold, ed. *William Shakespeare: Comedies and Romances*. New York, 1986.

Bradbury, Malcolm, and David Palmer, eds. *Shakespearian Comedy*. London, 1972.

Brown, John Russell. *Shakespeare and His Comedies*. London, 1957, 1968.

Brown, John Russell, and Bernard Harris, eds. *Early Shakespeare*. Stratford-upon-Avon Studies 3. London, 1961. (Including an essay by Frank Kermode on "The Mature Comedies.")

Bryant, J. A., Jr. *Shakespeare and the Uses of Comedy*. Lexington, Ky., 1986.

Burke, William Kenneth. *A New Approach to Shakespeare's Early Comedies: Theoretical Foundations*. New York, 1998.

Carroll, William C. *The Metamorphoses of Shakespearean Comedy*. Princeton, 1985.

Champion, Larry S. *The Evolution of Shakespeare's Comedy*. Cambridge, Mass., 1970.

Charlton, H. B. *Shakespearian Comedy*. London, 1938.

Charney, Maurice, ed. *Shakespearean Comedy*. New York, 1980.

Cody, Richard. *The Landscape of the Mind: Pastoralism and Platonic Theory in Tasso's "Aminta" and Shakespeare's Early Comedies*. Oxford, 1969.

Collins, Michael J., ed. *Shakespeare's Sweet Thunder: Essays on the Early Comedies*. Newark, Del., 1997.

Cook, Ann Jennalie. *Making a Match: Courtship in Shakespeare and His Society*. Princeton, 1991.

Cordner, Michael, Peter Holland, and John Kerrigan, eds. *English Comedy*. Cambridge, Eng., 1994.

Elam, Keir. *Shakespeare's Universe of Discourse: Language-Games in the Comedies*. Cambridge, Eng., 1984.

Evans, Bertrand. *Shakespeare's Comedies*. Oxford, 1960.

Freedman, Barbara. *Staging the Gaze: Postmodernism, Psychoanalysis, and Shakespearean Comedy*. Ithaca, N. Y., 1991.

Friedman, Michael D. *"The World Must Be Peopled": Shakespeare's Comedies of Forgiveness*. Madison, N. J., and London, 2002.

Frye, Northrop. "The Argument of Comedy," *English Institute Essays 1948*. New York, 1949.

——. *A Natural Perspective: The Development of Shakespearean Comedy and Romance*. New York, 1965.

Hall, Jonathan. *Anxious Pleasures: Shakespearean Comedy and the Nation-State*. Madison, N. J., 1995.

Hamilton, A. C. *The Early Shakespeare*. San Marino, Calif., 1967.

Hassel, R. Chris. *Faith and Folly in Shakespeare's Romantic Comedies*. Athens, Ga., 1980.

Hawkins, Sherman H. "The Two Worlds of Shakespearean Comedy," *ShakS 3* (1967), 62–80.

Hunter, Robert G. *Shakespeare and the Comedy of Forgiveness*. New York, 1965.

Huston, J. Dennis. *Shakespeare's Comedies of Play*. New York, 1981.

Leggatt, Alexander. *English Stage Comedy, 1490–1990: Five Centuries of a Genre*. London and New York, 1998.

——. *Shakespeare's Comedy of Love*. London and New York, 1974.

Lerner, Laurence, ed. *Shakespeare's Comedies: An Anthology of Modern Criticism*. Baltimore, 1967.

Levin, Richard A. *Love and Society in Shakespearean Comedy: A Study of Dramatic Form and Content*. Newark, Del., 1985.

Miola, Robert S. *Shakespeare and Classical Comedy: The Influence of Plautus and Terence*. Oxford, 1994.

Nevo, Ruth. *Comic Transformations in Shakespeare*. London, 1980.

Newman, Karen. *Shakespeare's Rhetoric of Comic Character*. New York and London, 1985.

Palmer, David J., and Malcolm Bradbury, eds. *Shakespearian Comedy*. Statford-upon-Avon Studies 1. London, 1972.

Palmer, John. *Comic Characters of Shakespeare*. London, 1946.

Pettet, E. C. *Shakespeare and the Romance Tradition*. London, 1949.

Phialas, Peter G. *Shakespeare's Romantic Comedies*. Chapel Hill, N.C., 1966.

Richmond, Hugh M. *Shakespeare's Sexual Comedy*. Indianapolis, 1971.

Salingar, Leo. *Shakespeare and the Traditions of Comedy*. Cambridge, Eng., 1974.

Shaheen, Naseeb. *Biblical References in Shakespeare's Comedies*. Newark, Del., 1993.

Smidt, Kristian. *Unconformities in Shakespeare's Early Comedies*. London, 1986.

Stevenson, David L. *The Love-Game Comedy*. New York, 1946.

Traversi, Derek. *Shakespeare: The Early Comedies*. London, 1960.

Turner, Robert Y. *Shakespeare's Apprenticeship*. Chicago, 1974.

Westlund, Joseph. *Shakespeare's Reparative Comedies: A Psychoanalytic View of the Middle Plays*. Chicago, 1984.

Wheeler, Richard P. "Deaths in the Family: The Loss of a Son and the Rise of Shakespearean Comedy." *SQ* 51 (2000), 127–53.

Williamson, Marilyn. *The Patriarchy of Shakespeare's Comedies*. Detroit, 1986.

The Problem Plays

Campbell, Oscar James. *Shakespeare's Satire*. London and New York, 1943, 1963.

Foakes, R. A. *Shakespeare, The Dark Comedies to the Last Plays: From Satire to Celebration*. Charlottesville, Va., 1971.

Frye, Northrop. *The Myth of Deliverance: Reflections on Shakespeare's Problem Comedies*. Toronto, 1983.

Jamieson, Michael. "The Problem Plays, 1920–1970: A Retrospect," *ShS* 25 (1972), 1–10.

Lawrence, W. W. *Shakespeare's Problem Comedies*. New York, 1931, 1960.

Maquerlot, Jean-Pierre. *Shakespeare and the Mannerist Tradition: A Reading of Five Problem Plays*. Cambridge, Eng., 1995. (Includes consideration of *Julius Caesar* and *Hamlet*.)

McCandless, David. *Gender and Performance in Shakespeare's Problem Comedies*. Bloomington, Ind., 1997.

Muir, Kenneth, and Stanley Wells, eds. *Aspects of Shakespeare's "Problem Plays": Articles Reprinted from "Shakespeare Survey."* Cambridge, Eng., 1982.

Schanzer, Ernest. *The Problem Plays of Shakespeare*. New York, 1963.

Thomas, Vivian. *The Moral Universe of Shakespeare's Problem Plays*. New York, 1987.

Tillyard, E. M. W. *Shakespeare's Problem Plays*. Toronto, 1949.

Wheeler, Richard P. *Shakespeare's Development and the Problem Comedies: Turn and Counter-Turn*. Berkeley, 1981.

Ure, Peter. *William Shakespeare: The Problem Plays*. London, 1961.

The Comedy of Errors

See also, under *Shakespeare Criticism Since 1980*, Hamilton (Chapter 3), and Parker; and under *The Comedies*, R. Berry, Charlton, Charney (essays by Shaw and Freedman), Cody, Collins (essays by Miola, Smith, and Thompson), Evans, Hamilton, Huston, Leggatt, Nevo, Pettet, Richmond, Salingar, Traversi, and Turner.

Barber, C. L. "Shakespearian Comedy in *The Comedy of Errors*," *College English* 25 (1964), 493–7.

Bishop, T. G. *Shakespeare and the Theatre of Wonder*. Cambridge, Eng., 1996.

Brooks, Charles. "Shakespeare's Romantic Shrews," *SQ* 11 (1960), 351–6.

Brooks, Harold. "Themes and Structure in *The Comedy of Errors*," *Early Shakespeare*, ed. John Russell Brown and Bernard Harris, pp. 55–71. Stratford-upon-Avon Studies 3. London, 1961.

Clubb, Louise G. "Italian Comedy and *The Comedy of Errors*," *Comparative Literature* 19 (1967), 240–51.

Elliott, C. R. "Weirdness in *The Comedy of Errors*," *University of Toronto Quarterly* 9 (1939), 95–106.

Enterline, Lynn. *The Tears of Narcissus: Melancholia and Masculinity in Early Modern Writing*. Stanford, 1995.

Fergusson, Francis. "Two Comedies: *The Comedy of Errors* and *Much Ado About Nothing*," *The Human Image in Dramatic Literature*, pp. 144–57. New York, 1957.

Freedman, Barbara. "Egeon's Debt: Self-Division and Self-Redemption in *The Comedy of Errors*," *English Literary Renaissance* 10 (1980), 360–83.

Hutson, Lorna. *The Usurer's Daughter: Male Friendship and Fictions of Women in Sixteenth-Century England*. London and New York, 1994.

Knight, G. Wilson. *The Shakespearian Tempest*. London, 1932, 1953.

Lea, Kathleen M. *Italian Popular Comedy: A Study in the Commedia dell' Arte, 1560–1620, with Special Reference to the English Stage*. Oxford, 1934.

Miola, Robert S., ed. *The Comedy of Errors: Critical Essays*. New York and London, 1997.

Salgādo, Gāmini. " 'Time's Deformed Hand': Sequence, Consequence, and Inconsequence in *The Comedy of Errors*," *ShS* 25 (1972), 81–91.

Love's Labor's Lost

See also, under *Shakespeare's Language*, Donawerth and Mahood; under *Shakespeare Criticism from the 1940s to the 1970s*, Calderwood and Hawkes; under *Shakespeare Criticism Since 1980*, Edwards et al. (essay by Hunter), Erickson and Kahn (essay by Levin), Kamps (essay by Maus), and Mazzio and Trevor (essay by Mazzio); and under *The Comedies*, Barber, R. Berry, Charlton, Cody, Collins (essay by Gilbert), Elam (Chapter 5), Hunter, Huston, Leggatt, Nevo, Palmer and Bradbury (essays by Hunt and Wells, Roberts, Swander, and Thompson), Smidt, and Stevenson.

Bevington, David. " 'Jack Hath Not Jill': Failed Courtship in Lyly and Shakespeare," *ShS* 42 (1990), 1–13.

Breitenberg, Mark. "The Anatomy of Masculine Desire in *Love's Labour's Lost*," *SQ* 43 (1992), 430–49.

Burnett, Mark Thornton. "Giving and Receiving: *Love's Labour's Lost* and the Politics of Exchange," *English Literary Renaissance* 23 (1993), 287–313.

Carroll, William C. *The Great Feast of Language in "Love's Labour's Lost."* Princeton, 1976.

Ellis, Herbert A. *Shakespeares's Lusty Punning in "Love's Labour's Lost" with Contemporary Analogues*. The Hague, 1973.

Erickson, Peter B. "The Failure of Relationship Between Men and Women in *Love's Labour's Lost*," *Women's Studies* 9 (1981): 65–81.

Evans, Malcolm. "Mercury Versus Apollo: A Reading of *Love's Labour's Lost*," *SQ* 26 (1975), 113–27.

Frye, Northrop. "Shakespeare's Experimental Comedy," *Stratford Papers on Shakespeare 1961*, ed. B. A. W. Jackson. Toronto, 1962.

Gilbert, Mariam. *Love's Labour's Lost*. Shakespeare in Performance Series. Manchester, Eng., 1993.

Goldstien, Neal L. "*Love's Labour's Lost* and the Renaissance Vision of Love," *SQ* 25 (1974), 335–50.

Greene, Thomas M. "*Love's Labour's Lost*: The Grace of Society," *SQ* 22 (1971), 315–28. Rpt. in *The Vulnerable Text: Essays on Renaissance Literature*. New York, 1986.

Harbage, Alfred. "*Love's Labor's Lost* and the Early Shakespeare," *Philological Quarterly* 41 (1962), 18–36.

Henderson, Diana E. "Shakespeare's Laboring Lovers: Lyric and Its Discontents," *Passion Made Public: Elizabethan Lyric, Gender, and Performance*, pp. 167–213. Urbana, Ill., 1995.

Hoy, Cyrus. "*Love's Labour's Lost* and the Nature of Comedy," *SQ* 13 (1962), 31–40.

Hunter, Robert G. "The Function of the Songs at the End of *Love's Labour's Lost*," *ShakS* 7 (1974), 55–64.

Lamb, Mary Ellen. "The Nature of Topicality in *Love's Labour's Lost*," *ShS* 38 (1985), 49–59.

Montrose, Louis Adrian. "Curious-knotted Garden": The Form, Themes and Contexts of Shakespeare's "Love's Labour's Lost." Salzburg, 1977.

———. " 'Sport by sport o'erthrown': *Love's Labour's Lost* and the Politics of Play," *Texas Studies in Literature and Language* 18 (1977), 528–52.

Proudfoot, Richard. "*Love's Labour's Lost*: Sweet Understanding and the Five Worthies," *Essays and Studies* n.s. 37 (1984), 16–30.

Parker, Patricia. "Preposterous Reversals: *Love's Labor's Lost*," *Modern Language Quarterly* 54 (1993), 435–82.

Westlund, Joseph. "Fancy and Achievement in *Love's Labour's Lost*," *SQ* 18 (1967), 37–46.

Wilders, John. "The Unresolved Conflicts of *Love's Labour's Lost*," *Essays in Criticism* 27 (1977), 20–33.

Yates, Frances A. *A Study of "Love's Labour's Lost."* Cambridge, Eng., 1936.

The Two Gentlemen of Verona

See also, under *The Comedies*, R. Berry, Bradbury and Palmer (essay by Ewbank), Champion, Charlton, Collins (essay by Carlisle and Derrick), Evans, Friedman, Hunter, Leggatt, Nevo, Pettet, and Salingar.

Brooks, Harold F. "Two Clowns in a Comedy (to Say Nothing of the Dog): Speed, Launce (and Crab) in *The Two Gentlemen of Verona*," *English Association Essays and Studies* n.s. 16 (1963), 91–100.

Danby, John F. "Shakespeare Criticism and *Two Gentlemen of Verona*," *Critical Quarterly* 2 (1960), 309–21.

Lindenbaum, Peter. "Education in *The Two Gentlemen of Verona*," *Studies in English Literature* 15 (1975), 229–44.

Morse, Ruth. "*Two Gentlemen* and the Cult of Friendship," *Neuphilologische Mitteilungen* 84:2 (1983), 214–24.

Rossky, William. "*The Two Gentlemen of Verona* as Burlesque," *English Literary Renaissance* 12 (1982), 210–19.

Schleiner, Louise. "Voice, Ideology, and Gendered Subjects: The Case of *As You Like It* and *Two Gentlemen*," *SQ* 50 (1999), 285–309.

Schlueter, June, ed. *"The Two Gentlemen of Verona": Critical Essays.* London and New York, 1996.

Slights, Camille Wells. "*The Two Gentlemen of Verona* and the Courtesy Book Tradition," *ShakS* 16 (1983), 13–31.

Stephenson, William E. "The Adolescent Dream-World of *The Two Gentlemen of Verona*," *SQ* 17:2 (1966), 165–8.

Weimann, Robert. "Laughing with the Audience: *The Two Gentlemen of Verona* and the Popular Tradition of Comedy," *ShS* 22 (1969), 35–42.

The Taming of the Shrew

See also, under *Shakespeare's Predecessors and Contemporaries*, Marrapodi (essay by Bevington); under *Shakespeare Criticism from the 1940s to the 1970s*, Garber; under *Shakespeare Criticism Since 1980*, Auden, Fumerton and Hunt (essay by Dolan), Kahn, Lenz et al. (essay by Bean), McDonald (essay by Boose), Novy (*Love's Argument*), and Parker and Hartman (essay by Fineman); under *Shakespeare in Performance*, Rutter; and under *The Comedies*, R. Berry, Charlton, Collins (essays by Dessen and Rutter), Evans, Hawkins, Huston, Leggatt, Nevo, and Stevenson.

Boose, Lynda E. " 'Scolding Brides and Bridling Scolds': Taming the Woman's Unruly Member," *SQ* 42 (1991), 179–213.

Brunvand, Jan Harold. "The Folktale Origin of *The Taming of the Shrew*," *SQ* 17 (1966), 345–59.

Dolan, Frances E., ed. *"The Taming of the Shrew": Text and Contexts.* New York, 1996.

Haring-Smith, Tori. *From Farce to Metadrama; A Stage History of "The Taming of the Shrew," 1594–1983.* Westport, Conn., 1985.

Hosley, Richard. "Was There a 'Dramatic Epilogue' to *The Taming of the Shrew?*" *Studies in English Literature* 1:2 (1961), 17–34.

Hutson, Lorna. *The Usurer's Daughter: Male Friendship and Fictions of Women in Sixteenth-Century England.* London and New York, 1994.

Jayne, Sears. "The Dreaming of *The Shrew*," *SQ* 17 (1966), 41–56.

Korda, Natasha. "Household Kates: Domesticating Commodities in *The Taming of the Shrew*," *SQ* 47 (1996), 109–31.

Maguire, Laurie E. "Cultural Control in *The Taming of the Shrew*," *Renaissance Drama* n.s. 26 (1995), 83–104.

Marcus, Leah. "The Shakespearean Editor as Shrew-Tamer," *English Literary Rennaisance* 22 (1922), 177–200.

Newman, Karen. "Renaissance Family Politics and Shakespeare's *The Taming of the Shrew*," *English Literary Renaissance* 16 (1986), 86–100.

Saccio, Peter. "Shrewd and Kindly Farce," *ShS* 37 (1984), 33–40.

Thompson, Ann, ed., *The Taming of the Shrew.* Cambridge, Eng., 1984.

Thorne, W. B. "Folk Elements in *The Taming of the Shrew*," *Queen's Quarterly* 75 (1968), 482–96.

A Midsummer Night's Dream

See also, under *Life in Shakespeare's England*, De Grazia, Quilligan, and Stallybrass (essay by Parker); under *Shakespeare Criticism from the 1940s to the 1970s*, Calderwood, Coghill, Garber, Granville-Barker, and Kott; under *Shakespeare Criticism Since 1980*, Callaghan (*A Feminist Companion*, essay by Loomba), Mazzio and Trevor (essay by Maus), Montrose, Parker, Paster, and Patterson (Chapter 3); and under *The Comedies*, Barber, Bloom (essay by Girard), Brown and Harris (essays by Kermode and Merchant), Carroll, Collins (essay by Halio), Evans, Huston, Leggatt, Lerner, Palmer and Bradbury (essay by Wells), and Smidt.

Bevington, David. " 'But We Are Spirits of Another Sort': The Dark Side of Love and Magic in *A Midsummer Night's Dream*," *Medieval and Renaissance Studies*, ed. Siegfried Wenzel. Chapel Hill, N.C., 1978.

Donaldson, E. Talbot. *The Swan at the Well: Shakespeare Reads Chaucer.* New Haven, 1985.

Garner, Shirley Nelson. "*A Midsummer Night's Dream*: 'Jack Shall Have Jill; Nought Shall Go Ill,' " *Women's Studies* 9 (1981), 47–63.

Girard, René. "Myth and Ritual in Shakespeare's *A Midsummer Night's Dream*," *Textual Strategies: Perspectives in Post-Structuralist Criticism*, ed. Josué V. Harari. Ithaca, N.Y., 1979.

Howard, Skiles. "Hands, Feet, and Bottoms: Decentering the Cosmic Dance in *A Midsummer Night's Dream*," *SQ* 44 (1993), 325–42.

Lamb, Mary Ellen. "*A Midsummer Night's Dream*: The Myth of Theseus and the Minotaur," *Texas Studies in Literature and Language* 21 (1979), 478–91.

———. " 'Taken by the Fairies': Fairy Practices and the Production of Popular Culture in *A Midsummer Night's Dream*," *SQ* 51 (2000), 277–312.

Montrose, Louis Adrian. " 'Shaping Fantasies': Figurations of Gender and Power in Elizabethan Culture," *Representations* 2 (1.2, Spring 1983), 61–94.

Nuttall, A. D. "*A Midsummer Night's Dream*: Comedy as *Apotrope* of Myth," *ShS* 53 (2000), 49–59.

Olson, Paul A. "*A Midsummer Night's Dream* and the Meaning of Court Marriage," *ELH* 24 (1957), 95–119.

Ormerod, David. "*A Midsummer Night's Dream*: The Monster in the Labyrinth," *ShakS* 11 (1978), 39–52.

Pearson, D'Orsay W. " 'Unkinde' Theseus: A Study in Renaissance Mythography," *English Literary Renaissance* 4 (1974), 276–98.

Wall, Wendy. "Why Does Puck Sweep?: Fairylore, Merry Wives, and Social Struggle," *SQ* 52 (2001), 67–106.

Warren, Roger. *"A Midsummer Night's Dream": Text and Performance.* Text and Performance. London, 1983.

Williams, Gary Jay. *Our Moonlight Revels: "A Midsummer Night's Dream" in the Theatre.* Ames, Iowa, 1997.

Young, David P. *Something of Great Constancy: The Art of "A Midsummer Night's Dream."* New Haven, 1966.

The Merchant of Venice

See also, under *Shakespeare's Predecessors and Contemporaries*, Rose (ed. *Renaissance Drama*, essay by Whigham); under *Shakespeare's Language*, Donawerth; under *Shakespeare Criticism from the 1940s to the 1970s*, Burkhardt, Fiedler, and Granville-Barker; under *Shakespeare Criticism Since 1980*, Auden, Callaghan (*A Feminist Companion*, essay by Singh), Dawson, Erickson and Kahn (essays by Kahn and Wheeler), Garber (*Cannibals*, essay by Mullaney), Grady (essays by Drakakis, Freinkel, and Mallin), Howard and O'Connor (essay by Moisan), Mazzio and Trevor (essay by Siemon), Novy (*Love's Argument*, Chapter 4), Rabkin, and Wayne (essay by Leventen); and under *The Comedies*, Barber, Bradbury and Palmer (essay by Palmer), Brown and Harris (essays by J. R. Brown and Kermode), Evans, Leggatt, Levin, Nevo, and Smidt.

Auden, W. H. "Brothers and Others," *"The Dyer's Hand" and Other Essays.* New York, 1948.

Berger, Harry, Jr. "Marriage and Mercifixion in *The Merchant of Venice:* The Casket Scene Revisited," *SQ* 32 (1981), 155–62.

Boose, Lynda E. "The Comic Contract and Portia's Golden Ring," *ShakS* 20 (1988), 241–54.

Bulman, James C. *The Merchant of Venice.* Shakespeare in Performance. Manchester, Eng., 1991.

Cohen, Walter. *"The Merchant of Venice* and the Possibilities of Historical Criticism," *ELH* 49 (1982), 765–89.

Danson, Lawrence. *The Harmonies of "The Merchant of Venice."* New Haven and London, 1978.

Dessen, Alan C. "The Elizabethan Stage Jew and Christian Example: Gerontus, Barabas, and Shylock," *Modern Language Quarterly* 35 (1974), 231–45.

Edelman, Charles. "Which is the Jew that Shakespeare Knew? Shylock on the Elizabethan Stage," *ShS* 52 (1999), 99–106.

Engle, Lars. " 'Thrift is Blessing': Exchange and Explanation in *The Merchant of Venice,*" *SQ* 37 (1986), 20–37.

Freud, Sigmund. "The Theme of the Three Caskets," *Complete Psychological Works of Sigmund Freud,* trans. James Strachey et al. London, 1973–4.

Girard, René. " 'To Entrap the Wisest': A Reading of *The Merchant of Venice,*" *Literature and Society.* Selected Papers from the English Institute, 1978, ed. Edward W. Said. Baltimore, 1980.

Hutson, Lorna. *The Usurer's Daughter: Male Friendship and Fictions of Women in Sixteenth-Century England.* London and New York, 1994.

Jardine, Lisa. "Cultural Confusion and Shakespeare's Learned Heroines: 'These Are Old Paradoxes,' " *SQ* 38 (1987), 1–18.

Lever, J. W. "Shylock, Portia, and the Values of Shakespearian Comedy," *SQ* 3 (1952), 383–6.

Lewalski, Barbara K. "Biblical Allusion and Allegory in *The Merchant of Venice,*" *SQ* 13 (1962), 327–43.

MacKay, Maxine. *"The Merchant of Venice:* A Reflection of the Early Conflict Between Courts of Law and Courts of Equity," *SQ* 15:4 (1964), 371–5.

Moody, A. D. *Shakespeare: "The Merchant of Venice."* London, 1964.

Newman, Karen. "Portia's Ring: Unruly Women and Structures of Exchange in *The Merchant of Venice,*" *SQ* 38 (1987), 19–33.

Normand, Lawrence. "Reading the Body in *The Merchant of Venice,*" *Textual Practice* 5 (1991), 55–73.

Overton, Bill. *"The Merchant of Venice": Text and Performance.* Atlantic Highlands, N.J., 1987.

Parten, Anne. "Re-establishing Sexual Order: The Ring Episode in *The Merchant of Venice,*" *Women's Studies* 9 (1982), 145–55.

Pettet, E. C. *"The Merchant of Venice* and the Problem of Usury," *English Association Essays and Studies* 31 (1945), 19–33.

Shapiro, James. *Shakespeare and the Jews.* New York, 1996.

Whigham, Frank. "Ideology and Class Conduct in *The Merchant of Venice,*" *Renaissance Drama* 10 (1979), 93–115.

Yaffe, Martin D. *Shylock and the Jewish Question.* Baltimore, 1997.

Much Ado About Nothing

See also, under *Shakespeare's Predecessors and Contemporaries,* Marrapodi (essay by Salingar); under *The Comedies,* R. Berry, Brown, Cordner et al. (essay by Everett), Evans, Hunter, Huston, Leggatt, Levin, Nevo, Newman, Salingar, and Stevenson; under *Shakespeare Criticism from the 1940s to the 1970s,* Rossiter; and under *Shakespeare Criticism Since 1980,* Howard and O'Connor (essay by Howard), Kirsch, Lenz et al. (essay by Hays), and Neely.

Barish, Jonas A. "Pattern and Purpose in the Prose of *Much Ado About Nothing,*" *Rice U. Studies* 60:2 (1974), 19–30.

Berger, Harry, Jr. "Against the Sink-a-Pace: Sexual and Family Politics in *Much Ado About Nothing,*" *SQ* 33 (1982), 302–13.

Cook, Carol. "'The Sign and Semblance of Her Honor': Reading Gender Difference in *Much Ado about Nothing,*" *PMLA* 101 (1986), 186–202.

Dawson, Anthony B. "Much Ado about Signifying," *Studies in English Literature* 22 (1982), 211–21.

Dusinberre, Juliet. "Much Ado about Lying," *Shakespeare Readers, Audiences, Players,* eds. R. S. White, Charles Edelman, and Christopher Wortham. Nedlands, Australia, 1998.

Everett, Barbara. *"Much Ado About Nothing,"* *Critical Quarterly* 3 (1961), 319–35.

Friedman, Michael D. "Male Bonds and Marriage in *All's Well* and *Much Ado,*" *Studies in English Literature* 35 (1995), 231–49.

Jorgensen, Paul A. *"Much Ado About Nothing,"* *SQ* 5 (1954), 287–95. Rpt. in *Redeeming Shakespeare's Words.* Berkeley, 1962.

Lane, Robert. " 'Foremost in report': Social Identity and Masculinity in *Much Ado About Nothing,*" *Upstart Crow* 16 (1996), 31–47.

Lewalski, Barbara K. "Love, Appearance, and Reality: Much Ado About Something," *Studies in English Literature* 8 (1968), 235–51.

Mason, Pamela. *"Much Ado About Nothing":* Text and Performance. Basingstoke, 1992.

Ormerod, David. "Faith and Fashion in *Much Ado About Nothing,*" *ShS* 25 (1972), 93–105.

Taylor, Michael. *"Much Ado About Nothing:* The Individual in Society," *Essays in Criticism* 23 (1973), 146–53.

The Merry Wives of Windsor

See also, under *Life in Shakespeare's England,* Helgerson; under *Shakespeare's Predecessors and Contemporaries,* Helgerson; under *Shakespeare Criticism Since 1980,* Erickson and Kahn (essay by Barton), Fumerton and Hunt (essay by Helgerson), Howard and O'Connor (essay by Erickson), Kahn (Chapter 5), Knowles (essay by Hall), Melchiori, and Parker; and under *The Comedies,* Anderson, R. Berry, Carroll, Charlton, Evans, and Nevo.

Bradley, A. C. "The Rejection of Falstaff," *Oxford Lectures on Poetry.* London, 1909, 1961.

Bryant, J. A., Jr. "Falstaff and the Renewal of Windsor," *PMLA* 89 (1974), 296–301.

Carroll, William. " 'A Received Belief': Imagination in *The Merry Wives of Windsor,*" *Studies in Philology* 74 (1977), 186–215.

Collington, Philip D. " 'I Would Thy Husband Were Dead': *The Merry Wives of Windsor* as Mock Domestic Tragedy," *English Literary Renaissance* 30 (2000), 184–212.

Green, William. *Shakespeare's "Merry Wives of Windsor."* Princeton, 1962.

Hinely, Jan Lawson. "Comic Scapegoats and the Falstaff of *The Merry Wives of Windsor,*" *ShakS* 15 (1982), 37–54.

Kegl, Rosemary. *The Rhetoric of Concealment: Figuring Gender and Class in Renaissance Literature.* Ithaca, N.Y., 1994.

Leggatt, Alexander. *Citizen Comedy in the Age of Shakespeare.* Toronto, 1973.

Parten, Anne. "Falstaff's Horns: Masculine Inadequacy and Feminine Mirth in *The Merry Wives of Windsor,*" *Studies in Philology* 82 (1985), 184–99.

Roberts, Jeanne Addison. *Shakespeare's English Comedy: "The Merry Wives of Windsor" in Context.* Lincoln, Neb. 1979.

Steadman, John M. "Falstaff as Actaeon: A Dramatic Emblem," *SQ* 14 (1963), 231–44.

Wall, Wendy. "Why Does Puck Sweep?: Fairylore, Merry Wives, and Social Struggle," *SQ* 52 (2001), 67–106.

———. " 'Household stuff': The Sexual Politics of Domesticity and the Advent of English Comedy," *ELH* 65 (1998), 1–45.

As You Like It

See also, under *The Comedies,* Barber, R. Berry, Bradbury and Palmer (essay by Anne Barton), Brown, Hunter, Leggatt, Nevo, and Salingar; and under *Shakespeare Criticism Since 1980,* Belsey, Callaghan (*A Feminist Companion,* essay by Neely), Erickson, Lenz et al. (essay by Park), Mahon and Pendleton (essay by Gibbons), and McDonald (essay by Wofford).

Alpers, Paul. *What Is Pastoral?* Chicago, 1996.

Barnet, Sylvan. "Strange Events: Improbability in *As You Like It,*" *ShakS* 4 (1968), 119–31.

Bono, Barbara J. "Mixed Gender, Mixed Genre in Shakespeare's *As You Like It,*" *Renaissance Genres: Essays on Theory, History, and Interpretation,* ed. Barbara Kiefer Lewalski. Cambridge, Mass., 1986.

Debax, Jean-Paul, and Yves Peyré, eds. *"As You Like It": Essais critiques.* Toulouse, 1998.

Doran, Madeleine. " 'Yet Am I Inland Bred,' " *SQ* 15:2 (1964), 99–114.

Fortin, René E. " 'Tongues in Trees': Symbolic Patterns in *As You Like it,*" *Texas Studies in Literature and Language* 14 (1973), 569–82.

Gardner, Helen. *"As You Like It," More Talking of Shakespeare*, ed. John Garrett. London and New York, 1959.

Halio, Jay L. " 'No Clock in the Forest': Time in *As You Like It,*" *Studies in English Literature* 2 (1962), 197–207.

Hayles, Nancy K. "Sexual Disguise in *As You Like It* and *Twelfth Night,*" *ShS* 32 (1979), 63–72.

Howard, Jean E. "Crossdressing, The Theatre, and Gender Struggle in Early Modern England," *SQ* 39 (1988), 418–40.

Kernan, Alvin B. *The Cankered Muse*. New Haven, 1959.

Knowles, Richard. "Myth and Type in *As You Like It,*" *ELH* 33 (1966), 1–22.

Marshall, Cynthia. "The Doubled Jaques and Constructions of Negation in *As You Like It,*" *SQ* 49 (1998), 375–92.

Montrose, Louis Adrian. " 'The Place of a Brother' in *As You Like It:* Social Process and Comic Form," *SQ* 32 (1981), 28–54.

Ronk, Martha. "Locating the Visual in *As You Like It,*" *SQ* 52 (2001), 255–76.

Schleiner, Louise. "Voice, Ideology, and Gendered Subjects: The Case of *As You Like It* and *Two Gentlemen,*" *SQ* 50 (1999), 285–309.

Young, David. *The Heart's Forest*. New Haven, 1972.

Twelfth Night

See also, under *The Comedies,* Barber, E. Berry, Bradbury and Palmer (essay by Anne Barton), Brown, Brown and Harris (essay by Kermode), Hunter, Leggatt, Levin, Nevo, and Salingar; and under *Shakespeare Criticism Since 1980,* Callaghan (*A Feminist Companion,* essay by Neely), Erickson and Kahn (essay by Booth), Greenblatt (*Shakespearean Negotiations,* Chapter 3), Hamilton (Chapter 4), Hawkes (essay by Elam), Howard, and Parker and Hartman (essay by Hartman).

Arlidge, Anthony. *Shakespeare and the Prince of Love: The Feast of Misrule in the Middle Temple*. London, 2000.

Auden, W. H. "Music in Shakespeare," *"The Dyer's Hand" and Other Essays*. New York, 1948.

Bloom, Harold, ed. *Modern Critical Interpretations of "Twelfth Night."* New York, 1987.

Booth, Stephen. *Precious Nonsense: The Gettysburg Address, Ben Jonson's Epitaphs on His Children, and "Twelfth Night."* Berkeley, 1998.

Brown, John Russell. "Directions for *Twelfth Night,* or What You Will," *Tulane Drama Review* 5:4 (1961), 77–88.

Downer, Alan S. "Feste's Night," *College English* 13 (1952), 258–65.

Eagleton, Terence. "Language and Reality in *Twelfth Night,*" *Critical Quarterly* 9 (1967), 217–28.

Elam, Keir. "The Fertile Eunuch: *Twelfth Night,* Early Modern Intercourse, and the Fruits of Castration," *SQ* 47 (1996), 1–36.

Hollander, John. "*Twelfth Night* and the Morality of Indulgence," *Sewanee Review* 67 (1959), 220–38.

Hutson, Lorna. "On Not Being Deceived: Rhetoric and the Body in *Twelfth Night,*" *Texas Studies in Literature and Language* 38 (1996), 140–74.

Kerrigan, John. "Secrecy and Gossip in *Twelfth Night,*" *ShS* 50 (1997), 65–80.

Leech, Clifford. *"Twelfth Night" and Shakespearian Comedy*. Toronto, 1965.

Lewalski, Barbara K. "Thematic Patterns in *Twelfth Night,*" *ShakS* 1 (1965), 168–81.

Potter, Lois. *"Twelfth Night": Text and Performance*. London, 1985.

Salingar, L. D. "The Design of *Twelfth Night,*" *SQ* 9 (1958), 117–39.

Shannon, Laurie J. "Nature's Bias: Renaissance Homonormativity and Elizabethan Likeness," *Modern Philology* 98 (2000), 183–210.

Wells, Stanley. *Royal Shakespeare*. Manchester, Eng., 1977. (Includes an account of John Barton's production of *Twelfth Night.*)

Welsford, Enid. *The Fool: His Social and Literary History*. London, 1935.

Williams, Porter, Jr. "Mistakes in *Twelfth Night* and Their Resolution," *PMLA* 76 (1961), 193–9.

All's Well That Ends Well

See also, under *The Comedies,* Hunter and Salingar: under *The Problem Plays,* Foakes, Frye, Muir and Wells, and Wheeler; under *The Tragedies,* Honigmann (Chapter 8); under *Shakespeare Criticism from the 1940s to the 1970s,* Rossiter; under *Shakespeare Criticism Since 1980,* Holland et al. (essay by Adelman), Kirsch, Mahon and Pendleton (essay by Nevo), and Neely; and under *Shakespeare's Language,* Donawerth.

Calderwood, James L. "Styles of Knowing in *All's Well,*" *Modern Language Quarterly* 25 (1964), 272–94.

Cole, Howard C. *The "All's Well" Story from Boccaccio to Shakespeare*. Urbana, Ill., 1981.

Desens, Marliss C. *The Bed-Trick in English Renaissance Drama: Explorations in Gender, Sexuality, and Power*. Newark, Del., 1994.

Donaldson, Ian. "*All's Well That Ends Well:* Shakespeare's Play of Endings," *Essays in Criticism* 27 (1977), 34–55.

Friedman, Michael D. "Male Bonds and Marriage in *All's Well* and *Much Ado,*" *Studies in English Literature* 35 (1995), 231–49.

Haley, David. *Shakespeare's Courtly Mirror: Reflexivity and Prudence in "All's Well That Ends Well."* Newark, Del., 1993.

Halio, Jay L. "*All's Well That Ends Well,*" *SQ* 15:1 (1964), 33–43.

Hodgdon, Barbara. "The Making of Virgins and Mothers: Sexual Signs, Substitute Scenes and Doubled Presences in *All's Well That Ends Well,*" *Philological Quarterly* 66 (1987), 47–71.

Kastan, David Scott. "*All's Well That Ends Well* and the Limits of Comedy," *ELH* 52 (1985), 575–89.

King, Walter N. "Shakespeare's 'Mingled Yarn,'" *Modern Language Quarterly* 21 (1960), 33–44.

Knight, G. Wilson. *The Sovereign Flower: On Shakespeare as the Poet of Royalism*. London, 1958.

Leech, Clifford. "The Theme of Ambition in *All's Well That Ends Well,*" *ELH* 21 (1954), 17–29.

Leggatt, Alexander. "*All's Well That Ends Well:* The Testing of Romance," *Modern Language Quarterly* 32 (1971), 21–41.

Lewis, Cynthia. " 'Derived Honesty and Achieved Goodness': Doctrines of Grace in *All's Well That Ends Well,*" *Renaissance and Reformation* (Spring, 1990), 147–70.

McCandless, David. "Helena's Bed-trick: Gender and Performance in *All's Well That Ends Well,*" *SQ* 45 (1994), 449–68.

Price, Joseph G. *The Unfortunate Comedy: A Study of "All's Well That Ends Well" and Its Critics*. Toronto, 1968.

Snyder, Susan. "*All's Well That Ends Well* and Shakespeare's Helens: Text and Subtext, Subject and Object," *English Literary Renaissance* 18 (1988), 66–77.

Styan, J. L. *Shakespeare in Performance: "All's Well That Ends Well."* Manchester, Eng., 1984.

Turner, Robert Y. "Dramatic Conventions in *All's Well That Ends Well,*" *PMLA* 75 (1960), 497–502.

Warren, Roger. "Why Does It End Well? Helena, Bertram, and the Sonnets," *ShS* 22 (1969), 79–92.

Measure for Measure

See also, under *The Comedies,* Hunter and Newman; under *The Problem Plays,* Frye, Schanzer, and Wheeler; under *Shakespeare Criticism from the 1940s to the 1970s,* Empson, Fly, Holland, Levin (pp. 171–93), and Sewell; and under *Shakespeare Criticism Since 1980,* Cox, Dollimore, Dollimore and Sinfield (essays by Dollimore and McLuskie), Drakakis (essay by Rose), Goldberg (Chapter 5), Grady (*Shakespeare and Modernity,* essay by Engle), Hamilton (Chapter 5), Holland et al. (essay by Adelman), Kirsch, Marcus, Mullaney (Chapter 4), and Skura (pp. 243–70).

Bennett, Josephine Waters. *"Measure for Measure" as Royal Entertainment*. New York, 1966.

Bennett, Robert B. *Romance and Reformation: The Erasmian Spirit of Shakespeare's "Measure for Measure."* Newark, Del., 2000.

Brown, Carolyn E. "The Wooing of Duke Vincentio and Isabella of *Measure for Measure:* 'The Image of It Gives [Them] Content,' " *ShakS* 22 (1994), 189–219.

Cacicedo, Alberto. " 'She is fast my wife': Sex, Marriage, and Ducal Authority in *Measure for Measure,*" *ShakS* 23 (1995), 187–209.

Chamberlain, Stephanie. "Defrocking Ecclesiastical Authority: *Measure for Measure* and the Struggle for Matrimonial Reform in Early Modern England," *Ben Jonson Journal* 7 (2000), 115–28.

Chambers, R. W. "The Jacobean Shakespeare and *Measure for Measure*," *Proceedings of the British Academy* 23 (1937), 135–92.

Coghill, Nevill. "Comic Form in *Measure for Measure*," *ShS* 8 (1955), 14–27.

Desens, Marliss C. *The Bed-Trick in English Renaissance Drama: Explorations in Gender, Sexuality, and Power.* Newark, Del., 1994.

Fergusson, Francis. *The Human Image in Dramatic Literature.* Garden City, N.Y., 1957.

Gless, Darryl. *"Measure for Measure," the Law, and the Convent.* Princeton, 1979.

Lascelles, Mary. *Shakespeare's "Measure for Measure."* London, 1953.

Leavis, F. R. "The Greatness of *Measure for Measure*," *Scrutiny* 10 (1942), 234–47.

Leggatt, Alexander. "Substitution in *Measure for Measure*," *SQ* 39 (1988), 342–59.

Nagarajan, S. *"Measure for Measure* and Elizabethan Betrothals," *SQ* 14 (1963), 115–19.

Shell, Marc. *The End of Kinship: "Measure for Measure," Incest, and the Ideal of Universal Siblinghood.* Stanford, 1988.

Stevenson, David L. *The Achievement of "Measure for Measure."* Ithaca, N.Y., 1966.

Wilson, Harold S. "Action and Symbol in *Measure for Measure* and *The Tempest*." *SQ* 4 (1953), 375–84.

Wood, Nigel. *"Measure for Measure."* Theory in Practice Series. Buckingham and Philadelphia, 1996.

Troilus and Cressida

See also, under *The Problem Plays*, especially Foakes and Frye; under *Shakespeare's Predecessors and Contemporaries*, Kernan and Ornstein; under *Shakespeare Criticism from the 1940s to the 1970s*, Colie, Council, Fly, Knights, Rossiter, Spencer, and Weimann; under *Shakespeare Criticism Since 1980*, Charnes, Dollimore, Eagleton (Chapter 3), Mallin, Novy (*Love's Argument*), Parker and Hartman (essays by Freund and Girard), Schwartz and Kahn (essay by Fineman), and Wheeler; and under *The Tragedies*, Honigmann.

Adamson, Jane. *"Troilus and Cressida."* Brighton, Sussex, 1987.

Adelman, Janet. "'This is and is Not Cressid': The Characterization of Cressida," *The (M)other Tongue: Essays in Feminist Psychoanalytic Interpretation,* ed. Shirley Nelson Garner, Claire Kehane, and Madelon Sprengnether. Ithaca, N.Y., 1985.

Bayley, John. "Time and the Trojans," *Essays in Criticism* 25 (1975), 55–73.

Bowen, Barbara E. *Gender in the Theater of War: Shakespeare's "Troilus and Cressida."* New York, 1993.

Campbell, Oscar James. *Comicall Satyre and Shakespeare's "Troilus and Cressida."* San Marino, Calif., 1938.

Cox, John D. "The Error of Our Eye in *Troilus and Cressida*," *Comparative Drama* 10 (1976), 147–71.

Elton, W. R. *Shakespeare's "Troilus and Cressida" and the Inns of Court Revels.* Aldershot, 2000.

Gil, Daniel Juan. "At the Limits of the Social World: Fear and Pride in *Troilus and Cressida*," *SQ* 52 (2001), 336–59.

Greenfield, Matthew A. "Fragments of Nationalism in *Troilus and Cressida*," *SQ* 51 (2000), 181–200.

Hillman, David. "The Gastric Epic: *Troilus and Cressida*," *SQ* 48 (1997), 295–313.

Kaula, David. "Will and Reason in *Troilus and Cressida*," *SQ* 12 (1961), 271–83.

Kermode, Frank. "'Opinion' in *Troilus and Cressida*," *Teaching the Text,* eds. Susanne Kappeler and Norman Bryson. London, 1983.

Kimbrough, Robert. *Shakespeare's "Troilus and Cressida" and its Setting.* Cambridge, Mass., 1964.

Knight, G. Wilson. *The Wheel of Fire.* London, 1930, 1965.

Levine, Laura. *Men in Women's Clothing: Anti-Theatricality and Effeminization, 1579–1642.* Cambridge, Eng., 1994.

Mallin, Eric. "Emulous Factions and the Collapse of Chivalry: *Troilus and Cressida*," *Representations* 29 (1990), 145–79.

Norbrook, David. "Rhetoric, Ideology, and the Elizabethan Picture," *Renaissance Rhetoric,* ed. Peter Mack. Basingstoke and New York, 1994.

Nowottny, Winifred M. T. "'Opinion' and 'Value' in *Troilus: and Cressida*," *Essays in Criticism* 4 (1954), 282–96.

Presson, Robert K. *Shakespeare's "Troilus and Cressida" and the Legends of Troy.* Madison, Wis., 1953.

Rabkin, Norman. *"Troilus and Cressida:* The Uses of the Double Plot," *ShakS* 1 (1965), 265–82.

Rutter, Carol Chillington. "Shakespeare, His Designers, and the Politics of Costume: Handing Over Cressida's Glove," *Essays in Theatre/Études théâtrales* 12 (1993–1994), 107–28.

Smith, Bruce R. "Rape, rap, rupture, rapture: R-rated futures on the global market," *Textual Practice* 9 (1995), 421–43.

Taylor, Gary. *"Troilus and Cressida:* Bibliography, Performance, and Interpretation," *ShakS* 15 (1982), 99–136.

Yoder, R. A. "'Sons and Daughters of the Game': An Essay on Shakespeare's *Troilus and Cressida*," *ShS* 25 (1972), 11–25.

The Histories

Alexander, Peter. *Shakespeare's, "Henry VI" and "Richard III."* Cambridge, Eng., 1929.

Berry, Edward I. *Patterns of Decay: Shakespeare's Early Histories.* Charlottesville, Va., 1975.

Blanpied, John W. *Time and the Artist in Shakespeare's English Histories.* Newark, Del., 1983.

Calderwood, James L. *Metadrama in Shakespeare's Henriad: "Richard II" to "Henry V."* Berkeley, 1979.

Campbell, Lily B. *Shakespeare's "Histories": Mirrors of Elizabethan Policy.* San Marino, Calif., 1947.

Champion, Larry S. *"The Noise of Threatening Drum": Dramatic Strategy and Political Ideology in Shakespeare and the English Chronicle Plays.* Newark, Del., 1990.

——. *Perspective in Shakespeare's English Histories.* Athens, Ga., 1980.

Dorius, R. J. "A Little More Than a Little," *SQ* 11 (1960), 13–26.

Edwards, Philip. "The Hidden King: Shakespeare's History Plays," *Threshold of a Nation: A Study in English and Irish Drama.* Cambridge, Eng., 1979.

Forker, Charles R. "Shakespeare's Chronicle Plays as Historical-Pastoral," *ShakS* 1 (1965), 85–104.

Hodgdon, Barbara. *The End Crowns All: Closure and Contradiction in Shakespeare's History.* Princeton, 1991.

Holderness, Graham. *Shakespeare's History.* New York, 1985. Largely reprinted in *Shakespeare Recycled: The Making of Historical Drama.* Hempstead, Eng., New York, 1992.

——, ed. *Shakespeare's History Plays: "Richard II" to "Henry V."* London, 1992.

Howard, Jean E., and Phyllis Rackin. *Engendering a Nation: A Feminist Account of Shakespeare's English Histories.* London and New York, 1997.

Jenkins, Harold. "Shakespeare's History Plays: 1900–1951," *ShS* 6 (1953), 1–15.

Jorgensen, Paul A. *Shakespeare's Military World.* Berkeley and Los Angeles, 1956.

Kastan, David Scott. *Shakespeare and the Shapes of Time.* Hanover, N. H., 1982.

Kelly, Henry A. *Divine Providence in the England of Shakespeare's Histories.* Cambridge, Mass., 1970.

Knights, L. C. "Shakespeare's Politics: With Some Reflections on the Nature of Tradition," *Proceedings of the British Academy* 43 (1957), 115–32.

Leggatt, Alexander. *Shakespeare's Political Drama: The History Plays and the Roman Plays.* London, 1988.

Levine, Nina S. *Women's Matters: Politics, Gender, and Nation in Shakespeare's Early History Plays.* Newark, Del., 1998.

Manheim, Michael. *The Weak King Dilemma in the Shakespearean History Play.* Syracuse, N.Y., 1973.

Norwich, John Julius. *Shakespeare's Kings: The Great Plays and the History of England in the Middle Ages: 1337–1485.* London, 1999; New York, 2000.

Ornstein, Robert. *A Kingdom for a Stage.* Cambridge, Mass., 1972.

Palmer, John. *Political Characters of Shakespeare.* London, 1945.

Paris, Bernard J. *Character as a Subversive Force in Shakespeare: The History and Roman Plays.* Rutherford, N.J., and London, 1991.

Patterson, Annabel. *Reading Holinshed's Chronicles.* Chicago, 1994.

Pierce, Robert B. *Shakespeare's History Plays: The Family and the State.* Columbus, Ohio, 1971.

Pilkington, Ace G. *Screening Shakespeare from "Richard II" to "Henry V."* Newark, Del., 1991.

Porter, Joseph. *The Drama of Speech Acts: Shakespeare's Lancastrian Tetralogy.* Berkeley, 1979.

Prior, Moody E. *The Drama of Power: Studies in Shakespeare's History Plays.* Evanston, Ill., 1973.

Pugliatti, Paola. *Shakespeare the Historian.* New York, 1996.

Pye, Christopher. *The Regal Phantasm: Shakespeare and the Politics of Spectacle.* London, 1990.

Rackin, Phyllis. "Anti-Historians: Women's Roles in Shakespeare's Histories," *Theatre Journal* 37 (1985), 329–44.

———. *Stages of History: Shakespeare's English Chronicles.* Ithaca, N.Y., 1990.

Reese, M. M. *The Cease of Majesty.* London and New York, 1961.

Ribner, Irving. *The English History Play in the Age of Shakespeare,* Rev. ed., London, 1965.

Rossiter, A. P. "Ambivalence: The Dialectic of the Histories," *Talking of Shakespeare,* ed. John Garrett. London, 1954.

Saccio, Peter. *Shakespeare's English Kings: History, Chronicle, and Drama.* New York, 1977.

Shaheen, Naseeb. *Biblical References in Shakespeare's History Plays.* Newark, Del., 1989.

Sprague, Arthur Colby. *Shakespeare's Histories: Plays for the Stage.* London, 1964.

Sterling, Eric. *The Movement Towards Subversion: The English History Play from Skelton to Shakespeare.* Lanham, Md., 1996.

Tillyard, E. M. W. *Shakespeare's History Plays.* London, 1944, 1961.

Traversi, Derek. *Shakespeare from "Richard II" to "Henry V."* London, 1957.

Velz, John W., ed. *Shakespeare's English Histories: A Quest for Form and Genre.* Binghamton, N.Y., 1996.

Winny, James. *The Player King: A Theme of Shakespeare's Histories.* London, 1968.

Yeats, William Butler. "At Stratford-upon-Avon," *Ideas of Good and Evil.* London, 1903.

The Henry VI Plays

See also, under *The Histories,* Alexander, Berry, Blanpied, Hodgdon, Kelly, Manheim, Ornstein, Prior, Ribner, Saccio, and Tillyard; under *Shakespeare Criticism from the 1940s to the 1970s,* Burckhardt, and Jones; under *Shakespeare Criticism Since 1980,* Cox, Edwards et al. (essay by Clemen), Kahn (Chapter 3), Marcus (Chapter 2), and Patterson (Chapter 2); and under *Richard III,* Torrey.

Berman, Ronald S. "Fathers and Sons in the Henry VI Plays," *SQ* 13 (1962), 487–97.

Bevington, David. "The Domineering Female in *1 Henry VI,*" *ShakS* 2 (1966). 51–8.

Candido, Joseph. "Getting Loose in the *Henry VI Plays,*" *SQ* 35 (1984), 392–406.

Clemen, Wolfgang H. "Anticipation and Foreboding in Shakespeare's Early Histories," *ShS* 6 (1953), 25–35.

Cox, John D. "*3 Henry VI:* Dramatic Convention and the Shakespearean History Play," *Comparative Drama* 12 (1978), 42–60.

French, A. L. "The Mills of God and Shakespeare's Early History Plays," *English Studies* 55 (1974), 313–24.

Greenblatt, Stephen. "Murdering Peasants, Status, Genre, and the Representation of Rebellion," *Representations* 1 (1983), 1–29.

Jackson, Gabriele Bernhard. "Topical Ideology: Witches, Amazons, and Shakespeare's Joan of Arc," *English Literary Renaissance* 18 (1988), 40–65.

Leech, Clifford. "The Two-Part Play: Marlowe and the Early Shakespeare," *Shakespeare Jahrbuch* 94 (1958), 90–106.

Price, Hereward T. *Construction in Shakespeare.* Ann Arbor, Mich., 1951.

Ricks, Don A. *Shakespeare's Emergent Form: A Study of the Structures of the Henry VI Plays.* Logan, Utah, 1968.

Riggs, David. *Shakespeare's Heroical Histories: "Henry VI" and its Literary Tradition.* Cambridge, Mass., 1971.

Rossiter, A. P., ed. *Woodstock, a Moral History.* London, 1946.

Watson, Donald G. *Shakespeare's Early History Plays: Politics at Play on the English Stage.* Athens, Ga., 1990.

Wilson, F. P. *Marlowe and the Early Shakespeare.* Oxford, 1953.

Richard III

See also, under *The Histories,* Alexander, Berry, Campbell, Kelly, Ornstein, Prior, Ribner, and Saccio; under *Shakespeare's Predecessors and Contemporaries,* Sanders; under *Shakespeare Criticism from the 1940s to the 1970s,* Jones, Rossiter, and Spivack; under *Shakespeare Criticism since 1980,* Dubrow and Strier (essay by Garber), and Lenz et al. (essay by Miner); under *The Tragedies,* Garner and Sprengnether (essay by Rackin), and Hunter; and under *The Henry VI Plays,* Watson.

Anderson, Judith H. "Shakespeare's *Richard III:* The Metamorphosis of Biographical Truth to Fiction," *Biographical Truth: The Representation of Historical Persons in Tudor-Stuart Writing.* New Haven, 1984.

Bevington, David. " 'Why Should Calamity Be Full of Words?' The Efficacy of Cursing in *Richard III,*" *Iowa State Journal of Research* 56:1 (1981), 9–21.

Colley, Scott. *"Richard's Himself Again": A Stage History of "Richard III."* New York, 1992.

French, A. L. 'The World of *Richard III,*" *ShakS* 4 (1968), 25–39.

Hankey, Julie, ed. *Plays in Performance: "Richard III."* Bristol, 1981; 2nd ed., 1988.

Hassel, R. Chris, Jr. *Songs of Death: Performance, Interpretation, and the Text of "Richard III."* Lincoln, Neb., 1987.

Hunter, Robert G. *Shakespeare and the Mystery of God's Judgments.* Athens, Ga., 1976.

Kendall, Paul Murray. *Richard the Third.* New York and London, 1956.

Krieger, Murray. "The Dark Generations of *Richard III,*" *Criticism* 1 (1959), 32–48.

Neill, Michael. "Shakespeare's Halle of Mirrors: Play, Politics, and Psychology in *Richard III,*" *ShakS* 8 (1975), 99–129.

Sher, Antony. *Year of the King: An Actor's Diary and Sketchbook.* London, 1985.

Torrey, Michael. " 'The plain devil and dissembling looks': Ambivalent Physiognomy and Shakespeare's *Richard III,*" *English Literary Renaissance* 30 (2000), 123–53.

Wheeler, Richard P. "History, Character, and Conscience in *Richard III,*" *Comparative Drama* 5 (1971–1972), 301–21.

King John

See also, under *Shakespeare's Language,* Donawerth; under *The Histories,* Blanpied, Campbell, Champion, Edwards, Ornstein, Pierce, Rackin (*Stages of History*), Reese, Ribner, Saccio, Sprague, and Tillyard; under *Shakespeare Criticism from the 1940s to the 1970s,* Burckhardt and Jones; and under *Shakespeare Criticism Since 1980,* Hamilton (Chapter 2).

Calderwood, James L. "Commodity and Honour in *King John,*" *University of Toronto Quarterly* 29 (1960), 341–56.

Cousin, Geraldine. *King John.* Shakespeare in Performance. Manchester, Eng., 1994.

Elliott, John R., Jr., "Shakespeare and the Double Image of King John," *ShakS* 1 (1965), 64–84.

Elson, John. "Studies in the *King John Plays,*" *J. Q. Adams Memorial Studies,* ed. J. McManaway et al., pp. 183–98. Washington, D.C., 1948.

Lane, Robert. " 'The sequence of posterity': Shakespeare's *King John* and the Succession Controversy," *Studies in Philology* 92 (1995), 460–81.

Levin, Carole. " 'I Trust I May Not Trust Thee': Women's Visions of the World in Shakespeare's *King John,*" *Ambiguous Realities: Women in the Middle Ages and Renaissance,* ed. Carole Levin and Jeanie Watson, pp. 219–34. Detroit, 1987.

Matchett, William H. "Richard's Divided Heritage in *King John,*" *Essays in Criticism* 12 (1962), 231–53.

Pettet, E. C. "Hot Irons and Fever: A Note on Some of the Imagery of *King John,*" *Essays in Criticism* 4 (1954), 128–44.

Waith, Eugene M. "*King John* and the Drama of History," *SQ* 29 (1978), 192–211.

Weimann, Robert. "Mingling Vice and 'Worthiness' in *King John,*" *ShakS* 27 (1999), 109–33.

Richard II

See also, under *The Histories*, Calderwood, Campbell, Dorius, Forker, Ornstein, Palmer, Porter, Reese, Ribner, Saccio and Tillyard; under *Shakespeare's Predecessors and Contemporaries*, Sanders; under *Shakespeare's Language*, Mahood; under *Shakespeare Criticism to the 1930s*, Coleridge (*Coleridge's Writings*); under *Shakespeare Criticism from the 1940s to the 1970s*, Bryant, Calderwood, Hawkes, Kernan (essay on the "Major History Plays"), and Rabkin (pp. 81–98); under *Shakespeare Criticism Since 1980*, Bergeron (essay by Black), Parker and Hartman (essay by Berger), and Woodbridge and Berry (essay by Liebler); under *Shakespeare in Performance*, McGuire and Samuelson (essay by McGuire); and under *The Tragedies*, Nevo.

Barkan, Leonard. "The Theatrical Consistency of *Richard II*," *SQ* 29 (1978), 5–19.

Berger, Harry, Jr. "Textual Dramaturgy: Representing the Limits of Theatre in *Richard II*," *Theatre Journal* 39 (1987), 135–55.

Bergeron, David M. "*Richard II*: Internal and External Evidence," *Practicing Renaissance Scholarship: Plays and Pageants, Patrons and Politics*. Pittsburgh, Pa., 2000.

Dorius, R. J. "A Little More Than a Little," *SQ* 11 (1960), 13–26.

Elliott, John R., Jr. "History and Tragedy in *Richard II*," *Studies in English Literature* 8 (1968), 253–71.

Forker, Charles. *Shakespeare: The Critical Tradition: Richard II*. London, 1998.

Gaudet, Paul. "The 'Parasitical' Counselors in Shakespeare's *Richard II*: A Problem in Dramatic Interpretation," *SQ* 33 (1982), 142–54.

Halvorson, John. "The Lamentable Comedy of Richard II," *English Literary Renaissance* 24 (1994), 343–69.

Harris, Kathryn Montgomery. "Sun and Water Imagery in *Richard II*: Its Dramatic Function," *SQ* 21 (1970), 157–65.

Heninger, S. K., Jr. "The Sun-King Analogy in *Richard II*," *SQ* 11 (1960), 319–27.

Humphreys, A. R. *Shakespeare: "Richard II."* London, 1967.

Kantorowicz, Ernst H. *The King's Two Bodies: A Study in Medieval Political Theology*. Princeton, 1957.

Lisak, Catherine. "In Search of *Richard II*: Shakespeare's Use of Eyewitness Accounts of the Revolution (1399–1400); Conflicting Tales and the Dramatic Structure of the Play," *Shakespeare et le Moyen-Âge*. Actes du colloque international de la Société française Shakespeare, gen. ed. Jean-Marie Maguin. Montpellier, France, 2002.

MacKenzie, Clayton G. "Paradise and Paradise Lost in *Richard II*," *SQ* 37 (1986), 318–39.

McMillin, Scott. "Shakespeare's *Richard II*: Eyes of Sorrow, Eyes of Desire," *SQ* 35 (1984), 40–52.

Page, Malcolm. Text and *Performance: "Richard II."* Atlantic Highlands, N.J., 1987.

Potter, Lois. "The Antic Disposition of Richard II," *ShS* 27 (1974), 33–41.

Schoenbaum, S. "*Richard II* and the Realities of Power," *ShS* 28 (1975), 1–13.

Shewring, Margaret. *Shakespeare in Performance: "King Richard II."* Manchester, Eng., 1996.

Stirling, Brents. "Bolingbroke's 'Decision,'" *SQ* 2 (1951), 27–34.

Yeats, W. B. "At Stratford-upon-Avon," *Ideas of Good and Evil*, collected in *Essays and Introductions*. New York, 1961.

Zitner, Sheldon P. "Aumerle's Conspiracy," *Studies in English Literature* 14 (1974), 239–57.

The Henry IV Plays

See also, under *The Histories*, Blanpied, Calderwood, Campbell, Dorius, Kelly, Manheim, Ornstein, Palmer, Porter, Prior, Reese, Saccio, Sprague, Tillyard, and Velz (essay by Rumrich); under *Shakespeare Criticism to the 1930s*, Johnson and Smith (*Eighteenth Century*, essay by Morgann); under *Shakespeare Criticism from the 1940s to the 1970s*, Bevington and Halio (essay by R. G. Hunter), Bryant, Burckhardt, Council, Goldman, Kernan (essay on the "Major History Plays"), Spivack, and Stewart; and under *Shakespeare Criticism Since 1980*, Auden, Dollimore and Sinfield (essay by Greenblatt, originally published by *Glyph* 8 and in *Shakespearean Negotiations*), Nuttall, and Watson; and under *The Comedies*, Barber.

Abrams, Richard. "Rumor's Reign in *2 Henry IV*: The Scope of a Personification," *English Literary Renaissance* 16 (1986), 467–95.

Auden, W. H. "The Prince's Dog," *"The Dyer's Hand" and Other Essays*. New York, 1948.

Barber, C. L. "Rule and Misrule in *Henry IV*," *Shakespeare's Festive Comedy*. Princeton, 1959.

Barish, Jonas A. "The Turning Away of Prince Hal," *ShakS* 1 (1965), 9–17.

Berger, Harry, Jr. "Sneak's Noise, or Rumor and Detextualization in *2 Henry IV*," *Kenyon Review* n.s. 6:4 (1984), 58–78.

Berry, Edward I. "The Rejection Scene in *2 Henry IV*," *Studies in English Literature* 17 (1977), 201–18.

Bradley, A. C. "The Rejection of Falstaff," *Oxford Lectures on Poetry*. London, 1909, 1961.

Bryant, J. A., Jr., "Prince Hal and the Ephesians," *Sewanee Review* 67 (1959), 204–19.

Cohen, Derek. "The Rite of Violence in *1 Henry IV*," *ShS* 38 (1985), 77–84.

Dessen, Alan. "Dual Protagonists in *1 Henry IV*," *Shakespeare and the Late Moral Plays*. Lincoln, Neb., 1986.

Doran, Madeleine. "Imagery in *Richard II* and in *Henry IV*," *Modern Language Review* 37 (1942), 113–22.

Dorius, R. J., ed. *Twentieth Century Interpretations of "Henry IV Part I."* Englewood Cliffs, N.J., 1970.

Empson, William. "Falstaff and Mr. Dover Wilson," *Kenyon Review* 15 (1953), 213–62.

Everett, Barbara. "The Fatness of Falstaff: Shakespeare and Character," *Proceedings of the British Academy* 76 (1990), 109–28.

Gottschalk, Paul A. "Hal and the 'Play Extempore' in *1 Henry IV*," *Texas Studies in Literature and Language* 15 (1974), 605–14.

Hawkins, Sherman H. "Virtue and Kingship in Shakespeare's *Henry IV*," *English Literary Renaissance* 5 (1975), 313–43.

Hodgdon, Barbara. *Shakespeare in Performance: "Henry IV, Part Two."* Manchester, Eng., 1993.

Hunter, G. K. "*Henry IV* and the Elizabethan Two-Part Play," *Review of English Studies* n.s. 5 (1954), 236–48.

———. "Shakespeare's Politics and the Rejection of Falstaff," *Critical Quarterly* 1 (1959), 229–36.

Jenkins, Harold. *The Structural Problem in Shakespeare's "Henry the Fourth."* London, 1956.

Jorgensen, Paul A. "The 'Dastardly Treachery' of Prince John of Lancaster," *PMLA* 76 (1961), 488–92.

Knowles, Richard. "Unquiet and the Double Plot of *2 Henry IV*," *ShakS* 2 (1966), 133–40.

Kris, Ernst. "Prince Hal's Conflict," *Psychoanalytic Explorations in Art*. New York, 1964.

Levine, Nina. "Extending Credit in the *Henry IV Plays*," *SQ* 51 (2000), 403–31.

Manley, Frank. "The Unity of Betrayal in *2 Henry IV*," *Studies in the Literary Imagination* 5:1 (1972), 91–110.

McAlindon, Tom. *Shakespeare's Tudor History: A Study of "Henry IV, Parts 1 and 2."* Aldershot, Eng., 2001.

McLuhan, Herbert Marshall. "*Henry IV*, A Mirror for Magistrates," *University of Toronto Quarterly* 17 (1947–1948), 152–60.

McMillin, Scott. *Shakespeare in Performance: "Henry IV, Part One."* Manchester, Eng., 1991.

Palmer, D. J. "Casting Off the Old Man: History and St. Paul in *Henry IV*," *Critical Quarterly* 12 (1970), 267–83.

Poole, Kristen. "Saints Alive! Falstaff, Martin Marprelate, and the Staging of Puritanism," *SQ* 46 (1995), 47–75.

Somerset, J. A. B. "Falstaff, the Prince, and the Pattern of *2 Henry IV*," *ShS* 30 (1977), 35–45.

Toliver, Harold E. "Falstaff, the Prince, and the History Play," *SQ* 16 (1965), 63–80.

Wharton, T. F. *"Henry the Fourth, Parts 1 and 2": Text and Performance*. London, 1983.

Wilson, J. Dover. *The Fortunes of Falstaff*. Cambridge, Eng., 1943.

Womersley, David. "Why Is Falstaff Fat?" *Review of English Studies* n.s. 47 (1996), 1–22.

Henry V

See also, under *The Histories*, Calderwood, Campbell, Jorgensen, Kastan, Ornstein, Porter, Prior, Reese, Ribner, Saccio, and Traversi; under *Shakespeare Criticism to the 1930s*, Hazlitt and Schlegel; under

Shakespeare Criticism from the 1940s to the 1970s, Burckhardt, Goddard, Goldman, and Kernan (essay on the "Major History Plays"); under *Shakespeare Criticism Since 1980*, Dollimore and Sinfield (essays by Greenblatt and Tennenhouse), Drakakis (essay by Dollimore and Sinfield), Erickson, Mahon and Pendleton (essay by Hammond), Patterson (Chapter 4), and Rabkin (Chapter 2); and under *Shakespeare in Performance*, Price (essay by Barton).

Altman, Joel B. " 'Vile Participation': The Amplification of Violence in the Theater of *Henry V*," *SQ* 42 (1991), 1–32.

Beauman, Sally, ed. *"King Henry V": The Royal Shakespeare Company's Production of "Henry V" for the Centenary Season at the Royal Shakespeare Theatre*. Oxford, 1976. (Includes information on Terry Hands's *Henry V*.)

Cubeta, Paul M. "Falstaff and the Art of Dying," *Studies in English Literature* 27 (1987), 197–211.

Eggert, Katherine. "Nostalgia and the Not Yet Late Queen: Refusing Female Rule in *Henry V*," *ELH* 61 (1994), 523–50.

Granville-Barker, Harley. "From *Henry V* to *Hamlet*," *Proceedings of the British Academy* 11 (1925), 283–309.

Gurr, Andrew. "*Henry V* and the Bees' Commonwealth," *ShS* 30 (1977): 61–72.

Levin, Richard. "Hazlitt on *Henry V*, and the Appropriation of Shakespeare," *SQ* 35 (1984), 134–41.

McEachern, Claire. *The Poetics of English Nationhood, 1590–1612*. Cambridge, Eng., 1996.

Henry VIII

See also, under *The Histories*, Saccio; under *Shakespeare Criticism Since 1980*, Dollimore and Sinfield (essay by Tennenhouse), Hamilton (Chapter 7), and Knowles (essay by McMullan); under *The Problem Plays*, Foakes, and under *The Romances*, Brown and Harris (essay by Harris), Felperin, Knight (*Crown of Life*), and Richards and Knowles (essays by Healy and McMullan).

Alexander, Peter. "Conjectural History, or Shakespeare's *Henry VIII*," *English Association Essays and Studies* 16 (1930), 85–120.

Anderson, Judith H. "Shakespeare's *Henry VIII*: The Changing Relation of Truth to Fiction," *Biographical Truth: The Representation of Historical Persons in Tudor-Stuart Writing*. New Haven, 1984.

Berry, Edward I. "*Henry VIII* and the Dynamics of Spectacle," *ShakS* 12 (1979), 229–46.

Bertram, Paul. "*Henry VIII*: The Conscience of the King," *In Defense of Reading*, ed. Reuben A. Brower and Richard Poirier. New York, 1962.

Bosman, Anston. "Seeing Tears: Truth and Sense in *All Is True*," *SQ* 50 (1999), 459–76.

Cespedes, Frank V. " 'We are one in fortunes': The Sense of History in *Henry VIII*," *English Literary Renaissance* 10 (1980), 413–38.

Cook, Albert. "The Ordering Effect of Dramatized History: Shakespeare and *Henry VIII*," *Centennial Review* 42 (1998), 211–27.

Cox, John D. "*Henry VIII* and the Masque," *ELH* 45 (1978), 390–409.

Kreps, Barbara. "When All Is True: Law, History, and Problems of Knowledge in *Henry VIII*," *ShS* 52 (1999), 166–82.

Leggatt, Alexander. "*Henry VIII* and the Ideal England," *ShS* 38 (1985), 131–43.

Monta, Susannah Brietz. " 'Thou fall'st a blessed martyr': Shakespeare's *Henry VIII* and the Politics of Conscience," *English Literary Renaissance* 30 (2000), 262–83.

Wasson, John. "In Defense of *King Henry VIII*," *Research Studies* (Washington State University) 32 (1964), 261–76.

Wegemer, Gerard. "Henry VIII on Trial: Confronting Malice and Conscience in Shakespeare's *All Is True*," *Renascence* 52 (2000), 111–30.

Wiley, Paul L. "Renaissance Exploitation of Cavendish's *Life of Wolsey*," *Studies in Philology* 43 (1946), 121–46.

The Tragedies

See also, under *Shakespeare's Predecessors and Contemporaries*, Belsey.

Armstrong, Philip. *Shakespeare's Visual Regime: Tragedy, Psychoanalysis, and the Gaze*. Basingstoke and New York, 2000.

Baldo, Jonathan. *The Unmasking of Drama: Contested Representation in Shakespeare's Tragedies*. Detroit, 1996.

Barker, Francis, ed. *The Culture of Violence: Essays on Tragedy and History*. Chicago, 1993.

Barroll, J. Leeds. *Artificial Persons: The Formation of Character in the Tragedies of Shakespeare*. Columbia, S. C., 1974.

Bayley, John. *Shakespeare and Tragedy*. London, 1981.

Bell, Millicent. *Shakespeare's Tragic Skepticism*. New Haven, 2002.

Berry, Philippa. *Shakespeare's Feminine Endings: Disfiguring Death in the Tragedies*. London and New York, 1999.

Berry, Ralph. *Tragic Instance: The Sequence of Shakespeare's Tragedies*. Newark, Del., 1999.

Bradley, A. C. *Shakespearean Tragedy*. London, 1904. (*Hamlet, Othello, King Lear, Macbeth*.)

Brooke, Nicholas. *Shakespeare's Early Tragedies*. London and New York, 1968.

Brown, John Russell, and Bernard Harris, eds. *Early Shakespeare*. London, 1961.

Bulman, James C. *The Heroic Idiom of Shakespearean Tragedy*. Newark, Del., 1985.

Bushnell, Rebecca. *Tragedies of Tyrants: Political Thought and Theater in the English Renaissance*. Ithaca, N.Y., 1990.

Campbell, Lily B. *Shakespeare's Tragic Heroes: Slaves of Passion*. Cambridge, Eng., 1930.

Champion, Larry S. *Shakespeare's Tragic Perspective*. Athens, Ga., 1976.

Charlton, H. B. *Shakespearian Tragedy*. Cambridge, Eng., 1948.

Cunningham, I. V. *Woe or Wonder: The Emotional Effect of Shakespearean Tragedy*.

Denver, 1951. Rpt. in *Tradition and Poetic Structure*. Denver, 1960.

Danson, Lawrence. *Tragic Alphabet: Shakespeare's Drama of Language*. New Haven and London, 1974.

Dickey, Franklin M. *Not Wisely But Too Well: Shakespeare's Love Tragedies*. San Marino, Calif., 1957.

Eliot, T. S. "Shakespeare and the Stoicism of Seneca," *Selected Essays, 1917–1932*. London, 1932.

Everett, Barbara. *Young Hamlet: Essays on Shakespeare's Tragedies*. Oxford, 1989.

Falco, Raphael. *Charismatic Authority in Early Modern English Tragedy*. Baltimore, 2000.

Farnham, Willard. *Shakespeare's Tragic Frontier*. Berkeley, 1950.

Frye, Northrop. *Fools of Time: Studies in Shakespearean Tragedy*. Toronto, 1967.

Gajowski, Evelyn. *The Art of Loving: Female Subjectivity and Male Discursive Traditions in Shakespeare's Tragedies*. Newark, Del., 1992.

Garner, Shirley Nelson, and Madelon Sprengnether, eds. *Shakespearean Tragedy and Gender*. Bloomington, Ind., 1996.

Goldman, Michael. *Acting and Action in Shakespearean Tragedy*. Princeton, 1985.

Grene, Nicholas. *Shakespeare's Tragic Imagination*. New York, 1992.

Hawkes, Terence. *Shakespeare and the Reason: A Study of the Tragedies and the Problem Plays*. London, 1964.

Held, George F. *The Good That Lives After Them: A Pattern in Shakespeare's Tragedies*. Heidelberg, 1995.

Holloway, John. *The Story of the Night: Studies in Shakespeare's Major Tragedies*. London and Lincoln, Neb., 1961.

Honigmann, E. A. J. *Myriad-Minded Shakespeare: Essays, Chiefly on the Tragedies and Problem Comedies*. New York, 1989.

———. *Shakespeare: Seven Tragedies Revisited: The Dramatist's Manipulation of Response*. London and New York, 1976. 2nd ed., 2002.

Hunter, Robert Grams. *Shakespeare and the Mystery of God's Judgments*. Athens, Ga., 1976.

Ide, Richard S. *Possessed with Greatness: The Heroic Tragedies of Chapman and Shakespeare*. Chapel Hill, N.C., 1980.

Kiefer, Frederick. *Fortune and Elizabethan Tragedy*. San Marino, Calif., 1983.

Kirsch, Arthur. *The Passions of Shakespeare's Tragic Heroes*. Charlottesville, Va., 1990.

Knight, G. Wilson. *The Wheel of Fire*. London, 1930, 1965.

Lawlor, John. *The Tragic Sense in Shakespeare*. London, 1960.

Leech, Clifford. *Shakespeare's Tragedies and Other Studies in Seventeenth-Century Drama*. London, 1950.

———, ed. *Shakespeare: The Tragedies*. Chicago, 1965.

Liebler, Naomi Conn. *Shakespeare's Festive Tragedy: The Ritual Foundations of Genre*. London and New York, 1995.

Mack, Maynard. *Everybody's Shakespeare: Reflections Chiefly on the Tragedies*. Lincoln, Neb., 1993.

———. "The Jacobean Shakespeare: Some Observations on the Construction of the Tragedies," *Jacobean Theatre*, ed. John Russell Brown and Bernard Harris. Stratford-upon-Avon Studies 1. London, 1960.

Mack, Maynard, Jr. *Killing the King: Three Studies in Shakespeare's Tragic Structure.* New Haven and London, 1973.

Margolies, David. *Monsters of the Deep: Social Dissolution in Shakespeare's Tragedies.* Manchester, Eng., 1992.

McAlindon, T. *Shakespeare's Tragic Cosmos.* Cambridge, Eng., 1991.

Miola, Robert S. *Shakespeare and Classical Tragedy: The Influence of Seneca.* Oxford, 1992.

Neill, Michael. *Issues of Death: Mortality and Identity in English Renaissance Tragedy.* Oxford, 1997.

Nevo, Ruth. *Tragic Form in Shakespeare.* Princeton, 1972.

Proser, Matthew N. *The Heroic Image in Five Shakespearean Tragedies.* Princeton, 1965.

Rackin, Phyllis. *Shakespeare's Tragedies.* New York, 1978.

Reid, Robert Lanier. *Shakespeare's Tragic Form: Spirit in the Wheel.* Newark, Del., 2000.

Ribner, Irving. *Patterns in Shakespearean Tragedy.* New York, 1960.

Rosen, William. *Shakespeare and the Craft of Tragedy.* Cambridge, Mass., 1960.

Sanders, Wilbur, and Howard Jacobson. *Shakespeare's Magnanimity: Four Tragic Heroes, Their Friends and Families.* Oxford, 1978.

Shaheen, Naseeb. *Biblical References in Shakespeare's Tragedies.* Newark, Del., 1987.

Smith, Molly. *The Darker World Within: Evil in the Tragedies of Shakespeare and His Successors.* Newark, Del., 1991.

Snyder, Susan. *The Comic Matrix of Shakespeare's Tragedies.* Princeton, 1979.

Spivack, Bernard. *Shakespeare and the Allegory of Evil.* New York, 1958.

Whitaker, Virgil. *The Mirror up to Nature.* San Marino, Calif., 1965.

Wilson, Harold S. *On the Design of Shakespearian Tragedy.* Toronto, 1957.

Young, David. *The Action to the Word: Structure and Style in Shakespearean Tragedy.* New Haven, 1990.

The Greek and Roman Tragedies

See also, under *Shakespeare Criticism Since 1980*, Paster (Chapter 3).

Brower, Reuben A. *Hero and Saint: Shakespeare and the Graeco-Roman Heroic Tradition.* New York and Oxford, 1971.

Cantor, Paul A. *Shakespeare's Rome: Republic and Empire.* Ithaca, N.Y., 1976.

Charney, Maurice, ed. *Discussions of Shakespeare's Roman Plays.* Boston, 1964.

———. *Shakespeare's Roman Plays: The Function of Imagery in the Drama.* Cambridge, Mass., 1961.

Knight, G. Wilson. *The Imperial Theme: Further Interpretations of Shakespeare's Tragedies Including the Roman Plays.* London, 1931, 1953.

Leggatt, Alexander. *Shakespeare's Political Drama: The History Plays and the Roman Plays.* London and New York, 1988.

MacCallum, M. W. *Shakespeare's Roman Plays and Their Background.* London, 1910.

Maxwell, J. C. "Shakespeare's Roman Plays: 1900–1956," *ShS* 10 (1957), 1–11.

Miles, Geoffrey. *Shakespeare and the Constant Romans.* Oxford, 1996.

Miola, Robert S. *Shakespeare's Rome.* Cambridge, Eng., 1983.

Nicoll, Allardyce, ed. *Shakespeare Survey 10* (1957).

Paris, Bernard J. *Character as a Subversive Force in Shakespeare: The History and Roman Plays.* Rutherford, N.J., and London, 1991.

Phillips, James E., Jr. *The State in Shakespeare's Greek and Roman Plays.* New York, 1940.

Simmons, J. L. *Shakespeare's Pagan World: The Roman Tragedies.* Charlottesville, Va., 1973.

Thomas, Vivian. *Shakespeare's Roman Worlds.* London, 1989.

Thomson, J. A. K. *Shakespeare and the Classics.* London, 1952.

Traversi, Derek. *Shakespeare: The Roman Plays.* Palo Alto, Calif., 1963.

Velz, John W. "The Ancient World in Shakespeare: Authenticity or Anachronism? A Retrospect," *ShS* 31 (1978), 1–12.

———. *Shakespeare and the Classical Tradition: A Critical Guide to Commentary, 1660–1960.* Minneapolis, 1968.

Titus Andronicus

See also, under *The Tragedies*, Brooke, Brown and Harris, Danson, and Spivack; under *The Greek and Roman Tragedies*, Brower (Chapter 4), Maxwell, Miola, and Thomson; under *Shakespeare's Predecessors and Contemporaries*, Bowers, and Hattaway (Chapter 8); under *Shakespeare Criticism from the 1940s to the 1970s*, Calderwood; under *Shakespeare Criticism Since 1980*, Wayne (essay by Wynne-Davies); and under *The Tragedies*, Garner and Sprengnether (essay by Eaton).

Barroll, J. Leeds. "Shakespeare and Roman History," *Modern Language Review* 53 (1958), 327–43.

Bartels, Emily C. "Making More of the Moor: Aaron, Othello, and Renaissance Refashionings of Race," *SQ* 41 (1990), 433–54.

Bradbrook, M. C. "Moral Heraldry: *Titus Andronicus, Rape of Lucrece, Romeo and Juliet*," in *Shakespeare and Elizabethan Poetry*. London, 1951.

Dessen, Alan C. *Titus Andronicus.* Shakespeare in Performance. Manchester, Eng., 1989.

Green, Douglas E. "Interpreting 'her martyr'd signs': Gender and Tragedy in *Titus Andronicus*," *SQ* 40 (1989), 317–26.

Liebler, Naomi Conn. "Getting It All Right: *Titus Andronicus* and Roman History," *SQ* 45 (1994), 263–78.

Lindroth, Mary. " 'Some Devise of Further Misery': Taymor's *Titus* Brings Shakespeare

to Film Audience with a Twist," *Literature and Film Quarterly* 29 (2002), 107–15.

Metz, G. Harold. "Stage History of *Titus Andronicus*," *SQ* 28 (1977), 154–69.

———. *Shakespeare's Earliest Tragedy: Studies in "Titus Andronicus."* Madison, N.J., London, 1996.

Nevo, Ruth. "Tragic Form in *Titus Andronicus*," *Further Studies in English Language and Literature*, ed. A. A. Mendilow. Jerusalem, 1973.

Palmer, D. J. "The Unspeakable in Pursuit of the Uneatable: Language and Action in *Titus Andronicus*," *Critical Quarterly* 14 (1972), 320–39.

Ray, Sid. " 'Rape, I Fear, was Root of Thy Annoy': The Politics of Consent in *Titus Andronicus*," *SQ* 49 (1998), 22–39.

Rowe, Katharine A. "Dismembering and Forgetting in *Titus Andronicus*," *SQ* 45 (1994), 279–303.

Royster, Francesca. "White-limed Walls: Whiteness and Gothic Extremism in Shakespeare's *Titus Andronicus*," *SQ* 51 (2000), 432–55.

Sommers, Alan. " 'Wilderness of Tigers': Structure and Symbolism in *Titus Andronicus*," *Essays in Criticism* 10 (1960), 275–89.

Tricomi, Albert H. "The Aesthetics of Mutilation in *Titus Andronicus*," *ShS* 27 (1974), 11–19.

———. "The Mutilated Garden in *Titus Andronicus*," *ShakS* 9 (1976), 89–105.

Waith, Eugene M. "The Metamorphosis of Violence in *Titus Andronicus*," *ShS* 10 (1957), 39–49.

Willbern, David. "Rape and Revenge in *Titus Andronicus*," *English Literary Renaissance* 8 (1978), 159–82.

Willis, Deborah. " 'The gnawing vulture': Revenge, Trauma Theory, and *Titus Andronicus*," *SQ* 53 (2002), 1–21.

Wilson, J. Dover. "*Titus Andronicus* on the Stage in 1595," *ShS* 1 (1948), 17–22.

Romeo and Juliet

See also, under *The Tragedies*, Brooke, Brown and Harris (essay by Lawlor), Charlton, Dickey, Nevo, Ribner, and Snyder; under *Shakespeare's Language*, Mahood; under *Shakespeare Criticism to the 1930s*, Hazlitt; under *Shakespeare Criticism from the 1940s to the 1970s*, Calderwood, Granville-Barker, and Rabkin (pp. 162–84); under *Shakespeare Criticism Since 1980*, Callaghan (*A Feminist Companion*, essay by Berry), Daileader, Edwards et al. (essay by Wells), Erickson and Kahn (essay by Snow), Lenz et al. (essay by Kahn), and Novy (*Love's Argument*); and under *Shakespeare in Performance*, Brockbank (essay by Brenda Bruce).

Appelbaum, Robert. " 'Standing to the wall': The Pressures of Masculinity in *Romeo and Juliet*," *SQ* 48 (1997), 251–72.

Auden, W. H. "Commentary on the Poetry and Tragedy of *Romeo and Juliet*." The Laurel

Shakespeare, gen. ed. Francis Fergusson. New York, 1958.

Evans, Bertrand. "The Brevity of Friar Lawrence," *PMLA* 65 (1950), 841–65.

Evans, Robert O. *The Osier Cage: Rhetorical Devices in "Romeo and Juliet."* Lexington, Ky., 1966.

Everett, Barbara. *"Romeo and Juliet:* The Nurse's Story," *Critical Quarterly* 14 (1972), 129–39.

Halio, Jay, ed. *"Romeo and Juliet": Texts, Contexts, and Interpretation.* Newark, Del., 1995.

Hosley, Richard. "The Use of the Upper Stage in *Romeo and Juliet," SQ* 5 (1954), 371–9.

Levenson, Jill L. *Shakespeare in Performance: "Romeo and Juliet."* Manchester, Eng., 1987.

Melchiori, Giorgio. "Peter, Balthasar, and Shakespeare's Art of Doubling," *Modern Language Review* 78 (1983), 777–92.

Williams, George W., ed. *The Most Excellent and Lamentable Tragedie of Romeo and Juliet.* Durham, N.C., 1964.

Julius Caesar

See also, under *The Greek and Roman Tragedies,* Brower, Charney (both titles), Knight, Miola, and Traversi; under *Shakespeare's Language,* Doran; under *Shakespeare Criticism to the 1930s,* Shaw; under *Shakespeare Criticism from the 1940s to the 1970s,* Burckhardt, Council, Goldman (Chapter 4), Granville-Barker, Kernan (essay by Mack), Rabkin (pp. 105–19), and Stirling; under *Shakespeare Criticism Since 1980,* Kahn; under *The Problem Plays,* Schanzer; and under *The Histories,* Palmer.

Blits, Jan H. *The End of the Ancient Republic: Essays on "Julius Caesar."* Durham, N.C., 1982.

Burke, Kenneth. "Antony in Behalf of the Play," *Southern Review* 1 (1935), 308–19. Rpt. in *The Philosophy of Literary Form.* Baton Rouge, La., 1941.

Knights, L. C. "Shakespeare and Political Wisdom: A Note on the Personalism of *Julius Caesar* and *Coriolanus," Sewanee Review* 61 (1953), 43–55.

Liebler, Naomi Conn. " 'Thou Bleeding Piece of Earth': The Ritual Ground of *Julius Caesar," ShakS* 14 (1981), 175–96.

Miola, Robert S. *"Julius Caesar* and the Tyrannicide Debate," *Renaissance Quarterly* 38 (1985), 271–89.

Ornstein, Robert. "Seneca and the Political Drama of *Julius Caesar," Journal of English and Germanic Philology* 57 (1958), 51–6.

Parker, Barbara L. " 'A Thing Unfirm': Plato's *Republic* and Shakespeare's *Julius Caesar," SQ* 44 (1993), 30–43.

Paster, Gail Kern. " 'In the spirit of men there is no blood': Blood as Trope of Gender in *Julius Caesar," SQ* 40 (1989), 284–98.

Ribner, Irving. "Political Issues in *Julius Caesar," Journal of English and Germanic Philology* 56 (1957), 10–22.

Ripley, John. *"Julius Caesar" on Stage in England and America, 1599–1973.* Cambridge, Eng., 1980.

Rose, Mark. "Conjuring Caesar: Ceremony, History, and Authority in 1599," *English Literary Renaissance* 19 (1989), 291–304.

Velz, John W. "Clemency, Will, and Just Cause in *Julius Caesar," ShS* 22 (1969), 109–18.

———. " 'If I Were Brutus Now . . . ': Role-Playing in *Julius Caesar," ShakS* 4 (1968), 149–59.

———. "Undular Structure in *Julius Caesar," Modern Language Review* 66 (1971), 21–30.

Hamlet

See also, under *Shakespeare's Language,* Donawerth; under *The Tragedies,* Barker, Bradley, Brooke, Goldman, Holloway, Kirsch, Mack, Mack Jr., Rosen, and Whitaker; under *The Greek and Roman Tragedies,* Brower; under *Shakespeare's Predecessors and Contemporaries,* Bowers, and Rabkin (essay by Booth); under *Shakespeare Criticism to the 1930s,* Coleridge (*Coleridge's Writings*); under *Shakespeare Criticism from the 1940s to the 1970s,* Granville-Barker, Hawkes, and Righter; under *Shakespeare Criticism Since 1980,* Cavell (Chapter 5), Drakakis (essay by Rose), Erickson, Garber (*Shakespeare's Ghost Writers,* Chapter 6), Loomba and Orkin (essay by Bertoldi), Mazzio and Trevor (essays by De Grazia and Guillory), McDonald (essay by Parker), Parker and Hartman (essays by Weimann, Ferguson, and Hawkes), Patterson (Chapters 1 and 5), and Schwartz and Kahn (essays by Fineman and Leverenz); under *Shakespeare in Performance,* Bevington; and under *The Problem Plays,* Tillyard.

Bertram, Paul, and Bernice W. Kliman, eds. *The Three-Text "Hamlet": Parallel Texts of the First and Second Quartos and First Folio.* New York, 1991.

Bowers, Fredson T. "Hamlet as Minister and Scourge," *PMLA* 70 (1955), 740–9.

Calderwood, James L. *To Be and Not to Be: Negation and Metadrama in "Hamlet."* New York, 1983.

Charney, Maurice. *Style in "Hamlet."* Princeton, 1969.

Clayton, Thomas, ed. *The "Hamlet" First Published (Q1, 1603): Origin, Form, Intertextualities.* Newark, Del., 1992.

Dawson, Anthony B. *Hamlet.* Shakespeare in Performance. Manchester, Eng., 1995.

Eliot, T. S. "Hamlet and His Problems," *Selected Essays, 1917–1932.* London and New York, 1932.

Erlich, Avi. *Hamlet's Absent Father.* Princeton, 1977.

Ewbank, Inga-Stina. "*Hamlet* and the Power of Words," *ShS* 30 (1977), 85–102.

Fergusson, Francis. *The Idea of a Theater.* Princeton, 1949.

Foakes, R. A. *"Hamlet" versus "Lear": Cultural Politics and Shakespeare's Art.* Cambridge, Eng., 1993.

Frye, Roland Mushat. *The Renaissance "Hamlet": Issues and Responses in 1600.* Princeton, 1984.

Greenblatt, Stephen. *Hamlet in Purgatory.* Princeton, 2001.

Heilbrun, Carolyn G. *Hamlet's Mother and Other Women.* New York, 1990.

James, D. G. *The Dream of Learning.* Oxford, 1951.

Jones, Ernest. *Hamlet and Oedipus.* Rev. ed. New York, 1949, 1954.

Joseph, Bertram. *Conscience and the King.* London, 1953.

Kerrigan, William. *Hamlet's Perfection.* Baltimore, 1994.

Kitto, H. D. F. *Form and Meaning in Drama.* London, 1956.

Knights, L. C. *An Approach to Hamlet.* London, 1960.

Lacan, Jacques. "Desire and the Interpretation of Desire in *Hamlet," Yale French Studies* 55/56 (1977), 11–52.

Lee, John. *Shakespeare's "Hamlet" and the Controversies of Self.* Oxford, 2000.

Levin, Harry. *The Question of Hamlet.* New York and London, 1959.

Lewis, C. S. "Hamlet: The Prince or the Poem?" *Proceedings of the British Academy* 28 (1942), 139–54.

Mack, Maynard. "The World of *Hamlet," Yale Review* 41 (1952), 502–23.

McCoy, Richard C. "A Wedding and Four Funerals: Conjunction and Commemoration in *Hamlet," ShS* 54 (2001), 122–39.

McGee, Arthur. *The Elizabethan Hamlet.* New Haven, 1987.

Muir, Kenneth, and Stanley Wells, eds., *Aspects of "Hamlet": Articles Reprinted from "Shakespeare Survey."* Cambridge, Eng., 1979. (Especially essay by Inga-Stina Ewbank.)

Murray, Gilbert. *Hamlet and Orestes.* Annual Shakespeare Lecture for the British Academy, 1914. London, 1919.

Nicoll, Allardyce, ed. *Shakespeare Survey 9* (1956).

Nietzsche, Friedrich. "The Birth of Tragedy or: Hellenism and Pessimism" (1872), *The Birth of Tragedy and The Case of Wagner,* trans. Walter Kaufmann. New York, 1967.

Rose, Mark. "*Hamlet* and the Shape of Revenge," *English Literary Renaissance* 1 (1971), 132–43.

Rosenberg, Marvin. *The Masks of "Hamlet."* Newark, Del., 1992.

Skulsky, Harold. " 'I Know My Course': Hamlet's Confidence," *PMLA* 89 (1974), 477–86.

States, Bert O. *"Hamlet" and the Concept of Character.* Baltimore, 1992.

Tronch-Pérez, Jesús. *A Synoptic "Hamlet": A Critical-Synoptic Edition of the Second Quarto and First Folio Texts of "Hamlet."* València, Spain, 2002.

Wilson, J. Dover. *What Happens in "Hamlet."* London and New York, 1935, 1951.

Wright, George T. "Hendiadys and *Hamlet*," *PMLA* 96 (1981), 168–93.

Young, David. "Hamlet, Son of Hamlet," *Perspectives on "Hamlet*," eds. William G. Holzberger and Peter B. Waldock. Lewisburg, Pa., and London, 1975.

Othello

See also, under *The Tragedies*, Philippa Berry, Bradley, Dickey, Garner and Sprengnether (essays by Orlin, Hendricks, and Rose), Goldman, Hawkes, Holloway, Knight, Snyder, and Spivack; under *Shakespeare's Language*, Doran; under *Shakespeare's Predecessors and Contemporaries*, Hendricks and Parker (essays by Boose and Parker); under *Shakespeare Criticism to the 1930s*, Coleridge (*Coleridge's Writings*) and Johnson; under *Shakespeare Criticism from the 1940s to the 1970s*, Empson, Fiedler, Granville-Barker, and Sewell; and under *Shakespeare Criticism Since 1980*, Cavell (Chapter 3), Daileder, Erickson, Erickson and Kahn (essay by Wheeler), Greenblatt (*Renaissance Self-Fashioning*, Chapter 6), Howard and O'Connor (essay by Newman), Kirsch, Lenz et al. (essay by Neely), Loomba and Orkin (essay by Burton), McDonald (essay by Parker), Novy (*Love's Argument*, Chapter 7), and Parker and Hartman (essays by Parker and Showalter).

Adamson, Jane. *"Othello" as Tragedy: Some Problems of Judgment and Feeling*. Cambridge, Eng., 1980.

Altman, Joel B. " 'Preposterous Conclusions': Eros, *Enargeia*, and the Composition of *Othello*," *Representations* 18 (1987), 129–57.

Bartels, Emily C. "Making More of the Moor: Aaron, Othello, and Renaissance Refashionings of Race," *SQ* 41 (1990), 433–54.

Bates, Catherine. "Weaving and Writing in *Othello*," *SQ* 46 (1995), 51–60.

Bayley, John. *The Characters of Love*. London, 1960.

Boose, Lynda E. "Othello's Handkerchief: 'The Recognizance and Pledge of Love'," *English Literary Renaissance* 5 (1975), 360–74.

Calderwood, James L. *The Properties of "Othello*." Amherst, Mass., 1989.

Dean, Leonard F., ed. *A Casebook on "Othello*." New York, 1961.

Evans, Robert C. "Friendship in Shakespeare's *Othello*," *Ben Jonson Journal* 6 (1999), 109–46.

Everett, Barbara. "Inside *Othello*." *ShS* 53 (2000), 184–95.

———. "Reflections on the Sentimentalist's *Othello*," *Critical Quarterly* 3 (1961), 127–39. (A comment on the Leavis article below.)

Garner, S. N. "Shakespeare's Desdemona," *ShakS* 9 (1976), 233–52.

Hankey, Julie, ed. *Plays in Performance: "Othello*." Bristol, 1987.

Heilman, Robert B. *Magic in the Web: Action and Language in "Othello*." Lexington, Ky., 1956.

Honigmann, E. A. J. *The Texts of "Othello" and Shakespearian Revision*. London, 1996.

Hyman, Stanley Edgar. *Iago: Some Approaches to the Illusion of His Motivation*. New York, 1970.

Jones, Eldred. *Othello's Countrymen: The African in English Renaissance Drama*. London, 1965.

Korda, Natasha. *Shakespeare's Domestic Economies: Gender and Property in Early Modern England*. Philadelphia, 2002 (Chapter 4).

Leavis, F. R. "Diabolic Intellect and the Noble Hero: Or The Sentimentalist's Othello," *The Common Pursuit*. London, 1952.

Muir, Kenneth, ed. *Shakespeare Survey 21* (1968).

Nowottny, Winifred M. T. "Justice and Love in *Othello*," *University of Toronto Quarterly* 21 (1952), 330–44.

Orkin, Martin. "Othello and the 'plain face' of Racism," *SQ* 38 (1987), 166–88.

Orlin, Lena Cowen. *Private Matters and Public Culture in Post-Reformation England*. Ithaca, N.Y., 1994.

Rosenberg, Marvin. *The Masks of "Othello*." Berkeley, 1961.

Seltzer, Daniel. "Elizabethan Acting in *Othello*," *SQ* 10 (1959), 201–10.

Snyder, Susan, ed. *"Othello": Critical Essays*. New York, 1988.

Stoll, E. E. *"Othello": An Historical and Comparative Study*. Minneapolis, 1915. Rpt. New York, 1964.

Wine, Martin L. *"Othello": Text and Performance*. London, 1984.

King Lear

See also, under *Life in Shakespeare's England*, De Grazia, Quilligan, and Stallybrass (essay by De Grazia); under *The Tragedies*, Bradley, Cunningham, Frye, Goldman, Holloway, Hunter, Kirsch, Knight, and Rosen; under *The Greek and Roman Tragedies*, Brower; under *Textual Criticism and Bibliography*, Blayney, and Taylor and Warren; under *Shakespeare's Language*, Doran; under *Shakespeare Criticism to the 1930s*, Hazlitt, Johnson, and Stoll; under *Shakespeare Criticism from the 1940s to the 1970s*, Bloom (essay by Jaffa), Burckhardt, Empson, Fly, Granville-Barker, Knights, Kott, and Sewell; under *Shakespeare Criticism Since 1980*, Auden, Boose, Cavell (Chapter 2, identical with the Cavell entry below), Dollimore, Dollimore and Sinfield (essay by McLuskie), Dubrow and Strier (essay by Strier), Erickson, Erickson and Kahn (essay by Berger), Garber (*Shakespeare's Ghost Writers*, Chapter 5), Greenblatt (*Shakespearean Negotiations*, Chapter 4), Loomba and Orkin (essay by Visser), Novy (*Love's Argument*), Patterson (Chapter 5), and Wayne (essay by Thompson); and under *The Romances*, Felperin and Young.

Alpers, Paul J. *"King Lear* and the Theory of the 'Sight Pattern'," *In Defense of Reading*, ed. Reuben A. Brower and Richard Poirier. New York, 1962.

Berger, Harry, Jr. *"King Lear*": The Lear Family Romance," *Centennial Review* 23 (1979), 348–76.

Booth, Stephen. *"King Lear," "Macbeth," Indefinition, and Tragedy*, New Haven, 1983.

Brownlow, F. W. *Shakespeare, Harsnett, and the Devils of Denham*. Newark, Del., 1993.

Cavell, Stanley. "The Avoidance of Love: A Reading of *King Lear*," *Must We Mean What We Say?* New York, 1969. Rpt. in *Disowning Knowledge in Six Plays of Shakespeare*. Cambridge, Eng., 1987.

Colie, Rosalie L., and F. T. Flahiff, eds. *Some Facets of "King Lear*." Toronto, 1974.

Danby, John F. *Shakespeare's Doctrine of Nature: A Study of "King Lear*." London, 1949.

Delany, Paul, *"King Lear" and the Decline of Feudalism*," *PMLA* 92 (1977), 429–40.

Elton, William R. *King Lear and the Gods*. San Marino, Calif., 1966. Rpt. Lexington, Ky., 1988.

Everett, Barbara. "The New *King Lear*," *Critical Quarterly* 2 (1960), 325–39.

Foakes, R. A. *"Hamlet" Versus "Lear": Cultural Politics and Shakespeare's Art*. Cambridge, Eng., 1993.

Freud, Sigmund. "The Theme of the Three Caskets," *Complete Psychological Works of Sigmund Freud* 12 (1911–1913), pp. 291–301. London, 1958.

Goldberg, S. L. *An Essay on "King Lear*." Cambridge, Eng., 1974.

Graham, Kenneth J. E. " 'Without the form of justice': Plainness and the Performance of Love in *King Lear*," *SQ* 42 (1991), 438–61.

Hardison, O. B., Jr. "Myth and History in *King Lear*," *SQ* 26 (1975), 227–42.

Heilman, Robert B. *This Great Stage: Image and Structure in "King Lear*." Baton Rouge, La., 1948. Rpt. Seattle, 1963.

Heinemann, Margot. " 'Demystifying the Mystery of State': *King Lear* and the World Upside Down," *ShS* 44 (1992), 75–83.

James, D. G. *The Dream of Learning*. Oxford, 1951.

Jorgensen, Paul A. *Lear's Self-Discovery*, Berkeley, 1967.

Kahn, Coppélia. "The Absent Mother in *King Lear*," *Rewriting the Renaissance: The Discourses of Sexual Difference in Early Modern Europe*, eds. Margaret W. Ferguson et al. Chicago, 1986.

Kernan, Alvin. "Formalism and Realism in Elizabethan Drama: The Miracles in *King Lear*," *Renaissance Drama* 9 (1966), 59–66.

Kirsch, Arthur. "The Emotional Landscape of *King Lear*," *SQ* 39 (1988), 154–70.

Kronenfeld, Judy. *King Lear and the Naked Truth: Rethinking the Language of Religion and Resistance*. Durham, N.C., 1998.

Leggatt, Alexander. *King Lear*. Shakespeare in Performance. Manchester, Eng., 1991.

Lothian, J. M. *"King Lear": A Tragic Reading of Life*. Toronto, 1949.

Lusardi, James P., and June Schlueter. *Reading Shakespeare in Performance: "King Lear*." Rutherford, N.J., 1991.

Mack, Maynard. *King Lear in Our Time*. Berkeley, 1965.

Maclean, Norman. "Episode, Scene, Speech, and Word: The Madness of Lear," *Critics and Criticism*, ed. R. S. Crane. Chicago, 1952.

Michie, Donald M., ed. *A Critical Edition of "The True Chronicle History of King Leir and His Three Daughters, Gonorill, Ragan and Cordella."* New York, 1991.

Murphy, John L. *Darkness and Devils: Exorcism and "King Lear."* Athens, Ohio, 1984.

Reibetanz, John. *The "Lear" World: A Study of "King Lear" in Its Dramatic Context.* Toronto, 1977.

Rosenberg, Marvin. *The Masks of "King Lear."* Berkeley, 1972.

Scott, William O. "Contracts of Love and Affection: Lear, Old Age, and Kingship," *ShS* 55 (2002), 36–42.

Sewall, Richard B. *The Vision of Tragedy.* New Haven, 1959.

Snyder, Susan. "*King Lear* and the Psychology of Dying," *SQ* 33 (1982), 449–60.

Soellner, Rolf. "*King Lear* and the Magic of the Wheel," *SQ* 35 (1984), 274–89.

Tate, Nahum. *The History of King Lear* (1681), ed. James Black. Lincoln, Neb. 1975.

Taylor, Gary, and Michael Warren, eds. *The Division of the Kingdoms: Shakespeare's Two Versions of "King Lear."* Oxford, 1983.

Urkowitz, Steven. *Shakespeare's Revision of "King Lear."* Princeton, 1980.

Warren, Michael, preparer. *The Parallel "King Lear," 1608–1623: Parallel Texts of the First Quarto (1608) and the First Folio (1623).* Berkeley, 1989.

Wittreich, Joseph. *"Image of that Horror": History, Prophecy, and Apocalypse in "King Lear."* San Marino, Calif., 1984.

Macbeth

See also, under *The Tragedies*, Berry, Bradley, Garner and Sprengnether (essay by Adelman), Goldman, Holloway, Hunter, Kirsch, Mack, Mack Jr., and Rosen; under *Shakespeare Criticism to the 1930s*, Smith (essay by De Quincey); under *Shakespeare Criticism from the 1940s to the 1970s*, Sanders and Sewell; under *Shakespeare Criticism Since 1980*, Garber (*Cannibals*, essay by Adelman), Howard and O'Connor (essay by Goldberg), Mullaney (Chapter 5), Schwartz and Kahn (essay by Gohlke), Watson, and Woodbridge and Berry (essay by Willis); and under *The Histories*, Pye.

Bartholomeusz, Dennis. *"Macbeth" and the Players.* Cambridge, Eng., 1969.

Booth, Stephen. *"King Lear," "Macbeth," Indefinition, and Tragedy.* New Haven, 1983.

Brooks, Cleanth. "The Naked Babe and the Cloak of Manliness," *The Well Wrought Urn.* New York, 1947.

Calderwood, James L. *If It Were Done: "Macbeth" and Tragic Action.* Amherst, 1986.

Driver, Tom. *The Sense of History in Greek and Shakespearean Drama.* New York, 1960.

Elliott, G. R. *Dramatic Providence in "Macbeth."* Princeton, 1958.

Fergusson, Francis. "*Macbeth* as the Imitation of an Action," *English Institute Essays 1951* (1952), 31–43.

Freud, Sigmund. "Some Character-Types Met with in Psycho-Analytic Work," trans. E. Cobern Mayne, *Collected Papers.* Vol. 4, pp. 326–32. London, 1925.

Gardner, Helen. "Milton's 'Satan' and the Theme of Damnation in Elizabethan Tragedy," *English Association Essays and Studies* n.s. 1 (1948), 46–66.

Jorgensen, Paul A. *Our Naked Frailties: Sensational Art and Meaning in "Macbeth."* Berkeley, 1971.

Kliman, Bernice W. *Macbeth.* Shakespeare in Performance. Manchester, Eng., 1992.

Knights, L. C. "How Many Children Had Lady Macbeth? An Essay in the Theory and Practice of Shakespeare Criticism," *Explorations.* London, 1946. Rpt. Westport, Conn., 1975.

Norbrook, David. "*Macbeth* and the Politics of Historiography," *Politics of Discourse: The Literature and History of Seventeenth-Century England*, eds. Kevin Sharpe and Steven Zwicker, pp. 78–116. Berkeley, 1987.

Orgel, Stephen. "Macbeth and the Antic Round," *ShS* 52 (1999), 143–53. Rpt. in Orgel, under *Shakespeare Criticism Since 1980*.

Paul, Henry N. *The Royal Play of Macbeth.* New York, 1950.

Purkiss, Diane. *The Witch in History: Early Modern and Twentieth-Century Representations.* London and New York, 1996.

Rosenberg, Marvin. *The Masks of "Macbeth."* Berkeley, 1978.

Sinfield, Alan. "*Macbeth*: History, Ideology and Intellectuals," *Critical Quarterly* 28 (1986), 63–77.

Spender, Stephen. "Time, Violence, and *Macbeth*," *Penguin New Writing*, 3. London, 1940–1941.

Williams, Raymond. "Monologue in *Macbeth*," *Teaching the Text*, eds. Susanne Kappeler and Norman Bryson. London, 1983.

Wills, Garry. *Witches and Jesuits: Shakespeare's "Macbeth."* Oxford, 1995.

Timon of Athens

See also, under *The Tragedies*, Knight; under *The Greek and Roman Tragedies*, generally; under *Shakespeare's Predecessors and Contemporaries*, Kernan; under *Shakespeare Criticism to the 1930s*, Hazlitt and Johnson; under *Shakespeare Criticism from the 1940s to the 1970s*, Burke, Empson, and Fly; under *Shakespeare Criticism Since 1980*, Paster (Chapter 4); and under *The Problem Plays*, Campbell.

Baldo, Jonathan. "The Shadow of Levelling in *Timon of Athens*," *Criticism* 35 (1993), 559–88.

Bevington, David, and David L. Smith. "James I and *Timon of Athens*," *Comparative Drama* 33 (1999), 56–87.

Cohen, Derek. "The Politics of Wealth: *Timon of Athens*," *Neophilologus* 77 (1993), 149–60.

Davidson, Clifford. "*Timon of Athens*: The Iconography of False Friendship," *Huntington Library Quarterly* 43 (1980), 181–200.

Fulton, Robert. "Timon, Cupid, and the Amazons," *ShakS* 9 (1976), 283–99.

Greene, Jody. " 'You must eat men': The Sodomistic Economy of Renaissance Patronage," *GLQ: A Journal of Lesbian and Gay Studies* 1 (1994), 163–87.

Kahn, Coppélia. " 'Magic of Bounty': *Timon of Athens*, Jacobean Patronage, and Maternal Power," *SQ* 38 (1987), 34–57.

Knights, L. C. "*Timon of Athens*," *The Morality of Art: Essays Presented to G. Wilson Knight*, ed. D. W. Jefferson. London, 1969.

Lancashire, Anne. "*Timon of Athens*: Shakespeare's *Dr. Faustus*," *SQ* 21 (1970), 35–44.

Miola, Robert S. "Timon in Shakespeare's Athens," *SQ* 31 (1980), 21–30.

O'Dair, Sharon. "The Statue of Class in Shakespeare: Or, Why Critics Love to Hate Capitalism," *Discontinuities: New Essays on Renaissance Literature and Criticism*, eds. Viviana Comensoli and Paul Stevens, pp. 201–23. Toronto, 1998.

Scott, William O. "The Paradox of Timon's Self-Cursing," *SQ* 35 (1984), 290–304.

Soellner, Rolf. *Timon of Athens: Shakespeare's Pessimistic Tragedy.* With a Stage History by Gary Jay Williams. Columbus, Ohio, 1979.

Walker, Lewis. "Fortune and Friendship in *Timon of Athens*," *Texas Studies in Literature and Language* 18 (1977), 577–600.

Waters, D. Douglas. "Shakespeare's *Timon of Athens* and Catharsis," *Upstart Crow* 8 (1988), 93–105.

Antony and Cleopatra

See also, under *The Tragedies*, Frye, Garner and Sprengnether (essays by Cook and Charnes), Goldman, Holloway, Mack, and Rosen; under *The Greek and Roman Tragedies*, Brower, Cantor, Charney, Miola, and Traversi; under *Shakespeare's Predecessors and Contemporaries*, Comensoli and Russell (essay by Adelman), and Waith; under *Shakespeare's Language*, Doran; under *Shakespeare Criticism to the 1930s*, Coleridge (*Coleridge's Writings*); under *Shakespeare Criticism from the 1940s to the 1970s*, Bethell, Burke, Colie, Granville-Barker, Kettle (essay by Nandy), McAlindon, and Van Laan; under *Shakespeare Criticism Since 1980*, Auden, Bamber, Cavell (pp. 18–37), Charnes, Dollimore (*Radical Tragedy*), Edwards et al. (essay by Hibbard), Erickson (Chapter 4), Holland et al. (essay by Sprengnether), and Neely; under *The Problem Plays*, Schanzer; under *The Histories*, Palmer; and under *The Romances*, Brown and Harris (essay by Ornstein), Danby, and Felperin.

Adelman, Janet. *The Common Liar: An Essay on "Antony and Cleopatra."* New Haven, 1973.

Barroll, J. Leeds. *Shakespearean Tragedy: Genre, Tradition, and Change in "Antony and Cleopatra."* Washington, D.C., 1984.

Bono, Barbara J. "The Shakespearean Synthesis: *Antony and Cleopatra*," *Literary Transvaluation: From Vergilian Epic to Shakespearean Tragicomedy.* Berkeley, 1984.

Bradley, A. C. *Oxford Lectures on Poetry*. London, 1909, 1961.

Drakakis, John, ed. *"Antony and Cleopatra."* Basingstoke, 1994.

Kaula, David. "The Time Sense of *Antony and Cleopatra*," *SQ* 15:3 (1964), 211–23.

Knights, L. C. *Some Shakespearean Themes*. London, 1959.

Lamb, Margaret. *"Antony and Cleopatra"* on the English Stage. Rutherford, N.J., and London, 1980.

Leavis, F. R. *"Antony and Cleopatra* and *All for Love*: A Critical Exercise," *Scrutiny* 5 (1936–1937), 158–69.

Levine, Laura. *Men in Women's Clothing: Anti-Theatricality and Effeminization, 1579–1642*. Cambridge, Eng., 1994.

Lloyd, Michael. "Cleopatra as Isis," *ShS 12* (1959), 88–94.

Mack, Maynard. *"Antony and Cleopatra*: The Stillness and the Dance," *Shakespeare's Art: Seven Essays*, ed. Milton Crane. Chicago, 1973.

Madelaine, Richard, ed. *Antony and Cleopatra*. Shakespeare in Production. Cambridge, Eng., 1998.

Markels, Julian. *The Pillar of the World: "Antony and Cleopatra" in Shakespeare's Development*. Columbus, Ohio, 1968.

Mayer, Jean-Christophe, ed. *Lectures de Shakespeare: "Antony and Cleopatra."* Rennes, France, 2000.

Rackin, Phyllis. "Shakespeare's Boy Cleopatra, the Decorum of Nature, and the Golden World of Poetry," *PMLA* 87 (1972), 201–12.

Reimer, A. P. *A Reading of Shakespeare's "Antony and Cleopatra."* Sydney, 1968.

Scott, Michael. *Antony and Cleopatra*. Text and Peformance. London, 1983.

Steppat, Michael. *The Critical Reception of Shakespeare's "Antony and Cleopatra" from 1607 to 1905*. Amsterdam, 1980.

Williamson, Marilyn L. *Infinite Variety: "Antony and Cleopatra" in Renaissance Drama and Earlier Tradition*. Mystic, Conn., 1974.

Wood, Nigel, ed. *"Antony and Cleopatra."* Theory in Practice. Buckingham and Philadelphia, 1996.

Yachnin, Paul. "Shakespeare's Politics of Loyalty: Sovereignty and Subjectivity in *Antony and Cleopatra*," *Studies in English Literature* 33 (1993), 343–63.

Coriolanus

See also, under *The Tragedies*, Brown and Harris (essays by Hunter and Wickham), Danson, Holloway, and Rosen; under *The Greek and Roman Tragedies*, Brower, Cantor, Charney, Miola, and Phillips; under *Shakespeare's Predecessors and Contemporaries*, Waith; under *Shakespeare Criticism to the 1930s*, Hazlitt; under *Shakespeare Criticism from the 1940s to the 1970s*, Burke, Granville-Barker, Knights, Kott, and Rossiter; and under *Shakespeare Criticism Since 1980*, Cavell (Chapter 4),

Dollimore, Goldberg (Chapter 4), Howard and O'Connor (essays by Bristol and Sorge), Kahn, Marcus (Chapter 4), Mazzio and Trevor (essay by Goldberg), Parker and Hartman (essay by Cavell), Patterson (Chapter 6), and Watson.

Adelman, Janet. "'Anger's My Meat': Feeding, Dependency, and Aggression in *Coriolanus*," *Shakespeare, Pattern of Excelling Nature*, eds. David Bevington and Jay L. Halio. Newark, Del., 1978.

Barton, Anne. "Livy, Machiavelli, and Shakespeare's *Coriolanus*," *ShS 38* (1985), 115–29.

Berry, Ralph. "The Metamorphoses of *Coriolanus*," *SQ* 26 (1975), 172–83.

———. "Sexual Imagery in *Coriolanus*," *Studies in English Literature* 13 (1973), 301–16.

Bloom, Harold, ed. *William Shakespeare's "Coriolanus."* New York, 1988. (Including an essay by Burke.)

Bradley, A. C. *A Miscellany*. London, 1929.

Brecht, Bertolt. *Coriolanus*, trans. Ralph Manheim, *Bertolt Brecht: Collected Plays*, Vol. 9, eds. Ralph Manheim and John Willett. New York, 1972.

Brockman, B. A., ed. *Shakespeare's "Coriolanus,": A Casebook*. London, 1977.

Browning, I. R. "*Coriolanus*: 'Boy of Tears'": *Essays in Criticism* 5 (1955), 18–31.

Calderwood, James L. "*Coriolanus*: Wordless Meanings and Meaningless Words," *Studies in English Literature* 6 (1966), 211–24.

Fish, Stanley. "How to Do Things with Austin and Searle: Speech-Act Theory and Literary Criticism," *Is There a Text In This Class?* Cambridge, Mass., 1980.

Jagendorf, Zvi. "*Coriolanus*: Body Politic and Private Parts," *SQ* 41 (1990), 455–69.

MacLure, Millar. "Shakespeare and the Lonely Dragon," *University of Toronto Quarterly* 24 (1955), 109–20.

Rabkin, Norman. "*Coriolanus*: The Tragedy of Politics," *SQ* 17 (1966), 195–212.

Ripley, John. *"Coriolanus" on Stage in England and America, 1609–1994*. Madison, N.J., and London, 1998.

Smith, Bruce R. "Rape, rap, rupture, rapture": R-rated futures on the global market," *Textual Practice* 9 (1995), 421–43.

Stockholder, Katherine. "The Other Coriolanus," *PMLA* 85 (1970), 228–36.

Vickers, Brian. *Shakespeare: "Coriolanus."* London, 1976.

The Romances

See also, under *Shakespeare Criticism Since 1980*, McMullan and Hope.

Bergeron, David M. *Shakespeare's Romances and the Royal Family*. Lawrence, Kans., 1985.

Brown, John Russell, and Bernard Harris, eds. *Later Shakespeare*. Stratford-upon-Avon Studies 8. London, 1966.

Danby, John F. *Poets on Fortune's Hill*. London, 1952. Reprinted as *Elizabethan and Jacobean Poets*. London, 1964.

Edwards, Philip. "Shakespeare's Romances: 1900–1957," *ShS 11* (1958), 1–18. See also other articles in this issue.

Fawkner, H. W. *Shakespeare's Miracle Plays: "Pericles," "Cymbeline," and "The Winter's Tale."* Rutherford, N.J., 1992.

Felperin, Howard. *Shakespearean Romance*. Princeton, 1972.

Foakes, R. A. *Shakespeare: From the Dark Comedies to the Last Plays*. London and Charlottesville, Va., 1971.

Frye, Northrop. *Anatomy of Criticism*. Princeton, 1957.

———. *A Natural Perspective: The Development of Shakespearean Comedy and Romance*. New York, 1965.

———. *The Secular Scripture: A Study of the Structure of Romance*. Cambridge, Mass., 1976.

Gesner, Carol. *Shakespeare and the Greek Romance: A Study of Origins*. Lexington, Ky., 1970.

Hartwig, Joan. *Shakespeare's Tragicomic Vision*. Baton Rouge, La., 1972.

Hunter, Robert Grams. *Shakespeare and the Comedy of Forgiveness*. New York, 1965.

James, D. G. "The Failure of the Ballad-Makers," *Scepticism and Poetry*. London, 1937.

Jordan, Constance. *Shakespeare's Monarchies: Ruler and Subject in the Romances*. Ithaca, N.Y., 1997.

Kermode, Frank. *William Shakespeare: The Final Plays*. London, 1963.

Knight, G. Wilson. *The Crown of Life*. London, 1947, 1966.

———. *The Shakespearian Tempest*. London, 1932, 1953.

Leavis, F. R. "A Criticism of Shakespeare's Last Plays," *Scrutiny* 10 (1942), 339–45. Rpt. in *The Common Pursuit*. London, 1952.

Marsh, D. R. C. *The Recurring Miracle: A Study of "Cymbeline" and the Last Plays*. Pietermaritzburg, Natal, 1962, 1964.

Marshall, Cynthia. *Last Things and Last Plays: Shakespearean Eschatology*. Carbondale, Ill., 1991.

Mincoff, Marco. *Things Supernatural and Causeless: Shakespearean Romance*. Newark, Del., 1992.

Mowat, Barbara A. *The Dramaturgy of Shakespeare's Romances*. Athens, Ga., 1976.

Nevo, Ruth. *Shakespeare's Other Language*. New York and London, 1987.

Palfrey, Simon. *Late Shakespeare: A New World of Words*. Oxford, 1997.

Peterson, Douglas L. *Time, Tide, and Tempest: A Study of Shakespeare's Romances*. San Marino, Calif., 1973.

Pettet, E. C. *Shakespeare and the Romance Tradition*. London, 1949.

Platt, Peter G. *Reason Diminished: Shakespeare and the Marvelous*. Lincoln, Neb., 1997.

Richards, Jennifer, and James Knowles, eds. *Shakespeare's Late Plays: New Readings*. Edinburgh, 1999.

Ryan, Kiernan, ed. *Shakespeare: The Late Plays*. New York, 1999.

Smith, Hallett. *Shakespeare's Romances*. San Marino, Calif., 1972.

Strachey, Lytton. "Shakespeare's Final Period," *Books and Characters*. London, 1922.

Traversi, Derek. *Shakespeare: The Last Phase.* New York, 1954.

Yates, Frances A. *Shakespeare's Last Plays: A New Approach.* London, 1975.

Young, David. *The Heart's Forest: A Study of Shakespeare's Pastoral Plays.* New Haven and London, 1972.

Pericles

See also, under *The Romances*, Bergeron, Brown and Harris (essay by Francis Berry), Danby, Felperin, Frye *(Natural Perspective)*, Kermode, Knight *(Crown of Life)*, Nevo, and Peterson; and under *Shakespeare Criticism Since 1980,* Edwards et al. (essay by Ewbank) and Mullaney (Chapter 6).

Barber, C. L. "'Thou That Beget'st Him That Did Thee Beget': Transformation in *Pericles* and *The Winter's Tale*," *ShS* 22 (1969), 59–67.

Bishop, T. G. *Shakespeare and the Theatre of Wonder.* Cambridge, Eng., 1996.

Brockbank, J. Philip. "*Pericles* and the Dream of Immortality," *ShS* 24 (1971), 105–16.

Dunbar, Mary Judith. "'To the Judgement of Your Eye': Iconography and the Theatrical Art of *Pericles*," *Shakespeare, Man of Theatre,* ed. Kenneth Muir et al., pp. 86–97. Newark, Del., 1983.

Edwards, Philip. "An Approach to the Problem of *Pericles*," *ShS* 5 (1952), 25–49.

Eliot, T. S. "Marina," *The Complete Poems and Plays, 1909–1950.* New York, 1952.

Helms, Lorraine. "The Saint in the Brothel: Or, Eloquence Rewarded," *SQ* 41 (1990), 319–32.

Hoeniger, F. David. "Gower and Shakespeare in *Pericles*," *SQ* 33 (1982), 461–79.

Lewis, Anthony J. "'I feed on mother's flesh': Incest and Eating in *Pericles*," *Essays in Literature* 15 (1988), 147–63.

Pitcher, John. "The Poet and Taboo: The Riddle of Shakespeare's *Pericles*," *English Association Essays and Studies* (1982), 14–29.

Skeele, David. *Thwarting the Wayward Seas: A Critical and Theatrical History of Shakespeare's "Pericles" in the Nineteenth and Twentieth Centuries.* Newark, Del., 1998.

Cymbeline

See also, under *The Romances*, Bergeron, Brown and Harris (essay by Harris), Felperin, Frye *(Natural Perspective)*, Hartwig, Hunter, Kermode, Marsh, Mowat, and Richards and Knowles (essays by Maley and Thorne); under *Shakespeare Criticism to the 1930s,* Shaw; under *Shakespeare Criticism from the 1940s to the 1970s,* Granville-Barker; under *Shakespeare Criticism Since 1980,* Adelman, Bergeron (essay by Wall), Dubrow and Strier (essay by Marcus), Hamilton (Chapter 7), James, Kahn, Kastan, Kirsch, Marcus (Chapter 3), Miola, and Schwartz and Kahn (essay by Skura); and under *The Greek and Roman Tragedies,* Miola.

Belsey, Catherine. "Marriage: Imogen's Bedchamber,"*Shakespeare and the Loss of Eden.* New Brunswick, N.J., 1999.

Freer, Coburn, *"Cymbeline," The Poetics of Jacobean Drama,* Chapter 4. Baltimore, 1981.

Gillies, John. "The Problem of Style in *Cymbeline*," *Southern Review* (University of Adelaide and Macquarie University) 15:3 (1982), 269–90.

Hoeniger, F. D. "Irony and Romance in *Cymbeline*," *Studies in English Literature 2* (1962), 219–28.

Kirsch, Arthur C. "*Cymbeline* and Coterie Dramaturgy," *ELH* 34 (1967), 285–306.

Lewis, Cynthia. "'With Simular Proof Enough': Modes of Misperception in *Cymbeline*," *Studies in English Literature* 31 (1991), 343–63.

Marcus, Leah. "*Cymbeline* and the Unease of Topicality," *The Historical Renaissance,* eds. Heather Dubrow and Richard Strier. Chicago, 1988.

Mikalachki, Jodi. "*Cymbeline* and the Masculine Romance of Roman Britain," *The Legacy of Boadicea.* London, 1998.

Olsen, Thomas G. "Iachimo's 'drug-damn'd Italy' and the Problem of British National Character in *Cymbeline*," *Shakespeare Yearbook* 10 (1999), 269–96.

Parker, Patricia. "Romance and Empire: Anachronistic *Cymbeline*," *Unfolded Tales: Essays on Renaissance Romance,* eds. Gordon Teskey and George M. Logan. Ithaca, N.Y., 1989.

Redmond, Michael J. "Rome, Italy, and the (Re) Construction of British National Identity," *Shakespeare Yearbook* 10 (1999), 297–316.

Simonds, Peggy Muñoz. *Myth, Emblem, and Music in Shakespeare's "Cymbeline."* Newark, Del., 1992.

Swander, Homer D. "*Cymbeline* and the 'Blameless Hero'," *ELH* 31 (1964), 259–70.

Warren, Roger. "Theatrical Virtuosity and Poetic Complexity in *Cymbeline*," *ShS 29* (1976), 41–50.

Woodbridge, Linda. "Palisading the Elizabethan Body Politic," *Texas Studies in Literature and Language* 33 (1991), 327–54.

The Winter's Tale

See also, under *The Romances*, Felperin, Foakes, Hartwig, Hunter, Knight (*Crown of Life*), Mowat, and Young; and under *Shakespeare Criticism Since 1980,* Cavell (Chapter 6), Erickson, Neely, and Parker and Hartman (essay by Felperin).

Alpers, Paul. *What Is Pastoral?* Chicago, 1996.

Barber, C. L. "'Thou That Beget'st Him That Did Thee Beget': Transformation in *Pericles* and *The Winter's Tale*," *ShS* 22 (1969), 59–67.

Bartholomeusz, Dennis. *"The Winter's Tale" in Performance in England and America, 1611–1976.* Cambridge, Eng., 1982.

Bethell, S. L. *The Winter's Tale: A Study.* London, 1947.

Bishop, T. G. *Shakespeare and the Theatre of Wonder.* Cambridge, Eng., 1996.

Coghill, Nevill. "Six Points of Stage-Craft in *The Winter's Tale*," *ShS* 11 (1958), 31–41.

Draper, R. P. *"The Winter's Tale": Text and Performance.* London, 1985.

Ewbank, Inga-Stina. "The Triumph of Time in *The Winter's Tale*," *Review of English Literature* 5:2 (1964), 83–100.

Frey, Charles. *Shakespeare's Vast Romance: A Study of "The Winter's Tale."* Columbia, Mo., 1980.

Frye, Northrop. "Recognition in *The Winter's Tale*," *Essays on Shakespeare and Elizabethan Drama in Honor of Hardin Craig,* ed. R. Hosley, pp. 235–46. Columbia, Mo., 1962.

Kaplan, Lindsay M., and Katherine Eggert. "'Good queen, my lord, good queen': Sexual Slanders and the Trials of Female Authority in *The Winter's Tale*," *Renaissance Drama* n.s. 25 (1994), 89–118.

Lindenbaum, Peter. "Time, Sexual Love, and the Uses of Pastoral in *The Winter's Tale*," *Modern Language Quarterly* 33 (1972), 3–22.

Matchett, William H. "Some Dramatic Techniques in *The Winter's Tale*," *ShS* 22 (1969), 93–107.

Siemon, James Edward. " 'But It Appears She Lives': Iteration in *The Winter's Tale*," *PMLA* 89 (1974), 10–16.

Snyder, Susan. "Mamillius and Gender Polarization in *The Winter's Tale*," *SQ* 50 (1999), 1–8.

Sokol, B. J. *Art and Illusion in "The Winter's Tale."* Manchester, Eng., 1994.

Tayler, Edward W. *Nature and Art in Renaissance Literature.* New York, 1964.

Wickham, Glynne. "Romance and Emblem: A Study in the Dramatic Structure of *The Winter's Tale*," *The Elizabethan Theatre III,* ed. David Galloway. Hamden, Conn., 1973.

Williams, John Anthony. *The Natural Work of Art: The Experience of Romance in Shakespeare's "Winter's Tale."* Cambridge, Mass., 1967.

The Tempest

See also, under *The Romances*, Brown and Harris (essay by Brockbank), Felperin, Frye *(Natural Perspective)*, Hartwig, Kermode, Mowat, Peterson, and Young; under *Shakespeare's Predecessors and Contemporaries,* Bevington and Holbrook (essay by Bevington); under *Shakespeare Criticism to the 1930s,* Coleridge (*Coleridge's Writings*); under *Shakespeare Criticism from the 1940s to the 1970s,* Fiedler, Kernan (*Playwright as Magician,* Chapter 6), and Kott; under *Shakespeare Criticism Since 1980,* Dollimore and Sinfield (essay by Brown), Drakakis (essay by Barker and Hulme), Garber (*Cannibals,* essay by Orgel), Greenblatt (*Shakespearean Negotiations,* Chapter 5), Hamlin, Howard and O'Connor (essay by Cartelli), Lenz et al. (essay by Leininger), Loomba and Orkin (essay by Brotton), McMullan and Hope (essay by Norbrook), and Schwartz and Kahn (essay by Sundelson); and under *The Comedies,* Palmer and Bradbury (essay by Wells).

Auden, W. H. "The Sea and the Mirror: A Commentary on Shakespeare's *The Tempest*," *The Collected Poetry*. New York, 1945.

Berger, Harry, Jr. "Miraculous Harp: A Reading of Shakespeare's *Tempest*," *ShakS 5* (1969), 253–83.

Demaray, John G. *Shakespeare and the Spectacles of Strangeness: "The Tempest" and the Transformation of Renaissance Theatrical Forms*. Pittsburgh, Pa., 1998.

Frey, Charles. "*The Tempest* and the New World," *SQ* 30 (1979), 29–41.

Hamilton, Donna. *Virgil and "The Tempest": The Politics of Imitation*. Columbus, Ohio, 1990.

Hulme, Peter, and William H. Sherman, eds. *"The Tempest" and Its Travels*. Philadelphia, 2000.

James, D. G. *The Dream of Prospero*. Oxford, 1967.

James, Henry. "Introduction to *The Tempest*." Rpt. in *Henry James: Selected Literary Criticism*, ed. Morris Shapiro. London, 1963.

Mebane, John S. *Renaissance Magic and the Return of the Golden Age: The Occult Tradition and Marlowe, Jonson, and Shakespeare*. Lincoln, Neb., 1989.

Mowat, Barbara A. "Prospero's Book," *SQ* 52 (2001), 1–33.

Orgel, Stephen. "New Uses of Adversity: Tragic Experience in *The Tempest*," *In Defense of Reading*, ed. Reuben A. Brower and Richard Poirier. New York, 1962.

———. "Prospero's Wife," *Representations* 8 (1984), 1–13. Rpt. in Orgel, under *Shakespeare Criticism Since 1980*.

Skura, Meredith Anne. "Discourse and the Individual: The Case of Colonialism in *The Tempest*," *SQ* 40 (1989), 42–69.

Strier, Richard. " 'I am Power': Normal and Magical Politics in *The Tempest*," in *Writing and Political Engagement in Seventeenth-Century England*, ed. Derek Hirst and Richard Strier. Cambridge, Eng., 1999.

Thompson, Ann. " 'Miranda, where's your sister?': Reading Shakespeare's *The Tempest*," *Feminist Criticism: Theory and Practice*, ed. Susan Sellers. New York, 1991.

Vaughan, Alden T. "Shakespeare's Indian: The Americanization of Caliban," *SQ* 39 (1988), 137–53.

Vaughan, Alden T., and Virginia Mason Vaughan. *Shakespeare's Caliban: A Cultural History*. Cambridge, Eng., 1991.

Vaughan, Virginia Mason, and Alden T. Vaughan, eds. *Critical Essays on Shakespeare's "The Tempest."* New York and London, 1998.

William, David. "*The Tempest* on the Stage," *Jacobean Theatre*, eds. John Russell Brown and Bernard Harris, pp. 133–57. Stratford-upon-Avon Studies 1. London, 1960.

The Two Noble Kinsmen

See also, under *The Romances*, Hartwig and Mowat; under *Textual Criticism and Bibliography*, Masten; and under *Shakespeare Criticism Since 1980*, Smith.

Abrams, Richard. "Gender Confusion and Sexual Politics in *The Two Noble Kinsmen*," *Themes in Drama 7: Drama, Sex and Politics*, ed. J. Redmond. Cambridge, Eng., 1985.

Berggren, Paula. " 'For what we lack, / We laugh': Incompletion and *The Two Noble Kinsmen*," *Modern Language Studies* 14 (1984), 3–17.

Bruster, Douglas. "The Jailer's Daughter and the Politics of Madwomen's Language," *SQ* 46 (1995), 277–300.

Edwards, Philip. "On the Design of *The Two Noble Kinsmen*," *A Review of English Literature* 5 (1964), 89–105.

Frey, Charles H., ed. *Shakespeare, Fletcher, and The Two Noble Kinsmen*. Columbia, Mo., 1989.

Hoy, Cyrus. "The Language of Fletcherian Tragicomedy," *Mirror up to Shakespeare*, ed. J. C. Gray, pp. 99–113. Toronto, 1984.

Lief, Madelon, and Nicholas F. Radel. "Linguistic Subversion and the Artifice of Rhetoric In *The Two Noble Kinsmen*," *SQ* 38 (1987), 405–25.

Mallette, Richard. "Same-Sex Friendship in *The Two Noble Kinsmen*," *Renaissance Drama* n.s. 26 (1995), 29–52.

McMullan, Gordon. "A Rose for Emilia: Collaborative Relations in *The Two Noble Kinsmen*," *Renaissance Configurations: Voices/Bodies/Spaces, 1580–1690*, ed. Gordon McMullan. Basingstoke and New York, 1998.

Potter, Lois. "Topicality or Politics? *The Two Noble Kinsmen, 1613–34*," *The Politics of Tragicomedy: Shakespeare and After*, eds. Gordon McMullan and Jonathan Hope. London, 1992.

Shannon, Laurie J. "Emilia's Argument: Friendship and 'Human Title' in *The Two Noble Kinsmen*," *ELH* 64 (1997), 657–82.

Waith, Eugene. "Shakespeare and Fletcher on Love and Friendship," *ShakS 18* (1986), 235–49.

The Poems

Dubrow, Heather. *Captive Victors: Shakespeare's Narrative Poems and Sonnets*. Ithaca, N.Y., 1987.

Hulse, Clarke. *Metamorphic Verse: The Elizabethan Minor Epic*. Princeton, 1981.

Shakespeare Survey 15 (1962). Devoted chiefly to the poems and music, including the sonnets.

Venus and Adonis

See also, under *The Poems*, Dubrow, and Hulse (pp. 143–75); under *Shakespeare Criticism from the 1940s to the 1970s*, Rabkin; and under *Shakespeare Criticism Since 1980*, Kahn (Chapter 2).

Allen, Michael J. B. "The Chase: The Development of a Renaissance Theme," *Comparative Literature* 20 (1968), 301–12. (Includes discussion of *Venus and Adonis*.)

Asals, Heather. "*Venus and Adonis*: The Education of a Goddess," *Studies in English Literature* 13 (1973), 31–51.

Beauregard, David N. "*Venus and Adonis*: Shakespeare's Representation of the Passions," *ShakS 8* (1975), 83–98.

Belsey, Catherine. "Love as Trompe-l'oeil: Taxonomies of Desire in *Venus and Adonis*," *SQ* 46 (1995), 257–76.

Hamilton, A. C. "*Venus and Adonis*," *Studies in English Literature* 1:1 (1961), 1–15.

Jahn, J. D. "The Lamb of Lust: The Role of Adonis in Shakespeare's *Venus and Adonis*," *ShakS 6* (1970), 11–25.

Keach, William. "*Venus and Adonis*," *Elizabethan Erotic Narratives: Irony and Pathos in the Ovidian Poetry of Shakespeare, Marlowe, and Their Contemporaries*. New Brunswick, N.J., 1977.

Mortimer, Anthony. *Variable Passions: A Reading of Shakespeare's "Venus and Adonis."* New York, 2000.

The Rape of Lucrece

See also, under *The Greek and Roman Tragedies*, Miola; under *Shakespeare's Language*, Lanham; and under *Shakespeare Criticism Since 1980*, Callaghan (*A Feminist Companion*, essay by Hendricks), Kahn, Little, Parker and Hartman (essay by Vickers), and Siemon (Chapter 2).

Belsey, Catherine. "Tarquin Dispossessed: Expropriation and Consent in *The Rape of Lucrece*," *SQ* 52 (2001), 315–35.

Donaldson, Ian. 'A Theme for Disputation': Shakespeare's Lucrece," *The Rapes of Lucretia: A Myth and Its Transformations*. Oxford, 1982.

Dubrow, Heather. " 'Full of forged lies': *The Rape of Lucrece*," *Captive Victors: Shakespeare's Narrative Poems and Sonnets*. Ithaca, N.Y., 1987.

Fineman, Joel. "Shakespeare's Will: The Temporality of Rape," *Representations* 20 (1987), 25–76.

Hulse, Clark. "*A Skilful Painting of Lucrece*," *Metamorphic Verse: The Elizabethan Minor Epic*. Princeton, 1981.

Kahn, Coppélia. "The Rape in Shakespeare's *Lucrece*," *ShakS 9* (1976), 45–72.

MacDonald, Joyce Green. "Speech, Silence, and History in *The Rape of Lucrece*," *ShakS 22* (1994), 77–103.

Maus, Katharine Eisaman. "Taking Tropes Seriously: Language and Violence in Shakespeare's *The Rape of Lucrece*," *SQ* 37 (1986), 66–82.

Newman, Jane O. " 'And Let Mild Women to Him Lose Their Mildness': Philomela, Female Violence, and Shakespeare's *The Rape of Lucrece*," *SQ* 45 (1994), 304–26.

Scholz, Susanne. "Textualizing the Body Politic: National Identity and the Female Body in *The Rape of Lucrece*," *Shakespeare Jahrbuch* 132 (1996), 103–13.

Williams, Carolyn D. " 'Silence, like a Lucrece knife': Shakespeare and the Meaning of Rape," *Yearbook of English Studies* 23 (1993), 93–110.

Wilson, R. Rawdon. "Shakespearean Narrative: *The Rape of Lucrece* Reconsidered," *Studies in English Literature* 28 (1988), 39–59.

The Phoenix and Turtle

See also, under *Shakespeare Criticism Since 1980,* Carey (essay by Buxton, pp. 44–55).

Alvarez, A. "William Shakespeare: *The Phoenix and the Turtle,*" *Interpretations,* ed. John Wain. London, 1955.

Arthos, John. *Shakespeare's Use of Dream and Vision,* Chapter 1. London and Totowa, N.J., 1977.

Ellrodt, Robert. "An Anatomy of *The Phoenix and the Turtle,*" *ShS 15* (1962), 99–110.

Empson, William. *"The Phoenix and the Turtle,"* *Essays in Criticism* 16 (1966), 147–53.

Garber, Marjorie. "Two Birds with One Stone: Lapidary Re-inscription in *The Phoenix and Turtle,*" *The Upstart Crow* 5 (1984), 5–19.

Honigmann, E. A. J. *"The Phoenix and the Turtle,"* *Shakespeare: The "Lost" Years,* pp. 90–113. Totowa, N.J., 1985.

Knight, G. Wilson. *The Mutual Flame: On Shakespeare's Sonnets and "The Phoenix and the Turtle."* London, 1955.

Matchett, William H. *"The Phoenix and the Turtle": Shakespeare's Poem and Chester's "Loues Martyr."* The Hague, 1965.

A Lover's Complaint

Jackson, MacD. P. *Shakespeare's "A Lover's Complaint": Its Date and Authenticity.* Auckland, N.Z., 1965.

Muir, Kenneth. "*A Lover's Complaint:* A Reconsideration." *Shakespeare 1564–1964,* ed. E. A. Bloom, pp. 154–66. Providence, 1964.

Underwood, Richard Allan. *Shakespeare on Love: The Poems and the Plays. Prolegomena to a Variorum Edition of "A Lover's Complaint."* Salzburg, 1985.

Warren, Roger. " 'A Lover's Complaint,' *All's Well,* and the Sonnets," *Notes and Queries* n.s. 17 (1970), 130–2.

Sonnets

See also, under. *The Poems,* Dubrow; under *Shakespeare's Predecessors and Contemporaries,* Rasmussen (essay by Alpers); under *Shakespeare Criticism from the 1940s to the 1970s,* Colie, and Kernan (*Playwright as Magician,* Chapter 2); and under *Shakespeare Criticism Since 1980,* Loomba and Orkin (essay by Hall), McDonald (essay by Vendler), Parker and Hartman (essay by Greene), and Wheeler (pp. 179–90).

Allen, Michael J. B. "Shakespeare's Man Descending a Staircase: Sonnets 126 to 154," *ShS 31* (1978), 127–38.

Booth, Stephen. *An Essay on Shakespeare's Sonnets.* New Haven, 1969.

———. ed. *Shakespeare's Sonnets, Edited with Analytic Commentary.* New Haven, 1977.

Bradley, A. C. *Oxford Lectures on Poetry.* London, 1909, 1961.

Cheney, Patrick. " 'O, let my books be . . . dumb presagers': Poetry and Theater in Shakespeare's Sonnets," *SQ 52* (2001), 222–54.

Clark, S. H. *Sordid Images: The Poetry of Masculine Desire.* London and New York, 1994.

Cousins, A. D. *Shakespeare's Sonnets and Narrative Poems.* Harlow, Eng., 2000.

De Grazia, Margreta. "The Scandal of Shakespeare's Sonnets," *ShS 46* (1994), 35–49.

Dubrow, Heather. *Echoes of Desire: English Petrarchism and Its Counterdiscourses.* Ithaca, N.Y., 1995.

Fineman, Joel. *Shakespeare's Perjured Eye: The Invention of Poetic Subjectivity in the Sonnets.* Berkeley, 1986.

Giroux, Robert. *The Book Known as Q: A Consideration of Shakespeare's Sonnets.* New York, 1982.

Hubler, Edward, Northrop Frye, Leslie A. Fiedler, Stephen Spender, and R. P. Blackmur. *The Riddle of Shakespeare's Sonnets.* New York, 1962.

Ingram, W. G., and Theodore Redpath, eds. *Shakespeare's Sonnets.* London, 1964.

Innes, Paul. *Shakespeare and the English Renaissance Sonnet: Verses of Feigning Love.* Basingstoke and New York, 1997.

Knight, G. Wilson. *The Mutual Flame: On Shakespeare's Sonnets and "The Phoenix and the Turtle."* London, 1955.

Krieger, Murray. *A Window to Criticism: Shakespeare's Sonnets and Modern Poetics.* Princeton, 1964.

Landry, Hilton. *Interpretations in Shakespeare's Sonnets.* Berkeley, 1963.

———. ed. *New Essays on Shakespeare's Sonnets.* New York, 1976.

Leishman, J. B. *Themes and Variations in Shakespeare's Sonnets.* London, 1961.

Lever, J. W. *The Elizabethan Love Sonnet.* London, 1956.

Melchiori, Giorgio. *Shakespeare's Dramatic Meditations: An Experiment in Criticism.* Oxford, 1976.

Muir, Kenneth. *Shakespeare's Sonnets.* London, 1979.

Pequigney, Joseph. *Such is My Love: A Study of Shakespeare's Sonnets.* Chicago, 1985.

Ramsay, Paul. *The Fickle Glass: A Study of Shakespeare's Sonnets.* New York, 1979.

Ransom, John Crowe. *The World's Body.* New York and London, 1938, 1968.

Schiffer, James, ed. *Shakespeare's Sonnets: Critical Essays.* New York, 1999.

Vendler, Helen. *The Art of Shakespeare's Sonnets.* Cambridge, Mass., 1997.

Textual Notes

These textual notes do not offer an historical collation, either of the early quartos and folios or of more recent editions; they are simply a record of departures in this edition from the copy text. For most plays the notes give the adopted reading of this edition in bold face, followed by the rejected reading in the relevant copy text. Where two substantive early texts are involved, or where a reading from some other earlier edition has been adopted, the notes provide information on the source of the reading in square brackets. In a few texts, adopted readings of editions more recent than the First Folio are indicated by [eds.]. Alterations in lineation are not indicated, nor are some minor and obvious typographical errors; changes in punctuation are indicated when the resulting change in meaning is substantive.

Abbreviations used:
F The First Folio
Q Quarto
O Octavo
s.d. stage direction
s.p. speech prefix

The Comedy of Errors

Copy text: the First Folio. Scene divisions not marked in the Folio are provided at 1.2, 2.2, 3.2, 4.2, 4.3, and 4.4.
1.1. 0.2 [and elsewhere] *Syracuse Siracusa* **1 [and elsewhere]** EGEON *Marchant* **41 [and throughout] Epidamnum** *Epidamium* **42 the** he **102 upon** vp **116 bark** backe **123 thee** they **151 health** helpe
1.2. 1 *Antipholus [of Syracuse] Antipholis Erotes* **[First]** *Merchant* a *Marchant* **1 [and elsewhere]** FIRST MERCHANT *Mer.* [also called *E. Mar.*] **4 arrival** a riuall **15 travel** trauaile **30 [and elsewhere] lose** loose **32 s.d.** *Exit Exeunt* **40 unhappy** vnhappie a **66 clock** cooke **94.1** *Exit Exeunt*
2.1. 0.1 *Antipholus of Ephesus Antipholis Sereptus* **11 o'door** adore **12 ill** thus **45 two** too **60 thousand** hundred **63 come home** come **71 errand** arrant **106 o' love** a loue **111 Wear** Where **115.1** *Exeunt Exit*
2.2. 0.1 *Antipholus of Syracuse Antipholus Errotis* **6.1.** *of Syracuse Siracusia* **12 didst** did didst **14 s.** ANTIPHOLUS *E. Ant.* **79 men** them **97 tiring** trying **101 e'en** in **135 off** of **174 stronger** stranger **185 offered** free'd **189 elves** Owles **193 drone** *Dromio* **194 not I** I not
3.1. 71 cake cake here **75 you** your **89 her** your **91 her** your **116 [and throughout] Porcupine** *Porpentine*

3.2. 110.1 *Luciana Iuliana* **1** LUCIANA *Iulia* **4 building** buildings **ruinous** ruinate **16 attaint** attaine **21 but** not **26 wife** wise **46 sister's** sister **49 bed** bud **them** thee **57 where** when **109 and** is **126 chalky** chalke **136 carracks** Carrects **162 [and elsewhere] lest** least
4.1. 1 [and elsewhere] SECOND MERCHANT *Mar.* **7 [and elsewhere]** ANGELO *Gold.* **13.1** *Enter . . . Ephesus Enter Antipholus Ephes. Dromio* **17 her** their **28 carat** charect **87 then** then sir
4.2. 6 Of Oh **34 One** On **48 That** Thus **61 'a** I **66 s.d.** *Exeunt Exit*
4.3. 1 s. ANTIPHOLUS [not in F] **58 if you** if **78 s.d.** *Exeunt Exit*
4.4. 42 to prophesy the prophesie **104 those** these **106.1–2.** *Enter . . . strives* [after line 105 in F] **113 his** this **130.1–3.** [after line 131 in F] *Manent Manet* **143.1–2.** *Enter . . . drawn Enter Antipholus Siracusia with his Rapier drawne, and Dromio Sirac.* **146.1 Run all out** [after "bound again" in line 146 in F]
5.1. 121 death depth **155 whither** whether **168** SERVANT [not in F] **175 scissors** Cizers **180** SERVANT *Mess.* **195** EGEON *Mar. Fat.* **283** EGEON *Fa.* [and elsewhere *Fath. and Father*] **330.1–2.** *Antipholus . . . Syracuse Antipholus Siracusa, and Dromio Sir.* **357–62** [these lines follow line 346 in F] **358 Antipholus'** *Antipholus* **403 ne'er** are **406 joy** go **408.1** *Manent Manet* **414.1** *Exeunt Exit*

Love's Labor's Lost

Copy text: the Quarto of 1598. The act and scene divisions here provided are not in Q. Act divisions are from F; scene divisions are editorial.
1.1. [and elsewhere] KING *Ferdinand* **18 schedule** sedule **23 too** to **24 three** thee **31 pomp** pome **62 feast** fast **70 quite** quit **79 losing** loosing **104 an** any **123 losing** loosing **127** BEROWNE [at line 132 (*Ber.*) in Q] **130 public** publibue **possibly** possible **165 One** On **168 umpire** vmpier **180 [and elsewhere]** DULL *Constab.* **188 [and elsewhere, except for lines 219 and 221]** COSTARD *Clowne* **188 contempts** Contempls **216 welkin's** welkis **227 besieged** besedged **245** KING [not in Q; also at lines 247, 249, 252] **254 with,** with *Which* with **264** DULL *Antho.* **273 worst** wost
1.2. 0.1 [and elsewhere] Mote *Moth* **3 [and elsewhere]** MOTE *Boy* **4 Why,** Why? **13–14 epitheton** apethaton **97 blushing** blush-in **126 deywoman** Day womand **128** JAQUENETTA *Maide* [and elsewhere Maid, *Ma.*] **139** DULL *Clo.* **172 duello** [F] *Duella*
2.1. 13 [and elsewhere] PRINCESS *Queene* **32 Importunes** Importuous **34 visaged** visage **36.1** *Exit Boyet* [at line 35 in Q] **39** A LORD *Lor.* [also at line 80] **Lord Longaville** *Longauill* **40** MARIA *1. Lady*

A-102

42–3 solemnizèd . . . Longaville. solemnized. In *Normandie* saw I this *Longauill,*   **44 parts** peerelsse   **53** MARIA *Lad.*   **56** KATHARINE 2. *Lad.*   **61 Alencon's** *Alansoes*   **64** ROSALINE 3. *Lad.*   **88 unpeopled** vnpeeled   **90 [and elsewhere]** KING *Nauar.*   **100 it—will** it will,   **115–26** ROSALINE *Kather.* or *Kath.*   **130 of** of, of   **142 demand** pemaund   **144 On** One   **180 mine own** my none   **190** *Non No*   **195 Katharine** *Rosalin*   **210 Rosaline** *Katherin*   **221** KATHARINE *La.* [also at lines 222 and 224]   **246 quote** coate   **254** ROSALINE *Lad.*   **255** MARIA *Lad.* 2   **256** KATHARINE *Lad.* 3   **257** MARIA *Lad.*   **258** KATHARINE *Lad.*

3.1. 1 [and elsewhere] ARMADO *Bra.*   **14 as if** if   **15 through the nose** through: nose   **18 thin-belly** thinbellies   **26 penny** penne   **65 voluble** volable   **69 [and elsewhere]** MOTE *Pag.*   **72 the mail** thee male   **plain** pline   **133 ounce** ouce   **136 remuneration** remuration   **138 carries it.** carries it   **141 My** [preceded by "O" in Q; also lines 145, 147, 149, 153, 155, 172]   **178 Junior** *Iunios*   **188 clock** Cloake   **202 sue** shue

4.1. 3 BOYET *Forr.*   **6 On** Ore   **42 God-i-good-e'en** God dig-you-den   **49 mistress** [F] Mistrs   **70–1 saw . . . saw** See . . . see   **71 overcame** couercame   **75 King's** King   **87 Adriano** Adriana   **Armado** Armatho   **128.1** *Exit* [at line 126 in Q]   **130 hit it** hit   **132 mete** meate   **134 ne'er** neare   **136 pin** is in   **144 o'th'one** ath toothen   **148 is a** is   **s.d.** *Shout* Shoot. [The s.d. follows line 149 in Q.]   **149 s.d.** *Exit Exeunt*

4.2. 3 [and elsewhere] HOLOFERNES *Ped.*   **8 [and elsewhere]** NATHANIEL *Curat. Nath.*   **14–15 explication; facere,** explication *facere:*   **29 of taste** taste   **30 indiscreet** indistreell   **36 Dictynna . . . Dictynna** *Dictisima . . . dictisima*   **51 ignorant** ignorault   **call I** cald   **53 scurrility** squirilitie   **65** HOLOFERNES *Nath.* [the subsequent speech prefixes in this scene of Holofernes and Nathaniel are reversed in Q through line 147, except that the speech at line 104 is correctly assigned to Nathaniel, at lines 118–20 to *Pedan.*, and at lines 135–42 to *Ped.*]   **69** *pia mater* primater   **71 in whom** whom   **72** NATHANIEL *Holo.*   **76 ingenious** ingenous   **78** *sapit sapis*   **81** HOLOFERNES *Nath.* [also at lines 85, 91]   **pierce-one** Person   **88 Person** Parson   **91** *Fauste Facile*   ***pecus pecas   omne omnia*   94–5** *Venezia . . . prezia vemchie, vencha, que non te vnde, que non te perreche*   **101** NATHANIEL *Holo.*   **102** HOLOFERNES *Nath.*   **stanza** stauze   **104** NATHANIEL [missing in Q]   **118 apostrophus** apostraphas   **119 canzonet** cangenet   **120 Here** [the rest of this speech is assigned to *Nath.* in Q]   **130** HOLOFERNES *Nath.*   **133 writing** written   **135 Sir Nathaniel** *Ped.* Sir *Holofernes*   **143** JAQUENETTA *Mayd*   **146** NATHANIEL *Holo.*   **148** HOLOFERNES *Ped.*   **156** *ben bien*

4.3. 12 melancholy mallicholie [also in line 13]   **13 here my** heare my   **35 wilt** will   **45** KING *Long.*   **69 lose** loose   **71 idolatry** ydotarie   **83 quoted** coted   **89 And I** And   **95 ode** Odo   **104 Wished** Wish   **108 thorn** throne   **151 coaches; in your tears** couches in your teares.   **157 mote . . . mote** Moth . . . Moth   **172 to . . . by** by . . . to   **176 like you** like   **178 Joan** Ione [Qb]; Loue [Qa]   **179 me? When** mee when   **184 s.d.** [after "God bless the king" in line 185 in Q]   **192 Where** [Q repeats the s.p. KING]   **255 and usurping** vsurping   **256 doters** dooters   **279 Nothing** O nothing   **291 And . . . maladies** [Q follows with the following twenty-three lines that appear to be a first draft of lines 292 ff.:

And where that you haue vowd to studie (Lordes)
In that each of you haue forsworne his Booke.
Can you still dreame and poare and thereon looke.
For when would you my Lord, or you, or you,
Haue found the ground of Studies excellence,
Without the beautie of a womans face?
From womens eyes this doctrine I deriue,
They are the Ground, the Bookes, the Achadems,
From whence doth spring the true *Promethean* fire.
Why vniuersall plodding poysons vp
The nimble sprites in the arteries,

As motion and long during action tyres
The sinnowy vigour of the trauayler.
Now for not looking on a womans face,
You haue in that forswone the vse of eyes:
And studie too, the causer of your vow.
For where is any Authour in the worlde,
Teaches such beautie as a womas eye:
Learning is but an adiunct to our selfe,
And where we are, our Learning likewise is.
Then when our selues we see in Ladies eyes,
With our selues.
Do we not likewise see our learning there?]

313 dainty Bacchus . . . taste. daintie, *Bachus . . .* taste,   **316 Subtle** Subtit   **333 authors** authour   **335 Let** Lets   **lose** loose [also in line 336]   **341 standards** standars   **356 betime** be time   **357** *Allons! Allons!* Alone alone   **359 forsworn** forsorne

5.1. 1 *quod* quid   **9** *hominem* hominum   **25 insanie** infamie   **27 bone** *bene*   **28 Bone . . . Priscian** *Bome boon for boon prescian*   **31** *gaudeo* gaudio   **33** *Quare Quari*   **38 lived** lyud   **56 wave** wane   **57 venue** vene we   **66** *manu vnum*   **73 wert** wart   **74** *dunghill dungil*   **76 Dunghill** *dunghel*   **90 choice** chose   **96 importunate** importunt   **101 mustachio** mustachie   **106 secrecy** secretie   **108 antic** antique [also at line 143]   **115 Nathaniel** *Holofernes*   **117 rendered** rended   **assistance** assistants   **148** *Allons* Alone

5.2. 13 ne'er neare   **17 ha' been a** a bin   **22 You'll Yole**   **28 cure . . . care** care . . . cure   **43 pencils, ho!** pensalls, How?   **53 [and at line 57]** MARIA *Marg.*   **53 pearls** Pearle   **65 hests** deuice   **67 pair-taunt-like** perttaunt like   **74 wantonness** wantons be   **80 stabbed** stable   **83 peace. Love** Peace Loue   **89 sycamore** Siccamone   **93 companions. Warily** companions warely,   **96 they** thy   **122 parle** parlee   **123 love suit** Loue-feat   **134 too** two   **148 her** his   **152 ne'er** are   **160.1 The . . . him** [after line 161 in Q]   **164 ever** *euen*   **176 strangers** stranges   **179 Princess** Princes   **198 travel** trauaile   **213 yet? No dance!** yet no dance: **217 The . . . it** [assigned in Q to *Rosa.*]   **223 measure! Be** measure be   **225 Price** Prise   **232 [and elsewhere]** PRINCESS *Quee.*   **243** KATHARINE *Maria* [also at lines 245, 248, 249, 250, 254, 256]   **260 sense, so sensible** sense so sensible,   **265.1** *Exeunt Exe*   **269 have; gross** haue grosse   **278 Non** No   **280 perhaps** perhapt   **298 vailing** varling   **300 woo** woe   **310 run** runs   **342 Construe** Consture   **353 unsullied** vnsallied   **375–7 foolish. When . . . eye, . . . light.** foolish when . . . eie: . . . light,   **397 lady. Dart** Ladie dart   **406 song** songue   **408 affectation** affection   **464 zany** saine   **479 allowed** aloude   **483 manage** nuage   **485** [Q supplies a s.p. here, "*Ber.*"]   **501 they** thy   **514 least** best   **529** *de la guerra* delaguar   **544 leopard's** Libbards   **554** PRINCESS *Lady*   **563 this** his   **582** [Q has "*Exit Curat.*"]   **591 Judas** *Pede.* Iudas   **596 proved** proud   **643 gilt** gift   **669 The . . . gone** [Q prints as a s.d. or as a part of Armado's speech]   **686 on, stir** or stir   **691 northern** Northren   **699 lose** loose   **746 wholesome** holdsome   **759 strange** straying   **764 gravities,** grauities.   **770 both—fair** both faire   **774 the ambassadors** embassadours   **778 this in** this   **782 quote** cote   **808 entitled** intiled   **812 hermit** herrite   **812 Hence . . . breast** [Q follows with the following six lines that appear to be a first draft of lines 813 ff.:

Berow. And what to me my Loue? and what to me?
Rosal. You must be purged to, your sinnes are rackt.
You are attaint with faultes and periurie:
Therefore if you my fauour meane to get,
A tweluemonth shall you spende and neuer rest,
But seeke the weery beddes of people sicke.]

814 A wife [assigned to *Kath.* in Q]   **881** [Q supplies a s.p. here, *Brag.*]   **883** [Q supplies a s.p. here, *B.*]   **884** SPRING [not in Q]   **885–6** [the second and third lines of the song are transposed in Q]   **906 foul** full   **918** ARMADO [not in Q]   **918–19 The . . . Apollo**

[printed in larger type in Q without s.p.; F adds s.p. *"Brag."* and "You that way: we this way," thus incorporating the ending into the text]

The Two Gentlemen of Verona

Copy text: the First Folio. Characters' name are grouped at the head of each scene. Act and scene divisions follow the Folio text throughout.
1.1. 26 swam swom   **66 leave** loue   **68 [and elsewhere] lose** loose   **78 I a** I   **141 testerned** cestern'd
1.2. 80–1 tune, . . . note. tune: . . . note,   **97 your** you
1.3. 16 travel trauaile   **16 [and elsewhere] whither** whether   **50** [here F repeats speech prefix *"Pro."*]   **88 father calls** Fathers call's   **91.1** *Exeunt Exeunt. Finis*
2.1. 109 stead steed   **136 What, are** What are
2.2. 18.1 [and elsewhere] *Panthino Panthion* [in F, grouped with characters' names at head of scene, as with entrance directions generally]
2.3. 27 wood would   **36 tied** tide [also at lines 37, 39, and 51]
2.4. 60 know knew   **106 mistress** a Mistresse   **114 SERVANT** *Thur.*   **118 to** too   **161 braggartism** Bragardisme   **163 makes** make   **188.1** [at line 187 in F]   **193 Is it mine eye** It is mine   **207 dazzlèd** dazel'd   **211 s.d.** *Exit Exeunt*
2.5. 1 Milan *Padua*   **37 that my** that that my
3.1. 56 tenor tenure   **280 master's ship** Mastership   **318 kissed fasting** fasting   **375.1** *Exit Exeunt*
4.1. 35 had often had   **49 An heir, and near** And heire and Neece,
4.2. 17.1. *Musicians Musitian* [grouped with characters' names at head of scene]   **38 MUSICIAN** [not in F]   **95 hast** has't   **110 his** her
4.3. 19 abhors abhor'd   **42 Recking** Wreaking
4.4. 54 hangman Hangmans   **68 thou** thee   **72 to** not   **105 woo** woe   **148 is.** is,   **149 well,** well;   **204 s.d.** *Exit Exeunt*
5.2. 7 JULIA *Pro.*   **13 JULIA** *Thu.*   **18 your** you   **47 you, stand not** you stand, not   **59 s.d.** *Exit Exeunt*
5.4. 26 this . . . hear! this? I see, and heare: **33 seizèd** ceazed   **49 me.** me,   **121 OUTLAWS** *Out-l.*

The Taming of the Shrew

Copy Text: The First Folio. The act and scene divisions are missing in the Folio except for Act 1 (before the first Induction), Act 3, Act 4 (at 4.3), and Act 5 (at 5.2).
Ind.1. 0.1 *Christopher Sly* [printed at the end of the s.d. in F as *"Christophero Sly"*]   **1 [and elsewhere] SLY** *Begger*   **10–11 thirdborough** Headborough   **16 Breathe** Brach   **21 [and elsewhere] FIRST HUNTSMAN** *Hunts.*   **81 FIRST PLAYER** *2. Player*   **87 SECOND PLAYER** *Sincklo*   **99 FIRST PLAYER** *Plai.*   **134 peasant.** peasant,
Ind. 2. 2 Lordship Lord   **18 Sly's** Sies   **26 [and elsewhere] THIRD SERVINGMAN** *3. Man*   **27 [and elsewhere] SECOND SERVINGMAN** *2 Man*   **47 [and elsewhere] FIRST SERVINGMAN** *1 Man*   **53 wi'th'** with   **93 Greet** Greece   **98 lose** loose   **99 [and elsewhere] PAGE** *Lady*   **125 SERVINGMAN** *Mes.*   **133 it. Is** it is
1.1. 3 fore for   **13 Vincentio** *Vincentio's*   **14 brought** brough   **24 satiety** sacietie   **25** *Mi perdonate Me Pardonato*   **33 Ovid be** *Ouid*   **146 s.d.** *Manent Manet*   **163 captum** captam   **208 colored** Conlord   **227 time.** time   **244 your** you   **248.2** *speak speakes*
1.2. 17.1 *wrings rings*   **18 masters** mistris   **24 Con . . . trovato** Contutti le core bene trobatto   **25 ben** bene   **26 Molto** multo   **onorato** honorata   **33 pip** peepe   **45 this's** this   **51 grows. But** growes but   **few,** few.   **72 me, were** she me. Were she is   **120 me and other more,** me. Other more   **171 help me** helpe one   **189 Antonio's** *Butonios*   **190 his** my   **212 ours** yours   **265 feat** seeke   **280** *ben Been*
2.1. 8 thee tell tel   **75–6 wooing.—Neighbors,** wooing neighbors: **79 unto you** vnto   **104 Pisa. By report** *Pisa* by report,   **153 struck** stroke   **157 rascal fiddler** Rascall, Fidler   **168 s.d.** *Exeunt Exit*   **186 bonny** bony   **244 askance** a sconce   **322 s.d.** *Exeunt Exit*   **328 in** me   **352 Valance** Vallens   **355 pail** pale   **373 Marseilles** Marcellus
3.1. 28 *Sigeia sigeria* [also at lines 33 and 42]   **43** *steterat staterat*   **47** [*Aside*] *Luc.*   **50 BIANCA** [not in F]   **51 LUCENTIO** *Bian.*

---

53 BIANCA *Hort.*   **74 B mi** Beeme   **76 clef** Cliffe   **80 change** charge   **odd** old   **81 SERVANT** *Nicke*
3.2. 13 behavior. behaviour,   **14 man,** man;   **29 of thy** of   **30 old news** newes   **33 hear** heard   **54 swayed** Waid   **56 cheeked** chekt   **60 velour** velure   **128 to love** Loue   **130 As I** As   **150 e'er** ere   **182 s.d.** *Music plays* [after line 183 in F]   **199 GREMIO** *Gra.*
4.1. 23 CURTIS *Gru.*   **59 Imprimis** Inprimis   **81 sleekly** slickely   **106 GRUMIO** *Gre.*   **168.1.** *Curtis Curtis a Seruant* [after line 169 in F]
4.2. 4 HORTENSIO *Luc.*   **6 LUCENTIO** *Hor.* [and at line 8]   **7 you? First resolve** you first, resolue   **8 read that I profess,** *The* reade, that I professe   **13 none** me   **31 her** them   **72 Take . . . alone** [assigned to *"Par."* in F]   **in** me
4.[3] [F has *"Actus Quartus. Scena Prima"* here]   **48 to** too   **62.1** *Enter Haberdasher* [after 61 in F]   **63 HABERDASHER** *Fel.*   **81 is a** is   **88 like a** like   **146 where,** where   **148 mete-yard** meat-yard   **177 account'st** accountedst
4.4. 0.2 [*booted*] [appears at line 18.2 in F]   **1 Sir** Sirs   **18.2 bareheaded** *booted and bare headed*   **68.1** *Exit* [after line 67 in F; F also adds a s.d., *"Enter Peter,"* after line 68]   **78 he's** has   **91 except** expect   **93** *solum solem*
4.5. 14 An And   **18 is** in   **35 make a** make the   **37 Whither** Whether   **where** whether   **77 she be** she
5.1. 4 [F has *"Exit"* here]   **6 master's** mistris   **42 brought** brough   **50 master's** Mistris   **62 copintank** copataine   **104.1** *Exeunt Exit*   **139 No** Mo   **143 than never** then ueuer
5.[2] [F has *"Actus Quintus"* here]   **2 done** come   **37 thee, lad** the lad   **39 butt** But   **40 butt! An** but an   **45 bitter** better   **two** too   **52 TRANIO** *Tri.*   **57 Oho** Oh, oh   **62 two** too   **65 for** sir   **93.1** *Enter Biondello* [after *"Do what you can"* in 93 in F]   **132 a** fiue   **136 you're** your   **152 maintenance commits** maintenance. Commits

A Midsummer Night's Dream

Copy text: the First Quarto of 1600. The act and scene divisions are absent from the Quarto; the Folio provides act divisions only.
1.1. 4 wanes waues   **10 New** Now   **19.1.** *Lysander Lysander and Helena*   **24 Stand forth, Demetrius** [printed as s.d. in Q]   **26 Stand forth, Lysander** [printed as s.d. in Q]   **74 their** there   **114 [and elsewhere] lose** loose   **132 Ay** Eigh   **133 hear** here   **136 low** loue   **187 Yours would** Your words   **191 I'd** ile   **216 sweet** sweld   **219 stranger companies** strange companions   **224 s.d.** *Exit Hermia* [after line 223 in Q]
2.1. 1 [and elsewhere] PUCK *Robin*   **61 [and elsewhere] TITANIA** *Qu.*   **61 Fairies** Fairy   **79 Aegles** Eagles   **109 thin** chinne   **158 the west** west   **183 off** of   **190 slay** stay   **slayeth** stayeth   **194 thee** the   **201 not** not not, not   **206 lose** loose   **246.1** [after line 247 in Q]
2.2. 4 leathern lethren   **9 FIRST FAIRY** [not in Q]   **13 CHORUS** [not in Q; also at line 24]   **44 comfort** comfor   **45 Be** Bet   **49 good** god   **53 is it** 63 human humane   **155 ate** eate
3.1. 52 BOTTOM *Cet.*   **72 PUCK** *Ro.*   **77 BOTTOM** *Pyra.* [also at lines 79 and 98]   **78 Odors, odors** Odours, odorous   **83 PUCK** *Quin.*   **84 FLUTE** *Thys.* [also at lines 88 and 97]   **120 ousel** Woosell   **144 own** owe   **156 [and elsewhere] Mote** *Moth*   **157–8 Ready . . . go** [assigned to FAIRIES in Q]   **170 PEASEBLOSSOM** *1. Fai.*   **171 COBWEB** [not in Q]   **172 MOTE** *2. Fair.*   **173 MUSTARDSEED** *3. Fai.*   **190 you of** you   **196.1.** *Exeunt Exit*
3.2. 0.1 [Q: *Enter King of Fairies, and* Robin goodfellow]   **3.1.** [See previous note.]   **6–7 love. / Near . . . bower,** loue, / Neere . . . bower.   **15–16 brake. / When . . . take,** brake, / When . . . take: **19 mimic** Minnick   **38 [and elsewhere] PUCK** *Rob.*   **80 I so** I   **85 sleep** slippe   **213 like** life   **215 rend** rent   **220 passionate words** words   **250 prayers** praise   **260 off** of   **299 gentlemen** gentleman   **313 too to** to   **326 but** hut   **344 s.d.** *Exit Exeunt*   **406 Speak! In some bush?** Speake in some bush.   **451 To your** your
4.1. 5 [and elsewhere] BOTTOM *Clown*   **20 courtesy** curtsie   **24 marvelous** maruailes   **54 flowerets'** flouriets   **64 off** of   **72 o'er** or   **81 five** fine   **82 ho** howe   **116 Seemed** Seeme   **127 this is** this

132 rite right   **137.2** *Wind . . . up they all start vp. Winde hornes*
171 saw see   **177 hear** here   **190 found** fonnd   **198 let us** lets
205 to expound expound   **208 a patched** patcht a   **213 ballad** Ballet
4.2. 0.1 [*Snout, and Starveling*] Thisby *and the rabble*   **3** STARVELLING
Flut.   **5** FLUTE *Thys.* [and at lines 9, 13, 19]   **29 no** not   **34 ribbons**
ribands
5.1. 34 our Or   **107** [and elsewhere] THESEUS *Duk*   **122 his** this
150.1 *Exeunt Exit* [after line 153 in Q]   **155 Snout** *Flute*   **190 up in**
thee now againe   **193 love! Thou art my** loue thou art, my   **205**
mural down Moon vsed   **209** [and elsewhere] HIPPOLYTA *Dutch.*
216 beasts in, a beasts, in a   **265.1** *Enter Pyramus* [after 267 in Q]
270 gleams beames   **309 before** before?   **315 mote** moth   **317 war-**
rant warnd   **325 tomb** tumbe   **347** BOTTOM *Lyon*   **363 gait** gate
(also at 411)   **366 lion** Lyons   **367 behowls** beholds   **414–15 And**
. . . rest [these lines are transposed in Q]

The Merchant of Venice

Copy text: the First Quarto of 1600 [Q]. The act and scene divisions are
absent from the Quarto; the Folio provides act divisions only.
1.1. 0.1 *Salerio Salaryno* [and also elsewhere *Salarino*, and abbreviated
Salar., Sala., and *Sal.*]   *Solanio Salanio* [and abbreviated elsewhere
Sola. and *Sol.*]   **19 Peering** Piring   **27 docked** docks   **84 alabaster**
Alablaster   **85 jaundice** *Iaundies*   **112 tongue** togue   **113 Is** It is
128 off of   **151 back** bake
1.2. 44 Palatine Palentine [and at line 57]   **53 Bone** *Boune*   **58 throstle**
Trassell   **119.1** *Enter a Servingman* [after line 120 in Q]
1.3. 28 [and elsewhere] SHYLOCK *Iew*   **76 compromised** compremyzd
82 peeled pyld   **110 spit** spet [also at lines 124 and 129]   **125 day,**
another time day another time,
2.1. 0.2 *Morocco Morochus*   **25 Sophy . . . prince,** Sophy, and a Persian
Prince   **31 thee** the   **35 page** rage
2.2. 1 [and elsewhere] LAUNCELOT *Clowne*   **3** [and elsewhere in this
scene] **Gobbo** *Iobbe*   **42 By** Be   **76 murder** muder   **91 fill horse**
philhorse   **94 last** lest   **165.1** *Exit Leonardo* [after line 164 in Q]
168 a suit sute   **180** [and elsewhere] **lose** loose
2.3. 11 did doe
2.4. 8 o'clock of clocke   **9** s.d. [after line 9 in Q]   **14 Love news,** Loue,
newes   **20.1** *Exit clown* [after line 23 in Q]   **39** s.d. *Exeunt Exit*
2.5. 44 Jewess' Iewes
2.6. 26 Ho! Who's Howe whose   **35 night, you** night you   **59 gentle-**
men gentleman   **61 Who's** Whose
2.7. 18 threatens. Men threatens men   **45 Spits** Spets   **69 tombs** timber
2.8. 8 gondola Gondylo   **39 Slubber** slumber
2.9. 6 rites rights   **48 chaff** chaft   **49 varnished** varnist   **64 judgment**
iudement   **73** [Q provides a s.p.: *Arrag.*]
3.1. 19 [and elsewhere] **lest** least   **21.1** *Enter Shylock* [after line 22 in
Q]   **46 courtesy** cursie   **70** MAN [not in Q]   **74.1** [Q repeats the s.d.
"*Enter Tuball*"]   **100 Heard** heere   **114 turquoise** Turkies
3.2. 23 eke ech   **61 live. With** liue with   **67 eyes** *eye*   **81 vice** voyce
84 stairs stayers   **99 Veiling** vailing   **101 Therefore** Therefore then
110 shuddering shyddring   **117 whether** whither   **199 loved; for**
intermission lou'd for intermission,   **204 roof** rough   **217.1–2** [after
line 219 in Q]   **315** BASSANIO [not in Q]   **336 e'er** ere
3.3 0.1 *Solanio Salerio*   **24** SOLANIO *Sal.*
3.4. 13 equal egall   **23 Hear other things:** heere other things
49 Padua Mantua   **50 cousin's** cosin   **53 traject** Tranect   **80 near**
nere   **81 my** my my
3.5. 20 enough enow   e'en in   **26 comes** come   **74 merit it,** meane it,
it   **81 a wife** wife   **85 howsome'er** how so mere   **87** s.d. *Exeunt Exit*
4.1. 30 his state this states   **31 flint** flints   **35** [and elsewhere in this
scene] SHYLOCK *Iewe*   **50 urine; for affection,** vrine for affection.
51 Mistress Maisters   **73 You may as well** well   **74 Why he hath**
made the the   **bleat** bleake   **75 pines of Pines** pines   **81 more** moe
100 is as   **123 sole . . . soul** soule . . . soule   **136 whilst** whilest
228 No, not Not not   **233 tenor** tenure   **270 off** of   **322 off** of
396 GRATIANO *Shy.*   **405.1** *Exeunt Exit*

5.1. 26 STEPHANO *Messen.* [also *Mess.* at lines 28 and 33]   **41 Lorenzo**
Lorenzo, &   **49 Sweet soul** [assigned in Q to Lancelot]   **51 Stephano**
Stephen   **62 choiring** quiring   **87 Erebus** *Terebus*   **106 wren** Renne
109 ho! how   **152 give it** giue   **233 my** mine

Much Ado About Nothing

Copy text: the Quarto of 1600. The act and scene divisions are missing
from the Quarto; the Folio provides act divisions only.
1.1. 0.1. *Messina Messina, Innogen, his wife*   **2 Pedro** Peter [also in line
9]   **40 bird-bolt** Burbolt   **84 Benedick** Benedict   **141 all, Leonato.**
Signor all: Leonato, signior   **194.1** *Pedro Pedro, Iohn the bastard*
239 [and elsewhere] **lose** loose
1.2. 3 [and elsewhere] ANTONIO *Old*   **6 event** euents   **25 skill** shill
1.3. 46 brother's bothers   **70** s.d. *Exeunt exit*
2.1. 0.1 *Hero his wife, Hero*   **0.3** *Ursula* [Q adds "*and a kinsman*"]
2 [and elsewhere] ANTONIO *brother*   **37 bearward** Berrord
44 Peter, for the heavens, Peter: for the heauens,   **50, 53 curtsy**
cursie   **67 hear** here   **79.3.** *and Don or dumb*   **80 a bout** about
94 BALTHASAR *Bene.* [also at lines 97 and 99]   **187 drover** Drouier
201.2 *Leonato Leonato, Iohn and Borachio, and Conrade*   **311** [and else-
where] DON PEDRO *Prince*   **369** s.d. *Exeunt exit*
2.3. 7 s.d. [at line 5 in Q]   **25 an** and   **35.1** *Claudio Claudio, Musicke*
61 BALTHASAR [not in Q]   **73–6 but . . . nonny** &c.   **84 lief** liue
91 s.d. [after line 90 in Q]   **139 us of** vs   **171 doffed** daft
3.1. 0.2. *Ursula Ursley*   **23** s.d. [after line 25 in Q]   **63 antic** antique
111 on; I on I
3.2. 27 can cannot   **51** DON PEDRO *Bene.*   **74** [and elsewhere] DON
JOHN *Bastard*   **75 e'en** den   **91–2 manifest. For my brother, I . . .**
heart hath manifest, for my brother (I . . . heart) hath   **108 her then,**
tomorrow her, then to morrow   **118 her, tomorrow** her to morrow
3.3. 17 SEACOAL *Watch* 2 [also at line 27]   **87** SEACOAL *Watch* [also at
lines 95, 105, 125]   **134 reechy** rechie   **161** SEACOAL *Watch* 1 [also at
line 165]   **162** FIRST WATCH *Watch* 2 [also at line 168]   **171** SEACOAL
[missing in Q]
3.4. 17 in it
3.5. 2 [and elsewhere] DOGBERRY *Const. Dog.*   **7** [and elsewhere]
VERGES *Headb.*   **9 off** of   **32 talking. As** talking as   **50** [Q provides
an "*exit*" at this point]
4.1. 4 FRIAR *Fran.*   **28** DON PEDRO *Princn*   **167 tenor** tenure
202 princes princesse
4.2. 0.1–3 [Q reads "*Enter the Constables, Borachio, and the Towne clearke in
gownes.*"]   **1** DOGBERRY *Keeper*   **2** [and elsewhere in this scene]
VERGES *Cowley*   **4** DOGBERRY *Andrew*   **9** [and elsewhere in this
scene] DOGBERRY *Kemp*   **18** CONRADE, BORACHIO *Both*   **39** SEACOAL
Watch 1 [also at line 53]   **47** FIRST WATCH *Watch* 2   **51** VERGES *Const.*
67 [and elsewhere] DOGBERRY *Constable*   **69** CONRADE [missing in
Q]   **67 off** of   **73** CONRADE *Couley*   **86.1** *Exeunt exit*
5.1. 16 Bid And   **97 anticly** antiquely, and   **98 off** of   **116 like** likt
167 there's theirs   **179 on** one   **189 Lackbeard there, he**
Lacke-beard, there hee   **201.1.2** [after line 197 in Q]   **251** VERGES *Con.* 2
5.2. 41.1 [after line 42 in Q]   **81 myself. So** my self so   **97** s.d. *Exeunt*
exit
5.3. 2 A LORD *Lord*   **3** CLAUDIO [missing in Q]   **10 dumb** dead   **11** [Q
provides a s.p. "*Claudio*" here]   **12** BALTHASAR [missing in Q]
22 CLAUDIO *Lo.*   **23 rite** right   **32 speed's** speeds
5.4. 53 ANTONIO *Leo.*   **96** BENEDICK *Leon.*

The Merry Wives of Windsor

Copy text: the First Folio. Act and scene divisions follow the Folio text
throughout. [Q] = readings taken from the First Quarto of 1602.
1.1. 0.1–2 [Entering characters are grouped at the heads of scenes
throughout the play.]   **30 compromises** compremises   **41 George**
Thomas   **56** SHALLOW *Slen.*   **84 Cotswold** *Cotsall*   **131 Garter** Gater
149 latten Latin   **164 careers** Car-eires   **165 Latin then, too** Latten

then to   **235 faul** fall   **236 the 'ort** the'ord [and in a few other instances dialect has been similarly regularized]
1.3. 14 lime [Q] liue   **47 well** [Q] will   **51 legion** [Q: legians] legend   **59 oeillades** illiads   **81 o'th' hoof** i'th' hoofe   **82 humor** [Q] honor   **93 Page** [Q] Ford   **94 Ford** [Q] *Page*   **98 Page** *Ford*
1.4. 21 whey face wee-face   **23 softly-spirited** softly-sprighted   **41** *un boîtier vert* vnboyteene verd   **46 Ma** *mai*   *fort chaud for ehando m'en vais* man voi   **47 la cour** le Court   *affaire affaires*   **49 mets-le à ma** mette le au mon   **53 and** [Q] aad   **57** *qu'ai-j'oublié que ay ie oublie*   **63** *Larron* La-roone   **82** *baille* ballow   **99 that, . . . mind:** that I know *Ans* mind,   **115 goodyear** good-ier   **134 [and elsewhere] lose** loose   **149 that I will** that wee will
2.1. have I haue   **23 i'th'** with The   **48 What? Thou liest!** What thou liest?   **55 praised** praise   **59–60 Hundredth Psalm** hundred Psalms   **130 and . . . of it** [Q; not in F]   **137 Cathayan** *Cataian*   **141 Whither** Whether [and at 3.3.139, 141]   **182 gentleman.** Gentleman   **199 FORD** [Q] *Shal.*   **201 Brook** [Q] *Broome* [and at line 203 and elsewhere]   **204 mynheers** An-heires   **216 s.d.** *Exeunt* [at line 223 in F]
2.2. 4 I will . . . equipage [Q; not in F]   **21 honor** honoror   **23, 50 [and elsewhere] God** [Q] heauen   **25 you, you** you   **196 jewel.** That Iewell, that   **224–5 exchange** enchange
2.3. 26 Galen *Galien*   **30 Castilian** Castalion   **34 Master Doctor. He** (M. Docto)rhe   **51 A word** [Q] a   **56 mush** much   **73 PAGE, SHALLOW, AND SLENDER** *All*   **77 But first** [Q; not in F]
3.1. 5 Petty-ward pittie-ward   **29 God** Heauen   **39 God save** [Q] 'Saue   **40 God pless** [Q] 'Plesse   **76–7 patience. In** patience in   **84–5 for . . . appointments** [Q; not in F]   **99–100 Give me . . . terrestrial; so** [Q; not in F]   **105 lads** Lad
3.2. 7 [and elsewhere] MRS. PAGE *M. Pa.* [used previously for *Page*]
3.3. 3 Robert *Robin*   **12 Datchet** Dotchet   **32 cue** *Qu*   **35 pumpkin** Pumpion   **54 By the Lord** [Q; not in F]   **58 not, Nature** not Nature   **62 thee there's** thee. Ther's   **68–9 Mistress** M.   **72 limekiln** Limekill [also at 4.2.51]   **141 whither** whether   **176 foolish** foolishion   **194 By** Be   **208 heartily** hartly
3.4. 12 FENTON [not in F]   **67 Fenton** *Fenton*   **109 s.d.** *Exit Exeunt*
3.5. 30 sperm Spersme   **57 he** be   **83 By the Lord** [Q] Yes   **142 s.d.** *Exit Exeunt*
4.1. 43 *hung hing*   **56** *Genitivo Genitiue*   **57 Jenny's** Ginyes   **62 "whorum"** *horum*   **64 lunatics** Lunaties   **73** *quae's* Ques
4.2. 10 who's whose   **51 MRS. PAGE** [not in F]   **59 MRS. PAGE** [Q] *Mist. Ford*   **68–9 [and elsewhere] Brentford** *Brainford*   **91 direct** direct direct   **95 misuse him** misuse   **106 as lief** liefe as   **111 ging** gin   **118 this** thi   **169 not strike** strike   **180 Jeshu** [Q] yea and no
4.3. 1 Germans desire Germane desires   **7 them** [Q] him   **9 house** [Q] houses
4.4. 7 cold gold   **25 MRS.** *M.*   **30 ragg'd horns** rag'd-hornes   **32 makes** make   **42** [Q, reading "Horne" for "Herne"; not in F]   **60 MRS. FORD** Ford   **65 ne'er** neu'r   **72 tire** time
4.5. 41 SIMPLE *Fal.*   **54 Thou art** [Q] Thou are   **75 Reading . . .** Colnbrook *Readins,* of *Maidenhead;* of *Cole-brooke*   **86 Hue** Huy [also in line 87]   **97 to say my prayers** [Q; not in F]   **118 is here** here is
4.6. 39 denote deuote
5.2. 3 my daughter my
5.3. 12 Hugh Herne
5.5. 2 hot-blooded hot-bloodied   **3 Jove** loue   **20 hail kissing-comfits** haile-kissing Comfits   **48 Bead** *Bede*   **65 ring.** ring,   **66 bears,** beares: **67 More** Mote   **70 sapphire, pearl** Saphire-pearle   **93 FAIRIES** [not in F]   **105 MRS.** *M.*   **179 what, son** what sonne   **193 white** greene   **197 green** white   **201** *un garçon* oon Garsoon   *un paysan* oon pesant   **203 green** white   **204 by** bee   By be

As You Like It

Copy text: the First Folio. Act and scene divisions follow the Folio text throughout.
1.1. 105 she hee   **154 OLIVER** [not in F]   **154 s.d.** *Exit* [at line 153 in F]

1.2. 3 I were were   **5 [and elsewhere] whither** whether   **51 goddesses and** goddesses   **55 [and elsewhere] TOUCHSTONE** *Clow.*   **56 father** farher   **80 CELIA** *Ros.*   **88 Le** the   **233 love** loue;   **251.1** [at line 249 in F]   **280 [and occasionally elsewhere] Rosalind** *Rosaline*
1.3. 55 likelihood likelihoods   **76 her** per   **87.1 with Lords** *&c*   **124 be** by   **135 we in** in we   **129 travel** trauaile   **131 [and elsewhere] woo** woe
2.1. 37 antique anticke   **49 much** must   **50 friends** friend   **59 of the** of
2.3. 10 some seeme   **16 ORLANDO** [not in F]   **29 ORLANDO** *Ad.*   **71 seventeen** seauentie
2.4. 1 weary merry   **42 thy wound** they would   **65 you,** your
2.5. 1 AMIENS [not in F; also at line 35]   **38.1** *All together here* [before line 35 in F]   **41–2 No . . . weather** *&c*   **46 JAQUES** Amy.
2.7. 0.1 Lords Lord   **38 brain** braiue   **55 Not to seem** Seeme   **87 comes** come   **161 treble, pipes** trebble pipes,   **173 AMIENS** [not in F]   **182 Then** *The*   **190–3 heigh-ho . . . jolly** *&c.*   **201 master** masters
3.2. 26 good pood   **115 graft** graffe [twice]   **123 a desert** *Desert*   **143 her** his   **190 whooping** hooping   **234 such fruit** fruite   **241 thy** the   **254 [and elsewhere] b'wi'you** buy you   **340 lectures** Lectors   **354 deifying** defying   **362 are** art
3.3. 52–3 so. Poor men alone? No so poore men alone: No   **88 TOUCHSTONE** *Ol.*   **99 s.d.** *Exit Exeunt*
3.4. 29 a lover Louer   **41 puny** puisny
3.5. 11 pretty, sure pretty sure   **65 hear** here   **105 erewhile** yere-while   **128 I have** Haue
4.1. 1 me be me   **18 my** by   **27 travel** trauaile   **36 gondola** Gundello   **44 thousandth** thousand   **72 warrant** warne   **148 hyena** Hyen   **202 it** in
4.2. 2 FIRST LORD Lord   **7 SECOND LORD** Lord   **10 SECOND LORD** [not in F]
4.3. 5.1 [after line 3 in F]   **8 bid** did bid   **12 tenor** tenure   **79–80 bottom; bottom** bottom   **104–5 itself:** it selfe   **143 In** I   **156 his** this
5.1. 14 gi' ye   **36 sir** sit   **55 policy** police
5.2. 7 nor her nor   **31 overcame** ouercome
5.3. 15 BOTH PAGES [not in F]   **18 In** *In the*   **ring** *rang*   **24–6 In . . . spring** *In spring time, &c* [also at lines 30–2 and 36–8]   **33–8** [this stanza comes after line 20 in F]
5.4. 25.1. *Exeunt Exit*   **34.1** [after line 33 in F]   **80 so to the** so ro   **113 her** his   **150 JAQUES DE BOYS** *2 Bro.* [also at line 182]   **163 them** him   **170 were** vvete   **196 rites** rights   **197 trust they'll end, in** trust, they'l end in   **197.1** *Exeunt Exit*

Twelfth Night

Copy text: the First Folio. Act and scene divisions follow the Folio text throughout.
1.1. 1 [and throughout] ORSINO *Duke*   **10–11 capacity** capacitie,   **11 sea, naught** sea. Nought   **22 s.d.** [after 22 in F]
1.2. 15 Arion *Orion*
1.3. 51 SIR ANDREW *Ma.*   **54 Mary Accost** *Mary,* accost   **96 curl by** coole my   **98 me we** we   **132 dun** dam'd   **set** sit   **136 That's** That
1.5. 5 [and throughout] FESTE *Clo.*   **85 gagged** gag'd [also at 5.1. 376]   **144 He's** Ha's   **163.1** *Viola Uiolenta*   **296 County's** Countes   **306 s.d.** [F adds *"Finis, Actus primus"*]
2.2. 20 That sure That   **31 our** O   **32 made of, such** made, if such
2.3. 3 *diluculo Deliculo*   **25 leman** Lemon   **39 FESTE (sings)** *Clowne sings.*   **119 stoop** stope   **133 a nayword** an ayword
2.4. 4 Metal *Mettle*   **51 FESTE** [not in F]   **53 Fly . . . fly** Fye . . . fie   **55 yew** Ew   **88 I** It
2.5. 112 staniel stallion   **118 portend?** portend,   **142 born** become   **achieve** atcheeues   **156–7 Unhappy." Daylight** vnhappy daylight   **173 dear** deero   **203 s.d.** [F adds *"Finis Actus secundus"*]
3.1. 8 king Kings   **68 wise men** wisemens   **91 all ready** already   **124 grece** grize
3.2. 7 thee the the   **64 nine** mine
3.4. 15.1–2 s.d. [at line 14 in F, after "hither"]   **25 OLIVIA** *Mal.*   **65.1** *Exeunt exit*   **72 tang** langer   **106 lose** loose   **175 You** Yon

222 thee the **228 sir. I am sure no** sir I am sure, no **249 competent** computent **397.1** *Exeunt Exit*
4.1. 34 struck stroke **101 b'wi'** buy
4.2. 6 in in **38 clerestories** cleere stores **71 sport to** sport
4.3. 1 SEBASTIAN [not in F] **35 s.d.** [F adds *"Finis Actus Quartus"*]
5.1. 5 freight fraught **141 Whither** Whether **173 He's** H'as **190.1** [after line 187 in F] **195 He's** has **200 pavane** panyn **205 help? An** helpe an **207 to** too **285 He's** has **389 *tiny*** tine **406 With hey** *hey*

All's Well That Ends Well

Copy text: the First Folio. Act divisions are from the Folio; scene divisions are editorially provided.

1.1. 1 [and elsewhere] COUNTESS *Mother* **3** [and elsewhere] BERTRAM *Ros.* **17** [and elsewhere] **losing** loosing **52** [and elsewhere] **to** too **lest** least **70 Farewell. My** Farewell my **130 got** goe **148 th'one** ten **159 wear** were
1.2. 3 [and elsewhere] FIRST LORD 1. *Lo. G.* **15** [and elsewhere] SECOND LORD 2. *Lo. E* **18 Rossillion** Rosignoll **52 him! He** him he **76.1** *Exeunt Exit*
1.3. 3 [and elsewhere] RINALDO *Ste.* **13** [and elsewhere] LAVATCH *Clo.* **19 I** w **74–5** [F indicates the repetition of the line by printing a single line, followed by *"bis"*] **112 Dian no queen** Queene **115 e'er** ere **124.2** [and elsewhere] *Helena* Hellen **125** [F has s.p. here, *Old. Cou.*, used subsequently in other s.p.] **127 rightly belong;** righlie belong **168 loneliness** louelinesse **174 th'one to th'other** 'ton tooth to th'other **180 forswear't. Howe'er,** forswear't how ere **199 intenible sieve** intemible Siue **233 Haply** Happily **247 day and** day, an
2.1. 3–4 gain all, / The gaine, all / The **5 FIRST LORD** *Lord. G* **15–16 it. When . . . shrinks, find** it, when . . . shrinkes: finde **18 SECOND LORD** *L.G* **25 SECOND LORD** 2 *Lo. E* **44 with his cicatrice** his sicatrice, with **63 fee** see **94.1** [and elsewhere] *Helena* Hellen **111 two, more dear.** I two: more deare I **146 fits** shifts **157 impostor** Impostrue **175 nay** ne **194 heaven** helpe **212 meed** deed **212.1** *Exeunt Exit*
2.2. 1 [and elsewhere in scene] COUNTESS *Lady* **60 An end, sir! To** An end sir to
2.3. 1 [and elsewhere] LAFEW *Ol. Laf.* **21 indeed. If** indeede if **34 minister, great** minister great **44 *Mort du vinaigre*** Mor du vinagre **51.1 *four*** 3 or 4 **65 ALL THE LORDS** *All* **70–1 choose; but, be refused, / Let** choose, but refused; / Let **76 s.d.** [below line 62 in F] **94 her** heere **96 HELENA** *La.* **99 LAFEW** *Ol. Lord* **125 when** whence **129 name; vileness** name? Vilenesse **130 it is** is is **137–8 word's a slave / Debauched** words, a slaue / Debosh'd **138–9 grave: / A** graue: / A **140–1 tomb / Of** Tombe. / Of **168 eyes. When** eies, when **170 it, I** it: I **213 lattice** Lettice **266.1** [at line 264 in F] **293 detested** detected **301.1** *Exeunt Exit*
2.4. 11 [and elsewhere] **whither** whether **16 fortunes** fortune **35 me?** [F adds a s.d., *Clo.*] **56 you.** you **s.d. Exit Parolles** [at line 55 in F] **s.d.** *Exeunt Exit*
2.5. 16 who's whose **27 End** And **29 one** on **31 heard** hard **89 BERTRAM** [at line 90 in F] **89 men, mousieur?** men? Monsieur,
3.1. 9 SECOND LORD *French E* **17 FIRST LORD** *Fren. G* **23 to the** to'th the
3.2. 9 sold hold **18 E'en** In **19 COUNTESS** [not in F] **45** [and throughout scene] SECOND LORD *French E* **47** [and throughout scene] FIRST LORD *French G* **64 COUNTESS** *Old La.* **65 engrossest all** engrossest, all **111 still-piecing** still-peering
3.4. 4 RINALDO [not in F] **9–10 hie. / Bless** hie, / Blesse **10 peace, whilst** peace. Whilst **18 COUNTESS** [not in F]
3.5. 0.2 *daughter* daughter, Violenta **10** [and elsewhere] MARIANA *Maria* **33 le** la **66 warrant** write **93.1.** *Exeunt Exit*
3.6. 1 [and throughout scene until line 109] FIRST LORD *Cap. E* **3** [and throughout scene until line 109] SECOND LORD *Cap. G* **36 his** this **37 metal** mettle **ore** ours **109 FIRST LORD** *Cap. G* **111, 117 SECOND LORD** *Cap. E*
3.7. 19 Resolved Resolue **41 steads** steeds **46 wicked** lawfull

4.1. 1 [and throughout scene] FIRST LORD 1. *Lord E* **69** [and throughout scene] FIRST SOLDIER *Inter.* **90 art** are **93 SECOND SOLDIER** *Sol.* [and at line 96] **97 s.d.** *Exeunt Exit*
4.2. 6 monument monument **31 least** lest **38 may** make **snare** scarre **56 bond** band
4.3 1 [and throughout scene] FIRST LORD *Cap. G* **2** [and throughout scene] SECOND LORD *Cap. E* **24 nobility, . . . stream** Nobility . . . streame, **81 FIRST LORD** *Ber.* **89 effected** affected **98 he's** ha s [also at line 268] **118 Hush, hush** [assigned in F to Bertram] **125 FIRST LORD** *Cap.* **138 All's one to him** [assigned in F to Parolles] **168 poll** pole **189 sheriff's** Shrieues **199 Lordship** Lord **242 our** your **316 BERTRAM** *Count*
4.4. 16 you, your
4.5. 21 grass grace **39 name** maine **46 of** off **70 home, I** home. I **80 Marseilles** Marcellus
5.1. 6 s.d. *a Gentleman* a gentle Astringer [after line 6 in F]
5.2. 1 Monsieur Mr **25 similes** smiles **33 under her** vnder
5.3. 50 warped warpe **59–60 carried, / To** carried / To **60 sender turns** sender, turnes **72 COUNTESS** [not in F] **102 Plutus** Platus **115 conjectural** connecturall **123 tax** taze **140 KING** [not in F] **148 toll** toule **154.1** [after line 152 in F] **155 since** sir **157 s.d. *Diana* Diana, *and Parolles*** [after line 157 in F] **183 them.** them: **Fairer prove** them fairer: proue **208 sickens but** sickens: but **217 infinite cunning** insuite comming **314 are** is
Epilogue 1 KING [not in F] **4 strife** strift

Measure for Measure

Copy text: the First Folio. Act and scene divisions are from the Folio except as indicated below.

The Names of All the Actors [at the end of the play in F]
1.1. 76 s.d. [at line 75 in F]
1.2. 58 [and elsewhere] MISTRESS OVERDONE *Bawd* **83.1** [after line 84 in F] **85** [and elsewhere] POMPEY *Clo.* **115** [F begins *"Scena Tertia"* here] **134 morality** mortality
1.3. [F labels as *"Scena Quarta"*] **20 steeds** weedes **27 Becomes more** More **48** [and elsewhere] **More** Moe **54.1** *Exeunt Exit*
1.4. [F labels as *"Scena Quinta"*] **0.1** [and elsewhere] *Isabella* Isabell **2** [and throughout] FRANCISCA *Nun* **5 sisterhood** Sisterstood **17 stead** steed [also at 3.2. 252] **54 givings-out** giuing-out **61–2 mind, study, and fast. / He** minde: Studie, and fast / He **72 He's** Has **78** [and elsewhere] **lose** loose
2.1. 12 your our **39 breaks** brakes **90** [and elsewhere] **prunes** prewyns **139.1** [at line 138 in F]
2.2. 63 back again againe **104 ere** here
2.3. 31 [and elsewhere] **lest** least
2.4. 9 sere feard **17 s.d. *Enter Servant*** [after line 17 in F] **30 s.d. *Enter Isabella*** [after line 30 in F] **48 metal** mettle **53 or** and **75 craftily** crafty **76 me be** be **94 all-binding** all-building
3.1. 29 thee sire, thee, fire **31 serpigo** Sapego **52 me to hear them** them to heare me **68 Though** Through **91 enew** emmew **96 damned'st** damnest **131 penury** periury **200 advisings. To . . . good a** aduisings, to . . . good; a **216 by oath** oath
3.2. 0 [not marked as a new scene in F] **8 law a** Law; a **9 on** and **26 eat, array** eate away **48 it clutched** clutch'd **74–5 bondage. If . . . patiently, why** bondage if . . . patiently: Why **109 ungenerative** generatiue **147 dearer** deare **214 See** Sea
4.1. 1 BOY [not in F] **49.1** [after line 48 in F] **61 quests** Quest **64 s.d. Enter . . . Isabella** [after line 64 in F]
4.2. 43–7 If . . . thief [assigned in F to Clo.] **58 yare** y'are **60.1** [at line 59 in F] **72 s.d. Enter Duke** [after line 72 in F] **100 This . . . man** [assigned in F to Duke] **Lordship's** Lords **101 DUKE** *Pro.* **120 PROVOST** [not in F]
4.3. 92.1 [at line 91 in F] **93 Varrius** Angelo **100 well** weale
4.4. 6 redeliver reliuer **15–16 proclaimed. Betimes** proclaim'd betimes **19 s.d.** [at line 18 in F]

4.5. 6 Flavius' *Flauia's*
5.1. 14 me we **34 hear!** heere. **173 s.d.** *Enter Mariana* [after line 173 in F] **174 her face** your face **226 promisèd** promis'd **268 s.d.** [at line 267 in F] **288.1** [after line 286 in F] **407 s.d.** *Mariana Maria* **431 confiscation** confutation **488.2** *Juliet Iulietta* **550 that's** that

Troilus and Cressida

Copy text: the Quarto of 1609. As a text seemingly based on Shake-speare's own manuscript, with many unsupplied or imprecise stage directions, mislineation, authorial punctuation, and the like, Q is a suitable copy text, even though the work of the Q compositors (three in number) reduces the reliability of that text's authority even in incidental matters. Substantively, the First Folio text (F) often gives what may perhaps be Shakespeare's later decisions in a manuscript that may also have been put to use in the theater. Some such manuscript was used to annotate a copy of Q for the Folio printers. At the same time one needs to be careful not to include in an edited text those changes in F that appear likely to have been sophistications or compositorial errors. For these limited reasons only, Q serves as copy text for these collation notes, even though many readings that substantively vary between Q and F are decided in favor of F. All adopted readings are from [F] unless otherwise indicated; [eds.] means that the reading is that of some editor since the First Folio. [Fa] refers to the first setting of the Folio text, [Fb] to the second setting. Act and scene divisions are not provided in the Quarto or the Folio. Some bracketed stage directions are from F.

Prologue [F; not in Q] **8 immures** emures [F] **12 barks** [eds.] Barke [F] **17 Antenorides** *Antenonidus* **19 Spar** [eds.] Stirre [F]
1.1. 4 [and elsewhere] Trojan [eds.] Troyan **26 the** [Q, Fa] of the [Fb] **27 [and elsewhere] ye** [eds.] yea **33 When she** [eds.] then she **is she** she is **38 [and elsewhere] Lest** [eds.] Least **55 Pour'st** [eds.] Powrest **55–7 heart / Her . . . voice; / Handlest . . . discourse— oh!—** [eds.] heart: / Her . . . voice, / Handlest . . . discourse: O **63 instead** [eds.] in steed **72 travail** [eds.] trauell **73 on of you** of you **78 not kin** [Fb] kin [Q, Fa] **79–80 what care** what **85 her. For** her for **99 woo** [eds.] woe **100 stubborn-chaste** stubborne, chast **104 resides** reides
1.2. 1 [and throughout] ALEXANDER *Man* **17 they** the **34 struck** [eds.] strooke **36.1** [F; not in Q] **48 ye** [eds.] yea **71 just . . . them; he** [eds.] iust, . . . them he **85 come** eome **87 wit** [eds.] will **117 lift** liste **125 valiantly** valianty **130 the** [eds.] thee **148 pot** por **177 s.d.** [at line 175 in Q] **180 Ilium** llion **189.1** [after line 190 in Q] **192 a man** man **205 man's** man **219 [and elsewhere] Who's** [eds.] Whose [Q, F] **225 [and elsewhere] hear** [eds.] here **236 ne'er** neuer **241.1** *Enter common soldiers* [F; not in Q] **245 i'th'eyes** in the eyes **249 among** amongst **256–7 so forth** such like **260 another** a **One** a man **269 too** two **280 I'll** I wil **281 bring, uncle?** [eds.] bring vncle: [Q] bring Vnkle. [F] **283.1** [F; not in Q] **291 prize** price **296 contents** content
1.3. 0.1 *Sennet* [F; not in Q] **2 the jaundice on** these Iaundies ore **13 every** euer **19 think** call **31 thy godly** the godlike **36 patient** ancient **48 herd** [eds.] heard **breese** Bryze **61 thy** the **67 On . . . ears** (On which heauen rides) knit all the Greekish eares **70–4** [F; not in Q] **75 basis** bases **92 ill . . . evil** influence of euill Planets **110 meets** melts **118 [and elsewhere] lose** [eds.] loose **119 includes** include **128 in** with **137 lives** stands **143 sinew** sinnow **149 awkward** sillie **159 unsquared** vnsquare **164 just** right **188 willed** wild **195 and** our **209 fineness** finesse **212 s.d.** *Tucket* [F; not in Q] **214.1** *Enter Aeneas* [F; not in Q] **219 ears** eyes **221 host** [eds.] heads **236 fame** same **238 Jove's** great *Ioues* **247 affair** affaires **250 him** with him **252 sense** seat **the** that **256 loud** alowd **262 this** his **267 That seeks** And feeds **276 compass** couple **289 or means** a meanes **294 One . . . one** A . . . no **297 this withered brawn** my withered braunes **298 will tell** tell **302 forbid** for-fend **youth** men **304 AGAMEMNON** [F; not in Q] **305 first** sir **309.1** [F; not in Q] **315 This 'tis** [F; not in Q] **324 The**

True the even as as **327 were** weare **333 Yes** Why **334 his honor** those honours **336 this** the **340 wild** vilde **343 indices** [eds.] *indexes* [Q, F] **352 from hence receives the** receiues from hence a **354–6** [F; not in Q] **354 his** [eds.] in his [F] **359 show our foulest wares** First shew foule wares **361–2 yet . . . better** shall exceed, / By shewing the worst first **368 wear** share **370 we** it **373 did** do **377 as the worthier** for the better **388 of it** thereof **391 tar** arre **their** a
2.1. 8 there would would **11 s.d.** [F; not in Q] **14 vinewed'st** [eds.] vnsalted [Q] whinid'st [F] **17 oration** oration without booke **18 learn a** learne **19 o' thy** [eds.] ath thy [Q] **24 a fool** foole **26–7 foot. An** foot, and **27 thee** the **38, 40, 41 THERSITES, AJAX, THERSITES** [F; not in Q] **45 Thou scurvy** you scuruy **55.1** [F; not in Q] **63 I do so** so do I **71 I will** It will **75 I'll** I **88 for a** the **101 an' a** and [Q] if the [F] **out at** **105 your** [eds.] their **nails on their toes** nailes **107 war** wars **111 wit as** as **114 brach** [eds.] brooch **122 fifth** first **130.1** [F; not in Q]
2.2. 3 damage domage **4 travail** trauell **7 struck** [eds.] stroke **14, 15 surety** surely **26 Weigh** Way **27 father** fathers **30 waist** [eds.] waste **33 at** of **34 them. Should . . . father** them should . . . father; **47 Let's** Sets **52 holding** keeping **58 inclinable** attributiue **64 shores** shore **67 chose** choose **70 spoiled** soild **71 sieve** siue **74 of** with **79 stale** pale **82 launched** lansh't **86 noble** worthy **96.1** *Enter . . . ears* Enter Cassandra rauing **97 shriek** shrike **104 old** elders **106 clamor** clamours **120 th'event** [eds.] euent **149 off** of **210 strike** shrike
2.3. 1 THERSITES [not in Q] **19 dependent** depending **21.1** *Enter Patroclus* [F; not in Q] **24 ha'** a **25 wouldst** couldst **31 art** art not **46 thyself** *Thersites* **49 mayst** must **54–9** [F; not in Q] **62–3 commanded of Agamemnon** commanded of the Prouer **68 Patroclus** Come *Patroclus* **69 s.d.** [F; not in Q] **73–4 Now . . . all** [F; not in Q] **73 serpigo** [eds.] Suppeago [F] **78 shent** [eds.] sent [F] sate [Q] **79 appertainments** appertainings **82 so say** say so **87 a** the **88 A word, my lord** [F; not in Q] **98 council that** composure **101.1** *Enter Patroclus* [F; not in Q] **111 Hear** Heere **129 pettish lunes** course, and time [Q] pettish lines [F] **his flows** and flowes **as** and **130 carriage of this action** streame of his commencement **135 Bring** [Q, Fb] ring [Fa] **140 enter you** entertaine **140.1** *Exit Ulysses* [F; not in Q] **151 it** pride **152 clearer, Ajax** cleerer **157 I hate** I do hate **166 Why, will** Why will **179 led** lead **186 do** doth **190 Must** Shall **stale** staule **192 titled** liked **200 this** his **202 pash** push **204 'a** he **211 let** tell **humors** humorous **214 o'** of **218 'twould** two'od **219 'A . . . shares** [assigned in Q to Ajax] **221 He's . . . warm** [assigned in Q to Ajax] **Farce** Force **222 praises** praiers **in; his** his **225 You** Yon **231 thus with us** with vs thus **241 beyond all** all thy **247 bourn** boord **248 Thy** This **255 ULYSSES** *Nest.* **262 cull** call
3.1. 0.1–2 *Music . . . Servant* [F] *Enter Pandarus* [Q] **1 not you** you not **3 [and elsewhere] SERVANT** *Man* **25 mean, friend** mean **31 who's** who is **33 visible** [eds.] inuisible [Q, F] **37 that thou** thou **38 Cressida** *Cressid* **41 There's** theirs **52 Nell, he** *Nel.* he **76 supper you** supper. You **90 poor disposer's** disposer's **106 lord** lad **107 hast** haste **113** [F; not in Q] **117 shaft confounds** shafts confound **120 Oh! Oh!** oh ho [and similarly in 122–5] **148 They're** Their **field** the field **149 woo** woe **151 these** this **159 thee** her
3.2. 3 he stays stayes **3.1** [F; not in Q] **8 a** to a **10 those** these **16 s.d.** [F; not in Q] **22 Swooning** [eds.] Sounding [Q, F] **23 Too subtle-potent** [eds.] To subtill, potent [Q, F] **28.1** [F; not in Q] **33.1** [F; not in Q] **37 unawares** vnwares **38.1** *Pandarus and Cressida* pandar and Cressid **45 thills** filles **61 Cressida** *Cressid* **67 fears** [eds.] teares **80 This is** This **91 crown it. No perfection** louer part no affection **98.1** [F; not in Q] **109 are** be **117 glance that ever—pardon** [eds.] glance; that euer pardon [Q, F] **121 grown** [eds.] grow [F] **131 Cunning** Comming **in** [eds.] from [Q, F] **132 My . . . from me** My very soule of councell **149–50 Where . . . what I** would be gone: / Where is my wit? I know not what I speake **156 might; that** might that **159 aye** age **175 similes, truth** simele's

truth   **179 Yet, after** After   **184 and** or   **197 witness. Here** [eds.]
witnes here [Q, F]   **199 pains** paine   **207 with a bed** [eds.; not in Q, F]
3.3. 0.2 *Calchas Chalcas*   **1 done you** done   **3 to your** to   **4 come** [eds.]
loue   **5 possessions** [eds.] possession   **29 off** of   **43 unplausive**
vnpaulsiue   **55 What, comes** [eds.] What comes [Q, F]   **69.1** *Exit*
[eds.] *Exeunt* [Q, F]   **73 use** [eds.] us'd   **101 shining** ayming   **111 mirrored** [eds.] married   **128 are.** are.   **129 abject** obiect   **141 on** one
142 shrinking shriking   **153 mail** [eds.] male [Q, F]   **156 one** on
159 hedge turne   **161 hindmost** him, most   **162–4 Or ... on** [F; not
in Q]   **163 rear** [eds.] neere [F]   **165 past** passe   **179 give** [eds.] goe
185 Than That   **not stirs** stirs not   **198 grain ... gold** thing
199 th'uncomprehensive deeps the vncomprehensiue depth
225 like a like   **234 we** they   **242 s.d.** *Enter Thersites* [after line 242 in
Q]   **267 ambassador to him** Ambassador   **275 the most** the
279 Grecian [not in Q]   **et cetera. Do** Do   **295–6 o'clock** of the clock
301 but he's but   **o'** of   **306 carry** beare
4.1. 0.1 *with a torch* [F; not in Q]   **0.2** [and elsewhere] *Diomedes*
[eds.] *Diomed* [Q, F]   **5 you** your   **18 But** Lul'd   **22–3 backward.
In humane gentleness,** back-ward, in humane gentlenesse:
39 Calchas' *Calcho's*   **42 do think** beleeue   **46 whereof** wherefore
52 s.d. [F; not in Q]   **54 the soul** soule   **55 merits** deserues   **most**
best   **58 soilure** soyle   **75 Hear** Here   **78 you** they
4.2. 15 gait [eds.] gate   **18 off** of   **21.1** [F; not in Q]   **32–3 Ah, poor
capoccia!** [eds.] a poore *chipochia*,   **35 s.d.** *One knocks* [after line 36
in Q, after 33 in F]   **56 Hoo!** [eds.] Who   **59.1** [F; not in Q]   **65 us;
and for him** him, and   **74 nature** neighbor *Pandar*   **79** CRESSIDA
[not in Q]   **87 wouldst** wouldest   **89–90 knees I beseech you** knees
110.1 [F; not in Q]
4.3. 0.2 and [F; not in Q]
4.4. 6 affection affections   **50 genius so** *Genius*   **51 "Come"** so
54 the root my throate   **58 my love** loue   **64 there's** there is
70 Wear were   **77** [F; not in Q]   **gifts** guift [F]   **78 flowing** swelling
79 person portion   **106 wear** were   **122 zeal** [eds.] seale   **135 I'll** I
139.1–2 *Sound trumpet* [F; not in Q]   **144–8** [F; not in Q]
144 DEIPHOBUS [eds.] *Dio.*   **148 s.d.** [after line 143 in Q, F]
4.5. 0.2 *Nestor* [eds.] *Nester, Calcas* [Q, F]   **2 time ... courage.** [eds.]
time. With starting courage, [Q, F]   **16 toe** too   **38** MENELAUS [eds.]
Patr.   **44 not** nor   **49 too.** [eds.] then. [Q] then? [F]   **60 accosting**
[eds.] a coasting [Q, F]   **64.1** *Exeunt* [F; not in Q]   **66 you** the
74 ACHILLES [eds.; not in Q, F]   **75 disprising** misprising   **95** [F; not
in Q]   **96** AGAMEMNON *Vlises*   **99 in deeds** deeds   **133 Of our rank
feud** [F; not in Q]   **134 drop** day   **162 mine** my   **164 of** all
166–71 [F; not in Q]   **179 Mock ... oath** (Mock not thy affect, the
vntraded earth)   **188 And seen thee scorning** Despising many
189 thy th'   **194 hemmed** shrupd   **200 Let** O let   **207** [F; not in Q]
253 the an   **256 stithied** stichied   **276 Beat ... taborins** To taste
your bounties   **282 on heaven nor on** vpon the heauen nor   **288 As**
But   **293 she loved** my Lord
5.1. 4 core curre   **12 need these** needs this   **14 boy** box   **15 thought**
said   **19 catarrhs** [F; not in Q]   **i'** in   **20 wheezing** whissing
26 mean'st meanes   **31 sarcenet** sacenet   **32 tassel** toslell
51 Here's her's   **54 brother** be   **56 hanging ... leg** at his bare
legge   **58 farced** [eds.] faced [F]   **59 he is** her's   **60 dog**
day   **mule** Moyle   **60 fitchew** Fichooke   **63 not** [F; not in Q]
66.1–3 *Enter ... lights* Enter *Agam: Vlysses, Nest: and Diomed with
lights*   **68 light** lights   **68 s.d.** [F; not in Q]   **71 good** God
77 sewer [eds.] sure   **78 both at once** both   **98 Calchas his** *Calcas*
5.2. 4.1 *Enter ... Ulysses* [F; not in Q]   **5 s.d.** *Enter Cressida* ["*Enter
Cressid*" after "to him" in line 6 in Q]   **11 clef** Cliff   **13** CRESSIDA
[eds.] *Cal.*   **16 should** shall   **35 one** a   **37 pray you** pray   **41 Nay**
Now   **42 distraction** distraction   **48 Why, how now, lord?** How
now my lord?   **49 Adieu, you** you   **57 tickles these** tickles
59 But will Will   **60 la** [eds.] lo   **63 sweet** my   **69** [F; not in Q]
70 CRESSIDA *Troy.*   **83 As I kiss thee** [eds.; continued as Cressida's
speech in Q, F]   **Nay ... me** [eds.; assigned to Diomedes in Q, F]
87 CRESSIDA [F; not in Q]   **92 one's** [eds.] on's [Q] one [F]   **94 By**
And by   **109 s.d.** *Exit* [F; not in Q]   **121 coact** Court   **126 had**

deceptious were deceptions   **137 soil** spoile   **146 is** was   **156 Ariachne's** *Ariachne's* [Qb] *Ariathna's* [Qa]   **161 five** finde   **164 bound**
giuen   **171 much as** [eds.] much
5.3. 14 CASSANDRA *Cres.*   **20–2** [F; not in Q]   **21 give** [eds.] count giue
[F]   **use** [eds.] as [F]   **23** CASSANDRA [F; not in Q]   **29 mean'st**
meanest   **45 mothers** Mother   **58** [F; not in Q]   **85 distraction**
distruction   **90 s.d.** [F; not in Q]   **93 of worth**   **96.1** *Pandarus* [eds.]
Pandar [Q, F]   **104 o' these** [eds.] ath's [Q] o'th's [F]   **112** [F follows
with an alternate version, slightly varied, of 5.10.32–4]
5.4. 0.1 *Alarum* [F, at 5.2.112; not in Q]   **4 young knave's** knaues
17.1 *Enter ... Troilus* [F; not in Q]   **26 art thou** art
5.5. 5 SERVANT *Man*   **5.1** *Enter Agamemnon* [after "proof" in line 5 in
Q]   **7 Margareton** [eds.] *Margaleron* [Q, F]   **11 Epistrophus** [eds.]
Epostropus   **Cedius** [eds.] *Cedus*   **12 Thoas** [eds.] *Thous*   **22 scalèd**
scaling   **schools** [eds.] sculls [Q] sculs [F]   **25 the** a   **41 luck** lust
43 AJAX [F; not in Q]
5.6. 1 AJAX [F; not in Q]   **2** DIOMEDES [F; not in Q]   **7 the** [eds.] thy [Q,
F]   **11.1** *Exit Troilus* [F; not in Q]   **11.2** *Enter Hector* [F; not in Q]
13 ACHILLES [F; not in Q]   **21 s.d.** *Enter Troilus* [eds.; after line 21 in
Q, F]   **26 reck** [eds.] wreake   **thou end** I end
5.7. 1 ACHILLES [F; not in Q]   **8 s.d.** *Exeunt* [eds.] *Exit*   **and** [F; not in
Q]   **10 'Loo** [eds.] lowe   **10–11 double-horned Spartan** [eds.]
double hen'd spartan [Q] double hen'd sparrow [F]   **12 s.d.** *Exeunt*
[eds.] *Exit*   **13** [and throughout scene] MARGARETON [eds.] *Bast.* [Q, F]
5.8. 3 good my   **4.2 his** [F; not in Q]   **11 Now** next, come   **15 part**
prat   **16** MYRMIDON [eds.] *One.* [Q] *Gree.* [F]   **Trojan trumpets**
Troyans trumpet
5.9. 0.1 *Sound retreat* [F; not in Q]   **0.3** *Shout* [F, at the end of scene 8;
not in Q]   **1 shout is that** is this   **3 slain! Achilles!** [F subst.] slaine
Achilles,   **6 a man as good** as good a man
5.10. 0.1 and [F; not in Q]   **2 Never** *Troy.* Neuer   **2.1** [placement as in
F; before line 2 in Q]   **3** TROILUS [F; not in Q]   **7 smite** [eds.] smile
[Q, F]   **20 Cold** Could [Q] Coole [F]   **21 Scare** [eds.] Scarre [Q, F]
21–2 But ... dead [F; not in Q]   **23 yet. You vile abominable tents,**
[F, subst.] yet you proud abhominable tents: [Q]   **33 broker-lackey!**
broker, lacky,   **Ignomy and** ignomyny   **36 world, world, world**
world, world   **39 desired** lou'd   **50 your** my   **51 hold-door**
hold-ore   **56 s.d.** *[Exit]* Exeunt [F; not in Q]

I Henry VI

Copy text: the First Folio. Act divisions are marked in F, except that Act 5
appears at 5.5; scene divisions, marked in Act 3, are otherwise editorially
supplied except as indicated below.
1.1. 57 FIRST MESSENGER *Mess.* [also at line 69]   **60 Rouen** [not in F]
65 [and elsewhere] **Rouen** Roan   **89** SECOND MESSENGER *Mess.*
92 [and elsewhere] **Dauphin** Dolphin   **94 Reignier** *Reynold*   **103** THIRD
MESSENGER *Mes.*   **141 slain? Then I** slaine then? I   **176 steal** send
1.2. 30 bred breed   **47** [and elsewhere] CHARLES *Dolph.*   **63.2** [and
elsewhere] **Pucelle** Puzel   **76 whilst** whilest   **99 five** fine
103.1 [and elsewhere] *la* [Q]   **113 rites** rights   **131 halcyon** *Halcyons*
1.3. 6 FIRST SERVINGMAN *Glost.* [Q]   **1.** *Man* [at line 8, 1. *Man*]
29 Humphrey *Vmpheir*   **30 Peeled** Piel'd   **74** OFFICER [not in F]
1.4. 10 Wont Went   **25 got'st** got's   **27 Duke** Earle   **28 Santrailles**
Santrayle   **29 ransomèd** ransom'd   **33 pilled** pil'd   **63 Glasdale**
Glansdale [also at line 67]   **69.1** *shoot* shot   **89 Bear ... bury it**
[before line 87 in F]   **95 Nero-like** like thee
1.5. 16 hungry starvèd hungry-starued
1.6. 21 pyramid Pyramis   **22 of** or
2.1. 5 A SENTINEL *Sent.*   **7.2 ladders** [F adds "*Their Drummes beating a
Dead March*"; see textual note at 2.2. 6 s.d.]   **29 all together**
altogether   **38** SENTINELS *Sent.*   **54** PUCELLE *Ioane* [also at line 72]
77.1–3 [F has *Exeunt* preceding this s.d.]
2.2. 6.2 their ... march [appears at 2.1.7 in F]   **20 Arc** Acre
38 Auvergne Ouergne
2.4. 1 PLANTAGENET *Yorke* [and thus through Act 3]   **57 law** you
117 wiped whipt   **132 gentlemen** gentle

2.5. 18 FIRST KEEPER *Keeper* [and at line 33] **35** [and elsewhere] PLANTAGENET *Rich.* **71 King Richard** *Richard* **84 Cambridge then,** Cambridge, then **121.1** *Exeunt Exit* **129 mine ill** my will

3.1. 52 SOMERSET [not in F] **53** WARWICK *Som.* **54** SOMERSET [not in F] **74** [F provides an s.p. here, "*King*"] **164 that** that all

3.2. 10 FIRST SOLDIER *Souldier* **13** *Qui là? Che la* **21–2 specify . . . in?** specifie? . . . in. **40.2** *Burgundy Burgonie* [also at lines 42 and 77, etc.] **41 Good** God **73 Good-bye** God b'uy **83 Coeur de Lion's** *Cordelions* **103.1** *Exeunt Exit* **123 gleeks** glikes

3.3. 46–8 foe . . . eyes, Foe, . . . Eyes.

3.4. 27.1 *Manent Manet*

4.1. 3 Exeter, Governor *and Gouernor Exeter* **14 thee** the **48 my Lord** Lord **151 umpire** Vmper **173.1** *Flourish* [at line 181 in F] *Manent Manet* **180 wist** wish

4.2. 3 calls call **15** GENERAL *Cap.*

4.3. 5 Talbot. As . . . along, *Talbot as he march'd along.* **17** [and throughout scene] LUCY 2 *Mes.* [*or Mes.*] **20 waist** waste **36 travel** trauaile **53 lands** Lauds

4.4. 13 Whither Whether **16 legions** Regions **27 Reignier** *Reignard* **31 horse** hoast

4.5. 55.1 *Exeunt Exit*

4.6. 57.1 *Exeunt Exit*

4.7. 18 antic antique **25 whether** whither **63 Wexford** Washford **64 Goodrich** *Goodrig* **89 have them** haue him **94 with them** with him **96 s.d.** *Exeunt Exit*

5.1. 0 [F here reads "*Scena secunda*"]

5.2. 0 [F here reads "*Scoena Tertia*"]

5.3. 57 her his **65** [and elsewhere in scene] **woo** woe **85 random** randon **106 in** iu **179 modestly** modestie **192 And** Mad

5.4. 28 suckedst suck'st **49 Arc** *Aire* **56 enough** enow **74 Machiavel** Macheuile **102 travail** trauell **123** CARDINAL *Win.* **127 breathe** breath **149 compromise** compremize

5.5. 0 [F here reads "*Actus Quintus*"] **60 That most** Most **82 love** Ioue

2 Henry VI

Copy text: the First Folio. Act and scene divisions, missing in F except for "*Actus Primus. Scoena Prima*" at 1.1. 0, are editorially provided.

1.1. 4 Princess Princes **37 s.d.** *kneeling kneel* **56** CARDINAL [Q] *Win.* **57 duchies** *Dutchesse* **72.1** *Exeunt Exit* **72.2** *Manent Manet* **91 had** hath **99 Razing** Racing **107 roast** rost **130** [and elsewhere] GLOUCESTER *Hum.* **166 all together** altogether **167 hoist** hoyse **176 Protector** [Q] Protectors **177.1** *Exeunt Exit* **190 thee** the **206 let's away** lets make hast away **211.1** *Exeunt Exit* **254 in** [Q] in in

1.2. 1 [and elsewhere] DUCHESS *Elia.* **19 hour** thought **22 dream** dreames **38 are** [Q] wer **60.1** *Exit Humphrey* [at line 59 in F]

1.3. 6 FIRST PETITIONER *Peter* **32 master** Mistresse **41 s.d.** *Exeunt Exit* **50 Pole** *Poole* **89 choir** Quier **100** [F has "*Exit*" here] **104 denied** denay'd **142 I'd** [Q] I could **187** [and throughout scene; also, 2.3] HORNER *Armorer* **212–13** [Q; not in F]

1.4. 25 MARGERY JORDAN *Witch* **25 Asnath** Asmath **62** *Aio te Aio* **63** *posse posso*

2.1. 30 Lord-Protectorship Lords Protectorship **48 Cardinal** [*aside to Gloucester*] **I am with you** Cardinall, I am with you [as part of Gloucester's speech] **59** TOWNSMAN *One* [also at line 61] **112 Alban** *Albones* **135 his** [Q] it

2.2. 45 was son was **46 son** Sonnes Sonne

2.3. 3 sins sinne **19 grave** ground **74 apron** Aporne

2.4. 88 too to

3.1. 211 strains strayes **218–19 eyes . . . good,** eyes; . . . good: **222.1** *Exeunt Exit* **328 Bristol** Bristow **333–4 art . . . death; it** art; . . . death, it

3.2. 14.2 Somerset *Suffolke, Somerset* **26 Meg** *Nell* **32.1** *swoons sounds* **75 leper** Leaper **79 Margaret** *Elianor* [also at lines 100 and 120] **113 losing** loosing **116 witch** watch **202 Lest** Least **278** COMMONS [not in F] **308 enemies** [Q] enemy **310 Could** [Q] Would **318 My** [Q] Mine **on** an **332 turn** turnes **391 breathe** breath

3.3. 8 CARDINAL [Q] *Beau.* **10 whe'er** where

4.1. 6 Clip Cleape **7 Breathe** Breath **18** WHITMORE *Lieu.* **48 Jove . . . I** [Q; not in F] **50** SUFFOLK [Q; at line 51 in F] **70** LIEUTENANT **Yes, Pole.** SUFFOLK **Pole?** [Q; not in F] **77 shalt** [Q] shall **85 mother's bleeding** Mother-bleeding **93 are** and **115–16** LIEUTENANT *Walter—/* WHITMORE *Lieu.* Water: W. **117** *Paene* Pine **119** WHITMORE *Wal.* [also at line 143] **133** SUFFOLK [at line 134 in F] **142 s.d.** *Exeunt Exit*

4.2. 33 [and elsewhere] DICK [Q] *But.* ["*Butch.*" or "*Butcher.*"] **34 fall** faile **46** [and elsewhere] SMITH *Weauer* [or "*Wea.*"] **99 an** a **131 this:** this **139.1** *Walter Water* **176.1** *Exeunt Exit*

4.4. 19 have huae **27** FIRST MESSENGER *Mes.* **49** SECOND MESSENGER *Mess.* **58 you be** you

4.5. 0.2 *enter enters*

4.6. 9 SMITH *But.* **13 Zounds** [Q] Come

4.7. 7 HOLLAND *Iohn* [also at line 15] **44 on** [Q] in **63 lose** loose **66 hands** hands? **67 But** Kent **you?** you, **79** BEVIS *Geo.* **86 caudle** Candle **132 s.d.** *Exeunt Exit*

4.8. 12 rebel rabble

4.9. 0.2 *terrace Tarras* **33 calmed** calme

4.10. 5 o'er on **20 waning** warning **24 Zounds** [Q; not in F] **28 I'll** He **46 far** farre **57 God** Ioue

5.1. 109 these thee **111 sons** [Q] sonne **113 for** of **149 bearherd** Berard [also at line 210] **160 lest** least **194 or** and **195** CLIFFORD *Old Clif.* [and at lines 198 and 208] **201 household** [Q] housed **207 to** [Q] io

5.2. 8 [F repeats s.p. "*War*"] **28** *oeuvres eumenes* **31** YOUNG CLIFFORD *Clif.* [also at line 84] **46 lose** loose

5.3. 29 faith [Q] hand

3 Henry VI

Copy text: the First Folio. Act and scene divisions, missing in F except for "*Actus Primus. Scoena Prima*" at 1.1.0, are editorially provided. "[O]"=Octavo.

1.1. 2 YORK *Pl.* [and elsewhere referred to in the s.p. as *Plan.* and *Plant.* as well as *Yorke*] **6–7 himself, . . . abreast,** himselfe . . . a-brest **19 hap** hope **21 I. Victorious . . . York,** I, victorious . . . Yorke. **43 lords. Be** Lords be **69** EXETER [O] *Westm.* **105 Thy** [O] My **107** [and elsewhere] **Dauphin** Dolphin **113** [and elsewhere] **lose** loose **120** NORTHUMBERLAND [O] *Henry* **259 with me** [O] me **261 from** [O] to **273.1** *Flourish* [at beginning of 1.2 in F] *Exeunt Exit*

1.2. 9 [and elsewhere] **Lest** Least **47.1** *a Messenger* [O] *Gabriel* **49** MESSENGER [O] *Gabriel* **75.1** *Exeunt Exit*

1.4. 108 whilst whilest **180.1** *Exeunt* [O] *Exit*

2.1. 94.1 *Montague Mountacute* **113 And . . . thought** [O; not in F] **124 spleen,** Spleene. **131 an idle** [O] a lazie **144 his** [O] the **170 more** moe

2.2. 89 Since *Cla.* Since **130 puts** put's **133** RICHARD [O] *War.* **163** [and elsewhere until 3.2] GEORGE [O] *Cla.*

2.3. 11 [and elsewhere] **Whither** whether

2.5. 54.1–2 [followed in F by "*and a Father that hath kill'd his Sonne at another doore*"] **78.1–2** [F reads: "*Enter Father, bearing of his Sonne*"] **89 stratagems** Stragems **119 E'en** Men

2.6. 6 fall, thy fall. Thy **commixture** [O] Commixtures **8 The common . . . flies** [O; not in F] **19 Had** [O] Hed **60 his** [O] is

3.1. 1 FIRST KEEPER *Sink.* [and similarly, or *Sin.* or *Sinklo*, throughout scene] **5** SECOND KEEPER *Hum.* [and similarly, throughout scene except at 12] **7 scare** scarre **12** SECOND KEEPER *Sink.* **17 wast** was **24 thee, sour adversity** the sower Aduersaries **30 Is** I: **55 thou that** [O] thou

3.2. 1 [and elsewhere] KING EDWARD *King* **8** [and throughout] GLOUCESTER *Rich.* **18** [and throughout] LADY GREY *Wid.* **28 whip me, then** [O] then whip me **123 honorably** [O] honourable **175 rends** rents

3.3. 11 state Seat **78** PRINCE EDWARD *Edw.* **124 eternal** [O] externall **161.1** [after line 160 in F] **228 I'll** [O] I

4.1. 67 QUEEN ELIZABETH [O: *Queen*] *Lady Grey*   93 **thy** [O] the
4.2. 15 **towns** Towne
4.3. 27.8 *fly flyes*   64 s.d. *Exeunt Exit*
4.4. 2 [and throughout scene] QUEEN ELIZABETH [O: *Queen*] *Gray*   4 **What? Loss** What losse   17 **wean** waine
4.5. 4 **stands** stand   8 **Comes** Come
4.6. 55 **goods be** Goods
4.8. 0.2 *Exeter Somerset*   50.1 *A Lancaster! A York! A* Lancaster, A Lancaster
5.1. 78 **an** in
5.3. 22–3 **augmented . . . along.** augmented: . . . along,
5.4. 27 **ragged** raged   46 **Lest** Least
5.5. 38 **thou** the   50 **The Tower** [O] Tower   77 **butcher** [O] butcher *Richard*   90 s.d. *Exeunt* [O] *Exit*
5.6. 7 **reckless** wreaklesse   43 **wast** was't   84 **keep'st** keept'st
5.7. 5 **renowned** [O] Renowne   25 **thou shalt** [O] that shalt   30 QUEEN ELIZABETH [O] *Cla.*   **Thanks** [O] Thanke   38 **Reignier** *Reynard*

Richard III

Copy text: the First Folio, except for two passages, 3.1.1–158 and 5.3.48 to end of play, for which Q1 is copy text. Unless otherwise indicated, the adopted readings are from the First Quarto of 1597 [Q1]. Act and scene divisions are marked in the copy text except as indicated below.

1.1. 1 RICHARD [not in F]   41.1. *Enter . . . Brackenbury* [eds.] *Enter Clarence, and Brackenbury, guarded*   45 **the** th'   52 **for** but   65 **tempers him to this** tempts him to this harsh   75 **to her for his** for her   88 **An 't** and   103 **I I** do   124 **the** this   133 **prey** play
1.2. 27 **life** [eds.] death   38 HALBERDIER [eds.] *Gen.*   39 **stand** Stand'st   78 **of a** of   80 **t'accuse** [eds.] to curse   94 **hand** hands   141 **thee** the   171 **words** word   204 RICHARD [not in F]   205 [not in F]   227.1 *Exeunt* [eds.] *Exit* [also at line 229]   228 RICHARD **Sirs . . . corpse** [not in F]   229.1 *Exeunt Exit*
1.3. 17 **come** comes   **lords** Lord   19 [and elsewhere] STANLEY *Der.*   54 **whom** who   69 [not in F]   109.1 [after line 110 in F]   114 [not in F]   155 **Ah, little** A little   160 **of** off   309 QUEEN ELIZABETH *Mar.*   342 FIRST MURDERER *Vil.* [also at lines 350 and 355]   351 **doers. Be assured** dooers, be assur'd:
1.4. 13 **Thence** There   22 **waters** water   22, 23 **my** mine   25 **Ten** A   39 **seek** find   41 **Which** Who   64 **my lord** Lord   99 s.d. *Exit* [at line 97 in F]   100 **I** we   122 **Faith** [not in F]   126 **Zounds** Come   147 **Zounds** [not in F]   152 **Tut** [not in F]   192 **to have redemption** for any goodnesse   193 [not in F]   240 [not in F]   242 **of** on   269 [in F, printed after line 263]   272 s.d. *Stabs him* [after line 272 in F]
2.1. 0.3. **Buckingham** [eds.] *Buckingham, Wooduill*   5 **in** to   7 **Rivers and Hastings** *Dorset* and *Riuers*   39 **God** heauen   57 **unwittingly** vnwillingly   59 **By** To   68 [F follows with a line: "Of you Lord *Wooduill*, and Lord *Scales* of you"]   93 **but** and   108 **at** and
2.2. 1 BOY *Edw.*   3 [and throughout scene] GIRL [eds.] *Daugh.*   3 **do you** do   26 **his** a   47 **have I** haue   83 **weep** weepes   84–5 **Clarence . . . they** *Clarence* weep, so do not they   87 **Pour** Power   142 **Ludlow** London [also at line 154]   145 [not in F]   145.1 *Manent* [eds.] *Manet*
2.3. 44 **Ensuing** Pursuing [but the catchword on page 184 in F is "Ensuing"]
2.4. 1 **hear** heard   9 **young** good   21 ARCHBISHOP *Car.* [Q1] *Yor.* [F]   65 **death** earth
3.1. 1–158 [based on Q1 as copy text]   2 [and elsewhere] RICHARD *Glo.*   60.1 [bracketed s.d. from F]   111 **With all** withall [Q1]   150.1 [*A sennet*] [from F]   150.2 *Hastings Hast. Dors.*   **Manent** [F2] *manet*
3.2. 20 **councils** Councell   78 **as you do** as
3.3. 1 [not in F]
3.4. 9 **methinks** we thinke   58 [not in F]   79.1 *Exeunt* [at line 78 in F]   *Manent Manet*   82 **raze** rowse
3.5. 4 **wert** were   20 **innocence** Innocencie   34 **Look . . . Mayor** [not in F; after line 26 in Q1]   56 **we** I   **hear** heard   66 **cause** case   74 **meet'st advantage** meetest vantage   104 **Penker** [eds.] *Peuker*   105.1. *Exeunt* [eds.] *Exit*   109 s.d. *Exit Exeunt*

3.7. 7 **insatiate** vnsatiate   20 **mine** my   33 **spake** spoke   40 **wisdoms** wisdome   43 [not in F]   44 RICHARD [not in F]   54 **we'll** we   83 **My lord** [not in F]   125 **her** his [also in lines 126 and 127]   214 **whe'er** where [also in line 229]   219 **Zounds! I'll** we will   220 [not in F]   224 **stone** Stones   240 **Richard** King *Richard*   241 MAYOR and CITIZENS *All*   247 **cousin** Cousins
4.1. 0.1–5. [F: *Enter the Queene, Anne Duchesse of Gloucester, the Duchesse of Yorke, and Marquesse Dorset*]   15 BRACKENBURY *Lieu.* [and at lines 18 and 26]
4.2. 36 **My Lord** [not in F]   72 **there** then   87 **to** vnto   90 **Hereford** Hertford   98–118 **perhaps . . . today** [not in F]
4.3. 0 [scene division not in F]   4 **whom** who   5 **ruthless** ruthfull   13 **Which** And   15 **once** one   20 **gone; with . . . remorse** gone with . . . Remorse,   31 **at** and   33 **thee** the   40 **Breton** Britaine   53 **leads** leds
4.4. 0 [*Scena Tertia* in F]   10 **unblown** vnblowed   39 [not in F]   **o'er over** [Q1]   41 **Harry** [eds.] Husband   45 **holp'st** hop'st   52–3 [lines reversed in F]   64 **Thy** The   112 **weary** wearied   118 **nights . . . days** night . . . day   128 **intestate** intestine   141 **Where** Where't   225 **lanced** [eds.] lanch'd   239 **or** and   268 **would I** I would   284 **This is** this   324 **Of ten** [eds.] Often   364–5 [lines reversed in F, and the s.p. *Queen Elizabeth* is missing]   366 KING RICHARD [not in F]   377 **God** God's Heanens   392 **in** with   396 **o'erpast** repast   417 **fond** found   430.1 *Exit Queen* [at line 429 in F]   431.1 *Enter Ratcliffe* [below line 432 in F]   444 **Ratcliffe** [eds.] *Catesby*   498 FIRST MESSENGER *Mess.*   503 SECOND MESSENGER *Mess.*   506 THIRD MESSENGER *Mess.* [also at lines 509 and 517]   518 FOURTH MESSENGER *Mess.*   534 **tidings** Newes, but
4.5. 0 [*Scena Quarta in* F]
5.1. 11 **is, my lord** is
5.2. 11 **center** Centry   12 **Near** Ne're   17 **swords** men
5.3. 0 [scene not marked in F]   20 **track** Tract   28 **you** [eds.] your   48 ff. [to the end of the play] [copy text is Q1]   54 **sentinels** [F] centinell [Q1]   59 CATESBY [eds.] *Rat.*   79 s.d. [F set [Q1]; also at line 131]   85 **that. The** that the [Q1]   100 **sundered** sundried [Q1]   107.1 [*Richmond remains*] [substantially from F]   119 **stabbed'st** stabst   139 GHOST OF RIVERS *King* [Q1]   141 GHOST OF GREY *Gray* [Q1]   142 GHOST OF VAUGHAN *Vaugh.* [Q1]   145 **Will** Wel [Q1]   145.2–150 [after line 158 in Q1]   151 GHOSTS [F] *Ghost* [Q1]   159 GHOST [not in Q1]   167 GHOST [not in Q1]   176 **fall** [F] fals [Q1]   183 **an** and [Q1]   209 **My** Ratcliffe, my   223 LORDS *Lo.* [Q1]   226, 235 A LORD *Lo.* [Q1]   243 **Richard except**, Richard, except   270.1 *Ratcliffe Rat. & c.*   299 **main** [F] matne [Q1]   301 **boot** bootes [Q1]   304 KING RICHARD [at line 306 ("*King*") in Q1]   324 **Brittany** Brittaine   351 **them! Victory** them victorie [Q1]
5.5. 13 STANLEY [not in Q1]   13 **Ferrers** *Ferri* [Q1]   15 **becomes** become [Q1]   41 s.d. *Exeunt* [F; not in Q1]

King John

Copy text: the First Folio. Act and scene markings are in F except as indicated below.

1.1. 30.1 *Exeunt Exit*   49 s.d. [after line 49 in F]   50 [and elsewhere] BASTARD *Philip*   75 **whe'er** where [also at 2.1.167]   79 **yourself.** your selfe   147 **I** It   188 **'Tis too** 'Tis two   189 **conversion. Now** conuersion, now   208 **smack** smoake   219.1 [after line 221 in F]   237 **he get** get   **me! Sir** me sir   257 **Thou** That
2.1. 0 [here F reads "*Scaena Secunda*"]   1 KING PHILIP *Lewis* [also at line 18]   37 **work. Our** worke our   63 **Ate** Ace   75.1 *Drum beats* [after line 77 in F]   89 [and elsewhere] KING PHILIP *Fran.*   106 **Geoffrey's. In** *Geffreyes* in   113 **breast** beast   120 [and elsewhere] ELEANOR *Queen*   127 **John in manners—** *Iohn*, in manners   144 **shows** shooes   149 **Philip** *Lewis*   150 KING PHILIP *Lew.*   152 **Anjou** *Angiers*   166 ELEANOR *Qu. Mo.*   187 **plague; her sin** plague her sinne: 215 **Confronts your** Comfort yours   232 **in, your** in. Your   252 **invulnerable** involuerable   259 **roundure** rounder   325 [and throughout remainder of scene] CITIZEN *Hubert* (or *Hub.*)   335 **run**

rome   362 **Who's** whose [also at 5.6.1]   368 CITIZEN *Fra.*
371 **Kinged** Kings   463 **cannon: fire** Cannon fire,   469 ELEANOR *Old Qu.*   488 **Anjou** *Angiers*   497 [and elsewhere] LEWIS *Dol.*
534 **well. Young** well young   540 **rites** rights   572 **lose** loose
3.1. 0 [here F reads "*Actus Secundus*"]   74 [following this line, F reads "*Actus Tertius, Scaena prima*"]   74.3 **Austria** *Austria, Constance*
110 **day** daies   148 **task** tast   155 **God** heauen   185 **too. When . . . right,** too, when . . . right.   196 **it** that   259 **chafèd** cased   283 **oath. The** oath the   317 [and elsewhere] LEWIS *Dolph.*   323 KING JOHN *Eng.*
3.2. 0. [F reads "*Scaena Secunda*"]   4.1 *Enter . . . Hubert* [after line 3 in F]   10.1 *Exeunt Exit*
3.3. 0. [scene not marked in F]
3.4. 0. [here F reads "*Scaena Tertia*"]   0.2 *Pandulph Pandulpho*
2 **armada** Armado   44 **not holy** holy   64 **friends** fiends
110 **world's** words   182 **make** makes
4.1. 6 FIRST EXECUTIONER *Exec.* [also at line 85]   7 **scruples! Fear** scruples feare   50 **lain** lyen   63 **his** this   80 **wince** winch   91 **mote** moth   120 **mercy-lacking** mercy, lacking
4.2. 1 **again crowned** against crown'd   42 **when** then   60–2 **exercise….occasions, let** exercise, . . . occasions: let   73 **Doth** Do
105.1 *Enter Messenger* [at line 103 in F]   143 **traveled** trauail'd
247 **blood and breath,** blood, and breathe   261 **haste** hast [also at line 269]
4.3. 33 **man** mans   142–3 **up! . . . royalty,** vp, . . . Royaltie?   155 **cincture** center   159.1 *Exeunt Exit*
5.1. 0 [here F reads "*Actus Quartus, Scaena prima*"]
5.2. 16 **metal** mettle   26 **Were** Was   36 **grapple** cripple   43 **hast thou** hast   63.1 *Pandulph Pandulpho*   133 **unhaired** vn-heard   135 **these** this   145 **his** this
5.3. 8 [and elsewhere] **Swinestead** *Swinsted*
5.5. 7 **wound** woon'd
5.6. 13 **eyeless** endles
5.7. 17 **mind** winde   21 **cygnet** Symet   60 **God** heauen   108 **give you** giue

Richard II

Copy text: the First Quarto of 1597 as press-corrected in all four extant copies [Q1]; and, for the deposition scene, 4.1. 155–321, the First Folio. Act and scene divisions, absent in Q1, are from F except that F provides no scene marking at 5.4 and labels 5.5 and 5.6 as "*Scaena Quarta*" and "*Scaena Quinta*," respectively.

1.1. 15 **presence. Face** presence face   19.1 [and throughout] *Bolingbroke Bullingbrooke*   118 **by my** [F] by   139 **But** Ah but
152 **gentlemen** [F] gentleman   162–3 **Harry, when? / Obedience bids** Harry? when obedience bids. / Obedience bids   176 **gage. My** gage, my   178 **reputation; that** Reputation that   192 **parle** parlee
205.1 *Exeunt Exit*
1.2. 25 **him. Thou** him, thou   42 **alas** [not in Q]   47 **sit** [F] set
48 **butcher** [Qb, F] butchers [Qa]   58 **it** [Q2–5, F] is   59 **empty** [Qb, F] emptines, [Qa]   60 **begun** begone   70 **hear** [F] cheere
1.3. 15 **thee** the   33 **comest** [Q5] comes   58 **thee** the   104 FIRST HERALD *Herald*   108 **his God** [F] God   128 **civil** [Qb, F] cruel [Qa]
133 **Draws** [Qb] Draw [Qa]   136 **wrathful iron** [Qb, F] harsh resounding [Qa]   172 **then but** [F] but   180 **you owe** [F] y'owe
193 **far** farre   222 **night** [Q4–5, F] nightes   239 **had it** had't
241 **sought** ought   269 **world** world:
1.4. 0.1 **Bagot** [F] *Bushie*   20 **our cousin,** [F] our Coosens   23 **Bagot here, and Green** [Q6; not in Q1]   27 **What** [Qb, F] With [Qa]
47 **hand. If** hand if   52.1 *Enter Bushy* [F] *Enter Bushie with newes*
53 **Bushy, what news** [F; not in Q1]   65 ALL [not in Q1]
2.1. 15 **life's** liues   18 **fond** found   30 [and elsewhere] **lose** loose
48 **as a** [Q4–5, F] as   68.1–2 [after line 70 in Q1]   70 **reined** ragde
102 **encagèd** [F] inraged   113 **not** not, not   124 **brother** brothers
156 **kerns** [Qb, F] kerne   161 **coin** [Qb, F] coines [Qa]   168 **my** [Qb, F] mine   177 **the** [F] a   209 **seize** cease   239 **more** mo   257 **King's**

[Q3–5, F] King   277 **Port le Blanc** le Port Blan   278 **Brittany** Brittaine [also in 285]   284 **Coint** Coines
2.2. 19 **Show** [Q6, F] Shows [Qa]   31 **though** [Q2–5, F] thought
53 **Harry** H.
2.3. 9 **Cotswold** Cotshall   30 **Lordship** Lo: 36 **Hereford** [Q3–5, F] Herefords   75 **raze** race   99 **the lord** [F] Lord   164 [and elsewhere] **Bristol** Bristow
2.4. 1 WELSH CAPTAIN *Welsh* [also at line 7]
3.2. 32 **succor** succors   40 **boldly** bouldy   72 **O'erthrows** [F] Ouerthrowes   86 **name! A** name a   170 **through** [Q2–5, F] thorough
3.3. 13 **brief with you** [F] briefe   31 **lord** [F] Lords   59 **rain** raigne.   60 **waters—on** water's on   100 **pastures'** pastors   119 **a prince and** princesse   127 **ourself** our selues
3.4. 11 **joy** griefe   26 **pins** [F] pines   27 **state, for** state for   28 **change; woe** change woe   29 **apricots** Aphricokes   34 **too** [F] two   48 **hath** htah   55 **seized** ceasde   57 **We at** at   80 **Cam'st** [Q2–5, F] Canst
4.1. 23 **him** [Q3–5, F] them   44 **Fitzwater** [F] Fitzwaters   55 **As** As it   56 **sun to sun** sinne to sinne   63 **true. You** true you   77 **my bond** [Q3–5, F] bond   110 **thee** [Q2–5, F] the   146 **you** yon   155–321 [This deposition scene is based on the First Folio text; Q1 has only: "Let it be so, and loe on wednesday next, / We solemnly proclaime our Coronation, / Lords be ready all." Unless otherwise indicated all the departures in F from lines 155–321 are taken from Q4.]   184 **and on on**   252 **and a**
256 **Nor** No, nor   297 **manners** manner   321.2 *Carlisle Caleil*
5.1. 11 **model** modle   41 **thee** [Q2–5, F] the   84 NORTHUMBERLAND [F] *King*
5.2. 2 **off** [F] of   11 **thee** [F] the [also at lines 17 and 94]   78 **my troth** by my troth   94 **thee the**   116 **An** And
5.3. 0.1 *King the King*   10 **While** Which   31 **the** my   36 **I may** [Q2–5, F] May   68 **And** An   75 **shrill-voiced** shril voice   111 KING HENRY *yorke*   135–6 **With . . . him** I pardon him with al my heart
5.4. 0.1 *Enter* [F] *Manet*   **Exton** *Exton, etc.*
5.5. 20 **through** [F] thorow   22 **cannot, die** cannot die   27 **sit** [Q3–5, F] set   33 **treason makes** treasons make   55 **sounds that tell** sound that telles   56 **that** which   58 **hours, and times** times, and houres
5.6. 8 **Salisbury, Spencer** [F] Oxford, Salisbury   12.1 *Fitzwater Fitzwaters*   43 **through the** [F] through

1 Henry IV

Copy text: the first complete Quarto of 1598 [Q1]; and, for 1.3.201 through 2.2.110, the fragment of an earlier Quarto [Q0]. The act and scene divisions, missing in Q0 and Q1, are based on F except that F provides no break at 5.3.

1.1. 22 **levy** leauy   39 **Herdfordshire** Herdforshire   62 **a dear** deere   69 **blood, did** bloud. Did   70 **plains. Of** plaines, of   76 **In faith, it is** [assigned in Q1 to King]
1.2. 16 **king** a king   33 **proof, now:** proofe. Now   78 **similes** smiles   154 **thou** the   158 **Peto, Bardolph** Haruey, Rossill
1.3. 12 **too** to,   137 [and throughout] **Bolingbroke** Bullingbrooke   194 **good night** god-night   201 HOTSPUR [missing in Q0–Q4]   222 **holler** hollow   238 **whipped** [Q1] whip [Q0]
2.1. 34 FIRST CARRIER *Car.*   48.1 [below line 47 in Q0]   56 **Weald** wild   70 **Trojans** Troyans
2.2. 0.1 **Poins, Peto, and** *Poines, and Peto &c*   12 **square** squire   16 **two-and-twenty** xxii: 20 **Bardolph** Bardol [and thus, or "Bardoll," throughout the play]   34 **mine** [Q1] my [Q0]   42 **Go hang** [F] Hang [Q0]   51 BARDOLPH **What news** [all assigned as continuation of Poins's speech in line 50]   52 GADSHILL *Bar.*   78 FIRST TRAVELER *Trauel.*   82 TRAVELERS *Trauel.*   86 TRAVELERS *Tra.*
2.3. 1 HOTSPUR [not in Q1]   4 **In** the   48 **thee** the   69 **A roan** Roane
2.4. 33 **precedent** present   36 POINS *Prin.*   121 **sun's** soanes
171 PRINCE *Gad*   172 GADSHILL *Ross.* [also at lines 174 and 178]
226 **keech** catch   242 **eel-skin** elsskin   322.1 [after line 321 in Q1]
337 **Owen** O   390 **tristful** trustfull   398 **yet** so   468 **lean** lane

518 Good God [also at line 519]   **526 s.d.** *pockets* pocket   **530** PETO [not in Q1]   **535** PRINCE [not in Q1]
3.1. 55 coz coose [also at line 75]   **97 cantle** scantle   **126 meter** miter   **129 on** an   **183 Loseth** Looseth   **261 hot Lord** Hot. Lord
3.2. 32 Council counsell   **59 won** wan   **84 gorged** gordge   **96 then** than   **145 northern** Northren   **161.1** [after line 162 in Q1]
3.3. 35 that's that   **57 tithe** tight   **119 no thing** nothing   **135 owed** ought   **173 guests** ghesse   **200 o'clock** of clocke
4.1. 1 [and elsewhere] HOTSPUR *Per.*   **20 lord** mind   **55 is** tis   **96 doffed** daft   **105 cuisses** cushes   **108 dropped** drop   **116 altar** altars   **123 ne'er** neare   **126 cannot** can   **127 yet** it   **134 merrily** merely
4.2. 3 Coldfield cop-hill   **15 yeomen's** Yeomans   **31 feazed** fazd   **33–4 tattered** tottered   **80 s.d.** *Exit Exeunt*
4.3. 23 horse horses   **74 heirs . . . followed** heires, as Pages followed   **84 country's** Countrey
4.4. 0.1 [and throughout] *Michael Mighell*   **18 o'erruled** ouerrulde   **36 not, ere** not ere   **37 power** he power, he
5.1. 0.2 *Lancaster Lancaster, Earle of Westmerland*   **2 bosky** bulky   **3 southern** Southren   **88 off** of   **138 will** it wil
5.2. 3 undone vnder one   **8 Suspicion** Supposition   **12 merrily** merely   **25.1** *Hotspur Percy*   **79** FIRST MESSENGER *Mes.*   **89** SECOND MESSENGER *Mes.*   **94–5 withal / . . . day.** withall. / . . . day,
5.3. 1 in the in   **22 A** Ah   **35–6 ragamuffins** rag of Muffins
5.4. 4 [and elsewhere] LANCASTER *P. John*   **68 Nor** Now   **76.1** *who he*   **92 enough. This** inough, this   **thee** thee
5.5. 36 bend you bend, you

2 Henry IV

Copy text: the Quarto of 1600, of which 2.4.340 through 3.2.104 exists in two states: the original printing by Valentine Sims [Qa], and a second version with six reset pages [Qb] that had been expanded to include 3.1, inadvertently omitted from Qa. Qa is the copy text for those portions that were reset, Qb for 3.1 itself. In addition, the First Folio is copy text for certain passages excised from Q, as indicated below. The act and scene divisions, missing in Q, are based on F, except that F labels 1.1 as "Scena Secunda," and so throughout Act 1; omits scene markings at 4.2, 4.3, and 4.5; and labels 4.4 as "Scena Secunda."
The Actors' Names [taken from F, at the end of the play]
Induction. 1 RUMOR [not in Q]   **35 hold** hole   **36 Where** [F] When   **40 s.d.** *Rumor Rumours*
1.1. 7 s.d. [and elsewhere] *Northumberland Earle*   **27.1** [at lines 25–6 in Q]   **96 slain, say so** [F] slaine   **126 Too** [F] So   **161** LORD BARDOLPH *Vmfr.*   **162** [assigned to *Bard.* in Q and F]   **164 Lean on your** [F] Leaue on you   **o'er** ore,   **165 passion,** passion   **166–179; 189–209** [F; not in Q]   **178 brought** bring [F]   **183 ventured, for . . . proposed** venturd for . . . proposde,   **201–2 religion.... thoughts,** Religion, . . . Thoughts:
1.2. 1 [and elsewhere] FALSTAFF *Iohn* [or *sir Iohn*]   **8 tends** [F] intends   **22 one of** [F] one off   **31** [and elsewhere] PAGE *Boy*   **36 rascally** [F] rascall: **48 Where's** Bardolph [F; in Q, follows "through it" in line 47]   **49 into** [F] in   **86 me so?** me, so   **87 me?** If me, if   **96 age** [F] an ague   **119** FALSTAFF [F] *Old.*   **142 waist slenderer** [F] waste slender   **159 on** [F] in   **168–9 bearward** Berod   **171 this** [F] his   **171–2 them, are** [F] the one   **177** [and elsewhere] CHIEF JUSTICE *Lo.*   **192 him! For** him for   **ear** yeere   **201–2 you and Prince Harry** [F] you
1.3. 0.2 *Hastings Hastings, Fauconbridge*   **1** [and elsewhere] ARCHBISHOP *Bishop*   **5** MOWBRAY *Marsh.*   **21–4, 36–55, 85–108** [F; not in Q]   **26 case** [F] cause   **28 on** [F] and   **29 with** [F] in   **58 one** [F] on   **59 through** [F] thorough   **66 a** [F] so   **71 Are** [F] And   **78 not** [F] not to   **79 To French** French   **84 'gainst** [F] against   **109** MOWBRAY [F] *Bish.*
2.1. 0.1–2 *two officers* [F] *an Officer or two*   **21 vice** [F] view   **25 continuantly** [F] continually   **43 Sir John, I** [F] I   **71–2 all, all** [F] al   **78 Fie, what** [F] what   **102 mad** [F] made   **117 done** [F] done with   **143 German** Iarman   **145 tapestries** [F] tapestrie   **163.1 Exeunt** exit

[after line 160 in Q]   **167, 171** GOWER *Mess.*   **167 Basingstoke** [F] Billingsgate
2.2. 0.1 *Poins Poynes, sir Iohn Russel, with other*   **15 viz.** [F] with   **16 ones** [F] once   **22 made a shift to eat** [F] eate   **75 e'en now** enow   **81 rabbit** [F] rabble   **90 him be** [F] him   **109 conceive. The** conceiue the   **110 borrower's** borowed   **118 Sure he** [F] He sure   **119** PRINCE [reads] [not in Q or F]   **126 familiars** [F] family   **149 heifers** Heicfors   **166 prince** pince
2.3. 5 [and elsewhere] LADY NORTHUMBERLAND *Wife*   **9** [and elsewhere] LADY PERCY *Kate*   **11 endeared** [F] endeere   **23–45 He . . . grave** [F; not in Q]
2.4. 0.1 *Drawer Drawer or two*   **4** SECOND DRAWER *Draw.*   **12.1** [below line 18 in Q]   **13** THIRD DRAWER *Dra.* [also at line 19]   **21** SECOND DRAWER [F] *Francis*   **22** [and elsewhere] HOSTESS *Quickly*   **30** [and elsewhere] DOLL *Tere.*   **43–4 them; I** [F] I   **50 know; to** know to   **63** DOLL *Dorothy*   **106** DOLL *Teresh.*   **108.1** BOY *Bardolfes boy*   **173 Die men** [F] Men   **190 Quoit** Quaite   **197 Untwine** vntwinde   **216 Ah, rogue** a rogue   **220 A rascally** Ah rascally   **253 the scales** [F] scales   **254 avoirdupois** haber de poiz   **259 poll** poule   **266 master's** [F] master   **276 It** [F] a   **279 so** [F] to   **295 light flesh** light, flesh   **301 even now** [F] now   **314 Not? To** Not to   **341–91** [copy text for this passage is Qa]   **382.1 Exit** [Qb; not in Qa]
3.1 [this scene appears in Qb, not in Qa]   **18 mast** [F] masse   **22 billows** [F] pillowes   **26 thy** [F] them   **27 sea-boy** [F] season   **36 letters** letter   **59 years** [F] yeare   **81 nature** [F] natures   **85 beginnings** [F] beginning
3.2. 1–104 [copy text for this passage is Qa]   **23 bona-robas** [F] bona robes   **39 Stamford** [F] Samforth   **45 fine** [Qb, F] fiue   **56** SHALLOW *Bardolfe* [Qa uncorr.; not in Qa corr. or Qb]   **67–8 accommodated** [F] accommodate   **82** SHALLOW *Iust.* [Qa]   **87 Surecard** [F] Soccard   **111** [Q prints as s.d.: *"Iohn prickes him"*]   **144 for his** [F] for   **175 prick me** [F] pricke   **195–6 good . . . that** [F] master Shallow   **250 Shadow** Sadow   **271 traverse** trauers   **272 Thus, thus, thus** [F] thas, thas, thas   **287 will** wooll   **299–331 On . . . end** [this speech assigned in Q to Shallow]   **312 invisible** inuincible   **314 ever** [F] ouer   **324 eelskin** [F, Q corr.] eele-shin [Q uncorr.]
4.1. 1 [and elsewhere] ARCHBISHOP *Bish.*   **9 tenor** tenure   **12 could** [F, Q corr.] would [Q uncorr.]   **30 Then, my lord** [F, Q corr.; not in Q uncorr.]   **34 rags** rage   **36 appeared** appeare   **45 figure** [F, Q corr.] figures [Q uncorr.]   **54 Briefly to this end: we** Briefly, to this end we   **55–79** [F; not in Q]   **93, 95 And . . . edge, To . . . cruelty** [Q uncorr.; not in Q corr. or F]   **103–39 O my . . . King** [F; not in Q]   **116 force** forc'd [F]   **139 indeed** and did [F]   **169–70 grievances . . . redressed,** grieuances, . . . redrest.   **175 to our** [F] our   **180 And** At   **182.1** [after "Which . . . it" in Q]   **185 not that.** not, that
4.2. 0.1 [appears below 4.1.226 in Q]   **8 Than** [F] That   **man** [F] man talking   **19 imagined** imagine   **24 Employ** [F] Imply   **25–6 name, / In deeds dishonorable? you** name: / In deedes dishonorable you   **48 this** [F] his   **67** PRINCE JOHN [F; not in Q]   **69** HASTINGS [F] *Prince*   **97.1** [at line 96 in Q]   **117 and such acts as yours** [F; not in Q]   **122 these traitors** [F] this traitour
4.3. 0.1–2 [Q: *"Alarum Enter Falstaffe excursions"*]   **25.1 retreat** [below line 23 in Q]   **41 I came** [F] there cosin, I came   **85 had but** had
4.4. 0.1 Warwick *Warwike, Kent*   **32 meting** [F] meeting   **51** [and elsewhere] CLARENCE *Tho.*   **52 Canst thou tell that** [F; not in Q]   **80 s.d. Enter Westmorland** [after line 80 in Q]   **93 s.d.** [after line 93 in Q]   **94 heaven** [F] heauens   **104 write** [F] wet   **letters** [F] termes   **112** [and elsewhere] GLOUCESTER *Hum.*   **120 and will break out** [F; not in Q]   **132 Softly, pray** [F; not in Q]
4.5. 1 KING [not in Q]   **13 altered** [F, Q corr.] vttred [Q uncorr.]   **48.1** [after line 47 in Q]   **75 thighs** [F] thigh   **78.1** [at line 81 in Q]   **80 have hands** [Q] hath [F]   **87.1** [at line 86 in Q]   **90** PRINCE *Harry*   **106 Which** [F] Whom   **147–8 bending.... me, when** bending, . . . me. When   **159 worst of** [F] worse then   **160 carat, is** [F] karrat   **176 Oh, my son** [F; not in Q]   **177 it in** [F] in   **203 my** thy   **219 My**

gracious liege [F; not in Q]   225 [and elsewhere] PRINCE JOHN *Lanc.*
5.1. 13 headland hade land   23 Hinckley [F] Hunkly   56 all my [F] my   65 of him [F] him
5.2. 0.1–2 [Q: "*Enter Warwike, duke Humphrey, L. chiefe Iustice, Thomas Clarence, Prince, Iohn Westmrland*"]   13.3 *Westmorland* [at 0.s.d. in Q]   21 GLOUCESTER, CLARENCE *Prin. ambo*   38–9 remission . . . me, remission, . . . me.   44 [and elsewhere] KING *Prince*   46 mix mixt   62 PRINCES *Bro.*   112 justice." You Iustice you   127 raze race   145 s.d. *Exeunt exit*
5.3. 5–6 a goodly . . . a rich goodly . . . rich   47 thee the   66 that. 'A that a   70 s.d. [at line 68 in Q]   83.1 [at line 82 in Q]   93 i' thy ith thy   103 Cophetua Couetua   128 knighthood [F] Knight   144.1 *Exeunt exit*
5.4. 0.1 *Beadle Sincklo*   4 [and throughout scene] BEADLE *Sincklo*   7 [and throughout scene] DOLL [F] *Whoore*   11 He [F] I
5.5. 1 FIRST GROOM 1 [and similarly in lines 2 and 3]   15 SHALLOW [F] *Pist.*   17, 19 SHALLOW *Pist.* [Q, F]   24 FALSTAFF [F; not in Q]   28 all in in   97 *spero me* [F] *spero* [Q]   97.1–2 [after line 96 Q]
Epilogue 23 before [F; not in Q]   30 died a [F] died   32–3 and so . . . queen [F; placed after line 15 in Q]

Henry V

Copy text: the First Folio. Act and scene divisions are for the most part editorially supplied; F marks "*Actus Secundus*" at Act 3, "*Actus Tertius*" at Act 4, "*Actus Quartus*" at 4.7, and "*Actus Quintus*" at Act 5.
Prologue. 1 CHORUS [not in F; also in prologues to other acts]
1.2. 38 *succedant* succedaul   45 Elbe Elue [also at line 52]   76 [and elsewhere] Lewis *Lewes*   82 Ermengard *Ermengare*   90–1 day, / Howbeit day. / Howbeit,   115 ELY *Bish.*   131 blood Bloods.   163 her their   166 A LORD *Bish. Ely*   197 majesty Maiesties   212 End [Q] And   221 [and elsewhere] Dauphin Dolphin   237 FIRST AMBASSADOR *Amb.* [also at line 245]   310.1 *Flourish* [at the beginning of 2.0 in F]
2.1. 23 mare [Q] name   28 NYM [Q; not in F]   42, 43 Iceland Island   73 thee defy [Q] defie thee   80 enough enough to   83 you your   105–6 [Q; not in F]   betting beating [Q]   116 that's that
2.2. 29 GREY *Kni.*   87 furnish him [Q] furnish   107 a an   108 whoop hoope   114 All And   139 mark the make thee   140 suspicion . . . thee; suspition, . . . thee.   147 Henry [Q] *Thomas*   148 Masham [Q] *Marsham*   159 Which I Which   176 have sought [Q] sought   181.1 *Exeunt Exit*
2.3. 16–17 'a babbled a Table   24 upward vp-peer'd   32 HOSTESS *Woman*   48 word world
2.4. 0.2 *Brittany Britaine*   1 [and elsewhere] FRENCH KING *King*   132 Louvre Louer   146.1 *Flourish* [at the beginning of 3.0 in F]
3.0. 6 fanning fayning   17 [and elsewhere in scene] Harfleur Harflew   35 eke eech
3.1. 7 conjure commune   17 noblest Noblish   24 men me   32 Straining Straying
3.2. 25 runs wins   67 [and elsewhere in scene] FLUELLEN *Welch*   82 [and elsewhere in scene] JAMY *Scot*   87 [and elsewhere in scene] MACMORRIS *Irish*   102 quite quit   112 Chrish Christ
3.3. 32 heady headly   35 Defile Desire   43 [here F has s.d. "*Enter Gouernour*"]   54 all. For all for
3.4. 2 parles *parlas* [throughout the play, the French has been somewhat modernized, besides the emendations listed here]   7 Elle *il*   8 Et les doigts [assigned to Alice in F]   9 ALICE *Kat.*   les doigts *e doyt*   10 souviendrai *souemeray*   12 KATHARINE *Alice*   13 j'ai *Kath. I'ay*   14 les *le*   16 Nous [not in F]   40 pas déjà *y desia*   42 Non *Nome*   46 Sauf *Sans*   51 les *le* [also in line 52]
3.5. 11 *de du*   26 "Poor" may Poore   43 Vaudemont Vandemont   45 Foix . . . Boucicault *Loys, Lestrale, Bouciquall*   46 knights Kings
3.6. 31 her [Q] his   37 is make [Q] makes   111–12 lenity Leuitie
3.7. 12 pasterns postures   14 *qui a* ches   59 lief liue   65 *et est* truie leuye

4.0. 16 name nam'd   20 cripple creeple   27 Presenteth Presented
4.1. 3 Good God   95 Thomas *Iohn*   158 deaths [Q] death   propose purpose   227 s.d. *Exeunt Exit* [at line 222 in F]   243 What is What? is   adoration Odoration   273 Hyperion *Hiperio*   289 reck'ning ere . . . numbers reckning of . . . numbers: 307 friends friend
4.2. 4 eaux ewes   6 Cieux Cein   11 dout doubt   47 drooping dropping   49 gimmaled lymold   52 all impatient all, impatient
4.3. 12 [placed after line 14 in F]   48 [Q; not in F]   124 'em vm
4.4. 15 Or for   36 *à cette heure* asture   37 *couper couppes*   54 *l'avez* layt a   57 *remercîments* remerciou   58 *j'ai tombé* Ie intombe   59 *très-distinguè* tres distinie   68 *Suivez-vous* Saaue vous
4.5. 2 *perdu . . . perdu* perdia . . . perdie   3 *Mort de* Mor Dieu   16 by a [Q] a base   24.1 *Exeunt Exit*
4.6. 34 mistful mixtfull   38 s.d. *Exeunt Exit*
4.7. 22 e'en in   69 [and elsewhere in this scene] MONTJOY *Her.*   77 the with   109 countryman Countrymen   114 God Good   123 'a live aliue   126 'a lived aliue   161 [and elsewhere] an't and
4.8. 77 Boucicault *Bouchiquald*   99 Foix *Foyes*   100 Vaudemont *Vandemont*   Lestrelles *Lestrale*   104 Keighley *Ketly*   110–11 loss / On . . . other? losse? / On . . . other,   113 we me   121 in my [Q] my   122 rites Rights
5.0. 29 but but by
5.1. 39 By Jesu [Q] I say   69 begun began   88 swear swore
5.2. 1 [and elsewhere] KING *King Henry*   12 [and throughout scene] QUEEN ISABEL *Quee.*   12 England Ireland   21 [also elsewhere] KING HENRY *Eng.*   45 fumitory Femetary   50 all withall   61 diffused defus'd   72 tenors Tenures   77 cursitory curselarie   93 Haply Happily   98 s.d. *Manent Manet*   114 [and elsewhere] ALICE *Lady*   190 meilleur melieus   255 grandeur grandeus   261 noces nopcese   264 les le   265 baiser buisse   267 entend entendre   323 hath never hath   332 then in in   364 paction Pation
Epilogue CHORUS [not in F]

Henry VIII

Copy text: the First Folio. Act and scene divisions are marked in the Folio except as indicated below.
1.1. 42–5 All . . . function [assigned in F to Buckingham]   47 as you guess [assigned in F to Norfolk]   63 web, 'a Web. O   64 way— way   69–70 that? . . . hell, the that, . . . Hell? The   79 council out, Councell, out   115 [and elsewhere] WOLSEY *Car.*   120 venom venom'd   200 Hereford Hertford   219 Perk *Pecke*   chancellor Councellour   221 Nicholas *Michael*   226 lord Lords
1.2. 8.1–3 A noise . . . Suffolk [F: *A noyse within crying roome for the Queene, vsher'd by the Duke of Norfolke. Enter the Queene, Norfolke and Suffolke: she kneels.*] [etc.]   9 [and elsewhere] KATHARINE *Queen*   36 to too   67 business basenesse   156 feared feare   164 confession's Commissions   170 To gain To   180 To For this to   190 Bulmer *Blumer*
1.3. 13 Or A   15 s.d. [after "*Lovell*" in line 16 in F]   34 oui wee   47 [and occasionally elsewhere] Sandys *Sands*   59 wherewithal: in him wherewithall in him;   66 [and at 1.4. 0.5 and elsewhere] Guildford *Guilford*
1.4. 50 s.d. [after line 49 in F]   68–9 assembly . . . here, they assembly, . . . heere they   82.1 *Whisper* [at "surrender it" in F]
2.1. 18 have him   20 Perk *Pecke*   41 attainder Attendure   86 mark make
2.2. 1 CHAMBERLAIN [not in F]   104 commanding, you commanding. You
2.3. 61 of you of you, to you   81 s.d. [after line 80 in F]
2.4. 7 come into the court & c [also in line 10]   11 KATHARINE [not in F]   125 GRIFFITH *Gent. Ush.*   131 s.d. *Exeunt Exit*   172 A And   217 summons. Unsolicited Summons vnsolicited.   237 return. With my approach, returne, with my approach:
3.1. 3 GENTLEWOMAN [not in F]   23 s.d. *Campeius Campian*   61 your our   83 profit. Can profit can   119 he's ha's
3.2. 143 glad gald   172 filed fill'd   234 commission, lords? Commission? Lords,   240 coarse course   293 Who Whom   344 Chattels Castles

4.1. 20 SECOND GENTLEMAN 1 **34 Kimbolton** Kymmalton **55** FIRST GENTLEMAN [not in F] **101 Stokesley** Stokeley
4.2. 4 led'st lead'st **7 think** thanke
5.1. 37 time Lime **42 you, I think—I** you) I thinke I **55.1** *Exeunt Exit* [after line 54 in F] **78.2** *Enter . . . Denny* [after line 79 in F] **139 precipice** Precepit **140 woo** woe **157** LOVELL *Gent. within*
5.2. s.d. *Enter* [*Door-*]*keeper* [after "Sure you know me?" in F] **8 piece** Peere
5.3. 0 [scene not marked in F] **86, 87** CHANCELLOR *Cham.* **133 this** his **171 brother-love** Brother; loue **173 heart** hearts
5.4. 0 [labeled "*Scena Tertia*" in F] **2 Paris** Parish **4, 27** ONE [not in F] **83 a way** away
5.5. 0 [labeled "*Scena Quarta*" in F] **38 ways** way
Epilogue 1 EPILOGUE [not in F]

Titus Andronicus

Copy text: the First Quarto of 1594, except for 3.2, based on F. Act and scene divisions are missing from the Quarto; act divisions alone are marked in the Folio.

1.1. 14 seat, to virtue consecrate, seate to vertue, consecrate. [The punctuation variations from the edited text are considerable in this play and are generally not recorded in these notes.] **18** MARCUS [not in Q] **35 the field** [Q follows with a half line and three more lines: "and at this day, / To the Monument of that *Androncy* / Done sacrifice of expiation, / And slaine the Noblest prisoner of the *Gothes*."] **55.1** *Exeunt Exit* **64** CAPTAIN [not in Q] **69.6** *three sons* two sonnes **78 rites** rights [also at line 143] **98** *manes* manus **129.1** *Exeunt Exit* **157** LAVINIA [not in Q] **164 Rome's** Roomes **193 Rome** Roome **227 Titan's** [F] *Tytus* **243 Pantheon** Pathan **265 chance** [F] change **281** *cuique* cuiqum **300 [and elsewhere]** SATURNINUS *Emperour* **317 Phoebe** *Thebe* **318 gallant'st** [F] gallanst **334 queen, Pantheon. Lords,** Queene: Panthean Lords **359** MARTIUS *Titus* two sonnes speakes QUINTUS [not in Q] **361** MARTIUS *Titus* sonne speakes **369** QUINTUS *3. Sonne* **370** MARTIUS *2. Sonne* [also at line 372] **389.1** *They all kneel* they all kneele and say **390** ALL [not in Q] **391.1** *Exeunt Exit* **392 dreary** dririe [Q] sudden [F] **399** [F; not in Q] **475** LUCIUS [F; not in Q] **476 mildly** mi'd ie
2.1. 37 [and elsewhere] AARON *Moore* **110 than** this
2.2. 1 morn [F] Moone **11** [Q provides a s.p.: *Titus*] **24 run** runnes
2.3. 13 snake [F] snakes **33 and** ann **43 lose** loose **69 try** [F] trie thy **72 swart** F (swarth) swartie [Q] **85 note** notice **88 [and elsewhere]** TAMORA *Queene* **131 ye desire** we desire **150 heard** hard **153 Some** So me **158 thee! For** thee for **160 ears** [F] yeares **175 their** there **180 satisfy** satisfice **192** AARON [not in Q] **208.1** *Exit* [at line 207 in Q] **210 unhallowed** [F] vnhollow **222 berayed in blood** bereaud in blood [Q, with marginal correction in contemporary handwriting: "heere reau'd of lyfe"] **231 Pyramus** [F] Priamus **236 Cocytus'** *Ocitus* **260 [and elsewhere]** SATURNINUS *King* **260 gripped** griude **276** [Q provides a s.p.: *King*] **291 fault** faults
2.4. 5 scrawl scrowle **11** MARCUS [not in Q] **27 him** them **30 three** their
3.1. 0.1 *over on* **17 urns** ruines **21 on thy** [F] out hy **67 handless** handles **146 his** her **225 blow** flow **281 employed:** imployde in these Armes [Q] employ'd in these things [F]
3.2 [the entire scene is missing in Q; copy text is F] **0.1** *banquet Bnaket* [F] **1 [and throughout scene]** TITUS *An.* **13 with outrageous** without ragious **38 mashed** mesh'd **39 complainer** complaynet **52 thy knife** knife **53 fly** Flys **54 thee, murderer!** the murderour: **55 are cloyed** cloi'd **72 myself** my selfes
4.1. 1 [and throughout] BOY [F] *Puer* **10** MARCUS [not in Q] **19 griefs** *greeues* **42** *Metamorphoses* Metamorphosis **46 s.d.** *Help her* [as dialogue in Q] **51 quotes** coats **54 Forced** Frocd **79** TITUS [not in Q] **89 hope** hop (?) I op (?)
4.2. 15 Lordships, that Lordships **51 Good** God **96 Alcides** *Alciades* **125 that** [F] your **154 Muly lives** Muliteus
4.3. 56 Saturn *Saturnine,* to **66 Jupiter** *Iubiter* [also at 79, 83, 84] **77 News . . . come** [assigned in Q to Clown] **96 from you** [Q fol-

lows with four lines: *Titus.* Tell mee, can you deliuer an Oration to the Em- / perour with a grace. / *Clowne.* Nay truelie sir, I could neuer say grace in all / my life.]
4.4. 5 know, as know know **43 good e'en** Godden **48 By 'r** be **93 feed** seede **98 ears** [F] yeares **105 on** [F] in
5.1. 9 A GOTH *Goth* [also at lines 121, 152, and 162] **17** ALL THE GOTHS [not in Q] **20** ANOTHER GOTH *Goth* **23 building, suddenly** building suddainely, **43 here's** [F] her's **53 Get me a ladder** [assigned in Q to Aaron] **113 extreme** extreanie **133 haystacks** haystalks
5.2. 18 it action [F] that accord **38 them out** the mout **49 globe** Globes **52 murderers** murder **caves** cares **56 Hyperion's** *Epeons* **61 Are they** Are them **65 worldly** wordlie **121.1** *Enter Marcus* [after line 120 in Q] **140 Yield** Yee'd **144 dam** Dame **196** [after line 203 in Q]
5.3. 3 A GOTH *Got.* **15.2** *Sound trumpets* [after line 16 in Q] **26 gracious lord** [F] Lord **36 Virginius** *Viginius* **124 witness, this is true.** witnes this is true, **125 cause** course **141** ALL *Marcus* **142** MARCUS [no s.p. here in Q; see previous note] **144 adjudged** [F] adiudge **146** ALL [not in Q] **154 bloodstained** blood slaine **163 Sung** Song **172** BOY [F] *Puer*

Romeo and Juliet

Copy text: the Second Quarto of 1599, except for 1.2.53–1.3.34, for which Q1 (the First Quarto) is the prior authority. Act and scene divisions are absent from the Second Quarto and the Folio.

1.1. 27 it in [Q1] it **38 side** sides **73** CITIZENS *Offi.* **76 CAPULET'S WIFE** *Wife* **92 Verona's** *Neronas* **120 drave** driue **147 his** is **153 sun** same **177 create** [Q1] created **179 well-seeming** [Q1] welseeing **189 grief to** [Q1] grief, too **192 lovers'** louing **202 Bid a** [Q1] A **make** [Q1] makes **206 markman** mark man **211 unharmed** [Q1] vncharmd **218 makes** make
1.2. 14 The earth Earth **32 on** one **38–9 written here** written. Here **46 One** [Q1] on **56 Good e'en** Goddess **57 God gi' good e'en** Godgigoden **70 and Livia** [Q1] Liuia [Q2] **79 thee** [Q1] you [Q2] **91 fires** fier [Q]
1.3. 12 an [Q2] a [Q1] **18 shall** [Q1] stal [Q2] **33 wi' th'** [Q1: *with*] *with the* [Q2] **50 [and elsewhere]** WIFE *Old La.* **66 disposition** [F] dispositions **67, 68 honor** [Q1] houre **100 it fly** [Q1] flie **105 [and elsewhere]** WIFE *Mo.*
1.4. 7–8 [Q1; not in Q2] **23** MERCUTIO *Horatio* **31 quote** cote **39 done** [Q1] dum **42 Of** Or **45 like lamps** [Q1] lights lights **47 five** fine **57 atomi** [Q1] ottamie **59–61** [these lines follow line 69 in Q2] **66 film** Philome **69 maid** [Q1] man **72 O'er** [Q1] On **74 on** one **76 breaths** [Q1] breath **80 parson's** Persons **81 dreams he** [Q1] he dreams **90 elflocks** Elklocks **111 forfeit** [Q1] fofreit
1.5. 0.1 [Q2 adds: "*Enter* Romeo"] **1** FIRST SERVINGMAN *Ser.* [also at lines 6 and 12] **3** SECOND SERVINGMAN 1 **7 court cupboard** Courtcubbert **11** THIRD SERVINGMAN 2 **14** FOURTH SERVINGMAN 3 **15 longest** longer **17** CAPULET 1. *Capu.* [also at lines 35 and 40] **18 a bout** about **57 antic** anticque **96 ready** [Q1] did readie
2.0. Chorus 1 CHORUS [not in Q2] **4 matched** match
2.1. 7 Nay . . . too [assigned in Q2 to Benvolio] **10 one** [Q1] on **11 Pronounce** [Q1] prouaunt **dove** [Q1] day **13 heir** [Q1] her **14 trim** [Q1] true **39 open-arse, and** open, or **pop'ring** Poprin
2.2. 16 do [Q1] to **20 eyes** [Q1] eye **41–2 nor any . . . name ô** be some other name / Belonging to a man **45 were** [Q1] wene **82 pilot** Pylat **83 washed** [Q1] washeth **92–3 false . . . They** false at louers periuries. / They **99 havior** behauiour **101 more cunning** coying **110 circled** [Q1] circle **146 [and elsewhere]** rite right **149, 151** NURSE [not in Q2] **150, 151** JULIET [not in Q2] **163 than mine** then **168 nyas** Neece **180 gyves** giues **187 Sleep . . . breast** [Q1; assigned in Q2 to Juliet] **189–90** [preceded in Q2 by an earlier version of lines 1–4 of the next scene, in which "fleckled darkness" reads "darknesse fleckted" and "and Titan's fiery wheels" reads "made by *Tytans* wheels"]
2.3. 2 Check'ring [Q1] Checking **22 sometime's** sometime **50 me me:** me: **51 wounded. Both our** wounded both, our **85 not. She whom** [Q1] me not, her

2.4. 18 BENVOLIO [Q1] *Ro.*   **28 antic** antique   **28–9 phantasimes** phantacies   **33 pardon-me's** pardons mees   **40 but a** a   **68 Switch . . . switch** Swits . . . swits   **113–14 for himself** [Q1] himself   **205 dog's** dog   **212 s.d.** *Exeunt* Exit
2.5. 11 three there   **15 And** *M.* And   **26 I had** [Q1] I
2.6. 18 gossamer gossamours   **27 music's** musicke
3.1. 2 Capels are *Capels*   **67 injured** iniuried   **73 stoccada** stucatho   **90 your houses** houses   **107 soundly too. Your** soundly, to your   **121 Alive** He gan   **123 fire-eyed** [Q1] fier end   **136** FIRST CITIZEN *Citti.*   **138** FIRST CITIZEN *Citi.*   **141 all** all: **165 agile** [Q1] aged   **183** MONTAGUE *Capu.*   **187 hate's** heart's   **191 I** [Q1] it   **196.1** *Exeunt* Exit
3.2. 1 JULIET [not in Q2]   **9 By** And by   **12 [and elsewhere] lose** loose   **15 grown** grow   **47 darting** arting   **49 shut** shot   **51 Brief sounds** Briefe, sounds,   **of my** my   **54 [and elsewhere] corpse** coarse   **60 one** on   **72 It . . . day it did** [assigned in Q2 to Juliet]   **73 O . . . face** [assigned in Q2 to Nurse]   **76 Dove-feathered** Rauenous doue-featherd   **79 damnèd** dimme   **143.1** *Exeunt* Exit
3.3. 0.1 [Q2 has "*Enter Friar and Romeo*"]   **39** [Q2 follows with a line: "This may flyes do, when I from this must flie"]   **43** [printed in Q2 before line 40]   **52 Thou** [Q1] Then   **61 madmen** [Q1] mad man   **70.1** *Knock Enter Nurse, and knocke*   **73 s.d.** *Knock They knocke*   **74** Who's whose   **75.1** *Knock Slud* knock   **80.1** *Enter Nurse* [below line 78 in Q2]   **110 denote** [Q1] deuote   **117 lives** [Q1] lies   **144 pout'st upon** puts vp   **168 disguised** disguise
3.4. 10 [and elsewhere] WIFE *La.*   **13 be** [Q1] me   **23 We'll keep** Well, keepe
3.5. 13 exhaled exhale   **19 the** the the   **31 changed** change   **36.1** *Enter Nurse Enter Madame and Nurse*   **54** JULIET *Ro.*   **67.1** [bracketed s.d. from Q1]   **82 pardon him** padon   **130–1 body . . . a bark** body? / Thou counterfeits. A Barke   **133–4 is, . . . flood;** is: . . . floud,   **139 gives** giue   **142 How? Will** How will   **151–2 proud . . . Thank** proud mistresse minion you? / Thanke   **160 [and elsewhere]** CAPULET *Fa.*   **172 CAPULET Oh, God-i'-good-e'en** Father, Godigeden   **173** NURSE [not in Q2]   **181 liened** liand
4.1. 7 talked [Q1] talke   **45 cure** [Q1] care   **46 Ah** [Q1] O   **72 slay** [Q1] stay   **78 off** [Q1] of   **83 chopless** [Q1] chapels   **85 his tomb** his   **98 breath** [Q1] breast   **100 To wanny** Too many   **110 In** Is [Q2 follows with a line: "Be borne to buriall in thy kindreds graue"]   **111 shalt** shall   **115 and he** an he   **116 waking** walking   **126 s.d.** *Exeunt* Exit
4.2. 3, 6 SERVINGMAN *Ser.*   **14 willed** wield   **26 becomèd** becomd   **38 [and elsewhere]** WIFE *Mo.*   **47.1** *Exeunt* Exit
4.3. 20 vial Violl   **49 wake** walke
4.4. 1 [and elsewhere] WIFE *La.*   **12.1** *Exeunt* Exit   **13.1–2** [after line 14 in Q2]   **15** FIRST SERVINGMAN *Fel.*   **18** SECOND SERVINGMAN *Fel.*   **21 Thou** Twou   **faith** father   **23 s.d.** [after line 21 in Q2]
4.5. 40 all; life all life   **41 long** [Q1] loue   **51 behold** bedold   **65 cure** care   **65–6 not . . . Heaven** not, / In these confusions heauen   **82 fond** some   **96** FIRST MUSICIAN *Musi.*   **98 s.d.** *Exit* Exit omnes [below line 99]   **99, 103** FIRST MUSICIAN *Fid.*   **99 by** [Q1] my   **99.1** *Enter Peter Enter Will Kemp*   **107** FIRST MUSICIAN Minstrels [and subsequently in this scene indicated by *Minst.* or *Minstrel*]   **123 Then . . . wit** [assigned in Q2 to *2 M*]   **127 And . . . oppress** [Q1; not in Q2]   **133, 136 Pretty** [Q1] Prates   **145 s.d.** *Exeunt* Exit
5.1. 15 fares my [Q1] doth my Lady   **17, 27, 32** BALTHASAR *Man*   **24 e'en** in   **defy** [Q1] denie   **33.1** [at line 32, after "good lord," in Q2]   **76 pay** [Q1] pray   **86 s.d.** *Exit Exeunt*
5.3. 3 yew [Q1] young   **21.2** [*Balthasar*] [Q1] Peter   **25 light. Upon** light vpon   **40, 43** BALTHASAR *Pet.*   **68 conjuration** commiration   **71** PAGE *Boy* [Q1; s.p. missing in Q2 and line treated as a s.d.]   **102 fair** faire? I will beleeue   **107 palace** pallat   **108** [Q2 has four undeleted lines here: "Depart againe, come lye thou in my arme, / Heer's to thy health, where ere thou tumblest in. / O true Appothecarie! / Thy drugs are quicke. Thus with a kisse I die."]   **123 [and elsewhere]** BALTHASAR *Man*   **137 yew** yong   **168** FIRST WATCH *Watch* [also at lines 172, 195, 199]   **171** PAGE *Watch boy*   **182** SECOND WATCH *Watch*

183, 187 FIRST WATCH *Chief. watch*   **187 too** too too   **190 shrieked** shrike   **194 our** your   **199 slaughtered** Slaughter   **201** [Q2 has a s.d. here: "*Enter Capulet and his wife*"]   **209 more early** [Q1] now earling   **232 that** thats   **274–5 place . . . This** place. To this same monument / This   **281** PAGE *Boy*   **299 raise** raie

Julius Caesar

Copy text: the First Folio. Act divisions are marked in the Folio; scene divisions are editorially supplied.

1.1. 0.1 [and elsewhere] *Marullus Murellus*   **37 Pompey? . . . oft** *Pompey* many a time and oft?   **61 [and elsewhere] whe'er** where
1.2. 0.1 [and elsewhere] *Calpurnia Calphurnia*   **24.1 Manent** Manet   **124 [and elsewhere] lose** loose   **254 like. He** like he   **301 digest** disgest
1.3. 129 In favor's like Is Fauors, like
2.1. 28 [and elsewhere] lest least   **40 ides** first   **67 of** of a   **83 put** path   **122 women, then,** women. Then   **136 oath, when** Oath. When   **214 eighth** eight   **268 his** hit   **281 the** tho   **310.1** *Enter Lucius and Ligarius* [after "with haste" in line 310 in F]   **314 [and through line 322]** LIGARIUS *Cai.*
2.2. 23 did neigh do neigh   **46 are** heare   **81 Of** And
2.3. 1 ARTEMIDORUS [not in F]   **120 to blame** too blame
3.1. 40 law lane   **114 states** State   **116 lies** lye   **201 [and elsewhere] corpse** Coarse [also Course and Corpes]   **256** ANTONY [not in F]   **277.1** *Octavius' Octauio's* [also at 5.2.4]   **285 for** from
3.2. 106 art are   **205** ALL [not in F]   **222 wit** writ   **260 s.d.** *Exeunt* Exit   **262 s.d.** *Enter Servant* [after "fellow" in F]
3.3. 6 Whither Whether
4.2. 34–6 FIRST, SECOND, THIRD SOLDIER [not in F]   **50 Lucius** *Lucillius*   **52 Lucilius** *Lucius*   **52.1 Manent** Manet
4.3. 209–10 off / If off. / If   **230 s.d.** *Enter Lucius* [before line 230 in F]   **244, 246 [and throughout] Claudius** *Claudio*   **246 [and throughout] Varro** *Varrus*   **252 will** will it   **303, 307** VARRO, CLAUDIUS *Both*
5.1. 42 teeth teethes   **67.1** *Exeunt* Exit   **70** [F has s.d.: "*Lucillius and Messala stand forth*"]   **71** LUCILIUS **(stands forth)** *Luc.*   **73** MESSALA **(stands forth)** *Messa.*   **99 rest** rests
5.3. 99 fare far   **104 Thasos** *Tharsus*   **108 Flavius** *Flauio*
5.4. 7 LUCILIUS [not in F]   **9 O** *Luc.* O   **12, 15** FIRST SOLDIER *Sold.*   **16.1** *Enter Antony* [before line 16 in F]   **17 the news** thee newes
5.5. 33 too, Strato to *Strato*   **77 With all** Withall

Hamlet

Copy text: the Second Quarto of 1604–1605 [Q2]. The First Folio text also represents an independently authoritative text; although seemingly not the correct choice for copy text, the Folio text is considerably less marred by typographical errors than is Q2. The adopted readings in these notes are from F unless otherwise indicated; [eds.] means that the adopted reading was first proposed by some editor since the time of F. Some readings also are supplied from the First Quarto of 1603 [Q1]. Act and scene divisions are missing in Q_q 1–2; the Folio provides such markings only through 1.3 and at Act 2.

1.1. 1 Who's Whose   **19 soldier** [F, Q1] souldiers   **44 off** [Q1] of   **48 harrows** horrowes   **67 sledded Polacks** [eds.] sleaded pollax   **77 why** [F, Q1] with   **cast** cost   **91 heraldry** [F, Q1] heraldy   **92 those** [F, Q1] these   **95 returned** returne   **97 cov'nant** comart   **98 designed** desseigne   **112 e'en so** [eds.] enso   **116 mote** [eds.] moth   **119 tenantless** tennatlesse   **125 feared** [eds.] feare   **142 you** [F, Q1] your   **144 at it** it   **181 conveniently** [F, Q1] conuenient
1.2. 0.2 [and elsewhere] *Gertrude Gertrad*   **1** KING *Claud.*   **67 so** so much   **77 good** coold   **82 shapes** [Q3] chapes   **83 denote** deuote   **96 a** or   **105 corpse** [eds.] course   **112 you. For** you for   **114 retrograde** retrogard   **129 sullied** [eds.] sallied [Q2] solid [F]   **132 self** seale   **133 weary** wary   **137 to this** thus   **140 satyr** [F4] satire   **143 would** [F, Q1] should   **149 even she** [F; not in Q2]   **175 to drink deep** [F, Q1] for to drinke   **178 to see** [F, Q1] to   **199 waste**

[F2] wast [Q2, F]   **206 jelly with . . . fear,** gelly, with . . . feare
210 Where, as [Q5] Whereas   **225 Indeed, indeed** [F, Q1] Indeede
241 Very like, very like [F, Q1] Very like   **242 hundred** hundreth
243 MARCELLUS, BERNARDO [eds.] *Both*   **247 tonight** to nigh
256 fare farre   **257 eleven** a leauen   **259.1** *Exeunt* [at line 258 in Q2]
262 Foul [F, Q1] fonde
1.3. 3 convoy is conuay, in   **12 bulk** bulkes   **18** [F; not in Q2]
29 weigh way   **49 like a** a   **74 Are** Or   **75 be** boy   **76 loan** loue
110 Running [eds.] Wrong [Q2] Roaming [F]   **116 springes** springs
126 tether tider   **130 implorators** imploratotors   **131 bawds** [eds.]
bonds   **132 beguile** beguide
1.4. 2 is a is   **6.1** *go off* [eds.] *goes of*   **17 revel** [Q3] reueale   **19 clepe**
clip   **36 evil** [eds.] eale [Q2] ease [Q3]   **37 often dout** [eds.] of a
doubt   **49 inurned** interr'd [Q2, Q1]   **61, 79 wafts** waues   **80 off** of
82 artery arture   **86.1** *Exeunt Exit*   **87 imagination** [F, Q1] imagion
1.5. 1 Whither [eds.] Whether   **20 on** [eds.] an   **21 fretful porcupine**
[F, Q1] fearfull Porpentine   **44 wit** [eds.] wits   **48 what a** what
56 lust [F, Q1] but   **angel** Angle   **57 sate** [F] sort   **59 scent** [eds.]
sent   **68 alleys** [eds.] allies   **69 posset** possesse   **96 stiffly** swiftly
119 bird and   **128 HORATIO, MARCELLUS** *Booth* [also at line 151]
heaven, my lord heauen   **138 Look you, I'll** I will   **157 s.d.** *cries*
Ghost cries   **179 some'er** so mere   **185 Well** well, well [Q1, Q2]
2.1 0.1 man [eds.] *man or two*   **3 marvelous** meruiles   **29 Faith, no**
Fayth   **41 warrant** wit   **42 sullies** sallies   **43 wi' th'** with   **60 o'er-**
took or tooke   **64 takes** take   **76 s.d.** *Exit Reynaldo. Enter Ophelia*
[after line 75 in Q2]   **107 passion** passions   **114 quoted** [eds.] coted
2.2. 0.1 [and elsewhere] *Rosencrantz Rosencraus*   **57 o'erhasty** hastie
73 three [F, Q1] threescore   **90 since brevity** breuitie   **125 This** [Q2
has a speech prefix: *Pol.* This]   **126 above** about   **137 winking** working
143 his her   **148 watch** wath   **149 to a** to   **151 'tis** [F, Q1; not in Q2]
170.1 [at line 169 in Q2] *Exeunt* [eds.] *Exit*   **210 sanity** sanctity
212–13 and suddenly . . . him [F; not in Q2]   **213 honorable lord** Lord
214 most humbly take take   **215 cannot, sir** cannot   **216 more** not
more   **224 excellent** extent   **228–9 overhappy. / On** euer happy
on   **229 cap** lap   **240–70 Let . . . attended** [F; not in Q2]
267 ROSENCRANTZ, GUILDENSTERN *Both* [Q1]   **273 even** euer   **288 could**
can   **292 off** of   **304 What a** What   **306–7 admirable, in action how**
. . . angel, in [F, subst.] admirable in action, how . . . Angell in   **310 no,**
nor nor   **314 you** yee   **321 of** on   **324–5 the clown . . . sear** [F; not in
Q2]   **tickle** [eds.] tickled [F]   **326 blank** black   **337–62 How . . . too**
[F; not in Q2]   **342 berattle** [eds.] be-ratled [F]   **349 most like** [eds.]
like most [F]   **373 lest my** let me   **381 too** to   **398–9 tragical-histori-**
cal, tragical-comical-historical-pastoral [F; not in Q2]   **401 light . . .**
these [eds.] light for the lawe of writ, and the liberty: these   **425 By 'r** by
429 e'en to 't ento't   **French falconers** friendly Fankners   **433 [and**
elsewhere] FIRST PLAYER *Player*   **436–7 caviare** cauiary   **443 affecta-**
tion affection   **446 tale** [F, Q1] talke   **456 heraldry** [F, Q1] heraldy
dismal. Head dismall head   **474 Then senseless Ilium** [F; not in
Q2]   **481 And, like** Like   **495 fellies** [F4] follies [Q2] Fallies [F]
504 "Moblèd queen" is good [F; not in Q2; F reads "Inobled"]
506 bisson *Bison*   **514 husband's** [F, Q1] husband   **519 whe'er**
where   **540 a** [F; not in Q2]   **541 or** [F, Q1] lines, or   **546 s.d.** *Exeunt*
players [see textual note at line 548.1]   **547 till** tell   **548.1** *Exeunt* [F;
Q2 has "*Exeunt Pol. and Players*" after line 547]   **554 his** the   **556 and**
an   **559 to Hecuba** [F, Q1] to her   **561 the cue** that   **582 Oh,**
vengeance [F; not in Q2]   **584 father** [Q1, Q3, Q4; not in Q2, F]
588 scullion [F] stallyon [Q2] scalion [Q1]   **600 the devil** a deale
the devil the deale
3.1. 1 And An   **28 too** two   **32 lawful espials** [F; not in Q2]   **33 Will**
Wee'le   **46 loneliness** lowlines   **to** too   **56 Let's withdraw**
with-draw   **56.2** *Enter Hamlet* [after line 55 in Q2]   **65 wished. To**
wisht to   **73 disprized** despiz'd   **84 of us all** [F, Q1; not in Q2]
86 sicklied sickled   **93 well, well, well** well   **100 the** these
108 your honesty you   **119 inoculate** euocutat   **122 to a** a   **130 knaves**
all knaues   **144 paintings too** [Q1] paintings   **146 jig, you amble** gig &
amble   **147 lisp** list   **148 your ignorance** [F, Q1] ignorance
155 Th'expectancy Th'expectation   **159 music** musickt   **160 that**

what   **161 tune** time   **162 feature** stature   **164** [Q2 has the
end of this line]   **191 unwatched** vnmatcht
3.2. 10 tatters totters   **split** [F, Q1] spleet   **27 of the** of   **29 praise**
praysd   **37 sir** [F; not in Q2]   **45.1** *Enter . . . Rosencrantz* [after line
47 in Q2]   **88 detecting** detected   **96 now. My lord,** now my Lord.
107 [and elsewhere] QUEEN *Ger.*   **108 metal** mettle   **112–13** [F; not
in Q2]   **127 devil** deule [Q2] Diuel [F]   **133.1 sound** [eds.] *sounds*
133.7 *Anon comes anon come*   **135 miching** [F, Q1] munching   **140**
keep counsel [F, Q1] keepe   **153 [and throughout scene]** PLAYER
KING *King*   **154 orbèd** orb'd the   **159 [and throughout scene]**
PLAYER QUEEN *Quee.*   **162 your** our   **164** [Q2 follows here with an
extraneous unrhymed line: "For women feare too much, euen as they
loue"]   **165 For** And   **166 In** Eyther none, in   **167 love** Lord   **179**
Wormwood, wormwood That's wormwood   **180 PLAYER QUEEN** [not
in Q2]   **188 like** the   **197 joys** joy   **217 An** And   **221 a widow** [F,
Q1] I be a widow   **be** [F] be a   **226.1** *Exit* [F, Q1] *Exeunt*   **240 wince**
[Q1] winch [Q2, F]   **241.1** [after line 242 in Q2]   **254 Confederate**
[F, Q1] Considerat   **256 infected** [F, Q1, Q4] inuected   **258 usurp**
vsurps   **264** [F; not in Q2]   **274 with two** with   **288.1** [F; after line
293 in Q2]   **308 start** stare   **317 of** my of   **343.1** [after line 341 in
Q2]   **357 thumb** the vmber   **366 to the top of** to   **370 can fret me**
[F] fret me not [Q2] can fret me, yet [Q1]   **371.1** [after line 372 in Q2]
385 POLONIUS [F; not in Q2]   **386 Leave me, friends** [so F; Q2 places
before "I will say so," and assigns both to Hamlet]   **388 breathes**
breakes   **390 bitter . . . day** business as the bitter day   **395 daggers**
[F, Q1] dagger
3.3. 19 huge hough   **22 ruin** raine   **23 but with** but   **35.1** *Exit* [after
"I know" in F]   **50 pardoned** pardon   **58 Offense's** [eds.] Offences
shove showe   **73 pat . . . a-praying** but now a is a praying
75 revenged reuendge   **79 hire and salary** base and silly   **81 With**
all Withall
3.4. 5–6 with him . . . Mother, Mother, Mother [F; not in Q2]   **7 war-**
rant wait   **8.1** *Enter Hamlet* [at line 5 in Q2]   **21 inmost** most
23 Help, ho! Helpe how   **43 off** of   **51 tristful** heated   **53** [assigned
in Q2 to Hamlet]   **60 heaven-kissing** heaue, a kissing   **89 panders**
pardons   **91 mine . . . soul** my very eyes into my soule   **92 grainèd**
greeued   **93 not leave** leaue there   **100 tithe** kyth   **146 Ecstasy** [F;
not in Q2]   **150 I** the the   **165 live** leaue   **172 Refrain tonight** to
refraine night   **193 ravel** rouell   **205 to breathe** [eds.] to breath
222 a [F, Q1] a most   **224.1** *Exeunt* [eds.] *Exit*
4.1. 32.1 [at 31 in Q2]
4.2. 0.1 [Q2: "Enter Hamlet, Rosencraus, and others."]   **2–3** [F; not in Q2;
the s.p. in F is "Gentlemen"]   **4 HAMLET** [not in Q2]   **5.1** [F; not in
Q2]   **7 Compounded** Compound   **18–19 an ape** [not in Q2]
31–2 Hide . . . after [F; not in Q2]
4.3. 44 With fiery quickness [F; not in Q2]   **56 and so** so   **72 were**
will   **begin** begin
4.4. 20–1 name. To name To
4.5. 16 Let . . . in [assigned in Q2 to Horatio]   **20.1** [after line 16 in Q2]
38 with all with   **52 clothes** close   **57 Indeed, la** Indeede   **62 to** too
83 in their in   **98** [F; not in Q2]   **100.1** [below line 97 in Q2]
103 impetuous [Q3, F2] impitious [Q2] impittious [F]   **109 They** The
146 swoopstake [eds.] soopstake [Q1 reads "Swoop-stake-like"]
158 Let her come in [assigned in Q2 to Laertes and placed before
"How now, what noyse is that?"]   **s.d.** *Enter Ophelia* [after line 157 in
Q2]   **162 Till** Tell   **165 an old** [F, Q1] a poore   **166–8, 170** [F; not in
Q2]   **186 must** [F, Q1] may   **191 affliction** [F, Q1] afflictions
199 All flaxen Flaxen   **203 Christian** [F] Christians   **souls, I**
pray God [F, Q1] soules   **204 you see** you   **217 trophy, sword**
trophe sword
4.6. 7, 9 FIRST SAILOR *Say.*   **9 an't** and   **22 good turn** turne   **26 bore**
bord   **30 He** So   **31 will give** will
4.7. 6 proceeded proceede   **7 crimeful** criminall   **15 conjunctive**
concliue   **22 gyves** Giues   **23 loud a wind** loued Arm'd   **25 had**
haue   **37 How . . . Hamlet** [F; not in Q2]   **38 This** These   **46–7 your**
pardon you pardon   **48 and more strange** [F; not in Q2]   **Hamlet** [F;
not in Q2]   **56 shall live** [F, Q1] liue   **62 checking** the King

78 ribbon [eds.] ribaud   **89 my** me   **101 escrimers** [eds.] Scrimures   **116 wick** [eds.] weeke   **123 spendthrift** [Q5] spend thirfts   **135 on** ore   **139 pass** pace   **141 for that** for   **151 shape. If** shape if   **157 ha 't** hate   **160 prepared** prefard   **168 hoar** horry   **172 cold** cull-cold   **192 douts** [F "doubts"] drownes
5.1. 1 [and throughout] FIRST CLOWN *Clowne*   **3** [and throughout] SECOND CLOWN *Other*   **9** *se offendendo* so offended   **12 and to** to   **Argal** or all   **34–7** SECOND CLOWN: Why . . . arms? [F; not in Q2]   **43 that frame** that   **55.1** [before line 65 in Q2]   **60 stoup** soope   **70 daintier** dintier   **85 meant** [F, Q1, Q3] went   **89 mazard** massene   **106–7 Is . . . recoveries** [F; not in Q2]   **107–8 Will his** will   **109 double ones too** doubles   **120 Oh** or   **121** [F; not in Q2]   **143 Of all** Of   **165 nowadays** [F; not in Q2]   **183 Let me see** [F; not in Q]   **192 chamber** [F, Q1] table   **208–9 As thus** [F; not in Q2]   **216 winter's** waters   **226, 235** PRIEST *Doct.*   **231 Shards, flints** Flints   **246 t' have** haue   **247 treble** double   **262 and rash** rash   **288 thus** this   **296.1** [*Exit*] *Horatio and Horatio*   **301 shortly** thereby   **302 Till** Tell
5.2. 5 Methought my thought   **6 bilboes** bilbo   **9 pall** fall   **17 unseal** vnfold   **19 Ah,** [eds.] A   **29 villainies** villaines   **30 Ere** Or   **43 "as"es** as sir   **52 Subscribed** Subscribe   **57, 68–80** [F; not in Q2]   **73 interim is** [eds.] *interim's* [F]   **78 court** [eds.] count [F]   **81** [and throughout] OSRIC *Cour.*   **82 humbly** humble   **93 Put your** your   **98 sultry** sully   **for** or   **107 gentleman** [eds.] gentlemen   **109 feelingly** [Q4] fellingly   **114 dozy** [eds.] dazzie   **yaw** [eds.] raw   **141 his** [eds.] this   **142 him by them,** him, by them   **149 hangers** hanger   **156 carriages** carriage   **159 might be** be might   **162 impawned, as** [eds.] all [Q2] impon'd, as [F]   **174 purpose, I** purpose; I   **181–2 Yours, yours. 'A does** Yours doo's   **186 comply** so sir   **190 yeasty** histy   **191 fanned** [eds.] prophane [Q2] fond [F] winnowed** trennowed   **210 But thou** thou   **218 be now** be   **220 will come** well come   **238** [F; not in Q2]   **248 To keep** To   **till** all   **252 foils. Come on** foiles.   **255 off** of   **261 bettered** better   **270 union** Vnice ["Onixe" in some copies]   **288 A touch, a touch, I** I   **302 afeard** sure   **316 Hamlet. Hamlet** *Hamlet*   **319 thy** [F, Q1] my   **327 murderous** [F; not in Q2]   **328 off** of   **thy union** [Q1] the Onixe   **345 ha 't** [eds.] hate [Q2] have 't [F]   **366 proud** prou'd   **369** FIRST AMBASSADOR *Embas.*   **381 th' yet** yet   **385 forced** for no   **394 on** no

Passages contained only in F and omitted from Q2 are noted in the textual notes above. Listed below are the more important instances in which Q2 contains words, lines, and passages omitted in F.
1.1. 112–29 BERNARDO I think . . . countrymen
1.2. 58–60 wrung . . . consent
1.3. 9 perfume and
1.4. 17–38 This heavy-headed . . . scandal   **75–8** The very . . . beneath
2.1. 122 Come
2.2. 17 Whether . . . thus   **217** except my life   **363** very   **366** 'Sblood (and some other profanity passim)   **371** then   **444–5** as wholesome . . . fine   **521–2** of this   **589** Hum
3.2. 169–70 Where . . . there   **216–17** To . . . scope
3.4. 72–7 Sense . . . difference   **79–82** Eyes . . . mope   **168–72** That monster . . . put on   **174–7** the next . . . potency   **187** One word . . . lady   **209–17** There's . . . meet
4.1. 4 Bestow . . . while   **41–4** Whose . . . air
4.2. 4 But soft
4.3. 26–9 KING Alas . . . worm
4.4. 9–67 Enter Hamlet . . . worth
4.5. 33 Oho
4.7. 68–82 LAERTES My lord . . . graveness   **101–3** Th' escrimers . . . them   **115–24** There . . . ulcer
5.1. 154 There
5.2. 106–42 here is . . . unfellowed (replaced in F by "you are not ignorant of what excellence Laertes is at his weapon")   **154–5** HORATIO [*to Hamlet*] I knew . . . done   **193–207** *Enter a Lord* . . . lose, my lord (replaced in F by "You will lose this wager, my lord")   **222** Let be

Othello

Copy text: the First Folio. The adopted readings are from the Quarto of 1622 [Q1], unless otherwise indicated; [eds.] means that the adopted reading was first proposed by some editor subsequent to the First Folio. Act and scene divisions are marked in the Folio with the exception of 2.3.
1.1. 1 Tush, never Neuer   **4 'Sblood, but** But   **16 And, in conclusion** [Q1; not in F]   **26 togaed** Tongued   **30 other** others   **34 God bless** blesse   **68 full** fall   **thick-lips** Thicks-lips   **74 changes** chances   **75** [and elsewhere] **lose** [eds.] loose   **81 Thieves, thieves, thieves** Theeues, Theeues   **83.1 *Brabantio above*** [in F, printed as a speech prefix to line 84]   **88 Zounds, sir** Sir [also at line 111]   **103 bravery** knauerie   **119 are now** are   **158 pains** apines   **161 sign. That** [eds.] signe) that   **186 night** might
1.2. 34 Duke Dukes   **50 carrack** Carract   **64 her!** [eds.] her   **69 darlings** Deareling   **89 I do** do
1.3. 1 There is There's   **these** this   **61** DUKE AND SENATORS [*All* Q1] *Sen.*   **101 maimed** main'd   **108 upon** vp on   **DUKE** [Q1; not in F]   **109 overt** ouer   **112** [and elsewhere] FIRST SENATOR *Sen.*   **124 till** tell   **132 battles** Battaile   **fortunes** Fortune   **141 travels'** Trauellours   **143 rocks, and** Rocks   **heads** head   **145 other** others   **146 Anthropophagi** *Antropophague*   **147 Do grow** Grew   **149 thence** hence   **157 intentively** instinctiuely   **161 sighs** kisses   **203 grece** grise   **204 Into your favor** [Q1; not in F]   **222 piercèd** pierc'd   **ear** eares   **227 sovereign** more soueraigne   **233 couch** [eds.] Coach [F] Cooch [Q1]   **237 These** [eds.] This   **244 Nor I. I would not** Nor would I   **251 did love** loue   **267 me** [eds.] my   **273 instruments** Instrument   **281** DESDEMONA **Tonight, my lord?** DUKE **This night** [Q1; not in F]   **285 With** And   **294** FIRST SENATOR *Sen.*   **296.1 *Exeunt*** Exit   **302 matters** matter   **303 the** the the   **329 beam** [eds.] braine [Q1] ballance [Q1]   **333–4 our unbitted** or vnbitted   **335 scion** [eds.] Seyen [F] syen [Q1]   **353 error** errors   **354 She . . . she must** [Q1; not in F]   **358 a supersubtle** super-subtle   **378–82** RODERIGO **What . . . purse** [Q1; not in F]   **386 a snipe** Snpe   **389 He's** [Ha's Q1] She ha's   **396 ear** eares
2.1. 35 prays praye   **36 heaven** Heauens   **42** THIRD GENTLEMAN *Gent.*   **44 arrivance** Arriuancie   **45 this** the   **58** SECOND GENTLEMAN *Gent.* [also at lines 61, 68, and 95]   **72 clog** enclogge   **84 And . . . comfort** [Q1; not in F]   **90 tell me** tell   **94 the sea** Sea   **96 their** this   **107 list** leaue   **111 doors** doore   **156** [and elsewhere] **ne'er** neu'r   **158 such wight** *such wightes*   **170 gyve** [eds.] giue   **174 An** and   **175 courtesy** Curtsie   **176 clyster pipes** Cluster-pipes   **214.1 *Exeunt*** [eds.] *Exit*   **216 hither** thither   **229 again** a game   **239 fortune** Forune   **241–2 compassing** compasse   **243–4 finder out** finder   **244 occasions** occasion   **has** he's   **263 mutualities** mutabilities   **300 for wife** for wift   **307 rank** right   **308 nightcap** Night-Cape
2.2. 6 addiction [eds.] addition   **10 Heaven bless** Blesse
2.3. 27 stoup [eds.] stope   **38 unfortunate** infortunate   **52 lads** else   **57 to put** put to   **61, 71 God** heauen   **76 Englishman** Englishmen   **91 Then . . . auld** [*Then . . . owd* Q1] *And take thy awl'd*   **93 'Fore God** Why   **97 God's** heau'ns   **106 God forgive** Forgiue   **110 speak I** speake   **123 the** his   **138 s.d. *Cry within*:** Help! Help! [from Q1: "Helpe, helpe, within"]   **139 Zounds, you** You   **152 God's will** Alas   **153 Montano—sir** *Montano*   **156 God's will, Lieutenant, hold** Fie, fie Lieutenant   **158 Zounds, I'll** I   **161 sense of place** [eds.] place of sense   **184 wont be** wont to be   **201 Zounds, if I** If I once   **212 leagued** [eds.] league   **218 Thus** This   **227 the** then   **246 well now** well   **250 vile** vil'd   **255 God** Heauen   **260 thought** had thought   **283 Oh, God** Oh   **308 I'll** I   **311 denotement** [eds.] deuotement   **325–6 me here** me   **337 were's** were   **356 s.d. *Enter Roderigo*** [after line 356 in F]   **369 hast** hath   **372 By the Mass** Introth   **378 on;** [on Q1] on   **379 the while** [eds.] a while
3.1. 1 *Musicians* [eds.] *Musicians, and Clowne*   **5** [and at lines 7, 9, and 15] A MUSICIAN *Mus.*   **21 s.d. *Exeunt*** [eds.] *Exit*   **22 hear** heare me   **26 General's wife** Generall   **31** CASSIO **Do, good my friend** [Q1; not in F]   **42 s.d. *Exit*** [at line 41 in F]   **52 To . . . front** [Q1; not in F]
3.3. 16 circumstance Circumstances   **41 you** your   **55 Yes, faith** I sooth   **66 or** on   **80 By'r Lady** Trust me   **103 you** he   **118 By heaven** Alas

124 In Of   **148 that all** that: All   **free to** free   **152 But some** Wherein
160 oft of   **161 wisdom then** wisdome   **175 By heaven, I'll** Ile
183 fondly [eds.] soundly [F] strongly [Q1]   **188 God** Heauen   **194 Is
once** Is   **196 blown** blow'd   **199 dances well** Dances   **216 God**
Heauen   **218 keep't** [eds.] keepe [Q1] kept [F]   **225 [and elsewhere]
to** too   **230 I'faith** Trust me   **232 my** your   **249 disproportion**
disproportions   **264 to hold** to   **275 qualities** Quantities
276 human humane   **289 of** to   **294 oh, then heaven mocks** Heauen
mock'd   **301 Faith** Why   **305.1** *Exit* [at line 304 in F]   **328 faith** but
345 s.d. *Enter Othello* [after "I did say so" in F]   **354 of her** in her
385 remorse; [remorce. Q1] remorse   **407 see, sir** see   **411 supervisor**
super-vision   **439 then laid** laid   **440 Over** ore   **sighed** sigh
kissed kisse   **441 Cried** cry   **455 any that was** [eds.] any, it was
468 mind perhaps minde   **471 Ne'er feels** [eds.] Neu'r keepes
3.4. 23 that the   **37 It yet** It   **56 faith** indeed   **77 I'faith** Indeed
79 God Heauen   **83 Heaven bless** Blesse   **88 can, sir** can
94–5 DESDEMONA I pray . . . Cassio. OTHELLO The handkerchief!
[Q1; not in F]   **99 I'faith** Insooth   **100 Zounds** Away   **142 s.d.** *Exit*
[after line 141 in F]   **164 that** the   **169.1** *Exit* [after line 168 in F]
172 I'faith Indeed   **182 friend.** [eds.] Friend,   **183 absence** [eds.]
absence, [Q1] Absence: [F]   **188 by my faith** in good troth
4.1. 32 Faith Why   **36 Zounds, that's** that's   **45 work** workes   **52 No,
forbear** [Q1; not in F]   **72 couch** [Coach Q1] Cowch;   **79 unsuiting**
[Q1 corrected] vnfitting [Q1 uncorrected] resulting [F]   **81 'scuse**
scuses   **97 clothes** Cloath   **103 conster** conserue   **105 you now** you
109 power dowre   **113 a woman** woman   **114 i'faith** indeed
121 Do you triumph, Roman? Do ye triumph, Romaine?
122 marry her marry   **125 win** winnes   **126 Faith** Why   **shall
marry** marry   **133 beckons** becomes   **138 by this hand, she** [Q1;
not in F]   **165 Faith, I** I   **167 Faith** Yes   **214.1** [after line 212 in F]
217 God save Saue   **240 By my troth** Trust me   **253 Truly, an** Truely
286 denote deonte [F uncorrected] deuote [F corrected]
4.2. 32 Nay May   **33 knees** knee   **35 But not the words** [Q1; not in F]
51 kinds kind   **56 A** The   **66 Ay, there** [eds.] I heere   **71 ne'er**
neuer   **83 Impudent strumpet** [Q1; not in F]   **96 keep** [eds.] keepes
s.d. *Enter Emilia* [after line 94 in F]   **155 O God** Alas   **162 them in**
[eds.] them: or   **174 And . . . you** [Q1; not in F]   **177 you to** to
190 Faith, I I   **for** and   **201 By this hand** Nay   **232 takes** taketh
236 of [Q1; not in F]
4.3. 10.1 *Exit* [after line 9 in F]   **22 favor in them** fauour   **25 faith**
Father   **26 before thee** before   **35 Barbary** *Braberie*   **43 sighing**
[eds.] *singing* [F corrected] *sining* [F uncorrected]   **73 Good troth**
Introth   **74 By my troth** Introth   **78 Uds pity** why   **107 God** Heauen
5.1. 1 bulk Barke   **22 Be't** But   **hear** heard   **36 Forth** For   **50 Did** Do
91 Oh, heaven Yes, 'tis   **106 out o'** o'   **113 'Las, what's . . . What's**
Alas, what is . . . What is   **116 dead** quite dead   **126 Faugh!** Fie Fie
5.2. 34 heaven Heauens   **37 say so** say   **56 Yes, presently** Presently
61 Then Lord O Heauen   **96 here** high   **104 Should** Did
108 s.d. *Enter Emilia* [after line 108 in F]   **121 Oh, Lord** Alas
131 heard heare   **148 Nay, had** had   **225 Oh, God! Oh, heavenly
God** Oh Heauen! oh heauenly Powres   **226 Zounds** Come
248 have here haue   **317 not. Here** [not: here Q1] not) heere
357 Indian Iudean

King Lear

Copy text: the First Folio, except for those 300 or so lines found only in
the First Quarto of 1608 [Q1]. Unless otherwise indicated, adopted readings are from the corrected state of Q1. A few readings are supplied from
the Second Quarto of 1619 [Q2]. All readings subsequent to 1619 are
marked as supplied by "eds." Act and scene divisions are as marked in F,
except that F does not mark 2.3 and 2.4, and omits 4.3 entirely, so that
4.4 is marked "*Scena Tertia*" and similarly with 4.5 and 4.6 (though 4.7 is
marked "*Scena Septima*").

1.1. 5 equalities qualities   **20–2 account . . . yet** [eds.] account, though
. . . for: yet   **35 liege** Lord   **55 words** word   **66 issue** issues
68 Speak [Q1; not in F]   **74 possesses** professes   **85 interested**

[eds.] interest   **104** [Q1; not in F]   **110 mysteries** [eds.] miseries [F]
mistresse [Q1]   **135 turns** turne   **156 as a** as   **157 nor** nere
161 LEAR *Kear*   **162 KENT** *Lent*   **165 CORNWALL** [eds.] *Cor.*   **166 the**
thy   **173 sentence** sentences   **191 GLOUCESTER** *Cor.*   **217 best
object** obiect   **229 well** will   **252 respects of fortune** respect and
Fortunes   **272 Ye** [eds.] The   **285 shame them** with shame
286.1 Exeunt [eds.] *Exit*   **293 hath not** hath   **306 hit** sit
1.2. 1 [and elsewhere] EDMUND *Bast.*   **21 top** [eds.] to'   **56 waked**
wake   **97–9 EDMUND Nor . . . earth** [Q1; not in F]   **134 Fut, I** I
136 Edgar [Q1; not in F]   **137 and pat** [eds.] Pat [F] and out [Q1]
147–55 as . . . come, [Q1; not in F]   **182 s.d.** [at line 181 in F]
1.3. 3 [and elsewhere] OSWALD [eds.] *Ste.*   **17–21** [Q1; not in F]
26–7 I would . . . speak [Q1; not in F]   **28 very** [Q1; not in F]
1.4. 1 well will   **31 canst** canst thou   **43.1** *Enter steward* [eds.; after
line 44 in F]   **50 daughter** Daughters   **76.1** *Enter steward* [eds.;
after line 77 in F]   **96 KENT** *Lear*   **Fool** my Boy   **135 Dost** Do'st thou
138–53 That . . . snatching [Q1; not in F]   **158 crown** Crownes
175 fools Foole   **195 nor crumb** not crum   **214 it had** it's had
229–32 [Q1; not in F]   **255 Oh . . . come** [Q1; not in F]   **303 Yea . . .
this** [Q1; not in F]   **343 You're** Your are   **attasked** at task
1.5. 0.1 *Kent Kent, Gentleman*   **51 s.d.** *Exit Exeunt*
2.1. 2 you your   **19.1** [after line 18 in F]   **39 stand 's** stand   **69 I should**
should I   **70 ay, though** though   **78 I never got him** [Q1; not in F]
78 s.d. [at line 76 in F, after "seeke it"]   **79 why** wher   **87 strange
news** strangenesse   **100 spoil** wast   **122 poise** prize   **125 least
thought** best though   **132** *Flourish. Exeunt* [eds.] *Exeunt. Flourish*
2.2. 22 clamorous clamours   **45 an** if   **52 What's** What is   **66 you'll**
you will   **78 Bring . . . their** Being . . . the   **79 Renege** Reuenge
80 gale gall   **83 Smile** Smoile   **84 an** if   **101 take't** take it   **109 flickering** flicking   **124 dread** dead   **127 their** there   **132 respect** respects
142.1 [at line 140 in F]   **144–8 His . . . with** [Q1; not in F]   **146 contemned'st** [eds.] temnest [Q1]   **148 King** King his Master, needs
153 [Q1; not in F]   **154 Come . . . away** [assigned in F to Cornwall]
good [Q1; not in F]   **154.1 Exeunt** [eds.] *Exit*   **155 Duke's** Duke
2.3. 18 sheepcotes Sheeps-Coates
2.4. 2 messenger Messengers   **9 man's** man   **18–19** [Q1; not in F]
30 panting painting   **33 whose** those   **56 Hysterica** [eds.] *Historica*
62 the the   **74 have** hause   **128 you** your   **130 mother's** Mother
183 s.d. [after line 182 in F]   **185.1** [at line 183 in F, after "Stockes"]
187 fickle fickly   **190 s.d.** [after line 188 in F]   **213 hot-blooded**
hot-bloodied   **285 s.d.** [after "weeping" in line 286 in F]   **297 s.d.** [after
line 296 in F]   **298 Whither** Whether [also in line 299]   **302 bleak** high
3.1. 7–15 tears . . . all [Q1; not in F]   **10 outstorm** [eds.] outscorne [Q1]
30–42 [Q1; not in F]
3.2. 3 drowned drown   **38.1** [after line 36 in F]   **50 pother** pudder
85–6 [these lines follow line 92 in F]
3.3. 17 for 't for it
3.4. 7 skin. So 'tis skinso: 'tis   **10 thy** they   **12 This** the   **27 s.d.** [at
line 26 in F]   **31 looped** lop'd   **38.1** *Enter Fool* [F, after line 36:
"*Enter Edgar, and Foole*"]   **44.1** [after line 36 in F]   **46 blows the cold
wind** blow the windes   **51 through** though Fire   **52 ford** Sword
57, 58 Bless Blisse   **90 deeply** deerely   **99 sessa** [eds.] *Sesey*
112.1 [after line 108 in F]   **114 fiend** [Q1; not in F]   **115 till the** at
116 squinnies [eds.] squints [F] squemes [Q1]   **134 stock-punished**
stockt, punish'd   **hath had** hath   **173 in th'** into th'
3.5. 11 he which hee   **26 dearer** deere
3.6. 5.1 Exit [at line 3 in F]   **17–55** [Q1; not in F]   **21 justicer** [eds.]
Iustice [Q1]   **22 Now** [Q2] no [Q1]   **24 eyes at trial, madam?** eyes,
at tral madam [Q1]   **25 burn** [eds.] broome [Q1]   **34 cushions** [eds.]
cushings [Q1]   **36 robèd** robbed   **51 joint** [eds.] ioyne [Q1]   **53 on**
[eds.] an [Q1]   **67 mongrel grim** Mongrill, Grim   **68 lym** [eds.]
Hym   **69 Bobtail tike or trundle-tail** Or Bobtaile tight, or Troudle
taile   **73 Sessa** sese   **76 makes** make   **85.1** [after line 80 in F]
97–101 KENT Oppressèd . . . behind [Q1; not in F]   **101 GLOUCESTER**
[not in F]   **102–15** [Q1; not in F]
3.7. 10 festinate [eds.] festiuate   **18 lord's dependents** Lords,
dependents   **23 s.d. Exeunt** [eds.] *Exit* [at line 22 in F]   **61 rash**

sticke   **66 dern** sterne   **75 FIRST SERVANT** *Seru.* [also *Seru.* or *Ser.* at lines 79, 82, 84]   **83** [F provides a stage direction: "*Killes him*"]   **102–10** [Q1; not in F]   **102 SECOND SERVANT** *Seruant* [and called "1 *Ser*" at line 106 in Q1]   **103 THIRD SERVANT** 2 *Seruant* [Q1]   **107 Roguish** [Qa; not in Qb]   **109 THIRD SERVANT** 2 *Ser.*   **110.1 Exeunt** *Exit*

4.1. 2 flattered. To be worst flattered to be worst,   **41 Then . . . gone** Get thee away   **57–62 Five . . . master** [Q1; not in F]   **60 Flibbertigibbet** [eds.] *Stiberdigebit* [Q1]   **60–1 mopping and mowing** [eds.] Mobing, & *Mohing* [Q1]

4.2. 0.1 Bastard *Bastard, and Steward*   **2 s.d. steward** [Q1; placed at scene beginning in F]   **30 whistling** whistle   **32–51 I fear . . . deep** [Q1; not in F]   **33 its** [eds.] ith [Q1]   **48 these** [eds.] this [Q1]   **54–60 that . . . so** [Q1; not in F]   **58 to threat** thereat [Q1 corrected]   **61 shows** seemes   **63–9, 70** [Q1; not in F]   **76 thereat enraged** threat-enrag'd   **80 justicers** [Q1 corrected] Iustices

4.3. 1–57 [scene omitted in F]   **11 sir** [eds.] say [Q1]   **16 strove** [eds.] streme [Q1]   **20 seemed** [eds.] seeme [Q1]   **22 dropped. In** dropt in   **32 then** her, then   **44 benediction, turned her** benediction turnd her,   **57 s.d. Exeunt** [eds.] *Exit* [Q1]

4.4 [F reads "*Scena Tertia*"]   **3 fumiter** [eds.] femiter [Q1] Fenitar [F]   **6 century** Centery   **18 distress** desires   **28 right** Rite

4.5 [F reads "*Scena Quarta*"]   **8 letters** Letter   **23 Something** Some things   **27 oeillades** [eds.] Eliads   **41 meet him** meet

4.6 [F reads "*Scena Quinta*"]   **17 walk** walk'd   **57 summit** Somnet   **66–7 strangeness. / Upon . . . cliff what** [eds.] strangenesse, / Vpon . . . Cliffe. What   **71 enridgèd** enraged   **83 coining** crying   **97 white** the white   **124 they're** they are   **161 thine** thy   **164 Through** Thorough   **small** great   **165 Plate sin** [eds.] Place sinnes   **197 Ay . . . dust** [Q1; not in F]   **205 one a**   **218.1 Exit** [after "moved on" in line 218 in F]   **235 Durst** Dar'st   **238 'cagion** 'casion   **263–4 not. / To** not / To   **269 done if . . . conqueror. Then** [eds.] *done. If . . . Conqueror then*   **274 and . . . venture** [Q1; not in F]   **275 indistinguish'd** indinguish'd   **288 s.d. Drum afar off** [after line 286 in F]

4.7. 25 doubt not doubt   **25–6 CORDELIA Very . . . there** [Q1; not in F]   **33 warring** iarring   **34–7 To stand . . . helm** [Q1; not in F]   **59 hands** hand   **60 No, sir** [Q1; not in F]   **83–4 and . . . lost** [Q1; not in F]   **91–103** [Q1; not in F]

5.1. 12–14 [Q1; not in F]   **18 me not** not   **19–20** [Q1; not in F]   **24–9 Where . . . nobly** [Q1; not in F]   **35** [Q1; not in F]   **41 s.d. Exeunt . . . armies** [after line 39 in F]   **48 love** loues

5.3. 13 and hear poor rogues and heare (poore Rogues)   **39–40** [Q1; not in F]   **49 and appointed guard** [Q1 corrected; not in F]   **56–61 At . . . place** [Q1; not in F]   **57 We** [Q1 corrected] mee [Q1 uncorrected]   **59 sharpness** [Q1 corrected] sharpes [Q1 uncorrected]   **72 GONERIL** *Alb.*   **85 attaint** arrest   **86 sister** Sisters   **87 bar** bare   **100 he is** hes   **105 EDMUND A herald, ho, a herald** [Q1; not in F]   **105.1 Enter a Herald** [after line 104 in F]   **106 ALBANY** [not in F]   **112 CAPTAIN Sound, trumpet** [Q1; not in F]   **118 EDMUND Sound** [Q1; not in F]   **124–5 lost, / By . . . canker-bit.** lost / By Treasons tooth: bare-gnawne, and Canker-bit,   **132 the** my priuiledge, The   **135 Despite** Despise   **146 tongue** some say of tongue (some say)   **149 those** these   **151 scarcely** scarely   **153.1 Fight** [eds.] Fights. ["*Alarums. Fights*" is opposite "Saue him, saue him," in line 154 in F.]   **155 arms** Warre   **158 stopple** stop   **163 GONERIL** *Bast.*   **163 s.d. Exit** [at line 162 after "for 't" in F]   **208–25 This . . . slave** [Q1; not in F]   **217 him** [eds.] me [Q1]   **241.1** [after line 234 in F]   **255 The captain** [Q1; not in F]   **262 you** your   **280 CAPTAIN** *Gent.*   **282 them** him   **294 You are** [eds.] Your are [F] You'r [Q1]   **299.1** [after "to him" in line 299 in F]   **320 rack** wracke

The above textual notes list all instances in which material not in F is included from Q1. To enable the reader to compare further the F and Q1 texts, a list is provided here of material not in Q1 that is to be found in F. There are some 100 lines in all.

1.1. 40–5 while . . . now   **49–50** Since . . . state   **64–5** and . . . rivers   **83–5** to whose . . . interested   **88–9** LEAR Nothing? CORDELIA Nothing   **165** ALBANY, CORNWALL Dear sir, forbear.

1.2. 112–17 This . . . graves   **169–75** I pray . . . brother

1.4. 260 ALBANY Pray . . . patient   **273** Of . . . you   **321–33** This . . . unfitness

2.4. 6 KENT No, my lord   **21** KENT By Juno . . . ay   **45–54** FOOL Winter's . . . year   **96–7** GLOUCESTER Well . . . man   **101–2** Are they . . . Fiery? The   **139–44** LEAR Say . . . blame   **298–9** CORNWALL Whither . . . horse

3.1. 22–9 Who . . . furnishings

3.2. 79–96 FOOL This . . . time. *Exit*

3.4. 17–18 In . . . endure   **26–7** In . . . sleep   **37–8** Fathom . . . Tom

3.6. 12–14 FOOL No . . . him   **85** FOOL And . . . noon

4.1. 6–9 Welcome . . . blasts

4.2. 26 Oh, the . . . man

4.6. 165–70 Plate . . . lips

5.2. 11 GLOUCESTER And . . . too

5.3. 78 Dispose . . . thine   **91** GONERIL An interlude   **147** What . . . delay   **226** ALBANY Speak, man   **316–17** Do you . . . look there

Macbeth

Copy text: the First Folio. Act and scene divisions follow the Folio text, except that 5.8 is not marked in the Folio.

1.1. 9 SECOND WITCH *All*   **10 THIRD WITCH** [not in F]   **11 ALL** [at line 9 in F]

1.2. 1 [and elsewhere] DUNCAN *King*   **13 gallowglasses** Gallowgrosses   **14 quarrel** Quarry   **21 ne'er** neu'r   **26 thunders break** Thunders

1.3. 32 Weird weyward [elsewhere in F spelled "weyard"]   **39 Forres** Soris   **97 death. As** death, as   **98 Came** Can   **111 lose** loose

1.4. 1 Are Or

1.5. 1 [and elsewhere] LADY MACBETH *Lady*   **12 lose** *loose*   **47 it** hit

1.6. 4 martlet Barlet   **9 most** must

1.7. 6 shoal Schoole   **48 do** no

2.1. 56 strides sides   **57 sure** sowre   **58 way they** they may

2.2. 13.1 [at line 8 in F, after "die"]

2.3. 41.1 [after line 40 in F]   **142 nea'er** neere

3.1. 76 MURDERERS *Murth.*   **116 BOTH MURDERERS** *Murth.* [also at line 141]   **142.1 Exeunt** [at line 144 in F]

3.3. 7 and end

3.4. 79 time times   **122.1 Exeunt** *Exit*

3.6. 24 son Sonnes   **38 the** their

4.1. 34 cauldron Cawdron   **38.1 to** and   **59 germens** Germaine   **93 Dunsinane** Dunsmane   **94 s.d. Descends** Descend   **98 Birnam** Byrnan [also spelled "Byrnam" at line 93 and "Birnan," "Byrnane," and "Birnane" in Act 5]   **119 eighth** eight

4.2. 1 [and throughout] LADY MACDUFF *Wife*   **22 none** moue   **70–1 ones . . . methinks,** ones / To fright you thus. Me thinkes   **80 s.d. Enter Murderers** [after "What are these faces" in F]   **81 [and throughout scene] FIRST MURDERER** *Mur.*   **84 shag-haired** shagge-ear'd

4.3. 4 downfall'n downfall   **15 deserve** discerne   **35 Fare** Far   **108 accurst** accust   **124 detraction, here** detraction. Heere   **134 thy** they   **144 essay** assay   **146.1** [after "amend" in F]   **161 not** nor   **237 tune** time

5.1. 37 fear who feare? who

5.3. 41 Cure her Cure   **54 pristine** pristiue   **57 senna** Cyme   **62.1 Exeunt** [at line 64 in F]

5.4. 16 SIWARD *Sey.*

Timon of Athens

Copy text: the First Folio. Act and scene divisions, missing in the Folio, are editorially supplied.

The Actors' Names [Supplied at the end of the play. F also lists Lucius as one of the "*Seruants to Vsurers*," and the order of names has been changed for Apemantus and Ventidius and some others.]

1.1. 0.1 and Merchant *Merchant, and Mercer*   **23 gum** Gowne   **oozes** vses   **27 chafes** chases   **43 man** men   **50 tax** wax   **77 conceived to**

scope. conceyu'd, to scope   **92 hands** hand   **slip** sit   **116 [and subsequently]** OLD ATHENIAN *Oldm.*   **160.1** *Exeunt* Exit   **184.1** *Enter Apemantus* Enter Apermantus [at line 182 in F]   **222 cost** cast   **227** APEMANTUS *pe.*   **234 feigned** fegin'd   **259 there!** their   **286 Come** Comes   **287 taste** raste   **296** FIRST LORD [not in F]

1.2. 0.2 [and elsewhere] *Ventidius Ventigius*   **30 ever** verie   **41 their** there   **91 thousands, did** thousands? Did   **98 'em, and** 'em? And   **105 Oh, joy's e'en** Oh ioyes, e'ne   **107 To forget their faults,** to forget their Faults.   **113 s.d.** *Sound tucket* [F continues: "*Enter the Maskers of Amazons with Lutes in their hands, dauncing and playing*"]   **114 s.d.** *Enter Servant* [after "How now?" in F]   **120.1** *Enter Cupid* [F continues: "*with the Maske of Ladies*"]   **124 Th'ear** There   **125 and smell** all   **129** FIRST LORD *Luc.*   **129.1–2** [see notes at lines 113 and 120 above]   **144.2** *singles* single   **151** FIRST LADY 1 *Lord*   **167 s.d.** *Enter Flavius* [at line 176, after "welcome," in F]   **181** SECOND SERVANT *Ser.*   **211 rode** rod   **213** THIRD LORD 1. *L.*

2.1. 34 Ay, go, sir. I go sir?   **35 in compt** in. Come

2.2. 1 [and elsewhere] FLAVIUS *Stew.*   **4 resumes** resume   **11 [and elsewhere]** VARRO'S SERVANT *Var.*   **13 [and elsewhere]** ISIDORE'S SERVANT *Isid.*   **41 broken** debt, broken   **64 [and elsewhere]** ALL THE SERVANTS *Al.* [or *All*]   **75, 104 mistress'** Masters   **81** PAGE *Boy*   **96 Ay. Would** I would   **132 proposed** propose   **139 found** sound   **160 of** or   **191 Flaminius** *Flauius*   **211 treasure, cannot** Treature cannot

3.1. 0.2 *Enter* enters   **1 [and elsewhere]** LUCULLUS'S SERVANT *Ser.*

3.2. 27 [and elsewhere] LUCIUS *Lucil.*   **35 [and elsewhere] He's** Has   **61.1** [at line 60 in F]

3.3. 5 Owe Owes   **23 I 'mongst** 'mong'st   **25 He'd** Had

3.4. 0.1 Men man   **1 [and elsewhere]** VARRO'S FIRST SERVANT *Var. man*   **2 [and elsewhere]** TITUS'S SERVANT *Tit.*   **[and elsewhere]** HORTENSIUS'S SERVANT *Hort.*   **3 [and elsewhere]** LUCIUS'S SERVANT *Luci.*   **6 [and elsewhere]** PHILOTUS'S SERVANT *Phil.*   **14 recoverable.** I fear recouerable, I feare: **15–16 purse;** / That is, purse, that is: **45 [and elsewhere]** VARRO'S SECOND SERVANT 2. *Varro*   **59 If** If't   **78 an answer** answer   **88** HORTENSIUS'S *Servant* 1. *Var.*   **89** BOTH VARRO'S SERVANTS 2. *Var.*   **112 Sempronius** *Sempronius Vllorxa*

3.5. 18 An And   **23 behave** behooue   **51 lion,** Lyon?   **felon** fellow   **52 judge,** Iudge?   **53 suffering.** suffering,   **66 Why, I** Why   **70 'em** him   **85 honors** Honour

3.6. 1 FIRST LORD 1 [and so throughout scene]   **19 here's** heares   **54** FIRST AND SECOND LORDS *Both*   **80 tag** *legge*   **87** OTHERS *other*   **91 with your** you with   **115** THIRD LORD 2   **116** SECOND LORD 3

4.1. 6 steads! To general filths steeds, to generall Filthes.   **8 fast;** fast   **9 back,** backe;   **13 Son** Some

4.3. 10 senator Senators   **12 pasture** Pastour   **13 lean** leaue   **16 grece** grize   **41 at, this** at. This   **88 tub-fast** Fubfast   **119 bars** Barne   **124 thy** the   **135 [and throughout scene]** PHRYNIA AND TIMANDRA *Both*   **158 scolds** scold'st   **187 thy human** the humane   **206 fortune** future   **225 mossed** moyst   **246 Outlives** Out-liues   **254 clasped** claspt: **255 swathe, proceeded** swath proceeded,   **257 drudges** drugges   **258 command,** command'st: **287 my** thy   **314 meddlers** Medlers   **368–9 thee.** beat thee, but thee, Ile beate thee; But   **387 son and sire** Sunne and fire   **401.1** [after line 402 in F]   **402 them** then   **414 [and throughout scene]** BANDITTI *All*   **439 villainy** Villaine   **439–40 do 't, Like workmen.** doo't. Like Workemen,   **458 us, not** vs not   **462.1** *Exeunt* Exit   **479 grant'st** grunt'st, **man, I** man. / I   **482 I; all** I all   **497 mild** wilde   **514 A** If not a

5.1. 5–6 Phrynia and Timandra *Phrinica* and *Timandylo*   **50 worship** worship   **66 go naked; men** go, / Naked men   **70 men** man   **115 in vain** vaine   **125 chance** chanc'd   **132 cauterizing** Cantherizing   **146 sense** since   **147 its own fail** it owne fall   **181 reverend'st** reuerends   **194 through** thorow

5.2. 1 [and throughout scene] THIRD SENATOR 1   **5 [and throughout scene]** FOURTH SENATOR 2   **14** FIRST SENATOR 3

5.3. 2 Who's Whose

5.4. 27 out. out,   **28 Shame . . . excess** (Shame that they wanted, cunning in excesse)   **55 Descend** Defend   **65** SOLDIER *Mes.*

Antony and Cleopatra

Copy text: the First Folio. Act and scene divisions, missing in the Folio, are editorially supplied.

1.1. 41 On One   **52 whose** who

1.2. 4 charge change   **41 fertile** fore-tell   **64–5 Alexas** [printed in F as s.p.]   **83 Saw** Saue   **90 Alexas** *Alexias*   **93 [and through line 118]** FIRST MESSENGER *Messen.* (or *Mess.*)   **116 minds** windes   **119 ho how**   **120** SECOND MESSENGER 1. *Mes.*   **121** THIRD MESSENGER 2. *Mes.*   **124** FOURTH MESSENGER 3. *Mes.*   **126** FOURTH MESSENGER *Mes.*   **137.1** *Enter Enobarbus* [after "hatch," line 137, in F]   **144 occasion** an occasion   **162 travel** Trauaile   **186 leave** loue   **191 Hath** Haue   **200 hair** heire   **202 place is** places   **requires** require

1.3. 2 who's Whose   **20 What, says** What sayes   **43 services** Seruicles   **63 vials** Violles   **80 blood. No more.** blood no more?   **82 by my** by my

1.4. 3 Our One   **8 Vouchsafed** vouchsafe   **9 abstract** abstracts   **34** FIRST MESSENGER *Mes.*   **44 deared** fear'd   **46 lackeying** lacking   **48** SECOND MESSENGER *Mes.*   **57 wassails** Vassailes   **58 Modena** *Medena*   **59 Pansa** *Pausa*   **77 we** me

1.5. 3 mandragora *Mandragoru*   **5 time** time: **35.1** *Alexas* Alexas *from Caesar*   **52 dumbed** dumbe   **53, What, was** What was   **64 man** mans

2.1. 2 [and throughout scene] MENAS *Mene.*   **22 joined** ioyne   **39 ne'er** neere   **42 warred** wan'd   **44–5 greater. . . . all,** greater, . . . all:

2.2. 77 Alexandria; you Alexandria you   **113 soldier only. Speak** Souldier, onely speak   **128 so** say   **129 reproof** proofe   **180.1** *Exeunt* Exit *omnes*   *Manent* Manet   **204 lovesick . . . The** Loue-sicke. With them the   **214 glow** gloue   **216 gentlewomen** Gentlewoman   **233 heard** hard

2.3. 23 afeard a feare   **25 thee; . . . to thee.** thee no more but: when to thee,   **31 away** alway   **32 [and elsewhere] Ventidius** *Ventigius*   **41 s.d.** *Enter Ventidius* [after "Ventigius," line 41, in F]

2.4. 6 th' Mount Mount   **9 MAECENAS, AGRIPPA** *Both*

2.5. 2 ALL *Omnes*   **10 river. There** Riuer there   **11 off, I** off. I   **12 finned** fine   **23 s.d.** *Enter a Messenger* [after "Italy," line 23, in F]   **28 him, there** him. / There   **44 is** 'tis   **85 s.d.** *Enter . . . again* [after "sir" line 85, in F]

2.6. 0.1 Menas [listed after *Agrippa* in F]   **16 th'all-honored** all-honor'd   **19 is** his   **39** CAESAR, ANTONY, LEPIDUS *Omnes*   **42–3 impatience. Though . . . telling,** impatience: though . . . telling.   **58 compostion** composition   **67 meanings** meaning   **71 more of** more   **83** CAESAR, ANTONY, LEPIDUS *All*   **83.1** *Manent* Manet

2.7. 1 their th'their   **4 colored** Conlord   **39 s.d.** *whispers in 's ear* [at line 41 in F]   **93 is** he is   **101 grows** grow   **113 bear** beate   **115** BOY [not in F]   **119 ALL** [not in F]   **122 off. Our** of our   **126 Splits** Spleet's   **130 father's** Father   **132 MENAS** [not in F]

3.1. 5 [and throughout scene] SILIUS *Romaine*   **8 [and elsewhere] whither** whether

3.2. 10 AGRIPPA *Ant.*   **16 figures** Figure   **49 full** the full   **60 wept** weepe

3.3. 2 s.d. *Enter . . . before* [after "sir," line 2, in F]   **19 looked'st** look'st

3.4. 8 them, then 9 **took't** look't   **24 yours** your   **30 Your** You   **38 has** he's

3.5. 13 world would   **hast** hadst   **chops** chaps   **15 grind the one** grind

3.6. 13 he there hither   **the kings** the King   **30 being, that** being that,   **62 obstruct** abstract   **73 Adallas** *Adullas*   **74 Manchus** *Mauchus*   **76 Comagene** Comageat   **Polemon** *Polemen*   **77 Lycaonia** Licoania

3.7. 4 it is it it   **14 Photinus, an** *Photinus* an   **19 s.d.** *Canidius Camidias* [also spelled "*Camidius*" in this scene and elsewhere]   **21 Brundusium** Brandusium   **23 Toryne** Troine   **29 [and elsewhere]** CANIDIUS *Cam.*   **36 muleteers** Militers   **52 Actium** Action   **57 impossible;** impossible   **67.1** *Exeunt* exit   **70 leader's** led Leaders leade   **73** CANIDIUS *Ven.*   **80 Well I** Well, I   **82 in** with

3.8. 6 s.d. *Exeunt* exit

3.9. 4 s.d. *Exeunt* exit
3.10. 0.5. *Enobarbus* Enobarbus and Scarus   **14 June** Inne   **28 he** his
3.11. 6 ALL Omnes   **19 that** them   **46 seize** cease   **50 led** lead   **57 tow** stowe   **58 Thy** The
3.12. 0.1. *Dolabella* Dollabello   **13 lessens** Lessons
3.13. 26 caparisons Comparisons   **34 alike. That** alike, that   **55 Caesar** Caesars   **74 deputation** disputation   **76 kneel / Till** kneele. / Tell him,   **94 s.d.** *Enter a Servant* [after "him," in line 94, in F]   **104 This** the   **114–15 eyes, / In . . . filth** eyes / In . . . filth,   **133 s.d.** *Enter . . . Thidias* [after "whipped," in line 133, in F]   **140 whipped . . . Henceforth** whipt. For following him, henceforth   **165 smite** smile   **168 discandying** discandering   **171 sits** sets   **202 on** in   **204 s.d.** *Exit* Exeunt
4.2. 1 Domitius Domitian   **20 ALL** Omnes
4.3. 8 THIRD 1   **25, 31 ALL** Omnes
4.4. 5 too too, *Anthony*   **6 ANTONY** [not in F, or mistakenly placed in line 5 as part of Cleopatra's speech]   **8 CLEOPATRA** [not in F]   **24 CAPTAIN** Alex.   **32–3 compliment . . . Now** Complement, Ile leaue thee. / Now
4.5. 1, 3, 6 SOLDIER Eros   **17 Dispatch.—Enobarbus** Dispatch Enobarbus   **17.1 Exeunt** Exit
4.6. 37–8 do 't . . . I doo't. I feele / I
4.7 3 s.d. *Exeunt* Exit   **8 s.d.** [after "heads," line 6, in F]
4.8. 2 gests guests   **18 My** Mine   **23 favoring** sauouring
4.12. 3 s.d. *Alarum . . . fight* [at 0.1 in F]   **4 augurers** Auguries   **21 spanieled** pannelled
4.13. 10 death. To death to'
4.14. 4 towered toward   **10 dislimns** dislimes   **19 Caesar** Caesars   **104 ho** how   **119 DERCETUS** Decre.   **145.1 Exeunt** Exit
4.15. 26–7 me. If . . . operation, me, if . . . operation.   **56 lived the** liued. The   **78 e'en** in   **96.1** *off of*
5.1 0.1 Maecenas Menas   **3.1 Dercetus** Decretas   **5, 13, 19 DERCETUS** Dec.   **5 Dercetus** Decretas   **26 you sad, friends?** you sad Friends,   **28, 31 AGRIPPA** Dol.   **48.1** [after "says," line 51, in F]   **54 intents** desires, desires,   **59 live** leaue
5.2. 26 dependency dependacie   **35** [F repeats s.p. *Pro.*]   **55 varletry** Varlotarie   **69.1** [after "to him" in F]   **80 O, the** o'th'   **86 autumn** 'twas *Anthony* it was   **102 success but** successe: But   **144 seal** seele   **156 soulless villain** Soule-lesse, Villain   **178 merits in our name,** merits, in our name   **207 s.d.** *Exit* [at line 206 in F]   **216 Ballad** Ballads   **223 my** mine   **228 Cydnus** Cidrus   **318 awry** away   **319.1** *in* in, *and Dolabella*   **342–3 diadem . . . mistress;** Diadem; . . . Mistris

Coriolanus

Copy text: the First Folio. Act divisions are from the Folio; scene divisions are from subsequent editorial tradition.

1.1. 7 [and throughout play] **Marcius** Martius   **15 on** one   **33 SECOND CITIZEN** All   **42–3 accusations. He** Accusations he   **55 FIRST CITIZEN** 2 Cit. [and so throughout scene]   **64 you. For your wants,** you for your wants.   **90 stale't** scale't   **105 you. With** you with   **108 tauntingly** taintingly   **123 you.** you,   **125 awhile,** awhile;   **171 geese. You are no** Geese you are: No   **214 Shouting** Shooting   **218 unroofed** vnroo'st   **227.1 Junius** Annius   **240 Lartius** Lucius   **242** [and at 1.1.246 and 1.5.21] **LARTIUS** Tit.   **245, 249** [and elsewhere] **FIRST SENATOR** Sen.   **252.2 Manent** Manet
1.2. 0.1 Corioles Coriolus   **4 on** one   **16 Whither** Whether   **27–8 Corioles. / . . . before's** Coriolus / If . . . before's;
1.3. 37 that's that   **44 sword, contemning.—Tell** sword. Contenning, tell   **82 VIRGILIA** Vlug.   **84 yarn** yearne   **85 Ithaca** Athica   **105 lady. . . . now,** Ladie, as she is now:
1.4. 0.3, 13.2 Corioles Coriolus   **18 up. Our** vp our   **20 s.d.** *Alarum far off* [after line 20 in F]   **32 herd of—Boils** Heard of Byles   **43 trenches. Follow 's** Trenches followes   **46.1 gates** Gati *and is shut in* [in F, this is part of the s.d. at line 43.2]   **57 left, Marcius.** left Martius,   **58 entire,** intire;   **59 Were** Weare   **60 Cato's** Calues

1.5. 3.3 Exeunt [before "*Alarum*" in line 3.1 in F]   **7 them,** them.   **8 up.** vp,   **9 him!** him
1.6. 9 s.d. [after line 9 in F]   **21 Who's** Whose   **22 flayed** Flead   **30 wooed, in heart** woo'd in heart;   **53 Antiates** Antients   **70 Lesser** Lessen   **73 alone, or** alone: Or   **84 I** foure
1.7. 7.1 Exeunt Exit
1.8. 11 masked. For maskt, for   **12 Wert** Wer't
1.9. 32 good . . . all good, and good store of all,   **41 May** [F provides a s.p., "*Mar.*"]   **49 shout** shoot   **64, 66** [and elsewhere] **Caius Marcius** Marcus Caius   **66 ALL** Omnes   **67, 78, 81, 89 CORIOLANUS** Martius   **93.1** *A flourish. Cornets.* [at the beginning of scene 10 in F]
1.10. 19 itself. Nor it selfe, nor
2.1. 18 with all withall   **24 how are** ho ware   **51 upon too** vppon, to   **57 cannot** can   **61 you you** you   **62 faces. If** faces, if   **64 bisson** beesome   **70–1 faucet-seller** Forcet-seller   **85 are. When . . . purpose,** are, when . . . purpose.   **106 VALERIA, VIRGILIA** 2. *Ladies*   **123 brows, Menenius.** Browes: *Menenius,*   **156 s.d.** [after line 156 in F]   **160.2** [and elsewhere] *Lartius* Latius   **164 "Coriolanus"** Martius Caius Coriolanus   **177 wear** were   **179 CORIOLANUS** Com.   **185 You** Yon   **203.2 Brutus** Enter Brutus   **Sicinius** Scicinius [and sometimes elsewhere]   **233 napless** Naples   **254 touch** teach
2.2. 25 ascent assent   **67** [and elsewhere] **FIRST SENATOR** Senat.   **81 one on 's** on ones   **91 chin** Shinne   **bristled** brizled   **108 took; from face to foot** tooke from face to foot: **155 Manent** Manet   **160 here. On the marketplace** heere on th' Market place,
2.3. 28 wedged wadg'd   **38–9 it. I say, if** it, I say. If   **52 tongue** tougne   **67 but not** but   **88, 91, 106 FOURTH CITIZEN** 1   **104 FIFTH CITIZEN** 2   **111 BOTH CITIZENS** Both   **114 hire** higher   **115 toge** tongue   **118 do't,** doo't?   **132 SIXTH CITIZEN** 1. *Cit.*   **134 SEVENTH CITIZEN** 2. *Cit.*
3.1. 46 suppliants for Suppliants: for   **60 abused, set on. This** abus'd: set on, this   **94 good God!** good God!   **129 Their** There   **137 poll** pole   **146 Where one** Whereon   **164 He's** Has [also at line 165]   **169 bench? In a rebellion,** Bench, in a rebellion: **176 s.d.** *Enter an Aedile* [after line 175 in F]   **181 ALL PATRICIANS** All   **187** [and elsewhere] **ALL PLEBEIANS** All   **189 ALL** [at line 191 in F]   **219 ALL PLEBEIANS** All Ple.   **233.1–2** [preceded in F by "*Exeunt*"]   **234 your** our   **235 CORIOLANUS** Com.   **242 COMINIUS** Corio.   **243 CORIOLANUS** Mene.   **245 MENENIUS** [not in F]   **283 comes 't** com'st   **315 SICINIUS** Menen.   **334 bring him** bring him in peace
3.2. 7 A PATRICIAN Noble   **14 s.d.** *Enter Volumnia* [after line 6 in F]   **23 thwartings** things   **34 herd** heart   **67 son, these . . . nobles;** Sonne: These . . . Nobles,   **80 With** Which   **103 bear? Well, I** beare well? I   **104 plot to lose,** Plot, to loose   **115 drum, into a pipe** Drumme into a pipe   **117 lulls** lull
3.3. 5 s.d. [after line 5 in F]   **34 for th'** fourth   **38 Throng** Through   **59 accents** Actions   **73 hell fold** hell. Fould   **76 clutched** clutcht: **77 numbers,** numbers.   **107 it;** in it. In   **118 for** from   **143–4 blows! Despising . . . city, thus** blowes, despising . . . City. Thus   **145.1 Cominius** Cominius, with Cumalijs   **147 Hoo! Hoo!** Hoo, oo   **147.1** [after line 145.1 in F]
4.1. 5 chances chances.   **24 thee** the   **34 wilt** will   **37 VIRGILIA** Corio.
4.2. 23 words, words.   **46 s.d.** *Exeunt* Exit   **55** [F has s.d. "*Exeunt*"]   **56 s.d.** *Exeunt* Exit
4.3. 9 approved appear'd   **32 will** well
4.4. 6 s.d. [after line 6 in F]   **23 hate** haue
4.5. 75 requited requitted: **83 Whooped** Hoop'd   **136 o'erbear't** o're-beate   **152.2 Two** Enter two   **169 on** one   **181, 185 FIRST AND SECOND SERVINGMEN** Both   **194 him, directly** him directly,   **195 Corioles;** Corioles,   **209 sowl** sole   **211 polled** poul'd   **233 sleepy** sleepe
4.6. 10 s.d. [after line 9 in F]   **21** [and elsewhere] **ALL CITIZENS** All   **36 lamentation** Lamention   **61 come** comming   **78 SECOND MESSENGER** Mes.   **127 BOTH TRIBUNES** Tri.   **144 one** oue   **146 ALL CITIZENS** Omnes   **151 us. That** vs, that   **165.1 Exeunt** Exit
4.7. 19 him. Although him, although   **21 fairly** fairely: **34 osprey** Aspray   **37 'twas** 'was   **39 defect** detect   **49 virtues** Vertue,   **55 falter** fouler

5.2. 65 by my my **76 our** your **88 pity note how much.** pitty: Note how much, **95.1 *Manent*** Manet

5.3. 15 accept. To accept, to **16 more, a** more: A **48 prate** pray **63 holp** hope **66 curded** curdied **127 YOUNG MARCIUS** *Boy* **149 fine** fiue **152 charge** change **163 clucked** clock'd **169 with our** with him with our **192 stead** steed

5.4. 40 [and throughout scene] SECOND MESSENGER *Mess.* **49.1 *all together*** altogether **51 cymbals** Symboles

5.5. 4 Unshout Vnshoot

5.6. 33 projects to accomplish, projects, to accomplish **43–4 it / For . . . him.** it: / For . . . him, **46 lies, he** Lies; he **56 second. When** second, when **57 way his** way. His **63 ALL LORDS** All **104 other** others **117 pieces, Volsces. Men** peeces Volces men **121 Fluttered** Flatter'd **136.1 *Draw*** Draw both

Pericles

Copy text: the First Quarto of 1609. Act and scene divisions, missing in the Quarto, are derived from subsequent editorial tradition.

1.0. 1 GOWER [not in Q; also in subsequent choruses throughout, except at 4.4, 5.2, and Epilogue] **6 holy-ales** Holydayes **11 these** those **39 a** of

1.1. 8 For th' For **18 razed** racte **23 the** th' **25 boundless** bondlesse **57 ANTIOCHUS** [not in Q; also at line 170] **63 advice** advise **100–1 clear . . . them. The** cleare: . . . them, the **106 know; . . . fit,** know, . . . fit; **112 our** your **114 cancel** counsell **128 you're** you **137 'schew** shew **160.1 *Enter a Messenger*** [after "done" in line 160 in Q]

1.2. 3 Be my By me **5 quiet?** quiet, **16 me: the** me the **20 honor him** honour him **25 th'ostent** the stint **30 am** once **41 blast** sparke **69–70 me . . . thyself.** me: . . . thy selfe, **72 Where, as** Whereas **80 seem** seemes **84 Bethought me** Bethought **85 fears** feare **87 doubt—as . . . he doth** doo't, as no doubt he doth **93 call't** call **122 word for faith,** word, for faith **123 will sure** will **124 we'll** will **126.1 *Exeunt*** Exit

1.3. 1 THALIARD [not in Q] **27 ears it** seas **please** please: **28 seas** Sea **30 HELICANUS** [not in Q] **34 betaken** betake **39.1 *Exeunt*** Exit

1.4. 5 aspire aspire? **13, 14 do** to **13 deep** deepe: **14 lungs** toungs **17 helps** helpers **36 they** thy **39 two summers** too sauers **44 loved.** lou'de, **58 thou** thee **67 Hath** That **these** the **69 men** mee **74 him 's** himnes **77 fear?** leaue **78 lowest,** lowest? **97 ALL** *Omnes* **106 ne'er** neare

2.0. 11 Tarsus Tharstill **12 speken** spoken **22 Sends word** Sau'd one **24 intent** in Tent **murder** murdred [some corrected copies of Q have "had . . . murder"]

2.1. 6 left me left my **12 ho** to **Pilch** pelch **31–2 devours** deuowre **39 THIRD FISHERMAN** 1 **48 finny** fenny **53 that?** that, **55 it.** it? **78 quotha** ke-tha **82 holidays** all day **83 moreo'er** more; or **91 your** you **100 is** I **122 pray** pary **123 yet** yeat **all thy** all **130 it.** it **131 thee from !—may 't** thee, Fame may **148 d' ye** di'e [Q uncorr.] do'e [Q corr.] **157 rapture** rupture **160 delightful** delight **167 equal** a Goale

2.2. 1 [and elsewhere] SIMONIDES *King* **4 daughter** daughter heere **27 *Piùe . . . forza*** Pue Per doleera kee per forsa **28 what's** with **29 chivalry** Chiually **30 *pompae*** Pompey **33 *Quod*** Qui

2.3. 3 To I **13 yours** your **39 Yon** You **40 tells me** tels **45 son's** sonne **52 stored** stur'd **53 you do** do you **109 s.d. *They dance*** [after "unclaspe" in Q] **113 to be** be **115 SIMONIDES** [not in Q]

2.4. 22 welcome. Happy welcome happy **34 death's** death **40 ALL** *Omnes*

2.5. 74 s.d. *Aside* [after line 75 in Q] **76 you, not** you not, **78 s.d. *Aside*** [after line 79 in Q] **92 BOTH** *Ambo*

3.0. 2 the house about about the house **6 'fore** from **7 crickets** Cricket **10 Where, by** Whereby **13 eche** each **17 coigns** Crignes **21 stead** steed **quest. At last from Tyre,** quest at last from *Tyre*: **29 appease** oppresse **35 Yravishèd** Iranyshed **46 Fortune's mood** fortune mou'd **57 not . . . told.** not? . . . told, **58 hold** hold:

3.1. 1 Thou The **7 Thou stormest** then storme **8 spit** speat **11 midwife** my wife **14 s.d. *Enter Lychorida*** [after "Lychorida" in Q] **34 Poor . . . nature** [Wilkins; not in Q] **38 MASTER** 1. *Sayl* [also in lines 43 and 47] **45 SAILOR** 2. *Sayl* **51 MASTER** 1 **52 custom easterne** 53 for . . . straight [printed in Q as part of the next line, after "As you think meet," the line assigned to Pericles] **60 in the ooze** in oare **62 And aye-** The ayre **65 paper** Taper **70 SAILOR** 2 **73 MASTER** 2 [also in line 76] **81 s.d. *Exeunt*** Exit

3.2. 6 ne'er neare **19 quit** quite **51 [and elsewhere] FIRST SERVANT** *Seru.* **58 bitumed** bottomed **61–2 open. / Soft!** open soft; **68–9 too! / Apollo** to *Apollo,* **79 even** euer **87 lain** lien **95 breathes** breath

3.3. 0.1 *at Tarsus* Artharsus **6 haunt** hant **31 Unscissored** vnsisterd hair heyre **32 ill** will **37 CLEON** *Cler.* **41 [and elsewhere] Lychorida** Lycherida

3.4. 0.1. *Thaisa* Tharsa **4 THAISA** *Thar.* **5 eaning** learning **9 vestal** vastall **11 CERIMON** *Cler.* **17.1 *Exeunt*** Exit

4.0. 8 music, letters Musicks letters **10 high** hie **14 Seeks** Seeke **15 hath our Cleon** our *Cleon* hath **16 wench full grown** full growne wench **17 ripe** right **rite** sight **21 she** they **25 to th'** too'th **26 bird** bed **29 Dian; still** *Dian* still, **32 With** [after "might" in Q] **35 given. This** giuen, this **38 murder** murderer **47 carry** carried **48 on** one

4.1. 5 inflaming love i'thy in flaming, thy loue **11 nurse's** Mistresse **25 me.** me? **27 On . . . margent** ere the sea marre it **36 here. When** here, when **40 courses. Go** courses, go **66 stem** sterne **76–7 killed? / Now** kild now? **99.1 *Exeunt*** Exit **105 aboard.** if aboord, if

4.2. 4 much much much **42 FIRST PIRATE** *Sayler* **73 was like** was **88–9 must stir** stir **103 i'th'** ethe **117–18 lovers; seldom but** Louers seldome, but **124 BAWD** *Mari.* **150 s.d. *Exeunt*** Exit

4.3. 1 are ere **6 A** O **12 fact** face **14–15 Fates; / To foster is** fates to foster it, **27 prime** prince **33 Marina's** *Marianas* **35 through** thorow

4.4. 3 your our **7 seem** seemes **8 i'th'** with **9 story.** storie **10 the** thy **13 along. Behind** along behind, **14 govern, if** gouerne it, **mind,** mind. **18 his** this **19 grow on** grone **20 gone.** gone **23 See** [Q adds an s.p. here: *Gowr.*] **24 true-owed** true olde **26 o'er-showered,** ore-showr'd. **27 embarks. He** imbarques, hee **29 puts** put **to sea. He bears** to Sea he beares, **48 scene** Steare

4.5. 9 s.d. *Exeunt* Exit

4.6. 0.1 *three bawds* Bawdes 3 **17 loon** Lowne **22 may so;** may, so **37 dignifies** dignities **69 name't** name **88 aloof** aloft **130 ways** way **137 She** He **154 ways** way **167 Coistrel** custerell **195 women** woman

5.0. 7 roses: Roses **8 twin** Twine **13 lost** left **20 fervor** [Q corr.] former [Q uncorr.]

5.1. 1 TYRIAN SAILOR 1. *Say* **7 TYRIAN SAILOR** 2. *Say* **12 TYRIAN SAILOR** 1. *Say* [Q corr.] Hell [Q uncorr.] **36 LYSIMACHUS** [not in Q] **37 Behold . . . person** [assigned to Lysimachus in Q] **38 Till Hell.** Till **night** wight **43 A LORD** *Lord* **48 deafened ports** defend parts **51 with her** her **is now** now **60 gods** God **68 presence** present **72 I'd** I do **wed** to wed **73 one** on **bounty** beautie **75 feat** fate **83 Marked** Marke **91 weighed.** wayde, **105 You're** your **countrywoman** Countrey women **106 Here** heare **shores . . . shores** shewes . . . shewes **114 cased** caste **124 palace** *Pallas* **126 make my** make **129 say** stay **134 thought'st** thoughts **143 thou them?** thou **166 dull** duld **182 imposter** imposture **185 PERICLES** Hell. **205 me but that,** me, but that **212 life** like **228–9 music? / Tell** Musicke tell, **230 doubt** doat **249 life** like **264 suit** sleight

5.2. 8 Mytilin Metalin. **9 King. So** King, so **14 interim, pray you, all** Interim pray, you all **15 filled** fild **16 willed** wild

5.3. 6 who whom **15 nun** mum **22 one** in **29–30 look! / If** looke if **38 Immortal** I, mortall **51 PERICLES** Hell. **71 I bless** blesse **79 credit, sir,** credit. Sir, **91 preserved** preferd **92 Led** Lead **98 deed to** deede,

Cymbeline

Copy text: the First Folio. Act and scene divisions are as in the Folio except as indicated below.

1.1. 2 courtiers' Courtiers: **30** [and elsewhere] **Cassibelan** *Cassibulan*   **59 swaddling-clothes the other,** swathing cloathes, the other   **70** [F begins "*Scena Secunda*" here]   **98 Philario's** *Filorio's*   **118 cere** seare   **160.1** *Enter Pisanio* [after *Exit*, line 160, in F]
1.2 [F labels "*Scena Tertia*"]
1.3 [F labels "*Scena Quarta*"]   **9 this** his
1.4 [F labels "*Scena Quinta*"]   **28 Briton** Britaine   **47 offend not** offend   **72 Britain.** Brittanie;   **others** others.   **74 but believe** beleeue   **84 purchase** purchases   **128 thousand** thousands   **137 preserve** preseure
1.5 [F labels "*Scena Sexta*"]   **3 s.d.** *Exeunt Exit*   **77 s.d.** *Exit Pisanio* [at line 76 in F]   **87 s.d.** *Exeunt* Exit
1.6 [F labels "*Scena Septima*"]   **7 desire** desires   **28 takes** take   **36 th'unnumbered** the number'd   **61, 67** [and elsewhere] **Briton** Britaine   **72 be, will . . . languish** be: will . . . languish: **104 Fixing** Fiering   **109 illustrous** illustrious   **169 men's** men   **170 descended** defended
2.1. 27 Your you   **34 tonight** night   **51.1** *Exeunt Exit*   **61 husband,** than Husband. Then   **62 divorce he'd make!** diuorce, heel'd make   **63 honor, keep** Honour. Keepe   **65 s.d.** *Exit Exeunt*
2.2. 1 *Helen La.* [also at line 2]   **49 bare** beare   **51.1** *Exeunt Exit*
2.3. 20 MUSICIAN [not in F]   **29** CLOTEN [not in F]   **30 vice** voyce   **32 amend** amed   **48 solicits** solicity   **130 envy, if** Enuie. If   **139 garment** Garments   **147 am** am   **156 you** your
2.4. 6 hopes hope   **18 legions** Legion   **24 mingled** wing-led   **34 through** thorough   **37** PHILARIO *Post.*   **48 not** note   **58 you** yon   **61 leaves** leaue   **63 near** nere   **138 the** her
2.5. [scene not marked in F]   **16 German one** Iarmen on   **27 have a name** name
3.1. 20 rocks Oakes   **53 be. We do say** be, we do. Say
3.2. 2 monster's her accuser Monsters her accuse   **67 score** store   **ride** rid   **78 here, nor** heere, not
3.3. 2 Stoop Sleepe   **23 bauble** Babe   **28 know** knowes   **31 known, well** knowne. Well   **34 for** or   **83 wherein they bow,** whereon the Bowe   **86 Polydore** Paladour   **106 Morgan** *Mergan*
3.4. 79 afore't a-foot   **90 make** makes   **102 blind first** first   **148** [and elsewhere] **haply** happily
3.5. 17.1 *Exeunt Exit*   **32 looks** looke   **40 strokes** stroke;,   **42** ATTENDANT *Mes.*   **44 loud'st** lowd   **55.1** *Exit* [after "days" in F]   **141–2 insultment** insulment
3.6. 27 [F begins "*Scena Septima*" here]   **89 Leonatus's** *Leonatus*
3.7 [F labels "*Scena Octaua*"]   **9 commends** commands
4.1. 18 her face thy face
4.2. 50–2 He . . . dieter [assigned in F to Arviragus]   **58 him** them   **59 Grow, patience** Grow patient   **124 thanks, ye** thanks the   **134 humor** Honor   **172 how** thou   **188 ingenious** ingenuous   **207 crare** care   **208 Might** Might'st   **226 ruddock** Raddocke   **293 is** are   **294** IMOGEN (*awakes*) [as stage direction in F]   **339 are** are heere   **393 wild-wood leaves** wild wood-leaves
4.3. 40 betid betide
4.4 2 find we we finde   **17 the** their   **27 hard** heard
5.1. 1 wished am wisht   **32–3 begin / The fashion:** begin, / The fashion
5.3. 24 harts hearts   **42 stooped** stopt   **43 they** the   **47 before, some** before some
5.4. 1 [and throughout scene] FIRST JAILER *Gao.*   **15 constrained. To** constrain'd, to   **50 deserved** d seru'd   **81 look** looke, looke   **165 Of** Oh, of   **169 sir** Sis   **197 s.d.** *Exeunt* [at line 206 in F]
5.5. 54 fine time   **62** LADIES *La.*   **65 heard** heare   **71 rased** rac'd   **128 saw** see   **136 On,** One   **207 got it** got   **264 from** fro   **277 truth** troth   **315 on 's** one's   **319 leave.** leaue   **338 mere** neere   **339 treason;** Treason   **382 ye** we   **390 brothers** Brother   **391 whither? These,** whether these?   **392 battle,** Battaile?   **395 to chance;** to chance?   **409 so** no   **439** SOOTHSAYER [not in F]   **473 this yet** yet this

The Winter's Tale

Copy text: the First Folio. Characters' names are groups at the heads of scenes throughout the play. Act and scene divisions are as marked in the Folio.

The Names of the Actors [printed in F at the end of the play]
ARCHIDAMUS [after *Autoclycus* in F]
1.1. 9 us, we vs: we
1.2. 104 And A   **121 hast** has't   **137–8 be?— / Affection, thy** be / Affection? thy   **148 What . . . brother** [assigned in F to Leontes]   **151–3 its folly, . . . Its tenderness, . . . bosoms!** it's folly? . . . It's tendernesse? . . . bosomes?   **158 do** do's   **202–3 powerful, think it, . . . south. Be** powrefull: thinke it: . . . South, be   **208 you, they** you   **253 forth. In . . . lord,** forth in . . . (my Lord.)   **275 hobbyhorse** Holy-Horse   **386 How? Caught** How caught   **461 off. Hence!** off, hence:
2.1. 2 [and throughout scene] FIRST LADY *Lady*   **91 fedarie** Federarie
2.2. 32–3 me. / If . . . blister me, / If . . . blister.
2.3. 2 thus, mere weakness. If thus: meere weaknesse, if   **39 What** Who   **61 good, so** good so,
3.2. 10 Silence [printed in F as a s.d.]   **10.1–2** *Hermione, as to her trial . . . Ladies* [at start of scene in F, as generally with the s.d. in this play]   **33 Who** Whom   **99 Starred** Star'd   **156 woo** woe
3.3. 64 scar'd scarr'd   **116 made** mad
4.2. 13 thee. Thou, thee, thou
4.3. 1 AUTOLYCUS [not in F]   **7 on** *an*   **10 With heigh, with heigh** *With heigh*   **38 currants** Currence
4.4. 12 Digest it Digest   **13 swoon** sworne   **60 a fire** o'fire   **83 bastards. Of** bastards) of   **93 scion** Sien   **98 your** you   **160 out** on't   **218** AUTOLYCUS [not in F]   **244 kilnhole** kill-hole   **297** AUTOLYCUS [in F, appears at line 298]   **299 Whither** Whether [and similarly throughout song]   **310 gentleman** Gent.   **316 cape** *Crpe*   **339 square** squire   **355 reply, at least** reply at least,   **361 who** whom   **421 acknowledged** acknowledge   **425 who** whom   **430 see** neuer see   **441 hoop** hope   **470 your** my   **473 sight as yet, I fear.** sight, as yet I feare;   **485–6 fancy. If . . . obedient, I** fancie, if . . . obedient: I   **503 our** her   **614 could** would   **filed** fill'd   **off** of   **644 flayed** fled   **708 know not** know   **738 to** at   **833 s.d.** *Exeunt* [at 845 in F]
5.1. 6 Whilst Whilest [also at line 169]   **59 Where . . . appear** (Where we Offendors now appeare)   **61 just** just such   **75 I have done** [assigned in F to Cleomenes]   **84 s.d.** *Gentleman Seruant*   **85** [and through line 110] GENTLEMAN, *Ser.*   **114 s.d.** *Exit* [after "us" in line 115 in F]   **160 his, parting** his parting
5.2. 113 s.d. *Exeunt Exit*
5.3. 18 Lonely Louely   **67 fixture** fixure

The Tempest

Copy text: the First Folio. Characters' names are groups at the heads of scenes throughout. Act and scene divisions are as marked in the Folio.
Names of the Actors [printed in F at the end of the play]
1.1. 8.1 *Ferdinand Ferdinando*   **34 s.d.** *Exeunt Exit*   **36** [and elsewhere] **wi' the** with   **38.1** [at line 37 in F]
1.2. 99 exact, like exact. Like   **166 steaded much.** steeded much,   **174 princes** Princesse   **201 bowsprit** Bore-spritt   **213 me. The** me the   **230 Bermudas** *Bermoothes*   **284 she** he   **288 service. Thou** service, thou   **330 forth at** for that   **377.5, 399.1 Ariel's** Ariel (or Ariell)   **385 s.d.** *Burden, dispersedly* [before "Hark, hark!" in line 384 in F]   **387** [F provides a speech prefix, *Ar.*]   **400** ARIEL [not in F]
2.1. 38 ANTONIO *Seb.*   **39** SEBASTIAN *Ant.*   **183 mettle** mettal   **232 throes** throwes
2.2. 9 mow moe   **116 spirits** sprights
3.1. 2 sets set
3.2. 51–2 isle; / From me he Isle / From me, he   **123 scout** *cout*
3.3. 15 travel trauaile   **17.1–2** *Solemn . . . invisible* [after "they are fresh" in F, and followed by the s.d. at line 19, *Enter . . . depart*]   **28 me** me?   **29 islanders?** Islands;   **33 human** humaine   **65 plume** plumbe

4.1. 9 off of   **13 gift** guest   **25 love as 'tis now, the** loue, as 'tis now the   **61 vetches** Fetches   **68 poll-clipped** pole-clipt   **74 Her** here   **110 CERES** [not in F]   **123 wife** wise   **124.1–2** [after line 127 in F]   **163.1** *Exeunt* Exit   **193 s.d.** *Enter Ariel . . . etc.* [after "on this line" in F, and followed by *Enter Caliban . . . all wet*]   **193 them on** on them   **232 Let't** let's

5.1. 60 boiled boile   **72 Didst** Did   **75 entertained** entertaine   **82 lies** ly   **88 ARIEL** [not in F]   **111 Whe'er** Where   **236 horrible,** horrible.   **238 her** our   **249 business. At** businesse, at   **250 Which . . . single** (Which shall be shortly single)   **260** *coraggio* Corasio

The Two Noble Kinsmen

Copy text: the Quarto of 1634. Act and scene divisions follow Q except at 2.1.48, where Q indicates "Scaena 2." Subsequently, "Scaena 3" and the first "Scaena 4" in the Q text of Act 2 are renumbered in this edition as scenes 2 and 3; the second "Scaena 4" in Q corresponds to scene 4 in this edition, perhaps suggesting that the earlier Q markings at "Scaena 3" and the first "Scaena 4" are in error. Act 3 scenes 5 and 6 are misnumbered "6" and "7" in Q, skipping "5" in error.

Prologue. 1 PROLOGUE [not in Q]   **26 tack** take   **29 travail** *travell*

1.1. 0.1 *Music* [after the s.d. in Q, together with indication of "The Song"]   **0.7** *Pirithous* Theseus   **1 BOY** [not in Q]   **6 thyme** *Time*   **7 firstborn child** *firstborne, child*   **13–14 children sweet / Lie** *children:sweete- / Ly*   **16 angel** *angle*   **20 chough hoar** *Clough hee*   **41 talons** Tallents   **59 Capaneus was your lord; the** *Capaneus, was your Lord the*   **68 Nemean** Nenuan   **90 thy** the   **104 willing way** willing, way   **112 pebbles** peobles   **glassy** glasse   **113 'em. Lady, lady, alack!** 'em (Lady, Lady, alacke)   **123 grief, indeed** greefe indeed   **132 longer** long   **138 move** mooves   **ospreys** Asprayes   **142 drams, precipitance** drams precipitance   **156 Rinsing** Wrinching   **159 Artesius** *Artesuis*   **178 twinning** twyning   **211 soldier.** [*To Artesius*] As before, hence Soldier (as before) hence   **212 Aulis** Anly   **218.1** [*The marriage . . . temple* Exeunt towards the Temple   **225.1** *Exeunt* [*in procession*] [no s.d. in Q; see textual note at 218.1]

1.2. 41 are here were are, here were   **42 be, mere** be meere   **55 canon** Cannon   **65 power there's nothing; almost** power: there's nothing, almost   **70 glory; one** glory on; [Q corr.], glory on [Q uncorr.]

1.3. 31 one ore   **54 eleven** a eleven   **Flavina** *Flauia*   **58–64** [Q, in left margin, prints: "2. Hearses rea- / dy with Pala- / mon: and Arci- / te: the 3. / Queenes: / Theseus: and / his Lordes / ready."]   **65 not, condemned—**not condemd   **73 happily her careless wear—**I happely, her careles, were, I   **75 one** on   **76 musical** misicall   **79 seely innocence** fury-innocent   **82 dividual** iudiuiduall   **out** ont

1.4. 13 s.d. [after 13 in Q]   **18 smeared** [Q corr.; succard, Q uncorr.]   **22 Wi'** We   **26** [Q prints s.d. in margin: "3. Hearses rea- / dy."]   **39 do—for** doe for   **40 friends' behests** friends, beheastes   **41 Love's provocations** Loves, provocations   **45 O'er-wrestling** Or wrastling   **49 'fore** for

1.5. 10 We convent . . . woes *We convent, &C.*

2.1. 16.1 *Enter . . . Daughter* [after "her?" in line 14 in Q]   **20 that now. So** that. / Now, so   **31 grece** greise   **51.1** *Enter . . . above* [after "the night" in line 50 in Q]

2.2. 0 [Q reads: "*Scaena 2. Enter Palamon, and Arcite in prison.*"]   **3 war; yet we** warre yet, we   **20 us. Our** us, our   **21 wore** were   **22 Ravished** Bravishd   **64 twinned** twyn'd   **118 This . . . in 't** [printed as the continuation of Arcite's speech in Q]   **129 will't** wilt   **132 was I** I was   **192 your blood** you blood   **223.1** *Jailer* Keeper [also in s.p. and s.d. at lines 227, 228, 230, 231 s.d., 249.1, and 251 to end of scene]   **243 apricot** Apricocke   **275 you** yon

2.3. 6 sins [Q corr.; fins, Q uncorr.]   **25 FIRST COUNTRYMAN 1** [and so throughout scene]   **44 ye** yet   **59 says** sees   **87 Well I** Well, I

2.4. 34 night; ere night, or

2.5. [Q marks as "Scaena 4"]   **0.1 [A]** This [s.d. is in margin in Q]   **28 For** Fo

2.6. 3 him. To him to   **12–13 it; / I** it / I   **15–16 dirge, / And** Dirge. / And

3.1. 2 laund land   **11 presence; in** presence, in   **13 thought! Thrice** thought, thrice   **36 looked, the** lookd the   **void'st** voydes   **36–7 honor / That** honour. That   **38 kin! Call'st** kin, call'st   **42 Not** Nor   **96.1 off.** *Cornets of Cornets* [s.d. is placed after line 95 in Q]   **97 muset** Mussicke   **107 not** nor   **108 s.d.** *Wind horns* [after line 106 in Q]   **112 'Tis** If

3.2. 1 mistook the brake mistooke; the Beake   **7 reck** wreake   **19 fed** feed   **25 dozens** dussons   **28 brine** bine

3.3. 3.1 [after line 1 in Q]   **12 sir!** &c.   **24 them** then   **53 Sirrah—** Sir ha:

3.4. 9 Open Vpon   **10 tack** take   **19 a foot** *afoote*   **20 e'e** *eie*   **22 He s' buy** He's buy

3.5. [Q marks as "Scaena 6"]   **0.1 six** 4   **0.2 babion** and Baum   **five** 2. or 3   **8 jean** iave   **21 figure, trace and** figure trace, and   **33 babion** *Bavian*   **60 From** [on previous line in Q; Q prints *"Daughter"* in margin]   **64–5** [Q prints "Chaire and / stooles out" in margin]   **65–6** [printed on one line in Q; also lines 70–1]   **66 I come** *come*   **68 he said** *sed*   **94 s.d.** *Wind horns* [opposite line 92 in Q]   **96 s.d.** *Exeunt . . . Schoolmaster* [after "Away, boys!" in line 94 in Q]   **101 THESEUS** *Per.*   **134 beest-eating** beast eating   **135 Babion** *Bavian*   **139 SCHOOLMASTER** [not in Q]   **139.1** *Music* [Q prints *"Musicke Dance"* after line 138]   **139.2–3** *Enter . . . a morris* [Q prints "Knocke for / Schoole.Enter / The Dance." in margin at lines 139–41]   **141 ye** thee   **144 thee** *three*   **153 you** yon   **159.1** *Wind horns* [after "made" in line 160 in Q]   **160** *deaeque* Deaeq;

3.6. Scaena 7.   **16 s.d.** *Enter . . . swords* [after "morrow" in line 16 in Q]   **armor** Armors   **39 spared. Your** spard, your   **86 strait** streight   **93 s.d.** *They . . . stand* [printed in margin at lines 93–5 in Q, keyed to an asterisk after "love" in line 93 in Q]   **112 die in. Gentle cousin,** dye in, gentle Cosen: **145 thine** this   **174–5 us; / As . . . valiant, for** us, / As . . . valiant; for   **228 it. If** it, if   **236 fail** fall   **240 name, opinion.** name; Opinion,   **242 prune** proyne   **272 must** muff   **279 PALAMON AND ARCITE** Both [also in line 280]   **285–6 excellent. / For** excellent / For

4.1. 11 oath o'th   **46 'Tis** [Q repeats s.p. here, "Woo."]   **63 sung** song   **84 wreath** wreake   **120 Far** For   **134 JAILER'S BROTHER** *Daugh.*   **141 SECOND FRIEND 1.** *Fr.*   **148 cheerly all.** cheerely. / *All.* [as s.p.]   **150 bowline** Bowling   **158 Tack** take

4.2. 16 Jove afire Love a fire   **25 such** sueh   **27 swart** swarth   **40 'em** 'em   **49–50 Palamon. / Stand** Palamon, / Stand   **54.1** *Enter a Gentleman* Enter Emil. and Gent: **55 How** Emil. How   **70.1** *Enter a Messenger* Enter Messengers. Curtis [after line 69 in Q]   **76 first** fitst   **81 fire** faire   **104 ivy-tods** Ivy tops   **109 court** corect   **152 stay,** stay.

4.3. 1–39 [lined as verse in Q]   **8.1** *Enter . . . Daughter* [placed in Q after "business" in line 8]   **22 spirits are—there's** spirits, as the'rs   **32 i'th'other** i'th / Thother   **39 enough.** enough. / Thother   **45 truth** troth   **punishment** [Q corr.; punishuent, Q uncorr.]   **49–50 engrafted** engraffed   **53 were** [Q corr.; weare, Q uncorr.]   **54 th'other** another   **55 behind** [Q corr.; behold, Q uncorr.]   **69 same** [Q corr.; Sawe, Q uncorr.]   **85 sweet flowers** [Q corr.; sweet, flowers, Q uncorr.]   **90 carve** crave   **96 falsehoods** fasehoods

5.1. 0.1 *Flourish* [before "*Exeunt*" at 4.3.104 in Q]   **7.1** *Flourish of cornets* [after line 5 in Q]   **17.1** *Exeunt* Exit   **33.1** *Exeunt . . . knights* [after "coz." in line 33 in Q]   **37 father of** farther off   **46 cistern** Cestron   **51 Whose . . . prewarn** Comets prewarne, whose havocke in vaste Feild   **54 armipotent** armenypotent   **68 design march** designe; march   **boldly.** boldly, [Q corr.; boldly, Q uncorr.]   **76 Her** [Q corr.; His, Q corr.]   **91 than his; the** then his the   **118 Brief, I** briefe I   **119 done, no companion;** done; no Companion   **120 not, a defier;** not; a defyer   **121 cannot, a rejoicer.** cannot; a Rejoycer,   **130 O thou** Pal. O thou   **136 s.d.** *They . . . bow* [at line 134 in Q]   **is** his   **151 maiden-hearted. A** mayden harted, a   **154 election. Of** election of

5.2. 3 kept hept   **37 Yes** Yet   **40.1** [*mad*] *Maide*   **41 humor** honour   **55 tune** turne   **85 two coarse** too corse

5.3. 0.1 *Flourish* [placed before *Exeunt* at 5.2.113 in Q]   **0.2** *attendants* Attendants, T. Tucke: Curtis   **3 decision. Ev'ry blow** decision. ev'ry; blow   **16 prize** price   **54 him** them   **66 s.d.** *Cornets . . . Palamon!* [after line 64 in Q]   *Enter Servant* [after line 66 in Q]   **75 in't else; chance** in't; else chance   **77 s.d.** *Another . . . cornets* [after line 75 in

Q]   89 s.d. *Cornets…. Arcite!"* [after line 88 in Q]   92 s.d.
Cornets…. Victory!" [after line 91 in Q]   121 all I all; I   136 lose
loose   139 your you   146.1 *Flourish* [after "deliver" in line 138 in Q]
5.4. 0.2 etc. *&c. Gard.*   1 PALAMON [not in Q]   10 unwappered, not
halting unwapper'd not, halting   35 quit quight   38 s.d. *lays Lies*
39 SECOND AND THIRD KNIGHTS 1.2.*K.*   47 rarely early   69 manège
mannadge   79 victor's [victors, Q corr.; victoros, Q uncorr.]
87 mighty, Arcite. If mightie *Arcite,* if   104 arrose arowze
107 Hath Hast   133–4 sorry, still / Are sorry still, / Are
Epilogue 1 EPILOGUE [not in Q]

Venus and Adonis

Copy text: the Quarto of 1593.
185 Souring So wring   208 Speak, fair, Speake fair   304 whe'er
where   457 marketh. marketh,   458 raineth, raineth: 570 woos
woos   621 shine when … fret; shine, when … fret   680 overshoot
ouer-shut   748 th' the th'   873 twine twin'd   1013 stories stories,
1027 falcon Faulcons   1031 as are   1054 was had

The Rape of Lucrece

Copy text: the corrected Quarto of 1594 [Q corr.]. A number of corrected
readings are however rejected as sophistications; see text notes below at
lines 31, 50, 125, 126.
24 morning's [Q corr., mornings] morning [Q uncorr.]   31 apology [Q
uncorr.] Apologies [Q corr.]   50 Collatium [Q uncorr., Colatium] Cola-
tia [Q corr.]   57 beauty, in … entitulèd Beautie in … entituled,
58 doves, doth … field. doues doth … field,   125 himself betakes
[Q uncorr.] themselues betake [Q corr.]   126 wakes [Q uncorr.] wake
[Q corr.]   550 blows blow   555 panteth pateth   560 wear were
650 sovereign, with … haste soueraigne with … hast,   688 lose
loose [also at lines 979 and 1158]   922 inclination inclination.
1126 Relish Ralish   1129 hair heare   1229 eyne, enforced eien
inforst,   1249 remain remaine.   1251 peep peepe,   1263–4 ensue /
By … wrong. insue. / By … wrong,   1312 schedule Cedule
1350 this pattern of the the patterne of this [in four copies of Q; it is
uncertain which is the corrected state]   1386 far-off farre of
1475 Thine Thy   1543 travail trauaile   1544 too to   1580 Losing
Loosing   1648 forbade forbod   1652 robbed rob'd   1660 here heare
1662 wreathèd wretched   1680 one woe on woe   1713 in it it in
1768 faltering foultring

A Lover's Complaint

Copy text: the Sonnet Quarto of 1609 [Q].
7 sorrow's sorrowes,   14 lattice lettice   37 beaded bedded   51 'gan
gaue   95 wear were   103 breathe breath   112 manage mannad'g

118 Came Can   131 Consents Consent's   164 forbade forbod
182 woo vovv   198 pallid palyd   204 hair heir   205 metal mettle
228 Hallowed Hollowed   251 immured enur'd   252 procured
procure   260 nun Sunne   293 Oh Or   303 strange straing

The Sonnets

Copy text: the Quarto of 1609 [Q].
2.4 tattered totter'd [also at 26.11]   2.14 cold could   6.4 beauty's
beautits   8.10 Strikes Strike [in some copies]   12.4 all or
13.7 Yourself You selfe   15.8 wear were   17.12 meter miter
17.14 twice, in it and twice in it, and   18.10 [and elsewhere] lose
loose   19.3 jaws yawes   20.2 Hast Haste   22.3 furrows forrwes
23.6 rite right   23.14 with wit   wit wiht   24.1 stelled steeld
25.9 fight worth   26.12 thy their [also at 27.10, 35.8 (twice), 37.7,
43.11, 45.12, 46.3, 46.8, 46.13, 46.14, 69.5, 70.6, 85.3, 128.11, 128.14]
27.2 travel trauaill   28.12 gild'st guil'st   28.14 strength length
31.8 thee there   34.2 travel trauaile   34.12 cross losse   34.13 sheds
sheeds   38.2 pour'st poor'st   38.3 too to   39.12 doth dost
41.7 woos woes   42.10 losing loosing   44.12 attend time's attend,
times   44.13 naught naughts   45.9 life's liues   46.9 'cide side
46.12 the he [in some copies]   47.2 other. other,   47.4 smother,
smother;   47.11 no nor   50.6 dully duly   51.10 perfect'st perfects
55.1 monuments monument   56.3 [and elsewhere] today too daie
58.7 patience-tame to suffrance, patience tame, to sufferance
59.6 hundred hundreth   59.11 whe'er where   61.14 off of   too to
62.10 chapped chopt   63.5 traveled trauaild   65.12 of or
67.6 seeming seeing   69.3 due end   69.14 soil sole   71.13 Lest
Least [also at 72.1, 72.9, and elsewhere]   73.4 ruined rn'wd   choirs
quiers   76.7 tell fel   77.1 wear were   77.10 blanks blacks
82.8 these the   83.7 too to   88.8 losing loosing   90.11 shall stall
91.9 better bitter   93.5 there their   98.11 were weare   99.4 dwells
dwells?   99.9 One Our   99.13 ate eate   102.8 her his   106.12 skill
still   111.1 with wish   112.14 are y'are   113.6 latch lack
113.13 more, replete with more repleat, with   113.14 mine eye
mine   116 [numbered 119 in Q]   117.10 surmise accumulate;
surmise, accumilate   118.5 ne'er-cloying nere cloying   118.10 were
not, grew were, not grew   119.4 losing loosing   121.11 bevel. beuel
125.6 rent, rent   125.7 sweet forgoing sweet; Forgoing   126.2 sickle
hour; sickle, hower: 126.8 minutes mynuit   127.2 were weare
127.10 brows eyes   129.9 Mad Made   129.10 quest to have, quest,
to haue   129.11 proved, a proud and   132.6 the east th' East
132.9 mourning morning   138.12 to have t' haue   140.5 were weare
144.6 side [adopted from *The Passionate Pilgrim*] sight   144.9 fiend
[adopted from *The Passionate Pilgrim*] finde   146.2 Thrall to My
sinfull earth   147.7 approve approoue.   153.14 eyes eye

Glossary

Shakespearean Words and Meanings of Frequent Occurrence

A

'A: he (unaccented form).

Abate: lessen, diminish; blunt, reduce; deprive; bar, leave out of account, except; depreciate; humble.

Abuse (N): insult, error, misdeed, offense, crime; imposture, deception; also the modern sense.

Abuse (V): deceive, misapply, put to a bad use; maltreat; frequently the modern sense.

Addition: something added to one's name to denote rank; mark of distinction; title.

Admiration: wonder; object of wonder.

Admire: wonder at.

Advantage (N): profit, convenience, benefit; opportunity, favorable opportunity; pecuniary profit; often shades toward the modern sense.

Advantage (V): profit, be of benefit to, benefit; augment.

Advice: reflection, consideration, deliberation, consultation.

Affect: aim at, aspire to, incline toward; be fond of, be inclined; love; act upon contagiously (as a disease). (PAST PART.) **Affected:** disposed, inclined, in love, loved.

Affection: passion, love; emotion, feeling, mental tendency, disposition; wish, inclination; affectation.

Alarum: signal calling soldiers to arms (in stage directions).

An: if; but; **an if:** if, though, even if.

Anon: at once, soon; presently, by and by.

Answer: return, requite; atone for; render an account of, account for; obey, agree with; also the modern sense.

Apparent: evident, plain; seeming.

Argument: subject, theme, reason, cause; story; excuse.

As: according as; as far as; namely; as if; in the capacity of; that; so that; that is, that they.

Assay: try, attempt; accost, address; challenge.

Atone: reconcile; set at one.

Attach: arrest, seize.

Aweful, awful: commanding reverential fear or respect; profoundly respectful or reverential.

B

Band: bond, fetters, manacle (leash for a dog). **Band** and **bond** are etymologically the same word; **band** was formerly used in both senses.

Basilisk: fabulous reptile said to kill by its look. The basilisk of popular superstition was a creature with legs, wings, a serpentine and winding tail, and a crest or comb somewhat like a cock. It was the offspring of a cock's egg hatched under a toad or serpent.

Bate: blunt, abate, reduce; deduct, except.

Battle: army; division of an army.

Beshrew: curse, blame; used as a mild curse, "Bad or ill luck to."

Bias: tendency, bent, inclination, swaying influence; term in bowling applied to the form of the bowl, the oblique line in which it runs, and the kind of impetus given to cause it to run obliquely.

Blood: nature, vigor; supposed source of emotion; passion; spirit, animation; one of the four humors (see **humor**).

Boot (N): advantage, profit; something given in addition to the bargain; booty, plunder.

Boot (V): profit, avail.

Brave (ADJ.): fine, gallant; splendid, finely arrayed, showy; ostentatiously defiant.

Brave (V): challenge, defy; make splendid.

Brook: tolerate, endure.

C

Can: can do; know; be skilled; sometimes used for *did*.

Capable: comprehensive; sensible, impressible, susceptible; capable of; gifted, intelligent.

Careful: anxious, full of care; provident; attentive.

Carry: manage, execute; be successful, win; conquer; sustain; endure.

Censure (N): judgment, opinion; critical opinion, unfavorable opinion.

Censure (V): judge, estimate; pass sentence or judgment.

Character (N): writing, printing, record; handwriting; cipher; face, features (bespeaking inward qualities).

Character (V): write, engrave, inscribe.

Check (N): reproof; restraint.

Check (V): reprove, restrain, keep from; control.

Circumstance: condition, state of affairs, particulars; adjunct details; detailed narration, argument, or discourse; formality, ceremony.

Clip: embrace; surround.

Close: secret, private; concealed; uncommunicative; enclosed.

Cog: cheat.

Coil: noise, disturbance, turmoil; fuss, to-do, bustle.

Color: appearance; pretext, pretense; excuse.

Companion: fellow (used contemptuously).

Complete: accomplished, fully endowed; perfect, perfect in quality; also frequently the modern sense.

Complexion: external appearance; temperament, disposition; the four complexions—sanguine, choleric, phlegmatic, and melancholy—corresponding to the four humors (see **humor**); also the modern sense.

Composition: compact, agreement, constitution.

Compound: settle, agree.

Conceit: conception, idea, thought; mental faculty, wit; fancy, imagination; opinion, estimate; device, invention, design.

Condition: temperament, disposition; characteristic, property, quality; social or official position, rank or status; covenant, treaty, contract.

Confound: waste, spend, invalidate, destroy; undo, ruin; mingle indistinguishably, mix, blend.

Confusion: destruction, overthrow, ruin; mental agitation.

Continent: that which contains or encloses; earth, globe; sum, summary.

Contrive: plot; plan; spend or pass (time).

Conversation: conduct, deportment; social intercourse, association.

Converse: hold intercourse; associate with, have to do with.

Cope: encounter, meet; have to do with.

Copy: model, pattern; example; minutes or memoranda.

Cousin: any relative not belonging to one's immediate family.

Cry you mercy: beg your pardon.

Cuckold: husband whose wife is unfaithful.

Curious: careful, fastidious; anxious, concerned; made with care, skillfully, intricately, or daintily wrought; particular.

Cursed, curst: shrewish, perverse, spiteful.

D

Dainty: minute; scrupulous, particular; particular about (with **of**); refined, elegant; also the modern sense.

Date: duration, termination, term of existence; limit or end of a term or period, term.

Dear: precious; best; costly; important; affectionate; hearty; grievous, dire; also the modern sense.

Debate: discuss; fight.

Decay (N): downfall, ruin; cause of ruin.

Decay (V): perish, be destroyed; destroy.

Defeat (N): destruction, ruin.

Defeat (V): destroy, disfigure, ruin.

Defy: challenge, challenge to a fight; reject; despise.

Demand (N): inquiry; request.

Demand (V): inquire, question; request.

Deny: refuse (to do something); refuse permission; refuse to accept; refuse admittance; disown.

Depart (N): departure.

Depart (V): part; go away from, leave, quit; take leave (of one another); **depart with, withal:** part with, give up.

Derive: gain, obtain; draw upon, direct (to); descend; pass by descent, be descended or inherited; trace the origin of.

Difference: diversity of opinion, disagreement, dissension, dispute; characteristic or distinguishing feature; alteration or addition to a coat of arms to distinguish a younger or lateral branch of a family.

Digest: arrange, perfect; assimilate, amalgamate; disperse, dissipate; comprehend, understand; put up with (FIG. from the physical sense of digesting food).

Discourse (N): reasoning, reflection; talk, act of conversing, conversation; faculty of conversing; familiar intercourse; relating (as by speech).

Discourse (V): speak, talk, converse; pass (the time) in talk; say, utter, tell, give forth; narrate, relate.

Discover: uncover, expose to view; divulge, reveal, make known; spy out, reconnoiter; betray; distinguish, discern; also the modern sense.

Dispose (N): disposal; temperament, bent of mind, disposition; external manner.

Dispose (V): distribute, manage, make use of; deposit, put or stow away; regulate, order, direct; come to terms. (PAST PART.) **Disposed:** in a good frame of mind; inclined to be merry.

Dispute: discuss, reason; strive against, resist.

Distemper (V): disturb; (N): disorder, ill humor; illness.

Doit: old Dutch coin, one-half an English farthing.

Doubt (N): suspicion, apprehension; fear, danger, risk; also the modern sense.

Doubt (V): suspect, apprehend; fear; also the modern sense.

Doubtful: inclined to suspect, suspicious, apprehensive; not to be relied on; almost certain.

Duty: reverence, respect, expression of respect; submission to authority, obedience; due.

E

Earnest: money paid as an installment to secure a bargain; partial payment; often used with *quibble* in the modern sense.

Ease: comfort, assistance, leisure; idleness, sloth, inactivity; also the modern sense.

Ecstasy: frenzy, madness, state of being beside oneself, excitement, bewilderment; swoon; rapture.

Element: used to refer to the simple substances of which all material bodies were thought to be composed; specifically earth, air, fire, and water, corresponding to the four humors (see **humor**); atmosphere, sky; atmospheric agencies or powers; that one of the four elements which is the natural abode of a creature; hence, natural surroundings, sphere.

Engage: pledge, pawn, mortgage; bind by a promise, swear to; entangle, involve; enlist; embark on an enterprise.

Engine: mechanical contrivance; artifice, device, plot.

Enlarge: give free scope to; set at liberty, release.

Entertain: keep up, maintain, accept; take into one's service; treat; engage (someone's) attention or thought; occupy, while or pass away pleasurably; engage (as an enemy); receive.

Envious: malicious, spiteful, malignant.

Envy: ill-will, malice, hate; also the modern sense.

Even: uniform; direct, straightforward; exact, precise; equable, smooth, comfortable; equal, equally balanced.

Event: outcome; affair, business; also frequently the modern sense.

Exclaim: protest, rail; accuse, blame (with **on**), reproach.

Excursion: stage battle or skirmish (in stage directions).

Excuse: seek to extenuate (a fault); maintain the innocence of; clear oneself, justify or vindicate oneself; decline.

F

Fact: deed, act; crime.

Faction: party, class, group, set (of persons); party strife, dissension; factious quarrel, intrigue.

Fail: die, die out; err, be at fault; omit, leave undone.

Fair (N): fair thing; one of the fair sex; someone beloved; beauty (the abstract concept).

Fair (ADJ.): just; clear, distinct; beautiful; of light complexion or color of hair.

Fair (ADV): fairly.

Fairly: beautifully, handsomely; courteously, civilly; properly, honorably, honestly; becomingly, appropriately; favorably, fortunately; softly, gently, kindly.

Fall: let fall, drop; happen, come to pass; befall; shades frequently toward the modern senses.

Falsely: wrongly; treacherously; improperly.

Fame: report; rumor; reputation.

Familiar (N): intimate friend; familiar or attendant spirit, demon associated with, and obedient to, a person.

Familiar (ADJ.): intimate, friendly; belonging to household or family, domestic; well-known; habitual, ordinary, trivial; plain, easily understood.

Fancy: fantasticalness; imaginative conception, flight of imagination; amorous inclination or passion, love; liking, taste.

Fantasy: fancy, imagination; caprice, whim.

Favor: countenance, face; complexion; aspect, appearance; leave, permission, pardon; attraction, charm, good will; **in favor:** benevolently.

Fear (N): dread, apprehension; dreadfulness; object of dread or fear.

Fear (V): be apprehensive or concerned about, mistrust, doubt; frighten, make afraid.

Fearful: exciting or inspiring fear, terrible, dreadful; timorous, apprehensive, full of fear.

Feature: shape or form of body, figure; shapeliness, comeliness.

Fellow: companion; partaker, sharer (of); equal, match; customary form of address to a servant or an inferior (sometimes used contemptuously or condescendingly).

Fine (N): end, conclusion; **in fine:** finally.

Fine (ADJ.): highly accomplished or skillful; exquisitely fashioned, delicate; refined, subtle; frequently the modern sense.

Flaw: fragment; crack, fissure; tempest, squall, gust of wind; outburst of passion.

Flesh (V): reward a hawk or hound with a piece of flesh of the game killed to excite its eagerness of the chase; hence, to inflame by a foretaste of success; initiate or inure to bloodshed (used for a first time in battle); harden, train.

Flourish: fanfare of trumpets (in stage directions).

Fond: foolish, doting; **fond of:** eager for; also the modern sense.

Fool: term of endearment and pity; frequently the modern sense.

For that, for why: because.

Forfend: forbid, avert.

Free: generous, magnanimous; candid, open; guiltless, innocent.

Front: forehead, face; foremost line of battle; beginning.

Furnish: equip, fit out (furnish forth); endow; dress, decorate, embellish.

G

Gear: apparel, dress; stuff, substance, thing, article; discourse, talk; matter, business, affair.

Get: beget.

Gloss: specious fair appearance; lustrous surface.

Go to: expression of remonstrance, impatience, disapprobation, or derision.

Grace (N): kindness, favor, charm, divine favor; fortune, luck; beneficent virtue; sense of duty or propriety; mercy, pardon; embellish; **do grace:** reflect credit on, do honor to, do a favor for.

Grace (V): gratify, delight; honor, favor.

Groat: coin equal to four pence.

H

Habit: dress, garb, costume; bearing, demeanor, manner; occasionally in the modern sense.

Happily: haply, perchance, perhaps; fortunately.

Hardly: with difficulty.

Have at: I shall come at (you) (i.e., listen to me), I shall attack (a person or thing); let me at.

Have with: I shall go along with; let me go along with; come along.

Having: possession, property, wealth, estate; endowments, accomplishments.

Head: armed force.

Hind: servant, slave; rustic, boor, clown.

His: its. **His** was historically the possessive form of both the masculine and neuter pronouns. **Its,** although not common in Shakespeare's time, occurs in the plays occasionally.

Holp: helped (archaic past tense).

Home: fully, satisfactorily, thoroughly, plainly, effectually; to the quick.

Honest: holding an honorable position, honorable, respectable; decent, kind, seemly, befitting, proper; chaste; genuine; loosely used as an epithet of approbation.

Humor: mood, temper, cast of mind, temperament, disposition; vagary, fancy, whim; moisture (the literal sense); a physiological and, by transference, a psychological term applied to the four chief fluids of the human body—phlegm, blood, bile or choler, and black bile or melancholy. A person's disposition and temporary state of mind were determined according to the relative proportions of these fluids in the body; consequently, a person was said to be phlegmatic, sanguine, choleric, or melancholy.

I

Image: likeness; visible form; representation; embodiment, type; mental picture, creation of the imagination.

Influence: supposed flowing from the stars or heavens of an ethereal fluid, acting upon the characters and destinies of men (used metaphorically).

Inform: take shape, give form to, imbue, inspire; instruct, teach; charge (against).

Instance: evidence, proof, sign, confirmation; motive, cause.

Invention: power of mental creation, the creative faculty; work of the imagination, artistic creation, premeditated design; device, plan, scheme.

J

Jar (N): discord in music; quarrel, discord.

Jar (V): be out of tune; be discordant, quarrel.

Jump: agree, tally, coincide, fit exactly; risk, hazard.

K

Keep: continue, carry on; dwell, lodge, guard, defend, care for, employ, be with; restrain, control; confine in prison.

Kind (N): nature, established order of things; manner, fashion, respect; race, class, kindred, family; **by kind:** naturally.

Kind (ADJ.): natural; favorable; affectionate.

Kindly (ADJ.): natural, appropriate; agreeable; innate; benign.

Kindly (ADV): naturally; gently, courteously.

L

Large: liberal, bounteous, lavish; free, unrestrained; **at large:** at length, in full; in full detail, as a whole, in general.

Late: lately.

Learn: teach; inform (someone of something); also the modern sense.

Let: hinder.

Level: aim; also shades toward the modern sense.

Liberal: possessed of the characteristics and qualities of wellborn persons; genteel, becoming, refined; free in speech; unrestrained by prudence or decorum; licentious.

Lie: be in bed; be still; be confined, be kept in prison; dwell, sojourn, reside, lodge.

Like: please, feel affection; liken, compare.

List (N): strip of cloth, selvedge; limit, boundary; desire.

List (V): choose, desire, please; listen to.

Liver: the seat of love and of violent passions generally (see also **spleen**).

'Long of: owing to, on account of.

Look: power to see; take care, see to it; expect; seek, search for.

M

Make: do; have to do (with); consider; go; be effective, make up, complete; also the modern sense.

Manage: management, conduct, administration; action and paces to which a horse is trained; short gallop at full speed.

Marry: mild interjection equivalent to "Indeed!" Originally, an oath by the Virgin Mary.

May: can; also frequently the modern sense to denote probability; **might** has corresponding meanings and uses.

Mean, means (N): instrument, agency, method; effort; opportunity (for doing something); something interposed or intervening; money, wealth (frequently in the plural form); middle position, medium; tenor or alto part in singing (usually in the singular form).

Mean (ADJ.): average, moderate, middle; of low degree, station, or position; undignified, base.

Measure (N): grave or stately dance, graceful motion; tune, melody, musical accompaniment; treatment meted out; moderation, proportion; limit; distance, reach.

Measure (V): judge, estimate; traverse.

Mere: absolute, sheer; pure, unmixed; downright, sincere.

Mew (up): coop up (as used of a hawk), shut up, imprison, confine.

Mind (N): thoughts, judgment, opinion, message; purpose, intention, desire; disposition; also the modern sense of the mental faculty.

Mind (V): remind; perceive, notice, attend; intend.

Minion: saucy woman, hussy; follower; favorite, favored person, darling (often used contemptuously).

Misdoubt (N): suspicion.

Misdoubt (V): mistrust, suspect.

Model: pattern, replica, likeness.

Modern: ordinary, commonplace, everyday.

Modest: moderate, marked by moderation, becoming; characterized by decency and propriety; chaste.

Moiety: half; share; small part, lesser share; portion, part of.

Mortal: fatal; deadly, of or for death; belonging to mankind; human, pertaining to human affairs.

Motion: power of movement; suggestion, proposal; movement of the soul; impulse, prompting; also the modern sense.

Move: make angry; urge, incite, instigate, arouse, prompt; propose, make a proposal to, apply to, appeal to, suggest; also the modern sense.

Muse: wonder, marvel; grumble, complain.

N

Napkin: handkerchief.

Natural: related by blood; having natural or kindly feeling; also the modern sense.

Naught: useless, worthless; wicked, naughty.

Naughty: wicked; good for nothing, worthless.

Nerves: sinews.

Nice: delicate; fastidious, dainty, particular, scrupulous; minute, subtle; shy, coy; reluctant, unwilling; unimportant, insignificant, trivial; accurate, precise; wanton, lascivious.

Nothing (ADJ.): not at all.

O

Of: from, away from; during; on; by; as regards; instead of; **out of:** compelled by; made from.

Offer: make an attack; menace; venture, dare, presume.

Opinion: censure; reputation or credit; favorable estimate of oneself; self-conceit, arrogance; self-confidence; public opinion, reputation; also the modern sense.

Or: before; also used conjunctively where no alternative is implied; **or . . . or:** either . . . or; whether . . . or.

Out (ADV): without, outside; abroad; fully, quite; at an end, finished; at variance, aligned the wrong way.

Out (INTERJ.): an expression of reproach, impatience, indignation, or anger.

Owe: own; also the modern sense.

P

Pack (V): load; depart, begone; conspire.

Pageant: show, spectacle, spectacular entertainment; device on a moving carriage.

Pain: punishment, penalty; labor, trouble, effort; also frequently the modern sense.

Painted: specious, unreal, counterfeit.

Parle (N): parley, conference, talk; bugle call for parley.

Part (V): depart, part from; divide.

Particular (N): detail; personal interest or concern; details of a private nature; single person.

Party: faction, side, part, cause; partner, ally.

Pass (V): pass through, traverse; exceed; surpass; pledge.

Passing (ADJ. and ADV.): surpassing, surpassingly, exceedingly.

Passion (N): powerful or violent feeling, violent sorrow or grief; painful affection or disorder of the body; sorrow; feelings or desires of love; passionate speech or outburst.

Passion (V): sorrow, grieve.

Peevish: silly, senseless, childish; perverse, obstinate, stubborn; sullen.

Perforce: by violence or compulsion; forcibly; necessarily.

Phoenix: mythical Arabian bird believed to be the only one of its kind; it lived five or six hundred years, after which it burned itself to ashes and reemerged to live through another cycle.

Physic: medical faculty; healing art, medical treatment; remedy, medicine, healing property.

Pitch: height; specifically, the height to which a falcon soars before swooping on its prey (often used figuratively); tarlike substance.

Policy: conduct of affairs (especially public affairs); prudent management; stratagem, trick; contrivance; craft, cunning.

Port: bearing, demeanor; state, style of living, social station; gate.

Possess: have or give possession or command (of something); inform, acquaint; also the modern sense.

Post (N): courier, messenger; post-horse; haste.

Post (V): convey swiftly; hasten, ignore through haste (with **over** or **off**).

Practice (N): execution; exercise (especially for instruction); stratagem, intrigue; conspiracy, plot, treachery.

Practice (V): perform, take part in; use stratagem, craft, or artifice; scheme, plot; play a joke on.

Pregnant: resourceful; disposed, inclined; clear, obvious.

Present (ADJ.): ready, immediate, prompt, instant.

Present (V): represent.

Presently: immediately, at once.

Prevent: forestall, anticipate, foresee; also the modern sense.

Process: drift, tenor, gist; narrative, story; formal command, mandate.

Proof: test, trial, experiment; experience; issue, result; proved or tested strength of armor or arms; also the modern sense.

Proper: (one's or its) own; peculiar, exclusive; excellent; honest, respectable; handsome, elegant, fine, good-looking.

Proportion: symmetry; size; form, carriage, appearance, shape; portion, allotment; rhythm.

Prove: make trial of; put to test; show or find out by experience.

Purchase (N): acquisition; spoil, booty.

Purchase (V): acquire, gain, obtain; strive, exert oneself; redeem, exempt.

Q

Quaint: skilled, clever; pretty, fine, dainty; handsome, elegant; carefully or ingeniously wrought or elaborated.

Quality: that which constitutes (something); essential being; good natural gifts; accomplishment, attainment, property; art, skill; rank, position; profession, occupation, business; party, side; manner, style; cause, occasion.

Quick: living (used substantively to mean "living flesh"); alive; lively, sharp, piercing; hasty, impatient; with child.

Quillets: verbal niceties, subtle distinctions.

Quit: requite, reward; set at liberty; acquit, remit; pay for, clear off.

R

Rack (V): stretch or strain beyond normal extent or capacity to endure; strain oneself; distort.

Rage (N): madness, insanity; vehement pain; angry disposition; violent passion or appetite; poetic enthusiasm; warlike ardor or fury.

Rage (V): behave wantonly or riotously; act with fury or violence; enrage; pursue furiously.

Range: extend or lie in the same plane (with); occupy a position; rove, roam; be inconstant; traverse.

Rank (ADJ.): coarsely luxuriant; puffed up, swollen, fat, abundant; full, copious; rancid; lustful; corrupt, foul.

Rate (N): estimate; value or worth; estimation, consideration; standard, style.

Rate (V): allot; calculate, estimate, compute; reckon, consider; be of equal value (with); chide, scold, berate; drive away by chiding or scolding.

Recreant (N): traitor, coward, cowardly wretch (also as ADJ.).

Remorse: pity, compassion; also the modern sense.

Remove: removal, absence; period of absence; change.

Require: ask, inquire of, request.

Resolve: dissolve, melt, dissipate; answer; free from doubt or uncertainty, convince; inform; decide; also the modern sense.

Respect (N): consideration, reflection, act of seeing, view; attention, notice; decency, modest deportment; also the modern sense.

Respect (V): esteem, value, prize; regard, consider; heed, pay attention to; also the modern sense.

Round: spherical; plain, direct, brusque; fair; honest.

Roundly: plainly, unceremoniously.

Rub: obstacle (a term in the game of bowls); unevenness; inequality.

S

Sack: generic term for Spanish and Canary wines; sweet white wine.

Sad: grave, serious; also the modern sense.

Sadness: seriousness; also the modern sense.

Sans: without (French preposition).

Scope: object, aim, limit; freedom, license; free play.

Seal: bring to completion or conclusion; conclude, confirm, ratify, stamp; also the modern sense.

Sennet: a series of notes sounded on a trumpet to herald the approach or departure of a procession (used in stage directions).

Sense: mental faculty, mind; mental perception, import, rational meaning; physical perception; sensual nature; **common sense:** ordinary or untutored perception, observation or knowledge.

Sensible: capable of physical feeling or perception, sensitive; capable of or exhibiting emotion; rational; capable of being perceived.

Serve: be sufficient; be favorable; succeed; satisfy the need for; serve a turn; answer the purpose.

Several: separate, distinct, different; particular, private; various.

Shadow: shade, shelter; reflection; likeness, image; ghost; representation, picture of the imagination, phantom; also the modern sense.

Shift: change; stratagem, strategy, trick, contrivance, device to serve a purpose; **make shift:** manage.

Shrewd: malicious, mischievous, ill-natured; shrewish; bad, of evil import, grievous; severe.

Sirrah: ordinary or customary form of address to inferiors or servants; disrespectful form of address.

Sith: since.

Smock: woman's undergarment; used typically for "a woman."

Something: somewhat.

Sometime: sometimes, from time to time; once, formerly; at times, at one time.

Speed (N): fortune, success; protecting and assisting power; also the modern sense.

Speed (V): fare (well or ill); succeed; be successful; assist, guard, favor.

Spleen: the seat of emotions and passions; violent passion; fiery temper; malice, anger, rage; impulse, fit of passion; caprice; impetuosity (see also **liver**).

Spoil: destruction, ruin; plunder; slaughter, massacre.

Starve: die of cold or hunger; be benumbed with cold; paralyze, disable; allow or cause to die.

State: degree, rank; social position, station; pomp, splendor, outward display, clothes; court, household of a great person; shades into the modern sense.

Stay: wait, wait for; sustain; stand; withhold, withstand; stop.

Stead: assist; be of use to, benefit, help.

Still: always, ever, continuously or continually, constant or constantly; silent, mute; also modern senses.

Stomach: appetite, inclination, disposition; resentment; angry temper, resentful feeling; proud spirit, courage.

Straight: immediately.

Strange: belonging to another country or person, foreign, unfriendly; new, fresh; ignorant; estranged.

Success: issue, outcome (good or bad); sequel, succession, descent (as from father to son).

Suggest: tempt; prompt; seduce.

Suggestion: temptation.

T

Table: memorandum, tablet; surface on which something is written or drawn.

Take: strike; bewitch; charm; infect; destroy; repair to for refuge; modern senses.

Tall: goodly, fine; strong in fight, valiant.

Target: shield.

Tax: censure, blame, accuse.

Tell: count; relate.

Thorough: through.

Throughly: thoroughly.

Toward: in preparation; forthcoming, about to take place; modern senses.

Toy: trifle, idle fancy; folly.

Train: lure, entice, allure, attract.

Trencher: wooden dish or plate.

Trow: think, suppose, believe; know.

U

Undergo: undertake, perform; modern sense.

Undo: ruin.

Unfold: disclose, tell, make known, reveal; communicate.

Unhappy: evil, mischievous; fatal, ill-fated; miserable.

Unjust: untrue, dishonest; unjustified, groundless; faithless, false.

Unkind: unnatural, cruel, faulty; compare **kind.**

Use (N): custom, habit; interest paid.

Use (V): make practice of; be accustomed; put out at interest.

V

Vail: lower, let fall.

Vantage: advantage; opportunity; benefit, profit; superiority.

Virtue: general excellence; valor, bravery; merit, goodness, honor; good accomplishment, excellence in culture; power; essence, essential part.

W

Want: lack; be in need of; be without.

Watch: be awake, lie awake, sit up at night, lose sleep; keep from sleep (TRANS.).

Weed: garment, clothes.

Welkin: sky, heavens.

Wink: close the eyes; close the eyes in sleep; have the eyes closed; seem not to see.

Withal: with; with it, this, or these; together with this; at the same time.

Wot: know.

Index

Clopton, Sir Hugh (d. 1496), Mayor of London, lii
Close, Glenn, actress, 1097
Cloten, son of Queen (*Cymb.*), 1476, 1477, 1478, 1479, 1480*n*, 1482*n*,
    1486*n*, 1490*n*, 1492*n*, 1493*n*, 1497*n*, 1503*n*, 1504*n*, 1508*n*, 1509*n*,
    1510*n*, 1511*n*, 1512*n*, 1523*n*, 1526*n*, A-56
Clotharius, King of ancient France, 931*n*
Clotho, fate, 178*n*, 846*n*, 1257
Clown (*Ant. and Cleo.*), 1335, 1381*n*
Clown (*Oth.*), 1156, 1181*n*
Clown (*Tit. And.*), 970, 995*n*, 996*n*
Clown, character in Morris dance, 1607, 1632*n*
Clown, Old Shepherd's son (*W.T.*), 1530, 1548*n*, 1551*n*, 1554*n*, 1559*n*,
    1561*n*, A-57
Clymene, wife of Merops, 94*n*
Cobham, Eleanor. *See* Eleanor, Duchess of Gloucester
Cobham, Henry Brooke, eighth Lord (d. 1619), 256, 269*n*, 872*n*, A-6,
    A-11, A-12
Cobweb, fairy (*Mids. Dr.*), 148, 152, 171*n*
Coincy, Gautier de, miracle play author, A-56
Colbrand the Giant, 706*n*, 962*n*
Cole, George, Warden of the Stationers' Company, xciv
Coleridge, Samuel Taylor (1772–1834), poet and critic, c–ci, cv, 645, 1093,
    1096, 1152
Coleville, Sir John, of rebels' party (*2 Hen. IV*), 826, 827, 830
Collatinus, husband of Lucretia (*Lucrece*), lxiii, 1672, 1678*n*, 1685*n*, 1695*n*
Collier, John Payne (1789–1883), editor, xcvii, A-6
Collins, Francis (*fl.* 1616), Shakespeare's lawyer, lxxvi
Combe, John and William (*fl.* 1602–1614), Stratford citizens, lxx, lxxvi
Combe, Thomas (*fl.* 1616), Stratford citizen, lxxvii
Comedy of Errors, The, xxxvii, xlvi, xlviii, l, lii, lv, lviii–lx, lxii–lxiii, lxxxi,
    lxxxviii, xciv, 2–5, **5–30**, 31, 75, 108, 109, 333, 363*n*, 1606, A-1, A-2,
    A-23–A-24, A-26, A-32, A-54, A-73
Cominius, general against Volscians (*Cor.*), 1385, 1392*n*, 1394*n*, 1396*n*,
    1399*n*, 1419*n*, 1427*n*, 1428*n*
Condell, Henry. *See* Heminges, John, and Henry Condell
Congreve, William (1670–1729), dramatist, 220, 222
Connor, Edric, singer, 1441
Conrade, follower of Don John (*Much Ado*), 223, 240*n*, 247*n*
Constable, Henry (1562–1613), *Diana*, 1708
Constable of France (*Hen. V*), 877, 899*n*
Constance, mother of Arthur (*K. John*), 700, 701, 703, 710*n*, 718*n*, 722*n*
Constant, Pierre, director, 1608
Constantine, Roman emperor, 517*n*
Cook, Ann Jennalie, scholar, cii
Cooke, George Frederick, actor, 184
Cook's Tale of Gamelyn, The, 294
"Cooper of Fife, The," Scottish folksong, A-26
Copernicus, Nicholas, astronomer, *De revolutionibus orbius coelestium*,
    xxv, ciii
Cophetua, King, ballad of, 40*n*, 49*n*, 779*n*, 869*n*, 1020*n*
Copland, Robert, translator of *Appolyn of Thyre*, A-54
Cordelia (*K. Lear*), lxxiv, ci, cvi, 1152, 1201, 1202, 1203, 1204, 1205, 1206,
    1207, 1208*n*, 1209*n*, 1215*n*, 1219*n*, 1240*n*, 1250*n*, 1254*n*, A-65, A-67,
    A-71
Corin, shepherd (*A.Y.L.*), 158*n*, 293–4, 298, 315*n*, A-31
Coriolanus, xlii, lxxviii, lxxxi, lxxxviii, xciv, 967, 1051, 1052, 1054, 1255,
    1294, 1384–7, **1388–1436**, 1604, A-1, A-19, A-53–A-54, A-67, A-72
Coriolanus, Caius Marcius (*Cor.*), lxv, lxxiv, 966, 997*n*, 1384, 1385, 1386,
    1387, 1388, 1396*n*, 1400*n*, 1401*n*, 1402*n*, 1405*n*, 1407*n*, 1410*n*, 1412*n*,
    1414*n*, 1422*n*, 1423*n*, 1424*n*, 1426*n*, 1427*n*, 1428*n*, 1429*n*, 1430*n*,
    1432*n*, 1433*n*, 1604, A-54
Corneille, Pierre (1606–1684), tragic dramatist, xxxviii, c
Cornelia, mother of Gracchi, 966, 990*n*
Cornelius, courtier (*Ham.*), 1097
Cornelius, physician (*Cymb.*), 1476, 1486*n*
Cornwall, Duke of (*K. Lear*), 1203, 1204, 1205, 1207, 1220*n*, 1223*n*,
    1224*n*, 1225*n*, 1237*n*, 1239*n*, 1240*n*, A-49, A-50
Corpus Christi play, xxx–xxxii, xxxiv, xliii, xlvii
Costard, clown (*L.L.L.*), 33, 34, 37*n*, 38*n*, 40*n*, 46*n*, 47*n*, 48*n*, 55*n*, 56*n*,
    70*n*, 71*n*, 72*n*, 294, A-24
Cotes, Thomas (*fl.* 1734–1739), printer, xcv

Countess of Rossillion (*All's Well*), 371–2, 374, 375*n*, 379*n*, 380*n*, 381*n*,
    393*n*, A-33
Court, soldier (*Hen. V*), 877
Courtesan (*Com. Er.*), 3, 5, 5*n*, 15*n*, 22*n*
Covell, William, Shakespeare allusions by, A-22
Coward, Noel, 222
Cowley, Richard (d. 1619), actor, lxx, A-5
Cox, Brian, actor, 1206
Cox, Captain (mentioned in *Laneham's Letter*), 261*n*
Cox, John D., editor, xci, xcvii
Craig, Hardin (1875–1968), scholar and editor, cii–ciii
Craig, W. J., editor, xcvii–xcviii
Crane, Milton, scholar, civ
Crane, Ralph (*fl.* 1616), scrivener, xc, xciv, A-3, A-6, A-7, A-17, A-19,
    A-20
Crane, Ronald S. (1886–1967), scholar and critic, civ
Cranmer, Thomas, Archbishop of Canterbury (*Hen. VIII*), xviii, xix, xxii,
    921, 922, 924, 943*n*, 959*n*, A-42
Crashaw, Richard (d. 1649), poet, 1673
Crassus, Marcus (d. 52 B.C.), member of first triumvirate, 1355*n*
Creed, Thomas (*fl.* 1594–1599), printer, A-5, A-6, A-8, A-13, A-14
Creon, King of Thebes, 1605, 1606, 1612*n*, 1615*n*, 1620*n*, A-58
Cressida, daughter of Calchas (*T. and C.*), lxxiii, 184, 214*n*, 252*n*, 264*n*,
    322*n*, 353*n*, 383*n*, 455–9, 460, 461*n*, 462*n*, 463*n*, 464*n*, 465*n*, 480*n*,
    481*n*, 488*n*, 489*n*, 490*n*, 491*n*, 500*n*, 885*n*, A-35, A-36
Créton, Jean, *Histoire du Roi d'Angleterre Richard*, A-39
Crews, Frederick, critic, cvi
Crimeston, Edward, translator of *De Rebus Burgundicis*, A-26
Cromwell, Thomas (1485?–1540), successor to Wolsey (*Hen. VIII*), xviii,
    xxi, 922, 924, 951*n*
Cronus. *See* Saturn
Crosby, Sir John, alderman and philanthropist, 654*n*
Crowne, John, adapter of *Henry VI* plays, *The Misery of Civil War*, A-65
Cupid, 47*n*, 54*n*, 60*n*, 77, 79*n*, 84*n*, 150, 155*n*, 172*n*, 224*n*, 225*n*, 237*n*,
    238*n*, 290*n*, 322*n*, 324*n*, 338*n*, 344*n*, 345*n*, 377*n*, 380*n*, 387*n*, 421*n*,
    517*n*, 578*n*, 917*n*, 1012*n*, 1016*n*, 1020*n*, 1025*n*, 1296, 1498*n*, 1553*n*,
    1596*n*, 1626*n*, 1640*n*, 1660*n*, 1661*n*, 1741*n*, 1744*n*, A-53
Curan, courtier (*K. Lear*), 1207
Cursor Mundi, Middle English epic, A-27
Curtain, The, playhouse, xliii–xliv, 878*n*
Curtis, servant of Petruchio (*Tam. Shrew*), 111, 133*n*
Cusack, Sinead, actress, 222
Cushman, Charlotte, actress, A-67
Cyclopes, 995*n*, 1117*n*
Cymbeline, xxxix, lxxiii–lxxv, lxxxi, lxxxiv–lxxxv, xc, xciv, xcix, 76, 221, 293,
    370, 920, 1203, 1439, 1440, 1475–9, **1479–1526**, 1527, 1528, 1571,
    1608, 1673, A-1, A-20, A-21, A-55–A-57
Cymbeline, King of Britain (*Cymb.*), 1475, 1476, 1477, 1478, 1479, 1480*n*,
    1481*n*, 1482*n*, 1483*n*, 1485*n*, 1490*n*, 1494*n*, 1496*n*, 1497*n*, 1498*n*,
    1503*n*, 1513*n*, 1517*n*, 1518*n*, 1519*n*, 1520*n*, A-48, A-55, A-56
Cynthia. *See* Diana
Cyrus, ruler of Persia (600?–529 B.C.), 524*n*
Cytherea (Venus), 108, 114*n*. *See also* Venus

Daedalus and Icarus, story of, 542*n*, 547*n*, 641*n*, 1632*n*
Dagonet, Sir, Arthur's fool, 853*n*
Damon and Pythias, story of, 1124*n*, 1605, A-25, A-60
Danae, mother of Perseus, lxxxii
Daniel, Samuel (1562–1619), lxxi
    The Complaint of Rosamond, 1672, A-60
    Delia, 1708
    The First Four Books of the Civil Wars, A-11, A-39, A-40, A-41
    Philotas, lxxiii
    The Tragedy of Cleopatra, lxxiii, 1331, A-19, A-53
Daniel, story of, xxix, 211*n*, 212*n*
Daniels, Ron, director, 1574, A-72
Dante Alighieri (1265–1321)
    Divine Comedy, xxiv, 1052, A-45
    Vita Nuova, 1710
Danter, John (*fl.* 1594), printer, A-13, A-14, A-15, A-42
Daphne, nymph beloved by Apollo, 114*n*, 160*n*, 462*n*

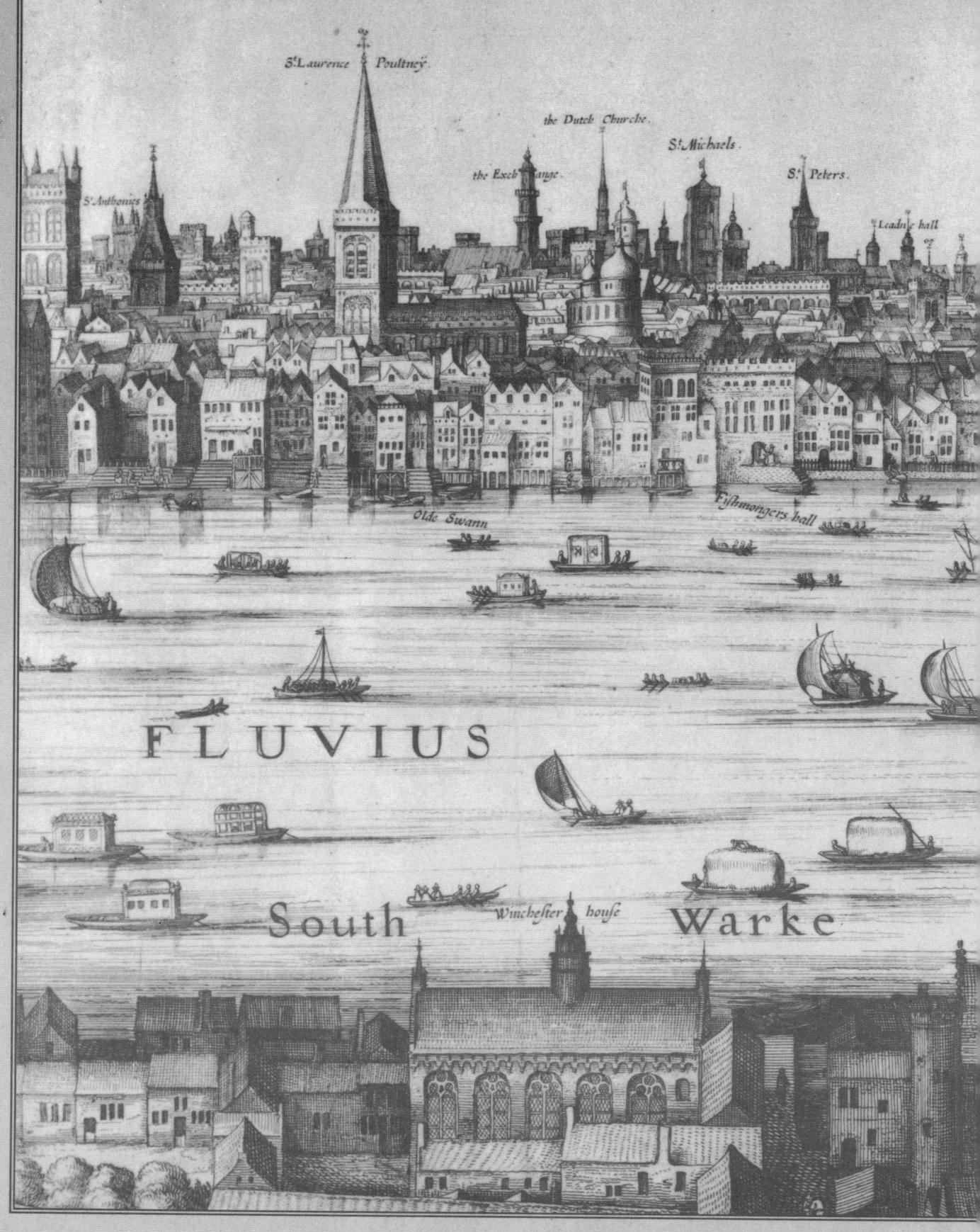

St. Laurence Poultney.

St. Anthonies.

the Dutch Churche.

the Exch ange.

St. Michaels.

St. Peters.

Leadne hall.

Olde Swann.

Fishmongers hall.

FLUVIUS

South   Winchester house   Warke